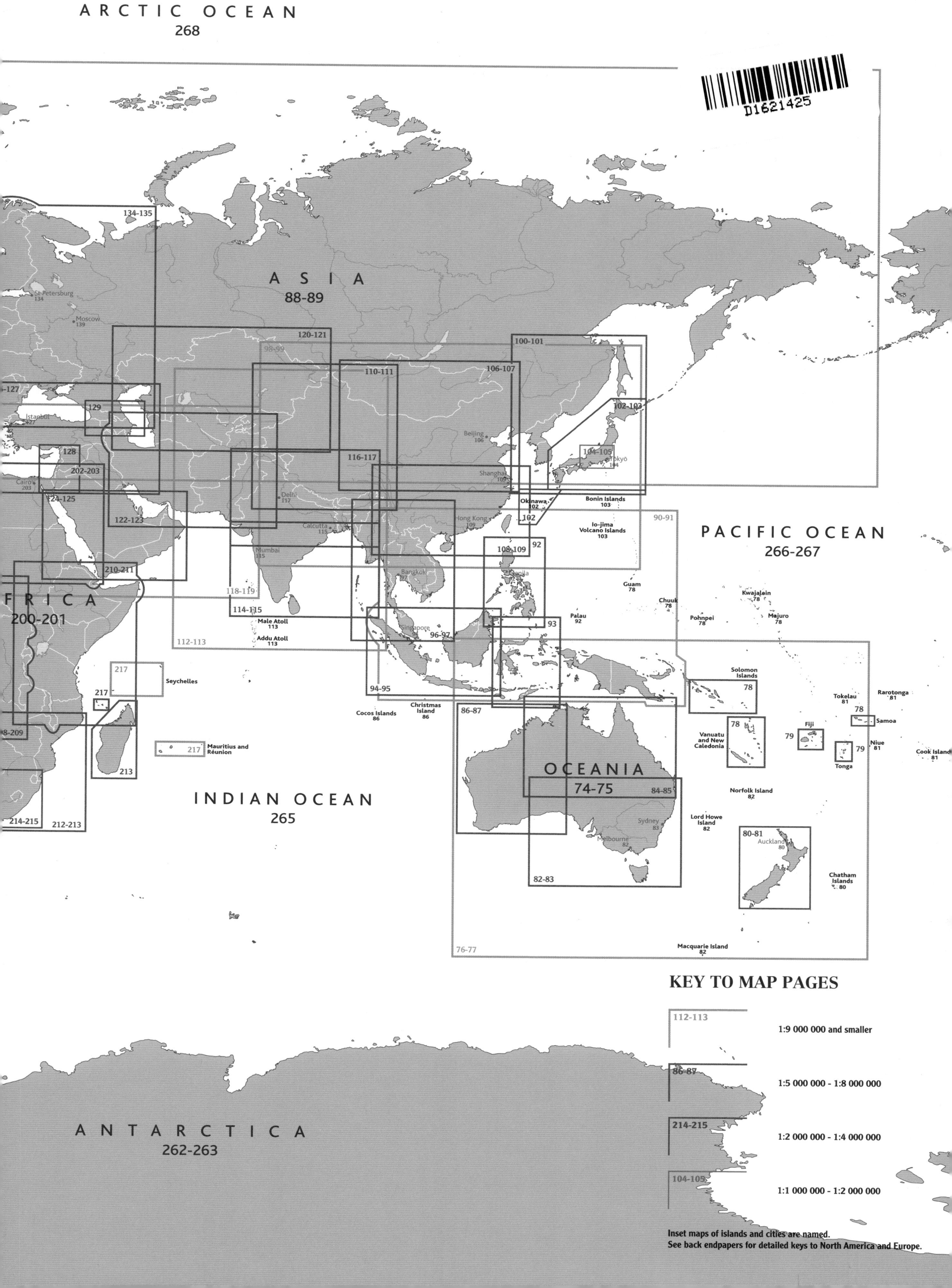
ARCTIC OCEAN
268
ASIA
88-89
St Petersburg 134
Moscow 139
134-135
120-121
98-99
110-111
106-107
100-101
102-103
104-105
Tokyo 104
Beijing 106
Shanghai 103
116-117
Delhi 117
Calcutta 115
Mumbai 115
Hong Kong 109
Okinawa 102
102
Bonin Islands 103
Io-jima Volcano Islands 103
90-91
108-109
92
Manila
Bangkok
Singapore
96-97
94-95
93
118-119
114-115
112-113
Male Atoll 113
Addu Atoll 113
Istanbul 127
129
128
202-203
Cairo 203
124-125
122-123
210-211
FRICA
200-201
217
Seychelles
217
213
Mauritius and Réunion
214-215
212-213
INDIAN OCEAN
265
Cocos Islands 86
Christmas Island 86
PACIFIC OCEAN
266-267
Guam 78
Palau 92
Chuuk 78
Pohnpei 78
Kwajalein 78
Majuro 78
Solomon Islands 78
Vanuatu and New Caledonia 78
Fiji 79
Tokelau 81
Rarotonga 81
Samoa 78
Niue 81
Tonga 79
Cook Islands 81
Norfolk Island 82
Lord Howe Island 82
86-87
OCEANIA
74-75
84-85
Sydney 83
Melbourne 82
82-83
80-81
Auckland 80
Chatham Islands 80
Macquarie Island 82
76-77
ANTARCTICA
262-263
KEY TO MAP PAGES
112-113 1:9 000 000 and smaller
86-87 1:5 000 000 - 1:8 000 000
214-215 1:2 000 000 - 1:4 000 000
104-105 1:1 000 000 - 1:2 000 000
Inset maps of islands and cities are named.
See back endpapers for detailed keys to North America and Europe.

THE TIMES

CONCISE ATLAS OF THE WORLD

Times Books, 77-85 Fulham Palace Road, London W6 8JB

First Edition 1972
Second Edition 1975
Third Edition 1978
Fourth Edition 1980
Fifth Edition 1986
Sixth Edition 1992
Seventh Edition 1995
Eighth Edition 2000
Ninth Edition 2004

Tenth Edition 2006

Printed and bound in Spain

British Library Cataloguing in Publication Data
A catalogue record for this book is available from the British Library

ISBN-13 978-0-00-722906-2
ISBN-10 0-00-722906-2

All mapping in this atlas is generated from Collins Bartholomew digital databases. Collins Bartholomew, the UK's leading independent geographical information supplier, can provide a digital, custom, and premium mapping service to a variety of markets. For further information:
Tel: +44 (0) 141 306 3752
e-mail: collinsbartholomew@harpercollins.co.uk

www.harpercollins.co.uk
Visit the book lover's website

THE TIMES

CONCISE ATLAS OF THE WORLD

TIMES BOOKS
London

THE WORLD TODAY

GEOGRAPHICAL INFORMATION

ATLAS OF THE WORLD

ASIA

EUROPE

AFRICA

OCEANIA

Australia and the vast expanse of the Pacific Ocean dominate this satellite image of Oceania. The islands of Indonesia lie to the northwest of Australia and New Guinea lies to the north, with the islands of the Solomon Island chain, Vanuatu and New Caledonia stretching southeast from New Guinea towards New Zealand. The Hawaiian Islands appear in the top right of the image.

The different colours on these images reveal a great variety of vegetation. This is particularly evident here in the contrasts between the highlands and lowlands of New Guinea and between the east coast, the Great Dividing Range and the complex interior of Australia.

See pages 74–75 for a map of Oceania.

Data from the 1km AVHRR Global Land dataset project by ESA, CEOS, IGBP, NASA, NOAA, USGS, IONIA processed by ESA/ESRIN distributed by Eurimage S.p.A.

ASIA

This image shows the continent of Asia from the Mediterranean Sea and the distinctive shape of The Gulf in the west, to Japan in the east, and from snow-covered Siberia in the north to the tropical islands of Indonesia in the south. The Black, Caspian and Aral Seas appear in the northwest.

The image illustrates a wide range of land cover – particularly in China, with great variation between the intricate patterns of vegetation in the southeast and the large, relatively featureless areas of the Tarim Pendi basin in the centre of the image. The snow covered Himalaya form a dominating feature of the image, stretching in a gentle white arc between the Indian sub-continent and China.

See pages 88–89 for a map of Asia.

Data from the 1km AVHRR Global Land dataset project by ESA, CEOS, IGBP, NASA, NOAA, USGS, IONIA processed by ESA/ESRIN distributed by Eurimage S.p.A.

EUROPE

The distinctive shapes of Scandinavia, the British Isles, Spain and Italy can be clearly seen on this image; Greenland lies to the northwest with Svalbard top centre. The huge land mass of the Russian Federation stretches from the Gulf of Bothnia and the Black Sea in the centre right of the image, northeast into Asia and beyond the horizon.

The colour combination used in the image shows areas such as agricultural crops, permanent grassland and deciduous woodland as green – evident over most of the British Isles and northwest Europe. Coniferous woodland, covering large areas of Scandinavia, appears dark purple/blue. Bare soil and deserts, such as those of the Middle East and parts of Spain and Turkey, appear yellow/brown. Snow and ice in the far northern areas and in such mountain ranges as the Alps and the Caucasus appear white. River valleys are also easily identified, most notably that of the Ob' in northern Russian Federation at the top of the image.

See pages 132–133 for a map of Europe.

Data from the 1km AVHRR Global Land dataset project by ESA, CEOS, IGBP, NASA, NOAA, USGS, IONIA processed by ESA/ESRIN distributed by Eurimage S.p.A.

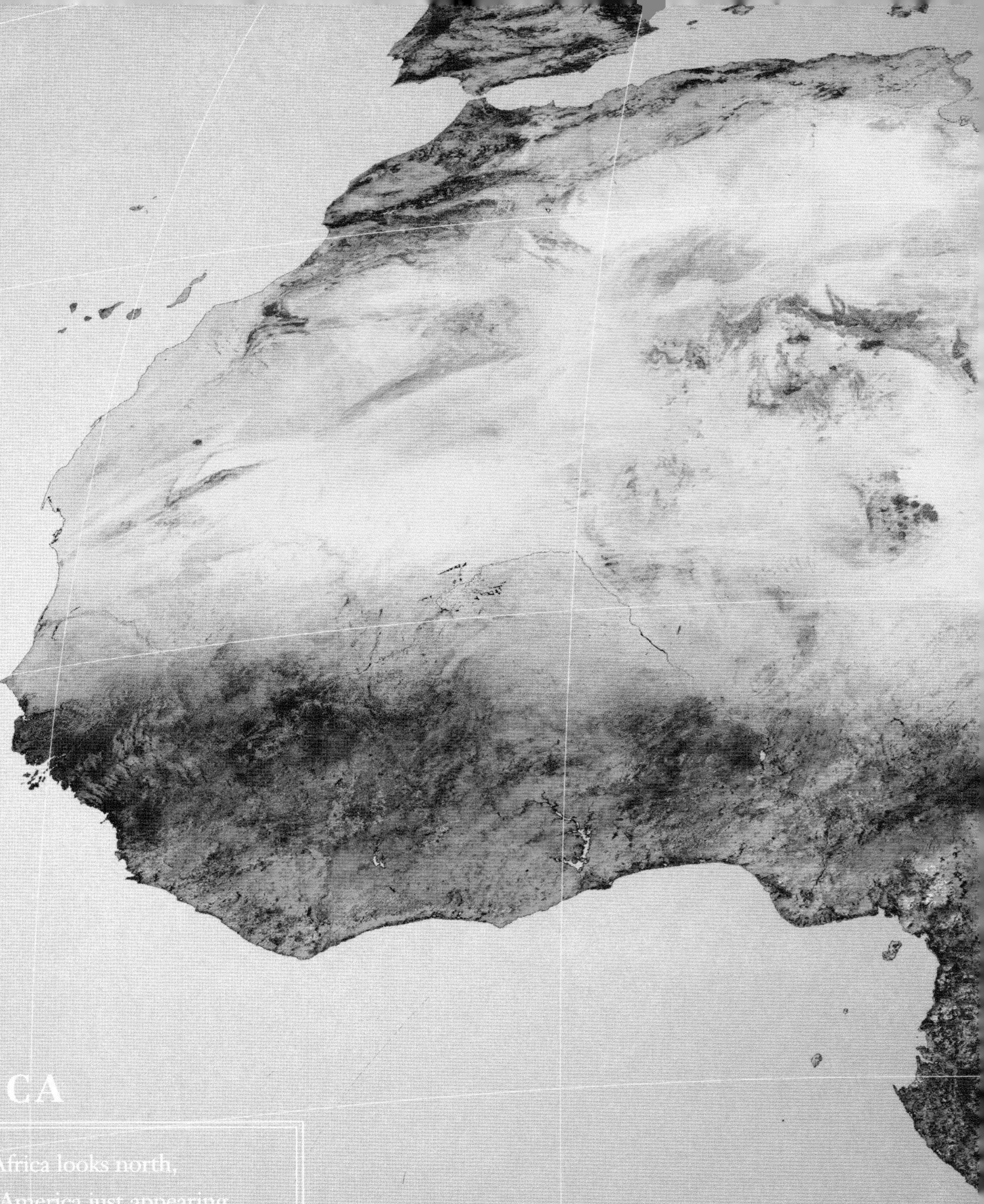

AFRICA

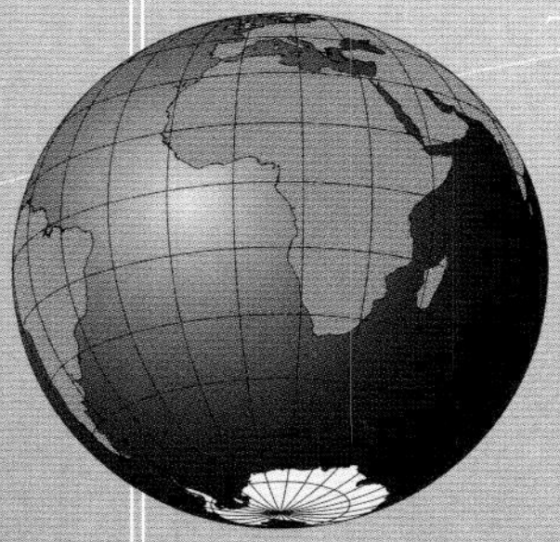

This view of Africa looks north, with South America just appearing in the southwest, the island of Madagascar to the southeast and the Arabian Peninsula and Asia to the northeast.

Subtle variations in vegetation are evident, particularly across the north of the continent and in the Sahara – an area of desert which could be expected to be more uniform in appearance. Also clearly shown are the variations in basic land cover with latitude. The gradations in colour southwards from the Sahara indicate a steady change in vegetation type through the equatorial regions. Sharp contrasts in land use are also clear along the northern coast of Africa with the cultivated area of the Nile valley and delta particularly impressive.

See pages 200–201 for a map of Africa.

Data from the 1km AVHRR Global Land dataset project by ESA, CEOS, IGBP, NASA, NOAA, USGS, IONIA processed by ESA/ESRIN distributed by Eurimage S.p.A.

NORTH AMERICA

This image views North America from above the centre of the continent and includes most of the Arctic Ocean. The Aleutian Islands in the northwest stretch in an arc toward the Kamchatka Peninsula in eastern Asia, while western Europe and northwest Africa appear to the northeast. The islands of the Caribbean lie east and south of Florida in the bottom right of the image.

The contrast between land and water areas is very clear, with the complex drainage patterns and coastlines of Alaska, northern Canada and Greenland shown in great detail. In northwest Canada the Great Slave Lake, Great Bear Lake and thousands of others in the far north are clearly visible, as is the Mackenzie river. The outlines of the Great Lakes are also impressively clear. The easy identification of specific variations in vegetation and land cover is also illustrated by the prominence of such features as the Mississippi river valley, and the San Joaquin and Sacramento valleys of California. The dominance of coniferous forest (dark purple/blue) across large areas of Canada, stretching in a wide band virtually across the whole continent, is also clearly seen.

See pages 218–219 for a map of North America.

Data from the 1km AVHRR Global Land dataset project by ESA, CEOS, IGBP, NASA, NOAA, USGS, IONIA processed by ESA/ESRIN distributed by Eurimage S.p.A.

SOUTH AMERICA

South and Central America appear in the centre of this image with the Pacific Ocean to the west, the Atlantic Ocean to the east, and Africa appearing on the northeast and southeast horizons. The Galapagos Islands lie off the coast of Ecuador and the Falkland Islands, South Georgia and the Antarctic Peninsula off the southern tip of the continent.

The great range of green and blue tones represent different types and conditions of vegetation across the Amazon basin. Although the data contains no information about surface height, it can indicate the underlying structure of the land. Here, the mountain ranges of the Andes are clearly evident. The small red areas on the east coast of Brazil, representing the major urban areas of São Paulo and Rio de Janeiro, illustrate the impressive level of detail available from this type of imagery.

See pages 248–249 for a map of South America.

Data from the 1km AVHRR Global Land dataset project by ESA, CEOS, IGBP, NASA, NOAA, USGS, IONIA processed by ESA/ESRIN distributed by Eurimage S.p.A.

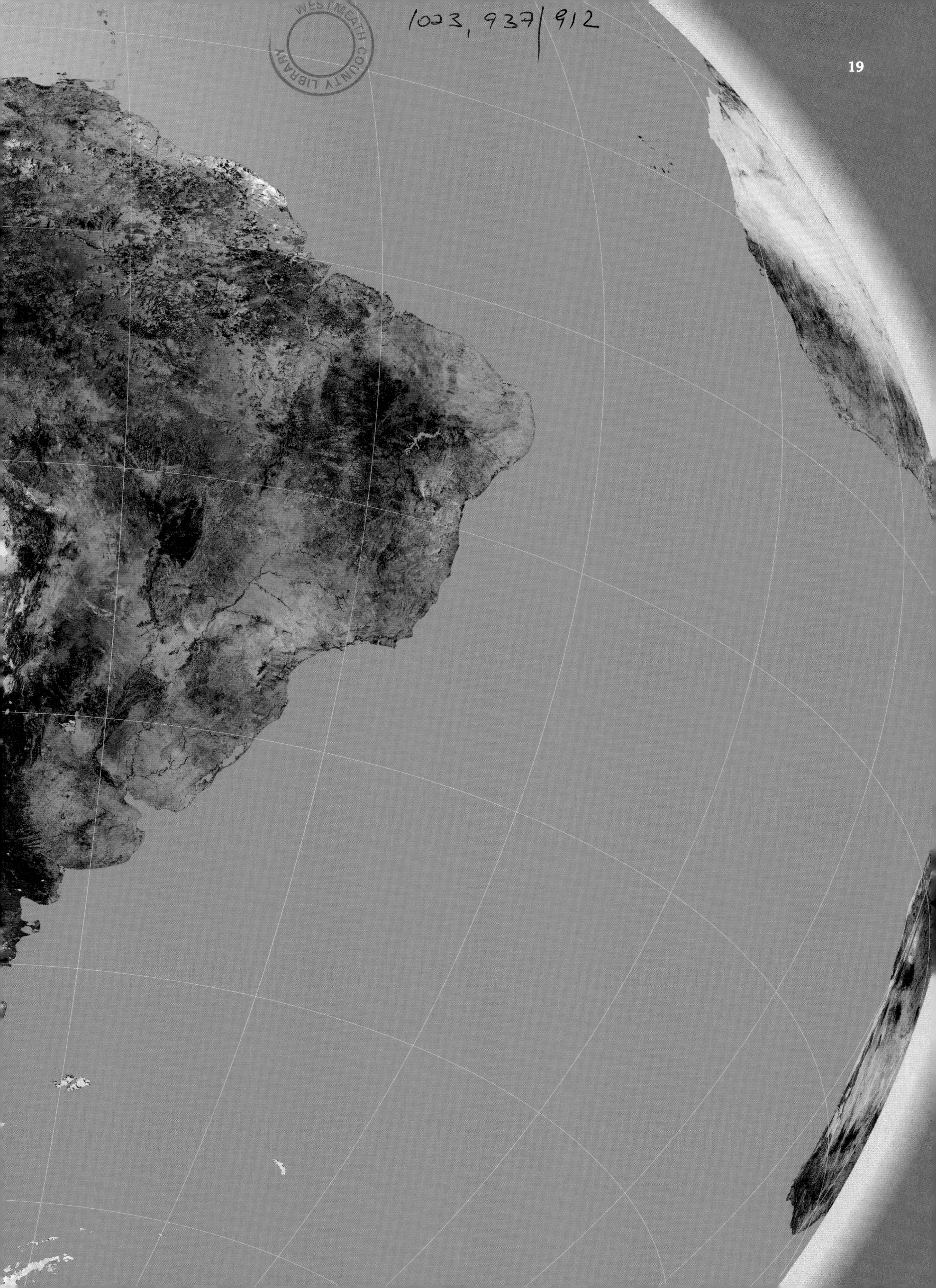

ANTARCTICA

This image positions the Antarctic continent with the Greenwich meridian to the top centre. The distinctive shape of the Antarctic Peninsula lies to the top left and the prominent Ross Ice Shelf can be identified to the bottom of the image, below the Transantarctic Mountains range.

Although not completely cloud-free – there is some cloud cover in the eastern area to the right of the image – the view is impressive in its depiction of the physical features of the continent. The Ronne Ice Shelf, including Berkner Island, and the Transantarctic Mountains are particularly spectacular. Floating ice is excluded from the image, resulting in a clear definition of the extent of the continental ice sheet in an austral summer.

See pages 262–263 for a continental map of Antarctica.

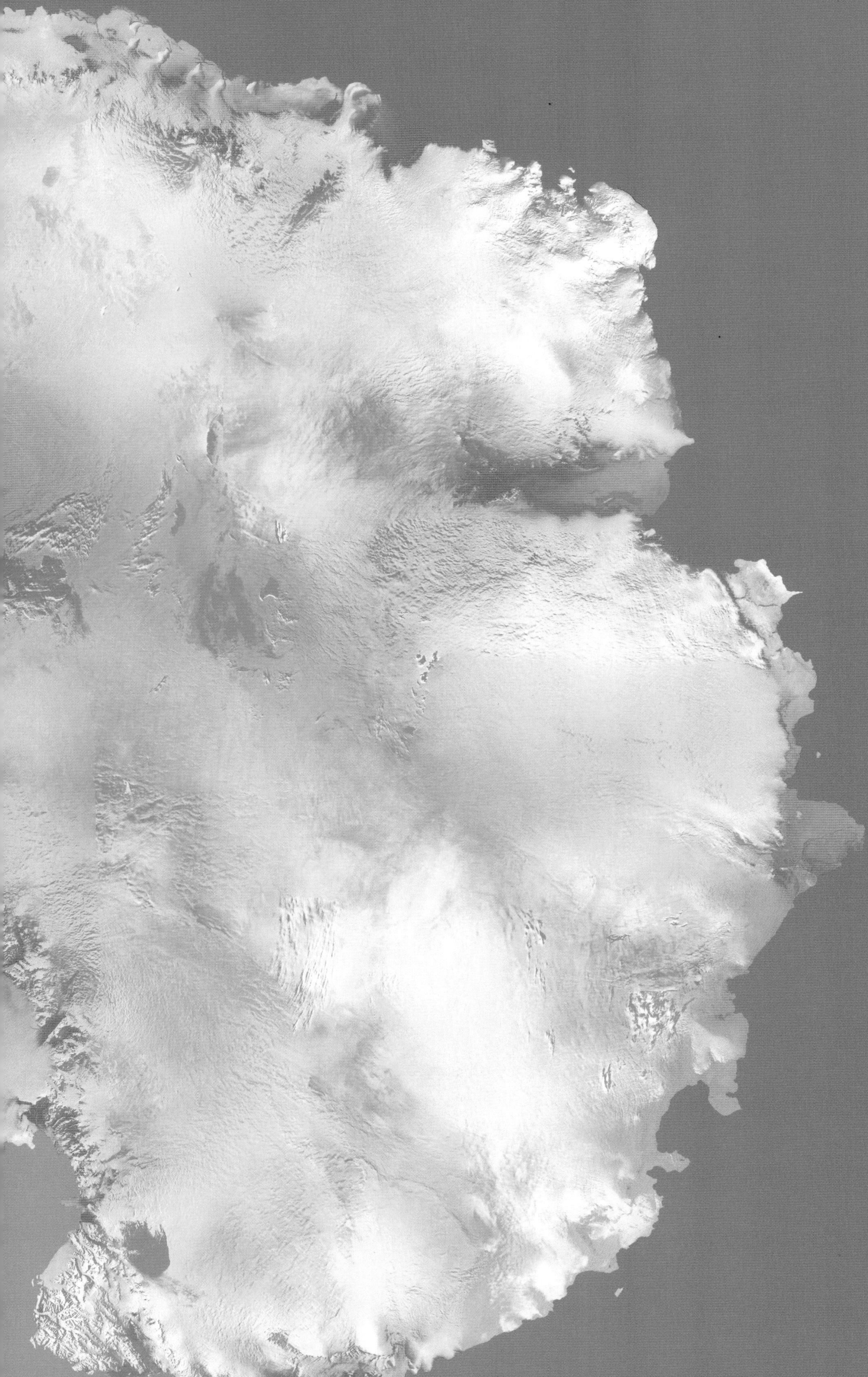

ORIGINS OF THE SOLAR SYSTEM

The nature and origin of our Solar System has been a subject of much debate. Early ideas of an Earth-centred system took many hundreds of years to be discarded in favour of Copernicus' heliocentric, or sun-centred model. More refined theories followed with Kepler's laws of orbital motion, and Newton's laws of gravity. The question of origin remained unanswered, and was regarded more as a philosophical matter.

The fact that the Sun and the planets rotate in a similar direction suggests a common formation mechanism – that of a large collapsing cloud or nebula. It is now believed that this did happen, about 4 600 million years ago. The nebula consisted of predominantly hydrogen and helium, but with a small amount of heavier elements. Over time, the cloud collapsed to form a rotating disk around a dense core. As core collapse continued and pressure in the core increased, material was heated enough to allow the nuclear fusion of hydrogen. Meanwhile as the disk cooled, the heavier elements began to condense and agglomerate. Larger bodies grew rapidly by sweeping up much of the remaining smaller material. As the core began to shine, its radiation pushed back much of the nearby volatile disk material into the outer Solar System, where it condensed and accumulated on the more distant planetary cores. This left the Inner Planets as small rocky bodies, and produced the Gas Giants of the outer system. Bombardment of the planets by a decreasing number of small bodies continued for several hundred million years, causing the craters now seen on many of the planets and moons.

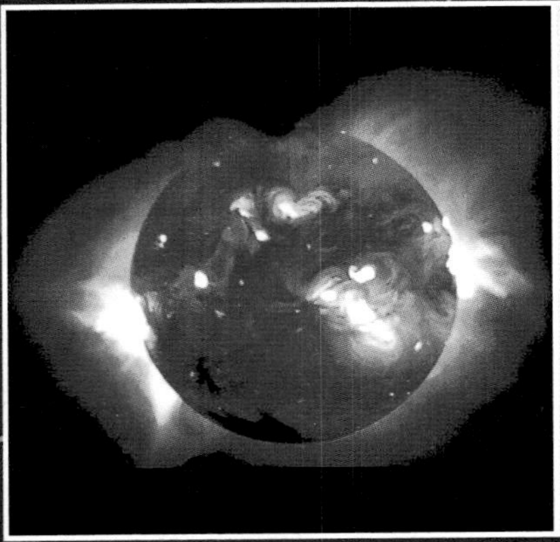

The Sun

The Sun is a typical star. It accounts for 99.85 per cent of the total mass contained within the Solar System, ensuring that it provides a dominating gravitational hold on its orbiting planets. The tremendous amount of heat and light produced by the Sun is the result of nuclear fusion reactions which occur in its core. In this process, hydrogen is converted into helium to produce a core temperature of roughly 15 million°C. Intense magnetic fields can induce cooling zones seen as dark sun spots on the Sun's surface. The Sun constantly emits a stream of charged particles which form the solar wind and cause auroral activity which can be seen on Earth.

	Sun	Mercury	Venus	Earth	Mars	Jupiter	Saturn	Uranus	Neptune	Pluto
Mass (Earth=1)	332 830	0.055	0.815	1 (6×10^{24})	0.107	317.82	95.161	14.371	17.147	0.002
Volume (Earth=1)	1 306 000	0.05	0.88	1	0.15	1 316	755	52	44	0.01
Density (Water=1)	1.41	5.43	5.24	5.52	3.94	1.33	0.70	1.30	1.76	1.10
Equatorial diameter (km)	1 392 000	4 879.4	12 103.6	12 756.3	6 794	142 984	120 536	51 118	49 528	2 390
Polar flattening	0	0	0	0.003	0.007	0.065	0.098	0.023	0.017	0
Surface gravity (Earth=1)	27.5	0.38	0.91	1	0.38	2.53	1.07	0.90	1.14	0.06
Number of satellites > 100 km	-	0	0	1	0	7	13	8	6	1
Total number of satellites	-	0	0	1	2	63	47	27	13	3
Rotation period (Earth days)	25–36	58.65	-243	23hr 56m 4s	1.03	0.41	0.44	-0.72	0.67	-6.39
Year (Earth days/years)	-	88 days	224.7 days	365.24 days	687 days	11.86 years	29.42 years	83.8 years	163.8 years	248 years
Mean orbital distance (million km)	-	57.9	108.2	149.6	227.9	778.4	1 426.7	2 871.0	4 498.3	5 906.4
Orbital eccentricity	-	0.2056	0.0068	0.0167	0.0934	0.0484	0.0542	0.0472	0.0086	0.2488
Mean orbital velocity (km/s)	-	47.87	35.02	29.79	24.13	13.07	9.67	6.84	5.48	4.75
Inclination of equator to orbit (deg.)	7.25	0	177.3	23.45	25.19	3.12	26.73	97.86	29.58	119.61
Orbital inclination (w.r.t. ecliptic)	-	7.005	3.395	0.00005	1.851	1.305	2.485	0.770	1.769	17.142
Mean surface temperature (°C)	5 700	167	457	15–20	-90– -5	-108	-139	-197	-200	-215.2
Atmospheric pressure (bars)	-	-	90	1	0.007–0.010	0.3	0.4	-	-	8×10^{-5}
Atmospheric composition (selected gas components)	H_2 92.1% He 7.8% O_2 0.061%	-	CO_2 96% N_2 3%	N_2 77% O_2 21% Ar 1.6%	CO_2 95.3% N_2 2.7%	H_2 90% He 10%	H_2 97% He 3%	H_2 83% He 15% CH_4 2%	H_2 85% He 13% CH_4 2%	N_2 CO CH_4

PLUTO
SATURN
VENUS
MERCURY
MARS
EARTH
JUPITER
URANUS

Mercury

Mercury's long period of rotation, close proximity to the Sun, and minimal atmosphere make its surface an extremely hostile environment with temperatures ranging from 427 to minus 173°C between its day and night side. Mercury is similar to Earth's Moon in size and appearance; its cratered surface was first photographed in detail in the mid-1970s by the Mariner 10 space probe. However the internal structure differs from the Moon; analysis of its magnetic field suggests that the core consists of molten iron, believed to be 40 per cent of the planet's volume. Mercury has a very eccentric orbit with its orbital distance varying from 46 to 70 million km.

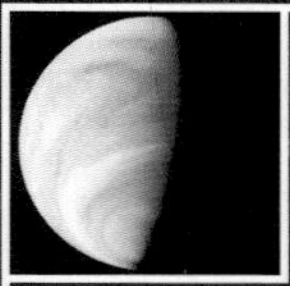

Venus

Venus' thick atmosphere of carbon dioxide and nitrogen creates not only a huge surface pressure of ninety times that on Earth but also a greenhouse effect producing temperatures in excess of 450°C. Traces of sulphur dioxide and water vapour form clouds of dilute sulphuric acid, making the atmosphere extremely corrosive. This atmosphere reflects almost all incident visible radiation and prevents direct observation of surface features. In 1990 use of radar imaging enabled the Magellan space probe to see through the cloud. Magellan mapped 98 per cent of the planet during three years to find a surface covered in craters, volcanoes, mountains and solidified lava flows. Venus is the brightest object in the sky after the Sun and Moon and is unusual in that its year is less than its rotation period.

Earth

Earth is the largest and densest of the Inner Planets. Created some 4 500 million years ago, the core, rocky mantle and crust are similar in structure to Venus. The Earth's core is composed almost entirely of iron and oxygen compounds which exist in a molten state at temperatures of around 5 000°C. Earth is the only planet with vast quantities of life-sustaining water, with the oceans covering 70.8 per cent of its surface. The action of plate tectonics has created vast mountain ranges and is responsible for volcanic activity. The Moon is Earth's only natural satellite and with a diameter of over one quarter that of the Earth's, makes the Earth-Moon system a near double-planet.

Mars

Named after the Roman god of war because of its blood-red appearance, Mars is the last of the Inner Planets. The red colour comes from the high concentration of iron oxides on its surface. Mars has impressive surface features, including the highest known peak in the Solar System, Olympus Mons, an inactive volcano reaching a height of 23 km above the surrounding plains, and Marineris, a 2 500 km long canyon four times as deep as the Grand Canyon. The Pathfinder mission in 1997 has shown that much of the Martian surface is shaped by intense dust storms which often engulf the entire planet. Mars has polar caps composed of water and carbon dioxide ice which partially evaporate during its summer.

Jupiter

Jupiter is by far the most massive of all the planets and is the dominant body in the Solar System after the Sun. It is the innermost of the Gas Giants. The dense surface atmosphere is predominantly hydrogen, with helium, water vapour, and methane. Below this is a layer of liquid hydrogen, then an even deeper layer of metallic hydrogen. Unlike solid bodies, Jupiter's rotation period is somewhat ill-defined, with equatorial regions rotating faster than the polar caps; this, combined with convection currents in lower layers, causes intense magnetic fields and rapidly varying surface features. Most notable of these is the Great Red Spot, a giant circular storm visible since the first observations of Jupiter's surface, which shows no signs of abating.

Saturn

Although only slightly smaller that Jupiter, Saturn is a mere one-third of Jupiter's mass, and the least dense of all the planets - less dense than water. The low mass, combined with a fast rotation rate, leads to the planet's significant polar flattening. Saturn exhibits a striking ring system, more than twice the diameter of the planet; the rings consist of countless small rock and ice clumps which vary in size from a grain of sand to tens of metres in diameter. It is believed that the rings were formed from a stray moon coming too close to Saturn, and being ripped apart by it. Distinct bands and gaps in the rings are the result of complex interactions between the planet and its closer moons. Recent rare opportunities to view Saturn's rings edgeways have yielded the discovery of at least two other moons.

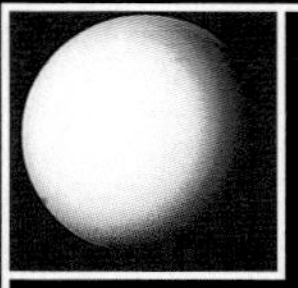

Uranus

Uranus has many surprising features; the most prominent of these is the tilt of its rotation axis by over 90 degrees caused by a series of large collisions in its early history. Like the other Gas Giants, Uranus is predominantly hydrogen and helium with a small proportion of methane and other gases. However, because Uranus is colder than Jupiter and Saturn, the methane forms ice crystals which give Uranus a featureless blue-green colour. The interior is also different from that expected. Instead of having a gaseous atmosphere above liquid and metallic hydrogen layers, Uranus has a super-dense gaseous atmosphere extending down to its core. Uranus' magnetic field is inclined at 60 degrees to the rotation axis, and is off centre by one third of the planet's radius, which suggests that it is not generated by the core. The system of eleven narrow rings around Uranus is prevented from spreading by the interaction of nearby 'shepherd' moons. Two new moons, Caliban and Sycorax, were discovered in 1997 although their large orbits indicate they are probably captured asteroids.

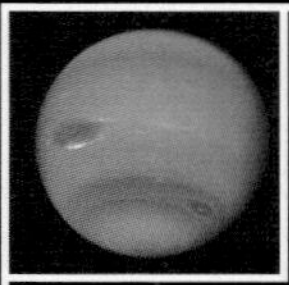

Neptune

Neptune has always been associated with Uranus because of its similar size, composition and appearance, but, unexpectedly, Neptune's atmosphere is more active than that of Uranus. This was shown by Voyager 2 in 1989 with the observation of the Great Dark Spot, Neptune's equivalent to Jupiter's Great Red Spot. Voyager 2 recorded the fastest winds ever seen in the Solar System, 2 000 km per hour, around the Dark Spot. This feature disappeared in 1994, but has been replaced by a similar storm in the northern polar cap. Like Uranus, Neptune has a magnetic field highly inclined to the planet's axis of rotation and off-centre by more than half of the planet's radius.
The cause of this magnetic field is convection currents in conducting fluid layers outside the core. Neptune's largest moon, Triton, is in an inclined retrograde orbit, indicating that it was captured by Neptune rather than formed alongside it. The slowly decaying orbit will one day bring Triton too close to Neptune, and it will be torn apart forming a spectacular ring.

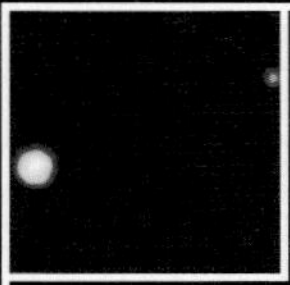

Pluto

Pluto's existence was predicted before its discovery in 1930 from studies of the motions of Neptune and Uranus. Its orbit is highly tilted with respect to the orbits of the other planets and is so eccentric that it occasionally comes inside Neptune's orbit. Its only moon, Charon, is unusually large. Unusually, minerals make up about 70 per cent of its total mass, with the rest being ice. Pluto, unlike Charon, has methane ice on its surface and this forms a tenuous yet deep atmosphere when Pluto is closest to the Sun.
These anomalies and, since 1992, the discovery of hundreds of other distant icy worlds, have often called Pluto's status as a planet into question. Astronomers now believe there are thousands of these icy mini-planets, many similar in size to Pluto and Charon. Most of them orbit in the Edgeworth-Kuiper belt which stretches from Neptune's orbit to about 7 500 million km from the Sun. A few objects travel even further away on very eccentric orbits. Beyond them lies only the Oort cloud of comets and the distant stars.

THE EARTH'S STRUCTURE

The interior of the Earth can be divided into three principal regions (*see 1*). The outermost region is known as the crust, which is extremely thin compared to the Earth as a whole. Under the continents the crust is about 33 km thick on average, only 0.5 per cent of the total radius of the Earth (6 370 km). Under the oceans the crust is even thinner: perhaps a third of its continental thickness. Over the course of geological time the Earth's crust has broken up into large fragments, which are known as lithospheric plates. These plates are slowly moving relative to one another at rates of a few centimetres per year – a process know as continental drift.

The next layer down is known as the mantle which is about 2 850 km thick. The distinction between the mantle and crust is made on the basis of composition and strength. There is a zone of the upper mantle, at depths between about 100 and 700 km, which behaves like a fluid when under stress. This weak zone is called the asthenosphere. The outermost 70 km or so of the mantle, together with the crust, is known as the lithosphere and is much stronger. The transition between the lithosphere and asthenosphere is due to variation in temperature, and is therefore gradual rather than being a distinct boundary.

Below the mantle is the Earth's core, which is about 3 470 km in radius, and is mainly made up of iron. The greater part of the core is completely liquid; however, there is a solid inner core, about 1 220 km in radius.

It is the dynamic processes operating in the upper parts of the Earth's interior which give rise to very dramatic and violent expressions of the huge energies involved: earthquakes and volcanoes. Both of these can be very destructive, even disastrous, in terms of both loss of life and economic impact. Consequently, study of these phenomena is very important if the natural disasters arising from them are to be mitigated.

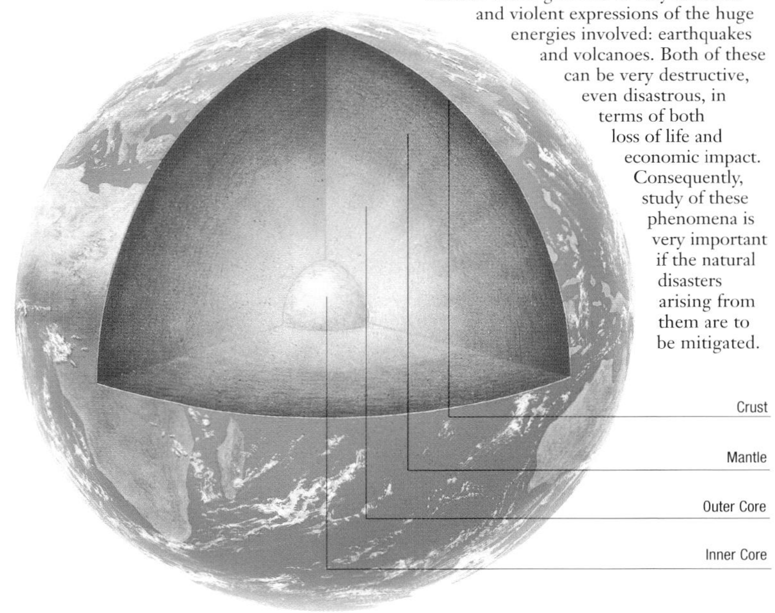

Crust
Mantle
Outer Core
Inner Core

1. THE EARTH'S INTERIOR

2. DISTRIBUTION OF MAJOR EARTHQUAKES AND VOLCANOES

Winkel Tripel Projection
scale 1:93 000 000

Arctic circle
EURASIAN PLATE
Liaoning
Gansu
Tangshan
Qinghai
Ningxia
Sichuan
Unzen-dake
Tokyo
O-yama
Yunnan/Sichuan
Tropic of Cancer
PHILIPPINE PLATE
Mt Pinatubo
Mayon
Sumatera
Equator
Rabaul
Gunung Galunggung
Bali
PA
PL
Tropic of Capricorn
INDO-AUSTRALIAN PLATE
Antarctic Circle

DISTRIBUTION OF EARTHQUAKES AND VOLCANOES

Any map showing the distribution of earthquakes and volcanoes (*see 2*) will inevitably look very similar to a map showing the boundaries of the tectonic plates (*see 3*). This is because both phenomena are largely controlled by the processes of plate tectonics. The vast majority of the world's earthquakes occur at plate boundaries as a result of one plate pushing past another along what is known as a constructive boundary, or under another at a destructive boundary, creating a subduction zone. Even those earthquakes which occur away from plate margins (intraplate earthquakes) are still mostly due to stresses in the rocks that result indirectly from plate movements.

Most major volcanoes occur along lines parallel to subduction zones, as for example, in the Andes. Other volcanoes can form along mid-ocean ridges where the asthenosphere is close to the surface; such volcanoes can produce what are known as fissure eruptions, where vast amounts of basaltic lava suddenly erupt on the surface, inundating huge areas.

3. TECTONIC PLATE BOUNDARIES

scale 1:271 000 000

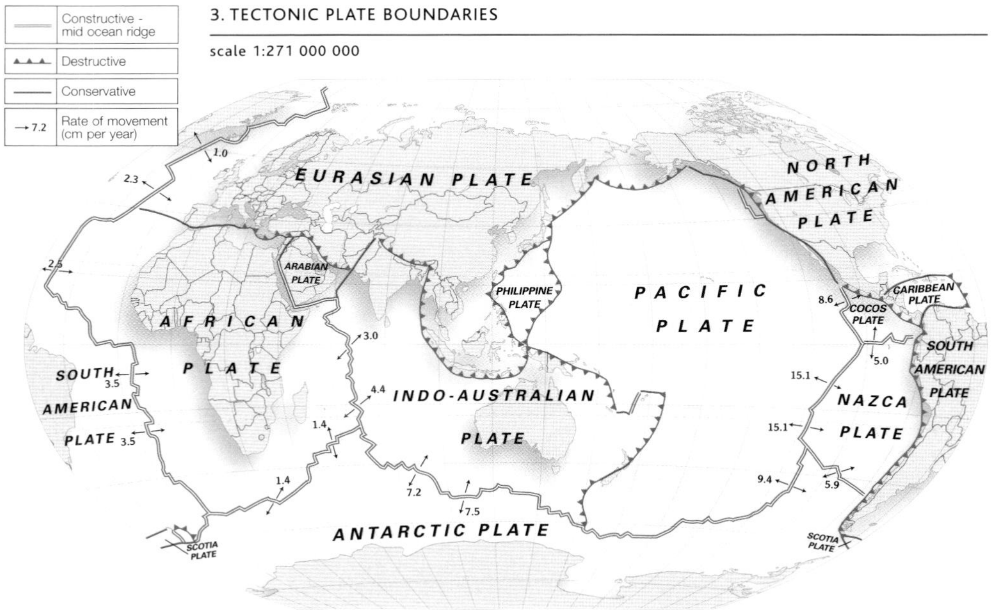

Constructive - mid ocean ridge
Destructive
Conservative
7.2 Rate of movement (cm per year)
EURASIAN PLATE
NORTH AMERICAN PLATE
ARABIAN PLATE
PHILIPPINE PLATE
PACIFIC PLATE
CARIBBEAN PLATE
COCOS PLATE
AFRICAN PLATE
SOUTH AMERICAN PLATE
INDO-AUSTRALIAN PLATE
NAZCA PLATE
ANTARCTIC PLATE
SCOTIA PLATE

VOLCANOES

In the simplest terms, a volcano is a vent at the surface of the Earth where molten rock (magma) from the interior can reach the surface. The magma originates in the Earth's mantle. It then erupts either as a stream of liquid rock (called lava when it appears at the surface) or as fine particles of ash or cinder. The erupted material builds up over time into a mountain, typically conical in shape. The exact shape of the volcano is controlled by the type of material erupted.

Plymouth, the capital of Montserrat, partially buried by volcanic ash after the eruption of Soufrière Hills in August 1997.

Volcanoes in oceanic locations (such as Hawaii) tend to erupt very basic (non-acidic) lava which flows relatively easily. Because it can run quite far before cooling, this produces a very flat volcano with gentle slopes, known as a shield volcano. Continental volcanoes produce more acidic lava which flows more slowly, and they produce more ash, and therefore have steeper-sided cones. Such volcanoes also tend to erupt more explosively, because of the greater amount of steam or gas in the lava, and are generally more dangerous. They can produce what is know as a pyroclastic flow, a fast-moving cloud of super-heated ash and gases, which is what destroyed Pompeii in AD79.

Volcanoes can also be classified according to their eruptive history. Active volcanoes are those that are currently erupting; an eruption can go on intermittently for years, and some volcanoes, such as Stromboli in Italy, are almost permanently active. However, most volcanoes erupt much less frequently, and those that have not erupted for tens or hundreds of years, but may be expected to erupt again, are said to be dormant. Volcanoes which were once active in response to the tectonic situation as it was millions of years ago, and which cannot possibly erupt again today, are said to be extinct.

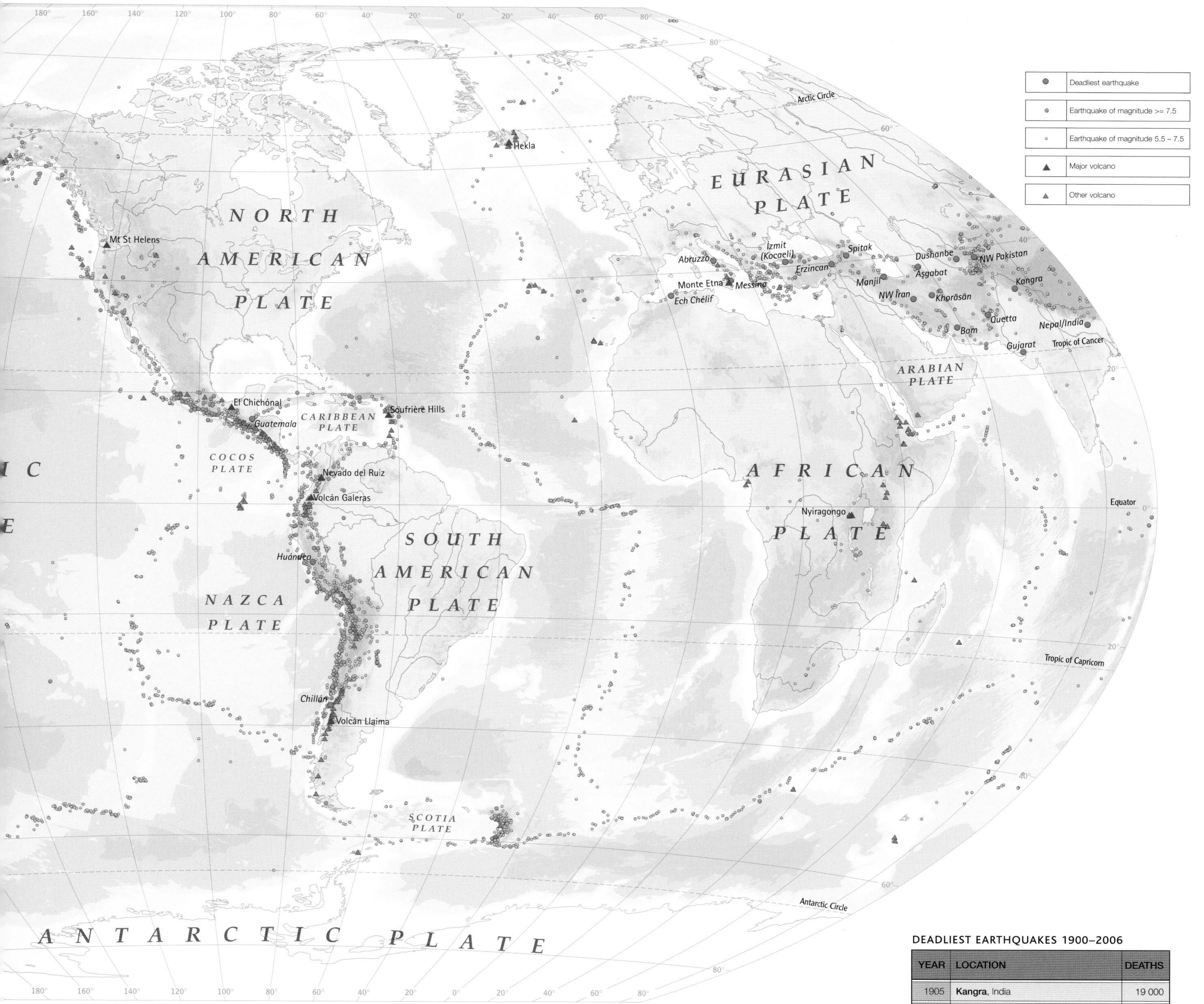
Deadliest earthquake
Earthquake of magnitude >= 7.5
Earthquake of magnitude 5.5 – 7.5
Major volcano
Other volcano
NORTH AMERICAN PLATE
EURASIAN PLATE
ARABIAN PLATE
AFRICAN PLATE
CARIBBEAN PLATE
COCOS PLATE
SOUTH AMERICAN PLATE
NAZCA PLATE
SCOTIA PLATE
ANTARCTIC PLATE
Arctic Circle
Tropic of Cancer
Equator
Tropic of Capricorn
Antarctic Circle
Hekla
Mt St Helens
El Chichónal
Guatemala
Soufrière Hills
Nevado del Ruiz
Volcán Galeras
Huánuco
Chillán
Volcán Llaima
Nyiragongo
Abruzzo
Izmit (Kocaeli)
Erzincan
Spitak
Monte Etna
Messina
Ech Chélif
Manjil
NW Iran
Dushanbe
Aşgabat
NW Pakistan
Khorāsān
Kangra
Quetta
Bam
Nepal/India
Gujarat

EARTHQUAKES

An earthquake is produced by a sudden breaking of rock in the Earth's crust as the stresses become too great for the strength of the rock to withstand. Naturally, this is most likely to happen where the rock is weakest. Where the rock breaks, a fracture line, known as a fault is left, and because there is now a break, future movements are likely to happen along the same weakness. The forces involved derive mostly from the movements of the tectonic plates; for example, between the upper surface of a subducting plate and the lower surface of the plate under which it is sliding – conditions which have caused some of the world's largest earthquakes.

The citadel of the ancient Iranian city of Bam, devastated by a major earthquake in December 2003.

The force with which the rock breaks releases a large amount of energy in the form of waves that travel through the Earth. These radiate outwards from where the fault has ruptured. The point on the fault at which the rupture begins is known as the hypocentre; this is usually at a depth of 10 to 30 km for shallow earthquakes; earthquakes in subduction zones can be as deep as 600 km below the Earth's surface. The point on the Earth's surface directly above the hypocentre is called the epicentre; this is what is usually shown on a map. The magnitude of an earthquake, the so-called Richter scale, is a logarithmic approximation of the total amount of energy released. A large earthquake which may be severely damaging at the epicentre, is less strongly felt by people at greater distances. The strength of shaking at any point is known as the intensity, and this decreases with distance from the epicentre.

The tsunami of December 2004 originated from a major earthquake of magnitude 9.0 off the coast of Sumatera. It caused over 225 000 deaths and widespread destruction in eleven countries around the Indian Ocean.

MAJOR VOLCANIC ERUPTIONS 1980–2006

YEAR	VOLCANO	COUNTRY
1980	**Mt St Helens**	USA
1982	**El Chichónal**	Mexico
1982	**Gunung Galunggung**	Indonesia
1983	**Kilauea**	Hawaii
1983	**Ō-yama**	Japan
1985	**Nevado del Ruiz**	Colombia
1991	**Mt Pinatubo**	Philippines
1991	**Unzen-dake**	Japan
1993	**Mayon**	Philippines
1993	**Volcán Galeras**	Colombia
1994	**Volcán Llaima**	Chile
1994	**Rabaul**	Papua New Guinea
1997	**Soufrière Hills**	Montserrat
2000	**Hekla**	Iceland
2001	**Monte Etna**	Italy
2002	**Nyiragongo**	Democratic Republic of the Congo

DEADLIEST EARTHQUAKES 1900–2006

YEAR	LOCATION	DEATHS
1905	**Kangra**, India	19 000
1908	**Messina**, Italy	110 000
1917	**Bali**, Indonesia	15 000
1920	**Ningxia Province**, China	200 000
1923	**Tōkyō**, Japan	142 807
1927	**Qinghai Province**, China	200 000
1932	**Gansu Province**, China	70 000
1935	**Quetta**, Pakistan	30 000
1939	**Chillán**, Chile	28 000
1939	**Erzincan**, Turkey	32 700
1948	**Aşgabat**, Turkmenistan	19 800
1970	**Huánuco Province**, Peru	66 794
1974	**Yunnan and Sichuan Provinces**, China	20 000
1976	central **Guatemala**	22 778
1976	**Tangshan**, Hebei Province, China	255 000
1978	**Khorāsān Province**, Iran	20 000
1988	**Spitak**, Armenia	25 000
1990	**Manjil**, Iran	50 000
1999	**İzmit (Kocaeli)**, Turkey	17 000
2001	**Gujarat**, India	20 000
2003	**Bam**, Iran	26 271
2004	**Sumatera**, Indonesia/Indian Ocean	>225 000
2005	**Northwest Pakistan**	87 000

OBSERVING THE OCEANS

The oceans cover 70.8 per cent of the surface of the Earth and exert an extraordinary influence on the physical processes of the Earth and its atmosphere. The circulation of water throughout the oceans is critical to world climate and climate change. Any study of these relationships relies upon a clear understanding of the role of the oceans and of the complex processes within them. Methods of direct and indirect observation of the oceans, particularly by sampling and through the application of satellite remote sensing, have developed enormously over the last forty years and continue to provide the data required to develop this understanding.

Until the advent of Earth-observation satellites in the late 1970s all ocean observations were made from ships. The first global survey of the oceans, their bathymetry and their physical and biological characteristics, was made by HMS Challenger between 1872 and 1876. Throughout the 20th century, comprehensive descriptions of the distributions of temperature and salinity were made through numerous regional and global expeditions. Analysis of the temperature and salinity characteristics of a water sample allowed its origins to be determined, and enabled overall patterns of water circulation to be deduced.

Until the 1960s there was no means of directly measuring currents below the ocean surface. Parallel developments produced two solutions to this problem. In the USA, current-recording meters were designed which returned records of current speed and direction, and water temperature. In the UK, devices were produced which could be made to drift with the currents at a predetermined depth and which could be tracked from an attendant ship. Such floats can now be used globally, independent of ships.

Earth observation satellites have become increasingly important in observing the oceans. Radiometers allow sea surface temperatures to be monitored and radar altimeters permit ocean surface currents to be inferred from measurements of sea surface height. Such developments meant that by the early 1990s routine monitoring of ocean surface currents was possible. The combination of satellite altimetry and other observation methods has also allowed a detailed picture of the ocean floor to be established (*see 1*).

1. GLOBAL SEAFLOOR TOPOGRAPHY

This image has been produced from a combination of shipboard depth soundings and gravity data derived from satellite altimetry from the ERS-1 and Geosat satellites. The range of colours represents different depths of the ocean – from orange and yellow on the shallow continental shelves to dark blues in the deepest ocean trenches. The heavily fractured mid-ocean ridges (ranging from green to yellow) are particularly prominent.

OCEAN CIRCULATION

Most of the Earth's incoming solar radiation is absorbed in the top few tens of metres of the ocean. Thus the upper ocean is warmed, the warming being greatest around the equator. Sea water has a high thermal capacity in comparison with the atmosphere or lithosphere and as a consequence, the ocean is an extremely effective store of thermal energy. Slow ocean currents play a major role in redistributing this heat around the globe and the oceans and their circulation are thus key elements in the climate system.

Estimates of the global transport of heat by the oceans (*see 2*) show a pattern of heat flow in the Indian and North Pacific Oceans away from the equator and towards the poles. However, the Atlantic Ocean has a clear northward flow throughout, decreasing from a maximum value of 1.4 petawatts (PW) at 24ºN to effectively zero in the Arctic Ocean. This decrease is indicative of the heat loss to the atmosphere which is responsible for the temperate climate of western Europe.

Ocean currents are influenced by winds, by density gradients and by the Earth's rotation. They are also constrained by the topography of the seafloor. Surface currents are usually strong, narrow, western-boundary currents flowing towards the poles. Some of these are well known, for example the Gulf Stream in the North Atlantic Ocean, the Kuroshio Current in the northwest Pacific, and the Brazil Current (*see 3*). These poleward flows are returned towards the equator in broad, slow, interior flows which complete a gyre in each hemisphere basin. Sea surface circulation is reflected in variations in sea surface height which can vary greatly across currents (*see 4*). For example, differences in sea surface height of over 1m are evident across the Kuroshio Current. At high latitudes, winter cooling produces high density water which sinks towards the ocean floor and flows towards the equator, being constrained by the sea floor topography (*see 5*). This fills the deep ocean basins with water at temperatures close to 0ºC.

2. OCEAN TRANSPORT OF HEAT

In petawatts (PW) (10^{15} watts). 1 PW is about sixty times the global consumption of energy.

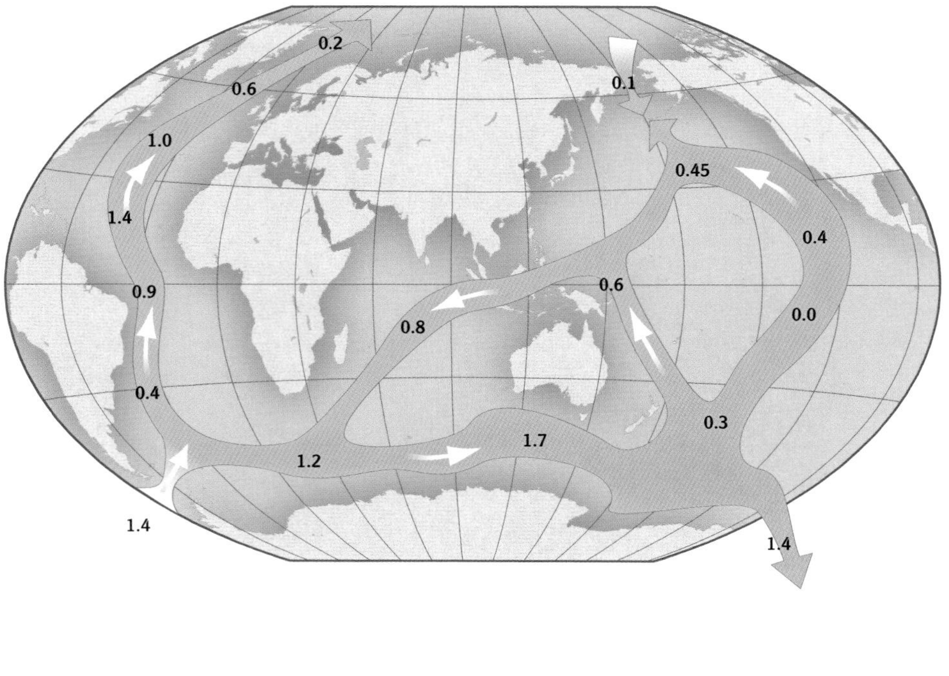

3. OCEAN SURFACE CURRENTS

scale 1 : 200 000 000

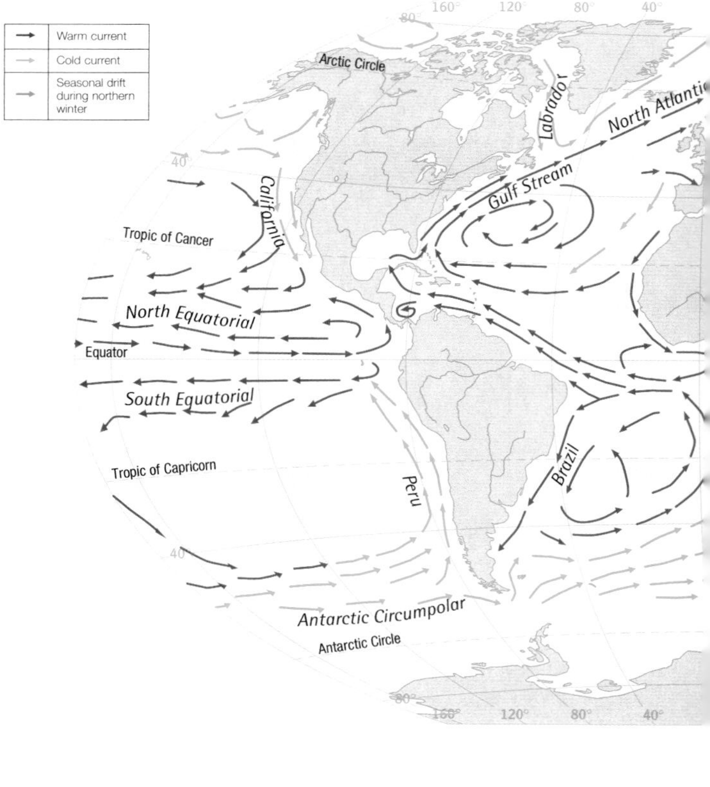

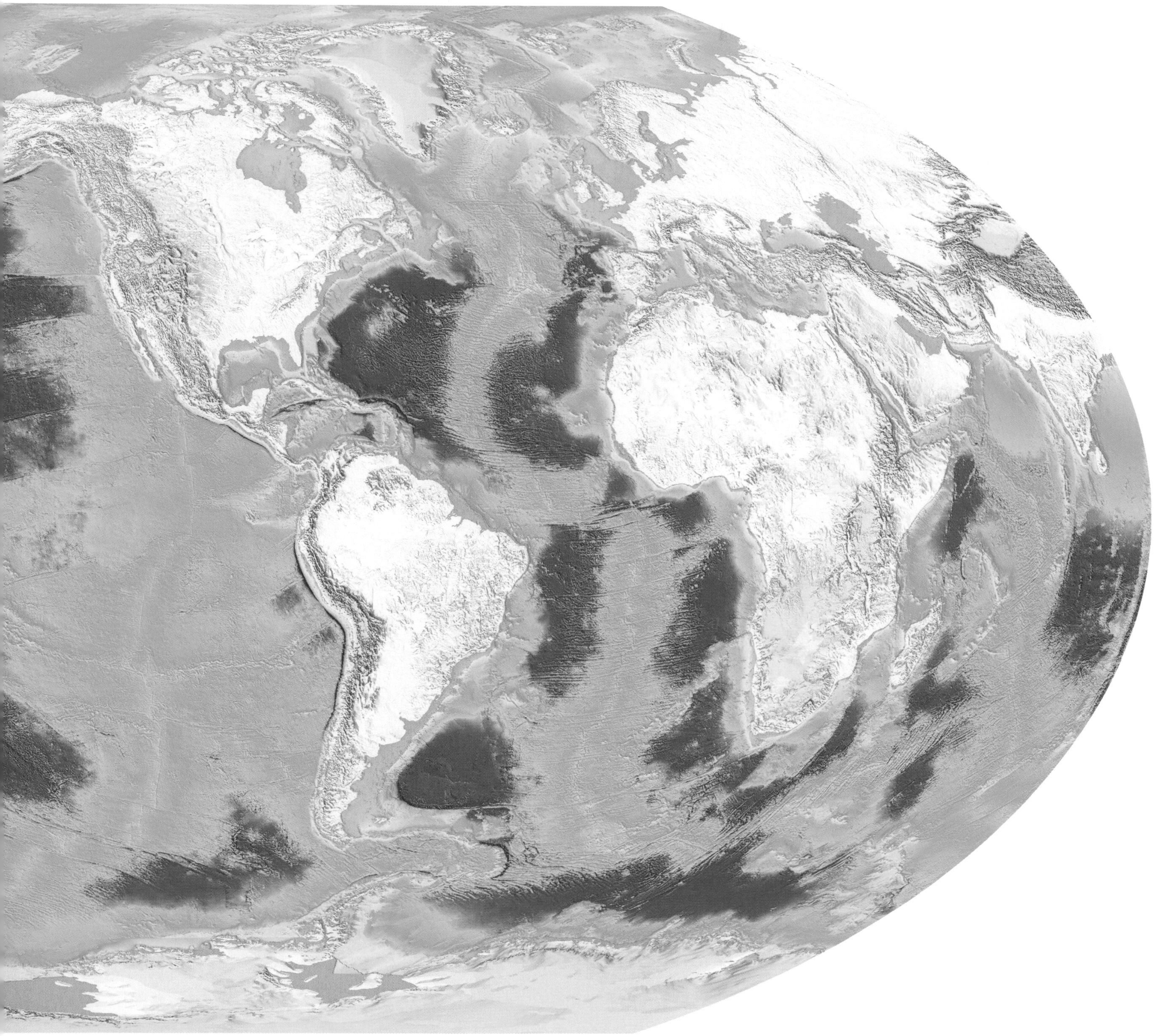

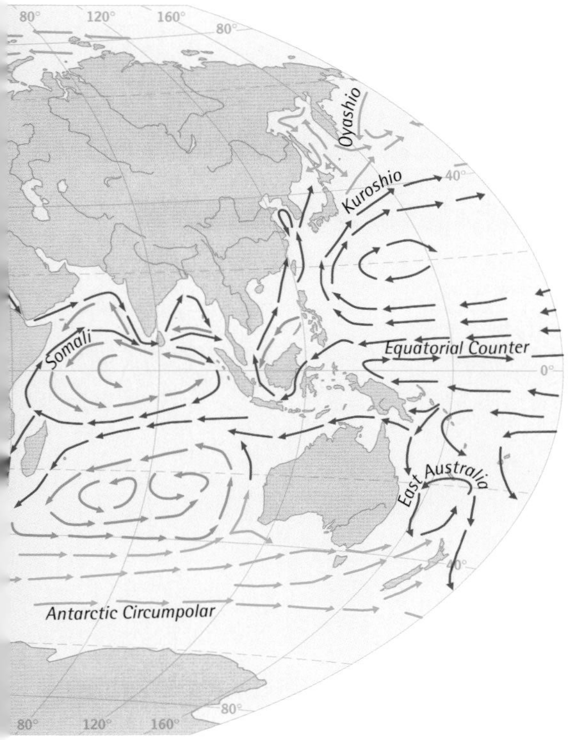

4. SEA SURFACE HEIGHT

From the TOPEX/POSEIDON satellite. Currents flow along the slopes and are strongest where the slopes are greatest.

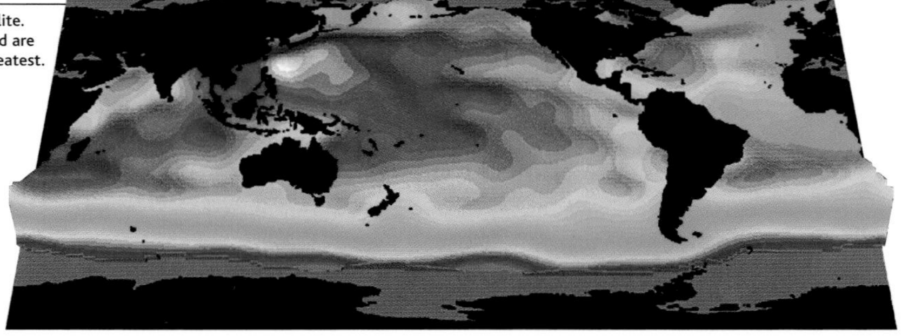

5. CROSS-SECTION OF SALINITY AND THE OCEAN FLOOR

Stretching 12 000 km across the Pacific Ocean from Antarctica (left) to Alaska (right) approximately along longitude 150°W. It shows water modified in the Antarctic descending to the ocean floor and into the ocean interior.

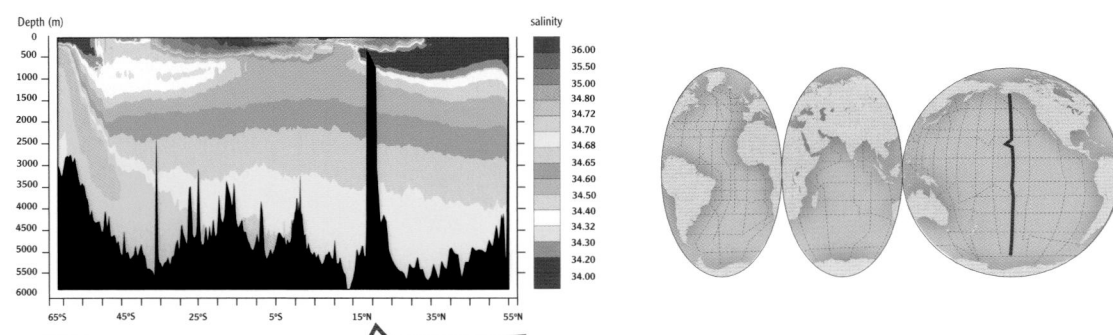

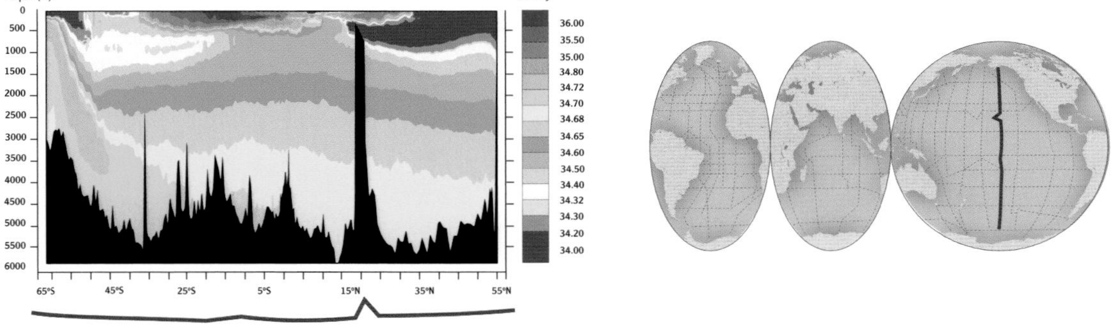

THE CLIMATE SYSTEM

The Earth's climate system is a highly complex interactive system involving the atmosphere, hydrosphere (oceans, lakes and rivers), biosphere (the Earth's living resources), cryosphere (particularly sea ice and polar ice caps) and lithosphere (the Earth's crust and upper mantle). This results in a great variety of climate types (*see 1*). Man's activities are affecting this system, and the monitoring of climate change, and of human influences upon it, is now a major issue.

Greenhouse gases such as carbon dioxide, methane and chlorofluorocarbons (CFCs) act to trap outgoing long-wave radiation, keeping the Earth's surface and lower atmosphere warmer than it would be otherwise. This is the phenomenon usually referred to as the greenhouse effect. Human activity has increased the atmospheric concentration of some of these gases and has therefore contributed to the effect. As a result of this, the world is about 0.6°C warmer than it was a hundred years ago with the three warmest years globally (in decreasing order) being 1998, 2002 and 2001 (*see 2*).

1. MAJOR CLIMATIC REGIONS AND SUB-TYPES

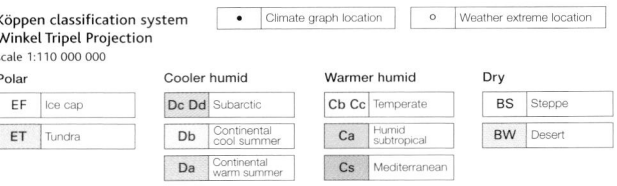

Köppen classification system
Winkel Tripel Projection
scale 1:110 000 000

• Climate graph location
○ Weather extreme location

Polar		Cooler humid		Warmer humid		Dry		Tropical humid	
EF	Ice cap	Dc Dd	Subarctic	Cb Cc	Temperate	BS	Steppe	Aw As	Savanna
ET	Tundra	Db	Continental cool summer	Ca	Humid subtropical	BW	Desert	Af Am	Rain forest
		Da	Continental warm summer	Cs	Mediterranean				

A Rainy climate with no winter: coolest month above 18°C (64.4°F).
B Dry climates; limits are defined by formulae based on rainfall effectiveness:
BS Steppe or semi-arid climate.
BW Desert or arid climate.
*C Rainy climates with mild winters: coolest month above 0°C (32°F), but below 18°C (64.4°F); warmest month above 10°C (50°F).
*D Rainy climates with severe winters: coldest month below 0°C (32°F); warmest month above 10°C (50°F).
E Polar climates with no warm season: warmest month below 10°C (50°F).
ET Tundra climate: warmest month below 10°C (50°F) but above 0°C (32°F).
EF Perpetual frost: all months below 0°C (32°F).

* Modification of Köppen definition

a Warmest month above 22°C (71.6°F).
b Warmest month below 22°C (71.6°F).
c Less than four months over 10°C (50°F).
d As 'c', but with severe cold: coldest month below -38°C (-36.4°F).
f Constantly moist rainfall throughout the year.
*h Warmer dry: all months above 0°C (32°F).
*k Cooler dry: at least one month below 0°C (32°F).
m Monsoon rain: short dry season, but is compensated by heavy rains during rest of the year.
n Frequent fog.
s Dry season in summer.
w Dry season in winter.

Arctic Circle
1. Nome
5. Victoria
Mount Rainier
BWh
Yuma
Tropic of Cancer
Mount Waialeale
BSh
Cb
Aw
Equator
Tropic of Capricorn
Antarctic Circle

CLIMATE GRAPHS

These graphs relate by number, name and colour to the selected stations on the map and present mean temperature and precipitation values for each month. Red bars show average daily maximum and minimum temperatures for each month in degrees centigrade and fahrenheit. Vertical blue columns depict precipitation in millimetres and inches, with the total mean annual precipitation shown under the graph. The altitude of each station above sea level is given in metres and feet.

Precipitation (average monthly total)
Temperature (average daily maximum and minimum)

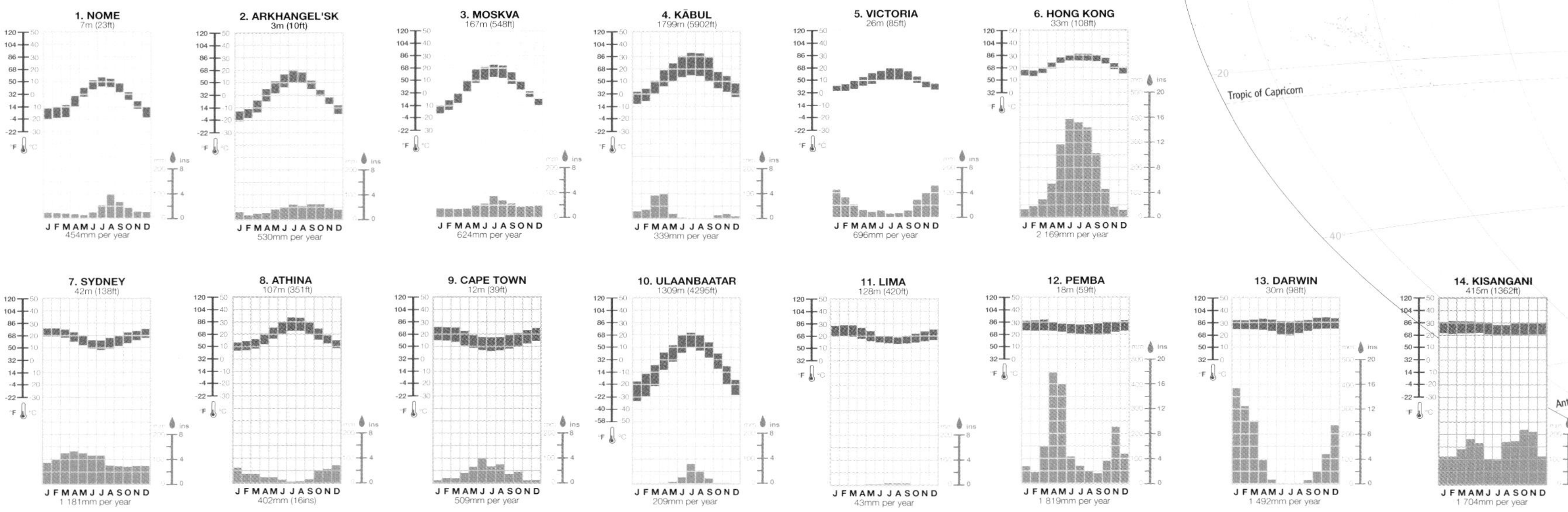
1. NOME 7m (23ft) 454mm per year
2. ARKHANGEL'SK 3m (10ft) 530mm per year
3. MOSKVA 167m (548ft) 624mm per year
4. KĀBUL 1799m (5902ft) 339mm per year
5. VICTORIA 26m (85ft) 696mm per year
6. HONG KONG 33m (108ft) 2 169mm per year
7. SYDNEY 42m (138ft) 1 181mm per year
8. ATHINA 107m (351ft) 402mm (16ins)
9. CAPE TOWN 12m (39ft) 509mm per year
10. ULAANBAATAR 1309m (4295ft) 209mm per year
11. LIMA 128m (420ft) 43mm per year
12. PEMBA 18m (59ft) 1 819mm per year
13. DARWIN 30m (98ft) 1 492mm per year
14. KISANGANI 415m (1362ft) 1 704mm per year
J F M A M J J A S O N D

CLIMATE CHANGE

Future climate change depends on how quickly and to what extent the concentration of greenhouse gases and aerosols in the atmosphere increases. If we assume that no action is taken to limit future greenhouse gas emissions, then a warming during the 21st century of 0.2 to 0.3°C per decade is likely. Such a rate of warming would be greater than anything that has occurred over the last 10 000 years.

The detailed climatic response to the increase in carbon dioxide and other greenhouse gases is predicted using complex mathematical models of the climate. One of the most advanced climate models in the world is that produced by the Hadley Centre of the UK Meteorological Office. This model has produced predictions of climatic change, including changes in temperature and precipitation (*see 3 and 4*). According to this model, some regions of the world will warm more quickly than others and precipitation will increase in some areas and decrease in others. Such changes are likely to have significant impacts on sea-level which could rise by as much as 50 cm over the next century. Human impacts would also be through the effects on water resources, food production and health.

2. COMBINED GLOBAL LAND, AIR AND SEA SURFACE TEMPERATURES 1860–2004

Relative to 1961–1990 average. The purple line is a smoothing of the annual values to suppress sub-decadal time-scale variations.

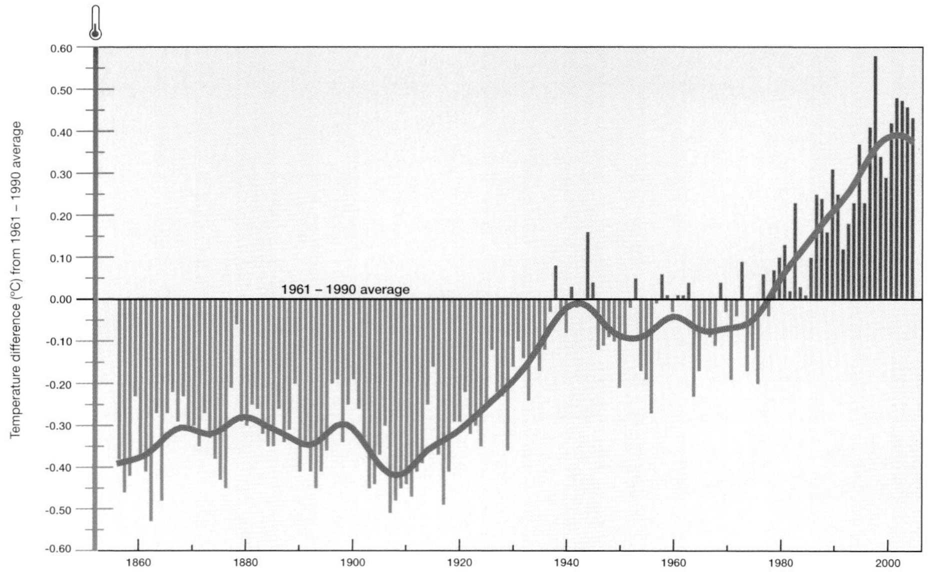
Temperature difference (°C) from 1961 – 1990 average
0.60
0.50
0.40
0.30
0.20
0.10
0.00
-0.10
-0.20
-0.30
-0.40
-0.50
-0.60
1961 – 1990 average
1860
1880
1900
1920
1940
1960
1980
2000

3. TEMPERATURE IN THE 2080s

Predicted annual mean temperature change

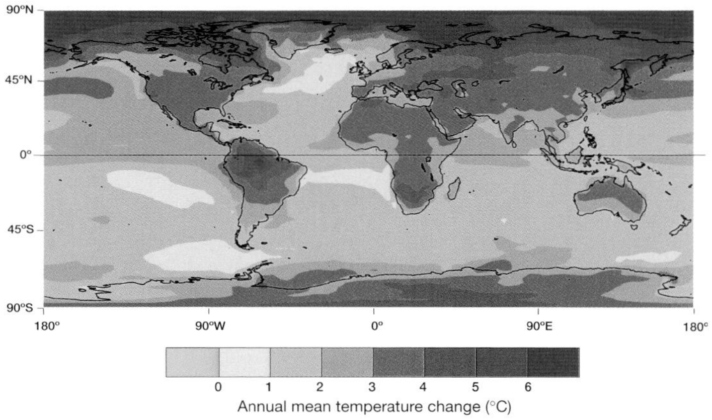
90°N
45°N
0°
45°S
90°S
180°
90°W
0°
90°E
180°
0 1 2 3 4 5 6
Annual mean temperature change (°C)

4. PRECIPITATION IN THE 2080s

Predicted average precipitation change

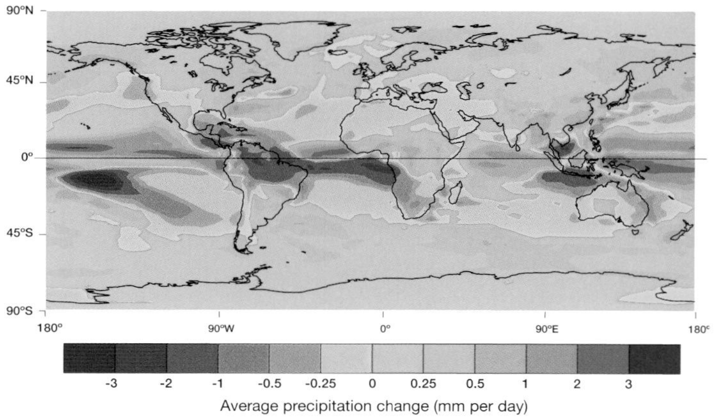
90°N
45°N
0°
45°S
90°S
180°
90°W
0°
90°E
180°
-3 -2 -1 -0.5 -0.25 0 0.25 0.5 1 2 3
Average precipitation change (mm per day)

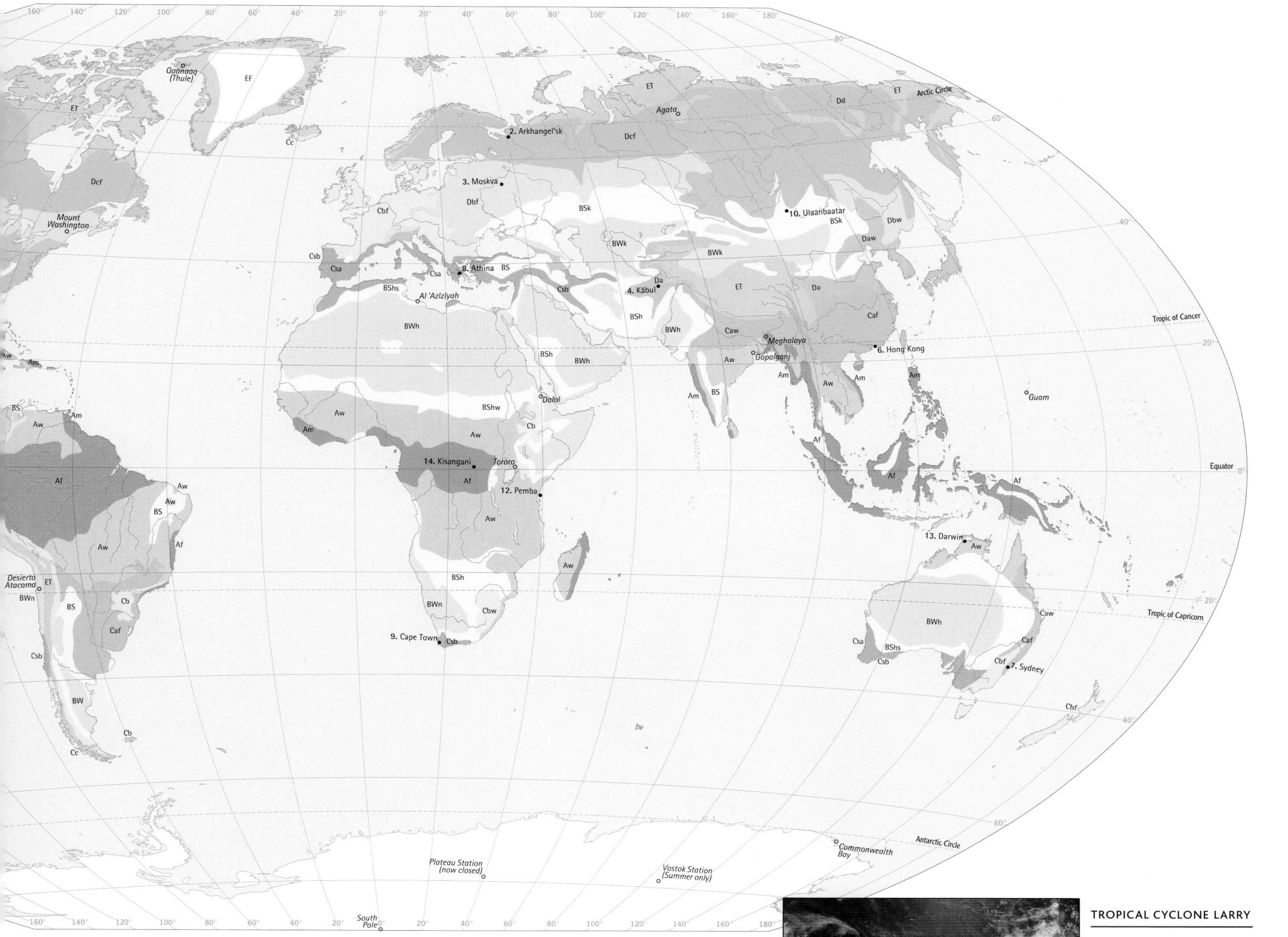
Qaanaaq (Thule)
EF
ET
Dcf
Mount Washington
Cc
Cbf
Csb
Csa
2. Arkhangel'sk
3. Moskva
Dbf
BSk
10. Ulaanbaatar
Dbw
Daw
BWk
8. Athina
BS
Al 'Azīzīyah
BShs
4. Kābul
Da
ET
Caf
BWh
BSh
Caw
Meghalaya
Gopalganj
6. Hong Kong
Aw
Am
Agata
Dd
Arctic Circle
Tropic of Cancer
Guam
Dalol
BShw
Cb
14. Kisangani
Tororo
Af
12. Pemba
Equator
13. Darwin
Desierto Atacama
BWn
Cbw
9. Cape Town
Tropic of Capricorn
7. Sydney
Cbf
BW
Antarctic Circle
Commonwealth Bay
Plateau Station (now closed)
Vostok Station (Summer only)
South Pole

TROPICAL CYCLONE LARRY

Tropical cyclone Larry developed off northeast Australia on 18 March 2006. It reached maximum intensity on 20 March with gusts of wind reaching 290 km per hour, causing considerable damage to coastal towns and sugar cane fields. Most of the Australian banana crop was lost and the indusrty may take years to recover.

TROPICAL STORMS

Tropical storms develop, and have different names, in different parts of the world: hurricanes in the north Atlantic and east Pacific; typhoons in the northwest Pacific; and cyclones in the Indian Ocean region. There are also many local names for these events – those affecting the northern coast of Australia are known colloquially as the 'Willy-willies' (*see 5*).

Tropical storms are among the most powerful and destructive weather systems on Earth. Of the eighty to one hundred which develop annually over the tropical oceans, many make landfall and cause considerable damage to property and loss of life as a result of high winds and heavy rain.

The majority of tropical storms originate in the northwest Pacific, where as typhoons they commonly affect areas from the Philippines through to China and Japan. They are also found as cyclones in the Bay of Bengal, either developing locally or on occasion being the remnants of typhoons which have moved westwards across Thailand. These storms bring heavy rains to eastern India or to the Ganges Delta in Bangladesh. In these places the land is so close to sea level that the rise in water levels has great potential for heavy loss of life.

The conditions required for the development of tropical storms – warm (over 26.5°C) ocean waters to a depth of at least 50 m; pre-existing cyclonic (low pressure) systems; thunderstorm activity; and moist layers of air in the mid-troposphere (around 5 km above the Earth's surface) – mean that most occur in mid- to late-summer in the areas concerned.

5. TRACKS OF TROPICAL STORMS

Wind speeds often over 160 km per hour
scale 1:295 000 000

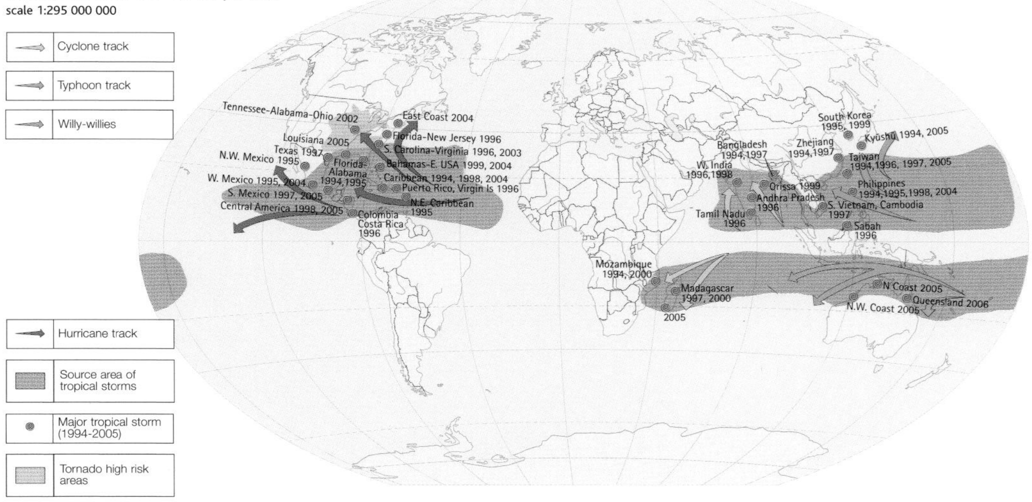
Cyclone track
Typhoon track
Willy-willies
Hurricane track
Source area of tropical storms
Major tropical storm (1994-2005)
Tornado high risk areas
Tennessee-Alabama-Ohio 2002
East Coast 2004
Louisiana 2005
Texas 1997
Florida-New Jersey 1996
S. Carolina-Virginia 1996, 2003
N.W. Mexico 1995
Bahamas-E. USA 1999, 2004
W. Mexico 1995, 2004
Caribbean 1994, 1998, 2004
S. Mexico 1997, 2005
Puerto Rico, Virgin Is 1996
Central America 1998, 2005
N.E. Caribbean 1995
Colombia 1996
Costa Rica
Bangladesh 1994,1997
W. India 1996,1998
Orissa 1999
Andhra Pradesh 1996
Tamil Nadu 1996
Zhejiang 1994,1997
South Korea 1995, 1999
Kyushu 1994, 2005
Taiwan 1994,1996, 1997, 2005
Philippines 1994,1995,1998, 2004
S. Vietnam, Cambodia 1997
Sabah 1996
Mozambique 1994, 2000
Madagascar 1997, 2000
2005
N.Coast 2005
Queensland 2006
N.W. Coast 2005

WORLD WEATHER EXTREMES

Highest shade temperature	57.8°C/136°F Al 'Azīzīyah, Libya (13th September 1922)
Hottest place – Annual mean	34.4°C/93.9°F Dalol, Ethiopia
Driest place – Annual mean	0.1 mm/0.004 inches Desierto de Atacama, Chile
Most sunshine – Annual mean	90% Yuma, Arizona, USA (over 4 000 hours)
Least sunshine	Nil for 182 days each year, South Pole
Lowest screen temperature	89.2°C/-128.6°F Vostok Station, Antarctica (21st July 1983)
Coldest place – Annual mean	-56.6°C/-69.9°F Plateau Station, Antarctica
Wettest place – Annual mean	11 873 mm/467.4 inches Meghalaya, India
Most rainy days	Up to 350 per year Mount Waialeale, Hawaii, USA
Windiest place	322 km per hour/200 miles per hour in gales, Commonwealth Bay, Antarctica
Highest surface wind speed High altitude	372 km per hour/231 miles per hour Mount Washington, New Hampshire, USA (12th April 1934)
Low altitude	333 km per hour/207 miles per hour Qaanaaq (Thule), Greenland 8th March 1972)
Tornado	512 km per hour/318 miles per hour Oklahoma City, Oklahoma, USA (3rd May 1999)
Greatest snowfall	31 102 mm/1 224.5 inches Mount Rainier, Washington, USA (19th February 1971 – 18th February 1972)
Heaviest hailstones	1 kg/2.21 lb Gopalganj, Bangladesh (14th April 1986)
Thunder-days Average	251 days per year Tororo, Uganda
Highest barometric pressure	1 083.8 mb Agata, Siberia, Russian Federation (31st December 1968)
Lowest barometric pressure	870 mb 483 km/300 miles west of Guam, Pacific Ocean (12th October 1979)

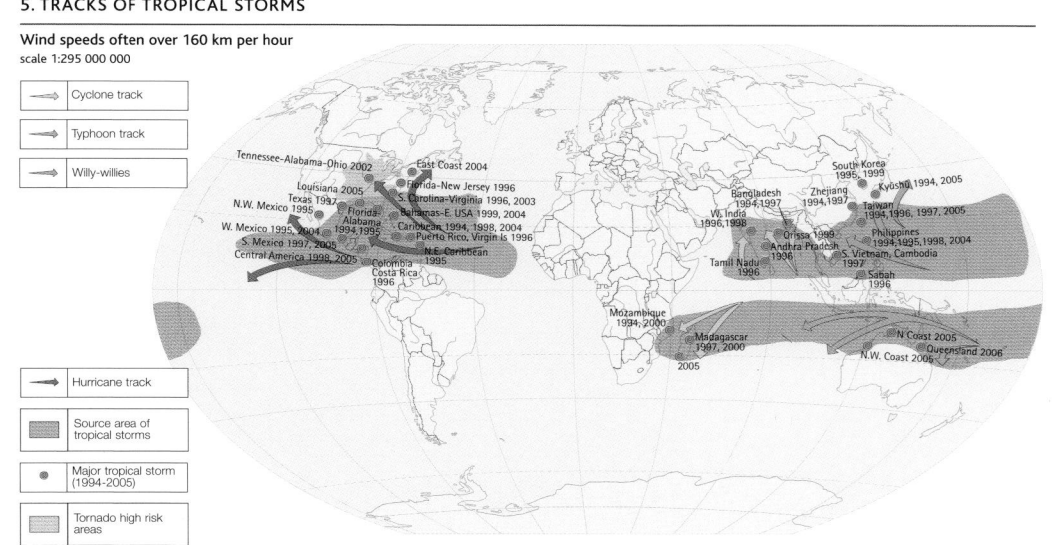

GLOBAL LAND COVER

Many existing global land cover maps show only a general idea of the actual conditions on the Earth's surface. In 1999, a partnership led by the European Commission's Joint Research Centre (JRC) started the preparation of a new database to document the state of the world's land cover at the turn of the Millennium – the Global Land Cover 2000 project (GLC2000). The resulting land cover map as shown here was completed in March 2003 and shows the Earth's land cover as it was in 2000 at a ground resolution of 1km. The high resolution of the imagery used to compile the data set and map allows detailed interpretation of land cover patterns across the world. An additional benefit of holding the data in digital form is the ease with which information on land cover on world and continental scales can be extracted and analysed (*see 2 and 3*).

The scarcity of wetland habitats show just how rare these precious, fragile ecosystems are. Only small, regularly flooded shrublands of Siberia and areas of tree cover liable to inundation in South America and central Africa are really evident on the global scale. In contrast, the concentration of the world's cultivated land in the northern hemisphere is obvious with the cereal belt in North America clearly visible. This contrasts with western Europe where the smaller field sizes and more common mixed farming lead to much of this region being classified as cropland/natural vegetation mosaics. The cereal belts of eastern Europe show the transition once again to extensive agriculture. One of the most striking features are the belts of herbaceous cover and grassland/shrubland south of the Sahara desert. This clearly shows the area which is most at risk from desertification as the Sahara encroaches southward. Humankind's influence on the Earth's land cover is apparent throughout the map. This is evident from the major cities (in red) most prominent in northern India, eastern China and eastern United States of America.

Tropical forest cover is far from the uniform, unbroken swath so often depicted on world vegetation maps. In all areas of the world the tropical forest margins show encroachment of cultivated or grassland in the wake of human activity (*see 4*), although parts of their interiors still remain largely untouched. In the light of such patterns, the global figures for tropical deforestation rates (typically around 0.5–1 per cent per year) become even more alarming. Deforestation is not uniform, so such figures hide far more rapid rates of loss in the forest margins.

2. GLOBAL LAND COVER COMPOSITION

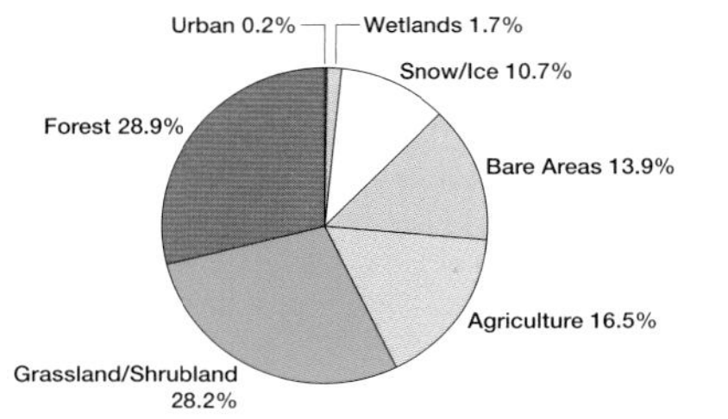

3. CONTINENTAL LAND COVER COMPOSITION

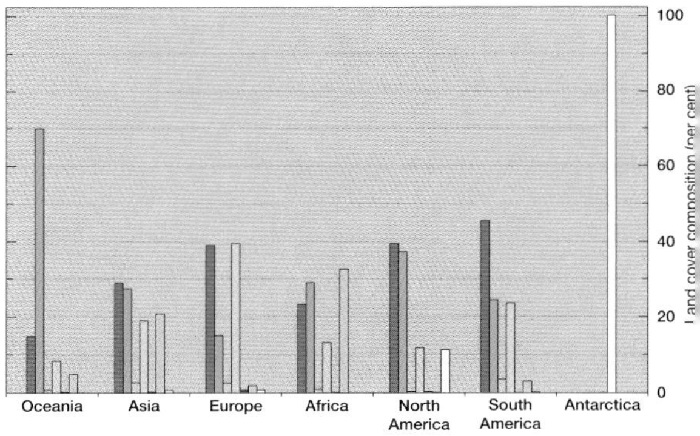

1. WORLD LAND COVER

Winkel Tripel Projection
scale 1:85 000 000

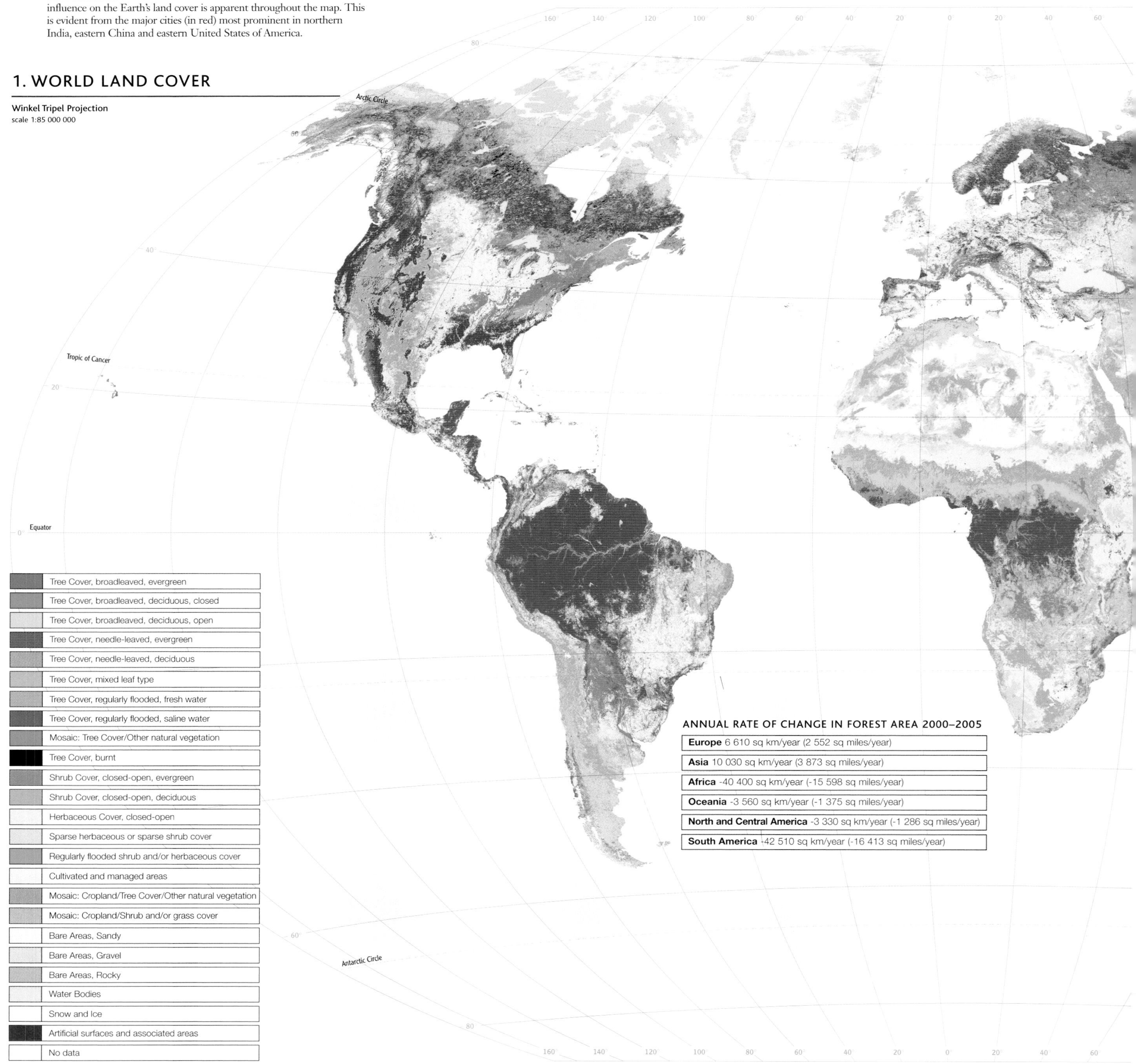

ANNUAL RATE OF CHANGE IN FOREST AREA 2000–2005

Europe 6 610 sq km/year (2 552 sq miles/year)
Asia 10 030 sq km/year (3 873 sq miles/year)
Africa -40 400 sq km/year (-15 598 sq miles/year)
Oceania -3 560 sq km/year (-1 375 sq miles/year)
North and Central America -3 330 sq km/year (-1 286 sq miles/year)
South America -42 510 sq km/year (-16 413 sq miles/year)

LAND COVER GRAPHS - CLASSIFICATION AND KEY

Class description	Global Land Cover class
Forest	Tree Cover, broadleaved, evergreen
	Tree Cover, broadleaved, deciduous, closed
	Tree Cover, broadleaved, deciduous, open
	Tree Cover, needle-leaved, evergreen
	Tree Cover, needle-leaved, deciduous
	Tree Cover, mixed leaf type
	Mosaic: Tree Cover/Other natural vegetation
	Tree Cover, burnt
Grass/Shrubland	Shrub Cover, closed-open, evergreen
	Shrub Cover, closed-open, deciduous
	Herbaceous Cover, closed-open
	Sparse herbaceous or sparse shrub cover
Wetlands	Tree Cover, regularly flooded, fresh water
	Tree Cover, regularly flooded, saline water
	Regularly flooded shrub and/or herbaceous cover
Agriculture	Cultivated and managed areas
	Mosaic: Cropland/Tree Cover/other natural vegetation
	Mosaic: Cropland/Shrub and/or grass cover
Urban	Artificial surfaces and associated areas
Snow/Ice	Water Bodies
	Snow and Ice
Bare Areas	Bare Areas

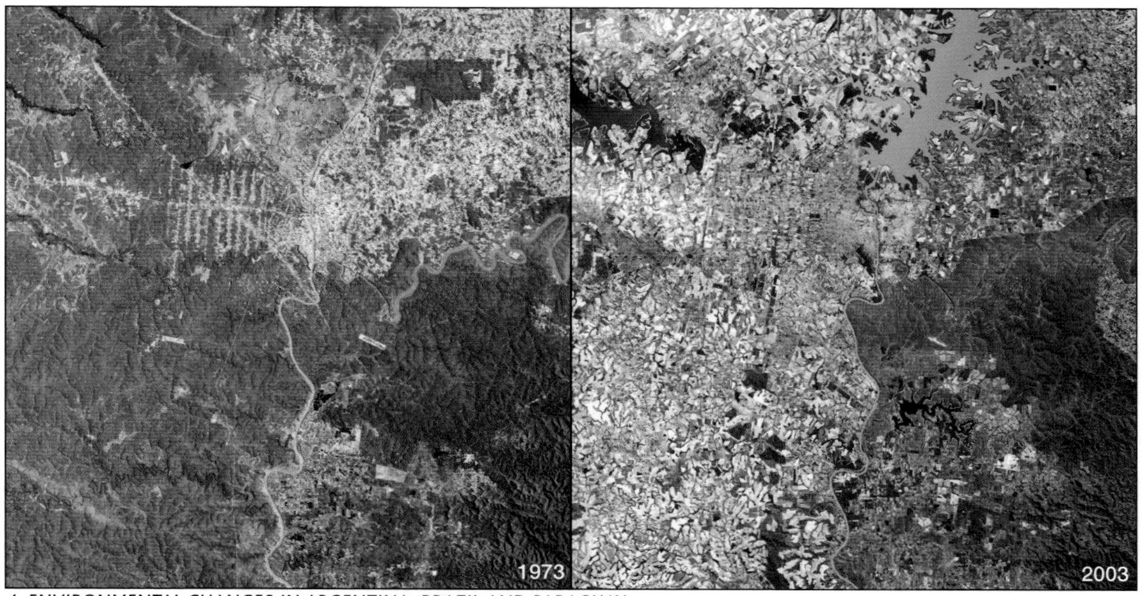
1973
2003

4. ENVIRONMENTAL CHANGES IN ARGENTINA, BRAZIL AND PARAGUAY

These two Landsat satellite images centre on the confluence of the Iguaçu and Paraná rivers in South America. Over the thirty-year time gap the Itaipu Dam was completed and the tremendous development in the area makes the Iguaçu National Park stand out clearly as an area where the native forest is being preserved.

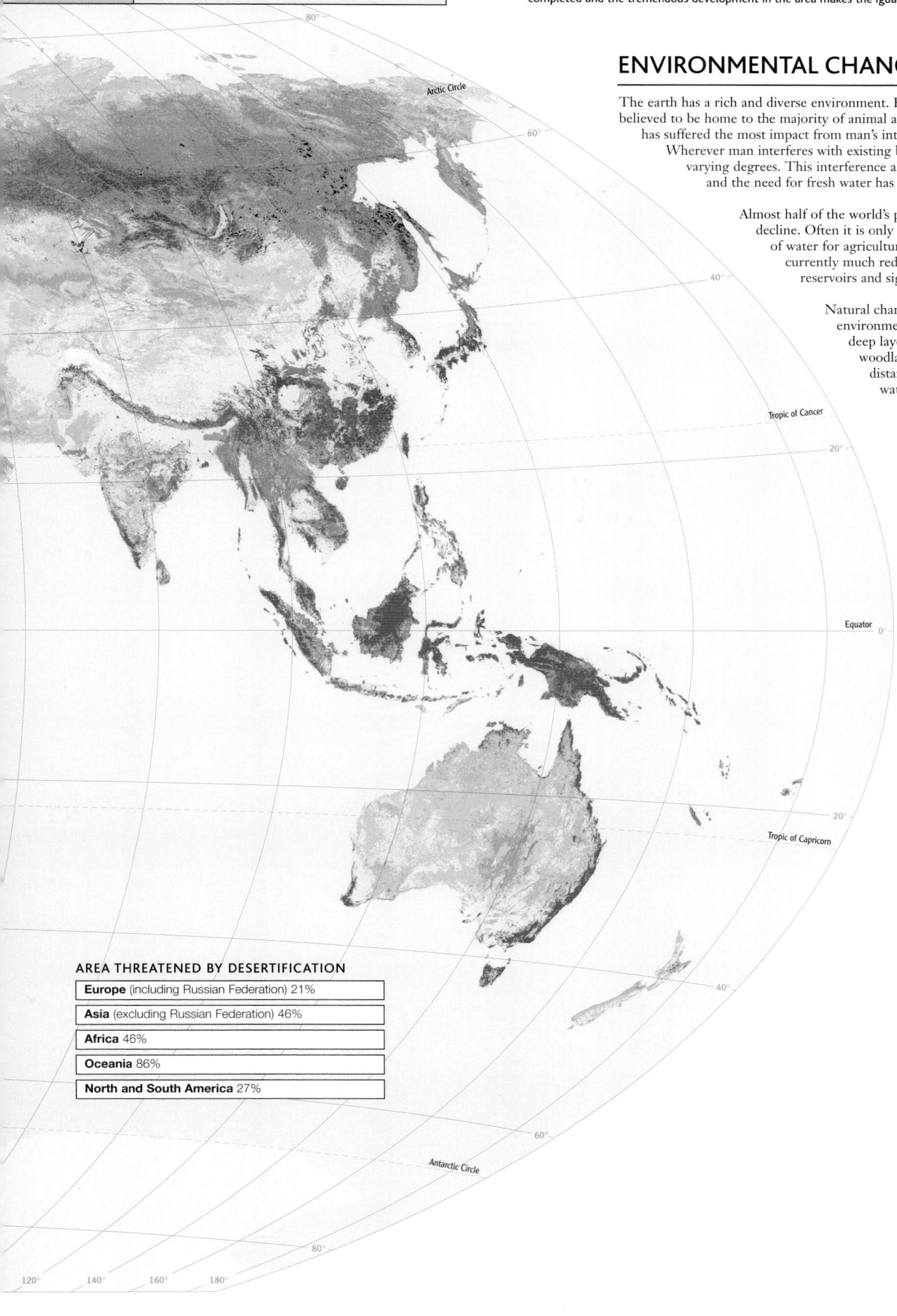
80°
Arctic Circle
60°
40°
Tropic of Cancer
20°
Equator
0°
20°
Tropic of Capricorn
40°
60°
Antarctic Circle
80°
120°
140°
160°
180°

AREA THREATENED BY DESERTIFICATION

Europe (including Russian Federation) 21%

Asia (excluding Russian Federation) 46%

Africa 46%

Oceania 86%

North and South America 27%

ENVIRONMENTAL CHANGE AND CONSERVATION

The earth has a rich and diverse environment. Forests and woodland form the predominant natural land cover with tropical rain forests believed to be home to the majority of animal and plant species. Grassland and scrub tend to have a lower natural species diversity but has suffered the most impact from man's intervention through conversion to agriculture, burning and the introduction of livestock. Wherever man interferes with existing biological and environmental processes, degradation of that environment occurs, to varying degrees. This interference also affects inland water and oceans where pollution, over-exploitation of marine resources and the need for fresh water has had major consequences for land and sea environments.

Almost half of the world's post-glacial forest has been cleared or degraded and old-growth forest continues to decline. Often it is only in protected areas (*see 4*) that the natural forest remains untouched. In other areas the use of water for agriculture can upset the natural cycle of events causing significant changes. Lake Chad is currently much reduced in size from thirty years ago (*see 5*). In other places man has built dams, created reservoirs and significantly changed the landscape by irrigation.

Natural changes to the planet's equilibrium can occur which can impact on the surrounding environment and on man's use of the land. For example, the eruption of Mt St Helens in 1980 left a deep layer of ash and pumice covering the area up to eight kilometres away as well as felling woodland as a result of the blast, leaving a barren wasteland. Dust storms can travel great distances, polluting the atmosphere while the failure of seasonal rains or the sudden excess of water can devastate a year's food resources for man and nature.

UNESCO adopted an international treaty in 1972 to recognize sites, both cultural and natural, of universal significance. Such places are unique, irreplaceable sites of inspiration of man's achievement or nature's creation. Presently there are 788 official sites, 154 natural and 23 mixed, but 35 of the 788 are cited as 'in danger' either due to civil conflicts or war, such as those in the Democratic Republic of the Congo or through pressure from agriculture and logging, as in Honduras.

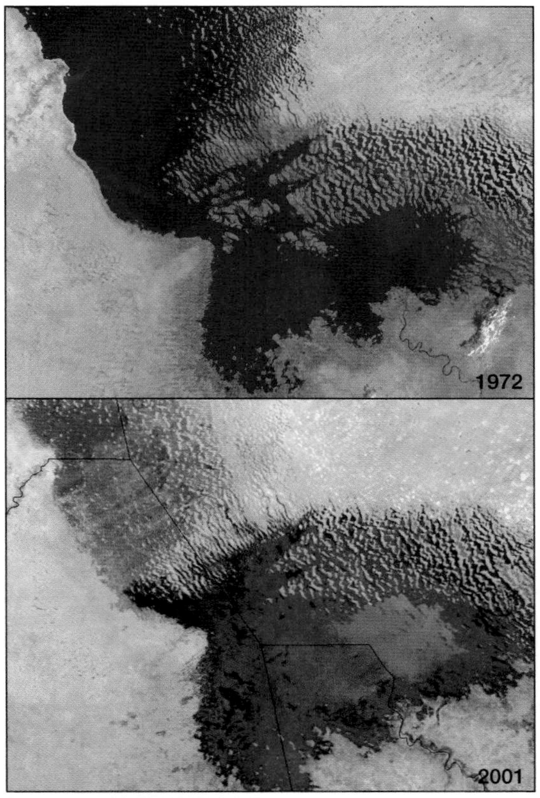
1972
2001

5. SHRINKING OF LAKE CHAD

Lake Chad is very shallow and the lake level has varied tremendously over time. During the past thirty-five years the climate has been dry and this coincided with increased human demand for water. The lake has shrunk dramatically as a result.

POPULATION DISTRIBUTION AND GROWTH

People are distributed very unevenly over the face of the planet. As shown on the main map *(see 1)*, over a quarter of the land area is uninhabited or has extremely low population density. Approximately a quarter of the land area is occupied at densities of 25 or more persons per square km, with the three largest concentrations of east Asia, the Indian subcontinent and Europe accounting for over half the world total. China and India dominate the scene, together accounting for nearly two-fifths of world population *(see 2)*.

Over the past half century world population has been growing faster than it has ever done before. Whereas world population did not pass the one billion mark until 1804 and took another 123 years to reach two billion in 1927, it then added the third billion in 33 years, the fourth in 14 years and the fifth in 13 years, with the 6 billion mark being passed only 12 years after this in 1999. It is expected that another three billion people will have been added to the world's population by 2050 *(see 3)*. Recent projections looking even further into the future estimate that the total will have risen to around 9 billion by 2300.

Population growth since 1950 has been spread very unevenly between the continents. While overall numbers have been growing extremely rapidly since 1950, a massive 89 per cent increase has taken place in the less developed regions, especially southern and eastern Asia, while Europe's population is now stationary and ageing rapidly. Africa was the second largest contributor and represents by far the highest growth rate of all the continents. The latest trends in population growth at country level *(see 4)* emphasize the continuing contrast between the more and less developed regions. Annual growth rates of 1.1 per cent or more are very common in Latin America, Africa and the southern half of Asia. A number of countries have rates in excess of 2.8 per cent, which if continued would lead to the doubling of their populations in 25 years or less.

2. TOP TEN COUNTRIES BY POPULATION AND POPULATION DENSITY

TOTAL POPULATION 2005	COUNTRY	RANK	COUNTRY	POPULATION DENSITY 2005 per sq mile	per sq km
1 323 345 000	China	1	Monaco	35 000	17 500
1 103 371 000	India	2	Singapore	17 514	6 770
298 213 000	USA	3	Malta	3 295	1 272
222 781 000	Indonesia	4	Maldives	2 861	1 104
186 405 000	Brazil	5	Vatican City	2 760	1 104
157 935 000	Pakistan	6	Bahrain	2 723	1 052
143 202 000	Russian Federation	7	Bangladesh	2 551	985
141 822 000	Bangladesh	8	Nauru	1 750	667
131 530 000	Nigeria	9	Taiwan	1 636	632
128 085 000	Japan	10	Barbados	1 627	628

3. WORLD POPULATION GROWTH BY CONTINENT 1750–2050

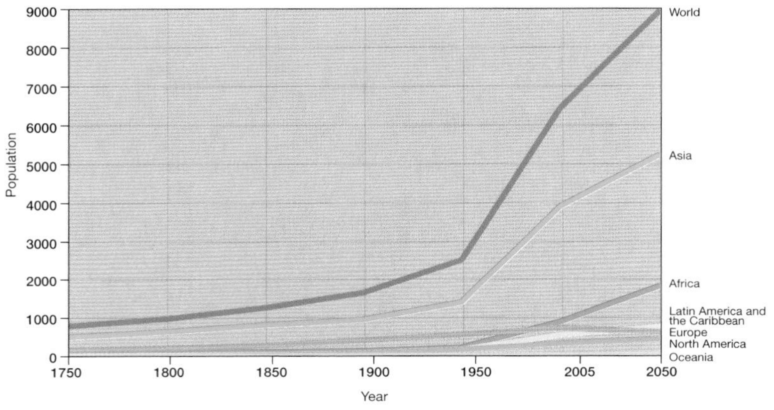

1. WORLD POPULATION DISTRIBUTION

Winkel Tripel Projection
scale 1:93 000 000

Population density

4. POPULATION CHANGE 2000–2005

Average annual rate of population change (per cent) and the top ten contributors to world population growth (net annual addition).
scale 1:255 000 000

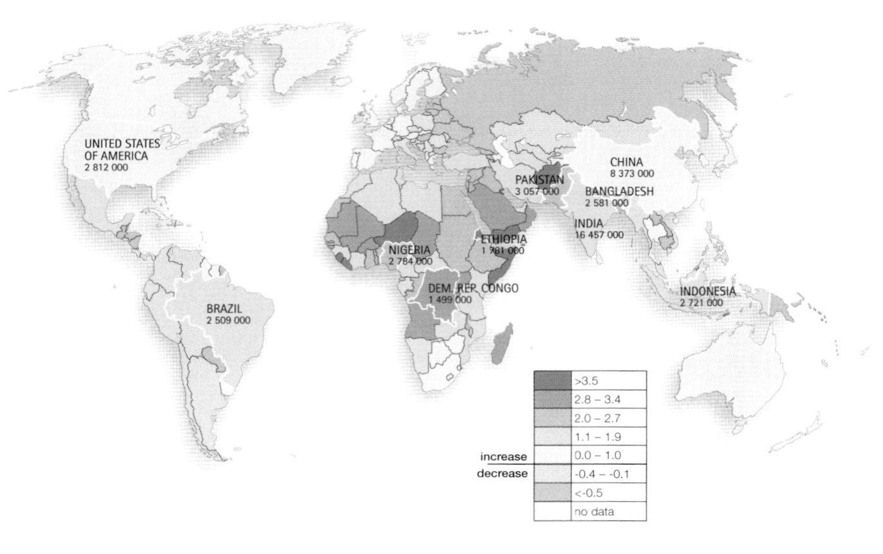

5. KEY POPULATION STATISTICS FOR MAJOR REGIONS

	Population 2005 (millions)	Growth (per cent)	Infant mortality rate	Total fertility rate	Life expectancy (years)	% aged 60 and over 2005	2050
World	6 453	1.21	57	2.65	65.4	10	22
More developed regions[1]	1 209	0.30	8	1.56	75.6	20	32
Less developed regions[2]	5 243	1.43	62	2.9	63.4	8	20
Africa	887	2.18	94	4.97	49.1	5	10
Asia	3 917	1.21	54	2.47	67.3	9	24
Europe[3]	725	0.00	9	1.4	73.7	21	35
Latin America and the Caribbean[4]	558	1.42	26	2.55	71.5	9	24
North America	332	0.97	7	1.99	77.6	17	27
Oceania	33	1.32	29	2.32	74	14	25

Except for population (2005), and % aged 60 and over figures, the data are annual averages projected for the period 2000–2005.

1. Europe, North America, Australia, New Zealand and Japan.
2. Africa, Asia (excluding Japan), Latin America and the Caribbean, and Oceania (excluding Australia and New Zealand).
3. Includes Russian Federation.
4. South America, Central America (including Mexico) and all Carribean Islands.

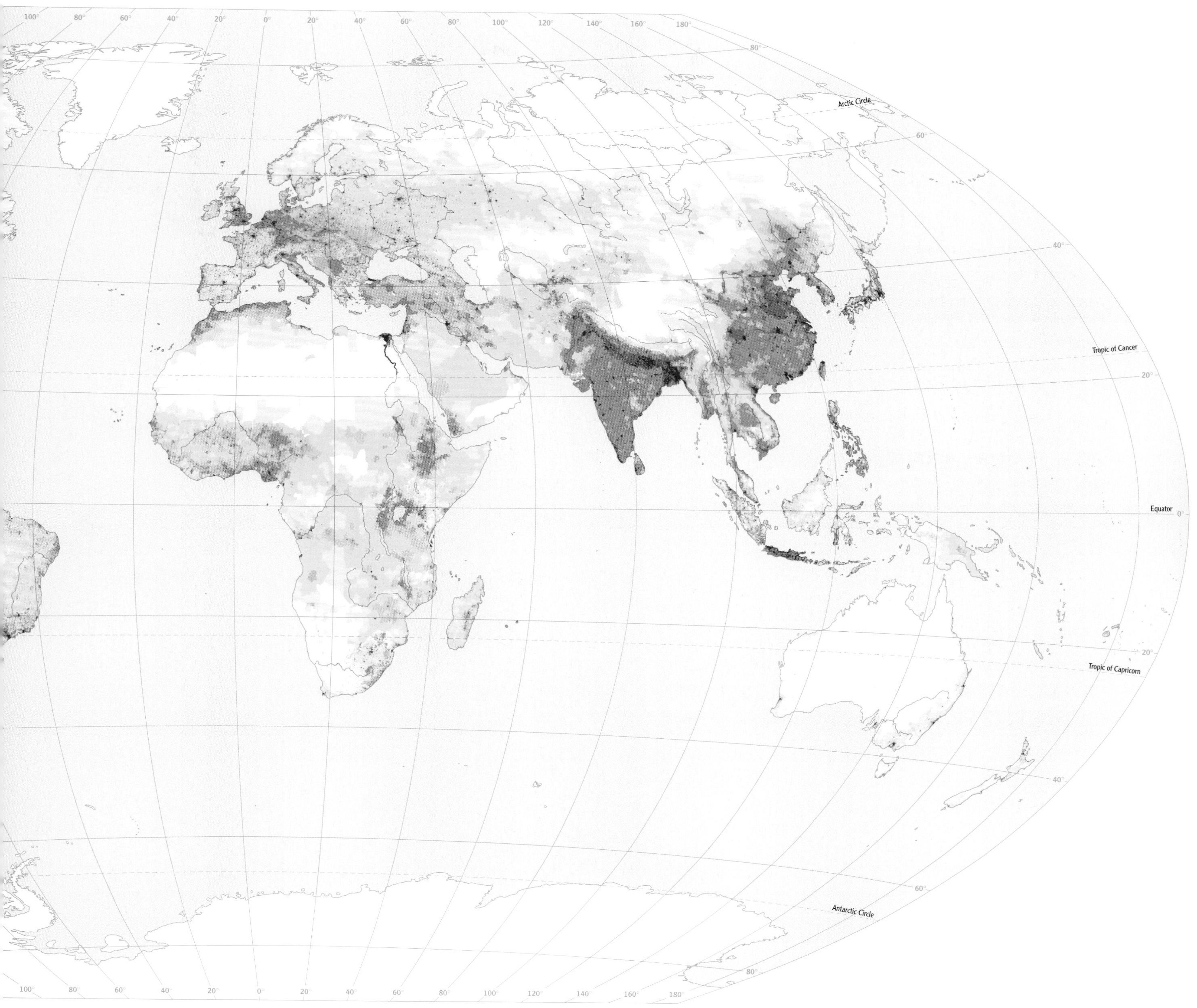
Arctic Circle
Tropic of Cancer
Equator
Tropic of Capricorn
Antarctic Circle

DEMOGRAPHIC TRANSITION

Behind patterns of population growth lies the 'demographic transition' process, where countries pass through a phase of falling death rates and then a phase of falling fertility. Most parts of the world have passed through the first phase, with the average life expectancy of 63.4 years in the less developed world now not far behind that of 75.6 years in the more developed regions *(see 5)*. Even so, infant mortality – a very good indicator of human development levels – remains a major challenge in the less developed regions *(see 6)*. Here, an average of sixty-two out of every one thousand babies die before their first birthday, compared to only eight out of every one thousand in the more developed regions. Sub-Saharan Africa started this transitional phase later than most other parts of the world and has so far seen life expectancy rise to only 45.7 years, with progress being hampered by continuing high levels of infant mortality and by rising numbers of AIDS-related deaths.

Reductions in fertility rate *(see 7)* hold the key to the successful completion of the transition and the future stabilization of population growth. Much of the more developed world is well advanced in this process. In particular, Europe's total fertility rate (broadly the average number of babies born to each woman) is now down to 1.4 – well below the 'replacement rate' of 2.1 needed to give a constant population in the long term. Predictions indicate that there will be a major increase in the number of older people throughout the world especially in less developed regions *(see 5)*. Europe's proportion of people aged 60 and over will rise from one-fifth to one-third whereas Latin America's will almost treble from 9 to 24 per cent.

6. INFANT MORTALITY RATE 2000–2005

Deaths of infants less than one year old per 1000 live births.
scale 1:315 000 000

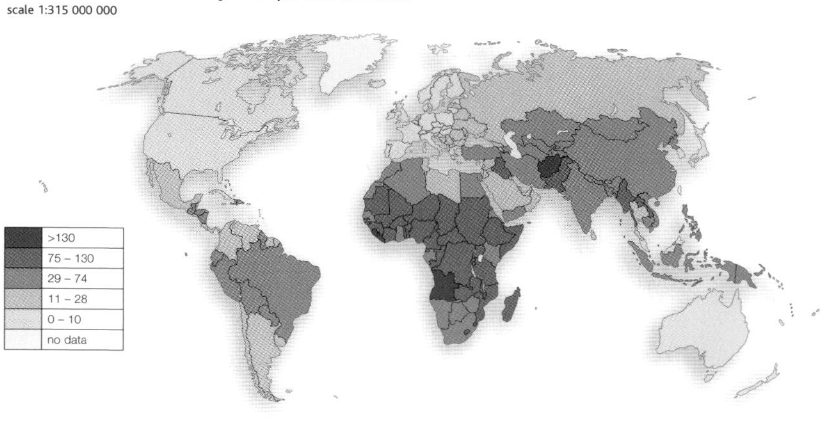
>130
75 – 130
29 – 74
11 – 28
0 – 10
no data

7. TOTAL FERTILITY RATE 2000–2005

Estimate of the number of children a woman will bear during her child-bearing years.
scale 1:315 000 000

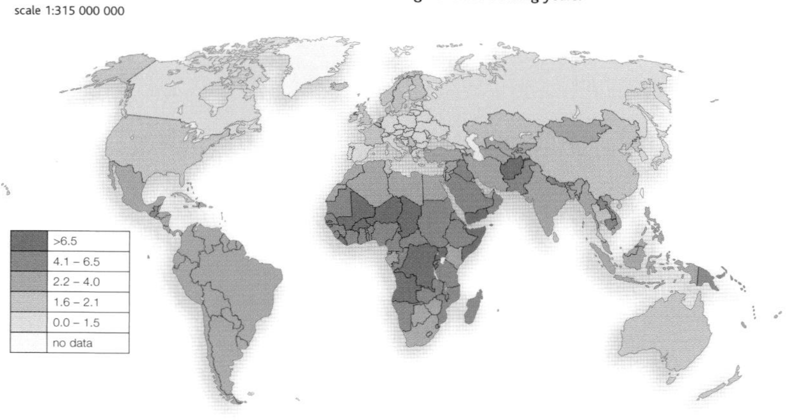
>6.5
4.1 – 6.5
2.2 – 4.0
1.6 – 2.1
0.0 – 1.5
no data

TOWARDS AN URBANIZED WORLD

World population is urbanizing rapidly but the current level of urbanization – the proportion of the population living in urban conditions – varies greatly across the world, as does its rate of increase. In the hundred years up to 1950 the greatest changes in urban population patterns took place in Europe and North America. Relatively few large cities developed elsewhere and most of these were in coastal locations with good trading connections with the imperial and industrial nations. This legacy is still highly visible on the world map of major cities (*see 1*). The main feature of the past half century has been the massive growth in the numbers of urban dwellers in the less developed regions. This process is still accelerating, posing an even greater logistical challenge during the next few decades than it did in the closing decades of the twentieth century.

The year 2007 is likely to be a momentous point in world history, when for the first time urban dwellers will outnumber those living in traditionally rural areas, according to UN projections. The annual rise in the percentage of the world's population living in cities has been accelerating steadily since the 1970s and will be running at unprecedentedly high levels until at least 2030. As a result, by then, 60.8 per cent of the world's population will be urbanites compared to 37.3 per cent in 1975 and 49.2 per cent in 2005 (*see 2*). In absolute terms, the global urban population more than doubled between 1970 and 2000 and is expected to grow by a further 2.1 billion by 2030 (*see 3*).

2. LEVEL OF URBANIZATION BY MAJOR REGION 1975–2030

Urban population as a percentage of total population

	1975	2005	2030
World	37.3	49.2	60.8
More developed regions[1]	67.2	74.9	81.7
Less developed regions[2]	26.9	43.2	57.1
Africa	25.3	39.7	53.5
Asia	24.0	39.9	54.5
Europe[3]	66.0	73.3	79.6
Latin America and the Caribbean[4]	61.2	77.6	84.6
North America	73.8	80.8	86.9
Oceania	71.7	73.3	74.9

1. Europe, North America, Australia, New Zealand and Japan.
2. Africa, Asia (excluding Japan), Latin America and the Caribbean, and Oceania (excluding Australia and New Zealand).
3. Includes Russian Federation.
4. South America, Central America (including Mexico) and all Caribbean Islands.

1. THE WORLD'S MAJOR CITIES

Urban agglomerations with over 1 million inhabitants
Winkel Tripel Projection
scale 1:111 000 000

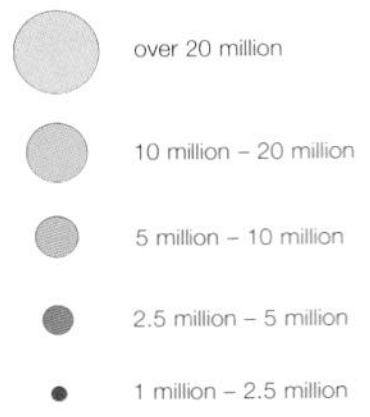

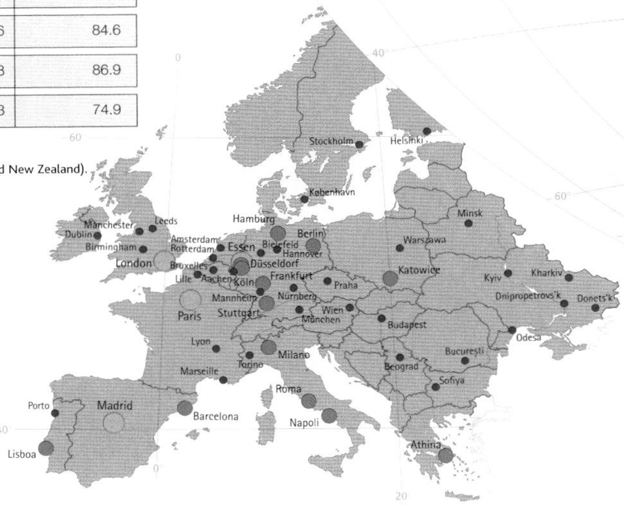

3. TOTAL URBAN POPULATION OF MAJOR REGIONS 1950–2030

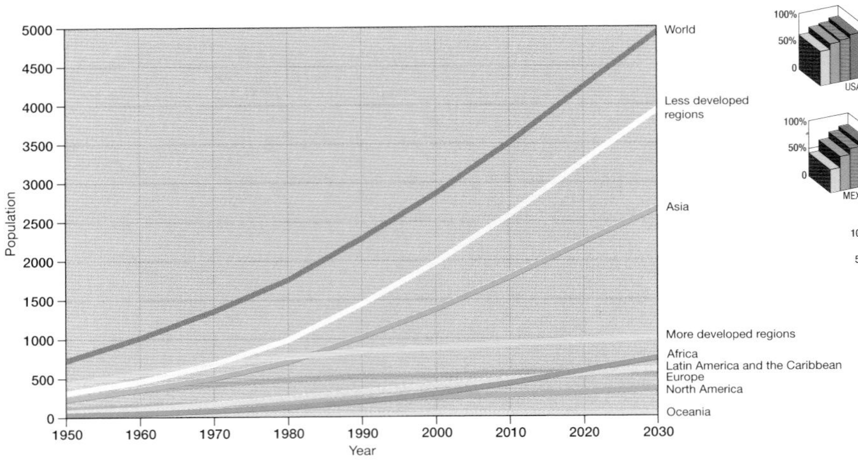

4. LEVEL OF URBANIZATION

Percentage of total population living in urban areas 2005 and growth in urbanization 1950–2025 (selected countries)
scale 1:280 000 000

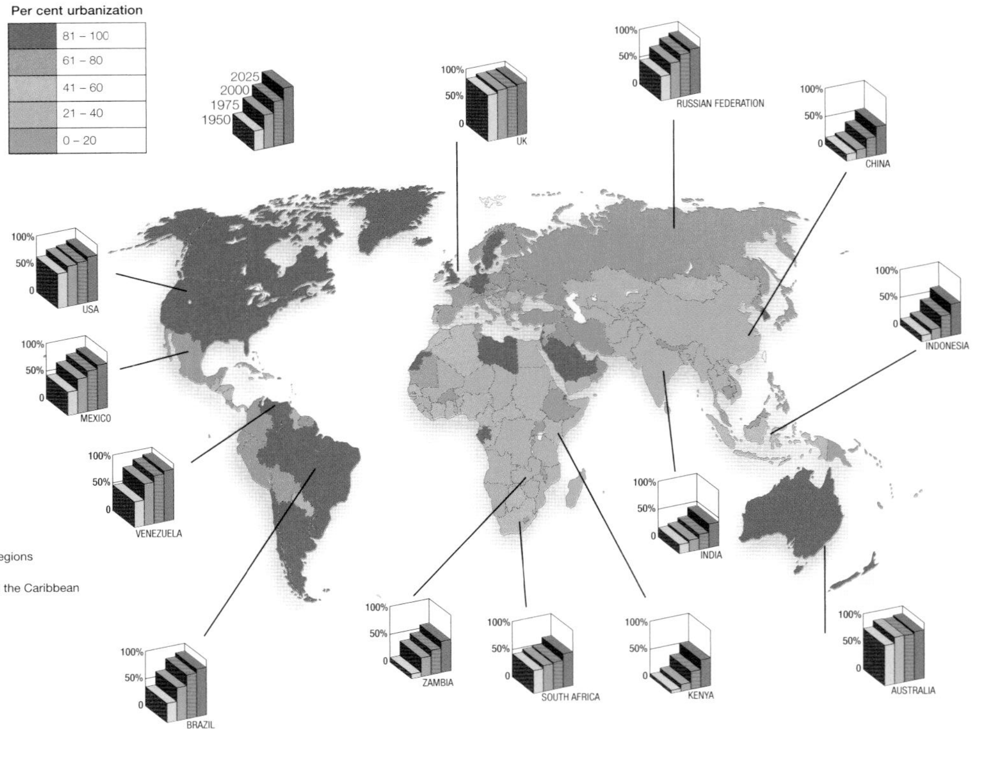

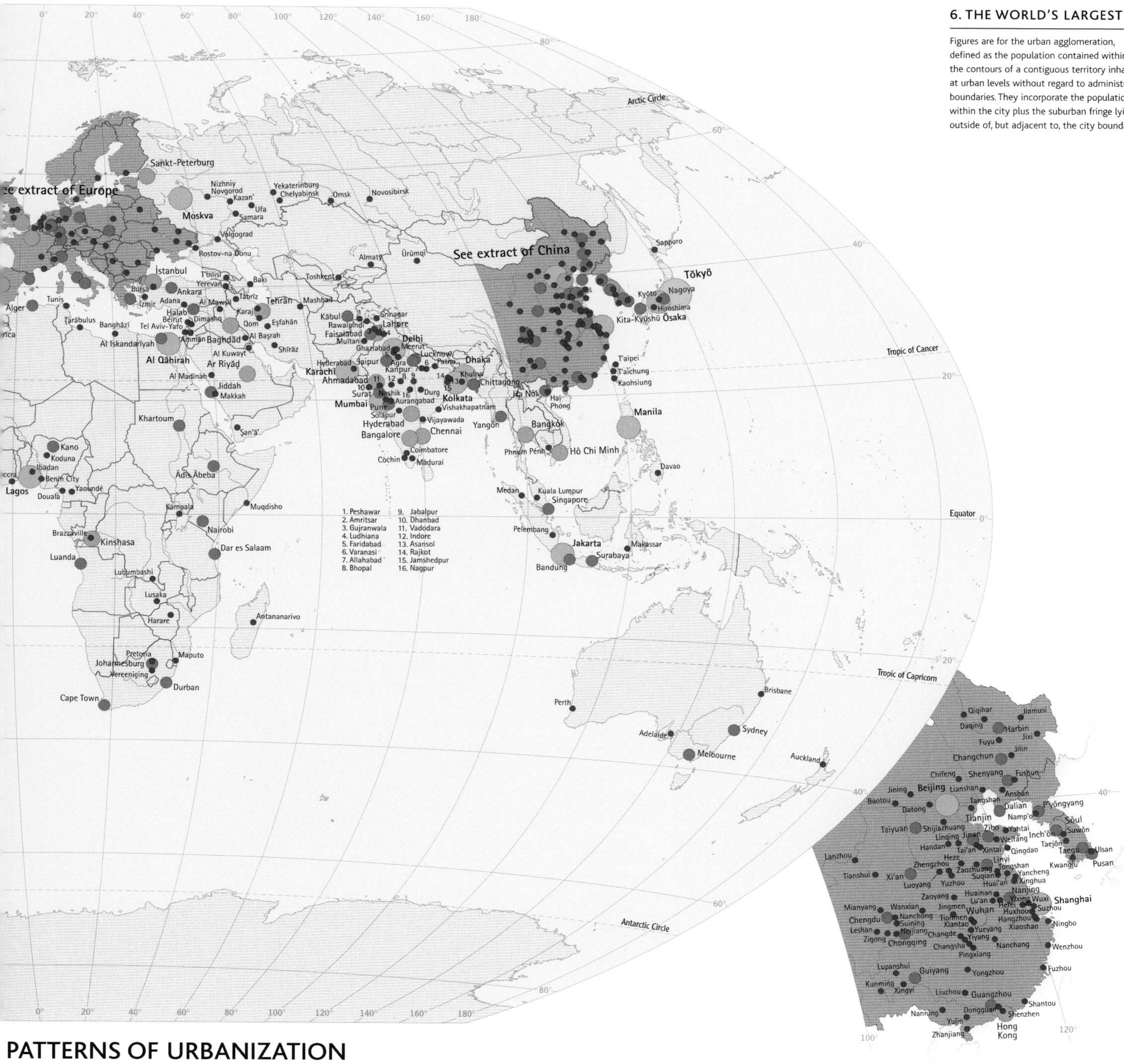

PATTERNS OF URBANIZATION

There is a broad contrast in the levels of urbanization between the more and less developed regions (*see 4*). In the more developed regions as a whole, three-quarters of the population now live in urban places. Excluding the smallest countries, levels range from 97 per cent for Belgium to under 50 per cent for Albania, Bosnia, Moldova and Slovenia. Many countries have seen very little increase in their level of urbanization over several decades, with some reporting renewed population growth in rural areas. Only 42.1 per cent of the population in the less developed regions are urbanites, but this represents a big jump from the 26.9 per cent figure for 1975. Africa and Asia both currently average less than this, but will be seeing the greatest changes in the future, with their urban proportions likely to pass the 50 per cent mark by 2025. Between 2000 and 2030, Africa and Asia are expected to account for 5 out of every 6 extra urbanites or around 453 and 1 300 million people in absolute terms.

Alongside the rise in the world's urban population has occurred a massive increase in the number and size of cities, especially of the very large cities or 'megacities'. In 1950, New York was the only agglomeration with over 10 million inhabitants, but the number of such cities had grown to six by 1980 and to twenty-one by 2000. There are expected to be twenty-five by 2015, according to United Nations figures (*see 5*). This increase has been principally an Asian phenomenon, as the additional four megacities are all in Asia. By 2000 North America's tally had risen to only two, and Latin America possessed four, but Asia had acquired twelve. This marked growth in the number of megacities in recent years is due to a combination of in-migration and natural increase, together with the physical outward expansion of their built-up areas and the incorporation of nearby settlements.

5. 10 MILLION CITIES

Dates by which cities attain 10 million population 1950–2015

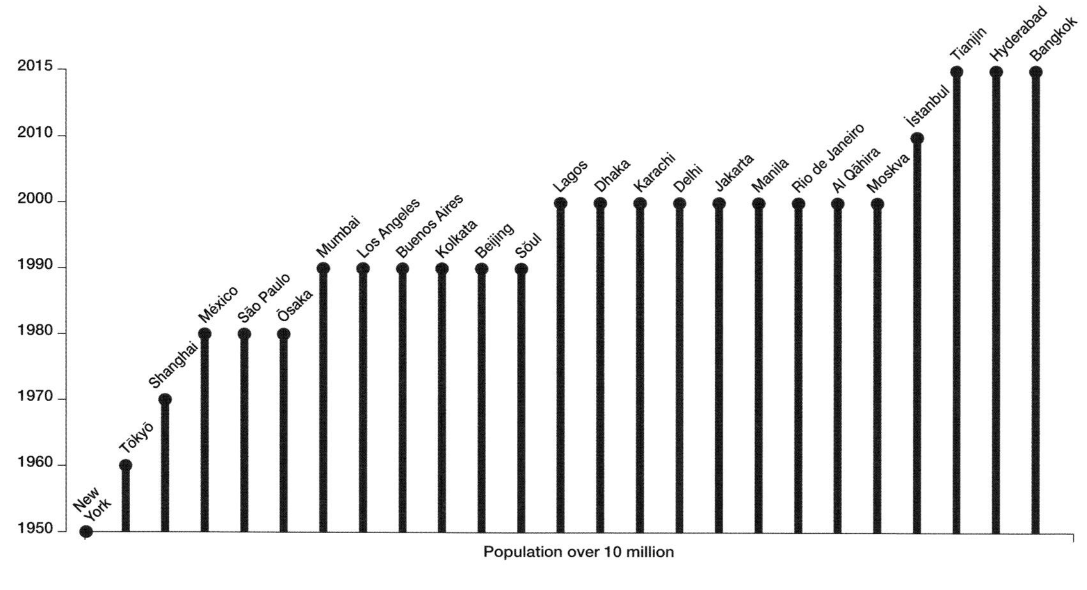

6. THE WORLD'S LARGEST CITIES 2005

Figures are for the urban agglomeration, defined as the population contained within the contours of a contiguous territory inhabited at urban levels without regard to administrative boundaries. They incorporate the population within the city plus the suburban fringe lying outside of, but adjacent to, the city boundaries.

City	Population
Cities>10 000 000 inhabitants	
Tōkyō Japan	35 327 000
México Mexico	19 013 000
New York USA	18 498 000
Mumbai India	18 336 000
São Paulo Brazil	18 333 000
Delhi India	15 334 000
Kolkata India	14 299 000
Buenos Aires Argentina	13 349 000
Jakarta Indonesia	13 194 000
Shanghai China	12 665 000
Dhaka Bangladesh	12 560 000
Los Angeles USA	12 146 000
Karachi Pakistan	11 819 000
Rio de Janeiro Brazil	11 469 000
Ōsaka Japan	11 286 000
Al Qāhirah Egypt	11 146 000
Lagos Nigeria	11 135 000
Beijing China	10 849 000
Manila Philippines	10 677 000
Moskva Russian Federation	10 672 000
Cities 5 000 000 – 10 000 000 inhabitants	
Paris France	9 854 000
İstanbul Turkey	9 760 000
Sŏul South Korea	9 592 000
Tianjin China	9 346 000
Chicago USA	8 711 000
Lima Peru	8 180 000
London United Kingdom	7 615 000
Bogotá Colombia	7 594 000
Tehrān Iran	7 352 000
Hong Kong China	7 182 000
Chennai India	6 915 000
Bangkok Thailand	6 604 000
Essen Germany	6 566 000
Bangalore India	6 532 000
LahorePakistan	6 373 000
Hyderabad India	6 145 000
Wuhan China	6 003 000
Baghdād Iraq	5 910 000
Kinshasa Democratic Rep. of the Congo	5 717 000
Santiago Chile	5 623 000
Ar Riyāḍ Saudi Arabia	5 514 000
Miami USA	5 380 000
Philadelphia USA	5 325 000
Sankt-Peterburg Russian Federation	5 315 000
Belo Horizonte Brazil	5 304 000
Ahmadabad India	5 171 000
Madrid Spain	5 145 000
Toronto Canada	5 060 000
Hô Chi Minh Vietnam	5 030 000
Cities 2 500 000 – 5 000 000 inhabitants	
Chongqing China	4 975 000
Shenyang China	4 916 000
Dallas USA	4 612 000
Khartoum Sudan	4 495 000
Pune India	4 485 000
Barcelona Spain	4 424 000
Sydney Australia	4 388 000
Singapore Singapore	4 372 000
Boston USA	4 313 000
Atlanta USA	4 284 000
Houston USA	4 283 000
Washington USA	4 190 000
Chittagong Bangladesh	4 171 000
Ha Nôi Vietnam	4 147 000
Yangôn Myanmar	4 082 000
Bandung Indonesia	4 020 000
Milano Italy	4 007 000
Detroit USA	3 980 000
Guadalajara Mexico	3 905 000
Guangzhou China	3 881 000
Jiddah Saudi Arabia	3 807 000
Porto Alegre Brazil	3 795 000
Al Iskandarīyah Egypt	3 760 000
Casablanca Morocco	3 743 000
Frankfurt am Main Germany	3 721 000
Surat India	3 671 000
Melbourne Australia	3 663 000
Ankara Turkey	3 593 000
Recife Brazil	3 527 000
Pusan South Korea	3 527 000
Monterrey Mexico	3 517 000
Abidjan Cote d'Ivoire	3 516 000
Montréal Canada	3 511 000
Chengdu China	3 478 000
Phoenix USA	3 393 000
San Francisco USA	3 342 000
Brasília Brazil	3 341 000
Salvador Brazil	3 331 000
Berlin Germany	3 328 000
Düsseldorf Germany	3 325 000
Johannesburg South Africa	3 288 000
Kābul Afghanistan	3 288 000
P'yŏngyang North Korea	3 284 000
Caracas Venezuela	3 276 000
Fortaleza Brazil	3 261 000
Alger Algeria	3 260 000
Xi'an China	3 256 000
Athina Greece	3 238 000
Medellín Colombia	3 236 000
Nagoya Japan	3 189 000
Cape Town South Africa	3 103 000
Changchun China	3 092 000
Köln Germany	3 084 000
Kanpur India	3 040 000
Tel Aviv-Yafo Israel	3 025 000
Seattle USA	2 959 000
Katowice Poland	2 914 000
Napoli Italy	2 905 000
Ādīs Ābeba Ethiopia	2 899 000
Harbin China	2 898 000
Kano Nigeria	2 884 000
Curitiba Brazil	2 871 000
Luanda Angola	2 839 000
San Diego USA	2 818 000
Nairobi Kenya	2 818 000
Kita-Kyūshū Japan	2 815 000
Nanjing China	2 806 000
Jaipur India	2 796 000
Zibo China	2 775 000
Surabaya Indonesia	2 735 000
Dalian China	2 709 000
Stuttgart Germany	2 705 000
Hamburg Germany	2 686 000
Dar es Salaam Tanzania	2 683 000
Jinan China	2 654 000
Durban South Africa	2 643 000
Inch'ŏn South Korea	2 642 000
Campinas Brazil	2 640 000
Roma Italy	2 628 000
Kyiv Ukraine	2 623 000
Lucknow India	2 589 000
Cali Colombia	2 583 000
Faisalabad Pakistan	2 533 000
Taiyuan China	2 516 000
Taegu South Korea	2 510 000
Ḥalab Syria	2 505 000
İzmir Turkey	2 500 000

THE DISTRIBUTION OF MINERALS

Geological processes have determined the distribution of mineral resources but the location of productive mines is the result of geological, economic and political factors. The map *(see 1)* shows the locations of the most important mines producing industrial and metallic minerals. The bulk of world reserves – those resources which can be extracted economically at a particular time – are located at the mines shown.

Many aspects of the distribution of mineral resources are related to the Earth's tectonic structure. For example, the numerous large copper mines around parts of the Pacific rim are related to the destructive plate margins in these areas *(see pages 24–25)*. Most iron ore now comes from giant sedimentary deposits which have been naturally enriched by near-surface processes. These occur in ancient 'cratons' which are areas of the crust which have been internally stable for more than half a billion years and are typified by western Australia, eastern Brazil and the Canadian and Eurasian 'shields'. Output from the main iron ore producers has varied over time, with China becoming the leading world producer in the 1990s *(see 2)*.

Another striking relationship of mineral resources to geography and climate is provided by the distribution of bauxite, the main ore of aluminium. With few exceptions, major bauxite deposits are situated in the tropics, because bauxite is formed by the weathering of rocks at the Earth's surface under tropical climatic conditions *(see 3)*.

1. LOCATION OF SIGNIFICANT MINES

Producing mines or major deposits in active development, 2002
See table below for index to sites
Winkel Tripel Projection
scale 1:100 000 000

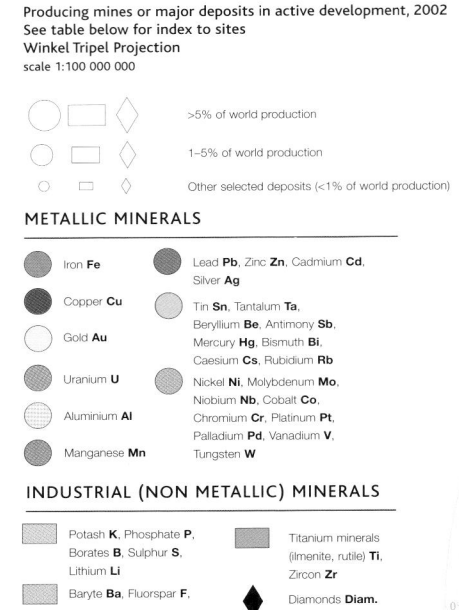

>5% of world production
1–5% of world production
Other selected deposits (<1% of world production)

METALLIC MINERALS

Iron **Fe**
Copper **Cu**
Gold **Au**
Uranium **U**
Aluminium **Al**
Manganese **Mn**
Lead **Pb**, Zinc **Zn**, Cadmium **Cd**, Silver **Ag**
Tin **Sn**, Tantalum **Ta**, Beryllium **Be**, Antimony **Sb**, Mercury **Hg**, Bismuth **Bi**, Caesium **Cs**, Rubidium **Rb**
Nickel **Ni**, Molybdenum **Mo**, Niobium **Nb**, Cobalt **Co**, Chromium **Cr**, Platinum **Pt**, Palladium **Pd**, Vanadium **V**, Tungsten **W**

INDUSTRIAL (NON METALLIC) MINERALS

Potash **K**, Phosphate **P**, Borates **B**, Sulphur **S**, Lithium **Li**
Baryte **Ba**, Fluorspar **F**, Asbestos **Asb**
Titanium minerals (ilmenite, rutile) **Ti**, Zircon **Zr**
Diamonds **Diam.**

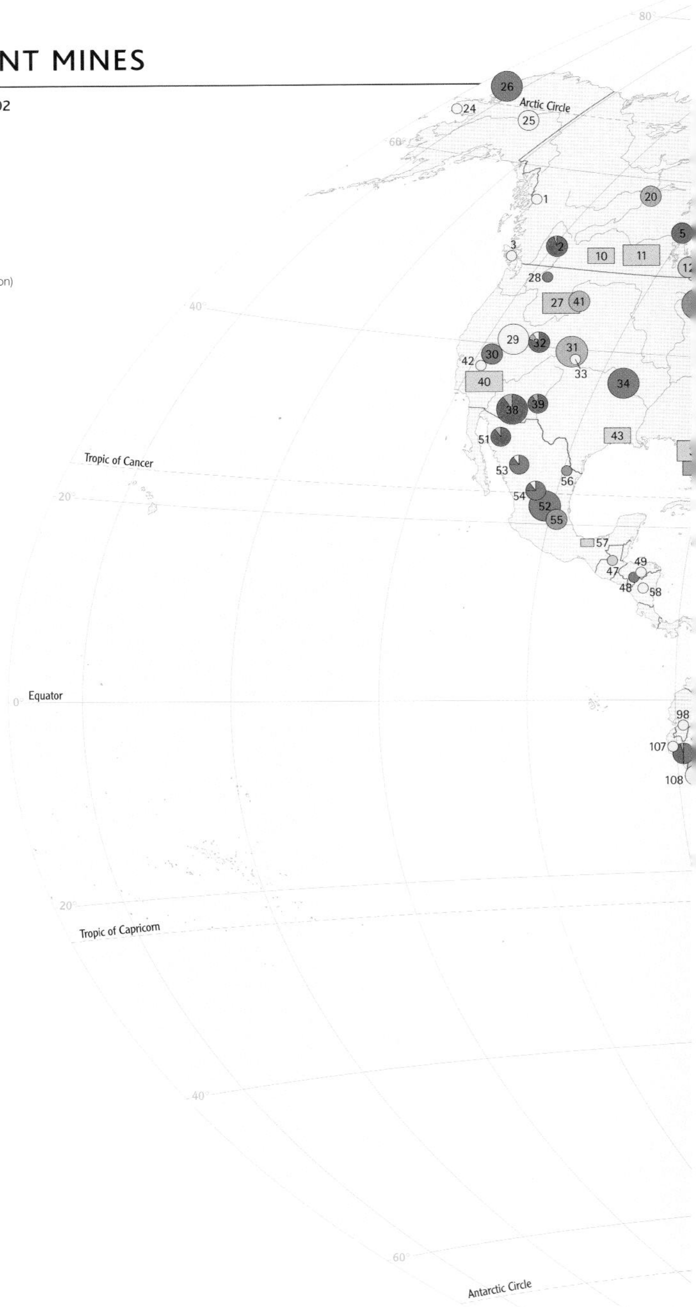
Arctic Circle
Tropic of Cancer
Equator
Tropic of Capricorn
Antarctic Circle

TYPES OF MINERALS

Minerals are usually grouped into four classes defined chiefly by their use:

Industrial minerals are minerals such as salt, fluorspar, barytes and sulphur, which are used in their natural state in industrial processes, and phosphate rock and potash which are vital constituents of fertilizers in addition to other uses. Gemstones are a special case in that, with the exception of industrial diamonds which are used as an abrasive, they are valued only for their aesthetic appearance.

Metallic minerals are mined to extract the metals they contain. Deposits of metallic minerals are evaluated chiefly on the costs of mining the ore and of extracting the metal from it.

Construction minerals such as sand, gravel, clay and gypsum, are used to make building materials. Their production costs are relatively low, but because their transport costs are high, they are normally used close to where they are produced. They are produced in most countries and are not shown on the map.

Energy minerals comprise coal, oil and natural gas, collectively known as 'fossil fuels', and uranium, the raw material for nuclear power. In terms of mass they are the most important traded minerals. Uranium is shown on the map; the others are shown on pages 38–39.

MINERAL PRODUCTION

Economies of scale have always been a strong influence on the geographic patterns of mineral production: a very large orebody is able to supply a significant proportion of world demand and can often be worked at a lower unit cost than a smaller deposit. Thus, for example, only a handful of giant mines in the Americas dominate the world supply of copper *(see 4)*. Similar geographical concentration of supply are marked also in other minerals, including chromium and nickel *(see 5 and 6)*. Production of gold *(see 7)* and diamonds was until fairly recently dominated by southern African countries but advances in exploration and processing technology have led to many new discoveries of both of these commodities in other continents, notably Australia and North America. China is the dominant producer of tungsten, antimony, tin, zinc and fluorspar *(see 8)*, having a large number of small to medium sized mines. The absence of mines of these materials elsewhere indicates not a lack of resources, but a lack of economic reserves.

2. IRON ORE PRODUCERS 1972–2005

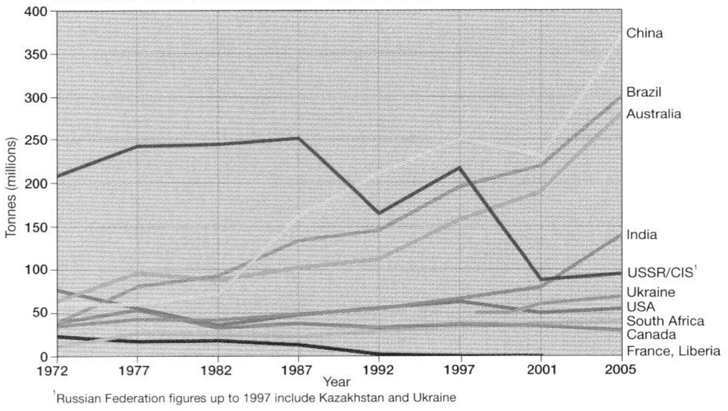
400
350
300
250
200
150
100
50
0
Tonnes (millions)
1972
1977
1982
1987
1992
1997
2001
2005
Year
China
Brazil
Australia
India
USSR/CIS[1]
Ukraine
USA
South Africa
Canada
France, Liberia

[1]Russian Federation figures up to 1997 include Kazakhstan and Ukraine

3. BAUXITE PRODUCTION 2005

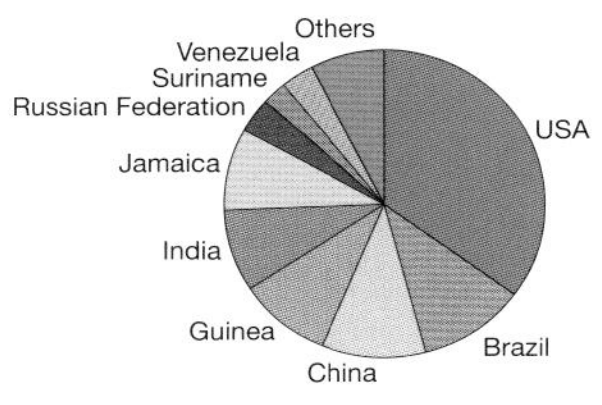
Others
Venezuela
Suriname
Russian Federation
Jamaica
India
Guinea
China
Brazil
USA

4. COPPER PRODUCTION 2005

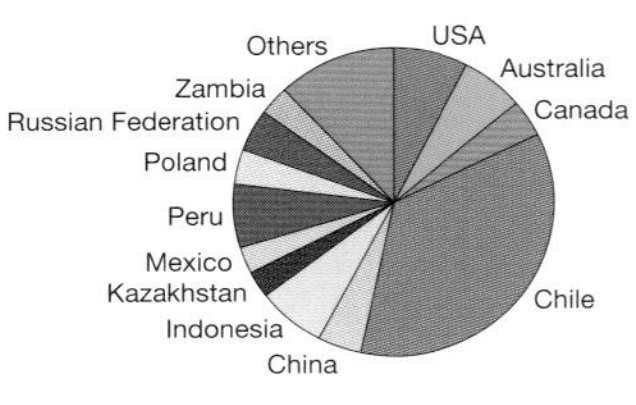
Others
USA
Australia
Canada
Zambia
Russian Federation
Poland
Peru
Mexico
Kazakhstan
Indonesia
China
Chile

INDEX TO SITES ON THE MAP

Key: Site number, Mine/*Province*/*District*/*Area*, **Minerals**

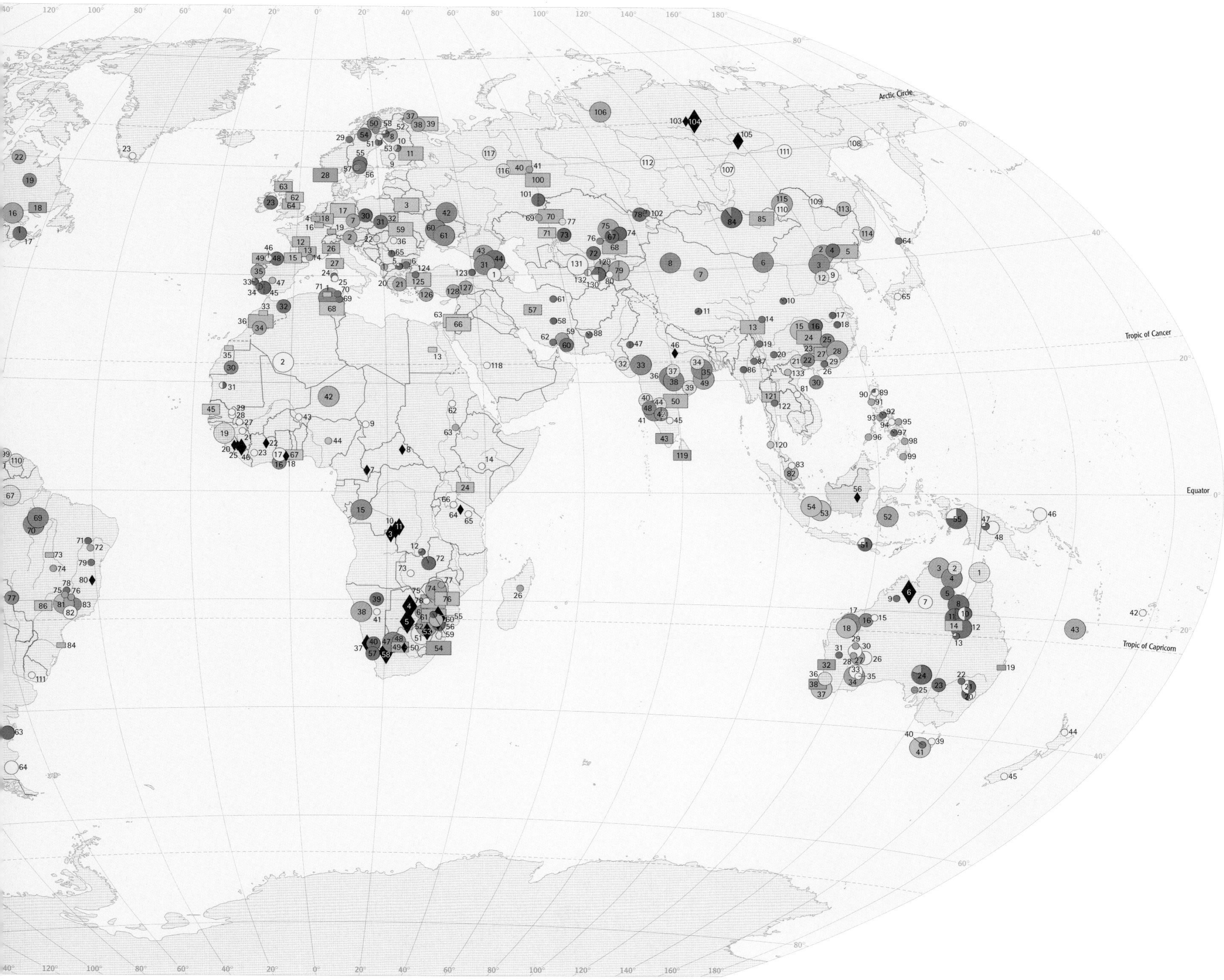
Arctic Circle
Tropic of Cancer
Equator
Tropic of Capricorn

5. CHROMIUM PRODUCTION 2005

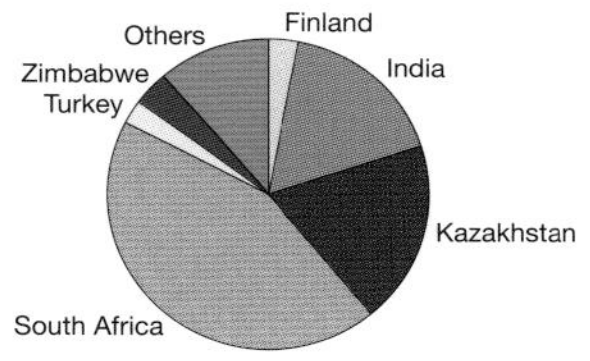
Others
Finland
Zimbabwe
India
Turkey
Kazakhstan
South Africa

6. NICKEL PRODUCTION 2005

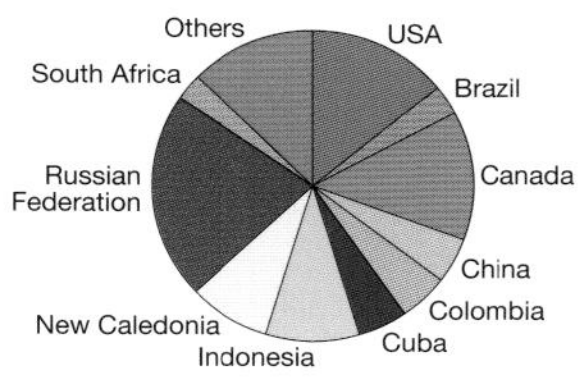
Others
USA
South Africa
Brazil
Russian Federation
Canada
China
New Caledonia
Colombia
Indonesia
Cuba

7. GOLD PRODUCTION 2005

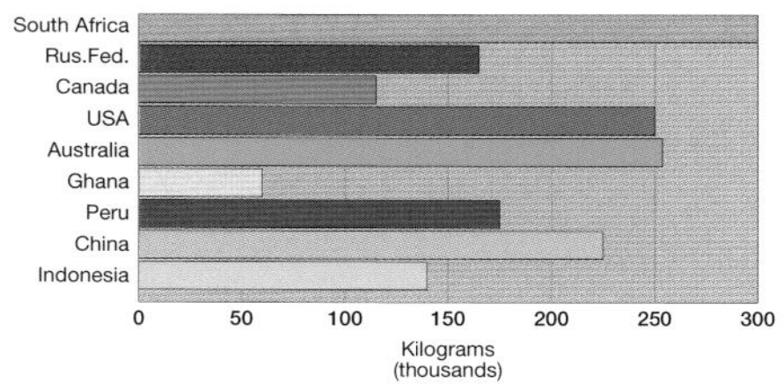
South Africa
Rus.Fed.
Canada
USA
Australia
Ghana
Peru
China
Indonesia
0
50
100
150
200
250
300
Kilograms (thousands)

8. FLUORSPAR PRODUCTION 2005

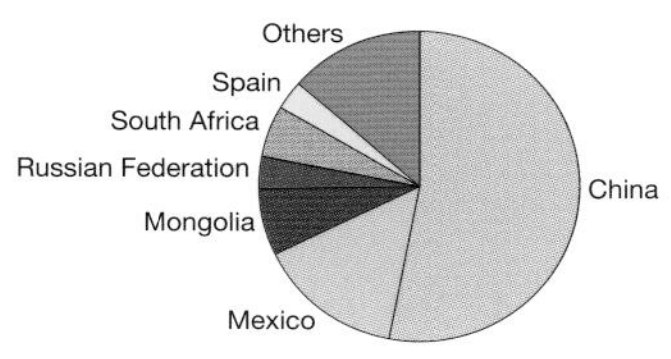
Others
Spain
South Africa
Russian Federation
Mongolia
China
Mexico

Au
, Au
Au

ania
(Fort-Gouraud), **Fe**
Moghrein, **Cu, Au**

co
t, Boubeker, **Pb, Zn, Ag**
Morocco, **P**
zer, **Co**
, **P**
rhoud, Jebel Zelmou,

ia
mund, **Diam.**
g, **U**
t, **Pb, Zn, Ag**
on, **Zn**
ab, **Au**

z Basin, **U**
, **Au**

Leone
Sanniquellie, Macenta,

Africa, Republic of
rn Cape, **Mn, Cu**
, **Fe**
land, **Asb**

50 Kimberley, **Diam.**
51 *Witwatersrand*, **Au, U**
52 *Bushveld*, **Cr, Pt, Ni, V, F**
53 Premier Mine, **Diam.**
54 Richards Bay, **Ti, Zr**
55 Murchison Range, **Sb**
56 Phalarborwa, **Cu, P**
57 Broken Hill, **Pb, Zn, Ag**
58 Finsch, **Diam.**
59 Messina, **Cu**
60 Venetia, **Diam.**
61 Vergenoeg, **F**

Sudan
62 Hassai, **Au**
63 Ingessana Hills, **Cr**

Tanzania
64 *Northern Tanzania*, **Diam.**
65 Golden Pride, **Au**
66 *Victoria Goldfields*, **Au**

Togo
67 *Hahotoé, Akoumapé*, **P**

Tunisia
68 *Djebel Onk and Gafsa Region*, **P**
69 *Northern Tunisia*, **Pb**
70 Bou Grine, **Zn, Pb**
71 Djerissa, **Fe**

Zambia
72 *Copperbelt*, **Cu, Co**
73 Dunrobin, **Au**

Zimbabwe
74 *Great Dyke*, **Cr, Pt, Pd**
75 Zvishavane, **Asb**
76 Bikita, **Li, Be, Sn**
77 Bindura, **Ni, Cu**
78 *Bulawayo*, **Au**

ASIA

Armenia
1 *Armenia*, **Cu, Mo, Au**

China
2 Jinzhou, **Mo**
3 Shijiaying, Shuicheng, **Fe**
4 Chengchengtsu, **Pb, Zn**
5 Liaoning & Shandong, **Talc**
6 Bayan Obo, **Fe**
7 Jinchuan, **Ni, Cu**
8 Xinjiang Uygur Zizhiqu (Sinkiang), **Fe**
9 Penglai, **Au**
10 Changduicheng, **Cu, Mo**
11 Xiaotieshan / Zheyaoshan, **Cu, Zn, Pb, Ag**
12 Zibo, **Al**
13 Sichuan, **Asb**
14 Cheng Xian, **Pb, Zn**
15 *Hunan-Sichuan*, **Hg, Sb**
16 Dexing, **Cu, Ag, Au**
17 Shinchao, **Cu**
18 Tongshankou, **Cu**
19 Lanping, **Pb, Zn**
20 Zhehai, **Pb, Zn**
21 Pingguo, **Al**
22 Mugui, **Mn**
23 *Hunan-Guangxi*, **Sn, W**
24 Gongxi (Xinhuang), **Ba**
25 Qidong, **Mn**
26 Fankou, **Pb, Zn**
27 *South China*, **Ba, F**
28 South Jiangxi, Guangdong, **W**
29 Guizhou, **Al**
30 Hainan, **Fe, Ti**

Georgia
31 Chiatura, **Mn**

India
32 Bhuj, **Al**
33 Panch Mahals, **Mn**
34 Ranchi, **Al**
35 Bihar, Orissa, **Fe, Mn**
36 Nagpur, Balaghat, **Mn**
37 Madhya Pradesh, **Al**
38 Rowghat, Bailadila, **Fe**
39 Koraput, **Al**
40 Maharashtra, **Al**
41 Supa, **Mn**
42 Karnataka, **Fe, Mn**
43 *Southeast Kerala* (*Travancore*), **Ti, Zr**
44 Hutti, **Al**
45 Kolar, **Au**
46 Majhgawan, **Diam.**
47 Rajasthan, **Cu, Zn, Pb, Ag**
48 Goa, **Fe**
49 *Cuttack*, **Cr**
50 Mangampet, **Ba**

Indonesia
51 Batu Hijau, **Cu, Au**
52 Pomalaa, **Ni**
53 Belitung (Billiton), **Sn**
54 Bangka, **Sn**
55 Grasberg, **Cu, Au**
56 Kalimantan, **Diam.**

Iran
57 *Iran*, **Ba**
58 Sar Cheshmeh, **Cu, Ag, Au, Mo**
59 *Faryab Area*, **Cr**
60 Angorhan, **Pb, Zn, Ag**
61 Nakhlak, **Pb, Zn, Ag**
62 Anguran, **Zn, Pb**

Israel
63 *Dead Sea Region*, **K, P**

Japan
64 Toyoha, **Pb, Zn, Ag**
65 Hishikari, **Au, Ag**

Jordan
66 *Dead Sea Region*, **K, P**

Kazakhstan
67 Balkhash, **Cu, Mo**
68 Kargayly, Zhayrem, **Ba**
69 Donskoy, **Cr**
70 Dzhetygara, **Asb**
71 Kara Tau, **P**
72 Achisay, **Pb, Zn, Ag**
73 Dzhezkazgan, **Cu, Mo**
74 Kounrad, **Cu, Mo**
75 Akchatau, **W, Mo**
76 Atasurda, **Mn**
77 Turgay, Krasnooktyabr, **Al**
78 Leninogorsk, **Zn, Pb**

Kyrgystan
79 *Kyrgyzstan*, **Hg, Sb, U**
80 Kumtor, **Au, Ag, Te, W**

Laos
81 Sepon, **Au, Ag**

Malaysia
82 Malaya, **Sn, Ti**
83 Penjom, **Au**

Mongolia
84 Erdenet, **Cu, Mo**
85 *Hentiy Province*, **F**

Myanmar
86 Monywa, **Cu**
87 Bawdwin, **Zn, Pb, Ag**

Pakistan
88 Saindak, **Cu, Au**

Philippines
89 Luzon, **Au, Cu**
90 Victoria, **Au**
91 *Zambales Mountains*, **Cr**
92 *Marinduque*, **Cu, Mo, Au**
93 Mindoro, **Ni, Co**
94 Masbate, **Au**
95 Samar, **Cr**
96 Palawan, **Ni, Co**
97 Cebu, **Cu, Mo, Au**
98 Northern Mindanao, **Ni, Co**
99 Southern Mindanao, **Ni, Co**

Russian Federation
100 Bazhenovskoye, **Asb**
101 *Central Urals*, **Cu, Zn, Au**
102 Altay, **Pb, Zn, Ag, Cu**
103 Alakit, **Diam.**
104 Daldyn, **Diam.**
105 Malaya Botuobiya, **Diam.**
106 Noril'sk, **Ni, Cu, Pt, Co**
107 *Lena, Vitim*, **Au**
108 *Magadan Region*, **Au**
109 *Amur*, **Au**
110 Zabaykal'sk, **Au**
111 Yakutsk, **Au**
112 Yenisey, **Au**
113 Birobidzhan, **Sn**
114 Primorskiy Kray, **Sn, W**
115 Chitinskaya, **W, Sn**
116 North-Ural Bauxite, **Al**
117 Timan Bauxite, **Al**

Saudi Arabia
118 Madh adh Dabh, **Au, Ag, Cu, Zn**

Sri Lanka
119 *Southern Sri Lanka*, **Ti, Zr**

Thailand
120 *Southern Thailand, Phuket*, **Sn, W**
121 *Northern Thailand*, **Ba, F**
122 Mae Sod, **Zn, Cd**

Turkey
123 Murgul, **Cu**
124 Biga Region, **Pb, Zn, Ag, Ba**
125 Balikesir, Emet, **B**
126 Fethiye-Köyceğiz, **Cr**
127 Gulema-Elaziğ, **Cr, Fe**
128 Karsanti, **Cr**

Uzbekistan/Tajikistan
129 *Almalyk*, **U, F**
130 *Southeast Uzbekistan/Tajikistan*, **Cu, Au, Pb, Zn,Ag**
131 Muruntau, Zarafshan, **Au**
132 Zarmitan, **Au, W**

Vietnam
133 *Vietnam*, **Sn**

OCEANIA

Australia
1 Weipa, **Al**
2 Gove, **Al**
3 Ranger, **U**
4 Groote Eylandt, **Mn**
5 McArthur River, **Pb, Zn, Ag**
6 Argyll, **Diam.**
7 The Granites / Tanami, **Au**
8 Century, **Zn, Pb, Ag**
9 *Lennard Shelf*, **Zn, Pb, Ag**
10 Ernest Henry, **Cu, Au**
11 *Mount Isa Region*, **Cu, Pb, Zn, Ag**
12 Cannington, **Pb, Ag, Zn**
13 Osborne, **Cu, Au**
14 Phosphate Hill, **P**
15 Telfer, **Au**
16 Woodie Woodie, **Mn**
17 Hamersley Range, **Fe**
18 Wodgina, **Ta, Sn**
19 *Sydney, Brisbane*, **Ti, Zr**
20 Cadia, **Au, Cu**
21 North Parkes, **Cu, Au, Ag**
22 Elura, **Zn, Pb**
23 Broken Hill, **Pb, Zn, Ag**
24 Olympic Dam, **Cu, U**
25 *Middleback Ranges*, **Fe**
26 Granny Smith / Wallaby, **Au**
27 Murrin Murrin, **Ni, Co**
28 Leinster, **Ni, Cu**
29 Mount Keith, **Ni, Cu**
30 Agnew, **Au**
31 Golden Grove, **Zn, Ag, Au, Cu**
32 Eneabba, **Ti, Zr**
33 *Kalgoorlie Region*, **Au, Ag**
34 Kambalda, **Ni, Cu, Co, Pt**
35 St Ives, **Au**
36 *Darling Ranges*, **Al**
37 Greenbushes, **Ta, Li**
38 *Capel*, **Ti, Zr**
39 Beaconsfield, **Au**
40 Rosebery, **Zn, Pb, Ag**
41 Renison Bell, **Sn**

Fiji
42 Viti Levu, Emperor, **Au**

New Caledonia
43 *New Caledonia*, **Ni, Co**

New Zealand
44 Martha Hill, **Au, Ag**
45 Macraes, **Au, Ag**

Papua New Guinea
46 Lihir, **Au**
47 Ok Tedi, **Cu, Au**
48 Porgera, **Au**

ENERGY PRODUCTION AND CONSUMPTION

The world's energy resources are unevenly distributed (*see 1*). Similarly, the geography of energy production and consumption is highly uneven, with three countries, the USA, the Russian Federation and China, dominating both the energy production and consumption of energy (*see 2 and 3*). Some countries – typically the oil-exporting states, such as Saudi Arabia, Iran and Nigeria – produce much more than they consume, but many of the most advanced industrial economies, such as the USA and Japan, as well as relatively newly industrialized countries such as South Korea and Taiwan, are net consumers. Peripheral countries, including Burkina, Chad and The Gambia, and some of the richest countries including Singapore are energy 'paupers' which produce no energy and are wholly reliant upon imports.

The USA is the largest primary energy consumer and, despite having only 5 per cent of the world's population, it consumes over a quarter of the world's energy. Together with Canada and Mexico, the USA's primary energy consumption increased by 15 per cent between 1992–2004, while the Middle East, South and Central America and Africa experienced higher growth rates from much lower base levels. Highest per capita energy consumption occurs in countries including Australia, Belgium and Canada as well as the USA. Lowest per capita energy consumption occurs in the world's poorest countries, including Benin, Burkina and Burundi. Uneven production and consumption mean that energy sources are the largest single items in international trade. Mexico and South and Central America, the Middle East, West and North Africa, Former Soviet Union and Canada are net oil exporters (*see 4*). The USA, Europe, eastern and South Africa, Australasia, China and Japan are net oil importers and generate wealth elsewhere to be able to pay for their imports.

2. ENERGY PRODUCTION

Thousand tonnes of oil equivalent

scale 1:295 000 000

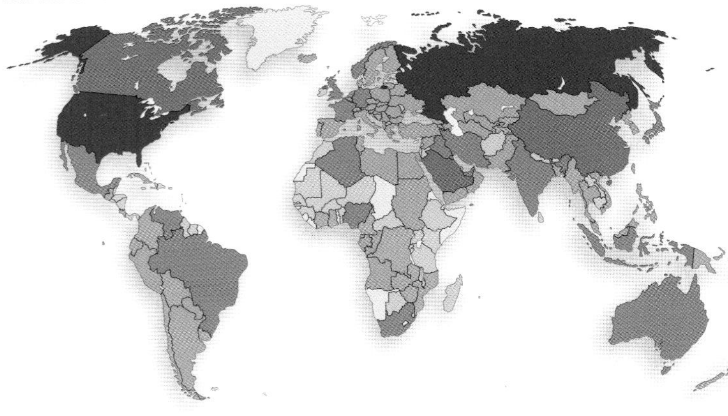

3. ENERGY CONSUMPTION

Thousand tonnes of oil equivalent

scale 1:295 000 000

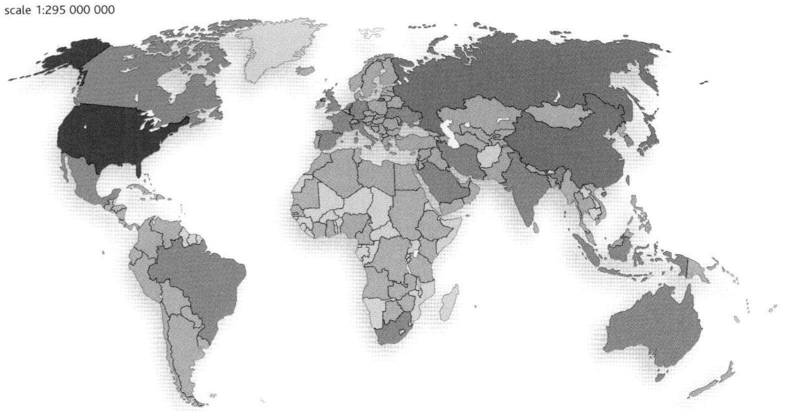

>1 000 000
400 000 – 999 999
100 000 – 399 999
10 000 – 99 999
1 000 – 9 999
1 – 999
0
no data

ENERGY RESERVES AND RATES OF CONSUMPTION

Proven energy reserves are also unevenly distributed (*see 5*). Nearly two-thirds of proven oil reserves are concentrated in the Middle East. Reserves in the USA and Russian Federation have declined and Europe's reserves are expected to dry up early this century. Central America and Africa are expected to cease oil exports around 2025. Major import-dependent regions will be reliant upon the Middle East, underlining issues of security of supply in the context of global geopolitical instability. Proven reserves of natural gas are dominated by the Former Soviet Union and the Middle East while coal reserves are more evenly distributed between the Asia-Pacific region, North America and the Former Soviet Union.

Global energy use has grown historically and further growth is expected due to developing world industrialization. Between 1992 and 2004, global primary energy consumption increased by 20 per cent (*see 6*), led by the Middle East with a 42 per cent increase. Elsewhere, relatively costly energy in Europe depressed consumption to the relatively low level of 8 per cent while the dissolution of the Soviet Union led to the collapse in consumption which is slowly recovering. If rates of energy consumption were to remain constant then it has been estimated that the proven oil reserves would last forty years, natural gas sixty years and coal three hundred years. However, energy consumption rates are increasing and these estimates need regular revision.

4. OIL IMPORTS AND EXPORTS 2004

Movements within the regions indicated are not included in the figures.

	Crude Exports (million tonnes)	Crude Imports (million tonnes)	Balance of Trade (million tonnes)
USA	1.9	501.2	-499.3
Canada	80.5	46.6	33.9
Mexico	99.9	0	99.9
South and Central America	106.7	37.8	68.9
Western Europe	45.6	507.8	-462.2
Former Soviet Union[1]	254.3	0.3	254
Middle East	853.8	9.2	844.6
North Africa	115.8	8.7	107.1
West Africa	196.7	2.7	194
Eastern and Southern Africa	11.5	25.4	-13.9
Australasia	7.8	23.5	-15.7
China	5.7	122.7	-117
Japan	0	208.9	-208.9
Other Asia-Pacific	48.7	360.1	-311.4
Unidentified	26	0	26
Total World	1855	1855	0

1. Comprises: Russian Federation, Estonia, Latvia, Lithuania, Belarus, Ukraine, Moldova, Georgia, Armenia, Azerbaijan, Kazakhstan, Uzbekistan, Turkmenistan, Tajikistan and Kyrgyzstan

5. PROVEN ENERGY RESERVES 2004

	Oil	%	Natural Gas	%	Coal	%
North America[1]	61.0	5.1	7.32	4.1	254 432	28.0
South and Central America	101.2	8.5	7.10	4.0	19 893	2.2
Europe	18.4	1.6	6.60	3.6	59 841	8.1
Former Soviet Union[2]	120.8	10.2	57.41	32.0	227 254	23.4
Middle East	733.9	61.7	72.83	40.6	419	-
Africa	112.2	9.4	14.06	7.8	50 336	5.6
Asia Pacific	41.1	3.5	14.21	7.9	296 889	32.7
World	1188.6	100	179.53	100	909 064	100

1. Canada, USA and Mexico.
2. See footnote for table 4.

Oil (thousand million barrels) Natural Gas (trillion cubic metres) Coal (million tonnes)

1. DISTRIBUTION OF RESOURCES

Winkel Tripel Projection
scale 1:94 000 000

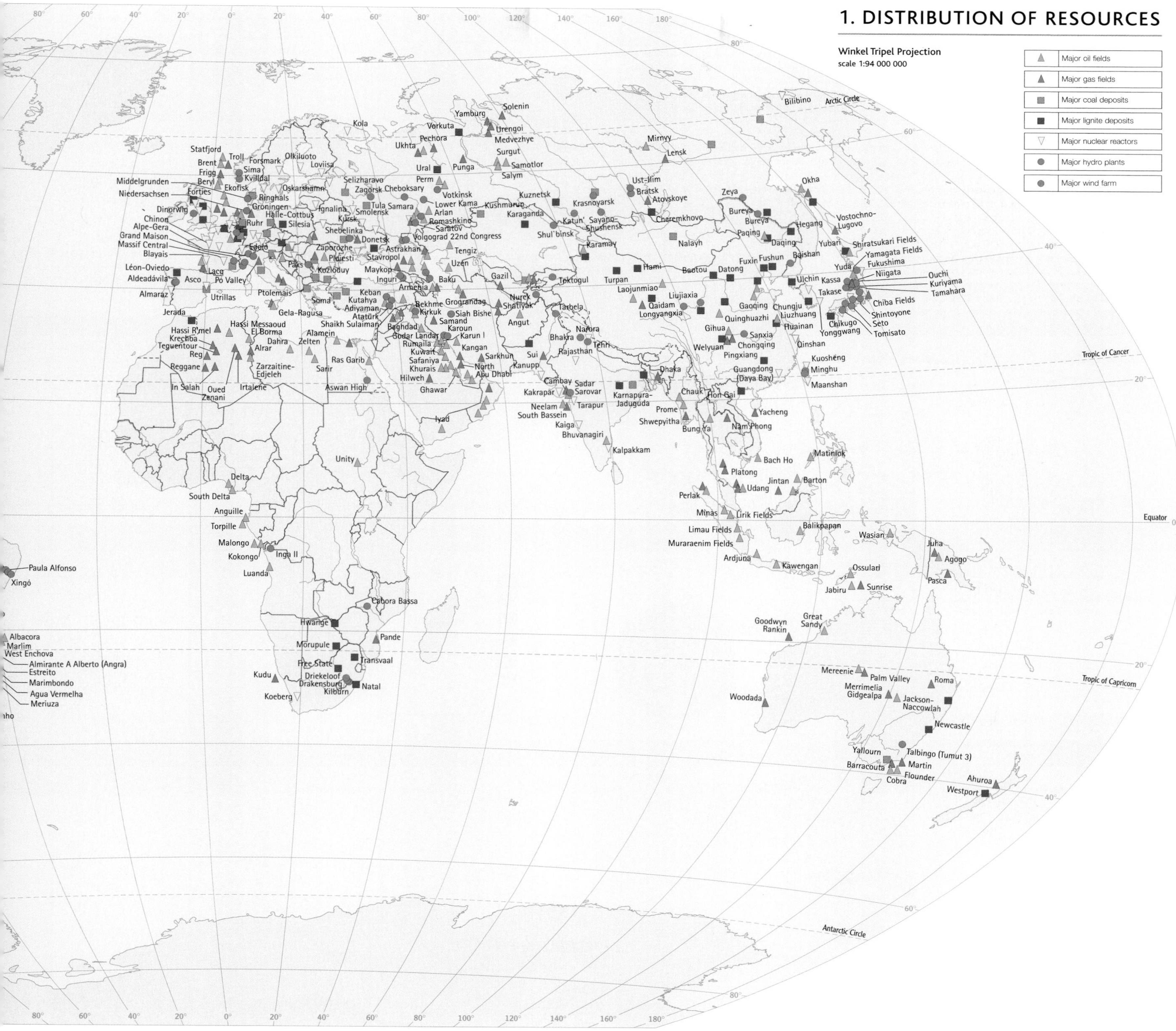

CONSERVATION AND RENEWABLE RESOURCES

Sustainability has underpinned the search for renewable energy sources that are less detrimental to environmental quality. Energy conservation aims to extend the life of non-renewable resources, reducing their environmental damage and increasing energy efficiency. Renewable energy sources may be another solution, although they currently only represent 11 per cent of world total primary energy supply (*see 8*).

Problems of cost and technical inefficiency are being addressed through technological advances and supportive government policy and growth is expected due to the longer-term constraints upon primary and non-renewable sources.

Biomass (wood and organic wastes) is prevalent in developing countries. Geothermal power is generated from underground water heated by the Earth's molten core. New Zealand utilizes this obtaining 10 per cent of its electricity from geothermal sources. Energy derived from water – hydroelectric power – is another renewable energy source. World hydroelectricity consumption has risen over 25 per cent between 1992 and 2004 (*see 9*). Solar energy has the benefit of being renewable on a daily basis and being available globally, although it varies by season and latitude. Currently Japan, the USA and Germany account for 80 per cent of installed generation capacity. Wind power requires the right conditions in terms of terrain and weather to be commercially viable. Installed generation capacity has increased more than tenfold in the last decade, concentrated in Germany, the USA, Spain and Denmark.

6. PRIMARY ENERGY CONSUMPTION

Million tonnes of oil equivalent.

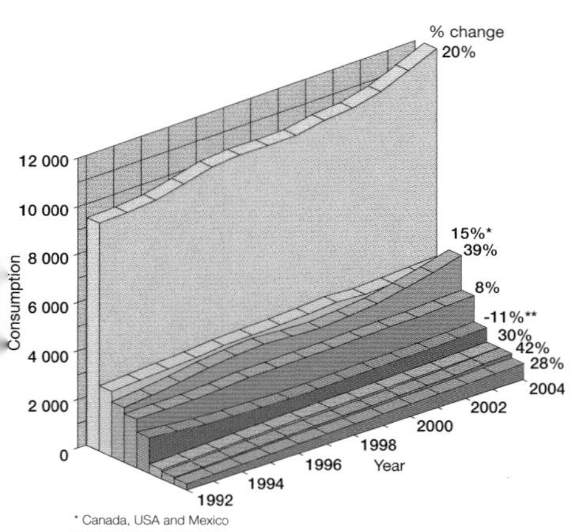

* Canada, USA and Mexico
** See footnote for table 4

7. NUCLEAR ENERGY CONSUMPTION

Million tonnes of oil equivalent.

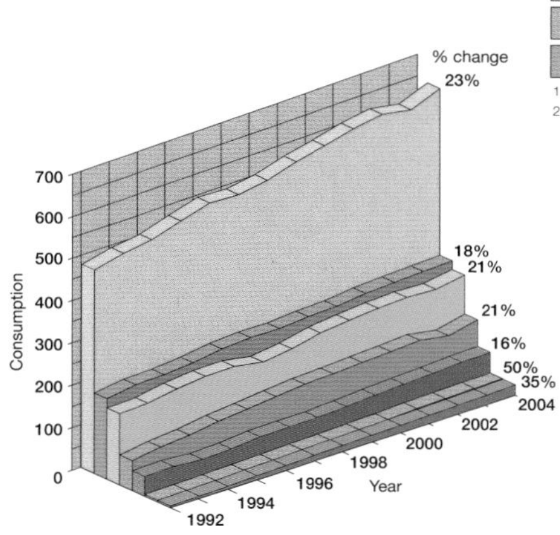

World	Former Soviet Union[2]
North America[1]	Middle East
South and Central America	Africa
Europe	Asia Pacific

1. Canada, USA and Mexico.
2. *See* footnote for table 4.

8. FUEL SHARES IN WORLD TOTAL PRIMARY ENERGY SUPPLY, 2003

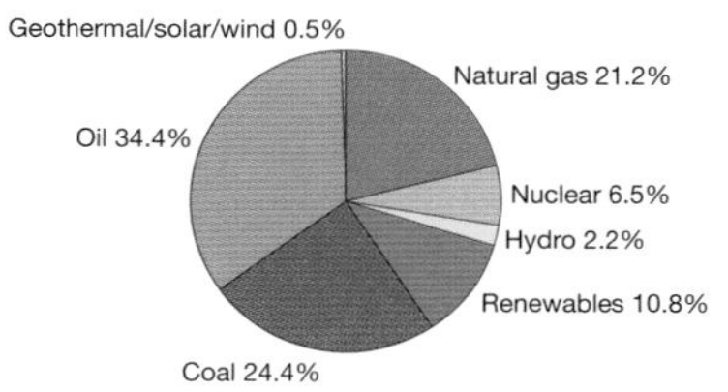

9. HYDROELECTRICITY CONSUMPTION

Million tonnes of oil equivalent.

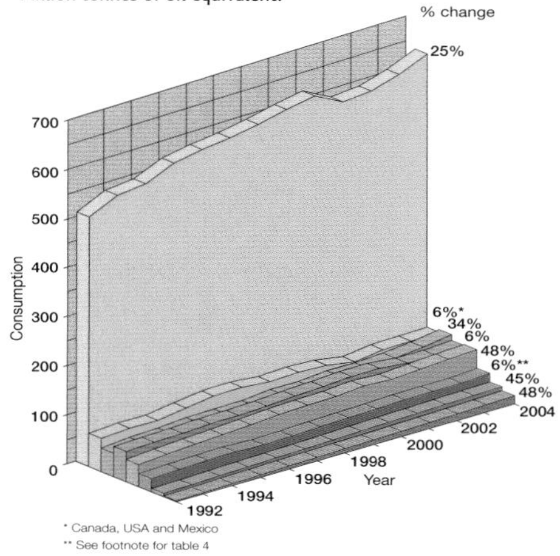

* Canada, USA and Mexico
** See footnote for table 4

INTERNATIONAL TELECOMMUNICATIONS

Increased availability and ownership of telecommunications equipment over the last thirty years has aided the globalization of the world economy. Over half of the world's fixed telephone lines have been installed since 1987, and the majority of the world's Internet hosts (computers on which World Wide Web sites are stored) have come on-line since 1997 (*see 1*). Network access is uneven, however. Nearly half of existing telephone lines and cellular phones are in North America and Europe. Internet users in Asia, North America and Europe make up over 88 per cent of the world total (*see 2*).

This means that there is strong competition in the traditional telephone market in many parts of the world. In North America and Europe consumers have a wide choice available to them. This is not the case everywhere. For example, in many African countries there is little or no competition and consumers have little choice in the service they subscribe to. This is also affecting the development of broadband internet access (*see 4*).

One measure of the perceived 'death of distance' is the steady rise in international telephone calls, which has increased by 381 per cent since 1991. The map (*see 3*) shows accessibility to telephone lines and telephone traffic between countries in different continents for routes using at least 100 million minutes of telecommunications time in 2004. In that year, these streams totalled 77 billion minutes, 39 per cent of global international traffic.

Changes are taking place in the international telephone market. Many people now access low cost or free international calls through the internet by means of specialist software. Others make use of satellite or cellular phones to make their international calls, or they send a text message or use electronic mail.

1. WORLD COMMUNICATIONS EQUIPMENT 1976–2004

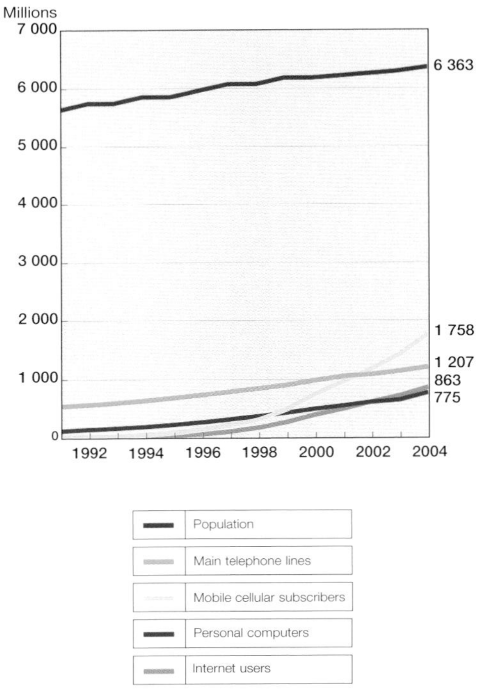

2. INTERNATIONAL TELECOMMUNICATIONS INDICATORS BY REGION 2004

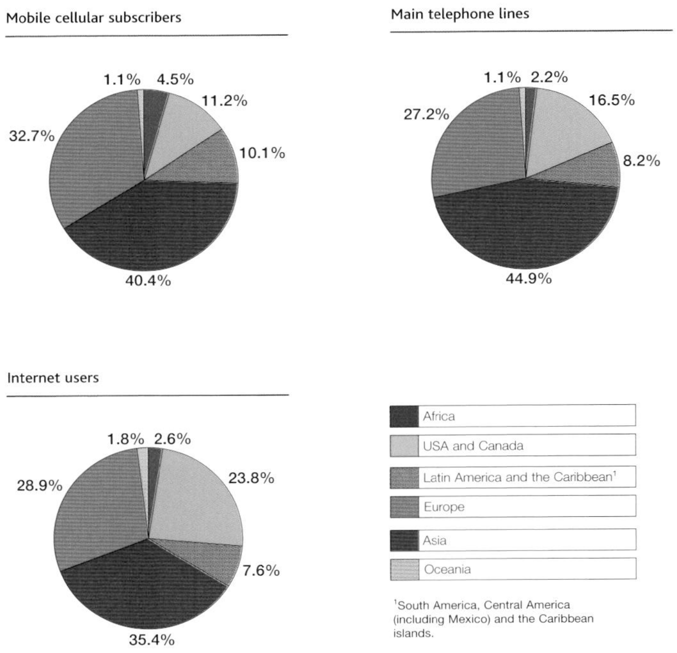

[1]South America, Central America (including Mexico) and the Caribbean islands.

4. TOP BROADBAND ECONOMIES 2004

Countries with the highest broadband penetration rate – subscribers per 100 inhabitants

	Top Economies	Rate
1	South Korea	24.8
2	Hong Kong, China	22.0
3	Netherlands	19.8
4	Denmark	19.1
5	Iceland	18.8
6	Canada	17.0
7	Taiwan	16.5
8	Switzerland	16.4
9	Belgium	15.6
10	Finland	15.3
11	Japan	15.3
12	Norway	14.9
13	Israel	14.0
14	Sweden	13.7
15	Liechtenstein	13.7
16	USA	12.9
17	United Kingdom	11.9
18	Singapore	11.9
19	France	11.2
20	Austria	10.0

3. INTERNATIONAL TELECOMMUNICATIONS TRAFFIC 2004

© Primetrica, Inc. Washington D.C. www.telegeography.com and www.primetrica.com

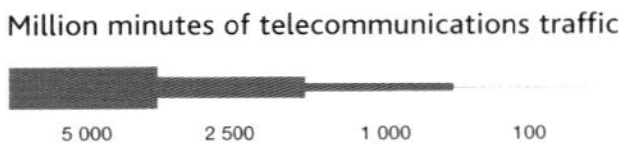

Each band is proportional to the total annual traffic on the public network in both directions between each pair of countries.

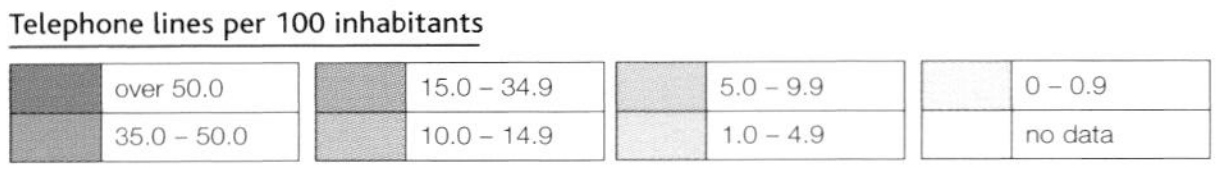

SATELLITE AND INTERNET COMMUNICATIONS

International telecommunications use either fibre-optic cables or satellites as transmission media. Although cables carry the vast majority of traffic around the world, communications satellites are important for person-to-person communication, including cellular telephones, and for broadcasting. Growing volumes of data traffic, particularly from the Internet (*see 5*), have boosted demand for international transmission capacity. Most traffic is routed over fibre-optic cables. In 1999, the world's trans-oceanic cables could carry approximately 250 gigabits per second (Gbps), which is equivalent to 17.5 million simultaneous phone calls. By 2003, international cable capacity had grown seventeen-fold and it continues to increase.

Unlike submarine cables, which must connect at fixed points, satellites can transmit information between Earth stations located anywhere within a satellite's radio beam, or 'footprint'. Geostationary satellites, which orbit at 36 000 kilometres above the Earth (*see 6*), may have footprints spanning over 1000 kilometres, thus providing a broad service area for point to multi-point voice, video and data communications. The positions of communications satellites are critical to their use, and reflect the demand for such communications in each part of the world. The satellites which are placed in 'geostationary' orbit sit above the equator. This means that they move at the same speed as the earth and remain fixed above a single point on the Earth's surface.

5. INTERNET USERS AND MAJOR INTERNET ROUTES

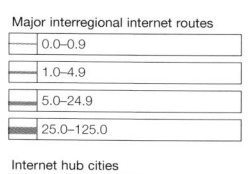

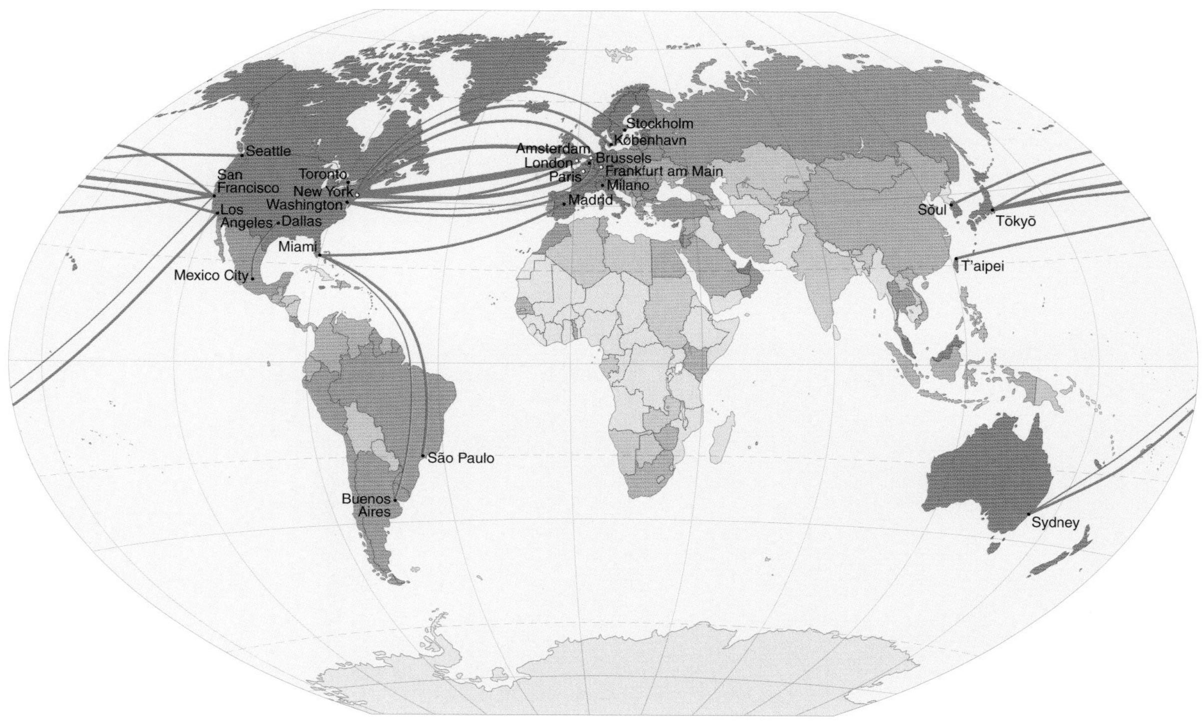
Seattle
San Francisco
Los Angeles
Dallas
Toronto
New York
Washington
Miami
Mexico City
São Paulo
Buenos Aires
Stockholm
København
Amsterdam
London
Brussels
Paris
Frankfurt am Main
Milano
Madrid
Sŏul
Tōkyō
T'aipei
Sydney
Internet users per 10 000 inhabitants 2004
3 000–8 000
1 000–2 999
400–999
200–399
0–199
no data
Major interregional internet routes
0.0–0.9
1.0–4.9
5.0–24.9
25.0–125.0
Internet hub cities
London

6. GEOSTATIONARY COMMUNICATIONS SATELLITES AND CELLULAR MOBILE SUBSCRIBERS

Cellular mobile subscribers per 100 inhabitants 2004
over 100
80–100
60–79.9
40–59.9
20–39.9
0–19.9
no data
Geostationary communications satellites
In service
Inclined orbit
Planned
Equator

PREHISTORIC AND CLASSICAL CARTOGRAPHY (500 BC – AD 500)

The evolution of mapping has been inextricably linked to people's knowledge of the world and to related scientific and technological developments. Mapping skills have been influenced by factors such as way of life and the nature of the physical environment, and maps can therefore provide an excellent insight into cultures and civilizations. Surviving examples of ancient maps are rare. Their limits of coverage tended to be the extent of the producers' accurate geographical knowledge. Beyond the local area, maps appeared to reflect a speculative or cosmological approach (*see 1*).

The most significant contribution of the Greeks to cartography was theoretical rather than practical. It is primarily the work of Claudius Ptolemy, a Greek mathematician, astronomer and geographer living in the 2nd century AD, which provides us with information about the level of geographical knowledge at this time. Ptolemy's work *Geographia* included theoretical principles of cartography, lists of place names and computed co-ordinates. Later maps, based on this work, show how he believed the world to look at that time (*see 2*).

1. MAP OF THE WORLD

Carved on a Babylonian clay tablet, *c.* 600 BC. Babylon is shown as a rectangle intersected by vertical lines representing the Euphrates river. Small circles show other cities and countries, and the world is encircled by an ocean – the 'Bitter River'.
British Museum, Department of Western Asiatic Antiquities, London, UK.

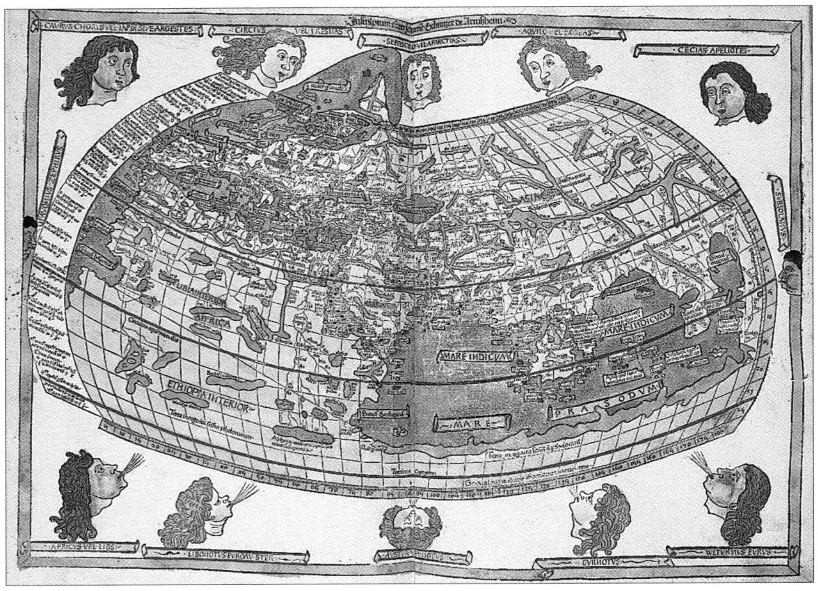

2. PTOLEMAIC WORLD MAP

Based on the work of Claudius Ptolemy, produced by Donis Nicolaus in Ulm, Germany, 1630. The map includes lines of latitude and longitude which give a sense of accuracy. The figures represent different wind directions.
British Library, London, UK.

AD 500–1600

Religious beliefs played an important part in the cartography of this period. One particularly significant product was the Madaba map (*c.* AD 550) – a Christian map in the form of a floor mosaic discovered in a church in Madaba, Jordan, depicting biblical Palestine (*see 3*). Also during this period, maps originating in the classical tradition were overlain with later Christian elements. Such maps were usually oval or circular in shape, schematic in content, and centred on Jerusalem. These world maps (*mappæmundi*) conveyed a Christian perspective of the world, and their detail ranged from the virtually diagrammatic to the highly complex (*see 4*).

Maps from the later medieval period include sea charts, town plans and local, district and route maps. Of these, portolan charts – sea charts designed primarily for navigation – were by far the most significant and provided impressively detailed and accurate information on coastlines, harbours and related navigational matters. Route maps, for the use of pilgrims and merchants travelling overland, also developed over this period, as exemplified by Matthew Paris' map of the route from London to Otranto, Italy produced around AD 1250 (*see 5*).

The 15th and 16th centuries were essentially the age of exploration and discovery, a period which witnessed an explosion of global knowledge and a veritable renaissance in cartography. The period saw a great development of world maps, many of which began to include the coastal detail of the earlier portolan charts and to show the latest geographical information resulting from the voyages of discovery. Rome and Venice dominated European map production from 1550 to 1570, but later in the period dominance in mapmaking passed to the Low Countries. This 'Golden Age' of Dutch cartography is exemplified by the first printed 'atlas' of map sheets by Abraham Ortelius in 1570 – the *Theatrum Orbis Terrarum*. The term 'atlas' was coined by Gerard Mercator the Flemish cartographer – perhaps the most widely known figure in the history of cartography. His work, in particular his map projection published in 1569, makes him the geographical colossus of the period.

4. THE HEREFORD MAPPAMUNDI

Produced on vellum, and attributed to Richard of Haldingham and Lafford, *c.* 1290. The map follows the form of a T-O map, centred on Jerusalem, with east to the top. The continents of Asia (top), Africa (lower right) and Europe (lower left) are separated by the Mediterranean Sea and the Nile and Don rivers.
Hereford Cathedral, Hereford, UK.

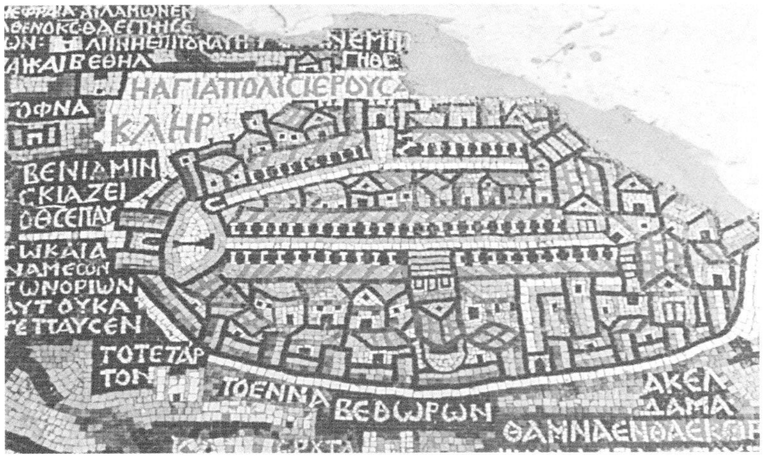

3. THE MADABA MOSAIC MAP

Detail from the Madaba map (*c.* AD 550) showing the walled city of Jerusalem and the surrounding area. Approximately a quarter of the original map, which covered 94 square metres of floor, is still intact.

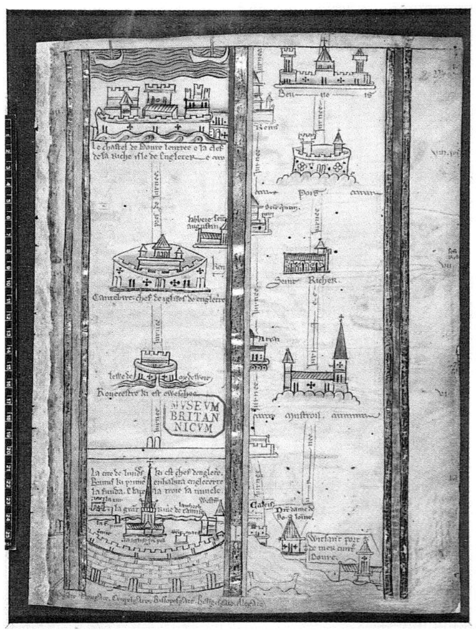

5. ITINERARY MAP OF A ROUTE FROM LONDON TO ITALY

Produced by Matthew Paris, *c.* 1250. This is a fine, early example of a road map in strip form. This extract includes Rochester, Canterbury and Dover.
British Library, London, UK.

1600–1900

Cartography in the earlier years of the 17th century was dominated by the Low Countries, epitomized by the Blaeu publishing house (*see 6*) but, by the late 17th century, the world centre for cartographic production had shifted from Amsterdam to Paris. France was one of the first countries to recognize the importance of establishing a national survey and mapping programme. There, the Cassini family established the national survey of France well ahead of other such surveys in western Europe (*see 7*).

The colonial scramble for North America, and the American War of Independence (1775–1783), drove the development of cartography in North America, and it was an age, too, when the exploration of Australia, Tasmania and New Zealand resulted in their appearance on world maps. Such exploration was aided by great developments in navigation and particularly the ability to establish longitude more precisely.

During the 19th century special maps appeared in greater numbers reflecting scientific and social observation and analysis. One significant example of this development of thematic mapping was the *Physikalischer Atlas* of Heinrich Berghaus, published in two volumes in 1845 and 1848 (*see 8*). Lithographic printing of maps was developed in the early years of the century allowing the production of multiple copies of maps very much more cheaply, stimulating a proliferation of maps for mass consumption and for educational purposes.

As the 19th century progressed, factors such as exploration and emigration were reflected in extended world coverage of maps and charts. Work on national surveys proceeded, one particularly notable national cartographic achievement being the Great Trigonometrical Survey (GTS) of India which facilitated the creation of extensive and detailed topographic maps of the sub-continent.

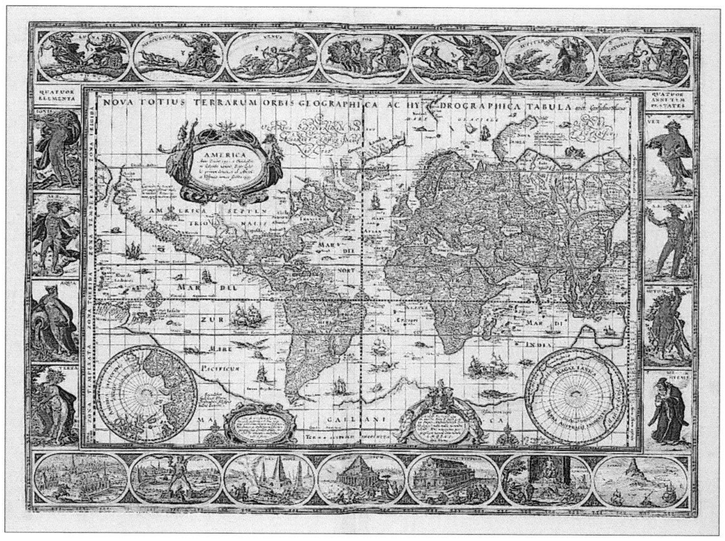

6. WORLD MAP

Produced in Amsterdam by Willem Blaeu, 1630. This is one of the finest examples of early maps on Mercator's projection. British Library, London, UK.

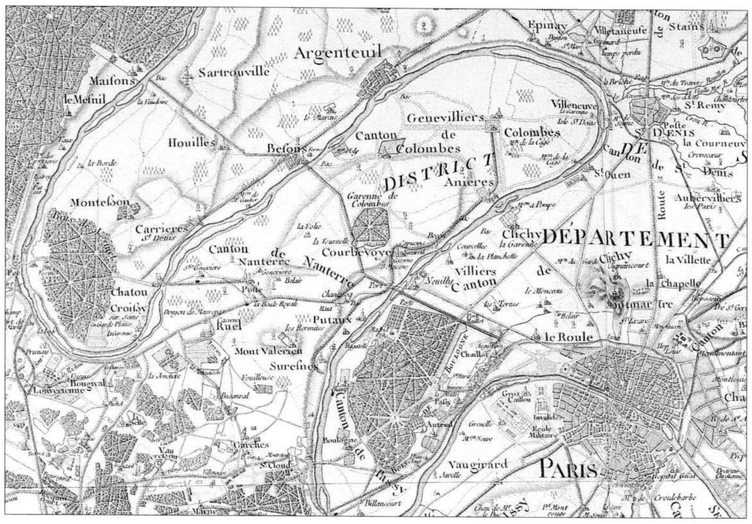

7. CARTE DE FRANCE

Detail from the first sheet – Sheet No. 1 Paris – by Cassini de Thury, 1736. Original scale 1:86 400. National Library of Scotland, Edinburgh, UK.

20TH CENTURY

War, politics and technological development were instrumental in prompting the expansion of map and chart coverage throughout the 20th century. The development of aviation and, in turn, space exploration, and photography and imagery possible through them, have been particularly significant in recent developments in cartography and have spawned a new age in map making. The development of the computer has led to the production of digital maps and the consequent development of Geographical Information Systems (GIS). New digital cartographic techniques allow users to combine and manipulate geographical data sets, and also support new forms of output and visualization (*see 9*).

There has been a significant increase in map coverage throughout the world, and yet the fact that comprehensive national topographic mapping has been produced does not mean that it is readily available to the public. Many countries, particularly in Africa and Asia, impose strict restrictions on the release of their mapping. The question of national map coverage and availability is complicated by the activities of external mapping organizations. The former USSR had extensive programmes producing topographic mapping of countries throughout the world (*see 10*). Easy access to this previously classified military mapping has recently served to extend map availability.

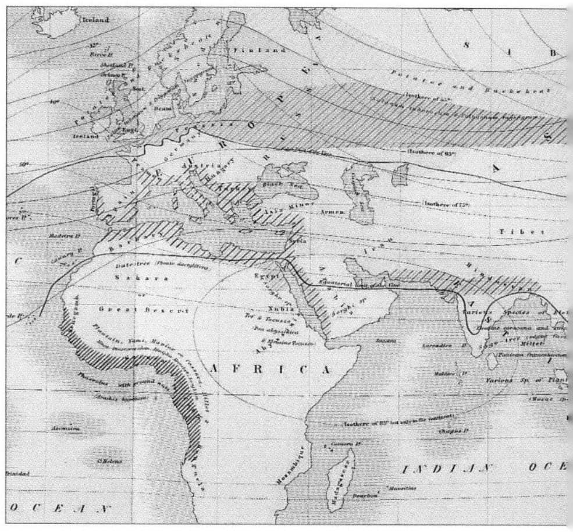

8. THEMATIC ATLAS MAP

Extract from a map of the *Survey of the geographical distribution and cultivation of the most important plants which are used as food for man: with indications of the isotheres and isokhimenes*, 1842. Published in the *Physikalischer Atlas* by Heinrich Berghaus, 1845 and 1848. This English language version appeared as Plate 44 in W & A K Johnston's *National Atlas of Historical, Commercial and Political Geography*, 1847. National Library of Scotland, Edinburgh, UK.

9. TERRAIN MODEL OF SOUTH AMERICA

A 3-D relief view of South America generated from a 1 km resolution digital elevation – or terrain – model.

10. GROZNYY, RUSSIAN FEDERATION

Extract from a Russian military topographic map 1:500 000, 1988.

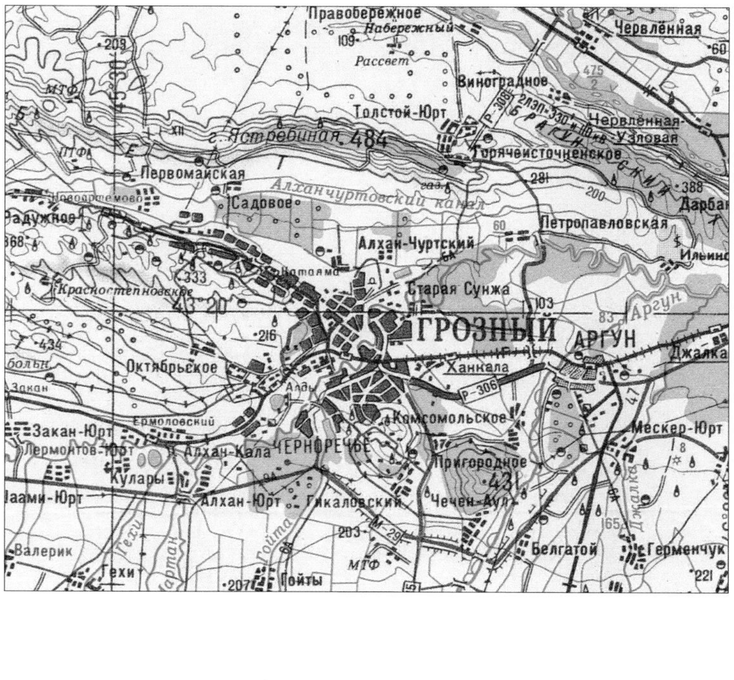

THE EARTH AND ITS REFERENCE SYSTEM

The earth was once believed to be stationary, flat, surrounded by water, and even the centre of the Universe. Belief in its spherical form arose from the ideas of the Greek philosopher Pythagoras (6th century BC) and, two centuries later, Aristotle's observations of how ships disappeared over the horizon. Important supporting evidence was also provided by astronomers noting the curved shadow cast by the Earth onto the Moon during an eclipse and by mariners' observations of stars rising and setting as they sailed their trade routes. The circumference of the globe was later determined in Alexandria by Eratosthenes (*c.* 250 BC), to within 1% of its true value.

Once knowledge of the Earth as a globe was established, there was a requirement for a reference system to permit the determination of geographical location. A graticule of meridians of longitude (stretching from pole to pole) and parallels of latitude (lines parallel to the Equator) is known to have existed in the 4th century BC. Early astronomers devised instruments to determine latitude on land and later the sextant was developed for use at sea. Determination of longitude proved more difficult. Techniques employed into the 18th century included using the eclipses of the sun and moon and of Jupiter's moons. But as longitude's angular value is directly related to the rotation of the earth, a precise way of measuring time was the key to solving this problem. John Harrison, an English inventor and horologist, made the crucial breakthrough in the mid-18th century with his H4 chronometer which was not only extremely accurate but also reliable at sea.

With the Equator as the reference for lines of latitude, a longitudinal standard was required. Such a prime meridian could in theory be placed anywhere, and in the past many cities, including London, Paris, Cadiz and Stockholm had their own national reference. Not until the International Meridian Conference in Washington, DC in 1884, was the Greenwich Meridian established as the world-wide reference (*see 1*).

1. THE GREENWICH MERIDIAN

The Greenwich Meridian line at the Royal Observatory, Greenwich, London illuminated at night. This is the universally recognized 'prime meridian' marking the position of 0° longitude and the basis of Greenwich Mean Time.

MAP PROJECTIONS

One of the main challenges of cartography is how to depict a sphere on a plane surface. It is impossible to do this while preserving correct shapes and areas and compromises have to be reached. Transformations of the globe onto a flat surface are referred to as projections. The earliest examples (6th – 1st centuries BC) were vaguely 'cylindrical' (i.e. constructed as if the Earth's graticule is projected onto a cylinder of paper wrapped around the globe). These produce a rectangular pattern of lines of latitude and longitude. Ptolemy's written work of the 2nd century AD contained some of the most detailed cartographic instructions and in his Geography he also describes simple conic projections (produced as if projected onto a cone). The other main type of projection is azimuthal, with the graticule 'projected' onto a flat piece of paper in contact with, or cutting through the globe. Perhaps the most famous projection of all time is that of Mercator. Cylindrical in form, the lines of latitude are spaced to allow loxodromes (lines of constant compass bearing) to appear as straight lines to satisfy the convenience of the mariner who navigates by compass. This projection and variations of it are still used today for detailed topographic mapping. Although the projection does preserve shape around each point, areas, especially in high latitudes, are very distorted. Thus when the whole world is depicted, a hectare of forest in northern Canada would appear over 1000% larger than the equivalent ground area in central Africa. For this reason its use in an atlas to depict the world distribution of forest cover, for example, could be justly criticized. Today there are numerous map projections to choose from (*see 2*), many of which are appropriate for small-scale world maps.

2. WORLD MAP PROJECTIONS

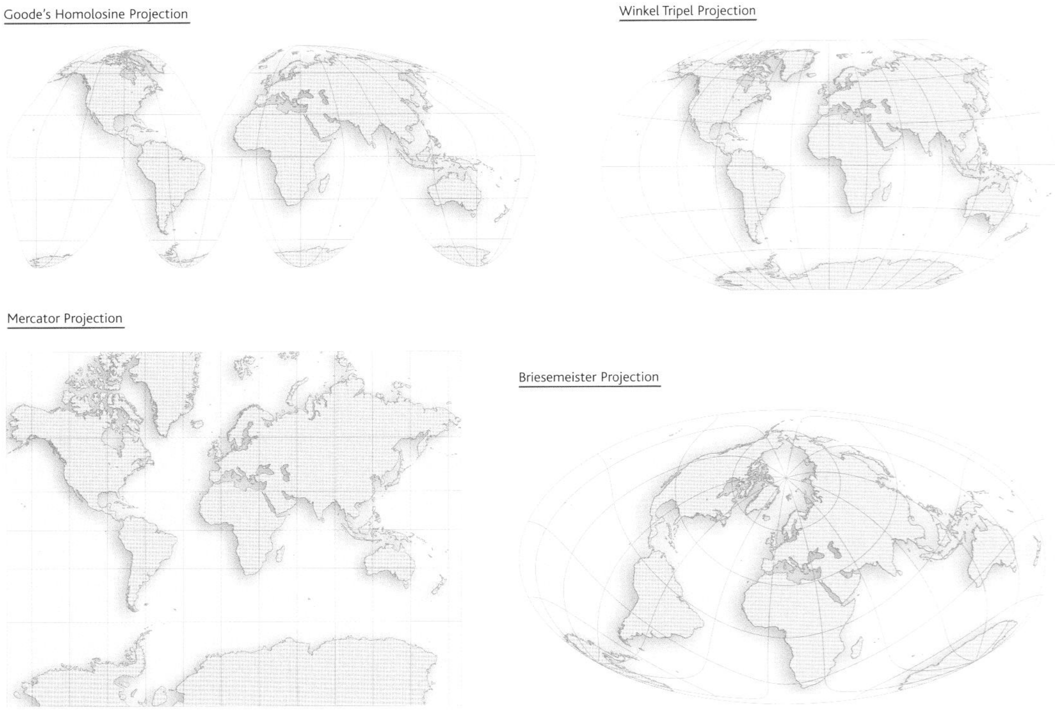
Goode's Homolosine Projection
Winkel Tripel Projection
Mercator Projection
Briesemeister Projection

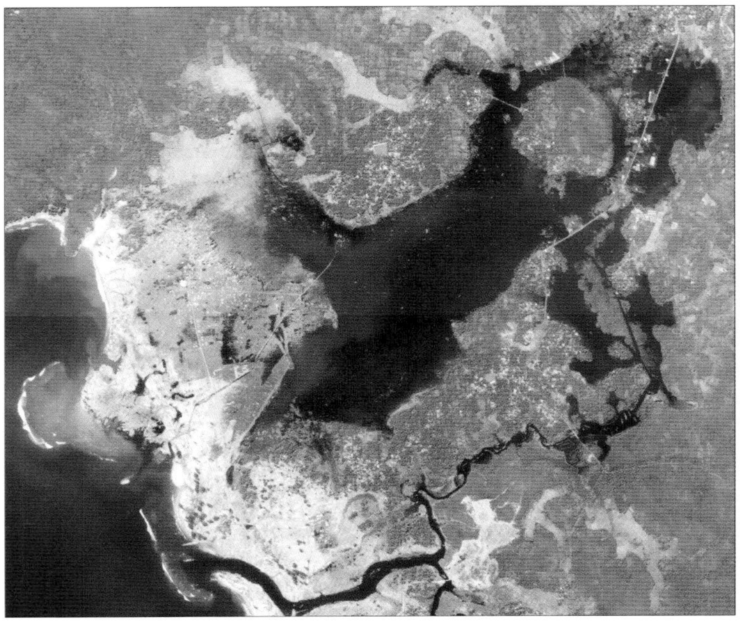

3. SATELLITE IMAGE OF SUMATRA

This satellite image taken on 29 December 2004, shows some of the damage done by the tsunami of 26 December 2004. The coastal area has been stripped of vegetation and buildings except for the mosque. Low-lying areas inland are flooded with salty water. Such imagery is an invaluable tool for assessing and mapping geological and environmental phenomena.

CARTOGRAPHIC DATA

Following the Dark Ages (AD 500–1300) mapping expanded both within Europe and globally with the growth of colonialism and world trade. The development of printing in the 15th century increased the demand from mariners for sea charts, and from the military for topographic maps of the land. Survey accuracy, an essential characteristic of such products, requires the measurement procedure of working from the whole (control frameworks at global and regional scales) to the part (detailed mapping at local level). With horizontal and vertical control in place, mapping progressed, initially with ground surveying techniques but later using aerial photography and photogrammetry (taking measurements from stereographic aerial photographs). New technologies such as satellite Global Positioning Systems (GPS), originally developed in the USA for military use, are now employed for navigation, establishing control and for detailed survey work. While topographic base maps are essential for many purposes, the growing need to map and monitor global issues has led to the employment of advanced techniques including radar imagery and satellite imaging systems (*see 3*). Recent high-resolution (sub-metre) scanners on the Quick Bird and IKONOS satellites (*see 4*) are even adding fine metric data and permitting these images to act directly as map substitutes for some tasks. With the development of digital systems in recent decades the storage, manipulation, transmission and visualization of all this data are becoming much simpler and more routine. Such data, essential for producing accurate maps, are therefore much in demand by environmental scientists and planners.

Recently these high resolution images have become more accessible to the general public via the internet permitting the user to view high resolution satellite images of many major towns and cities throughout the world.

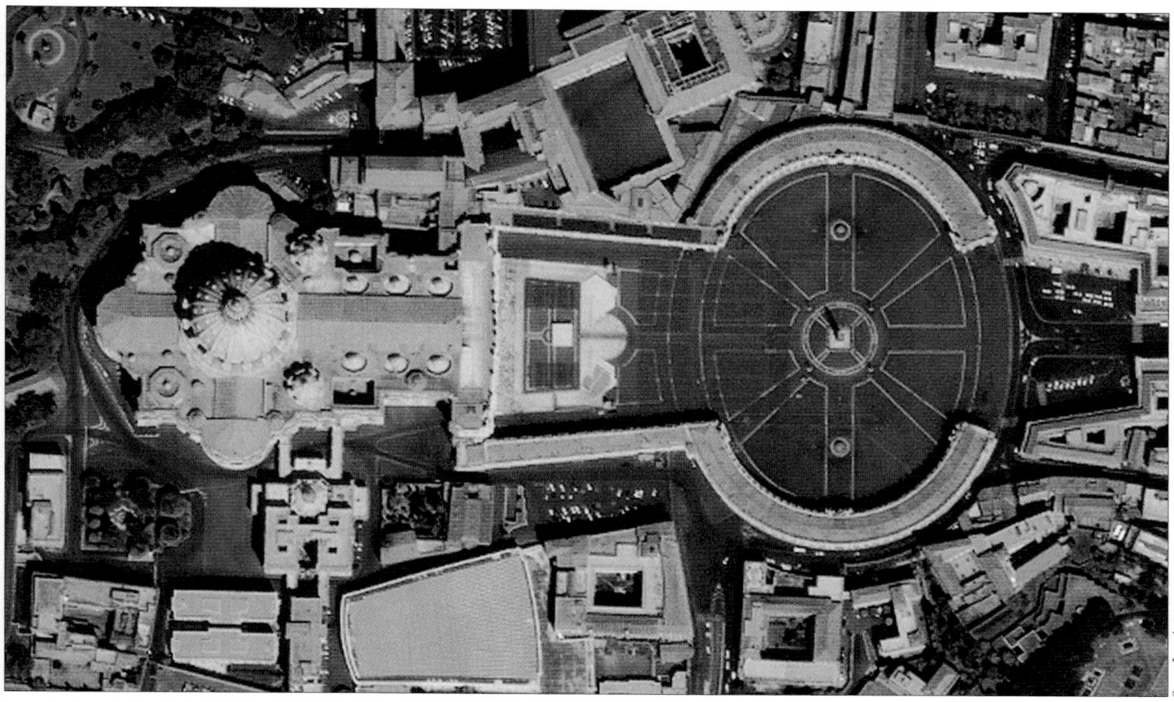

Space Imaging

4. SATELLITE IMAGE OF VATICAN CITY

High resolution satellite images such as this one of Vatican City can provide huge amounts of data for cartographers and urban planners. They can serve as source material for the compilation of large-scale maps, or may sometimes be used directly as a map base.

5. SAND MAP

Members of the US Pennsylvania National Guard examine a rudimentary map drawn in sand before an exercise. Maps can be 'externalized' in many ways using the most convenient and readily available media.

INTERACTING WITH GEOGRAPHIC INFORMATION

Spatial knowledge of the environment, structured as cognitive (mental) maps, is essential for human survival and routine activities. Although some people can retain complex geographies in their minds, most require external (for example, printed) maps for them to examine their surroundings and consider spatial problems or tasks in more detail. Cognitive maps can be externalized in several ways, for example verbally, through hand gestures (such as pointing) or through sketch maps, whether on paper or in sand (*see 5*). The last of these provide continuity between our instinctive abilities to make and use maps and what has become the professional discipline of cartography.

In the past, maps were used for both data storage and visualization. Once compiled, designed and printed they were normally sold and archived. However, because of the time-lapse introduced by these processes, maps can often be out of date or may not contain exactly the information required. Fundamental changes have followed the introduction of computers. Maps and geographic information are now stored in digital databases which can be constantly maintained, with direct updating possible from survey and satellite data. This procedure is increasingly being employed by national and commercial mapping agencies where maps, particularly at large scales, are compiled digitally and printed on demand rather than as part of a publishing programme or printed series. This means that choices are now available for the provision of geographic or cartographic information – through printing or via computer-based mapping systems on CD-ROM or the Internet.

The latter may carry some disadvantages (such as the need for the latest hardware, and the restricted view of a monitor screen) but these systems can also offer revolutionary advantages for the viewer. Not only can geographic information be selected and combined at will but the user may also have interactive control over the design and content of the image (*see 6*). Animation may also be provided as well as hyper-links to other parts of the database for images, video-clips or sounds.

Geographic information systems (GIS) – combining software and hardware for the manipulation and analysis of spatial data – develop these ideas much farther and are now used extensively within government, industry and commerce. Digital geographic data and cartographic facilities are now also being employed in what are often referred to as location-based services (LBS), including in-car navigation systems (*see 7*), mobile phones and personal digital assistants. These can incorporate GPS receivers and respond to geographic triggers such as the input of a town name, street name or postcode. The precise position of the user can then be identified and route guidance and local information provided directly. However, new technology need not change completely how we access and use maps. We still travel on foot, by bicycle, motorcar or aircraft as circumstances demand. Thus the future can be interpreted as offering a wider spectrum of cartographic sources and facilities for different uses – from high quality publications produced by cartographic specialists, to personal interactive experiences.

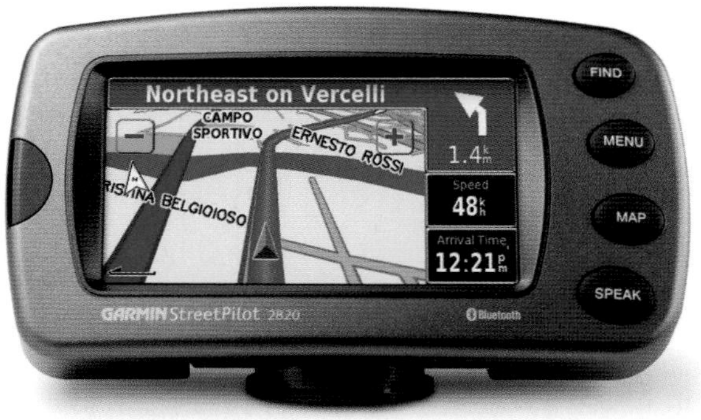

7. MOBILE MAPPING

The Garmin iQue was the first personal digital assistant (PDA) to include Global Positioning System (GPS) technology and carried map data and mapping software. It was capable of automatic route calculation and turn-by turn voice guidance. The latest in-car systems use Bluetooth technology to facilitate 'hands-free' navigation, and real-time traffic information is also now available. This permits routes to be calculated around traffic bottlenecks, and road incidents affecting traffic are graphically represented on-screen as icons on the navigation map. It is also possible for the user to load customized points of interest (POIs) such as speed cameras to add to a pre-loaded POI database.

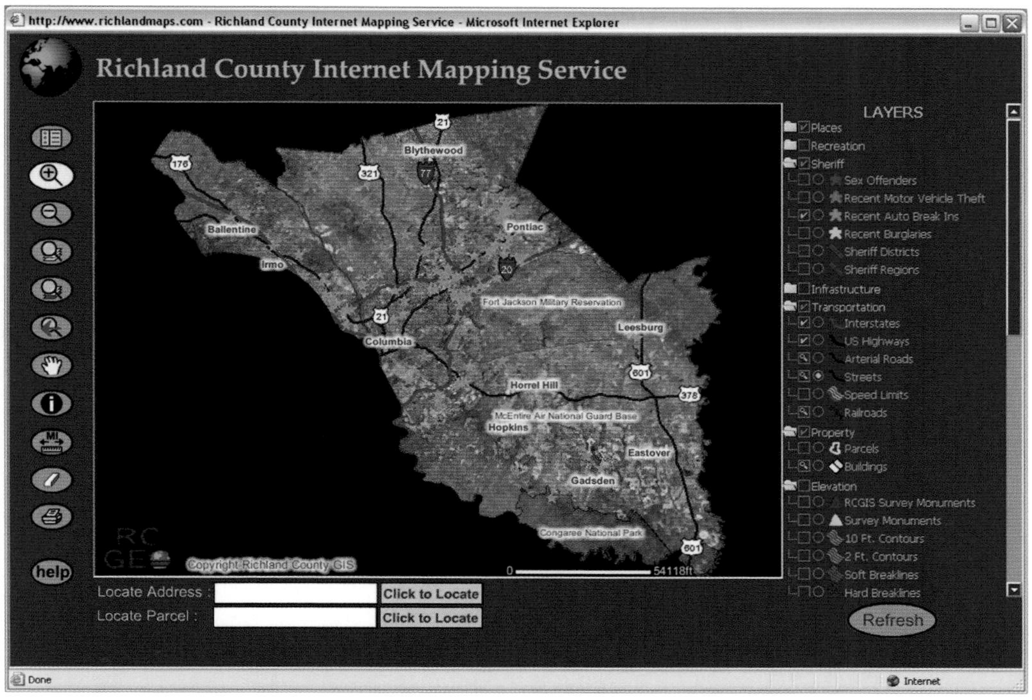

6. INTERACTIVE WEB MAPPING

Richland County Geographic Information Systems (RC GEO), South Carolina, use data from across several departments to develop spatial databases and mapping services for use by local government, the general public and businesses. Integration of the data within a geographic information system (GIS) allows each point on a map to become an index to cultural, environmental, demographic and political information about that location, and allows users to manipulate and output maps for their specific needs.

AUSTRALASIA Total Land Area 8 844 516 sq km / 3 414 887 sq miles (includes New Guinea and Pacific Island nations)

Puncak Jaya, Indonesia

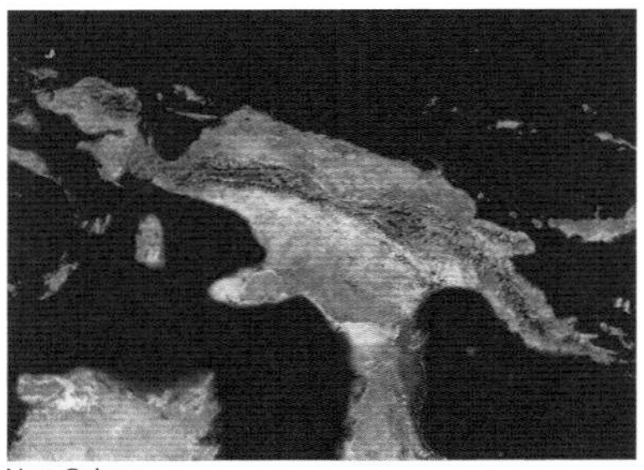
New Guinea

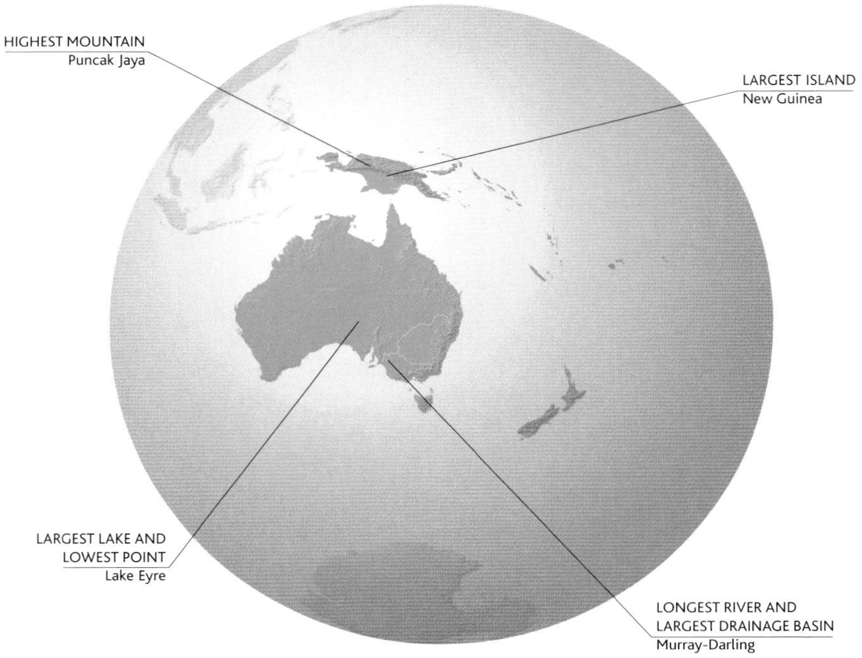
HIGHEST MOUNTAIN
Puncak Jaya
LARGEST ISLAND
New Guinea
LARGEST LAKE AND
LOWEST POINT
Lake Eyre
LONGEST RIVER AND
LARGEST DRAINAGE BASIN
Murray-Darling

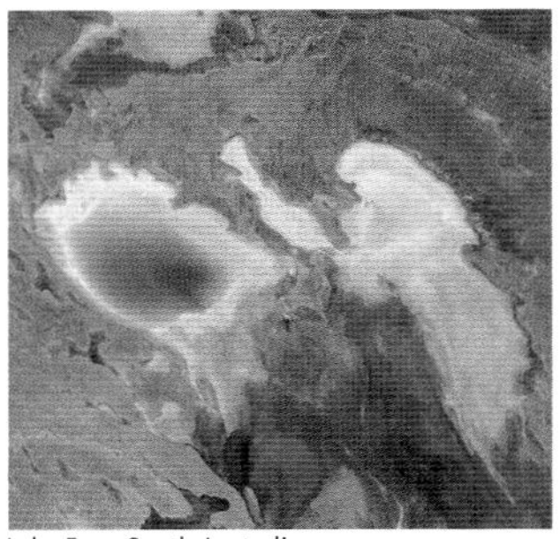
Lake Eyre, South Australia

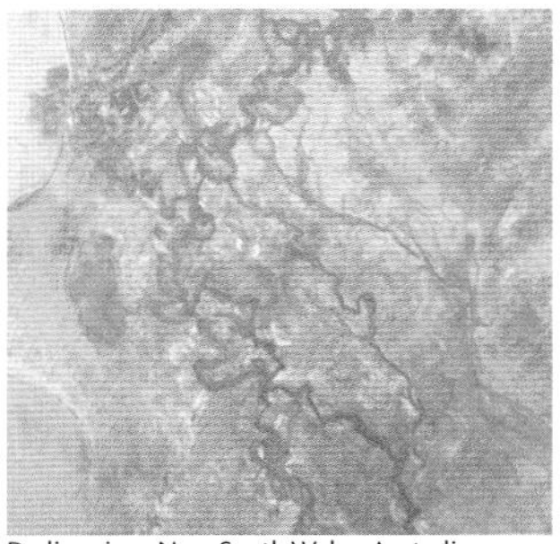
Darling river, New South Wales, Australia

HIGHEST MOUNTAINS	metres	feet	Location
Puncak Jaya	5 030	16 502	Indonesia
Puncak Trikora	4 730	15 518	Indonesia
Puncak Mandala	4 700	15 420	Indonesia
Puncak Yamin	4 595	15 075	Indonesia
Mt Wilhelm	4 509	14 793	Papua New Guinea
Mt Kubor	4 359	14 301	Papua New Guinea

LARGEST ISLANDS	sq km	sq miles
New Guinea	808 510	312 167
South Island, New Zealand	151 215	58 384
North Island, New Zealand	115 777	44 702
Tasmania	67 800	26 178

LONGEST RIVERS	km	miles
Murray-Darling	3 750	2 330
Darling	2 739	1 702
Murray	2 589	1 608
Murrumbidgee	1 690	1 050
Lachlan	1 480	919
Macquarie	950	590

LARGEST LAKES	sq km	sq miles
Lake Eyre	0–8 900	0–3 436
Lake Torrens	0–5 780	0–2 232

ASIA Total Land Area 45 036 492 sq km / 17 388 686 sq miles

Mt Everest, China/Nepal

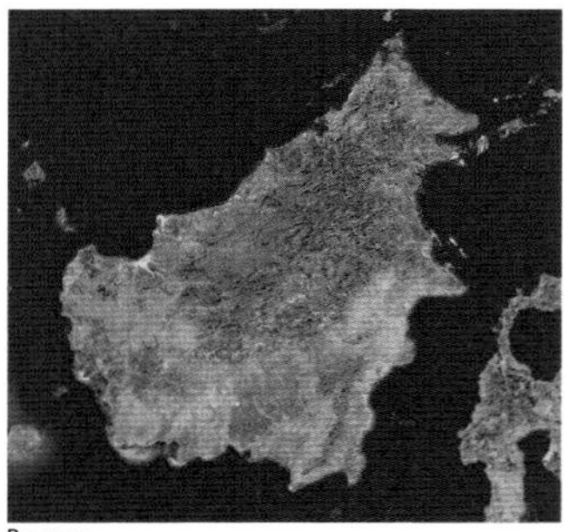
Borneo

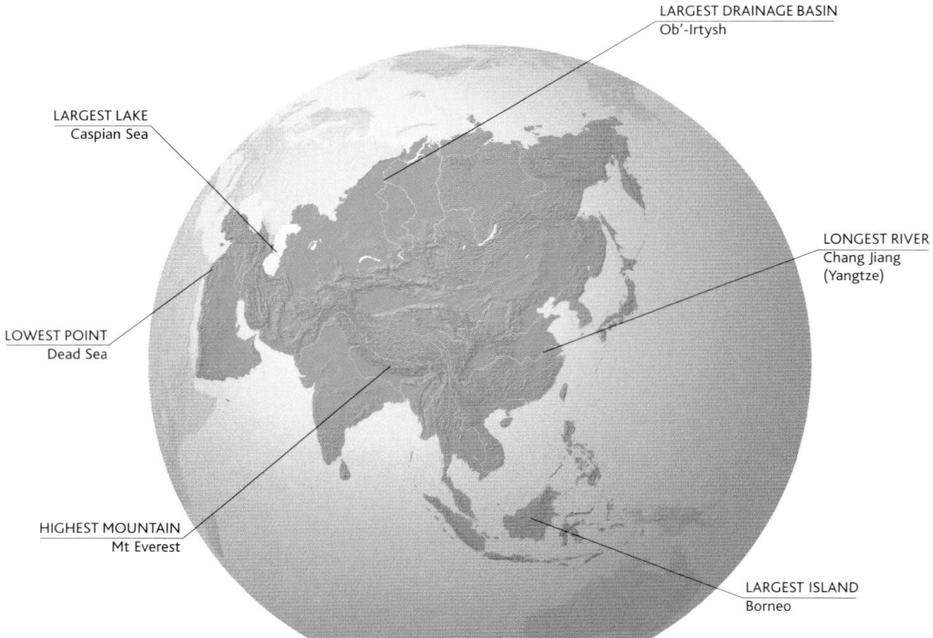
LARGEST DRAINAGE BASIN
Ob'-Irtysh
LARGEST LAKE
Caspian Sea
LONGEST RIVER
Chang Jiang
(Yangtze)
LOWEST POINT
Dead Sea
HIGHEST MOUNTAIN
Mt Everest
LARGEST ISLAND
Borneo

Aral Sea

Chang Jiang (Yangtze), China

HIGHEST MOUNTAINS	metres	feet	Location
Mt Everest (Sagarmatha/ Qomolangma Feng)	8 848	29 028	China/Nepal
K2 (Qogir Feng)	8 611	28 251	China/Jammu and Kashmir
Kangchenjunga	8 586	28 169	India/Nepal
Lhotse	8 516	27 939	China/Nepal
Makalu	8 463	27 765	China/Nepal
Cho Oyu	8 201	26 906	China/Nepal

LARGEST ISLANDS	sq km	sq miles
Borneo	745 561	287 863
Sumatera (Sumatra)	473 606	182 860
Honshū	227 414	87 805
Sulawesi (Celebes)	189 216	73 057
Jawa (Java)	132 188	51 038
Luzon	104 690	40 421

LONGEST RIVERS	km	miles
Chang Jiang (Yangtze)	6 380	3 965
Ob'-Irtysh	5 568	3 460
Yenisey-Angara-Selenga	5 550	3 448
Huang He (Yellow River)	5 464	3 395
Irtysh	4 440	2 759
Mekong	4 425	2 749

LARGEST LAKES	sq km	sq miles
Caspian Sea	371 000	143 244
Ozero Baykal (Lake Baikal)	30 500	11 776
Ozero Balkhash	17 400	6 718
Aral Sea (Aral'skoye More)	17 158	6 625
Ysyk-Köl	6 200	2 393

EUROPE Total Land Area 9 908 599 sq km / 3 825 731 sq miles

El'brus, Russian Federation

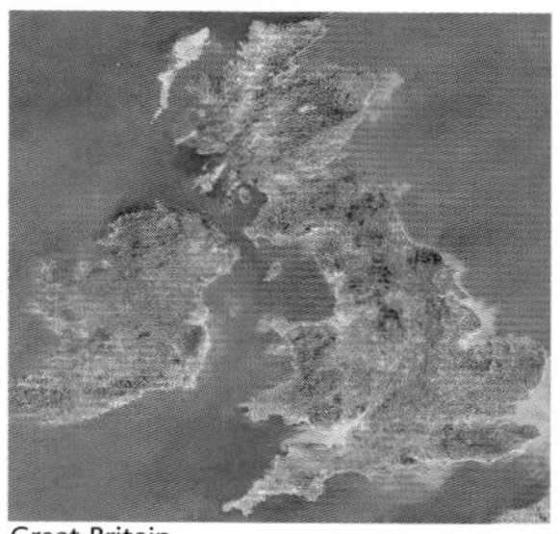
Great Britain

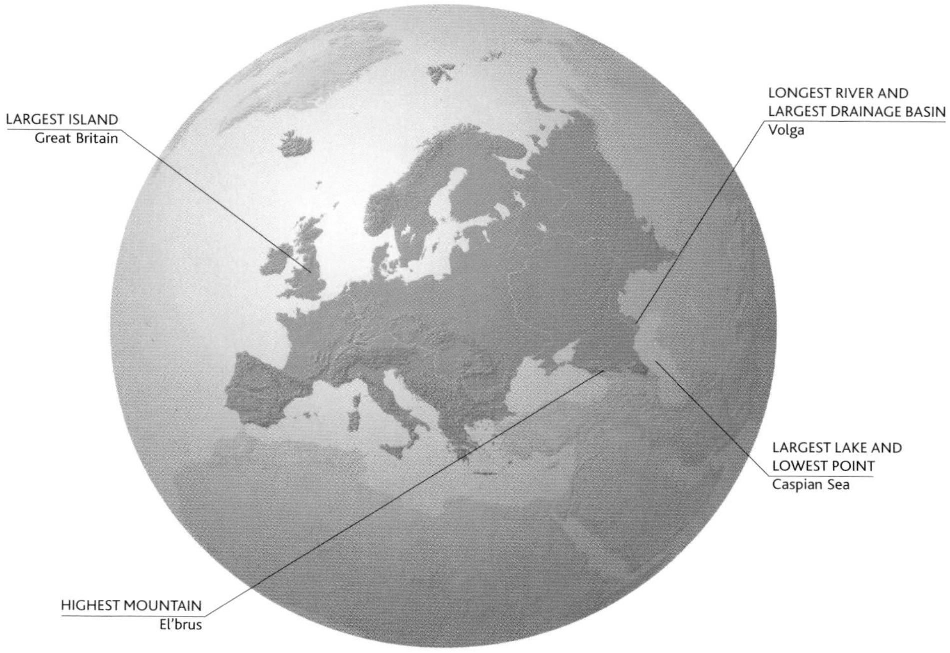
LARGEST ISLAND
Great Britain
LONGEST RIVER AND
LARGEST DRAINAGE BASIN
Volga
LARGEST LAKE AND
LOWEST POINT
Caspian Sea
HIGHEST MOUNTAIN
El'brus

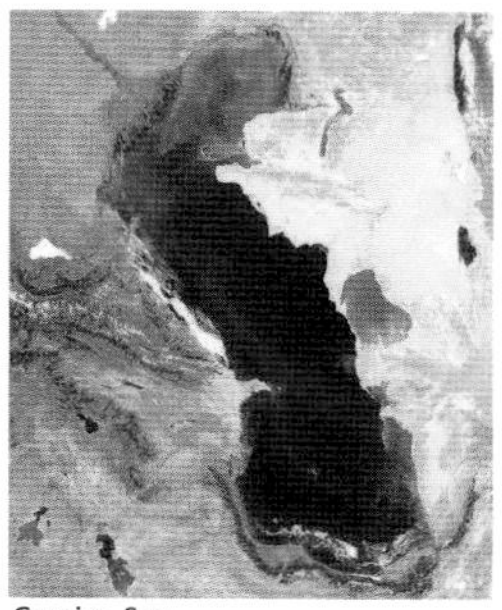
Caspian Sea

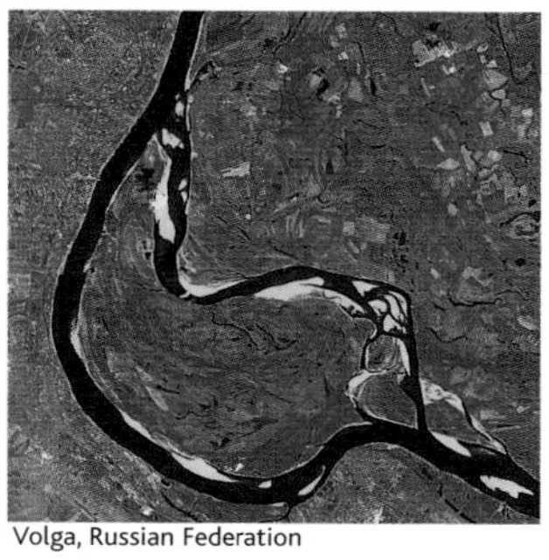
Volga, Russian Federation

HIGHEST MOUNTAINS	metres	feet	Location
El'brus	5 642	18 510	Russian Federation
Gora Dykh-Tau	5 204	17 073	Russian Federation
Shkhara	5 201	17 063	Georgia/Russian Federation
Kazbek	5 047	16 558	Georgia/Russian Federation
Mont Blanc	4 808	15 774	France/Italy
Dufourspitze	4 634	15 203	Italy/Switzerland

LARGEST ISLANDS	sq km	sq miles
Great Britain	218 476	84 354
Iceland	102 820	39 699
Novaya Zemlya	90 650	35 000
Ireland	83 045	32 064
Spitsbergen	37 814	14 600
Sicilia (Sicily)	25 426	9 817

LONGEST RIVERS	km	miles
Volga	3 688	2 291
Danube	2 850	1 770
Dnieper	2 285	1 419
Kama	2 028	1 260
Don	1 931	1 199
Pechora	1 802	1 119

LARGEST LAKES	sq km	sq miles
Caspian Sea	371 000	143 243
Ladozhskoye Ozero (Lake Ladoga)	18 390	7 100
Onezhskoye Ozero (Lake Onega)	9 600	3 706
Vänern	5 585	2 156
Rybinskoye Vodokhranilishche	5 180	2 000

AFRICA Total Land Area 30 343 578 sq km / 11 715 721 sq miles

Kilimanjaro, Tanzania

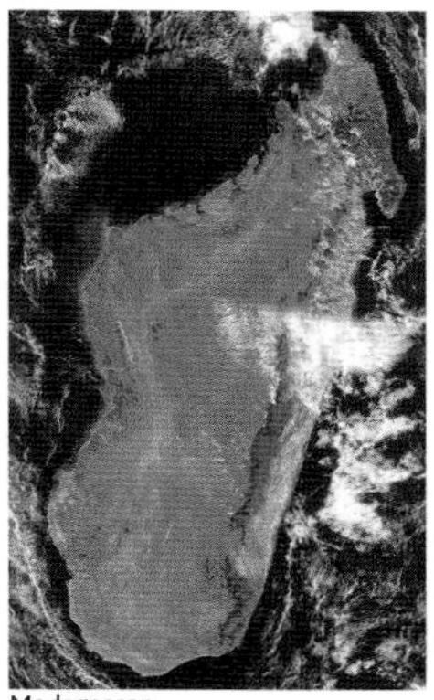
Madagascar

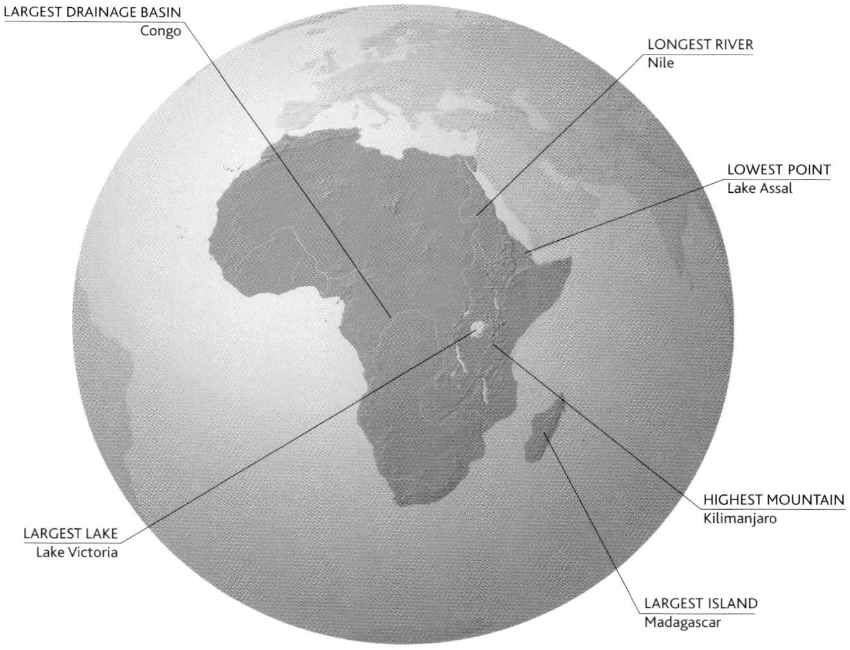
LARGEST DRAINAGE BASIN
Congo
LONGEST RIVER
Nile
LOWEST POINT
Lake Assal
HIGHEST MOUNTAIN
Kilimanjaro
LARGEST LAKE
Lake Victoria
LARGEST ISLAND
Madagascar

Lake Victoria, Kenya/Tanzania/Uganda

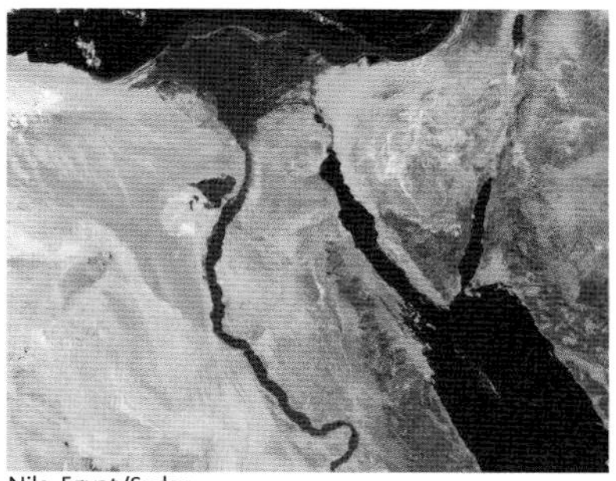
Nile, Egypt/Sudan

HIGHEST MOUNTAINS	metres	feet	Location
Kilimanjaro	5 892	19 331	Tanzania
Kirinyaga (Mt Kenya)	5 199	17 057	Kenya
Margherita Peak (Mt Stanley)	5 110	16 765	Democratic Republic of the Congo/Uganda
Meru	4 565	14 977	Tanzania
Ras Dejen	4 533	14 872	Ethiopia
Mt Karisimbi	4 510	14 796	Rwanda

LARGEST ISLANDS	sq km	sq miles
Madagascar	587 040	226 657

LONGEST RIVERS	km	miles
Nile	6 695	4 160
Congo	4 667	2 900
Niger	4 184	2 599
Zambezi (Zambeze)	2 736	1 700
Webi Shabeelle	2 490	1 547
Ubangi	2 250	1 398

LARGEST LAKES	sq km	sq miles
Lake Victoria	68 800	26 564
Lake Tanganyika	32 900	12 702
Lake Nyasa (Lake Malawi)	30 044	11 600
Lake Volta	8 485	3 276
Lake Turkana	6 475	2 500
Lake Albert	5 600	2 162

NORTH AMERICA

Total Land Area 24 680 331 sq km / 9 529 129 sq miles (including Hawaiian Islands)

Mt McKinley, United States of America

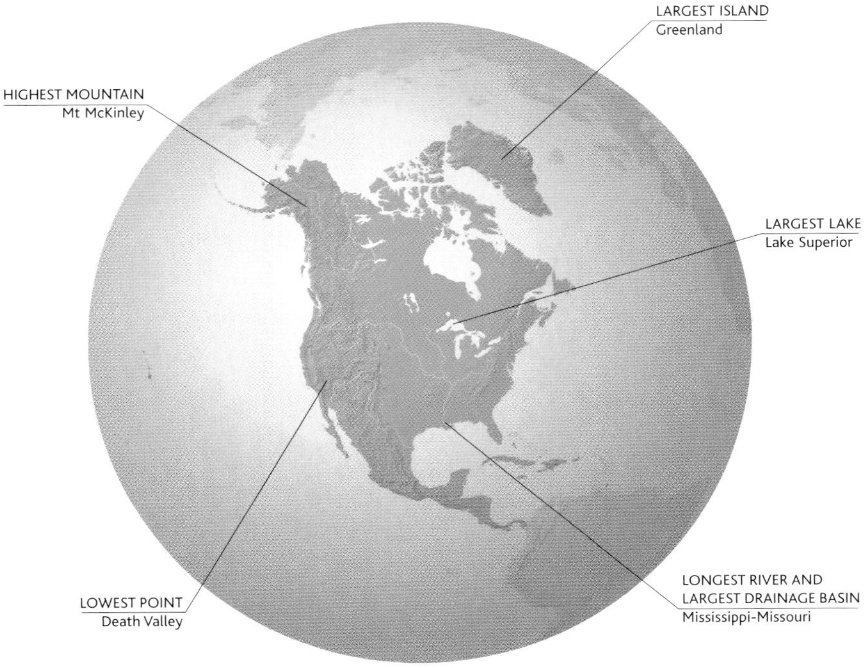
HIGHEST MOUNTAIN
Mt McKinley
LARGEST ISLAND
Greenland
LARGEST LAKE
Lake Superior
LOWEST POINT
Death Valley
LONGEST RIVER AND
LARGEST DRAINAGE BASIN
Mississippi-Missouri

Lake Superior, USA/Canada

Greenland

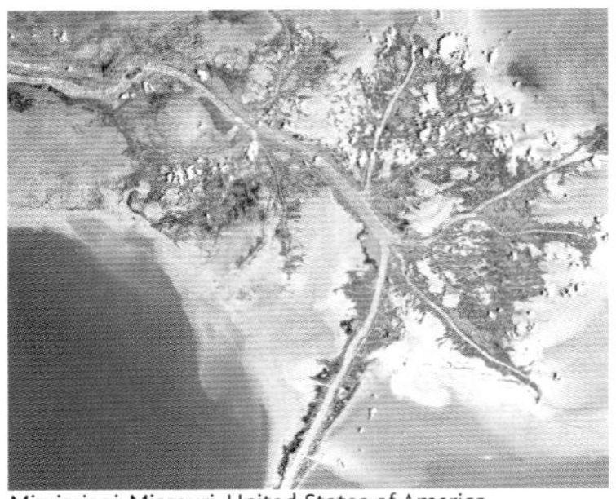

Mississippi-Missouri, United States of America

HIGHEST MOUNTAINS	metres	feet	Location
Mt McKinley	6 194	20 321	USA
Mt Logan	5 959	19 550	Canada
Pico de Orizaba	5 747	18 855	Mexico
Mt St Elias	5 489	18 008	USA
Volcan Popocatépetl	5 452	17 887	Mexico
Mt Foraker	5 303	17 398	USA

LARGEST ISLANDS	sq km	sq miles
Greenland	2 175 600	840 004
Baffin Island	507 451	195 928
Victoria Island	217 291	83 897
Ellesmere Island	196 236	75 767
Cuba	110 860	42 803
Newfoundland	108 860	42 031
Hispaniola	76 192	29 418

LONGEST RIVERS	km	miles
Mississippi-Missouri	5 969	3 709
Mackenzie-Peace-Finlay	4 241	2 635
Missouri	4 086	2 539
Mississippi	3 765	2 339
Yukon	3 185	1 979
Rio Grande (Río Bravo del Norte)	3 057	1 899

LARGEST LAKES	sq km	sq miles
Lake Superior	82 100	31 699
Lake Huron	59 600	23 012
Lake Michigan	57 800	22 317
Great Bear Lake	31 328	12 095
Great Slave Lake	28 568	11 030
Lake Erie	25 700	9 922
Lake Winnipeg	24 387	9 415
Lake Ontario	18 960	7 320

SOUTH AMERICA

Total Land Area 17 815 420 sq km / 6 878 572 sq miles

Cerro Aconcagua, Argentina

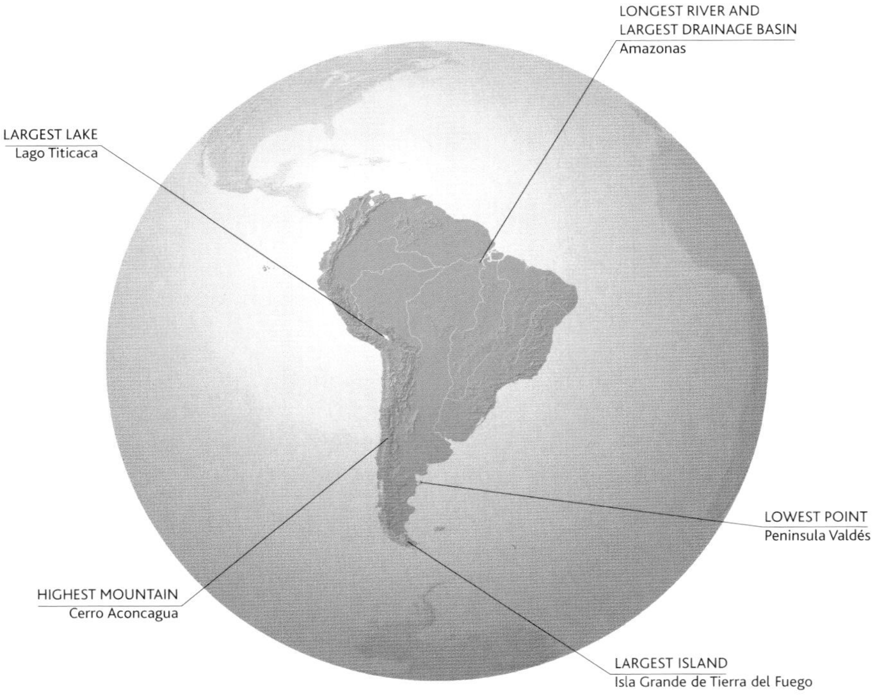
LONGEST RIVER AND
LARGEST DRAINAGE BASIN
Amazonas
LARGEST LAKE
Lago Titicaca
LOWEST POINT
Peninsula Valdés
HIGHEST MOUNTAIN
Cerro Aconcagua
LARGEST ISLAND
Isla Grande de Tierra del Fuego

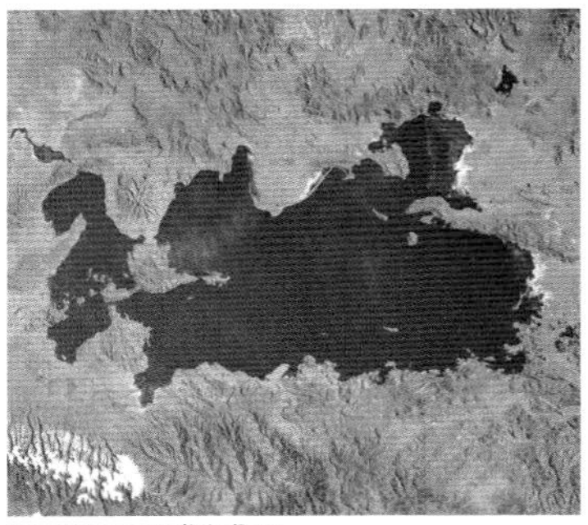

Lago Titicaca, Bolivia/Peru

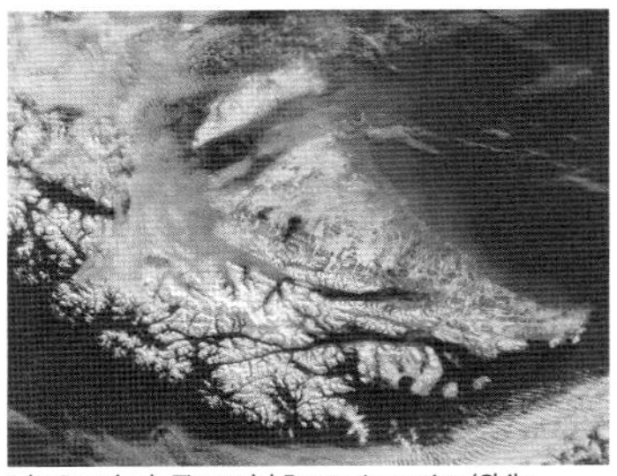

Isla Grande de Tierra del Fuego, Argentina/Chile

Amazonas (Amazon)

HIGHEST MOUNTAINS	metres	feet	Location
Cerro Aconcagua	6 959	22 831	Argentina
Nevado Ojos del Salado	6 908	22 664	Argentina/Chile
Cerro Bonete	6 872	22 546	Argentina
Cerro Pissis	6 858	22 500	Argentina
Cerro Tupungato	6 800	22 309	Argentina/Chile
Cerro Mercedario	6 770	22 211	Argentina

LARGEST ISLANDS	sq km	sq miles
Isla Grande de Tierra del Fuego	47 000	18 147
Isla de Chiloé	8 394	3 240
East Falkland	6 760	2 610
West Falkland	5 413	2 090

LONGEST RIVERS	km	miles
Amazonas (Amazon)	6 516	4 049
Río de la Plata-Paraná	4 500	2 796
Purus	3 218	1 999
Madeira	3 200	1 988
São Francisco	2 900	1 802
Tocantins	2 750	1 708

LARGEST LAKES	sq km	sq miles
Lago Titicaca	8 340	3 220

OCEANS AND POLES

Vinson Massif, West Antarctica

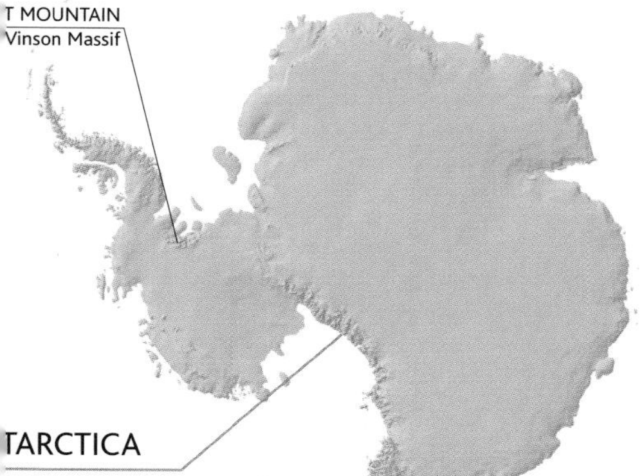
T MOUNTAIN
Vinson Massif

TARCTICA
Land Area 12 093 000 sq km /
9 133 sq miles (excluding ice shelves)

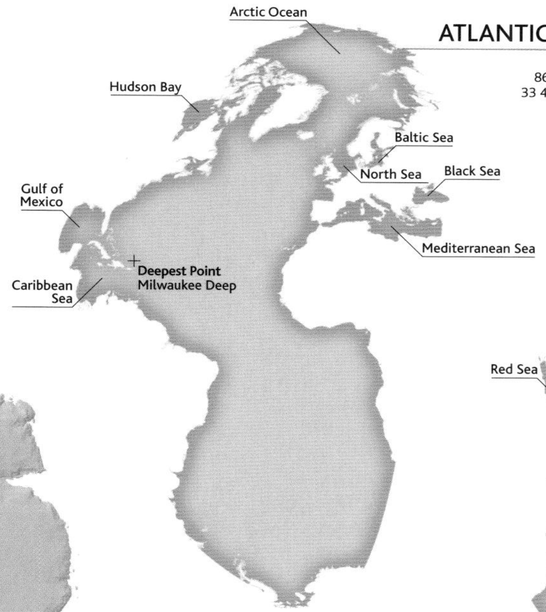
Arctic Ocean
Hudson Bay
Baltic Sea
North Sea
Black Sea
Gulf of Mexico
Mediterranean Sea
Deepest Point
Milwaukee Deep
Caribbean Sea

ATLANTIC OCEAN
Total Area
86 557 000 sq km
33 420 000 sq miles

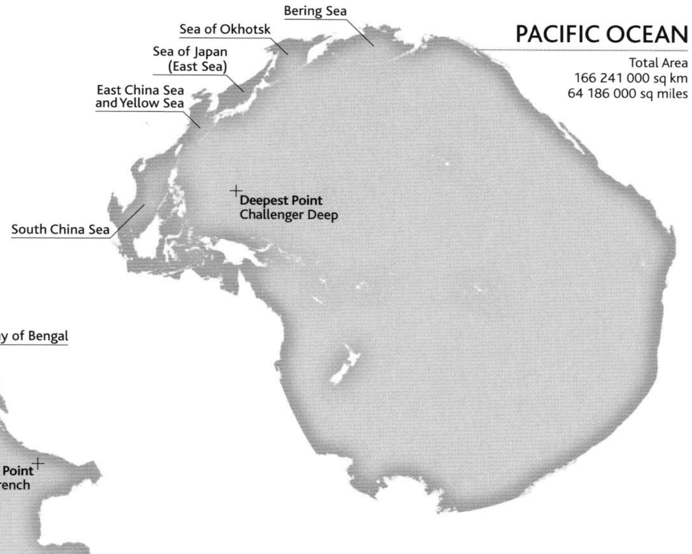
Bering Sea
Sea of Okhotsk
Sea of Japan
(East Sea)
East China Sea
and Yellow Sea
Deepest Point
Challenger Deep
South China Sea

PACIFIC OCEAN
Total Area
166 241 000 sq km
64 186 000 sq miles

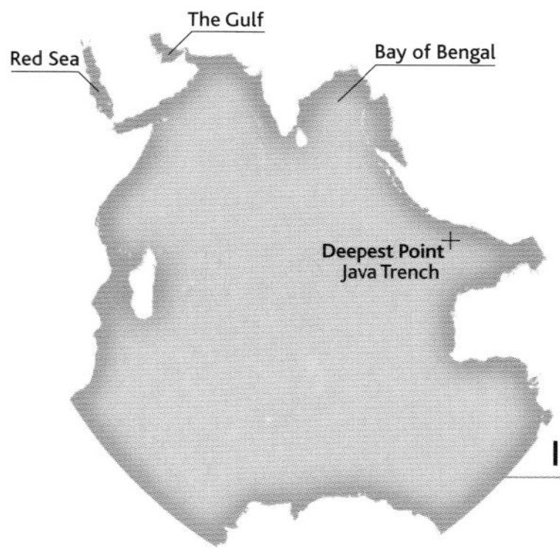
The Gulf
Red Sea
Bay of Bengal
Deepest Point
Java Trench

INDIAN OCEAN
Total Area
73 427 000 sq km
28 350 000 sq miles

EST NTAINS	metres	feet
n Massif	4 897	16 066
ree	4 852	15 918
rkpatrick	4 528	14 855
arkham	4 351	14 275
ckson	4 190	13 747
dley	4 181	13 717

ATLANTIC OCEAN	Area sq km	sq miles	Deepest Point metres	feet
Extent	86 557 000	33 420 000	8 605	28 231
Arctic Ocean	9 485 000	3 662 000	5 450	17 880
Caribbean Sea	2 512 000	970 000	7 680	25 196
Mediterranean Sea	2 510 000	969 000	5 121	16 800
Gulf of Mexico	1 544 000	596 000	3 504	11 495
Hudson Bay	1 233 000	476 000	259	849
North Sea	575 000	222 000	661	2 168
Black Sea	508 000	196 000	2 245	7 365
Baltic Sea	382 000	147 000	460	1 509

INDIAN OCEAN	Area sq km	sq miles	Deepest Point metres	feet
Extent	73 427 000	28 350 000	7 125	23 376
Bay of Bengal	2 172 000	839 000	4 500	14 763
Red Sea	453 000	175 000	3 040	9 973
The Gulf	238 000	92 000	73	239

PACIFIC OCEAN	Area sq km	sq miles	Deepest Point metres	feet
Extent	166 241 000	64 186 000	10 920	35 826
South China Sea	2 590 000	1 000 000	5 514	18 090
Bering Sea	2 261 000	873 000	4 150	13 615
Sea of Okhotsk	1 392 000	537 000	3 363	11 033
Sea of Japan (East Sea)	1 013 000	391 000	3 743	12 280
East China Sea and Yellow Sea	1 202 000	464 000	2 717	8 913

WORLD

HIGHEST MOUNTAINS	metres	feet	Location
Mt Everest	8 848	29 028	China/Nepal
K2	8 611	28 251	China/Jammu and Kashmir
Kangchenjunga	8 586	28 169	India/Nepal
Lhotse	8 516	27 939	China/Nepal
Makalu	8 463	27 765	China/Nepal
Cho Oyu	8 201	26 906	China/Nepal
Dhaulagiri	8 167	26 794	Nepal
Manaslu	8 163	26 781	Nepal
Nanga Parbat	8 126	26 660	Jammu and Kashmir
Annapurna I	8 091	26 545	Nepal
Gasherbrum I	8 068	26 469	China/Jammu and Kashmir
Broad Peak	8 047	26 401	China/Jammu and Kashmir
Gasherbrum II	8 035	26 361	China/Jammu and Kashmir
Xixabangma Feng	8 012	26 286	China
Annapurna II	7 937	26 040	Nepal
Nuptse	7 885	25 869	Nepal
Himalchul	7 864	25 800	Nepal
Masherbrum	7 821	25 659	Jammu and Kashmir
Nandi Devi	7 816	25 643	India
Rakaposhi	7 788	25 551	Jammu and Kashmir

LARGEST ISLANDS	sq km	sq miles	Continent
Greenland	2 175 600	840 004	North America
New Guinea	808 510	312 167	Australasia
Borneo	745 561	287 863	Asia
Madagascar	587 040	266 657	Africa
Baffin Island	507 451	195 928	North America
Sumatera	473 606	182 860	Asia
Honshū	227 414	87 805	Asia
Great Britain	218 476	84 354	Europe
Victoria Island	217 291	83 897	North America
Ellesmere Island	196 236	75 767	North America
Sulawesi (Celebes)	189 216	73 057	Asia
South Island, New Zealand	151 215	58 384	Australasia
Jawa (Java)	132 188	51 038	Asia
North Island, New Zealand	115 777	44 702	Australasia
Cuba	110 860	42 803	North America
Newfoundland	108 860	42 031	North America
Luzon	104 690	40 421	Asia
Iceland	102 820	39 699	Europe
Mindanao	94 630	36 537	Asia
Novaya Zemlya	90 650	35 000	Europe

LONGEST RIVERS	km	miles	Continent
Nile	6 695	4 160	Africa
Amazonas (Amazon)	6 516	4 049	South America
Chang Jiang (Yangtze)	6 380	3 965	Asia
Mississippi-Missouri	5 969	3 709	North America
Ob'-Irtysh	5 568	3 460	Asia
Yenisey-Angara-Selenga	5 550	3 449	Asia
Huang He (Yellow River)	5 464	3 395	Asia
Congo	4 667	2 900	Africa
Río de la Plata-Paraná	4 500	2 796	South America
Irtysh	4 440	2 759	Asia
Mekong	4 425	2 750	Asia
Heilong Jiang (Amur)-Argun'	4 416	2 744	Asia
Lena-Kirenga	4 400	2 734	Asia
MacKenzie-Peace-Finlay	4 241	2 635	North America
Niger	4 184	2 600	Africa
Yenisey	4 090	2 542	Asia
Missouri	4 086	2 539	North America
Mississippi	3 765	2 340	North America
Murray-Darling	3 750	2 330	Australasia
Ob'	3 701	2 300	Asia

LARGEST DRAINAGE BASINS	sq km	sq miles	Continent
Amazonas (Amazon)	7 050 000	2 722 000	South America
Congo	3 700 000	1 429 000	Africa
Nile	3 349 000	1 293 000	Africa
Mississippi-Missouri	3 250 000	1 255 000	North America
Río de la Plata-Paraná	3 100 000	1 197 000	South America
Ob'-Irtysh	2 990 000	1 154 000	Asia
Yenisey-Angara-Selenga	2 580 000	996 000	Asia
Lena-Kirenga	2 490 000	961 000	Asia
Chang Jiang (Yangtze)	1 959 000	756 000	Asia
Niger	1 890 000	730 000	Africa
Heilong Jiang (Amur)-Argun'	1 855 000	716 000	Asia
Mackenzie-Peace-Finlay	1 805 000	697 000	North America
Ganga (Ganges)-Brahmaputra	1 621 000	626 000	Asia
St Lawrence-St Louis	1 463 000	565 000	North America
Volga	1 380 000	533 000	Europe
Zambezi (Zambeze)	1 330 000	514 000	Africa
Indus	1 166 000	450 000	Asia
Nelson-Saskatchewan	1 150 000	444 000	North America
Shaṭṭ al'Arab	1 114 000	430 000	Asia
Murray-Darling	1 058 000	408 000	Australasia

LARGEST LAKES	sq km	sq miles	Continent
Caspian Sea	371 000	143 244	Asia/Europe
Lake Superior	82 100	31 699	North America
Lake Victoria	68 800	26 564	Africa
Lake Huron	59 600	23 012	North America
Lake Michigan	57 800	22 317	North America
Lake Tanganyika	32 900	12 702	Africa
Great Bear Lake	31 328	12 095	North America
Ozero Baykal (Lake Baikal)	30 500	11 776	Asia
Lake Nyasa (Lake Malawi)	30 044	11 600	Africa
Great Slave Lake	28 568	11 030	North America
Lake Erie	25 700	9 922	North America
Lake Winnipeg	24 387	9 415	North America
Lake Ontario	18 960	7 320	North America
Ladozhskoye Ozero (Lake Ladoga)	18 390	7 100	Europe
Ozero Balkhash	17 400	6 718	Asia
Aral Sea (Aral'skoye More)	17 158	6 625	Asia
Onezhskoye Ozero (Lake Onega)	9 600	3 706	Europe
Lake Volta	8 485	3 276	Africa
Lake Titicaca	8 340	3 220	South America
Lago de Nicaragua	8 150	3 147	North America

EARTH'S DIMENSIONS	
Mass	5.974 X 10^{21} tonnes
Total area	509 450 000 sq km / 196 672 000 sq miles
Land area	149 450 000 sq km / 57 688 000 sq miles
Water area	360 000 000 sq km / 138 984 000 sq miles
Volume	1 083 207 x 10^6 cubic km / 259 875 x 10^6 cubic miles
Equatorial diameter	12 756 km / 7 926 miles
Polar diameter	12 714 km / 7 900 miles
Equatorial circumference	40 075 km / 24 903 miles
Meridional circumference	40 008 km / 24 861 miles

All 194 independent countries and all populated dependent and disputed territories are included in this list of the states and territories of the world; the list is arranged in alphabetical order by the conventional name form. For independent states, the full name is given below the conventional name, if this is different; for territories, the status is given. The capital city name is given in the local form as shown on the reference maps.

Area and population statistics are the latest available and include estimates. The information on languages and religions is based on the latest information on 'de facto' speakers of the language or 'de facto' adherents of the religion. This varies greatly from country to country because some countries include questions in censuses while others do not, in which case best estimates are used. The order of the languages and religions reflects their relative importance within the country; generally, languages or religions are included when more than one per cent of the population are estimated to be speakers or adherents.

Membership of selected international organizations is shown by the abbreviations below; dependent territories do not normally have separate memberships of these organizations.

APEC	Asia-Pacific Economic Cooperation
ASEAN	Association of Southeast Asian Nations
CARICOM	Caribbean Community
CIS	Commonwealth of Independent States
Comm.	The Commonwealth
EU	European Union
NATO	North Atlantic Treaty Organization
OECD	Organisation for Economic Co-operation and Development
OPEC	Organization of Petroleum Exporting Countries
SADC	Southern African Development Community
UN	United Nations

AFGHANISTAN
Islamic State of Afghanistan

Area Sq Km	652 225	**Currency**	Afghani
Area Sq Miles	251 825	**Languages**	Dari, Pushtu, Uzbek, Turkmen
Population	29 863 000	**Religions**	Sunni Muslim, Shi'a Muslim
Capital	Kābul	**Organizations**	UN

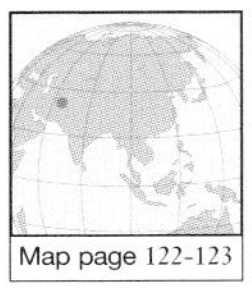

Map page 122–123

A landlocked country in central Asia with central highlands bordered by plains in the north and southwest, and by the Hindu Kush mountains in the northeast. The climate is dry continental. Over the last thirty years war has disrupted the economy, which is highly dependent on farming and livestock rearing. Most trade is with the former USSR, Pakistan and Iran.

ALBANIA
Republic of Albania

Area Sq Km	28 748	**Currency**	Lek
Area Sq Miles	11 100	**Languages**	Albanian, Greek
Population	3 130 000	**Religions**	Sunni Muslim, Orthodox, Roman Catholic
Capital	Tiranë	**Organizations**	UN

Albania lies in the western Balkan Mountains in southeastern Europe, bordering the Adriatic Sea. It is mountainous, with coastal plains where half the population lives. The economy is based on agriculture and mining. Albania is one of the poorest countries in Europe and relies heavily on foreign aid.

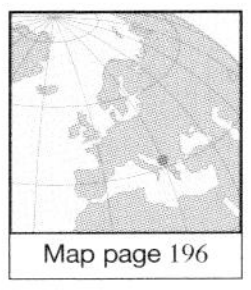

Map page 196

ALGERIA
People's Democratic Republic of Algeria

Area Sq Km	2 381 741	**Currency**	Algerian dinar
Area Sq Miles	919 595	**Languages**	Arabic, French, Berber
Population	32 854 000	**Religions**	Sunni Muslim
Capital	Alger (Algiers)	**Organizations**	OPEC, UN

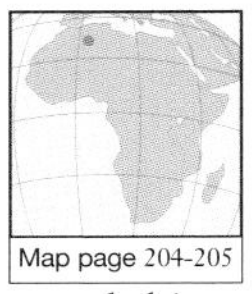

Map page 204–205

Algeria, the second largest country in Africa, lies on the Mediterranean coast of northwest Africa and extends southwards to the Atlas Mountains and the dry sandstone plateau and desert of the Sahara. The climate ranges from Mediterranean on the coast to semi-arid and arid inland. The most populated areas are the coastal plains and the fertile northern slopes of the Atlas Mountains. Oil, natural gas and related products account for over ninety-five per cent of export earnings. Agriculture employs about a quarter of the workforce, producing mainly food crops. Algeria's main trading partners are Italy, France and the USA.

American Samoa
United States Unincorporated Territory

Area Sq Km	197	**Currency**	United States dollar
Area Sq Miles	76	**Languages**	Samoan, English
Population	65 000	**Religions**	Protestant, Roman Catholic
Capital	Fagatogo		

Lying in the south Pacific Ocean, American Samoa consists of five main islands and two coral atolls. The largest island is Tutuila. Tuna and tuna products are the main exports, and the main trading partner is the USA.

Map page 78

ANDORRA
Principality of Andorra

Area Sq Km	465	**Currency**	Euro
Area Sq Miles	180	**Languages**	Spanish, Catalan, French
Population	67 000	**Religions**	Roman Catholic
Capital	Andorra la Vella	**Organizations**	UN

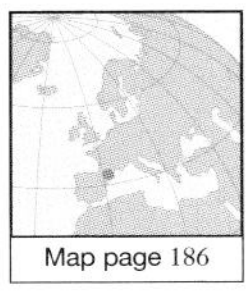

Map page 186

A landlocked state in southwest Europe, Andorra lies in the Pyrenees mountain range between France and Spain. It consists of deep valleys and gorges, surrounded by mountains. Tourism, encouraged by the development of ski resorts, is the mainstay of the economy. Banking is also an important economic activity.

ANGOLA
Republic of Angola

Area Sq Km	1 246 700	**Currency**	Kwanza
Area Sq Miles	481 354	**Languages**	Portuguese, Bantu, local languages
Population	15 941 000	**Religions**	Roman Catholic, Protestant, traditional beliefs
Capital	Luanda	**Organizations**	SADC, UN

Angola lies on the Atlantic coast of south central Africa. Its small northern province, Cabinda, is separated from the rest of the country by part of the Democratic Republic of the Congo. Much of Angola is high plateau. In the west is a narrow coastal plain and in the southwest is desert. The climate is equatorial in the north but desert in the south. Over eighty per cent of the population relies on subsistence agriculture. Angola is rich in minerals (particularly diamonds), and oil accounts for approximately ninety per cent of export earnings. The USA, South Korea and Portugal are its main trading partners.

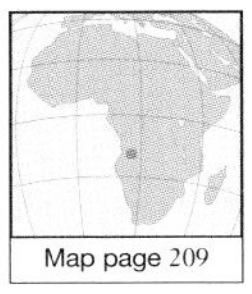

Map page 209

Anguilla
United Kingdom Overseas Territory

Area Sq Km	155	**Currency**	East Caribbean dollar
Area Sq Miles	60	**Languages**	English
Population	12 000	**Religions**	Protestant, Roman Catholic
Capital	The Valley		

Anguilla lies at the northern end of the Leeward Islands in the eastern Caribbean. Tourism and fishing form the basis of the economy.

Map page 247

ANTIGUA AND BARBUDA

Area Sq Km	442	**Currency**	East Caribbean dollar
Area Sq Miles	171	**Languages**	English, creole
Population	81 000	**Religions**	Protestant, Roman Catholic
Capital	St John's	**Organizations**	CARICOM, Comm., UN

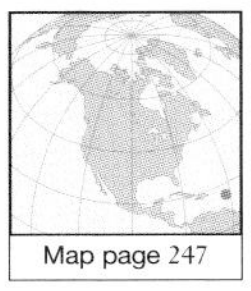

Map page 247

The state comprises the islands of Antigua, Barbuda and the tiny rocky outcrop of Redonda, in the Leeward Islands in the eastern Caribbean. Antigua, the largest and most populous island, is mainly hilly scrubland, with many beaches. The climate is tropical, and the economy relies heavily on tourism. Most trade is with other eastern Caribbean states and the USA.

ARGENTINA
Argentine Republic

Area Sq Km	2 766 889	**Currency**	Argentinian peso
Area Sq Miles	1 068 302	**Languages**	Spanish, Italian, Amerindian languages
Population	38 747 000	**Religions**	Roman Catholic, Protestant
Capital	Buenos Aires	**Organizations**	UN

Argentina, the second largest state in South America, extends from Bolivia to Cape Horn and from the Andes mountains to the Atlantic Ocean. It has four geographical regions: subtropical forests and swampland in the northeast; temperate fertile plains or Pampas in the centre; the wooded foothills and valleys of the Andes in the west; and the cold, semi-arid plateaus of Patagonia in the south. The highest mountain in South America, Cerro Aconcagua, is in Argentina. Nearly ninety per cent of the population lives in towns and cities. The country is rich in natural resources including petroleum, natural gas, ores and precious metals. Agricultural products dominate exports, which also include motor vehicles and crude oil. Most trade is with Brazil and the USA.

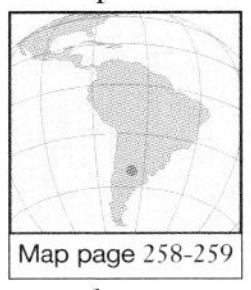

Map page 258–259

ARMENIA
Republic of Armenia

Area Sq Km	29 800	**Currency**	Dram
Area Sq Miles	11 506	**Languages**	Armenian, Azeri
Population	3 016 000	**Religions**	Armenian Orthodox
Capital	Yerevan (Erevan)	**Organizations**	CIS, UN

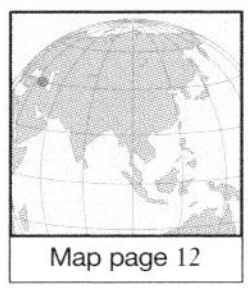

Map page 12

A landlocked state in southwest Asia, Armenia lies in the south of the Lesser Caucasus mountains. It is a mountainous country with a continental climate. One-third of the population lives in the capital, Yerevan. Exports include diamonds, scrap metal and machinery. Many Armenians depend on remittances from abroad.

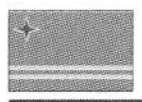

Aruba
Self-governing Netherlands Territory

Area Sq Km	193	**Currency**	Aruban florin
Area Sq Miles	75	**Languages**	Papiamento, Dutch, English
Population	99 000	**Religions**	Roman Catholic, Protestant
Capital	Oranjestad		

The most southwesterly of the islands in the Lesser Antilles in the Caribbean, Aruba lies just off the coast of Venezuela. Tourism, offshore finance and oil refining are the most important sectors of the economy. The USA is the main trading partner.

Map page 247

Ascension Dependency of St Helena

Area Sq Km (Miles)	88 (34)	**Population**	1 122	**Capital**	Georgetown

A volcanic island in the south Atlantic Ocean about 1 300 kilometres (800 miles) northwest of St Helena.

Map page 216

AUSTRALIA
Commonwealth of Australia

Area Sq Km	7 692 024	**Currency**	Australian dollar
Area Sq Miles	2 969 907	**Languages**	English, Italian, Greek
Population	20 155 000	**Religions**	Protestant, Roman Catholic, Orthodox
Capital	Canberra	**Organizations**	APEC, Comm., OECD, UN

Australia, the world's sixth largest country, occupies the smallest, flattest and driest continent. The western half of the continent is mostly arid plateaus, ridges and vast deserts. The central eastern area comprises the lowlands of river systems draining into Lake Eyre, while to the east is the Great Dividing Range, a belt of ridges and plateaus running from Queensland to Tasmania. Climatically, more than two-thirds of the country is arid or semi-arid. The north is tropical monsoon, the east subtropical, and the southwest and southeast temperate. The majority of Australia's highly urbanized population lives along the east, southeast and southwest coasts. Australia has vast mineral deposits and various sources of energy. It is among the world's leading producers of iron ore, bauxite, nickel, copper and uranium. It is a major producer of coal, and oil and natural gas are also being exploited. Although accounting for only five per cent of the workforce, agriculture continues to be an important sector of the economy, with food and agricultural raw materials making up most of Australia's export earnings. Fuel, ores and metals, and manufactured goods, account for the remainder of exports. Japan and the USA are Australia's main trading partners.

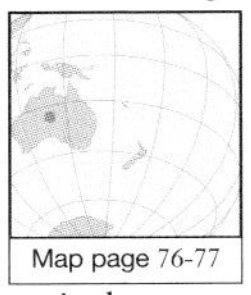

Map page 76–77

Australian Capital Territory (Federal territory)					
Area Sq Km (Miles)	2 358 (910)	**Population**	321 680	**Capital**	Canberra
Jervis Bay Territory (Territory)					
Area Sq Km (Miles)	73 (28)	**Population**	611	**Capital**	
New South Wales (State)					
Area Sq Km (Miles)	800 642 (309 130)	**Population**	6 609 304	**Capital**	Sydney
Northern Territory (Territory)					
Area Sq Km (Miles)	1 349 129 (520 902)	**Population**	200 019	**Capital**	Darwin
Queensland (State)					
Area Sq Km (Miles)	1 730 648 (668 207)	**Population**	3 635 121	**Capital**	Brisbane
South Australia (State)					
Area Sq Km (Miles)	983 482 (379 725)	**Population**	1 514 854	**Capital**	Adelaide
Tasmania (State)					
Area Sq Km (Miles)	68 401 (26 410)	**Population**	472 931	**Capital**	Hobart
Victoria (State)					
Area Sq Km (Miles)	227 416 (87 806)	**Population**	4 822 663	**Capital**	Melbourne
Western Australia (State)					
Area Sq Km (Miles)	2 529 875 (976 790)	**Population**	1 906 114	**Capital**	Perth

AUSTRIA
Republic of Austria

Area Sq Km	83 855	**Currency**	Euro
Area Sq Miles	32 377	**Languages**	German, Croatian, Turkish
Population	8 189 000	**Religions**	Roman Catholic, Protestant
Capital	Wien (Vienna)	**Organizations**	EU, OECD, UN

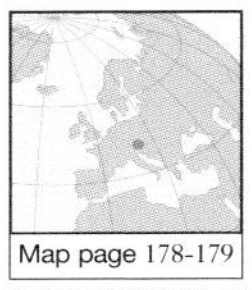

Map page 178–179

Two-thirds of Austria, a landlocked state in central Europe, lies within the Alps, with lower mountains to the north. The only lowlands are in the east. The Danube river valley in the northeast contains almost all the agricultural land and most of the population. Although the climate varies with altitude, in general summers are warm and winters cold with heavy snowfalls. Manufacturing industry and tourism are the most important sectors of the economy. Exports are dominated by manufactured goods. Germany is Austria's main trading partner.

AZERBAIJAN
Republic of Azerbaijan

Area Sq Km	86 600	**Currency**	Azerbaijani manat
Area Sq Miles	33 436	**Languages**	Azeri, Armenian, Russian, Lezgian
Population	8 411 000	**Religions**	Shi'a Muslim, Sunni Muslim, Orthodox
Capital	Bakı (Baku)	**Organizations**	CIS, UN

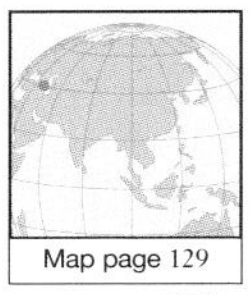

Map page 129

Azerbaijan lies to the southeast of the Caucasus mountains, on the Caspian Sea. Its region of Naxçivan is separated from the rest of the country by part of Armenia. It has mountains in the northeast and west, valleys in the centre, and a low coastal plain. The climate is continental. It is rich in energy and mineral resources. Oil production, onshore and offshore, is the main industry and the basis of heavy industries. Agriculture is important, with cotton and tobacco the main cash crops.

THE BAHAMAS
Commonwealth of the Bahamas

Area Sq Km	13 939	**Currency**	Bahamian dollar
Area Sq Miles	5 382	**Languages**	English, creole
Population	323 000	**Religions**	Protestant, Roman Catholic
Capital	Nassau	**Organizations**	CARICOM, Comm., UN

The Bahamas, an archipelago made up of approximately seven hundred islands and over two thousand cays, lies to the northeast of Cuba and east of the Florida coast of the USA. Twenty-two islands are inhabited, and two-thirds of the population lives on the main island of

New Providence. The climate is warm for much of the year, with heavy rainfall in the summer. Tourism is the islands' main industry. Offshore banking, insurance and ship registration are also major foreign exchange earners.

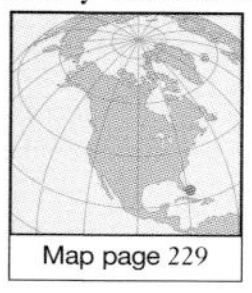
Map page 229

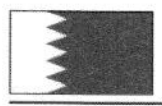

BAHRAIN
Kingdom of Bahrain

Area Sq Km	691	**Currency**	Bahraini dinar
Area Sq Miles	267	**Languages**	Arabic, English
Population	727 000	**Religions**	Shi'a Muslim, Sunni Muslim, Christian
Capital	Al Manāmah (Manama)	**Organizations**	UN

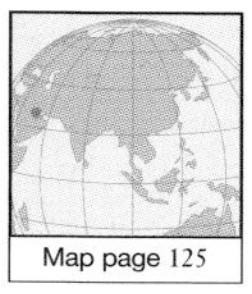
Map page 125

Bahrain consists of more than thirty islands lying in a bay in The Gulf, off the coasts of Saudi Arabia and Qatar. Bahrain Island, the largest island, is connected to other islands and to the mainland of Arabia by causeways. Oil production and processing are the main sectors of the economy.

BANGLADESH
People's Republic of Bangladesh

Area Sq Km	143 998	**Currency**	Taka
Area Sq Miles	55 598	**Languages**	Bengali, English
Population	141 822 000	**Religions**	Sunni Muslim, Hindu
Capital	Dhaka	**Organizations**	Comm., UN

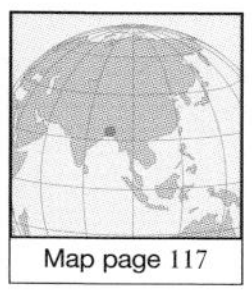
Map page 117

The south Asian state of Bangladesh is in the northeast of the Indian subcontinent, on the Bay of Bengal. It consists almost entirely of the low-lying alluvial plains and deltas of the Ganges and Brahmaputra rivers. The southwest is swampy, with mangrove forests in the delta area. The north, northeast and southeast have low forested hills. Bangladesh is one of the world's most densely populated and least developed countries. The economy is based on agriculture, though the garment industry is the main export sector. Floods and cyclones during the summer monsoon season often cause devastating flooding and crop destruction. The country relies on large-scale foreign aid and remittances from workers abroad.

BARBADOS

Area Sq Km	430	**Currency**	Barbados dollar
Area Sq Miles	166	**Languages**	English, creole
Population	270 000	**Religions**	Protestant, Roman Catholic
Capital	Bridgetown	**Organizations**	CARICOM, Comm., UN

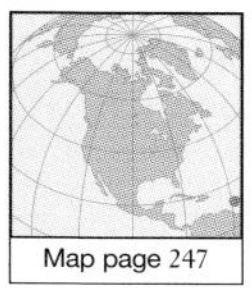
Map page 247

The most easterly of the Caribbean islands, Barbados is small and densely populated. It has a tropical climate and is subject to hurricanes. The economy is based on tourism, financial services, light industries and sugar production.

BELARUS
Republic of Belarus

Area Sq Km	207 600	**Currency**	Belarus rouble
Area Sq Miles	80 155	**Languages**	Belorussian, Russian
Population	9 755 000	**Religions**	Belorussian Orthodox, Roman Catholic
Capital	Minsk	**Organizations**	CIS, UN

Belarus, a landlocked state in eastern Europe, consists of low hills and plains, with many lakes, rivers and, in the south, extensive marshes. Forests cover approximately one-third of the country. It has a continental climate. Agriculture contributes one-third of national income, with beef cattle and grains as the major products. Manufacturing industries produce a range of items, from construction equipment to textiles. The Russian Federation and Ukraine are the main trading partners.

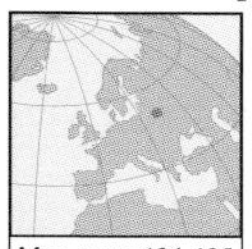
Map page 134–135

BELGIUM
Kingdom of Belgium

Area Sq Km	30 520	**Currency**	Euro
Area Sq Miles	11 784	**Languages**	Dutch (Flemish), French (Walloon), German
Population	10 419 000	**Religions**	Roman Catholic, Protestant
Capital	Bruxelles/Brussel (Brussels)	**Organizations**	EU, NATO, OECD, UN

Belgium lies on the North Sea coast of western Europe. Beyond low sand dunes and a narrow belt of reclaimed land, fertile plains extend to the Sambre-Meuse river valley. The land rises to the forested Ardennes plateau in the southeast. Belgium has mild winters and cool summers. It is densely populated and has a highly urbanized population. With few mineral resources, Belgium imports raw materials for processing and manufacture. The agricultural sector is small, but provides for most food needs. A large services sector reflects Belgium's position as the home base for over eight hundred international institutions. The headquarters of the European Union are in the capital, Brussels.

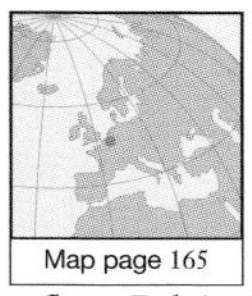
Map page 165

BELIZE

Area Sq Km	22 965	**Currency**	Belize dollar
Area Sq Miles	8 867	**Languages**	English, Spanish, Mayan, creole
Population	270 000	**Religions**	Roman Catholic, Protestant
Capital	Belmopan	**Organizations**	CARICOM, Comm., UN

Belize lies on the Caribbean coast of central America and includes numerous cays and a large barrier reef offshore. The coastal areas are flat and swampy. To the southwest are the Maya Mountains. Tropical jungle covers much of the country and the climate is humid tropical, but tempered by sea breezes. A third of the population lives in the capital. The economy is based primarily on agriculture, forestry and fishing, and exports include raw sugar, orange concentrate and bananas.

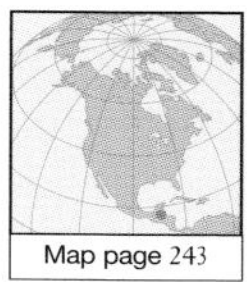
Map page 243

BENIN
Republic of Benin

Area Sq Km	112 620	**Currency**	CFA franc
Area Sq Miles	43 483	**Languages**	French, Fon, Yoruba, Adja, local languages
Population	8 439 000	**Religions**	Traditional beliefs, Roman Catholic, Sunni Muslim
Capital	Porto-Novo	**Organizations**	UN

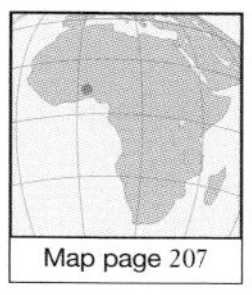
Map page 207

Benin is in west Africa, on the Gulf of Guinea. The climate is tropical in the north, equatorial in the south. The economy is based mainly on agriculture and transit trade. Agricultural products account for two-thirds of export earnings. Oil, produced offshore, is also a major export.

Bermuda
United Kingdom Overseas Territory

Area Sq Km	54	**Currency**	Bermuda dollar
Area Sq Miles	21	**Languages**	English
Population	64 000	**Religions**	Protestant, Roman Catholic
Capital	Hamilton		

In the Atlantic Ocean to the east of the USA, Bermuda comprises a group of small islands with a warm and humid climate. The economy is based on tourism, insurance and shipping.

Map page 231

BHUTAN
Kingdom of Bhutan

Area Sq Km	46 620	**Currency**	Ngultrum, Indian rupee
Area Sq Miles	18 000	**Languages**	Dzongkha, Nepali, Assamese
Population	2 163 000	**Religions**	Buddhist, Hindu
Capital	Thimphu	**Organizations**	UN

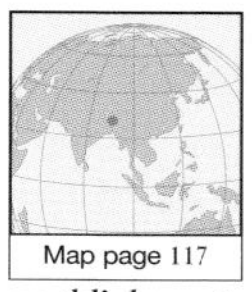
Map page 117

Bhutan lies in the eastern Himalaya mountains, between China and India. It is mountainous in the north, with fertile valleys. The climate ranges between permanently cold in the far north and subtropical in the south. Most of the population is involved in livestock rearing and subsistence farming. Bhutan is the world's largest producer of cardamom. Tourism is an increasingly important foreign currency earner.

BOLIVIA
Republic of Bolivia

Area Sq Km	1 098 581	**Currency**	Boliviano
Area Sq Miles	424 164	**Languages**	Spanish, Quechua, Aymara
Population	9 182 000	**Religions**	Roman Catholic, Protestant, Baha'i
Capital	La Paz/Sucre	**Organizations**	UN

Map page 252–253

Bolivia is a landlocked state in central South America. Most Bolivians live on the high plateau within the Andes mountains. The lowlands range between dense rainforest in the northeast and semi-arid grasslands in the southeast. Bolivia is rich in minerals (zinc, tin and gold), and sales generate approximately half of export income. Natural gas, timber and soya beans are also exported. The USA is the main trading partner.

Bonaire part of Netherlands Antilles

Area Sq Km (Miles) 288 (111) **Population** 10 114 **Capital** Kralendijk

An island in the Caribbean Sea off the north coast of Venezuela, known for its fine beaches; tourism is the mainstay of the economy.

Map page 247

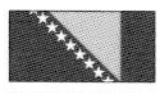

BOSNIA-HERZEGOVINA
Republic of Bosnia and Herzegovina

Area Sq Km	51 130	**Currency**	Marka
Area Sq Miles	19 741	**Languages**	Bosnian, Serbian, Croatian
Population	3 907 000	**Religions**	Sunni Muslim, Orthodox, Roman Catholic, Protestant
Capital	Sarajevo	**Organizations**	UN

Bosnia-Herzegovina lies in the western Balkan Mountains of southern Europe, on the Adriatic Sea. It is mountainous, with ridges running northwest–southeast. The main lowlands are around the Sava valley in the north. Summers are warm, but winters can be very cold. The economy relies heavily on overseas aid.

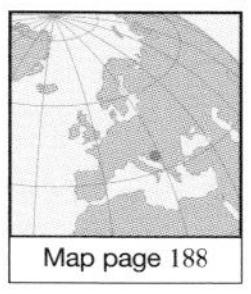
Map page 188

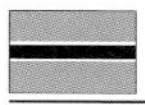

BOTSWANA
Republic of Botswana

Area Sq Km	581 370	**Currency**	Pula
Area Sq Miles	224 468	**Languages**	English, Setswana, Shona, local languages
Population	1 765 000	**Religions**	Traditional beliefs, Protestant, Roman Catholic
Capital	Gaborone	**Organizations**	Comm., SADC, UN

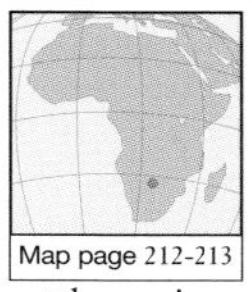
Map page 212–213

Botswana is a landlocked state in southern Africa. Over half of the country lies within the Kalahari Desert, with swamps to the north and salt-pans to the northeast. Most of the population lives near the eastern border. The climate is subtropical, but drought-prone. The economy was founded on cattle rearing, and although beef remains an important export, the economy is now based on mining. Diamonds account for seventy per cent of export earnings. Copper-nickel matte is also exported. Most trade is with members of the South African Customs Union.

BRAZIL
Federative Republic of Brazil

Area Sq Km	8 514 879	**Currency**	Real
Area Sq Miles	3 287 613	**Languages**	Portuguese
Population	186 405 000	**Religions**	Roman Catholic, Protestant
Capital	Brasília	**Organizations**	UN

Brazil, in eastern South America, covers almost half of the continent, and is the world's fifth largest country. The northwest contains the vast basin of the Amazon, while the centre-west is largely a vast plateau of savanna and rock escarpments. The northeast is mostly semi-arid plateaus, while to the east and south are rugged mountains, fertile valleys and narrow, fertile coastal plains. The Amazon basin is hot, humid and wet; the rest of the country is cooler and drier, with seasonal variations. The northeast is drought-prone. Most Brazilians live in urban areas along the coast and on the central plateau. Brazil has well-developed agricultural, mining, and service sectors, and the economy is larger than that of all other South American countries combined. Brazil is the world's biggest producer of coffee, and other agricultural crops include grains and sugar cane. Mineral production includes iron, aluminium and gold. Manufactured goods include food products, transport equipment, machinery and industrial chemicals. The main trading partners are the USA and Argentina. Despite its natural wealth, Brazil has a large external debt and a growing poverty gap.

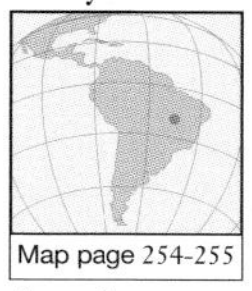
Map page 254–255

British Indian Ocean Territory
United Kingdom Overseas Territory

Area Sq Km (Miles) 60 (23) **Population** uninhabited

The territory consists of the Chagos Archipelago in the central Indian Ocean. The islands are uninhabited apart from the joint British-US military base on Diego Garcia.

Map page 88

BRUNEI
Brunei Darussalam

Area Sq Km	5 765	**Currency**	Brunei dollar
Area Sq Miles	2 226	**Languages**	Malay, English, Chinese
Population	374 000	**Religions**	Sunni Muslim, Buddhist, Christian
Capital	Bandar Seri Begawan	**Organizations**	APEC, ASEAN, Comm., UN

The Southeast Asian oil-rich state of Brunei lies on the northwest coast of the island of Borneo, on the South China Sea. Its two enclaves are surrounded by the Malaysian state of Sarawak. Tropical rainforest covers over two-thirds of the country. The economy is dominated by the oil and gas industries.

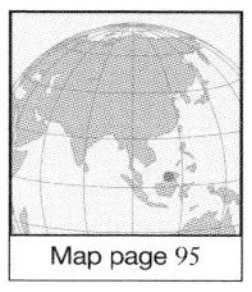
Map page 95

BULGARIA
Republic of Bulgaria

Area Sq Km	110 994	**Currency**	Lev
Area Sq Miles	42 855	**Languages**	Bulgarian, Turkish, Romany, Macedonian
Population	7 726 000	**Religions**	Bulgarian Orthodox, Sunni Muslim
Capital	Sofiya (Sofia)	**Organizations**	NATO, UN

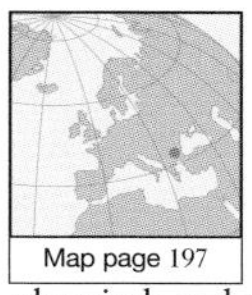
Map page 197

Bulgaria, in southern Europe, borders the western shore of the Black Sea. The Balkan Mountains separate the Danube plains in the north from the Rhodope Mountains and the lowlands in the south. The economy has a strong agricultural base. Manufacturing industries include machinery, consumer goods, chemicals and metals. Most trade is with the Russian Federation, Italy and Germany.

BURKINA
Democratic Republic of Burkina Faso

Area Sq Km	274 200	**Currency**	CFA franc
Area Sq Miles	105 869	**Languages**	French, Moore (Mossi), Fulani, local languages
Population	13 228 000	**Religions**	Sunni Muslim, traditional beliefs, Roman Catholic
Capital	Ouagadougou	**Organizations**	UN

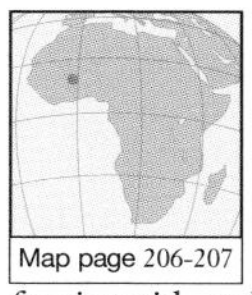
Map page 206–207

Burkina, a landlocked country in west Africa, lies within the Sahara desert to the north and semi-arid savanna to the south. Rainfall is erratic, and droughts are common. Livestock rearing and farming are the main activities, and cotton, livestock, groundnuts and some minerals are exported. Burkina relies heavily on foreign aid, and is one of the poorest and least developed countries in the world.

BURUNDI
Republic of Burundi

Area Sq Km	27 835	**Currency**	Burundian franc
Area Sq Miles	10 747	**Languages**	Kirundi (Hutu, Tutsi), French
Population	7 548 000	**Religions**	Roman Catholic, traditional beliefs, Protestant
Capital	Bujumbura	**Organizations**	UN

The densely populated east African state of Burundi consists of high plateaus rising from the shores of Lake Tanganyika in the southwest. It has a tropical climate and depends on subsistence farming. Coffee is its main export, and its main trading partners are Germany and Belgium. The country has been badly affected by internal conflict since the early 1990s.

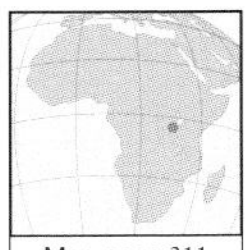
Map page 211

CAMBODIA
Kingdom of Cambodia

Area Sq Km	181 000	**Currency**	Riel
Area Sq Miles	69 884	**Languages**	Khmer, Vietnamese
Population	14 071 000	**Religions**	Buddhist, Roman Catholic, Sunni Muslim
Capital	Phnum Pénh	**Organizations**	ASEAN, UN

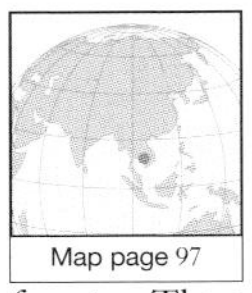
Map page 97

Cambodia lies in Southeast Asia on the Gulf of Thailand, and occupies the Mekong river basin, with the Tônlé Sap (Great Lake) at its centre. The climate is tropical monsoon. Forests cover half the country. Most of the population lives on the plains and is engaged in farming (chiefly rice growing), fishing and forestry. The economy is recovering slowly following the devastation of civil war in the 1970s.

CAMEROON
Republic of Cameroon

Area Sq Km	475 442	**Currency**	CFA franc
Area Sq Miles	183 569	**Languages**	French, English, Fang, Bamileke, local languages
Population	16 322 000	**Religions**	Roman Catholic, traditional beliefs, Sunni Muslim, Protestant
Capital	Yaoundé	**Organizations**	Comm., UN

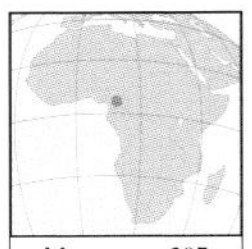
Map page 207

Cameroon is in west Africa, on the Gulf of Guinea. The coastal plains and southern and central plateaus are covered with tropical forest. Despite oil resources and favourable agricultural conditions Cameroon still faces problems of underdevelopment. Oil, timber and cocoa are the main exports. France is the main trading partner.

CANADA

Area Sq Km	9 984 670	**Currency**	Canadian dollar
Area Sq Miles	3 855 103	**Languages**	English, French, local languages
Population	32 268 000	**Religions**	Roman Catholic, Protestant, Orthodox, Jewish
Capital	Ottawa	**Organizations**	APEC, Comm., NATO, OECD, UN

The world's second largest country, Canada covers the northern two-fifths of North America and has coastlines on the Atlantic, Arctic and Pacific Oceans. In the west are the Coast Mountains, the Rocky Mountains and interior plateaus. In the centre lie the fertile Prairies. Further east, covering about half the total land area, is the Canadian Shield, a relatively flat area of infertile lowlands around Hudson Bay, extending to Labrador on the east coast. The Shield is bordered to the south by the fertile Great Lakes-St Lawrence lowlands. In the far north climatic conditions are polar, while the rest has a continental climate. Most Canadians live in the urban areas of the Great Lakes-St Lawrence basin. Canada is rich in mineral and energy resources. Only five per cent of land is arable . Canada is among the world's leading producers of wheat, of wood from its vast coniferous forests, and of fish and seafood from its Atlantic and Pacific fishing grounds. It is a major producer of nickel, uranium, copper, iron ore, zinc and other minerals, as well as oil and natural gas. Its abundant raw materials are the basis for many manufacturing industries. Main exports are machinery, motor vehicles, oil, timber, newsprint and paper, wood pulp and wheat. Since the 1989 free trade agreement with the USA and the 1994 North America Free Trade Agreement, trade with the USA has grown and now accounts for around seventy-five per cent of imports and around eighty-five per cent of exports.

Map page 220-221

Province / Territory	Area Sq Km (Miles)	Population	Capital
Alberta (Province)	661 848 (255 541)	3 113 600	Edmonton
British Columbia (Province)	944 735 (364 764)	4 141 300	Victoria
Manitoba (Province)	647 797 (250 116)	1 150 800	Winnipeg
New Brunswick (Province)	72 908 (28 150)	756 700	Fredericton
Newfoundland and Labrador (Province)	405 212 (156 453)	531 600	St John's
Northwest Territories (Province)	1 346 106 (519 734)	41 400	Yellowknife
Nova Scotia (Province)	55 284 (21 345)	944 800	Halifax
Nunavut (Territory)	2 093 190 (808 185)	28 700	Iqaluit
Ontario (Province)	1 076 395 (415 598)	12 068 300	Toronto
Prince Edward Island (Province)	5 660 (2 185)	139 900	Charlottetown
Québec (Province)	1 542 056 (595 391)	7 455 200	Québec
Saskatchewan (Province)	651 036 (251 366)	1 011 800	Regina
Yukon Territory (Territory)	482 443 (186 272)	29 900	Whitehorse

CAPE VERDE
Republic of Cape Verde

Area Sq Km	4 033	**Currency**	Cape Verde escudo
Area Sq Miles	1 557	**Languages**	Portuguese, creole
Population	507 000	**Religions**	Roman Catholic, Protestant
Capital	Praia	**Organizations**	UN

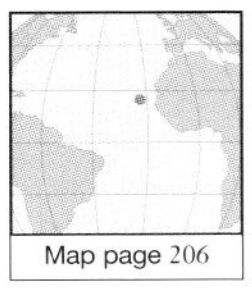
Map page 206

Cape Verde is a group of semi-arid volcanic islands lying off the coast of west Africa. The economy is based on fishing and subsistence farming but relies on emigrant workers' remittances and foreign aid.

Cayman Islands
United Kingdom Overseas Territory

Area Sq Km	259	**Currency**	Cayman Islands dollar
Area Sq Miles	100	**Languages**	English
Population	45 000	**Religions**	Roman Catholic, Protestant
Capital	George Town	**Organizations**	UN

A group of islands in the Caribbean, northwest of Jamaica. There are three main islands: Grand Cayman, Little Cayman and Cayman Brac. The Cayman Islands are one of the world's major offshore financial centres. Tourism is also important to the economy.

Map page 246

CENTRAL AFRICAN REPUBLIC

Area Sq Km	622 436	**Currency**	CFA franc
Area Sq Miles	240 324	**Languages**	French, Sango, Banda, Baya, local languages
Population	4 038 000	**Religions**	Protestant, Roman Catholic, trad. beliefs, Muslim
Capital	Bangui	**Organizations**	UN

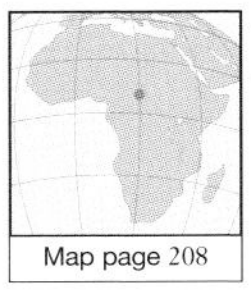
Map page 208

A landlocked country in central Africa, the Central African Republic is mainly savanna plateau, drained by the Ubangi and Chari river systems, with mountains to the east and west. The climate is tropical, with high rainfall. Most of the population lives in the south and west, and a majority of the workforce is involved in subsistence farming. Some cotton, coffee, tobacco and timber are exported, but diamonds account for around half of export earnings.

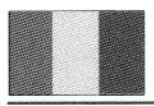

CHAD
Republic of Chad

Area Sq Km	1 284 000	**Currency**	CFA franc
Area Sq Miles	495 755	**Languages**	Arabic, French, Sara, local languages
Population	9 749 000	**Religions**	Sunni Muslim, Roman Catholic, Protestant
Capital	Ndjamena	**Organizations**	UN

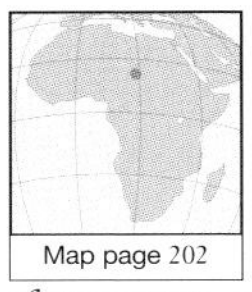
Map page 202

Chad is a landlocked state of north-central Africa. It consists of plateaus, the Tibesti mountains in the north and the Lake Chad basin in the west. Climatic conditions range between desert in the north and tropical forest in the southwest. With few natural resources, Chad relies on subsistence farming, exports of raw cotton, and foreign aid. The main trading partners are France, Portugal and Cameroon.

CHILE
Republic of Chile

Area Sq Km	756 945	**Currency**	Chilean peso
Area Sq Miles	292 258	**Languages**	Spanish, Amerindian languages
Population	16 295 000	**Religions**	Roman Catholic, Protestant
Capital	Santiago	**Organizations**	APEC, UN

Chile lies along the Pacific coast of the southern half of South America. Between the Andes in the east and the lower coastal ranges is a central valley, with a mild climate, where most Chileans live. To the north is the arid Atacama Desert and to the south is cold, wet forested grassland. Chile has considerable mineral resources and is the world's leading exporter of copper. Nitrates, molybdenum, gold and iron ore are also mined. Agriculture (particularly viticulture), forestry and fishing are also important to the economy.

Map page 258-259

CHINA
People's Republic of China

Area Sq Km	9 584 492	**Currency**	Yuan, Hong Kong dollar, Macao pataca
Area Sq Miles	3 700 593	**Languages**	Mandarin, Wu, Cantonese, Hsiang, regional languages
Population	1 323 345 000	**Religions**	Confucian, Taoist, Buddhist, Christian, Muslim
Capital	Beijing	**Organizations**	APEC, UN

China, the world's most populous and fourth largest country, occupies a large part of east Asia, borders fourteen states and has coastlines on the Yellow, East China and South China Seas. It has a huge variety of landscapes. The southwest contains the high Plateau of Tibet, flanked by the Himalaya and Kunlun Shan mountains. The north is mountainous with arid basins and extends from the Tien Shan and Altai Mountains and the vast Taklimakan Desert in the west to the plateau and Gobi Desert in the centre-east. Eastern China is predominantly lowland and is divided broadly into the basins of the Huang He (Yellow River) in the north, the Chang Jiang (Yangtze) in the centre and the Xi Jiang (Pearl River) in the southeast. Climatic conditions and vegetation are as diverse as the topography: much of the country experiences temperate conditions, while the southwest has an extreme mountain climate and the southeast enjoys a moist, warm subtropical climate. Nearly seventy per cent of China's huge population lives in rural areas, and agriculture employs around half of the working population. The main crops are rice, wheat, soya beans, peanuts, cotton, tobacco and hemp. China is rich in coal, oil and natural gas and has the world's largest potential in hydroelectric power. It is a major world producer of iron ore, molybdenum, copper, asbestos and gold. Economic reforms from the early 1980s led to an explosion in manufacturing development concentrated on the 'coastal economic open region'. The main exports are machinery, textiles, footwear, toys and sports goods. Japan and the USA are China's main trading partners.

Map page 98

Province / Region	Area Sq Km (Miles)	Population	Capital
Anhui (Province)	139 000 (53 668)	59 860 000	Hefei
Beijing (Municipality)	16 800 (6 487)	13 820 000	Beijing
Chongqing (Municipality)	23 000 (8 880)	30 900 000	Chongqing
Fujian (Province)	121 400 (46 873)	34 710 000	Fuzhou
Gansu (Province)	453 700 (175 175)	25 620 000	Lanzhou
Guangdong (Province)	178 000 (68 726)	86 420 000	Guangzhou
Guangxi Zhuangzu Zizhiqu (Autonomous Region)	236 000 (91 120)	44 890 000	Nanning
Guizhou (Province)	176 000 (67 954)	35 250 000	Guiyang
Hainan (Province)	34 000 (13 127)	7 870 000	Haikou
Hebei (Province)	187 700 (72 471)	67 440 000	Shijiazhuang
Heilongjiang (Province)	454 600 (175 522)	36 890 000	Harbin
Henan (Province)	167 000 (64 479)	92 560 000	Zhengzhou
Hong Kong (Special Administrative Region)	1 075 (415)	6 780 000	Hong Kong
Hubei (Province)	185 900 (71 776)	60 280 000	Wuhan
Hunan (Province)	210 000 (81 081)	64 400 000	Changsha
Jiangsu (Province)	102 600 (39 614)	74 380 000	Nanjing
Jiangxi (Province)	166 900 (64 440)	41 400 000	Nanchang
Jilin (Province)	187 000 (72 201)	27 280 000	Changchun
Liaoning (Province)	147 400 (56 911)	42 380 000	Shenyang
Macao (Special Administrative Region)	17 (7)	440 000	Macao
Nei Mongol Zizhiqu (Inner Mongolia) (Autonomous Region)	1 183 000 (456 759)	23 760 000	Huhhot
Ningxia Huizu Zizhiqu (Autonomous Region)	66 400 (25 637)	5 620 000	Yinchuan
Qinghai (Province)	721 000 (278 380)	5 180 000	Xining
Shaanxi (Province)	205 600 (79 383)	36 050 000	Xi'an
Shandong (Province)	153 300 (59 189)	90 790 000	Jinan
Shanghai (Municipality)	6 300 (2 432)	16 740 000	Shanghai
Shanxi (Province)	156 300 (60 348)	32 970 000	Taiyuan
Sichaun (Province)	569 000 (219 692)	83 290 000	Chengdu
Tianjin (Municipality)	11 300 (4 363)	10 010 000	Tianjin
Xinjiang Uygur Zizhiqu (Sinkiang) (Autonomous Region)	1 600 000 (617 763)	19 250 000	Ürümqi
Xizang Zizhiqu (Tibet) (Autonomous Region)	1 228 400 (474 288)	2 620 000	Lhasa
Yunnan (Province)	394 000 (152 124)	42 880 000	Kunming
Zhejiang (Province)	101 800 (39 305)	46 770 000	Hangzhou

Christmas Island
Australian External Territory

Area Sq Km	135	**Currency**	Australian dollar
Area Sq Miles	52	**Languages**	English
Population	1 508	**Religions**	Buddhist, Sunni Muslim, Protestant, Roman Catholic
Capital	The Settlement		

The island is situated in the east of the Indian Ocean, to the south of Indonesia. The economy was formerly based on phosphate extraction, although reserves are now nearly depleted. Tourism is developing and is a major employer.

Map page 86

Cocos Islands (Keeling Islands)
Australian External Territory

Area Sq Km	14	**Currency**	Australian dollar
Area Sq Miles	5	**Languages**	English
Population	621	**Religions**	Sunni Muslim, Christian
Capital	West Island		

The Cocos Islands consist of numerous islands on two coral atolls in the eastern Indian Ocean between Sri Lanka and Australia. Most of the population lives on West Island or Home Island. Coconuts are the only cash crop, and the main export.

Map page 86

COLOMBIA
Republic of Colombia

Area Sq Km	1 141 748	**Currency**	Colombian peso
Area Sq Miles	440 831	**Languages**	Spanish, Amerindian languages
Population	45 600 000	**Religions**	Roman Catholic, Protestant
Capital	Bogotá	**Organizations**	APEC, UN

A state in northwest South America, Colombia has coastlines on the Pacific Ocean and the Caribbean Sea. Behind coastal plains lie three ranges of the Andes mountains, separated by high valleys and plateaus where most Colombians live. To the southeast are grasslands and the forests of the Amazon. The climate is tropical, although temperatures vary with altitude. Only five per cent of land is cultivable. Coffee (Colombia is the world's second largest producer), sugar, bananas, cotton and flowers are exported. Coal, nickel, gold, silver, platinum and emeralds (Colombia is the world's largest producer) are mined. Oil and its products are the main export. Industries include the processing of minerals and crops. The main trade partner is the USA. Internal violence – both politically motivated and relating to Colombia's leading role in the international trade in illegal drugs – continues to hinder development.

Map page 250

COMOROS
Union of the Comoros

Area Sq Km	1 862	**Currency**	Comoros franc
Area Sq Miles	719	**Languages**	Comorian, French, Arabic
Population	798 000	**Religions**	Sunni Muslim, Roman Catholic
Capital	Moroni	**Organizations**	UN

This state, in the Indian Ocean off the east African coast, comprises three volcanic islands of Njazidja, Nzwani and Mwali, and some coral atolls. These tropical islands are mountainous, with poor soil and few natural resources. Subsistence farming predominates. Vanilla, cloves and ylang-ylang (an essential oil) are exported, and the economy relies heavily on workers' remittances from abroad.

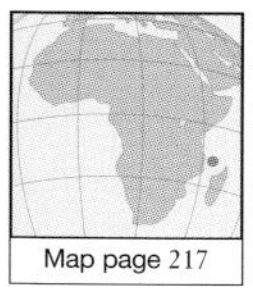
Map page 217

CONGO
Republic of the Congo

Area Sq Km	342 000	**Currency**	CFA franc
Area Sq Miles	132 047	**Languages**	French, Kongo, Monokutuba, local languages
Population	3 999 000	**Religions**	Roman Catholic, Protestant, trad. beliefs, Muslim
Capital	Brazzaville	**Organizations**	UN

Congo, in central Africa, is mostly a forest or savanna-covered plateau drained by the Ubangi-Congo river systems. Sand dunes and lagoons line the short Atlantic coast. The climate is hot and tropical. Most Congolese live in the southern third of the country. Half of the workforce are farmers, growing food and cash crops including sugar, coffee, cocoa and oil palms. Oil and timber are the mainstays of the economy, and oil generates over fifty per cent of export revenues.

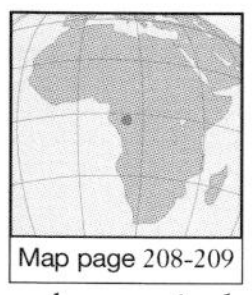
Map page 208-209

CONGO, DEMOCRATIC REPUBLIC OF THE

Area Sq Km	2 345 410	**Currency**	Congolese franc
Area Sq Miles	905 568	**Languages**	French, Lingala, Swahili, Kongo, local languages
Population	52 549 000	**Religions**	Christian, Sunni Muslim
Capital	Kinshasa	**Organizations**	SADC, UN

This central African state, formerly Zaire, consists of the basin of the Congo river flanked by plateaus, with high mountain ranges to the east and a short Atlantic coastline to the west. The climate is tropical, with rainforest close to the Equator and savanna to the north and south. Fertile land allows a range of food and cash crops to be grown, chiefly coffee. The country has vast mineral resources, with copper, cobalt and diamonds being the most important.

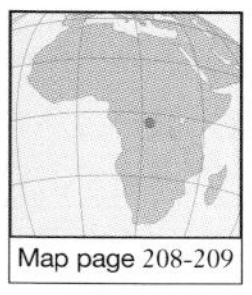
Map page 208-209

Cook Islands
New Zealand Overseas Territory

Area Sq Km	293	**Currency**	New Zealand dollar
Area Sq Miles	113	**Languages**	English, Maori
Population	18 000	**Religions**	Protestant, Roman Catholic
Capital	Avarua		

These consist of groups of coral atolls and volcanic islands in the southwest Pacific Ocean. The main island is Rarotonga. Distance from foreign markets and restricted natural resources hinder development.

Map page 81

COSTA RICA
Republic of Costa Rica

Area Sq Km	51 100	**Currency**	Costa Rican colón
Area Sq Miles	19 730	**Languages**	Spanish
Population	4 327 000	**Religions**	Roman Catholic, Protestant
Capital	San José	**Organizations**	UN

Costa Rica, in central America, has coastlines on the Caribbean Sea and Pacific Ocean. From tropical coastal plains, the land rises to mountains and a temperate central plateau, where most of the population lives. The economy depends on agriculture and tourism, with ecotourism becoming increasingly important. Main exports are textiles, coffee and bananas, and almost half of all trade is with the USA.

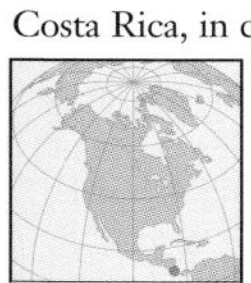
Map page 242

CÔTE D'IVOIRE (Ivory Coast)
Republic of Côte d'Ivoire

Area Sq Km	322 463	**Currency**	CFA franc
Area Sq Miles	124 504	**Languages**	French, creole, Akan, local languages
Population	18 154 000	**Religions**	Muslim, Roman Catholic, trad. beliefs, Protestant
Capital	Yamoussoukro	**Organizations**	UN

Côte d'Ivoire (Ivory Coast) is in west Africa, on the Gulf of Guinea. In the north are plateaus and savanna; in the south are low undulating plains and rainforest, with sand-bars and lagoons on the coast. Temperatures are warm, and rainfall is heavier in the south. Most of the workforce is engaged in farming. Côte d'Ivoire is a major producer of cocoa and coffee, and agricultural products (also including cotton and timber) are the main exports. Oil and gas have begun to be exploited.

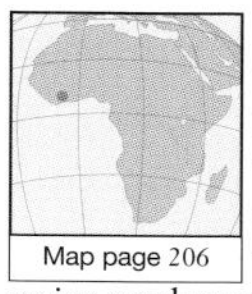
Map page 206

CROATIA
Republic of Croatia

Area Sq Km	56 538	**Currency**	Kuna
Area Sq Miles	21 829	**Languages**	Croatian, Serbian
Population	4 551 000	**Religions**	Roman Catholic, Serbian Orthodox, Sunni Muslim
Capital	Zagreb	**Organizations**	UN

The southern European state of Croatia has a long coastline on the Adriatic Sea, with many offshore islands. Coastal areas have a Mediterranean climate; inland is cooler and wetter. Croatia was once strong agriculturally and industrially, but conflict in the early 1990s, and associated loss of markets and a fall in tourist revenue, caused economic difficulties from which recovery has been slow.

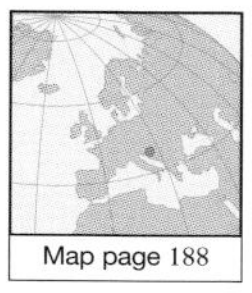
Map page 188

CUBA
Republic of Cuba

Area Sq Km	110 860	**Currency**	Cuban peso
Area Sq Miles	42 803	**Languages**	Spanish
Population	11 269 000	**Religions**	Roman Catholic, Protestant
Capital	La Habana (Havana)	**Organizations**	UN

The country comprises the island of Cuba (the largest island in the Caribbean), and many islets and cays. A fifth of Cubans live in and around Havana. Cuba is slowly recovering from the withdrawal of aid and subsidies from the former USSR. Sugar remains the basis of the economy, although tourism is developing and is, together with remittances from workers abroad, an important source of revenue.

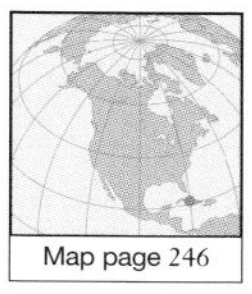
Map page 246

Curaçao part of Netherlands Antilles

Area Sq Km (Miles)	444 (171)	**Population**	126 816	**Capital**	Willemstad

An island in the Caribbean Sea off the north coast of Venezuela, it is the largest and most populous island of the Netherlands Antilles. Oil refining and tourism form the basis of the economy.

Map page 247

CYPRUS
Republic of Cyprus

Area Sq Km	9 251	**Currency**	Cyprus pound
Area Sq Miles	3 572	**Languages**	Greek, Turkish, English
Population	835 000	**Religions**	Greek Orthodox, Sunni Muslim
Capital	Lefkosia (Nicosia)	**Organizations**	Comm., EU, UN

The eastern Mediterranean island of Cyprus has hot dry summers and mild winters. The economy of the Greek south is based mainly on specialist agriculture and tourism, though shipping and offshore banking are also major sources of income. The Turkish north depends on agriculture, tourism and aid from Turkey. Cyprus joined the European Union in May 2004.

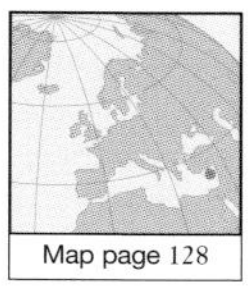
Map page 128

CZECH REPUBLIC

Area Sq Km	78 864	**Currency**	Czech koruna
Area Sq Miles	30 450	**Languages**	Czech, Moravian, Slovakian
Population	10 220 000	**Religions**	Roman Catholic, Protestant
Capital	Praha (Prague)	**Organizations**	EU, NATO, UN

The landlocked Czech Republic in central Europe consists of rolling countryside, wooded hills and fertile valleys. The climate is continental. The country has substantial reserves of coal and lignite, timber and some minerals, chiefly iron ore. It is highly industrialized, and major manufactured goods include industrial machinery, consumer goods, cars, iron and steel, chemicals and glass. Germany is the main trading partner. The Czech Republic joined the European Union in May 2004.

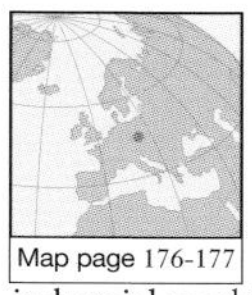
Map page 176-177

DENMARK
Kingdom of Denmark

Area Sq Km	43 075	**Currency**	Danish krone
Area Sq Miles	16 631	**Languages**	Danish
Population	5 431 000	**Religions**	Protestant
Capital	København (Copenhagen)	**Organizations**	EU, NATO, OECD, UN

In northern Europe, Denmark occupies the Jutland (Jylland) peninsula and nearly five hundred islands in and between the North and Baltic Seas. The country is low-lying, with long, indented coastlines. The climate is cool and temperate, with rainfall throughout the year. A fifth of the population lives in and around the capital, Copenhagen (København), on the largest of the islands, Zealand (Sjælland). The country's main natural resource is its agricultural potential: two-thirds of the total area is fertile farmland or pasture. Agriculture is high-tech, and with forestry and fishing employs only around six per cent of the workforce. Denmark is self-sufficient in oil and natural gas, produced from fields in the North Sea. Manufacturing, largely based on imported raw materials, accounts for over half of all exports, which include machinery, food, furniture, and pharmaceuticals. The main trading partners are Germany and Sweden.

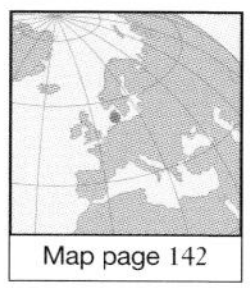
Map page 142

DJIBOUTI
Republic of Djibouti

Area Sq Km	23 200	**Currency**	Djibouti franc
Area Sq Miles	8 958	**Languages**	Somali, Afar, French, Arabic
Population	793 000	**Religions**	Sunni Muslim, Christian
Capital	Djibouti	**Organizations**	UN

Djibouti lies in northeast Africa, on the Gulf of Aden at the entrance to the Red Sea. Most of the country is semi-arid desert with high temperatures and low rainfall. More than two-thirds of the population lives in the capital. There is some camel, sheep and goat herding, but with few natural resources the economy is based on services and trade. Djibouti serves as a free trade zone for northern Africa, and the capital's port is a major transhipment and refuelling destination. It is linked by rail to Addis Ababa in Ethiopia.

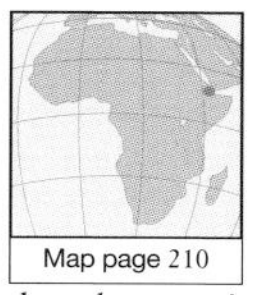
Map page 210

DOMINICA
Commonwealth of Dominica

Area Sq Km	750	**Currency**	East Caribbean dollar
Area Sq Miles	290	**Languages**	English, creole
Population	79 000	**Religions**	Roman Catholic, Protestant
Capital	Roseau	**Organizations**	CARICOM, Comm., UN

Dominica is the most northerly of the Windward Islands, in the eastern Caribbean. It is very mountainous and forested, with a coastline of steep cliffs. The climate is tropical and rainfall is abundant. Approximately a quarter of Dominicans live in the capital. The economy is based on agriculture, with bananas (the major export), coconuts and citrus fruits the most important crops. Tourism is a developing industry.

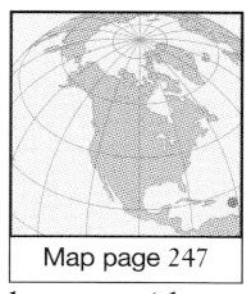
Map page 247

DOMINICAN REPUBLIC

Area Sq Km	48 442	**Currency**	Dominican peso
Area Sq Miles	18 704	**Languages**	Spanish, creole
Population	8 895 000	**Religions**	Roman Catholic, Protestant
Capital	Santo Domingo	**Organizations**	UN

The state occupies the eastern two-thirds of the Caribbean island of Hispaniola (the western third is Haiti). It has a series of mountain ranges, fertile valleys and a large coastal plain in the east. The climate is hot tropical, with heavy rainfall. Sugar, coffee and cocoa are the main cash crops. Nickel (the main export), and gold are mined, and there is some light industry. The USA is the main trading partner. Tourism is the main foreign exchange earner.

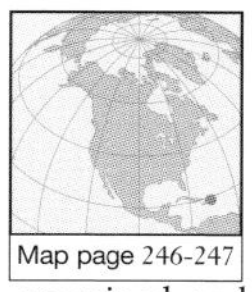
Map page 246-247

EAST TIMOR
Democratic Republic of Timor-Leste

Area Sq Km	14 874	**Currency**	United States dollar
Area Sq Miles	5 743	**Languages**	Portuguese, Tetun, English
Population	947 000	**Religions**	Roman Catholic
Capital	Dili	**Organizations**	UN

The island of Timor is part of the Indonesian archipelago, to the north of Western Australia. East Timor occupies the eastern section of the island, and a small coastal enclave (Ocussi) to the west. A referendum in 1999 ended Indonesia's occupation, after which the country was under UN transitional administration until full independence was achieved in 2002. The economy is in a poor state and East Timor is heavily dependent on foreign aid.

Map page 93

ECUADOR
Republic of Ecuador

Area Sq Km	272 045	**Currency**	United States dollar
Area Sq Miles	105 037	**Languages**	Spanish, Quechua, and other Amerindian languages
Population	13 228 000	**Religions**	Roman Catholic
Capital	Quito	**Organizations**	APEC, UN

Ecuador is in northwest South America, on the Pacific coast. It consists of a broad coastal plain, high mountain ranges in the Andes, and part of the forested upper Amazon basin to the east. The climate is tropical, moderated by altitude. Most people live on the coast or in the mountain valleys. Ecuador is one of South America's main oil producers, and mineral reserves include gold. Most of the workforce depends on agriculture. Petroleum, bananas, shrimps, coffee and cocoa are exported. The USA is the main trading partner.

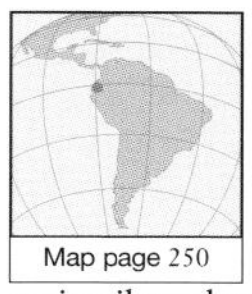
Map page 250

EGYPT
Arab Republic of Egypt

Area Sq Km	1 000 250	**Currency**	Egyptian pound
Area Sq Miles	386 199	**Languages**	Arabic
Population	74 033 000	**Religions**	Sunni Muslim, Coptic Christian
Capital	Al Qāhirah (Cairo)	**Organizations**	UN

Egypt, on the eastern Mediterranean coast of north Africa, is low-lying, with areas below sea level in the Qattara depression. It is a land of desert and semi-desert, except for the Nile valley, where ninety-nine per cent of Egyptians live. The Sinai peninsula in the northeast of the country forms the only land bridge between Africa and Asia. The summers are hot, the winters mild and rainfall is negligible. Less than four per cent of land (chiefly around the Nile floodplain and delta) is cultivated. Farming employs about one-third of the workforce; cotton is the main cash crop. Egypt imports over half its food needs. There are oil and natural gas reserves, although nearly a

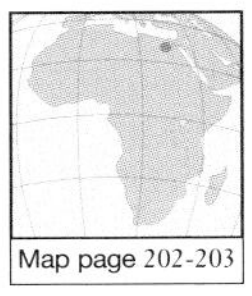
Map page 202-203

quarter of electricity comes from hydroelectric power. Main exports are oil and oil products, cotton, textiles and clothing.

EL SALVADOR
Republic of El Salvador

Area Sq Km	21 041	**Currency**	El Salvador colón, United States dollar
Area Sq Miles	8 124	**Languages**	Spanish
Population	6 881 000	**Religions**	Roman Catholic, Protestant
Capital	San Salvador	**Organizations**	UN

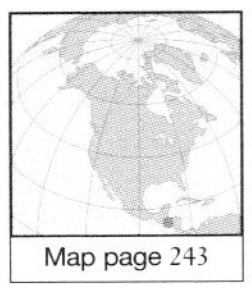
Map page 243

Located on the Pacific coast of central America, El Salvador consists of a coastal plain and volcanic mountain ranges which enclose a densely populated plateau area. The coast is hot, with heavy summer rainfall; the highlands are cooler. Coffee (the chief export), sugar and cotton are the main cash crops. The main trading partners are the USA and Guatemala.

EQUATORIAL GUINEA
Republic of Equatorial Guinea

Area Sq Km	28 051	**Currency**	CFA franc
Area Sq Miles	10 831	**Languages**	Spanish, French, Fang
Population	504 000	**Religions**	Roman Catholic, traditional beliefs
Capital	Malabo	**Organizations**	UN

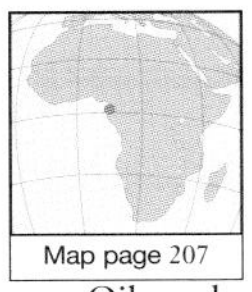
Map page 207

The state consists of Rio Muni, an enclave on the Atlantic coast of central Africa, and the islands of Bioco, Annobón and the Corisco group. Most of the population lives on the coastal plain and upland plateau of Rio Muni. The capital city, Malabo, is on the fertile volcanic island of Bioco. The climate is hot, humid and wet. Oil production started in 1992, and oil is now the main export, along with timber. The economy depends heavily on foreign aid.

ERITREA
State of Eritrea

Area Sq Km	117 400	**Currency**	Nakfa
Area Sq Miles	45 328	**Languages**	Tigrinya, Tigre
Population	4 401 000	**Religions**	Sunni Muslim, Coptic Christian
Capital	Asmara	**Organizations**	UN

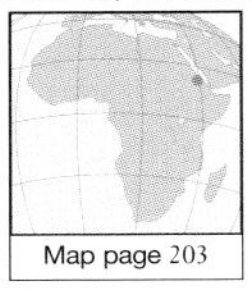
Map page 203

Eritrea, on the Red Sea coast of northeast Africa, consists of a high plateau in the north with a coastal plain which widens to the south. The coast is hot; inland is cooler. Rainfall is unreliable. The agriculture-based economy has suffered from over thirty years of war and occasional poor rains. Eritrea is one of the least developed countries in the world.

ESTONIA
Republic of Estonia

Area Sq Km	45 200	**Currency**	Kroon
Area Sq Miles	17 452	**Languages**	Estonian, Russian
Population	1 330 000	**Religions**	Protestant, Estonian and Russian Orthodox
Capital	Tallinn	**Organizations**	EU, NATO, UN

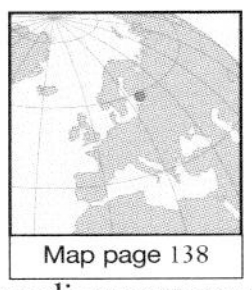
Map page 138

Estonia is in northern Europe, on the Gulf of Finland and the Baltic Sea. The land, over one-third of which is forested, is generally low-lying with many lakes. Approximately one-third of Estonians live in the capital, Tallinn. Exported goods include machinery, wood products, textiles and food products. The main trading partners are the Russian Federation, Finland and Sweden. Estonia joined the European Union in May 2004.

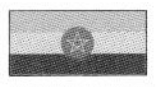

ETHIOPIA
Federal Democratic Republic of Ethiopia

Area Sq Km	1 133 880	**Currency**	Birr
Area Sq Miles	437 794	**Languages**	Oromo, Amharic, Tigrinya, local languages
Population	77 431 000	**Religions**	Ethiopian Orthodox, Muslim, trad. beliefs
Capital	Ādīs Ābeba	**Organizations**	UN

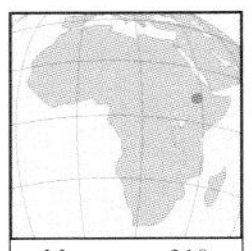
Map page 210

A landlocked country in northeast Africa, Ethiopia comprises a mountainous region in the west which is traversed by the Great Rift Valley. The east is mostly arid plateau land. The highlands are warm with summer rainfall. Most people live in the central–northern area. In recent years civil war, conflict with Eritrea and poor infrastructure have hampered economic development. Subsistence farming is the main activity, although droughts have led to frequent famines. Coffee is the main export and there is some light industry. Ethiopia is one of the least developed countries in the world.

Falkland Islands
United Kingdom Overseas Territory

Area Sq Km	12 170	**Currency**	Falkland Islands pound
Area Sq Miles	4 699	**Languages**	English
Population	3 000	**Religions**	Protestant, Roman Catholic
Capital	Stanley		

Map page 259

Lying in the southwest Atlantic Ocean, northeast of Cape Horn, two main islands, West Falkland and East Falkland and many smaller islands, form the territory of the Falkland Islands. The economy is based on sheep farming and the sale of fishing licences.

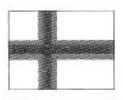

Faroe Islands
Self-governing Danish Territory

Area Sq Km	1 399	**Currency**	Danish krone
Area Sq Miles	540	**Languages**	Faroese, Danish
Population	47 000	**Religions**	Protestant
Capital	Tórshavn	**Organizations**	UN

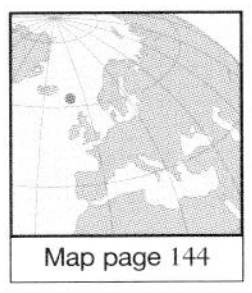
Map page 144

A self-governing territory, the Faroe Islands lie in the north Atlantic Ocean between the UK and Iceland. The islands benefit from the North Atlantic Drift, which has a moderating effect on the climate. The economy is based on deep-sea fishing.

FIJI
Republic of the Fiji Islands

Area Sq Km	18 330	**Currency**	Fiji dollar
Area Sq Miles	7 077	**Languages**	English, Fijian, Hindi
Population	848 000	**Religions**	Christian, Hindu, Sunni Muslim
Capital	Suva	**Organizations**	Comm., UN

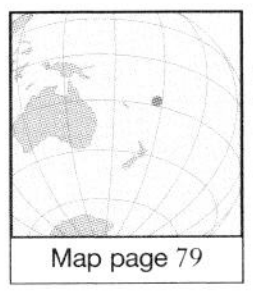
Map page 79

The southwest Pacific republic of Fiji comprises two mountainous and volcanic islands, Vanua Levu and Viti Levu, and over three hundred smaller islands. The climate is tropical and the economy is based on agriculture (chiefly sugar, the main export), fishing, forestry, gold mining and tourism.

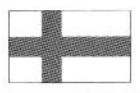

FINLAND
Republic of Finland

Area Sq Km	338 145	**Currency**	Euro
Area Sq Miles	130 559	**Languages**	Finnish, Swedish
Population	5 249 000	**Religions**	Protestant, Greek Orthodox
Capital	Helsinki	**Organizations**	EU, OECD, UN

Finland is in northern Europe, and nearly one-third of the country lies north of the Arctic Circle. Forests cover over seventy per cent of the land area, and ten per cent is covered by lakes. Summers are short and warm, and winters are long and severe, particularly in the north. Most of the population lives in the southern third of the country, along the coast or near the lakes. Timber is a major resource and there are important minerals, chiefly chromium. Main industries include metal working, electronics, paper and paper products, and chemicals. The main trading partners are Germany, Sweden and the UK.

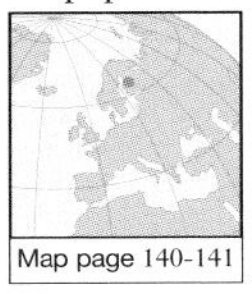
Map page 140-141

FRANCE
French Republic

Area Sq Km	543 965	**Currency**	Euro
Area Sq Miles	210 026	**Languages**	French, Arabic
Population	60 496 000	**Religions**	Roman Catholic, Protestant, Sunni Muslim
Capital	Paris	**Organizations**	EU, NATO, OECD, UN

France lies in western Europe and has coastlines on the Atlantic Ocean and the Mediterranean Sea. It includes the Mediterranean island of Corsica. Northern and western regions consist mostly of flat or rolling countryside, and include the major lowlands of the Paris basin, the Loire valley and the Aquitaine basin, drained by the Seine, Loire and Garonne river systems respectively. The centre-south is dominated by the hill region of the Massif Central. To the east are the Vosges and Jura mountains and the Alps. In the southwest, the Pyrenees form a natural border with Spain. The climate is temperate with warm summers and cool winters, although the Mediterranean coast has hot, dry summers and mild winters. Over seventy per cent of the population lives in towns, with almost a sixth of the population living in the Paris area. The French economy has a substantial and varied agricultural base. It is a major producer of both fresh and processed food. There are relatively few mineral resources; it has coal reserves, and some oil and natural gas, but it relies heavily on nuclear and hydroelectric power and imported fuels. France is one of the world's major industrial countries. Main industries include food processing, iron, steel and aluminium production, chemicals, cars, electronics and oil refining. The main exports are transport equipment, plastics and chemicals. Tourism is a major source of revenue and employment. Trade is predominantly with other European Union countries.

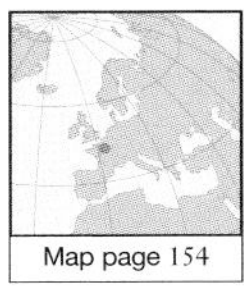
Map page 154

French Guiana
French Overseas Department

Area Sq Km	90 000	**Currency**	Euro
Area Sq Miles	34 749	**Languages**	French, creole
Population	187 000	**Religions**	Roman Catholic
Capital	Cayenne		

French Guiana, on the north coast of South America, is densely forested. The climate is tropical, with high rainfall. Most people live in the coastal strip, and agriculture is mostly subsistence farming. Forestry and fishing are important, but mineral resources are largely unexploited and industry is limited. French Guiana depends on French aid. The main trading partners are France and the USA.

Map page 251

FRENCH POLYNESIA
French Overseas Country

Area Sq Km	3 265	**Currency**	CFP franc
Area Sq Miles	1 261	**Languages**	French, Tahitian, Polynesian languages
Population	257 000	**Religions**	Protestant, Roman Catholic
Capital	Papeete		

Extending over a vast area of the southeast Pacific Ocean, French Polynesia comprises more than one hundred and thirty islands and coral atolls. The main island groups are the Marquesas Islands, the Tuamotu Archipelago and the Society Islands. The capital, Papeete, is on Tahiti in the Society Islands. The climate is subtropical, and the economy is based on tourism. The main export is cultured pearls.

Map page 79

French Southern and Antarctic Lands
French Overseas Territory

Area Sq Km (Miles) 439 580 (169 723) **Population** uninhabited

This territory includes the Crozet Islands, Kerguelen, Amsterdam Island and St Paul Island. All are uninhabited apart from scientific research staff. In accordance with the Antarctic Treaty, French (and all other) territorial claims in Antarctica have been suspended.

Map page 73

GABON
Gabonese Republic

Area Sq Km	267 667	**Currency**	CFA franc
Area Sq Miles	103 347	**Languages**	French, Fang, local languages
Population	1 384 000	**Religions**	Roman Catholic, Protestant, traditional beliefs
Capital	Libreville	**Organizations**	UN

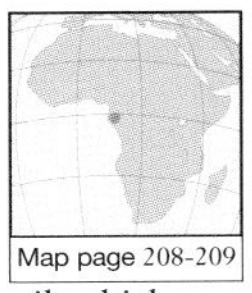
Map page 208-209

Gabon, on the Atlantic coast of central Africa, consists of low plateaus and a coastal plain lined by lagoons and mangrove swamps. The climate is tropical and rainforests cover over three-quarters of the land area. Over seventy per cent of the population lives in towns. The economy is heavily dependent on oil, which accounts for around seventy-five per cent of exports; manganese, uranium and timber are the other main exports. Agriculture is mainly at subsistence level.

THE GAMBIA
Republic of The Gambia

Area Sq Km	11 295	**Currency**	Dalasi
Area Sq Miles	4 361	**Languages**	English, Malinke, Fulani, Wolof
Population	1 517 000	**Religions**	Sunni Muslim, Protestant
Capital	Banjul	**Organizations**	Comm., UN

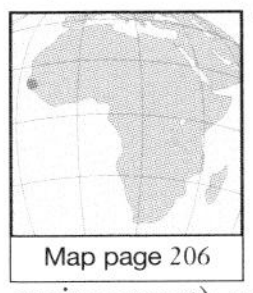
Map page 206

The Gambia, on the coast of west Africa, occupies a strip of land along the lower Gambia river. Sandy beaches are backed by mangrove swamps, beyond which is savanna. The climate is tropical, with most rainfall in the summer. Over seventy per cent of Gambians are farmers, growing chiefly groundnuts (the main export), cotton, oil palms and food crops. Livestock rearing and fishing are important, while manufacturing is limited. Re-exports, mainly from Senegal, and tourism are major sources of income.

Gaza Semi-autonomous region

Area Sq Km	363	**Currency**	Israeli shekel
Area Sq Miles	140	**Languages**	Arabic
Population	1 406 423	**Religions**	Sunni Muslim, Shi'a Muslim
Capital	Gaza		

Gaza is a narrow strip of land on the southeast corner of the Mediterranean Sea, between Egypt and Israel. This Palestinian territory has internal autonomy, but Israel exerts full control over its border with Israel. All Israeli settlers were evacuated in 2005. Hostilities between the two parties continue to restrict its economic development.

Map page 128

GEORGIA
Republic of Georgia

Area Sq Km	69 700	**Currency**	Lari
Area Sq Miles	26 911	**Languages**	Georgian, Russian, Armenian, Azeri, Ossetian, Abkhaz
Population	4 474 000	**Religions**	Georgian Orthodox, Russian Orthodox, Sunni Muslim
Capital	T'bilisi	**Organizations**	CIS, UN

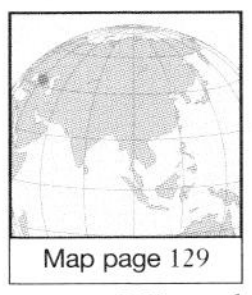
Map page 129

Georgia is in the northwest Caucasus area of southwest Asia, on the eastern coast of the Black Sea. Mountain ranges in the north and south flank the Kura and Rioni valleys. The climate is generally mild, and along the coast it is subtropical. Agriculture is important, with tea, grapes, and citrus fruits the main crops. Mineral resources include manganese ore and oil, and the main industries are steel, oil refining and machine building. The main trading partners are the Russian Federation and Turkey.

GERMANY
Federal Republic of Germany

Area Sq Km	357 022	**Currency**	Euro
Area Sq Miles	137 847	**Languages**	German, Turkish
Population	82 689 000	**Religions**	Protestant, Roman Catholic
Capital	Berlin	**Organizations**	EU, NATO, OECD, UN

The central European state of Germany borders nine countries and has coastlines on the North and Baltic Seas. Behind the indented coastline, and covering about one-third of the country, is the north German plain, a region of fertile farmland and sandy heaths drained by the country's major rivers. The central highlands are a belt of forested hills and plateaus which stretch from the Eifel region in the west to the mountains of the Erzgebirge along the border with the Czech Republic. Farther south the land rises to the Swabian Alps (Schwäbische Alb), with the high rugged and forested Black Forest (Schwarzwald) in the southwest. In the far south the Bavarian Alps form the border with Austria. The climate is temperate, with continental conditions in eastern areas. The population is highly

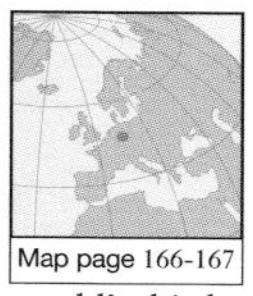

Map page 166-167

urbanized, with over eighty-five per cent living in cities and towns. With the exception of coal, lignite, potash and baryte, Germany lacks minerals and other industrial raw materials. It has a small agricultural base, although a few products (chiefly wines and beers) enjoy an international reputation. Germany is the world's third ranking economy after the USA and Japan. Its industries are amongst the world's most technologically advanced. Exports include machinery, vehicles and chemicals. The majority of trade is with other countries in the European Union, the USA and Japan.

Baden-Württemberg (State)
Area Sq Km (Miles) 35 752 (13 804) **Population** 10 601 000 **Capital** Stuttgart

Bayern (State)
Area Sq Km (Miles) 70 550 (27 240) **Population** 12 330 000 **Capital** München

Berlin (State)
Area Sq Km (Miles) 892 (344) **Population** 3 388 000 **Capital** Berlin

Brandenburg (State)
Area Sq Km (Miles) 29 476 (11 381) **Population** 2 593 000 **Capital** Potsdam

Bremen (State)
Area Sq Km (Miles) 404 (156) **Population** 660 000 **Capital** Bremen

Hamburg (State)
Area Sq Km (Miles) 755 (292) **Population** 1 726 000 **Capital** Hamburg

Hessen (State)
Area Sq Km (Miles) 21 114 (8 152) **Population** 6 078 000 **Capital** Wiesbaden

Mecklenburg-Vorpommern (State)
Area Sq Km (Miles) 23 173 (8 947) **Population** 1 760 000 **Capital** Schwerin

Niedersachsen (State)
Area Sq Km (Miles) 47 616 (18 385) **Population** 7 956 000 **Capital** Hannover

Nordrhein-Westfalen (State)
Area Sq Km (Miles) 34 082 (13 159) **Population** 18 052 000 **Capital** Düsseldorf

Rheinland-Pfalz (State)
Area Sq Km (Miles) 19 847 (7 663) **Population** 4 049 000 **Capital** Mainz

Saarland (State)
Area Sq Km (Miles) 2 568 (992) **Population** 1 066 000 **Capital** Saarbrücken

Sachsen (State)
Area Sq Km (Miles) 18 413 (7 109) **Population** 4 384 000 **Capital** Dresden

Sachsen-Anhalt (State)
Area Sq Km (Miles) 20 447 (7 895) **Population** 2 581 000 **Capital** Magdeburg

Schleswig-Holstein (State)
Area Sq Km (Miles) 15 761 (6 085) **Population** 2 804 000 **Capital** Kiel

Thüringen (State)
Area Sq Km (Miles) 16 172 (6 244) **Population** 2 411 000 **Capital** Erfurt

GHANA
Republic of Ghana

Area Sq Km	238 537	**Currency**	Cedi
Area Sq Miles	92 100	**Languages**	English, Hausa, Akan, local languages
Population	22 113 000	**Religions**	Christian, Sunni Muslim, traditional beliefs
Capital	Accra	**Organizations**	Comm., UN

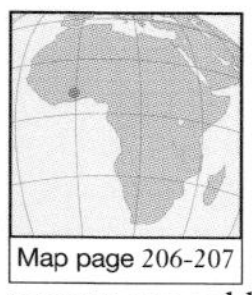

Map page 206-207

A west African state on the Gulf of Guinea, Ghana is a land of plains and low plateaus covered with savanna and rainforest. In the east is the Volta basin and Lake Volta. The climate is tropical, with the highest rainfall in the south, where most of the population lives. Agriculture employs around sixty per cent of the workforce. Main exports are gold, timber, cocoa, bauxite and manganese ore.

Gibraltar
United Kingdom Overseas Territory

Area Sq Km	7	**Currency**	Gibraltar pound
Area Sq Miles	3	**Languages**	English, Spanish
Population	28 000	**Religions**	Roman Catholic, Protestant, Sunni Muslim
Capital	Gibraltar		

Gibraltar lies on the south coast of Spain at the western entrance to the Mediterranean Sea. The economy depends on tourism, offshore banking and shipping services.

Map page 185

GREECE
Hellenic Republic

Area Sq Km	131 957	**Currency**	Euro
Area Sq Miles	50 949	**Languages**	Greek
Population	11 120 000	**Religions**	Greek Orthodox, Sunni Muslim
Capital	Athina (Athens)	**Organizations**	EU, NATO, OECD, UN

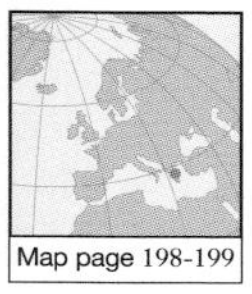

Map page 198-199

Greece comprises a mountainous peninsula in the Balkan region of southeastern Europe and many islands in the Ionian, Aegean and Mediterranean Seas. The islands make up over one-fifth of its area. Mountains and hills cover much of the country. The main lowland areas are the plains of Thessaly in the centre and around Thessaloniki in the northeast. Summers are hot and dry while winters are mild and wet, but colder in the north with heavy snowfalls in the mountains. One-third of Greeks live in the Athens area. Employment in agriculture accounts for approximately twenty per cent of the workforce, and exports include citrus fruits, raisins, wine, olives and olive oil. Aluminium and nickel are mined and a wide range of manufactures are produced, including food products and tobacco, textiles, clothing, and chemicals. Tourism is an important industry and there is a large services sector. Most trade is with other European Union countries.

GREENLAND
Self-governing Danish Territory

Area Sq Km	2 175 600	**Currency**	Danish krone
Area Sq Miles	840 004	**Languages**	Greenlandic, Danish
Population	57 000	**Religions**	Protestant
Capital	Nuuk (Godthåb)		

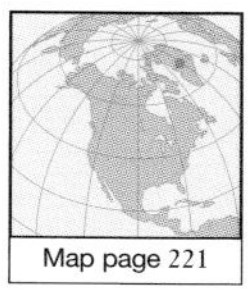

Map page 221

Situated to the northeast of North America between the Atlantic and Arctic Oceans, Greenland is the largest island in the world. It has a polar climate and over eighty per cent of the land area is covered by permanent ice cap. The economy is based on fishing and fish processing.

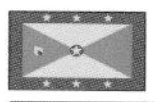

GRENADA

Area Sq Km	378	**Currency**	East Caribbean dollar
Area Sq Miles	146	**Languages**	English, creole
Population	103 000	**Religions**	Roman Catholic, Protestant
Capital	St George's	**Organizations**	CARICOM, Comm., UN

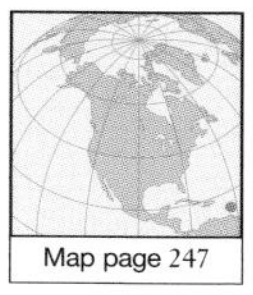

Map page 247

The Caribbean state comprises Grenada, the most southerly of the Windward Islands, and the southern islands of the Grenadines. Grenada has wooded hills, with beaches in the southwest. The climate is warm and wet. Agriculture is the main activity, with bananas, nutmeg and cocoa the main exports. Tourism is the main foreign exchange earner.

Guadeloupe
French Overseas Department

Area Sq Km	1 780	**Currency**	Euro
Area Sq Miles	687	**Languages**	French, creole
Population	448 000	**Religions**	Roman Catholic
Capital	Basse-Terre		

Guadeloupe, in the Leeward Islands in the Caribbean, consists of two main islands (Basse-Terre and Grande-Terre, connected by a bridge), Marie-Galante, and a few outer islands. The climate is tropical, but moderated by trade winds. Bananas, sugar and rum are the main exports and tourism is a major source of income.

Map page 247

Guam
United States Unincorporated Territory

Area Sq Km	541	**Currency**	United States dollar
Area Sq Miles	209	**Languages**	Chamorro, English, Tagalog
Population	170 000	**Religions**	Roman Catholic
Capital	Hagåtña (Agana)		

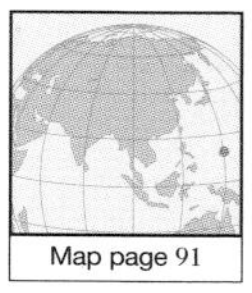

Map page 91

Lying at the south end of the Northern Mariana Islands in the western Pacific Ocean, Guam has a humid tropical climate. The island has a large US military base and the economy relies on that and on tourism, which has grown rapidly.

GUATEMALA
Republic of Guatemala

Area Sq Km	108 890	**Currency**	Quetzal, United States dollar
Area Sq Miles	42 043	**Languages**	Spanish, Mayan languages
Population	12 599 000	**Religions**	Roman Catholic, Protestant
Capital	Guatemala	**Organizations**	UN

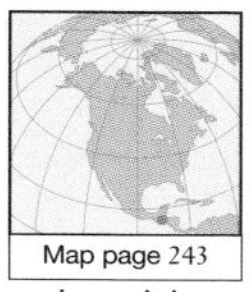

Map page 243

The most populous country in Central America after Mexico, Guatemala has long Pacific and short Caribbean coasts separated by a mountain chain which includes several active volcanoes. The climate is hot tropical in the lowlands and cooler in the highlands, where most of the population lives. Farming is the main activity and coffee, sugar and bananas are the main exports. There is some manufacturing of clothing and textiles. The main trading partner is the USA.

Guernsey
United Kingdom Crown Dependency

Area Sq Km	78	**Currency**	Pound sterling
Area Sq Miles	30	**Languages**	English, French
Population	62 692	**Religions**	Protestant, Roman Catholic
Capital	St Peter Port		

Guernsey is one of the Channel Islands, lying off northern France. The dependency also includes the nearby islands of Alderney, Sark and Herm. Financial services are an important part of the island's economy.

Map page 158

GUINEA
Republic of Guinea

Area Sq Km	245 857	**Currency**	Guinea franc
Area Sq Miles	94 926	**Languages**	French, Fulani, Malinke, local languages
Population	9 402 000	**Religions**	Sunni Muslim, traditional beliefs, Christian
Capital	Conakry	**Organizations**	UN

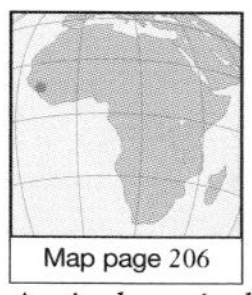

Map page 206

Guinea is in west Africa, on the Atlantic Ocean. There are mangrove swamps along the coast, while inland are lowlands and the Fouta Djallon mountains and plateaus. To the east are savanna plains drained by the upper Niger river system. The southeast is hilly. The climate is tropical, with high coastal rainfall. Agriculture is the main activity, employing nearly eighty per cent of the workforce, with coffee, bananas and pineapples the chief cash crops. There are huge reserves of bauxite, which accounts for more than seventy per cent of exports. Other exports include aluminium oxide, gold, coffee and diamonds.

GUINEA-BISSAU
Republic of Guinea-Bissau

Area Sq Km	36 125	**Currency**	CFA franc
Area Sq Miles	13 948	**Languages**	Portuguese, crioulo, local languages
Population	1 586 000	**Religions**	Traditional beliefs, Sunni Muslim, Christian
Capital	Bissau	**Organizations**	UN

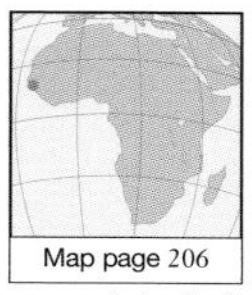

Map page 206

Guinea-Bissau is on the Atlantic coast of west Africa. The mainland coast is swampy and contains many estuaries. Inland are forested plains, and to the east are savanna plateaus. The climate is tropical. The economy is based mainly on subsistence farming. There is little industry, and timber and mineral resources are largely unexploited. Cashews account for seventy per cent of exports. Guinea-Bissau is one of the least developed countries in the world.

GUYANA
Co-operative Republic of Guyana

Area Sq Km	214 969	**Currency**	Guyana dollar
Area Sq Miles	83 000	**Languages**	English, creole, Amerindian languages
Population	751 000	**Religions**	Protestant, Hindu, Roman Catholic, Sunni Muslim
Capital	Georgetown	**Organizations**	CARICOM, Comm., UN

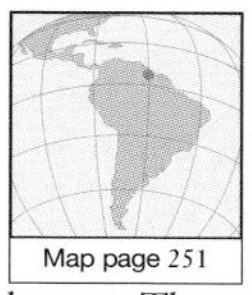

Map page 251

Guyana, on the northeast coast of South America, consists of highlands in the west and savanna uplands in the southwest. Most of the country is densely forested. A lowland coastal belt supports crops and most of the population. The generally hot, humid and wet conditions are modified along the coast by sea breezes. The economy is based on agriculture, bauxite, and forestry. Sugar, bauxite, gold, rice and timber are the main exports.

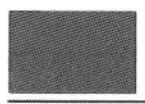

HAITI
Republic of Haiti

Area Sq Km	27 750	**Currency**	Gourde
Area Sq Miles	10 714	**Languages**	French, creole
Population	8 528 000	**Religions**	Roman Catholic, Protestant, Voodoo
Capital	Port-au-Prince	**Organizations**	CARICOM, UN

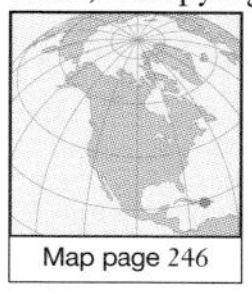

Map page 246

Haiti, occupying the western third of the Caribbean island of Hispaniola, is a mountainous state with small coastal plains and a central valley. The Dominican Republic occupies the rest of the island. The climate is tropical, and is hottest in coastal areas. Haiti has few natural resources, is densely populated and relies on exports of local crafts and coffee, and remittances from workers abroad.

HONDURAS
Republic of Honduras

Area Sq Km	112 088	**Currency**	Lempira
Area Sq Miles	43 277	**Languages**	Spanish, Amerindian languages
Population	7 205 000	**Religions**	Roman Catholic, Protestant
Capital	Tegucigalpa	**Organizations**	UN

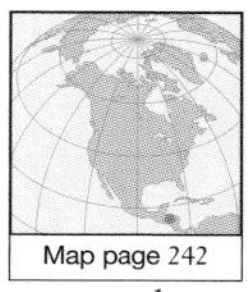

Map page 242

Honduras, in central America, is a mountainous and forested country with lowland areas along its long Caribbean and short Pacific coasts. Coastal areas are hot and humid with heavy summer rainfall; inland is cooler and drier. Most of the population lives in the central valleys. Coffee and bananas are the main exports, along with shellfish and zinc. Industry involves mainly agricultural processing.

HUNGARY
Republic of Hungary

Area Sq Km	93 030	**Currency**	Forint
Area Sq Miles	35 919	**Languages**	Hungarian
Population	10 098 000	**Religions**	Roman Catholic, Protestant
Capital	Budapest	**Organizations**	EU, NATO, OECD, UN

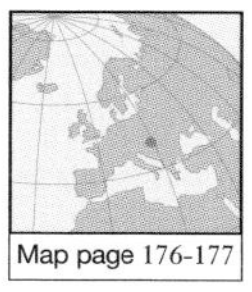

Map page 176-177

The Danube river flows north-south through central Hungary, a landlocked country in eastern Europe. In the east lies a great plain, flanked by highlands in the north. In the west low mountains and Lake Balaton separate a smaller plain and southern uplands. The climate is continental. Sixty per cent of the population lives in urban areas, and one-fifth lives in the capital, Budapest. Some minerals and energy resources are exploited, chiefly bauxite, coal and natural gas. Hungary has an industrial economy based on metals, machinery, transport equipment, chemicals and food products. The main trading partners are Germany and Austria. Hungary joined the European Union in May 2004.

ICELAND
Republic of Iceland

Area Sq Km	102 820	**Currency**	Icelandic króna
Area Sq Miles	39 699	**Languages**	Icelandic
Population	295 000	**Religions**	Protestant
Capital	Reykjavík	**Organizations**	NATO, OECD, UN

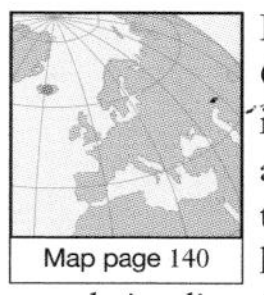

Map page 140

Iceland lies in the north Atlantic Ocean near the Arctic Circle, to the northwest of Scandinavia. The landscape is volcanic, with numerous hot springs, geysers, and approximately two hundred volcanoes. One-tenth of the country is covered by ice caps. Only coastal lowlands are cultivated and settled, and over half the population lives in the Reykjavík area. The climate is mild, moderated by the North Atlantic Drift ocean current and by southwesterly winds. The mainstays of the economy are fishing and fish processing, which account for seventy per cent of exports. Agriculture involves mainly sheep and dairy farming. Hydroelectric and geothermal energy resources are considerable. The main industries produce aluminium, ferro-silicon and fertilizers. Tourism, including ecotourism, is growing in importance.

INDIA
Republic of India

Area Sq Km	3 064 898	**Currency**	Indian rupee
Area Sq Miles	1 183 364	**Languages**	Hindi, English, many regional languages
Population	1 103 371 000	**Religions**	Hindu, Sunni Muslim, Shi'a Muslim, Sikh, Christian
Capital	New Delhi	**Organizations**	Comm., UN

The south Asian country of India occupies a peninsula that juts out into the Indian Ocean between the Arabian Sea and Bay of Bengal. The heart of the peninsula is the Deccan plateau, bordered on either side by ranges of hills, the Western Ghats and the lower Eastern Ghats, which fall away to narrow coastal plains. To the north is a broad plain, drained by the Indus, Ganges and Brahmaputra rivers and their tributaries. The plain is intensively farmed and is the most populous region. In the west is the Thar Desert. The mountains of the Himalaya form India's northern border, together with parts of the Karakoram and Hindu Kush ranges in the northwest. The climate shows marked seasonal variation: a hot season from March to June; a monsoon season from June to October; and a cold season from November to February.

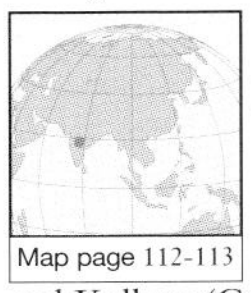
Map page 112-113

Rainfall ranges between very high in the northeast Assam region to negligible in the Thar Desert. Temperatures range from very cold in the Himalaya to tropical heat over much of the south. Over seventy per cent of the huge population – the second largest in the world – is rural, although Delhi, Mumbai (Bombay) and Kolkata (Calcutta) all rank among the ten largest cities in the world. Agriculture, forestry and fishing account for a quarter of national output and two-thirds of employment. Much of the farming is on a subsistence basis and involves mainly rice and wheat. India is a major world producer of tea, sugar, jute, cotton and tobacco. Livestock is reared mainly for dairy products and hides. There are major reserves of coal, reserves of oil and natural gas, and many minerals, including iron, manganese, bauxite, diamonds and gold. The manufacturing sector is large and diverse – mainly chemicals and chemical products, textiles, iron and steel, food products, electrical goods and transport equipment; software and pharmaceuticals are also important. All the main manufactured products are exported, together with diamonds and jewellery. The USA, Germany, Japan and the UK are the main trading partners.

INDONESIA
Republic of Indonesia

Area Sq Km	1 919 445	**Currency**	Rupiah
Area Sq Miles	741 102	**Languages**	Indonesian, local languages
Population	222 781 000	**Religions**	Sunni Muslim, Protestant, Roman Catholic
Capital	Jakarta	**Organizations**	APEC, ASEAN, OPEC, UN

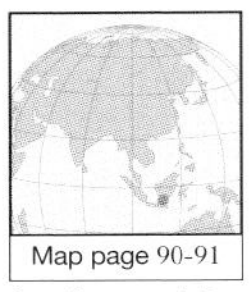
Map page 90-91

Indonesia, the largest and most populous country in Southeast Asia, consists of over thirteen thousand islands extending between the Pacific and Indian Oceans. Sumatra, Java, Sulawesi, Kalimantan (two-thirds of Borneo) and Papua (formerly Irian Jaya, western New Guinea) make up ninety per cent of the land area. Most of Indonesia is mountainous and covered with rainforest or mangrove swamps, and there are over three hundred volcanoes, many active. Two-thirds of the population lives in the lowland areas of the islands of Java and Madura. The climate is tropical monsoon. Agriculture is the largest sector of the economy and Indonesia is among the world's top producers of rice, palm oil, tea, coffee, rubber and tobacco. Many goods are produced, including textiles, clothing, cement, tin, fertilizers and vehicles. Main exports are oil, natural gas, timber products and clothing. Main trading partners are Japan, the USA and Singapore. Indonesia is a relatively poor country, and ethnic tensions and civil unrest often hinder economic development.

IRAN
Islamic Republic of Iran

Area Sq Km	1 648 000	**Currency**	Iranian rial
Area Sq Miles	636 296	**Languages**	Farsi, Azeri, Kurdish, regional languages
Population	69 515 000	**Religions**	Shi'a Muslim, Sunni Muslim
Capital	Tehrān	**Organizations**	OPEC, UN

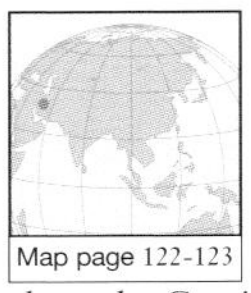
Map page 122-123

Iran is in southwest Asia, and has coasts on The Gulf, the Caspian Sea and the Gulf of Oman. In the east is a high plateau, with large salt pans and a vast sand desert. In the west the Zagros Mountains form a series of ridges, and to the north lie the Elburz Mountains. Most farming and settlement is on the narrow plain along the Caspian Sea and in the foothills of the north and west. The climate is one of extremes, with hot summers and very cold winters. Most of the light rainfall is in the winter months. Agriculture involves approximately one-third of the workforce. Wheat is the main crop, but fruit (especially dates) and pistachio nuts are grown for export. Petroleum (the main export) and natural gas are Iran's leading natural resources. Manufactured goods include carpets, clothing, food products and construction materials.

IRAQ
Republic of Iraq

Area Sq Km	438 317	**Currency**	Iraqi dinar
Area Sq Miles	169 235	**Languages**	Arabic, Kurdish, Turkmen
Population	28 807 000	**Religions**	Shi'a Muslim, Sunni Muslim, Christian
Capital	Baghdād	**Organizations**	OPEC, UN

Iraq, in southwest Asia, has at its heart the lowland valley of the Tigris and Euphrates rivers. In the southeast, where the two rivers join, are the Mesopotamian marshes and the Shaṭṭ al 'Arab waterway. Northern Iraq is hilly, while western Iraq is desert. Summers are hot and dry, while winters are mild with light, unreliable rainfall. One in five of the population lives in the capital, Baghdād. The economy has

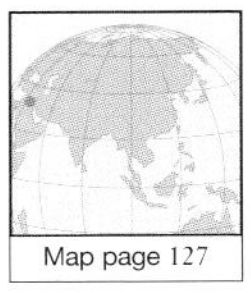
Map page 127

suffered following the 1991 Gulf War and the invasion of US-led coalition forces in 2005. The latter resulted in the overthrow of the dictator Saddam Hussein, but there is continuing internal instability. Oil is normally the main export.

IRELAND

Area Sq Km	70 282	**Currency**	Euro
Area Sq Miles	27 136	**Languages**	English, Irish
Population	4 148 000	**Religions**	Roman Catholic, Protestant
Capital	Dublin	**Organizations**	EU, OECD, UN

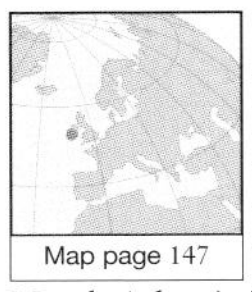
Map page 147

The Irish Republic occupies some eighty per cent of the island of Ireland, in northwest Europe. It is a lowland country of wide valleys, lakes and peat bogs, with isolated mountain ranges around the coast. The west coast is rugged and indented with many bays. The climate is mild due to the modifying effect of the North Atlantic Drift ocean current and rainfall is plentiful, although highest in the west. Nearly sixty per cent of the population lives in urban areas, Dublin and Cork being the main cities. Resources include natural gas, peat, lead and zinc. Agriculture, the traditional mainstay, now employs less than ten per cent of the workforce, while industry employs nearly thirty per cent. The main industries are electronics, pharmaceuticals and engineering as well as food processing, brewing and textiles. Service industries are expanding, with tourism a major earner. The UK is the main trading partner.

Isle of Man
United Kingdom Crown Dependency

Area Sq Km	572	**Currency**	Pound sterling
Area Sq Miles	221	**Languages**	English
Population	77 000	**Religions**	Protestant, Roman Catholic
Capital	Douglas		

The Isle of Man lies in the Irish Sea between England and Northern Ireland. The island is self-governing, although the UK is responsible for its defence and foreign affairs. It is not part of the European Union, but has a special relationship with the EU which allows for free trade. Eighty per cent of the economy is based on the service sector, particularly financial services.

Map page 148

ISRAEL
State of Israel

Area Sq Km	20 770	**Currency**	Shekel
Area Sq Miles	8 019	**Languages**	Hebrew, Arabic
Population	6 725 000	**Religions**	Jewish, Sunni Muslim, Christian, Druze
Capital	Jerusalem (Yerushalayim) (El Quds) De facto capital. Disputed	**Organizations**	UN

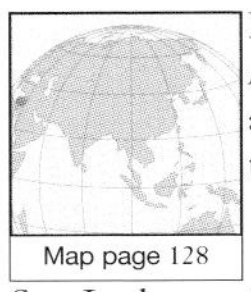
Map page 128

Israel lies on the Mediterranean coast of southwest Asia. Beyond the coastal Plain of Sharon are the hills and valleys of Samaria, with the Galilee highlands to the north. In the east is a rift valley, which extends from Lake Tiberias (Sea of Galilee) to the Gulf of Aqaba and contains the Jordan river and the Dead Sea. In the south is the Negev, a triangular semi-desert plateau. Most of the population lives on the coastal plain or in northern and central areas. Much of Israel has warm summers and mild, wet winters. The south is hot and dry. Agricultural production was boosted by the occupation of the West Bank in 1967. Manufacturing makes the largest contribution to the economy, and tourism is also important. Israel's main exports are machinery and transport equipment, software, diamonds, clothing, fruit and vegetables. The country relies heavily on foreign aid. Security issues relating to the West Bank and Gaza have still to be resolved.

ITALY
Italian Republic

Area Sq Km	301 245	**Currency**	Euro
Area Sq Miles	116 311	**Languages**	Italian
Population	58 093 000	**Religions**	Roman Catholic
Capital	Roma (Rome)	**Organizations**	EU, NATO, OECD, UN

Most of the southern European state of Italy occupies a peninsula that juts out into the Mediterranean Sea. It includes the islands of Sicily and Sardinia and approximately seventy much smaller islands in the surrounding seas. Italy is mountainous, dominated by the Alps, which form its northern border, and the various ranges of the Apennines, which run almost the full length of the peninsula. Many of Italy's mountains are of volcanic origin, and its active volcanoes are

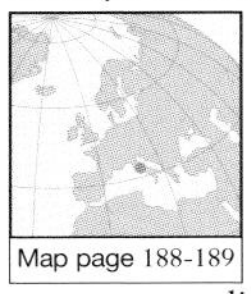
Map page 188-189

Vesuvius, near Naples, Etna and Stromboli. The main lowland area, the Po river valley in the northeast, is the main agricultural and industrial area and is the most populous region. Italy has a Mediterranean climate, although the north experiences colder, wetter winters, with heavy snow in the Alps. Natural resources are limited, and only about twenty per cent of the land is suitable for cultivation. The economy is fairly diversified. Some oil, natural gas and coal are produced, but most fuels and minerals used by industry are imported. Agriculture is important, with cereals, vines, fruit and vegetables the main crops. Italy is the world's largest wine producer. The north is the centre of Italian industry, especially around Turin, Milan and Genoa. Leading manufactures include industrial and office equipment, domestic appliances, cars, textiles, clothing, leather goods, chemicals and metal products. There is a strong service sector, and with over twenty-five million visitors a year, tourism is a major employer and accounts for five per cent of the national income. Finance and banking are also important. Most trade is with other European Union countries.

JAMAICA

Area Sq Km	10 991	**Currency**	Jamaican dollar
Area Sq Miles	4 244	**Languages**	English, creole
Population	2 651 000	**Religions**	Protestant, Roman Catholic
Capital	Kingston	**Organizations**	CARICOM, Comm., UN

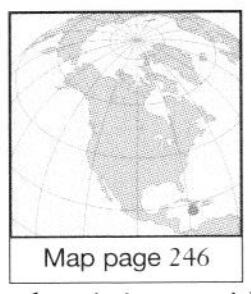
Map page 246

Jamaica, the third largest Caribbean island, has beaches and densely populated coastal plains traversed by hills and plateaus rising to the forested Blue Mountains in the east. The climate is tropical, but cooler and wetter on high ground. The economy is based on tourism, agriculture, mining and light manufacturing. Bauxite, aluminium oxide, sugar and bananas are the main exports. The USA is the main trading partner. Foreign aid is also significant.

Jammu and Kashmir
Disputed territory (India, Pakistan, China)

Area Sq Km (Miles) 222 236 (85 806) **Population** 13 000 000 **Capital** Srinagar

A disputed region in the north of the Indian subcontinent, to the west of the Karakoram and Himalaya mountains. The 'Line of Control' separates the northwestern, Pakistani-controlled area and the southeastern, Indian-controlled area. China occupies the Himalayan section known as the Aksai Chin, which is also claimed by India.

Map page 116

JAPAN

Area Sq Km	377 727	**Currency**	Yen
Area Sq Miles	145 841	**Languages**	Japanese
Population	128 085 000	**Religions**	Shintoist, Buddhist, Christian
Capital	Tōkyō	**Organizations**	APEC, OECD, UN

Japan lies in the Pacific Ocean off the coast of eastern Asia and consists of four main islands – Hokkaidō, Honshū, Shikoku and Kyūshū – and more than three thousand smaller islands in the surrounding Sea of

Map page 102-103

Japan, East China Sea and Pacific Ocean. The central island of Honshū accounts for sixty per cent of the total land area and contains eighty per cent of the population. Behind the long and deeply indented coastline, nearly three-quarters of the country is mountainous and heavily forested. Japan has over sixty active volcanoes, and is subject to frequent earthquakes and typhoons. The climate is generally temperate maritime, with warm summers and mild winters, except in western Hokkaidō and northwest Honshū, where the winters are very cold with heavy snow. Only fourteen per cent of the land area is suitable for cultivation, and its few raw materials (coal, oil, natural gas, lead, zinc and copper) are insufficient for its industry. Most materials must be imported, including about ninety per cent of energy requirements. Yet Japan has the world's second largest industrial economy, with a range of modern heavy and light industries centred mainly around the major ports of Yokohama, Ōsaka and Tōkyō. It is the world's largest manufacturer of cars, motorcycles and merchant ships, and a major producer of steel, textiles, chemicals and cement. It is also a leading producer of many consumer durables, such as washing machines, and electronic equipment, chiefly office equipment and computers. Japan has a strong service sector, banking and finance being particularly important, and Tōkyō has one of the world's major stock exchanges. Owing to intensive agricultural production, Japan is seventy per cent self-sufficient in food. The main food crops are rice, barley, fruit, wheat and soya beans. Livestock rearing (chiefly cattle, pigs and chickens) and fishing are also important, and Japan has one of the largest fishing fleets in the world. A major trading nation, Japan has trade links with many countries in Southeast Asia and in Europe, although its main trading partner is the USA.

Jersey
United Kingdom Crown Dependency

Area Sq Km	116	**Currency**	Pound sterling
Area Sq Miles	45	**Languages**	English, French
Population	87 500	**Religions**	Protestant, Roman Catholic
Capital	St Helier		

One of the Channel Islands lying off the west coast of the Cherbourg peninsula in northern France. Financial services are the most important part of the economy.

Map page 148

JORDAN
Hashemite Kingdom of Jordan

Area Sq Km	89 206	**Currency**	Jordanian dinar
Area Sq Miles	34 443	**Languages**	Arabic
Population	5 703 000	**Religions**	Sunni Muslim, Christian
Capital	'Ammān	**Organizations**	UN

Map page 128

Jordan, in southwest Asia, is landlocked apart from a short coastline on the Gulf of Aqaba. Much of the country is rocky desert plateau. To the west of the mountains, the land falls below sea level to the Dead Sea and the Jordan river. The climate is hot and dry. Most people live in the northwest. Phosphates, potash, pharmaceuticals, fruit and vegetables are the main exports. The tourist industry is important, and the economy relies on workers' remittances from abroad and foreign aid.

KAZAKHSTAN
Republic of Kazakhstan

Area Sq Km	2 717 300	**Currency**	Tenge
Area Sq Miles	1 049 155	**Languages**	Kazakh, Russian, Ukrainian, German, Uzbek, Tatar
Population	14 825 000	**Religions**	Sunni Muslim, Russian Orthodox, Protestant
Capital	Astana (Akmola)	**Organizations**	CIS, UN

Stretching across central Asia, Kazakhstan covers a vast area of steppe land and semi-desert. The land is flat in the west, with large lowlands

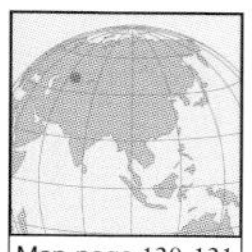
Map page 120-121

around the Caspian Sea, rising to mountains in the southeast. The climate is continental. Agriculture and livestock rearing are important, and cotton and tobacco are the main cash crops. Kazakhstan is very rich in minerals, including coal, chromium, gold, molybdenum, lead and zinc, and has substantial reserves of oil and gas. Mining, metallurgy, machine building and food processing are major industries. Oil, gas and minerals are the main exports, and the Russian Federation is the dominant trading partner.

KENYA
Republic of Kenya

Area Sq Km	582 646	**Currency**	Kenyan shilling
Area Sq Miles	224 961	**Languages**	Swahili, English, local languages
Population	34 256 000	**Religions**	Christian, traditional beliefs
Capital	Nairobi	**Organizations**	Comm., UN

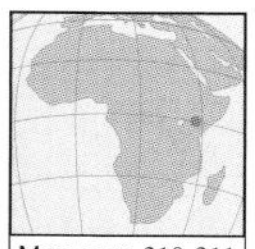
Map page 210-211

Kenya is in east Africa, on the Indian Ocean. Inland beyond the coastal plains the land rises to plateaus interrupted by volcanic mountains. The Great Rift Valley runs north-south to the west of the capital, Nairobi. Most of the population lives in the central area. Conditions are tropical on the coast, semi-desert in the north and savanna in the south. Hydroelectric power from the Upper Tana river provides most of the country's electricity. Agricultural products, mainly tea, coffee, fruit and vegetables, are the main exports. Light industry is important, and tourism, oil refining and re-exports for landlocked neighbours are major foreign exchange earners.

KIRIBATI
Republic of Kiribati

Area Sq Km	717	**Currency**	Australian dollar
Area Sq Miles	277	**Languages**	Gilbertese, English
Population	99 000	**Religions**	Roman Catholic, Protestant
Capital	Bairiki	**Organizations**	Comm., UN

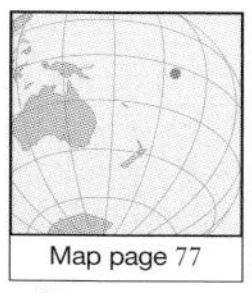
Map page 77

Kiribati, in the Pacific Ocean, straddles the Equator and comprises coral islands in the Gilbert, Phoenix and Line Island groups and the volcanic island of Banaba. Most people live on the Gilbert Islands, and the capital, Bairiki, is on Tarawa island in this group. The climate is hot, and wetter in the north. Copra and fish are exported. Kiribati relies on remittances from workers abroad and foreign aid.

KUWAIT
State of Kuwait

Area Sq Km	17 818	**Currency**	Kuwaiti dinar
Area Sq Miles	6 880	**Languages**	Arabic
Population	2 687 000	**Religions**	Sunni Muslim, Shi'a Muslim, Christian, Hindu
Capital	Al Kuwayt (Kuwait)	**Organizations**	OPEC, UN

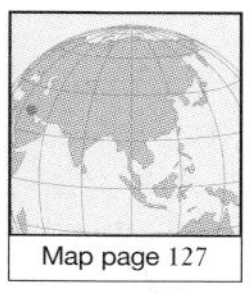
Map page 127

Kuwait lies on the northwest shores of The Gulf in southwest Asia. It is mainly low-lying desert, with irrigated areas along the bay, Kuwait Jun, where most people live. Summers are hot and dry, and winters are cool with some rainfall. The oil industry, which accounts for eighty per cent of exports, has largely recovered from the damage caused by the Gulf War in 1991. Income is also derived from extensive overseas investments. Japan and the USA are the main trading partners.

KYRGYZSTAN
Kyrgyz Republic

Area Sq Km	198 500	**Currency**	Kyrgyz som
Area Sq Miles	76 641	**Languages**	Kyrgyz, Russian, Uzbek
Population	5 264 000	**Religions**	Sunni Muslim, Russian Orthodox
Capital	Bishkek (Frunze)	**Organizations**	CIS, UN

Map page 121

A landlocked central Asian state, Kyrgyzstan is rugged and mountainous, lying to the west of the Tien Shan mountain range. Most of the population lives in the valleys of the north and west. Summers are hot and winters cold. Agriculture (chiefly livestock farming) is the main activity. Some oil and gas, coal, gold, antimony and mercury are produced. Manufactured goods include machinery, metals and metal products, which are the main exports. Most trade is with Germany, the Russian Federation, Kazakhstan and Uzbekistan.

LAOS
Lao People's Democratic Republic

Area Sq Km	236 800	**Currency**	Kip
Area Sq Miles	91 429	**Languages**	Lao, local languages
Population	5 924 000	**Religions**	Buddhist, traditional beliefs
Capital	Viangchan (Vientiane)	**Organizations**	ASEAN, UN

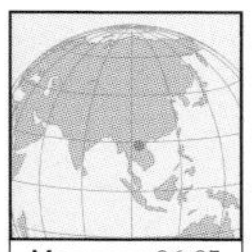
Map page 96-97

A landlocked country in Southeast Asia, Laos is a land of mostly forested mountains and plateaus. The climate is tropical monsoon. Most of the population lives in the Mekong valley and the low plateau in the south, where food crops, chiefly rice, are grown. Hydroelectricity from a plant on the Mekong river, timber, coffee and tin are exported. Laos relies heavily on foreign aid.

LATVIA
Republic of Latvia

Area Sq Km	63 700	**Currency**	Lats
Area Sq Miles	24 595	**Languages**	Latvian, Russian
Population	2 307 000	**Religions**	Protestant, Roman Catholic, Russian Orthodox
Capital	Rīga	**Organizations**	EU, NATO, UN

Latvia is in northern Europe, on the Baltic Sea and the Gulf of Riga. The land is flat near the coast but hilly with woods and lakes inland. The country has a modified continental climate. One-third of the

Map page 138

people live in the capital, Rīga. Crop and livestock farming are important. There are few natural resources. Industries and main exports include food products, transport equipment, wood and wood products and textiles. The main trading partners are the Russian Federation and Germany. Latvia joined the European Union in May 2004.

LEBANON
Republic of Lebanon

Area Sq Km	10 452	**Currency**	Lebanese pound
Area Sq Miles	4 036	**Languages**	Arabic, Armenian, French
Population	3 577 000	**Religions**	Shi'a Muslim, Sunni Muslim, Christian
Capital	Beirut	**Organizations**	UN

Map page 128

Lebanon lies on the Mediterranean coast of southwest Asia. Beyond the coastal strip, where most of the population lives, are two parallel mountain ranges, separated by the Bekaa Valley (El Beq'a). The economy and infrastructure have been recovering since the 1975-1991 civil war crippled the traditional sectors of financial services and tourism. Italy, France and the UAE are the main trading partners.

LESOTHO
Kingdom of Lesotho

Area Sq Km	30 355	**Currency**	Loti, South African rand
Area Sq Miles	11 720	**Languages**	Sesotho, English, Zulu
Population	1 795 000	**Religions**	Christian, traditional beliefs
Capital	Maseru	**Organizations**	Comm., SADC, UN

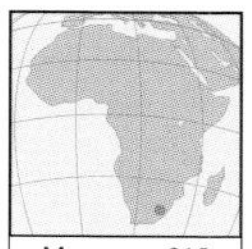
Map page 215

Lesotho is a landlocked state surrounded by the Republic of South Africa. It is a mountainous country lying within the Drakensberg mountain range. Farming and herding are the main activities. The economy depends heavily on South Africa for transport links and employment. A major hydroelectric plant completed in 1998 allows the sale of water to South Africa. Exports include manufactured goods (mainly clothing and road vehicles), food, live animals, wool and mohair.

LIBERIA
Republic of Liberia

Area Sq Km	111 369	**Currency**	Liberian dollar
Area Sq Miles	43 000	**Languages**	English, creole, local languages
Population	3 283 000	**Religions**	Traditional beliefs, Christian, Sunni Muslim
Capital	Monrovia	**Organizations**	UN

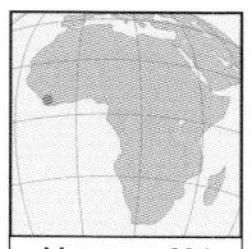
Map page 206

Liberia is on the Atlantic coast of west Africa. Beyond the coastal belt of sandy beaches and mangrove swamps the land rises to a forested plateau and highlands along the Guinea border. A quarter of the population lives along the coast. The climate is hot with heavy rainfall. Liberia is rich in mineral resources and forests. The economy is based on the production and export of basic products. Exports include diamonds, iron ore, rubber and timber. Liberia has a huge international debt and relies heavily on foreign aid.

LIBYA
Great Socialist People's Libyan Arab Jamahiriya

Area Sq Km	1 759 540	**Currency**	Libyan dinar
Area Sq Miles	679 362	**Languages**	Arabic, Berber
Population	5 853 000	**Religions**	Sunni Muslim
Capital	Ṭarābulus (Tripoli)	**Organizations**	OPEC, UN

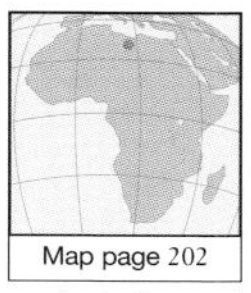
Map page 202

Libya lies on the Mediterranean coast of north Africa. The desert plains and hills of the Sahara dominate the landscape and the climate is hot and dry. Most of the population lives in cities near the coast, where the climate is cooler with moderate rainfall. Farming and herding, chiefly in the northwest, are important but the main industry is oil. Libya is a major producer, and oil accounts for virtually all of its export earnings. Italy and Germany are the main trading partners.

LIECHTENSTEIN
Principality of Liechtenstein

Area Sq Km	160	**Currency**	Swiss franc
Area Sq Miles	62	**Languages**	German
Population	35 000	**Religions**	Roman Catholic, Protestant
Capital	Vaduz	**Organizations**	UN

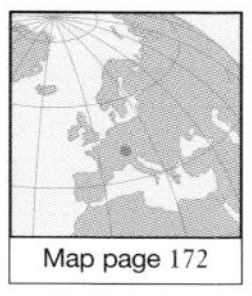
Map page 172

A landlocked state between Switzerland and Austria, Liechtenstein has an industrialized, free-enterprise economy. Low business taxes have attracted companies to establish offices which provide approximately one-third of state revenues. Banking is also important. Major products include precision instruments, ceramics and textiles.

LITHUANIA
Republic of Lithuania

Area Sq Km	65 200	**Currency**	Litas
Area Sq Miles	25 174	**Languages**	Lithuanian, Russian, Polish
Population	3 431 000	**Religions**	Roman Catholic, Protestant, Russian Orthodox
Capital	Vilnius	**Organizations**	EU, NATO, UN

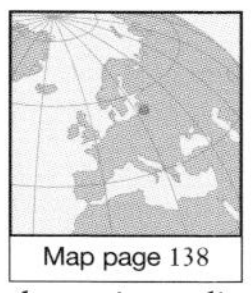
Map page 138

Lithuania is in northern Europe on the eastern shores of the Baltic Sea. It is mainly lowland with many lakes, rivers and marshes. Agriculture, fishing and forestry are important, but manufacturing dominates the economy. The main exports are machinery, mineral products and chemicals. The Russian Federation and Germany are the main trading partners. Lithuania joined the European Union in May 2004.

LUXEMBOURG
Grand Duchy of Luxembourg

Area Sq Km	2 586	**Currency**	Euro
Area Sq Miles	998	**Languages**	Letzeburgish, German, French
Population	465 000	**Religions**	Roman Catholic
Capital	Luxembourg	**Organizations**	EU, NATO, OECD, UN

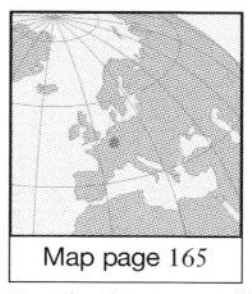
Map page 165

Luxembourg, a small landlocked country in western Europe, borders Belgium, France and Germany. The hills and forests of the Ardennes dominate the north, with rolling pasture to the south, where the main towns, farms and industries are found. The iron and steel industry is still important, but light industries (including textiles, chemicals and food products) are growing. Luxembourg is a major banking centre. Main trading partners are Belgium, Germany and France.

MACEDONIA (F.Y.R.O.M.)
Republic of Macedonia

Area Sq Km	25 713	**Currency**	Macedonian denar
Area Sq Miles	9 928	**Languages**	Macedonian, Albanian, Turkish
Population	2 034 000	**Religions**	Macedonian Orthodox, Sunni Muslim
Capital	Skopje	**Organizations**	UN

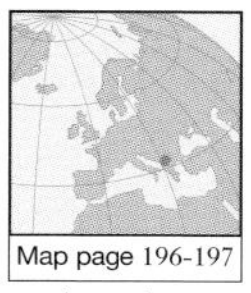
Map page 196-197

The Former Yugoslav Republic of Macedonia is a landlocked state in southern Europe. Lying within the southern Balkan Mountains, it is traversed northwest-southeast by the Vardar valley. The climate is continental. The economy is based on industry, mining and agriculture, but conflicts in the region have reduced trade and caused economic difficulties. Foreign aid and loans are now assisting in modernization and development of the country.

MADAGASCAR
Republic of Madagascar

Area Sq Km	587 041	**Currency**	Malagasy ariary, Malagasy franc
Area Sq Miles	226 658	**Languages**	Malagasy, French
Population	18 606 000	**Religions**	Traditional beliefs, Christian, Sunni Muslim
Capital	Antananarivo	**Organizations**	SADC, UN

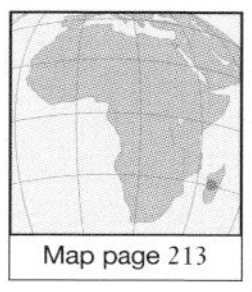
Map page 213

Madagascar lies off the east coast of southern Africa. The world's fourth largest island, it is mainly a high plateau, with a coastal strip to the east and scrubby plain to the west. The climate is tropical, with heavy rainfall in the north and east. Most of the population lives on the plateau. Although the amount of arable land is limited, the economy is based on agriculture. The main industries are agricultural processing, textile manufacturing and oil refining. Foreign aid is important. Exports include coffee, vanilla, cotton cloth, sugar and shrimps. France is the main trading partner.

MALAWI
Republic of Malawi

Area Sq Km	118 484	**Currency**	Malawian kwacha
Area Sq Miles	45 747	**Languages**	Chichewa, English, local languages
Population	12 884 000	**Religions**	Christian, traditional beliefs, Sunni Muslim
Capital	Lilongwe	**Organizations**	Comm., SADC, UN

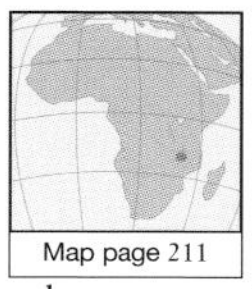
Map page 211

Landlocked Malawi in central Africa is a narrow hilly country at the southern end of the Great Rift Valley. One-fifth is covered by Lake Nyasa. Most of the population lives in rural areas in the southern regions. The climate is mainly subtropical, with varying rainfall. The economy is predominantly agricultural, with tobacco, tea and sugar the main exports. Malawi is one of the world's least developed countries and relies heavily on foreign aid. South Africa is the main trading partner.

MALAYSIA
Federation of Malaysia

Area Sq Km	332 965	**Currency**	Ringgit
Area Sq Miles	128 559	**Languages**	Malay, English, Chinese, Tamil, local languages
Population	25 347 000	**Religions**	Sunni Muslim, Buddhist, Hindu, Christian
Capital	Kuala Lumpur (Putrajaya)	**Organizations**	APEC, ASEAN, Comm., UN

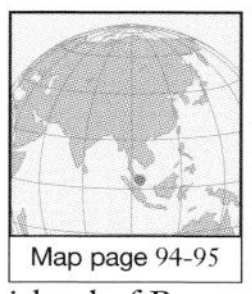
Map page 94-95

Malaysia, in Southeast Asia, comprises two regions, separated by the South China Sea. The western region occupies the southern Malay Peninsula, which has a chain of mountains dividing the eastern coastal strip from wider plains to the west. East Malaysia, consisting of the states of Sabah and Sarawak in the north of the island of Borneo, is mainly rainforest-covered hills and mountains with mangrove swamps along the coast. Both regions have a tropical climate with heavy rainfall. About eighty per cent of the population lives in Peninsular Malaysia. The country is rich in natural resources and has reserves of minerals and fuels. It is an important producer of tin, oil, natural gas and tropical hardwoods. Agriculture remains a substantial part of the economy, but industry is the most important sector. The main exports are transport and electronic equipment, oil, chemicals, palm oil, wood and rubber. The main trading partners are Japan, the USA and Singapore.

MALDIVES
Republic of the Maldives

Area Sq Km	298	**Currency**	Rufiyaa
Area Sq Miles	115	**Languages**	Divehi (Maldivian)
Population	329 000	**Religions**	Sunni Muslim
Capital	Male	**Organizations**	Comm., UN

The Maldive archipelago comprises over a thousand coral atolls (around two hundred of which are inhabited), in the Indian Ocean, southwest of India. Over eighty per cent of the land area is less than one metre above sea level. The main atolls are North and South Male

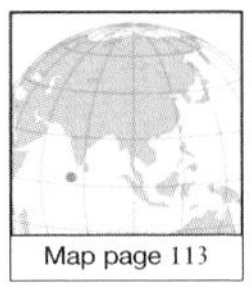
Map page 113

and Addu. The climate is hot, humid and monsoonal. There is little cultivation and almost all food is imported. Tourism has expanded rapidly and is the most important sector of the economy.

MALI
Republic of Mali

Area Sq Km	1 240 140	**Currency**	CFA franc
Area Sq Miles	478 821	**Languages**	French, Bambara, local languages
Population	13 518 000	**Religions**	Sunni Muslim, traditional beliefs, Christian
Capital	Bamako	**Organizations**	UN

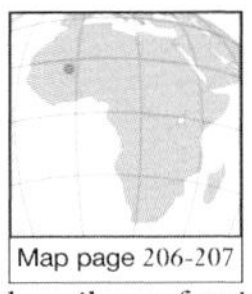
Map page 206–207

A landlocked state in west Africa, Mali is generally low-lying. Northern regions lie within the Sahara desert. To the south are marshes and savanna grassland. Rainfall is unreliable. Most of the population lives along the Niger and Falémé rivers. Exports include cotton, livestock and gold. Mali relies heavily on foreign aid.

MALTA
Republic of Malta

Area Sq Km	316	**Currency**	Maltese lira
Area Sq Miles	122	**Languages**	Maltese, English
Population	402 000	**Religions**	Roman Catholic
Capital	Valletta	**Organizations**	Comm., EU, UN

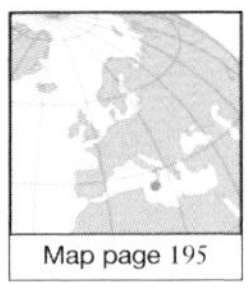
Map page 195

The islands of Malta and Gozo lie in the Mediterranean Sea, off the coast of southern Italy. The islands have hot, dry summers and mild winters. The economy depends on foreign trade, tourism and the manufacture of electronics and textiles. Main trading partners are the USA, France and Italy. Malta joined the European Union in May 2004.

MARSHALL ISLANDS
Republic of the Marshall Islands

Area Sq Km	181	**Currency**	United States dollar
Area Sq Miles	70	**Languages**	English, Marshallese
Population	62 000	**Religions**	Protestant, Roman Catholic
Capital	Delap-Uliga-Djarrit	**Organizations**	UN

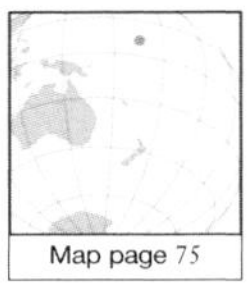
Map page 75

The Marshall Islands consist of over a thousand atolls and islands in the north Pacific Ocean. The main atolls are Majuro (home to half the population), Kwajalein, Jaluit, Enewetak and Bikini. The climate is tropical. About half the workforce is employed in farming or fishing. Tourism is a small source of foreign exchange and the islands depend heavily on aid from the USA.

Martinique
French Overseas Department

Area Sq Km	1 079	**Currency**	Euro
Area Sq Miles	417	**Languages**	French, creole
Population	396 000	**Religions**	Roman Catholic, traditional beliefs
Capital	Fort-de-France		

Martinique, one of the Caribbean Windward Islands, has volcanic peaks in the north, a populous central plain, and hills and beaches in the south. Tourism is a major source of income, and substantial aid comes from France. The main trading partners are France and Guadeloupe.

Map page 247

MAURITANIA
Islamic Arab and African Republic of Mauritania

Area Sq Km	1 030 700	**Currency**	Ouguiya
Area Sq Miles	397 955	**Languages**	Arabic, French, local languages
Population	3 069 000	**Religions**	Sunni Muslim
Capital	Nouakchott	**Organizations**	UN

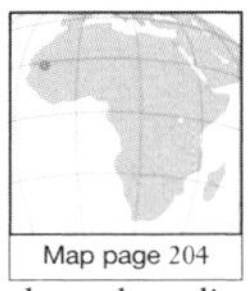
Map page 204

Mauritania is on the Atlantic coast of northwest Africa and lies almost entirely within the Sahara desert. Oases and a fertile strip along the Senegal river to the south are the only areas suitable for cultivation. The climate is generally hot and dry. About a quarter of Mauritanians live in the capital, Nouakchott. Most of the workforce depends on livestock rearing and subsistence farming. There are large deposits of iron ore which account for more than half of total exports. Mauritania's coastal waters are among the richest fishing grounds in the world. The main trading partners are France, Japan and Italy.

MAURITIUS
Republic of Mauritius

Area Sq Km	2 040	**Currency**	Mauritius rupee
Area Sq Miles	788	**Languages**	English, creole, Hindi, Bhojpuri, French
Population	1 245 000	**Religions**	Hindu, Roman Catholic, Sunni Muslim
Capital	Port Louis	**Organizations**	Comm., SADC, UN

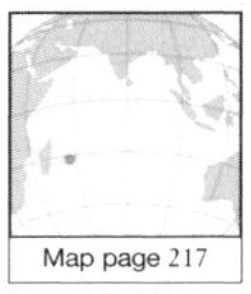
Map page 217

The state comprises Mauritius, Rodrigues and some twenty small islands in the Indian Ocean, east of Madagascar. The main island of Mauritius is volcanic in origin and has a coral coast, rising to a central plateau. Most of the population lives on the north and west sides of the island. The climate is warm and humid. The economy is based on sugar production, light manufacturing (chiefly clothing) and tourism.

Mayotte
French Departmental Collectivity

Area Sq Km	373	**Currency**	Euro
Area Sq Miles	144	**Languages**	French, Mahorian
Population	186 026	**Religions**	Sunni Muslim, Christian
Capital	Dzaoudzi		

Lying in the Indian Ocean off the east coast of central Africa, Mayotte is geographically part of the Comoro archipelago. The economy is based on agriculture, but Mayotte depends heavily on aid from France.

Map page 217

MEXICO
United Mexican States

Area Sq Km	1 972 545	**Currency**	Mexican peso
Area Sq Miles	761 604	**Languages**	Spanish, Amerindian languages
Population	107 029 000	**Religions**	Roman Catholic, Protestant
Capital	México	**Organizations**	APEC, OECD, UN

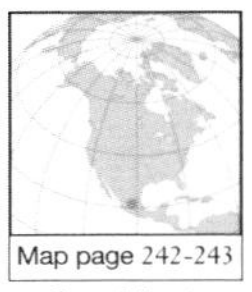
Map page 242–243

The largest country in Central America, Mexico extends south from the USA to Guatemala and Belize. Most of the country is high plateau flanked by the Sierra Madre mountains. The principal lowland is the Yucatán peninsula in the southeast. The climate is hot and humid in the lowlands, warm on the plateau and cool with cold winters in the mountains. The north is arid, while the far south has heavy rainfall. Mexico City is the second largest conurbation in the world and the country's economic centre. Agriculture involves a fifth of the workforce; crops include grains, coffee, cotton and vegetables. Mexico is rich in minerals, including copper, zinc, lead, tin, sulphur, and silver. It is one of the world's largest producers of oil, from vast reserves in the Gulf of Mexico. The oil and petrochemical industries still dominate the economy, but a variety of goods are produced, including iron and steel, motor vehicles, textiles, chemicals and food and tobacco products. Over three-quarters of all trade is with the USA.

MICRONESIA, FEDERATED STATES OF

Area Sq Km	701	**Currency**	United States dollar
Area Sq Miles	271	**Languages**	English, Chuukese, Pohnpeian, local languages
Population	110 000	**Religions**	Roman Catholic, Protestant
Capital	Palikir	**Organizations**	UN

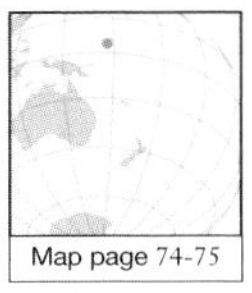
Map page 74–75

Micronesia comprises over six hundred atolls and islands of the Caroline Islands in the north Pacific Ocean. A third of the population lives on Pohnpei. The climate is tropical, with heavy rainfall. Fishing and subsistence farming are the main activities. Fish, garments and bananas are the main exports. Income is also derived from tourism and the licensing of foreign fishing fleets. The islands depend heavily on aid from the USA.

MOLDOVA
Republic of Moldova

Area Sq Km	33 700	**Currency**	Moldovan leu
Area Sq Miles	13 012	**Languages**	Romanian, Ukrainian, Gagauz, Russian
Population	4 206 000	**Religions**	Romanian Orthodox, Russian Orthodox
Capital	Chişinău	**Organizations**	CIS, UN

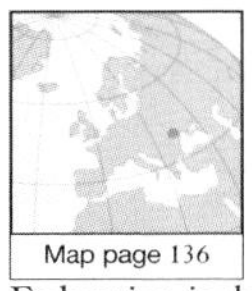
Map page 136

Moldova lies between Romania and Ukraine in eastern Europe. It consists of hilly steppe land, drained by the Prut and Dniester rivers. The economy is mainly agricultural, with sugar beet, tobacco, wine and fruit the chief products. Food processing, machinery and textiles are the main industries. The Russian Federation is the main trading partner.

MONACO
Principality of Monaco

Area Sq Km	2	**Currency**	Euro
Area Sq Miles	1	**Languages**	French, Monégasque, Italian
Population	35 000	**Religions**	Roman Catholic
Capital	Monaco-Ville	**Organizations**	UN

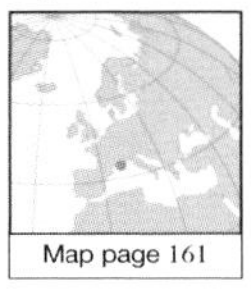
Map page 161

The principality occupies a rocky peninsula and a strip of land on France's Mediterranean coast. Monaco's economy depends on service industries (chiefly tourism, banking and finance) and light industry.

MONGOLIA

Area Sq Km	1 565 000	**Currency**	Tugrik (tögrög)
Area Sq Miles	604 250	**Languages**	Khalka (Mongolian), Kazakh, local languages
Population	2 646 000	**Religions**	Buddhist, Sunni Muslim
Capital	Ulaanbaatar	**Organizations**	UN

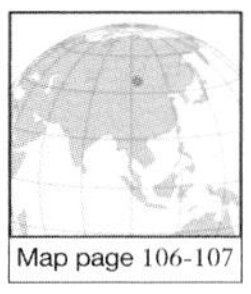
Map page 106–107

Mongolia is a landlocked country in eastern Asia between the Russian Federation and China. Much of it is high steppe land, with mountains and lakes in the west and north. In the south is the Gobi desert. Mongolia has long, cold winters and short, mild summers. A quarter of the population lives in the capital, Ulaanbaatar. Livestock breeding and agricultural processing are important. There are substantial mineral resources. Copper and textiles are the main exports.

MONTENEGRO
Republic of Montenegro

Area Sq Km	13 812	**Currency**	Euro
Area Sq Miles	5 333	**Languages**	Serbian (Montenegrin), Albanian
Population	620 145	**Religions**	Montenegrin Orthodox, Sunni Muslim
Capital	Podgorica		

Map page 196

Montenegro was the last constituent republic of the former Yugoslavia to become an independent nation, in June 2006. At that time it opted to split from the state union of Serbia and Montenegro. Montenegro separates the much larger Serbia from the Adriatic coast.

Montserrat
United Kingdom Overseas Territory

Area Sq Km	100	**Currency**	East Caribbean dollar
Area Sq Miles	39	**Languages**	English
Population	4 000	**Religions**	Protestant, Roman Catholic
Capital	Plymouth	**Organizations**	CARICOM

An island in the Leeward Islands group in the Lesser Antilles, in the Caribbean. From 1995 to 1997 the volcanoes in the Soufrière Hills erupted for the first time since 1630. Over sixty per cent of the island was covered in volcanic ash and the capital was virtually destroyed. Many people emigrated, and the remaining population moved to the north of the island. Reconstruction is being funded by aid from the UK.

Map page 247

MOROCCO
Kingdom of Morocco

Area Sq Km	446 550	**Currency**	Moroccan dirham
Area Sq Miles	172 414	**Languages**	Arabic, Berber, French
Population	31 478 000	**Religions**	Sunni Muslim
Capital	Rabat	**Organizations**	UN

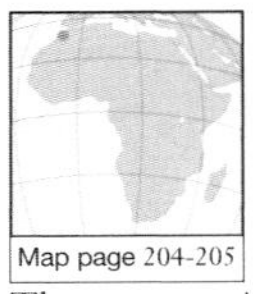
Map page 204–205

Lying in the northwest corner of Africa, Morocco has both Atlantic and Mediterranean coasts. The Atlas Mountains separate the arid south and disputed region of Western Sahara from the fertile regions of the west and north, which have a milder climate. Most Moroccans live on the Atlantic coastal plain. The economy is based on agriculture, phosphate mining and tourism; the most important industries are food processing, textiles and chemicals. France is the main trading partner.

MOZAMBIQUE
Republic of Mozambique

Area Sq Km	799 380	**Currency**	Metical
Area Sq Miles	308 642	**Languages**	Portuguese, Makua, Tsonga, local languages
Population	19 792 000	**Religions**	Traditional beliefs, Roman Catholic, Sunni Muslim
Capital	Maputo	**Organizations**	Comm., SADC, UN

Map page 213

Mozambique lies on the east coast of southern Africa. The land is mainly a savanna plateau drained by the Zambezi and Limpopo rivers, with highlands to the north. Most of the population lives on the coast or in the river valleys. In general the climate is tropical with winter rainfall, but droughts occur. The economy is based on subsistence agriculture. Exports include shrimps, cashews, cotton and sugar, but Mozambique relies heavily on aid, and remains one of the least developed countries in the world.

MYANMAR (Burma)
Union of Myanmar

Area Sq Km	676 577	**Currency**	Kyat
Area Sq Miles	261 228	**Languages**	Burmese, Shan, Karen, local languages
Population	50 519 000	**Religions**	Buddhist, Christian, Sunni Muslim
Capital	Naypyidaw/Yangôn (Rangoon)	**Organizations**	ASEAN, UN

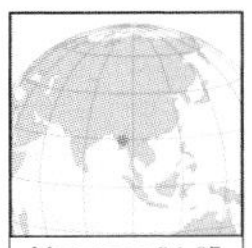
Map page 96–97

Myanmar (Burma) is in Southeast Asia, bordering the Bay of Bengal and the Andaman Sea. Most of the population lives in the valley and delta of the Irrawaddy river, which is flanked by mountains and high plateaus. The climate is hot and monsoonal, and rainforest covers much of the land. Most of the workforce is employed in agriculture. Myanmar is rich in minerals, including zinc, lead, copper and silver. Political and social unrest and lack of foreign investment have affected economic development.

NAMIBIA
Republic of Namibia

Area Sq Km	824 292	**Currency**	Namibian dollar
Area Sq Miles	318 261	**Languages**	English, Afrikaans, German, Ovambo, local languages
Population	2 031 000	**Religions**	Protestant, Roman Catholic
Capital	Windhoek	**Organizations**	Comm., SADC, UN

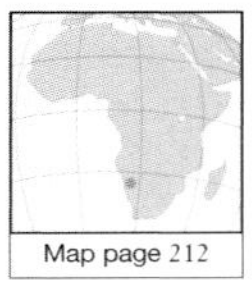
Map page 212

Namibia lies on the Atlantic coast of southern Africa. Mountain ranges separate the coastal Namib Desert from the interior plateau, bordered to the south and east by the Kalahari Desert. The country is hot and dry, but some summer rain in the north supports crops and livestock. Most of the workforce is employed in agriculture, although the economy is based on mineral extraction –predominantly diamonds, but also uranium, lead, zinc and silver. Fishing is increasingly important. The economy is closely linked to that of the Republic of South Africa.

NAURU
Republic of Nauru

Area Sq Km	21	**Currency**	Australian dollar
Area Sq Miles	8	**Languages**	Nauruan, English
Population	14 000	**Religions**	Protestant, Roman Catholic
Capital	Yaren	**Organizations**	Comm., UN

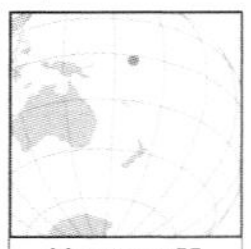
Map page 77

Nauru is a coral island near the Equator in the Pacific Ocean. It has a fertile coastal strip and a barren central plateau. The climate is tropical. The economy is based on phosphate mining, but reserves are near exhaustion and replacement of this income is a serious long-term problem.

NEPAL
Kingdom of Nepal

Area Sq Km	147 181	**Currency**	Nepalese rupee
Area Sq Miles	56 827	**Languages**	Nepali, Maithili, Bhojpuri, English, local languages
Population	27 133 000	**Religions**	Hindu, Buddhist, Sunni Muslim
Capital	Kathmandu	**Organizations**	UN

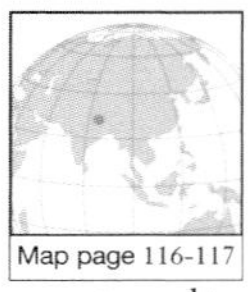
Map page 116–117

Nepal lies in the eastern Himalaya mountains between India and China. High mountains (including Everest) dominate the north. Most people live in the temperate central valleys and subtropical southern plains. The economy is based largely on agriculture and forestry. There is some manufacturing, chiefly of textiles and carpets, and tourism is important. Nepal relies heavily on foreign aid.

NETHERLANDS
Kingdom of the Netherlands

Area Sq Km	41 526	**Currency**	Euro
Area Sq Miles	16 033	**Languages**	Dutch, Frisian
Population	16 299 000	**Religions**	Roman Catholic, Protestant, Sunni Muslim
Capital	Amsterdam/ 's-Gravenhage (The Hague)	**Organizations**	EU, NATO, OECD, UN

The Netherlands lies on the North Sea coast of western Europe. Apart from low hills in the far southeast, the land is flat and low-lying, much of it below sea level. The coastal region includes the delta of five rivers and polders (reclaimed land), protected by sand dunes, dykes and canals. The climate is temperate, with cool summers and mild winters. Rainfall is spread evenly throughout the year. The Netherlands is a densely populated and highly urbanized country, with the majority of the population living in the cities of Amsterdam, Rotterdam and The Hague. Horticulture and dairy farming are important activities, although they employ less than four per cent of the workforce. The Netherlands ranks as the world's third agricultural exporter, and is a leading producer and exporter of natural gas from reserves in the North Sea. The economy is based mainly on international trade and manufacturing industry. The main industries produce food products, chemicals, machinery, electrical and electronic goods and transport equipment. Germany is the main trading partner, followed by other European Union countries.

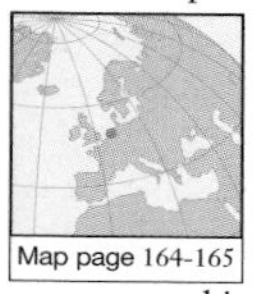
Map page 164-165

Netherlands Antilles
Self-governing Netherlands Territory

Area Sq Km	800	**Currency**	Netherlands Antilles guilder
Area Sq Miles	309	**Languages**	Dutch, Papiamento, English
Population	183 000	**Religions**	Roman Catholic, Protestant
Capital	Willemstad		

The territory comprises two separate island groups: Curaçao and Bonaire off the northern coast of Venezuela, and Saba, Sint Eustatius and the southern part of St-Martin (Sint Maarten) in the Lesser Antilles. Tourism, oil refining and offshore finance are the mainstays of the economy. The main trading partners are the USA, Venezuela and Mexico.

Map page 247

New Caledonia
French Overseas Country

Area Sq Km	19 058	**Currency**	CFP franc
Area Sq Miles	7 358	**Languages**	French, local languages
Population	237 000	**Religions**	Roman Catholic, Protestant, Sunni Muslim
Capital	Nouméa		

An island group lying in the southwest Pacific, with a sub-tropical climate. New Caledonia has over one-fifth of the world's nickel reserves, and the main economic activity is metal mining. Tourism is also important. New Caledonia relies on aid from France.

Map page 78

NEW ZEALAND

Area Sq Km	270 534	**Currency**	New Zealand dollar
Area Sq Miles	104 454	**Languages**	English, Maori
Population	4 028 000	**Religions**	Protestant, Roman Catholic
Capital	Wellington	**Organizations**	APEC, Comm., OECD, UN

New Zealand comprises two main islands separated by the narrow Cook Strait, and a number of smaller islands. North Island, where three-quarters of the population lives, has mountain ranges, broad fertile valleys and a central plateau with hot springs and active volcanoes. South Island is also mountainous, with the Southern Alps running its entire length. The only major lowland area is the Canterbury Plains in the centre-east. The climate is generally temperate, although South Island has colder winters. Farming is the mainstay of the economy. New Zealand is one of the world's leading producers of meat (beef, lamb and mutton), wool and dairy products; fruit and fish are also important. Hydroelectric and geothermal power provide much of the country's energy needs. Other industries produce timber, wood pulp, iron, aluminium, machinery and chemicals. Tourism is the fastest growing sector of the economy. The main trading partners are Australia, the USA and Japan.

Map page 80-81

NICARAGUA
Republic of Nicaragua

Area Sq Km	130 000	**Currency**	Córdoba
Area Sq Miles	50 193	**Languages**	Spanish, Amerindian languages
Population	5 487 000	**Religions**	Roman Catholic, Protestant
Capital	Managua	**Organizations**	UN

Nicaragua lies at the heart of Central America, with both Pacific and Caribbean coasts. Mountain ranges separate the east, which is largely rainforest, from the more developed western regions, which include Lake Nicaragua and some active volcanoes. The highest land is in the north. The climate is tropical. Nicaragua is one of the western hemisphere's poorest countries, and the economy is largely agricultural. Exports include coffee, seafood, cotton and bananas. The USA is the main trading partner. Nicaragua has a huge national debt, and relies heavily on foreign aid.

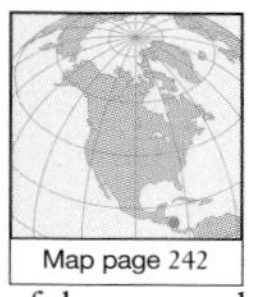
Map page 242

NIGER
Republic of Niger

Area Sq Km	1 267 000	**Currency**	CFA franc
Area Sq Miles	489 191	**Languages**	French, Hausa, Fulani, local languages
Population	13 957 000	**Religions**	Sunni Muslim, traditional beliefs
Capital	Niamey	**Organizations**	UN

A landlocked state of west Africa, Niger lies mostly within the Sahara desert, but with savanna in the south and in the Niger valley area. The mountains of the Massif de l'Aïr dominate central regions. Much of the country is hot and dry. The south has some summer rainfall, although droughts occur. The economy depends on subsistence farming and herding, and uranium exports, but Niger is one of the world's least developed countries and relies heavily on foreign aid. France is the main trading partner.

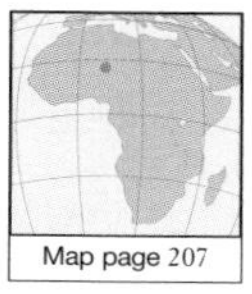
Map page 207

NIGERIA
Federal Republic of Nigeria

Area Sq Km	923 768	**Currency**	Naira
Area Sq Miles	356 669	**Languages**	English, Hausa, Yoruba, Ibo, Fulani, local languages
Population	131 530 000	**Religions**	Sunni Muslim, Christian, traditional beliefs
Capital	Abuja	**Organizations**	Comm., OPEC, UN

Nigeria is in west Africa, on the Gulf of Guinea, and is the most populous country in Africa. The Niger delta dominates coastal areas, fringed with sandy beaches, mangrove swamps and lagoons. Inland is a belt of rainforest which gives way to woodland or savanna on high plateaus. The far north is the semi-desert edge of the Sahara. The climate is tropical, with heavy summer rainfall in the south but low rainfall in the north. Most of the population lives in the coastal lowlands or in the west. About half the workforce is involved in agriculture, mainly growing subsistence crops. Agricultural production, however, has failed to keep up with demand, and Nigeria is now a net importer of food. Cocoa and rubber are the only significant export crops. The economy is heavily dependent on vast oil resources in the Niger delta and in shallow offshore waters, and oil accounts for over ninety per cent of export earnings. Nigeria also has natural gas reserves and some mineral deposits, but these are largely undeveloped. Industry involves mainly oil refining, chemicals (chiefly fertilizers), agricultural processing, textiles, steel manufacture and vehicle assembly. Political instability in the past has left Nigeria with heavy debts, poverty and unemployment.

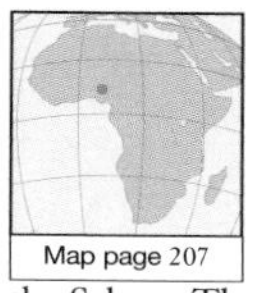
Map page 207

Niue
Self-governing New Zealand Overseas Territory

Area Sq Km	258	**Currency**	New Zealand dollar
Area Sq Miles	100	**Languages**	English, Niuean
Population	1 000	**Religions**	Christian
Capital	Alofi		

Niue, one of the largest coral islands in the world, lies in the south Pacific Ocean about 500 kilometres (300 miles) east of Tonga. The economy depends on aid and remittances from New Zealand. The population is declining because of migration to New Zealand.

Map page 81

Norfolk Island
Australian External Territory

Area Sq Km	35	**Currency**	Australian dollar
Area Sq Miles	14	**Languages**	English
Population	2 601	**Religions**	Protestant, Roman Catholic
Capital	Kingston		

In the south Pacific Ocean, Norfolk Island lies between Vanuatu and New Zealand. Tourism has increased steadily and is the mainstay of the economy and provides revenues for agricultural development.

Map page 82

Northern Mariana Islands
United States Commonwealth

Area Sq Km	477	**Currency**	United States dollar
Area Sq Miles	184	**Languages**	English, Chamorro, local languages
Population	81 000	**Religions**	Roman Catholic
Capital	Capitol Hill		

A chain of islands in the northwest Pacific Ocean, extending over 550 kilometres (350 miles) north to south. The main island is Saipan. Tourism is a major industry, employing approximately half the workforce.

Map page 74

NORTH KOREA
People's Democratic Republic of Korea

Area Sq Km	120 538	**Currency**	North Korean won
Area Sq Miles	46 540	**Languages**	Korean
Population	22 488 000	**Religions**	Traditional beliefs, Chondoist, Buddhist
Capital	P'yŏngyang	**Organizations**	UN

Occupying the northern half of the Korean peninsula in eastern Asia, North Korea is a rugged and mountainous country. The principal lowlands and the main agricultural areas are the plains in the southwest. More than half the population lives in urban areas, mainly on the coastal plains. North Korea has a continental climate, with cold, dry winters and hot, wet summers. Approximately one-third of the workforce is involved in agriculture, mainly growing food crops on cooperative farms. Various minerals, notably iron ore, are mined and are the basis of the country's heavy industries. Exports include minerals (lead, magnesite and zinc) and metal products (chiefly iron and steel). The economy declined after 1991, when ties to the former USSR and eastern bloc collapsed, and there have been serious food shortages.

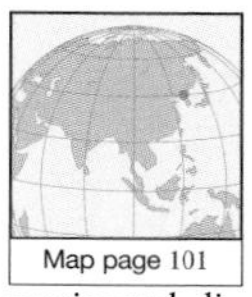
Map page 101

NORWAY
Kingdom of Norway

Area Sq Km	323 878	**Currency**	Norwegian krone
Area Sq Miles	125 050	**Languages**	Norwegian
Population	4 620 000	**Religions**	Protestant, Roman Catholic
Capital	Oslo	**Organizations**	NATO, OECD, UN

Norway stretches along the north and west coasts of Scandinavia, from the Arctic Ocean to the North Sea. Its extensive coastline is indented with fjords and fringed with many islands. Inland, the terrain is mountainous, with coniferous forests and lakes in the south. The only major lowland areas are along the southern North Sea and Skagerrak coasts, where most of the population lives. The climate is modified by the effect of the North Atlantic Drift ocean current. Norway has vast petroleum and natural gas resources in the North Sea. It is one of western Europe's leading producers of oil and gas, and exports of oil account for approximately half of total export earnings. Related industries include engineering (oil and gas platforms) and petrochemicals. More traditional industries process local raw materials, particularly fish, timber and minerals. Agriculture is limited, but fishing and fish farming are important. Norway is the world's leading exporter of farmed salmon. Merchant shipping and tourism are major sources of foreign exchange.

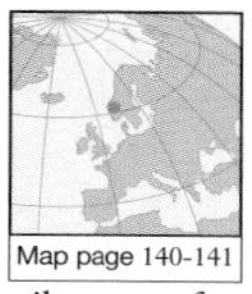
Map page 140-141

OMAN
Sultanate of Oman

Area Sq Km	309 500	**Currency**	Omani riyal
Area Sq Miles	119 499	**Languages**	Arabic, Baluchi, Indian languages
Population	2 567 000	**Religions**	Ibadhi Muslim, Sunni Muslim
Capital	Masqaṭ (Muscat)	**Organizations**	UN

In southwest Asia, Oman occupies the east and southeast coasts of the Arabian Peninsula and an enclave north of the United Arab Emirates. Most of the land is desert, with mountains in the north and south. The climate is hot and mainly dry. Most of the population lives on the coastal strip on the Gulf of Oman. The majority depend on farming and fishing, but the oil and gas industries dominate the economy with around eighty per cent of export revenues coming from oil.

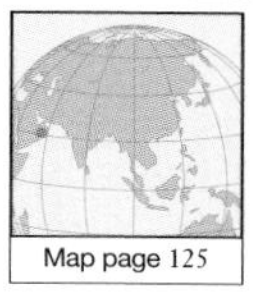
Map page 125

PAKISTAN
Islamic Republic of Pakistan

Area Sq Km	803 940	**Currency**	Pakistani rupee
Area Sq Miles	310 403	**Languages**	Urdu, Punjabi, Sindhi, Pushtu, English
Population	157 935 000	**Religions**	Sunni Muslim, Shi'a Muslim, Christian, Hindu
Capital	Islamabad	**Organizations**	Comm., UN

Pakistan is in the northwest part of the Indian subcontinent in south Asia, on the Arabian Sea. The east and south are dominated by the great basin of the Indus river system. This is the main agricultural area and contains most of the predominantly rural population. To the north the land rises to the mountains of the Karakoram, Hindu Kush and Himalaya mountains. The west is semi-desert plateaus and mountain ranges. The climate ranges between dry desert, and arctic tundra on the mountain tops. Temperatures are generally warm and rainfall is monsoonal. Agriculture is the main sector of the economy, employing approximately half of the workforce, and is based on extensive irrigation schemes. Pakistan is one of the world's leading producers of cotton and a major exporter of rice. Pakistan produces natural gas and has a variety of mineral deposits including coal and gold, but they are little developed. The main industries are textiles and clothing manufacture and food processing, with fabrics and ready-made clothing the leading exports. Pakistan also produces leather goods, fertilizers, chemicals, paper and precision instruments. The country depends heavily on foreign aid and remittances from workers abroad.

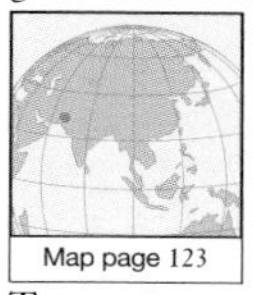
Map page 123

PALAU
Republic of Palau

Area Sq Km	497	**Currency**	United States dollar
Area Sq Miles	192	**Languages**	Palauan, English
Population	20 000	**Religions**	Roman Catholic, Protestant, traditional beliefs
Capital	Koror	**Organizations**	UN

Palau comprises over three hundred islands in the western Caroline Islands, in the west Pacific Ocean. The climate is tropical. The economy is based on farming, fishing and tourism, but Palau is heavily dependent on aid from the USA.

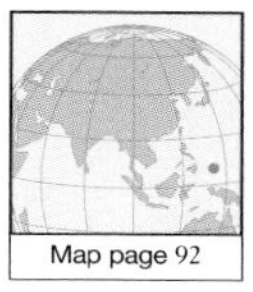
Map page 92

PANAMA
Republic of Panama

Area Sq Km	77 082	**Currency**	Balboa
Area Sq Miles	29 762	**Languages**	Spanish, English, Amerindian languages
Population	3 232 000	**Religions**	Roman Catholic, Protestant, Sunni Muslim
Capital	Panamá	**Organizations**	UN

Panama is the most southerly state in central America and has Pacific and Caribbean coasts. It is hilly, with mountains in the west and jungle near the Colombian border. The climate is tropical. Most of the population lives on the drier Pacific side. The economy is based mainly on services related to the Panama Canal: shipping, banking and tourism. Exports include bananas, shrimps, coffee, clothing and fish products. The USA is the main trading partner.

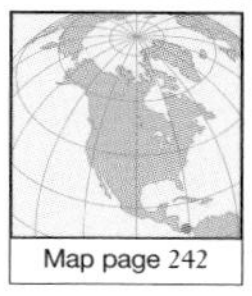
Map page 242

PAPUA NEW GUINEA
Independent State of Papua New Guinea

Area Sq Km	462 840	**Currency**	Kina
Area Sq Miles	178 704	**Languages**	English, Tok Pisin (creole), local languages
Population	5 887 000	**Religions**	Protestant, Roman Catholic, traditional beliefs
Capital	Port Moresby	**Organizations**	Comm., UN

Papua New Guinea occupies the eastern half of the island of New Guinea and includes many island groups. It has a forested and mountainous interior, bordered by swampy plains, and a tropical monsoon climate. Most of the workforce are farmers. Timber, copra, coffee and cocoa are important, but exports are dominated by minerals, chiefly gold and copper. The country depends on foreign aid. Australia, Japan and Singapore are the main trading partners.

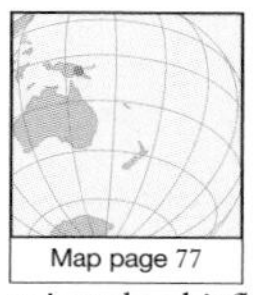
Map page 77

PARAGUAY
Republic of Paraguay

Area Sq Km	406 752	**Currency**	Guaraní
Area Sq Miles	157 048	**Languages**	Spanish, Guaraní
Population	6 158 000	**Religions**	Roman Catholic, Protestant
Capital	Asunción	**Organizations**	UN

Map page 253

Paraguay is a landlocked country in central South America, bordering Bolivia, Brazil and Argentina. The Paraguay river separates a sparsely populated western zone of marsh and flat alluvial plains from a more developed, hilly and forested region to the east and south. The climate is subtropical. Virtually all electricity is produced by hydroelectric plants, and surplus power is exported to Brazil and Argentina. The hydroelectric dam at Itaipú is one of the largest in the world. The mainstay of the economy is agriculture and related industries. Exports include cotton, soya bean and edible oil products, timber and meat. Brazil and Argentina are the main trading partners.

PERU
Republic of Peru

Area Sq Km	1 285 216	**Currency**	Sol
Area Sq Miles	496 225	**Languages**	Spanish, Quechua, Aymara
Population	27 968 000	**Religions**	Roman Catholic, Protestant
Capital	Lima	**Organizations**	APEC, UN

Map page 252

Peru lies on the Pacific coast of South America. Most Peruvians live on the coastal strip and on the plateaus of the high Andes mountains. East of the Andes is the Amazon rainforest. The coast is temperate with low rainfall while the east is hot, humid and wet. Agriculture involves one-third of the workforce and fishing is also important. Agriculture and fishing have both been disrupted by the El Niño climatic effect in recent years. Sugar, cotton, coffee and, illegally, coca are the main cash crops. Copper and copper products, fishmeal, zinc products, coffee, petroleum and its products, and textiles are the main exports. The USA and the European Union are the main trading partners.

PHILIPPINES
Republic of the Philippines

Area Sq Km	300 000	**Currency**	Philippine peso
Area Sq Miles	115 831	**Languages**	English, Filipino, Tagalog, Cebuano, local languages
Population	83 054 000	**Religions**	Roman Catholic, Protestant, Sunni Muslim
Capital	Manila	**Organizations**	APEC, ASEAN, UN

Map page 92

The Philippines, in Southeast Asia, consists of over seven thousand islands and atolls lying between the South China Sea and the Pacific Ocean. The islands of Luzon and Mindanao account for two-thirds of the land area. They and nine other fairly large islands are mountainous and forested. There are active volcanoes, and earthquakes and tropical storms are common. Most of the population lives in the plains on the larger islands or on the coastal strips. The climate is hot and humid with heavy monsoonal rainfall. Rice, coconuts, sugar cane, pineapples and bananas are the main agricultural crops, and fishing is also important. Main exports are electronic equipment, machinery and transport equipment, garments and coconut products. Foreign aid and remittances from workers abroad are important to the economy, which faces problems of high population growth rate and high unemployment. The USA and Japan are the main trading partners.

Pitcairn Islands
United Kingdom Overseas Territory

Area Sq Km	45	**Currency**	New Zealand dollar
Area Sq Miles	17	**Languages**	English
Population	47	**Religions**	Protestant
Capital	Adamstown		

An island group in the southeast Pacific Ocean consisting of Pitcairn Island and three uninhabited islands. It was originally settled by mutineers from *HMS Bounty* in 1790.

Map page 75

POLAND
Polish Republic

Area Sq Km	312 683	**Currency**	Złoty
Area Sq Miles	120 728	**Languages**	Polish, German
Population	38 530 000	**Religions**	Roman Catholic, Polish Orthodox
Capital	Warszawa (Warsaw)	**Organizations**	EU, NATO, OECD, UN

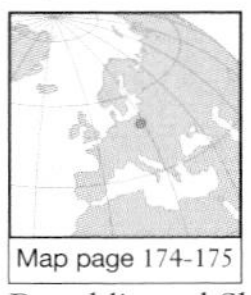
Map page 174-175

Poland lies on the Baltic coast of eastern Europe. The Oder (Odra) and Vistula (Wisła) river deltas dominate the coast. Inland, much of the country is low-lying, with woods and lakes. In the south the land rises to the Sudeten Mountains and the western part of the Carpathian Mountains, which form the borders with the Czech Republic and Slovakia respectively. The climate is continental. Around a quarter of the workforce is involved in agriculture, and exports include livestock products and sugar. The economy is heavily industrialized, with mining and manufacturing accounting for forty per cent of national income. Poland is one of the world's major producers of coal, and also produces copper, zinc, lead, sulphur and natural gas. The main industries are machinery and transport equipment, shipbuilding, and metal and chemical production. Exports include machinery and transport equipment, manufactured goods, food and live animals. Germany is the main trading partner. Poland joined the European Union in May 2004.

PORTUGAL
Portuguese Republic

Area Sq Km	88 940	**Currency**	Euro
Area Sq Miles	34 340	**Languages**	Portuguese
Population	10 495 000	**Religions**	Roman Catholic, Protestant
Capital	Lisboa (Lisbon)	**Organizations**	EU, NATO, OECD, UN

Map page 180

Portugal lies in the western part of the Iberian peninsula in southwest Europe, has an Atlantic coastline and is bordered by Spain to the north and east. The island groups of the Azores and Madeira are parts of Portugal. On the mainland, the land north of the river Tagus (Tejo) is mostly highland, with extensive forests of pine and cork. South of the river is undulating lowland. The climate in the north is cool and moist; the south is warmer, with dry, mild winters. Most Portuguese live near the coast, and more than one-third of the total population lives around the capital, Lisbon (Lisboa). Agriculture, fishing and forestry involve approximately ten per cent of the workforce. Mining and manufacturing are the main sectors of the economy. Portugal produces kaolin, copper, tin, zinc, tungsten and salt. Exports include textiles, clothing and footwear, electrical machinery and transport equipment, cork and wood products, and chemicals. Service industries, chiefly tourism and banking, are important to the economy, as are remittances from workers abroad. Most trade is with other European Union countries.

PUERTO RICO
United States Commonwealth

Area Sq Km	9 104	**Currency**	United States dollar
Area Sq Miles	3 515	**Languages**	Spanish, English
Population	3 955 000	**Religions**	Roman Catholic, Protestant
Capital	San Juan		

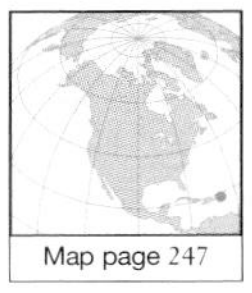
Map page 247

The Caribbean island of Puerto Rico has a forested, hilly interior, coastal plains and a tropical climate. Half of the population lives in the San Juan area. The economy is based on manufacturing (chiefly chemicals, electronics and food), tourism and agriculture. The USA is the main trading partner.

QATAR
State of Qatar

Area Sq Km	11 437	**Currency**	Qatari riyal
Area Sq Miles	4 416	**Languages**	Arabic
Population	813 000	**Religions**	Sunni Muslim
Capital	Ad Dawḩah (Doha)	**Organizations**	OPEC, UN

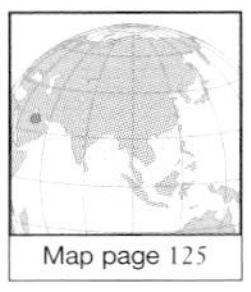
Map page 125

Qatar occupies a peninsula in southwest Asia that extends northwards from east-central Saudi Arabia into The Gulf. The land is flat and barren with sand dunes and salt pans. The climate is hot and mainly dry. Most people live in the area of the capital, Doha. The economy is heavily dependent on oil and natural gas production and the oil-refining industry. Income also comes from overseas investment. Japan is the largest trading partner.

Réunion
French Overseas Department

Area Sq Km	2 551	**Currency**	Euro
Area Sq Miles	985	**Languages**	French, creole
Population	785 000	**Religions**	Roman Catholic
Capital	St-Denis		

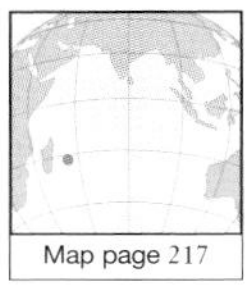
Map page 217

The Indian Ocean island of Réunion is mountainous, with coastal lowlands and a warm climate. The economy depends on tourism, French aid, and exports of sugar. Several widely-dispersed and uninhabited islets to the west are administered from Réunion.

ROMANIA

Area Sq Km	237 500	**Currency**	Romanian leu
Area Sq Miles	91 699	**Languages**	Romanian, Hungarian
Population	21 711 000	**Religions**	Romanian Orthodox, Protestant, Roman Catholic
Capital	Bucureşti (Bucharest)	**Organizations**	NATO, UN

Map page 196-197

Romania lies in eastern Europe, on the northwest coast of the Black Sea. Mountains separate the Transylvanian Basin in the centre of the country from the populous plains of the east and south and from the Danube delta. The climate is continental. Romania has mineral resources (zinc, lead, silver and gold) and oil and natural gas reserves. Economic development has been slow and sporadic, but measures to accelerate change were introduced in 1999. Agriculture employs over one-third of the workforce. The main exports are textiles, mineral products, chemicals, machinery and footwear. The main trading partners are Germany and Italy.

RUSSIAN FEDERATION

Area Sq Km	17 075 400	**Currency**	Russian rouble
Area Sq Miles	6 592 849	**Languages**	Russian, Tatar, Ukrainian, local languages
Population	143 202 000	**Religions**	Russian Orthodox, Sunni Muslim, Protestant
Capital	Moskva (Moscow)	**Organizations**	APEC, CIS, UN

The Russian Federation occupies much of eastern Europe and all of northern Asia, and is the world's largest country. It borders fourteen countries to the west and south and has long coastlines on the Arctic and Pacific Oceans to the north and east. European Russia lies west of the Ural Mountains. To the south the land rises to uplands and the Caucasus mountains on the border with Georgia and Azerbaijan. East of the Urals lies the flat West Siberian Plain and the Central Siberian Plateau. In the south-east is Lake Baikal, the world's deepest lake, and the Sayan ranges on the border with Kazakhstan and Mongolia. Eastern Siberia is rugged and mountainous, with many active volcanoes in the Kamchatka Peninsula. The country's major rivers are the Volga in the west and the Ob', Irtysh, Yenisey, Lena and Amur in Siberia. The climate and

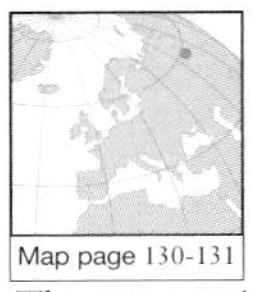
Map page 130-131

vegetation range between arctic tundra in the north and semi-arid steppe towards the Black and Caspian Sea coasts in the south. In general, the climate is continental with extreme temperatures. The majority of the population (the eighth largest in the world), and industry and agriculture are concentrated in European Russia. The economy is dependent on exploitation of raw materials and on heavy industry. Russia has a wealth of mineral resources, although they are often difficult to exploit because of climate and remote locations. It is one of the world's leading producers of petroleum, natural gas and coal as well as iron ore, nickel, copper, bauxite, and many precious and rare metals. Forests cover over forty per cent of the land area and supply an important timber, paper and pulp industry. Approximately eight per cent of the land is suitable for cultivation, but farming is generally inefficient and food, especially grains, must be imported. Fishing is important and Russia has a large fleet operating around the world. The transition to a market economy has been slow and difficult, with considerable underemployment. As well as mining and extractive industries there is a wide range of manufacturing industry, from steel mills to aircraft and space vehicles, shipbuilding, synthetic fabrics, plastics, cotton fabrics, consumer durables, chemicals and fertilizers. Exports include fuels, metals, machinery, chemicals and forest products. The most important trading partners include Germany, the USA and Belarus.

RWANDA
Republic of Rwanda

Area Sq Km	26 338	**Currency**	Rwandan franc
Area Sq Miles	10 169	**Languages**	Kinyarwanda, French, English
Population	9 038 000	**Religions**	Roman Catholic, traditional beliefs, Protestant
Capital	Kigali	**Organizations**	UN

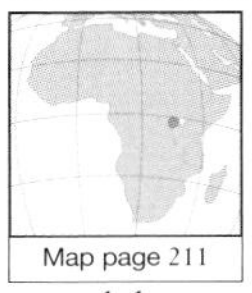
Map page 211

Rwanda, the most densely populated country in Africa, is situated in the mountains and plateaus to the east of the western branch of the Great Rift Valley in east Africa. The climate is warm with a summer dry season. Rwanda depends on subsistence farming, coffee and tea exports, light industry and foreign aid. The country is slowly recovering from serious internal conflict which caused devastation in the early 1990s.

Saba part of Netherlands Antilles

Area Sq Km (Miles) 13 (5) **Population** 1 387 **Capital** Bottom

An island in the Leeward Islands in the Lesser Antilles, in the Caribbean to the south of St-Martin.

Map page 247

St-Barthélemy Dependency of Guadeloupe (France)

Area Sq Km (Miles) 21 (8) **Population** 6 852 **Capital** Gustavia

An island in the Leeward Islands in the Lesser Antilles, in the Caribbean south of St-Martin. Tourism is the main economic activity.

Map page 247

St Helena
United Kingdom Overseas Territory

Area Sq Km	121	**Currency**	St Helena pound
Area Sq Miles	47	**Languages**	English
Population	5 000	**Religions**	Protestant, Roman Catholic
Capital	Jamestown		

St Helena and its dependencies Ascension and Tristan da Cunha are isolated island groups lying in the south Atlantic Ocean. St Helena is a rugged island of volcanic origin. The main activity is fishing, but the economy relies on financial aid from the UK. Main trading partners are the UK and South Africa.

Map page 216

ST KITTS AND NEVIS
Federation of St Kitts and Nevis

Area Sq Km	261	**Currency**	East Caribbean dollar
Area Sq Miles	101	**Languages**	English, creole
Population	43 000	**Religions**	Protestant, Roman Catholic
Capital	Basseterre	**Organizations**	CARICOM, Comm., UN

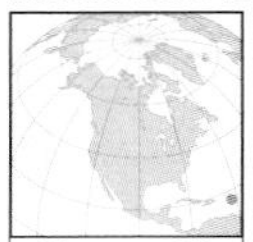
Map page 247

St Kitts and Nevis are in the Leeward Islands, in the Caribbean. Both volcanic islands are mountainous and forested, with sandy beaches and a warm, wet climate. About three-quarters of the population lives on St Kitts. Agriculture is the main activity, with sugar the main product. Tourism and manufacturing (chiefly garments and electronic components) and offshore banking are important activities.

ST LUCIA

Area Sq Km	616	**Currency**	East Caribbean dollar
Area Sq Miles	238	**Languages**	English, creole
Population	161 000	**Religions**	Roman Catholic, Protestant
Capital	Castries	**Organizations**	CARICOM, Comm., UN

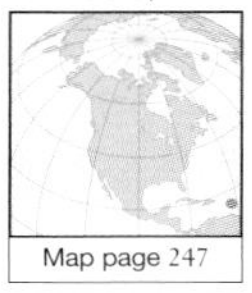
Map page 247

St Lucia, one of the Windward Islands in the Caribbean Sea, is a volcanic island with forested mountains, hot springs, sandy beaches and a wet tropical climate. Agriculture is the main activity, with bananas accounting for approximately forty per cent of export earnings. Tourism, agricultural processing and light manufacturing are increasingly important.

St-Martin Dependency of Guadeloupe (France)

Area Sq Km (Miles) 54 (21) **Population** 29 078 **Capital** Marigot

The northern part of one of the Leeward Islands, in the Caribbean. The other part of the island is part of the Netherlands Antilles (Sint Maarten). Tourism is the main source of income.

Map page 247

St Pierre and Miquelon
French Territorial Collectivity

Area Sq Km	242	**Currency**	Euro
Area Sq Miles	93	**Languages**	French
Population	6 000	**Religions**	Roman Catholic
Capital	St-Pierre		

A group of islands off the south coast of Newfoundland in eastern Canada. The islands are largely unsuitable for agriculture, and fishing and fish processing are the most important activities. The islands rely heavily on financial assistance from France.

Map page 225

ST VINCENT AND THE GRENADINES

Area Sq Km	389	**Currency**	East Caribbean dollar
Area Sq Miles	150	**Languages**	English, creole
Population	119 000	**Religions**	Protestant, Roman Catholic
Capital	Kingstown	**Organizations**	CARICOM, Comm., UN

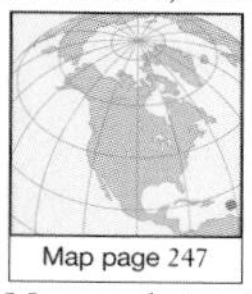
Map page 247

St Vincent, whose territory includes islets and cays in the Grenadines, is in the Windward Islands, in the Caribbean. St Vincent itself is forested and mountainous, with an active volcano, Soufrière. The climate is tropical and wet. The economy is based mainly on agriculture and tourism. Bananas account for approximately one-third of export earnings and arrowroot is also important. Most trade is with the USA and other CARICOM countries.

SAMOA
Independent State of Samoa

Area Sq Km	2 831	**Currency**	Tāla
Area Sq Miles	1 093	**Languages**	Samoan, English
Population	185 000	**Religions**	Protestant, Roman Catholic
Capital	Apia	**Organizations**	Comm., UN

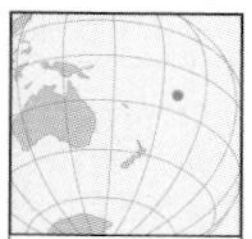
Map page 78

Samoa consists of two larger mountainous and forested islands, Savai'i and Upolu, and seven smaller islands, in the south Pacific Ocean. Over half the population lives on Upolu. The climate is tropical. The economy is based on agriculture, with some fishing and light manufacturing. Traditional exports are coconut products, fish and beer. Tourism is increasing, but the islands depend on workers' remittances and foreign aid.

SAN MARINO
Republic of San Marino

Area Sq Km	61	**Currency**	Euro
Area Sq Miles	24	**Languages**	Italian
Population	28 000	**Religions**	Roman Catholic
Capital	San Marino	**Organizations**	UN

Map page 191

Landlocked San Marino lies in northeast Italy. A third of the people live in the capital. There is some agriculture and light industry, but most income comes from tourism. Italy is the main trading partner.

SÃO TOMÉ AND PRÍNCIPE
Democratic Republic of São Tomé and Príncipe

Area Sq Km	964	**Currency**	Dobra
Area Sq Miles	372	**Languages**	Portuguese, creole
Population	157 000	**Religions**	Roman Catholic, Protestant
Capital	São Tomé	**Organizations**	UN

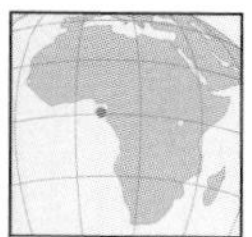
Map page 207

The two main islands and adjacent islets lie off the coast of west Africa in the Gulf of Guinea. São Tomé is the larger island, with over ninety per cent of the population. Both São Tomé and Príncipe are mountainous and tree-covered, and have a hot and humid climate. The economy is heavily dependent on cocoa, which accounts for around ninety per cent of export earnings.

SAUDI ARABIA
Kingdom of Saudi Arabia

Area Sq Km	2 200 000	**Currency**	Saudi Arabian riyal
Area Sq Miles	849 425	**Languages**	Arabic
Population	24 573 000	**Religions**	Sunni Muslim, Shi'a Muslim
Capital	Ar Riyāḍ (Riyadh)	**Organizations**	OPEC, UN

Map page 118-119

Saudi Arabia occupies most of the Arabian Peninsula in southwest Asia. The terrain is desert or semi-desert plateaus, which rise to mountains running parallel to the Red Sea in the west and slope down to plains in the southeast and along The Gulf in the east. Over eighty per cent of the population lives in urban areas. There are around four million foreign workers in Saudi Arabia, employed mainly in the oil and service industries. Summers are hot, winters are warm and rainfall is low. Saudi Arabia has the world's largest reserves of oil and significant natural gas reserves, both onshore and in The Gulf. Crude oil and refined products account for over ninety per cent of export earnings. Other industries and irrigated agriculture are being encouraged, but most food and raw materials are imported. Saudi Arabia has important banking and commercial interests. Japan and the USA are the main trading partners.

SENEGAL
Republic of Senegal

Area Sq Km	196 720	**Currency**	CFA franc
Area Sq Miles	75 954	**Languages**	French, Wolof, Fulani, local languages
Population	11 658 000	**Religions**	Sunni Muslim, Roman Catholic, traditional beliefs
Capital	Dakar	**Organizations**	UN

Senegal lies on the Atlantic coast of west Africa. The north is arid semi-desert, while the south is mainly fertile savanna bushland. The climate is tropical with summer rains, although droughts occur. One-fifth of the population lives in and around Dakar, the capital and main port. Fish, groundnuts and phosphates are the main exports. France is the main trading partner.

Map page 206

SERBIA
Republic of Serbia

Area Sq Km	88 361	**Currency**	Serbian dinar, euro
Area Sq Miles	34 116	**Languages**	Serbian, Albanian, Hungarian
Population	9 379 437	**Religions**	Serbian Orthodox, Sunni Muslim
Capital	Beograd (Belgrade)	**Organizations**	UN

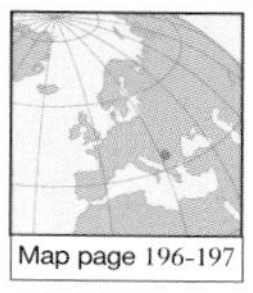
Map page 196-197

The southern European republic of Serbia was separated in 2006 from its neighbour, Montenegro – the two becoming independent countries. The state union of Serbia and Montenegro had retained the name Yugoslavia until 2003. The southern province of Kosovo, is under UN administration. After 1991 the economy was seriously affected by civil war and economic sanctions. The landscape is for the most part rugged, mountainous and forested. Northern Serbia is low-lying and is drained by the Danube river system.

SEYCHELLES
Republic of the Seychelles

Area Sq Km	455	**Currency**	Seychelles rupee
Area Sq Miles	176	**Languages**	English, French, creole
Population	81 000	**Religions**	Roman Catholic, Protestant
Capital	Victoria	**Organizations**	Comm., UN

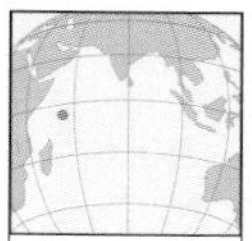
Map page 217

The Seychelles comprises an archipelago of over one hundred granitic and coral islands in the western Indian Ocean. Over ninety per cent of the population lives on the main island, Mahé. The climate is hot and humid with heavy rainfall. The economy is based mainly on tourism, fishing and light manufacturing.

SIERRA LEONE
Republic of Sierra Leone

Area Sq Km	71 740	**Currency**	Leone
Area Sq Miles	27 699	**Languages**	English, creole, Mende, Temne, local languages
Population	5 525 000	**Religions**	Sunni Muslim, traditional beliefs
Capital	Freetown	**Organizations**	Comm., UN

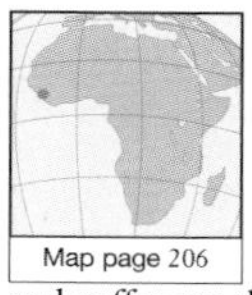
Map page 206

Sierra Leone lies on the Atlantic coast of west Africa. Its coastline is heavily indented and is lined with mangrove swamps. Inland is a forested area rising to savanna plateaus, with mountains to the northeast. The climate is tropical and rainfall is heavy. Most of the workforce is involved in subsistence farming. Cocoa and coffee are the main cash crops. Diamonds and rutile (titanium ore) are the main exports. Sierra Leone is one of the world's poorest countries, and the economy relies on substantial foreign aid.

SINGAPORE
Republic of Singapore

Area Sq Km	639	**Currency**	Singapore dollar
Area Sq Miles	247	**Languages**	Chinese, English, Malay, Tamil
Population	4 326 000	**Religions**	Buddhist, Taoist, Sunni Muslim, Christian, Hindu
Capital	Singapore	**Organizations**	APEC, ASEAN, Comm., UN

Map page 94

The state comprises the main island of Singapore and over fifty other islands, lying off the southern tip of the Malay Peninsula in Southeast Asia. Singapore is generally low-lying and includes land reclaimed from swamps and the sea. It is hot and humid, with heavy rainfall throughout the year. There are fish farms and vegetable gardens in the north and east of the island, but most food is imported. Singapore also lacks mineral and energy resources. Manufacturing industries and services are the main sectors of the economy. Their rapid development has fuelled the nation's impressive economic growth during recent decades. Main industries include electronics, oil refining, chemicals, pharmaceuticals, ship repair, food processing and textiles. Singapore is also a major financial centre. Its port is one of the world's largest and busiest and acts as an entrepôt for neighbouring states. Tourism is also important. Japan, the USA and Malaysia are the main trading partners.

Sint Eustatius part of Netherlands Antilles

Area Sq Km (Miles)	21 (8)	**Population**	2 829	**Capital**	Oranjestad

An island in the Leeward Islands, in the Caribbean south of St-Martin (Sint Maarten). It has a developing tourism industry.

Map page 247

Sint Maarten part of Netherlands Antilles

Area Sq Km (Miles)	34 (13)	**Population**	31 882	**Capital**	Philipsburg

The southern part of one of the Leeward Islands, in the Caribbean; the other part of the island is a dependency of France. Tourism and fishing are the most important industries.

Map page 247

SLOVAKIA
Slovak Republic

Area Sq Km	49 035	**Currency**	Slovakian koruna
Area Sq Miles	18 933	**Languages**	Slovakian, Hungarian, Czech
Population	5 401 000	**Religions**	Roman Catholic, Protestant, Orthodox
Capital	Bratislava	**Organizations**	EU, NATO, OECD, UN

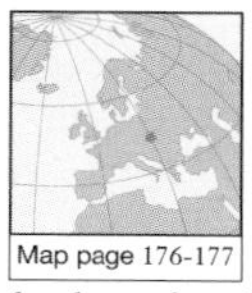
Map page 176-177

A landlocked country in central Europe, Slovakia is mountainous in the north, but low-lying in the southwest. The climate is continental. There is a range of manufacturing industries, and the main exports are machinery and transport equipment, but in recent years there have been economic difficulties and growth has been slow. Slovakia joined the European Union in May 2004. Most trade is with other EU countries, especially the Czech Republic.

SLOVENIA
Republic of Slovenia

Area Sq Km	20 251	**Currency**	Tólar
Area Sq Miles	7 819	**Languages**	Slovenian, Croatian, Serbian
Population	1 967 000	**Religions**	Roman Catholic, Protestant
Capital	Ljubljana	**Organizations**	EU, NATO, UN

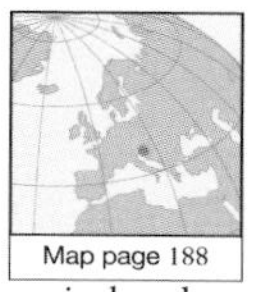
Map page 188

Slovenia lies in the northwest Balkan Mountains of southern Europe and has a short coastline on the Adriatic Sea. It is mountainous and hilly, with lowlands on the coast and in the Sava and Drava river valleys. The climate is generally continental inland and Mediterranean nearer the coast. The main agricultural products are potatoes, grain and sugar beet; the main industries include metal processing, electronics and consumer goods. Trade has been re-orientated towards western markets and the main trading partners are Germany and Italy. Slovenia joined the European Union in May 2004.

SOLOMON ISLANDS

Area Sq Km	28 370	**Currency**	Solomon Islands dollar
Area Sq Miles	10 954	**Languages**	English, creole, local languages
Population	478 000	**Religions**	Protestant, Roman Catholic
Capital	Honiara	**Organizations**	Comm., UN

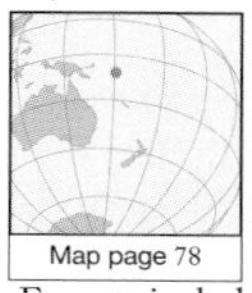
Map page 78

The state consists of the Solomon, Santa Cruz and Shortland Islands in the southwest Pacific Ocean. The six main islands are volcanic, mountainous and forested, although Guadalcanal, the most populous, has a large lowland area. The climate is generally hot and humid. Subsistence farming, forestry and fishing predominate. Exports include timber products, fish, copra and palm oil. The islands depend on foreign aid.

SOMALIA
Somali Democratic Republic

Area Sq Km	637 657	**Currency**	Somali shilling
Area Sq Miles	246 201	**Languages**	Somali, Arabic
Population	8 228 000	**Religions**	Sunni Muslim
Capital	Muqdisho (Mogadishu)	**Organizations**	UN

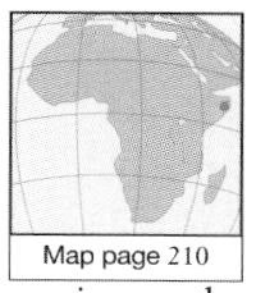
Map page 210

Somalia is in northeast Africa, on the Gulf of Aden and Indian Ocean. It consists of a dry scrubby plateau, rising to highlands in the north. The climate is hot and dry, but coastal areas and the Jubba and Webi Shabeelle river valleys support crops and most of the population. Subsistence farming and livestock rearing are the main activities. Exports include livestock and bananas. Frequent drought and civil war have prevented economic development. Somalia is one of the poorest, most unstable and least developed countries in the world.

SOUTH AFRICA, REPUBLIC OF

Area Sq Km	1 219 090	**Currency**	Rand
Area Sq Miles	470 689	**Languages**	Afrikaans, English, nine other official languages
Population	47 432 000	**Religions**	Protestant, Roman Catholic, Sunni Muslim, Hindu
Capital	Pretoria/ Cape Town	**Organizations**	Comm., SADC, UN

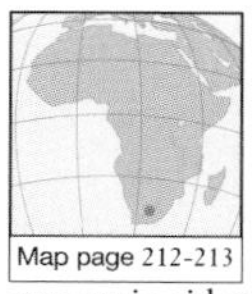
Map page 212-213

The Republic of South Africa occupies most of the southern part of Africa. It surrounds Lesotho and has a long coastline on the Atlantic and Indian Oceans. Much of the land is a vast plateau, covered with grassland or bush and drained by the Orange and Limpopo river systems. A fertile coastal plain rises to mountain ridges in the south and east, including Table Mountain near Cape Town and the Drakensberg range in the east. Gauteng is the most populous province, with Johannesburg and Pretoria its main cities. South Africa has warm summers and mild winters. Most of the country has the majority of its rainfall in summer, but the coast around Cape Town has winter rains. South Africa has the largest economy in Africa, although wealth is unevenly distributed and unemployment is very high. Agriculture employs approximately one-third of the workforce, and crops include fruit, wine, wool and maize. The country is the world's leading producer of gold and chromium and an important producer of diamonds. Many other minerals are also mined. The main industries are mineral and food processing, chemicals, electrical equipment, textiles and motor vehicles. Financial services are also important.

SOUTH KOREA
Republic of Korea

Area Sq Km	99 274	**Currency**	South Korean won
Area Sq Miles	38 330	**Languages**	Korean
Population	47 817 000	**Religions**	Buddhist, Protestant, Roman Catholic
Capital	Sŏul (Seoul)	**Organizations**	APEC, UN

The state consists of the southern half of the Korean Peninsula in eastern Asia and many islands lying off the western and southern coasts in the Yellow Sea. The terrain is mountainous, although less

© Collins Bartholomew Ltd

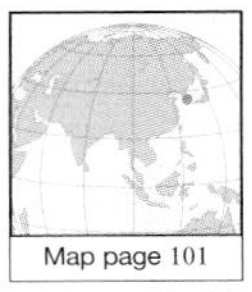

Map page 101

rugged than that of North Korea. Population density is high and the country is highly urbanized; most of the population lives on the western coastal plains and in the river basins of the Han-gang in the northwest and the Naktong-gang in the southeast. The climate is continental, with hot, wet summers and dry, cold winters. Arable land is limited by the mountainous terrain, but because of intensive farming South Korea is nearly self-sufficient in food. Sericulture (silk) is important, as is fishing, which contributes to exports. South Korea has few mineral resources, except for coal and tungsten. It has achieved high economic growth based mainly on export manufacturing. The main manufactured goods are cars, electronic and electrical goods, ships, steel, chemicals and toys, as well as textiles, clothing, footwear and food products. The USA and Japan are the main trading partners.

SPAIN
Kingdom of Spain

Area Sq Km	504 782	**Currency**	Euro
Area Sq Miles	194 897	**Languages**	Spanish, Catalan, Galician, Basque
Population	43 064 000	**Religions**	Roman Catholic
Capital	Madrid	**Organizations**	EU, NATO, OECD, UN

Map page 180-181

Spain occupies the greater part of the Iberian peninsula in southwest Europe, with coastlines on the Atlantic Ocean and Mediterranean Sea. It includes the Balearic Islands in the Mediterranean, the Canary Islands in the Atlantic, and two enclaves in north Africa (Ceuta and Melilla). Much of the mainland is a high plateau drained by the Douro (Duero), Tagus (Tajo) and Guadiana rivers. The plateau is interrupted by a low mountain range and bounded to the east and north also by mountains, including the Pyrenees, which form the border with France and Andorra. The main lowland areas are the Ebro basin in the northeast, the eastern coastal plains and the Guadalquivir basin in the southwest. Over three-quarters of the population lives in urban areas. The plateau experiences hot summers and cold winters. Conditions are cooler and wetter to the north, and warmer and drier to the south. Agriculture involves about ten per cent of the workforce, and fruit, vegetables and wine are exported. Fishing is an important industry, and Spain has a large fishing fleet. Mineral resources include lead, copper, mercury and fluorspar. Some oil is produced, but Spain has to import most energy needs. The economy is based mainly on manufacturing and services. The principal products are machinery, transport equipment, motor vehicles and food products, with a wide variety of other manufactured goods. With approximately fifty million visitors a year, tourism is a major industry. Banking and commerce are also important. Approximately seventy per cent of trade is with other European Union countries.

SRI LANKA
Democratic Socialist Republic of Sri Lanka

Area Sq Km	65 610	**Currency**	Sri Lankan rupee
Area Sq Miles	25 332	**Languages**	Sinhalese, Tamil, English
Population	20 743 000	**Religions**	Buddhist, Hindu, Sunni Muslim, Roman Catholic
Capital	Sri Jayewardenepura Kotte	**Organizations**	Comm., UN

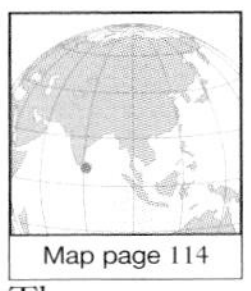

Map page 114

Sri Lanka lies in the Indian Ocean off the southeast coast of India in south Asia. It has rolling coastal plains, with mountains in the centre-south. The climate is hot and monsoonal. Most people live on the west coast. Manufactures (chiefly textiles and clothing), tea, rubber, copra and gems are exported. The economy relies on foreign aid and workers' remittances. The USA and the UK are the main trading partners.

SUDAN
Republic of the Sudan

Area Sq Km	2 505 813	**Currency**	Sudanese dinar
Area Sq Miles	967 500	**Languages**	Arabic, Dinka, Nubian, Beja, Nuer, local languages
Population	36 233 000	**Religions**	Sunni Muslim, traditional beliefs, Christian
Capital	Khartoum	**Organizations**	UN

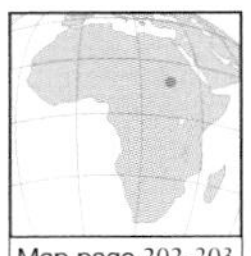

Map page 202-203

Africa's largest country, the Sudan is in the northeast of the continent, on the Red Sea. It lies within the upper Nile basin, much of which is arid plain but with swamps to the south. Mountains lie to the northeast, west and south. The climate is hot and arid with light summer rainfall, and droughts occur. Most people live along the Nile and are farmers and herders. Cotton, gum arabic, livestock and other agricultural products are exported. The government is working with foreign investors to develop oil resources, but civil war in the south continues to restrict the growth of the economy. Main trading partners are Saudi Arabia, China and Libya.

SURINAME
Republic of Suriname

Area Sq Km	163 820	**Currency**	Suriname guilder
Area Sq Miles	63 251	**Languages**	Dutch, Surinamese, English, Hindi
Population	449 000	**Religions**	Hindu, Roman Catholic, Protestant, Sunni Muslim
Capital	Paramaribo	**Organizations**	CARICOM, UN

Map page 251

Suriname, on the Atlantic coast of northern South America, consists of a swampy coastal plain (where most of the population lives), central plateaus, and highlands in the south. The climate is tropical, and rainforest covers much of the land. Bauxite mining is the main industry, and alumina and aluminium are the chief exports, with shrimps, rice, bananas and timber also exported. The main trading partners are the Netherlands, Norway and the USA.

SWAZILAND
Kingdom of Swaziland

Area Sq Km	17 364	**Currency**	Emalangeni, South African rand
Area Sq Miles	6 704	**Languages**	Swazi, English
Population	1 032 000	**Religions**	Christian, traditional beliefs
Capital	Mbabane	**Organizations**	Comm., SADC, UN

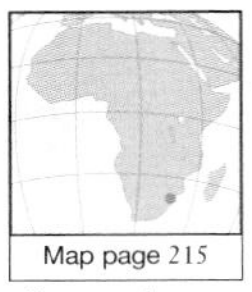

Map page 215

Landlocked Swaziland in southern Africa lies between Mozambique and the Republic of South Africa. Savanna plateaus descend from mountains in the west towards hill country in the east. The climate is subtropical, but temperate in the mountains. Subsistence farming predominates. Asbestos and diamonds are mined. Exports include sugar, fruit and wood pulp. Tourism and workers' remittances are important to the economy. Most trade is with South Africa.

SWEDEN
Kingdom of Sweden

Area Sq Km	449 964	**Currency**	Swedish krona
Area Sq Miles	173 732	**Languages**	Swedish
Population	9 041 000	**Religions**	Protestant, Roman Catholic
Capital	Stockholm	**Organizations**	EU, OECD, UN

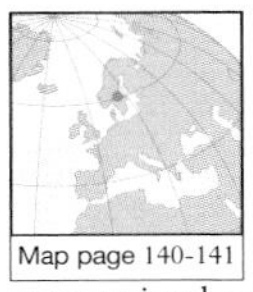

Map page 140-141

Sweden occupies the eastern part of the Scandinavian peninsula in northern Europe and borders the Baltic Sea, the Gulf of Bothnia, and the Kattegat and Skagerrak, connecting with the North Sea. Forested mountains cover the northern half, part of which lies within the Arctic Circle. The southern part of the country is a lowland lake region where most of the population lives. Sweden has warm summers and cold winters, which are more severe in the north. Natural resources include coniferous forests, mineral deposits and water resources. Some dairy products, meat, cereals and vegetables are produced in the south. The forests supply timber for export and for the important pulp, paper and furniture industries. Sweden is an important producer of iron ore and copper. Zinc, lead, silver and gold are also mined. Machinery and transport equipment, chemicals, pulp and wood, and telecommunications equipment are the main exports. The majority of trade is with other European Union countries.

SWITZERLAND
Swiss Confederation

Area Sq Km	41 293	**Currency**	Swiss franc
Area Sq Miles	15 943	**Languages**	German, French, Italian, Romansch
Population	7 252 000	**Religions**	Roman Catholic, Protestant
Capital	Bern	**Organizations**	OECD, UN

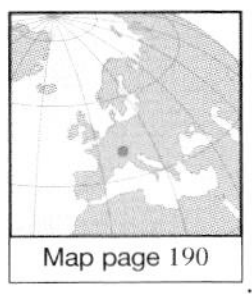

Map page 190

Switzerland is a mountainous landlocked country in west central Europe. The southern regions lie within the Alps, while the northwest is dominated by the Jura mountains. The rest of the land is a high plateau, where most of the population lives. The climate varies greatly, depending on altitude and relief, but in general summers are mild and winters are cold with heavy snowfalls. Switzerland has one of the highest standards of living in the world, yet it has few mineral resources, and most food and industrial raw materials are imported. Manufacturing makes the largest contribution to the economy. Engineering is the most important industry, producing precision instruments and heavy machinery. Other important industries are chemicals and pharmaceuticals. Banking and financial services are very important, and Zürich is one of the world's leading banking cities. Tourism, and international organizations based in Switzerland, are also major foreign currency earners. Germany is the main trading partner.

SYRIA
Syrian Arab Republic

Area Sq Km	185 180	**Currency**	Syrian pound
Area Sq Miles	71 498	**Languages**	Arabic, Kurdish, Armenian
Population	19 043 000	**Religions**	Sunni Muslim, Shi'a Muslim, Christian
Capital	Dimashq (Damascus)	**Organizations**	UN

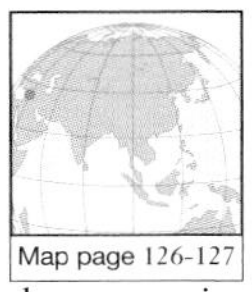

Map page 126-127

Syria is in southwest Asia, has a short coastline on the Mediterranean Sea, and stretches inland to a plateau traversed northwest-southeast by the Euphrates river. Mountains flank the southwest borders with Lebanon and Israel. The climate is Mediterranean in coastal regions, hotter and drier inland. Most Syrians live on the coast or in the river valleys. Cotton, cereals and fruit are important products, but the main exports are petroleum and related products, and textiles.

TAIWAN

Area Sq Km	36 179	**Currency**	Taiwan dollar
Area Sq Miles	13 969	**Languages**	Mandarin, Min, Hakka, local languages
Population	22 858 000	**Religions**	Buddhist, Taoist, Confucian, Christian
Capital	T'aipei	**Organizations**	APEC

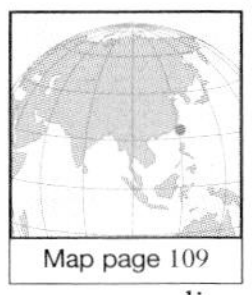

Map page 109

The east Asian state consists of the island of Taiwan, separated from mainland China by the Taiwan Strait, and several much smaller islands. Much of Taiwan is mountainous and forested. Densely populated coastal plains in the west contain the bulk of the population and most economic activity. Taiwan has a tropical monsoon climate, with warm, wet summers and mild winters. Agriculture is highly productive. The country is virtually self-sufficient in food and exports some products. Coal, oil and natural gas are produced and a few minerals are mined, but none of them are of great significance to the economy. Taiwan depends heavily on imports of raw materials and exports of manufactured goods. The main manufactures are electrical and electronic goods, including television sets, personal computers and calculators, textiles, fertilizers, clothing, footwear and toys. The main trading partners are the USA, Japan and Germany.

TAJIKISTAN
Republic of Tajikistan

Area Sq Km	143 100	**Currency**	Somoni
Area Sq Miles	55 251	**Languages**	Tajik, Uzbek, Russian
Population	6 507 000	**Religions**	Sunni Muslim
Capital	Dushanbe	**Organizations**	CIS, UN

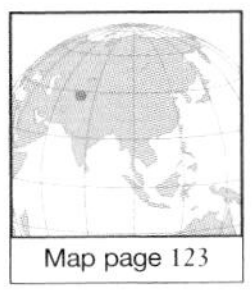

Map page 123

Landlocked Tajikistan in central Asia is a mountainous country, dominated by the mountains of the Alai Range and the Pamir. In the less mountainous western areas summers are warm, although winters are cold. Agriculture is the main sector of the economy, chiefly cotton growing and cattle breeding. Mineral deposits include lead, zinc, and uranium. Metal processing, textiles and clothing are the main manufactured goods; the main exports are aluminium and cotton. Uzbekistan, Kazakhstan and the Russian Federation are the main trading partners.

TANZANIA
United Republic of Tanzania

Area Sq Km	945 087	**Currency**	Tanzanian shilling
Area Sq Miles	364 900	**Languages**	Swahili, English, Nyamwezi, local languages
Population	38 329 000	**Religions**	Muslim, traditional beliefs, Christian
Capital	Dodoma	**Organizations**	Comm., SADC, UN

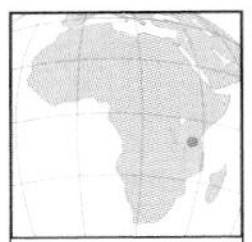

Map page 211

Tanzania lies on the coast of east Africa and includes the island of Zanzibar in the Indian Ocean. Most of the mainland is a savanna plateau lying east of the Great Rift Valley. In the north, near the border with Kenya, is Kilimanjaro, the highest mountain in Africa. The climate is tropical. The economy is predominantly based on agriculture, which employs an estimated ninety per cent of the workforce. Agricultural processing and gold and diamond mining are the main industries, although tourism is growing. Coffee, cotton, cashew nuts and tobacco are the main exports, with cloves from Zanzibar. Most export trade is with India and the UK. Tanzania depends heavily on foreign aid.

THAILAND
Kingdom of Thailand

Area Sq Km	513 115	**Currency**	Baht
Area Sq Miles	198 115	**Languages**	Thai, Lao, Chinese, Malay, Mon-Khmer language
Population	64 233 000	**Religions**	Buddhist, Sunni Muslim
Capital	Bangkok	**Organizations**	APEC, ASEAN, UN

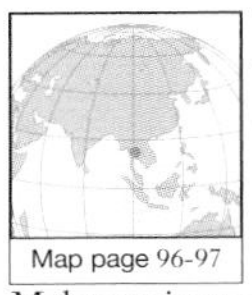

Map page 96-97

The largest country in the Indo-China peninsula, Thailand has coastlines on the Gulf of Thailand and Andaman Sea. Central Thailand is dominated by the Chao Phraya river basin, which contains Bangkok, the capital city and centre of most economic activity. To the east is a dry plateau drained by tributaries of the Mekong river, while to the north, west and south, extending down most of the Malay peninsula, are forested hills and mountains. Many small islands line the coast. The climate is hot, humid and monsoonal. About half the workforce is involved in agriculture. Fishing and fish processing are important. Thailand produces natural gas, some oil and lignite, minerals (chiefly tin, tungsten and baryte) and gemstones. Manufacturing is the largest contributor to national income, with electronics, textiles, clothing and footwear, and food processing the main industries. With around seven million visitors a year, tourism is the major source of foreign exchange. Thailand is one of the world's leading exporters of rice and rubber, and a major exporter of maize and tapioca. Japan and the USA are the main trading partners.

TOGO
Republic of Togo

Area Sq Km	56 785	**Currency**	CFA franc
Area Sq Miles	21 925	**Languages**	French, Ewe, Kabre, local languages
Population	6 145 000	**Religions**	Traditional beliefs, Christian, Sunni Muslim
Capital	Lomé	**Organizations**	UN

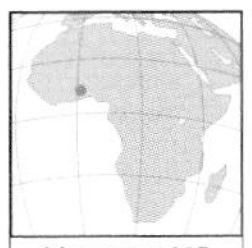

Map page 207

Togo is a long narrow country in west Africa with a short coastline on the Gulf of Guinea. The interior consists of plateaus rising to mountainous areas. The climate is tropical, and is drier inland. Agriculture is the mainstay of the economy. Phosphate mining and food processing are the main industries. Cotton, phosphates, coffee and cocoa are the main exports. Lomé, the capital, is an entrepôt trade centre.

Tokelau New Zealand Overseas Territory

Area Sq Km (Miles) 10 (4) **Population** 1 000

Tokelau consists of three atolls, Atafu, Nukunonu and Fakaofa, lying in the Pacific Ocean north of Samoa. Subsistence agriculture is the main activity, and the islands rely on aid from New Zealand and remittances from workers overseas.

Map page 81

TONGA
Kingdom of Tonga

Area Sq Km	748	**Currency**	Pa'anga
Area Sq Miles	289	**Languages**	Tongan, English
Population	102 000	**Religions**	Protestant, Roman Catholic
Capital	Nuku'alofa	**Organizations**	Comm., UN

Tonga comprises some one hundred and seventy islands in the south Pacific Ocean, northeast of New Zealand. The three main groups are Tongatapu (where sixty per cent of Tongans live), Ha'apai and Vava'u.

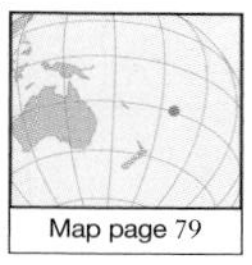
Map page 79

The climate is warm and wet, and the economy relies heavily on agriculture. Tourism and light industry are also important to the economy. Exports include squash, fish, vanilla beans and root crops. Most trade is with New Zealand, Japan and Australia.

TRINIDAD AND TOBAGO
Republic of Trinidad and Tobago

Area Sq Km	5 130	**Currency**	Trinidad and Tobago dollar
Area Sq Miles	1 981	**Languages**	English, creole, Hindi
Population	1 305 000	**Religions**	Roman Catholic, Hindu, Protestant, Sunni Muslim
Capital	Port of Spain	**Organizations**	CARICOM, Comm., UN

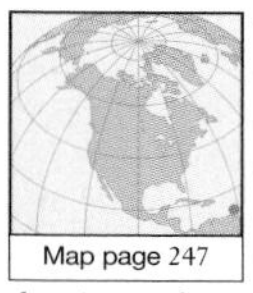
Map page 247

Trinidad, the most southerly Caribbean island, lies off the Venezuelan coast. It is hilly in the north, with a central plain. Tobago, to the northeast, is smaller, more mountainous and less developed. The climate is tropical. The main crops are cocoa, sugar cane, coffee, fruit and vegetables. Oil and petrochemical industries dominate the economy. Tourism is also important. The USA is the main trading partner.

Tristan da Cunha Dependency of St Helena

Area Sq Km (Miles) 98 (38) **Population** 284 **Capital** Settlement of Edinburgh

A group of volcanic islands in the south Atlantic Ocean: the other main islands in the group are Nightingale Island and Inaccessible Island. The group is over 2 000 kilometres (1 250 miles) south of St Helena. The economy is based on fishing, fish processing and agriculture. Ecotourism is increasingly important.

Map page 216

TUNISIA
Tunisian Republic

Area Sq Km	164 150	**Currency**	Tunisian dinar
Area Sq Miles	63 379	**Languages**	Arabic, French
Population	10 102 000	**Religions**	Sunni Muslim
Capital	Tunis	**Organizations**	UN

Map page 205

Tunisia is on the Mediterranean coast of north Africa. The north is mountainous with valleys and coastal plains, has a Mediterranean climate and is the most populous area. The south is hot and arid. Oil and phosphates are the main resources, and the main crops are olives and citrus fruit. Tourism is an important industry. Exports include petroleum products, textiles, fruit and phosphorus. Most trade is with European Union countries.

TURKEY
Republic of Turkey

Area Sq Km	779 452	**Currency**	Turkish lira
Area Sq Miles	300 948	**Languages**	Turkish, Kurdish
Population	73 193 000	**Religions**	Sunni Muslim, Shi'a Muslim
Capital	Ankara	**Organizations**	NATO, OECD, UN

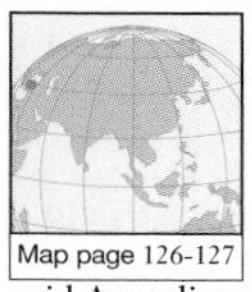
Map page 126-127

Turkey occupies a large peninsula of southwest Asia and has coastlines on the Black, Mediterranean and Aegean Seas. It includes eastern Thrace, which is in southeastern Europe and separated from the rest of the country by the Bosporus, the Sea of Marmara and the Dardanelles. The Asian mainland consists of the semi-arid Anatolian plateau, flanked to the north, south and east by mountains. Over forty per cent of Turks live in central Anatolia and on the Marmara and Aegean coastal plains. The coast has a Mediterranean climate, but inland conditions are more extreme with hot, dry summers and cold, snowy winters. Agriculture involves about forty per cent of the workforce, and products include cotton, grain, tobacco, fruit, nuts and livestock. Turkey is a leading producer of chromium, iron ore, lead, tin, borate, and baryte. Coal is also mined. The main manufactured goods are clothing, textiles, food products, steel and vehicles. Tourism is a major industry, with nine million visitors a year. Germany and the USA are the main trading partners. Remittances from workers abroad are important to the economy.

TURKMENISTAN
Republic of Turkmenistan

Area Sq Km	488 100	**Currency**	Turkmen manat
Area Sq Miles	188 456	**Languages**	Turkmen, Uzbek, Russian
Population	4 833 000	**Religions**	Sunni Muslim, Russian Orthodox
Capital	Aşgabat	**Organizations**	CIS, UN

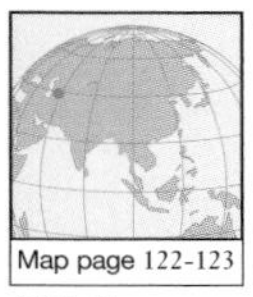
Map page 122-123

Turkmenistan, in central Asia, comprises the plains of the Karakum Desert, the foothills of the Kopet Dag mountains in the south, the Amudar'ya valley in the north and the Caspian Sea plains in the west. The climate is dry, with extreme temperatures. The economy is based mainly on irrigated agriculture (chiefly cotton growing), and natural gas and oil. Main exports are natural gas, oil and cotton fibre. Ukraine, Iran, Turkey and the Russian Federation are the main trading partners.

Turks and Caicos Islands
United Kingdom Overseas Territory

Area Sq Km (Miles) 430 (166) **Population** 26 000 **Capital** Grand Turk

The state consists of over forty low-lying islands and cays in the northern Caribbean. Only eight islands are inhabited, and two-fifths of the people live on Grand Turk and Salt Cay. The climate is tropical, and the economy is based on tourism, fishing and offshore banking.

Map page 246

TUVALU

Area Sq Km	25	**Currency**	Australian dollar
Area Sq Miles	10	**Languages**	Tuvaluan, English
Population	10 000	**Religions**	Protestant
Capital	Vaiaku	**Organizations**	Comm., UN

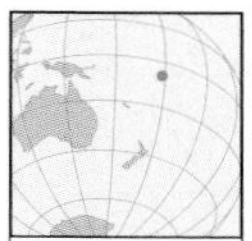
Map page 77

Tuvalu comprises nine low-lying coral atolls in the south Pacific Ocean. One-third of the population lives on Funafuti, and most people depend on subsistence farming and fishing. The islands export copra, stamps and clothing, but rely heavily on foreign aid. Most trade is with Fiji, Australia and New Zealand.

UGANDA
Republic of Uganda

Area Sq Km	241 038	**Currency**	Ugandan shilling
Area Sq Miles	93 065	**Languages**	English, Swahili, Luganda, local languages
Population	28 816 000	**Religions**	Roman Catholic, Protestant, Muslim, trad. beliefs
Capital	Kampala	**Organizations**	Comm., UN

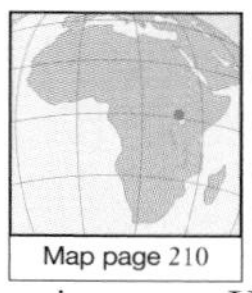
Map page 210

A landlocked country in east Africa, Uganda consists of a savanna plateau with mountains and lakes. The climate is warm and wet. Most people live in the southern half of the country. Agriculture employs around eighty per cent of the workforce and dominates the economy. Coffee, tea, fish and fish products are the main exports. Uganda relies heavily on aid.

UKRAINE

Area Sq Km	603 700	**Currency**	Hryvnia
Area Sq Miles	233 090	**Languages**	Ukrainian, Russian
Population	46 481 000	**Religions**	Orthodox, Ukrainian Catholic, Roman Catholic
Capital	Kyiv (Kiev)	**Organizations**	CIS, UN

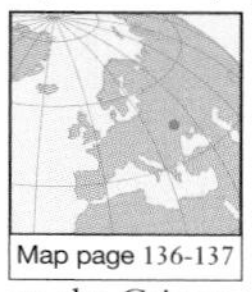
Map page 136-137

The country lies on the Black Sea coast of eastern Europe. Much of the land is steppe, generally flat and treeless, but with rich black soil, and it is drained by the river Dnieper. Along the border with Belarus are forested, marshy plains. The only uplands are the Carpathian Mountains in the west and smaller ranges on the Crimean peninsula. Summers are warm and winters are cold, with milder conditions in the Crimea. About a quarter of the population lives in the mainly industrial areas around Donets'k, Kiev and Dnipropetrovs'k. The Ukraine is rich in natural resources: fertile soil, substantial mineral and natural gas deposits, and forests. Agriculture and livestock rearing are important, but mining and manufacturing are the dominant sectors of the economy. Coal, iron and manganese mining, steel and metal production, machinery, chemicals and food processing are the main industries. The Russian Federation is the main trading partner.

UNITED ARAB EMIRATES
Federation of Emirates

Area Sq Km	77 700	**Currency**	United Arab Emirates dirham
Area Sq Miles	30 000	**Languages**	Arabic,English
Population	4 496 000	**Religions**	Sunni Muslim, Shi'a Muslim
Capital	Abū Ẓabī (Abu Dhabi)	**Organizations**	OPEC, UN

Map page 125

The UAE lies on the Gulf coast of the Arabian Peninsula. Six emirates are on The Gulf, while the seventh, Fujairah, is on the Gulf of Oman. Most of the land is flat desert with sand dunes and salt pans. The only hilly area is in the northeast. Over eighty per cent of the population lives in three of the emirates - Abu Dhabi, Dubai and Sharjah. Summers are hot and winters are mild, with occasional rainfall in coastal areas. Fruit and vegetables are grown in oases and irrigated areas, but the Emirates' wealth is based on hydrocarbons found in Abu Dhabi, Dubai, Sharjah and Ras al Khaimah. The UAE is one of the major oil producers in the Middle East. Dubai is an important entrepôt trade centre. The main trading partner is Japan.

Abū Ẓabī (Abu Dhabi) (Emirate)
Area Sq Km (Miles) 67 340 (26 000) **Population** 1 248 000 **Capital** Abu Dhabi

'Ajman (Emirate)
Area Sq Km (Miles) 259 (100) **Population** 189 000 **Capital** Ajman

Dubayy (Dubai) (Emirate)
Area Sq Km (Miles) 3 885 (1 500) **Population** 971 000 **Capital** Dubai

Al Fujayrah (Emirate)
Area Sq Km (Miles) 1 165 (450) **Population** 103 000 **Capital** Al Fujayrah

Ra's al Khaymah (Emirate)
Area Sq Km (Miles) 1 684 (650) **Population** 179 000 **Capital** Ras al Khaymah

Ash Shāriqah (Sharjah) (Emirate)
Area Sq Km (Miles) 2 590 (1 000) **Population** 551 000 **Capital** Sharjah

Umm al Qaywayn (Emirate)
Area Sq Km (Miles) 777 (300) **Population** 49 000 **Capital** Umm al Qaywayn

UNITED KINGDOM
United Kingdom of Great Britain and Northern Ireland

Area Sq Km	243 609	**Currency**	Pound sterling
Area Sq Miles	94 058	**Languages**	English, Welsh, Gaelic
Population	59 668 000	**Religions**	Protestant, Roman Catholic, Muslim
Capital	London	**Organizations**	Comm., EU, NATO, OECD, UN

The United Kingdom, in northwest Europe, occupies the island of Great Britain, part of Ireland, and many small adjacent islands. Great Britain comprises England, Scotland and Wales. England covers over half the land area and supports over four-fifths of the population, at its densest in the southeast. The English landscape is flat or rolling with some uplands, notably the Cheviot Hills on the Scottish border, the

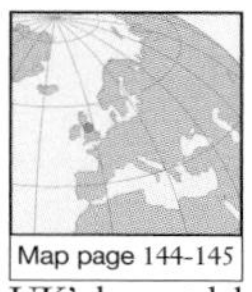
Map page 144-145

Pennines in the centre-north, and the hills of the Lake District in the northwest. Scotland consists of southern uplands, central lowlands, the Highlands (which include the UK's highest peak) and many islands. Wales is a land of hills, mountains and river valleys. Northern Ireland contains uplands, plains and the UK's largest lake, Lough Neagh. The climate of the UK is mild, wet and variable. There are few mineral deposits, but important energy resources. Agricultural activities involve sheep and cattle rearing, dairy farming, and crop and fruit growing in the east and southeast. Productivity is high, but approximately one-third of food is imported. The UK produces petroleum and natural gas from reserves in the North Sea and is self-sufficient in energy in net terms. Major manufactures are food and drinks, motor vehicles and parts, aerospace equipment, machinery, electronic and electrical equipment, and chemicals and chemical products. However, the economy is dominated by service industries, including banking, insurance, finance and business services. London, the capital, is one of the world's major financial centres. Tourism is also a major industry, with approximately twenty-five million visitors a year. International trade is also important, equivalent to one-third of national income. Over half of the UK's trade is with other European Union countries.

England (Constituent country)
Area Sq Km (Miles) 130 433 (50 360) **Population** 49 138 831 **Capital** London

Northern Ireland (Province)
Area Sq Km (Miles) 13 576 (5 242) **Population** 1 685 267 **Capital** Belfast

Scotland (Constituent country)
Area Sq Km (Miles) 78 822 (30 433) **Population** 5 062 011 **Capital** Edinburgh

Wales (Principality)
Area Sq Km (Miles) 20 778 (8 022) **Population** 2 903 085 **Capital** Cardiff

UNITED STATES OF AMERICA
Federal Republic

Area Sq Km	9 826 635	**Currency**	United States dollar
Area Sq Miles	3 794 085	**Languages**	English, Spanish
Population	298 213 000	**Religions**	Protestant, Roman Catholic, Sunni Muslim, Jewish
Capital	Washington D.C.	**Organizations**	APEC, NATO, OECD, UN

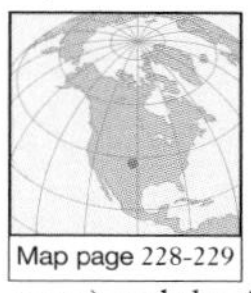
Map page 228-229

The USA comprises forty-eight contiguous states in North America, bounded by Canada and Mexico, plus the states of Alaska, to the northwest of Canada, and Hawaii, in the north Pacific Ocean. The populous eastern states cover the Atlantic coastal plain (which includes the Florida peninsula and the Gulf of Mexico coast) and the Appalachian Mountains. The central states occupy a vast interior plain drained by the Mississippi-Missouri river system. To the west lie the Rocky Mountains, separated from the Pacific coastal ranges by intermontane plateaus. The Pacific coastal zone is also mountainous, and prone to earthquakes. Hawaii is a group of some twenty volcanic islands. Climatic conditions range between arctic in Alaska to desert in the intermontane plateaus. Most of the USA has a temperate climate, although the interior has continental conditions. There are abundant natural resources, including major reserves of minerals and energy resources. The USA has the largest and most technologically advanced economy in the world, based on manufacturing and services. Although agriculture accounts for approximately two per cent of national income, productivity is high and the USA is a net exporter of food, chiefly grains and fruit. Cotton is the major industrial crop. The USA produces iron ore, copper, lead, zinc, and many other minerals. It is a major producer of coal, petroleum and natural gas, although being the world's biggest energy user it imports significant quantities of petroleum and its products. Manufacturing is diverse. The main industries are petroleum, steel, motor vehicles, aerospace, telecommunications, electronics, food processing, chemicals and consumer goods. Tourism is a major foreign currency earner, with approximately forty-five million visitors a year. Other important service industries are banking and finance, Wall Street in New York being one of the world's major stock exchanges. Canada and Mexico are the main trading partners.

Alabama (State)
Area Sq Km (Miles) 135 765 (52 419) **Population** 4 486 508 **Capital** Montgomery

Alaska (State)
Area Sq Km (Miles) 1 717 854 (663 267) **Population** 643 786 **Capital** Juneau

Arizona (State)
Area Sq Km (Miles) 295 253 (113 998) **Population** 5 456 453 **Capital** Phoenix

Arkansas (State)
Area Sq Km (Miles) 137 733 (53 179) **Population** 2 710 079 **Capital** Little Rock

California (State)
Area Sq Km (Miles) 423 971 (163 696) **Population** 35 116 033 **Capital** Sacramento

Colorado (State)
Area Sq Km (Miles) 269 602 (104 094) **Population** 4 506 542 **Capital** Denver

Connecticut (State)
Area Sq Km (Miles) 14 356 (5 543) **Population** 3 460 503 **Capital** Hartford

Delaware (State)
Area Sq Km (Miles) 6 446 (2 489) **Population** 807 385 **Capital** Dover

District of Columbia (District)
Area Sq Km (Miles) 176 (68) **Population** 570 898 **Capital** Washington

Florida (State)
Area Sq Km (Miles) 170 305 (65 755) **Population** 16 713 149 **Capital** Tallahassee

Georgia (State)
Area Sq Km (Miles) 153 910 (59 425) **Population** 8 560 310 **Capital** Atlanta

Hawaii (State)
Area Sq Km (Miles) 28 311 (10 931) **Population** 1 244 898 **Capital** Honolulu

Idaho (State)
Area Sq Km (Miles) 216 445 (83 570) **Population** 1 341 131 **Capital** Boise

Illinois (State)
Area Sq Km (Miles) 149 997 (57 914) **Population** 12 600 620 **Capital** Springfield

Indiana (State)
Area Sq Km (Miles) 94 322 (36 418) **Population** 6 159 068 **Capital** Indianapolis

Iowa (State)
Area Sq Km (Miles) 145 744 (56 272) **Population** 2 936 760 **Capital** Des Moines

Kansas (State)
Area Sq Km (Miles) 213 096 (82 277) **Population** 2 715 884 **Capital** Topeka

Kentucky (State)
Area Sq Km (Miles) 104 659 (40 409) **Population** 4 092 891 **Capital** Frankfort

Louisiana (State)
Area Sq Km (Miles) 134 265 (51 840) **Population** 4 482 646 **Capital** Baton Rouge

Maine (State)
Area Sq Km (Miles) 91 647 (35 385) **Population** 1 294 464 **Capital** Augusta

Maryland (State)
Area Sq Km (Miles) 32 134 (12 407) **Population** 5 458 137 **Capital** Annapolis

Massachusetts (State)
Area Sq Km (Miles) 27 337 (10 555) **Population** 6 427 801 **Capital** Boston

Michigan (State)
Area Sq Km (Miles) 250 493 (96 716) **Population** 10 050 446 **Capital** Lansing

Minnesota (State)
Area Sq Km (Miles) 225 171 (86 939) **Population** 5 019 720 **Capital** St Paul

Mississippi (State)
Area Sq Km (Miles) 125 433 (48 430) **Population** 2 871 782 **Capital** Jackson

Missouri (State)
Area Sq Km (Miles) 180 533 (69 704) **Population** 5 672 579 **Capital** Jefferson City

Montana (State)
Area Sq Km (Miles) 380 837 (147 042) **Population** 909 453 **Capital** Helena

Nebraska (State)
Area Sq Km (Miles) 200 346 (77 354) **Population** 1 729 180 **Capital** Lincoln

Nevada (State)
Area Sq Km (Miles) 286 352 (110 561) **Population** 2 173 491 **Capital** Carson City

New Hampshire (State)
Area Sq Km (Miles) 24 216 (9 350) **Population** 1 275 056 **Capital** Concord

New Jersey (State)
Area Sq Km (Miles) 22 587 (8 721) **Population** 8 590 300 **Capital** Trenton

New Mexico (State)
Area Sq Km (Miles) 314 914 (121 589) **Population** 1 855 059 **Capital** Santa Fe

New York (State)
Area Sq Km (Miles) 141 299 (54 556) **Population** 19 157 532 **Capital** Albany

North Carolina (State)
Area Sq Km (Miles) 139 391 (53 819) **Population** 8 320 146 **Capital** Raleigh

North Dakota (State)
Area Sq Km (Miles) 183 112 (70 700) **Population** 634 110 **Capital** Bismarck

Ohio (State)
Area Sq Km (Miles) 116 096 (44 825) **Population** 11 421 267 **Capital** Columbus

Oklahoma (State)
Area Sq Km (Miles) 181 035 (69 898) **Population** 3 493 714 **Capital** Oklahoma City

Oregon (State)
Area Sq Km (Miles) 254 806 (98 381) **Population** 3 521 515 **Capital** Salem

Pennsylvania (State)
Area Sq Km (Miles) 119 282 (46 055) **Population** 12 335 091 **Capital** Harrisburg

Rhode Island (State)
Area Sq Km (Miles) 4 002 (1 545) **Population** 1 069 725 **Capital** Providence

South Carolina (State)
Area Sq Km (Miles) 82 931 (32 020) **Population** 4 107 183 **Capital** Columbia

South Dakota (State)
Area Sq Km (Miles) 199 730 (77 116) **Population** 761 063 **Capital** Pierre

Tennessee (State)
Area Sq Km (Miles) 109 150 (42 143) **Population** 5 797 289 **Capital** Nashville

Texas (State)
Area Sq Km (Miles) 695 622 (268 581) **Population** 21 779 893 **Capital** Austin

Utah (State)
Area Sq Km (Miles) 219 887 (84 899) **Population** 2 316 256 **Capital** Salt Lake City

Vermont (State)
Area Sq Km (Miles) 24 900 (9 614) **Population** 616 592 **Capital** Montpelier

Virginia (State)
Area Sq Km (Miles) 110 784 (42 774) **Population** 7 293 542 **Capital** Richmond

Washington (State)
Area Sq Km (Miles) 184 666 (71 300) **Population** 6 068 996 **Capital** Olympia

West Virginia (State)
Area Sq Km (Miles) 62 755 (24 230) **Population** 1 801 873 **Capital** Charleston

Wisconsin (State)
Area Sq Km (Miles) 169 639 (65 498) **Population** 5 441 196 **Capital** Madison

Wyoming (State)
Area Sq Km (Miles) 253 337 (97 814) **Population** 498 703 **Capital** Cheyenne

URUGUAY
Oriental Republic of Uruguay

Area Sq Km	176 215	**Currency**	Uruguayan peso
Area Sq Miles	68 037	**Languages**	Spanish
Population	3 463 000	**Religions**	Roman Catholic, Protestant, Jewish
Capital	Montevideo	**Organizations**	UN

Map page 258

Uruguay, on the Atlantic coast of central South America, is a low-lying land of prairies. The coast and the River Plate estuary in the south are fringed with lagoons and sand dunes. Almost half the population lives in the capital, Montevideo. Uruguay has warm summers and mild winters. The economy is based on cattle and sheep ranching, and the main industries produce food products, textiles, and petroleum products. Meat, wool, hides, textiles and agricultural products are the main exports. Brazil and Argentina are the main trading partners.

UZBEKISTAN
Republic of Uzbekistan

Area Sq Km	447 400	**Currency**	Uzbek som
Area Sq Miles	172 742	**Languages**	Uzbek, Russian, Tajik, Kazakh
Population	26 593 000	**Religions**	Sunni Muslim, Russian Orthodox
Capital	Toshkent	**Organizations**	CIS, UN

A landlocked country of central Asia, Uzbekistan consists mainly of the flat Kyzylkum Desert. High mountains and valleys are found towards the southeast borders with Kyrgyzstan and Tajikistan. Most settlement is in the Fergana basin. The climate is hot and dry. The economy is based mainly on irrigated agriculture, chiefly cotton production.

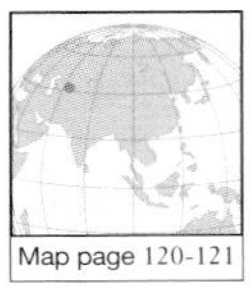
Map page 120-121

Uzbekistan is rich in minerals, including gold, copper, lead, zinc and uranium, and it has one of the largest gold mines in the world. Industry specializes in fertilizers and machinery for cotton harvesting and textile manufacture. The Russian Federation is the main trading partner.

VANUATU
Republic of Vanuatu

Area Sq Km	12 190	**Currency**	Vatu
Area Sq Miles	4 707	**Languages**	English, Bislama (creole), French
Population	211 000	**Religions**	Protestant, Roman Catholic, traditional beliefs
Capital	Port Vila	**Organizations**	Comm., UN

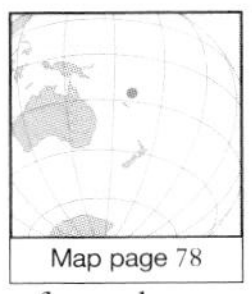
Map page 78

Vanuatu occupies an archipelago of approximately eighty islands in the southwest Pacific. Many of the islands are mountainous, of volcanic origin and densely forested. The climate is tropical, with heavy rainfall. Half of the population lives on the main islands of Éfaté and Espíritu Santo, and the majority of people are employed in agriculture. Copra, beef, timber, vegetables, and cocoa are the main exports. Tourism is becoming important to the economy. Australia, Japan and Germany are the main trading partners.

VATICAN CITY
Vatican City State or Holy See

Area Sq Km	0.5	**Currency**	Euro
Area Sq Miles	0.2	**Languages**	Italian
Population	552	**Religions**	Roman Catholic
Capital	Vatican City		

Map page 193

The world's smallest sovereign state, the Vatican City occupies a hill to the west of the river Tiber within the Italian capital, Rome. It is the headquarters of the Roman Catholic church, and income comes from investments, voluntary contributions and tourism.

VENEZUELA
Republic of Venezuela

Area Sq Km	912 050	**Currency**	Bolívar
Area Sq Miles	352 144	**Languages**	Spanish, Amerindian languages
Population	26 749 000	**Religions**	Roman Catholic, Protestant
Capital	Caracas	**Organizations**	OPEC, UN

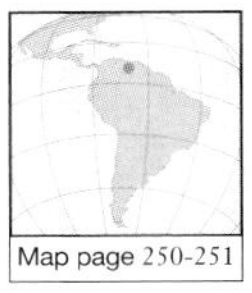
Map page 250-251

Venezuela is in northern South America, on the Caribbean. Its coast is much indented, with the oil-rich area of Lake Maracaibo at the western end, and the swampy Orinoco Delta to the east. Mountain ranges run parallel to the coast, and turn southwestwards to form a northern extension of the Andes. Central Venezuela is an area of lowland grasslands drained by the Orinoco river system. To the south are the Guiana Highlands, which contain the Angel Falls, the world's highest waterfall. Almost ninety per cent of the population lives in towns, mostly in the coastal mountain areas. The climate is tropical, with most rainfall in summer. Farming is important, particularly cattle ranching and dairy farming; coffee, maize, rice and sugar cane are the main crops. Venezuela is a major oil producer, and oil accounts for about seventy-five per cent of export earnings. Aluminium, iron ore, copper and gold are also mined, and manufactures include petrochemicals, aluminium, steel, textiles and food products. The USA and Puerto Rico are the main trading partners.

VIETNAM
Socialist Republic of Vietnam

Area Sq Km	329 565	**Currency**	Dong
Area Sq Miles	127 246	**Languages**	Vietnamese, Thai, Khmer, Chinese, local languages
Population	84 238 000	**Religions**	Buddhist, Taoist, Roman Catholic, Cao Dai, Hoa Hao
Capital	Ha Nôi	**Organizations**	APEC, ASEAN, UN

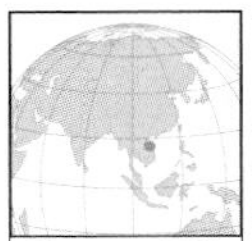
Map page 96-97

Vietnam lies in Southeast Asia on the west coast of the South China Sea. The Red River delta lowlands in the north are separated from the huge Mekong delta in the south by long, narrow coastal plains backed by the mountainous and forested terrain of the Annam Highlands. Most of the population lives in the river deltas. The climate is tropical, with summer monsoon rains. Over three-quarters of the workforce is involved in agriculture, forestry and fishing. Coffee, tea and rubber are important cash crops, but Vietnam is the world's second largest rice exporter. Oil, coal and copper are produced, and other main industries are food processing, clothing and footwear, cement and fertilizers. Exports include oil, coffee, rice, clothing, fish and fish products. Japan and Singapore are the main trading partners.

Virgin Islands (U.K.)
United Kingdom Overseas Territory

Area Sq Km	153	**Currency**	United States dollar
Area Sq Miles	59	**Languages**	English
Population	22 000	**Religions**	Protestant, Roman Catholic
Capital	Road Town		

The Caribbean territory comprises four main islands and over thirty islets at the eastern end of the Virgin Islands group. Apart from the flat coral atoll of Anegada, the islands are volcanic in origin and hilly. The climate is subtropical, and tourism is the main industry.

Map page 247

Virgin Islands (U.S.A.)
United States Unincorporated Territory

Area Sq Km	352	**Currency**	United States dollar
Area Sq Miles	136	**Languages**	English, Spanish
Population	112 000	**Religions**	Protestant, Roman Catholic
Capital	Charlotte Amalie		

The territory consists of three main islands and over fifty islets in the Caribbean's western Virgin Islands. The islands are hilly, of volcanic origin, and the climate is subtropical. The economy is based on tourism, with some manufacturing, including a major oil refinery on St Croix.

Map page 247

Wallis and Futuna Islands
French Overseas Territory

Area Sq Km	274	**Currency**	CFP franc
Area Sq Miles	106	**Languages**	French, Wallisian, Futunian
Population	15 000	**Religions**	Roman Catholic
Capital	Matā'utu		

The south Pacific territory comprises the volcanic islands of the Wallis archipelago and the Hoorn Islands. The climate is tropical. The islands depend on subsistence farming, the sale of licences to foreign fishing fleets, workers' remittances from abroad and French aid.

Map page 75

West Bank
Disputed Territory

Area Sq Km	5 860	**Currency**	Jordanian dinar, Israeli shekel
Area Sq Miles	2 263	**Languages**	Arabic, Hebrew
Population	2 421 491	**Religions**	Sunni Muslim, Jewish, Shi'a Muslim, Christian

The territory consists of the west bank of the river Jordan and parts of Judea and Samaria. The land was annexed by Israel in 1967, but some areas have been granted autonomy under agreements between Israel and the Palestinian Authority. Conflict between the Israelis and the Palestinians continues to restrict economic development.

Map page 128

Western Sahara
Disputed Territory (Morocco)

Area Sq Km	266 000	**Currency**	Moroccan dirhamr
Area Sq Miles	102 703	**Languages**	Arabic
Population	341 000	**Religions**	Sunni Muslim
Capital	Laâyoune		

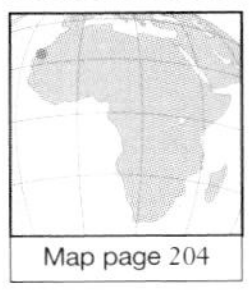
Map page 204

Situated on the northwest coast of Africa, the territory of the Western Sahara is now effectively controlled by Morocco. The land is low, flat desert with higher land in the northeast. There is little cultivation and only about twenty per cent of the land is pasture. Livestock herding, fishing and phosphate mining are the main activities. All trade is controlled by Morocco.

YEMEN
Republic of Yemen

Area Sq Km	527 968	**Currency**	Yemeni riyal
Area Sq Miles	203 850	**Languages**	Arabic
Population	20 975 000	**Religions**	Sunni Muslim, Shi'a Muslim
Capital	Şan'ā'	**Organizations**	UN

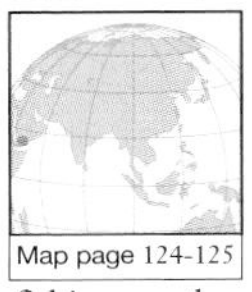
Map page 124-125

Yemen occupies the southwestern part of the Arabian Peninsula, on the Red Sea and the Gulf of Aden. Beyond the Red Sea coastal plain the land rises to a mountain range and then descends to desert plateaus. Much of the country is hot and arid, but there is more rainfall in the west, where most of the population lives. Farming and fishing are the main activities, with cotton the main cash crop. The main exports are crude oil, fish, coffee and dried fruit. Despite some oil resources Yemen is one of the poorest countries in the Arab world. Main trading partners are Thailand, China, South Korea and Saudi Arabia.

ZAMBIA
Republic of Zambia

Area Sq Km	752 614	**Currency**	Zambian kwacha
Area Sq Miles	290 586	**Languages**	English, Bemba, Nyanja, Tonga, local languages
Population	11 668 000	**Religions**	Christian, traditional beliefs
Capital	Lusaka	**Organizations**	Comm., SADC, UN

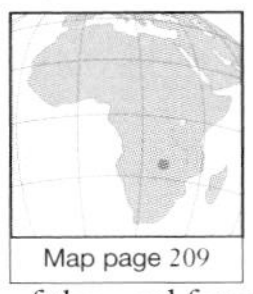
Map page 209

A landlocked state in south central Africa, Zambia consists principally of high savanna plateaus and is bordered by the Zambezi river in the south. Most people live in the Copperbelt area in the centre-north. The climate is tropical, with a rainy season from November to May. Agriculture employs approximately eighty per cent of the workforce, but is mainly at subsistence level. Copper mining is the mainstay of the economy, although reserves are declining. Copper and cobalt are the main exports. Most trade is with South Africa.

ZIMBABWE
Republic of Zimbabwe

Area Sq Km	390 759	**Currency**	Zimbabwean dollar
Area Sq Miles	150 873	**Languages**	English, Shona, Ndebele
Population	13 010 000	**Religions**	Christian, traditional beliefs
Capital	Harare	**Organizations**	SADC, UN

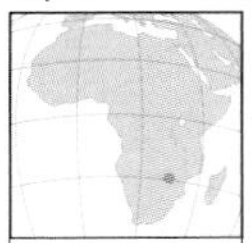
Map page 213

Zimbabwe, a landlocked state in south-central Africa, consists of high plateaus flanked by the Zambezi river valley and Lake Kariba in the north and the Limpopo river in the south. Most of the population lives in the centre of the country. There are significant mineral resources, including gold, nickel, copper, asbestos, platinum and chromium. Agriculture is a major sector of the economy, with crops including tobacco, maize, sugar cane and cotton. Beef cattle are also important. Exports include tobacco, gold, ferroalloys, nickel and cotton. South Africa is the main trading partner. The economy has suffered recently through significant political unrest and instability.

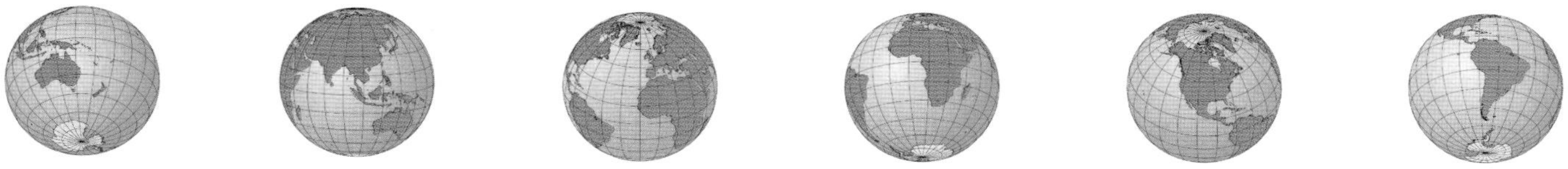

ATLAS OF THE WORLD

ATLAS MAPPING

The Atlas of the World includes a variety of styles and scales of mapping which together provide comprehensive coverage of all parts of the world; the map styles and editorial policies followed are introduced here. The area covered by each map is shown on the front and back endpapers.

Each continent is introduced by a politically coloured map followed by reference maps of sub-continental regions and then more detailed reference mapping of regions and individual countries. Scales for continental maps (*see 1*) range between 1:15 000 000 and 1:27 000 000 and regional maps (*see 2*) are in the range 1:11 000 000 to 1:13 000 000. Mapping for most countries is at scales between 1:3 000 000 and 1:7 500 000 (*see 3*) although selected, more densely populated areas of Europe, North America and Asia are mapped at larger scales, up to 1:1 000 000 (*see 4*). Large-scale city plans of a selection of the world's major cities (*see 5*), are included on the appropriate map pages. A suite of maps covering the world's oceans and poles (*see 6*) at a variety of scales, concludes the main reference map section.

The symbols and place name abbreviations used on the maps are fully explained on pages 68–69 and a glossary of geographical terms is included at the back of the atlas on pages 269–272. The alphanumeric reference system used in the index is based on latitude and longitude, and the number and letter for each graticule square are shown within each map frame, in red. The numbers of adjoining or overlapping pages are shown by arrows in the page frame and accompanying numbers in the margin.

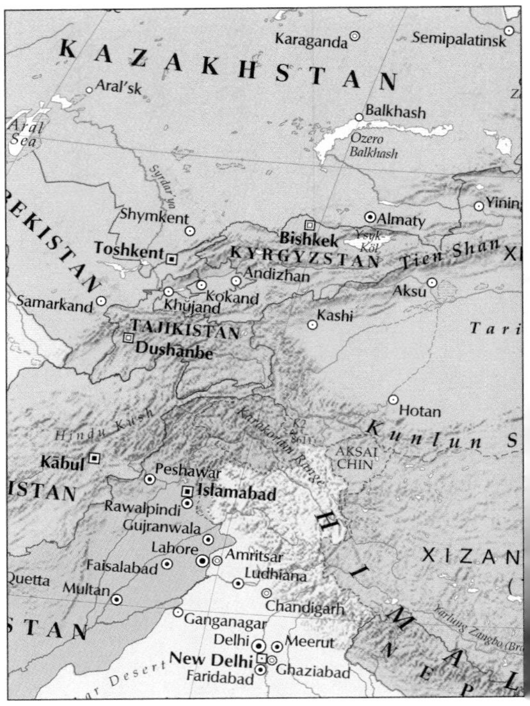

1. CONTINENTAL MAP OF ASIA (extract from pages 88–89)

BOUNDARIES

The status, names and boundaries of nations are shown in this atlas as they are at the time of going to press, as far as can be ascertained. Where an international boundary symbol appears in the sea or ocean it does not necessarily infer a legal maritime boundary, but shows which off-shore islands belong to which country.

Where international boundaries are the subject of dispute it may be that no portrayal of them will meet with the approval of any of the countries involved, but it is not seen as the function of this atlas to try to adjudicate between the rights and wrongs of political issues. The atlas aims to take a neutral viewpoint of all such cases. Although reference mapping at atlas scales is not the ideal medium for indicating territorial claims, every reasonable attempt is made to show where an active territorial dispute exists, and where there is an important difference between 'de facto' (existing in fact, on the ground) and 'de jure' (according to law) boundaries. This is done by the use of a different symbol where international boundaries are disputed, or where the alignment is unconfirmed, to that used for settled international boundaries. Cease-fire lines are also shown by a separate symbol. For clarity, disputed boundaries and areas are annotated where this is considered necessary but it is impossible to represent all the complexities of territorial disputes on maps at atlas scales.

The latest internal administrative division boundaries are shown on the maps for selected countries where the combination of map scale and the number of divisions permits, with recent changes to local government systems being taken into account as far as possible. Towns which are first-order and second-order administrative centres are also symbolized where scale permits.

2. SOUTHEAST ASIA 1:13 000 000 (extract from pages 90–91)

3. EAST CENTRAL AFRICA 1:7 500 000 (extract from pages 210–211)

PLACE NAMES

NAME FORM POLICY

The spelling of place names on maps has always been a matter of great complexity, because of the variety of the world's languages and the systems used to write them down. There is no standard way of spelling names or of converting them from one alphabet, or symbol set, to another. Instead, conventional ways of spelling have evolved in each of the world's major languages, and the results often differ significantly from the name as it is spelled in the original language. Familiar examples of English conventional names include Munich (München), Florence (Firenze) and Moscow (from the transliterated form, Moskva).

In this atlas, local name forms are used where they are in the Roman alphabet. These local forms are those which are recognized by the government of the country concerned, usually as represented by its official mapping agency. This is a basic principle laid down by the United Kingdom government's Permanent Committee on Geographical Names for British Official Use (PCGN).

For languages in non-Roman alphabets or symbol sets, names need to be 'Romanized' through a process of transliteration (the conversion of characters or symbols from one alphabet into another) or transcription (conversion of names based on pronunciation). Different systems often exist for this process, but PCGN and its United States counterpart, the Board on Geographic Names (BGN), usually follow the same Romanization principles, and the general policy for this atlas is to follow their lead. One notable change in this edition is that PCGN and BGN principles are now followed for Arabic names in Egypt ('Al' style – for example Al Qāhirah for Cairo), where previous editions followed PCGN's former policy of using a local Survey of Egypt system ('El' style – El Qâhira).

Local name form mapping is the nearest that the cartographer can achieve to an international standard. It is in fact impossible, and perhaps unnecessary, to provide English names for the majority of mapped features, and translating names into English is fraught with linguistic hazards. Consequently, a local name form map is more internally consistent than a partly-anglicized one.

Although local forms in this atlas are given precedence, prominent English-language conventional names and historic names are not neglected. The names of countries, continents, oceans, seas and underwater features in international waters appear in English throughout the atlas, as do those of other international features where such an English form exists. Significant superseded names and other alternative spellings are included in brackets on the maps where space permits, and variants and former names are cross-referenced in the index.

NAME CHANGES

Continuing changes in official languages, in writing systems and in Romanization methods, have to be taken into account by cartographers. In many countries different languages are in use in different regions or side-by-side in the same region, and there is potential for widely varying name forms even within a single country. A worldwide trend towards national, regional and ethnic self-determination is operating at the same time as pressure towards increased international standardization.

Place names are, to an extent, a mirror for the changes that continue to transform the political world. Changes of territorial control may have a significant effect on name forms. Yet even in countries where name forms could be expected to have long been largely standardized, there are sometimes continuing issues for the cartographer to address. In the UK, for example, there is a trend for more Gaelic and Welsh-language names to be given official recognition. Similarly, there has been an increase in the official recognition and use of indigenous name forms in for instance New Zealand (Maori) and Canada (Inuit and Indian names). Name spelling issues are, in fact, likely to emerge in almost any part of the world.

Reflecting trends across the world, systematic alterations affecting various countries are reflected in this atlas. The dissolution of the

MAP PROJECTIONS

The creation of computer-generated maps presents the opportunity to select projections specifically for the area and scale of each map. As the only way to show the Earth with absolute accuracy is on a globe, all map projections are compromises. Some projections seek to maintain correct area relationships (equal area projections), true distances and bearings from a point (equidistant projections) or correct angles and shapes (conformal projections); others attempt to achieve a balance between these properties. The choice of projections used in this atlas has been made on an individual continental and regional basis. Projections used, and their individual parameters, have been defined to minimize distortion and to reduce scale errors (shown as percentage figures in the accompanying diagrams) as much as possible.

For world maps, the Bartholomew version of the Winkel Tripel Projection is used. This projection combines elements of conformality with that of equal area, and shows, over the world as a whole, relatively true shapes and reasonably equal areas. The Mercator Projection (*see 7*) has been selected for the regional maps of southeast Asia along the Equator , while in higher latitudes, particularly in Europe and to some extent in North America, the Conic Equidistant Projection (*see 8*) has been used extensively for regional mapping. The Lambert Azimuthal Equal Area Projection (*see 9*) has been employed in both South America and Australia.

MERCATOR PROJECTION

s rectangular or cylindrical projection is constructed on the basis of a cylinder in tact with the globe, in this case around the Equator. Scale is correct along the ator and distortion increases away from it in both directions.

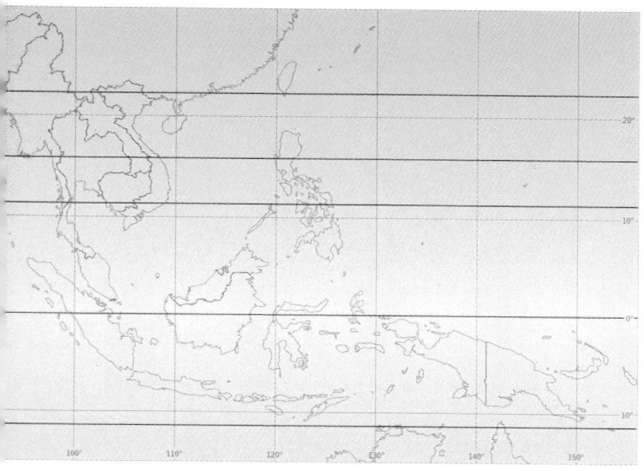

8. CONIC EQUIDISTANT PROJECTION

Constructed on the basis of a cone intersecting the globe along two standard parallels (55°N and 75°N in this illustration), along both of which scale is correct. Lines of equal scale error are parallel to the standard lines, with distortion increasing away from each.

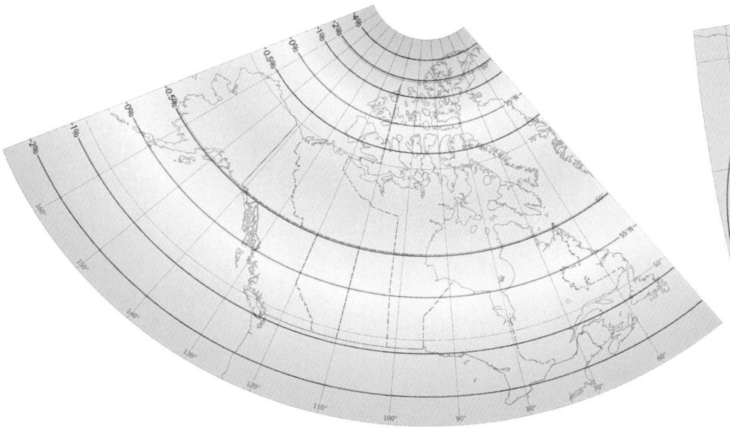

9. LAMBERT AZIMUTHAL EQUAL AREA PROJECTION

Points are projected onto a plane in contact with the globe at the centre point (25°S, 135°E in this illustration). Scale is correct at the centre, and scale errors increase in concentric circles away from it. Areas are true in relation to the corresponding areas on the globe.

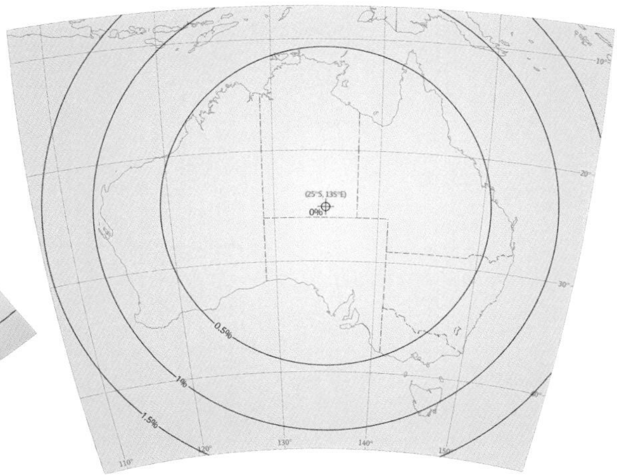

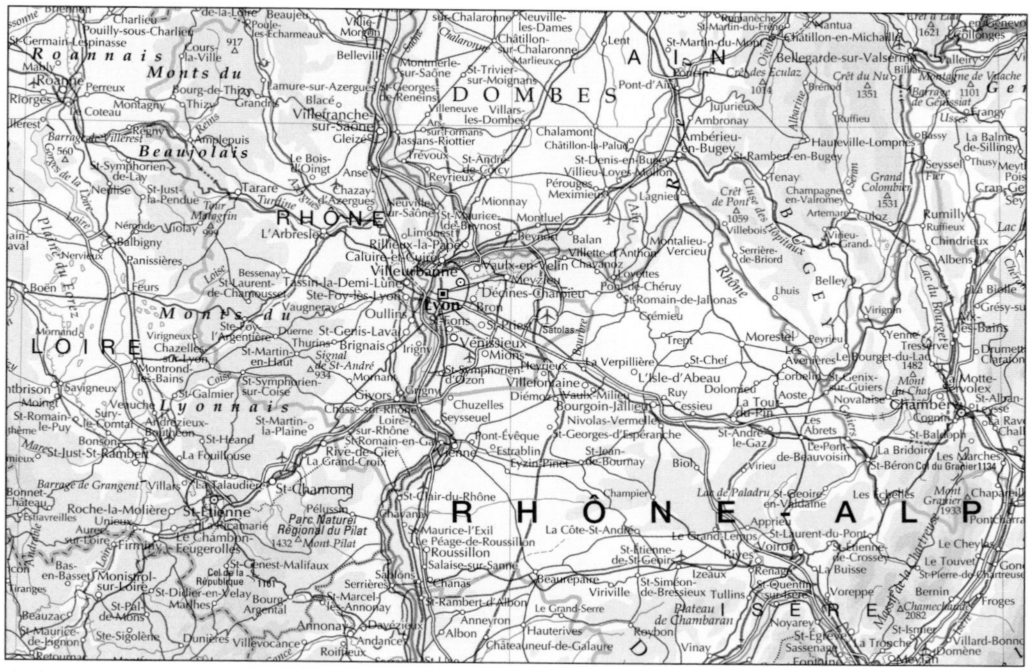

4. SOUTHEAST FRANCE 1:1 200 000 (extract from pages 160–161)

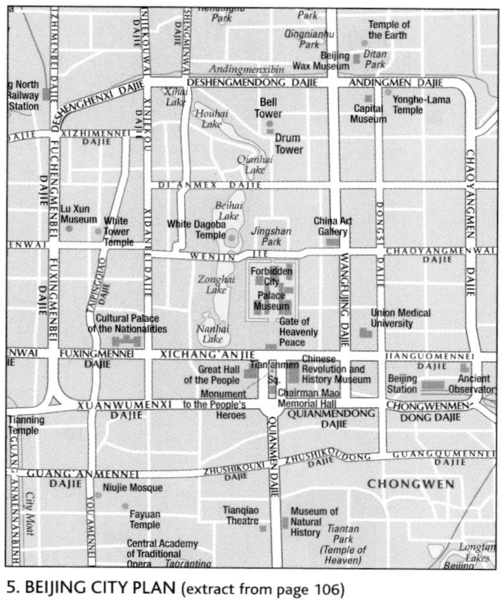

5. BEIJING CITY PLAN (extract from page 106)

former USSR has given rise to the greatest changes in recent years, and this atlas continues the policy established in the previous edition of names being converted from Russian to the main national language in Belarus, Ukraine, Moldova, Armenia, Georgia, Azerbaijan, Kyrgyzstan and Tajikistan. Uzbekistan is the latest to have been converted in this way, using the new Uzbek Roman alphabet. Russian naturally continues to be used as the main form in the Russian Federation and also continues to be used as the prime language on maps of Kazakhstan. Here, local-language name forms (derived from Kazakh Cyrillic) are included for main place names where space permits on the maps, with additional alternatives in the index. In Turkmenistan, main Turkmen Cyrillic-derived names are similarly covered, but native sources are starting to apply a finalized Roman alphabet, pointing the way to a future in which Cyrillic names will be dropped entirely. Main examples of new Turkmen forms are included as cross-references in the index.

In Spain, account is taken of the official prominence now given to Catalan, Galician and some Basque spellings, which results in name forms such as Eivissa for Ibiza and A Coruña for La Coruña. Reflecting these changes, many names are now represented in dual form on official Spanish mapping. Depending on their specific treatment on local mapping, some of these are shown in this atlas as hyphenated (for example Donostia-San Sebastián, Gijón-Xixón, Elche-Elx) while others include the second forms as alternative names.

Chinese name forms, which were fully converted to the official Pinyin Romanization system some years ago in earlier editions of this atlas, continue to change. Name forms have been brought into line with the latest official sources, continuing to follow the principle whereby numerous towns which are the centres of administrative units such as the county or 'xian' officially take the name of the county itself. The alternative place name in common local use is shown in brackets on the map. The index also includes numerous cross-references for Chinese name forms as they were before the introduction of Pinyin – taking account of the main so-called 'Post Office' spellings such as Tientsin (now Tianjin), and more particularly of the long-familiar Wade-Giles Romanization, which gives, for instance, Pei-ching as against the Pinyin form Beijing.

As well as systematic changes in name forms such as those outlined above, occasionally places are given entirely new names for a variety of reasons. This atlas accounts for any such recent changes. One significant example is the official renaming of Calcutta as Kolkata, following earlier changes by the Indian authorities to Bombay (now Mumbai) and Madras (now Chennai).

6. ANTARCTICA 1:18 000 000 (extract from pages 262–263)

REFERENCE MAPS

CITIES AND TOWNS

Population	National Capital	Administrative Capital Shown for selected countries only.		Other City or Town
		First order	Second order Scales larger than 1:9 000 000.	
over 10 million	TŌKYŌ ▣	Karachi ▣	Los Angeles ◉	New York ◉
5 million to 10 million	SANTIAGO ▣	Tianjin ▣	Chicago ◉	Hong Kong ◉
1 million to 5 million	KĀBUL ▣	Sydney ▣	Tangshan ◉	Kaohsiung ◉
500 000 to 1 million	BANGUI ▣	Trujillo ▣	Agra ◉	Jiddah ◉
100 000 to 500 000	WELLINGTON ▣	Mansa ▣	Naogaon ◉	Apucarana ◉
50 000 to 100 000	PORT OF SPAIN ▢	Potenza ▢	Trier ○	Arecibo ○
10 000 to 50 000	MALABO ▢	Chinhoyi ▢	Willimantic ○	Ceres ○
1 000 to 10 000	VALLETTA ▢	Ati ▢	Nepalganj ○	Abla ○
under 1000 Scales 1: 4 000 000 and larger		Chhukha ▢	Carmel ○	Lopigna ○

Built-up area

MISCELLANEOUS FEATURES

---------- National park ················ Regional park ··············· Reserve or special land area ∴ Site of specific interest ⌒⌒⌒⌒⌒ Wall

RELIEF

Contour intervals used in layer-colouring for land height and sea depth

Scales 1:4 000 000 and larger	Scales 1:4 000 000 and larger (Europe only)	Scales smaller than 1:4 000 000	Oceans and Antarctica (Pages 262–268)

METRES FEET

Scales 1:4 000 000 and larger:
6000 / 19686
5000 / 16404
4000 / 13124
3000 / 9843
2000 / 6562
1500 / 4921
1000 / 3281
500 / 1640
200 / 656
100 / 328
0 / 0
LAND BELOW SEA LEVEL
200 / 656
1000 / 3281
2000 / 6562

Scales 1:4 000 000 and larger (Europe only):
6000 / 19686
5000 / 16404
4000 / 13124
3000 / 9843
2000 / 6562
1500 / 4921
1000 / 3281
500 / 1640
200 / 656
100 / 328
0 / 0
LAND BELOW SEA LEVEL
50 / 164
200 / 656
1000 / 3281
2000 / 6562

Scales smaller than 1:4 000 000:
6000 / 19686
5000 / 16404
4000 / 13124
3000 / 9843
2000 / 6562
1000 / 3281
500 / 1640
200 / 656
0 / 0
LAND BELOW SEA LEVEL
200 / 656
2000 / 6562
4000 / 13124
6000 / 19686

Oceans and Antarctica:
4000 / 13124
2000 / 6562
1000 / 3281
500 / 1640
200 / 656
0 / 0
200 / 656
2000 / 6562
3000 / 9843
4000 / 13124
5000 / 16404
6000 / 19686
7000 / 22967
9000 / 29529

12:34 △ Summit Height in metres

-123 • Spot height Surface height in metres for depressions and areas below sea level.

5678 • Ocean deep In metres. Ocean pages only.

LAND AND SEA FEATURES

Rock desert

Sand desert / Dunes

⌄ Oasis

Lava field

1234 ▲ Volcano Height in metres.

Marsh

Ice cap / Glacier

Nunatak

Coral reef

·············· Escarpment

············· Flood dyke

) [123 Pass Height in metres.

Ice shelf

LAKES AND RIVERS

Lake

Impermanent lake

Salt lake or lagoon

Impermanent salt lake

Dry salt lake or salt pan

123 Lake height Surface height above sea level, in metres.

——— River

- - - - Impermanent river

– – – Wadi or watercourse

Waterfall

| Dam

Barrage

BOUNDARIES

▪-▪-▪- International boundary

▪▪▪▪ Disputed international boundary or alignment unconfirmed

Undefined international boundary in the sea. All land within this boundary is part of state or territory named.

------- Administrative boundary, first order internal division. Scales 1:4 000 000 and larger. Shown for selected countries only.

——— Administrative boundary, first order internal division. Scales smaller than 1:4 000 000. Shown for selected countries only.

——— Administrative boundary, second order internal division. Scales 1:4 000 000 and larger. Shown for selected countries only.

-▪-◇-▪- Disputed administrative boundary Scales 1:4 000 000 and larger. Shown for selected countries only.

●●●●●● Ceasefire line or other boundary described on the map

STYLES OF LETTERING

Cities and towns are explained separately

	Physical features	
Country — **FRANCE**	Island	*Gran Canaria*
Overseas Territory/Dependency — **Guadeloupe**		
Disputed Territory — AKSAI CHIN	Lake	*LAKE ERIE*
Administrative name, first order internal division Shown for selected countries only. — **SCOTLAND**	Mountain	*Mt Blanc*
Administrative name, second order internal division Scales 1:4 000 000 and larger. Shown for selected countries only. — MANCHE	River	*Thames*
Area name — ARTOIS	Region	*PAMPAS*

TRANSPORT

═══ under construction ════ Motorway Scales 1:4 000 000 and larger.

——— under construction Main road

——— under construction Secondary road

═╪═╪═ Motorway tunnel

–▪–▪–▪ Road tunnel

- - - - Track

——— under construction - - - - Main railway

——— under construction - - - - Secondary railway

–▪–▪–▪ under construction Railway tunnel

——— Canal

——— Minor canal

⊕ Main airport

✈ Regional airport

CITY PLANS

▒	Built-up area
▒	Cemetery
▒	Park
▪	Place of worship
▪	General place of interest
▪	Transport location
▪	Academic / municipal building

CONTINENTAL MAPS

BOUNDARIES

———	International boundary
-------	Disputed international boundary or alignment unconfirmed
/——	Undefined international boundary in the sea. All land within this boundary is part of state or territory named.
••••••••	Ceasefire line
- - - - -	Administrative boundary Shown for selected countries only.

CITIES AND TOWNS

Population	National Capital	Other City or Town
over 10 million	México ▣	Mumbai ◉
5 million to 10 million	London ▣	Belo Horizonte ◉
1 million to 5 million	Kābul ▣	Kaohsiung ◉
500 000 to 1 million	Bangui ⧈	Khulna ◎
100 000 to 500 000	Wellington ⊡	Iquitos ⊙
50 000 to 100 000	Port of Spain □	Naga ○
10 000 to 50 000	Malabo ▫	Ushuaia ○
under 10 000	Valletta ▫	Arviat ∘

ABBREVIATIONS

A.C.T.	Australian Capital Territory		
Arch.	Archipelago		
	Archipiélago	Spanish	**archipelago**
B.	Bay		
	Bahia, Baía	Portuguese	**bay**
	Bahía	Spanish	**bay**
	Baie	French	**bay**
Bol.	Bol'shaya, Bol'shoy, Bol'shoye	Russian	**big**
C.	Cape		
	Cabo	Portuguese, Spanish	**cape, headland**
	Cap	Catalan, French	**cape, headland**
Cach.	Cachoeira	Portuguese	**waterfall, rapids**
Can.	Canal	French, Portuguese, Spanish	**canal, channel**
Cd	Ciudad	Spanish	**city, town**
Chan.	Channel		
Co	Cerro	Spanish	**hill, mountain, peak**
Cord.	Cordillera	Spanish	**mountain range**
Cr.	Creek		
Cuch.	Cuchilla	Spanish	**hills, mountain range**
D.	Dağ, Dağı	Turkish	**mountain**
	Dāgh	Farsi	**mountain, mountains**
	Dağları	Turkish	**mountain range**
	Danau	Indonesian, Malay	**lake**
Div.	Division		
Dr	Doctor		
E.	East, Eastern		
Emb.	Embalse	Spanish	**reservoir**
Est.	Estero	Spanish	**estuary, inlet**
	Estrecho	Spanish	**strait**
Fj.	Fjörður	Icelandic	**fjord, inlet**
Ft	Fort		
G.	Gebel	Arabic	**hill, mountain**
	Golfo	Italian, Spanish	**gulf, bay**
	Gora	Russian	**mountain**
	Gunung	Indonesian, Malay	**hill, mountain**
Gd	Grand	French	**big**
Gde	Grande	French, Italian, Portuguese, Spanish	**big**
Geb.	Gebergte	Afrikaans, Dutch	**mountain range**
Gen.	General		
Gl.	Glacier		
Gp	Group		
Gt	Great		
Harb.	Harbour		
Hd	Head		
I.	Island, Isle		
	Ilha	Portuguese	**island**
	Isla	Spanish	**island**
Î.	Île	French	**island**
im.	imeni	Russian	**'in the name of'**
Ind. Res.	Indian Reservation		
Ing.	Ingeniero	Spanish	**engineer**
Is	Islands, Isles		
	Islas	Spanish	**islands**
Îs	Îles	French	**islands**
J.	Jabal, Jebel	Arabic	**mountain, mountains**
Kep.	Kepulauan	Indonesian, Malay	**archipelago, islands**
Khr.	Khrebet	Russian	**mountain range**
L.	Lake		
	Loch	(Scotland)	**lake**
	Lough	(Ireland)	**lake**
	Lac	French	**lake**
	Lago	Portuguese, Spanish	**lake**
Lag.	Laguna	Spanish	**lagoon**
M.	Mys	Russian	**cape, point**
Mt	Mount		
	Mont	French	**hill, mountain**
Mt.	Mountain		
Mte	Monte	Portuguese, Spanish	**hill, mountain**
Mts	Mountains		
	Monts	French	**hills, mountains**
N.	North, Northern		
Nev.	Nevado	Spanish	**peak**
Nat.	National		
Nat. Park	National Park		
Nat. Res.	Nature Reserve		
Nizh.	Nizhniy, Nizhnyaya	Russian	**lower**
N.E.	Northeast, Northeastern		
N.H.S.	National Heritage Site		
N.W.	Northwest, Northwestern		
O.	Ostrov	Russian	**island**
O-va	Ostrova	Russian	**islands**
Oz.	Ozero	Russian, Ukrainian	**lake**
P.	Paso	Spanish	**pass**
	Pulau	Indonesian, Malay	**island**
Pass.	Passage		
Peg.	Pegunungan	Indonesian, Malay	**mountain range**
Pen.	Peninsula		
	Península	Spanish	**peninsula**
Pk	Peak		
	Puncak	Indonesian	**mountain, peak**
P-ov	Poluostrov	Russian	**peninsula**
P. P.	Pulau-pulau	Indonesian	**islands**
Psa	Presa	Spanish	**reservoir**
Pt	Point		
Pta	Punta	Italian, Spanish	**cape, point**
Pte	Pointe	French	**cape, point**
Pto	Porto	Portuguese	**harbour, port**
	Puerto	Spanish	**harbour, port**
R.	River		
	Rio	Portuguese	**river**
	Río	Spanish	**river**
	Rivière	French	**river**
	Rūd	Farsi	**river**
Ra.	Range		
Rec.	Recreation		
Res.	Reservation, Reserve		
Resr	Reservoir		
S.	South, Southern		
	Salar, Salina, Salinas	Spanish	**salt pan, salt pans**
Sa	Serra	Portuguese	**mountain range**
	Sierra	Spanish	**mountain range**
Sd	Sound		
S.E.	Southeast, Southeastern		
Serr.	Serranía	Spanish	**mountain range**
Sk.	Shuiku	Chinese	**reservoir**
Sr.	Sredniy, Srednyaya	Russian	**middle, central**
St	Saint		
	Sankt	German, Russian	**saint**
	Sint	Dutch	**saint**
Sta	Santa	Italian, Portuguese, Spanish	**saint**
Ste	Sainte	French	**saint**
Sto	Santo	Italian, Portuguese, Spanish	**saint**
Str.	Strait		
S.W.	Southwest, Southwestern		
Tg	Tanjong, Tanjung	Indonesian, Malay	**cape, point**
Tk	Teluk, Telukan	Indonesian, Malay	**bay, gulf**
Tte	Teniente	Spanish	**lieutenant**
Va	Villa	Spanish	**town**
Vdkhr.	Vodokhranilishche	Russian	**reservoir**
Verkh.	Verkhniy, Verkhnyaya	Russian	**upper**
Vol.	Volcano		
	Volcan	French	**volcano**
	Volcán	Spanish	**volcano**
Vozv.	Vozvyshennost'	Russian	**hills, upland**
W.	West, Western		
	Wadi, Wâdi, Wādī	Arabic	**watercourse**

Winkel Tripel Projection

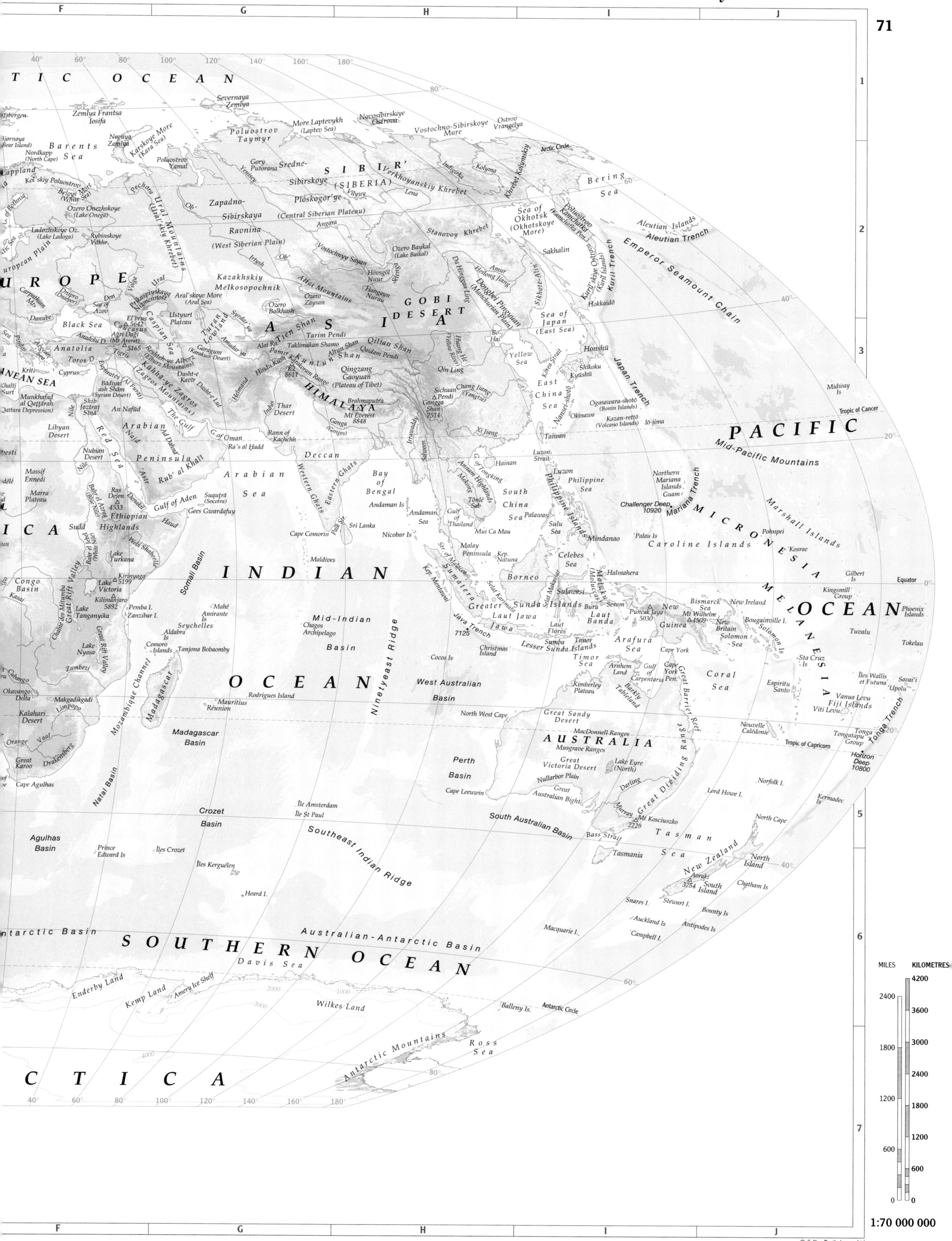
F
G
H
I
J
1
2
3
4
5
6
7
T I C O C E A N
Severnaya Zemlya
Zemlya Frantsa Iosifa
Novaya Zemlya
Karskoye More (Kara Sea)
Barents Sea
Nordkapp (North Cape)
Lappland
Kol'skiy Poluostrov
Beloye More (White Sea)
Ozero Onezhskoye (Lake Onega)
Ladozhskoye Oz. (Lake Ladoga)
Rybinskoye Vdkhr.
Poluostrov Taymyr
More Laptevykh (Laptev Sea)
Novosibirskiye Ostrova
Vostochno-Sibirskoye More
Ostrov Vrangelya
Arctic Circle
Poluostrov Yamal
Gory Putorana
Sredne-Sibirskoye Ploskogor'ye
(Central Siberian Plateau)
S I B I R' (SIBERIA)
Verkhoyanskiy Khrebet
Khrebet Kolymskiy
Kolyma
Indigirka
Lena
Vilyuy
Yenisey
Angara
Pechora
Ural Mountains (Ural'skiy Khrebet)
Ob'
Zapadno-Sibirskaya Ravnina (West Siberian Plain)
Irtysh
Bering Sea
Sea of Okhotsk (Okhotskoye More)
Poluostrov Kamchatka (Kamchatka Pen.)
Aleutian Islands
Aleutian Trench
Emperor Seamount Chain
Stanovoy Khrebet
Ozero Baykal (Lake Baikal)
Vostochnyy Sayan
Sakhalin
Kuril'skiye Ostrova (Kuril Islands)
Kuril Trench
Hokkaidō
Sikhote-Alin'
Amur
Heilong Jiang
Da Hinggan Ling
Dongbei Pingyuan (Manchurian Plain)
Hövsgöl Nuur
Hangayn Nuruu
Altai Mountains
Ozero Zaysan
G O B I D E S E R T
Kazakhskiy Melkosopochnik
Ozero Balkhash
Ural
Volga
Prikaspiyskaya Nizmennost'
Aral'skoye More (Aral Sea)
Ustyurt Plateau
Caspian Sea
Turan Lowland
Syrdar'ya
Amudar'ya
Garagum (Karakum Desert)
E U R O P E
European Plain
Carpathian Mts
Dnipro (Dnieper)
Don
Sea of Azov
Danube
Black Sea
Caucasus
El'brus 5642
Ağrı Dağı (Mt Ararat) 5165
Anadolu D.
Anatolia
Toros D.
Kriti
Cyprus
NEAN SEA
Tigris
Euphrates
Reshteh-ye Alborz (Elburz Mountains)
Dasht-e Kavir
Dasht-e Lut
Kūhhā-ye Zagros (Zagros Mountains)
Bādiyat ash Shām (Syrian Desert)
An Nafūd
The Gulf
Munkhafad al Qaţţārah (Qattara Depression)
Shib Jazīrat Sīnā'
Nile
Libyan Desert
Arabian Peninsula
Najd
Ad Dahnā'
Rub' al Khālī
G. of Oman
Ra's al Ḩadd
Red Sea
Nubian Desert
A S I A
Tien Shan
Tarim Pendi
Taklimakan Shamo
Alai Ra.
Pamir
Hindu Kush
Karakoram Range
K2 8611
Kunlun Shan
Altun Shan
Qaidam Pendi
Qilian Shan
Qingzang Gaoyuan (Plateau of Tibet)
H I M A L A Y A
Helmand
Indus
Thar Desert
Rann of Kachchh
Brahmaputra
Mt Everest 8848
Ganga (Ganges)
Chang Jiang (Yangtze)
Sichuan Pendi
Gongga Shan 7514
Qin Ling
Huang He (Yellow River)
Bo Hai
Yellow Sea
Korea Strait
Sea of Japan (East Sea)
Honshū
Shikoku
Kyūshū
Japan Trench
East China Sea
Nansei-shotō
Okinawa
Ogasawara-shotō (Bonin Islands)
Kazan-rettō (Volcano Islands)
Iō-jima
Midway Is
Tropic of Cancer
P A C I F I C
Mid-Pacific Mountains
Xi Jiang
Taiwan
Luzon Strait
Luzon
Hainan
G. of Tongking
Annam Highlands
Mekong
Tônlé Sab
South China Sea
Philippine Sea
Philippine Islands
Palawan
Sulu Sea
Mindanao
Northern Mariana Islands
Guam
Mariana Trench
Challenger Deep 10920
M I C R O N E S I A
Marshall Islands
Pohnpei
Kosrae
Caroline Islands
Palau Is
Irrawaddy
Salween
Deccan
Western Ghats
Eastern Ghats
Bay of Bengal
Andaman Is
Andaman Sea
Gulf of Thailand
Mui Ca Mau
Nicobar Is
Sri Lanka
Palk Str.
Cape Comorin
Arabian Sea
Gulf of Aden
Suquţrā (Socotra)
Gees Gwardafuy
Ras Dejen 4533
Ethiopian Highlands
Haud
Denakil
Asīr
Bahr el Azraq (Blue Nile)
Bahr el Jebel (White Nile)
Sudd
Marra Plateau
Massif Emmedi
I C A
Lake Turkana
Webi Shabeelle
Somali Basin
Kirinyaga 5199
Lake Victoria
Kilimanjaro 5892
Congo Basin
Kasai
Great Rift Valley
Chaîne des Mitumba
Lake Tanganyika
Lake Nyasa
Zambezi
Pemba I.
Zanzibar I.
Mahé
Amirante Is
Seychelles
Aldabra Is
Comoro Islands
Tanjona Bobaomby
Madagascar
Mozambique Channel
Okavango Delta
Makgadikgadi
Limpopo
Kalahari Desert
Orange
Vaal
Drakensberg
Great Karoo
Cape Agulhas
Madagascar Basin
Mauritius
Réunion
Rodrigues Island
Natal Basin
Agulhas Basin
Prince Edward Is
Îles Crozet
Crozet Basin
Îles Kerguélen
Heard I.
Île Amsterdam
Île St Paul
I N D I A N
O C E A N
Maldives
Mid-Indian Basin
Chagos Archipelago
Ninetyeast Ridge
Southeast Indian Ridge
Malay Peninsula
Str. of Malacca
Kep. Natuna
Borneo
Celebes Sea
Sumatera
Kep. Mentawai
Selat Karimata
Selat Makassar
Sulawesi
Halmahera
Maluku (Moluccas)
Greater Sunda Islands
Laut Jawa
Jawa
Java Trench 7125
Christmas Island
Cocos Is
Lesser Sunda Islands
Sumba
Flores
Laut Flores
Timor
Timor Sea
Buru
Seram
Laut Banda
Puncak Jaya 5030
New Guinea
Bismarck Sea
New Ireland
Mt Wilhelm 4509
New Britain
Bougainville I.
Solomon Sea
Solomon Is
Arafura Sea
Cape York
Cape York Pen.
Gulf of Carpentaria
Arnhem Land
Barkly Tableland
Great Barrier Reef
Coral Sea
Kimberley Plateau
West Australian Basin
North West Cape
Great Sandy Desert
MacDonnell Ranges
A U S T R A L I A
Musgrave Ranges
Great Victoria Desert
Lake Eyre (North)
Great Dividing Range
Nullarbor Plain
Great Australian Bight
Darling
Murray
Mt Kosciuszko 2229
Perth Basin
Cape Leeuwin
South Australian Basin
Bass Strait
Tasmania
Tasman Sea
Lord Howe I.
Norfolk I.
North Cape
North Island
New Zealand
Aoraki 3754
South Island
Chatham Is
Snares I.
Stewart I.
Bounty Is
Auckland Is
Antipodes Is
Campbell I.
Macquarie I.
Kermadec Is
Tonga Trench
Tonga
Tongatapu Group
Horizon Deep 10800
Tropic of Capricorn
Nouvelle Calédonie
Espiritu Santo
Vanua Levu
Viti Levu
Fiji Islands
Îles Wallis et Futuna
Savai'i
'Upolu
Tokelau
Tuvalu
Sta Cruz Is
M E L A N E S I A
O C E A N
Phoenix Islands
Kingsmill Group
Gilbert Is
Equator
Antarctic Basin
S O U T H E R N O C E A N
Australian-Antarctic Basin
Davis Sea
Enderby Land
Kemp Land
Amery Ice Shelf
Wilkes Land
Balleny Is.
Antarctic Circle
Antarctic Mountains
Ross Sea
C T I C A
MILES
KILOMETRES
2400
1800
1200
600
0
4200
3600
3000
2400
1800
1200
600
0

1:70 000 000

© Collins Bartholomew Ltd

A.	ANDORRA	LITH.	LITHUANIA
AL.	ALBANIA	M.	MACEDONIA
ARM.	ARMENIA	MOL.	MOLDOVA
AUST.	AUSTRIA	MO.	MONTENEGRO
AZER.	AZERBAIJAN	NETH.	NETHERLANDS
B.	BURUNDI	R.	RWANDA
BEL.	BELGIUM	R.F.	RUSSIAN FEDERATION
B.H.	BOSNIA-HERZEGOVINA	ROM.	ROMANIA
BULG.	BULGARIA	S.	SERBIA
CR.	CROATIA	SL.	SLOVENIA
CZ.R.	CZECH REPUBLIC	SLA.	SLOVAKIA
EST.	ESTONIA	SUR.	SURINAME
GEOR.	GEORGIA	SW.	SWITZERLAND
HUN.	HUNGARY	TAJIK.	TAJIKISTAN
ISR.	ISRAEL	TURKM.	TURKMENISTAN
JOR.	JORDAN	U.A.E.	UNITED ARAB EMIRATES
L.	LUXEMBOURG	U.S.A.	UNITED STATES OF AMERICA
LAT.	LATVIA	UZBEK.	UZBEKISTAN
LEB.	LEBANON		

Winkel Tripel Projection

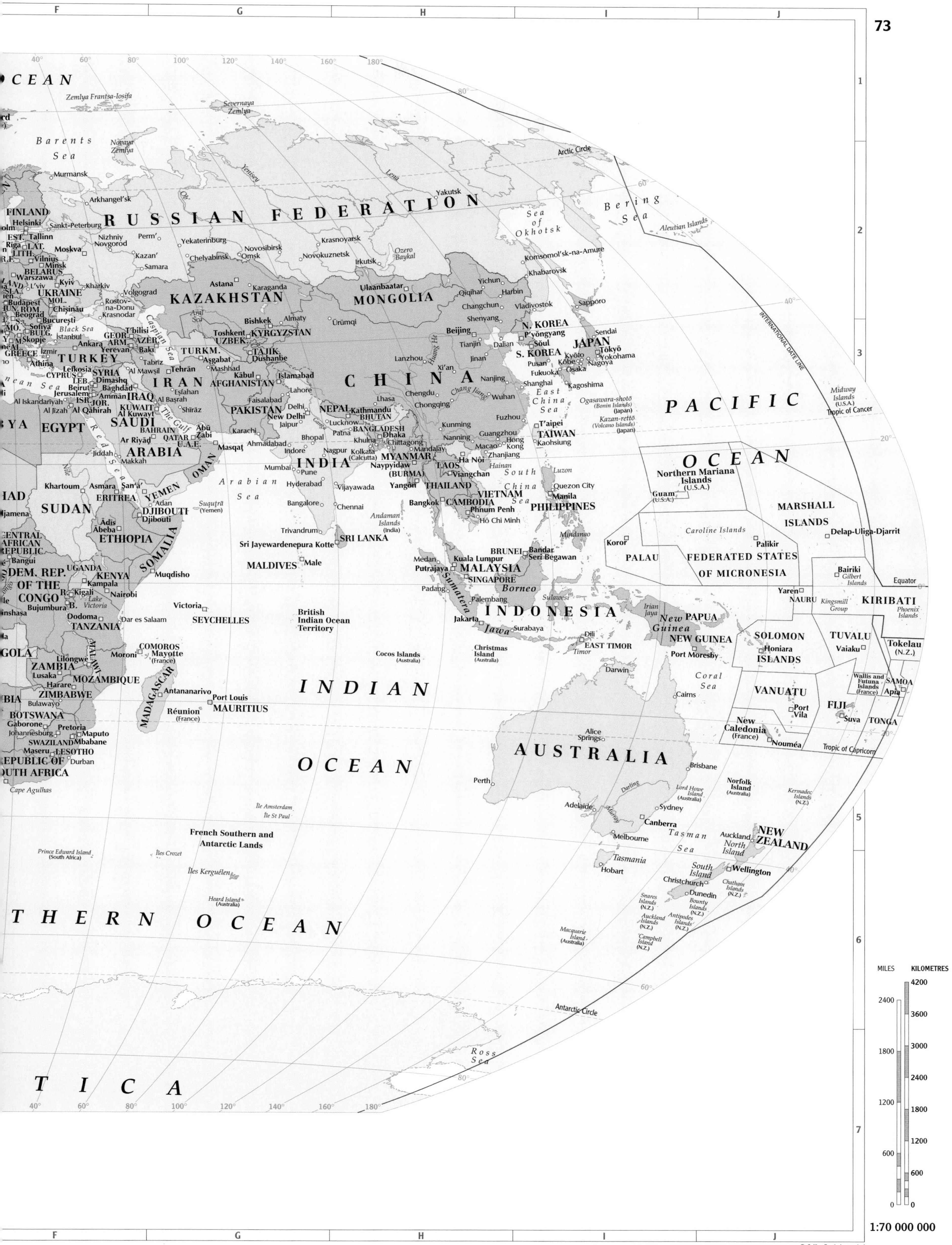
OCEAN
Zemlya Frantsa-Iosifa
Severnaya Zemlya
Barents Sea
Novaya Zemlya
Murmansk
Arkhangel'sk
RUSSIAN FEDERATION
Yakutsk
Lena
Yenisey
Ob'
Sea of Okhotsk
Bering Sea
Aleutian Islands
Arctic Circle
FINLAND
Helsinki
EST. Tallinn
Riga LAT.
LITH. Vilnius
Sankt-Peterburg
Moskva
Nizhniy Novgorod
Perm'
Yekaterinburg
Novosibirsk
Krasnoyarsk
Novokuznetsk
Irkutsk
Ozero Baykal
Chelyabinsk
Omsk
Kazan'
Samara
BELARUS
Minsk
Warszawa
UKRAINE
Kyiv
L'viv
Kharkiv
Volgograd
Rostov-na-Donu
Krasnodar
MOL.
Chişinău
Budapest
ROM.
Beograd
Bucureşti
Sofiya
BULG.
Skopje
GREECE
Athina
Izmir
Ankara
İstanbul
Black Sea
TURKEY
GEOR.
T'bilisi
ARM.
AZER.
Yerevan
Bakı
Caspian Sea
KAZAKHSTAN
Astana
Karaganda
Aral Sea
Bishkek
Almaty
KYRGYZSTAN
Toshkent
UZBEK.
TURKM.
Aşgabat
TAJIK.
Dushanbe
Ürümqi
Ulaanbaatar
MONGOLIA
Komsomol'sk-na-Amure
Khabarovsk
Yichun
Harbin
Qiqihar
Changchun
Vladivostok
Shenyang
Sapporo
N. KOREA
P'yŏngyang
Sendai
JAPAN
Beijing
Tianjin
Dalian
Sŏul
S. KOREA
Tōkyō
Yokohama
Kyōto
Kōbe
Ōsaka
Nagoya
Pusan
Fukuoka
Kagoshima
Jinan
Lanzhou
Huang He
Xi'an
CHINA
Nanjing
Shanghai
Chang Jiang
Wuhan
Chengdu
Chongqing
East China Sea
Ogasawara-shotō (Bonin Islands) (Japan)
Kazan-rettō (Volcano Islands) (Japan)
Lefkosia
CYPRUS
SYRIA
LEB.
Dimashq
Beirut
Jerusalem
ISR.
'Amman
JOR.
Baghdad
IRAQ
Al Mawşil
Tabrīz
Tehrān
Mashhad
IRAN
Eşfahan
Shīrāz
Al Başrah
KUWAIT
Al Kuwayt
The Gulf
BAHRAIN
QATAR
Abū Zabi
U.A.E.
Masqaţ
OMAN
Ar Riyāḑ
SAUDI ARABIA
Makkah
Jiddah
Al Iskandarīyah
Al Jīzah
Al Qāhirah
EGYPT
Nile
Red Sea
Kābul
AFGHANISTAN
Islamabad
Lahore
Faisalabad
PAKISTAN
Karachi
Delhi
New Delhi
Jaipur
Ganga
Lucknow
NEPAL
Kathmandu
BHUTAN
Lhasa
BANGLADESH
Dhaka
Khulna
Chittagong
Patna
Bhopal
Ahmadabad
Indore
Nagpur
Kolkata (Calcutta)
INDIA
Mumbai
Pune
Hyderabad
Vijayawada
Bangalore
Chennai
Trivandrum
SRI LANKA
Sri Jayewardenepura Kotte
Arabian Sea
Suqutrā (Yemen)
MALDIVES
Male
Andaman Islands (India)
MYANMAR
Mandalay
Naypyidaw
(BURMA)
Yangon
THAILAND
Bangkok
LAOS
Viangchan
Ha Nôi
CAMBODIA
Phnum Penh
VIETNAM
Hô Chi Minh
Kunming
Nanning
Guangzhou
Hong Kong
Macao
Zhanjiang
Hainan
Fuzhou
T'aipei
TAIWAN
Kaohsiung
South China Sea
Luzon
Quezon City
Manila
PHILIPPINES
Mindanao
BRUNEI
Bandar Seri Begawan
Medan
Kuala Lumpur
Putrajaya
MALAYSIA
SINGAPORE
Borneo
Padang
Sumatera
Palembang
Sulawesi
INDONESIA
Jakarta
Jawa
Surabaya
Dili
EAST TIMOR
Timor
Christmas Island (Australia)
Cocos Islands (Australia)
Irian Jaya
New Guinea
PAPUA NEW GUINEA
Port Moresby
PACIFIC OCEAN
Midway Islands (U.S.A.)
Tropic of Cancer
INTERNATIONAL DATE LINE
Northern Mariana Islands (U.S.A.)
Guam (U.S.A.)
MARSHALL ISLANDS
Delap-Uliga-Djarrit
Caroline Islands
Palikir
Koror
PALAU
FEDERATED STATES OF MICRONESIA
Bairiki
Gilbert Islands
Equator
Yaren
NAURU
Kingsmill Group
KIRIBATI
Phoenix Islands
SOLOMON ISLANDS
Honiara
TUVALU
Vaiaku
Tokelau (N.Z.)
Wallis and Futuna Islands (France)
SAMOA
Apia
VANUATU
Port Vila
FIJI
Suva
TONGA
New Caledonia (France)
Nouméa
Tropic of Capricorn
Coral Sea
Darwin
Cairns
Alice Springs
AUSTRALIA
Brisbane
Perth
Darling
Murray
Adelaide
Sydney
Canberra
Melbourne
Tasmania
Hobart
Lord Howe Island (Australia)
Norfolk Island (Australia)
Kermadec Islands (N.Z.)
Tasman Sea
Auckland
North Island
NEW ZEALAND
Wellington
South Island
Christchurch
Dunedin
Chatham Islands (N.Z.)
Snares Islands (N.Z.)
Bounty Islands (N.Z.)
Auckland Islands (N.Z.)
Antipodes Islands (N.Z.)
Campbell Island (N.Z.)
Macquarie Island (Australia)
Khartoum
SUDAN
Asmara
ERITREA
Şan'ā'
YEMEN
Adan
DJIBOUTI
Djibouti
Ādīs Ābeba
ETHIOPIA
SOMALIA
Muqdisho
UGANDA
KENYA
Kampala
Nairobi
Kigali
Lake Victoria
Bujumbura
DEM. REP. OF THE CONGO
Bangui
Dodoma
Dar es Salaam
TANZANIA
SEYCHELLES
Victoria
British Indian Ocean Territory
COMOROS
Moroni
Mayotte (France)
MALAWI
Lilongwe
ZAMBIA
Lusaka
Harare
ZIMBABWE
MOZAMBIQUE
Bulawayo
BOTSWANA
Gaborone
Pretoria
Maputo
Johannesburg
SWAZILAND
Mbabane
Maseru
LESOTHO
Durban
REPUBLIC OF SOUTH AFRICA
Cape Agulhas
MADAGASCAR
Antananarivo
Port Louis
MAURITIUS
Réunion (France)
INDIAN OCEAN
Île Amsterdam
Île St Paul
French Southern and Antarctic Lands
Prince Edward Island (South Africa)
Îles Crozet
Îles Kerguélen
Heard Island (Australia)
SOUTHERN OCEAN
Antarctic Circle
Ross Sea
ANTARCTICA
F
G
H
I
J
1
2
3
4
5
6
7
MILES
KILOMETRES
2400
1800
1200
600
0
4200
3600
3000
2400
1800
1200
600
0
1:70 000 000

A
B
C
D
E
1
2
3
4
5
6
7
Hokkaidō
Kuril'ski
Sea of Japan
Honshū
Shikoku
Kyūshū
Ogasawara-shotō
Kazan-rettō
East China Sea
Nansei-shotō
A S I A
Chang Jiang
Taiwan Strait
Luzon Strait
Luzon
Xun Jiang
Hainan
Tropic of Cancer
Pagan
Tinian
Saipan
Rota
Northern Mariana Islands (U.S.A.)
Guam (U.S.A.)
Hagåtña
Ulithi
Fais
Yap
Sorol
Faraulep
Pikelot
Chuuk
Ngulu
Caroline Islands
Eauripik
Palau Islands
Samar
Panay
Negros
Palawan
Mindanao
Sulu Sea
FEDERATED S
Mussau Island
Admiralty Islands
New Hanov
Bismarck Sea
Rabaul
Irrawaddy
Mekong
South China Sea
Celebes Sea
Laut Maluku
Halmahera
Vanimo
Wewak
Sepik
Madang
New Britain
Mt Wilhelm
Goroka
Lae
PAPUA NEW GUINEA
Kerema
Balimo
Gulf of Papua
Daru
Port Moresby
D'Ent Islan
Louisiade
New Guinea
Bay of Bengal
Gulf of Thailand
Borneo
Makassar Strait
Sulawesi
Laut Banda
Arafura Sea
Torres Strait
Cape York
Coral Sea Islands Territory (Australia)
Strait of Malacca
Sumatera
Laut Jawa
Laut Flores
Timor
Flores
Sumbawa
Bali
Sumba
Jawa (Java)
Kepulauan Mentawai
Melville Island
Wessel Islands
Cape Arnhem
Gulf of Carpentaria
Cape York Peninsula
Great Barrier Reef
Bathurst Island
Darwin
Arnhem Land
Groote Eylandt
Cooktown
Timor Sea
Ashmore and Cartier Islands (Australia)
Cape Londonderry
Wellesley Islands
Mitchell
Gilbert
Cairns
Normanton
Townsville
Wyndham
Mackay
INDIAN OCEAN
Equator
Christmas Island (Australia)
Cocos Islands (Australia)
Cape Lévêque
Broome
Halls Creek
NORTHERN TERRITORY
Mount Isa
Cloncurry
Great Dividing Range
QUEENSLAND
Longreach
Rock
Port Hedland
Karratha
Great Sandy Desert
Lake Mackay
Mount Liebig 1524
Alice Springs
AUSTRALIA
Diamantina
Cooper Creek (Barcoo Creek)
Charleville
Barrow Island
North West Cape
Newman
Lake Disappointment
Lake Amadeus
Oodnadatta
Toowoomba
Balonne
Paraburdoo
WESTERN AUSTRALIA
Great Victoria Desert
Lake Eyre (North)
SOUTH AUSTRALIA
Darling
NEW SOUTH WALES
Meekatharra
Mount Magnet
Leonora
Woomera
Port Augusta
Broken Hill
Lachlan
Orange
Lithgo
Geraldton
Lake Moore
Kalgoorlie
Ceduna
Whyalla
Port Pirie
Wagga Wagga
A.C.T.
Canber
Great Australian Bight
Port Lincoln
Cape Carnot
Adelaide
Murray
Albury
Bendigo
VICTORIA
Melbourne
Geelong
Perth
Fremantle
Bunbury
Esperance
Kangaroo Island
Mount Gambier
Bass Strait
Flinders Islan
Cape Leeuwin
Albany
King Island
Devonport
Launceston
TASMANIA
Hobart
South East Cape
Tropic of Capricorn
60°
30°
75°
90°
45°
105°
120°
135°
150°

F
G
H
I
J
1
2
3
4
5
6
7
165°
180°
45°
150°
135°
120°
30°
15°
0°
Hawaiian Islands
Kure Atoll
Midway Islands
Pearl and Hermes Atoll
Lisianski Island
Laysan Island
Gardner Pinnacles
Necker Island
Kaua'i
O'ahu
Maui
Hawai'i
Tropic of Cancer
INTERNATIONAL DATE LINE
Wake Island (U.S.A.)
MARSHALL ISLANDS
Ralik Chain
Ratak Chain
Kwajalein
Maloelap
Majuro
Delap-Uliga-Djarrit
Jaluit
Mili
Palikir
Kosrae
MICRONESIA
Johnston Atoll (U.S.A.)
PACIFIC OCEAN
Gilbert Islands
Tarawa
Bairiki
Yaren
NAURU
Banaba
Aranuka
Nonouti
Tabiteuea
Beru
Nikunau
Onotoa
Tamana
Kingsmill Group
Arorae
Howland Island (U.S.A.)
Baker Island (U.S.A.)
Kingman Reef (U.S.A.)
Palmyra Atoll (U.S.A.)
Teraina
Tabuaeran
Kiritimati
Line Islands
Jarvis Island (U.S.A.)
Ontong Java Atoll
Santa Isabel
SOLOMON ISLANDS
Malaita
Honiara
Guadalcanal
San Cristobal
Rennell
Duff Islands
Ndeni
Santa Cruz Islands
Nanumea
Nanumanga
Niutao
TUVALU
Nui
Vaitupu
Nukufetau
Funafuti
Vaiaku
Nukulaelae
Niulakita
Phoenix Islands
McKean
Kanton
Nikumaroro
Orona
Rawaki
Manra
KIRIBATI
Banks Islands
Espiritu Santo
VANUATU
Maéwo
Pentecost I.
Malakula
Ambrym
Epi
Port Vila
Éfaté
Erromango
Tanna
Anatom
Chesterfield (France)
New Caledonia (France)
Nouméa
Îles Loyauté (France)
Matthew I.
Hunter I.
Île des Pins
Rotuma (Fiji)
Wallis and Futuna Islands (France)
Îles Wallis
Matā'utu
Île de Hoorn
Yasawa Group
Vanua Levu
Viti Levu
Koro
Ovalau
Gau
Suva
FIJI
Moala
Kadavu
Totoya
Ceva-i-Ra (Conway Reef)
Ono-i-Lau
Atafu
Nukunono
Fakaofo
Tokelau (New Zealand)
Swains Island
SAMOA
Savai'i
Apia
'Upolu
American Samoa
Tutuila
Fagatogo
Manu'a Islands
Rose Island
Pukapuka
Nassau
Niuafo'ou
Tafahi
Vava'u Group
Tofua
TONGA
Nuku'alofa
Tongatapu Group
Ata
Alofi
Niue (New Zealand)
Rakahanga
Manihiki
Penrhyn
Suwarrow
Malden Island
Starbuck Island
Vostok Island
Flint Island
Caroline Island (Millennium Island)
Equator
Palmerston
Aitutaki
Cook Islands (New Zealand)
Atiu
Mauke
Rarotonga
Mangaia
Motu One
Îles du Roi Georges
Rangiroa
Archipel des Tuamotu
Papeete
Moorea
Tahiti
Fakarava
Anaa
Archipel de la Société
French Polynesia
Nuku Hiva
Îles Marquises
Hiva Oa
Îles du Désappointement
Raroia
Pukapuka
Maria
Rimatara
Rurutu
Îles Australes
Tubuai
Raivavae
Hereheretue
Îles du Duc de Gloucester
Hao
Mururoa
Groupe Actéon
Rapa
Marotiri
Îles Gambier
Adamstown
Pitcairn Islands (U.K.)
Pitcairn Island
Henderson I.
Ducie I.
Tropic of Capricorn
Norfolk Island (Australia)
Lord Howe Island (Australia)
Raoul Island
Kermadec Islands (New Zealand)
Cape Maria van Diemen
Whangarei
Great Barrier Island
North Island
Auckland
Manukau
TASMAN SEA
Hamilton
New Plymouth
Lake Taupo
Gisborne
NEW ZEALAND
Cape Farewell
Napier
Nelson
Palmerston North
Wellington
Greymouth
Blenheim
South Island
Aoraki
Southern Alps
Christchurch
Timaru
Cape Providence
Dunedin
Oamaru
Stewart Island
Invercargill
Chatham Islands (New Zealand)
Pitt Island
Snares Islands (New Zealand)
Bounty Islands (New Zealand)
Auckland Islands (New Zealand)
Antipodes Islands (New Zealand)
Campbell Island (New Zealand)
Macquarie Island (Australia)
MILES
KILOMETRES
1000
750
500
250
0
1500
1250
1000
750
500
250
0

1:27 000 000

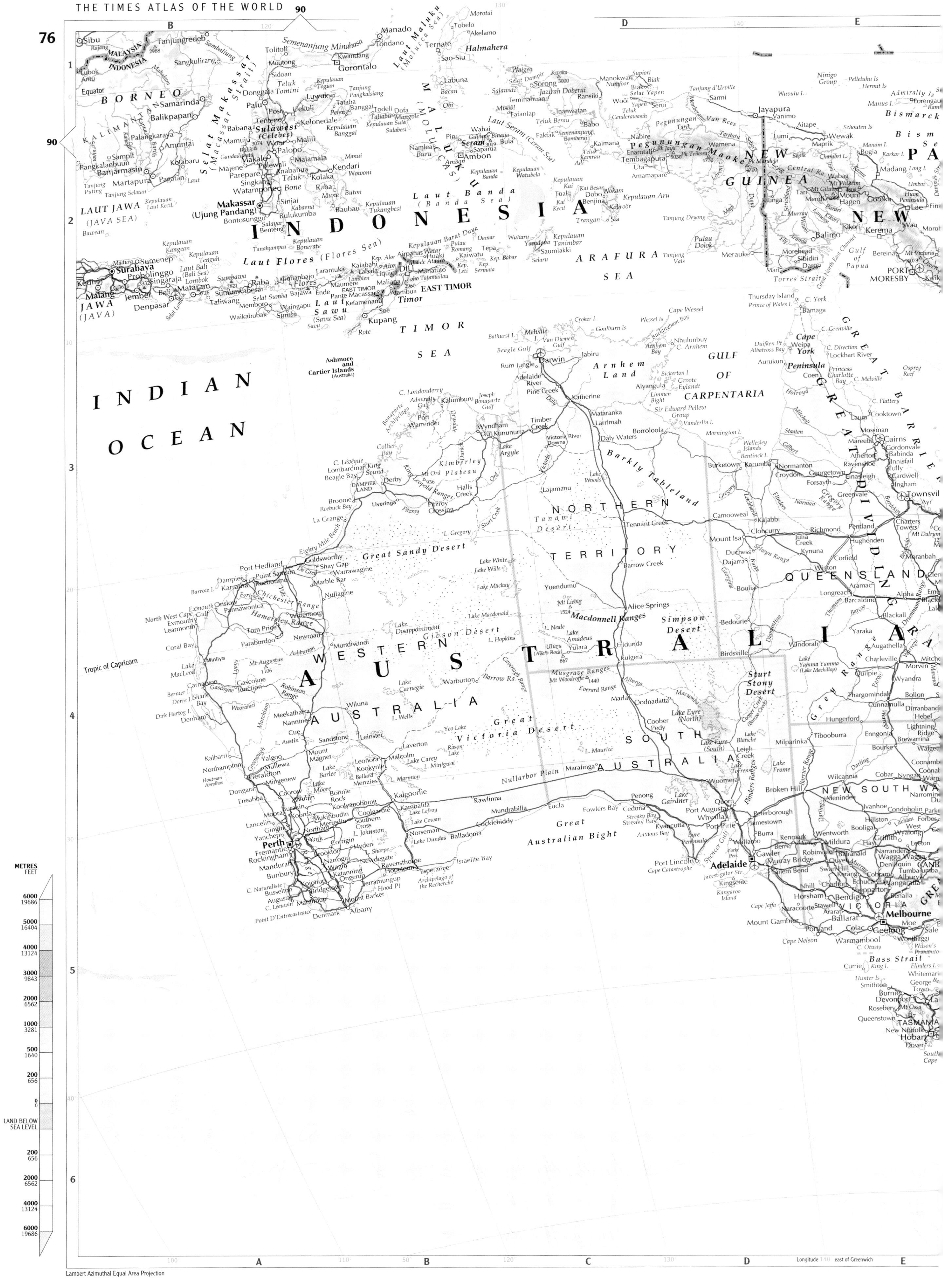
INDIAN OCEAN
INDONESIA
AUSTRALIA
BORNEO
KALIMANTAN
MALAYSIA
Sulawesi (Celebes)
Selat Makassar (Macassar Strait)
LAUT JAWA (JAVA SEA)
JAWA (JAVA)
Laut Flores (Flores Sea)
Laut Sawu (Savu Sea)
Laut Banda (Banda Sea)
Laut Seram (Ceram Sea)
Laut Maluku (Molucca Sea)
MALUKU (MOLUCCAS)
Halmahera
EAST TIMOR
Timor
TIMOR SEA
ARAFURA SEA
GULF OF CARPENTARIA
NEW GUINEA
PAPUA NEW GUINEA
Gulf of Papua
PORT MORESBY
Jayapura
Torres Strait
Cape York Peninsula
GREAT BARRIER REEF
GREAT DIVIDING RANGE
Arnhem Land
Darwin
Katherine
Barkly Tableland
NORTHERN TERRITORY
Tanami Desert
Tennant Creek
Alice Springs
Macdonnell Ranges
Simpson Desert
Kimberley Plateau
Great Sandy Desert
Gibson Desert
Great Victoria Desert
Nullarbor Plain
WESTERN AUSTRALIA
SOUTH AUSTRALIA
QUEENSLAND
NEW SOUTH WALES
VICTORIA
TASMANIA
Lake Eyre (North)
Lake Eyre (South)
Lake Torrens
Lake Gairdner
Flinders Ranges
Musgrave Ranges
Sturt Stony Desert
Great Australian Bight
Bass Strait
Perth
Fremantle
Kalgoorlie
Esperance
Albany
Geraldton
Carnarvon
Port Hedland
Broome
Derby
Wyndham
Adelaide
Port Augusta
Whyalla
Port Lincoln
Broken Hill
Mount Isa
Cairns
Townsville
Melbourne
Geelong
Hobart
Makassar (Ujung Pandang)
Surabaya
Manado
Ambon
Kupang
Dili
Tropic of Capricorn
Equator
Lambert Azimuthal Equal Area Projection
Longitude east of Greenwich
METRES
FEET
6000
19686
5000
16404
4000
13124
3000
9843
2000
6562
1000
3281
500
1640
200
656
0
0
LAND BELOW SEA LEVEL
200
656
2000
6562
4000
13124
6000
19686

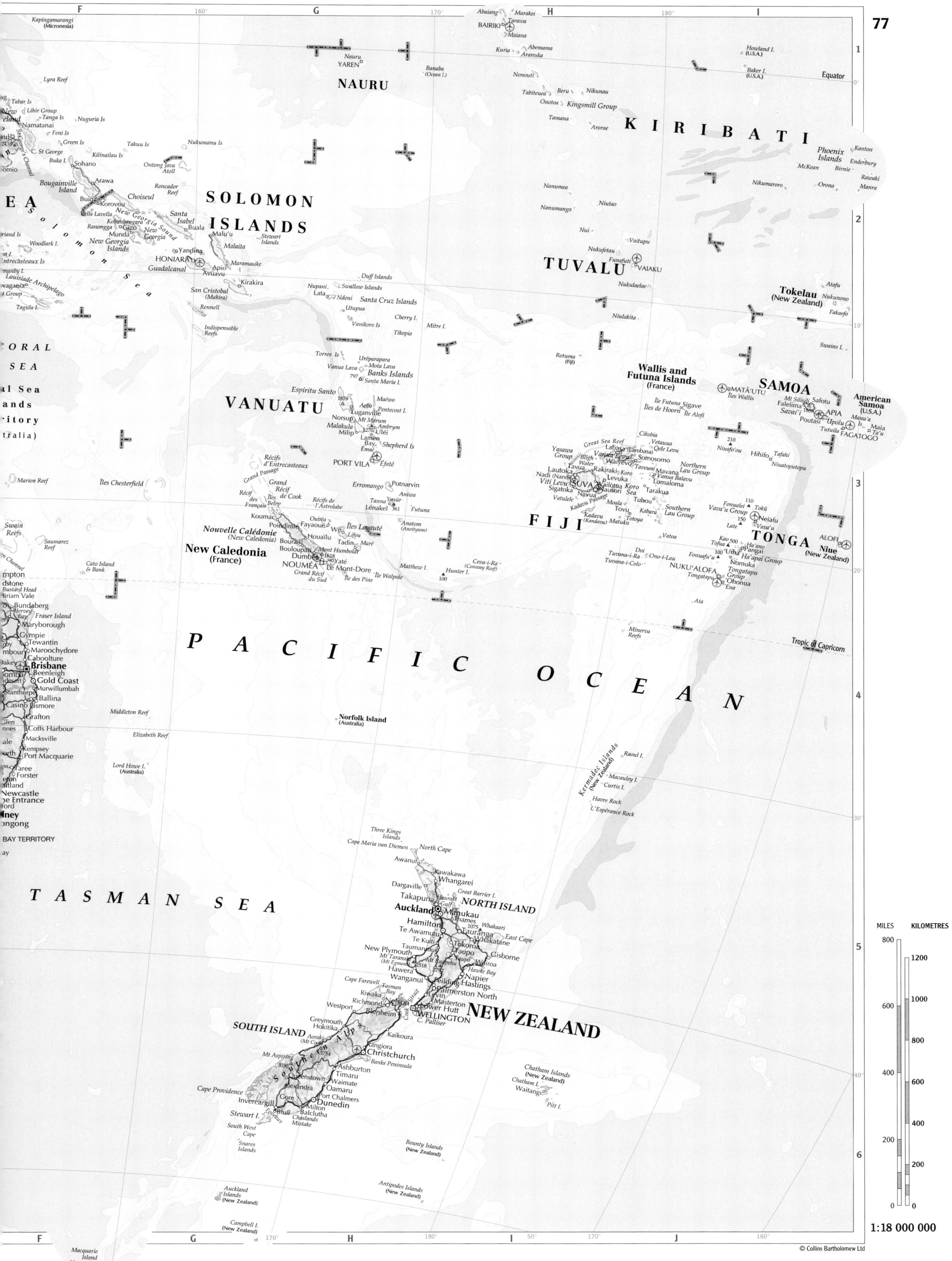
NAURU
Nauru
YAREN
Banaba (Ocean I.)
BAIRIKI
Tarawa
Equator
K I R I B A T I
Kingsmill Group
Phoenix Islands
Howland I. (U.S.A.)
Baker I. (U.S.A.)
SOLOMON ISLANDS
HONIARA
Guadalcanal
Malaita
Santa Isabel
Choiseul
Bougainville Island
New Georgia Islands
Ontong Java Atoll
Solomon Sea
Santa Cruz Islands
TUVALU
Funafuti
VAIAKU
Tokelau (New Zealand)
Wallis and Futuna Islands (France)
SAMOA
APIA
American Samoa (U.S.A.)
FAGATOGO
VANUATU
PORT VILA
Espíritu Santo
Banks Islands
FIJI
SUVA
Viti Levu
Vanua Levu
Lau Group
TONGA
NUKU'ALOFA
Niue (New Zealand)
ALOFI
Nouvelle Calédonie (New Caledonia)
New Caledonia (France)
NOUMÉA
Îles Loyauté
Îles Chesterfield
CORAL SEA
Tropic of Capricorn
P A C I F I C   O C E A N
Norfolk Island (Australia)
Lord Howe I. (Australia)
Middleton Reef
Elizabeth Reef
Kermadec Islands (New Zealand)
Raoul I.
Minerva Reefs
T A S M A N   S E A
Brisbane
Gold Coast
Bundaberg
Maryborough
Gympie
Grafton
Coffs Harbour
Port Macquarie
Newcastle
NEW ZEALAND
NORTH ISLAND
SOUTH ISLAND
Auckland
Manukau
Hamilton
Tauranga
Rotorua
New Plymouth
Napier
Hastings
Palmerston North
WELLINGTON
Nelson
Blenheim
Christchurch
Dunedin
Invercargill
Queenstown
Southern Alps
Stewart I.
Chatham Islands (New Zealand)
Bounty Islands (New Zealand)
Antipodes Islands (New Zealand)
Auckland Islands (New Zealand)
Campbell I. (New Zealand)
Macquarie Island (Australia)
MILES
KILOMETRES
1:18 000 000

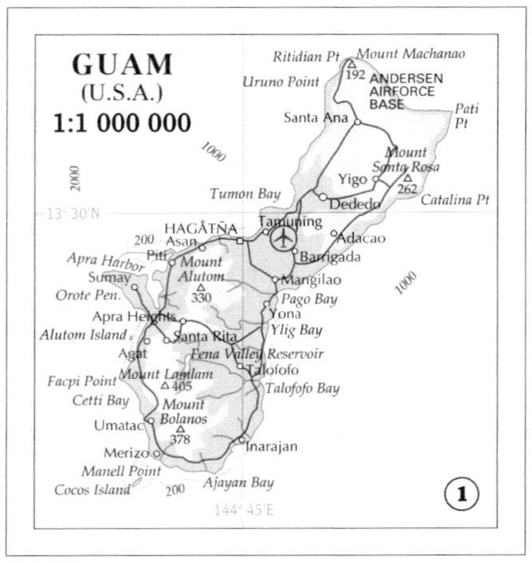
GUAM
(U.S.A.)
1:1 000 000
Ritidian Pt
Mount Machanao
Uruno Point
ANDERSEN AIRFORCE BASE
Pati Pt
Santa Ana
Yigo
Mount Santa Rosa
Tumon Bay
Dededo
Catalina Pt
13°30'N
HAGÅTÑA
Asan
Tamuning
Adacao
Barrigada
Apra Harbor
Piti
Sumay
Orote Pen.
Mount Alutom
Mangilao
Pago Bay
Apra Heights
Yona
Alutom Island
Santa Rita
Ylig Bay
Agat
Fena Valley Reservoir
Facpi Point
Mount Lamlam
Talofofo
Talofofo Bay
Cetti Bay
Umatac
Mount Bolanos
Inarajan
Merizo
Manell Point
Cocos Island
Ajayan Bay
144°45'E
1

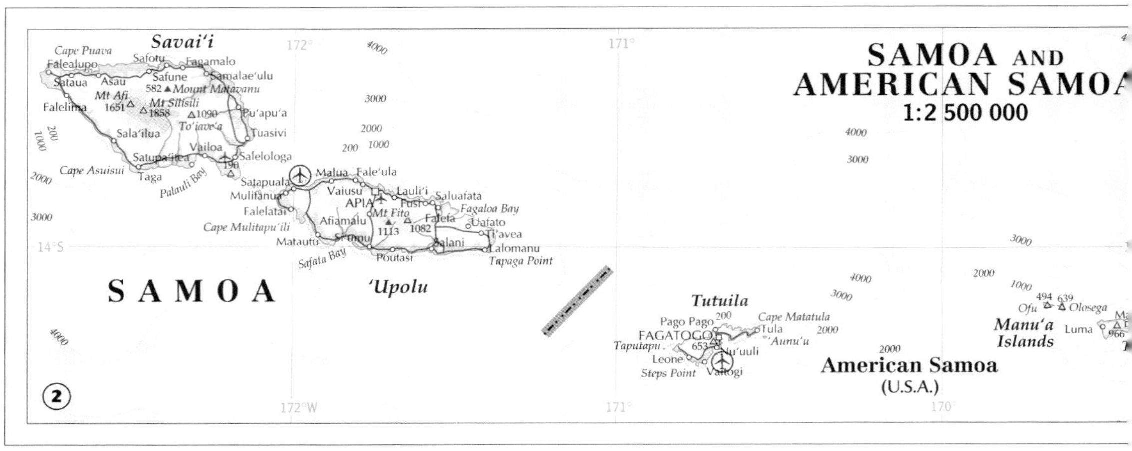
Savai'i
SAMOA AND AMERICAN SAMOA
1:2 500 000
Cape Puava
Falealupo
Salotu
Fagamalo
Sataua
Asau
Safune
Samalae'ulu
Mt Afi
Mount Mata'ava
Mt Silisili
Falelima
Pu'apu'a
Sala'ilua
To'iavea
Tuasivi
Vailoa
Satupa'itea
Salelologa
Cape Asuisui
Taga
Palauli Bay
Malua
Fale'ula
Satapuala
Mulifanua
Vaiusu
Lauli'i
Falelatai
APIA
Saluafata
Fagaloa Bay
Cape Mulitapu'ili
Afiamalu
Mt Fito
Falefa
Ti'avea
Matautu
Siumu
Lalomanu
Safata Bay
Poutasi
Tapaga Point
SAMOA
'Upolu
Tutuila
Pago Pago
Cape Matatula
FAGATOGO
Tula
Taputapu
Leone
Aunu'u
Steps Point
Vaitogi
Manu'a Islands
Ofu
Olosega
Luma
American Samoa
(U.S.A.)
14°S
172°W
171°
170°
2

167°E
Roi-Namur
Ennumennet
Ennugarret
Mellu Pass.
Mellu
Edgigen
Ebadon
Oreba
Biggerann
Etcharai
Bigi
Mejatto
Marsugalt
Biggarenn
Boggerik
Tabik Channel
Tabik
Kwajalein Lagoon
Yabbenohr
Boggenatjen
Gellinam
Eru
Nell
Onemak
Nell Passage
Enniwetak
Eller
Ambo Channel
Legan
Mann
Bigej
Gehh
Bigej Channel
Ninai
Gugegwe
Ennylabagan
South Pass.
Ebeye
Ennubuj
Kwajalein
MARSHALL ISLANDS
Kwajalein
1:2 000 000
167°30'E
9°N
3a

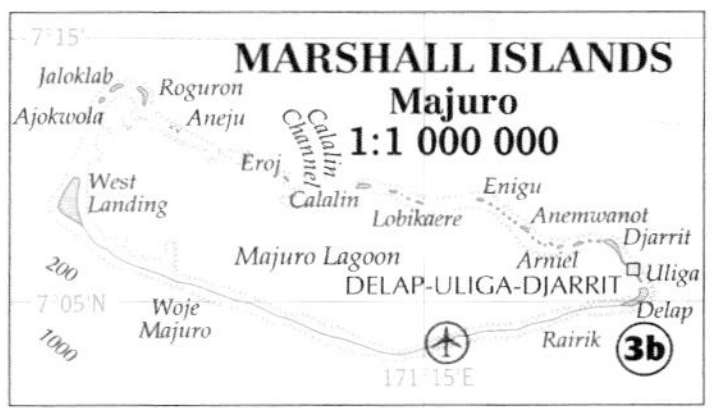
MARSHALL ISLANDS
Majuro
1:1 000 000
7°15'
Jaloklab
Roguron
Ajokwola
Aneju
Calalin Channel
Eroj
West Landing
Enigu
Calalin
Lobikaere
Anemwanot
Djarrit
Majuro Lagoon
Arniel
Uliga
DELAP-ULIGA-DJARRIT
Delap
7°05'N
Woje
Majuro
Rairik
171°15'E
3b

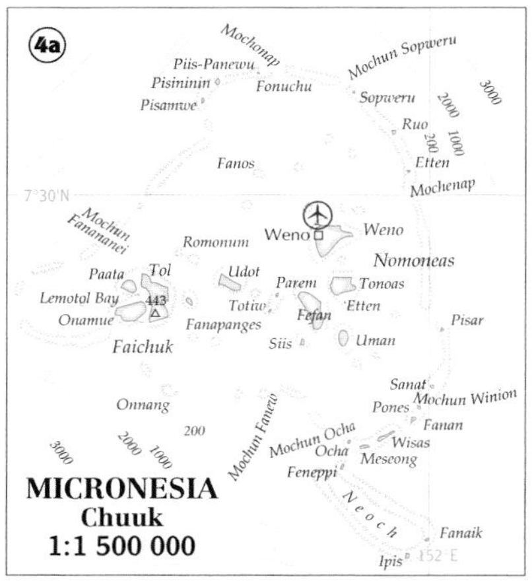
4a
Mochonap
Mochun Sopweru
Piis-Panewu
Pisininin
Fonuchu
Pisamwe
Sopweru
Ruo
Fanos
Etten
Mochenap
7°30'N
Mochun Fanamanu
Weno
Weno
Romonum
Nomoneas
Paata
Tol
Udot
Parem
Tonoas
Lemotol Bay
Totiw
Etten
Onamue
Fanapanges
Fefan
Pisar
Faichuk
Siis
Uman
Sanat
Onnang
Pones
Mochun Winiton
Fanan
Mochun Ocha
Ocha
Wisas
Mochun Fanere
Feneppi
Meseong
Neoch
Fanaik
Ipis
152°E
MICRONESIA
Chuuk
1:1 500 000

MICRONESIA
Pohnpei
1:1 000 000
4b
Parempei
7°N
Palikir Passage
Dekehtik
Sokehs
Kolonia
Dehpehk
PALIKIR
Alohkapw
Temwetemwensekir
Tauak Passage
Pwel Weite
Nanlaud
Dolohmwar
Temwen
Tamworohi
Sekeren Iap
Pwok
Kepidau en Pohnahtik
158°15'E

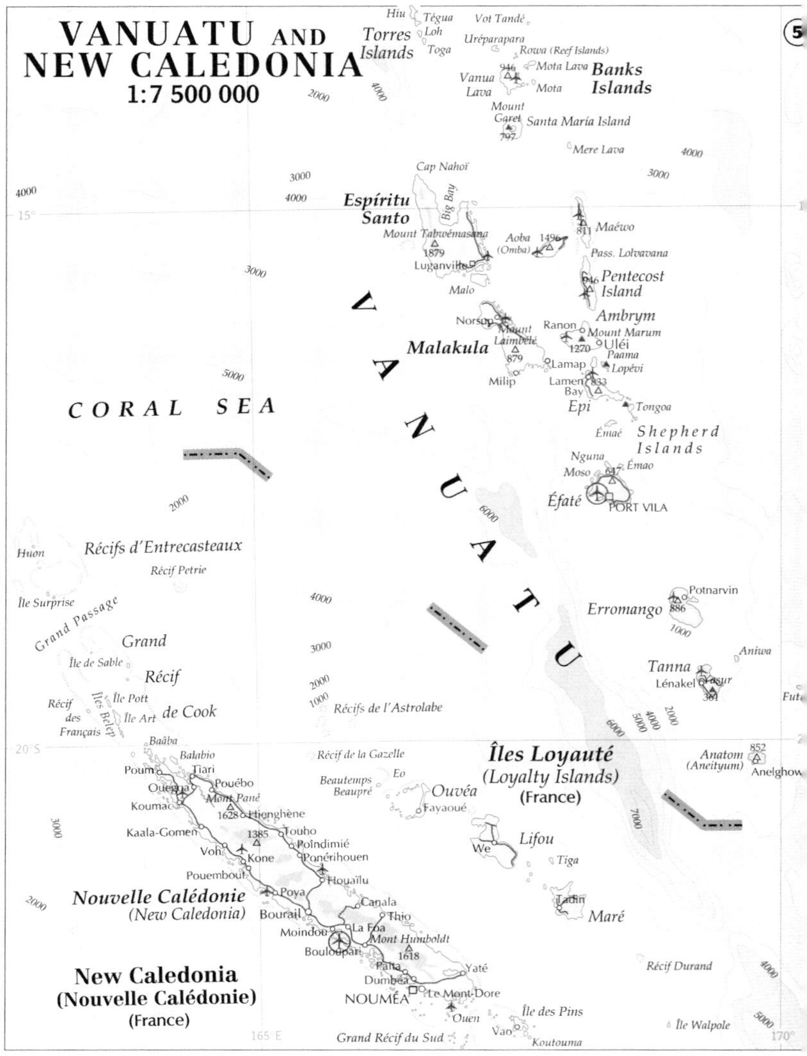
VANUATU AND NEW CALEDONIA
1:7 500 000
5
Hiu
Tégua
Vot Tandé
Torres Islands
Loh
Toga
Uréparapara
Rowa (Reef Islands)
Vanua Lava
Mota Lava
Banks Islands
Mota
Mount Garet
Santa Maria Island
Mere Lava
Cap Nahoï
Big Bay
Espíritu Santo
Mount Tabwémasana
Aoba (Omba)
Maéwo
Luganville
Pass. Loluwana
Pentecost Island
Malo
Norsup
Mount Lambéte
Ranon
Ambrym
Mount Marum
Uléi
Malakula
Lamap
Paama
Lopévi
Milip
Lamen Bay
Epi
Tongoa
Émaé
Shepherd Islands
Nguna
Moso
Émao
Éfaté
PORT VILA
VANUATU
CORAL SEA
Huon
Récifs d'Entrecasteaux
Récif Petrie
Île Surprise
Grand Passage
Erromango
Potnarvin
Grand Récif de Cook
Île de Sable
Récif des Français
Île Pott
Île Art
Îles Belep
Récifs de l'Astrolabe
Tanna
Lénakel
Aniwa
Futuna
Anatom (Aneityum)
Anelghowhat
Baaba
Balabio
Récif de la Gazelle
Îles Loyauté
(Loyalty Islands)
(France)
Poum
Ouégoa
Tiari
Pouébo
Beautemps Beaupré
Ouvéa
Fayaoué
Mont Panié
Koumac
Hienghène
Kaala-Gomen
Touho
Poindimié
Voh
Kone
Ponérihouen
Lifou
We
Tiga
Pouembout
Houaïlu
Poya
Nouvelle Calédonie
(New Caledonia)
Canala
Thio
Bourail
Maré
Tadin
Moindou
La Foa
Mont Humboldt
Boulouparis
Yaté
Récif Durand
Dumbéa
New Caledonia
(Nouvelle Calédonie)
(France)
NOUMÉA
Le Mont-Dore
Ouen
Île des Pins
Vao
Île Walpole
Grand Récif du Sud
Koutouma
20°S
15°
165°E
170°

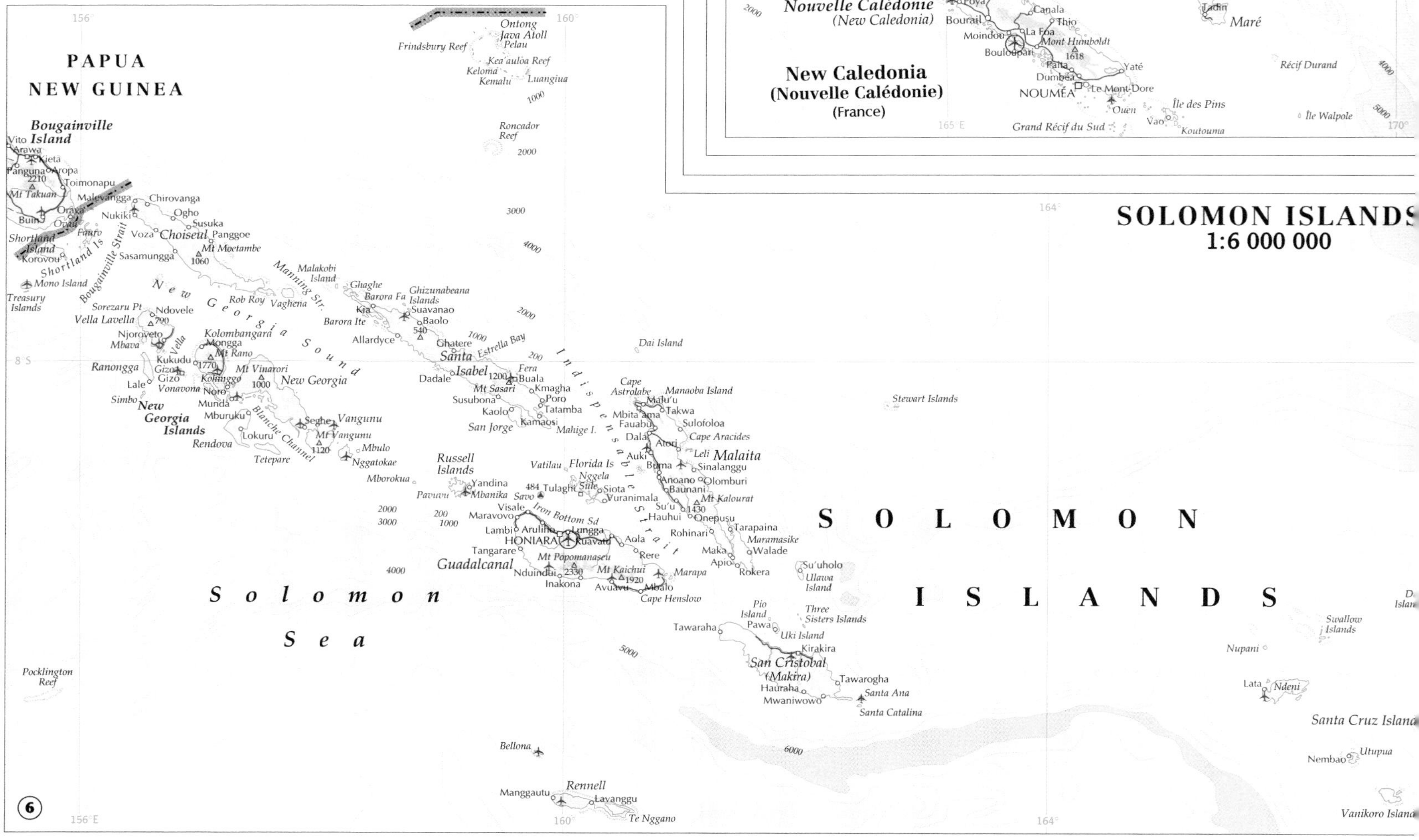
SOLOMON ISLANDS
1:6 000 000
PAPUA NEW GUINEA
156°
160°
164°
Ontong Java Atoll
Pelau
Frindsbury Reef
Kea'auloa Reef
Keloma
Luangiua
Kemalu
Roncador Reef
Bougainville Island
Vito
Arawa
Kieta
Panguna
Aropa
Toimonapu
Mt Takuan
Buin
Malevangga
Chirovanga
Nukiki
Ogho
Susuka
Oaza
Fauro
Voza
Choiseul
Panggoe
Shortland Island
Korovou
Shortland Is
Bougainville Strait
Sasamungga
Mt Maetambe
Manning Str.
Malakobi Island
Mono Island
Treasury Islands
Sorezaru Pt
Vella Lavella
Ndovele
New Georgia Sound
Rob Roy
Vaghena
Ghaghe
Barora Fa
Ghizunabeana Islands
Kia
Suavanao
Baolo
Barora Ite
Allardyce
Njoroveto
Mbava
Kolombangara
Mongga
Mt Rano
Vella
Ranongga
Gizo
Gizo
Lale
Vonavona
Mt Vinarori
Kolinggo
Noro
New Georgia
Simbo
Munda
New Georgia Islands
Mburuku
Blanche Channel
Rendova
Lokuru
Seghe
Vangunu
Mt Vangunu
Tetepare
Mbulo
Nggatokae
Ghatere
Santa Isabel
Estrella Bay
Buala
Fera
Dadale
Kmagha
Susubona
Poro
Kaolo
Tatamba
San Jorge
Kamaosi
Mahige I.
Indispensable Strait
Dai Island
Cape Astrolabe
Manaoba Island
Malu'u
Takwa
Mbita'ama
Fauabu
Sulofoloa
Dala
Cape Aracides
Auki
Atori
Malaita
Leli
Buma
Sinalanggu
Anoano
Olomburi
Baunani
Mt Kalourat
Su'u
Hauhui
Onepusu
Stewart Islands
Russell Islands
Yandina
Mbanika
Vatilau
Florida Is
Nggela
Tulaghi
Siota
Vuranimala
Mborokua
Pavuvu
Savo
Iron Bottom Sd
Visale
Maravovo
Lambi
Aruliho
HONIARA
Lungga
Kuvavu
Aola
Tangarare
Mt Popomanaseu
Rere
Guadalcanal
Nduindi
Mt Kaichui
Marapa
Inakona
Avuavu
Mbalo
Cape Henslow
Rohinari
Tarapaina
Maramasike
Walade
Maka
Apio
Rokera
Su'uholo
Ulawa Island
Three Sisters Islands
Pio Island
Pawa
Uki Island
Tawaraha
Kirakira
San Cristobal (Makira)
Tawarogha
Hauraha
Mwaniwowo
Santa Ana
Santa Catalina
Solomon Sea
SOLOMON ISLANDS
Pocklington Reef
Bellona
Rennell
Manggautu
Lavanggu
Te Nggano
Swallow Islands
Nupani
Lata
Ndeni
Santa Cruz Islands
Utupua
Nembao
Vanikoro Islands
8°S
156°E
6

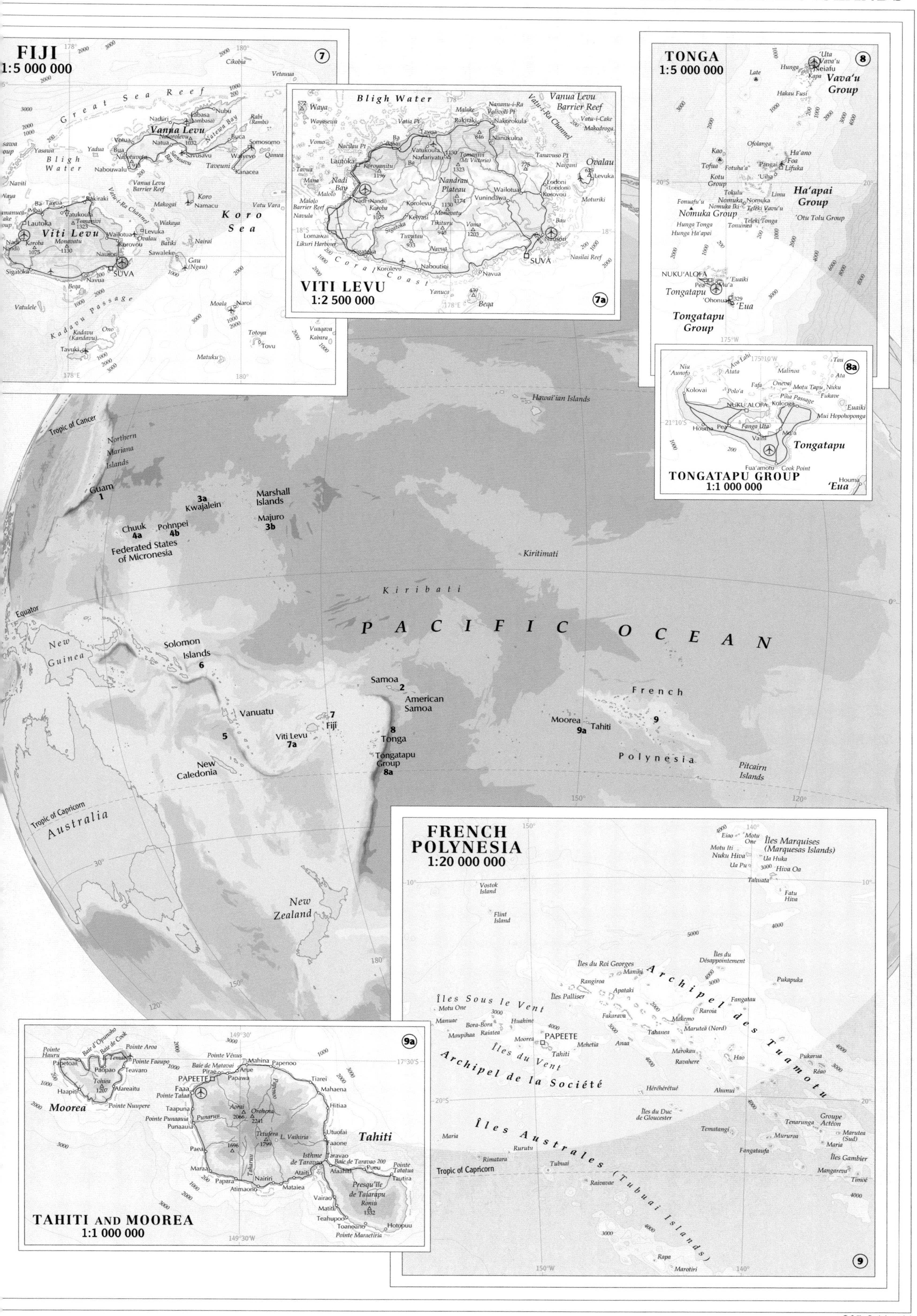
FIJI
1:5 000 000
7
Great Sea Reef
Vanua Levu
Viti Levu
Bligh Water
Koro Sea
Kadavu Passage
Lautoka
Nadi
SUVA
Labasa
Savusavu
Taveuni
Levuka
Ovalau
Koro
Gau (Ngau)
Kadavu (Kandavu)
Nausori
Sigatoka
Rakiraki
Vatu-i-Ra Channel
Natewa Bay
Cikobia
Vetauua
Rabi (Rambi)
Yadua
Beqa
Vatulele
Moala
Totoya
Matuku
178°E
180°
VITI LEVU
1:2 500 000
7a
Bligh Water
Vanua Levu Barrier Reef
Vatu-i-Ra Channel
Nadi Bay
Coral Coast
Nandrau Plateau
Tomanivi (Mt Victoria) 1323
Lautoka
Nadi (Nandi)
SUVA
Sigatoka
Korolevu
Navua
Nausori
Rakiraki
Tavua
Vatukoula
Ba
Ovalau
Levuka
Nasilai Reef
Beqa
Yanuca
Waya
Lomawai
Likuri Harbour
Malolo Barrier Reef
TONGA
1:5 000 000
8
Vava'u Group
Neiafu
Ha'apai Group
Nomuka Group
Tongatapu Group
Tongatapu
NUKU'ALOFA
'Eua
'Otu Tolu Group
Late
Hunga
Kao
Tofua
Lifuka
Hunga Tonga
Hunga Ha'apai
175°W
20°S
TONGATAPU GROUP
1:1 000 000
8a
Tongatapu
NUKU'ALOFA
Kolovai
Kolonga
Mu'a
Fua'amotu
Houma
'Eua
Eua'iki
Malinoa
Atata
Piha Passage
Fanga Uta
Cook Point
21°10'S
175°10'W
Hawai'ian Islands
Tropic of Cancer
Northern Mariana Islands
Guam
1
3a
Kwajalein
Marshall Islands
Majuro
3b
Chuuk
4a
Pohnpei
4b
Federated States of Micronesia
Kiritimati
Kiribati
Equator
PACIFIC OCEAN
New Guinea
Solomon Islands
6
Samoa
2
American Samoa
French Polynesia
9
Moorea
9a
Tahiti
Vanuatu
5
7
Fiji
Viti Levu
7a
8
Tonga
Tongatapu Group
8a
New Caledonia
Pitcairn Islands
Tropic of Capricorn
Australia
New Zealand
150°
120°
180°
30°
FRENCH POLYNESIA
1:20 000 000
9
Îles Marquises (Marquesas Islands)
Nuku Hiva
Ua Huka
Ua Pu
Hiva Oa
Fatu Hiva
Vostok Island
Flint Island
Îles du Roi Georges
Îles du Désappointement
Rangiroa
Pukapuka
Archipel des Tuamotu
Îles Sous le Vent
Îles du Vent
Archipel de la Société
Bora-Bora
Raiatea
Huahine
Moorea
PAPEETE
Tahiti
Makemo
Hao
Îles du Duc de Gloucester
Îles Australes (Tubuai Islands)
Rurutu
Tubuai
Raivavae
Rapa
Marotiri
Groupe Actéon
Îles Gambier
Mangareva
Mururoa
Fangataufa
Tropic of Capricorn
150°W
140°
10°
20°S
TAHITI AND MOOREA
1:1 000 000
9a
Moorea
Tahiti
PAPEETE
Faaa
Papeete
Pointe Vénus
Mahina
Papenoo
Tiarei
Hitiaa
Taravao
Isthme de Taravao
Presqu'île de Taiarapu
Teahupoo
Papara
Paea
Punaauia
Orohena 2241
Aorai 2066
Tetufera 1799
Pointe Maraetiria
17°30'S
149°30'W

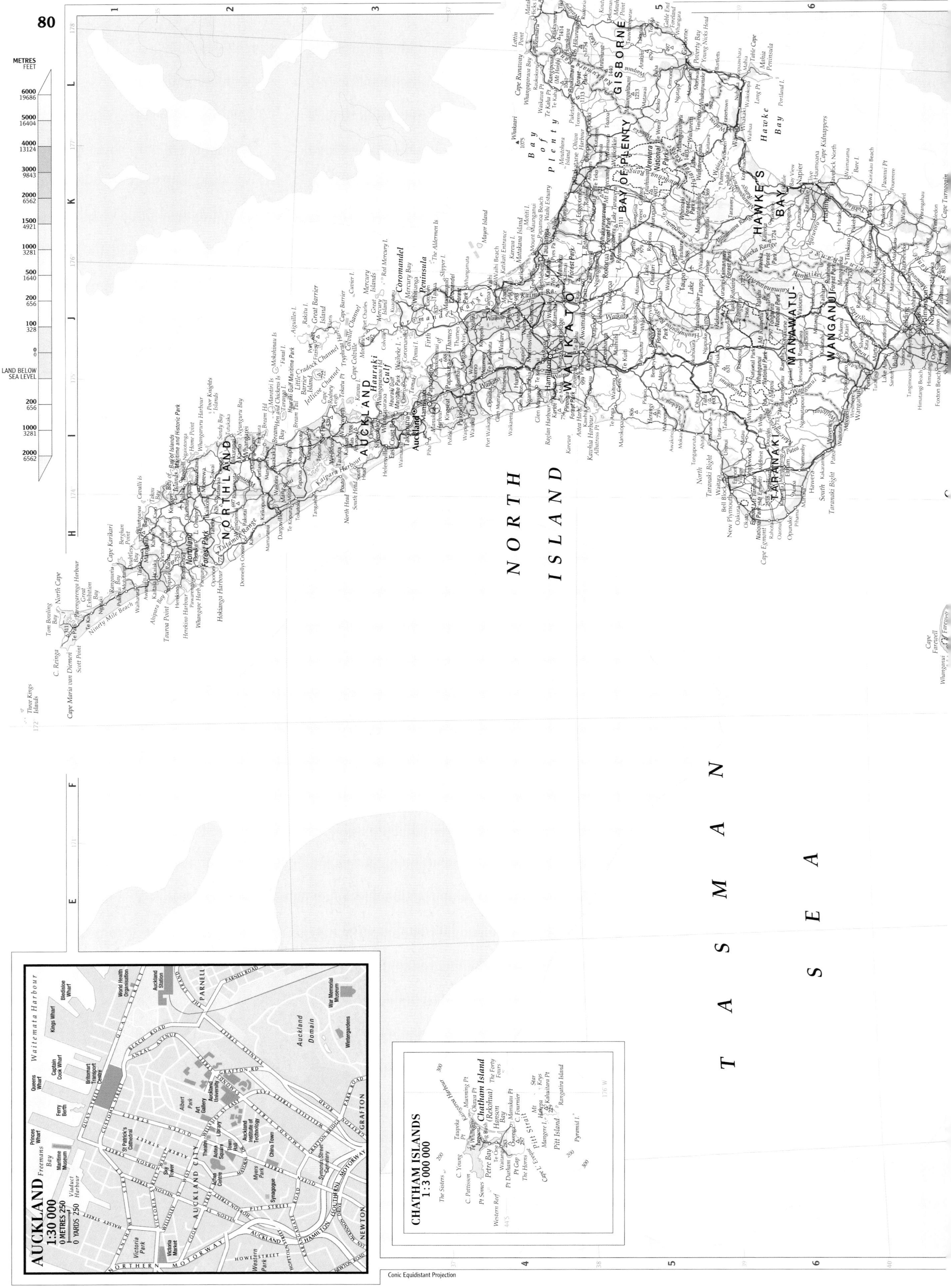
AUCKLAND
1:30 000
0 METRES 250
0 YARDS 250
Waitemata Harbour
Auckland Domain
CHATHAM ISLANDS
1:3 000 000
Chatham Island (Rekohua)
Pitt Island
METRES
FEET
6000
19686
5000
16404
4000
13124
3000
9843
2000
6562
1500
4921
1000
3281
500
1640
200
656
100
328
0
0
LAND BELOW
SEA LEVEL
200
656
1000
3281
2000
6562
NORTH ISLAND
TASMAN SEA
NORTHLAND
AUCKLAND
WAIKATO
BAY OF PLENTY
GISBORNE
HAWKE'S BAY
TARANAKI
MANAWATU-WANGANUI
Bay of Plenty
Hawke Bay
Hauraki Gulf
Coromandel Peninsula
North Taranaki Bight
South Taranaki Bight
Conic Equidistant Projection

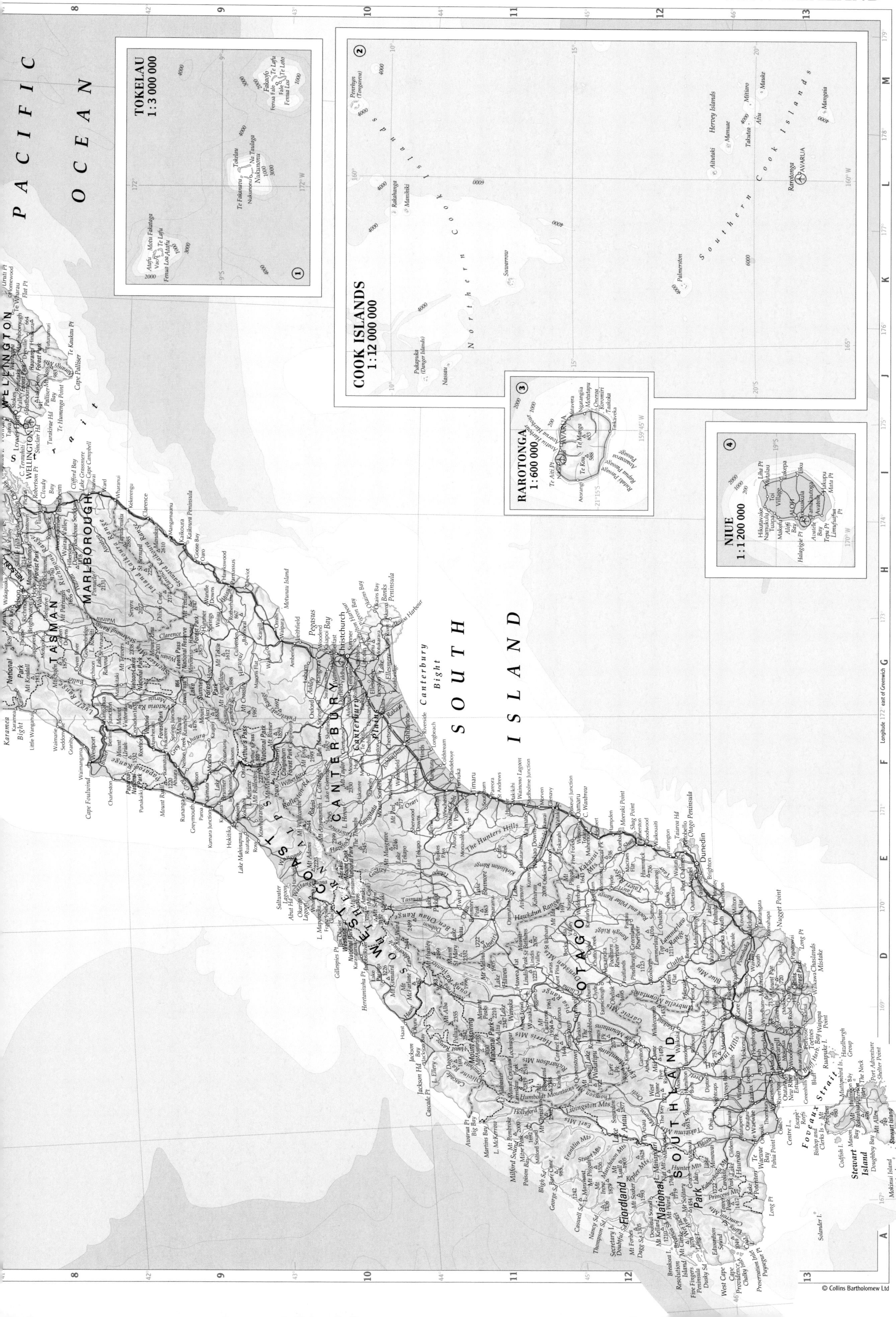
PACIFIC OCEAN
TOKELAU
1:3 000 000
COOK ISLANDS
1:12 000 000
RAROTONGA
1:600 000
NIUE
1:1 200 000
Northern Cook Islands
Southern Cook Islands
SOUTH ISLAND
Canterbury Bight
Foveaux Strait
Stewart Island
WELLINGTON
Christchurch
Dunedin
MARLBOROUGH
CANTERBURY
OTAGO
SOUTHLAND
TASMAN
WEST COAST
Longitude 172 east of Greenwich

MILES KILOMETRES

1:3 000 000

© Collins Bartholomew Ltd

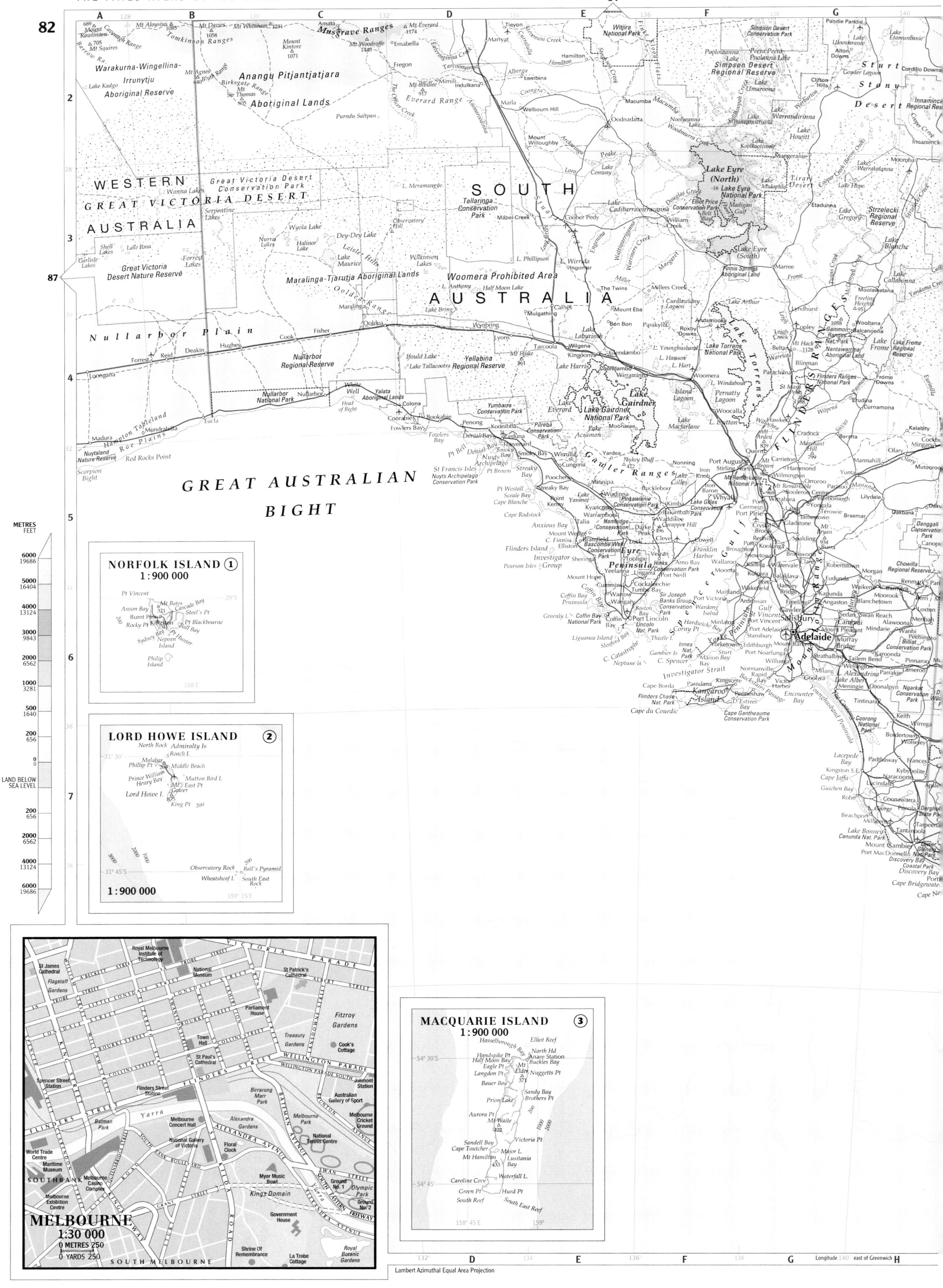
84
87
SOUTH AUSTRALIA
WESTERN AUSTRALIA
GREAT VICTORIA DESERT
GREAT AUSTRALIAN BIGHT
Nullarbor Plain
Musgrave Ranges
Tomkinson Ranges
Anangu Pitjantjatjara Aboriginal Lands
Warakurna-Wingellina-Irrunytju Aboriginal Reserve
Great Victoria Desert Conservation Park
Great Victoria Desert Nature Reserve
Maralinga-Tjarutja Aboriginal Lands
Woomera Prohibited Area
Tallaringa Conservation Park
Nullarbor Regional Reserve
Nullarbor National Park
Yellabina Regional Reserve
Lake Eyre (North)
Lake Eyre National Park
Lake Eyre (South)
Simpson Desert Regional Reserve
Simpson Desert Conservation Park
Witjira National Park
Sturt Stony Desert
Tirari Desert
Strzelecki Regional Reserve
Lake Torrens
Lake Torrens National Park
Lake Gairdner
Lake Gairdner National Park
Gawler Ranges
FLINDERS RANGES
Flinders Ranges National Park
Eyre Peninsula
Spencer Gulf
Gulf St Vincent
Yorke Peninsula
Kangaroo Island
Investigator Strait
Adelaide
Salisbury
Port Augusta
Whyalla
Port Pirie
Port Lincoln
Coober Pedy
Oodnadatta
Marree
Woomera
Tarcoola
Ceduna
Eucla
Mount Gambier
Murray Bridge
Coorong National Park
Lambert Azimuthal Equal Area Projection
Longitude 140 east of Greenwich
METRES FEET
6000 19686
5000 16404
4000 13124
3000 9843
2000 6562
1000 3281
500 1640
200 656
0 0
LAND BELOW SEA LEVEL
200 656
2000 6562
4000 13124
6000 19686
NORFOLK ISLAND ① 1:900 000
Pt Vincent
Mt Bates 321
Anson Bay
Cascade Bay
Steel's Pt
Burnt Pine
Kingston
Pt Blackbourne
Rocky Pt
Ball Bay
Sydney Bay
Pt Hunter
Nepean Island
Philip Island
LORD HOWE ISLAND ② 1:900 000
North Rock
Admiralty Is
Roach I.
Malabar
Phillip Pt
Middle Beach
Prince William Henry Bay
Mutton Bird I.
Mt Gower 875
East Pt
Lord Howe I.
King Pt
Observatory Rock
Ball's Pyramid
Wheatsheaf I.
South East Rock
1:900 000
MACQUARIE ISLAND ③ 1:900 000
Elliot Reef
Hasselborough Bay
North Hd
Anare Station
Handspike Pt
Half Moon Bay
Buckles Bay
Eagle Pt
Langdon Pt
Mt Elder 371
Nuggetts Pt
Bauer Bay
Sandy Bay
Brothers Pt
Prion Lake
Aurora Pt
Mt Waite 322
Victoria Pt
Sandell Bay
Cape Toutcher
Mt Hamilton 433
Major L.
Lusitania Bay
Waterfall L.
Caroline Cove
Green Pt
Hurd Pt
South Reef
South East Reef
MELBOURNE 1:30 000
0 METRES 250
0 YARDS 250
Royal Melbourne Institute of Technology
St James Cathedral
Flagstaff Gardens
National Museum
St Patrick's Cathedral
Parliament House
Fitzroy Gardens
Treasury Gardens
Cook's Cottage
Town Hall
St Paul's Cathedral
Spencer Street Station
Flinders Street Station
Jolimont Station
Australian Gallery of Sport
Birrarung Marr Park
Melbourne Cricket Ground
Melbourne Park
National Tennis Centre
Melbourne Concert Hall
Alexandra Gardens
National Gallery of Victoria
Floral Clock
World Trade Centre
Maritime Museum
Melbourne Casino Complex
Melbourne Exhibition Centre
SOUTHBANK
Myer Music Bowl
Kings Domain
Olympic Park
Government House
Shrine Of Remembrance
La Trobe Cottage
Royal Botanic Gardens
SOUTH MELBOURNE
Yarra

85
QUEENSLAND
NEW SOUTH WALES
VICTORIA
TASMANIA
GREAT DIVIDING RANGE
GREY RANGE
TASMAN SEA
Bass Strait
Banks Strait
AUSTRALIAN CAPITAL TERRITORY
JERVIS BAY TERRITORY
CANBERRA
Brisbane
Sydney
Melbourne
Hobart
Newcastle
Wollongong
Gold Coast
Geelong
Launceston
Toowoomba
Darling Downs
Fraser Island
Furneaux Group
Flinders Island
King Island
Kent Group
Hunter Islands
MILES
KILOMETRES
1:6 000 000
SYDNEY
1:45 000
METRES
YARDS
Sydney Harbour
Port Jackson
Darling Harbour
THE ROCKS
MILLERS POINT
POTTS POINT
WOOLLOOMOOLOO
KINGS CROSS
DARLINGHURST
PADDINGTON
SURRY HILLS
ULTIMO
Sydney Opera House
Royal Botanic Gardens
The Domain
Hyde Park
Central Station

© Collins Bartholomew Ltd

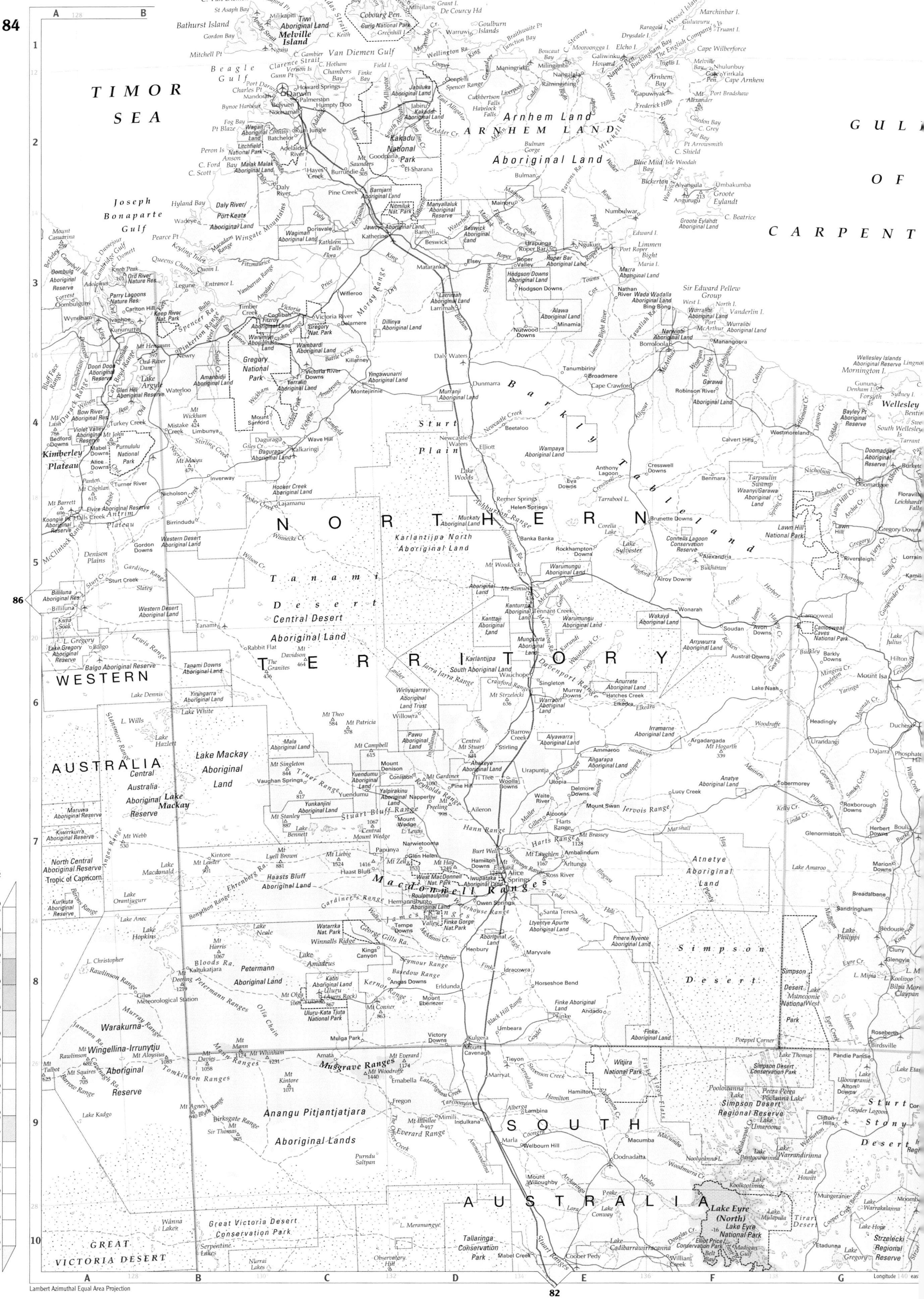
TIMOR SEA
Joseph Bonaparte Gulf
Beagle Gulf
Van Diemen Gulf
Bathurst Island
Melville Island
Tiwi Aboriginal Land
Darwin
Arnhem Land
ARNHEM LAND
Aboriginal Land
Kakadu National Park
GULF OF CARPENTARIA
Groote Eylandt
Katherine
Sturt Plain
Barkly Tableland
NORTHERN TERRITORY
Tanami Desert
Central Desert Aboriginal Land
Tennant Creek
Alice Springs
Macdonnell Ranges
Simpson Desert
WESTERN AUSTRALIA
Lake Mackay Aboriginal Land
Kimberley Plateau
Musgrave Ranges
Anangu Pitjantjatjara Aboriginal Lands
SOUTH AUSTRALIA
GREAT VICTORIA DESERT
Great Victoria Desert Conservation Park
Lake Eyre (North)
Lake Eyre National Park
Mount Isa
Uluru (Ayers Rock)
Uluru-Kata Tjuta National Park
METRES
FEET
6000
19686
5000
16404
4000
13124
3000
9843
2000
6562
1000
3281
500
1640
200
656
0
0
LAND BELOW SEA LEVEL
200
656
2000
6562
4000
13124
6000
19686
86
82
Longitude 140 east
Lambert Azimuthal Equal Area Projection

PAPUA NEW GUINEA
CORAL SEA
Coral Sea Islands Territory
GREAT BARRIER REEF
Great Barrier Reef Marine Park (Far North Section)
Great Barrier Reef Marine Park (Cairns Section)
Great Barrier Reef Marine Park (Central Section)
Great Barrier Reef Marine Park (Capricorn Section)
CAPE YORK PENINSULA
GREAT DIVIDING RANGE
QUEENSLAND
Gregory Range
Grey Range
Drummond Range
Warrego Range
Darling Downs
Capricorn Channel
Swain Reefs
Tropic of Capricorn
Cape York
Torres Strait
Cooktown
Cairns
Townsville
Mackay
Rockhampton
Gladstone
Bundaberg
Maryborough
Fraser Island
Brisbane
Toowoomba
Charters Towers
Hughenden
Winton
Longreach
Barcaldine
Emerald
Roma
Charleville
Cunnamulla
Quilpie
MILES
KILOMETRES
1:6 000 000

© Collins Bartholomew Ltd

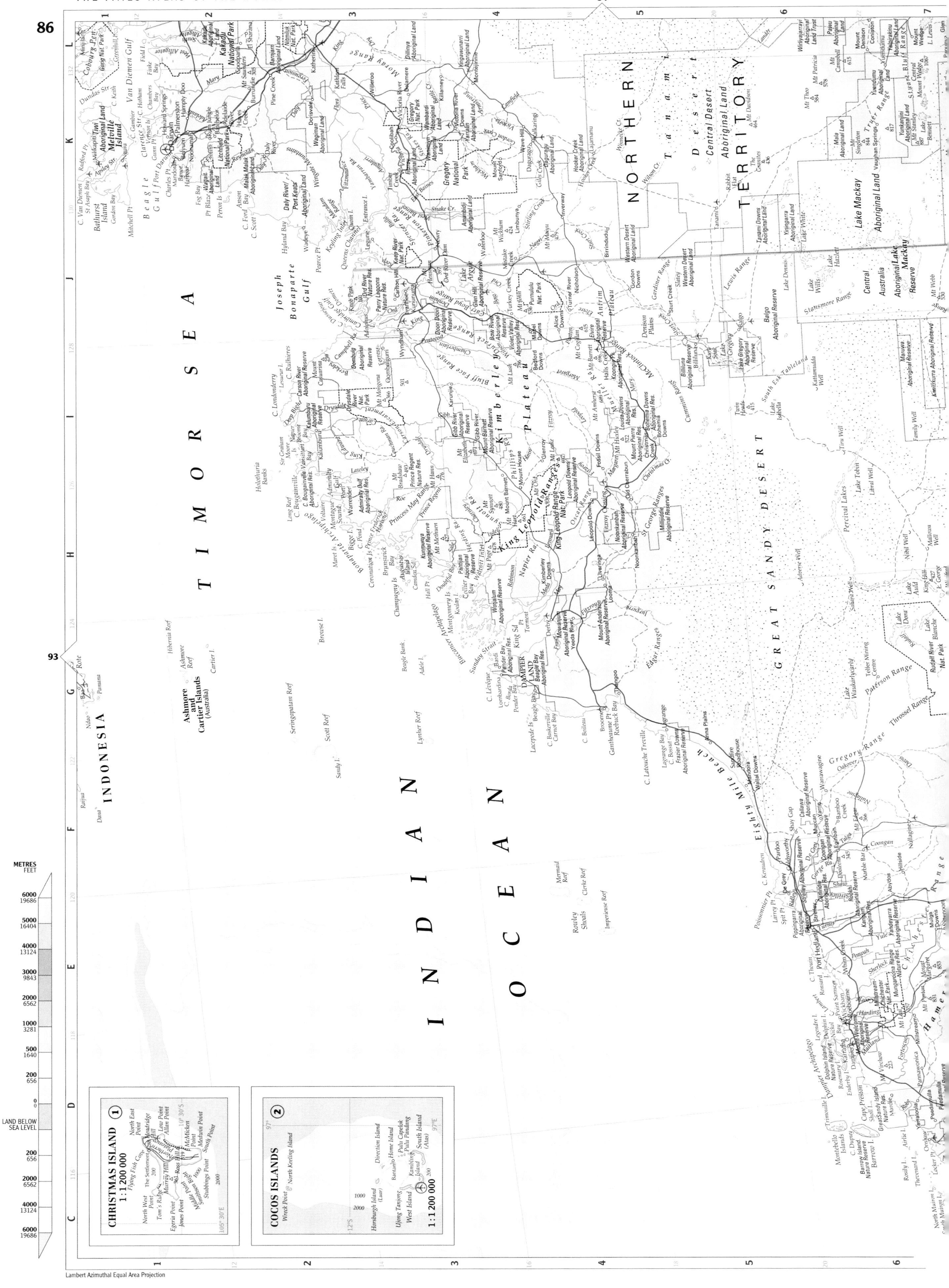
84
93
TIMOR SEA
INDIAN OCEAN
INDONESIA
NORTHERN TERRITORY
GREAT SANDY DESERT
Tanami Desert
Joseph Bonaparte Gulf
Kimberley Plateau
Ashmore and Cartier Islands (Australia)
Melville Island
Bathurst Island
Van Diemen Gulf
Beagle Gulf
Darwin
Kakadu National Park
Eighty Mile Beach
Port Hedland
Broome
Derby
Wyndham
Kununurra
Lake Mackay
Central Desert Aboriginal Land
CHRISTMAS ISLAND 1:1 200 000
COCOS ISLANDS 1:1 200 000
METRES
FEET
6000
19686
5000
16404
4000
13124
3000
9843
2000
6562
1000
3281
500
1640
200
656
0
0
LAND BELOW SEA LEVEL
200
656
2000
6562
4000
13124
6000
19686

82
WESTERN AUSTRALIA
SOUTH AUSTRALIA
GREAT VICTORIA DESERT
Nullarbor Plain
GREAT AUSTRALIAN BIGHT
Gibson Desert Nature Reserve
Great Victoria Desert Nature Reserve
Nullarbor National Park
Nullarbor Regional Reserve
Perth
Kalgoorlie
Geraldton
Carnarvon
Shark Bay
Houtman Abrolhos
Tropic of Capricorn
Longitude 120° east of Greenwich

MILES KILOMETRES

1:6 000 000

© Collins Bartholomew Ltd

A
B
C
D
E
1
2
3
4
5
6
7
EUROPE
RUSSIAN
ARCT
Karskoye More
Beloye More
Arctic Circle
Gulf of Bothnia
Baltic Sea
Ural'skiy Khrebet (Ural Mountains)
Urengoy
Surgut
Tobol'sk
Yekaterinburg
Chelyabinsk
Omsk
Novosibirsk
Tomsk
Novokuznetsk
Barnaul
Pavlodar
Astana
Semipalatinsk
Karaganda
Ust'-Kamenogorsk
Alps
Carpathian Mountains
Sea of Azov
Volga
Ural'sk
Aktobe
Atyrau
KAZAKHSTAN
Aral'sk
Aral Sea
Balkhash
Ozero Balkhash
Ozero Zaysan
Altay
Altai Mountains
Tacheng
Black Sea
Caucasus
Caspian Sea
Aktau
UZBEKISTAN
Shymkent
Almaty
Yining
Ürümqi
Turpan
Bursa
Samsun
T'bilisi
GEORGIA
Ankara
TURKEY
İzmir
Sivas
Yerevan
ARMENIA
AZERBAIJAN
Baki
Konya
Kayseri
Erzurum
Antalya
Adana
Malatya
Gaziantep
Garabogazköl Aylagy
Türkmenbaşy
TURKMENISTAN
Aşgabat
Toshkent
Bishkek
KYRGYZSTAN
Tien Shan
XINJIANG UYGUR ZIZHIQU
(SINKIANG)
Andizhan
Kokand
Khujand
Samarkand
TAJIKISTAN
Dushanbe
Aksu
Korla
Kashi
Tarim Pendi
Lop Nur
Lefkosia
CYPRUS
LEBANON
Beirut
SYRIA
Halab
Tabrīz
Ardabīl
Al Mawşil
Arbīl
Kirkūk
Mediterranean Sea
ISRAEL
Tel Aviv-Yafo
Dimashq
Gaza
'Ammān
Jerusalem
JORDAN
IRAQ
Baghdād
Kermānshāh
Tehrān
Mashhad
Gorgān
Qom
Dasht-e Kavīr
Borūjerd
Eşfahān
IRAN
Birjand
Herāt
Hindu Kush
Kābul
AFGHANISTAN
Kandahār
Peshawar
Islamabad
Rawalpindi
Gujranwala
Lahore
Amritsar
Ludhiana
Chandigarh
Faisalabad
Multan
Quetta
PAKISTAN
Hotan
Kunlun Shan
AKSAI CHIN
HIMALAYA
XIZANG ZIZHIQU
(TIBET)
An Najaf
Al Başrah
Ahvāz
Ābādān
Al Kuwayt
KUWAIT
Shīrāz
Būshehr
Kermān
Zāhedān
Bandar-e 'Abbās
An Nafūd
The Gulf
Ad Dammām
Al Manāmah
BAHRAIN
Al Hufūf
QATAR
Ad Dawhah
Dubayy
Abū Zabī
UNITED ARAB EMIRATES
Gulf of Oman
Masqat
Al Madīnah
Ar Riyāḍ
SAUDI ARABIA
Jiddah
Makkah
Red Sea
Nile
Libyan Desert
Tropic of Cancer
Rub' al Khālī
OMAN
'Ibrā'
Şūr
Maşīrah
Pasni
Karachi
Hyderabad
Indus
Thar Desert
Jodhpur
Ganganagar
Delhi
Meerut
New Delhi
Ghaziabad
Faridabad
Jaipur
Agra
Lucknow
Kanpur
Gorakhpur
Kathmandu
NEPAL
Mount Everest
Thimphu
BHUTAN
Darjiling
Xigazê
Lhasa
Beawar
Kota
Gwalior
Allahabad
Varanasi
Patna
Guwahati
Shillong
BANGLADESH
Dhaka
Khulna
Chittagong
Ahmadabad
Vadodara
Indore
Bhopal
Jabalpur
Ranchi
Asansol
Jamshedpur
Calcutta (Kolkata)
Mouths of the Ganges
Surat
Nagpur
Nashik
INDIA
Cuttack
Thane
Mumbai
Ulhasnagar
Aurangabad
Pune
Solapur
Deccan
Hyderabad
Vishakhapatnam
BAY OF BENGAL
Sittwe
Al Hudaydah
Şan'ā'
YEMEN
Şalālah
Ta'izz
Al Mukallā
'Adan
Gulf of Aden
Suquţrā (Yemen)
ARABIAN SEA
Dharwad
Kurnool
Vijayawada
Nellore
Mangalore
Bangalore
Chennai
Mysore
Salem
Calicut
Coimbatore
Tiruchchirappalli
Cochin
Madurai
Jaffna
Trincomalee
Trivandrum
Gulf of Mannar
SRI LANKA
Kandy
Colombo
Sri Jayewardenepura Kotte
Laccadive Islands (India)
Male
MALDIVES
AFRICA
Equator
Lake Victoria
INDIAN OCEAN
Mahé
Seychelles
Coëtivy
British Indian Ocean Territory
Chagos Archipelago
Diego Garcia
Lake Nyasa
Aldabra Islands (Seychelles)
Farquhar Islands (Seychelles)
Njazidja
Comoros
Mayotte
Agalega Islands (Mauritius)
30°
45°
60°
75°
90°
15°

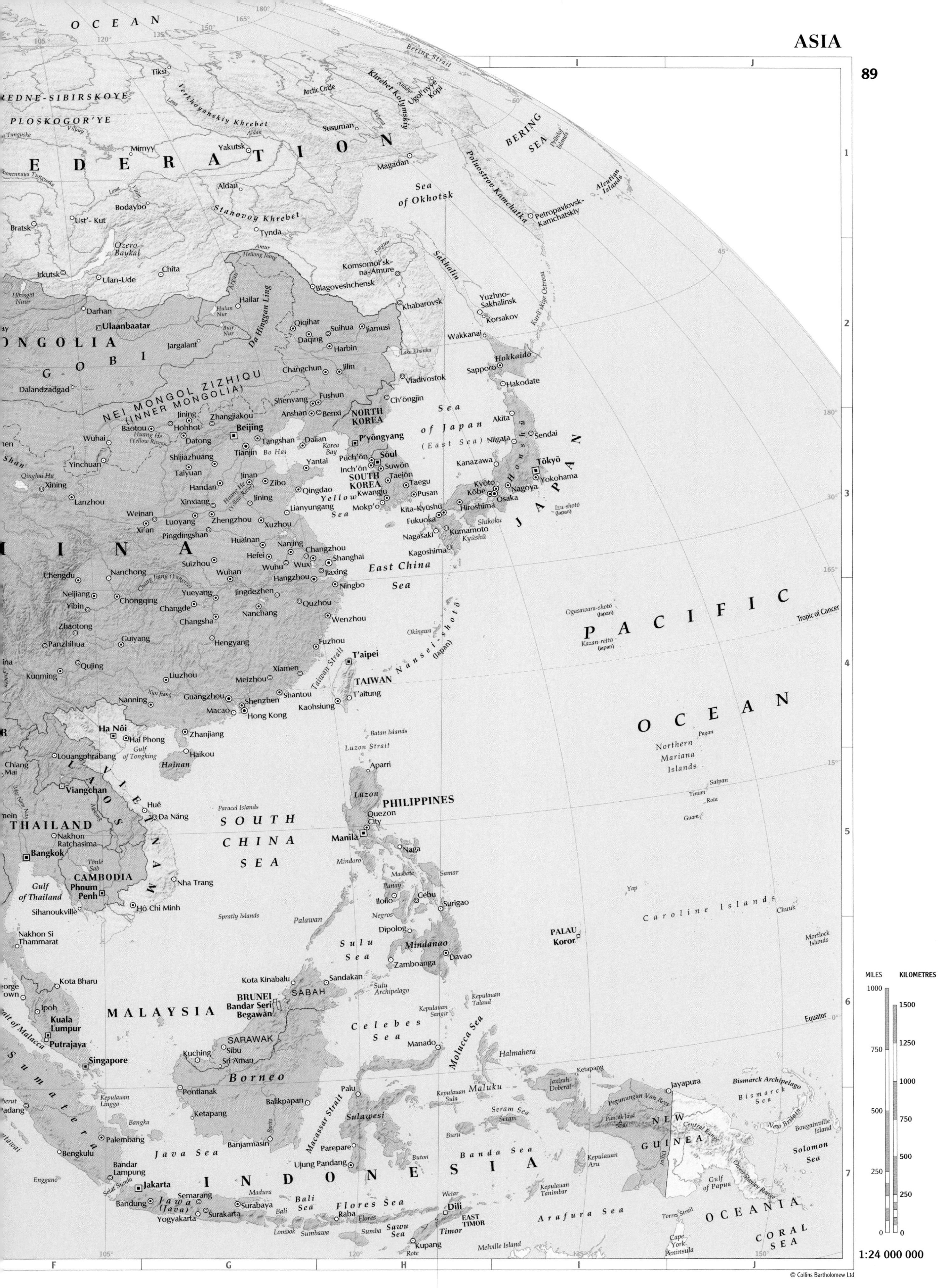
O C E A N
Bering Strait
Tiksi
Verkhoyanskiy Khrebet
Arctic Circle
Khrebet Kolymskiy
Ugol'nyye Kopi
Susuman
Yakutsk
Mirnyy
Magadan
Aldan
Sea of Okhotsk
Bodaybo
Ust'-Kut
Bratsk
Stanovoy Khrebet
Tynda
Ozero Baykal
Irkutsk
Ulan-Ude
Chita
Komsomol'sk-na-Amure
Blagoveshchensk
Khabarovsk
Sakhalin
Yuzhno-Sakhalinsk
Korsakov
BERING SEA
Pribilof Islands
Poluostrov Kamchatka
Petropavlovsk-Kamchatskiy
Aleutian Islands
Kuril'skiye Ostrova
Darhan
Ulaanbaatar
Hailar
Da Hinggan Ling
Qiqihar
Daqing
Suihua
Jiamusi
Harbin
Jargalant
Wakkanai
Hokkaidō
Sapporo
Hakodate
Changchun
Jilin
Vladivostok
Dalandzadgad
NEI MONGOL ZIZHIQU (INNER MONGOLIA)
Shenyang
Fushun
Anshan
Benxi
Ch'ŏngjin
NORTH KOREA
P'yŏngyang
Sea of Japan (East Sea)
Akita
Sendai
Niigata
Jining
Zhangjiakou
Baotou
Hohhot
Beijing
Datong
Tangshan
Tianjin
Dalian
Bo Hai
Korea Bay
Wuhai
Yinchuan
Shijiazhuang
Taiyuan
Yantai
Puch'ŏn
Inch'ŏn
Sŏul
Suwŏn
Taejŏn
SOUTH KOREA
Taegu
Kwangju
Pusan
Mokp'o
Kanazawa
Tōkyō
Yokohama
Kyōto
Kōbe
Ōsaka
Nagoya
Honshū
JAPAN
Hiroshima
Kita-Kyūshū
Fukuoka
Kumamoto
Nagasaki
Kyūshū
Kagoshima
Shikoku
Izu-shotō (Japan)
Xining
Lanzhou
Handan
Jinan
Zibo
Qingdao
Xinxiang
Jining
Yellow Sea
Lianyungang
Weinan
Xi'an
Luoyang
Zhengzhou
Xuzhou
Pingdingshan
Huainan
Nanjing
Changzhou
Shanghai
Hefei
Wuhu
Wuxi
Jiaxing
Hangzhou
Ningbo
East China Sea
CHINA
Suizhou
Wuhan
Chengdu
Nanchong
Neijiang
Yibin
Chongqing
Yueyang
Jingdezhen
Changde
Nanchang
Quzhou
Wenzhou
Zhaotong
Changsha
Panzhihua
Guiyang
Hengyang
Fuzhou
Okinawa
Nansei-shotō (Japan)
Ogasawara-shotō (Japan)
Kazan-rettō (Japan)
PACIFIC OCEAN
Tropic of Cancer
Qujing
Kunming
Liuzhou
Meizhou
Xiamen
Taiwan Strait
T'aipei
TAIWAN
T'aitung
Kaohsiung
Shantou
Nanning
Guangzhou
Shenzhen
Macao
Hong Kong
Ha Nôi
Hai Phong
Zhanjiang
Gulf of Tongking
Haikou
Hainan
Batan Islands
Luzon Strait
Aparri
Louangphrabang
LAOS
VIETNAM
Viangchan
Huê
Da Năng
Paracel Islands
SOUTH CHINA SEA
Luzon
PHILIPPINES
Quezon City
Manila
Naga
Mindoro
Northern Mariana Islands
Pagan
Saipan
Tinian
Rota
Guam
THAILAND
Nakhon Ratchasima
Bangkok
Tônlé Sab
CAMBODIA
Phnum Penh
Gulf of Thailand
Nha Trang
Hô Chi Minh
Sihanoukville
Spratly Islands
Masbate
Samar
Panay
Iloilo
Cebu
Negros
Surigao
Palawan
Dipolog
Mindanao
Davao
Zamboanga
Sulu Sea
Yap
Caroline Islands
Chuuk
PALAU
Koror
Mortlock Islands
Nakhon Si Thammarat
Kota Bharu
Kota Kinabalu
Sandakan
SABAH
Sulu Archipelago
BRUNEI
Bandar Seri Begawan
MALAYSIA
Ipoh
Kuala Lumpur
Putrajaya
Singapore
Kepulauan Talaud
Kepulauan Sangir
Celebes Sea
Molucca Sea
Manado
Equator
SARAWAK
Kuching
Sibu
Sri Aman
Borneo
Halmahera
Ketapang
Jazirah Doberai
Jayapura
Bismarck Archipelago
Bismarck Sea
New Britain
Bougainville Island
Sumatera
Pontianak
Balikpapan
Palu
Kepulauan Sula
Maluku
Seram Sea
Seram
Pegunungan Van Rees
Puncak Jaya
NEW GUINEA
Central Range
Kepulauan Lingga
Bangka
Ketapang
Macassar Strait
Sulawesi
Buru
Digul
Solomon Sea
Palembang
Bengkulu
Banjarmasin
Parepare
Java Sea
Ujung Pandang
Buton
Banda Sea
Kepulauan Aru
Gulf of Papua
Owen Stanley Range
Bandar Lampung
INDONESIA
Enggano
Selat Sunda
Jakarta
Madura
Semarang
Bandung
Jawa (Java)
Surabaya
Surakarta
Yogyakarta
Bali Sea
Bali
Lombok
Sumbawa
Flores Sea
Flores
Raba
Sumba
Sawu Sea
Wetar
Dili
EAST TIMOR
Timor
Kupang
Rote
Kepulauan Tanimbar
Arafura Sea
Melville Island
Torres Strait
Cape York Peninsula
OCEANIA
CORAL SEA
MILES
KILOMETRES
1000
750
500
250
0
1500
1250
1000
750
500
250
0
1:24 000 000
F
G
H
I
J
1
2
3
4
5
6
7

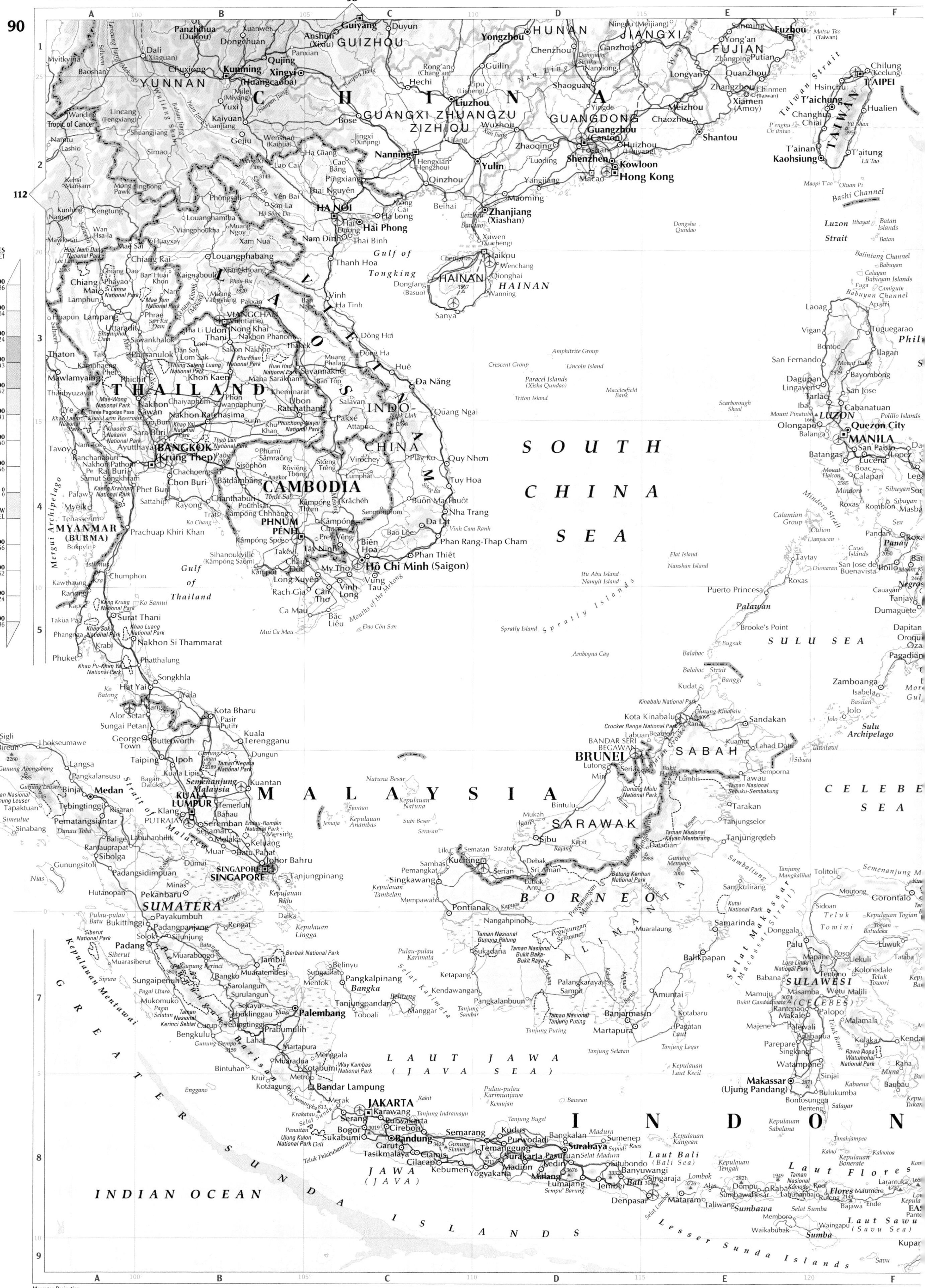
98
112
METRES
FEET
6000
19686
5000
16404
4000
13124
3000
9843
2000
6562
1000
3281
500
1640
200
656
0
0
LAND BELOW SEA LEVEL
200
656
2000
6562
4000
13124
6000
19686
C H I N A
YUNNAN
GUIZHOU
HUNAN
JIANGXI
FUJIAN
GUANGXI ZHUANGZU ZIZHIQU
GUANGDONG
HAINAN
TAIWAN
T'AIPEI
Kunming (Huangcaoba)
Guiyang
Nanning
Guangzhou (Canton)
Shenzhen
Kowloon
Hong Kong
Macao
Kaohsiung
Fuzhou
Xiamen (Amoy)
Haikou
Zhanjiang (Xiashan)
Tropic of Cancer
MYANMAR (BURMA)
LAOS
VIETNAM
THAILAND
CAMBODIA
INDO-CHINA
HA NOI
Hai Phong
VIANGCHAN (Vientiane)
BANGKOK (Krung Thep)
PHNUM PÉNH
Hô Chi Minh (Saigon)
Đa Năng
Gulf of Tongking
Gulf of Thailand
Mergui Archipelago
SOUTH CHINA SEA
Paracel Islands (Xisha Qundao)
Spratly Islands
LUZON
MANILA
Quezon City
Luzon Strait
Bashi Channel
Palawan
SULU SEA
Sulu Archipelago
CELEBES SEA
MALAYSIA
KUALA LUMPUR
PUTRAJAYA
SINGAPORE
Strait of Malacca
Medan
Banda Aceh
SUMATERA
Palembang
Bandar Lampung
Padang
BRUNEI
BANDAR SERI BEGAWAN
SABAH
SARAWAK
Kota Kinabalu
Kuching
BORNEO
KALIMANTAN
Pontianak
Banjarmasin
Balikpapan
Samarinda
Selat Makassar (Macassar Strait)
SULAWESI (CELEBES)
Makassar (Ujung Pandang)
LAUT JAWA (JAVA SEA)
JAKARTA
Bandung
Semarang
Surabaya
JAWA (JAVA)
Bali
Denpasar
Lombok
Mataram
Sumbawa
Flores
Sumba
Laut Bali (Bali Sea)
Laut Flores
Laut Sawu (Savu Sea)
Lesser Sunda Islands
GREATER SUNDA ISLANDS
Kepulauan Mentawai
INDIAN OCEAN
I N D O N
A B C D E F
100 105 110 115 120
1 2 3 4 5 6 7 8 9

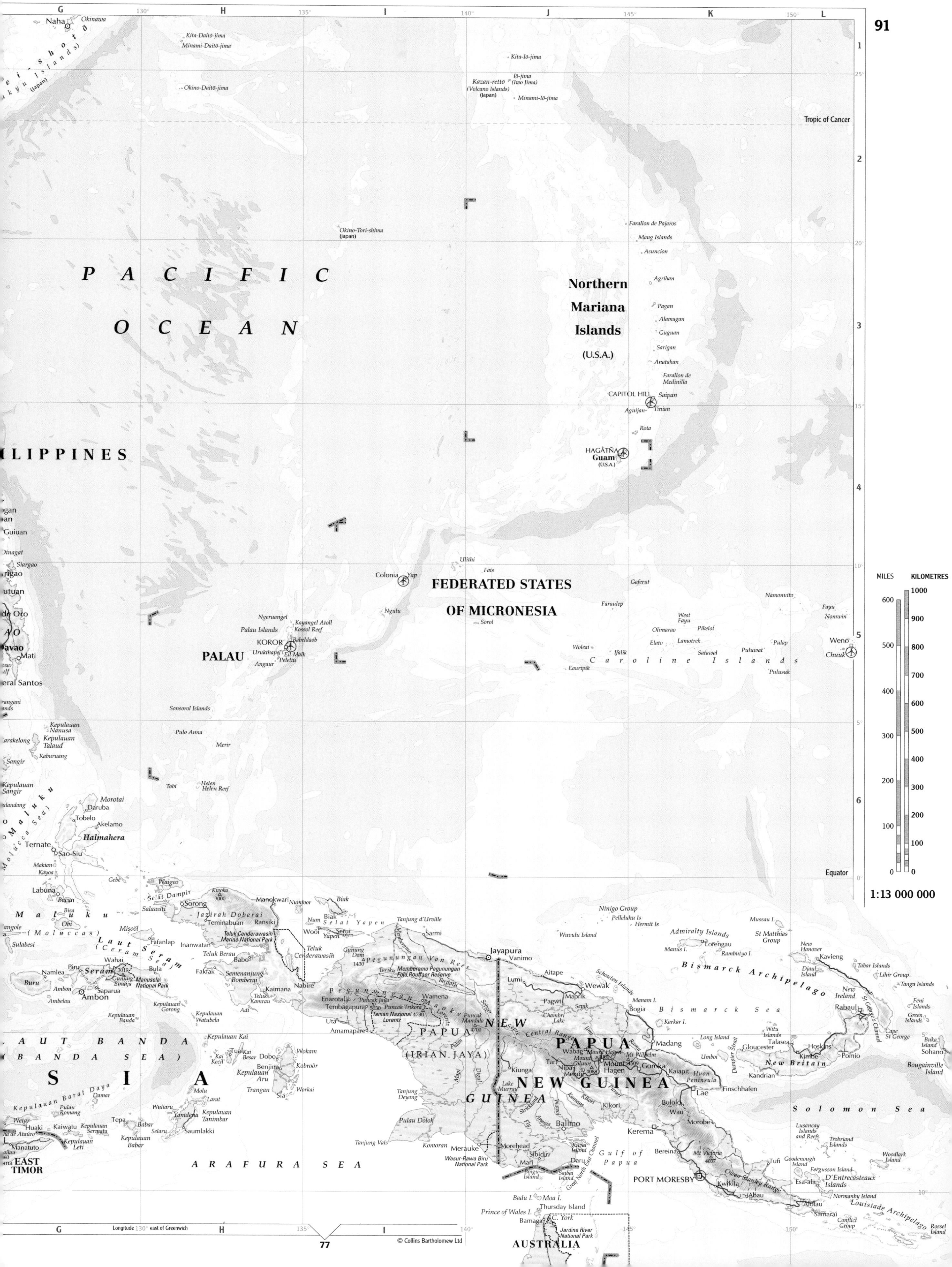
Naha
Okinawa
Kita-Daitō-jima
Minami-Daitō-jima
Oki-Daitō-jima
Kita-Iō-jima
Kazan-rettō (Volcano Islands) (Japan)
Iō-jima (Iwo Jima)
Minami-Iō-jima
Tropic of Cancer
Okino-Tori-shima (Japan)
Farallon de Pajaros
Maug Islands
Asuncion
Agrihan
Pagan
Alamagan
Guguan
Sarigan
Anatahan
Farallon de Medinilla
P A C I F I C
O C E A N
Northern Mariana Islands (U.S.A.)
CAPITOL HILL
Saipan
Tinian
Aguijan
Rota
HAGÅTÑA
Guam (U.S.A.)
PHILIPPINES
Siargao
Davao
Mati
Ulithi
Fais
Colonia
Yap
Ngulu
FEDERATED STATES OF MICRONESIA
Sorol
Gaferut
Faraulep
Namonuito
West Fayu
Pikelot
Olimarao
Elato
Lamotrek
Satawal
Puluwat
Pulap
Woleai
Ifalik
Eauripik
Caroline Islands
Pulusuk
Fayu
Nomwin
Weno
Chuuk
Ngeruangel
Kayangel Atoll
Kossol Reef
Palau Islands
KOROR
Babeldaob
Urukthapel
Eil Malk
Peleliu
Angaur
PALAU
Sonsorol Islands
Pulo Anna
Merir
Tobi
Helen
Helen Reef
Kepulauan Nanusa
Kepulauan Talaud
Kaburuang
Sangir
Kepulauan Sangir
Morotai
Daruba
Tobelo
Akelamo
Halmahera
Ternate
Sao-Siu
Makian
Kayoa
Molucca Sea
Equator
MILES
KILOMETRES
1:13 000 000
Labuha
Bacan
Obi
Gebe
Waigeo
Kwoka 3000
Selat Dampir
Sorong
Salawati
Jazirah Doberai
Teminabuan
Manokwari
Numfoor
Biak
Ransiki
Teluk Cenderawasih Marine National Park
Selat Yapen
Yapen
Serui
Woo
Tanjung d'Urville
Sarmi
Misoöl
Fafanlap
Inanwatan
Teluk Berau
Babo
Laut Seram (Ceram Sea)
Teluk Cenderawasih
Gunung Dom 1430
Pegunungan Van Rees
Memberamo Pegunungan Foja Rouffaer Reserve
Jayapura
Vanimo
Sulabesi
Namlea
Buru
Seram
Wahai
Bula
Gunung Binaiya 3019
Manusela National Park
Saparua
Ambon
Ambelau
Fakfak
Semenanjung Bomberai
Kaimana
Nabire
Enarotali
Puncak Jaya
Tembagapura
Puncak Trikora 4730
Taman Nasional Lorentz
Wamena
Puncak Mandala 4700
PAPUA (IRIAN JAYA)
Uta
Amamapare
Kepulauan Gorong
Kepulauan Watubela
Teluk Kamrau
Adi
Kepulauan Banda
Laut Banda (Banda Sea)
Kepulauan Kai
Tual
Kai Besar
Kai Kecil
Dobo
Wokam
Kobroör
Benjina
Kepulauan Aru
Trangan
Sia
Workai
ASIA
Kepulauan Barat Daya
Damar
Molu
Larat
Yamdena
Kepulauan Tanimbar
Wuliaru
Saumlakki
Selaru
Tepa
Babar
Kepulauan Babar
Wetar
Huaki
Kaiwatu
Kepulauan Sermata
Kepulauan Leti
Pulau Romang
Manatuto
EAST TIMOR
A R A F U R A S E A
Tanjung Vals
Pulau Dolok
Tanjung Deyong
Komoran
Merauke
Wasur-Rawa Biru National Park
Morehead
Sibidiri
Mari
Boigu Island
Saibai Island
Daru
Kiwai Island
Great North East Channel
Gulf of Papua
NEW GUINEA
PAPUA NEW GUINEA
Lake Murray
Kiunga
Tari
Mendi
Mount Hagen
Wabag
Mount Giluwe 4368
Mt Wilhelm 4509
Goroka
Lumi
Aitape
Wewak
Maprik
Pagwi
Chambri Lake
Sepik
Central Range
Ninigo Group
Pelleluhu Is
Hermit Is
Wuvulu Island
Admiralty Islands
Manus I.
Lorengau
Rambutyo I.
Mussau I.
St Matthias Group
New Hanover
Kavieng
Tabar Islands
Lihir Group
Tanga Islands
Djaul Island
Bismarck Archipelago
Schouten Islands
Manam I.
Bogia
Bismarck Sea
Karkar I.
Madang
Kaiapit
Huon Peninsula
Finschhafen
Lae
Bulolo
Wau
Morobe
Kerema
Kikori
Balimo
Bereina
Mt Victoria 4073
Owen Stanley Range
PORT MORESBY
Kwikila
Abau
Tufi
Long Island
Umboi
Dampier Strait
Gloucester
Talasea
Witu Islands
Kimbe
Hoskins
Pomio
Kandrian
New Britain
Rabaul
New Ireland
St George's Channel
Cape St George
Feni Islands
Green Islands
Buka Island
Sohano
Bougainville Island
Solomon Sea
Lusancay Islands and Reefs
Trobriand Islands
Woodlark Island
Goodenough Island
Fergusson Island
D'Entrecasteaux Islands
Esa-ala
Normanby Island
Alotau
Samarai
Louisiade Archipelago
Conflict Group
Rossel Island
Badu I.
Moa I.
Thursday Island
Prince of Wales I.
Bamaga
Cape York
Jardine River National Park
AUSTRALIA
Longitude 130° east of Greenwich
77
© Collins Bartholomew Ltd

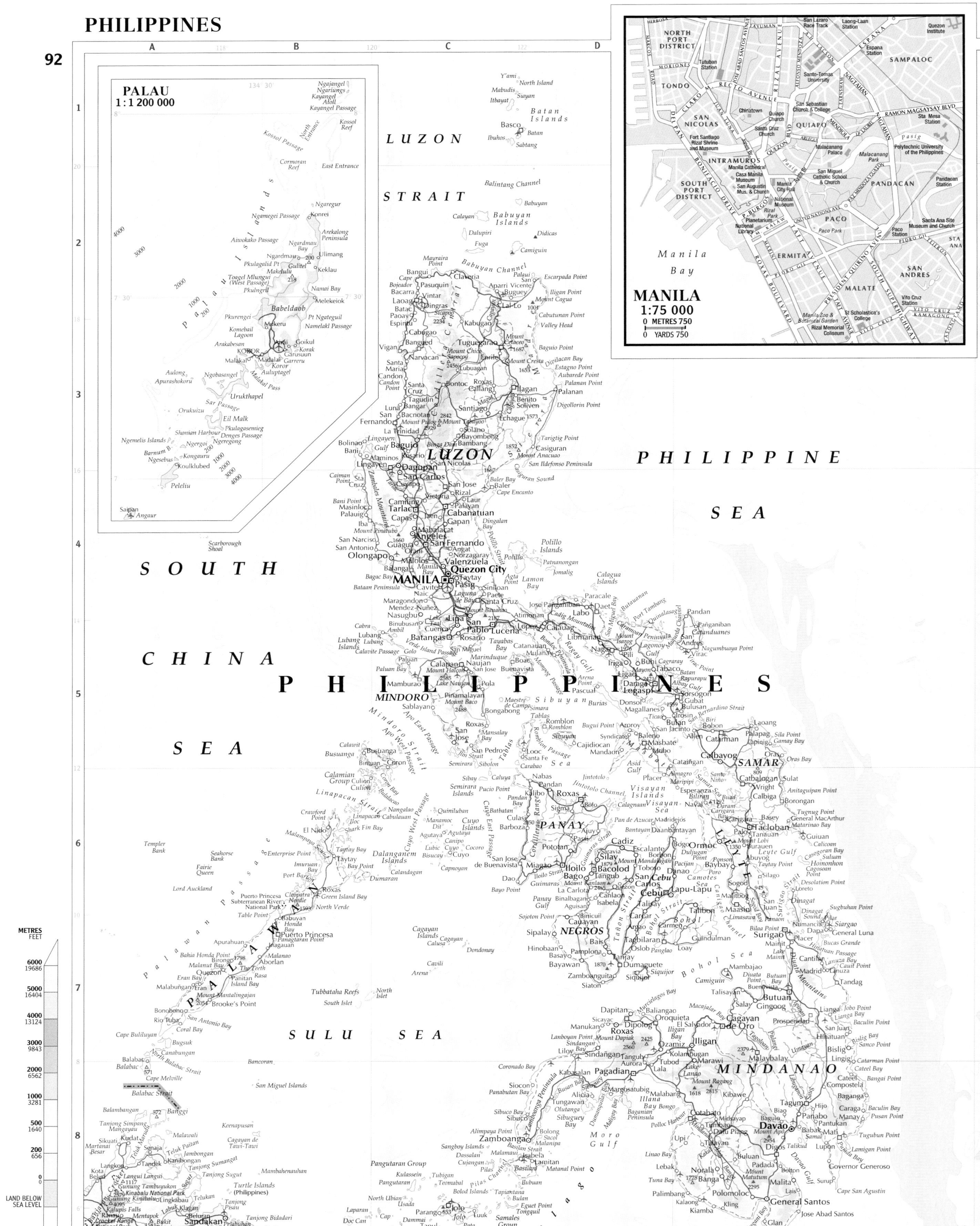
PALAU
1 : 1 200 000
Babeldaob
Koror
Peleliu
Angaur
Palau Islands
MANILA
1:75 000
METRES 750
YARDS 750
NORTH PORT DISTRICT
TONDO
SAN NICOLAS
INTRAMUROS
SOUTH PORT DISTRICT
QUIAPO
SAMPALOC
PANDACAN
PACO
ERMITA
MALATE
SAN ANDRES
Manila Bay
LUZON STRAIT
Babuyan Islands
Batan Islands
Babuyan Channel
LUZON
PHILIPPINE SEA
SOUTH CHINA SEA
PHILIPPINES
MANILA
Quezon City
Baguio
Dagupan
San Fernando
Angeles
Olongapo
Batangas
Lucena
Legaspi
Naga
Sibuyan Sea
MINDORO
PANAY
NEGROS
Cebu
Iloilo
Bacolod
Tacloban
SAMAR
LEYTE
Bohol
Visayan Sea
Bohol Sea
Surigao
Butuan
Cagayan de Oro
Iligan
MINDANAO
Davao
Zamboanga
Pagadian
Cotabato
General Santos
Moro Gulf
Mindoro Strait
Palawan Passage
PALAWAN
Puerto Princesa
SULU SEA
Sulu Archipelago
Jolo
CELEBES SEA
SABAH
MALAYSIA
Sandakan
INDONESIA
METRES
FEET
6000
19686
5000
16404
4000
13124
3000
9843
2000
6562
1000
3281
500
1640
200
656
0
0
LAND BELOW SEA LEVEL
200
656
2000
6562
4000
13124
6000
19686
Longitude 124 east of Greenwich
Mercator Projection

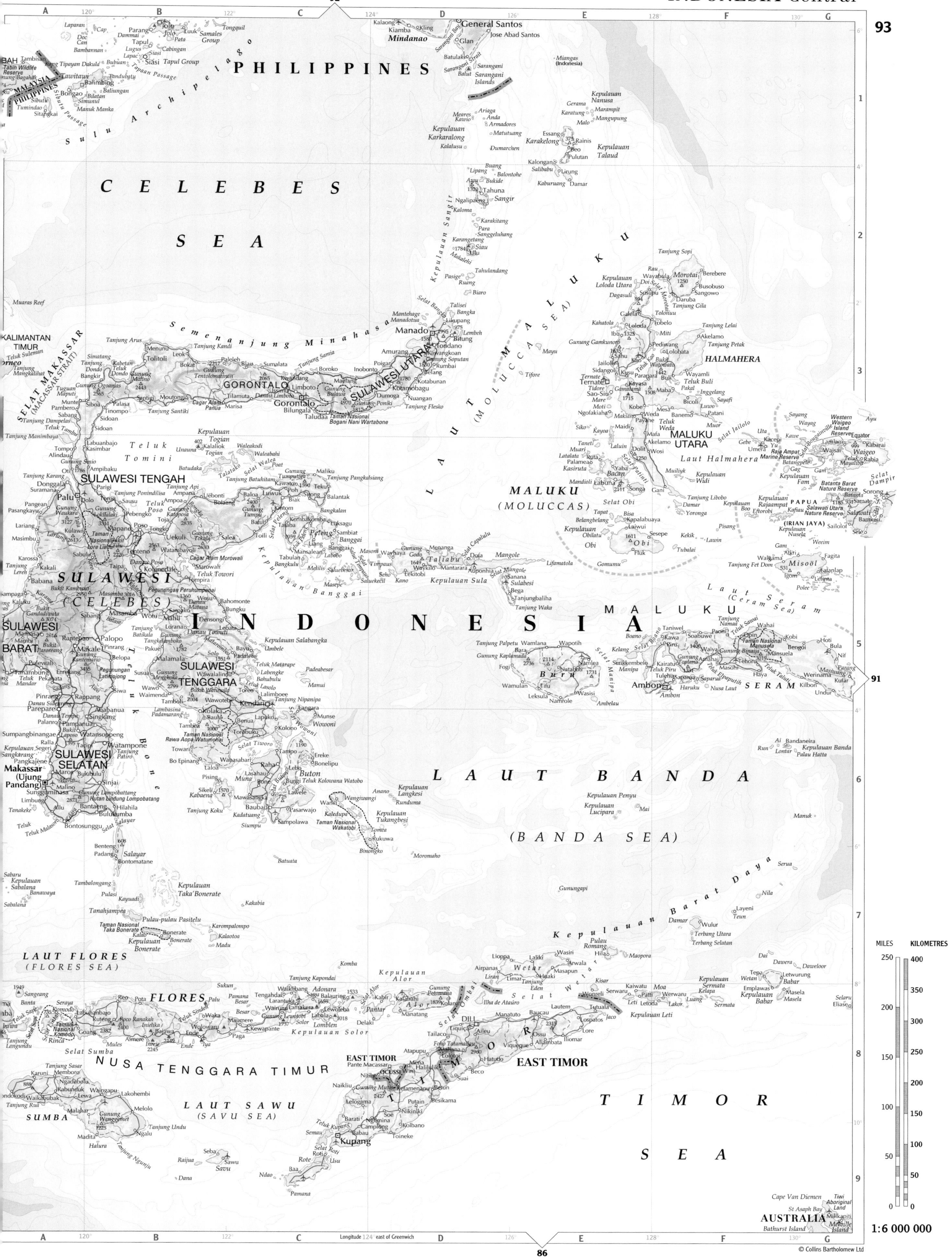
PHILIPPINES
CELEBES SEA
Sulu Archipelago
Mindanao
General Santos
Kepulauan Sangir
Kepulauan Talaud
Semenanjung Minahasa
Manado
GORONTALO
Gorontalo
SULAWESI UTARA
LAUT MALUKU (MOLUCCA SEA)
Morotai
HALMAHERA
MALUKU UTARA
Ternate
Laut Halmahera
MALUKU (MOLUCCAS)
Obi
Waigeo
Misoöl
PAPUA (IRIAN JAYA)
KALIMANTAN TIMUR
SELAT MAKASSAR (MAKASSAR STRAIT)
Teluk Tomini
SULAWESI TENGAH
Palu
Poso
Kepulauan Banggai
Kepulauan Sula
SULAWESI (CELEBES)
INDONESIA
MALUKU
Laut Seram (Ceram Sea)
Buru
SERAM
Ambon
SULAWESI BARAT
SULAWESI TENGGARA
Kendari
Teluk Bone
SULAWESI SELATAN
Makassar (Ujung Pandang)
Buton
Kepulauan Tukangbesi
LAUT BANDA (BANDA SEA)
Kepulauan Banda
Salayar
LAUT FLORES (FLORES SEA)
Kepulauan Barat Daya
Wetar
Alor
FLORES
NUSA TENGGARA TIMUR
Kepulauan Solor
DILI
EAST TIMOR
TIMOR
Kupang
LAUT SAWU (SAVU SEA)
SUMBA
Sawu
Rote
TIMOR SEA
AUSTRALIA
Bathurst Island
Melville Island
MILES
KILOMETRES
1:6 000 000

97
ANDAMAN SEA
SOUTH
INDIAN OCEAN
STRAIT OF MALACCA
THAILAND
MALAYSIA
KEDAH
PERAK
KELANTAN
TERENGGANU
PAHANG
SELANGOR
KUALA LUMPUR
PUTRAJAYA
NEGERI SEMBILAN
MELAKA
JOHOR
SINGAPORE
ACEH
SUMATERA UTARA
SUMATERA BARAT
RIAU
KEPULAUAN RIAU
JAMBI
BENGKULU
SUMATERA SELATAN
LAMPUNG
BANTEN
SUMATERA
PEGUNUNGAN BARISAN
INDO
Medan
Banda Aceh
Padang
Pekanbaru
Jambi
Palembang
Bandar Lampung
Pangkalpinang
Kuantan
Kota Bharu
Kuala Terengganu
Johor Bahru
Pinang
Ipoh
Simeulue
Nias
Kepulauan Mentawai
Selat Mentawai
Siberut
Enggano
Bangka
Kepulauan Lingga
Equator
Selat Sunda
Strait of Singapore
SINGAPORE
1:300 000
MALAYSIA
Johor Bahru
WOODLANDS
SEMBAWANG
YISHUN
MANDAI
BUKIT PANJANG
BUKIT BATOK
BUKIT TIMAH
ANG MO KIO
HOUGANG
PUNGGOL
SELETAR
TAMPINES
BEDOK
CHANGI
JURONG
CLEMENTI
QUEENSTOWN
TANGLIN
SINGAPORE
TELOK BLANGAH
TOA PAYOH
GEYLANG
KALLANG
KATONG
SIGLAP
TUAS
Jurong Island
Sentosa
Pulau Ubin
Selat Johor
Strait of Singapore
Selat Pandan
METRES
FEET
6000 19686
5000 16404
4000 13124
3000 9843
2000 6562
1000 3281
500 1640
200 656
0 0
LAND BELOW SEA LEVEL
200 656
2000 6562
4000 13124
6000 19686
Longitude 104 east of Greenwich
Mercator Projection
Christmas Island (Australia)

SULU SEA
PHILIPPINES
CHINA SEA
SABAH
BRUNEI
BANDAR SERI BEGAWAN
LABUAN
Kota Kinabalu
Sandakan
Tawau
SARAWAK
Kuching
Sibu
Bintulu
Miri
MALAYSIA
KALIMANTAN TIMUR
KALIMANTAN BARAT
KALIMANTAN TENGAH
KALIMANTAN SELATAN
BORNEO
KALIMANTAN
Pontianak
Samarinda
Balikpapan
Banjarmasin
Palangkaraya
Tarakan
Equator
CELEBES SEA
SELAT MAKASSAR (MACASSAR STRAIT)
SULAWESI (CELEBES)
SULAWESI BARAT
SULAWESI TENGAH
SULAWESI SELATAN
Makassar (Ujung Pandang)
Palu
LAUT JAWA (JAVA SEA)
JAWA (JAVA)
JAWA TENGAH
JAWA TIMUR
YOGYAKARTA
Semarang
Surabaya
Madura
BALI
Denpasar
Lombok
Mataram
SUMBAWA
NUSA TENGGARA BARAT
LAUT BALI (BALI SEA)
LAUT FLORES (FLORES SEA)
Sumba
Belitung
Natuna Besar
92
93
MILES
KILOMETRES

1:6 000 000

© Collins Bartholomew Ltd

METRES
FEET
6000
19686
5000
16404
4000
13124
3000
9843
2000
6562
1000
3281
500
1640
200
656
0
0
LAND BELOW SEA LEVEL
200
656
2000
6562
4000
13124
6000
19686
109
108
111
117
115
CHINA
MYANMAR (BURMA)
LAOS
VIETNAM
THAILAND
INDIA
BANGLADESH
YUNNAN
GUIZHOU
GUANGXI ZHUANGZU ZIZHIQU
SICHUAN
HUNAN
HAINAN
KACHIN
SAGAING
SHAN
MANDALAY
MAGWE
PEGU
YANGON
IRRAWADDY
ARAKAN
CHIN
KAYAH
KAYIN
MON
MANIPUR
NAGALAND
ASSAM
ARUNACHAL PRADESH
MEGHALAYA
TRIPURA
MIZORAM
GULF OF TONGKING
BAY OF BENGAL
Kunming
Guiyang
Nanning
Ha Noi
Hai Phong
Mandalay
Yangon (Rangoon)
Naypyidaw
Vientiane
Chiang Mai
Luang Phrabang
Chittagong
Haikou
Zhanjiang
Liuzhou
Guilin
Yulin
Dali
Panzhihua
Tropic of Cancer
Mercator Projection

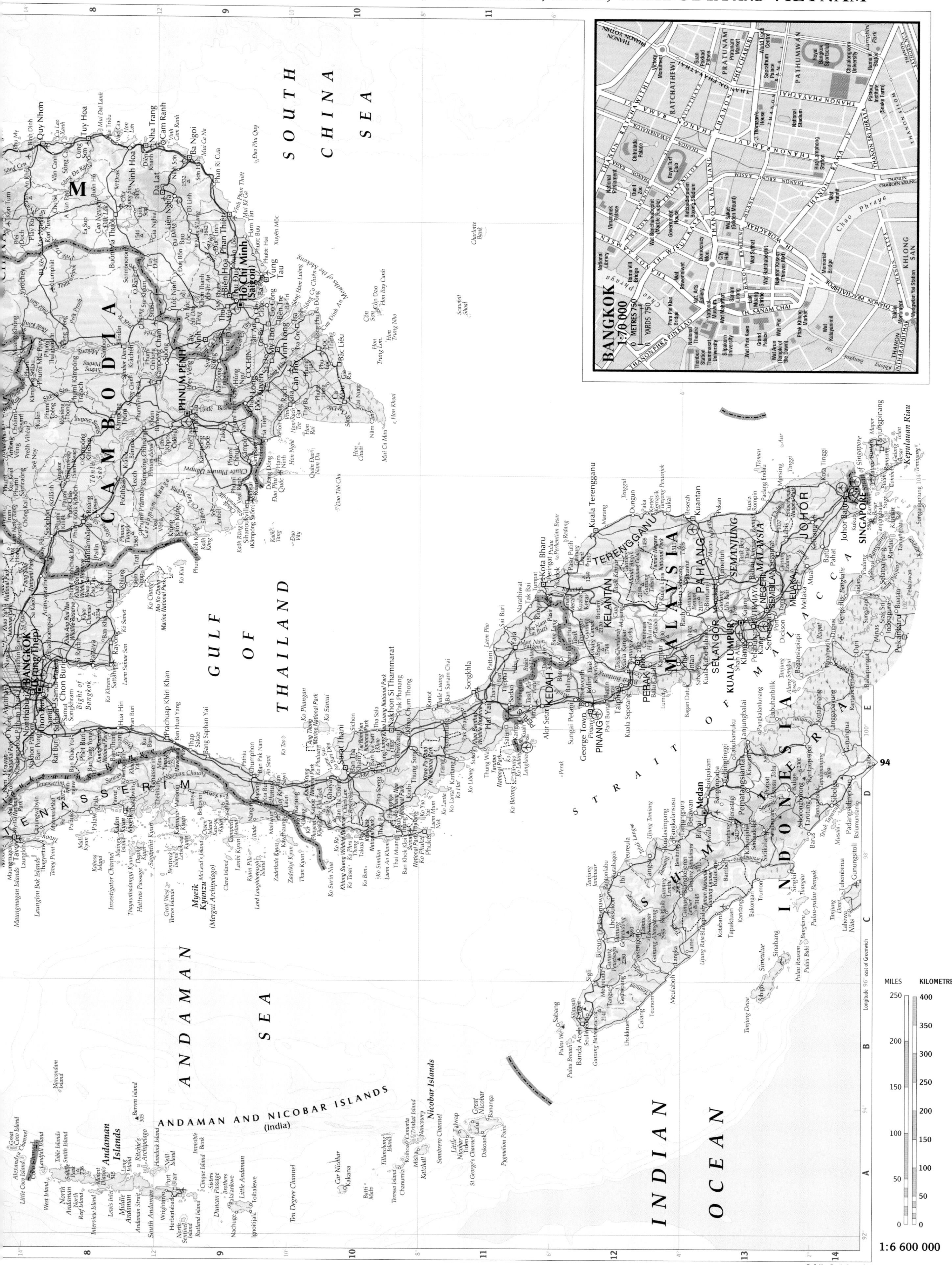
SOUTH CHINA SEA
GULF OF THAILAND
ANDAMAN SEA
INDIAN OCEAN
STRAIT OF MALACCA
ANDAMAN AND NICOBAR ISLANDS
(India)
CAMBODIA
MALAYSIA
INDONESIA
SUMATERA
BANGKOK
PHNUM PENH
KUALA LUMPUR
SINGAPORE
Hô Chi Minh (Saigon)
Medan
George Town
BANGKOK
1:70 000
MILES
KILOMETRES
1:6 600 000

© Collins Bartholomew Ltd

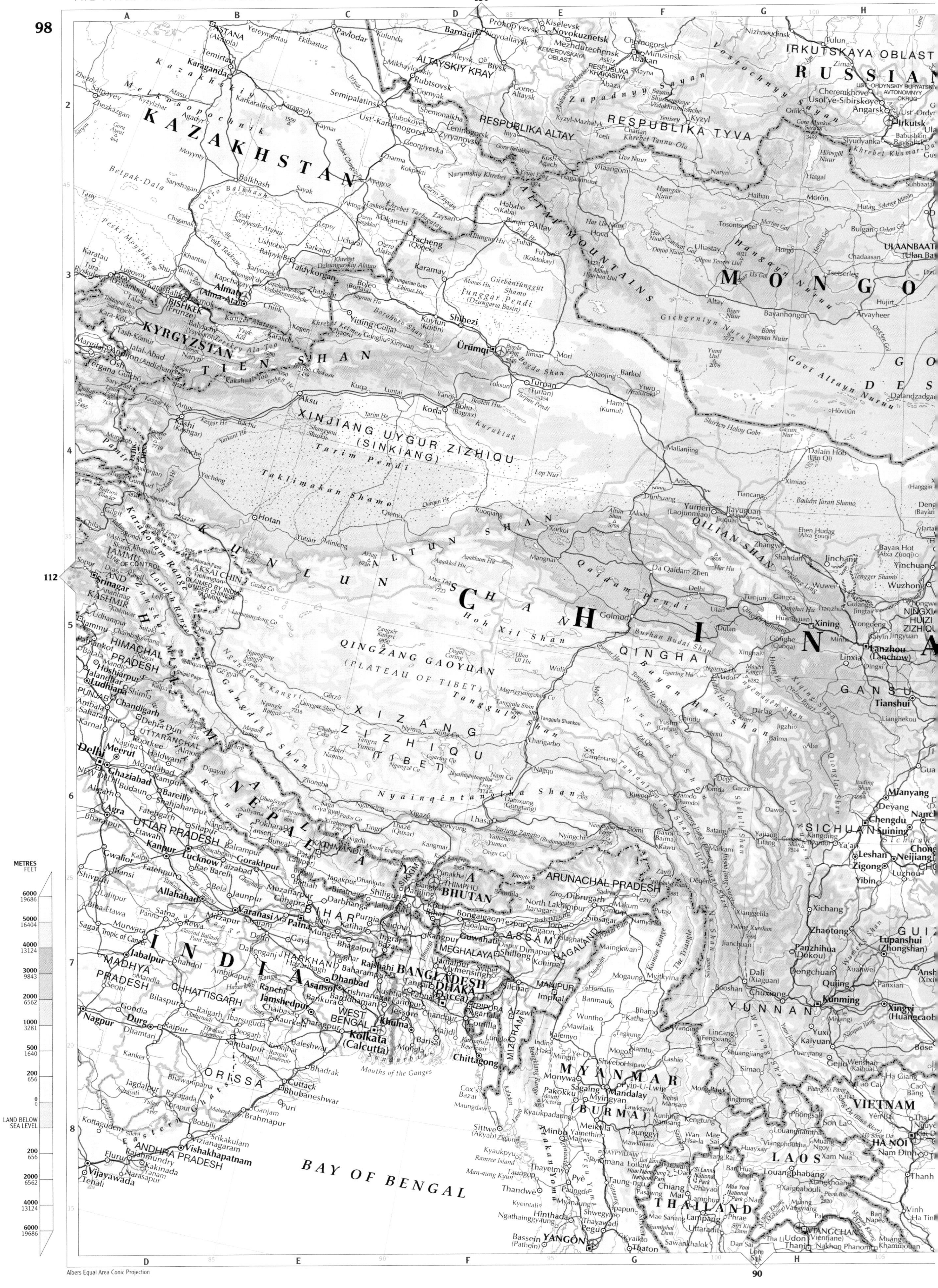
KAZAKHSTAN
KYRGYZSTAN
TIEN SHAN
RUSSIA
MONGOLIA
CHINA
XINJIANG UYGUR ZIZHIQU (SINKIANG)
Tarim Pendi
Taklimakan Shamo
KUNLUN SHAN
ALTUN SHAN
QILIAN SHAN
QINGHAI
QINGZANG GAOYUAN (PLATEAU OF TIBET)
XIZANG ZIZHIQU (TIBET)
GANSU
SICHUAN
YUNNAN
ALTAI MOUNTAINS
RESPUBLIKA ALTAY
RESPUBLIKA TYVA
ALTAYSKIY KRAY
IRKUTSKAYA OBLAST
INDIA
NEPAL
BHUTAN
BANGLADESH
MYANMAR (BURMA)
LAOS
VIETNAM
THAILAND
JAMMU AND KASHMIR
HIMACHAL PRADESH
UTTARANCHAL
UTTAR PRADESH
BIHAR
JHARKHAND
WEST BENGAL
ORISSA
CHHATTISGARH
MADHYA PRADESH
ANDHRA PRADESH
ARUNACHAL PRADESH
ASSAM
MEGHALAYA
NAGALAND
MANIPUR
TRIPURA
MIZORAM
SIKKIM
PUNJAB
BAY OF BENGAL
Mouths of the Ganges
Tropic of Cancer
Astana (Akmola)
Almaty (Alma-Ata)
Bishkek (Frunze)
Ürümqi
Delhi
New Delhi
Kathmandu
Thimphu
Dhaka (Dacca)
Kolkata (Calcutta)
Lhasa
Xining
Lanzhou (Lanchow)
Chengdu
Kunming
Mandalay
Yangon
Naypyidaw
Vientiane
Ha Nôi
Irkutsk
Barnaul
Novosibirsk
Ulaanbaatar (Ulan Bator)
METRES
FEET
6000 19686
5000 16404
4000 13124
3000 9843
2000 6562
1000 3281
500 1640
200 656
0 0
LAND BELOW SEA LEVEL
200 656
2000 6562
4000 13124
6000 19686

131

SEA OF OKHOTSK
(OKHOTSKOYE MORE)
SEA OF JAPAN
(EAST SEA)
JAPAN
NORTH KOREA
SOUTH KOREA
Bo Hai
Yellow Sea
(Huang Hai)
EAST CHINA SEA
(DONG HAI)
PACIFIC OCEAN
SOUTH CHINA SEA
TAIWAN
PHILIPPINES
HEILONGJIANG
JILIN
LIAONING
NEI MONGOL ZIZHIQU
(INNER MONGOLIA)
HEBEI
SHANXI
SHANDONG
HENAN
JIANGSU
ANHUI
HUBEI
ZHEJIANG
JIANGXI
HUNAN
FUJIAN
GUANGDONG
HAINAN
AMURSKAYA OBLAST'
KHABAROVSKIY KRAY
PRIMORSKIY KRAY
SAKHALINSKAYA OBLAST'
CHITINSKAYA OBLAST'
BEIJING
(Peking)
Shanghai
Hong Kong
Sapporo
TŌKYŌ
Yokohama
Nagoya
Ōsaka
Kyōto
Kōbe
Hiroshima
Fukuoka
SŎUL
(Seoul)
P'YŎNGYANG
Pusan
(Busan)
Vladivostok
Khabarovsk
Harbin
Changchun
Shenyang
Dalian
(Lüda)
Tianjin
(Tientsin)
Qingdao
(Tsingtao)
Nanjing
Hangzhou
Wuhan
Fuzhou
Xiamen
(Amoy)
Guangzhou (Canton)
T'AIPEI
Kaohsiung
Tropic of Cancer
Luzon Strait
Bashi Channel
Taiwan Strait
Korea Strait
Nansei-shotō
(Ryukyu Islands)
(Japan)
Kuril'skiye Ostrova
(Kuril Islands)
ADMINISTERED BY RUSSIAN FEDERATION, CLAIMED BY JAPAN
Tatarskiy Proliv
La Pérouse Strait
LUZON

MILES | KILOMETRES

1:13 000 000

© Collins Bartholomew Ltd

91

RUSSIAN FEDERATION
CHINA
SAKHALIN
SAKHALINSKAYA OBLAST'
KHABAROVSKIY KRAY
AMURSKAYA OBLAST'
YEVREYSKAYA AVTONOMNAYA OBLAST'
PRIMORSKIY KRAY
CHITINSKAYA OBLAST'
HEILONGJIANG
JILIN
NEI MONGOL ZIZHIQU (INNER MONGOLIA)
DONGBEI (MANCHURIA)
HOKKAIDŌ
Tatarskiy Proliv
La Pérouse Strait
Khabarovsk
Komsomol'sk-na-Amure
Blagoveshchensk
Yuzhno-Sakhalinsk
Vladivostok
Harbin
Changchun
Qiqihar
Jiamusi
Daqing
Mudanjiang
Hegang
Sapporo
Otaru
Ussuriysk
Heihe
Jixi
Yichun
Jilin
Hulun Buir (Hailar)
Ulanhot
Tongliao
Baicheng
Xiao Hinggan Ling

131

METRES
FEET

6000
19686
5000
16404
4000
13124
3000
9843
2000
6562
1000
3281
500
1640
200
656
0
0
LAND BELOW
SEA LEVEL
200
656
2000
6562
4000
13124
6000
19686

Conic Equidistant Projection

107

MILES KILOMETRES

250 200 150 100 50 0

400 350 300 250 200 150 100 50 0

1:6 000 000

109

© Collins Bartholomew Ltd

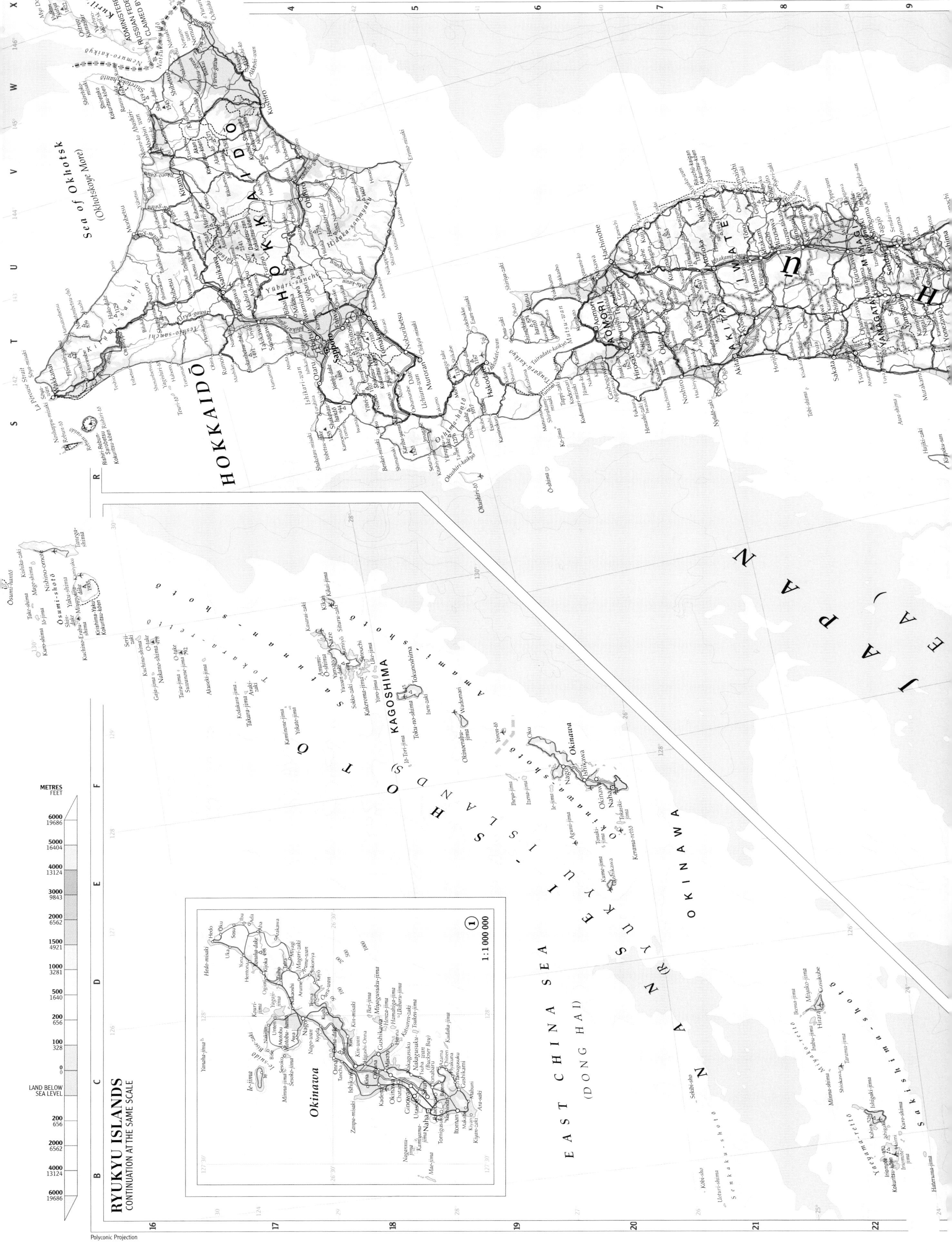
HOKKAIDŌ
Sea of Okhotsk
(Okhotskoye More)
Kuril'skiye Ostrova
(Kuril Islands)
ADMINISTERED BY RUSSIAN FEDERATION, CLAIMED BY JAPAN
La Pérouse Strait
Nemuro-kaikyō
Tsugaru-kaikyō
JAPAN
SEA OF JAPAN (EAST SEA)
RYUKYU ISLANDS
CONTINUATION AT THE SAME SCALE
1:1 000 000
Okinawa
OKINAWA
KAGOSHIMA
EAST CHINA SEA
(DONG HAI)
NANSEI-SHOTO (RYUKYU ISLANDS)
Ōsumi-shotō
Tokara-rettō
Amami-shotō
Okinawa-shotō
Sakishima-shotō
Senkaku-shotō
Yaeyama-rettō
Miyako-rettō
METRES
FEET
6000
19686
5000
16404
4000
13124
3000
9843
2000
6562
1500
4921
1000
3281
500
1640
200
656
100
328
0
LAND BELOW SEA LEVEL
200
656
2000
6562
4000
13124
6000
19686

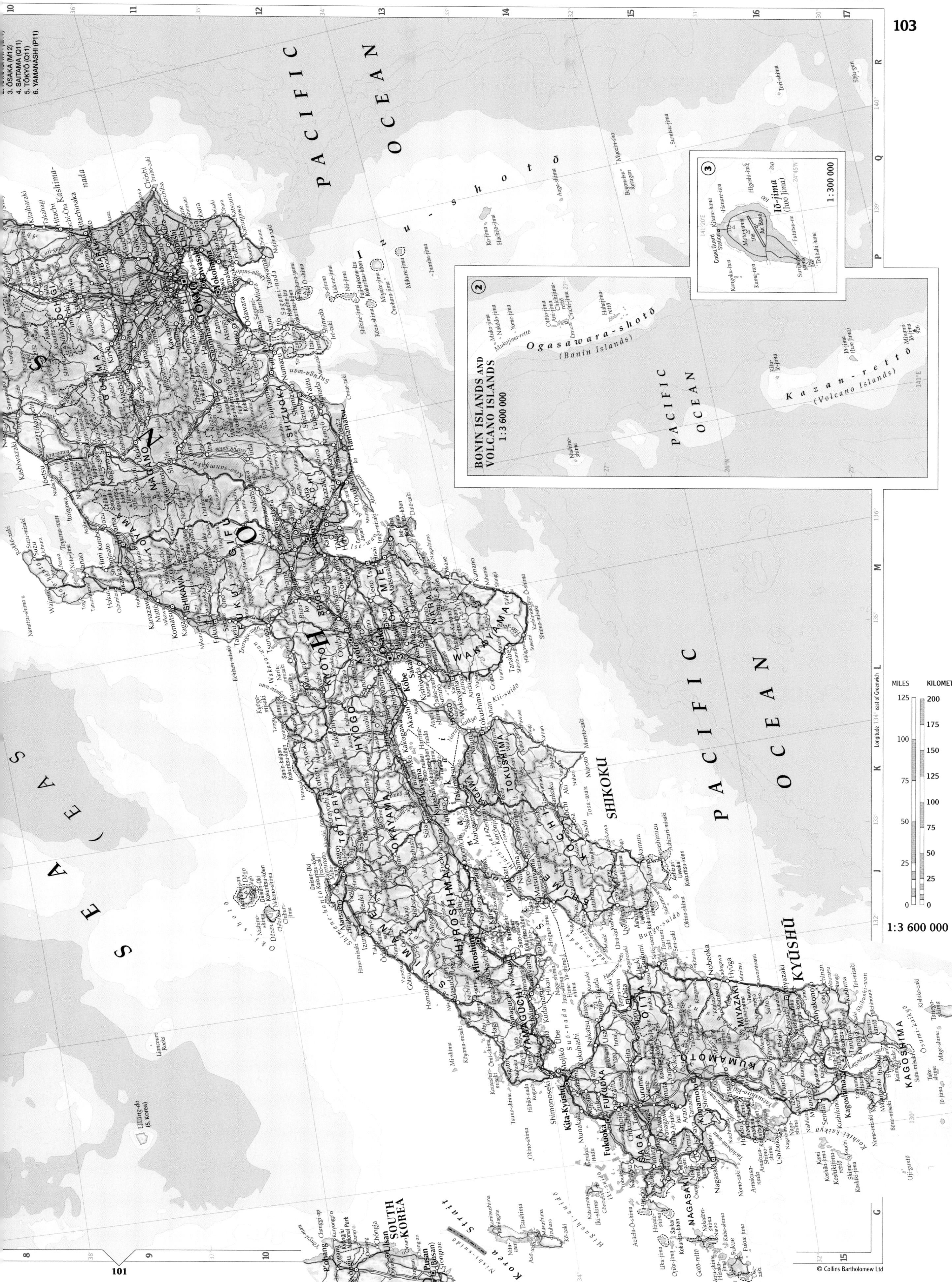
3. ŌSAKA (M12)
4. SAITAMA (Q11)
5. TŌKYŌ (Q11)
6. YAMANASHI (P11)
PACIFIC OCEAN
SEA OF JAPAN
SHIKOKU
KYŪSHŪ
SOUTH KOREA
Korea Strait
BONIN ISLANDS AND VOLCANO ISLANDS
1:3 600 000
Ogasawara-shotō
(Bonin Islands)
Kazan-rettō
(Volcano Islands)
Iō-jima
(Iwo Jima)
1:300 000
Tōkyō
Yokohama
Kawasaki
Chiba
Nagoya
Kōbe
Hiroshima
Kita-Kyūshū
Fukuoka
Kumamoto
Nagasaki
Kagoshima
Shizuoka
Hamamatsu
Wakayama
Pusan (Busan)
Ulsan
MILES
KILOMETRES
1:3 600 000
Longitude 134 east of Greenwich

101

© Collins Bartholomew Ltd

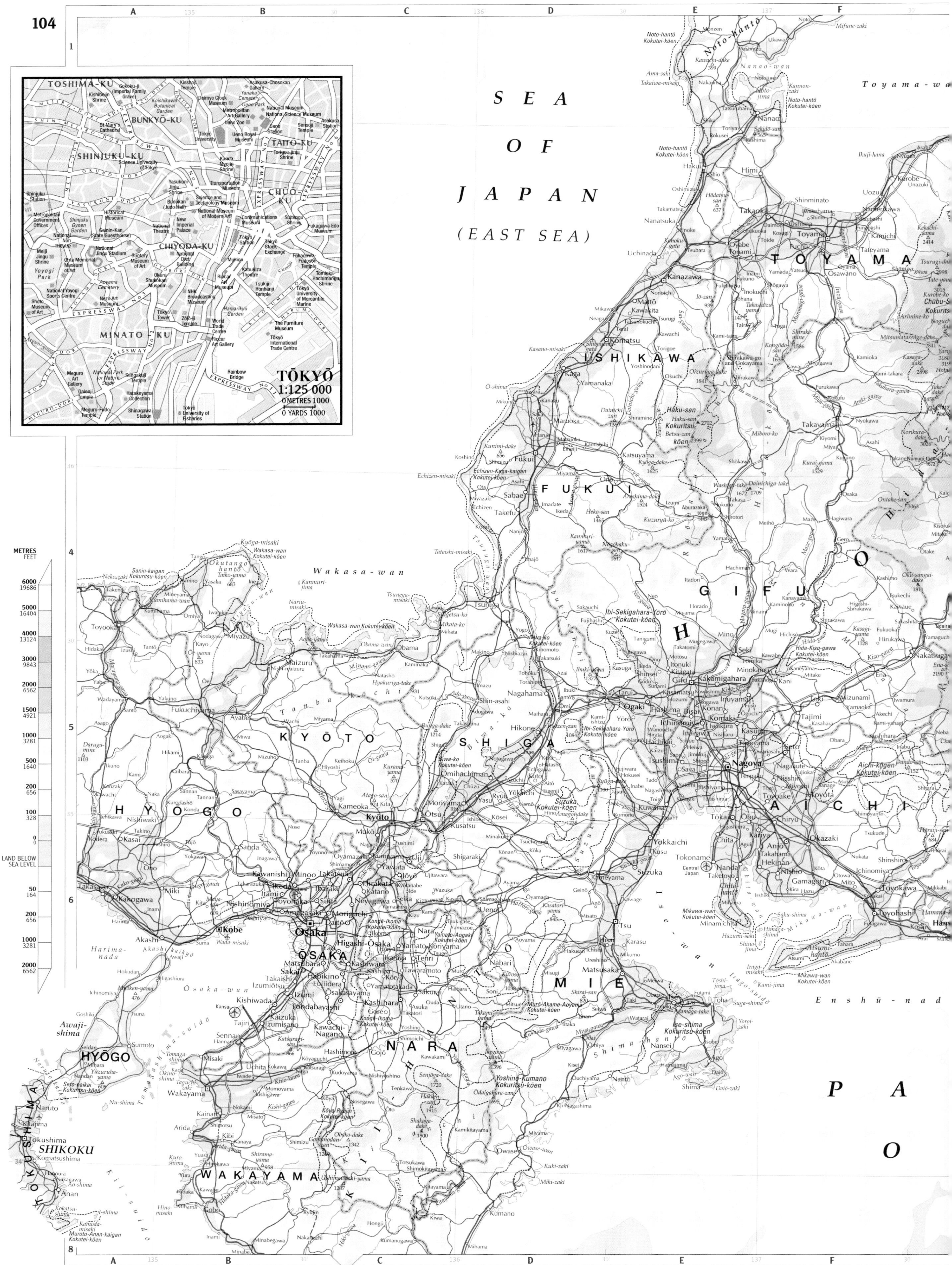
SEA OF JAPAN
(EAST SEA)
TŌKYŌ
1:125 000
0 METRES 1000
0 YARDS 1000
TOSHIMA-KU
BUNKYŌ-KU
SHINJUKU-KU
TAITO-KU
CHUO-KU
CHIYODA-KU
MINATO KU
METRES
FEET
6000 19686
5000 16404
4000 13124
3000 9843
2000 6562
1500 4921
1000 3281
500 1640
200 656
100 328
0 0
LAND BELOW SEA LEVEL
50 164
200 656
1000 3281
2000 6562
TOYAMA
ISHIKAWA
FUKUI
GIFU
SHIGA
KYŌTO
HYŌGO
ŌSAKA
NARA
MIE
AICHI
WAKAYAMA
SHIKOKU
TOKUSHIMA
Noto-hantō
Toyama-wan
Wakasa-wan
Ōsaka-wan
Ise-wan
Enshū-nada
Kii-suidō
Harima-nada
Awaji-shima
Kanazawa
Fukui
Kyōto
Ōsaka
Kōbe
Nagoya
Nara
Wakayama
Tsu
Gifu
Toyama
Ōtsu
Tokushima
Kii-hantō
Shima-hantō

102
NIIGATA
FUKUSHIMA
GUNMA
TOCHIGI
IBARAKI
SAITAMA
TOKYO
CHIBA
KANAGAWA
YAMANASHI
SHIZUOKA
NAGANO
Jōetsu
Nagano
Ueda
Matsumoto
Maebashi
Takasaki
Utsunomiya
Mito
Hitachi
Iwaki
Kumagaya
Kawagoe
Hachiōji
TŌKYŌ
Kawasaki
Yokohama
Chiba
Funabashi
Sagamihara
Fuchū
Kōfu
Odawara
Fuji
Numazu
Shizuoka
Shimizu
Yokosuka
Narita
Chōshi
Kashima-nada
Tōkyō-wan
Sagami-wan
Sagami-nada
Suruga-wan
Izu-hantō
Bōsō-hantō
Ō-shima
Nii-jima
Kōzu-shima
Miyake-jima
Mikura-jima
Fuji-Hakone-Izu Kokuritsu-kōen
Nikkō Kokuritsu-kōen
Chichibu-Tama Kokuritsu-kōen
Jōshinetsu-kōgen Kokuritsu-kōen
Minami-Bōsō Kokutei-kōen
Suigō-Tsukuba Kokutei-kōen
F I C
A N
MILES
KILOMETRES
1:1 200 000
Longitude 138° east of Greenwich

© Collins Bartholomew Ltd

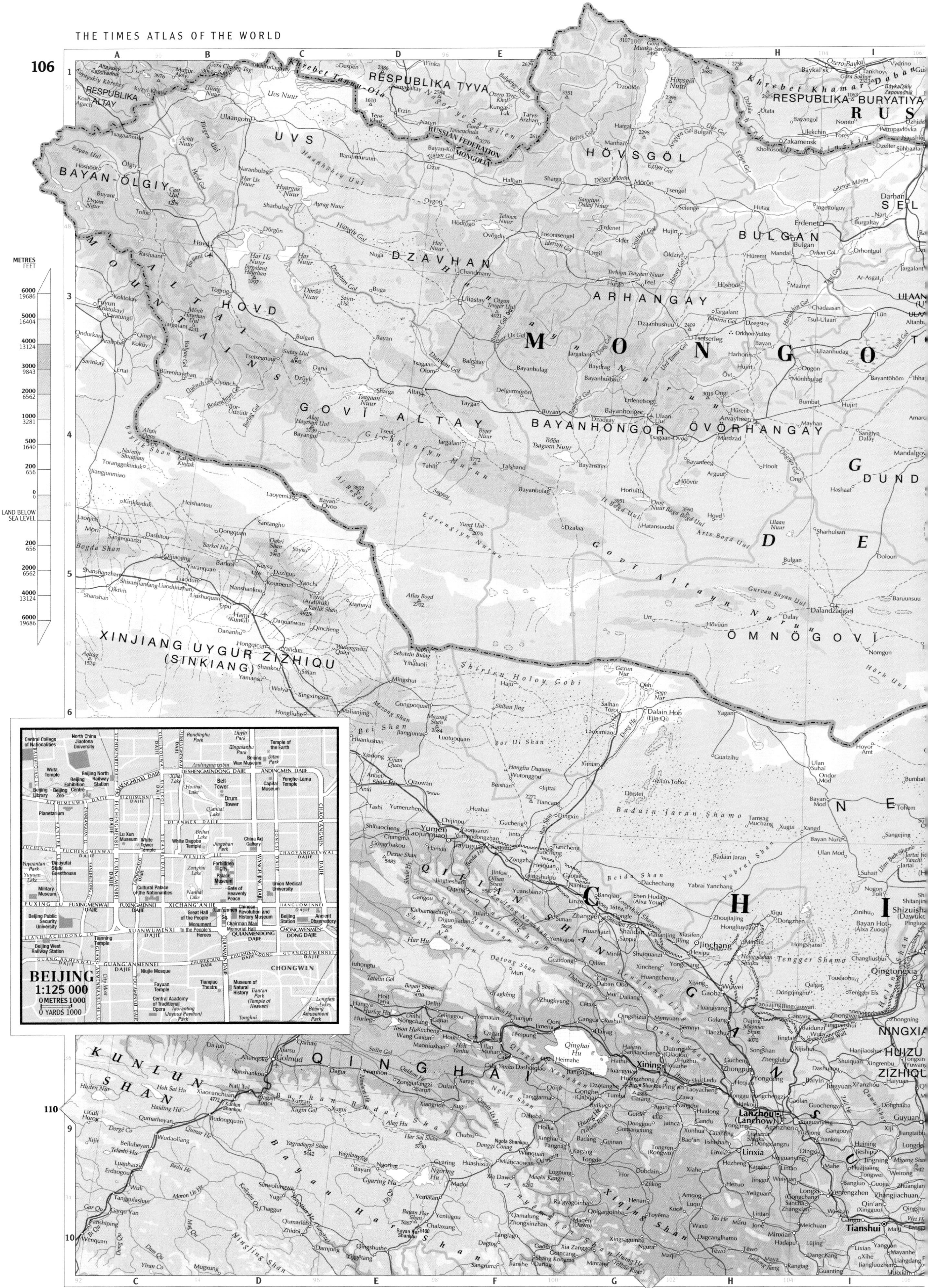
METRES
FEET
6000
19686
5000
16404
4000
13124
3000
9843
2000
6562
1000
3281
500
1640
200
656
0
0
LAND BELOW
SEA LEVEL
200
656
2000
6562
4000
13124
6000
19686
RESPUBLIKA TYVA
RESPUBLIKA ALTAY
RESPUBLIKA BURYATIYA
RUS
RUSSIAN FEDERATION
MONGOLIA
UVS
BAYAN-ÖLGIY
HÖVSGÖL
DZAVHAN
HOVD
ARHANGAY
BULGAN
SEL
MONGOL
GOVĬ-ALTAY
BAYANHONGOR
ÖVÖRHANGAY
DUND
GOVĬ
ÖMNÖGOVĬ
XINJIANG UYGUR ZIZHIQU
(SINKIANG)
CHI
NE
NINGXIA
HUIZU
ZIZHIQU
QINGHAI
GANSU
KUNLUN SHAN
Uvs Nuur
Ulaangom
Hovd
Ölgiy
Mörön
Uliastay
Altay
Bayanhongor
Erdenet
Dalandzadgad
Hami
(Kumul)
Barkol
Yumen
Jiayuguan
Jiuquan
Zhangye
Jinchang
Wuwei
Xining
Qinghai Hu
Lanzhou
(Lanchow)
Linxia
Tianshui
Golmud
Shiren Holoy Gobi
Badain Jaran Shamo
Tengger Shamo
Gobi Altay Nuruu
Qilian Shan
Bayan Har Shan
BEIJING
1:125 000
0 METRES 1000
0 YARDS 1000
Forbidden City
Palace Museum
Tiananmen Sq.
Temple of Heaven
Beijing Station
CHONGWEN
110
Conic Equidistant Projection

131
100
101
109
FEDERATION
AGINSKIY BURYATSKIY AVT. OKRUG
CHITINSKAYA OBLAST
DORNOD
HENTIY
SÜHBAATAR
DORNOGOVĬ
NEI MONGOL ZIZHIQU
HEILONGJIANG
JILIN
LIAONING
BEIJING
TIANJIN
HEBEI
SHANXI
SHANDONG
HENAN
ANHUI
JIANGSU
SHAANXI
BO HAI
Bohai Wan
Bohai Haixia
Liaodong Wan
YELLOW SEA
(HUANG HAI)
Manzhouli
Hulun Buir (Hailar)
Choybalsan
Qiqihar
Ulanhot
Baicheng
Tongliao
Xilinhot
Erenhot
Chifeng (Ulanhad)
Fuxin
Shenyang
Fushun
Anshan
Benxi
Jinzhou
Huludao
Yingkou
Dalian (Lüda)
Qinhuangdao
Tangshan
Beijing (Peking)
Tianjin (Tientsin)
Zhangjiakou (Kalgan)
Datong
Hohhot
Baotou
Jining (Tsining)
Baoding
Shijiazhuang
Taiyuan
Handan
Linfen
Changzhi
Anyang (Zhangde)
Xinxiang
Jiaozuo
Zhengzhou
Kaifeng
Luoyang
Xi'an
Xianyang
Weinan
Yan'an
Jinan
Zibo
Weifang
Qingdao (Tsingtao)
Yantai
Weihai
Dongying
Dezhou
Liaocheng
Tai'an
Xintai
Jining
Linyi
Rizhao (Shijiusuo)
Zaozhuang
Xuzhou
Huaibei
Lianyungang
Yancheng
Heze (Mudan)
Shangqiu
Pingdingshan
Zhoukou
MILES
KILOMETRES
1:6 000 000

106
111
96
96
METRES
FEET
6000
19686
5000
16404
4000
13124
3000
9843
2000
6562
1000
3281
500
1640
200
656
0
0
LAND BELOW
SEA LEVEL
200
656
2000
6562
4000
13124
6000
19686
QINGHAI
GANSU
SHAANXI
XIZANG ZIZHIQU
(TIBET)
SICHUAN
CHONGQING
CHINA
GUIZHOU
YUNNAN
GUANGXI ZHUANGZU ZIZHIQU
HAINAN
KACHIN
MYANMAR
(BURMA)
SHAN
THAILAND
LAOS
VIETNAM
TONKIN
GULF OF
TONGKING
INDIA
MYANMAR
Tianshui
Baoji
Xianyang
Xi'an
Weinan
Hanzhong
Ankang
Guangyuan
Mianyang
Deyang
Chengdu
Nanchong
Suining
Dazhou
Wanxian
Leshan
Neijiang
Zigong
Chongqing
Yibin
Xichang
Panzhihua
(Dukou)
Zhaotong
Zunyi
Guiyang
Anshun
Lupanshui
(Zhongshan)
Dali
(Xiaguan)
Kunming
Qujing
Chuxiong
Xingyi
(Huangcaoba)
Gejiu
Kaiyuan
Liuzhou
Nanning
Beihai
Zhanjiang
Yulin
HA NOI
Hai Phong
Nam Dinh
Thanh Hoa
Vinh
Luang Phabang
VIANGCHAN
(Vientiane)
Chiang Mai
Lampang
Enshi
Jishou
Huaihua
Kaili
Duyun
Hechi
Baise
Bose
THREE GORGES
DAM PROJECT
Tropic of Cancer
Fengtongzai Giant Panda Reserve
Wolong Reserve
XISHUANGBANNA
Mouths of the Hong
Conic Equidistant Projection

107
101
YELLOW SEA
(HUANG HAI)
EAST CHINA SEA
(DONG HAI)
SOUTH KOREA
JAPAN
HENAN
HUBEI
ANHUI
JIANGSU
SHANDONG
ZHEJIANG
JIANGXI
FUJIAN
GUANGDONG
TAIWAN
HONG KONG
Taiwan Strait
Tropic of Cancer
Shanghai
Pudong
Nanjing
Hefei
Wuhan
Hangzhou
Ningbo
Nanchang
Changsha
Fuzhou
Xiamen
Guangzhou (Canton)
Shenzhen
Kowloon
Hong Kong
Macao
Shantou
T'aipei
Kaohsiung
MILES
KILOMETRES
1:6 000 000

SHANGHAI
1:75 000
0 METRES 750
0 YARDS 750
JINGAN
HUANGPU
NANSHI
LUWAN
PUDONG
Huangpu Jiang

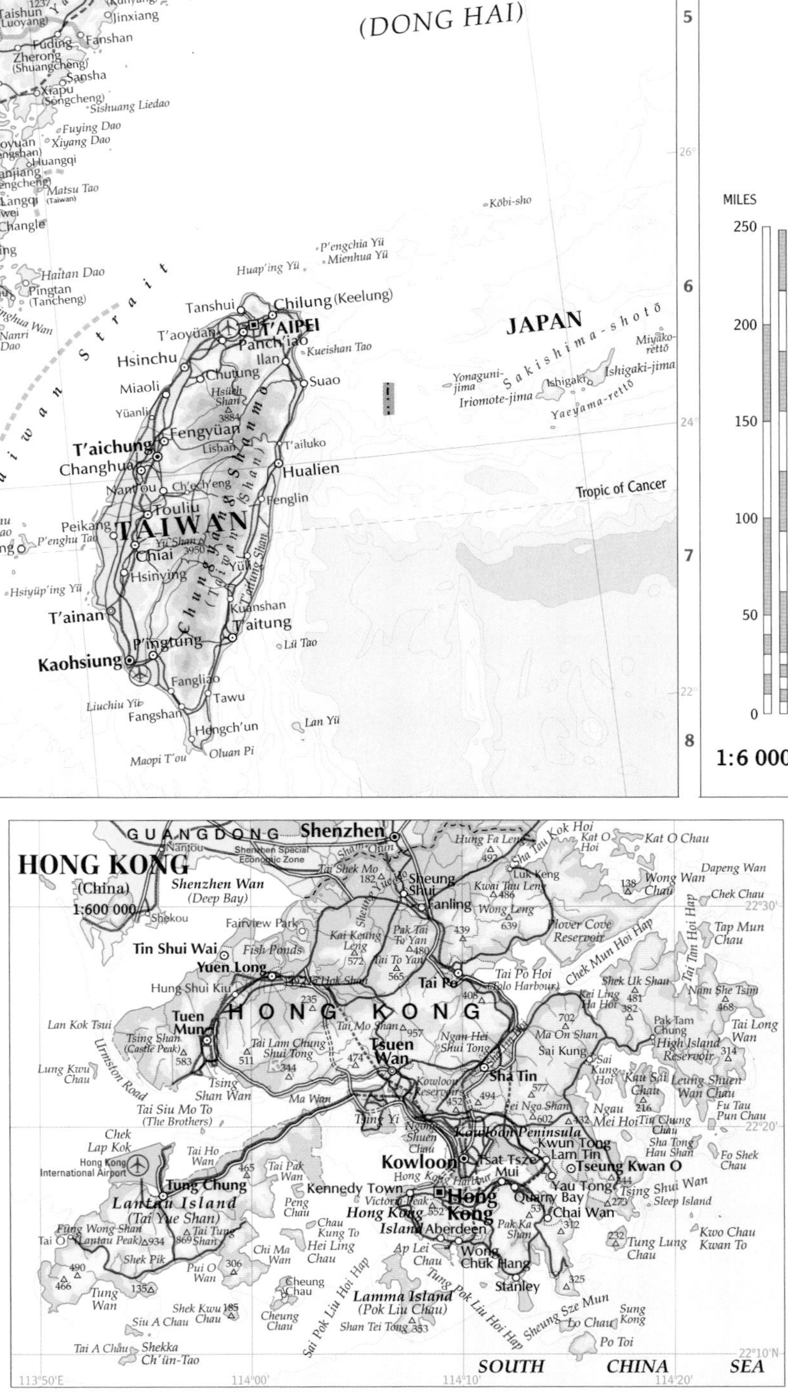
HONG KONG
(China)
1:600 000
GUANGDONG
Shenzhen
HONG KONG
Kowloon
Hong Kong Island
Lantau Island
Lamma Island
SOUTH CHINA SEA

Longitude 112° east of Greenwich

© Collins Bartholomew Ltd

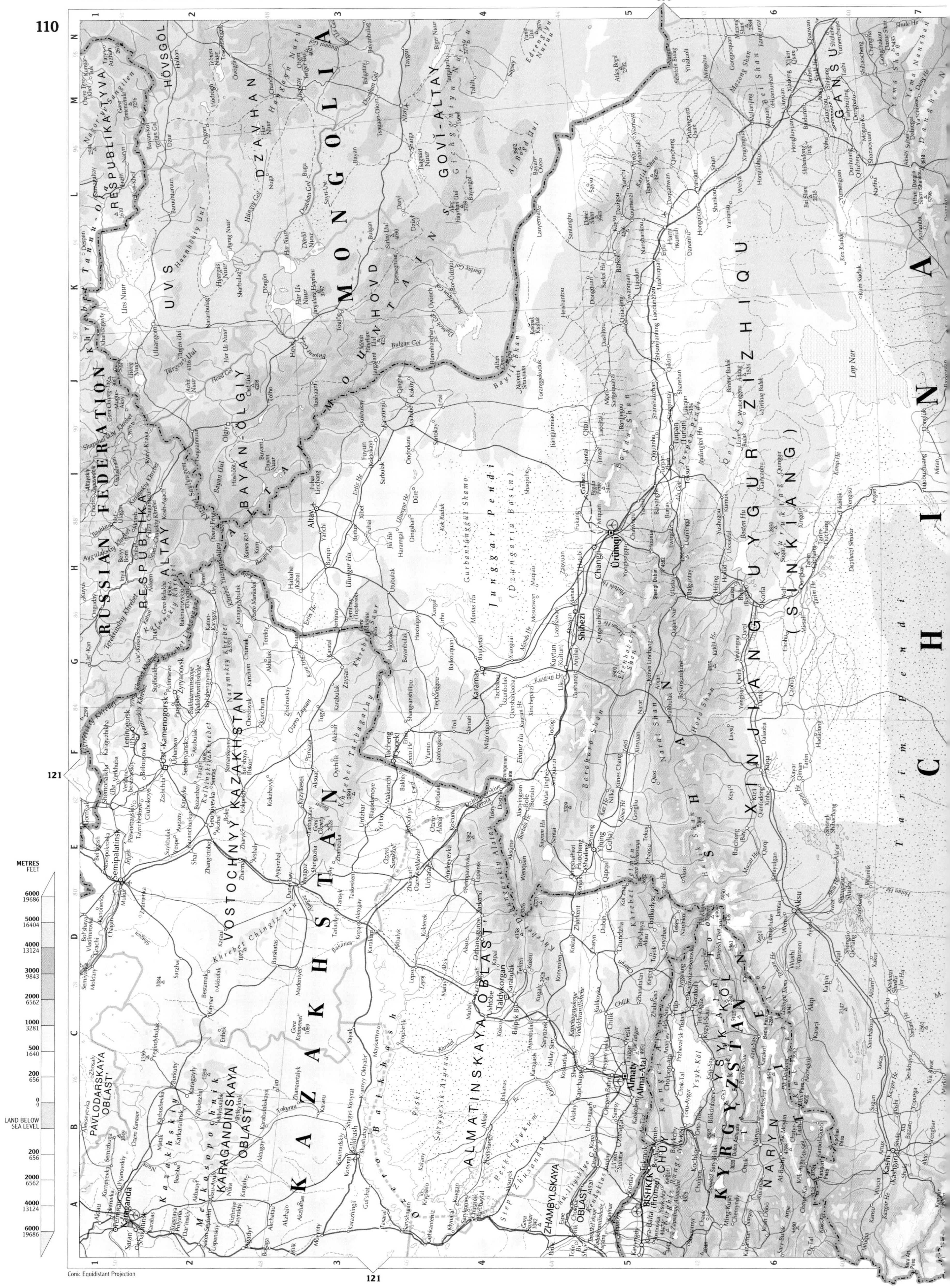
METRES
FEET
6000
19686
5000
16404
4000
13124
3000
9843
2000
6562
1000
3281
500
1640
200
656
0
0
LAND BELOW SEA LEVEL
200
656
2000
6562
4000
13124
6000
19686
106
121
KAZAKHSTAN
MONGOLIA
CHINA
RUSSIAN FEDERATION
RESPUBLIKA ALTAY
RESPUBLIKA TYVA
XINJIANG UYGUR ZIZHIQU (SINKIANG)
KYRGYZSTAN
VOSTOCHNYY KAZAKHSTAN
KARAGANDINSKAYA OBLAST'
PAVLODARSKAYA OBLAST'
ALMATINSKAYA OBLAST'
ZHAMBYLSKAYA OBLAST'
CHUY
NARYN
UVS
HÖVSGÖL
DZAVHAN
HOVD
BAYAN-ÖLGIY
GOVĬ-ALTAY
GANSU
Semipalatinsk
Ust'-Kamenogorsk
Karaganda
Almaty (Alma-Ata)
Bishkek (Frunze)
Ürümqi
Karamay
Aksu
Kashi (Kashgar)
Hami (Kumul)
Turpan
Korla
Tacheng (Qoqek)
Lop Nur
Tarim Pendi
Junggar Pendi
Ysyk-Köl

Conic Equidistant Projection

108

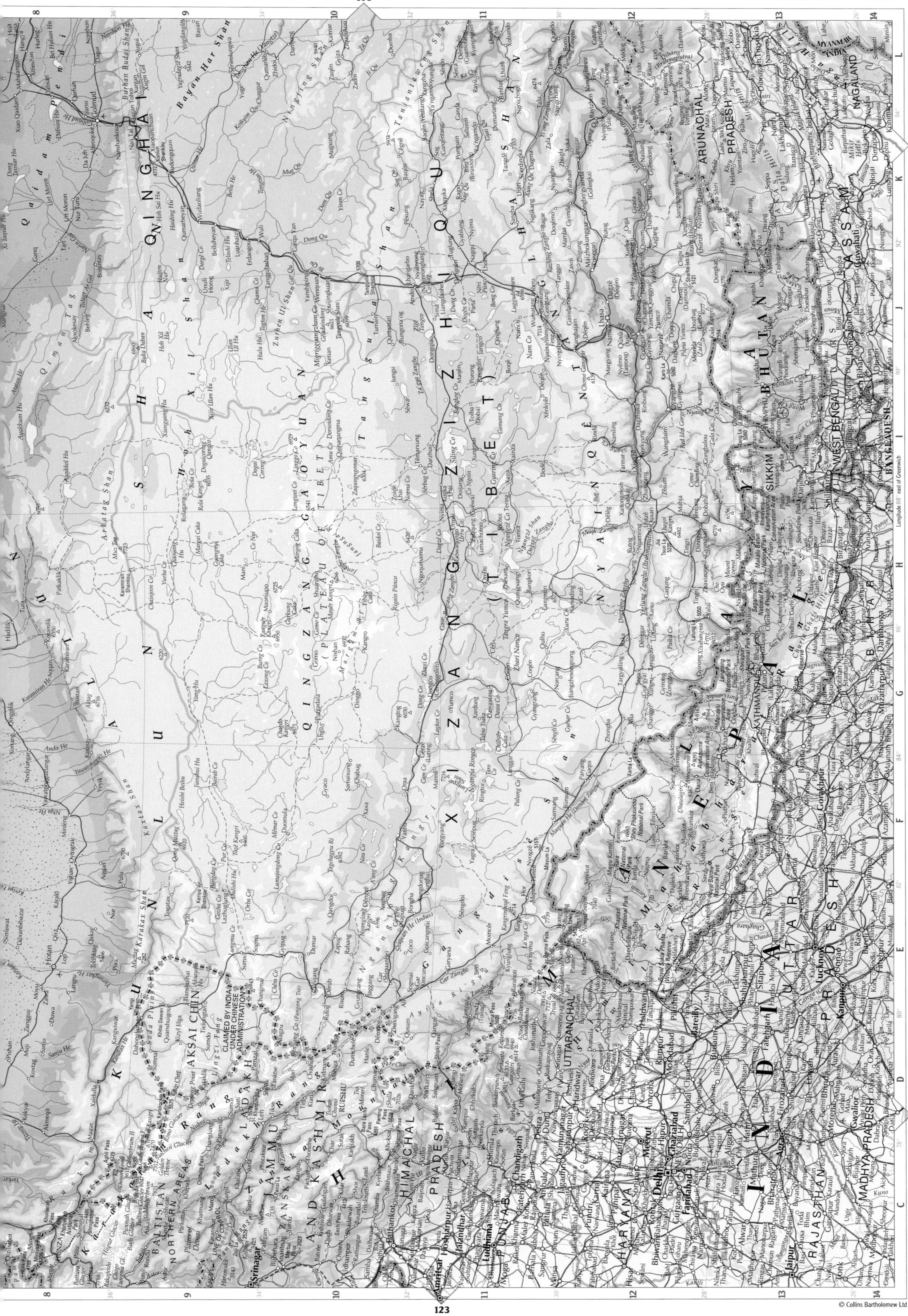

117

116

MILES KILOMETRES

250 200 150 100 50 0

400 350 300 250 200 150 100 50 0

1:6 000 000

123

© Collins Bartholomew Ltd

98

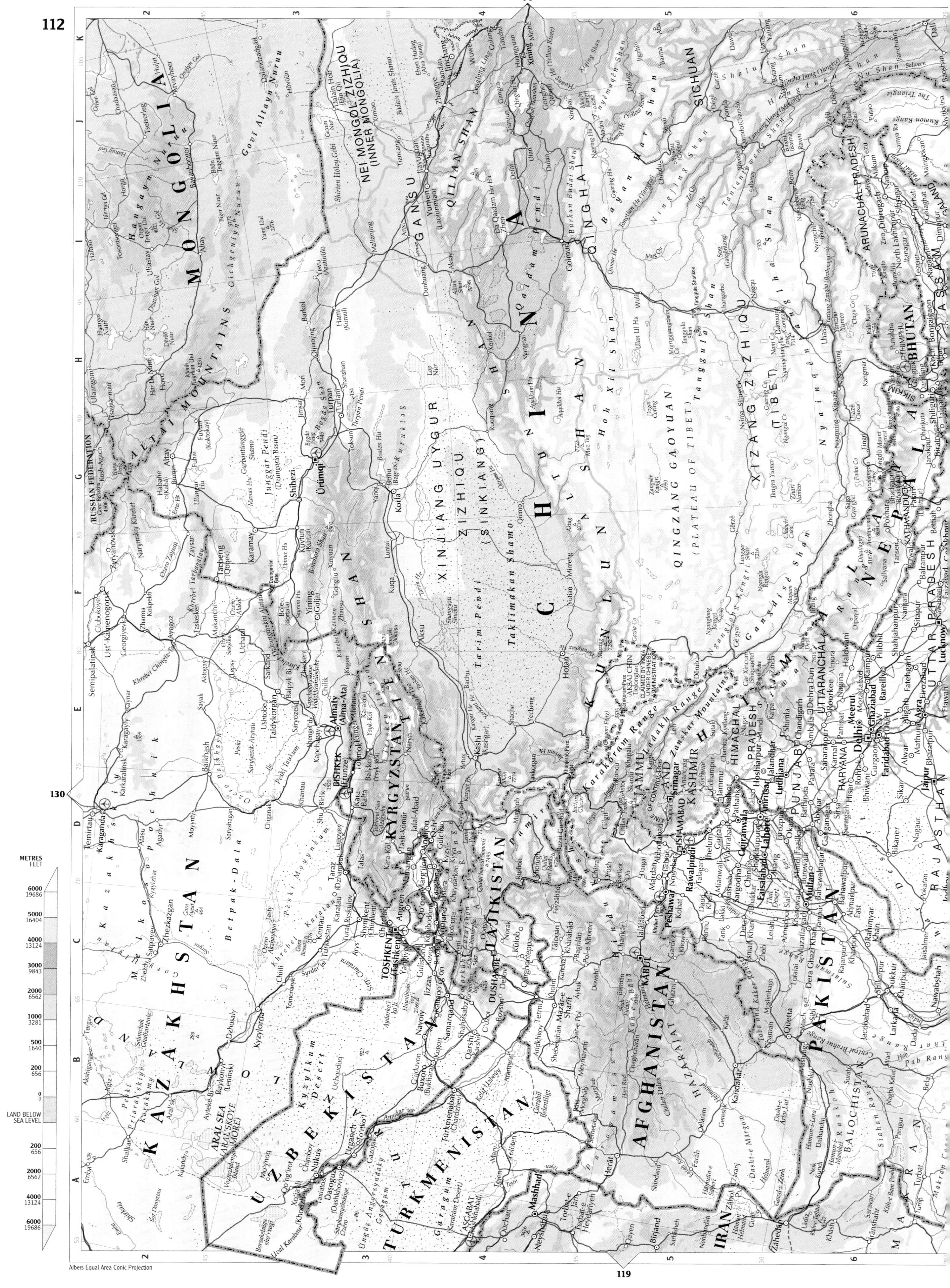
METRES
FEET
6000
19686
5000
16404
4000
13124
3000
9843
2000
6562
1000
3281
500
1640
200
656
0
0
LAND BELOW
SEA LEVEL
200
656
2000
6562
4000
13124
6000
19686
MONGOLIA
KAZAKHSTAN
UZBEKISTAN
TURKMENISTAN
KYRGYZSTAN
TAJIKISTAN
AFGHANISTAN
PAKISTAN
CHINA
NEPAL
BHUTAN
IRAN
RUSSIAN FEDERATION
NEI MONGOL ZIZHIQU (INNER MONGOLIA)
XINJIANG UYGUR ZIZHIQU (SINKIANG)
XIZANG ZIZHIQU (TIBET)
QINGZANG GAOYUAN (PLATEAU OF TIBET)
QINGHAI
GANSU
SICHUAN
ARUNACHAL PRADESH
ASSAM
UTTAR PRADESH
UTTARANCHAL
HIMACHAL PRADESH
HARYANA
PUNJAB
RAJASTHAN
JAMMU AND KASHMIR
BALOCHISTAN
HAZARAJAT
ALTAI MOUNTAINS
TIEN SHAN
KUNLUN SHAN
QILIAN SHAN
Taklimakan Shamo
Tarim Pendi
Qaidam Pendi
Junggar Pendi (Dzungarian Basin)
Betpak-Dala
Kyzylkum Desert
Garagum (Karakum Desert)
Karakoram Range
Hindu Kush
ARAL SEA (ARAL'SKOYE MORE)
Ürümqi
Almaty (Alma-Ata)
BISHKEK (Frunze)
TOSHKENT (Tashkent)
DUSHANBE
KABUL
ISLAMABAD
New Delhi
KATHMANDU
THIMPHU
AŞGABAT (Ashkhabad)
Karaganda
Samarqand
Mashhad
Herāt
Kandahār
Quetta
Lahore
Rawalpindi
Srinagar
Kashi (Kashgar)
Hotan
Lhasa
Xining
Golmud
Hami (Kumul)
Lucknow
Agra

130

119

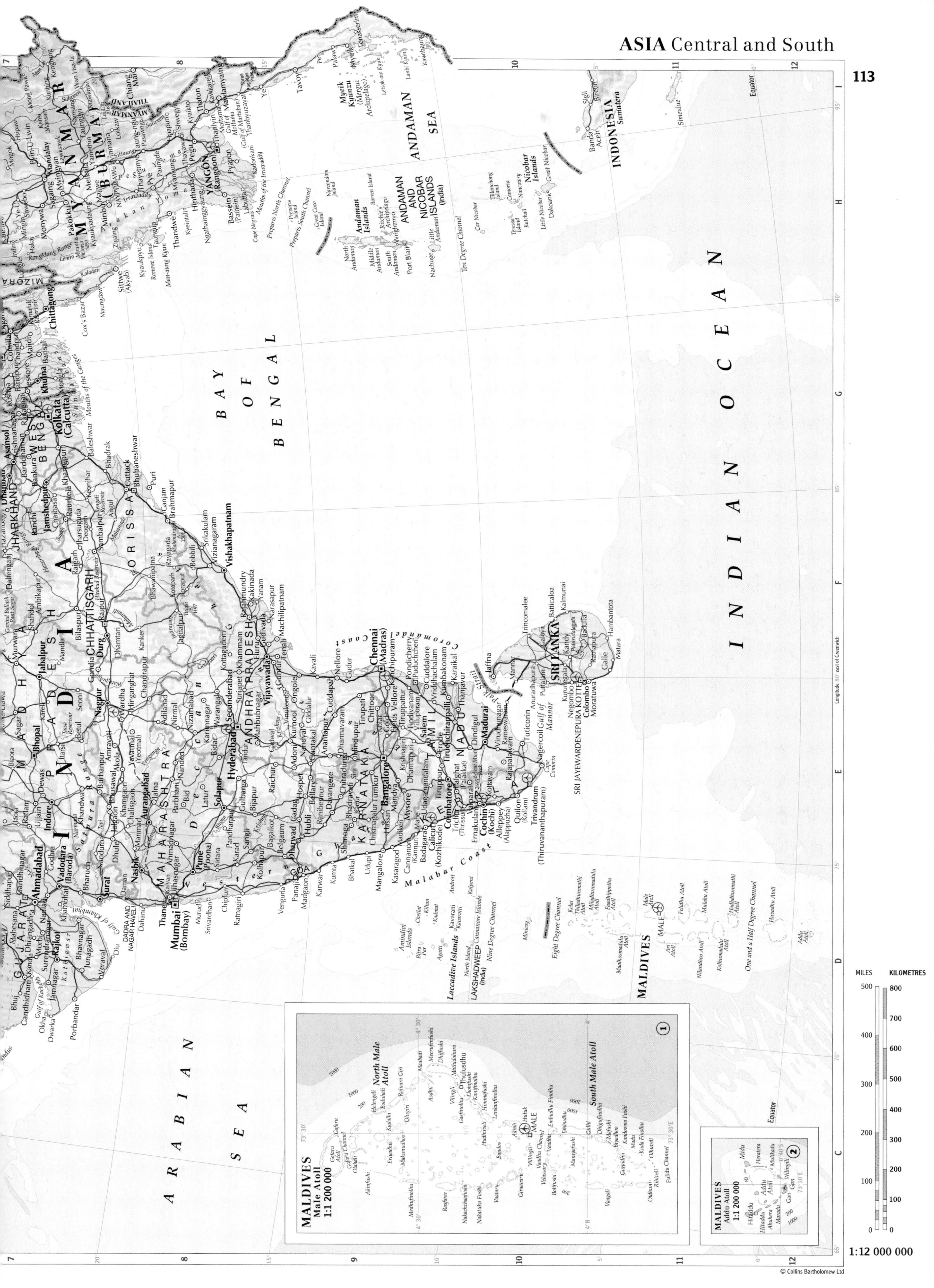
ARABIAN SEA
BAY OF BENGAL
INDIAN OCEAN
ANDAMAN SEA
MYANMAR (BURMA)
THAILAND
INDONESIA
Sumatera
SRI LANKA
MALDIVES
INDIA
MAHARASHTRA
KARNATAKA
TAMIL NADU
ANDHRA PRADESH
ORISSA
CHHATTISGARH
JHARKHAND
GUJARAT
MADHYA PRADESH
WEST BENGAL
ANDAMAN AND NICOBAR ISLANDS (India)
LAKSHADWEEP (India)
Laccadive Islands
DADRA AND NAGAR HAVELI
Andaman Islands
Nicobar Islands
Mumbai (Bombay)
Pune (Poona)
Hyderabad
Bangalore
Chennai (Madras)
Kolkata (Calcutta)
Vishakhapatnam
Vijayawada
Nagpur
Ahmadabad
Surat
Vadodara (Baroda)
Rajkot
Bhopal
Indore
Jabalpur
Solapur
Aurangabad
Nashik
Madurai
Coimbatore
Cochin (Kochi)
Trivandrum (Thiruvananthapuram)
Mysore
Salem
Colombo
SRI JAYEWARDENEPURA KOTTE
Jaffna
Trincomalee
Kandy
Galle
YANGON (Rangoon)
Mandalay
Chittagong
Khulna
Dhaka
Port Blair
Banda Aceh
MALE
Gulf of Mannar
Gulf of Khambhat
Gulf of Kachchh
Palk Strait
Malabar Coast
Coromandel Coast
Ten Degree Channel
Nine Degree Channel
Eight Degree Channel
One and a Half Degree Channel
Equator
Longitude 80° east of Greenwich
MALDIVES Male Atoll 1:1 200 000
North Male Atoll
South Male Atoll
MALDIVES Addu Atoll 1:1 200 000
Addu Atoll
MILES
KILOMETRES
1:12 000 000

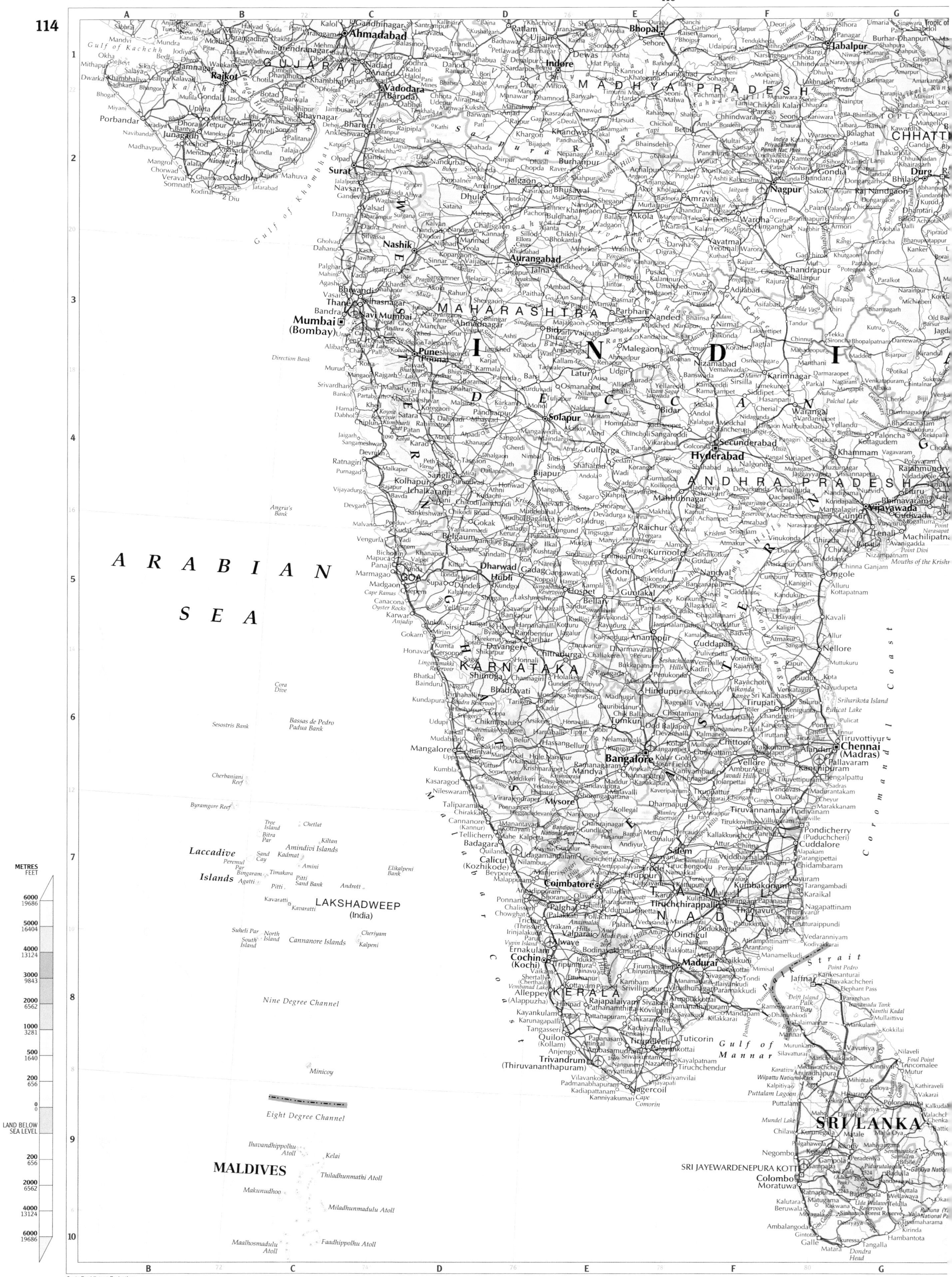
116
ARABIAN SEA
INDIA
GUJARAT
MADHYA PRADESH
MAHARASHTRA
ANDHRA PRADESH
KARNATAKA
KERALA
TAMIL NADU
GOA
DECCAN
WESTERN GHATS
EASTERN GHATS
SRI LANKA
MALDIVES
LAKSHADWEEP (India)
Laccadive Islands
Gulf of Kachchh
Gulf of Khambhat
Malabar Coast
Coromandel Coast
Palk Strait
Gulf of Mannar
Nine Degree Channel
Eight Degree Channel
Mumbai (Bombay)
Ahmadabad
Vadodara
Surat
Rajkot
Bhopal
Indore
Jabalpur
Nagpur
Aurangabad
Nashik
Pune (Poona)
Solapur
Hyderabad
Secunderabad
Vijayawada
Bangalore
Chennai (Madras)
Mysore
Mangalore
Calicut (Kozhikode)
Coimbatore
Cochin (Kochi)
Madurai
Trivandrum (Thiruvananthapuram)
Pondicherry (Puduchcheri)
Colombo
SRI JAYEWARDENEPURA KOTTE
Jaffna
Kandy
METRES
FEET
6000 19686
5000 16404
4000 13124
3000 9843
2000 6562
1000 3281
500 1640
200 656
0 0
LAND BELOW SEA LEVEL
200 656
2000 6562
4000 13124
6000 19686

BAY OF BENGAL
INDIAN OCEAN
BANGLADESH
MYANMAR (BURMA)
BIHAR
WEST BENGAL
ORISSA
KHULNA
BARISAL
DHAKA
CHITTAGONG
CHIN
SAGAING
MANDALAY
MAGWE
RAKHINE
PEGU
IRRAWADDY
YANGON
Ranchi
Jamshedpur
Kolkata (Calcutta)
Khulna
Chittagong
Cox's Bazar
Sittwe (Akyab)
Cuttack
Bhubaneshwar
Puri
Brahmapur
Vishakhapatnam
Bassein (Pathein)
Yangon (Rangoon)
Mouths of the Ganges
Mouths of the Irrawaddy
Andaman Islands
Nicobar Islands
ANDAMAN AND NICOBAR ISLANDS (India)
Port Blair
Ten Degree Channel
Sombrero Channel
Preparis North Channel
Preparis South Channel
Administrative divisions in India numbered on the map:
1. DADRA AND NAGAR HAVELI (C2)
2. DAMAN AND DIU (B2, C2)
3. PONDICHERRY (D7, F7, H4)
KOLKATA
1:70 000
0 METRES 750
0 YARDS 750
HOWRAH
SHIBPUR
Hooghly
The Maidan
Fort William
HASTINGS
WATGUNGE
KIDDERPORE
ALIPORE
BALLYGUNGE
TALTALA
ENTALLY
BENIAPUKUR
BITAKHANA
TIRETTA
B.B.D. BAG
JORASANKO
MACHUABAZAR
MUMBAI
1:90 000
0 METRES 1000
0 YARDS 1000
Arabian Sea
Back Bay
Mumbai Harbour
BYCULLA
MAZAGAON
TARDEO
KAMATIPURA
UMARKHADI
KHETWADI
BHULESHWAR
MANDVI
MALABAR HILL
FORT
COTTON GREEN
MILES
KILOMETRES
1:6 000 000
Longitude 84° east of Greenwich
© Collins Bartholomew Ltd

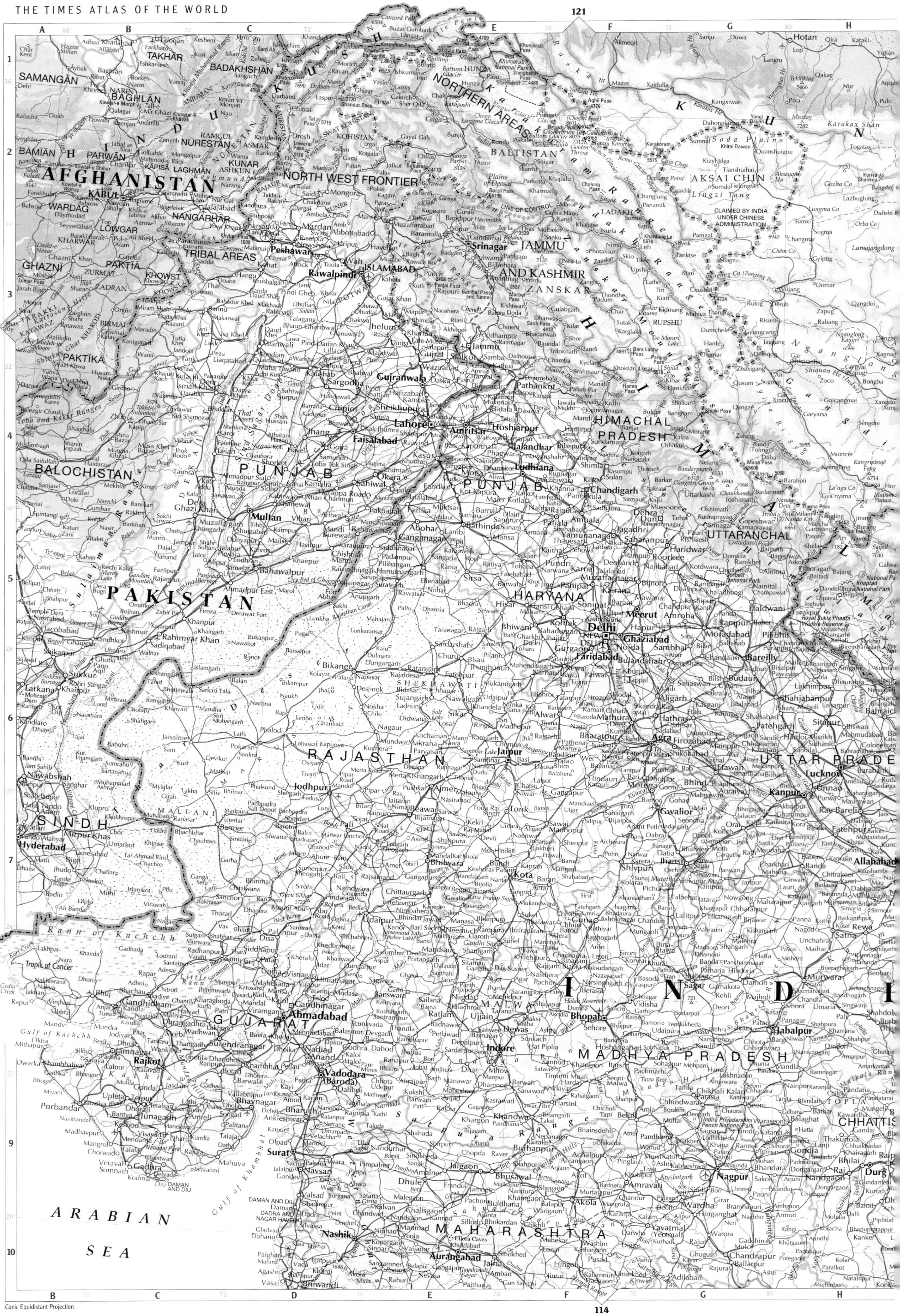
121
123
114
AFGHANISTAN
PAKISTAN
INDIA
ARABIAN SEA
NORTHERN AREAS
NORTH WEST FRONTIER
TRIBAL AREAS
BALOCHISTAN
PUNJAB
SINDH
JAMMU AND KASHMIR
HIMACHAL PRADESH
UTTARANCHAL
HARYANA
RAJASTHAN
GUJARAT
MADHYA PRADESH
MAHARASHTRA
UTTAR PRADESH
AKSAI CHIN
CLAIMED BY INDIA UNDER CHINESE ADMINISTRATION
LINE OF CONTROL
Kabul
Islamabad
Rawalpindi
Peshawar
Lahore
Amritsar
Faisalabad
Multan
Srinagar
Leh
Delhi
New Delhi
Jaipur
Agra
Lucknow
Kanpur
Ahmadabad
Gandhinagar
Vadodara
Surat
Nashik
Aurangabad
Nagpur
Jabalpur
Bhopal
Indore
Hyderabad
Rajkot
Jodhpur
Bikaner
Chandigarh
Meerut
Tropic of Cancer
Gulf of Kachchh
Gulf of Khambhat
Rann of Kachchh
THAR DESERT
DAMAN AND DIU
DADRA AND NAGAR HAVELI
Karakoram Range
Hindu Kush
Himalaya

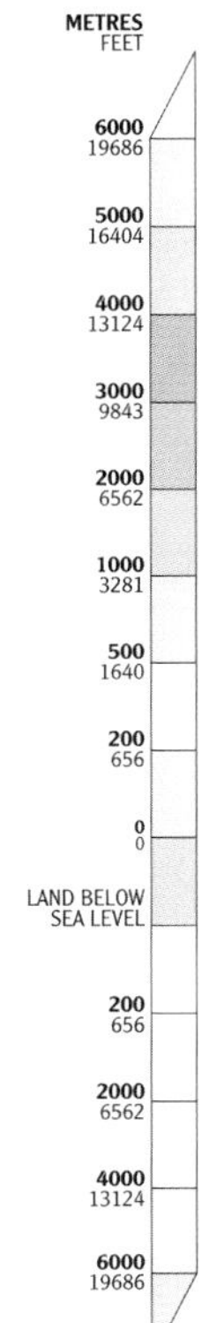
METRES
FEET
6000
19686
5000
16404
4000
13124
3000
9843
2000
6562
1000
3281
500
1640
200
656
0
0
LAND BELOW SEA LEVEL
200
656
2000
6562
4000
13124
6000
19686

Conic Equidistant Projection

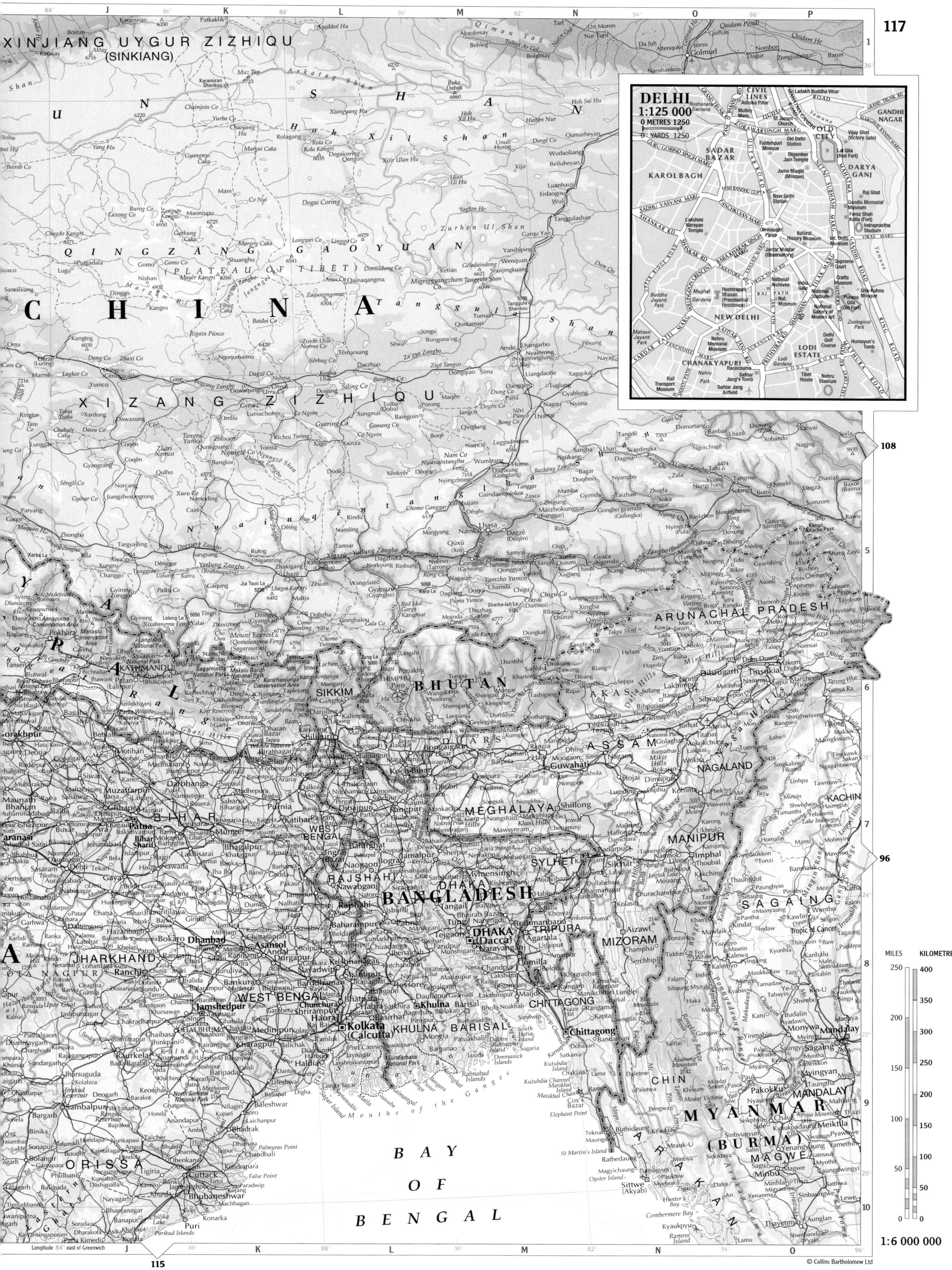
XINJIANG UYGUR ZIZHIQU
(SINKIANG)
CHINA
QINGZANG GAOYUAN
(PLATEAU OF TIBET)
XIZANG ZIZHIQU
DELHI
1:125 000
NEW DELHI
OLD CITY
KAROLBAGH
SADAR BAZAR
CIVIL LINES
DARYA GANJ
CHANAKYAPURI
LODI ESTATE
NEPAL
BHUTAN
SIKKIM
ARUNACHAL PRADESH
ASSAM
NAGALAND
MEGHALAYA
MANIPUR
MIZORAM
TRIPURA
BIHAR
JHARKHAND
WEST BENGAL
ORISSA
BANGLADESH
RAJSHAHI
DHAKA
KHULNA
BARISAL
CHITTAGONG
SYLHET
Dhaka (Dacca)
Kolkata (Calcutta)
Chittagong
Patna
Ranchi
Guwahati
Lhasa
Golmud
Mandalay
MYANMAR (BURMA)
SAGAING
MAGWE
CHIN
ARAKAN
KACHIN
BAY OF BENGAL
Mouths of the Ganges
Tropic of Cancer
MILES
KILOMETRES
Longitude 84° east of Greenwich
108
96
115

1:6 000 000

© Collins Bartholomew Ltd

135
199
202
210

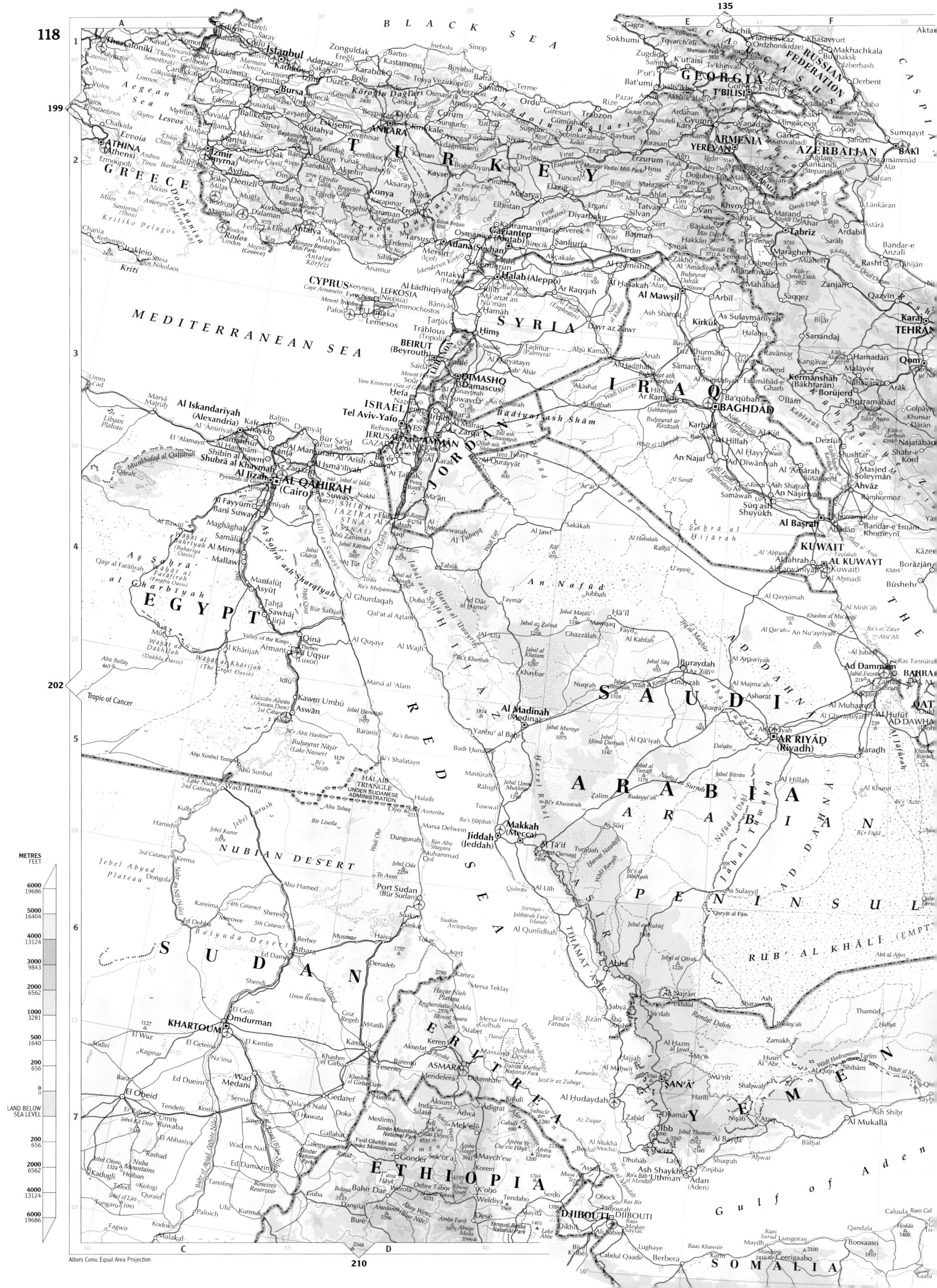

BLACK SEA
CASPIAN
MEDITERRANEAN SEA
Aegean Sea
RED SEA
Gulf of Aden
GREECE
TURKEY
GEORGIA
ARMENIA
AZERBAIJAN
RUSSIAN FEDERATION
CYPRUS
SYRIA
LEBANON
ISRAEL
JORDAN
IRAQ
KUWAIT
EGYPT
SUDAN
ERITREA
ETHIOPIA
DJIBOUTI
SOMALIA
YEMEN
SAUDI ARABIA
ARABIAN PENINSULA
NUBIAN DESERT
RUB' AL KHĀLĪ
An Nafūd
Tropic of Cancer
HALAIB TRIANGLE UNDER SUDANESE ADMINISTRATION
ATHINA (Athens)
Thessaloniki
İstanbul
ANKARA
İzmir (Smyrna)
Bursa
Konya
Adana (Seyhan)
Gaziantep (Aintab)
T'BILISI
YEREVAN
BAKI
TEHRAN
LEFKOSIA (Nicosia)
Halab (Aleppo)
Ḥimṣ
BEIRUT (Beyrouth)
DIMASHQ (Damascus)
Tel Aviv-Yafo
JERUSALEM
'AMMĀN
Al Mawṣil
Kirkūk
BAGHDĀD
Al Baṣrah
AL KUWAYT (Kuwait)
Al Iskandarīyah (Alexandria)
AL QĀHIRAH (Cairo)
Al Jīzah
Aswān
Al Uqṣur (Luxor)
Al Madīnah (Medina)
Makkah (Mecca)
Jiddah (Jeddah)
AR RIYĀḌ (Riyadh)
Port Sudan
KHARTOUM
Omdurman
ASMARA
SAN'Ā'
Adan (Aden)
DJIBOUTI
METRES
FEET
6000 19686
5000 16404
4000 13124
3000 9843
2000 6562
1000 3281
500 1640
200 656
0 0
LAND BELOW SEA LEVEL
200 656
2000 6562
4000 13124
6000 19686

Albers Conic Equal Area Projection

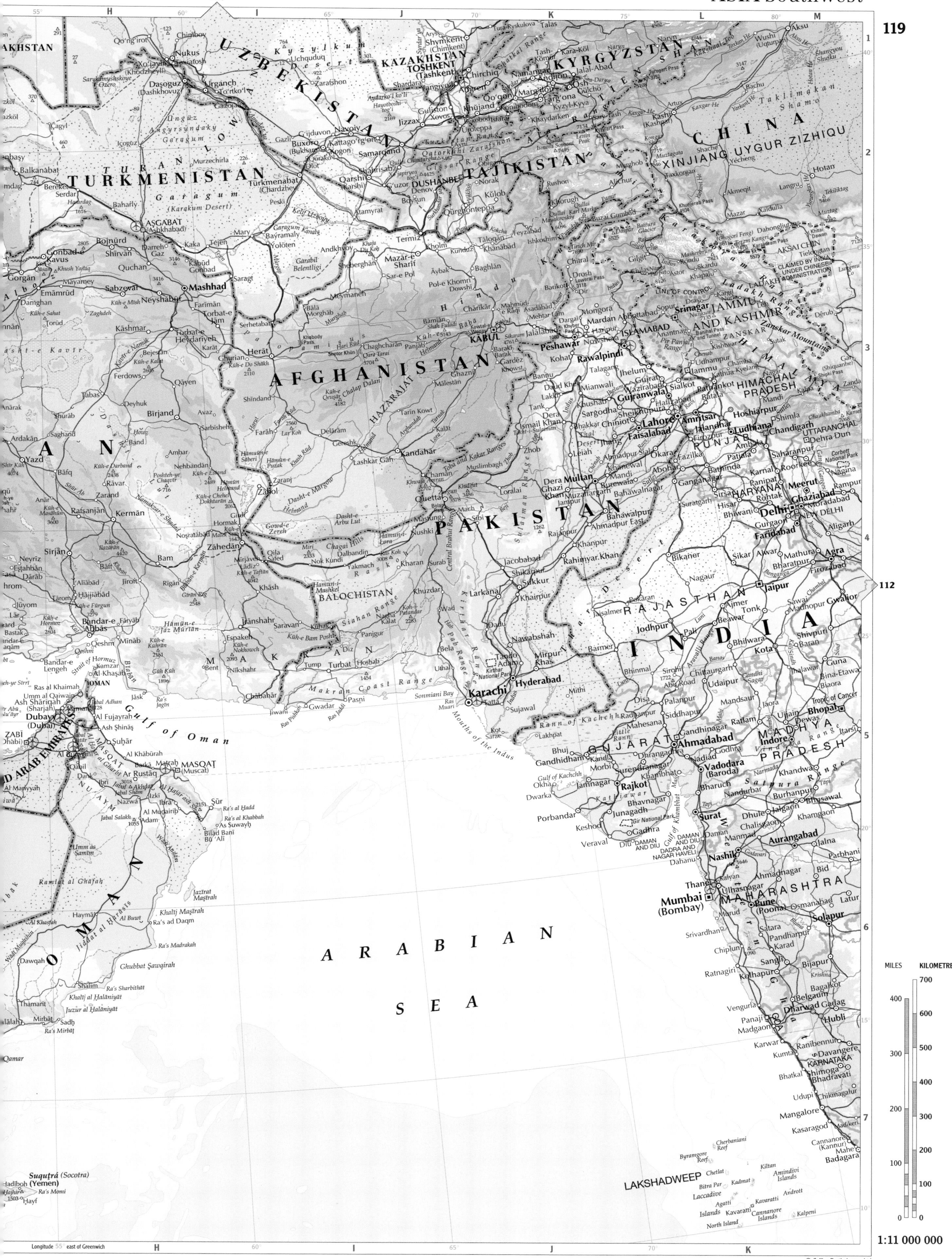
120
112
TURKMENISTAN
UZBEKISTAN
KAZAKHSTAN
KYRGYZSTAN
TAJIKISTAN
AFGHANISTAN
PAKISTAN
INDIA
CHINA
XINJIANG UYGUR ZIZHIQU
JAMMU AND KASHMIR
HIMACHAL PRADESH
UTTARANCHAL
HARYANA
PUNJAB
RAJASTHAN
GUJARAT
MADHYA PRADESH
MAHARASHTRA
KARNATAKA
LAKSHADWEEP
BALOCHISTAN
OMAN
UNITED ARAB EMIRATES
ARABIAN SEA
Gulf of Oman
Strait of Hormuz
Gulf of Kachchh
Mouths of the Indus
Kyzylkum Desert
Garagum (Karakum Desert)
Thar Desert
Hindu Kush
Karakoram Range
Himalaya
Makran Coast Range
TOSHKENT (Tashkent)
DUSHANBE
AŞGABAT (Ashkhabad)
KABUL
ISLAMABAD
NEW DELHI
MASQAT (Muscat)
Mashhad
Herāt
Kandahār
Quetta
Karachi
Hyderabad
Lahore
Faisalabad
Rawalpindi
Peshawar
Multan
Amritsar
Delhi
Jaipur
Agra
Ahmadabad
Vadodara (Baroda)
Surat
Mumbai (Bombay)
Pune
Thane
Srinagar
Samarqand
Zāhedān
Kermān
Yazd
Dubayy (Dubai)
Suquṭrā (Socotra)
AKSAI CHIN
CLAIMED BY INDIA UNDER CHINESE ADMINISTRATION
LINE OF CONTROL
MILES
KILOMETRES
Longitude 55° east of Greenwich

1:11 000 000

© Collins Bartholomew Ltd

134

METRES
FEET
6000
19686
5000
16404
4000
13124
3000
9843
2000
6562
1000
3281
500
1640
200
656
0
0
LAND BELOW
SEA LEVEL
200
656
2000
6562
4000
13124
6000
19686
RUSSIAN FEDERATION
RESPUBLIKA BASHKORTOSTAN
SAMARSKAYA OBLAST'
SARATOVSKAYA OBLAST'
ORENBURGSKAYA OBLAST'
CHELYABINSKAYA OBLAST'
KOSTANAYSKAYA OBLAST'
ZAPADNYY KAZAKHSTAN
AKTYUBINSKAYA OBLAST
ATYRAUSKAYA OBLAST'
ASTRAKHANSKAYA OBLAST
MANGISTAUSKAYA OBLAST'
KYZYLORDINSKAYA OBLAS
KAZAKHSTAN
Prikaspiyskaya Nizmennost' (Caspian Lowland)
Ryn-Peski
Obshchiy Syrt
Turgayskaya Stolovaya Strana
Ustyurt Plateau
CASPIAN SEA
ARAL SEA (Aral'skoye More)
Vozrozhdenya Island
Garabogazköl Aýlagy
QORAQALPOG'ISTON RESPUBLIKASI (RESPUBLIKA KARAKALPAKSTAN)
UZBEKISTAN
NAVOIY
BUXORO
KYZYLKUM DESERT
TURKMENISTAN
BALKAN
DAŞOGUZ
AHAL
MARY
GARAGUM (Karakum Desert)
RESPUBLIKA DAGESTAN
AZERBAIJAN
BAKI
IRAN
GOLESTAN
KHORASAN-E SHEMALI
MAZANDARAN
SEMNAN
Samara (Kuybyshev)
Saratov
Orenburg
Ural'sk
Aktobe (Aktyubinsk)
Atyrau (Gur'yev)
Astrakhan'
Aktau (Shevchenko)
Makhachkala
Derbent
Sumqayıt
Nukus
Dasoguz (Dashkhovuz)
Urganch
Türkmenbaşy
Balkanabat
Aşgabat (Ashkhabad)
Buxoro (Bukhara)
Türkmenabat (Chardzhev)
Kostanay
Orsk
Magnitogorsk
Baykonyr (Leninsk)
Administrative divisions in Uzbekistan numbered on the map:
1. ANDIJON (O7)
2. FARG'ONA (N7)
3. NAMANGAN (N7)
Conic Equidistant Projection

122

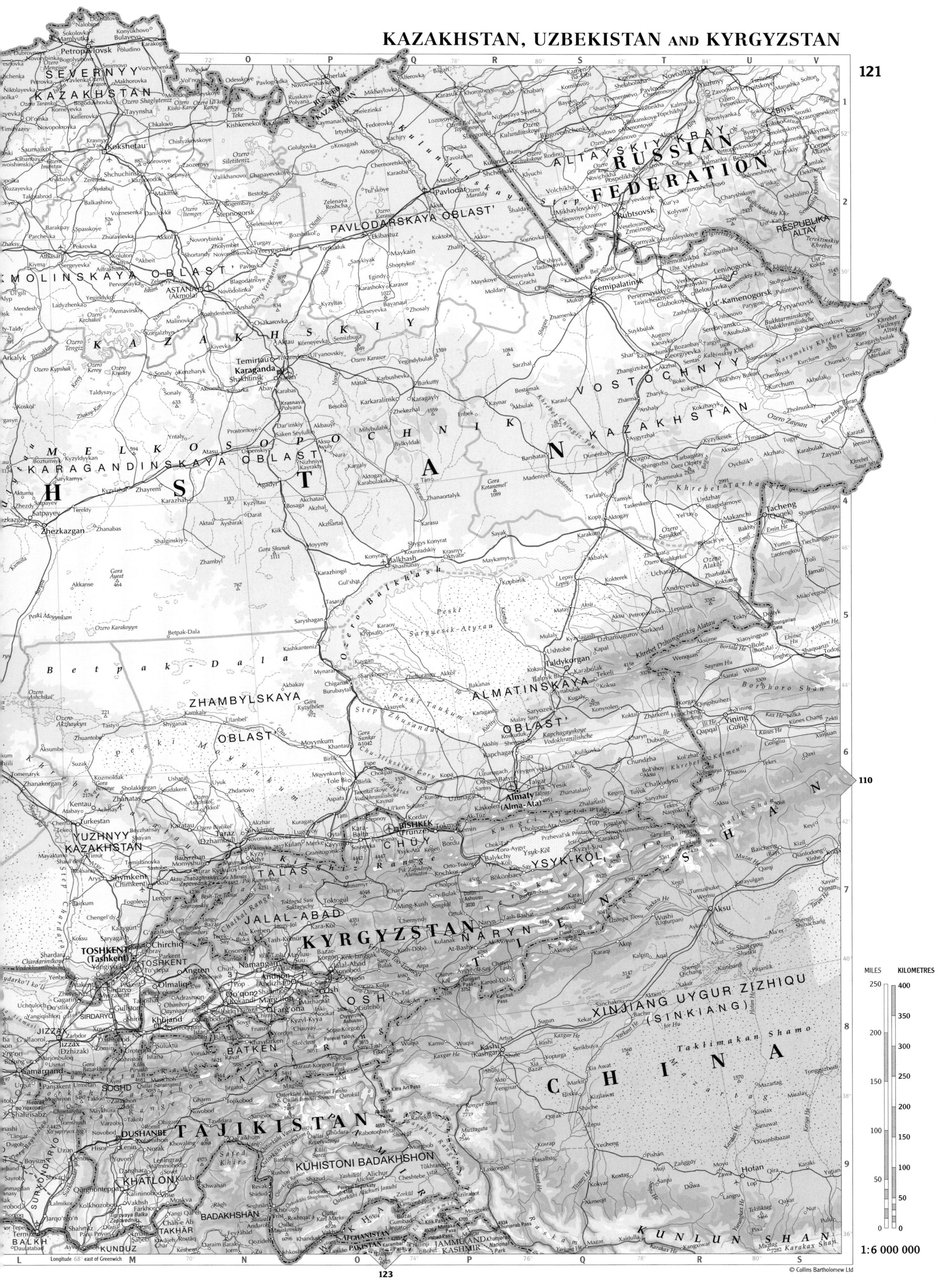
SEVERNYY KAZAKHSTAN
AKMOLINSKAYA OBLAST'
ASTANA (Akmola)
PAVLODARSKAYA OBLAST'
Pavlodar
KARAGANDINSKAYA OBLAST'
Karaganda
VOSTOCHNYY KAZAKHSTAN
Semipalatinsk
Ust'-Kamenogorsk
KAZAKHSTAN
RUSSIAN FEDERATION
ALTAYSKIY KRAY
RESPUBLIKA ALTAY
Kulundinskaya Step'
MELKOSOPOCHNIK
Betpak-Dala
Ozero Balkhash
Balkhash
ZHAMBYLSKAYA OBLAST'
ALMATINSKAYA OBLAST'
Almaty (Alma-Ata)
Taraz (Dzhambul)
YUZHNYY KAZAKHSTAN
Shymkent (Chimkent)
TOSHKENT (Tashkent)
BISHKEK (Frunze)
CHÜY
TALAS
YSYK-KÖL
Ysyk-Köl
JALAL-ABAD
NARYN
OSH
BATKEN
KYRGYZSTAN
TAJIKISTAN
DUSHANBE
SOGHD
KHATLON
KŬHISTONI BADAKHSHON
SAMARQAND
SIRDARYO
JIZZAX
SURXONDARYO
CHINA
XINJIANG UYGUR ZIZHIQU (SINKIANG)
Taklimakan Shamo
TIAN SHAN
KUNLUN SHAN
Kashi (Kashgar)
Aksu
Hotan
PAKISTAN
AFGHANISTAN
JAMMU AND KASHMIR
BADAKHSHĀN
TAKHĀR
KUNDUZ
BALKH
MILES
KILOMETRES
1:6 000 000
Longitude 68° east of Greenwich
110
123

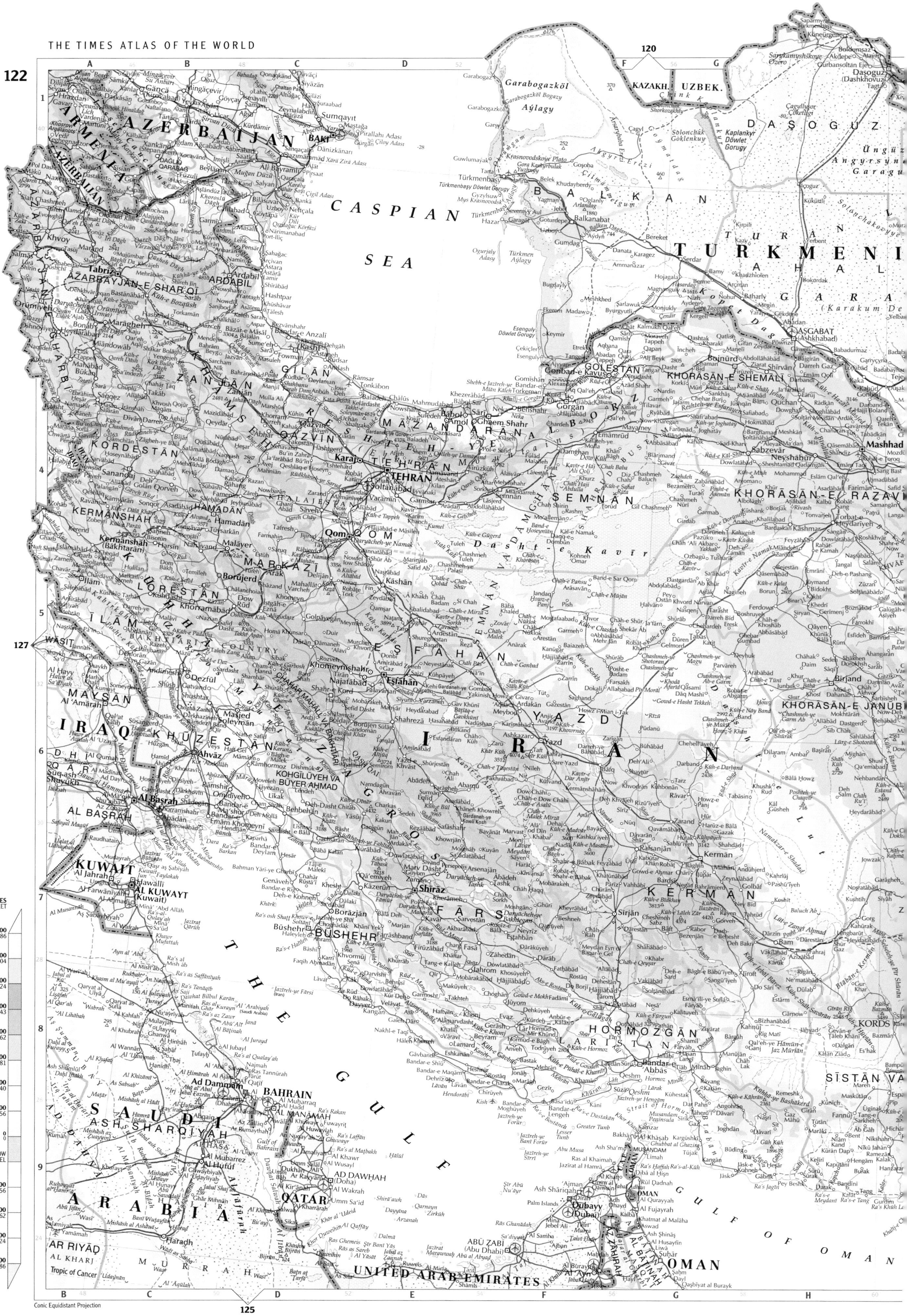
CASPIAN SEA
TURKMENI
DAŞOGUZ
BALKAN
AHAL
AZERBAIJAN
ARMENIA
IRAN
IRAQ
KUWAIT
SAUDI ARABIA
BAHRAIN
QATAR
UNITED ARAB EMIRATES
OMAN
THE GULF
GULF OF OMAN
KAZAKH.
UZBEK.
TEHRAN
Mashhad
Eşfahān
Shīrāz
Kermān
Yazd
Tabrīz
Ahvāz
Al Başrah
AL KUWAYT (Kuwait)
Ad Dammām
AL MANĀMAH
AD DAWHAH (Doha)
ABŪ ZABI (Abu Dhabi)
Dubayy (Dubai)
BAKI
Aşgabat (Ashkhabad)
Strait of Hormuz
Tropic of Cancer
Dasht-e Kavīr
Dasht-e Lut
ZAGROS MOUNTAINS
METRES
FEET
6000 19686
5000 16404
4000 13124
3000 9843
2000 6562
1000 3281
500 1640
200 656
0
LAND BELOW SEA LEVEL
200 656
2000 6562
4000 13124
6000 19686

120
127
125

Conic Equidistant Projection

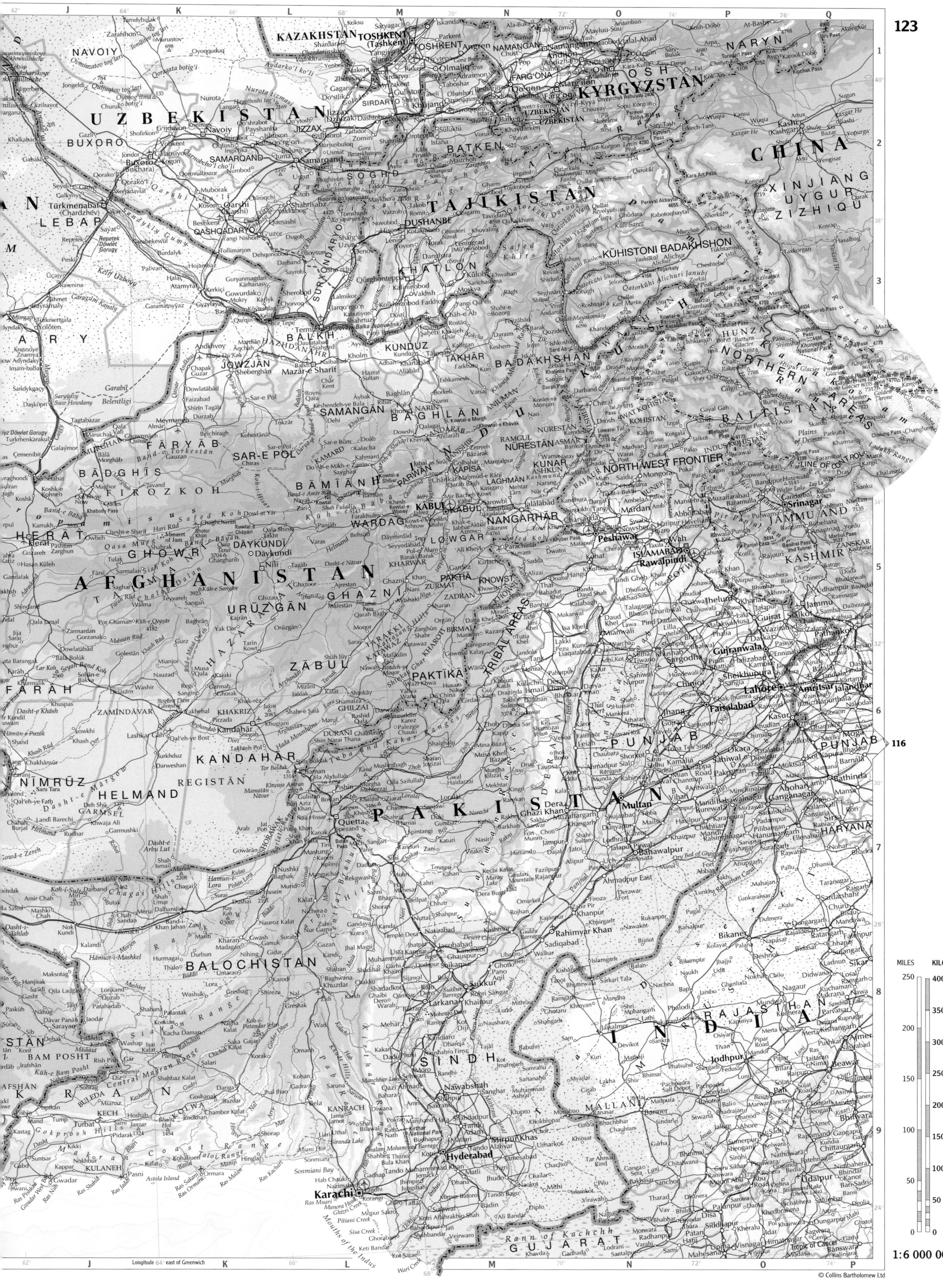
UZBEKISTAN
KAZAKHSTAN
KYRGYZSTAN
TAJIKISTAN
CHINA
XINJIANG UYGUR ZIZHIQU
AFGHANISTAN
PAKISTAN
INDIA
NAVOIY
BUXORO
SAMARQAND
QASHQADARYO
SURXONDARYO
SIRDARYO
JIZZAX
TOSHKENT (Tashkent)
NAMANGAN
FARG'ONA
ANDIJON
OSH
JALAL-ABAD
NARYN
BATKEN
SOGHD
KHATLON
KŬHISTONI BADAKHSHON
DUSHANBE
LEBAP
Türkmenabat (Chardzhev)
BALKH
JOWZJĀN
KUNDUZ
TAKHĀR
BADAKHSHĀN
SAMANGĀN
BAGHLĀN
FĀRYĀB
SAR-E POL
BĀDGHĪS
HERĀT
GHOWR
DĀYKUNDĪ
BĀMĪĀN
PARWĀN
KAPĪSA
LAGHMĀN
NŪRESTĀN
KUNAR
NANGARHĀR
KABUL
WARDAG
LOWGAR
PAKTĪĀ
KHOWST
GHAZNĪ
URŪZGĀN
ZĀBUL
PAKTĪKĀ
FARĀH
KANDAHĀR
HELMAND
NĪMRŪZ
REGISTĀN
NORTH WEST FRONTIER
TRIBAL AREAS
NORTHERN AREAS
BALTISTAN
HUNZA
JAMMU AND KASHMIR
LINE OF CONTROL
Srinagar
Peshawar
ISLAMABAD
Rawalpindi
PUNJAB
Lahore
Amritsar
Faisalabad
Multan
Quetta
BALOCHISTAN
SINDH
Hyderabad
Karachi
RAJASTHAN
HARYANA
GUJARAT
Jodhpur
Bikaner
Rann of Kachchh
Mouths of the Indus
Hindu Kush
Longitude 64° east of Greenwich
MILES
KILOMETRES
116
1:6 000 000
© Collins Bartholomew Ltd

128

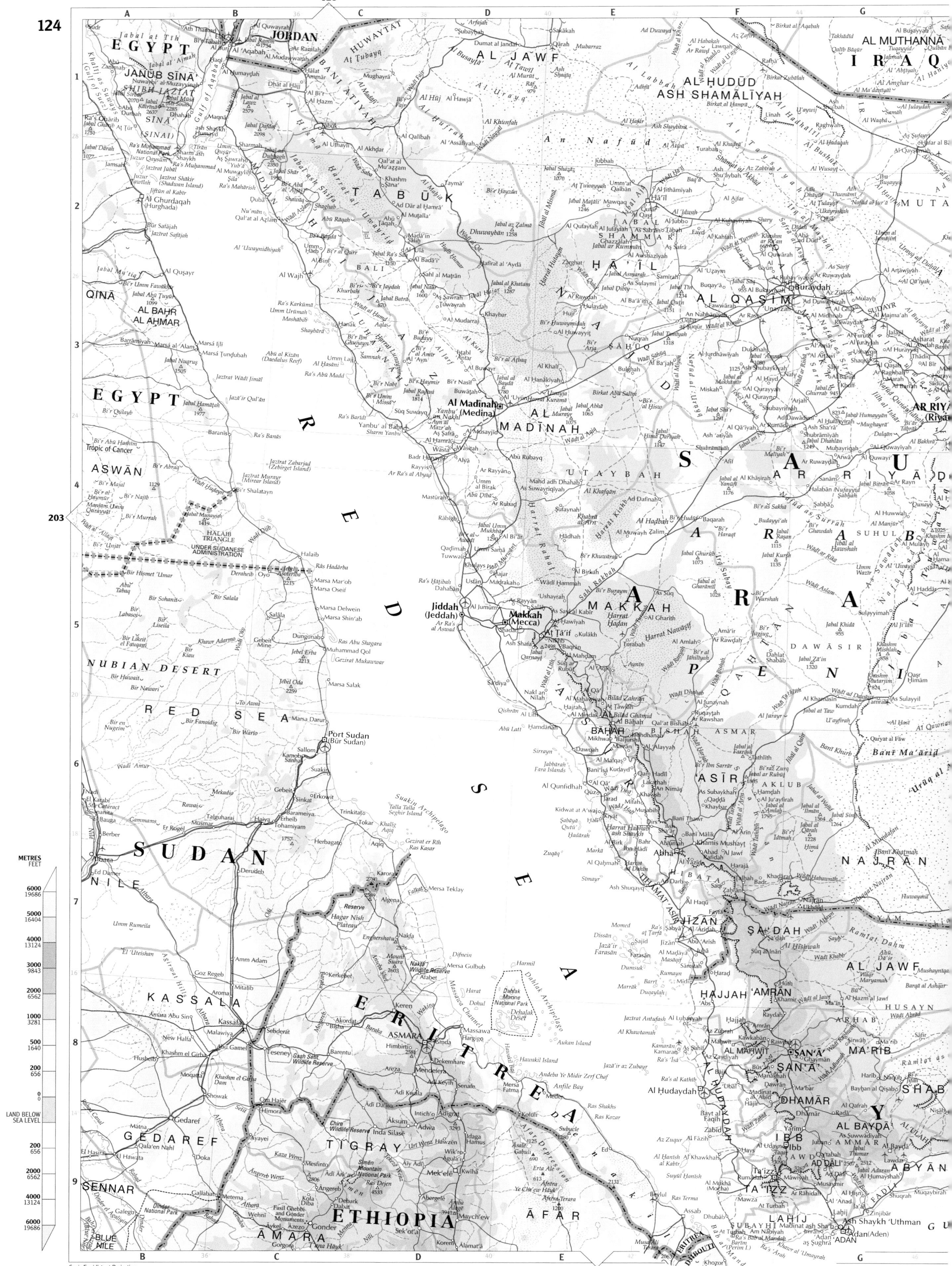

203

Conic Equidistant Projection

210

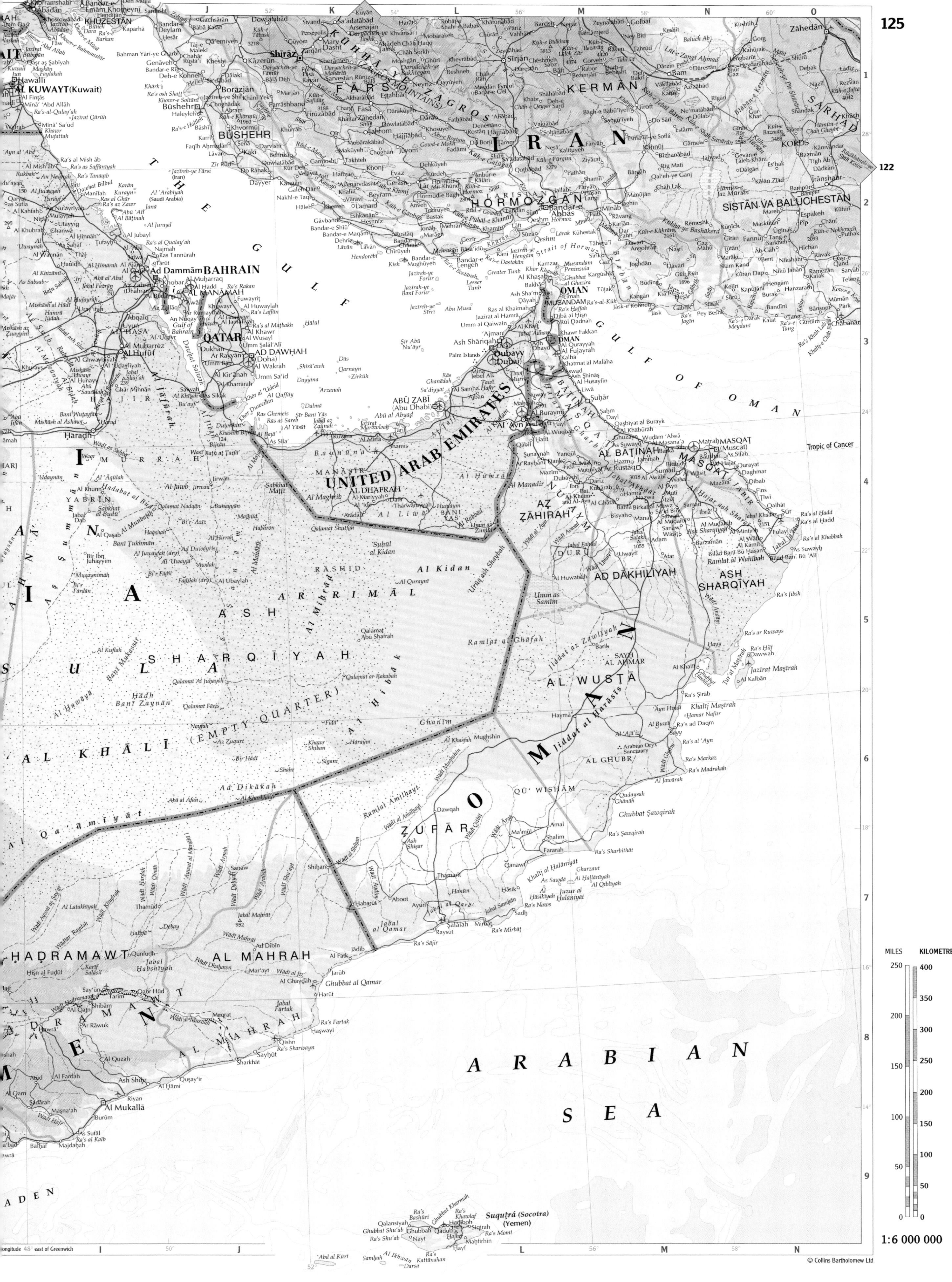
IRAN
KHUZESTĀN
FĀRS
KERMĀN
HORMOZGĀN
SĪSTĀN VA BALŪCHESTĀN
BŪSHEHR
ZAGROS MOUNTAINS
Shīrāz
Bandar-e 'Abbās
Strait of Hormuz
THE GULF
GULF OF OMAN
AL KUWAYT (Kuwait)
BAHRAIN
Al Manāmah
Ad Dammām
QATAR
AD DAWḤAH (Doha)
UNITED ARAB EMIRATES
ABŪ ZABĪ (Abu Dhabi)
Dubayy (Dubai)
Ash Shāriqah
OMAN
MUSANDAM
MASQAṬ (Muscat)
AL BĀṬINAH
AZ ZĀHIRAH
AD DAKHILIYAH
ASH SHARQĪYAH
AL WUSṬĀ
ZUFĀR
Ṣalālah
AR RUB' AL KHĀLĪ (EMPTY QUARTER)
ASH SHARQĪYAH
YEMEN
ḤAḌRAMAWT
AL MAHRAH
Al Mukallā
Tropic of Cancer
ARABIAN SEA
Suquṭrā (Socotra) (Yemen)
MILES
KILOMETRES
1:6 000 000

© Collins Bartholomew Ltd

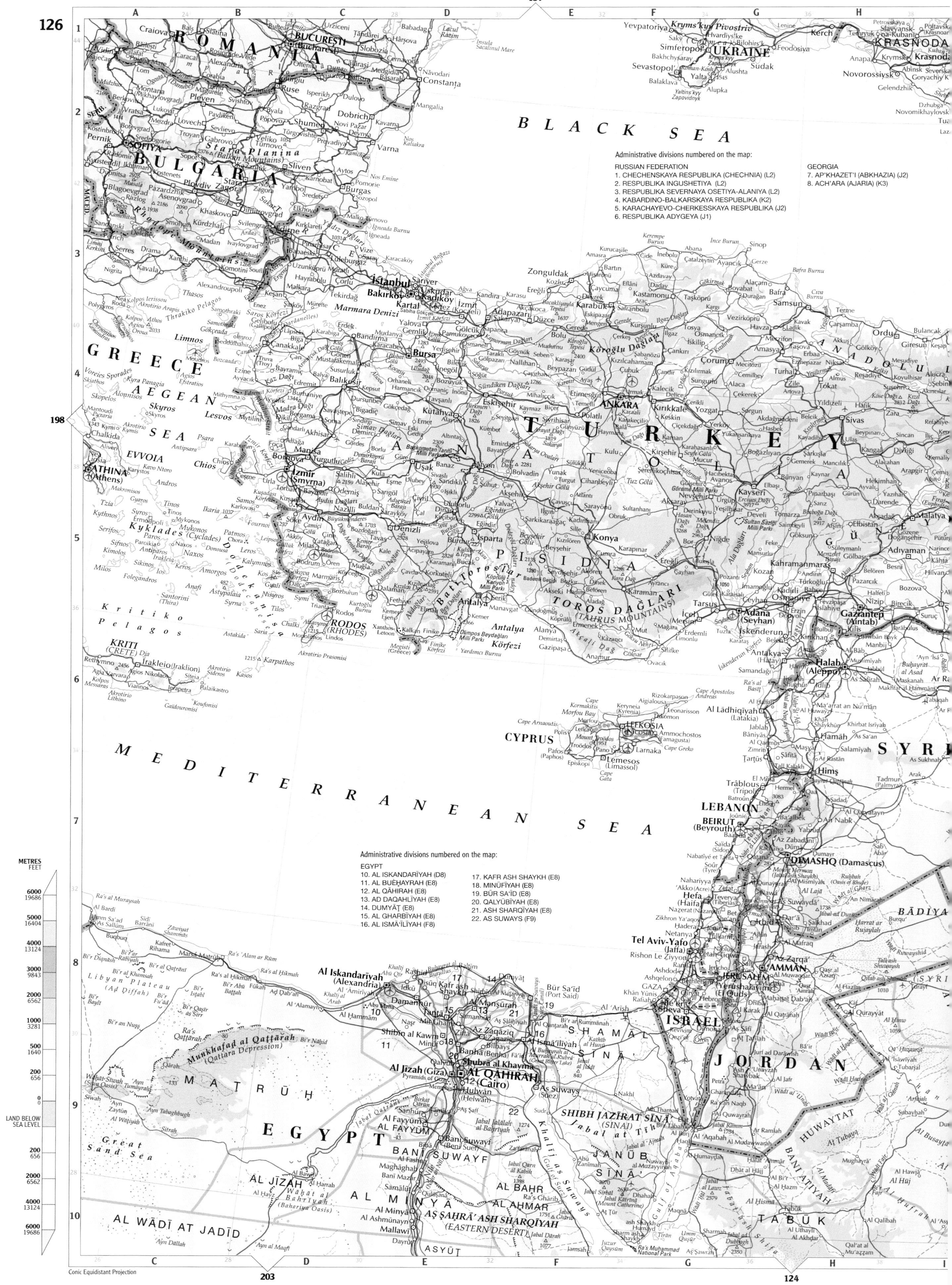
137
198
203
124
BLACK SEA
Administrative divisions numbered on the map:
RUSSIAN FEDERATION
1. CHECHENSKAYA RESPUBLIKA (CHECHNIA) (L2)
2. RESPUBLIKA INGUSHETIYA (L2)
3. RESPUBLIKA SEVERNAYA OSETIYA-ALANIYA (L2)
4. KABARDINO-BALKARSKAYA RESPUBLIKA (K2)
5. KARACHAYEVO-CHERKESSKAYA RESPUBLIKA (J2)
6. RESPUBLIKA ADYGEYA (J1)
GEORGIA
7. AP'KHAZET'I (ABKHAZIA) (J2)
8. ACH'ARA (AJARIA) (K3)
ROMANIA
BULGARIA
UKRAINE
GREECE
AEGEAN SEA
TURKEY
CYPRUS
MEDITERRANEAN SEA
LEBANON
SYRIA
ISRAEL
JORDAN
EGYPT
Administrative divisions numbered on the map:
EGYPT
10. AL ISKANDARĪYAH (D8)
11. AL BUḨAYRAH (E8)
12. AL QĀHIRAH (E8)
13. AD DAQAHLĪYAH (E8)
14. DUMYĀṬ (E8)
15. AL GHARBĪYAH (E8)
16. AL ISMĀ'ĪLĪYAH (F8)
17. KAFR ASH SHAYKH (E8)
18. MINŪFĪYAH (E8)
19. BŪR SA'ĪD (E8)
20. QALYŪBĪYAH (E8)
21. ASH SHARQĪYAH (E8)
22. AS SUWAYS (F9)
METRES
FEET
6000 19686
5000 16404
4000 13124
3000 9843
2000 6562
1000 3281
500 1640
200 656
0
LAND BELOW SEA LEVEL
200 656
2000 6562
4000 13124
6000 19686
Conic Equidistant Projection

RUSSIAN FEDERATION
STAVROPOL'SKIY KRAY
GEORGIA
T'BILISI
ARMENIA
YEREVAN
AZERBAIJAN
BAKI
RESPUBLIKA DAGESTAN
CASPIAN SEA
KAZAKHSTAN
MANGISTAUSKAYA OBLAST'
UZBEKISTAN
TURKMENISTAN
BALKAN
Garabogazköl Aýlagy
IRAN
TEHRAN
Tabriz
ĀZARBĀYJĀN-E SHARQĪ
ĀZARBĀYJĀN-E GHARBĪ
ARDABĪL
GĪLĀN
MĀZANDARĀN
GOLESTĀN
SEMNĀN
QAZVĪN
ZANJĀN
HAMADĀN
KORDESTĀN
KERMĀNSHĀH
LORESTĀN
ĪLĀM
KHŪZESTĀN
FĀRS
BŪSHEHR
Van Gölü (Lake Van)
IRAQ
BAGHDĀD
Al Mawşil
Arbil
Kirkūk
NĪNAWÁ
DAHŪK
AT TA'MĪM
AS SULAYMĀNĪYAH
ŞALĀḤ AD DĪN
DIYĀLÁ
AL ANBĀR
WĀSIŢ
BĀBIL
KARBALĀ'
AL QĀDISĪYAH
AN NAJAF
DHĪ QĀR
MAYSĀN
AL BAŞRAH
AL MUTHANNÁ
KUWAIT
AL KUWAYT (Kuwait)
SAUDI ARABIA
AL ḤUDŪD ASH SHAMĀLĪYAH
ASH SHARQĪYAH
THE GULF
ZAGROS MOUNTAINS
MILES
KILOMETRES
1:6 000 000
Longitude 44° east of Greenwich
© Collins Bartholomew Ltd
120
122
125
ISTANBUL
1:60 000
METRES 750
YARDS 750
BEYOĞLU
KARAKÖY
EMINÖNÜ
ÜSKÜDAR
Boğaziçi (Bosporus)
Haliç (Golden Horn)
Topkapı Palace
Ayasofya Museum (Hagia Sophia)
Sultan Ahmet Mosque (Blue Mosque)
Dolmabahçe Palace
Galata Tower

METRES
FEET

METRES	FEET
6000	19686
5000	16404
4000	13124
3000	9843
2000	6562
1500	4921
1000	3281
500	1640
200	656
100	328
0	0
LAND BELOW SEA LEVEL	
50	164
200	656
1000	3281
2000	6562

1:3 000 000

Conic Equidistant Projection

MILES KILOMETRES

1:3 000 000

Equidistant Projection

© Collins Bartholomew Ltd

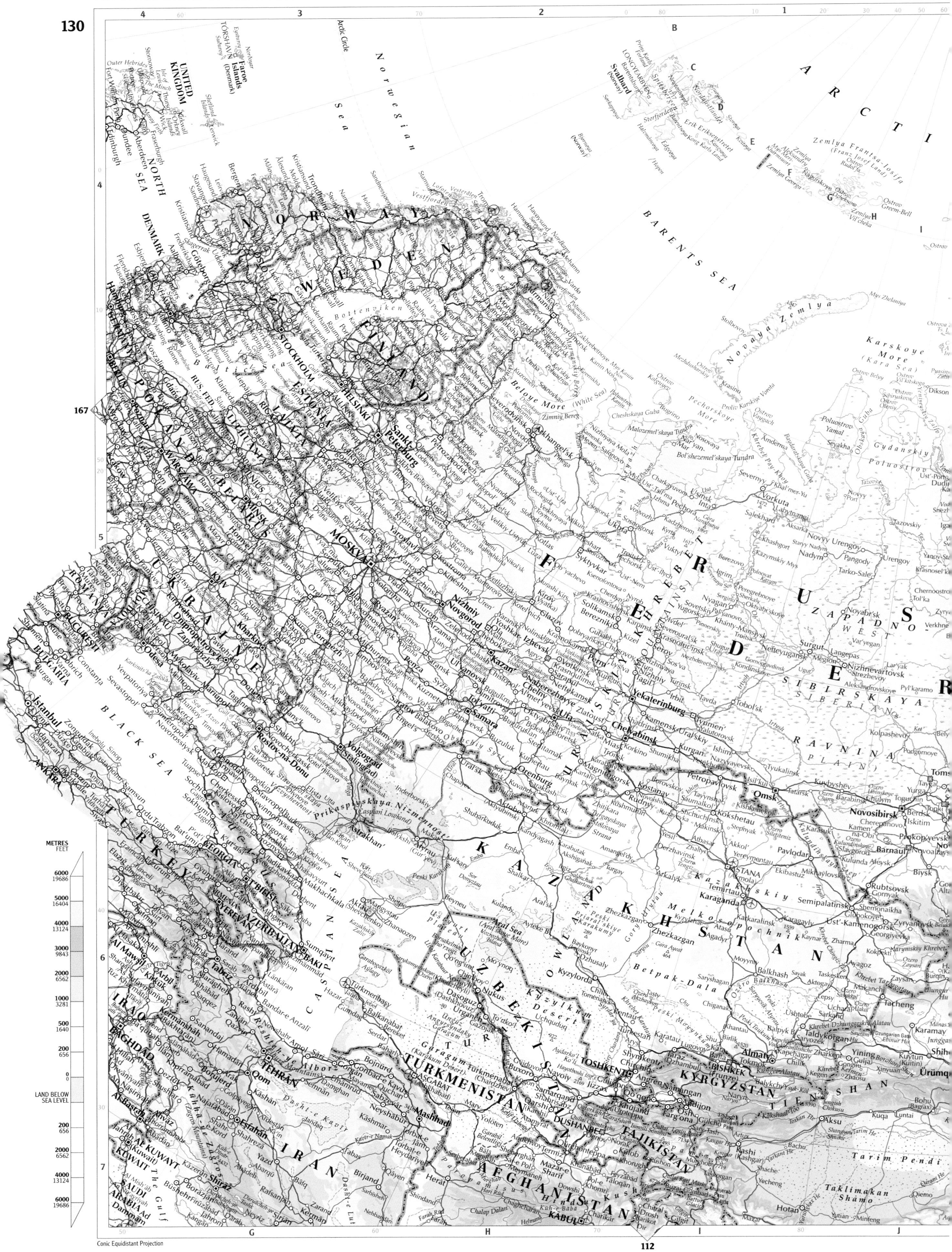

Conic Equidistant Projection

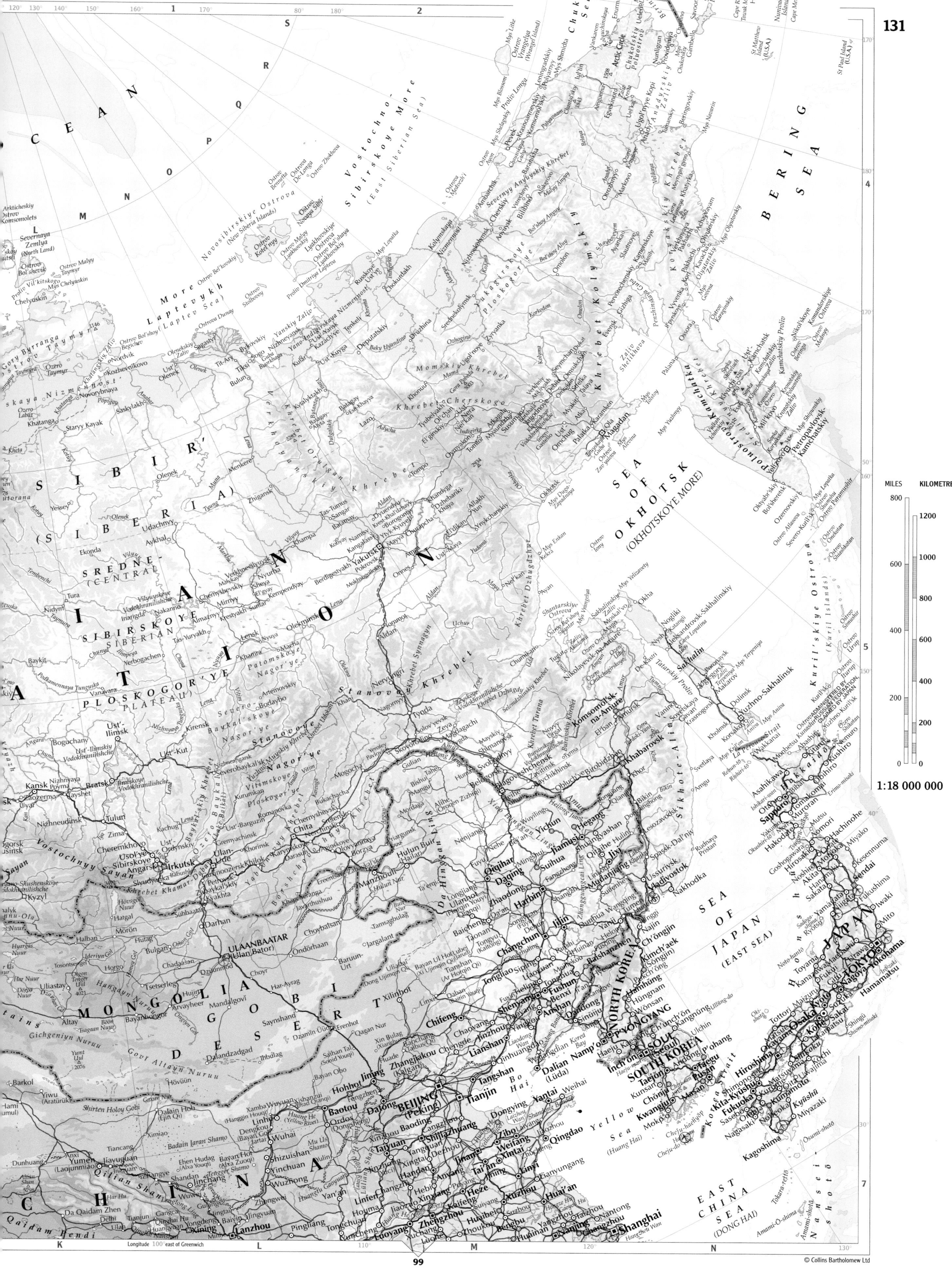
SEA OF OKHOTSK (OKHOTSKOYE MORE)
BERING SEA
SEA OF JAPAN (EAST SEA)
Yellow Sea (Huang Hai)
EAST CHINA SEA (DONG HAI)
Laptevykh More (Laptev Sea)
Vostochno-Sibirskoye More (East Siberian Sea)
Chukchi Sea
SIBIR' (SIBERIA)
SREDNE-SIBIRSKOYE PLOSKOGOR'YE (CENTRAL SIBERIAN PLATEAU)
MONGOLIA
GOBI DESERT
CHINA
JAPAN
NORTH KOREA
SOUTH KOREA
ULAANBAATAR (Ulan Bator)
BEIJING (Peking)
P'YONGYANG
SOUL (Seoul)
TOKYO
Yakutsk
Magadan
Khabarovsk
Vladivostok
Irkutsk
Chita
Harbin
Shanghai
Sapporo
Petropavlovsk-Kamchatskiy
Yuzhno-Sakhalinsk
Sakhalin
Kuril'skiye Ostrova (Kuril Islands)
Novosibirskiye Ostrova (New Siberia Islands)
Ostrov Vrangelya (Wrangel Island)
MILES
KILOMETRES
1:18 000 000
Longitude 100° east of Greenwich
99

NORTH AMERICA
Baffin Bay
Greenland
Arctic Circle
Denmark Strait
Jan Mayen (Norway)
Svalbard (Norway)
Nordaustlandet
Spitsbergen
Longyearbyen
Zemlya Frantsa-Iosifa
Greenland Sea
Bjørnøya (Norway)
BARENTS S
Nordkapp
ICELAND
Reykjavík
NORWEGIAN SEA
Trondheim
NORWAY
SWEDEN
Faroe Islands (Denmark)
Tórshavn
Shetland Islands
Orkney Islands
Outer Hebrides
Bergen
Oslo
Vänern
Skagerrak
Kattegat
Göteb
Ålborg
DENMARK
København
Odense
SCOTLAND
Glasgow
Edinburgh
NORTHERN IRELAND
Belfast
UNITED KINGDOM
NORTH SEA
Dublin
IRELAND
Manchester
Liverpool
Leeds
Birmingham
WALES
ENGLAND
Cardiff
London
English Channel
Channel Islands
NETHERLANDS
Amsterdam
's-Gravenhage
Rotterdam
Hambu
Bremen
Hannover
Bielefeld
GERM
Essen
Düsseldorf
Köln
Bonn
Aachen
Bruxelles
BELGIUM
Lille
LUXEMBOURG
Luxembourg
Frankfurt am Mai
Mannhe
Rhein
Seine
Paris
Brest
Rennes
Orléans
Loire
Strasbourg
Dijon
Nantes
FRANCE
Zürich
Bern
SWITZERLA
Genève
Lyon
Milano
Torin
Rhône
Bay of Biscay
Bordeaux
Toulouse
Marseille
Nice
MON
Cor
Pyrenees
Andorra la Vella
ANDORRA
Barcelona
A Coruña
Bilbao
Ebro
Zaragoza
Porto
Salamanca
Madrid
Tajo
SPAIN
PORTUGAL
Lisboa
Valencia
Islas Baleares
Menorca
Mallorca
Eivissa
Sardeg
Córdoba
Sevilla
Cartagena
Cádiz
Málaga
Gibraltar (U.K.)
Ceuta (Spain)
Melilla (Spain)
ATLANTIC OCEAN
Arquipélago dos Açores
Corvo
Flores
São Jorge
Faial
Pico
Terceira
Azores (Portugal)
São Miguel
Ponta Delgada
Santa Maria
Arquipélago da Madeira
Madeira (Portugal)
Ilha de Porto Santo
Funchal
AFRICA
ME
A B C D E
1 2 3 4 5 6 7

Orthographic Projection

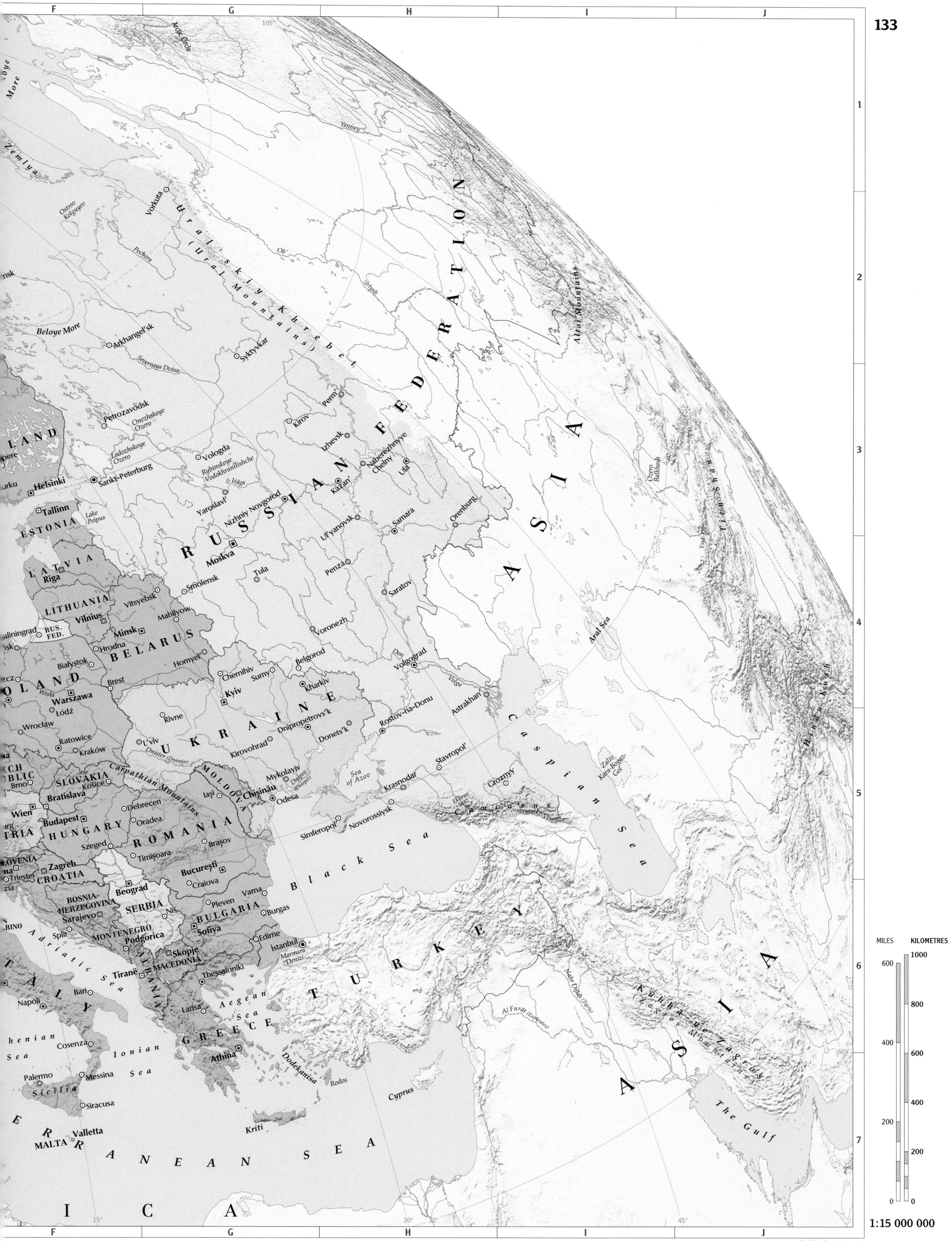

F
G
H
I
J
1
2
3
4
5
6
7
Arctic Circle
RUSSIAN FEDERATION
ASIA
Ural'skiy Khrebet (Ural Mountains)
Vorkuta
Ostrov Kolguyev
Pechora
Ob'
Yenisey
Irtysh
Altai Mountains
Beloye More
Arkhangel'sk
Syktyvkar
Severnaya Dvina
Petrozavodsk
Onezhskoye Ozero
Ladozhskoye Ozero
Vologda
Rybinskoye Vodokhranilishche
Volga
Sankt-Peterburg
Helsinki
Tallinn
Lake Peipus
ESTONIA
Yaroslavl'
Nizhniy Novgorod
Kirov
Perm'
Izhevsk
Naberezhnyye Chelny
Ufa
Kazan'
Samara
Orenburg
Ul'yanovsk
Moskva
Tula
Penza
Saratov
Smolensk
LATVIA
Riga
LITHUANIA
Vilnius
Vitsyebsk
Mahilyow
Minsk
BELARUS
Hrodna
Homyel'
Kaliningrad
RUS. FED.
Voronezh
Belgorod
Kharkiv
Chernihiv
Sumy
Kyiv
Brest
Białystok
POLAND
Warszawa
Wisła
Łódź
Wrocław
Katowice
Kraków
Rivne
L'viv
UKRAINE
Dnipropetrovs'k
Donets'k
Kirovohrad
Dniester (Dniester)
Don
Volgograd
Rostov-na-Donu
Astrakhan'
Aral Sea
Ozero Balkhash
Tien Shan
Ysyk-Köl
Hindu Kush
Caspian Sea
Zaliv Kara-Bogaz-Gol
Stavropol'
Sea of Azov
Krasnodar
Elbrus
Caucasus
Groznyy
Mykolayiv
Dnipro (Dnieper)
Odesa
Chişinău
Iaşi
MOLDOVA
Carpathian Mountains
SLOVAKIA
Košice
Bratislava
Brno
CZECH REPUBLIC
Wien
AUSTRIA
Budapest
Debrecen
Oradea
HUNGARY
ROMANIA
Braşov
Szeged
Timişoara
Simferopol'
Novorossiysk
Black Sea
Bucureşti
Craiova
SLOVENIA
Zagreb
Trieste
CROATIA
BOSNIA-HERZEGOVINA
Beograd
SERBIA
Niš
Pleven
Varna
Burgas
BULGARIA
Sofiya
Sarajevo
MONTENEGRO
Podgorica
Split
Adriatic Sea
SAN MARINO
Skopje
MACEDONIA
Tiranë
ALBANIA
Edirne
İstanbul
Marmara Denizi
Thessaloniki
TURKEY
ITALY
Bari
Napoli
Larisa
Aegean Sea
GREECE
Tyrrhenian Sea
Cosenza
Ionian Sea
Athina
Dodekanisa
Rodos
Palermo
Messina
Sicilia
Siracusa
Kriti
Cyprus
MALTA
Valletta
MEDITERRANEAN SEA
AFRICA
Nahr Dijlah (Tigris)
Al Furāt (Euphrates)
Kūhhā-ye Zāgros (Zagros Mountains)
The Gulf
90°
105°
15°
30°
45°
60°
MILES
KILOMETRES
600
400
200
0
1000
800
600
400
200
0

1:15 000 000

© Collins Bartholomew Ltd

130

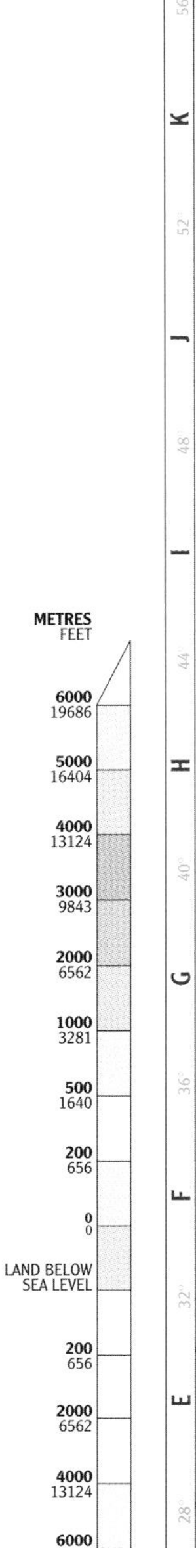
METRES
FEET
6000
19686
5000
16404
4000
13124
3000
9843
2000
6562
1000
3281
500
1640
200
656
0
0
LAND BELOW
SEA LEVEL
200
656
2000
6562
4000
13124
6000
19686

BARENTS SEA
BELOYE MORE
(WHITE SEA)
BALTIC SEA
Gulf of Finland
RUSSIA
FINLAND
SWEDEN
ESTONIA
LATVIA
LITHUANIA
RESPUBLIKA KARELIYA
MURMANSKAYA OBLAST'
ARKHANGEL'SKAYA OBLAST'
NENETSKIY AVTONOMNYY OKRUG
RESPUBLIKA KOMI
KHANTY-MANSIYSKIY AVTONOMNYY OKRUG-YUGRA
SVERDLOVSKAYA OBLAST'
PERMSKIY KRAY
KIROVSKAYA OBLAST'
VOLOGODSKAYA OBLAST'
LENINGRADSKAYA OBLAST'
NOVGORODSKAYA OBLAST'
PSKOVSKAYA OBLAST
TVERSKAYA OBLAST'
YAROSLAVSKAYA OBLAST'
KOSTROMSKAYA OBLAST'
IVANOVSKAYA
UDMURTSKAYA RESPUBLIKA
RESPUBLIKA MARIY EL
URAL MOUNTAINS
Arkhangel'sk
Murmansk
Sankt-Peterburg
HELSINKI
(Helsingfors)
TALLINN
RIGA
STOCKHOLM
Perm'
Syktyvkar
Petrozavodsk
Kirov
Vologda
Yaroslavl'
Kostroma
Ivanovo
Cherepovets
Velikiy Novgorod
Pskov
Tartu
Tampere
Turku
Oulu
Vorkuta
Severodvinsk
Kotlas
Ukhta
Naryan-Mar
Izhevsk
Nizhniy Novgorod
Arctic Circle
Åland
D E F G H I J K L M N
1 2 3 4
ST PETERSBURG
1:125 000
0 METRES 1000
0 YARDS 1000
Neva
VIBORGSKAYA STORONA
Finland Station
Smol'nyy
Aleksandr Nevskiy Monastery
Summer Palace of Peter I
Russian Museum
Peter and Paul Fortress
The Hermitage
Admiralty
Kazan Cathedral
St Isaac's Cathedral
State University
Moscow Station
Vitebsk Station
Warsaw Station
Baltic Station
Planetarium
Artillery Museum
Lenin Stadium
Vasil'yevskiy Ostrov
Petrogradskiy Ostrov
Kamennyy Ostrov
Krestovskiy Ostrov
Yelagin Ostrov
Dekabristov Ostrov
Gutuevskiy Ostrov
Kirov Stadium
Volkovskoye Cemetery
Smolenskoye Cemetery
Ekaterinhof Park
NEVSKIY PROSPEKT
MOSKOVSKIY PROSPEKT
KAMENNOOSTROVSKIY PROSPEKT
BOL'SHOY SAMPSONIYEVSKIY PROSPEKT
LITEYNYY PROSPEKT
ZAGORODNYY PROSPEKT

140

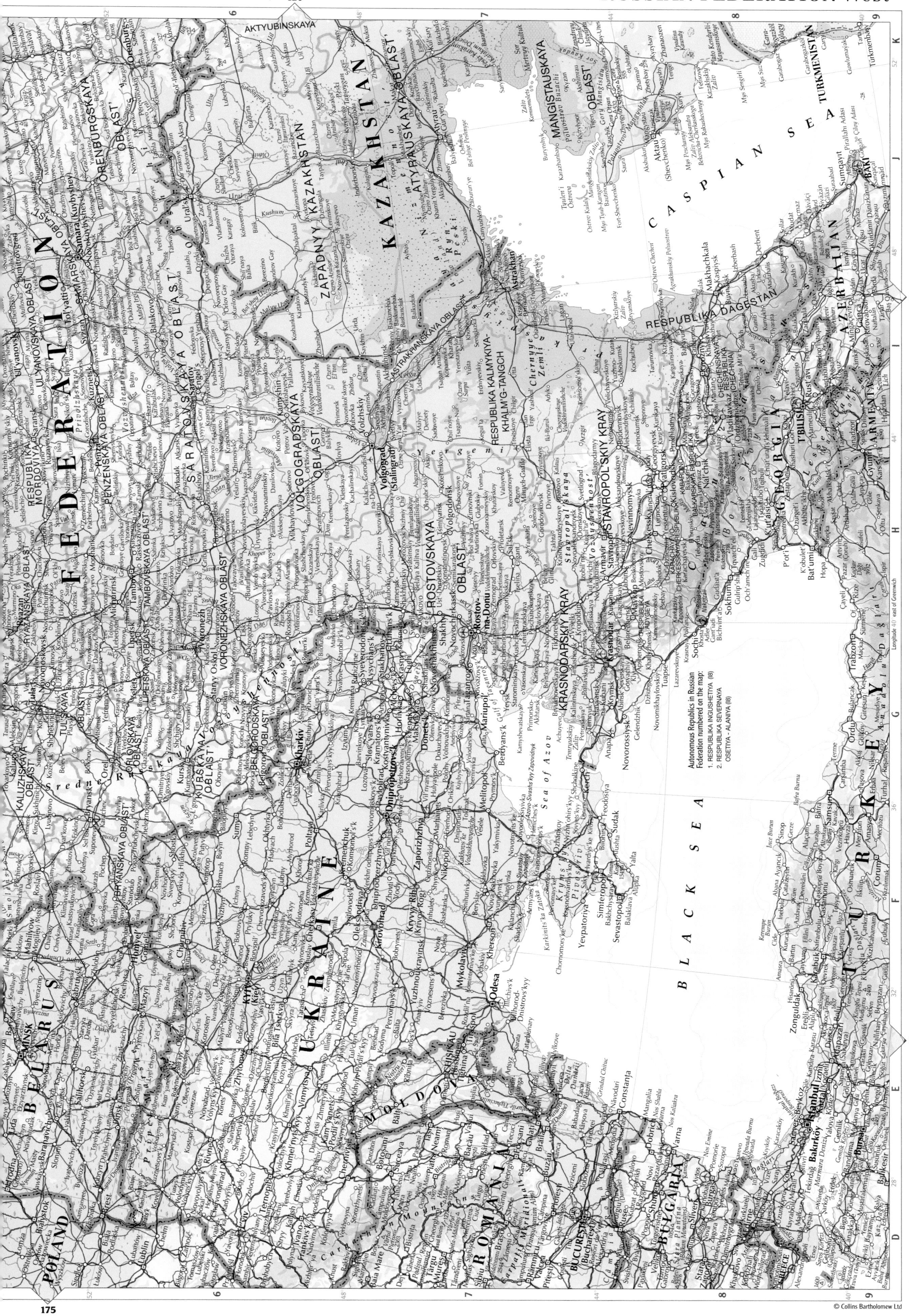
120
122
126
175
RUSSIAN FEDERATION
KAZAKHSTAN
UKRAINE
BELARUS
MOLDOVA
ROMANIA
BULGARIA
TURKEY
GEORGIA
ARMENIA
AZERBAIJAN
TURKMENISTAN
POLAND
GREECE
CASPIAN SEA
BLACK SEA
Sea of Azov
Autonomous Republics in Russian Federation numbered on the map:
1. RESPUBLIKA INGUSHETIYA (8)
2. RESPUBLIKA SEVERNAYA OSETIYA - ALANIYA (8)
Longitude 40 east of Greenwich

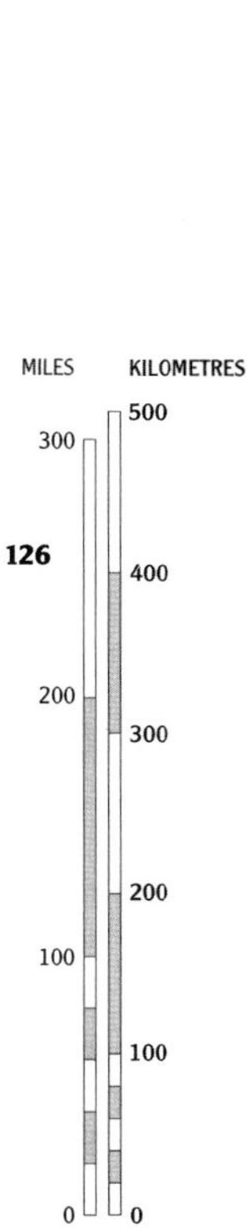
MILES
KILOMETRES
300
200
100
0
500
400
300
200
100
0

1:7 200 000

© Collins Bartholomew Ltd

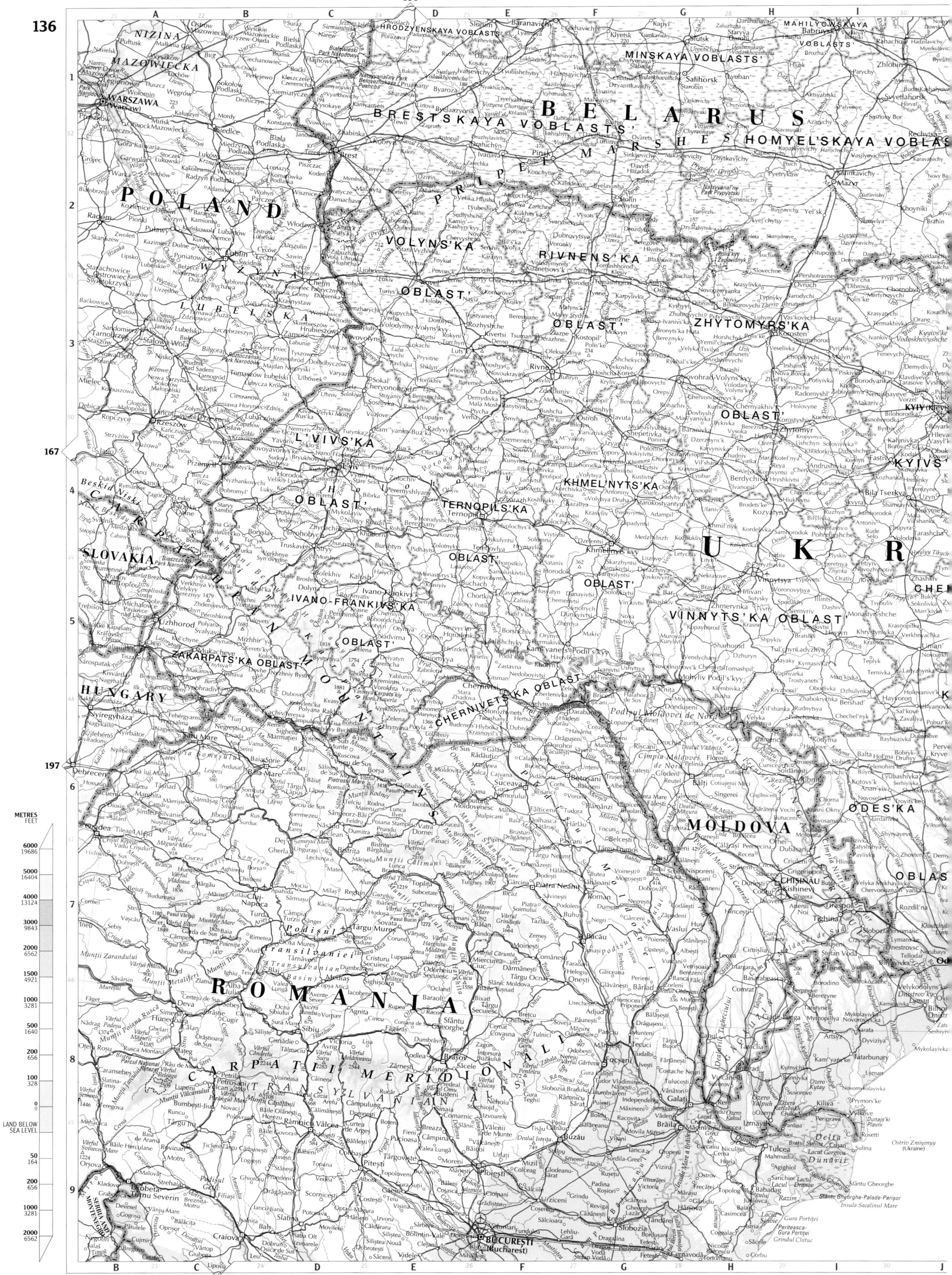
138
197
167
POLAND
BELARUS
UKR
SLOVAKIA
HUNGARY
ROMANIA
MOLDOVA
SERBIA AND MONTENEGRO
MAZOWIECKA
HRODZYENSKAYA VOBLASTS'
MINSKAYA VOBLASTS'
MAHILYOWSKAYA VOBLASTS'
BRESTSKAYA VOBLASTS'
HOMYEL'SKAYA VOBLAS
PRIPET MARSHES
VOLYNS'KA OBLAST'
RIVNENS'KA OBLAST'
ZHYTOMYRS'KA OBLAST'
L'VIVS'KA OBLAST'
TERNOPIL'S'KA OBLAST'
KHMEL'NYTS'KA OBLAST'
IVANO-FRANKIVS'KA OBLAST'
VINNYTS'KA OBLAST'
ZAKARPATS'KA OBLAST'
CHERNIVETS'KA OBLAST'
ODES'KA OBLAS
KYIVS'
CARPATHIAN MOUNTAINS
CARPAȚII MERIDIONALI
WARSZAWA (Warsaw)
BUCUREȘTI (Bucharest)
CHIȘINĂU (Kishinev)
METRES
FEET
6000
19686
5000
16404
4000
13124
3000
9843
2000
6562
1500
4921
1000
3281
500
1640
200
656
100
328
0
0
LAND BELOW SEA LEVEL
50
164
200
656
1000
3281
2000
6562
Conic Equidistant Projection

RUSSIAN
FEDERATION
BRYANSKAYA OBLAST'
ORLOVSKAYA OBLAST'
LIPETSKAYA OBLAST'
TAMBOVSKAYA OBLAST'
KURSKAYA OBLAST'
VORONEZHSKAYA OBLAST'
BELGORODSKAYA OBLAST'
SUMS'KA OBLAST'
POLTAVS'KA OBLAST'
KHARKIVS'KA OBLAST'
LUHANS'KA OBLAST'
DONETS'KA OBLAST'
DNIPROPETROVS'KA OBLAST'
ZAPORIZ'KA OBLAST'
KHERSONS'KA OBLAST'
ROSTOVSKAYA OBLAST'
KRASNODARSKIY KRAY
RESPUBLIKA KRYM (CRIMEA)
Sea of Azov
Kharkiv
Dnipropetrovs'k
Zaporizhzhya
Donets'k
Luhans'k
Poltava
Sumy
Kursk
Belgorod
Voronezh
Orel
Kremenchuk
Kirovohrad
Mykolayiv
Kherson
Melitopol'
Mariupol'
Rostov-na-Donu
Taganrog
Krasnodar
Novorossiysk
Kerch
Simferopol'
Sevastopol'
Yalta
Gulf of Taganrog
Karkinits'ka Zatoka
Temryukskiy Zaliv
Kosa Arabats'ka Strilka
BLACK SEA
MILES
KILOMETRES
1:3 000 000
Longitude 32° east of Greenwich
139
135

© Collins Bartholomew Ltd

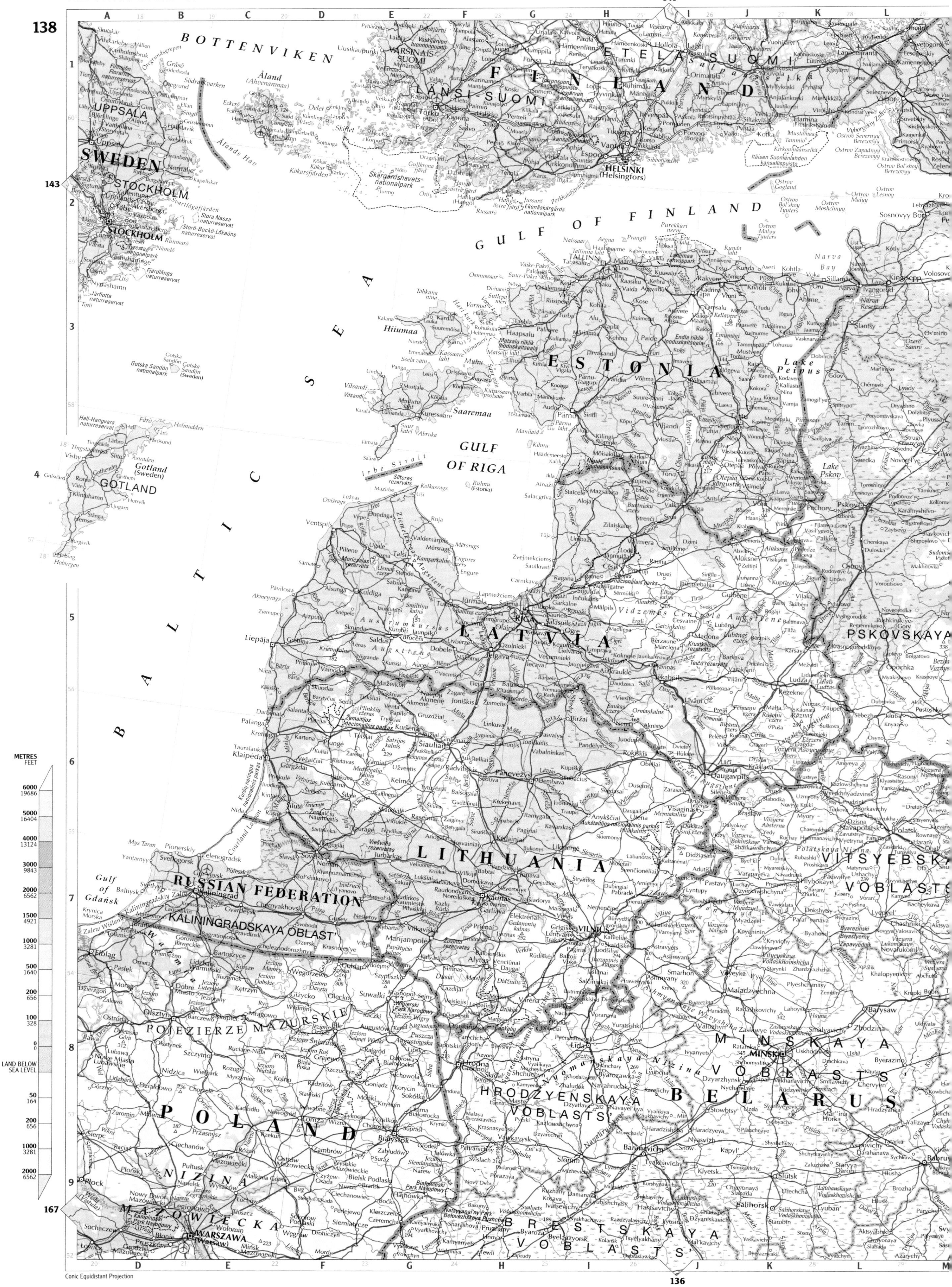
BOTTENVIKEN
FINLAND
LÄNSI-SUOMI
ETELÄ-SUOMI
SWEDEN
UPPSALA
STOCKHOLM
HELSINKI (Helsingfors)
GULF OF FINLAND
TALLINN
ESTONIA
BALTIC SEA
GULF OF RIGA
GOTLAND
Lake Peipus
Lake Pskov
LATVIA
RIGA
PSKOVSKAYA
LITHUANIA
RUSSIAN FEDERATION
KALININGRADSKAYA OBLAST'
VITSYEBSKAYA VOBLASTS'
MINSKAYA VOBLASTS'
BELARUS
HRODZYENSKAYA VOBLASTS'
BRESTSKAYA VOBLASTS'
POLAND
POJEZIERZE MAZURSKIE
NIZINA MAZOWIECKA
WARSZAWA (Warsaw)
MINSK
VILNIUS
Gulf of Gdańsk
METRES
FEET
6000 19686
5000 16404
4000 13124
3000 9843
2000 6562
1500 4921
1000 3281
500 1640
200 656
100 328
0 0
LAND BELOW SEA LEVEL
50 164
200 656
1000 3281
2000 6562
141
143
167
136

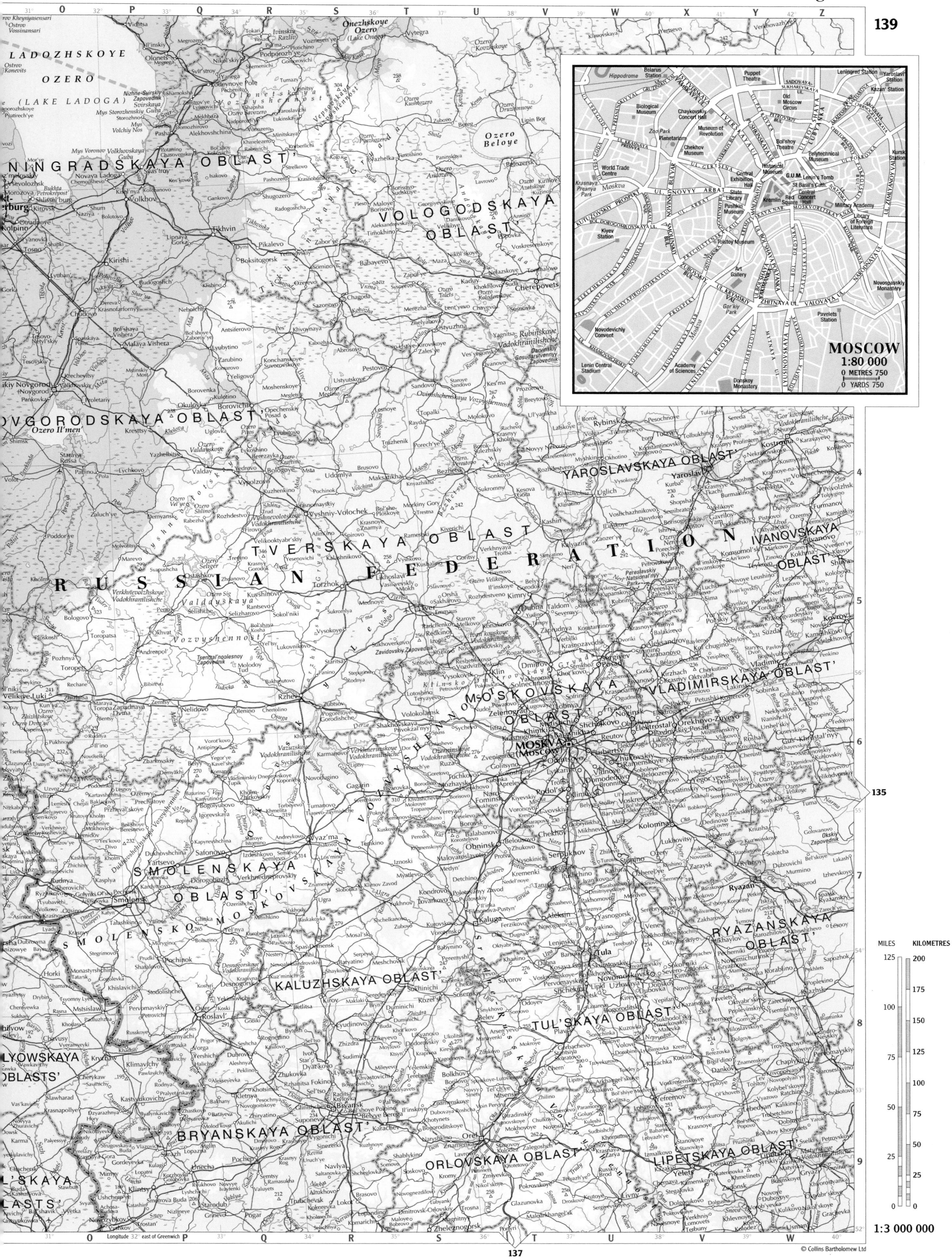
RUSSIAN FEDERATION
LADOZHSKOYE OZERO
(LAKE LADOGA)
Onezhskoye Ozero
(Lake Onega)
Ozero Beloye
NOVGORODSKAYA OBLAST'
VOLOGODSKAYA OBLAST'
YAROSLAVSKAYA OBLAST'
TVERSKAYA OBLAST
IVANOVSKAYA OBLAST'
MOSKOVSKAYA OBLAST'
VLADIMIRSKAYA OBLAST'
SMOLENSKAYA OBLAST'
KALUZHSKAYA OBLAST'
RYAZANSKAYA OBLAST'
TUL'SKAYA OBLAST'
BRYANSKAYA OBLAST'
ORLOVSKAYA OBLAST'
LIPETSKAYA OBLAST'
Moskva (Moscow)
MOSCOW
1:80 000
METRES 750
YARDS 750
Kremlin
Red Square
Bol'shoy Theatre
G.U.M.
St Basil's Cath.
Belarus Station
Leningrad Station
Kiyev Station
Pavelets Station
Novodevichiy Convent
Gor'kiy Park
MILES
KILOMETRES
135

© Collins Bartholomew Ltd

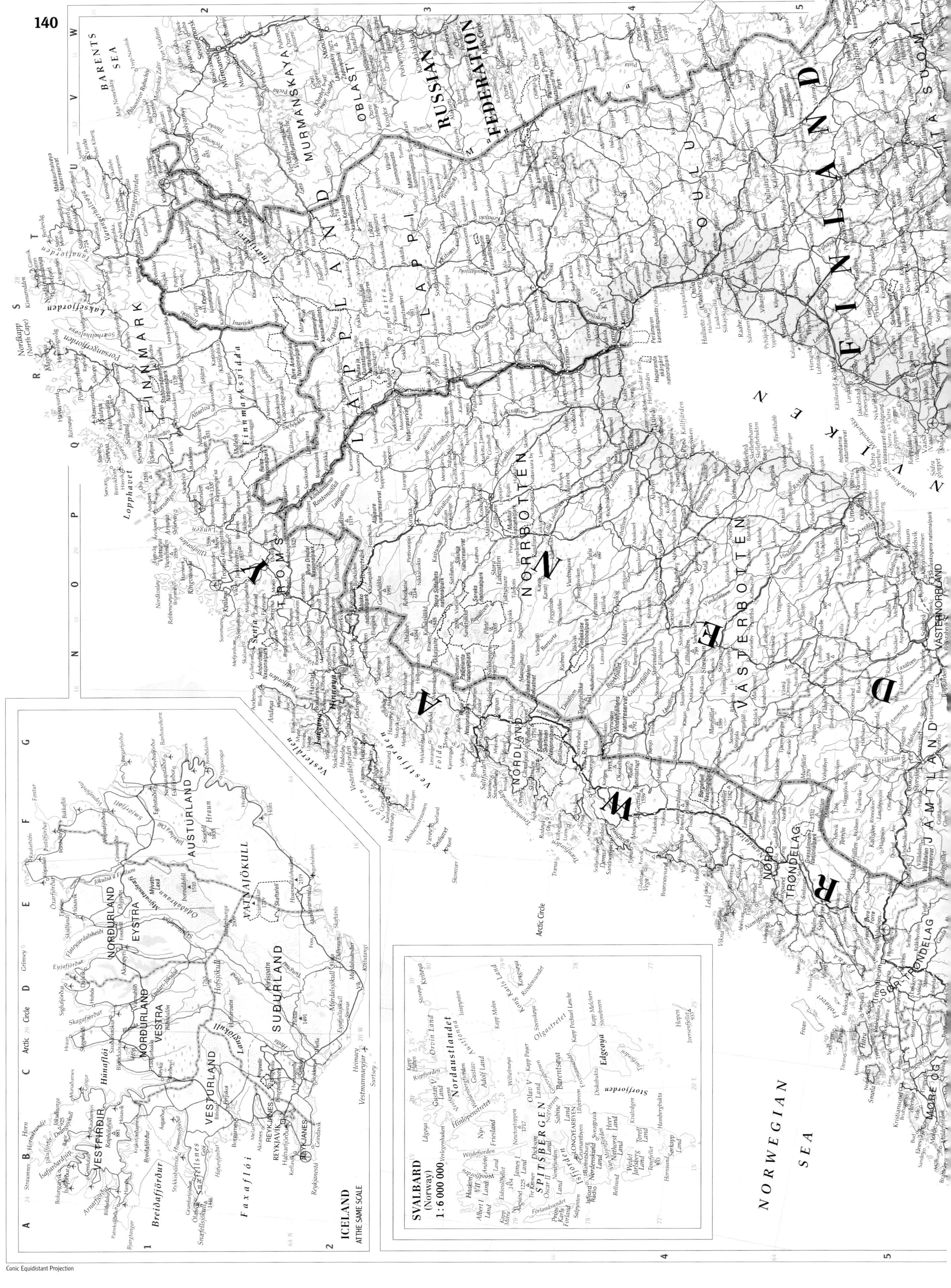
BARENTS SEA
RUSSIAN FEDERATION
MURMANSKAYA OBLAST'
FINLAND
LAPPI
OULU
FINNMARK
TROMS
NORRBOTTEN
VÄSTERBOTTEN
NORDLAND
NORD TRØNDELAG
SØR TRØNDELAG
JÄMTLAND
NORWEGIAN SEA
Arctic Circle
SVALBARD (Norway) 1: 6 000 000
ICELAND AT THE SAME SCALE

METRES
FEET
3000
9843
2000
6562
1500
4921
1000
3281
500
1640
200
656
100
328
0
0
LAND BELOW SEA LEVEL
50
164
200
656
1000
3281
2000
6562
MILES
KILOMETRES
1:4 000 000
167
GULF OF FINLAND
GULF OF RIGA
BALTIC SEA
SKAGERRAK
KATTEGAT
ESTONIA
LATVIA
LITHUANIA
BELARUS
RUSSIAN FEDERATION
POLAND
GERMANY
DENMARK
HELSINKI (Helsingfors)
TALLINN
STOCKHOLM
OSLO
KØBENHAVN (Copenhagen)
VILNIUS
Gotland (Sweden)
Bornholm (Denmark)
Åland (Ahvenanmaa)

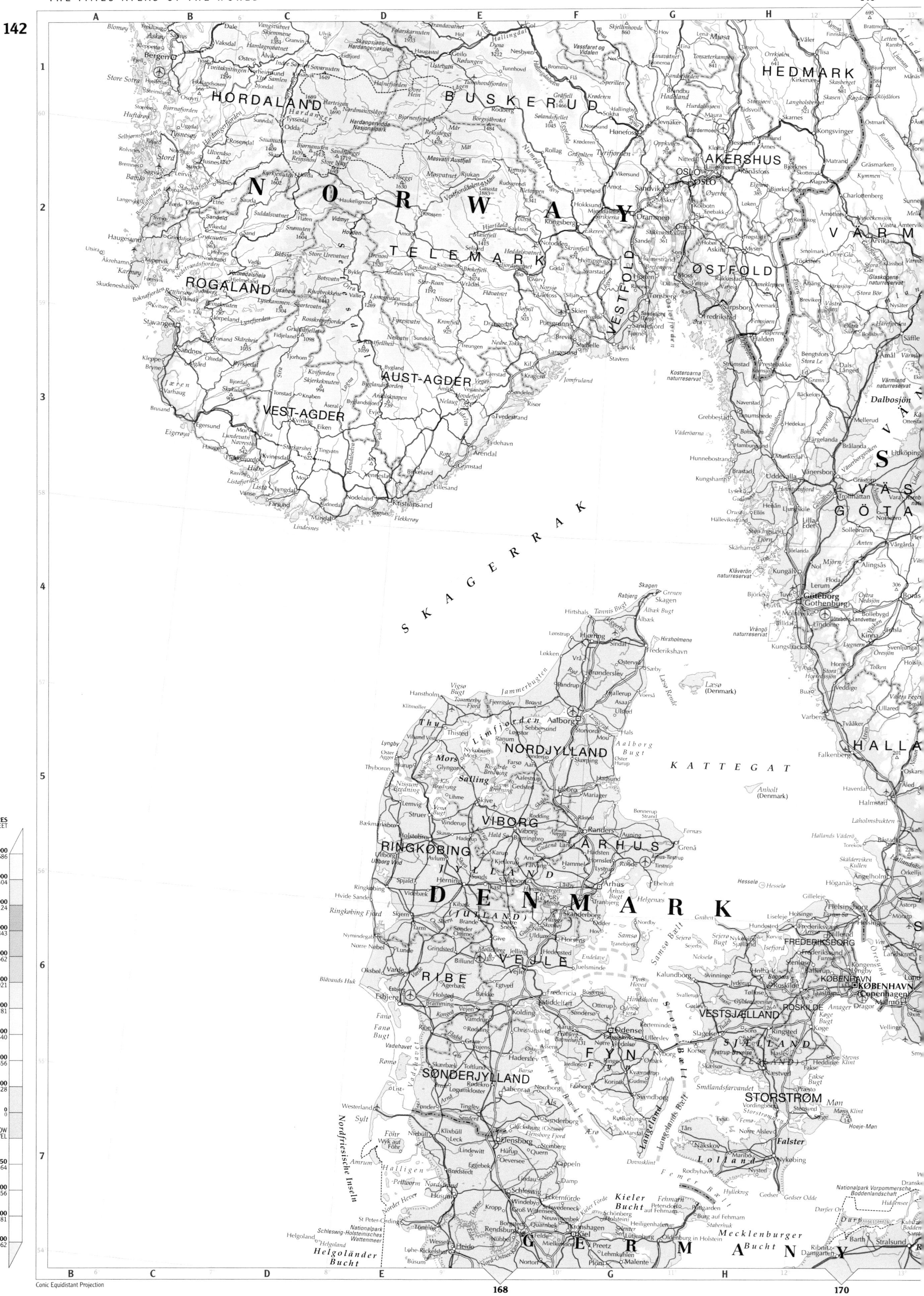
140
A
B
C
D
E
F
G
H
NORWAY
HORDALAND
BUSKERUD
HEDMARK
AKERSHUS
OSLO
TELEMARK
ROGALAND
ØSTFOLD
VESTFOLD
AUST-AGDER
VEST-AGDER
VÄRM
SKAGERRAK
KATTEGAT
DENMARK
JYLLAND
NORDJYLLAND
VIBORG
ÅRHUS
RINGKØBING
VEJLE
RIBE
SØNDERJYLLAND
FYN
VESTSJÆLLAND
SJÆLLAND
(ZEALAND)
FREDERIKSBORG
KØBENHAVN
(Copenhagen)
ROSKILDE
STORSTRØM
HALLA
GÖTA
VÄS
GERMANY
Bergen
Stavanger
Haugesund
Kristiansand
Arendal
Skagen
Aalborg
Århus
Odense
Esbjerg
Göteborg
Gothenburg
Helsingborg
Kiel
Flensburg
Lolland
Falster
Møn
Læsø
(Denmark)
Anholt
(Denmark)
Kieler Bucht
Helgoländer Bucht
Mecklenburger Bucht
168
170
METRES
FEET
6000
19686
5000
16404
4000
13124
3000
9843
2000
6562
1500
4921
1000
3281
500
1640
200
656
100
328
0
0
LAND BELOW SEA LEVEL
50
164
200
656
1000
3281
2000
6562

GÄVLEBORG
UPPSALA
Uppland
VÄSTMANLAND
STOCKHOLM
ÖREBRO
SÖDERMANLAND
ÖSTERGOTLAND
JÖNKÖPING
KALMAR
KRONOBERG
BLEKINGE
BORNHOLM
Bornholm (Denmark)
Bornholmsgattet
Hanöbukten
GOTLAND
GOTLAND (Sweden)
Gotska Sandön (Sweden)
ÖLAND
Kalmarsund
Ålands Hav
Åland (Ahvenanmaa)
FINLAND
LÄNSI-SUOMI
Skärgårdshavets nationalpark
ESTONIA
Hiiumaa
Saaremaa
Irbe Strait
LATVIA
LITHUANIA
RUSSIAN FEDERATION
Courland Lagoon
Gulf of Gdańsk
POLAND
BALTIC SEA
Gävle
Uppsala
Västerås
Örebro
Eskilstuna
Södertälje
Nyköping
Norrköping
Linköping
Västervik
Kalmar
Växjö
Karlskrona
Visby
Ventspils
Liepāja
Klaipėda
Kaliningrad
Gdańsk
Gdynia
Słupsk
Koszalin
Elbląg
Turku (Åbo)
Mariehamn
Rønne
MILES
KILOMETRES
1:2 250 000
138
175

METRES
FEET
6000 19686
5000 16404
4000 13124
3000 9843
2000 6562
1500 4921
1000 3281
500 1640
200 656
100 328
0 0
LAND BELOW SEA LEVEL
50 164
200 656
1000 3281
2000 6562

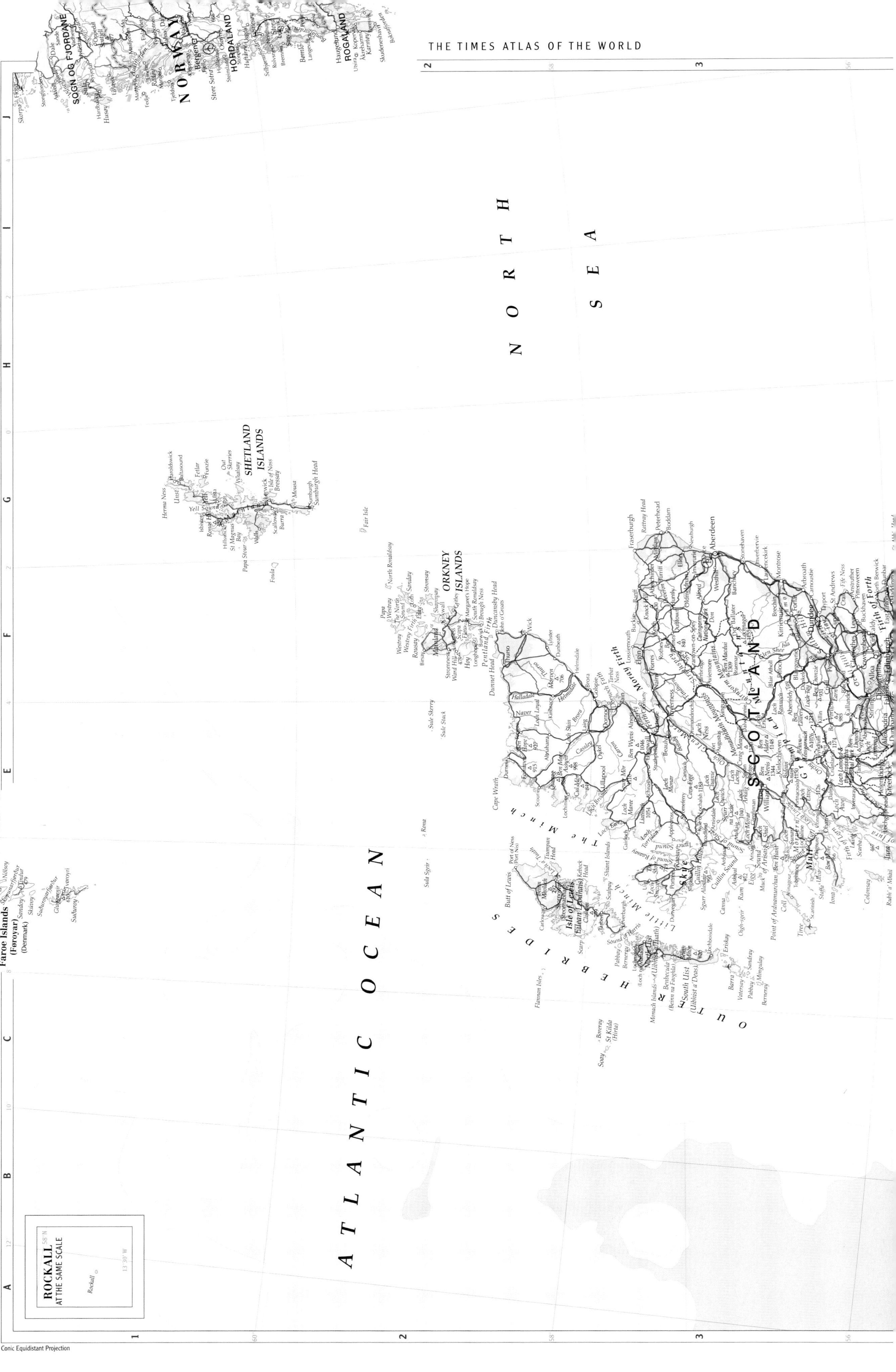

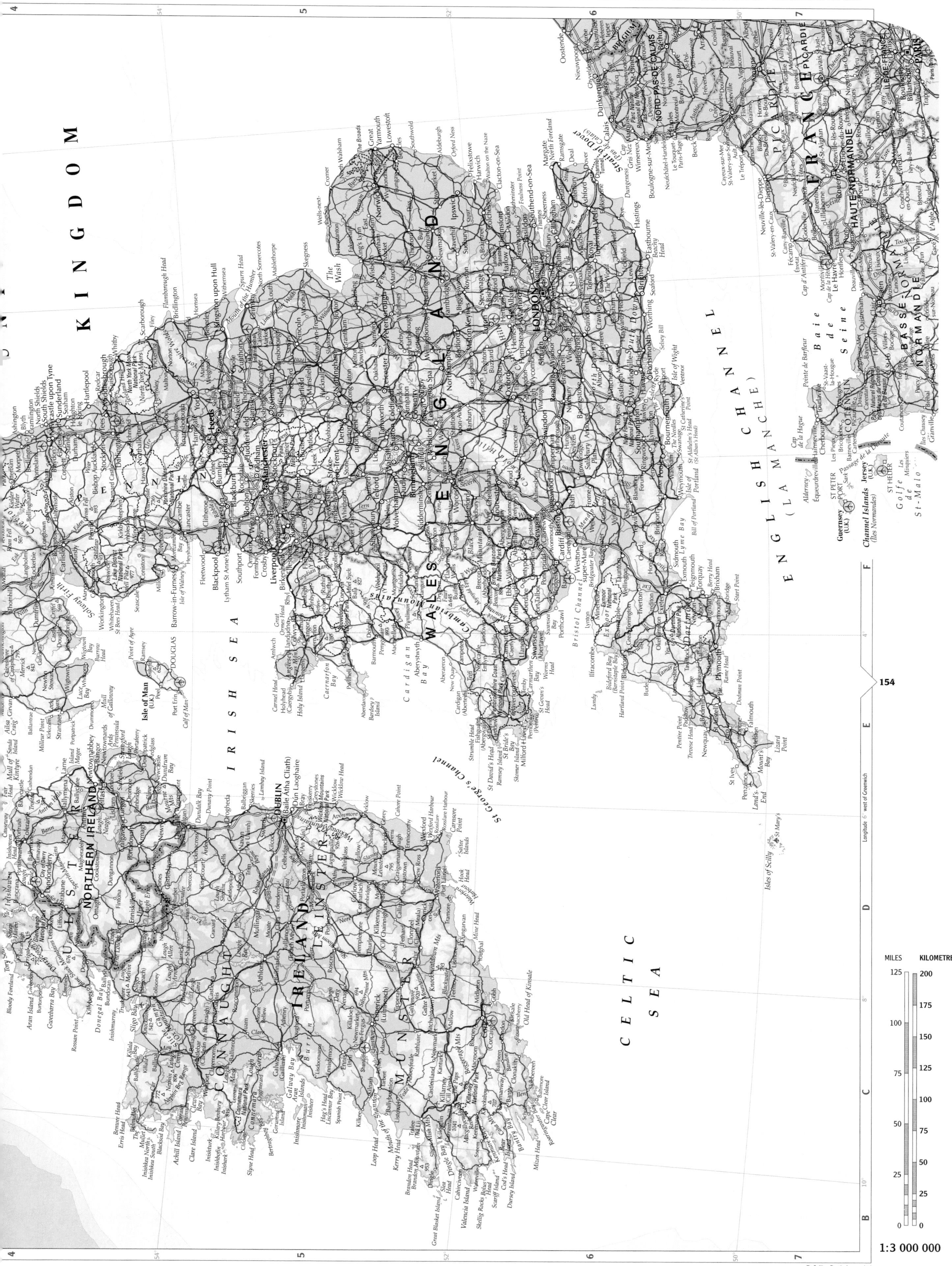
UNITED KINGDOM
ENGLAND
WALES
NORTHERN IRELAND
IRELAND
ULSTER
CONNAUGHT
LEINSTER
MUNSTER
FRANCE
BELGIUM
IRISH SEA
CELTIC SEA
ENGLISH CHANNEL (LA MANCHE)
St George's Channel
Bristol Channel
Strait of Dover
Baie de Seine
Channel Islands (Îles Normandes)
Isle of Man (U.K.)
DOUGLAS
LONDON
DUBLIN (Baile Átha Cliath)
Cardiff
Belfast
Isles of Scilly
MILES
KILOMETRES
1:3 000 000
154
© Collins Bartholomew Ltd

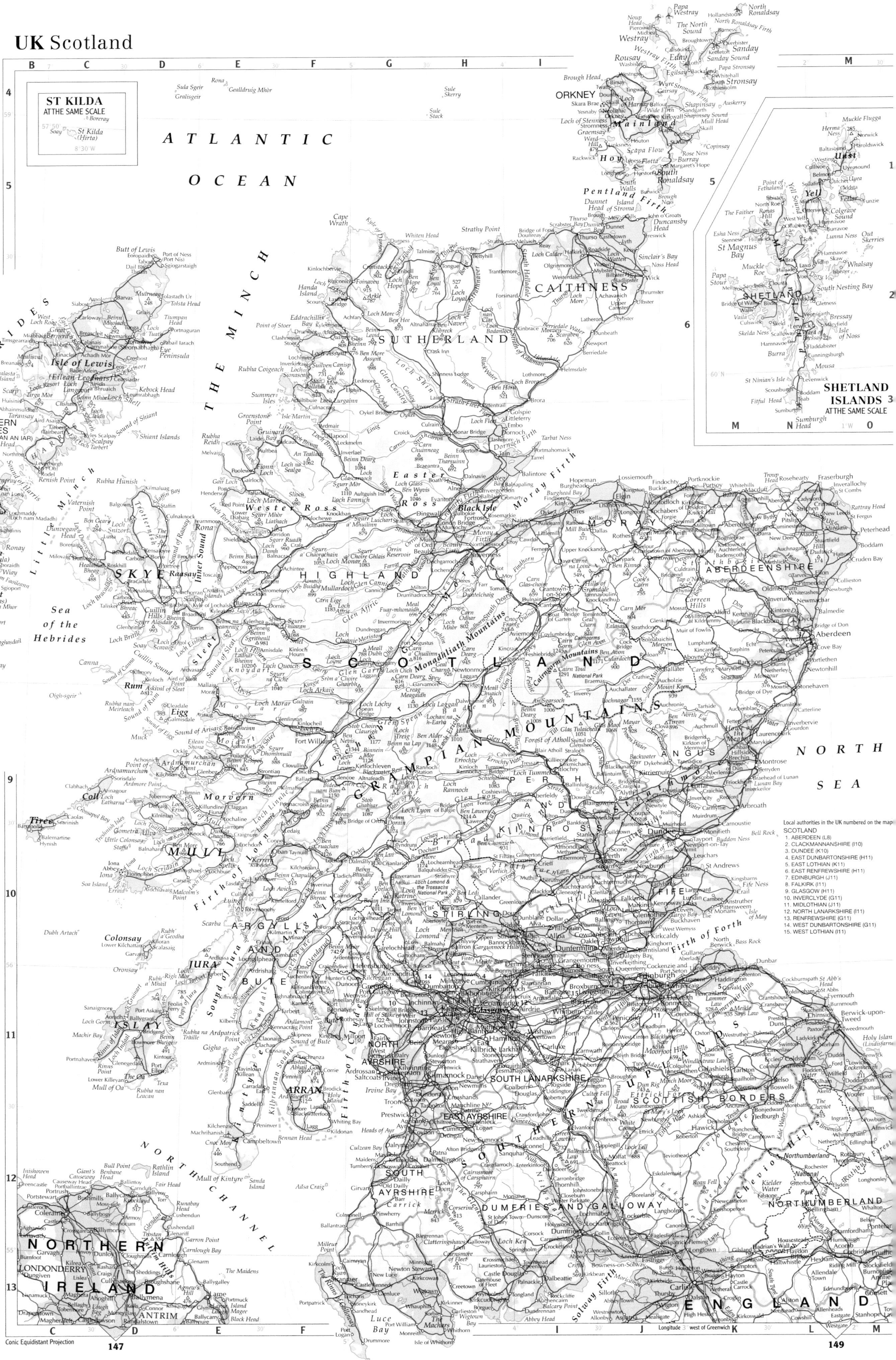
ST KILDA
AT THE SAME SCALE
St Kilda (Hirta)
ATLANTIC OCEAN
ORKNEY
Mainland
Pentland Firth
CAITHNESS
SUTHERLAND
THE MINCH
OUTER HEBRIDES
WESTERN ISLES (NA H-EILEANAN AN IAR)
Isle of Lewis (Eilean Leòdhais)
North Uist (Uibhist a' Tuath)
Benbecula (Beinn na Faoghla)
South Uist (Uibhist a' Deas)
Barra (Barraigh)
Little Minch
Sea of the Hebrides
SKYE
Raasay
HIGHLAND
Wester Ross
Easter Ross
Moray Firth
Black Isle
MORAY
ABERDEENSHIRE
Aberdeen
SCOTLAND
GRAMPIAN MOUNTAINS
Monadhliath Mountains
Cairngorm Mountains
ANGUS
PERTH AND KINROSS
Dundee
FIFE
Firth of Forth
Edinburgh
STIRLING
ARGYLL AND BUTE
MULL
JURA
ISLAY
Coll
Tiree
Colonsay
ARRAN
Firth of Clyde
Glasgow
NORTH AYRSHIRE
EAST AYRSHIRE
SOUTH AYRSHIRE
SOUTH LANARKSHIRE
SOUTHERN UPLANDS
SCOTTISH BORDERS
DUMFRIES AND GALLOWAY
Solway Firth
NORTHUMBERLAND
Cheviot Hills
ENGLAND
NORTH SEA
NORTH CHANNEL
NORTHERN IRELAND
ANTRIM
LONDONDERRY
SHETLAND ISLANDS
AT THE SAME SCALE
SHETLAND
Mainland
Yell
Unst
Local authorities in the UK numbered on the map
SCOTLAND
1. ABERDEEN (L8)
2. CLACKMANNANSHIRE (I10)
3. DUNDEE (K10)
4. EAST DUNBARTONSHIRE (H11)
5. EAST LOTHIAN (K11)
6. EAST RENFREWSHIRE (H11)
7. EDINBURGH (J11)
8. FALKIRK (I11)
9. GLASGOW (H11)
10. INVERCLYDE (G11)
11. MIDLOTHIAN (J11)
12. NORTH LANARKSHIRE (I11)
13. RENFREWSHIRE (G11)
14. WEST DUNBARTONSHIRE (G11)
15. WEST LOTHIAN (I11)
Longitude west of Greenwich
Conic Equidistant Projection
147
149

METRES / FEET
6000 / 19686
5000 / 16404
4000 / 13124
3000 / 9843
2000 / 6562
1500 / 4921
1000 / 3281
500 / 1640
200 / 656
100 / 328
0 / 0
LAND BELOW SEA LEVEL
50 / 164
200 / 656
1000 / 3281
2000 / 6562

1:1 500 000

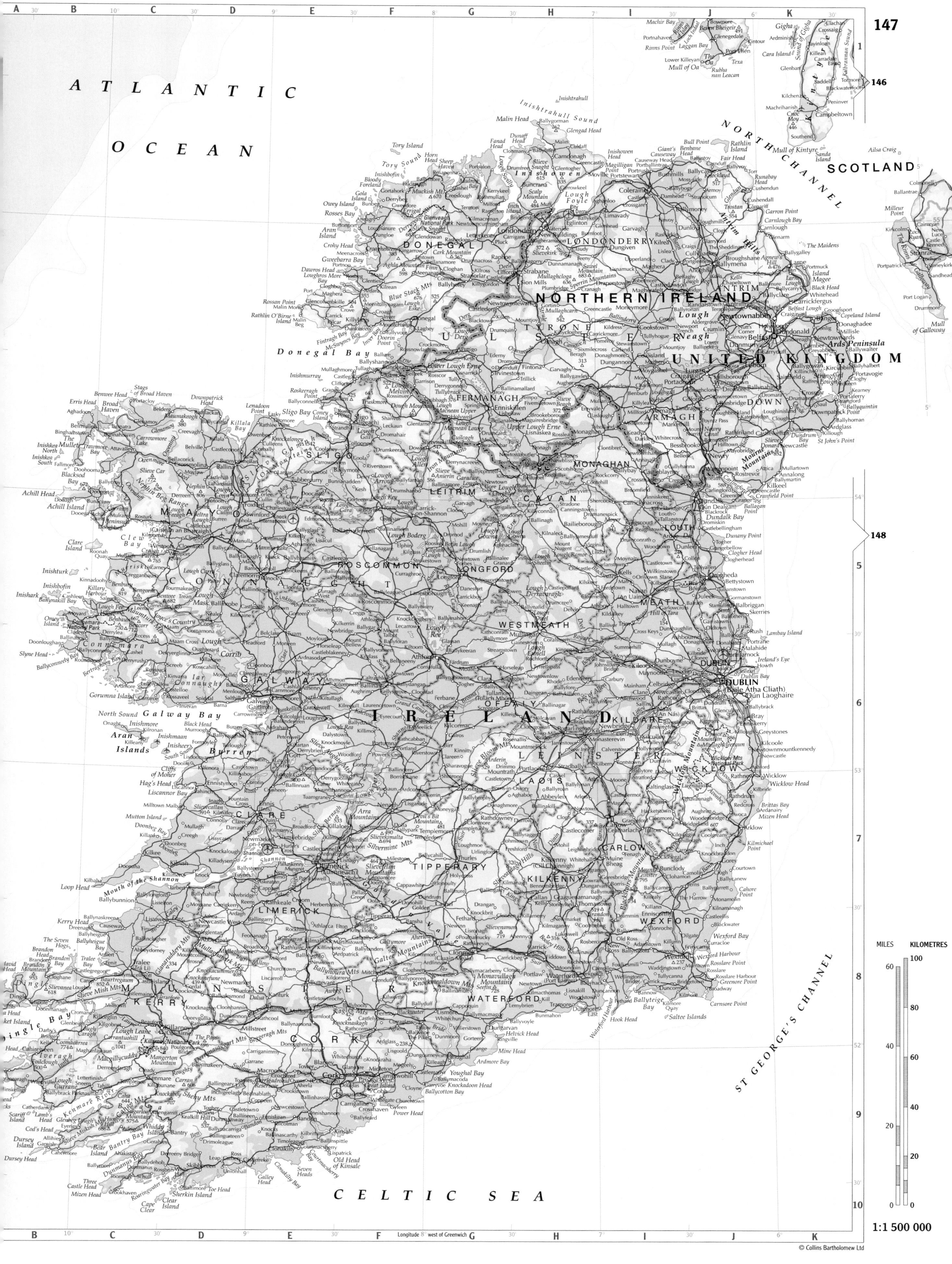
ATLANTIC
OCEAN
SCOTLAND
NORTH CHANNEL
NORTHERN IRELAND
UNITED KINGDOM
IRELAND
ULSTER
CONNAUGHT
LEINSTER
MUNSTER
DONEGAL
LONDONDERRY
ANTRIM
TYRONE
FERMANAGH
ARMAGH
DOWN
MONAGHAN
CAVAN
LEITRIM
SLIGO
MAYO
ROSCOMMON
LONGFORD
WESTMEATH
MEATH
LOUTH
GALWAY
OFFALY
KILDARE
DUBLIN
WICKLOW
LAOIS
CARLOW
KILKENNY
WEXFORD
TIPPERARY
CLARE
LIMERICK
KERRY
CORK
WATERFORD
Belfast
Londonderry
Dublin (Baile Átha Cliath)
Cork
Limerick
Galway
Waterford
Donegal Bay
Galway Bay
Dingle Bay
ST GEORGE'S CHANNEL
CELTIC SEA
146
148
MILES
KILOMETRES
1:1 500 000
Longitude 8° west of Greenwich
© Collins Bartholomew Ltd

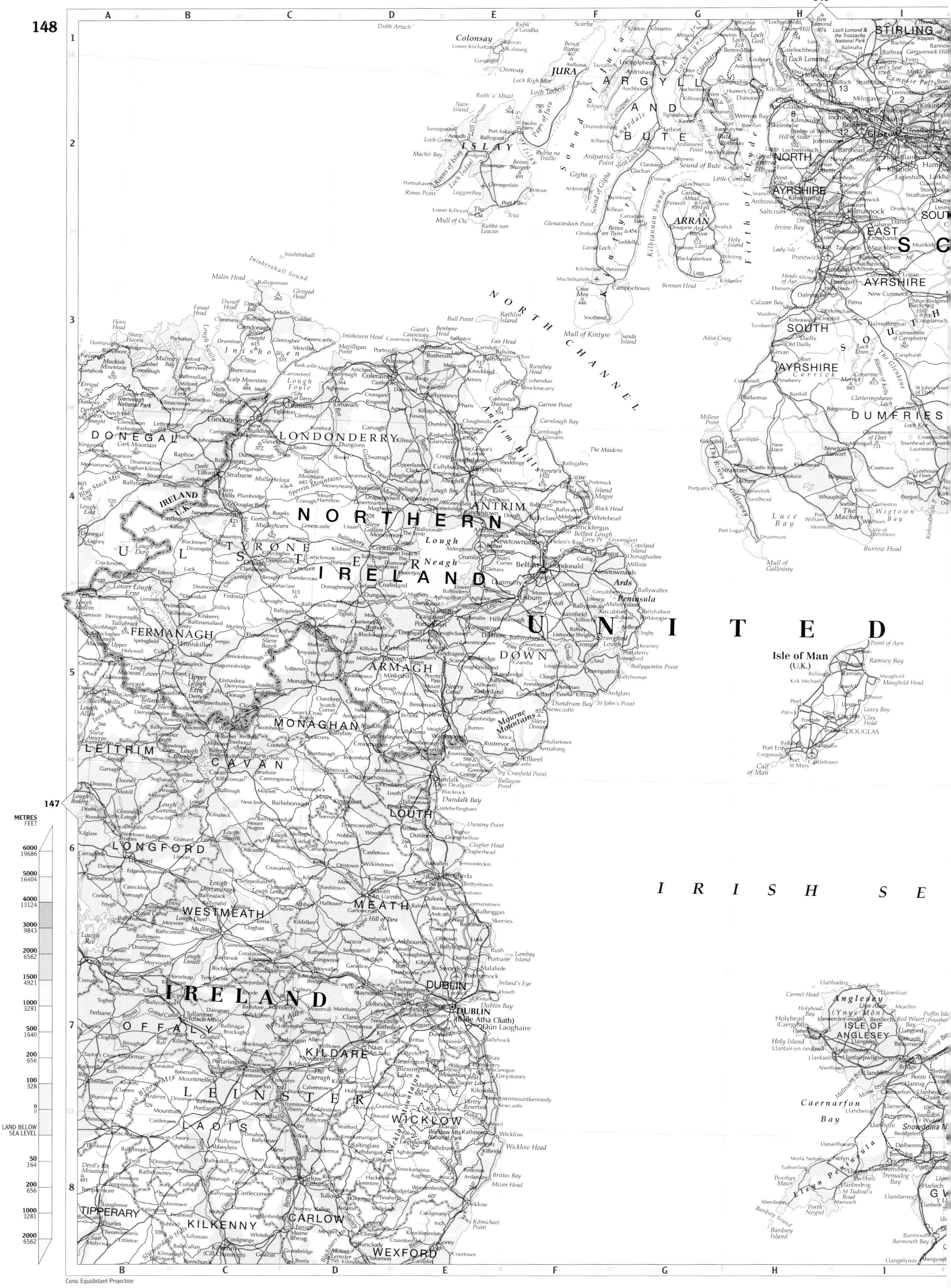
146
147
NORTHERN IRELAND
UNITED
IRELAND
DONEGAL
LONDONDERRY
TYRONE
ULSTER
FERMANAGH
ARMAGH
DOWN
ANTRIM
MONAGHAN
CAVAN
LEITRIM
LONGFORD
WESTMEATH
MEATH
LOUTH
DUBLIN
OFFALY
KILDARE
LEINSTER
LAOIS
WICKLOW
CARLOW
KILKENNY
WEXFORD
TIPPERARY
ARGYLL AND BUTE
NORTH AYRSHIRE
SOUTH AYRSHIRE
EAST AYRSHIRE
DUMFRIES
STIRLING
ISLAY
JURA
ARRAN
Colonsay
Isle of Man
(U.K.)
DOUGLAS
NORTH CHANNEL
IRISH SEA
Lough Neagh
Belfast
Londonderry
Glasgow
DUBLIN
(Baile Átha Cliath)
Anglesey
(Ynys Môn)
ISLE OF ANGLESEY
Caernarfon Bay
METRES
FEET
6000
19686
5000
16404
4000
13124
3000
9843
2000
6562
1500
4921
1000
3281
500
1640
200
656
100
328
0
0
LAND BELOW SEA LEVEL
50
164
200
656
1000
3281
2000
6562

Conic Equidistant Projection

Local authorities in the UK numbered on the map:
SCOTLAND
1. CLACKMANNANSHIRE (J1)
2. EAST DUNBARTONSHIRE (I2)
3. EAST LOTHIAN (L2)
4. EAST RENFREWSHIRE (I2)
5. EDINBURGH (K2)
6. FALKIRK (J2)
7. GLASGOW (I2)
8. INVERCLYDE (H2)
9. MIDLOTHIAN (K2)
10. NORTH LANARKSHIRE (J2)
11. PERTH AND KINROSS (K1)
12. RENFREWSHIRE (H2)
13. WEST DUNBARTONSHIRE (H2)
14. WEST LOTHIAN (J2)
ENGLAND
15. BLACKPOOL (K6)
16. DARLINGTON (N4)
17. HARTLEPOOL (O4)
18. KINGSTON UPON HULL (Q6)
19. MIDDLESBROUGH (O4)
20. NORTH EAST LINCOLNSHIRE (Q6)
21. STOCKTON-ON-TEES (O4)
22. STOKE-ON-TRENT (M7)
NORTH SEA
MILES
KILOMETRES
Greenwich 0° meridian

1:1 200 000

151

© Collins Bartholomew Ltd

149
150
147
IRISH SEA
CARDIGAN BAY
St George's Channel
Bristol Channel
IRELAND
WALES
UNITED
DUBLIN (Baile Átha Cliath)
ISLE OF ANGLESEY
CONWY
GWYNEDD
DENBIGHSHIRE
FLINTSHIRE
CHESHIRE
SHROPSHIRE
CEREDIGION
POWYS
HEREFORDSHIRE
PEMBROKESHIRE
CARMARTHENSHIRE
MONMOUTHSHIRE
SWANSEA
NEATH PORT TALBOT
VALE OF GLAMORGAN
SOMERSET
DEVON
CORNWALL
DORSET
ISLES OF SCILLY
CONTINUATION AT THE SAME SCALE
Local authorities in the UK numbered on the map:
ENGLAND
1. BATH AND N.E. SOMERSET (H5)
2. BRACKNELL FOREST (K5)
3. BRIGHTON AND HOVE (L6)
4. BRISTOL (G5)
5. BOURNEMOUTH (I6)
6. GREATER MANCHESTER (H1)
7. LUTON (L4)
8. MILTON KEYNES (K3)
9. NOTTINGHAM (J2)
10. PLYMOUTH (D7)
11. POOLE (I6)
12. PORTSMOUTH (J6)
13. READING (J5)
14. SLOUGH (K4)
15. SOUTHAMPTON (J6)
16. SOUTHEND (N4)
17. STOKE-ON-TRENT (H1)
18. SWINDON (I4)
19. THURROCK (M5)
20. TORBAY (E7)
21. WEST MIDLANDS (I3)
22. WINDSOR AND MAIDENHEAD (K5)
23. WOKINGHAM (K5)
WALES
24. BLAENAU GWENT (F4)
25. BRIDGEND (E4)
26. CAERPHILLY (F4)
27. CARDIFF (F5)
28. MERTHYR TYDFIL (F4)
29. NEWPORT (G4)
30. RHONDDA CYNON TAFF (F4)
31. TORFAEN (F4)
METRES
FEET
6000 19686
5000 16404
4000 13124
3000 9843
2000 6562
1500 4921
1000 3281
500 1640
200 656
100 328
0 0
LAND BELOW SEA LEVEL
50 164
200 656
1000 3281
2000 6562

Conic Equidistant Projection

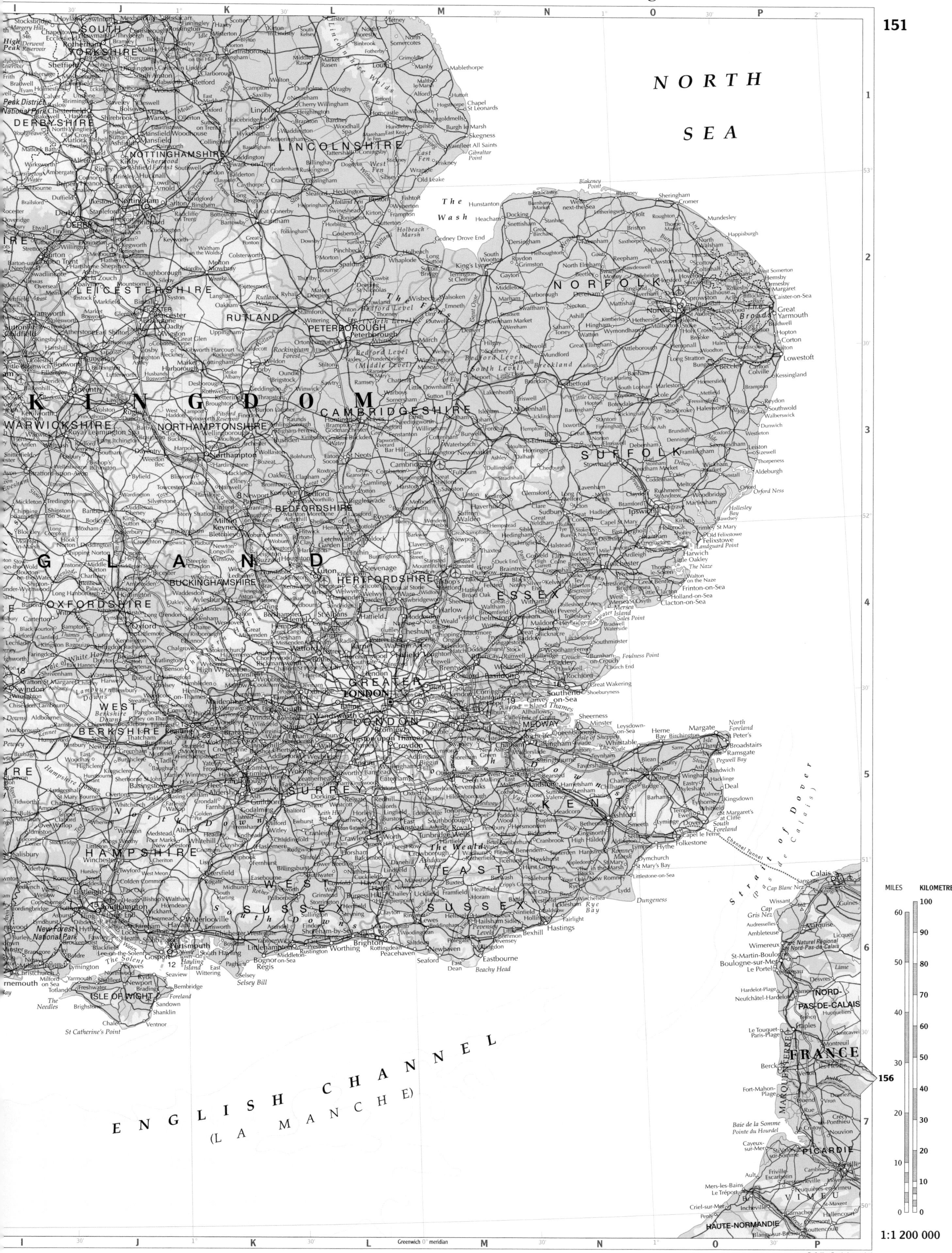

1:1 200 000

156

© Collins Bartholomew Ltd

NORTH SEA
ENGLISH CHANNEL
(LA MANCHE)
Strait of Dover
(Pas de Calais)
The Wash
KINGDOM
ENGLAND
FRANCE
LONDON
GREATER LONDON
LINCOLNSHIRE
NORFOLK
SUFFOLK
ESSEX
KENT
CAMBRIDGESHIRE
NORTHAMPTONSHIRE
BEDFORDSHIRE
HERTFORDSHIRE
BUCKINGHAMSHIRE
OXFORDSHIRE
WEST BERKSHIRE
HAMPSHIRE
SURREY
WEST SUSSEX
EAST SUSSEX
ISLE OF WIGHT
LEICESTERSHIRE
RUTLAND
NOTTINGHAMSHIRE
DERBYSHIRE
SOUTH YORKSHIRE
WARWICKSHIRE
NORD-PAS-DE-CALAIS
PICARDIE
HAUTE-NORMANDIE
MILES
KILOMETRES

CENTRAL LONDON
1:30 000
REDBRIDGE
WALTHAM FOREST
NEWHAM
GREENWICH
TOWER HAMLETS
HACKNEY
ISLINGTON
HARINGEY
CAMDEN
WESTMINSTER
KENSINGTON AND CHELSEA
HAMMERSMITH AND FULHAM
SOUTHWARK
LEWISHAM
BROMLEY
LAMBETH
WANDSWORTH
MERTON
SUTTON
CROYDON
BRENT
EALING
HOUNSLOW
RICHMOND UPON THAMES
KINGSTON UPON THAMES
SURREY
Heathrow Airport (London)
Richmond Park
London City Airport
YARDS
METRES
1:125 000
© Collins Bartholomew

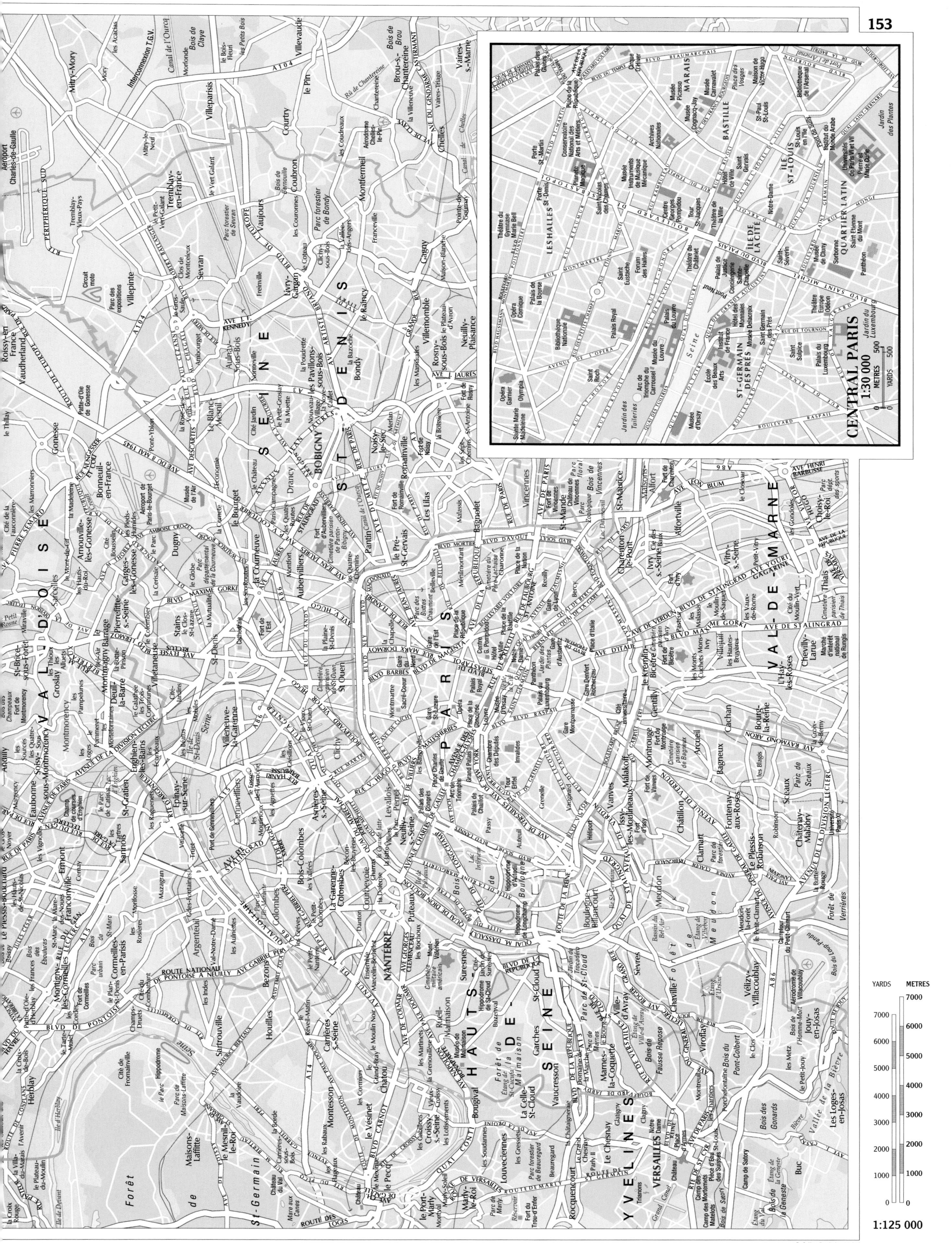
CENTRAL PARIS
1:30 000
METRES 0 500
YARDS 0 500
PARIS
HAUTS-DE-SEINE
SEINE-ST-DENIS
VAL-DE-MARNE
VAL-D'OISE
YVELINES
YARDS
METRES
0
1000
2000
3000
4000
5000
6000
7000

1:125 000

© Collins Bartholomew Ltd

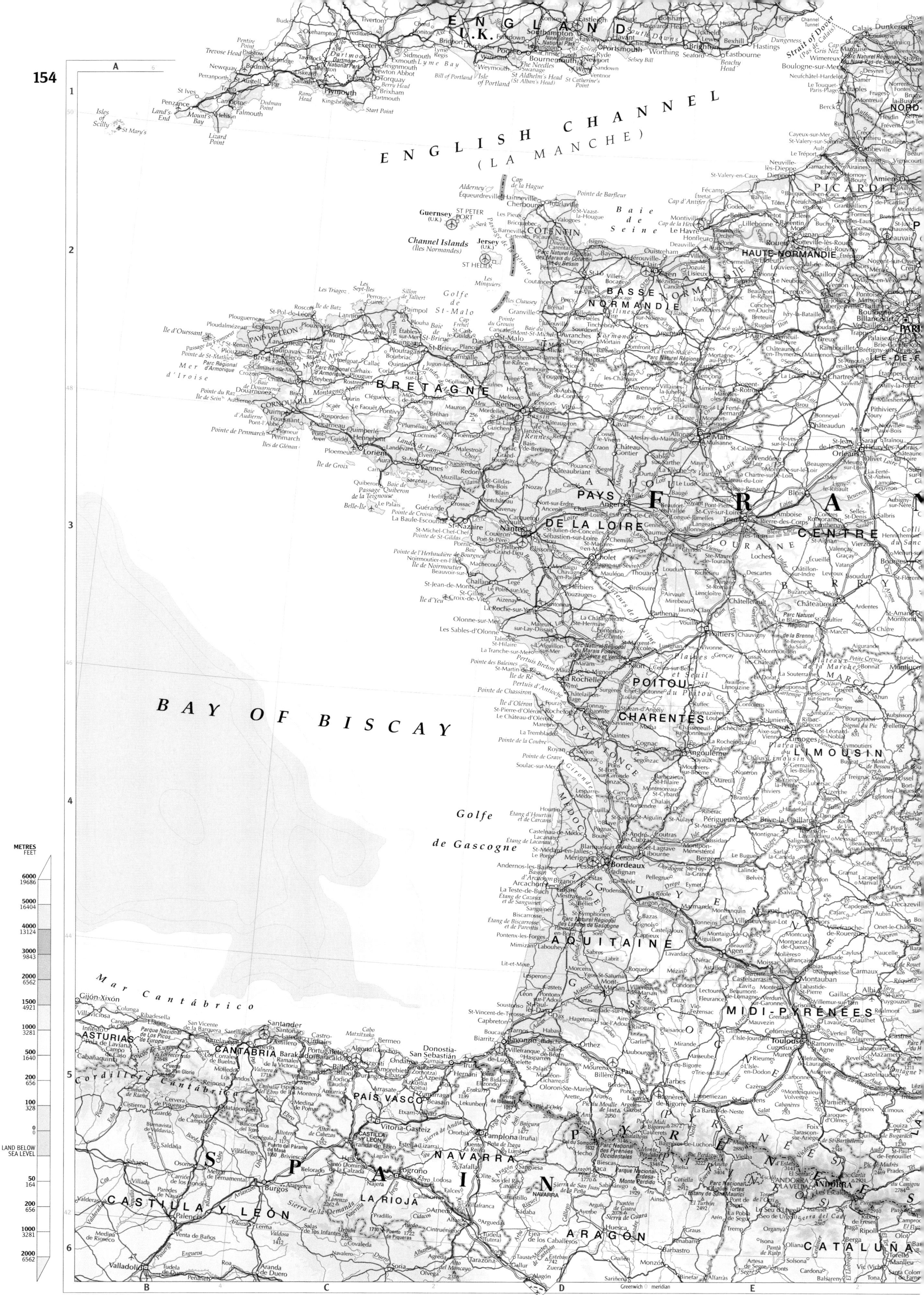
ENGLAND
U.K.
ENGLISH CHANNEL
(LA MANCHE)
Strait of Dover
(Pas de Calais)
Channel Islands
(Îles Normandes)
Guernsey (U.K.)
Jersey (U.K.)
Golfe de St-Malo
Baie de Seine
PICARDIE
HAUTE-NORMANDIE
BASSE NORMANDIE
BRETAGNE
PAYS DE LA LOIRE
CENTRE
ÎLE-DE-FRANCE
POITOU-CHARENTES
LIMOUSIN
AQUITAINE
MIDI-PYRÉNÉES
FRANCE
BAY OF BISCAY
Golfe de Gascogne
Mar Cantábrico
ASTURIAS
CANTABRIA
PAÍS VASCO
NAVARRA
LA RIOJA
CASTILLA Y LEÓN
ARAGÓN
CATALUÑA
ANDORRA
SPAIN
PYRENEES
Paris
Bordeaux
Toulouse
Nantes
Rennes
Brest
Le Mans
Tours
Orléans
Poitiers
Limoges
La Rochelle
Bilbao
Donostia-San Sebastián
Vitoria-Gasteiz
Pamplona (Iruña)
Burgos
Santander
Valladolid
Plymouth
Southampton
Brighton
METRES
FEET
6000 19686
5000 16404
4000 13124
3000 9843
2000 6562
1500 4921
1000 3281
500 1640
200 656
100 328
0 0
LAND BELOW SEA LEVEL
50 164
200 656
1000 3281
2000 6562

Conic Equidistant Projection

181

166
188
G
H
I
J
K
1
2
3
4
5
6
BELGIUM
BRUXELLES (Brussels)
LUXEMBOURG
GERMANY
NORDRHEIN-WESTFALEN
HESSEN
RHEINLAND-PFALZ
SAARLAND
BADEN-WÜRTTEMBERG
BAYERN
CZECH REPUBLIC
AUSTRIA
LIECHTENSTEIN
SWITZERLAND
ALPS
ITALY
TRENTINO-ALTO ADIGE
VENETO
LOMBARDIA
VALLE D'AOSTA
PIEMONTE
LIGURIA
EMILIA-ROMAGNA
TOSCANA
FRANCE
CHAMPAGNE
ARDENNE
LORRAINE
ALSACE
VOSGES
JURA
FRANCHE-COMTÉ
BOURGOGNE
RHÔNE-ALPES
PROVENCE-ALPES-CÔTE D'AZUR
MONACO
CORSE (CORSICA) (France)
LIGURIAN SEA
MEDITERRANEAN SEA
GOLFE DU LION
Golfo di Genova
MILES
KILOMETRES
1:3 000 000
© Collins Bartholomew Ltd

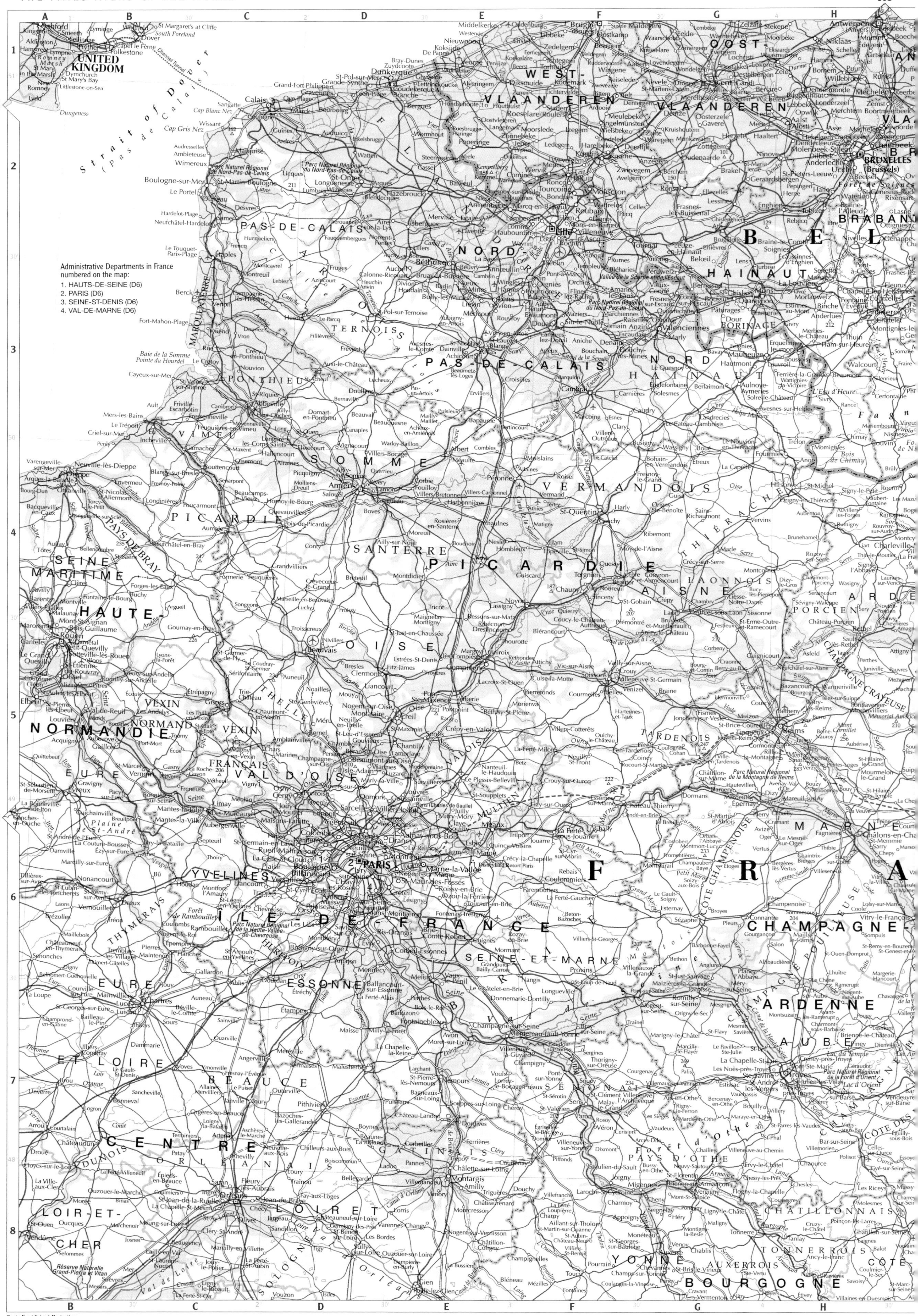
165
156
151
159
UNITED KINGDOM
Strait of Dover (Pas de Calais)
Administrative Departments in France numbered on the map:
1. HAUTS-DE-SEINE (D6)
2. PARIS (D6)
3. SEINE-ST-DENIS (D6)
4. VAL-DE-MARNE (D6)
METRES
FEET
6000
19686
5000
16404
4000
13124
3000
9843
2000
6562
1500
4921
1000
3281
500
1640
200
656
100
328
0
0
LAND BELOW SEA LEVEL
50
164
200
656
1000
3281
2000
6562
WEST-VLAANDEREN
OOST-VLAANDEREN
HAINAUT
BRABANT
NORD-PAS-DE-CALAIS
PAS-DE-CALAIS
NORD
SOMME
PICARDIE
AISNE
OISE
SEINE-MARITIME
HAUTE-NORMANDIE
EURE
VAL D'OISE
YVELINES
ÎLE-DE-FRANCE
ESSONNE
SEINE-ET-MARNE
EURE-ET-LOIR
CENTRE
LOIRET
LOIR-ET-CHER
MARNE
CHAMPAGNE-ARDENNE
AUBE
YONNE
BOURGOGNE
FRANCE
PARIS
BRUXELLES (Brussels)
Conic Equidistant Projection

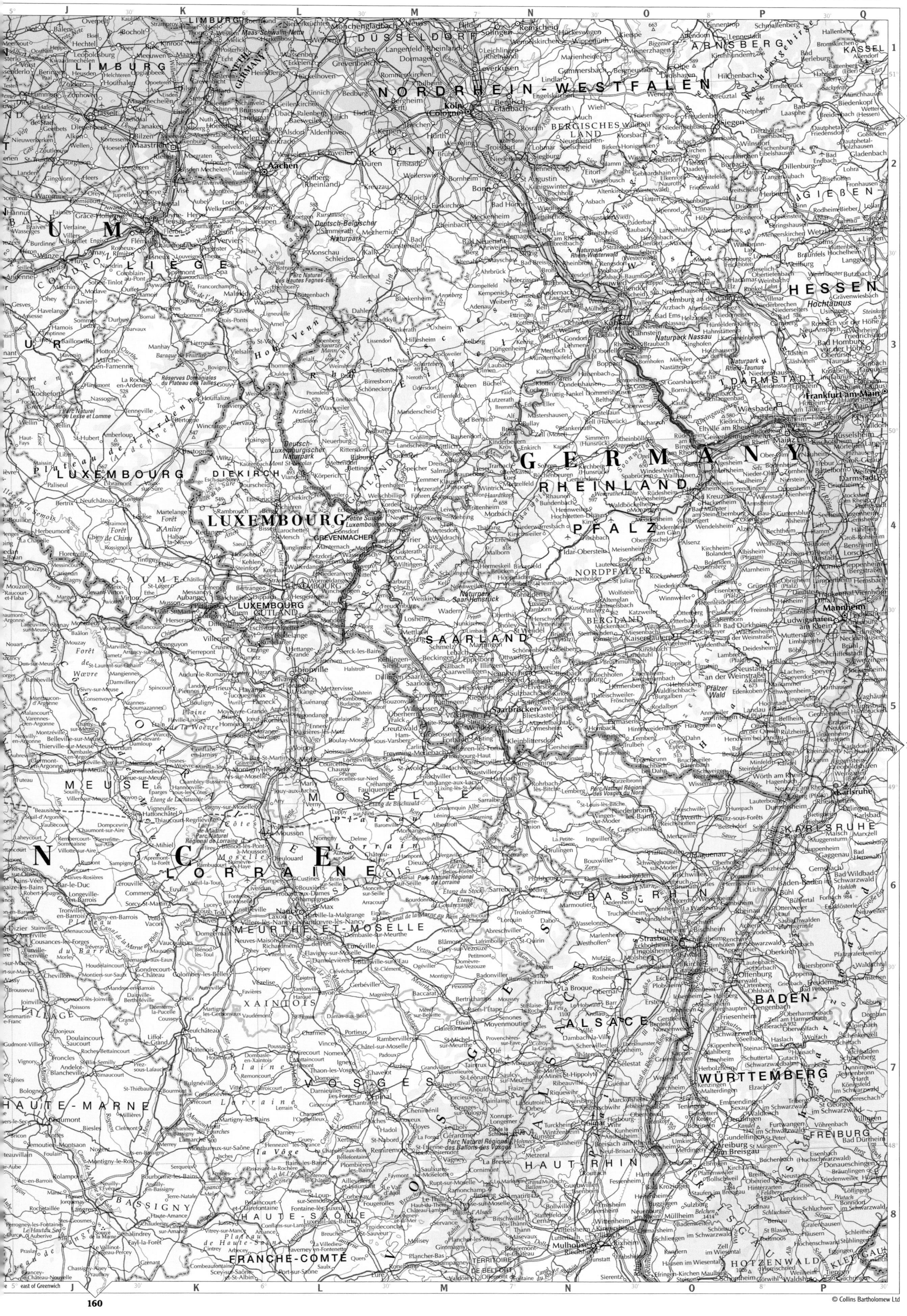

MILES 0 10 20 30 40 50 60

KILOMETRES 0 10 20 30 40 50 60 70 80 90 100

1:1 200 000

© Collins Bartholomew Ltd

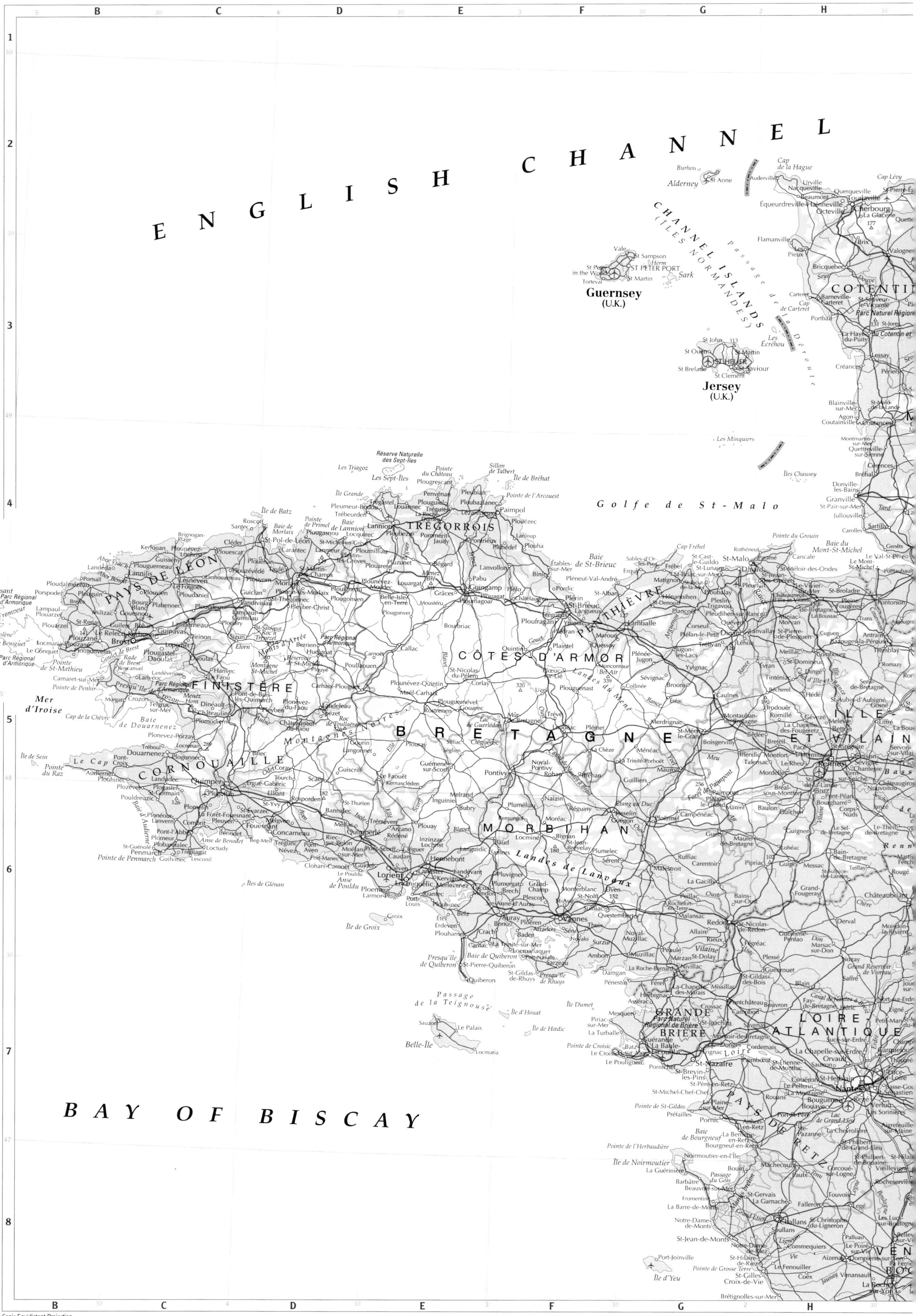

Conic Equidistant Projection

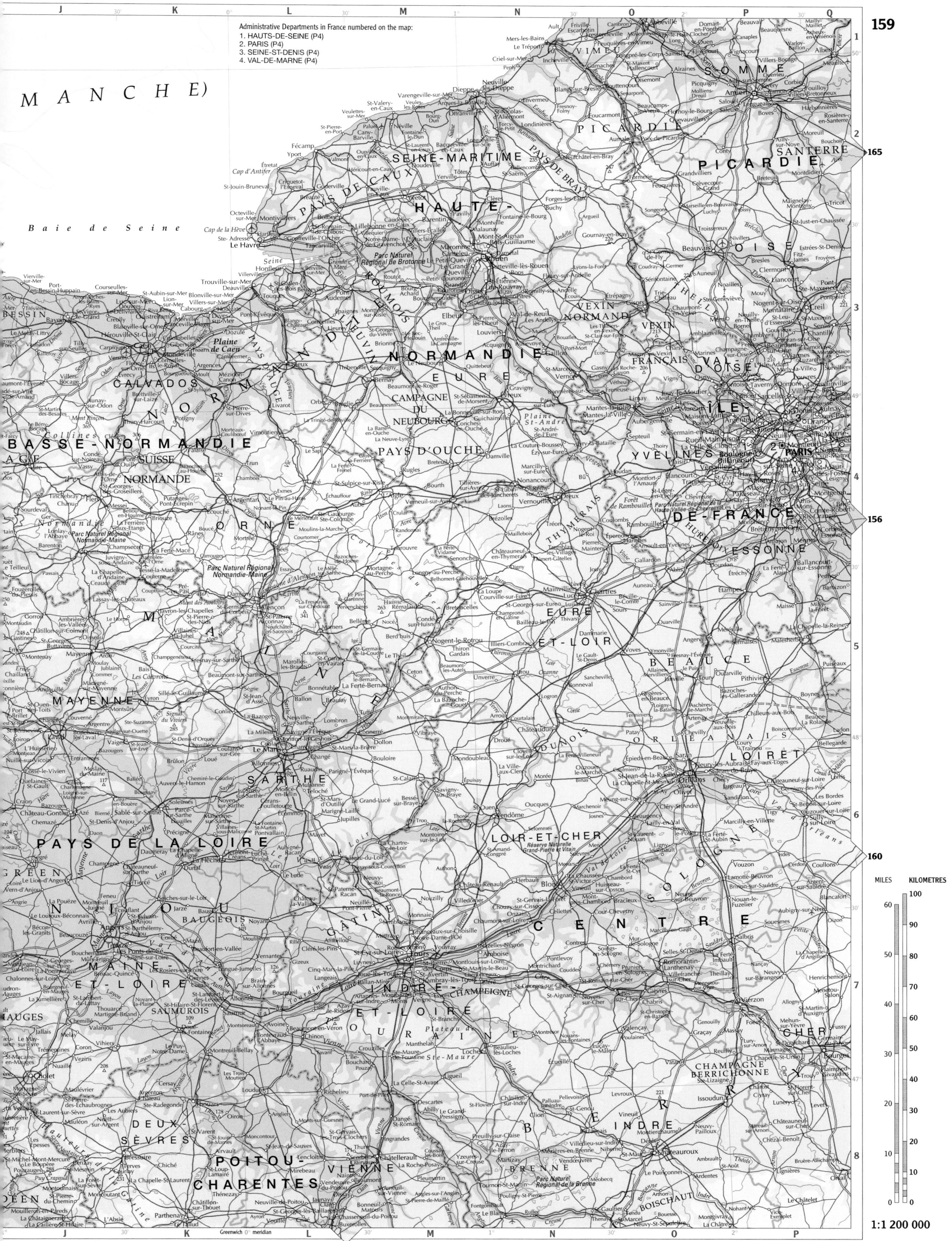
Administrative Departments in France numbered on the map:
1. HAUTS-DE-SEINE (P4)
2. PARIS (P4)
3. SEINE-ST-DENIS (P4)
4. VAL-DE-MARNE (P4)
MANCHE)
Baie de Seine
PICARDIE
SOMME
SEINE-MARITIME
HAUTE-NORMANDIE
OISE
CALVADOS
BASSE-NORMANDIE
EURE
ÎLE-DE-FRANCE
YVELINES
ESSONNE
ORNE
MAYENNE
SARTHE
PAYS DE LA LOIRE
EURE-ET-LOIR
LOIRET
LOIR-ET-CHER
CENTRE
MAINE-ET-LOIRE
INDRE-ET-LOIRE
CHER
INDRE
DEUX-SÈVRES
VIENNE
POITOU-CHARENTES
PARIS
Rouen
Le Havre
Caen
Amiens
Beauvais
Chartres
Le Mans
Orléans
Tours
Angers
Blois
Bourges
Châteauroux
165
156
160
162
MILES
KILOMETRES

1:1 200 000

172

156

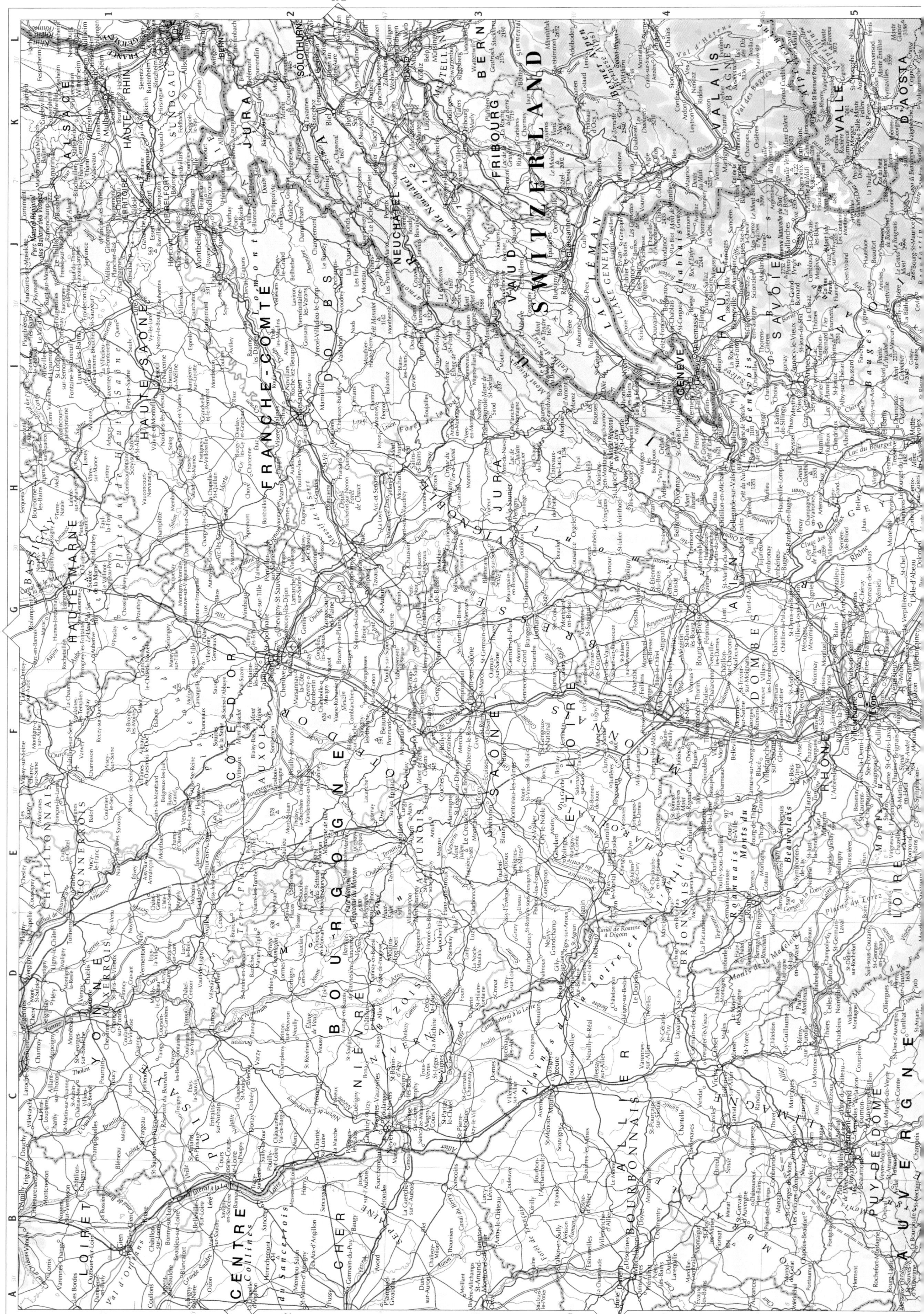

METRES FEET
6000 19686
5000 16404
4000 13124
3000 9843
2000 6562
1500 4921
1000 3281
500 1640
200 656
100 328
0 0
LAND BELOW SEA LEVEL
50 164
200 656
1000 3281
2000 6562

Conic Equidistant Projection

159

162

MILES

KILOMETRES

1:1 200 000

© Collins Bartholomew Ltd

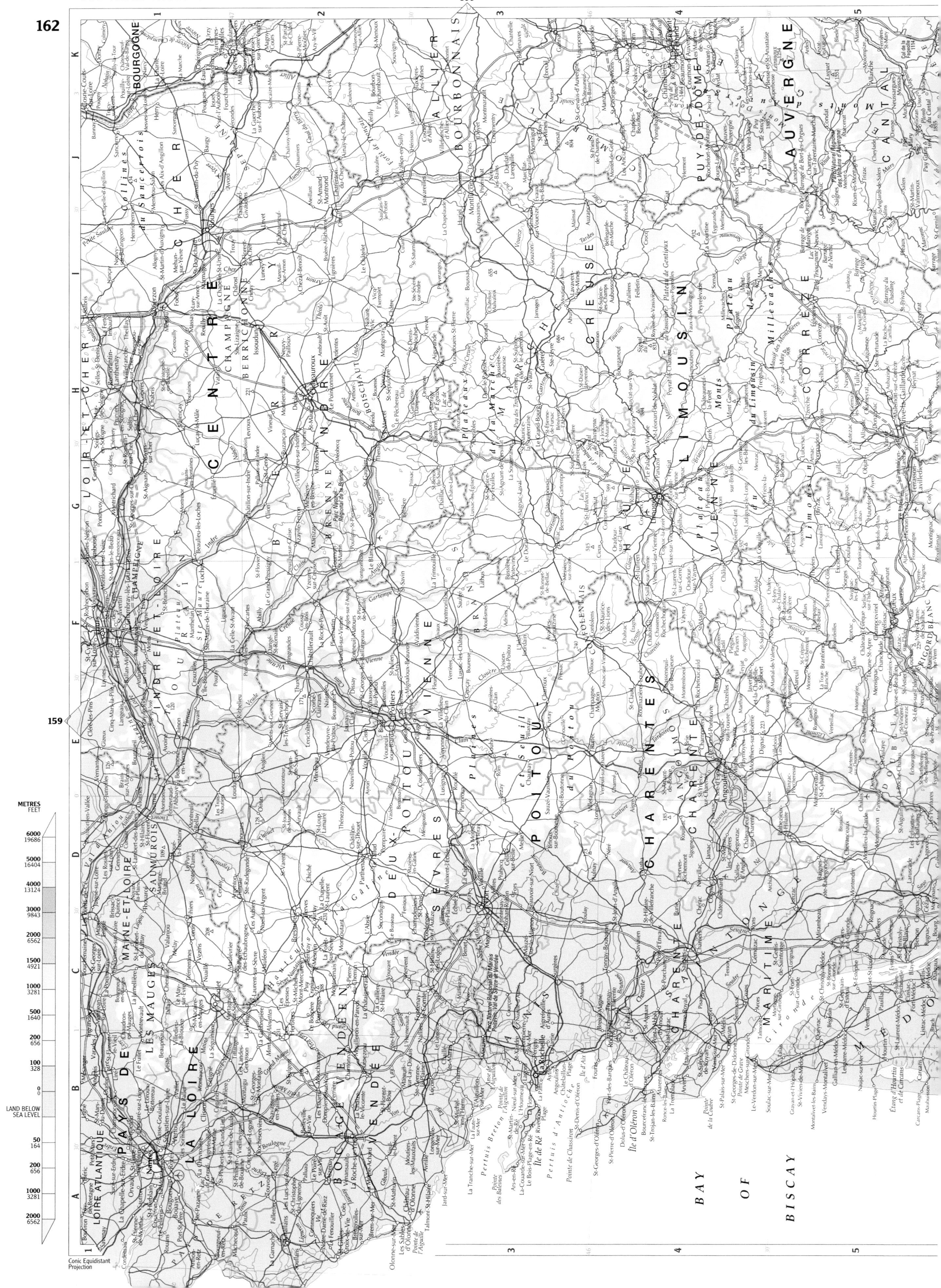
160
159
METRES
FEET
6000
19686
5000
16404
4000
13124
3000
9843
2000
6562
1500
4921
1000
3281
500
1640
200
656
100
328
0
0
LAND BELOW
SEA LEVEL
50
164
200
656
1000
3281
2000
6562
Conic Equidistant
Projection
BAY OF BISCAY
CENTRE
LIMOUSIN
AUVERGNE
POITOU-CHARENTES
PAYS DE LA LOIRE
BOURGOGNE
BOURBONNAIS
CHARENTE-MARITIME
DEUX-SÈVRES
VIENNE
HAUTE-VIENNE
CREUSE
CORRÈZE
CANTAL
PUY-DE-DÔME
ALLIER
CHER
INDRE
INDRE-ET-LOIRE
LOIR-ET-CHER
MAINE-ET-LOIRE
VENDÉE
LOIRE-ATLANTIQUE
GIRONDE
DORDOGNE
CHARENTE

161

FRANCE Southwest

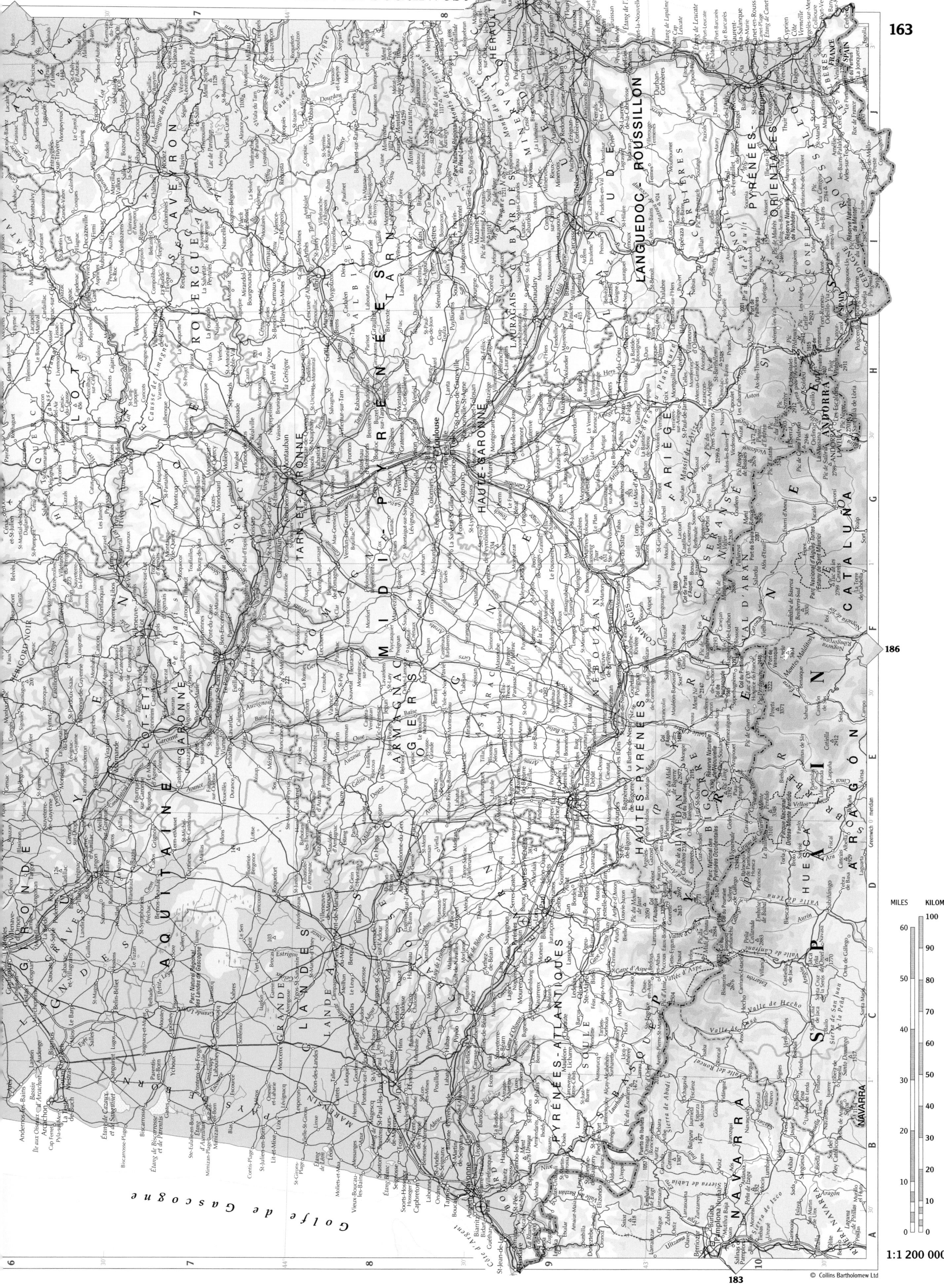

186

183

1:1 200 000

© Collins Bartholomew Ltd

168

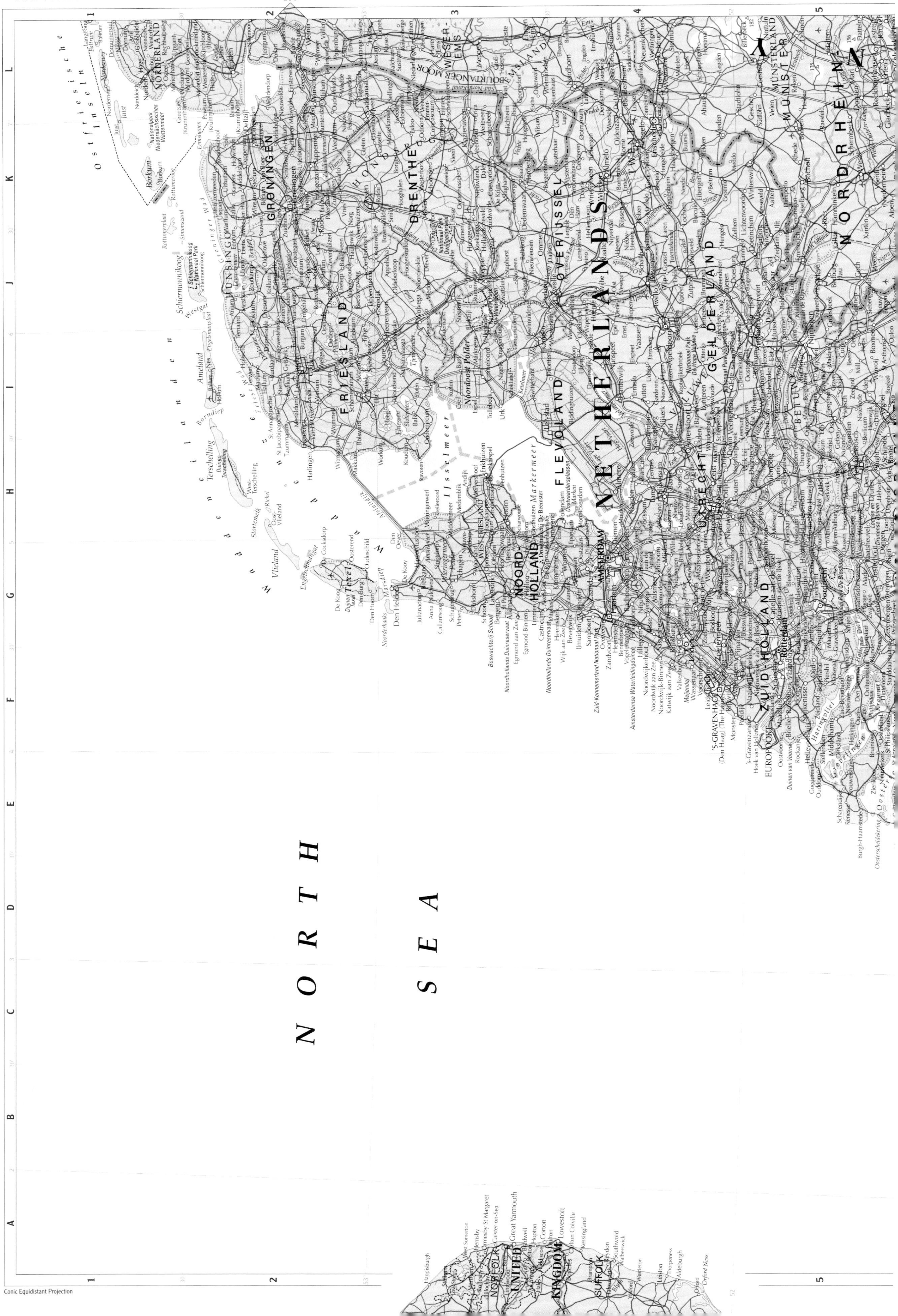
NORTH SEA
NETHERLANDS
FRIESLAND
GRONINGEN
DRENTHE
OVERIJSSEL
FLEVOLAND
GELDERLAND
UTRECHT
NOORD-HOLLAND
ZUID-HOLLAND
AMSTERDAM
Rotterdam
'S-GRAVENHAGE (Den Haag) (The Hague)
IJsselmeer
Markermeer
Waddenzee
Noordoost Polder
NIEDERSACHSEN
MÜNSTERLAND
NORDRHEIN
Münster
UNITED KINGDOM
NORFOLK
SUFFOLK
Great Yarmouth
Lowestoft
Texel
Vlieland
Terschelling
Ameland
Schiermonnikoog
Borkum
Juist
Ostfriesische Inseln

METRES / FEET

METRES	FEET
6000	19686
5000	16404
4000	13124
3000	9843
2000	6562
1500	4921
1000	3281
500	1640
200	656
100	328
0	0
LAND BELOW SEA LEVEL	
50	164
200	656
1000	3281
2000	6562

Conic Equidistant Projection

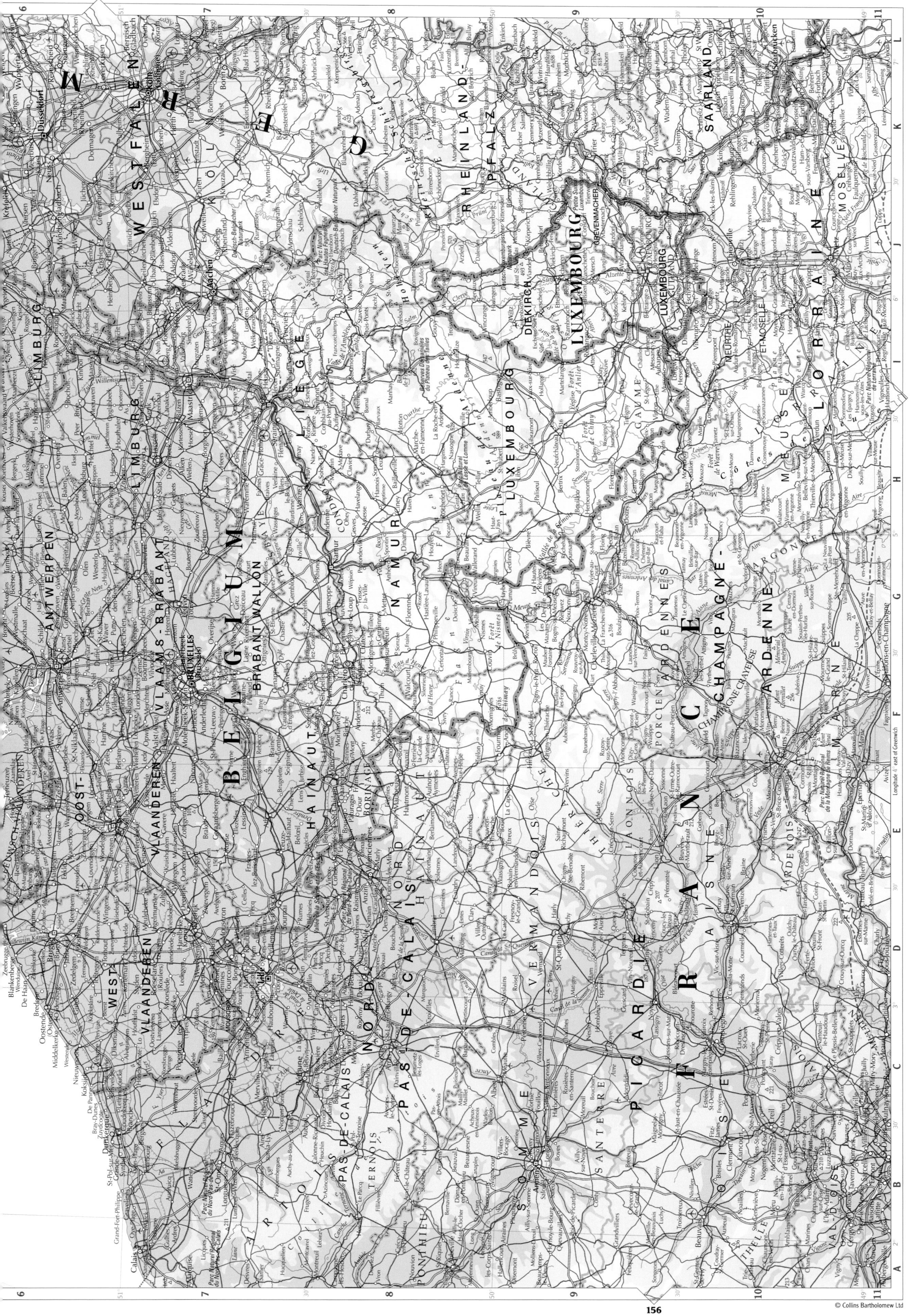
169
157
156
BELGIUM
LUXEMBOURG
FRANCE
ANTWERPEN
LIMBURG
LIÈGE
NAMUR
HAINAUT
BRABANT WALLON
VLAAMS-BRABANT
OOST-VLAANDEREN
WEST-VLAANDEREN
NORD
PAS-DE-CALAIS
PICARDIE
CHAMPAGNE-ARDENNE
LORRAINE
SAARLAND
RHEINLAND-PFALZ
BRUXELLES
LUXEMBOURG
DIEKIRCH
GREVENMACHER
Longitude 4° east of Greenwich

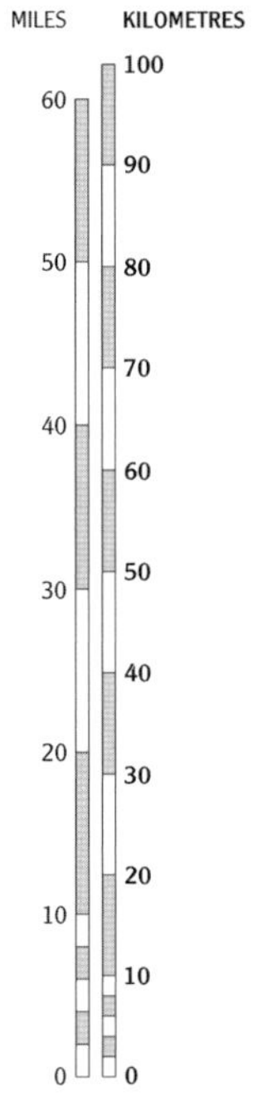
MILES
KILOMETRES
0
10
20
30
40
50
60
70
80
90
100

1:1 200 000

NORTH SEA
DENMARK
NETHERLANDS
BELGIUM
GERMANY
FRANCE
SWITZERLAND
AUSTRIA
ITALY
ALPS
NIEDERSACHSEN
SCHLESWIG-HOLSTEIN
MECKLENBURG-VORPOMMERN
NORDRHEIN-WESTFALEN
HESSEN
THÜRINGEN
SACHSEN-ANHALT
RHEINLAND-PFALZ
SAARLAND
BADEN-WÜRTTEMBERG
BAYERN
LORRAINE
ALSACE
CHAMPAGNE-ARDENNE
NORD-PAS-DE-CALAIS
PICARDIE
BOURGOGNE
FRANCHE-COMTÉ
RHÔNE-ALPES
LUXEMBOURG
LIECHTENSTEIN
TRENTINO-ALTO ADIGE
LOMBARDIA
PIEMONTE
VENETO
METRES
FEET
6000 19686
5000 16404
4000 13124
3000 9843
2000 6562
1500 4921
1000 3281
500 1640
200 656
100 328
0
LAND BELOW SEA LEVEL
50 164
200 656
1000 3281
2000 6562
142
155

Conic Equidistant Projection

BALTIC SEA
Gulf of Gdańsk
Pomeranian Bay
RUSSIAN FEDERATION
LITHUANIA
BELARUS
UKRAINE
POLAND
CZECH REPUBLIC
SLOVAKIA
HUNGARY
ROMANIA
SERBIA
CROATIA
SLOVENIA
CARPATHIAN MOUNTAINS
POJEZIERZE POMORSKIE
POJEZIERZE MAZURSKIE
NIZINA MAZOWIECKA
WYŻYNA LUBELSKA
WYŻYNA MAŁOPOLSKA
WARSZAWA (Warsaw)
PRAHA (Prague)
WIEN (Vienna)
BRATISLAVA
BUDAPEST
Kraków
Wrocław
Poznań
Gdańsk
Łódź
Katowice
Lublin
Białystok
Szczecin
Kaliningrad
Debrecen
Miskolc
Brno
Ostrava
Košice
Balaton
MILES
KILOMETRES
1:3 000 000
© Collins Bartholomew Ltd
134
136
196

170

142

NORTH SEA
HAMBURG
BREMEN
GRONINGEN
SCHLESWIG-HOLSTEIN
MECKLENBURG-VORPOMMERN
NIEDERSACHSEN
FRIESLAND
DRENTHE
OSTFRIESLAND
LÜNEBURGER HEIDE
Nordfriesische Inseln
Ostfriesische Inseln
Waddeneilanden
Helgoländer Bucht
Kieler Bucht
Mecklenburger Bucht
Lübecker Bucht
Femer Bælt
Lille Bælt
Langelands Bælt
Lolland
Langeland
Ærø
Fehmarn
Sylt
Föhr
Borkum
Ameland
Schiermonnikoog
Helgoland
Lübeck
Kiel
Flensburg
Oldenburg
Emden
Bremerhaven
Cuxhaven
Wilhelmshaven
Neumünster
Rendsburg
Lüneburg
Celle
Husum
Heide
Itzehoe
Uelzen
Leer
Aurich
Norden
Jever
Delmenhorst
Stade
Wadden Zee
Halligen

METRES
FEET

Metres	Feet
6000	19686
5000	16404
4000	13124
3000	9843
2000	6562
1500	4921
1000	3281
500	1640
200	656
100	328
0	0
LAND BELOW SEA LEVEL	
50	164
200	656
1000	3281
2000	6562

Conic Equidistant Projection

171

173

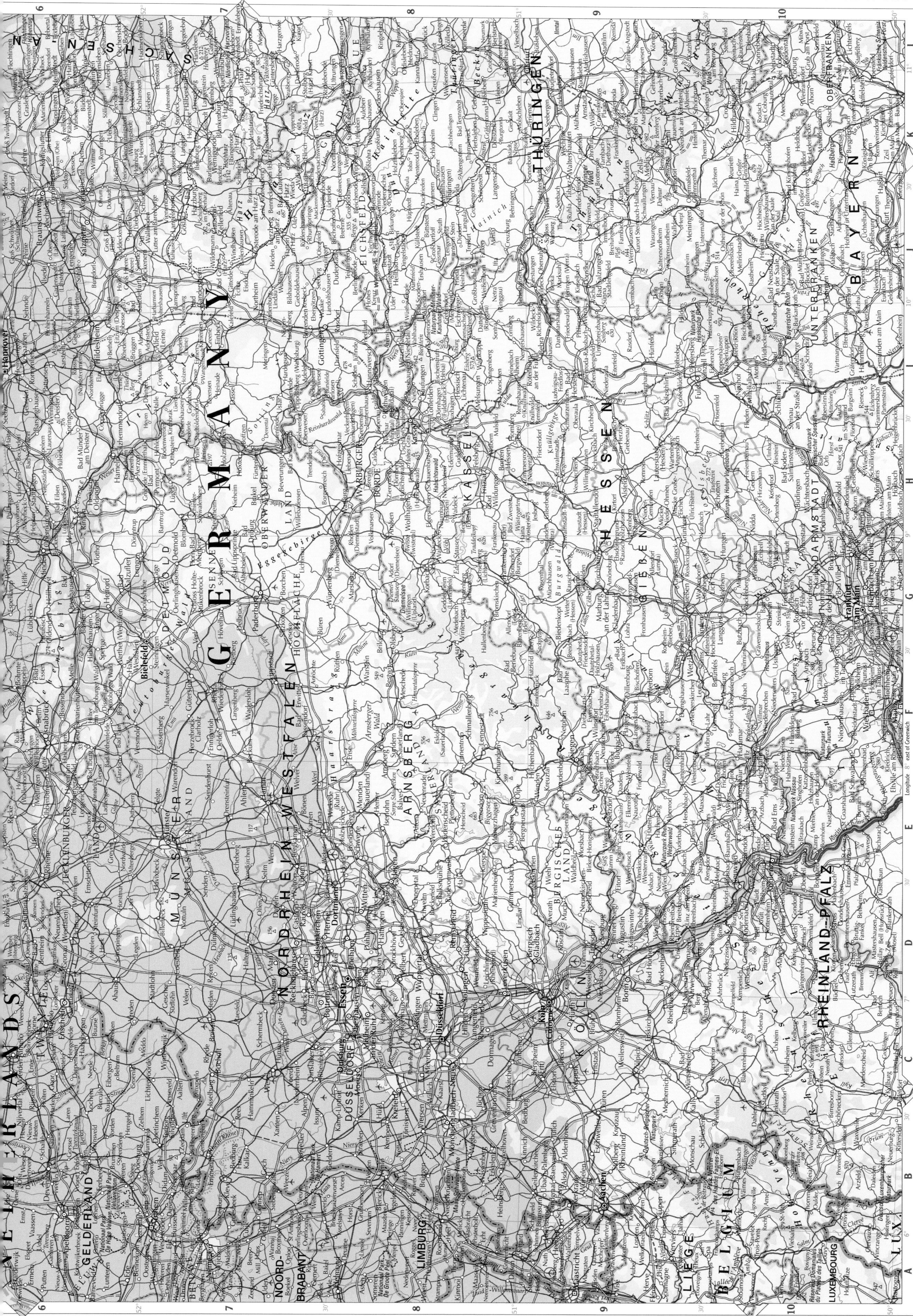
GERMANY
NETHERLANDS
BELGIUM
LUX.
NORDRHEIN-WESTFALEN
HESSEN
THÜRINGEN
BAYERN
RHEINLAND-PFALZ
SACHSEN
Hannover
Bielefeld
Dortmund
Essen
Düsseldorf
Köln
Bonn
Aachen
Kassel
Göttingen
Frankfurt am Main
Wiesbaden
Koblenz
Münster
Osnabrück
Braunschweig
Hildesheim
Paderborn
Siegen
Marburg
Fulda
Erfurt
LIÈGE
LIMBURG
GELDERLAND
NOORD-BRABANT
LUXEMBOURG
UNTERFRANKEN
OBERFRANKEN

172

MILES | KILOMETRES

0 10 20 30 40 50 60 (miles)

0 10 20 30 40 50 60 70 80 90 100 (kilometres)

1:1 200 000

164

157

© Collins Bartholomew Ltd

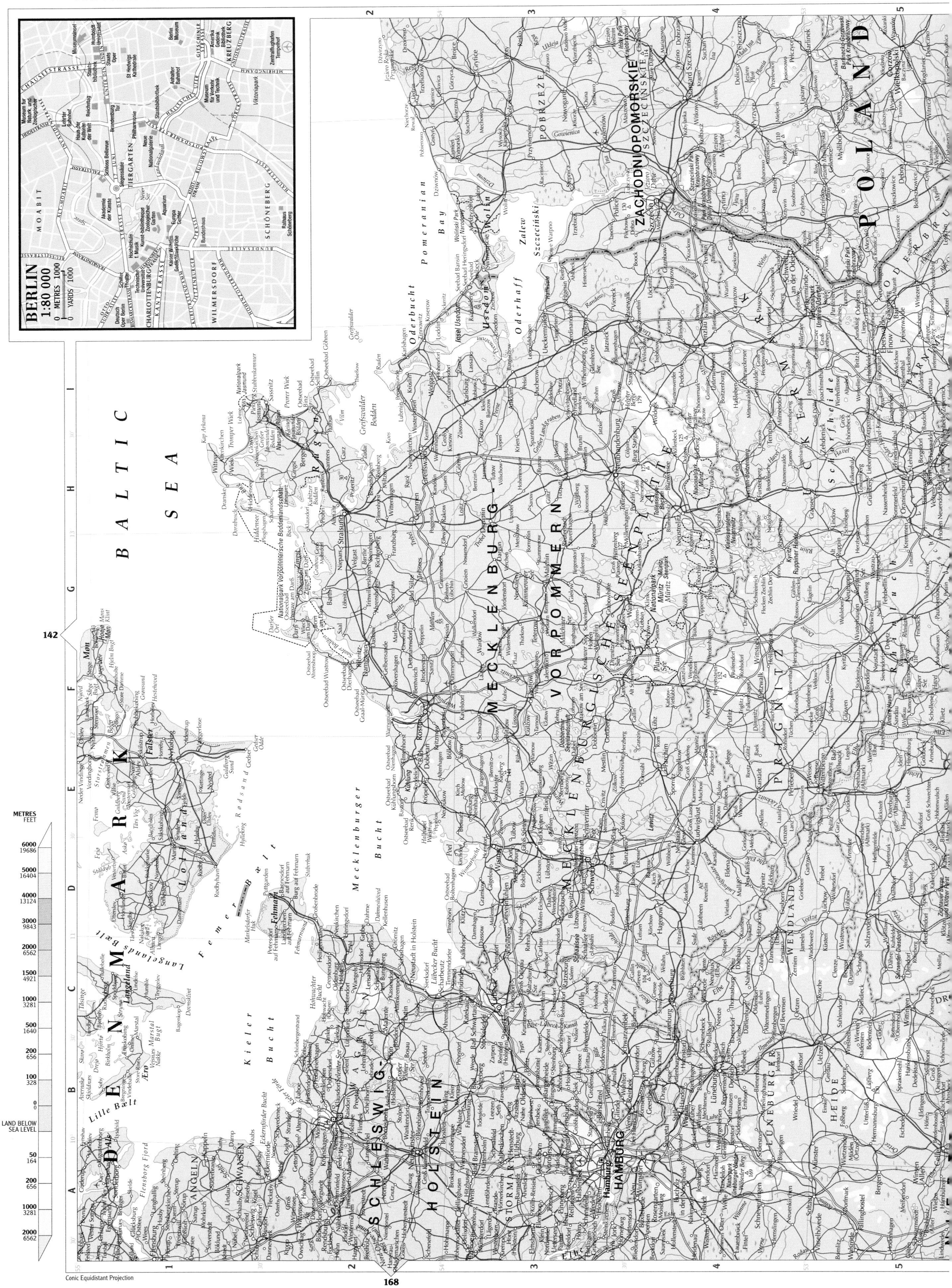
BALTIC SEA
DENMARK
POLAND
MECKLENBURG-VORPOMMERN
MECKLENBURGISCHE SEENPLATTE
SCHLESWIG-HOLSTEIN
HAMBURG
ZACHODNIOPOMORSKIE
Pomeranian Bay
Mecklenburger Bucht
Kieler Bucht
Lolland
Falster
Møn
Fehmarn
Rügen
Usedom
Wolin
Stralsund
Rostock
Lübeck
Kiel
Schwerin
Szczecin
BERLIN
1:80 000
METRES 1000
YARDS 1000
MOABIT
TIERGARTEN
CHARLOTTENBURG
WILMERSDORF
SCHÖNEBERG
KREUZBERG
METRES
FEET
6000 19686
5000 16404
4000 13124
3000 9843
2000 6562
1500 4921
1000 3281
500 1640
200 656
100 328
0 0
LAND BELOW SEA LEVEL
50 164
200 656
1000 3281
2000 6562
Conic Equidistant Projection

142

168

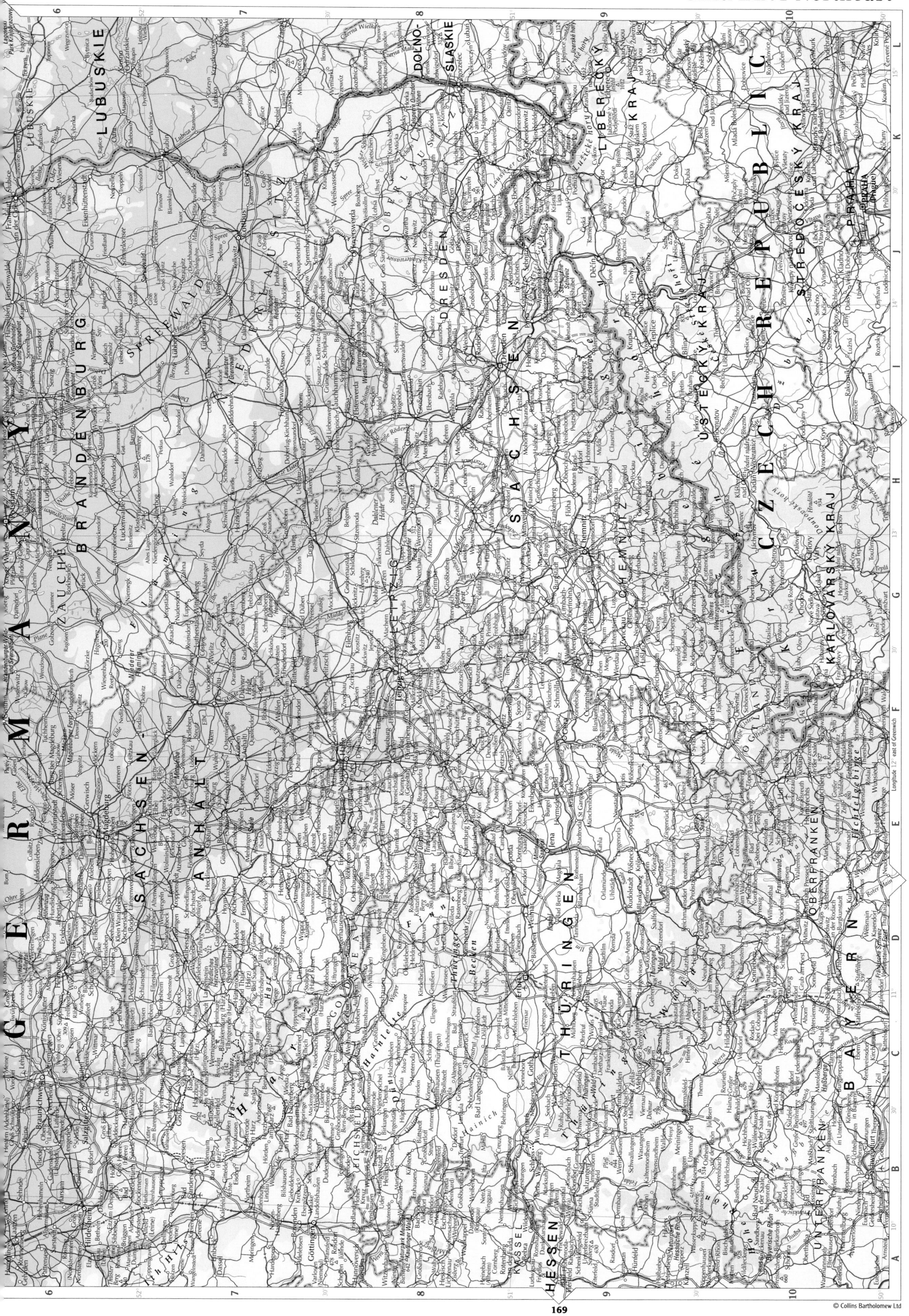

MILES KILOMETRES

1:1 200 000

© Collins Bartholomew Ltd

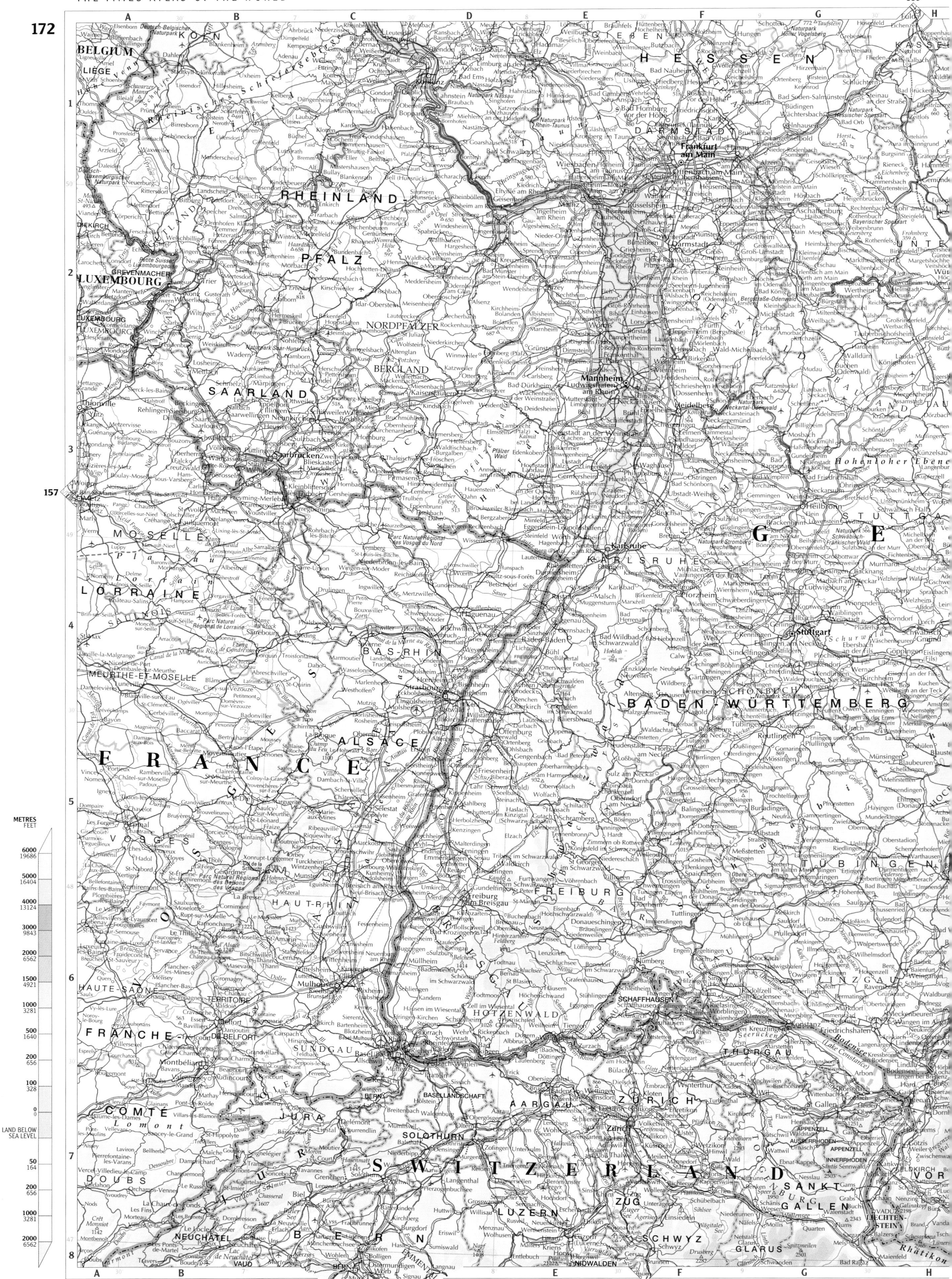
169
172
157
190
A
B
C
D
E
F
G
H
1
2
3
4
5
6
7
8
METRES
FEET
6000
19686
5000
16404
4000
13124
3000
9843
2000
6562
1500
4921
1000
3281
500
1640
200
656
100
328
0
0
LAND BELOW
SEA LEVEL
50
164
200
656
1000
3281
2000
6562
BELGIUM
LIÈGE
LUXEMBOURG
GREVENMACHER
DIEKIRCH
KÖLN
HESSEN
DARMSTADT
Frankfurt am Main
Offenbach am Main
Wiesbaden
Mainz
RHEINLAND-PFALZ
NORDPFALZER BERGLAND
SAARLAND
Saarbrücken
Trier
Mannheim
Ludwigshafen am Rhein
Heidelberg
Karlsruhe
KARLSRUHE
Stuttgart
STUTTGART
BADEN-WÜRTTEMBERG
TÜBINGEN
FREIBURG
Freiburg im Breisgau
MOSELLE
LORRAINE
MEURTHE-ET-MOSELLE
VOSGES
BAS-RHIN
Strasbourg
ALSACE
HAUT-RHIN
Mulhouse
FRANCE
HAUTE-SAÔNE
TERRITOIRE DE BELFORT
FRANCHE-COMTÉ
DOUBS
JURA
SUNDGAU
Basel
HOTZENWALD
SCHAFFHAUSEN
ZÜRICH
Zürich
AARGAU
SOLOTHURN
BASELLANDSCHAFT
SWITZERLAND
BERN
LUZERN
ZUG
SCHWYZ
NIDWALDEN
GLARUS
SANKT GALLEN
APPENZELL
THURGAU
LIECHTENSTEIN
VADUZ
NEUCHÂTEL
VAUD
Konstanz
Bodensee (Lake Constance)
Conic Equidistant Projection

THÜRINGEN
OBERFRANKEN
MITTELFRANKEN
OBERPFALZ
NIEDERBAYERN
OBERBAYERN
SCHWABEN
BAYERN
(BAVARIA)
CZECH REPUBLIC
KARLOVARSKÝ KRAJ
PLZEŇSKÝ KRAJ
ÚSTECKÝ KRAJ
STŘEDOČESKÝ KRAJ
JIHOČESKÝ KRAJ
AUSTRIA
OBERÖSTERREICH
SALZBURG
TIROL
KÄRNTEN
OSTTIROL
ITALY
Nürnberg
Regensburg
Ingolstadt
Augsburg
München
(Munich)
Landshut
Passau
Rosenheim
Salzburg
Innsbruck
Plzeň
Longitude 12° east of Greenwich
171
174
176
178

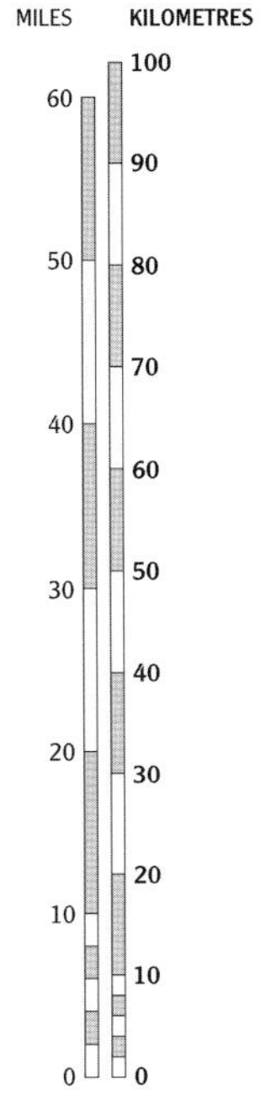
MILES
KILOMETRES

1:1 200 000

© Collins Bartholomew Ltd

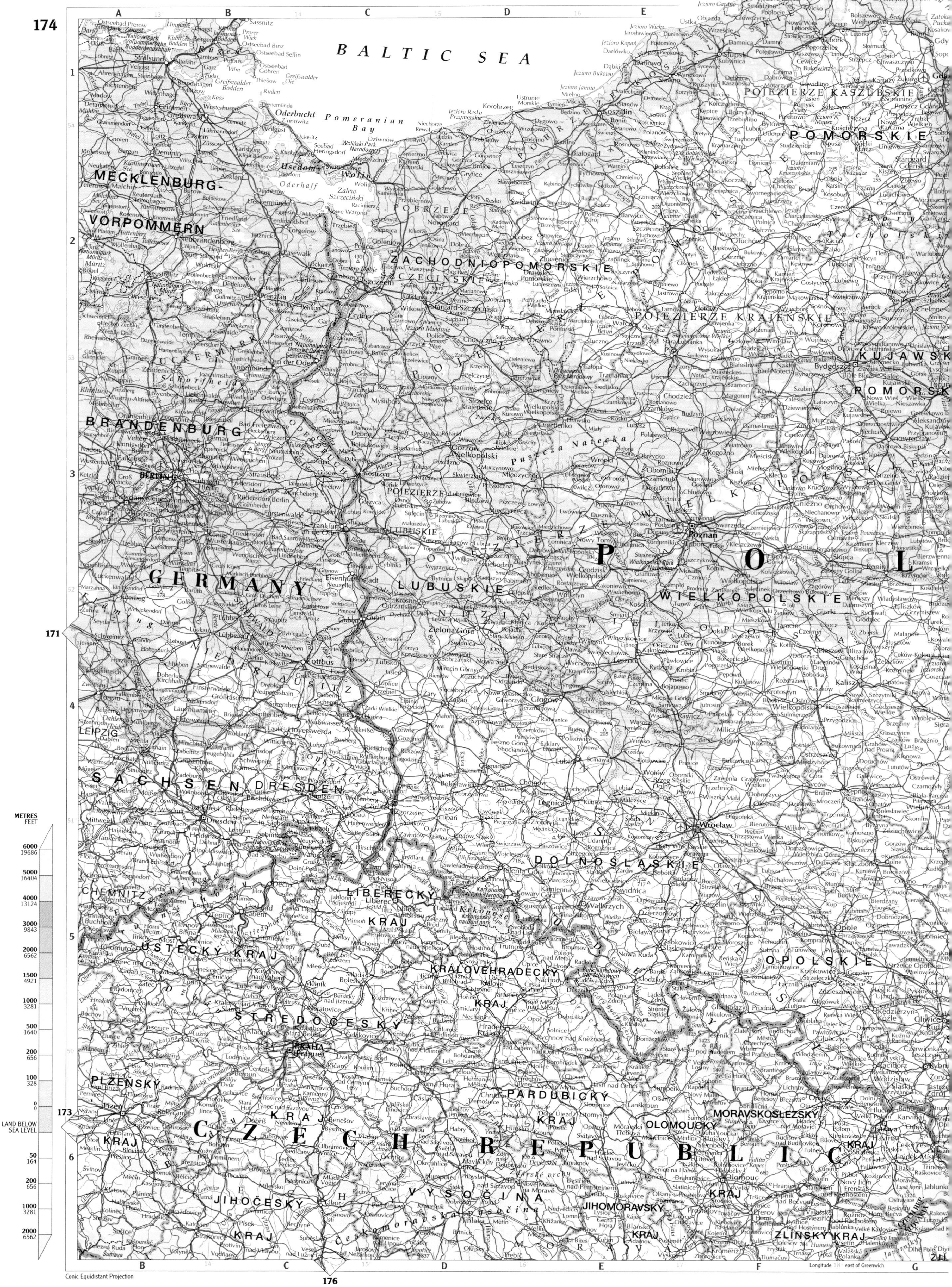
BALTIC SEA
Pomeranian Bay
MECKLENBURG-VORPOMMERN
BRANDENBURG
GERMANY
SACHSEN
BERLIN
Dresden
LEIPZIG
CHEMNITZ
ZACHODNIOPOMORSKIE
POMORSKIE
POJEZIERZE KASZUBSKIE
POJEZIERZE KRAJEŃSKIE
KUJAWSKO-POMORSKIE
WIELKOPOLSKIE
LUBUSKIE
DOLNOŚLĄSKIE
OPOLSKIE
POL
Poznań
Szczecin
Wrocław
Gdańsk
Bydgoszcz
CZECH REPUBLIC
PRAHA (Prague)
LIBERECKÝ KRAJ
ÚSTECKÝ KRAJ
KRÁLOVÉHRADECKÝ KRAJ
STŘEDOČESKÝ KRAJ
PLZEŇSKÝ KRAJ
PARDUBICKÝ KRAJ
OLOMOUCKÝ KRAJ
MORAVSKOSLEZSKÝ KRAJ
JIHOČESKÝ KRAJ
VYSOČINA
JIHOMORAVSKÝ KRAJ
ZLÍNSKÝ KRAJ
METRES
FEET
6000 19686
5000 16404
4000 13124
3000 9843
2000 6562
1500 4921
1000 3281
500 1640
200 656
100 328
0 0
LAND BELOW SEA LEVEL
50 164
200 656
1000 3281
2000 6562
171
173
Longitude 18 east of Greenwich

138
RUSSIAN FEDERATION
LITHUANIA
WARMIŃSKO-MAZURSKIE
POJEZIERZE MAZURSKIE
HRODZYENSKAYA VOBLASTS'
PODLASKIE
BELARUS
NIZINA
MAZOWIECKIE
PODLASKA
BRESTSKAYA VOBLASTS'
WARSZAWA (Warsaw)
MAZOWIECKA
LUBELSKIE
WYŻYNA LUBELSKA
WYŻYNA MAŁOPOLSKA
ŚWIĘTOKRZYSKIE
UKRAINE
MAŁOPOLSKIE
PODKARPACKIE
CARPATHIAN MOUNTAINS
PREŠOVSKÝ KRAJ
136
177
MILES
KILOMETRES
1:1 800 000

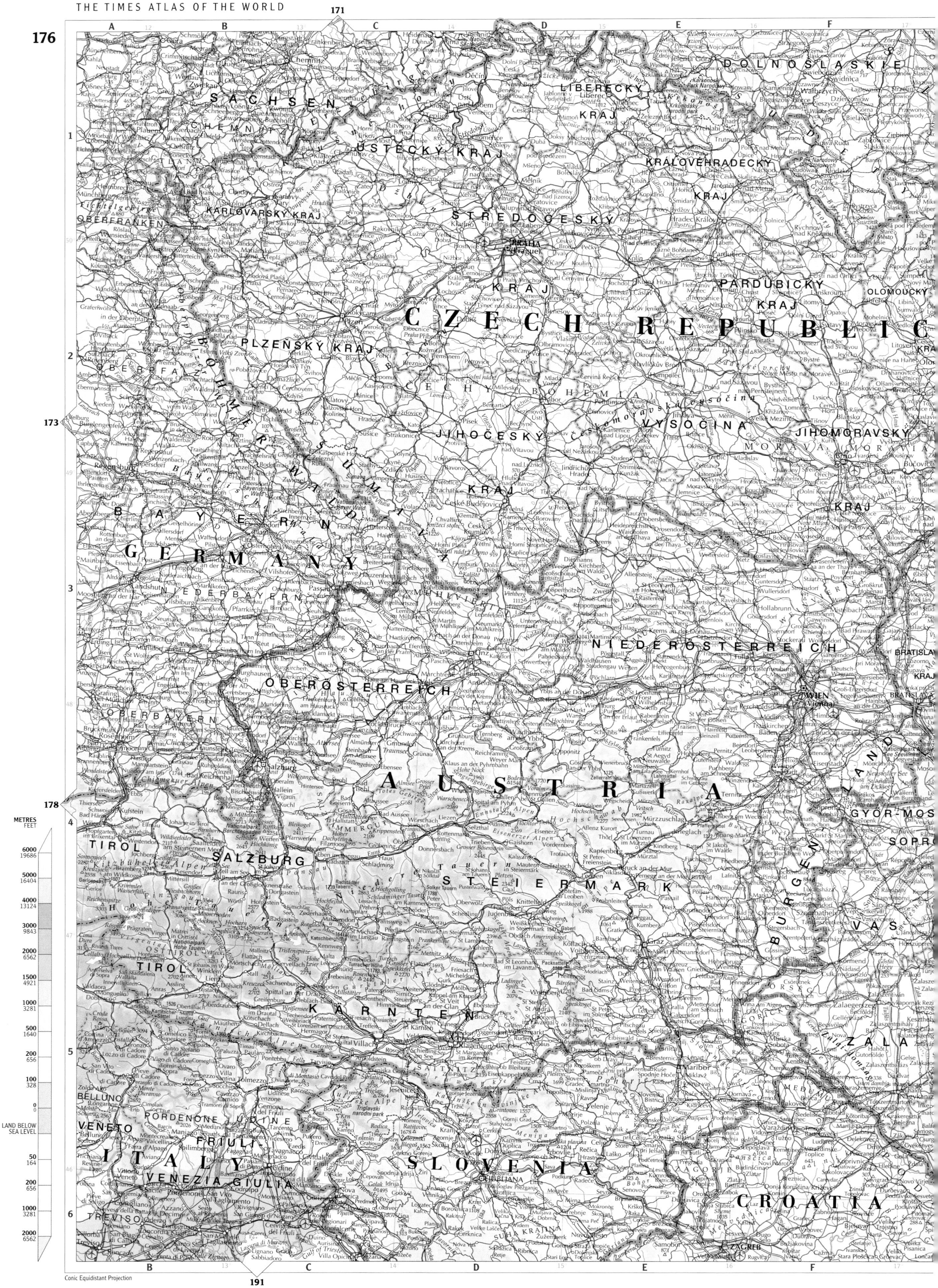
171
191
173
178
METRES
FEET
6000
19686
5000
16404
4000
13124
3000
9843
2000
6562
1500
4921
1000
3281
500
1640
200
656
100
328
0
0
LAND BELOW SEA LEVEL
50
164
200
656
1000
3281
2000
6562
CZECH REPUBLIC
AUSTRIA
GERMANY
SLOVENIA
CROATIA
ITALY
PRAHA (Prague)
WIEN Vienna
LJUBLJANA
ZAGREB
SACHSEN
CHEMNITZ
BAYERN
OBERFRANKEN
OBERPFALZ
NIEDERBAYERN
OBERBAYERN
KARLOVARSKÝ KRAJ
ÚSTECKÝ KRAJ
LIBERECKÝ KRAJ
KRÁLOVÉHRADECKÝ KRAJ
STŘEDOČESKÝ KRAJ
PARDUBICKÝ KRAJ
PLZEŇSKÝ KRAJ
JIHOČESKÝ KRAJ
VYSOČINA
JIHOMORAVSKÝ KRAJ
OLOMOUCKÝ
DOLNOŚLĄSKIE
ČECHY BOHEMIA
MORAVA MORAVIA
NIEDERÖSTERREICH
OBERÖSTERREICH
SALZBURG
TIROL
STEIERMARK
KÄRNTEN
BURGENLAND
BRATISLAVA
GYŐR-MOSON
VAS
ZALA
VENETO
FRIULI-VENEZIA GIULIA
BELLUNO
PORDENONE
UDINE
TREVISO
Conic Equidistant Projection

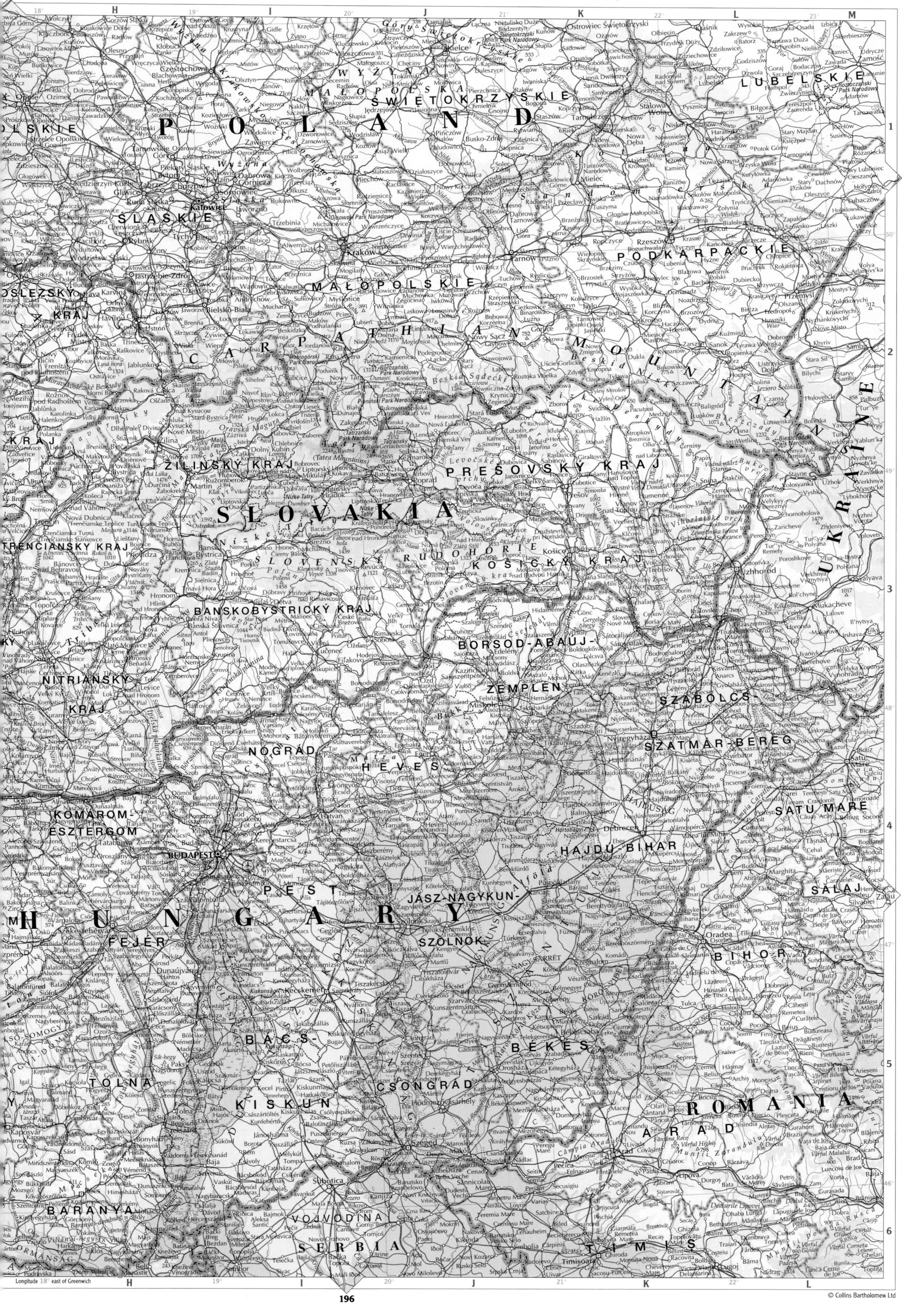
174
136
197
196
H
I
J
K
L
M
1
2
3
4
5
6
POLAND
SLOVAKIA
HUNGARY
ROMANIA
UKRAINE
SERBIA
CARPATHIAN MOUNTAINS
ŚWIĘTOKRZYSKIE
LUBELSKIE
PODKARPACKIE
MAŁOPOLSKIE
ŚLĄSKIE
ŽILINSKÝ KRAJ
PREŠOVSKÝ KRAJ
KOŠICKÝ KRAJ
TRENČIANSKY KRAJ
BANSKOBYSTRICKÝ KRAJ
NITRIANSKY KRAJ
BORSOD-ABAÚJ-ZEMPLÉN
SZABOLCS-SZATMÁR-BEREG
NÓGRÁD
HEVES
KOMÁROM-ESZTERGOM
PEST
JÁSZ-NAGYKUN-SZOLNOK
HAJDÚ-BIHAR
SATU MARE
SĂLAJ
BIHOR
FEJÉR
BÁCS-KISKUN
BÉKÉS
CSONGRÁD
TOLNA
BARANYA
ARAD
TIMIŞ
VOJVODINA
BUDAPEST
Kraków
Katowice
Rzeszów
Debrecen
Košice
Szeged
Timişoara
Oradea
Longitude 18° east of Greenwich

MILES KILOMETRES

1:1 800 000

© Collins Bartholomew Ltd

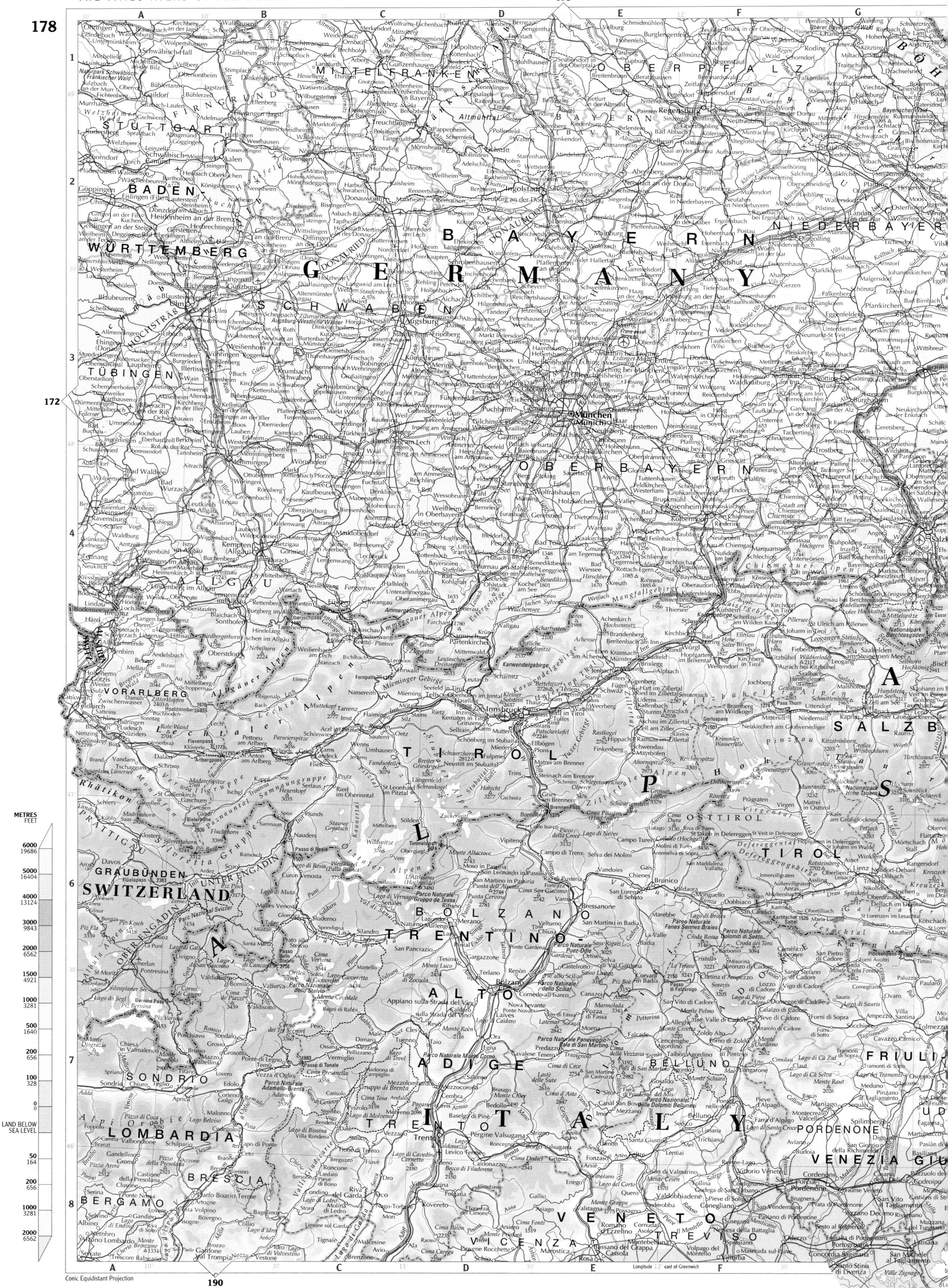

Conic Equidistant Projection

173
GERMANY
BAYERN
MITTELFRANKEN
OBERPFALZ
NIEDERBAYERN
OBERBAYERN
SCHWABEN
BADEN
WÜRTTEMBERG
STUTTGART
TÜBINGEN
ALLGÄU
München (Munich)
Augsburg
Ingolstadt
Regensburg
Innsbruck
AUSTRIA
TIROL
OSTTIROL
SALZBURG
VORARLBERG
SWITZERLAND
GRAUBÜNDEN
ITALY
ALTO ADIGE
TRENTINO
BOLZANO
TRENTO
BELLUNO
VENETO
TREVISO
VICENZA
LOMBARDIA
BERGAMO
BRESCIA
SONDRIO
PORDENONE
FRIULI-VENEZIA GIULIA
Alpen
METRES
FEET
6000 19686
5000 16404
4000 13124
3000 9843
2000 6562
1500 4921
1000 3281
500 1640
200 656
100 328
0
LAND BELOW SEA LEVEL
50 164
200 656
1000 3281
2000 6562
Longitude 12° east of Greenwich
172
190

MILES
KILOMETRES

1:1 200 000

© Collins Bartholomew Ltd

A
B
C
D
Mar Cantábrico
BAY
ATLANTIC OCEAN
PORTUGAL
SPAIN
GALICIA
ASTURIAS
CANTABRIA
CORDILLERA CANTÁBRICA
CASTILLA Y LEÓN
EXTREMADURA
ANDALUCÍA
SIERRA MORENA
MINHO
VIANA DO CASTELO
BRAGA
VILA REAL
BRAGANÇA
TRÁS-OS-MONTES
PORTO
AVEIRO
VISEU
BEIRA ALTA
GUARDA
COIMBRA
CASTELO BRANCO
LEIRIA
SANTARÉM
LISBOA
PORTALEGRE
ÉVORA
SETÚBAL
BEJA
ALGARVE
FARO
MOROCCO
TANGER-TETOUAN
TAZA-AL-HOCEIMA-TAOUNATE
A Coruña (La Coruña)
Santiago de Compostela
Lugo
Ourense (Orense)
Pontevedra
Vigo
Oviedo
Gijón-Xixón
Santander
León
Burgos
Palencia
Valladolid
Zamora
Salamanca
Segovia
Ávila
MADRID
Toledo
Cáceres
Badajoz
Mérida
Ciudad Real
Porto (Oporto)
Coimbra
LISBOA (Lisbon)
Setúbal
Évora
Huelva
Sevilla
Córdoba
Jaén
Granada
Málaga
Cádiz
Jerez de la Frontera
Gibraltar (U.K.)
Ceuta (Spain)
Tanger (Tangier)
Tétouan
Golfo de Cádiz
Costa de la Luz
Costa del Sol
Strait of Gibraltar
Cabo Fisterra (Cape Finisterre)
Cabo de São Vicente
Cabo da Roca
Cabo Espichel
Cabo Trafalgar
Cabo Ortegal
Punta de Tarifa
Punta Almina
Cabo Negro
Parque Nacional de Doñana
Parque Nacional de los Picos de Europa
Sierra de Gredos
Sierra de Guadarrama
Montes de León
Sierra de Aracena
Serra da Estrela
METRES
FEET
6000 19686
5000 16404
4000 13124
3000 9843
2000 6562
1500 4921
1000 3281
500 1640
200 656
100 328
0 0
LAND BELOW SEA LEVEL
50 164
200 656
1000 3281
2000 6562
Longitude 8 west of Greenwich
Conic Equidistant Projection

204

154

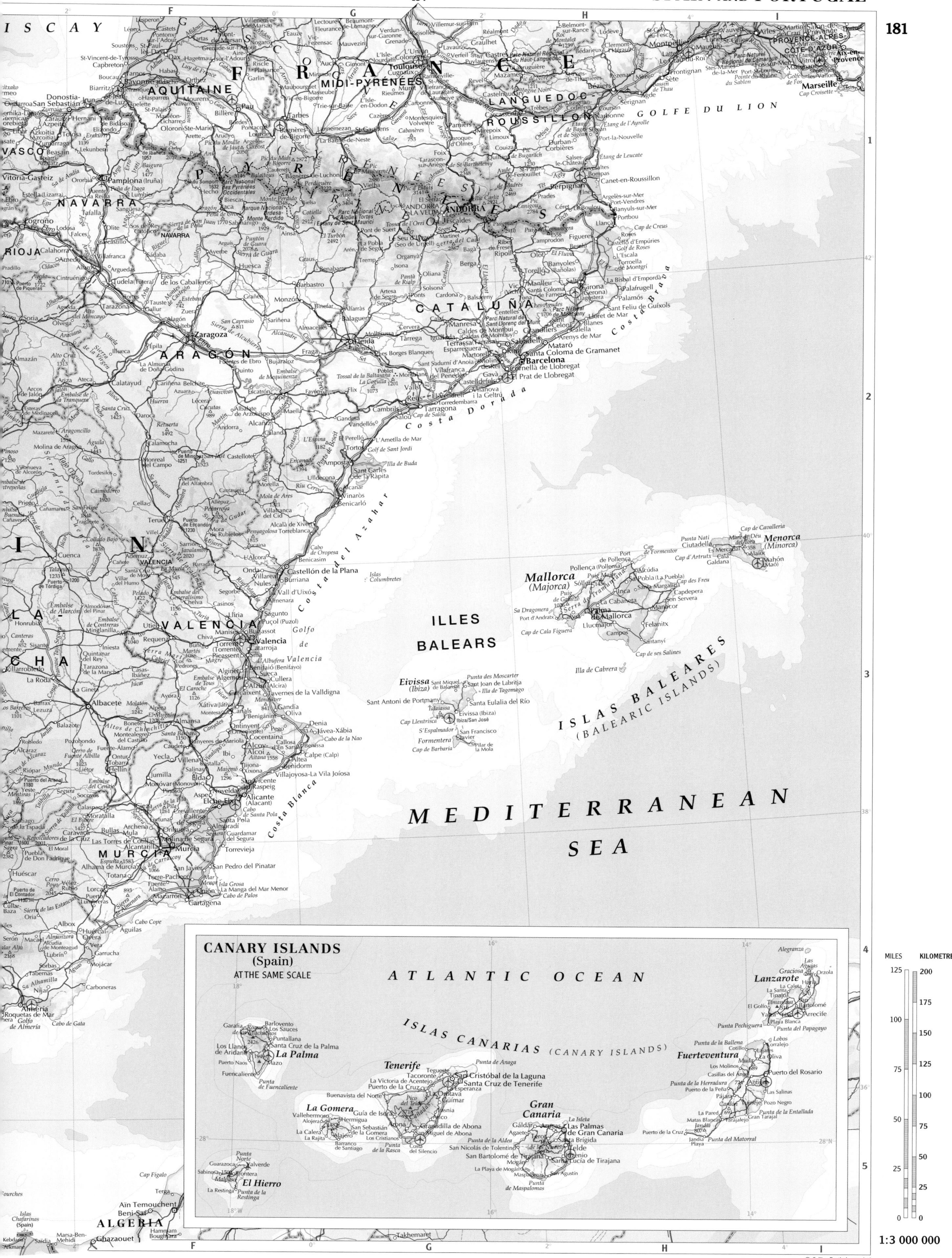
F
G
H
I
FRANCE
AQUITAINE
MIDI-PYRÉNÉES
LANGUEDOC-ROUSSILLON
PROVENCE-ALPES-CÔTE-D'AZUR
GOLFE DU LION
PYRÉNÉES
ANDORRA
NAVARRA
RIOJA
ARAGÓN
CATALUÑA
Costa Brava
Costa Dorada
Costa del Azahar
Costa Blanca
VALENCIA
MURCIA
Golfo de Valencia
ILLES BALEARS
ISLAS BALEARES (BALEARIC ISLANDS)
Mallorca (Majorca)
Menorca (Minorca)
Eivissa (Ibiza)
Formentera
MEDITERRANEAN SEA
ALGERIA
Toulouse
Marseille
Montpellier
Perpignan
Pamplona (Iruña)
Zaragoza
Lleida (Lérida)
Barcelona
Tarragona
Castellón de la Plana
Valencia
Alicante (Alacant)
Murcia
Cartagena
Almería
Albacete
Palma de Mallorca
Mahón (Maó)
CANARY ISLANDS
(Spain)
AT THE SAME SCALE
ATLANTIC OCEAN
ISLAS CANARIAS (CANARY ISLANDS)
La Palma
El Hierro
La Gomera
Tenerife
Gran Canaria
Fuerteventura
Lanzarote
Santa Cruz de Tenerife
Las Palmas de Gran Canaria
Puerto del Rosario
Arrecife
MILES
KILOMETRES
1:3 000 000

© Collins Bartholomew Ltd

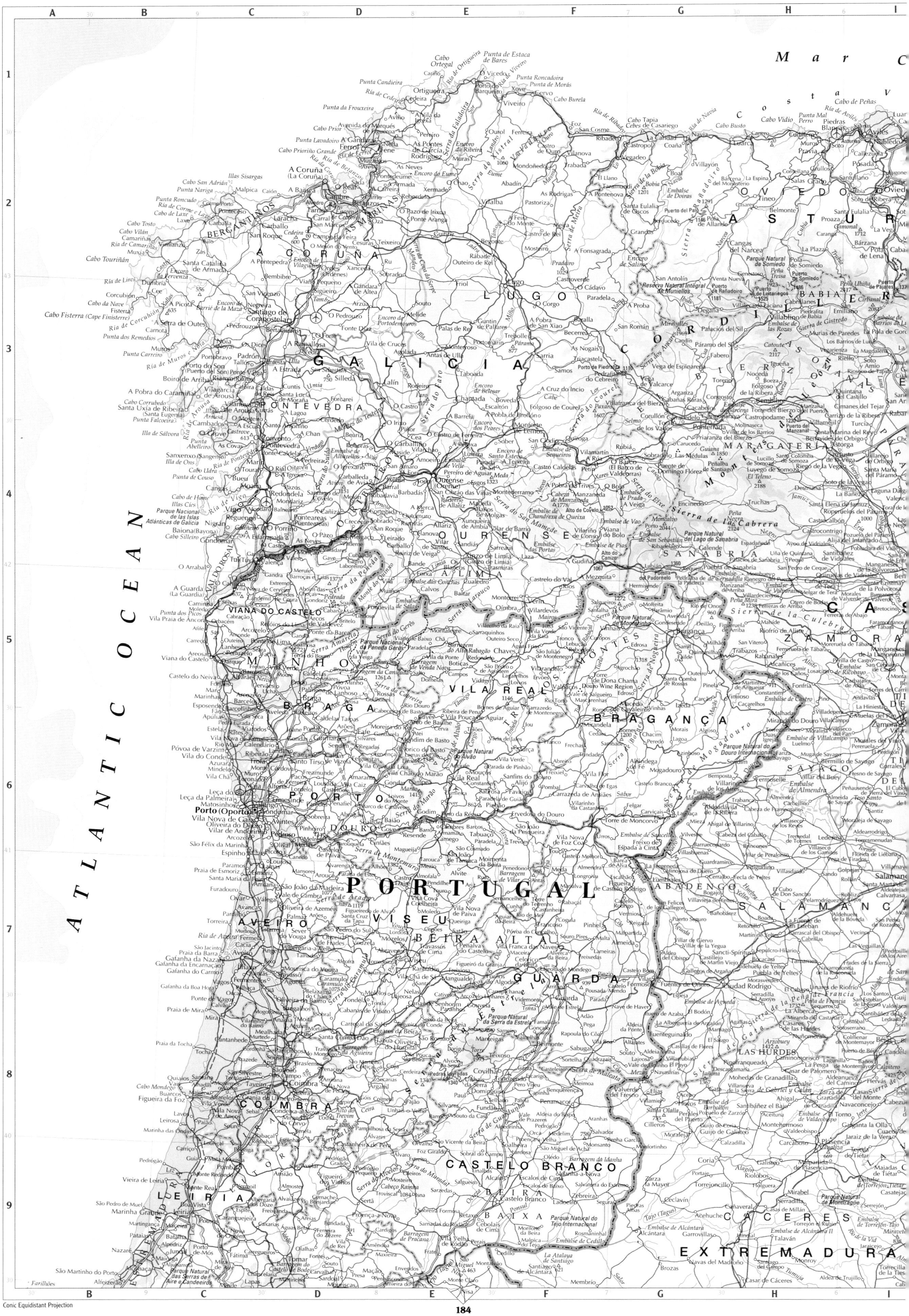

METRES / FEET

METRES	FEET
6000	19686
5000	16404
4000	13124
3000	9843
2000	6562
1500	4921
1000	3281
500	1640
200	656
100	328
0	0
LAND BELOW SEA LEVEL	
50	164
200	656
1000	3281
2000	6562

Conic Equidistant Projection

184

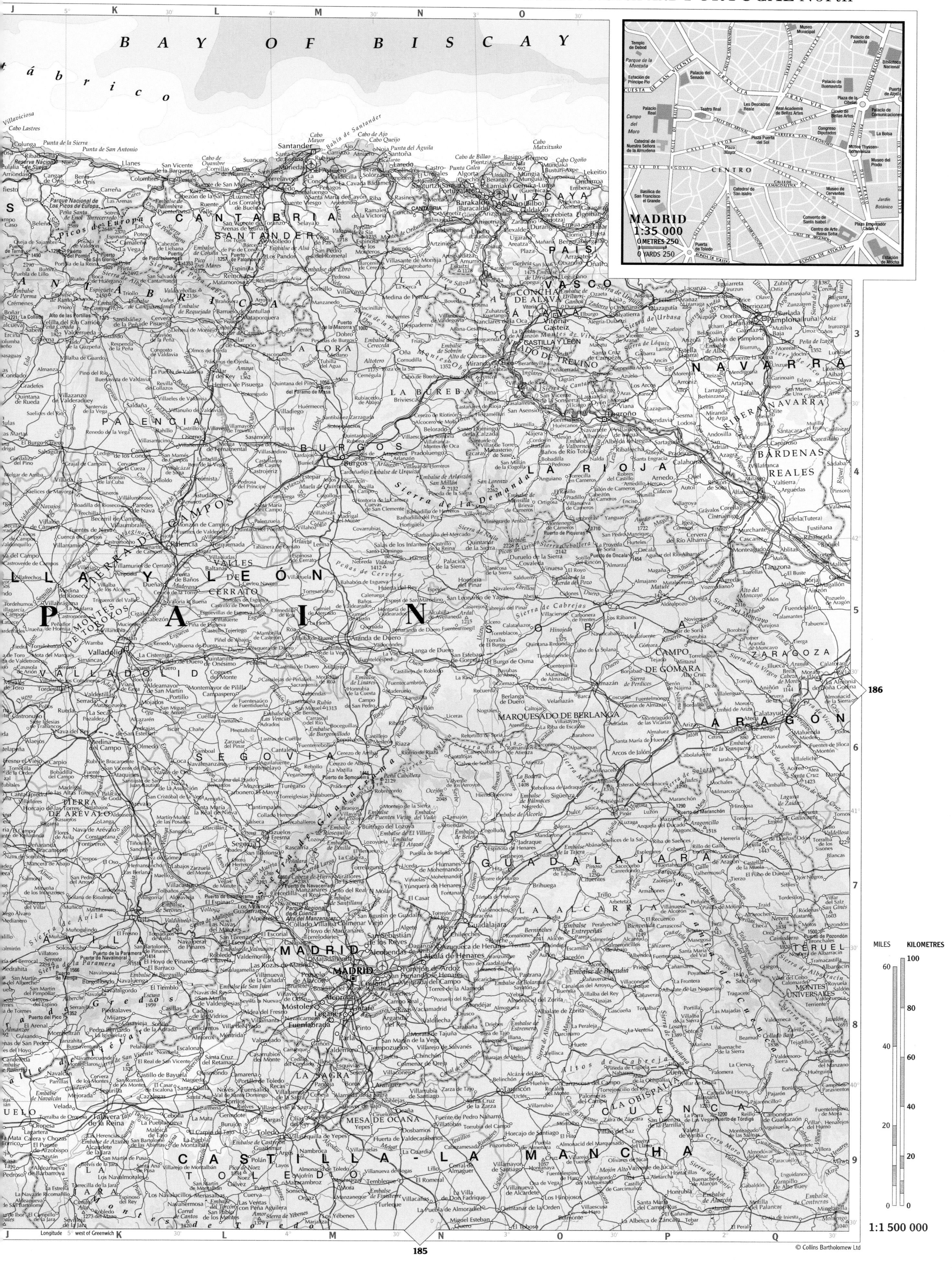
BAY OF BISCAY
MADRID 1:35 000
CANTABRIA
SANTANDER
PAIS VASCO
ÁLAVA
NAVARRA
LA RIOJA
BURGOS
PALENCIA
CASTILLA Y LEÓN
SPAIN
SORIA
VALLADOLID
SEGOVIA
ZARAGOZA
ARAGÓN
GUADALAJARA
MADRID
ÁVILA
TERUEL
CUENCA
TOLEDO
CASTILLA - LA MANCHA
Santander
Bilbao (Bilbo)
Vitoria Gasteiz
Pamplona (Iruña)
Logroño
Burgos
Palencia
Valladolid
Soria
Segovia
Guadalajara
Alcalá de Henares
Toledo
Cuenca
Teruel
Ávila
MILES
KILOMETRES
1:1 500 000
Longitude 5° west of Greenwich

186

185

182

184

PORTUGAL
LEIRIA
CASTELO BRANCO
SANTARÉM
PORTALEGRE
LISBOA
Lisboa (Lisbon)
ÉVORA
SETÚBAL
BEJA
FARO
ALGARVE
RIBATEJO
BEIRA BAIXA
EXTREMADURA
CÁCERES
BADAJOZ
HUELVA
CÁDIZ
EL ANDÉVALO
CONDADO DE NIEBLA
EL ALJARAFE
LLANOS DE OLIVENZA
TIERRA DE BARROS
Sevilla
Huelva
Badajoz
Cáceres
Mérida
Jerez de la Frontera
Tanger (Tangier)
GOLFO DE CÁDIZ
Costa de la Luz
Baía de Setúbal
Sierra de Aracena
Sierra de San Pedro
Parque Nacional de Doñana
Las Marismas
Cabo da Roca
Cabo de São Vicente
Cabo Trafalgar
Cabo Espichel
Cabo de Sines
Cabo de Santa Maria
Strait
MADEIRA
(Portugal)
1:1 250 000
Arquipélago da Madeira
Ilha da Madeira
Ilha de Porto Santo
Ilhas Desertas
Deserta Grande
Bugio
FUNCHAL
METRES
FEET
6000
19686
5000
16404
4000
13124
3000
9843
2000
6562
1500
4921
1000
3281
500
1640
200
656
100
328
0
0
LAND BELOW SEA LEVEL
50
164
200
656
1000
3281
2000
6562

Conic Equidistant Projection

183
187
SPAIN
CASTILLA-LA MANCHA
LA MANCHA
ANDALUCÍA
TOLEDO
CIUDAD REAL
CUENCA
ALBACETE
MURCIA
CÓRDOBA
JAÉN
GRANADA
ALMERÍA
MÁLAGA
SIERRA MORENA
CAMPO DE CALATRAVA
VALLE DE ALCUDIA
MESA DE OCAÑA
CAMPO DE DALÍAS
Costa del Sol
MEDITERRANEAN SEA
Golfo de Almería
Sierra Nevada
Toledo
Ciudad Real
Albacete
Córdoba
Jaén
Granada
Almería
Málaga
Marbella
Estepona
Gibraltar (U.K.)
Ceuta (Spain)
Isla de Alborán (Spain)
Cabo de Gata
GIBRALTAR (U.K.)
1:100 000
North Mole
Eastern Beach
Gibraltar Harbour
Bay of Gibraltar
The Rock
Catalan Bay (Caleta)
St Abb's Hd
Shirley Cove
Sandy Bay
Rosia Bay
Camp Bay
Little Bay
Europa Pt
36°08'N
5°21'W
Longitude 5° west of Greenwich
MILES
KILOMETRES
1:1 500 000

© Collins Bartholomew Ltd

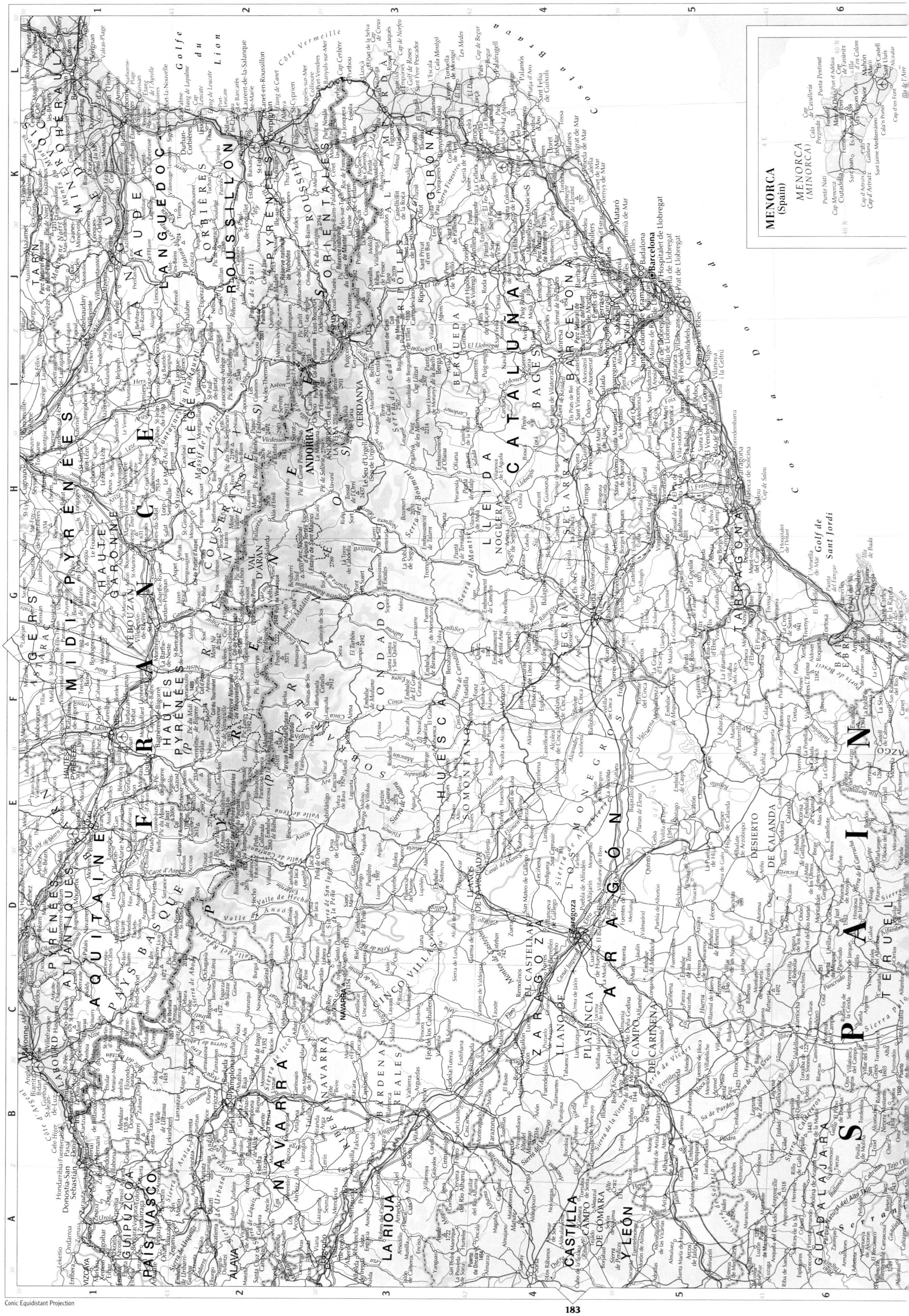
FRANCE
SPAIN
ANDORRA
MENORCA (Spain)
MIDI-PYRÉNÉES
AQUITAINE
LANGUEDOC-ROUSSILLON
CATALUÑA
ARAGÓN
NAVARRA
PAÍS VASCO
LA RIOJA
CASTILLA Y LEÓN
Golfe du Lion
Barcelona
Zaragoza

163

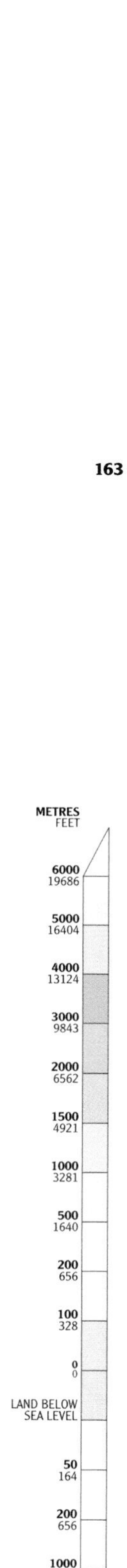
METRES
FEET
6000
19686
5000
16404
4000
13124
3000
9843
2000
6562
1500
4921
1000
3281
500
1640
200
656
100
328
0
LAND BELOW SEA LEVEL
50
164
200
656
1000
3281
2000
6562

Conic Equidistant Projection

183

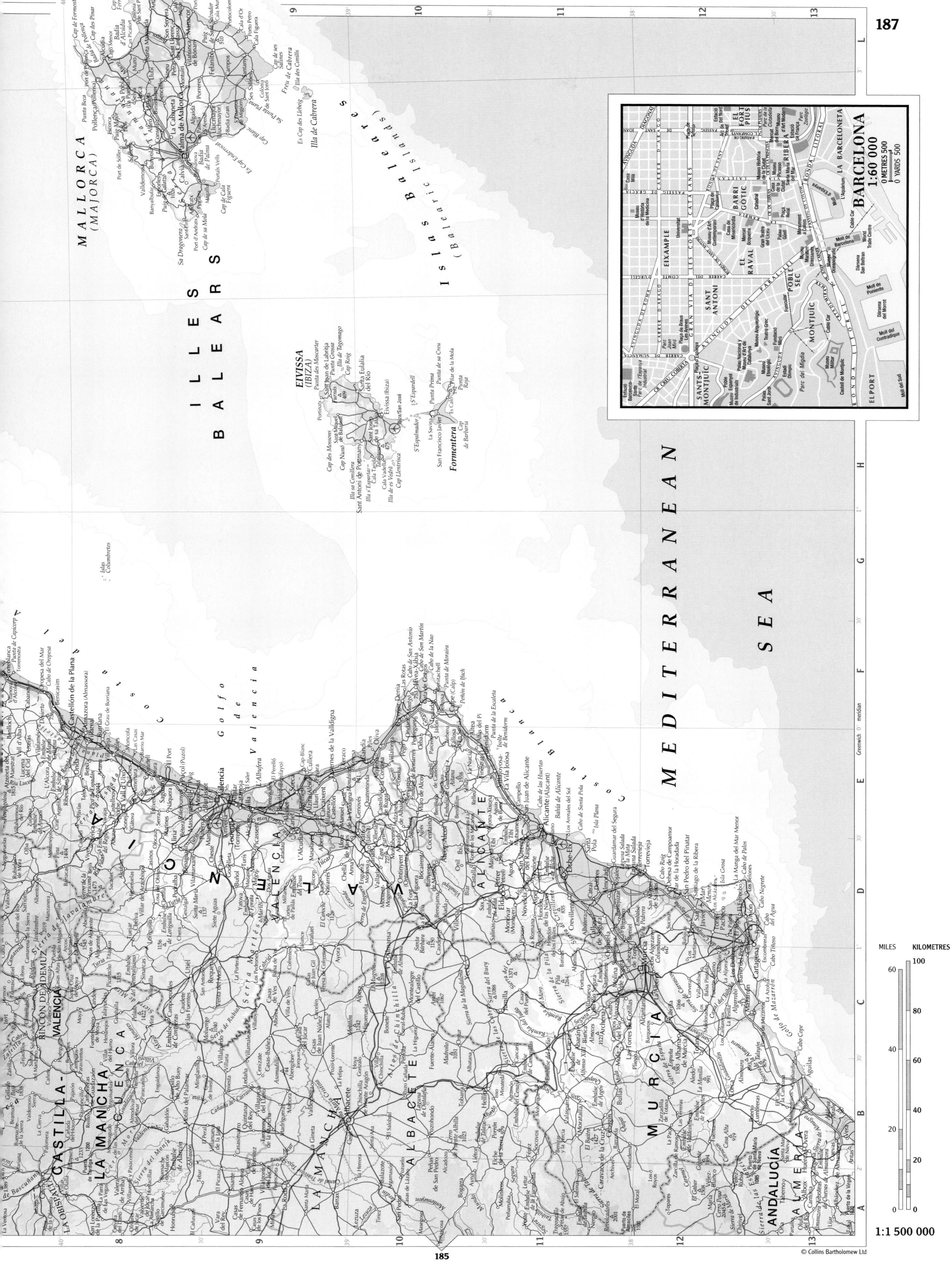
MEDITERRANEAN SEA
ILLES BALEARS
Islas Baleares
(Balearic Islands)
MALLORCA
(MAJORCA)
Palma de Mallorca
EIVISSA
(IBIZA)
Formentera
Illa de Cabrera
Golfo de Valencia
Costa Blanca
Valencia
Alicante
Murcia
Cartagena
Albacete
CASTILLA-LA MANCHA
CUENCA
VALENCIA
ALICANTE
ALBACETE
MURCIA
ANDALUCÍA
ALMERÍA
BARCELONA
1:60 000
MILES
KILOMETRES
1:1 500 000

185

© Collins Bartholomew Ltd

196

167

166

METRES
FEET
6000
19686
5000
16404
4000
13124
3000
9843
2000
6562
1500
4921
1000
3281
500
1640
200
656
100
328
0
0
LAND BELOW
SEA LEVEL
50
164
200
656
1000
3281
2000
6562
SLOVAKIA
HUNGARY
BOSNIA-HERZEGOVINA
REPUBLIKA SRPSKA
FEDERACIJA BOSNA I HERCEGOVINA
DAYTON ACCORD LINE 1995
MONTENEGRO
CROATIA
SLOVENIA
AUSTRIA
GERMANY
BAYERN
BADEN-WÜRTTEMBERG
SWITZERLAND
LIECHTENSTEIN
FRANCE
ALSACE
LORRAINE
FRANCHE-COMTÉ
RHÔNE-ALPES
PROVENCE-ALPES-CÔTE D'AZUR
MONACO
ITALY
PIEMONTE
VALLE D'AOSTA
LOMBARDIA
TRENTINO-ALTO ADIGE
VENETO
FRIULI-VENEZIA GIULIA
EMILIA-ROMAGNA
LIGURIA
TOSCANA
UMBRIA
MARCHE
SAN MARINO
ADRIATIC SEA
LIGURIAN SEA
Gulf of Venice
Golfo di Genova
BUDAPEST
BRATISLAVA
WIEN (Vienna)
ZAGREB
LJUBLJANA
SARAJEVO
München (Munich)
Milano (Milan)
Torino (Turin)
Genova (Genoa)
Venezia (Venice)
Firenze (Florence)
BERN
VADUZ
Conic Equidistant Projection

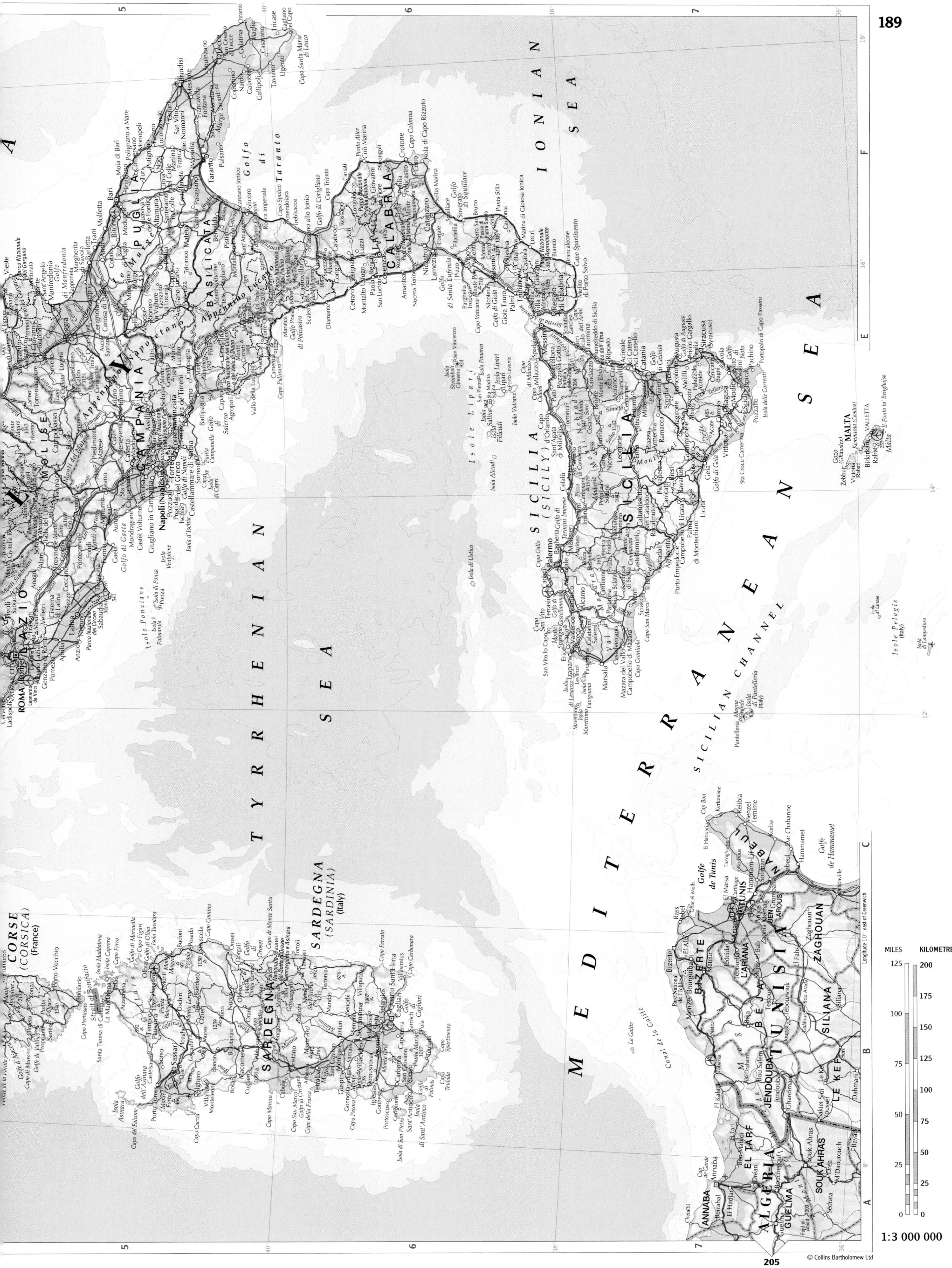
TYRRHENIAN SEA
MEDITERRANEAN SEA
IONIAN SEA
SICILIAN CHANNEL
Golfo di Taranto
CORSE (CORSICA) (France)
SARDEGNA (SARDINIA) (Italy)
SICILIA (SICILY)
CALABRIA
BASILICATA
PUGLIA
CAMPANIA
MOLISE
LAZIO
ROMA
Napoli (Naples)
Palermo
Catania
Messina
Cagliari
Sassari
Taranto
Brindisi
Bari
MALTA
VALLETTA
Isole Pelagie (Italy)
Isola di Pantelleria (Italy)
Isole Lipari
TUNISIA
TUNIS
ALGERIA
ANNABA
MILES
KILOMETRES
1:3 000 000

172

160

161

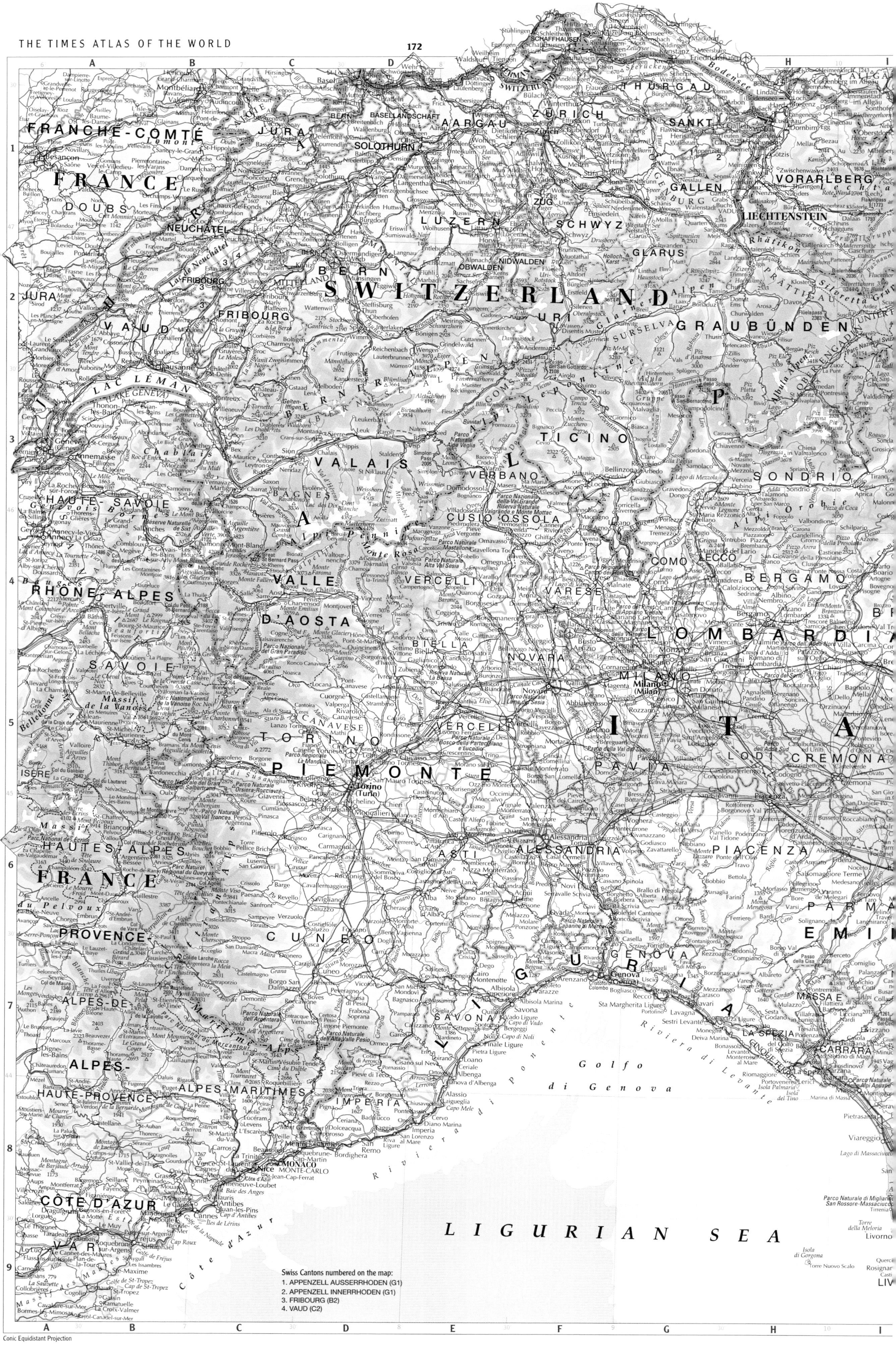
FRANCHE-COMTÉ
FRANCE
DOUBS
JURA
VAUD
FRIBOURG
NEUCHÂTEL
SOLOTHURN
BASELLANDSCHAFT
AARGAU
ZÜRICH
THURGAU
SANKT GALLEN
VORARLBERG
LIECHTENSTEIN
LUZERN
ZUG
SCHWYZ
GLARUS
NIDWALDEN
OBWALDEN
BERN
SWITZERLAND
URI
GRAUBÜNDEN
LAC LÉMAN
(LAKE GENEVA)
VALAIS
TICINO
SONDRIO
HAUTE-SAVOIE
RHÔNE-ALPES
VALLE D'AOSTA
VERBANO-CUSIO-OSSOLA
COMO
LECCO
BERGAMO
VARESE
LOMBARDIA
BIELLA
NOVARA
MILANO
SAVOIE
VERCELLI
ITALIA
LODI
CREMONA
TORINO
PIEMONTE
PAVIA
ISÈRE
HAUTES-ALPES
FRANCE
ASTI
ALESSANDRIA
PIACENZA
PARMA
PROVENCE-
CUNEO
GENOVA
EMI
ALPES-DE-
HAUTE-PROVENCE
LIGURIA
SAVONA
MASSA E CARRARA
ALPES-MARITIMES
IMPERIA
Golfo di Genova
Riviera di Ponente
Riviera di Levante
MONACO
CÔTE D'AZUR
VAR
LIGURIAN SEA
Swiss Cantons numbered on the map:
1. APPENZELL AUSSERRHODEN (G1)
2. APPENZELL INNERRHODEN (G1)
3. FRIBOURG (B2)
4. VAUD (C2)

METRES / FEET
6000 19686
5000 16404
4000 13124
3000 9843
2000 6562
1500 4921
1000 3281
500 1640
200 656
100 328
0 0
LAND BELOW SEA LEVEL
50 164
200 656
1000 3281
2000 6562

Conic Equidistant Projection

178

AUSTRIA
SALZBURG
STEIERMARK
TIROL
OSTTIROL
KÄRNTEN
BAYERN
SLOVENIA
CROATIA
BOLZANO
TRENTINO-
ALTO ADIGE
TRENTO
BELLUNO
FRIULI-
VENEZIA GIULIA
UDINE
PORDENONE
GORIZIA
TREVISO
VICENZA
VENETO
VERONA
PADOVA
VENEZIA
ROVIGO
FERRARA
ROMAGNA
MODENA
BOLOGNA
RAVENNA
FORLÌ-
CESENA
RIMINI
SAN MARINO
PESARO
E URBINO
ANCONA
MARCHE
MACERATA
PERUGIA
UMBRIA
AREZZO
SIENA
FIRENZE
TOSCANA
Gulf of Venice
Gulf of Trieste
ADRIATIC SEA
Istra
Ljubljana
Trieste
Rijeka
Venezia
Bologna
Ancona
Longitude 11° east of Greenwich

176
196
193

MILES
KILOMETRES
1:1 500 000

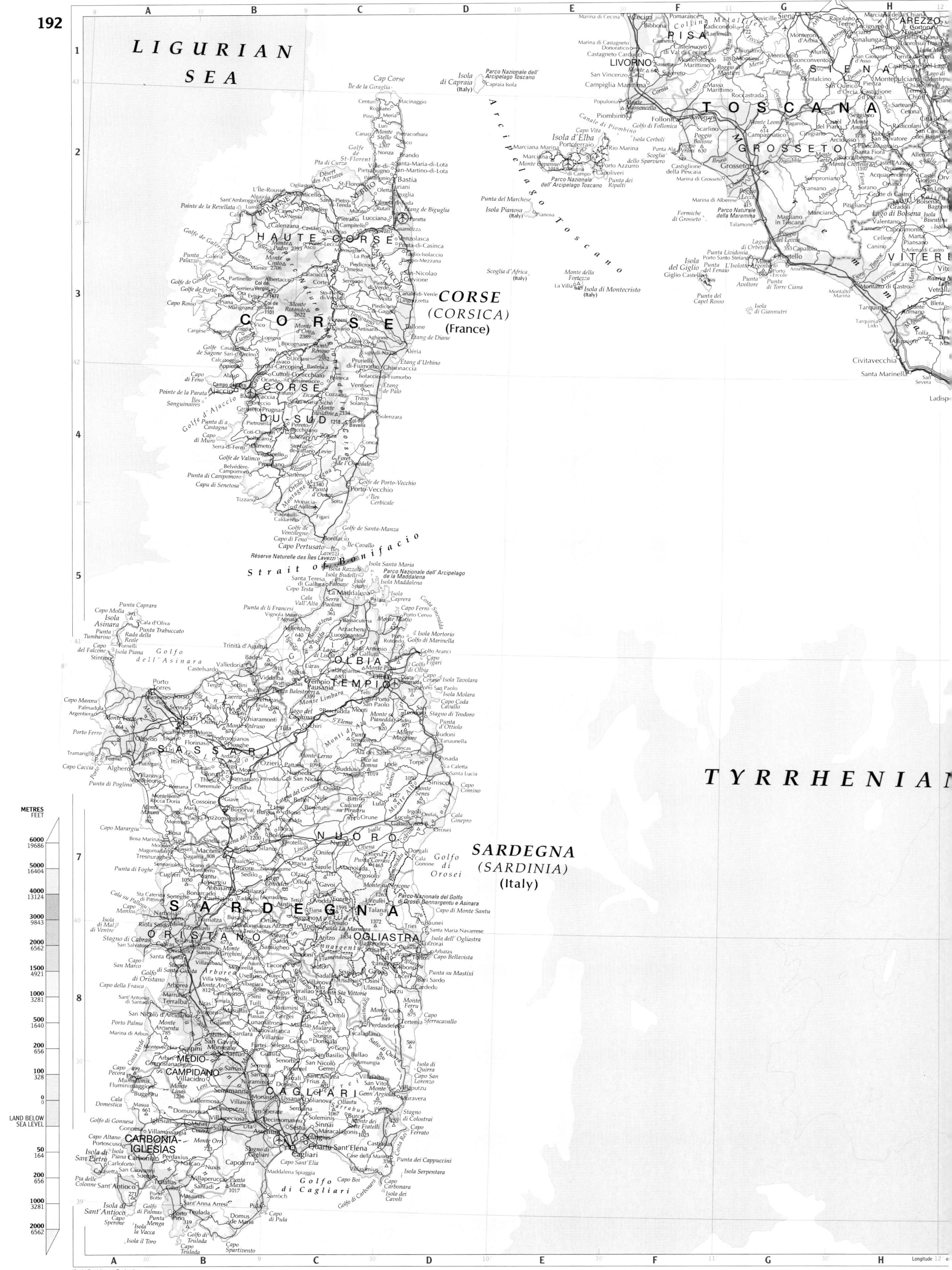
LIGURIAN SEA
TYRRHENIAN
CORSE
(CORSICA)
(France)
SARDEGNA
(SARDINIA)
(Italy)
HAUTE-CORSE
CORSE-DU-SUD
SASSARI
OLBIA-TEMPIO
NUORO
ORISTANO
OGLIASTRA
MEDIO CAMPIDANO
CARBONIA-IGLESIAS
CAGLIARI
TOSCANA
PISA
LIVORNO
SIENA
GROSSETO
AREZZO
VITERBO
Strait of Bonifacio
Arcipelago Toscano
Isola d'Elba
Golfo di Cagliari
Golfo dell'Asinara
Golfo di Orosei
Bastia
Ajaccio
Porto-Vecchio
Sassari
Alghero
Olbia
Nuoro
Oristano
Cagliari
Grosseto
Piombino
Civitavecchia
METRES
FEET
6000 19686
5000 16404
4000 13124
3000 9843
2000 6562
1500 4921
1000 3281
500 1640
200 656
100 328
0 0
LAND BELOW SEA LEVEL
50 164
200 656
1000 3281
2000 6562
Longitude
Conic Equidistant Projection

CROATIA
ADRIATIC SEA
MARCHE
MACERATA
ASCOLI PICENO
TERAMO
PESCARA
ABRUZZO
L'AQUILA
CHIETI
RIETI
ITALY
LAZIO
ROMA
FROSINONE
LATINA
ISERNIA
MOLISE
CAMPOBASSO
FOGGIA
PUGLIA
BARI
BENEVENTO
CASERTA
AVELLINO
CAMPANIA
NAPOLI
Napoli (Naples)
SALERNO
BASILICATA
POTENZA
MATERA
COSENZA
CALABRIA
Golfo di Gaeta
Golfo di Napoli
Golfo di Salerno
Golfo di Policastro
Golfo di Manfredonia
Isole Tremiti (Italy)
Palagruža (Croatia)
Isole Ponziane
Isola d'Ischia
Isola di Capri
Pescara
Termoli
Barletta
Trani
Bisceglie
Molfetta
Giovinazzo
Terlizzi
Corato
Ruvo di Puglia
Altamura
Manfredonia
Vieste
Foggia
Salerno
Paestum
Agropoli
Cosenza
Paola
ROME 1:50 000
0 METRES 500
0 YARDS 500
VATICAN CITY
TRASTEVERE
SALARIO
TRIONFALE
Villa Borghese
Colosseo
Foro Romano
Circo Massimo
MILES
KILOMETRES
1:1 500 000
195
© Collins Bartholomew Ltd

193

TYRRHENIAN SEA
SICILIAN CHANNEL
SICILIA
(SICILY)
TUNISIA
Cap Bon
El Haouaria
Kerkouane
Kelibia
Isola di Pantelleria (Italy)
Pantelleria
Scauri
Tracino
Isola Palmarola
Isola Zannone
Isola di Gavi
Isola di Ponza
Ponza
Isole Ponziane
Isola Ventotene
Isola di Ustica
Ustica
Isola Alicudi
Isola Filicudi
Filicudi Porto
Isole Lip
Mondragone
Castèl Volturno
Giugliano in Campania
Napoli (Naples)
Pozzuoli
Golfo di Napoli
Isola d'Ischia
Ischia
Procida
Torre del Greco
Castellammare di Stabia
Vico Equense
Sorrento
Massa Lubrense
Anacapri
Capri
Isola di Capri
Punta Campanella
Amalfi
Praiano
Golf di Sale
CASERTA
Caserta
BENEVE
Benevento
NAPOLI
Capo San Vito
San Vito lo Capo
Golfo di Castellammare
Punta Raisi
Capo Gallo
Golfo di Palermo
Palermo
Capo Zafferano
Golfo di Termini Imerese
Bagheria
Termini Imerese
Cefalù
Trapani
Erice
Isola Marettimo
Marettimo
Isola di Levanzo
Levanzo
Isola Favignana
Favignana
Isola Grande
Marsala
Petrosino
Capo Feto
Mazara del Vallo
Campobello di Mazara
Granitola Torretta
Capo Granitola
Castelvetrano
Menfi
Sciacca
Capo San Marco
Ribera
Capo Bianco
Siculiana
Realmonte
Agrigento
Porto Empedocle
Favara
Canicattì
Licata
Gela
Golfo di Gela
Vittoria
Scoglitti
Sta Croce Camerina
Marina di Ragusa
Sampieri
Niscemi
Caltagirone
Piazza Armerina
Enna
Leonforte
Nicosia
Caltanissetta
Corleone
Alcamo
Partinico
Carini
Monreale
Bisacquino
Lercara Friddi
Madonie
Capo d'Orlando
Sant'Agata di Militello
TRAPANI
PALERMO
AGRIGENTO
CALTANISSETTA
ENNA
RAGUSA
Monti Nebrodi
Sicilia
Conic Equidistant Projection
METRES
FEET
6000 19686
5000 16404
4000 13124
3000 9843
2000 6562
1500 4921
1000 3281
500 1640
200 656
100 328
0 0
LAND BELOW SEA LEVEL
50 164
200 656
1000 3281
2000 6562

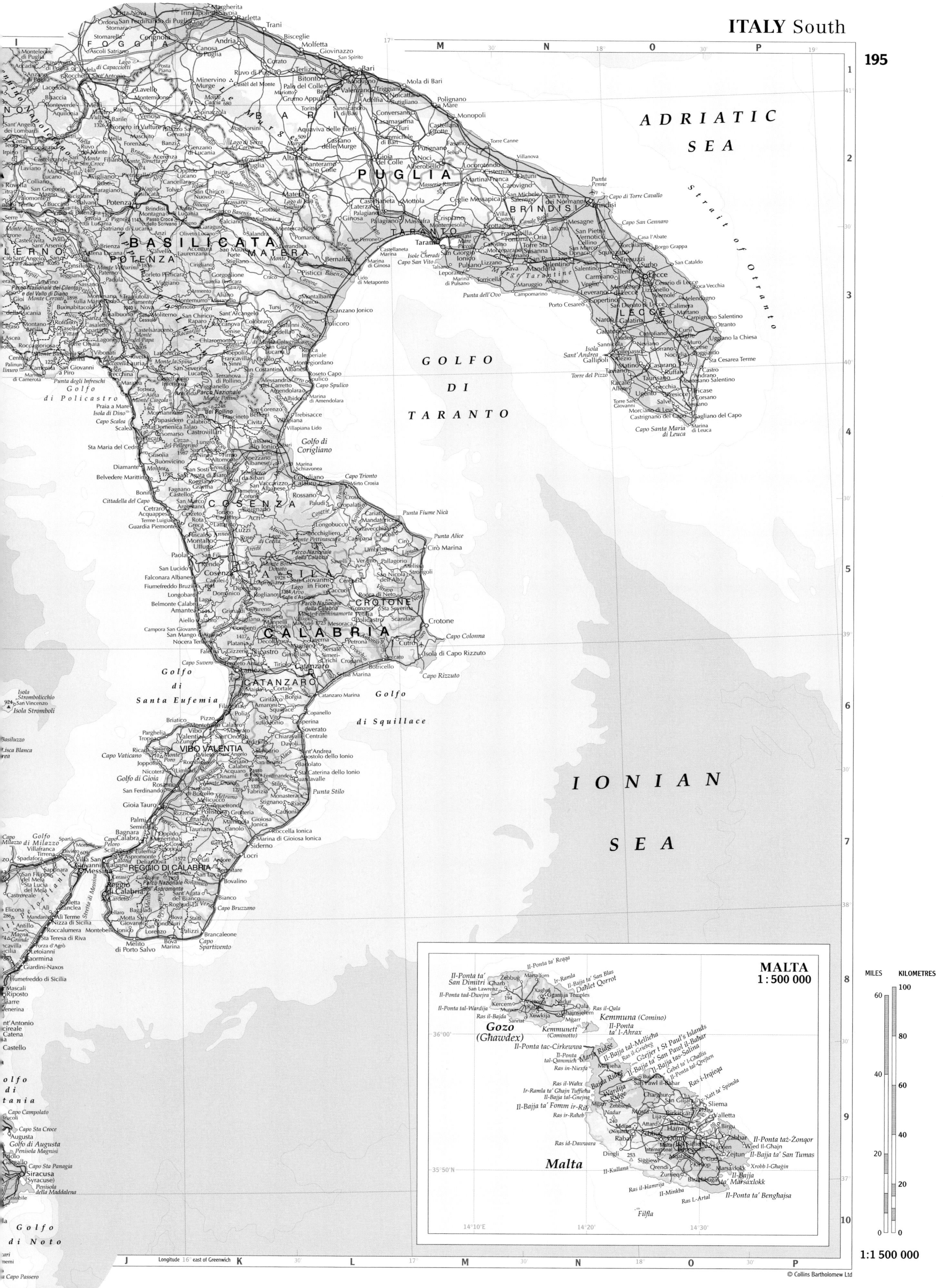
ADRIATIC SEA
Strait of Otranto
GOLFO DI TARANTO
IONIAN SEA
Golfo di Policastro
Golfo di Santa Eufemia
Golfo di Squillace
Golfo di Corigliano
Golfo di Gioia
Golfo di Catania
Golfo di Noto
PUGLIA
BASILICATA
CALABRIA
FOGGIA
BARI
BRINDISI
TARANTO
LECCE
POTENZA
MATERA
COSENZA
CROTONE
CATANZARO
VIBO VALENTIA
REGGIO DI CALABRIA
LA SILA
Bari
Brindisi
Taranto
Lecce
Potenza
Matera
Cosenza
Crotone
Catanzaro
Messina
Reggio di Calabria
Otranto
Gallipoli
Capo Santa Maria di Leuca
Capo Colonna
Capo Rizzuto
Capo Spartivento
Capo Vaticano
Punta Stilo
Punta Alice
MALTA
1 : 500 000
Gozo (Għawdex)
Kemmuna (Comino)
Malta
Valletta
Sliema
Rabat
Mdina
Filfla
Marfa Ridge
St Paul's Islands
MILES
KILOMETRES
Longitude 16° east of Greenwich
1:1 500 000

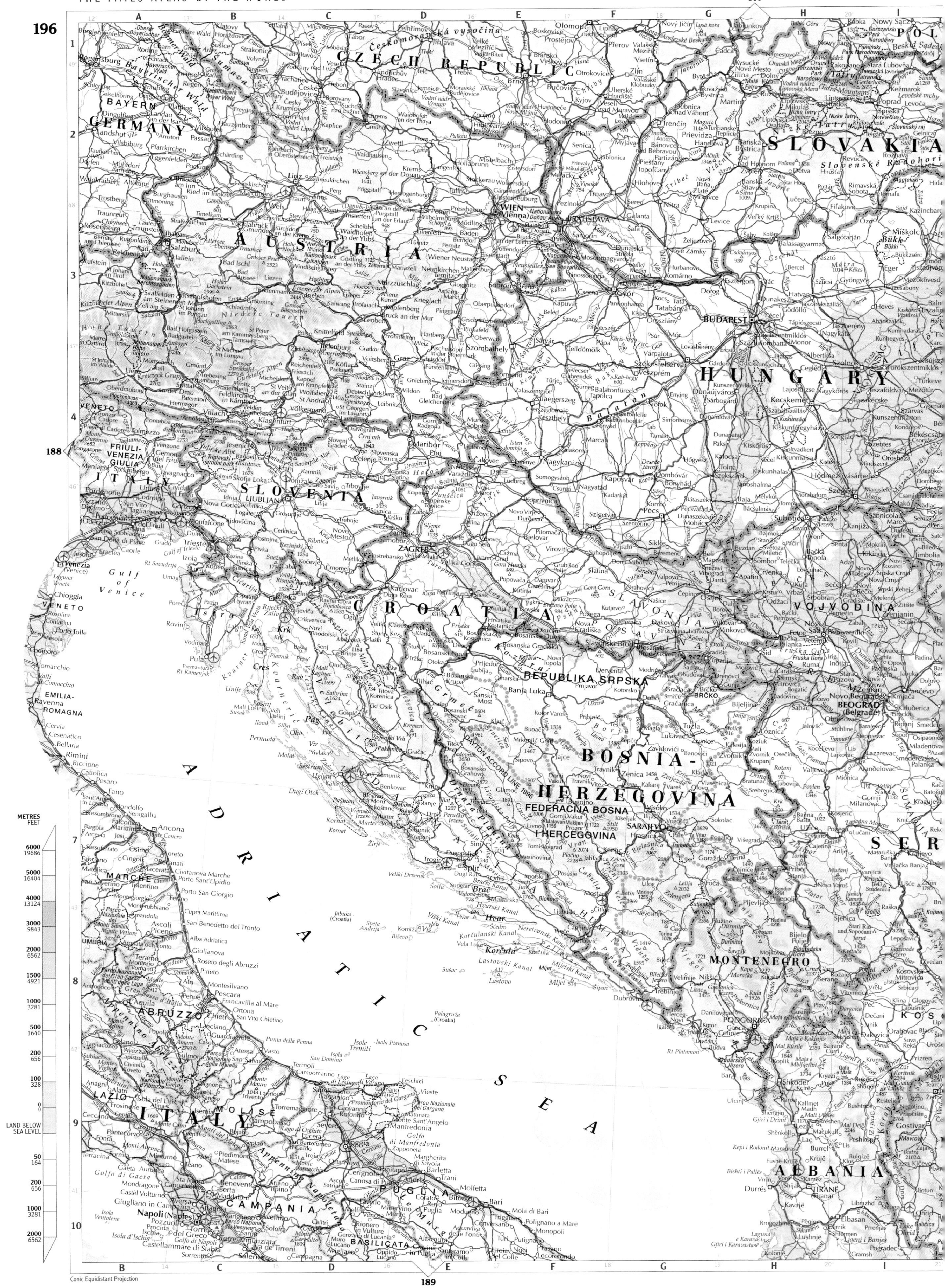
167
CZECH REPUBLIC
SLOVAKIA
POLAND
GERMANY
BAYERN
AUSTRIA
HUNGARY
SLOVENIA
CROATIA
BOSNIA-HERZEGOVINA
REPUBLIKA SRPSKA
FEDERACNA BOSNA I HERCEGOVINA
DAYTON ACCORD LINE 1996
VOJVODINA
SERBIA
MONTENEGRO
KOSOVO
ALBANIA
ITALY
FRIULI-VENEZIA GIULIA
VENETO
EMILIA-ROMAGNA
MARCHE
UMBRIA
ABRUZZO
LAZIO
MOLISE
CAMPANIA
PUGLIA
BASILICATA
Gulf of Venice
ADRIATIC SEA
188
METRES
FEET
6000
19686
5000
16404
4000
13124
3000
9843
2000
6562
1500
4921
1000
3281
500
1640
200
656
100
328
0
0
LAND BELOW SEA LEVEL
50
164
200
656
1000
3281
2000
6562
Conic Equidistant Projection
189

UKRAINE
MOLDOVA
ROMANIA
BULGARIA
GREECE
TURKEY
BLACK SEA
CARPATHIAN MOUNTAINS
CARPAŢII MERIDIONALI
TRANSYLVANIAN ALPS
STARA PLANINA
BALKAN MOUNTAINS
RHODOPE MOUNTAINS
Marmara Denizi
Thrakiko Pelagos
BUCUREŞTI (Bucharest)
SOFIYA
CHIŞINĂU
İstanbul
Odesa
MILES
KILOMETRES
east of Greenwich
136
198

1:3 000 000

© Collins Bartholomew Ltd

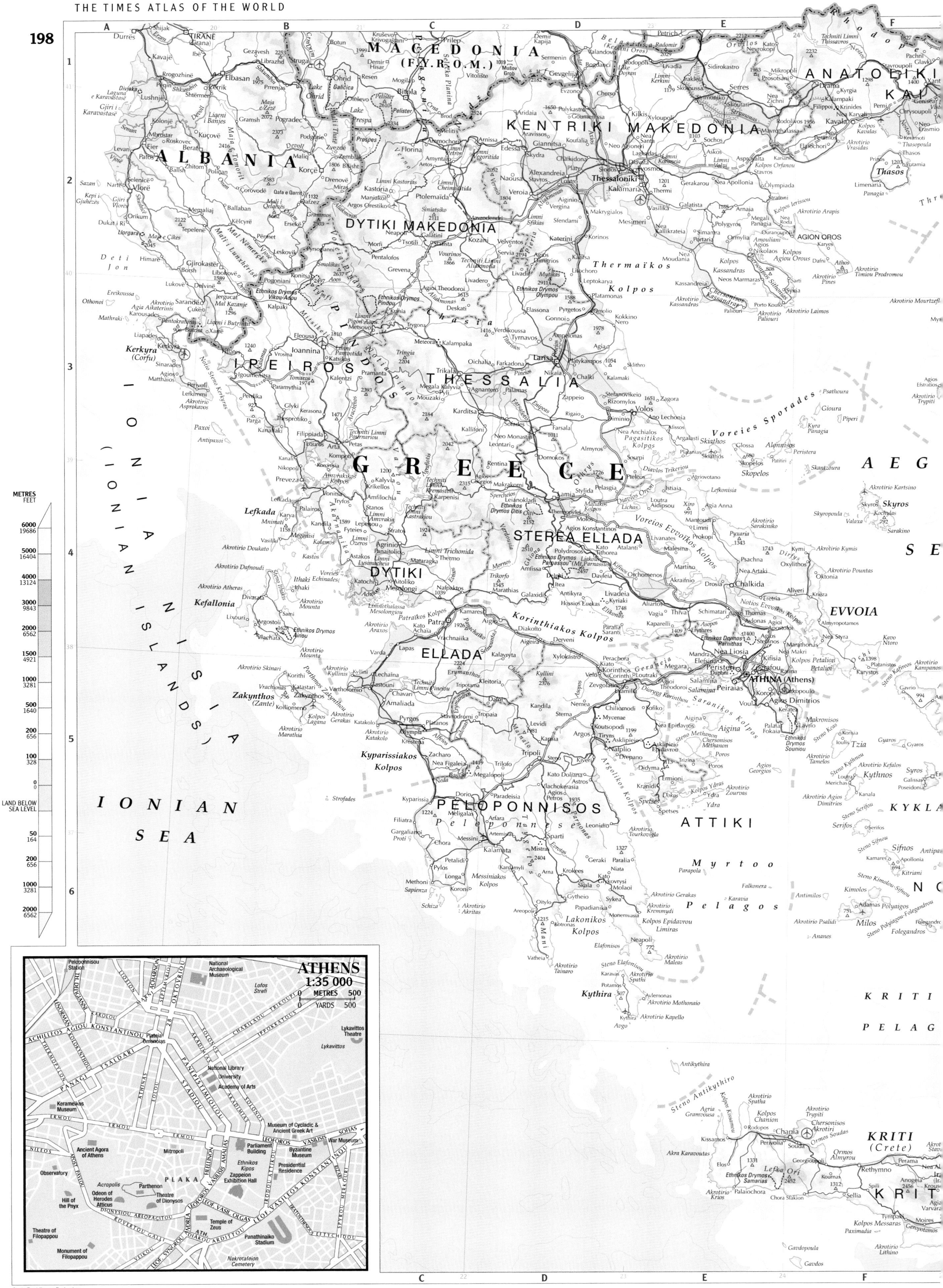
ALBANIA
MACEDONIA (F.Y.R.O.M.)
KENTRIKI MAKEDONIA
DYTIKI MAKEDONIA
ANATOLIKI
IPEIROS
THESSALIA
GREECE
STEREA ELLADA
DYTIKI ELLADA
PELOPONNISOS
ATTIKI
EVVOIA
KRITI (Crete)
IONIA NISIA (IONIAN ISLANDS)
IONIAN SEA
AEGEAN SEA
Myrtoo Pelagos
Thermaïkos Kolpos
Korinthiakos Kolpos
Voreies Sporades
Thessaloniki
Larisa
Volos
Lamia
Patra
ATHINA (Athens)
Peiraias
Tripoli
Kalamata
Chania
Rethymno
Kerkyra (Corfu)
Ioannina
Kefallonia
Zakynthos (Zante)
Lefkada
Kythira
Thasos
Skyros
METRES FEET
6000 19686
5000 16404
4000 13124
3000 9843
2000 6562
1500 4921
1000 3281
500 1640
200 656
100 328
0 0
LAND BELOW SEA LEVEL
50 164
200 656
1000 3281
2000 6562
ATHENS
1:35 000
0 METRES 500
0 YARDS 500
National Archaeological Museum
Pelopponisou Station
Lofos Strefi
Plateia Omonias
Lykavittos Theatre
Lykavittos
National Library
University
Academy of Arts
Kerameikos Museum
Museum of Cycladic & Ancient Greek Art
Parliament Building
Byzantine Museum
War Museum
Ancient Agora of Athens
Mitropoli
Presidential Residence
Ethnikos Kipos
Zappeion Exhibition Hall
Observatory
Acropolis
Parthenon
Odeon of Herodes Atticus
Theatre of Dionysos
PLAKA
Hill of the Pnyx
Temple of Zeus
Panathinaiko Stadium
Theatre of Filopappou
Monument of Filopappou
Nekrotafeion Cemetery

Conic Equidistant Projection

197

BLACK SEA
BULGARIA
EDİRNE
TEKİRDAĞ
İSTANBUL
İstanbul
Kadıköy
Bakırköy
KOCAELİ
İzmit
SAKARYA
Adapazarı
DÜZCE
BOLU
ANKARA
Marmara Denizi
Saros Körfezi
Gelibolu
Çanakkale
ÇANAKKALE
Gökçeada
BURSA
Bursa
BİLECİK
ESKİŞEHİR
Eskişehir
BALIKESİR
Balıkesir
KÜTAHYA
Kütahya
LESVOS
VOREIO AIGAIO
Edremit Körfezi
TURKEY
ANATOLIA
MANİSA
Manisa
AFYON
Afyon
UŞAK
Uşak
İzmir
İZMİR
Chios
Samos
Ikaria
Kuşadası Körfezi
AYDIN
Aydın
DENİZLİ
Denizli
ISPARTA
Isparta
Eğirdir Gölü
BURDUR
Burdur
MUĞLA
Muğla
Güllük Körfezi
Gökova Körfezi
DODEKANISA (DODECANESE)
Kos
Patmos
Leros
Kalymnos
Astypalaia
Tilos
Symi
Naxos
AIGAIO
ANTALYA
Antalya
ANTALYA KÖRFEZİ
LYCIA
RODOS (RHODES)
Karpathos
Kasos
Steno Karpathou
MEDITERRANEAN SEA
MILES
KILOMETRES
1:2 250 000
Longitude 26° east of Greenwich

126

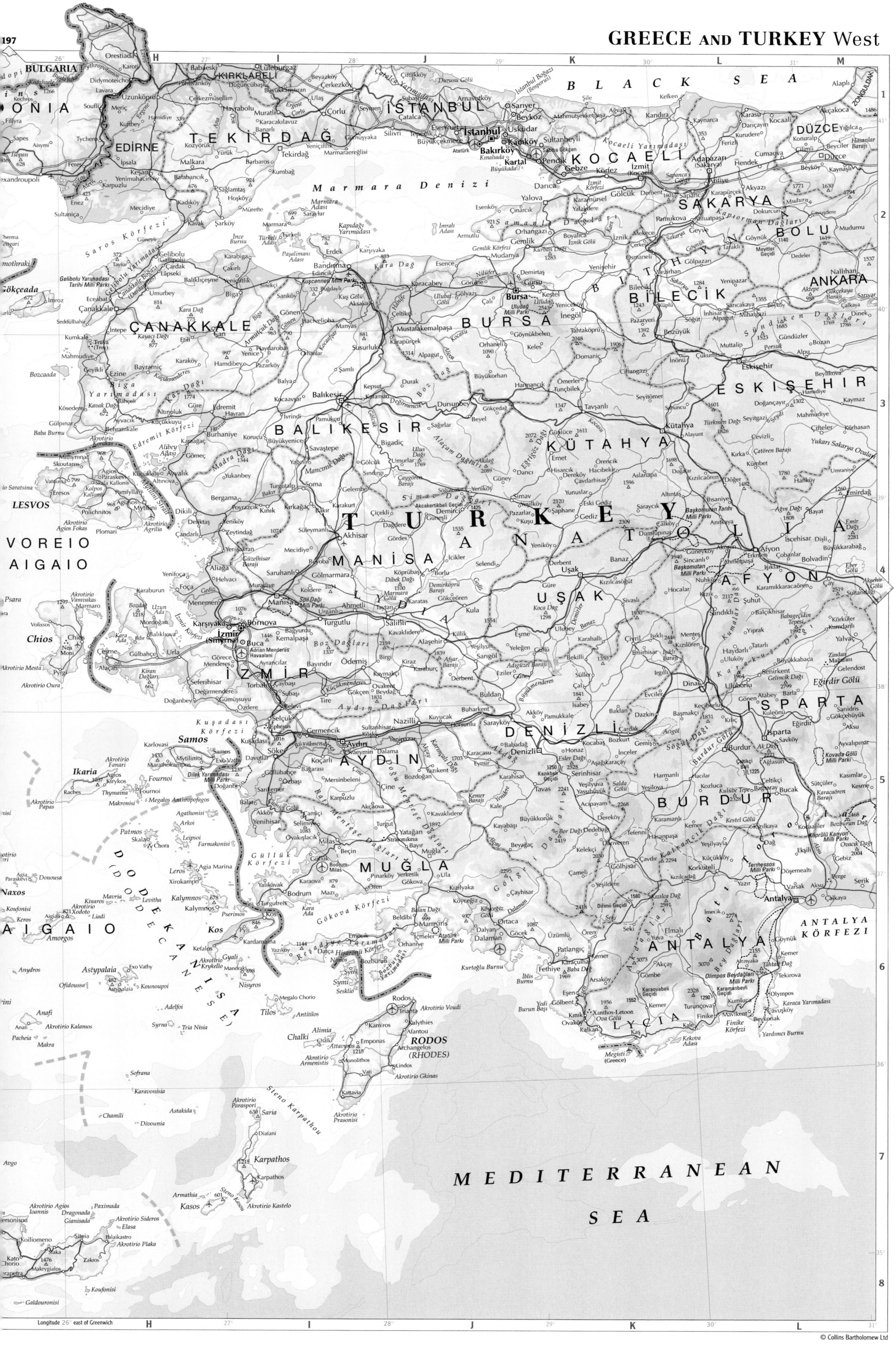

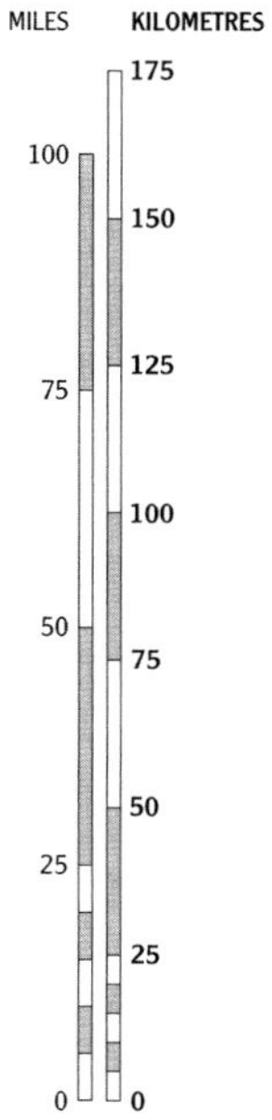

A
B
C
D
E
1
2
3
4
5
6
7
Pyrenees
Corse
Sardegna
Alger
Bejaïa
Skikda
Annaba
Ech Chélif
Constantine
Gabès
TUNI
Laghouat
Tanger
Str. of Gibraltar
Oran
Sidi Bel Abbès
Rabat
Fès
Casablanca
MOROCCO
Beni Mellal
Béchar
Marrakech
ATLAS MOUNTAINS
ALGERIA
Arquipélago dos Açores
Arquipélago da Madeira
Islas Canarias (Spain)
Tenerife
Las Palmas de Gran Canaria
Lanzarote
Islas Canarias
Gran Canaria
Laâyoune
WESTERN SAHARA
Hoggar
Mt Tahat 2918
SAHARA
Nouâdhibou
MAURITANIA
MALI
NI
Agadez
Nouakchott
Gao
Sénégal
St Louis
Niger
Mopti
Niamey
Zind
Tropic of Cancer
Santo Antão
Boa Vista
CAPE VERDE
Santiago
Praia
Fogo
Dakar
SENEGAL
Kayes
Ségou
BURKINA
Sokoto
Kano
Kaolack
Bamako
Ouagadougou
THE GAMBIA
Banjul
Bobo-Dioulasso
Kainji Reservoir
Shiroro Reservoir
Kaduna
GUINEA-BISSAU
Bissau
Fouta Djallon
GUINEA
Kankan
BENIN
NIGER
Parakou
Abuja
White Volta
Black Volta
Tamale
TOGO
CÔTE D'IVOIRE
GHANA
Ogbomosho
Conakry
SIERRA LEONE
Freetown
Lac de Kossou
Bouaké
Lake Volta
Porto-Novo
Ibadan
Lagos
Onitsha
Yamoussoukro
Kumasi
Volta
Lomé
Accra
Warri
Nkongsamba
Monrovia
LIBERIA
Abidjan
Cape Coast
Port Harcourt
Gulf of Guinea
Malabo
Bioco
EQUATORIAL GUINEA
Príncipe
SÃO TOMÉ AND PRÍNCIPE
São Tomé
Port-Gentil
Annobón (Equatorial Guinea)
ATLANTIC OCEAN
Poin
Equator
Ascension (U.K.)
St Helena (U.K.)
SOUTH AMERICA
Ilha da Trindade
Ilhas Martin Vaz
Tropic of Capricorn
30°
15°
0°
45°
60°

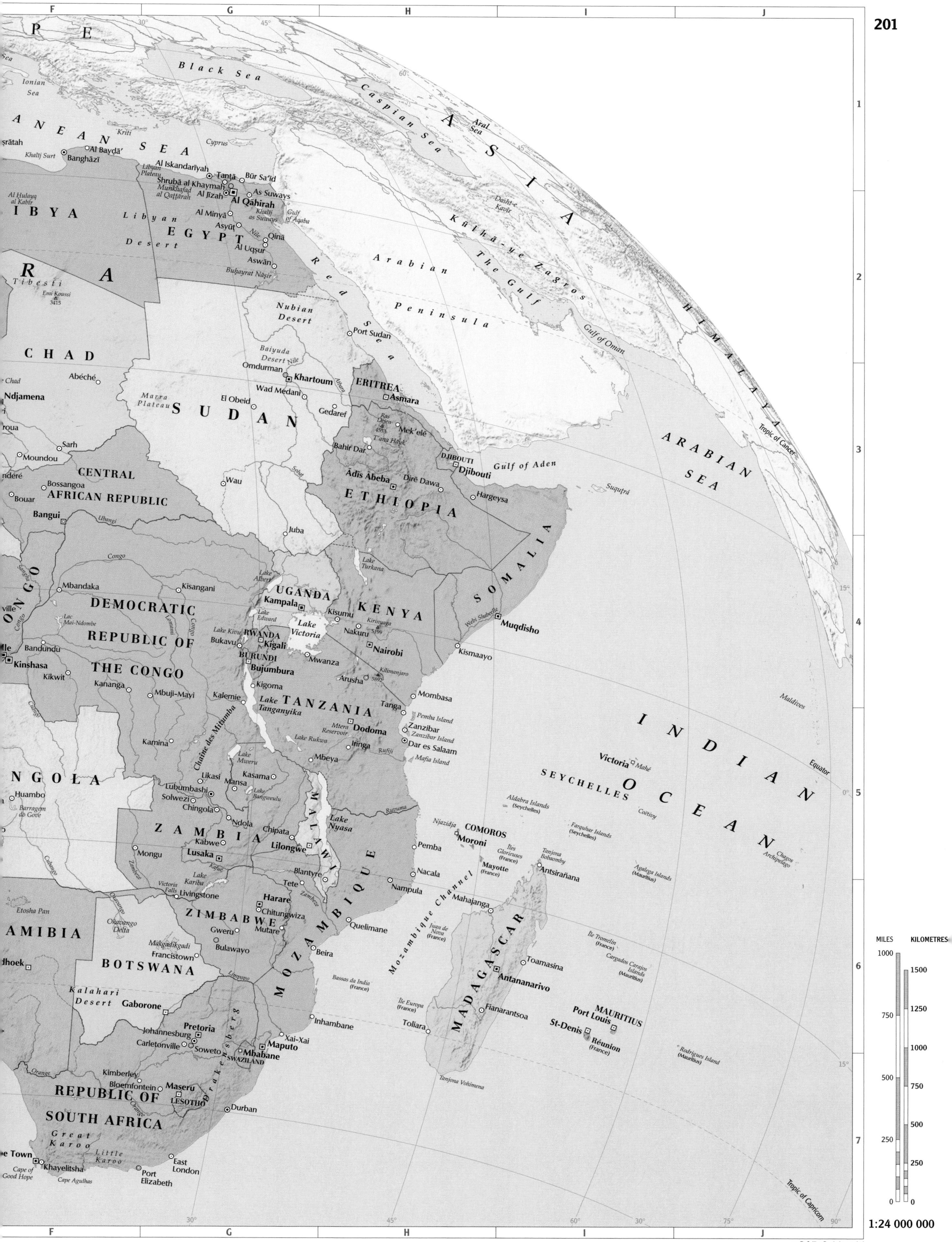
F
G
H
I
J
1
2
3
4
5
6
7
Black Sea
Ionian Sea
Caspian Sea
Aral Sea
ASIA
MEDITERRANEAN SEA
Kriti
Cyprus
Khalīj Surt
Al Bayḑā'
Banghāzī
Libyan Plateau
Al Iskandarīyah
Ṭanṭā
Būr Sa'īd
Shubrā al Khaymah
Munkhafaḑ al Qaţţārah
Al Jīzah
As Suways
Al Qāhirah
Al Hulayq al Kabīr
LIBYA
Libyan Desert
Al Minyā
Asyūţ
Khalīj as Suways
Gulf of Aqaba
EGYPT
Nile
Qinā
Al Uqşur
Aswān
Buḩayrat Nāşir
Tibesti
Emi Koussi 3415
Dasht-e Kavīr
Kūhhā-ye Zagros
The Gulf
Arabian Peninsula
Red Sea
Nubian Desert
Port Sudan
Gulf of Oman
HIMALAYA
CHAD
Baiyuda Desert
Nile
Omdurman
Khartoum
Abéché
Lake Chad
Ndjamena
Marra Plateau
SUDAN
El Obeid
Wad Medanī
ERITREA
Asmara
Gedaref
Ras Dejen 4533
Mek'elē
T'ana Hāyk'
Bahir Dar
Tropic of Cancer
ARABIAN SEA
Moundou
Sarh
DJIBOUTI
Djibouti
Gulf of Aden
Suquţrā
CENTRAL AFRICAN REPUBLIC
Bossangoa
Bouar
Wau
Sobat
Ādīs Ābeba
Dīrē Dawa
Hargeysa
ETHIOPIA
Bangui
Ubangi
Juba
SOMALIA
Lake Turkana
Congo
Lake Albert
Mbandaka
Kisangani
UGANDA
Kampala
KENYA
CONGO
DEMOCRATIC REPUBLIC OF THE CONGO
Lac Mai-Ndombe
Lake Edward
Kisumu
Lake Victoria
Kirinyaga 5199
Nakuru
Webi Shabeelle
Muqdisho
Lake Kivu
RWANDA
Kigali
Bukavu
Nairobi
Kinshasa
Bandundu
BURUNDI
Bujumbura
Mwanza
Kismaayo
Kikwit
Kananga
Mbuji-Mayi
Kigoma
Kilimanjaro 5892
Arusha
Kalemie
Lake Tanganyika
TANZANIA
Tanga
Mombasa
Maldives
Pemba Island
Zanzibar
Zanzibar Island
Dar es Salaam
Mtera Reservoir
Dodoma
Lake Rukwa
Iringa
Rufiji
Mafia Island
Kamina
Chaîne des Mitumba
INDIAN OCEAN
Victoria
Mahé
SEYCHELLES
Equator
Lake Mweru
Mbeya
ANGOLA
Likasi
Mansa
Kasama
Lake Bangweulu
Huambo
Lubumbashi
Solwezi
Chingola
Barragem do Gove
Aldabra Islands (Seychelles)
Coëtivy
Ndola
Ruvuma
Lake Nyasa
MALAWI
Njazidja
COMOROS
Moroni
Farquhar Islands (Seychelles)
ZAMBIA
Kabwe
Chipata
Lilongwe
Pemba
Mongu
Lusaka
Kafue
Îles Glorieuses (France)
Tanjona Bobaomby
Antsirañana
Chagos Archipelago
Agalega Islands (Mauritius)
Zambeze
Lake Kariba
Blantyre
Nacala
Mayotte (France)
Victoria Falls
Livingstone
Tete
Nampula
Mozambique Channel
Mahajanga
Etosha Pan
Okavango
Harare
Chitungwiza
MOZAMBIQUE
NAMIBIA
Okavango Delta
ZIMBABWE
Mutare
Quelimane
Juan de Nova (France)
Gweru
Île Tromelin (France)
Makgadikgadi
Bulawayo
Francistown
Beira
Cargados Carajos Islands (Mauritius)
Windhoek
BOTSWANA
Toamasina
Antananarivo
Limpopo
MADAGASCAR
Kalahari Desert
Gaborone
Bassas da India (France)
Île Europa (France)
Fianarantsoa
Drakensberg
Pretoria
Johannesburg
Carletonville
Soweto
Inhambane
Toliara
MAURITIUS
Port Louis
St-Denis
Réunion (France)
SWAZILAND
Mbabane
Maputo
Xai-Xai
Rodrigues Island (Mauritius)
Orange
Kimberley
Bloemfontein
Maseru
Tanjona Vohimena
REPUBLIC OF SOUTH AFRICA
LESOTHO
Durban
Great Karoo
Little Karoo
Cape Town
Khayelitsha
Cape of Good Hope
Cape Agulhas
Port Elizabeth
East London
Tropic of Capricorn
MILES
KILOMETRES
1000
750
500
250
0
1500
1250
1000
750
500
250
0
1:24 000 000

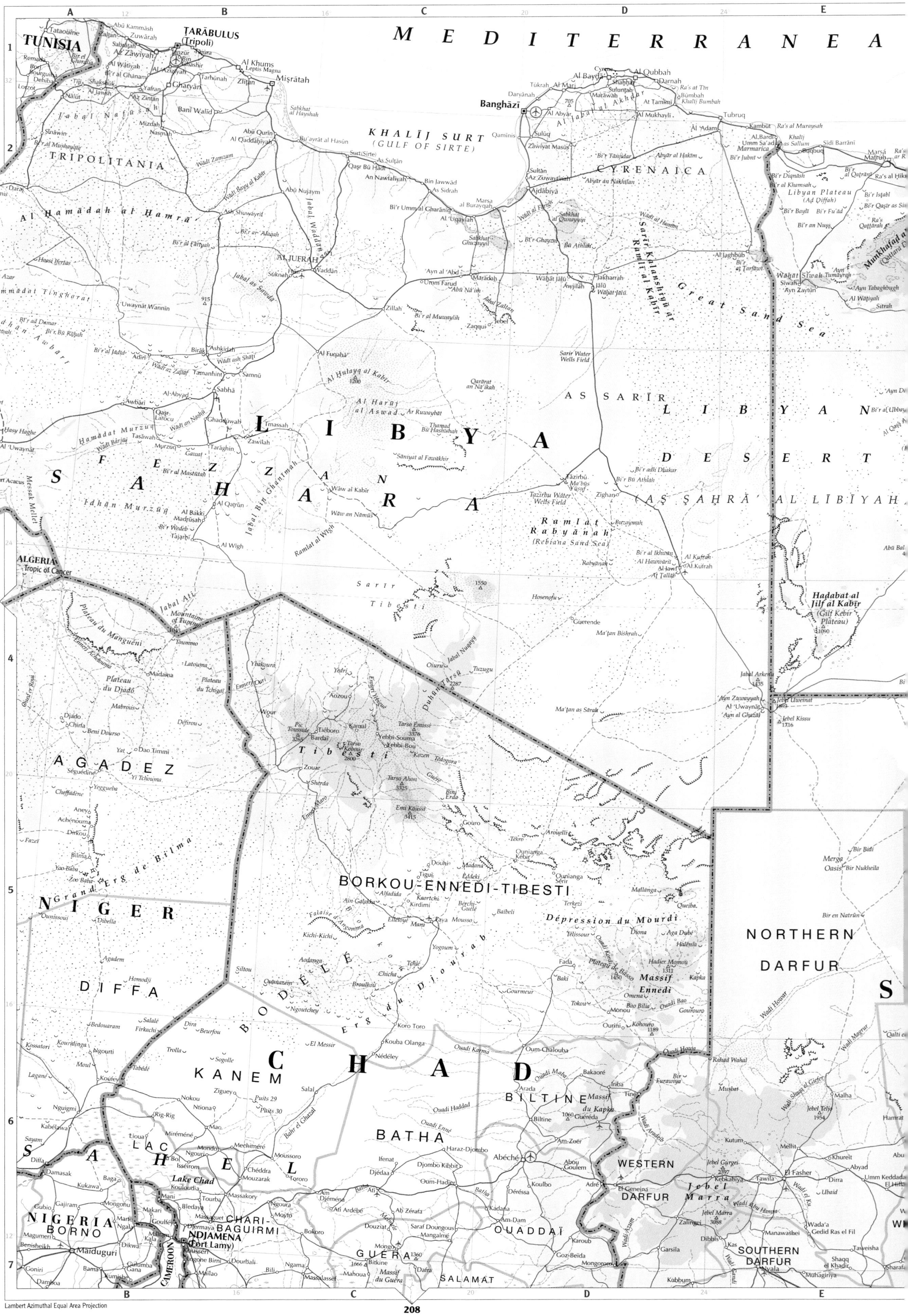
MEDITERRANEAN
TUNISIA
ṬARĀBULUS (Tripoli)
Al Khums
Leptis Magna
Miṣrātah
Zlīṭan
Az Zāwiyah
Gharyān
Banī Walīd
Mizdah
Nālūt
Jabal Nafūsah
TRIPOLITANIA
KHALĪJ SURT (GULF OF SIRTE)
Surt (Sirte)
Banghāzī
Al Bayḍā
Cyrene
Al Qubbah
Darnah
Al Jabal al Akhḍar
Al Mukhaylī
Tubruq
Al Marj
Ajdābiyā
CYRENAICA
Marmarica
As Sallum
Sīdī Barrānī
Marsá Maṭrūḥ
Libyan Plateau (Ad Diffah)
Qattara Depression
Munkhafaḍ al Qaṭṭārah
Siwah
Wāḥāt Sīwah
Al Jaghbūb
Great Sand Sea
Ghadāmis
Al Ḥamādah al Ḥamrā'
Ḥammādat Tinghrat
Idhān Awbārī
AL JUFRAH
Hūn
Waddān
Sūknah
Jabal as Sawdā'
Zillah
Awjilah
Jālū
Wāḥat Jālū
Marādah
Al Fuqahā
Al Hulayq al Kabīr
Al Harūj al Aswad
Sabhā
Awbārī
Ghāt
Jabal Akakus
Murzuq
Ḥamādat Murzuq
Idhān Murzuq
Messak Mellet
Al Qaṭrūn
Tajarḥī
Ramlat al Wīgh
AS SARĪR
LIBYAN DESERT
(AṢ ṢAḤRĀ' AL LĪBĪYAH)
LIBYA
SAHARA
FEZZAN
Tāzirbū
Ramlat Rabyānah (Rebiana Sand Sea)
Al Kufrah
Al Jawf
Sarīr Tibesti
Jabal al 'Uwaynāt
Jabal Arkanū
Hadabat al Jilf al Kabīr (Gilf Kebir Plateau)
ALGERIA
Tropic of Cancer
Plateau du Manguéni
Plateau du Djado
Djado
AGADEZ
Séguédine
Bilma
Grand Erg de Bilma
NIGER
DIFFA
Agadem
Tibesti
Pic Toussidé 3265
Bardaï
Tarso Emissi 3376
Emi Koussi 3415
Aozou
Zouar
Ounianga Kébir
BORKOU-ENNEDI-TIBESTI
Faya
Dépression du Mourdi
Plateau de Basso
Massif Ennedi
Fada
Bodélé
Erg du Djourab
Koro Toro
Kouba Olanga
NORTHERN DARFUR
Merga Oasis
KANEM
CHAD
BILTINE
Massif du Kapka
Biltine
BATHA
Abéché
OUADDAÏ
Oum-Hadjer
Ati
WESTERN DARFUR
Jebel Marra 3088
El Geneina
El Fasher
SOUTHERN DARFUR
Nyala
Zalingei
LAC
SAHEL
Lake Chad
Nguigmi
Mao
Bol
NIGERIA
BORNO
Maiduguri
CAMEROON
NDJAMENA (Fort Lamy)
CHARI-BAGUIRMI
Massakory
GUERA
Massif du Guéra
Mongo
SALAMAT
Lambert Azimuthal Equal Area Projection

METRES
FEET

METRES	FEET
6000	19686
5000	16404
4000	13124
3000	9843
2000	6562
1000	3281
500	1640
200	656
0	0
LAND BELOW SEA LEVEL	
200	656
2000	6562
4000	13124
6000	19686

205
208

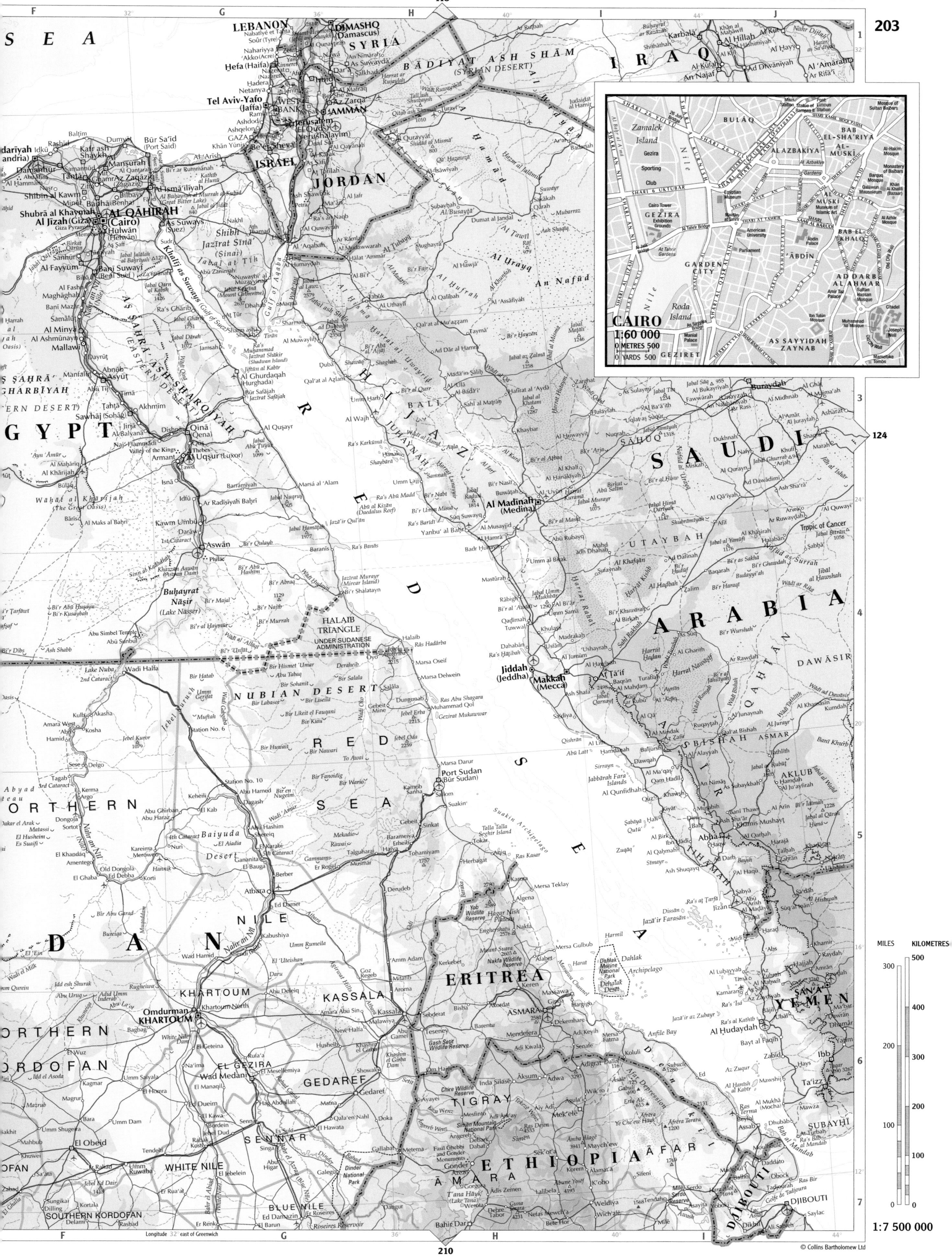
CAIRO
1:60 000
EGYPT
SAUDI ARABIA
JORDAN
ISRAEL
LEBANON
SYRIA
IRAQ
ERITREA
ETHIOPIA
YEMEN
DJIBOUTI
RED SEA
NUBIAN DESERT
HALAIB TRIANGLE
UNDER SUDANESE ADMINISTRATION
KHARTOUM
Port Sudan
Jiddah
Makkah
Al Madīnah
Aswān
Al Qāhirah (Cairo)
Tropic of Cancer
MILES
KILOMETRES
1:7 500 000
Longitude 32° east of Greenwich

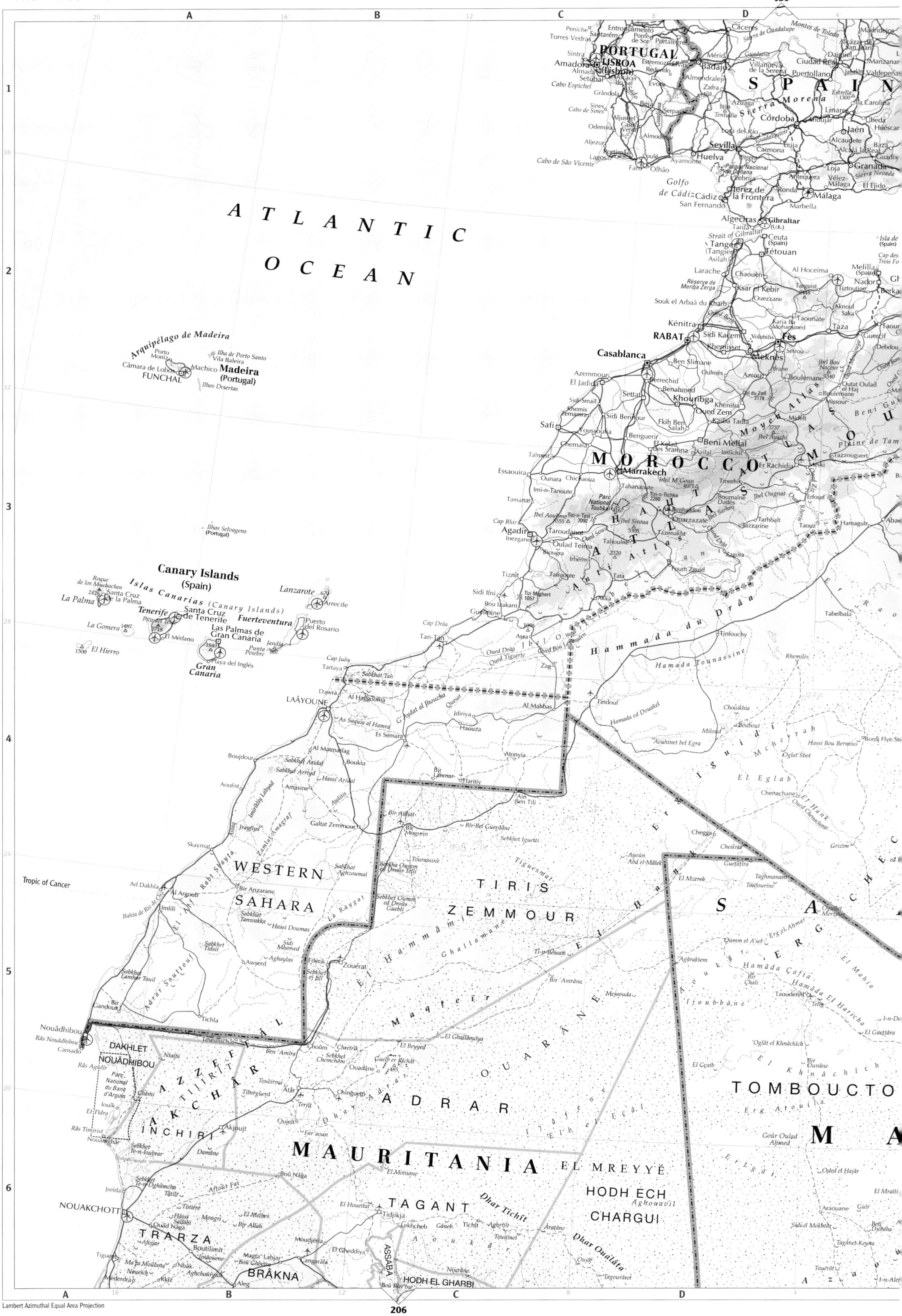
180
A
B
C
D
1
2
3
4
5
6
ATLANTIC
OCEAN
PORTUGAL
LISBOA
(Lisbon)
SPAIN
Sierra Morena
Córdoba
Sevilla
Huelva
Granada
Málaga
Golfo de Cádiz
Cádiz
Gibraltar (U.K.)
Strait of Gibraltar
Ceuta (Spain)
Tanger (Tangier)
Tétouan
Melilla (Spain)
Kénitra
RABAT
Fès
Meknès
Casablanca
El Jadida
Safi
MOROCCO
Marrakech
Essaouira
Agadir
HAUT ATLAS
MOYEN ATLAS
ANTI ATLAS
Arquipélago de Madeira
Madeira (Portugal)
FUNCHAL
Ilhas Selvagens (Portugal)
Canary Islands (Spain)
Islas Canarias (Canary Islands)
La Palma
Tenerife
Santa Cruz de Tenerife
La Gomera
El Hierro
Gran Canaria
Las Palmas de Gran Canaria
Fuerteventura
Lanzarote
Arrecife
Tan-Tan
Tarfaya
LAÂYOUNE
Boujdour
WESTERN SAHARA
Ad Dakhla
Tropic of Cancer
Hammada du Drâa
Tindouf
TIRIS ZEMMOUR
Zouérat
Nouâdhibou
DAKHLET NOUÂDHIBOU
Parc National du Banc d'Arguin
ADRAR
INCHIRI
Akjoujt
MAURITANIA
NOUAKCHOTT
TRARZA
BRÂKNA
TAGANT
Tidjikja
ASSABA
HODH EL GHARBI
HODH ECH CHARGUI
EL MREYYÉ
TOMBOUCTOU
SAHARA
Taoudenni
A
B
C
D
206
Lambert Azimuthal Equal Area Projection

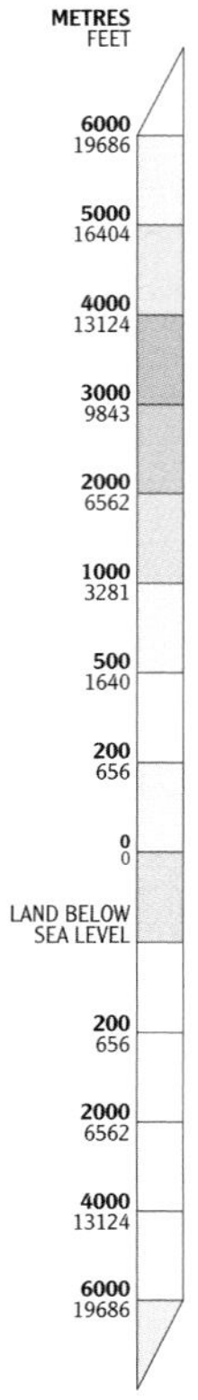
METRES
FEET
6000
19686
5000
16404
4000
13124
3000
9843
2000
6562
1000
3281
500
1640
200
656
0
0
LAND BELOW SEA LEVEL
200
656
2000
6562
4000
13124
6000
19686

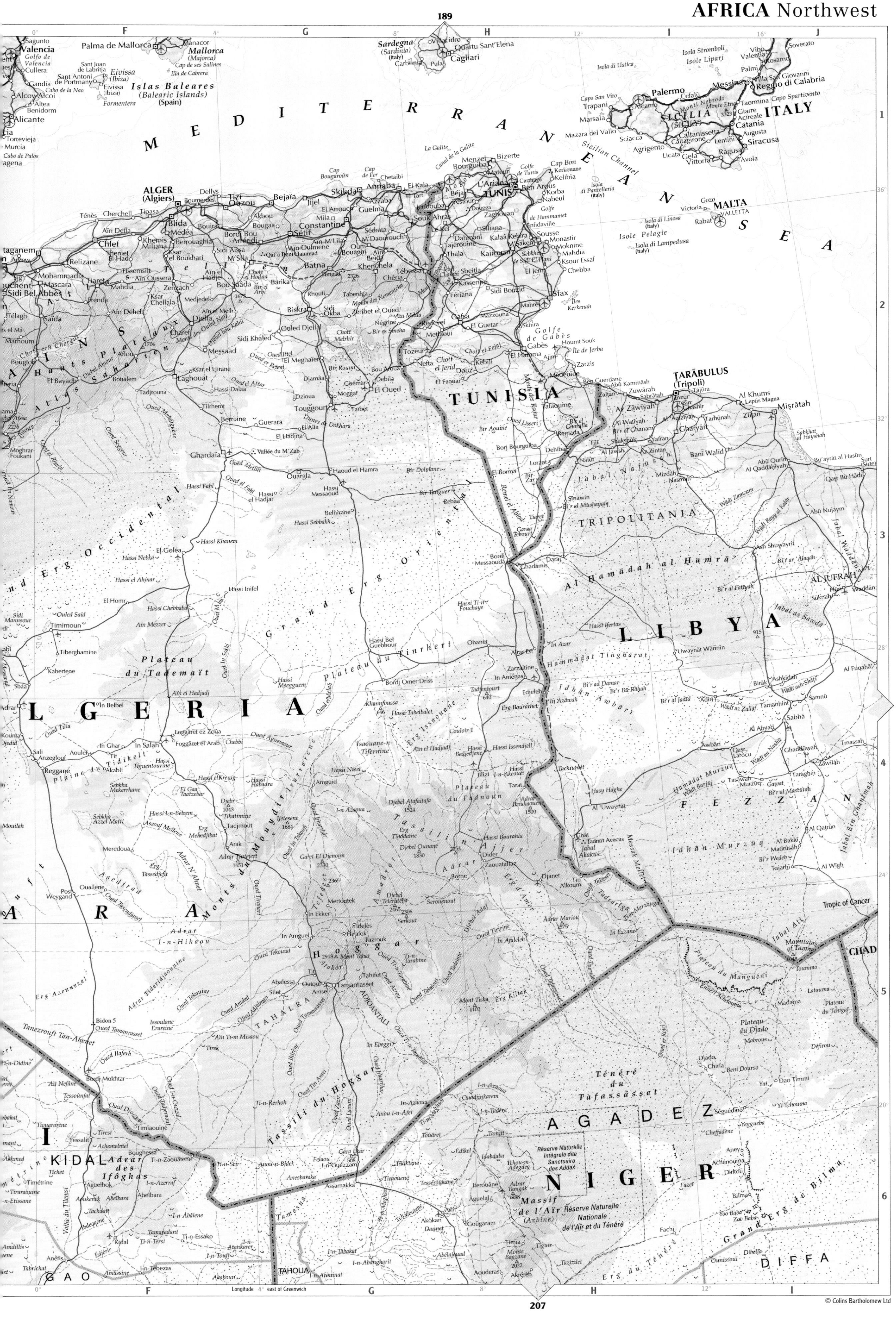
189
MEDITERRANEAN SEA
Sardegna (Sardinia) (Italy)
Cagliari
Palma de Mallorca
Mallorca (Majorca)
Islas Baleares (Balearic Islands) (Spain)
Eivissa (Ibiza)
Valencia
Alicante
Murcia
SICILIA (SICILY)
ITALY
Palermo
Messina
Catania
Siracusa
Reggio di Calabria
MALTA
VALLETTA
Sicilian Channel
ALGER (Algiers)
Oran
Tizi Ouzou
Bejaïa
Skikda
Annaba
Constantine
Sétif
Blida
Médéa
Chlef
Batna
Tébessa
Biskra
Djelfa
Laghouat
Ghardaïa
Ouargla
Touggourt
El Oued
Hassi Messaoud
El Goléa
Timimoun
Adrar
In Salah
Reggane
Tamanrasset
Djanet
Bordj Mokhtar
Tinzaouatene
TUNISIA
TUNIS
Bizerte
Sousse
Monastir
Mahdia
Kairouan
Sfax
Gabès
Gafsa
Tozeur
Nefta
Kebili
Medenine
Tataouine
Golfe de Gabès
Golfe de Tunis
Île de Jerba
ṬARĀBULUS (Tripoli)
Al Khums
Mişrātah
Zuwārah
Az Zāwiyah
Gharyān
Nālūt
Ghadāmis
Sabhā
Ubārī
Murzuq
Ghāt
Waddān
AL JUFRAH
LIBYA
TRIPOLITANIA
FEZZAN
Al Ḥamādah al Ḩamrā'
Jabal Nafūsah
Ḩamādat Tinghārat
Idhān Awbārī
Idhān Murzuq
ALGERIA
SAHARA
Hauts Plateaux
Atlas Saharien
Grand Erg Occidental
Grand Erg Oriental
Plateau du Tademaït
Plateau du Tinrhert
Tassili n'Ajjer
Hoggar
Tassili du Hoggar
Adrar des Ifôghas
KIDAL
GAO
TAHOUA
AGADEZ
NIGER
Massif de l'Aïr
Réserve Naturelle Intégrale dite Sanctuaire des Addax
Réserve Naturelle Nationale de l'Aïr et du Ténéré
Ténéré du Tafassâsset
Grand Erg de Bilma
Plateau du Djado
Plateau du Manguéni
Tropic of Cancer
CHAD
DIFFA
Bilma
202
207
Longitude 4° east of Greenwich
F G H I J
1 2 3 4 5 6

MILES KILOMETRES

1:7 500 000

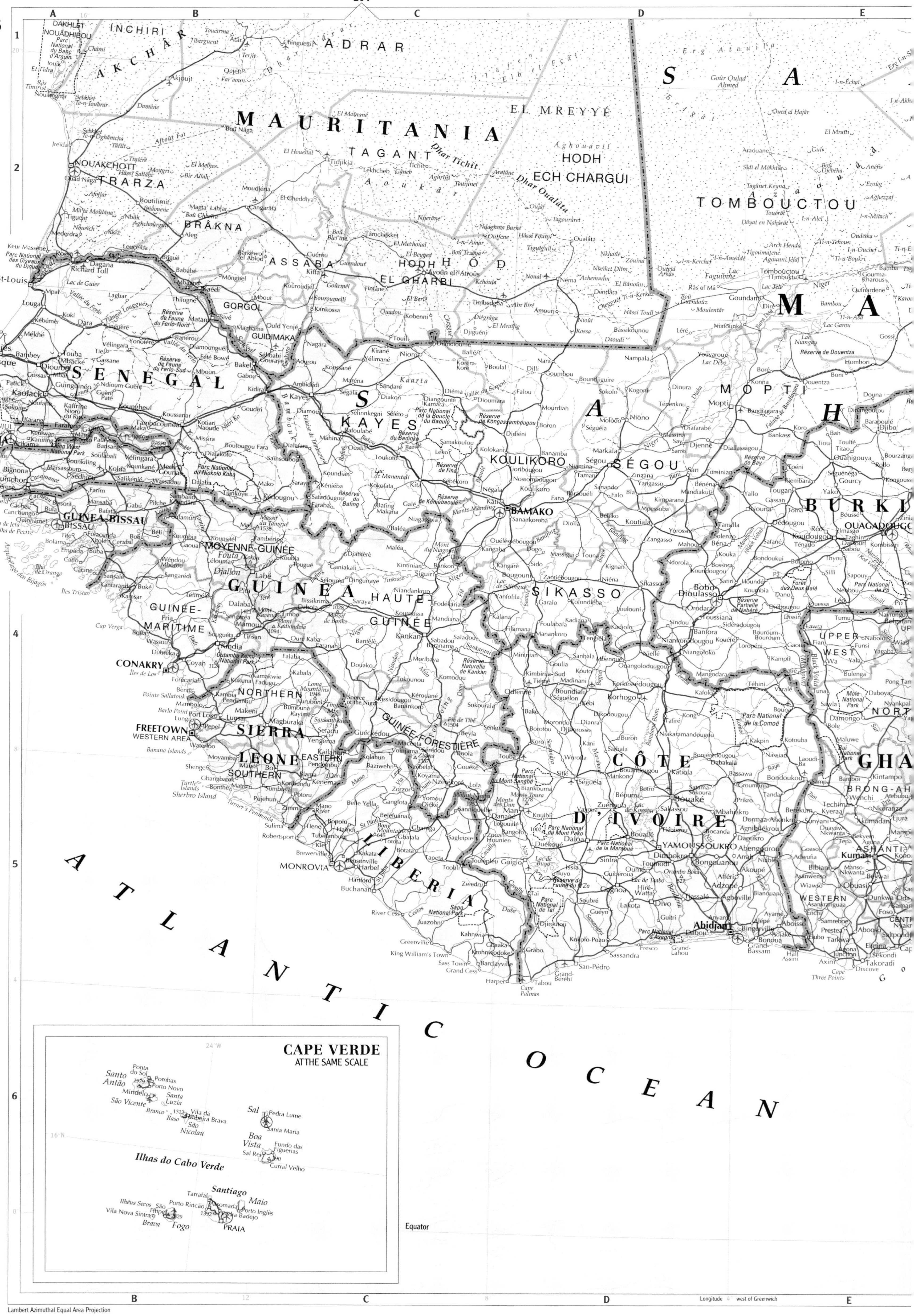
204
MAURITANIA
SENEGAL
THE GAMBIA
GUINEA-BISSAU
GUINEA
SIERRA LEONE
LIBERIA
CÔTE D'IVOIRE
BURKI
GHA
ATLANTIC OCEAN
INCHIRI
ADRAR
AKCHÂR
TAGANT
TRARZA
BRÂKNA
ASSABA
HODH EL GHARBI
HODH ECH CHARGUI
GORGOL
GUIDIMAKA
EL MREYYÉ
TOMBOUCTOU
MOPTI
KAYES
KOULIKORO
SÉGOU
SIKASSO
MOYENNE-GUINÉE
HAUTE-GUINÉE
GUINÉE-MARITIME
GUINÉE-FORESTIÈRE
NORTHERN
EASTERN
SOUTHERN
WESTERN AREA
UPPER WEST
BRONG-AHAFO
ASHANTI
WESTERN
NOUAKCHOTT
DAKAR
BANJUL
BISSAU
CONAKRY
FREETOWN
MONROVIA
BAMAKO
YAMOUSSOUKRO
OUAGADOUGOU
Abidjan
St-Louis
Kaolack
Ziguinchor
Kankan
Bouaké
Kumasi
Bobo Dioulasso
Mopti
Ségou
Kayes
Tombouctou
CAPE VERDE
AT THE SAME SCALE
Ilhas do Cabo Verde
Santo Antão
São Vicente
Mindelo
São Nicolau
Sal
Boa Vista
Maio
Santiago
PRAIA
Fogo
Brava
Equator
METRES
FEET
6000
19686
5000
16404
4000
13124
3000
9843
2000
6562
1000
3281
500
1640
200
656
0
0
LAND BELOW SEA LEVEL
200
656
2000
6562
4000
13124
6000
19686
Longitude 4 west of Greenwich

Lambert Azimuthal Equal Area Projection

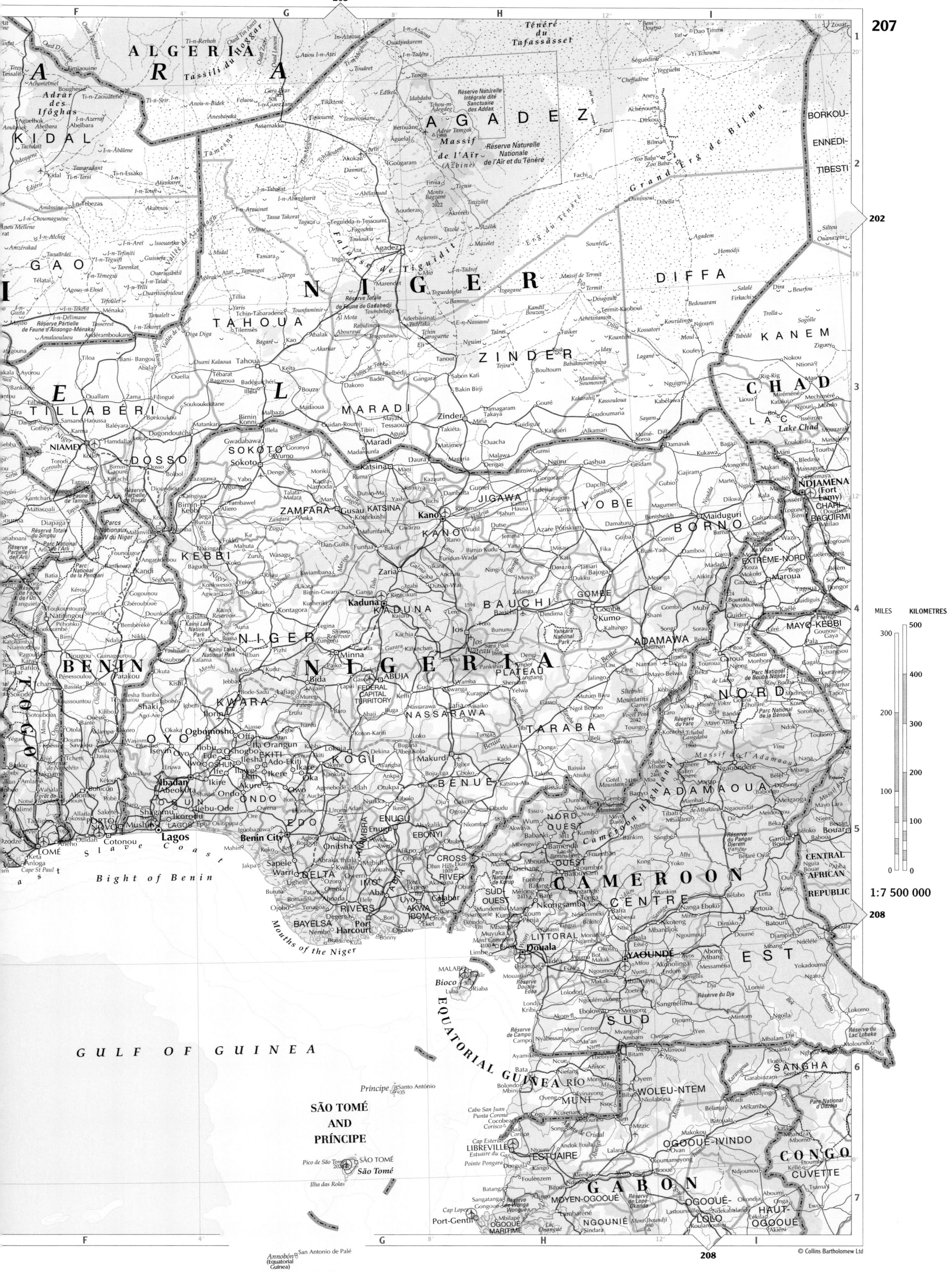
ALGERIA
KIDAL
GAO
AGADEZ
NIGER
TAHOUA
ZINDER
DIFFA
MARADI
TILLABÉRI
DOSSO
NIAMEY
CHAD
KANEM
LAC
Lake Chad
BORKOU-ENNEDI-TIBESTI
NDJAMENA (Fort Lamy)
BENIN
TOGO
NIGERIA
SOKOTO
ZAMFARA
KATSINA
KANO
JIGAWA
YOBE
BORNO
KEBBI
KADUNA
BAUCHI
GOMBE
ADAMAWA
NIGER
KWARA
FEDERAL CAPITAL TERRITORY
ABUJA
PLATEAU
NASSARAWA
TARABA
OYO
OSUN
EKITI
ONDO
OGUN
KOGI
BENUE
EDO
ENUGU
EBONYI
ANAMBRA
DELTA
IMO
ABIA
CROSS RIVER
AKWA IBOM
RIVERS
BAYELSA
Lagos
Ibadan
Benin City
Port Harcourt
Kano
Kaduna
CAMEROON
EXTRÊME-NORD
NORD
ADAMAOUA
NORD OUEST
OUEST
SUD OUEST
LITTORAL
CENTRE
EST
SUD
YAOUNDÉ
Douala
MAYO-KEBBI
CENTRAL AFRICAN REPUBLIC
EQUATORIAL GUINEA
RÍO MUNI
MALABO
Bioco
GABON
ESTUAIRE
LIBREVILLE
WOLEU-NTEM
OGOOUÉ-IVINDO
MOYEN-OGOOUÉ
OGOOUÉ-LOLO
HAUT-OGOOUÉ
NGOUNIÉ
OGOOUÉ MARITIME
Port-Gentil
CONGO
CUVETTE
SANGHA
SÃO TOMÉ AND PRÍNCIPE
SÃO TOMÉ
Príncipe
Annobón (Equatorial Guinea)
GULF OF GUINEA
Bight of Benin
Slave Coast
Mouths of the Niger
MILES
KILOMETRES
1:7 500 000
205
202
208

© Collins Bartholomew Ltd

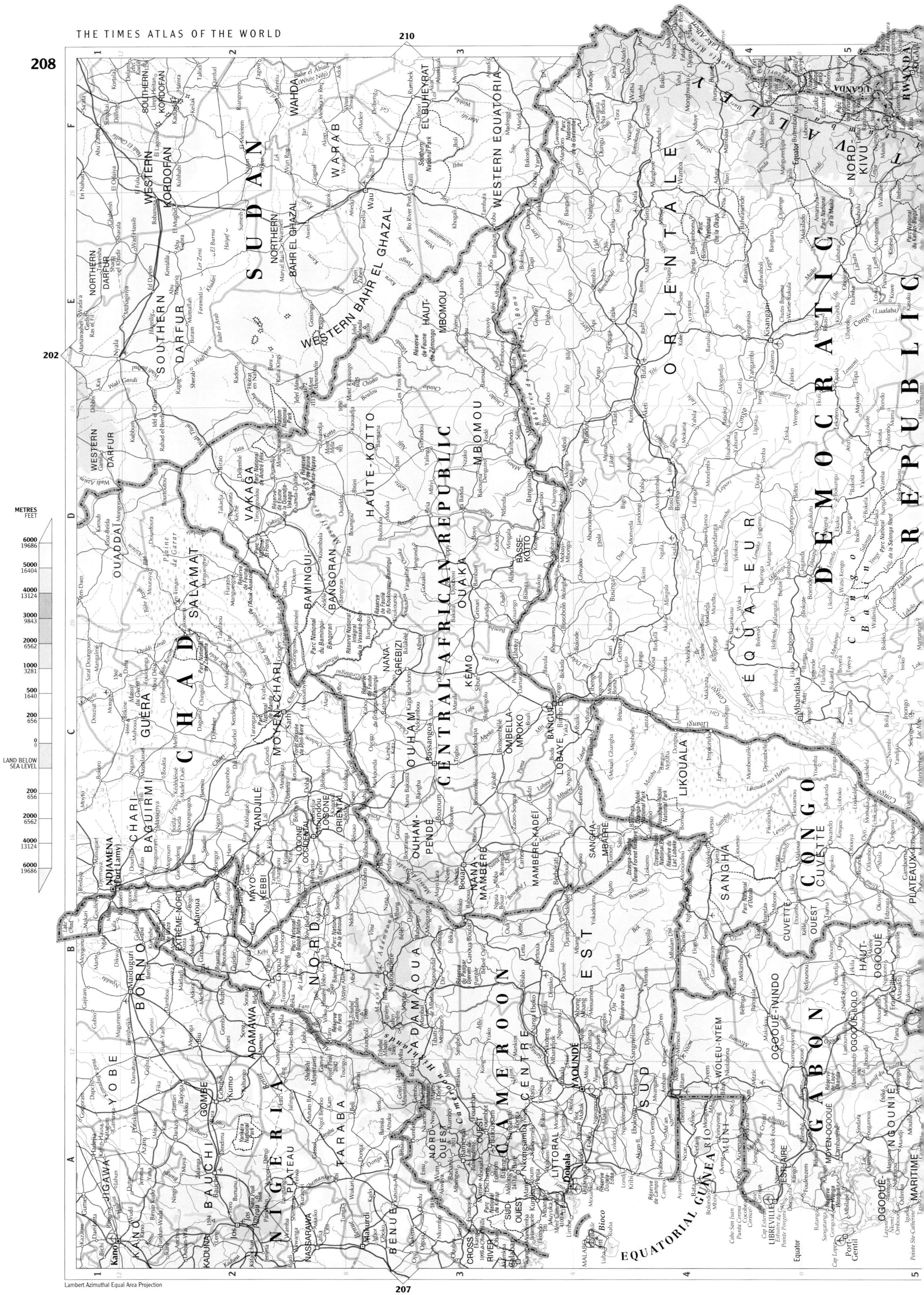
210
202
207
METRES
FEET
6000
19686
5000
16404
4000
13124
3000
9843
2000
6562
1000
3281
500
1640
200
656
0
0
LAND BELOW
SEA LEVEL
200
656
2000
6562
4000
13124
6000
19686
SUDAN
CHAD
CENTRAL AFRICAN REPUBLIC
CAMEROON
NIGERIA
GABON
CONGO
DEMOCRATIC REPUBLIC
EQUATORIAL GUINEA
UGANDA
RWANDA
NORTHERN DARFUR
WESTERN DARFUR
SOUTHERN DARFUR
NORTHERN KORDOFAN
WESTERN KORDOFAN
SOUTHERN KORDOFAN
NORTHERN BAHR EL GHAZAL
WESTERN BAHR EL GHAZAL
WARAB
WAHDA
EL BUHEYRAT
WESTERN EQUATORIA
ORIENTALE
EQUATEUR
NORD-KIVU
LIKOUALA
SANGHA
CUVETTE
CUVETTE OUEST
PLATEAUX
ESTUAIRE
MOYEN-OGOOUÉ
OGOOUÉ-IVINDO
NGOUNIÉ
WOLEU-NTEM
LITTORAL
CENTRE
SUD
EST
ADAMAOUA
NORD
EXTRÊME-NORD
OUADDAÏ
SALAMAT
GUÉRA
CHARI-BAGUIRMI
MOYEN-CHARI
TANDJILÉ
MAYO-KEBBI
LOGONE ORIENTAL
LOGONE OCCIDENTAL
VAKAGA
BAMINGUI-BANGORAN
HAUTE-KOTTO
HAUT-MBOMOU
MBOMOU
OUAKA
KÉMO
NANA-GRÉBIZI
OUHAM
OUHAM-PENDÉ
NANA-MAMBÉRÉ
MAMBÉRÉ-KADEÏ
SANGHA MBAÉRÉ
LOBAYE
OMBELLA MPOKO
BASSE-KOTTO
BORNO
YOBE
JIGAWA
KANO
BAUCHI
GOMBE
ADAMAWA
TARABA
PLATEAU
NASSARAWA
BENUE
KADUNA
N'DJAMENA (Fort Lamy)
BANGUI
YAOUNDÉ
Douala
LIBREVILLE
MALABO
Kisangani
Mbandaka
Equator
Lambert Azimuthal Equal Area Projection

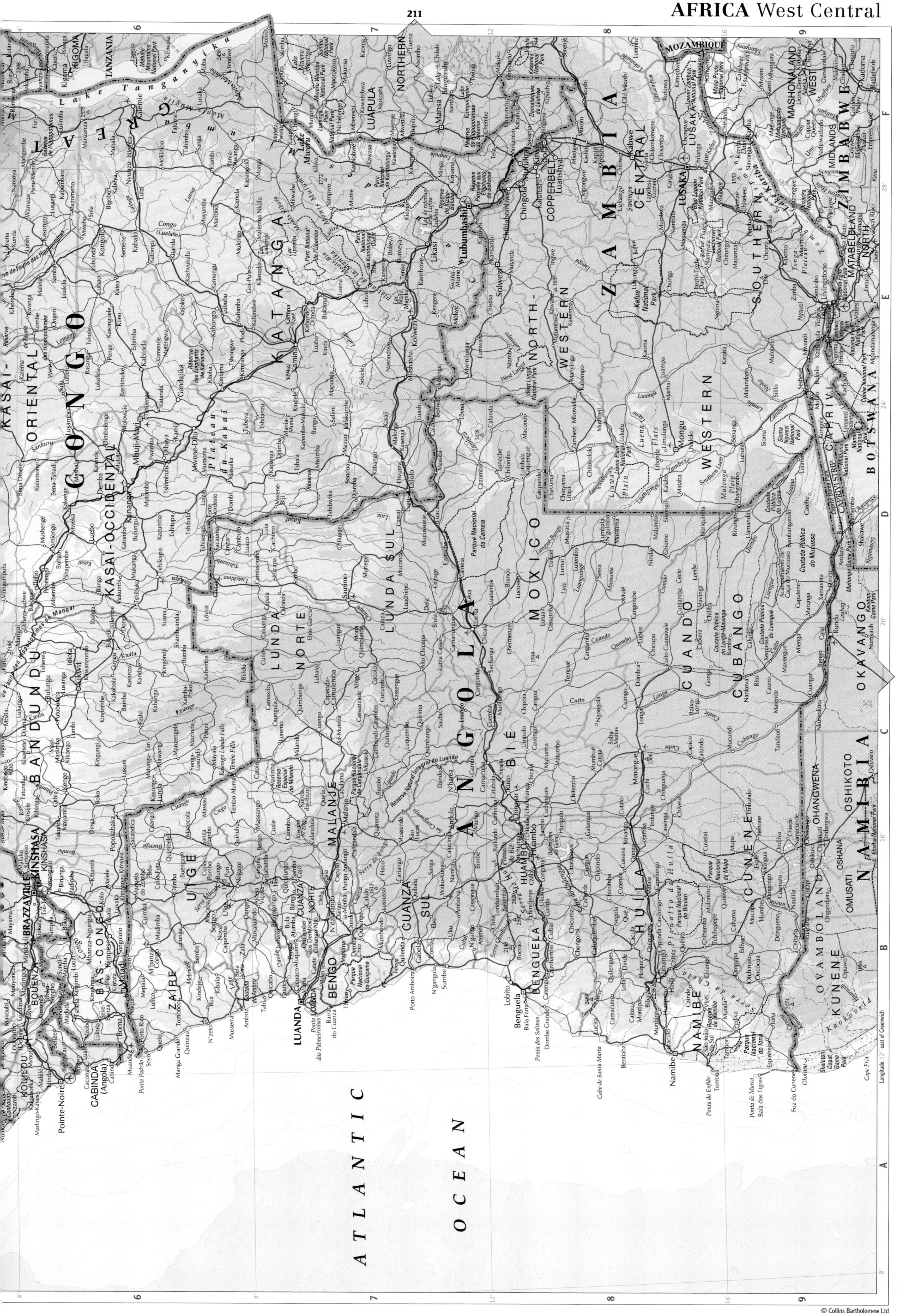

MILES
KILOMETRES
300
200
100
0
500
400
300
200
100
0

1:7 500 000

© Collins Bartholomew Ltd

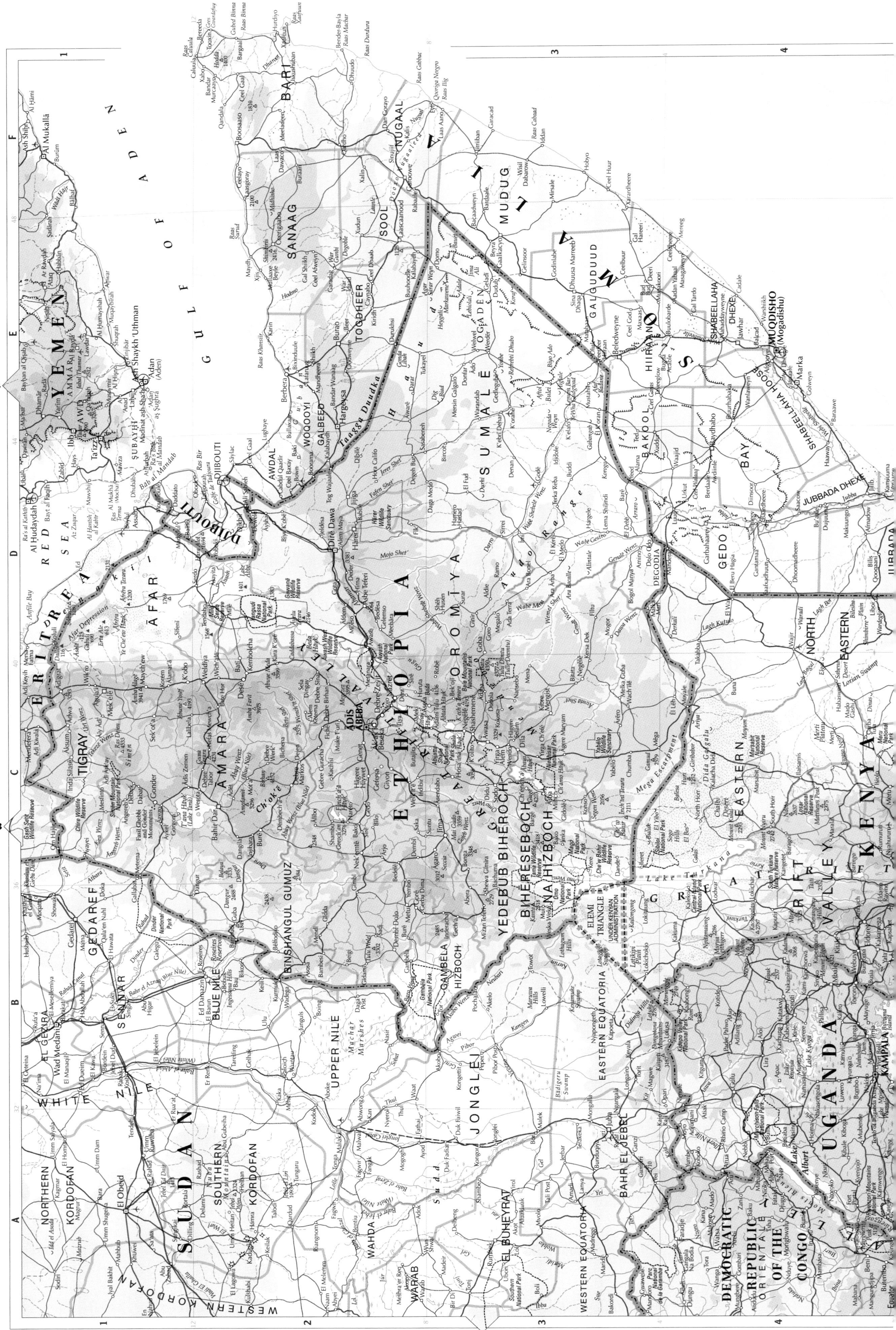

METRES / FEET

Metres	Feet
6000	19686
5000	16404
4000	13124
3000	9843
2000	6562
1000	3281
500	1640
200	656
0	0
LAND BELOW SEA LEVEL	
200	656
2000	6562
4000	13124
6000	19686

Lambert Azimuthal Equal Area Projection

208

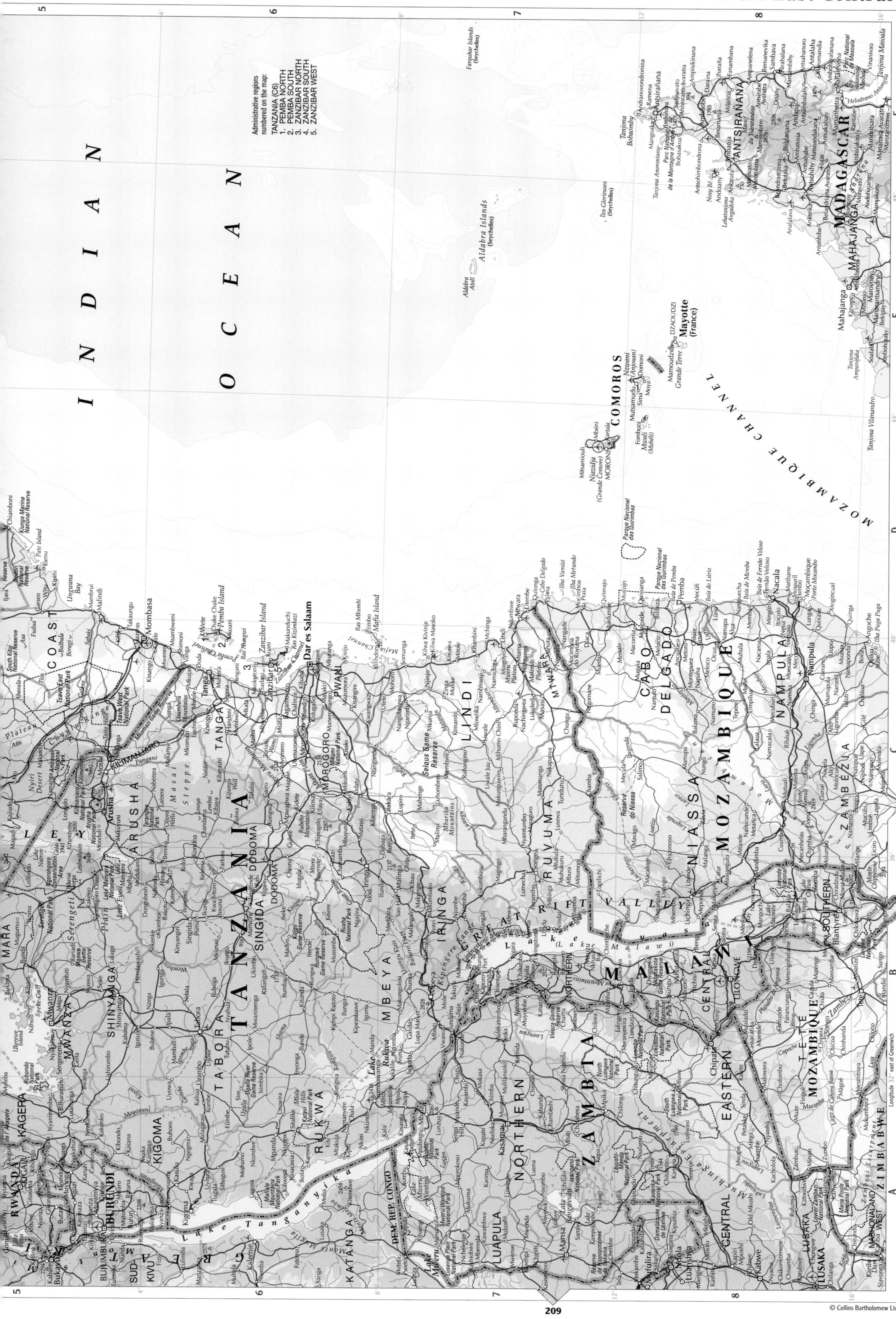
INDIAN OCEAN
Administrative regions numbered on the map:
TANZANIA (C6)
1. PEMBA NORTH
2. PEMBA SOUTH
3. ZANZIBAR NORTH
4. ZANZIBAR SOUTH
5. ZANZIBAR WEST
MOZAMBIQUE CHANNEL
TANZANIA
MOZAMBIQUE
ZAMBIA
MALAWI
MADAGASCAR
COMOROS
Mayotte (France)
DZAOUDZI
MORONI
Dar es Salaam
Zanzibar
Mombasa
Dodoma
Lilongwe
Lusaka
Blantyre
Nampula
Mahajanga
Antsiranana
Lake Malawi
Lake Tanganyika
Aldabra Islands (Seychelles)
Farquhar Islands (Seychelles)
Îles Glorieuses (Seychelles)
GREAT RIFT VALLEY
DEM. REP. CONGO
BURUNDI
RWANDA
ZIMBABWE
Longitude 32° east of Greenwich
213

MILES | KILOMETRES

1:7 500 000

© Collins Bartholomew Ltd

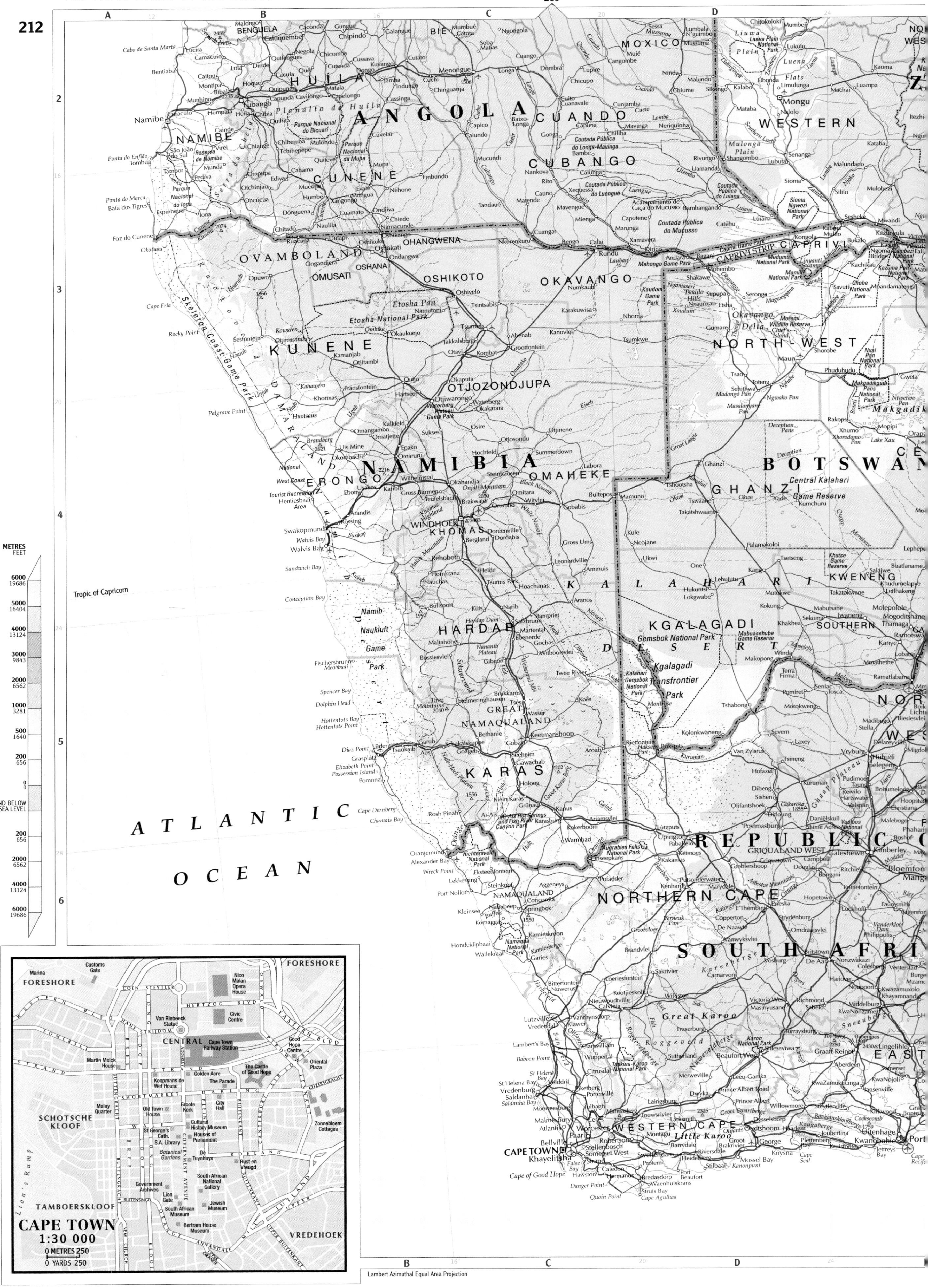
209
ANGOLA
NAMIBIA
BOTSWANA
REPUBLIC OF SOUTH AFRICA
ATLANTIC OCEAN
HUÍLA
NAMIBE
CUNENE
CUANDO CUBANGO
MOXICO
WESTERN
OVAMBOLAND
OHANGWENA
OMUSATI
OSHANA
OSHIKOTO
OKAVANGO
CAPRIVI
KUNENE
OTJOZONDJUPA
ERONGO
OMAHEKE
KHOMAS
HARDAP
KARAS
GREAT NAMAQUALAND
NORTH-WEST
GHANZI
KGALAGADI
KWENENG
SOUTHERN
KALAHARI DESERT
NORTHERN CAPE
WESTERN CAPE
NAMAQUALAND
GRIQUALAND WEST
Great Karoo
Little Karoo
Etosha National Park
Skeleton Coast Game Park
Namib-Naukluft Game Park
Central Kalahari Game Reserve
Kgalagadi Transfrontier Park
Tropic of Capricorn
Namibe
Benguela
Lubango
Menongue
Ondjiva
Windhoek
Swakopmund
Walvis Bay
Lüderitz
Keetmanshoop
Rundu
Maun
Ghanzi
Upington
Kimberley
Springbok
CAPE TOWN
Cape of Good Hope
Cape Agulhas
METRES
FEET
6000
19686
5000
16404
4000
13124
3000
9843
2000
6562
1000
3281
500
1640
200
656
0
LAND BELOW SEA LEVEL
FORESHORE
CENTRAL
SCHOTSCHE KLOOF
TAMBOERSKLOOF
VREDEHOEK
Cape Town Railway Station
The Castle of Good Hope
Nico Malan Opera House
Civic Centre
Houses of Parliament
South African National Gallery
CAPE TOWN
1:30 000
0 METRES 250
0 YARDS 250

211
MILES
KILOMETRES
1:7 500 000
MOZAMBIQUE CHANNEL
INDIAN OCEAN
Tropic of Capricorn
MOZAMBIQUE
ZIMBABWE
MALAWI
SWAZILAND
LESOTHO
NIASSA
CABO DELGADO
NAMPULA
ZAMBÉZIA
TETE
SOFALA
MANICA
INHAMBANE
GAZA
MAPUTO
EASTERN
CENTRAL
LUSAKA
SOUTHERN
MASHONALAND CENTRAL
MASHONALAND EAST
MASHONALAND WEST
MIDLANDS
MANICALAND
MASVINGO
MATABELELAND SOUTH
LIMPOPO
MPUMALANGA
KWAZULU-NATAL
EASTERN CAPE
HARARE
Bulawayo
Lilongwe
Blantyre
Beira
Quelimane
Nampula
Nacala
Pemba
Inhambane
Xai-Xai
Maputo
Johannesburg
Vereeniging
Pietermaritzburg
Durban
East London
Lake Nyasa
Lake Malawi
Lake Kariba
Lago de Cahora Bassa
Juan de Nova (France)
Bassas da India (France)
Ilha do Bazaruto
Greater St Lucia Wetland Park
MADAGASCAR
AT THE SAME SCALE
ANTSIRAÑANA
MAHAJANGA
TOAMASINA
ANTANANARIVO
FIANARANTSOA
TOLIARA
Antananarivo
Mahajanga
Toamasina
Antsirabe
Fianarantsoa
Toliara
Tôlañaro
Antsirañana
Tanjona Bobaomby
Tanjona Vohimena
Parc National de Masoala
east of Greenwich

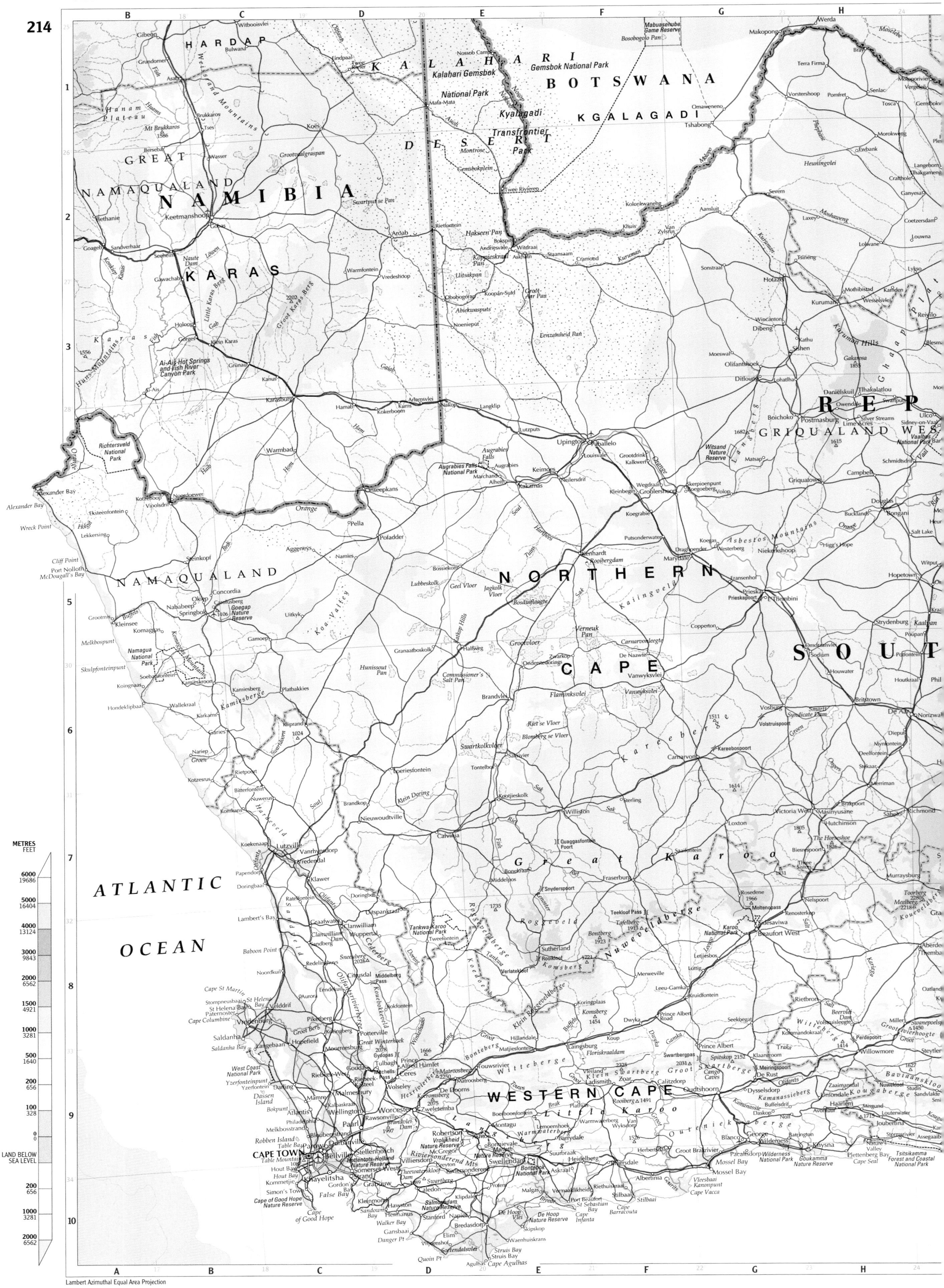
NAMIBIA
BOTSWANA
NORTHERN CAPE
WESTERN CAPE
ATLANTIC OCEAN
KALAHARI DESERT
Kgalagadi Transfrontier Park
GREAT NAMAQUALAND
NAMAQUALAND
KARAS
HARDAP
KGALAGADI
Great Karoo
Little Karoo
CAPE TOWN
Keetmanshoop
Upington
Cape of Good Hope
Cape Agulhas
Lambert Azimuthal Equal Area Projection

215

MPUMALANGA
GAUTENG
PRETORIA
Tshwane
Johannesburg
Soweto
Vereeniging
MAPUTO
MOZAMBIQUE
SWAZILAND
MBABANE
LESOTHO
MASERU
FREE STATE
Bloemfontein
KWAZULU-NATAL
Pietermaritzburg
Durban
EASTERN CAPE
East London
Port Elizabeth
INDIAN
OCEAN
Maputo
MILES
KILOMETRES
1:3 300 000
Longitude 26° east of Greenwich

© Collins Bartholomew Ltd

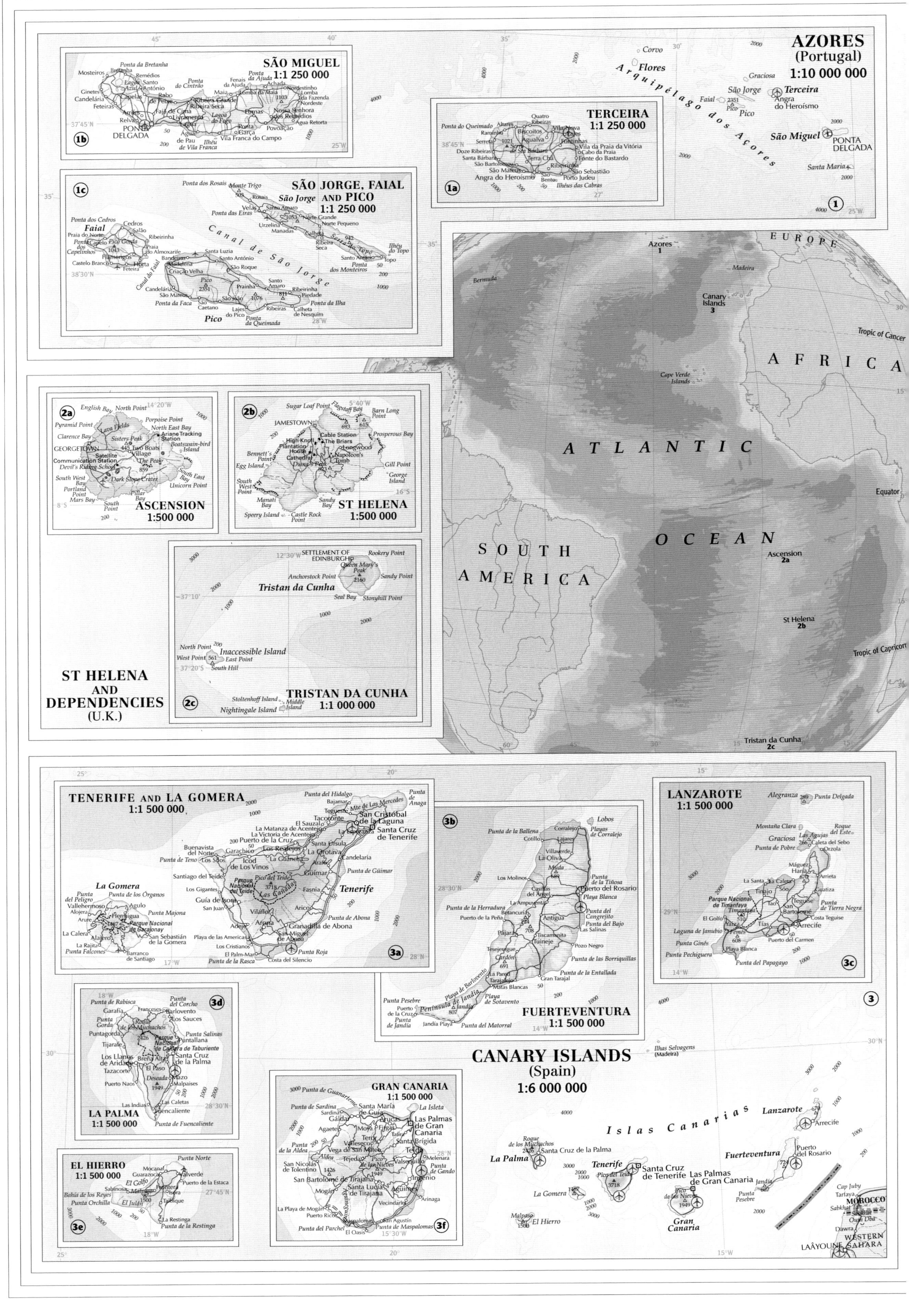

AZORES
(Portugal)
1:10 000 000
Arquipélago dos Açores
Corvo
Flores
Graciosa
São Jorge
Terceira
Angra do Heroísmo
Faial
Pico
São Miguel
PONTA DELGADA
Santa Maria
SÃO MIGUEL
1:1 250 000
TERCEIRA
1:1 250 000
SÃO JORGE, FAIAL AND PICO
1:1 250 000
Canal de São Jorge
Canal do Faial
EUROPE
AFRICA
ATLANTIC OCEAN
SOUTH AMERICA
Tropic of Cancer
Equator
Tropic of Capricorn
Azores
Bermuda
Madeira
Canary Islands
Cape Verde Islands
Ascension
St Helena
Tristan da Cunha
ASCENSION
1:500 000
ST HELENA
1:500 000
TRISTAN DA CUNHA
1:1 000 000
Tristan da Cunha
Inaccessible Island
Nightingale Island
ST HELENA AND DEPENDENCIES
(U.K.)
TENERIFE AND LA GOMERA
1:1 500 000
La Gomera
Tenerife
FUERTEVENTURA
1:1 500 000
LANZAROTE
1:1 500 000
LA PALMA
1:1 500 000
EL HIERRO
1:1 500 000
GRAN CANARIA
1:1 500 000
CANARY ISLANDS
(Spain)
1:6 000 000
Islas Canarias
Lanzarote
Arrecife
Fuerteventura
Puerto del Rosario
La Palma
Santa Cruz de la Palma
Tenerife
Santa Cruz de Tenerife
Las Palmas de Gran Canaria
La Gomera
El Hierro
Gran Canaria
Ilhas Selvagens (Madeira)
MOROCCO
WESTERN SAHARA
LAÂYOUNE

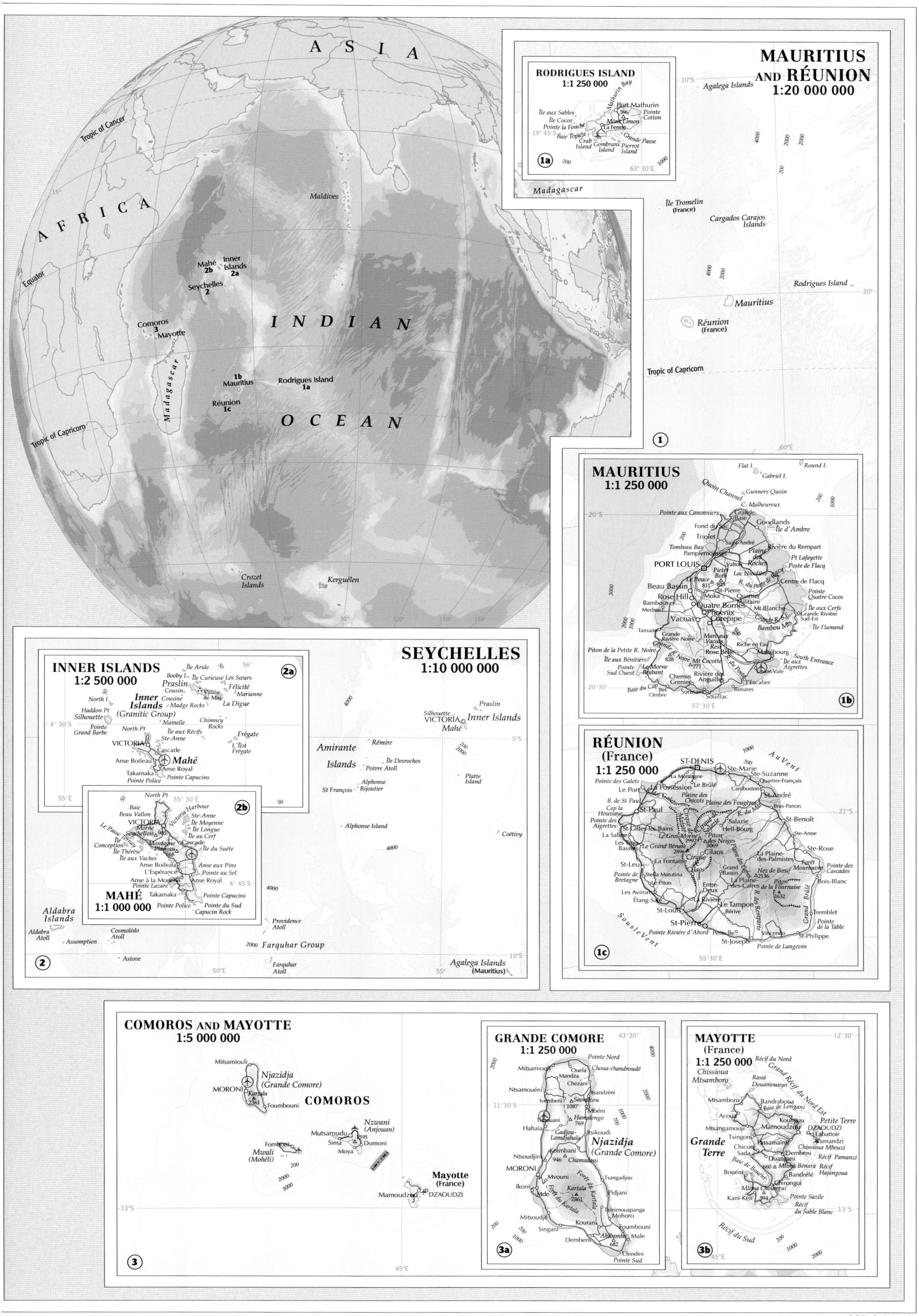
ASIA
AFRICA
INDIAN
OCEAN
Tropic of Cancer
Equator
Tropic of Capricorn
Maldives
Mahé 2b
Inner Islands 2a
Seychelles 2
Comoros 3
Mayotte
Madagascar
1b Mauritius
Réunion 1c
Rodrigues Island 1a
Crozet Islands
Kerguélen
MAURITIUS AND RÉUNION
1:20 000 000
Agalega Islands
Madagascar
Île Tromelin (France)
Cargados Carajos Islands
Rodrigues Island
Mauritius
Réunion (France)
Tropic of Capricorn
RODRIGUES ISLAND
1:1 250 000
Mathurin Bay
Port Mathurin
Île aux Sables
Île Cocos
Pointe la Fouche
Baie Topaze
Mont Limon
La Ferme
Pointe Cotton
Grande Passe
Crab Island
Gombrani Island
Pierrot Island
MAURITIUS
1:1 250 000
Flat I.
Gabriel I.
Round I.
Quoin Channel
Gunners Quoin
C. Malheureux
Pointe aux Canonniers
Grande Baie
Goodlands
Île d'Ambre
Fond du Sac
Triolet
Tombeau Bay
Pamplemousses
Rivière du Rempart
Pt Lafayette
Poste de Flacq
PORT LOUIS
Plaine des Roches
Lac Nicolière
Centre de Flacq
Beau Bassin
Rose Hill
Moka
Quartier Militaire
Pointe Quatre Cocos
Bambous
Quatre Bornes
Phoenix
Vacoas
Curepipe
Mt Blanche
Île aux Cerfs
Grande Rivière Sud-Est
Île Flamand
Tamarin
Grande Rivière Noire
Mare aux Vacoas Res.
Rose Belle
Riche en Eau
Mahébourg
Piton de la Petite R. Noire
Île aux Bénitiers
Le Morne Brabant
Pointe Sud Ouest
Mt Cocotte
Rivière des Anguilles
Chemin Grenier
Souillac
Plaisance
Île aux Aigrettes
South Entrance
Baie du Cap
Bel Ombre
Surinam
L'Escalier
Benares
RÉUNION (France)
1:1 250 000
Au Vent
Sous le Vent
ST-DENIS
Ste-Marie
Ste-Suzanne
Quartier-Français
Pointe des Galets
Le Port
La Possession
Le Brûlé
Cambuston
St-André
Bras-Panon
St-Paul
Plaine des Chicots
Plaine des Fougères
St-Benoît
St-Gilles-les-Bains
Salazie
Hell-Bourg
Piton des Neiges 3069
Ste-Anne
Ste-Rose
Cilaos
La Plaine-des-Palmistes
Pointe des Cascades
St-Leu
Nez de Bœuf 2136
Piton de la Fournaise 2632
Bois-Blanc
Les Avirons
Étang-Salé
Entre-Deux
Le Tampon
Tremblet
St-Louis
St-Pierre
Pointe de la Table
St-Philippe
Pointe Rivière d'Abord
St-Joseph
Vincendo
Pointe de Langevin
SEYCHELLES
1:10 000 000
Praslin
Silhouette
VICTORIA
Inner Islands
Mahé
Amirante Islands
Rémire
Île Desroches
Poivre Atoll
Alphonse
Bijoutier
St François
Platte Island
Alphonse Island
Coëtivy
Aldabra Islands
Aldabra Atoll
Assomption
Cosmoledo Atoll
Astove
Providence Atoll
Farquhar Group
Farquhar Atoll
Agalega Islands (Mauritius)
INNER ISLANDS
1:2 500 000
Île Aride
Booby I.
Île Curieuse
Les Sœurs
Praslin
Cousin
Vallée de Mai
Félicité
Marianne
Cousine
La Digue
North I.
Inner Islands (Granitic Group)
Madge Rocks
Silhouette
Mamelle
Chimney Rocks
Île aux Récifs
Frégate
Ste-Anne
L'Îlot Frégate
VICTORIA
Cascade
Anse Boileau
Mahé
Anse Royal
Takamaka
Pointe Capucins
Pointe Police
MAHÉ
1:1 000 000
North Pt
Victoria Harbour
Baie Beau Vallon
Ste-Anne
Île Moyenne
Île Longue
Île au Cerf
Le Passe Pernay
Morne Seychellois 905
Conception
Île Thérèse
Île aux Vaches
Montagne Planeau
Cascade
Île du Suète
Anse Boileau
Anse aux Pins
L'Espérance
Pointe au Sel
Anse à la Mouche
Anse Royal
Pointe Lazare
Takamaka
Pointe Capucins
Pointe Police
Pointe du Sud
Capucin Rock
COMOROS AND MAYOTTE
1:5 000 000
Mitsamiouli
Njazidja (Grande Comore)
MORONI
Kartala 2361
Foumbouni
COMOROS
Nzwani (Anjouan)
Mutsamudu
Sima
Domoni
Moya
Fomboni
Mwali (Mohéli)
Mayotte (France)
Mamoudzou
DZAOUDZI
GRANDE COMORE
1:1 250 000
Pointe Nord
Mitsamiouli
Ouela
Choua-chandroudé
Mandza
Chezani
Ntsaoueni
Itsandzéni
Ivembeni
Sada Tsou
Mbéni
Hamalengo
Hahaïa
Gadjou-Lamdjahalé
Itsikoudi
Njazidja (Grande Comore)
Ntsoudjini
Koimbani
MORONI
Chamadori
Tsangadjou
Mvouni
Foret du Karthala
Ikoni
Karthala 2361
Idjani
Mitsoudjé
Itsinimouapanga
Mohoro
Singani
Kourani
Foumbouni
Dembeni
Malé
Chindini
Pointe Sud
MAYOTTE (France)
1:1 250 000
Récif du Nord
Chissioua Mtsamboro
Grand Récif du Nord Est
Rassi Douamounyo
Mtsamboro
Bandraboua
Baie de Longani
Acoua
Koungou
Petite Terre
Mtsangamouji
Mamoudzou
DZAOUDZI
Labattoir
Grande Terre
Tsingoni
Passamainti
Pamandzi
Chissioua Mbouzi
Chiconi
Sada
Dembeni
Récif Pamanzi
Ouangani
Mtima Bénara 660
Récif Hajangoua
Baie de Boueni
Bandrélé
Boueni
Chirongui
Mlima Choungui
Kani-Kéli 594
Pointe Sazile
Récif du Sable Blanc
Récif du Sud

A
B
C
D
E
1
2
3
4
5
6
7
ASIA
ARCTIC OCEAN
Arctic Circle
Chukchi Sea
BERING SEA
Bering Strait
Point Hope
Barrow
BEAUFORT SEA
Prince Patrick Island
McClure Strait
Banks Island
Sachs Harbour
Mackenzie Bay
Inuvik
Amundsen Gulf
Nome
Norton Sound
St Lawrence Island
St Matthew Island
Attu Island
Pribilof Islands
Nunivak Island
Brooks Range
ALASKA
Yukon
Kuskokwim Mts
Mount McKinley
Alaska Range
Anchorage
Iliamna Lake
Bristol Bay
Aleutian Range
Aleutian Islands
Andreanof Islands
Fox Islands
Kodiak Island
Wrangell Mountains
Mount Logan
Gulf of Alaska
Richardson Mountains
Ogilvie Mountains
Mackenzie Mountains
Selwyn Mountains
YUKON TERRITORY
Whitehorse
NORTHWEST TERRITORIES
Great Bear Lake
Déline
Hottah L.
Coronation Gulf
Napaktulik Lake
Bathurst Inlet
Yellowknife
MacKay Lake
Aylmer Lake
Fort Simpson
Great Slave Lake
Trout Lake
Watson Lake
Cassiar Mountains
Juneau
Alexander Archipelago
COAST MOUNTAINS
Fort Nelson
BRITISH COLUMBIA
Williston Lake
Dawson Creek
Prince Rupert
Queen Charlotte Islands
Hecate Str.
Queen Charlotte Sound
Prince George
Fraser
ALBERTA
Peace
L. Claire
Lake Athabasca
Fort McMurray
Grande Prairie
Lesser Slave Lake
Edmonton
Jasper
N. Saskatchewan
SASKATCHEWAN
Prince Albert
Lloydminster
Saskatoon
Kamloops
Calgary
Medicine Hat
Lethbridge
ROCKY MOUNTAINS
Vancouver Island
Vancouver
Victoria
Seattle
Olympia
WASHINGTON
Spokane
Portland
Salem
Columbia
Eugene
OREGON
Cascade Range
Coast Ranges
Bitterroot Range
MONTANA
Great Falls
Helena
Billings
Bighorn Mountains
IDAHO
Boise
Snake
Twin Falls
WYOMING
Casper
Great Salt Lake
Salt Lake City
Uinta Mountains
Reno
NEVADA
Carson City
Great Basin
UTAH
COLORADO
Sacramento
San Francisco
San Jose
Sierra Nevada
Mount Whitney
UNITED STATES
Colorado Plateau
CALIFORNIA
Las Vegas
Los Angeles
Riverside
San Diego
ARIZONA
Albuquerque
Santa Fe
NEW MEXICO
Phoenix
Tijuana
Mexicali
Ensenada
Tucson
El Paso
Ciudad Juárez
Sacramento Mts
Rio Grande
Hermosillo
Chihuahua
Baja California
Golfo de California
Sierra Madre Occidental
Guadalupe (Mexico)
Villa Insurgentes
La Paz
Los Mochis
Torreón
MEXICO
Durango
Mazatlán
Tepic
Guadalajara
Islas Revillagigedo (Mexico)
Île Clipperton (France)
PACIFIC OCEAN
Midway Islands (U.S.A.)
Tropic of Cancer
Kaua'i
O'ahu
Honolulu
HAWAII
Maui
Hawai'ian Islands (U.S.A.)
Hawai'i
Equator
Line Islands
Administrative regions abbreviated on the map:
U.S.A.
CONN. CONNECTICUT
DEL. DELAWARE
MD MARYLAND
MASS. MASSACHUSETTS
N.H. NEW HAMPSHIRE
N.J. NEW JERSEY
R.I. RHODE ISLAND
VER. VERMONT
W. VIRG. WEST VIRGINIA
CANADA
P.E.I. PRINCE EDWARD ISLAND

Orthographic Projection

EUROPE
AFRICA
SOUTH AMERICA
ATLANTIC OCEAN
Greenland (Kalaallit Nunaat) (Denmark)
Greenland Sea
Denmark Strait
Iceland
Arctic Circle
Baffin Bay
Baffin Island
Davis Strait
Labrador Sea
Hudson Strait
HUDSON BAY
Nuuk
Station Nord
Daneborg
Uummannaq
Nuussuaq
Ilulissat
Ammassalik
Nanortalik
Clyde River
Iqaluit
Cape Dorset
Coral Harbour
Repulse Bay
Arviat
Nain
Péninsule d'Ungava
NEWFOUNDLAND AND LABRADOR
QUÉBEC
ONTARIO
Gander
St John's
St Pierre and Miquelon (France)
Gulf of St Lawrence
NOVA SCOTIA
Halifax
Québec
Montréal
Ottawa
Toronto
Boston
New York
Philadelphia
Washington
Chicago
Detroit
Atlanta
Jacksonville
Miami
New Orleans
Houston
Bermuda (U.K.)
Arquipélago dos Açores
Arquipélago da Madeira
Islas Canarias
Ilhas do Cabo Verde
Tropic of Cancer
Equator
GULF OF MEXICO
THE BAHAMAS
Nassau
CUBA
La Habana
HAITI
Port-au-Prince
DOMINICAN REPUBLIC
Santo Domingo
Puerto Rico (U.S.A.)
San Juan
JAMAICA
Kingston
CARIBBEAN SEA
Greater Antilles
Lesser Antilles
Leeward Islands
Windward Islands
TRINIDAD AND TOBAGO
Port of Spain
BARBADOS
BELIZE
Belmopan
GUATEMALA
Guatemala
HONDURAS
Tegucigalpa
EL SALVADOR
San Salvador
NICARAGUA
Managua
COSTA RICA
San José
PANAMA
Panamá
F
G
H
I
J
1
2
3
4
5
6
7

MILES | KILOMETRES

1:27 000 000

131
BERING SEA
ARCTIC OCEAN
BEAUFORT SEA
Chukchi Sea
RUSSIAN FEDERATION
ALEUTIAN ISLANDS
Andreanof Islands
Fox Islands
Pribilof Islands
U.S.A.
ALASKA
Brooks Range
Kuskokwim Mountains
Alaska Range
Philip Smith Mountains
GULF OF ALASKA
PACIFIC OCEAN
YUKON TERRITORY
NORTHWEST TERRITORIES
BRITISH COLUMBIA
ALBERTA
SASKATCHEWAN
CANADA
ROCKY MOUNTAINS
COAST MOUNTAINS
Mackenzie Mountains
WASHINGTON
OREGON
IDAHO
MONTANA
WYOMING
NEVADA
UTAH
CALIFORNIA
NORTH DAKOTA
SOUTH DAKOTA
NEBRASKA
UNITED STATES OF AMERICA
Anchorage
Fairbanks
Whitehorse
Yellowknife
Edmonton
Calgary
Vancouver
Victoria
Seattle
Portland
Boise
Salt Lake City
Sacramento
San Francisco
San Jose
Regina
Saskatoon
Great Slave Lake
Great Bear Lake
Queen Charlotte Islands
Vancouver Island
METRES
FEET
6000 19686
5000 16404
4000 13124
3000 9843
2000 6562
1000 3281
500 1640
200 656
0 0
LAND BELOW SEA LEVEL
200 656
2000 6562
4000 13124
6000 19686
Lambert Conformal Conic Projection
228

MILES KILOMETRES

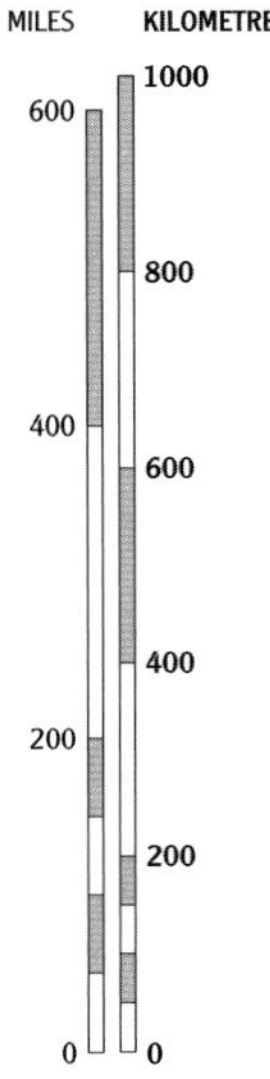

1:15 000 000

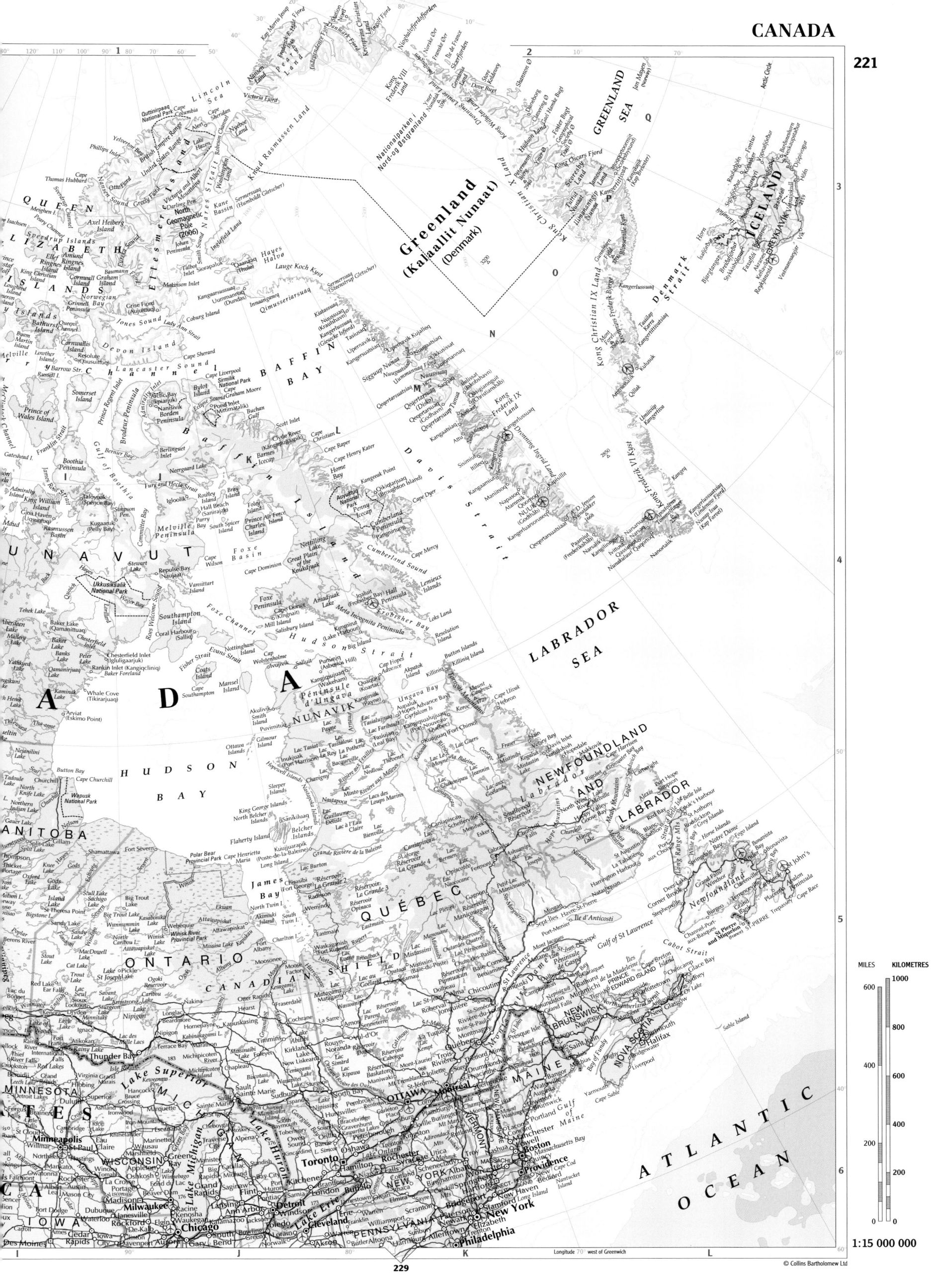

© Collins Bartholomew Ltd

220

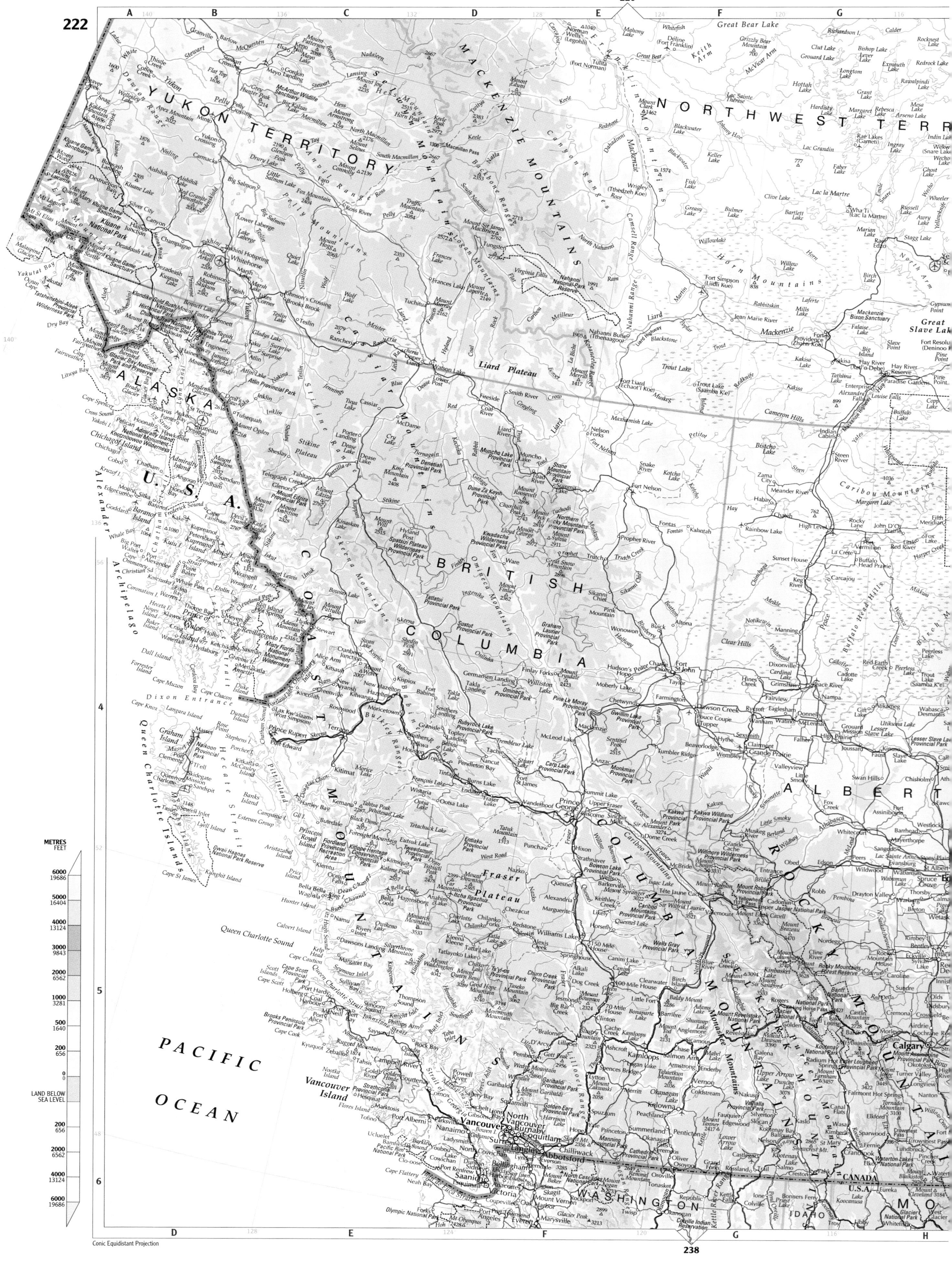
YUKON TERRITORY
NORTHWEST TERR
ALASKA
U.S.A.
BRITISH COLUMBIA
ALBERT
WASHINGTON
IDAHO
MO
CANADA
U.S.A.
PACIFIC OCEAN
MACKENZIE MOUNTAINS
COAST MOUNTAINS
COLUMBIA MOUNTAINS
ROCKY MOUNTAINS
SELKIRK MOUNTAINS
Selwyn Mountains
Cassiar Mountains
Omineca Mountains
Skeena Mountains
Stikine Plateau
Liard Plateau
Fraser Plateau
Horn Mountains
Caribou Mountains
Cariboo Mountains
Franklin Mountains
Alexander Archipelago
Queen Charlotte Islands
Queen Charlotte Sound
Hecate Strait
Dixon Entrance
Vancouver Island
Great Bear Lake
Great Slave Lake
Whitehorse
Juneau
Prince Rupert
Prince George
Kamloops
Kelowna
Vancouver
Victoria
Calgary
Fort Nelson
Fort St John
Dawson Creek
Grande Prairie
Fort Simpson
Watson Lake
Yellowknife
Peace
Liard
Mackenzie
Fraser
Stikine
Skeena
Yukon
Kluane National Park
Glacier Bay National Park and Preserve
Pacific Rim National Park
Jasper National Park
Banff National Park
Olympic National Park
A
B
C
D
E
F
G
H
4
5
6
140
136
132
128
124
120
116
60
56
52
48
METRES
FEET
6000 19686
5000 16404
4000 13124
3000 9843
2000 6562
1000 3281
500 1640
200 656
0 0
LAND BELOW SEA LEVEL
200 656
2000 6562
4000 13124
6000 19686

MILES KILOMETRES

1:6 000 000

© Collins Bartholomew Ltd

HUDSON BAY
James Bay
ONTARIO
CANADIAN SHIELD
MANITOBA
MINNESOTA
WISCONSIN
MICHIGAN
NEW YORK
CANADA
U.S.A.
LAKE SUPERIOR
LAKE MICHIGAN
LAKE HURON
LAKE ERIE
LAKE ONTARIO
Georgian Bay
North Channel
Lake Nipigon
Lake of the Woods
Belcher Islands
Akimiski Island
Manitoulin Island
Isle Royale
Wapusk National Park
Polar Bear Provincial Park
Woodland Caribou Provincial Park
Quetico Provincial Park
Pukaskwa National Park
Lake Superior Provincial Park
Algonquin Provincial Park
Pictured Rocks National Lakeshore
Apostle Islands National Lakeshore
Seney National Wildlife Refuge
Churchill
Thunder Bay
Sault Sainte Marie
Sudbury
Timmins
Moosonee
Kapuskasing
North Bay
Ottawa
Toronto
Hamilton
London
Windsor
Detroit
Chicago
Milwaukee
Duluth
Green Bay
Grand Rapids
Lansing
Flint
Toledo
Cleveland
Buffalo
Rochester
Syracuse
Kingston
Kenora
Dryden
Hearst
Cochrane
Rouyn-Noranda
Val-d'Or
Inukjuak (Port Harrison)
Kuujjuarapik (Poste-de-la-Baleine)
Chisasibi (Fort George)
Réservoir La Grande 2
Réservoir Opinaca
Adirondack Mountains
METRES
FEET
6000
19686
5000
16404
4000
13124
3000
9843
2000
6562
1000
3281
500
1640
200
656
0
LAND BELOW SEA LEVEL
Conic Equidistant Projection
236
230

Ungava Bay
Torngat Mountains
LABRADOR SEA
NEWFOUNDLAND AND LABRADOR
Smallwood Reservoir
Lake Melville
Mealy Mountains
Strait of Belle Isle
Long Range Mountains
NEWFOUNDLAND
St Pierre and Miquelon (France)
GULF OF ST LAWRENCE
Île d'Anticosti
Péninsule de Gaspé
Cabot Strait
PRINCE EDWARD ISLAND
NEW BRUNSWICK
NOVA SCOTIA
Cape Breton Island
Bay of Fundy
Gulf of Maine
MAINE
NEW HAMPSHIRE
White Mountains
ATLANTIC OCEAN
Sable Island
Québec
Halifax
Boston
Portland
Saint John
Fredericton
Moncton
Charlottetown
Sydney
Schefferville
Labrador City
Goose Bay
Nain
Hopedale
Sept-Îles
Chicoutimi
MILES
KILOMETRES
longitude 72° west of Greenwich

1:6 000 000

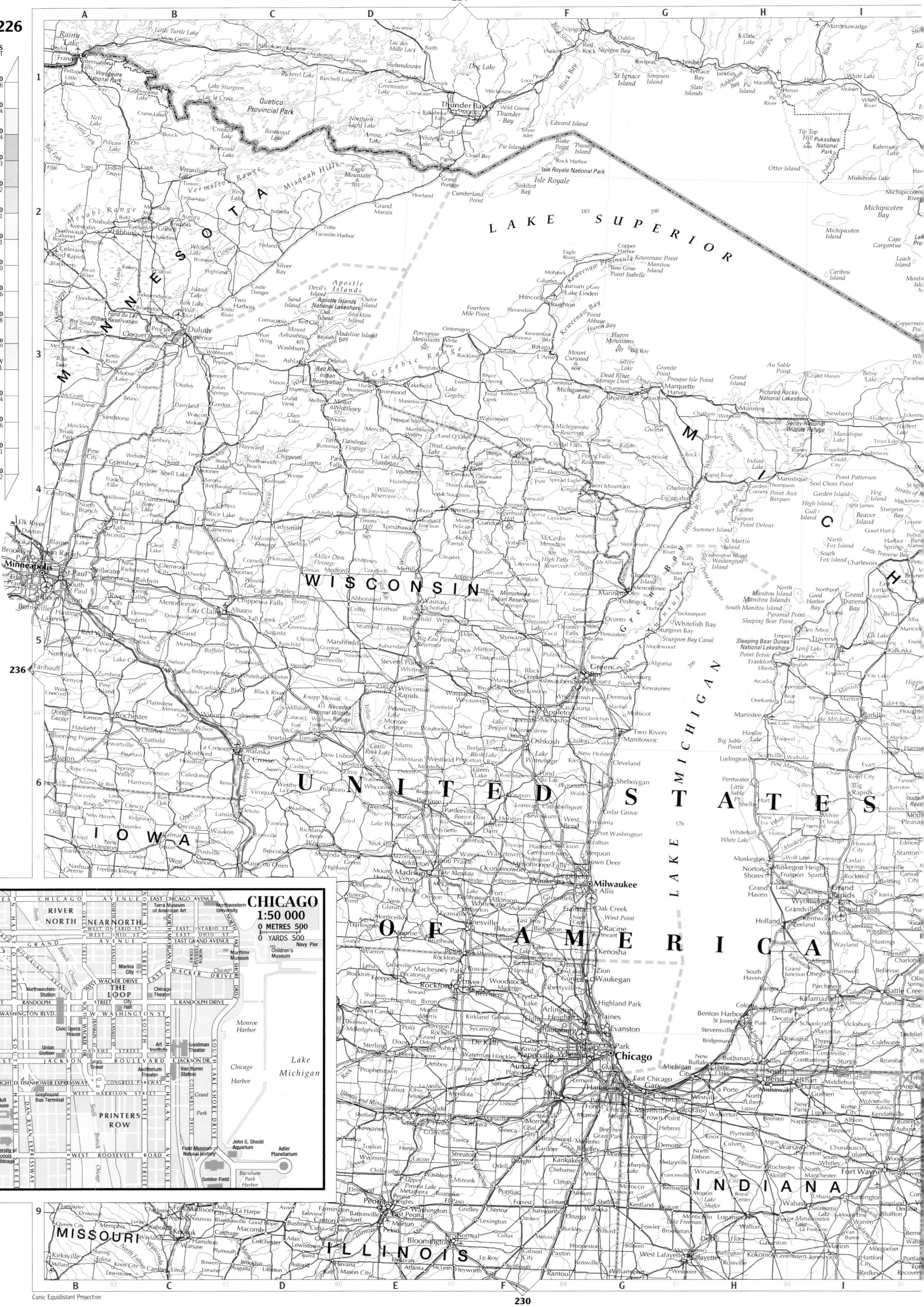
224
METRES
FEET
LAND BELOW SEA LEVEL
MINNESOTA
WISCONSIN
UNITED STATES OF AMERICA
IOWA
ILLINOIS
INDIANA
MISSOURI
MICHIGAN
LAKE SUPERIOR
LAKE MICHIGAN
Quetico Provincial Park
Voyageurs National Park
Isle Royale
Isle Royale National Park
Apostle Islands
Apostle Islands National Lakeshore
Thunder Bay
Duluth
Superior
Minneapolis
St Paul
Milwaukee
Chicago
Green Bay
Madison
Rochester
Grand Rapids
CHICAGO
1:50 000
METRES 500
YARDS 500
RIVER NORTH
NEAR NORTH
THE LOOP
PRINTERS ROW
Navy Pier
Monroe Harbor
Chicago Harbor
Lake Michigan
Burnham Park Harbor
Adler Planetarium
Soldier Field
236
230
Conic Equidistant Projection

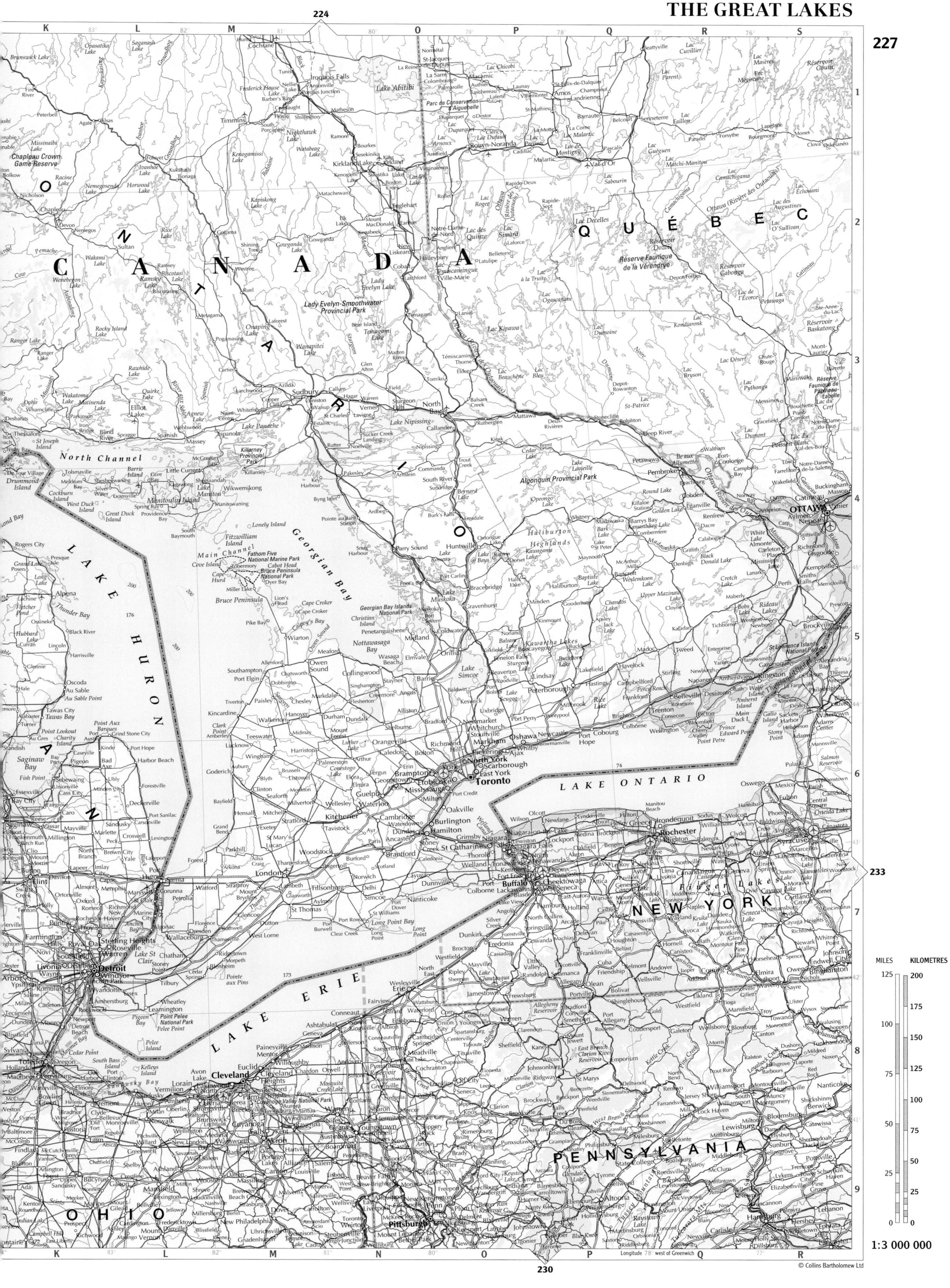
224
230
233
CANADA
ONTARIO
QUÉBEC
NEW YORK
PENNSYLVANIA
OHIO
LAKE HURON
LAKE ONTARIO
LAKE ERIE
Georgian Bay
North Channel
Main Channel
Lake Nipissing
Lake Simcoe
Lake Abitibi
Saginaw Bay
Thunder Bay
Long Point Bay
Finger Lakes
Algonquin Provincial Park
Lady Evelyn-Smoothwater Provincial Park
Réserve Faunique de la Vérendrye
Chapleau Crown Game Reserve
Haliburton Highlands
Kawartha Lakes
Bruce Peninsula
Manitoulin Island
Toronto
OTTAWA
Sudbury
Timmins
North Bay
Rouyn-Noranda
Val-d'Or
Kingston
Hamilton
London
Mississauga
Oshawa
Detroit
Windsor
Toledo
Cleveland
Buffalo
Rochester
Syracuse
Erie
Pittsburgh
Akron
Youngstown
Harrisburg
Binghamton
Sarnia
Flint
MILES
KILOMETRES
125
100
75
50
25
0
200
175
150
125
100
75
50
25
0
1:3 000 000
Longitude 78° west of Greenwich
© Collins Bartholomew Ltd

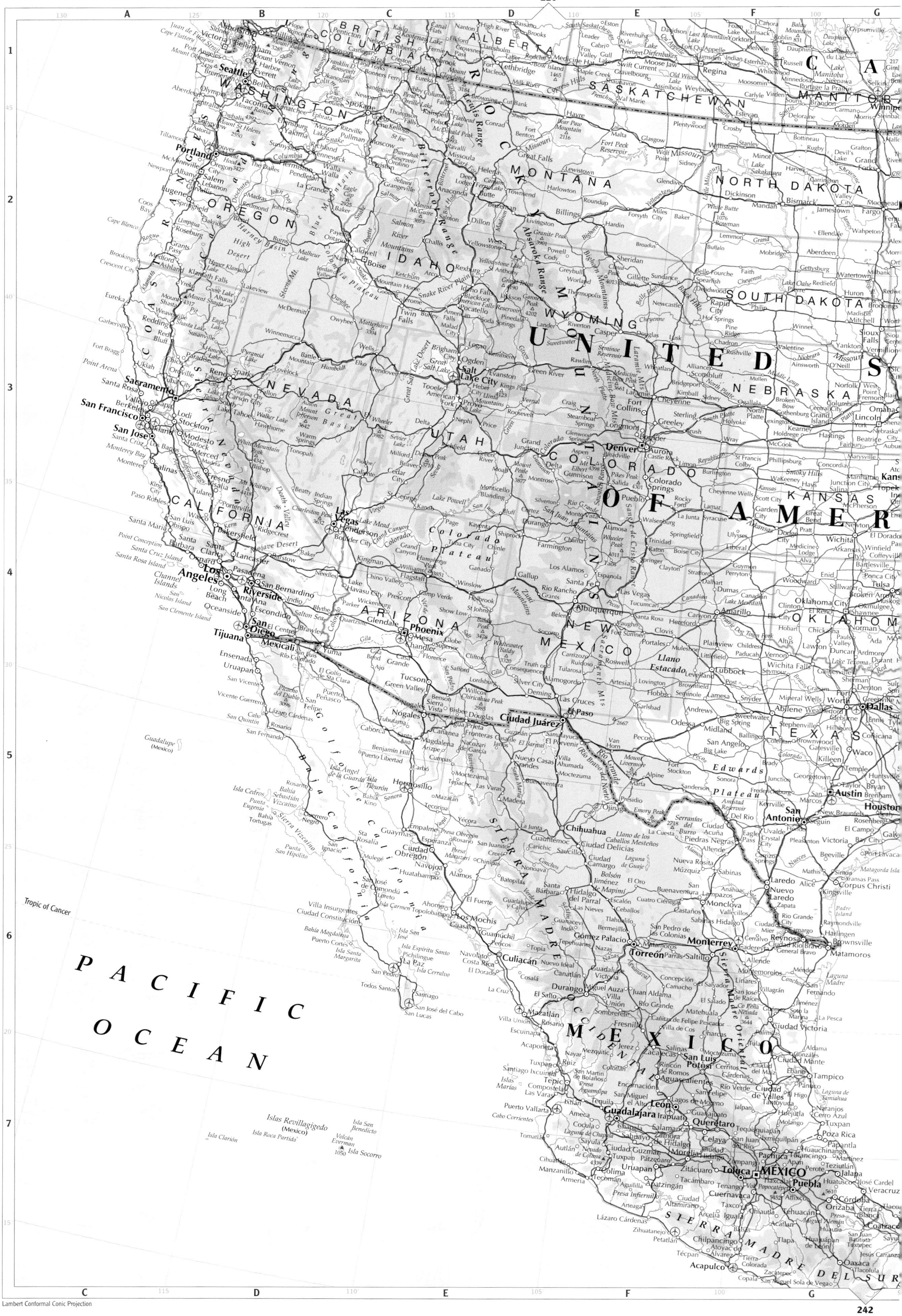

METRES / FEET

METRES	FEET
6000	19686
5000	16404
4000	13124
3000	9843
2000	6562
1000	3281
500	1640
200	656
0	0
LAND BELOW SEA LEVEL	
200	656
2000	6562
4000	13124
6000	19686

Lambert Conformal Conic Projection

221
246
247
CANADA
UNITED STATES
ONTARIO
QUÉBEC
NEW BRUNSWICK
NOVA SCOTIA
PRINCE EDWARD ISLAND
MAINE
VERMONT
NEW HAMPSHIRE
MASSACHUSETTS
CONNECTICUT
RHODE ISLAND
NEW YORK
PENNSYLVANIA
NEW JERSEY
DELAWARE
MARYLAND
WASHINGTON
WEST VIRGINIA
VIRGINIA
NORTH CAROLINA
SOUTH CAROLINA
GEORGIA
FLORIDA
ALABAMA
MISSISSIPPI
TENNESSEE
KENTUCKY
OHIO
INDIANA
ILLINOIS
MICHIGAN
WISCONSIN
Lake Superior
Lake Michigan
Lake Huron
Lake Erie
Lake Ontario
Gulf of St Lawrence
Gulf of Maine
Bay of Fundy
APPALACHIAN MOUNTAINS
ATLANTIC OCEAN
GULF OF MEXICO
CARIBBEAN SEA
Straits of Florida
Tropic of Cancer
Bermuda (U.K.)
HAMILTON
THE BAHAMAS
NASSAU
WEST INDIES
GREATER ANTILLES
CUBA
LA HABANA (Havana)
JAMAICA
KINGSTON
HISPANIOLA
HAITI
PORT-AU-PRINCE
DOMINICAN REPUBLIC
SANTO DOMINGO
Puerto Rico (U.S.A.)
Turks and Caicos Islands (U.K.)
Cayman Islands (U.K.)
YUCATÁN
BELIZE
GUATEMALA
Chicago
Detroit
Toronto
Montréal
OTTAWA
Boston
New York
Philadelphia
Baltimore
Pittsburgh
Cleveland
Columbus
Indianapolis
Cincinnati
St Louis
Memphis
Nashville
Atlanta
Charlotte
Richmond
Norfolk
Jacksonville
Orlando
Tampa
Miami
New Orleans
Milwaukee
Halifax
Québec
MILES
KILOMETRES
0
100
200
300
400
500
600
700
800
Longitude 90° west of Greenwich

1:12 000 000

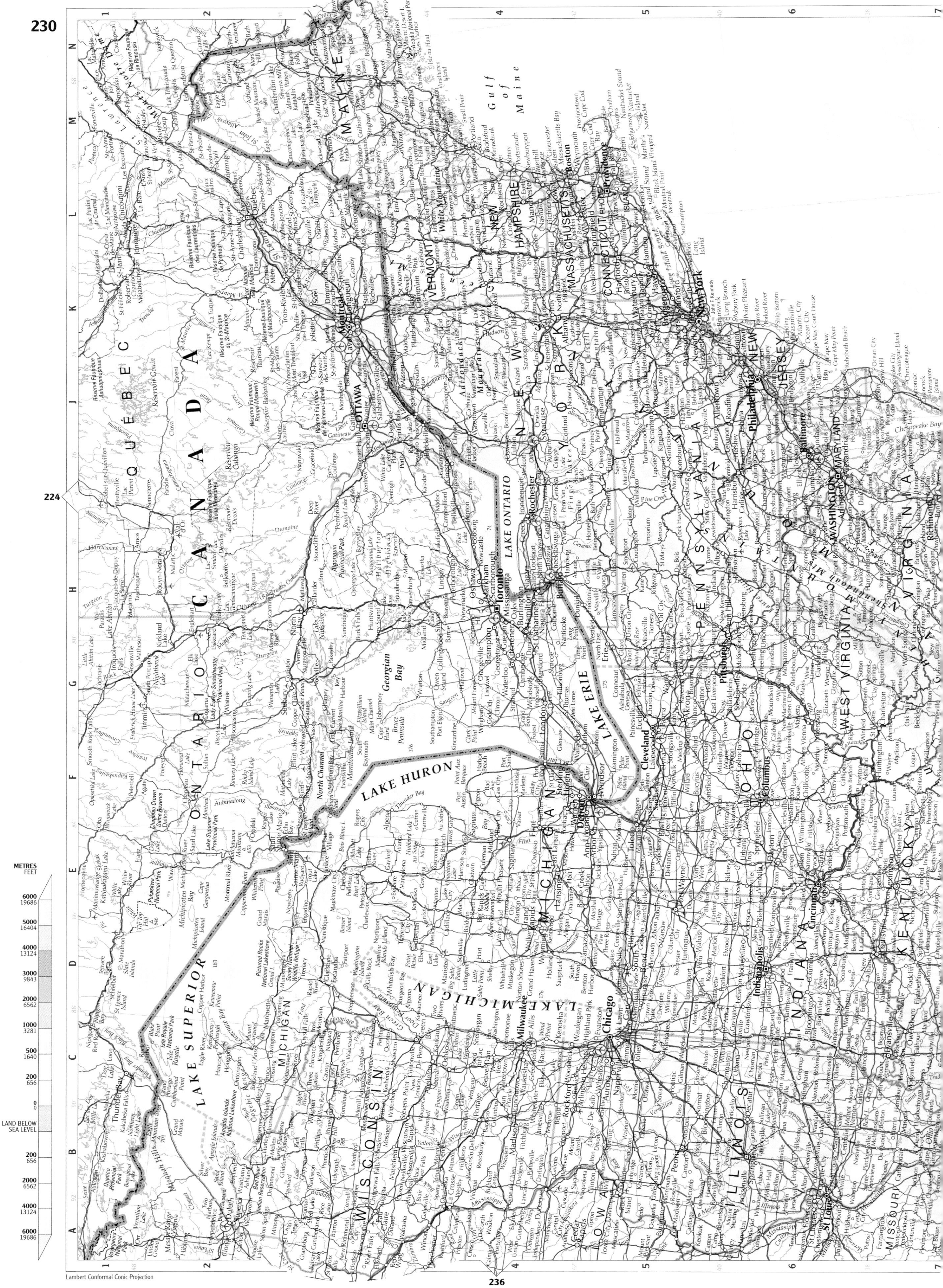

Lambert Conformal Conic Projection

224

236

NORTH ATLANTIC OCEAN
GULF OF MEXICO
THE BAHAMAS
BERMUDA (U.K.) 1:500 000
NEW PROVIDENCE (The Bahamas) 1: 500 000
FLORIDA
GEORGIA
ALABAMA
MISSISSIPPI
TENNESSEE
NORTH CAROLINA
SOUTH CAROLINA
Straits of Florida
Tropic of Cancer
Great Bahama Bank
Grand Bahama
Great Abaco
Andros
Eleuthera
NASSAU
Miami
Fort Lauderdale
West Palm Beach
Orlando
Tampa
Jacksonville
Tallahassee
Savannah
Charleston
Atlanta
Montgomery
Birmingham
Mobile
New Orleans
Memphis
Jackson
Columbus
Macon
Augusta
Charlotte
Raleigh
Wilmington
Knoxville
Chattanooga
Pensacola

246
237

MILES KILOMETRES

1:6 000 000

224
226
231

METRES
FEET
6000
19686
5000
16404
4000
13124
3000
9843
2000
6562
1500
4921
1000
3281
500
1640
200
656
100
328
0
0
LAND BELOW SEA LEVEL
200
656
1000
3281
2000
6562
A
B
C
D
E
F
G
H
4
5
6
7
10
11
12
MICHIGAN
ONTARIO
OHIO
PENNSYLVANIA
WEST VIRGINIA
KENTUCKY
VIRGINIA
TENNESSEE
NORTH CAROLINA
LAKE HURON
LAKE ERIE
LAKE ONTARIO
Georgian Bay
Saginaw Bay
CANADA
U.S.A.
APPALACHIAN MOUNTAINS
BLUE RIDGE
ALLEGHENY MOUNTAINS
Toronto
Detroit
Cleveland
Pittsburgh
Columbus
Cincinnati
Buffalo
Rochester
Toledo
Richmond
WASHINGTON
Charleston
Hamilton
London
Lansing
Erie
Roanoke

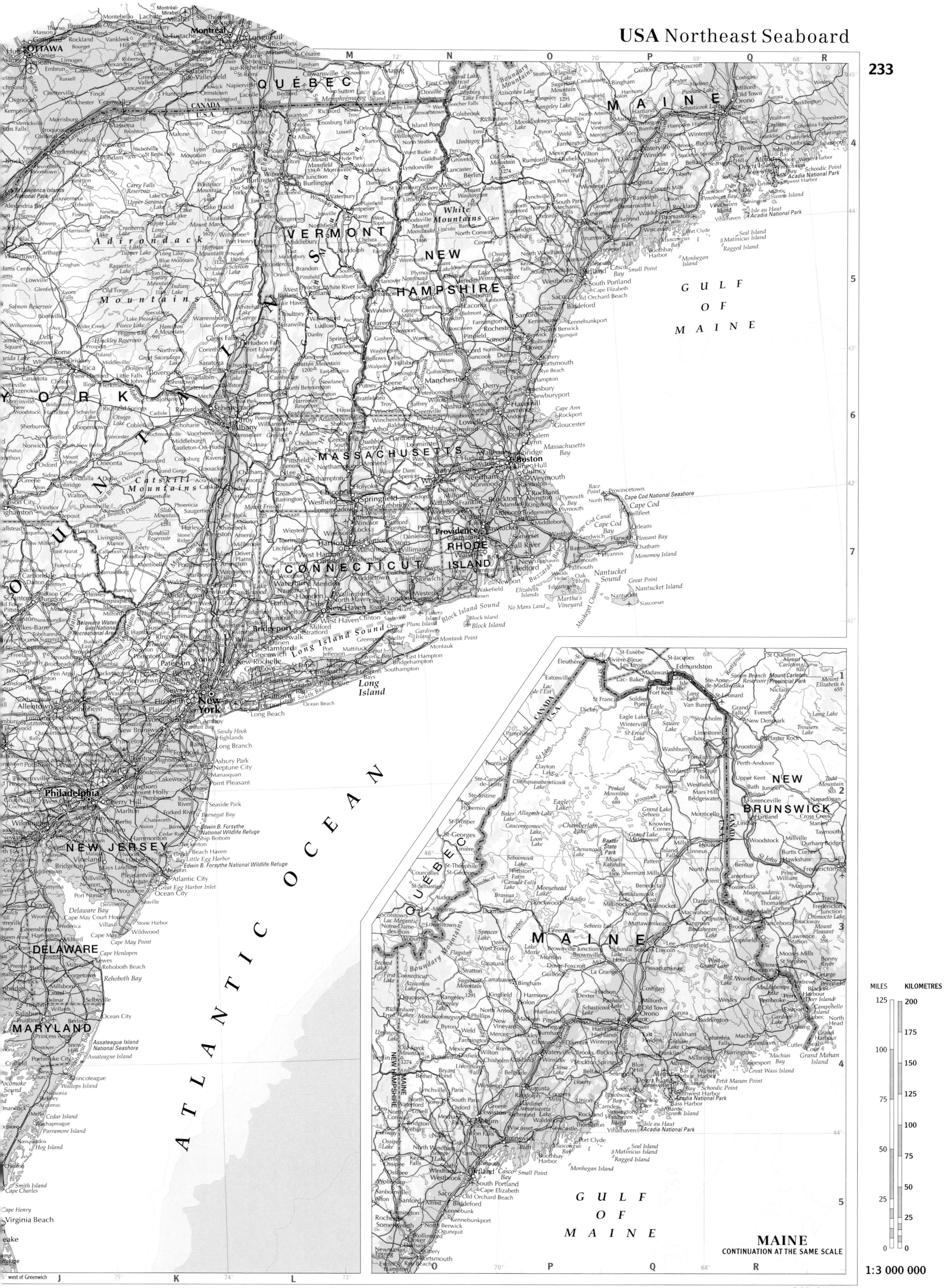
QUÉBEC
CANADA
U.S.A.
MAINE
VERMONT
NEW HAMPSHIRE
MASSACHUSETTS
RHODE ISLAND
CONNECTICUT
NEW YORK
NEW JERSEY
DELAWARE
MARYLAND
NEW BRUNSWICK
GULF OF MAINE
ATLANTIC OCEAN
Adirondack Mountains
Catskill Mountains
White Mountains
Green Mountains
Long Island Sound
Long Island
Cape Cod
Nantucket Sound
Martha's Vineyard
Nantucket Island
Montréal
Ottawa
Boston
Providence
New York
Philadelphia
MAINE
CONTINUATION AT THE SAME SCALE
MILES
KILOMETRES
1:3 000 000
west of Greenwich

© Collins Bartholomew Ltd

233

A B C D E F

PENNSYLVANIA

APPALACHIAN MOUNTAINS

MARYLAND

DELAWARE

TIOGA COUNTY

BRADFORD COUNTY

WAYNE COUNTY

SULLIVAN COUNTY

WYOMING COUNTY

LACKAWANNA COUNTY

LYCOMING COUNTY

PIKE COUNTY

LUZERNE COUNTY

COLUMBIA COUNTY

MONTOUR COUNTY

UNION COUNTY

MONROE COUNTY

SUSSEX COUNTY

WARREN COUNTY

CARBON COUNTY

NORTHUMBERLAND COUNTY

SNYDER COUNTY

SCHUYLKILL COUNTY

NORTHAMPTON COUNTY

JUNIATA COUNTY

LEHIGH COUNTY

HUNTERDON COUNTY

PERRY COUNTY

BERKS COUNTY

BUCKS COUNTY

LEBANON COUNTY

DAUPHIN COUNTY

MONTGOMERY COUNTY

CUMBERLAND COUNTY

LANCASTER COUNTY

CHESTER COUNTY

PHILADELPHIA COUNTY

Philadelphia

ADAMS COUNTY

YORK COUNTY

DELAWARE COUNTY

CAMDEN COUNTY

GLOUCESTER COUNTY

CARROLL COUNTY

HARFORD COUNTY

CECIL COUNTY

NEW CASTLE COUNTY

SALEM COUNTY

BALTIMORE COUNTY

ATLANTIC COUNTY

BALTIMORE CITY

Baltimore

HOWARD COUNTY

KENT COUNTY

CUMBERLAND COUNTY

ANNE ARUNDEL COUNTY

QUEEN ANNE'S COUNTY

MONTGOMERY COUNTY

CAPE MAY COUNTY

Delaware Bay

Chesapeake Bay

DISTRICT OF COLUMBIA

Washington

PRINCE GEORGE'S COUNTY

CAROLINE COUNTY

TALBOT COUNTY

METRES / FEET

6000 / 19686

5000 / 16404

4000 / 13124

3000 / 9843

2000 / 6562

1500 / 4921

1000 / 3281

500 / 1640

200 / 656

100 / 328

0 / 0

LAND BELOW SEA LEVEL

50 / 164

200 / 656

1000 / 3281

2000 / 6562

A B C D E F

Conic Equidistant Projection

233

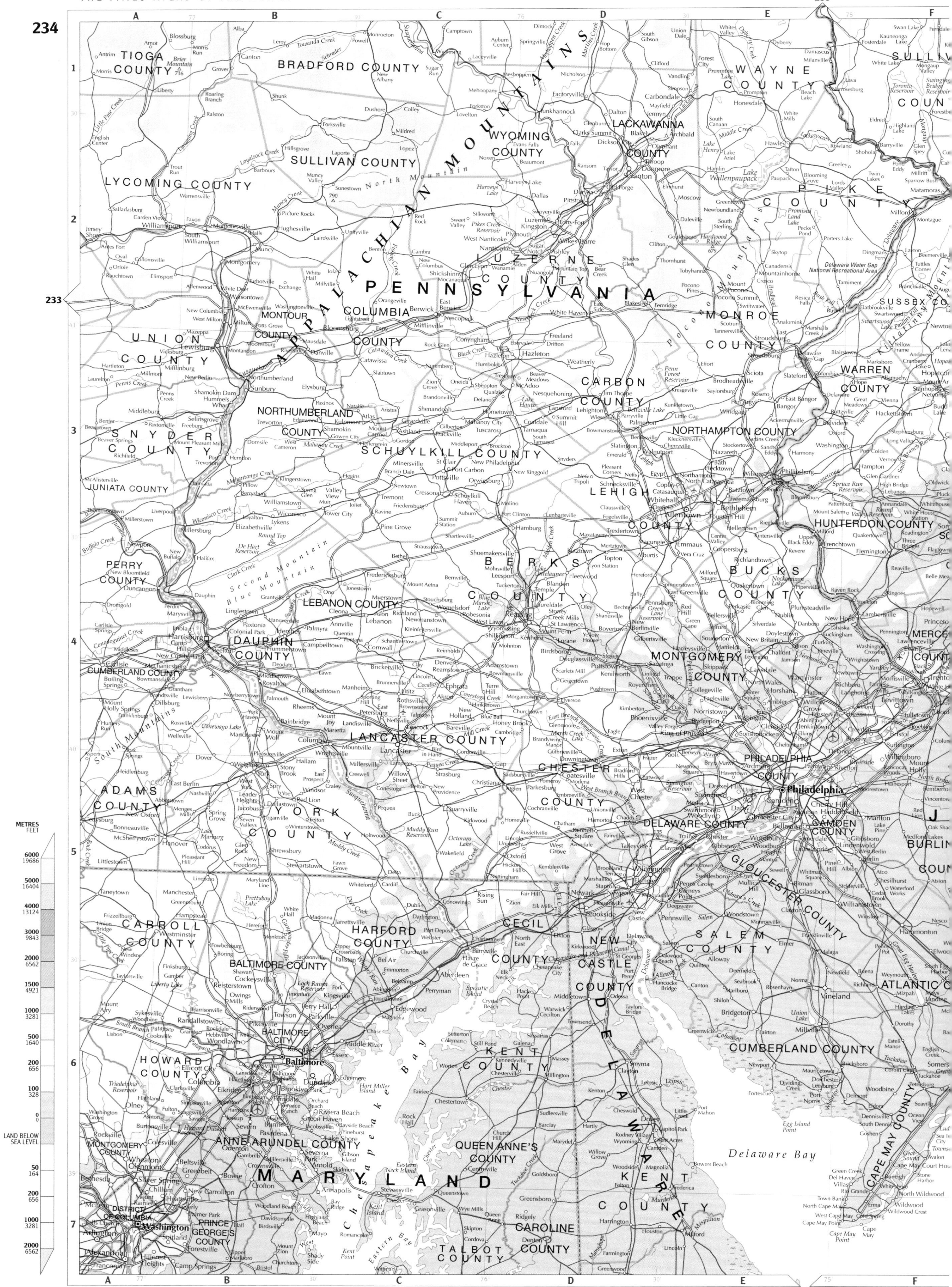

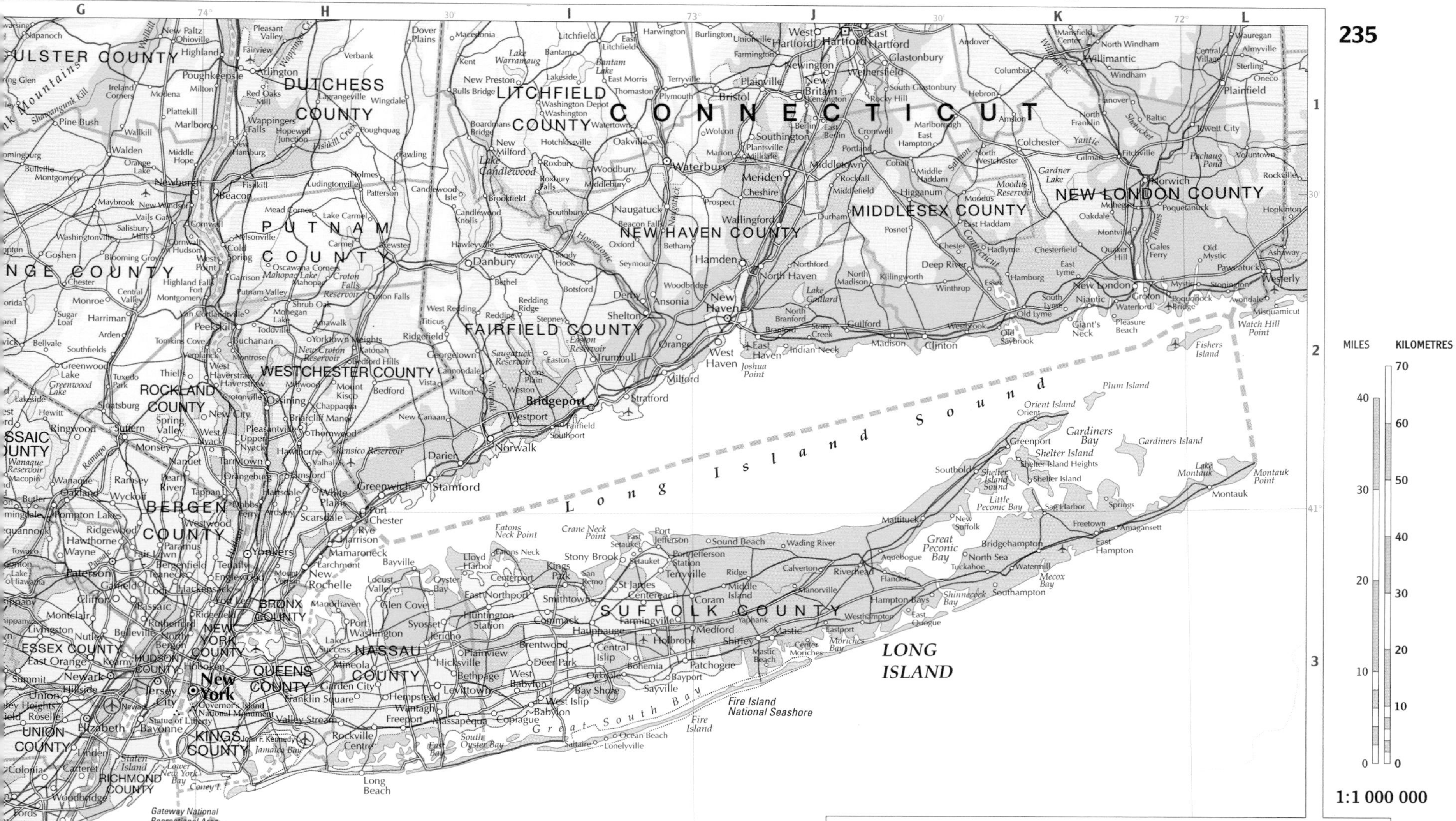
ULSTER COUNTY
DUTCHESS COUNTY
LITCHFIELD COUNTY
CONNECTICUT
PUTNAM COUNTY
NEW HAVEN COUNTY
MIDDLESEX COUNTY
NEW LONDON COUNTY
FAIRFIELD COUNTY
WESTCHESTER COUNTY
ROCKLAND COUNTY
BERGEN COUNTY
BRONX COUNTY
NEW YORK COUNTY
QUEENS COUNTY
NASSAU COUNTY
SUFFOLK COUNTY
KINGS COUNTY
RICHMOND COUNTY
ESSEX COUNTY
HUDSON COUNTY
UNION COUNTY
MONMOUTH COUNTY
Long Island Sound
LONG ISLAND
New York
Hartford
New Haven
Bridgeport
Stamford
Waterbury
New London
Fire Island National Seashore
Great South Bay
Gateway National Recreational Area
Edwin B. Forsythe National Wildlife Refuge
ATLANTIC OCEAN
MILES
KILOMETRES
1:1 000 000
Longitude 74° west of Greenwich
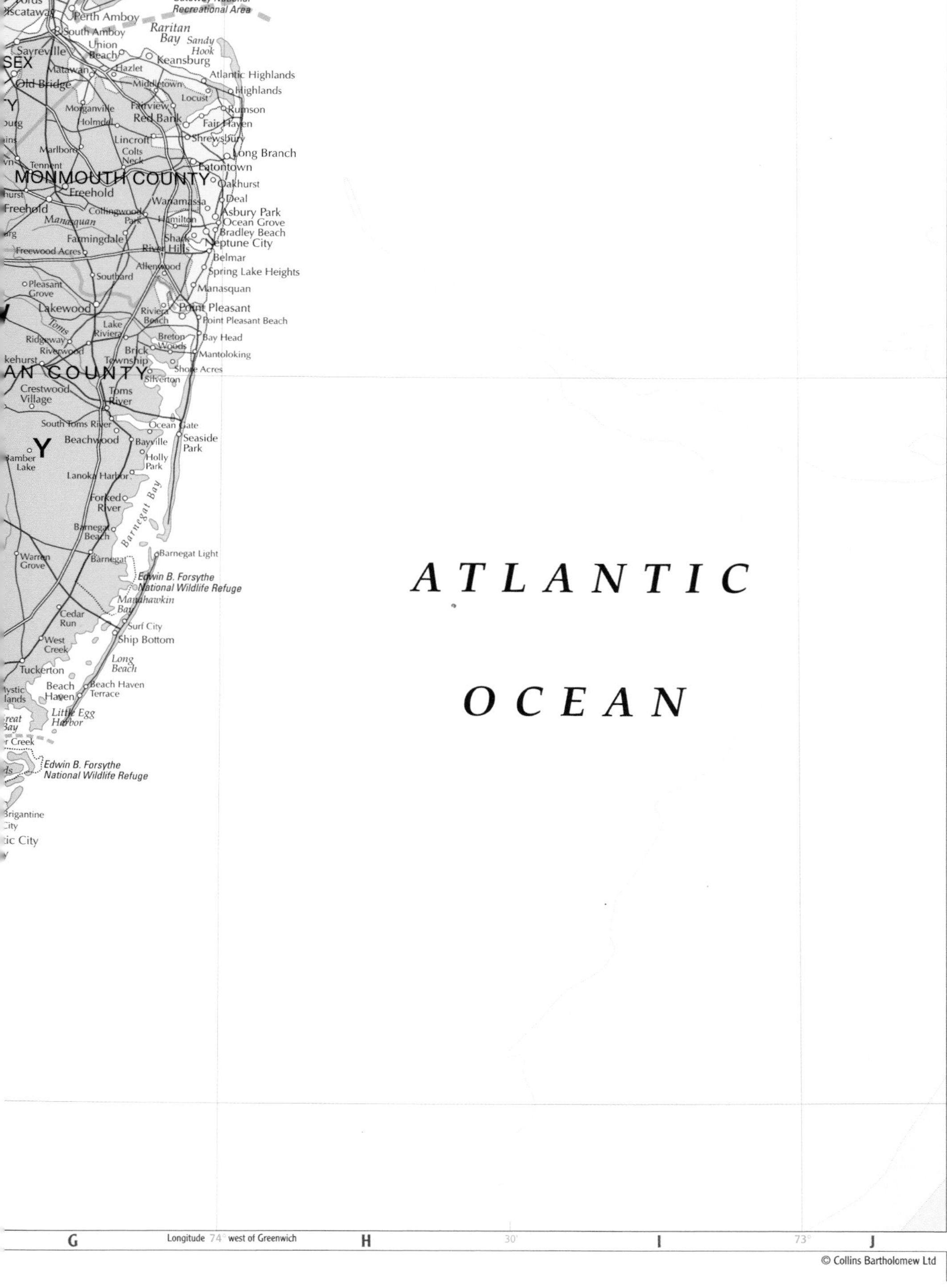

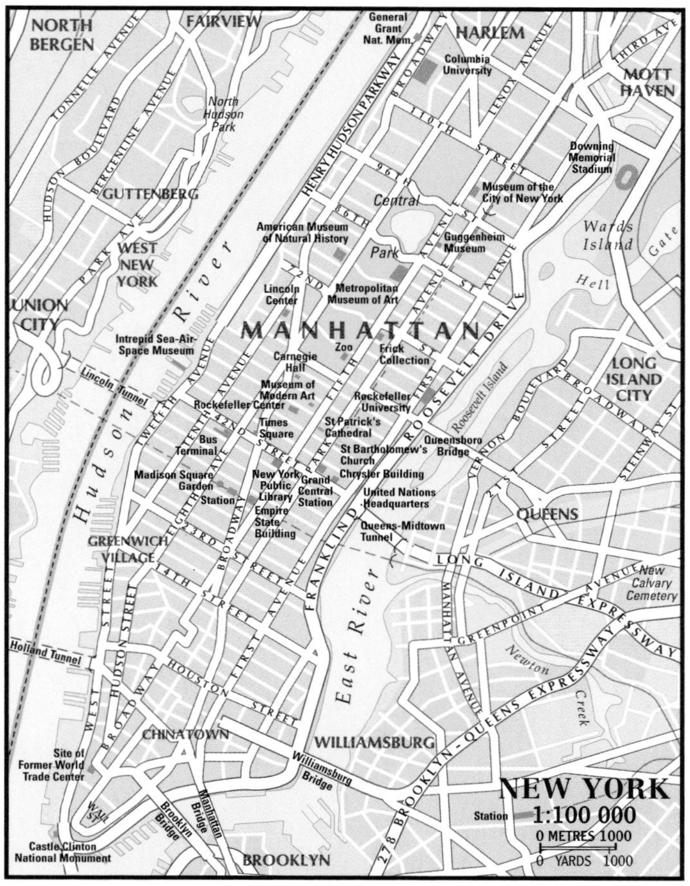
NORTH BERGEN
FAIRVIEW
HARLEM
MOTT HAVEN
GUTTENBERG
WEST NEW YORK
UNION CITY
MANHATTAN
LONG ISLAND CITY
QUEENS
GREENWICH VILLAGE
CHINATOWN
WILLIAMSBURG
BROOKLYN
Hudson River
East River
Central Park
Holland Tunnel
Lincoln Tunnel
NEW YORK
1:100 000
0 METRES 1000
0 YARDS 1000

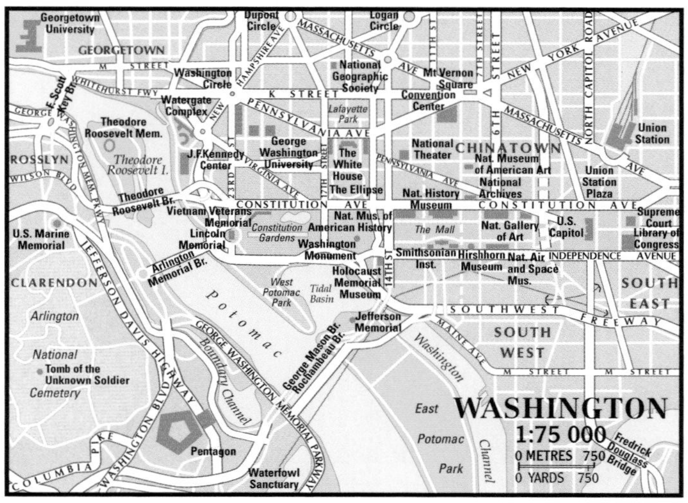
Georgetown University
GEORGETOWN
Dupont Circle
Logan Circle
ROSSLYN
CLARENDON
Arlington
CHINATOWN
The White House
U.S. Capitol
Lincoln Memorial
Washington Monument
Jefferson Memorial
Pentagon
National Tomb of the Unknown Soldier Cemetery
Potomac
SOUTH WEST
SOUTH EAST
WASHINGTON
1:75 000
0 METRES 750
0 YARDS 750

230

223

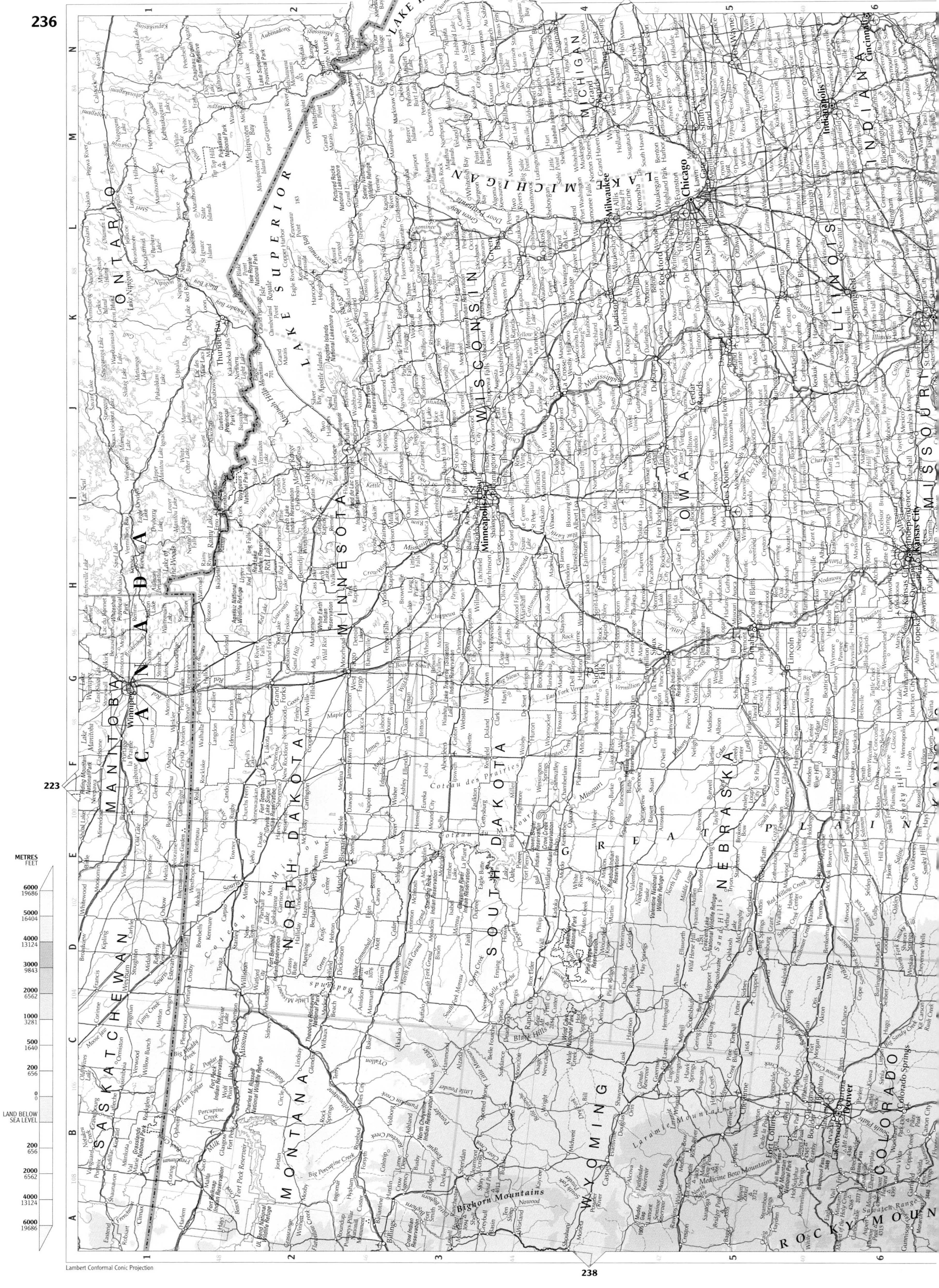
METRES
FEET
6000
19686
5000
16404
4000
13124
3000
9843
2000
6562
1000
3281
500
1640
200
656
0
0
LAND BELOW
SEA LEVEL
200
656
2000
6562
4000
13124
6000
19686
ONTARIO
MANITOBA
SASKATCHEWAN
CANADA
LAKE SUPERIOR
LAKE HURON
LAKE MICHIGAN
MICHIGAN
WISCONSIN
MINNESOTA
NORTH DAKOTA
SOUTH DAKOTA
MONTANA
WYOMING
NEBRASKA
IOWA
ILLINOIS
INDIANA
MISSOURI
COLORADO
GREAT PLAINS
ROCKY MOUNTAINS
Bighorn Mountains
Black Hills
Winnipeg
Thunder Bay
Duluth
Minneapolis
Milwaukee
Chicago
Indianapolis
Cincinnati
Des Moines
Omaha
Lincoln
Kansas City
Topeka
Denver
Colorado Springs
Springfield
Madison
Bismarck
Pierre
Cheyenne

238

231

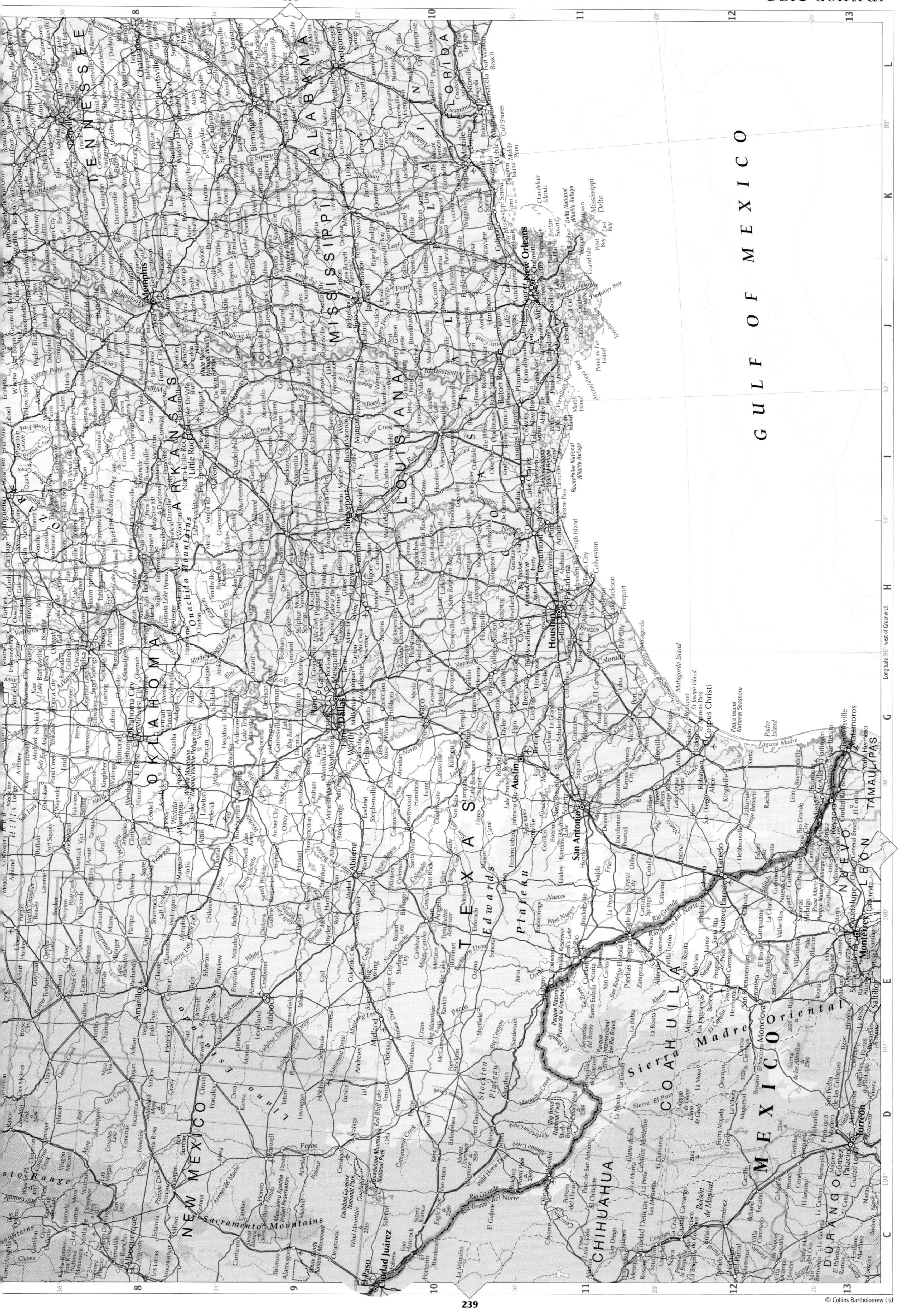
GULF OF MEXICO
TENNESSEE
ALABAMA
MISSISSIPPI
LOUISIANA
ARKANSAS
OKLAHOMA
TEXAS
NEW MEXICO
FLORIDA
MEXICO
COAHUILA
CHIHUAHUA
DURANGO
NUEVO LEÓN
TAMAULIPAS
Edwards Plateau
Sierra Madre Oriental
Llano Estacado
Ouachita Mountains
Sacramento Mountains
New Orleans
Houston
Dallas
San Antonio
Austin
Memphis
Monterrey
Longitude 96° west of Greenwich

243

MILES KILOMETRES

1:6 000 000

239

© Collins Bartholomew Ltd

236

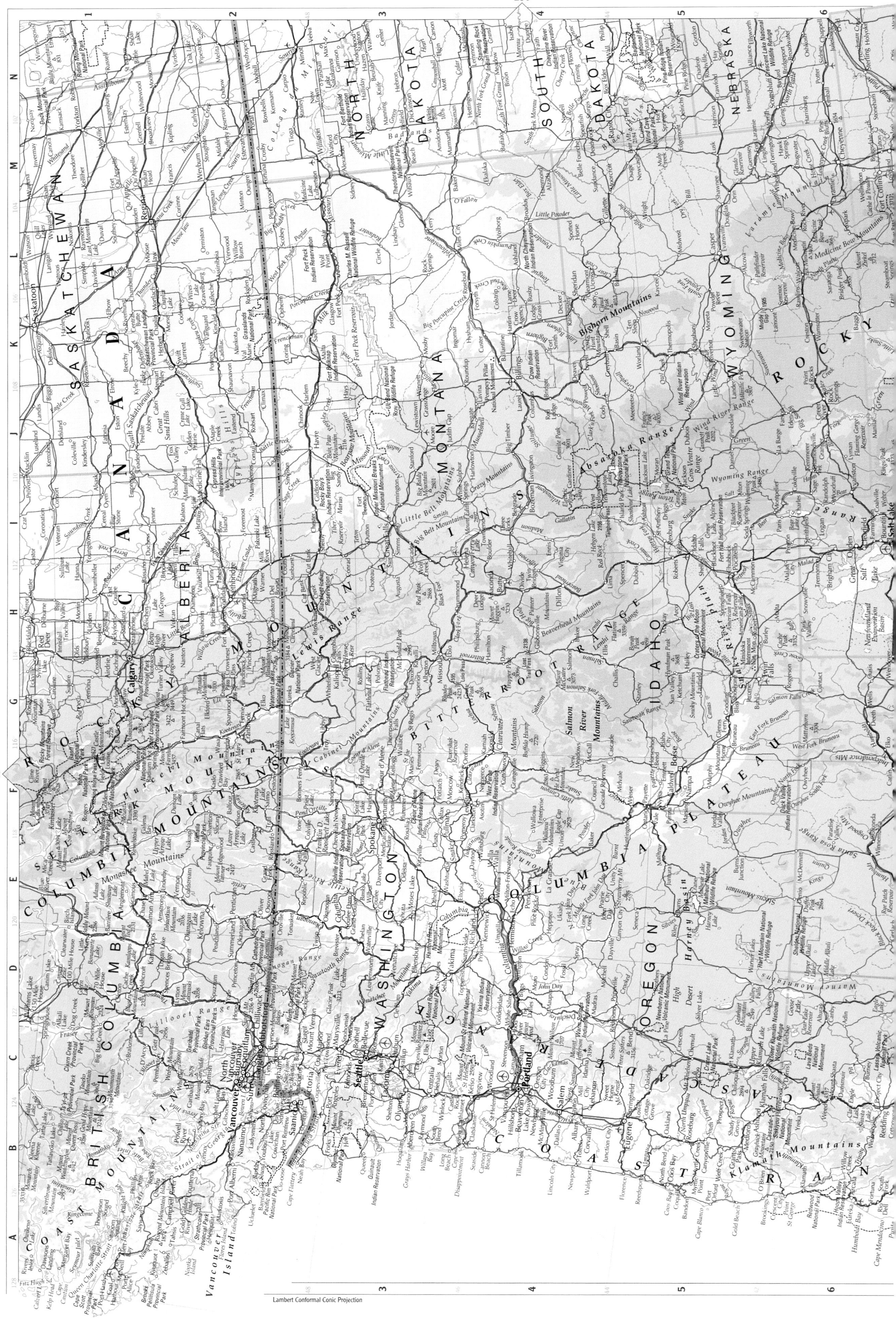

222

METRES
FEET
6000 19686
5000 16404
4000 13124
3000 9843
2000 6562
1000 3281
500 1640
200 656
0 0
LAND BELOW SEA LEVEL
200 656
2000 6562
4000 13124
6000 19686

Lambert Conformal Conic Projection

242
MILES
KILOMETRES
1:6 000 000
LOS ANGELES
1:60 000
SAN FRANCISCO
1:125 000
PACIFIC
OCEAN
NEVADA
UTAH
COLORADO
ARIZONA
NEW MEXICO
TEXAS
CALIFORNIA
BAJA CALIFORNIA
SONORA
CHIHUAHUA
MEXICO
Golfo de California

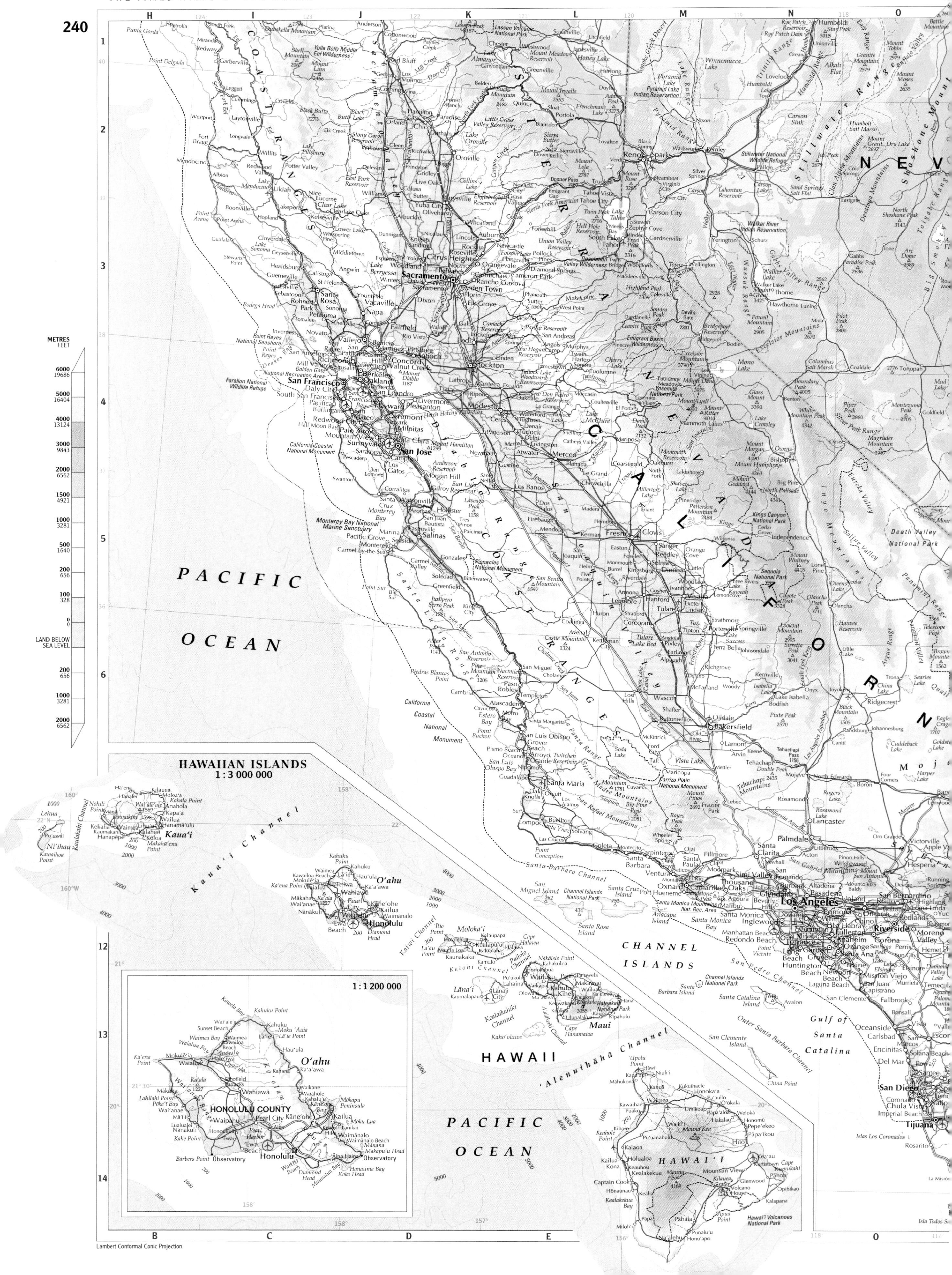

Lambert Conformal Conic Projection

PACIFIC OCEAN
COAST RANGES
SIERRA NEVADA
CALIFORNIA
NEV
HAWAIIAN ISLANDS
1 : 3 000 000
1 : 1 200 000
HONOLULU COUNTY
O'ahu
Kaua'i
Ni'ihau
Moloka'i
Lāna'i
Maui
HAWAII
HAWAI'I
Kaua'i Channel
'Alenuihāhā Channel
CHANNEL ISLANDS
Santa Barbara Channel
San Pedro Channel
Outer Santa Barbara Channel
Gulf of Santa Catalina
San Francisco
Oakland
San Jose
Sacramento
Stockton
Modesto
Fresno
Bakersfield
Los Angeles
San Diego
Tijuana
Reno
Honolulu
Monterey Bay National Marine Sanctuary
California Coastal National Monument
Yosemite National Park
Kings Canyon National Park
Sequoia National Park
Death Valley National Park
Channel Islands National Park
Hawai'i Volcanoes National Park
METRES
FEET
6000 19686
5000 16404
4000 13124
3000 9843
2000 6562
1500 4921
1000 3281
500 1640
200 656
100 328
0 0
LAND BELOW SEA LEVEL
200 656
1000 3281
2000 6562

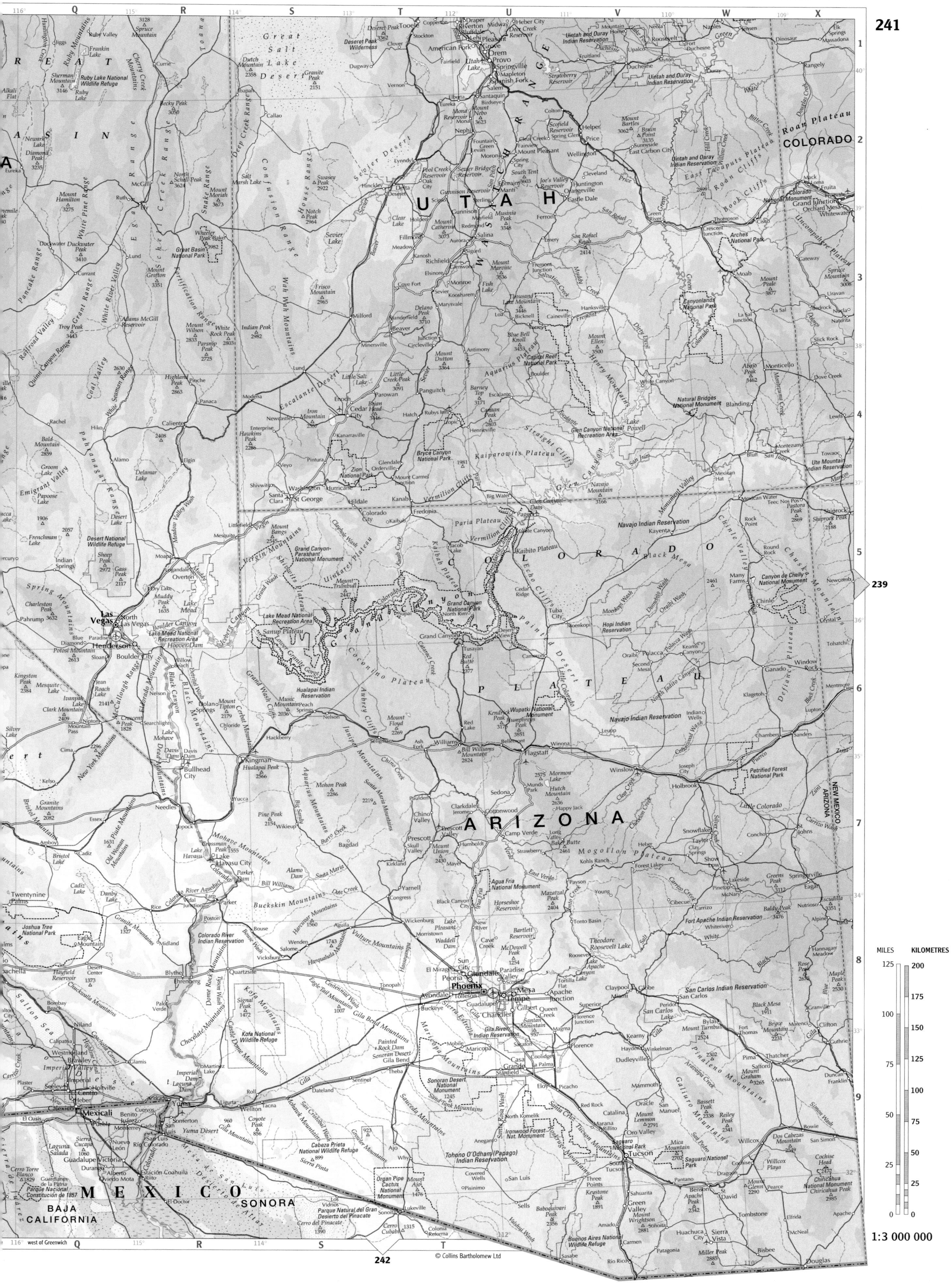
UTAH
ARIZONA
COLORADO
NEW MEXICO
ARIZONA
MEXICO
BAJA CALIFORNIA
SONORA
C O L O R A D O
P L A T E A U
GREAT BASIN
Great Salt Lake Desert
WASATCH RANGE
Salt Lake City
Provo
Orem
Springville
Spanish Fork
Nephi
Price
Moab
Green River
Richfield
Cedar City
St George
Kanab
Page
Las Vegas
North Las Vegas
Henderson
Boulder City
Kingman
Flagstaff
Williams
Winslow
Holbrook
Prescott
Sedona
Phoenix
Glendale
Mesa
Tempe
Chandler
Scottsdale
Tucson
Yuma
Mexicali
Calexico
El Centro
Nogales
Douglas
Bisbee
Sierra Vista
Grand Canyon
Grand Canyon National Park
Lake Mead
Lake Mead National Recreation Area
Lake Powell
Glen Canyon National Recreation Area
Canyonlands National Park
Arches National Park
Capitol Reef National Park
Bryce Canyon National Park
Zion National Park
Great Basin National Park
Petrified Forest National Park
Canyon de Chelly National Monument
Natural Bridges National Monument
Navajo Indian Reservation
Hopi Indian Reservation
Fort Apache Indian Reservation
San Carlos Indian Reservation
Tohono O'Odham (Papago) Indian Reservation
Saguaro National Park
Organ Pipe Cactus National Monument
Kofa National Wildlife Refuge
Cabeza Prieta National Wildlife Refuge
Joshua Tree National Park
Salton Sea
Mogollon Plateau
Kaibab Plateau
Coconino Plateau
Painted Desert
Black Mesa
Colorado
Gila
Salt
Sonoran Desert National Monument
Yuma Desert
Theodore Roosevelt Lake
MILES
KILOMETRES
1:3 000 000

239

242

© Collins Bartholomew Ltd

Lambert Conformal Conic Projection

239
242
250
ARIZONA
NEW MEXICO
UNITE
SONORA
CHIHUAHUA
SINALOA
DURANGO
NAYARIT
JALISCO
COLIMA
ZACATEC
BAJA CALIFORNIA
BAJA CALIFORNIA SUR
Golfo de California
SIERRA MADRE OCCIDENTAL
PACI
Tropic of Cancer
Tijuana
Mexicali
Ensenada
Yuma
Tucson
Nogales
Hermosillo
Guaymas
Ciudad Obregón
Los Mochis
Culiacán
Mazatlán
Durango
Torreón
Chihuahua
Ciudad Juárez
El Paso
Las Cruces
La Paz
Santa Rosalía
Tepic
Puerto Vallarta
Islas Marías
Guadalupe
CENTRAL AMERICA
CONTINUATION AT THE SAME SCALE
BELIZE
GUATEMALA
HONDURAS
EL SALVADOR
NICARAGUA
COSTA RICA
PANAMA
COLOMBIA
TEGUCIGALPA
MANAGUA
SAN JOSÉ
PANAMÁ
San Pedro Sula
León
Granada
Colón
David
Gulf of Honduras
Golfo de Fonseca
Lago de Nicaragua
MOSQUITIA
COSTA DE MOSQUITOS
CARIBBEAN SEA
PACIFIC OCEAN
Golfo de Panamá
Golfo de los Mosquitos
Golfo de Chiriquí
METRES
FEET
6000 19686
5000 16404
4000 13124
3000 9843
2000 6562
1000 3281
500 1640
200 656
0 0
LAND BELOW SEA LEVEL
200 656
2000 6562
4000 13124
6000 19686

237
237
UNITED STATES OF AMERICA
TEXAS
LOUISIANA
MISSISSIPPI
ALABAMA
FLORIDA
Dallas
Fort Worth
Austin
San Antonio
Houston
Galveston
Corpus Christi
Laredo
Baton Rouge
New Orleans
Mobile
Pensacola
Jackson
Shreveport
GULF OF MEXICO
Tropic of Cancer
Bahía de Campeche
Yucatan Channel
NUEVO LEÓN
Monterrey
TAMAULIPAS
Matamoros
SAN LUIS POTOSÍ
Tampico
VERACRUZ
Veracruz
HIDALGO
QUERÉTARO
MÉXICO
Puebla
PUEBLA
TLAXCALA
MORELOS
GUERRERO
Acapulco
OAXACA
Oaxaca
SIERRA MADRE DEL SUR
Istmo de Tehuantepec
Golfo de Tehuantepec
TABASCO
Villahermosa
CHIAPAS
CAMPECHE
Campeche
YUCATÁN
Mérida
QUINTANA ROO
Cancún
BELIZE
BELMOPAN
GUATEMALA
HONDURAS
EL SALVADOR
SAN SALVADOR
Gulf of Honduras
PACIFIC OCEAN
Longitude 100° west of Greenwich
MILES
KILOMETRES
1:6 600 000

© Collins Bartholomew Ltd

242

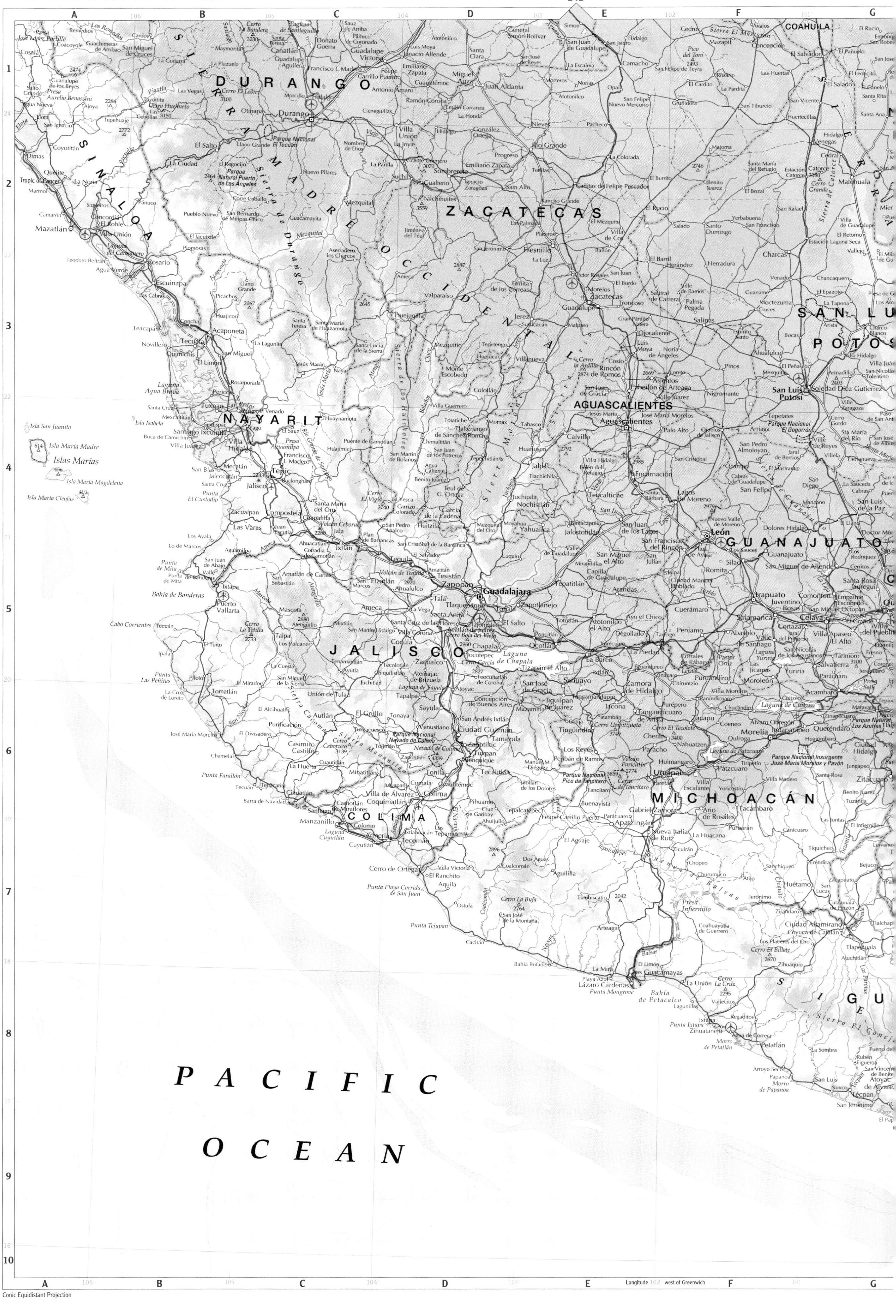

DURANGO
SINALOA
SIERRA MADRE OCCIDENTAL
ZACATECAS
NAYARIT
AGUASCALIENTES
JALISCO
GUANAJUATO
COLIMA
MICHOACÁN
SAN LUIS POTOSÍ
COAHUILA
PACIFIC OCEAN
Durango
Mazatlán
Zacatecas
Aguascalientes
Tepic
Guadalajara
León
San Luis Potosí
Colima
Morelia
Uruapan
Puerto Vallarta
Manzanillo
Islas Marías
Bahía de Banderas
Laguna de Chapala
Tropic of Cancer
A
B
C
D
E
F
G
1
2
3
4
5
6
7
8
9
10

METRES / FEET

METRES	FEET
6000	19686
5000	16404
4000	13124
3000	9843
2000	6562
1500	4921
1000	3281
500	1640
200	656
100	328
0	0
LAND BELOW SEA LEVEL	
200	656
1000	3281
2000	6562
4000	13124

Longitude 102 west of Greenwich

Conic Equidistant Projection

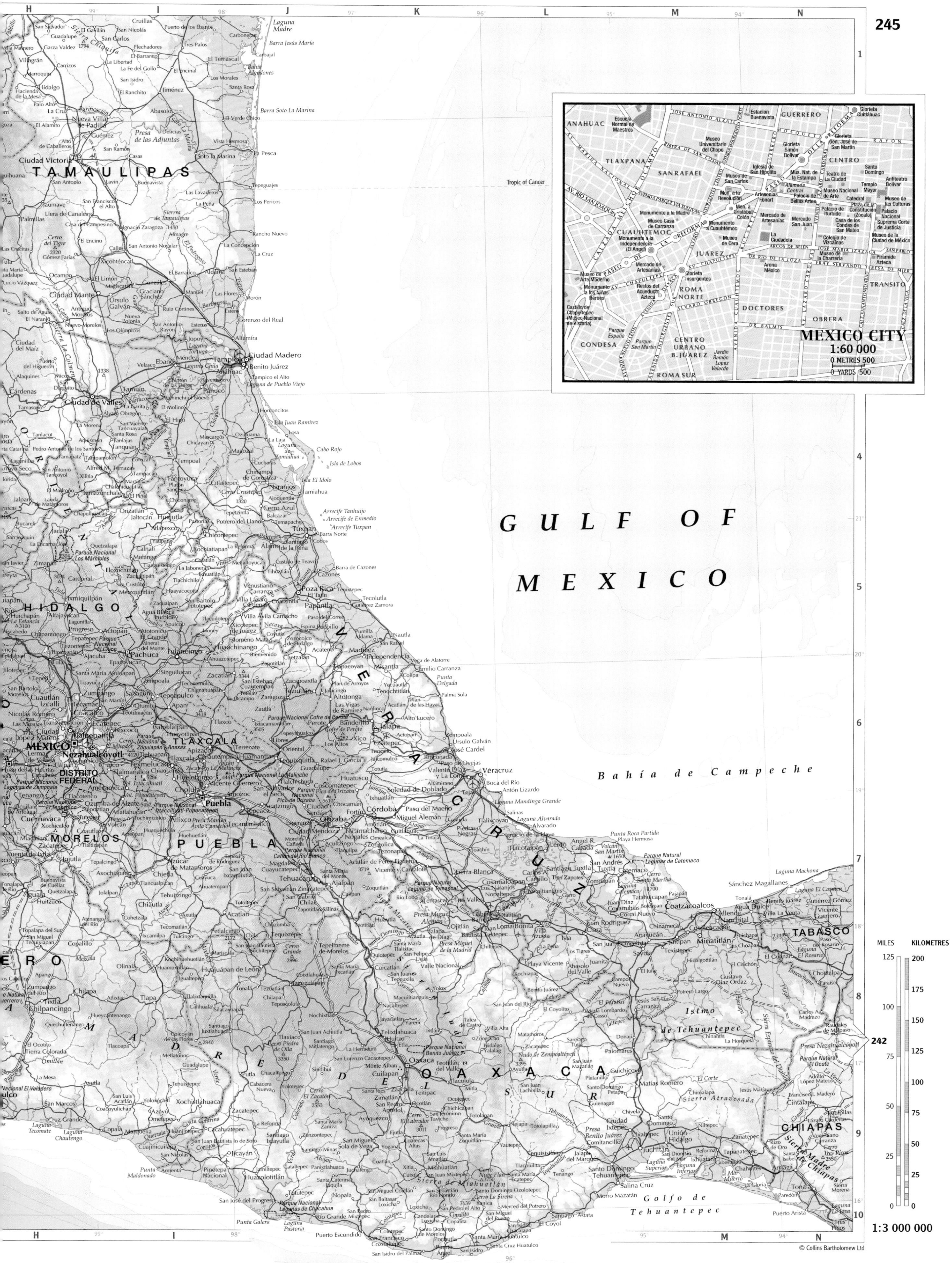
GULF OF MEXICO
Bahía de Campeche
Golfo de Tehuantepec
Tropic of Cancer
TAMAULIPAS
HIDALGO
VERACRUZ
PUEBLA
TLAXCALA
MORELOS
DISTRITO FEDERAL
MÉXICO
OAXACA
CHIAPAS
TABASCO
SIERRA MADRE DEL SUR
Istmo de Tehuantepec
Ciudad Victoria
Ciudad Madero
Tampico
Ciudad Mante
Ciudad de Valles
Poza Rica
Tuxpan
Pachuca
Jalapa
Veracruz
Puebla
Orizaba
Córdoba
Cuernavaca
Chilpancingo
Oaxaca
Coatzacoalcos
Minatitlán
Juchitán
Salina Cruz
Puerto Escondido
Santa María Huatulco
Laguna Madre
Cabo Rojo
Laguna de Tamiahua
Laguna de Términos
MEXICO CITY
1:60 000
0 METRES 500
0 YARDS 500
ANAHUAC
TLAXPANA
SAN RAFAEL
GUERRERO
CENTRO
CUAUHTEMOC
JUAREZ
ROMA NORTE
DOCTORES
OBRERA
CONDESA
CENTRO URBANO B.JUAREZ
ROMA SUR
TRANSITO
MILES
KILOMETRES
1:3 000 000
242

© Collins Bartholomew Ltd

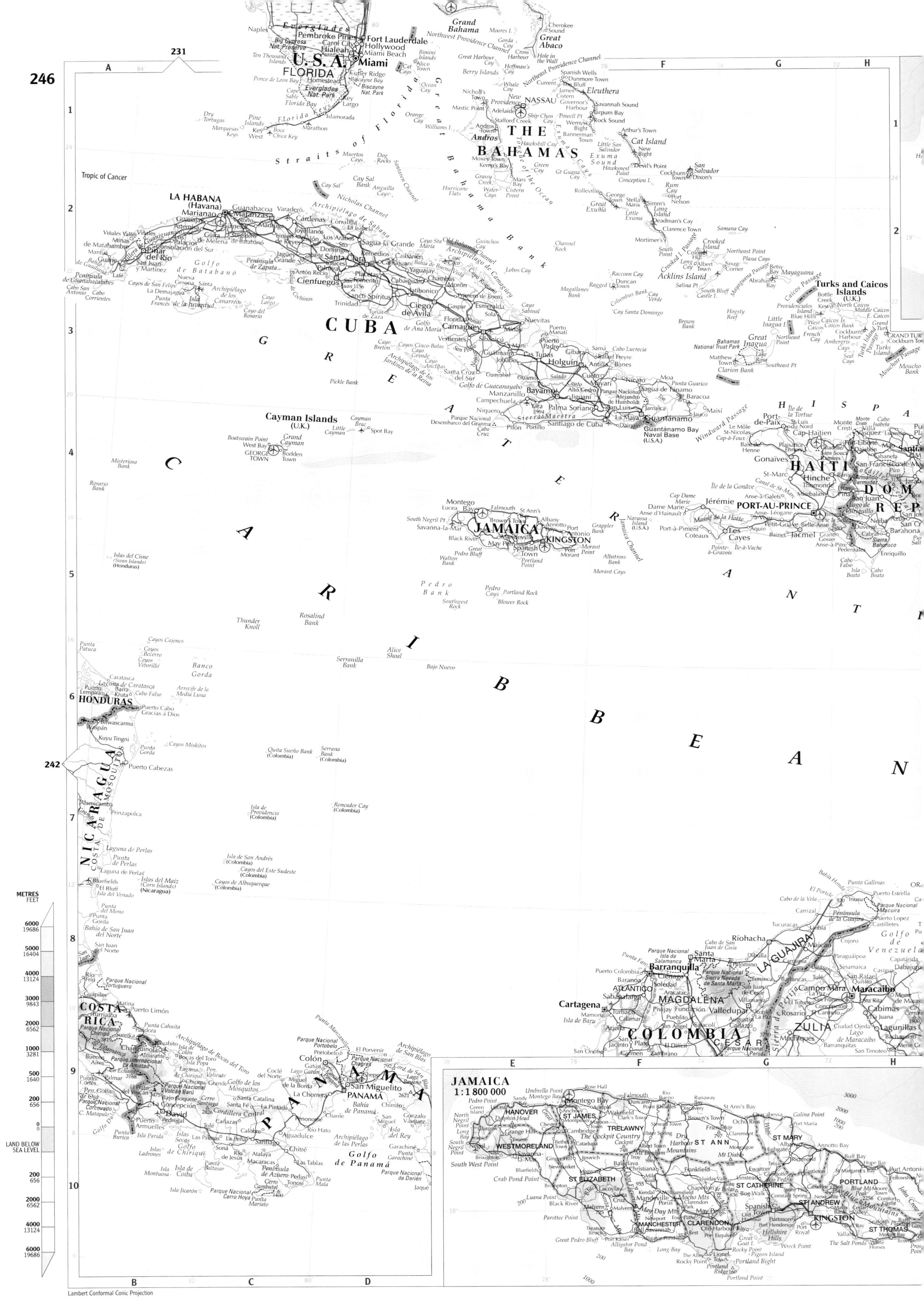
CUBA
LA HABANA
(Havana)
THE BAHAMAS
NASSAU
U.S.A.
FLORIDA
Miami
Fort Lauderdale
Hollywood
Hialeah
Miami Beach
Pembroke Pines
Carol City
Naples
Everglades
Grand Bahama
Great Abaco
Eleuthera
Andros
Cat Island
San Salvador
Acklins Island
Mayaguana
Turks and Caicos Islands
(U.K.)
Great Inagua
Straits of Florida
Great Bahama Bank
Tropic of Cancer
Pinar del Río
Matanzas
Cárdenas
Santa Clara
Cienfuegos
Sancti Spíritus
Ciego de Ávila
Camagüey
Las Tunas
Holguín
Bayamo
Manzanillo
Santiago de Cuba
Guantánamo
Guantánamo Bay Naval Base
(U.S.A.)
Cayman Islands
(U.K.)
Grand Cayman
GEORGE TOWN
Little Cayman
Cayman Brac
JAMAICA
KINGSTON
Montego Bay
Spanish Town
Mandeville
HAITI
PORT-AU-PRINCE
Cap-Haïtien
Gonaïves
Jacmel
Les Cayes
Jérémie
Windward Passage
DOM. REP.
CARIBBEAN
Pedro Bank
Rosalind Bank
Thunder Knoll
Serranilla Bank
Alice Shoal
Bajo Nuevo
Quita Sueño Bank
(Colombia)
Serrana Bank
(Colombia)
Roncador Cay
(Colombia)
Isla de Providencia
(Colombia)
Isla de San Andrés
(Colombia)
Islas del Maíz
(Corn Islands)
(Nicaragua)
HONDURAS
NICARAGUA
Puerto Cabezas
Bluefields
COSTA RICA
Puerto Limón
PANAMA
PANAMÁ
Colón
San Miguelito
David
Golfo de Panamá
COLOMBIA
Barranquilla
Cartagena
Santa Marta
Riohacha
LA GUAJIRA
MAGDALENA
ATLÁNTICO
CESAR
Valledupar
ZULIA
Maracaibo
Golfo de Venezuela
JAMAICA
1:1 800 000
HANOVER
ST JAMES
TRELAWNY
ST ANN
ST MARY
WESTMORELAND
ST ELIZABETH
MANCHESTER
CLARENDON
ST CATHERINE
ST ANDREW
PORTLAND
ST THOMAS
KINGSTON
Montego Bay
Mandeville
Spanish Town
Port Antonio
METRES
FEET
6000
19686
5000
16404
4000
13124
3000
9843
2000
6562
1000
3281
500
1640
200
656
0
0
LAND BELOW SEA LEVEL
200
656
2000
6562
4000
13124
6000
19686

Lambert Conformal Conic Projection

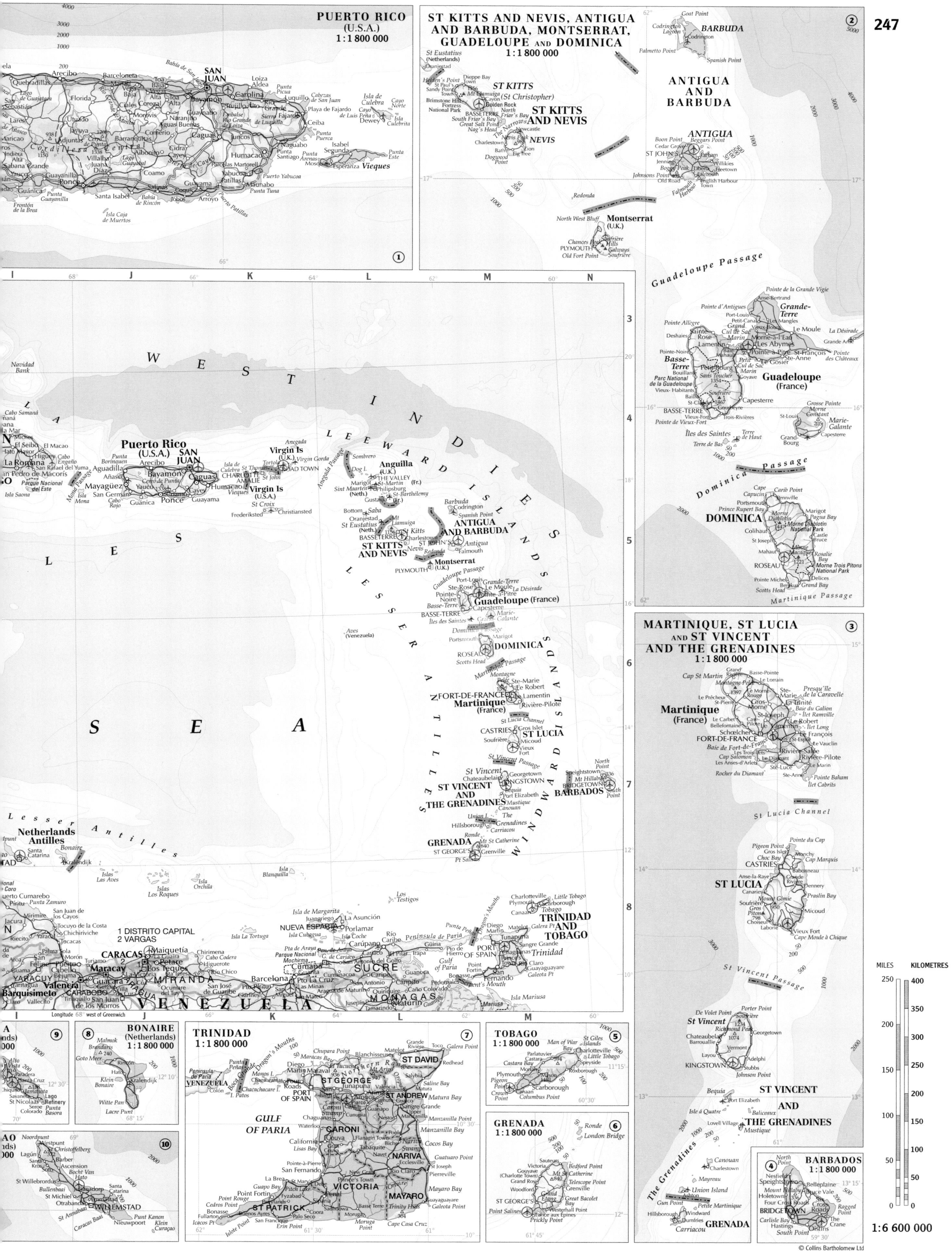
PUERTO RICO (U.S.A.) 1:1 800 000
SAN JUAN
Bayamón
Caguas
Ponce
Vieques
ST KITTS AND NEVIS, ANTIGUA AND BARBUDA, MONTSERRAT, GUADELOUPE AND DOMINICA 1:1 800 000
ST KITTS (St Christopher)
ST KITTS AND NEVIS
NEVIS
BASSETERRE
ANTIGUA AND BARBUDA
BARBUDA
ANTIGUA
ST JOHN'S
Montserrat (U.K.)
PLYMOUTH
Guadeloupe Passage
Grande-Terre
Basse-Terre
Guadeloupe (France)
BASSE-TERRE
Marie-Galante
Îles des Saintes
Dominica Passage
DOMINICA
ROSEAU
Martinique Passage
W E S T I N D I E S
L E E W A R D I S L A N D S
L E S S E R A N T I L L E S
W I N D W A R D I S L A N D S
Puerto Rico (U.S.A.)
Virgin Is (U.K.)
ROAD TOWN
Virgin Is (U.S.A.)
CHARLOTTE AMALIE
Anguilla (U.K.)
THE VALLEY
Aves (Venezuela)
FORT-DE-FRANCE
Martinique (France)
CASTRIES
ST LUCIA
ST VINCENT AND THE GRENADINES
KINGSTOWN
BARBADOS
BRIDGETOWN
GRENADA
ST GEORGE'S
TRINIDAD AND TOBAGO
PORT OF SPAIN
Netherlands Antilles
Lesser Antilles
S E A
CARACAS
Maracay
Valencia
Barquisimeto
Barcelona
Cumaná
SUCRE
MONAGAS
MIRANDA
V E N E Z U E L A
1 DISTRITO CAPITAL
2 VARGAS
Isla de Margarita
MARTINIQUE, ST LUCIA AND ST VINCENT AND THE GRENADINES 1:1 800 000
St Lucia Channel
St Vincent Passage
BONAIRE (Netherlands) 1:1 800 000
Kralendijk
TRINIDAD 1:1 800 000
GULF OF PARIA
Dragon's Mouths
Serpent's Mouth
TOBAGO 1:1 800 000
Scarborough
GRENADA 1:1 800 000
BARBADOS 1:1 800 000
WILLEMSTAD
MILES
KILOMETRES
1:6 600 000

NORTH AMERICA
Gulf of Mexico
Yucatan Channel
Cuba
Greater A
Jamaica
CARIBBEA
Bahía de Campeche
Yucatán
Golfo de California
Baja California
Sierra Madre del Sur
Golfo de Tehuantepec
Lago de Nicaragua
Barranquilla
Cartagena
Golfo del Darién
Montería
Golfo de Panamá
Medellín
Ibagué
Bogo
COLOM
Cali
Neiva
Pasto
Isla de Coco
Isla de Malpelo (Colombia)
Islas Revillagigedo
Île Clipperton
Tropic of Cancer
Esmeraldas
Quito
Manta
ECUADOR
Guayaquil
Golfo de Guayaquil
Cuenca
Machala
Islas Galápagos (Ecuador)
Piura
Chiclayo
Tarapoto
Trujillo
Pucallpa
PERU
Callao
Lima
Huancayo
Ica
PACIFIC
OCEAN
Equator
Islas de los Desventurados (Chile)
Isla San Félix
Isla San Ambrosio
Îles Marquises
Hiva Oa
Îles du Désappointement
Isla Sala y Gómez
Isla de Pascua (Easter Island) (Rapa Nui)
Archipiélago Juan Fernández (Chile)
Concepción
Valdivia
Puerto Montt
Isla de Chiloé
Archipiélago de los Chonos
Golfo de Penas
Îles du Roi Georges
Archipel des Tuamotu
Hao
Rangiroa
Tahiti
Archipel de la Société
Mururoa
Îles Gambier
Henderson Island
Pitcairn Island
OCEANIA
Îles Australes
Tropic of Capricorn
A
B
C
D
E
1
2
3
4
5
6
7

F
G
H
I
J
1
2
3
4
5
6
7
Anguilla
Virgin Is
Barbuda
Antigua
St Kitts-Nevis
Montserrat
Guadeloupe
Dominica
Martinique
St Lucia
Barbados
Grenada
St Vincent and the Grenadines
Tobago
Trinidad
Lesser Antilles
Caracas
Cumaná
Ciudad Bolívar
Orinoco
VENEZUELA
Guiana Highlands
Georgetown
GUYANA
Paramaribo
SURINAME
Cayenne
French Guiana
Boa Vista
Branco
Macapá
Mouths of the Amazon
Negro
Manaus
Amazonas (Amazon)
Santarém
Xingu
Belém
Carauari
Purus
Madeira
Tapajós
Iriri
São Luís
Represa Tucuruí
Parnaíba
Marabá
Tocantins
Teresina
Fortaleza
Porto Velho
BRAZIL
Araguaína
Natal
João Pessoa
Recife
Barragem de Sobradinho
Juàzeiro
Floresta
Maceió
Aracaju
Palmas
Guaporé
Trinidad
Mamoré
BOLIVIA
Santa Cruz
Sucre
Cuiabá
Paraguai
Araguaia
Paraná
Represa Serra da Mesa
São Francisco
Brasília
Goiânia
Salvador
Ilhéus
Tarija
Campo Grande
PARAGUAY
Uberaba
Patos de Minas
Teófilo Otôni
Araçatuba
Pedro Juan Caballero
Ribeirão Preto
Belo Horizonte
Vitória
San Salvador de Jujuy
Gran Chaco
Maringá
Campinas
San Miguel de Tucumán
Asunción
Coronel Oviedo
São Paulo
Santos
Rio de Janeiro
Formosa
Resistencia
Iguaçu
Encarnación
Curitiba
Corrientes
Posadas
Salinas de Ambargasta
Florianópolis
Laguna Mar Chiquita
Santa Maria
Santa Fé
Concórdia
Lagoa dos Patos
Porto Alegre
Paraná
Rosario
Paysandú
San Luis
URUGUAY
Rio Grande
Buenos Aires
Montevideo
ARGENTINA
La Plata
Río de la Plata
Pampas
Mar del Plata
Bahía Blanca
Negro
Viedma
Golfo San Matías
Trelew
Comodoro Rivadavia
Golfo de San Jorge
Falkland Islands (U.K.)
Stanley
Isla de los Estados
Cabo de Hornos
Drake Passage
Shag Rocks
South Georgia (U.K.)
South Shetland Islands
Antarctic Peninsula
South Orkney Islands
South Sandwich Islands (U.K.)
Traversay Islands
Candlemas Island
Saunders Island
Montagu Island
Bristol Island
Southern Thule
Arquipélago da Madeira
Islas Canarias
Gran Canaria
Santo Antão
Ilhas do Cabo Verde
Boa Vista
Santiago
Tropic of Cancer
Sénégal
Niger
São Pedro e São Paulo (Brazil)
Atol das Rocas
Fernando de Noronha (Brazil)
AFRICA
Gulf of Guinea
Equator
Ascension
ATLANTIC OCEAN
Ilha da Trindade (Brazil)
Ilhas Martin Vaz (Brazil)
St Helena
Tropic of Capricorn
Tristan da Cunha
Orange
Cape of Good Hope

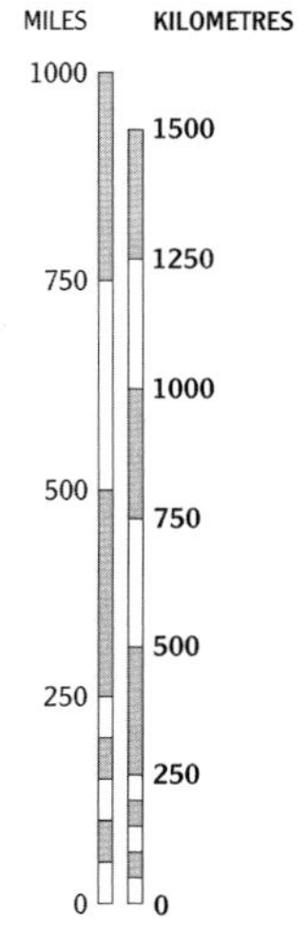

MILES
KILOMETRES
1000
750
500
250
0
1500
1250
1000
750
500
250
0

1:27 000 000

Administrative regions numbered on the map:

COLOMBIA
1. SANTAFÉ DE BOGOTÁ (C3)

ECUADOR
2. BOLÍVAR (B5)
3. CHIMBORAZO (B5)
4. TUNGURAHUA (B5)
5. ZAMORA-CHINCHIPE (B5)

VENEZUELA
1. DISTRITO CAPITAL (E2)
2. VARGAS (E2)

GALÁPAGOS ISLANDS
(Ecuador)
AT THE SAME SCALE

ISLAS GALÁPAGOS

METRES
FEET

6000
19686

5000
16404

4000
13124

3000
9843

2000
6562

1000
3281

500
1640

200
656

0

LAND BELOW
SEA LEVEL

200
656

2000
6562

4000
13124

6000
19686

Lambert Azimuthal Equal Area Projection

247

ATLANTIC
OCEAN
GRENADA
TRINIDAD AND TOBAGO
PORT OF SPAIN
Tobago
Trinidad
NUEVA ESPARTA
SUCRE
MONAGAS
ANZOÁTEGUI
DELTA AMACURO
Ciudad Guayana
Ciudad Bolívar
BOLÍVAR
GUYANA
GEORGETOWN
SURINAME
PARAMARIBO
French Guiana
CAYENNE
Serra Tumucumaque
AMAPÁ
Macapá
Equator
Mouths of the Amazon
Ilha de Marajó
RORAIMA
Boa Vista
Pakaraima Mountains
Manaus
AMAZONAS
BRAZIL
Santarém
Óbidos
Altamira
Tucuruí
Itaituba
PARÁ
Porto Velho
RONDÔNIA
MATO GROSSO
Humaitá
Serra do Cachimbo
Serra dos Carajás
MILES
KILOMETRES
1:7 500 000
Longitude 64° west of Greenwich

254

253

© Collins Bartholomew Ltd

250

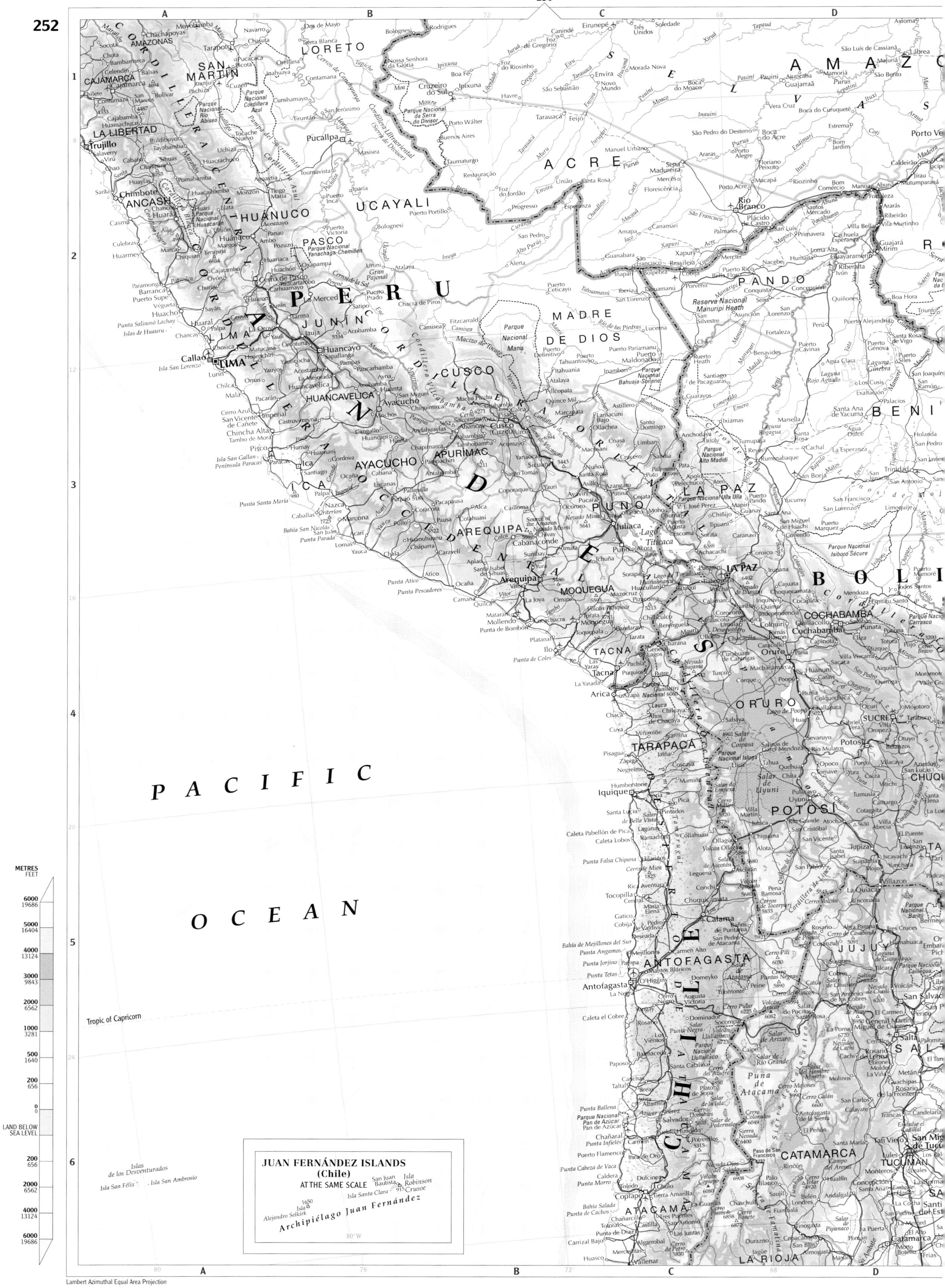

Lambert Azimuthal Equal Area Projection

251

PARÁ
TOCANTINS
MATO GROSSO
BRAZIL
Planalto do Mato Grosso
GOIÁS
DISTRITO FEDERAL
BRASÍLIA
Goiânia
MINAS GERAIS
MATO GROSSO DO SUL
Campo Grande
Cuiabá
Corumbá
SÃO PAULO
São Paulo
Campinas
Santos
Tropic of Capricorn
PARANÁ
Curitiba
SANTA CATARINA
Florianópolis
RIO GRANDE DO SUL
PARAGUAY
ASUNCIÓN
MISIONES
CORRIENTES
Corrientes
CHACO
FORMOSA
SANTA FE
ARGENTINA
SANTA CRUZ
Pantanal
Parque Indígena do Xingu
Ilha do Bananal
ATLANTIC OCEAN
Longitude 60° west of Greenwich

254

MILES KILOMETRES
1:7 500 000

258

© Collins Bartholomew Ltd

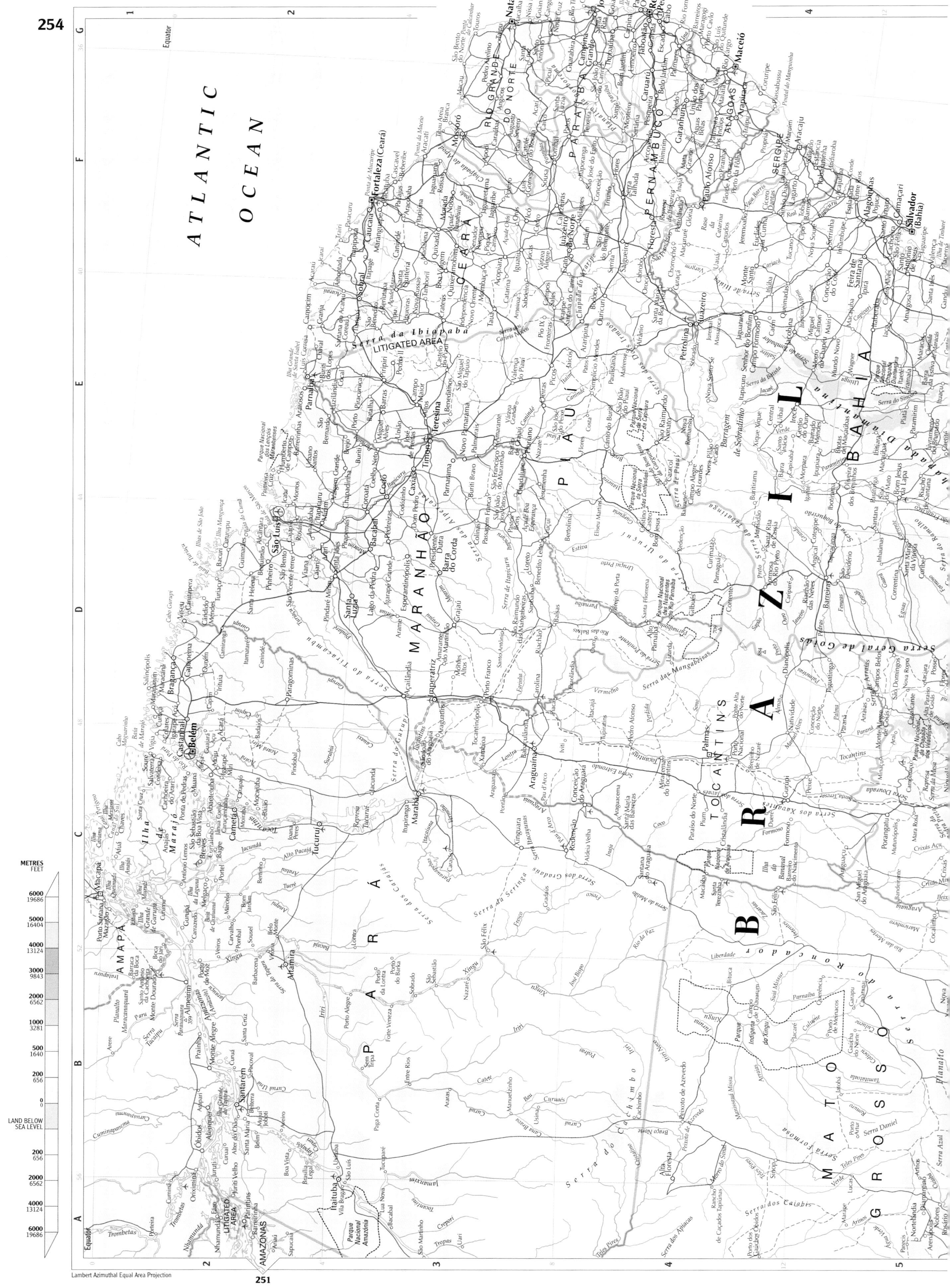
ATLANTIC
OCEAN
Equator
BRAZIL
PARÁ
MARANHÃO
PIAUÍ
CEARÁ
RIO GRANDE DO NORTE
PARAÍBA
PERNAMBUCO
ALAGOAS
SERGIPE
BAHIA
TOCANTINS
MATO GROSSO
AMAPÁ
AMAZONAS
Ilha de Marajó
LITIGATED AREA
Belém
São Luís
Fortaleza (Ceará)
Natal
João Pessoa
Recife (Pernambuco)
Maceió
Aracaju
Salvador (Bahia)
Teresina
Macapá
Santarém
Marabá
Imperatriz
Palmas
Serra da Ibiapaba
Serra Geral de Goiás
Serra do Roncador
METRES
FEET
6000
19686
5000
16404
4000
13124
3000
9843
2000
6562
1000
3281
500
1640
200
656
0
0
LAND BELOW SEA LEVEL
200
656
2000
6562
4000
13124
6000
19686

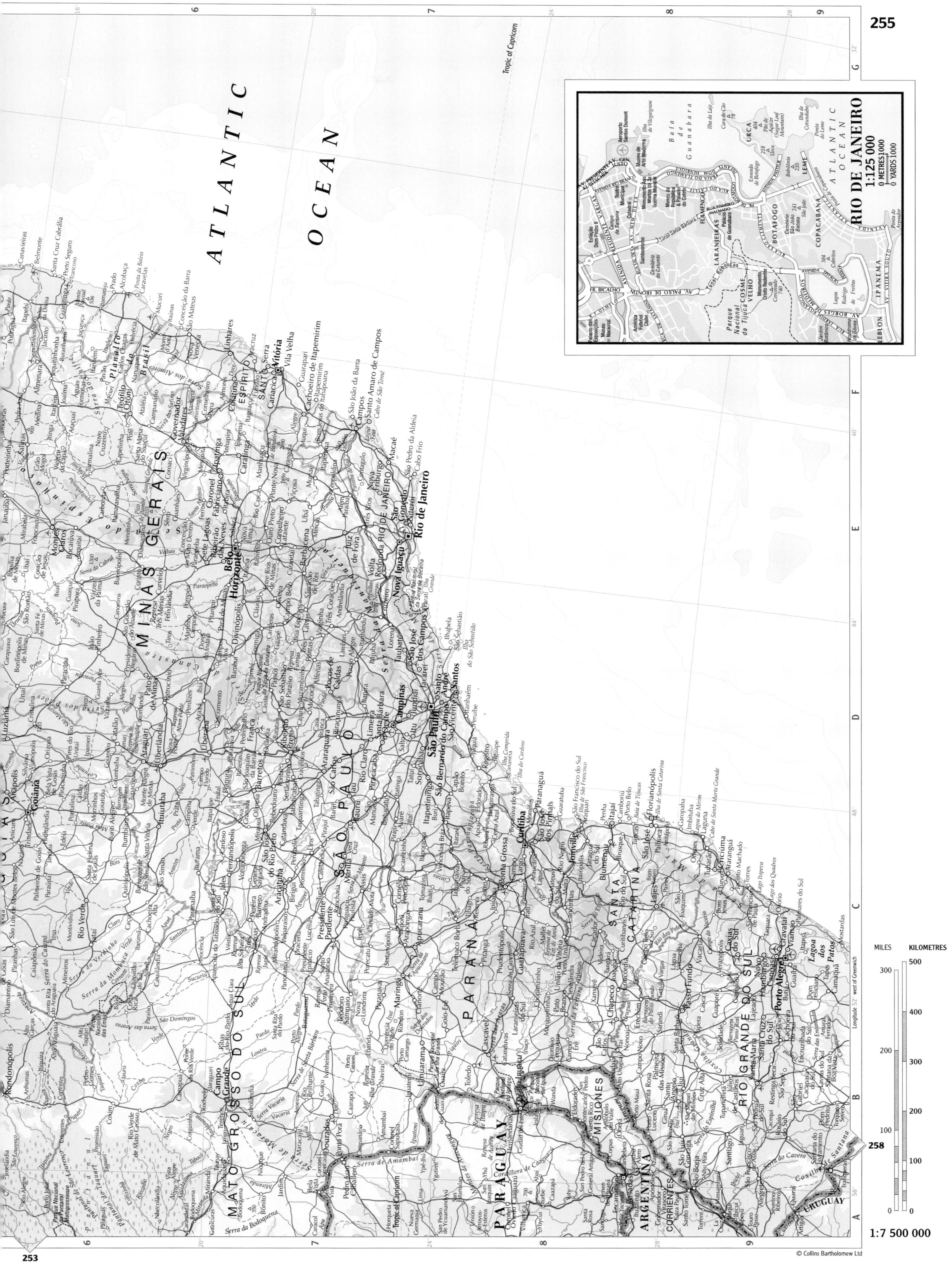
ATLANTIC
OCEAN
Tropic of Capricorn
RIO DE JANEIRO
1:125 000
MINAS GERAIS
SÃO PAULO
PARANÁ
SANTA CATARINA
RIO GRANDE DO SUL
MATO GROSSO DO SUL
RIO DE JANEIRO
ESPÍRITO SANTO
MISIONES
CORRIENTES
ARGENTINA
PARAGUAY
URUGUAY
Belo Horizonte
Rio de Janeiro
São Paulo
Curitiba
Porto Alegre
Vitória
Goiânia
Campo Grande
Florianópolis
Lagoa dos Patos
MILES
KILOMETRES
258
253
1:7 500 000

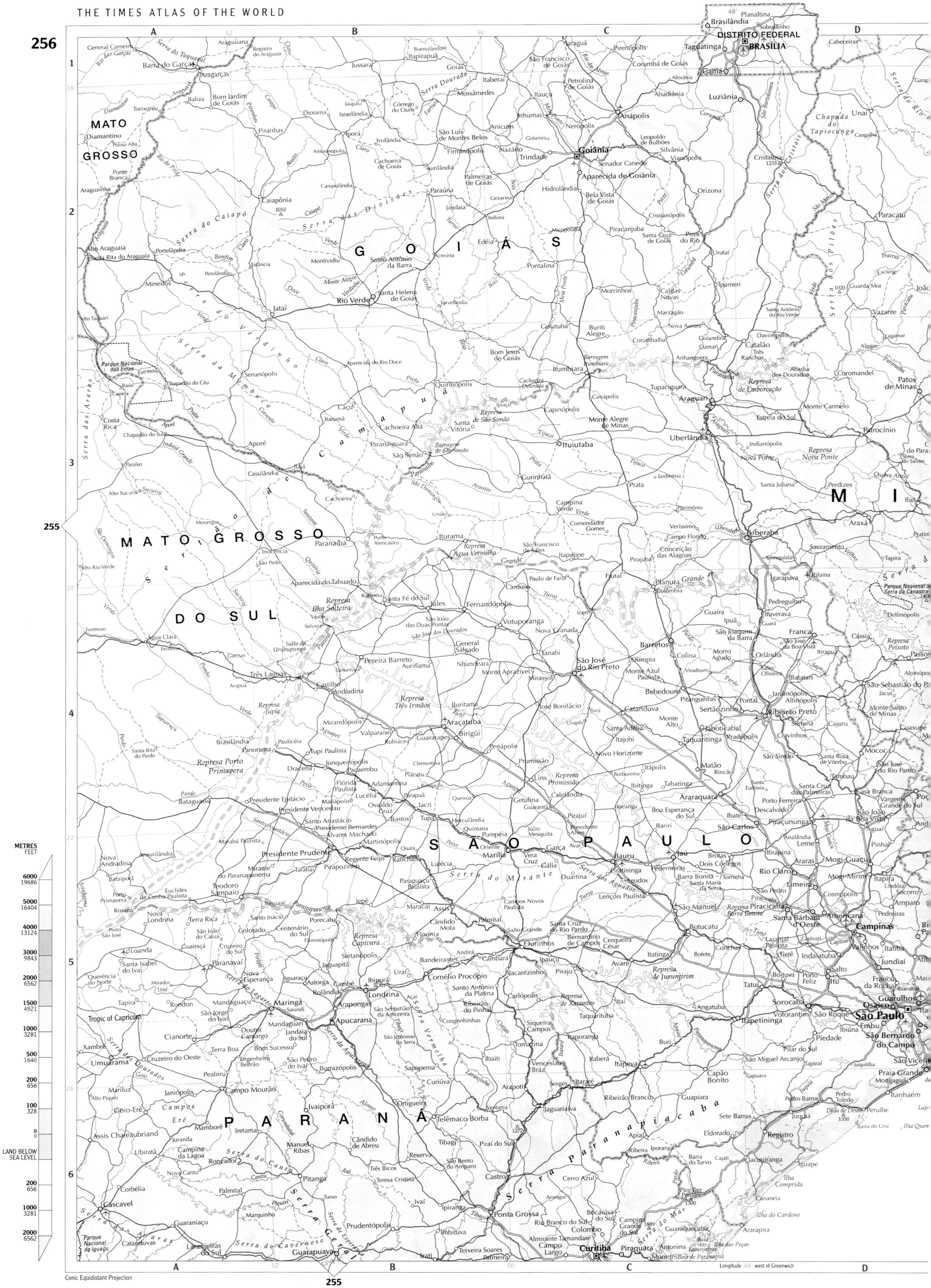
GOIÁS
MATO GROSSO
MATO GROSSO DO SUL
SÃO PAULO
PARANÁ
MI
DISTRITO FEDERAL
BRASÍLIA
Goiânia
Anápolis
Uberlândia
Uberaba
Ribeirão Preto
Campinas
São Paulo
Curitiba
Londrina
Maringá
Ponta Grossa
Bauru
Marília
Presidente Prudente
Araçatuba
São José do Rio Preto
Rio Verde
Jataí
Catalão
Araguari
Sorocaba
Guarulhos
Osasco
Serra do Caiapó
Serra das Divisões
Serra do Mirante
Serra Geral
Serra do Mar
Serra Paranapiacaba
Tropic of Capricorn
METRES
FEET
6000
19686
5000
16404
4000
13124
3000
9843
2000
6562
1500
4921
1000
3281
500
1640
200
656
100
328
0
0
LAND BELOW SEA LEVEL
200
656
1000
3281
2000
6562
Longitude 48 west of Greenwich

Conic Equidistant Projection

255

257

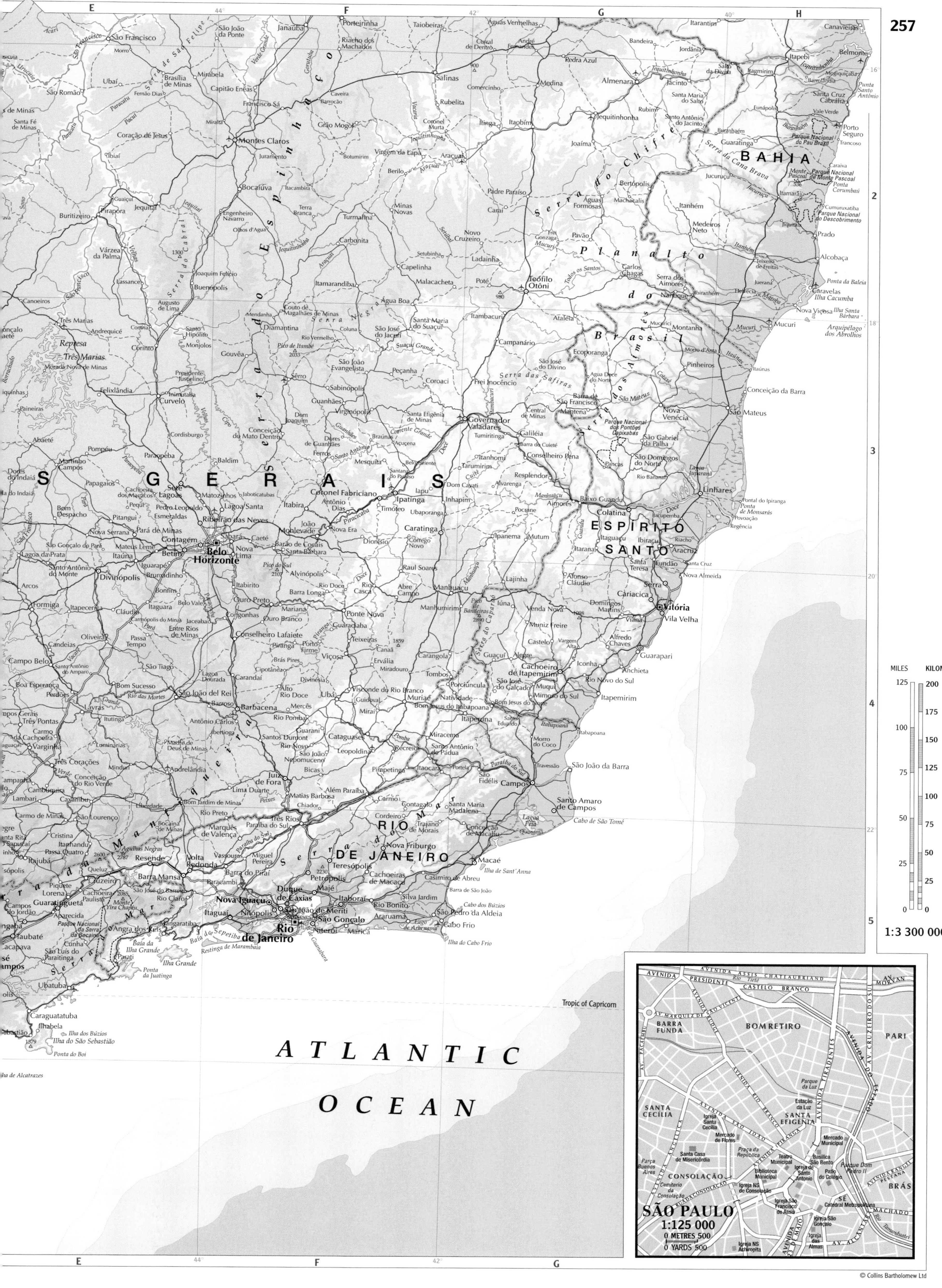
BAHIA
MINAS GERAIS
ESPÍRITO SANTO
RIO DE JANEIRO
ATLANTIC OCEAN
Tropic of Capricorn
Belo Horizonte
Vitória
Rio de Janeiro
Montes Claros
Governador Valadares
Teófilo Otôni
Juiz de Fora
Campos
Niterói
Nova Iguaçu
Duque de Caxias
Petrópolis
Nova Friburgo
Vila Velha
Cariacica
Serra
Colatina
Linhares
São Mateus
Ipatinga
Coronel Fabriciano
Contagem
Betim
Divinópolis
Barbacena
São João del Rei
Volta Redonda
Barra Mansa
Resende
Ubatuba
Caraguatatuba
Ilhabela
Angra dos Reis
Parati
Cabo Frio
Macaé
Porto Seguro
Caravelas
Arquipélago dos Abrolhos
Serra do Espinhaço
Serra da Mantiqueira
Serra do Mar
Planalto do Brasil
Serra do Chifre
Serra dos Aimorés
Cabo de São Tomé
Ilha Grande
Ilha de São Sebastião
MILES
KILOMETRES
1:3 300 000
SÃO PAULO
1:125 000
0 METRES 500
0 YARDS 500
BOM RETIRO
BARRA FUNDA
PARI
SANTA CECÍLIA
SANTA EFIGÊNIA
CONSOLAÇÃO
BRÁS
SÉ
Catedral Metropolitana
Parque da Luz
Estação da Luz
Mercado Municipal
Praça da República
Teatro Municipal
Biblioteca Municipal
Parque Dom Pedro II
AVENIDA PRESIDENTE CASTELO BRANCO
AVENIDA ASSIS CHATEAUBRIAND
AVENIDA SÃO JOÃO
AVENIDA RIO BRANCO
AVENIDA TIRADENTES
AVENIDA IPIRANGA

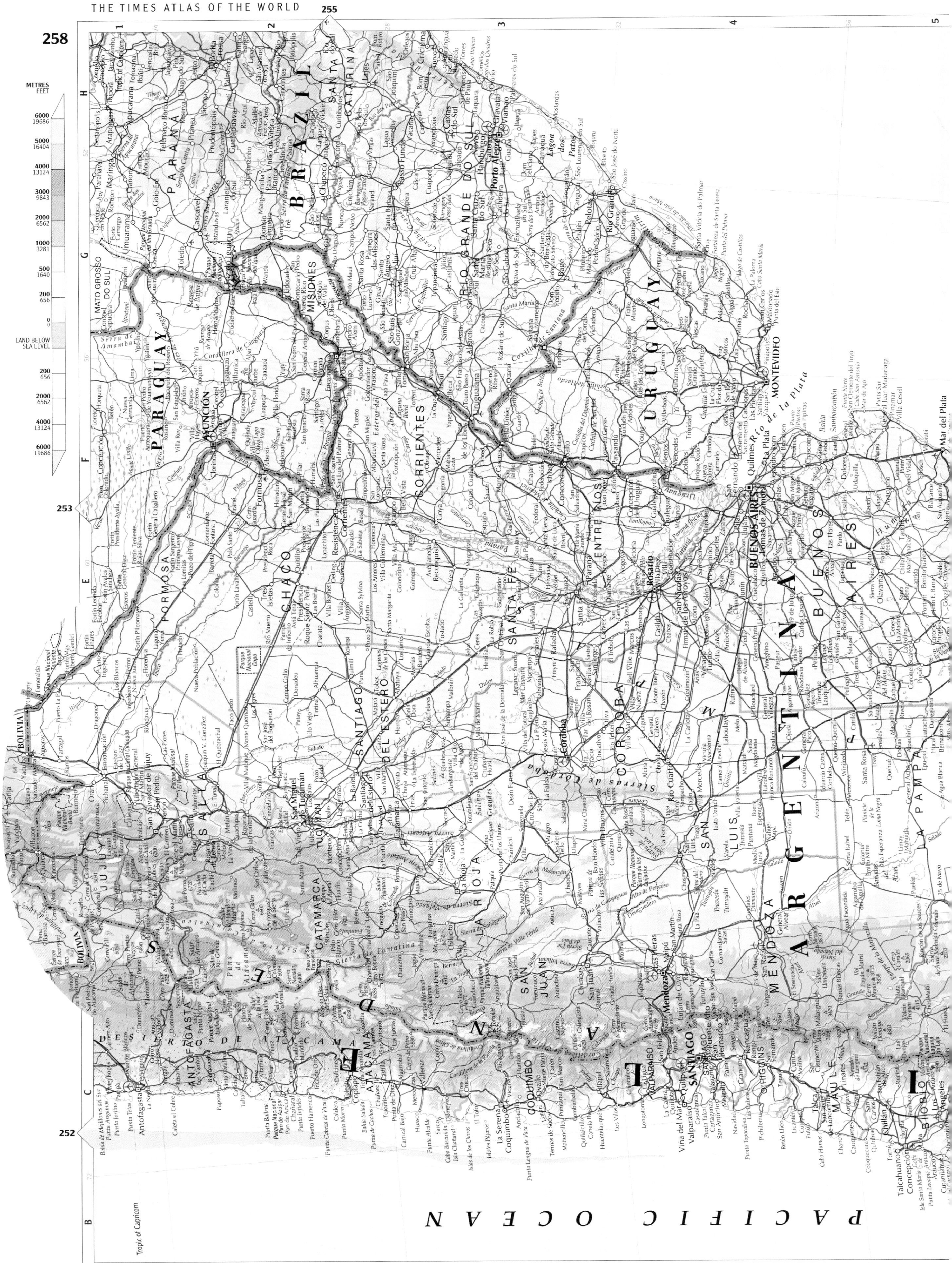
METRES
FEET
6000 19686
5000 16404
4000 13124
3000 9843
2000 6562
1000 3281
500 1640
200 656
0
LAND BELOW SEA LEVEL
200 656
2000 6562
4000 13124
6000 19686
255
253
252
PACIFIC OCEAN
BRAZIL
PARAGUAY
URUGUAY
ARGENTINA
CHILE
BOLIVIA
BUENOS AIRES
MONTEVIDEO
ASUNCIÓN
SANTIAGO
Tropic of Capricorn
Río de la Plata

BUENOS AIRES
1:125 000
SOUTH GEORGIA
(U.K.)
AT THE SAME SCALE
ATLANTIC
OCEAN
Falkland Islands
(U.K.)
West Falkland
East Falkland
STANLEY
MILES
KILOMETRES
1:7 500 000
RÍO NEGRO
CHUBUT
SANTA CRUZ
AISÉN
LOS LAGOS
MAGALLANES Y ANTÁRTICA CHILENA
TIERRA DEL FUEGO
Golfo San Jorge
Comodoro Rivadavia
Longitude 76° west of Greenwich

258

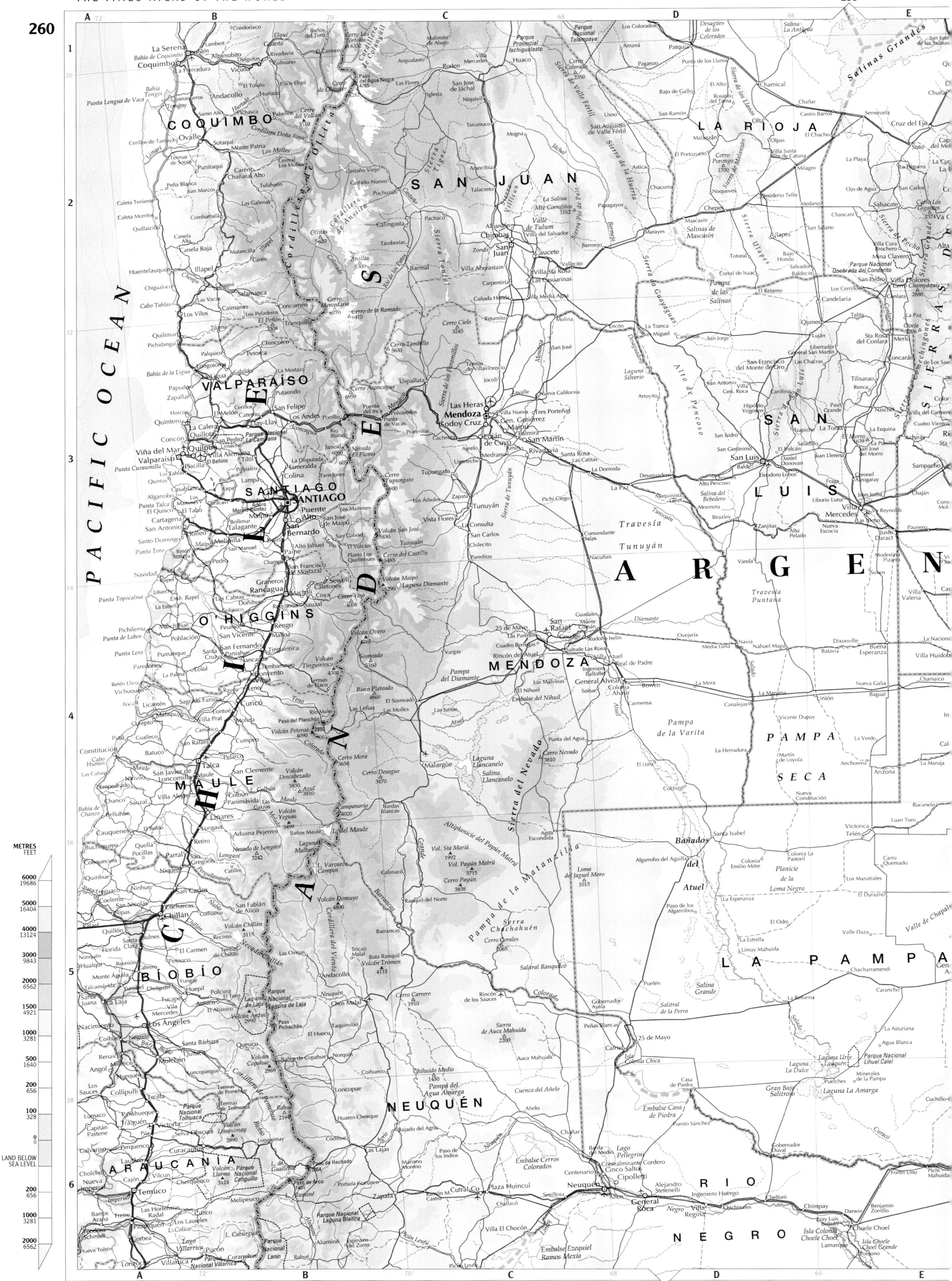
PACIFIC OCEAN
ANDES
CHILE
ARGEN
COQUIMBO
VALPARAÍSO
SANTIAGO
O'HIGGINS
MAULE
BÍOBÍO
ARAUCANÍA
SAN JUAN
LA RIOJA
SAN LUIS
MENDOZA
NEUQUÉN
LA PAMPA
RIO NEGRO
Salinas Grandes
Travesía Tunuyán
Travesía Puntana
PAMPA SECA
Pampa de la Varita
Pampa del Diamante
Sierra del Nevado
Cordillera de Olivares
Cordillera de Ansilta
La Serena
Coquimbo
Valparaíso
Viña del Mar
Santiago
Rancagua
Curicó
Talca
Linares
Chillán
Concepción
Los Angeles
Temuco
Mendoza
San Juan
San Luis
San Rafael
Neuquén
Cerro Aconcagua
Cerro Tupungato
METRES
FEET
6000
19686
5000
16404
4000
13124
3000
9843
2000
6562
1500
4921
1000
3281
500
1640
200
656
100
328
0
0
LAND BELOW SEA LEVEL
200
656
1000
3281
2000
6562
A
B
C
D
E
1
2
3
4
5
6
72
70
68
66
30
32
34
36
38
Conic Equidistant Projection

259

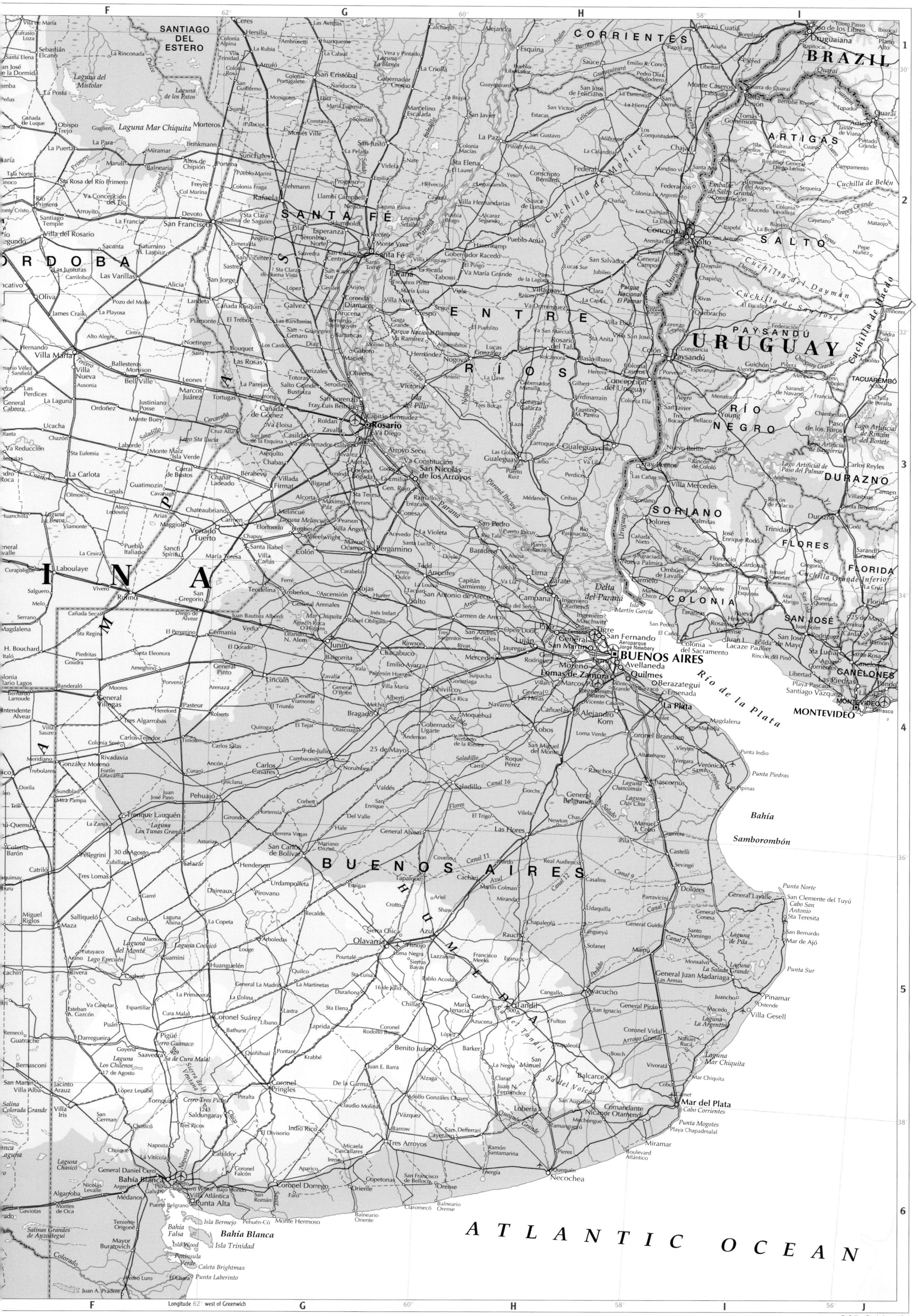
SANTIAGO DEL ESTERO
CORRIENTES
BRAZIL
ARTIGAS
SANTA FÉ
SALTO
CÓRDOBA
ENTRE RÍOS
PAYSANDÚ
URUGUAY
TACUAREMBÓ
RÍO NEGRO
DURAZNO
SORIANO
FLORES
FLORIDA
COLONIA
SAN JOSÉ
CANELONES
MONTEVIDEO
BUENOS AIRES
Río de la Plata
Bahía Samborombón
Rosario
Santa Fé
Paraná
Concordia
Salto
Paysandú
La Plata
Mar del Plata
Bahía Blanca
Necochea
Tandil
Olavarría
Azul
Junín
Pergamino
San Nicolás de los Arroyos
Laguna Mar Chiquita
Bahía Blanca
Isla Trinidad
ATLANTIC OCEAN
258
Longitude 62° west of Greenwich
© Collins Bartholomew Ltd

MILES KILOMETRES

1:3 300 000

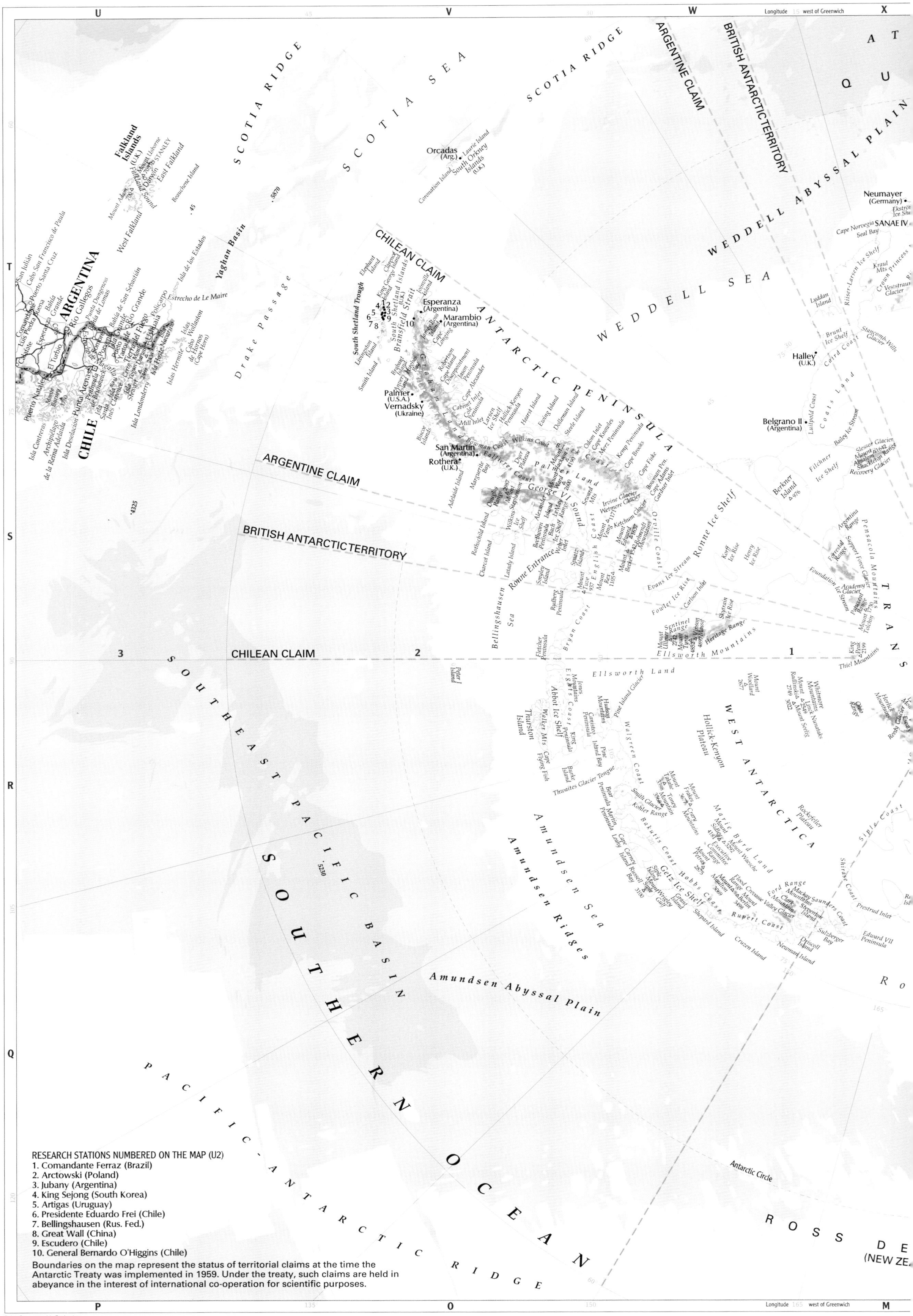

METRES / FEET

METRES	FEET
4000	13124
3000	9843
2000	6562
1000	3281
500	1640
200	656
0	0
LAND BELOW SEA LEVEL	
200	656
2000	6562
3000	9843
4000	13124
5000	16404
6000	19686
7000	22967
9000	29529

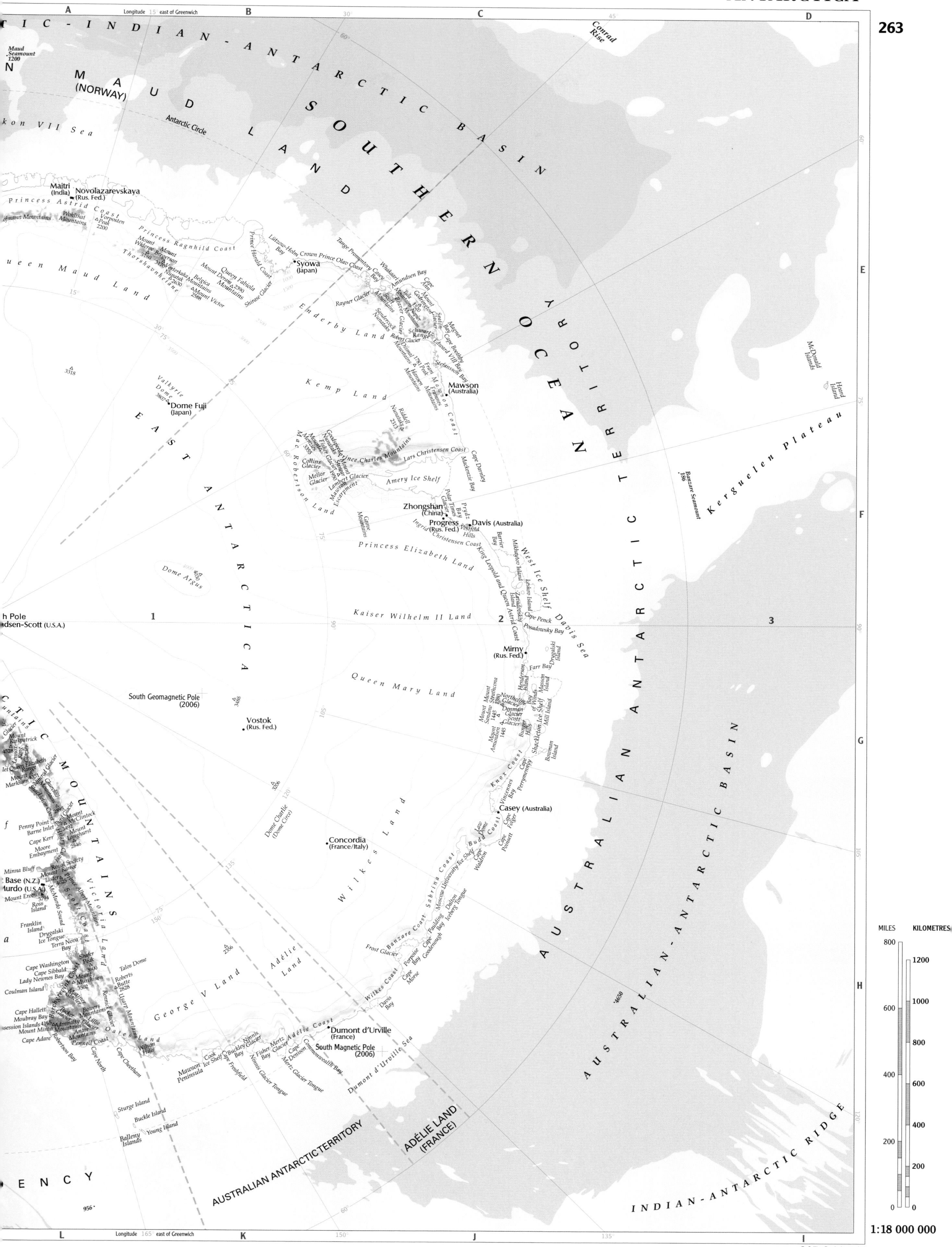
Longitude 15° east of Greenwich
Longitude 165° east of Greenwich
A
B
C
D
E
F
G
H
I
J
K
L
1
2
3
SOUTHERN OCEAN
ATLANTIC-INDIAN-ANTARCTIC BASIN
QUEEN MAUD LAND (NORWAY)
Antarctic Circle
Maud Seamount 1200
Conrad Rise
Maitri (India)
Novolazarevskaya (Rus. Fed.)
Princess Astrid Coast
Princess Ragnhild Coast
Queen Maud Land
Prince Harald Coast
Lützow-Holm Bay
Syowa (Japan)
Crown Prince Olav Coast
Queen Fabiola Mountains
Belgica Mountains
Mount Victor 2588
Shirase Glacier
Enderby Land
Amundsen Bay
Rayner Glacier
Kemp Land
Mawson (Australia)
Edward VIII Bay
Stefansson Bay
Cape Boothby
AUSTRALIAN ANTARCTIC TERRITORY
Valkyrie Dome
Dome Fuji (Japan)
EAST ANTARCTICA
Prince Charles Mountains
Lars Christensen Coast
Mac. Robertson Land
Amery Ice Shelf
Lambert Glacier
Cape Darnley
Mackenzie Bay
Zhongshan (China)
Progress (Rus. Fed.)
Davis (Australia)
Prydz Bay
Vestfold Hills
Ingrid Christensen Coast
Princess Elizabeth Land
Kerguelen Plateau
McDonald Islands
Heard Island
Banzare Seamount 186
Dome Argus
Kaiser Wilhelm II Land
West Ice Shelf
Davis Sea
King Leopold and Queen Astrid Coast
Cape Penck
Posadowsky Bay
Mirny (Rus. Fed.)
Farr Bay
Drygalski Island
Queen Mary Land
Henderson Island
Masson Island
Shackleton Ice Shelf
Mill Island
Denman Glacier
Scott Glacier
Bowman Island
Knox Coast
South Geomagnetic Pole (2006)
Vostok (Rus. Fed.)
Dome Charlie (Dome Circe)
Concordia (France/Italy)
Wilkes Land
Casey (Australia)
Vincennes Bay
Cape Poinsett
Law Dome
Budd Coast
Sabrina Coast
Moscow University Ice Shelf
Banzare Coast
Frost Glacier
Porpoise Bay
Cape Morse
Wilkes Coast
Davis Bay
AUSTRALIAN-ANTARCTIC BASIN
INDIAN-ANTARCTIC RIDGE
Adélie Land
George V Land
Adélie Coast
Dumont d'Urville (France)
South Magnetic Pole (2006)
Dumont d'Urville Sea
Commonwealth Bay
Cape Denison
Mertz Glacier Tongue
Ninnis Glacier Tongue
Fisher Bay
Cape Freshfield
Cook Ice Shelf
Buckley Bay
Mawson Peninsula
ADÉLIE LAND (FRANCE)
AUSTRALIAN ANTARCTIC TERRITORY
Oates Land
Wilson Hills
Pennell Coast
Cape North
Cape Cheetham
Sturge Island
Buckle Island
Young Island
Balleny Islands
TRANSANTARCTIC MOUNTAINS
Victoria Land
Mount Kirkpatrick 4528
Queen Elizabeth Range
Mount Markham 4351
Penny Point
Barnee Inlet
Cape Kerr
Moore Embayment
Minna Bluff
Scott Base (N.Z.)
McMurdo (U.S.A.)
Mount Erebus 3794
Ross Island
McMurdo Sound
Franklin Island
Drygalski Ice Tongue
Terra Nova Bay
Talos Dome
Cape Washington
Cape Sibbald
Lady Newnes Bay
Coulman Island
Cape Hallett
Moubray Bay
Possession Islands
Cape Adare
Robertson Bay
Admiralty Mountains
Usarp Mountains
South Pole
Amundsen-Scott (U.S.A.)
ROSS DEPENDENCY
MILES
KILOMETRES
1:18 000 000

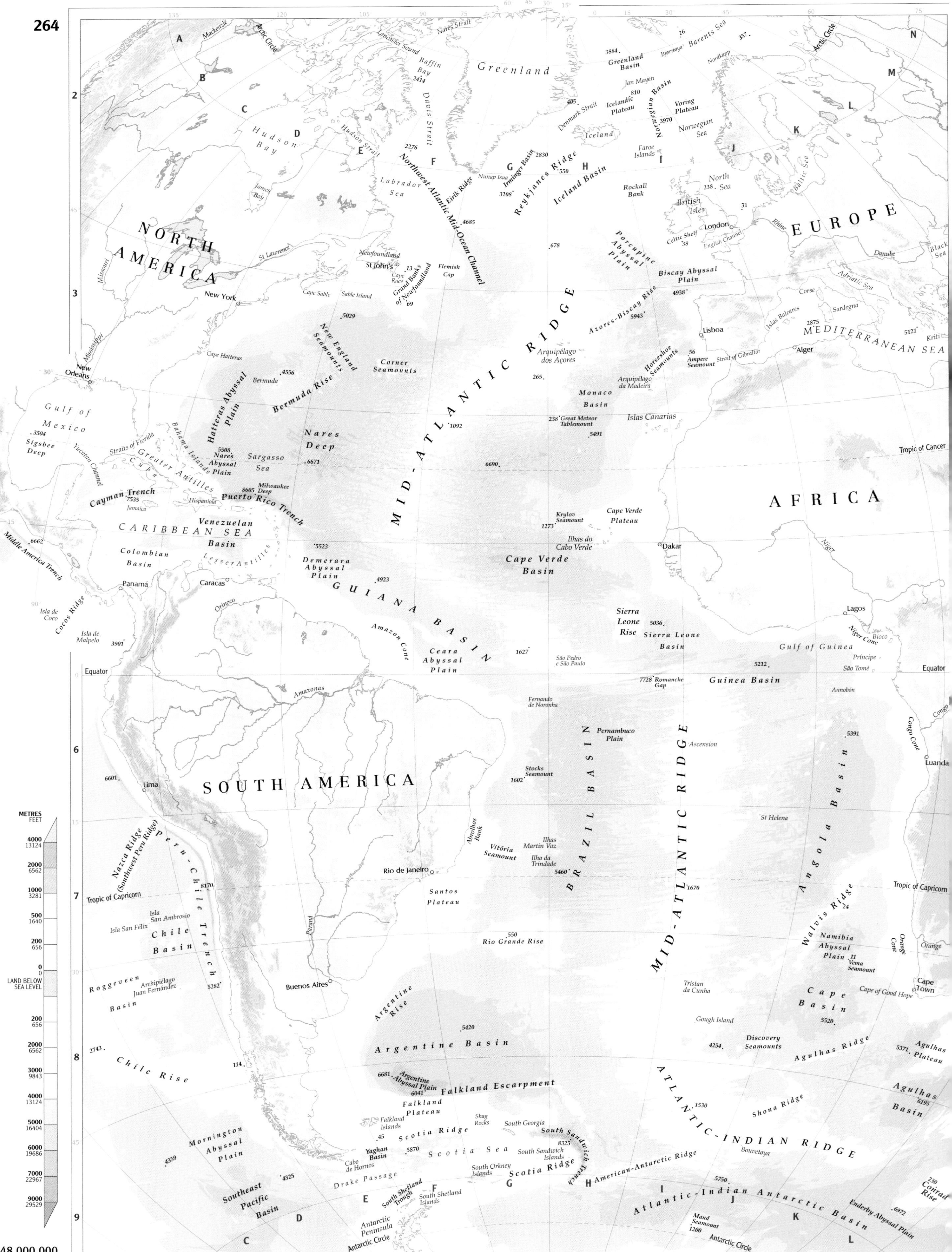

1:48 000 000

Lambert Azimuthal Equal Area Projection

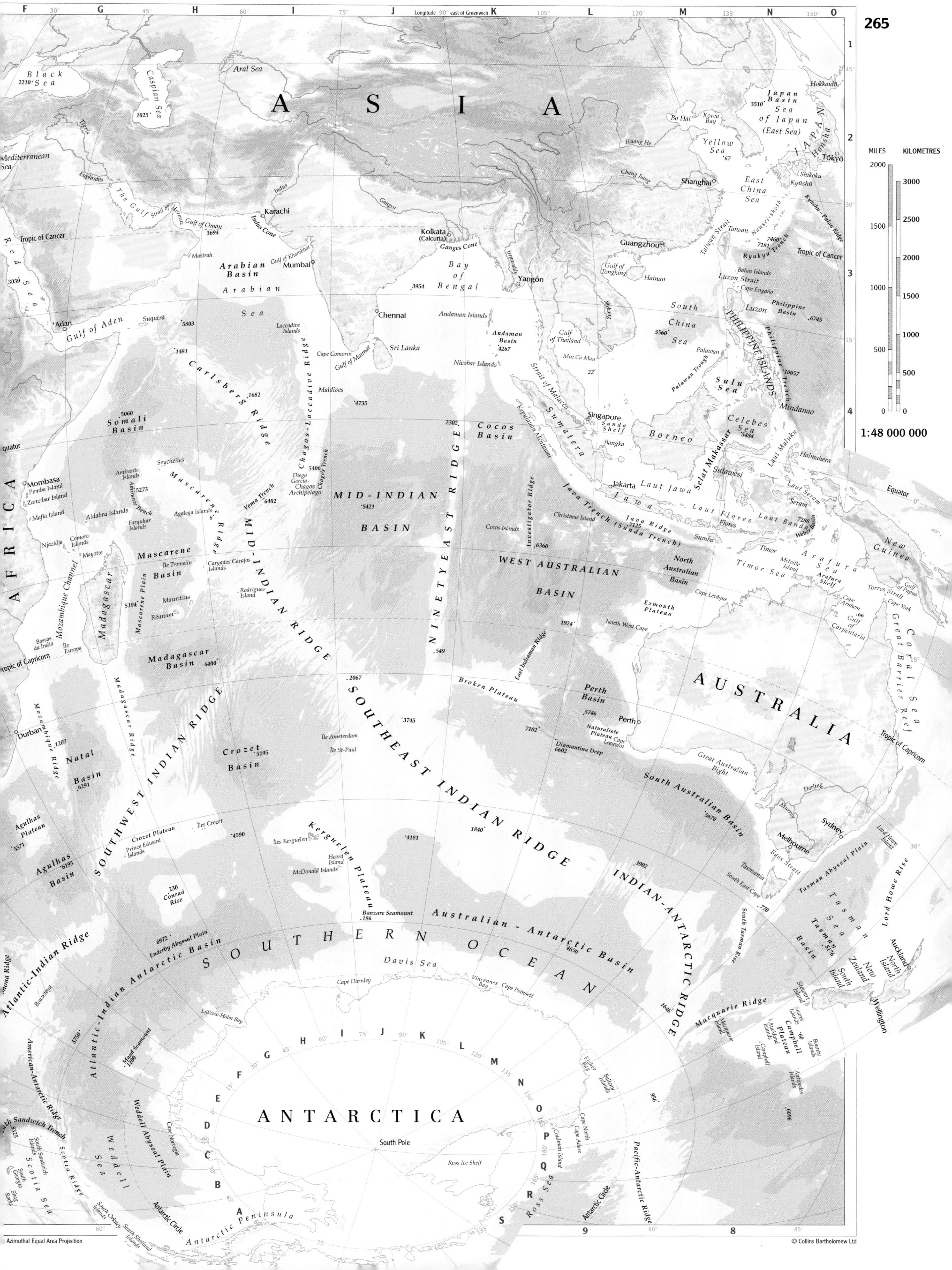
Longitude 90° east of Greenwich
MILES
KILOMETRES
1:48 000 000
ASIA
AFRICA
AUSTRALIA
ANTARCTICA
SOUTHERN OCEAN
Black Sea
Caspian Sea
Aral Sea
Mediterranean Sea
Red Sea
The Gulf
Strait of Hormuz
Gulf of Oman
Gulf of Aden
Suquṭrā
Arabian Basin
Arabian Sea
Karachi
Indus
Indus Cone
Gulf of Khambhat
Mumbai
Mastrah
Ganges
Kolkata (Calcutta)
Ganges Cone
Bay of Bengal
Chennai
Sri Lanka
Cape Comorin
Gulf of Mannar
Laccadive Islands
Maldives
Chagos-Laccadive Ridge
Carlsberg Ridge
Somali Basin
Seychelles
Amirante Islands
Amirante Trench
Mascarene Ridge
Mascarene Basin
Mascarene Plain
Aldabra Islands
Agalega Islands
Farquhar Islands
Comoro Islands
Njazidja
Mayotte
Mombasa
Pemba Island
Zanzibar Island
Mafia Island
Mozambique Channel
Madagascar
Bassas da India
Île Europa
Île Tromelin
Cargados Carajos Islands
Rodrigues Island
Mauritius
Réunion
Madagascar Basin
Madagascar Ridge
Mozambique Ridge
Natal Basin
Durban
Agulhas Plateau
Agulhas Basin
Diego Garcia
Chagos Archipelago
Chagos Trench
Vema Trench
MID-INDIAN BASIN
MID-INDIAN RIDGE
NINETYEAST RIDGE
Cocos Basin
Cocos Islands
Andaman Islands
Andaman Basin
Nicobar Islands
Yangôn
Irrawaddy
Gulf of Thailand
Mui Ca Mau
Mekong
Strait of Malacca
Sumatera
Kepulauan Mentawai
Singapore
Sunda Shelf
Bangka
Borneo
Jakarta
Laut Jawa
Jawa
Java Trench (Sunda Trench)
Java Ridge
Christmas Island
Investigator Ridge
WEST AUSTRALIAN BASIN
North Australian Basin
Exmouth Plateau
North West Cape
Cape Lévêque
East Indiaman Ridge
Broken Plateau
Perth Basin
Perth
Naturaliste Plateau
Cape Leeuwin
Diamantina Deep
Great Australian Bight
South Australian Basin
Darling
Murray
Sydney
Melbourne
Bass Strait
Tasmania
South East Cape
SOUTHEAST INDIAN RIDGE
SOUTHWEST INDIAN RIDGE
Crozet Basin
Crozet Plateau
Îles Crozet
Prince Edward Islands
Conrad Rise
Île Amsterdam
Île St-Paul
Îles Kerguelen
Kerguelen Plateau
Heard Island
McDonald Islands
Banzare Seamount
Australian - Antarctic Basin
INDIAN-ANTARCTIC RIDGE
Atlantic-Indian Ridge
Atlantic-Indian Antarctic Basin
Enderby Abyssal Plain
Davis Sea
Cape Darnley
Vincennes Bay
Cape Poinsett
Lützow-Holm Bay
Maud Seamount
American-Antarctic Ridge
South Sandwich Trench
South Sandwich Islands
Scotia Ridge
Scotia Sea
South Georgia
Shag Rocks
South Orkney Islands
South Shetland Islands
Weddell Sea
Weddell Abyssal Plain
Cape Norvegia
Antarctic Peninsula
Antarctic Circle
South Pole
Ross Ice Shelf
Ross Sea
Coulman Island
Cape Adare
Cape North
Balleny Islands
Fisher Bay
Pacific-Antarctic Ridge
Macquarie Ridge
Macquarie Island
Campbell Plateau
Campbell Island
Auckland Islands
Antipodes Islands
Bounty Islands
Snares Islands
Stewart Island
South Island
North Island
New Zealand
Wellington
Auckland
South Tasman Rise
Tasman Basin
Tasman Sea
Tasman Abyssal Plain
Lord Howe Rise
Lord Howe Island
Coral Sea
Great Barrier Reef
Tropic of Capricorn
Tropic of Cancer
Equator
Cape York
Torres Strait
Gulf of Papua
New Guinea
Gulf of Carpentaria
Cape Arnhem
Arafura Sea
Arafura Shelf
Melville Island
Timor Sea
Timor
Sumba
Flores
Laut Flores
Laut Banda
Weber Basin
Seram
Laut Seram
Halmahera
Laut Maluku
Sulawesi
Selat Makassar
Celebes Sea
Sulu Sea
Mindanao
Palawan
Palawan Trough
PHILIPPINE ISLANDS
Philippine Trench
Philippine Basin
Luzon
Luzon Strait
Cape Engaño
Batan Islands
South China Sea
Hainan
Gulf of Tongking
Guangzhou
Taiwan
Taiwan Strait
Ryukyu Trench
Nansei-shotō
East China Sea
Shanghai
Chang Jiang
Huang He
Yellow Sea
Bo Hai
Korea Bay
Japan Basin
Sea of Japan (East Sea)
JAPAN
Hokkaidō
Honshū
Tōkyō
Shikoku
Kyūshū
Kyushu - Palau Ridge
Tigris
Euphrates
Adan

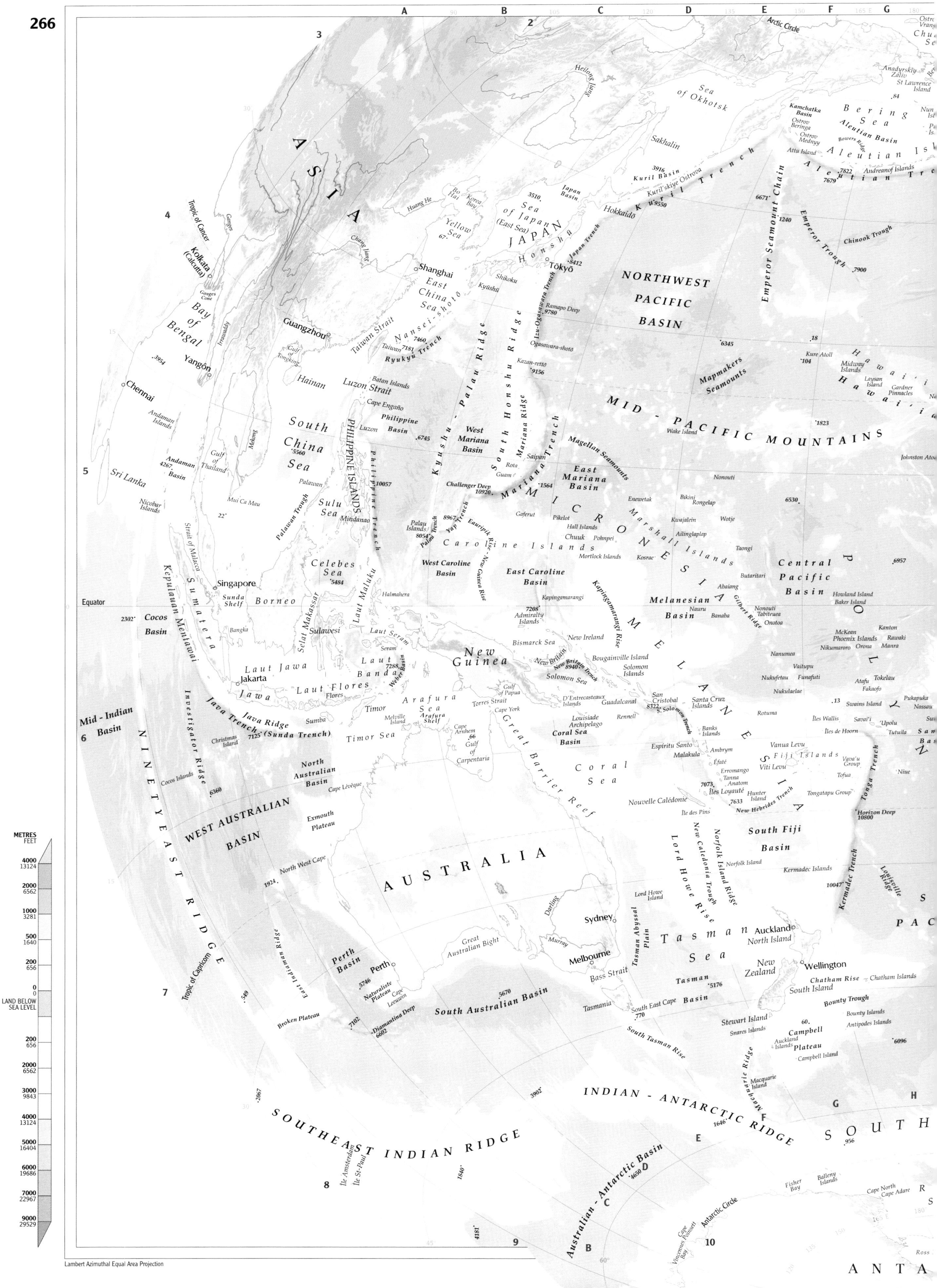
A
B
C
D
E
F
G
Arctic Circle
ASIA
Sea of Okhotsk
Kamchatka Basin
Bering Sea
Aleutian Basin
Aleutian Islands
Aleutian Trench
Kuril Basin
Kuril'skiye Ostrova
Kuril Trench
Sakhalin
Heilong Jiang
Japan Basin
Sea of Japan (East Sea)
JAPAN
Honshū
Hokkaidō
Tōkyō
Japan Trench
Shikoku
Kyūshū
Yellow Sea
Bo Hai
Korea Bay
Huang He
Chang Jiang
Shanghai
East China Sea
Nansei-shotō
Taiwan Strait
Taiwan
Ryukyu Trench
Guangzhou
Gulf of Tongking
Hainan
Luzon Strait
Batan Islands
Cape Engaño
Luzon
Philippine Basin
PHILIPPINE ISLANDS
Philippine Trench
South China Sea
Palawan
Palawan Trough
Sulu Sea
Mindanao
Celebes Sea
Laut Maluku
Halmahera
Borneo
Sunda Shelf
Singapore
Sumatera
Kepulauan Mentawai
Strait of Malacca
Selat Makassar
Sulawesi
Laut Seram
Seram
Laut Banda
Weber Basin
Laut Jawa
Jakarta
Jawa
Laut Flores
Flores
Sumba
Timor
Timor Sea
Arafura Sea
Arafura Shelf
Java Ridge
Java Trench (Sunda Trench)
Christmas Island
Cocos Islands
Cocos Basin
Investigator Ridge
Mid-Indian Basin
NINETYEAST RIDGE
North Australian Basin
WEST AUSTRALIAN BASIN
Exmouth Plateau
Cape Lévêque
North West Cape
AUSTRALIA
Perth Basin
Perth
Naturaliste Plateau
Cape Leeuwin
Diamantina Deep
Broken Plateau
South Australian Basin
Great Australian Bight
East Indiaman Ridge
Tropic of Capricorn
Tropic of Cancer
Kolkata (Calcutta)
Ganges
Ganges Cone
Bay of Bengal
Irrawaddy
Yangôn
Chennai
Andaman Islands
Andaman Basin
Gulf of Thailand
Mekong
Mui Ca Mau
Sri Lanka
Nicobar Islands
Equator
Kyushu-Palau Ridge
South Honshu Ridge
Izu-Ogasawara Trench
Ramapo Deep
Ogasawara-shotō
Kazan-rettō
West Mariana Basin
Mariana Ridge
Mariana Trench
Saipan
Rota
Guam
Challenger Deep
East Mariana Basin
Magellan Seamounts
MICRONESIA
Palau Islands
Palau Trench
Yap Trench
Eauripik Rise
Gaferut
Caroline Islands
West Caroline Basin
East Caroline Basin
Chuuk
Pohnpei
Mortlock Islands
Kosrae
Pikelot
Hall Islands
Marshall Islands
Enewetak
Bikini
Rongelap
Kwajalein
Ailinglaplap
Wotje
Taongi
Kapingamarangi
Kapingamarangi Rise
Admiralty Islands
New Guinea
Bismarck Sea
New Ireland
New Britain
New Britain Trench
Bougainville Island
Solomon Islands
Solomon Sea
Gulf of Papua
Torres Strait
Cape York
Cape Arnhem
Gulf of Carpentaria
Great Barrier Reef
Coral Sea
Coral Sea Basin
Louisiade Archipelago
D'Entrecasteaux Islands
Guadalcanal
Rennell
San Cristobal
Solomon Trench
Santa Cruz Islands
Banks Islands
Espiritu Santo
Malakula
Ambrym
Éfaté
Erromango
Tanna
Anatom
Îles Loyauté
Nouvelle Calédonie
Île des Pins
New Hebrides Trench
Hunter Island
MELANESIA
Melanesian Basin
Nauru
Banaba
Gilbert Ridge
Abaiang
Butaritari
Nonouti
Tabiteuea
Onotoa
Central Pacific Basin
Howland Island
Baker Island
Kanton
Phoenix Islands
McKean
Rawaki
Nikumaroro
Orona
Manra
Nanumea
Vaitupu
Nukufetau
Funafuti
Nukulaelae
Atafu
Tokelau
Fakaofo
Swains Island
Rotuma
Îles Wallis
Îles de Hoorn
Savai'i
'Upolu
Tutuila
Vanua Levu
Fiji Islands
Viti Levu
Vava'u Group
Tofua
Tongatapu Group
Tonga Trench
Horizon Deep
'Niue
South Fiji Basin
Norfolk Island
Norfolk Island Ridge
New Caledonia Trough
Lord Howe Rise
Lord Howe Island
Kermadec Islands
Kermadec Trench
Louisville Ridge
Tasman Abyssal Plain
Tasman Sea
Tasman Basin
Sydney
Darling
Murray
Melbourne
Bass Strait
Tasmania
South East Cape
South Tasman Rise
Auckland
North Island
New Zealand
Wellington
South Island
Chatham Rise
Chatham Islands
Bounty Trough
Bounty Islands
Antipodes Islands
Stewart Island
Snares Islands
Auckland Islands
Campbell Plateau
Campbell Island
Macquarie Ridge
Macquarie Island
NORTHWEST PACIFIC BASIN
Emperor Seamount Chain
Emperor Trough
Chinook Trough
Hawaiian Islands
Kure Atoll
Midway Islands
Laysan Island
Gardner Pinnacles
Mapmakers Seamounts
MID-PACIFIC MOUNTAINS
Wake Island
Johnston Atoll
Nonouti
Anadyrskiy Zaliv
St Lawrence Island
Ostrov Beringa
Ostrov Mednyy
Bowers Ridge
Attu Island
Andreanof Islands
INDIAN-ANTARCTIC RIDGE
SOUTHEAST INDIAN RIDGE
Île Amsterdam
Île St-Paul
Australian-Antarctic Basin
Antarctic Circle
Cape Poinsett
Vincennes Bay
Fisher Bay
Balleny Islands
Cape North
Cape Adare
Ross
ANTA
SOUTH
PAC
1
2
3
4
5
6
7
8
9
10
H
METRES
FEET
4000
13124
2000
6562
1000
3281
500
1640
200
656
0
0
LAND BELOW SEA LEVEL
200
656
2000
6562
3000
9843
4000
13124
5000
16404
6000
19686
7000
22967
9000
29529

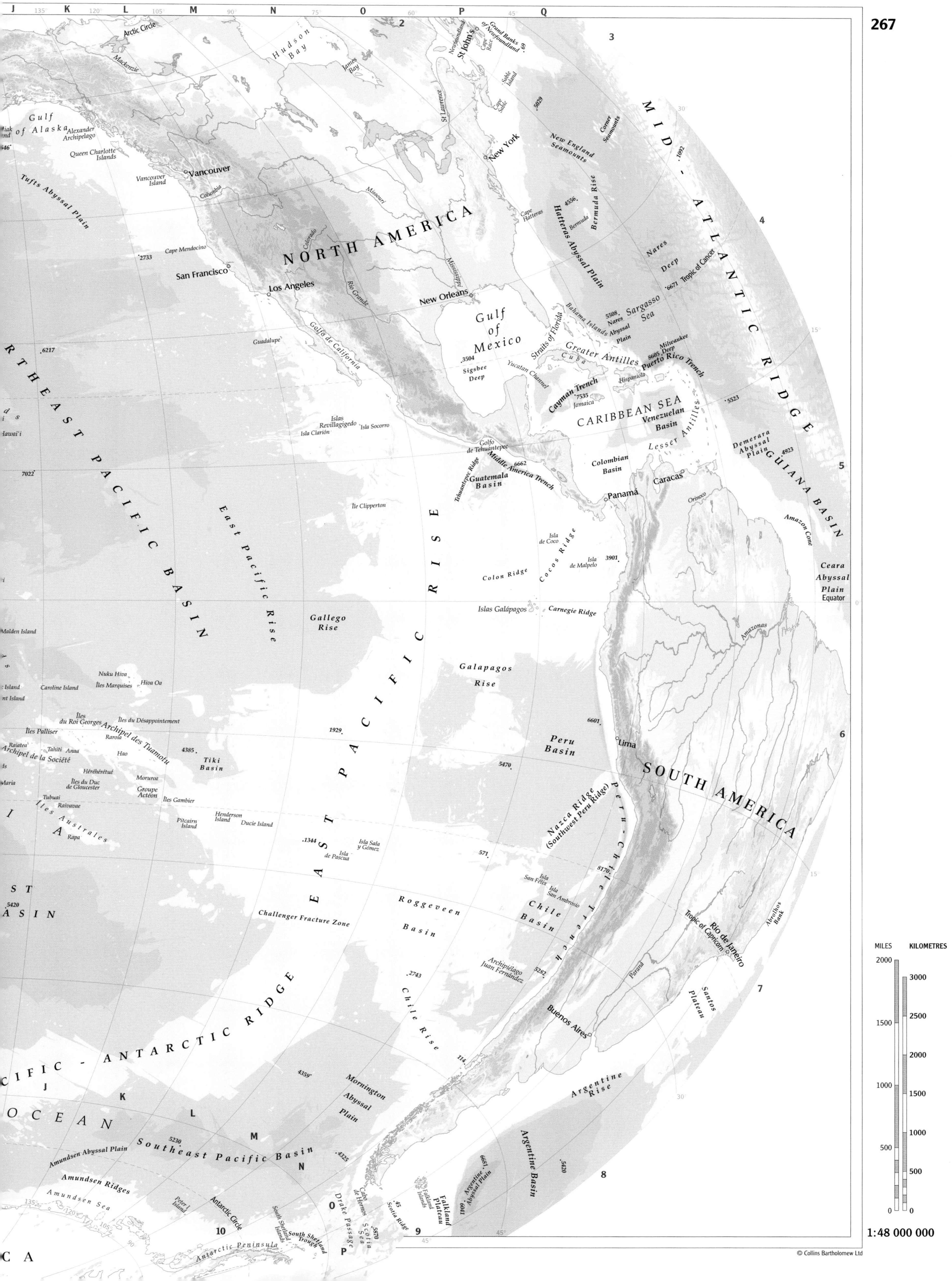
NORTH AMERICA
SOUTH AMERICA
Arctic Circle
Hudson Bay
James Bay
Mackenzie
Gulf of Alaska
Alexander Archipelago
Queen Charlotte Islands
Vancouver Island
Vancouver
Columbia
Tufts Abyssal Plain
Missouri
Colorado
Cape Mendocino
2733
San Francisco
Los Angeles
Rio Grande
Mississippi
New Orleans
St Lawrence
New York
Newfoundland
St John's
Grand Banks of Newfoundland
Cape Race
Sable Island
Cape Sable
5029
Corner Seamounts
New England Seamounts
1092
Cape Hatteras
Bermuda
Bermuda Rise
4556
Hatteras Abyssal Plain
Nares Deep
Tropic of Cancer
6671
MID - ATLANTIC RIDGE
Gulf of Mexico
Straits of Florida
Bahama Islands
5508
Nares Abyssal Plain
Sargasso Sea
Greater Antilles
Cuba
Milwaukee Deep
8605
Puerto Rico Trench
Hispaniola
Sigsbee Deep
3504
Yucatan Channel
Cayman Trench
7535
Jamaica
CARIBBEAN SEA
Venezuelan Basin
Lesser Antilles
5523
Demerara Abyssal Plain
4923
GUIANA BASIN
Golfo de California
Guadalupe
6217
Islas Revillagigedo
Isla Socorro
Isla Clarión
Golfo de Tehuantepec
Tehuantepec Ridge
6662
Middle America Trench
Guatemala Basin
Colombian Basin
Panamá
Caracas
Orinoco
Amazon Cone
Ceara Abyssal Plain
Equator
Île Clipperton
7022
Hawai'i
NORTHEAST PACIFIC BASIN
East Pacific Rise
EAST PACIFIC RISE
Isla de Coco
Cocos Ridge
Isla de Malpelo
3901
Colon Ridge
Islas Galápagos
Carnegie Ridge
Gallego Rise
Malden Island
Galapagos Rise
Amazonas
Nuku Hiva
Îles Marquises
Hiva Oa
Caroline Island
Îles du Roi Georges
Îles du Désappointement
Îles Palliser
Archipel des Tuamotu
Raroia
Raiatea
Tahiti
Anaa
Hao
Archipel de la Société
1929
4385
Tiki Basin
Héréhérétué
Îles du Duc de Gloucester
Moruroa
Groupe Actéon
Îles Gambier
Tubuai
Raivavae
Îles Australes
Rapa
Pitcairn Island
Henderson Island
Ducie Island
6601
Lima
Peru Basin
5470
Nazca Ridge (Southwest Peru Ridge)
Peru - Chile Trench
1344
Isla de Pascua
Isla Sala y Gómez
571
Isla San Félix
Isla San Ambrosio
8170
5420
Challenger Fracture Zone
Roggeveen Basin
Chile Basin
Tropic of Capricorn
Rio de Janeiro
Abrolhos Bank
Paraná
Archipiélago Juan Fernández
5282
2743
Chile Rise
Santos Plateau
Buenos Aires
PACIFIC - ANTARCTIC RIDGE
114
4359
Mornington Abyssal Plain
Argentine Rise
SOUTHERN OCEAN
5230
Southeast Pacific Basin
4325
Amundsen Abyssal Plain
Amundsen Ridges
Amundsen Sea
Peter I Island
Antarctic Circle
Argentine Basin
6681
Argentine Abyssal Plain
5420
Falkland Plateau
Falkland Islands
Cabo de Hornos
Drake Passage
Scotia Ridge
Scotia Sea
5870
South Shetland Islands
South Shetland Trough
Antarctic Peninsula
1949
MILES
KILOMETRES
2000
1500
1000
500
0
3000
2500
2000
1500
1000
500
0

1:48 000 000

© Collins Bartholomew Ltd

ARCTIC OCEAN

1:24 000 000

MILES / KILOMETRES

METRES / FEET: 4000 13124; 2000 6562; 1000 3281; 500 1640; 200 656; 0 0; LAND BELOW SEA LEVEL; 200 656; 2000 6562; 3000 9843; 4000 13124; 5000 16404; 6000 19686; 7000 22967; 9000 29529

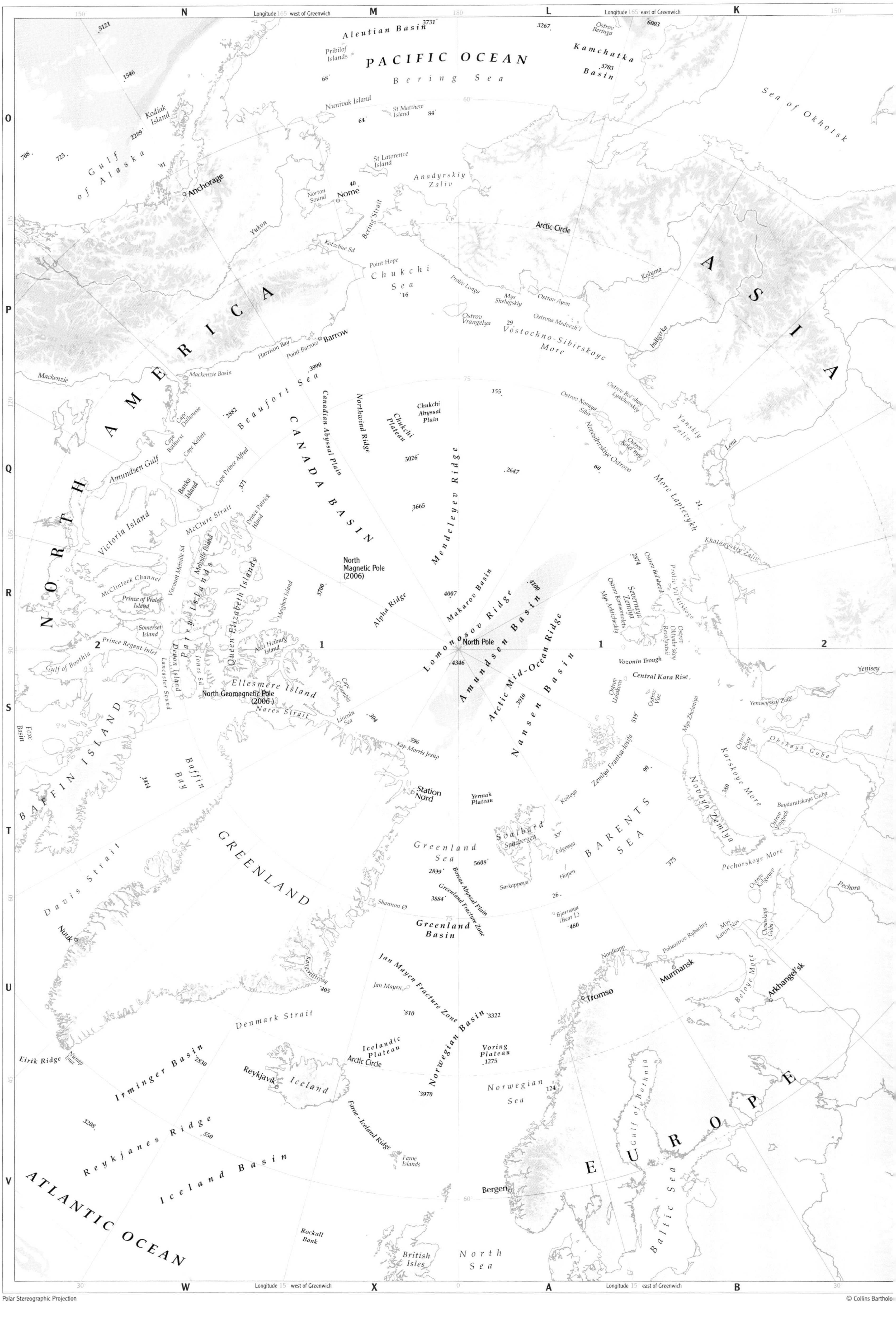
Longitude 165 west of Greenwich
Longitude 165 east of Greenwich
PACIFIC OCEAN
Bering Sea
Aleutian Basin
Pribilof Islands
Kamchatka Basin
Sea of Okhotsk
Nunivak Island
St Matthew Island
Kodiak Island
Gulf of Alaska
Anchorage
St Lawrence Island
Anadyrskiy Zaliv
Norton Sound
Nome
Yukon
Bering Strait
Kotzebue Sd
Arctic Circle
Point Hope
Chukchi Sea
Proliv Longa
Mys Shelagskiy
Ostrov Ayon
Kolyma
Ostrov Vrangelya
Ostrova Medvezh'i
Vostochno-Sibirskoye More
Indigirka
ASIA
NORTH AMERICA
Harrison Bay
Point Barrow
Barrow
Mackenzie
Mackenzie Basin
Beaufort Sea
Canadian Abyssal Plain
Northwind Ridge
Chukchi Plateau
Chukchi Abyssal Plain
Ostrov Bol'shoy Lyakhovskiy
Ostrov Novaya Sibir
Novosibirskiye Ostrova
Ostrov Kotel'nyy
Yanskiy Zaliv
Lena
Cape Dalhousie
Cape Bathurst
Cape Kellett
Amundsen Gulf
Cape Prince Alfred
Banks Island
CANADA BASIN
Mendeleyev Ridge
More Laptevykh
Victoria Island
McClure Strait
Prince Patrick Island
Melville Island
Viscount Melville Sd
McClintock Channel
Prince of Wales Island
Parry Islands
Queen Elizabeth Islands
Meighen Island
North Magnetic Pole (2006)
Alpha Ridge
Makarov Basin
Lomonosov Ridge
North Pole
Amundsen Basin
Arctic Mid-Ocean Ridge
Nansen Basin
Khatangskiy Zaliv
Proliv Vil'kitskogo
Ostrov Bol'shevik
Severnaya Zemlya
Ostrov Komsomolets
Mys Arkticheskiy
Ostrov Oktyabr'skoy Revolyutsii
Vozonin Trough
Central Kara Rise
Ostrov Ushakova
Ostrov Vize
Yenisey
Yeniseyskiy Zaliv
Somerset Island
Prince Regent Inlet
Gulf of Boothia
Devon Island
Lancaster Sound
Jones Sd
Axel Heiburg Island
Ellesmere Island
North Geomagnetic Pole (2006)
Nares Strait
Cape Columbia
Lincoln Sea
Kap Morris Jesup
Zemlya Frantsa-Iosifa
Mys Zhelaniya
Ostrov Belyy
Obskaya Guba
Karskoye More
Foxe Basin
BAFFIN ISLAND
Baffin Bay
Station Nord
Yermak Plateau
Kvitøya
Novaya Zemlya
Baydaratskaya Guba
Ostrov Vaygach
Svalbard
Spitsbergen
Edgeøya
BARENTS SEA
Greenland Sea
Boreas Abyssal Plain
Greenland Fracture Zone
Hopen
Sørkappøya
Pechorskoye More
Ostrov Kolguyev
Pechora
Davis Strait
GREENLAND
Shannon Ø
Greenland Basin
Bjørnøya (Bear I.)
Nuuk
Poluostrov Rybachiy
Mys Kanin Nos
Cheshskaya Guba
Nordkapp
Murmansk
Beloye More
Arkhangel'sk
Kangertittivaq
Jan Mayen Fracture Zone
Jan Mayen
Tromsø
Denmark Strait
Norwegian Basin
Icelandic Plateau
Arctic Circle
Voring Plateau
Eirik Ridge
Nunap Isua
Irminger Basin
Reykjavík
Iceland
Norwegian Sea
Gulf of Bothnia
Faroe-Iceland Ridge
Faroe Islands
Reykjanes Ridge
Iceland Basin
EUROPE
ATLANTIC OCEAN
Bergen
Baltic Sea
Rockall Bank
British Isles
North Sea
Longitude 15 west of Greenwich
Longitude 15 east of Greenwich

© Collins Bartholomew

GLOSSARY

Geographical term	Language	Meaning
A		
-á	Icelandic	river
-å	Danish	river
Āb	Farsi	river
Abajo	Spanish	lower
Abbaye	French	abbey
Abhainn	Gaelic	river
Abyār	Arabic	wells
Açude	Portuguese	reservoir
Adası	Azeri, Turkish	island
Adrar	Berber	hills, mountains
Agia, Agios	Greek	saint
Agioi	Greek	saints
Aiguille	French	peak
Ain, 'Ain, 'Aîn, Aïn, 'Aïn	Arabic	spring, well
Akra	Greek	cape, point
Ala-	Finnish	lower
Allt	Gaelic	river
Alpi	Italian	mountain range
Alpe	Slovene	mountain range
Alpen	German	mountain range
Alpes	French	mountain range
Alt-	German	old
Alta	Italian, Portuguese, Spanish	upper
Altiplanicie	Spanish	high plain
Alto	Italian, Portuguese, Spanish	upper
Alto	Spanish	summit
-älv, -älven	Swedish	river
Ano	Greek	upper
Anou, Ânou	Berber	well
Anse	French	bay
Ao	Thai	bay
Archipel	French	archipelago
Archipiélago	Spanish	archipelago
Arenas	Spanish	sands
Argelanots'	Armenian	reserve
Arkhipelag	Russian	archipelago
Arquipélago	Portuguese	archipelago
Arrecife	Spanish	reef
Arriba	Spanish	upper
Arroio	Portuguese	watercourse
Arroyo	Spanish	watercourse
Augstiene	Latvian	hill region
Aust-	Norwegian	east, eastern
Austur-	Icelandic	east, eastern
Avtonomnaya, Avtonomnyy	Russian	autonomous
Āw	Kurdish	river
'Ayn	Arabic	spring, waterhole, well
B		
Baai, -baai	Afrikaans, Dutch	bay
Bāb	Arabic	strait
Bad	German	spa
Badia	Catalan	bay
Bādiyah	Arabic	desert
Bælt	Danish	strait
Bagh	Gaelic	bay
Bahia	Portuguese	bay
Bahía	Spanish	bay
Bahr, Baḩr, Baḩr	Arabic	bay, lake, canal, river, watercourse
Bahra, Baḩra	Arabic	lagoon, lake
Baía	Portuguese	bay
Baie	French	bay
Baixa, Baixo	Portuguese	lower
Baja	Spanish	lower
Bajja	Maltese	bay
Bajo	Spanish	depression, lower
Bālā	Farsi	upper
Ban	Laotian, Thai	village
Banc	Welsh	hill
Banco	Spanish	shoal
Bandao	Chinese	peninsula
Bandar	Arabic, Farsi, Somali	anchorage, inlet, port, harbour
Bandar	Malay	port, town
Banī	Arabic	desert
Banjaran	Malay	mountain range
Baraj, Barajı	Turkish	dam
Barat	Indonesian, Malay	west, western
Barra	Portuguese, Spanish	sandbank, sandbar, spit
Barrage	French	dam
Barragem	Portuguese	dam, reservoir
Barranco	Spanish	gorge, ravine
Baruun	Mongolian	west, western
Bas, Basse	French	lower
Bassin	French	basin
Bāţin, Baţn	Arabic	depression
-beek	Afrikaans, Dutch	river
Beg, Beag	Gaelic, Irish	small
Bei	Chinese	north, northern
bei	German	at, near
Beinn	Gaelic	mountain
Belogor'ye	Russian	mountain range
Ben	Gaelic	mountain
Bereg	Russian	coastal area
-berg, -berge	German, Norwegian, Swedish, Afrikaans	mountain, mountains
Besar	Indonesian, Malay	big
Bi'ār	Arabic	wells
Bir, Bi'r, Bîr	Arabic	waterhole, well
Birkat	Arabic	waterhole, well
-bjerg	Danish	hill
Boca	Portuguese, Spanish	mouth
Bodden	German	bay
Boğazı	Turkish	strait, pass
Bois	French	forest, wood
Boloto	Russian	marsh
Bol'shaya, Bol'shiye, Bol'shoy, Bol'shoye	Russian	big
-bong	Korean	mountain
Boquerón	Spanish	pass
Bory	Polish	woods
-botn	Norwegian	valley floor
-botten	Swedish	valley floor
Böyük	Azeri	big
Braţul	Romanian	arm, branch
-bre, -breen	Norwegian	glacier
Bredning	Danish	bay
Breg	Croatian, Serbian	hill
-bron	Afrikaans	spring, well
Brücke	German	bridge
Bucht	German	bay
Bugt	Danish	bay
-bugten	Danish	bay
Bukhta	Russian	bay
Bukit	Indonesian, Malay	hill, mountain
-bukt, -bukta	Norwegian	bay
-bukten	Swedish	bay
Bulag	Mongolian	spring
Bulak	Russian, Uighur	spring
Bum	Burmese	mountain
Burnu, Burun	Turkish	cape, point
Büyük	Turkish	big
Bwlch	Welsh	pass
C		
Cabo	Portuguese, Spanish	cape, point
Cachoeira	Portuguese	waterfall
Caka	Tibetan	salt lake
Cala	Catalan, Italian	bay
Caleta	Spanish	inlet
Câmpia	Romanian	plain
Campo	Italian, Spanish	plain
Cañada, Cañadón	Spanish	ravine, gorge
Canal	French, Portuguese, Spanish	canal, channel
Caño	Spanish	river
Cañon	Spanish	canyon
Caol	Gaelic	hill
Cap	Catalan, French	cape, point
Capo	Italian	cape, point
Carn	Welsh	hill
Castell	Catalan	castle
Causse	French	limestone plateau
Çay, -çay, Çayı, -çayı	Azeri, Turkish	river
Cayo	Spanish	island
Cefn	Welsh	hill, ridge
Cerro	Spanish	hill, mountain, peak
Česká, České, Český	Czech	Czech
Chaco	Spanish	plain
Chāh	Farsi	river
Chaîne	French	mountain range
Cham	Kurdish	river
Chapada	Portuguese	hills, uplands
Château	French	castle, palace
Chau	Chinese	island
Chaung	Burmese	river
Chāy	Kurdish	river
Chhu	Dzongkha (Bhutan)	river
Chiang	Thai	town
Chink	Russian	hill range
Chiyā	Kurdish	mountain, hill range
Chott	Arabic	salt lake
Chuan	Chinese	river
Chuŏr Phnum	Cambodian	mountain range
Ci	Indonesian	river
Ciénaga	Spanish	marshy lake
Cima	Italian	peak
Cime	French	peak
Città	Italian	city
Ciudad	Spanish	town, city
Cnoc	Gaelic	hill
Co	Tibetan	lake
Col	French	pass
Collado	Spanish	mountain
Colle	Italian	pass
Colline	French	hill
Cona	Tibetan	lake
Cordillera	Spanish	mountain range
Corno	Italian	peak
Coronel	Spanish	colonel
Costa	Catalan, Italian, Portuguese, Spanish	coastal area
Côte	French	coast, hill region, slope
Coutada	Portuguese	reserve
Coxilha	Portuguese	mountain pasture
Cratère	French	crater
Creag	Gaelic	mountain
Cruz	Spanish	cross
Cu Lao	Vietnamese	island
Cuchilla	Spanish	mountain range
Cuenca	Spanish	deep valley, river basin
Cueva	Spanish	cave
Cumbre	Spanish	mountain
-cun	Chinese	village
D		
Da	Chinese	big
Da	Vietnamese	river
Dağ, Dağı	Azeri, Turkish	hill(s), mountain(s)
Dāgh	Farsi	mountain(s)
Dağları	Turkish	mountains
-dake	Japanese	hill, mountain
-dal	Afrikaans, Danish, Swedish	valley
-dal, -dalen	Norwegian	valley
-dalur	Icelandic	valley
-dan	Korean	cape, point
Danau	Indonesian, Malay	lake
Dao	Chinese	island
Đao	Vietnamese	island
Daqq	Farsi	salt flat, salt lake
-dara	Tajik	river
Darreh	Farsi	valley
Dar'ya	Russian	river
Daryācheh	Farsi	lake
Dashan	Chinese	mountain
Dasht	Farsi	desert
Dataran Tinggi	Malay	plateau
Davan	Kazakh	pass
Dawḩat	Arabic	bay
Dayr	Arabic	monastery
Dealul	Romanian	hill, mountain
Dealurile	Romanian	hills
Deh	Farsi	village
Deir	Arabic	monastery
Denizi	Turkish	sea
Deresi	Turkish	river
Desierto	Spanish	desert
Détroit	French	channel
-diep	Dutch	channel
Dingzi	Chinese	hill, small mountain
Djebel	Arabic	mountain
-do	Korean	island
Dolna, Dolni	Bulgarian	lower
Dolna, Dolne, Dolny	Polish	lower
Dolní	Czech	lower
Dong	Chinese	east, eastern
-dong	Korean	village
Donja, Donji	Croatian, Serbian	lower
Dorf	German	village
-dorp	Afrikaans, Dutch	village
Druim	Gaelic	hill, mountain
Dund	Mongolian	middle, central
Düzü	Azeri	plain
-dyngja	Icelandic	hill, mountain
Dzüün	Mongolian	east, eastern
E		
Eilean	Gaelic	island
-elv, -elva	Norwegian	river
Embalse	Spanish	reservoir
'Emeq	Hebrew	plain
Ensenada	Spanish	bay
Erg, 'Erg, 'Erg	Arabic	sand dunes
Eski	Turkish	old
Estany	Catalan	pond
Estero	Spanish	estuary, inlet, lagoon
Estrada	Spanish	bay
Estrecho	Spanish	strait
Étang	French	lagoon, lake
-ey, -eyjar	Icelandic	island, islands
-eyri	Icelandic	sandbar
ežeras	Lithuanian	lake
ezers	Latvian	lake
F		
Falaise	French	cliff, escarpment
Farihy	Malagasy	lake
Fayḑat	Arabic	waterhole
-fell	Icelandic	hill, mountain
Fels	German	rock
Feng	Chinese	mountain
Fiume	Italian	river

Geographical term	Language	Meaning
-fjäll, -fjällen, -fjället	Swedish	hill(s), mountain(s)
-fjallgarður	Icelandic	mountains
-fjara	Icelandic	beach
-fjell, -fjellet	Norwegian	mountain
-fjöll	Icelandic	hill(s), mountain(s)
Fjord, -fjord, -fjorden	Danish, Norwegian, Swedish	fjord
-fjörður	Icelandic	fjord
Fliegu	Maltese	channel
-fljót	Icelandic	river
-flói	Icelandic	bay
-főcsatorna	Hungarian	canal
Foel	Welsh	hill
Förde	German	inlet
Forêt	French	forest
Forst	German	forest
-foss	Icelandic	waterfall
-foss, -fossen	Norwegian	rapids, waterfall
Fuente	Spanish	source, well
Fulayj	Arabic	watercourse

G

Geographical term	Language	Meaning
-gan	Japanese	rock
Gang	Dzongkha (Bhutan)	mountain
Gang	Chinese	bay, river
-gang	Korean	river
Gaoyuan	Chinese	plateau
Gardaneh	Farsi	pass
-gat	Dutch	channel
-gata	Japanese	inlet, lagoon, lake
Gau	German	district
Gave	French	torrent
-gawa	Japanese	river
Gebel	Arabic	mountain
Gebergte	Dutch	mountain range
Gebiet	German	district, region
Gebirge	German	mountains
Geodha	Gaelic	inlet
Gezâ'ir	Arabic	islands
Gezirat	Arabic	island
Ghard	Arabic	sand dunes
Ghubba	Arabic	bay
Gjiri	Albanian	bay
Gletscher	German	glacier
Gobernador	Spanish	governor
Gobi	Mongolian	desert
Gol	Mongolian	river
Göl	Azeri	lake
Golets	Russian	mountain
Golf	Catalan	gulf
Golfe	French	bay, gulf
Golfo	Italian, Spanish	bay, gulf
Gölü	Azeri, Turkish	lake
Gora	Bulgarian, Croatian, Russian, Serbian	mountain(s)
Gorges	French	gorge
Górka	Polish	hill
Gornja, Gornje, Gornji	Croatian, Serbian	upper
Gorno-	Russian	mountainous
Gory	Russian	mountains
Góry	Polish	mountains
Gou	Chinese	river
Graben	German	trench
-grad	Bulgarian, Croatian, Russian, Serbian	town
Grand, Grande	French	big
-gród	Polish	town
Groot	Afrikaans, Dutch	big
Gross, Grosse, Grossen, Grosser (also Groß-)	German	big
Grotta	Italian	cave
Grotte	French	cave
Grotte	Italian	caves
Groupe	French	group
Grund	German	ground, valley
Gruppo	Italian	group
Gryada	Russian	mountains
Guan	Chinese	pass
Guba	Russian	bay, gulf
Gubed	Somali	bay
-guntō	Japanese	islands
Gunung	Indonesian, Malay	mountain
Guri	Albanian	peak

H

Geographical term	Language	Meaning
Ḥafar	Arabic	wells
Hafen	German	port, harbour
Haff	German	bay
Hai	Chinese	lake, sea
Haixia	Chinese	channel, strait
-háls	Icelandic	ridge
-halvøya	Norwegian	peninsula
Hamada, Hammada	Arabic	plateau
-hamn	Norwegian, Swedish	port, harbour
-hamrar	Icelandic	cliffs
Hāmūn	Farsi	marsh, salt pan
-hantō	Japanese	peninsula
Har	Hebrew	mountain
Hara	Belorussian	hill
Hardt	German	wooded hills
Ḥarrat, Ḥarrāt	Arabic	lava field
Hassi	Arabic	well
-haug, -haugen	Norwegian	hill
-havn	Danish, Faroese, Norwegian	bay, harbour, port
Hawr	Arabic	lake, impermanent lake, marsh
Häyk'	Amharic	lake
He	Chinese	river
-hegység	Hungarian	hills, mountains
-hei	Norwegian	heath, moor
-heide	Dutch	heath, marsh
Heide	German	heath, moor
-heiði	Icelandic	heath
Helodrano	Malagasy	bay
Higashi-	Japanese	east, eastern
-hisar	Turkish	castle
Ḥiṣn	Arabic	fort
Hka	Burmese	river
-hnjúkur	Icelandic	hill
-ho	Korean	lake
-hø	Norwegian	peak
Hoch	German	high
Hoek	Dutch	cape, point
-höfði	Icelandic	hill, mountain
-höfn	Icelandic	cove
Hög	Swedish	height, high
-högda	Norwegian	height
Höhe	German	height
Hohen-	German	high
Hoi, Hoi Hap	Chinese	bay, channel, harbour, inlet
-høj, -høje	Danish	hill, hills
Hon	Vietnamese	island
Hoog	Dutch	high
Hora, Hory	Czech, Ukrainian	mountain(s)
-horn	Icelandic	cape, point, peak
Horn, -horn	German	mountain, peak
Horná, Horné, Horní, Horný	Czech	upper
Ḥorvot	Hebrew	ruins
-hot	Mongolian	town
-hrad	Czech	town
-hraun	Icelandic	lava field
Hu	Chinese	lake

I

Geographical term	Language	Meaning
Idd	Arabic	well
Île	French	island
Ilha, Ilhéu	Portuguese	island
Illa	Catalan	island
im	German	in
imeni	Russian	in the name of
Inish	Irish	island
Insel, Inseln	German	island, islands
Insula	Romanian	island
Irq, 'Irq	Arabic	hill, sand dune, sand dunes
Isla	Spanish	island
Iso-	Finnish	big
Isola, Isole	Italian	island, islands
Isolte	Catalan	island
Isthme	French	isthmus
Istmo	Spanish	isthmus
-iwa	Japanese	island

J

Geographical term	Language	Meaning
Jabal	Arabic	mountain
järv	Estonian	lake
-järvi	Finnish	lake
Jasiired	Somali	island
Jaun-	Latvian	new
-jaure	Lappish	lake
Jazīrah, Jazīreh, Jazīrat	Arabic	island
Jbel, Jebel	Arabic	mountain
Jezero, jezero	Croatian, Serbian, Slovene	lake
Jezioro	Polish	lake
Jiang	Chinese	river
Jiao	Chinese	cape, point
Jibāl	Arabic	mountains
-jima	Japanese	island
Jing	Chinese	well
-jõgi	Estonian	river
-joki	Finnish	river
-jokka	Lappish	river
-jökull, jökullen	Icelandic, Norwegian	glacier, ice cap

K

Geographical term	Language	Meaning
Kaap	Afrikaans	cape, point
-kai	Japanese	bay, channel
-kaigan	Japanese	coastal area
-kaikyō	Japanese	channel, strait
Kali	Indonesian, Malay	river
kalnas, kalnis	Lithuanian	hill
Kalns	Latvian	hill
Kamen'	Russian	rock
Kamm	German	ridge, crest
Kâmpóng	Cambodian	town, village
-kanaal	Dutch	canal
Kanal	German, Russian	canal
Kanał	Polish	canal
Kanalı	Azeri	canal
Kaôh	Cambodian	island
Kap	Danish	cape, point
Kapp	Norwegian	cape, point
Karang	Indonesian, Malay	reef
Kato	Greek	lower
Kavīr	Farsi	salt desert
-kawa	Japanese	river
Kecil	Indonesian, Malay	small
K'edi	Georgian	hills
Kefar	Hebrew	village
Kepi	Albanian	cape, point
Kepulauan	Indonesian	islands
Keski-	Finnish	middle, central
Khabrah, Khabrat	Arabic	impermanent lake
Khalīg, Khalīj	Arabic	bay, gulf
Khao	Thai	peak
Khashm	Arabic	hill
Khawr	Arabic	bay, channel
Khor, Khōr	Arabic	bay
Khowr	Farsi	bay, inlet
Khrebet	Russian	mountain range
Kis-	Hungarian	small
Kita-	Japanese	north, northern
Klein	Afrikaans	small
Klein, Kleine, Kleiner	German	small
Klint	Danish	cliff
-kloof	Afrikaans	pass
Knock	Irish	hill
-ko	Japanese	lake
Ko	Thai	island
-kōchi, -kōgen	Japanese	plateau
Koh	Farsi	mountain
Kok	Chinese	cape, point
Köl	Kazakh, Kyrgyz	lake
Kolpos	Greek	gulf
Koog	German	polder (reclaimed land)
-kop	Afrikaans	hill, mountain
Kopf	German	hill
Körfezi	Turkish	bay, gulf
kõrgustik	Estonian	upland
Kosa	Russian, Ukrainian	spit
Kou	Chinese	river mouth
-köy	Turkish	village
Kraj	Croatian, Czech, Polish, Serbian	region
Krajobrazowy	Polish	regional
Kray	Russian	territory
Kryazh	Russian	hills, ridge
Kuala	Malay	river mouth
Küçük	Turkish	small
Kuduk	Uighur	well
Kūh	Farsi	mountain
Kūhhā	Farsi	mountain range
Kul'	Russian	lake
-kūl	Tajik	lake
-küla	Estonian	village
Kum	Russian	sandy desert
-kundo	Korean	islands
Kuppe	German	hill top
kurk	Estonian	channel, strait
K'vemo	Georgian	upper
-kvísl, kvíslar	Icelandic	river, rivers
-kylä	Finnish	village
Kyun	Burmese	island

L

Geographical term	Language	Meaning
La	Tibetan	pass
Lac	French	lake
Lacul	Romanian	lake
Laem	Thai	cape, point
Lago	Italian, Portuguese, Spanish	lake
Lagoa	Portuguese	lagoon
Laguna	Spanish	lagoon, lake
Lagune	French	lagoon
laht	Estonian	bay
-laid	Estonian	island
Lam	Thai	river
Län	Swedish	county
Land	German	province
Lande	French	heath, sandy moor
Las	Polish	wood, forest
Laut	Indonesian, Malay	sea
Lerr	Armenian	mountain
Lerrnashght'a	Armenian	mountains
Lich	Armenian	lake
Liedao	Chinese	islands
Liel-	Latvian	big
Lille	Danish, Norwegian	small
Liman	Russian	bay, lagoon, lake
Limni	Greek	lagoon, lake
Limnothalassa	Greek	inlet, lagoon
Ling	Chinese	mountain range
Liqeni	Albanian	lake
Llano	Spanish	plain, prairie
Llyn	Welsh	lake
Loch, Lochan	Gaelic	lake, small lake
Lohatanjona	Malagasy	cape, point
Loi	Burmese	mountain
looduskaitseala	Estonian	reserve
Luonnonpuisto	Finnish	nature reserve
-luoto	Finnish	rocky island
Lyman	Ukrainian	bay, lake

M

Geographical term	Language	Meaning
Macizo	Spanish	mountain range
Madh	Albanian	big
Madīnat	Arabic	town
Mae, Mae Nam	Thai	river
mägi	Estonian	hill
Măgura	Romanian	hill, mountain
Maḥaṭṭat	Arabic	station
Maja	Albanian	mountain
Mal	Albanian	mountain(s)
Mala	Croatian, Serbian	small
Malá	Czech, Slovak	small
Mali	Albanian	mountain
Mali	Croatian, Serbian, Ukrainian	small
Malo	Croatian, Serbian	small
Maloye	Russian	small
Maly, Malyya	Belorussian	small
-man	Korean	bay
Mar	Spanish	lagoon, lake
Marais	French	marsh, swamp
Mare	Italian	sea
Mare	Romanian	big
marios	Lithuanian	lake
Marsa	Arabic	anchorage, bay, inlet
Marsch	German	fen, marsh
Masabb	Arabic	estuary
Massif	French	mountains, upland
Ma'ṭan	Arabic	well
Mayor	Spanish	higher, larger
Maz-	Latvian	small
Meall	Gaelic	hill, mountain
Meer	Dutch, German	lake
Mega, Megalo-	Greek	big
Men	Chinese	gate

Geographical term	Language	Meaning
Menor	Portuguese, Spanish	smaller, lesser
Mersa	Arabic	anchorage, inlet
Mesa, Meseta	Spanish	tableland
Mesto	Croatian, Serbian	town
Město	Czech	town
Mets	Armenian	big
Mezzo	Italian	middle, central
Miao	Chinese	temple
Miasto	Polish	town
Mic, Mica	Romanian	small
Mikra, Mikri	Greek	small
Mīnā'	Arabic	port, harbour
Minami-	Japanese	south, southern
-mine	Japanese	mountain
-misaki	Japanese	cape, point
Mishāsh	Arabic	well
Mittel-, Mitten-	German	middle, central
Moel	Welsh	hill
Monasterio	Spanish	monastery
Moni	Greek	monastery
Mont	French	hill, mountain
Montagna	Italian	mountain
Montagne	French	mountain
Monte	Italian, Portuguese, Spanish	hill, mountain
Monti	Italian	mountains
Moor	German	marsh, moor, swamp
Moos	German	marsh, moss
More	Russian	sea
Mörön	Mongolian	river
Morro	Portuguese	hill
Morro	Spanish	cape, point
-mose	Danish	marsh, moor
Moyen	French	middle, central
Mt'a	Georgian	mountain
Muang	Laotian, Thai	town
Muara	Indonesian, Malay	estuary
Mui	Vietnamese	cape, point
Mun	Chinese	channel
Munţii	Romanian	mountains
Mynydd	Welsh	mountain
-mýri	Icelandic	marsh
Mys	Russian	cape, point

N

Geographical term	Language	Meaning
na	Croatian, Czech, Russian, Serbian, Slovak, Slovene	on
Nacional	Portuguese, Spanish	national
nacionalinis	Lithuanian	national
nad	Czech, Polish, Slovak	above, over
-nada	Japanese	bay, gulf
Nafūd	Arabic	desert, sand dunes
Nagor'ye	Russian	mountains, plateau
Nagy-	Hungarian	big
Nahr	Arabic	river
Nakhon	Thai	town
Nakrdzali	Georgian	reserve
Nam	Burmese, Laotian	river
Nam	Korean, Vietnamese	south, southern
Nan	Chinese	south, southern
Nanshan	Chinese	mountain range
Narodowy	Polish	national
Nationaal	Dutch	national
Naturreservat	Norwegian, Swedish	nature reserve
Natuurreservaat	Dutch	nature reserve
Naviglio	Italian	canal
Nawa-	Urdu	new
Nazionale	Italian	national
Neder-	Dutch	lower
Nehri	Turkish	river
Nei	Chinese	inner
Nek	Afrikaans	pass
-nes	Icelandic	cape, point
Neu-	German	new
Neuf, Neuve	French	new
Nevado, Nevada	Spanish	snow-covered mountain(s)
Nieder-	German	lower
Nieuw, Nieuwe, Nieuwer	Dutch	new
nina	Estonian	cape, point
Nishi-	Japanese	west, western
Nizhneye, Nizhniy, Nizhniye, Nizhnyaya	Russian	lower
Nizina	Belorussian	lowland
Nízke	Slovak	low
Nizmennost'	Russian	lowland
Nižní	Czech	lower
Nižný	Slovak	lower
Noguera	Catalan	river
Noord	Dutch	north, northern
Nord	French, German	north, northern
Nord-, Nordre	Danish	north, northern
Norður	Icelandic	north, northern
Norra	Swedish	north, northern
Nørre	Danish	north, northern
Norte	Portuguese, Spanish	north, northern
Nos	Bulgarian, Russian	cape, point, spit
Nosy	Malagasy	island
Nou	Romanian	new
Nouveau, Nouvelle	French	new
Nova	Bulgarian, Croatian, Portuguese, Serbian, Slovene, Ukrainian	new
Nová	Czech	new
Novaya	Russian	new
Nové	Czech, Slovak	new
Novi	Bulgarian, Croatian, Serbian, Ukrainian	new
Novo	Portuguese, Slovene	new
Novo-, Novoye	Russian	new
Novy	Belorussian	new
Nový	Czech	new
Novyy, Novyye	Russian, Ukrainian	new
Novyya	Belorussian	new
Nowa, Nowe, Nowy	Polish	new
Nueva, Nuevo	Spanish	new
-numa	Japanese	lake

Geographical term	Language	Meaning
-núpur	Icelandic	hill
Nur	Chinese, Mongolian	lake
Nuruu	Mongolian	mountain range
Nuur	Mongolian	lake
Ny-	Danish, Norwegian, Swedish	new

O

Geographical term	Language	Meaning
-ø	Danish	island
-ö	Swedish	island
oaivi, oaivve	Lappish	hill, mountain
Obanbari	Tajik	reservoir
Ober-	German	upper
Oblast'	Russian, Ukrainian	administrative division
-odde	Danish, Norwegian	cape, point
Oeste	Spanish	west, western
Okrug	Russian	administrative district
-ön	Swedish	island
Öndör-	Mongolian	upper
-oog	German	island
Oost, Ooster	Dutch	east, eastern
-öræfi	Icelandic	lava field
Oriental	Spanish	east, eastern
Ormos	Greek	bay
Oros	Greek	mountain
-ós	Icelandic	river mouth
Ost-	German	east, eastern
Øster-	Danish, Norwegian	east, eastern
Östra-	Swedish	east, eastern
Ostriv	Ukrainian	island
Ostrov, Ostrova	Russian	island, islands
Oud, Oude, Ouden, Ouder	Dutch	old
Oued	Arabic	watercourse
Ovası	Turkish	plain
Over-	Danish, Dutch	upper
Över-, Övre-	Norwegian, Swedish	upper
-oy	Faroese	island
Ozero	Russian, Ukrainian	lake

P

Geographical term	Language	Meaning
-pää	Finnish	hill
Pampa	Spanish	plain
Pantà	Catalan	reservoir
Pantanal	Portuguese	marsh
Pao	Chinese	small lake
Parbat	Urdu	mountain
Parc	French	park
Parc Naturel	French	nature reserve
Parco	Italian	park
parkas	Lithuanian	park
Parque	Portuguese, Spanish	park
-pas	Afrikaans	pass
Paso	Spanish	pass
Paß	German	pass
Passage	French	channel
Passe	French	channel
Passo	Italian	pass
Pasul	Romanian	pass
Pegunungan	Indonesian, Malay	mountain range
Pelabuhan	Malay	port, harbour
Pen	Welsh	hill
Peña	Spanish	cliff, rock
Pendi	Chinese	basin
Península	Spanish	peninsula
Péninsule	French	peninsula
Penisola	Italian	peninsula
Pereval	Russian	pass
Pervo-, Pervyy	Russian	first
Peski	Russian	desert
Petit, Petite	French	small
Phou	Laotian	mountain
Phu	Thai, Vietnamese	mountain
Phumĭ	Cambodian	town, village
Pic	Catalan, French	peak
Picacho	Spanish	peak
Pico	Spanish	peak
Pik	Russian	peak
Pingyuan	Chinese	plain
Pivostriv	Ukrainian	peninsula
Pizzo	Italian	peak
-plaat	Dutch	flat, sandbank, shoal
Plage	French	beach
Plaine	French	plain
Planalto	Portuguese	plateau
Planina	Bulgarian, Croatian, Serbian	mountain(s)
Platforma	Romanian	plateau
Plato	Bulgarian, Russian	plateau
Playa	Spanish	beach
Plaza	Spanish	market-place, square
Ploskogor'ye	Russian	plateau
Po	Chinese	lake
pod	Czech, Russian, Slovak	under, sub-, near
Podişul	Romanian	plateau
Pointe	French	cape, point
Pojezierze	Polish	area of lakes
Polje	Croatian, Serbian	plain
Poluostrov	Russian	peninsula
Pont	French	bridge
Ponta	Maltese, Portuguese	cape, point
Ponte	Portuguese	bridge
poolsaar	Estonian	peninsula
Porogi	Russian	rapids
Port	Catalan, French, Maltese, Russian	port, harbour
Portella	Italian	pass
Portillo	Spanish	gap, pass
Porto	Italian, Portuguese, Spanish	bay, port, harbour, pass
Pradesh	Hindi	state

Geographical term	Language	Meaning
Praia	Portuguese	beach, shore
Prêk	Cambodian	lake, river
près	French	near, beside
Presa	Spanish	reservoir
Presqu'île	French	peninsula
Pri-	Russian	near, by
Proliv	Russian	channel, strait
Protoka	Russian	channel, watercourse
Pueblo	Spanish	village
Puente	Spanish	bridge
Puerta	Spanish	narrow pass
Puerto	Spanish	pass, port, harbour
Puig	Catalan	hill, mountain
Puk-	Korean	north, northern
Pulau	Indonesian, Malay	island
Pulau-pulau	Indonesian, Malay	islands
Puncak	Indonesian, Malay	hill, mountain, summit
Punta	Italian, Spanish	cape, point
Punta	Italian	hill, mountain
Puntan	Marshallese	cape, point
Puy	French	peak

Q

Geographical term	Language	Meaning
Qā'	Arabic	depression, salt flat, impermanent lake
Qabr	Arabic	tomb
Qafa	Albanian	pass
Qala	Maltese	bay
Qalamat	Arabic	well
Qalti	Arabic	well
Qâret	Arabic	hill
Qatorkŭhi	Tajik	mountain range
Qi	Chinese	banner (administrative division)
Qiao	Chinese	bridge
Qiryat	Hebrew	town
Qolleh	Farsi	mountain
Qoor, Qooriga	Somali	bay
qoruğu	Azeri	reserve
Qu	Tibetan	river
Quan	Chinese	spring, well
Quebrada	Spanish	ravine, river
Qullai	Tajik	mountain
Qundao	Chinese	islands

R

Geographical term	Language	Meaning
Raas	Somali	cape, point
Rade	French	harbour
rags	Latvian	cape, point
Rambla	Catalan	river
Ramla	Maltese	bay, harbour
Ramlat	Arabic	sandy desert
-rani	Icelandic	spur
Ras	Arabic, Maltese	cape, point
Ra's	Arabic, Farsi	cape, point
Râs, Rās	Arabic	cape, point
Ravnina	Russian	plain
Récif	French	reef
Represa	Portuguese, Spanish	reservoir
Reserva	Portuguese, Spanish	reserve
Réserve de Faune, Réserve Faunique	French	wildlife reserve
Réserve Naturelle	French	nature reserve
Reshteh	Farsi	mountain range
Respublika	Russian	republic
-rettō	Japanese	island chain, island group
rezervatas	Lithuanian	reserve
-ri	Korean	village
Ri	Tibetan	mountain
Ría	Spanish	estuary, inlet, river mouth
Ribeirão, Ribeiro	Portuguese	river
Rio	Portuguese	river
Río	Spanish	river
Riserva	Italian	reserve
-rivier	Afrikaans	river
Riviera	Italian	coastal area
Rivière	French	river
Roca	Spanish	rock
Rocher	French	rock
Rt	Croatian, Serbian	cape, point
Rū, Ŗūbār	Kurdish	river
Rubh', Rubha	Gaelic	cape, point
Rūd, Rūdkhāneh	Farsi	river
Rujm	Arabic	hill

S

Geographical term	Language	Meaning
-saar	Estonian	island
-saari	Finnish	island
Sabkhat, Sabkhet	Arabic	impermanent lake, salt flat, salt marsh
Sadd, Saddat	Arabic	dam
Sagar, Sagara	Hindi	lake
Şaghîr, Şaghīr	Arabic	small
Şaḩrā'	Arabic	desert
-saki	Japanese	cape, point
Salar, Salina	Spanish	salt pan
Salto	Portuguese, Spanish	waterfall
San	Italian, Maltese, Portuguese, Spanish	saint
San	Laotian	mountain
-san	Japanese, Korean	mountain
-sanchi	Japanese	mountain range
-sandur	Icelandic	sandy area
Sankt	German, Russian	saint
-sanmaek	Korean	mountain range
-sanmyaku	Japanese	mountain range
Sant	Catalan	saint
Sant'	Italian	saint

Geographical term	Language	Meaning
Santa	Italian, Portuguese, Spanish	saint
Santo	Italian, Portuguese, Spanish	saint
São	Portuguese	saint
Sar	Kurdish	mountain
Sarīr	Arabic	desert
Satu	Romanian	village
Say	Kyrgyz	river
Schloß	German	castle, mansion
Scoglio	Italian	reef, rock
Sebkha, Sebkhet	Arabic	salt flat, salt marsh
See, -see	German	lake
-şehir	Turkish	town
Selat	Indonesian, Malay	channel, strait
Selatan	Indonesian, Malay	south, southern
-selkä	Finnish	lake, open water, ridge
Selo	Croatian, Russian, Serbian	village
Selva	Portuguese, Spanish	forest
Semenanjung	Indonesian, Malay	peninsula
Seno	Spanish	bay, sound
Serra	Catalan, Portuguese	hills, mountains
Serranía	Spanish	mountain range
-seter	Norwegian	mountain pasture
-seto	Japanese	channel, strait
Severnaya, Severnoye, Severnyy, Severo-	Russian	north, northern
Sfântu	Romanian	saint
Sgeir	Gaelic	island
Sgor, Sgorach, Sgorr, Sgurr	Gaelic	hill
Shahr	Farsi	town
Sha'īb, Sha'īān	Arabic	watercourse
Shamo	Chinese	desert
Shan	Chinese	hill(s), mountain(s)
Shang	Chinese	next to, upper
Shankou	Chinese	pass
Sharm	Arabic	bay
Shaţţ	Arabic	estuary, river mouth, watercourse
Shën-	Albanian	saint
Shet'	Amharic	watercourse
Shi	Chinese	city
-shima	Japanese	island
-sho	Japanese	island
-shotō	Japanese	islands
Shui	Chinese	river
Shui Tong	Chinese	reservoir
Shuiku	Chinese	reservoir
Sierra	Spanish	mountain range
Silsiläsi	Azeri	hills
-sjø	Norwegian	lake
-sjö, -sjön	Swedish	lake
-sjór	Icelandic	lake
-sker	Icelandic	island
-skog	Norwegian	wood
Slieau	Manx	hill, mountain
Slieve	Irish	hill, mountain
Sloboda	Russian	large village
Sø	Danish, Norwegian	lake
Söder, Södra	Swedish	south, southern
Solonchak	Russian	salt lake
Sommet	French	peak, summit
Sønder-, Søndre	Danish	south, southern
Sông	Vietnamese	river
Sopka	Russian	hill, mountain, volcano
Sør-	Norwegian	south, southern
Sor	Russian	salt pan
sous	French	under
Sovkhoz	Russian	state farm
Spitze	German	peak
Sredna, Sredno	Bulgarian	middle, central
Sredne-, Sredneye, Sredniy, Srednyaya	Russian	middle, central
Sron	Gaelic	hill
Stac	Gaelic	hill, stack
-stad	Afrikaans, Norwegian, Swedish	town
-stadt	German	town
-staður	Icelandic	town
Stagno	Italian	lagoon, lake
Stara, Stari	Croatian, Serbian, Ukrainian	old
Stará, Staré, Starý	Czech	old
Staraya, Stary, Staryya	Belorussian	old
Staraya, Staroye, Staryy, Staryye	Russian	old
Stare, Staro-, Staryy	Ukrainian	old
Stausee	German	reservoir
Steno	Greek	strait
Step'	Russian	plain, steppe
Stob	Gaelic	hill, mountain
Stœ̆ng	Cambodian	river
Stór-, Stóra, Stóri	Icelandic	big
Stor, Stora	Swedish	big
Store	Danish	big
Strand	Danish, German	beach
-strand	Norwegian, Swedish	beach
Straße	German	street
Stretta	Italian	strait
-strönd	Icelandic	beach
Sud	French	south, southern
Süd-, Süder-	German	south, southern
Suður-	Icelandic	south, southern
Suid	Afrikaans	south, southern
-suidō	Japanese	channel, strait
Sul	Portuguese	south, southern
sul, sull'	Italian	on
Sund	Swedish	strait, sound
Sungai	Indonesian, Malay	river
-suo	Finnish	marsh, swamp
Superior	Spanish	upper
Sūq	Arabic	market
Sur	Spanish	south, southern
sur	French	on
Suur	Estonian	big
Sveti	Croatian, Serbian	saint
Syðra, Syðri	Icelandic	south, southern
sýsla	Icelandic	county
Szent-	Hungarian	saint
-sziget	Hungarian	island

T

Geographical term	Language	Meaning
-tag	Uighur	mountain
-take	Japanese	hill, mountain
Tal	German	valley
Tall	Arabic	hill
Tanjona	Malagasy	cape, point
Tanjong, Tanjung	Indonesian, Malay	cape, point
Tao	Chinese	island
Tassili	Berber	plateau
Tau	Russian	mountain(s)
Taung	Burmese	mountain
Tba	Georgian	lake
Techniti Limni	Greek	reservoir
tekojärvi	Finnish	reservoir
Tell	Arabic	hill, mountain
Teluk, Telukan	Indonesian, Malay	bay, gulf
Tengah	Indonesian, Malay	middle, central
Teniente	Spanish	lieutenant
Tepe, Tepesi	Turkish	hill, mountain
Terara	Amharic	mountain
Terre	French	land
Thale	Thai	lake
Thamad	Arabic	well
Tierra	Spanish	land
Timur	Indonesian, Malay	east, eastern
-tind, -tinden	Norwegian	peak
-tindar	Icelandic	peak
-tindur	Faroese, Icelandic	peak
Tir'at	Arabic	canal, river, watercourse
Tizi	Berber	pass
-tjåkkå	Lappish	mountain
-tjärro	Lappish	mountain
-tó	Hungarian	lake
-tō	Japanese	island
-to	Korean	island
-tōge	Japanese	pass
-tong	Korean	village
Tônlé	Cambodian	lake, river
Too	Kyrgyz	mountain range
-topp, -toppen	Norwegian	peak
T'ou	Chinese	cape, point
Tsentral'nyy	Russian	central
Tso	Tibetan	lake
Tsqalsats'avi	Georgian	reservoir
Tsui	Chinese	cape, point
Túnel	Spanish	tunnel
-tunturi	Finnish	treeless mountain

U

Geographical term	Language	Meaning
Über-	German	upper
-udden	Swedish	cape, point
Ugheltekhili	Georgian	pass
Új-	Hungarian	new
Ujung	Indonesian	cape, point
Unter-, unter	German	below, lower
'Uqlat	Arabic	well
-ura	Japanese	inlet
'Urayq, 'Urūq	Arabic	sand dunes
Ust'-, Ust'ye	Russian	river mouth
Utara	Indonesian, Malay	north, northern
Uttar	Hindi	north, northern
Uul	Mongolian	mountain range
Uval	Russian	hills
'Uyūn	Arabic	springs

V

Geographical term	Language	Meaning
v	Czech	in
-vaara, -vaarat	Finnish	hill(s), mountain(s)
Vaart, -vaart	Dutch	canal
-vaðall	Icelandic	inlet
-våg	Norwegian	bay
-vágur	Faroese	bay
Väike-	Estonian	small
väin	Estonian	bay, channel, strait
Val	French, Portuguese, Spanish	valley
Vale	Portuguese, Romanian	valley
Vall	Catalan, Spanish	valley
Valle	Italian, Spanish	valley
Vallée	French	valley
Valli	Italian	valleys
Vallon	French	small valley
Vârful	Romanian	hill, mountain
-város	Hungarian	town
-varre	Norwegian	mountain
Väster, Västra	Swedish	west, western
-vatn	Icelandic	lake
-vatn, -vatnet	Norwegian	lake
-vatten, -vattnet	Swedish	lake
Vaux	French	valleys
Vechi	Romanian	old
veehoidla	Estonian	lake
-veld	Afrikaans	field
Velha, Velho	Portuguese	old
Velika	Croatian, Slovene, Serbian	big
Velikaya, Velikiy, Velikiye	Russian	big
Velike	Slovene	big
Veliki	Croatian, Serbian	big
Velká, Velké, Velký	Czech	big
Veľká, Veľké, Veľký	Slovak	big
-vellir	Icelandic	plain
Velyka	Ukrainian	big
Verkhne-, Verkhneye, Verkhniy, Verkhnyaya	Russian	upper
-vesi	Finnish	lake, water
Viaduc	French	viaduct
-vidda	Norwegian	plateau
Vieja, Viejo	Spanish	old
Vieux	French	old
Vig	Danish	bay
-vík	Icelandic	bay
-vik	Norwegian	bay, inlet
Vila	Portuguese	small town
Ville	French	town
Vinh	Vietnamese	bay
-víz	Hungarian	river
-víztároló	Hungarian	reservoir
-vlei	Afrikaans	lake, salt pan
-vloer	Afrikaans	salt pan
Voblasts'	Belorussian	province
Vodaskhovishcha	Belorussian	reservoir
Vodná nádrž	Slovak	reservoir
Vodní nádrž	Czech	reservoir
Vodokhranilishche	Russian	reservoir
Vodoskhovyshche	Ukrainian	reservoir
-vogur	Icelandic	bay
Volcán	Spanish	volcano
Vostochno-, Vostochnyy	Russian	east, eastern
-vötn	Icelandic	lakes
Vozvyshennost'	Russian	hills, upland
Vozyera	Belorussian	lake
Vpadina	Russian	depression
Vrchovina	Czech	hills, mountain region
Vrŭkh	Bulgarian	hill, mountain
Vulkan	Russian	volcano
Vyalikaya, Vyalikaye, Vyaliki, Vyalikiya	Belorussian	big
Vyerkhnya	Belorussian	upper
Vysokaya, Vysokoye	Russian	upper

W

Geographical term	Language	Meaning
-waard	Dutch	polder (reclaimed land)
Wad	Dutch	sandflat
Wadi, Wâdi, Wādī	Arabic	watercourse
Wai	Chinese	outer
Wald	German	forest
Wan	Chinese	bay
-wan	Japanese	bay
Wand	German	cliff
Wasser	German	water
Wāw	Arabic	well
Webi	Somali	river
Wenz	Amharic	river, watercourse
Wielka, Wielki, Wielkie, Wielko-	Polish	big
-woud	Dutch	wood, forest
Wysoka, Wysoki, Wysokie	Polish	upper
Wyżna	Polish	lowland
Wzvyshsha	Belorussian	upland

X

Geographical term	Language	Meaning
Xé	Vietnamese	river
Xi	Chinese	river, west, western
Xia	Chinese	gorge, lower
Xian	Chinese	county
Xiao	Chinese	small

Y

Geographical term	Language	Meaning
Yam	Hebrew	lake, sea
-yama	Japanese	mountain
Yang	Chinese	channel
Yangi	Russian	new
Yarımadası	Azeri, Turkish	peninsula
Yazovir	Bulgarian	reservoir
Ye	Burmese	island
Yeni	Turkish	new
Yli-	Finnish	upper
Ynys	Welsh	island
Yoma	Burmese	mountain range
You	Chinese	right
Ytra-, Ytri-	Icelandic	outer
Ytre-	Norwegian	outer
Ytter-	Norwegian, Swedish	outer
Yuan	Chinese	spring
Yumco	Tibetan	lake
Yunhe	Chinese	canal
Yuzhno-, Yuzhnyy	Russian	south, southern

Z

Geographical term	Language	Meaning
Za-	Russian	behind, beyond
-zaki	Japanese	cape, point
Zalew	Polish	bay
Zaliv	Russian	bay, gulf, inlet
-zan	Japanese	mountain
Zand	Dutch	sandbank, sandhill
Zangbo	Tibetan	river
Zapadnaya, Zapadno-, Zapadnyy	Russian	west, western
Zapavyednik	Belorussian	reserve
Zapovednik	Russian	reserve
Zapovidnyk	Ukrainian	reserve
Zatoka	Polish, Ukrainian	bay, gulf, lagoon
-zee	Dutch	lake, sea
Zemlya	Russian	land
Zemo	Georgian	upper
Zhen	Chinese	town
Zhong	Chinese	middle, central
Zhou	Chinese	island
Zizhiqu	Chinese	autonomous region
Zuid, Zuider	Dutch	south, southern
Zuo	Chinese	left

INTRODUCTION TO THE INDEX

The index includes names shown on the maps in the Atlas of the World. Each entry includes the country or geographical area in which the feature is located, a page number and an alphanumeric reference. Additional details within the entries are explained below. Abbreviations used in the index are explained in the table below.

Referencing

Names are referenced by page number, the first element of each entry, and by a grid reference. The grid reference correlates to the alphanumeric values which appear within each map frame. These reflect the graticule on the map – the letter relates to longitude divisions, the number to latitude divisions.

Names are generally referenced to the largest scale map page on which they appear. For large geographical features, including countries, the reference is to the largest scale map on which the feature appears in its entirety, or on which the majority of it appears.

Rivers are referenced to their lowest downstream point – either their mouth or their confluence with another river. The river name will generally be positioned as close to this point as possible, but may not necessarily be in the same grid square.

Alternative Names

Alternative names or name forms appear as cross-references and refer the user to the entry for the map form of the name.

For rivers with multiple names – for example those which flow through several countries – all alternative name forms are included within the main index entries, with details of the countries in which each form applies. Different types of name used are: alternative forms or spellings currently in use (alt.); English conventional name forms normally used in English-language contexts (conv.); and long names – full forms of names which are most commonly used in the abbreviated form.

Administrative Qualifiers

Entries within the following countries include the main administrative division in which they occur: Australia, Canada, China, India, Serbia, UK and USA. Administrative divisions are also included to differentiate duplicate names – entries of exactly the same name and feature type within the one country – where these division names are shown on the maps. In such cases, duplicate names are alphabetized in the order of the administrative division names.

Additional qualifiers are included for names within selected geographical areas, to indicate more clearly their location. In particular, this has been applied to island nations to indicate the island group, or individual island, on which a feature occurs.

Descriptors

Entries, other than those for towns and cities, include a descriptor indicating the type of geographical feature. Descriptors are not included where the type of feature is implicit in the name itself, unless there is a town or city of exactly the same name.

Insets

Entries relating to names appearing on insets are indicated by a small box symbol: ▫, followed by an inset number if there is more than one inset on the page, or by a grid reference if the inset has its own alphanumeric values.

Name Forms and Alphabetical Order

Name forms are as they appear on the maps, with additional alternative forms included as cross-references. Names appear in full in the index, although they may appear in abbreviated form on the maps.

The Icelandic characters Þ and þ are transliterated and alphabetized as 'Th' and 'th'. The German character ß is alphabetized as 'ss'. Names beginning with Mac or Mc are alphabetized exactly as they appear. The terms Saint, Sainte, etc, are abbreviated to St, Ste, etc, but alphabetized as if in the full form.

Name form policies are explained in the Introduction to the Atlas (pp 66-67).

Numerical Entries

Entries beginning with numerals appear at the beginning of the index, in numerical order. Elsewhere, numerals appear before 'a'.

Permuted terms

Names beginning with generic, geographical terms are permuted – the descriptive term is placed after, and the index alphabetized by, the main part of the name. For example, Lake Superior is indexed as Superior, Lake; Mount Everest as Everest, Mount. This policy is applied to all languages. Permuting has not been applied to names of towns, cities or administrative divisions beginning with such geographical terms. These remain in their full form, for example, Lake Isabella, California, USA. The definite article, for example La, Le, Les (French); El, Las, Los (Spanish); Al, Ar, As (Arabic), is not permuted in any language.

Index Abbreviations

A.C.T.	Australian Capital Territory
admin. dist.	administrative district
admin. div.	administrative division
admin. reg.	administrative region
Afgh.	Afghanistan
AK	Alaska
AL	Alabama
Alg.	Algeria
alt.	alternative name form
Alta	Alberta
Andhra Prad.	Andhra Pradesh
AR	Arkansas
Arg.	Argentina
Arun. Prad.	Arunachal Pradesh
Austr.	Australia
aut. comm.	autonomous community
aut. div.	autonomous division
aut. prov.	autonomous province
aut. reg.	autonomous region
aut. rep.	autonomous republic
AZ	Arizona
Azer.	Azerbaijan
b.	bay
Bangl.	Bangladesh
B.C.	British Columbia
B.I.O.T.	British Indian Ocean Territory
Bol.	Bolivia
Bos.-Herz.	Bosnia-Herzegovina
Bulg.	Bulgaria
c.	cape
CA	California
Can.	Canada
C.A.R.	Central African Republic
CO	Colorado
Col.	Colombia
conv.	conventional name form
CT	Connecticut
Czech Rep.	Czech Republic
DC	District of Columbia
DE	Delaware
Dem. Rep. Congo	Democratic Republic of the Congo
depr.	depression
dept	department
des.	desert
Dom. Rep.	Dominican Republic
E.	East, Eastern
Equat. Guinea	Equatorial Guinea
esc.	escarpment
est.	estuary
Eth.	Ethiopia
Fin.	Finland
FL	Florida
for.	forest
Fr. Guiana	French Guiana
Fr. Polynesia	French Polynesia
g.	gulf
GA	Georgia
Gd Bahama	Grand Bahama
Ger.	Germany
Guat.	Guatemala
hd	headland
Heilong.	Heilongjiang
HI	Hawaii
Hima. Prad.	Himachal Pradesh
H.K.	Hong Kong
Hond.	Honduras
i.	island
is	islands
IA	Iowa
ID	Idaho
IL	Illinois
imp. l.	impermanent lake
IN	Indiana
Indon.	Indonesia
isth.	isthmus
Kazakh.	Kazakhstan
KS	Kansas
KY	Kentucky
Kyrg.	Kyrgyzstan
l.	lake
LA	Louisiana
lag.	lagoon
Lith.	Lithuania
Lux.	Luxembourg
MA	Massachusetts
Madag.	Madagascar
Madh. Prad.	Madhya Pradesh
Mahar.	Maharashtra
Man.	Manitoba
Maur.	Mauritania
MD	Maryland
ME	Maine
Mex.	Mexico
MI	Michigan
MN	Minnesota
MO	Missouri
Moz.	Mozambique
MS	Mississippi
MT	Montana
mt.	mountain
mts	mountains
mun.	municipality
N.	North
N.B.	New Brunswick
NC	North Carolina
ND	North Dakota
NE	Nebraska
Neth.	Netherlands
Nfld.	Newfoundland
NH	New Hampshire
Nic.	Nicaragua
NJ	New Jersey
NM	New Mexico
N.S.	Nova Scotia
N.S.W.	New South Wales
N.T.	Northern Territory
NV	Nevada
N.W.T.	Northwest Territories
NY	New York
N.Z.	New Zealand
OH	Ohio
OK	Oklahoma
Ont.	Ontario
OR	Oregon
PA	Pennsylvania
Pak.	Pakistan
Para.	Paraguay
P.E.I.	Prince Edward Island
pen.	peninsula
Phil.	Philippines
plat.	plateau
P.N.G.	Papua New Guinea
Pol.	Poland
Port.	Portugal
pref.	prefecture
prov.	province
Qld	Queensland
Que.	Québec
r.	river
r. mouth	river mouth
reg.	region
Rep.	Republic
research stn	research station
resr	reservoir
rf	reef
RI	Rhode Island
Rus. Fed.	Russian Federation
S.	South
S.A.	South Australia
Sask.	Saskatchewan
SC	South Carolina
SD	South Dakota
sea chan.	sea channel
Sing.	Singapore
str.	strait
Switz.	Switzerland
Tajik.	Tajikistan
Tanz.	Tanzania
Tas.	Tasmania
terr.	territory
Thai.	Thailand
TN	Tennessee
Trin. and Tob.	Trinidad and Tobago
tun.	tunnel
Turkm.	Turkmenistan
TX	Texas
U.A.E.	United Arab Emirates
U.K.	United Kingdom
Ukr.	Ukraine
Uru.	Uruguay
U.S.A.	United States of America
UT	Utah
Uttar Prad.	Uttar Pradesh
Uzbek.	Uzbekistan
VA	Virginia
val.	valley
Venez.	Venezuela
Vic.	Victoria
vol.	volcano
vol. crater	volcanic crater
VT	Vermont
W.	West, Western
W.A.	Western Australia
WA	Washington
WI	Wisconsin
WV	West Virginia
WY	Wyoming
Y.T.	Yukon Territory

1

203 G3 1st Cataract rapids Egypt
85 J2 1st Three Mile Opening sea chan. Qld Austr.
203 F4 2nd Cataract rapids Sudan
85 I2 2nd Three Mile Opening sea chan. Qld Austr.
203 F5 3rd Cataract rapids Sudan
203 G5 4th Cataract rapids Sudan
203 G5 5th Cataract rapids Sudan
261 G4 9 de Julio Arg.
261 G5 16 de Julio Arg.
261 F5 17 de Agosto Arg.
261 G4 25 de Mayo Buenos Aires Arg.
260 D5 25 de Mayo La Pampa Arg.
260 C4 25 de Mayo Mendoza Arg.
261 I4 25 de Mayo Uru.
129 K6 26 Bakı Komissari Azer.
261 F5 30 de Agosto Arg.
215 N4 42nd Hill S. Africa
222 F5 70 Mile House B.C. Can.
222 F5 100 Mile House B.C. Can.
222 F4 150 Mile House B.C. Can.

A

156 D1 Aa r. France
169 B7 Aa r. Ger.
169 E7 Aa r. Ger.
142 F6 Aabenraa Denmark
172 F6 Aach Ger.
172 G6 Aach r. Ger.
169 B9 Aachen Ger.
210 E4 Aadan Yabaal Somalia
190 F1 Aadorf Switz.
143 K6 Aakirkeby Bornholm Denmark
142 F4 Aalborg Denmark
142 G5 Aalborg Bugt b. Denmark
173 I4 Aalen Ger.
142 F5 Aalestrup Denmark
Aalesund Norway see Ålesund
Aaley Lebanon see Aley
164 G4 Aalsmeer Neth.
165 F7 Aalst Belgium
165 H6 Aalst Neth.
164 K5 Aalten Neth.
165 D6 Aalter Belgium
Aanaar Fin. see Inari
140 R5 Äänekoski Fin.
214 G2 Aansluit S. Africa
Aar r. Switz. see Aare
113 □1 Aarah i. N. Male Maldives
190 E1 Aarau Switz.
190 C1 Aarberg Switz.
190 D1 Aarburg Switz.
165 D6 Aardenburg Neth.
190 E1 Aare r. Switz.
140 Q3 Aareavaara Sweden
190 E1 Aargau canton Switz.
Aarhus Denmark see Århus
164 I6 Aarle Neth.
Aarlen Belgium see Arlon
182 D2 A Armada Spain
142 F5 Aars Denmark
165 G7 Aarschot Belgium
165 F6 Aartselaar Belgium
142 G6 Aarup Denmark
172 D7 Aarwangen Switz.
221 M3 Aasiaat Greenland
Aath Belgium see Ath
140 Q3 Aavasaksa Fin.
108 C2 Aba Sichuan China
208 F4 Aba Dem. Rep. Congo
177 H4 Aba Hungary
207 G5 Aba Nigeria
124 G2 Abā ad Dūd Saudi Arabia
125 J6 Abā al Afan oasis Saudi Arabia
128 D9 Abā al Hinshan Saudi Arabia
251 G6 Abacaxis r. Brazil
122 C6 Ābādān Iran
122 H2 Abadan Turkm.
122 C6 Ābādān, Jazīrah i. Iran/Iraq
122 F3 Abadan Tappeh Iran
122 E6 Ābādeh Iran
122 E7 Ābādeh Ṭashk Iran
182 G7 Abadengo reg. Spain
183 L7 Abades Spain
256 D3 Abadia dos Dourados Brazil
256 C2 Abadiânia Brazil
182 F2 Abadín Spain
204 E3 Abadla Alg.
177 J4 Abádszalók Hungary
129 B1 Abadzekhskaya Rus. Fed.
257 E3 Abaeté Brazil
257 E3 Abaeté r. Brazil
254 C2 Abaetetuba Brazil
107 O2 Abagaytuy Rus. Fed.
Abagnar Qi Nei Mongol China see Xilinhot
Abag Qi Nei Mongol China see Xin Hot
253 G6 Abaí Para.
77 H1 Abaiang atoll Kiribati
182 D2 A Baiuca Spain
207 G4 Abaji Nigeria
241 W4 Abajo Peak UT U.S.A.
207 H5 Abakaliki Nigeria
98 F1 Abakan Rus. Fed.
98 E1 Abakanskiy Khrebet mts Rus. Fed.
208 B5 Abala Congo
207 F3 Abala Niger
207 G3 Abalak Niger
205 G5 Abalessa Alg.
138 N7 Abalyanka r. Belarus
126 G3 Abana Turkey
183 P7 Abánades Spain
252 B3 Abancay Peru
208 A5 Abanga r. Gabon
187 C11 Abanilla Spain
191 L5 Abano Terme Italy
252 E4 Abapó Bol.
187 C11 Abarán Spain
Abariringa atoll Phoenix Is Kiribati see Kanton
122 E6 Abarkūh, Kavīr-e des. Iran
122 E6 Abarqū Iran
182 E3 A Barrela Spain
Abarshahr Iran see Neyshābūr
177 J4 Abasár Hungary
129 D3 Abasha Georgia
102 V2 Abashiri Japan
102 V3 Abashiri-ko l. Japan
102 V2 Abashiri-wan b. Japan
244 F5 Abasolo Guanajuato Mex.
245 I1 Abasolo Tamaulipas Mex.
245 L8 Abasolo del Valle Mex.
129 D4 Abast'umani Georgia
211 C5 Abasula waterhole Kenya
91 K9 Abau P.N.G.
177 K3 Abaújszántó Hungary
138 E4 Abava r. Latvia
121 O3 Abay Karagandinskaya Oblast' Kazakh.
Abay Vostochnyy Kazakhstan Kazakh. see Karaul
Abaya, Lake Eth. see Ābaya Hāyk'
210 C3 Ābaya Hāyk' l. Eth.
Abay Bazar Kazakh. see Abay
210 B2 Ābay Wenz r. Eth. alt. Azraq, Bahr el (Sudan), conv. Blue Nile
98 F1 Abaza Rus. Fed.
208 B3 Abba C.A.R.
192 H2 Abbadia San Salvatore Italy
127 P8 Abbāsābād Fārs Iran
122 H5 Abbāsābād Khorāsān Iran
122 G3 'Abbāsābad Iran
122 F5 Abbāsābād Mehr Jān Iran
192 B7 Abbasanta Sardegna Italy
Abbatis Villa France see Abbeville
226 F3 Abbaye, Point MI U.S.A.
210 D2 Abbe, Lake Djibouti/Eth.
151 N4 Abberton Reservoir England U.K.
156 C3 Abbeville France
231 E10 Abbeville AL U.S.A.
231 F10 Abbeville GA U.S.A.
237 I11 Abbeville LA U.S.A.
231 F8 Abbeville SC U.S.A.
223 I5 Abbey Sask. Can.
147 C8 Abbeydorney Ireland
147 D8 Abbeyfeale Ireland
146 I13 Abbey Head Scotland U.K.
147 H7 Abbeyleix Ireland
149 K4 Abbey Town Cumbria, England U.K.
190 F5 Abbiategrasso Italy
140 O4 Abborrträsk Sweden
85 K6 Abbot, Mount Qld Austr.
85 K5 Abbot Bay Qld Austr.
262 R2 Abbot Ice Shelf Antarctica
151 I2 Abbots Bromley Staffordshire, England U.K.
150 G6 Abbotsbury Dorset, England U.K.
222 F5 Abbotsford B.C. Can.
226 D5 Abbotsford WI U.S.A.
151 L4 Abbots Langley Hertfordshire, England U.K.
234 B5 Abbotstown PA U.S.A.
239 L8 Abbott NM U.S.A.
232 E11 Abbott VA U.S.A.
232 E10 Abbott WV U.S.A.
123 O4 Abbottabad Pak.
138 M7 Abchuha Belarus
164 G4 Abcoude Neth.
177 G4 Abda Hungary
127 J5 'Abd al 'Azīz, Jabal hill Syria
125 K9 'Abd al Kūrī i. Yemen
127 N9 'Abd Allah, Khawr sea chan. Iraq/Kuwait
128 G8 Abd al Ma'asīr well Saudi Arabia
122 B5 Ābdānān Iran
134 J5 Abdi Rus. Fed.
122 G4 Abdolabād Iran
122 G3 Abdollāhābād Khorāsān Iran
122 E4 Abdollāhābād Semnān Iran
120 E1 Abdulino Rus. Fed.
202 D6 Abéché Chad
122 G5 Ab-e Garm, Chashmeh-ye spring Iran
105 H6 Abe-gawa r. Japan
207 F2 Abeïbara Mali
207 F2 Abeïbara well Mali
183 O5 Abejar Spain
187 D8 Abejuela Spain
207 G5 Abejukolo Nigeria
184 B4 Abela Port.
207 G2 Abélajouad well Niger
206 E2 Abelbod well Mali
165 C7 Abele Belgium
182 C4 Abelleiro, Punta pt Spain
Abellinum Italy see Avellino
81 H7 Abel Tasman National Park South I. N.Z.
140 K4 Abelvær Norway
77 H1 Abemama atoll Gilbert Is Kiribati
212 C3 Abenab Namibia
173 J3 Abenberg Ger.
185 P2 Abengibre Spain
206 E5 Abengourou Côte d'Ivoire
185 K3 Abenójar Spain
Åbenrå Denmark see Aabenraa
173 L4 Abens r. Ger.
173 L4 Abensberg Ger.
207 F5 Abeokuta Nigeria
210 B3 Abera Eth.
150 D3 Aberaeron Ceredigion, Wales U.K.
150 F4 Aberaman Rhondda Cynon Taff, Wales U.K.
150 E4 Aberavon Neath Port Talbot, Wales U.K.
158 B4 Aber Benoît inlet France
150 F4 Abercanaid Merthyr Tydfil, Wales U.K.
150 B4 Abercastle Pembrokeshire, Wales U.K.
146 K7 Aberchirder Aberdeenshire, Scotland U.K.
Abercorn Zambia see Mbala
83 L5 Abercrombie r. N.S.W. Austr.
83 L6 Abercrombie River National Park N.S.W. Austr.
150 F4 Abercynon Rhondda Cynon Taff, Wales U.K.
150 F4 Aberdare Rhondda Cynon Taff, Wales U.K.
210 C5 Aberdare National Park Kenya
150 C2 Aberdaron Gwynedd, Wales U.K.
Aberdaugleddau Pembrokeshire, Wales U.K. see Milford Haven
83 M5 Aberdeen N.S.W. Austr.
109 □J7 Aberdeen H.K. China
214 I8 Aberdeen S. Africa
146 L8 Aberdeen Aberdeen, Scotland U.K.
146 L8 Aberdeen admin. div. Scotland U.K.
234 C6 Aberdeen MD U.S.A.
237 K9 Aberdeen MS U.S.A.
232 B10 Aberdeen OH U.S.A.
236 F3 Aberdeen SD U.S.A.
238 C3 Aberdeen WA U.S.A.
Aberdeen Island H.K. China see Ap Lei Chau
223 L1 Aberdeen Lake Nunavut Can.
214 I8 Aberdeen Road S. Africa
146 K8 Aberdeenshire admin. div. Scotland U.K.
146 J10 Aberdour Fife, Scotland U.K.
150 D2 Aberdovey Gwynedd, Wales U.K.
Aberdyfi Gwynedd, Wales U.K. see Aberdovey
146 I9 Aberfeldy Perth and Kinross, Scotland U.K.
150 D1 Aberffraw Isle of Anglesey, Wales U.K.
149 O6 Aberford West Yorkshire, England U.K.
146 H10 Aberfoyle Stirling, Scotland U.K.
150 F4 Abergavenny Monmouthshire, Wales U.K.
210 C1 Ābergelē Eth.
150 E1 Abergele Conwy, Wales U.K.
Abergwaun Pembrokeshire, Wales U.K. see Fishguard
150 E3 Abergwesyn Powys, Wales U.K.
150 E2 Abergynolwyn Gwynedd, Wales U.K.
Aberhonddu Powys, Wales U.K. see Brecon
150 E4 Aberkenfig Bridgend, Wales U.K.
146 K10 Aberlady East Lothian, Scotland U.K.
146 K9 Aberlemno Angus, Scotland U.K.
146 J8 Aberlour Moray, Scotland U.K.
Abermaw Gwynedd, Wales U.K. see Barmouth
Abermaw Wales U.K. see Barmouth
237 E9 Abernathy TX U.S.A.
146 J10 Abernethy Perth and Kinross, Scotland U.K.
Aberpennar Wales U.K. see Mountain Ash
150 C3 Aberporth Ceredigion, Wales U.K.
150 C2 Abersoch Gwynedd, Wales U.K.
150 F4 Abersychan Torfaen, Wales U.K.
176 B1 Abertamy Czech Rep.
Abertawe Swansea, Wales U.K. see Swansea
Aberteifi Ceredigion, Wales U.K. see Cardigan
150 F4 Abertillery Blaenau Gwent, Wales U.K.
184 H2 Abertura Spain
146 I10 Aberuthven Perth and Kinross, Scotland U.K.
158 B4 Aber Vrac'h inlet France
150 D3 Aberystwyth Ceredigion, Wales U.K.
Abeshr Chad see Abéché
134 M2 Abez' Rus. Fed.
178 G6 Abfaltersbach Austria
122 H8 Āb Gāh Iran
135 I6 Abganerovo Rus. Fed.
124 F6 Abhā Saudi Arabia
124 E3 Abhā, Jabal hill Saudi Arabia
146 B7 Abhainnsuidhe Western Isles, Scotland U.K.
116 H9 Abhanpur Chhattisgarh India
122 C3 Abhar Iran
122 C4 Abhar Rūd r. Iran
207 G5 Abia state Nigeria
203 G6 Abiad, Bahr el r. Sudan/Uganda alt. Jebel, Bahr el conv. White Nile
183 P8 Abia de la Obispalía Spain
210 C3 Ābīata Hāyk' l. Eth.
250 B2 Abibe, Serranía de mts Col.
206 D5 Abidjan Côte d'Ivoire
186 E3 Abiego Spain
214 E3 Abiekwasputs salt pan S. Africa
210 C3 Abijatta-Shalla National Park Eth.
105 L4 Abiko Japan
168 G1 Abild Denmark
236 G6 Abilene KS U.S.A.
237 F9 Abilene TX U.S.A.
159 M8 Abilly France
151 J4 Abingdon Oxfordshire, England U.K.
234 C6 Abingdon MD U.S.A.
232 C12 Abingdon VA U.S.A.
Abingdon Island Islas Galápagos Ecuador see Pinta, Isla
146 I12 Abington South Lanarkshire, Scotland U.K.
233 O6 Abington MA U.S.A.
234 E4 Abington PA U.S.A.
85 L5 Abington Reef Coral Sea Is Terr. Austr.
135 G7 Abinsk Rus. Fed.
183 N5 Abión r. Spain
Ab-i-Panja r. Afgh./Tajik. see Panj
140 O2 Abisko nationalpark nat. park Sweden
223 J2 Abitau Lake N.W.T. Can.
224 D3 Abitibi r. Ont. Can.
224 D3 Abitibi, Lake Ont./Que. Can.
Abkhazia aut. rep. Georgia see Ap'khazet'i
122 G4 Ab Khūr Iran
185 N6 Abla Spain
156 C6 Ablis France
183 Q5 Ablitas Spain
203 F3 Abnūb Egypt
Åbo Fin. see Turku
186 C2 Abodi, Sierra de mts Spain
116 E4 Abohar Punjab India
182 D5 Aboim das Choças Port.
206 E5 Aboisso Côte d'Ivoire
210 B2 Aboke Sudan
207 F5 Abomey Benin
216 □3a Abona, Punta de pt Tenerife Canary Is
160 J4 Abondance France
94 B2 Abongabong, Gunung mt. Indon.
207 I6 Abong Mbang Cameroon
177 J4 Abony Hungary
206 E5 Abooso Ghana
125 K7 Aboot Oman
92 B7 Aborlan Palawan Phil.
104 G3 Abō-tōge pass Japan
208 C2 Abou Déia Chad
202 D6 Abou Goulem Chad
208 B5 Aboumi Gabon
208 E2 Abourasséin, Mont mt. C.A.R.
207 G3 Abouraya well Niger
129 F5 Abovyan Armenia
146 K8 Aboyne Aberdeenshire, Scotland U.K.
125 I3 Abqaiq Saudi Arabia
259 B9 Abra, Canal sea chan. Chile
259 E6 Abra, Laguna del l. Arg.
124 H8 Abrād, Wādī watercourse Yemen
182 D6 Abragão Port.
246 G2 Abraham's Bay Mayaguana Bahamas
207 G5 Abraka Nigeria
177 L4 Abram Romania
149 L6 Abram Greater Manchester, England U.K.
134 H2 Abramov, Mys pt Rus. Fed.
137 U2 Abramovka Rus. Fed.
226 F5 Abrams WI U.S.A.
177 L4 Abrămuț Romania
184 C2 Abrantes Port.
258 D1 Abra Pampa Arg.
129 G6 Äbraqunis Azer.
137 Q9 Abrau Dyurso Rus. Fed.
182 E7 Abraveses Port.
257 F4 Abre Campo Brazil
182 F6 Abreiro Port.
242 C4 Abreojos, Punta pt Mex.
186 I4 Abrera Spain
157 N6 Abreschviller France
160 C4 Abrest France
203 F4 'Abri Sudan
161 J7 Abriès France
257 H3 Abrolhos, Arquipélago dos is Brazil
264 G7 Abrolhos Bank sea feature S. Atlantic Ocean
139 S3 Abrosovo Rus. Fed.
185 N6 Abrucena Spain
197 L4 Abrud Romania
138 F3 Abruka i. Estonia
Abruzzi admin. reg. Italy see Abruzzo
193 L3 Abruzzo admin. reg. Italy
193 L4 Abruzzo, Parco Nazionale d' nat. park Italy
124 F7 'Abs Yemen
262 W1 Absalom, Mount Antarctica
178 E5 Absam Austria
238 I4 Absaroka Range mts WY U.S.A.
173 J3 Absberg Ger.
179 M3 Absdorf Austria
235 G6 Absecon NJ U.S.A.
235 G6 Absecon Bay NJ U.S.A.
129 K5 Abşeron Yarımadası pen. Azer.
138 K6 Absterna, Vozyera l. Belarus
128 F4 Abtar, Jabal al hills Syria
179 H4 Abtenau Austria
172 H4 Abtsgmünd Ger.
103 I12 Abu Japan
128 F3 Abū aḍ Ḍuhūr Syria
125 K3 Abū al Abyaḍ i. U.A.E.
128 G6 Abū al Ḥusayn, Qā' imp. l. Jordan
125 I2 Abū 'Alī i. Saudi Arabia
124 C3 Abū al Kizān rf Saudi Arabia
128 E8 Abū 'Āmūd, Wādī watercourse Jordan
124 F7 Abū 'Arīsh Saudi Arabia
202 E3 Abū Ballāṣ hill Egypt
124 G7 Abū Dā'ir des. Yemen
203 G6 Abu Deleiq Sudan
Abu Dhabi U.A.E. see Abū Ẓabī
124 D4 Abū Ḍībā' waterhole Saudi Arabia
128 G2 Abū Du'ān Syria
128 B10 Abū Durbah Egypt
251 F6 Abufari Brazil
208 E2 Abu Gabra Sudan
203 H6 Abu Gamel Sudan
203 G5 Abu Ghirban Sudan
210 A2 Abu Gubeiha Sudan
128 B10 Abū Ḥād, Wādī watercourse Egypt
128 G6 Abū Ḥafnah, Wādī watercourse Jordan
128 E7 Abū Ḥallūfah, Jabal hill Jordan
203 G5 Abu Hamed Sudan
202 E6 Abu Hamra, Wadi watercourse Sudan
203 G5 Abu Haraz Sudan
203 G5 Abu Hashim Sudan
128 B10 Abū Ḥaṣwah, Jabal hill Egypt
113 □2 Abuhera i. Addu Atoll Maldives
203 G6 Abu Higar Sudan
207 G4 Abuja Nigeria
128 C10 Abū Jalūm, Ra's pt Egypt
125 H3 Abū Jifān well Saudi Arabia
128 D8 Ābū Jurdhān Jordan
127 J6 Abū Kamāl Syria
202 A1 Abū Kammāsh Libya
175 M2 Abukhava Belarus
105 L1 Abukuma-gawa r. Japan
105 M2 Abukuma-kōchi plat. Japan
203 F6 Abu La'ot watercourse Sudan
124 E6 Abū Latt i. Saudi Arabia
124 C3 Abū Madd, Ra's hd Saudi Arabia
208 E2 Abu Matariq Sudan
126 D8 Abu Mena tourist site Egypt
208 D4 Abumombazi Dem. Rep. Congo
125 L3 Abu Musa i. The Gulf
Abū Mūsá, Jazīreh-ye i. The Gulf see Abu Musa
252 D2 Abunã r. Bol.
252 D2 Abunã Brazil
250 E5 Abunai Brazil
202 C2 Abū Nā'im well Libya
210 C1 Ābune Yosēf mt. Eth.
202 B2 Abū Nujaym Libya
128 F4 Abū Qa'ṭūr Syria
126 E8 Abū Qīr, Khalīj b. Egypt
202 B2 Abū Qurīn Libya
124 C2 Abū Rāqah well Saudi Arabia
128 C9 Abū Rawthah, Jabal mt. Egypt
104 E4 Aburazaka-tōge pass Japan
208 F4 Aburo mt. Dem. Rep. Congo
116 D7 Abu Road Rajasthan India
124 D4 Abū Rubayq Saudi Arabia
128 B10 Abū Rudays Egypt
128 G4 Abū Rujmayn, Jabal mts Syria
124 E3 Abū Salīm, Birkat waterhole Saudi Arabia
128 F10 Abū Sallah, Wādī watercourse Saudi Arabia
125 I3 Abū Sawādah well Saudi Arabia
203 H4 Abu Shagara, Ras pt Sudan
202 E6 Abu Shanab Sudan
203 F4 Abu Simbel Temple tourist site Egypt
127 L8 Abū Şukhayr Iraq
203 F4 Abū Sunbul Egypt
102 R4 Abuta Japan
203 G4 Abu Tabaq well Sudan
124 C2 Abū Ṭāqah Saudi Arabia
128 B9 Abū Ṭarfā', Wādī watercourse Egypt
81 E10 Abut Head South I. N.Z.
203 F3 Abū Tīj Egypt
203 G3 Abū Ṭuyūr, Jabal mt. Egypt
203 F6 Abu Uruq well Sudan
128 C8 Abū 'Uwayqilah well Egypt
210 C2 Abuye Meda mt. Eth.
92 E6 Abuyog Leyte Phil.
203 F6 Abu Zabad Sudan
125 L3 Abū Ẓabī U.A.E.
122 C6 Abūzam Iran
203 G2 Abū Zanīmah Egypt
122 D5 Abū Zeydābād Iran
210 B2 Abwong Sudan
143 M3 Åby Sweden
202 E6 Abyad Sudan
128 F4 Abyaḍ, Jabal al mts Syria
124 G9 Abyān governorate Yemen
202 D2 Abyār al Hakīm well Libya
202 D2 Abyār an Nakhīlan well Libya
86 E6 Abydos W.A. Austr.
208 F2 Abyei Sudan
127 O5 Ābyek Iran
140 P4 Åbyn Sweden
Abyssinia country Africa see Ethiopia
120 H1 Abzakovo Rus. Fed.
120 G2 Abzanovo Rus. Fed.
202 C6 Ab Zérafa Chad
250 C4 Acacias Col.
Acacus, Jabal mts Libya see Akakus, Jabal
Academician Vernadskiy research stn Antarctica see Vernadsky
Academy Bay Rus. Fed. see Akademii, Zaliv
262 T1 Academy Glacier Antarctica
Acadia prov. Can. see Nova Scotia
233 □Q4 Acadia National Park ME U.S.A.
256 B5 Açaí Brazil
254 D3 Açailândia Brazil
254 F4 Acajutiba Brazil
243 O11 Acajutla El Salvador
243 M9 Acala Mex.
Acamarachi mt. Chile see Pili, Cerro
244 G5 Acambaro Mex.
245 H6 Acambay Mex.
209 D9 Acampamento de Caça do Mucusso Angola
243 O7 Acancéh Mex.
250 B2 Acandí Col.
182 D4 A Cañiza Spain
244 B3 Acaponeta Mex.
244 B3 Acaponeta r. Mex.
245 H9 Acapulco Mex.
Acapulco de Juárez Mex. see Acapulco
254 C2 Acará Brazil
254 C2 Acará r. Brazil
251 F6 Acará, Lago l. Brazil
251 G4 Acarai Mountains hills Brazil/Guyana
254 C2 Acará Miri r. Brazil
254 E2 Acaraú Brazil
254 E2 Acaraú r. Brazil
253 G6 Acaray, Represa de resr Para.
182 C2 A Carballa Spain
254 F3 Acarí Brazil
257 E1 Acari r. Brazil
252 B3 Acarí Peru
252 B3 Acarí r. Peru
250 D2 Acarigua Venez.
182 D2 A Carreira Spain
197 K3 Acâș Romania
194 G9 Acate Sicilia Italy
245 J5 Acateno Mex.
245 I7 Acatlan Mex.
245 K6 Acatlán Mex.
244 D5 Acatlán de Juárez Mex.
245 K7 Acatlán de Pérez Figueroa Mex.
245 J7 Acatzingo Mex.
258 D2 Acay, Nevado de mt. Arg.
245 M8 Acayucán Mex.
193 O5 Accadia Italy
190 B7 Acceglio Italy
193 Q7 Accettura Italy
Accho Israel see 'Akko
193 L3 Acciano Italy
233 J11 Accomac VA U.S.A.
Accomack VA U.S.A. see Accomac
163 C10 Accous France
206 E5 Accra Ghana
149 M6 Accrington Lancashire, England U.K.
193 K2 Accumoli Italy
261 G3 Aceba Arg.
182 G8 Acebo Spain
184 H2 Acedera Spain
183 P3 Acedo Spain
258 G3 Aceguá Brazil
94 B2 Aceh admin. dist. Indon.
182 G9 Acehuche Spain
182 H8 Aceituna Spain
183 Q6 Acered Spain
193 P6 Acerenza Italy
193 O6 Acerno Italy
193 M6 Acerra Italy
184 G3 Aceuchal Spain
261 G3 Acevedo Arg.
178 G3 Ach Austria
173 K4 Ach r. Ger.
173 K6 Ach r. Ger.
252 C4 Achacachi Bol.
216 □1b Achada São Miguel Azores
184 □ Achadas da Cruz Madeira
146 C6 Achadh Mòr Western Isles, Scotland U.K.
250 D3 Achaguas Venez.
116 F9 Achalpur Mahar. India
114 F4 Achampet Andhra Prad. India
100 J4 Achan Rus. Fed.
182 D4 A Chan Spain
114 G4 Achanta Andhra Prad. India
261 I3 Achar Uru.
129 D4 Ach'ara aut. rep. Georgia
146 E9 Acharacle Highland, Scotland U.K.
129 C4 Acharistsqali r. Georgia
146 J6 Achavanich Highland, Scotland U.K.
131 S3 Achayvayam Rus. Fed.
202 A5 Achegour well Niger
Acheh admin. dist. Indon. see Aceh
165 H6 Achel Belgium
198 C4 Acheloos r. Greece
205 F5 Achemelmel well Mali
206 D2 Achemmîm well Maur.
100 E6 Acheng Heilong. China
178 E4 Achenkirch Austria
207 I2 Achénouma Niger
178 E5 Achensee l. Austria
172 E4 Achern Ger.
207 H3 Achétinamou well Niger
156 E3 Acheux-en-Amiénois France
146 G6 Achfary Highland, Scotland U.K.
116 H9 Achhota Chhattisgarh India
104 G5 Achi Japan
156 E3 Achicourt France
129 C3 Ach'igvara Georgia
129 F1 Achikulak Rus. Fed.
147 B5 Achill Head Ireland
147 B5 Achill Island Ireland
147 C5 Achill Sound Ireland
146 F6 Achiltibuie Highland, Scotland U.K.
168 H4 Achim Ger.
Achin admin. dist. Indon. see Aceh
131 K4 Achinsk Rus. Fed.
146 F8 Achintee Highland, Scotland U.K.
260 E3 Achiras Arg.
121 M6 Achisay Kazakh.
129 I3 Achisu Rus. Fed.
134 L4 Achit Rus. Fed.
106 B2 Achit Nuur l. Mongolia
129 G2 Achkhoy-Martan Rus. Fed.
199 G6 Achlada, Akrotirio pt Greece
128 B3 Achna Cyprus
146 F7 Achnasheen Highland, Scotland U.K.
139 O9 Achosa-Rudnya Belarus
146 D9 Achosnich Highland, Scotland U.K.
173 N4 Achslach Ger.
172 H5 Achstetten Ger.
168 H1 Achtrup Ger.
135 G7 Achuyevo Rus. Fed.
195 I8 Aci Castello Sicilia Italy
195 I8 Aci Catena Sicilia Italy
199 K5 Acıgöl l. Turkey
129 H4 Acınohur depr. Azer.
199 K5 Acıpayam Turkey
195 I8 Acireale Sicilia Italy
195 I8 Aci Sant'Antonio Sicilia Italy
237 K9 Ackerman MS U.S.A.
234 E3 Ackermanville PA U.S.A.
236 I4 Ackley IA U.S.A.
246 F2 Acklins Island Bahamas
149 O6 Ackworth Moor Top West Yorkshire, England U.K.
151 P2 Acle Norfolk, England U.K.
252 B3 Acobamba Huancavelica Peru
252 B2 Acobamba Junín Peru
160 C3 Acolin r. France
252 C3 Acomayo Cusco Peru
252 A2 Acomayo Huánuco Peru
149 M4 Acomb Northumberland, England U.K.
260 B3 Aconcagua r. Chile
260 B3 Aconcagua, Cerro mt. Arg.
254 F3 Acopiara Brazil
252 C3 Acora Peru
216 □1 Açores, Arquipélago dos is N. Atlantic Ocean
182 D2 A Coruña Spain
182 D2 A Coruña prov. Spain
252 B3 Acostambo Peru
217 □3b Acoua Mayotte
242 □Q12 Acoyapa Nic.
194 H6 Acquacalda Isole Lipari Italy
191 N8 Acqualagna Italy
195 L4 Acquaniti r. Italy
192 H2 Acquapendente Italy
193 P9 Acquappesa Italy
195 K6 Acquaro Italy
190 F3 Acquarossa Switz.
193 K2 Acquasanta Terme Italy
193 J2 Acquasparta Italy
193 L2 Acquaviva Picena Italy
194 H7 Acquedolci Sicilia Italy
156 B5 Acquigny France
190 E6 Acqui Terme Italy
233 K6 Acra NY U.S.A.
Acragas Sicilia Italy see Agrigento
82 E5 Acraman, Lake salt flat S.A. Austr.
252 D2 Acre r. Brazil
252 C2 Acre state Brazil
Acre Israel see 'Akko
256 B2 Acreúna Brazil
195 K5 Acri Italy
182 F3 A Cruz do Incio Spain
177 H4 Ács Hungary
177 I4 Acsa Hungary
Actaeon Group is Arch. des Tuamotu Fr. Polynesia see Actéon, Groupe
79 □9 Actéon, Groupe is Arch. des Tuamotu Fr. Polynesia
245 I7 Acteopan Mex.
227 N6 Acton Ont. Can.
151 N3 Acton Suffolk, England U.K.
240 N7 Acton CA U.S.A.
245 I5 Actopán Mex.
245 K6 Actopan Mex.
252 D1 Açuã r. Brazil
257 F3 Açuçena Brazil
245 H5 Aculco de Espinosa Mex.
245 J7 Acultzingo Mex.
261 I1 Acuña Arg.
256 C6 Acungui Brazil
Acunum Acusio France see Montélimar
207 H6 Acurenam Equat. Guinea
253 F3 Açurizal Brazil
193 K4 Acuto Italy
207 F5 Ada Ghana
196 I5 Ada Vojvodina Serbia
236 G2 Ada MN U.S.A.
232 B8 Ada OH U.S.A.
237 G8 Ada OK U.S.A.
210 C3 Ādaba Eth.
Adabazar Turkey see Adapazarı
78 □1 Adacao Guam
205 H5 Adaf, Djebel mts Alg.
137 Q8 Adagum r. Rus. Fed.
186 E3 Adahuesca Spain
226 D9 Adair IL U.S.A.
183 K5 Adaja r. Spain
140 O4 Adak Sweden
220 A4 Adak AK U.S.A.
220 A4 Adak Island AK U.S.A.
129 B6 Adaklı Bingöl Turkey
128 F1 Adaklı Gaziantep Turkey
210 E3 Adale well Eth.
Adalia Turkey see Antalya
125 M4 Adam Oman
259 F8 Adam, Mount hill Falkland Is
256 B4 Adamantina Brazil
207 I5 Adamaoua prov. Cameroon
207 I5 Adamaoua, Massif de l' mts Cameroon
198 F6 Adamas Milos Greece
207 H4 Adamawa state Nigeria
197 P6 Adamclisi Romania
190 J3 Adamello mt. Italy
190 I3 Adamello-Brenta, Parco Naturale nature res. Italy
83 L7 Adaminaby N.S.W. Austr.
210 C3 Ādamī Tulu Eth.
174 E6 Adamov Czech Rep.
120 H2 Adamovka Rus. Fed.
175 K4 Adamów Lubelskie Pol.
175 L5 Adamów Lubelskie Pol.
175 K5 Adamówka Pol.
136 G4 Adampil' Ukr.
232 C10 Adams KY U.S.A.
233 L6 Adams MA U.S.A.
226 B6 Adams MN U.S.A.
233 I5 Adams NY U.S.A.
226 E6 Adams WI U.S.A.
262 T2 Adams, Cape Antarctica
81 E10 Adams, Mount South I. N.Z.
114 F8 Adam's Bridge sea feature India/Sri Lanka
233 I5 Adams Center NY U.S.A.
234 A5 Adams County county PA U.S.A.
222 G5 Adams Lake B.C. Can.
241 Q3 Adams McGill Reservoir NV U.S.A.
222 D4 Adams Mountain AK U.S.A.
Adam's Peak Sri Lanka see Sri Pada
240 L2 Adams Peak CA U.S.A.
147 I8 Adamstown Ireland
234 C4 Adamstown PA U.S.A.
185 J4 Adamuz Spain
124 G9 'Adan Yemen
124 G9 'Adan governorate Yemen
126 G5 Adana Turkey
128 D1 Adana prov. Turkey
Adana Yemen see 'Adan
124 G9 'Adan aş Şughrá Yemen
197 O3 Adâncata Romania
177 H5 Ádánd Hungary
183 K7 Adanero Spain
95 L5 Adang, Teluk b. Indon.
207 G5 Adani Nigeria
182 F8 Adão Port.
199 L2 Adapazarı Turkey
124 G9 Adaran, Jabal mt. Yemen
147 E7 Adare Ireland
263 L2 Adare, Cape Antarctica
124 B5 Adarmo, Khawr watercourse Sudan
102 R9 Adatara-san vol. Japan
210 D3 Ada Terra Eth.
85 J8 Adavale Qld Austr.
138 H4 Ādaži Latvia
123 M3 Adban Afgh.
117 I9 Adbhar Chhattisgarh India
190 H5 Adda r. Italy
202 F2 Aḍ Ḍab'ah Egypt
Ad Dabbah Sudan see Ed Debba
124 E4 Ad Dafīnah Saudi Arabia
127 L7 Ad Daghghārah Iraq
124 H5 Ad Dahnā' des. Saudi Arabia
125 M5 Ad Dākhilīyah admin. reg. Oman
204 B5 Ad Dakhla Western Sahara
124 G9 Aḍ Ḍāli' Yemen
124 G9 Aḍ Ḍāli' governorate Yemen
Ad Damir Sudan see Ed Damer
125 J2 Ad Dammām Saudi Arabia
114 F5 Addanki Andhra Prad. India
190 H4 Adda Nord, Parco dell' park Italy
126 E8 Ad Daqahlīyah governorate Egypt
124 C2 Ad Dār al Ḥamrā' Saudi Arabia
124 F7 Ad Darb Saudi Arabia
190 H5 Adda Sud, Parco dell' park Italy
114 H4 Addatigala Andhra Prad. India
124 G3 Ad Dawādimī Saudi Arabia
125 J3 Ad Dawḥah Qatar
127 K6 Ad Dawr Iraq
128 F4 Ad Daww plain Syria
207 H2 Addax, Réserve Naturelle Intégrale dite Sanctuaire des nature res. Niger
127 M8 Ad Dayr Iraq
151 J3 Adderbury Oxfordshire, England U.K.
124 H2 Ad Dibdibah plain Saudi Arabia
125 J7 Ad Dibīn Yemen
Aḍ Ḍiffah plat. Egypt/Libya see Libyan Plateau
125 J6 Ad Dikākah des. Saudi Arabia
125 H4 Ad Dilam Saudi Arabia
149 N6 Addingham West Yorkshire, England U.K.
124 H3 Ad Dir'īyah Saudi Arabia
Addis Ababa Eth. see Ādīs Ābeba
232 H6 Addison NY U.S.A.
127 L8 Ad Dīwānīyah Iraq
Ad Dīwānīyah governorate Iraq see Al Qādisīyah
151 L5 Addlestone Surrey, England U.K.
215 J9 Addo S. Africa
215 J9 Addo Elephant National Park S. Africa
113 □2 Addu Atoll Maldives
127 K8 Ad Duwayd well Saudi Arabia
124 G2 Ad Duwayḥirah Saudi Arabia
Ad Duwaym Sudan see Ed Dueim
125 J4 Ad Duwayris well Saudi Arabia
216 □3a Adeje Tenerife Canary Is
231 F10 Adel GA U.S.A.
236 H5 Adel IA U.S.A.
82 G6 Adelaide S.A. Austr.
84 C2 Adelaide r. N.T. Austr.
246 E1 Adelaide New Prov. Bahamas
215 K8 Adelaide S. Africa
262 T2 Adelaide Island Antarctica
84 C2 Adelaide River N.T. Austr.
190 D3 Adelboden Switz.
169 I7 Adelebsen Ger.
86 G3 Adele Island W.A. Austr.
195 L1 Adelfia Italy
199 H6 Adelfoi i. Greece
168 J5 Adelheidsdorf Ger.
261 E3 Adelia María Arg.
Adélie Coast reg. Antarctica see Adélie Land
263 J2 Adélie Land reg. Antarctica
172 H4 Adelmannsfelden Ger.
83 L6 Adelong N.S.W. Austr.
87 F10 Adelong Aboriginal Reserve W.A. Austr.
246 □ Adelphi Jamaica
247 □3 Adelphi St Vincent
173 K4 Adelschlag Ger.
173 J2 Adelsdorf Ger.
172 G3 Adelsheim Ger.
173 J5 Adelsried Ger.
173 K5 Adelzhausen Ger.
187 C7 Ademuz Spain
Aden Yemen see 'Adan
118 F7 Aden, Gulf of Somalia/Yemen
232 E8 Adena OH U.S.A.
169 C10 Adenau Ger.
168 J4 Adendorf Ger.
214 I8 Adendorp S. Africa
169 I7 Adenstedt Ger.
207 G3 Aderbissinat Niger
Aderno Sicilia Italy see Adrano
116 C8 Adesar Gujarat India
210 C2 Ādēt Eth.
Adhámas Milos Greece see Adamas
125 M3 Adhan, Jabal mt. U.A.E.
124 G8 Adhanah, Wādī watercourse Yemen
125 L3 Adh Dhayd U.A.E.
124 G2 Adh Dhāyūf well Saudi Arabia
127 J9 'Adhfā' well Saudi Arabia
123 N5 Adhi Kot Pak.
128 E8 'Ādhirīyāt, Jibāl al mts Jordan
116 C8 Adhoi Gujarat India
91 H7 Adi i. Papua Indon.
206 E5 Adiaké Côte d'Ivoire
210 C1 Ādī Ārk'ay Eth.
184 E4 Adiça, Serra da hills Port.
250 D2 Adícora Venez.
124 D8 Ādī Da'iro Eth.
203 F6 'Adid Umm Inderab well Sudan
191 M5 Adige r. Italy
Adigey Autonomous Oblast aut. rep. Rus. Fed. see Adygeya, Respublika
210 C1 Ādīgrat Eth.
199 K4 Adıgüzel Barajı resr Turkey
203 H6 Adi Keyih Eritrea
203 H6 Adi Kwala Eritrea
114 F3 Adilabad Andhra Prad. India
210 B4 Adilang Uganda
127 K4 Adilcevaz Turkey
238 D6 Adin CA U.S.A.
Adîncata Romania see Adâncata
165 C6 Adinkerke Belgium
202 B3 Adīrī Libya
233 K4 Adirondack Mountains NY U.S.A.
210 C2 Ādīs Ābeba Eth.
210 C1 Ādīs Zemen Eth.
Adi Ugri Eritrea see Mendefera
126 I5 Adıyaman Turkey
Adjaria aut. rep. Georgia see Ach'ara
205 F5 Adjelman, Oued watercourse Alg.
197 P4 Adjud Romania
210 A4 Adjumani Uganda
247 □1 Adjuntas Puerto Rico
245 I2 Adjuntas, Presa de las resr Mex.
225 J2 Adlavik Islands Nfld and Lab. Can.
129 A2 Adler Rus. Fed.
149 L6 Adlington Lancashire, England U.K.
190 F1 Adliswil Switz.
173 M4 Adlkofen Ger.
86 H3 Admiralty Gulf W.A. A[...]
86 H3 Admiralty Gulf Aborig[...] Reserve W.A. Austr.
221 J2 Admiralty Inlet Nunav[...]
221 H3 Admiralty Island Nuna[...]
220 E4 Admiralty Island AK U[...]
220 E4 Admiralty Island Nati[...] Monument-Kootznoo[...] Wilderness nat. park A[...]
82 □2 Admiralty Islands Lord Howe I. Austr.
91 K7 Admiralty Islands P.N[...]
263 L2 Admiralty Mountains Antarctica
179 J4 Admont Austria
199 I4 Adnan Menderes Hav[...] airport Turkey
210 E3 Ādo Eth.
207 G5 Ado-Ekiti Nigeria
104 D5 Adogawa Japan
104 D5 Ado-gawa r. Japan
208 F2 Adok Sudan
261 G6 Adolfo Gonzáles Cha[...]
245 N9 Adolfo López Mateos
140 N3 Adolfsström Sweden
86 J3 Adolphus Island W.A.
93 C8 Adonara i. Indon.
114 E5 Adoni Andhra Prad. Ind[...]
177 H4 Adony Hungary
171 F10 Adorf Sachsen Ger.
171 G9 Adorf Sachsen Ger.
169 G8 Adorf (Diemelsee) Ge[...]
184 A2 A-dos-Cunhados Port[...]
100 M3 Ado-Tymovo Sakhalin R[...]
182 E6 Adoufe Port.
163 A8 Adour r. France
117 K8 Adra W. Bengal India
185 M7 Adra Spain
185 N7 Adra r. Spain
128 E5 'Adrā' Syria
183 P6 Adradas Spain
183 L6 Adrados Spain
Adramyttium Turkey s[...] Edremit
Adramyttium, Gulf of see Edremit Körfezi
194 H8 Adrano Sicilia Italy
205 E4 Adrar Alg.
205 G4 Adrar mts Alg.
Adrar hills Mali see Ifôghas, Adrar des
204 C5 Adrar admin. reg. Mau[...]
Adrar des Iforas hills Ifôghas, Adrar des
205 G5 Adrar Tedjorart well A[...]
128 B2 Adras Dağı mt. Turkey
123 J5 Adraskand r. Afgh.
123 M1 Adrasmon Tajik.
202 D6 Adré Chad
191 M5 Adria Italy
227 J8 Adrian MI U.S.A.
237 D8 Adrian TX U.S.A.
Adrianople Turkey see[...]
Adrianopolis Turkey se[...]
188 D3 Adriatic Sea Europe
162 F3 Adriers France
147 C9 Adrigole Ireland
Adua Eth. see Ādwa
260 B5 Aduana Pejerrey Chil[...]
164 J2 Aduard Neth.
190 G3 Adula Gruppe mts Sw[...]
Adunara i. Indon. see [...]
114 E8 Adur Kerala India
208 F4 Adusa Dem. Rep. Con[...]
202 E5 Adusa, Qalti el well S[...]
138 J6 Adutiškis Lith.
Aduwa Eth. see Ādwa
86 G6 Adverse Well W.A. Au[...]
210 C1 Ādwa Eth.
149 O6 Adwick le Street South Yorkshire, Englan[...]
206 E5 Adwufia Ghana
131 O3 Adycha r. Rus. Fed.
129 C1 Adyge-Khabl' Rus. Fe[...]
Adygeya aut. rep. Rus[...] see Adygeya, Respubl[...]
129 B1 Adygeya, Respublika Rus. Fed.
135 G7 Adygeysk Rus. Fed.
Adygeyskaya Avtono[...] Oblast' aut. rep. Rus. [...] Adygeya, Respublika
135 I7 Adyk Rus. Fed.
187 E10 Adzaneta de Albaida
137 L5 Adzhamka Ukr.
Adzharia aut. rep. Ge[...] Ach'ara
206 E5 Adzopé Côte d'Ivoire
134 M2 Adz'va r. Rus. Fed.
134 L2 Adz'vavom Rus. Fed.
199 F4 Aegean Sea Greece/T[...]
Aegeri, Lake of Switz[...] Ägerisee
Aegina i. Greece see A[...]
138 H2 Aegna i. Estonia
138 I2 Aegviidu Estonia
Aegyptus country Afri[...] Egypt
Aela Jordan see Al 'Ac[...]
Aelana Jordan see Al [...]
Aelia Capitolina Israel/West Bank see Je[...]
Aelönlaplap atoll Mar[...] see Ailinglaplap
Aenus Turkey see Ene[...]
142 G7 Ærø i. Denmark
137 N8 Aeroflots'kyy Ukr.
150 D3 Aeron r. Wales U.K.
168 J1 Ærøskøbing Denmark
169 H6 Aerzen Ger.
182 C3 A Escusa Spain
Aesernia Italy see Ise[...]
182 C4 A Esfarrapada Spain
182 D3 A Estrada Spain
198 C2 Aetos Greece
141 Q6 Äetsä Fin.
79 □9a Afaahiti Tahiti Fr. Poly[...]
203 H5 Afabet Eritrea
210 E3 Afaf Badane well Eth.
Afal watercourse Saud[...] see 'Ifāl, Wādī
127 L5 Afan Iran
137 R3 Afanas'yevka Rus. Fe[...]
134 K4 Afanas'yevo Rus. Fed[...]
Afándou Rodos Greec[...] Afantou
199 J6 Afantou Rodos Greece
210 D1 Āfar admin. reg. Eth.
125 M4 Afar Oman
203 I6 Afar Depression Eritr[...]
79 □9a Afareaitu Moorea Fr. F[...]
210 D2 Āfdem Eth.
182 E2 A Feira do Monte Spa[...]
158 G6 Aff r. France
206 E5 Afféri Côte d'Ivoire
193 K4 Affile Italy
173 J5 Affing Ger.
190 E1 Affoltern am Albis Sw[...]
Affreville Alg. see Khemis Miliana
146 F8 Affric, Loch l. Scotlan[...]
Afghānestān country Afghanistan
123 K5 Afghanistan country [...]
210 E4 Afgooye Somalia
78 □2 Afi, Mount Samoa
78 □2 Afiamalu Samoa
124 F4 'Afif Saudi Arabia
182 C5 Afife Port.
207 G5 Afikpo Nigeria
139 R4 Afim'ino Rus. Fed.
137 R9 Afipskiy Rus. Fed.
128 D6 Afiq Syria
198 E3 Afissos Greece
Afiun Karahissar Turk[...] Afyon
122 D4 Afjeh Iran
140 K5 Åfjord Norway
165 D6 Afleidingskanaal van[...] canal Belgium
179 L4 Aflenz Kurort Austria
205 F2 Aflou Alg.
210 D4 Afmadow Somalia
220 C4 Afognak Island AK U.[...]
206 B2 Afojjar well Maur.
182 F2 A Fonsagrada Spain
257 G4 Afonso Cláudio Brazil

A Forxa Galicia Spain
Afra r. Italy
Afragola Italy
Afrânio Brazil
Āfrēra Terara vol. Eth.
Āfrēra YeChe'ew Hāyk' l. Eth.
Africa continent
Africa Nova country Africa see Tunisia
'Afrīn Syria
'Afrīn, Nahr r. Syria/Turkey
Afritz Austria
Afşar Barajı resr Turkey
Afşin Turkey
Afsluitdijk barrage Neth.
Aftar Iran
Aftol well Eth.
Afton NY U.S.A.
Afton WY U.S.A.
Afton Bridgend East Ayrshire, Scotland U.K.
Afṭoût Faï depr. Maur.
Afuá Brazil
'Afula Israel
Afyon Turkey
Afyon prov. Turkey
Afyonkarahisar Turkey see Afyon
Aga Ger.
Aga Rus. Fed.
Aga r. Rus. Fed.
Aga-Buryat Autonomous Okrug admin. div. Rus. Fed. see Aginskiy Buryatskiy Avtonomnyy Okrug
Agadem well Niger
Agadès Niger see Agadez
Agadez Niger
Agadez dept Niger
Agadir Morocco
Agâdîr, Râs pt Maur.
Aga Dubé well Chad
Agadyr' Kazakh.
Agaete Gran Canaria Canary Is
Agaie Nigeria
Agalega Islands Mauritius
Agallas Spain
Agalta nat. park Hond.
Agalta, Sierra de mts Hond.
Agana Guam see Hagåtña
A Gándara Galicia Spain
A Gándara de Altea Galicia Spain
Aganzhen Gansu China
Agapovka Rus. Fed.
Agar Madh. Prad. India
Agara Georgia
Agârak well Niger
Agâraktem well Mali
Āgaro Eth.
Agar Sarar Weyn well Eth.
Agartala Tripura India
Ágasegyháza Hungary
Agashi Mahar. India
Agassiz National Wildlife Refuge nature res. MN U.S.A.
Agat Guam
Agate Ont. Can.
Agathe France see Agde
Agathonisi i. Greece
Agatsuma Japan
Agatsuma-gawa r. Japan
Agatti i. India
Agawa r. Ont. Can.
Agayani Georgia see Aghaiani
Agbor Bojiboji Nigeria
Agboville Côte d'Ivoire
Ağcabädi Azer.
Ağcaşar Turkey
Ağdam Azer.
Ağdam Azer.
Ağdärä Dağlıq Qarabağ Azer.
Ağdärä Azer.
Ağdaş Azer.
Agdash Azer. see Ağdaş
Agde France
Agdzhabedi Azer. see Ağcabädi
Agedabia Libya see Ajdābiyā
Agematsu Japan
Agen France
Agenais reg. France
Agenebode Nigeria
Agenois reg. France see Agenais
Ageo Japan
Àger Spain
Agerbæk Denmark
Āgere Maryam Eth.
Ägerisee l. Switz.
Ageyevo Rus. Fed.
Ágfalva Hungary
Aggeneys S. Africa
Agger r. Ger.
Aggershus county Norway see Akershus
Aggius Sardegna Italy
Ağgöl salt flat Azer.
Ağgöl Qoruğu nature res. Azer.
Aggsbach Markt Austria
Aggteleki nat. park Hungary
Aghaboe Ireland
Aghadoon Ireland
Aghagallon Northern Ireland U.K.
Aghaiani Georgia
Āghā Jārī Iran
Aghalee Northern Ireland U.K.
Aghamore Ireland
Aghanloo Northern Ireland U.K.
Aghavannagh Ireland
Aghaylas well Western Sahara
Aghchoûrguit well Maur.
Aghern Ireland
Aghezzaf well Mali
Aghil Pass China/Jammu and Kashmir
Aghione Corse France
Aghireşu Romania
Aghla Mountain hill Ireland
Aghnacliff Ireland
Aghnjadzor Armenia
Aghouavil des. Maur.
Aghrîjît well Maur.
Aghstev r. Armenia
Aghzoumal, Sabkhat salt pan Western Sahara
Agia Greece
Agia Aikaterinis, Akrotirio pt Kerkyra Greece
Agia Anna Greece
Agiabampo Mex.
Agia Eirinis, Akrotirio pt Limnos Greece
Agia Marina Greece
Agia Paraskevi Greece
Agiasos Lesvos Greece
Agia Varvara Kriti Greece
Agigea Romania
Agighiol Romania
Agiguan i. N. Mariana Is see Aguijan
Ağın Turkey
Agincourt France see Azincourt
Ağın Dağı mt. Turkey
Aginskiy Buryatskiy Avtonomnyy Okrug admin. div. Rus. Fed.
Aginskoye Rus. Fed.
Aginum France see Agen
Agioi Apostoloi Greece
Agioi Theodoroi Dytiki Makedonia Greece
Agioi Theodoroi Peloponnisos Greece
Agion Oros admin. div. Greece
Agios Charalampos Greece
Agios Dimitrios Attiki Greece
Agios Dimitrios Kentriki Makedonia Greece
Agios Dimitrios, Akrotirio pt Kythnos Greece
Agios Efstratios Greece
Agios Efstratios i. Greece
Agios Fokas, Akrotirio pt Lesvos Greece
Agios Georgios Greece
Agios Georgios i. Greece
Agios Ioannis, Akrotirio pt Kriti Greece
Agios Kirykos Ikaria Greece
198 D4 Agios Konstantinos Greece
198 A3 Agios Matthaios Kerkyra Greece
198 E2 Agios Nikolaos Kentriki Makedonia Greece
199 G7 Agios Nikolaos Kriti Greece
199 H3 Agios Paraskevi Lesvos Greece
198 D5 Agios Petros Greece
128 B3 Agios Sergios Cyprus
198 E4 Agios Stefanos Greece
128 C3 Agios Theodoros Cyprus
198 E4 Agios Thomas Greece
198 E2 Agiou Orous, Kolpos b. Greece
194 H8 Agira Sicilia Italy
203 G5 Agirwat Hills Sudan
215 J2 Agisanang S. Africa
148 D3 Agivey Northern Ireland U.K.
172 F3 Aglasterhausen Ger.
199 L5 Ağlasun Turkey
191 K8 Agliana Italy
192 C5 Aglientu Sardegna Italy
163 K10 Agly r. France
190 H5 Agnadello Italy
198 C3 Agnantero Greece
159 I3 Agneaux France
161 J7 Agnel, Col pass France
193 L5 Agnena r. Italy
82 B2 Agnes, Mount hill S.A. Austr.
87 F10 Agnew W.A. Austr.
227 M3 Agnew Lake Ont. Can.
147 K3 Agnew's Hill Northern Ireland U.K.
206 E5 Agnibilékrou Côte d'Ivoire
197 M5 Agnita Romania
100 K3 Agniye-Afanas'yevsk Rus. Fed.
191 K4 Agno r. Italy
190 F3 Agno Switz.
193 M4 Agnone Italy
104 E7 Ago Japan
207 F4 Ago-Are Nigeria
190 F5 Agogna r. Italy
206 E5 Agogo Ghana
Agoitz Spain see Aoiz
182 D3 Agolada Spain
206 E5 Agona Ghana
162 F5 Agonac France
206 E5 Agona Junction Ghana
158 H3 Agon-Coutainville France
106 G8 Agong Qinghai China
191 M3 Agordo Italy
117 I7 Agori Uttar Prad. India
105 J4 Agose Japan
187 D11 Agost Spain
163 D9 Agos-Vidalos France
177 K4 Ágotapuszta nature res. Hungary
206 E2 Agounni Jefal well Mali
240 N7 Agoura CA U.S.A.
207 F2 Agous-n-Ehsel well Mali
163 H8 Agout r. France
104 E7 Ago-wan b. Japan
129 A1 Agoy Rus. Fed.
116 G6 Agra Uttar Prad. India
261 H3 Agraciada Uru.
198 C4 Agrafiotis r. Greece
129 I2 Agrakhanskiy Poluostrov pen. Rus. Fed.
Agram Croatia see Zagreb
185 P4 Agramón Spain
186 H4 Agramunt Spain
190 G4 Agrate Brianza Italy
183 Q5 Agreda Spain
260 C3 Agrelo Arg.
187 E10 Agrés Spain
193 R7 Agri r. Italy
127 K4 Ağrı Turkey
129 E6 Ağrı prov. Turkey
198 E7 Agria Gramvousa i. Greece
192 C2 Agriates, Désert des hills Corse France
129 F6 Ağrı Dağı mt. Turkey
Agrigan i. N. Mariana Is see Agrihan
194 F9 Agrigento Sicilia Italy
194 E8 Agrigento prov. Sicilia Italy
Agrigentum Sicilia Italy see Agrigento
91 K3 Agrihan i. N. Mariana Is
197 L3 Agrii r. Romania
199 H3 Agrilia, Akrotirio pt Lesvos Greece
198 C4 Agrinio Greece
260 C6 Agrio r. Arg.
184 G5 Agrio, Embalse de resr Spain
198 E3 Agriovotano Greece
182 F5 Agrochão Port.
193 N7 Agropoli Italy
134 K4 Agryz Rus. Fed.
140 L3 Ågskaret Norway
129 G4 Ağstafa Azer.
129 J5 Ağsu Azer.
92 C4 Agta Point Phil.
215 J8 Agter Sneeuberg S. Africa
215 J6 Agtertang S. Africa
187 D12 Agua, Cabo del c. Spain
184 H4 Agua, Sierra del hills Spain
260 C6 Agua Amarga, Pampa del plain Arg.
260 E5 Agua Blanca Arg.
245 I5 Agua Blanca Iturbide Mex.
257 F2 Água Boa Brazil
244 B3 Agua Brava, Laguna lag. Mex.
244 D4 Agua Caliente Mex.
252 D3 Agua Clara Bol.
256 A4 Água Clara Brazil
250 C3 Aguaclara Col.
243 N8 Aguada Mex.
247 □1 Aguada Puerto Rico
247 I8 Aguada Grande Venez.
250 C3 Aguadas Col.
244 F8 Agua de Correra Mex.
216 □1b Água de Pau São Miguel Azores
247 □1 Aguadilla Puerto Rico
259 D6 Aguado Cecilio Arg.
257 G3 Agua Doce do Norte Brazil
256 C5 Aguados, Serra dos mts Brazil
252 D3 Agua Dulce Bol.
245 M7 Agua Dulce Mex.
242 □S13 Aguadulce Panama
185 J6 Aguadulce Andalucía Spain
185 N7 Aguadulce Andalucía Spain
260 C5 Agua Escondida Arg.
241 T8 Agua Fria r. AZ U.S.A.
241 T7 Agua Fria National Monument nat. park AZ U.S.A.
256 D5 Aguaí Brazil
216 □1a Agualva Terceira Azores
244 B5 Aguamilpa Mex.
244 C4 Aguamilpa, Presa l. Mex.
244 D1 Aguanaval r. Mex.
184 E5 Água Negra hill Port.
260 C2 Agua Negra, Paso del pass Arg./Chile
240 P8 Aguanga CA U.S.A.
242 □P11 Aguanqueterique Hond.
242 F5 Agua Nueva Mex.
225 I3 Aguanus r. Que. Can.
253 F4 Aguapeí Brazil
256 B4 Aguapeí r. Brazil
253 F3 Aguapeí r. Brazil
253 F4 Aguapeí, Serra hills Brazil
242 E2 Agua Prieta Mex.
252 E5 Aguaragüe, Cordillera de mts Bol.
258 E1 Aguaray Arg.
182 C5 A Guarda Spain
216 □1b Agua Retorta São Miguel Azores
250 E2 Aguaro-Guariquito, Parque Nacional nat. park Venez.
186 C5 Aguarón Spain
242 F5 Aguaruto Mex.
186 E3 Aguas Spain
185 P6 Aguas r. Spain
254 F4 Águas Belas Brazil
182 D9 Águas Belas Port.
247 □1 Aguas Buenas Puerto Rico
244 E4 Aguascalientes Mex.
244 E4 Aguascalientes state Mex.
261 I4 Aguas Corrientes Uru.
187 E10 Aguas de Busot Spain
257 G2 Águas Formosas Brazil
182 F5 Águas Frias Port.
257 G1 Águas Vermelhas Brazil
186 E5 Aguasvivas r. Spain
253 F3 Água Verde r. Brazil
244 B3 Agua Verde Mex.
256 B3 Água Vermelha, Represa resr Brazil
186 E6 Aguaviva Spain
252 B2 Aguaytia Peru
182 F4 A Gudiña Spain
185 J3 Agudo Spain
256 C5 Agudos Brazil
182 D7 Águeda Port.
182 G6 Águeda r. Port./Spain
182 H7 Agueda, Embalse de resr Spain
207 H2 Âguelal Niger
207 F2 Aguelhok Mali
205 F4 Aguemour, Oued watercourse Alg.
183 N2 Agüera r. Spain
161 C8 Aguessac France
207 H2 Aguessis well Niger
191 O8 Agugliano Italy
104 E6 Agui Japan
184 D4 Aguiar Port.
182 E7 Aguiar da Beira Port.
207 G3 Aguié Niger
182 D8 Aguieira, Barragem da resr Port.
91 K4 Aguijan i. N. Mariana Is
183 Q7 Águila mt. Spain
241 S8 Aguila AZ U.S.A.
183 N2 Águila, Punta del pt Spain
183 L6 Aguilafuente Spain
239 L8 Aguilar CO U.S.A.
186 D6 Aguilar de Alfambra Spain
183 L3 Aguilar de Campóo Spain
183 L3 Aguilar de Campóo, Embalse de resr Spain
185 J5 Aguilar de la Frontera Spain
183 Q5 Aguilar del Río Alhama Spain
185 P6 Águilas Spain
244 E7 Aguililla Mex.
182 D8 Aguim Port.
216 □3f Agüimes Gran Canaria Canary Is
216 □3f Aguineguin r. Gran Canaria Canary Is
92 D6 Aguisan Negros Phil.
183 N6 Aguisejo r. Spain
210 C1 Āgula'i Eth.
184 □ Agulha, Ponta da pt Madeira
214 E10 Agulhas S. Africa
214 E10 Agulhas, Cape S. Africa
264 K9 Agulhas Basin sea feature Southern Ocean
257 E5 Agulhas Negras mt. Brazil
265 F7 Agulhas Plateau sea feature Southern Ocean
264 J8 Agulhas Ridge sea feature S. Atlantic Ocean
186 K3 Agullana Spain
187 D10 Agullent Spain
216 □3a Agulo La Gomera Canary Is
102 □E20 Aguni-jima i. Nansei-shotō Japan
Aguntum Italy see San Candido
92 E7 Agusan r. Mindanao Phil.
261 G4 Agustín Roca O'Higgins Arg.
92 C6 Agutaya Phil.
92 C6 Agutaya i. Phil.
199 K1 Ağva Turkey
129 H3 Agvali Rus. Fed.
207 G4 Agwarra Nigeria
210 B3 Agwei r. Sudan
129 I4 Ağyazı Azer.
Agyrium Sicilia Italy see Agira
102 □1 Aha Okinawa Japan
124 F6 Ahad Rafidah Saudi Arabia
Ahaggar plat. Alg. see Hoggar
84 D7 Ahakeye Aboriginal Land res. N.T. Austr.
147 C9 Ahakista Ireland
122 H2 Ahal admin. div. Turkm.
173 M4 Aham Ger.
122 I5 Āhangarān Iran
122 B2 Ahar Iran
81 F9 Ahaura South I. N.Z.
81 F9 Ahaura r. South I. N.Z.
169 D6 Ahaus Ger.
168 H4 Ahausen Ger.
147 H8 Ahenny Ireland
147 E9 Aherla Ireland
147 G8 Aherlow r. Ireland
217 □3a Ahibambo hill Njazidja Comoros
182 H8 Ahigal Spain
182 H6 Ahigal de Villarino Spain
185 K5 Ahillo mt. Spain
184 H4 Ahillones Spain
80 K5 Ahimanawa Range mts North I. N.Z.
136 E1 Ahinski, Kanal canal Belarus
80 H2 Ahipara North I. N.Z.
80 H2 Ahipara Bay North I. N.Z.
114 G3 Ahiri Mahar. India
80 I5 Ahititi North I. N.Z.
138 K3 Ahja r. Estonia
220 B4 Ahklun Mountains AK U.S.A.
127 K4 Ahlat Turkey
170 J3 Ahlbeck Ger.
170 J3 Ahlbeck, Seebad Ger.
168 I5 Ahlden (Aller) Ger.
169 E7 Ahlen Ger.
168 H4 Ahlerstedt Ger.
168 F5 Ahlhorn Ger.
171 D7 Ahlsdorf Ger.
116 D8 Ahmadabad Gujarat India
127 P8 Ahmadābād Iran
122 H4 Aḥmadābād Khorāsān Iran
122 I4 Aḥmadābād Khorāsān Iran
128 D9 Aḥmad al Bāqir, Jabal mt. Jordan
129 I6 Āhmädbäyli Azer.
114 D3 Ahmadnagar Mahar. India
114 E3 Ahmadpur Mahar. India
123 N7 Ahmadpur East Pak.
123 N6 Ahmadpur Sial Pak.
210 D2 Ahmar mts Eth.
Ahmedabad Gujarat India see Ahmadabad
Ahmednagar Mahar. India see Ahmadnagar
199 I4 Ahmetli Turkey
199 L4 Ahmetpaşa Turkey
168 J5 Ahnsbeck Ger.
207 G5 Ahoada Nigeria
147 J3 Ahoghill Northern Ireland U.K.
242 E5 Ahome Mex.
116 D7 Ahore Rajasthan India
169 K10 Ahorn Ger.
178 E5 Ahornspitze mt. Austria
231 I7 Ahoskie NC U.S.A.
169 D9 Ahr r. Ger.
122 D7 Ahram Iran
Ahrâmât el Jîzah tourist site Egypt see Pyramids of Giza
137 N8 Ahrarne Ukr.
117 I7 Ahraura Uttar Prad. India
122 E6 Āhravān Iran
195 □ Ahrax, Il-Ponta ta' l- pt Malta
169 C10 Ahrbrück Ger.
168 K2 Ahrensbök Ger.
168 J3 Ahrensburg Ger.
170 I5 Ahrensfelde Ger.
170 G2 Ahrenshagen Ger.
170 F2 Ahrenshoop, Ostseebad Ger.
169 E7 Ahse r. Ger.
134 D3 Ähtäri Fin.
138 K2 Ahtme Estonia
122 C6 Āhū Iran
244 C4 Ahuacatlán Mex.
243 O11 Ahuachapán El Salvador
244 D5 Ahualulco Jalisco Mex.
244 F3 Ahualulco San Luis Potosí Mex.
245 I7 Ahuatempan Mex.
245 I5 Ahuazotepec Mex.
244 D6 Ahuijullo Mex.
162 I3 Ahun France
138 K3 Ahunapalu Estonia
79 □9 Ahunui atoll Arch. des Tuamotu Fr. Polynesia
81 E11 Ahuriri r. South I. N.Z.
80 I3 Ahuroa North I. N.Z.
143 K6 Åhus Sweden
122 C6 Ahvāz Iran
Ahvenanmaa is Åland Fin. see Åland
116 D9 Ahwa Gujarat India
124 H9 Aḥwar Yemen
Ahwāz Iran see Ahvāz
207 F3 Ahzar, Vallée de l' watercourse Niger
93 F6 Ai i. Maluku Indon.
212 C5 Ai-Ais Namibia
212 C5 Ai-Ais Hot Springs and Fish River Canyon Park nature res. Namibia
251 F6 Aiapuá, Lago l. Brazil
250 D4 Aiari r. Brazil
107 L5 Aibag Gol r. China
183 R3 Aibar Spain
102 T3 Aibetsu Japan
179 L6 Aibl Austria
247 □1 Aibonito Puerto Rico
173 K5 Aichach Ger.
172 E5 Aichhalden Ger.
104 F6 Aichi pref. Japan
104 F5 Aichi-kōgen Kokutei-kōen park Japan
173 I6 Aichstetten Ger.
116 F7 Aichwara Madh. Prad. India
232 C10 Aid OH U.S.A.
103 L12 Aida Japan
173 O4 Aidenbach Ger.
169 J10 Aidhausen Ger.
194 G9 Aidone Sicilia Italy
240 □D12 'Aiea HI U.S.A.
193 Q9 Aiello Calabro Italy
193 P8 Aieta Italy
162 D3 Aiffres France
198 D4 Aigeira Greece
179 J4 Aigen im Ennstal Austria
179 I2 Aigen im Mühlkreis Austria
199 G6 Aigiali Greece
128 C3 Aigialousa Cyprus
198 E5 Aigina Greece
198 E5 Aigina i. Greece
198 D2 Aiginio Greece
198 D4 Aigio Greece
190 B3 Aigle Switz.
162 I5 Aigle, Barrage de l' dam France
161 J7 Aigle de Chambeyron mt. France
161 I8 Aiglun France
163 E8 Aignan France
156 I8 Aignay-le-Duc France
161 D8 Aigoual, Mont mt. France
162 E4 Aigre France
162 C3 Aigrefeuille-d'Aunis France
158 I7 Aigrefeuille-sur-Maine France
217 □1b Aigrettes, Île aux i. Mauritius
217 □1c Aigrettes, Pointe des pt Réunion
182 D4 A Igrexa Spain
258 G4 Aiguá Uru.
160 F2 Aigue, Mont hill France
160 I5 Aiguebelle France
227 P1 Aiguebelle, Parc de Conservation d' nature res. Que. Can.
160 J5 Aigueblanche France
160 C4 Aigueperse France
161 F8 Aigues r. France
161 E9 Aigues-Mortes France
161 D10 Aigues-Mortes, Golfe d' b. France
186 G2 Aigües Tortes i Estany de Sant Maurici, Parc Nacional d' nat. park Spain
161 B10 Aigues-Vives Languedoc-Roussillon France
161 E9 Aigues-Vives Languedoc-Roussillon France
163 H10 Aigues-Vives Midi-Pyrénées France
161 H7 Aiguille, Mont mt. France
162 A3 Aiguille, Pointe de l' pt France
160 K5 Aiguille d'Argentière mt. France/Switz.
160 K5 Aiguille de la Grande Sassière mt. France
161 J6 Aiguille de Péclet mt. France
161 J6 Aiguille de Scolette mt. France/Italy
160 J5 Aiguille du Midi mt. France
161 J7 Aiguilles France
161 I6 Aiguilles d'Arves mts France
160 J5 Aiguilles des Glaciers mts France
80 J3 Aiguilles Island North I. N.Z.
160 J5 Aiguille Verte mt. France
163 E7 Aiguillon France
162 B3 Aiguillon, Anse de l' b. France
162 B3 Aiguillon, Pointe de l' pt France
162 H3 Aigurande France
101 D8 Ai He r. China
Aihua Yunnan China see Yunxian
Aihui Heilong. China see Heihe
Aihui Heilong. China see Heihe
252 A2 Aija Peru
Aijal Mizoram India see Aizawl
105 J4 Aikawa Kanagawa Japan
102 P8 Aikawa Niigata Japan
231 G9 Aiken SC U.S.A.
108 C6 Ailao Shan mts Yunnan China
84 D7 Aileron N.T. Austr.
93 D8 Aileu East Timor
242 □T13 Ailigandi Panama
108 G6 Ailing Guangxi China
Ailinglabelab atoll Marshall Is see Ailinglaplap
266 G6 Ailinglaplap atoll Marshall Is
156 F8 Aillant-sur-Tholon France
163 D7 Aillas France
161 J10 Aille r. France
157 L8 Aillevillers-et-Lyaumont France
156 C3 Ailly-le-Haut-Clocher France
156 D4 Ailly-sur-Noye France
156 D4 Ailly-sur-Somme France
227 M6 Ailsa Craig Ont. Can.
146 F12 Ailsa Craig i. Scotland U.K.
161 E9 Aimargues France
160 J5 Aime France
Aimeo i. Fr. Polynesia see Moorea
93 B8 Aimere Flores Indon.
258 D3 Aimogasta Arg.
257 G3 Aimorés Brazil
257 G2 Aimorés, Serra dos hills Brazil
160 G4 Ain dept France
160 G5 Ain r. France
240 □D12 'Āina Haina HI U.S.A.
160 B3 Ainay-le-Château France
138 H4 Ainaži Latvia
205 G2 Aïn Beïda Alg.
204 E2 Aïn Beni Mathar Morocco
204 C4 'Aïn Ben Tili Maur.
206 C2 Aïn Biré well Maur.
205 F1 Aïn Defla Alg.
205 F2 Aïn Deheb Alg.
173 J4 Aindling Ger.
189 B7 Aïn Draham Tunisia
205 F3 Aïn el Hadjadj well Alg.
205 G4 Aïn el Hadjadj well Alg.
205 F2 Aïn el Hadjel Alg.
205 G2 Aïn el Melh Alg.
178 G6 Ainet Austria
202 C5 Aïn Galakka spring Chad
163 B9 Ainhoa France
205 G2 Aïn Mdila well Alg.
205 F3 Aïn Mezzer well Alg.
205 G1 Aïn-M'Lila Alg.
Aïn Mokra Alg. see Berrahal
198 B4 Ainou, Ethnikos Drymos nat. park Kefallonia Greece
205 G2 Aïn Oulmene Alg.
205 F2 Aïn Oussera Alg.
173 N6 Ainring Ger.
186 F3 Ainsa Spain
Ain Salah Alg. see In Salah
149 K6 Ainsdale Merseyside, England U.K.
205 E2 Aïn Sefra Alg.
225 I4 Ainslie, Lake N.S. Can.
236 F4 Ainsworth NE U.S.A.
Aintab Turkey see Gaziantep
205 E2 Aïn Temouchent Alg.
205 F5 Aïn Ti-m Misaou well Alg.
149 L7 Aintree Merseyside, England U.K.
183 R5 Ainzón Spain
103 L12 Aioi Japan
250 C4 Aipe Col.
252 D4 Aiquile Bol.
94 G3 Air i. Indon.
207 H2 Aïr, Massif de l' mts Niger
92 □ Airai Palau
156 C4 Airaines France
251 F5 Airão Brazil
190 C6 Airasca Italy
94 C4 Airbangis Sumatera Indon.
146 C7 Aird Asaig Western Isles, Scotland U.K.
146 E8 Aird of Sleat Highland, Scotland U.K.
222 H5 Airdrie Alta Can.
146 I11 Airdrie North Lanarkshire, Scotland U.K.
157 I5 Aire r. France
156 E2 Aire, Canal d' France
186 □ Aire, Illa de l' i. Spain
149 N6 Airedale val. England U.K.
163 D8 Aire-sur-l'Adour France
156 D2 Aire-sur-la-Lys France
207 H2 Aïr et du Ténéré, Réserve Naturelle Nationale de l' nature res. Niger
221 K3 Air Force Island Nunavut Can.
107 L5 Airgin Sum Nei Mongol China
95 I6 Airhitam r. Indon.
95 I6 Airhitam, Teluk b. Indon.
146 C6 Airidh a'Bhruaich Western Isles, Scotland U.K.
85 L6 Airlie Beach Qld Austr.
86 C6 Airlie Island W.A. Austr.
94 D1 Air Muda, Tasik l. Malaysia
193 N5 Airola Italy
190 F2 Airolo Switz.
93 D7 Airpanas Maluku Indon.
94 D1 Air Pedu, Tasik l. Malaysia
223 J4 Air Ronge Sask. Can.
146 I10 Airth Falkirk, Scotland U.K.
149 M5 Airton North Yorkshire, England U.K.
162 D2 Airvault France
96 A4 Aisatung Mountain Myanmar
173 K2 Aisch r. Ger.
259 B7 Aisén admin. reg. Chile
156 I8 Aisey-sur-Seine France
251 G4 Aishalton Guyana
107 Q8 Ai Shan hill Shandong China
222 B2 Aishihik Y.T. Can.
222 B2 Aishihik Lake Y.T. Can.
Aisími Greece see Aisymi
173 I4 Aislingen Ger.
156 G4 Aisne dept France
157 E5 Aisne r. France
205 E2 Aïssa, Djebel mt. Alg.
160 I2 Aïssey France
199 G1 Aisymi Greece
160 E1 Aisy-sur-Armançon France
140 R3 Aitamännikkö Fin.
187 E10 Aitana mt. Spain
91 J7 Aitape P.N.G.
204 D3 Aït Benhaddou tourist site Morocco
173 N4 Aiterach r. Ger.
173 N4 Aiterhofen Ger.
146 K4 Aith Orkney, Scotland U.K.
236 I2 Aitkin MN U.S.A.
205 F5 Aït Nefâne well Mali
104 D5 Aitō Japan
198 C4 Aitoliko Greece
186 F5 Aitona Spain
120 F1 Aitova Rus. Fed.
173 I6 Aitrach Ger.
173 J6 Aitrang Ger.
81 □2 Aitutaki i. Cook Is
197 L4 Aiud Romania
138 I5 Aiviekste r. Latvia
92 □ Aiwokako Passage Palau
Aix France see Aix-en-Provence
160 E5 Aix r. France
162 B3 Aix, Île d' i. France
156 G7 Aix-en-Othe France
161 G9 Aix-en-Provence France
162 G4 Aixe-sur-Vienne France
Aix-la-Chapelle Ger. see Aachen
160 H5 Aix-les-Bains France
210 C1 Āīy Ādī Eth.
Aiyiáli Greece see Aigiali
Aíyina i. Greece see Aigina
Aiyínion Greece see Aiginio
Aíyion Greece see Aigio
Aíyira Greece see Aigeira
117 N8 Aizawl Mizoram India
158 H8 Aizenay France
138 I5 Aizkraukle Latvia
183 Q3 Aizpún Spain
138 E5 Aizpute Latvia
103 Q9 Aizu-Wakamatsu Japan
124 E2 Ajā, Jibāl mts Saudi Arabia
122 A3 'Ajab Shīr Iran
192 B4 Ajaccio Corse France
Ajaccio airport Corse France see Campo dell'Oro
192 B4 Ajaccio, Golfe d' b. Corse France
245 H5 Ajacuba Mex.
116 H7 Ajaigarh Madh. Prad. India
250 C4 Ajajú r. Col.
177 L3 Ajak Hungary
245 J7 Ajalpán Mex.
129 D3 Ajamet'is Nakrdzali nature res. Georgia
116 E9 Ajanta Mahar. India
Ajanta Range hills India see Sahyadriparvat Range
207 G5 Ajaokuta Nigeria
Ajaria aut. rep. Georgia see Ach'ara
207 G4 Ajasse Nigeria
162 G5 Ajat France
227 O6 Ajax Ont. Can.
81 G9 Ajax, Mount South I. N.Z.
Ajayameru Rajasthan India see Ajmer
78 □1 Ajayan Bay Guam
125 L3 Ajban U.A.E.
106 D4 Aj Bogd Uul mts Mongolia
202 D2 Ajdābiyā Libya
188 D3 Ajdovščina Slovenia
a-Jiddét des. Oman see Ḥarāsīs, Jiddat al
102 R6 Ajigasawa Japan
205 H2 Ajim Tunisia
117 L7 Ajimganj W. Bengal India
105 J5 Ajiro Japan
177 G4 Ajka Hungary
128 D6 'Ajlūn Jordan
124 B1 'Ajmah, Jabal al mts Egypt
128 B9 'Ajmah, Jabal al plat. Egypt
125 L3 'Ajman U.A.E.
116 E6 Ajmer Rajasthan India
Ajmer-Merwara Rajasthan India see Ajmer
116 E4 Ajnala Punjab India
183 M2 Ajo Spain
241 T9 Ajo AZ U.S.A.
183 M1 Ajo, Cabo de c. Spain
241 T9 Ajo, Mount AZ U.S.A.
183 M9 Ajofrín Spain
190 B1 Ajoie reg. Switz.
78 □3b Ajokwola i. Majuro Marshall Is
245 J4 Ajoquentla Mex.
244 A1 Ajoya Mex.
114 D4 Ajra Mahar. India
123 L5 Ajrestan Afgh.
244 G7 Ajuchitlán Mex.
216 □1b Ajuda, Ponta da pt São Miguel Azores
252 D1 Ajuricaba Brazil
92 D6 Ajuy Panay Phil.
122 F3 Ajyyap Turkm.
104 F6 Akabane Japan
102 T3 Akabira Japan
205 F4 Akabli Alg.
105 J3 Akabori Japan
207 F2 Akaboun well Mali
100 K1 Akademii, Zaliv b. Rus. Fed.
Akademii Nauk, Khrebet mt. Tajik. see Akademiyai Fanho, Qatorkŭhi
123 N2 Akademiyai Fanho, Qatorkŭhi mt. Tajik.
103 P9 Akadomari Japan
102 Q8 Aka-gawa r. Japan
211 A5 Akagera, Parc National de l' nat. park Rwanda
Akagera, Parc National de l' nat. park Rwanda see Akagera, Parc National de l'
105 J2 Akagi Gunma Japan
103 J12 Akagi Shimane Japan
105 J2 Akagi-yama vol. Japan
105 H5 Akaishi-dake mt. Japan
105 G6 Akaishi-sanmyaku mts Japan
210 C2 Āk'ak'ī Beseka Eth.
202 A3 Akakus, Jabal mts Libya
114 E4 Akalkot Mahar. India
Akama, Akra c. Cyprus see Arnaoutis, Cape
Akamagaseki Japan see Shimonoseki
207 H5 Akamkpa Nigeria
102 V3 Akan Japan
102 U3 Akan-ko l. Japan
102 V3 Akan Kokuritsu-kōen nat. park Japan
207 G3 Akarkar well Niger
198 B4 Akarnanika mts Greece
81 G10 Akaroa South I. N.Z.
81 G10 Akaroa Harbour South I. N.Z.
117 N6 Akas reg. India
103 K11 Akasaki Japan
203 F4 Akasha Sudan
118 D3 'Akāshāt Iraq
127 I7 Akāshat Iraq
104 A6 Akashi Japan
104 A6 Akashi-kaikyō str. Japan
105 G3 Akashina Japan
215 M1 Akasia S. Africa
140 Q3 Äkäsjoki r. Fin.
140 Q3 Äkäsjokisuu Fin.
177 I5 Akasztó Hungary
81 J8 Akatarawa North I. N.Z.
129 C5 Akbaba Turkey
121 O5 Akbakay Kazakh.
121 R4 Akbalyk Kazakh.
123 M4 Akbar Afgh.
122 E7 Akbarābād Iran
116 H6 Akbarpur Uttar Prad. India
117 I6 Akbarpur Uttar Prad. India
120 I4 Akbasty Kazakh.
121 P3 Akbauyr Kazakh.
Akbaytal Kŭhistoni Badakhshon Tajik. see Rabotoqbaytal
123 O2 Akbaytal, Pereval pass Tajik.
121 N2 Akbeit Kazakh.
128 E2 Akbez Turkey
205 G1 Akbou Alg.
121 R3 Akbulak Kazakh.
121 U3 Akbulak Kazakh.
120 F2 Akbulak Rus. Fed.
129 A4 Akçaabat Turkey
126 H4 Akçadağ Turkey
129 E6 Akça Dağ mt. Turkey
126 I5 Akçakale Turkey
199 J3 Akcakertikbeli Geçidi pass Turkey
199 M1 Akçakoca Turkey
128 F2 Akçakoyunlu Turkey
126 F5 Akçali Dağ mt. Turkey
128 A2 Akçalı Dağları mts Turkey
199 I5 Akçaova Turkey
199 K6 Akçay Antalya Turkey
129 E5 Akçay Kars Turkey
199 J5 Akçay r. Turkey
206 B2 Akchâr reg. Maur.
121 O4 Akchatau Kazakh.
Akchi Kazakh. see Akshiy
129 C6 Akdağ mt. Turkey
199 J3 Akdağ mt. Turkey
199 J5 Akdağ mts Turkey
199 L5 Ak Dağı mt. Turkey
199 K6 Akdağlar mts Turkey
126 G4 Akdağmadeni Turkey
129 E5 Akdam Turkey
122 H1 Akdepe Turkm.
128 B2 Akdere Turkey
Akdoğan Cyprus see Lysi
129 C6 Akdoğan Dağı mts Turkey
104 F5 Akechi Japan
93 E4 Akelamo Halmahera Indon.
93 F3 Akelamo Halmahera Indon.
149 M2 Akeld Northumberland, England U.K.
124 D8 Akele Guzai prov. Eritrea
210 B3 Akelo Sudan
171 F7 Aken Ger.
105 L3 Akeno Ibaraki Japan
105 H4 Akeno Yamanashi Japan
143 O2 Åkersberga Sweden
142 H1 Akershus county Norway
164 G3 Akersloot Neth.
143 N2 Åkers styckebruk Sweden
141 K6 Åkerstrømmen Norway
120 I4 Akespe Kazakh.
208 D4 Aketi Dem. Rep. Congo
Akgyr Erezi hills Turkm. see Akgyr Erezi
122 F1 Akgyr Erezi hills Turkm.
122 E5 Ā Khakh Iran
129 F3 Akhalgori Georgia
Akhali-Afoni Georgia see Akhali Ap'oni
129 B2 Akhali Ap'oni Georgia
129 E4 Akhalk'alak'i Georgia
Akhal Oblast admin. div. Turkm. see Ahal
129 D4 Akhalts'ikhe Georgia
202 D2 Akhḍar, Al Jabal al mts Libya
125 M4 Akhḍar, Jabal mts Oman
128 E10 Akhḍar, Wādī al watercourse Saudi Arabia
Akhelóös r. Greece see Acheloos
197 P8 Akheloy Bulg.
199 I4 Akhisar Turkey
129 F4 Akhk'erp'i Georgia
129 G3 Akhmeta Georgia
129 C1 Akhmetovskaya Rus. Fed.
203 F3 Akhmīm Egypt
116 E3 Akhnoor Jammu and Kashmir
129 E3 Akhsau Rus. Fed.
Akhsu Azer. see Ağsu
Akhta Armenia see Hrazdan
127 P10 Akhtar Iran
128 F2 Akhtarīn Syria
135 I6 Akhtubinsk Rus. Fed.
129 I4 Akhty Rus. Fed.
Akhtyrka Ukr. see Okhtyrka
137 R9 Akhtyrskiy Rus. Fed.
120 H1 Akhunovo Rus. Fed.
129 I4 Akhvay, Gora mt. Azer./Rus. Fed.
103 K13 Aki Japan
208 B5 Akiéni Gabon
224 D2 Akimiski Island Nunavut Can.
Akıncılar İzmir Turkey see Selçuk
126 I3 Akıncılar Sivas Turkey
113 □1 Akinfushi i. N. Male Maldives
105 J4 Akiruno Japan
105 J4 Akishima Japan
100 H2 Akishma r. Rus. Fed.
102 R7 Akita Japan
102 R7 Akita pref. Japan
80 K7 Akitio North I. N.Z.
105 K3 Akiyama-gawa r. Japan
206 B2 Akjoujt Maur.
204 C3 Akka Morocco
120 J3 Akkabak Kazakh.
140 N3 Akkajaure l. Sweden
121 M4 Akkanse Kazakh.
129 C4 Akkaya Turkey
110 H1 Akkem Rus. Fed.
Akkerman Ukr. see Bilhorod-Dnistrovs'kyy
120 H2 Akkermanovka Rus. Fed.
102 V3 Akkeshi Japan
102 W3 Akkeshi-ko l. Japan
102 V4 Akkeshi-wan b. Japan
120 D4 Akkistau Kazakh.
128 D6 'Akko Israel
121 N1 Akkol' Akmolinskaya Oblast' Kazakh.
121 P5 Akkol' Almatinskaya Oblast' Kazakh.
135 J7 Akkol' Atyrauskaya Oblast' Kazakh.
121 N6 Akkol' Zhambylskaya Oblast' Kazakh.
199 I5 Akköy Aydın Turkey
199 K5 Akköy Denizli Turkey
164 I2 Akkrum Neth.
121 Q2 Akku Kazakh.
Akkul' Kazakh. see Akkol'
120 K5 Akkum Kazakh.
126 H3 Akkuş Turkey
207 F4 Aklampa Benin
220 E3 Aklavik N.W.T. Can.
116 F7 Aklera Rajasthan India
Akli well Mali see I-n-Akli
124 G6 Aklub reg. Saudi Arabia
Ak-Mechet Kazakh. see Kyzylorda
138 F6 Akmena r. Lith.
138 F5 Akmenė Lith.
138 E5 Akmeņrags pt Latvia
111 C8 Akmeqit Xinjiang China
121 N3 Akmeshit Kazakh.
Akmola Kazakh. see Astana
Akmola Oblast admin. div. Kazakh. see Akmolinskaya Oblast'
Akmolinsk Kazakh. see Astana
121 N2 Akmolinskaya Oblast' admin. div. Kazakh.
121 Q7 Ak-Moyun Kyrg.
138 I5 Aknīste Latvia
204 E2 Aknoul Morocco
103 L12 Akō Japan
210 B3 Akobo Sudan
210 B3 Akobo Wenz r. Eth./Sudan
116 F8 Akodia Madh. Prad. India
207 G2 Akokan Niger
114 D3 Akola Mahar. India
116 F9 Akola Mahar. India
207 H6 Akom II Cameroon
110 C6 Akongkür Xinjiang China
207 I6 Akonolinga Cameroon
208 F2 Akop Sudan
203 H6 Akordat Eritrea
199 L4 Akören Afyon Turkey
126 F5 Akören Konya Turkey
116 F9 Akot Mahar. India
208 F3 Akot Sudan
206 E5 Akoupé Côte d'Ivoire
221 L3 Akpatok Island Nunavut Can.
110 D6 Akqi Xinjiang China
198 E4 Akraifnio Greece
140 □B1 Akranes Iceland
142 B2 Åkrehamn Norway
207 H2 Akrérèb Niger
198 C6 Akritas, Akrotirio pt Greece
236 D5 Akron CO U.S.A.
226 H8 Akron IN U.S.A.
232 G5 Akron NY U.S.A.
232 D7 Akron OH U.S.A.
234 C4 Akron PA U.S.A.
198 F7 Akrotiri, Chersonisos pen. Kriti Greece
Akrotiri Bay Cyprus see Akrotirion Bay
128 B4 Akrotirion Bay Cyprus
Akrotiriou, Kolpos b. Cyprus see Akrotirion Bay
128 A4 Akrotiri Sovereign Base Area military base Cyprus
111 D9 Aksai Chin terr. Asia
199 J2 Aksakal Turkey
197 P7 Aksakovo Bulg.
135 K5 Aksakovo Rus. Fed.
126 G4 Aksaray Turkey
130 H3 Aksarka Rus. Fed.
129 C2 Aksaut r. Rus. Fed.
110 L7 Aksay Gansu China
120 E2 Aksay Kazakh.
121 P7 Ak-Say r. Kyrg.
135 G7 Aksay Rostovskaya Oblast' Rus. Fed.
135 I7 Aksay Volgogradskaya Oblast' Rus. Fed.
137 S6 Aksay r. Rus. Fed.
111 D9 Aksayqin Hu l. Aksai Chin
126 E4 Akşehir Turkey
199 M4 Akşehir Gölü l. Turkey
126 E5 Akseki Turkey
120 F1 Aksenovo Rus. Fed.
122 F7 Aks-e Rostam r. Iran
107 M1 Aksha Rus. Fed.
120 F3 Akshatau Kazakh.
120 J3 Akshiganak Kazakh.
120 E5 Akshimrau Kazakh.
121 Q6 Akshiy Kazakh.
120 D6 Akshukur Kazakh.
110 E5 Aksu Xinjiang China
110 E6 Aksu Xinjiang China
121 N1 Aksu Akmolinskaya Oblast' Kazakh.
121 R5 Aksu Almatinskaya Oblast' Kazakh.
121 Q1 Aksu Pavlodarskaya Oblast' Kazakh.
121 M6 Aksu Kazakh.
120 E2 Aksu Zapadnyy Kazakhstan Kazakh.
121 R4 Aksu r. Kazakh.
Aksu r. Tajik. see Oqsu
199 L6 Aksu Antalya Turkey
129 B5 Aksu Erzurum Turkey
199 M5 Aksu Isparta Turkey
199 L6 Aksu r. Turkey
120 K2 Aksuat Kostanayskaya Oblast' Kazakh.
121 T4 Aksuat Vostochnyy Kazakhstan Kazakh.
Aksuat, Ozero salt l. Kazakh. see Bol'shoy Aksuat, Ozero
121 O3 Aksu-Ayuly Kazakh.
135 J5 Aksubayevo Rus. Fed.
110 E6 Aksu He r. China
210 C1 Āksum Eth.
121 L5 Aksumbe Kazakh.
110 E4 Aksüme Xinjiang China
121 P5 Aksuyek Kazakh.
121 N6 Aksu-Zhabaglinskiy Zapovednik nature res. Kazakh.
111 G8 Aktag mt. Xinjiang China
110 D7 Aktam Xinjiang China
134 K5 Aktanysh Rus. Fed.
121 L3 Aktas Kazakh.
128 E2 Aktaş Hatay Turkey
129 B4 Aktaş Rize Turkey
127 L4 Aktas Dağı mt. Turkey
110 H1 Aktash Rus. Fed.
129 I2 Aktash r. Rus. Fed.
Aktash Uzbek. see Oqtosh
121 N4 Aktau Karagandinskaya Oblast' Kazakh.
121 O2 Aktau Karagandinskaya Oblast' Kazakh.
120 D6 Aktau Mangistauskaya Oblast' Kazakh.
128 E2 Aktepe Turkey
199 M2 Aktepe hill Turkey
110 C7 Akto Xinjiang China
120 G2 Aktobe Aktyubinskaya Oblast' Kazakh.
121 P3 Aktogay Karagandinskaya Oblast' Kazakh.
121 P1 Aktogay Pavlodarskaya Oblast' Kazakh.
121 R4 Aktogay Vostochnyy Kazakhstan Kazakh.
128 F1 Aktoprak Turkey
139 N6 Aktsyabrskaya Belarus
138 L9 Aktsyabrski Homyel'skaya Voblasts' Belarus
138 M7 Aktsyabrski Vitsyebskaya Voblasts' Belarus
121 L3 Aktuma Kazakh.
120 G4 Aktumsyk Kazakh.
120 H5 Aktumsyk, Mys pt Uzbek.
121 P6 Ak-Tüz Kyrg.
Aktyubinsk Aktyubinskaya Oblast' Kazakh. see Aktobe
120 H3 Aktyubinskaya Oblast' admin. div. Kazakh.
Aktyubinsk Oblast admin. div. Kazakh. see Aktyubinskaya Oblast'
Aktyuz Kyrg. see Ak-Tüz
140 S2 Akujärvi Fin.
208 D4 Akula Dem. Rep. Congo
139 Q8 Akulichi Rus. Fed.
221 K3 Akulivik Que. Can.
206 E5 Akumadan Ghana
103 H14 Akune Japan
210 B4 Akur mt. Uganda
129 G4 Akura Georgia
207 G5 Akure Nigeria
114 G9 Akuressa Sri Lanka
140 □D1 Akureyri Iceland
102 □G17 Akuseki-jima i. Nansei-shotō Japan
129 I3 Akusha Rus. Fed.
220 B4 Akutan AK U.S.A.
207 G5 Akwa Ibom state Nigeria
207 H4 Akwanga Nigeria
207 H5 Akwaya Cameroon
111 J8 Akxokesay Qinghai China
Akyab Myanmar see Sittwe
129 E5 Akyaka Turkey
120 H2 Ak"yar Rus. Fed.
128 D2 Akyatan Gölü salt l. Turkey
199 L2 Akyazı Turkey
121 O4 Akzhal Karagandinskaya Oblast' Kazakh.

Alice, Punta pt Italy
Alice Arm B.C. Can.
Alicedale S. Africa
Alice Downs W.A. Austr.
Alice Shoal sea feature Caribbean Sea
Alice Springs N.T. Austr.
Alice Town Bahamas
Aliceville AL U.S.A.
Aliçeyrek Turkey
Alichur Tajik.
Alichur r. Tajik.
Alichuri Janubí, Qatorkŭhi mts Tajik.
Alicia Arg.
Alicia Mindanao Phil.
Alick Creek r. Qld Austr.
Alicudi, Isola i. Isole Lipari Italy
Alicún de Ortega Spain
Al 'Idd U.A.E.
Al 'Idwah well Saudi Arabia
Aliero Nigeria
Alife Italy
Alifuatpaşa Turkey
Aligarh Rajasthan India
Aligarh Uttar Prad. India
Alīgūdarz Iran
Alihe Nei Mongol China
Alija del Infantado Spain
Alija de los Melones Spain see Alija del Infantado
Alijó Port.
Alījūq, Kūh-e mt. Iran
Alikamerli Turkey
Alikazgan r. Rus. Fed.
'Alī Kheyl Afgh.
Al Ikhwān is Yemen
Alikovo Rus. Fed.
Alima r. Congo
Al Imārāt al 'Arabīyah at Muttaḥidah country Asia see United Arab Emirates
Alimena Sicilia Italy
Alimia i. Greece
A Limia reg. Spain
Aliminusa Sicilia Italy
Alimpaya Point Mindanao Phil.
Alindao C.A.R.
Alindau Sulawesi Indon.
Alinghar r. Afgh.
Alingsås Sweden
Alintale well Eth.
Aliova r. Turkey
Alipur Mahar. India
Alipur Pak.
Alipur Duar W. Bengal India
Aliquippa PA U.S.A.
Alirajpur Madh. Prad. India
Ali Sabieh Djibouti
Al 'Īsāwīyah Saudi Arabia
Aliseda Spain
Alise-Ste-Reine France
Alī Shah Iran
Al Iskandarīyah Egypt
Al Iskandarīyah governorate Egypt
Al Iskandarīyah Iraq
Aliskerovo Rus. Fed.
Al Ismā'īlīyah Egypt
Al Ismā'īlīyah governorate Egypt
Alisofu Turkey
Aliste r. Spain
Alitåive mt. Sweden
Ali Terme Sicilia Italy
Al Ittihab Yemen see Madīnat ash Sha'b
Aliveri Greece
Aliwal Punjab India
Aliwal North S. Africa
Alix Alta Can.
Aliyaha r. Ukr.
Alizai Pak.
Alizay France
Al Jafr Jordan
Al Jāfūrah des. Saudi Arabia
Al Jaghbūb Libya
Al Jahrah Kuwait
Al Jamalīyah Qatar
Aljaraque Spain
Al Jarāwī well Saudi Arabia
Al Jarf mts Saudi Arabia
Al Jauf Saudi Arabia see Dumat al Jandal
Al Jawārah well Oman
Al Jawb reg. Saudi Arabia
Al Jawf Libya
Al Jawf 'Asīr Saudi Arabia
Al Jawf Saudi Arabia
Al Jawf prov. Saudi Arabia
Al Jawf governorate Yemen
Al Jawlān hills Syria see Golan
Al Jawsh Libya
Al Jaza'ir Alg. see Alger
Alj Beyk Iran
Aljezur Port.
Al Jībān reg. Saudi Arabia
Aljibe mt. Spain
Al Ji'lān hills Saudi Arabia
Al Jilh esc. Saudi Arabia
Al Jithāmīyah Saudi Arabia
Al Jīzah Egypt
Al Jīzah governorate Egypt
Al Jīzah Jordan
Al Ju'ayfirah Saudi Arabia
Aljubarrota Port.
Al Jubayl Saudi Arabia
Al Jubayl hills Saudi Arabia
Al Jubaylah Saudi Arabia
Al Jubb Saudi Arabia
Aljucén Spain
Aljucén r. Spain
Al Jufayfah Saudi Arabia
Al Jufrah oasis Libya
Al Julaydah well Saudi Arabia
Al Julayqah well Saudi Arabia
Al Jumah Saudi Arabia
Al Jumūm Saudi Arabia
Al Junaynah Saudi Arabia
Al Jurayd i. Saudi Arabia
Al Jurayfah Saudi Arabia
Al Jurayr well Saudi Arabia
Al Jurdhāwīyah Saudi Arabia
Aljustrel Port.
Al Juwayf depr. Syria
Al Juwayfah well Saudi Arabia
Al Kahfah Al Qaşīm Saudi Arabia
Al Kahfah Ash Sharqīyah Saudi Arabia
Al Kalbān Oman
Alkali Lake B.C. Can.
Alkaliya r. Ukr.
Alkamari Niger
Al Kāmil Oman
Al Karak Jordan
Al Karāmah Jordan
Al Kāẓimīyah Iraq
Alken Belgium
Al Khābūrah Oman
Al Khaḍrā' well Saudi Arabia
Al Khafaq well Saudi Arabia
Al Khafqān salt pan Saudi Arabia
Al Khafţ U.A.E.
Al Khalf Saudi Arabia
Al Khalīf Oman
Al Khalīl West Bank see Hebron
Al Khāliş Iraq
Al Khamāsīn Saudi Arabia
Al Kharfah Saudi Arabia
Al Khārijah Egypt
Al Kharj reg. Saudi Arabia
Al Kharkhayr oasis Saudi Arabia
Al Kharrārah Qatar
Al Kharrūbah Egypt
Al Khaşab Oman
Al Khasfah well Oman
Al Khāşirah Saudi Arabia
Al Khatam reg. U.A.E.
Al Khaţimī vol. Saudi Arabia
Al Khawkhah Yemen
Al Khawr Qatar
Al Khawtamah i. Yemen
Al Khiḍr Iraq
Al Khīşah well Saudi Arabia
Al Khizāmī well Saudi Arabia
Al Khobar Saudi Arabia
Al Khubrah Saudi Arabia
124 G3 Al Khuff reg. Saudi Arabia
202 B1 Al Khums Libya
124 D1 Al Khunfah sand area Saudi Arabia
125 I4 Al Khunn Saudi Arabia
128 D5 Al Khushnīyah Syria
125 J2 Al Khuwayr Qatar
125 L4 Al Kidan well Saudi Arabia
127 L7 Al Kifl Iraq
125 J3 Al Kir'ānah Qatar
128 E5 Al Kiswah Syria
164 G3 Alkmaar Neth.
179 J3 Alkoven Austria
128 A8 Al Kūbrī Egypt
127 L7 Al Kūfah Iraq
125 I5 Al Kuflah well Saudi Arabia
202 D3 Al Kufrah Libya
202 D3 Al Kufrah oasis Libya
124 F2 Al Kuhayfīyah Saudi Arabia
127 M7 Al Kumayt Iraq
128 C9 Al Kuntillah Egypt
124 D3 Al Kurá lava field Saudi Arabia
128 G7 Al Kusūr hills Saudi Arabia
127 L7 Al Kūt Iraq
Al Kuwayt country Asia see Kuwait
127 M9 Al Kuwayt Kuwait
128 D8 Al La'bān Jordan
127 J9 Al Labbah plain Saudi Arabia
207 F5 Allada Benin
128 D3 Al Lādhiqīyah Syria
128 D3 Al Lādhiqīyah governorate Syria
114 F5 Allagadda Andhra Prad. India
233 □P1 Allagash r. ME U.S.A.
233 □P2 Allagash Lake ME U.S.A.
116 H7 Allahabad Uttar Prad. India
129 D5 Allahüekber Dağları mts Turkey
129 D5 Allahüekber Tepe mt. Turkey
192 B8 Allai Sardegna Italy
156 E4 Allaines France
156 C7 Allaines-Mervilliers France
158 G6 Allaire France
128 E6 Al Lajā lava field Syria
220 C3 Allakaket AK U.S.A.
131 O3 Allakh-Yun' Rus. Fed.
234 F3 Allamuchy NJ U.S.A.
161 F7 Allan France
161 B6 Allanche France
215 L4 Allandale S. Africa
86 □1 Allan Point Christmas I.
215 K3 Allanridge S. Africa
148 J2 Allanton North Lanarkshire, Scotland U.K.
114 G3 Allapalli Mahar. India
203 G4 'Allāqī, Wādī al watercourse Egypt
129 J6 Allar Azer.
225 H4 Allardville N.B. Can.
78 □6 Allardyce Sta Isabel Solomon Is
182 E4 Allariz Spain
157 N7 Allarmont France
162 G5 Allassac France
125 I7 Al Latakhīyah well Yemen
161 G10 Allauch France
213 F4 Alldays S. Africa
190 C1 Alle Switz.
226 I7 Allegan MI U.S.A.
232 G6 Allegany NY U.S.A.
191 M3 Alleghe Italy
232 F8 Allegheny r. PA U.S.A.
232 C12 Allegheny Mountains U.S.A.
232 G7 Allegheny Reservoir PA U.S.A.
161 D6 Allègre France
247 □2 Allègre, Pointe pt Guadeloupe
161 G9 Alleins France
215 L4 Allemanskraaldam resr S. Africa
161 I6 Allemond France
260 D6 Allen Arg.
92 E5 Allen Samar Phil.
148 D7 Allen Ireland
232 A7 Allen MI U.S.A.
147 F4 Allen, Lough l. Ireland
81 B14 Allen, Mount hill Stewart I. N.Z.
231 G9 Allendale SC U.S.A.
149 M4 Allendale Town Northumberland, England U.K.
243 I3 Allende Coahuila Mex.
243 I5 Allende Nuevo León Mex.
245 M7 Allende Veracruz Mex.
169 G8 Allendorf (Eder) Ger.
169 G9 Allendorf (Lumda) Ger.
227 M5 Allenford Ont. Can.
149 M4 Allenheads Northumberland, England U.K.
172 G6 Allensbach Ger.
Allenstein Pol. see Olsztyn
232 C9 Allensville OH U.S.A.
232 H8 Allensville PA U.S.A.
234 F4 Allentown NJ U.S.A.
234 D3 Allentown PA U.S.A.
179 L2 Allentsteig Austria
147 I6 Allenwood Ireland
235 G4 Allenwood NJ U.S.A.
234 B2 Allenwood PA U.S.A.
114 E8 Alleppey Kerala India
186 D7 Allepuz Spain
168 H5 Aller r. Ger.
160 F3 Allerey-sur-Saône France
192 H2 Allerona Italy
173 K3 Allersberg Ger.
173 L5 Allershausen Ger.
161 I6 Allevard France
161 F7 Allex France
173 I6 Allgäu reg. Ger.
178 B5 Allgäuer Alpen mts Austria
151 N5 Allhallows Medway, England U.K.
251 H3 Allianc Suriname
236 D4 Alliance NE U.S.A.
232 D8 Alliance OH U.S.A.
156 H6 Allibaudières France
Al Lībīyah country Africa see Libya
160 C4 Allier dept France
160 C3 Allier r. France
127 K8 Al Lifīyah well Iraq
85 H4 Alligator Point Qld Austr.
246 □ Alligator Pond Jamaica
246 □ Alligator Pond Bay Jamaica
160 E2 Alligny-en-Morvan France
125 H2 Al Lihābah well Saudi Arabia
147 B9 Allihies Ireland
114 E3 Allikher Karnataka India
160 I4 Allinges France
143 K6 Allinge-Sandvig Bornholm Denmark
124 H2 Al Lişāfah well Saudi Arabia
128 D7 Al Lisān pen. Jordan
236 I4 Allison IA U.S.A.
195 O4 Alliste Italy
227 O5 Alliston Ont. Can.
124 E5 Al Līth Saudi Arabia
125 K4 Al Liwā' oasis U.A.E.
172 H5 Allmendingen Ger.
183 P3 Allo Spain
146 I10 Alloa Clackmannanshire, Scotland U.K.
159 P7 Allogny France
149 K4 Allonby Cumbria, England U.K.
162 E1 Allonnes Pays de la Loire France
159 L6 Allonnes Pays de la Loire France
163 D7 Allons France
83 N3 Allora Qld Austr.
161 J8 Allos France
161 J8 Allos, Col d' pass France
162 F3 Alloue France
226 F5 Allouez WI U.S.A.
147 E8 Allow r. Ireland
146 G12 Alloway South Ayrshire, Scotland U.K.
234 E5 Alloway NJ U.S.A.
234 D6 Alloway Creek r. NJ U.S.A.
183 Q3 Alloz, Embalse de resr Spain
186 D6 Alloza Spain
190 D1 Allschwil Switz.
171 D8 Allstedt Ger.
93 A6 Allu Sulawesi Indon.
124 F8 Al Luḥayyah Yemen
227 Q4 Allumettes, Île aux i. Que. Can.
192 H3 Allumiere Italy
114 G5 Allur Andhra Prad. India
114 G5 Alluru Kottapatnam Andhra Prad. India
127 K8 Al Lussuf well Iraq
160 D2 Alluy France
225 G3 Alma Que. Can.
231 F10 Alma GA U.S.A.
236 G6 Alma KS U.S.A.
226 J6 Alma MI U.S.A.
236 F5 Alma NE U.S.A.
127 K8 Al Ma'ānīyah Iraq
Alma-Ata Kazakh. see Almaty
Alma-Ata Oblast admin. div. Kazakh. see Almatinskaya Oblast'
186 F4 Almacelles Spain
185 K7 Almáchar Spain
185 O5 Almaciles, Puerto de pass Spain
184 A3 Almada Port.
124 C1 Al Madāfi' plat. Saudi Arabia
127 L9 Al Ma'danīyāt well Iraq
124 F7 Al Maḍāyā Saudi Arabia
85 J4 Almaden Qld Austr.
185 J3 Almadén Spain
184 G5 Almadén de la Plata Spain
185 J3 Almadenejos Spain
185 P4 Almadenes, Embalse de resr Spain
122 B6 Al Madīnah Iraq
124 D3 Al Madīnah Saudi Arabia
124 E3 Al Madīnah prov. Saudi Arabia
128 E6 Al Mafraq Jordan
261 E3 Almafuerte Arg.
125 K4 Al Maghrib reg. U.A.E.
245 I2 Almagre Mex.
92 E6 Almagro i. Phil.
185 L3 Almagro Spain
187 B13 Almagro, Sierra de hills Spain
125 J4 Al Mahākīk reg. Saudi Arabia
203 F3 Al Maḥāriq Egypt
124 E5 Al Maḥāwiyah Saudi Arabia
204 C4 Al Mahbas Western Sahara
124 E5 Al Mahḍam Saudi Arabia
128 F2 Al Mahdum Syria
124 D2 Al Maḥiā depr. Saudi Arabia
127 L7 Al Maḥmūdīyah Iraq
125 J7 Al Mahrah governorate Yemen
125 J8 Al Mahrah reg. Yemen
124 F8 Al Maḥwīt Yemen
124 F8 Al Maḥwīt governorate Yemen
125 J4 Al Majann ridge Saudi Arabia
183 P5 Almajano Spain
124 G3 Al Majma'ah Saudi Arabia
197 K6 Almăjului, Munţii mts Romania
203 F3 Al Maks al Baḥrī Egypt
129 H4 Almalı Azer.
125 I3 Al Malsūnīyah reg. Saudi Arabia
183 P6 Almaluez Spain
Almalyk Uzbek. see Olmaliq
125 L4 Al Manadir reg. Oman
125 J2 Al Manāmah Bahrain
124 G4 Al Manjūr well Saudi Arabia
240 K1 Almanor, Lake CA U.S.A.
187 C10 Almansa Spain
187 C10 Almansa, Embalse de resr Spain
184 C6 Almansil Port.
184 B3 Almansor r. Port.
203 F2 Al Manşūrah Egypt
127 L6 Al Manşūrīyah Iraq
183 J3 Almanza Spain
183 J8 Almanzor mt. Spain
185 P6 Almanzora r. Spain
124 E6 Al Ma'qaş Saudi Arabia
127 M8 Al Ma'qil Iraq
123 K4 Almār Afgh.
183 J7 Almar r. Spain
182 I9 Almaraz Spain
185 I6 Almargen Spain
125 K4 Al Mariyyah U.A.E.
202 D1 Al Marj Libya
128 B9 Al Markhah spring Egypt
183 P5 Almarza Spain
254 D4 Almas Brazil
177 L5 Almaş Romania
197 L3 Almaş r. Romania
256 C1 Almas, Rio das r. Brazil
125 M4 Al Masana'a Oman
177 H4 Almásfüzitő Hungary
177 G6 Almás-patak r. Hungary
Almassora Valencia Spain see Almazora
126 F8 Al Maţarīyah Egypt
121 Q5 Almatinskaya Oblast' admin. div. Kazakh.
204 B4 Al Matmarfag Western Sahara
121 Q6 Almaty Kazakh.
Almaty Oblast admin. div. Kazakh. see Almatinskaya Oblast'
Almaty Oblysy admin. div. Kazakh. see Almatinskaya Oblast'
127 K5 Al Mawşil Iraq
127 J6 Al Mayādīn Syria
183 O6 Almazán Spain
128 B7 Al Mazār Egypt
131 M3 Almaznyy Rus. Fed.
187 E8 Almazora Spain
128 D7 Al Mazra'ah Jordan
183 P5 Almazul Spain
173 P4 Alm Berg mt. Ger.
169 G7 Alme r. Ger.
187 C11 Almeces mt. Spain
185 N3 Almedina Spain
185 K6 Almedinilla Spain
182 G7 Almeida Port.
182 H6 Almeida de Sayago Spain
251 H5 Almeirim Brazil
184 B2 Almeirim Port.
164 K4 Almelo Neth.
186 G4 Almenar Spain
257 G2 Almenara Brazil
187 E8 Almenara Spain
187 B12 Almenara hill Spain
187 B12 Almenara, Sierra de hills Spain
185 O3 Almenaras mt. Spain
183 P5 Almenar de Soria Spain
182 F6 Almendra Port.
182 H6 Almendra Spain
182 H6 Almendra, Embalse de resr Spain
184 F3 Almendral Spain
184 G3 Almendralejo Spain
185 P6 Almendricos Spain
164 H4 Almere Neth.
185 O7 Almería Spain
185 O6 Almería prov. Spain
185 O7 Almería, Golfo de b. Spain
185 N7 Almerimar Spain
Almetievsk Rus. Fed. see Al'met'yevsk
135 K5 Al'met'yevsk Rus. Fed.
143 K5 Älmhult Sweden
124 G3 Al Midhnab Saudi Arabia
125 K5 Al Miḥrāḍ reg. Saudi Arabia
185 L7 Almijara, Sierra de mts Spain
185 I9 Almina, Punta pt Ceuta Spain
124 E5 Al Mindak Saudi Arabia
125 N4 Al Mintirib Oman
203 F2 Al Minyā Egypt
126 E9 Al Minyā governorate Egypt
259 C9 Almirantazgo, Seno del sea chan. Chile
242 □R13 Almirante Panama
256 C6 Almirante Tamandaré Brazil
125 K3 Al Mirfa U.A.E.
Almirós Greece see Almyros
125 I1 Al Mish'āb Saudi Arabia
128 E5 Al Mismīyah Syria
164 G5 Almkerk Neth.
184 C5 Almodôvar Port.
183 M8 Almodóvar hill Spain
184 H8 Almodóvar r. Spain
185 K3 Almodóvar del Campo Spain
183 Q9 Almodóvar del Pinar Spain
185 I5 Almodóvar del Río Spain
182 E7 Almofala Port.
185 J7 Almogía Spain
184 B5 Almograve Port.
183 O8 Almoguera Spain
184 G2 Almoharín Spain
244 G7 Almoloya Mex.
183 R6 Almonacid de la Sierra Spain
183 O9 Almonacid del Marquesado Spain
183 O8 Almonacid del Zorita Spain
183 M9 Almonacid de Toledo Spain
184 F5 Almonaster la Real Spain
146 J10 Almond r. Scotland U.K.
146 I10 Almondbank Perth and Kinross, Scotland U.K.
150 G4 Almondsbury South Gloucestershire, England U.K.
227 K7 Almont MI U.S.A.
227 R4 Almonte Ont. Can.
184 F6 Almonte Spain
182 H9 Almonte r. Spain
116 G5 Almora Uttaranchal India
187 D11 Almoradí Spain
185 I3 Almorchón Spain
183 L8 Almorox Spain
177 K4 Álmosd Hungary
182 D9 Almoster Port.
184 B2 Almoster r. Port.
207 G3 Al Mota well Niger
207 F2 Almoustarat Mali
179 I4 Almsee l. Austria
169 I6 Almstedt Ger.
128 G9 Al Mu'ayzīlah hill Saudi Arabia
125 I3 Al Mubarrez Saudi Arabia
125 N4 Al Muḍaibī Oman
125 N4 Al Muḍairib Oman
124 D3 Al Mudarraj Saudi Arabia
128 E9 Al Mudawwarah Jordan
185 P4 Almudema Spain
186 D3 Almudévar Spain
125 J2 Al Muḥarraq Bahrain
128 E10 Al Muḥtaṭab depr. Saudi Arabia
125 I8 Al Mukallā Yemen
124 F9 Al Mukhā Yemen
202 D1 Al Mukhaylī Libya
124 G4 Al Mulayḥ Saudi Arabia
125 I4 Al Munbaṭiḥ des. Saudi Arabia
124 G6 Al Mundafan pass Saudi Arabia
185 L7 Almuñécar Spain
186 E4 Almuniente Spain
179 I4 Almünster Austria
127 L7 Al Muqdādīyah Iraq
185 M3 Álmuradiel Spain
Al Mūrītānīyah country Africa see Mauritania
184 D2 Almuro r. Port.
127 I9 Al Murūt well Saudi Arabia
126 H3 Almus Turkey
124 H1 Al Musannāh ridge Saudi Arabia
124 D3 Al Musayjīd Saudi Arabia
187 E9 Almussafes Spain
124 C2 Al Muṭalla' Saudi Arabia
127 L8 Al Muthanná governorate Iraq
128 E7 Al Muwaqqar Jordan
124 E4 Al Muwayh Saudi Arabia
124 B2 Al Muwayliḥ Saudi Arabia
198 F4 Almyropotamos Greece
198 D3 Almyros Greece
198 F7 Almyrou, Ormos b. Kriti Greece
235 L1 Almyville CT U.S.A.
146 H7 Alness Highland, Scotland U.K.
Alness r. Scotland U.K. see Averon
149 N3 Alnmouth Northumberland, England U.K.
149 N3 Alnwick Northumberland, England U.K.
187 C7 Alobras Spain
183 O7 Alocén Spain
81 □4 Alofi Niue
77 I3 Alofi, Île i. Wallis and Futuna Is
81 □4 Alofi Bay Niue
78 □4b Alohkapw Pohnpei Micronesia
210 B4 Aloi Uganda
138 H4 Aloja Latvia
216 □3a Alojera La Gomera Canary Is
138 M5 Alol' Rus. Fed.
138 L5 Alolya r. Rus. Fed.
117 O5 Along Arun. Prad. India
100 B3 Alongshan Nei Mongol China
198 E3 Alonnisos i. Greece
256 B6 Alonso r. Brazil
93 D8 Alor i. Indon.
93 D8 Alor, Kepulauan is Indon.
93 C8 Alor, Selat sea chan. Indon.
185 J7 Álora Spain
94 D1 Alor Setar Malaysia
Alor Star Malaysia see Alor Setar
186 H2 Alós d'Ensil Spain
184 E5 Alosno Spain
Alost Belgium see Aalst
116 E8 Alot Madh. Prad. India
252 D5 Alota Bol.
91 L9 Alotau P.N.G.
159 J8 Alouettes, Mont des hill France
183 N7 Alovera Spain
160 F2 Aloxe-Corton France
87 J9 Aloysius, Mount W.A. Austr.
185 J7 Alozaina Spain
134 E2 Alozero Rus. Fed.
186 I3 Alp Spain
261 F5 Alpachiri Arg.
260 E3 Alpa Corral Arg.
199 J3 Alpagut Bursa Turkey
199 L2 Alpagut Eskişehir Turkey
184 D2 Alpalhão Port.
183 O6 Alpanseque Spain
240 M6 Alpaugh CA U.S.A.
178 E5 Alpbach Austria
183 L7 Alpedrete Spain
182 F8 Alpedrinha Port.
182 C9 Alpedriz Port.
169 C7 Alpen Ger.
227 K4 Alpena MI U.S.A.
169 E9 Alpenrod Ger.
186 J3 Alpens Spain
187 C10 Alpera Spain
254 D3 Alpercatas, Serra das hills Brazil
161 I8 Alpes-de-Haute-Provence dept France
161 K9 Alpes-Maritimes dept France
Alpes Maritimes mts France/Italy see Maritime Alps
178 D6 Alpetta, Punta dell' mt. Italy
190 E3 Alpe Veglia, Parco Naturale nature res. Italy
85 K7 Alpha Qld Austr.
215 P3 Alpha S. Africa
85 K7 Alpha Creek r. Qld Austr.
268 P1 Alpha Ridge sea feature Arctic Ocean
164 G6 Alphen Neth.
164 G4 Alphen aan den Rijn Neth.
217 □2 Alphonse i. Seychelles
217 □2 Alphonse Island Seychelles
190 I7 Alpi Apuane, Parco Naturale delle nature res. Italy
184 B2 Alpiarça Port.
186 G4 Alpicat Spain
Alpi Dolomitiche mts Italy see Dolomiti
161 F9 Alpilles hills France
161 F9 Alpilles, Canal des France
Alpi Marittime mts France/Italy see Maritime Alps
241 W8 Alpine AZ U.S.A.
240 P9 Alpine CA U.S.A.
227 R7 Alpine NY U.S.A.
237 D10 Alpine TX U.S.A.
238 I5 Alpine WY U.S.A.
83 K7 Alpine National Park Vic. Austr.
256 D4 Alpinópolis Brazil
172 E5 Alpirsbach Ger.
190 E2 Alpnach Switz.
179 O5 Alpokalja mts Hungary
191 K5 Alpone r. Italy
184 D6 Alportel r. Port.
190 B5 Alps mts Europe
199 L3 Alpu Turkey
187 D8 Alpuente Spain
128 B10 Al Qā' val. Egypt
124 E5 Al Qā' Makkah Saudi Arabia
124 E6 Al Qā' Makkah Saudi Arabia
125 H7 Al Qa'āmīyāt reg. Saudi Arabia
202 B2 Al Qaddāḥīyah Libya
127 L8 Al Qādisīyah governorate Iraq
128 E3 Al Qadmūs Syria
125 K3 Al Qaffāy i. U.A.E.
124 G8 Al Qafrah Yemen
203 F2 Al Qāhirah Egypt
126 E9 Al Qāhirah governorate Egypt
124 E6 Al Qaḥmah Saudi Arabia
124 F3 Al Qā'īyah Saudi Arabia
124 G2 Al Qā'īyah well Saudi Arabia
124 C1 Al Qalībah Saudi Arabia
127 J5 Al Qāmishlī Syria
203 G2 Al Qanṭarah Egypt
124 H2 Al Qar'ah well Saudi Arabia
128 E6 Al Qar'ah lava field Syria
128 E3 Al Qardāḥah Syria
203 I5 Al Qarḥah Saudi Arabia
125 H8 Al Qarn Yemen
128 F7 Al Qarqar Saudi Arabia
128 F4 Al Qaryatayn Syria
124 G3 Al Qaşab Ar Riyāḍ Saudi Arabia
125 I4 Al Qaşab Ash Sharqīyah Saudi Arabia
124 F3 Al Qaşīm prov. Saudi Arabia
203 F3 Al Qaşr Egypt
124 E2 Al Qaşr Saudi Arabia
202 E3 Al Qaşş Abū Sa'īd plat. Egypt
125 J2 Al Qaţīf Saudi Arabia
125 I8 Al Qaţn Yemen
128 E7 Al Qaţrānah Jordan
202 B3 Al Qaţrūn Libya
124 G5 Al Qawnas reg. Saudi Arabia
124 H1 Al Qayşūmah Saudi Arabia
127 K9 Al Qāyşūmah well Saudi Arabia
125 M7 Al Qiblīyah i. Oman
202 D1 Al Qubbah Darnah Libya
187 E10 Alquería de la Condesa Spain
184 D4 Alqueva Port.
184 E4 Alqueva, Barragem de resr Port.
186 F3 Alquézar Spain
124 E2 Al Qufayfah Saudi Arabia
185 M6 Alquife Spain
125 I1 Al-Qulay'ah, Ra's- pt Kuwait
Al Qumur country Africa see Comoros
128 D5 Al Qunayţirah Syria
128 D5 Al Qunayţirah governorate Syria
124 E6 Al Qunfidhah Saudi Arabia
124 F3 Al Qurayn Saudi Arabia
125 K5 Al Quraynī oasis Saudi Arabia
124 F3 Al Qurayyah Saudi Arabia
125 M3 Al Qurayyah U.A.E.
126 H8 Al Qurayyāt Saudi Arabia
127 M8 Al Qurnah Iraq
128 C8 Al Quşaymah Egypt
203 G3 Al Quşayr Egypt
127 L8 Al Qusayr Iraq
128 E4 Al Quşayr Syria
128 E5 Al Quţayfah Syria
124 F2 Al Quwārah Saudi Arabia
124 G4 Al Quwayi' Saudi Arabia
124 G3 Al Quwayīyah Saudi Arabia
128 D9 Al Quwayrah Jordan
125 I8 Al Quzah Yemen
125 L4 Al Rabbād reg. U.A.E.
161 B8 Alrance France
205 H3 Alrar Est Alg.
151 O4 Alresford Essex, England U.K.
151 I2 Alrewas Staffordshire, England U.K.
84 F5 Alroy Downs N.T. Austr.
142 F6 Als i. Denmark
183 M2 Alsa, Embalse de resr Spain
157 N7 Alsace admin. reg. France
157 N7 Alsace reg. France
157 N8 Alsace, Plaine d' val. France
149 M7 Alsager Cheshire, England U.K.
122 F9 Al Samha U.A.E.
127 K8 Al Samīt well Iraq
223 I5 Alsask Sask. Can.
Alsasua Spain see Altsasu
Alsatia reg. France see Alsace
172 F2 Alsbach Ger.
169 B9 Alsdorf Ger.
222 B3 Alsek r. AK U.S.A.
172 D3 Alsenborn Ger.
190 H6 Alseno Italy
172 D2 Alsenz Ger.
169 H9 Alsfeld Ger.
168 I1 Als Fjord inlet Denmark
146 E8 Alsh, Loch sea chan. Scotland U.K.
172 E2 Alsheim Ger.
261 H3 Alsina Arg.
100 J1 Al'skiy Khrebet mt. Rus. Fed.
171 E7 Alsleben (Saale) Ger.
177 I4 Alsónémedi Hungary
177 G4 Alsóörs Hungary
177 J3 Alsóvadász Hungary
177 J3 Alsózsolca Hungary
143 M5 Alsterån r. Sweden
143 L5 Alstermo Sweden
157 M5 Alsting France
149 M4 Alston Cumbria, England U.K.
83 N3 Alstonville N.S.W. Austr.
138 E5 Alsunga Latvia
138 J4 Alsviķi Latvia
140 Q2 Alta Norway
143 O2 Älta Sweden
81 C11 Alta, Mount South I. N.Z.
190 H1 Altach Austria
191 K2 Altacroce, Monte mt. Italy
240 N7 Altadena CA U.S.A.
140 Q2 Altaelva r. Norway
140 Q1 Altafjorden sea chan. Norway
253 F2 Alta Floresta Brazil
186 H5 Altafulla Spain
260 E2 Alta Gracia Arg.
242 □Q12 Alta Gracia Nic.
110 H2 Altai Mountains Asia
261 E4 Alta Italia Arg.
231 G10 Altamaha r. GA U.S.A.
250 E4 Altamira Amazonas Brazil
251 H5 Altamira Pará Brazil
258 C2 Altamira Chile
250 C4 Altamira Col.
242 □Q12 Altamira Costa Rica
245 J3 Altamíra Mex.
183 L2 Altamira, Cuevas de tourist site Spain
185 I1 Altamira, Sierra de mts Spain
261 H4 Altamirano Arg.
243 M9 Altamirano Chiapas Mex.
245 K6 Altamirano Veracruz Mex.
231 G11 Altamonte Springs City FL U.S.A.
186 K3 Alt Ampordà reg. Spain
193 R6 Altamura Italy
107 K2 Altan Chitinskaya Oblast' Rus. Fed.
107 L2 Altan Chitinskaya Oblast' Rus. Fed.
106 J3 Altanbulag Mongolia
107 O2 Altan Emel Nei Mongol China
192 A9 Altano, Capo c. Sardegna Italy
106 B4 Altan Ovoo mt. China/Mongolia
107 K7 Altan Shiret Nei Mongol China
Altan Xiret Nei Mongol China see Altan Shiret
254 D5 Alta Paraiso de Goiás Brazil
251 E2 Altapirire Venez.
242 D2 Altar Mex.
239 I11 Altar r. Mex.
242 B1 Altar, Desierto de des. Mex.
190 E7 Altare Italy
216 □1a Altares Terceira Azores
242 F5 Altata Mex.
179 I4 Altaussee Austria
179 I4 Altausseer See l. Austria
190 D7 Alta Valle Pesio, Parco Naturale dell' nature res. Italy
190 D4 Alta Val Sesia, Parco Naturale nature res. Italy
194 H2 Altavilla Irpina Italy
193 O6 Altavilla Silentina Italy
232 F11 Altavista VA U.S.A.
110 I3 Altay Xinjiang China
106 E3 Altay Mongolia
106 A1 Altay, Respublika aut. rep. Rus. Fed.
Altay Kray admin. div. Rus. Fed. see Altayskiy Kray
121 U2 Altayskiy Rus. Fed.
Altayskiy Khrebet mts Asia see Altai Mountains
121 T2 Altayskiy Kray admin. div. Rus. Fed.
106 A1 Altayskiy Zapovednik nature res. Rus. Fed.
171 J7 Altdöbern Ger.
173 M4 Altdorf Ger.
190 F2 Altdorf Switz.
173 K3 Altdorf bei Nürnberg Ger.
168 I2 Alt Duvenstedt Ger.
184 C6 Alte Port.
187 E10 Altea Spain
170 D4 Alte Elde r. Ger.
170 H2 Altefähr Ger.
173 M4 Alteglofsheim Ger.
140 Q1 Alteidet Norway
169 E8 Altena Ger.
169 C9 Altenahr Ger.
169 J7 Altenau Ger.
169 G7 Altenbeken Ger.
171 I9 Altenberg Ger.
169 D6 Altenberge Ger.
168 G3 Altenbruch-Westerende Ger.
172 G2 Altenbuch Ger.
171 F9 Altenburg Ger.
169 E10 Altendiez Ger.
169 K9 Altenfeld Ger.
179 I3 Altenfelden Austria
172 C2 Altenglan Ger.
169 K8 Altengottern Ger.
170 E2 Altenhagen Ger.
172 D5 Altenheim Ger.
170 I5 Altenhof Ger.
168 J2 Altenholz Ger.
170 H1 Altenkirchen Ger.
169 E9 Altenkirchen (Westerwald) Ger.
168 K2 Altenkrempe Ger.
173 N5 Altenmarkt an der Alz Ger.
179 M3 Altenmarkt an der Triesting Austria
179 K4 Altenmarkt bei Sankt Gallen Austria
179 H5 Altenmarkt im Pongau Austria
168 K4 Altenmedingen Ger.
173 J5 Altenmünster Ger.
106 D8 Altenqoke Qinghai China
173 I5 Altenstadt Bayern Ger.
173 J6 Altenstadt Bayern Ger.
169 G10 Altenstadt Hessen Ger.
173 M2 Altenstadt an der Waldnaab Ger.
172 F4 Altensteig Ger.
170 H3 Altentreptow Ger.
171 E7 Altenweddingen Ger.
170 J5 Alte Oder r. Ger.
251 H5 Alter do Chão Brazil
184 D2 Alter do Chão Port.
184 D2 Alter Pedroso hill Port.
171 H6 Altes Lager Ger.
140 O2 Altevatnet l. Norway
173 M5 Altfraunhofen Ger.
173 K5 Althegnenberg Ger.
178 H3 Altheim Austria
172 G5 Altheim Ger.
173 I4 Altheim (Alb) Ger.
172 F4 Althengstett Ger.
179 J6 Althofen Austria
129 J5 Altıağaç Azer.
161 D8 Altier France
161 D8 Altier r. France
129 A6 Altınbasak Turkey
129 A5 Altındere park Turkey
135 F8 Altınkaya Barajı resr Turkey
127 L6 Altin Köprü Iraq
199 H3 Altınoluk Turkey
256 D4 Altinópolis Brazil
199 H3 Altınova Balıkesir Turkey
128 F1 Altınova Şanlıurfa Turkey
128 E2 Altınözü Turkey
199 L3 Altıntaş Turkey
199 L6 Altınyaka Turkey
252 C4 Altiplano plain Bol.
129 E6 Altıyol Turkey
160 K1 Altkirch France
171 F9 Altkirchen Ger.
170 D4 Alt Krenzlin Ger.
170 I5 Altlandsberg Ger.
173 L4 Altmannstein Ger.
170 D5 Altmark reg. Ger.
171 G9 Altmittweida Ger.
173 L4 Altmühl r. Ger.
173 K4 Altmühltal park Ger.
146 G9 Altnafeadh Highland, Scotland U.K.
146 H6 Altnaharra Highland, Scotland U.K.
226 I7 Alto MI U.S.A.
191 L5 Alto, Monte hill Italy
261 F3 Alto Alegre Arg.
256 A2 Alto Araguaia Brazil
246 F3 Alto Cedro Cuba
209 C7 Alto Chicapa Angola
183 P5 Alto Cruz mt. Spain
243 N10 Alto Cuchumatanes mts Guat.
245 H2 Alto de Caballeros Mex.
183 N3 Alto de Cabezas mt. Spain
182 F4 Alto de Covelo pass Spain
183 K3 Alto de las Portillas pass Spain
183 Q5 Alto del Moncayo mt. Spain
182 I3 Alto del Rabizo pass Spain
260 D3 Alto de Pencoso hills Arg.
185 M6 Alto de San Juan mt. Spain
182 F4 Alto do Canizo pass Spain
182 D8 Alto do Trevim mt. Port.
182 F5 Alto Douro Wine Region reg. Port.
194 E7 Altofonte Sicilia Italy
255 B6 Alto Garças Brazil
260 B3 Alto Jahuel Chile
213 H2 Alto Ligonha Moz.
245 K6 Alto Lucero Mex.
252 C3 Alto Madidi, Parque Nacional nat. park Bol.
183 O8 Altomira, Sierra de mts Spain
213 H2 Alto Molócuè Moz.
193 Q8 Altomonte Italy
173 K5 Altomünster Ger.
151 K5 Alton Hampshire, England U.K.
151 I2 Alton Staffordshire, England U.K.
236 J6 Alton IL U.S.A.
237 J7 Alton MO U.S.A.
233 □N5 Alton NH U.S.A.
222 F3 Altona B.C. Can.
223 L5 Altona Man. Can.
82 G2 Alton Downs S.A. Austr.
259 B7 Alto Nevado mt. Chile
232 G8 Altoona PA U.S.A.
226 C5 Altoona WI U.S.A.
251 I5 Alto Pacajá r. Brazil
254 D4 Alto Parnaíba Brazil
191 J8 Altopascio Italy
260 D3 Alto Pelado Arg.
260 D3 Alto Pencoso Arg.
256 A6 Alto Piquiri Brazil
252 C2 Alto Purús r. Peru
182 E5 Alto Rabagão, Barragem do resr Port.
257 F4 Alto Rio Doce Brazil
259 C7 Alto Río Senguerr Arg.
256 A3 Alto Rio Verde Brazil
186 F4 Altorricón Spain
254 E3 Altos Brazil
183 O8 Altos de Cabrejas mts Spain
252 C4 Altos de Chacaya Chile
185 P3 Altos de Chinchilla mts Spain
261 F2 Altos de Chipión Arg.
256 A3 Alto Sucuriú Brazil
183 P7 Alto Tajo, Parque Natural del nature res. Spain
256 A2 Alto Taquarí Brazil
183 M3 Altotero mt. Spain
245 J6 Altotonga Mex.
173 N5 Altötting Ger.
255 B8 Alto Uruguai Brazil
247 □9 Alto Vista hill Aruba
170 J5 Altranft Ger.
172 B2 Altrich Ger.
149 M7 Altrincham Greater Manchester, England U.K.
170 G5 Alt Ruppin Ger.
183 P3 Altsasu Spain
170 F3 Alt Schwerin Ger.
172 H6 Altshausen Ger.
190 H1 Altstätten Switz.
129 E2 Altud Rus. Fed.
139 R9 Altukhovo Rus. Fed.
129 B6 Altunkent Turkey
110 K7 Altun Shan mt. Qinghai China
111 H8 Altun Shan mts China
187 E8 Altura Spain
238 D6 Alturas CA U.S.A.
237 F8 Altus OK U.S.A.
173 I6 Altusried Ger.
169 J6 Alt Wallmoden Ger.
137 M2 Altynivka Ukr.
Altyn-Topkan Tajik. see Oltintopkan
138 H2 Alu Estonia
213 H2 Alua Moz.
208 F3 Aluakluak Sudan
125 J4 Al Ubaylah Saudi Arabia
126 I3 Alucra Turkey
125 I3 Al 'Uḍaylīyah Saudi Arabia
124 F9 Al Udayn Yemen
138 K4 Alūksne Latvia
138 K4 Alūksnes l. Latvia
124 C2 Al 'Ulā Saudi Arabia
124 G8 Al'ulah reg. Yemen
122 C5 Alūm Iran
232 E9 Alum Bridge WV U.S.A.
232 C8 Alum Creek Lake OH U.S.A.
260 B6 Aluminé Arg.
260 B6 Aluminé r. Arg.
260 B6 Aluminé, Lago l. Arg.
143 O1 Alunda Sweden
197 M4 Aluniş Romania
137 N9 Alupka Ukr.
202 C2 Al 'Uqaylah Libya
Al 'Uqaylah Saudi Arabia see An Nabk
125 J3 Al 'Uqayr Saudi Arabia
203 G3 Al Uqşur Egypt
114 E5 Alur Andhra Prad. India
126 I9 Al Urayq des. Saudi Arabia
Al 'Urdun country Asia see Jordan
Alur Setar Malaysia see Alor Setar
137 N9 Alushta Ukr.
183 Q7 Alustante Spain
122 A4 'Ālūt Iran
124 C1 Al Uthaylī Saudi Arabia
78 □1 Alutom, Mount hill Guam
78 □1 Alutom Island Guam
Aluva Kerala India see Alwaye
124 G4 Al 'Uwayjā' well Saudi Arabia
125 J4 Al 'Uwayjā' well Saudi Arabia
125 I2 Al 'Uwaynah well Saudi Arabia
202 E4 Al 'Uwaynāt Al Kufrah Libya
202 A3 Al 'Uwaynāt Awbārī Libya
124 C2 Al 'Uwaynidhiyah i. Saudi Arabia
127 K8 Al 'Uwayqīlah Saudi Arabia
124 H3 Al Uyainah Saudi Arabia
128 E10 Al 'Uyaynah well Saudi Arabia
124 D3 Al 'Uyūn Al Madīnah Saudi Arabia
124 F2 Al 'Uyūn Al Qaşīm Saudi Arabia
124 F2 Al 'Uẓaym Saudi Arabia
127 M8 Al 'Uzayr Iraq
182 D8 Alva r. Port.
146 I10 Alva Clackmannanshire, Scotland U.K.
237 F7 Alva OK U.S.A.
182 D9 Alvaiázere Port.
184 C5 Alvalade Port.
129 I5 Älvänd Azer.
122 C4 Alvand, Kūh-e mt. Iran
190 H2 Alvaneu Switz.
182 E6 Alvão, Parque Natural do nature res. Port.
182 E6 Alvão, Serra de mts Spain
129 C6 Alvar Turkey
245 L7 Alvarado Mex.
237 G9 Alvarado TX U.S.A.
245 L7 Alvarado, Laguna lag. Mex.
251 E5 Alvarães Brazil
182 C5 Alvarães Port.
257 G3 Alvarenga Brazil
182 D7 Alvarenga Port.
182 D8 Álvares Port.
256 B5 Álvares Machado Brazil
261 G3 Alvarez Arg.
182 E9 Álvaro Port.
244 F6 Álvaro Obregón Mex.
245 I4 Álvaro Obregón Mex.
141 M6 Älvdalen Sweden
141 J1 Alvdalen val. Sweden
151 I3 Alvechurch Worcestershire, England U.K.
182 D2 Alvedro airport Spain
184 C2 Alvega Port.
150 H3 Alveley Shropshire, England U.K.
182 D9 Alvelos, Serra de mts Port.
184 A3 Alverca Port.
182 F7 Alverca da Beira Port.
165 C6 Alveringem Belgium
146 J7 Alves Moray, Scotland U.K.
168 I3 Alveslohe Ger.
143 K5 Alvesta Sweden
150 G4 Alveston South Gloucestershire, England U.K.
193 I2 Alviano Italy
146 I8 Alvie Highland, Scotland U.K.
163 H6 Alvignac France
142 C1 Ålvik Norway
141 N5 Alvik Sweden
237 H11 Alvin TX U.S.A.
226 F4 Alvin WI U.S.A.
257 F4 Alvinópolis Brazil
182 E7 Alvite Port.
193 L4 Alvito Italy
184 D4 Alvito Port.
184 D4 Alvito, Barragem do resr Port.
143 N1 Älvkarleby Sweden
193 P6 Alvo r. Italy
182 E8 Alvoco da Serra Port.
184 B6 Alvor Port.
140 P4 Älvsbyn Sweden
126 C10 Al Wādī at Jadīd governorate Egypt
125 N4 Al Wāfī Oman
127 M9 Al Wafrah Kuwait
124 C2 Al Wajh Saudi Arabia
125 J3 Al Wakrah Qatar
125 I2 Al Wannān Saudi Arabia
124 G1 Al Waqbá well Saudi Arabia
116 F6 Alwar Rajasthan India
125 H2 Al Warī'ah Saudi Arabia
125 N4 Al Wāsiţ Oman
202 E2 Al Wāţiyah well Egypt
202 A1 Al Watīyah Libya
114 E7 Alwaye Kerala India
150 E1 Alwen Reservoir Wales U.K.
175 H5 Alwernia Pol.
127 J7 Al Widyān plat. Iraq/Saudi Arabia
202 B3 Al Wīgh Libya
125 M4 Al Wuqbah Oman
125 J3 Al Wusayl Qatar
124 G1 Al Wusayţ well Saudi Arabia
125 M5 Al Wusţá admin. reg. Oman
Alxa Youqi Nei Mongol China see Ehen Hudag
Alxa Zuoqi Nei Mongol China see Bayan Hot
124 D4 'Alyā Saudi Arabia
125 H3 Al Yamāmah Saudi Arabia
84 F2 Alyangula N.T. Austr.
125 J3 Al Yāsāt i. U.A.E.
84 E6 Alyawarra Aboriginal Land res. N.T. Austr.
124 F6 Āl Yazīd Saudi Arabia
121 L2 Alyp Kazakh.
146 J9 Alyth Perth and Kinross, Scotland U.K.
138 H7 Alytus Lith.
173 N5 Alz r. Ger.
238 L4 Alzada MT U.S.A.
261 H5 Alzaga Arg.
190 H4 Alzano Lombardo Italy
169 H10 Alzenau in Unterfranken Ger.
165 J9 Alzette r. Lux.
172 E2 Alzey Ger.
187 E9 Alzira Spain
161 C9 Alzon France
163 I9 Alzonne France
215 L8 Amabele S. Africa
250 D5 Amacayacu, Parque Nacional nat. park Col.
245 H8 Amacuzac r. Mex.
141 M6 Åmådalen Sweden
84 C8 Amadeus, Lake salt flat N.T. Austr.
208 F3 Amadi Sudan
221 K3 Amadjuak Lake Nunavut Can.
241 U10 Amado AZ U.S.A.
184 A3 Amadora Port.
205 G4 Amadror plain Alg.
250 C3 Amaga Col.
105 I5 Amaga-dake mt. Japan
235 K3 Amagansett NY U.S.A.
104 B6 Amagasaki Japan
142 I6 Amager i. Denmark
103 H13 Amagi Japan
105 I6 Amagi-san vol. Japan
105 I6 Amagi-tōge pass Japan
105 I6 Amagiyugashima Japan
156 I4 Amagne France
104 D5 Amagoi-dake mt. Japan
93 F5 Amahai Seram Indon.
124 F5 Amā'ir Saudi Arabia
186 C1 Amaiur-Maia Spain
245 I4 Amajac r. Mex.

Anivorano Avaratra Madag.
Aniwa WI U.S.A.
Aniwa i. Vanuatu
Anizy-le-Château France
Anjad Madh. Prad. India
Anjadip i. India
Anjafy mt. Madag.
Anjalankoski Fin.
Anjangaon Mahar. India
Anjar Gujarat India
Anjengo Kerala India
Anji Zhejiang China
Anji Mahar. India
Anjiang Hunan China see Qianyang
Anjihai Xinjiang China
Anjir Avand Iran
Anjō Japan
Anjoman Iran
Anjou reg. France
Anjou, Val d' val. France
Anjouan i. Comoros see Nzwani
Anjozorobe Madag.
Anjŭ N. Korea
Anjum Neth.
Anjuman reg. Afgh.
Anka Nigeria
Ankaboa, Tanjona pt Madag.
Ankang Shaanxi China
Ankara Turkey
Ankara prov. Turkey
Ankaran Slovenia
Ankaratra mts Madag.
Ankarsrum Sweden
Ankarsund Sweden
Ankatafa Madag.
Ankavandra Madag.
Ankazoabo Madag.
Ankazobe Madag.
Ankazomiriotra Madag.
Ankeny IA U.S.A.
Ankerika Madag.
Ankershagen Ger.
An Khê Vietnam
Ankiliabo Madag.
Anklam Ger.
Ankleshwar Gujarat India
Anklesvar Gujarat India see Ankleshwar
Ankofa mt. Madag.
Ankogel mt. Austria
Ankola Karnataka India
Ankouzhen Gansu China
An'kovo Rus. Fed.
Ankpa Nigeria
Ankum Ger.
Anlaby East Riding of Yorkshire, England U.K.
Anlauter r. Ger.
Anlezy France
Anlier, Forêt d' for. Belgium
Anling Henan China see Yanling
An Lôc Vietnam
Anloga Ghana
Anlong Guizhou China
Ânlong Vêng Cambodia
Anlu Hubei China
Anmoore WV U.S.A.
An Muileann gCearr Ireland see Mullingar
Anmyŏn-do i. S. Korea
Ann, Cape Antarctica
Ann, Cape MA U.S.A.
Anna Rus. Fed.
Anna Spain
Anna OH U.S.A.
Anna, Lake VA U.S.A.
Anna, Pulo i. Palau
Annaba Alg.
Annaba prov. Alg.
Annaberg Austria
Annaberg-Buchholtz Ger.
An Nabhānīyah Saudi Arabia
An Nabk Saudi Arabia
An Nabk Syria
Annaburg Ger.
Annacotty Ireland
An Nafūd des. Saudi Arabia
Annagry Ireland
Annahütte Ger.
Annai Guyana
An Najaf Iraq
An Najaf governorate Iraq
Annaka Japan
Annalee r. Ireland
Annalong Northern Ireland U.K.
Annam reg. Vietnam
Annam Highlands mts Laos/Vietnam
Annamoe Ireland
Annan Dumfries and Galloway, Scotland U.K.
Annan r. Scotland U.K.
'Annān, Wādī al watercourse Syria
Annanba Gansu China
Annandale val. Scotland U.K.
Annandale NJ U.S.A.
Annandale VA U.S.A.
Anna Paulowna Neth.
Anna Plains W.A. Austr.
Annapolis MD U.S.A.
Annapolis Royal N.S. Can.
Annapurna Conservation Area nature res. Nepal
Annapurna I mt. Nepal
An Naqīrah well Saudi Arabia
Ann Arbor MI U.S.A.
Anna Regina Guyana
Annarode Ger.
An Nás Ireland see Naas
An Nashū, Wādī watercourse Libya
An Nāşirīyah Iraq
Annaspan imp. l. S. Africa
An Naşrānī, Jabal mts Syria
An Nawfalīyah Libya
Annayalla Ireland
Annbank South Ayrshire, Scotland U.K.
Annea r. Italy
Annean, Lake salt flat W.A. Austr.
Anne Arundel County county MD U.S.A.
Anne Arundel Town MD U.S.A. see Annapolis
Annecy France
Annecy, Lac d' l. France
Annecy-le-Vieux France
Annel Fin. see Angeli
Anne Marie Lake Nfld and Lab. Can.
Annemasse France
Annen Neth.
Annesse-et-Beaulieu France
Annet i. England U.K.
Annette Island AK U.S.A.
Anneyron France
Annfield Plain Durham, England U.K.
Annick r. Scotland U.K.
Annie r. Qld Austr.
Annikvere Estonia
An Nimārah Syria
An Nimāş Saudi Arabia
Anning Yunnan China
Anning He r. Sichuan China
Annino Lipetskaya Oblast' Rus. Fed.
Annino Vologodskaya Oblast' Rus. Fed.
An Nīr, Jabal hills Saudi Arabia
Anniston AL U.S.A.
Annobón i. Equat. Guinea
Annœullin France
Annonay France
Annone, Lago di l. Italy
Annot France
Annotto Bay Jamaica
Annsborough Northern Ireland U.K.
An Nu'ayrīyah Saudi Arabia
An Nu'mānīyah Iraq
An Nuqay'ah Qatar
An Nuşayrīyah, Jabal mts Syria
Annville KY U.S.A.
234 B4 Annville PA U.S.A.
172 D3 Annweiler am Trifels Ger.
104 D6 Anō Japan
78 □6 Anoano Malaita Solomon Is
186 A1 Anoeta Spain
198 F7 Anogeia Kriti Greece
226 A4 Anoka MN U.S.A.
198 E3 Ano Lechonia Greece
183 Q5 Añón Spain
Anonima atoll Micronesia see Namonuito
139 X6 Anopino Rus. Fed.
156 H4 Anor France
185 J4 Añora Spain
251 F5 Anori Brazil
211 F8 Anorontany, Tanjona hd Madag.
213 □K3 Anosibe An'Ala Madag.
205 G5 Anou I-n-Atei well Alg.
157 M7 Anould France
207 F2 Ânou Mellene well Mali
205 G6 Anou-n-Bidek well Alg.
183 M9 Añover de Tajo Spain
Anóyia Kriti Greece see Anogeia
109 I5 Anping Hunan China
108 H8 Anpu Guangdong China
108 G8 Anpu Gang b. China
109 K3 Anqing Anhui China
107 P8 Anqiu Shandong China
183 P7 Anquela del Ducado Spain
178 G6 Anras Austria
109 I5 Anren Hunan China
169 F7 Anröchte Ger.
An Rubha pen. Scotland U.K. see Eye Peninsula
165 I7 Ans Belgium
142 F5 Ans Denmark
162 F4 Ansac-sur-Vienne France
107 K8 Ansai Shaanxi China
173 J3 Ansbach Ger.
160 F5 Anse France
246 G4 Anse-à-Galets Haiti
217 □2b Anse à la Mouche Mahé Seychelles
246 H4 Anse-à-Pitre Haiti
246 G4 Anse-à-Veau Haiti
124 C7 Anseba Shet watercourse Eritrea
247 □2 Anse-Bertrand Guadeloupe
217 □2b Anse Boileau Mahé Seychelles
246 F4 Anse d'Hainault Haiti
192 G3 Ansedonia Italy
247 □3 Anse-la-Raye St Lucia
165 G8 Anseremme Belgium
83 K8 Anser Group is Tas. Austr.
250 C3 Anserma Col.
217 □2b Anse Royal Mahé Seychelles
179 J3 Ansfelden Austria
146 I9 An Sgarsoch mt. Scotland U.K.
107 R6 Anshan Liaoning China
108 E5 Anshun Guizhou China
108 D4 Anshunchang Sichuan China
182 D9 Ansião Port.
191 M3 Ansiei r. Italy
260 C2 Ansilta mt. Arg.
260 C2 Ansilta, Cordillera de mts Arg.
258 G3 Ansina Uru.
126 H8 An Sirhān, Wādī watercourse Saudi Arabia
140 N5 Ansjö Sweden
236 F5 Ansley NE U.S.A.
186 D2 Ansó Spain
186 D2 Ansó, Valle de val. Spain
237 F9 Anson TX U.S.A.
84 C2 Anson Bay N.T. Austr.
82 □1 Anson Bay Norfolk I.
207 F3 Ansongo Mali
207 F3 Ansongo-Ménaka, Réserve Partielle de Faune d' nature res. Mali
235 I2 Ansonia CT U.S.A.
232 A8 Ansonia OH U.S.A.
224 D3 Ansonville Ont. Can.
171 H9 Ansprung Ger.
232 D10 Ansted WV U.S.A.
146 K10 Anstruther Fife, Scotland U.K.
Ansu Hebei China see Xushui
151 P2 Ant r. England U.K.
116 F7 Anta Rajasthan India
252 B3 Anta Peru
252 B3 Antabamba Peru
126 H5 Antakya Turkey
213 □K2 Antalaha Madag.
199 L6 Antalya Turkey
199 L5 Antalya prov. Turkey
199 L6 Antalya Körfezi g. Turkey
213 □K3 Antanambao Manampotsy Madag.
213 □K3 Antanambe Madag.
213 □J3 Antananarivo Madag.
213 □J3 Antananarivo prov. Madag.
213 □J3 Antanifotsy Madag.
213 □J5 Antanimora Atsimo Madag.
An tAonach Ireland see Nenagh
262 Antarctica continent
262 T2 Antarctic Peninsula Antarctica
213 □J5 Antaritarika Madag.
182 F7 Antas Port.
185 P6 Antas Spain
185 P6 Antas r. Spain
182 E3 Antas de Ulla Spain
146 F7 An Teallach mt. Scotland U.K.
261 G3 Antelo Arg.
241 P2 Antelope Range mts NV U.S.A.
142 I3 Anten l. Sweden
162 D4 Antenne r. France
185 J6 Antequera Spain
178 F6 Anterselva di Sopra Italy
234 A2 Antes Fort PA U.S.A.
161 J10 Anthéor France
178 H4 Anthering Austria
160 D2 Anthien France
237 F7 Anthony KS U.S.A.
239 K10 Anthony NM U.S.A.
82 D3 Anthony, Lake salt flat S.A. Austr.
84 E4 Anthony Lagoon N.T. Austr.
204 C3 Anti Atlas mts Morocco
161 K9 Antibes France
161 K9 Antibes, Cap d' c. France
225 I3 Anticosti, Île d' i. Que. Can.
Anticosti Island Que. Can. see Anticosti, Île d'
159 L2 Antifer, Cap d' c. France
226 E4 Antigo WI U.S.A.
225 I4 Antigonish N.S. Can.
247 □2 Antigua i. Antigua and Barbuda
216 □3b Antigua Fuerteventura Canary Is
Antigua Guat. see Antigua Guatemala
Antigua country West Indies see Antigua and Barbuda
247 □2 Antigua and Barbuda country West Indies
243 N10 Antigua Guatemala Guat.
247 □2 Antigues, Pointe d' pt Guadeloupe
245 H3 Antiguo-Morelos Mex.
198 D4 Antikyra Greece
198 E7 Antikythira i. Greece
198 E7 Antikythiro, Steno sea chan. Greece
Anti Lebanon mts Lebanon/Syria see Sharqī, Jabal ash
258 D2 Antilla Arg.
246 F3 Antilla Cuba
195 I8 Antillo Sicilia Italy
198 F6 Antimilos i. Greece
241 U3 Antimony UT U.S.A.
An tInbhear Mór Ireland see Arklow
240 K3 Antioch CA U.S.A.
226 F7 Antioch IL U.S.A.
128 A2 Antiocheia ad Cragum tourist site Turkey
Antiochia Turkey see Antakya
250 C3 Antioquia Col.
250 C3 Antioquia dept Col.
198 G5 Antiparos i. Greece
198 B3 Antipaxoi i. Greece
139 Q6 Antipino Rus. Fed.
77 H6 Antipodes Islands N.Z.
199 G4 Antipsara i. Greece
192 C3 Antisanti Corse France
199 I6 Antitilos i. Greece
Antium Italy see Anzio
237 H8 Antlers OK U.S.A.
An t-Ob Western Isles, Scotland U.K. see Leverburgh
252 C5 Antofagasta Chile
252 C5 Antofagasta admin. reg. Chile
258 D2 Antofagasta de la Sierra Arg.
165 D7 Antoing Belgium
177 H3 Antol Slovakia
190 G6 Antola, Monte mt. Italy
213 □J2 Antonhibe Madag.
256 C6 Antonina Brazil
136 F4 Antoniny Ukr.
195 L5 Antonio r. Italy
244 C1 Antonio Amaro Mex.
257 F4 Antônio Carlos Brazil
259 D7 Antonio de Biedma Arg.
257 F3 Antônio Dias Brazil
António Enes Moz. see Angoche
251 I5 Antônio Lemos Brazil
136 I4 Antoniv Ukr.
137 L3 Antonivka Chernihivs'ka Oblast' Ukr.
137 L7 Antonivka Khersons'ka Oblast' Ukr.
177 L3 Antonivka Zakarpats'ka Oblast' Ukr.
137 O6 Antonivka Zaporiz'ka Oblast' Ukr.
245 L6 Antón Lizardo Mex.
162 F5 Antonne-et-Trigonant France
246 C2 Antón Recio Cuba
156 D6 Antony France
136 D1 Antopal' Belarus
161 E7 Antraigues-sur-Volane France
158 I5 Antrain France
137 S5 Antratsyt Ukr.
147 J3 Antrim Northern Ireland U.K.
147 J3 Antrim county Northern Ireland U.K.
234 A1 Antrim PA U.S.A.
147 J2 Antrim Hills Northern Ireland U.K.
86 J5 Antrim Plateau W.A. Austr.
193 K3 Antrodoco Italy
134 H4 Antropovo Rus. Fed.
213 □K2 Antsahabe Madag.
213 □K2 Antsahanoro Madag.
213 □K2 Antsakabary Madag.
213 □J3 Antsalova Madag.
213 □K2 Antsambalahy Madag.
Antseranana Madag. see Antsirañana
139 Q3 Antsiferovo Rus. Fed.
213 □J3 Antsirabe Madag.
213 □K2 Antsirabe Avaratra Madag.
213 □K2 Antsirañana Madag.
213 □K2 Antsirañana prov. Madag.
138 J4 Antsla Estonia
213 □J2 Antsohihy Madag.
213 □K2 Antsohimbondrona Madag.
213 □J3 Antsondrodava Madag.
140 Q3 Anttis Sweden
141 S6 Anttola Fin.
Antu Jilin China see Songjiang
An Tuc Vietnam see An Khê
260 B5 Antuco Chile
260 B5 Antuco, Volcán vol. Chile
124 F8 Antufash, Jazīrat i. Yemen
Antufush Island Yemen see Antufash, Jazīrat
160 E3 Antully France
Antunnacum Ger. see Andernach
Antwerp Belgium see Antwerpen
233 J4 Antwerp NY U.S.A.
165 F6 Antwerpen Belgium
165 G6 Antwerpen prov. Belgium
186 A1 Antzuola Spain
An Uaimh Ireland see Navan
224 F1 Anuc, Lac l. Que. Can.
100 H7 Anuchino Rus. Fed.
259 C6 Anueque, Sierra mts Arg.
101 E11 Anŭi S. Korea
116 D5 Anupgarh Rajasthan India
114 G8 Anuradhapura Sri Lanka
84 E6 Anurrete Aboriginal Land res. N.T. Austr.
122 F8 Anveh Iran
Anvers Belgium see Antwerpen
262 T2 Anvers Island Antarctica
222 C2 Anvil Range mts Y.T. Can.
156 D3 Anvin France
109 L6 Anxi Fujian China
106 D6 Anxi Gansu China
Anxian Sichuan China see Anchang
108 E3 Anxian Sichuan China
109 I4 Anxiang Hunan China
107 N7 Anxin Hebei China
82 E5 Anxious Bay S.A. Austr.
Anxur Italy see Terracina
206 D5 Anyama Côte d'Ivoire
Anyang Guangxi China see Du'an
107 N8 Anyang Henan China
101 E10 Anyang S. Korea
94 F8 Anyar Jawa Indon.
199 G6 Anydros i. Greece
106 F9 A'nyêmaqên Shan mts China
109 J4 Anyi Jiangxi China
138 I6 Anykščiai Lith.
215 O3 Anysspruit S. Africa
109 I5 Anyuan Jiangxi China
109 J6 Anyuan Jiangxi China
134 L3 An'yudin Rus. Fed.
108 E3 Anyue Sichuan China
100 J4 Anyuy r. Rus. Fed.
131 R3 Anyuysk Rus. Fed.
190 E3 Anza r. Italy
223 I3 Anzac Alta Can.
222 F4 Anzac B.C. Can.
186 D3 Anzánigo Spain
193 O5 Anzano di Puglia Italy
161 C6 Anzat-le-Luguet France
107 M8 Anze Shanxi China
165 D7 Anzegem Belgium
205 F4 Anzeglouf Alg.
173 L2 Anzelberg hill Ger.
160 K4 Anzère Switz.
130 J4 Anzhero-Sudzhensk Rus. Fed.
208 D5 Anzi Dem. Rep. Congo
193 P6 Anzi Italy
156 F3 Anzin France
176 A3 Anzing Ger.
193 J5 Anzio Italy
261 F6 Anzoátegui Arg.
251 E2 Anzoátegui state Venez.
261 F6 Anzoátegui, Salinas Grandes de salt pan Arg.
185 J6 Anzur r. Spain
105 K4 Aoba Japan
78 □5 Aoba i. Vanuatu
104 B4 Aoba-yama hill Japan
202 C5 Aodanga well Chad
104 B5 Aogaki Japan
103 Q14 Aoga-shima i. Japan
Aohan Qi Nei Mongol China see Xinhui
183 R3 Aoiz Spain
97 D10 Ao Kham, Laem pt Thai.
105 H3 Aoki Japan
78 □6 Aola Guadalcanal Solomon Is
Aomen Macau China see Macao
102 R6 Aomori Japan
102 S6 Aomori pref. Japan
146 F8 Aonach Buidhe hill Scotland U.K.
111 E10 A'ong Co l. Xizang China
198 B2 Aoos r. Greece
97 D10 Ao Phang Nga National Park Thai.
146 D11 Aoradh Argyll and Bute, Scotland U.K.
79 □9a Aorai mt. Tahiti Fr. Polynesia
81 E10 Aoraki South I. N.Z.
81 E10 Aoraki mt. South I. N.Z.
81 E10 Aoraki/Mount Cook National Park South I. N.Z.
97 G8 Aôral, Phnum mt. Cambodia
Aorangi mt. South I. N.Z. see Aoraki
81 J8 Aorangi Mountains North I. N.Z.
81 G7 Aorere r. South I. N.Z.
183 R3 Aós Spain
104 A8 Ao-shima i. Japan
190 C4 Aosta Italy
160 H5 Aoste France
80 I5 Aotea Harbour North I. N.Z.
Aotearoa country Oceania see New Zealand
207 H2 Aouderas Niger
204 B4 Aoufist Western Sahara
204 D4 Aouhinet bel Egra well Alg.
208 C2 Aouk, Bahr r. C.A.R./Chad
208 D2 Aoukalé r. C.A.R./Chad
208 D2 Aouk-Aoakole, Réserve de Faune de l' nature res. C.A.R.
204 D5 Aoukâr reg. Mali/Maur.
207 F2 Aoukenek well Mali
205 F4 Aoulef Alg.
204 C3 Aoulime, Jbel mt. Morocco
206 C3 Aourou Mali
161 G7 Aouste-sur-Sye France
Aoxi Jiangxi China see Le'an
103 L11 Aoya Japan
104 D6 Aoyama Japan
Aoyang Jiangxi China see Shanggao
202 C4 Aozou Chad
253 F5 Apa r. Brazil
197 L3 Apa Romania
210 B4 Apac Uganda
179 M6 Apače Slovenia
241 W10 Apache AZ U.S.A.
237 F8 Apache OK U.S.A.
241 U8 Apache, Lake AZ U.S.A.
241 U8 Apache Junction AZ U.S.A.
241 V10 Apache Peak AZ U.S.A.
252 D5 Apagado, Volcán vol. Bol.
177 K4 Apagy Hungary
197 L4 Apahida Romania
256 C5 Apaiai r. Brazil
Apaiang atoll Kiribati see Abaiang
177 I4 Apaj Hungary
231 E11 Apalachee Bay FL U.S.A.
231 E11 Apalachicola FL U.S.A.
231 E11 Apalachicola r. FL U.S.A.
231 E11 Apalachicola Bay FL U.S.A.
206 E5 Apam Ghana
Apamama atoll Gilbert Is Kiribati see Abemama
Apamea Turkey see Dinar
245 I6 Apan Mex.
157 L8 Apance r. France
245 H8 Apango Mex.
250 D5 Apaporis r. Col.
95 L6 Apar, Teluk b. Indon.
129 F5 Aparan Armenia
257 E5 Aparecida Brazil
256 C2 Aparecida de Goiânia Brazil
256 B3 Aparecida do Rio Doce Brazil
256 B4 Aparecida do Tabuado Brazil
177 H5 Aparhant Hungary
261 G6 Aparico Arg.
Aparima South I. N.Z. see Riverton
81 C13 Aparima r. South I. N.Z.
92 C2 Aparri Luzon Phil.
251 F3 Aparurén Venez.
259 D6 Apas, Sierra hills Arg.
138 H5 Apaščia r. Lith.
244 G5 Apaseo El Grande Mex.
79 □9 Apataki atoll Arch. des Tuamotu Fr. Polynesia
177 K5 Apateu Romania
177 J5 Apátfalva Hungary
196 G5 Apatin Vojvodina Serbia
134 F2 Apatity Rus. Fed.
251 H3 Apatou Fr. Guiana
179 O7 Apatovac Croatia
244 E6 Apatzingán Mex.
245 H7 Apaxtla Mex.
138 J4 Ape Latvia
191 M8 Apecchio Italy
253 E2 Apediá r. Brazil
182 D4 A Pedreira Spain
164 I4 Apeldoorn Neth.
169 H6 Apelern Ger.
168 E4 Apen Ger.
170 D5 Apenburg Ger.
168 I4 Apensen Ger.
252 D3 Apere r. Bol.
182 E4 A Peroxa Spain
222 B2 Apex Mountain Y.T. Can.
208 E4 Api Dem. Rep. Congo
116 H4 Api mt. Nepal
Api i. Vanuatu see Epi
93 B4 Api, Tanjung pt Indon.
250 C3 Apia Col.
Apia atoll Kiribati see Abaiang
78 □2 Apia Samoa
253 F2 Apiacas, Serra dos hills Brazil
256 C6 Apiaí Brazil
251 F4 Apiaú, Serra do mts Brazil
193 N5 Apice Italy
182 C3 A Picota Spain
78 □6 Apio Malaita Solomon Is
245 H7 Apipilulco Mex.
191 O9 Apiro Italy
237 D6 Apishapa r. CO U.S.A.
80 J6 Apiti North I. N.Z.
245 I6 Apizaco Mex.
242 H5 Apizolaya Mex.
129 C2 Ap'khazet'i aut. rep. Georgia
252 B4 Aplao Peru
109 □J7 Ap Lei Chau i. H.K. China
92 E8 Apo, Mount vol. Mindanao Phil.
182 F3 A Pobla de Brollón Spain
182 F3 A Pobra de San Xiao Spain
182 F4 A Pobra de Trives Spain
182 C3 A Pobra do Caramiñal Spain
137 Q2 Apochka r. Rus. Fed.
254 F3 Apodi Brazil
254 F3 Apodi, Chapada do hills Brazil
92 C5 Apo East Passage Phil.
251 G3 Apoera Suriname
171 E8 Apolda Ger.
Apollinopolis Magna Egypt see Idfū
83 I8 Apollo Bay Vic. Austr.
Apollonia Bulg. see Sozopol
198 F6 Apollonia Sifnos Greece
252 C3 Apolo Bol.
182 F2 A Pontenova Spain
182 C2 A Pontepedra Spain
231 G11 Apopka FL U.S.A.
255 B6 Aporé Goiás Brazil
256 B3 Aporé Mato Grosso do Sul Brazil
256 B3 Aporé r. Brazil
251 I4 Aporema Brazil
177 H5 Apostag Hungary
226 D3 Apostle Islands WI U.S.A.
226 D2 Apostle Islands National Lakeshore nature res. WI U.S.A.
221 N3 Apostolens Tommelfinger mt. Greenland
258 G2 Apóstoles Arg.
128 C3 Apostolos Andreas, Cape Cyprus
137 M6 Apostolove Ukr.
251 G3 Apoteri Guyana
Apoucaroua atoll Arch. des Tuamotu Fr. Polynesia see Pukarua
92 C5 Apo West Passage Phil.
232 C12 Appalachia VA U.S.A.
232 B12 Appalachian Mountains U.S.A.
Appalla i. Fiji see Kabara
164 J3 Appelscha Neth.
Appenines mts Italy
Appennino mts Italy see Appenines
193 K3 Appennino Abruzzese mts Italy
193 M4 Appennino Campano mts Italy
193 P6 Appennino Lucano mts Italy
193 O5 Appennino Napoletano mts Italy
191 I8 Appennino Tosco-Emiliano mts Italy
191 M9 Appennino Umbro-Marchigiano mts Italy
172 D4 Appenweier Ger.
190 G1 Appenzell Switz.
190 G1 Appenzell Ausserrhoden canton Switz.
190 G1 Appenzell Innerrhoden canton Switz.
191 K3 Appiano sulla Strada del Vino Italy
192 B3 Appietto Corse France
191 O9 Appignano Italy
164 K2 Appingedam Neth.
149 M4 Appleby-in-Westmorland Cumbria, England U.K.
146 E8 Applecross Highland, Scotland U.K.
150 D5 Appledore Devon, England U.K.
151 N5 Appledore Kent, England U.K.
236 G3 Appleton MN U.S.A.
226 F5 Appleton WI U.S.A.
149 L7 Appleton Thorn Warrington, England U.K.
240 O7 Apple Valley CA U.S.A.
156 G8 Appoigny France
232 G11 Appomattox VA U.S.A.
161 G6 Apprieu France
78 □1 Apra Harbor inlet Guam
78 □1 Apra Heights Guam
139 U6 Aprelevka Rus. Fed.
160 H2 Apremont France
157 K6 Apremont-la-Forêt France
190 I3 Aprica Italy
193 O4 Apricena Italy
195 K5 Aprigliano Italy
193 J4 Aprilia Italy
182 G3 A Proba Spain
117 O5 Aprunyi Arun. Prad. India
129 A1 Apsheronsk Rus. Fed.
Apsheronskaya Rus. Fed. see Apsheronsk
Apsheronskiy Poluostrov pen. Azer. see Abşeron Yarımadası
82 H7 Apsley Vic. Austr.
227 P5 Apsley Ont. Can.
84 C1 Apsley Strait N.T. Austr.
161 G9 Apt France
190 I7 Apuane, Alpi mts Italy
240 □F14 'Apua Point HI U.S.A.
256 B5 Apucarana Brazil
256 B5 Apucarana, Serra da hills Brazil
245 I5 Apulco Mex.
182 C6 Apúlia Port.
Apulum Romania see Alba Iulia
92 B7 Apurahuan Palawan Phil.
92 □ Apurashokoru i. Palau
250 E3 Apure r. Venez.
250 D3 Apure state Venez.
252 B3 Apurímac dept Peru
252 B3 Apurimac r. Peru
250 D3 Apurito Venez.
Aq"a Georgia see Sokhumi
'Aqaba Jordan see Al 'Aqabah
124 B1 'Aqaba, Gulf of Asia
127 K8 'Aqabah, Birkat al well Iraq
128 B8 'Aqabah, Wādī al watercourse Egypt
Aqadyr Kazakh. see Agadyr'
110 D6 Aqal Xinjiang China
Aqbalyq Kazakh. see Akbalyk
Aqbaüyr Kazakh. see Akbauyr
Aqbeyit Kazakh. see Akbeit
123 L3 Āqchah Afgh.
127 L4 Aq Chai r. Iran
122 E5 'Aqdā Iran
122 B3 Aqdoghmish r. Iran
127 N5 Āq Gadūk, Gardaneh-ye pass Iran
203 H5 Aqiq Sudan
124 D6 Aqiq, Khalīg b. Sudan
124 E3 Aqiq, Wādī al watercourse Saudi Arabia
106 B6 Aqitag mt. Xinjiang China
Aqköl Akmolinskaya Oblast' Kazakh. see Akkol'
Aqköl Atyrauskaya Oblast' Kazakh. see Akkol'
124 C3 Aqla well Saudi Arabia
Aqmola Kazakh. see Astana
Aqmola Oblysy admin. div. Kazakh. see Akmolinskaya Oblast'
122 F3 Āq Qal'eh Iran
111 E8 Aqqan Xinjiang China
111 G8 Aqqan Xinjiang China
111 I8 Aqqikkol Hu salt l. China
Aqqystaū Kazakh. see Akkistau
128 D6 'Aqraba West Bank
127 K5 'Aqrah Iraq
128 G7 'Aqran hill Saudi Arabia
Aqsay Kazakh. see Aksay
Aqsayqin Hit terr. Asia see Aksai Chin
Aqshataū Kazakh. see Akchatau
Aqshī Kazakh. see Akshiy
120 H6 Aqsho'laq Uzbek.
Aqshuqyr Kazakh. see Akshukur
Aqsū Akmolinskaya Oblast' Kazakh. see Aksu
Aqsū Almatinskaya Oblast' Kazakh. see Aksu
Aqsū Pavlodarskaya Oblast' Kazakh. see Aksu
Aqsūat Kazakh. see Aksuat
Aqsū-Ayuly Kazakh. see Aksu-Ayuly
Aqtas Kazakh. see Aktas
Aqtaū Kazakh. see Aktau
Aqtöbe Kazakh. see Aktobe
Aqtöbe Oblysy admin. div. Kazakh. see Aktyubinskaya Oblast'
Aqtoghay Karagandinskaya Oblast' Kazakh. see Aktogay
Aqtoghay Pavlodarskaya Oblast' Kazakh. see Aktogay
Aquae Grani Ger. see Aachen
Aquae Gratianae France see Aix-les-Bains
Aquae Mortuae France see Aigues-Mortes
Aquae Sextiae France see Aix-en-Provence
Aquae Statiellae Italy see Acqui Terme
241 S7 Aquarius Mountains AZ U.S.A.
241 U4 Aquarius Plateau UT U.S.A.
195 L2 Aquaviva delle Fonti Italy
235 J3 Aquebogue NY U.S.A.
253 F5 Aquidabánmi r. Para.
253 G5 Aquidauana Brazil
253 F4 Aquidauana r. Brazil
244 D7 Aquila Mex.
179 H8 Aquileia Italy
242 F3 Aquiles Mex.
193 O6 Aquilonia Italy
186 E3 Aquilué Spain
246 G4 Aquin Haiti
Aquincum Hungary see Budapest
193 L5 Aquino Italy
Aquinum Italy see Aquino
Aquiry r. Brazil see Acre
Aquisgranum Ger. see Aachen
245 H4 Aquismón Mex.
163 D7 Aquitaine admin. reg. France
Aqzhal Kazakh. see Akzhal
Aqzhar Kazakh. see Akzhar
Aqzhayqyn Köli salt l. Kazakh. see Akzhaykyn, Ozero
117 J7 Ara Bihar India
186 F3 Ara r. Spain
210 D3 Āra Ārba Eth.
123 K6 Arab Afgh.
231 D8 Arab AL U.S.A.
208 F2 Arab, Bahr el watercourse Sudan
203 F2 'Arab, Khalīj al b. Egypt
122 G5 'Arabābād Iran
210 D3 Ara Bacalle well Eth.
128 A9 'Arabah, Wādī watercourse Egypt
125 J7 'Arabah, Wādī r. Yemen
128 D9 'Arabah, Wādī al watercourse Israel/Jordan
128 D3 'Arab al Mulk Syria
137 N8 Arabats'ka Strilka, Kosa spit Ukr.
Arabatskaya Strelka spit Ukr. see Arabats'ka Strilka, Kosa
137 O8 Arabats'ka Zatoka b. Ukr.
251 E3 Arabelo Venez.
187 C10 Arabí mt. Spain
265 I4 Arabian Basin sea feature Indian Ocean
Arabian Gulf Asia see The Gulf
125 M6 Arabian Oryx Sanctuary tourist site Saudi Arabia
125 J5 Arabian Peninsula Asia
119 J6 Arabian Sea Indian Ocean
129 J4 Arablinskoye Rus. Fed.
210 D3 Ara Bonel Eth.
251 F3 Arabopó Venez.
129 J5 Ārāb Qubalı Azer.
163 G10 Arac r. France
126 F3 Araç Turkey
251 F5 Araça r. Brazil
254 F4 Aracaju Brazil
253 G6 Aracanguy, Montes de hills Para.
258 D2 Aracar, Volcán vol. Arg.
246 F8 Aracataca Col.
254 F3 Aracati Brazil
254 E5 Aracatu Brazil
256 B4 Araçatuba Brazil
184 F5 Aracena Spain
184 G5 Aracena, Embalse de resr Spain
259 C9 Aracena, Isla i. Chile
184 E5 Aracena, Sierra de hills Spain
198 C3 Arachthos r. Greece
78 □6 Aracides, Cape Malaita Solomon Is
197 J8 Aračinovo Macedonia
254 F3 Aracoiaba Brazil
257 G3 Aracruz Brazil
257 F2 Araçuaí Brazil
257 F2 Araçuaí r. Brazil
128 D7 'Arad Israel
196 J4 Arad Romania
177 K5 Arad county Romania
202 D6 Arada Chad
182 D7 Arada, Serra de mts Port.
125 K4 'Arādah U.A.E.
122 E4 Arādān Iran
184 B6 Arade r. Port.
184 C6 Arade, Barragem de resr Port.
202 D6 Aradeib, Wadi watercourse Sudan
195 O3 Aradeo Italy
177 J5 Aradului, Câmpia plain Romania
216 □3a Arafo Tenerife Canary Is
105 I3 Arafune-yama mt. Japan
76 D2 Arafura Sea Austr./Indon.
266 D6 Arafura Shelf sea feature Austr./Indon.
256 A1 Aragarças Brazil
129 F5 Aragats Lerr mt. Armenia
105 H1 Ara-gawa r. Japan
105 K4 Ara-gawa r. Japan
163 E10 Aragnouet France
183 Q6 Aragón aut. comm. Spain
183 Q4 Aragón r. Spain
186 C4 Aragón, Canal Imperial de Spain
194 F9 Aragona Sicilia Italy
183 P7 Aragoncillo Spain
183 P7 Aragoncillo mt. Spain
250 E2 Aragua state Venez.
254 C4 Araguacema Brazil
254 C5 Araguaçu Brazil
251 E2 Aragua de Barcelona Venez.
251 F2 Aragua de Maturín Venez.
256 C Araguaia r. Brazil
254 C4 Araguaia, Parque Nacional de nat. park Brazil
256 B1 Araguaiana Brazil
254 C3 Araguaína Brazil
256 A2 Araguainha Brazil
253 H1 Araguana Brazil
251 F2 Araguao, Boca r. mouth Venez.
251 F2 Araguapiche, Punta pt Venez.
256 C3 Araguari Brazil
256 C3 Araguari r. Brazil
251 I4 Araguari r. Brazil
254 C3 Araguatins Brazil
129 F4 Aragvi r. Georgia
124 F9 'Araḩ, Ra's pt Yemen
125 L7 'Araḩ, Wādī r. Oman
254 D5 Arai Brazil
105 H2 Arai Niigata Japan
104 G6 Arai Shizuoka Japan
183 P3 Araia Spain
254 E2 Araiosos Brazil
205 F4 Arak Alg.
122 C4 Arāk Iran
128 G4 Arak Syria
105 K1 Arakai-yama mt. Japan
251 F3 Arakaka Guyana
96 A4 Arakan state Myanmar
96 B4 Arakan Yoma mts Myanmar
102 □1 Arakawa Okinawa Japan
Arakhthos r. Greece see Arachthos
104 F3 Araki-gawa r. Japan
80 M5 Arakihi hill North I. N.Z.
114 F6 Arakkonam Tamil Nadu India
129 B5 Araklı Turkey
129 F6 Arak's r. Armenia alt. Aras Nehri (Turkey), alt. Araz (Azerbaijan/Iran), conv. Aras, hist. Araxes
129 I4 Arakul Rus. Fed.
111 J7 Aral Qinghai China
Aral Kazakh. see Aral'sk
Aral Tajik. see Vose
186 A1 Aralar, Sierra de mts Spain
129 F6 Aralık Turkey
120 I5 Aral Sea salt l. Kazakh./Uzbek.
120 I4 Aral'sk Kazakh.
Aral'skoye More salt l. Kazakh./Uzbek. see Aral Sea
120 C3 Aralsor, Ozero l. Kazakh.
120 E3 Aralsor, Ozero salt l. Kazakh.
Aral Tengizi salt l. Kazakh./Uzbek. see Aral Sea
106 B3 Araltobe Xinjiang China
85 J7 Aramac Qld Austr.
85 J7 Aramac Creek watercourse Qld Austr.
124 H3 Aramah plat. Saudi Arabia
182 C3 A Ramallosa Spain
245 H1 Aramberri Mex.
254 D3 Arame Brazil
91 J8 Aramia r. P.N.G.
163 C9 Aramits France
161 F9 Aramon France
129 H5 Aran Azer.
114 F3 Aran r. India
186 G2 Aran, Val d' reg. Spain
185 M6 Arana, Sierra mts Spain
129 I6 Ārānchī Iran
260 C2 Arancibia Arg.
183 R5 Aranda r. Spain
183 M5 Aranda de Duero Spain
183 Q5 Aranda de Moncayo Spain
127 M6 Arandān Iran
244 E5 Arandas Mex.
196 I6 Arandelovac Serbia
212 B4 Arandis Namibia
116 I9 Arang Chhattisgarh India
182 F8 Aranhas Port.
114 F6 Arani Tamil Nadu India
147 E3 Aran Island Ireland
147 C6 Aran Islands Ireland
183 M8 Aranjuez Spain
261 F5 Arano Arg.
212 C5 Aranos Namibia
237 G12 Aransas Pass TX U.S.A.
114 F7 Arantangi Tamil Nadu India
256 B3 Arantes r. Brazil
182 I9 Arañuelo, Campo reg. Spain
77 H1 Aranuka atoll Gilbert Is Kiribati
97 F8 Aranyaprathet Thai.
177 L3 Aranyosapáti Hungary
183 N8 Aranzueque Spain
103 H14 Arao Japan
206 E2 Araouane Mali
237 F8 Arapaho OK U.S.A.
236 F5 Arapahoe NE U.S.A.
251 H5 Arapari Brazil
81 I8 Arapawa Island South I. N.Z.
261 I2 Arapey Grande r. Uru.
126 I4 Arapgir Turkey
250 B5 Arapicos Ecuador
182 I7 Arapiles Spain
254 F4 Arapiraca Brazil
198 F2 Arapis, Akrotirio pt Greece
256 B5 Arapongas Brazil
256 C6 Arapoti Brazil
Arapsun Turkey see Gülşehir
256 A4 Arapuá Brazil
80 J5 Arapuni North I. N.Z.
255 C8 Araquari Brazil
127 J8 'Ar'ar Saudi Arabia
127 K8 'Ar'ar, Wādī watercourse Iraq/Saudi Arabia
251 F5 Arara r. Brazil
250 C5 Araracuara Col.
250 C5 Araracuara, Cerros de hills Col.
117 J6 Araraj Bihar India
255 C9 Araranguá Brazil
256 C6 Ararapira Brazil
256 C4 Araraquara Brazil
252 C2 Araras Amazonas Brazil
251 H6 Araras Pará Brazil
252 D2 Ararás Brazil
256 D5 Araras São Paulo Brazil
254 E3 Araras, Açude resr Brazil
256 A3 Araras, Serra das hills Brazil
256 A6 Araras, Serra das mts Brazil
129 F6 Ararat Armenia
83 I7 Ararat Vic. Austr.
Ararat, Mount Turkey see Ağrı Dağı
254 D2 Arari Brazil
117 K6 Araria Bihar India
254 E3 Araripe Brazil
254 E3 Araripe, Chapada do hills Brazil
254 E3 Araripina Brazil
257 F5 Araruama Brazil
257 F5 Araruama, Lago de lag. Brazil
127 L4 Aras r. Asia alt. Arak's (Armenia), alt. Aras Nehri (Turkey), alt. Araz (Azerbaijan/Iran), hist. Araxes
183 P3 Aras Spain
127 K4 Aras Turkey
102 □1 Ara-saki c. Okinawa Japan
122 F4 Arāsavān Iran
187 C8 Aras de Alpuente Spain
106 I2 Ar-Asgat Mongolia
129 G6 Aras Govşaghyuyn resr Azer./Iran
129 D6 Aras Güneyi Dağları mts Turkey
104 E4 Arashima-dake mt. Japan
247 □9 Arasji Aruba
129 C6 Aras Nehri r. Turkey alt. Arak's (Armenia), alt. Araz (Azerbaijan/Iran), conv. Aras, hist. Araxes
260 E4 Arata Arg.
255 F5 Arataca Brazil
206 C2 Aratâne well Maur.
251 I5 Arataú r. Brazil
Aratürük Xinjiang China see Yiwu
94 D1 Arau Malaysia
252 D2 Arauã r. Brazil
251 F6 Arauá r. Brazil
251 F6 Arauá r. Brazil
250 D3 Arauca Col.
250 D3 Arauca dept Col.
250 E3 Arauca r. Venez.
260 A6 Araucanía admin. reg. Chile
255 C8 Araucária Brazil
258 B5 Arauco Chile
258 B5 Arauco, Golfo de b. Chile
161 E6 Araules France
250 D3 Arauquita Col.
250 D2 Araure Venez.
241 V9 Aravaipa Creek watercourse AZ U.S.A.
116 D7 Aravalli Range mts India
138 I2 Aravete Estonia
183 P5 Araviana r. Spain
160 I5 Aravis mts France
160 I5 Aravis, Col des pass France
198 D2 Aravissos Greece
78 □6 Arawa P.N.G.
211 D5 Arawale National Reserve nature res. Kenya
Arawata r. South I. N.Z. see Arawhata
80 L5 Arawhana mt. North I. N.Z.
81 C11 Arawhata r. South I. N.Z.
256 D3 Araxá Brazil
198 C4 Araxos, Akrotirio pt Greece
Araya Spain see Araia
251 E2 Araya, Península de pen. Venez.
247 K8 Araya, Punta de pt Venez.
126 E4 Arayıt Dağı mt. Turkey
129 J6 Araz r. Azer. alt. Arak's (Armenia), alt. Aras Nehri (Turkey), conv. Aras, hist. Araxes
182 C8 Arazede Port.
186 C4 Arba r. Spain
186 C3 Arba de Biel r. Spain
186 C3 Arba de Luesia r. Spain
Arbailu Iraq see Arbīl
210 C3 Ārba Minch Eth.
163 F10 Arbas France
127 L6 Arbat Iraq
192 D8 Arbatax Sardegna Italy
134 J4 Arbazh Rus. Fed.
186 G4 Arbeca Spain
157 K8 Arbecey France
190 G3 Arbedo Switz.
Arbela Iraq see Arbīl
160 H4 Arbent France
163 D10 Arbéost France
173 J3 Arberg Ger.
Arberth Pembrokeshire, Wales U.K. see Narberth
179 K2 Arbesbach Austria
183 P7 Arbeteta Spain
191 K9 Arbia r. Italy
127 L5 Arbīl Iraq
127 K6 Arbīl governorate Iraq
183 P3 Arbizu Spain
143 L2 Arboga Sweden
160 H3 Arbois France
185 O6 Arboleas Spain
261 G5 Arboledas Arg.
250 B2 Arboletes Col.
261 I3 Arbolito Uru.
190 G1 Arbon Switz.
192 B8 Arborea Sardegna Italy
192 B8 Arborea reg. Sardegna Italy
223 K4 Arborfield Sask. Can.
223 L5 Arborg Man. Can.
190 E5 Arborio Italy
141 N6 Arbrå Sweden
146 K9 Arbroath Angus, Scotland U.K.
186 K4 Arbúcies Spain
240 J2 Arbuckle CA U.S.A.
123 J7 Arbu Lut, Dasht-e des. Afgh.
163 C9 Arbus France
192 B8 Arbus Sardegna Italy
137 K6 Arbuzynka Ukr.
161 G9 Arc r. France
161 I5 Arc r. France
163 B6 Arcachon France
163 B6 Arcachon, Bassin d' inlet France
232 G6 Arcade NY U.S.A.
231 G12 Arcadia FL U.S.A.
237 I9 Arcadia LA U.S.A.
226 H5 Arcadia MI U.S.A.
232 G8 Arcadia PA U.S.A.
226 C5 Arcadia WI U.S.A.
160 I5 Arcalod, Pointe d' mt. France
232 A9 Arcanum OH U.S.A.
243 N7 Arcas, Cayos is Mex.
238 B6 Arcata CA U.S.A.
240 O3 Arc Dome mt. NV U.S.A.
193 L4 Arce Italy
244 G7 Arcelia Mex.
164 J6 Arcen Neth.
157 J8 Arc-en-Barrois France
162 C4 Arces France
156 G7 Arces-Dilo France
160 H2 Arc-et-Senans France
191 N8 Arcevia Italy
Archangel Rus. Fed. see Arkhangel'sk
Archangel Oblast admin. div. Rus. Fed. see Arkhangel'skaya Oblast'
199 J6 Archangelos Rodos Greece
197 K7 Archar r. Bulg.
234 D2 Archbald PA U.S.A.
232 A7 Archbold OH U.S.A.
187 C11 Archena Spain
85 H2 Archer r. Qld Austr.
85 I2 Archer Bend National Park Qld Austr.
237 F9 Archer City TX U.S.A.
157 M7 Arches France
241 W3 Arches National Park UT U.S.A.

Ascheberg Ger.
Ascheberg (Holstein) Ger.
Aschenstein hill Ger.
Aschères-le-Marché France
Aschersleben Ger.
Aschheim Ger.
Asciano Italy
Ascione, Colle d' pass Italy
Asco Corse France
Ascochinga Arg.
Ascoli Piceno Italy
Ascoli Piceno prov. Italy
Ascoli Satriano Italy
Ascona Switz.
Ascot Windsor and Maidenhead, England U.K.
Ascotán Chile
Ascotán, Salar de salt flat Chile
Ascou France
As Covas Spain
Asculum Italy see Ascoli Piceno
Asculum Picenum Italy see Ascoli Piceno
Ascutney VT U.S.A.
Asdhu i. N. Male Maldives
Asdu i. N. Male Maldives see Asdhu
Åse Norway
Āseb Eritrea see Assab
Åseda Sweden
Asedjrad plat. Alg.
Asekeyevo Rus. Fed.
Āsela Eth.
Åsele Sweden
Åsen Sweden
Āsendabo Eth.
Asendorf Niedersachsen Ger.
Asendorf Niedersachsen Ger.
Asenovgrad Bulg.
Åseral Norway
Aseri Estonia
A Serra de Outes Spain
Aserradero los Charcos Mex.
Aşfāk Iran
Aşfar, Jabal al mt. Jordan
Aşfar, Tall al hill Syria
Asfeld France
Asfordby Leicestershire, England U.K.
Aşgabat Turkm.
Ásgarður Iceland
Ash Kent, England U.K.
Ash Surrey, England U.K.
Asha Rus. Fed.
Ashahi-dake mt. Japan
Ashanti admin. reg. Ghana
Ashap Rus. Fed.
Asharat Saudi Arabia
Ash 'arīyah Saudi Arabia
Ashaway RI U.S.A.
Ashbourne Ireland
Ashbourne Derbyshire, England U.K.
Ashburn GA U.S.A.
Ashburton watercourse W.A. Austr.
Ashburton South I. N.Z.
Ashburton r. South I. N.Z.
Ashburton Devon, England U.K.
Ashburton Bay Ont. Can.
Ashburton Range hills N.T. Austr.
Ashbury Oxfordshire, England U.K.
Ashby de la Zouch Leicestershire, England U.K.
Ashchikol', Ozero salt l. Kazakh.
Ashchikol', Ozero salt l. Kazakh.
Ashchurch Gloucestershire, England U.K.
Ashchysay Kazakh. see Achisay
Ashcott Somerset, England U.K.
Ashcroft B.C. Can.
Ashdod Israel
Ashdown AR U.S.A.
Ashdown Forest reg. England U.K.
Asheboro NC U.S.A.
Asher OK U.S.A.
Ashern Man. Can.
Asheville NC U.S.A.
Ashevo Rus. Fed.
Asheweig r. Ont. Can.
Ashford N.S.W. Austr.
Ashford Ireland
Ashford r. Ireland
Ashford Hampshire, England U.K.
Ashford Kent, England U.K.
Ashford Surrey, England U.K.
Ash Fork AZ U.S.A.
Ashhurst North I. N.Z.
Ashibetsu Japan
Ashigawa Japan
Ashikaga Japan
Ashikita Japan
Ashill Norfolk, England U.K.
Ashington Northumberland, England U.K.
Ashino-ko l. Japan
Ashio Japan
Ashio-sanchi mts Japan
Ashippun WI U.S.A.
Ashiro Japan
Ashiwada Japan
Ashiya Japan
Ashizuri-misaki pt Japan
Ashizuri-Uwakai Kokuritsu-kōen nat. park Japan
Ashkazar Iran
Ashkelon Israel see Ashqelon
Ashkhabad Turkm. see Aşgabat
Ashkhabadskaya Oblast' admin. div. Turkm. see Ahal
Ashkīdah Libya
Ashkirk Scottish Borders, Scotland U.K.
Ashkum IL U.S.A.
Ashkun reg. Afgh.
Ashland AL U.S.A.
Ashland KS U.S.A.
Ashland KY U.S.A.
Ashland ME U.S.A.
Ashland MS U.S.A.
Ashland MT U.S.A.
Ashland NE U.S.A.
Ashland NH U.S.A.
Ashland OH U.S.A.
Ashland OR U.S.A.
Ashland PA U.S.A.
Ashland VA U.S.A.
Ashland WI U.S.A.
Ashland City TN U.S.A.
Ashley N.S.W. Austr.
Ashley r. South I. N.Z.
Ashley Cambridgeshire, England U.K.
Ashley IN U.S.A.
Ashley MI U.S.A.
Ashley ND U.S.A.
Ashley OH U.S.A.
Ashley PA U.S.A.
Ashmore and Cartier Islands terr. Austr.
Ashmore Reef Ashmore & Cartier Is Austr.
Ashmyanskaye Wzvyshsha hills Belarus
Ashmyany Hrodzyenskaya Voblasts' Belarus
Ashmyany Hrodzyenskaya Voblasts' Belarus
Ashoknagar Madh. Prad. India
Ashoro Japan
Ashots'k' Armenia
Ashqar, Barqā al reg. Yemen
Ashqelon Israel
Ash Sha'ār Saudi Arabia
Ash Shabakah Iraq
Ash Shabb well Egypt
Ash Shaddādah Syria
Ash Shafa Saudi Arabia
Ash Shallūfah Egypt
Ash Sham Syria see Dimashq
Ash Sha'm U.A.E.

127 L8 Ash Shanāfīyah Iraq
127 J9 Ash Shaqīq well Saudi Arabia
124 G3 Ash Sha'rā' Saudi Arabia
128 D8 Ash Sharāh mts Jordan
125 H7 Ash Sharawrah Saudi Arabia
125 L3 Ash Shāriqah U.A.E.
127 K6 Ash Sharqāţ Iraq
126 E8 Ash Sharqīyah governorate Egypt
125 N5 Ash Sharqīyah admin. reg. Oman
125 N4 Ash Sharqīyah reg. Oman
125 J5 Ash Sharqīyah prov. Saudi Arabia
127 M8 Ash Shaţrah Iraq
128 A9 Ash Shaţţ Egypt
128 D8 Ash Shawbak Jordan
124 E1 Ash Shaybānī well Saudi Arabia
124 B1 ash Shaykh Humayd Saudi Arabia
128 G3 Ash Shaykh Ibrāhīm Syria
124 G9 Ash Shaykh 'Uthman Yemen
128 F9 Ash Shiblīyāt hill Saudi Arabia
125 I8 Ash Shiḩr Yemen
125 M3 Ash Şhināş Oman
125 K6 Ash Shişar well Oman
124 F2 Ash Shu'āybah Saudi Arabia
124 G1 Ash Shu'bah Saudi Arabia
124 F3 Ash Shubaykīyah Saudi Arabia
125 H2 Ash Shumlūl Saudi Arabia
124 F7 Ash Shuqayq Saudi Arabia
Ash Shurayf Saudi Arabia see Khaybar
202 B2 Ash Shuwayrif Libya
116 F8 Ashta Madh. Prad. India
114 D4 Ashta Mahar. India
232 E7 Ashtabula OH U.S.A.
129 F5 Ashtarak Armenia
114 D3 Ashti Mahar. India
114 F3 Ashti Mahar. India
116 G9 Ashti Mahar. India
214 E9 Ashton S. Africa
247 □3 Ashton St Vincent
149 L7 Ashton Cheshire, England U.K.
238 I4 Ashton ID U.S.A.
226 E8 Ashton IL U.S.A.
234 A6 Ashton MD U.S.A.
149 M7 Ashton-under-Lyne Greater Manchester, England U.K.
129 I4 Ashty Rus. Fed.
225 H2 Ashuanipi r. Nfld and Lab. Can.
225 H2 Ashuanipi Lake Nfld and Lab. Can.
230 K1 Ashuapmushuan r. Que. Can.
224 F3 Ashuapmushuan, Réserve Faunique nature res. Que. Can.
Ashur Iraq see Ash Sharqāţ
151 I6 Ashurst Hampshire, England U.K.
151 M5 Ashurst Kent, England U.K.
231 D9 Ashville AL U.S.A.
233 □Q4 Ashville ME U.S.A.
232 G8 Ashville PA U.S.A.
226 D3 Ashwabay, Mount hill WI U.S.A.
226 F5 Ashwaubenon WI U.S.A.
150 G5 Ashwick Somerset, England U.K.
128 E4 'Āşī r. Lebanon alt. 'Āşī, Nahr al (Syria), alt. Asi (Turkey), hist. Orontes
128 E3 Asi r. Turkey alt. 'Āşī (Lebanon), alt. 'Āşī, Nahr al (Syria), hist. Orontes
128 E2 'Āşī, Nahr al r. Syria alt. 'Āşī (Lebanon), alt. Asi (Turkey), hist. Orontes
88 Asia continent
191 L4 Asiago Italy
92 D5 Asid Gulf Masbate Phil.
244 E3 Asientos Mex.
114 F3 Asifabad Andhra Prad. India
115 I3 Asika Orissa India
141 R6 Asikkala Fin.
204 D2 Asilah Morocco
252 C3 Asillo Peru
198 G7 Asimi Kriti Greece
186 C3 Asín Spain
192 B6 Asinara, Golfo dell' b. Sardegna Italy
192 A5 Asinara, Isola i. Sardegna Italy
116 E7 Asind Rajasthan India
130 J4 Asino Rus. Fed.
139 N7 Asintorf Belarus
138 L8 Asipovichy Belarus
122 E8 Asīr Iran
124 E5 'Asīr prov. Saudi Arabia
124 E5 'Asīr reg. Saudi Arabia
Asisium Italy see Assisi
138 E1 Askainen Fin.
116 E2 Askale Jammu and Kashmir
127 J4 Aşkale Turkey
137 M7 Askaniya Nova Ukr.
137 M7 Askaniya Nova Zapovidnyk nature res. Ukr.
120 H1 Askarovo Rus. Fed.
147 E7 Askeaton Ireland
215 L7 Askeaton S. Africa
142 G2 Asker Norway
129 A7 Asker Dağı mt. Turkey
149 O6 Askern South Yorkshire, England U.K.
143 K3 Askersund Sweden
214 E2 Askham S. Africa
147 F4 Askill Ireland
142 H2 Askim Norway
127 K5 Askī Mawşil Iraq
134 L4 Askino Rus. Fed.
207 I4 Askira Nigeria
146 D9 Askival hill Scotland U.K.
98 F1 Askiz Rus. Fed.
198 E5 Asklipieio Greece
198 E5 Asklipieio Epidavrou tourist site Greece
168 L1 Askø i. Denmark
141 R6 Askola Fin.
143 M2 Äsköping Sweden
198 E2 Askos Greece
116 H5 Askot Uttaranchal India
142 B1 Askøy i. Norway
214 E10 Askraal S. Africa
141 H6 Askvoll Norway
129 H6 Askyaran Azer.
124 G5 Aslam, Wādī watercourse Saudi Arabia
199 K3 Aslanapa Turkey
122 B2 Aşlāndūz Iran
138 M8 Aslik r. Belarus
Aslóközpont Hungary see Mórahalom
123 N4 Asmar Afgh.
123 N4 Asmar reg. Afgh.
124 F6 Asmar reg. Saudi Arabia
203 H6 Asmara Eritrea
124 E2 Asmarah, Jabal mts Saudi Arabia
182 D2 As Mariñas reg. Spain
Āsmera Eritrea see Asmara
143 K5 Åsnen l. Sweden
182 D2 As Neves Galicia Spain
182 D4 As Neves Galicia Spain
182 F3 As Nogais Spain
193 L1 Aso r. Italy
105 L4 Asō Japan
251 G4 Asoenangka Brazil
103 I14 Aso-Kuju Kokuritsu-kōen nat. park Japan
190 I5 Asola Italy
191 L4 Asolo Italy
185 P2 Asomadilla hill Spain
117 O5 Asonli Arun. Prad. India
198 D5 Asopos r. Greece
198 E4 Asopos r. Greece
210 B2 Āsosa Eth.
103 I14 Aso-san vol. Japan
203 H4 Asoteriba, Jebel mt. Sudan
238 F3 Asotin WA U.S.A.
177 I5 Ásotthalom Hungary
103 G12 Asō-wan b. Japan
134 L4 Aspa Rus. Fed.
179 H3 Aspach Austria
179 N4 Aspang-Markt Austria
122 C3 Aspar Iran
121 O6 Aspara Kazakh.
179 N2 Asparn an der Zaya Austria
197 P8 Asparukhovo Bulg.
140 M5 Aspås Sweden
149 K4 Aspatria Cumbria, England U.K.
187 D11 Aspe Spain

163 C10 Aspe, Vallée d' val. France
140 N5 Aspeå Sweden
239 K7 Aspen CO U.S.A.
164 H5 Asperen Neth.
142 H2 Asperen l. Norway
172 G4 Asperg Ger.
237 E9 Aspermont TX U.S.A.
234 A5 Aspers PA U.S.A.
163 F9 Aspet France
163 E10 Aspin, Col d' pass France
129 E4 Aspindza Georgia
161 C9 Aspiran France
81 C11 Aspiring, Mount South I. N.Z.
182 E2 As Pontes de García Rodríguez Spain
161 H7 Aspremont France
161 H7 Aspres-sur-Buëch France
163 I6 Asprières France
Aspro, Cape Cyprus see Aspron, Cape
198 B3 Asprokavos, Akrotirio pt Kerkyra Greece
195 J7 Aspromonte, Parco Nazionale dell' nat. park Italy
128 A4 Aspron, Cape Cyprus
Aspropotamos r. Greece see Acheloos
198 E2 Asprovalta Greece
116 E8 Aspur Rajasthan India
223 J4 Asquith Sask. Can.
182 F2 As Rodrigas Spain
191 K4 Assa r. Italy
204 C3 Assa Morocco
129 G2 Assa r. Rus. Fed.
128 F3 As Sa'an Syria
203 I6 Assab Eritrea
206 C2 Assaba admin. reg. Maur.
124 E2 Aš Sab'ān Saudi Arabia
128 H3 As Sabkhah Syria
125 I2 As Sabsab well Saudi Arabia
102 R5 Assabu Japan
128 E5 Aş Şafā lava field Syria
Aş Şafāqis Tunisia see Sfax
203 F2 Aş Şaff Egypt
128 D7 Aş Şāfī Jordan
128 F2 As Safirah Syria
124 D3 Aş Şafrā Saudi Arabia
124 F2 Aş Şafrā Saudi Arabia
125 I2 Aş Şahāf Saudi Arabia
124 F8 Aş Şahīf Yemen
Aş Şahrā' des. Egypt/Libya see Libyan Desert
203 F3 Aş Şahrā' al Gharbīyah des. Egypt
203 G3 Aş Şahrā' ash Sharqīyah des. Egypt
207 H4 Assaiko Nigeria
Assake Uzbek. see Asaka
120 G6 Assake-Audan, Vpadina depr. Uzbek.
203 I7 'Assal, Lac l. Djibouti
125 H3 As Salamiyah Saudi Arabia
126 F8 Aş Şāliḩīyah Egypt
127 J6 Aş Şāliḩīyah Syria
126 B8 As Sallūm Egypt
127 L8 As Salmān Iraq
128 D6 As Salţ Jordan
117 M6 Assam state India
207 G2 Assamakka Niger
127 L8 As Samāwah Iraq
128 E6 As Samrā' Jordan
172 H3 Assamstadt Ger.
125 J5 Aş Şanām reg. Saudi Arabia
128 E5 Aş Şanamayn Syria
204 B4 Assaq watercourse Western Sahara
204 B4 As Saquia al Hamra watercourse Western Sahara
124 G2 As Sarīf well Saudi Arabia
202 D3 As Sarīr reg. Libya
163 D9 Assat France
233 J10 Assateague Island MD U.S.A.
233 J11 Assateague Island National Seashore nature res. VA U.S.A.
124 G4 As Sawādah reg. Saudi Arabia
125 L7 As Sawdā i. Oman
124 D2 Aş Şawrah Al Madīnah Saudi Arabia
124 B2 Aş Şawrah Tabūk Saudi Arabia
124 H4 As Sayḩ Saudi Arabia
124 E5 As Sayl al Kabīr Saudi Arabia
165 F7 Asse Belgium
161 H9 Asse r. France
214 I9 Assegaaibos S. Africa
192 C9 Assemini Sardegna Italy
164 K2 Assen Neth.
164 G4 Assendelft Neth.
165 E6 Assenede Belgium
142 F6 Assens Denmark
158 G7 Assérac France
193 L3 Assergi Italy
165 H8 Assesse Belgium
202 C2 As Sidrah Libya
163 H6 Assier France
125 N4 As Sīfah Oman
225 H2 Assigny, Lac l. Nfld and Lab. Can.
125 J3 As Sikak Saudi Arabia
125 J4 As Sila' U.A.E.
223 J5 Assiniboia Sask. Can.
223 L5 Assiniboine r. Man./Sask. Can.
222 H5 Assiniboine, Mount Alta/B.C. Can.
224 F3 Assinica, Réserve Faunique nature res. Que. Can.
256 B5 Assis Brazil
256 A6 Assis Chateaubriand Brazil
193 J1 Assisi Italy
169 F9 Aßlar Ger.
178 G6 Assling Austria
173 M6 Aßling Ger.
190 G4 Asso Italy
206 □ Assomada Santiago Cape Verde
217 □2 Assomption i. Aldabra Is Seychelles
163 D9 Asson France
194 G8 Assoro Sicilia Italy
205 F4 Assouf Mellene watercourse Alg.
127 M9 Aş Şubayḩīyah Kuwait
124 F6 As Subaykhah Saudi Arabia
125 I8 As Sufāl Yemen
124 G1 Aş Şufayrī well Saudi Arabia
128 G4 As Sukhnah Syria
127 L6 As Sulaymānīyah Iraq
127 L6 As Sulaymānīyah governorate Iraq
124 E2 As Sulaymī Saudi Arabia
124 G5 As Sulayyil Saudi Arabia
125 I3 Aş Şulb reg. Saudi Arabia
202 C2 As Sulţān Libya
184 E2 Assumar Port.
124 H2 Aş Şummān plat. Saudi Arabia
125 I5 Aş Şummān plat. Saudi Arabia
124 E5 As Sūq Saudi Arabia
As Sūrīyah country Asia see Syria
127 J6 Aş Şuwar Syria
128 E6 As Suwaydā' Syria
128 E6 As Suwaydā' governorate Syria
125 N4 As Suwayḩ Oman
125 M4 As Suwayq Oman
127 L7 Aş Şuwayrah Iraq
124 E4 As Suwayriqīyah Saudi Arabia
203 G2 As Suways Egypt
128 A9 As Suways governorate Egypt
124 G8 As Suwwādīyah Yemen
146 F6 Assynt, Loch l. Scotland U.K.
141 K6 Asta r. Norway
191 L3 Asta, Cima d' mt. Italy
Astacus Turkey see İzmit
163 F7 Astaffort France
199 H7 Astakida i. Greece
198 C4 Astakos Greece
Astalu Island Pak. see Astola Island
121 N2 Astana Kazakh.
122 C3 Astaneh Iran
122 C2 Āstārā Iran
163 E8 Astarac reg. France
163 F9 Astarac, Barrage de l' dam France
142 J1 Åsteby Sweden
179 J3 Asten Austria
165 I6 Asten Neth.
Asterabad Iran see Gorgān
190 E6 Asti Italy
190 E6 Asti prov. Italy
260 D2 Astica Arg.

191 L4 Astico r. Italy
177 L4 Aştileu Romania
252 C3 Astillero Peru
Astin Tag mts China see Altun Shan
Astipálaia i. Greece see Astypalaia
123 J9 Astola Island Pak.
163 H10 Aston r. France
215 I10 Aston Bay S. Africa
151 K4 Aston Clinton Buckinghamshire, England U.K.
116 E2 Astor Jammu and Kashmir
123 P4 Astor r. Pak.
256 B5 Astorga Brazil
182 H4 Astorga Spain
226 D9 Astoria IL U.S.A.
238 C3 Astoria OR U.S.A.
142 I5 Åstorp Sweden
217 □2 Astove i. Aldabra Is Seychelles
259 D7 Astra Arg.
Astrabad Iran see Gorgān
Astrakhan' Kazakh. see Astrakhanka
120 C4 Astrakhan' Rus. Fed.
Astrakhan' Bazar Azer. see Cälilabad
121 M2 Astrakhanka Kazakh.
137 O7 Astrakhanka Ukr.
Astrakhan Oblast admin. div. Rus. Fed. see Astrakhanskaya Oblast'
120 B4 Astrakhanskaya Oblast' admin. div. Rus. Fed.
138 I7 Astravyets Belarus
129 J5 Astraxanka Azer.
Astrida Rwanda see Butare
78 □6 Astrolabe, Cape Malaita Solomon Is
78 □5 Astrolabe, Récifs de l' rf New Caledonia
198 D5 Astros Greece
138 M6 Astrowna Belarus
138 H8 Astryna Belarus
139 O8 Astsyer r. Belarus
183 L4 Astudillo Spain
193 J5 Astura r. Italy
261 F5 Asturias Arg.
182 H1 Asturias airport Spain
182 H2 Asturias aut. comm. Spain
Asturica Augusta Spain see Astorga
151 I3 Astwood Bank Worcestershire, England U.K.
199 H6 Astypalaia Greece
199 H6 Astypalaia i. Greece
121 T3 Asubulak Kazakh.
Asūbulaq Kazakh. see Asubulak
78 □2 Asuisui, Cape Samoa
104 C7 Asuka Japan
104 F5 Asuke Japan
252 D2 Asunción Bol.
239 H11 Asunción r. Mex.
91 K3 Asuncion i. N. Mariana Is
253 F6 Asunción Para.
243 O10 Asunción Mita Guat.
143 O4 Asunden i. Sweden
142 J4 Åsunden l. Sweden
143 L4 Åsunden l. Sweden
192 B8 Asuni Sardegna Italy
104 D3 Asuwa-gawa r. Japan
138 L5 Asvyeya Belarus
138 L5 Asvyeyskaye, Vozyera l. Belarus
210 A4 Aswa r. Uganda
125 M3 Aswad Oman
124 D5 Aswad, Ar Ra's al pt Saudi Arabia
125 L5 Aswad, Wādī watercourse Oman
203 G3 Aswān Egypt
124 A3 Aswān governorate Egypt
203 G3 Aswān, Khazzān dam Egypt
Aswan Dam Egypt see Aswān, Khazzān
203 F3 Asyūţ Egypt
126 E10 Asyūţ governorate Egypt
177 J3 Aszaló Hungary
79 □8a Ata i. Tonga
250 E3 Atabapo r. Col./Venez.
121 M6 Atabay Kazakh.
199 L5 Atabey Turkey
258 C2 Atacama admin. reg. Chile
258 C2 Atacama, Desierto de des. Chile
258 D2 Atacama, Puna de plat. Arg.
252 C5 Atacama, Salar de salt flat Chile
250 B4 Atacames Ecuador
250 C4 Ataco Col.
205 G4 Atafaitafa, Djebel mt. Alg.
81 □1 Atafu atoll Tokelau
81 □1 Atafu i. Tokelau
104 C5 Atago-san hill Japan
105 K5 Atago-yama hill Japan
79 □9a Ataiti Tahiti Fr. Polynesia
121 M7 Atakent Kazakh.
128 C2 Atakent Turkey
129 J5 Atakişili Azer.
205 G5 Atakor mts Alg.
207 F4 Atakora, Chaîne de l' mts Benin
207 F5 Atakpamé Togo
254 G4 Atalaia Brazil
184 B4 Atalaia hill Port.
184 B6 Atalaia, Ponta da pt Port.
250 D6 Atalaia do Norte Brazil
Atalándi Greece see Atalanti
198 E4 Atalanti Greece
242 □S13 Atalaya Panama
252 C3 Atalaya Madre de Dios Peru
252 B2 Atalaya Ucayali Peru
185 P6 Atalaya Arabe hill Spain
257 G3 Ataléia Brazil
76 C2 Atambua Timor Indon.
105 J5 Atami Japan
258 E3 Atamisqui Arg.
221 M3 Atammik Greenland
123 K3 Atamyrat Turkm.
Ataniya Turkey see Adana
177 J4 Átány Hungary
183 M4 Atapuerca tourist site Spain
93 D8 Atapupu Timor Indon.
124 H8 'Ataq Yemen
128 A9 'Atāqah, Jabal hill Egypt
183 K6 Ataquines Spain
204 B5 Atâr Maur.
96 C6 Ataran r. Myanmar
245 H4 Atarjea Mex.
Atas i. Cocos Is see South Island
240 L6 Atascadero CA U.S.A.
237 F11 Atascosa watercourse TX U.S.A.
121 N3 Atasu Kazakh.
79 □8a Atata i. Tonga
111 I7 Atatan He r. China
126 D3 Atatürk airport Turkey
199 J6 Atatürk Milli Parkı nat. park Turkey
93 D8 Ataúro, Ilha de i. East Timor
Atáviros mt. Rodos Greece see Attavyros
122 H1 Ataýap Turkm.
128 B2 Atayurt Turkey
203 G5 Atbara Sudan
203 G5 Atbara r. Sudan
121 M2 Atbasar Kazakh.
121 P7 At-Bashy Kyrg.
237 J11 Atchafalaya Bay LA U.S.A.
236 H6 Atchison KS U.S.A.
234 F5 Atco NJ U.S.A.
183 Q6 Atea Spain
206 E5 Atebubu Ghana
183 Q6 Ateca Spain
182 E6 Atei Port.
182 F4 A Teixeira Spain
193 M4 Ateleta Italy
193 P6 Atella Italy
193 P6 Atella r. Italy
244 D5 Atemajac de Brizuela Mex.
105 I1 Atema-yama mt. Japan
252 C3 Aten Bol.
193 P7 Atena Lucana Italy
245 H7 Atenango del Río Mex.
244 C4 Atengo r. Mex.
244 C5 Atenguillo Mex.
244 C5 Atenguillo r. Mex.
244 D6 Atenquique Mex.
Ateransk Kazakh. see Atyrau
193 L3 Aterno r. Italy

122 E4 Āteshān Iran
123 I5 Āteshkhāneh, Kūh-e hill Afgh.
193 M3 Atessa Italy
124 G7 'Aţfayn, Wādī watercourse Yemen
234 D5 Atglen PA U.S.A.
165 E7 Ath Belgium
222 H4 Athabasca Alta Can.
222 I3 Athabasca r. Alta Can.
223 I3 Athabasca, Lake Alta/Sask. Can.
223 I3 Athabasca Sand Dunes Wilderness Provincial Park nature res. Sask. Can.
117 J9 Athagarh Orissa India
232 C10 Athalia OH U.S.A.
223 K4 Athapapuskow Lake Man. Can.
123 O6 Atharan Hazari Pak.
147 I5 Athboy Ireland
147 D8 Athea Ireland
Athenae Greece see Athina
147 E6 Athenry Ireland
227 S5 Athens Ont. Can.
Athens Greece see Athina
231 D8 Athens AL U.S.A.
231 F9 Athens GA U.S.A.
233 L6 Athens NY U.S.A.
232 C9 Athens OH U.S.A.
232 I7 Athens PA U.S.A.
231 E8 Athens TN U.S.A.
237 H9 Athens TX U.S.A.
169 K7 Athenstedt Ger.
198 B4 Atheras, Akrotirio pt Kefallonia Greece
150 D6 Atherington Devon, England U.K.
151 I2 Atherstone Warwickshire, England U.K.
85 J4 Atherton Qld Austr.
149 M6 Atherton Greater Manchester, England U.K.
211 C5 Athi r. Kenya
156 E4 Athies France
156 G4 Athies-sous-Laon France
198 E5 Athina Greece
Athínai Greece see Athina
211 C5 Athi River Kenya
159 K4 Athis-de-l'Orne France
156 D6 Athis-Mons France
147 E8 Athlacca Ireland
147 F5 Athleague Ireland
147 G6 Athlone Ireland
128 G6 Athnā', Wādī al watercourse Jordan
114 D4 Athni Karnataka India
81 C12 Athol South I. N.Z.
233 M6 Athol MA U.S.A.
231 □2 Athol Island New Prov. Bahamas
146 H9 Atholl, Forest of reg. Scotland U.K.
198 F2 Athos mt. Greece
Athos, Mount admin. div. Greece see Agion Oros
203 G2 Ath Thamad Egypt
127 K6 Ath Tharthār, Wādī r. Iraq
128 E9 Ath Thāyat mt. Saudi Arabia
124 G2 Ath Thumāmī well Saudi Arabia
147 I7 Athy Ireland
202 C6 Ati Chad
202 B4 Ati, Jabal mts Libya
122 H4 Aţīābād Iran
210 B4 Atiak Uganda
80 K5 Atiamuri North I. N.Z.
202 C6 Ati Ardébé Chad
256 D5 Atibaia Brazil
252 B4 Atico Peru
252 B4 Atico, Punta pt Peru
208 E3 Atiedo Sudan
183 O6 Atienza Spain
244 F7 Atijo Mex.
223 L5 Atikaki Provincial Wilderness Park Man. Can.
222 H4 Atikameg Alta Can.
224 D2 Atikameg r. Ont. Can.
223 M4 Atik Lake Man. Can.
224 B3 Atikokan Ont. Can.
225 H2 Atikonak Lake Nfld and Lab. Can.
79 □9a Atimaono Tahiti Fr. Polynesia
92 C4 Atimonan Luzon Phil.
193 L4 Atina Italy
243 O10 Atiquizaya El Salvador
114 F7 Atirampattinam Tamil Nadu India
243 N10 Atitlán Guat.
243 N10 Atitlán, Parque Nacional nat. park Guat.
81 □2 Atiu i. Cook Is
Atjeh admin. dist. Indon. see Aceh
124 H2 'Atk, Wādī al watercourse Saudi Arabia
131 Q3 Atka Rus. Fed.
220 A4 Atka AK U.S.A.
220 A4 Atka Island AK U.S.A.
177 I4 Atkár Hungary
135 I6 Atkarsk Rus. Fed.
237 I8 Atkins AR U.S.A.
93 G4 Atkri Papua Indon.
245 H6 Atlacomulco Mex.
215 L1 Atlanta S. Africa
231 E9 Atlanta GA U.S.A.
226 E9 Atlanta IL U.S.A.
227 J4 Atlanta MI U.S.A.
237 H9 Atlanta TX U.S.A.
126 F4 Atlantı Turkey
236 H5 Atlantic IA U.S.A.
233 □Q4 Atlantic ME U.S.A.
231 I8 Atlantic NC U.S.A.
233 K9 Atlantic City NJ U.S.A.
234 F6 Atlantic County county NJ U.S.A.
235 G4 Atlantic Highlands NJ U.S.A.
262 X2 Atlantic-Indian-Antarctic Basin sea feature S. Atlantic Ocean
263 H3 Atlantic-Indian-Antarctic Basin sea feature S. Atlantic Ocean
265 D8 Atlantic-Indian Ridge sea feature Southern Ocean
250 C2 Atlántico dept Col.
264 Atlantic Ocean
238 J5 Atlantic Peak WY U.S.A.
214 C9 Atlantis S. Africa
245 I4 Atlapexco Mex.
234 C3 Atlas PA U.S.A.
106 E5 Atlas Bogd mt. Mongolia
Atlas Méditerranéen mts Alg. see Atlas Tellien
204 D3 Atlas Mountains Africa
131 Q4 Atlasova, Ostrov i. Kuril'skiye O-va Rus. Fed.
205 F2 Atlas Saharien mts Alg.
205 F2 Atlas Tellien mts Alg.
245 I7 Atlatlahucan Mex.
222 C3 Atlin B.C. Can.
222 C3 Atlin Lake B.C./Y.T. Can.
222 C3 Atlin Provincial Park B.C. Can.
128 C6 'Atlit Israel
245 I7 Atlixco Mex.
245 I8 Atlixtac Mex.
114 F5 Atmakur Andhra Prad. India
114 F5 Atmakur Andhra Prad. India
231 D10 Atmore AL U.S.A.
141 K6 Atna Norway
116 F9 Atner Madh. Prad. India
84 F7 Atnetye Aboriginal Land res. N.T. Austr.
114 E4 Atnur Karnataka India
103 I12 Atō Japan
252 D5 Atocha Bol.
237 G8 Atoka OK U.S.A.
209 B7 Atome Angola
204 C4 Atonyia Western Sahara
78 □6 Atori Malaita Solomon Is
245 I5 Atotonico El Grande Mex.
244 D1 Atotonilco Durango Mex.
244 E1 Atotonilco Zacatecas Mex.
244 E5 Atotonilco el Alto Mex.
96 H6 Atouat mt. Laos
184 A2 Atouguia da Baleia Port.
204 D5 Atouila, Erg des. Mali
244 D5 Atoyac Mex.
245 I7 Atoyac r. Mex.
245 J9 Atoyac r. Mex.
245 K6 Atoyac r. Mex.
244 G8 Atoyac de Álvarez Mex.
114 D4 Atpadi Mahar. India

Atqan Xinjiang China see Aqqan
220 C2 Atqasuk AK U.S.A.
117 L7 Atrai r. India
Atrak, Rūd-e r. Turkm. see Atrek
122 G3 Ätran r. Sweden
142 I5 Atranh Uttar Prad. India
116 G6 Atrato r. Col.
250 B2 Atravesada, Sierra mts Mex.
245 M9 Atrek r. Iran
122 G3 Atri Italy
193 L2 Atria Italy see Adria
Atripalda Italy
193 N6 Atropatene country Asia see Azerbaijan
129 D3 Ats'ana Georgia
198 G3 Atsiki Limnos Greece
234 F5 Atsion NJ U.S.A.
105 J5 Atsugi Japan
207 H5 Atsuku Nigeria
104 F6 Atsumi Aichi Japan
102 Q8 Atsumi Yamagata Japan
104 F6 Atsumi-hantō pen. Japan
102 S3 Atsuta Japan
125 L3 Aţ Ţaff reg. U.A.E.
128 D8 Aţ Ţafīlah Jordan
124 E5 Aţ Ţā'if Saudi Arabia
177 H5 Attala Hungary
Attalea Turkey see Antalya
Attalia Turkey see Antalya
231 D8 Attalla AL U.S.A.
202 D3 Aţ Ţallāb oasis Libya
127 K6 At Ta'mīm governorate Iraq
202 D1 At Tamīmī Libya
148 C8 Attanagh Ireland
97 H7 Attapu Laos
205 G2 Attar, Oued el watercourse Alg.
195 □ Attard Malta
147 C4 Attavalley Ireland
199 I6 Attavyros mt. Rodos Greece
224 D2 Attawapiskat Ont. Can.
224 D2 Attawapiskat r. Ont. Can.
224 C2 Attawapiskat Lake Ont. Can.
203 H2 Aţ Ţawīl mts Saudi Arabia
124 E5 Aţ Ţāwlah Saudi Arabia
124 F1 At Taysīyah plat. Saudi Arabia
128 D8 Aţ Ţayyibah Jordan
80 H7 Attempt Hill South I. N.Z.
169 E8 Attendorn Ger.
173 L4 Attenkirchen Ger.
215 M1 Atteridgeville S. Africa
179 I4 Attersee Austria
179 I4 Attersee l. Austria
165 I9 Attert Belgium
165 J9 Attert r. Lux.
147 J4 Attica Northern Ireland U.K.
230 D5 Attica IN U.S.A.
232 G6 Attica NY U.S.A.
232 C7 Attica OH U.S.A.
156 F5 Attichy France
193 I2 Attigliano Italy
160 G4 Attignat France
156 I5 Attigny France
225 H2 Attikamagen Lake Nfld and Lab. Can.
198 E5 Attiki admin. reg. Greece
128 A7 Aţ Ţīnah Egypt
114 E8 Attingal Kerala India
233 N7 Attleboro MA U.S.A.
151 O2 Attleborough Norfolk, England U.K.
151 O2 Attlebridge Norfolk, England U.K.
179 I3 Attnang Austria
123 O5 Attock City Pak.
Attopeu Laos see Attapu
221 M3 Attu Greenland
126 H9 Aţ Ţubayq reg. Saudi Arabia
266 G2 Attu Island AK U.S.A.
124 G2 Aţ Ţulayḩī well Saudi Arabia
83 M4 Attunga N.S.W. Austr.
At Tūnisīyah country Africa see Tunisia
203 G2 Aţ Ţūr Egypt
114 E7 Attur Tamil Nadu India
114 F7 Attur Tamil Nadu India
124 F9 At Turbah Ta'izz Yemen
124 G9 At Turbah Ta'izz Yemen
124 E2 Aţ Ţuwayyah well Saudi Arabia
147 E6 Attymon Ireland
261 H3 Atucha Arg.
125 I8 Atūd Yemen
260 D5 Atuel r. Arg.
162 F5 Atur France
143 L3 Åtvidaberg Sweden
117 L6 Atwari Bangl.
240 L4 Atwater CA U.S.A.
236 E6 Atwood KS U.S.A.
135 I5 Atyashevo Rus. Fed.
120 D4 Atyrau Kazakh.
Atyrau Oblast admin. div. Kazakh. see Atyrauskaya Oblast'
Atyraū Oblysy admin. div. Kazakh. see Atyrauskaya Oblast'
120 D4 Atyrauskaya Oblast' admin. div. Kazakh.
135 H5 Atyur'yevo Rus. Fed.
137 L2 Atyusha Ukr.
192 C8 Atzara Sardegna Italy
179 M3 Atzenbrugg Austria
171 E7 Atzendorf Ger.
187 E7 Atzeneta del Maestrat Spain
178 A5 Au Austria
190 H1 Au Switz.
250 E5 Auati-Paraná r. Brazil
173 I2 Aub Ger.
169 H10 Aubach r. Ger.
161 H10 Aubagne France
161 E9 Aubais France
165 I9 Aubange Belgium
92 D3 Aubarede Point Luzon Phil.
162 H5 Aubazines France
159 M4 Aube France
156 H7 Aube dept France
156 G6 Aube r. France
213 H3 Aúbe Moz.
165 I7 Aubel Belgium
161 E7 Aubenas France
156 H4 Aubenton France
156 C6 Aubergenville France
156 H5 Aubérive France
157 J8 Auberive France
162 E5 Aubeterre-sur-Dronne France
156 F6 Aubetin r. France
156 B5 Aubevoye France
163 F8 Aubiet France
161 G8 Aubignan France
159 L6 Aubigné-Racan France
161 H8 Aubignosc France
156 E3 Aubigny-en-Artois France
159 P7 Aubigny-sur-Nère France
163 I6 Aubin France
224 D4 Aubinadong r. Ont. Can.
163 D10 Aubisque, Col d' pass France
190 A2 Aubonne Switz.
161 E9 Aubord France
157 K5 Auboué France
161 B7 Aubrac mts France
157 J5 Aubreville France
241 T6 Aubrey Cliffs mts AZ U.S.A.
220 F3 Aubry Lake N.W.T. Can.
85 M8 Auburn r. Qld Austr.
227 M6 Auburn Ont. Can.
231 E9 Auburn AL U.S.A.
240 K3 Auburn CA U.S.A.
236 K6 Auburn IL U.S.A.
230 E5 Auburn IN U.S.A.
233 N6 Auburn MA U.S.A.
233 □O4 Auburn ME U.S.A.
227 J6 Auburn MI U.S.A.
236 H5 Auburn NE U.S.A.
232 I6 Auburn NY U.S.A.
234 C3 Auburn PA U.S.A.
238 C3 Auburn WA U.S.A.
234 C1 Auburn Center PA U.S.A.
226 D5 Auburndale WI U.S.A.
85 M8 Auburn Range hills Qld Austr.
162 I4 Aubusson France
156 F3 Auby France
260 C5 Auca Mahuida Arg.
260 C5 Auca Mahuida, Sierra de mt. Arg.
163 G8 Aucamville France
138 F5 Auce Latvia
163 F8 Auch France
146 J9 Auchallater Aberdeenshire, Scotland U.K.
148 G2 Auchbraad Argyll and Bute, Scotland U.K.

96 C2 Auche Myanmar
156 D2 Auchel France
146 L9 Auchenblae Aberdeenshire, Scotland U.K.
146 F11 Auchenbreck Argyll and Bute, Scotland U.K.
146 I13 Auchencairn Dumfries and Galloway, Scotland U.K.
146 L11 Auchencrow Scottish Borders, Scotland U.K.
207 G5 Auchi Nigeria
146 H12 Auchinleck East Ayrshire, Scotland U.K.
146 K9 Auchmull Angus, Scotland U.K.
146 L8 Auchnagatt Aberdeenshire, Scotland U.K.
146 J8 Aucholzie Aberdeenshire, Scotland U.K.
146 K9 Auchronie Angus, Scotland U.K.
146 I10 Auchterarder Perth and Kinross, Scotland U.K.
146 J10 Auchtermuchty Fife, Scotland U.K.
156 D2 Auchy-au-Bois France
80 I3 Auckland North I. N.Z.
80 I3 Auckland admin. reg. North I. N.Z.
77 G6 Auckland Islands N.Z.
163 D10 Aucun France
161 A10 Aude dept France
161 C10 Aude r. France
224 C3 Auden Ont. Can.
Audenarde Belgium see Oudenaarde
163 B6 Audenge France
158 H2 Auderville France
233 □O3 Audet Que. Can.
160 H2 Audeux France
158 B5 Audierne France
158 C6 Audierne, Baie d' b. France
160 J2 Audincourt France
150 G2 Audlem Cheshire, England U.K.
149 M7 Audley Staffordshire, England U.K.
210 D3 Audo mts Eth.
163 C8 Audon France
156 C2 Audresselles France
138 H3 Audru Estonia
156 D2 Audruicq France
236 H5 Audubon IA U.S.A.
234 E5 Audubon NJ U.S.A.
157 K5 Audun-le-Roman France
171 G9 Aue Ger.
168 E4 Aue r. Ger.
169 J5 Aue r. Ger.
173 O4 Auerbach Bayern Ger.
171 F9 Auerbach Sachsen Ger.
171 G9 Auerbach Sachsen Ger.
173 L2 Auerbach in der Oberpfalz Ger.
171 G10 Auersberg mt. Ger.
179 O3 Auersthal Austria
171 G9 Auerswalde Ger.
121 S3 Auezov Kazakh.
156 B4 Auffay France
173 M4 Aufhausen Ger.
85 K8 Augathella Qld Austr.
147 H4 Augher Northern Ireland U.K.
147 I4 Aughnacloy Northern Ireland U.K.
147 F6 Aughrim Galway Ireland
147 J7 Aughrim Wicklow Ireland
149 L6 Aughton Lancashire, England U.K.
149 O7 Aughton South Yorkshire, England U.K.
162 F4 Augignac France
Augila Libya see Awjilah
214 E4 Augrabies S. Africa
214 E4 Augrabies Falls S. Africa
214 E4 Augrabies Falls National Park S. Africa
227 K5 Au Gres MI U.S.A.
173 J5 Augsburg Ger.
178 C3 Augsburg airport Ger.
173 J5 Augsburg-Westliche Wälder park Ger.
138 I4 Augšlīgatne Latvia
138 J5 Augšzemes augstiene hills Latvia
87 C13 Augusta W.A. Austr.
195 I9 Augusta Sicilia Italy
237 J8 Augusta AR U.S.A.
231 F9 Augusta GA U.S.A.
226 D9 Augusta IL U.S.A.
237 G7 Augusta KS U.S.A.
232 A10 Augusta KY U.S.A.
233 □P4 Augusta ME U.S.A.
238 H3 Augusta MT U.S.A.
234 F2 Augusta NJ U.S.A.
226 C5 Augusta WI U.S.A.
232 G9 Augusta WV U.S.A.
195 I9 Augusta, Golfo di b. Sicilia Italy
Augusta Auscorum France see Auch
Augusta Taurinorum Italy see Torino
Augusta Treverorum Ger. see Trier
252 C6 Augusta Victoria Chile
Augusta Vindelicorum Ger. see Augsburg
168 I1 Augustenborg Denmark
246 G8 Augustin Cadazzi Col.
220 C4 Augustine Island AK U.S.A.
227 S2 Augustines, Lac des l. Que. Can.
Augusto Cardosa Moz. see Metangula
257 E3 Augusto de Lima Brazil
Augustodunum France see Autun
254 F3 Augusto Severo Brazil
175 K2 Augustów Pol.
175 L3 Augustowo Pol.
175 L2 Augustowska, Puszcza for. Pol.
175 L2 Augustowski, Kanał canal Pol.
87 D8 Augustus, Mount W.A. Austr.
171 H9 Augustusburg Ger.
86 H3 Augustus Island W.A. Austr.
169 H6 Auhagen Ger.
173 L4 Au in der Hallertau Ger.
157 I7 Aujon r. France
Aujuittuq Nunavut Can. see Grise Fiord
124 E8 Aukan Island Eritrea
222 C3 Auke Bay AK U.S.A.
78 □6 Auki Malaita Solomon Is
168 I2 Aukrug Ger.
138 J6 Aukštaitijos nacionalinis parkas nat. park Lith.
138 G6 Aukštelkai Lith.
138 G6 Aukštelkė Lith.
140 O4 Auktsjaur Sweden
220 G2 Aulavik National Park N.W.T. Can.
86 G7 Auld, Lake salt flat W.A. Austr.
146 I7 Auldearn Highland, Scotland U.K.
169 K8 Auleben Ger.
190 H7 Aulella r. Italy
172 H6 Aulendorf Ger.
193 O6 Auletta Italy
Auliye Ata Kazakh. see Taraz
120 K1 Auliyekol' Kazakh.
190 H7 Aulla Italy
192 C4 Aullène Corse France
160 C5 Aulnat France
160 C5 Aulnat airport France
162 D3 Aulnay France
156 E6 Aulnay-sous-Bois France
158 C5 Aulne r. France
223 M5 Aulneau Peninsula Ont. Can.
157 L6 Aulnois sur-Seille France
156 G3 Aulnoye-Aymeries France
Aulon Albania see Vlorë
163 F9 Aulon France
92 □ Aulong i. Palau
170 E5 Aulosen Ger.
156 B3 Ault France
146 E7 Aultbea Highland, Scotland U.K.
146 G7 Aultguish Inn Highland, Scotland U.K.
92 □ Auluptagel i. Palau
163 G10 Aulus-les-Bains France
171 E9 Auma Ger.
156 C4 Aumale France
160 B3 Aumance r. France
157 K5 Aumetz France
160 H3 Aumont France
161 C7 Aumont-Aubrac France

B

163 E9 Beaudéan France
85 N9 Beaudesert Qld Austr.
Beauduc, Golfe de b. France see Stes Maries, Golfe des
159 L5 Beaufay France
83 I7 Beaufort Vic. Austr.
160 G3 Beaufort Franche-Comté France
160 J5 Beaufort Rhône-Alpes France
95 K2 Beaufort Sabah Malaysia
147 C8 Beaufort Ireland
231 I8 Beaufort NC U.S.A.
231 G9 Beaufort SC U.S.A.
162 D1 Beaufort-en-Vallée France
160 J5 Beaufortin mts France
Beaufort Island H.K. China see Lo Chau
220 F2 Beaufort Sea Can./U.S.A.
214 G8 Beaufort West S. Africa
156 C8 Beaugency France
233 L3 Beauharnois Que. Can.
161 I8 Beaujeu Provence-Alpes-Côte d'Azur France
160 F4 Beaujeu Rhône-Alpes France
160 E4 Beaujolais, Monts du hills France
161 E9 Beaulieu France
159 N7 Beaulieu-lès-Loches France
162 H6 Beaulieu-sur-Dordogne France
160 B1 Beaulieu-sur-Loire France
160 D3 Beaulon France
146 H8 Beauly Highland, Scotland U.K.
146 H8 Beauly r. Scotland U.K.
146 H8 Beauly Firth est. Scotland U.K.
163 E8 Beaumarchés France
150 D1 Beaumaris Isle of Anglesey, Wales U.K.
145 E5 Beaumaris Castle tourist site Wales U.K.
161 G8 Beaumes-de-Venise France
159 M3 Beaumesnil France
156 E3 Beaumetz-lès-Loges France
165 F8 Beaumont Belgium
163 F6 Beaumont Aquitaine France
160 C5 Beaumont Auvergne France
158 H2 Beaumont Basse-Normandie France
159 L8 Beaumont Poitou-Charentes France
81 D12 Beaumont South I. N.Z.
240 P8 Beaumont CA U.S.A.
237 K10 Beaumont MS U.S.A.
234 D2 Beaumont PA U.S.A.
237 H10 Beaumont TX U.S.A.
163 F8 Beaumont-de-Lomagne France
161 H9 Beaumont-de-Pertuis France
157 J4 Beaumont-en-Argonne France
159 L7 Beaumont-en-Véron France
159 M6 Beaumont-la-Ronce France
159 M3 Beaumont-le-Roger France
159 M5 Beaumont-les-Autels France
161 F7 Beaumont-lès-Valence France
156 D5 Beaumont-sur-Oise France
159 L5 Beaumont-sur-Sarthe France
160 F2 Beaune France
156 D7 Beaune-La Rolande France
159 J7 Beaupréau France
156 D3 Beauquesne France
165 G8 Beauraing Belgium
160 K5 Beauregard, Lago di l. Italy
161 G6 Beaurepaire France
160 G3 Beaurepaire-en-Bresse France
161 H7 Beaurières France
223 L5 Beauséjour Man. Can.
157 J6 Beausite France
161 K9 Beausoleil France
78 □5 Beautemps Beaupré atoll Îles Loyauté New Caledonia
156 F4 Beautor France
156 D5 Beauvais France
223 J4 Beauval Sask. Can.
156 D3 Beauval France
217 □2b Beau Vallon, Baie b. Mahé Seychelles
161 J8 Beauvezer France
163 F7 Beauville France
158 G8 Beauvoir-sur-Mer France
162 D3 Beauvoir-sur-Niort France
161 E9 Beauvoisin France
161 E6 Beauzac France
163 G8 Beauzelle France
223 J4 Beaver r. Alta/Sask. Can.
224 C2 Beaver r. Ont. Can.
222 C2 Beaver r. Y.T. Can.
222 E3 Beaver r. Y.T. Can.
237 E7 Beaver OK U.S.A.
241 T3 Beaver UT U.S.A.
237 E7 Beaver r. OK U.S.A.
241 T2 Beaver r. UT U.S.A.
236 F5 Beaver City NE U.S.A.
222 A2 Beaver Creek Y.T. Can.
237 I7 Beaver Creek r. MO U.S.A.
238 K2 Beaver Creek r. MT U.S.A.
236 E2 Beaver Creek r. ND U.S.A.
236 F5 Beaver Creek r. NE U.S.A.
230 D7 Beaver Dam KY U.S.A.
226 F6 Beaver Dam WI U.S.A.
226 F6 Beaver Dam Lake WI U.S.A.
232 E8 Beaver Falls PA U.S.A.
263 D2 Beaver Glacier Antarctica
238 H4 Beaverhead r. MT U.S.A.
238 H4 Beaverhead Mountains MT U.S.A.
223 H4 Beaverhill Lake Alta Can.
223 M4 Beaver Hill Lake Man. Can.
223 J2 Beaverhill Lake N.W.T. Can.
226 I4 Beaver Island MI U.S.A.
237 I7 Beaver Lake resr AR U.S.A.
222 G4 Beaverlodge Alta Can.
234 D3 Beaver Meadows PA U.S.A.
232 F8 Beaver Run Reservoir PA U.S.A.
234 A3 Beaver Springs PA U.S.A.
224 E4 Beaverton Ont. Can.
226 J6 Beaverton MI U.S.A.
238 C4 Beaverton OR U.S.A.
234 A3 Beavertown PA U.S.A.
116 E6 Beawar Rajasthan India
260 D3 Beazley Arg.
177 J5 Beba Veche Romania
260 D3 Bebedero, Salina del salt pan Arg.
208 C2 Bébédjia Chad
256 C4 Bebedouro Brazil
254 F3 Beberibe Brazil
171 D6 Bebertal Ger.
149 K7 Bebington Merseyside, England U.K.
208 C2 Bébôto Chad
169 I9 Bebra Ger.
108 A3 Bêca Qinghai China
187 K8 Beca, Punta pt Spain
160 J5 Becca du Lac mt. France
151 P3 Beccles Suffolk, England U.K.
191 K4 Becco di Filadonna mt. Italy
182 I8 Becedas Spain
186 F6 Beceite Spain
196 I5 Bečej Vojvodina Serbia
182 F3 Becerreá Spain
185 J6 Becerrero hill Spain
183 K4 Becerril de Campos Spain
242 □R10 Becerro, Cayos is Hond.
204 E3 Béchar Alg.
234 C4 Becharof Lake AK U.S.A.
172 D2 Becherbach Ger.
158 H5 Bécherel France
134 G4 Bechevinka Rus. Fed.
173 J3 Bechhofen Bayern Ger.
172 C3 Bechhofen Rheinland-Pfalz Ger.
171 J10 Bechlín Czech Rep.
234 D4 Bechtelsville PA U.S.A.
172 E2 Bechtheim Ger.
Bechuanaland country Africa see Botswana
176 D2 Bechyně Czech Rep.
177 K6 Becicherecu Mic Romania
183 J4 Becilla de Valderaduey Spain
199 I5 Beçin Turkey
168 I4 Beckdorf Ger.
169 H6 Beckedorf Ger.
168 G5 Beckeln Ger.
262 T1 Becker, Mount Antarctica
172 B3 Beckingen Ger.
149 P7 Beckingham Nottinghamshire, England U.K.
232 D11 Beckley WV U.S.A.
177 G3 Beckov Slovakia
81 D11 Becks South I. N.Z.
169 F7 Beckum Ger.
241 R2 Becky Peak NV U.S.A.
197 M3 Beclean Romania
93 D8 Beco East Timor
159 J7 Bécon-les-Granits France
171 I10 Bečov Czech Rep.
176 B1 Bečov nad Teplou Czech Rep.
176 F5 Becsehely Hungary
176 F5 Becsvölgye Hungary
177 G2 Bečva r. Czech Rep.
210 D2 Beda Hāyk' l. Eth.
149 N5 Bedale North Yorkshire, England U.K.
208 C2 Bédan Chad
161 C9 Bédarieux France
161 F8 Bédarrides France
169 C9 Bedburg Ger.
169 E7 Bedburg-Hau Ger.
150 F4 Beddau Rhondda Cynon Taff, Wales U.K.
150 D1 Beddgelert Gwynedd, Wales U.K.
151 M6 Beddingham East Sussex, England U.K.
233 □Q4 Beddington ME U.S.A.
Bedeau Alg. see Râs el Ma
158 H5 Bédée France
179 M7 Bedekovčina Croatia
Bedel', Pereval pass China/Kyrg. see Bedel Pass
210 C2 Bedelē Eth.
110 D6 Bedel Pass China/Kyrg.
210 D2 Bedēsa Eth.
134 L5 Bedeyeva Polyana Rus. Fed.
225 I4 Bedford N.S. Can.
233 M3 Bedford Que. Can.
215 K8 Bedford Eastern Cape S. Africa
215 O4 Bedford KwaZulu-Natal S. Africa
151 L3 Bedford Bedfordshire, England U.K.
236 H5 Bedford IA U.S.A.
230 D6 Bedford IN U.S.A.
230 E6 Bedford KY U.S.A.
235 H2 Bedford NY U.S.A.
232 G8 Bedford PA U.S.A.
232 F11 Bedford VA U.S.A.
85 J3 Bedford, Cape Qld Austr.
86 I4 Bedford Downs W.A. Austr.
232 D7 Bedford Heights OH U.S.A.
235 H2 Bedford Hills NY U.S.A.
151 L3 Bedford Level (Middle Level) lowland England U.K.
151 L2 Bedford Level (North Level) lowland England U.K.
151 M3 Bedford Level (South Level) lowland England U.K.
247 □6 Bedford Point Grenada
151 L3 Bedfordshire admin. div. England U.K.
83 K5 Bedgerebong N.S.W. Austr.
116 C8 Bedi Gujarat India
129 F4 Bediani Georgia
94 G6 Bedinggong Indon.
175 H4 Będków Pol.
116 D7 Bedla Rajasthan India
149 N3 Bedlington Northumberland, England U.K.
175 H3 Bedlno Pol.
185 M5 Bedmar Spain
179 M7 Bednja Croatia
188 F2 Bednja r. Croatia
161 G8 Bédoin France
94 □ Bedok Sing.
94 □ Bedok, Sungai r. Sing.
94 □ Bedok Jetty Sing.
94 □ Bedok Reservoir Sing.
191 K3 Bedollo Italy
190 H6 Bedonia Italy
207 I3 Bedouaram well Niger
84 G8 Bedourie Qld Austr.
163 C9 Bedous France
241 X3 Bedrock CO U.S.A.
163 H6 Béduer France
164 K2 Bedum Neth.
150 F4 Bedwas Caerphilly, Wales U.K.
151 J3 Bedworth Warwickshire, England U.K.
175 H5 Będzin Pol.
174 D1 Będzino Pol.
146 B8 Bee, Loch l. Scotland U.K.
85 J9 Beechal Creek watercourse Qld Austr.
226 G8 Beecher IL U.S.A.
233 N3 Beecher Falls VT U.S.A.
232 C10 Beech Fork Lake WV U.S.A.
83 K7 Beechworth Vic. Austr.
223 J5 Beechy Sask. Can.
168 J5 Beedenbostel Ger.
149 Q6 Beeford East Riding of Yorkshire, England U.K.
164 I5 Beek Gelderland Neth.
164 I5 Beek Noord-Brabant Neth.
164 I4 Beekbergen Neth.
87 C10 Beekeepers Nature Reserve W.A. Austr.
171 G6 Beelitz Ger.
234 F2 Beemerville NJ U.S.A.
171 D6 Beendorf Ger.
85 N9 Beenleigh Qld Austr.
170 H4 Beenz Ger.
210 E2 Beer Somalia
150 F6 Beer Devon, England U.K.
172 F2 Beerfelden Ger.
87 D10 Beeringnurding, Mount hill W.A. Austr.
128 D8 Be'ér Menuḥa Israel
165 D6 Beernem Belgium
128 C9 Be'ér Ora Israel
164 I5 Beers Neth.
165 G6 Beerse Belgium
165 F7 Beersel Belgium
Beersheba Israel see Be'ér Sheva'
128 C7 Be'ér Sheva' Israel
128 C7 Be'ér Sheva' watercourse Israel
165 C6 Beerst Belgium
164 L2 Beerta Neth.
214 H9 Beervlei Dam S. Africa
171 E7 Beesenstedt Ger.
171 J6 Beeskow Ger.
215 L1 Beestekraal S. Africa
169 E6 Beesten Ger.
151 J2 Beeston Nottinghamshire, England U.K.
84 D4 Beetaloo N.T. Austr.
262 T2 Beethoven Peninsula Antarctica
151 N2 Beetley Norfolk, England U.K.
164 J2 Beetsterzwaag Neth.
170 D5 Beetzendorf Ger.
171 G6 Beetzsee l. Ger.
237 G11 Beeville TX U.S.A.
208 D4 Befale Dem. Rep. Congo
213 □I4 Befandriana Atsimo Madag.
213 □K2 Befandriana Avaratra Madag.
213 □J4 Befasy Madag.
208 D4 Befori Dem. Rep. Congo
213 □J4 Befotaka Fianarantsoa Madag.
213 □K2 Befotaka Mahajanga Madag.
147 J3 Beg, Lough l. Northern Ireland U.K.
83 L7 Bega N.S.W. Austr.
93 D5 Bega Maluku Indon.
197 J5 Bega r. Romania
163 G8 Bégaar France
162 C5 Bégadan France
117 M8 Begamganj Bangl.
158 E4 Bégard France
123 M7 Begari r. Pak.
177 K5 Begécsivíztároló resr Hungary
247 □2 Beggars Point Antigua and Barbuda
Begicheva, Ostrov i. Rus. Fed. see Bol'shoy Begichev, Ostrov
185 L5 Begíjar Spain
165 G6 Begijnendijk Belgium
163 C6 Bègles France
158 D6 Beg-Meil France
142 G1 Begna r. Norway
182 E2 Begonte Spain
206 E5 Begoro Ghana
Begovat Uzbek. see Bekobod
116 E7 Begun Rajasthan India
186 L4 Begur Spain
186 L4 Begur, Cap de c. Spain
117 K7 Begusarai Bihar India
122 H5 Behābād Iran
251 I3 Béhague, Pointe pt Fr. Guiana
213 □J5 Behara Madag.
122 D6 Behbehān Iran
111 J8 Behleg Qinghai China
168 K3 Behlendorf Ger.
222 D4 Behm Canal sea chan. AK U.S.A.
199 H3 Behramkale Turkey
262 T2 Behrendt Mountains Antarctica
157 M5 Behren-lès-Forbach France
170 G2 Behren-Lübchin Ger.
169 K8 Behringen Ger.
122 E7 Behrūsī Iran
122 E3 Behshahr Iran
123 L4 Behsūd Afgh.
215 I8 Behulpsaam S. Africa
100 E4 Bei'an Heilong. China
Bei'ao Zhejiang China see Dongtou
108 F2 Beiba Shaanxi China
108 F4 Beibei Chongqing China
108 E3 Beichuan Sichuan China
Beida Libya see Al Bayḍā'
106 F7 Beida He r. Gansu China
106 G7 Beida Shan mts Nei Mongol China
171 G9 Beierfeld Ger.
Beigang Taiwan see Peikang
149 O7 Beighton South Yorkshire, England U.K.
210 B2 Beigi Eth.
190 F7 Beigua, Monte mt. Italy
108 G8 Beihai Guangxi China
111 L8 Bei Hulsan Hu salt l. Qinghai China
109 I7 Bei Jiang r. China
107 O7 Beijing Beijing China
107 O6 Beijing mun. China
164 K3 Beilen Neth.
108 H7 Beiliu Guangxi China
173 K3 Beilngries Ger.
171 H7 Beilrode Ger.
172 G3 Beilstein Ger.
111 K9 Beilu He r. Qinghai China
106 C9 Beiluheyan Qinghai China
172 H5 Beimerstetten Ger.
208 B2 Béinamar Chad
190 D5 Beinasco Italy
156 H5 Beine-Nauroy France
190 D7 Beinette Italy
107 Q6 Beining Liaoning China
148 F2 Beinn an Tuirc hill Scotland U.K.
146 E8 Beinn Bhan hill Scotland U.K.
146 D11 Beinn Bheigeir hill Scotland U.K.
148 F1 Beinn Bhreac hill Argyll and Bute, Scotland U.K.
146 F10 Beinn Bhreac hill Argyll and Bute, Scotland U.K.
146 F11 Beinn Bhreac hill Argyll and Bute, Scotland U.K.
146 D8 Beinn Bhreac hill Highland, Scotland U.K.
146 G10 Beinn Bhuidhe hill Scotland U.K.
146 F10 Beinn Chapull hill Scotland U.K.
146 G7 Beinn Dearg mt. Highland, Scotland U.K.
146 I9 Beinn Dearg mt. Perth and Kinross, Scotland U.K.
146 G9 Beinn Dorain mt. Scotland U.K.
144 E3 Beinn Heasgarnich mt. Scotland U.K.
146 G10 Beinn Ime mt. Scotland U.K.
146 D9 Beinn Leoid hill Scotland U.K.
146 C6 Beinn Mholach hill Scotland U.K.
146 F10 Beinn Mhòr hill Scotland U.K.
146 B8 Beinn Mhòr hill Western Isles, Scotland U.K.
146 C7 Beinn Mhòr hill Western Isles, Scotland U.K.
Beinn na Faoghla i. Scotland U.K. see Benbecula
146 G9 Beinn na Lap hill Scotland U.K.
146 E8 Beinn na Seamraig hill Scotland U.K.
146 E9 Beinn Resipol hill Scotland U.K.
146 E8 Beinn Sgritheall hill Scotland U.K.
146 F9 Beinn Sgulaird hill Scotland U.K.
146 H7 Beinn Tharsuinn hill Scotland U.K.
146 H9 Beinn Udlamain mt. Scotland U.K.
190 E1 Beinwil Switz.
108 F6 Beipan Jiang r. Guizhou China
107 Q6 Beipiao Liaoning China
213 G3 Beira Moz.
Beira prov. Moz. see Sofala
184 E2 Beirã Port.
182 E7 Beira Alta reg. Port.
182 F9 Beira Baixa reg. Port.
182 D8 Beira Litoral reg. Port.
183 Q4 Beire Spain
109 J2 Beiru He r. China
128 D5 Beirut Lebanon
222 H5 Beiseker Alta Can.
106 F6 Beishan Nei Mongol China
106 D6 Bei Shan mts China
107 M7 Beitai Ding mts China
213 F4 Beitbridge Zimbabwe
146 G11 Beith North Ayrshire, Scotland U.K.
128 D7 Beit Jālā West Bank
140 K5 Beitstadfjorden sea chan. Norway
110 H3 Beitun Xinjiang China
197 K4 Beiuș Romania
100 D4 Beixing Heilong. China
Beizhen Liaoning China see Beining
254 C2 Beja Brazil
184 D4 Beja Port.
184 C5 Beja admin. dist. Port.
205 H1 Béja Tunisia
189 B7 Béja admin. div. Tunisia
205 G1 Bejaïa Alg.
182 I8 Béjar Spain
122 H4 Bejestān Iran
123 M7 Beji r. Pak.
187 D8 Bejís Spain
244 G7 Bejucos Mex.
247 I8 Bejuma Venez.
207 I6 Bek r. Cameroon
207 I5 Béka Adamaoua Cameroon
207 I5 Béka Est Cameroon
207 I4 Béka Nord Cameroon
Bekabad Uzbek. see Bekobod
114 D6 Bekal Kerala India
213 □J3 Bekapaika Madag.
94 G8 Bekasi Jawa Indon.
120 E4 Bekbike Kazakh.
209 E7 Beke Dem. Rep. Congo
177 K5 Békés Hungary
177 K5 Békés county Hungary
177 J5 Békéscsaba Hungary
177 J5 Békéssámson Hungary
177 J5 Békésszentandrás Hungary
134 G3 Beketovskaya Rus. Fed.
137 L7 Bekhtery Ukr.
199 K4 Bekilli Turkey
213 □J5 Bekily Madag.
213 □J3 Bekipay Madag.
213 □J5 Bekitro Madag.
102 W3 Bekkai Japan
119 J1 Bekobod Uzbek.
213 □J3 Bekodoka Madag.
210 C3 BeK'ojī Eth.
213 □J3 Bekopaka Madag.
213 □I4 Bekoropoka-Antongo Madag.
135 H5 Bekovo Rus. Fed.
206 E5 Bekwai Ghana
206 E5 Bekyem Ghana
117 J7 Bela Bihar India
116 H7 Bela Uttar Prad. India
123 L8 Bela Pak.
177 H2 Belá Slovakia
123 M7 Belab r. Pak.
213 F5 Bela-Bela S. Africa
207 I5 Bélabo Cameroon
162 G2 Bélâbre France
196 J6 Bela Crkva Vojvodina Serbia
177 H3 Beladice Slovakia
177 H2 Belá-Dulice Slovakia
95 J3 Belaga Sarawak Malaysia
121 S2 Bel'agash Kazakh.
158 F5 Bel Air hill France
234 C5 Bel Air MD U.S.A.
208 D5 Belaka Dem. Rep. Congo
185 I3 Belalcázar Spain
176 B2 Bělá nad Radbuzou Czech Rep.
93 D3 Belang Sulawesi Indon.
93 E4 Belangbelang i. Maluku Indon.
197 K7 Bela Palanka Serbia
177 J3 Bélapátfalva Hungary
176 D1 Bělá pod Bezdězem Czech Rep.
176 G1 Bělá pod Pradědem Czech Rep.
114 D3 Belapur Mahar. India
135 E5 Belarus country Europe
183 Q3 Belascoáin Spain
Belasica mts Bulg./Macedonia see Belasitsa
197 K9 Belasitsa mts Bulg./Macedonia
Belau country N. Pacific Ocean see Palau
209 B6 Bela Vista Bengo Angola
Bela Vista Huambo Angola see Katchiungo
250 E4 Bela Vista Amazonas Brazil
253 F5 Bela Vista Mato Grosso do Sul Brazil
213 G5 Bela Vista Moz.
256 C2 Bela Vista de Goiás Brazil
94 C3 Belawan Sumatera Indon.
210 C2 Belaya mt. Eth.
137 O2 Belaya Rus. Fed.
131 S3 Belaya r. Rus. Fed.
137 S8 Belaya r. Rus. Fed.
137 M1 Belaya Berezka Rus. Fed.
135 H7 Belaya Glina Rus. Fed.
135 H6 Belaya Kalitva Rus. Fed.
134 J4 Belaya Kholunitsa Rus. Fed.
95 L5 Belayan r. Indon.
95 K4 Belayan, Gunung mt. Indon.
139 W5 Belaya Rechka Rus. Fed.
Belaya Tserkva Ukr. see Bila Tserkva
182 D7 Belazaima do Chão Port.
207 G3 Belbédji Niger
190 F6 Belbo r. Italy
163 H10 Belcaire France
234 C6 Belcamp MD U.S.A.
163 I7 Belcastel France
197 P3 Belceşti Romania
175 H4 Bełchatów Pol.
172 D6 Belchen mt. Ger.
232 C11 Belcher KY U.S.A.
224 E1 Belcher Islands Nunavut Can.
123 K4 Belchiragh Afgh.
186 D5 Belchite Spain
176 D2 Bělčice Czech Rep.
126 H4 Belcik Turkey
147 E6 Belclare Ireland
227 Q1 Belcourt Que. Can.
117 L8 Beldanga W. Bengal India
175 J2 Bełdany, Jezioro l. Pol.
240 K1 Belden CA U.S.A.
147 C4 Belderg Ireland
199 J6 Beldibi Turkey
226 I6 Belding MI U.S.A.
Beleapani rf India see Cherbaniani Reef
120 F1 Belebey Rus. Fed.
176 G4 Beled Hungary
210 E3 Beledweyne Somalia
206 C5 Belefuanai Liberia
191 Q6 Belej Croatia
122 E2 Belek Turkm.
206 D3 Béléko Mali
207 I5 Bélèl Cameroon
207 I4 Belel Nigeria
254 C2 Belém Brazil
208 B2 Belém Chad
258 D2 Belén Arg.
253 F5 Belén Para.
128 A2 Belen Antalya Turkey
126 H5 Belen Hatay Turkey
261 I2 Belén Uru.
239 K9 Belen NM U.S.A.
261 I2 Belén, Cuchilla de hills Uru.
183 N7 Beleña, Embalse de resr Spain
244 E4 Belén del Refugio Mex.
197 N7 Belene Bulg.
137 P3 Belenikhino Rus. Fed.
183 J2 Beleño Spain
78 □5 Belep, Îles is New Caledonia
182 E3 Belesar, Encoro de resr Spain
163 H10 Bélesta France
139 T8 Belev Rus. Fed.
199 I4 Belevi Turkey
176 F5 Belezna Hungary
81 G10 Belfast South I. N.Z.
215 O1 Belfast S. Africa
147 K3 Belfast Northern Ireland U.K.
233 □P4 Belfast ME U.S.A.
232 G6 Belfast NY U.S.A.
148 E4 Belfast International airport Northern Ireland U.K.
147 K3 Belfast Lough inlet Northern Ireland U.K.
165 J6 Belfeld Neth.
236 D2 Belfield ND U.S.A.
210 B2 Bēlfodiyo Eth.
149 N2 Belford Northumberland, England U.K.
160 J1 Belfort France
163 H7 Belfort-du-Quercy France
193 K1 Belforte del Chienti Italy
114 D5 Belgaum Karnataka India
161 I10 Belgentier France
171 H8 Belgern Ger.
171 G8 Belgershain Ger.
Belgian Congo country Africa see Congo, Democratic Republic of the
Belgicafjella mts Antarctica see Belgica Mountains
263 C2 Belgica Mountains Antarctica
België country Europe see Belgium
190 G5 Belgioioso Italy
Belgique country Europe see Belgium
165 F7 Belgium country Europe
192 C2 Belgodère Corse France
135 G6 Belgorod Rus. Fed.
Belgorod-Dnestrovskyy Ukr. see Bilhorod-Dnistrovs'kyy
Belgorod Oblast admin. div. Rus. Fed. see Belgorodskaya Oblast'
135 G6 Belgorodskaya Oblast' admin. div. Rus. Fed.
Belgrade Serbia see Beograd
233 □P4 Belgrade ME U.S.A.
238 I4 Belgrade MT U.S.A.
262 V1 Belgrano II research stn Antarctica
81 G8 Belgrove South I. N.Z.
163 C7 Belhade France
205 G3 Belhirane Alg.
156 B6 Belhomert-Guéhouville France
191 Q5 Beli Croatia
206 B4 Beli Guinea-Bissau
207 H5 Beli Nigeria
186 H4 Belianes Spain
179 O7 Belica Croatia
194 D8 Belice r. Sicilia Italy
184 E6 Beliche r. Port.
194 F8 Belici r. Sicilia Italy
196 I8 Beli Drim r. Albania/Serbia
129 J4 Belidzhi Rus. Fed.
Beliliou i. Palau see Peleliu
197 O7 Beli Lom r. Bulg.
188 G3 Beli Manastir Croatia
94 F7 Belimbing Sumatera Indon.
97 I14 Belimbing, Tanjung pt Indon.
163 C7 Belin-Béliet France
183 N8 Belinchón Spain
208 B4 Bélinga Gabon
232 F9 Belington WV U.S.A.
Belingwe Zimbabwe see Mberengwa
135 H5 Belinskiy Rus. Fed.
197 J5 Belinț Romania
94 F5 Belinyu Indon.
197 K6 Beli Timok r. Serbia
175 N2 Belitsa Belarus
197 L9 Belitsa Bulg.
137 Q2 Belitsa Rus. Fed.
95 H6 Belitung i. Indon.
177 L5 Beliu Romania
209 B6 Belize Angola
243 O9 Belize Belize
243 O9 Belize country Central America
251 H3 Bélizon Fr. Guiana
Beljak Austria see Villach
197 J6 Beljanica mt. Serbia
131 O2 Bel'kovskiy, Ostrov i. Novosibirskiye O-va Rus. Fed.
85 M9 Bell Qld Austr.
83 L5 Bell r. N.S.W. Austr.
224 E3 Bell r. Que. Can.
169 D10 Bell Ger.
215 L9 Bell S. Africa
169 D10 Bell (Hunsrück) Ger.
82 D5 Bell, Point S.A. Austr.
193 P6 Bella Italy
222 D4 Bella Bella B.C. Can.
162 G3 Bellac France
160 I5 Bellacha, Mont mt. France
261 I3 Bellaco Uru.
222 E4 Bella Coola B.C. Can.
222 E4 Bella Coola r. B.C. Can.
147 C4 Bellacorick Ireland
252 D2 Bella Flor Bol.
147 I3 Bellaghy Northern Ireland U.K.
190 G4 Bellagio Italy
147 E5 Bellahy Ireland
226 I5 Bellaire MI U.S.A.
237 H11 Bellaire TX U.S.A.
147 F5 Bellanagare Ireland
147 G4 Bellanaleck Northern Ireland U.K.
147 F3 Bellanamore Ireland
147 F6 Bellaneeny Ireland
190 G3 Bellano Italy
193 L2 Bellante Italy
191 M7 Bellaria Italy
114 E5 Bellary Karnataka India
83 L3 Bellata N.S.W. Austr.
261 I2 Bella Unión Uru.
148 B5 Bellavally Gap pass Ireland
147 D5 Bellavary Ireland
258 F3 Bella Vista Corrientes Arg.
259 C8 Bella Vista Santa Cruz Arg.
253 E3 Bella Vista Bol.
253 F5 Bella Vista Para.
250 B6 Bellavista Cajamarca Peru
250 C5 Bellavista Loreto Peru
192 D8 Bellavista, Capo c. Sardegna Italy
252 C5 Bella Vista, Salar de salt flat Chile
80 I6 Bell Block North I. N.Z.
85 M6 Bell Cay rf Qld Austr.
186 G4 Bellcaire d'Urgell Spain
232 D10 Belle WV U.S.A.
246 G4 Belle-Anse Haiti
171 E7 Belleben Ger.
161 H6 Belledonne mts France
147 F4 Belleek Northern Ireland U.K.
147 J4 Belleek Northern Ireland U.K.
157 L7 Bellefontaine France
247 □3 Bellefontaine Martinique
232 B8 Bellefontaine OH U.S.A.
232 H8 Bellefonte PA U.S.A.
236 D3 Belle Fourche SD U.S.A.
236 D3 Belle Fourche r. SD U.S.A.
156 D8 Bellegarde Centre France
161 F9 Bellegarde Languedoc-Roussillon France
162 I4 Bellegarde-en-Marche France
160 H4 Bellegarde-sur-Valserine France
231 G12 Belle Glade FL U.S.A.
158 E7 Belle-Île i. France
225 K3 Belle Isle i. Nfld and Lab. Can.
225 J3 Belle Isle, Strait of Nfld and Lab. Can.
158 E4 Belle-Isle-en-Terre France
159 M5 Bellême France
234 F4 Belle Mead NJ U.S.A.
241 U6 Bellemont AZ U.S.A.
160 C4 Bellenaves France
173 I5 Bellenberg Ger.
156 B4 Bellencombre France
247 □4 Belleplaine Barbados
160 C4 Bellerive-sur-Allier France
157 M6 Belles-Forêts France
224 E4 Belleterre Que. Can.
156 F5 Belleu France
160 J4 Bellevaux France
160 G3 Bellevesvre France
224 E4 Belleville Ont. Can.
160 F4 Belleville France
236 G6 Belleville KS U.S.A.
235 G3 Belleville NJ U.S.A.
160 B1 Belleville-sur-Loire France
157 J5 Belleville-sur-Meuse France
158 I8 Belleville-sur-Vie France
230 B4 Bellevue IA U.S.A.
226 I7 Bellevue MI U.S.A.
236 H5 Bellevue NE U.S.A.
232 C7 Bellevue OH U.S.A.
238 C3 Bellevue WA U.S.A.
161 D6 Bellevue-la-Montagne France
160 H5 Belley France
206 C5 Belle Yella Liberia
226 F9 Bellflower IL U.S.A.
172 E3 Bellheim Ger.
160 J2 Bellherbe France
160 H4 Bellignat France
Bellin Que. Can. see Kangirsuk
83 N4 Bellingen N.S.W. Austr.
149 M3 Bellingham Northumberland, England U.K.
238 C2 Bellingham WA U.S.A.
262 U2 Bellingshausen research stn Antarctica
Bellingshausen Island atoll Arch. de la Société Fr. Polynesia see Motu One
262 S2 Bellingshausen Sea Antarctica
164 L2 Bellingwolde Neth.
190 F4 Bellinzago Novarese Italy
190 G3 Bellinzona Switz.
225 K3 Bell Island Nfld and Lab. Can.
222 D4 Bell Island Hot Springs AK U.S.A.
193 N6 Bellizzi Italy
234 E5 Bellmawr NJ U.S.A.
250 C3 Bello Col.
183 R7 Bello Spain
163 C8 Bellocq France
78 □6 Bellona i. Solomon Is
159 K4 Bellou-en-Houlme France
233 M5 Bellows Falls VT U.S.A.
123 M7 Bellpat Pak.
186 H4 Bellpuig Spain
146 L10 Bell Rock i. Scotland U.K.
146 H11 Bellshill North Lanarkshire, Scotland U.K.
140 □ Bellsund inlet Svalbard
191 M3 Belluno Italy
191 M3 Belluno prov. Italy
114 E6 Belluru Karnataka India
235 G2 Bellvale NY U.S.A.
186 I3 Bellver de Cerdanya Spain
261 F3 Bell Ville Arg.
214 C9 Bellville S. Africa
232 C8 Bellville OH U.S.A.
237 G11 Bellville TX U.S.A.
232 G8 Bellwood PA U.S.A.
222 H5 Belly r. Alta Can.
169 F6 Belm Ger.
235 G4 Belmar NJ U.S.A.
177 K5 Bélmegyer Hungary
185 I4 Bélmez Spain
185 M5 Bélmez de la Moraleda Spain
83 M5 Belmont N.S.W. Austr.
163 E8 Belmont France
214 I5 Belmont S. Africa
146 □O1 Belmont Shetland, Scotland U.K.
233 N5 Belmont NH U.S.A.
232 G6 Belmont NY U.S.A.
160 E4 Belmont-de-la-Loire France
257 H1 Belmonte Brazil
182 F8 Belmonte Port.
182 H2 Belmonte Asturias Spain
183 O9 Belmonte Castilla-La Mancha Spain
193 Q9 Belmonte Calabro Italy
193 M4 Belmonte del Sannio Italy
193 J3 Belmonte in Sabina Italy
194 E7 Belmonte Mezzagno Sicilia Italy
161 B9 Belmont-sur-Rance France
243 O9 Belmopan Belize
85 H5 Belmore Creek r. Qld Austr.
147 C4 Belmullet Ireland
213 □J4 Belo Madag.
255 E5 Belo Campo Brazil
165 E7 Belœil Belgium
121 T1 Beloglazovo Rus. Fed.
100 F3 Belogorsk Rus. Fed.
Belogorsk Ukr. see Bilohirs'k
137 T3 Belogor'ye Rus. Fed.
197 K7 Belogradchik Bulg.
213 □J5 Beloha Madag.
250 E5 Belo Horizonte Amazonas Brazil
257 F3 Belo Horizonte Minas Gerais Brazil
236 F6 Beloit KS U.S.A.
226 E7 Beloit WI U.S.A.
254 F4 Belo Jardim Brazil
Belokamensk Ukr. see Inkerman
208 B3 Béloko C.A.R.
121 U2 Belokurikha Rus. Fed.
217 □1b Bel Ombre Mauritius
251 I5 Belo Monte Pará Brazil
Belo Monte Piauí Brazil see Batalha
134 F2 Belomorsk Rus. Fed.
117 M8 Belonia Tripura India
139 W7 Beloomut Rus. Fed.
257 F3 Belo Oriente Brazil
Beloozersk Belarus see Byelaazyorsk
139 V6 Beloozerskiy Rus. Fed.
93 B5 Belopa Sulawesi Indon.
Belopol'ye Ukr. see Bilopillya
183 N4 Belorado Spain
135 G7 Belorechensk Rus. Fed.
Belorechenskaya Rus. Fed. see Belorechensk
126 H5 Belören Adıyaman Turkey
126 F5 Belören Konya Turkey
120 H1 Beloretsk Rus. Fed.
Belorussia country Europe see Belarus
Belorusskaya S.S.R. country Europe see Belarus
197 P7 Beloslav Bulg.
Belostok Pol. see Białystok
129 F3 Belot'i Georgia
177 G2 Bělotín Czech Rep.
197 K7 Belotintsi Bulg.
213 □J3 Belo Tsiribihina Madag.
121 T2 Belousovka Kazakh.
139 T6 Belousovo Rus. Fed.
257 E4 Belo Vale Brazil
197 M8 Belovo Bulg.
100 F3 Beloyarovo Rus. Fed.
134 G2 Beloye Rus. Fed.
139 U1 Beloye, Ozero l. Rus. Fed.
140 V3 Beloye More Rus. Fed.
134 G2 Beloye More sea Rus. Fed.
134 K4 Beloyevo Rus. Fed.
120 F1 Belozerka Rus. Fed.
139 U1 Belozersk Rus. Fed.
Belozerskoye Ukr. see Bilozers'ke
190 C2 Belp Switz.
172 D8 Belp airport Switz.
194 H8 Belpasso Sicilia Italy
163 H9 Belpech France
149 O7 Belper Derbyshire, England U.K.
232 D9 Belpre OH U.S.A.
149 N3 Belsay Northumberland, England U.K.
175 I4 Belsk Duży Pol.
139 X7 Bel'skoye Rus. Fed.
82 G4 Beltana S.A. Austr.
82 F3 Belt Bay salt flat S.A. Austr.
241 P4 Belted Range mts NV U.S.A.
251 H5 Belterra Brazil
106 F1 Beltes Gol r. Mongolia
169 D10 Beltheim Ger.
179 N6 Beltinci Slovenia
177 L4 Beltiug Romania
151 P2 Belton Norfolk, England U.K.
236 H6 Belton MO U.S.A.
237 G10 Belton TX U.S.A.
120 I6 Beltov Uzbek.
147 D5 Beltra Mayo Ireland
147 E4 Beltra Sligo Ireland
147 D5 Beltra Lough l. Ireland
164 K4 Beltrum Neth.
Bel'ts' Moldova see Bălți
234 B6 Beltsville MD U.S.A.
Bel'tsy Moldova see Bălți
147 H4 Belturbet Ireland
234 D3 Beltzville Lake PA U.S.A.
192 B8 Belu r. Sardegna Italy
112 G2 Belukha, Gora mt. Kazakh./Rus. Fed.
114 D6 Belur Karnataka India
95 L2 Beluran Sabah Malaysia
177 H2 Beluša Slovakia
134 I2 Belush'ye Rus. Fed.
232 D10 Belva WV U.S.A.
192 B4 Belvédère-Campomoro Corse France
193 P8 Belvedere Marittimo Italy
184 D1 Belver Port.
186 F4 Belver de Cinca Spain
163 G6 Belvès France
163 I9 Belvèze-du-Razès France
161 E8 Belvézet France
226 F7 Belvidere IL U.S.A.
234 E3 Belvidere NJ U.S.A.
147 D4 Belville Ireland
183 K9 Belvís de la Jara Spain
178 B7 Belviso, Lago l. Italy
85 K6 Belyando r. Qld Austr.
85 K6 Belyando Crossing Qld Austr.
120 G2 Belyayevka Rus. Fed.
Belyayevka Ukr. see Bilyayivka
139 O6 Belyayevo Rus. Fed.
84 C2 Belyuen N.T. Austr.
139 P6 Belyy Rus. Fed.
130 I2 Belyy, Ostrov i. Rus. Fed.
110 H1 Belyy Bom Rus. Fed.
139 R8 Belyye Berega Rus. Fed.
139 U6 Belyye Stolby Rus. Fed.
139 U5 Belyy Gorodok Rus. Fed.
137 R3 Belyy Kolodez' Rus. Fed.
130 J4 Belyy Yar Rus. Fed.
158 E6 Belz France
136 D3 Belz Ukr.
175 L5 Bełżec Pol.
171 G6 Belzig Ger.
237 J9 Belzoni MS U.S.A.
175 K4 Bełżyce Pol.
213 □K2 Bemanevika Madag.
213 □J3 Bemaraha, Plateau du Madag.
209 B6 Bembe Angola
207 F4 Bembèrèkè Benin
185 I5 Bembézar r. Spain
185 I5 Bembézar, Embalse del resr Spain
182 H3 Bembibre Castilla y León Spain
182 C2 Bembibre Galicia Spain
209 C7 Bembo Angola
151 J6 Bembridge Isle of Wight, England U.K.
236 H2 Bemidji MN U.S.A.
237 K8 Bemis TN U.S.A.
164 I5 Bemmel Neth.
184 H6 Bemposta Bragança Port.
184 C2 Bemposta Santarém Port.
149 Q5 Bempton East Riding of Yorkshire, England U.K.
206 D3 Béna Burkina
186 F3 Benabarre Spain
209 D6 Bena Dibele Dem. Rep. Congo
95 K5 Benagin Kalimantan Indon.
187 D8 Benaguasil Spain
185 O7 Benahadux Spain
185 I7 Benahavís Spain
204 D2 Benahmed Morocco
146 J7 Ben Aigan hill Scotland U.K.
185 I4 Benajarafe r. Spain
146 H9 Ben Alder mt. Scotland U.K.
83 J7 Benalla Vic. Austr.
185 J7 Benalmádena Spain
185 M6 Benalúa de Guadix Spain
185 L6 Benalúa de las Villas Spain
184 H8 Benalup de Sidonia Spain
185 K7 Benamargosa Spain
185 N5 Benamaurel Spain
185 J6 Benamejí Spain
204 B5 Ben 'Amîra well Maur.
185 K7 Benamocarra Spain
185 I7 Benaocaz Spain
185 I7 Benaoján Spain
Benares Uttar Prad. In Varanasi
217 □1b Benares Mauritius
205 H1 Ben Arous Tunisia
189 B7 Ben Arous admin. div
187 E7 Benasal Spain
187 E10 Benasau Spain
186 G2 Benasque Spain
162 E2 Benassay France
161 I10 Bénat, Cap c. France
176 D1 Benátky nad Jizerou Czech Rep.
209 D6 Bena-Tshadi Dem. Rep. Congo
184 B3 Benavente Port.
182 I4 Benavente Spain
252 D3 Benavides Bol.
182 I4 Benavides de Orbigo
184 D2 Benavila Port.
146 J8 Ben Avon mt. Scotlan
147 J2 Benbane Head Northe Ireland U.K.
147 C5 Benbaun hill Ireland
146 B8 Benbecula i. Scotland
83 M7 Ben Boyd National P N.S.W. Austr.
147 F4 Benbulben hill Ireland
147 I4 Benburb Northern Irel
147 C5 Benbury hill Ireland
184 E3 Bencatel Port.
109 M2 Bencha Jiangsu China
Bencheng Hebei Chin Luannan
146 I10 Ben Chonzie hill Scot
147 C5 Bencorr hill Ireland
146 F10 Ben Cruachan mt. Scotland U.K.
87 D11 Bencubbin W.A. Aust
238 D4 Bend OR U.S.A.
215 L7 Bendearg mt. S. Afric
209 C5 Bendela Dem. Rep. C
83 M4 Bendemeer N.S.W. A
Bender Moldova see
210 F2 Bender-Bayla Somali
226 G5 Benderville WI U.S.A.
Bendery Moldova see
168 I4 Bendestorf Ger.
82 G4 Bendieuta watercours Austr.
83 J7 Bendigo Vic. Austr.
83 L7 Bendoc Vic. Austr.
169 E10 Bendorf Ger.
Bendzin Pol. see Będ
138 G5 Bēne Latvia
213 G2 Bene Moz.
164 H5 Beneden-Leeuwen N
225 J2 Benedict, Mount hill Nfld and Lab. Can.
233 □Q3 Benedicta ME U.S.A.
173 K6 Benediktbeuren Ger.
173 K6 Benediktenwand mt.
184 B2 Benedita Port.
254 E3 Beneditinos Brazil
254 D3 Benedito Leite Brazil
182 I5 Benegiles Spain
163 D9 Bénéjacq France
187 D10 Benejama Spain
187 D11 Benejúzar Spain
206 D3 Bénéna Mali
151 N5 Benenden Kent, Engla
213 □J4 Benenitra Madag.
176 D2 Benešov Czech Rep.
179 K2 Benešov nad Černou Czech Rep.
176 D1 Benešov nad Ploučni Czech Rep.
163 B8 Bénesse-Maremne F
195 K7 Benestare Italy
157 M6 Bénestroff France
162 C3 Benet France
192 C7 Benetutti Sardegna It
190 D6 Bene Vagienna Italy
162 H3 Bénévent-l'Abbaye F
193 N5 Benevento Italy
193 N5 Benevento prov. Italy
Beneventum Italy see Benevento
232 G7 Benezette PA U.S.A.
157 O7 Benfeld France
234 A3 Benfer PA U.S.A.
184 B2 Benfica do Ribatejo
96 E5 Beng, Nam r. Laos
Benga i. Fiji see Beqa
211 B8 Benga Malawi
113 G8 Bengal, Bay of sea Indian Ocean
208 E4 Bengamisa Dem. Rep
207 I6 Bengbis Cameroon
109 K2 Bengbu Anhui China
146 C7 Ben Geary hill Scotlan
195 □ Bengħajsa, Il-Ponta Malta
Benghazi Libya see Ba
107 P9 Beng He r. China
Bengħisa Point Malta
Bengħajsa, Il-Ponta ta
94 E4 Bengkalis Sumatera In
94 E4 Bengkalis i. Indon.
95 H4 Bengkayang Kalimant
94 E6 Bengkulu Sumatera In
94 D6 Bengkulu prov. Indon.
95 L6 Bengkung Kalimantan
209 C9 Bengo Cuando Cuban Angola
209 B7 Bengo Uíge Angola
209 B7 Bengo prov. Angola
93 G5 Bengoi Seram Indon.
147 C5 Bengorm hill Ireland
142 I2 Bengtsfors Sweden
209 B8 Benguela Angola
209 B8 Benguela prov. Angola
205 H2 Ben Guerdane Tunisia
204 D2 Benguerir Morocco
213 G4 Benguérua, Ilha i. Mo
Benha Qalyūbīyah Egy Banhā
146 G6 Ben Hee hill Scotland
146 D9 Ben Hiant hill Scotlan
146 G6 Ben Hope hill Scotlan
146 H6 Ben Horn hill Scotland
252 D3 Beni dept Bol.
252 D2 Beni r. Bol.
208 F4 Beni Dem. Rep. Cong
117 I5 Beni Nepal
204 E3 Beni-Abbès Alg.
183 K2 Benia de Onís Spain
223 H2 Beniah Lake N.W.T. C
187 E10 Beniarrés Spain
187 E10 Beniarrés, Embalse d Spain
180 D5 Beni Boufrah Morocc
186 F7 Benicarló Spain
187 F7 Benicasim Spain
240 J3 Benicia CA U.S.A.
187 E10 Benidorm Spain
187 E10 Benidorm, Isolte de i.
207 I1 Beni Dourso well Nige
187 D11 Beniel Spain
187 E9 Benifaió Spain
186 G6 Benifallet Spain
187 E10 Benifallim Spain
Benifayo Valencia Spa Benifaió
181 F3 Benigánim Spain
158 B5 Beniguet, Île de i. Fra
204 E2 Beni Guil reg. Morocc
187 E10 Benilloba Spain
204 D2 Beni Mellal Morocco
207 F4 Benin country Africa
207 G5 Benin r. Nigeria
207 F5 Benin, Bight of g. Afri
207 G5 Benin City Nigeria
205 E3 Beni-Ounif Alg.
205 E2 Beni-Saf Alg.
207 I4 Benisheikh Nigeria
187 F10 Benissa Spain
186 G5 Benissanet Spain
Beni Suef Banī Suway see Banī Suwayf
187 F10 Benitachell Spain
114 E4 Benithora r. India
217 □1b Bénitiers, Île aux i. M
Benito r. Equat. Guinea Mbini
242 B3 Benito, Islas is Mex.
261 H5 Benito Juárez Arg.
241 R9 Benito Juárez Baja California Mex.
244 G6 Benito Juarez Michoacán Mex.

Benito Juarez San Luis Potosí Mex.
Benito Juárez Tabasco Mex.
Benito Juárez Veracruz Mex.
Benito Juárez Veracruz Mex.
Benito Juárez Zacatecas Mex.
Benito Juárez, Parque Nacional nat. park Mex.
Benito Juárez, Presa resr Mex.
Benito Soliven Luzon Phil.
Benizalón Spain
Benizar y la Tercia Spain
Benjamim Constant Brazil
Benjamin TX U.S.A.
Benjamin, Isla i. Chile
Benjamín Hill Mex.
Benjamin Zorrillo Arg.
Benjina Maluku Indon.
Benkei-misaki pt Japan
Benkelman NE U.S.A.
Benken Switz.
Ben Klibreck hill Scotland U.K.
Benkovac Croatia
Benkovski Bulg.
Ben Lawers mt. Scotland U.K.
Ben Ledi hill Scotland U.K.
Benllech Isle of Anglesey, Wales U.K.
Benlloch Spain
Ben Lomond mt. N.S.W. Austr.
Ben Lomond hill Scotland U.K.
Ben Lomond CA U.S.A.
Ben Lomond National Park Tas. Austr.
Ben Loyal hill Scotland U.K.
Ben Lui mt. Scotland U.K.
Ben Macdhui mt. Lesotho
Ben Macdui mt. Scotland U.K.
Ben Mahidi Alg.
Benmara N.T. Austr.
Ben More mt. South I. N.Z.
Ben More hill Scotland U.K.
Ben More mt. Scotland U.K.
Benmore, Lake South I. N.Z.
Ben More Assynt hill Scotland U.K.
Benmore Peak South I. N.Z.
Bennan Head Scotland U.K.
Benndorf Ger.
Bennebroek Neth.
Benneckenstein (Harz) Ger.
Bennekom Neth.
Bennett B.C. Can.
Bennett WI U.S.A.
Bennett, Lake salt flat N.T. Austr.
Bennetta, Ostrov i. Novosibirskiye O-va Rus. Fed.
Bennett Island Novosibirskiye O-va Rus. Fed. see **Bennetta, Ostrov**
Bennett Lake B.C. Can.
Bennettsbridge Ireland
Bennett's Point St Helena
Bennettsville SC U.S.A.
Ben Nevis mt. Scotland U.K.
Benneydale North I. N.Z.
Bennington NH U.S.A.
Bennington VT U.S.A.
Bennstedt Ger.
Bennungen Ger.
Bénodet France
Benodet, Anse de b. France
Ben Ohau Range mts South I. N.Z.
Benoi Basin dock Sing.
Benoni S. Africa
Bénoué r. Cameroon
Bénoué, Parc National de la nat. park Cameroon
Bénoye Chad
Benquerença Port.
Benquet France
Ben Rinnes hill Scotland U.K.
Bensafrim Port.
Bensdorf Ger.
Benshausen Ger.
Bensheim Ger.
Ben Slimane Morocco
Benson Oxfordshire, England U.K.
Benson AZ U.S.A.
Benson MN U.S.A.
Bensonville Liberia
Bens Run WV U.S.A.
Ben Starav mt. Scotland U.K.
Bent Iran
Benta Seberang Malaysia
Bentelo Neth.
Benteng Sulawesi Indon.
Ben Thuy Vietnam
Benti Guinea
Bentiaba Angola
Ben Tieb Morocco
Bentinck Island Qld Austr.
Bentinck Island Myanmar
Ben Tirran hill Scotland U.K.
Bentiu Sudan
Bent Jbaïl Lebanon
Bentley Alta Can.
Bentley South Yorkshire, England U.K.
Bentleyville PA U.S.A.
Bento Gomes r. Brazil
Benton N.B. Can.
Benton AR U.S.A.
Benton CA U.S.A.
Benton IL U.S.A.
Benton KY U.S.A.
Benton LA U.S.A.
Benton MO U.S.A.
Benton PA U.S.A.
Benton TN U.S.A.
Bentong Malaysia see **Bentung**
Benton Harbor MI U.S.A.
Bentonville AR U.S.A.
Bentonville OH U.S.A.
Bên Tre Vietnam
Bentsy Rus. Fed.
Bentung Malaysia
Bentwisch Ger.
Bentzin Ger.
Benua Sulawesi Indon.
Benua i. Indon.
Benuamartinus Kalimantan Indon.
Benue r. Nigeria
Benue state Nigeria
Benum, Gunung mt. Malaysia
Beňuš Slovakia
Ben Vorlich hill Argyll and Bute, Scotland U.K.
Ben Vorlich hill Perth and Kinross/Stirling, Scotland U.K.
Benwa Zambia
Benwee hill Ireland
Benwee Head Ireland
Benwood WV U.S.A.
Ben Wyvis mt. Scotland U.K.
Benxi Liaoning China
Ben Zireg Alg.
Benzu Morocco
Beo Sulawesi Indon.
Beograd Serbia
Beohari Madh. Prad. India
Béoumi Côte d'Ivoire
Bepagut, Gunung mt. Indon.
Beppu Japan
Beppu-wan b. Japan
Beqa i. Fiji
Bequia i. St Vincent
Bequimão Brazil
Bera Bangl.
Bera, Tasik l. Malaysia
Berabevú Arg.
Berach r. India
Bera de Bidasoa Spain
Beragh Northern Ireland U.K.
Beraketa Madag.
Beramanja Madag.
Berane Montenegro
Beranga Spain
Berangas Kalimantan Indon.
Berango Spain
Berantevilla Spain
Bérard, Lac l. Que. Can.
Berasia Madh. Prad. India
Berastagi Sumatera Indon.
Berat Albania
Bérat France
95 L5 **Beratus, Gunung** mt. Indon.
173 L3 **Beratzhausen** Ger.
95 L3 **Berau** r. Indon.
91 H7 **Berau, Teluk** b. Papua Indon.
213 □J3 **Beravina** Madag.
261 H4 **Berazategui** Arg.
94 F5 **Berbak, Taman Nasional** nat. park Indon.
186 E4 **Berbegal** Spain
203 G5 **Berber** Sudan
210 E2 **Berbera** Somalia
208 B3 **Berbérati** C.A.R.
215 P3 **Berbice** S. Africa
183 Q3 **Berbinzana** Spain
183 N2 **Bercedo** Spain
177 I4 **Bercel** Hungary
156 G7 **Bercenay-en-Othe** France
183 J5 **Bercero** Spain
190 H6 **Berceto** Italy
165 E7 **Berchem** Belgium
190 B2 **Bercher** Switz.
192 C6 **Berchidda** Sardegna Italy
202 C5 **Berchi-Guélé** well Chad
173 K3 **Berching** Ger.
120 H3 **Berchogur** Kazakh.
173 O6 **Berchtesgaden** Ger.
173 N6 **Berchtesgaden, Nationalpark** nat. park Ger.
173 N6 **Berchtesgadener Alpen** mts Ger.
185 M7 **Bérchules** Spain
182 I4 **Bercianos del Páramo** Spain
156 C3 **Berck** France
177 L4 **Bercu** Romania
129 G5 **Berd** Armenia
137 P7 **Berda** r. Ukr.
210 D4 **Berdaale** Somalia
159 M5 **Berd'huis** France
Berdichev Ukr. see **Berdychiv**
131 N3 **Berdigestyakh** Rus. Fed.
130 J4 **Berdsk** Rus. Fed.
182 G2 **Berducedo** Spain
186 D2 **Berdún** Spain
137 P7 **Berdyans'k** Ukr.
137 P7 **Berdyans'ka Kosa** spit Ukr.
Berdyanskaya Kosa spit Ukr. see **Berdyans'ka Kosa**
137 P7 **Berdyans'ka Zatoka** b. Ukr.
136 H4 **Berdychiv** Ukr.
208 C2 **Béré** Chad
232 A11 **Berea** KY U.S.A.
232 D7 **Berea** OH U.S.A.
150 D7 **Bere Alston** Devon, England U.K.
93 F2 **Berebere** Maluku Indon.
Béréby Côte d'Ivoire see **Grand-Bérébi**
210 F2 **Bereeda** Somalia
150 D7 **Bere Ferrers** Devon, England U.K.
139 U1 **Bereg** Rus. Fed.
177 L3 **Beregdaróc** Hungary
Beregovo Ukr. see **Berehove**
100 E1 **Beregovoy** Rus. Fed.
190 G5 **Bereguardo** Italy
136 E5 **Berehomet** Ukr.
137 O8 **Berehove** Respublika Krym Ukr.
136 B5 **Berehove** Zakarpats'ka Oblast' Ukr.
91 K8 **Bereina** P.N.G.
179 O8 **Berek** Croatia
137 P4 **Bereka** Ukr.
137 P4 **Bereka** r. Ukr.
177 K4 **Berekböszörmény** Hungary
122 F2 **Bereket** Turkm.
213 □J4 **Bereketa** Madag.
177 J4 **Berekfürdő** Hungary
211 B6 **Bereku** Tanz.
247 □2 **Berekua** Dominica
206 E5 **Berekum** Ghana
121 V3 **Berel'** Kazakh.
177 H6 **Beremend** Hungary
139 W5 **Berendeyevo** Rus. Fed.
252 C4 **Berenguela** Bol.
Berenice Libya see **Banghāzī**
223 L4 **Berens** r. Man. Can.
223 L4 **Berens Island** Man. Can.
223 L4 **Berens River** Man. Can.
213 □J4 **Berenty** Madag.
150 H6 **Bere Regis** Dorset, England U.K.
225 H4 **Beresford** N.B. Can.
236 G4 **Beresford** SD U.S.A.
136 E3 **Berestechko** Ukr.
197 P4 **Berești** Romania
137 M3 **Berestivka** Ukr.
137 O4 **Berestova** r. Ukr.
137 P5 **Berestove** Kharkivs'ka Oblast' Ukr.
137 P6 **Berestove** Zaporiz'ka Oblast' Ukr.
137 O4 **Berestoven'ka** Ukr.
137 L2 **Berestovets'** Ukr.
136 E3 **Berestyane** Ukr.
177 K4 **Berettyó** r. Hungary
177 K4 **Berettyóújfalu** Hungary
213 □J3 **Berevo** Madag.
213 □J3 **Berevo-Ranobe** Madag.
Bereza Belarus see **Byaroza**
137 K3 **Berezan'** Ukr.
137 K7 **Berezanka** Ukr.
137 S8 **Berezanskaya** Rus. Fed.
137 K7 **Berezans'kiy Lyman** l. Ukr.
139 Q4 **Berezayka** Rus. Fed.
136 G3 **Berezdiv** Ukr.
197 Q4 **Berezeni** Romania
136 D4 **Berezhany** Ukr.
Berezino Minskaya Voblasts' Belarus see **Byerazino**
Berezino Vitsyebskaya Voblasts' Belarus see **Byerazino**
120 C2 **Berezino** Kazakh.
137 L3 **Berezivka** Chernihivs'ka Oblast' Ukr.
137 L6 **Berezivka** Kirovohrads'ka Oblast' Ukr.
136 J6 **Berezivka** Odes'ka Oblast' Ukr.
136 G4 **Berezivka** Zhytomyrs'ka Oblast' Ukr.
136 H3 **Berezivka** Zhytomyrs'ka Oblast' Ukr.
137 K2 **Berezna** Ukr.
136 F2 **Berezne** Ukr.
137 L6 **Bereznehuvate** Ukr.
134 H3 **Bereznik** Rus. Fed.
134 L4 **Berezniki** Rus. Fed.
136 G3 **Bereznyky** Ukr.
Berezov Rus. Fed. see **Berezovo**
134 L3 **Berezovaya** r. Rus. Fed.
136 G2 **Berezove** Ukr.
134 I3 **Berezovik** Rus. Fed.
Berezovka Belarus see **Byarozawka**
100 E3 **Berezovka** Amurskaya Oblast' Rus. Fed.
139 V8 **Berezovka** Lipetskaya Oblast' Rus. Fed.
120 H1 **Berezovka** Orenburgskaya Oblast' Rus. Fed.
134 L4 **Berezovka** Permskaya Oblast' Rus. Fed.
Berezovka Ukr. see **Berezivka**
130 H3 **Berezovo** Rus. Fed.
100 I3 **Berezovyy** Rus. Fed.
136 I7 **Berezyne** Ukr.
172 H6 **Berg** Baden-Württemberg Ger.
171 E10 **Berg** Bayern Ger.
173 K6 **Berg** Bayern Ger.
169 C9 **Berg** Rheinland-Pfalz Ger.
165 J9 **Berg** Lux.
172 E4 **Berg (Pfalz)** Ger.
171 D8 **Berga** Sachsen-Anhalt Ger.
171 F9 **Berga** Thüringen Ger.
186 I3 **Berga** Spain
199 I3 **Bergama** Turkey
190 H4 **Bergamo** Italy
190 H4 **Bergamo** prov. Italy
186 E6 **Bergantes, Riu** r. Spain
182 C2 **Bergantiños** reg. Spain
183 P2 **Bergara** Spain
172 H6 **Bergatreute** Ger.
173 K3 **Berg bei Neumarkt in der Oberpfalz** Ger.
179 I2 **Berg bei Rohrbach** Austria
141 N6 **Bergby** Sweden
170 E4 **Berge** Brandenburg Ger.
168 E5 **Berge** Niedersachsen Ger.
186 E6 **Berge** Spain
190 E7 **Bergeggi** Italy
173 N6 **Bergen** Bayern Ger.
170 H2 **Bergen** Mecklenburg-Vorpommern Ger.
168 I5 **Bergen** Niedersachsen Ger.
164 G3 **Bergen** Neth.
142 B1 **Bergen** Norway
215 O3 **Bergen** S. Africa
232 H5 **Bergen** NY U.S.A.
168 K5 **Bergen (Dumme)** Ger.
235 G3 **Bergen County** county NJ U.S.A.
235 H3 **Bergenfield** NJ U.S.A.
164 F6 **Bergen op Zoom** Neth.
164 K3 **Bergentheim** Neth.
163 E6 **Bergerac** France
156 H6 **Bergères-lès-Vertus** France
263 B2 **Bergerson, Mount** Antarctica
160 F4 **Bergesserin** France
165 H6 **Bergeyk** Neth.
170 H5 **Bergfelde** Ger.
80 H1 **Berghan Point** North I. N.Z.
164 I5 **Bergharen** Neth.
172 D5 **Berghaupten** Ger.
178 H4 **Bergheim** Austria
173 K4 **Bergheim** Ger.
169 H8 **Bergheim (Edertal)** Ger.
169 C9 **Bergheim (Erft)** Ger.
164 I5 **Berghem** Neth.
171 H6 **Bergholz-Rehbrücke** Ger.
172 H5 **Berghülen** Ger.
178 H6 **Berg im Drautal** Austria
169 D9 **Bergisches Land** reg. Ger.
169 D9 **Bergisch Gladbach** Ger.
169 E7 **Bergkamen** Ger.
173 K5 **Bergkirchen** Ger.
212 C4 **Bergland** Namibia
226 E3 **Bergland** MI U.S.A.
140 N4 **Bergnäs** Sweden
140 O3 **Bergnäsviken** Sweden
169 E8 **Bergneustadt** Ger.
Bergomum Italy see **Bergamo**
232 E10 **Bergoo** WV U.S.A.
169 J10 **Bergrheinfeld** Ger.
143 O2 **Bergshamra** Sweden
141 N6 **Bergsjö** Sweden
172 G2 **Bergstraße-Odenwald** park Ger.
140 P4 **Bergsviken** Sweden
173 I2 **Bergtheim** Ger.
186 I3 **Bergueda** reg. Spain
183 N3 **Berguenda** Spain
156 D2 **Bergues** France
190 H2 **Bergün** Switz.
215 N4 **Bergville** S. Africa
171 G7 **Bergwitz** Ger.
107 L3 **Berh** Mongolia
94 E5 **Berhala, Selat** sea chan. Indon.
Berhampur W. Bengal India see **Baharampur**
197 P4 **Berheci** r. Romania
177 H4 **Berhida** Hungary
94 G6 **Berikat, Tanjung** pt Indon.
129 J3 **Berikey** Rus. Fed.
257 F2 **Berilo** Brazil
131 R4 **Beringa, Ostrov** i. Rus. Fed.
87 D8 **Beringarra** W.A. Austr.
165 I6 **Beringe** Neth.
184 D4 **Beringel** Port.
165 H6 **Beringen** Belgium
220 B3 **Bering Land Bridge National Preserve** nature res. AK U.S.A.
131 S3 **Beringovskiy** Rus. Fed.
220 A4 **Bering Sea** N. Pacific Ocean
220 B3 **Bering Strait** Rus. Fed./U.S.A.
151 J4 **Berinsfield** Oxfordshire, England U.K.
123 I9 **Berīs, Ra's** pt Iran
Berislav Ukr. see **Beryslav**
217 □1c **Bérive** Réunion
136 J6 **Berizky** Ukr.
185 N7 **Berja** Spain
169 J9 **Berka** Ger.
140 K5 **Berkåk** Norway
204 E2 **Berkane** Morocco
164 F5 **Berkel** Neth.
164 J4 **Berkel** r. Neth.
86 I3 **Berkeley** r. W.A. Austr.
150 H4 **Berkeley** Gloucestershire, England U.K.
240 J4 **Berkeley** CA U.S.A.
235 G3 **Berkeley Heights** NJ U.S.A.
232 G9 **Berkeley Springs** WV U.S.A.
168 K3 **Berkenthin** Ger.
151 K4 **Berkhamsted** Hertfordshire, England U.K.
173 I5 **Berkheim** Ger.
164 H3 **Berkhout** Neth.
262 U1 **Berkner Island** Antarctica
197 L7 **Berkovitsa** Bulg.
234 D4 **Berks County** county PA U.S.A.
151 J5 **Berkshire Downs** hills England U.K.
233 L6 **Berkshire Hills** MA U.S.A.
151 I3 **Berkswell** West Midlands, England U.K.
164 J3 **Berkum** Neth.
165 G6 **Berlaar** Belgium
156 G3 **Berlaimont** France
222 G4 **Berland** r. Alta Can.
184 H4 **Berlanga** Spain
183 O6 **Berlanga de Duero** Spain
165 F6 **Berlare** Belgium
184 A2 **Berlenga** i. Port.
140 T1 **Berlevåg** Norway
164 H5 **Berlicum** Neth.
164 I2 **Berlikum** Neth.
170 H5 **Berlin** Ger.
171 H5 **Berlin** land Ger.
235 J1 **Berlin** CT U.S.A.
233 J10 **Berlin** MD U.S.A.
233 □N4 **Berlin** NH U.S.A.
234 F5 **Berlin** NJ U.S.A.
232 D8 **Berlin** OH U.S.A.
232 G9 **Berlin** PA U.S.A.
226 F6 **Berlin** WI U.S.A.
262 O1 **Berlin, Mount** Antarctica
169 J8 **Berlingerode** Ger.
221 J2 **Berlinguet Inlet** Nunavut Can.
81 F8 **Berlins** South I. N.Z.
234 D3 **Berlinsville** PA U.S.A.
196 J6 **Berlişte** Romania
171 D8 **Berlstedt** Ger.
83 M7 **Bermagui** N.S.W. Austr.
172 G6 **Bermatingen** Ger.
122 G2 **Berme** Turkm.
259 E6 **Bermeja, Punta** pt Arg.
185 I8 **Bermeja, Sierra** mts Spain
185 L7 **Bermejales, Embalse de los** resr Spain
242 H5 **Bermejíllo** Mex.
260 D2 **Bermejo** Arg.
260 D3 **Bermejo** r. Arg.
258 F2 **Bermejo** r. Arg./Bol.
252 D5 **Bermejo** Bol.
261 G6 **Bermejo, Isla** i. Arg.
225 G2 **Bermen, Lac** l. Que. Can.
183 O2 **Bermeo** Spain
182 H6 **Bermillo de Sayago** Spain
231 □1 **Bermuda** terr. N. Atlantic Ocean
264 E4 **Bermuda Rise** sea feature N. Atlantic Ocean
190 C2 **Bern** Switz.
190 D2 **Bern** canton Switz.
261 I2 **Bernabé Rivera** Uru.
163 E9 **Bernac-Dessus** France
195 L3 **Bernalda** Italy
239 K9 **Bernalillo** NM U.S.A.
161 J9 **Bernarde, Sommet de la** mt. France
256 C5 **Bernardino de Campos** Brazil
227 O4 **Bernard Lake** Ont. Can.
261 G3 **Bernardo de Irigoyen** Arg.
261 F4 **Bernardo Larroude** Arg.
259 B8 **Bernardo O'Higgins, Parque Nacional** nat. park Chile
183 L6 **Bernardos** Spain
234 F3 **Bernardsville** NJ U.S.A.
176 D2 **Bernartice** Czech Rep.
261 F5 **Bernasconi** Arg.
172 E6 **Bernau** Baden-Württemberg Ger.
170 I5 **Bernau** Brandenburg Ger.
173 M6 **Bernau am Chiemsee** Ger.
161 J6 **Bernaude, Roche** mt. France/Italy
156 D3 **Bernaville** France
159 M3 **Bernay** France
173 J6 **Bernbeuren** Ger.
171 E7 **Bernburg (Saale)** Ger.
179 N4 **Berndorf** Austria
168 F4 **Berne** Ger.
Berne Switz. see **Bern**
226 J9 **Berne** IN U.S.A.
177 H3 **Bernecebaráti** Hungary
183 P3 **Bernedo** Spain
190 C3 **Berner Alpen** mts Switz.
146 B7 **Berneray** i. Western Isles, Scotland U.K.
146 A9 **Berneray** i. Western Isles, Scotland U.K.
Bernese Alps mts Switz. see **Berner Alpen**
182 I4 **Bernesga** r. Spain
160 J4 **Bernex** France
173 K3 **Berngau** Ger.
179 O2 **Bernhardsthal** Austria
173 M3 **Bernhardswald** Ger.
221 J2 **Bernier Bay** Nunavut Can.
87 B8 **Bernier Island** W.A. Austr.
161 H6 **Bernin** France
190 I3 **Bernina Pass** Switz.
183 O7 **Berninches** mt. Spain
146 D8 **Bernisdale** Highland, Scotland U.K.
165 E8 **Bernissart** Belgium
170 E3 **Bernitt** Ger.
172 C2 **Bernkastel-Kues** Ger.
163 D7 **Bernos-Beaulac** France
173 K6 **Bernried** Bayern Ger.
173 N4 **Bernried** Bayern Ger.
171 J8 **Bernsdorf** Ger.
173 I4 **Bernstadt** Baden-Württemberg Ger.
171 K8 **Bernstadt** Sachsen Ger.
232 A11 **Bernstadt** KY U.S.A.
179 N5 **Bernstein** Austria
234 C4 **Bernville** PA U.S.A.
Beroea Greece see **Veroia**
Beroea Syria see **Ḥalab**
190 E1 **Beromünster** Switz.
213 □J4 **Beroroha** Madag.
176 D2 **Beroun** Czech Rep.
176 D2 **Berounka** r. Czech Rep.
Berovina Madag. see **Beravina**
197 K9 **Berovo** Macedonia
191 L6 **Berra** Italy
189 A7 **Berrahal** Alg.
161 B10 **Berre** r. France
161 G10 **Berre, Étang de** lag. France
204 D2 **Berrechid** Morocco
161 G10 **Berre-l'Étang** France
82 H6 **Berri** S.A. Austr.
205 F2 **Berriane** Alg.
161 E8 **Berrias-et-Casteljau** France
83 L7 **Berridale** N.S.W. Austr.
146 I6 **Berriedale** Highland, Scotland U.K.
146 I6 **Berriedale Water** r. Scotland U.K.
158 D5 **Berrien** France
83 J6 **Berrigan** N.S.W. Austr.
183 Q3 **Berriozar** Spain
184 F5 **Berrocal** Spain
260 E3 **Berrotarán** Arg.
205 F1 **Berrouaghia** Alg.
150 F5 **Berrow** Somerset, England U.K.
156 H5 **Berru** France
83 M6 **Berry** N.S.W. Austr.
162 H2 **Berry** reg. France
160 B3 **Berry, Canal du** France
156 G5 **Berry-au-Bac** France
223 I5 **Berry Creek** r. Alta Can.
240 J3 **Berryessa, Lake** CA U.S.A.
150 F7 **Berry Head** England U.K.
246 E1 **Berry Islands** Bahamas
234 B3 **Berrysburg** PA U.S.A.
237 I7 **Berryville** AR U.S.A.
232 H9 **Berryville** VA U.S.A.
214 B2 **Berseba** Namibia
168 E5 **Bersenbrück** Ger.
136 I5 **Bershad'** Ukr.
162 C5 **Berson** France
191 J4 **Bersone** Italy
171 I7 **Berste** r. Ger.
120 I1 **Bersuat** Rus. Fed.
129 C4 **Berta** r. Turkey
94 E2 **Bertam** Malaysia
182 C3 **Bertamirans** Spain
225 G3 **Berté, Lac** l. Que. Can.
171 J8 **Berthelsdorf** Ger.
161 B8 **Bertholène** France
156 E3 **Bertincourt** France
251 I5 **Bertinho** Brazil
191 M7 **Bertinoro** Italy
165 I8 **Bertogne** Belgium
254 E3 **Bertolinía** Brazil
257 G2 **Bertópolis** Brazil
207 I5 **Bertoua** Cameroon
147 C6 **Bertraghboy Bay** Ireland
165 J9 **Bertrange** Lux.
157 M7 **Bertrichamps** France
165 H9 **Bertrix** Belgium
191 M6 **Bertuzzi, Valle** lag. Italy
77 H2 **Beru** atoll Gilbert Is Kiribati
168 D3 **Berumbur** Ger.
120 I7 **Beruniy** Uzbek.
251 F5 **Beruri** Brazil
114 F9 **Beruwala** Sri Lanka
197 K3 **Berveni** Romania
146 L9 **Bervie Water** r. Scotland U.K.
159 L3 **Berville-sur-Mer** France
83 J8 **Berwick** Vic. Austr.
233 O5 **Berwick** ME U.S.A.
227 R8 **Berwick** PA U.S.A.
149 M2 **Berwick-upon-Tweed** Northumberland, England U.K.
150 F2 **Berwyn** hills Wales U.K.
234 E4 **Berwyn** PA U.S.A.
137 M7 **Beryslav** Ukr.
Berytus Lebanon see **Beirut**
197 J6 **Berzasca** Romania
138 J5 **Bērzaune** Latvia
138 G6 **Beržė** r. Lith.
176 G5 **Berzence** Hungary
175 L1 **Berźniki** Pol.
185 I2 **Berzocana** Spain
138 K5 **Bērzpils** Latvia
161 C7 **Bès** r. France
95 L3 **Besah** Kalimantan Indon.
213 □J3 **Besalampy** Madag.
186 K3 **Besalú** Spain
160 I2 **Besançon** France
183 K3 **Besande** Spain
93 C8 **Besar** i. Indon.
95 K6 **Besar, Gunung** mt. Indon.
94 D2 **Besar, Gunung** mt. Malaysia
183 L2 **Besaya** r. Spain
120 F4 **Besbay** Kazakh.
160 D3 **Besbre** r. France
186 K4 **Bescanó** Spain
139 O9 **Besed'** r. Rus. Fed.
137 P2 **Besedino** Rus. Fed.
169 F10 **Beselich-Obertiefenbach** Ger.
177 H3 **Bešeňov** Slovakia
177 J4 **Besenyőtelek** Hungary
177 J4 **Besenyszög** Hungary
94 E3 **Beserah** Malaysia
121 N7 **Beshariq** Uzbek.
Besharyk Uzbek. see **Beshariq**
120 K8 **Beshkent** Uzbek.
116 F8 **Beshnagar** Madh. Prad. India
122 F7 **Beshneh** Iran
129 F4 **Besht'asheni** Georgia
Besh-Ter, Gora mt. Kyrg./Uzbek. see **Besh-Ter Toosu**
121 N6 **Besh-Ter Toosu** mt. Kyrg./Uzbek.
Beshtor Toghi mt. Kyrg./Uzbek. see **Besh-Ter Toosu**
186 G2 **Besiberri Sud** mt. Spain
93 D8 **Besikama** Timor Indon.
120 K8 **Beşir** Turkm.
127 J5 **Beşiri** Turkey
94 C2 **Besitang** Sumatera Indon.
175 J6 **Beskid Niski** hills Pol.
175 I6 **Beskid Sądecki** mts Pol.
Beskra Alg. see **Biskra**
177 H2 **Beskydy** park Czech Rep.
129 F2 **Beslan** Rus. Fed.
197 L9 **Beslet** mt. Bulg.
197 K8 **Besna Kobila** mt. Serbia
223 J4 **Besnard Lake** Sask. Can.
126 H5 **Besni** Turkey
121 P3 **Besoba** Kazakh.
128 C7 **Besor** watercourse Israel
190 F4 **Besozzo** Italy
Beşparmak Dağları mts Cyprus see **Pentadaktylos Range**
139 U7 **Besputa** r. Rus. Fed.
149 O6 **Bessacarr** South Yorkshire, England U.K.
Bessa Monteiro Angola see **Kindeje**
208 B3 **Bessan** C.A.R.
161 C10 **Bessan** France
208 B3 **Béssao** Chad
Bessarabka Moldova see **Basarabeasca**
160 C4 **Bessay-sur-Allier** France
121 M6 **Bessaz, Gora** mt. Kazakh.
147 J4 **Bessbrook** Northern Ireland U.K.
161 I6 **Besse** France
160 B5 **Besse-et-St-Anastaise** France
161 E8 **Bessèges** France
231 D9 **Bessemer** AL U.S.A.
226 D3 **Bessemer** MI U.S.A.
232 E8 **Bessemer** PA U.S.A.
160 F5 **Bessenay** France
172 G2 **Bessenbach** Ger.
159 M6 **Bessé-sur-Braye** France
161 I10 **Besse-sur-Issole** France
120 E5 **Besshoky, Gora** hill Kazakh.
163 H8 **Bessières** France
159 J3 **Bessin** reg. France
162 G3 **Bessines-sur-Gartempe** France
129 C1 **Besskorbnaya** Rus. Fed.
137 P3 **Bessonovka** Belgorodskaya Oblast' Rus. Fed.
135 I5 **Bessonovka** Penzenskaya Oblast' Rus. Fed.
162 I4 **Bessou, Mont de** hill France
164 H5 **Best** Neth.
120 F3 **Bestamak** Aktyubinskaya Oblast' Kazakh.
121 R3 **Bestamak** Vostochnyy Kazakhstan Kazakh.
171 I6 **Bestensee** Ger.
215 N4 **Besters** S. Africa
121 O1 **Bestobe** Kazakh.
143 L3 **Bestorp** Sweden
134 H3 **Bestuzhevo** Rus. Fed.
169 F8 **Bestwig** Ger.
84 D3 **Beswick** N.T. Austr.
84 D3 **Beswick Aboriginal Land** res. N.T. Austr.
213 □J3 **Betafo** Madag.
213 □J3 **Betanantanana** Madag.
216 □3b **Betancuria** Fuerteventura Canary Is
252 D4 **Betanzos** Bol.
182 D2 **Betanzos** Spain
182 D2 **Betanzos, Ría de** est. Spain
207 I5 **Bétaré Oya** Cameroon
250 B3 **Beté** Col.
226 G2 **Bete Grise** MI U.S.A.
210 C2 **Bete Hor** Eth.
186 B1 **Betelu** Spain
187 E8 **Bétera** Spain
207 F4 **Bétérou** Benin
94 F5 **Betet** i. Indon.
183 P7 **Beteta** Spain
128 C7 **Bet Guvrin** Israel
204 D2 **Beth, Oued** r. Morocco
215 N2 **Bethal** S. Africa
212 C5 **Bethanie** Namibia
235 J2 **Bethany** CT U.S.A.
236 H5 **Bethany** MO U.S.A.
237 G8 **Bethany** OK U.S.A.
117 I6 **Bethari** Nepal
177 K6 **Bethausen** Romania
220 B3 **Bethel** AK U.S.A.
235 I2 **Bethel** CT U.S.A.
233 □O4 **Bethel** ME U.S.A.
232 A10 **Bethel** OH U.S.A.
234 C4 **Bethel** PA U.S.A.
169 I6 **Betheln** Ger.
232 E8 **Bethel Park** PA U.S.A.
215 J9 **Bethelsdorp** S. Africa
246 □ **Bethel Town** Jamaica
156 H5 **Bétheny** France
151 N5 **Bethersden** Kent, England U.K.
150 D1 **Bethesda** Gwynedd, Wales U.K.
234 A7 **Bethesda** MD U.S.A.
232 D8 **Bethesda** OH U.S.A.
215 I7 **Bethesdaweg** S. Africa
156 E5 **Béthisy-St-Pierre** France
80 K4 **Bethlehem** North I. N.Z.
215 M4 **Bethlehem** S. Africa
234 E3 **Bethlehem** PA U.S.A.
128 D7 **Bethlehem** West Bank
163 G10 **Bethmale** France
156 G6 **Bethon** France
235 I3 **Bethpage** NY U.S.A.
215 J6 **Bethulie** S. Africa
156 E2 **Béthune** France
156 B4 **Béthune** r. France
123 M7 **Beti** Pak.
250 D2 **Betijoque** Venez.
257 E3 **Betim** Brazil
213 □J4 **Betioky** Madag.
95 J9 **Betiri, Gunung** mt. Indon.
Bet Lehem West Bank see **Bethlehem**
139 Q7 **Betlitsa** Rus. Fed.
116 E8 **Betma** Madh. Prad. India
156 F6 **Beton-Bazoches** France
95 I4 **Betong** Sarawak Malaysia
97 E12 **Betong** Thai.
84 H8 **Betoota** Qld Austr.
210 C2 **Beto Shet'** r. Eth.
208 C4 **Bétou** Congo
121 N4 **Betpak-Dala** Kazakh.
121 N5 **Betpak-Dala** plain Kazakh.
213 □J3 **Betrandraka** Madag.
213 □J4 **Betroka** Madag.
157 O6 **Betschdorf** France
128 D6 **Bet She'an** Israel
225 G3 **Betsiamites** Que. Can.
225 G3 **Betsiamites** r. Que. Can.
213 □J2 **Betsiboka** r. Madag.
226 H5 **Betsie, Point** MI U.S.A.
104 E3 **Betsu-zan** mt. Japan
246 G2 **Betsy Bay** Mayaguana Bahamas
226 I3 **Betsy Lake** MI U.S.A.
157 L5 **Bettelainville** France
178 E5 **Bettelwurf** mt. Austria
165 J9 **Bettembourg** Lux.
165 J9 **Bettendorf** Lux.
234 C6 **Betterton** MD U.S.A.
117 J6 **Bettiah** Bihar India
215 N2 **Bettiesdam** S. Africa
172 A2 **Bettingen** Ger.
143 M3 **Bettna** Sweden
190 H6 **Bettola** Italy
158 H5 **Betton** France
193 J1 **Bettona** Italy
146 H5 **Bettyhill** Highland, Scotland U.K.
147 J5 **Bettystown** Ireland
116 F9 **Betul** Madh. Prad. India
93 D8 **Betun** Timor Indon.
95 J4 **Betung Kerihun National Park** Indon.
164 I5 **Betuwe** reg. Neth.
116 G7 **Betwa** r. India
150 E1 **Betws-y-coed** Conwy, Wales U.K.
187 E8 **Betxi** Spain
138 G6 **Betygala** Lith.
174 E2 **Betyń, Jezioro** l. Pol.
156 E5 **Betz** France
169 E9 **Betzdorf** Ger.
165 J9 **Betzdorf** Lux.
173 K2 **Betzenstein** Ger.
173 I6 **Betzigau** Ger.
209 B6 **Béu** Angola
161 J8 **Beuil** France
83 I6 **Beulah** Vic. Austr.
150 E3 **Beulah** Powys, Wales U.K.
226 H5 **Beulah** MI U.S.A.
236 E2 **Beulah** ND U.S.A.
151 M5 **Beult** r. England U.K.
164 I5 **Beuningen** Neth.
169 J8 **Beuren** Ger.
202 B6 **Beurfou** well Chad
172 F5 **Beuron** Ger.
157 I7 **Beurville** France
Beuthen Pol. see **Bytom**
160 E3 **Beuvray, Mont** hill France
160 D2 **Beuvron** r. France
159 N7 **Beuvron** r. France
156 E2 **Beuvry** France
159 L3 **Beuzeville** France
193 J2 **Bevagna** Italy
190 B2 **Bevaix** Switz.
169 E6 **Bever** r. Ger.
161 L9 **Bévéra** r. France
87 D12 **Beverley** W.A. Austr.
149 Q6 **Beverley** East Riding of Yorkshire, England U.K.
233 O6 **Beverly** MA U.S.A.
234 F4 **Beverly** NJ U.S.A.
232 D9 **Beverly** OH U.S.A.
240 N7 **Beverly Hills** CA U.S.A.
223 K1 **Beverly Lake** Nunavut Can.
169 H7 **Bevern** Ger.
168 G4 **Beverstedt** Ger.
169 H7 **Beverungen** Ger.
164 G4 **Beverwijk** Neth.
156 C7 **Béville-le-Comte** France
150 H3 **Bewdley** Worcestershire, England U.K.
151 M5 **Bewl Water** resr England U.K.
190 C3 **Bex** Switz.
172 C3 **Bexbach** Ger.
151 M6 **Bexhill** East Sussex, England U.K.
199 J5 **Beyağaç** Turkey
127 M6 **Beyānlū** Iran
199 I1 **Beyazköy** Turkey
Beyce Turkey see **Orhaneli**
163 D6 **Beychac-et-Caillau** France
199 M2 **Beyciler** Turkey
199 J4 **Beydağ** Turkey
199 L6 **Bey Dağları** mts Turkey
129 B7 **Beydoğan** Turkey
199 J3 **Beyel** Turkey
171 E6 **Beyendorf** Ger.
199 L6 **Beykonak** Turkey
199 M2 **Beyköy** Bolu Turkey
199 L2 **Beyköy** Eskişehir Turkey
199 K1 **Beykoz** Turkey
206 C4 **Beyla** Guinea
Beylagan Azer. see **Beyläqan**
129 I6 **Beyläqan** Azer.
199 M3 **Beylikova** Turkey
203 I6 **Beylul** Eritrea
163 G6 **Beynac-et-Cazenac** France
162 H5 **Beynat** France
165 I7 **Beyne-Heusay** Belgium
120 F5 **Beyneu** Kazakh.
160 G5 **Beynost** France
199 I4 **Beyoba** Turkey
103 Q15 **Beyoneisu-retsugan** i. Japan
103 Q15 **Beyoneisu Retugan** i. Japan
126 E3 **Beypazarı** Turkey
126 H4 **Beypınarı** Turkey
114 D7 **Beypore** Kerala India
210 E3 **Beyra** Somalia
122 E8 **Beyram** Iran
Beyrouth Lebanon see **Beirut**
126 E5 **Beyşehir** Turkey
126 E5 **Beyşehir Gölü** l. Turkey
137 S8 **Beysug** Rus. Fed.
137 R7 **Beysug** r. Rus. Fed.
137 R7 **Beysugskiy Liman** lag. Rus. Fed.
137 R8 **Beysuzhek** r. Rus. Fed.
100 D2 **Beytonovo** Rus. Fed.
127 K5 **Beytüşşebap** Turkey
161 G7 **Bez** r. France
122 G4 **Bezameh** Iran
187 C7 **Bezas** Spain
178 A5 **Bezau** Austria
134 J4 **Bezbozhnik** Rus. Fed.
196 G5 **Bezdan** Vojvodina Serbia
160 G2 **Bèze** France
129 E2 **Bezengi** Rus. Fed.
122 G7 **Bezenjān** Iran
176 G4 **Bezenye** Hungary
138 M5 **Bezhanitskaya Vozvyshennost'** hills Rus. Fed.
138 M5 **Bezhanitsy** Rus. Fed.
197 M7 **Bezhanovo** Bulg.
139 T4 **Bezhetsk** Rus. Fed.
139 T4 **Bezhetskiy Verkh** reg. Rus. Fed.
129 H3 **Bezhta** Rus. Fed.
161 C10 **Béziers** France
175 I1 **Bezledy** Pol.
Bezmein Turkm. see **Abadan**
161 F9 **Bezouce** France
177 L3 **Bežovce** Slovakia
Bezwada Andhra Prad. India see **Vijayawada**
116 C7 **Bhabhar** Gujarat India
117 I7 **Bhabhua** Bihar India
116 E8 **Bhabra** Madh. Prad. India
116 C8 **Bhachau** Gujarat India
116 C7 **Bhachbhar** Rajasthan India
116 B9 **Bhadar** r. India
116 E3 **Bhadarwah** Jammu and Kashmir
123 P6 **Bhadaur** Punjab India
116 F7 **Bhadaura** Madh. Prad. India
117 J6 **Bhadgaon** Nepal
117 I7 **Bhadohi** Uttar Prad. India
116 E5 **Bhadra** Rajasthan India
114 G4 **Bhadrachalam** Andhra Prad. India
Bhadrachalam Road Station Andhra Prad. India see **Kottagudem**
116 D7 **Bhadrajan** Rajasthan India
117 K9 **Bhadrak** Orissa India
114 D6 **Bhadra Reservoir** India
114 D6 **Bhadravati** Karnataka India
123 L7 **Bhag** Pak.
111 C10 **Bhaga** r. India
117 K7 **Bhagalpur** Bihar India
117 L8 **Bhagirathi** r. India
114 E3 **Bhainsa** Andhra Prad. India
116 F9 **Bhainsdehi** Madh. Prad. India
117 M7 **Bhairab Bazar** Bangl.
117 I6 **Bhairawa** Nepal
Bhairawaha Nepal see **Bhairawa**
119 I4 **Bhairi Hol** mt. Pak.
123 N6 **Bhakkar** Pak.
Bhaktapur Nepal see **Bhadgaon**
Bhaleshear i. Scotland U.K. see **Baleshare**
114 E3 **Bhalki** Karnataka India
123 O5 **Bhalwal** Pak.
116 F9 **Bhamgarh** Madh. Prad. India
96 C2 **Bhamo** Myanmar
114 G3 **Bhamragarh** Mahar. India
116 G9 **Bhandara** Mahar. India
116 G7 **Bhander** Madh. Prad. India
116 H6 **Bhangaha** Uttar Prad. India
116 B8 **Bhangor** Gujarat India
115 I3 **Bhanjanagar** Orissa India
116 E7 **Bhanpura** Madh. Prad. India
116 G8 **Bhanrer Range** hills Madh. Prad. India
116 H9 **Bhanupratappur** Chhattisgarh India
Bharat country Asia see **India**
116 F6 **Bharatpur** Rajasthan India
117 J6 **Bharatpur** Nepal
117 N6 **Bhareli** r. India
123 J9 **Bhari** r. Pak.
116 G6 **Bharthana** Uttar Prad. India
116 D9 **Bharuch** Gujarat India
116 H9 **Bhatapara** Chhattisgarh India
Bhatarsaigh i. Scotland U.K. see **Vatersay**
114 C3 **Bhatghar Lake** India
117 L8 **Bhatiapara Ghat** Bangl.
Bhatinda Punjab India see **Bathinda**
114 D6 **Bhatkal** Karnataka India
Bhatnair Rajasthan India see **Hanumangarh**
117 L8 **Bhatpara** W. Bengal India
123 O5 **Bhaun Gharibwal** Pak.
114 E7 **Bhavani** Tamil Nadu India
114 E7 **Bhavani** r. India
114 E7 **Bhavani Sagar** l. India
116 D9 **Bhavnagar** Gujarat India
123 O6 **Bhawana** Pak.
115 H3 **Bhawanipatna** Orissa India
Bhearnaraigh, Eilean i. Western Isles, Scotland U.K. see **Berneray**
Bheemavaram Andhra Prad. India see **Bhimavaram**
215 O3 **Bhekuzulu** S. Africa
116 H7 **Bhelki** Madh. Prad. India
123 O5 **Bhera** Pak.
116 H5 **Bheri** r. Nepal
114 D3 **Bhigvan** Mahar. India
116 H9 **Bhilai** Chhattisgarh India
116 D7 **Bhildi** Gujarat India
116 E7 **Bhilwara** Rajasthan India
114 E4 **Bhima** r. India
116 C6 **Bhimar** Rajasthan India
114 G4 **Bhimavaram** Andhra Prad. India
123 P5 **Bhimbar** Pak.
116 H8 **Bhimlath** Madh. Prad. India
117 K6 **Bhimnagar** Bihar India
117 J6 **Bhimphedi** Nepal
116 G6 **Bhind** Madh. Prad. India
116 E7 **Bhindar** Rajasthan India
116 H6 **Bhinga** Uttar Prad. India
114 D3 **Bhingar** Mahar. India
116 D7 **Bhinmal** Rajasthan India
114 C3 **Bhiwandi** Mahar. India
116 F5 **Bhiwani** Haryana India
116 G6 **Bhogaipur** Uttar Prad. India
116 B9 **Bhogat** Gujarat India
116 F8 **Bhojpur** Madh. Prad. India
117 K6 **Bhojpur** Nepal
116 E9 **Bhokardan** Mahar. India
117 M8 **Bhola** Bangl.
116 G6 **Bhongaon** Uttar Prad. India
114 F4 **Bhongir** Andhra Prad. India
215 N6 **Bhongweni** S. Africa
116 F8 **Bhopal** Madh. Prad. India
114 G3 **Bhopalpatnam** Chhattisgarh India
114 C3 **Bhor** Mahar. India
Bhrigukaccha Gujarat India see **Bharuch**
117 J9 **Bhuban** Orissa India
117 J9 **Bhubaneshwar** Orissa India
Bhubaneswar Orissa India see **Bhubaneshwar**
117 N7 **Bhuban Hills** India
116 B8 **Bhuj** Gujarat India
96 D6 **Bhumiphol Dam** Thai.
215 P2 **Bhunya** Swaziland
116 E9 **Bhusawal** Mahar. India
117 M6 **Bhutan** country Asia
116 C6 **Bhuttewala** Rajasthan India
114 F7 **Bhuvanagiri** Tamil Nadu India
250 E5 **Biá** r. Brazil
209 E7 **Bia, Monts** mts Dem. Rep. Congo
96 F5 **Bia, Phou** mt. Laos
122 G8 **Bīabān** mts Iran
210 E3 **Biad** well Eth.
174 F4 **Biadki** Pol.
111 B9 **Biafo Glacier** Jammu and Kashmir
Biafra, Bight of g. Africa see **Benin, Bight of**
91 I7 **Biak** Papua Indon.
93 C4 **Biak** Sulawesi Indon.
91 I7 **Biak** i. Papua Indon.
174 F5 **Biała** Pol.
175 I5 **Biała** r. Pol.
174 F5 **Biała** r. Pol.
174 G4 **Biała-Parcela Pierwsza** Pol.
175 K2 **Biała Piska** Pol.
175 L3 **Biała Podlaska** Pol.
175 I4 **Biała Rawska** Pol.
174 F2 **Białe Błota** Pol.
175 K4 **Białka** r. Pol.
175 I4 **Białobrzegi** Mazowieckie Pol.
175 K5 **Białobrzegi** Podkarpackie Pol.
174 D2 **Białogard** Pol.
174 F2 **Białośliwie** Pol.
175 L3 **Białowieski Park Narodowy** nat. park Pol.
175 L3 **Białowieża** Pol.
174 E2 **Biały Bór** Pol.
175 I6 **Biały Dunajec** Pol.
175 L2 **Białystok** Pol.
194 F9 **Bianca, Punta** pt Sicilia Italy
194 H8 **Biancavilla** Sicilia Italy
195 K7 **Bianco** Italy
191 L5 **Bianco, Canale** canal Italy
194 E9 **Bianco, Capo** c. Sicilia Italy
190 D4 **Bianco, Corno** mt. Italy
Bianco, Monte mt. France/Italy see **Blanc, Mont**
107 Q9 **Biandangang Kou** r. mouth China
190 E5 **Biandrate** Italy
208 D3 **Bianga** C.A.R.
206 D5 **Biankouma** Côte d'Ivoire
206 E5 **Bianouan** Côte d'Ivoire
160 I3 **Bians-les-Usiers** France
190 E5 **Bianzè** Italy
107 R4 **Bianzhao** Jilin China
Bianzhuang Shandong China see **Cangshan**
92 E8 **Biao** Mindanao Phil.
116 F8 **Biaora** Madh. Prad. India
187 D10 **Biar** Spain
122 F3 **Bīārjmand** Iran
93 D2 **Biaro** i. Indon.
163 A9 **Biarritz** France
Biarritz airport France see **Parme**
163 B8 **Biarrotte** France
162 H6 **Biars-sur-Cère** France
124 G3 **Bi'ār Tabrāk** well Saudi Arabia
163 B7 **Bias** Aquitaine France
163 F7 **Bias** Aquitaine France
190 F3 **Biasca** Switz.
261 I2 **Biassini** Uru.
177 H4 **Biatorbágy** Hungary
203 F2 **Bibā** Egypt
102 S3 **Bibai** Japan
209 B8 **Bibala** Angola
208 A4 **Bibas** Gabon
83 L7 **Bibbenluke** N.S.W. Austr.
191 L8 **Bibbiena** Italy
191 J9 **Bibbona** Italy
223 M2 **Bibby Island** Nunavut Can.
207 I4 **Bibémi** Cameroon
172 E5 **Biberach** Ger.
172 H5 **Biberach an der Riß** Ger.
173 J4 **Biberbach** Ger.
173 J3 **Bibert** r. Ger.
206 E5 **Bibiani** Ghana
114 G9 **Bibile** Sri Lanka
191 O4 **Bibione** Italy
139 P5 **Bibirevo** Rus. Fed.
117 M7 **Bibiyana** r. Bangl.
172 E2 **Biblis** Ger.
Biblos Lebanon see **Jbail**
136 D4 **Bibrka** Ukr.
151 I4 **Bibury** Gloucestershire, England U.K.
138 J5 **Bicānu ezers** l. Latvia
257 F4 **Bicas** Brazil
177 M4 **Bicaz** Maramureș Romania
197 O4 **Bicaz** Neamț Romania
193 O5 **Biccari** Italy
126 E4 **Biçer** Turkey
151 J4 **Bicester** Oxfordshire, England U.K.
116 D7 **Bichabhera** Rajasthan India
247 □7 **Biche** Trin. and Tob.
210 C2 **Bichena** Eth.
Bicheng Chongqing China see **Bishan**
83 L9 **Bicheno** Tas. Austr.
100 I5 **Bichevaya** Rus. Fed.
207 H3 **Bichi** Nigeria
100 K2 **Bichi** r. Rus. Fed.
173 K6 **Bichl** Ger.
178 C5 **Bichlbach** Austria
114 C5 **Bicholim** Goa India
117 J6 **Bichraltar** Nepal
107 J1 **Bichura** Rus. Fed.
129 B2 **Bichvint'a** Georgia
129 B2 **Bichvint'is Konts'khi** pt Georgia
172 F2 **Bickenbach** Ger.
151 I3 **Bickenhill** West Midlands, England U.K.
84 F2 **Bickerton Island** N.T. Austr.
150 D7 **Bickleigh** Devon, England U.K.
150 E6 **Bickleigh** Devon, England U.K.
151 N4 **Bicknacre** Essex, England U.K.
241 U3 **Bicknell** UT U.S.A.
129 J5 **Bico** Azer.
93 F3 **Bicoli** Halmahera Indon.
187 D9 **Bicorp** Spain
184 C5 **Bicos** Port.
177 H4 **Bicske** Hungary
150 G2 **Bicton** Shropshire, England U.K.
209 B8 **Bicuari, Parque Nacional do** nat. park Angola
114 D3 **Bid** Mahar. India
207 G4 **Bida** Nigeria
163 B9 **Bidache** France
95 M2 **Bidadari, Tanjung** pt Malaysia
114 E4 **Bidar** Karnataka India
163 A9 **Bidart** France
116 E6 **Bidasar** Rajasthan India
125 N4 **Bidbid** Oman

233 □O5 Biddeford ME U.S.A.
151 N5 Biddenden Kent, England U.K.
164 I4 Biddinghuizen Neth.
149 M7 Biddulph Staffordshire, England U.K.
146 F9 Bidean nam Bian mt. Scotland U.K.
150 D5 Bideford Devon, England U.K.
Bideford Bay England U.K. see Barnstaple Bay
191 M7 Bidente r. Italy
151 I3 Bidford-on-Avon Warwickshire, England U.K.
140 Q2 Bidjovagge Norway
122 G7 Bīdkhan, Kūh-e mt. Iran
122 H4 Bīdokht Iran
205 F5 Bidon 5 tourist site Alg.
163 C9 Bidos France
176 B3 Bidouze r. France
177 K3 Bidovce Slovakia
100 G5 Bidzhan Rus. Fed.
100 H5 Bidzhar r. Rus. Fed.
Bié Angola see Kuito
209 C8 Bié prov. Angola
209 B8 Bié, Planalto do plat. Angola
169 H10 Bieber Ger.
172 E2 Biebesheim am Rhein Ger.
175 K2 Biebrza r. Pol.
175 K2 Biebrzański Park Narodowy nat. park Pol.
175 J6 Biecz Pol.
169 G9 Biedenkopf Ger.
171 E6 Biederitz Ger.
186 D3 Biel Spain
190 C1 Biel Switz.
177 I1 Bielańsko-Tyniecki Park Krajobrazowy Pol.
175 K3 Bielany-Żyłaki Pol.
175 E1 Bielawa Pol.
169 G6 Bielefeld Ger.
177 H2 Biele Karpaty park Slovakia
178 B6 Bielerhöhe pass Austria
190 C1 Bieler See l. Switz.
174 C2 Bielice Pol.
175 I5 Bieliny Kapitulne Pol.
Bielitz Pol. see Bielsko-Biała
190 E4 Biella Italy
190 E4 Biella prov. Italy
163 D9 Bielle France
186 F2 Bielsa Spain
175 H3 Bielsk Pol.
175 H6 Bielsko-Biała Pol.
175 L3 Bielsk Podlaski Pol.
169 I8 Bielstein hill Ger.
168 J4 Bienenbüttel Ger.
97 H9 Biên Hoa Vietnam
174 D4 Bieniów Pol.
160 H4 Bienne r. France
Bienne Switz. see Biel
190 I4 Bienno Italy
185 N3 Bienservida Spain
184 G4 Bienvenida Spain
184 G4 Bienvenida hill Spain
183 P7 Bienvenida mt. Spain
245 J5 Bienvenido Mex.
251 H4 Bienvenue Fr. Guiana
225 F2 Bienville, Lac l. Que. Can.
177 H1 Bierawa Pol.
174 G5 Bierawka r. Pol.
85 J9 Bierbank Qld Austr.
174 G5 Bierdzany Pol.
171 E7 Biere Ger.
190 A2 Bière Switz.
186 E3 Bierge Spain
159 J6 Bierné France
163 G10 Biert France
175 H5 Bieruń Pol.
174 F4 Bierutów Pol.
174 G3 Bierzwienna-Długa Pol.
174 D2 Bierzwnik Pol.
186 E2 Biescas Spain
170 E5 Biese r. Ger.
170 I5 Biesenthal Ger.
174 E1 Biesiekierz Pol.
215 J2 Biesiesvlei S. Africa
157 J7 Biesles France
175 H1 Biesowice Pol.
214 H7 Biesrespoort S. Africa
173 J6 Biessenhofen Ger.
175 K6 Bieszczady mts Pol.
175 K6 Bieszczadzki Park Narodowy nat. park Pol.
172 E4 Bietigheim Ger.
172 G4 Bietigheim-Bissingen Ger.
170 I4 Bietikow Ger.
190 D3 Bietschhorn mt. Switz.
165 H9 Bièvre Belgium
175 H3 Bieżuń Pol.
193 O4 Biferno r. Italy
208 A5 Bifoun Gabon
140 □C1 Bifröst Iceland
102 T2 Bifuka Japan
240 I2 Big r. CA U.S.A.
199 I2 Biga Turkey
199 I2 Biga r. Turkey
199 J3 Bigadiç Turkey
261 G3 Bigand Arg.
163 C6 Biganos France
187 D11 Bigastro Spain
199 H3 Biga Yarımadası pen. Turkey
238 I3 Big Baldy Mountain MT U.S.A.
222 F5 Big Bar Creek B.C. Can.
81 C11 Big Bay b. South I. N.Z.
226 G3 Big Bay MI U.S.A.
78 □5 Big Bay b. Vanuatu
226 G4 Big Bay de Noc MI U.S.A.
240 P7 Big Bear Lake CA U.S.A.
238 I3 Big Belt Mountains MT U.S.A.
215 P2 Big Bend Swaziland
237 D11 Big Bend National Park TX U.S.A.
237 J9 Big Black r. MS U.S.A.
236 G6 Big Blue r. NE U.S.A.
150 E7 Bigbury Bay England U.K.
150 E7 Bigbury-on-Sea Devon, England U.K.
80 □ Big Bush Chatham Is S. Pacific Ocean
237 E11 Big Canyon watercourse TX U.S.A.
246 C1 Big Cypress National Preserve nature res. FL U.S.A.
231 G13 Big Cypress National Preserve nature res. FL U.S.A.
82 H6 Big Desert Wilderness Park nature res. Vic. Austr.
226 E5 Big Eau Pleine Reservoir WI U.S.A.
78 □3a Bigej i. Kwajalein Marshall Is
78 □3a Bigej Channel Kwajalein Marshall Is
234 D5 Big Elk Creek r. MD U.S.A.
106 E4 Biger Nuur salt l. Mongolia
236 I1 Big Falls MN U.S.A.
226 A1 Big Fork r. MN U.S.A.
223 J4 Biggar Sask. Can.
146 I11 Biggar South Lanarkshire, Scotland U.K.
224 F3 Biggar, Lac l. Que. Can.
78 □3a Biggarenn i. Kwajalein Marshall Is
215 N4 Biggarsberg S. Africa
86 H3 Bigge Island W.A. Austr.
85 N8 Biggenden Qld Austr.
222 B3 Bigger, Mount B.C. Can.
78 □3a Biggerann i. Kwajalein Marshall Is
169 E8 Biggesee l. Ger.
151 M5 Biggin Hill Greater London, England U.K.
151 L3 Biggleswade Bedfordshire, England U.K.
240 K2 Biggs CA U.S.A.
238 D4 Biggs OR U.S.A.
238 H4 Big Hole r. MT U.S.A.
238 K3 Bighorn r. MT/WY U.S.A.
238 K4 Bighorn Mountains WY U.S.A.
208 D4 Bigi Dem. Rep. Congo
78 □3a Bigi i. Kwajalein Marshall Is
139 W8 Bigil'dino Rus. Fed.
129 I5 Bığır Azer.
221 K3 Big Island i. Nunavut Can.
222 G2 Big Island i. N.W.T. Can.
233 F11 Big Island VA U.S.A.
222 C2 Big Kalzas Lake Y.T. Can.
237 E10 Big Lake TX U.S.A.
236 I1 Big Lake l. ME U.S.A.
238 H5 Big Lost r. ID U.S.A.
Big Moggy Island Stewart I. N.Z. see Mokinui Island
238 L2 Big Muddy Creek r. MT U.S.A.
158 F6 Bignan France
190 F3 Bignasco Switz.
206 A3 Bignona Senegal
209 E6 Bigobo Dem. Rep. Congo
163 D10 Bigorre reg. France
232 F11 Big Otter r. VA U.S.A.
240 N4 Big Pine CA U.S.A.
240 M7 Big Pine Peak CA U.S.A.
238 K3 Big Porcupine Creek r. MT U.S.A.
222 C3 Big Port Walter AK U.S.A.
226 I6 Big Rapids MI U.S.A.
226 E5 Big Rib r. WI U.S.A.
223 J4 Big River Sask. Can.
226 H5 Big Sable Point MI U.S.A.
222 C2 Big Salmon Y.T. Can.
222 C2 Big Salmon r. Y.T. Can.
223 L3 Big Sand Lake Man. Can.
238 I2 Big Sandy MT U.S.A.
238 J6 Big Sandy r. WY U.S.A.
241 S7 Big Sandy watercourse AZ U.S.A.
236 D6 Big Sandy Creek r. CO U.S.A.
223 J4 Big Sandy Lake Sask. Can.
226 A3 Big Sandy Lake MN U.S.A.
236 G4 Big Sioux r. SD U.S.A.
240 O3 Big Smokey Valley NV U.S.A.
81 B14 Big South Cape Island Stewart I. N.Z.
237 E9 Big Spring TX U.S.A.
236 D5 Big Springs NE U.S.A.
223 I5 Big Stone Alta Can.
236 G3 Big Stone City SD U.S.A.
232 C12 Big Stone Gap VA U.S.A.
223 M4 Bigstone Lake Man. Can.
237 J5 Big Sunflower r. MS U.S.A.
240 K5 Big Sur CA U.S.A.
237 H10 Big Thicket National Preserve nature res. TX U.S.A.
238 J4 Big Timber MT U.S.A.
224 B2 Big Trout Lake Ont. Can.
224 B2 Big Trout Lake l. Ont. Can.
186 G2 Bigüézal Spain
192 C2 Biguglia Corse France
192 C2 Biguglia, Étang de lag. Corse France
222 H4 Big Valley Alta Can.
241 U4 Big Water UT U.S.A.
227 O4 Bigwin Ont. Can.
188 E3 Bihać Bos.-Herz.
117 J7 Bihar state India
177 K4 Biharia Romania
117 K7 Bihariganj Bihar India
177 K4 Biharkeresztes Hungary
177 K4 Biharnagybajom Hungary
117 J7 Bihar Sharif Bihar India
177 K5 Biharugra Hungary
177 K5 Biharugraihalastavak lakes Hungary
177 L5 Bihor county Romania
197 K4 Bihor, Vârful mt. Romania
102 V3 Bihoro Japan
177 L5 Bihorului, Munții mts Romania
117 N6 Bihpuriagaon Assam India
120 F4 Biikzhal Kazakh.
116 E9 Bijagarh Madh. Prad. India
206 A4 Bijagós, Arquipélago dos is Guinea-Bissau
116 E7 Bijainagar Rajasthan India
116 F6 Bijaipur Madh. Prad. India
114 D4 Bijapur Karnataka India
122 B4 Bījār Iran
114 G3 Bijarpur Chhattisgarh India
116 G7 Bijawar Madh. Prad. India
116 E3 Bijbehara Jammu and Kashmir
188 G3 Bijeljina Bos.-Herz.
188 E3 Bijelolasica mt. Croatia
196 H7 Bijelo Polje Montenegro
116 H8 Bijeraghogarh Madh. Prad. India
Bijiang Yunnan China see Zhiziluo
108 E5 Bijie Guizhou China
114 G3 Bijji Chhattisgarh India
117 M6 Bijni Assam India
116 G5 Bijnor Uttar Prad. India
123 N7 Bijnot Pak.
116 E7 Bijolia Rajasthan India
217 □2 Bijoutier i. Seychelles
125 J3 Bijrān well Saudi Arabia
125 J3 Bijrān, Khashm hill Saudi Arabia
116 D6 Bikampur Rajasthan India
116 D5 Bikaner Rajasthan India
120 J5 Bikbauli Kazakh.
128 D5 Bikfaiya Lebanon
100 I5 Bikin Rus. Fed.
100 I5 Bikin r. Rus. Fed.
213 F4 Bikita Zimbabwe
210 B2 Bikori Sudan
208 C5 Bikoro Dem. Rep. Congo
108 E2 Bikou Gansu China
108 E2 Bikou Shuiku resr Gansu China
177 I6 Bikovo Vojvodina Serbia
117 J7 Bikramganj Bihar India
137 R4 Bila r. Ukr.
137 S4 Bila r. Ukr.
92 E7 Bilaa Point Mindanao Phil.
129 K5 Biläcarı Azer.
125 N5 Bilād Banī Bū 'Alī Oman
125 N4 Bilād Banī Bū Ḩasan Oman
124 E5 Bilād Ghāmid reg. Saudi Arabia
124 E5 Bilād Zahrān reg. Saudi Arabia
137 M6 Bila Krynytsya Ukr.
129 B7 Bilaloğlu Turkey
207 E3 Bilanga Burkina
95 M4 Bilangbilangan i. Indon.
116 D6 Bilara Rajasthan India
116 G5 Bilari Uttar Prad. India
116 I8 Bilaspur Chhattisgarh India
116 F4 Bilaspur Hima. Prad. India
129 J6 Biläsuvar Azer.
129 J6 Biläsuvar Azer.
92 C9 Bilatan i. Phil.
136 J4 Bila Tserkva Ukr.
97 D7 Bilauktaung Range mts Myanmar/Thai.
183 O2 Bilbao Spain
203 F2 Bilbays Egypt
Bilbo Spain see Bilbao
197 N3 Bilbor Romania
146 J6 Bilbster Highland, Scotland U.K.
107 L1 Bil'chir Rus. Fed.
140 □B1 Bíldudalur Iceland
175 M6 Bile Ukr.
188 G4 Bileća Bos.-Herz.
199 K2 Bilecik Turkey
199 L2 Bilecik prov. Turkey
188 G4 Bilećko Jezero resr Bos.-Herz./Montenegro
196 I5 Biled Romania
129 J6 Bīleh Savār Iran
177 G2 Bílé Karpaty park Czech Rep.
137 Q5 Bilen'ke Donets'ka Oblast' Ukr.
137 O6 Bilen'ke Zaporiz'ka Oblast' Ukr.
210 D4 Bilesha Plain Kenya
175 K5 Biłgoraj Pol.
211 A5 Bilharamulo Tanz.
116 H6 Bilhaur Uttar Prad. India
136 J7 Bilhorod-Dnistrovs'kyy Ukr.
208 C2 Bili Chad
208 E3 Bili Dem. Rep. Congo
208 D3 Bili r. Dem. Rep. Congo
131 R3 Bilibino Rus. Fed.
211 D8 Bilibiza Moz.
129 B6 Bilice Turkey
Bilikōl l. Kazakh. see Biylikol', Ozero
96 C6 Bilin Myanmar
176 C1 Bílina Czech Rep.
193 Q6 Bilioso r. Italy
92 E6 Biliran i. Phil.
198 B2 Bilisht Albania
210 D4 Bilis Qooqaani Somalia
95 M2 Bilit Sabah Malaysia
107 R7 Biliu He r. China
177 M3 Bilky Ukr.
238 L5 Bill WY U.S.A.
87 C9 Billabalong W.A. Austr.
Billabong Creek r. N.S.W. Austr. see Moulamein Creek
87 C9 Billabong Roadhouse W.A. Austr.
183 O2 Billao, Cabo de c. Spain
142 H4 Billdal Sweden
168 J3 Bille r. Ger.
169 D7 Billerbeck Ger.
163 D9 Billère France
151 M4 Billericay Essex, England U.K.
160 H4 Billiat France
82 H6 Billiat Conservation Park nature res. S.A. Austr.
172 G3 Billigheim Ger.
86 I5 Billiluna W.A. Austr.
86 I5 Billiluna Aboriginal Reserve W.A. Austr.
264 J2 Billingford Norfolk, England U.K.
149 O4 Billingham Stockton-on-Tees, England U.K.
149 Q7 Billinghay Lincolnshire, England U.K.
238 J4 Billings MT U.S.A.
151 L5 Billingshurst West Sussex, England U.K.
Billiton i. Indon. see Belitung
151 P2 Billockby Norfolk, England U.K.
150 G6 Bill of Portland hd England U.K.
160 C5 Billom France
142 F6 Billund Denmark
141 J9 Billund airport Denmark
241 R7 Bill Williams r. AZ U.S.A.
241 T6 Bill Williams Mountain AZ U.S.A.
160 C4 Billy France
207 I2 Bilma Niger
210 C2 Bīlo Eth.
85 M8 Biloela Qld Austr.
176 F5 Bilo Gora hills Croatia
137 N8 Bilohirs'k Ukr.
136 F3 Bilohir"ya Ukr.
136 F4 Bilohorodka Khmel'nyts'ka Oblast' Ukr.
136 J3 Bilohorodka Kyivs'ka Oblast' Ukr.
251 G4 Biloku Guyana
137 R4 Bilokurakyne Ukr.
114 E3 Biloli Mahar. India
137 S4 Biloluts'k Ukr.
137 N2 Bilopillya Ukr.
136 F3 Bilotyn Ukr.
137 L3 Bilousivka Ukr.
177 H2 Bílovec Czech Rep.
177 G2 Bílovice Czech Rep.
137 S4 Bilovods'k Ukr.
237 K10 Biloxi MS U.S.A.
137 L7 Bilozerka Ukr.
137 Q5 Bilozers'ke Ukr.
84 G8 Bilpa Morea Claypan salt flat Qld Austr.
169 J7 Bilshausen Ger.
136 D4 Bil'shivtsi Ukr.
116 G5 Bilsi Uttar Prad. India
137 N3 Bil's'k Ukr.
136 E2 Bil's'ka Volya Ukr.
146 J11 Bilston Midlothian, Scotland U.K.
164 H4 Bilthoven Neth.
202 D6 Biltine Chad
202 D6 Biltine pref. Chad
140 P2 Bilto Norway
149 Q6 Bilton East Riding of Yorkshire, England U.K.
96 C6 Bilugyun Island Myanmar
137 O4 Bilukhivka Ukr.
93 C3 Bilungala Sulawesi Indon.
242 □R10 Bilwascarma Nic.
136 J7 Bilyayivka Ukr.
175 K6 Bilychi Ukr.
137 N4 Bilyky Ukr.
136 I4 Bilylivka Ukr.
136 I6 Bilyne Ukr.
137 Q5 Bilyts'ke Ukr.
136 D5 Bilyy Cheremosh r. Ukr.
137 Q3 Bilyy Kolodyaz' Ukr.
165 I7 Bilzen Belgium
208 E4 Bima r. Dem. Rep. Congo
95 M9 Bima Sumbawa Indon.
95 M9 Bima, Teluk b. Sumbawa Indon.
209 B7 Bimbe Angola
207 F4 Bimbila Ghana
208 C3 Bimbo C.A.R.
246 D1 Bimini Islands Bahamas
115 H4 Bimlipatam Andhra Prad. India
129 H6 Binä Dağlıq Qarabağ Azer.
129 L5 Binä Azer.
173 N5 Bina r. Ger.
177 H4 Bíňa Slovakia
127 N5 Bināb Iran
186 F4 Binaced Spain
116 G7 Bina-Etawa Madh. Prad. India
93 F5 Binaija, Gunung mt. Seram Indon.
92 D6 Binalbagan Negros Phil.
122 H3 Bīnālūd, Kūh-e mts Iran
209 B6 Binanga Dem. Rep. Congo
122 H4 Binar pass Iran
175 J6 Binarowa Pol.
156 B8 Binas France
190 G5 Binasco Italy
95 I3 Binatang Sarawak Malaysia
85 K6 Binbee Qld Austr.
126 H4 Binboğa Daği mt. Turkey
149 Q7 Binbrook Lincolnshire, England U.K.
165 F8 Binche Belgium
107 P8 Bincheng Shandong China
Bincheng Shandong China see Binzhou
108 C6 Binchuan Yunnan China
208 B2 Binder Chad
116 H6 Bindki Uttar Prad. India
173 L2 Bindlach Ger.
85 L9 Bindle Qld Austr.
Bindloe Island Islas Galápagos Ecuador see Marchena, Isla
209 C6 Bindu Dem. Rep. Congo
213 F3 Bindura Zimbabwe
186 F4 Binefar Spain
148 D3 Binevenagh hill Northern Ireland U.K.
213 E3 Binga Zimbabwe
213 G3 Binga, Monte mt. Moz.
83 M3 Bingara N.S.W. Austr.
114 C7 Bingaram i. India
84 F3 Bing Bong N.T. Austr.
106 H8 Bingcaowan Gansu China
172 G5 Bingen Ger.
172 D2 Bingen am Rhein Ger.
164 J5 Bingerden Neth.
206 E5 Bingerville Côte d'Ivoire
151 K2 Bingham Nottinghamshire, England U.K.
233 □P3 Bingham ME U.S.A.
147 B4 Binghamstown Ireland
233 J6 Binghamton NY U.S.A.
202 B3 Bin Ghanīmah, Jabal hills Libya
202 B1 Bin Ghashir Libya
149 N6 Bingley West Yorkshire, England U.K.
Bingmei Guizhou China see Congjiang
127 J4 Bingöl Turkey
129 B6 Bingöl prov. Turkey
127 J4 Bingol Dağı mt. Turkey
129 C6 Bingöl Dağları mts Turkey
Bingxi Jiangxi China see Yushan
108 B4 Bingzhongluo Yunnan China
97 I8 Binh Đinh Vietnam
96 H4 Binh Gia Vietnam
158 F4 Binic France
92 D7 Binicuil Negros Phil.
202 C4 Bini Erda well Chad
186 D2 Biniés Spain
117 I9 Binika Orissa India
187 K8 Binissalem Spain
94 C3 Binjai Sumatera Indon.
202 C2 Bin Jawwād Libya
210 F2 Binna, Raas pt Somalia
83 L4 Binnaway N.S.W. Austr.
146 G9 Binnein Mòr mt. Scotland U.K.
168 H5 Binnen Ger.
93 D7 Binongko i. Indon.
129 D6 Binpınar Turkey
117 K8 Binpur W. Bengal India
81 F10 Binser, Mount South I. N.Z.
210 B2 Bīnshangul Gumuz admin. reg. Eth.
173 J4 Binswangen Ger.
94 F4 Bintan i. Indon.
94 D2 Bintang, Bukit mts Malaysia
92 C5 Bintuan Phil.
94 E7 Bintuhan Sumatera Indon.
95 J3 Bintulu Sarawak Malaysia
92 C5 Binubusan Luzon Phil.
100 E6 Binxian Heilong. China
107 K9 Binxian Shaanxi China
Binxian Shandong China see Bincheng
108 G7 Binyang Guangxi China
207 G4 Bin-Yauri Nigeria
170 I2 Binz, Ostseebad Ger.
172 D6 Binzen Ger.
Binzhou Guangxi China see Binyang
Binzhou Heilong. China see Binxian
107 P8 Binzhou Shandong China
260 A5 Biobío admin. reg. Chile
260 A5 Biobío r. Chile
207 H6 Bioco i. Equat. Guinea
188 E4 Biograd na Moru Croatia
196 H8 Biogradska Gora nat. park Montenegro
Bioko i. Equat. Guinea see Bioco
188 F4 Biokovo park Croatia
160 G6 Biol France
190 C4 Bionaz Italy
186 H4 Biosca Spain
161 K9 Biot France
186 C3 Biota Spain
204 C3 Biougra Morocco
168 E5 Bippen Ger.
111 K10 Bi Qu r. Qinghai China
257 E3 Biquinhas Brazil
Bir Mahar. India see Bid
210 D2 Bir, Ras pt Djibouti
100 H4 Bira Rus. Fed.
100 H4 Bira r. Rus. Fed.
124 C2 Bi'r Abā al 'Ajjāj well Saudi Arabia
203 G4 Bi'r Abraq well Egypt
126 C8 Bi'r Abū Baṭṭah well Egypt
128 A9 Bi'r Abū Daraj well Egypt
203 F5 Bir Abu Garad well Sudan
203 G4 Bi'r Abū Hashīm well Egypt
203 F4 Bi'r Abū Ḩuṣayn well Egypt
128 G2 Bi'r Abū Jady oasis Syria
202 E3 Bi'r Abū Minqār well Egypt
202 A3 Bi'r ad Damar well Libya
128 A8 Bi'r ad Duwaydār well Egypt
202 D3 Bi'r adh Dhakar well Libya
123 I8 Bīrag, Kūh-e mts Iran
204 C4 Bîr Aïdiat well Maur.
202 B3 Birāk Libya
100 G4 Birakan Rus. Fed.
128 B7 Bi'r al 'Abd Egypt
124 D3 Bi'r al Amīr well Saudi Arabia
124 D3 Bi'r al Aṭbaq well Saudi Arabia
124 D4 Bi'r al 'Awādī well Saudi Arabia
202 B2 Bi'r al Fātīyah well Libya
202 B1 Bi'r al Ghanam Libya
128 G4 Bi'r al Ḩalbā well Syria
203 G4 Bi'r al Ḩaymūr well Egypt
124 E3 Bi'r al Ḩisw well Saudi Arabia
202 D3 Bi'r al Ikhwān well Libya
202 B3 Bi'r al Jadīd well Libya
124 F5 Bi'r al Jāhilīyah well Saudi Arabia
128 B8 Bi'r al Jifjāfah well Egypt
202 E2 Bi'r al Khamsah well Egypt
206 B2 Bir Allah well Maur.
128 B9 Bi'r al Māliḩah well Egypt
203 H3 Bi'r al Mashī well Saudi Arabia
202 B3 Bi'r al Mastūtah well Libya
127 J7 Bī'r al Mulūsi Iraq
128 G4 Bi'r al Munbaṭiḩ well Syria
202 A2 Bi'r al Mushayqīq well Libya
202 C2 Bi'r al Muwaylih well Libya
202 E2 Bi'r al Qaṭrānī well Egypt
124 C2 Bi'r al Qurr well Saudi Arabia
202 E3 Bi'r al Ubbayiḑ well Egypt
128 C10 Bi'r al 'Udayd well Egypt
204 C5 Bir 'Amrâne well Maur.
134 G3 Birandozero Rus. Fed.
202 E2 Bi'r an Nuṣṣ well Egypt
204 B5 Bir Anzarane Western Sahara
208 D2 Birao C.A.R.
205 H2 Bir Aouine well Tunisia
202 B2 Bi'r ar 'Alaqah well Libya
124 E3 Bi'r 'Arja well Saudi Arabia
126 B8 Bi'r ar Rābiyah well Egypt
203 G2 Bi'r ar Rummānah Egypt
124 F4 Bi'r as Sakhā well Saudi Arabia
128 C9 Bi'r as Sawrah well Egypt
110 J6 Biratar Bulak spring China
117 K6 Biratnagar Nepal
102 T4 Biratori Japan
202 E2 Bi'r aṭ Ṭarfāwī well Libya
125 J4 Bi'r 'Azīz well Saudi Arabia
124 F6 Bi'raz Zurq well Saudi Arabia
128 F4 Bī'r Başīrī well Syria
128 C8 Bi'r Bayḑā' well Egypt
124 C2 Bi'r Baydā well Saudi Arabia
202 E2 Bi'r Baylī well Egypt
204 C4 Bîr Bel Guerdâne well Maur.
204 E4 Bir Ben Takoul well Alg.
202 E5 Bir Bidi well Sudan
202 D3 Bi'r Bū Athlah well Libya
124 D3 Bi'r Budayy well Saudi Arabia
202 A3 Bi'r Bū Rāḩah well Libya
124 E5 Bi'r Buraym well Saudi Arabia
126 I5 Bi'r Buṭaymān Syria
222 H3 Birch r. Alta Can.
204 D5 Bir Chali well Mali
223 J4 Birch Hills Sask. Can.
151 O5 Birchington Kent, England U.K.
83 I6 Birchip Vic. Austr.
177 L6 Birchiș Romania
222 G5 Birch Island B.C. Can.
222 G2 Birch Lake N.W.T. Can.
223 M5 Birch Lake Ont. Can.
223 I4 Birch Lake Sask. Can.
226 C2 Birch Lake MN U.S.A.
222 H3 Birch Mountains Y.T. Can.
223 K4 Birch River Man. Can.
232 E10 Birch River WV U.S.A.
227 K6 Birch Run MI U.S.A.
226 C4 Birchwood WI U.S.A.
210 D3 Bircot Eth.
175 K6 Bircza Pol.
147 F7 Birdhill Ireland
208 F3 Bir Di Sudan
203 F4 Bi'r Dibs well Egypt
234 C4 Bird in Hand PA U.S.A.
202 E2 Bi'r Diqnāsh well Egypt
Bird Island N. Mariana Is see Farallon de Medinilla
205 H3 Bir Dolmane well Alg.
234 D4 Birdsboro PA U.S.A.
241 U2 Birdseye UT U.S.A.
84 G8 Birdsville Qld Austr.
234 B7 Birdsville MD U.S.A.
84 D3 Birdum r. N.T. Austr.
126 H5 Birecik Turkey
204 E4 Bir ed Deheb well Alg.
205 G2 Bir el Arbi well Alg.
205 H2 Bir el Ghoralia well Tunisia
205 E4 Bir El Hadjaj well Alg.
Birendranagar Nepal see Surkhet
211 A5 Birenga Rwanda
202 E5 Bir en Natrûn well Sudan
203 G5 Bir en Nugeim well Sudan
205 G2 Bir es Smeha well Alg.
94 B2 Bireun Sumatera Indon.
125 I4 Bi'r Fāḑil well Saudi Arabia
124 C1 Bi'r Fajr well Saudi Arabia
203 G5 Bir Fanoidig well Sudan
125 I4 Bi'r Fardān well Saudi Arabia
202 E2 Bi'r Fu'ād well Egypt
202 D6 Bir Furawiya well Sudan
204 A5 Bir Gandouz Western Sahara
124 G4 Bi'r Ghawdah well Saudi Arabia
202 D2 Bi'r Ghayzal well Libya
199 J4 Birgi Turkey
195 □ Birgu Malta
125 J6 Bir Hādī oasis Saudi Arabia
128 H4 Bi'r Ḩajal well Syria
210 C2 Birhan mt. Eth.
124 F4 Bi'r Haraqī well Saudi Arabia
128 B8 Bi'r Ḩasanah well Egypt
203 G4 Bir Hatab well Sudan
124 D3 Bi'r Ḩaymir well Saudi Arabia
124 D2 Bi'r Ḩayzān well Saudi Arabia
203 G4 Bir Hismet 'Umar well Sudan
124 F4 Bi'r Ḩudūf well Saudi Arabia
203 G4 Bir Huwait well Sudan
124 E3 Bi'r Ḩuwaymidah well Saudi Arabia
92 E5 Biri i. Phil.
124 C3 Bi'r Ibn Ghunayn well Saudi Arabia
Bi'r Ibn Hirmās Saudi Arabia see Al Bi'r
125 I4 Bir Ibn Juhayyim Saudi Arabia
124 F6 Bi'r Ibn Sarrār well Saudi Arabia
124 G6 Bi'r Īdīmah well Saudi Arabia
256 B4 Birigüi Brazil
128 E3 Bīrīn Syria
129 G4 Birinci Şıxlı Azer.
208 D3 Birini C.A.R.
202 E2 Bi'r Isṭabl well Egypt
122 H5 Bīrjand Iran
124 C2 Bi'r Jaydah well Saudi Arabia
124 G8 Bi'r Jifah well Yemen
202 E2 Bi'r Jubnī well Libya
124 F5 Bi'r Jugjug well Saudi Arabia
125 M4 Birkat al Mawz Oman
142 E3 Birkeland Norway
172 F2 Birkenau Ger.
172 F4 Birkenfeld Baden-Württemberg Ger.
172 H2 Birkenfeld Bayern Ger.
172 C2 Birkenfeld Rheinland-Pfalz Ger.
149 K7 Birkenhead Merseyside, England U.K.
169 E9 Birken-Honigsessen Ger.
170 H5 Birkenwerder Berlin Ger.
168 L1 Birket Denmark
179 M5 Birkfeld Austria
168 J1 Birkholm i. Denmark
124 C2 Bi'r Khurbah well Saudi Arabia
124 E4 Bi'r Khuwārah well Saudi Arabia
203 G4 Bir Kiau well Sudan
127 L5 Bīrkim Iraq
195 □ Birkirkara Malta
82 C2 Birksgate Range hills S.A. Austr.
169 J8 Birkungen Ger.
203 F4 Bi'r Kusaybah well Egypt
137 N3 Birky Ukr.
203 G4 Bir Labasoi well Sudan
Bîrlad Romania see Bârlad
128 B7 Bi'r Lahfān well Egypt
204 C4 Bir Lahmar Western Sahara
121 O5 Birlik Zhambylskaya Oblast' Kazakh.
121 O6 Birlik Zhambylskaya Oblast' Kazakh.
203 G4 Bir Likeit el Fauqani well Sudan
203 G4 Bir Liseila well Sudan
203 G4 Bi'r Majal well Egypt
123 M5 Birmal reg. Afgh.
124 F4 Bi'r Malīyah well Saudi Arabia
151 I3 Birmingham West Midlands, England U.K.
231 D9 Birmingham AL U.S.A.
202 E4 Bi'r Misāḩa well Egypt
117 J8 Birmitrapur Orissa India
204 C4 Bîr Mogreïn Maur.
128 G4 Bi'r Muḩaymid al Wazwaz well Syria
128 D9 Bi'r Mujayfil well Saudi Arabia
203 G4 Bi'r Murrah well Egypt
124 C3 Bi'r Nabt well Saudi Arabia
203 F2 Bi'r Nāḩid oasis Egypt
203 G4 Bi'r Najīb well Egypt
124 D3 Bi'r Nasīf Saudi Arabia
203 G4 Bir Nawari well Sudan
178 G6 Birnbaum Austria
178 G5 Birnhorn mt. Austria
207 F4 Birni Benin
78 □5 Birnie i. Kiribati
207 F3 Birnin-Gaouré Niger
207 G4 Birnin-Gwari Nigeria
207 G3 Birnin-Kebbi Nigeria
207 G3 Birnin Konni Niger
207 H4 Birnin Kudu Nigeria
207 H3 Birniwa Nigeria
202 E5 Bir Nukheila well Sudan
100 H4 Birobidzhan Rus. Fed.
100 H4 Birofel'd Rus. Fed.
163 F6 Biron France
92 B7 Birong Palawan Phil.
204 E4 Bir Ould Brini well Alg.
204 E5 Bir Ounâne well Mali
117 K6 Birpur Bihar India
202 E2 Bi'r Qaşīr as Sirr well Egypt
203 G3 Bi'r Qulayb well Egypt
147 G6 Birr Ireland
128 B8 Bi'r Rawḑ Sālim well Egypt
169 C10 Birresborn Ger.
83 K3 Birrie r. N.S.W. Austr.
84 B5 Birrindudu N.T. Austr.
205 G2 Bir Roumi well Alg.
127 K7 Bi'r Sābil Iraq
203 F4 Bi'r Şafşaf well Egypt
203 F4 Bi'r Şaḩrā' well Egypt
203 G4 Bir Salala well Sudan
Bîrsana Romania see Bârsana
146 J4 Birsay Orkney, Scotland U.K.
190 D1 Birse r. Switz.
203 G4 Bi'r Shalatayn Egypt
128 H2 Bi'r Shamandūr well Syria
Birshoghyr Kazakh. see Berchogur
134 K5 Birsk Rus. Fed.
203 G4 Bir Sohanit well Sudan
151 J2 Birstall Leicestershire, England U.K.
169 H10 Birstein Ger.
138 H7 Birštonas Lith.
128 C9 Bi'r Tābah Egypt
124 H4 Bir Ṭalḩah well Saudi Arabia
205 H3 Bir Tanguer well Alg.
202 D2 Bi'r Tānjidar well Libya
203 F4 Bi'r Ṭarfāwī well Egypt
140 P2 Birtavarre Norway
128 B9 Bi'r Thāl well Egypt
85 I2 Birthday Mountain hill Qld Austr.
223 K5 Birtle Man. Can.
149 N4 Birtley Tyne and Wear, England U.K.
111 K11 Biru Xizang China
128 A9 Bi'r Udayb well Egypt
136 H6 Biruința Moldova
Biruintsa Moldova see Ştefan Vodă
202 C2 Bi'r Umm al Gharānīq Libya
124 A3 Bi'r Umm Fawākhīr well Egypt
124 C3 Bi'r Umm Missā well Saudi Arabia
Biruni Uzbek. see Beruniy
203 G4 Bi'r 'Unjāt well Egypt
114 D6 Birur Karnataka India
124 H4 Bi'r Usaylīlah well Saudi Arabia
203 G5 Bir Wario well Sudan
202 B3 Bi'r Wedeb well Libya
124 F5 Bi'r Wurshah well Saudi Arabia
137 R3 Biryuch Rus. Fed.
129 I2 Biryuchek Rus. Fed.
138 H5 Biržai Lith.
205 H3 Bir Zar well Tunisia
195 □ Birżebbuġa Malta
179 M6 Biš Slovenia
93 E4 Bisa i. Maluku Indon.
193 O5 Bisaccia Italy
194 E8 Bisacquino Sicilia Italy
104 E5 Bisai Japan
116 G5 Bisalpur Uttar Prad. India
116 E5 Bisau Rajasthan India
186 D2 Bisaurín mt. Spain
241 W10 Bisbee AZ U.S.A.
Biscari Sicilia Italy see Acate
163 B7 Biscarrosse France
163 B7 Biscarrosse et de Parentis, Étang de l. France
163 B7 Biscarrosse-Plage France
154 B4 Biscay, Bay of sea France/Spain
264 I3 Biscay Abyssal Plain sea feature N. Atlantic Ocean
231 G13 Biscayne Bay FL U.S.A.
231 G13 Biscayne National Park FL U.S.A.
193 R5 Bisceglie Italy
173 J2 Bischberg Ger.
172 G2 Bischbrunn Ger.
157 O6 Bischheim France
169 F9 Bischoffen Ger.
169 J8 Bischofferode Ger.
173 L1 Bischofsgrün Ger.
172 E2 Bischofsheim Ger.
169 J10 Bischofsheim an der Rhön Ger.
178 H5 Bischofshofen Austria
173 O4 Bischofsmais Ger.
171 J8 Bischofswerda Ger.
173 N6 Bischofswiesen Ger.
190 G1 Bischofszell Switz.
157 M6 Bischwald, Étang de l. France
157 O6 Bischwiller France
262 T2 Biscoe Islands Antarctica
216 □1a Biscoitos Terceira Azores
224 D4 Biscotasi Lake Ont. Can.
224 D4 Biscotasing Ont. Can.
102 □1 Bise Okinawa Japan
208 E3 Bisellia Sudan
193 L2 Bisenti Italy
192 H2 Bisentina, Isola i. Italy
134 L4 Biser Rus. Fed.
134 K4 Biserovo Rus. Fed.
134 L4 Bisert' r. Rus. Fed.
197 O7 Bisertsi Bulg.
188 E4 Biševo i. Croatia
102 □1 Bise-zaki pt Okinawa Japan
108 D7 Bisezhai Yunnan China
203 H6 Bisha Eritrea
124 F6 Bīshah reg. Saudi Arabia
124 G5 Bīshah, Wādī watercourse Saudi Arabia
108 F4 Bishan Chongqing China
Bishbek Kyrg. see Bishkek
127 N7 Bīsheh Iran
117 P5 Bishemnagar Arun. Prad. India
121 P6 Bishkek Kyrg.
117 K8 Bishnupur W. Bengal India
215 L8 Bisho S. Africa
240 N4 Bishop CA U.S.A.
81 B13 Bishop and Clerks Islands Stewart I. N.Z.
149 N4 Bishop Auckland Durham, England U.K.
146 H11 Bishopbriggs East Dunbartonshire, Scotland U.K.
222 G1 Bishop Lake N.W.T. Can.
150 G3 Bishop's Castle Shropshire, England U.K.
150 H4 Bishop's Cleeve Gloucestershire, England U.K.
150 F5 Bishop's Hull Somerset, England U.K.
151 J3 Bishop's Itchington Warwickshire, England U.K.
150 F5 Bishop's Lydeard Somerset, England U.K.
151 M4 Bishop's Stortford Hertfordshire, England U.K.
150 D5 Bishop's Tawton Devon, England U.K.
150 E6 Bishopsteignton Devon, England U.K.
151 J6 Bishop's Waltham Hampshire, England U.K.
146 H11 Bishopton Renfrewshire, Scotland U.K.
231 G8 Bishopville SC U.S.A.
126 I6 Bishrī, Jabal hills Syria
100 C2 Bishui Heilong. China
Bishui Henan China see Biyang
215 N6 Bisi S. Africa
193 Q8 Bisignano Italy
250 D3 Bisinaca Col.
172 F5 Bisingen Ger.
205 G2 Biskra Alg.
175 K4 Biskupice Lubelskie Pol.
174 G4 Biskupice Opolskie Pol.
177 I3 Biskupice Slovakia
175 H2 Biskupiec Warmińsko-Mazurskie Pol.
175 I2 Biskupiec Warmińsko-Mazurskie Pol.
150 H4 Bisley Gloucestershire, England U.K.
92 F7 Bislig Mindanao Phil.
92 F7 Bislig Bay Mindanao Phil.
236 E2 Bismarck ND U.S.A.
91 K7 Bismarck Archipelago is P.N.G.
76 E2 Bismarck Range mts P.N.G.
91 K7 Bismarck Sea P.N.G.
170 E5 Bismark (Altmark) Ger.
127 J5 Bismil Turkey
141 J6 Bismo Norway
236 D3 Bison SD U.S.A.
122 B4 Bīsotūn Iran
140 N5 Bispgården Sweden
168 J4 Bispingen Ger.
115 H3 Bissamcuttak Orissa India
206 B4 Bissau Guinea-Bissau
207 H5 Bissaula Nigeria
165 J9 Bissen Lux.
169 F6 Bissendorf Ger.
168 I5 Bissendorf (Wedemark) Ger.
223 M5 Bissett Man. Can.
206 C4 Bissikrima Guinea
178 C7 Bissina, Lago di l. Italy
173 J4 Bissingen Ger.
206 B3 Bissorã Guinea-Bissau
190 E6 Bistagno Italy
222 G3 Bistcho Lake Alta Can.
196 I9 Bistra mt. Macedonia
196 I8 Bistra mt. Macedonia/Serbia
197 K5 Bistra r. Romania
197 L7 Bistreț Romania
197 L7 Bistreț, Lacul l. Romania
179 M7 Bistrica Šmarje pri Jelšah Slovenia
179 J7 Bistrica Tržič Slovenia
197 M3 Bistrița Romania
197 M3 Bistrița r. Romania
197 O4 Bistrița r. Romania
197 M3 Bistrița Bârgăului Romania
197 N3 Bistriței, Munții mts Romania
197 L9 Bistritsa r. Bulg.
92 C6 Bisucay i. Phil.
116 H6 Biswan Uttar Prad. India
125 M4 Bīsyah Oman
143 Q7 Bisztynek Pol.
113 □1 Bitadhoo i. S. Male Maldives
Bitadoo i. S. Male Maldives see Bitadhoo
208 A4 Bitam Gabon
210 C3 Bitata Eth.
172 B2 Bitburg Ger.
157 N5 Bitche France
195 L1 Bitetto Italy
116 H6 Bithur Uttar Prad. India
199 K2 Bithynia reg. Turkey
120 D2 Bitik Kazakh.
208 E3 Bitilifondi C.A.R.
208 C2 Bitkine Chad
127 K4 Bitlis Turkey
196 J9 Bitola Macedonia
Bitolj Macedonia see Bitola
195 L1 Bitonto Italy
124 G4 Bitrān, Jabal hill Saudi Arabia
114 C7 Bitra Par rf India
157 N8 Bitschwiller-lès-Thann France
241 W2 Bitter Creek r. UT U.S.A.
238 J6 Bitter Creek r. WY U.S.A.
171 F7 Bitterfeld Ger.
214 C7 Bitterfontein S. Africa
238 G3 Bitterroot r. MT U.S.A.
238 G3 Bitterroot Range mts ID U.S.A.
240 L5 Bitterwater CA U.S.A.
192 C7 Bitti Sardegna Italy
171 E6 Bittkau Ger.
150 H5 Bitton South Gloucestershire, England U.K.
207 E4 Bittou Burkina
254 B4 Bituca Brazil
93 D3 Bitung Sulawesi Indon.
215 M7 Bityi S. Africa
135 G6 Bityug r. Rus. Fed.
172 G5 Bitz Ger.
207 I4 Biu Nigeria
209 D7 Biula Angola
183 Q3 Biurrun Spain
215 P3 Bivane r. S. Africa
190 H3 Bivio Switz.
197 P3 Bivolari Romania
194 E8 Bivona Sicilia Italy
226 B2 Biwabik MN U.S.A.
104 C5 Biwa-ko l. Japan
104 D5 Biwa-ko Kokutei-kōen park Japan
Biwmares Wales U.K. Beaumaris
197 N4 Bixad Romania
210 E2 Bixinduule Somalia
146 □N2 Bixter Shetland, Scotl
121 U1 Biya r. Rus. Fed.
Biyang Anhui China se
109 I2 Biyang Henan China
210 D2 Bīye K'obē Eth.
121 N6 Biylikol', Ozero l. Ka
210 E3 Biyo Ado well Eth.
121 U1 Biysk Rus. Fed.
215 N6 Bizana S. Africa
161 B10 Bizanet France
163 D9 Bizanos France
178 A5 Bizau Austria
161 B10 Bize-Minervois Franc
103 L12 Bizen Japan
Bizerta Tunisia see Bi
205 H1 Bizerte Tunisia
189 B7 Bizerte admin. div. Tu
122 H8 Bīzhanābād Iran
140 □A1 Bjargtangar hd Icelar
140 N2 Bjarkøy Norway
143 J5 Bjärnum Sweden
143 J6 Bjärsjölagård Swede
140 O5 Bjästa Sweden
196 H8 Bjelasica mts Monter
188 G4 Bjelašnica mts Bos.-
188 F3 Bjelovar Croatia
140 N2 Bjerkvik Norway
168 K1 Bjerreby Denmark
142 F5 Bjerringbro Denmark
140 M3 Bjøllånes Norway
142 G1 Bjoneroa Norway
143 K1 Björbo Sweden
142 C3 Bjordal Norway
140 K5 Bjørgan Norway
142 H2 Bjørkelangen Norway
140 N3 Björkfjället mts Swec
140 O2 Björkliden Sweden
143 N1 Björklinge Sweden
142 H1 Bjørknes Akershus No
140 T2 Bjørknes Finnmark No
142 H4 Björkö Sweden
143 P2 Björkö i. Sweden
140 O4 Björksele Sweden
141 J5 Bjorli Norway
140 O5 Björna Sweden
142 B1 Bjørnafjorden b. Nor
142 C2 Bjørnanuten mt. Norw
Björneborg Fin. see P
142 D1 Bjornesfjorden l. Nor
140 T2 Bjørnevatn Norway
140 O2 Bjørnfjell Norway
268 B2 Bjørnøya i. Arctic Oce
140 U2 Bjørnstad Norway
142 I1 Bjurberget Sweden
140 O5 Bjurholm Sweden
140 P4 Bjuröklubb pt Swede
143 L1 Bjursås Sweden
206 D3 Bla Mali
146 D8 Bla Bheinn hill Scotla
160 F4 Blacé France
196 I8 Blace Kosovo Serbia
196 J7 Blace Serbia
174 G5 Blachownia Pol.
223 L5 Black r. Man. Can.
224 D3 Black r. Ont. Can.
226 H1 Black r. Ont. Can.
246 □ Black r. Jamaica
Black Mauritius see Grande Rivière Noire
229 H3 Black r. AR U.S.A.
237 J8 Black r. AR U.S.A.
241 V8 Black r. AZ U.S.A.
227 L7 Black r. MI U.S.A.
231 H9 Black r. SC U.S.A.
226 C5 Black r. WI U.S.A.
146 L11 Blackadder Water r. Scotland U.K.
85 J8 Blackall Qld Austr.
224 B3 Black Bay Ont. Can.
223 I3 Black Bay Sask. Can.
224 B2 Blackbear r. Ont. Car
226 A2 Blackberry MN U.S.A
223 J3 Black Birch Lake Sas
82 □1 Blackbourne, Point N
151 I4 Black Bourton Oxfor
England U.K.
85 H4 Blackbull Qld Austr.
148 E7 Black Bull Ireland
146 L8 Blackburn Aberdeens
Scotland U.K.
149 M6 Blackburn Blackburn Darwen, England U.K.
146 I11 Blackburn West Lothi
Scotland U.K.
149 M6 Blackburn with Darw
admin. div. England U.
85 N9 Blackbutt Qld Austr.
240 J2 Black Butte mt. CA U
240 J2 Black Butte Lake CA
241 R6 Black Canyon gorge AZ U.S.A.
241 T7 Black Canyon City A.
239 K7 Black Canyon of the Gunnison National P
CO U.S.A.
262 T2 Black Coast Antarctic
149 K5 Black Combe hill Eng
148 I3 Blackcraig Hill Scotla
226 F5 Black Creek WI U.S.A
234 C2 Black Creek r. PA U.S
241 W6 Black Creek waterco
AZ U.S.A.
222 E4 Black Dome mt. B.C.
227 R4 Black Donald Lake C
150 F6 Black Down Hills England U.K.
85 L7 Blackdown Tablelan
National Park Qld Au
236 H2 Blackduck MN U.S.A.
143 M2 Blacken b. Sweden
222 H4 Blackfalds Alta Can.
238 H2 Blackfeet Indian Res
res. MT U.S.A.
151 J6 Blackfield Hampshire,
England U.K.
238 H5 Blackfoot ID U.S.A.
238 H3 Black Foot r. MT U.S.
238 I5 Blackfoot Reservoir
146 I10 Blackford Perth and K
Scotland U.K.
Black Forest mts Ger
Schwarzwald
147 D6 Black Head Ireland
150 B7 Black Head England U
147 K3 Black Head Northern Ireland U.K.
149 N6 Black Hill England U.K
84 D8 Black Hill Range hills
N.T. Austr.
220 H5 Black Hills SD U.S.A.
238 L4 Black Hills SD U.S.A.
146 J11 Blackhope Scar hill Scotland U.K.
223 L5 Black Island Man. Ca
146 H7 Black Isle pen. Scotla
223 J3 Black Lake Sask. Can
223 J3 Black Lake l. Sask. Ca
227 J4 Black Lake l. MI U.S.A
148 B5 Blacklion Ireland
146 J9 Blacklunans Perth an
Kinross, Scotland U.K.
247 □4 Blackman's Barbados
241 W8 Black Mesa mt. AZ U
241 V5 Black Mesa ridge AZ
150 E5 Blackmoor Gate Dev
England U.K.
151 M4 Blackmore Essex, Engl
150 E4 Black Mountain hills Wales U.K.
240 O6 Black Mountain CA U
232 C12 Black Mountain KY U
150 F4 Black Mountains hills
Wales U.K.
241 R6 Black Mountains AZ
212 C4 Black Nossob waterc
Namibia
151 N4 Black Notley Essex, England U.K.
Black Pagoda Orissa
Konarka
Black Point H.K. Chin
Lan Kok Tsui
149 K6 Blackpool Blackpool, England U.K.
83 I7 Black Range State P
nature res. Vic. Austr.
246 □ Black River Jamaica

134 I5 Bol'shoye Murashkino Rus. Fed.
140 V2 Bol'shoye Ozerko Rus. Fed.
139 R8 Bol'shoye Polpino Rus. Fed.
139 W9 Bol'shoye Popovo Rus. Fed.
134 G4 Bol'shoye Selo Rus. Fed.
137 O2 Bol'shoye Soldatskoye Rus. Fed.
121 R1 Bol'shoye Topol'noye, Ozero salt l. Rus. Fed.
139 Q3 Bol'shoye Zaborov'ye Rus. Fed.
139 V7 Bol'shoye Zhokovo Rus. Fed.
120 F2 Bol'shoy Ik r. Rus. Fed.
120 B2 Bol'shoy Irgiz r. Rus. Fed.
100 H7 Bol'shoy Kamen' Rus. Fed.
Bol'shoy Kavkaz mts Asia/Europe see Caucasus
139 W9 Bol'shoy Khomutets Rus. Fed.
139 Q1 Bol'shoy Kokovichi Rus. Fed.
129 F1 Bol'shoy Levoberezhnyy, Kanal canal Rus. Fed.
131 P2 Bol'shoy Lyakhovskiy, Ostrov i. Novosibirskiye O-va Rus. Fed.
134 L2 Bol'shoy Patok r. Rus. Fed.
131 K3 Bol'shoy Porog Rus. Fed.
131 O4 Bol'shoy Shantar, Ostrov i. Rus. Fed.
Bol'shoy Tokmak Kyrg. see Tokmok
Bol'shoy Tokmak Ukr. see Tokmak
139 O4 Bol'shoy Tuder r. Rus. Fed.
138 K2 Bol'shoy Tyuters, Ostrov i. Estonia
120 C3 Bol'shoy Uzen' r. Kazakh./Rus. Fed.
129 C1 Bol'shoy Zelenchuk r. Rus. Fed.
242 G4 Bolsón de Mapimí des. Mex.
149 O7 Bolsover Derbyshire, England U.K.
164 I2 Bolsward Neth.
174 G1 Bolszewo Pol.
186 F3 Boltaña Spain
149 O5 Boltby North Yorkshire, England U.K.
170 D3 Boltenhagen, Ostseebad Ger.
150 E7 Bolt Head England U.K.
190 C2 Boltigen Switz.
227 O6 Bolton Ont. Can.
92 E8 Bolton Mindanao Phil.
149 M6 Bolton Greater Manchester, England U.K.
149 L5 Bolton-le-Sands Lancashire, England U.K.
139 P7 Boltutino Rus. Fed.
137 N5 Boltyshka Ukr.
126 E3 Bolu Turkey
199 M2 Bolu prov. Turkey
140 □B1 Bolungarvík Iceland
111 K8 Boluntay Qinghai China
109 J7 Boluo Guangdong China
147 B9 Bolus Head Ireland
139 R8 Bolva r. Rus. Fed.
199 M4 Bolvadin Turkey
150 C6 Bolventor Cornwall, England U.K.
177 H6 Bóly Hungary
197 O8 Bolyarovo Bulg.
191 K3 Bolzano Italy
191 K2 Bolzano prov. Italy
209 B6 Boma Dem. Rep. Congo
83 M6 Bomaderry N.S.W. Austr.
207 G5 Bomadi Nigeria
108 B4 Bomai Sichuan China
165 I8 Bomal Belgium
208 C4 Bomassa Congo
193 M3 Bomba Italy
83 L7 Bombala N.S.W. Austr.
184 A2 Bombarral Port.
Bombay Mahar. India see Mumbai
80 I4 Bombay North I. N.Z.
241 Q8 Bombay Beach CA U.S.A.
91 H7 Bomberai, Semenanjung pen. Papua Indon.
209 B5 Bombo r. Dem. Rep. Congo
210 B4 Bombo Uganda
207 G6 Bom Bom, Ilha i. São Tomé and Príncipe
208 C4 Bomboma Dem. Rep. Congo
252 D2 Bom Comércio Brazil
257 E3 Bom Despacho Brazil
117 N6 Bomdila Arun. Prad. India
150 G2 Bomere Heath Shropshire, England U.K.
111 L12 Bomi Xizang China
208 E4 Bomili Dem. Rep. Congo
252 D2 Bom Jardim Amazonas Brazil
251 I5 Bom Jardim Pará Brazil
254 G3 Bom Jardim Pernambuco Brazil
256 A2 Bom Jardim de Goiás Brazil
257 E4 Bom Jardim de Minas Brazil
209 B7 Bom Jesus Angola
254 D4 Bom Jesus Piauí Brazil
255 C9 Bom Jesus Rio Grande do Sul Brazil
254 E4 Bom Jesus da Gurgueia, Serra do hills Brazil
254 E5 Bom Jesus da Lapa Brazil
256 C3 Bom Jesus de Goiás Brazil
257 G4 Bom Jesus do Itabapoana Brazil
257 G4 Bom Jesus do Norte Brazil
142 B2 Bomlafjorden sea chan. Norway
168 I5 Bomlitz Ger.
142 B2 Bømlo i. Norway
208 E4 Bomokandi r. Dem. Rep. Congo
208 C4 Bomongo Dem. Rep. Congo
163 J10 Bompas France
194 F9 Bompensiere Sicilia Italy
194 G8 Bompietro Sicilia Italy
255 C8 Bom Retiro Brazil
257 E4 Bom Sucesso Minas Gerais Brazil
256 B5 Bom Sucesso Paraná Brazil
208 D3 Bomu, Réserve de Faune de la nature res. Dem. Rep. Congo
205 H1 Bon, Cap c. Tunisia
97 C10 Bon, Ko i. Thai.
Bona Alg. see Annaba
160 C2 Bona France
122 B3 Bonāb Iran
163 F10 Bonac-Irazein France
190 G2 Bonaduz Switz.
232 H11 Bon Air VA U.S.A.
247 □8 Bonaire i. Neth. Antilles
83 N3 Bonalbo N.S.W. Austr.
195 K7 Bonamico r. Italy
94 C4 Bonandolok Sumatera Indon.
242 □Q11 Bonanza Nic.
184 G7 Bonanza Spain
246 H4 Bonao Dom. Rep.
86 H3 Bonaparte Archipelago is W.A. Austr.
222 F5 Bonaparte Lake B.C. Can.
183 J3 Boñar Spain
146 H7 Bonar Bridge Highland, Scotland U.K.
192 B7 Bonarcado Sardegna Italy
247 □7 Bonasse Trin. and Tob.
190 H7 Bonassola Italy
225 K3 Bonavista Nfld and Lab. Can.
225 K3 Bonavista Bay Nfld and Lab. Can.
160 H2 Bonboillon France
82 E4 Bon Bon S.A. Austr.
159 J5 Bonchamp-lès-Laval France
146 K12 Bonchester Bridge Scottish Borders, Scotland U.K.
190 C1 Boncourt Switz.
137 S4 Bondarevo Rus. Fed.
135 H5 Bondari Rus. Fed.
191 K6 Bondeno Italy
208 D5 Bondo Équateur Dem. Rep. Congo
208 D4 Bondo Orientale Dem. Rep. Congo
92 D5 Bondoc Peninsula Luzon Phil.
93 A8 Bondokodi Sumba Indon.
172 F4 Bondorf Ger.
206 E4 Bondoukou Côte d'Ivoire
206 E4 Bondoukui Burkina
95 J8 Bondowoso Jawa Indon.
231 I13 Bonds Cay i. Bahamas
226 F5 Bonduel WI U.S.A.
156 F2 Bondues France
134 K3 Bondyug Rus. Fed.
Bondyuzhskiy Rus. Fed. see Mendeleyevsk
Bône Alg. see Annaba
93 C6 Bone Sulawesi Indon.
93 B6 Bone, Teluk b. Indon.
168 J2 Bönebüttel Ger.
207 G6 Bone de Jókei, Ilha i. São Tomé and Príncipe
231 □2 Bonefish Pond New Prov. Bahamas
193 N4 Bonefro Italy
214 E7 Bonekraal S. Africa
226 B4 Bone Lake WI U.S.A.
93 C6 Bonelipu Sulawesi Indon.
169 E7 Bönen Ger.
163 F7 Bon-Encontre France
93 B7 Bonerate Sulawesi Indon.
93 B7 Bonerate i. Indon.
93 B7 Bonerate, Kepulauan is Indon.
146 I10 Bo'ness Falkirk, Scotland U.K.
236 F4 Bonesteel SD U.S.A.
187 C10 Bonete Spain
258 C2 Bonete, Cerro mt. Arg.
257 E4 Bonfim Brazil
256 A2 Bonfim r. Brazil
257 E2 Bonfinópolis de Minas Brazil
210 C3 Bonga Eth.
92 C5 Bongabong Mindoro Phil.
117 M6 Bongaigaon Assam India
208 D4 Bongandanga Dem. Rep. Congo
214 H5 Bongani S. Africa
92 B9 Bongao Phil.
85 N9 Bongaree Qld Austr.
111 E10 Bongba Xizang China
111 J11 Bong Co l. China
93 B4 Bongka r. Indon.
206 C5 Bong Mountains hills Liberia
209 D6 Bongo Dem. Rep. Congo
92 E8 Bongo i. Phil.
208 D2 Bongo, Massif des mts C.A.R.
209 B7 Bongo, Serra do mts Angola
213 □J3 Bongolava mts Madag.
208 B2 Bongor Chad
206 D5 Bongouanou Côte d'Ivoire
208 B5 Bongoville Gabon
97 I7 Bông Son Vietnam
237 G9 Bonham TX U.S.A.
140 O5 Bönhamn Sweden
206 E3 Boni Mali
183 Q9 Boniches Spain
206 D4 Boniérédougou Côte d'Ivoire
174 G3 Boniewo Pol.
192 C5 Bonifacio Corse France
Bonifacio, Bocche di str. France/Italy see Bonifacio, Strait of
Bonifacio, Bouches de str. France/Italy see Bonifacio, Strait of
192 B5 Bonifacio, Strait of France/Italy
193 P8 Bonifati Italy
231 E10 Bonifay FL U.S.A.
190 D2 Bönigen Switz.
174 E1 Bonin Pol.
211 D5 Boni National Reserve nature res. Kenya
Bonin Islands N. Pacific Ocean see Ogasawara-shotō
231 G12 Bonita Springs FL U.S.A.
253 F5 Bonito Brazil
256 B2 Bonito r. Brazil
146 K12 Bonjedward Scottish Borders, Scotland U.K.
94 D4 Bonjol Sumatera Indon.
207 F3 Bonkoukou Niger
169 D9 Bonn Ger.
Bonna Ger. see Bonn
163 H9 Bonnac France
192 B6 Bonnanaro Sardegna Italy
162 H3 Bonnat France
160 F3 Bonnay France
172 E6 Bonndorf im Schwarzwald Ger.
161 H7 Bonne r. France
234 A5 Bonneauville PA U.S.A.
163 E9 Bonnefont France
238 F2 Bonners Ferry ID U.S.A.
142 G5 Bønnerup Strand Denmark
223 M5 Bonnet, Lac du resr Man. Can.
159 L5 Bonnétable France
159 M8 Bonneuil-Matours France
156 B7 Bonneval Centre France
160 J5 Bonneval Rhône-Alpes France
161 K6 Bonneval-sur-Arc France
160 I3 Bonnevaux France
160 I4 Bonneville France
82 H7 Bonney, Lake S.A. Austr.
156 C5 Bonnières-sur-Seine France
87 E11 Bonnie Rock W.A. Austr.
161 G9 Bonnieux France
214 E9 Bonnievale S. Africa
172 G3 Bönnigheim Ger.
168 I3 Bönningstedt Ger.
163 C8 Bonnut France
207 G5 Bonny Nigeria
146 I10 Bonnybridge Falkirk, Scotland U.K.
85 J4 Bonny Glen Aboriginal Holding res. Qld Austr.
215 N6 Bonny Ridge S. Africa
146 J11 Bonnyrigg Midlothian, Scotland U.K.
233 □S3 Bonny River N.B. Can.
160 B1 Bonny-sur-Loire France
223 I4 Bonnyville Alta Can.
158 F6 Bono France
192 C7 Bono Sardegna Italy
92 A7 Bonobono Palawan Phil.
103 H15 Bōno-misaki pt Japan
Bononia Italy see Bologna
192 B7 Bonorva Sardegna Italy
206 E5 Bonoua Côte d'Ivoire
261 I1 Bonpland Arg.
81 C11 Bonpland, Mount South I. N.Z.
240 O8 Bonsall CA U.S.A.
160 I4 Bons-en-Chablais France
83 M3 Bonshaw N.S.W. Austr.
160 E5 Bonson France
95 L4 Bontang Kalimantan Indon.
214 F8 Bontberg mt. S. Africa
214 D9 Bonteberg mts S. Africa
214 E10 Bontebok National Park S. Africa
206 B5 Bonthe Sierra Leone
92 C3 Bontoc Luzon Phil.
93 B7 Bontomatane Sulawesi Indon.
93 A6 Bontosunggu Sulawesi Indon.
215 N6 Bontrand S. Africa
215 J9 Bontrug S. Africa
177 G4 Bőny Hungary
177 H5 Bonyhád Hungary
84 B7 Bonython Range hills N.T. Austr.
143 O2 Boo Sweden
93 F4 Boo, Kepulauan is Papua Indon.
217 □2a Booby Island Inner Islands Seychelles
170 J4 Boock Ger.
87 G8 Boodie Boodie Range hills W.A. Austr.
82 D4 Bookabie S.A. Austr.
241 W2 Book Cliffs ridge UT U.S.A.
208 D5 Booke Dem. Rep. Congo
237 E7 Booker TX U.S.A.
206 C4 Boola Guinea
83 L3 Boolba Qld Austr.
82 G5 Booleroo Centre S.A. Austr.
147 H8 Booley Hills Ireland
83 J5 Booligal N.S.W. Austr.
87 C8 Boologooro W.A. Austr.
83 L3 Boomi N.S.W. Austr.
226 I5 Boon MI U.S.A.
85 N9 Boonah Qld Austr.
239 L7 Boone CO U.S.A.
236 I4 Boone IA U.S.A.
231 G7 Boone NC U.S.A.
232 C12 Boone Lake TN U.S.A.
232 F11 Boones Mill VA U.S.A.
237 I8 Booneville AR U.S.A.
232 B11 Booneville KY U.S.A.
237 K8 Booneville MS U.S.A.
247 □2 Boon Point Antigua and Barbuda
215 L1 Boons S. Africa
232 H9 Boonsboro MD U.S.A.
235 G3 Boonton NJ U.S.A.
106 F4 Böön Tsagaan Nuur salt l. Mongolia
240 I3 Boonville CA U.S.A.
230 D6 Boonville IN U.S.A.
236 I6 Boonville MO U.S.A.
233 J5 Boonville NY U.S.A.
252 D3 Boopi r. Bol.
87 F11 Boorabin National Park W.A. Austr.
210 D2 Boorama Somalia
83 J6 Booroorban N.S.W. Austr.
83 L6 Boorowa N.S.W. Austr.
83 I7 Boort Vic. Austr.
165 G7 Boortmeerbeek Belgium
156 B5 Boos France
173 I5 Boos Ger.
210 F2 Boosaaso Somalia
168 J2 Boostedt Ger.
233 □P5 Boothbay Harbor ME U.S.A.
263 D2 Boothby, Cape Antarctica
221 J3 Boothia, Gulf of Nunavut Can.
221 I2 Boothia Peninsula Nunavut Can.
149 K5 Bootle Cumbria, England U.K.
149 L7 Bootle Merseyside, England U.K.
208 A5 Booué Gabon
173 I4 Bopfingen Ger.
206 C5 Bopolu Liberia
169 E10 Boppard Ger.
111 J11 Boqê Xizang China
258 G3 Boqueirão Brazil
254 D5 Boqueirão, Serra do hills Brazil
247 □1 Boquerón Puerto Rico
242 G4 Boquilla, Presa de la resr Mex.
242 H3 Boquillas del Carmen Mex.
242 H5 Boquillas del Refugio Mex.
176 B2 Bor Czech Rep.
134 I4 Bor Rus. Fed.
197 K6 Bor Serbia
210 A3 Bor Sudan
126 G5 Bor Turkey
210 D4 Bor, Lagh watercourse Kenya/Somalia
79 □9 Bora-Bora is Arch. de la Société Fr. Polynesia
129 J7 Boradigah Azer.
211 C5 Boragi waterhole Kenya
213 □K3 Boraha, Nosy i. Madag.
238 H4 Borah Peak ID U.S.A.
116 H9 Borai Chhattisgarh India
215 L1 Borakalalo Nature Reserve S. Africa
Boran Kazakh. see Buran
156 D5 Boran-sur-Oise France
96 E7 Boraphet, Bung l. Thai.
Boraraigh i. Western Isles, Scotland U.K. see Boreray
142 I4 Borås Sweden
117 I9 Borasambar Orissa India
122 D7 Borāzjān Iran
251 G6 Borba Brazil
184 E3 Borba Port.
190 F6 Borbera r. Italy
182 G8 Borbollón, Embalse del resr Spain
92 E6 Borbon Cebu Phil.
190 E6 Borbore r. Italy
256 C4 Borborema Brazil
254 F3 Borborema, Planalto da plat. Brazil
197 N3 Borca Romania
197 P6 Borcea, Brațul watercourse Romania
Borchalo Georgia see Marneuli
169 G7 Borchen Ger.
263 K2 Borchgrevink Coast Antarctica
127 J3 Borçka Turkey
164 K4 Borculo Neth.
86 G4 Borda, Cape W.A. Austr.
256 D5 Borda da Mata Brazil
199 K5 Bor Dağı mt. Turkey
183 P6 Bordalba Spain
177 I5 Bordány Hungary
163 C6 Bordeaux France
116 G8 Bordehi Madh. Prad. India
203 G6 Bordein Sudan
184 B6 Bordeira Port.
168 G1 Bordelum Ger.
87 E13 Borden W.A. Austr.
225 I4 Borden-Carleton P.E.I. Can.
221 G2 Borden Island N.W.T. Can.
221 J2 Borden Peninsula Nunavut Can.
234 F4 Bordentown NJ U.S.A.
163 E10 Bordères-Louron France
163 E9 Bordères-sur-l'Échez France
83 N3 Border Ranges National Park N.S.W. Austr.
Borders admin. div. Scotland U.K. see Scottish Borders
82 H7 Bordertown S.A. Austr.
163 D9 Bordes Aquitaine France
163 E9 Bordes Midi-Pyrénées France
168 J2 Bordesholm Ger.
140 □C1 Borðeyri Iceland
190 D8 Bordighera Italy
186 K3 Bordils Spain
194 D8 Bordino r. Sicilia Italy
205 G1 Bordj Bou Arréridj Alg.
204 E4 Bordj Flye Ste-Marie Alg.
205 H3 Bordj Messaouda Alg.
205 F5 Bordj Mokhtar Alg.
Bordj Omar Driss Alg. see Bordj Omer Driss
205 G3 Bordj Omer Driss Alg.
186 E6 Bordón Spain
144 D1 Borðoy i. Faroe Is
121 P6 Bordu Kyrg.
Bordunskiy Kyrg. see Bordu
197 P6 Bordușani Romania
190 H6 Bore Italy
206 E3 Boré Mali
262 X2 Boreas Nunatak Antarctica
151 N4 Boreham Essex, England U.K.
151 L4 Borehamwood Hertfordshire, England U.K.
173 O3 Borek hill Czech Rep.
175 I5 Borek Pol.
174 F5 Borek Strzeliński Pol.
174 F4 Borek Wielkopolski Pol.
225 G1 Borel r. Que. Can.
146 J12 Boreland Dumfries and Galloway, Scotland U.K.
136 E3 Boremel' Ukr.
143 L3 Boren l. Sweden
143 L3 Borensberg Sweden
146 C8 Boreraig Highland, Scotland U.K.
146 B7 Boreray i. Western Isles, Scotland U.K.
146 □1 Boreray i. Western Isles, Scotland U.K.
179 O2 Bořetice Czech Rep.
172 A2 Borg Ger.
Borgå Fin. see Porvoo
140 M4 Borgafjäll Sweden
140 □G1 Borgarfjörður Iceland
140 □C1 Borgarnes Iceland
140 L4 Børgefjell Nasjonalpark nat. park Norway
169 H7 Borgentreich Ger.
168 E5 Börger Ger.
164 K3 Borger Neth.
237 E8 Borger TX U.S.A.
187 L8 Borges r. Spain
190 F6 Borghetto di Borbera Italy
143 M5 Borgholm Öland Sweden
169 F6 Borgholzhausen Ger.
195 L6 Borgia Italy
146 H5 Borgie r. Scotland U.K.
165 H7 Borgloon Belgium
192 C2 Borgo Corse France
191 J8 Borgo a Mozzano Italy
190 E5 Borgo d'Ale Italy
191 J5 Borgoforte Italy
190 D4 Borgofranco d'Ivrea Italy
195 O3 Borgo Grappa Italy
190 F5 Borgo-lavezzaro Italy
190 E4 Borgomanero Italy
190 D8 Borgomaro Italy
190 C5 Borgone Susa Italy
190 G5 Borgonovo Val Tidone Italy
191 K6 Borgo Panigale airport Italy
193 K3 Borgorose Italy
190 C7 Borgo San Dalmazzo Italy
191 K8 Borgo San Lorenzo Italy
190 F5 Borgo San Martino Italy
190 E4 Borgosesia Italy
191 L7 Borgo Tossignano Italy
190 H7 Borgo Val di Taro Italy
191 K3 Borgo Valsugana Italy
193 K3 Borgo Velino Italy
190 E5 Borgo Vercelli Italy
170 H5 Borgsdorf Ger.
142 E1 Borgsjåbrotet mt. Norway
168 I2 Borgstedt Ger.
146 H13 Borgue Dumfries and Galloway, Scotland U.K.
116 E8 Bori Madh. Prad. India
116 G9 Bori Mahar. India
116 E9 Bori r. India
207 G5 Bori Nigeria
96 F5 Borikhan Laos
Börili Kazakh. see Burli
139 S8 Borilovo Rus. Fed.
165 E8 Borinage reg. Belgium
234 B5 Boring MD U.S.A.
197 M9 Borino Bulg.
247 □1 Borinquen, Punta pt Puerto Rico
139 W9 Borinskoye Rus. Fed.
Borislav Ukr. see Boryslav
135 H6 Borisoglebsk Rus. Fed.
139 W4 Borisoglebskiy Rus. Fed.
Borisov Belarus see Barysaw
135 G6 Borisovka Rus. Fed.
139 T6 Borisovo Rus. Fed.
139 T2 Borisovo-Sudskoye Rus. Fed.
Borispol' Ukr. see Boryspil'
208 E3 Bo River Post Sudan
213 □J2 Boriziny Madag.
188 F3 Borja mts Bos.-Herz.
250 B6 Borja Peru
183 Q5 Borja Spain
183 P5 Borjabad Spain
122 G4 Borjak Iran
179 H7 Borjana Slovenia
Borjas Blancas Spain see Les Borges Blanques
205 H2 Borj Bourguiba Tunisia
129 E4 Borjomi Georgia
129 E4 Borjomis Nakrdzali nature res. Georgia
138 L6 Borkavichy Belarus
123 M3 Borkeh Afgh.
169 C7 Borken Ger.
169 H8 Borken (Hessen) Ger.
140 N2 Borkenes Norway
171 G6 Borkheide Ger.
175 M3 Borki Belarus
175 K4 Borki Pol.
137 R1 Borki Rus. Fed.
202 C5 Borkou reg. Chad
202 C5 Borkou-Ennedi-Tibesti pref. Chad
134 J2 Borkovskaya Rus. Fed.
175 I4 Borkowice Pol.
168 C3 Borkum Ger.
168 C3 Borkum i. Ger.
143 L1 Borlänge Sweden
141 I6 Borlaug Norway
199 J4 Borlu Turkey
161 I10 Bormes, Rade de inlet France
161 I10 Bormes-les-Mimosas France
190 F6 Bormida r. Italy
190 I3 Bormio Italy
171 D6 Born Ger.
171 G8 Borna Sachsen Ger.
171 H8 Borna Sachsen Ger.
170 G2 Born am Darß Ger.
169 J8 Born-Berge hill Ger.
164 I2 Borndiep sea chan. Neth.
205 G4 Borne Alg.
160 I4 Borne r. France
164 K4 Borne Neth.
156 D5 Bornel France
165 F6 Bornem Belgium
90 D6 Borneo i. Asia
164 K4 Bornerbroek Neth.
160 J5 Bornes mts France
182 G6 Bornes Port.
182 F6 Bornes, Serra de mts Port.
182 E5 Bornes de Aguiar Port.
174 E2 Borne Sulinowo Pol.
169 C9 Bornheim Ger.
169 E10 Bornhofen Ger.
143 K6 Bornholm county Denmark
143 L7 Bornholm i. Bornholm Denmark
143 K6 Bornholmsgattet str. Denmark/Sweden
168 J2 Bornhöved Ger.
169 E10 Bornich Ger.
207 I4 Borno state Nigeria
184 H7 Bornos Spain
184 H7 Bornos, Embalse de resr Spain
183 O7 Bornova r. Spain
199 I4 Bornova Turkey
168 J4 Börnsen Ger.
171 D8 Bornstedt Ger.
183 Q5 Borobia Spain
95 H8 Borobudur tourist site Indon.
177 L5 Borod Romania
137 N5 Borodayivka Ukr.
130 J3 Borodino Krasnoyarskiy Kray Rus. Fed.
139 S6 Borodino Moskovskaya Oblast' Rus. Fed.
139 S6 Borodino Moskovskaya Oblast' Rus. Fed.
136 I7 Borodino Ukr.
138 M1 Borodinskoye Rus. Fed.
136 I3 Borodyanka Ukr.
131 O3 Borogontsy Rus. Fed.
110 F4 Borohoro Shan mts China
176 F1 Borohrádek Czech Rep.
139 V3 Borok Rus. Fed.
93 C3 Boroko Sulawesi Indon.
139 T4 Borok-Sulezhskiy Rus. Fed.
208 D2 Boromata C.A.R.
137 N3 Boromlya Ukr.
137 O3 Boromlya r. Ukr.
206 E4 Boromo Burkina
206 D4 Boron Côte d'Ivoire
206 D3 Boron Mali
240 O7 Boron CA U.S.A.
114 H3 Borondi Orissa India
92 E6 Borongan Samar Phil.
174 G5 Boronów Pol.
192 B7 Borore Sardegna Italy
85 M8 Bororen Qld Austr.
174 G5 Boroszów Pol.
177 I5 Borota Hungary
206 D4 Borotou Côte d'Ivoire
149 O5 Boroughbridge North Yorkshire, England U.K.
151 M5 Borough Green Kent, England U.K.
137 Q4 Borova Kharkivs'ka Oblast' Ukr.
136 J3 Borova Kyivs'ka Oblast' Ukr.
137 R5 Borova r. Ukr.
197 L7 Borovan Bulg.
176 D3 Borovany Czech Rep.
136 E2 Borove Rivnens'ka Oblast' Ukr.
136 G2 Borove Rivnens'ka Oblast' Ukr.
139 Q3 Borovenka Rus. Fed.
139 Q3 Borovichi Rus. Fed.
121 U1 Borovlyanka Rus. Fed.
179 J8 Borovnica Slovenia
188 G3 Borovo Selo Croatia
134 J4 Borovoy Kirovskaya Oblast' Rus. Fed.
134 F2 Borovoy Respublika Kareliya Rus. Fed.
134 K3 Borovoy Respublika Komi Rus. Fed.
121 N1 Borovoye Kazakh.
139 T6 Borovsk Rus. Fed.
120 K1 Borovskoy Kazakh.
175 J5 Borów Pol.
175 J5 Borowa Pol.
175 J4 Borowie Pol.
183 M8 Borox Spain
257 E3 Borrachudo r. Brazil
256 B5 Borrazópolis Brazil
143 K6 Borrby Sweden
170 F1 Borre Denmark
241 P8 Borrego Springs CA U.S.A.
170 G3 Borrentin Ger.
162 G6 Borrèze France
187 E7 Borriol Spain
216 □3b Borriquillas, Punta de las pt Fuerteventura Canary Is
147 I7 Borris Ireland
147 G7 Borris-in-Ossory Ireland
147 F7 Borrisokane Ireland
84 F4 Borroloola N.T. Austr.
149 K4 Borrowdale Cumbria, England U.K.
177 K4 Borș Romania
140 K5 Børsa Norway
197 L4 Borșa Cluj Romania
197 M3 Borșa Maramureș Romania
177 K3 Borša Slovakia
116 D8 Borsad Gujarat India
120 G6 Borsakelmas sho'rxogi salt marsh Uzbek.
165 G6 Borsbeek Belgium
171 G8 Borsdorf Ger.
197 N4 Borsec Romania
140 R1 Børselv Norway
198 A2 Borsh Albania
137 T2 Borshchevskiye Peski Rus. Fed.
136 I6 Borshchi Ukr.
136 F5 Borshchiv Ukr.
136 E4 Borshchivka Ukr.
107 K2 Borshchovochnyy Khrebet mts Rus. Fed.
175 M6 Borshchovychi Ukr.
127 L7 Borsippa tourist site Iraq
120 D1 Borskoye Rus. Fed.
Borský Jur Slovakia see Borský Svätý Jur
179 P2 Borský Svätý Jur Slovakia
177 K3 Borsod-Abaúj-Zemplén county Hungary
177 J3 Borsodbóta Hungary
177 J3 Borsodnádasd Hungary
177 J3 Borsodszentgyörgy Hungary
165 E6 Borssele Neth.
169 K6 Börßum Ger.
168 G5 Borstel Ger.
171 H9 Borstendorf Ger.
Bortala Xinjiang China see Bole
110 F4 Bortala He r. China
150 D3 Borth Ceredigion, Wales U.K.
192 B7 Bortigali Sardegna Italy
192 C6 Bortigiadas Sardegna Italy
162 I5 Bort-les-Orgues France
162 J5 Bort-les-Orgues, Barrage de dam France
106 C4 Bor-Üdzüür Mongolia
122 D6 Borūjen Iran
122 C5 Borūjerd Iran
106 F6 Bor Ul Shan mts China
122 H4 Borun Iran
197 N8 Borushtitsa Bulg.
192 B6 Borutta Sardegna Italy
146 D8 Borve Highland, Scotland U.K.
136 B4 Borynya Ukr.
136 C4 Boryslav Ukr.
136 J3 Boryspil' Ukr.
175 K4 Borzechów Pol.
174 F4 Borzęciczki Pol.
137 L2 Borzenka r. Ukr.
136 B5 Borzhava r. Ukr.
Borzhomi Georgia see Borjomi
137 L2 Borzna Ukr.
190 G7 Borzonasca Italy
177 H4 Börzsöny hills Hungary
177 H4 Börzsönyi park Hungary
107 O1 Borzya Rus. Fed.
107 N1 Borzya r. Rus. Fed.
174 F1 Borzytuchom Pol.
192 B7 Bosa Sardegna Italy
177 G3 Bošáca Slovakia
121 O4 Bosaga Kazakh.
Bosagha Kazakh. see Bosaga
Bosaginskiy Kazakh. see Bosaga
192 A7 Bosa Marina Sardegna Italy
197 O3 Bosanci Romania
188 F3 Bosanska Dubica Bos.-Herz.
188 F3 Bosanska Gradiška Bos.-Herz.
188 F3 Bosanska Kostajnica Bos.-Herz.
188 F3 Bosanska Krupa Bos.-Herz.
188 G3 Bosanski Brod Bos.-Herz.
188 F3 Bosanski Novi Bos.-Herz.
188 F3 Bosanski Petrovac Bos.-Herz.
188 G3 Bosanski Šamac Bos.-Herz.
188 F3 Bosansko Grahovo Bos.-Herz.
177 H3 Bošany Slovakia
176 G4 Bősárkány Hungary
168 J2 Bosau Ger.
215 K4 Bosberg mt. S. Africa
150 H3 Bosbury Herefordshire, England U.K.
150 C6 Boscastle Cornwall, England U.K.
233 N5 Boscawen NH U.S.A.
Boscawen Island Tonga see Niuatoputopu
261 H5 Bosch Arg.
193 I1 Bosco Italy
226 D6 Boscobel WI U.S.A.
191 K4 Bosco Chiesanuova Italy
190 E5 Bosco della Partecipiano e Lucedio, Parco Naturale nature res. Italy
190 F6 Bosco Marengo Italy
193 M6 Boscotrecase Italy
168 J2 Bösdorf Ger.
214 E5 Bosduiflaagte salt pan S. Africa
108 F7 Bose Guangxi China
168 E4 Bösel Ger.
244 G6 Bosencheve, Parque Nacional nat. park Mex.
151 K6 Bosham West Sussex, England U.K.
Boshchakul' Kazakh. see Bozshakol'
100 M4 Boshnyakovo Sakhalin Rus. Fed.
215 L1 Boshoek S. Africa
215 J4 Boshof S. Africa
122 G5 Boshruyeh Iran
197 K8 Bosilegrad Serbia
Bosiljgrad Serbia see Bosilegrad
172 F5 Bösingen Ger.
120 I1 Boskol' Kazakh.
164 G4 Boskoop Neth.
176 F2 Boskovice Czech Rep.
251 H3 Boslanti Suriname
188 G3 Bosna r. Bos.-Herz.
197 P8 Bosna hills Bulg.
Bosna i Hercegovina country Europe see Bosnia-Herzegovina
Bosna Saray Bos.-Herz. see Sarajevo
Bosnia and Herzegovina, Federation of aut. div. Bos.-Herz. see Federacija Bosna i Hercegovina
188 F3 Bosnia-Herzegovina country Europe
208 D4 Boso Dem. Rep. Congo
214 G1 Bosobogolo Pan salt pan Botswana
208 C3 Bosobolo Dem. Rep. Congo
105 L5 Bōsō-hantō pen. Japan
208 D3 Bososama Dem. Rep. Congo
Bosost Spain see Bòssòst
179 O1 Bošovice Czech Rep.
215 K2 Bospoort S. Africa
Bosporus str. Turkey see İstanbul Boğazı
Bossaga Turkm. see Basaga
208 C3 Bossangoa C.A.R.
141 M6 Bössbod Sweden
208 C3 Bossembélé C.A.R.
Bossemptélé C.A.R. see Bossentélé
208 C3 Bossentélé C.A.R.
162 E6 Bosset France
214 E5 Bossiekom S. Africa
237 I9 Bossier City LA U.S.A.
212 C5 Bossiesvlei Namibia
206 D4 Bossora Burkina
186 G2 Bòssòst Spain
215 L1 Bosspruit S. Africa
86 F5 Bossut, Cape W.A. Austr.
111 G8 Bostan Xinjiang China
122 B6 Bostān Iran
123 L6 Bostan Pak.
120 C3 Bostandyk Kazakh.
122 F8 Bostāneh, Ra's-e pt Iran
110 H6 Bosten Hu l. China
147 E6 Boston Ireland
151 L2 Boston Lincolnshire, England U.K.
233 N6 Boston MA U.S.A.
82 E6 Boston Bay S.A. Austr.
227 O1 Boston Creek Ont. Can.
237 H8 Boston Mountains AR U.S.A.
149 O6 Boston Spa West Yorkshire, England U.K.
188 G3 Bosut r. Croatia
164 G3 Boswachterij Schoorl nature res. Neth.
226 G9 Boswell IN U.S.A.
232 F8 Boswell PA U.S.A.
116 C8 Botad Gujarat India
137 M8 Botanichne Ukr.
206 C5 Botata Liberia
140 N5 Boteå Sweden
215 Q2 Boteler Point S. Africa
197 N5 Boteni Romania
151 O3 Botesdale Suffolk, England U.K.
212 E4 Boteti r. Botswana
135 D8 Botev mt. Bulg.
197 L8 Botevgrad Bulg.
215 K3 Bothaville S. Africa
168 I4 Bothel Ger.
149 K4 Bothel Cumbria, England U.K.
238 C3 Bothell WA U.S.A.
150 G6 Bothenhampton Dorset, England U.K.
141 O6 Bothnia, Gulf of Fin./Sweden
83 K10 Bothwell Tas. Austr.
227 M7 Bothwell Ont. Can.
182 E5 Boticas Port.
188 G4 Botin mt. Bos.-Herz.
179 M8 Botinec Stupnički Croatia
137 O7 Botiyeve Ukr.
177 L4 Botiz Romania
232 A8 Botkins OH U.S.A.
135 I6 Botkul', Ozero l. Kazakh./Rus. Fed.
129 H3 Botlikh Rus. Fed.
207 H6 Bot Makak Cameroon
136 I7 Botna r. Moldova
186 C4 Botorrita Spain
197 O3 Botoșani Romania
107 O7 Botou Hebei China
195 L6 Botricello Italy
206 D5 Botro Côte d'Ivoire
215 J1 Botsalano Game Reserve nature res. S. Africa
235 I2 Botsford CT U.S.A.
215 K5 Botshabelo S. Africa
140 P4 Botsmark Sweden
142 D2 Botsvatn l. Norway
212 D5 Botswana country Africa
195 K5 Botte Donato, Monte mt. Italy
169 G8 Bottendorf (Burgwald) Ger.
168 K5 Bottendorf (Obernholz) Ger.
140 Q4 Bottenviken g. Fin./Sweden
151 K2 Bottesford Leicestershire, England U.K.
149 P6 Bottesford North Lincolnshire, England U.K.
192 C7 Bottidda Sardegna Italy
236 E1 Bottineau ND U.S.A.
246 G3 Bottle Creek Turks and Caicos Is
247 L5 Bottom Saba Neth. Antilles
169 C7 Bottrop Ger.
256 C5 Botucatu Brazil
257 F2 Botumirim Brazil
196 I9 Botun Macedonia
Botushany Moldova see Butuceni
225 K3 Botwood Nfld and Lab. Can.
172 D5 Bötzingen Ger.
206 D5 Bouaflé Côte d'Ivoire
156 B5 Bouafles France
180 D5 Bou Ahmed Morocco
206 D5 Bouaké Côte d'Ivoire
205 F2 Boualem Alg.
206 D4 Bouandougou Côte d'Ivoire
208 C5 Bouanga Congo
208 B3 Bouar C.A.R.
189 B7 Bou Arada Tunisia
204 E2 Bouârfa Morocco
205 G2 Bou Aroua Alg.
158 H7 Bouaye France
207 I4 Bouba Ndjida, Parc National de nat. park Cameroon
176 C2 Boubín mt. Czech Rep.
206 C2 Boû Bleï'îne well Maur.
204 D4 Boubout well Alg.
208 C3 Bouca C.A.R.
163 B8 Boucau France
84 E2 Boucaut Bay N.T. Austr.
161 G10 Bouc-Bel-Air France
159 K4 Boucé France
156 F3 Bouchain France
189 A7 Bouchegouf Alg.
159 J7 Bouchemaine France
Boucher, Île i. Îles Loyauté New Caledonia see Tiga
233 L3 Boucherville Que. Can.
161 G9 Bouches-du-Rhône dept France
227 S3 Bouchette Que. Can.
156 E4 Bouchoir France
206 C3 Boucle du Baoulé, Parc National de la nat. park Mali
225 H4 Bouctouche N.B. Can.
208 A5 Bouda Gabon
165 D6 Boudewijn Kanaal canal Belgium
117 J9 Boudh Orissa India
180 E5 Boudinar Morocco
206 E2 Boû Djébéha well Mali
208 C3 Boudoua C.A.R.
190 B2 Boudry Switz.
156 G3 Boué France
217 □3b Bouéni Mayotte
217 □3b Bouéni, Baie de b. Mayotte
209 B6 Bouenza admin. reg. Congo
209 B6 Bouenza r. Congo
159 K6 Bouessay France
159 O8 Bouesse France
208 C3 Boufore C.A.R.
205 G1 Bougaa Alg.
86 I2 Bougainville, Cape W.A. Austr.
93 G4 Bougainville, Selat sea chan. Papua Indon.
91 L8 Bougainville Island P.N.G.
85 K3 Bougainville Reef Coral Sea Is Terr. Austr.
78 □6 Bougainville Strait Solomon Is
205 G1 Bougaroûn, Cap c. Alg.
206 B2 Boû Ghbeïra spring Maur.
207 F2 Boughessa Mali
Bougie Alg. see Bejaïa
163 E7 Bouglon France
208 B2 Bougoumen Chad
206 D4 Bougouni Mali
205 F2 Bougtob Alg.
158 H7 Bouguenais France
206 D2 Boû Guendoûz well Mali
163 G8 Bouillac France
247 □2 Bouillante Guadeloupe
161 E9 Bouillargues France
165 H9 Bouillon Belgium
156 G7 Bouilly France
158 G8 Bouin France
205 F1 Bouira Alg.
204 C3 Bou Izakarn Morocco
160 I3 Boujailles France
161 C10 Boujan-sur-Libron France
204 B4 Boujdour Western Sahara
205 F2 Bou Kahil, Djebel mts Alg.
207 F4 Boukoumbé Benin
204 B4 Boukra Western Sahara
208 C2 Boukta Chad
208 C2 Boula Bouda Chad
206 C3 Boulal Mali
157 L5 Boulay-Moselle France
162 F5 Boulazac France
161 F9 Boulbon France
87 F11 Boulder W.A. Austr.
238 L6 Boulder CO U.S.A.
238 H3 Boulder MT U.S.A.
241 U4 Boulder UT U.S.A.
241 R5 Boulder Canyon gorge NV U.S.A.
241 R6 Boulder City NV U.S.A.
204 C3 Bou Legmaden, Oued watercourse Alg./Morocco
204 D2 Boulemane Fez-Boulmane Morocco
204 D2 Boulemane Fez-Boulmane Morocco
241 P9 Boulevard CA U.S.A.
261 H6 Boulevard Atlántico Arg.
207 F3 Boulgou Burkina
Boulhaut Morocco see Ben Slimane
84 G7 Boulia Qld Austr.
157 K5 Bouligny France
163 G8 Bouloc France
Boulogne France see Boulogne-sur-Mer
158 H7 Boulogne r. France
156 D6 Boulogne-Billancourt
163 F9 Boulogne-sur-Gesse
156 C2 Boulogne-sur-Mer Fra
159 M6 Bouloire France
208 E3 Boulou r. C.A.R.
208 D3 Boulouba C.A.R.
77 G4 Bouloupari New Caled
161 J10 Boulouris France
206 E3 Boulsa Burkina
149 M6 Boulsworth Hill Englar
157 I5 Boult-aux-Bois France
207 H3 Boultoum Niger
156 I4 Boulzicourt France
204 D3 Boumalne Dadès Mor
208 B5 Boumango Gabon
207 I6 Boumba r. Cameroon
208 B3 Boumbé I r. C.A.R.
205 F1 Boumerdes Alg.
186 H3 Boumort mt. Spain
186 H3 Boumort, Serra del m
206 E4 Bouna Côte d'Ivoire
204 E2 Bou Naceur, Jbel mt. Morocco
206 B2 Boû Nâga Maur.
233 □O3 Boundary Mountains ME U.S.A.
240 N4 Boundary Peak NV U.
234 F3 Bound Brook NJ U.S.
206 D4 Boundiali Côte d'Ivoire
208 B5 Boundji Congo
206 D3 Boundjiguire Mali
208 D3 Boungou C.A.R.
208 D3 Boungou r. C.A.R.
163 F6 Bouniagues France
206 B3 Bounkiling Senegal
96 E4 Boun Nua Laos
238 I6 Bountiful UT U.S.A.
84 G4 Bountiful Island Qld
77 H6 Bounty Islands N.Z.
266 G9 Bounty Trough sea fe S. Pacific Ocean
261 G3 Bouquet Arg.
78 □5 Bourail New Caledoni
205 H4 Bourarhet, Erg des.
160 E4 Bourbince r. France
Bourbon reg. France s Bourbonnais
Bourbon terr. Indian C see Réunion
160 D3 Bourbon-Lancy Franc
160 C3 Bourbon-l'Archamba France
160 B4 Bourbonnais reg. Fra
157 K8 Bourbonne-les-Bains
156 D2 Bourbourg France
160 G5 Bourbre r. France
158 E5 Bourbriac France
162 B4 Bourcefranc-le-Chap France
161 G7 Bourdeaux France
162 F5 Bourdeilles France
160 C1 Bourdon, Réservoir d France
157 M6 Bourdonnay France
206 E2 Bourem Mali
Bouressa Mali see Bo
162 F3 Bouresse France
162 C5 Bourg France
159 M3 Bourg-Achard France
162 H4 Bourganeuf France
161 F6 Bourg-Argental Franc
158 H6 Bourgbarré France
158 B5 Bourg-Blanc France
161 G6 Bourg-de-Péage Fran
160 E4 Bourg-de-Thizy Franc
163 F7 Bourg-de-Visa France
156 A4 Bourg-Dun France
160 G4 Bourg-en-Bresse Fra
162 I1 Bourges France
233 J3 Bourget Ont. Can.
160 H5 Bourget, Lac du l. Fra
156 G5 Bourg-et-Comin Fran
160 B5 Bourg-Lastic France
161 F7 Bourg-lès-Valence F
163 H11 Bourg-Madame Fran
227 S1 Bourgmont Que. Can.
158 G7 Bourgneuf, Baie de b
159 J7 Bourgneuf-en-Mauge France
158 H7 Bourgneuf-en-Retz F
156 H5 Bourgogne France
156 G8 Bourgogne admin. re
156 H8 Bourgogne, Canal de
160 G5 Bourgoin-Jallieu Fra
161 F8 Bourg-St-Andéol Fra
163 H8 Bourg-St-Bernard Fr
160 J5 Bourg-St-Maurice Fr
159 M3 Bourgtheroulde-Infre France
159 K3 Bourguébus France
159 L7 Bourgueil France
83 J4 Bourke N.S.W. Austr.
227 N1 Bourkes Ont. Can.
157 K7 Bourmont France
161 G6 Bourne r. France
151 L2 Bourne Lincolnshire, England U.K.
151 I6 Bournemouth Bourne England U.K.
151 I6 Bournemouth admin. England U.K.
159 I8 Bournezeau France
161 C6 Bournoncle-St-Pierr
182 D5 Bouro Port.
160 J1 Bourogne France
204 E2 Bou Rouhat, Oued watercourse Morocco
206 E4 Bouroum-Bouroum E
207 I4 Bourrah Cameroon
163 E7 Bourran France
163 D7 Bourriot-Bergonce F
165 J9 Bourscheid Lux.
164 L2 Bourtange Neth.
168 D5 Bourtanger Moor reg
159 M4 Bourth France
150 H5 Bourton Dorset, Engla
151 I4 Bourton-on-the-Wate Gloucestershire, Englar
208 D2 Bourtoutou Chad
206 E3 Bourzanga Burkina
205 G2 Bou Saâda Alg.
189 B7 Bou Salem Tunisia
241 R8 Bouse AZ U.S.A.
241 R7 Bouse Wash waterco AZ U.S.A.
162 I3 Boussac France
206 E3 Boussé Burkina
163 F9 Boussens France
160 H2 Boussières France
208 C2 Bousso Chad
156 H3 Boussois France
165 E8 Boussu Belgium
165 G7 Boutersem Belgium
206 C2 Boû Tezâya well Mau
206 B2 Boutilimit Maur.
162 C4 Boutonne r. France
206 B3 Boutougou Fara Sen
156 C4 Bouttencourt France
190 B3 Bouveret Switz.
Bouvet Island terr. S. Ocean see Bouvetøya
264 J9 Bouvetøya terr. S. Atlantic Ocean
161 G7 Bouvières France
158 H7 Bouvron France
157 L6 Bouxières-aux-Dame
157 N6 Bouxwiller France
156 H5 Bouy France
204 E3 Bou Yala Alg.
207 G3 Bouza Niger
159 N8 Bouzanne r. France
157 M5 Bouzonville France
156 H5 Bouzy France
195 J7 Bova Italy
195 K7 Bovalino Italy
195 J8 Bova Marina Italy
179 I7 Bovec Slovenia
182 F3 Bóveda Galicia Spain
183 N3 Boveda País Vasco Sp
190 I4 Bovegno Italy
169 I7 Bovenden Ger.
Boven Kapuas Mour Indon./Malaysia see K Hulu, Pegunungan
164 H3 Bovenkarspel Neth.
164 J3 Bovensmilde Neth.
156 D4 Boves France
190 D7 Boves Italy
150 E6 Bovey r. England U.K.
226 A2 Bovey MN U.S.A.

Bovey Tracey Devon, England U.K.
Boviel Northern Ireland U.K.
Bovigny Belgium
Boville Ernica Italy
Bovington Camp Dorset, England U.K.
Bovino Italy
Bovolone Italy
Bovril Arg.
Bovrup Denmark
Bovtyshka Ukr.
Bow r. W.A. Austr.
Bow r. Alta Can.
Bow r. Alta Can.
Bowa Sichuan China see Muli
Bowbells ND U.S.A.
Bowburn Durham, England U.K.
Bowden Jamaica
Bowden WV U.S.A.
Bowditch atoll Tokelau see Fakaofo
Bowen Arg.
Bowen Qld Austr.
Bowen r. Qld Austr.
Bowen IL U.S.A.
Bowen, Mount Vic. Austr.
Bowen Downs Qld Austr.
Bowen Island B.C. Can.
Bowen Mountains Vic. Austr.
Bowen Strait N.T. Austr.
Bowenville Qld Austr.
Bowers Beach DE U.S.A.
Bowers Mountains Antarctica
Bowers Ridge sea feature Bering Sea
Bowes Durham, England U.K.
Bowie Qld Austr.
Bowie AZ U.S.A.
Bowie MD U.S.A.
Bowie TX U.S.A.
Bow Island Alta Can.
Bowland, Forest of reg. England U.K.
Bowling Green KY U.S.A.
Bowling Green MO U.S.A.
Bowling Green OH U.S.A.
Bowling Green VA U.S.A.
Bowling Green, Cape Qld Austr.
Bowling Green Bay Qld Austr.
Bowling Green Bay National Park Qld Austr.
Bowman ND U.S.A.
Bowman, Mount B.C. Can.
Bowman Coast Antarctica
Bowman Island Antarctica
Bowman Peninsula Antarctica
Bowmansdale PA U.S.A.
Bowmanstown PA U.S.A.
Bowmansville PA U.S.A.
Bowmanville Ont. Can.
Bowmont Water r. England/Scotland U.K.
Bowmore Argyll and Bute, Scotland U.K.
Bown Somalia
Bowness-on-Solway Cumbria, England U.K.
Bowness-on-Windermere Cumbria, England U.K.
Bowo Sichuan China see Bomai
Bowo Xizang China see Bomi
Bowraville N.S.W. Austr.
Bow River Aboriginal Reserve W.A. Austr.
Bowron r. B.C. Can.
Bowron Lake Provincial Park B.C. Can.
Bowser Lake B.C. Can.
Box Wiltshire, England U.K.
Boxberg Baden-Württemberg Ger.
Boxberg Sachsen Ger.
Boxdorf Ger.
Box Elder SD U.S.A.
Box Elder r. SD U.S.A.
Boxholm Sweden
Boxing Shandong China
Boxmeer Neth.
Boxtel Neth.
Boyabat Turkey
Boyacá dept Col.
Boyadzhik Bulg.
Boyalıca Turkey
Boyalık Turkey see Çiçekdağı
Boyana tourist site Bulg.
Boyang Jiangxi China
Boyanovichi Rus. Fed.
Boyanovo Bulg.
Boyanup W.A. Austr.
Boyarka Ukr.
Boyd r. N.S.W. Austr.
Boyd Lagoon salt flat W.A. Austr.
Boyd Lake N.W.T. Can.
Boydton VA U.S.A.
Boyer r. IA U.S.A.
Boyera Dem. Rep. Congo
Boyertown PA U.S.A.
Boykins VA U.S.A.
Boykov Liman l. Rus. Fed.
Boyle Alta Can.
Boyle Ireland
Boyne r. Qld Austr.
Boyne r. Qld Austr.
Boyne r. Ireland
Boyne City MI U.S.A.
Boynes France
Boyni Qara Afgh.
Boyo C.A.R.
Boyoma, Chutes waterfall Dem. Rep. Congo
Boysun Uzbek.
Boyuibe Bol.
Böyük Dähnä Azer.
Böyük Hinaldağ mt. Azer.
Böyük İşıqlı Dağ mt. Armenia
Boyup Brook W.A. Austr.
Bozan Turkey
Bozanbay Kazakh.
Bozan Dağı mt. Turkey
Bozashy Tübegi pen. Kazakh. see Buzachi, Poluostrov
Bozburun Turkey
Bozburun Dağ mt. Turkey
Bozburun Yarımadası pen. Turkey
Bozcaada i. Turkey
Bozdağ mt. Turkey
Bozdağ mt. Turkey
Boz Dağ mts Turkey
Bozdag, Khrebet hills Azer. see Bozdağ Silsiläsi
Boz Dağları mts Turkey
Bozdağ Silsiläsi hills Azer.
Bozdağ Tepe mt. Turkey
Bozdoğan Turkey
Bozeat Northamptonshire, England U.K.
Bozel France
Bozeman MT U.S.A.
Bozen Italy see Bolzano
Bożewo Pol.
Bozhou Anhui China
Božice Czech Rep.
Božjakovina Croatia
Bozkır Turkey
Bozköl Kazakh. see Boskol'
Bozkurt Turkey
Boznābād Iran
Bozoglan mts Turkey see Bolkar Dağları
Bozouls France
Bozoum C.A.R.
Bozova Turkey
Bozovici Romania
Bozqūsh, Kūh-e mts Iran
Bozshakol' Kazakh.
Boztumsyk Kazakh.
Bozüyük Turkey
Bozyazı Turkey
Bozzolo Italy
Bra Italy
Braaid Isle of Man
Braan r. Scotland U.K.
Braås Sweden
Brabant Island Antarctica
Brabant Wallon prov. Belgium
Brač i. Croatia
Bracadale Highland, Scotland U.K.
146 C8 Bracadale, Loch b. Scotland U.K.
Bracara Port. see Braga
192 I3 Bracciano Italy
192 I3 Bracciano, Lago di l. Italy
224 E4 Bracebridge Ont. Can.
149 P7 Bracebridge Heath Lincolnshire, England U.K.
162 C5 Brach France
169 E9 Brachbach Ger.
225 G3 Brachet, Lac au l. Que. Can.
159 O6 Bracieux France
148 C7 Brackagh Ireland
140 M5 Bräcke Sweden
168 J4 Brackel Ger.
172 G3 Brackenheim Ger.
237 E11 Brackettville TX U.S.A.
188 F4 Bracki Kanal sea chan. Croatia
151 J3 Brackley Northamptonshire, England U.K.
147 H6 Bracknagh Ireland
151 K5 Bracknell Bracknell Forest, England U.K.
151 K5 Bracknell Forest admin. div. England U.K.
253 G2 Braço Norte r. Brazil
197 K4 Brad Romania
193 R7 Bradano r. Italy
231 F12 Bradenton FL U.S.A.
227 O5 Bradford Ont. Can.
149 N6 Bradford West Yorkshire, England U.K.
232 A8 Bradford OH U.S.A.
232 G7 Bradford PA U.S.A.
233 M5 Bradford VT U.S.A.
234 C1 Bradford County county PA U.S.A.
234 D4 Bradford Hills PA U.S.A.
150 H5 Bradford-on-Avon Wiltshire, England U.K.
151 J6 Brading Isle of Wight, England U.K.
226 G8 Bradley IL U.S.A.
235 G4 Bradley Beach NJ U.S.A.
232 B7 Bradner OH U.S.A.
150 F6 Bradninch Devon, England U.K.
150 G6 Bradpole Dorset, England U.K.
149 M6 Bradshaw Greater Manchester, England U.K.
232 D11 Bradshaw WV U.S.A.
86 H3 Bradshaw, Mount hill W.A. Austr.
149 N7 Bradwell Derbyshire, England U.K.
151 P2 Bradwell Norfolk, England U.K.
151 N4 Bradwell Waterside Essex, England U.K.
237 F10 Brady TX U.S.A.
237 F10 Brady Creek r. TX U.S.A.
222 B3 Brady Glacier AK U.S.A.
175 L4 Bradzyatsin Belarus
146 □N2 Brae Shetland, Scotland U.K.
146 H7 Braeantra Highland, Scotland U.K.
146 K9 Braehead of Lunan Angus, Scotland U.K.
82 G5 Braemar S.A. Austr.
146 J8 Braemar Aberdeenshire, Scotland U.K.
194 G9 Braemi r. Sicilia Italy
182 D5 Braga Port.
182 D5 Braga admin. dist. Port.
261 G4 Bragado Arg.
254 D2 Bragança Brazil
182 G5 Bragança Port.
182 G5 Bragança admin. dist. Port.
256 D5 Bragança Paulista Brazil
226 A4 Braham MN U.S.A.
136 J2 Brahin Belarus
136 J2 Brahinka r. Belarus
168 K4 Brahlstorf Ger.
117 P6 Brahmakund Arun. Prad. India
117 M8 Brahmanbaria Bangl.
117 K9 Brahmani r. India
115 I3 Brahmapur Orissa India
117 M8 Brahmaputra r. Asia alt. Dihang (India), alt. Jamuna (Bangladesh), alt. Yarlung Zangbo (China)
116 F3 Brahmaur Hima. Prad. India
83 L6 Braidwood N.S.W. Austr.
226 F8 Braidwood IL U.S.A.
178 F6 Braies, Lago di l. Italy
197 P5 Brăila Romania
197 P6 Brăilei, Insula Mare a i. Romania
151 I2 Brailsford Derbyshire, England U.K.
156 G5 Braine France
165 F7 Braine-l'Alleud Belgium
165 F7 Braine-le-Comte Belgium
236 H2 Brainerd MN U.S.A.
159 L7 Brain-sur-Allonnes France
151 N4 Braintree Essex, England U.K.
149 K4 Braithwaite Cumbria, England U.K.
84 D1 Braithwaite Point N.T. Austr.
165 H7 Braives Belgium
213 F4 Brak r. Limpopo S. Africa
214 E9 Brak r. Western Cape S. Africa
214 C4 Brak watercourse S. Africa
168 F4 Brake (Unterweser) Ger.
165 E7 Brakel Belgium
169 H7 Brakel Ger.
164 H5 Brakel Neth.
206 B2 Brâkna admin. reg. Maur.
143 L5 Bräkneån r. Sweden
215 M2 Brakpan S. Africa
214 H7 Brakpoort S. Africa
215 K2 Brakspruit S. Africa
212 C4 Brakwater Namibia
142 I3 Brålanda Sweden
174 F4 Bralin Pol.
190 G6 Brallo di Pregola Italy
222 F5 Bralorne B.C. Can.
163 I9 Bram France
161 J6 Bramans France
178 F5 Bramberg am Wildkogel Austria
82 E5 Bramfield S.A. Austr.
151 O3 Bramford Suffolk, England U.K.
116 G9 Bramhapuri Mahar. India
149 O7 Bramley South Yorkshire, England U.K.
142 E6 Bramming Denmark
134 B3 Brämön i. Sweden
224 E5 Brampton Ont. Can.
151 L3 Brampton Cambridgeshire, England U.K.
149 L4 Brampton Cumbria, England U.K.
151 P3 Brampton Suffolk, England U.K.
169 D6 Bramsche Niedersachsen Ger.
169 F6 Bramsche Niedersachsen Ger.
143 N1 Bramsöfjärden l. Sweden
168 G4 Bramstedt Ger.
85 I2 Bramwell Qld Austr.
182 I2 Braña Caballo mt. Spain
171 I9 Braňany Czech Rep.
177 H3 Branč Slovakia
195 K8 Brancaleone Italy
151 N2 Brancaster Norfolk, England U.K.
225 K4 Branch Nfld and Lab. Can.
234 C3 Branch Dale PA U.S.A.
234 F2 Branchville NJ U.S.A.
209 D8 Branco Angola
251 F5 Branco r. Roraima Brazil
253 E2 Branco r. Brazil
206 □ Branco i. Cape Verde
178 A5 Brand Austria
173 L2 Brand Ger.
247 □8 Brandaris hill Bonaire Neth. Antilles
212 B4 Brandberg mt. Namibia
141 N5 Brändbo Sweden
142 G1 Brandbu Norway
142 F6 Brande Denmark
168 I3 Brande-Hörnerkirchen Ger.
178 E5 Brandenberg Austria
171 G6 Brandenburg Ger.
171 H5 Brandenburg land Ger.
230 D7 Brandenburg KY U.S.A.
171 F6 Brandenburger Wald- und Seengebiet park Ger.
171 H9 Brand-Erbisdorf Ger.
162 F3 Brandes reg. France
149 Q6 Brandesburton East Riding of Yorkshire, England U.K.
215 K4 Brandfort S. Africa
171 H7 Brandis Brandenburg Ger.
171 G8 Brandis Sachsen Ger.
214 D7 Brandkop S. Africa
179 L2 Brand-Nagelberg Austria
141 P6 Brändö Åland Fin.
192 C2 Brando Corse France
85 K5 Brandon Qld Austr.
223 L5 Brandon Man. Can.
147 B8 Brandon Ireland
149 N4 Brandon Durham, England U.K.
151 N3 Brandon Suffolk, England U.K.
237 K9 Brandon MS U.S.A.
236 G4 Brandon SD U.S.A.
233 L5 Brandon VT U.S.A.
147 B8 Brandon Bay Ireland
147 B8 Brandon Head Ireland
147 I7 Brandon Hill Ireland
147 B8 Brandon Mountain hill Ireland
234 C3 Brandonville PA U.S.A.
232 F9 Brandonville WV U.S.A.
170 H2 Brandshagen Ger.
234 A4 Brandtsville PA U.S.A.
214 E6 Brandvlei S. Africa
214 D9 Brandvlei Dam resr S. Africa
140 O2 Brandvoll Norway
176 D1 Brandýs nad Labem-Stará Boleslav Czech Rep.
234 D5 Brandywine Creek, East Branch r. PA U.S.A.
234 D5 Brandywine Creek, West Branch r. DE U.S.A.
234 D4 Brandywine Manor PA U.S.A.
235 J2 Branford CT U.S.A.
231 F11 Branford FL U.S.A.
160 G3 Branges France
94 □ Brani, Pulau i. Sing.
179 I8 Branica r. Slovenia
143 P7 Braniewo Pol.
179 I8 Branik Slovenia
177 L6 Brănișca Romania
156 F8 Branlin r. France
140 P4 Brännberg Sweden
163 D6 Branne France
173 M6 Brannenburg Ger.
183 L3 Brañosera Spain
262 T2 Bransfield Strait Antarctica
151 I6 Bransgore Hampshire, England U.K.
175 K3 Brańsk Pol.
237 D7 Branson CO U.S.A.
149 Q7 Branston Lincolnshire, England U.K.
175 J3 Brańszczyk Pol.
95 J8 Brantas r. Indon.
224 D5 Brantford Ont. Can.
151 O4 Brantham Suffolk, England U.K.
177 G1 Brantice Czech Rep.
231 D10 Brantley AL U.S.A.
162 F5 Brantôme France
137 O3 Brantsivka Ukr.
226 D4 Brantwood WI U.S.A.
137 K3 Branytsya Ukr.
190 H3 Branzi Italy
183 M6 Braojos Spain
190 I4 Braone Italy
251 G5 Brás Brazil
161 H10 Bras France
196 J8 Brasaljce Kosovo Serbia
225 I4 Bras d'Or Lake N.S. Can.
182 D8 Brasfemes Port.
250 D6 Brasil Brazil
Brasil country S. America see Brazil
257 G2 Brasil, Planalto do plat. Brazil
256 A4 Brasilândia Mato Grosso do Sul Brazil
256 C1 Brasilândia Minas Gerais Brazil
257 D2 Brasilândia Minas Gerais Brazil
252 C2 Brasileia Brazil
256 D1 Brasília Brazil
257 E2 Brasília de Minas Brazil
251 H5 Brasília Legal Brazil
138 H4 Brasla r. Latvia
Braslav Belarus see Braslaw
138 K6 Braslaw Belarus
197 N5 Brașov Romania
139 R9 Brasovo Rus. Fed.
217 □1c Bras-Panon Réunion
257 F4 Brás Pires Brazil
207 G5 Brass Nigeria
163 I8 Brassac France
161 C6 Brassac-les-Mines France
165 F6 Brasschaat Belgium
95 L2 Brassey, Banjaran mts Malaysia
84 E7 Brassey, Mount N.T. Austr.
87 G8 Brassey Range hills W.A. Austr.
233 □P3 Brassua Lake ME U.S.A.
160 D2 Brassy France
142 H3 Brastad Sweden
173 P2 Břasy Czech Rep.
197 N8 Bratan mt. Bulg.
197 K4 Bratca Romania
176 G3 Bratislava Slovakia
176 G3 Bratislavský kraj admin. reg. Slovakia
175 J5 Bratkowice Pol.
131 L4 Bratsk Rus. Fed.
137 K6 Brats'ke Mykolayivs'ka Oblast' Ukr.
137 M8 Brats'ke Respublika Krym Ukr.
Bratskoye Rus. Fed. see Nogamirzin-Yurt
131 L4 Bratskoye Vodokhranilishche resr Rus. Fed.
136 H5 Bratslav Ukr.
233 M6 Brattleboro VT U.S.A.
142 I1 Brattmon Sweden
150 H5 Bratton Wiltshire, England U.K.
140 I5 Brattvåg Norway
188 G3 Bratunac Bos.-Herz.
169 E10 Braubach Ger.
162 C5 Braud-et-St-Louis France
242 □R12 Braulio Carrillo, Parque Nacional nat. park Costa Rica
257 F3 Braúnas Brazil
178 H3 Braunau am Inn Austria
172 B2 Brauneberg Ger.
169 F9 Braunfels Ger.
169 K7 Braunlage Ger.
172 E6 Bräunlingen Ger.
172 H3 Braunsbach Ger.
171 E8 Braunsbedra Ger.
169 K6 Braunschweig Ger.
151 J3 Braunston Northamptonshire, England U.K.
151 J2 Braunstone Leicestershire, England U.K.
150 D5 Braunton Devon, England U.K.
215 L7 Braunville S. Africa
206 □ Brava i. Cape Verde
185 O5 Bravatas r. Spain
232 E9 Brave PA U.S.A.
136 H6 Bravicea Moldova
143 M3 Bråviken inlet Sweden
143 N3 Bråvikens naturreservat nature res. Sweden
252 D4 Bravo, Cerro mt. Bol.
243 K5 Bravo del Norte, Río r. Mex./U.S.A. alt. Rio Grande
184 B6 Bravura, Barragem da resr Port.
241 Q9 Brawley CA U.S.A.
147 J6 Bray Ireland
214 H1 Bray S. Africa
151 K4 Bray Windsor and Maidenhead, England U.K.
150 E6 Bray r. England U.K.
156 E1 Bray-Dunes France
159 M6 Braye r. France
147 B9 Bray Head Ireland
136 H4 Brayiliv Ukr.
221 K3 Bray Island Nunavut Can.
156 F7 Bray-sur-Seine France
149 O6 Brayton North Yorkshire, England U.K.
185 K3 Brazatortas Spain
222 H4 Brazeau r. Alta Can.
222 G4 Brazeau, Mount Alta Can.
215 N7 Brazen Head S. Africa
160 G2 Brazey-en-Plaine France
177 L5 Brazii Romania
254 C4 Brazil country S. America
230 D6 Brazil IN U.S.A.
264 H7 Brazil Basin sea feature S. Atlantic Ocean
237 H11 Brazos r. TX U.S.A.
209 B6 Brazzaville Congo
188 G3 Brčko Bos.-Herz.
174 G2 Brda r. Pol.
174 G3 Brdów Pol.
176 C2 Brdy hills Czech Rep.
Bré Ireland see Bray
183 Q5 Brea Spain
84 G7 Breadalbane Qld Austr.
146 H10 Breadalbane reg. Scotland U.K.
87 H8 Breaden, Lake salt flat W.A. Austr.
183 N8 Brea de Tajo Spain
215 K9 Breakfast Vlei S. Africa
81 A12 Breaksea Island South I. N.Z.
81 A12 Breaksea Sound inlet South I. N.Z.
85 N8 Breaksea Spit Qld Austr.
158 H5 Bréal-sous-Montfort France
150 G4 Bream Gloucestershire, England U.K.
80 I2 Bream Bay North I. N.Z.
80 I2 Bream Head North I. N.Z.
149 M2 Breamish r. England U.K.
80 I3 Bream Tail c. North I. N.Z.
146 B6 Breanais Western Isles, Scotland U.K.
258 C2 Breas Chile
146 C6 Breascleit Western Isles, Scotland U.K.
151 J2 Breaston Derbyshire, England U.K.
159 L2 Bréauté France
197 N5 Breaza Romania
95 H8 Brebes Jawa Indon.
95 H8 Brebes, Tanjung pt Indon.
161 K9 Brec d'Utelle mt. France
158 I4 Brécey France
158 F6 Brech France
156 D5 Brêche r. France
150 D4 Brechfa Carmarthenshire, Wales U.K.
146 K9 Brechin Angus, Scotland U.K.
165 G6 Brecht Belgium
239 K7 Breckenridge CO U.S.A.
236 G2 Breckenridge MN U.S.A.
237 F9 Breckenridge TX U.S.A.
169 D8 Breckerfeld Ger.
151 N3 Breckland lowland England U.K.
259 B9 Brecknock, Península pen. Chile
232 D7 Brecksville OH U.S.A.
176 F3 Břeclav Czech Rep.
150 F4 Brecon Powys, Wales U.K.
150 F4 Brecon Beacons reg. Wales U.K.
150 F4 Brecon Beacons National Park Wales U.K.
164 G5 Breda Neth.
186 K4 Breda Spain
143 J4 Bredaryd Sweden
214 E10 Bredasdorp S. Africa
83 L6 Bredbo N.S.W. Austr.
168 E5 Breddenberg Ger.
170 F5 Breddin Ger.
168 H4 Breddorf Ger.
142 E6 Brede r. Denmark
151 N6 Brede r. England U.K.
165 C6 Bredene Belgium
170 H4 Bredereiche Ger.
150 H3 Bredon Worcestershire, England U.K.
168 G1 Bredstedt Ger.
140 O5 Bredträsk Sweden
140 M3 Bredviken Sweden
120 I1 Bredy Rus. Fed.
165 I6 Bree Belgium
214 E10 Breede r. S. Africa
170 E4 Breese Ger.
164 G3 Breezand Neth.
232 G9 Breezewood PA U.S.A.
172 F6 Breg r. Ger.
197 J9 Bregalnica r. Macedonia
179 M8 Bregana Croatia
191 L4 Breganze Italy
178 A4 Bregenz Austria
178 A5 Bregenzer Wald mts Austria
168 J1 Bregninge Denmark
197 K6 Bregovo Bulg.
191 J4 Breguzzo Italy
158 H4 Bréhal France
158 F5 Bréhan France
158 F4 Bréhat, Île de i. France
169 J8 Brehme Ger.
171 F7 Brehna Ger.
140 □A1 Breiðafjörður b. Iceland
140 B1 Breiðafjörður nature res. Iceland
140 □F1 Breiðdalsvík Iceland
157 N5 Breidenbach France
169 F9 Breidenbach Ger.
236 E2 Breien ND U.S.A.
168 I2 Breiholz Ger.
190 G2 Breil Switz.
161 L9 Breil-sur-Roya France
215 K6 Breipaal S. Africa
172 D5 Breisach am Rhein Ger.
172 D6 Breisgau reg. Ger.
190 D1 Breitenbach Switz.
169 I9 Breitenbach am Herzberg Ger.
178 E5 Breitenbach am Inn Austria
173 P4 Breitenberg Ger.
173 I5 Breitenbrunn Bayern Ger.
173 L3 Breitenbrunn Bayern Ger.
168 I3 Breitenburg Ger.
168 K3 Breitenfelde Ger.
171 E7 Breitenhagen Ger.
178 C5 Breitenwang Austria
169 J8 Breitenworbis Ger.
178 D5 Breiter Grieskogel mt. Austria
170 H4 Breiter Luzinsee l. Ger.
172 E6 Breitnau Ger.
169 F9 Breitscheid Hessen Ger.
169 D9 Breitscheid Rheinland-Pfalz Ger.
169 J9 Breitungen Ger.
140 Q1 Breivikbotn Norway
140 O2 Breivikeidet Norway
184 B6 Brejeira, Serra da mts Port.
254 C4 Brejinho de Nazaré Brazil
254 E2 Brejo Brazil
254 E4 Brejo r. Brazil
254 D4 Brejo da Porta Brazil
168 G1 Breklum Ger.
140 J5 Brekstad Norway
158 B5 Brélès France
190 H4 Brembo r. Italy
168 G4 Bremen Ger.
168 G4 Bremen land Ger.
231 E9 Bremen GA U.S.A.
226 H8 Bremen IN U.S.A.
232 C9 Bremen OH U.S.A.
87 E13 Bremer Bay W.A. Austr.
87 E13 Bremer Bay b. W.A. Austr.
168 G3 Bremerhaven Ger.
87 F12 Bremer Range hills W.A. Austr.
Bremersdorp Swaziland see Manzini
238 C3 Bremerton WA U.S.A.
168 H4 Bremervörde Ger.
190 E1 Bremgarten Switz.
169 D10 Bremm Ger.
142 B2 Bremnes Norway
162 A2 Brem-sur-Mer France
175 J5 Breń r. Pol.
185 J5 Breña, Embalse de la resr Spain
216 □3d Breña Alta La Palma Canary Is
150 F5 Brendon Hills England U.K.
184 H5 Brenes Spain
237 G10 Brenham TX U.S.A.
184 E4 Brenhas r. Port.
150 E1 Brenig, Llyn resr Wales U.K.
140 L4 Brenna Norway
174 G6 Brenna Pol.
160 G3 Brenne r. France
159 M7 Brenne r. France
159 N8 Brenne reg. France
162 G2 Brenne, Parc Naturel Régional de la nature res. France
191 L2 Brennero Italy
Brennero, Passo di pass Austria/Italy see Brenner Pass
Brennerpaß pass Austria/Italy see Brenner Pass
178 E6 Brenner Pass pass Austria/Italy
140 P2 Brennes Norway
140 P2 Brennfjell Norway
190 I4 Breno Italy
160 H4 Brénod France
163 H8 Brens France
172 F2 Brensbach Ger.
224 E4 Brent Ont. Can.
191 M5 Brenta r. Italy
191 J3 Brenta, Gruppo di mts Italy
150 G5 Brent Knoll Somerset, England U.K.
151 M4 Brentwood Essex, England U.K.
235 I3 Brentwood NY U.S.A.
173 I4 Brenz r. Ger.
191 J4 Brenzone Italy
190 I4 Brescia Italy
190 I4 Brescia prov. Italy
165 E6 Breskens Neth.
Breslau Pol. see Wrocław
156 B3 Bresle r. France
156 D5 Bresles France
225 G2 Brésolles, Lac l. Que. Can.
190 G5 Bressana Bottarone Italy
191 L2 Bressanone Italy
146 □N2 Bressay i. Scotland U.K.
160 G4 Bresse reg. France
163 G8 Bressols France
162 D2 Bressuire France
136 C1 Brest Belarus
158 C5 Brest France
158 C5 Brest, Rade de inlet France
179 L8 Brestanica Slovenia
179 M6 Bresternica Slovenia
Brest-Litovsk Belarus see Brest
Brest Oblast admin. div. Belarus see Brestskaya Voblasts'
197 J7 Brestovac Serbia
177 K6 Brestovăț Romania
Brestskaya Oblast' admin. div. Belarus see Brestskaya Voblasts'
138 I9 Brestskaya Voblasts' admin. div. Belarus
158 F5 Bretagne admin. reg. France
217 □1c Bretagne, Pointe de pt Réunion
163 E8 Bretagne-d'Armagnac France
250 C6 Bretana Peru
142 G2 Bretangen b. Norway
216 □1b Bretanha São Miguel Azores
216 □1b Bretanha, Ponta da pt São Miguel Azores
197 O4 Brețcu Romania
158 H5 Breteil France
163 H6 Bretenoux France
159 M4 Breteuil Haute-Normandie France
156 D4 Breteuil Picardie France
158 H8 Brétignolles-sur-Mer France
156 D6 Brétigny-sur-Orge France
171 J8 Bretnig Ger.
182 I5 Bretocino Spain
222 H4 Breton Alta Can.
246 D3 Breton, Cayo i. Cuba
159 M5 Bretoncelles France
237 K11 Breton Sound b. LA U.S.A.
235 G4 Breton Woods NJ U.S.A.
172 F3 Bretten Ger.
150 G1 Bretton Flintshire, Wales U.K.
159 K3 Brettville-sur-Laize France
172 D2 Bretzenheim Ger.
172 G3 Bretzfeld Ger.
252 B2 Breu r. Brazil/Peru
172 G2 Breuberg-Neustadt Ger.
157 L8 Breuches France
157 L8 Breuchin r. France
94 A2 Breueh, Pulau i. Indon.
164 I5 Breugel Neth.
190 D4 Breuil-Cervinia Italy
162 C4 Breuil-Magné France
156 B6 Breuilpont France
164 H4 Breukelen Neth.
169 H8 Breuna Ger.
157 K7 Breuvannes-en-Bassigny France
231 F8 Brevard NC U.S.A.
251 I5 Breves Brazil
142 F2 Brevik Norway
142 I2 Breviken Sweden
160 J4 Brévon r. France
169 H7 Brevörde Ger.
83 K3 Brewarrina N.S.W. Austr.
233 □Q4 Brewer ME U.S.A.
206 C5 Brewerville Liberia
150 H2 Brewood Staffordshire, England U.K.
236 F5 Brewster NE U.S.A.
235 H2 Brewster NY U.S.A.
232 D8 Brewster OH U.S.A.
238 E2 Brewster WA U.S.A.
Brewster, Kap c. Greenland see Kangikajik
83 J5 Brewster, Lake imp. l. N.S.W. Austr.
231 D10 Brewton AL U.S.A.
215 N2 Breyten S. Africa
139 U3 Breytovo Rus. Fed.
177 I2 Breza Slovakia
179 L7 Breze Slovenia
Brezhnev Rus. Fed. see Naberezhnyye Chelny
176 F3 Březí Czech Rep.
188 E3 Brežice Slovenia
179 N7 Breznica Croatia
177 K2 Breznica Slovakia
176 C2 Březnice Czech Rep.
197 K8 Breznik Bulg.
197 L6 Breznița-Motru Romania
197 L9 Breznitsa Bulg.
171 H10 Březno Czech Rep.
177 I3 Brezno Slovakia
156 B6 Brézolles France
177 G2 Březová Czech Rep.
177 G3 Brezová pod Bradlom Slovakia
177 L3 Brezovec Slovakia
179 J7 Brezovica Slovenia
197 N8 Brezovo Bulg.
188 F3 Brezovo Polje plain Croatia
208 D3 Bria C.A.R.
100 I2 Briakan Rus. Fed.
162 G4 Briance r. France
161 J7 Briançon France
241 T4 Brian Head mt. UT U.S.A.
150 E3 Brianne, Llyn resr Wales U.K.
235 H2 Briarcliff Manor NY U.S.A.
160 B1 Briare France
156 E8 Briare, Canal de France
163 H8 Briatexte France
195 K6 Briatico Italy
85 N9 Bribie Island Qld Austr.
161 K7 Bric Bouchet mt. France/Italy
136 G5 Briceni Moldova
161 J7 Bric Froid mt. France/Italy
Brichany Moldova see Briceni
190 C6 Bricherasio Italy
147 E5 Brickeens Ireland
234 C4 Brickerville PA U.S.A.
234 F6 Bricksboro NJ U.S.A.
235 G4 Brick Township NJ U.S.A.
157 I7 Bricon France
158 H3 Bricquebec France
147 G8 Bride r. Ireland
161 J6 Brides-les-Bains France
151 O5 Bridge Kent, England U.K.
235 K3 Bridgehampton NY U.S.A.
147 I7 Bridgeland Ireland
226 H8 Bridgeman MI U.S.A.
147 H2 Bridgend Ireland
146 K9 Bridgend Angus, Scotland U.K.
146 D11 Bridgend Argyll and Bute, Scotland U.K.
150 E4 Bridgend Bridgend, Wales U.K.
146 J8 Bridgend Moray, Scotland U.K.
150 E4 Bridgend admin. div. Wales U.K.
146 I10 Bridge of Allan Stirling, Scotland U.K.
146 H9 Bridge of Balgie Perth and Kinross, Scotland U.K.
146 J9 Bridge of Cally Perth and Kinross, Scotland U.K.
146 J9 Bridge of Craigisla Angus, Scotland U.K.
146 L8 Bridge of Don Aberdeen, Scotland U.K.
146 K9 Bridge of Dun Angus, Scotland U.K.
146 K9 Bridge of Dye Aberdeenshire, Scotland U.K.
146 J10 Bridge of Earn Perth and Kinross, Scotland U.K.
146 I5 Bridge of Forss Highland, Scotland U.K.
146 G9 Bridge of Orchy Argyll and Bute, Scotland U.K.
146 □M2 Bridge of Walls Shetland, Scotland U.K.
146 G11 Bridge of Weir Renfrewshire, Scotland U.K.
231 E8 Bridgeport AL U.S.A.
240 M3 Bridgeport CA U.S.A.
233 L7 Bridgeport CT U.S.A.
227 K6 Bridgeport MI U.S.A.
236 D5 Bridgeport NE U.S.A.
234 E4 Bridgeport PA U.S.A.
237 G9 Bridgeport TX U.S.A.
240 M3 Bridgeport Reservoir CA U.S.A.
238 J4 Bridger MT U.S.A.
238 K6 Bridger Peak WY U.S.A.
234 E6 Bridgeton NJ U.S.A.
87 D12 Bridgetown W.A. Austr.
247 □4 Bridgetown Barbados
225 H4 Bridgetown N.S. Can.
147 I8 Bridgetown Ireland
233 J10 Bridgeville DE U.S.A.
83 K10 Bridgewater Tas. Austr.
225 H4 Bridgewater N.S. Can.
233 O7 Bridgewater MA U.S.A.
233 □R2 Bridgewater ME U.S.A.
233 J6 Bridgewater NY U.S.A.
232 G10 Bridgewater VA U.S.A.
82 H8 Bridgewater, Cape Vic. Austr.
150 H2 Bridgnorth Shropshire, England U.K.
233 □O4 Bridgton ME U.S.A.
150 F5 Bridgwater Somerset, England U.K.
150 F5 Bridgwater Bay England U.K.
176 G2 Břidličná Czech Rep.
149 Q5 Bridlington East Riding of Yorkshire, England U.K.
149 Q5 Bridlington Bay England U.K.
83 K9 Bridport Tas. Austr.
150 G6 Bridport Dorset, England U.K.
162 E4 Brie France
156 E7 Brie reg. France
158 D5 Briec France
156 E6 Brie-Comte-Robert France
169 D10 Briedel Ger.
Brieg Pol. see Brzeg
164 F5 Brielle Neth.
156 I7 Brienne-le-Château France
160 E4 Briennon France
156 G7 Brienon-sur-Armançon France
190 E2 Brienz Switz.
193 P7 Brienza Italy
190 E2 Brienzer Rothorn mt. Switz.
190 D2 Brienzer See l. Switz.
158 G7 Brière, Parc Naturel Régional de nature res. France
234 A1 Brier Mountain hill PA U.S.A.
232 E10 Briery Knob mt. WV U.S.A.
171 J6 Briescht Ger.
170 G5 Brieselang Ger.
171 J6 Briesen Ger.
171 I8 Brieske Ger.
171 K6 Brieskow-Finkenheerd Ger.
171 K7 Briesnig Ger.
168 J4 Brietlingen Ger.
157 I5 Brieuilles-sur-Bar France
183 O4 Brieva de Cameros Spain
157 K5 Briey France
190 D3 Brig Switz.
172 F6 Brigach r. Ger.
261 I2 Brigadier General Diego Lamas Uru.
235 G6 Brigantine NJ U.S.A.
149 Q6 Brigg North Lincolnshire, England U.K.
238 L6 Briggsdale CO U.S.A.
226 E6 Briggsville WI U.S.A.
149 K4 Brigham Cumbria, England U.K.
238 H6 Brigham City UT U.S.A.
149 N6 Brighouse West Yorkshire, England U.K.
151 J6 Brighstone Isle of Wight, England U.K.
83 K7 Bright Vic. Austr.
151 O4 Brightlingsea Essex, England U.K.
261 F6 Brightman, Caleta inlet Arg.
227 Q5 Brighton Ont. Can.
81 E12 Brighton South I. N.Z.
151 L6 Brighton Brighton and Hove, England U.K.
238 L7 Brighton CO U.S.A.
227 K7 Brighton MI U.S.A.
232 H5 Brighton NY U.S.A.
232 C10 Brighton WV U.S.A.
151 L6 Brighton and Hove admin. div. England U.K.
85 H7 Brighton Downs Qld Austr.
81 H8 Brightwater South I. N.Z.
160 F5 Brignais France
163 F8 Brignemont France
158 C4 Brignogan-Plage France
161 I10 Brignoles France
146 H10 Brig o'Turk Stirling, Scotland U.K.
151 K3 Brigstock Northamptonshire, England U.K.
183 O7 Brihuega Spain
191 P6 Brijuni nat. park Croatia
206 A3 Brikama Gambia
226 F5 Brillion WI U.S.A.
157 J6 Brillon-en-Barrois France
169 G8 Brilon Ger.
149 O7 Brimington Derbyshire, England U.K.
226 J3 Brimley MI U.S.A.
140 □G1 Brimnes Iceland
226 C2 Brimson MN U.S.A.
247 □2 Brimstone Hill Fortress National Park St Kitts and Nevis
184 D4 Brinches Port.
182 H6 Brincones Spain
195 N2 Brindisi Italy
195 N2 Brindisi prov. Italy
193 P6 Brindisi Montagna Italy
82 D4 Bring, Lake salt flat S.A. Austr.
188 E3 Brinje Croatia
237 J8 Brinkley AR U.S.A.
261 F2 Brinkmann Arg.
168 E4 Brinkum Niedersachsen Ger.
168 G4 Brinkum Niedersachsen Ger.
82 G5 Brinkworth S.A. Austr.
160 C2 Brinon-sur-Beuvron France
159 P6 Brinon-sur-Sauldre France
149 O7 Brinsley Nottinghamshire, England U.K.
157 L6 Brin-sur-Seille France
149 O7 Brinsworth South Yorkshire, England U.K.
161 C7 Brion France
225 I4 Brion, Île i. Que. Can.
183 O3 Briones Spain
160 E4 Brionnais reg. France
159 M3 Brionne France
161 C6 Brioude France
162 D3 Brioux-sur-Boutonne France
159 K4 Briouze France
225 G2 Brisay Que. Can.
85 N9 Brisbane Qld Austr.
191 L7 Brisighella Italy
159 K7 Brissac-Quincé France
233 □R2 Bristol N.B. Can.
150 G5 Bristol Bristol, England U.K.
150 G5 Bristol admin. div. England U.K.
233 M7 Bristol CT U.S.A.
231 E10 Bristol FL U.S.A.
234 B7 Bristol MD U.S.A.
233 N5 Bristol NH U.S.A.
234 F4 Bristol PA U.S.A.
233 N7 Bristol RI U.S.A.
232 C12 Bristol TN U.S.A.
233 L4 Bristol VT U.S.A.
220 B4 Bristol Bay AK U.S.A.
150 D5 Bristol Channel est. England U.K.
249 G7 Bristol Island S. Sandwich Is
241 Q7 Bristol Lake CA U.S.A.
241 P7 Bristol Mountains CA U.S.A.
151 O2 Briston Norfolk, England U.K.
237 G8 Bristow OK U.S.A.
150 G6 Brit r. England U.K.
Britannia Island Îles Loyauté New Caledonia see Maré
182 D5 Britelo Port.
262 S2 British Antarctic Territory Antarctica
222 F5 British Columbia prov. Can.
221 J1 British Empire Range mts Nunavut Can.
British Guiana country S. America see Guyana
88 C7 British Indian Ocean Territory terr. Indian Ocean
264 J6 British Isles N. Atlantic Ocean
British Solomon Islands country S. Pacific Ocean see Solomon Islands
179 J7 Britof Slovenia
Brito Godins Angola see Kiwaba N'zogi
215 L1 Brits S. Africa
214 H6 Britstown S. Africa
147 J6 Brittas Ireland
147 J7 Brittas Bay Ireland
146 D8 Brittle, Loch b. Scotland U.K.
236 G3 Britton SD U.S.A.
170 I5 Britz Ger.
162 H5 Brive-la-Gaillarde France
161 D6 Brives-Charensac France
183 N3 Briviesca Spain
158 H2 Brix France
178 F5 Brixen im Thale Austria
150 E7 Brixham Torbay, England U.K.
Brixia Italy see Brescia
178 E5 Brixlegg Austria
151 K3 Brixworth Northamptonshire, England U.K.
191 P4 Brkini reg. Slovenia
Brlik Zhambylskaya Oblast' Kazakh. see Birlik
171 K9 Brniště Czech Rep.
176 F2 Brno Czech Rep.
143 N2 Bro Sweden
Broach Gujarat India see Bharuch
231 G8 Broad r. SC U.S.A.
233 K5 Broadalbin NY U.S.A.
87 F11 Broad Arrow W.A. Austr.
224 E3 Broadback r. Que. Can.
150 F6 Broadclyst Devon, England U.K.
83 J7 Broadford Vic. Austr.
147 E7 Broadford Clare Ireland
147 E8 Broadford Limerick Ireland
146 E8 Broadford Highland, Scotland U.K.
147 C4 Broad Haven b. Ireland
150 B4 Broad Haven Pembrokeshire, Wales U.K.
150 H3 Broadheath Worcestershire, England U.K.
146 J12 Broad Law hill Scotland U.K.
150 H6 Broadmayne Dorset, England U.K.
84 E4 Broadmere N.T. Austr.
151 N6 Broad Oak East Sussex, England U.K.
123 Q4 Broad Peak China/Jammu and Kashmir
85 L7 Broad Sound sea chan. Qld Austr.
85 M7 Broad Sound Channel Qld Austr.
85 L7 Broadsound Range hills Qld Austr.
151 O5 Broadstairs Kent, England U.K.
238 L4 Broadus MT U.S.A.
223 K5 Broadview Sask. Can.
83 N3 Broadwater N.S.W. Austr.
236 D5 Broadwater NE U.S.A.
147 J8 Broadway Ireland
151 I3 Broadway Worcestershire, England U.K.
232 G10 Broadway VA U.S.A.
150 H6 Broadwey Dorset, England U.K.
150 G6 Broadwindsor Dorset, England U.K.
80 H2 Broadwood North I. N.Z.
168 I1 Broager Denmark
143 K5 Broby Sweden
190 C2 Broc Switz.
163 C7 Brocas France
138 F5 Brocēni Latvia
146 D8 Brochel Highland, Scotland U.K.
223 K3 Brochet Man. Can.
223 K3 Brochet, Lac l. Man. Can.
149 L6 Brock r. England U.K.
168 I4 Brockel Ger.
168 J5 Bröckel Ger.
169 K7 Brocken mt. Ger.
151 I6 Brockenhurst Hampshire, England U.K.
221 G2 Brock Island N.W.T. Can.
86 D7 Brockman, Mount W.A. Austr.
232 H5 Brockport NY U.S.A.
232 G7 Brockport PA U.S.A.
233 N6 Brockton MA U.S.A.
234 C3 Brockton PA U.S.A.
169 F6 Brockum Ger.
224 F4 Brockville Ont. Can.
233 □R3 Brockway N.B. Can.
232 G7 Brockway PA U.S.A.
150 H4 Brockworth Gloucestershire, England U.K.
232 F6 Brocton NY U.S.A.
174 E2 Broczyno Pol.
198 C2 Brod Macedonia
196 J9 Brod Macedonia
176 G2 Brodek u Přerova Czech Rep.
Broderick Falls Kenya see Webuye
170 F2 Broderstorf Ger.
136 H4 Brodets'ke Ukr.
221 J2 Brodeur Peninsula Nunavut Can.
226 E7 Brodhead WI U.S.A.
234 E3 Brodhead r. PA U.S.A.
234 E3 Brodheadsville PA U.S.A.
146 F11 Brodick North Ayrshire, Scotland U.K.
232 G12 Brodnax VA U.S.A.
175 H2 Brodnica Kujawsko-Pomorskie Pol.
174 E3 Brodnica Wielkopolskie Pol.
167 I2 Brodnicki Park Krajobrazowy Pol.
176 G3 Brodské Slovakia
174 C4 Brody Lubuskie Pol.
174 D3 Brody Lubuskie Pol.
136 E3 Brody Ukr.
215 J2 Broedersput S. Africa
164 J6 Broekhuizenvorst Neth.
215 J6 Broekpoort r. S. Africa
159 M3 Broglie France
169 D10 Brohl Ger.
170 I3 Brohm Ger.
160 G2 Broin France
174 D3 Brójce Pol.
174 D2 Brojce Pol.
175 J3 Brok Pol.
175 J3 Brok r. Pol.
168 H3 Brokdorf Ger.
142 E2 Brokefjell mt. Norway
87 D13 Broke Inlet W.A. Austr.
237 H7 Broken Arrow OK U.S.A.
83 M5 Broken Bay N.S.W. Austr.
236 F5 Broken Bow NE U.S.A.
237 H8 Broken Bow OK U.S.A.
237 H8 Broken Bow Reservoir OK U.S.A.
232 H10 Brokenburg VA U.S.A.
223 L5 Brokenhead r. Man. Can.
82 H4 Broken Hill N.S.W. Austr.
Broken Hill Zambia see Kabwe
265 K7 Broken Plateau sea feature Indian Ocean
251 H3 Brokopondo Suriname
Brokopondo Stuwmeer resr Suriname see Professor van Blommestein Meer
168 I3 Brokstedt Ger.
194 H7 Brolo Sicilia Italy
173 J3 Brombachsee l. Ger.
Bromberg Pol. see Bydgoszcz
168 K5 Brome Ger.
150 G3 Bromfield Shropshire, England U.K.
151 K3 Bromham Bedfordshire, England U.K.
150 H5 Bromham Wiltshire, England U.K.
151 L5 Bromley Greater London, England U.K.
142 F1 Bromma Norway
161 B7 Brommat France
143 J3 Brommö i. Sweden
140 O1 Bromnes Norway
95 J8 Bromo Tengger Semeru, Taman Nasional nat. park Indon.
246 □ Brompton Jamaica

149 O5 Brompton North Yorkshire, England U.K.
149 N5 Brompton on Swale North Yorkshire, England U.K.
143 M5 Brömsebro Sweden
150 H3 Bromsgrove Worcestershire, England U.K.
169 G8 Bromskirchen Ger.
150 G3 Bromyard Herefordshire, England U.K.
160 F5 Bron France
150 E2 Bronaber Gwynedd, Wales U.K.
183 Q7 Bronchales Spain
142 F4 Brønderslev Denmark
206 E5 Brong-Ahafo admin. reg. Ghana
190 G5 Broni Italy
171 K7 Bronice Pol.
215 M1 Bronkhorstspruit S. Africa
139 V6 Bronnitsy Rus. Fed.
140 L4 Brønnøysund Norway
231 F11 Bronson FL U.S.A.
226 I8 Bronson MI U.S.A.
194 H8 Bronte Sicilia Italy
235 H3 Bronx County county NY U.S.A.
136 G3 Bronyts'ka Huta Ukr.
190 H4 Bronzone, Monte mt. Italy
151 O2 Brooke Norfolk, England U.K.
232 H10 Brooke VA U.S.A.
147 H4 Brookeborough Northern Ireland U.K.
92 A7 Brooke's Point Palawan Phil.
235 I1 Brookfield CT U.S.A.
236 I6 Brookfield MO U.S.A.
226 F6 Brookfield WI U.S.A.
237 J10 Brookhaven MS U.S.A.
238 B5 Brookings OR U.S.A.
236 G3 Brookings SD U.S.A.
234 D5 Brookland Terrace DE U.S.A.
233 N6 Brookline MA U.S.A.
226 D9 Brooklyn IL U.S.A.
227 J7 Brooklyn MI U.S.A.
234 B6 Brooklyn Park MD U.S.A.
226 A4 Brooklyn Park MN U.S.A.
232 G11 Brookneal VA U.S.A.
226 A4 Brook Park MN U.S.A.
223 I5 Brooks Alta Can.
233 □P4 Brooks ME U.S.A.
232 E11 Brooks WV U.S.A.
262 T2 Brooks, Cape Antarctica
222 C2 Brooks Brook Y.T. Can.
234 D5 Brookside DE U.S.A.
222 E5 Brooks Peninsula Provincial Park B.C. Can.
220 D3 Brooks Range mts AK U.S.A.
226 H9 Brookston IN U.S.A.
226 B3 Brookston MN U.S.A.
231 F11 Brooksville FL U.S.A.
232 A10 Brooksville KY U.S.A.
87 D12 Brookton W.A. Austr.
233 □R3 Brookton ME U.S.A.
230 E6 Brookville IN U.S.A.
232 F7 Brookville PA U.S.A.
146 F7 Broom, Loch inlet Scotland U.K.
86 G4 Broome W.A. Austr.
87 D12 Broomehill W.A. Austr.
147 I4 Broomfield Ireland
151 M4 Broomfield Essex, England U.K.
158 G5 Broons France
161 B8 Broquiès France
146 I6 Brora Highland, Scotland U.K.
146 I6 Brora r. Scotland U.K.
146 I6 Brora, Loch l. Scotland U.K.
143 K6 Brösarp Sweden
150 H2 Broseley Shropshire, England U.K.
136 D5 Broshniv Osada Ukr.
147 D8 Brosna Ireland
147 G6 Brosna r. Ireland
162 D5 Brossac France
140 N2 Brøstadbotn Norway
197 N3 Broșteni Romania
232 F12 Brosville VA U.S.A.
256 C5 Brotas Brazil
184 C3 Brotas Port.
254 E5 Brotas de Macaúbas Brazil
115 M7 Brothers is Andaman & Nicobar Is India
238 D5 Brothers OR U.S.A.
82 □3 Brothers Point S. Pacific Ocean
186 E2 Broto Spain
159 M3 Brotonne, Parc Naturel Régional de nature res. France
157 J7 Brottes France
149 P4 Brotton Redcar and Cleveland, England U.K.
156 B7 Brou France
149 M4 Brough Cumbria, England U.K.
149 P6 Brough East Riding of Yorkshire, England U.K.
146 J5 Brough Highland, Scotland U.K.
148 B7 Broughal Ireland
146 J4 Brough Head Scotland U.K.
146 K5 Brough Ness pt Scotland U.K.
147 J3 Broughshane Northern Ireland U.K.
150 G1 Broughton Flintshire, Wales U.K.
151 K3 Broughton Northamptonshire, England U.K.
149 P6 Broughton North Lincolnshire, England U.K.
146 J11 Broughton Scottish Borders, Scotland U.K.
151 J2 Broughton Astley Leicestershire, England U.K.
149 K5 Broughton in Furness Cumbria, England U.K.
Broughton Island Nunavut Can. see Qikiqtarjuaq
146 K4 Broughtown Orkney, Scotland U.K.
202 C5 Broulkou well Chad
176 F1 Broumov Czech Rep.
157 I7 Brousseval France
157 M7 Brouvelieures France
164 E5 Brouwershaven Neth.
136 J3 Brovary Ukr.
85 M9 Brovinia Qld Austr.
142 F4 Brovst Denmark
236 H2 Browerville MN U.S.A.
87 E11 Brown, Lake salt flat W.A. Austr.
82 G5 Brown, Mount hill S.A. Austr.
82 D5 Brown, Point S.A. Austr.
246 F3 Brown Bank sea feature Bahamas
227 L6 Brown City MI U.S.A.
85 I4 Brown Creek r. Qld Austr.
226 G6 Brown Deer WI U.S.A.
149 M7 Brown Edge Staffordshire, England U.K.
87 H8 Browne Range hills W.A. Austr.
237 D9 Brownfield TX U.S.A.
151 I2 Brownhills West Midlands, England U.K.
238 H2 Browning MT U.S.A.
240 O6 Brown Mountain CA U.S.A.
226 B6 Brownsdale MN U.S.A.
234 F5 Browns Mills NJ U.S.A.
246 □ Brown's Town Jamaica
230 D6 Brownstown IN U.S.A.
234 C4 Brownstown PA U.S.A.
236 G3 Browns Valley MN U.S.A.
230 D7 Brownsville KY U.S.A.
232 F8 Brownsville PA U.S.A.
237 K8 Brownsville TN U.S.A.
237 G13 Brownsville TX U.S.A.
251 H3 Brownsweg Suriname
233 □P3 Brownville ME U.S.A.
233 □P3 Brownville Junction ME U.S.A.
237 F10 Brownwood TX U.S.A.
243 J2 Brownwood, Lake TX U.S.A.
86 G3 Browse Island W.A. Austr.
146 J11 Broxburn West Lothian, Scotland U.K.
190 C2 Broye r. Switz.
156 G6 Broyes France
171 J10 Brozany Czech Rep.
182 G9 Brozas Spain
138 M9 Brozha Belarus
190 I4 Brozzo Italy
176 E2 Brtnice Czech Rep.
146 I9 Bruar Water r. Scotland U.K.
156 E3 Bruay-la-Bussière France
Bruce Barbados see Bruce Vale
237 K9 Bruce MS U.S.A.
226 C4 Bruce WI U.S.A.
86 E7 Bruce, Mount W.A. Austr.
226 E3 Bruce Crossing MI U.S.A.
227 M5 Bruce Peninsula Ont. Can.
227 M4 Bruce Peninsula National Park Ont. Can.
87 E11 Bruce Rock W.A. Austr.
247 □4 Bruce Vale Barbados
157 O6 Bruche r. France
168 H5 Bruchhausen-Vilsen Ger.
169 G10 Bruchköbel Ger.
172 C3 Bruchmühlbach Ger.
172 F3 Bruchsal Ger.
172 D3 Bruchweiler-Bärenbach Ger.
171 G6 Brück Ger.
178 G5 Bruck an der Großglocknerstraße Austria
179 O3 Bruck an der Leitha Austria
179 L5 Bruck an der Mur Austria
173 L4 Bruckberg Ger.
172 C2 Brücken Ger.
172 C3 Brücken (Pfalz) Ger.
173 M3 Bruck in der Oberpfalz Ger.
179 K6 Brückl Austria
173 L6 Bruckmühl Ger.
195 I9 Brucoli Sicilia Italy
175 H3 Brudzeń Duży Pol.
167 I2 Brudzeński Park Krajobrazowy Pol.
174 G3 Brudzew Pol.
150 G5 Brue r. England U.K.
161 H9 Brue-Auriac France
170 E3 Brüel Ger.
159 P8 Bruère-Allichamps France
165 E7 Brugelette Belgium
Bruges Belgium see Brugge
190 E1 Brugg Switz.
165 D6 Brugge Belgium
169 I6 Brüggen Niedersachsen Ger.
169 B8 Brüggen Nordrhein-Westfalen Ger.
190 H7 Brugnato Italy
191 N4 Brugnera Italy
163 G8 Bruguières France
140 I5 Bruhagen Norway
172 F3 Brühl Baden-Württemberg Ger.
169 C9 Brühl Nordrhein-Westfalen Ger.
232 B10 Bruin KY U.S.A.
232 F7 Bruin PA U.S.A.
164 F5 Bruinisse Neth.
241 V2 Bruin Point mt. UT U.S.A.
117 P5 Bruint Arun. Prad. India
212 C5 Brukkaros Namibia
214 B1 Brukkaros, Mount Namibia
222 G4 Brûlé Alta Can.
226 C3 Brule WI U.S.A.
225 I2 Brûlé, Lac l. Que. Can.
159 K6 Brûlon France
165 G9 Brûly Belgium
257 E4 Brumadinho Brazil
254 E5 Brumado Brazil
157 O6 Brumath France
85 M1 Brumer Islands P.N.G.
164 J4 Brummen Neth.
177 H2 Brumov-Bylnice Czech Rep.
177 G1 Brumovice Czech Rep.
141 K6 Brumunddal Norway
192 F2 Bruna r. Italy
147 J5 Brú Na Bóinne tourist site Ireland
170 D5 Brunau Ger.
151 O2 Brundall Norfolk, England U.K.
151 O3 Brundish Suffolk, England U.K.
Brundisium Italy see Brindisi
238 G5 Bruneau ID U.S.A.
238 G5 Bruneau r. ID U.S.A.
238 G5 Bruneau, East Fork r. ID/NV U.S.A.
238 G5 Bruneau, West Fork r. ID/NV U.S.A.
156 H4 Brunehamel France
95 K2 Brunei country Asia
Brunei Brunei see Bandar Seri Begawan
95 K2 Brunei Bay Malaysia
183 M8 Brunete Spain
84 E5 Brunette Downs N.T. Austr.
225 K4 Brunette Island Nfld and Lab. Can.
140 M5 Brunflo Sweden
191 L2 Brunico Italy
163 H7 Bruniquel France
179 L6 Brunn Austria
Brünn Czech Rep. see Brno
170 H3 Brunn Ger.
143 N2 Brunna Sweden
179 N3 Brunn am Gebirge Austria
190 F1 Brunnen Switz.
81 F9 Brunner, Lake South I. N.Z.
234 C4 Brunnerville PA U.S.A.
223 J4 Bruno Sask. Can.
226 B3 Bruno MN U.S.A.
168 H3 Brunsbüttel Ger.
165 I7 Brunssum Neth.
157 N8 Brunstatt France
Brunswick Ger. see Braunschweig
231 G10 Brunswick GA U.S.A.
232 H9 Brunswick MD U.S.A.
233 □P5 Brunswick ME U.S.A.
236 I6 Brunswick MO U.S.A.
232 D7 Brunswick OH U.S.A.
259 C9 Brunswick, Península de pen. Chile
86 H3 Brunswick Bay W.A. Austr.
83 N3 Brunswick Heads N.S.W. Austr.
87 C12 Brunswick Junction W.A. Austr.
224 D3 Brunswick Lake Ont. Can.
176 G2 Bruntál Czech Rep.
262 W2 Brunt Ice Shelf Antarctica
215 O5 Bruntville S. Africa
83 K10 Bruny Island Tas. Austr.
196 J7 Brus Serbia
Brusa Turkey see Bursa
178 D7 Brusago Italy
142 B3 Brusand Norway
134 H3 Brusenets Rus. Fed.
170 D3 Brüsewitz Ger.
236 D5 Brush CO U.S.A.
233 K4 Brushton NY U.S.A.
190 I3 Brusio Switz.
177 I3 Brusno Slovakia
139 S4 Brusovo Rus. Fed.
255 C8 Brusque Brazil
161 B9 Brusque France
Brussel Belgium see Bruxelles
Brussels Belgium see Bruxelles
227 M6 Brussels Ont. Can.
170 J4 Brüssow Ger.
177 L4 Brusturi Romania
197 O3 Brusturi-Drăgănești Romania
174 F2 Brusy Pol.
136 I3 Brusyliv Ukr.
83 K7 Bruthen Vic. Austr.
150 H5 Bruton Somerset, England U.K.
169 D10 Bruttig-Fankel Ger.
165 F7 Bruxelles Belgium
157 M7 Bruyères France
156 G4 Bruyères-et-Montbérault France
158 H5 Bruz France
250 D2 Bruzual Venez.
195 K7 Bruzzano, Capo c. Italy
177 H2 Brvnište Slovakia
175 I3 Brwinów Pol.
236 M5 Bryan OH U.S.A.
237 G10 Bryan TX U.S.A.
82 G5 Bryan, Mount hill S.A. Austr.
262 S2 Bryan Coast Antarctica
137 R5 Bryanka Ukr.
139 R8 Bryansk Rus. Fed.
129 I1 Bryanskaya Kosa, Mys pt Rus. Fed.
139 Q8 Bryanskaya Oblast' admin. div. Rus. Fed.
Bryansk Oblast admin. div. Rus. Fed. see Bryanskaya Oblast'
129 H1 Bryanskoye Rus. Fed.
237 I8 Bryant AR U.S.A.
226 E4 Bryant WI U.S.A.
237 I7 Bryant Creek r. MO U.S.A.
233 □O4 Bryant Pond ME U.S.A.
241 T4 Bryce Canyon National Park UT U.S.A.
241 W8 Bryce Mountain AZ U.S.A.
150 □ Bryher i. England U.K.
137 M7 Brylivka Ukr.
150 F1 Brymbo Wrexham, Wales U.K.
139 S8 Bryn' Rus. Fed.
150 E4 Brynamman Carmarthenshire, Wales U.K.
Brynbuga Wales U.K. see Usk
142 B3 Bryne Norway
150 F1 Brynford Flintshire, Wales U.K.
175 H5 Brynica r. Pol.
135 G7 Bryn'kovskaya Rus. Fed.
150 F4 Brynmawr Blaenau Gwent, Wales U.K.
234 E4 Bryn Mawr PA U.S.A.
227 Q3 Bryson, Lac l. Que. Can.
231 F8 Bryson City NC U.S.A.
135 G7 Bryukhovetskaya Rus. Fed.
136 C4 Bryukhovychi Ukr.
196 I5 Brzava r. Serbia
174 F5 Brzeg Pol.
174 E4 Brzeg Dolny Pol.
174 G3 Brześć Kujawski Pol.
Brześć nad Bugiem Belarus see Brest
175 I6 Brzesko Pol.
175 H6 Brzeszcze Pol.
174 G3 Brzezie Kujawsko-Pomorskie Pol.
174 E2 Brzezie Pomorskie Pol.
175 H4 Brzeziny Łódzkie Pol.
175 J6 Brzeziny Podkarpackie Pol.
174 G4 Brzeziny Wielkopolskie Pol.
175 H6 Brzeźnica Małopolskie Pol.
175 J5 Brzeźnica Podkarpackie Pol.
174 G4 Brzeźnio Pol.
175 L4 Brzeźno Lubelskie Pol.
174 G3 Brzeźno Wielkopolskie Pol.
174 D2 Brzeźno Zachodniopomorskie Pol.
175 J6 Brzostek Pol.
177 J3 Brzotín Slovakia
175 J4 Brzóza Pol.
175 K6 Brzozów Pol.
175 K2 Brzozówka r. Pol.
175 H2 Brzuze Pol.
175 K5 Brzyska Wola Pol.
156 C6 Bû France
124 G7 Bū well Yemen
209 B6 Bua Angola
79 □7 Bua Vanua Levu Fiji
142 I4 Bua Sweden
210 D4 Bu'aale Somalia
92 E6 Buad i. Phil.
159 J4 Buais France
78 □6 Buala Sta Isabel Solomon Is
Buandougou Côte d'Ivoire see Bouandougou
93 D2 Buang i. Indon.
182 C8 Buarcos Port.
94 D4 Buatan Sumatera Indon.
202 D2 Bū Athlah well Libya
125 J3 Bu'ayj well Saudi Arabia
202 B2 Bu'ayrāt al Hasūn Libya
206 B4 Buba Guinea-Bissau
186 E2 Búbal, Embalse de resr Spain
211 A5 Bubanza Burundi
173 K2 Bubenreuth Ger.
213 F4 Bubi r. Zimbabwe
127 N9 Būbiyān, Jazīrat i. Kuwait
158 E6 Bubry France
92 C8 Bubuan i. Phil.
92 C9 Bubuan i. Phil.
149 P6 Bubwith East Riding of Yorkshire, England U.K.
79 □7 Buca Vanua Levu Fiji
199 I4 Buca Turkey
199 L5 Bucak Turkey
177 G3 Bučany Slovakia
129 I4 Bucaq Azer.
250 C3 Bucaramanga Col.
245 H4 Bucareli Mex.
92 E7 Bucas Grande i. Phil.
86 G4 Buccaneer Archipelago is W.A. Austr.
194 H9 Buccheri Sicilia Italy
193 M3 Bucchianico Italy
191 K7 Bucciana, Monte mt. Italy
190 G5 Buccinasco Italy
193 O6 Buccino Italy
197 O3 Bucecea Romania
197 N5 Bucegi, Munții mts Romania
184 A3 Bucelas Port.
160 H2 Bucey-lès-Gy France
173 I5 Buch Ger.
136 E4 Buchach Ukr.
173 M5 Buch am Erlbach Ger.
83 L7 Buchan Vic. Austr.
84 F5 Buchanan watercourse N.T. Austr.
206 C5 Buchanan Liberia
231 E9 Buchanan GA U.S.A.
226 H8 Buchanan MI U.S.A.
235 H2 Buchanan NY U.S.A.
232 F11 Buchanan VA U.S.A.
85 J6 Buchanan, Lake salt flat Qld Austr.
87 G8 Buchanan, Lake salt flat W.A. Austr.
237 F10 Buchanan, Lake TX U.S.A.
221 K2 Buchan Gulf Nunavut Can.
225 J3 Buchans Nfld and Lab. Can.
Bucharest Romania see București
173 M5 Buchbach Ger.
178 A5 Buchboden Austria
169 D10 Büchel Ger.
168 K4 Büchen Ger.
172 G2 Buchen (Odenwald) Ger.
172 E6 Buchenbach Ger.
173 K3 Büchenbach Ger.
173 I6 Buchenberg Ger.
172 C2 Büchenbeuren Ger.
170 F4 Buchholz Ger.
168 I5 Buchholz (Aller) Ger.
169 D9 Buchholz (Westerwald) Ger.
179 J3 Buchkirchen Austria
173 P4 Büchlberg Ger.
173 J5 Buchloe Ger.
176 G2 Buchlovice Czech Rep.
146 H10 Buchlyvie Stirling, Scotland U.K.
168 I4 Bucholz in der Nordheide Ger.
240 L6 Buchon, Point CA U.S.A.
190 G1 Buchs Switz.
260 A5 Buchupureo Chile
156 B4 Buchy France
197 N4 Bucin, Pasul pass Romania
191 L9 Bucine Italy
234 C5 Buck PA U.S.A.
237 E10 Buckburn Draw watercourse TX U.S.A.
151 L3 Buckden Cambridgeshire, England U.K.
149 M5 Buckden North Yorkshire, England U.K.
169 H6 Bückeburg Ger.
168 H5 Bücken Ger.
241 T8 Buckeye AZ U.S.A.
150 E7 Buckfastleigh Devon, England U.K.
232 E10 Buckhannon WV U.S.A.
232 F9 Buckhannon r. WV U.S.A.
146 J10 Buckhaven Fife, Scotland U.K.
227 P5 Buckhorn Ont. Can.
227 P5 Buckhorn Lake Ont. Can.
146 K7 Buckie Moray, Scotland U.K.
227 S4 Buckingham Que. Can.
244 C4 Buckingham Mex.
151 K3 Buckingham Buckinghamshire, England U.K.
234 E4 Buckingham PA U.S.A.
232 G11 Buckingham VA U.S.A.
84 E2 Buckingham Bay N.T. Austr.
151 K4 Buckinghamshire admin. div. England U.K.
220 B3 Buckland AK U.S.A.
214 H5 Bucklands S. Africa
85 L8 Buckland Tableland reg. Qld Austr.
82 F5 Buckleboo S.A. Austr.
151 J5 Bucklebury West Berkshire, England U.K.
263 K2 Buckle Island Antarctica
82 □3 Buckles Bay S. Pacific Ocean
84 F6 Buckley watercourse Qld Austr.
150 F1 Buckley Flintshire, Wales U.K.
226 F9 Buckley IL U.S.A.
263 J2 Buckley Bay Antarctica
179 M4 Bucklige Welt reg. Austria
237 F7 Bucklin KS U.S.A.
Buckner Bay Okinawa Japan see Nakagusuku-wan
170 J5 Buckow Märkische Schweiz Ger.
146 L8 Bucksburn Aberdeen, Scotland U.K.
234 E4 Bucks County county PA U.S.A.
241 S7 Buckskin Mountains AZ U.S.A.
240 K2 Bucks Mountain CA U.S.A.
233 □Q4 Bucksport ME U.S.A.
170 F5 Bückwitz Ger.
176 G2 Bučovice Czech Rep.
209 B6 Buco-Zau Angola
177 K4 Bucsa Hungary
197 N6 Bucșani Romania
197 O6 București Romania
156 G4 Bucy-lès-Pierrepont France
232 C8 Bucyrus OH U.S.A.
175 H4 Buczek Pol.
140 I5 Bud Norway
139 R8 Buda Rus. Fed.
186 G6 Buda, Illa de i. Spain
171 L6 Budachów Pol.
177 H4 Budai park Hungary
139 N9 Buda-Kashalyova Belarus
177 H4 Budakeszi Hungary
96 B3 Budalin Myanmar
177 H4 Budaörs Hungary
177 I4 Budapest Hungary
116 G5 Budaun Uttar Prad. India
83 M6 Budawang National Park N.S.W. Austr.
124 F4 Budayyi'ah well Saudi Arabia
210 E3 Bud Bud Somalia
87 C10 Budd, Mount hill W.A. Austr.
83 J4 Budda N.S.W. Austr.
263 H2 Budd Coast Antarctica
171 D6 Büddenstedt Ger.
210 D3 Buddi Eth.
234 F3 Budd Lake NJ U.S.A.
146 K10 Buddon Ness pt Scotland U.K.
192 C6 Buddusò Sardegna Italy
150 C6 Bude Cornwall, England U.K.
237 J10 Bude MS U.S.A.
150 C6 Bude Bay England U.K.
165 I6 Budel Neth.
192 C5 Budelli, Isola i. Sardegna Italy
168 I2 Büdelsdorf Ger.
136 E5 Budenets' Ukr.
169 F10 Budenheim Ger.
129 F1 Budennovsk Rus. Fed.
Budennoye Rus. Fed. see Krasnogvardeyskoye
184 B6 Budens Port.
85 N9 Buderim Qld Austr.
197 O6 Budești Romania
123 M9 Budhapur Pak.
123 P7 Budhlada Punjab India
183 O7 Budia Spain
177 I3 Budiná Slovakia
122 G8 Būdīng Iran
169 H10 Büdingen Ger.
179 N7 Budinšćina Croatia
177 G2 Budišov nad Budišovkou Czech Rep.
128 B9 Budīyah, Jabal hills Egypt
128 B9 Budīyah, Jabal mt. Egypt
208 C4 Budjala Dem. Rep. Congo
174 F5 Budkowiczanka r. Pol.
150 F6 Budleigh Salterton Devon, England U.K.
139 P2 Budogoshch' Rus. Fed.
191 N3 Budoia Italy
106 C9 Budongquan Qinghai China
192 D6 Budoni Sardegna Italy
191 L6 Budrio Italy
175 J1 Budry Pol.
Büdszentmihály Hungary see Tiszavasvári
125 I4 Budū, Ḩadabat al plain Saudi Arabia
125 I4 Budū', Sabkhat al salt pan Saudi Arabia
197 K4 Budureasa Romania
177 L4 Buduslău Romania
196 G8 Budva Montenegro
175 K1 Būdviečiai Lith.
Budweis Czech Rep. see České Budějovice
171 J10 Budyně nad Ohří Czech Rep.
138 M6 Budzilava Belarus
175 H4 Budziszewice Pol.
175 H6 Budzów Pol.
174 E3 Budzyń Pol.
207 H5 Buea Cameroon
161 H8 Buëch r. France
240 L7 Buellton CA U.S.A.
186 C6 Bueña Spain
234 F5 Buena NJ U.S.A.
183 P9 Buenache de Alarcón Spain
183 P8 Buenache de la Sierra Spain
260 E4 Buena Esperanza Arg.
250 B4 Buenaventura Col.
242 F3 Buenaventura Mex.
183 K8 Buenaventura Spain
252 E4 Buena Vista Bol.
185 □ Buena Vista Gibraltar
244 E6 Buenavista Michoacán Mex.
245 I2 Buenavista Tamaulipas Mex.
Buena Vista i. N. Mariana Is see Tinian
92 E7 Buenavista Mindanao Phil.
92 C5 Buenavista Phil.
239 K7 Buena Vista CO U.S.A.
231 E9 Buena Vista GA U.S.A.
232 F11 Buena Vista VA U.S.A.
246 D2 Buena Vista, Bahía de b. Cuba
245 H7 Buenavista de Cuéllar Mex.
216 □3a Buenavista del Norte Tenerife Canary Is
183 K3 Buenavista de Valdavia Spain
183 O8 Buendía Spain
183 O8 Buendia, Embalse de resr Spain
209 B6 Buenga r. Angola
209 B6 Buengas Angola
256 B1 Buenolândia Brazil
257 E2 Buenópolis Brazil
261 H4 Buenos Aires Arg.
261 G5 Buenos Aires prov. Arg.
252 B2 Buenos Aires Brazil
250 D5 Buenos Aires Amazonas Col.
250 C4 Buenos Aires Guaviare Col.
242 □R13 Buenos Aires Costa Rica
259 B7 Buenos Aires, Lago l. Arg./Chile
241 U10 Buenos Aires National Wildlife Refuge nature res. AZ U.S.A.
247 □7 Buenos Ayres Trin. and Tob.
259 C7 Buen Pasto Arg.
259 C8 Buen Tiempo, Cabo c. Arg.
255 F5 Buerarema Brazil
250 B4 Buesaco Col.
160 J4 Buet, Le Mont mt. France
182 C4 Bueu Spain
185 M3 Buey, Cabeza de mt. Spain
187 C11 Buey, Sierra del mts Spain
242 G4 Búfalo Mex.
222 H2 Buffalo r. Alta/N.W.T. Can.
236 I3 Buffalo MN U.S.A.
237 I7 Buffalo MO U.S.A.
232 G6 Buffalo NY U.S.A.
232 D9 Buffalo OH U.S.A.
237 F7 Buffalo OK U.S.A.
236 D3 Buffalo SD U.S.A.
237 G10 Buffalo TX U.S.A.
226 C5 Buffalo WI U.S.A.
238 K4 Buffalo WY U.S.A.
237 I7 Buffalo r. AR U.S.A.
231 D8 Buffalo r. TN U.S.A.
226 C5 Buffalo r. WI U.S.A.
234 A4 Buffalo Creek r. PA U.S.A.
222 G3 Buffalo Head Hills Y.T. Can.
222 G3 Buffalo Head Prairie Alta Can.
238 G4 Buffalo Hump mt. ID U.S.A.
222 H2 Buffalo Lake N.W.T. Can.
223 I4 Buffalo Narrows Sask. Can.
213 F4 Buffalo Range Zimbabwe
240 O1 Buffalo Valley NV U.S.A.
246 □ Buff Bay Jamaica
215 O4 Buffels r. KwaZulu-Natal S. Africa
214 E9 Buffels r. Western Cape S. Africa
214 B5 Buffels watercourse S. Africa
214 G9 Buffelsdrif S. Africa
213 E4 Buffels Drift S. Africa
160 F4 Buffières France
169 K8 Bufleben Ger.
231 E8 Buford GA U.S.A.
197 N6 Buftea Romania
170 H1 Bug pen. Ger.
175 L4 Bug r. Pol.
250 B4 Buga Col.
106 D3 Buga Mongolia
207 G4 Buga Nigeria
Buga Buga i. Vanuatu see Toga
177 I5 Bugac Hungary
210 B5 Bugala Island Uganda
83 L4 Bugaldie N.S.W. Austr.
207 G5 Bugana Nigeria
107 J2 Bugant Mongolia
163 I10 Bugarach, Pic de mt. France
Bugaz Ukr. see Zatoka
151 J3 Bugbrooke Northamptonshire, England U.K.
210 E3 Bugda Acable Somalia
199 I2 Buğdaylı Turkey
122 F2 Bugdaýly Turkm.
162 H4 Bugeat France
95 I8 Bugel, Tanjung pt Indon.
160 H5 Bugey reg. France
165 F6 Buggenhout Belgium
192 A9 Buggerru Sardegna Italy
172 D6 Buggingen Ger.
195 □ Buġibba Malta
184 □ Bugio i. Madeira
129 C7 Buğlan Geçidi pass Turkey
193 L3 Bugnara Italy
163 C9 Bugnein France
188 F3 Bugojno Bos.-Herz.
140 T2 Bugøyfjord Norway
134 J1 Bugrino Rus. Fed.
92 A7 Bugsuk i. Phil.
107 Q2 Bugt Nei Mongol China
92 C2 Buguey Luzon Phil.
92 D5 Bugui Point Masbate Phil.
135 K5 Bugul'ma Rus. Fed.
120 I4 Bugun' Kazakh.
Bügür Xinjiang China see Luntai
120 E1 Buguruslan Rus. Fed.
177 I4 Bugyi Hungary
117 N6 Buha Arun. Prad. India
122 F6 Būhābād Iran
199 J5 Buharkent Turkey
213 F3 Buhera Zimbabwe
106 F8 Buh He r. China
92 D5 Buhi Luzon Phil.
172 E4 Bühl Ger.
238 G5 Buhl ID U.S.A.
226 B2 Buhl MN U.S.A.
172 E4 Bühlertal Ger.
172 H3 Bühlertann Ger.
172 H3 Bühlerzell Ger.
169 K7 Bühne Ger.
211 A6 Buhoro Tanz.
211 B7 Buhoro Flats plain Tanz.
136 F3 Buhryn Ukr.
127 K5 Bühtan r. Turkey
211 B6 Buhu r. Tanz.
197 O4 Buhuși Romania
191 O3 Buia Italy
222 F3 Buick B.C. Can.
146 E10 Buie, Loch b. Scotland U.K.
150 F3 Builth Wells Powys, Wales U.K.
260 B3 Buin Chile
122 D4 Bū'īn Iran
78 □6 Buin P.N.G.
206 E4 Bui National Park Ghana
135 J5 Buinsk Rus. Fed.
122 B4 Bu'in Soflā Iran
122 D4 Bu'in Zahrā Iran
107 O3 Buir Nur l. Mongolia
161 G8 Buis-les-Baronnies France
164 J2 Buitenpost Neth.
212 C4 Buitepos Namibia
183 M7 Buitrago del Lozoya Spain
138 I7 Būivydžiai Lith.
185 K5 Bujalance Spain
197 J8 Bujanovac Serbia
186 E5 Bujaraloz Spain
191 P5 Buje Croatia
197 N7 Bujoru Romania
211 A5 Bujumbura Burundi
179 O5 Bük Hungary
174 E3 Buk Pol.
99 K1 Bukachacha Rus. Fed.
175 M6 Bukachivtsi Ukr.
111 J8 Buka Daban mt. Qinghai/Xinjiang China
91 L8 Buka Island P.N.G.
212 E3 Bukalo Namibia
209 E7 Bukama Dem. Rep. Congo
122 B3 Būkān Iran
139 R8 Bukan' Rus. Fed.
122 E6 Būkand Iran
121 S1 Bukanskoye Rus. Fed.
208 F5 Bukavu Dem. Rep. Congo
209 C6 Bukedi Dem. Rep. Congo
211 B6 Bukene Tanz.
209 E7 Bukeya Dem. Rep. Congo
Bukhara Buxoro Uzbek. see Buxoro
Bukhara Oblast admin. div. Uzbek. see Buxoro
138 M6 Bukhava Belarus
Bukhoro Uzbek. see Buxoro
Bukhoro Wiloyati admin. div. Uzbek. see Buxoro
100 B1 Bukhta Rus. Fed.
121 U3 Bukhtarminskoye Vodokhranilishche resr Kazakh.
93 D2 Bukide i. Indon.
211 B5 Bukima Tanz.
95 J5 Bukit Baka-Bukit Raya, Taman Nasional nat. park Indon.
95 J6 Bukitlidi Kalimantan Indon.
94 □ Bukit Timah Sing.
94 D5 Bukittinggi Sumatera Indon.
177 J3 Bükk mts Hungary
177 J4 Bükkábrány Hungary
177 J4 Bükkalja hills Hungary
114 E5 Bukkapatnam Andhra Prad. India
177 J3 Bükki nat. park Hungary
177 G5 Bükkösd Hungary
177 J4 Bükkzsérc Hungary
171 F7 Buko Ger.
211 A5 Bukoba Tanz.
138 H6 Bukonys Lith.
177 H2 Bukovec Czech Rep.
179 J8 Bukovje Slovenia
177 L2 Bukovské vrchy hills Slovakia
175 K5 Bukowa r. Pol.
174 F3 Bukowe Pol.
174 F4 Bukowice Pol.
174 G2 Bukowiec Kujawsko-Pomorskie Pol.
174 D3 Bukowiec Lubuskie Pol.
171 L6 Bukowiec hill Pol.
174 F1 Bukowina Pol.
175 I6 Bukowina Tatrzańska Pol.
174 G4 Bukownica Pol.
175 H5 Bukowno Pol.
174 F2 Bukowo Pol.
143 M7 Bukowo, Jezioro lag. Pol.
175 K6 Bukowsko Pol.
Bükreș Romania see București
94 F5 Buku, Tanjung pt Indon.
107 L2 Bukukun Rus. Fed.
94 □ Bukum, Pulau i. Sing.
136 J4 Buky Ukr.
122 E6 Būl, Kūh-e mt. Iran
206 B3 Bula Guinea-Bissau
93 G5 Bula Seram Indon.
209 B7 Bula Atumba Angola
190 F1 Bülach Switz.
107 K2 Bulag Mongolia
107 J2 Bulagtay Mongolia
83 N5 Bulahdelah N.S.W. Austr.
92 C6 Bulalacao i. Phil.
94 E4 Bulan i. Indon.
92 D5 Bulan Luzon Phil.
92 C8 Bulan i. Phil.
126 I3 Bulancak Turkey
116 F5 Bulandshahr Uttar Prad. India
127 K4 Bulanık Turkey
120 F1 Bulanovo Rus. Fed.
203 F3 Būlāq Egypt
100 L3 Bulava Rus. Fed.
93 C3 Bulawa, Gunung mt. Indon.
213 F4 Bulawayo Zimbabwe
121 N1 Bulayevo Kazakh.
126 H5 Bulbul Syria
208 E2 Bulbul, Wadi watercourse Sudan
211 C5 Bulbula waterhole Kenya
199 J4 Buldan Turkey
116 F9 Buldhana Mahar. India
252 A2 Buldibuyo Peru
220 A4 Buldir Island AK U.S.A.
116 F4 Buldur Hima. Prad. India
120 E2 Buldurta Kazakh.
Buldyrty Kazakh. see Buldurta
123 J8 Buleda reg. Pak.
210 E3 Bulei well Eth.
215 P1 Bulembu Swaziland
206 E4 Bulenga Ghana
151 I5 Bulford Wiltshire, England U.K.
106 H2 Bulgan Bulgan Mongolia
Bulgan Hovd Mongolia see Bürenhayrhan
106 C3 Bulgan Hovd Mongolia
106 G1 Bulgan Hövsgöl Mongolia
106 H4 Bulgan Ömnögovĭ Mongolia
106 H2 Bulgan prov. Mongolia
106 B3 Bulgan Gol r. Mongolia
Bulgar Rus. Fed. see Bolgar
197 Q7 Bŭlgarevo Bulg.
197 N8 Bulgaria country Europe
Bŭlgariya country Europe see Bulgaria
124 E3 Bulghah Saudi Arabia
193 O7 Bulgheria, Monte mt. Italy
157 K7 Bulgnéville France
129 D5 Bulgurlu Turkey
137 M9 Bulhanak r. Ukr.
93 F3 Buli Halmahera Indon.
93 F3 Buli, Teluk b. Halmahera Indon.
92 A7 Bulilüyan, Cape Palawan Phil.
210 A4 Bulisa Uganda
168 G3 Bülkau Ger.
151 J3 Bulkington Warwickshire, England U.K.
222 D4 Bulkley Ranges mts B.C. Can.
175 I3 Bulkowo Pol.
Bulla, Ostrov is Azer. see Xärä Zirä Adası
185 K3 Bullaque r. Spain
185 P4 Bullas Spain
85 I9 Bullawarra, Lake salt flat Qld Austr.
210 E2 Bullaxaar Somalia
169 D10 Bullay Ger.
246 □ Bull Bay Jamaica
190 C2 Bulle Switz.
83 H4 Bullea, Lake salt flat N.S.W. Austr.
247 □10 Bullenbaai b. Curaçao Neth. Antilles
81 F8 Buller r. South I. N.Z.
85 I4 Bulleringa National Park Qld Austr.
87 E11 Bullfinch W.A. Austr.
241 R6 Bullhead City AZ U.S.A.
83 M6 Bulli N.S.W. Austr.
165 J8 Büllingen Belgium
241 P7 Bullion Mountains CA U.S.A.
140 P4 Bullmark Sweden
84 B3 Bullo r. N.T. Austr.
183 P7 Bullones r. Spain
83 I3 Bulloo watercourse Qld Austr.
83 I3 Bulloo Downs Qld Austr.
83 I3 Bulloo Lake salt flat Qld Austr.
147 J2 Bull Point Northern Ireland U.K.
80 J7 Bulls North I. N.Z.
246 □ Bull Savannah Jamaica
235 I1 Bulls Bridge CT U.S.A.
237 I7 Bull Shoals Lake AR U.S.A.
212 C5 Büllsport Namibia
235 G1 Bullville NY U.S.A.
156 E3 Bully-les-Mines France
84 E2 Bulman N.T. Austr.
84 E2 Bulman Gorge N.T. Austr.
222 F2 Bulmer Lake N.W.T. Can.
151 N3 Bulmer Tye Essex, England U.K.
260 A5 Bulnes Chile
94 □ Buloh, Pulau i. Sing.
83 I7 Buloke, Lake dry lake Vic. Austr.
91 K8 Bulolo P.N.G.
196 I9 Bulqizë Albania
192 C7 Bultei Sardegna Italy
215 K4 Bultfontein S. Africa
95 L3 Bulu, Gunung mt. Indon.
92 E8 Buluan Mindanao Phil.
93 B6 Bulubulu Sulawesi Indon.
210 C3 Buluk well Kenya
93 B6 Bulukumba Sulawesi Indon.
208 D5 Bulukutu Dem. Rep. Congo
131 N2 Bulun Rus. Fed.
123 P2 Bulungkol Xinjiang China
209 C6 Bulungu Bandundu Dem. Rep. Congo
209 D6 Bulungu Kasaï-Occidental Dem. Rep. Congo
129 E2 Bulungu Rus. Fed.
121 L8 Bulung'ur Uzbek.
92 E5 Bulusan Luzon Phil.
214 C1 Bulwana Namibia
215 N5 Bulwer S. Africa
177 L5 Bulz Romania
192 B6 Bulzi Sardegna Italy
78 □6 Buma Malaita Solomon Is
209 C6 Bumba Bandundu Dem. Rep. Congo
208 D4 Bumba Équateur Dem. Rep. Congo
202 D1 Būmbah Libya
202 D1 Bumbah, Khalīj b. Libya
106 I6 Bumbat Nei Mongol China
106 I3 Bumbat Mongolia
197 L5 Bumbești-Jiu Romania
206 C4 Bumbuna Sierra Leone
96 C1 Bumhkang Myanmar
96 C1 Bumpha Bum mt. Myanmar
209 C5 Buna Dem. Rep. Congo
210 C4 Buna Kenya
147 C5 Bunacurry Ireland
125 J4 Bunayyān well Saudi Arabia
211 A5 Bunazi Tanz.
147 F2 Bunbeg Ireland
87 C12 Bunbury W.A. Austr.
149 L7 Bunbury Cheshire, England U.K.
147 I7 Bunclody Ireland
147 H2 Buncrana Ireland
211 B5 Bunda Tanz.
85 N8 Bundaberg Qld Austr.
83 K3 Bundaleer Qld Austr.
83 M4 Bundarra N.S.W. Austr.
168 D4 Bunde Ger.
169 G6 Bünde Ger.
172 C2 Bundenbach Ger.
168 D4 Bunderhee Ger.
84 E6 Bundey watercourse N.T. Austr.
116 E7 Bundi Rajasthan India
210 A4 Bundibugyo Uganda
83 N3 Bundjalung National Park N.S.W. Austr.
147 F4 Bundoran Ireland
117 J8 Bundu Jharkhand India
210 A3 Bunduqiya Sudan
196 H9 Bunë r. Albania/Montenegro
122 C6 Būneh i. Iran
125 I1 Būneh Dara b. Iran
123 O4 Buner reg. Pak.
207 H3 Bunga r. Nigeria
104 C5 Bunga-dake mt. Japan
94 C6 Bungalaut, Selat sea chan. Indon.
151 O3 Bungay Suffolk, England U.K.
83 L6 Bungendore N.S.W. Austr.
263 G2 Bunger Hills Antarctica
93 C6 Bungi Sulawesi Indon.
85 L9 Bungil Creek r. Qld Austr.
93 B5 Bungku Sulawesi Indon.
Bungle Bungle National Park W.A. Austr. see Purnululu National Park
209 B6 Bungo Angola
210 B4 Bungoma Kenya
111 J10 Bungona'og Xizang China
103 J13 Bungo-suidō sea chan. Japan
103 I13 Bungo-Takada Japan
Bunguran, Kepulauan is Indon. see Natuna, Kepulauan
Bunguran, Pulau i. Indon. see Natuna Besar
94 G8 Buni, Ci r. Indon.
208 F4 Bunia Dem. Rep. Congo
183 M4 Buniel Spain
177 L6 Bunila Romania
87 G11 Buningonia well W.A. Austr.
207 I4 Buni-Yadi Nigeria
116 E2 Bunji Jammu and Kashmir
237 J7 Bunker MO U.S.A.
85 N7 Bunker Group atolls Q…
209 E7 Bunkeya Dem. Rep. Co…
237 I10 Bunkie LA U.S.A.
141 L6 Bunkris Sweden
147 H8 Bunmahon Ireland
147 C4 Bunnahowen Ireland
147 E4 Bunnanadden Ireland
231 G11 Bunnell FL U.S.A.
164 H4 Bunnik Neth.
147 D4 Bunnyconnellan Irelan…
80 J7 Bunnythorpe North I. N…
187 D9 Buñol Spain
164 H4 Bunschoten-Spakenbu…
111 F11 Bünsum Xizang China
207 G3 Bunsuru watercourse …
177 L5 Buntești Romania
87 D10 Buntine W.A. Austr.
151 L4 Buntingford Hertfordsh… England U.K.
95 K5 Buntok Kalimantan Ind…
95 K5 Buntokecil Kalimantan …
183 R5 Buñuel Spain
207 H4 Bununu Nigeria
85 M9 Bunya Mountains Nat… Park Qld Austr.
126 G4 Bünyan Turkey
187 K8 Bunyola Spain
95 L3 Bunyu i. Indon.
207 G3 Bunza Nigeria
188 F3 Buoač Bos.-Herz.
Buoddobohki Fin. see Patoniva
193 P7 Buonabitacolo Italy
193 N5 Buonalbergo Italy
192 G1 Buonconvento Italy
97 I8 Buôn Hô Vietnam
97 I8 Buôn Ma Thuột Vietna…
193 P8 Buonvicino Italy
131 O2 Buorkhaya, Guba b. R…
111 H12 Bup r. China
124 F2 Buqay'ā Saudi Arabia
Buqayq Saudi Arabia s… Abqaiq
202 E2 Buqbuq Egypt
Buqtyrma Bögeni resr Kazakh. see Bukhtarmi… Vodokhranilishche
211 C5 Bura Kenya
210 F2 Buraan Somalia
122 H9 Burak Iran
87 D11 Burakin W.A. Austr.
208 E2 Buram Sudan
121 U3 Buran Kazakh.
94 □ Buran Darat rf Sing.
116 H4 Burang Xizang China
257 G2 Buranhaém Brazil
257 H2 Buranhaém r. Brazil
120 F2 Burannoye Rus. Fed.
191 N8 Burano r. Italy
128 E5 Burāq Syria
92 E6 Burauen Leyte Phil.
123 O4 Burawai Pak.
116 E9 Buray r. India
124 F2 Buraydah Saudi Arabia
134 K5 Burayevo Rus. Fed.
169 F9 Burbach Ger.
151 I5 Burbage Wiltshire, Eng… U.K.
186 C5 Burbáguena Spain
240 N7 Burbank CA U.S.A.
192 C9 Burcei Sardegna Italy
137 O6 Burchak Ukr.
226 D1 Burchell Lake Ont. Ca…
83 K5 Burcher N.S.W. Austr.
210 E2 Burco Somalia
164 I2 Burdaard Neth.
123 K2 Burdalyk Turkm.
85 K5 Burdekin r. Qld Austr.
85 K6 Burdekin Falls Qld Au…
160 H4 Burdet, Mont mt. Fran…
Burdigala France see Bordeaux
165 H7 Burdinne Belgium
199 L5 Burdur Turkey
199 L5 Burdur prov. Turkey
199 L5 Burdur Gölü l. Turkey
Burdwan W. Bengal Inc… Barddhaman
210 C2 Burē Āmara Eth.
210 B2 Burē Oromīya Eth.
151 P2 Bure r. England U.K.
161 H7 Bure, Pic de mt. Franc…
140 P4 Bureå Sweden
100 H3 Bureinskiy Khrebet m… Rus. Fed.
203 F5 Bureiqa well Sudan
183 L3 Burejo r. Spain
182 F1 Burela, Cabo c. Spain
169 G7 Büren Ger.
164 H5 Buren Neth.
190 C1 Büren an der Aare Sw…
106 B3 Bürenhayrhan Mongo…
107 L3 Bürentsogt Mongolia
260 A5 Bureo r. Chile
151 N4 Bures Suffolk, England …
100 F4 Bureya r. Rus. Fed.
Bureya-Pristan' Rus. … Novobureyskiy
Bureya Range mts Ru… see Bureinskiy Khrebe…
100 I3 Bureyinski Zapovedni… nature res. Rus. Fed.
227 N6 Burford Ont. Can.
151 I4 Burford Oxfordshire, England U.K.
128 A7 Būr Fu'ād Egypt
163 E9 Burg France
171 J7 Burg Ger.
168 H3 Burg (Dithmarschen) …
106 I2 Burgaltay Mongolia
182 I5 Burganes de Valverde…
197 P8 Burgas Bulg.
179 N5 Burgau Austria
173 I5 Burgau Ger.
184 B6 Burgau Port.
170 D2 Burg auf Fehmarn Ge…
231 I8 Burgaw NC U.S.A.
171 E6 Burg bei Magdeburg …
173 I6 Burgberg im Allgäu G…
173 I3 Burgbernheim Ger.
169 D10 Burgbrohl Ger.
169 J6 Burgdorf Niedersachse…
169 J6 Burgdorf Niedersachse…
190 D1 Burgdorf Switz.
173 J2 Burgebrach Ger.
171 E9 Bürgel Ger.
179 N5 Burgenland land Austr…
225 J4 Burgeo Nfld and Lab. C…
215 K6 Burgersdorp S. Africa
213 F5 Burgersfort S. Africa
214 I6 Burgerville S. Africa
87 F11 Burges, Mount hill W.A…
233 I11 Burgess VA U.S.A.
151 L6 Burgess Hill West Suss… England U.K.
202 E4 Burget Tuyur waterho…
173 J2 Burghaslach Ger.
169 I9 Burghaun Ger.
173 N5 Burghausen Ger.
149 K4 Burgh by Sands Cumb… England U.K.
151 J5 Burghclere Hampshire, England U.K.
146 J7 Burghead Moray, Scotla…
146 I7 Burghead Bay Scotlan…
173 K4 Burgheim Ger.
151 J5 Burghfield Common … Berkshire, England U.K.
164 E5 Burgh-Haamstede Ne…
150 G3 Burghill Herefordshire, England U.K.
149 R7 Burgh le Marsh Lincol… England U.K.
194 E8 Burgio Sicilia Italy
194 H9 Burgio, Serra di hill Si… Italy
178 H3 Burgkirchen Austria
173 N5 Burgkirchen an der A…
171 D10 Burgkunstadt Ger.
190 G1 Bürglen Thurgau Switz
190 F2 Bürglen Uri Switz.
173 M3 Burglengenfeld Ger.
173 J3 Burgoberbach Ger.
183 K8 Burgohondo Spain
183 M6 Burgomillodo, Embals… resr Spain
192 B7 Burgos Sardegna Italy
243 J5 Burgos Mex.
183 M4 Burgos Spain
183 M4 Burgos prov. Spain
169 K10 Burgpreppach Ger.

Burgrieden Ger.
Burgsalach Ger.
Burgsinn Ger.
Bürgstadt Ger.
Burgstädt Ger.
Burg Stargand Ger.
Burgsvik Gotland Sweden
Burgthann Ger.
Burgtonna Ger.
Burgui Spain
Burguillo, Embalse de resr Spain
Burguillos Spain
Burguillos del Cerro Spain
Burgum Neth.
Burgwald for. Ger.
Burgwindheim Ger.
Burhabalanga r. India
Burhan Budai Shan mts China
Burhaniye Turkey
Burhanpur Madh. Prad. India
Burhanuddin Bangl.
Burhar-Dhanpuri Madh. Prad. India
Burhave (Butjadingen) Ger.
Burhi Gandak r. India
Burhou i. Channel Is
Buri Brazil
Buriai Indon.
Burias i. Phil.
Buriasco Italy
Buriat-Mongol Republic aut. rep. Rus. Fed. see Buryatiya, Respublika
Buribay Rus. Fed.
13 Burica, Punta pt Costa Rica
Burie France
Buri Gandak r. Nepal
Burin Nfld and Lab. Can.
Burin Peninsula Nfld and Lab. Can.
Buriram Thai.
Buritama Brazil
Buriti Brazil
Buriti r. Brazil
Buriti Alegre Brazil
Buriti Bravo Brazil
Buriti dos Lopes Brazil
Buritirama Brazil
Buritis Brazil
Buritizeiro Brazil
Burjassot Spain
Burjay Xinjiang China
Burj Aziz Khan Pak.
Burjuc Romania
Burk Ger.
Burkan-Suu r. Kyrg.
Burkardroth Ger.
Burkburnett TX U.S.A.
Burke watercourse Qld Austr.
Burke SD U.S.A.
Burke Channel B.C. Can.
Burke Island Antarctica
Burkes Pass South I. N.Z.
Burkesville KY U.S.A.
Burketown Qld Austr.
Burkeville VA U.S.A.
Burkhala Rus. Fed.
Burkina country Africa
Burkina Faso country Africa see Burkina
Burk's Falls Ont. Can.
Burkutty Kazakh.
Burla Rus. Fed.
Burla r. Rus. Fed.
Burlada Spain
Burladingen Ger.
Burlats France
Burleigh Qld Austr.
Burleigh NJ U.S.A.
Burley Hampshire, England U.K.
Burley ID U.S.A.
Burley Gate Herefordshire, England U.K.
Burley in Wharfedale West Yorkshire, England U.K.
Burli Kazakh.
Burlin Kazakh.
Burlingame CA U.S.A.
Burlington Ont. Can.
Burlington CO U.S.A.
Burlington CT U.S.A.
Burlington IA U.S.A.
Burlington IN U.S.A.
Burlington KS U.S.A.
Burlington KY U.S.A.
Burlington NC U.S.A.
Burlington NJ U.S.A.
Burlington VT U.S.A.
Burlington WA U.S.A.
Burlington WI U.S.A.
Burlington County county NJ U.S.A.
Burly Rus. Fed.
Burma country Asia see Myanmar
Burmakino Kirovskaya Oblast' Rus. Fed.
Burmakino Yaroslavskaya Oblast' Rus. Fed.
Burmantovo Rus. Fed.
Burminka Rus. Fed.
Bürmoos Austria
Burnaby B.C. Can.
Burnchurch Ireland
Burness Orkney, Scotland U.K.
Burnet TX U.S.A.
Burnett r. Qld Austr.
Burnett Heads Qld Austr.
Burney CA U.S.A.
Burney, Monte vol. Chile
Burnfoot Ireland
Burnfoot Northern Ireland U.K.
Burnham South I. N.Z.
Burnham Buckinghamshire, England U.K.
Burnham ME U.S.A.
Burnham PA U.S.A.
Burnham Market Norfolk, England U.K.
Burnham-on-Crouch Essex, England U.K.
Burnham-on-Sea Somerset, England U.K.
Burnhouse North Ayrshire, Scotland U.K.
Burnie Tas. Austr.
Burning Springs KY U.S.A.
Burniston North Yorkshire, England U.K.
Burnley Lancashire, England U.K.
Burnmouth Scottish Borders, Scotland U.K.
Burnopfield Durham, England U.K.
Burnoye Kazakh. see Bauyrzhan Momyshuly
Burns OR U.S.A.
Burnside r. Nunavut Can.
Burnside, Lake salt flat W.A. Austr.
Burns Junction OR U.S.A.
Burns Lake B.C. Can.
Burnsville MN U.S.A.
Burnsville WV U.S.A.
Burnsville Lake WV U.S.A.
Burnt r. OR U.S.A.
Burntisland Fife, Scotland U.K.
Burnt Lake Que. Can. see Brûlé, Lac
Burnt Pine Norfolk I.
Burntwood r. Man. Can.
Burntwood Green Staffordshire, England U.K.
Burntwood Lake Man. Can.
Burog Co l. Xizang China
Buron r. Que. Can.
Buron Rus. Fed.
Burón Spain
Buronzo Italy
Buros France
Burow Ger.
Burqin Xinjiang China
Burqin He r. China
Burqu' Jordan
Burra S.A. Austr.
Burra i. Scotland U.K.
Burravoe Shetland, Scotland U.K.
146 K5 Burray i. Scotland U.K.
196 I9 Burrel Albania
240 M5 Burrel CA U.S.A.
146 J9 Burrelton Perth and Kinross, Scotland U.K.
147 D6 Burren Ireland
147 D5 Burren Ireland
147 D6 Burren reg. Ireland
148 E5 Burren Northern Ireland U.K.
83 L5 Burrendong, Lake resr N.S.W. Austr.
83 L4 Burren Junction N.S.W. Austr.
83 M6 Burrewarra Point N.S.W. Austr.
187 E8 Burriana Spain
83 L6 Burrinjuck Reservoir N.S.W. Austr.
243 H3 Burro, Serranías del mts Mex.
226 C6 Burr Oak IA U.S.A.
232 C9 Burr Oak Reservoir OH U.S.A.
241 S7 Burro Creek watercourse AZ U.S.A.
148 I4 Burrow Head Scotland U.K.
84 C2 Burrundie N.T. Austr.
258 D2 Burruyacú Arg.
150 D4 Burry Inlet Wales U.K.
150 D4 Burry Port Carmarthenshire, Wales U.K.
178 A5 Bürs Austria
199 K2 Bursa Turkey
199 J2 Bursa prov. Turkey
203 G3 Būr Safājah Egypt
203 G2 Būr Sa'īd Egypt
126 F8 Būr Sa'īd governorate Egypt
149 L6 Burscough Lancashire, England U.K.
149 L6 Burscough Bridge Lancashire, England U.K.
169 I7 Bursfelde Ger.
136 D4 Burshtyn Ukr.
100 G3 Bursinskoye Vodokhranilishche resr Rus. Fed.
172 E2 Bürstadt Ger.
151 L5 Burstow Surrey, England U.K.
Būr Sudan Sudan see Port Sudan
82 H5 Burta N.S.W. Austr.
128 A9 Būr Tawfīq Egypt
173 I5 Burtenbach Ger.
226 J4 Burt Lake MI U.S.A.
138 I4 Burtnieku ezers l. Latvia
151 I6 Burton Dorset, England U.K.
227 K7 Burton MI U.S.A.
224 E2 Burton, Lac l. Que. Can.
150 G6 Burton Bradstock Dorset, England U.K.
149 L5 Burton-in-Kendal Cumbria, England U.K.
151 K3 Burton Latimer Northamptonshire, England U.K.
149 O5 Burton Leonard North Yorkshire, England U.K.
147 F3 Burtonport Ireland
234 B6 Burtonsville MD U.S.A.
149 P6 Burton upon Stather North Lincolnshire, England U.K.
151 I2 Burton upon Trent Staffordshire, England U.K.
140 P4 Burträsk Sweden
233 □S2 Burtts Corner N.B. Can.
83 I5 Burtundy N.S.W. Austr.
84 D7 Burt Well N.T. Austr.
93 E5 Buru i. Maluku Indon.
121 O5 Burubaytal Kazakh.
183 L9 Burujón Spain
128 B8 Burūk, Wādī al watercourse Egypt
137 N8 Burul'cha r. Ukr.
126 E8 Burullus, Buḩayrat al lag. Egypt
Burullus, Lake lag. Egypt see Burullus, Buḩayrat al
Burultokay Xinjiang China see Fuhai
125 I8 Burūm Yemen
128 B7 Burūn, Ra's pt Egypt
211 A5 Burundi country Africa
Burunniy Rus. Fed. see Tsagan Aman
211 A5 Bururi Burundi
207 G5 Burutu Nigeria
150 G3 Burwarton Shropshire, England U.K.
151 M6 Burwash East Sussex, England U.K.
222 B2 Burwash Landing Y.T. Can.
151 M3 Burwell Cambridgeshire, England U.K.
236 F5 Burwell NE U.S.A.
146 K5 Burwick Orkney, Scotland U.K.
149 M6 Bury Greater Manchester, England U.K.
Buryatia aut. rep. Rus. Fed. see Buryatiya, Respublika
106 H1 Buryatiya, Respublika aut. rep. Rus. Fed.
Buryatskaya Mongolskaya A.S.S.R. aut. rep. Rus. Fed. see Buryatiya, Respublika
Būrylbaytal Kazakh. see Burubaytal
137 M2 Buryn' Ukr.
120 D5 Burynshyk Kazakh.
151 N3 Bury St Edmunds Suffolk, England U.K.
261 H4 Burzaco Arg.
174 G4 Burzenin Pol.
161 E7 Burzet France
116 E2 Burzil Pass Jammu and Kashmir
192 B7 Busachi Sardegna Italy
190 F6 Busalla Italy
Busan Pusan-si S. Korea see Pusan
124 F8 Būs'ān Yemen
190 I7 Busana Italy
92 D8 Busan Bay Mindanao Phil.
208 D5 Busanga Dem. Rep. Congo
238 K4 Busby MT U.S.A.
190 C6 Busca Italy
179 N2 Buschberg hill Austria
170 G5 Buschow Ger.
168 I2 Busdorf Ger.
Buseire Syria see Al Buşayrah
194 D7 Buseto Palizzolo Sicilia Italy
148 D3 Bush r. Northern Ireland U.K.
136 H5 Busha Ukr.
136 F3 Bushcha Ukr.
122 D7 Būshehr Iran
122 D7 Būshehr prov. Iran
210 A5 Bushenyi Uganda
151 L4 Bushey Hertfordshire, England U.K.
Bushire Iran see Būshehr
234 E2 Bushkill PA U.S.A.
234 F2 Bush Kill r. PA U.S.A.
147 I2 Bushmills Northern Ireland U.K.
231 F11 Bushnell FL U.S.A.
226 D9 Bushnell IL U.S.A.
196 I9 Bushtricë Albania
210 B4 Busia Kenya
156 F3 Busigny France
177 I3 Bušince Slovakia
94 □ Busing, Pulau i. Sing.
208 D4 Businga Dem. Rep. Congo
208 C5 Busira r. Dem. Rep. Congo
142 J1 Busjön l. Sweden
136 D4 Bus'k Ukr.
142 E1 Buskerud county Norway
175 I5 Busko-Zdrój Pol.
Buskul' Kazakh. see Boskol'
174 E2 Buślary Pol.
93 F2 Busobuso Maluku Indon.
128 E6 Buşrá ash Shām Syria
157 M8 Bussang France
100 E3 Busse Rus. Fed.
87 C12 Busselton W.A. Austr.
193 P7 Bussento r. Italy
208 F3 Busseri watercourse Sudan
190 I5 Busseto Italy
162 F4 Bussière-Badil France
162 H3 Bussière-Dunoise France
162 G4 Bussière-Galant France
162 F3 Bussière-Poitevine France
190 B2 Bussigny Switz.
193 L3 Bussi sul Tirino Italy
171 D9 Büßleben Ger.
191 J5 Bussolengo Italy
190 C5 Bussoleno Italy
164 H4 Bussum Neth.
156 G7 Bussy-en-Othe France
160 F1 Bussy-le-Grand France
243 I4 Bustamante Nuevo León Mex.
245 H2 Bustamante Tamaulipas Mex.
Bustandyk Kazakh. see Bostandyk
77 F4 Bustard Head Qld Austr.
197 N5 Buşteni Romania
242 F3 Bustillos, Lago l. Mex.
261 G3 Bustinza Arg.
182 H1 Busto, Cabo c. Spain
190 F4 Busto Arsizio Italy
183 O2 Busturi-Axpe Spain
92 B5 Busuanga Phil.
92 B5 Busuanga i. Phil.
208 D4 Busu-Djanoa Dem. Rep. Congo
168 G2 Büsum Ger.
208 C4 Busu Modanda Dem. Rep. Congo
191 O3 But r. Italy
208 E4 Buta Dem. Rep. Congo
210 C2 Butajīra Eth.
123 J7 Butak Pak.
197 L7 Butan Bulg.
260 C5 Buta Ranquil Arg.
211 A5 Butare Rwanda
266 G6 Butaritari atoll Kiribati
92 D4 Butauanan pt Luzon Phil.
146 F11 Bute i. Scotland U.K.
146 F11 Bute, Sound of sea chan. Scotland U.K.
197 O3 Butea Romania
222 D4 Butedale B.C. Can.
222 E5 Bute Inlet B.C. Can.
208 F4 Butembo Dem. Rep. Congo
177 L5 Buteni Romania
194 G9 Butera Sicilia Italy
165 J8 Bütgenbach Belgium
215 M4 Butha-Buthe Lesotho
Butha Qi Nei Mongol China see Zalantun
96 A4 Buthidaung Myanmar
160 K5 Buthier di Valpelline r. Italy
255 C9 Butiá Brazil
210 A4 Butiaba Uganda
168 F3 Butjadingen reg. Ger.
237 K9 Butler AL U.S.A.
231 E9 Butler GA U.S.A.
226 J8 Butler IN U.S.A.
232 A10 Butler KY U.S.A.
236 H6 Butler MO U.S.A.
235 G2 Butler NJ U.S.A.
232 F8 Butler PA U.S.A.
147 H4 Butlers Bridge Ireland
93 C6 Buton i. Indon.
93 C6 Buton, Selat sea chan. Indon.
136 I6 Butor Moldova
137 P3 Butovo Rus. Fed.
170 F4 Bütow Ger.
184 G4 Butrera mt. Spain
175 M1 Butrimonys Alytus Lith.
138 I7 Butrimonys Vilnius Lith.
198 B3 Butrint tourist site Albania
198 B3 Butrintit, Liqeni i l. Albania
175 I2 Butryny Pol.
190 G1 Bütschwil Switz.
175 M4 Butsyn Ukr.
237 K9 Buttahatchee r. MS U.S.A.
114 G9 Buttala Sri Lanka
238 H3 Butte MT U.S.A.
236 F4 Butte NE U.S.A.
172 F2 Büttelborn Ger.
171 D8 Buttelstedt Ger.
173 K2 Buttenheim Ger.
173 J4 Buttenwiesen Ger.
149 K4 Buttermere Cumbria, England U.K.
226 D3 Butternut WI U.S.A.
149 Q5 Butterwick North Yorkshire, England U.K.
94 D2 Butterworth Malaysia
215 M8 Butterworth S. Africa
240 L2 Buttes, Sierra mt. CA U.S.A.
147 E8 Buttevant Ireland
172 H2 Bütthard Ger.
146 D5 Butt of Lewis hd Scotland U.K.
223 M3 Button Bay Man. Can.
221 L3 Button Islands Nunavut Can.
240 M6 Buttonwillow CA U.S.A.
171 D8 Buttstädt Ger.
169 J8 Büttstedt Ger.
87 F12 Butty Head W.A. Austr.
234 E3 Buttzville NJ U.S.A.
92 E7 Butuan Mindanao Phil.
92 E7 Butuan Bay Mindanao Phil.
136 I6 Butuceni Moldova
108 D5 Butuo Sichuan China
135 H6 Buturlinovka Rus. Fed.
117 I6 Butwal Nepal
Butysh Rus. Fed. see Kama
169 G10 Butzbach Ger.
170 E3 Bützow Ger.
234 E3 Butztown PA U.S.A.
210 E2 Buuhoodle Somalia
210 E4 Buulobarde Somalia
Buurakan r. Kyrg. see Burkan-Suu
211 D5 Buur Gaabo Somalia
210 E4 Buurhabaka Somalia
164 K4 Buurse Neth.
140 M2 Buvåg Norway
210 B4 Buvuma Island Uganda
128 C10 Buwārah, Jabal mt. Saudi Arabia
124 D3 Buwāţah Saudi Arabia
117 J7 Buxar Bihar India
159 L8 Buxerolles France
173 K4 Buxheim Ger.
160 B4 Buxières-les-Mines France
120 K8 Buxoro Buxoro Uzbek.
120 J7 Buxoro admin. div. Uzbek.
151 M6 Buxted East Sussex, England U.K.
168 I4 Buxtehude Ger.
149 N7 Buxton Derbyshire, England U.K.
160 F3 Buxy France
134 H4 Buy Rus. Fed.
134 K4 Buy r. Rus. Fed.
106 F3 Buyant Bayanhongor Mongolia
106 A2 Buyant Bayan-Ölgiy Mongolia
107 L3 Buyant Hentiy Mongolia
106 B2 Buyant Gol r. Mongolia
106 E3 Buyant Gol r. Mongolia
107 J4 Buyant-Ovoo Mongolia
107 L4 Buyant-Uhaa Mongolia
226 B1 Buyck MN U.S.A.
129 I3 Buynaksk Rus. Fed.
136 H2 Buynavichy Belarus
206 D5 Buyo Côte d'Ivoire
206 D5 Buyo, Lac de l. Côte d'Ivoire
108 C8 Buyuan Jiang r. Yunnan China
199 K2 Büyükada i. Turkey
127 L4 Büyük Ağrı Dağı mt. Turkey
129 E5 Büyükçatak Turkey
199 J1 Büyükçekmece Turkey
129 B6 Büyükgeçit Turkey
128 G1 Büyükhan Turkey
199 L4 Büyükkabaca Turkey
199 M4 Büyükkarabağ Turkey
199 I1 Büyükkarıştıran Turkey
199 K5 Büyükkonak Turkey
199 I5 Büyükmenderes r. Turkey
199 J3 Büyükorhan Turkey
128 F2 Büyükşahinbey Turkey
199 I3 Büyükyenice Turkey
107 R6 Buyun Shan mt. Liaoning China
120 D5 Buzachi, Poluostrov pen. Kazakh.
123 P3 Buzai Gumbad Afgh.
162 G2 Buzançais France
157 I5 Buzancy France
197 O5 Buzău Romania
197 O5 Buzău r. Romania
197 P5 Buzău r. Romania
202 D3 Buzaymah oasis Libya
135 K5 Buzdyak Rus. Fed.
191 P5 Buzet Croatia
163 E7 Buzet-sur-Baïse France
163 H8 Buzet-sur-Tarn France
139 X6 Buzha r. Rus. Fed.
213 G3 Búzi Moz.
213 G3 Búzi r. Moz.
197 J5 Buziaş Romania
177 K3 Buzica Slovakia
257 G5 Búzios, Cabo dos c. Brazil
257 E5 Búzios, Ilha dos i. Brazil
Büzmeyin Turkm. see Abadan
129 L5 Buzovna Azer.
121 L2 Buzuluk Kazakh.
120 E1 Buzuluk Rus. Fed.
135 H6 Buzuluk r. Rus. Fed.
163 D9 Buzy France
233 O7 Buzzards Bay MA U.S.A.
91 L9 Bwagaoia P.N.G.
211 A5 Bwanga Tanz.
Bwcle Flintshire, Wales U.K. see Buckley
208 F5 Bwindi National Park Uganda
114 D5 Byadgi Karnataka India
138 L7 Byahoml' Belarus
Byakar Bhutan see Jakar
197 N7 Byala Ruse Bulg.
197 P8 Byala Varna Bulg.
199 H1 Byala Reka r. Bulg.
197 L7 Byala Slatina Bulg.
138 M8 Byalynichy Belarus
139 P8 Byalynkavichy Belarus
Byam Martin atoll Arch. des Tuamotu Fr. Polynesia see Ahunui
221 H2 Byam Martin Island Nunavut Can.
138 I8 Byarezina r. Belarus
138 N9 Byarezina r. Belarus
138 L7 Byarezinski Biyasfyerny Zapavyednik nature res. Belarus
138 H9 Byaroza Belarus
138 I8 Byarozawka Belarus
175 M3 Byarozna Belarus
128 D4 Byblos tourist site Lebanon
175 K4 Bychawa Pol.
174 G5 Bycina Pol.
174 G4 Byczyna Pol.
174 F2 Bydgoski, Kanał canal Pol.
174 G2 Bydgoszcz Pol.
138 I9 Byelaazyorsk Belarus
136 F2 Byelavusha Belarus
175 L3 Byelavyezhski Belarus
175 M2 Byelaye, Vozyera l. Belarus
137 P8 Byelins'ke Ukr.
139 N9 Byelitsk Belarus
138 K6 Byel'ki Belarus
Byelorussia country Europe see Belarus
175 N1 Byenyakoni Belarus
Byerastavitsa Belarus see Pahranichny
138 L8 Byerazino Minskaya Voblasts' Belarus
138 L7 Byerazino Vitsyebskaya Voblasts' Belarus
138 K9 Byeraznyaki Belarus
238 L7 Byers CO U.S.A.
138 H8 Byershty Belarus
138 M6 Byeshankovichy Belarus
232 D9 Byesville OH U.S.A.
139 O9 Byesyedz' r. Belarus
85 M7 Byfield Qld Austr.
151 J3 Byfield Northamptonshire, England U.K.
85 M7 Byfield National Park Qld Austr.
151 L5 Byfleet Surrey, England U.K.
140 P4 Bygdeå Sweden
140 P4 Bygdsiljum Sweden
142 D3 Bygland Norway
142 D3 Byglandsfjord Norway
142 D3 Byglandsfjorden l. Norway
171 J7 Byhleguhre Ger.
137 P5 Byk r. Ukr.
139 N8 Bykhaw Belarus
Bykhov Belarus see Bykhaw
136 G3 Bykivka Ukr.
142 D2 Bykle Norway
137 P3 Bykovka Rus. Fed.
137 Q2 Bykovo Kurskaya Oblast' Rus. Fed.
135 I6 Bykovo Volgogradskaya Oblast' Rus. Fed.
131 N2 Bykovskiy Rus. Fed.
241 V8 Bylas AZ U.S.A.
150 E1 Bylchau Conwy, Wales U.K.
168 H1 Bylderup-Bov Denmark
121 P3 Bylkyldak Kazakh.
221 K2 Bylot Island Nunavut Can.
129 D2 Bylym Rus. Fed.
227 N4 Byng Inlet Ont. Can.
85 H4 Bynoe r. Qld Austr.
84 C2 Bynoe Harbour N.T. Austr.
114 B7 Byramgore Reef India
263 K1 Byrd Glacier Antarctica
107 P1 Byrka Rus. Fed.
142 C3 Byrkjedal Norway
141 I6 Byrkjelo Norway
137 L3 Byrlivka Ukr.
83 K4 Byrock N.S.W. Austr.
226 E7 Byron IL U.S.A.
233 □O4 Byron ME U.S.A.
232 B6 Byron MI U.S.A.
83 N3 Byron, Cape N.S.W. Austr.
83 N3 Byron Bay N.S.W. Austr.
Byron Island Gilbert Is Kiribati see Nikunau
131 K2 Byrranga, Gory mts Rus. Fed.
137 M1 Byryne Ukr.
136 I3 Byshiv Ukr.
176 D1 Byšice Czech Rep.
140 P4 Byske Sweden
140 P4 Byskeälven r. Sweden
100 G2 Byssa Rus. Fed.
100 G2 Byssa r. Rus. Fed.
175 H6 Bystra Pol.
177 I2 Bystrá mt. Slovakia
176 F2 Bystré Czech Rep.
177 K2 Bystré Slovakia
138 L4 Bystretsovo Rus. Fed.
177 H3 Bystričany Slovakia
177 H2 Bystřice Moravskoslezský kraj Czech Rep.
176 D2 Bystřice Středočeský kraj Czech Rep.
176 E1 Bystřice r. Czech Rep.
176 F2 Bystřice nad Pernštejnem Czech Rep.
177 G2 Bystřice pod Hostýnem Czech Rep.
107 L2 Bystrinskiy Golets, Gora mt. Rus. Fed.
Bystrovka Kyrg. see Kemin
136 D5 Bystrytsya Ukr.
136 C4 Bystrytsya r. Ukr.
121 U1 Bystryy Istok Rus. Fed.
134 K5 Bystryy Tanyp r. Rus. Fed.
174 F5 Bystrzyca Pol.
174 E4 Bystrzyca r. Pol.
175 K4 Bystrzyca r. Pol.
174 E5 Bystrzyca Kłodzka Pol.
176 F1 Bystrzyckie, Góry mts Czech Rep./Pol.
131 O3 Bytantay r. Rus. Fed.
177 H2 Bytča Slovakia
174 D3 Bytnica Pol.
174 G5 Bytom Pol.
174 D4 Bytom Odrzański Pol.
139 R8 Bytosh' Rus. Fed.
143 N7 Bytów Pol.
211 A5 Byumba Rwanda
122 F2 Byurgyutli Turkm.
136 J2 Byval'ki Belarus
143 N4 Byxelkrok Öland Sweden
Byzantium Turkey see İstanbul
176 G3 Bzenec Czech Rep.
129 B2 Bzip'i r. Georgia
129 B2 Bzip'is K'edi hills Georgia
175 I3 Bzura r. Pol.
129 A2 Bzych Rus. Fed.

C

96 G5 Ca, Sông r. Vietnam
253 F6 Caacupé Para.
253 F6 Caaguazú Para.
253 G6 Caaguazú, Cordillera de hills Para.
209 B8 Caála Angola
251 F5 Caapiranga Brazil
253 F6 Caapucú Para.
255 B7 Caarapó Brazil
257 E2 Caatinga Brazil
253 F6 Caazapá Para.
210 F3 Cabaad, Raas pt Somalia
253 F3 Cabaçal r. Brazil
245 J9 Cabacera Nueva Mex.
186 G5 Cabacés Spain
246 D2 Cabaiguán Cuba
163 D10 Cabaliros, Pic de mt. France
252 B3 Caballas Peru
185 M6 Caballo mt. Spain
250 D5 Caballococha Peru
239 K10 Caballo Reservoir NM U.S.A.
242 G3 Caballos Mesteños, Llano de los plain Mex.
252 A2 Cabana Ancash Peru
252 B3 Cabana Ayacucho Peru
163 E9 Cabanac France
163 C6 Cabanac-et-Villagrains France
252 C3 Cabanaconde Peru
182 D5 Cabana Maior Port.
182 I2 Cabañaquinta Spain
184 D6 Cabanas Port.
185 N5 Cabañas mt. Spain
182 I9 Cabañas del Castillo Spain
182 E8 Cabanas de Viriato Port.
182 G3 Cabañas Raras Spain
92 C4 Cabanatuan Luzon Phil.
150 E3 Caban Coch Reservoir Wales U.K.
163 G9 Cabanères hill France
187 F7 Cabanes Spain
161 F9 Cabannes France
225 G4 Cabano Que. Can.
188 E3 Čabar Croatia
163 I9 Cabardès reg. France
161 I10 Cabasse France
210 D2 Cabdul Qaadir Somalia
182 E4 Cabe r. Spain
184 D5 Cabeça Gorda Port.
184 C3 Cabeção Port.
253 G3 Cabeceira Rio Manso Brazil
256 D1 Cabeceiras Brazil
182 E5 Cabeceiras de Basto Port.
184 D2 Cabeço de Vide Port.
182 E9 Cabeço Rainha mt. Port.
254 G3 Cabedelo Brazil
163 J10 Cabestany France
177 L5 Căbeşti Romania
245 M9 Cabestrada Mex.
182 H6 Cabeza de Framontanos Spain
259 C6 Cabeza del Buey Arg.
185 I3 Cabeza del Buey Spain
182 G6 Cabeza del Caballo Spain
258 C2 Cabeza de Vaca, Punta pt Chile
184 G4 Cabeza la Vaca Spain
183 N9 Cabezamesada Spain
241 S9 Cabeza Prieta National Wildlife Refuge nature res. AZ U.S.A.
185 K3 Cabezarados Spain
253 E4 Cabezas Bol.
183 J7 Cabezas del Villar Spain
247 □1 Cabezas de San Juan pt Puerto Rico
184 E5 Cabezas Rubias Spain
183 Q6 Cabezo de Morés mt. Spain
187 C11 Cabezo de Torres Spain
184 E5 Cabezo Gordo hill Spain
183 K5 Cabezón Spain
183 O4 Cabezón de Cameros Spain
183 L2 Cabezón de la Sal Spain
183 K2 Cabezón de Liébana Spain
182 I8 Cabezuela del Valle Spain
Cabicorp, Punta pt Spain see Capicorp, Punta de
261 G6 Cabildo Arg.
260 B3 Cabildo Chile
250 D2 Cabimas Venez.
209 B6 Cabinda Angola
209 B6 Cabinda prov. Angola
262 T2 Cabinet Inlet Antarctica
238 G2 Cabinet Mountains MT U.S.A.
92 C9 Cabingan i. Phil.
177 K2 Čabiny Slovakia
Cabistra Turkey see Ereğli
226 C3 Cable WI U.S.A.
231 □2 Cable Beach New Prov. Bahamas
254 G4 Cabo Brazil
259 D7 Cabo Blanco Arg.
216 □1a Cabo da Praia Terceira Azores
213 H2 Cabo Delgado prov. Moz.
257 F5 Cabo Frio Brazil
257 G5 Cabo Frio, Ilha do i. Brazil
183 P6 Cabolafuente Spain
183 M6 Cabollera, Peña mt. Spain
224 E4 Cabonga, Réservoir resr Que. Can.
237 I7 Cabool MO U.S.A.
85 N9 Caboolture Qld Austr.
251 I4 Cabo Orange, Parque Nacional de nat. park Brazil
250 C5 Cabo Pantoja Peru
Cabora Bassa, Lake resr Moz. see Cahora Bassa, Lago de
259 D7 Cabo Raso Arg.
242 C2 Caborca Mex.
247 □1 Cabo Rojo Puerto Rico
227 M4 Cabot Head Ont. Can.
225 I4 Cabot Strait Nfld and Lab./N.S. Can.
159 K3 Cabourg France
Cabo Verde country N. Atlantic Ocean see Cape Verde
206 □ Cabo Verde, Ilhas do is N. Atlantic Ocean
Cabo Yubi Morocco see Tarfaya
92 C5 Cabra i. Phil.
185 K6 Cabra Spain
185 J5 Cabra r. Spain
182 C5 Cabração Port.
186 H5 Cabra del Camp Spain
185 M5 Cabra del Santo Cristo Spain
187 D7 Cabra de Mora Spain
246 H4 Cabral Dom. Rep.
257 E2 Cabral, Serra do mts Brazil
192 B8 Cabras Sardegna Italy
244 G4 Cabras Mex.
185 K6 Cabras mt. Spain
207 G6 Cabras, Ilha das i. São Tomé and Príncipe
216 □1a Cabras, Ilhéus das is Azores
184 H7 Cabras, Sierra de las mts Spain
187 C11 Cabras, Sierra de las mts Spain
192 A8 Cabras, Stagno di l. Sardegna Italy
244 F4 Cabras de Guadalupe Mex.
129 I6 Căbrayıl Azer.
161 H7 Cabre, Col de pass France
261 I1 Cabred Arg.
182 D5 Cabreira, Serra da mts Port.
183 O5 Cabrejas, Sierra de mts Spain
183 O5 Cabrejas del Pinar Spain
184 C3 Cabrela Port.
184 B3 Cabrela r. Port.
246 I4 Cabrera Dom. Rep.
185 K4 Cabrera r. Spain
187 K9 Cabrera, Freu de sea chan. Spain
187 K9 Cabrera, Illa de i. Spain
185 O6 Cabrera, Sierra mts Spain
182 G4 Cabrera, Sierra de la mts Spain
163 H6 Cabrerets France
260 A5 Cabrero Chile
223 I5 Cabri Sask. Can.
183 R10 Cabriel r. Spain
161 H9 Cabrières-d'Aigues France
182 E8 Cabril Port.
182 H3 Cabrillanes Spain
182 H7 Cabrillas Spain
183 P7 Cabrillas r. Spain
186 E6 Cabrillas, Puerto de pass Spain
247 □3 Cabrits, Îlet i. Martinique
254 F4 Cabrobó Brazil
250 E3 Cabruta Venez.
92 C3 Cabugao Luzon Phil.
92 C6 Cabulauan i. Phil.
188 F4 Čabulja mt. Bos.-Herz.
242 E2 Cabullona Mex.
177 G6 Cabuna Croatia
260 B6 Caburgua, Lago l. Chile
92 D2 Cabutunan Point Luzon Phil.
182 G3 Cacabelos Spain
255 C8 Caçador Brazil
Cacagoin Sichuan China see Qagca
245 I9 Cacahuatepec Mex.
196 I7 Čačak Serbia
244 G8 Cacalutla Mex.
251 H3 Cacao Fr. Guiana
257 E5 Cacapava Brazil
255 B9 Cacapava do Sul Brazil
232 G9 Cacapon r. WV U.S.A.
182 H5 Caçarelhos Port.
250 C3 Cácares Col.
244 D7 Cacbán Mex.
194 F8 Caccamo Sicilia Italy
192 A6 Caccia, Capo c. Sardegna Italy
193 Q5 Caccia, Monte hill Italy
195 L5 Caccuri Italy
122 I3 Çäçe Turkm.
184 A3 Cacém Port.
255 B9 Cacequi Brazil
253 F4 Cáceres Brazil
184 G2 Cáceres Spain
182 H9 Cáceres prov. Spain
184 G2 Cáceres, Embalse de resr Spain
252 D3 Cachal Bol.
261 H5 Cachari Arg.
237 K7 Cache r. IL U.S.A.
206 A3 Cacheau r. Guinea-Bissau
222 F5 Cache Creek B.C. Can.
240 K3 Cache Creek r. CA U.S.A.
238 L6 Cache la Poudre r. CO U.S.A.
238 H5 Cache Peak ID U.S.A.
206 A3 Cacheu Guinea-Bissau
260 C3 Cacheuta Arg.
258 D2 Cachi Arg.
258 D2 Cachi, Nevados de mts Arg.
254 B4 Cachimbo Brazil
254 B4 Cachimbo, Serra do hills Brazil
209 D7 Cachimo Angola
258 C2 Cachina r. Chile
209 C8 Cachingues Angola
250 C3 Cáchira Col.
254 F5 Cachoeira Bahia Brazil
256 B3 Cachoeira Mato Grosso do Sul Brazil
256 B3 Cachoeira Alta Brazil
256 B2 Cachoeira de Goiás Brazil
254 C2 Cachoeira do Arari Brazil
257 E3 Cachoeira dos Macacos Brazil
255 B9 Cachoeira do Sul Brazil
257 E5 Cachoeira Paulista Brazil
257 F5 Cachoeiras de Macacu Brazil
257 G4 Cachoeiro de Itapemirim Brazil
184 D6 Cachopo Port.
258 C2 Cachos, Punta de pt Chile
177 G3 Čachtice Slovakia
252 D2 Cachuela Esperanza Bol.
182 C7 Cacia Port.
185 L6 Cacín Spain
185 K6 Cacín r. Spain
206 B4 Cacine Guinea-Bissau
251 I4 Caciporé, Cabo c. Brazil
209 C7 Cacolo Angola
244 B5 Cacoma, Sierra mts Mex.
209 B8 Caconda Angola
209 B6 Cacongo Angola
237 D7 Cactus TX U.S.A.
240 O4 Cactus Range mts NV U.S.A.
256 B3 Caçu Brazil
209 B7 Cacuaco Angola
209 B8 Cacula Angola
209 C7 Caculama Angola
254 E5 Caculé Brazil
257 H2 Cacumba, Ilha i. Brazil
209 B7 Cacuso Angola
184 A2 Cadafais Port.
150 E2 Cadair Idris hills Wales U.K.
210 E4 Cadale Somalia
163 H8 Cadalen France
183 L8 Cadalso de los Vidrios Spain
148 B7 Cadamstown Ireland
186 L3 Cadaqués Spain
184 A2 Cadaval Port.
177 G6 Čađavica Croatia
177 H2 Čadca Slovakia
210 D2 Caddabassa l. Eth.
151 L4 Caddington Bedfordshire, England U.K.
237 I9 Caddo Lake TX U.S.A.
191 J6 Cadelbosco di Sopra Italy
84 E2 Cadell r. N.T. Austr.
85 H7 Cadell Creek watercourse Qld Austr.
190 F3 Cadenazzo Switz.
168 H3 Cadenberge Ger.
161 G9 Cadenet France
190 H6 Cadeo Italy
243 I5 Cadereyta Nuevo León Mex.
245 H5 Cadereyta Querétaro Mex.
Cader Idris hills Wales U.K. see Cadair Idris
161 F8 Caderousse France
Cadí mt. Spain see Torre de Cadí
186 I3 Cadí, Serra del mts Spain
186 I3 Cadí, Túnel de tun. Spain
185 M7 Cádiar Spain
82 E3 Cadibarrawirracanna, Lake salt flat S.A. Austr.
92 D4 Cadig Mountains Luzon Phil.
227 P1 Cadillac Que. Can.
223 J5 Cadillac Sask. Can.
163 D6 Cadillac France
226 I5 Cadillac MI U.S.A.
129 D4 Çadır Dağı mt. Turkey
129 B6 Çadırkaya Turkey
92 D6 Cadiz Negros Phil.
184 G7 Cádiz Spain
184 H8 Cádiz prov. Spain
241 Q7 Cadiz CA U.S.A.
230 D7 Cadiz KY U.S.A.
232 E8 Cadiz OH U.S.A.
184 G7 Cádiz, Bahía de b. Spain
184 E7 Cádiz, Golfo de g. Spain
241 Q7 Cadiz Lake CA U.S.A.
173 J3 Cadolzburg Ger.
222 G4 Cadomin Alta Can.
191 L5 Cadoneghe Italy
191 M3 Cadore reg. Italy
226 C5 Cadott WI U.S.A.
222 G3 Cadotte r. Alta Can.
222 G3 Cadotte Lake Alta Can.
163 G8 Cadours France
87 D11 Cadoux W.A. Austr.
254 E4 Caém Brazil
159 K3 Caen France
159 K3 Caen, Plaine de plain France
150 F5 Caerau Cardiff, Wales U.K.
Caerdydd Cardiff, Wales U.K. see Cardiff
Caere Italy see Cerveteri
Caerffili Caerphilly, Wales U.K. see Caerphilly
Caerfyrddin Carmarthenshire, Wales U.K. see Carmarthen
150 F1 Caergwrle Flintshire, Wales U.K.
Caergybi Isle of Anglesey, Wales U.K. see Holyhead
150 E1 Caerhun Conwy, Wales U.K.
150 G4 Caerleon Newport, Wales U.K.
150 D1 Caernarfon Gwynedd, Wales U.K.
150 C1 Caernarfon Bay Wales U.K.
Caernarvon Gwynedd, Wales U.K. see Caernarfon
150 F4 Caerphilly Caerphilly, Wales U.K.
150 F4 Caerphilly admin. div. Wales U.K.
150 F2 Caersws Powys, Wales U.K.
150 G4 Caerwent Monmouthshire, Wales U.K.
Caesaraugusta Spain see Zaragoza
Caesarea Alg. see Cherchell
128 C6 Caesarea tourist site Israel
Caesarea Cappadociae Turkey see Kayseri
Caesarea Philippi Syria see Bāniyās
Caesarodunum France see Tours
Caesaromagus Essex, England U.K. see Chelmsford
257 F3 Caeté Brazil
252 C2 Caeté r. Brazil
254 E5 Caetité Brazil
190 D5 Cafasse Italy
258 D2 Cafayate Arg.
256 C4 Cafelândia Brazil
Caffa Ukr. see Feodosiya
204 D5 Çafia, Ḩamâda des. Mali
250 D3 Cafifi Col.
217 □1c Cafres, Plaine des hills Réunion
251 G4 Cafuini r. Brazil
184 □ Cágado, Ponta do pt Madeira
92 C7 Cagayan i. Phil.
92 C2 Cagayan r. Luzon Phil.
92 E7 Cagayan de Oro Mindanao Phil.
92 B8 Cagayan de Tawi-Tawi i. Phil.
92 C7 Cagayan Islands Phil.
193 P6 Caggiano Italy
191 N8 Cagli Italy
192 C9 Cagliari Sardegna Italy
192 C9 Cagliari prov. Sardegna Italy
192 C9 Cagliari, Golfo di b. Sardegna Italy
192 B9 Cagliari, Stagno di l. Sardegna Italy
192 B4 Cagna, Montagne de mts Corse France
163 I8 Cagnac-les-Mines France
193 P4 Cagnano Varano Italy
161 K9 Cagnes-sur-Mer France
92 E6 Cagosoan Point Phil.
92 D2 Cagua, Mount vol. Phil.
250 C5 Caguán r. Col.
247 □1 Caguas Puerto Rico
122 F1 Çagyl Turkm.
122 H1 Çagyllyşor Çöketligi depr. Turkm.
147 C9 Caha hill Ireland
231 D9 Cahaba r. AL U.S.A.
209 B9 Cahama Angola
147 C9 Caha Mountains hills Ireland
147 E7 Caher Ireland
147 B9 Cahermore Ireland
Cahersiveen Ireland see Cahirciveen
147 G8 Cahir Ireland
147 B9 Cahirciveen Ireland
234 F2 Cahoonzie NY U.S.A.
213 F2 Cahora Bassa, Lago de resr Moz.
147 J7 Cahore Point Ireland
163 G7 Cahors France
250 B6 Cahuapanas Peru
242 □R13 Cahuita, Punta pt Costa Rica
136 H8 Cahul Moldova
163 H8 Cahuzac-sur-Vère France
213 G3 Caia Moz.
184 E3 Caia Port.
184 E3 Caia r. Port.
184 E2 Caia, Barragem do resr Port.
253 F3 Caiabis, Serra dos hills Brazil
209 D7 Caianda Angola
256 B1 Caiapó r. Brazil
256 A2 Caiapó, Serra do mts Brazil
256 B2 Caiapônia Brazil
209 D7 Caiaza Angola
193 M5 Caiazzo Italy
246 D2 Caibarién Cuba
96 H4 Cai Bâu, Đao i. Vietnam
97 H9 Cai Be Vietnam
251 E3 Caicara Venez.
254 F3 Caicó Brazil
246 H3 Caicos Bank sea feature Turks and Caicos Is
246 H3 Caicos Islands Turks and Caicos Is
246 G3 Caicos Passage Bahamas/Turks and Caicos Is
109 J3 Caidian Hubei China
Caidu Henan China see Shangcai
209 D7 Caifuche Angola
87 H12 Caiguna W.A. Austr.
108 H3 Caihua Hubei China
252 C3 Cailloma Peru
244 A3 Caimanero, Laguna del lag. Mex.
260 B2 Caimanes Chile
92 B4 Caiman Point Luzon Phil.
209 B8 Caimbambo Angola
183 Q7 Caimodorro mt. Spain
136 H6 Căinar r. Moldova
209 B8 Cainde Angola
197 M5 Câineni Romania
241 U3 Caineville UT U.S.A.
108 D2 Cainnyigoin Sichuan China
97 G10 Cai Nước Vietnam
182 C2 Caión Spain
258 C2 Caipe Arg.
161 F8 Cairanne France
262 W1 Caird Coast Antarctica
Cairinis Scotland U.K. see Carinish
146 F10 Cairnbaan Argyll and Bute, Scotland U.K.
146 G10 Cairndow Argyll and Bute, Scotland U.K.
146 I10 Cairneyhill Fife, Scotland U.K.
146 I8 Cairn Gorm mt. Scotland U.K.
146 I8 Cairngorm Mountains Scotland U.K.
146 I8 Cairngorms National Park Scotland U.K.
146 F13 Cairnryan Dumfries and Galloway, Scotland U.K.
85 J4 Cairns Qld Austr.
146 H12 Cairnsmore of Carsphairn hill Scotland U.K.
146 H13 Cairnsmore of Fleet hill Scotland U.K.
146 I8 Cairn Toul mt. Scotland U.K.
Cairo Egypt see Al Qāhirah
231 E10 Cairo GA U.S.A.
237 K7 Cairo IL U.S.A.
193 L4 Cairo, Monte mt. Italy
190 E7 Cairo Montenotte Italy
Caisleán an Bharraigh Ireland see Castlebar
161 E9 Caissargues France
146 F11 Caisteal Abhail hill Scotland U.K.
151 P2 Caister-on-Sea Norfolk, England U.K.
149 Q7 Caistor Lincolnshire, England U.K.
146 J6 Caithness reg. Scotland U.K.
209 B8 Caitou Angola
209 C8 Caiundo Angola
83 J3 Caiwarro Qld Austr.
109 K6 Caixi Fujian China
Caiyuanzhen Zhejiang China see Shengsi
252 D5 Caiza Bol.
109 K3 Caizi Hu l. China
252 A1 Cajabamba Peru
247 □1 Caja de Muertos, Isla i. Puerto Rico
252 A1 Cajamarca Peru
250 B6 Cajamarca dept Peru
254 D2 Cajapió Brazil
163 H7 Cajarc France
254 D2 Cajari Brazil
252 A2 Cajatambo Peru
256 C6 Cajati Brazil
254 F3 Cajàzeiras Brazil
196 H7 Čajetina Serbia
92 D5 Cajidiocan Phil.
177 H3 Čajkov Slovakia
188 G4 Čajniče Bos.-Herz.
260 A6 Cajón Chile
242 □R9 Cajones, Cayos is Hond.
245 L8 Cajonos r. Mex.
252 D4 Cajuata Bol.
256 D4 Cajuru Brazil
197 N3 Cajvana Romania
106 F8 Çaka Qinghai China
177 H3 Čakajovce Slovakia
Caka'lho Xizang China see Yanjing
106 F8 Caka Yanhu l. Qinghai China
129 A7 Cakırkaş Turkey
199 I2 Çakırlı Turkey
129 E5 Çakmak Turkey
129 D6 Çakmak Dağı mts Turkey
188 F2 Čakovec Croatia
199 K4 Çal Denizli Turkey
Çal Hakkâri Turkey see Çukurca
215 L7 Cala S. Africa
184 G5 Cala Spain
184 G5 Cala r. Spain
184 G5 Cala, Embalse de resr Spain
207 H5 Calabar Nigeria
187 B13 Calabardina Spain
227 R4 Calabogie Ont. Can.
250 E2 Calabozo Venez.
193 Q9 Calabria admin. reg. Italy

Cantil CA U.S.A.
Cantilan Mindanao Phil.
Cantillana Spain
Cantimpalos Spain
Canto do Buriti Brazil
Cantoira Italy
Canton Guangdong China see Guangzhou
Canton Cardiff, Wales U.K.
Canton GA U.S.A.
Canton IL U.S.A.
Canton MO U.S.A.
Canton MS U.S.A.
Canton NJ U.S.A.
Canton NY U.S.A.
Canton OH U.S.A.
Canton PA U.S.A.
Canton SD U.S.A.
Canton TX U.S.A.
Canton WI U.S.A.
Canton Island atoll Phoenix Is Kiribati see Kanton
Cantoria Spain
Cantos Negros hill Spain
Cantu r. Brazil
Cantù Italy
Cantu, Serra do hills Brazil
Cantuaria Kent, England U.K. see Canterbury
Canudos Amazonas Brazil
Canudos Bahia Brazil
Cañuelas Arg.
Canumã Amazonas Brazil
Canumã Amazonas Brazil
Canunda National Park S.A. Austr.
Canusium Italy see Canosa di Puglia
Canutama Brazil
Canutillo Mex.
Canvastown South I. N.Z.
Canvey Island Essex, England U.K.
Canwood Sask. Can.
Canxixe Moz.
Cany-Barville France
Cànyoles r. Spain
Canyon Y.T. Can.
Canyon TX U.S.A.
Canyon City OR U.S.A.
Canyon Creek r. CA U.S.A.
Canyondam CA U.S.A.
Canyon de Chelly National Monument nat. park AZ U.S.A.
Canyon Ferry Lake MT U.S.A.
Canyon Lake AZ U.S.A.
Canyonlands National Park UT U.S.A.
Canyon Ranges mts N.W.T. Can.
Canyonville OR U.S.A.
Canzar Angola
Cao Băng Vietnam
Caocheng Shandong China see Caoxian
Cao Daban Qinghai China
Caohai Guizhou China see Weining
Caohe Hubei China see Qichun
Cao He r. China
Caohu Xinjiang China
Caohu Xinjiang China
Caojiahe Hubei China see Qichun
Caojian Yunnan China
Caolas Argyll and Bute, Scotland U.K.
Caolas Scalpaigh Western Isles, Scotland U.K. see Kyles Scalpay
Caolisport, Loch inlet Scotland U.K.
Caombo Angola
Caorame r. Italy
Caorle Italy
Caoxian Shandong China
Caozhou Shandong China see Heze
Cap i. Phil.
Cap, Baie du b. Mauritius
Cap, Pointe du pt St Lucia
Capac MI U.S.A.
Capaccio Italy
Capacciotti, Lago di l. Italy
Capaci Sicilia Italy
Cap-à-Foux c. Haiti
Capaia Angola
Çapakçur Turkey see Bingöl
Capalbio Italy
Căpâlna Romania
Capalulu, Selat sea chan. Indon.
Capana Brazil
Capanaparo r. Venez.
Capanema Brazil
Capanne, Monte mt. Italy
Capanne di Marcarolo, Parco Naturale delle nature res. Italy
Capannoli Italy
Capannori Italy
Capão Bonito Brazil
Caparaó, Serra do mts Brazil
Caparica Port.
Caparo r. Venez.
Caparrosa Port.
Caparroso Spain
Capas Luzon Phil.
Căpăţânii, Munţii mts Romania
Capatárida Venez.
Cap-aux-Meules Que. Can.
Cap-Blanc Spain
Capbreton France
Cap-Chat Que. Can.
Capcir reg. France
Cap d'Agde France
Cap d'Artrutx Spain
Cap-de-la-Madeleine Que. Can.
Capdenac France
Capdenac-Gare France
Cap d'en Font Spain
Capdepera Spain
Cape r. Qld Austr.
Cape Arid National Park W.A. Austr.
Cape Bald N.B. Can. see Cap-Pelé
Cape Barren Island Tas. Austr.
Cape Basin sea feature S. Atlantic Ocean
Cape Borda S.A. Austr.
Cape Bougainville Aboriginal Reserve W.A. Austr.
Cape Breton Highlands National Park N.S. Can.
Cape Breton Island N.S. Can.
Cape Charles Nfld and Lab. Can.
Cape Charles VA U.S.A.
Cape Coast Ghana
Cape Coast Castle Ghana see Cape Coast
Cape Cod Bay MA U.S.A.
Cape Cod Canal MA U.S.A.
Cape Cod National Seashore nature res. MA U.S.A.
Cape Coral FL U.S.A.
Cape Crawford N.T. Austr.
Cape Croker Ont. Can.
Cape Dorset Nunavut Can.
Cape Elizabeth ME U.S.A.
Cape Fanshaw AK U.S.A.
Cape Fear r. NC U.S.A.
Cape Gantheaume Conservation Park nature res. S.A. Austr.
Cape George N.S. Can.
Cape Girardeau MO U.S.A.
Cape Juby Morocco see Tarfaya
Cape Krusenstern National Monument nat. park AK U.S.A.
Capel W.A. Austr.
Capel Kent, England U.K.
Capel Surrey, England U.K.
Capela Brazil
Capelas São Miguel Azores
Capel Curig Conwy, Wales U.K.
87 G12 Cape Le Grand National Park W.A. Austr.
257 F2 Capelinha Brazil
216 □1c Capelinhos, Ponta dos pt Faial Azores
184 E3 Capelins Port.
85 L7 Capella Qld Austr.
164 G5 Capelle aan de IJssel Neth.
151 O5 Capel le Ferne Kent, England U.K.
165 J9 Capellen Lux.
216 □1c Capelo Faial Azores
86 □2 Capelok, Pulu i. Cocos Is
209 B8 Capelongo Huíla Angola
Capelongo Huíla Angola see Kuvango
192 F3 Capel Rosso, Punta del Italy
151 O3 Capel St Mary Suffolk, England U.K.
234 F7 Cape May NJ U.S.A.
234 F6 Cape May County county NJ U.S.A.
234 F6 Cape May Court House NJ U.S.A.
234 F7 Cape May Point NJ U.S.A.
234 F7 Cape May Point pt NJ U.S.A.
85 J3 Cape Melville National Park Qld Austr.
209 C7 Capenda-Camulemba Angola
163 J9 Capendu France
214 C10 Cape of Good Hope Nature Reserve S. Africa
85 L6 Cape Palmerston National Park Qld Austr.
86 B7 Cape Range hills W.A. Austr.
86 B7 Cape Range National Park W.A. Austr.
231 H9 Cape Romain National Wildlife Refuge nature res. SC U.S.A.
225 H5 Cape Sable Island N.S. Can.
225 J3 Cape St George Nfld and Lab. Can.
222 D5 Cape Scott Provincial Park B.C. Can.
161 C10 Capestang France
247 □2 Capesterre Guadeloupe
193 L3 Capestrano Italy
214 C9 Cape Town S. Africa
85 J3 Cape Tribulation National Park Qld Austr.
85 K5 Cape Upstart National Park Qld Austr.
206 □ Cape Verde country N. Atlantic Ocean
264 G5 Cape Verde Basin sea feature N. Atlantic Ocean
264 G4 Cape Verde Plateau sea feature N. Atlantic Ocean
233 I4 Cape Vincent NY U.S.A.
225 H4 Cape Wolfe P.E.I. Can.
85 I2 Cape York Peninsula Qld Austr.
163 B6 Cap Ferret France
246 G4 Cap-Haïtien Haiti
250 E4 Capibara Venez.
209 C8 Capico Angola
187 F7 Capicorp, Punta de pt Spain
185 M7 Capileira Spain
185 I3 Capilla Spain
244 E5 Capilla de Guadalupe Mex.
260 E2 Capilla del Monte Arg.
261 H4 Capilla del Señor Arg.
254 D2 Capim Brazil
254 C2 Capim r. Brazil
182 F8 Capinha Port.
256 C3 Capinópolis Brazil
252 D4 Capinota Bol.
193 K4 Capistrello Italy
239 L10 Capitan NM U.S.A.
261 G3 Capitán Bermudez Arg.
260 A6 Capitán Pastene Chile
261 H4 Capitán Sarmiento Arg.
257 F2 Capitão Enéas Brazil
251 F6 Capitari Brazil
234 D6 Capitol Park DE U.S.A.
241 U3 Capitol Reef National Park UT U.S.A.
256 B5 Capivara, Represa resr Brazil
256 D5 Capivari Brazil
256 D5 Capivari r. Brazil
254 F5 Capivari r. Brazil
254 E4 Capixaba Brazil
194 G8 Capizzi Sicilia Italy
177 L4 Căpleni Romania
188 F4 Čapljina Bos.-Herz.
186 I3 Cap Llitzet mt. Spain
92 C6 Capnoyan i. Phil.
213 G2 Capoche r. Moz./Zambia
192 H2 Capodimonte Italy
190 I3 Capo di Ponte Italy
193 M6 Capodochino airport Italy
194 H7 Capo d'Orlando Sicilia Italy
251 G6 Capoeira Brazil
251 G6 Capoeiras, Cachoeira das waterfall Brazil
192 E2 Capoliveri Italy
191 L8 Capolona Italy
195 I10 Capo Passero, Isola i. Sicilia Italy
193 O6 Caposele Italy
192 B9 Capoterra Sardegna Italy
163 H10 Capoulet France
193 K3 Cappadocia Italy
147 E7 Cappagh Ireland
147 F7 Cappamore Ireland
147 F7 Cappawhite Ireland
168 G3 Cappel Ger.
225 H4 Cap-Pelé N.B. Can.
193 M3 Cappelle sul Tavo Italy
168 F5 Cappeln (Oldenburg) Ger.
146 J12 Capplegill Dumfries and Galloway, Scotland U.K.
147 G8 Cappoquin Ireland
192 D9 Cappuccini, Punta dei pt Sardegna Italy
193 M4 Capracotta Italy
192 D1 Capraia, Isola di i. Italy
193 P3 Capraia, Isole is Italy
192 D1 Capraia Isola Italy
192 I3 Capranica Italy
192 A5 Caprara, Punta pt Sardegna Italy
192 I3 Caprarola Italy
192 C5 Caprera, Isola i. Sardegna Italy
193 M6 Capri Italy
193 M6 Capri, Isola di i. Italy
193 M5 Capriati a Volturno Italy
85 M7 Capricorn, Cape Qld Austr.
85 M7 Capricorn Channel Qld Austr.
85 N7 Capricorn Group atolls Qld Austr.
190 G4 Caprino Bergamasco Italy
191 J4 Caprino Veronese Italy
212 D3 Caprivi admin. reg. Namibia
212 D3 Caprivi Game Park nature res. Namibia
Capsa Tunisia see Gafsa
240 □F14 Captain Cook HI U.S.A.
163 D7 Captieux France
232 E9 Captina r. OH U.S.A.
193 M5 Capua Italy
256 D6 Capuava Brazil
247 □2 Capucin, Cape Dominica
217 □2b Capucin Rock i. Mahé Seychelles
217 □2b Capucins, Pointe pt Mahé Seychelles
245 H6 Capulhuac Mex.
244 G4 Capulín Mex.
209 C8 Capuna Angola
209 B8 Capunda Cavilongo Angola
209 D9 Caputene Angola
171 G6 Caputh Ger.
146 J9 Caputh Perth and Kinross, Scotland U.K.
163 E9 Capvern-les-Bains France
250 C4 Caquetá dept Col.
250 D5 Caquetá r. Col. alt. Japurá (Brazil)
250 C3 Cáqueza Col.
183 N8 Carabaña Spain
92 C5 Carabao i. Phil.
252 C3 Carabaya, Cordillera de mts Peru
261 G4 Carabelas Arg.
251 F5 Carabinani r. Brazil
250 E2 Carabobo state Venez.
197 M6 Caracal Romania
251 F4 Caracarai Brazil
250 E2 Caracas Venez.
247 □10 Caracas Baai b. Curaçao Neth. Antilles
253 F5 Caracol Mato Grosso do Sul Brazil
254 E4 Caracol Piauí Brazil
252 D2 Caracol Rondônia Brazil
246 G8 Caracolí Col.
252 D4 Caracollo Bol.
244 F6 Carácuaro Mex.
185 K3 Caracuel de Calatrava Spain
92 F8 Caraga Mindanao Phil.
83 K5 Caragabal N.S.W. Austr.
147 C8 Caragh, Lough l. Ireland
190 C7 Caraglio Italy
257 E5 Caraguatatuba Brazil
259 B5 Carahue Chile
257 G2 Caraí Brazil
147 K1 Cara Island Scotland U.K.
257 H2 Caraiva Brazil
251 H6 Carajari Brazil
251 I6 Carajás, Serra dos hills Brazil
Carales Sardegna Italy see Cagliari
Caralis Sardegna Italy see Cagliari
Caralps Spain see Queralbs
163 H8 Caraman France
193 M3 Caramanico Terme Italy
185 P5 Caramel r. Spain
92 D5 Caramoan Peninsula Luzon Phil.
182 D7 Caramulo Port.
182 D7 Caramulo mt. Port.
182 D8 Caramulo, Serra do mts Port.
253 F3 Caraná r. Brazil
252 D3 Caranavi Bol.
260 E5 Carancho Arg.
177 L5 Cărand Romania
257 F4 Carandaí Brazil
253 E5 Carandaiti Bol.
253 F4 Carandazal Brazil
182 H2 Caranga Spain
257 F4 Carangola Brazil
182 C9 Caranguejeira Port.
197 K5 Caransebeş Romania
158 D4 Carantec France
163 F10 Carants, Tuc de les mt. Spain
251 I5 Carapajó Brazil
250 C5 Cara Paraná r. Col.
253 F6 Carapeguá Para.
193 P5 Carapelle Italy
193 P5 Carapelle r. Italy
193 P5 Carapellotto r. Italy
82 F5 Carappee Hill S.A. Austr.
225 H4 Caraquet N.B. Can.
250 C3 Carare r. Col.
190 G7 Carasco Italy
197 J5 Caraşova Romania
177 L4 Carastelec Romania
94 F6 Carat, Tanjung pt Indon.
242 □R10 Caratasca Hond.
242 □R10 Caratasca, Laguna de lag. Hond.
257 F3 Caratinga Brazil
250 D5 Caratué r. Col.
233 □P3 Caratunk ME U.S.A.
250 E6 Carauari Brazil
254 F3 Caraúbas Brazil
Carauná mt. Brazil see Grande, Serra
185 P4 Caravaca de la Cruz Spain
190 H5 Caravaggio Italy
257 H2 Caravelas Brazil
252 B3 Caravelí Peru
247 □3 Caravelle, Presqu'île de la pen. Martinique
245 J1 Carbajal Mex.
182 I5 Carbajales de Alba Spain
182 D4 Carballeda de Avia Spain
182 C2 Carballo Galicia Spain
182 E4 Carballo Galicia Spain
182 H6 Carbellino Spain
223 L5 Carberry Man. Can.
261 H3 Carbo Arg.
242 D3 Carbó Mex.
194 D8 Carboi r. Sicilia Italy
192 D9 Carbonara, Capo c. Sardegna Italy
192 C9 Carbonara, Golfo di b. Sardegna Italy
194 G8 Carbonara, Pizzo mt. Italy
163 D6 Carbon-Blanc France
234 D3 Carbon County county PA U.S.A.
239 K7 Carbondale CO U.S.A.
237 K7 Carbondale IL U.S.A.
234 D1 Carbondale PA U.S.A.
225 K4 Carbonear Nfld and Lab. Can.
183 O5 Carbonera de Frentes Spain
245 J1 Carboneras Mex.
185 P7 Carboneras Spain
183 Q9 Carboneras de Guadazaón Spain
183 L6 Carbonero El Mayor Spain
185 L4 Carboneros Spain
192 B9 Carbonia Sardegna Italy
192 B9 Carbonia-Iglesias prov. Sardegna Italy
191 M2 Carbonin Italy
257 F2 Carbonita Brazil
163 G9 Carbonne France
146 D8 Carbost Highland, Scotland U.K.
146 D8 Carbost Highland, Scotland U.K.
147 I6 Carbury Ireland
182 H8 Carcaboso Spain
185 K6 Carcabuey Spain
187 E9 Carcaixent Spain
222 G3 Carcajou Alta Can.
222 D1 Carcajou r. N.W.T. Can.
197 Q5 Carcaliu Romania
162 B5 Carcans France
162 B5 Carcans-Plage France
182 G5 Carção Port.
92 D6 Carcar Cebu Phil.
261 G3 Carcaraña r. Arg.
190 E7 Carcare Italy
163 I9 Carcassonne France
183 R4 Carcastillo Spain
187 C9 Carcelén Spain
161 I10 Carcès France
187 C11 Carche, Sierra del mts Spain
185 L5 Carchelejo Spain
250 B4 Carchi prov. Ecuador
190 E4 Carcoforo Italy
149 O6 Carcroft South Yorkshire, England U.K.
222 C2 Carcross Y.T. Can.
163 H6 Cardaillac France
199 H2 Çardak Çanakkale Turkey
199 K5 Çardak Denizli Turkey
261 I4 Cardal Uru.
Cardamomes, Chaîne des mts Cambodia see Cardamom Range
114 E7 Cardamom Hills India
96 F8 Cardamom Range mts Cambodia
186 J4 Cardedeu Spain
192 D8 Cardedu Sardegna Italy
185 K4 Cardeña Spain
183 M4 Cardeñadijo Spain
246 C2 Cárdenas Cuba
245 H3 Cárdenas San Luis Potosí Mex.
243 M8 Cárdenas Tabasco Mex.
183 Q9 Cardenete Spain
183 K7 Cardeñosa Spain
83 I3 Cardenyabba watercourse N.S.W. Austr.
195 J7 Cardeto Italy
Çardi Turkey see Harmancık
259 C8 Cardiel, Lago l. Arg.
150 F5 Cardiff Cardiff, Wales U.K.
150 F4 Cardiff admin. div. Wales U.K.
234 C5 Cardiff MD U.S.A.
150 F5 Cardiff International airport Wales U.K.
150 C3 Cardigan Ceredigion, Wales U.K.
150 C2 Cardigan Bay Wales U.K.
182 D9 Cardigos Port.
233 J4 Cardinal Ont. Can.
195 K6 Cardinale Italy
222 G3 Cardinal Lake Alta Can.
232 C8 Cardington OH U.S.A.
193 L4 Cardito Italy
216 □3b Cardón hill Fuerteventura Canary Is
242 C4 Cardón, Cerro hill Mex.
186 I4 Cardona Spain
261 I3 Cardona Uru.
245 H5 Cardonal Mex.
186 I4 Cardoner r. Spain
244 B1 Cardos Mex.
256 C4 Cardoso Brazil
256 D6 Cardoso, Ilha do i. Brazil
81 D11 Cardrona South I. N.Z.
81 C11 Cardrona, Mount South I. N.Z.
146 G11 Cardross Argyll and Bute, Scotland U.K.
222 H5 Cardston Alta Can.
85 K5 Cardwell Qld Austr.
257 E5 Careaçu Brazil
223 I3 Careen Lake Sask. Can.
191 K4 Carega, Cima mt. Italy
197 K3 Carei Romania
177 L4 Careilor, Câmpia plain Romania
251 G5 Careiro Brazil
251 F5 Careiro do Castanho Brazil
260 B2 Carén Coquimbo Chile
260 B2 Carén Coquimbo Chile
183 Q6 Carenas Spain
158 I3 Carentan France
158 G6 Carentoir France
183 K2 Cares r. Spain
179 O7 Carevdar Croatia
232 B8 Carey OH U.S.A.
87 G10 Carey, Lake salt flat W.A. Austr.
87 C8 Carey Downs W.A. Austr.
223 K2 Carey Lake N.W.T. Can.
217 □1 Cargados Carajos Islands Mauritius
146 I12 Cargenbridge Dumfries and Galloway, Scotland U.K.
192 B3 Cargèse Corse France
158 D5 Carhaix-Plouguer France
252 A2 Carhuamayo Peru
261 F5 Carhué Arg.
182 F8 Caria Port.
254 F4 Cariacá r. Brazil
257 G4 Cariacica Brazil
247 L8 Cariaco Venez.
247 K8 Cariaco, Golfo de b. Venez.
250 B6 Cariamanga Ecuador
209 B7 Cariango Angola
195 L5 Cariati Italy
246 B4 Caribbean Sea N. Atlantic Ocean
222 F4 Cariboo Mountains B.C. Can.
222 F4 Cariboo Mountains Provincial Park B.C. Can.
223 M3 Caribou r. Man. Can.
222 E2 Caribou r. N.W.T. Can.
233 □Q2 Caribou ME U.S.A.
226 I2 Caribou Island Ont. Can.
222 H2 Caribou Islands N.W.T. Can.
224 B3 Caribou Lake Ont. Can.
222 H3 Caribou Mountains Alta Can.
247 □2 Carib Point Dominica
242 F4 Carichic Mex.
92 E6 Carigara Leyte Phil.
92 E6 Carigara Bay Leyte Phil.
157 J4 Carignan France
190 D6 Carignano Italy
83 K4 Carinda N.S.W. Austr.
186 C5 Cariñena Spain
186 C5 Cariñena, Campo de reg. Spain
254 E5 Carinhanha Brazil
254 E5 Carinhanha r. Brazil
194 E7 Carini Sicilia Italy
146 B7 Carinish Western Isles, Scotland U.K.
182 E1 Cariño Spain
193 L5 Carinola Italy
Carinthia land Austria see Kärnten
209 D8 Caripande Angola
254 D4 Cariparé Brazil
251 F2 Caripe Venez.
251 F2 Caripito Venez.
254 E3 Cariris Novos, Serra dos hills Brazil
251 F2 Caris r. Venez.
190 E5 Carisio Italy
191 J3 Carisolo Italy
253 E2 Caritianas Brazil
177 L6 Cârjiţi Romania
147 G3 Cark Mountain hill Ireland
163 G9 Carla-Bayle France
Carlabhagh Scotland U.K. see Carloway
Carlabhagh Western Isles, Scotland U.K. see Carloway
147 I3 Carland Northern Ireland U.K.
147 I5 Carlanstown Ireland
193 N4 Carlantino Italy
161 B7 Carlat France
195 I9 Carlentini Sicilia Italy
187 D9 Carlet Spain
227 K7 Carleton MI U.S.A.
225 H4 Carleton, Mount hill N.B. Can.
224 E4 Carleton Place Ont. Can.
215 L2 Carletonville S. Africa
197 N3 Cârlibaba Romania
238 F6 Carlin NV U.S.A.
86 E6 Carlindie Aboriginal Reserve W.A. Austr.
157 M5 Carling France
147 J4 Carlingford Ireland
147 J4 Carlingford Lough inlet Ireland/U.K.
236 K6 Carlinville IL U.S.A.
149 L4 Carlisle Cumbria, England U.K.
232 A10 Carlisle KY U.S.A.
233 K6 Carlisle NY U.S.A.
227 Q9 Carlisle PA U.S.A.
247 □4 Carlisle Bay Barbados
215 K9 Carlisle Bridge S. Africa
87 I10 Carlisle Lakes salt flat W.A. Austr.
234 A4 Carlisle Springs PA U.S.A.
163 H10 Carlit, Pic mt. France
192 A9 Carloforte Sardegna Italy
195 K5 Carlopoli Italy
256 C5 Carlópolis Brazil
146 J11 Carlops Scottish Borders, Scotland U.K.
245 L7 Carlos A. Carrillo Mex.
245 N8 Carlos A. Madrazo Mex.
261 G4 Carlos Casares Arg.
257 G2 Carlos Chagas Brazil
261 I3 Carlos Reyles Uru.
261 G4 Carlos Salas Arg.
261 F4 Carlos Tejedor Arg.
168 K3 Carlow Ger.
147 I7 Carlow Ireland
147 I7 Carlow county Ireland
146 C6 Carloway Western Isles, Scotland U.K.
Carlsbad Czech Rep. see Karlovy Vary
240 O8 Carlsbad CA U.S.A.
239 L10 Carlsbad NM U.S.A.
237 E10 Carlsbad TX U.S.A.
239 L10 Carlsbad Caverns National Park NM U.S.A.
172 E3 Carlsberg Ger.
265 H4 Carlsberg Ridge sea feature Indian Ocean
171 G10 Carlsfeld Ger.
262 S1 Carlson Inlet Antarctica
215 I7 Carlton S. Africa
151 J2 Carlton Nottinghamshire, England U.K.
226 B3 Carlton MN U.S.A.
151 P3 Carlton Colville Suffolk, England U.K.
86 J3 Carlton Hill W.A. Austr.
215 I7 Carlton Hills S. Africa
149 O7 Carlton in Lindrick Nottinghamshire, England U.K.
146 I11 Carluke South Lanarkshire, Scotland U.K.
163 G6 Carlux France
223 K5 Carlyle Sask. Can.
236 K6 Carlyle IL U.S.A.
236 K6 Carlyle Lake IL U.S.A.
222 B2 Carmacks Y.T. Can.
190 D6 Carmagnola Italy
223 L5 Carman Man. Can.
Carmana Iran see Kermān
150 D4 Carmarthen Carmarthenshire, Wales U.K.
150 C4 Carmarthen Bay Wales U.K.
150 D4 Carmarthenshire admin. div. Wales U.K.
163 I7 Carmaux France
230 D6 Carmel IN U.S.A.
233 □P4 Carmel ME U.S.A.
233 L7 Carmel NY U.S.A.
Carmel, Mount hill Israel see Karmel, Har
240 K5 Carmel-by-the-Sea CA U.S.A.
150 C1 Carmel Head Wales U.K.
243 N9 Carmelita Guat.
261 H3 Carmelo Uru.
240 K5 Carmel Valley CA U.S.A.
261 G3 Carmen Arg.
258 C2 Carmen Chile
250 C2 Carmen Col.
243 I5 Carmen Mex.
242 F2 Carmen r. Mex.
92 E7 Carmen Bohol Phil.
261 I3 Carmen Uru.
241 U10 Carmen AZ U.S.A.
242 D5 Carmen, Isla i. Mex.
243 N8 Carmen, Isla del i. Mex.
183 L9 Carmena Spain
252 C5 Carmen Alto Chile
261 H4 Carmen de Areco Arg.
253 F6 Carmen del Paraná Para.
259 E6 Carmen de Patagones Arg.
182 I3 Cármenes Spain
260 D4 Carmensa Arg.
236 K6 Carmi IL U.S.A.
195 O3 Carmiano Italy
231 □2 Carmichael New Prov. Bahamas
240 K3 Carmichael CA U.S.A.
85 L6 Carmila Qld Austr.
257 F4 Carmo Brazil
257 E4 Carmo da Cachoeira Brazil
257 E5 Carmo de Minas Brazil
256 D3 Carmo do Paranaíba Brazil
87 E12 Carmody, Lake salt flat W.A. Austr.
Carmona Angola see Uíge
242 □Q13 Carmona Hond.
184 H6 Carmona Spain
184 G2 Carmonita Spain
257 E4 Carmópolis do Minas Brazil
146 K9 Carmyllie Angus, Scotland U.K.
158 E6 Carnac France
146 G8 Carn a' Chuilinn hill Scotland U.K.
147 I4 Carnagh Northern Ireland U.K.
87 C10 Carnamah W.A. Austr.
87 B8 Carnarvon W.A. Austr.
214 G6 Carnarvon S. Africa
214 F6 Carnarvonleegte salt pan S. Africa
85 K8 Carnarvon National Park Qld Austr.
87 F8 Carnarvon Range hills W.A. Austr.
85 L8 Carnarvon Range mts Qld Austr.
146 K10 Carnbee Fife, Scotland U.K.
146 G7 Carn Chuinneag hill Scotland U.K.
146 G8 Carn Dearg hill Highland, Scotland U.K.
146 H8 Carn Dearg hill Highland, Scotland U.K.
147 H2 Carndonagh Ireland
147 J2 Carnduff Northern Ireland U.K.
146 J8 Carn Ealasaid hill Scotland U.K.
150 E1 Carnedd Llywelyn mt. Wales U.K.
150 E2 Carnedd y Filiast hill Wales U.K.
87 G8 Carnegie W.A. Austr.
87 G9 Carnegie, Lake salt flat W.A. Austr.
267 N6 Carnegie Ridge sea feature S. Pacific Ocean
146 F8 Carn Eige mt. Scotland U.K.
146 I8 Carne na Loine hill Scotland U.K.
258 B5 Carnero, Bahía del b. Chile
185 I8 Carnero, Punta del pt Spain
82 E4 Carnes S.A. Austr.
231 F8 Carnesville GA U.S.A.
147 J7 Carnew Ireland
226 G4 Carney MI U.S.A.
262 P2 Carney Island Antarctica
234 E5 Carneys Point NJ U.S.A.
146 K8 Carnferg hill Scotland U.K.
149 L5 Carnforth Lancashire, England U.K.
146 I8 Carn Glas-choire hill Scotland U.K.
115 M8 Car Nicobar i. Andaman & Nicobar Is India
156 F3 Carnières France
138 H4 Carnikava Latvia
147 K3 Carnlough Northern Ireland U.K.
147 K2 Carnlough Bay Northern Ireland U.K.
146 J8 Carn Mòr hill Scotland U.K.
147 E6 Carnmore Ireland
150 E2 Carno Powys, Wales U.K.
146 H8 Carn Odhar hill Scotland U.K.
158 D5 Carnoët France
161 D9 Carnon-Plage France
208 B3 Carnot C.A.R.
76 D5 Carnot, Cape S.A. Austr.
182 B3 Carnota Spain
86 G4 Carnot Bay W.A. Austr.
161 I10 Carnoules France
146 K9 Carnoustie Angus, Scotland U.K.
161 H10 Carnoux-en-Provence France
147 J8 Carnsore Point Ireland
148 D5 Carnteel Northern Ireland U.K.
146 I11 Carnwath South Lanarkshire, Scotland U.K.
227 K6 Caro MI U.S.A.
251 F4 Caroaebe r. Brazil
Caroch mt. Spain see El Caroche
85 N5 Carola Cay rf Coral Sea Is Terr. Austr.
231 G13 Carol City FL U.S.A.
193 Q9 Carolei Italy
260 D3 Carolina Arg.
254 D3 Carolina Brazil
247 □1 Carolina Puerto Rico
215 O2 Carolina S. Africa
231 I8 Carolina Beach NC U.S.A.
222 H4 Caroline Alta Can.
234 D7 Caroline County county MD U.S.A.
82 □3 Caroline Cove b. S. Pacific Ocean
267 I6 Caroline Island atoll Kiribati
266 E5 Caroline Islands N. Pacific Ocean
81 B12 Caroline Peak South I. N.Z.
158 H4 Carolles France
214 B5 Carolusberg S. Africa
161 G8 Caromb France
190 H3 Carona Italy
250 B4 Carondelet Ecuador
247 □7 Caroni Trinidad Trin. and Tob.
247 □7 Caroni Trinidad Trin. and Tob.
247 □7 Caroni county Trin. and Tob.
251 F2 Caroní r. Venez.
194 G7 Caronia Sicilia Italy
247 □7 Caroni Swamp Trin. and Tob.
250 D2 Carora Venez.
197 R5 C. A. Rosetti Romania
195 M3 Carosino Italy
195 N2 Carovigno Italy
193 M4 Carovilli Italy
227 R4 Carp Ont. Can.
190 H6 Carpaneto Piacentino Italy
177 I2 Carpathian Mountains Europe
Carpaţii mts Europe see Carpathian Mountains
197 K5 Carpaţii Meridionali mts Romania
191 M8 Carpegna Italy
190 I5 Carpenedolo Italy
84 G3 Carpentaria, Gulf of N.T./Qld Austr.
85 J5 Carpentaria Downs Qld Austr.
260 C2 Carpentiría Arg.
161 G8 Carpentras France
191 J6 Carpi Italy
195 O3 Carpignano Salentino Italy
190 E4 Carpignano Sesia Italy
254 G3 Carpina Brazil
191 M9 Carpina r. Italy
177 L5 Cărpinet Romania
190 I7 Carpineti Italy
193 K4 Carpineto Romano Italy
196 I5 Cărpiniş Romania
193 P4 Carpino Italy
193 M4 Carpinone Italy
240 M7 Carpinteria CA U.S.A.
183 J6 Carpio Spain
236 E1 Carpio ND U.S.A.
159 K3 Carpiquet France
222 F4 Carp Lake Provincial Park B.C. Can.
158 I7 Carquefou France
161 I10 Carqueiranne France
184 F2 Carquesa hill Spain
147 D5 Carra, Lough l. Ireland
233 □O3 Carrabassett ME U.S.A.
231 E11 Carrabelle FL U.S.A.
147 E5 Carracastle Ireland
182 G3 Carracedelo Spain
146 F11 Carradale East Argyll and Bute, Scotland U.K.
Carraig na Siuire Ireland see Carrick-on-Suir
250 C2 Carraipía Col.
182 D2 Carral Spain
147 D9 Carran hill Ireland
183 M8 Carranque Spain
147 C9 Carrantuohill mt. Ireland
184 B6 Carrapateira Port.
182 F7 Carrapichana Port.
190 I7 Carrara Italy
147 C6 Carraroe Ireland
186 E6 Carrascal mt. Spain
182 I7 Carrascal del Obispo Spain
183 M6 Carrascal del Río Spain
252 D4 Carrasco, Parque Nacional nat. park Bol.
183 P7 Carrascosa Spain
183 O8 Carrascosa del Campo Spain
187 C12 Carrascoy, Sierra de mts Spain
83 J6 Carrathool N.S.W. Austr.
185 J7 Carratraca Spain
182 F6 Carrazeda de Ansiães Port.
251 I5 Carrazedo Brazil
182 F5 Carrazedo de Montenegro Port.
86 J4 Carr Boyd Range hills W.A. Austr.
146 I8 Carrbridge Highland, Scotland U.K.
182 C5 Carreço Port.
184 B2 Carregado Port.
182 E8 Carregal do Sal Port.
182 D9 Carregueiros Port.
182 B3 Carreiro, Punta pt Spain
184 D5 Carreiros r. Port.
183 K2 Carreña Spain
260 C5 Carrero, Cerro mt. Arg.
163 C9 Carresse-Cassaber France
261 I4 Carreta Quemada Uru.
Carrhae Turkey see Harran
247 □3 Carriacou i. Grenada
183 M2 Carriazo Spain
147 E3 Carrick Donegal Ireland
147 I8 Carrick Wexford Ireland
146 G12 Carrick reg. Scotland U.K.
147 H8 Carrickbeg Ireland
147 G5 Carrickboy Ireland
147 K3 Carrickfergus Northern Ireland U.K.
147 I5 Carrickmacross Ireland
147 H3 Carrickmore Northern Ireland U.K.
147 F5 Carrick-on-Shannon Ireland
147 H8 Carrick-on-Suir Ireland
182 C9 Carriço Port.
82 G5 Carrieton S.A. Austr.
147 E9 Carrigadrohid Reservoir Ireland
147 F9 Carrigaline Ireland
147 G5 Carrigallen Ireland
147 D9 Carriganimmy Ireland
147 H3 Carrigans Ireland
147 D8 Carrigkerry Ireland
147 F9 Carrigtwohill Ireland
261 H4 Carril Arg.
242 H4 Carrillo Mex.
261 F2 Carrilobo Arg.
236 F2 Carrington ND U.S.A.
182 D2 Carrio Spain
183 K4 Carrion r. Spain
185 L2 Carrión de Calatrava Spain
184 G6 Carrión de los Céspedes Spain
183 K4 Carrión de los Condes Spain
250 C2 Carrizal Col.
242 F2 Carrizal Mex.
258 C3 Carrizal Bajo Chile
261 G3 Carrizales Arg.
241 V7 Carrizo AZ U.S.A.
244 D4 Carrizo Colorado Mex.
237 D7 Carrizo Creek r. TX U.S.A.
241 V8 Carrizo Creek watercourse AZ U.S.A.
241 Q8 Carrizo Creek watercourse CA U.S.A.
182 I3 Carrizo de la Ribera Spain
240 M7 Carrizo Plain National Monument nat. park CA U.S.A.
245 H1 Carrizos Mex.
185 N3 Carrizosa Spain
237 F11 Carrizo Springs TX U.S.A.
241 W7 Carrizo Wash watercourse AZ/NM U.S.A.
239 L10 Carrizozo NM U.S.A.
185 O2 Carro hill Spain
186 F3 Carrodilla, Sierra de mts Spain
236 H4 Carroll IA U.S.A.
234 A5 Carroll County county MD U.S.A.
237 K9 Carrollton AL U.S.A.
231 E9 Carrollton GA U.S.A.
236 J6 Carrollton IL U.S.A.
230 E6 Carrollton KY U.S.A.
236 I6 Carrollton MO U.S.A.
237 K9 Carrollton MS U.S.A.
232 D8 Carrollton OH U.S.A.
232 G8 Carrolltown PA U.S.A.
85 H4 Carron r. Qld Austr.
146 H7 Carron r. Highland, Scotland U.K.
146 E8 Carron, Loch inlet Scotland U.K.
146 I12 Carronbridge Dumfries and Galloway, Scotland U.K.
260 E5 Carro Quemado Arg.
161 K9 Carros France
223 K4 Carrot r. Sask. Can.
223 K4 Carrot River Sask. Can.
159 K4 Carrouges France
147 H2 Carrowkeel Ireland
147 E6 Carrowmore Ireland
147 C4 Carrowmore Lake Ireland
147 E4 Carrowneden Ireland
232 I12 Carrsville VA U.S.A.
190 D7 Carrù Italy
223 K2 Carruthers Lake Nunavut Can.
237 K7 Carruthersville MO U.S.A.
147 K3 Carryduff Northern Ireland U.K.
233 K4 Carry Falls Reservoir NY U.S.A.
161 G10 Carry-le-Rouet France
162 C5 Cars France
163 G6 Carsac-Aillac France
146 E10 Carsaig Argyll and Bute, Scotland U.K.
126 H3 Çarşamba Turkey
129 A4 Çarşıbaşı Turkey
149 N7 Carsington Water resr England U.K.
193 K3 Carsoli Italy
86 I3 Carson r. W.A. Austr.
236 E2 Carson ND U.S.A.
240 M2 Carson r. NV U.S.A.
226 J6 Carson City MI U.S.A.
240 M2 Carson City NV U.S.A.
86 I3 Carson Escarpment W.A. Austr.
240 N2 Carson Lake NV U.S.A.
86 I3 Carson River Aboriginal Reserve W.A. Austr.
240 N2 Carson Sink l. NV U.S.A.
227 L6 Carsonville MI U.S.A.
160 K1 Carspach France
146 H12 Carsphairn Dumfries and Galloway, Scotland U.K.
146 I11 Carstairs South Lanarkshire, Scotland U.K.
Carstensz-top mt. Papua Indon. see Jaya, Puncak
223 I3 Carswell Lake Sask. Can.
260 B3 Cartagena Chile
250 C2 Cartagena Col.
187 D12 Cartagena Spain
250 C3 Cartago Col.
242 □R13 Cartago Costa Rica
185 J7 Cártama Spain
184 B2 Cartaxo Port.
184 E6 Cartaya Spain
161 J10 Cartaya, Cap c. France
162 C5 Cartelègue France
85 I2 Carter, Mount hill Qld Austr.
158 H3 Carteret France
235 G3 Carteret NJ U.S.A.
158 H3 Carteret, Cap de c. France
Carteret Group is P.N.G. see Kilinailau Islands
Carteret Island Solomon Is see Malaita
85 H7 Carters Range hills Qld Austr.
231 E8 Cartersville GA U.S.A.
81 J8 Carterton North I. N.Z.
151 I4 Carterton Oxfordshire, England U.K.
183 L2 Cartes Spain
205 H1 Carthage tourist site Tunisia
226 C9 Carthage IL U.S.A.
237 H7 Carthage MO U.S.A.
231 C9 Carthage MS U.S.A.
231 H8 Carthage NC U.S.A.
233 J5 Carthage NY U.S.A.
231 E7 Carthage TN U.S.A.
237 H9 Carthage TX U.S.A.
Carthago tourist site Tunisia see Carthage
Carthago Nova Spain see Cartagena
227 M3 Cartier Ont. Can.
86 G2 Cartier Island Ashmore & Cartier Is Austr.
149 L5 Cartmel Cumbria, England U.K.
191 N8 Cartoceto Italy
223 L5 Cartwright Man. Can.
225 J2 Cartwright Nfld and Lab. Can.
251 F2 Caruachi Venez.
254 G4 Caruarú Brazil
254 C2 Caruçambaba Brazil
182 G4 Carucedo Spain
193 N4 Carunchio Italy
197 O4 Cărunta, Vârful mt. Romania
251 F2 Carúpano Venez.
254 D2 Carutapera Brazil
182 D9 Carvalhal Santarém Port.
184 B4 Carvalhal Setúbal Port.
251 I5 Carvalho Brazil
182 F6 Carvalho de Egas Port.
232 B11 Carver KY U.S.A.
182 G6 Carviçais Port.
156 E3 Carvin France
184 A2 Carvoeira Port.
251 F5 Carvoeiro Brazil
184 C6 Carvoeiro Port.
184 A2 Carvoeiro, Cabo c. Port.
85 K8 Carwell Qld Austr.
129 J4 Çarxı Azer.
231 H8 Cary NC U.S.A.
83 I3 Caryapundy Swamp Qld Austr.
232 A12 Caryville TN U.S.A.
226 C5 Caryville WI U.S.A.
185 P5 Casa Alta hill Spain
185 K7 Casabermeja Spain
258 D1 Casabindo, Cerro de mt. Arg.
260 B3 Casablanca Chile
204 D2 Casablanca Morocco
256 D4 Casa Branca Brazil
184 C3 Casa Branca Évora Port.
184 D3 Casa Branca Portalegre Port.
193 N4 Casacalenda Italy
247 □7 Casa Cruz, Cape Trin. and Tob.
242 E2 Casa de Janos Mex.
245 I2 Casa del Campesino Mex.
185 K3 Casa de Michos Spain
260 D6 Casa de Piedra Arg.
260 D6 Casa de Piedra, Embalse resr Arg.
193 M5 Casagiove Italy
192 B3 Casaglione Corse France
241 U9 Casa Grande AZ U.S.A.
195 O3 Casa l'Abate Italy
193 M3 Casalanguida Italy
183 O3 Casalarreina Spain
193 N3 Casalbordino Italy
193 O5 Casalbore Italy
193 P7 Casalbuono Italy
190 H5 Casalbuttano ed Uniti Italy
190 F6 Casàl Cermelli Italy
191 K7 Casalecchio di Reno Italy
261 G3 Casalegno Arg.
190 E5 Casale Monferrato Italy
193 P7 Casaletto Spartano Italy
191 L7 Casalfiumanese Italy
191 J6 Casalgrande Italy
190 D6 Casalgrasso Italy
184 B2 Casalinho Port.
261 H5 Casalins Arg.
190 I6 Casalmaggiore Italy
193 O4 Casalnuovo Monterotaro Italy
190 H5 Casalpusterlengo Italy
253 E3 Casalvasco Brazil
193 O4 Casalvecchio di Puglia Italy
193 O7 Casàl Velino Italy
206 A3 Casamance r. Senegal
195 L2 Casamassima Italy
192 C2 Casamozza Corse France
250 D3 Casanare dept Col.
250 D3 Casanare r. Col.
185 J7 Casarabonela Spain
195 O3 Casarano Italy
182 H9 Casar de Cáceres Spain
182 H8 Casar de Palomero Spain
183 N5 Casarejos Spain
242 □P12 Casares Nic.
185 I8 Casares Spain
182 H2 Casares Spain
182 H8 Casares de las Hurdes Spain
185 J6 Casariche Spain
183 L8 Casarrubios del Monte Spain
191 N4 Casarsa della Delizia Italy
190 G7 Casarza Ligure Italy
245 I2 Casas Mex.
187 C7 Casas Altas Spain
185 O2 Casas de Benítez Spain
185 I2 Casas de Don Pedro Spain
185 O2 Casas de Fernando Alonso Spain
185 O2 Casas de Haro Spain
187 C9 Casas de Juan Gil Spain
185 P2 Casas de Juan Núñez Spain
185 O3 Casas de Lázaro Spain
182 I8 Casas del Monte Spain
185 O2 Casas de los Pinos Spain
187 C11 Casas del Puerto Spain
182 H9 Casas de Millán Spain
187 C9 Casas de Ves Spain
242 F2 Casas Grandes Mex.
242 F2 Casas Grandes r. Mex.
185 Q2 Casas-Ibáñez Spain
185 O2 Casasimarro Spain
184 E3 Casas Novas de Mares Port.
183 J5 Casasola de Arión Spain
182 I9 Casatejada Spain
190 G4 Casatenovo Italy
183 K8 Casavieja Spain
261 F5 Casbas Arg.
255 B9 Casca Brazil
242 E3 Cascada de Bassaseachic, Parque Nacional nat. park Mex.
87 F12 Cascade W.A. Austr.
81 C11 Cascade r. South I. N.Z.
217 □2b Cascade Mahé Seychelles
236 J4 Cascade IA U.S.A.
238 F4 Cascade ID U.S.A.
238 I3 Cascade MT U.S.A.
82 □1 Cascade Bay Norfolk I.
81 C11 Cascade Point South I. N.Z.
228 B2 Cascade Range mts Can./U.S.A.
238 F4 Cascade Reservoir ID U.S.A.
217 □1c Cascades, Pointe des pt Réunion
238 D5 Cascade-Siskiyou National Monument nat. park OR U.S.A.
184 A3 Cascais Port.
242 □Q12 Cascal, Paso del pass Nic.
183 Q4 Cascante Spain
187 C7 Cascante del Río Spain
225 H3 Cascapédia r. Que. Can.
254 F3 Cascavel Ceará Brazil
256 A6 Cascavel Paraná Brazil
193 K2 Cascia Italy
191 J8 Casciana Terme Italy
190 J8 Cascina Italy

197 O6 **Căscioarele** Romania
226 G5 **Casco** *WI* U.S.A.
233 □P5 **Casco Bay** *ME* U.S.A.
184 B3 **Casebres** Port.
183 R3 **Cáseda** Spain
192 D9 **Case della Marina** *Sardegna* Italy
190 F5 **Casei Gerola** Italy
170 J4 **Casekow** Ger.
190 F6 **Casella** Italy
193 P7 **Caselle in Pittari** Italy
190 D5 **Caselle Torinese** Italy
191 N3 **Cà Selva, Lago di** *l.* Italy
195 L2 **Case Perrone** Italy
247 □3 **Case-Pilote** Martinique
193 M5 **Caserta** Italy
193 M5 **Caserta** *prov.* Italy
184 C5 **Casével** Port.
227 K6 **Caseville** *MI* U.S.A.
263 H2 **Casey** *research stn* Antarctica
263 D2 **Casey Bay** Antarctica
Cas-gwent *Wales* U.K. *see* **Chepstow**
147 G2 **Cashel** *Donegal* Ireland
147 E5 **Cashel** *Galway* Ireland
147 C6 **Cashel** *Galway* Ireland
147 H7 **Cashel** *Laois* Ireland
147 G7 **Cashel** *Tipperary* Ireland
147 E6 **Cashla** Ireland
147 B5 **Cashleen** Ireland
85 L9 **Cashmere** *Qld* Austr.
226 D6 **Cashton** *WI* U.S.A.
250 D2 **Casigua** *Falcón* Venez.
250 C2 **Casigua** *Zulia* Venez.
92 D3 **Casiguran** *Luzon* Phil.
92 C3 **Casiguran Sound** *sea chan.* *Luzon* Phil.
261 G3 **Casilda** Arg.
183 K8 **Casillas** Spain
182 G8 **Casillas de Flores** Spain
216 □3b **Casillas del Ángel** *Fuerteventura* Canary Is
197 Q6 **Casimcea** Romania
197 Q6 **Casimcea** *r.* Romania
244 C6 **Casimiro Castillo** Mex.
257 F5 **Casimiro de Abreu** Brazil
190 I6 **Casina** Italy
83 N3 **Casino** *N.S.W.* Austr.
187 D8 **Casinos** Spain
239 I11 **Casita** Mex.
176 E2 **Čáslav** Czech Rep.
252 A2 **Casma** Peru
Casnewydd *Newport, Wales* U.K. *see* **Newport**
226 I6 **Casnovia** *MI* U.S.A.
92 E6 **Casogoran Bay** Phil.
182 G4 **Casoio** *r.* Spain
190 I7 **Casola in Lunigiana** Italy
191 L7 **Casola Valsenio** Italy
191 K9 **Casole d'Elsa** Italy
193 M3 **Casoli** Italy
96 G5 **Ca, Sòng** *r.* Vietnam
193 M6 **Casoria** Italy
186 E5 **Caspe** Spain
186 E5 **Caspe, Embalse de** *resr* Spain
238 K5 **Casper** *WY* U.S.A.
226 F3 **Caspian** *MI* U.S.A.
Caspian Lowland Kazakh./Rus. Fed. *see* **Prikaspiyskaya Nizmennost'**
120 C5 **Caspian Sea** *l.* Asia/Europe
232 F10 **Cass** *WV* U.S.A.
227 K6 **Cass** *r. MI* U.S.A.
213 G2 **Cassacatiza** Moz.
232 F6 **Cassadaga** *NY* U.S.A.
186 K4 **Cassà de la Selva** Spain
163 F9 **Cassagnabère-Tournas** France
163 J7 **Cassagnes-Bégonhès** France
209 D7 **Cassai** Angola
209 D8 **Cassamba** Angola
163 I6 **Cassaniouze** France
193 Q8 **Cassano allo Ionio** Italy
195 L2 **Cassano delle Murge** Italy
190 F4 **Cassano Magnano** Italy
190 F6 **Cassano Spinola** Italy
209 C7 **Cassanzade** Angola
253 E3 **Cassara** Brazil
194 H9 **Cassaro** *Sicilia* Italy
227 K6 **Cass City** *MI* U.S.A.
156 D2 **Cassel** France
224 F4 **Casselman** *Ont.* Can.
236 G2 **Casselton** *ND* U.S.A.
163 F7 **Casseneuil** France
186 I3 **Casserres** Spain
256 D4 **Cássia** Brazil
222 D3 **Cassiar** *B.C.* Can.
222 D3 **Cassiar Mountains** *B.C.* Can.
195 I10 **Cassibile** *Sicilia* Italy
195 I10 **Cassibile** *r. Sicilia* Italy
256 B3 **Cassilândia** Brazil
83 L5 **Cassilis** *N.S.W.* Austr.
190 F6 **Cassine** Italy
209 C8 **Cassinga** Angola
258 G4 **Cassino** Brazil
193 L5 **Cassino** Italy
161 H10 **Cassis** France
236 H2 **Cass Lake** *MN* U.S.A.
146 G7 **Cassley** *r. Scotland* U.K.
191 L4 **Cassola** Italy
209 B7 **Cassongue** Angola
226 H8 **Cassopolis** *MI* U.S.A.
161 B7 **Cassuéjouls** France
237 I7 **Cassville** *MO* U.S.A.
176 G3 **Častá** Slovakia
190 F4 **Castagliona Olona** Italy
192 B4 **Castagna, Punta di a** *pt Corse* France
191 K5 **Castagnaro** Italy
192 F1 **Castagneto Carducci** Italy
192 C3 **Castagniccia** *reg. Corse* France
190 E6 **Castagnole delle Lanze** Italy
190 E6 **Castagnole Monferrato** Italy
187 D10 **Castalla** Spain
183 J9 **Castañar de Ibor** Spain
183 O3 **Castañares de Rioja** Spain
163 H8 **Castanet-Tolosan** France
251 F6 **Castanhal** *Amazonas* Brazil
254 D2 **Castanhal** *Pará* Brazil
182 F7 **Castanheira** Port.
184 □ **Castanheira, Ponta da** *pt* Madeira
182 D8 **Castanheira de Pêra** Port.
251 E5 **Castanheiro** Brazil
253 E1 **Castanho** Brazil
260 C2 **Castaño** *r.* Arg.
184 F4 **Castaño, Sierra del** *hills* Spain
260 C2 **Castaño Nuevo** Arg.
190 F4 **Castano Primo** Italy
243 I4 **Castaños** Mex.
260 C2 **Castaño Viejo** Arg.
247 □5 **Castara** Trin. and Tob.
247 □5 **Castara Bay** Trin. and Tob.
190 H3 **Castasegna** Switz.
190 G5 **Casteggio** Italy
183 Q4 **Castejón** Spain
186 C4 **Castejón, Montes de** *mts* Spain
186 F4 **Castejón del Puente** Spain
186 E4 **Castejón de Monegros** Spain
186 F2 **Castejón de Sos** Spain
186 D4 **Castejón de Valdejasa** Spain
193 O5 **Castèl Baronia** Italy
191 O9 **Castelbellino** Italy
191 L7 **Castèl Bolognese** Italy
194 G8 **Castelbuono** *Sicilia* Italy
193 O7 **Castelcivita** Italy
194 F7 **Casteldaccia** *Sicilia* Italy
191 J5 **Castèl d'Ario** Italy
190 C6 **Casteldelfino** Italy
193 L3 **Castèl del Monte** Italy
195 K1 **Castèl del Monte** *tourist site* Italy
192 H2 **Castèl del Piano** Italy
191 L7 **Castèl del Rio** Italy
194 H9 **Castèl di Iudica** *Sicilia* Italy
193 L2 **Castèl di Lama** Italy
194 G8 **Castèl di Lucio** *Sicilia* Italy
193 M4 **Castèl di Sangro** Italy
182 F8 **Casteleiro** Port.
191 P9 **Castelfidardo** Italy
191 J8 **Castelfiorentino** Italy
186 E4 **Castelflorite** Spain
191 L8 **Castèl Focognano** Italy
193 L5 **Castelforte** Italy
193 O6 **Castelfranci** Italy
191 L8 **Castelfranco di Sopra** Italy
191 J8 **Castelfranco di Sotto** Italy
191 K6 **Castelfranco Emilia** Italy
193 O5 **Castelfranco in Miscano** Italy
191 L4 **Castelfranco Veneto** Italy
193 M3 **Castèl Frentano** Italy
192 H2 **Castèl Giorgio** Italy
190 I5 **Castèl Goffredo** Italy
193 O6 **Castelgrande** Italy
163 E7 **Casteljaloux** France
173 I2 **Castell** Ger.
190 E6 **Castell'Alfero** Italy
193 L2 **Castellalto** Italy
194 D7 **Castellammare, Golfo di** *b. Sicilia* Italy
194 D7 **Castellammare del Golfo** *Sicilia* Italy
193 M6 **Castellammare di Stabia** Italy
190 D5 **Castellamonte** Italy
195 M2 **Castellana Grotte** Italy
161 J9 **Castellane** France
195 L2 **Castellaneta** Italy
195 L3 **Castellaneta Marina** Italy
185 N3 **Castellanos** *mt.* Spain
183 L4 **Castellanos de Castro** Spain
185 I8 **Castellar de la Frontera** Spain
183 Q7 **Castellar de la Muela** Spain
186 H3 **Castellar de la Ribera** Spain
185 M3 **Castellar de Santiago** Spain
185 M4 **Castellar de Santisteban** Spain
190 H6 **Castell'Arquato** Italy
192 H2 **Castell'Azzara** Italy
190 F6 **Castellazzo Bormida** Italy
186 G5 **Castelldans** Spain
186 F6 **Castell de Cabres** Spain
187 E10 **Castell de Castells** Spain
186 I5 **Castelldefels** Spain
185 M7 **Castell de Ferro** Spain
190 H5 **Castelleone** Italy
190 F4 **Castelletto sopra Ticino** Italy
186 K3 **Castellfollit de la Roca** Spain
186 E6 **Castellfort** Spain
261 I5 **Castelli** *Buenos Aires* Arg.
258 E2 **Castelli** *Chaco* Arg.
191 K9 **Castellina in Chianti** Italy
191 J9 **Castellina Marittima** Italy
193 L4 **Castelliri** Italy
Castell-nedd *Neath Port Talbot, Wales* U.K. *see* **Neath**
Castell Newydd Emlyn *Ceredigion, Wales* U.K. *see* **Newcastle Emlyn**
187 E8 **Castellnovo** Spain
161 K7 **Castello, Lago di** *l.* Italy
187 E8 **Castelló, Plana de** *plain* Spain
191 K6 **Castello d'Argile** Italy
Castello de Ampurias Spain *see* **Castelló d'Empúries**
186 L3 **Castelló d'Empúries** Spain
187 E10 **Castelló de Rugat** Spain
190 E6 **Castello di Annone** Italy
187 E8 **Castellón de la Plana** Spain
187 E7 **Castellón de la Plana** *prov.* Spain
186 E6 **Castellote** Spain
191 L3 **Castello Tesino** Italy
186 G4 **Castellserá** Spain
186 J4 **Castellterçol** Spain
191 J5 **Castellucchio** Italy
193 O5 **Castelluccio dei Sauri** Italy
193 P7 **Castelluccio Inferiore** Italy
193 O5 **Castellucio Valmaggiore** Italy
194 H7 **Castell'Umberto** *Sicilia* Italy
194 D7 **Castelluzzo** *Sicilia* Italy
193 J4 **Castèl Madama** Italy
191 K6 **Càstel Maggiore** Italy
190 C7 **Castelmagno** Italy
191 K5 **Castelmassa** Italy
163 E7 **Castelmoron-sur-Lot** France
194 G1 **Castèl Morrone** Italy
163 G9 **Castelnau** France
163 F8 **Castelnau-Barbarens** France
163 H9 **Castelnaudary** France
163 E8 **Castelnau-d'Auzan** France
163 F6 **Castelnaud-de-Gratecambe** France
163 J8 **Castelnau-de-Brassac** France
162 C5 **Castelnau-de-Médoc** France
163 H8 **Castelnau-de-Montmiral** France
163 G8 **Castelnau d'Estréfonds** France
161 D9 **Castelnau-le-Lez** France
163 F9 **Castelnau-Magnoac** France
163 G7 **Castelnau-Montratier** France
163 D8 **Castelnau-Rivière-Basse** France
191 J6 **Castelnovo di Sotto** Italy
190 I7 **Castelnovo ne'Monti** Italy
191 L9 **Castelnuovo Berardenga** Italy
193 O4 **Castelnuovo della Daunia** Italy
190 I7 **Castelnuovo di Garfagnana** Italy
192 F1 **Castelnuovo di Val di Cecina** Italy
190 D5 **Castelnuovo Don Bosco** Italy
190 F6 **Castelnuovo Scrivia** Italy
257 G4 **Castelo** Brazil
182 G7 **Castelo Bom** Port.
216 □1c **Castelo Branco** *Faial* Azores
182 G6 **Castelo Branco** *Bragança* Port.
182 F9 **Castelo Branco** *Castelo Branco* Port.
182 F8 **Castelo Branco** *admin. dist.* Port.
182 D9 **Castelo de Bode, Barragem do** *resr* Port.
182 D6 **Castelo de Paiva** Port.
184 E2 **Castelo de Vide** Port.
182 C5 **Castelo do Neiva** Port.
254 E3 **Castelo do Piauí** Brazil
182 D6 **Castelões** Port.
182 F6 **Castelo Melhor** Port.
182 G7 **Castelo Mendo** Port.
182 G7 **Castelo Rodrigo** Port.
191 O9 **Castelplanio** Italy
191 O9 **Castelraimondo** Italy
193 J2 **Castèl Ritaldi** Italy
191 L2 **Castelrotto** Italy
163 F7 **Castelsagrat** France
190 G5 **Castèl San Giovanni** Italy
191 L8 **Castèl San Niccolò** Italy
191 L7 **Castèl San Pietro Terme** Italy
193 K3 **Castèl Sant'Angelo** Italy
193 K2 **Castelsantangelo sul Nera** Italy
193 P7 **Castelsaraceno** Italy
192 B6 **Castelsardo** *Sardegna* Italy
163 G7 **Castelsarrasin** France
186 E6 **Castelseras** Spain
194 F8 **Casteltermini** *Sicilia* Italy
190 H5 **Castelverde** Italy
193 N5 **Castelvetere in Val Fortore** Italy
194 D8 **Castelvetrano** *Sicilia* Italy
190 H5 **Castelvetro Placentino** Italy
192 I2 **Castèl Viscardo** Italy
193 L5 **Castèl Volturno** Italy
191 K6 **Castenaso** Italy
163 E8 **Castéra-Verduzan** France
82 H7 **Casterton** *Vic.* Austr.
163 C9 **Castetnau-Camblong** France
163 B8 **Castets** France
192 D9 **Castiadas** *Sardegna* Italy
187 C7 **Castielfabib** Spain
186 D2 **Castiello de Jaca** Spain
192 C2 **Castifao** *Corse* France
190 I9 **Castiglioncello** Italy
191 K7 **Castiglione dei Pepoli** Italy
192 I1 **Castiglione del Lago** Italy
192 F2 **Castiglione della Pescaia** Italy
190 I5 **Castiglione della Stiviere** Italy
192 H1 **Castiglione d'Orcia** Italy
192 I2 **Castiglione in Teverina** Italy
193 M4 **Castiglione Messer Marino** Italy
191 L9 **Castiglion Fiorentino** Italy
193 L2 **Castignano** Italy
225 G1 **Castignon, Lac** *l. Que.* Can.
185 I2 **Castilblanco** Spain
184 H5 **Castilblanco de los Arroyos** Spain
232 G6 **Castile** *NY* U.S.A.
256 B4 **Castilho** Brazil
183 R4 **Castiliscar** Spain
258 C2 **Castilla** Chile
250 A6 **Castilla** Peru
183 L4 **Castilla, Canal de** Spain
183 N10 **Castilla-La Mancha** *aut. comm.* Spain
183 L5 **Castilla y León** *aut. comm.* Spain
184 G6 **Castilleja de la Cuesta** Spain
185 N5 **Castillejar** Spain
183 J6 **Castillejo** *hill* Spain
251 F3 **Castillejo** Venez.
182 G7 **Castillejo de Martin Viejo** Spain
183 M6 **Castillejo de Mesleón** Spain
183 N5 **Castillejo de Robledo** Spain
250 D2 **Castilletes** Col.
259 B8 **Castillo, Canal del** *sea chan.* Chile
260 C3 **Castillo, Cerro del** *mt.* Arg.
259 C7 **Castillo, Pampa del** *hills* Arg.
183 K8 **Castillo de Bayuela** Spain
183 P9 **Castillo de Garcimuñoz** Spain
185 L5 **Castillo de Locubín** Spain
245 J5 **Castillo de Teavo** Mex.
161 J9 **Castillon, Barrage de** *dam* France
163 G10 **Castillon-en-Couserans** France
163 D6 **Castillon-la-Bataille** France
163 F6 **Castillonnès** France
186 C2 **Castillo-Nuevo** Spain
258 G4 **Castillos** *Rocha* Uru.
261 I3 **Castillos** *Soriano* Uru.
258 G4 **Castillos, Lago de** *l.* Uru.
183 P5 **Castilruiz** Spain
190 I4 **Castione della Presolana** Italy
178 H8 **Castiòns di Strada** Italy
147 D5 **Castlebar** Ireland
146 B9 **Castlebay** *Western Isles, Scotland* U.K.
147 J5 **Castlebellingham** Ireland
147 F6 **Castleblakeney** Ireland
147 I4 **Castleblayney** Ireland
151 I2 **Castle Bromwich** *West Midlands, England* U.K.
247 □2 **Castle Bruce** Dominica
149 L4 **Castle Carrock** *Cumbria, England* U.K.
150 G5 **Castle Cary** *Somerset, England* U.K.
147 H7 **Castlecomer** Ireland
147 E7 **Castleconnell** Ireland
147 D4 **Castleconor** Ireland
241 U2 **Castle Dale** *UT* U.S.A.
226 C2 **Castle Danger** *MN* U.S.A.
147 I3 **Castledawson** *Northern Ireland* U.K.
147 G3 **Castlederg** *Northern Ireland* U.K.
147 I7 **Castledermot** Ireland
241 R8 **Castle Dome Mountains** *AZ* U.S.A.
151 J2 **Castle Donington** *Leicestershire, England* U.K.
146 I13 **Castle Douglas** *Dumfries and Galloway, Scotland* U.K.
147 J8 **Castleellis** Ireland
147 G3 **Castlefinn** Ireland
149 O6 **Castleford** *West Yorkshire, England* U.K.
147 E9 **Castlefreke** Ireland
147 F4 **Castlegal** Ireland
222 G5 **Castlegar** *B.C.* Can.
147 B8 **Castlegregory** Ireland
231 □1 **Castle Harbour** *b.* Bermuda
147 D4 **Castlehill** Ireland
246 F2 **Castle Island** Bahamas
147 D8 **Castleisland** Ireland
148 C7 **Castlejordan** Ireland
146 G13 **Castle Kennedy** *Dumfries and Galloway, Scotland* U.K.
147 F8 **Castlelyons** Ireland
83 J7 **Castlemaine** *Vic.* Austr.
147 C8 **Castlemaine** Ireland
150 B4 **Castlemartin** *Pembrokeshire, Wales* U.K.
147 F9 **Castlemartyr** Ireland
222 H5 **Castle Mountain** *Alta* Can.
240 L6 **Castle Mountain** *CA* U.S.A.
Castle Peak *hill H.K.* China *see* **Tsing Shan**
Castle Peak Bay *H.K.* China *see* **Tsing Shan Wan**
81 K7 **Castlepoint** *North I.* N.Z.
147 H5 **Castlepollard** Ireland
147 F5 **Castlerea** Ireland
83 K4 **Castlereagh** *r. N.S.W.* Austr.
147 K3 **Castlereagh** *Northern Ireland* U.K.
147 I2 **Castlerock** *Northern Ireland* U.K.
239 L7 **Castle Rock** *CO* U.S.A.
238 C3 **Castle Rock** *WA* U.S.A.
226 D6 **Castle Rock Lake** *WI* U.S.A.
216 □2b **Castle Rock Point** St Helena
147 I2 **Castleroe** *Northern Ireland* U.K.
149 N4 **Castleside** *Durham, England* U.K.
246 □ **Castleton** Jamaica
149 P5 **Castleton** *North Yorkshire, England* U.K.
233 L6 **Castleton-On-Hudson** *NY* U.S.A.
148 H5 **Castletown** Isle of Man
147 D6 **Castletown** *Clare* Ireland
147 E9 **Castletown** *Cork* Ireland
147 H7 **Castletown** *Laois* Ireland
147 I5 **Castletown** *Meath* Ireland
146 J5 **Castletown** *Highland, Scotland* U.K.
147 F8 **Castletownroche** Ireland
147 D5 **Castleville** Ireland
147 K4 **Castlewellan** *Northern Ireland* U.K.
223 I4 **Castor** *Alta* Can.
224 E2 **Castor, Rivière du** *r. Que.* Can.
237 I10 **Castor Creek** *r. LA* U.S.A.
Castra Regina Ger. *see* **Regensburg**
183 L9 **Castrejón, Embalse de** *resr* Spain
183 K3 **Castrejón de la Peña** Spain
182 F5 **Castrelo do Val** Spain
163 I8 **Castres** France
164 G3 **Castricum** Neth.
161 D9 **Castries** France
247 □3 **Castries** St Lucia
195 O4 **Castrignano del Capo** Italy
185 N5 **Castril** Spain
185 N5 **Castril** *r.* Spain
183 L5 **Castrillo de Don Juan** Spain
183 L5 **Castrillo de Duero** Spain
183 N5 **Castrillo de la Reina** Spain
183 M5 **Castrillo de la Vega** Spain
183 L4 **Castrillo de Villavega** Spain
183 L5 **Castrillo Tejeriego** Spain
256 C6 **Castro** Brazil
259 B6 **Castro** Chile
195 O3 **Castro** Italy
182 B2 **Castro** *r.* Spain
182 H5 **Castro, Embalse de** *resr* Spain
254 F5 **Castro Alves** Brazil
260 E2 **Castro Barros** Arg.
183 N2 **Castrobarto** Spain
182 I4 **Castrocalbón** Spain
182 F4 **Castro Caldelas** Spain
191 L7 **Castrocaro Terme** Italy
182 H4 **Castrocontrigo** Spain
182 E7 **Castro Daire** Port.
193 L4 **Castro dei Volsci** Italy
185 K5 **Castro del Río** Spain
182 F1 **Castro de Ouro** Spain
182 F2 **Castro de Rei** Spain
194 F9 **Castrofilippo** *Sicilia* Italy
182 I5 **Castrogonzalo** Spain
183 L4 **Castrojeriz** Spain
182 D4 **Castro Laboreiro** Port.
184 E6 **Castro Marim** Port.
183 K4 **Castromocho** Spain
183 J5 **Castromonte** Spain
182 I5 **Castronuevo** Spain
183 J6 **Castronuño** Spain
194 F8 **Castronuovo di Sicilia** *Sicilia* Italy
193 N4 **Castropignano** Italy
182 H3 **Castropodame** Spain
182 F1 **Castropol** Spain
169 D7 **Castrop-Rauxel** Ger.
195 I7 **Castroreale** *Sicilia* Italy
183 N2 **Castro-Urdiales** Spain
182 C4 **Castrove** *hill* Spain
184 C5 **Castro Verde** Port.
182 F2 **Castroverde** Spain
183 J5 **Castroverde de Campos** Spain
193 Q8 **Castrovillari** Italy
240 K5 **Castroville** *CA* U.S.A.
252 B3 **Castrovirreyna** Peru
184 H3 **Castuera** Spain
106 B2 **Cast Uul** *mt.* Mongolia
86 I3 **Casuarina, Mount** *hill W.A.* Austr.
81 B11 **Caswell Sound** *inlet South I.* N.Z.
127 J4 **Çat** Turkey
209 C8 **Catabola** Angola
242 □Q10 **Catacamas** Hond.
250 A6 **Catacaos** Peru
250 B6 **Catacocha** Ecuador
187 D9 **Catadau** Spain
246 □ **Catadupa** Jamaica
257 F4 **Cataguases** Brazil
237 I10 **Catahoula Lake** *LA* U.S.A.
92 D5 **Cataiñgan** *Masbate* Phil.
128 B2 **Çatak** *İçel* Turkey
127 K5 **Çatak** *Van* Turkey
129 C7 **Çataklı** Turkey
185 □ **Catalan Bay** Gibraltar
256 D3 **Catalão** Brazil
199 J1 **Çatalca** Turkey
199 J1 **Çatalca Yarımadası** *pen.* Turkey
241 V9 **Catalina** *AZ* U.S.A.
78 □1 **Catalina Point** Guam
Catalonia *aut. comm.* Spain *see* **Cataluña**
186 I4 **Cataluña** *aut. comm.* Spain
Catalunya *aut. comm.* Spain *see* **Cataluña**
126 G3 **Çatalzeytin** Turkey
83 K10 **Catamaran** *Tas.* Austr.
258 D3 **Catamarca** Arg.
258 D2 **Catamarca** *prov.* Arg.
Catambia Moz. *see* **Catandica**
Catana *Sicilia* Italy *see* **Catania**
92 D5 **Catanauan** *Luzon* Phil.
213 G3 **Catandica** Moz.
92 E5 **Catanduanes** *i.* Phil.
256 C4 **Catanduva** Brazil
256 A6 **Catanduvas** Brazil
195 I9 **Catania** *Sicilia* Italy
194 H9 **Catania** *prov. Sicilia* Italy
195 I9 **Catania, Golfo di** *g. Sicilia* Italy
259 C5 **Catán Lil** Arg.
195 L6 **Catanzaro** Italy
195 L6 **Catanzaro** *prov.* Italy
195 L6 **Catanzaro Marina** Italy
253 E2 **Cataqueamã** Brazil
226 D5 **Cataract** *WI* U.S.A.
241 T5 **Cataract Creek** *watercourse AZ* U.S.A.
254 F3 **Catarina** Brazil
237 F11 **Catarina** *TX* U.S.A.
243 I5 **Catarino Rodriguez** Mex.
92 E5 **Catarman** *Samar* Phil.
92 F8 **Catarman Point** *Mindanao* Phil.
187 E9 **Catarroja** Spain
234 E3 **Catasauqua** *PA* U.S.A.
82 E6 **Catastrophe, Cape** *S.A.* Austr.
209 B8 **Catata Nova** Angola
250 C2 **Catatumbo Bari** *nat. park* Col.
252 D4 **Catavi** Bol.
226 D4 **Catawba** *WI* U.S.A.
231 G8 **Catawba** *r. SC* U.S.A.
227 R9 **Catawissa** *PA* U.S.A.
234 C3 **Catawissa Creek** *r. PA* U.S.A.
96 H4 **Cat Ba, Đao** *i.* Vietnam
92 E6 **Catbalogan** *Samar* Phil.
246 D1 **Cat Cays** *is* Bahamas
92 F8 **Cateel** *Mindanao* Phil.
92 F8 **Cateel Bay** *Mindanao* Phil.
209 D9 **Catehu** Angola
245 L7 **Catemaco** Mex.
245 L7 **Catemaco, Laguna** *l.* Mex.
215 Q2 **Catembe** Moz.
260 B3 **Catemu** Chile
192 C7 **Catena del Goceano** *mts Sardegna* Italy
192 B7 **Catena del Marghine** *mts Sardegna* Italy
194 H8 **Catenanuova** *Sicilia* Italy
209 B8 **Catengue** Angola
151 L5 **Caterham** *Surrey, England* U.K.
192 B2 **Cateri** *Corse* France
209 B7 **Catete** Angola
251 H6 **Catete** *r.* Brazil
83 L7 **Cathcart** *N.S.W.* Austr.
215 L8 **Cathcart** S. Africa
241 P8 **Cathedral City** *CA* U.S.A.
215 N4 **Cathedral Peak** Lesotho
222 F5 **Cathedral Provincial Park** *B.C.* Can.
147 B9 **Catherdaniel** Ireland
231 D9 **Catherine** *AL* U.S.A.
Catherine, Mount Egypt *see* **Kātrīnā, Jabal**
241 T3 **Catherine, Mount** *UT* U.S.A.
246 □ **Catherine's Peak** *hill* Jamaica
240 L4 **Catheys Valley** *CA* U.S.A.
238 C3 **Cathlamet** *WA* U.S.A.
186 F7 **Catí** Spain
193 L3 **Catignano** Italy
260 B5 **Catillo** Chile
206 B4 **Catió** Guinea-Bissau
251 F3 **Catisimiña** Venez.
246 F1 **Cat Island** Bahamas
182 E7 **Cativelos** Port.
129 C6 **Çatkale** Turkey
224 B3 **Cat Lake** *Ont.* Can.
232 C10 **Catlettsburg** *KY* U.S.A.
81 D13 **Catlins Forest Park** *nature res. South I.* N.Z.
243 P7 **Catoche, Cabo** *c.* Mex.
182 C3 **Catoira** Spain
77 F4 **Cato Island and Bank** *rf Coral Sea Is Terr.* Austr.
254 F3 **Catolé do Rocha** Brazil
209 C7 **Catolo** Angola
149 L5 **Caton** *Lancashire, England* U.K.
195 J7 **Catona** *r.* Italy
234 B6 **Catonsville** *MD* U.S.A.
244 G2 **Catorce** Mex.
244 G2 **Catorce, Sierra de** *mts* Mex.
199 L3 **Çatören Barajı** *resr* Turkey
209 C8 **Catota** Angola
182 H3 **Catoute** *mt.* Spain
187 D11 **Catral** Spain
191 N9 **Catria, Monte** *mt.* Italy
260 D5 **Catriel** Arg.
261 F5 **Catriló** Arg.
251 F4 **Catrimani** Brazil
251 F4 **Catrimani** *r.* Brazil
146 H11 **Catrine** *East Ayrshire, Scotland* U.K.
150 H3 **Catshill** *Worcestershire, England* U.K.
233 L6 **Catskill** *NY* U.S.A.
233 K6 **Catskill Mountains** *NY* U.S.A.
157 L5 **Cattenom** France
169 K9 **Catterfeld** Ger.
149 N5 **Catterick** *North Yorkshire, England* U.K.
149 N5 **Catterick Garrison** *North Yorkshire, England* U.K.
146 L9 **Catterline** *Aberdeenshire, Scotland* U.K.
81 E11 **Cattle Creek** *South I.* N.Z.
191 N8 **Cattolica** Italy
194 E9 **Cattolica Eraclea** *Sicilia* Italy
258 D1 **Catúa** Arg.
213 G5 **Catuane** Moz.
213 G2 **Catur** Moz.
163 G6 **Catus** France
194 F8 **Catuso, Monte** *mt.* Italy
177 L4 **Căuaș** Romania
254 C2 **Cauaxi** *r.* Brazil
92 D7 **Cauayan** *Negros* Phil.
225 I1 **Caubvick, Mount** *Nfld and Lab.* Can.
250 B4 **Cauca** *dept* Col.
250 C2 **Cauca** *r.* Col.
254 F2 **Caucaia** Brazil
250 C3 **Caucasia** Col.
129 B2 **Caucasus** *mts* Asia/Europe
260 C2 **Caucete** Arg.
258 D1 **Cauchari, Salar de** *salt flat* Arg.
223 L4 **Cauchon Lake** *Man.* Can.
233 □P2 **Caucomgomoc Lake** *ME* U.S.A.
158 E6 **Caudan** France
162 F6 **Caudau** *r.* France
159 M2 **Caudebec-en-Caux** France
163 F7 **Caudecoste** France
187 D10 **Caudete** Spain
187 C8 **Caudete de las Fuentes** Spain
187 D8 **Caudiel** Spain
163 I10 **Caudiès de-Fenouillèdes** France
156 F3 **Caudry** France
96 G5 **Câu Giat** Vietnam
92 F7 **Cauit Point** *Mindanao* Phil.
163 G9 **Caujac** France
158 G5 **Caulnes** France
195 K7 **Caulonia** Italy
163 G7 **Caumont** *Midi-Pyrénées* France
163 G9 **Caumont** *Midi-Pyrénées* France
159 J3 **Caumont-l'Éventé** France
161 F9 **Caumont-sur-Durance** France
246 D2 **Caunao** *r.* Cuba
163 J9 **Caunes-Minervois** France
209 C7 **Caungula** Angola
209 C9 **Cauno** Angola
260 A4 **Cauquenes** Chile
251 E3 **Caura** *r.* Venez.
251 F5 **Caurés** *r.* Brazil
192 B4 **Cauro** *Corse* France
225 H3 **Causapscal** *Que.* Can.
136 I7 **Căușeni** Moldova
147 C8 **Causeway** Ireland
147 I2 **Causeway Head** *Northern Ireland* U.K.
163 H7 **Caussade** France
252 D3 **Cautário** *r.* Brazil
163 D10 **Cauterets** France
222 E5 **Caution, Cape** *B.C.* Can.
246 E3 **Cauto** *r.* Cuba
129 J5 **Cavad** Azer.
193 N6 **Cava de'Tirreni** Italy
182 C5 **Cávado** *r.* Port.
190 E5 **Cavaglià** Italy
161 G9 **Cavaillon** France
161 J10 **Cavalaire-sur-Mer** France
254 D5 **Cavalcante** *Goiás* Brazil
252 E2 **Cavalcante** *Rondônia* Brazil
184 B5 **Cavaleiro** Port.
191 K3 **Cavalese** Italy
236 G1 **Cavalier** *ND* U.S.A.
186 □ **Cavalleria, Cap de** *c.* Spain
190 D6 **Cavallermaggiore** Italy
80 H1 **Cavalli Islands** *North I.* N.Z.
191 N5 **Cavallino** Italy
192 C5 **Cavallo, Île** *i. Corse* France
193 N3 **Cavalluccio, Punta** *pt* Italy
206 D5 **Cavally** *r.* Côte d'Ivoire
190 G5 **Cava Manara** Italy
147 H5 **Cavan** Ireland
147 H5 **Cavan** *county* Ireland
261 F3 **Cavanagh** Arg.
190 G3 **Cavargna** Italy
191 M5 **Cavarzere** Italy
191 O3 **Cavazzo Carnico** Italy
199 K3 **Çavdarhisar** Turkey
199 K5 **Çavdır** Turkey
81 E11 **Cave** *South I.* N.Z.
237 J7 **Cave City** *AR* U.S.A.
230 E7 **Cave City** *KY* U.S.A.
241 U8 **Cave Creek** *AZ* U.S.A.
191 P3 **Cave del Predil** Italy
191 J3 **Cavedine, Lago di** *l.* Italy
257 F2 **Caveira** Brazil
161 E9 **Caveirac** France
87 J9 **Cavenagh Range** *hills W.A.* Austr.
83 I7 **Cavendish** *Vic.* Austr.
255 B9 **Cavera, Serra do** *hills* Brazil
256 A6 **Cavernoso, Serra do** *mts* Brazil
150 H2 **Caverswall** *Staffordshire, England* U.K.
232 B10 **Cave Run Lake** *KY* U.S.A.
182 E5 **Cavês** Port.
191 K6 **Cavezzo** Italy
251 I4 **Caviana, Ilha** *i.* Brazil
162 D5 **Cavignac** France
92 C7 **Cavili** *rf* Phil.
92 C4 **Cavite** *Luzon* Phil.
191 Q5 **Čavle** Croatia
197 L3 **Cavnic** Romania
193 J4 **Cavo, Monte** *hill* Italy
192 D9 **Cavoli, Isola dei** *i. Sardegna* Italy
195 L3 **Cavone** *r.* Italy
209 C8 **Cavongo** Angola
190 C6 **Cavour** Italy
226 F4 **Cavour** *WI* U.S.A.
190 E5 **Cavour, Canale** *canal* Italy
191 J6 **Cavriago** Italy
191 K8 **Cavriglia** Italy
126 E4 **Çavuşçu** Turkey
199 M2 **Çavuşdere** Turkey
199 L6 **Çavuşköy** Turkey
146 I7 **Cawdor** *Highland, Scotland* U.K.
83 H5 **Cawndilla Lake** *imp. l. N.S.W.* Austr.
Cawnpore *Uttar Prad.* India *see* **Kanpur**
149 O6 **Cawood** *North Yorkshire, England* U.K.
232 B12 **Cawood** *KY* U.S.A.
151 O2 **Cawston** *Norfolk, England* U.K.
257 E4 **Caxambu** Brazil
182 C9 **Caxarias** Port.
250 D6 **Caxias** *Amazonas* Brazil
254 E3 **Caxias** *Maranhão* Brazil
255 C9 **Caxias do Sul** Brazil
209 B7 **Caxito** Angola
251 I5 **Caxiuana, Baía de** *l.* Brazil
199 M4 **Çay** Turkey
250 B5 **Cayambe-Coca, Reserva Ecológica** *nat. park* Ecuador
129 D5 **Çayarası** Turkey
261 G2 **Cayastá** Arg.
199 I4 **Çaybaşı** *İzmir* Turkey
Çaybaşı *Rize* Turkey *see* **Çayeli**
231 G9 **Cayce** *SC* U.S.A.
126 F3 **Çaycuma** Turkey
127 J3 **Çayeli** Turkey
251 H3 **Cayenne** Fr. Guiana
261 I2 **Cayetano** Uru.
156 C3 **Cayeux-sur-Mer** France
247 □1 **Cayey** Puerto Rico
247 □1 **Cayey, Sierra de** *hills* Puerto Rico
199 J3 **Çaygören Barajı** *resr* Turkey
126 G5 **Çayhan** Turkey
199 J6 **Çayhisar** Turkey
126 E3 **Çayırhan** Turkey
129 B6 **Çayırlı** Turkey
129 B5 **Çaykara** Turkey
129 H6 **Çaylaqqala** Azer.
163 H7 **Caylus** France
246 D4 **Cayman Brac** *i.* Cayman Is
246 C4 **Cayman Islands** *terr.* West Indies
264 D4 **Cayman Trench** *sea feature* Caribbean Sea
210 E2 **Caynabo** Somalia
150 G3 **Caynham** *Shropshire, England* U.K.
161 J8 **Cayolle, Col de la** *pass* France
247 □2 **Cayon** St Kitts and Nevis
231 □2 **Cay Point** *New Prov.* Bahamas
129 G5 **Çay Räsullu** Azer.
161 D7 **Cayres** France
246 C2 **Cay Sal** *i.* Bahamas
246 C2 **Cay Sal Bank** *sea feature* Bahamas
246 F3 **Cay Santa Domingo** *i.* Bahamas
149 P7 **Caythorpe** *Lincolnshire, England* U.K.
149 Q5 **Cayton** *North Yorkshire, England* U.K.
240 L6 **Cayucos** *CA* U.S.A.
227 O7 **Cayuga** *Ont.* Can.
232 I6 **Cayuga Heights** *NY* U.S.A.
232 I6 **Cayuga Lake** *NY* U.S.A.
246 F2 **Cay Verde** *i.* Bahamas
209 D7 **Cazage** Angola
Cazaje Angola *see* **Cazage**
183 K8 **Cazalegas** Spain
184 H5 **Cazalla de la Sierra** Spain
163 G6 **Cazals** *Midi-Pyrénées* France
163 H7 **Cazals** *Midi-Pyrénées* France
197 P6 **Căzănești** Romania
258 F3 **Caza Pava** Arg.
163 D8 **Cazaubon** France
163 B7 **Cazaux et de Sanguinet, Étang de** *l.* France
111 H11 **Cazê** *Xizang* China
233 J6 **Cazenovia** *NY* U.S.A.
163 G9 **Cazères** France
163 G7 **Cazes-Mondenard** France
163 I9 **Cazilhac** France
188 F3 **Cažma** Croatia
209 D7 **Cazombo** Angola
245 J5 **Cazones** Mex.
245 J5 **Cazones** *r.* Mex.
185 N5 **Cazorla** Spain
185 M5 **Cazorla, Sierra de** *mts* Spain
163 G6 **Cazoulès** France
191 N3 **Cà Zul, Lago di** *l.* Italy
213 G2 **Cazula** Moz.
183 K4 **Cea** *Castilla y León* Spain
182 E4 **Cea** *Galicia* Spain
183 I4 **Cea** *r.* Spain
Ceadâr-Lunga Moldova *see* **Ciadîr-Lunga**
Ceanannus Mór Ireland *see* **Kells**
146 B7 **Ceann a' Bhàigh** *Western Isles, Scotland* U.K.
Ceará Brazil *see* **Fortaleza**
254 F3 **Ceará** *state* Brazil
264 G6 **Ceara Abyssal Plain** *sea feature* S. Atlantic Ocean
146 C6 **Cearsiadar** *Western Isles, Scotland* U.K.
197 Q5 **Ceatalchioi** Romania
Ceatharlach Ireland *see* **Carlow**
159 J5 **Ceaucé** France
161 D6 **Céaux-d'Allègre** France
242 G4 **Ceballos** Mex.
182 G1 **Cebes, Cabo** *c.* Spain
128 A2 **Cebireis Dağı** *mt.* Turkey
182 E9 **Cebolais de Cima** Port.
183 K9 **Cebolla** Spain
258 D3 **Cebollar** Arg.
183 O4 **Cebollera, Sierra** *mts* Spain
244 C6 **Ceboruco, Cerro** *mt.* Mex.
244 C4 **Ceboruco, Volcán** *vol.* Mex.
177 I3 **Čebovce** Slovakia
183 L8 **Cebreros** Spain
92 D6 **Cebu** *Cebu* Phil.
92 D6 **Cebu** *i.* Phil.
193 K4 **Ceccano** Italy
177 H5 **Cece** Hungary
178 E7 **Cece, Cima di** *mt.* Italy
182 D2 **Cecebre, Encoro de** *resr* Spain
177 K3 **Čečejovce** Slovakia
176 E2 **Čechtice** Czech Rep.
176 D2 **Čechy** *reg.* Czech Rep.
177 H3 **Čechynce** Slovakia
226 F5 **Cecil** *WI* U.S.A.
234 D5 **Cecil County** *county MD* U.S.A.
85 M9 **Cecil Plains** *Qld* Austr.
87 F8 **Cecil Rhodes, Mount** *hill W.A.* Austr.
234 D6 **Cecilton** *MD* U.S.A.
191 J9 **Cecina** Italy
191 I9 **Cecina** *r.* Italy
195 K5 **Cecita, Lago di** *l.* Italy
182 G9 **Ceclavín** Spain
182 F6 **Cedães** Port.
226 J6 **Cedar** *r. MI* U.S.A.
236 E2 **Cedar** *r. ND* U.S.A.
236 G5 **Cedar** *r. NE* U.S.A.
232 D11 **Cedar Bluff** *VA* U.S.A.
234 F5 **Cedar Brook** *NJ* U.S.A.
241 S4 **Cedar City** *UT* U.S.A.
237 G9 **Cedar Creek Reservoir** *TX* U.S.A.
239 K7 **Cedaredge** *CO* U.S.A.
236 I4 **Cedar Falls** *IA* U.S.A.
247 □2 **Cedar Grove** Antigua and Barbuda
240 N5 **Cedar Grove** *CA* U.S.A.
226 G6 **Cedar Grove** *WI* U.S.A.
232 D10 **Cedar Grove** *WV* U.S.A.
233 J11 **Cedar Island** *VA* U.S.A.
223 K4 **Cedar Lake** *Man.* Can.
227 P3 **Cedar Lake** *Ont.* Can.
232 B7 **Cedar Point** *OH* U.S.A.
230 B5 **Cedar Rapids** *IA* U.S.A.
241 U5 **Cedar Ridge** *AZ* U.S.A.
226 G4 **Cedar River** *MI* U.S.A.
235 G5 **Cedar Run** *NJ* U.S.A.
227 L7 **Cedar Springs** *Ont.* Can.
226 I6 **Cedar Springs** *MI* U.S.A.
231 E8 **Cedartown** *GA* U.S.A.
246 □ **Cedar Valley** Jamaica
215 N6 **Cedarville** S. Africa
226 E7 **Cedarville** *IL* U.S.A.
227 J4 **Cedarville** *MI* U.S.A.
232 B9 **Cedarville** *OH* U.S.A.
190 I3 **Cedegolo** Italy
182 D1 **Cedeira** Spain
182 C2 **Cedeira** *hill* Spain
182 D1 **Cedeira, Ría de** *inlet* Spain
183 L9 **Cedena** *r.* Spain
242 □P11 **Cedeño** Hond.
214 C8 **Cederberg** *mts* S. Africa
182 F9 **Cedillo** Spain
182 F9 **Cedillo, Embalse de** *resr* Port./Spain
183 M8 **Cedillo del Condado** Spain
243 P7 **Cedral** *Quintana Roo* Mex.
244 G2 **Cedral** *San Luis Potosí* Mex.
186 D7 **Cedrillas** Spain
192 D7 **Cedrino** *r. Sardegna* Italy
254 F3 **Cedro** Brazil
216 □1c **Cedros** *Faial* Azores
242 □P10 **Cedros** Hond.
242 E4 **Cedros** *Sonora* Mex.
244 F1 **Cedros** *Zacatecas* Mex.
242 B3 **Cedros, Isla** *i.* Mex.
216 □1c **Cedros, Ponta dos** *pt Faial* Azores
247 □7 **Cedros Point** Trin. and Tob.
174 G1 **Cedry Wielkie** Pol.
82 D5 **Ceduna** *S.A.* Austr.
174 C3 **Cedynia** Pol.
170 J5 **Cedyński Park Krajobrazowy** Pol.
182 B3 **Cee** Spain
210 E2 **Ceel Afweyn** Somalia
210 F2 **Ceelayo** Somalia
210 D2 **Ceel Baxay** Somalia
210 E3 **Ceelbuur** Somalia
210 E2 **Ceel Dhaab** Somalia
210 E4 **Ceeldheere** Somalia
210 D2 **Ceel Gaal** *Awdal* Somalia
210 F2 **Ceel Gaal** *Bari* Somalia
210 E3 **Ceel Garas** *well* Somalia
210 E3 **Ceel God** Somalia
210 F3 **Ceel Huur** Somalia
210 D4 **Ceel Walaaq** *well* Somalia
210 E2 **Ceerigaabo** Somalia
177 K5 **Cefa** Romania
194 G7 **Cefalù** *Sicilia* Italy
Cefn Bychan *Caerphilly, Wales* U.K. *see* **Newbridge**
150 F2 **Cefn-mawr** *Wrexham, Wales* U.K.
183 K5 **Cega** *r.* Spain
191 N4 **Ceggia** Italy
177 I4 **Cegléd** Hungary
177 I4 **Ceglédbercel** Hungary
195 N2 **Ceglie Messapica** Italy
175 J3 **Cegłów** Pol.
111 K10 **Cêgnê** *Xizang* China
196 I9 **Čegrane** Macedonia
177 L4 **Cehal** Romania
185 P4 **Cehegín** Spain
108 E6 **Ceheng** *Guizhou* China
196 G7 **Čehotina** *r.* Montenegro
197 L3 **Cehu Silvaniei** Romania
247 □1 **Ceiba** Puerto Rico
261 H3 **Ceibas** Arg.
177 L5 **Ceica** Romania
161 C9 **Ceilhes-et-Rocozels** France
Ceinewydd *Ceredigion, Wales* U.K. *see* **New Quay**
183 J4 **Ceinos de Campos** Spain
157 L6 **Ceintrey** France
182 D8 **Ceira** Port.
182 D8 **Ceira** *r.* Port.
176 F3 **Čejč** Czech Rep.
177 K3 **Čejkov** Slovakia
179 O2 **Čejkovice** Czech Rep.
174 G2 **Cekcyn** Pol.
126 G3 **Çekerek** Turkey
122 E3 **Çekiçler** Turkm.
174 G4 **Ceków-Kolonia** Pol.
186 C7 **Celadas** Spain
Celah, Gunung *mt.* Malaysia *see* **Mandi Angin, Gunung**
176 D1 **Čelákovice** Czech Rep.
193 L3 **Celano** Italy
182 E4 **Celanova** Spain
243 O10 **Celaque, Parque Naci**[...] *nat. park* Hond.
244 G5 **Celaya** Mex.
147 I6 **Celbridge** Ireland
163 H7 **Célé** *r.* France
Celebes *i.* Indon. *see* **S**[...]
93 B2 **Celebes Sea** Indon./Ph[...]
129 E7 **Çelebibağı** Turkey
182 D5 **Celeiros** Port.
184 H8 **Celemin, Embalse de** Spain
250 B6 **Celendín** Peru
193 N4 **Celenza Valfortore** Ital[...]
243 N7 **Celestún** Mex.
195 K5 **Celico** Italy
129 D6 **Çelikli** Turkey
236 M5 **Celina** *OH* U.S.A.
231 E7 **Celina** *TN* U.S.A.
188 E2 **Celje** Slovenia
186 C7 **Cella** Spain
176 G4 **Celldömölk** Hungary
168 J5 **Celle** Ger.
192 H3 **Cellere** Italy
165 D7 **Celles** Belgium
163 H10 **Celles** France
162 D3 **Celles-sur-Belle** Franc[...]
160 D5 **Celles-sur-Durolle** Fra[...]
156 H7 **Celles-sur-Ource** Fran[...]
159 N6 **Cellettes** France
191 N3 **Cellina** *r.* Italy
193 L2 **Cellino Attanasio** Italy
195 N3 **Cellino San Marco** Ital[...]
193 L5 **Cellole** Italy
193 P4 **Celone** *r.* Italy
182 F7 **Celorico da Beira** Port[...]
182 E6 **Celorico de Basto** Por[...]
Celovec Austria *see* **Klagenfurt**
186 K3 **Celrà** Spain
145 D6 **Celtic Sea** Ireland/U.K.
264 I2 **Celtic Shelf** *sea feature* N. Atlantic Ocean
199 L5 **Çeltikçi** *Burdur* Turkey
199 J2 **Çeltikçi** *Bursa* Turkey
199 L5 **Çeltikçi Beli** *pass* Turk[...]
150 E2 **Celyn, Llyn** *l. Wales* U.[...]
129 D6 **Cem** *r.* Turkey
95 K4 **Cemaru, Gunung** *mt.* [...]
191 K3 **Cembra** Italy
123 J4 **Çemenibit** Turkm.
126 G3 **Çemilbey** Turkey
126 I4 **Çemişgezek** Turkey
150 E2 **Cemmaes** *Powys, Wale*[...]
95 M9 **Cempi, Teluk** *b. Sumb*[...] Indon.
179 K7 **Čemšeniška planina** *r*[...] Slovenia
163 G6 **Cénac-et-St-Julien** Fr[...]
196 I4 **Cenad** Romania
185 P4 **Cenajo, Embalse del** [...] Spain
191 L3 **Cencenighe Agordino**[...]
91 I7 **Cenderawasih, Teluk** [...] *Papua* Indon.
122 F2 **Çendir** *r.* Turkm.
161 E8 **Cendras** France
162 F6 **Cendrieux** France
196 I5 **Cenei** Romania
191 K5 **Ceneselli** Italy
190 E7 **Cengio** Italy
183 O4 **Cenicero** Spain
183 L8 **Ceniclentos** Spain
161 J6 **Cenis, Col du Mont** *pa*[...] France
185 P2 **Cenizate** Spain
129 A6 **Cennetpınar** Turkey
190 I6 **Ceno** *r.* Italy
163 C6 **Cenon** France
184 □ **Cenouras, Ilhéu das** *i.* Madeira
93 A5 **Cenrana** *Sulawesi Bara*[...]
196 I5 **Čenta** *Vojvodina* Serbia
190 D6 **Centallo** Italy
Centane S. Africa *see* [...]
81 C11 **Centaur Peak** *South I.*
Centellas Spain *see* **Ce**[...]
186 J4 **Centelles** Spain
260 C6 **Centenario** Arg.
256 B5 **Centenário do Sul** Bra[...]
213 F3 **Centenary** Zimbabwe
241 T8 **Centennial Wash** *wate*[...] *AZ* U.S.A.
236 E2 **Center** *ND* U.S.A.
236 G4 **Center** *NE* U.S.A.
237 H10 **Center** *TX* U.S.A.
232 C8 **Centerburg** *OH* U.S.A.
235 I3 **Centereach** *NY* U.S.A.
231 E8 **Center Hill Lake** *resr T*[...]
235 J3 **Center Moriches** *NY* [...]
233 □N5 **Center Ossipee** *NH* U[...]
231 D9 **Center Point** *AL* U.S.A.
235 I3 **Centerport** *NY* U.S.A.
234 E4 **Center Square** *PA* U.S[...]
234 E3 **Center Valley** *PA* U.S.A.
236 I5 **Centerville** *IA* U.S.A.
237 J7 **Centerville** *MO* U.S.A.
232 C10 **Centerville** *OH* U.S.A.
232 F7 **Centerville** *PA* U.S.A.
232 F8 **Centerville** *PA* U.S.A.
231 D8 **Centerville** *TN* U.S.A.
237 H10 **Centerville** *TX* U.S.A.
232 E9 **Centerville** *WV* U.S.A.
191 K6 **Cento** Italy
193 O7 **Centola** Italy
251 G3 **Centraal Suriname Natuurreservaat** *natur*[...] Suriname
Centrafricaine, Répub[...] *country* Africa *see* **Central African Republ**[...]
212 E4 **Central** *admin. dist.* Bo[...]
254 E4 **Central** Brazil
252 C5 **Central** Chile
206 E5 **Central** *admin. reg.* Gh[...]
210 C5 **Central** *prov.* Kenya
211 B8 **Central** *admin. reg.* Ma[...]
239 J10 **Central** *NM* U.S.A.
209 F8 **Central** *prov.* Zambia
252 D4 **Central, Cordillera** *mt*[...]
250 B4 **Central, Cordillera** *mt*[...]
246 H4 **Central, Cordillera** *mt*[...] Dom. Rep.
242 □S13 **Central, Cordillera** *mt*[...] Panama
252 A2 **Central, Cordillera** *mt*[...]
92 C3 **Central, Cordillera** *mt*[...] Phil.
247 □1 **Central, Cordillera** *mt*[...] Puerto Rico
Central African Empi[...] *country* Africa *see* **Central African Republ**[...]
208 D3 **Central African Repub**[...] *country* Africa
86 J6 **Central Australia Abo**[...] **Reserve** *W.A.* Austr.
123 L7 **Central Brahui Range** Pak.
223 J5 **Central Butte** *Sask.* Ca[...]
236 J4 **Central City** *IA* U.S.A.
236 F5 **Central City** *NE* U.S.A.
232 G8 **Central City** *PA* U.S.A.
257 G3 **Central de Minas** Braz[...]
84 C6 **Central Desert Aborig**[...] **Land** *res. N.T.* Austr.
233 N7 **Central Falls** *RI* U.S.A.
236 K6 **Centralia** *IL* U.S.A.
238 C3 **Centralia** *WA* U.S.A.
210 C4 **Central Island Nationa**[...] Kenya
235 I3 **Central Islip** *NY* U.S.A.
104 E6 **Central Japan Interna**[...] **Airport** *airport Aichi* Ja[...]
212 D4 **Central Kalahari Gam**[...] **Reserve** *nature res.* Bo[...]
260 B2 **Central Los Molles** Ch[...]
123 K8 **Central Makran Range** Pak.
84 D6 **Central Mount Stuart** Austr.
84 C7 **Central Mount Wedge** Austr.
266 G5 **Central Pacific Basin** *sea feature* Pacific Oce[...]
83 K9 **Central Plateau Conservation Area** *na*[...] *Tas.* Austr.
Central Provinces *stat*[...] *see* **Madhya Pradesh**

Central Range mts Lesotho
Central Range mts P.N.G.
Central Russian Upland hills Rus. Fed. see Sredne-Russkaya Vozvyshennost'
Central Siberian Plateau Rus. Fed. see Sredne-Sibirskoye Ploskogor'ye
Central Square NY U.S.A.
Central Valley NY U.S.A.
Central Village CT U.S.A.
Centre prov. Cameroon
Centre admin. reg. France
Centre AL U.S.A.
Centre, Canal du France
Centre de Flacq Mauritius
Centre Island South I. N.Z.
Centreville AL U.S.A.
Centreville MD U.S.A.
Centreville MI U.S.A.
Centreville VA U.S.A.
Centuri Corse France
Centurion S. Africa
Centuripe Sicilia Italy
Century FL U.S.A.
Cenxi Guangxi China
Ceos i. Greece see Tzia
Ceos Scotland U.K. see Keose
Céou r. France
Cepagatti Italy
Cephaloedium Sicilia Italy see Cefalù
Cephalonia i. Greece see Kefallonia
Čepin Croatia
Čepkelių nature res. Lith.
Cepões Port.
Čepovan Slovenia
Cepoy France
Ceppaloni Italy
Ceprano Italy
Cepu Jawa Indon.
Cer hills Serbia
Ceram i. Maluku Indon. see Seram
Cerami Sicilia Italy
Cerami r. Sicilia Italy
Ceram Sea Indon. see Seram, Laut
Cerano Italy
Ceranów Pol.
Cérans-Foulletourte France
Cerasi Italy
Ceraso Italy
Ceraso, Capo c. Sardegna Italy
Cerbăl Romania
Cerbat Mountains AZ U.S.A.
Cerbère France
Cerbère, Cap c. France/Spain
Cerbicale, Îles is Corse France
Cerbol r. Spain see Cervol, Riu
Cerboli, Isola i. Italy
Cercal Lisboa Port.
Cercal Setúbal Port.
Cercal hill Port.
Cercal, Serra do mts Port.
Čerčany Czech Rep.
Cercedilla Spain
Cercemaggiore Italy
Cerchio Italy
Čerchov mt. Czech Rep.
Cercy-la-Tour France
Cerda Sicilia Italy
Cerdagne reg. France
Cerdaña reg. France see Cerdagne
Cerdanya reg. Spain
Cerdanyola del Vallès Spain
Cerdedo Spain
Cerdeira Port.
Cerdon France
Cère r. France
Cerea Italy
Cereal Alta Can.
Cereales Arg.
Cereceda, Embalse de resr Spain
Cered Hungary
Ceredigion admin. div. Wales U.K.
Ceregnano Italy
Cerekwica Pol.
Cérences France
Cerenzia Italy
Ceres Arg.
Ceres Brazil
Ceres Italy
Ceres S. Africa
Ceres CA U.S.A.
Ceresole, Lago di l. Italy
Ceresole Reale Italy
Ceresone r. Italy
Céreste France
Céret France
Cereté Col.
Cerezo de Abajo Spain
Cerezo de Arriba Spain
Cerezo de Riotirón Spain
Cerf, Île au i. Inner Islands Seychelles
Cerf, Lac du l. Que. Can.
Cerfontaine Belgium
Cerfs, Îles aux is Mauritius
Čergov mts Slovakia
Cergy France
Cerhenice Czech Rep.
Cêri Xizang China
Ceriale Italy
Ceriana Italy
Cerignola Italy
Cerigo i. Greece see Kythira
Çerikli Turkey
Cerillos Chile
Cerillos de Tamaya Chile
Cérilly France
Cêringgolêb Xizang China see Dongco
Cerisiers France
Cerisy-la-Forêt France
Cerisy-la-Salle France
Cerizay France
Cerk mt. Slovenia
Çerkeş Turkey
Çerkeşli Turkey
Çerkezköy Turkey
Çerkezmüsellim Turkey
Cerklje Brežice Slovenia
Cerklje Kranj Slovenia
Cerknica Slovenia
Cerkniško jezero l. Slovenia
Cerkno Slovenia
Cerkwica Pol.
Çerme Turkey
Cermei Romania
Cermignano Italy
Çermik Turkey
Cerna Romania
Cerna r. Romania
Cerna r. Romania
Cerna r. Romania
Cernache do Bonjardim Port.
Cernadilla, Embalse de resr Spain
Černá Hora Czech Rep.
Černá hora mt. Czech Rep.
Cernat Romania
Cernăuți Ukr. see Chernivtsi
Cernavodă Romania
Cernay France
Cernay-en-Dormois France
Černčice Czech Rep.
Cernégula Spain
Černelavci Slovenia
Cernier Switz.
Černík Slovakia
Černiny hill Slovakia
Cernobbio Italy
Černošice Czech Rep.
Černošín Czech Rep.
Černovice Czech Rep.
Cérou r. France
Cerovica Croatia
Cerovlje Croatia
Cerovo Slovakia
Cerqueira César Brazil
Cerralbo Spain
Cerralvo Mex.
Cerralvo, Isla i. Mex.
Cerrato, Valles de reg. Spain
190 I7 Cerreto, Passo del pass Italy
191 N9 Cerreto d'Esi Italy
193 J2 Cerreto di Spoleto Italy
193 N5 Cerreto Sannita Italy
150 E1 Cerrigydrudion Conwy, Wales U.K.
196 H9 Cërrik Albania
258 D2 Cerrillos Arg.
244 G5 Cerritos Guanajuato Mex.
244 G3 Cerritos San Luis Potosí Mex.
193 M4 Cerro al Volturno Italy
256 C6 Cerro Azul Brazil
245 J4 Cerro Azul Mex.
252 A3 Cerro Azul Peru
184 H5 Cerro del Hiero Spain
244 D7 Cerro de Ortega Mex.
252 A2 Cerro de Pasco Peru
244 G4 Cerro Gordo Mex.
242 □S14 Cerro Hoya, Parque Nacional nat. park Panama
259 C9 Cerro Manantiales Chile
185 M7 Cerrón mt. Spain
250 D2 Cerrón, Cerro mt. Venez.
252 C5 Cerro Negro Chile
242 F4 Cerro Prieto Mex.
260 C6 Cerros Colorados, Embalse resr Arg.
250 A5 Cerros de Amotape, Parque Nacional nat. park Peru
159 K7 Cersay France
193 Q7 Cersosimo Italy
191 K8 Certaldo Italy
197 K5 Certeju de Sus Romania
177 K2 Čertižne Slovakia
190 G5 Certosa di Pavia Italy
190 D7 Certosa di Pesio Italy
Ceru Colorado Aruba see Seroe Colorado
182 E6 Cerva Port.
182 C5 Cervães Port.
183 J9 Cervales mt. Spain
87 C11 Cervantes W.A. Austr.
259 B8 Cervantes, Cerro mt. Arg.
193 L5 Cervaro Italy
193 P4 Cervaro r. Italy
193 O7 Cervati, Monte mt. Italy
183 K4 Cervatos de la Cueza Spain
176 F1 Červená Voda Czech Rep.
171 L10 Červené Pečky Czech Rep.
197 N7 Cervenia Romania
176 G2 Červenka Czech Rep.
186 H4 Cervera Spain
186 F6 Cervera, Rambla de r. Spain
183 Q6 Cervera de la Cañada Spain
183 P9 Cervera del Llano Spain
183 K8 Cervera de los Montes Spain
183 Q4 Cervera del Río Alhama Spain
183 L3 Cervera de Pisuerga Spain
192 I4 Cerveteri Italy
191 M7 Cervia Italy
193 O6 Cervialto, Monte mt. Italy
191 O4 Cervignano del Friuli Italy
191 K2 Cervina, Punta mt. Italy
193 N5 Cervinara Italy
176 E2 Červiná Řečice Czech Rep.
192 C3 Cervione Corse France
190 E8 Cervo Italy
190 E5 Cervo r. Italy
182 F1 Cervo Spain
186 G7 Cervol, Riu r. Spain
160 D2 Cervon France
193 Q9 Cerzeto Italy
191 O8 Cesano r. Italy
250 C2 Cesar dept Col.
250 C2 Cesar r. Col.
194 H8 Cesarò Sicilia Italy
178 F8 Cesen, Monte mt. Italy
191 M7 Cesena Italy
191 M7 Cesenatico Italy
190 D7 Cesio Italy
138 I4 Cēsis Latvia
176 D1 Česká Kamenice Czech Rep.
176 D1 Česká Lípa Czech Rep.
Česká Republika country Europe see Czech Republic
176 F1 Česká Skalice Czech Rep.
177 I3 České Brezovo Slovakia
176 D3 České Budějovice Czech Rep.
176 C1 České Středohoří hills Czech Rep.
179 K2 České Velenice Austria
176 D2 Českomoravská vysočina hills Czech Rep.
176 D1 Český Brod Czech Rep.
171 K9 Český Dub Czech Rep.
176 D3 Český Krumlov Czech Rep.
176 B2 Český les mts Czech Rep./Ger.
176 E1 Český Ráj park Czech Rep.
179 L1 Český Rudolec Czech Rep.
177 H2 Český Těšín Czech Rep.
188 F3 Česma r. Croatia
199 H4 Çeşme Turkey
182 I7 Cespedosa Spain
191 N4 Cessalto Italy
161 B10 Cesse r. France
161 C10 Cessenon-sur-Orb France
160 G5 Cessieu France
83 M5 Cessnock N.S.W. Austr.
158 H5 Cesson-Sévigné France
163 C6 Cestas France
206 C5 Cestos r. Liberia
182 D2 Cesuras Spain
138 J5 Cesvaine Latvia
92 D3 Cetaceo, Mount Phil.
106 G8 Cêtar Qinghai China
177 L4 Cetariu Romania
197 L6 Cetate Romania
Cetatea Albă Ukr. see Bilhorod-Dnistrovs'kyy
188 F4 Cetina r. Croatia
183 Q6 Cetina Spain
196 G8 Cetinje Montenegro
190 I3 Ceto Italy
159 M5 Ceton France
192 H2 Cetona Italy
193 P8 Cetraro Italy
163 C10 Cette-Eygun France
78 □1 Cetti Bay Guam
161 H7 Céüse France
161 H7 Céüse, Montagne de mt. France
180 D5 Ceuta N. Africa
187 C11 Ceutí Spain
190 E7 Ceva Italy
77 H4 Ceva-i-Ra rf Fiji
191 J3 Cevedale, Monte mt. Italy
161 C9 Cévennes mts France
161 D8 Cévennes, Parc National des nat. park France
Čevetjävri Fin. see Sevettijärvi
183 L5 Cevico de la Torre Spain
183 L5 Cevico Navero Spain
160 I5 Cevins France
190 F3 Cevio Switz.
129 C5 Cevizli Erzurum Turkey
199 L3 Cevizli Eskişehir Turkey
128 F2 Cevizli Gaziantep Turkey
Cevizlik Turkey see Maçka
174 F1 Cewice Pol.
175 K5 Cewków Pol.
126 G5 Ceyhan Turkey
128 D2 Ceyhan r. Turkey
128 D2 Ceyhan Boğazı r. mouth Turkey
127 J5 Ceylanpınar Turkey
129 K5 Çeyldağ Azer.
Ceylon country Asia see Sri Lanka
129 K5 Ceyranbatan Azer.
161 H10 Ceyreste France
160 G4 Ceyzériat France
162 D5 Cézac France
161 F8 Cèze r. France
182 E5 Chã Port.
164 G6 Chaam Neth.
122 I9 Chābahār Iran
162 F4 Chabanais France
261 G3 Chabas Arg.
161 H8 Chabestan France
161 G7 Chabeuil France
175 H4 Chabielice Pol.
160 J4 Chablais mts France
243 N9 Chablé Mex.
156 G8 Chablis France
162 F4 Chabrac France
161 H8 Chabre ridge France
160 D5 Chabreloche France
159 O7 Chabris France
Chabrol i. Îles Loyauté New Caledonia see Lifou
111 L13 Chabua Assam India
111 F10 Chabug Xizang China
111 G11 Chabyêr Caka salt l. China
252 C4 Chaca Chile
261 G4 Chacabuco Arg.
247 □7 Chacachacare Island Trin. and Tob.
245 L7 Chacaltianguis Mex.
245 J8 Chacaltongo Mex.
252 C4 Chacarilla Bol.
250 B6 Chachapoyas Peru
260 E5 Chacharramendi Arg.
116 F7 Chachaura-Binaganj Madh. Prad. India
Chāche Turkm. see Çäçe
139 N9 Chachersk Belarus
138 M8 Chachevichy Belarus
97 E8 Chachoengsao Thai.
123 N9 Chachro Pak.
182 G6 Chacim Port.
258 E2 Chaco prov. Arg.
253 F5 Chaco Boreal reg. Para.
239 K8 Chaco Culture National Historical Park nat. park NM U.S.A.
222 C4 Chacon, Cape AK U.S.A.
251 G6 Chacorão, Cachoeira da waterfall Brazil
252 B2 Chacra de Piros Peru
202 C6 Chad country Africa
202 B6 Chad, Lake Africa
106 H3 Chadaasan Mongolia
98 F1 Chadan Rus. Fed.
231 □1 Chaddock Bar rf Bermuda
234 D5 Chadds Ford PA U.S.A.
213 G2 Chadiza Zambia
161 D6 Chadrac France
236 D4 Chadron NE U.S.A.
Chadyr-Lunga Moldova see Ciadîr-Lunga
96 D5 Chae Hom Thai.
121 P7 Chaek Kyrg.
101 D9 Chaeryŏng N. Korea
96 D5 Chae Son National Park Thai.
181 E5 Chafarinas, Islas is N. Africa
207 G4 Chafe Nigeria
237 K7 Chaffee MO U.S.A.
259 B7 Chaffers, Isla i. Chile
226 B3 Chaffey WI U.S.A.
250 C4 Chafurray Col.
123 K7 Chagai Pak.
123 J7 Chagai Hills Afgh./Pak.
114 F5 Chagalamarri Andhra Prad. India
120 K5 Chagan Kyzylordinskaya Oblast' Kazakh.
121 R2 Chagan Vostochnyy Kazakhstan Kazakh.
110 I1 Chaganuzun Rus. Fed.
111 G9 Chagdo Kangri mt. China
150 E6 Chagford Devon, England U.K.
111 L9 Chaggur Qinghai China
122 D6 Chaghā Khūr mt. Iran
123 K4 Chaghcharān Afgh.
121 M1 Chaglinka r. Kazakh.
160 F3 Chagny France
139 S2 Chagoda Rus. Fed.
139 S2 Chagoda r. Rus. Fed.
139 T3 Chagodoshcha r. Rus. Fed.
265 I5 Chagos Archipelago is B.I.O.T.
265 I5 Chagos-Laccadive Ridge sea feature Indian Ocean
265 I5 Chagos Trench sea feature Indian Ocean
100 F2 Chagoyan Rus. Fed.
120 C1 Chagra r. Rus. Fed.
Chagrayskoye Plato plat. Kazakh. see Shagyray, Plato
242 □T13 Chagres, Parque Nacional nat. park Panama
247 □7 Chaguanas Trin. and Tob.
247 □7 Chaguaramas Trin. and Tob.
250 E2 Chaguaramas Venez.
122 E1 Chagyllyshor, Vpadina depr. Turkm.
136 I8 Chaha r. Ukr.
123 J6 Chahah Burjal Afgh.
122 H5 Chāhak Iran
122 H5 Chāh Ākhvor Iran
122 E6 Chah 'Ali Iran
122 G4 Chāh 'Ali Akbar Iran
123 N4 Chaharbagh Afgh.
122 D5 Chahār Maḩāll va Bakhtīārī prov. Iran
122 D7 Chahār Rūstā'ī Iran
122 B3 Chahār Ţāq Iran
122 F4 Chah Baba well Iran
122 E5 Chāh Badam Iran
122 I9 Chāh Bahār, Khalīj-e b. Iran
122 I3 Chahchaheh Turkm.
123 M3 Chāh-e Āb Afgh.
122 E6 Chāh-e Dow Chāhī Iran
122 G5 Chāh-e Khoshāb Iran
122 F5 Chāh-e Nūklok Iran
122 F7 Chāh-e Rāh Iran
123 I5 Chah-e Rig Afgh.
122 F5 Chāh-e Shūr Iran
122 I7 Chah Gheybī, Hāmūn-e salt pan Iran
122 F7 Chāh Ḩaqq Iran
122 E6 Chāh Kūh Iran
122 G8 Chāh Lak Iran
123 J7 Chah Sandan Pak.
122 E4 Chah Shirin Iran
122 E7 Chāh Sorkh Iran
245 M9 Chahuites Mex.
117 J8 Chaibasa Jharkhand India
225 H2 Chaigneau, Lac l. Que. Can.
Chaigoubu Hebei China see Huai'an
100 B5 Chaihe Nei Mongol China
100 C7 Chai He r. China
123 M9 Chailar Pak.
151 L6 Chailey East Sussex, England U.K.
162 G3 Chaillac France
159 J5 Chailland France
162 B3 Chaillé-les-Marais France
156 G7 Chailley France
208 A5 Chaillu, Massif du mts Gabon
96 E7 Chainat Thai.
161 D6 Chaîne du Devès mts France
111 H9 Chainjoin Co l. Xizang China
156 H6 Chaintrix-Bierges France
96 D5 Chai Prakan Thai.
97 E8 Chai Si r. Thai.
259 B6 Chaitén Chile
109 □J7 Chai Wan H.K. China
110 H5 Chaiwopu Xinjiang China
97 D10 Chaiya Thai.
96 E7 Chaiyaphum Thai.
260 E3 Chaján Arg.
261 I2 Chajarí Arg.
117 K7 Chakai Bihar India
123 O4 Chakai Pak.
123 P5 Chak Amru Pak.
123 M7 Chakar r. Pak.
213 F3 Chakari Zimbabwe
117 N9 Chakaria Bangl.
123 O4 Chakdarra Pak.
211 C6 Chake Chake Tanz.
123 J6 Chakhānsūr Afgh.
117 I7 Chakia Uttar Prad. India
123 O6 Chak Jhumra Pak.
123 L8 Chakku Pak.
225 G1 Chakonipau, Lac l. Que. Can.
117 J8 Chakradharpur Jharkhand India
117 K8 Chakulia Jharkhand India
129 C4 Ch'ak'vi Georgia
123 O5 Chakwal Pak.
252 B3 Chala Peru
211 A6 Chala Tanz.
211 A7 Chalabesa Zambia
163 I10 Chalabre France
Chaladidi Georgia see Sabazho
160 H3 Chalain, Lac de l. France
162 E5 Chalais France
190 D3 Chalais Switz.
160 G4 Chalamont France
123 K5 Chalap Dalan mts Afgh.
160 F4 Chalaronne r. France
242 □O10 Chalatenango El Salvador
213 H3 Chaláua Moz.
106 E9 Chalaxung Qinghai China
210 C4 Chalbi Desert Kenya
Chalcedon Turkey see Kadıköy
244 D2 Chalchihuites Mex.
245 I6 Chalco Mex.
100 A2 Chaldonka Rus. Fed.
151 J6 Chale Isle of Wight, England U.K.
162 F4 Chaleix France
161 F7 Chalencon France
111 K7 Chalengkou Qinghai China
156 E7 Châlette-sur-Loing France
225 H3 Chaleur Bay inlet N.B./Que. Can.
Chaleurs, Baie de inlet N.B./Que. Can. see Chaleur Bay
234 E4 Chalfont PA U.S.A.
151 K4 Chalfont St Peter Buckinghamshire, England U.K.
150 H4 Chalford Gloucestershire, England U.K.
151 J4 Chalgrove Oxfordshire, England U.K.
259 C8 Chalía r. Arg.
175 H3 Chalin Pol.
157 J8 Chalindrey France
109 I5 Chaling Hunan China
211 C6 Chalinze Tanz.
116 E9 Chalisgaon Mahar. India
114 E7 Chalisseri Kerala India
160 B3 Chalivoy-Milon France
Chalkar, Ozero salt l. Kazakh. see Shalkar, Ozero
199 I6 Chalki Notio Aigaio Greece
198 D3 Chalki Thessalia Greece
199 I6 Chalki i. Greece
198 E4 Chalkida Greece
198 D2 Chalkidona Greece
121 R6 Chalkudysu Kazakh.
81 A13 Chalky Inlet South I. N.Z.
260 C6 Challacó Arg.
114 E5 Challakere Karnataka India
158 H8 Challans France
252 D4 Challapata Bol.
266 E5 Challenger Deep sea feature N. Pacific Ocean
267 L8 Challenger Fracture Zone sea feature S. Pacific Ocean
156 I5 Challerange France
160 H5 Challes-les-Eaux France
238 G4 Challis ID U.S.A.
237 K11 Chalmette LA U.S.A.
134 G2 Chal'mny-Varre Rus. Fed.
160 D3 Chalmoux France
160 E3 Chaloire r. France
162 C1 Chalonnes-sur-Loire France
156 H6 Châlons-en-Champagne France
Châlons-sur-Marne France see Châlons-en-Champagne
160 F3 Chalon-sur-Saône France
163 C8 Chalosse reg. France
129 E3 Chalovani Georgia
116 E1 Chalt Jammu and Kashmir
129 J5 Chaltan Pass Azer.
137 S6 Chaltyr' Rus. Fed.
100 D7 Chaluhe Jilin China
215 L9 Chalumna S. Africa
162 F4 Châlus France
122 D3 Chālūs Iran
122 D3 Chālūs, Rūd-e r. Iran
173 N3 Cham Ger.
190 E1 Cham Switz.
96 I7 Cham, Cu Lao i. Vietnam
122 D5 Cham, Kūh-e hill Iran
239 K8 Chama NM U.S.A.
239 K8 Chama r. NM U.S.A.
211 B7 Chama Zambia
217 □3a Chamadani hill Njazidja Comoros
260 E4 Chamaico Arg.
212 B5 Chamais Bay Namibia
160 C5 Chamalières France
161 G7 Chamaloc France
211 B6 Chamamba Tanz.
123 L6 Chaman Pak.
122 G3 Chaman Bid Iran
97 E8 Chamao, Khao mt. Thai.
173 N3 Chamb r. Ger.
116 F3 Chamba Hima. Prad. India
213 H2 Chamba Moz.
211 C7 Chamba Tanz.
116 G6 Chambal r. India
129 G5 Chambarak Armenia
161 G6 Chambaran, Plateau de France
246 D2 Chambas Cuba
225 G2 Chambeaux, Lac l. Que. Can.
162 H4 Chamberet France
160 H4 Chambéria France
86 I4 Chamberlain r. W.A. Austr.
223 J5 Chamberlain Sask. Can.
261 I3 Chamberlain Uru.
236 F4 Chamberlain SD U.S.A.
233 □P2 Chamberlain Lake ME U.S.A.
241 W6 Chambers AZ U.S.A.
84 C2 Chambers Bay N.T. Austr.
232 H9 Chambersburg PA U.S.A.
226 G4 Chambers Island WI U.S.A.
160 H5 Chambéry France
211 A7 Chambeshi Zambia
205 H2 Chambi, Jebel mt. Tunisia
250 C6 Chambira r. Peru
157 K5 Chambley-Bussières France
156 D5 Chambly France
159 L4 Chambois France
160 F2 Chambolle-Musigny France
162 H3 Chambon, Lac de l. France
160 B5 Chambon-sur-Lac France
162 I3 Chambon-sur-Voueize France
225 F3 Chambord Que. Can.
159 O6 Chambord France
123 K8 Chambor Kalat Pak.
162 H5 Chamboulive France
159 M7 Chambray-lès-Tours France
91 J7 Chambri Lake P.N.G.
156 G4 Chambry France
127 L6 Chamchamāl Iraq
117 M5 Chamda Xizang China
Chamdo Xizang China see Qamdo
242 □T13 Chame Panama
161 H6 Chamechaude mt. France
122 C5 Cham-e Ḩannā Iran
244 B6 Chamela Mex.
173 N3 Chamerau Ger.
156 I8 Chamesson France
213 G3 Chametengo Moz.
162 H5 Chameyrat France
204 B5 Châmi well Maur.
260 D2 Chamical Arg.
199 H7 Chamili i. Greece
129 B1 Chamlykskaya Rus. Fed.
210 C3 Ch'amo Hāyk' l. Eth.
190 D4 Chamois Italy
Chamoli Uttaranchal India see Gopeshwar
160 J5 Chamonix-Mont-Blanc France
Chamouchouane r. Que. Can. see Ashuapmushuan
161 H8 Chamouse, Montagne de mt. France
160 I5 Chamoux-sur-Gelon France
260 B3 Champa Chile
117 I8 Champa Chhattisgarh India
162 I5 Champagnac France
162 F5 Champagnac-de-Belair France
161 D6 Champagnac-le-Vieux France
222 B2 Champagne Y.T. Can.
159 L5 Champagné France
156 H6 Champagne-Ardenne admin. reg. France
159 O7 Champagne Berrichonne reg. France
215 N5 Champagne Castle mt. S. Africa
156 H5 Champagne Crayeuse reg. France
160 H5 Champagne-en-Valromey France
156 H7 Champagne Humide reg. France
162 E4 Champagne-Mouton France
156 G7 Champagne Pouilleuse reg. France
156 D5 Champagne-sur-Oise France
156 E7 Champagne-sur-Seine France
157 M8 Champagney France
160 H3 Champagnole France
86 H3 Champagny Islands W.A. Austr.
230 C5 Champaign IL U.S.A.
149 J2 Champany Falkirk, Scotland U.K.
260 E2 Champaqui, Cerro mt. Arg.
252 A2 Champara mt. Peru
97 G7 Champasak Laos
156 G6 Champaubert France
116 H5 Champawat Uttaranchal India
162 F5 Champcevinel France
162 D3 Champdeniers-St-Denis France
160 E1 Champ-d'Oiseau France
225 H2 Champdoré, Lac l. Que. Can.
157 N7 Champ du Feu mt. France
159 M7 Champeigne reg. France
160 C5 Champeix France
190 B3 Champéry Switz.
190 C3 Champex Switz.
160 F3 Champforgeuil France
159 K5 Champgenéteux France
117 N8 Champhai Mizoram India
161 G6 Champier France
159 J6 Champigné France
156 F8 Champignelles France
157 L6 Champigneulles France
156 I7 Champignol-lez-Mondeville France
156 F7 Champigny France
222 H5 Champion Alta Can.
226 G3 Champion MI U.S.A.
233 L4 Champlain NY U.S.A.
232 I10 Champlain VA U.S.A.
224 F4 Champlain, Lake Can./U.S.A.
233 L5 Champlain Canal NY U.S.A.
160 C2 Champlemy France
160 H1 Champlitte France
227 Q1 Champneuf Que. Can.
162 E4 Champniers France
161 I7 Champoléon France
160 D5 Champoly France
243 N8 Champotón Mex.
156 B7 Champrond-en-Gâtine France
159 J4 Champsecret France
161 B6 Champs-sur-Tarentaine-Marchal France
156 G8 Champs-sur-Yonne France
161 H6 Champ-sur-Drac France
161 I8 Champtercier France
158 I7 Champtoceaux France
160 G2 Champvans France
114 E7 Chamrajnagar Karnataka India
161 H6 Chamrousse France
122 D6 Cham Siyāh Iran
111 J9 Chamu Co l. Qinghai China
184 C2 Chamusca Port.
Chamyndy Naryn Kyrg. see Chemyndy
135 I5 Chamzinka Rus. Fed.
97 E11 Chana Thai.
161 C8 Chanac France
Chanak Turkey see Çanakkale
243 M9 Chanal Mex.
261 H2 Chañar Entre Ríos Arg.
260 E2 Chañar La Rioja Arg.
260 C6 Chañar Neuquén Arg.
258 C2 Chañaral Chile
258 C3 Chañaral, Isla i. Chile
260 B2 Chañaral Alto Chile
122 H3 Chanārān Iran
258 C2 Chañarcillo Chile
261 F3 Chañar Ladeado Arg.
251 F3 Chanaro, Cerro mt. Venez.
161 F6 Chanas France
184 D2 Chança Port.
Chança r. Port./Spain see Chanza
260 E2 Chancani Arg.
244 G3 Chancaquero Mex.
252 A2 Chancay Peru
160 F1 Chanceaux France
159 M7 Chanceaux-sur-Choisille France
162 F5 Chancelade France
182 C9 Chancelaria Port.
247 □2 Chances Peak vol. Montserrat
243 O8 Chanchén Mex.
260 A4 Chanco Chile
260 A4 Chanco, Bahía de b. Chile
252 A2 Chancos Peru
Chanda Mahar. India see Chandrapur
220 D3 Chandalar r. AK U.S.A.
211 C6 Chandama Tanz.
116 H5 Chandan Chauki Uttar Prad. India
117 I9 Chandarpur Chhattisgarh India
116 G5 Chandausi Uttar Prad. India
117 K9 Chandbali Orissa India
117 O7 Chandel Manipur India
237 K11 Chandeleur Islands LA U.S.A.
116 G7 Chanderi Madh. Prad. India
116 H8 Chandia Madh. Prad. India
116 F4 Chandigarh Chandigarh India
116 F4 Chandigarh union terr. India
117 K8 Chandil Jharkhand India
225 H3 Chandler Que. Can.
241 U8 Chandler AZ U.S.A.
237 G8 Chandler OK U.S.A.
252 C2 Chandless r. Brazil
106 E2 Chandmany Mongolia
227 Q5 Chandos Lake Ont. Can.
117 M8 Chandpur Bangl.
116 G5 Chandpur Uttar Prad. India
114 F6 Chandragiri Andhra Prad. India
114 F3 Chandrapur Mahar. India
182 F4 Chandrexa de Queixa, Embalse de resr Spain
116 G9 Chandur Mahar. India
116 E9 Chandvad Mahar. India
183 L6 Chañe Spain
122 I8 Chānf Iran
97 F8 Chang, Ko i. Thai.
215 Q2 Changalane Moz.
Chang'an Guangxi China see Rong'an
107 K9 Chang'an Shaanxi China
103 G11 Chang-an S. Korea
213 G5 Changane r. Moz.
213 G3 Changara Moz.
101 F8 Changbai Jilin China
101 E8 Changbai Shan mts China/N. Korea
Chang Cheng research stn Antarctica see Great Wall
108 G9 Changcheng Hainan China
108 G9 Changcheng Hainan China
Changchow Fujian China see Zhangzhou
Changchow Jiangsu China see Changzhou
100 D7 Changchun Jilin China
107 Q8 Changdao Shandong China
109 H4 Changde Hunan China
159 J5 Changé Pays de la Loire France
159 L6 Changé Pays de la Loire France
109 K2 Changfeng Anhui China
107 M9 Changge Henan China
101 F10 Changgi-ap pt S. Korea
111 G12 Changgo Xizang China
109 I3 Chang Hu l. China
109 M6 Changhua Taiwan
108 G9 Changhua Jiang r. China
101 E11 Changhŭng S. Korea
94 □ Changi Sing.
94 □ Changi Airport airport Sing.
110 H5 Changji Xinjiang China
108 G9 Changjiang Hainan China
99 L5 Chang Jiang r. China alt. Jinsha Jiang, alt. Tongtian He, conv. Yangtze, long Yangtze Kiang
109 M3 Changjiang Kou r. mouth China
101 E8 Changjin N. Korea
101 E8 Changjin-gang r. N. Korea
Changkiang Guangdong China see Zhanjiang
111 L13 Changlang Arun. Prad. India
109 L6 Changle Fujian China
Changleng Jiangxi China see Xinjian
107 P7 Changli Hebei China
107 R4 Changling Jilin China
106 I7 Changliushui Nei Mongol China
94 D1 Changlun Malaysia
116 F2 Changlung Jammu and Kashmir
106 E7 Changma Gansu China
111 E9 Changmar Xizang China
109 I5 Changning Hunan China
Changning Jiangxi China see Xunwu
108 E4 Changning Sichuan China
108 B6 Changning Yunnan China
101 D9 Changnyŏn N. Korea
Ch'ang-pai Shan mts China/N. Korea see Changbai Shan
107 O6 Changping Beijing China
Changpu Hunan China see Suining
101 D9 Changsan-got pt N. Korea
109 I4 Changsha Hunan China
109 L4 Changshan Zhejiang China
107 R7 Changshan Qundao is China
108 E5 Changshi Guizhou China
108 F4 Changshou Chongqing China
109 I4 Changshoujie Hunan China
109 M3 Changshu Jiangsu China
101 E11 Changsŏng S. Korea
109 K6 Changtai Fujian China
Changteh Hunan China see Changde
109 K6 Changting Fujian China
100 F6 Changting Heilong. China
100 D7 Changtu Liaoning China
242 □R13 Changuinola Panama
111 K7 Changweiliang Qinghai China
101 F11 Ch'angwŏn S. Korea
107 J9 Changwu Shaanxi China
109 L3 Changxing Zhejiang China
107 Q7 Changxing Dao i. China
160 E4 Changy France
109 H3 Changyang Hubei China
107 P8 Changyi Shandong China
101 D9 Changyŏn N. Korea
Changyuan Chongqing China see Rongchang
107 N9 Changyuan Henan China
107 M8 Changzhi Shanxi China
107 M9 Changzhi Shanxi China
109 L3 Changzhou Jiangsu China
258 D2 Chañi, Nevado de mt. Arg.
198 F7 Chania Kriti Greece
162 C4 Chaniers France
198 E7 Chanion, Kolpos b. Kriti Greece
106 I9 Chankou Gansu China
96 I6 Chân Mây Đông, Mui pt Vietnam
114 D5 Channagiri Karnataka India
114 E6 Channapatna Karnataka India
158 F3 Channel Islands English Chan.
240 M8 Channel Islands CA U.S.A.
240 M7 Channel Islands National Park CA U.S.A.
225 J4 Channel-Port-aux-Basques Nfld and Lab. Can.
246 E2 Channel Rock i. Bahamas
145 H6 Channel Tunnel France/U.K.
226 F3 Channing MI U.S.A.
237 D8 Channing TX U.S.A.
116 D7 Chanod Rajasthan India
182 E3 Chantada Spain
131 S3 Chantal'skiy mt. Rus. Fed.
160 C4 Chantelle France
158 H5 Chantepie France
97 F8 Chanthaburi Thai.
156 D5 Chantilly France
162 B2 Chantonnay France
157 L7 Chantraine France
160 I2 Chantrans France
159 J4 Chanu France
115 M8 Chanumla Andaman & Nicobar Is India
237 H7 Chanute KS U.S.A.
123 O5 Chanuwala Pak.
130 I4 Chany, Ozero salt l. Rus. Fed.
184 D5 Chanza r. Port./Spain
252 A2 Chao Peru
184 □ Chão, Ilhéu i. Madeira
109 K7 Chao'an Guangdong China
107 O7 Chaobai Xinhe r. China
109 K3 Chaohu Anhui China
109 K3 Chao Hu l. China
97 E8 Chao Phraya r. Thai.
107 Q2 Chaor Nei Mongol China
204 D2 Chaouèn Morocco
180 D5 Chaouèn prov. Morocco
156 H7 Chaource France
109 K7 Chaoyang Guangdong China
Chaoyang Heilong. China see Jiayin
Chaoyang Jilin China see Huinan
107 Q6 Chaoyang Liaoning China
107 S2 Chaoyangcun Nei Mongol China
111 H9 Chaoyang Hu l. Xizang China
107 Q1 Chaozhong Nei Mongol China
109 K7 Chaozhou Guangdong China
254 E5 Chapada Diamantina, Parque Nacional nat. park Brazil
253 G3 Chapada dos Guimarães Brazil
254 D5 Chapada dos Veadeiros, Parque Nacional da nat. park Brazil
256 A3 Chapadão do Céu Brazil
255 B6 Chapadão do Sul Brazil
254 E2 Chapadinha Brazil
224 F3 Chapais Que. Can.
123 K3 Chapak Guzar Afgh.
244 D5 Chapala Mex.
244 D5 Chapala, Laguna de l. Mex.
260 E5 Chapalcó, Valle de val. Arg.
261 H5 Chapaleofú Arg.
244 C4 Chapalilla Mex.
245 H5 Chapantongo Mex.
252 D3 Chapare r. Bol.
161 H6 Chapareillan France
123 K4 Chāpārī, Kowtal-e pass Afgh.
252 B3 Cháparra Peru
250 C4 Chaparral Col.
120 D2 Chapayev Kazakh.
137 O4 Chapayeve Ukr.
137 L4 Chapayevka Ukr.
120 C1 Chapayevsk Rus. Fed.
121 O1 Chapayevskoye Kazakh.
160 B5 Chapdes-Beaufort France
255 B8 Chapecó Brazil
255 B8 Chapecó r. Brazil
149 N7 Chapel-en-le-Frith Derbyshire, England U.K.
149 M4 Chapelfell Top hill England U.K.
231 H8 Chapel Hill NC U.S.A.
165 F8 Chapelle-lez-Herlaimont Belgium
149 R7 Chapel St Leonards Lincolnshire, England U.K.
246 □ Chapelton Jamaica
147 J3 Chapeltown Northern Ireland U.K.
149 O7 Chapeltown South Yorkshire, England U.K.
261 I2 Chapicuy Uru.
252 B3 Chapimarca Peru
183 L8 Chapinería Spain
100 M5 Chaplanovo Rus. Fed.
224 D4 Chapleau Ont. Can.
224 D3 Chapleau Crown Game Reserve nature res. Ont. Can.
223 J5 Chaplin Sask. Can.
Chaplinka Ukr. see Chaplynka
223 J5 Chaplin Lake Sask. Can.
131 T3 Chaplino Rus. Fed.
137 M2 Chapliyivka Ukr.
139 W8 Chaplygin Rus. Fed.
137 P5 Chaplyne Ukr.
137 M7 Chaplynka Ukr.
137 M7 Chaplyns'kyy Kanal canal Ukr.
137 Q2 Chaplyzhnoye Rus. Fed.
222 G5 Chapman, Mount B.C. Can.
232 F7 Chapmanville PA U.S.A.
232 C11 Chapmanville WV U.S.A.
235 H2 Chappaqua NY U.S.A.
236 D5 Chappell NE U.S.A.
83 K9 Chappell Islands Tas. Austr.
Chapra Bihar India see Chhapra
245 I4 Chapulhuacán Mex.
261 G3 Chapuy Arg.
116 F3 Char Jammu and Kashmir
258 F2 Charadai Arg.
253 E4 Charagua Bol.
252 C4 Charana Bol.
250 C5 Charapita Col.
258 E2 Charata Arg.
242 E4 Charay Mex.
160 E3 Charbonnat France
161 K6 Charbonnel, Pointe de mt. France
244 F2 Charcas Mex.
160 H2 Charcenne France
160 H4 Charchilla France
244 G3 Charco Blanco Mex.
262 S2 Charcot Island Antarctica
223 I4 Chard Alta Can.
150 G6 Chard Somerset, England U.K.
Chardara Kazakh. see Shardara
121 L7 Chardara, Step' plain Kazakh.
121 M7 Chardarinskoye Vodokhranilishche resr Kazakh./Uzbek.
122 B5 Chardāvol Iran
122 F3 Chardeh Iran
232 D7 Chardon OH U.S.A.
150 G6 Chardstock Devon, England U.K.
Chardzhev Lebapskaya Oblast' Turkm. see Türkmenabat
Chardzhou Turkm. see Türkmenabat
Chardzhouskaya Oblast' admin. div. Turkm. see Lebap
205 F2 Charef Alg.
204 E2 Charef, Oued watercourse Morocco
162 E4 Charente dept France
162 C4 Charente r. France
162 C4 Charente-Maritime dept France
160 B3 Charenton-du-Cher France
159 M3 Charentonne r. France
129 F5 Ch'arents'avan Armenia
150 H4 Charfield South Gloucestershire, England U.K.
122 E7 Charg Iran
160 H2 Chargey-lès-Gray France
208 B1 Chari r. Cameroon/Chad
122 G6 Chārī Iran
208 C2 Chari-Baguirmi pref. Chad
123 M4 Chārīkār Afgh.
117 K6 Charikot Nepal
151 N5 Charing Kent, England U.K.
236 I5 Chariton IA U.S.A.
236 I6 Chariton r. IA U.S.A.
227 K5 Charity Island MI U.S.A.
137 M6 Charivne Ukr.
Chärjew Turkm. see Türkmenabat
127 O8 Charkas Iran
134 K2 Charkayuvom Rus. Fed.
123 L3 Chār Kent Afgh.
116 G7 Charkhari Uttar Prad. India
116 F5 Charkhi Dadri Haryana India
Charkhlik Xinjiang China see Ruoqiang
151 J4 Charlbury Oxfordshire, England U.K.
215 N2 Charl Cilliers S. Africa
147 I4 Charlemont Northern Ireland U.K.
165 F8 Charleroi Belgium
233 J11 Charles, Cape VA U.S.A.
225 G4 Charlesbourg Que. Can.
226 B6 Charles City IA U.S.A.
232 H11 Charles City VA U.S.A.
Charles Island Islas Galápagos Ecuador see Santa María, Isla
223 I3 Charles Lake Alta Can.
238 K3 Charles M. Russell National Wildlife Refuge nature res. MT U.S.A.
84 C2 Charles Point N.T. Austr.
81 F8 Charleston South I. N.Z.
237 H8 Charleston AR U.S.A.
226 C9 Charleston IA U.S.A.
236 K6 Charleston IL U.S.A.
237 K7 Charleston MO U.S.A.
237 J8 Charleston MS U.S.A.
231 H9 Charleston SC U.S.A.
232 D10 Charleston WV U.S.A.
241 Q5 Charleston Peak NV U.S.A.
147 E5 Charlestown Ireland
215 N3 Charlestown S. Africa
247 □2 Charlestown St Kitts and Nevis
247 □3 Charlestown St Vincent
234 D5 Charlestown MD U.S.A.
233 M5 Charlestown NH U.S.A.
233 N7 Charlestown RI U.S.A.
232 H9 Charles Town WV U.S.A.
Charlestown of Aberlour Moray, Scotland U.K. see Aberlour
85 K9 Charleville Qld Austr.
Charleville Ireland see Rathluirc
156 I4 Charleville-Mézières France
226 I4 Charlevoix MI U.S.A.
222 F3 Charlie Lake B.C. Can.
160 E4 Charlieu France
226 J7 Charlotte MI U.S.A.
231 G8 Charlotte NC U.S.A.
247 K4 Charlotte Amalie Virgin Is (U.S.A.)
95 G1 Charlotte Bank sea feature S. China Sea
232 G11 Charlotte Court House VA U.S.A.
231 F12 Charlotte Harbor b. FL U.S.A.
222 E4 Charlotte Lake B.C. Can.
142 I2 Charlottenberg Sweden
232 G10 Charlottesville VA U.S.A.
225 I4 Charlottetown P.E.I. Can.
Charlotte Town Grenada see Gouyave
247 □5 Charlotteville Trin. and Tob.
83 I7 Charlton Vic. Austr.
151 J5 Charlton Hampshire, England U.K.
150 H4 Charlton Wiltshire, England U.K.
224 E2 Charlton Island Nunavut Can.
150 H4 Charlton Kings Gloucestershire, England U.K.
151 L5 Charlwood Surrey, England U.K.
156 F6 Charly France
162 E4 Charmé France
157 L7 Charmes France
161 F7 Charmes-sur-Rhône France
190 C2 Charmey Switz.
150 H6 Charminster Dorset, England U.K.
157 L7 Charmois-l'Orgueilleux France
156 H7 Charmont-sous-Barbuise France
150 G6 Charmouth Dorset, England U.K.
156 F8 Charmoy France
160 F4 Charnay-lès-Mâcon France
184 A3 Charneca Port.
139 N7 Charnitsa r. Belarus
86 H4 Charnley r. W.A. Austr.
156 F8 Charny France
175 M4 Charnyany Belarus
157 J5 Charny-sur-Meuse France
160 E4 Charollais reg. France
160 E4 Charolles France
138 K6 Charomkhava Belarus
159 P8 Chârost France
134 G3 Charozero Rus. Fed.
160 J2 Charquemont France
190 C3 Charrat Switz.
156 I8 Charrey-sur-Seine France
160 D3 Charrin France
223 M4 Charron Lake Man. Can.
162 E3 Charroux France
156 C5 Chars France
123 N4 Charsadda Pak.
Charsk Kazakh. see Shar
138 L6 Charstsvyatskaye, Vozyera l. Belarus
175 H5 Charsznica Pol.
232 B10 Charters KY U.S.A.
85 K6 Charters Towers Qld Austr.
151 O5 Chartham Kent, England U.K.
156 B7 Chartres France
161 H6 Chartreuse, Massif de la mts France
190 C4 Charvensod Italy
160 I4 Charvonnex France

121 R6 Charyn Kazakh.
121 R6 Charyn r. Kazakh.
121 T1 Charysh r. Rus. Fed.
121 T2 Charyshskoye Rus. Fed.
174 F2 Charzykowskie, Jezioro l. Pol.
174 F2 Charzykowy Pol.
174 D1 Charzyno Pol.
261 H4 Chas Arg.
117 K8 Chas Jharkhand India
182 D7 Chãs mt. Port.
258 C2 Chaschuil Arg.
261 H4 Chascomús Arg.
261 H4 Chascomús, Laguna l. Arg.
222 G5 Chase B.C. Can.
234 C6 Chase MD U.S.A.
226 I6 Chase MI U.S.A.
232 G12 Chase City VA U.S.A.
123 I3 Chashkent Turkm.
122 F4 Chashmeh Baluch Iran
122 G4 Chashmeh Nūrī Iran
122 E4 Chashmeh Tuleh Iran
122 E4 Chashmeh-ye Palasi Iran
138 M7 Chashniki Belarus
127 P6 Chāsht Khvāran Iran
198 C3 Chasia reg. Greece
261 F6 Chasicó Arg.
259 D6 Chasico Arg.
261 F6 Chasicó, Laguna l. Arg.
137 Q5 Chasiv Yar Ukr.
236 I3 Chaska MN U.S.A.
81 D13 Chaslands Mistake c. South I. N.Z.
101 E8 Chasŏng N. Korea
100 A2 Chasovaya Rus. Fed.
134 H2 Chasovenskaya Arkhangel'skaya Oblast' Rus. Fed.
139 Q1 Chasovenskaya Leningradskaya Oblast' Rus. Fed.
159 L8 Chasseneuil-du-Poitou France
162 E4 Chasseneuil-sur-Bonnieure France
162 F4 Chassenon France
161 D7 Chasseradès France
190 C1 Chasseral mt. Switz.
160 F5 Chasse-sur-Rhône France
161 E8 Chassezac r. France
157 J8 Chassigny-Aisey France
159 K5 Chassillé France
162 B3 Chassiron, Pointe de pt France
122 F5 Chastab, Kūh-e mts Iran
162 I5 Chastang, Barrage du dam France
165 G7 Chastre Belgium
134 K4 Chastyye Rus. Fed.
250 B6 Chasuta Peru
122 F3 Chāt Iran
160 H5 Chat, Mont du mt. France
163 I6 Châtaigneraie reg. France
226 E9 Chatauqua Lake IL U.S.A.
158 E4 Château, Pointe du pt France
161 H8 Château-Arnoux France
247 □3 Chateaubelair St Vincent
162 D4 Châteaubernard France
158 I5 Châteaubourg France
261 G3 Chateaubriand Arg.
158 I6 Châteaubriant France
160 D2 Château-Chinon France
190 C3 Château-d'Oex Switz.
162 A2 Château-d'Olonne France
159 L6 Château-du-Loir France
156 B7 Châteaudun France
160 C5 Châteaugay France
233 K4 Chateaugay NY U.S.A.
158 H5 Châteaugiron France
159 J6 Château-Gontier France
233 L3 Châteauguay Que. Can.
225 G1 Châteauguay r. Que. Can.
225 G1 Châteauguay, Lac l. Que. Can.
156 E7 Château-Landon France
159 L6 Château-la-Vallière France
162 F5 Château-l'Évêque France
158 C5 Châteaulin France
161 F9 Châteauneuf-de-Gadagne France
161 F6 Châteauneuf-de-Galaure France
161 D7 Châteauneuf-de-Randon France
158 H4 Châteauneuf-d'Ille-et-Vilaine France
158 D5 Châteauneuf-du-Faou France
161 F8 Châteauneuf-du-Pape France
161 F8 Châteauneuf-du-Rhône France
156 B6 Châteauneuf-en-Thymerais France
162 H4 Châteauneuf-la-Forêt France
160 B4 Châteauneuf-les-Bains France
161 G10 Châteauneuf-les-Martigues France
162 D4 Châteauneuf-sur-Charente France
159 P8 Châteauneuf-sur-Cher France
156 D8 Châteauneuf-sur-Loire France
159 K6 Châteauneuf-sur-Sarthe France
160 C2 Châteauneuf-Val-de-Bargis France
225 J2 Chateau Pond l. Nfld and Lab. Can.
162 G3 Châteauponsac France
156 H4 Château-Porcien France
161 I8 Châteauredon France
156 E8 Châteaurenard Centre France
161 F9 Châteaurenard Provence-Alpes-Côte d'Azur France
160 G3 Châteaurenaud France
159 M6 Château-Renault France
162 H2 Châteauroux Centre France
161 J7 Châteauroux Provence-Alpes-Côte d'Azur France
157 M6 Château-Salins France
156 F5 Château-Thierry France
157 I7 Châteauvillain France
247 □2 Châteaux, Pointe des pt Guadeloupe
222 G3 Chateh Alta Can.
160 J4 Châtel France
162 B3 Châtelaillon-Plage France
158 F4 Châtelaudren France
160 D1 Châtel-Censoir France
160 D5 Châteldon France
165 G8 Châtelet Belgium
160 E1 Châtel-Gérard France
160 C5 Châtelguyon France
162 F2 Châtellerault France
160 D4 Châtel-Montagne France
160 D4 Châtelperron France
190 B2 Châtel-St-Denis Switz.
157 L7 Châtel-sur-Moselle France
162 I3 Châtelus-Malvaleix France
157 N7 Châtenois Alsace France
157 K7 Châtenois Lorraine France
160 J1 Châtenois-les-Forges France
160 F3 Châtenoy-le-Royal France
226 B6 Chatfield MN U.S.A.
232 C8 Chatfield OH U.S.A.
224 D5 Chatham Ont. Can.
151 N5 Chatham Medway, England U.K.
222 C3 Chatham AK U.S.A.
233 P7 Chatham MA U.S.A.
226 H3 Chatham MI U.S.A.
235 G3 Chatham NJ U.S.A.
233 L6 Chatham NY U.S.A.
234 D5 Chatham PA U.S.A.
232 F12 Chatham VA U.S.A.
259 B8 Chatham, Isla i. Chile
Chatham Island Islas Galápagos Ecuador see San Cristóbal, Isla
Chatham Island Samoa see Savai'i
80 □ Chatham Island Chatham Is S. Pacific Ocean
80 □ Chatham Islands S. Pacific Ocean
266 H8 Chatham Rise sea feature S. Pacific Ocean
222 D4 Chatham Sound sea chan. B.C. Can.
222 C3 Chatham Strait AK U.S.A.
165 I9 Châtillon Belgium
190 D4 Châtillon Italy
156 E8 Châtillon-Coligny France
160 D2 Châtillon-en-Bazois France
161 G7 Châtillon-en-Diois France
160 H4 Châtillon-en-Michaille France
160 G5 Châtillon-la-Palud France
156 I8 Châtillonnais reg. France
160 F4 Châtillon-sur-Chalaronne France
159 J5 Châtillon-sur-Colmont France
162 G2 Châtillon-sur-Indre France
160 B1 Châtillon-sur-Loire France
156 G5 Châtillon-sur-Marne France
156 I8 Châtillon-sur-Seine France
159 K8 Châtillon-sur-Thouet France
121 N7 Chatkal r. Kyrg.
121 N7 Chatkal Range mts Kyrg.
237 K10 Chatom AL U.S.A.
117 J7 Chatra Jharkhand India
117 K6 Chatra Nepal
116 E6 Chatsu Rajasthan India
84 H6 Chatsworth Qld Austr.
227 N5 Chatsworth Ont. Can.
231 E8 Chatsworth GA U.S.A.
226 F9 Chatsworth IL U.S.A.
234 F5 Chatsworth NJ U.S.A.
213 F3 Chatsworth Zimbabwe
Chattagam Bangl. see Chittagong
231 E10 Chattahoochee FL U.S.A.
231 E10 Chattahoochee r. GA U.S.A.
231 E8 Chattanooga TN U.S.A.
161 G6 Chatte France
151 M3 Chatteris Cambridgeshire, England U.K.
Chattisgarh state India see Chhattisgarh
81 D12 Chatto Creek South I. N.Z.
149 N2 Chatton Northumberland, England U.K.
96 E7 Chatturat Thai.
161 G7 Chatuzange-le-Goubet France
234 D5 Chatwood PA U.S.A.
Chatyrkël', Ozero l. Kyrg. see Chatyr-Köl
121 P7 Chatyr-Köl l. Kyrg.
121 Q7 Chatyr-Tash Kyrg.
123 N6 Chaubara Pak.
185 L6 Chauchina Spain
137 O8 Chauda, Mys pt Ukr.
157 K8 Chaudenay France
161 C7 Chaudes-Aigues France
161 D7 Chaudeyrac France
165 I7 Chaudfontaine Belgium
97 G9 Châu Đôc Vietnam
159 J7 Chaudron-en-Mauges France
160 E4 Chauffailles France
161 I7 Chauffayer France
116 C7 Chauhtan Rajasthan India
96 B4 Chauk Myanmar
116 H6 Chauka r. India
116 G4 Chaukhamba mts Uttaranchal India
109 □J7 Chau Kung To i. H.K. China
114 C3 Chaul Mahar. India
156 E4 Chaulnes France
160 D2 Chaumeçon, Barrage de dam France
160 G3 Chaumergy France
157 J7 Chaumont France
156 C5 Chaumont-en-Vexin France
156 H4 Chaumont-Porcien France
157 J6 Chaumont-sur-Aire France
159 N7 Chaumont-sur-Loire France
162 E3 Chaunay France
232 C9 Chauncey OH U.S.A.
97 D8 Chaungwabyin Myanmar
131 R3 Chaunskaya Guba b. Rus. Fed.
156 F4 Chauny France
96 I7 Châu Ô Vietnam
Chau Phu Vietnam see Châu Đôc
116 G8 Chaurai Madh. Prad. India
162 D3 Chauray France
158 H4 Chausey, Îles is France
160 G3 Chaussin France
104 G5 Chausu-yama mt. Japan
Chausy Belarus see Chavusy
232 F6 Chautauqua, Lake NY U.S.A.
245 H9 Chautengo, Laguna l. Mex.
123 L6 Chauter Pak.
121 O7 Chauvay Kyrg.
162 F2 Chauvigny France
223 I4 Chauvin Alta Can.
160 H2 Chaux, Forêt de for. France
158 I8 Chavagnes-en-Paillers France
114 G8 Chavakachcheri Sri Lanka
254 E2 Chaval Brazil
161 F6 Chavanay France
134 G2 Chavan'ga Rus. Fed.
156 I6 Chavanges France
161 D6 Chavaniac-Lafayette France
160 G5 Chavanoz France
122 B5 Chavār Iran
198 C5 Chavari Greece
157 L7 Chavelot France
251 I5 Chaves Brazil
182 F5 Chaves Port.
250 B6 Chaves Valdivia Peru
224 F1 Chavigny, Lac l. Que. Can.
250 C3 Chaviva Col.
209 D8 Chavuma Zambia
139 N8 Chavusy Belarus
123 L7 Chawal r. Pak.
97 D10 Chawang Thai.
96 G4 Chay, Sông r. Vietnam
Chayan Kazakh. see Shayan
252 D4 Chayanta r. Bol.
100 J2 Chayatyn, Khrebet ridge Rus. Fed.
Chayek Kyrg. see Chaek
139 U3 Chayevo Rus. Fed.
Ch'ayk'end Armenia see Dprabak
134 K4 Chaykovskiy Rus. Fed.
Chăyul Xizang China see Qayü
160 F5 Chazay-d'Azergues France
162 E4 Chazelles France
160 E5 Chazelles-sur-Lyon France
134 K3 Chazhegovo Rus. Fed.
261 F3 Chazón Arg.
245 J7 Chazumba Mex.
233 L4 Chazy NY U.S.A.
149 M7 Cheadle Greater Manchester, England U.K.
151 I2 Cheadle Staffordshire, England U.K.
232 F9 Cheat r. WV U.S.A.
176 B1 Cheb Czech Rep.
226 G8 Chebanse IL U.S.A.
205 H2 Chebba Tunisia
205 F4 Chebbi salt l. Alg.
134 I4 Cheboksarskoye Vodokhranilishche resr Rus. Fed.
134 I4 Cheboksary Rus. Fed.
226 J4 Cheboygan MI U.S.A.
183 Q7 Checa Spain
136 I5 Chechel'nyk Ukr.
129 I2 Chechen', Ostrov i. Rus. Fed.
109 M7 Ch'ech'eng Taiwan
129 G2 Chechenskaya Respublika aut. rep. Rus. Fed.
215 M5 Cheche Pass Lesotho
Chechnia aut. rep. Rus. Fed. see Chechenskaya Respublika
Chechnya aut. rep. Rus. Fed. see Chechenskaya Respublika
101 F10 Chech'ŏn S. Korea
136 D5 Chechva r. Ukr.
175 I5 Chęciny Pol.
237 H8 Checotah OK U.S.A.
156 D8 Chécy France
107 Q8 Chedao Shandong China
151 N3 Chedburgh Suffolk, England U.K.
150 G5 Cheddar Somerset, England U.K.
149 M7 Cheddleton Staffordshire, England U.K.
202 C6 Chéddra Chad
96 A5 Cheduba Strait Myanmar
157 I6 Chée r. France
147 I8 Cheekpoint Ireland
232 G6 Cheektowaga NY U.S.A.
224 D3 Cheepash r. Ont. Can.
85 J9 Cheepie Qld Austr.
263 K2 Cheetham, Cape Antarctica
162 D3 Chef-Boutonne France
207 I2 Cheffadène well Niger
Chefoo Shandong China see Yantai
220 B3 Chefornak AK U.S.A.
100 H3 Chegdomyn Rus. Fed.
Chegem 1 Rus. Fed. see Chegem Pervyy
129 E2 Chegem r. Rus. Fed.
129 E2 Chegem Pervyy Rus. Fed.
204 D4 Chegga Maur.
206 C2 Cheggué watercourse Maur.
206 D2 Chegguet Ti-n-Kerkâz des. Maur.
213 F3 Chegutu Zimbabwe
238 C3 Chehalis WA U.S.A.
238 C3 Chehalis r. WA U.S.A.
122 G3 Chehar Burj Iran
122 G5 Cheharden Iran
127 M7 Chehariz tourist site Iraq
122 B4 Chehel Chashmeh, Kūh-e hill Iran
122 I6 Chehel Dokhtarān, Kūh-e mt. Iran
122 G6 Chehell'āyeh Iran
204 D4 Cheikria well Alg.
197 J5 Cheil Nerei-Beușnița nat. park Romania
198 C2 Cheimaditida, Limni l. Greece
161 J9 Cheiron, Cime du mt. France
101 E12 Cheju S. Korea
101 E12 Cheju-do i. S. Korea
101 E12 Cheju-haehyŏp sea chan. S. Korea
139 T7 Chekalin Rus. Fed.
134 K5 Chekan Rus. Fed.
109 □J7 Chek Chau i. H.K. China
Chek Chue H.K. China see Stanley
139 U6 Chekhov Moskovskaya Oblast' Rus. Fed.
100 L5 Chekhov Sakhalin Rus. Fed.
Chekiang prov. China see Zhejiang
Chekichler Turkm. see Çekiçler
94 □ Chek Jawa, Tanjong pt Sing.
109 □I7 Chek Lap Kok reg. H.K. China
109 □J7 Chek Mun Hoi Hap sea chan. H.K. China
134 H4 Chekshino Rus. Fed.
100 H3 Chekunda Rus. Fed.
209 B9 Chela, Serra da mts Angola
163 F9 Chélan France
238 D3 Chelan WA U.S.A.
238 D2 Chelan, Lake WA U.S.A.
137 R7 Chelbas r. Rus. Fed.
137 S8 Chelbasskaya Rus. Fed.
184 A3 Cheleiros Port.
184 A3 Cheleiros r. Port.
184 E3 Cheles Spain
260 D6 Chelforó Arg.
213 G4 Cheline Moz.
120 D2 Chelkar Zapadnyy Kazakhstan Kazakh.
187 D9 Chella Spain
175 L4 Chełm Pol.
175 H5 Chełmek Pol.
151 N4 Chelmer r. England U.K.
175 I6 Chełmiec Pol.
174 G2 Chełmno Kujawsko-Pomorskie Pol.
174 G3 Chełmno Wielkopolskie Pol.
198 D5 Chelmos mt. Greece
151 M4 Chelmsford Essex, England U.K.
233 N6 Chelmsford MA U.S.A.
Chelmsford Dam S. Africa see Ntshingwayo Dam
215 N3 Chelmsford Public Resort Nature Reserve S. Africa
136 C2 Chełmski Park Krajobrazowy Pol.
176 F1 Chełmy, Park Krajobrazowy Pol.
174 G2 Chełmża Pol.
227 J7 Chelsea MI U.S.A.
233 M5 Chelsea VT U.S.A.
80 J7 Cheltenham North I. N.Z.
150 H4 Cheltenham Gloucestershire, England U.K.
234 E4 Cheltenham PA U.S.A.
187 D8 Chelva Spain
130 H4 Chelyabinsk Rus. Fed.
120 I1 Chelyabinskaya Oblast' admin. div. Rus. Fed.
Chelyabinsk Oblast admin. div. Rus. Fed. see Chelyabinskaya Oblast'
137 P8 Chelyadinove Ukr.
232 D10 Chelyan WV U.S.A.
131 L2 Chelyuskin Rus. Fed.
131 L2 Chelyuskin, Mys c. Rus. Fed.
204 C2 Chemaïa Morocco
243 P7 Chemax Mex.
159 J6 Chemazé France
213 G3 Chemba Moz.
209 F7 Chembe Zambia
204 B5 Chemchâm, Sebkhet salt flat Maur.
111 D9 Chêm Co l. China
136 F4 Chemerivtsi Ukr.
159 N7 Chémery France
175 M6 Chemeryntsi Ukr.
157 I4 Chémery-sur-Bar France
162 C1 Chemillé France
160 G3 Chemin France
217 □1b Chemin Grenier Mauritius
157 I6 Cheminon France
159 K6 Chemiré-le-Gaudin France
Chemmis Egypt see Akhmīm
171 G9 Chemnitz Ger.
171 G9 Chemnitz admin. reg. Ger.
233 □P2 Chemquasabamticook Lake ME U.S.A.
Chemulpo S. Korea see Inch'ŏn
238 D5 Chemult OR U.S.A.
227 R8 Chemung r. NY U.S.A.
121 P7 Chemyndy Naryn Kyrg.
116 C5 Chenab r. India/Pak.
204 D4 Chenachane Alg.
204 E4 Chenachane, Oued watercourse Alg.
233 J6 Chenango r. NY U.S.A.
233 J6 Chenango Bridge NY U.S.A.
160 F4 Chénas France
210 C3 Ch'ench'a Eth.
94 D2 Chenderoh, Tasik resr Malaysia
Chendir r. Turkm. see Çendir
160 H2 Chenecey-Buillon France
162 I3 Chénérailles France
237 G7 Cheney Reservoir KS U.S.A.
114 G6 Chengalpattu Tamil Nadu India
114 F6 Chengam Tamil Nadu India
107 N8 Cheng'an Hebei China
108 F6 Chengbihe Shuiku resr China
108 H5 Chengbu Hunan China
107 K9 Chengcheng Shaanxi China
Chengchow Henan China see Zhengzhou
107 O6 Chengde Hebei China
107 P6 Chengde Hebei China
108 E3 Chengdu Sichuan China
Chengel'dy Almatinskaya Oblast' Kazakh. see Shengel'dy
Chengel'dy Kyzylordinskaya Oblast' Kazakh. see Shengel'dy
121 M7 Chengel'dy Kazakh.
117 P5 Chengele Arun. Prad. India
108 D6 Chenggong Yunnan China
109 K7 Chenghai Guangdong China
108 C5 Cheng Hai l. China
Chengjiang Jiangxi China see Taihe
108 D6 Chengjiang Yunnan China
108 G3 Chengkou Chongqing China
108 H9 Chengmai Hainan China
107 O9 Chengqian Shandong China
Chengqiao Shanghai China see Chongming
Chengshou Sichuan China see Yingshan
Chengtu Sichuan China see Chengdu
107 N9 Chengwu Shandong China
108 E2 Chengxian Gansu China
Chengxian Guizhou China see Fuquan
Chengxiang Chongqing China see Wuxi
Chengxiang Jiangxi China see Quannan
Chengyang Shandong China see Juxian
Chengzhong Guangxi China see Ningming
108 A6 Chengzi Yunnan China
157 M7 Cheniménil France
107 P9 Cheniu Shan i. China
114 G9 Chenkaladi Sri Lanka
114 G6 Chennai Tamil Nadu India
226 F9 Chenoa IL U.S.A.
159 N7 Chenonceaux France
160 G2 Chenôve France
109 N3 Chenqian Shan i. China
100 E4 Chenqing Heilong. China
Chenqingqiao Heilong. China see Chenqing
Chenstokhov Pol. see Częstochowa
107 J2 Chentejn Nuruu mts Mongolia
94 □ Chenting, Tanjong pt Sing.
108 H5 Chenxi Hunan China
156 G8 Cheny France
Chenyang Hunan China see Chenxi
Chenying Jiangxi China see Wannian
109 I6 Chenzhou Hunan China
107 N7 Chenzhuang Hebei China
Cheom Ksan Cambodia see Chŏâm Khsant
197 M9 Chepelare Bulg.
250 B6 Chepén Peru
260 D2 Chepes Arg.
137 P4 Chepil' Ukr.
139 O6 Chepli Rus. Fed.
242 □T13 Chepo Panama
150 G4 Chepstow Monmouthshire, Wales U.K.
134 J4 Cheptsa r. Rus. Fed.
156 H6 Chepy France
122 B5 Cheqād Kabūd Iran
226 D3 Chequamegon Bay WI U.S.A.
159 P7 Cher dept France
162 E1 Cher r. France
Chera state India see Kerala
187 D8 Chera Spain
162 D4 Chérac France
195 M3 Cheradi, Isole is Italy
160 H5 Chéran r. France
244 F6 Cherán Mex.
210 B4 Cherangany Hills Kenya
190 D6 Cherasco Italy
123 N5 Cherat Pak.
163 C9 Chéraute France
231 H8 Cheraw SC U.S.A.
114 B6 Cherbaniani Reef India
158 H2 Cherbourg France
205 F1 Cherchell Alg.
Cherchen Xinjiang China see Qiemo
135 J5 Cherdakly Rus. Fed.
121 T3 Cherdoyak Kazakh.
134 L3 Cherdyn' Rus. Fed.
158 H6 Chère r. France
Chereapani rf India see Byramgore Reef
177 L4 Cherechiu Romania
129 F2 Cherek r. Rus. Fed.
138 L4 Cherekha r. Rus. Fed.
135 G6 Cheremisinovo Rus. Fed.
98 H1 Cheremkhovo Rus. Fed.
121 T1 Cheremnoye Rus. Fed.
100 I6 Cheremshany Rus. Fed.
134 J4 Cheremukhovka Rus. Fed.
192 B6 Cheremule Sardegna Italy
130 J4 Cherepanovo Rus. Fed.
Cherepkovo Moldova see Ciripcău
139 U2 Cherepovets Rus. Fed.
134 I3 Cherevkovo Rus. Fed.
205 E2 Chergui, Chott ech imp. l. Alg.
205 G2 Chéria Alg.
114 F4 Cherial Andhra Prad. India
190 H4 Cherio r. Italy
151 J5 Cheriton Hampshire, England U.K.
233 J11 Cheriton VA U.S.A.
114 C7 Cheriyam atoll India
136 K4 Cherkas'ka Oblast' admin. div. Ukr.
137 O5 Cherkas'ke Dnipropetrovs'ka Oblast' Ukr.
137 Q5 Cherkas'ke Donets'ka Oblast' Ukr.
Cherkas'ke Luhans'ka Oblast' Ukr. see Zymohir"ya
Cherkasskaya Oblast' admin. div. Ukr. see Cherkas'ka Oblast'
Cherkasskoye Ukr. see Zymohir"ya
Cherkassy Ukr. see Cherkasy
137 L4 Cherkasy Ukr.
Cherkasy Oblast admin. div. Ukr. see Cherkas'ka Oblast'
129 D1 Cherkessk Rus. Fed.
139 W5 Cherkutino Rus. Fed.
114 G3 Cherla Andhra Prad. India
121 P1 Cherlak Rus. Fed.
136 F5 Cherlenivka Ukr.
129 F2 Chermen Rus. Fed.
209 D8 Chermenze Angola
134 L4 Chermoz Rus. Fed.
139 T8 Chern' Rus. Fed.
139 T8 Chern' r. Rus. Fed.
121 M6 Chernak Kazakh.
139 V9 Chernava Lipetskaya Oblast' Rus. Fed.
139 W8 Chernava Ryazanskaya Oblast' Rus. Fed.
134 L1 Chernaya Rus. Fed.
134 L1 Chernaya r. Rus. Fed.
138 K3 Chernaya r. Rus. Fed.
137 T3 Chernaya Kalitva r. Rus. Fed.
134 J4 Chernaya Kholunitsa Rus. Fed.
137 M2 Chernecha Sloboda Ukr.
Chernenko Moldova see Şoldăneşti
137 O4 Cherneshchyna Ukr.
139 V7 Chernevo Moskovskaya Oblast' Rus. Fed.
138 L3 Chernevo Pskovskaya Oblast' Rus. Fed.
Chernigov Ukr. see Chernihiv
100 H6 Chernigovka Rus. Fed.
Chernigov Oblast admin. div. Ukr. see Chernihivs'ka Oblast'
129 A1 Chernigovskaya Rus. Fed.
Chernigovskaya Oblast' admin. div. Ukr. see Chernihivs'ka Oblast'
129 A1 Chernigovskoye Rus. Fed.
137 K2 Chernihiv Ukr.
Chernihiv Oblast admin. div. Ukr. see Chernihivs'ka Oblast'
137 L2 Chernihivs'ka Oblast' admin. div. Ukr.
197 N7 Cherni Lom r. Bulg.
137 P6 Cherninivka Ukr.
175 M6 Cherniv Ukr.
136 F5 Chernivets'ka Oblast' admin. div. Ukr.
Chernivetskaya Oblast' admin. div. Ukr. see Chernivets'ka Oblast'
197 L8 Cherni Vrŭkh mt. Bulg.
136 E5 Chernivtsi Chernivets'ka Oblast' Ukr.
136 H5 Chernivtsi Vinnyts'ka Oblast' Ukr.
Chernivtsi Oblast admin. div. Ukr. see Chernivets'ka Oblast'
136 D5 Cherniyiv Ukr.
Chernobyl' Ukr. see Chornobyl'
98 F1 Chernogorsk Rus. Fed.
129 E1 Chernolesskoye Rus. Fed.
130 J3 Chernoostrovskoye Rus. Fed.
134 K3 Chernorechenskiy Rus. Fed.
129 G2 Chernorech'ye Rus. Fed.
121 Q1 Chernoretskoye Kazakh.
139 P1 Chernoushevo Rus. Fed.
134 I4 Chernovskoye Rus. Fed.
Chernovtsy Ukr. see Chernivtsi
Chernovtsy Oblast admin. div. Ukr. see Chernivets'ka Oblast'
Chernoye More sea Asia/Europe see Black Sea
134 L4 Chernushka Rus. Fed.
136 H3 Chernyakhiv Ukr.
138 E7 Chernyakhovsk Rus. Fed.
135 G6 Chernyanka Rus. Fed.
100 D2 Chernyayeve Rus. Fed.
129 I2 Chernyayevskiy Rus. Fed.
139 N7 Chernyewka Belarus
120 H5 Chernysheva, Zaliv b. Kazakh.
99 K1 Chernyshevsk Rus. Fed.
131 M3 Chernyshevskiy Rus. Fed.
135 H6 Chernyshkovskiy Rus. Fed.
137 M8 Chernyshove Ukr.
135 I7 Chernyye Zemli reg. Rus. Fed.
Chernyy Irtysh r. China/Kazakh. see Ertix He
120 F2 Chernyy Otrog Rus. Fed.
134 F3 Chernyy Porog Rus. Fed.
Chernyy Rynok Rus. Fed. see Kochubey
135 I6 Chernyy Yar Rus. Fed.
236 H4 Cherokee IA U.S.A.
237 F7 Cherokee OK U.S.A.
231 F7 Cherokee Lake TN U.S.A.
237 H7 Cherokees, Lake o' the OK U.S.A.
246 E1 Cherokee Sound Gt Abaco Bahamas
156 F7 Chéroy France
139 N5 Cherpessa Rus. Fed.
260 A6 Cherquenco Chile
117 M7 Cherrapunji Meghalaya India
149 Q6 Cherry Burton East Riding of Yorkshire, England U.K.
236 E3 Cherry Creek r. SD U.S.A.
241 R1 Cherry Creek Mountains NV U.S.A.
233 □R4 Cherryfield ME U.S.A.
234 E5 Cherry Hill NJ U.S.A.
77 G3 Cherry Island Solomon Is
240 M3 Cherry Lake CA U.S.A.
227 Q6 Cherry Valley Ont. Can.
234 D3 Cherryville PA U.S.A.
149 Q7 Cherry Willingham Lincolnshire, England U.K.
138 L4 Cherskaya Rus. Fed.
131 R3 Cherskiy Rus. Fed.
Cherskiy Range mts Rus. Fed. see Cherskogo, Khrebet
107 L1 Cherskogo, Khrebet mts Rus. Fed.
131 P3 Cherskogo, Khrebet mts Rus. Fed.
198 D1 Cherso Greece
190 C6 Chersogno, Monte mt. Italy
186 F6 Chert Spain
Cherta Spain see Xerta
Cherthala Kerala India see Shertally
Chertkov Ukr. see Chortkiv
135 H6 Chertkovo Rus. Fed.
139 Q5 Chertolino Rus. Fed.
81 F10 Chertsey South I. N.Z.
151 K5 Chertsey Surrey, England U.K.
139 X6 Cherusti Rus. Fed.
162 G5 Cherveix-Cubas France
197 M7 Cherven Bryag Bulg.
162 D4 Cherves-Richemont France
129 G2 Chervlennaya Rus. Fed.
129 G1 Chervlennyye Buruny Rus. Fed.
137 M5 Chervona Kam"yanka Ukr.
137 N2 Chervone Sums'ka Oblast' Ukr.
136 H4 Chervone Zhytomyrs'ka Oblast' Ukr.
137 Q6 Chervone Pole Ukr.
137 K3 Chervoni Partyzany Ukr.
Chervonoarmeyskoye Ukr. see Vil'nyans'k
Chervonoarmiys'k Donets'ka Oblast' Ukr. see Krasnoarmiys'k
Chervonoarmiys'k Rivnens'ka Oblast' Ukr. see Radyvyliv
136 H3 Chervonoarmiys'k Zhytomyrs'ka Oblast' Ukr.
137 N7 Chervonoarmiys'ke Ukr.
Chervonograd Ukr. see Chervonohrad
136 D3 Chervonohrad Ukr.
137 N6 Chervonohryhorivka Ukr.
137 Q4 Chervonooskil's'ke Vodoskhovyshche resr Ukr.
Chervonopartizansk Ukr. see Chervonopartyzans'k
137 S5 Chervonopartyzans'k Ukr.
137 M3 Chervonozavods'ke Ukr.
136 J6 Chervonoznam"yanka Ukr.
137 P4 Chervonyy Donets' Ukr.
137 M7 Chervonyy Mayak Ukr.
138 L8 Chervyen' Belarus
151 J4 Cherwell r. England U.K.
139 O8 Cherykaw Belarus
227 J6 Chesaning MI U.S.A.
233 I12 Chesapeake VA U.S.A.
234 D5 Chesapeake and Delaware Canal DE U.S.A.
234 C7 Chesapeake Bay MD/VA U.S.A.
232 I10 Chesapeake Beach MD U.S.A.
234 D5 Chesapeake City MD U.S.A.
151 K4 Chesham Buckinghamshire, England U.K.
149 M7 Cheshire admin. div. England U.K.
235 J2 Cheshire CT U.S.A.
233 L6 Cheshire MA U.S.A.
149 L7 Cheshire Plain England U.K.
122 G7 Cheshmeh Sabz Iran
123 I2 Cheshme Vtoroy Turkm.
129 G3 Chesho Georgia
134 I2 Cheshskaya Guba b. Rus. Fed.
123 P3 Cheshtebe Tajik.
123 J4 Chesht-e Sharīf Afgh.
151 L4 Cheshunt Hertfordshire, England U.K.
150 G6 Chesil Beach England U.K.
234 F5 Chesilhurst NJ U.S.A.
227 M5 Chesley Ont. Can.
156 H8 Chesley France
120 I1 Chesma Rus. Fed.
Chesnokovka Rus. Fed. see Novoaltaysk
156 G7 Chessy-les-Prés France
187 D9 Cheste Spain
225 H4 Chester N.S. Can.
149 L7 Chester Cheshire, England U.K.
240 K1 Chester CA U.S.A.
235 K2 Chester CT U.S.A.
236 K7 Chester IL U.S.A.
234 C7 Chester MD U.S.A.
238 I2 Chester MT U.S.A.
234 F3 Chester NJ U.S.A.
235 G2 Chester NY U.S.A.
232 D9 Chester OH U.S.A.
234 E5 Chester PA U.S.A.
231 G8 Chester SC U.S.A.
232 H11 Chester VA U.S.A.
234 C7 Chester r. MD U.S.A.
246 □ Chester Castle Jamaica
234 D4 Chester County county PA U.S.A.
149 O7 Chesterfield Derbyshire, England U.K.
235 K2 Chesterfield CT U.S.A.
236 J6 Chesterfield MO U.S.A.
231 G8 Chesterfield SC U.S.A.
232 H11 Chesterfield VA U.S.A.
77 F3 Chesterfield, Îles is New Caledonia
223 N2 Chesterfield Inlet Nunavut Can.
223 M2 Chesterfield Inlet inlet Nunavut Can.
149 N4 Chester-le-Street Durham, England U.K.
146 K12 Chesters Scottish Borders, Scotland U.K.
234 C6 Chestertown MD U.S.A.
233 L5 Chestertown NY U.S.A.
233 J3 Chesterville Ont. Can.
234 D6 Chesterville MD U.S.A.
232 F8 Chestnut Ridge PA U.S.A.
233 □P2 Chesuncook Lake ME U.S.A.
234 D6 Cheswold DE U.S.A.
205 G1 Chetaïbi Alg.
226 C4 Chetek WI U.S.A.
225 I4 Chéticamp N.S. Can.
114 C7 Chetlat i. India
237 H7 Chetopa KS U.S.A.
243 O8 Chetumal Mex.
81 I7 Chetwode Islands South I. N.Z.
222 F4 Chetwynd B.C. Can.
100 G3 Cheugda Rus. Fed.
109 □J7 Cheung Chau H.K. China
109 □J7 Cheung Chau H.K. China
161 I8 Cheval Blanc, Sommet du mt. France
162 D5 Chevanceaux France
156 G8 Chevannes France
241 V7 Chevelon Creek r. AZ U.S.A.
177 K6 Cheverešu Mare Romania
234 B7 Cheverly MD U.S.A.
160 G2 Chevigny-St-Sauveur France
157 J6 Chevillon France
156 C7 Chevilly France
81 H9 Cheviot South I. N.Z.
232 A9 Cheviot OH U.S.A.
149 L3 Cheviot Hills England U.K.
85 I8 Cheviot Range hills Qld Austr.
158 B5 Chèvre, Cap de la c. France
224 F2 Chevreulx r. Que. Can.
156 D6 Chevreuse France
210 C3 Che'w Bahir salt l. Eth.
210 C3 Che'w Bahir Wildlife Reserve nature res. Eth.
238 F2 Chewelah WA U.S.A.
150 G5 Chew Magna Bath and North East Somerset, England U.K.
150 G5 Chew Valley Lake resr England U.K.
237 F8 Cheyenne OK U.S.A.
238 L6 Cheyenne WY U.S.A.
236 E3 Cheyenne r. SD U.S.A.
236 E3 Cheyenne River Indian Reservation res. SD U.S.A.
236 D6 Cheyenne Wells CO U.S.A.
161 B6 Cheylade France
87 E13 Cheyne Bay W.A. Austr.
114 G6 Cheyur Tamil Nadu India
114 F6 Cheyyar r. India
222 E4 Chezacut B.C. Can.
159 P8 Chezal-Benoît France
217 □3a Chezani Njazidja Comoros
163 D10 Chèze France
116 F7 Chhabra Rajasthan India
116 E6 Chhapar Rajasthan India
117 J7 Chhapra Bihar India
116 F6 Chhata Uttar Prad. India
117 M7 Chhatak Bangl.
117 J7 Chhatarpur Jharkhand India
116 G7 Chhatarpur Madh. Prad. India
123 M7 Chhatr Pak.
115 I3 Chhatrapur Orissa India
116 H9 Chhattisgarh state India
97 F9 Chhay Arêng, Stœng r. Cambodia
116 G6 Chhibramau Uttar Prad. India
116 G8 Chhindwara Madh. Prad. India
116 F7 Chhipa Barod Rajasthan India
116 G4 Chhitkul Hima. Prad. India
97 G8 Chhlong, Prêk r. Cambodia
116 G8 Chhota Chhindwara Madh. Prad. India
116 E8 Chhota Udepur Gujarat India
116 H9 Chhuikhadan Chhattisgarh India
Chhuk Cambodia see Phumĭ Chhuk
117 L6 Chhukha Bhutan
97 F7 Chi, Lam r. Thai.
96 G7 Chi, Mae Nam r. Thai.
257 F4 Chiador Brazil
109 M7 Chiai Taiwan
101 F10 Ch'iak-san National Park S. Korea
211 D5 Chiamboni Kenya
191 K4 Chiampo Italy
191 K5 Chiampo r. Italy
192 H1 Chianciano Terme Italy
96 D5 Chiang Dao Thai.
209 B8 Chiange Angola
96 E5 Chiang Kham Thai.
96 E6 Chiang Khan Thai.
96 D5 Chiang Mai Thai.
96 D5 Chiang Rai Thai.
96 E4 Chiang Saen Thai.
192 I2 Chiani r. Italy
191 J8 Chianni Italy
243 M9 Chiapa Mex.
245 N9 Chiapas state Mex.
243 M9 Chiapilla Mex.
194 H9 Chiaramonte Gulfi Sicilia Italy
192 B6 Chiaramonti Sardegna Italy
191 O8 Chiaravalle Italy
195 K6 Chiaravalle Centrale Italy
190 H4 Chiari Italy
193 Q7 Chiaromonte Italy
191 O3 Chiarso r. Italy
191 M9 Chiascio r. Italy
190 G4 Chiasso Italy
129 E3 Chiat'ura Georgia
245 I6 Chiautempan Mex.
245 I7 Chiautla Mex.
245 I6 Chiautzingo Mex.
190 G7 Chiavari Italy
190 H5 Chiavenna r. Italy
190 G3 Chiavenno Italy
105 L4 Chiba Japan
105 L5 Chiba pref. Japan
213 G4 Chibabava Moz.
102 □1 Chibana Okinawa Japan
209 B8 Chibemba Angola
109 I4 Chibi Hubei China
Chibi Zimbabwe see Chivi
209 B8 Chibia Angola
110 H1 Chibit Rus. Fed.
Chibizovka Rus. Fed. see Zherdevka
213 G4 Chiboma Moz.
224 F3 Chibougamau Que. Can.
224 F3 Chibougamau r. Que. Can.
224 F3 Chibougamau, Lac l. Que. Can.
103 K10 Chibu Japan
103 K11 Chiburi-jima i. Japan
213 G5 Chibuto Moz.
209 F8 Chibwe Zambia
260 E2 Chica, Sierra mts Arg.
Chicacole Andhra Prad. India see Srikakulam
226 G8 Chicago IL U.S.A.
226 G8 Chicago Heights IL U.S.A.
226 G8 Chicago O'Hare airport IL U.S.A.
209 C8 Chicala Bié Angola
209 C7 Chicala Moxico Angola
213 G3 Chicamba Moz.
209 D6 Chicapa r. Angola
245 I4 Chicayan Mex.
245 I3 Chicayán r. Mex.
225 H3 Chic-Chocs, Monts mts Que. Can.
225 H3 Chic-Chocs, Réserve Faunique des nature res. Que. Can.
197 M5 Chicera Hamba hill Romania
202 C5 Chicha well Chad
222 B3 Chichagof AK U.S.A.
220 E4 Chichagof Island AK U.S.A.
123 K8 Chichak r. Pak.
204 C3 Chichaoua Morocco
252 D5 Chichas, Cordillera de mts Bol.
159 K8 Chiché France
107 N6 Chicheng Hebei China
Chicheng Sichuan China see Pengxi
243 O7 Chichén Itzá tourist site Mex.
151 K6 Chichester West Sussex, England U.K.
86 E7 Chichester Range mts W.A. Austr.
116 H9 Chichgarh Mahar. India
105 J4 Chichibu Japan
105 J3 Chichibu-gawa r. Japan
105 I4 Chichibu-Tama Kokuritsu-kōen nat. park Japan
245 K9 Chichicapan Mex.
245 H8 Chichihualco Mex.
103 □2 Chichi-jima i. Ogasawara-shotō Japan
103 □2 Chichijima-rettō is Ogasawara-shotō Japan
260 D6 Chichinales Arg.
250 D2 Chichiriviche Venez.
116 F9 Chicholi Madh. Prad. India
232 I11 Chickahominy r. VA U.S.A.
231 E8 Chickamauga Lake TN U.S.A.
237 K10 Chickasawhay r. MS U.S.A.
237 G8 Chickasha OK U.S.A.
150 G6 Chickerell Dorset, England U.K.
261 G4 Chiclana Arg.
184 G8 Chiclana de la Fronte[...] Spain
250 B6 Chiclayo Peru
261 G6 Chico r. Arg.
259 C6 Chico r. Arg.
259 C8 Chico r. Arg.
259 D7 Chico r. Arg.
244 D3 Chico r. Mex.
240 K2 Chico CA U.S.A.
213 G2 Chicoa Moz.
Chicobea i. Fiji see Cik[...]
227 P1 Chicobi, Lac l. Que. Ca[...]
209 B8 Chicomba Angola
213 G5 Chicomo Moz.
243 M10 Chicomucelo Mex.
245 I4 Chiconamel Mex.
217 □3b Chiconi Mayotte
211 B8 Chiconono Moz.
245 I4 Chicontepec Mex.
233 M6 Chicopee MA U.S.A.
92 C3 Chico Sapocoy, Moun[...] Luzon Phil.
217 □1c Chicots, Plaine des h[...] Réunion
225 G3 Chicoutimi Que. Can.
225 G3 Chicoutimi r. Que. Can[...]
213 F4 Chicualacuala Moz.
209 B8 Chicuma Angola
209 C8 Chicupo Angola
114 F7 Chidambaram Tamil Na[...] India
151 K5 Chiddingfold Surrey, England U.K.
213 G5 Chidenguele Moz.
221 L3 Chidley, Cape Nfld and Lab./Nunavut Can.
Chido Xizang China see[...]
101 E11 Chido S. Korea
209 C9 Chiede Angola
231 F11 Chiefland FL U.S.A.
212 D3 Chief's Island Botswa[...]
173 M6 Chiemgauer Alpen m[...]
173 N6 Chieming Ger.
173 M6 Chiemsee l. Ger.
191 L2 Chienes Italy
209 F7 Chiengi Zambia
Chiengmai Thai. see Chiang Mai
191 P9 Chienti r. Italy
97 D10 Chieo Lan Reservoir [...]
190 D5 Chieri Italy
157 J4 Chiers r. France
190 H3 Chiesa in Valmalenco[...]
177 L4 Chieșd Romania
191 I5 Chiese r. Italy
193 M3 Chieti Italy
193 M3 Chieti prov. Italy
193 O4 Chieuti Italy
151 J5 Chieveley West Berksh[...] England U.K.
165 E7 Chièvres Belgium
107 P5 Chifeng Nei Mongol Ch[...]
257 G2 Chifre, Serra do mts B[...]
213 G2 Chifunde Moz.
121 O5 Chiganak Kazakh.
105 J5 Chigasaki Japan
Chigil, Ostrov i. Azer. s[...] Çigil Adası
220 C4 Chiginagak Volcano, [...] AK U.S.A.
137 T2 Chigla r. Rus. Fed.
245 I6 Chignahuapán Mex.
225 H4 Chignecto Bay N.B./N[...]
225 H4 Chignecto Game Sanc[...] nature res. N.S. Can.
220 C4 Chignik AK U.S.A.
160 I5 Chignin France
250 B3 Chigorodó Col.
111 J12 Chigu Xizang China
260 B2 Chigualoco Chile
252 D5 Chiguana Bol.
213 G4 Chigubo Moz.
111 J12 Chigu Co l. China
151 M4 Chigwell Essex, Englan[...]
242 F3 Chihuahua Mex.
242 F3 Chihuahua state Mex.
260 C6 Chihuido Medio mt. A[...]
121 L5 Chiili Kazakh.
106 E6 Chijinpu Gansu China
129 G4 Chikaani Georgia
116 F9 Chikalda Mahar. India
108 H8 Chikan Guangdong Chi[...]
237 G7 Chikaskia r. KS U.S.A.
114 E6 Chik Ballapur Karnatak[...]
138 M4 Chikhachevo Rus. Fed[...]
116 G8 Chikhali Kalan Parasi[...] Prad. India
116 F9 Chikhli Mahar. India
Chikishlyar Turkm. see Çekiçler
114 D6 Chikmagalur Karnataka[...]
114 D4 Chikodi Karnataka India[...]
114 D4 Chikodi Road Karnatak[...]
129 E2 Chikola Rus. Fed.
209 F8 Chikonkomene Zambi[...]
106 J1 Chikoy Rus. Fed.
107 J1 Chikoy r. Rus. Fed.
103 H13 Chikugo Japan
105 I1 Chikuma-gawa r. Japa[...]
105 K6 Chikura Japan
103 H13 Chikushino Japan
211 B7 Chikwa Zambia
211 B8 Chikwawa Malawi
102 S4 Chikyū-misaki pt Japa[...]
209 B8 Chila Angola
245 J8 Chila Mex.
245 I3 Chila, Laguna l. Mex.
209 F8 Chilanga Zambia
222 F4 Chilanko r. B.C. Can.
222 E4 Chilanko Forks B.C. C[...]
245 H8 Chilapa Guerrero Mex.
245 J8 Chilapa Oaxaca Mex.
116 E2 Chilas Jammu and Kas[...]
114 F9 Chilaw Sri Lanka
252 A3 Chilca Peru
252 C4 Chilcaya Chile
187 E8 Chilches Spain
150 G5 Chilcompton Somerset, England U.K.
222 F5 Chilcotin r. B.C. Can.
85 M4 Chilcott Island Coral S[...] Terr. Austr.
85 N8 Childers Qld Austr.
237 E8 Childress TX U.S.A.
151 J4 Childrey Oxfordshire, England U.K.
259 B7 Chile country S. Americ[...]
267 N8 Chile Basin sea feature[...] S. Pacific Ocean
259 C7 Chile Chico Chile
258 D3 Chilecito La Rioja Arg.
260 C3 Chilecito Mendoza Arg.
209 B8 Chilengue, Serra do m[...] Angola
267 N8 Chile Rise sea feature S. Pacific Ocean
252 A1 Chilete Peru
135 I7 Chilgir Rus. Fed.
151 N5 Chilham Kent, England [...]
232 D12 Chilhowie VA U.S.A.
Chilia-Nouă Ukr. see Ki[...]
197 R5 Chilia Veche Romania
209 D8 Chiliba Angola
250 B2 Chilibre Panama
121 R6 Chilik Kazakh.
121 R6 Chilik r. Kazakh.
115 I3 Chilika Lake India
209 E8 Chililabombwe Zambia[...]
Chilimanzi Zimbabwe s[...] Chirumanzu
198 D5 Chiliomodi Greece
222 C3 Chilkat r. Can./U.S.A.
222 F4 Chilko r. B.C. Can.
222 E5 Chilko Lake B.C. Can.
220 E4 Chilkoot Trail National[...] Historic Site nat. park AK U.S.A.
85 J4 Chillagoe Qld Austr.
260 A5 Chillán Chile
260 A5 Chillán r. Chile
260 B5 Chillán, Nevado mts Ch[...]
260 B5 Chillán, Volcán vol. Chi[...]
261 H5 Chillar Arg.
156 D7 Chilleurs-aux-Bois Fra[...]
226 E9 Chillicothe IL U.S.A.
236 I6 Chillicothe MO U.S.A.
232 C9 Chillicothe OH U.S.A.
252 C4 Chilliculco Peru
116 E1 Chillinji Jammu and Ka[...]
222 F5 Chilliwack B.C. Can.
185 J3 Chillón Spain

Chilluévar Spain
Chillum *MD* U.S.A.
Chilmari Bangl.
Chilo *Rajasthan* India
Chiloé, Isla de *i.* Chile
Chiloé, Isla Grande de *i.* Chile *see* Chiloé, Isla de
Chiloeches Spain
Chilombo Angola
Chilonga Zambia
Chiloquin *OR* U.S.A.
Chilpancingo Mex.
Chilpi *Chhattisgarh* India
Chilson *MI* U.S.A.
Chiltepec Mex.
Chiltern *Vic.* Austr.
Chiltern Hills *England* U.K.
Chilton *WI* U.S.A.
Chiluage Angola
Chilubi Zambia
Chilumba Malawi
Chilung Taiwan
Chilwa, Lake Malawi
Chimala Tanz.
Chimalapa Mex.
0 Chimaltenango Guat.
Chimaltitán Mex.
13 Chimán Panama
Chimanimani Zimbabwe
7 Chi Ma Wan *H.K.* China
Chimay Belgium
Chimay, Bois de *for.* Belgium
Chimba Zambia
Chimbarongo Chile
Chimbas Arg.
Chimbay Uzbek. *see* Chimboy
Chimborazo *mt.* Ecuador
Chimbote Peru
Chimboy Uzbek.
Chimeneas Spain
Chimian Pak.
Chimichaguá Col.
Chimishliya Moldova *see* Cimişlia
Chimkent Kazakh. *see* Shymkent
Chimkentskaya Oblast' *admin. div.* Kazakh. *see* Yuzhnyy Kazakhstan
Chimney Rocks *is* Inner Islands Seychelles
Chimoio Moz.
Chimorra *hill* Spain
Chimorra, Sierra *mts* Spain
Chimpay Arg.
Chimtarga, Qullai *mt.* Tajik.
Chimtorga, Gora *mt.* Tajik. *see* Chimtargha, Qullai
Chimyon Uzbek.
Chin *state* Myanmar
China *country* Asia
China Mex.
China, Republic of *country* Asia *see* Taiwan
China Bakir *r.* Myanmar *see* To
Chinacates Mex.
Chinajá Guat.
China Lake *CA* U.S.A.
4 China Lake *ME* U.S.A.
Chinameca Mex.
Chinampa de Gorostiza Mex.
Chinandega Italy
11 Chinandega Nic.
Chinantla Mex.
China Point *CA* U.S.A.
2 Chinati Peak *TX* U.S.A.
Chinaz Uzbek. *see* Chinoz
Chinca Ecuador
Chincha Alta Peru
Chinchaga *r.* Alta Can.
Chinchilla *Qld* Austr.
Chinchilla de Monte Aragón Spain
Chincholi *Karnataka* India
Chinchón Spain
Chinchorro, Banco *sea feature* Mex.
Chincolco Chile
Chincoteague *VA* U.S.A.
Chincoteague Bay *MD/VA* U.S.A.
Chinde Moz.
Chindini *Njazidja* Comoros
Chindo S. Korea
Chin-do *i.* S. Korea
Chindrieux France
Chindu *Qinghai* China
Chindwin *r.* Myanmar
Chinen *Okinawa* Japan
Chineni Jammu and Kashmir
Chinese Turkestan *aut. reg.* China *see* Xinjiang Uygur Zizhiqu
Chinga Moz.
Chingaza, Parque Nacional *nat. park* Col.
Chingford *Greater London, England* U.K.
Chinghai *prov.* China *see* Qinghai
Chinghwa N. Korea
Chingirlau Kazakh.
Chingiz-Tau, Khrebet *mts* Kazakh.
Chingleput *Tamil Nadu* India *see* Chengalpattu
Chingola Zambia
Chinguanja Angola
Chinguar Angola
Chinguețți Maur.
Chinguil Chad
Chinhae S. Korea
Chinhanda Moz.
Chinhoyi Zimbabwe
Chini *Hima. Prad.* India *see* Kalpa
Chinijo Bol.
Chining *Shandong* China *see* Jining
Chiniot Pak.
Chinipas Mex.
Chinit, Stœng *r.* Cambodia
Chinju S. Korea
Chinko *r.* C.A.R.
Chinle *AZ* U.S.A.
Chinle Valley *AZ* U.S.A.
Chinle Wash *watercourse AZ* U.S.A.
Chinmen Taiwan
Chinmen Tao *i.* Taiwan
Chinna Ganjam *Andhra Prad.* India
Chinnamanur *Tamil Nadu* India
Chinnamp'o N. Korea *see* Namp'o
Chinna Salem *Tamil Nadu* India
Chinnor *Oxfordshire, England* U.K.
Chinnur *Andhra Prad.* India
Chino Japan
Chino *CA* U.S.A.
Chino Creek *watercourse* U.S.A.
2 Chinocup, Lake *salt flat W.A.* Austr.
2 Chinocup Nature Reserve *W.A.* Austr.
Chinon France
Chinook *MT* U.S.A.
Chinook Trough *sea feature* N. Pacific Ocean
Chino Valley *AZ* U.S.A.
Chinoz Uzbek.
Chinsali Zambia
Chintalnar *Chhattisgarh* India
Chintamani *Karnataka* India
Chinteni Romania
Chintheche Malawi
Chintón de las Flores Mex.
Chinú Col.
Chiny Belgium
Chiny, Forêt de *for.* Belgium
Chinyama Litapi Zambia
Chin'yavoryk Rus. Fed.
Chioco Moz.
Chioggia Italy
Chiomonte Italy
Chiona Tanz.
Chios *Chios* Greece
Chios *i.* Greece
Chios Strait Greece
243 N10 Chipam Guat.
213 G3 Chipanga Moz.
211 B8 Chipata Zambia
111 C9 Chip Chap *r.* China/India
259 C6 Chipchihua, Sierra de *mts* Arg.
213 G2 Chipera Moz.
209 C8 Chipeta Angola
97 H9 Chiphu Cambodia
209 F7 Chipili Zambia
209 B8 Chipindo Angola
107 O8 Chiping *Shandong* China
Chipinga Zimbabwe *see* Chipinge
213 G4 Chipinge Zimbabwe
184 G7 Chipiona Spain
231 E10 Chipley *FL* U.S.A.
114 C4 Chiplun *Mahar.* India
225 H4 Chipman *N.B.* Can.
211 C6 Chipogolo Tanz.
209 C8 Chipoia Angola
150 H5 Chippenham *Wiltshire, England* U.K.
213 G3 Chipperone, Monte *mt.* Moz.
236 H3 Chippewa *r. MN* U.S.A.
226 B5 Chippewa *r. WI* U.S.A.
226 C4 Chippewa, Lake *WI* U.S.A.
226 C5 Chippewa Falls *WI* U.S.A.
151 I3 Chipping Campden *Gloucestershire, England* U.K.
151 I4 Chipping Norton *Oxfordshire, England* U.K.
151 M4 Chipping Ongar *Essex, England* U.K.
150 H4 Chipping Sodbury *South Gloucestershire, England* U.K.
190 D3 Chippis Switz.
186 E5 Chiprana Spain
197 K7 Chiprovtsi Bulg.
209 F8 Chipundu *Central* Zambia
209 F8 Chipundu *Luapula* Zambia
Chipuriro Zimbabwe *see* Guruve
115 H3 Chipurupalle *Andhra Prad.* India
115 H4 Chipurupalle *Andhra Prad.* India
233 □R3 Chiputneticook Lakes Can./U.S.A.
252 A2 Chiquian Peru
243 O9 Chiquibul National Park Belize
243 P7 Chiquilá Mex.
244 D5 Chiquilistlán Mex.
243 O10 Chiquimula Guat.
250 C3 Chiquinquira Col.
252 B3 Chiquintirca Peru
261 G4 Chiquita, Mar *l.* Arg.
245 H1 Chiquita, Sierra *mts* Mex.
244 F7 Chiquito *r.* Mex.
253 E4 Chiquitos, Llanos de *plain* Bol.
135 H6 Chir *r.* Rus. Fed.
161 C7 Chirac France
114 G5 Chirada *Andhra Prad.* India
211 B8 Chiradzulu Malawi
129 I4 Chiragdzhun Rus. Fed.
129 J4 Chirakhchay *r.* Rus. Fed.
114 D7 Chirakkal *Kerala* India
114 G5 Chirala *Andhra Prad.* India
213 G3 Chiramba Moz.
250 B3 Chirambirá, Punta *pt* Col.
123 K4 Chiras Afgh.
111 B12 Chirawa *Rajasthan* India
150 F2 Chirbury *Shropshire, England* U.K.
121 M7 Chirchiq Uzbek.
121 M7 Chirchiq *r.* Uzbek.
213 F4 Chiredzi Zimbabwe
210 C1 Chire Wildlife Reserve *nature res.* Eth.
202 B4 Chirfa Niger
250 E2 Chirgua *r.* Venez.
241 W9 Chiricahua National Monument *nat. park AZ* U.S.A.
241 W10 Chiricahua Peak *AZ* U.S.A.
250 C2 Chiriguaná Col.
220 C4 Chirikof Island *AK* U.S.A.
247 J8 Chirimena Venez.
250 B6 Chirinos Peru
242 □R13 Chiriquí, Golfo de *b.* Panama
242 □R13 Chiriquí, Laguna de *b.* Panama
246 C9 Chiriquí, Punta *pt* Panama
242 □R13 Chiriquí Grande Panama
101 E11 Chiri-san *mt.* S. Korea
101 E11 Chiri-san National Park S. Korea
185 O5 Chirivel Spain
129 G2 Chiri-Yurt Rus. Fed.
150 F2 Chirk *Wrexham, Wales* U.K.
146 L11 Chirnside *Scottish Borders, Scotland* U.K.
217 □3b Chirongui Mayotte
121 L6 Chiroqchi Uzbek.
160 F4 Chiroubles France
78 □6 Chirovanga *Choiseul* Solomon Is
197 N8 Chirpan Bulg.
242 □R13 Chirripó, Parque Nacional *nat. park* Costa Rica
213 F3 Chirumanzu Zimbabwe
213 F3 Chirundu Zimbabwe
244 F5 Chiruntzio Mex.
122 E8 Chirūyeh Iran
104 F5 Chiryū Japan
209 F8 Chisamba Zambia
209 E8 Chisasa Zambia
224 E2 Chisasibi *Que.* Can.
261 I4 Chis Chis, Laguna *l.* Arg.
243 N10 Chisec Guat.
209 E9 Chisekesi Zambia
151 I4 Chiseldon *Swindon, England* U.K.
197 O6 Chiselet Romania
211 B7 Chisenga Malawi
Chishima-retto *is* Rus. Fed. *see* Kuril'skiye Ostrova
135 K5 Chishmy Rus. Fed.
222 H4 Chisholm *Alta* Can.
233 □O4 Chisholm *ME* U.S.A.
226 B2 Chisholm *MN* U.S.A.
123 O7 Chishtian Mandi Pak.
108 E4 Chishui *Guizhou* China
108 E5 Chishuihe *Sichuan* China
108 E4 Chishui He *r.* China
Chisimaio Somalia *see* Kismaayo
136 H6 Chişinău Moldova
177 L5 Chişindia Romania
197 J4 Chişineu-Criş Romania
177 L4 Chişineu-Criş Romania
116 E2 Chisi Vi Chisholm Zambia
190 D6 Chisola *r.* Italy
190 C6 Chisone *r.* Italy
217 □3b Chissioua Mbouzi *i.* Mayotte
217 □3b Chissioua Mtsamboro *i.* Mayotte
134 J5 Chistopol' Rus. Fed.
121 L1 Chistopol'ye Kazakh.
Chistyakovo Ukr. *see* Torez
121 N1 Chistyakovskoye Kazakh.
175 K1 Chistye-Prudy Rus. Fed.
252 D5 Chita Bol.
250 C3 Chita Col.
104 E6 Chita Japan
99 J1 Chita Rus. Fed.
211 B7 Chita Tanz.
122 D6 Chitab Iran
209 B9 Chitado Angola
104 E6 Chita-hantō *pen.* Japan
Chitaldrug *Karnataka* India *see* Chitradurga
116 C7 Chitalwana *Rajasthan* India
211 A8 Chitambo Zambia
107 L1 Chitanga Rus. Fed.
Chita Oblast *admin. div.* Rus. Fed. *see* Chitinskaya Oblast'
209 D6 Chitato Angola
104 E6 Chita-wan *b.* Japan
134 J3 Chitayevo Rus. Fed.
223 J4 Chitek *Sask.* Can.
223 L4 Chitek Lake *l. Man.* Can.
209 C8 Chitembo Angola
191 L8 Chitignano Italy
100 A3 Chitinskaya Oblast' *admin. div.* Rus. Fed.
211 B7 Chitipa Malawi
Chitkul *Hima. Prad.* India *see* Chitkul
213 G4 Chitobe Moz.
209 D8 Chitokoloki Zambia
209 E9 Chitongo Zambia
Chitor *Rajasthan* India *see* Chittaurgarh
102 S4 Chitose Japan
114 E5 Chitradurga *Karnataka* India
116 H7 Chitrakoot *Uttar Prad.* India
123 N4 Chitral Pak.
123 N4 Chitral *r.* Pak.
114 F5 Chitravati *r.* India
242 □S14 Chitré Panama
116 C8 Chitrod *Gujarat* India
117 M8 Chittagong Bangl.
117 M8 Chittagong *admin. div.* Bangl.
117 K8 Chittaranjan *W. Bengal* India
116 E7 Chittaurgarh *Rajasthan* India
114 F6 Chittoor *Andhra Prad.* India
Chittorgarh *Rajasthan* India *see* Chittaurgarh
114 E7 Chittur *Kerala* India
211 B8 Chitungulu Zambia
213 F3 Chitungwiza Zimbabwe
211 C7 Chiulezi *r.* Moz.
Chiu Lung *H.K.* China *see* Kowloon
209 D8 Chiume Angola
213 H2 Chiúre Novo Moz.
190 H3 Chiuro Italy
191 L2 Chiusa Italy
190 D7 Chiusa di Pesio Italy
191 O3 Chiusaforte Italy
194 E8 Chiusa Sclafani *Sicilia* Italy
190 D8 Chiusavecchia Italy
192 G1 Chiusdino Italy
190 D5 Chiusella *r.* Italy
192 H1 Chiusi Italy
192 H1 Chiusi, Lago di *l.* Italy
191 L8 Chiusi della Verna Italy
213 G2 Chiúta Moz.
187 D9 Chiva Spain
190 D5 Chivasso Italy
242 D4 Chivato, Punta *pt* Mex.
252 C3 Chivay Peru
252 C3 Chive Bol.
209 C8 Chiveio Angola
245 M9 Chivela Mex.
213 F3 Chivhu Zimbabwe
213 F4 Chivi Zimbabwe
261 G4 Chivilcoy Arg.
109 I8 Chixi *Guangdong* China
Chiyirchik, Pereval *pass* Kyrg. *see* Chyyyrchyk Ashuusu
105 J3 Chiyoda *Gunma* Japan
105 L3 Chiyoda *Ibaraki* Japan
105 K3 Chiyogawa Japan
213 E3 Chizarira Hills Zimbabwe
213 E3 Chizarira National Park Zimbabwe
162 D3 Chizé France
134 I2 Chizha Rus. Fed.
120 C2 Chizha Vtoraya Kazakh.
109 K3 Chizhou *Anhui* China
103 L11 Chizu Japan
Chkalov Rus. Fed. *see* Orenburg
137 N6 Chkalove Ukr.
121 N1 Chkalovo Kazakh.
Chkalovo Rus. Fed. *see* Kurchaloy
134 H4 Chkalovsk Rus. Fed.
Chkalovskaya Oblast' *admin. div.* Rus. Fed. *see* Orenburgskaya Oblast'
137 P4 Chkalovs'ke Ukr.
100 H6 Chkalovskoye Rus. Fed.
129 D3 Ch'khari Georgia
177 G2 Chlebičov Czech Rep.
177 I2 Chlebnice Slovakia
174 C3 Chlebowo Pol.
205 F1 Chlef Alg.
175 I4 Chlewiska Pol.
177 K3 Chlmec *r.* Slovakia
174 C3 Chłopice Pol.
241 R6 Chloride *AZ* U.S.A.
174 E3 Chludowo Pol.
173 O2 Chlumčany Czech Rep.
176 C1 Chlumec Czech Rep.
176 E1 Chlumec nad Cidlinou Czech Rep.
176 D3 Chlum u Třeboně Czech Rep.
100 L2 Chlya, Ozero *l.* Rus. Fed.
177 H2 Chmelová *hill* Slovakia
175 I5 Chmielnik Pol.
174 E2 Chmielno Pol.
175 K4 Chmiel Pierwszy Pol.
94 □ Choa Chu Kang Sing.
94 □ Choa Chu Kang *hill* Sing.
97 G7 Chŏam Khsant Cambodia
260 B2 Choapa Chile
260 B2 Choapa *r.* Chile
212 E3 Choabe *admin. dist.* Botswana
212 E3 Chobe National Park Botswana
174 E4 Chobienia Pol.
174 D3 Chobienice Pol.
96 G4 Chŏ Bo Vietnam
245 J6 Chocamán Mex.
247 □3 Choc Bay St Lucia
176 F1 Choceň Czech Rep.
175 H3 Choceń Pol.
101 E10 Choch'iwŏn S. Korea
177 G3 Chocholná-Velčice Slovakia
96 G4 Chợ Chu Vietnam
174 D4 Chocianów Pol.
174 D2 Chociwel Pol.
250 B3 Chocó *dept* Col.
241 Q8 Chocolate Mountains *AZ/CA* U.S.A.
250 C3 Choconta Col.
231 D10 Choctawhatchee *r. FL* U.S.A.
174 F4 Chocz Pol.
174 F1 Choczewo Pol.
114 G4 Chodavaram *Andhra Prad.* India
175 H3 Chodecz Pol.
175 K4 Chodel Pol.
175 J4 Chodelka *r.* Pol.
101 D9 Cho-do *i.* N. Korea
173 O2 Chodov Czech Rep.
176 B2 Chodová Planá Czech Rep.
175 K3 Chodów *Mazowieckie* Pol.
175 H3 Chodów *Wielkopolskie* Pol.
110 I1 Chodro Rus. Fed.
174 E3 Chodzież Pol.
260 F6 Choele Choel Arg.
260 E6 Choele Choel Grande, Isla *i.* Arg.
213 F2 Chofombo Moz.
105 K4 Chōfu Japan
122 D7 Choghādak Iran
122 F7 Choghān Iran
116 E2 Chogo Lungma Glacier Jammu and Kashmir
Chogori Feng *mt.* China/Jammu and Kashmir *see* K2
135 I7 Chograyskoye Vodokhranilishche *resr* Rus. Fed.
223 J4 Choiceland *Sask.* Can.
261 F6 Choique Arg.
78 □6 Choiseul *i.* Solomon Is
247 □3 Choiseul St Lucia
259 F8 Choiseul Sound *sea chan.* Falkland Is
160 I5 Choisey France
242 E4 Choix Mex.
174 C3 Chojna Pol.
174 F2 Chojnice Pol.
174 D4 Chojnów Pol.
136 A1 Chojnowski Park Krajobrazowy Pol.
102 R7 Chōkai-san *vol.* Japan
210 C2 Ch'ok'ē *mts* Eth.
129 D3 Ch'okhatauri Georgia
121 P6 Chokpar Kazakh.
121 Q6 Chok-Tal Kyrg.
Chokue Moz. *see* Chókwè
131 P2 Chokurdakh Rus. Fed.
213 G5 Chókwè Moz.
108 B3 Cho La *pass Sichuan* China
240 L6 Cholame *CA* U.S.A.
240 L6 Cholame Creek *r. CA* U.S.A.
108 B2 Chola Shan *mts Sichuan* China
260 A6 Cholchol Chile
162 C1 Cholet France
260 A5 Cholguan Chile
242 □P10 Choloma Hond.
121 P6 Cholpon Kyrg.
121 Q6 Cholpon-Ata Kyrg.
151 J4 Cholsey *Oxfordshire, England* U.K.
245 I6 Cholula Mex.
242 □P11 Choluteca Hond.
209 E9 Choma Zambia
101 F10 Chŏmch'ŏn S. Korea
161 D6 Chomelix France
161 F7 Chomérac France
111 I12 Chomo Ganggar *mt. Xizang* China
96 G4 Chợ Moi Vietnam
117 L6 Chomo Lhari *mt.* Bhutan
96 D5 Chom Thong Thai.
116 E6 Chomun *Rajasthan* India
176 C1 Chomutov Czech Rep.
176 C1 Chomutovka *r.* Czech Rep.
131 L3 Chona *r.* Rus. Fed.
105 L5 Chōnan Japan
101 E10 Ch'ŏnan S. Korea
97 E8 Chon Buri Thai.
259 B6 Chonchi Chile
250 A5 Chone Ecuador
Chong'an *Fujian* China *see* Wuyishan
101 D9 Ch'ŏngch'ŏn-gang *r.* N. Korea
101 F11 Ch'ongdo S. Korea
Chonggye *Xizang* China *see* Qonggyai
103 G11 Chŏngja S. Korea
101 F8 Ch'ŏngjin N. Korea
101 D9 Chŏngju N. Korea
101 E10 Ch'ŏngju S. Korea
97 F8 Chong Kal Cambodia
107 N6 Chongli *Hebei* China
Chonglong *Sichuan* China *see* Zizhong
109 M3 Chongming *Shanghai* China
109 M3 Chongming Dao *i.* China
209 B8 Chongoroi Angola
101 E9 Chŏngp'yŏng N. Korea
108 F4 Chongqing *Chongqing* China
Chongqing *Sichuan* China *see* Chongzhou
108 F3 Chongqing *mun.* China
109 J5 Chongren *Jiangxi* China
101 E11 Chŏngŭp S. Korea
209 F8 Chongwe Zambia
109 J4 Chongyang *Hubei* China
109 L5 Chongyang Xi *r.* China
109 J6 Chongyi *Jiangxi* China
108 D3 Chongzhou *Sichuan* China
108 F7 Chongzuo *Guangxi* China
137 N7 Chonhar, Pivostriv *pen.* Ukr.
101 E11 Chŏnju S. Korea
107 N4 Chonogol Mongolia
259 B7 Chonos, Archipiélago de los *is* Chile
245 N8 Chontalpa Mex.
97 H9 Chon Thanh Vietnam
117 K5 Cho Oyu *mt.* China/Nepal
157 I3 Chooz France
136 B5 Chop Ukr.
117 I7 Chopan *Uttar Prad.* India
116 E9 Chopda *Mahar.* India
255 B8 Chopimzinho Brazil
136 H3 Chopovychi Ukr.
233 I10 Choptank *r. MD* U.S.A.
122 C6 Choqāy Zanbil *tourist site* Iran
252 D4 Choquecamata Bol.
123 M9 Chor Pak.
198 G6 Chora Greece
198 G6 Chora Greece
198 C5 Chora Greece
198 C5 Chora *tourist site* Greece
199 H5 Chora *tourist site* Greece
199 F7 Chora Sfakion *Kriti* Greece
161 I7 Chorges France
185 K2 Chorito, Sierra del *mts* Spain
149 L6 Chorley *Lancashire, England* U.K.
151 K4 Chorleywood *Hertfordshire, England* U.K.
136 I6 Chorna Ukr.
137 M9 Chorna *r.* Ukr.
136 D5 Chorna Tysa Ukr.
136 E1 Chornaye, Vozyera *l.* Belarus
175 M5 Chorniyiv Ukr.
137 L4 Chornobay Ukr.
136 J2 Chornobyl' Ukr.
177 L3 Chornoholova Ukr.
137 J7 Chornomors'ke *Odes'ka Oblast'* Ukr.
135 F7 Chornomors'ke *Respublika Krym* Ukr.
137 K7 Chornomors'kyy Zapovidnyk *nature res.* Ukr.
136 I4 Chornorudka Ukr.
137 L3 Chornukhy Ukr.
137 J5 Chornyy Tashlyk *r.* Ukr.
129 C4 Chorokhi *r.* Georgia/Turkey
258 C3 Choros, Islas de los *is* Chile
175 K2 Choroszcz Pol.
85 I7 Chorregon *Qld* Austr.
254 F4 Chorrochó Brazil
136 E4 Chortkiv Ukr.
136 G4 Chorvoq Uzbek.
121 M7 Chorvoq suv ombori *resr* Kazakh./Uzbek.
116 C9 Chorwad *Gujarat* India
101 E9 Ch'ŏrwŏn S. Korea
175 I2 Chorzele Pol.
175 I4 Chorzów Pol.
101 D8 Ch'osan N. Korea
Chōsen-kaikyō *sea chan.* Japan/S. Korea *see* Nishi-suidō
105 M4 Chōshi Japan
259 B5 Choshuenco, Volcán *vol.* Chile
252 A2 Chosica Peru
260 B5 Chos Malal Arg.
260 D3 Chosmes Arg.
174 D2 Choszczno Pol.
250 B6 Chota Peru
117 I8 Chota Nagpur *reg. Chhattisgarh* India
177 K2 Chotča Slovakia
238 H3 Choteau *MT* U.S.A.
176 E2 Chotěboř Czech Rep.
176 C2 Chotěšov Czech Rep.
123 N7 Choti Pak.
116 C8 Chotila *Gujarat* India
177 H4 Chotín Slovakia
217 □3a Choua-chandroudé *i.* Comoros
204 D4 Chouikia *well* Alg.
156 H5 Chouilly France
204 B5 Choûm Maur.
184 C2 Chouto Port.
159 N6 Chouzy-sur-Cisse France
240 L4 Chowchilla *CA* U.S.A.
114 D7 Chowghat *Kerala* India
82 H5 Chowilla Regional Reserve *nature res.* S.A. Austr.
222 G4 Chown, Mount *Alta* Can.
258 D3 Choya Arg.
121 V2 Choya Rus. Fed.
107 N3 Choybalsan Mongolia
160 H2 Choye France
107 K3 Choyr Mongolia
182 I3 Chozas de Abajo Spain
Chozas de la Sierra Spain *see* Soto del Real
211 B7 Chozi Zambia
176 E2 Chrast Czech Rep.
176 C2 Chrást Czech Rep.
176 D1 Chrastava Czech Rep.
204 B5 Chreïrik *well* Maur.
171 J9 Chřibská Czech Rep.
176 G2 Chřiby *hills* Czech Rep.
236 L6 Chrisman *IL* U.S.A.
215 O2 Chrissiesmeer S. Africa
81 G10 Christchurch *South I.* N.Z.
151 I6 Christchurch *Dorset, England* U.K.
221 L2 Christian, Cape *Nunavut* Can.
246 □ Christiana Jamaica
215 J3 Christiana S. Africa
234 D5 Christiana *PA* U.S.A.
Christiania Norway *see* Oslo
227 N5 Christian Island *Ont.* Can.
232 E11 Christiansburg *VA* U.S.A.
142 F6 Christiansfeld Denmark
Christianshåb Greenland *see* Qasigiannguit
143 L6 Christiansø *i.* Denmark
222 C4 Christian Sound *sea chan. AK* U.S.A.
247 K5 Christiansted Virgin Is (U.S.A.)
226 D5 Christie *WI* U.S.A.
223 I3 Christie Bay *N.W.T.* Can.
223 I3 Christina *r. Alta* Can.
81 C11 Christina, Mount *South I.* N.Z.
149 L7 Christleton *Cheshire, England* U.K.
86 H5 Christmas Creek *W.A.* Austr.
86 H5 Christmas Creek *r. W.A.* Austr.
86 □1 Christmas Island *terr.* Indian Ocean
Christmas Island *atoll* Kiribati *see* Kiritimati
149 N2 Christon Bank *Northumberland, England* U.K.
87 I8 Christopher, Lake *salt flat W.A.* Austr.
176 E2 Chrudim Czech Rep.
175 H3 Chruślin Pol.
128 A3 Chrysochou Bay Cyprus
Chrysochous, Kolpos *b.* Cyprus *see* Chrysochou Bay
198 F2 Chrysoupoli Greece
148 I2 Chryston *North Lanarkshire, Scotland* U.K.
175 H5 Chrzanów Pol.
174 F4 Chrząstowa Wielka Pol.
174 G5 Chrząstowice Pol.
174 G3 Chrzypsko Wielkie Pol.
Chu Kazakh. *see* Shu
121 L5 Chu *r.* Kazakh.
117 L8 Chuadanga Bangl.
Chuanhui *Henan* China *see* Zhoukou
109 M3 Chuansha *Shanghai* China
108 B4 Chubalung *Sichuan* China
137 P6 Chubarivka Ukr.
Chubarovka Ukr. *see* Polohy
139 T6 Chubarovo Rus. Fed.
Chubartau Kazakh. *see* Barshatas
238 H5 Chubbuck *ID* U.S.A.
137 R7 Chuburka *r.* Rus. Fed.
104 G3 Chūbu-Sangaku Kokuritsu-kōen *nat. park* Japan
259 C6 Chubut *prov.* Arg.
259 D6 Chubut *r.* Arg.
106 F9 Chubxi *Qinghai* China
244 F6 Chucándiro Mex.
177 H2 Chuchelná Czech Rep.
135 H5 Chuchkovo Rus. Fed.
241 Q8 Chuckwalla Mountains *CA* U.S.A.
261 E3 Chucul Arg.
260 D2 Chucuma Arg.
242 □U13 Chucunaque *r.* Panama
150 E6 Chudleigh *Devon, England* U.K.
136 H3 Chudniv Ukr.
174 G5 Chudoba Pol.
139 O2 Chudovo Rus. Fed.
Chudskoye, Ozero *l.* Estonia/Rus. Fed. *see* Peipus, Lake
138 J9 Chudzin Belarus
220 D3 Chugach Mountains *AK* U.S.A.
103 J12 Chūgoku-sanchi *mts* Japan
Chugqênsumdo *Qinghai* China *see* Jigzhi
Chuguchak *Xinjiang* China *see* Tacheng
Chuguyev Ukr. *see* Chuhuyiv
100 H6 Chuguyevka Rus. Fed.
238 L6 Chugwater *WY* U.S.A.
Chuhai *Guangdong* China *see* Zhuhai
137 P4 Chuhuyiv Ukr.
121 P5 Chu-Iliyskiye Gory *mts* Kazakh.
Chuimatan *Gansu* China *see* Jishishan
Chujiang *Hunan* China *see* Shimen
108 B4 Chuka *Xizang* China
Chukai Malaysia *see* Cukai
100 J2 Chukchagirskoye, Ozero *l.* Rus. Fed.
Chukchi Peninsula Rus. Fed. *see* Chukotskiy Poluostrov
268 M1 Chukchi Plateau *sea feature* Arctic Ocean
220 A3 Chukchi Sea Rus. Fed./U.S.A.
134 H4 Chukhloma Rus. Fed.
131 T3 Chukotskiy, Mys *c.* Rus. Fed.
131 T3 Chukotskiy Poluostrov *pen.* Rus. Fed.
137 L7 Chulakivka Ukr.
Chulakkurgan Kazakh. *see* Sholakkorgan
Chulaktau Kazakh. *see* Karatau
96 E6 Chulaphon Reservoir Thai.
134 I2 Chulasa Rus. Fed.
240 O9 Chula Vista *CA* U.S.A.
187 D8 Chulilla Spain
139 T8 Chulkovo Rus. Fed.
185 I8 Chullera, Punta de la *pt* Spain
150 E6 Chulmleigh *Devon, England* U.K.
252 C6 Chulo Chile
250 A6 Chulucanas Peru
123 Q4 Chulung Pass Pak.
106 G2 Chuluut Gol *r.* Mongolia
130 J4 Chulym Rus. Fed.
110 H1 Chulyshman *r.* Rus. Fed.
134 M2 Chum Rus. Fed.
252 C3 Chuma Bol.
137 N6 Chumak Ukr.
116 G3 Chumar Jammu and Kashmir
210 C3 Chumba Eth.
258 D3 Chumbicha Arg.
108 A2 Chumda *Qinghai* China
124 H6 Chumek Kazakh.
197 N8 Chumerna *mt.* Bulg.
100 I1 Chumikan Rus. Fed.
129 C4 Ch'umlaqi Georgia
96 F6 Chum Phae Thai.
97 D9 Chumphon Thai.
96 E7 Chum Saeng Thai.
260 E2 Chuña Arg.
131 K4 Chuna *r.* Rus. Fed.
261 E1 Chuña Huasi Arg.
109 L4 Chun'an *Zhejiang* China
140 V3 Chuna-Tundra *plain* Rus. Fed.
101 E10 Ch'unch'ŏn S. Korea
117 L8 Chunchura *W. Bengal* India
121 R6 Chundzha Kazakh.
209 E8 Chunga Zambia
Chung-hua Jen-min Kung-ho-kuo *country* Asia *see* China
Chung-hua Min-kuo *country* Asia *see* Taiwan
101 E10 Ch'ungju S. Korea
Chungking *Chongqing* China *see* Chongqing
Ch'ungmu S. Korea *see* T'ongyŏng
101 D9 Chŭngsan N. Korea
211 C7 Chungu Tanz.
109 M7 Chungyang Shanmo *mts* Taiwan
100 G7 Chunhua *Jilin* China
108 G1 Chunhua *Shaanxi* China
243 O8 Chunhuhux Mex.
Chunxi *Jiangsu* China *see* Gaochun
131 K3 Chunya *r.* Rus. Fed.
211 B7 Chunya Tanz.
97 G10 Chuōi, Hon *i.* Vietnam
Chuosijia *Sichuan* China *see* Guanyinqiao
134 F2 Chupa Rus. Fed.
137 N3 Chupakhivka Ukr.
247 □7 Chupara Point Trin. and Tob.
122 B3 Chūplū Iran
136 J4 Chupyra Ukr.
252 C5 Chuquicamata Chile
252 D5 Chuquisaca *dept* Bol.
Chuqung *Qinghai* China *see* Chindu
Chur Switz.
190 H2 Chur Switz.
117 N7 Churachandpur *Manipur* India
134 K4 Churaki Rus. Fed.
122 F7 Chūrān Iran
131 O3 Churapcha Rus. Fed.
139 I5 Churapcha Rus. Fed.
151 M3 Church End *Essex, England* U.K.
148 B4 Church Hill Ireland
234 D6 Church Hill *MD* U.S.A.
232 C12 Church Hill *TN* U.S.A.
223 M3 Churchill *Man.* Can.
225 I2 Churchill *r. Nfld and Lab.* Can.
223 M3 Churchill, Cape *Man.* Can.
225 I2 Churchill Falls *Nfld and Lab.* Can.
223 I4 Churchill Lake *Sask.* Can.
263 K1 Churchill Mountains Antarctica
222 E3 Churchill Peak *B.C.* Can.
224 E1 Churchill Sound *sea chan. Nunavut* Can.
149 M7 Church Lawton *Cheshire, England* U.K.
236 F1 Churchs Ferry *ND* U.S.A.
150 G2 Church Stretton *Shropshire, England* U.K.
234 B7 Churchton *MD* U.S.A.
147 E8 Churchtown *Cork* Ireland
147 F9 Churchtown *Cork* Ireland
234 D4 Churchtown *PA* U.S.A.
234 C5 Churchville *MD* U.S.A.
232 F10 Churchville *VA* U.S.A.
106 B1 Chureg-Tag, Gora *mt.* Rus. Fed.
117 J6 Churia Ghati Hills Nepal
139 N6 Churilovo Rus. Fed.
252 A2 Churin Peru
129 H3 Churkey Rus. Fed.
129 H3 Churkeyskoye Vodokhranilishche *resr* Rus. Fed.
222 F5 Churn Creek Provincial Park *B.C.* Can.
134 I4 Churovichi Rus. Fed.
137 L1 Churovichi Rus. Fed.
116 E5 Churu *Rajasthan* India
Churubay Nura Kazakh. *see* Abay
226 I8 Churubusco *IN* U.S.A.
250 D2 Churuguara Venez.
102 U4 Chūrui Japan
123 K1 Churuk Uzbek.
244 F7 Churumuco Mex.
190 H2 Churwalden Switz.
137 N7 Churyuk, Ostriv *i.* Ukr.
97 I8 Chư Sê Vietnam
116 G3 Chushul Jammu and Kashmir
241 W5 Chuska Mountains *NM* U.S.A.
134 L4 Chusovaya *r.* Rus. Fed.
134 L3 Chusovoy Rus. Fed.
134 L3 Chusovskoye Rus. Fed.
Chust Ukr. *see* Khust
121 N7 Chust Uzbek.
225 G3 Chute-des-Passes *Que.* Can.
227 R3 Chute-Rouge *Que.* Can.
117 N6 Chutia *Assam* India
137 O4 Chutove Ukr.
109 M6 Chutung Taiwan
78 □4a Chuuk *is* Micronesia
134 L3 Chuval Rus. Fed.
Chuvashia *aut. rep.* Rus. Fed. *see* Chuvashskaya Respublika
Chuvashskaya A.S.S.R. *aut. rep.* Rus. Fed. *see* Chuvashskaya Respublika
135 I5 Chuvashskaya Respublika *aut. rep.* Rus. Fed.
129 I4 Chuvek Rus. Fed.
101 F10 Chuwang-san National Park S. Korea
108 C6 Chuxiong *Yunnan* China
121 P6 Chüy *admin. div.* Kyrg.
258 G4 Chuy Uru.
Chuyskaya Oblast' *admin. div.* Kyrg. *see* Chüy
160 F5 Chuzelles France
105 J2 Chūzenji-ko *l.* Japan
109 L2 Chuzhou *Anhui* China
109 L2 Chuzhou *Jiangsu* China
104 D5 Chūzu Japan
176 D3 Chvalšiny Czech Rep.
127 L6 Chwārtā Iraq
174 G1 Chwaszczyno Pol.
Chwitffordd *Flintshire, Wales* U.K. *see* Whitford
Chwitffordd *Wales* U.K. *see* Whitford
174 G6 Chybie Pol.
136 K6 Chychyklyya *r.* Ukr.
138 M8 Chyhirynskaye Vodaskhovishcha *resr* Belarus
137 L4 Chyhyryn Ukr.
Chymyshliya Moldova *see* Cimişlia
136 B5 Chynadiyeve Ukr.
171 J10 Chyňava Czech Rep.
175 J4 Chynów Pol.
175 M2 Chyrvonae Syalo Belarus
138 K9 Chyrvonaya Slabada Belarus
138 K9 Chyrvonaya Slabada Belarus
136 G1 Chyrvonaye, Vozyera *l.* Belarus
Chysten'ke Ukr.
137 N9 Chystopillya Ukr.
137 P8 Chystyakove Ukr. *see* Torez
Chyulu Range *mts* Kenya
211 C5 Chyyyrchyk Ashuusu *pass* Kyrg.
121 O7 Chyzhykiv Ukr.
175 M6 Ciacova Romania
196 J5 Ciadâr-Lunga Moldova *see* Ciadîr-Lunga
Ciadîr-Lunga Moldova
136 H7 Ciadoux France
163 F9 Ciagola, Monte *mt.* Italy
193 P8 Ciales Puerto Rico
247 □1 Ciamannacce *Corse* France
192 C4 Ciamis *Jawa* Indon.
95 H8 Ciampino Italy
193 J4 Ciampino *airport* Italy
193 J4 Cianciana *Sicilia* Italy
194 E8 Cianjur *Jawa* Indon.
94 G8 Cianorte Brazil
256 A5 Ciang *r.* France
161 K9 Cians *r.* France
175 J5 Ciasna Pol.
174 F3 Ciążeń Pol.
94 G8 Cibadak *Jawa* Indon.
177 J5 Cibakháza Hungary
95 H8 Cibatu *Jawa* Indon.
241 V7 Cibecue *AZ* U.S.A.
94 G8 Cibinong *Jawa* Indon.
211 A5 Cibitoke Burundi
237 G11 Cibolo Creek *r. TX* U.S.A.
184 C3 Ciborro Port.
242 D2 Cibuta Mex.
242 D2 Cibuta, Sierra *mt.* Mex.
190 G7 Cicagna Italy
196 E4 Čićarija *mts* Croatia
190 D2 Cicciano Italy
126 G4 Çiçekdağı Turkey
128 D2 Çiçekli *İçel* Turkey
128 D2 Çiçekli *Manisa* Turkey
199 J3 Cicerale Italy
193 O7 Cicero *IL* U.S.A.
226 G8 Cicero Dantas Brazil
254 F4 Cićevac Serbia
196 J7 Cicha Woda *r.* Pol.
174 E4 Cicibór Duży Pol.
175 L3 Čičov Slovakia
177 G4 Cidacos *r.* Spain
183 Q4 Cidaun *Jawa* Indon.
94 G8 Cide Turkey
126 F3 Cidlina *r.* Czech Rep.
176 E1 Cidones Spain
185 O1 Cidra Puerto Rico
247 □1 Ciechanów Pol.
175 I3 Ciechanowiec Pol.
175 K3 Ciechocinek Pol.
174 G3 Ciego de Ávila Cuba
246 D3 Ciemas *Jawa* Indon.
175 I4 Cielądz Pol.
260 C3 Cielo, Cerro *mt.* Arg.
94 G8 Ciemas *Jawa* Indon.
183 M8 Ciempozuelos Spain
250 C2 Ciénaga Col.
250 D2 Ciénagas del Catatumbo *nat. park* Venez.
243 I5 Ciénega Mex.
246 C2 Cieneguillas Mex.
246 C2 Cienfuegos Cuba
174 F3 Cienin Zaborny Pol.
175 J4 Ciepielów Pol.
175 H3 Ciepłowody Pol.
163 F10 Cier-de-Luchon France
177 G3 Čierna Voda Slovakia
177 H3 Čierna voda *r.* Slovakia
177 K3 Čierne Kľačany Slovakia
177 I3 Čierny Balog Slovakia
163 F10 Cierp-Gaud France
174 F2 Cierznie Pol.
182 C4 Cies, Illas *is* Spain
175 I4 Cieszanów Pol.
174 G6 Cieszków Pol.
Cieszyn *Śląskie* Pol.
174 F4 Cieszyn *Wielkopolskie* Pol.
163 E9 Cieutat France
162 G4 Cieux France
187 C11 Cieza Spain
175 I6 Ciężkowice Pol.
128 F2 Çiftlikköy Turkey
199 M3 Çifteler Turkey
Çiftlik Turkey *see* Kelkit
129 C6 Çiftlikköy *Erzurum* Turkey
199 J1 Çiftlikköy *İstanbul* Turkey
183 O7 Cifuentes Spain
183 K5 Cigales Spain
177 K3 Cigánd Hungary
129 C6 Çiğdemli Turkey
94 F8 Cigeulis *Jawa* Indon.
129 K6 Çigil Adası *i.* Azer.
190 E5 Cigliano Italy
183 M10 Cigüela *r.* Spain
126 F4 Cihanbeyli Turkey
199 K3 Cihangazi Turkey
244 C6 Cihuatlán Mex.
185 J2 Cijara, Embalse de *resr* Spain
117 J6 Čik *r.* Serbia
Cikai *Yunnan* China *see* Gongshan
95 H8 Cikalong *Jawa* Indon.
198 A2 Çikes, Maja e *mt.* Albania
79 □7 Cikobia *i.* Fiji
188 F4 Čikola *r.* Croatia
95 H8 Cilacap *Jawa* Indon.
94 G8 Cilangkahan *Jawa* Indon.
217 □1c Cilaos Réunion
217 □1c Cilaos, Cirque de *vol. crater* Réunion
127 K3 Çıldır Turkey
127 K3 Çıldır Gölü *l.* Turkey
128 F2 Çıldıroba Turkey
95 H8 Ciledug *Jawa* Indon.
193 O7 Cilento e del Vallo di Diano, Parco Nazionale del *nat. park* Italy
129 A5 Çilhorozdağı Geçidi *pass* Turkey
109 H4 Cili *Hunan* China
128 B2 Cilicia *reg.* Turkey
Cilician Gates *pass* Turkey *see* Gülek Boğazı
197 M7 Cilieni Romania
199 M2 Cilimli Turkey
Cill Airne Ireland *see* Killarney
183 Q7 Cillas Spain
Cill Chainnigh Ireland *see* Kilkenny
146 B8 Cille Bhrighde *Western Isles, Scotland* U.K.
182 G8 Cilleros Spain
129 F6 Çilli Geçidi *pass* Turkey
Cill Mhantáin Ireland *see* Wicklow
122 F1 Çilmämmetgum *des.* Turkm.
127 L5 Cilo Dağı *mt.* Turkey
129 L5 Çiloy Azer.
129 L5 Çiloy Adası *i.* Azer.
150 E4 Cilybebyll *Neath Port Talbot, Wales* U.K.
150 E3 Cilycwm *Carmarthenshire, Wales* U.K.
241 Q6 Cima *CA* U.S.A.
184 □ Cima, Ilhéu de *i.* Madeira
94 G8 Cimahi *Jawa* Indon.
182 I3 Cimanes del Tejar Spain
237 E7 Cimarron *KS* U.S.A.
239 L8 Cimarron *NM* U.S.A.
237 G7 Cimarron *r. OK* U.S.A.
239 L8 Cimarron Creek *r. CO* U.S.A.
183 Q6 Cimballa Spain
194 F8 Ciminna *Sicilia* Italy
192 I3 Cimino, Monte *mt.* Italy
136 H7 Cimişlia Moldova
191 M3 Cimolais Italy
191 J7 Cimone, Monte *mt.* Italy
Cîmpeni Romania *see* Câmpeni
Cîmpia Turzii Romania *see* Câmpia Turzii
Cîmpina Romania *see* Câmpina
Cîmpulung Romania *see* Câmpulung
Cîmpulung la Tisa Romania *see* Câmpulung la Tisa
Cîmpulung Moldovenesc Romania *see* Câmpulung Moldovenesc
94 F7 Cina, Tanjung *c.* Indon.
127 J5 Çınar Turkey
199 K2 Çınarcık Turkey
250 E3 Cinaruco *r.* Venez.
250 E3 Cinaruco-Capanaparo, Parque Nacional *nat. park* Venez.
186 F3 Cinca *r.* Spain
186 F5 Cinca *r.* Spain
188 F4 Cincar *mt.* Bos.-Herz.
236 M6 Cincinnati *OH* U.S.A.
233 J6 Cincinnatus *NY* U.S.A.
246 D3 Cinco-Balas, Cayos *is* Cuba
185 M2 Cinco Casas Spain
Cinco de Outubro Angola *see* Xá-Muteba
260 C5 Cinco Saltos Arg.
186 C5 Cinco Villas *reg.* Spain
186 E6 Cinctorres Spain
197 M5 Cincu Romania
150 H4 Cinderford *Gloucestershire, England* U.K.
199 J5 Çine Turkey
199 J5 Çine *r.* Turkey
199 I5 Cinera Spain
182 I3 Ciney Belgium
165 H8 Cinfães Port.
182 D6 Cingoli Italy
191 O9 Cinigiano Italy
192 G2 Cinisello Balsamo Italy
190 G4 Cinisi *Sicilia* Italy
194 E7 Cinobaña Slovakia
177 I3 Cinq-Mars-la-Pile France
159 L7 Cinquefrondi Italy
195 K7 Cinque Island *Andaman & Nicobar Is* India
115 M7 Cinque Terre *reg.* Italy
190 H7 Cintalapa Mex.
245 N9 Cintegabelle France
163 H9 Cinto, Monte *mt.* France
192 B3 Cintra Arg.
261 F3 Cintrão, Ponta do *pt São Miguel* Azores
216 □1b Cintrey France
157 K8 Cintruénigo Spain
183 Q4 Cintsa S. Africa
215 M8 Cinzas *r.* Brazil
256 B5 Ciolpani Romania
197 O6 Ciordan, Dealul *hill* Romania
177 L6 Čiovo *i.* Croatia
188 F4 Cipatuja *Jawa* Indon.
95 H8 Ciping *Jiangxi* China *see* Jinggangshan
254 F4 Cipó Brazil
257 E3 Cipó *r.* Brazil
260 D6 Cipolletti Arg.
257 F4 Cipotânea Brazil
129 H5 Çıraqdärä Azer.
187 C7 Cirat Spain
94 G8 Cirata, Waduk *resr Jawa* Indon.
182 I3 Cirbanal *mt.* Spain
193 N5 Circello Italy
193 K5 Circeo, Monte *hill* Italy
193 J5 Circeo, Parco Nazionale del *nat. park* Italy
220 D3 Circle *AK* U.S.A.
238 L3 Circle *MT* U.S.A.
232 C9 Circleville *OH* U.S.A.
241 T3 Circleville *UT* U.S.A.
95 H8 Cirebon *Jawa* Indon.
151 I4 Cirencester *Gloucestershire, England* U.K.
Cirene *tourist site* Libya *see* Cyrene
94 D5 Cirenti *Sumatera* Indon.
157 I7 Cirey-sur-Blaise France
157 M6 Cirey-sur-Vezouze France
183 Q5 Ciria Spain
190 D5 Ciriè Italy
193 Q7 Cirigliano Italy
136 H5 Ciripcău Moldova
138 J5 Ciriss *l.* Latvia
195 □ Cirkewwa, Il-Ponta tac- *pt* Malta
195 M5 Cirò Italy
177 K3 Cirocha *r.* Slovakia

195 M5 Cirò Marina Italy
163 D6 Ciron r. France
225 I1 Cirque Mountain Nfld and Lab. Can.
Cirta Alg. see Constantine
183 M9 Ciruelos Spain
160 E3 Ciry-le-Noble France
190 H7 Cisa, Passo della pass Italy
190 E7 Cisano sul Neva Italy
241 W3 Cisco UT U.S.A.
178 E7 Cismòn r. Italy
175 K6 Cisna Pol.
197 M5 Cisnădie Romania
246 B5 Cisne, Islas del is Caribbean Sea
183 K4 Cisneros Spain
258 E3 Cisnes, Lagunas de los lakes Arg.
191 M4 Cisòn di Valmarino Italy
177 J1 Cisowsko-Orłowiński Park Krajobrazowy Pol.
159 L8 Cissé France
193 J4 Cisterna di Latina Italy
195 M2 Cisternino Italy
246 E2 Cistern Point Andros Bahamas
183 J3 Cistierna Spain
246 G4 Citadelle/Sans Souci/Ramiers tourist site Haiti
191 M9 Citerna Italy
245 J4 Citlaltepec Mex.
Citlaltépetl vol. Mex. see Orizaba, Pico de
188 F4 Čitluk Bos.-Herz.
163 J9 Citou France
237 K10 Citronelle AL U.S.A.
214 D8 Citrusdal S. Africa
240 K3 Citrus Heights CA U.S.A.
191 L4 Cittadella Italy
193 P8 Cittadella del Capo c. Italy
192 I2 Città della Pieve Italy
191 M9 Città di Castello Italy
190 D5 Città di Torino airport Italy
193 J3 Cittaducale Italy
195 K7 Cittanova Italy
193 K2 Cittareale Italy
193 M2 Città Sant'Angelo Italy
190 F4 Cittiglio Italy
147 H2 City of Derry airport Northern Ireland U.K.
197 N5 Ciucaş, Vârful mt. Romania
197 K4 Ciucea Romania
243 I3 Ciudad Acuña Mex.
244 G7 Ciudad Altamirano Mex.
251 F2 Ciudad Bolívar Venez.
242 G4 Ciudad Camargo Mex.
242 D5 Ciudad Constitución Baja California Sur Mex.
243 N10 Ciudad Cuauhtémoc Mex.
243 N8 Ciudad del Carmen Mex.
253 G6 Ciudad del Este Para.
242 G3 Ciudad Delicias Mex.
245 H3 Ciudad del Maíz Mex.
245 H4 Ciudad de Valles Mex.
251 F2 Ciudad Guayana Venez.
244 D6 Ciudad Guzmán Mex.
244 G6 Ciudad Hidalgo Mex.
245 L9 Ciudad Ixtepec Mex.
242 F2 Ciudad Juárez Mex.
242 H5 Ciudad Lerdo Mex.
245 H6 Ciudad López Mateos Mex.
245 J3 Ciudad Madero Mex.
245 I3 Ciudad Mante Mex.
244 F5 Ciudad Manuel Doblado Mex.
245 J7 Ciudad Mendoza Mex.
243 J4 Ciudad Mier Mex.
242 E4 Ciudad Obregón Mex.
246 H8 Ciudad Ojeda Venez.
251 F3 Ciudad Piar Venez.
185 L3 Ciudad Real Spain
185 M3 Ciudad Real prov. Spain
243 J5 Ciudad Río Bravo Mex.
182 G7 Ciudad Rodrigo Spain
245 J7 Ciudad Serdán Mex.
243 M10 Ciudad Tecún Uman Guat.
Ciudad Trujillo Dom. Rep. see Santo Domingo
245 H2 Ciudad Victoria Mex.
197 J5 Ciudanoviţa Romania
177 L4 Ciuhoi Romania
136 G6 Ciuhur r. Moldova
136 H6 Ciulucal de Mijloc r. Moldova
197 N4 Ciumani Romania
177 K5 Ciumeghiu Romania
186 □ Ciutadella Spain
126 H3 Cıva Burnu pt Turkey
162 F3 Civaux France
191 M3 Civetta, Monte mt. Italy
191 O3 Cividale del Friuli Italy
193 Q8 Civita Italy
193 I3 Civita Castellana Italy
193 K4 Civita d'Antino Italy
191 P9 Civitanova Marche Italy
193 L3 Civitaquana Italy
192 H3 Civitavecchia Italy
192 H2 Civitella, Monte mt. Italy
193 L3 Civitella Casanova Italy
192 I2 Civitella d'Agliano Italy
191 L7 Civitella di Romagna Italy
191 L9 Civitella in Val di Chiana Italy
193 K4 Civitella Roveto Italy
159 P8 Civray Centre France
162 E3 Civray Poitou-Charentes France
199 K4 Çivril Turkey
192 C9 Cixerri r. Sardegna Italy
109 M3 Cixi Zhejiang China
107 N8 Cixian Hebei China
107 O9 Ciyao Shandong China
177 L4 Cizer Romania
Cizhou Hebei China see Cixian
171 J10 Čížkovice Czech Rep.
127 K5 Cizre Turkey
176 C2 Čkyně Czech Rep.
146 C9 Clabhach Argyll and Bute, Scotland U.K.
146 E11 Clachan Argyll and Bute, Scotland U.K.
146 D8 Clachan Highland, Scotland U.K.
Clachan Strachur Scotland U.K. see Strachur
238 C4 Clackamas r. OR U.S.A.
146 I10 Clackmannanshire admin. div. Scotland U.K.
151 O4 Clacton-on-Sea Essex, England U.K.
146 F10 Cladich Argyll and Bute, Scotland U.K.
148 B4 Clady Northern Ireland U.K.
147 I3 Clady Northern Ireland U.K.
150 E3 Claerwen Reservoir Wales U.K.
146 E9 Claggan Highland, Scotland U.K.
146 C7 Claidh, Loch inlet Scotland U.K.
162 F2 Clain r. France
163 E7 Clairac France
223 H3 Claire, Lake Alta Can.
238 C6 Clair Engle Lake resr CA U.S.A.
222 G4 Clairmont Alta Can.
156 E5 Clairoix France
163 I7 Clairvaux-d'Aveyron France
160 H3 Clairvaux-les-Lacs France
162 F2 Claise r. France
161 H6 Claix France
160 D2 Clamecy France
226 D3 Clam Lake WI U.S.A.
148 C4 Clanabogan Northern Ireland U.K.
240 O2 Clan Alpine Mountains NV U.S.A.
81 F11 Clandeboye South I. N.Z.
147 I6 Clane Ireland
151 I4 Clanfield Oxfordshire, England U.K.
161 K8 Clans France
231 D9 Clanton AL U.S.A.
215 L7 Clanville S. Africa
214 C8 Clanwilliam S. Africa
214 C8 Clanwilliam Dam S. Africa
146 F11 Claonaig Argyll and Bute, Scotland U.K.
151 L3 Clapham Bedfordshire, England U.K.
149 M5 Clapham North Yorkshire, England U.K.
146 H6 Clar, Loch nan l. Scotland U.K.
261 H2 Clara Arg.
85 H5 Clara r. Qld Austr.
147 G6 Clara Ireland
259 D6 Clara, Punta pt Arg.
97 C9 Clara Island Myanmar
85 H5 Claraville Qld Austr.
261 H5 Claraz Arg.
149 P7 Clarborough Nottinghamshire, England U.K.
83 I5 Clare N.S.W. Austr.
82 G5 Clare S.A. Austr.
147 E7 Clare county Ireland
147 D6 Clare r. Ireland
151 N3 Clare Suffolk, England U.K.
226 J6 Clare MI U.S.A.
147 E7 Clarecastle Ireland
147 G6 Clareen Ireland
147 E6 Claregalway Ireland
147 B5 Clare Island Ireland
246 □ Claremont Jamaica
233 M5 Claremont NH U.S.A.
85 I2 Claremont Isles Qld Austr.
237 H7 Claremore OK U.S.A.
147 E5 Claremorris Ireland
83 N3 Clarence r. N.S.W. Austr.
81 H9 Clarence South I. N.Z.
81 H9 Clarence r. South I. N.Z.
259 C9 Clarence, Isla i. Chile
216 □2a Clarence Bay Ascension S. Atlantic Ocean
262 U2 Clarence Island Antarctica
84 C1 Clarence Strait N.T. Austr.
222 C3 Clarence Strait AK U.S.A.
246 F2 Clarence Town Long I. Bahamas
246 □ Clarendon parish Jamaica
81 E13 Clarendon South I. N.Z.
237 J8 Clarendon AR U.S.A.
232 F7 Clarendon PA U.S.A.
237 E8 Clarendon TX U.S.A.
246 □ Clarendon Park Jamaica
215 M4 Clarens S. Africa
225 K3 Clarenville Nfld and Lab. Can.
222 H5 Claresholm Alta Can.
161 D9 Claret Languedoc-Roussillon France
161 H8 Claret Provence-Alpes-Côte d'Azur France
187 E9 Clariano r. Spain
85 H4 Clarina Creek r. Qld Austr.
236 H5 Clarinda IA U.S.A.
247 K9 Clarines Venez.
232 E9 Clarington OH U.S.A.
236 I4 Clarion IA U.S.A.
232 F7 Clarion PA U.S.A.
232 F7 Clarion r. PA U.S.A.
228 D7 Clarión, Isla i. Mex.
246 G3 Clarion Bank sea feature Bahamas
80 J3 Claris North I. N.Z.
236 G3 Clark SD U.S.A.
222 F1 Clark, Mount N.W.T. Can.
234 B4 Clark Creek r. PA U.S.A.
241 T7 Clarkdale AZ U.S.A.
85 J5 Clarke r. Qld Austr.
215 M7 Clarkebury S. Africa
83 L9 Clarke Island Tas. Austr.
85 K6 Clarke Range mts Qld Austr.
85 J5 Clarke River Qld Austr.
85 H4 Clarkes Creek r. Qld Austr.
225 K3 Clarke's Head Nfld and Lab. Can.
231 F8 Clarkesville GA U.S.A.
238 F2 Clark Fork r. ID U.S.A.
238 F2 Clark Fork r. MT U.S.A.
231 F9 Clark Hill Reservoir GA/SC U.S.A.
241 Q6 Clark Mountain CA U.S.A.
262 O1 Clark Mountains Antarctica
224 D4 Clark Point Ont. Can.
235 G4 Clarksburg NJ U.S.A.
232 E9 Clarksburg WV U.S.A.
237 J8 Clarksdale MS U.S.A.
238 J4 Clark's Fork Yellowstone r. MT U.S.A.
81 E12 Clarks Junction South I. N.Z.
214 I10 Clarkson S. Africa
234 D1 Clarks Summit PA U.S.A.
238 F3 Clarkston WA U.S.A.
246 □ Clark's Town Jamaica
237 I8 Clarksville AR U.S.A.
234 B6 Clarksville MD U.S.A.
231 D7 Clarksville TN U.S.A.
237 H9 Clarksville TX U.S.A.
232 G12 Clarksville VA U.S.A.
256 B1 Claro r. Brazil
256 B3 Claro r. Brazil
190 G3 Claro Switz.
261 G6 Claromecó Arg.
156 F3 Clary France
146 H7 Clashmore Highland, Scotland U.K.
146 F6 Clashnessie Highland, Scotland U.K.
238 C3 Clatskanie OR U.S.A.
146 H12 Clatteringshaws Loch l. Scotland U.K.
237 E8 Claude TX U.S.A.
257 E4 Cláudio Brazil
261 G6 Claudio Molina Arg.
147 H3 Claudy Northern Ireland U.K.
171 H9 Clausnitz Ger.
234 D3 Claussville PA U.S.A.
169 J7 Clausthal-Zellerfeld Ger.
191 N3 Claut Italy
191 N3 Clauzetto Italy
92 C2 Claveria Luzon Phil.
151 M4 Clavering Essex, England U.K.
221 P2 Clavering Ø i. Greenland
150 H2 Claverley Shropshire, England U.K.
165 H8 Clavier Belgium
231 G9 Claxton GA U.S.A.
234 C4 Clay PA U.S.A.
232 D10 Clay WV U.S.A.
233 L4 Clayburg NY U.S.A.
236 G6 Clay Center KS U.S.A.
236 F5 Clay Center NE U.S.A.
232 B11 Clay City KY U.S.A.
149 O7 Clay Cross Derbyshire, England U.K.
151 O3 Claydon Suffolk, England U.K.
156 E6 Claye-Souilly France
148 I5 Clay Head Isle of Man
241 S4 Clayhole Wash watercourse AZ U.S.A.
234 E5 Claymont DE U.S.A.
149 P7 Claypole Lincolnshire, England U.K.
241 V8 Claypool AZ U.S.A.
241 V7 Clay Springs AZ U.S.A.
151 L6 Clayton West Sussex, England U.K.
231 E10 Clayton AL U.S.A.
234 D6 Clayton DE U.S.A.
231 F8 Clayton GA U.S.A.
234 E5 Clayton NJ U.S.A.
237 D7 Clayton NM U.S.A.
233 I4 Clayton NY U.S.A.
237 H8 Clayton OK U.S.A.
233 □P2 Clayton Lake ME U.S.A.
149 M6 Clayton-le-Moors Lancashire, England U.K.
232 E11 Claytor Lake VA U.S.A.
261 H3 Clé r. Arg.
146 D9 Cleadale Highland, Scotland U.K.
149 O4 Cleadon Tyne and Wear, England U.K.
147 C9 Cleady Ireland
147 C10 Clear, Cape Ireland
232 E10 Clearco WV U.S.A.
227 N7 Clear Creek Ont. Can.
241 U2 Clear Creek UT U.S.A.
241 V7 Clear Creek r. AZ U.S.A.
238 K4 Clear Creek r. WY U.S.A.
232 G7 Clearfield PA U.S.A.
238 H6 Clearfield UT U.S.A.
237 F9 Clear Fork Brazos r. TX U.S.A.
222 G3 Clear Hills Y.T. Can.
147 D10 Clear Island Ireland
236 I4 Clear Lake IA U.S.A.
236 G3 Clear Lake SD U.S.A.
226 B4 Clear Lake WI U.S.A.
240 J2 Clear Lake l. CA U.S.A.
241 T2 Clear Lake l. UT U.S.A.
240 J2 Clearlake Oaks CA U.S.A.
238 D6 Clear Lake Reservoir CA U.S.A.
238 K4 Clearmont WY U.S.A.
232 H9 Clear Spring MD U.S.A.
222 G5 Clearwater B.C. Can.
222 H4 Clearwater r. Alta Can.
223 I3 Clearwater r. Alta/Sask. Can.
231 F12 Clearwater FL U.S.A.
238 F3 Clearwater r. ID U.S.A.
236 G2 Clearwater r. MN U.S.A.
Clear Water Bay H.K. China see Tsing Shui Wan
223 K4 Clearwater Lake l. Man. Can.
226 E4 Clearwater Lake WI U.S.A.
223 K4 Clearwater Lake Provincial Park Man. Can.
238 G4 Clearwater Mountains ID U.S.A.
223 I3 Clearwater River Provincial Park Sask. Can.
149 J4 Cleator Moor Cumbria, England U.K.
237 G9 Cleburne TX U.S.A.
159 K4 Clécy France
158 C4 Cléder France
150 G3 Cleehill Shropshire, England U.K.
238 D3 Cle Elum WA U.S.A.
149 Q6 Cleethorpes North East Lincolnshire, England U.K.
157 K7 Clefmont France
158 E6 Cléguer France
158 E5 Cléguérec France
150 G3 Clehonger Herefordshire, England U.K.
197 N6 Clejani Romania
161 H7 Clelles France
165 I9 Clémency Lux.
251 H4 Clément Fr. Guiana
94 □ Clementi Sing.
256 B4 Clementina Brazil
231 F8 Clemson SC U.S.A.
232 D10 Clendenin WV U.S.A.
232 D8 Clendening Lake OH U.S.A.
168 K5 Clenze Ger.
150 H3 Cleobury Mortimer Shropshire, England U.K.
156 B5 Cléon France
234 C4 Cleona PA U.S.A.
161 F7 Cléon-d'Andran France
92 B6 Cleopatra Needle mt. Palawan Phil.
159 L7 Cléré-les-Pins France
156 B4 Clères France
156 H7 Clérey France
Clerf Lux. see Clervaux
227 P1 Cléricy Que. Can.
161 F6 Clérieux France
81 A12 Clerke, Mount South I. N.Z.
86 E4 Clerke Reef W.A. Austr.
160 F4 Clermain France
85 K7 Clermont Qld Austr.
163 G9 Clermont Midi-Pyrénées France
156 D5 Clermont Picardie France
215 O5 Clermont S. Africa
231 G11 Clermont FL U.S.A.
159 K6 Clermont-Créans France
162 F6 Clermont-de-Beauregard France
Clermont de Tonnère atoll Arch. des Tuamotu Fr. Polynesia see Reao
157 J5 Clermont-en-Argonne France
160 C5 Clermont-Ferrand France
161 C9 Clermont-l'Hérault France
160 J2 Clerval France
165 J8 Clervaux Lux.
165 J9 Clervé r. Lux.
156 E7 Cléry r. France
156 C8 Cléry-St-André France
191 K3 Cles Italy
82 F5 Cleve S.A. Austr.
150 G5 Clevedon North Somerset, England U.K.
231 F8 Cleveland GA U.S.A.
237 J9 Cleveland MS U.S.A.
232 D7 Cleveland OH U.S.A.
231 E8 Cleveland TN U.S.A.
237 H10 Cleveland TX U.S.A.
241 V2 Cleveland UT U.S.A.
232 C12 Cleveland VA U.S.A.
226 G6 Cleveland WI U.S.A.
85 K5 Cleveland, Cape Qld Austr.
238 H2 Cleveland, Mount MT U.S.A.
85 K5 Cleveland Bay Qld Austr.
232 D7 Cleveland Heights OH U.S.A.
149 O5 Cleveland Hills England U.K.
255 B8 Clevelândia Brazil
222 C4 Cleveland Peninsula AK U.S.A.
149 K6 Cleveleys Lancashire, England U.K.
Cleves Ger. see Kleve
147 C5 Clew Bay Ireland
215 N1 Clewer S. Africa
231 G12 Clewiston FL U.S.A.
81 B13 Clifden South I. N.Z.
147 B6 Clifden Ireland
84 G4 Cliffdale r. Qld Austr.
151 M5 Cliffe Medway, England U.K.
151 M5 Cliffe Woods Medway, England U.K.
147 F4 Cliffoney Ireland
215 L7 Clifford S. Africa
234 D1 Clifford PA U.S.A.
81 I8 Clifford Bay South I. N.Z.
214 A5 Cliff Point S. Africa
232 E10 Clifftop WV U.S.A.
85 M9 Clifton Qld Austr.
231 □2 Clifton New Prov. Bahamas
151 L3 Clifton Bedfordshire, England U.K.
241 W8 Clifton AZ U.S.A.
226 G9 Clifton IL U.S.A.
236 G6 Clifton KS U.S.A.
235 G3 Clifton NJ U.S.A.
234 D2 Clifton PA U.S.A.
85 J4 Clifton Beach Qld Austr.
232 F11 Clifton Forge VA U.S.A.
82 G2 Clifton Hills S.A. Austr.
233 L6 Clifton Park NY U.S.A.
231 □2 Clifton Point New Prov. Bahamas
223 I5 Climax Sask. Can.
226 I7 Climax MI U.S.A.
232 B12 Clinch r. TN U.S.A.
232 C11 Clinchco VA U.S.A.
232 C12 Clinch Mountain mts TN/VA U.S.A.
232 C12 Clinchport VA U.S.A.
222 G4 Cline River Alta Can.
165 F6 Clinge Neth.
169 K8 Clingen Ger.
222 F5 Clinton B.C. Can.
224 D5 Clinton Ont. Can.
81 D13 Clinton South I. N.Z.
237 I8 Clinton AR U.S.A.
235 J2 Clinton CT U.S.A.
230 B5 Clinton IA U.S.A.
236 K5 Clinton IL U.S.A.
237 K7 Clinton KY U.S.A.
237 J10 Clinton LA U.S.A.
233 □P4 Clinton ME U.S.A.
227 K7 Clinton MI U.S.A.
236 I6 Clinton MO U.S.A.
237 J9 Clinton MS U.S.A.
231 H8 Clinton NC U.S.A.
233 J5 Clinton NY U.S.A.
232 D8 Clinton OH U.S.A.
237 F8 Clinton OK U.S.A.
231 E7 Clinton TN U.S.A.
223 J1 Clinton-Colden Lake N.W.T. Can.
226 F5 Clintonville WI U.S.A.
232 E11 Clintonville WV U.S.A.
232 C11 Clintwood VA U.S.A.
231 E10 Clio AL U.S.A.
227 K6 Clio MI U.S.A.
159 N8 Clion France
218 E7 Clipperton, Île terr. N. Pacific Ocean
146 C7 Clisham hill Scotland U.K.
158 I7 Clisson France
149 M6 Clitheroe Lancashire, England U.K.
80 K6 Clive North I. N.Z.
222 G2 Clive Lake N.W.T. Can.
252 D4 Cliza Bol.
87 B7 Cloates, Point W.A. Austr.
215 L4 Clocolan S. Africa
147 H7 Clogh Kilkenny Ireland
147 J7 Clogh Wexford Ireland
147 J3 Clogh Northern Ireland U.K.
147 G3 Cloghan Donegal Ireland
147 G6 Cloghan Offaly Ireland
148 C6 Cloghan Westmeath Ireland
147 B8 Cloghane Ireland
147 E3 Cloghboy Ireland
147 G8 Clogheen Ireland
147 D5 Clogher Ireland
147 H4 Clogher Northern Ireland U.K.
147 J5 Clogherhead Ireland
147 J5 Clogher Head Ireland
147 L4 Cloghy Northern Ireland U.K.
147 I7 Clohamon Ireland
158 D6 Clohars-Carnoët France
85 H6 Clonagh Qld Austr.
147 E9 Clonakilty Ireland
147 E9 Clonakilty Bay Ireland
147 H6 Clonare Ireland
148 B7 Clonaslee Ireland
84 H6 Cloncurry Qld Austr.
85 H5 Cloncurry r. Qld Austr.
147 J6 Clondalkin Ireland
147 H8 Clonea Ireland
147 J6 Clonee Ireland
147 G8 Cloneen Ireland
147 I7 Clonegal Ireland
147 H4 Clones Ireland
147 H2 Clonmany Ireland
147 G8 Clonmel Ireland
147 H5 Clonmellon Ireland
147 I7 Clonmore Carlow Ireland
147 G7 Clonmore Tipperary Ireland
147 G6 Clonony Ireland
147 G7 Clonoulty Ireland
147 I8 Clonroche Ireland
147 J6 Clontarf Ireland
147 I4 Clontibret Ireland
147 H6 Clonygowan Ireland
147 E4 Cloonacool Ireland
147 D8 Cloonbannin Ireland
147 D6 Cloonboo Ireland
147 G5 Cloone Ireland
148 B6 Clooneagh Ireland
147 E5 Cloonfad Roscommon Ireland
147 F6 Cloonfad Roscommon Ireland
147 D5 Cloonkeen Ireland
147 E5 Cloontia Ireland
222 E5 Clo-oose B.C. Can.
168 F5 Cloppenburg Ger.
226 B3 Cloquet MN U.S.A.
226 B2 Cloquet r. MN U.S.A.
258 F2 Clorinda Arg.
146 I12 Closeburn Dumfries and Galloway, Scotland U.K.
226 E1 Cloud Bay Ont. Can.
220 H5 Cloud Peak WY U.S.A.
238 K4 Cloud Peak WY U.S.A.
81 I8 Cloudy Bay South I. N.Z.
162 E3 Clouère r. France
147 K4 Clough Northern Ireland U.K.
147 J2 Cloughmills Northern Ireland U.K.
149 Q5 Cloughton North Yorkshire, England U.K.
146 □N2 Clousta Shetland, Scotland U.K.
224 F3 Clova Que. Can.
146 J9 Clova Angus, Scotland U.K.
150 D5 Clovelly Devon, England U.K.
146 K11 Clovenfords Scottish Borders, Scotland U.K.
241 T1 Clover UT U.S.A.
240 I3 Cloverdale CA U.S.A.
240 M5 Clovis CA U.S.A.
237 D8 Clovis NM U.S.A.
146 F9 Clovullin Highland, Scotland U.K.
149 O7 Clowne Derbyshire, England U.K.
156 B8 Cloyes-sur-le-Loir France
227 Q5 Cloyne Ont. Can.
147 F9 Cloyne Ireland
Cluain Meala Ireland see Clonmel
146 F8 Cluanie, Loch l. Scotland U.K.
223 I3 Cluff Lake Mine Sask. Can.
162 H2 Cluis France
197 L4 Cluj-Napoca Romania
161 I8 Clumanc France
150 F3 Clun Shropshire, England U.K.
150 G3 Clun r. England U.K.
146 G9 Clunes Highland, Scotland U.K.
84 G8 Cluny Qld Austr.
160 F4 Cluny France
160 G5 Cluse des Hôpitaux gorge France
160 J4 Cluses France
Clusium Italy see Chiusi
190 H4 Clusone Italy
232 G12 Cluster Springs VA U.S.A.
81 D13 Clutha r. South I. N.Z.
222 G1 Clut Lake N.W.T. Can.
87 I8 Clutterbuck Hills W.A. Austr.
150 G5 Clutton Bath and North East Somerset, England U.K.
150 F1 Clwydian Range hills Wales U.K.
150 E4 Clydach Swansea, Wales U.K.
150 F4 Clydach Vale Rhondda Cynon Taff, Wales U.K.
222 H4 Clyde Alta Can.
81 D12 Clyde South I. N.Z.
146 H11 Clyde r. Scotland U.K.
232 I5 Clyde NY U.S.A.
232 C7 Clyde OH U.S.A.
146 G12 Clyde, Firth of est. Scotland U.K.
146 H11 Clydebank West Dunbartonshire, Scotland U.K.
221 L2 Clyde River Nunavut Can.
146 I11 Clydesdale val. Scotland U.K.
81 D13 Clydevale South I. N.Z.
226 F6 Clyman WI U.S.A.
232 F8 Clymer PA U.S.A.
150 C4 Clynderwen Carmarthenshire, Wales U.K.
150 F3 Clyro Powys, Wales U.K.
150 E3 Clywedog Reservoir, Llyn Wales U.K.
175 J5 Ćmielów Pol.
146 I8 Cnoc Fraing hill Scotland U.K.
146 E12 Cnoc Moy hill Scotland U.K.
Cnossus tourist site Greece see Knosos
182 F6 Côa r. Port.
245 H6 Coacalco Mex.
241 P8 Coachella CA U.S.A.
241 P8 Coachella Canal CA U.S.A.
147 E9 Coachford Ireland
244 A1 Coacoyole Mex.
245 I9 Coacoyulichán Mex.
147 I3 Coagh Northern Ireland U.K.
244 F7 Coahuayutla de Guerrero Mex.
242 H4 Coahuila state Mex.
222 E3 Coal r. Y.T. Can.
146 I11 Coalburn South Lanarkshire, Scotland U.K.
226 F8 Coal City IL U.S.A.
244 D7 Coalcomán Mex.
244 D7 Coalcomán r. Mex.
223 H5 Coaldale Alta Can.
240 O3 Coaldale NV U.S.A.
234 D3 Coaldale PA U.S.A.
237 G8 Coalgate OK U.S.A.
232 C10 Coal Grove OH U.S.A.
222 E5 Coal Harbour B.C. Can.
240 L5 Coalinga CA U.S.A.
81 A13 Coal Island South I. N.Z.
147 I3 Coalisland Northern Ireland U.K.
232 G8 Coalport PA U.S.A.
222 E3 Coal River B.C. Can.
241 Q4 Coal Valley NV U.S.A.
215 N2 Coalville S. Africa
151 J2 Coalville Leicestershire, England U.K.
238 I6 Coalville UT U.S.A.
247 □1 Coamo Puerto Rico
182 G1 Coaña Spain
251 F6 Coari Brazil
251 F6 Coari r. Brazil
251 F6 Coari, Lago l. Brazil
163 D9 Coarraze France
240 M4 Coarsegold CA U.S.A.
252 C3 Coasa Peru
211 D5 Coast prov. Kenya
Coast admin. reg. Tanz. see Pwani
197 O2 Coasta Ibăneştilor ridge Romania
237 H10 Coastal Plain U.S.A.
222 E4 Coast Mountains B.C. Can.
85 M8 Coast Range hills Qld Austr.
240 I1 Coast Ranges mts CA U.S.A.
146 H11 Coatbridge North Lanarkshire, Scotland U.K.
245 K9 Coatecas Altas Mex.
245 K6 Coatepec Mex.
245 H7 Coatepec Harinas Mex.
243 N10 Coatepeque Guat.
234 D5 Coatesville PA U.S.A.
225 G4 Coaticook Que. Can.
245 K9 Coatlán Mex.
221 J3 Coats Island Nunavut Can.
262 V1 Coats Land reg. Antarctica
245 M7 Coatzacoalcos Mex.
245 M7 Coatzacoalcos r. Mex.
245 J5 Coatzintla Mex.
197 Q6 Cobadin Romania
227 O2 Cobalt Ont. Can.
235 J1 Cobalt CT U.S.A.
243 N10 Cobán Guat.
129 G4 Çobandağ hill Azer./Georgia
199 L4 Çobanlar Turkey
129 B6 Çobantaş Geçidi pass Turkey
83 J4 Cobar N.S.W. Austr.
83 L7 Cobargo N.S.W. Austr.
87 I8 Cobb, Lake salt flat W.A. Austr.
83 I8 Cobden Vic. Austr.
227 R4 Cobden Ont. Can.
183 M8 Cobeja Spain
183 P7 Cobeta Spain
147 F9 Cobh Ireland
223 M4 Cobham r. Man./Ont. Can.
151 L5 Cobham Surrey, England U.K.
252 C2 Cobija Bol.
252 C5 Cobija Chile
Coblenz Ger. see Koblenz
233 K6 Cobleskill NY U.S.A.
148 D7 Coblinstown Ireland
261 I5 Cobo Arg.
222 C3 Cobol AK U.S.A.
245 J5 Cobos Mex.
224 E5 Cobourg Ont. Can.
84 D1 Cobourg Peninsula N.T. Austr.
260 A5 Cobquecura Chile
87 D8 Cobra W.A. Austr.
83 J6 Cobram Vic. Austr.
252 D5 Cobres Arg.
184 D5 Cobres r. Port.
211 B8 Cóbuè Moz.
169 K10 Coburg Ger.
221 K2 Coburg Island Nunavut Can.
250 B5 Coca Orellana Ecuador
183 K6 Coca Spain
190 I3 Coca, Pizzo di mt. Italy
252 C4 Cocachacra Peru
254 E2 Cocal Brazil
234 C4 Cocalico Creek r. PA U.S.A.
254 C5 Cocalinho Brazil
Cocanada Andhra Prad. India see Kakinada
252 D4 Cocapata Bol.
193 P7 Coccovello, Monte mt. Italy
187 E10 Cocentaina Spain
252 D4 Cochabamba Bol.
252 D4 Cochabamba dept Bol.
259 B6 Cochamó Chile
260 A5 Cocharcas Chile
251 F2 Coche, Isla i. Venez.
169 D10 Cochem Ger.
260 D4 Cochicó Arg.
261 F5 Cochicó, Laguna l. Arg.
97 H10 Co Chiên, Sông r. mouth Vietnam
114 E8 Cochin Kerala India
97 G9 Cochin reg. Vietnam
246 C2 Cochinos, Bahía de b. Cuba
241 W9 Cochise AZ U.S.A.
241 W9 Cochise Head mt. AZ U.S.A.
231 F9 Cochran GA U.S.A.
222 H5 Cochrane Alta Can.
224 D3 Cochrane Ont. Can.
223 K3 Cochrane r. Sask. Can.
259 B7 Cochrane Chile
259 B7 Cochrane, Lago l. Arg./Chile
232 E7 Cochranton PA U.S.A.
234 D5 Cochranville PA U.S.A.
171 D7 Cochstedt Ger.
177 L5 Cociuba Mare Romania
82 E6 Cockaleechie S.A. Austr.
146 J8 Cock Bridge Aberdeenshire, Scotland U.K.
82 H5 Cockburn S.A. Austr.
246 H3 Cockburn Harbour Turks and Caicos Is
224 D4 Cockburn Island Ont. Can.
146 L11 Cockburnspath Scottish Borders, Scotland U.K.
246 F1 Cockburn Town San Salvador Bahamas
Cockburn Town Turks and Caicos Is see Grand Turk
149 N2 Cockenheugh hill England U.K.
146 K11 Cockenzie and Port Seton East Lothian, Scotland U.K.
149 J4 Cocker r. England U.K.
149 L6 Cockerham Lancashire, England U.K.
149 K4 Cockermouth Cumbria, England U.K.
150 E4 Cockett Swansea, Wales U.K.
234 B6 Cockeysville MD U.S.A.
87 I12 Cocklebiddy W.A. Austr.
246 □ Cockpit hill Jamaica
215 I9 Cockscomb mt. S. Africa
242 □S13 Coclé del Norte Panama
254 C4 Coco r. Brazil
242 □R10 Coco r. Hond./Nic.
246 D2 Coco, Cayo i. Cuba
267 N5 Coco, Isla de i. N. Pacific Ocean
Cocoa Island Rodrigues I. Mauritius see Cocos, Île
208 A4 Cocobeach Gabon
115 M6 Coco Channel India
242 F3 Cocomórachic Mex.
241 S6 Coconino Plateau AZ U.S.A.
83 K6 Cocopara National Park N.S.W. Austr.
83 K5 Cocoparra Range hills N.S.W. Austr.
250 C3 Cocorná Col.
92 C6 Cocoro i. Phil.
254 D5 Cocos Brazil
217 □1a Cocos, Île i. Rodrigues I. Mauritius
265 K4 Cocos Basin sea feature Indian Ocean
247 □7 Cocos Bay Trin. and Tob.
78 □1 Cocos Island Guam
86 □2 Cocos Islands terr. Indian Ocean
267 N5 Cocos Ridge sea feature N. Pacific Ocean
217 □1b Cocotte, Mont hill Mauritius
244 D5 Cocula Mex.
163 E7 Cocumont France
233 O7 Cod, Cape MA U.S.A.
192 D6 Coda Cavallo, Capo c. Sardegna Italy
197 P4 Codăeşti Romania
251 F5 Codajás Brazil
149 O5 Cod Beck r. England U.K.
151 O3 Coddenham Suffolk, England U.K.
149 P7 Coddington Nottinghamshire, England U.K.
251 E2 Codera, Cabo c. Venez.
223 J5 Coderre Sask. Can.
191 M5 Codevigo Italy
81 B13 Codfish Island Stewart I. N.Z.
192 D8 Codi, Monte hill Italy
151 L4 Codicote Hertfordshire, England U.K.
191 M6 Codigoro Italy
260 B6 Codihue Arg.
225 I1 Cod Island Nfld and Lab. Can.
197 N5 Codlea Romania
149 O7 Codnor Derbyshire, England U.K.
254 E3 Codó Brazil
190 H5 Codogno Italy
234 B5 Codorus PA U.S.A.
183 R6 Codos Spain
254 D3 Codózinho Brazil
247 □2 Codrington Antigua and Barbuda
263 D2 Codrington, Mount Antarctica
247 □2 Codrington Lagoon Antigua and Barbuda
191 N4 Codroipo Italy
192 B6 Codrongianos Sardegna Italy
136 H7 Codru Moldova
177 L5 Codru-Moma, Munţii mts Romania
150 H2 Codsall Staffordshire, England U.K.
147 B9 Cod's Head Ireland
238 J4 Cody WY U.S.A.
232 C12 Coeburn VA U.S.A.
215 J9 Coega S. Africa
260 A5 Coelemu Chile
254 E3 Coelho Neto Brazil
85 I2 Coen Qld Austr.
85 I2 Coen r. Qld Austr.
244 F6 Coeneo Mex.
215 J9 Coerney S. Africa
251 G4 Coeroeni r. Suriname
169 D7 Coesfeld Ger.
217 □2 Coëtivy i. Seychelles
215 I8 Coetzeesberg mts S. Africa
214 I2 Coetzersdam S. Africa
238 F3 Coeur d'Alene ID U.S.A.
238 F3 Coeur d'Alene r. ID U.S.A.
238 F3 Coeur d'Alene Indian Reservation res. ID U.S.A.
238 F3 Coeur d'Alene Lake ID U.S.A.
164 K3 Coevorden Neth.
158 H8 Coëx France
215 N7 Coffee Bay S. Africa
222 B2 Coffee Creek Y.T. Can.
237 K9 Coffeeville MS U.S.A.
237 H7 Coffeyville KS U.S.A.
82 E6 Coffin Bay S.A. Austr.
82 E6 Coffin Bay b. S.A. Austr.
82 E6 Coffin Bay National Park S.A. Austr.
82 E6 Coffin Bay Peninsula S.A. Austr.
83 N4 Coffs Harbour N.S.W. Austr.
215 L8 Cofimvaba S. Africa
242 □O10 Cofradía Hond.
244 C5 Cofradia de Camotlán Mex.
245 J6 Cofre de Perote mt. Mex.
245 J6 Cofre de Perote, Parque Nacional nat. park Mex.
187 C9 Cofrentes Spain
Cogălniceanu airport Romania see Kogălniceanu
Cogâlniceni Moldova see Cogîlniceni
197 Q6 Cogealac Romania
183 L5 Cogeces del Monte Spain
151 N4 Coggeshall Essex, England U.K.
192 B3 Coggia Corse France
190 E4 Coggiola Italy
192 B6 Coghinas r. Italy
192 C6 Coghinas, Lago del l. Sardegna Italy
215 M7 Coghlan S. Africa
86 I5 Coghlan, Mount hill W.A. Austr.
186 G3 Cogigar r. Spain
136 H6 Cogîlniceni Moldova
162 D4 Cognac France
162 G4 Cognac-la-Forêt France
190 C4 Cogne Italy
160 H5 Cognin France
207 H6 Cogo Equat. Guinea
258 F2 Cogoi Arg.
190 F7 Cogoleto Italy
161 J10 Cogolin France
183 M4 Cogollos Spain
183 L4 Cogollos r. Spain
185 L6 Cogollos Vega Spain
183 N7 Cogolludo Spain
108 C4 Cogsum Sichuan China
182 F7 Cogula Port.
213 G5 Coguno Moz.
234 E6 Cohansey r. NJ U.S.A.
245 I7 Cohetzala Mex.
183 L2 Cohilla, Embalse de resr Spain
140 R2 Čohkarášša mt. Norway
Čohkkiras Sweden see Jukkasjärvi
232 H6 Cohocton r. NY U.S.A.
233 L6 Cohoes NY U.S.A.
83 J6 Cohuna Vic. Austr.
242 □S14 Coiba, Isla de i. Panama
245 I8 Coicoyán de las Flores Mex.
262 T3 Coig r. Arg.
146 F6 Coigeach, Rubha pt Scotland U.K.
259 B7 Coihaique Chile
259 C7 Coihaique Alto Chile
260 A5 Coihüe Chile
260 B5 Coihueco Arg.
260 B5 Coihueco Chile
114 E7 Coimbatore Tamil Nadu India
182 D8 Coimbra Port.
182 D8 Coimbra admin. dist. Port.
185 J7 Coín Spain
156 F5 Coincy France
252 C4 Coipasa, Salar de salt flat Bol.
Coire Switz. see Chur
161 F7 Coiron, Plateau du France
160 E5 Coise r. France
245 J8 Coixtlahuaca Mex.
182 E8 Coja Port.
197 N6 Cojasca Romania
252 C3 Cojata Peru
250 D2 Cojedes state Venez.
250 A4 Cojimíes Ecuador
250 D2 Cojoro Venez.
259 C7 Cojudo Blanco, Cerro mt. Arg.
177 J6 Čoka Vojvodina Serbia
238 I5 Cokeville WY U.S.A.
83 I8 Colac Vic. Austr.
81 B13 Colac South I. N.Z.
Colair Lake India see Kolleru Lake
260 C1 Colangüil, Cordillera de mts Arg.
128 H2 Colap watercourse Turkey
254 C2 Colares Brazil
257 G3 Colatina Brazil
245 I5 Colatlán Mex.
163 F7 Colayrac-St-Cirq France
169 G9 Cölbe Ger.
Colbert Alg. see Aïn Oulmene
171 E6 Colbitz Ger.
191 N8 Colbordola Italy
227 Q6 Colborne Ont. Can.
260 B4 Colbún Chile
260 B4 Colbún, Lago l. Chile
236 E6 Colby KS U.S.A.
226 D5 Colby WI U.S.A.
252 B3 Colca r. Peru
197 O6 Colceag Romania
215 J9 Colchester S. Africa
151 N4 Colchester Essex, England U.K.
235 K1 Colchester CT U.S.A.
226 D9 Colchester IL U.S.A.
220 B4 Cold Bay AK U.S.A.
151 J6 Colden Common Hampshire, England U.K.
146 L11 Coldingham Scottish Borders, Scotland U.K.
171 G8 Colditz Ger.
171 G8 Colditzer Forst park Ger.
223 I4 Cold Lake Alta Can.
223 I4 Cold Lake l. Alta/Sask. Can.
234 F7 Cold Spring NJ U.S.A.
235 H2 Cold Spring NY U.S.A.
237 H10 Coldspring TX U.S.A.
240 O2 Cold Springs NV U.S.A.
222 G5 Coldstream B.C. Can.
81 F11 Coldstream South I. N.Z.
146 L11 Coldstream Scottish Borders, Scotland U.K.
227 O5 Coldwater Ont. Can.
237 F7 Coldwater KS U.S.A.
226 J8 Coldwater MI U.S.A.
237 J8 Coldwater r. MS U.S.A.
237 E7 Coldwater Creek r. OK U.S.A.
226 H1 Coldwell Ont. Can.
233 N4 Colebrook NH U.S.A.
215 N5 Coleford S. Africa
150 G4 Coleford Gloucestershire, England U.K.
150 H5 Coleford Somerset, England U.K.
85 H3 Coleman r. Qld Austr.
234 C6 Coleman MD U.S.A.
226 J6 Coleman MI U.S.A.
237 F10 Coleman TX U.S.A.
226 F4 Coleman WI U.S.A.
Çölemerik Turkey see Hakkâri
215 N4 Colenso S. Africa
197 N6 Colentina r. Romania
262 T2 Cole Peninsula Antarctica
82 H7 Coleraine Vic. Austr.
147 I2 Coleraine Northern Ireland U.K.
226 A2 Coleraine MN U.S.A.
81 F10 Coleridge, Lake South I. N.Z.
150 H5 Colerne Wiltshire, England U.K.
114 F7 Coleroon r. India
252 C4 Coles, Punta de pt Peru
83 L10 Coles Bay Tas. Austr.
215 J6 Colesberg S. Africa
151 I2 Coleshill Warwickshire England U.K.
234 A6 Colesville MD U.S.A.
234 F2 Colesville NJ U.S.A.
223 I5 Coleville Sask. Can.
240 M3 Coleville CA U.S.A.
240 L2 Colfax CA U.S.A.
226 F9 Colfax IL U.S.A.
237 I10 Colfax LA U.S.A.
238 F3 Colfax WA U.S.A.
226 C5 Colfax WI U.S.A.
117 K7 Colgong Bihar India
146 □O1 Colgrave Sound str. Scotland U.K.
259 C7 Colhué Huapí, Lago l.
260 B4 Coliauco Chile
197 M6 Colibaşi Romania
190 G3 Colico Italy
260 B6 Colico, Lago l. Chile
160 G4 Coligny France
215 K2 Coligny S. Africa
247 □2 Colihaut Dominica
164 E5 Colijnsplaat Neth.
244 D6 Colima Mex.
244 D6 Colima state Mex.
244 D6 Colima, Nevado de vo
256 C4 Colina Brazil
260 B3 Colina Chile
254 D3 Colinas Brazil
183 N2 Colindres Spain
146 F11 Colintraive Argyll and Scotland U.K.
245 K6 Colipa Mex.
254 B5 Coliseu r. Brazil
146 C9 Coll i. Scotland U.K.
183 Q8 Collado Bajo mt. Spai
183 M6 Collado Hermoso Spa
183 M7 Collado Villalba Spain
190 I7 Collagna Italy
252 C5 Collahuasi Chile
178 F6 Collalto mt. Austria/Ita
182 I2 Collanzo Spain
186 E2 Collarada, Peña mt. S
83 L3 Collarenebri N.S.W. A
193 L3 Collarmele Italy
193 I2 Collazzone Italy
190 I6 Collecchio Italy
193 L2 Colledara Italy
191 K9 Colle di Val d'Elsa Ita
213 F4 Colleen Dawn Zimbab
193 K4 Colleferro Italy
231 E9 College Park GA U.S.
237 G10 College Station TX U.
234 E4 Collegeville PA U.S.A.
190 D5 Collegno Italy
191 K2 Colle Isarco Italy
193 L4 Collelongo Italy
193 K4 Collepardo Italy
195 O3 Collepasso Italy
83 K3 Collerina N.S.W. Austr
190 I8 Collesalvetti Italy
193 N5 Colle Sannita Italy
194 F8 Collesano Sicilia Italy
193 N4 Colletorto Italy
234 C1 Colley PA U.S.A.
193 O6 Colliano Italy
193 M4 Colli a Volturno Italy
83 L4 Collie N.S.W. Austr.
87 D12 Collie W.A. Austr.
86 H4 Collier Bay W.A. Austr
87 E8 Collier Range hills W.A
87 E8 Collier Range Nation W.A. Austr.
237 K8 Collierville TN U.S.A.
146 M8 Collieston Aberdeensh Scotland U.K.
150 C6 Colliford Reservoir England U.K.
146 I12 Collin Dumfries and Ga Scotland U.K.
192 B8 Collinas Sardegna Italy
158 F5 Collinée France
149 P7 Collingham Nottinghar England U.K.
168 E4 Collinghorst (Rhauderf
224 D4 Collingwood Ont. Can
80 G7 Collingwood South I. N
235 G4 Collingwood Park NJ
237 K10 Collins MS U.S.A.
263 E2 Collins Glacier Antarc
240 K2 Collins Lake CA U.S.A
221 H2 Collinson Peninsula Nunavut Can.
85 K6 Collinsville Qld Austr.
231 E8 Collinsville AL U.S.A.
237 H7 Collinsville OK U.S.A.
232 F12 Collinsville VA U.S.A.
178 B8 Collio Italy
163 K10 Collioure France
260 A5 Collipulli Chile
171 H8 Collmberg hill Ger.
161 I10 Collobrières France
190 B3 Collombey Switz.
234 A2 Collomsville PA U.S.A.
147 J5 Collon Ireland
160 H4 Collonges France
162 H5 Collonges-la-Rouge F
147 F4 Collooney Ireland
157 N7 Colmar France
261 F2 Col Marina Arg.
161 J8 Colmars France
173 I3 Colmberg Ger.
182 E8 Colmeal Port.
258 E3 Colmena Arg.
185 K7 Colmenar Spain
182 I8 Colmenar de Monten Spain
183 N8 Colmenar de Oreja Sp
183 M7 Colmenar Viejo Spain
160 C2 Colméry France
146 G12 Colmonell South Ayrsh Scotland U.K.
151 I4 Coln r. England U.K.
146 J8 Colnabaichin Aberdee Scotland U.K.
151 K5 Colnbrook Windsor an Maidenhead, England U
149 M6 Colne Lancashire, Engla
151 N4 Colne r. England U.K.
151 L4 Colney Heath Hertford England U.K.
168 F5 Colnrade Ger.
83 M5 Colo r. N.S.W. Austr.
195 K3 Colobraro Italy
191 K5 Cologna Veneta Italy
163 F8 Cologne France
Cologne Ger. see Köln
234 F6 Cologne NJ U.S.A.
186 □ Colom, Illa d'en i. Spa
226 H7 Coloma MI U.S.A.
226 E5 Coloma WI U.S.A.
Colomb-Béchar Alg. s Béchar
159 K3 Colombelles France
156 D6 Colombes France
157 K6 Colombey-les-Belles
157 I7 Colombey-les Deux-É France
256 C4 Colômbia Brazil
250 C4 Colombia Col.
243 J4 Colombia Mex.
250 C4 Colombia country S. A
264 D5 Colombian Basin sea S. Atlantic Ocean
190 B2 Colombier Switz.
160 I5 Colombier, Mont mt. F
163 I7 Colombiès France
256 C6 Colombo Brazil
114 F9 Colombo Sri Lanka
227 O1 Colombourg Que. Can
183 K2 Colombres Spain
185 L6 Colomera Spain
185 L6 Colomera r. Spain
185 L6 Colomera, Embalse d Spain
186 K3 Colomers Spain
163 G8 Colomiers France
261 G3 Colón Buenos Aires Arg
261 H3 Colón Entre Ríos Arg.
246 C2 Colón Cuba
244 G5 Colón Mex.
242 □T13 Colón Panama
226 I8 Colon MI U.S.A.
247 □7 Colón Venez.
Colón, Archipiélago d Pacific Ocean see Galápagos, Islas
242 □R13 Colón, Isla de i. Panan
82 D4 Colona S.A. Austr.

Colonelganj Uttar Prad. India
Colonel Hill Bahamas
Colonet, Cabo c. Mex.
Colonia Arg.
Colonia Yap Micronesia
Colonia dept Uru.
Colonia NJ U.S.A.
Colonia Agrippina Ger. see Köln
Colonia Alpina Arg.
Colonia Alvear Arg.
Colonia Barón Arg.
Colonia Biagorria Arg.
Colonia Caseros Arg.
Colonia Chica, Isla i. Arg.
Colonia Choele Choel, Isla i. Arg.
Colonia del Sacramento Uru.
Colònia de Sant Jordi Spain
Colònia de Sant Pere Spain
Colonia Díaz Mex.
Colonia Dora Arg.
Colonia Elía Arg.
Colonia Emilio Mitre Arg.
Colonia Fraga Arg.
Colonia Hilario Lagos Arg.
Colonia Julia Fenestris Italy see Fano
Colonia La Argentina Arg.
Colonia La Pastoril Arg.
Colonia Las Heras Arg.
Colonia Lavalleja Uru.
Colonial Heights VA U.S.A.
Colonial Park PA U.S.A.
Colonia Macías Arg.
Colonia Portugalete Arg.
Colonia Reforma Mex.
Colonia Rosa Arg.
Colonia Seré Arg.
Colonia Suiza Uru.
Colonna, Capo c. Italy
Colonne, Punta delle pt Sardegna Italy
Colonnella Italy
Colon Ridge sea feature Pacific Ocean
Colonsay i. Scotland U.K.
Colorada Grande, Salina salt l. Arg.
Colorado r. Arg.
Colorado r. Arg.
Colorado r. Arg.
Colorado Brazil
Colorado r. Chile
Colorado r. Mex.
Colorado r. Mex./U.S.A.
Colorado r. TX U.S.A.
Colorado state U.S.A.
Colorado, Cerro mt. Arg.
Colorado, Delta del Río Arg.
Colorado City AZ U.S.A.
Colorado City TX U.S.A.
Colorado Desert CA U.S.A.
Colorado National Monument nat. park CO U.S.A.
Colorado Plateau CO U.S.A.
Colorado River Aqueduct canal CA U.S.A.
Colorado River Indian Reservation res. AZ/CA U.S.A.
Colorados, Cerro mt. Arg.
Colorado Springs CO U.S.A.
Colorno Italy
Colos Port.
Colossae Turkey see Honaz
Colostrai, Stagno di lag. Sardegna Italy
Colostre r. France
Colotepec Mex.
Colotepec r. Mex.
Colotlán Mex.
Cölpin Ger.
Colquechaca Bol.
Colquhar Scottish Borders, Scotland U.K.
Colquiri Bol.
Colquitt GA U.S.A.
Çölquşçu Azer.
Colroy-la-Grande France
Colson KY U.S.A.
Colsterworth Lincolnshire, England U.K.
Colstrip MT U.S.A.
Coltishall Norfolk, England U.K.
Colton CA U.S.A.
Colton NY U.S.A.
Colton UT U.S.A.
Colts Neck NJ U.S.A.
Columbares hill Spain
Columbia CT U.S.A.
Columbia KY U.S.A.
Columbia LA U.S.A.
Columbia MD U.S.A.
Columbia MO U.S.A.
Columbia MS U.S.A.
Columbia NC U.S.A.
Columbia NJ U.S.A.
Columbia PA U.S.A.
Columbia SC U.S.A.
Columbia TN U.S.A.
Columbia r. WA U.S.A.
Columbia, Cape Nunavut Can.
Columbia, District of admin. dist. U.S.A.
Columbia, Mount Alta/B.C. Can.
Columbia, Sierra mts Mex.
Columbia City IN U.S.A.
Columbia County county PA U.S.A.
Columbia Falls ME U.S.A.
Columbia Falls MT U.S.A.
Columbia Mountains B.C. Can.
Columbiana AL U.S.A.
Columbiana OH U.S.A.
Columbia Plateau U.S.A.
Columbine, Cape S. Africa
Columbretes, Islas is Spain
Columbus GA U.S.A.
Columbus IN U.S.A.
Columbus KS U.S.A.
Columbus MS U.S.A.
Columbus MT U.S.A.
Columbus NC U.S.A.
Columbus NE U.S.A.
Columbus NJ U.S.A.
Columbus NM U.S.A.
Columbus OH U.S.A.
Columbus PA U.S.A.
Columbus TX U.S.A.
Columbus WI U.S.A.
Columbus Bank sea feature Bahamas
Columbus Grove OH U.S.A.
Columbus Point Trin. and Tob.
Columbus Salt Marsh NV U.S.A.
Coluna Brazil
Colunga Spain
Colusa CA U.S.A.
Colville North I. N.Z.
Colville WA U.S.A.
Colville r. AK U.S.A.
Colville, Cape North I. N.Z.
Colville, Lake salt flat W.A. Austr.
Colville Channel North I. N.Z.
Colville Indian Reservation res. WA U.S.A.
Colville Lake N.W.T. Can.
Colwich Staffordshire, England U.K.
Colwyn Bay Conwy, Wales U.K.
Coly France
Colyton Devon, England U.K.
Comacchio Italy
Comacchio, Valli di lag. Italy
Comacho, Puerto pass Spain
Comai Xizang China
Comala Mex.
Comalcalco Mex.
Comales r. Mex.
Comallo Arg.
Comana Romania
Comana de Sus Romania
Comanche TX U.S.A.
Comandante Ferraz research stn Antarctica
Comandante Fontana Arg.
Comandante Luis Piedra Buena Arg.
261 I6 Comandante Nicanor Otamendi Arg.
260 C3 Comandante Salas Arg.
181 H1 Comanegra, Puig de mt. Spain
197 O4 Comănești Romania
186 H2 Coma Pedrosa, Pic de mt. Andorra
197 N5 Comarnic Romania
242 □P10 Comayagua Hond.
231 G9 Combahee r. SC U.S.A.
260 B2 Combarbalá Chile
157 K8 Combeaufontaine France
160 I5 Combe de Savoie val. France
150 D5 Combe Martin Devon, England U.K.
147 K3 Comber Northern Ireland U.K.
227 Q4 Combermere Ont. Can.
96 A5 Combermere Bay Myanmar
151 M3 Comberton Cambridgeshire, England U.K.
150 G6 Combe St Nicholas Somerset, England U.K.
165 I8 Comblain-au-Pont Belgium
160 F2 Comblanchien France
156 E3 Combles France
160 J5 Combloux France
94 E4 Combol i. Indon.
190 I3 Combolo, Monte mt. Italy/Switz.
158 H5 Combourg France
160 A4 Combraille reg. France
158 C6 Combrit France
160 C5 Combronde France
260 E3 Comechingones, Sierra de mts Arg.
191 N2 Comeglians Italy
191 N2 Comèlico Superiore Italy
224 F3 Comencho, Lac l. Que. Can.
184 D2 Comenda Port.
256 C3 Comendador Gomes Brazil
257 G2 Comercinho Brazil
247 □1 Comerio Puerto Rico
191 M8 Comero, Monte mt. Italy
85 L7 Comet Qld Austr.
85 L7 Comet r. Qld Austr.
237 F10 Comfort TX U.S.A.
232 D10 Comfort WV U.S.A.
246 □ Comfort Castle Jamaica
117 M8 Comilla Bangl.
183 L2 Comillas Spain
165 C7 Comines Belgium
Comino i. Malta see Kemmuna
192 D6 Comino, Capo c. Sardegna Italy
Cominotto i. Malta see Kemmunett
194 H10 Comiso Sicilia Italy
245 L9 Comitancillo Mex.
243 M9 Comitán de Domínguez Mex.
194 F9 Comitini Sicilia Italy
177 J6 Comloșu Mare Romania
235 I3 Commack NY U.S.A.
227 O4 Commanda Ont. Can.
147 G3 Commeen Ireland
160 G3 Commenailles France
163 C7 Commensacq France
160 B4 Commentry France
158 H8 Commequiers France
159 J5 Commer France
157 K6 Commercy France
163 F10 Comminges reg. France
231 □1 Commissioner's Point Bermuda
214 D6 Commissioner's Salt Pan S. Africa
221 J3 Committee Bay Nunavut Can.
215 O3 Commondale S. Africa
263 J2 Commonwealth Bay Antarctica
Commonwealth Territory admin. div. Austr. see Jervis Bay Territory
190 G4 Como Italy
190 G4 Como prov. Italy
190 G4 Como, Lago di l. Italy
Como, Lake Italy see Como, Lago di
245 L7 Comoapan Mex.
111 I12 Como Chamling l. China
260 B3 Comodoro Arturo Merino Benitez airport Chile
259 D7 Comodoro Rivadavia Arg.
Comoé r. Côte d'Ivoire see Komoé
206 E4 Comoé, Parc National de la nat. park Côte d'Ivoire
244 G5 Comonfort Mex.
Comores country Africa see Comoros
114 E8 Comorin, Cape India
217 □3 Comoros country Africa
222 E5 Comox B.C. Can.
185 L7 Cómpeta Spain
190 H6 Compiano Italy
156 E5 Compiègne France
163 I7 Compolibat France
184 B4 Comporta Port.
244 C4 Compostela Mex.
92 F8 Compostela Mindanao Phil.
162 G4 Compreignac France
256 D6 Comprida, Ilha i. Brazil
161 J9 Comps-sur-Artuby France
240 N8 Compton CA U.S.A.
226 E8 Compton IL U.S.A.
183 K3 Compuerto, Embalse de resr Spain
136 H7 Comrat Moldova
146 I10 Comrie Perth and Kinross, Scotland U.K.
237 E11 Comstock TX U.S.A.
193 K2 Comunanza Italy
194 G9 Comunelli r. Sicilia Italy
96 G5 Con, Sông r. Vietnam
97 I8 Con, Sông r. Vietnam
111 J13 Cona Xizang China
191 M5 Cona Italy
128 E1 Çona Turkey
206 B4 Conakry Guinea
250 B5 Conambo Ecuador
250 B5 Conambo r. Ecuador
259 D6 Cona Niyeo Arg.
83 K9 Conara Junction Tas. Austr.
258 C3 Conay Chile
192 C4 Conca Corse France
191 N8 Conca r. Italy
260 E3 Concarán Arg.
158 D6 Concarneau France
192 D6 Concas Sardegna Italy
251 F5 Conceição Amazonas Brazil
253 F1 Conceição Mato Grosso Brazil
254 F3 Conceição Paraíba Brazil
253 E2 Conceição Rondônia Brazil
251 F4 Conceição Roraima Brazil
256 E2 Conceição r. Brazil
184 D6 Conceição Port.
257 H3 Conceição da Barra Brazil
256 C3 Conceição das Alagoas Brazil
257 G5 Conceição de Macabu Brazil
254 C4 Conceição do Araguaia Brazil
254 F4 Conceição do Coité Brazil
257 F3 Conceição do Mato Dentro Brazil
251 G4 Conceição do Maú Brazil
254 D5 Conceição do Norte Brazil
257 E4 Conceição do Rio Verde Brazil
258 F3 Concepción Corrientes Arg.
258 D2 Concepción Tucumán Arg.
252 D2 Concepción Beni Bol.
253 E4 Concepción Santa Cruz Bol.
258 B5 Concepción Chile
244 F1 Concepción Mex.
242 C2 Concepción r. Mex.
253 F5 Concepción Para.
250 D2 Concepción Venez.
259 B8 Concepción, Canal sea chan. Chile
242 D4 Concepción, Punta pt Mex.
244 D6 Concepción de Buenos Aires Mex.
261 H3 Concepción del Uruguay Arg.
217 □2b Conception, Île i. Inner Islands Seychelles
240 L7 Conception, Point CA U.S.A.
212 B4 Conception Bay Namibia
246 F2 Conception Island Bahamas
190 I4 Concesio Italy
213 F3 Concession Zimbabwe
244 B3 Concha Mex.
183 N2 Concha Spain
183 O3 Concha de Álava reg. Spain
256 C5 Conchas Brazil
239 L9 Conchas NM U.S.A.
182 E5 Conchas, Embalse das resr Spain
239 L9 Conchas Lake NM U.S.A.
156 A6 Conches-en-Ouche France
252 C5 Conchi Chile
242 G4 Concho Mex.
241 W7 Concho AZ U.S.A.
237 F10 Concho r. TX U.S.A.
243 K5 Conchos r. Nuevo León/Tamaulipas Mex.
242 G3 Conchos r. Mex.
260 B3 Concón Chile
240 J4 Concord CA U.S.A.
226 J7 Concord MI U.S.A.
231 G8 Concord NC U.S.A.
233 N5 Concord NH U.S.A.
232 H8 Concord PA U.S.A.
232 G11 Concord VA U.S.A.
233 N4 Concord VT U.S.A.
262 I2 Concordia research stn Antarctica
261 I2 Concordia Arg.
250 E6 Concórdia Amazonas Brazil
255 B8 Concórdia Santa Catarina Brazil
250 C3 Concordia Antioquia Col.
250 C4 Concordia Meta Col.
244 A2 Concordiá Mex.
250 C6 Concordia Peru
214 B5 Concordia S. Africa
236 G6 Concordia KS U.S.A.
191 N4 Concordia Sagittaria Italy
123 O3 Concord Peak Afgh.
163 G6 Concorès France
163 H7 Concots France
260 B2 Concumén Chile
96 G5 Con Cuông Vietnam
209 B7 Conda Angola
186 F3 Condado reg. Spain
184 G6 Condado de Niebla reg. Spain
183 O3 Condado de Treviño reg. Spain
85 M9 Condamine Qld Austr.
85 L9 Condamine r. Qld Austr.
97 H10 Côn Đao Vietnam
161 B6 Condat France
162 G4 Condat-sur-Vienne France
254 F4 Conde Brazil
156 G5 Condé-en-Brie France
242 □P11 Condega Nic.
254 C2 Condeixa Brazil
182 D8 Condeixa-a-Nova Port.
159 M5 Condé-sur-Huisne France
156 G3 Condé-sur-l'Escaut France
159 J4 Condé-sur-Noireau France
159 I3 Condé-sur-Vire France
255 E5 Condeúba Brazil
191 J4 Condino Italy
83 K5 Condobolin N.S.W. Austr.
213 G3 Condoe Moz.
195 J7 Condofuri Italy
163 E8 Condom France
238 D4 Condon OR U.S.A.
250 B6 Condor, Cordillera del mts Ecuador/Peru
260 B1 Condoriaco Chile
190 C5 Condove Italy
150 G2 Condover Shropshire, England U.K.
165 G8 Condroz reg. Belgium
231 D10 Conecuh r. AL U.S.A.
191 M4 Conegliano Italy
242 H4 Conejos Mex.
239 K8 Conejos CO U.S.A.
239 L8 Conejos r. CO/NM U.S.A.
227 O9 Conemaugh r. PA U.S.A.
191 P8 Conero, Monte hill Italy
261 G3 Conesa Arg.
234 C5 Conestoga PA U.S.A.
234 C4 Conestoga Creek r. PA U.S.A.
227 N6 Conestogo Lake Ont. Can.
232 H6 Conesus Lake NY U.S.A.
232 D8 Conesville OH U.S.A.
234 B4 Conewago Creek r. PA U.S.A.
234 B4 Conewago Lake PA U.S.A.
157 L8 Coney r. France
231 □1 Coney Island Bermuda
147 E4 Coney Island Ireland
Coney Island Sing. see Serangoon, Pulau
235 H3 Coney Island NY U.S.A.
157 K5 Conflans-en-Jarnisy France
157 L8 Conflans-sur-Lanterne France
163 I10 Conflent reg. France
193 Q9 Conflenti Italy
91 L9 Conflict Group is P.N.G.
232 F9 Confluence PA U.S.A.
Confoederatio Helvetica country Europe see Switzerland
162 F3 Confolens France
162 F4 Confolentais reg. France
241 S3 Confusion Range mts UT U.S.A.
253 F6 Confuso r. Para.
147 D5 Cong Ireland
108 B3 Conga Xizang China
150 D6 Congdon's Shop Cornwall, England U.K.
111 H12 Congdü Xizang China
109 I7 Conghua Guangdong China
108 G6 Congjiang Guizhou China
149 M7 Congleton Cheshire, England U.K.
208 B5 Congo country Africa
209 B6 Congo r. Congo/Dem. Rep. Congo
Congo (Brazzaville) country Africa see Congo
Congo (Kinshasa) country Africa see Congo, Democratic Republic of the
208 D5 Congo, Democratic Republic of the country Africa
Congo, Republic of country Africa see Congo
208 D5 Congo Basin Dem. Rep. Congo
264 J6 Congo Cone sea feature S. Atlantic Ocean
Congo Free State country Africa see Congo, Democratic Republic of the
257 F4 Congonhas Brazil
256 B5 Congonhinhas Brazil
182 H3 Congosto Spain
183 K3 Congosto de Valdavia Spain
150 G5 Congresbury North Somerset, England U.K.
241 T7 Congress AZ U.S.A.
159 I6 Congrier France
260 B6 Conguillo, Parque Nacional nat. park Chile
260 E5 Conhelo Arg.
243 O8 Conhuas Mex.
81 E12 Conical Peak hill South I. N.Z.
259 C6 Cónico, Cerro mt. Arg.
156 B7 Conie r. France
184 G8 Conil de la Frontera Spain
187 H10 Conillera, Illa sa i. Spain
187 K9 Conills, Illa des i. Spain
149 Q7 Coningsby Lincolnshire, England U.K.
149 O7 Conisbrough South Yorkshire, England U.K.
84 D7 Coniston N.T. Austr.
224 D4 Coniston Ont. Can.
149 K5 Coniston Cumbria, England U.K.
149 K5 Coniston Water l. England U.K.
85 J5 Conjuboy Qld Austr.
185 M7 Conjuros hill Spain
243 O7 Conkal Mex.
223 I4 Conklin Alta Can.
209 A5 Conkouati, Réserve de Faune nature res. Congo
260 E3 Conlara Arg.
260 E3 Conlara r. Arg.
159 K5 Conlie France
160 H3 Conliège France
147 K3 Conlig Northern Ireland U.K.
224 E2 Conn r. Que. Can.
147 D4 Conn, Lough l. Ireland
Connacht reg. Ireland see Connaught
150 F1 Connah's Quay Flintshire, Wales U.K.
156 G6 Connantre France
227 N1 Connaught Ont. Can.
147 D5 Connaught reg. Ireland
161 F8 Connaux France
232 E7 Conneaut OH U.S.A.
232 E7 Conneaut Lake PA U.S.A.
232 E7 Conneautville PA U.S.A.
235 K2 Connecticut r. CT U.S.A.
233 M7 Connecticut state U.S.A.
146 F10 Connel Argyll and Bute, Scotland U.K.
84 F5 Connells Lagoon Conservation Reserve nature res. N.T. Austr.
232 F8 Connellsville PA U.S.A.
85 I8 Connemara Qld Austr.
147 C6 Connemara reg. Ireland
147 C5 Connemara National Park Ireland
84 C8 Conner, Mount hill N.T. Austr.
159 L5 Connerré France
230 E6 Connersville IN U.S.A.
147 D7 Connolly Ireland
222 C2 Connolly, Mount Y.T. Can.
146 D13 Connor Northern Ireland U.K.
85 L6 Connors Range hills Qld Austr.
83 J5 Conoble N.S.W. Austr.
234 B4 Conodoguinet Creek r. PA U.S.A.
250 C5 Cononaco Ecuador
250 C5 Cononaco r. Ecuador
146 H7 Conon Bridge Highland, Scotland U.K.
177 K5 Conop Romania
177 I6 Čonoplja Vojvodina Serbia
226 E3 Conover WI U.S.A.
170 H4 Conow Ger.
234 C5 Conowingo MD U.S.A.
163 I6 Conques France
163 I9 Conques-sur-Orbiel France
252 D2 Conquista Bol.
256 D3 Conquista Brazil
185 J4 Conquista Spain
238 I2 Conrad MT U.S.A.
264 L9 Conrad Rise sea feature Southern Ocean
237 H10 Conroe TX U.S.A.
237 H10 Conroe, Lake TX U.S.A.
191 L6 Consandolo Italy
261 H2 Conscripto Bernardi Arg.
165 J9 Consdorf Lux.
227 Q5 Consecon Ont. Can.
243 O8 Consejo Belize
257 F4 Conselheiro Lafaiete Brazil
257 G3 Conselheiro Pena Brazil
191 L6 Conselice Italy
187 K8 Consell Spain
157 J5 Consenvoye France
149 N4 Consett Durham, England U.K.
234 E4 Conshohocken PA U.S.A.
246 B2 Consolación del Sur Cuba
97 H10 Côn Sơn, Đao i. Vietnam
223 I4 Consort Alta Can.
Constance Ger. see Konstanz
Constance, Lake Ger./Switz. see Bodensee
184 C2 Constância Port.
261 H3 Constancia Uru.
251 F6 Constância dos Baetas Brazil
197 Q6 Constanța Romania
Constanța airport Romania see Kogălniceanu
186 H5 Constantí Spain
Constantia tourist site Cyprus see Salamis
Constantia Ger. see Konstanz
182 H5 Constantim Bragança Port.
182 E6 Constantim Vila Real Port.
184 H5 Constantina Spain
205 G1 Constantine Alg.
150 B7 Constantine Cornwall, England U.K.
226 I8 Constantine MI U.S.A.
220 C4 Constantine, Cape AK U.S.A.
Constantinople Turkey see İstanbul
246 □ Constant Spring Jamaica
261 G2 Constanza Arg.
183 K7 Constanzana Spain
260 A4 Constitución Chile
261 I2 Constitución Uru.
242 B1 Constitución de 1857, Parque Nacional nat. park Mex.
185 L2 Consuegra Spain
85 L8 Consuelo Qld Austr.
253 E3 Consuelo Brazil
223 I5 Consul Sask. Can.
223 K1 Consul r. Nunavut Can.
238 G6 Contact NV U.S.A.
257 F4 Contagalo Brazil
257 E3 Contagem Brazil
252 B1 Contamana Peru
191 M5 Contarina Italy
254 F5 Contas r. Brazil
192 A7 Conte, Porto b. Sardegna Italy
215 I4 Content S. Africa
194 E8 Contessa Entellina Sicilia Italy
190 C3 Conthey Switz.
193 J3 Contigliano Italy
146 G7 Contin Highland, Scotland U.K.
232 A7 Continental OH U.S.A.
163 B7 Contis-Plage France
233 N5 Contoocook r. NH U.S.A.
243 P7 Contoy, Isla i. Mex.
260 C6 Contralmirante Cordero Arg.
194 G8 Contrasto, Colle del pass Italy
250 C3 Contratacion Col.
185 M7 Contraviesa, Sierra de mts Spain
183 Q9 Contreras, Embalse de resr Spain
259 B8 Contreras, Isla i. Chile
162 G1 Contres France
157 K7 Contrexéville France
257 E3 Contria Brazil
193 O6 Controne Italy
258 B5 Contulmo Chile
252 A1 Contumazá Peru
193 O6 Contursi Terme Italy
223 I1 Contwoyto Lake N.W.T./Nunavut Can.
156 D4 Conty France
250 C2 Convención Col.
237 J10 Convent LA U.S.A.
260 B4 Convento Viejo Chile
195 M2 Conversano Italy
232 A8 Convoy OH U.S.A.
215 J7 Conway S. Africa
Conway Conwy, Wales U.K. see Conwy
237 I8 Conway AR U.S.A.
232 A11 Conway KY U.S.A.
236 G1 Conway ND U.S.A.
233 □N5 Conway NH U.S.A.
231 H9 Conway SC U.S.A.
85 L6 Conway, Cape Qld Austr.
82 E3 Conway, Lake salt flat S.A. Austr.
85 L6 Conway National Park Qld Austr.
Conway Reef Fiji see Ceva-i-Ra
237 G7 Conway Springs KS U.S.A.
150 E1 Conwy Conwy, Wales U.K.
150 E1 Conwy admin. div. Wales U.K.
150 E1 Conwy r. Wales U.K.
150 D1 Conwy Bay Wales U.K.
234 C3 Conyngham PA U.S.A.
193 O6 Conza, Lago di l. Italy
82 E3 Coober Pedy S.A. Austr.
Cooch Behar W. Bengal India see Koch Bihar
85 L9 Coogoon r. Qld Austr.
82 C4 Cook S.A. Austr.
226 B2 Cook MN U.S.A.
259 C9 Cook, Bahía de b. Chile
79 □9a Cook, Baie de b. Moorea Fr. Polynesia
222 E5 Cook, Cape B.C. Can.
78 □5 Cook, Grand Récif de rf New Caledonia
222 B2 Cook, Mount Can./U.S.A.
Cook, Mount South I. N.Z. see Aoraki
Cook Atoll Kiribati see Tarawa
239 K10 Cookes Peak NM U.S.A.
231 E7 Cookeville TN U.S.A.
151 K4 Cookham Windsor and Maidenhead, England U.K.
215 J8 Cookhouse S. Africa
263 K2 Cook Ice Shelf Antarctica
220 C3 Cook Inlet sea chan. AK U.S.A.
81 □2 Cook Islands S. Pacific Ocean
150 H3 Cookley Worcestershire, England U.K.
79 □8a Cook Point Tongatapu Tonga
Cook's Bay Moorea Fr. Polynesia see Cook, Baie de
233 K6 Cooksburg NY U.S.A.
146 J8 Cook's Cairn hill Scotland U.K.
225 K3 Cook's Harbour Nfld and Lab. Can.
85 J3 Cooks Passage Qld Austr.
147 I3 Cookstown Northern Ireland U.K.
81 I7 Cook Strait South I. N.Z.
234 A6 Cooksville MD U.S.A.
85 J3 Cooktown Qld Austr.
147 F4 Coola Ireland
83 K4 Coolabah N.S.W. Austr.
85 J9 Cooladdi Qld Austr.
83 L4 Coolah N.S.W. Austr.
83 M4 Coolah Tops National Park N.S.W. Austr.
83 K6 Coolamon N.S.W. Austr.
147 E4 Coolaney Ireland
156 H6 Coole France
156 H6 Coole r. France
148 C6 Coole Ireland
87 F11 Coolgardie W.A. Austr.
147 H7 Coolgrange Ireland
147 J7 Coolgreany Ireland
84 C3 Coolibah N.T. Austr.
241 U9 Coolidge AZ U.S.A.
87 C10 Coolimba W.A. Austr.
147 J6 Coolock Ireland
85 N9 Cooloola National Park Qld Austr.
147 H8 Coolroebeg Ireland
85 N9 Coolum Beach Qld Austr.
83 L7 Cooma N.S.W. Austr.
147 B9 Coomacarrea hill Ireland
82 H5 Coombah N.S.W. Austr.
150 C6 Coombe Cornwall, England U.K.
151 I5 Coombe Bissett Wiltshire, England U.K.
83 L4 Coonabarabran N.S.W. Austr.
82 G6 Coonalpyn S.A. Austr.
83 L4 Coonamble N.S.W. Austr.
87 G11 Coonana W.A. Austr.
87 G11 Coonana Aboriginal Reserve W.A. Austr.
82 H7 Coonawarra S.A. Austr.
82 E4 Coondambo S.A. Austr.
Coondapoor Karnataka India see Kundapura
86 E6 Coongan r. W.A. Austr.
86 E6 Coongan Aboriginal Reserve W.A. Austr.
85 J9 Coongoola Qld Austr.
82 E2 Coongra watercourse S.A. Austr.
226 A4 Coon Rapids MN U.S.A.
84 D2 Cooper r. N.T. Austr.
237 H9 Cooper TX U.S.A.
82 F3 Cooper Creek watercourse Qld/S.A. Austr.
232 C8 Cooperdale OH U.S.A.
83 N4 Coopernook N.S.W. Austr.
234 E3 Coopersburg PA U.S.A.
233 □P4 Coopers Mills ME U.S.A.
231 I12 Cooper's Town Bahamas
236 F2 Cooperstown ND U.S.A.
233 K6 Cooperstown NY U.S.A.
83 L7 Coopracambra National Park Vic. Austr.
247 □7 Coora Trin. and Tob.
82 D4 Coorabie S.A. Austr.
87 D8 Coor-de-Wandy hill W.A. Austr.
82 G7 Coorong National Park S.A. Austr.
87 D10 Coorow W.A. Austr.
85 N9 Cooroy Qld Austr.
231 D9 Coosa r. AL U.S.A.
238 B5 Coos Bay OR U.S.A.
238 B5 Coos Bay b. OR U.S.A.
83 L6 Cootamundra N.S.W. Austr.
147 H4 Cootehill Ireland
114 G6 Cooum r. India
85 M9 Cooyar Qld Austr.
258 D3 Copacabana Arg.
177 L5 Copăcel Romania
260 B5 Copahue, Volcán vol. Chile
243 M9 Copainalá Mex.
245 I9 Copala Mex.
245 H7 Copalillo Mex.
245 K10 Copalita Mex.
245 K10 Copalita r. Mex.
250 C5 Copal Urcu Peru
242 □O10 Copán tourist site Hond.
195 L6 Copanello Italy
236 D6 Cope CO U.S.A.
187 C13 Cope, Cabo c. Spain
147 L3 Copeland Island Northern Ireland U.K.
226 I5 Copemish MI U.S.A.
Copenhagen Denmark see København
253 E4 Copere Bol.
195 O3 Copertino Italy
261 G6 Copetonas Arg.
83 M3 Copeton Reservoir N.S.W. Austr.
96 G6 Cô Pi, Phou mt. Laos/Vietnam
235 I3 Copiague NY U.S.A.
258 C2 Copiapó Chile
258 C2 Copiapo, Volcán vol. Chile
146 K5 Copinsay i. Scotland U.K.
234 E3 Coplay PA U.S.A.
82 G4 Copley S.A. Austr.
149 N4 Copley Durham, England U.K.
149 O6 Copmanthorpe York, England U.K.
253 E6 Copo, Parque Nacional nat. park Arg.
186 I4 Copons Spain
252 C3 Coporaque Peru
190 G5 Coppa r. Italy
191 L6 Copparo Italy
147 E9 Coppeen Ireland
251 G3 Coppename r. Suriname
169 I6 Coppenbrügge Ger.
169 I7 Coppengrave Ger.
209 E8 Copperbelt prov. Zambia
224 D4 Copper Cliff Ont. Can.
85 I4 Copperfield r. Qld Austr.
226 G2 Copper Harbor MI U.S.A.
Coppermine Nunavut Can. see Kugluktuk
220 G3 Coppermine r. Nunavut Can.
224 C4 Coppermine Point Ont. Can.
213 F3 Copper Queen Zimbabwe
214 G5 Copperton S. Africa
241 T1 Copperton UT U.S.A.
222 H2 Copp Lake N.W.T. Can.
150 E6 Copplestone Devon, England U.K.
197 M4 Copșa Mică Romania
151 L5 Copthorne Surrey, England U.K.
151 I6 Copythorne Hampshire, England U.K.
111 G11 Coqên Xizang China
111 G11 Coqên Xizang China
247 □1 Coqui Puerto Rico
Coquilhatville Dem. Rep. Congo see Mbandaka
Coquille i. Micronesia see Pikelot
238 B5 Coquille OR U.S.A.
244 D6 Coquimatlán Mex.
260 B1 Coquimbo Chile
260 B2 Coquimbo admin. reg. Chile
260 B1 Coquimbo, Bahía de b. Chile
222 F5 Coquitlam B.C. Can.
197 M7 Corabia Romania
257 E2 Coração de Jesus Brazil
195 L6 Corace r. Italy
Coracesium Turkey see Alanya
252 B3 Coracora Peru
183 J3 Corada, Peña mt. Spain
114 C6 Cora Dive sea feature India
83 N3 Coraki N.S.W. Austr.
87 B7 Coral Bay W.A. Austr.
92 A7 Coral Bay b. Palawan Phil.
79 □7a Coral Coast Fiji
260 C5 Corales, Cerro mt. Arg.
231 □2 Coral Harbour New Prov. Bahamas
221 J3 Coral Harbour Nunavut Can.
231 □2 Coral Heights New Prov. Bahamas
78 □5 Coral Sea S. Pacific Ocean
266 F6 Coral Sea Basin S. Pacific Ocean
77 F3 Coral Sea Islands Territory terr. Austr.
147 H6 Coralstown Ireland
235 I3 Coram NY U.S.A.
83 I8 Corangamite, Lake Vic. Austr.
258 D1 Coranzuli Arg.
232 E8 Coraopolis PA U.S.A.
129 K5 Corat Azer.
193 Q5 Corato Italy
158 D5 Coray France
186 D7 Corbalán Spain
147 D4 Corbally Ireland
192 I2 Corbara, Lago di l. Italy
156 D6 Corbeil-Essonnes France
156 E7 Corbeilles France
256 A6 Corbélia Brazil
160 H5 Corbelin France
157 L8 Corbenay France
156 G5 Corbeny France
186 F5 Corbera d'Ebre Spain
261 G4 Corbett Arg.
223 M2 Corbett Inlet Nunavut Can.
116 G5 Corbett National Park India
156 E4 Corbie France
163 I10 Corbières reg. France
190 C2 Corbières Switz.
160 D2 Corbigny France
232 A12 Corbin KY U.S.A.
234 F6 Corbin City NJ U.S.A.
186 G4 Corbins Spain
191 M5 Corbola Italy
185 H5 Corbones r. Spain
149 M4 Corbridge Northumberland, England U.K.
197 Q6 Corbu Romania
151 K3 Corby Northamptonshire, England U.K.
186 L4 Corçà Spain
Corcaigh Ireland see Cork
160 G2 Corcelles-lès-Cîteaux France
193 I3 Corchiano Italy
216 □3d Corcho, Punta del pt La Palma Canary Is
193 I1 Corciano Italy
157 M7 Corcieux France
185 M2 Córcoles r. Spain
240 M5 Corcoran CA U.S.A.
158 H8 Corcoué-sur-Logne France
259 C6 Corcovado Arg.
259 B6 Corcovado, Golfo de sea chan. Chile
242 □R13 Corcovado, Parque Nacional nat. park Costa Rica
182 B3 Corcubión Spain
182 B3 Corcubión, Ría de b. Spain
Corcyra i. Greece see Kerkyra
147 D8 Cordal Ireland
85 N8 Cordalba Qld Austr.
257 F5 Cordeiro Brazil
231 F10 Cordele GA U.S.A.
240 J3 Cordelia CA U.S.A.
237 F8 Cordell OK U.S.A.
158 H7 Cordemais France
191 N4 Cordenòns Italy
163 H7 Cordes France
191 M3 Cordevole r. Italy
191 M4 Cordignano Italy
252 B1 Cordillera Azul, Parque Nacional nat. park Peru
250 C4 Cordillera de los Picachos, Parque Nacional nat. park Col.
92 D6 Cordilleras Range mts Panay Phil.
82 H2 Cordillo Downs S.A. Austr.
182 C8 Cordinhã Port.
257 E3 Cordisburgo Brazil
261 E2 Córdoba Córdoba Arg.
259 C6 Córdoba Río Negro Arg.
261 F3 Córdoba prov. Arg.
250 C2 Córdoba dept Col.
242 H4 Córdoba Durango Mex.
245 K7 Córdoba Veracruz Mex.
185 J5 Córdoba Spain
185 J4 Córdoba prov. Spain
185 J5 Córdoba, Sierra de hills Spain
260 E3 Córdoba, Sierras de mts Arg.
185 J6 Cordobilla, Embalse de resr Spain
184 G2 Cordobilla de Lácara Spain
252 B3 Cordova Peru
Cordova Spain see Córdoba
220 D3 Cordova AK U.S.A.
234 D7 Cordova MD U.S.A.
222 C4 Cordova Bay AK U.S.A.
183 O4 Cordovín Spain
Corduba Spain see Córdoba
183 Q7 Corduente Spain
254 E2 Coreaú Brazil
191 J7 Coreglia Antelminelli Italy
85 H5 Corella r. Qld Austr.
183 Q4 Corella Spain
84 E5 Corella Lake salt flat N.T. Austr.
182 I5 Coreses Spain
150 H6 Corfe Castle Dorset, England U.K.
150 H6 Corfe Mullen Dorset, England U.K.
85 I6 Corfield Qld Austr.
193 L3 Corfinio Italy
Corfu i. Ionioi Nisoi Greece see Kerkyra
232 G6 Corfu NY U.S.A.
182 E6 Corgo r. Port.
255 B6 Corguinho Brazil
193 J4 Cori Italy
182 G9 Coria Spain
184 G6 Coria del Río Spain
191 N8 Coriano Italy
254 D5 Coribe Brazil
83 M5 Coricudgy mt. N.S.W. Austr.
195 L4 Corigliano, Golfo di b. Italy
195 L4 Corigliano Calabro Italy
191 O8 Corinaldo Italy
85 M4 Coringa Islands Coral Sea Is Terr. Austr.
Corinium Gloucestershire, England U.K. see Cirencester
83 J9 Corinna Tas. Austr.
223 J5 Corinne Sask. Can.
Corinth Peloponnisos Greece see Korinthos
237 K8 Corinth MS U.S.A.
233 L5 Corinth NY U.S.A.
Corinth, Gulf of sea chan. Greece see Korinthiakos Kolpos
Corinthus Greece see Korinthos
257 E3 Corinto Brazil
242 □P11 Corinto Nic.
185 I7 Coripe Spain
207 H6 Corisco i. Equat. Guinea
253 F4 Corixa Grande r. Bol./Brazil
253 F4 Corixinha r. Brazil
147 F9 Cork Ireland
147 E8 Cork county Ireland
158 E5 Corlay France
148 B6 Corlea Ireland
147 D4 Corlee Ireland
194 E8 Corleone Sicilia Italy
193 Q7 Corleto Perticara Italy
199 I1 Çorlu Turkey
199 I1 Çorlu r. Turkey
160 F3 Cormatin France
182 B2 Corme e Laxe, Ría de b. Spain
159 L3 Cormeilles France
159 K3 Cormelles-le-Royal France
182 C2 Corme Porto Spain
162 C4 Corme-Royal France
156 G5 Cormicy France
191 O4 Cormons Italy
251 H4 Cormontibo Fr. Guiana
156 H5 Cormontreuil France
191 O4 Cormor r. Italy
92 □ Cormoran Reef Palau
223 K4 Cormorant Man. Can.
223 K4 Cormorant Lake Man. Can.
223 K4 Cormorant Provincial Forest nature res. Man. Can.
193 O5 Cornacchia, Monte mt. Italy
147 G6 Cornafulla Ireland
183 P4 Cornago Spain
147 D5 Cornamona Ireland
190 G4 Cornaredo Italy
161 F7 Cornas France
168 F5 Cornau Ger.
169 I8 Cornberg Ger.
159 K7 Corné France
191 K3 Cornedo all'Isarco Italy
163 J10 Corneilla-del-Vercol France
215 M3 Cornelia S. Africa
256 B5 Cornélio Procópio Brazil
258 H3 Cornélios Brazil
251 G3 Corneliskondre Suriname
226 C4 Cornell WI U.S.A.
186 J5 Cornellà de Llobregat Spain
186 K3 Cornellà de Terri Spain
182 H2 Cornellana Spain
225 J3 Corner Brook Nfld and Lab. Can.
83 K8 Corner Inlet b. Vic. Austr.
185 P5 Corneros r. Spain
264 F3 Corner Seamounts sea feature N. Atlantic Ocean
136 H6 Cornești Moldova
Corneto Italy see Tarquinia
191 K4 Cornetto mt. Italy
232 B11 Cornettsville KY U.S.A.
177 L6 Cornetu, Vârful hill Romania
146 K7 Cornhill Aberdeenshire, Scotland U.K.
149 M2 Cornhill-on-Tweed Northumberland, England U.K.
149 M6 Cornholme West Yorkshire, England U.K.
197 O3 Corni Romania
192 F2 Cornia r. Italy
190 I7 Corniglio Italy
156 H5 Cornillet, Mont hill France
157 M8 Cornimont France
237 J7 Corning AR U.S.A.
240 J2 Corning CA U.S.A.
236 H5 Corning IA U.S.A.
232 H6 Corning NY U.S.A.
232 C9 Corning OH U.S.A.
85 J7 Cornish watercourse Qld Austr.
259 B7 Cornish, Estrada b. Chile
Corn Islands is Nic. see Maíz, Islas del
193 J2 Corno r. Italy
193 L3 Corno, Monte mt. Italy
190 I3 Corno di Campo mt. Italy/Switz.
158 C5 Cornouaille reg. France
226 C3 Cornucopia WI U.S.A.
191 M4 Cornuda Italy
183 N3 Cornudilla Spain
161 C9 Cornus France
224 F4 Cornwall Ont. Can.
225 I4 Cornwall P.E.I. Can.
246 □ Cornwall reg. Jamaica
150 C6 Cornwall admin. div. England U.K.
235 G2 Cornwall NY U.S.A.
234 C4 Cornwall PA U.S.A.
150 □ Cornwall, Cape England U.K.
221 I2 Cornwallis Island Nunavut Can.
221 I2 Cornwall Island Nunavut Can.
235 G2 Cornwall on Hudson NY U.S.A.
82 F6 Corny Point S.A. Austr.
250 D2 Coro Venez.
182 F5 Coroa, Serra da mts Port.
257 F3 Coroaci Brazil
254 D3 Coroatá Brazil
252 C4 Corocoro Bol.
251 F2 Corocoro, Isla i. Venez.
147 D7 Corofin Ireland
80 J3 Coroglen North I. N.Z.
252 D4 Coroico Bol.
256 D3 Coromandel Brazil
80 J3 Coromandel North I. N.Z.
114 G7 Coromandel Coast India
80 J4 Coromandel Forest Park nature res. North I. N.Z.
80 J3 Coromandel Peninsula North I. N.Z.
80 J3 Coromandel Range hills North I. N.Z.
159 J7 Coron France
92 C5 Coron Phil.
184 C4 Corona r. Port.
183 R3 Corona mt. Spain
240 O8 Corona CA U.S.A.
239 L9 Corona NM U.S.A.
207 H6 Corona, Punta pt Equat. Guinea
182 C6 Coronado Port.
240 O9 Coronado CA U.S.A.
242 □R13 Coronado, Bahía de b. Costa Rica
92 D8 Coronado Bay Mindanao Phil.
259 B6 Coronados, Golfo de los b. Chile
223 I4 Coronation Alta Can.
220 G3 Coronation Gulf Nunavut Can.
262 U2 Coronation Island S. Orkney Is Atlantic Ocean
222 C4 Coronation Island AK U.S.A.
86 H3 Coronation Islands W.A. Austr.
92 C6 Coron Bay Phil.
261 G2 Coronda Arg.
260 E3 Coronel Alzogaray Arg.
261 G3 Coronel Bogada Arg.
261 H4 Coronel Brandsen Arg.
261 G6 Coronel Dorrego Arg.
257 F3 Coronel Fabriciano Brazil
261 G6 Coronel Falcón Arg.
259 D6 Coronel Francisco Sosa Arg.
261 E6 Coronel Juliá y Echarrán Arg.
260 E3 Coronel Moldes Córdoba Arg.
258 D2 Coronel Moldes Salta Arg.
257 F2 Coronel Murta Brazil
253 F6 Coronel Oviedo Para.
253 G3 Coronel Ponce Brazil
250 B5 Coronel Portillo Peru
261 G5 Coronel Pringles Arg.
261 G5 Coronel Rodolfo Bunge Arg.
253 G5 Coronel Sapucaia Mato Grosso do Sul Brazil
261 G5 Coronel Suárez Arg.
261 I5 Coronel Vidal Arg.
244 G5 Coroneo Mex.
81 C11 Coronet Peak South I. N.Z.
198 B2 Çorovodë Albania
83 K6 Corowa N.S.W. Austr.
243 O8 Corozal Belize
245 I4 Corozal Mex.
247 □1 Corozal Puerto Rico
251 F2 Corozal Venez.
250 E2 Corozo Pando Venez.
259 C8 Corpen Aike Arg.
161 H7 Corps France
158 H6 Corps-Nuds France
258 G2 Corpus Arg.
237 G12 Corpus Christi TX U.S.A.
237 G11 Corpus Christi, Lake TX U.S.A.
252 D4 Corque Bol.
259 B5 Corral Chile
182 I7 Corral mt. Spain
183 N9 Corral de Almaguer Spain
261 F3 Corral de Bustos Arg.
185 K3 Corral de Calatrava Spain
183 L9 Corral de Cantos mt. Spain
260 D2 Corral de Isaac Arg.
216 □3b Corralejo Fuerteventura Canary Is
237 C13 Corrales Mex.
182 I6 Corrales Spain
244 F5 Corrales de Rábago Mex.
246 C2 Corralilla Cuba
240 K5 Corralitos CA U.S.A.
260 D2 Corralitos, Monte mt. Arg.
245 L7 Corral Nuevo Mex.
185 Q3 Corral-Rubio Spain
87 C8 Corrandibby Range hills W.A. Austr.
213 H2 Corrane Moz.
192 C7 Corrasi, Punta mt. Sardegna Italy
147 C5 Corraun Peninsula Ireland
157 L8 Corre France
244 C2 Corre Caballo Mex.
146 K8 Correen Hills Scotland U.K.
191 J6 Correggio Italy
256 B2 Córrego do Ouro Brazil
257 F3 Córrego Novo Brazil
254 D4 Corrente Brazil
256 B3 Corrente r. Brazil
254 E5 Corrente r. Brazil
257 F3 Corrente Grande r. Brazil
255 B6 Correntes Brazil
253 G4 Correntes r. Brazil
189 E7 Correnti, Isola delle i. Sicilia Italy
254 D5 Correntina Brazil

Correntina r. Brazil see Éguas
162 H5 Corrèze France
162 H5 Corrèze dept France
162 G5 Corrèze r. France
147 D6 Corrib, Lough l. Ireland
191 P9 Corridonia Italy
146 F11 Corrie North Ayrshire, Scotland U.K.
258 F2 Corrientes Arg.
261 H1 Corrientes prov. Arg.
258 F3 Corrientes r. Arg.
250 C5 Corrientes r. Peru
261 I6 Corrientes, Cabo c. Arg.
250 B3 Corrientes, Cabo c. Col.
246 A3 Corrientes, Cabo c. Cuba
244 B5 Corrientes, Cabo c. Mex.
237 H10 Corrigan TX U.S.A.
87 D12 Corrigin W.A. Austr.
151 M4 Corringham Thurrock, England U.K.
150 E2 Corris Gwynedd, Wales U.K.
251 G3 Corriverton Guyana
156 G6 Corrobert France
182 B3 Corrubedo, Cabo c. Spain
232 F7 Corry PA U.S.A.
83 K7 Corryong Vic. Austr.
190 D7 Corsaglia r. Italy
195 O4 Corsano Italy
192 C3 Corse admin. reg. France
192 A3 Corse i. France
192 C1 Corse, Cap c. Corse France
192 B2 Corse, Parc Naturel Régional de la nature res. Corse France
192 B4 Corse-du-Sud dept Corse France
146 H12 Corserine hill Scotland U.K.
158 G5 Corseul France
150 H5 Corsham Wiltshire, England U.K.
Corsica i. France see Corse
237 G9 Corsicana TX U.S.A.
190 G5 Corsico Italy
208 A4 Corsico, Baie de b. Gabon
146 I12 Corsock Dumfries and Galloway, Scotland U.K.
234 F6 Corson's Inlet NJ U.S.A.
Cort Adelaer, Kap c. Greenland see Kangeq
195 K6 Cortale Italy
244 G5 Cortazar Mex.
192 C3 Corte Corse France
184 F3 Corte de Peleas Spain
182 D4 Cortegada Spain
184 F5 Cortegana Spain
190 E6 Cortemilia Italy
190 I3 Corteno Golgi Italy
190 G5 Corteolona Italy
183 R5 Cortes Spain
Cortes, Sea of g. Mex. see California, Golfo de
186 D6 Cortes de Aragón Spain
185 N5 Cortes de Baza Spain
185 I7 Cortes de la Frontera Spain
184 H7 Cortes de la Frontera, Reserva Nacional de nature res. Spain
187 D9 Cortes de Pallás Spain
239 J8 Cortez CO U.S.A.
241 P1 Cortez Mountains NV U.S.A.
184 C3 Cortiçadas do Lavre Port.
186 G5 Cortiella r. Spain
185 K2 Cortijo de Arriba Spain
245 I9 Cortijos r. Mex.
185 N4 Cortijos Nuevos Spain
191 M2 Cortina d'Ampezzo Italy
233 I6 Cortland NY U.S.A.
232 E7 Cortland OH U.S.A.
178 E8 Corto, Lago del l. Italy
151 P2 Corton Suffolk, England U.K.
191 L9 Cortona Italy
206 B4 Corubal r. Guinea-Bissau
184 B3 Coruche Port.
Çoruh Turkey see Artvin
129 C4 Çoruh r. Turkey
127 J3 Çoruh r. Turkey
182 G3 Corullón Spain
126 G3 Çorum Turkey
253 F4 Corumbá Brazil
256 C3 Corumbá r. Brazil
256 C1 Corumbá de Goiás Brazil
256 C3 Corumbaíba Brazil
256 B5 Corumbataí r. Brazil
257 H2 Corumbaú, Ponta pt Brazil
182 D2 Coruña, Ría da b. Spain
197 N4 Corund Romania
177 L4 Corund r. Romania
232 C6 Corunna Ont. Can.
Corunna Spain see A Coruña
227 J7 Corunna MI U.S.A.
254 F4 Coruripe Brazil
238 C4 Corvallis OR U.S.A.
191 L2 Corvara in Badia Italy
150 G3 Corve Dale val. England U.K.
187 C12 Corvera Spain
224 F2 Corvette, Lac de la l. Que. Can.
193 J4 Corvia, Colle hill Italy
216 □1 Corvo i. Azores
150 F2 Corwen Denbighshire, Wales U.K.
236 I5 Corydon IA U.S.A.
230 D6 Corydon IN U.S.A.
151 N4 Coryton Thurrock, England U.K.
232 G7 Coryville PA U.S.A.
Cos i. Greece see Kos
186 C6 Cosa Spain
244 A1 Cosalá Mex.
245 L7 Cosamaloapan Mex.
129 A5 Coşandere Turkey
151 J2 Cosby Leicestershire, England U.K.
252 C4 Coscaya Chile
193 J2 Coscerno, Monte mt. Italy
195 L4 Coscile r. Italy
245 J6 Coscomatepec Mex.
183 P6 Coscurita Spain
Cosentia Italy see Cosenza
193 Q9 Cosenza Italy
193 Q9 Cosenza prov. Italy
197 O6 Coşereni Romania
195 L4 Coserie r. Italy
146 I9 Coshieville Perth and Kinross, Scotland U.K.
232 D8 Coshocton OH U.S.A.
244 E3 Cosío Mex.
190 D7 Cosio di Arroscia Italy
183 M8 Coslada Spain
217 □2 Cosmoledo Atoll Aldabra Is Seychelles
87 G10 Cosmo Newbery Aboriginal Reserve W.A. Austr.
256 D5 Cosmópolis Brazil
160 B2 Cosne-Cours-sur-Loire France
160 B4 Cosne-d'Allier France
245 M8 Cosoleacaque Mex.
195 J7 Cosoleto Italy
260 E2 Cosquín Arg.
190 E4 Cossato Italy
171 I8 Cossebaude Ger.
159 J6 Cossé-le-Vivien France
192 B7 Cossoine Sardegna Italy
156 B8 Cosson r. France
190 B2 Cossonay Switz.
254 E3 Costa Brazil
184 A4 Costa Bela coastal area Port.
187 E11 Costa Blanca coastal area Spain
186 L5 Costa Brava coastal area Spain
191 N9 Costacciaro Italy
197 P5 Costache Negri Romania
184 A3 Costa da Caparica Port.
184 B4 Costa da Galé coastal area Port.
186 G6 Costa de Fora coastal area Spain
184 E6 Costa de la Luz coastal area Spain
187 E8 Costa del Azahar coastal area Spain
216 □3a Costa del Silencio Tenerife Canary Is
185 I8 Costa del Sol coastal area Spain
242 □R11 Costa de Mosquitos coastal area Nic.
184 A3 Costa do Estoril coastal area Port.
186 J5 Costa Dorada coastal area Spain
184 A3 Costa do Sol coastal area Port.
261 G3 Costa Grande Arg.
252 D3 Costa Marques Brazil
192 D9 Costa Rei coastal area Sardegna Italy
256 A3 Costa Rica Brazil
246 A8 Costa Rica country Central America
242 F5 Costa Rica Mex.
192 D5 Costa Smeralda coastal area Sardegna Italy
216 □3c Costa Teguise Lanzarote Canary Is
192 A9 Costa Verde coastal area Sardegna Italy
182 G1 Costa Verde coastal area Spain
190 I4 Costa Volpino Italy
177 K6 Coşteiu Romania
147 C6 Costelloe Ireland
Costermansville Dem. Rep. Congo see Bukavu
151 O2 Costessey Norfolk, England U.K.
136 G6 Costeşti Moldova
197 M6 Costeşti Argeş Romania
197 P4 Costeşti Vaslui Romania
233 □Q3 Costigan ME U.S.A.
223 J3 Costigan Lake Sask. Can.
190 E6 Costigliole d'Asti Italy
190 C6 Costigliole Saluzzo Italy
186 C5 Cosuenda Spain
197 L6 Coşuştea r. Romania
171 I8 Coswig Sachsen Ger.
171 F7 Coswig Sachsen-Anhalt Ger.
252 B3 Cotabambas Peru
92 E8 Cotabato Mindanao Phil.
252 D4 Cotacajes r. Bol.
252 D5 Cotagaita Bol.
252 B3 Cotahuasi Peru
257 G3 Cotaxé r. Brazil
245 K7 Cotaxtla Mex.
222 D3 Cote, Mount AK U.S.A.
236 F3 Coteau des Prairies slope SD U.S.A.
236 D1 Coteau du Missouri slope ND U.S.A.
236 E3 Coteau du Missouri slope SD U.S.A.
233 K3 Coteau Station Que. Can.
246 F4 Coteaux Haiti
156 G6 Côte Champenoise reg. France
163 A9 Côte d'Argent coastal area France
161 K9 Côte d'Azur airport France
161 K9 Côte d'Azur coastal area France
156 H7 Côte des Bars reg. France
206 D5 Côte d'Ivoire country Africa
156 I8 Côte-d'Or dept France
160 F3 Côte d'Or reg. France
Côte Française de Somalis country Africa see Djibouti
254 D4 Cotegipe Brazil
158 I3 Cotentin pen. France
158 F5 Côtes-d'Armor dept France
157 I4 Côtes de Meuse ridge France
157 K6 Côtes de Moselle hills France
Côtes-du-Nord dept France see Côtes-d'Armor
163 K10 Côte Vermeille coastal area France
150 D4 Cothi r. Wales U.K.
252 D2 Coti r. Brazil
Cotiaeum Turkey see Kütahya
192 B4 Coti-Chiavari Corse France
186 F2 Cotiella mt. Spain
161 I9 Cotignac France
191 L7 Cotignola Italy
244 E6 Cotija Mex.
216 □3b Cotillo Fuerteventura Canary Is
251 F4 Cotingo r. Brazil
136 H6 Cotiujeni Moldova
136 H6 Cotiujenii Mici Moldova
197 M6 Cotmeana r. Romania
96 H4 Cô Tô, Quân Đao is Vietnam
Coton, Pointe pt Rodrigues I. Mauritius see Cotton, Pointe
184 G5 Coto Nacional de la Pata del Caballo nature res. Spain
207 F5 Cotonou Benin
250 B5 Cotopaxi prov. Ecuador
250 B5 Cotopaxi, Volcán vol. Ecuador
246 B2 Cotorro Cuba
Cotovsc Moldova see Hînceşti
195 L5 Cotronei Italy
150 H4 Cotswold Hills England U.K.
238 C5 Cottage Grove OR U.S.A.
193 J3 Cottanello Italy
171 J7 Cottbus Ger.
114 G6 Cotteliar r. India
151 M3 Cottenham Cambridgeshire, England U.K.
151 K2 Cottesmore Rutland, England U.K.
161 J8 Cottian Alps mts France/Italy
251 H4 Cottica Suriname
Cottiennes, Alpes mts France/Italy see Cottian Alps
149 Q6 Cottingham East Riding of Yorkshire, England U.K.
151 K2 Cottingham Northamptonshire, England U.K.
226 B2 Cotton MN U.S.A.
217 □1a Cotton, Pointe pt Rodrigues I. Mauritius
84 G7 Cottonbush Creek watercourse Qld Austr.
241 T7 Cottonwood AZ U.S.A.
240 J1 Cottonwood CA U.S.A.
238 F3 Cottonwood ID U.S.A.
236 G6 Cottonwood r. KS U.S.A.
236 H3 Cottonwood r. MN U.S.A.
237 D10 Cottonwood Creek watercourse TX U.S.A.
236 G6 Cottonwood Falls KS U.S.A.
241 V7 Cottonwood Wash watercourse AZ U.S.A.
246 H4 Cotuí Dom. Rep.
237 F11 Cotulla TX U.S.A.
197 O2 Coţuşca Romania
161 D6 Coubon France
162 B4 Coubre, Pointe de la pt France
160 F3 Couches France
86 I3 Couchman Range hills W.A. Austr.
184 C3 Couço Port.
161 D7 Coucouron France
156 F4 Coucy-le-Château-Auffrique France
159 N7 Couddes France
156 D1 Coudekerque-Branche France
232 G7 Coudersport PA U.S.A.
225 G4 Coudres, Île aux i. Que. Can.
82 F7 Couedic, Cape du S.A. Austr.
158 H7 Couëron France
158 H4 Couesnon r. France
163 G10 Couflens France
163 H8 Coufouleux France
162 E3 Couhé France
163 I10 Couiza France
159 L5 Coulaines France
156 G8 Coulanges-la-Vineuse France
160 C2 Coulanges-lès-Nevers France
160 D1 Coulanges-sur-Yonne France
159 L5 Coulans-sur-Gée France
162 F5 Coulaures France
238 E3 Coulee City WA U.S.A.
238 E3 Coulee Dam WA U.S.A.
160 B3 Couleuvre France
159 P6 Coullons France
263 L2 Coulman Island Antarctica
156 H8 Coulmier-le-Sec France
156 C8 Coulmiers France
156 C2 Coulogne France
156 G5 Coulognes-Cohan France
205 H4 Couloir 1 well Alg.
162 E3 Coulombiers France
156 C6 Coulombs France
156 F6 Coulommiers France
161 F9 Coulon r. France
224 E4 Coulonge r. Que. Can.
162 C3 Coulonges-sur-l'Autize France
162 F5 Coulounieix-Chamiers France
146 G10 Coulport Argyll and Bute, Scotland U.K.
240 L4 Coulterville CA U.S.A.
238 F4 Council ID U.S.A.
236 H5 Council Bluffs IA U.S.A.
236 G6 Council Grove KS U.S.A.
83 J8 Councillor Island Tas. Austr.
151 J2 Countesthorpe Leicestershire, England U.K.
146 J9 Coupar Angus Perth and Kinross, Scotland U.K.
238 C2 Coupeville WA U.S.A.
161 B9 Coupiac France
159 K5 Couptrain France
182 C5 Coura Port.
223 I1 Courageous Lake N.W.T. Can.
251 G3 Courantyne r. Guyana
165 F8 Courcelles Belgium
233 □O3 Courcelles Que. Can.
157 L5 Courcelles-Chaussy France
157 L5 Courcelles-sur-Nied France
160 J1 Courchaton France
161 J6 Courchevel France
159 N6 Cour-Cheverny France
159 K5 Courcité France
162 C3 Courçon France
156 H5 Courcy France
182 F4 Courel, Serra do mts Spain
159 L5 Courgains France
156 G7 Courgenay France
190 C1 Courgenay Switz.
138 E6 Courland Lagoon b. Lith./Rus. Fed.
160 G3 Courlaoux France
159 J8 Courlay France
156 F7 Courlon-sur-Yonne France
190 B4 Courmayeur Italy
156 F5 Courmelles France
160 C5 Cournon-d'Auvergne France
161 D9 Cournonterral France
161 G10 Couronne, Cap c. France
160 D5 Courpière France
190 C1 Courrendlin Switz.
163 E8 Courrensan France
156 E3 Courrières France
160 B2 Cours France
162 F5 Coursac France
161 C10 Coursan France
161 K9 Coursegoules France
159 K3 Courseulles-sur-Mer France
160 E4 Cours-la-Ville France
160 C1 Courson-les-Carrières France
190 C1 Court Switz.
156 B7 Courtalain France
190 C1 Courtelary Switz.
160 K1 Courtelevant France
222 E5 Courtenay B.C. Can.
156 F7 Courtenay France
161 F8 Courthézon France
156 I6 Courtisols France
232 H12 Courtland VA U.S.A.
147 E9 Courtmacsherry Ireland
147 E9 Courtmacsherry Bay Ireland
159 L4 Courtomer France
147 J7 Courtown Ireland
Courtrai Belgium see Kortrijk
165 G7 Court-St-Etienne Belgium
156 B7 Courville-sur-Eure France
160 G3 Cousance France
157 J6 Cousances-les-Forges France
163 F10 Couserans reg. France
237 I9 Coushatta LA U.S.A.
160 D1 Cousin r. France
217 □2a Cousin i. Inner Islands Seychelles
217 □2a Cousine i. Inner Islands Seychelles
182 C4 Couso, Punta de pt Spain
162 G4 Coussac-Bonneval France
159 M8 Coussay-les-Bois France
156 H8 Coussegrey France
157 K7 Coussey France
161 G9 Coustellet France
163 J11 Coustouges France
158 I3 Coutances France
159 K4 Couterne France
Coutinho Moz. see Ulongue
257 F3 Couto de Magalhães de Minas Brazil
162 D5 Coutras France
223 I5 Coutts Alta Can.
162 E4 Couture r. France
247 □7 Couva Trin. and Tob.
190 B2 Couvet Switz.
165 G8 Couvin Belgium
156 G4 Couvron-et-Aumencourt France
163 F6 Couze r. France
163 F6 Couze-et-St-Front France
162 G4 Couzeix France
182 I8 Covacha del Losar mt. Spain
182 E3 Cova da Serpe, Sierra da mts Spain
183 O5 Covaleda Spain
183 N4 Covarrubias Spain
177 K5 Covăsinţ Romania
197 O5 Covasna Romania
146 E7 Cove Highland, Scotland U.K.
146 L8 Cove Bay Aberdeen, Scotland U.K.
241 T3 Cove Fort UT U.S.A.
227 M4 Cove Island Ont. Can.
261 H5 Covello Arg.
240 I2 Covelo CA U.S.A.
232 G9 Cove Mountains hills PA U.S.A.
250 C2 Coveñas Col.
252 D3 Covendo Bol.
151 I3 Coventry West Midlands, England U.K.
149 N5 Cover r. England U.K.
150 B7 Coverack Cornwall, England U.K.
241 T9 Covered Wells AZ U.S.A.
187 F7 Coves de Sant Miquel, Riu de les r. Spain
232 G11 Covesville VA U.S.A.
182 F8 Covilhã Port.
231 F9 Covington GA U.S.A.
230 D5 Covington IN U.S.A.
232 A9 Covington KY U.S.A.
237 J10 Covington LA U.S.A.
226 F3 Covington MI U.S.A.
232 A8 Covington OH U.S.A.
237 K8 Covington TN U.S.A.
232 E11 Covington VA U.S.A.
227 K2 Cow r. Ont. Can.
83 K5 Cowal, Lake dry lake N.S.W. Austr.
232 B10 Cowan KY U.S.A.
87 F11 Cowan, Lake salt flat W.A. Austr.
225 F4 Cowansville Que. Can.
151 L2 Cowbit Lincolnshire, England U.K.
150 F5 Cowbridge Vale of Glamorgan, Wales U.K.
87 D11 Cowcowing Lakes salt flat W.A. Austr.
146 J10 Cowdenbeath Fife, Scotland U.K.
82 F5 Cowell S.A. Austr.
232 E10 Cowen WV U.S.A.
83 J8 Cowes Vic. Austr.
151 J6 Cowes Isle of Wight, England U.K.
151 L6 Cowfold West Sussex, England U.K.
149 M4 Cow Green Reservoir England U.K.
146 I10 Cowie Stirling, Scotland U.K.
85 J9 Cowley Qld Austr.
149 M6 Cowling North Yorkshire, England U.K.
238 C3 Cowlitz r. WA U.S.A.
232 F11 Cowpasture r. VA U.S.A.
83 L5 Cowra N.S.W. Austr.
149 M4 Cowshill Durham, England U.K.
84 E3 Cox r. N.T. Austr.
163 G8 Cox France
Coxen Hole Hond. see Roatán
151 M5 Coxheath Kent, England U.K.
149 N4 Coxhoe Durham, England U.K.
258 G3 Coxilha de Santana hills Brazil/Uru.
255 B9 Coxilha Grande hills Brazil
255 B6 Coxim Brazil
255 B6 Coxim r. Brazil
233 L6 Coxsackie NY U.S.A.
117 M9 Cox's Bazar Bangl.
149 O5 Coxwold North Yorkshire, England U.K.
260 B4 Coya Chile
206 B4 Coyah Guinea
259 C8 Coy Aike Arg.
237 C11 Coyame Mex.
237 D10 Coyanosa Creek watercourse TX U.S.A.
150 E4 Coychurch Bridgend, Wales U.K.
146 H12 Coylton South Ayrshire, Scotland U.K.
146 I8 Coylumbridge Highland, Scotland U.K.
239 H11 Coyote r. Mex.
242 D5 Coyote, Punta pt Mex.
240 P6 Coyote Lake CA U.S.A.
241 R9 Coyote Peak hill AZ U.S.A.
240 N5 Coyote Peak CA U.S.A.
244 G5 Coyotillos Mex.
244 A2 Coyotitán Mex.
244 G9 Coyuca, Laguna l. Mex.
244 G8 Coyuca de Benítez Mex.
244 G7 Coyuca de Catalán Mex.
245 J5 Coyutla Mex.
236 F5 Cozad NE U.S.A.
185 M3 Cózar Spain
162 C4 Cozes France
197 M5 Cozia, Vârful mt. Romania
Cozie, Alpi mts France/Italy see Cottian Alps
243 P7 Cozumel Mex.
243 P7 Cozumel, Isla de i. Mex.
192 C4 Cozzano Corse France
193 Q8 Cozzo del Pellegrino mt. Italy
148 E8 Craanford Ireland
85 I1 Crab Island Qld Austr.
217 □1a Crab Island Rodrigues I. Mauritius
246 □ Crab Pond Point Jamaica
158 E6 Crach France
193 Q7 Craco Italy
Cracovia Pol. see Kraków
85 M8 Cracow Qld Austr.
Cracow Pol. see Kraków
83 K9 Cradle Mountain Lake St Clair National Park Tas. Austr.
150 H3 Cradley Herefordshire, England U.K.
82 G4 Cradock S.A. Austr.
215 J8 Cradock S. Africa
80 J3 Cradock Channel North I. N.Z.
190 J4 Craffaro r. Italy
214 I2 Crafthole S. Africa
146 K9 Craichie Angus, Scotland U.K.
177 L4 Craidorolţ Romania
146 F8 Craig Highland, Scotland U.K.
222 C4 Craig AK U.S.A.
238 K6 Craig CO U.S.A.
147 K3 Craigavad Northern Ireland U.K.
147 J4 Craigavon Northern Ireland U.K.
146 H12 Craigdarroch East Ayrshire, Scotland U.K.
146 F11 Craigendive Argyll and Bute, Scotland U.K.
83 J7 Craigieburn Vic. Austr.
81 F10 Craigieburn South I. N.Z.
81 F10 Craigieburn Forest Park nature res. South I. N.Z.
146 E10 Craignure Argyll and Bute, Scotland U.K.
147 J3 Craigs Northern Ireland U.K.
232 F10 Craigsville VA U.S.A.
232 E10 Craigsville WV U.S.A.
146 K10 Crail Fife, Scotland U.K.
173 I3 Crailsheim Ger.
197 L6 Craiova Romania
177 K5 Craiva Romania
234 B5 Craley PA U.S.A.
156 G6 Cramant France
149 N3 Cramlington Northumberland, England U.K.
214 F3 Cramond S. Africa
163 H9 Crampagna France
148 C3 Crana r. Ireland
149 M7 Cranage Cheshire, England U.K.
147 H3 Cranagh Northern Ireland U.K.
222 D4 Cranberry Junction B.C. Can.
234 F3 Cranberry Lake NJ U.S.A.
233 K4 Cranberry Lake l. NY U.S.A.
223 K4 Cranberry Portage Man. Can.
150 H6 Cranborne Chase for. England U.K.
83 J8 Cranbourne Vic. Austr.
87 D13 Cranbrook W.A. Austr.
222 H5 Cranbrook B.C. Can.
151 N5 Cranbrook Kent, England U.K.
235 F4 Cranbury NJ U.S.A.
226 F4 Crandon WI U.S.A.
238 E5 Crane OR U.S.A.
237 D10 Crane TX U.S.A.
223 I5 Crane Lake l. Sask. Can.
226 B1 Crane Lake MN U.S.A.
235 I3 Crane Neck Point NY U.S.A.
151 K3 Cranfield Bedfordshire, England U.K.
147 J4 Cranfield Point Northern Ireland U.K.
148 B3 Cranford Ireland
160 I5 Cran-Gevrier France
151 L5 Cranleigh Surrey, England U.K.
163 I6 Cransac France
146 L11 Cranshaws Scottish Borders, Scotland U.K.
190 C3 Crans-sur-Sierre Switz.
146 G6 Cranstackie hill Scotland U.K.
232 B10 Cranston KY U.S.A.
233 N7 Cranston RI U.S.A.
149 Q7 Cranwell Lincolnshire, England U.K.
Cranz Rus. Fed. see Zelenogradsk
254 D3 Craolândia Brazil
159 J6 Craon France
156 G5 Craonne France
197 Q5 Crapina, Lacul l. Romania
161 D6 Craponne-sur-Arzon France
262 M1 Crary Ice Rise Antarctica
262 P1 Crary Mountains Antarctica
146 G6 Crask Inn Highland, Scotland U.K.
197 K3 Crasna Romania
197 K3 Crasna r. Romania
136 I7 Crasnoe Moldova
238 C5 Crater Lake National Park OR U.S.A.
238 H5 Craters of the Moon National Monument nat. park ID U.S.A.
254 E3 Crateús Brazil
146 J8 Crathie Aberdeenshire, Scotland U.K.
193 Q8 Crati r. Italy
254 F3 Crato Brazil
184 D2 Crato Port.
161 F9 Crau reg. France
147 E6 Craughwell Ireland
190 E4 Cravagliana Italy
160 J1 Cravanche France
156 G8 Cravant France
253 F3 Cravari r. Brazil
150 G3 Craven Arms Shropshire, England U.K.
256 D4 Cravinhos Brazil
250 D3 Cravo Norte Col.
236 D4 Crawford NE U.S.A.
238 F2 Crawford Bay B.C. Can.
146 I12 Crawfordjohn South Lanarkshire, Scotland U.K.
92 B6 Crawford Point Palawan Phil.
84 D6 Crawford Range hills N.T. Austr.
81 F9 Crawford Range mts South I. N.Z.
230 D5 Crawfordsville IN U.S.A.
231 E10 Crawfordville FL U.S.A.
231 F9 Crawfordville GA U.S.A.
169 K9 Crawinkel Ger.
151 L5 Crawley West Sussex, England U.K.
238 I3 Crazy Mountains MT U.S.A.
Creag Ghoraidh Scotland U.K. see Creagorry
146 G9 Creag Meagaidh mt. Scotland U.K.
146 B8 Creagorry Western Isles, Scotland U.K.
158 H3 Créances France
160 F2 Créancey France
223 J4 Crean Lake Sask. Can.
182 D4 Crecente Spain
160 F4 Crêches-sur-Saône France
156 C3 Crécy-en-Ponthieu France
156 E6 Crécy-la-Chapelle France
156 G4 Crécy-sur-Serre France
150 G3 Credenhill Herefordshire, England U.K.
150 E6 Crediton Devon, England U.K.
223 J3 Cree r. Sask. Can.
150 F5 Creech St Michael Somerset, England U.K.
239 K8 Creede CO U.S.A.
147 D7 Creegh Ireland
242 F4 Creel Mex.
223 J3 Cree Lake Sask. Can.
227 N5 Creemore Ont. Can.
147 G2 Creeslough Ireland
146 H13 Creetown Dumfries and Galloway, Scotland U.K.
147 D4 Creevagh Ireland
147 H3 Creggan Northern Ireland U.K.
147 I4 Creggan Northern Ireland U.K.
147 C5 Cregganbaun Ireland
147 F5 Creggs Ireland
173 I3 Creglingen Ger.
148 H5 Cregneash Isle of Man
157 M5 Créhange France
223 K4 Creighton Sask. Can.
215 N6 Creighton S. Africa
156 D5 Creil France
164 I3 Creil Neth.
161 C8 Creissels France
190 H5 Crema Italy
160 D5 Cremeaux France
183 J3 Crémenes Spain
160 G5 Crémieu France
169 K6 Cremlingen Ger.
222 H5 Cremona Alta Can.
190 I5 Cremona Italy
190 I5 Cremona prov. Italy
156 H7 Creney-près-Troyes France
179 N6 Črenšovci Slovenia
163 D6 Créon France
157 K6 Crépey France
251 G6 Crepori r. Brazil
156 G4 Crépy France
156 E5 Crépy-en-Valois France
146 F9 Creran, Loch inlet Scotland U.K.
188 E3 Cres Croatia
188 E3 Cres i. Croatia
238 D5 Crescent OR U.S.A.
238 B6 Crescent City CA U.S.A.
231 G11 Crescent City FL U.S.A.
90 D3 Crescent Group is Paracel Is
83 N4 Crescent Head N.S.W. Austr.
190 E5 Crescentino Italy
241 W3 Crescent Junction UT U.S.A.
236 D5 Crescent Lake National Wildlife Refuge nature res. NE U.S.A.
241 Q6 Crescent Peak NV U.S.A.
240 P1 Crescent Valley NV U.S.A.
226 B6 Cresco IA U.S.A.
234 E2 Cresco PA U.S.A.
190 G5 Crespi d'Adda tourist site Italy
191 L6 Crespino Italy
261 G3 Crespo Arg.
183 K7 Crespos Spain
162 H5 Cressensac France
172 C7 Cressier Switz.
234 C3 Cressona PA U.S.A.
84 E5 Cresswell watercourse N.T. Austr.
84 E4 Cresswell Downs N.T. Austr.
83 I8 Cressy Vic. Austr.
161 G7 Crest France
92 D3 Cresta, Mount Phil.
Crest Hill H.K. China see Tai Shek Mo
232 C8 Crestline OH U.S.A.
222 G5 Creston B.C. Can.
236 H5 Creston IA U.S.A.
238 K6 Creston WY U.S.A.
231 D10 Crestview FL U.S.A.
160 J5 Crest-Voland France
235 G5 Crestwood Village NJ U.S.A.
149 O7 Creswell Derbyshire, England U.K.
234 C5 Creswell PA U.S.A.
83 I7 Creswick Vic. Austr.
Creta i. Kriti Greece see Kriti
191 N2 Creta Forata, Monte mt. Italy
186 F6 Cretas Spain
160 H4 Crêt de la Neige mt. France
160 G5 Crêt de Pont mt. France
160 H4 Crêt des Eculaz mt. France
160 H4 Crêt du Nu mt. France
Crete i. Kriti Greece see Kriti
236 G5 Crete NE U.S.A.
156 D6 Créteil France
160 I2 Crêt Monniot mt. France
159 J3 Creully France
186 L3 Creus, Cap de c. Spain
162 I3 Creuse dept France
162 F1 Creuse r. France
173 L2 Creußen Ger.
173 L2 Creußen r. Ger.
157 M5 Creutzwald France
169 J8 Creuzburg Ger.
160 C4 Creuzier-le-Vieux France
191 K6 Crevalcore Italy
162 H3 Crevant France
262 O1 Crevasse Valley Glacier Antarctica
157 L6 Crévéchamps France
156 D4 Crèvecœur-le-Grand France
187 D11 Crevillente Spain
187 D11 Crevillente, Sierra de mts Spain
149 M7 Crewe Cheshire, England U.K.
232 G11 Crewe VA U.S.A.
150 G6 Crewkerne Somerset, England U.K.
163 F6 Creysse France
216 □1c Criação Velha Pico Azores
146 G10 Crianlarich Stirling, Scotland U.K.
150 D2 Criccieth Gwynedd, Wales U.K.
255 C9 Criciúma Brazil
150 F4 Crickhowell Powys, Wales U.K.
151 I4 Cricklade Wiltshire, England U.K.
136 H6 Cricova Moldova
197 O6 Cricovu Sărat r. Romania
232 A8 Cridersville OH U.S.A.
146 I10 Crieff Perth and Kinross, Scotland U.K.
156 B3 Criel-sur-Mer France
146 I13 Criffel hill Scotland U.K.
149 N6 Crigglestone West Yorkshire, England U.K.
188 E3 Crikvenica Croatia
222 B3 Crillon, Mount AK U.S.A.
148 D5 Crilly Northern Ireland U.K.
Crimea aut. rep. Ukr. see Krym, Respublika
Crimea pen. Ukr. see Kryms'kyy Pivostriv
Crimean Republic aut. rep. Ukr. see Krym, Respublika
171 F9 Crimmitschau Ger.
146 M7 Crimond Aberdeenshire, Scotland U.K.
146 E10 Crinan Argyll and Bute, Scotland U.K.
151 O2 Cringleford Norfolk, England U.K.
171 I7 Crinitz Ger.
239 L7 Cripple Creek CO U.S.A.
151 N6 Cripp's Corner East Sussex, England U.K.
159 L2 Criquetot-l'Esneval France
197 R5 Crişan Romania
233 J11 Crisfield MD U.S.A.
195 M2 Crispiano Italy
190 C6 Crissolo Italy
256 D2 Cristais, Serra dos mts Brazil
208 A4 Cristal, Monts de mts Equat. Guinea/Gabon
254 C4 Cristalândia Brazil
256 D2 Cristalina Brazil
Cristalino r. Brazil see Mariembero
253 G2 Cristalino r. Brazil
191 M2 Cristallo mt. Italy
256 C2 Cristianópolis Brazil
257 E5 Cristina Brazil
254 D4 Cristino Castro Brazil
177 L5 Criştioru de Jos Romania
182 I8 Cristóbal Spain
190 F7 Cristoforo Colombo airport Italy
197 N4 Cristuru Secuiesc Romania
197 J4 Crişul Alb r. Romania
197 J4 Crişul Negru r. Romania
197 J3 Crişul Repede r. Romania
197 J4 Crişurilor, Câmpia plain Romania
252 B3 Criterión mt. Peru
136 I6 Criuleni Moldova
170 E3 Crivitz Ger.
226 F4 Crivitz WI U.S.A.
254 C5 Crixás Brazil
254 C5 Crixás Açu r. Brazil
254 C5 Crixás Mirim r. Brazil
197 J9 Crna r. Macedonia
179 K7 Črna Slovenia
177 J6 Crna Bara Vojvodina Serbia
196 H8 Crna Glava mt. Montenegro
196 J8 Crna Gora mts Macedonia/Serbia
Crna Gora country Europe see Montenegro
191 Q6 Crna Pta, Rt pt Croatia
197 K8 Crna Trava Serbia
196 I9 Crni Drim r. Macedonia
191 R5 Crni Lug Croatia
197 K7 Crni Timok r. Serbia
188 E2 Črni vrh mt. Slovenia
188 E3 Črnomelj Slovenia
197 K8 Crnook mt. Serbia
147 F3 Croagh Ireland
147 F3 Croagheheen hill Ireland
147 C5 Croagh Patrick hill Ireland
83 L7 Croajingolong National Park Vic. Austr.
188 E3 Croatia country Europe
195 L6 Crocchio r. Italy
195 K7 Crocco, Monte mt. Italy
191 K3 Croce, Monte mt. Italy
193 P6 Croce dello Scrivano, Passo pass Italy
193 I2 Croce di Serra, Monte hill Italy
169 K10 Crock Ger.
95 K2 Crocker, Banjaran mts Malaysia
95 L2 Crocker Range National Park Malaysia
146 I12 Crocketford Dumfries and Galloway, Scotland U.K.
237 H10 Crockett TX U.S.A.
147 G3 Crockmore Ireland
162 I4 Crocq France
191 M2 Croda dei Toni mt. Italy
191 M2 Croda Rossa mt. Italy
190 E3 Crodo Italy
150 E4 Croeserw Neath Port Talbot, Wales U.K.
150 B4 Croesgoch Pembrokeshire, Wales U.K.
149 O6 Crofton West Yorkshire, England U.K.
234 B6 Crofton MD U.S.A.
236 G4 Crofton NE U.S.A.
150 D4 Crofty Swansea, Wales U.K.
147 F5 Croghan Ireland
233 J5 Croghan NY U.S.A.
149 L4 Croglin Cumbria, England U.K.
193 K2 Crognaleto Italy
147 F3 Crohy Head Ireland
146 G7 Croick Highland, Scotland U.K.
161 G10 Croisette, Cap c. France
158 F7 Croisic, Pointe de pt France
156 E3 Croisilles France
81 H8 Croisilles Harbour South I. N.Z.
190 A5 Croix de Fer, Col de la pass France
161 H7 Croix-Haute, Col de la pass France
190 C5 Croix-Rousse mt. Italy
84 D1 Croker, Cape N.T. Austr.
227 N5 Croker, Cape Ont. Can.
84 D1 Croker Island N.T. Austr.
147 C8 Cromane Ireland
146 H7 Cromarty Highland, Scotland U.K.
146 H7 Cromarty Firth est. Scotland U.K.
146 I8 Cromdale, Hills of Scotland U.K.
151 O2 Cromer Norfolk, England U.K.
150 H4 Cromhall South Gloucestershire, England U.K.
81 D12 Cromwell South I. N.Z.
235 J1 Cromwell CT U.S.A.
226 B3 Cromwell MN U.S.A.
81 F9 Cronadun South I. N.Z.
160 D3 Cronat France
161 C6 Cronce r. France
151 K5 Crondall Hampshire, England U.K.
149 N4 Crook Durham, England U.K.
238 D4 Crooked r. OR U.S.A.
Crooked Harbour b. H.K. China see Kat O Hoi
246 F2 Crooked Island Bahamas
Crooked Island H.K. China see Kat O Chau
246 F2 Crooked Island Passage Bahamas
226 C1 Crooked Lake Can./U.S.A.
223 K4 Crooked River Sask. Can.
147 C10 Crookhaven Ireland
236 G2 Crookston MN U.S.A.
147 E9 Crookstown Ireland
232 C9 Crooksville OH U.S.A.
83 L6 Crookwell N.S.W. Austr.
147 E7 Croom Ireland
195 L4 Cropalati Italy
195 L6 Cropani Italy
83 M3 Croppa Creek N.S.W. Austr.
85 I3 Crosbie r. Qld Austr.
146 D6 Crosbost Western Isles, Scotland U.K.
149 K7 Crosby Merseyside, England U.K.
149 P6 Crosby North Lincolnshire, England U.K.
236 I2 Crosby MN U.S.A.
236 D1 Crosby ND U.S.A.
149 L4 Crosby Ravensworth Cumbria, England U.K.
237 E9 Crosbyton TX U.S.A.
195 L4 Crosia Italy
207 H5 Cross r. Nigeria
158 G7 Crossac France
146 F11 Crossaig Argyll and Bute, Scotland U.K.
148 C6 Crossakeel Ireland
146 C9 Crossapol Bay Scotland U.K.
223 M2 Cross Bay Nunavut Can.
149 K4 Crosscanonby Cumbria, England U.K.
231 F11 Cross City FL U.S.A.
233 □S2 Cross Creek N.B. Can.
147 H5 Crossdoney Ireland
237 I9 Crossett AR U.S.A.
149 M4 Cross Fell hill England U.K.
222 H5 Crossfield Alta Can.
146 I11 Crossford South Lanarkshire, Scotland U.K.
147 K4 Crossgar Northern Ireland U.K.
147 I2 Crossgare Northern Ireland U.K.
150 F3 Crossgates Powys, Wales U.K.
146 H11 Crosshands East Ayrshire, Scotland U.K.
246 E1 Cross Harbour b. Gt Abaco Bahamas
147 F9 Crosshaven Ireland
146 G12 Crosshill South Ayrshire, Scotland U.K.
148 H2 Crosshouse East Ayrshire, Scotland U.K.
150 D3 Cross Inn Ceredigion, Wales U.K.
148 C7 Crosskeys Ireland
147 I5 Cross Keys Ireland
223 L4 Cross Lake Man. Can.
223 L4 Cross Lake l. Man. Can.
232 I5 Cross Lake l. NY U.S.A.
81 G9 Crossley, Mount South I. N.Z.
147 I4 Crossmaglen Northern Ireland U.K.
241 R7 Crossman Peak AZ U.S.A.
146 I13 Crossmichael Dumfries and Galloway, Scotland U.K.
147 D4 Crossmolina Ireland
207 H5 Cross River state Nigeria
222 B3 Cross Sound sea chan. AK U.S.A.
231 E8 Crossville TN U.S.A.
150 F3 Crossway Powys, Wales U.K.
191 J6 Crostolo r. Italy
149 L6 Croston Lancashire, England U.K.
227 L6 Croswell MI U.S.A.
227 R5 Crotch Lake Ont. Can.
Croton Italy see Crotone
195 M5 Crotone Italy
195 L5 Crotone prov. Italy
235 H2 Croton Falls NY U.S.A.
235 H2 Croton Falls Reservo[ir] NY U.S.A.
235 H2 Crotonville NY U.S.A.
161 I7 Crots France
171 G10 Crottendorf Ger.
261 G5 Crotto Arg.
151 N4 Crouch r. England U.K.
151 J4 Croughton Northampt[onshire,] England U.K.
162 E2 Croutelle France
156 F5 Crouy France
156 F5 Crouy-sur-Ourcq Fra[nce]
159 L7 Crouzilles France
147 E3 Crove Ireland
222 E3 Crow r. B.C. Can.
238 K4 Crow Agency MT U.S[.A.]
83 K4 Crowal watercourse N.S.W. Austr.
151 M5 Crowborough East Su[ssex,] England U.K.
238 L6 Crow Creek r. CO U.S[.A.]
236 F3 Crow Creek Indian Reservation res. SD U[.S.A.]
83 N4 Crowdy Bay National [Park] N.S.W. Austr.
237 F8 Crowell TX U.S.A.
150 G4 Crow Hill Herefordshir[e,] England U.K.
238 K4 Crow Indian Reserva[tion] MT U.S.A.
83 J5 Crowl watercourse N.S.W. Austr.
151 L2 Crowland Lincolnshire[,] England U.K.
149 P6 Crowle North Lincolns[hire,] England U.K.
237 I10 Crowley LA U.S.A.
240 N4 Crowley, Lake CA U.S[.A.]
146 E8 Crowlin Islands Scotl[and U.K.]
247 □5 Crown Point pt Trin. a[nd Tob.]
230 D5 Crown Point IN U.S.A.
239 J9 Crownpoint NM U.S.A.
233 L5 Crown Point NY U.S.A.
263 C2 Crown Prince Olav C[oast] Antarctica
262 W1 Crown Princess Mar[tha] Coast Antarctica
234 B6 Crownsville MD U.S.A.
85 N9 Crows Nest Qld Austr.
222 H5 Crowsnest Pass Alta [Can.]
222 H5 Crowsnest Pass pass Alta/B.C. Can.
151 K5 Crowthorne Bracknell [Forest,] England U.K.
236 H2 Crow Wing r. MN U.S.[A.]
146 H7 Croy Highland, Scotlar[nd U.K.]
150 D5 Croyde Devon, Englan[d U.K.]
85 I5 Croydon Qld Austr.
151 L5 Croydon Greater Lond[on,] England U.K.
234 F4 Croydon PA U.S.A.
162 H3 Crozant France
232 G10 Crozet VA U.S.A.
265 H8 Crozet, Îles is Indian [Ocean]
217 □1 Crozet Basin sea feat[ure] Indian Ocean
265 G7 Crozet Plateau sea fe[ature] Indian Ocean
220 F2 Crozier Channel N.W[.T. Can.]
158 C5 Crozon France
158 B5 Crozon, Presqu'île de France
161 F7 Cruas France
197 N3 Crucea Romania
252 C3 Crucero Peru
246 C2 Cruces Cuba
244 F3 Cruces Mex.
250 B3 Cruces, Punta pt Col.
185 O3 Crucetillas, Puerto d[e] pass Spain
195 L5 Crucoli Italy
146 M8 Cruden Bay Aberdeen[shire,] Scotland U.K.
245 I1 Cruillas Mex.
146 C6 Crùlabhig Western Isle[s,] Scotland U.K.
159 M4 Crulai France
232 C11 Crum WV U.S.A.
150 F4 Crumlin Caerphilly, Wa[les U.K.]
147 J3 Crumlin Northern Irela[nd U.K.]
149 K4 Crummock Water l. England U.K.
160 I4 Cruseilles France
147 E7 Crusheen Ireland
157 K5 Crusnes France
157 K5 Crusnes r. France
245 J4 Crustepec, Cerro mt.
183 O9 Cruz mt. Spain
251 E2 Cruz Venez.
246 E4 Cruz, Cabo c. Cuba
261 G3 Cruz Alta Arg.
255 B9 Cruz Alta Brazil
244 D6 Cruz de Garibay Mex
260 E2 Cruz del Eje Arg.
257 E5 Cruzeiro Brazil
256 A5 Cruzeiro do Oeste Br[azil]
252 B1 Cruzeiro do Sul Acre
256 A5 Cruzeiro do Sul Paran[á]
262 O2 Cruzen Island Antarct[ica]
245 H9 Cruz Grande Mex.
161 B10 Cruzy France
156 H8 Cruzy-le-Châtel Franc[e]
196 H5 Crvenka Vojvodina Se[rbia]
222 D3 Cry Lake B.C. Can.
150 C4 Crymych Pembrokeshi[re,] Wales U.K.
222 F4 Crysdale, Mount B.C.
241 X5 Crystal NM U.S.A.
234 D6 Crystal Beach MD U.S.
82 G5 Crystal Brook S.A. Au[str.]
223 L5 Crystal City Man. Can
236 J6 Crystal City MO U.S.A
237 F11 Crystal City TX U.S.A.
226 F3 Crystal Falls MI U.S.A
226 F7 Crystal Lake IL U.S.A.
231 F11 Crystal River FL U.S.A
237 J10 Crystal Springs MS U
177 J5 Csabacsűd Hungary
176 G4 Csabrendek Hungary
177 J5 Csaj-tó l. Hungary
176 F5 Csákánydoroszló Hur[ngary]
177 H4 Csákvár Hungary
177 J5 Csanádapáca Hungary
177 J5 Csanádi-hát hills Hung[ary]
177 J5 Csanádpalota Hungar[y]
177 J5 Csanytelek Hungary
177 H4 Császár Hungary
177 I5 Császártöltés Hungar[y]
177 H5 Csátalja Hungary
177 I5 Csávoly Hungary
177 I4 Csécse Hungary
177 I4 Csemő Hungary
177 I5 Csengele Hungary
177 L4 Csenger Hungary
177 J5 Csépa Hungary
176 F4 Csepreg Hungary
177 J3 Cserehát mts Hungary
177 I4 Cserhát hills Hungary
177 I4 Cserhátsurány Hunga[ry]
177 J5 Cserkeszőlő Hungary
177 J3 Csernely Hungary
176 G5 Cserszegtomaj Hunga[ry]
179 O6 Cserta r. Hungary
176 F5 Csesztreg Hungary
177 G4 Csetény Hungary
Csév Hungary see Pilis[csév]
177 I5 Csikéria Hungary
177 H4 Csókakő Hungary
177 K4 Csökmő Hungary
177 G5 Csököly Hungary
176 G5 Csokonyavisonta Hun[gary]
177 J3 Csokvaomány Hungar[y]
177 H4 Csolnok Hungary
177 I5 Csólyospálos Hungary
177 I4 Csömör Hungary
177 J5 Csongrád Hungary
177 J5 Csongrád county Hung[ary]
177 G5 Csopak Hungary
177 H4 Csór Hungary
176 G4 Csorna Hungary
176 F5 Csörnyeföld Hungary
176 F5 Csörötnek Hungary
177 J5 Csorvás Hungary
177 H4 Csősz Hungary
177 G4 Csót Hungary
177 H4 Csóványos hill Hungar[y]
176 G5 Csurgó Hungary
127 L7 Ctesiphon tourist site [Iraq]
182 G3 Cua r. Spain
247 J8 Cúa Venez.

Cuacos de Yuste Spain
Cuadrada, Sierra hills Arg.
Cuadro Berregas Arg.
Cuadros Spain
Cuajinicuilapa Mex.
Cuale Angola
Cualedro Spain
Cuamato Angola
Cuamba Moz.
Cuando r. Angola/Zambia
Cuando Cubango prov. Angola
Cuangar Angola
Cuango Cuando Cubango Angola
Cuango Lunda Norte Angola
Cuango Uíge Angola
Cuango r. Angola alt. Kwango (Dem. Rep. Congo)
Cuanza r. Angola
Cuanza Norte prov. Angola
Cuanza Sul prov. Angola
Cuareim r. Uru.
Cuaró Uru.
Cuaro r. Uru.
Cuarte de Huerva Spain
Cuarto r. Arg.
Cuatir r. Angola
Cuatretonda Spain see Quatretonda
Cuatro Ciénegas Mex.
Cuatro Ojos Bol.
Cuatro Vientos Arg.
Cuauhtémoc Chihuahua Mex.
Cuauhtémoc Colima Mex.
Cuauhtémoc Durango Mex.
Cuautitlán Mex.
Cuautla Mex.
Cuautlán Izcalli Mex.
Cuayuca Mex.
Cuba Port.
Cuba IL U.S.A.
Cuba NM U.S.A.
Cuba NY U.S.A.
Cuba OH U.S.A.
Cuba country West Indies
Cubabi, Cerro mt. Mex.
Cubagua, Isla i. Venez.
Cubal Angola
Cubal r. Angola
Cubalhão Port.
Cubango r. Angola/Namibia
Cubara Col.
Cubatão Brazil
Cubells Spain
Cub Hills Sask. Can.
Cubia r. Spain
Cubillas r. Spain
Cubillo r. Spain
Cubjac France
Cubla Spain
Cubo de Bureba Spain
Cubo de la Solana Spain
Cubolta r. Moldova
Çubuk Turkey
Cubulco Guat.
Cubzac-les-Ponts France
Cucalón Spain
Cucao Chile
Cucapa, Sierra mts Mex.
Cucco, Monte mt. Italy
Cuccuru su Pirastru hill Sardegna Italy
Cucharas Mex.
Cuchi Angola
Cuchilla de Peralta Uru.
Cuchilla Grande hills Uru.
Cuchilla Grande Inferior hills Uru.
Cuchillo-Có Arg.
Cuckfield West Sussex, England U.K.
Cuckmere r. England U.K.
Cucu, Vârful mt. Romania
Cucuí Brazil
Cucumbi Angola
Cucuron France
Cucurpe Mex.
Cucurrupí Col.
Cúcuta Col.
Cucutas hill Spain
Cudalbi Romania
Cudarebe pt Aruba
Cuddalore Tamil Nadu India
Cuddapah Andhra Prad. India
Cuddapan, Lake salt flat Qld Austr.
Cuddeback Lake CA U.S.A.
Cuddebackville NY U.S.A.
Cuddia r. Sicilia Italy
Cuddington Cheshire, England U.K.
Cudi watercourse Turkey
Cudi Dağı hill Turkey
Cudillero Spain
Cudos France
Cudworth Sask. Can.
Cudworth South Yorkshire, England U.K.
Cue W.A. Austr.
Cuebe r. Angola
Cueio r. Angola
Cuelebrita, Isla i. Puerto Rico
Cuéllar Spain
Cuemba Angola
Cuenca Ecuador
Cuenca Luzon Phil.
Cuenca Spain
Cuenca prov. Spain
Cuenca, Serranía de mts Spain
Cuenca Alta del Manzanares, Parque Regional de la park Spain
Cuenca de Balsas basin Mex.
Cuenca de Campos Spain
Cuenca del Añelo reg. Arg.
Cuencamé Mex.
Cuerámaro Mex.
Cuerda del Pozo, Embalse de la resr Spain
Cuerda Larga ridge Spain
Cuernavaca Mex.
Cuero TX U.S.A.
Cuers France
Cuerva Spain
Cuervo r. Spain
Cuervos Mex.
Cueto Cuba
Cuetzalán Mex.
Cuevas Altas hill Spain
Cuevas Bajas Spain
Cuevas de Almanzora Spain
Cuevas de Almanzora, Embalse resr Spain
Cuevas del Becerro Spain
Cuevas del Campo Spain
Cuevas de San Clemente Spain
Cuevas Labradas Spain
Cuevo Bol.
Cueza r. Spain
Cuffley Hertfordshire, England U.K.
Cugand France
Cuges-les-Pins France
Cugir Romania
Cugir r. Romania
Cuglieri Sardegna Italy
Cugnaux France
Cugo r. Angola
Cuguen France
Cuiabá Brazil
Cuiabá r. Brazil
Cuicatlan Mex.
Cuichapa Mex.
Cuihua Yunnan China see Daguan
Cuijiang Fujian China see Ninghua
Cuijk Neth.
Cuilapa Guat.
Cuilapan Mex.
Cuilcagh hill Ireland/U.K.
Cuillin Hills Scotland U.K.
Cuillin Sound sea chan. Scotland U.K.
Cuilo Angola
Cuilo-Futa Angola
Cuilo Pombo Angola
Cuiluan Heilong. China
209 B6 Cuimba Angola
160 G4 Cuiseaux France
156 F5 Cuise-la-Motte France
160 F3 Cuisery France
257 G3 Cuité r. Brazil
245 K7 Cuitláhuac Mex.
209 D9 Cuito r. Angola
209 C8 Cuito Cuanavale Angola
244 F6 Cuitzeo Mex.
244 F6 Cuitzeo, Laguna de l. Mex.
251 F5 Cuiuni r. Brazil
236 J6 Cuivre r. MO U.S.A.
245 K9 Cuixtla Mex.
92 C8 Cujangan i. Phil.
197 K6 Cujmir Romania
94 E2 Cukai Malaysia
198 B3 Çukë Albania
129 E6 Çukurbağ Turkey
127 K5 Çukurca Turkey
129 A5 Çukurçayır Turkey
199 L3 Çukurhisar Turkey
129 A6 Çukurköy Turkey
128 D2 Çukurova plat. Turkey
136 H6 Cula r. Moldova
107 O8 Culai Shan mt. Shandong China
162 I2 Culan France
146 J8 Culardoch hill Scotland U.K.
92 D6 Culasi Panay Phil.
238 L2 Culbertson MT U.S.A.
236 E5 Culbertson NE U.S.A.
146 H7 Culbokie Highland, Scotland U.K.
83 K6 Culcairn N.S.W. Austr.
177 M4 Culciu Romania
147 H2 Culdaff Ireland
146 K8 Culdrain Aberdeenshire, Scotland U.K.
247 □1 Culebra, Isla de i. Puerto Rico
182 H5 Culebra, Sierra de la mts Spain
252 A2 Culebras Peru
247 □1 Culebrinas r. Puerto Rico
164 H5 Culemborg Neth.
129 G7 Culfa Azer.
242 F5 Culiacán Mex.
92 B6 Culion Phil.
92 B6 Culion i. Phil.
148 B5 Culkey Northern Ireland U.K.
187 E7 Culla Spain
148 C8 Cullahill Ireland
185 N5 Cullar r. Spain
185 N5 Cúllar-Baza Spain
147 I4 Cullaville Northern Ireland U.K.
147 D4 Culleens Ireland
146 K7 Cullen Moray, Scotland U.K.
237 I9 Cullen LA U.S.A.
85 H1 Cullen Point Qld Austr.
187 E9 Cullera Spain
146 H7 Cullicudden Highland, Scotland U.K.
147 D5 Cullin Ireland
147 D5 Cullin, Lough l. Ireland
215 M1 Cullinan S. Africa
146 E10 Cullipool Argyll and Bute, Scotland U.K.
146 □N1 Cullivoe Shetland, Scotland U.K.
231 D8 Cullman AL U.S.A.
85 J7 Culloden Creek watercourse Qld Austr.
150 F6 Cullompton Devon, England U.K.
190 B3 Cully Switz.
147 J3 Cullybackey Northern Ireland U.K.
147 I4 Cullyhanna Northern Ireland U.K.
146 F6 Cul Mòr hill Scotland U.K.
147 H2 Culmore Northern Ireland U.K.
150 F6 Culmstock Devon, England U.K.
146 F7 Culnacraig Highland, Scotland U.K.
146 D7 Culnaknock Highland, Scotland U.K.
185 N7 Culo de Perro, Punta pt Spain
160 H5 Culoz France
232 H10 Culpeper VA U.S.A.
250 □ Culpepper, Isla i. Islas Galápagos Ecuador
146 H7 Culrain Highland, Scotland U.K.
146 □M2 Culswick Shetland, Scotland U.K.
146 I11 Culter Fell hill Scotland U.K.
146 L8 Cults Aberdeen, Scotland U.K.
254 B4 Culuene r. Brazil
226 H8 Culver IN U.S.A.
87 H12 Culver, Point W.A. Austr.
81 G9 Culverden South I. N.Z.
146 G12 Culzean Bay Scotland U.K.
254 D2 Cumã, Baía do inlet Brazil
129 E6 Cumaçay Turkey
251 E2 Cumaná Venez.
247 L8 Cumanacoa Venez.
199 L2 Cumaova Turkey
256 C3 Cumari Brazil
129 H4 Cumay Azer.
250 B4 Cumbal, Nevado de vol. Col.
232 C12 Cumberland KY U.S.A.
232 G9 Cumberland MD U.S.A.
232 D9 Cumberland OH U.S.A.
232 G11 Cumberland VA U.S.A.
226 B4 Cumberland WI U.S.A.
232 B12 Cumberland r. KY U.S.A.
Cumberland, Cape Vanuatu see Nahoï, Cap
230 E7 Cumberland, Lake KY U.S.A.
259 □ Cumberland Bay S. Georgia
234 E6 Cumberland County county NJ U.S.A.
234 A4 Cumberland County county PA U.S.A.
223 K4 Cumberland House Sask. Can.
85 L6 Cumberland Islands Qld Austr.
223 K4 Cumberland Lake Sask. Can.
232 B12 Cumberland Mountains KY/TN U.S.A.
221 L3 Cumberland Peninsula Nunavut Can.
231 E8 Cumberland Plateau KY/TN U.S.A.
226 E2 Cumberland Point MI U.S.A.
221 L3 Cumberland Sound sea chan. Nunavut Can.
146 I11 Cumbernauld North Lanarkshire, Scotland U.K.
183 K9 Cumbre Alta mt. Spain
259 C7 Cumbre Negro mt. Arg.
242 F3 Cumbres de Majalca, Parque Nacional nat. park Mex.
243 I5 Cumbres de Monterey, Parque Nacional nat. park Mex.
184 F4 Cumbres de San Bartolomé Spain
184 F4 Cumbres Mayores Spain
149 K4 Cumbria admin. div. England U.K.
114 F5 Cumbum Andhra Prad. India
184 C6 Cumeada Port.
190 C6 Cumiana Italy
182 E6 Cumieira Port.
251 G5 Cuminá Brazil
251 H5 Cuminapanema r. Brazil
146 L7 Cuminestown Aberdeenshire, Scotland U.K.
170 E4 Cumlosen Ger.
231 E8 Cumming GA U.S.A.
240 I2 Cummings CA U.S.A.
82 E6 Cummins S.A. Austr.
86 I5 Cummins Range hills W.A. Austr.
83 L5 Cumnock N.S.W. Austr.
146 H12 Cumnock East Ayrshire, Scotland U.K.
151 J4 Cumnor Oxfordshire, England U.K.
242 E2 Cumpas Mex.
260 B4 Cumpeo Chile
126 F5 Çumra Turkey
242 E3 Cumuripa Mex.
257 H2 Cumuruxatiba Brazil
247 □7 Cumuto Trin. and Tob.
251 I4 Cunani Brazil
250 C4 Cuñaré Col.
159 K7 Cunault France
260 A6 Cunco Chile
87 G11 Cundeelee Aboriginal Reserve W.A. Austr.
87 D11 Cunderdin W.A. Austr.
250 C3 Cundinamarca dept Col.
215 N4 Cundycleugh S. Africa
163 E6 Cunegès France
243 N10 Cunén Guat.
209 B9 Cunene prov. Angola
209 A9 Cunene r. Angola/Namibia alt. Kunene
190 D7 Cuneo Italy
190 D7 Cuneo prov. Italy
171 K8 Cunewalde Ger.
156 I7 Cunfin France
82 E5 Cungena S.A. Austr.
97 I8 Cung Sơn Vietnam
126 I4 Çüngüş Turkey
257 E5 Cunha Brazil
182 F7 Cunha Port.
209 C8 Cunhinga Angola
136 H6 Cunicea Moldova
186 I5 Cunit Spain
209 D8 Cunjamba Angola
160 D5 Cunlhat France
83 J3 Cunnamulla Qld Austr.
231 □2 Cunningham, Lake New Prov. Bahamas
146 □N2 Cunningsburgh Shetland, Scotland U.K.
252 B1 Cunshamayo Peru
182 C3 Cuntis Spain
197 J6 Cununa mt. Romania
247 □7 Cunupia Trin. and Tob.
190 D5 Cuorgnè Italy
146 J10 Cupar Fife, Scotland U.K.
251 H5 Cupari r. Brazil
177 L4 Cupari, Dealul hill Romania
136 G5 Cupcina Moldova
193 N3 Cupello Italy
250 B3 Cupica Col.
193 L1 Cupra Marittima Italy
191 O9 Cupramontana Italy
196 J7 Ćuprija Serbia
242 D5 Cupula, Pico mt. Mex.
163 H8 Cuq-Toulza France
244 D5 Cuquio Mex.
251 F6 Curaça Brazil
254 F4 Curaçá Brazil
250 D6 Curaçá r. Brazil
247 □10 Curaçao i. Neth. Antilles
260 B6 Curacautín Chile
260 B3 Curacavi Chile
260 E6 Curacó r. Arg.
209 B8 Curaculo Angola
252 C4 Curahuara de Carangas Bol.
261 F5 Cura Malal Arg.
261 F5 Cura Malal, Sierra de hills Arg.
258 B5 Curanilahue Chile
252 C2 Curanja r. Peru
261 F4 Curapaligüe Arg.
250 C5 Curaray r. Ecuador
260 B6 Curarrehue Chile
261 F4 Curarú Arg.
251 F3 Curatabaca Venez.
177 L5 Curăţele Romania
260 B3 Curaumilla, Punta pt Chile
258 F3 Curaya r. Arg.
82 F4 Curdlawidny Lagoon salt flat S.A. Austr.
250 D5 Curé r. Col.
160 D1 Cure r. France
190 E4 Cureggio Italy
217 □1b Curepipe Mauritius
260 A4 Curepto Chile
160 E3 Curgy France
Curia Switz. see Chur
251 F2 Curiapo Venez.
260 B4 Curicó Chile
250 E5 Curicuriari, Serra hill Brazil
250 E5 Curieuriari r. Brazil
217 □2a Curieuse, Île i. Inner Islands Seychelles
254 D4 Curimata Brazil
195 K6 Curinga Italy
250 C4 Curiplaya Col.
256 C6 Curitiba Brazil
255 C8 Curitibanos Brazil
256 B6 Curiúva Brazil
83 M4 Curlewis N.S.W. Austr.
82 G4 Curnamona S.A. Austr.
209 A8 Curoca r. Angola
190 F5 Curone r. Italy
191 J2 Curon Venosta Italy
182 F5 Curopos Port.
83 M4 Currabubula N.S.W. Austr.
147 J8 Curracloe Ireland
147 I6 Curragh Ireland
147 F5 Curraghroe Ireland
147 E5 Curragh West Ireland
147 F8 Curraglass Ireland
184 □ Curral das Freiras Madeira
257 G1 Curral de Dentro Brazil
251 I5 Curralinho Brazil
82 E2 Curralulla watercourse S.A. Austr.
206 □ Curral Velho Cape Verde
227 K5 Curran MI U.S.A.
147 B9 Currane, Lough l. Ireland
241 Q3 Currant NV U.S.A.
83 J4 Curranyalpa N.S.W. Austr.
182 C3 Currás Spain
85 H8 Currawilla Qld Austr.
83 J3 Currawinya National Park Qld Austr.
246 E1 Current Eleuthera Bahamas
237 J7 Current r. MO U.S.A.
83 I8 Currie Tas. Austr.
241 R1 Currie NV U.S.A.
231 I7 Currituck NC U.S.A.
147 E5 Curry Ireland
150 G5 Curry Rivel Somerset, England U.K.
195 O3 Cursi Italy
177 L6 Curtea Romania
197 M5 Curtea de Argeş Romania
196 J4 Curtici Romania
87 G11 Curtin W.A. Austr.
85 N8 Curtis Channel Qld Austr.
83 K8 Curtis Group is Tas. Austr.
85 M7 Curtis Island Qld Austr.
77 I5 Curtis Island N.Z.
177 L4 Curtuişeni Romania
251 H5 Curuá Brazil
251 H6 Curuá r. Brazil
251 I4 Curuá, Ilha i. Brazil
254 B3 Curuaés r. Brazil
251 H5 Curuaí Brazil
251 H5 Curuapanema r. Brazil
251 H5 Curuá Una r. Brazil
254 D2 Curuçá Brazil
251 I5 Curumu Brazil
94 E6 Curup Sumatera Indon.
251 F5 Curupira Brazil
251 E4 Curupira, Serra mts Brazil/Venez.
253 E3 Cururú Bol.
253 F1 Cururu r. Brazil
254 D2 Cururupu Brazil
251 F3 Curutú, Cerro mt. Venez.
261 H1 Curuzú Cuatiá Arg.
257 E3 Curvelo Brazil
226 F3 Curwood, Mount hill MI U.S.A.
192 C2 Curza, Punta di pt Corse France
193 N5 Cusano Mutri Italy
252 C3 Cusco Peru
252 B3 Cusco dept Peru
147 J2 Cushendall Northern Ireland U.K.
147 J2 Cushendun Northern Ireland U.K.
148 C7 Cushina Ireland
237 G7 Cushing OK U.S.A.
190 I7 Cusna, Monte mt. Italy
162 F4 Cussac France
162 C5 Cussac-Fort-Médoc France
161 D7 Cussac-sur-Loire France
212 B2 Cussava Angola
160 C4 Cusset France
231 E9 Cusseta GA U.S.A.
160 E2 Cussy-les-Forges France
238 K3 Custer MT U.S.A.
236 D4 Custer SD U.S.A.
157 L6 Custines France
194 D7 Custonaci Sicilia Italy
209 C8 Cutato Angola
238 H2 Cut Bank MT U.S.A.
238 H2 Cut Bank Creek r. MT U.S.A.
212 B2 Cutenda Angola
231 E10 Cuthbert GA U.S.A.
84 D2 Cuthbertson Falls N.T. Austr.
191 J7 Cutigliano Italy
240 M5 Cutler CA U.S.A.
233 □R4 Cutler ME U.S.A.
231 G13 Cutler Ridge FL U.S.A.
194 H8 Cutò r. Sicilia Italy
237 J11 Cut Off LA U.S.A.
147 E6 Cutra, Lough l. Ireland
260 C6 Cutral-Co Arg.
195 L5 Cutro Italy
195 O3 Cutrofiano Italy
83 J3 Cuttaburra Creek r. Qld Austr.
117 J9 Cuttack Orissa India
192 B4 Cuttoli-Corticchiato Corse France
244 G7 Cutzamala r. Mex.
244 G7 Cutzamala de Pinzón Mex.
209 B8 Cuvelai Angola
208 B5 Cuvette admin. reg. Congo
208 B5 Cuvette Ouest admin. reg. Congo
87 B8 Cuvier, Cape W.A. Austr.
80 J3 Cuvier Island North I. N.Z.
227 R1 Cuvillier, Lac l. Que. Can.
163 I9 Cuxac-Cabardès France
161 B10 Cuxac-d'Aude France
129 J6 Çuxanlı Azer.
168 G3 Cuxhaven Ger.
129 J5 Çuxuryurd Azer.
252 C4 Cuya Chile
232 D7 Cuyahoga Falls OH U.S.A.
232 D7 Cuyahoga Valley National Park OH U.S.A.
240 M7 Cuyama CA U.S.A.
240 L7 Cuyama r. CA U.S.A.
92 C4 Cuyapo Luzon Phil.
92 C6 Cuyo Phil.
92 C6 Cuyo i. Phil.
92 C6 Cuyo East Passage Phil.
92 C6 Cuyo Islands Phil.
92 C6 Cuyo West Passage Phil.
251 G3 Cuyuni r. Guyana
Cuyutingni Nic. see Kuyu Tingni
244 C7 Cuyutlán Mex.
244 C7 Cuyutlán, Laguna lag. Mex.
162 H6 Cuzance France
Cuzco Cusco Peru see Cusco
252 A1 Cuzco San Martín Peru
185 J4 Cuzna r. Spain
163 F6 Cuzorn France
171 K9 Cvikov Czech Rep.
150 F4 Cwm Blaenau Gwent, Wales U.K.
150 E4 Cwmafan Neath Port Talbot, Wales U.K.
150 F3 Cwmbach Powys, Wales U.K.
150 F4 Cwmbrân Torfaen, Wales U.K.
150 E4 Cwmllynfell Neath Port Talbot, Wales U.K.
211 A5 Cyangugu Rwanda
174 C3 Cybinka Pol.
174 D2 Cybowo Pol.
170 K5 Cychry Pol.
Cyclades is Greece see Kyklades
175 L4 Cyców Pol.
Cydonia Kriti Greece see Chania
Cydweli Carmarthenshire, Wales U.K. see Kidwelly
Cydweli Wales U.K. see Kidwelly
83 K10 Cygnet Tas. Austr.
232 B7 Cygnet OH U.S.A.
Cymru admin. div. U.K. see Wales
150 E3 Cynghordy Carmarthenshire, Wales U.K.
150 D4 Cynin r. Wales U.K.
232 A10 Cynthiana KY U.S.A.
150 D4 Cynwyl Elfed Carmarthenshire, Wales U.K.
223 I5 Cypress Hills Sask. Can.
223 I5 Cypress Hills Interprovincial Park B.C. Can.
128 B3 Cyprus country Asia
202 D3 Cyrenaica reg. Libya
202 D1 Cyrene tourist site Libya
156 F2 Cysoing France
Cythera i. Greece see Kythira
150 D4 Cywyn r. Wales U.K.
174 E3 Czacz Pol.
174 G4 Czajków Pol.
174 E2 Czaplinek Pol.
223 I4 Czar Alta Can.
175 J5 Czarna Podkarpackie Pol.
175 K5 Czarna Podkarpackie Pol.
175 H4 Czarna r. Pol.
175 H5 Czarna r. Pol.
175 J5 Czarna r. Pol.
175 L2 Czarna Białostocka Pol.
174 F1 Czarna Dąbrówka Pol.
175 K6 Czarna Górna Pol.
175 L2 Czarna Hańcza r. Pol.
175 I5 Czarna Nida r. Pol.
174 G3 Czarna Struga r. Pol.
174 G2 Czarna Woda Pol.
175 H5 Czarnca Pol.
174 E2 Czarne Pol.
175 J2 Czarnia Pol.
174 E3 Czarnków Pol.
170 K5 Czarnów Pol.
174 G4 Czarnożyły Pol.
175 H6 Czarny Dunajec Pol.
177 I2 Czarny Dunajec r. Pol.
174 G4 Czastary Pol.
175 I6 Czchów Pol.
175 H6 Czechowice-Dziedzice Pol.
176 E2 Czech Republic country Europe
174 E2 Czechy Pol.
175 J4 Czekarzewice Pol.
175 K4 Czemierniki Pol.
174 E3 Czempiń Pol.
175 L3 Czeremcha Pol.
174 F4 Czermin Pol.
174 D4 Czerna Mała r. Pol.
174 D4 Czerna Wielka r. Pol.
174 F4 Czernica Pol.
174 E2 Czernica r. Pol.
175 I2 Czernice Borowe Pol.
174 F3 Czerniejewo Pol.
175 I4 Czerniewice Pol.
174 G3 Czernikowo Pol.
174 E4 Czernina Pol.
Czernowitz Ukr. see Chernivtsi
174 F2 Czersk Pol.
174 D3 Czerwieńsk Pol.
175 J3 Czerwin Pol.
175 I3 Czerwińsk nad Wisłą Pol.
174 G5 Czerwionka-Leszczyny Pol.
174 E3 Czerwonak Pol.
171 L8 Czerwona Woda Pol.
175 J3 Czerwonka Włościańska Pol.
175 H4 Czestków Pol.
175 H5 Częstochowa Pol.
174 F4 Czeszów Pol.
174 E2 Człopa Pol.
174 F2 Człuchów Pol.
174 F3 Czmoń Pol.
171 K8 Czorneboh hill Ger.
175 I6 Czorsztyn, Jezioro resr Pol.
175 I3 Czosnów Pol.
175 J6 Czudec Pol.
175 L3 Czyże Pol.
175 K3 Czyżew-Osada Pol.

D

96 G4 Đa, Sông r. Vietnam
169 E9 Daaden Ger.
107 S4 Da'an Jilin China
92 D6 Daanbantayan Phil.
164 K4 Daarle Neth.
111 D11 Daba Xizang China
128 D7 Ḑabāb, Jabal aḑ mt. Jordan
211 B7 Dabaga Tanz.
250 D2 Dabajuro Venez.
206 D4 Dabakala Côte d'Ivoire
107 P5 Daban Nei Mongol China
106 G8 Daban Shan mts China
108 D4 Dabao Sichuan China
177 I4 Dabas Hungary
108 G2 Daba Shan mts China
210 C1 Dabat Eth.
Dabba Sichuan China see Daocheng
250 B3 Dabeiba Col.
96 C6 Dabein Myanmar
170 E3 Dabel Ger.
116 D8 Dabhoi Gujarat India
114 C4 Dabhol Mahar. India
128 E7 Ḑab'ī, Wādī aḑ watercourse Jordan
174 D3 Dąbie Lubuskie Pol.
174 G3 Dąbie Wielkopolskie Pol.
174 C2 Dąbie, Jezioro l. Pol.
106 D7 Dabiegai Gansu China
109 J3 Dabie Shan mts China
143 M7 Dąbki Pol.
128 E9 Dabl, Wādī watercourse Saudi Arabia
157 N6 Dabo France
116 G7 Daboh Madh. Prad. India
206 C4 Dabola Guinea
206 D5 Dabou Côte d'Ivoire
206 E4 Daboya Ghana
107 K7 Dabqig Nei Mongol China
116 G7 Dabra Madh. Prad. India
138 J9 Dabraslawka Belarus
175 M3 Dabravolya Belarus
174 C3 Dąbroszyn Lubuskie Pol.
174 G3 Dąbroszyn Wielkopolskie Pol.
174 F3 Dąbrowa Kujawsko-Pomorskie Pol.
174 F5 Dąbrowa Opolskie Pol.
174 F5 Dąbrowa Opolskie Pol.
175 L2 Dąbrowa Białostocka Pol.
174 G3 Dąbrowa Biskupia Pol.
174 G2 Dąbrowa Chełmińska Pol.
175 H5 Dąbrowa Górnicza Pol.
175 I5 Dąbrowa Tarnowska Pol.
175 H3 Dąbrowice Pol.
174 D3 Dąbrówka Wielkopolska Pol.
175 I2 Dąbrówno Pol.
106 D8 Dabsan Qinghai China
111 L8 Dabsan Hu salt l. Qinghai China
109 K6 Dabu Guangdong China
Dabu Guangxi China see Liucheng
175 M3 Dabuchyn Belarus
197 M7 Dăbuleni Romania
Dacca Bangl. see Dhaka
173 K5 Dachau Ger.
173 K5 Dachauer Moos marsh Ger.
106 G7 Dachechang Nei Mongol China
107 P6 Dachengzi Liaoning China
114 F4 Dachepalle Andhra Prad. India
175 L5 Dachnów Pol.
169 J8 Dachrieden Ger.
173 J2 Dachsbach Ger.
179 I4 Dachstein Gruppe mts Austria
Dachuan Sichuan China see Dazhou
176 E2 Dačice Czech Rep.
227 R4 Dacre Ont. Can.
149 L4 Dacre Cumbria, England U.K.
177 H4 Dad Hungary
175 I2 Dadaj, Jezioro l. Pol.
78 □6 Dadale Sta Isabel Solomon Is
251 G4 Dadanawa Guyana
129 C6 Dadaş Turkey
128 F2 Dādāt Syria
126 F3 Daday Turkey
210 D1 Daddato Djibouti
231 F11 Dade City FL U.S.A.
231 E9 Dadeville AL U.S.A.
123 L7 Dadhar Pak.
122 I8 Dādkān Iran
Dadong Liaoning China see Donggang
163 H8 Dadou r. France
116 D9 Dadra Dadra India
Dadra Mahar. India see Achalpur
116 D9 Dadra and Nagar Haveli union terr. India
123 L8 Dadu Pak.
108 D4 Dadu He r. Sichuan China
Daedalus Reef Saudi Arabia see Abū al Kizān
Daegu S. Korea see Taegu
Daejŏn S. Korea see Taejŏn
92 D4 Daet Luzon Phil.
108 E5 Dafang Guizhou China
109 M2 Dafeng Jiangsu China
100 E7 Dafengman Jilin China
125 K4 Dafīr U.A.E.
117 N6 Dafla Hills India
114 D4 Daflapur Mahar. India
198 D5 Dafni Dytiki Ellas Greece
198 F2 Dafni Kentriki Makedonia Greece
198 B4 Dafnoudi, Akrotirio pt Kefallonia Greece
223 M4 Dafoe r. Man. Can.
208 C2 Dafra Chad
226 J3 Dafter MI U.S.A.
177 H4 Dág Hungary
116 E8 Dag Rajasthan India
199 L5 Dağ Turkey
210 D3 Daga Medo Eth.
206 B2 Dagana Senegal
183 N7 Daganzo de Arriba Spain
210 B2 Daga Post Sudan
203 G5 Dagash Sudan
93 E2 Dagasuli i. Maluku Indon.
106 H9 Dagcanglhamo Gansu China
129 G5 Dağ Cäyir Azer.
129 D5 Dağcı Turkey
138 K5 Dagda Latvia
199 J4 Dağdere Turkey
Dage Hebei China see Fengning
168 G1 Dagebüll Ger.
Dagenraad atoll Arch. des Tuamotu Fr. Polynesia see Manihi
129 I3 Dagestan, Respublika aut. rep. Rus. Fed.
Dagestanskaya A.S.S.R. aut. rep. Rus. Fed. see Dagestan, Respublika
129 J3 Dagestanskiye Ogni Rus. Fed.
129 I1 Dagestanskiy Zapovednik nature res. Rus. Fed.
Dagezhen Hebei China see Fengning
215 J8 Daggaboersnek S. Africa
81 A12 Dagg Sound inlet South I. N.Z.
Daghestan aut. rep. Rus. Fed. see Dagestan, Respublika
125 N4 Daghmar Oman
163 G6 Daglan France
129 H6 Dağlıq Qarabağ aut. reg. Azer.
111 J12 Daglung Xizang China
111 K11 Dagma Xizang China
108 A3 Dagmala Shan mts Xizang China
166 C5 Dagmersellen Luzern Switz.
190 D1 Dagmersellen Luzern Switz.
Dagö i. Estonia see Hiiumaa
129 A2 Dagomys Rus. Fed.
Dagon Myanmar see Yangôn
81 C11 Dagon mt. South I. N.Z.
206 E4 Dagonkadi Ghana
129 B5 Dağönü Turkey
128 B2 Dağpazarı Turkey
129 E5 Dağpınar Turkey
111 H11 Dagrag Zangbo r. Xizang China
108 B2 Dagtog Qinghai China
107 O7 Dagu Tianjin China
108 D5 Daguan Yunnan China
208 C2 Daguéla Chad
107 Q8 Dagu He r. China
100 F6 Daguokui Shan hill Heilong. China
92 C3 Dagupan Luzon Phil.
106 D8 Dagur Qinghai China
84 C4 Daguragu N.T. Austr.
84 C4 Daguragu Aboriginal Land res. N.T. Austr.
96 C5 Dagwin Myanmar
Dagxoi Sichuan China see Yidun
Dagxoi Sichuan China see Sowa
111 J12 Dagzê Xizang China
111 H11 Dagzê Co salt l. China
111 I12 Dagzhuka Xizang China
124 D5 Dahabān Saudi Arabia
222 E2 Dahadinni r. N.W.T. Can.
Dahalach, Isole is Eritrea see Dahlak Archipelago
Dahana des. Saudi Arabia see Ad Dahnā'
114 C3 Dahanu Mahar. India
Dahe Guangxi China see Ziyuan
106 F9 Daheba Qinghai China
100 F5 Daheiding Shan mt. China
107 L6 Dahei He r. China
106 C5 Dahei Shan mt. Xinjiang China
100 D7 Dahei Shan mts China
109 L6 Daheng Fujian China
Daheyan Xinjiang China see Turpan Zhan
100 H5 Dahezhen Heilong. China
124 E7 Dahīn, Ḩarrat ad lava field Saudi Arabia
107 O5 Da Hinggan Ling mts China
114 D4 Dahivadi Mahar. India
124 G5 Daḩl, Nafūd ad des. Saudi Arabia
203 I6 Dahlak Archipelago is Eritrea
203 I5 Dahlak Marine National Park Eritrea
125 H2 Daḩl al Furayy well Saudi Arabia
124 F5 Daḩlat Shabāb Saudi Arabia
169 C10 Dahlem Ger.
171 H8 Dahlen Ger.
168 K4 Dahlenburg Ger.
171 H8 Dahlener Heide reg. Ger.
171 E6 Dahlenwarsleben Ger.
195 □ Dahlet Qorrot b. Gozo Malta
125 H2 Daḩl Iftākh well Saudi Arabia
231 F8 Dahlonega GA U.S.A.
171 I5 Dahlwitz-Hoppegarten Ger.
124 G7 Dahm, Ramlat des. Saudi Arabia/Yemen
205 H2 Dahmani Tunisia
171 H7 Dahme Brandenburg Ger.
170 D2 Dahme Schleswig-Holstein Ger.
171 I6 Dahme r. Ger.
170 D2 Dahmeshöved hd Ger.
172 D3 Dahn Ger.
116 E8 Dahod Gujarat India
Dahomey country Africa see Benin
111 D9 Dahongliutan Aksai Chin
Dahra Senegal see Dara
168 K5 Dähre Ger.
108 G7 Dahua Guangxi China
127 K5 Dahūk Iraq
127 K5 Dahūk governorate Iraq
127 K5 Dahūk, Buḩayrat l. Iraq
125 J7 Ḑaḩyah, Wādī r. Yemen
93 F7 Dai i. Maluku Indon.
105 I4 Daibosatsu-rei mt. Japan
107 O7 Daicheng Hebei China
Daido r. N. Korea see Taedong-gang
105 L2 Daigo Japan
107 M6 Dai Hai l. China
78 □6 Dai Island Solomon Is
94 F5 Daik Indon.
140 N4 Daikanvik Sweden
96 C6 Daik-U Myanmar
97 I8 Đai Lanh, Mui pt Vietnam
Dail Bho Thuath Scotland U.K. see North Dell
116 H5 Dailekh Nepal
232 F10 Dailey WV U.S.A.
146 G12 Dailly South Ayrshire, Scotland U.K.
122 H5 Daim Iran
103 K10 Daimanji-san hill Japan
185 L2 Daimiel Spain
104 F2 Daimon Japan
105 H3 Daimon-tōge pass Japan
105 H5 Daimugen-zan mt. Japan
175 M1 Dainava Lith.
147 H6 Daingean Ireland
237 H9 Daingerfield TX U.S.A.
104 E3 Dainichiga-take vol. Japan
104 E3 Dainichi-gawa r. Japan
104 D3 Dainichi-zan mt. Japan
108 A2 Dainkog Sichuan China
85 J4 Daintree Qld Austr.
85 J4 Daintree National Park Qld Austr.
156 E3 Dainville France
157 K7 Dainville-Bertheléville France
104 E7 Daiō Japan
104 E7 Daiō-zaki pt Japan
246 F4 Daiquiri Cuba
261 G5 Daireaux Arg.
Dairen Liaoning China see Dalian
146 K10 Dairsie Fife, Scotland U.K.
235 F1 Dairyland NY U.S.A.
226 B3 Dairyland WI U.S.A.
103 K11 Dai-sen vol. Japan
103 K11 Daisen-Oki Kokuritsu-kōen nat. park Japan
102 T3 Daisetsu-zan Kokuritsu-kōen nat. park Japan
109 N3 Daishan Zhejiang China
104 C6 Daitō Ōsaka Japan
105 H6 Daitō Shizuoka Japan
105 K2 Daiya-gawa r. Japan
Daiyue Shanxi China see Shanyin
109 L6 Daiyun Shan mts China
246 H4 Dajabón Dom. Rep.
123 N7 Dajal Pak.
104 E5 Dajan Japan
84 G6 Dajarra Qld Austr.
Dajie Yunnan China see Jiangchuan
108 C3 Dajin Chuan r. Sichuan China
106 H8 Dajing Gansu China
106 D8 Da Juh Qinghai China
206 A3 Dakar Senegal
203 F5 Dakar el Arak well Sudan
128 A10 Dakhal, Wādī ad watercourse Egypt
203 F3 Dākhilah, Wāḩāt ad oasis Egypt
117 M8 Dakhin Shahbazpur Island Bangl.
Dakhla Western Sahara see Ad Dakhla
Dakhla Oasis Egypt see Dākhilah, Wāḩāt ad
204 A5 Dakhlet Nouâdhibou admin. reg. Maur.
129 B1 Dakhovskaya Rus. Fed.
207 G4 Dakingari Nigeria
107 K2 Dakituy Rus. Fed.
97 I8 Đăk Lăk, Cao Nguyên plat. Vietnam
115 M9 Dakoank Andaman & Nicobar Is India
138 L9 Dakol'ka r. Belarus
116 D8 Dakor Gujarat India
207 G3 Dakoro Niger
236 H4 Dakota City IA U.S.A.
236 G4 Dakota City NE U.S.A.
196 I8 Đakovica Kosovo Serbia
188 G3 Đakovo Croatia
100 E2 Daktuy Rus. Fed.
209 D7 Dala Angola
177 J5 Đala Vojvodina Serbia
78 □6 Dala Malaita Solomon Is
178 B5 Dalaas Austria
206 B4 Dalaba Guinea
206 B3 Dalaba Senegal
146 B8 Dalabrog Western Isles, Scotland U.K.
Dalad Qi Nei Mongol China see Shulinzhao
Dalai Jilin China see Da'an
106 G6 Dalain Hob Nei Mongol China
107 O5 Dalai Nur l. China
122 B4 Dālā Khānī, Kūh-e mt. Iran
122 D7 Dālakī Iran
122 D7 Dālakī, Rūd-e r. Iran
128 B10 Ḑalāl, Jabal mt. Egypt
143 N1 Dalälven r. Sweden
199 J5 Dalama Turkey
107 M6 Dalamamiao Nei Mongol China
199 J6 Dalaman Turkey
199 J6 Dalaman r. Turkey
106 I5 Dalandzadgad Mongolia
92 C6 Dalanganem Islands Phil.
110 F6 Dalaoba Xinjiang China
Dalap-Uliga-Darrit Majuro Marshall Is see Delap-Uliga-Djarrit
143 K1 Dalarna county Sweden
141 L6 Dalarna reg. Sweden
95 I3 Dalat Sarawak Malaysia
97 I9 Đa Lat Vietnam
Dalatando Angola see N'dalatando
116 E8 Dalauda Madh. Prad. India
106 H5 Dalay Mongolia
123 K7 Dalbandin Pak.
146 I13 Dalbeattie Dumfries and Galloway, Scotland U.K.
85 K6 Dalbeg Qld Austr.
170 D3 Dalberg-Wendelstorf Ger.
226 A4 Dalbo MN U.S.A.
142 I3 Dalbosjön l. Sweden
85 M9 Dalby Qld Austr.
148 H5 Dalby Isle of Man
142 J6 Dalby Sweden
259 B6 Dalcahue Chile
142 B1 Dale Hordaland Norway
141 H6 Dale Sogn og Fjordane Norway
150 B4 Dale Pembrokeshire, Wales U.K.
232 H10 Dale City VA U.S.A.
229 I3 Dale Hollow Lake TN U.S.A.
169 B10 Daleiden Ger.
137 M8 Daleke Ukr.
164 K3 Dalen Neth.
179 N1 Dalešice, Vodní nádrž resr Czech Rep.
215 M2 Daleside S. Africa
175 I5 Daleszyce Pol.
96 A5 Dalet Myanmar
96 A4 Daletme Myanmar
231 E10 Daleville AL U.S.A.
234 D2 Daleville PA U.S.A.
141 M6 Dalfors Sweden
164 J3 Dalfsen Neth.
122 H8 Dalgān Iran
87 D9 Dalgaranger, Mount hill W.A. Austr.
83 L7 Dalgety N.S.W. Austr.
87 C8 Dalgety r. W.A. Austr.
146 J10 Dalgety Bay Fife, Scotland U.K.
151 N3 Dalham Suffolk, England U.K.
237 D7 Dalhart TX U.S.A.
225 H3 Dalhousie N.B. Can.
116 F3 Dalhousie Hima. Prad. India
220 F2 Dalhousie, Cape N.W.T. Can.
107 L9 Dali Shaanxi China
108 C6 Dali Yunnan China
128 B3 Dali Cyprus
107 Q7 Dalian Liaoning China
Daliang Guangdong China see Shunde
106 G8 Daliang Qinghai China
108 D4 Daliang Shan mts Sichuan China
107 Q7 Dalian Wan b. China
185 N7 Dalías Spain
185 N7 Dalías, Campo de reg. Spain
Daliburgh Western Isles, Scotland U.K. see Dalabrog
129 H6 Dälidağ mt. Azer.
107 L8 Dali He r. China
175 H4 Dalików Pol.
129 H5 Dälilär Azer.
129 H5 Dälimämmädli Azer.
107 R5 Dalin Nei Mongol China
Dalinghe Liaoning China see Linghai
107 Q6 Daling He r. China
101 E8 Dalizi Jilin China
188 G3 Dalj Croatia
146 J11 Dalkeith Midlothian, Scotland U.K.
117 K7 Dalkola W. Bengal India
85 N8 Dallarnil Qld Austr.
146 J7 Dallas Moray, Scotland U.K.
238 C4 Dallas OR U.S.A.
234 D2 Dallas PA U.S.A.
237 G9 Dallas TX U.S.A.
226 C9 Dallas City IL U.S.A.
234 B5 Dallastown PA U.S.A.
Dalles City OR U.S.A. see The Dalles
170 H5 Dallgow Ger.
116 H9 Dalli Chhattisgarh India
220 E4 Dall Island AK U.S.A.
210 D1 Dallol vol. Eth.
207 F3 Dallol Bosso watercourse Mali/Niger
125 K3 Dalmā i. U.A.E.
188 E3 Dalmacija reg. Croatia
261 F3 Dalmacio Vélez Sarsfield Arg.
146 G10 Dalmally Argyll and Bute, Scotland U.K.
177 H5 Dalmand Hungary
225 G2 Dalmas, Lac l. Que. Can.
Dalmatia reg. Croatia see Dalmacija
234 B3 Dalmatia PA U.S.A.
116 H6 Dalmau Uttar Prad. India
146 H12 Dalmellington East Ayrshire, Scotland U.K.
223 J4 Dalmeny Sask. Can.
117 K8 Dalmi Jharkhand India
190 H4 Dalmine Italy
146 H7 Dalnavie Highland, Scotland U.K.
100 I6 Dal'negorsk Rus. Fed.
100 H6 Dal'nerechensk Rus. Fed.
134 I5 Dal'neye Konstantinovo Rus. Fed.
134 G1 Dal'niye Zelentsy Rus. Fed.
Dalny Liaoning China see Dalian
206 D5 Daloa Côte d'Ivoire
85 M1 Daloloia Group is P.N.G.
108 F5 Dalou Shan mts China
171 G10 Dalovice Czech Rep.
124 G3 Dalqān well Saudi Arabia
146 G11 Dalry North Ayrshire, Scotland U.K.
146 G12 Dalrymple East Ayrshire, Scotland U.K.
85 K6 Dalrymple, Lake Qld Austr.
85 L6 Dalrymple, Mount Qld Austr.
138 F1 Dalsbruk Fin.
142 I3 Dals Långed Sweden
157 L5 Dalstein France
149 L4 Dalston Cumbria, England U.K.
117 J7 Daltenganj Jharkhand India
224 C3 Dalton Ont. Can.
215 O5 Dalton S. Africa
231 E8 Dalton GA U.S.A.
233 L6 Dalton MA U.S.A.
232 D8 Dalton OH U.S.A.
234 D1 Dalton PA U.S.A.
Daltonganj Jharkhand India see Daltenganj
263 I2 Dalton Iceberg Tongue Antarctica
149 K5 Dalton-in-Furness Cumbria, England U.K.
227 J1 Dalton Mills Ont. Can.
147 E8 Dalua r. Ireland
94 D4 Daludalu Sumatera Indon.
101 C9 Dalu Dao i. China
161 J8 Daluis France
108 C8 Daluo Yunnan China
109 I7 Daluo Shan mt. Guangdong China
92 C2 Dalupiri i. Phil.
140 □D1 Dalvík Iceland
87 D11 Dalwallinu W.A. Austr.
146 H9 Dalwhinnie Highland, Scotland U.K.
84 C2 Daly r. N.T. Austr.
199 J6 Dalyan Turkey
240 J4 Daly City CA U.S.A.
138 J6 Dalyokiya Belarus
84 C2 Daly River N.T. Austr.
84 C3 Daly River/Port Keats Aboriginal Land res. N.T. Austr.
147 F6 Dalystown Ireland
84 D4 Daly Waters N.T. Austr.
136 C2 Damachava Belarus
207 H3 Damagaram Takaya Niger
129 D4 Damal Turkey
209 F8 Damalisques de Leshwe nature res. Dem. Rep. Congo
116 D9 Daman Daman India
116 C9 Daman and Diu union terr. India
138 I9 Damanava Belarus
206 B2 Damâne well Maur.
122 D5 Dāmaneh Iran
203 F2 Damanhūr Egypt
223 J2 Damant Lake N.W.T. Can.
Damão Daman India see Daman
122 C4 Damaq Iran
107 N6 Damaqun Shan mts China
93 E2 Damar Sulawesi Indon.
93 F4 Damar i. Maluku Indon.
93 F7 Damar i. Maluku Indon.
129 C4 Damar Turkey
208 C3 Damara C.A.R.
212 C4 Damaraland reg. Namibia
233 □P4 Damariscotta Lake ME U.S.A.
94 □ Damar Laut, Pulau i. Sing.
Damas Syria see Dimashq
207 I3 Damasak Nigeria

Delbrück Ger.
Delburne Alta Can.
Del Campillo Arg.
Delčevo Macedonia
Delden Neth.
Dêlêg Xizang China
Delegate N.S.W. Austr.
Deleitosa Spain
Đelekovec Croatia
Délembé C.A.R.
Delémont Switz.
Delet b. Fin.
Delevan CA U.S.A.
Delevan NY U.S.A.
Delfinópolis Brazil
Delft Neth.
Delft Island Sri Lanka
Delfzijl Neth.
Delgada, Point CA U.S.A.
Delgada, Punta pt Mex.
Delgado, Cabo c. Moz.
Delgermörön Mongolia
Delger Mörön r. Mongolia
Delgo Sudan
Del Haven NJ U.S.A.
Delhi Ont. Can.
Delhi Qinghai China
Delhi Delhi India
Delhi admin. div. India
Delhi CA U.S.A.
Delhi CO U.S.A.
Delhi LA U.S.A.
Delhi NY U.S.A.
Delhi Nongchang Qinghai China
Deli i. Indon.
Deli r. Turkey
Delia Sicilia Italy
Delia r. Sicilia Italy
Delianuova Italy
Delice Turkey
Delice r. Turkey
Delices Dominica
Délices Fr. Guiana
Deliceto Italy
Delicias Mex.
Delījān Iran
Deliktaş Turkey
Déline N.W.T. Can.
Delingha Qinghai China see Delhi
Delingha Nongchang Qinghai China see Delhi Nongchang
Delingsdorf Ger.
Delisle Sask. Can.
Delitua Sumatera Indon.
Delitzsch Ger.
Dellach Austria
Dellach im Drautal Austria
Delle France
Delligsen Ger.
Dello Italy
Dell Rapids SD U.S.A.
Dellys Alg.
Del Mar CA U.S.A.
Delmar DE U.S.A.
Delmas S. Africa
Delme France
Delmenhorst Ger.
Delmont NJ U.S.A.
Delmont PA U.S.A.
Delmore Downs N.T. Austr.
Delnice Croatia
Del Norte CO U.S.A.
De-Longa, Ostrova is Novosibirskiye O-va Rus. Fed.
De Long Islands Novosibirskiye O-va Rus. Fed. see De-Longa, Ostrova
De Long Mountains AK U.S.A.
De Long Strait Rus. Fed. see Longa, Proliv
Deloraine Tas. Austr.
Deloraine Man. Can.
Delph Greater Manchester, England U.K.
Delphi tourist site Greece
Delphi IN U.S.A.
Delphos OH U.S.A.
Delportshoop S. Africa
Delray Beach FL U.S.A.
Del Río Mex.
Del Rio TX U.S.A.
Delsbo Sweden
Delta state Nigeria
Delta CO U.S.A.
Delta OH U.S.A.
Delta PA U.S.A.
Delta UT U.S.A.
Delta Amacuro state Venez.
Delta Downs Qld Austr.
Delta du Saloum, Parc National du nat. park Senegal
Delta Junction AK U.S.A.
Delta National Wildlife Refuge nature res. LA U.S.A.
Delta Reservoir NY U.S.A.
Deltebre Spain
Deltona FL U.S.A.
Delungra N.S.W. Austr.
De Lutte Neth.
Delvada Gujarat India
Del Valle Arg.
Delve Ger.
Delvin Ireland
Delvinë Albania
Delyatyn Ukr.
Dema r. Rus. Fed.
Demak Jawa Indon.
Demanda, Sierra de la mts Spain
Demange-aux-Eaux France
Demavend mt. Iran see Damāvand, Qolleh-ye
Demba Dem. Rep. Congo
Demba Chio Angola
Dembava Lith.
Dembech'a Eth.
Dembeni Njazidja Comoros
Dembeni Mayotte
Dembī Eth.
Dembia C.A.R.
Dembī Dolo Eth.
Demecser Hungary
De Meern Neth.
Demen Ger.
Demer r. Belgium
Demerara Guyana see Georgetown
Demerara Abyssal Plain sea feature S. Atlantic Ocean
Demerdzhi mt. Ukr.
Demidov Rus. Fed.
Demidovo Rus. Fed.
Demigny France
Deming NM U.S.A.
Demini r. Brazil
Demini, Serras do mts Brazil
Demirci Manisa Turkey
Demirci Trabzon Turkey
Demir Hisar Macedonia
Demir Kapija Macedonia
Demirkent Turkey
Demirköprü Barajı resr Turkey
Demirköy Turkey
Demirler r. Turkey
Demirözü Turkey
Demirtaş Antalya Turkey
Demirtaş Bursa Turkey
Demistkraal S. Africa
Demmin Ger.
Democracia Brazil
Demonte Italy
Demopolis AL U.S.A.
Demotte IN U.S.A.
Dempo, Gunung vol. Indon.
Dempster, Point W.A. Austr.
Dêmqog Jammu and Kashmir
Dému France
Demuryne Ukr.
Demyakhi Rus. Fed.
Dem'yanovka Kazakh. see Uzynkol'
Dem'yanovo Rus. Fed.
Demyansk Rus. Fed.
Demydiv Ukr.
Demydivka Ukr.
Demydove Ukr.
Demyno-Oleksandrivka Ukr.
De Naawte S. Africa
Denain France
240 L4 Denair CA U.S.A.
203 I6 Denakil reg. Eritrea/Eth.
Denali mt. AK U.S.A. see McKinley, Mount
220 C3 Denali National Park and Preserve AK U.S.A.
210 D3 Denan Eth.
223 K4 Denare Beach Sask. Can.
163 I8 Dénat France
224 E4 Denbigh Ont. Can.
150 F1 Denbigh Denbighshire, Wales U.K.
150 F1 Denbighshire admin. div. Wales U.K.
164 F5 Den Bommel Neth.
Den Bosch Neth. see 's-Hertogenbosch
164 G2 Den Burg Neth.
149 N6 Denby Dale West Yorkshire, England U.K.
96 E6 Den Chai Thai.
95 G6 Dendang Indon.
206 D2 Dendâra Maur.
165 F7 Denderleeuw Belgium
165 F6 Dendermonde Belgium
164 H4 Den Dolder Neth.
165 F6 Dendre r. Belgium
164 H5 Den Dungen Neth.
164 L4 Denekamp Neth.
196 J8 Đeneral Jankovič Kosovo Serbia
222 E3 Denetiah Provincial Park nat. park B.C. Can.
134 L3 Denezhkin Kamen', Gora mt. Rus. Fed.
207 H3 Dengas Niger
207 G3 Denge Nigeria
92 □ Denges Passage Palau
107 M9 Dengfeng Henan China
111 G12 Dênggar Xizang China
207 H4 Dengi Nigeria
Dengjiabu Jiangxi China see Yujiang
Dêngka Gansu China see Têwo
Dêngkagoin Gansu China see Têwo
107 J6 Dengkou Nei Mongol China
111 L11 Dêngqên Xizang China
109 J7 Dengta Guangdong China
163 D9 Denguin France
208 D3 Denguiro C.A.R.
Dengxian Henan China see Dengzhou
111 E10 Dêngzê Xizang China
109 I2 Dengzhou Henan China
Dengzhou Shandong China see Penglai
Den Haag Neth. see 's-Gravenhage
87 B8 Denham W.A. Austr.
86 J3 Denham r. W.A. Austr.
164 K4 Den Ham Neth.
151 L4 Denham Buckinghamshire, England U.K.
246 □ Denham, Mount hill Jamaica
84 G4 Denham Island Qld Austr.
85 L7 Denham Range mts Qld Austr.
87 B8 Denham Sound sea chan. W.A. Austr.
164 G3 Den Helder Neth.
223 I4 Denholm Sask. Can.
146 K12 Denholm Scottish Borders, Scotland U.K.
149 N6 Denholme West Yorkshire, England U.K.
164 G2 Den Hoorn Neth.
187 F10 Denia Spain
82 D5 Denial Bay S.A. Austr.
82 D5 Denial Bay b. S.A. Austr.
83 J6 Deniliquin N.S.W. Austr.
117 P6 Dening Arun. Prad. India
Deninoo Kue N.W.T. Can. see Fort Resolution
238 E6 Denio NV U.S.A.
137 K1 Deniskovichi Rus. Fed.
236 H4 Denison IA U.S.A.
237 G9 Denison TX U.S.A.
263 J2 Denison, Cape Antarctica
86 J5 Denison Plains W.A. Austr.
120 I1 Denisovka Kazakh.
114 G9 Deniyaya Sri Lanka
199 K5 Denizli Turkey
199 K5 Denizli prov. Turkey
161 J8 Denjuan, Sommet de mt. France
172 G4 Denkendorf Baden-Württemberg Ger.
173 K4 Denkendorf Bayern Ger.
172 F5 Denkingen Baden-Württemberg Ger.
172 G6 Denkingen Baden-Württemberg Ger.
173 J6 Denklingen Ger.
169 K6 Denkte Ger.
83 M5 Denman N.S.W. Austr.
263 G2 Denman Glacier Antarctica
87 D13 Denmark W.A. Austr.
142 G5 Denmark country Europe
226 G5 Denmark WI U.S.A.
Denmark Fjord inlet Greenland see Danmark Fjord
221 P3 Denmark Strait Greenland/Iceland
151 J6 Denmead Hampshire, England U.K.
247 □3 Dennery St Lucia
171 H7 Dennewitz Ger.
215 N1 Dennilton S. Africa
151 O3 Dennington Suffolk, England U.K.
86 J6 Dennis, Lake salt flat W.A. Austr.
232 D8 Dennison OH U.S.A.
234 F6 Dennisville NJ U.S.A.
146 I10 Denny Falkirk, Scotland U.K.
164 H3 Den Oever Neth.
121 L8 Denov Uzbek.
Denow Uzbek. see Denov
95 K9 Denpasar Bali Indon.
93 B5 Densongi Sulawesi Indon.
170 H4 Densow Ger.
190 D3 Dent Blanche mt. Switz.
161 E8 Dent de Rez hill France
165 D7 Dentergem Belgium
173 I3 Dentlein am Forst Ger.
149 M7 Denton Greater Manchester, England U.K.
234 D7 Denton MD U.S.A.
237 G9 Denton TX U.S.A.
161 J6 Dent Parrachée mt. France
87 C13 D'Entrecasteaux, Point W.A. Austr.
77 G3 D'Entrecasteaux, Récifs rf New Caledonia
91 L8 D'Entrecasteaux Islands P.N.G.
87 C13 D'Entrecasteaux National Park W.A. Austr.
190 B3 Dents du Midi mt. Switz.
151 M2 Denver Norfolk, England U.K.
238 L7 Denver CO U.S.A.
234 C4 Denver PA U.S.A.
224 E2 Denys r. Que. Can.
136 I2 Denysovychi Ukr.
172 D5 Denzlingen Ger.
117 J7 Deo Bihar India
116 F5 Deoband Uttar Prad. India
115 H3 Deobhog Chhattisgarh India
234 B4 Deodate PA U.S.A.
117 I7 Deogaon Uttar Prad. India
116 G9 Deogarh Madh. Prad. India
117 J9 Deogarh Orissa India
116 D7 Deogarh Rajasthan India
116 G7 Deogarh Uttar Prad. India
116 I8 Deogarh mt. Madh. Prad. India
117 K7 Deoghar Jharkhand India
116 G9 Deoli Mahar. India
117 K8 Deoli Orissa India
116 E7 Deolia Rajasthan India
162 H2 Déols France
116 G8 Deori Madh. Prad. India
117 I6 Deoria Uttar Prad. India
116 E2 Deosai, Plains of Jammu and Kashmir
116 I8 Deosil Chhattisgarh India
117 M6 Deothang Bhutan
100 E2 Dep r. Rus. Fed.
116 E8 Depalpur Madh. Prad. India
165 C6 De Panne Belgium
225 H2 De Pas, Rivière r. Que. Can.
226 F5 De Pere WI U.S.A.
232 G6 Depew NY U.S.A.
233 J6 Deposit NY U.S.A.
227 R2 Depot-Forbes Que. Can.
227 Q3 Depot-Rowanton Que. Can.
111 D9 Depsang Point hill Aksai Chin
226 E8 Depue IL U.S.A.
131 O3 Deputatskiy Rus. Fed.
111 J11 Dêqên Xizang China
111 J12 Dêqên Xizang China
Dêqên Xizang China see Dagzê
108 B4 Dêqên Yunnan China
109 H7 Deqing Guangdong China
109 M3 Deqing Zhejiang China
237 H8 De Queen AR U.S.A.
237 I10 De Quincy LA U.S.A.
156 I6 Der, Lac du l. France
210 C2 Dera Eth.
116 F4 Dera Hima. Prad. India
123 M7 Dera Bugti Pak.
123 N6 Dera Ghazi Khan Pak.
203 G4 Deraheib reg. Sudan
123 N6 Dera Ismail Khan Pak.
123 N6 Derajat reg. Pak.
263 C2 Deram, Mount Antarctica
123 N7 Derawar Fort Pak.
136 F3 Derazhne Ukr.
136 G4 Derazhnya Ukr.
171 E6 Derben Ger.
129 J3 Derbent Rus. Fed.
199 L2 Derbent Kocaeli Turkey
199 J4 Derbent Manisa Turkey
199 K4 Derbent Uşak Turkey
Derbent Uzbek. see Darband
Derbesiye Turkey see Şenyurt
100 B3 Derbur Nei Mongol China
83 K9 Derby Tas. Austr.
86 G4 Derby W.A. Austr.
215 L1 Derby S. Africa
151 J2 Derby Derby, England U.K.
151 J2 Derby admin. div. England U.K.
235 I2 Derby CT U.S.A.
237 G7 Derby KS U.S.A.
233 M3 Derby Line VT U.S.A.
149 N7 Derbyshire admin. div. England U.K.
129 C5 Derebaşı Turkey
177 K4 Derecske Hungary
151 N2 Dereham Norfolk, England U.K.
128 A1 Dereiçi Turkey
177 J5 Derekegyház Hungary
128 A2 Dereköy Antalya Turkey
199 K5 Dereköy Denizli Turkey
199 K3 Dereköy Kütahya Turkey
169 K7 Derenburg Ger.
169 H7 Derental Ger.
202 D6 Déréssa Chad
139 P2 Dereva Rus. Fed.
137 O5 Derezuvate Ukr.
147 H3 Derg r. Ireland/U.K.
147 G3 Derg, Lough l. Ireland
147 F7 Derg, Lough l. Ireland
120 C2 Dergachi Rus. Fed.
Dergachi Ukr. see Derhachi
82 H7 Dergholm State Park nature res. Vic. Austr.
137 P3 Derhachi Ukr.
116 G7 Deri Uttar Prad. India
237 I10 De Ridder LA U.S.A.
164 G3 De Rijp Neth.
127 J5 Derik Turkey
129 B6 Derinçay Turkey
129 B6 Derindere Turkey
126 G4 Derinkuyu Turkey
137 M5 Deriyivka Ukr.
210 D4 Derkali well Kenya
137 S5 Derkul r. Rus. Fed./Ukr.
169 J9 Dermbach Ger.
120 J5 Dermentobe Kazakh.
Derna Libya see Darnah
177 L4 Derna Romania
212 B5 Dernberg, Cape Namibia
129 B5 Dernekpazarı Turkey
136 E3 Derno Ukr.
108 B4 Dêrong Sichuan China
158 G3 Déroute, Passage de la str. Channel Is/France
120 C9 Derow Iran
147 H5 Derravaragh, Lough l. Ireland
213 H3 Derre Moz.
147 D4 Derreen Ireland
147 C9 Derreendaragh Ireland
147 D9 Derreeny Bridge Ireland
147 F4 Derry Ireland
147 I7 Derry r. Ireland
Derry Northern Ireland U.K. see Londonderry
233 N6 Derry NH U.S.A.
147 F2 Derrybeg Ireland
147 E6 Derrybrien Ireland
147 D6 Derryerglinna Ireland
147 G4 Derrygonnelly Northern Ireland U.K.
147 F7 Derrygoolin Ireland
147 C6 Derrylea Ireland
148 B5 Derrylin Northern Ireland U.K.
147 G4 Derrynacreeve Ireland
147 D9 Derrynasaggart Mountains hills Ireland
148 C5 Derrynawilt Northern Ireland U.K.
147 C6 Derryrush Ireland
148 E5 Derrytrasna Northern Ireland U.K.
147 F3 Derryveagh Mountains hills Ireland
197 O3 Dersca Romania
151 N2 Dersingham Norfolk, England U.K.
107 M5 Derst Nei Mongol China
106 G6 Derstei Nei Mongol China
168 D5 Dersum Ger.
111 D10 Dêrub Xizang China
203 H5 Derudeb Sudan
214 G9 De Rust S. Africa
193 I2 Deruta Italy
146 D9 Dervaig Argyll and Bute, Scotland U.K.
158 H6 Derval France
198 D4 Derveni Greece
188 F3 Derventa Bos.-Herz.
190 G3 Dervio Italy
83 K10 Derwent r. Tas. Austr.
151 J2 Derwent r. Derbyshire, England U.K.
149 P6 Derwent r. England U.K.
149 N7 Derwent Reservoir Derbyshire, England U.K.
149 N4 Derwent Reservoir Durham/Northumberland, England U.K.
149 K4 Derwent Water l. England U.K.
137 O1 Deryugino Rus. Fed.
139 R5 Derza r. Rus. Fed.
120 E1 Derzhavino Rus. Fed.
121 L2 Derzhavinsk Kazakh.
Derzhavinskiy Kazakh. see Derzhavinsk
197 L7 Desa Romania
260 D3 Desaguadero Arg.
260 D4 Desaguadero r. Arg.
252 C4 Desaguadero r. Bol.
260 C4 Desague, Cerro mt. Arg.
260 D1 Desagües de los Colorados marsh Arg.
161 F7 Désaignes France
190 E5 Desana Italy
79 □9 Désappointement, Îles du is Arch. des Tuamotu Fr. Polynesia
237 J8 Des Arc AR U.S.A.
240 O2 Desatoya Mountains NV U.S.A.
227 K3 Desbarats Ont. Can.
151 K3 Desborough Northamptonshire, England U.K.
260 B4 Descabezado, Volcán vol. Chile
253 F4 Descalvado Mato Grosso Brazil
256 D4 Descalvado São Paulo Brazil
182 H8 Descargamaría Spain
162 F2 Descartes France
223 K4 Deschambault Lake Sask. Can.
223 K4 Deschambault Lake l. Sask. Can.
238 D4 Deschutes r. OR U.S.A.
257 H2 Descombrimento, Parque Nacional do nat. park Brazil
210 C2 Desē Eth.
216 □3d Deseada vol. La Palma Canary Is
252 C5 Deseada Chile
259 D7 Deseado Arg.
259 D7 Deseado r. Arg.
177 G5 Deseda-tározó l. Hungary
246 B2 Desembarco del Granma National Park tourist site Cuba
242 C2 Desemboque Mex.
259 D8 Desengaño, Punta pt Arg.
191 J5 Desenzano del Garda Italy
241 T2 Deseret UT U.S.A.
241 T1 Deseret Peak UT U.S.A.
241 T1 Deseret Peak Wilderness nature res. UT U.S.A.
227 Q5 Deseronto Ont. Can.
227 R3 Désert, Lac l. Que. Can.
184 □ Deserta Grande i. Madeira
184 □ Desertas, Ilhas is Madeira
123 M7 Desert Canal Pak.
241 Q8 Desert Center CA U.S.A.
241 P8 Desert Hot Springs CA U.S.A.
160 B4 Désertines France
239 G8 Desert Lake NV U.S.A.
148 D4 Desertmartin Northern Ireland U.K.
241 Q5 Desert National Wildlife Refuge nature res. NV U.S.A.
241 U5 Desert View AZ U.S.A.
185 M4 Desesperada mt. Spain
161 C6 Desges France
247 □2 Deshaies i. Guadeloupe
232 B7 Deshler OH U.S.A.
116 D6 Deshnok Rajasthan India
260 D2 Desiderio Tello Arg.
187 F7 Desierto hill Spain
242 B3 Desierto Central de Baja California, Parque Natural del nature res. Mex.
190 G4 Desio Italy
198 C3 Deskati Greece
179 I7 Deskle Slovenia
236 G3 De Smet SD U.S.A.
236 I5 Des Moines IA U.S.A.
237 D7 Des Moines NM U.S.A.
228 H2 Des Moines r. IA U.S.A.
136 H4 Desna r. Rus. Fed./Ukr.
137 J3 Desna r. Rus. Fed./Ukr.
136 J3 Desna Ukr.
197 L7 Desnățui r. Romania
139 Q7 Desnogorsk Rus. Fed.
139 Q7 Desnogorskoye Vodokhranilishche resr Rus. Fed.
259 C7 Desnudo, Cerro mt. Arg.
259 B9 Desolación, Isla i. Chile
92 E6 Desolation Point Phil.
240 L3 Desolation Valley Wilderness nature res. CA U.S.A.
226 C6 DeSoto WI U.S.A.
215 J9 Despatch S. Africa
106 C1 Despen Rus. Fed.
260 E2 Despeñaderos Arg.
226 G7 Des Plaines IL U.S.A.
196 J6 Despotovac Serbia
217 □2 Desroches, Île i. Seychelles
171 F7 Dessau Ger.
165 H6 Dessel Belgium
160 J2 Dessoubre r. France
Dessye Eth. see Desē
164 J4 De Steeg Neth.
165 E6 Destelbergen Belgium
227 P1 Destor Que. Can.
82 F6 D'Estrees Bay S.A. Austr.
182 H4 Destriana Spain
222 B2 Destruction Bay Y.T. Can.
192 C7 Desulo Sardegna Italy
252 A6 Desventurados, Islas de los is S. Pacific Ocean
156 C2 Desvres France
174 D3 Deszczno Pol.
177 J5 Deszk Hungary
196 J5 Deta Romania
222 H2 Detah N.W.T. Can.
139 T7 Detchino Rus. Fed.
213 E3 Dete Zimbabwe
168 E4 Detern Ger.
198 A2 Deti Jon b. Albania/Greece
196 I7 Đetinja r. Serbia
177 J4 Detk Hungary
177 G6 Detkovac Croatia
169 G7 Detmold Ger.
169 G7 Detmold admin. reg. Ger.
226 H4 Detour, Point MI U.S.A.
227 K4 De Tour Village MI U.S.A.
241 R5 Detrital Wash watercourse AZ U.S.A.
227 K7 Detroit MI U.S.A.
227 K8 Detroit Beach MI U.S.A.
236 H2 Detroit Lakes MN U.S.A.
Dett Zimbabwe see Dete
173 I2 Dettelbach Ger.
172 G4 Dettingen an der Erms Ger.
173 I5 Dettingen an der Iller Ger.
170 G2 Dettmannsdorf Ger.
169 K6 Dettum Ger.
157 N6 Dettwiller France
97 G7 Det Udom Thai.
177 I3 Detva Slovakia
83 L6 Deua National Park N.S.W. Austr.
171 F8 Deuben Ger.
156 E2 Deûle, Canal de la r. France
169 J8 Deuna Ger.
165 I6 Deurne Neth.
165 J8 Deutsch-Belgischer Naturpark nature res. Belgium
168 J4 Deutsch Evern Ger.
179 L5 Deutschfeistritz Austria
179 M6 Deutsch Goritz Austria
179 J6 Deutsch-Griffen Austria
170 G5 Deutschhof Ger.
179 N5 Deutsch Kaltenbrunn Austria
179 O4 Deutschkreutz Austria
Deutschland country Europe see Germany
179 L6 Deutschlandsberg Austria
169 B11 Deutsch-Luxemburgischer Naturpark nature res. Ger.
171 H9 Deutschneudorf Ger.
179 O3 Deutsch-Wagram Austria
171 F8 Deutzen Ger.
227 P3 Deux-Rivières Ont. Can.
159 K8 Deux-Sèvres dept France
197 K5 Deva Romania
183 K2 Deva r. Spain
Deva Cheshire, England U.K. see Chester
114 E4 Devadurga Karnataka India
114 F8 Devakottai Tamil Nadu India
237 J8 De Valls Bluff AR U.S.A.
Devana Aberdeen, Scotland U.K. see Aberdeen
114 E6 Devanhalli Karnataka India
114 F4 Devarkonda Andhra Prad. India
177 J4 Dévaványa Hungary
177 J4 Dévaványai park Hungary
Deve Bair pass Macedonia see Velbŭzhdki Prokhod
176 G4 Devecser Hungary
126 G4 Develi Turkey
164 J4 Deventer Neth.
190 E3 Devero r. Italy
146 K7 Deveron r. Scotland U.K.
197 K6 Devesel Romania
129 E6 Devetaş Turkey
176 E2 Devét Skal hill Czech Rep.
116 D8 Devgadh Bariya Gujarat India
114 C4 Devgarh Mahar. India
Devghar Jharkhand India see Deoghar
116 C6 Devikot Rajasthan India
156 I4 Deville France
81 G7 Devil River Peak South I. N.Z.
237 E11 Devils r. TX U.S.A.
81 H8 Devil's Backbone mt. South I. N.Z.
147 G7 Devil's Bit Mountain hill Ireland
150 E3 Devil's Bridge Ceredigion, Wales U.K.
240 M3 Devil's Gate pass CA U.S.A.
226 D2 Devil's Island WI U.S.A.
236 F1 Devil's Lake ND U.S.A.
237 E11 Devil's Lake l. TX U.S.A.
220 E4 Devil's Paw mt. AK U.S.A.
240 M4 Devil's Peak CA U.S.A.
246 F1 Devil's Point Cat I. Bahamas
216 □2a Devil's Riding School vol. crater Ascension S. Atlantic Ocean
222 C3 Devil's Thumb mt. Can./U.S.A.
197 M9 Devin Bulg.
237 F11 Devine TX U.S.A.
137 R2 Devitsa r. Rus. Fed.
151 I5 Devizes Wiltshire, England U.K.
116 E7 Devli Rajasthan India
226 A1 Devlin Ont. Can.
197 P7 Devnya Bulg.
247 □3 De Volet Point St Vincent
196 H10 Devoll r. Albania
161 H7 Dévoluy mts France
227 K2 Devon Ont. Can.
215 M2 Devon S. Africa
150 E6 Devon admin. div. England U.K.
149 P7 Devon r. England U.K.
146 I10 Devon r. Scotland U.K.
221 I2 Devon Island Nunavut Can.
83 K9 Devonport Tas. Austr.
240 O7 Devore CA U.S.A.
261 F2 Devoto Arg.
126 E3 Devrek Turkey
135 F8 Devrekâni Turkey
126 G3 Devrez r. Turkey
114 C4 Devrukh Mahar. India
94 A3 Dewa, Tanjung pt Indon.
95 M7 Dewakang Besar i. Indon.
117 L7 Dewanganj Bangl.
116 F8 Dewas Madh. Prad. India
164 J3 De Weerribben, Nationaal Park nat. park Neth.
210 D2 Dewelē Eth.
215 K5 Dewetsdorp S. Africa
247 □1 Dewey Puerto Rico
164 J3 De Wijk Neth.
237 J8 De Witt AR U.S.A.
236 J5 De Witt IA U.S.A.
233 I5 DeWitt NY U.S.A.
149 N6 Dewsbury West Yorkshire, England U.K.
109 K4 Dexing Jiangxi China
111 L12 Dêxing Xizang China
233 □P3 Dexter ME U.S.A.
227 K7 Dexter MI U.S.A.
226 B6 Dexter MN U.S.A.
237 K7 Dexter MO U.S.A.
239 L10 Dexter NM U.S.A.
233 I4 Dexter NY U.S.A.
226 D5 Dexterville WI U.S.A.
108 E3 Deyang Sichuan China
82 C3 Dey-Dey Lake salt flat S.A. Austr.
122 G5 Deyhuk Iran
137 N3 Deykalivka Ukr.
122 C3 Deylaman Iran
143 R7 Deyma r. Rus. Fed.
Deynau Turkm. see Galkynyş
91 I8 Deyong, Tanjung pt Papua Indon.
122 C6 Dez r. Iran
122 C5 Dez, Sadd-e resr Iran
183 P6 Deza Spain
182 D3 Deza r. Spain
222 B2 Dezadeash Y.T. Can.
222 B2 Dezadeash Lake Y.T. Can.
122 C5 Dezfūl Iran
131 U3 Dezhneva, Mys c. Rus. Fed.
107 O8 Dezhou Shandong China
Dezhou Sichuan China see Dechang
Dezh Shāhpūr Iran see Marīvān
177 L5 Dezna Romania
190 I4 Dezzo r. Italy
129 D3 Dghnorisa Georgia
129 D4 Dghvani Georgia
117 I6 Dhabarau Uttar Prad. India
117 J6 Dhading Nepal
203 G2 Dhahab Egypt
128 C10 Dhahab, Marsá b. Egypt
124 F5 Dhahab, Wādī watercourse Saudi Arabia
128 D6 Dhahab, Wādī adh r. Syria
125 J7 Dhaḩawn, Wādī r. Yemen
128 C7 Dhāhiriya West Bank
124 G3 Dhahlān, Jabal hill Saudi Arabia
Dhahran Saudi Arabia see Az Ẓahrān
117 M8 Dhaka Bangl.
117 M8 Dhaka admin. div. Bangl.
117 K8 Dhalbhum reg. Jharkhand India
117 M8 Dhaleswari r. Bangl.
117 N7 Dhaleswari r. India
114 D4 Dhalgaon Mahar. India
Dhali Cyprus see Dali
124 G8 Dhamār Yemen
124 G8 Dhamār governorate Yemen
117 K9 Dhamara Orissa India
116 E8 Dhamnod Madh. Prad. India
116 G7 Dhamoni Madh. Prad. India
116 G5 Dhampur Uttar Prad. India
116 H9 Dhamtari Chhattisgarh India
123 M9 Dhana Pak.
123 N6 Dhana Sar Pak.
117 K8 Dhanbad Jharkhand India
116 D8 Dhandhuka Gujarat India
116 D7 Dhanera Gujarat India
116 H5 Dhangarhi Nepal
116 H5 Dhang Range mts Nepal
117 K6 Dhankuta Nepal
116 E5 Dhansia Rajasthan India
114 F8 Dhanushkodi Tamil Nadu India
116 F3 Dhaola Dhar mts India
116 E9 Dhaoli Madh. Prad. India
116 E8 Dhar Madh. Prad. India
206 B2 Ḍhar Adrar hills Maur.
115 I3 Dharakota Orissa India
116 D9 Dharampur Gujarat India
117 K6 Dharan Bazar Nepal
114 E7 Dharapuram Tamil Nadu India
123 M8 Dhareja Pak.
116 C9 Dhari Gujarat India
117 N7 Dharmanagar Tripura India
114 F6 Dharmapuri Tamil Nadu India
114 E5 Dharmavaram Andhra Prad. India
117 I8 Dharmjaygarh Chhattisgarh India
116 E4 Dharmkot Punjab India
117 K9 Dharmsala Orissa India
210 F2 Dharoor watercourse Somalia
206 D2 Ḍhar Oualâta hills Maur.
206 C2 Ḍhar Tîchît hills Maur.
83 M5 Dharug National Park N.S.W. Austr.
114 E3 Dharur Mahar. India
114 D5 Dharwad Karnataka India
Dharwar Karnataka India see Dharwad
116 F3 Dharwas Hima. Prad. India
116 C9 Dhasa Gujarat India
116 G7 Dhasan r. Madh. Prad. India
126 H9 Dhāt al Ḥājj Saudi Arabia
117 I5 Dhaulagiri mt. Nepal
116 G7 Dhaura Uttar Prad. India
116 H6 Dhaurahra Uttar Prad. India
Dhávlia Greece see Davleia
Dhawlagiri mt. Nepal see Dhaulagiri
Dhebar Lake India see Jaisamand Lake
128 B3 Dhekelia Sovereign Base Area military base Cyprus
117 N6 Dhekiajuli Assam India
117 O6 Dhemaji Assam India
117 J9 Dhenkanal Orissa India
Dheskáti Greece see Deskati
Dhiafánion Karpathos Greece see Diafani
Dhiakoptón Greece see Diakofto
128 D7 Dhībān Jordan
Dhídhima Greece see Didyma
Dhidhimótikhon Greece see Didymoteicho
113 □1 Dhiffushi i. N. Male Maldives
113 □1 Dhigufinolhu i. S. Male Maldives
117 N6 Dhing Assam India
Dhíorix Korínthou b. Greece see Korinthou, Dioryga
127 M8 Dhī Qār governorate Iraq
128 E7 Dhirwah, Wādī adh watercourse Jordan
Dhodhekánisos is Greece see Dodekanisa
Dhofar admin. reg. Oman see Ẓufār
Dhokós i. Greece see Dokos
116 C9 Dhola Gujarat India
116 D8 Dholera Gujarat India
116 D8 Dholka Gujarat India
116 F6 Dholpur Rajasthan India
Dhomokós Greece see Domokos
114 E5 Dhone Andhra Prad. India
210 D4 Dhoomadheere Somalia
148 I5 Dhoon Isle of Man
116 C9 Dhoraji Gujarat India
116 B8 Dhori Gujarat India
Dhragonádha i. Greece see Dragonada
Dhragónisos i. Greece see Tragonisi
116 C8 Dhrangadhra Gujarat India
116 C8 Dhrol Gujarat India
172 B2 Dhron Ger.
Dhrosiá Greece see Drosia
124 F9 Dhubāb Yemen
117 L7 Dhubri Assam India
Dhuburi Assam India see Dhubri
123 O5 Dhudial Pak.
116 E9 Dhule Mahar. India
Dhulia Mahar. India see Dhule
117 K7 Dhulian W. Bengal India
123 O5 Dhulian Pak.
116 G8 Dhuma Madh. Prad. India
117 J6 Dhunche Nepal
210 F2 Dhuudo Somalia
210 E3 Dhuusa Marreeb Somalia
124 D2 Dhuwaybān basin Saudi Arabia
Dhytikí Ellás admin. reg. Greece see Dytiki Ellada
Dhytikí Makedhonía admin. reg. Greece see Dytiki Makedonia
198 G7 Dia i. Greece
161 K8 Diable, Cime du mt. France
246 □ Diablo, Mount hill Jamaica
240 K4 Diablo, Mount CA U.S.A.
242 B2 Diablo, Picacho del mt. Mex.
240 K4 Diablo Range mts CA U.S.A.
211 C7 Diaca Moz.
199 I7 Diafani Karpathos Greece
206 D3 Diafarabé Mali
260 B2 Diaguitas Chile
206 D3 Diaka r. Mali
198 D4 Diakofto Greece
206 C3 Diakon Mali
177 G3 Diakovce Slovakia
206 C3 Dialafara Mali
206 B3 Dialakoto Senegal
206 E3 Diallassagou Mali
247 □3 Diamant, Rocher du i. Martinique
261 G3 Diamante Arg.
260 D4 Diamante r. Arg.
193 P8 Diamante Italy
260 C4 Diamante, Laguna l. Arg.
260 C4 Diamante, Pampa del plain Arg.
261 G3 Diamante, Parque Nacional nat. park Arg.
85 G9 Diamantina watercourse Qld Austr.
251 F6 Diamantina Amazonas Brazil
257 F3 Diamantina Minas Gerais Brazil
254 E5 Diamantina, Chapada plat. Brazil
265 K7 Diamantina Deep sea feature Indian Ocean
85 H7 Diamantina Gates National Park Qld Austr.
85 H7 Diamantina Lakes Qld Austr.
256 A2 Diamantino Mato Grosso Brazil
253 F3 Diamantino Mato Grosso Brazil
256 A2 Diamantino r. Brazil
117 L8 Diamond Harbour W. Bengal India
240 □D12 Diamond Head HI U.S.A.
240 □D12 Diamond Head HI U.S.A.
85 M4 Diamond Islets Coral Sea Is Terr. Austr.
241 Q2 Diamond Peak NV U.S.A.
240 L3 Diamond Springs CA U.S.A.
240 O8 Diamond Valley Lake resr CA U.S.A.
238 I6 Diamondville WY U.S.A.
206 C3 Diamou Mali
206 B3 Diamounguél Senegal
216 □2b Diana's Peak hill St Helena
109 H8 Dianbai Guangdong China
Dianbu Anhui China see Feidong
108 C6 Diancang Shan mt. Yunnan China
108 D6 Dian Chi l. China
206 C3 Diandioumé Mali
192 D3 Diane, Étang de lag. Corse France
85 L3 Diane Bank sea feature Coral Sea Is Terr. Austr.
206 C3 Diangounté Kamara Mali
206 C5 Diani r. Guinea
108 F3 Dianjiang Chongqing China
190 E6 Diano d'Alba Italy
190 E8 Diano Marina Italy
254 D4 Dianópolis Brazil
206 D4 Dianra Côte d'Ivoire
Dianyang Yunnan China see Shidian
107 R5 Diaobingshan Liaoning China
107 P8 Diaokou Shandong China
100 G6 Diaoling Heilong. China
207 F3 Diapaga Burkina
128 A4 Diarizos r. Cyprus
206 C4 Diatifèrè Guinea
198 D2 Diavata Greece
115 M6 Diavolo, Mount hill Andaman & Nicobar Is India
261 G3 Diaz Arg.
212 B5 Diaz Point Namibia
125 M3 Dibā al Ḥiṣn U.A.E.
125 N4 Ḍibab Oman
Dibang r. India see Dingba Qu
209 D6 Dibaya Dem. Rep. Congo
209 C6 Dibaya-Lubwe Dem. Rep. Congo
202 E6 Dibbis Sudan
151 J6 Dibden Hampshire, England U.K.
199 J4 Dibek Dağı mt. Turkey
207 I2 Dibella well Niger
214 G3 Dibeng S. Africa
210 D2 Dībīlē Eth.
124 E2 Ḍibīy, Jabal hills Saudi Arabia
217 □3a Dibouani Njazidja Comoros
136 I2 Dibrova Kyivs'ka Oblast' Ukr.
136 G2 Dibrova Zhytomyrs'ka Oblast' Ukr.
117 O6 Dibrugarh Assam India
Dibse Syria see Dibsī
128 G3 Dibsī Syria
250 C2 Dibulla Col.
168 F5 Dickel Ger.
237 E9 Dickens TX U.S.A.
233 □P1 Dickey ME U.S.A.
236 D2 Dickinson ND U.S.A.
231 D7 Dickson TN U.S.A.
234 D2 Dickson City PA U.S.A.
140 □ Dickson Land reg. Svalbard
127 K5 Dicle r. Turkey alt. Dijlah, Nahr (Iraq/Syria), conv. Tigris
191 L8 Dicomano Italy
210 C4 Dida Galgalu reg. Kenya
124 G2 Dīdah well Saudi Arabia
164 J5 Didam Neth.
151 J4 Didcot Oxfordshire, England U.K.
169 J6 Didderse Ger.
205 H4 Dider Alg.
129 G3 Didi Borbalo, Mt'a Georgia
92 D2 Didicas i. Phil.
206 C3 Didiéni Mali
129 D3 Didi Inch'khuri Georgia
129 D3 Didi Jikhaishi Georgia
129 F4 Didi Lilo Georgia
210 B3 Didinga Hills Sudan
136 I3 Didivshchyna Ukr.
211 D5 Dido waterhole Kenya
222 H5 Didsbury Alta Can.
210 C3 Didu Eth.
116 E6 Didwana Rajasthan India
213 □K3 Didy Madag.
198 E5 Didyma Greece
199 H1 Didymoteicho Greece
138 J6 Didžiasalis Lith.
138 H7 Didžiulis l. Lith.
161 G7 Die France
169 D10 Dieblich Ger.
206 E4 Diébougou Burkina
172 F2 Dieburg Ger.
177 L5 Dieci Romania
Dieciséis de Julio Arg. see 16 de Julio
Diecisiete de Agosto Arg. see 17 de Agosto
Diedenhofen France see Thionville
173 J5 Diedorf Bayern Ger.
169 J8 Diedorf Thüringen Ger.
223 I5 Diefenbaker, Lake Sask. Can.
162 I5 Diège r. France
183 J7 Diego Álvaro Spain
259 B8 Diego de Almagro, Isla i. Chile
261 F4 Diego de Alvear Arg.
265 I5 Diego Garcia atoll B.I.O.T.
247 □7 Diego Martin Trin. and Tob.
259 C9 Diego Ramirez, Islas is Chile
Diégo Suarez Madag. see Antsirañana
206 C3 Diégrâga well Maur.
206 C5 Diéké Guinea
170 F3 Diekhof Ger.
169 I6 Diekholzen Ger.
165 J9 Diekirch Lux.
165 I9 Diekirch admin. dist. Lux.
190 E1 Dielsdorf Switz.
206 C3 Diéma Mali
206 A3 Diembéreng Senegal
169 H7 Diemel r. Ger.
169 G8 Diemelsee park Ger.
169 G8 Diemel-Stausee resr Ger.
164 G4 Diemen Neth.
160 G5 Diémoz France
Điên Biên Vietnam see Điên Biên Phu
96 F4 Điên Biên Phu Vietnam
96 G5 Diên Châu Vietnam
172 E2 Dienheim Ger.
97 I8 Diên Khanh Vietnam
161 B6 Dienne France
138 H5 Dienvidsusēja r. Latvia
156 I7 Dienville France
169 G6 Diepenau Ger.
165 H7 Diepenbeek Belgium
164 K4 Diepenheim Neth.
164 J4 Diepenveen Neth.
168 F5 Diepholz Ger.
156 B4 Dieppe France
247 □2 Dieppe Bay Town St Kitts and Nevis
214 H6 Dieput S. Africa
169 E9 Dierdorf Ger.
164 J4 Dieren Neth.
170 F2 Dierhagen, Ostseebad Ger.
237 H8 Dierks AR U.S.A.
106 J7 Di'er Nonchang Qu r. China
100 D6 Di'er Songhua Jiang r. China
168 K5 Diesdorf Ger.
171 F8 Dieskau Ger.
173 J2 Diespeck Ger.
164 H6 Diessen Neth.
173 K6 Dießen am Ammersee Ger.
190 F1 Diessenhofen Switz.
165 H7 Diest Belgium
179 J3 Dietachdorf Austria
173 I5 Dietenheim Ger.
173 J3 Dietenhofen Ger.
173 N4 Dietersburg Ger.
173 L3 Dietfurt an der Altmühl Ger.
190 E1 Dietikon Switz.
172 F5 Dietingen Ger.
179 K2 Dietmanns Niederösterreich Austria
179 L2 Dietmanns Niederösterreich Austria
173 I6 Dietmannsried Ger.
173 L6 Dietramszell Ger.
169 G10 Dietzenbach Ger.
169 F9 Dietzhölztal-Ewersbach Ger.
157 J5 Dieue-sur-Meuse France
161 G7 Dieulefit France
157 L6 Dieulouard France
157 M6 Dieuze France
138 I7 Dieveniškės Lith.
164 J3 Diever Neth.
179 K6 Diex Austria
169 F10 Diez Ger.
185 M6 Diezma Spain
207 I3 Diffa Niger
207 I2 Diffa dept Niger
165 I9 Differdange Lux.
124 D7 Difnein i. Eritrea
210 E3 Dig well Eth.
207 F3 Diga Diga well Niger
115 I3 Digapahandi Orissa India
208 E3 Digba Dem. Rep. Congo
117 O6 Digboi Assam India
225 H4 Digby N.S. Can.
141 M6 Digerbergen hill Sweden
142 J1 Digerberget hill Sweden
116 E6 Diggi Rajasthan India
117 K9 Digha W. Bengal India
129 F4 Dighomi Georgia
236 E6 Dighton KS U.S.A.
114 E3 Diglur Mahar. India
162 E4 Dignac France
191 N3 Dignano Italy
161 I8 Digne-les-Bains France
156 B6 Digny France
160 D4 Digoin France
92 D3 Digollorin Point Luzon Phil.
191 N2 Digòn r. Italy
129 E5 Digor Turkey
129 F2 Digora Rus. Fed.
92 E8 Digos Mindanao Phil.
116 F9 Digras Mahar. India
123 M9 Digri Pak.
91 I8 Digul r. Papua Indon.
106 F7 Diguojiadan Qinghai China
206 E5 Digya National Park Ghana
111 L13 Dihang r. India alt. Jamuna (Bangladesh), alt. Yarlung Zangbo (China), conv. Brahmaputra
225 H1 Dihourse, Lac l. Que. Can.
175 M5 Dihtiv Ukr.
137 L3 Dihtyari Ukr.
124 C4 Diib, Wadi watercourse Sudan
207 I4 Diibao Cameroon
210 D4 Diinsoor Somalia
127 M8 Dijlah, Nahr r. Iraq/Syria alt. Dicle (Turkey), conv. Tigris
165 G7 Dijle r. Belgium
160 G2 Dijon France
Dijon airport France see Longvic
208 C2 Dik Chad
140 N4 Dikanäs Sweden
129 I6 Dīkdāsh Iran
116 E7 Diken Madh. Prad. India
210 D2 Dikhil Djibouti
117 O6 Dikho r. India
199 H3 Dikili Turkey
165 C7 Dikkebus Belgium
129 G3 Diklosmta mt. Rus. Fed.
129 D5 Dikmeköyü Turkey
206 D4 Dikodougou Côte d'Ivoire
165 C6 Diksmuide Belgium
130 J2 Dikson Rus. Fed.
207 I3 Dikwa Nigeria
210 C3 Dīla Eth.
185 L6 Dilar Spain
185 L6 Dilar r. Spain
122 H6 Dilaram Iran
165 F7 Dilbeek Belgium
129 B5 Dilek Dağı mt. Turkey
199 I5 Dilek Yarımadası Milli Parkı nat. park Turkey
208 E4 Dili Dem. Rep. Congo
93 D8 Dili East Timor
207 I3 Dilia watercourse Niger
129 F5 Dilijan Armenia
129 F5 Dilijan Argelanots' nature res. Armenia
97 I9 Di Linh Vietnam
81 H9 Dilion Cone mt. South I. N.Z.
129 E4 Dilit'i Georgia
Dilizhan Armenia see Dilijan
169 F9 Dillenburg Ger.
237 F11 Dilley TX U.S.A.
206 D3 Dilli Mali
142 G2 Dilling Norway
203 F6 Dilling Sudan
172 B3 Dillingen (Saar) Ger.
173 I4 Dillingen an der Donau Ger.
220 C4 Dillingham AK U.S.A.

84 D3 **Dillinya Aboriginal Land** *res.* *N.T.* Austr.
223 I4 **Dillon** *Sask.* Can.
223 I4 **Dillon** *r. Alta/Sask.* Can.
238 H4 **Dillon** *MT* U.S.A.
231 H8 **Dillon** *SC* U.S.A.
227 Q9 **Dillsburg** *PA* U.S.A.
232 G11 **Dillwyn** *VA* U.S.A.
209 D7 **Dilolo** Dem. Rep. Congo
199 G5 **Dilos** *i.* Greece
165 I6 **Dilsen** Belgium
127 L7 **Diltāwa** Iraq
207 I5 **Dimako** Cameroon
117 N7 **Dimapur** *Nagaland* India
191 J3 **Dimaro** Italy
244 A2 **Dimas** Mex.
128 E5 **Dimashq** Syria
128 F5 **Dimashq** *governorate* Syria
209 D6 **Dimbelenge** Dem. Rep. Congo
206 D5 **Dimbokro** Côte d'Ivoire
83 I7 **Dimboola** *Vic.* Austr.
85 J4 **Dimbulah** *Qld* Austr.
198 D3 **Diminio** Greece
Dimitrov Ukr. *see* **Dymytrov**
197 N8 **Dimitrovgrad** Bulg.
135 J5 **Dimitrovgrad** Rus. Fed.
197 K7 **Dimitrovgrad** Serbia
Dimitrovo Bulg. *see* **Pernik**
237 D8 **Dimmitt** *TX* U.S.A.
234 D1 **Dimock** *PA* U.S.A.
128 D7 **Dīmona** Israel
92 E6 **Dinagat** *i.* Phil.
92 E7 **Dinagat Sound** *sea chan.* Phil.
117 L7 **Dinajpur** Bangl.
195 K6 **Dinami** Italy
158 G5 **Dinan** France
116 E3 **Dinanagar** *Punjab* India
206 E3 **Dinangourou** Mali
165 G8 **Dinant** Belgium
117 J7 **Dinapur** *Bihar* India
199 L4 **Dinar** Turkey
122 D6 **Dīnār, Kūh-e** *mt.* Iran
188 F3 **Dinara** *mt.* Bos.-Herz.
188 F3 **Dinara Planina** *mts* Bos.-Herz./Croatia
158 G4 **Dinard** France
Dinaric Alps *mts* Bos.-Herz./Croatia *see* Dinara Planina
210 C4 **Dinas** *well* Kenya
150 C3 **Dinas Head** *Wales* U.K.
150 F5 **Dinas Powys** *Vale of Glamorgan, Wales* U.K.
Dinbych *Denbighshire, Wales* U.K. *see* **Denbigh**
Dinbych-y-Pysgod *Pembrokeshire, Wales* U.K. *see* **Tenby**
209 B8 **Dinde** Angola
203 G6 **Dinder** *r.* Sudan
124 B9 **Dinder el Agaliyin** *r.* Sudan
203 G6 **Dinder National Park** Sudan
114 F4 **Dindi** *r.* India
114 E7 **Dindigul** *Tamil Nadu* India
207 H4 **Dindima** Nigeria
213 G4 **Dindiza** Moz.
116 H8 **Dindori** *Madh. Prad.* India
116 D9 **Dindori** *Mahar.* India
158 C5 **Dinéault** France
199 M3 **Dinek** *Eskişehir* Turkey
126 F5 **Dinek** *Konya* Turkey
209 C6 **Dinga** Dem. Rep. Congo
123 O5 **Dinga** Pak.
92 C4 **Dingalan Bay** *Luzon* Phil.
108 H9 **Ding'an** *Hainan* China
117 O6 **Dingba Qu** *r.* India
107 J8 **Dingbian** *Shaanxi* China
109 J3 **Dingbujie** *Anhui* China
Dingcheng *Anhui* China *see* Dingyuan
Dingcheng *Hainan* China *see* Ding'an
209 B6 **Dinge** Angola
158 H5 **Dingé** France
169 J8 **Dingelstädt** Ger.
111 G10 **Dinggo** *Xizang* China
94 E6 **Dingin, Bukit** *mt.* Indon.
117 K6 **Dingla** Nepal
147 B8 **Dingle** Ireland
147 B8 **Dingle** *pen.* Ireland
147 B8 **Dingle Bay** Ireland
195 □ **Dingli** Malta
234 F2 **Dingmans Ferry** *PA* U.S.A.
109 J6 **Dingnan** *Jiangxi* China
85 L7 **Dingo** *Qld* Austr.
173 N4 **Dingolfing** Ger.
Dingping *Sichuan* China *see* Linshui
108 B4 **Ding Qu** *r. Sichuan* China
92 C2 **Dingras** *Luzon* Phil.
110 H3 **Dingshan** *Xinjiang* China
107 N9 **Dingtao** *Shandong* China
206 C4 **Dinguiraye** Guinea
225 I4 **Dingwall** *N.S.* Can.
146 H7 **Dingwall** *Highland, Scotland* U.K.
106 I9 **Dingxi** *Gansu* China
Dingxian *Hebei* China *see* Dingzhou
107 M7 **Dingxiang** *Shanxi* China
106 F6 **Dingxin** *Gansu* China
107 N7 **Dingxing** *Hebei* China
109 K2 **Dingyuan** *Anhui* China
107 N7 **Dingzhou** *Hebei* China
107 Q8 **Dingzi Gang** *b.* China
110 K7 **Dingzikou** *Qinghai* China
97 H10 **Đinh An, Cưa** *r. mouth* Vietnam
117 L6 **Dinhata** *W. Bengal* India
96 H4 **Dinh Lâp** Vietnam
91 J8 **Dini, Mount** P.N.G.
147 H7 **Dinin** *r.* Ireland
164 K3 **Dinkel** *r.* Neth.
173 I3 **Dinkelsbühl** Ger.
173 J5 **Dinkelscherben** Ger.
168 F5 **Dinklage** Ger.
241 U6 **Dinnebito Wash** *watercourse AZ* U.S.A.
146 K8 **Dinnet** *Aberdeenshire, Scotland* U.K.
111 H12 **Dinngyê** *Xizang* China
149 O7 **Dinnington** *South Yorkshire, England* U.K.
193 P8 **Dino, Isola di** *i.* Italy
212 E4 **Dinokwe** Botswana
241 W1 **Dinosaur** *CO* U.S.A.
238 J6 **Dinosaur National Monument** *nat. park CO* U.S.A.
137 S8 **Dinskaya** Rus. Fed.
169 C7 **Dinslaken** Ger.
164 F5 **Dinteloord** Neth.
164 H5 **Dinther** Neth.
94 F7 **Dintiteladas** *Sumatera* Indon.
240 M5 **Dinuba** *CA* U.S.A.
232 H11 **Dinwiddie** *VA* U.S.A.
164 J5 **Dinxperlo** Neth.
206 D3 **Dioïla** Mali
161 G7 **Diois, Massif du** *mts* France
206 C4 **Dion** *r.* Guinea
202 D5 **Diona** *well* Chad
257 F3 **Dionísio** Brazil
255 B8 **Dionísio Cerqueira** Brazil
161 E9 **Dions** France
256 B2 **Diorama** Brazil
Dioscurias Georgia *see* **Sokhumi**
177 H4 **Diósd** Hungary
197 K3 **Diosig** Romania
177 I4 **Diósjenő** Hungary
Diospolis Magna *tourist site* Egypt *see* **Thebes**
160 D3 **Diou** France
206 A3 **Diouloulou** Senegal
206 C3 **Dioumara** Mali
207 F3 **Dioundiou** Niger
206 D3 **Dioura** Mali
206 A3 **Diourbel** Senegal
123 O6 **Dipalpur** Pak.
116 H5 **Dipayal** Nepal
117 N7 **Diphu** *Assam* India
193 Q9 **Dipignano** Italy
Dipkarpaz Cyprus *see* **Rizokarpason**
123 M9 **Diplo** Pak.
92 D7 **Dipolog** *Mindanao* Phil.
165 J9 **Dippach** Lux.
85 L6 **Dipperu National Park** *Qld* Austr.
169 I9 **Dipperz** Ger.
171 I9 **Dippoldiswalde** Ger.
81 C12 **Dipton** *South I.* N.Z.
Dipu *Zhejiang* China *see* **Anji**
207 I5 **Dir** Cameroon
123 N4 **Dir** Pak.
123 O4 **Dir** *reg.* Pak.
202 B6 **Dira** *well* Chad
125 L3 **Dīrah** U.A.E.
117 N6 **Dirang** *Arun. Prad.* India
206 E2 **Diré** Mali
85 I2 **Direction, Cape** *Qld* Austr.
114 C3 **Direction Bank** *sea feature* India
86 □2 **Direction Island** Cocos Is
210 D2 **Dirē Dawa** Eth.
198 E4 **Dirfys** *mts* Greece
138 G2 **Dirhami** Estonia
242 □P12 **Diriamba** Nic.
209 D9 **Dirico** Angola
194 G9 **Dirillo** *r. Sicilia* Italy
199 K6 **Dirimii Geçidi** *pass* Turkey
158 C5 **Dirinon** France
87 B8 **Dirk Hartog Island** *W.A.* Austr.
207 I2 **Dirkou** Niger
164 G3 **Dirkshorn** Neth.
164 F5 **Dirksland** Neth.
173 J5 **Dirlewang** Ger.
172 E2 **Dirmstein** Ger.
202 E6 **Dirra** Sudan
83 L3 **Dirranbandi** *Qld* Austr.
149 M2 **Dirrington Great Law** *hill Scotland* U.K.
124 F6 **Ḍirs** Saudi Arabia
Dirschau Pol. *see* **Tczew**
122 C6 **Dīrsīyeh** Iran
241 V4 **Dirty Devil** *r. UT* U.S.A.
116 D7 **Disa** *Gujarat* India
117 O6 **Disang** *r.* India
262 T2 **Disappointment, Cape** Antarctica
259 □ **Disappointment, Cape** S. Georgia
238 B3 **Disappointment, Cape** *WA* U.S.A.
87 G7 **Disappointment, Lake** *salt flat W.A.* Austr.
Disappointment Islands *Arch. des Tuamotu* Fr. Polynesia *see* **Désappointement, Îles du**
225 I2 **Disappointment Lake** *Nfld and Lab.* Can.
173 I4 **Dischingen** Ger.
82 H8 **Discovery Bay** *b. Vic.* Austr.
Discovery Bay *b. H.K.* China *see* **Tai Pak Wan**
246 □ **Discovery Bay** Jamaica
82 H8 **Discovery Bay Coastal Park** *nature res. Vic.* Austr.
264 J8 **Discovery Seamounts** *sea feature* S. Atlantic Ocean
190 F2 **Disentis Muster** Switz.
190 H3 **Disgrazia, Monte** *mt.* Italy
122 D6 **Dishmūk** Iran
203 G3 **Dishnā** Egypt
Disko *i.* Greenland *see* **Qeqertarsuaq**
Disko Bugt *b.* Greenland *see* **Qeqertarsuup Tunua**
140 □ **Diskobukta** *b.* Svalbard
199 M4 **Dişli** Turkey
84 H5 **Dismal Creek** *r. Qld* Austr.
263 D2 **Dismal Mountains** Antarctica
233 I12 **Dismal Swamp** *VA* U.S.A.
156 E6 **Disneyland Resort Paris** *tourist site* France
195 O3 **Diso** Italy
165 I7 **Dison** Belgium
112 H6 **Dispur** *Assam* India
232 H11 **Disputanta** *VA* U.S.A.
225 G4 **Disraëli** *Que.* Can.
151 O3 **Diss** *Norfolk, England* U.K.
124 E7 **Dissān** *i.* Saudi Arabia
159 L8 **Dissay** France
159 L6 **Dissay-sous-Courcillon** France
169 F6 **Dissen am Teutoburger Wald** Ger.
206 E4 **Dissin** Burkina
149 J4 **Distington** *Cumbria, England* U.K.
250 E2 **Distrito Capital** *admin. dist.* Venez.
256 D1 **Distrito Federal** *admin. dist.* Brazil
245 H6 **Distrito Federal** *admin. dist.* Mex.
126 E8 **Disūq** Egypt
92 C6 **Dit** *i.* Phil.
171 D7 **Ditfurt** Ger.
214 G4 **Ditloung** S. Africa
194 I9 **Dittaino** *r. Sicilia* Italy
169 J10 **Dittelbrunn** Ger.
173 J3 **Dittenheim** Ger.
151 M5 **Ditton** *Kent, England* U.K.
172 G4 **Ditzingen** Ger.
116 C9 **Diu** *Daman* India
92 E7 **Diuata Mountains** *Mindanao* Phil.
92 E7 **Diuata Point** *Mindanao* Phil.
179 I8 **Divača** Slovenia
122 B4 **Dīvān Darreh** Iran
198 B4 **Divarata** *Kefallonia* Greece
Divehi *country* Indian Ocean *see* **Maldives**
208 B5 **Divénié** Congo
190 E3 **Diveria** *r.* Italy
159 K3 **Dives** *r.* France
159 K3 **Dives-sur-Mer** France
135 H5 **Diveyevo** Rus. Fed.
114 G5 **Divi, Point** India
Divichi Azer. *see* **Däväçi**
238 H4 **Divide** *MT* U.S.A.
234 E6 **Dividing Creek** *NJ* U.S.A.
195 I7 **Divieto** *Sicilia* Italy
92 D3 **Divilacan Bay** *Luzon* Phil.
177 I3 **Divín** Slovakia
177 H2 **Divina** Slovakia
257 F4 **Divinésia** Brazil
257 E4 **Divinópolis** Brazil
156 E3 **Divion** France
256 B2 **Divisões, Serra das** *mts* Brazil
Divisor, Sierra de *mts* Peru *see* **Ultraoriental, Cordillera**
198 A2 **Divjaka** *nat. park* Albania
135 H7 **Divnoye** Rus. Fed.
137 O7 **Divnyns'ke** Ukr.
206 D5 **Divo** Côte d'Ivoire
139 O6 **Divo** Rus. Fed.
160 I4 **Divonne-les-Bains** France
184 C3 **Divor** *r.* Port.
184 D3 **Divor, Barragem do** *resr* Port.
199 H7 **Divounia** *i.* Greece
126 I4 **Divriği** Turkey
209 D7 **Divuma** Dem. Rep. Congo
134 L4 **Div'ya** Rus. Fed.
123 L8 **Diwana** Pak.
Diwaniyah Iraq *see* **Ad Dīwānīyah**
190 C3 **Dix, Lac des** *l.* Switz.
206 E5 **Dixcove** Ghana
233 □O4 **Dixfield** *ME* U.S.A.
156 F7 **Dixmont** France
233 □P4 **Dixmont** *ME* U.S.A.
240 K3 **Dixon** *CA* U.S.A.
226 E8 **Dixon** *IL* U.S.A.
238 G3 **Dixon** *MT* U.S.A.
220 E4 **Dixon Entrance** *sea chan.* Can./U.S.A.
246 F1 **Dixon's** *San Salvador* Bahamas
260 E4 **Dixonville** Arg.
222 G3 **Dixonville** *Alta* Can.
233 N3 **Dixville** *Que.* Can.
127 K4 **Diyadin** Turkey
127 L6 **Diyālá** *governorate* Iraq
127 L7 **Diyālá, Nahr** *r.* Iraq
127 J5 **Diyarbakır** Turkey
116 C7 **Diyodar** *Gujarat* India
123 J8 **Diz** Pak.
Dizak Iran *see* **Dāvar Panāh**
207 H6 **Dizangué** Cameroon
122 F4 **Diz Chah** Iran
Dize Turkey *see* **Yüksekova**
108 H4 **Dizhuang** *Hunan* China
232 B12 **Dizney** *KY* U.S.A.
156 G5 **Dizy** France
156 H4 **Dizy-le-Gros** France
207 I6 **Dja** *r.* Cameroon
207 I6 **Dja, Réserve du** *nature res.* Cameroon
202 B4 **Djado** Niger
202 B4 **Djado, Plateau du** Niger
Djakarta *Jawa* Indon. *see* **Jakarta**
Djakovica *Kosovo* Serbia *see* **Đakovica**
205 G2 **Djamâa** Alg.
209 D7 **Djamba** *Katanga* Dem. Rep. Congo
209 D7 **Djamba** *Katanga* Dem. Rep. Congo
208 B5 **Djambala** Congo
208 C5 **Djampie** Dem. Rep. Congo
207 I5 **Djampiel** Cameroon
205 H4 **Djanet** Alg.
78 □3b **Djarrit** *i. Majuro* Marshall Is
Djarrit-Uliga-Dalap *Majuro* Marshall Is *see* **Delap-Uliga-Djarrit**
91 L7 **Djaul Island** P.N.G.
205 F4 **Djebr** *mt.* Alg.
208 C2 **Djébrène** Chad
202 C6 **Djédaa** Chad
205 E4 **Djedid** *well* Alg.
205 F2 **Djelfa** Alg.
208 E3 **Djéma** C.A.R.
208 C2 **Djèmber** Chad
Djeneral Jankovič *Kosovo* Serbia *see* **Đeneral Jankovič**
206 D3 **Djenné** Mali
197 K6 **Djerdap** *nat. park* Serbia
202 B6 **Djermaya** Chad
209 D5 **Djia** Dem. Rep. Congo
206 E3 **Djibo** Burkina
206 D4 **Djiborosso** Côte d'Ivoire
210 D2 **Djibouti** *country* Africa
210 D2 **Djibouti** Djibouti
Djidjelli Alg. *see* **Jijel**
206 C3 **Djiguéni** Maur.
206 D5 **Djiroutou** Côte d'Ivoire
207 I5 **Djohong** Cameroon
208 C2 **Djoli-Kera, Forêt classée de** *nature res.* Chad
208 D4 **Djolu** Dem. Rep. Congo
202 C6 **Djombo Kibbit** Chad
208 B4 **Djoua** *r.* Congo/Gabon
208 D3 **Djoubissi** C.A.R.
147 J6 **Djouce Mountain** *hill* Ireland
205 F5 **Djoúdem, Oued** *watercourse* Alg.
207 F4 **Djougou** Benin
207 I6 **Djoum** Cameroon
208 C4 **Djoumbélé** Congo
208 B3 **Djoumboli** Cameroon
202 C6 **Djourab, Erg du** *des.* Chad
208 F4 **Djugu** Dem. Rep. Congo
209 C6 **Djuma** Dem. Rep. Congo
140 □F1 **Djúpivogur** Iceland
143 L1 **Djurås** Sweden
142 J3 **Djurö nationalpark** *nat. park* Sweden
143 M3 **Djursö** *i.* Sweden
116 E4 **Dlairi** *Punjab* India
177 K3 **Dlhé Klčovo** Slovakia
177 H2 **Dlhé Pole** Slovakia
176 G2 **Dlouhá Loučka** Czech Rep.
174 I5 **Dłubnia** *r.* Pol.
177 I1 **Dłubniański Park Krajobrazowy** Pol.
174 F4 **Długołęka** *Dolnośląskie* Pol.
175 K2 **Długołęka** *Podlaskie* Pol.
175 J3 **Długosiodło** Pol.
171 L6 **Długoszyn** Pol.
175 H4 **Dłutów** Pol.
131 P2 **Dmitriya Lapteva, Proliv** *sea chan.* Rus. Fed.
120 D1 **Dmitriyevka** *Samarskaya Oblast'* Rus. Fed.
135 H5 **Dmitriyevka** *Tambovskaya Oblast'* Rus. Fed.
135 F5 **Dmitriyev-L'govskiy** Rus. Fed.
Dmitriyevsk Ukr. *see* **Makiyivka**
139 U7 **Dmitriyevskoye** Rus. Fed.
139 U5 **Dmitrov** Rus. Fed.
139 Q8 **Dmitrovo** Rus. Fed.
139 W6 **Dmitrovskiy Pogost** Rus. Fed.
139 S9 **Dmitrovsk-Orlovskiy** Rus. Fed.
137 S1 **Dmitryashevka** Rus. Fed.
137 L3 **Dmytrivka** *Chernihivs'ka Oblast'* Ukr.
137 N6 **Dmytrivka** *Dnipropetrovs'ka Oblast'* Ukr.
137 P5 **Dmytrivka** *Dnipropetrovs'ka Oblast'* Ukr.
137 M7 **Dmytrivka** *Khersons'ka Oblast'* Ukr.
137 L5 **Dmytrivka** *Kirovohrads'ka Oblast'* Ukr.
137 K7 **Dmytrivka** *Mykolayivs'ka Oblast'* Ukr.
137 O8 **Dmytrivka** *Respublika Krym* Ukr.
137 P7 **Dmytrivka** *Zaporiz'ka Oblast'* Ukr.
Dmytriyevs'k Ukr. *see* **Makiyivka**
139 N7 **Dnepr** *r.* Rus. Fed.
alt. **Dnipro (Ukraine),**
alt. **Dnyapro (Belarus),**
conv. **Dnieper**
Dneprodzerzhinsk Ukr. *see* **Dniprodzerzhyns'k**
Dnepropetrovsk Ukr. *see* **Dnipropetrovs'k**
Dnepropetrovskaya Oblast' *admin. div.* Ukr. *see* **Dnipropetrovs'ka Oblast'**
Dnepropetrovsk Oblast *admin. div.* Ukr. *see* **Dnipropetrovs'ka Oblast'**
Dneprorudnoye Ukr. *see* **Dniprorudne**
139 Q6 **Dneprovskoye** Rus. Fed.
136 I7 **Dnestrovsc** Moldova
135 F7 **Dnieper** *r.* Europe
alt. **Dnepr (Rus. Fed.),**
alt. **Dnipro (Ukraine),**
alt. **Dnyapro (Belarus)**
136 J7 **Dniester** *r.* Ukr./Moldova
alt. **Dnister (Ukraine),**
alt. **Nistru (Moldova)**
137 L7 **Dnipro** *r.* Ukr.
alt. **Dnepr (Rus. Fed.),**
alt. **Dnyapro (Belarus),**
conv. **Dnieper**
137 N4 **Dnipro-Donbas, Kanal** *canal* Ukr.
137 N5 **Dniprodzerzhyns'k** Ukr.
137 M5 **Dniprodzerzhyns'ke Vodoskhovyshche** *resr* Ukr.
137 M6 **Dnipro-Kryvyy Rih, Kanal** *canal* Ukr.
137 O5 **Dnipropetrovs'k** Ukr.
137 O5 **Dnipropetrovs'ka Oblast'** *admin. div.* Ukr.
Dnipropetrovsk Oblast *admin. div.* Ukr. *see* **Dnipropetrovs'ka Oblast'**
137 N6 **Dniprorudne** Ukr.
137 N8 **Dniprovka** *Respublika Krym* Ukr.
137 N6 **Dniprovka** *Zaporiz'ka Oblast'* Ukr.
137 O5 **Dniprovs'ke Vodoskhovyshche** *resr* Ukr.
137 K7 **Dniprovs'kyy Lyman** *b.* Ukr.
137 M7 **Dnipryany** Ukr.
136 J7 **Dnister** *r.* Ukr.
alt. **Nistru (Moldova),**
conv. **Dniester**
136 J7 **Dnistrov'ky Lyman** *l.* Ukr.
138 M4 **Dno** Rus. Fed.
139 O7 **Dnyapro** *r.* Belarus
alt. **Dnepr (Rus. Fed.),**
alt. **Dnipro (Ukraine),**
conv. **Dnieper**
136 D1 **Dnyaprowska-Buhski, Kanal** *canal* Belarus
213 G3 **Doa** Moz.
123 L4 **Doāb** Afgh.
123 N5 **Doaba** Pak.
123 L4 **Do Āb-e Mīkh-e Zarrīn** Afgh.
147 J3 **Doagh** *Northern Ireland* U.K.
148 C3 **Doagh Isle** *pen.* Ireland
225 H4 **Doaktown** *N.B.* Can.
95 L7 **Doangdoangan Besar** *i.* Indon.
95 L7 **Doangdoangan Kecil** *i.* Indon.
96 G4 **Doan Hung** Vietnam
213 □K2 **Doany** Madag.
163 C8 **Doazit** France
208 C2 **Doba** Chad
177 L4 **Doba** Romania
138 N9 **Dobasna** *r.* Belarus
170 F3 **Dobbertin** Ger.
170 F3 **Dobbertiner Seenlandschaft** *park* Ger.
191 M2 **Dobbiaco** Italy
227 M5 **Dobbinton** *Ont.* Can.
235 H2 **Dobbs Ferry** *NY* U.S.A.
175 I6 **Dobczyce** Pol.
106 G9 **Dobdain** *Qinghai* China
138 G5 **Dobele** Latvia
171 H8 **Döbeln** Ger.
91 H7 **Doberai, Jazirah** *pen. Papua* Indon.
Doberai Peninsula *Papua* Indon. *see* **Doberai, Jazirah**
171 I7 **Doberlug-Kirchhain** Ger.
171 K7 **Döbern** Ger.
179 L2 **Dobersberg** Austria
168 J2 **Dobersdorf** Ger.
171 J8 **Dobershau** Ger.
174 D3 **Dobiegniew** Pol.
175 J4 **Dobieszyn** Pol.
179 L6 **Dobl** Austria
261 E5 **Doblas** Arg.
91 H8 **Dobo** *Maluku* Indon.
188 G3 **Doboj** Bos.-Herz.
122 F7 **Do Borjī** Iran
179 M8 **Dobova** Slovenia
177 K5 **Doboz** Hungary
175 I6 **Dobra** *Małopolskie* Pol.
174 G4 **Dobra** *Wielkopolskie* Pol.
174 C2 **Dobra** *Zachodniopomorskie* Pol.
174 D2 **Dobra** *Zachodniopomorskie* Pol.
177 L6 **Dobra** Romania
171 E10 **Döbraberg** *hill* Ger.
177 I3 **Dobrá Niva** Slovakia
176 C2 **Dobřany** Czech Rep.
179 L2 **Dobra Stausee** *resr* Austria
179 K2 **Dobrá Voda** Czech Rep.
174 G3 **Dobre** *Kujawsko-Pomorskie* Pol.
175 J3 **Dobre** *Mazowieckie* Pol.
137 L6 **Dobre** Ukr.
143 Q8 **Dobre Miasto** Pol.
197 K4 **Dobreşti** Romania
197 P7 **Dobrich** Bulg.
135 H5 **Dobrinka** Rus. Fed.
176 D2 **Dobříš** Czech Rep.
171 F6 **Dobritz** Ger.
173 P2 **Dobřív** Czech Rep.
179 L7 **Dobrna** Slovenia
179 K8 **Dobrnič** Slovenia
183 M3 **Dobro** Spain
174 G5 **Dobrodzień** Pol.
177 H5 **Döbrököz** Hungary
174 E5 **Dobromierz** Pol.
136 B4 **Dobromyl'** Ukr.
175 H4 **Dobroń** Pol.
177 L3 **Dobron'** Ukr.
176 E2 **Dobronín** Czech Rep.
137 Q5 **Dobropillya** Ukr.
Dobropol'ye Ukr. *see* Dobropillya
175 L5 **Dobrosyn** Ukr.
174 F4 **Dobroszyce** Pol.
197 M6 **Dobroteşti** Romania
175 M5 **Dobrotvir** Ukr.
197 P4 **Dobrovăţ** Romania
171 K10 **Dobrovice** Czech Rep.
137 P5 **Dobrovillya** Ukr.
179 N6 **Dobrovnik** Slovenia
138 F7 **Dobrovol'sk** Rus. Fed.
175 I5 **Dobrowoda** Pol.
139 W9 **Dobroye** Rus. Fed.
138 K3 **Dobruchi** Rus. Fed.
197 P7 **Dobrudzhansko Plato** *plat.* Bulg.
197 M6 **Dobrun** Romania
137 K1 **Dobrush** Belarus
137 M8 **Dobrushyne** Ukr.
176 F1 **Dobruška** Czech Rep.
134 L4 **Dobryanka** Rus. Fed.
137 K1 **Dobryanka** Ukr.
139 U6 **Dobrynikha** Rus. Fed.
175 I3 **Dobrzankowo** Pol.
174 D2 **Dobrzany** Pol.
174 F5 **Dobrzeń Wielki** Pol.
174 F4 **Dobrzyca** Pol.
174 E2 **Dobrzyca** *r.* Pol.
175 H3 **Dobrzyków** Pol.
175 H3 **Dobrzyń nad Wisłą** Pol.
177 J3 **Dobšiná** Slovakia
175 J1 **Dobskie, Jezioro** *l.* Pol.
81 F9 **Dobson** *South I.* N.Z.
81 D11 **Dobson** *r. South I.* N.Z.
231 G7 **Dobson** *NC* U.S.A.
150 C7 **Dobwalls** *Cornwall, England* U.K.
111 I12 **Dobzha** *Xizang* China
177 J5 **Dóc** Hungary
96 H6 **Đôc, Mui** *pt* Vietnam
92 B9 **Doc Can** *rf* Phil.
256 B3 **Doce** *r.* Brazil
257 H3 **Doce** *r.* Brazil
146 H10 **Dochart** *r. Scotland* U.K.
146 H8 **Dochgarroch** *Highland, Scotland* U.K.
123 M6 **Do China Qala** Afgh.
151 N2 **Docking** *Norfolk, England* U.K.
169 C10 **Dockweiler** Ger.
Doc Penfro *Pembrokeshire, Wales* U.K. *see* **Pembroke Dock**
244 G2 **Doctor Arroyo** Mex.
242 F3 **Doctor Belisario Domínguez** Mex.
237 F13 **Doctor Coss** Mex.
87 H10 **Doctor Hicks Range** *hills W.A.* Austr.
244 G4 **Doctor Mora** Mex.
Doctor Petru Groza Romania *see* **Ştei**
211 C6 **Doda** Tanz.
123 M7 **Dodapur** Pak.
114 E6 **Dod Ballapur** *Karnataka* India
151 M4 **Doddinghurst** *Essex, England* U.K.
149 M2 **Doddington** *Northumberland, England* U.K.
111 I11 **Dodê** *Xizang* China
Dodecanese *is* Greece *see* Dodekanisa
199 I7 **Dodekanisa** *is* Greece
164 I5 **Dodewaard** Neth.
226 B5 **Dodge Center** *MN* U.S.A.
237 E7 **Dodge City** *KS* U.S.A.
226 D7 **Dodgeville** *WI* U.S.A.
191 K4 **Dodici, Cima** *mt.* Italy
150 C7 **Dodman Point** *England* U.K.
210 C3 **Dodola** Eth.
211 B6 **Dodoma** Tanz.
211 B6 **Dodoma** *admin. reg.* Tanz.
211 D5 **Dodori National Reserve** *nature res.* Kenya
223 I5 **Dodsland** *Sask.* Can.
232 B9 **Dodsonville** *OH* U.S.A.
164 J4 **Doesburg** Neth.
164 J5 **Doetinchem** Neth.
93 D4 **Dofa** *Maluku* Indon.
197 N5 **Doftana** *r.* Romania
224 B3 **Dog** *r. Ont.* Can.
111 I9 **Dogai Coring** *salt l.* China
111 I9 **Dogaicoring Qangco** *salt l.* China
199 L3 **Doğalar** Turkey
199 I5 **Doğanbey** *Aydın* Turkey
199 H4 **Doğanbey** *İzmir* Turkey
199 L3 **Doğançayır** Turkey
126 H4 **Doğanşehir** Turkey
129 D6 **Doğansu** Turkey
222 F5 **Dog Creek** *B.C.* Can.
149 Q7 **Dogdyke** *Lincolnshire, England* U.K.
111 J11 **Dogên Co** *l.* China
105 J2 **Dōgen-ko** *l.* Japan
199 L3 **Döğer** Turkey
172 E6 **Dogern** Ger.
122 I4 **Doghārūn** Iran
247 L4 **Dog Island** Anguilla
225 I1 **Dog Island** *Nfld and Lab.* Can.
223 L5 **Dog Lake** *Man.* Can.
224 B3 **Dog Lake** *Ont.* Can.
224 C3 **Dog Lake** *Ont.* Can.
190 D6 **Dogliani** Italy
197 J5 **Dognecea** Romania
103 K10 **Dōgo** *i.* Japan
206 D4 **Dogo** Mali
210 E2 **Dogoble** *well* Somalia
207 G3 **Dogondoutchi** Niger
208 C2 **Dogoumbo** Chad
103 K11 **Dōgo-yama** *mt.* Japan
246 D1 **Dog Rocks** *is* Bahamas
127 L4 **Doğubeyazıt** Turkey
129 B5 **Doğu Karadeniz Dağları** *mts* Turkey
199 J5 **Doğu Menteşe Dağları** *mts* Turkey
247 □2 **Dogwood Point** St Kitts and Nevis
111 H12 **Dogxung Zangbo** *r. Xizang* China
Doha Qatar *see* **Ad Dawḥah**
Dohad *Gujarat* India *see* **Dahod**
117 N8 **Dohazari** Bangl.
171 E10 **Döhlau** Ger.
171 I9 **Dohna** Ger.
215 L8 **Dohne** S. Africa
168 E5 **Dohren** Ger.
111 F13 **Dohrighat** *Uttar Prad.* India
124 D8 **Dohul** *i.* Eritrea
77 I4 **Doi** *i.* Fiji
93 E2 **Doi** *i. Maluku* Indon.
96 D5 **Doi Inthanon National Park** Thai.
111 I11 **Doijang** *Xizang* China
96 D5 **Doi Khuntan National Park** Thai.
96 D5 **Doi Luang National Park** Thai.
Doïranis, Limni *l.* Greece/Macedonia *see* **Dojran, Lake**
182 G2 **Doiras, Embalse de** *resr* Spain
Doire *Northern Ireland* U.K. *see* **Londonderry**
96 D5 **Doi Saket** Thai.
117 J8 **Doisanagar** *Jharkhand* India
165 G8 **Doische** Belgium
256 C5 **Dois Córregos** Brazil
254 E4 **Dois Irmãos, Serra dos** *hills* Brazil
184 A2 **Dois Portos** Port.
96 D5 **Doi Suthep-Pui National Park** Thai.
176 G3 **Dojč** Slovakia
197 K9 **Dojran, Lake** Greece/Macedonia
Dojransko Ezero *l.* Greece/Macedonia *see* **Dojran, Lake**
203 G6 **Doka** Sudan
122 F5 **Dokali** Iran
127 L6 **Dokan, Sadd** *dam* Iraq
205 G2 **Dokhara, Dunes de** *des.* Alg.
141 K6 **Dokka** Norway
140 P3 **Dokkas** Sweden
164 I2 **Dokkum** Neth.
164 I2 **Dokkumer Ee** *r.* Neth.
206 C4 **Doko** Guinea
108 C3 **Dokog He** *r. Sichuan* China
198 E5 **Dokos** *i.* Greece
123 M8 **Dokri** Pak.
Dokshukino Rus. Fed. *see* **Nartkala**
138 K7 **Dokshytsy** Belarus
176 D1 **Doksy** *Liberecký kraj* Czech Rep.
171 J10 **Doksy** *Středočeský kraj* Czech Rep.
102 X2 **Dokuchayeva, Mys** *c.* *Kuril'skiye O-va* Rus. Fed.
137 Q6 **Dokuchayevs'k** Ukr.
129 C5 **Dokumacılar** Turkey
199 L2 **Dokurcun** Turkey
236 F3 **Doland** *SD* U.S.A.
150 F2 **Dolanog** *Powys, Wales* U.K.
241 R6 **Dolan Springs** *AZ* U.S.A.
259 D6 **Dolavón** Arg.
225 F3 **Dolbeau** *Que.* Can.
150 D2 **Dolbenmaen** *Gwynedd, Wales* U.K.
190 D8 **Dolceacqua** Italy
158 H4 **Dol-de-Bretagne** France
160 G2 **Dole** France
191 R4 **Dolenja Vas** Slovenia
179 L8 **Dolenjske Toplice** Slovenia
160 K5 **Dolent, Mont** *mt.* France/Italy
150 F3 **Dolfor** *Powys, Wales* U.K.
150 E1 **Dolgarrog** *Conwy, Wales* U.K.
137 Q7 **Dolgaya, Kosa** *spit* Rus. Fed.
150 E2 **Dolgellau** *Gwynedd, Wales* U.K.
170 H4 **Dolgen** Ger.
233 K5 **Dolgeville** *NY* U.S.A.
134 K1 **Dolgiy, Ostrov** *i.* Rus. Fed.
134 L1 **Dolgiy, Ostrov** *i.* Rus. Fed.
137 O2 **Dolgiye Budy** Rus. Fed.
175 I1 **Dolgorukovo** *Kaliningradskaya Oblast'* Rus. Fed.
139 V9 **Dolgorukovo** *Lipetskaya Oblast'* Rus. Fed.
139 W8 **Dolgoye** *Lipetskaya Oblast'* Rus. Fed.
135 G5 **Dolgoye** *Orlovskaya Oblast'* Rus. Fed.
139 V9 **Dolgusha** Rus. Fed.
197 O3 **Dolhasca** Romania
175 M5 **Dołhobyczów** Pol.
192 C9 **Dolianova** *Sardegna* Italy
174 D2 **Dolice** Pol.
Dolina Ukr. *see* **Dolyna**
143 N7 **Dolina Słupi, Park Krajobrazowy** Pol.
177 I1 **Dolinki Krakowskie, Park Krajobrazowy** Pol.
129 E1 **Dolinovka** Rus. Fed.
100 M5 **Dolinsk** *Sakhalin* Rus. Fed.
167 G3 **Doliny Bobru, Park Krajobrazowy** Pol.
170 J4 **Doliny Dolnej Odry, Park Krajobrazowy** Pol.
Dolisie *Loubomo* Congo *see* **Loubomo**
93 E4 **Dolit** *Halmahera* Indon.
197 J7 **Doljevac** Serbia
147 F7 **Dolla** Ireland
146 I10 **Dollar** *Clackmannanshire, Scotland* U.K.
168 D4 **Dollart** Ger.
171 E6 **Dolle** Ger.
262 T2 **Dolleman Island** Antarctica
157 N8 **Doller** *r.* France
168 I3 **Dollern** Ger.
171 F8 **Döllnitz** Ger.
173 K4 **Dollnstein** Ger.
159 M5 **Dollon** France
169 K8 **Döllstädt** Ger.
169 J9 **Dolmar** *hill* Ger.
121 M1 **Dolmatovo** Kazakh.
197 N7 **Dolna Lipnitska** Bulg.
177 I3 **Dolná Strehová** Slovakia
177 H3 **Dolné Vestenice** Slovakia
177 H2 **Dolní Benešov** Czech Rep.
171 J10 **Dolní Beřkovice** Czech Rep.
179 P2 **Dolní Bojanovice** Czech Rep.
176 E1 **Dolní Bousov** Czech Rep.
179 K1 **Dolní Bukovsko** Czech Rep.
197 P8 **Dolni Chiflik** Bulg.
197 M7 **Dolni Dŭbnik** Bulg.
179 O2 **Dolní Dunajovice** Czech Rep.
176 D3 **Dolní Dvořiště** Czech Rep.
176 F2 **Dolní Kounice** Czech Rep.
177 G3 **Dolní Němčí** Czech Rep.
176 D1 **Dolní Podluží** Czech Rep.
171 J9 **Dolní Poustevna** Czech Rep.
176 F2 **Dolní Újezd** Czech Rep.
176 B1 **Dolní Žandov** Czech Rep.
197 L8 **Dolno Kamartsi** Bulg.
197 M8 **Dolno Levski** Bulg.
174 E4 **Dolnośląskie** *prov.* Pol.
177 I2 **Dolný Kubín** Slovakia
Dolný Peter Slovakia *see* **Svätý Peter**
177 H3 **Dolný Pial** Slovakia
177 G4 **Dolný Štál** Slovakia
93 A4 **Dolo** *Sulawesi* Indon.
191 M5 **Dolo** Italy
190 J7 **Dolo** *r.* Italy
78 □4b **Dolohmwar** *hill Pohnpei* Micronesia
91 I8 **Dolok, Pulau** *i. Papua* Indon.
160 H5 **Dolomieu** France
Dolomites *mts* Italy *see* Dolomiti
191 L4 **Dolomiti** *mts* Italy
191 L3 **Dolomiti Bellunesi, Parco Nazionale delle** *nat. park* Italy
191 M2 **Dolomiti di Sesto, Parco Naturale** *nature res.* Italy
Dolon, Pereval *pass* Kyrg. *see* **Dolon Ashuusu**
121 P7 **Dolon Ashuusu** *pass* Kyrg.
107 O5 **Dolonnur** *Nei Mongol* China
210 D3 **Dolo Odo** Eth.
106 I4 **Doloon** Mongolia
261 I5 **Dolores** Arg.
243 O9 **Dolores** Guat.
242 D5 **Dolores** Mex.
187 D11 **Dolores** Spain
261 H3 **Dolores** Uru.
241 W3 **Dolores** *r. CO* U.S.A.
244 G4 **Dolores Hidalgo** Mex.
196 I6 **Dolovo** *Vojvodina* Serbia
259 F8 **Dolphin, Cape** Falkland Is
220 G3 **Dolphin and Union Strait** *Nunavut* Can.
246 □ **Dolphin Head** *hill* Jamaica
212 B5 **Dolphin Head** Namibia
86 D6 **Dolphin Island** *W.A.* Austr.
86 D6 **Dolphin Island Nature Reserve** *W.A.* Austr.
149 K2 **Dolphinton** *South Lanarkshire, Scotland* U.K.
178 G6 **Dölsach** Austria
174 F4 **Dolsk** Pol.
175 M4 **Dol's'k** Ukr.
175 K3 **Dołubowo** Pol.
96 G5 **Đô Lương** Vietnam
162 B4 **Dolus-d'Oléron** France
136 C5 **Dolyna** Ukr.
137 L5 **Dolyns'ka** Ukr.
137 Q7 **Dolzhanskaya** Rus. Fed.
137 O2 **Dolzhenkovo** Rus. Fed.
138 M3 **Dolzhitsy** Rus. Fed.
91 I7 **Dom, Gunung** *mt. Papua* Indon.
177 J3 **Domaháza** Hungary
116 G5 **Domaila** *Uttaranchal* India
199 K3 **Domaniç** Turkey
175 K3 **Domanice** Pol.
193 Q9 **Domanico** Italy
175 H3 **Domaniewice** *Łódzkie* Pol.
175 I4 **Domaniewice** *Mazowieckie* Pol.
177 H2 **Domaniža** Slovakia
117 L6 **Domar** Bangl.
111 E10 **Domar** *Xizang* China
175 J6 **Domaradz** Pol.
111 L11 **Domartang** *Xizang* China
156 D3 **Domart-en-Ponthieu** France
179 O7 **Domašinec** Croatia
177 J5 **Domaszek** Hungary
174 E5 **Domaszków** Pol.
174 F4 **Domaszowice** Pol.
190 G2 **Domat Ems** Switz.
156 F7 **Domats** France
176 B2 **Domažlice** Czech Rep.
111 L10 **Domba** *Qinghai* China
122 B5 **Dom Bākh** Iran
120 H2 **Dombarovskiy** Rus. Fed.
141 J5 **Dombås** Norway
157 J5 **Dombasle-en-Argonne** France
157 K7 **Dombasle-en-Xaintois** France
157 L6 **Dombasle-sur-Meurthe** France
129 C2 **Dombay** Rus. Fed.
213 G3 **Dombe** Moz.
209 B8 **Dombe Grande** Angola
177 K5 **Dombegyház** Hungary
160 F4 **Dombes** *reg.* France
209 D6 **Dombi** Dem. Rep. Congo
177 H5 **Dombóvár** Hungary
209 C8 **Dombra** Angola
177 K3 **Dombrád** Hungary
Dombrau Pol. *see* **Dąbrowa Górnicza**
190 B1 **Dombresson** Switz.
Dombrovitsa Ukr. *see* **Dubrovytsya**
Dombrowa Pol. *see* **Dąbrowa Górnicza**
164 E5 **Domburg** Neth.
257 F3 **Dom Cavati** Brazil
Domda *Qinghai* China *see* **Qingshuihe**
160 B5 **Dôme, Monts** *mts* France
263 F1 **Dome Argus** *ice feature* Antarctica
263 H2 **Dome Charlie** *ice feature* Antarctica
Dome Circe *ice feature* Antarctica *see* **Dome Charlie**
222 F4 **Dome Creek** *B.C.* Can.
263 C1 **Dome Fuji** *research stn* Antarctica
178 F7 **Domegge di Cadore** Italy
138 G7 **Domeikava** Lith.
Domel Island Myanmar *see* **Letsok-aw Kyun**
161 H6 **Domène** France
160 B4 **Domérat** France
241 R8 **Dome Rock Mountains** *AZ* U.S.A.
171 D6 **Domersleben** Ger.
192 A9 **Domestica, Cala** *b. Sardegna* Italy
86 J3 **Domett, Cape** *W.A.* Austr.
81 G8 **Domett, Mount** *South I.* N.Z.
157 K6 **Domèvre-en-Haye** France
157 M6 **Domèvre-sur-Vezouze** France
252 C5 **Domeyko** *Antofagasta* Chile
258 C3 **Domeyko** *Atacama* Chile
163 C9 **Domezaine-Berraute** France
255 B9 **Dom Feliciano** Brazil
159 J4 **Domfront** France
157 K6 **Domgermain** France
252 C6 **Dominador** Chile
257 G4 **Domingos Martins** Brazil
182 E8 **Dominguiso** Port.
247 □2 **Dominica** *country* West Indies
242 □R13 **Dominical** Costa Rica
Dominicana, República *country* West Indies *see* **Dominican Republic**
246 H4 **Dominican Republic** *country* West Indies
247 □2 **Dominica Passage** Dominica/Guadeloupe
221 K3 **Dominion, Cape** *Nunavut* Can.
Dominique *i.* Fr. Polynesia *see* **Hiva Oa**
209 D6 **Domiongo** Dem. Rep. Congo
170 D4 **Dömitz** Ger.
257 F3 **Dom Joaquim** Brazil
117 M6 **Domkhar** Bhutan
157 I7 **Dommartin-le-Franc** France
156 I6 **Dommartin-Varimont** France
163 G6 **Domme** France
164 H5 **Dommel** *r.* Neth.
169 D10 **Dommershausen** Ger.
171 G7 **Dommitzsch** Ger.
197 M5 **Domneşti** *Argeş* Romania
197 N6 **Domneşti** *Bucureşti* Romania
170 E5 **Dömnitz** *r.* Ger.
175 I1 **Domnovo** Rus. Fed.
210 E3 **Domo** Eth.
139 U6 **Domodedovo** Rus. Fed.
190 E3 **Domodossola** Italy
198 D3 **Domokos** Greece
217 □3 **Domoni** *Nzwani* Comoros
156 D5 **Domont** France
177 H4 **Dömös** Hungary
139 Q1 **Domozhirovo** Rus. Fed.
157 L7 **Dompaire** France
157 J6 **Dompcevrin** France
255 B9 **Dom Pedrito** Brazil
254 D3 **Dom Pedro** Brazil
160 E4 **Dompierre-les-Ormes** France
160 D3 **Dompierre-sur-Besbre** France
162 B3 **Dompierre-sur-Mer** France
158 I8 **Dompierre-sur-Yon** France
95 M9 **Dompu** *Sumbawa* Indon.
157 K7 **Domrémy-la-Pucelle** France
177 I4 **Dömsöd** Hungary
170 E4 **Domsühl** Ger.
192 B10 **Domus de Maria** *Sardegna* Italy
192 B9 **Domusnovas** *Sardegna* Italy
260 B5 **Domuyo, Volcán** *vol.* Arg.
137 O7 **Domuzla** *r.* Ukr.
83 M3 **Domville, Mount** *hill Qld* Austr.
188 E2 **Domžale** Slovenia
85 L5 **Don** *r. Qld* Austr.
158 H6 **Don** *r.* France
114 E4 **Don** *r.* India
242 E4 **Don** Mex.
139 L8 **Don** *r.* Rus. Fed.
146 L8 **Don** *r. Scotland* U.K.
96 G7 **Don, Xé** *r.* Laos
147 J6 **Donabate** Ireland
191 M5 **Donada** Italy
258 E2 **Donadeu** Arg.
147 H4 **Donagh** *Northern Ireland* U.K.
147 K3 **Donaghadee** *Northern Ireland* U.K.
147 J4 **Donaghcloney** *Northern Ireland* U.K.
147 G7 **Donaghmore** *Laois* Ire
147 J6 **Donaghmore** *Meath* I
147 I3 **Donaghmore** *Norther Ireland* U.K.
245 L8 **Donaji** Mex.
83 I7 **Donald** *Vic.* Austr.
237 J10 **Donaldsonville** *LA* U.
258 C2 **Donalnes, Cerro** *mt.*
231 E10 **Donalsonville** *GA* U.S
184 G3 **Don Álvaro** Spain
185 P2 **Doña María Cristina,** de Spain
185 K5 **Doña Mencía** Spain
184 G7 **Doñana, Parque Nac** *nat. park* Spain
147 I6 **Donard** Ireland
260 B2 **Doña Rosa, Cordiller** Chile
244 C1 **Donato Guerra** Mex.
178 E2 **Donau** *r.* Austria/Ger.
alt. **Duna (Hungary),**
alt. **Dunaj (Slovakia)**
alt. **Dunărea (Romar**
alt. **Dunav (Serbia),**
conv. **Danube**
179 O3 **Donau-Auen, Nation** *nat. park* Austria
172 E6 **Donaueschingen** Ge
173 K4 **Donaumoos** *reg.* Ger.
173 I4 **Donauried** *reg.* Ger.
173 M3 **Donaustauf** Ger.
173 J4 **Donauwörth** Ger.
184 H3 **Don Benito** Spain
122 D5 **Donbī** Iran
149 O6 **Doncaster** *South York England* U.K.
157 I4 **Donchery** France
209 B7 **Dondo** Angola
213 G3 **Dondo** Moz.
93 B3 **Dondo, Tanjung** *pt* In
93 B3 **Dondo, Teluk** *b.* Indo
92 C7 **Dondonay** *i.* Phil.
114 G10 **Dondra Head** Sri Lan
136 G5 **Donduşeni** Moldova
Dondyushany Moldo Donduşeni
147 F3 **Donegal** Ireland
147 F3 **Donegal** *county* Irelar
147 F3 **Donegal Bay** Ireland
Dönenbay Kazakh. *se* Dunenbay
137 S5 **Donetsk** Rus. Fed.
137 Q6 **Donets'k** Ukr.
137 Q5 **Donets'ka Oblast'** *admin. div.* Ukr.
Donetskaya Oblast' *admin. div.* Ukr. *see* Donets'ka Oblast'
137 P2 **Donetskaya Seymits** Rus. Fed.
Donetsko-Amrovsiye *see* **Amvrosiyivka**
Donetsk Oblast *adm* Ukr. *see* **Donets'ka Ob**
137 R5 **Donets'kyy** Ukr.
137 Q5 **Donets'kyy Kryazh** *h* Rus. Fed./Ukr.
186 B1 **Doneztebe** Spain
210 E3 **Donfar** Eth.
246 □ **Don Figuerero Moun** *hills* Jamaica
141 J6 **Dønfoss** Norway
207 H4 **Donga** *r.* Cameroon/N
207 H5 **Donga** Nigeria
109 H5 **Dong'an** *Hunan* China
87 C10 **Dongara** *W.A.* Austr.
116 H9 **Dongargaon** *Chhattis*
116 H9 **Dongargarh** *Chhattis*
110 L6 **Dongbatu** *Gansu* Chi
99 M2 **Dongbei** *reg. Heilong.*
107 Q5 **Dongbei Pingyuan** *p*
Dongbo *Xizang* China Mêdog
Dongcheng *Guangdo see* **Yangdong**
Dongchuan *Yunnan* C Yao'an
108 D5 **Dongchuan** *Yunnan* C
111 G10 **Dongco** *Xizang* China
111 G10 **Dong Co** *l. Xizang* Ch
Dongcun *Shandong* C Haiyang
Dongcun *Shanxi* Chin Lanxian
108 F8 **Đông Đăng** Vietnam
107 O8 **Dong'e** *Shandong* Chi
164 G5 **Dongen** Neth.
158 G7 **Donges** France
108 G9 **Dongfang** *Hainan* Chi
100 H5 **Dongfanghong** *Heilo*
100 D7 **Dongfeng** *Jilin* China
93 A4 **Donggala** *Sulawesi* In
101 D9 **Donggang** *Liaoning* C
107 P9 **Donggang** *Shandong*
106 F9 **Donggi Conag** *l. Qing*
Donggou *Liaoning* Ch Donggang
106 G9 **Donggou** *Qinghai* Chi
109 J5 **Donggu** *Jiangxi* China
109 I7 **Dongguan** *Guangdon*
96 H6 **Đông Ha** Vietnam
107 P9 **Donghai** *Jiangsu* Chir
Dong Hai *sea* N. Paci *see* **East China Sea**
106 I8 **Donghaiba** *Ningxia* Cl
108 H8 **Donghai Dao** *i.* China
108 F3 **Dong He** *r.* China
106 G5 **Dong He** *watercourse*
96 H6 **Đông Hơi** Vietnam
107 K8 **Donghuachi** *Gansu* C
Donghuang *Guizhou* Xishui
109 I7 **Dong Jiang** *r.* China
90 D1 **Dongjiang Shuiku** *re* China
100 F6 **Dongjingcheng** *Heilo*
93 A5 **Dongkait, Tanjung** *p*
111 J12 **Dongkar** *Xizang* Chin
108 H5 **Dongkou** *Hunan* Chin
108 F6 **Donglan** *Guangxi* Chi
106 G7 **Dongle** *Gansu* China
107 R5 **Dongliao He** *r.* China
110 I7 **Donglük** *Xinjiang* Chir
Dongmen *Guangxi* Ch Luocheng
107 N9 **Dongming** *Shandong*
100 G6 **Dongning** *Heilong.* Ch
209 B8 **Dongo** Angola
209 C6 **Dongo** Dem. Rep. Co
190 G3 **Dongo** Italy
211 B6 **Dongobesh** Tanz.
203 F5 **Dongola** Sudan
210 B3 **Dongotona Mountai**
208 C4 **Dongou** Congo
Dong Phaya Yen Rar Thai. *see* Phang Hoei, San Kha
96 E7 **Dong Phraya Yen** *es*
109 I8 **Dongping** *Guangdong*
Dongping *Hunan* Chi Anhua
107 O8 **Dongping Hu** *l.* China
Dongpo *Sichuan* Chin Meishan
111 J11 **Dongqiao** *Xizang* Chir
106 I8 **Dongqinghu** *Nei Mon*
111 K10 **Dong Qu** *r. Qinghai* C
106 C5 **Dongquan** *Xinjiang* C
109 K7 **Dongshan** *Fujian* Chi
108 H8 **Dongshan** *Guangdon*
109 L3 **Dongshan** *Jiangsu* Ch
109 M3 **Dongshan** *Jiangsu* Ch
Dongshan *Jiangxi* Chi Shangyou
109 J5 **Dongshao** *Jiangxi* Ch
90 E2 **Dongsha Qundao** *is*
Dongsheng *Nei Mong see* **Ordos**
Dongshuan *Yunnan* C Tangdan
109 M2 **Dongtai** *Jiangsu* Chin
109 M2 **Dongtai He** *r.* China
111 L8 **Dong Taijnar Hu** *l. Qi* China
109 I4 **Dongting Hu** *l.* China
109 M5 **Dongtou** *Zhejiang* Chi
96 H4 **Đông Triêu** Vietnam
209 B9 **Donguena** Angola
208 A4 **Donguila** Gabon
Dong Ujimqin Qi *Nei* China *see* **Uliastai**

197 N5 **Dumbrăviţa** Braşov Romania
177 K6 **Dumbrăviţa** Timiş Romania
182 B2 **Dumbría** Spain
116 G3 **Dumchele** Jammu and Kashmir
94 G4 **Dumdum** i. Indon.
117 O6 **Dum Duma** Assam India
197 P4 **Dumeşti** Romania
158 F7 **Dumet, Île** i. France
247 □3 **Dumfries** Grenada
146 I12 **Dumfries** Dumfries and Galloway, Scotland U.K.
146 I12 **Dumfries and Galloway** admin. div. Scotland U.K.
139 S8 **Duminichi** Kaluzhskaya Oblast' Rus. Fed.
139 S8 **Duminichi** Kaluzhskaya Oblast' Rus. Fed.
197 M3 **Dumitra** Romania
117 K7 **Dumka** Jharkhand India
129 C5 **Dumlu** Turkey
129 C5 **Dumlu Dağı** mt. Turkey
128 A2 **Dumlugöze** Turkey
199 K4 **Dumlupınar** Turkey
114 G4 **Dummagudem** Andhra Prad. India
168 F5 **Dümmer** l. Ger.
169 F5 **Dümmer, Naturpark** nature res. Ger.
170 F3 **Dummerstorf** Ger.
93 D3 **Dumoga** Sulawesi Indon.
224 E4 **Dumoine** r. Que. Can.
227 Q3 **Dumoine, Lac** l. Que. Can.
227 R3 **Dumont, Lac** l. Que. Can.
263 J2 **Dumont d'Urville** research stn Antarctica
263 I2 **Dumont d'Urville Sea** Antarctica
169 C10 **Dümpelfeld** Ger.
117 J7 **Dumraon** Bihar India
124 F7 **Dumsuk** i. Saudi Arabia
203 F2 **Dumyāţ** Egypt
126 E8 **Dumyāţ** governorate Egypt
163 H9 **Dun** France
169 J8 **Dün** ridge Ger.
188 G3 **Duna** r. Hungary alt. **Donau (Austria/Germany),** alt. **Dunaj (Slovakia),** alt. **Dunărea (Romania),** alt. **Dunav (Serbia),** conv. **Danube**
177 H4 **Dunaalmás** Hungary
Dünaburg Latvia see **Daugavpils**
177 H5 **Dunaegyháza** Hungary
177 H5 **Dunafalva** Hungary
147 G2 **Dunaff Head** Ireland
177 H5 **Dunaföldvár** Hungary
177 I4 **Dunaharaszti** Hungary
188 F2 **Dunaj** r. Slovakia alt. **Donau (Austria/Germany),** alt. **Duna (Hungary),** alt. **Dunărea (Romania),** alt. **Dunav (Serbia),** conv. **Danube**
175 I5 **Dunajec** r. Pol.
176 G3 **Dunajská Lužná** Slovakia
177 G4 **Dunajská Streda** Slovakia
136 I8 **Dunajs'ki Plavni** nature res. Ukr.
177 I4 **Dunakeszi** Hungary
176 G4 **Dunakiliti** Hungary
83 K10 **Dunalley** Tas. Austr.
Dunanbay Kazakh. see **Dunenbay**
147 J5 **Dunany Point** Ireland
177 I5 **Dunapataj** Hungary
197 R5 **Dunărea** r. Romania alt. **Donau (Austria/Germany),** alt. **Duna (Hungary),** alt. **Dunaj (Slovakia),** alt. **Dunav (Serbia),** conv. **Danube**
197 R5 **Dunării, Delta** Romania
177 G4 **Dunaszeg** Hungary
177 H5 **Dunaszekcső** Hungary
177 H5 **Dunaszentgyörgy** Hungary
176 G4 **Dunasziget** Hungary
177 I5 **Dunatetétlen** Hungary
177 I5 **Duna-Tisza Köze** reg. Hungary
177 H5 **Dunaújváros** Hungary
197 P6 **Dunav** r. Serbia alt. **Donau (Austria/Germany),** alt. **Duna (Hungary),** alt. **Dunaj (Slovakia),** alt. **Dunărea (Romania),** conv. **Danube**
177 I4 **Dunavarsány** Hungary
177 H5 **Dunavecse** Hungary
197 K7 **Dunavtsi** Bulg.
131 N2 **Dunay, Ostrova** is Rus. Fed.
136 F4 **Dunayivtsi** Khmel'nyts'ka Oblast' Ukr.
136 F5 **Dunayivtsi** Khmel'nyts'ka Oblast' Ukr.
81 E12 **Dunback** South I. N.Z.
85 I4 **Dunbar** Qld Austr.
146 K10 **Dunbar** East Lothian, Scotland U.K.
232 F9 **Dunbar** PA U.S.A.
226 F4 **Dunbar** WI U.S.A.
232 D10 **Dunbar** WV U.S.A.
146 J6 **Dunbeath** Highland, Scotland U.K.
146 I10 **Dunblane** Stirling, Scotland U.K.
147 J6 **Dunboyne** Ireland
222 F5 **Duncan** B.C. Can.
241 W9 **Duncan** AZ U.S.A.
237 G8 **Duncan** OK U.S.A.
224 D2 **Duncan, Cape** Nunavut Can.
224 E2 **Duncan, Lac** l. Que. Can.
222 G5 **Duncan Lake** B.C. Can.
222 H2 **Duncan Lake** N.W.T. Can.
147 I8 **Duncannon** Ireland
227 Q9 **Duncannon** PA U.S.A.
147 D8 **Duncannon Bridge** Ireland
115 M7 **Duncan Passage** Andaman & Nicobar Is India
246 □ **Duncans** Jamaica
146 J5 **Duncansby Head** Scotland U.K.
246 F2 **Duncan Town** Bahamas
151 J3 **Dunchurch** Warwickshire, England U.K.
147 I8 **Duncormick** Ireland
138 F4 **Dundaga** Latvia
146 E10 **Dun da Ghaoithe** hill Scotland U.K.
227 N5 **Dundalk** Ont. Can.
147 J4 **Dundalk** Ireland
234 B6 **Dundalk** MD U.S.A.
147 J5 **Dundalk Bay** Ireland
224 E5 **Dundas** Ont. Can.
Dundas Greenland see **Uummannaq**
87 F12 **Dundas, Lake** salt flat W.A. Austr.
222 D4 **Dundas Island** B.C. Can.
87 G12 **Dundas Nature Reserve** W.A. Austr.
220 G2 **Dundas Peninsula** N.W.T. Can.
84 C1 **Dundas Strait** N.T. Austr.
107 L3 **Dundbürd** Mongolia
Dún Dealgan Ireland see **Dundalk**
215 O4 **Dundee** S. Africa
146 K10 **Dundee** Dundee, Scotland U.K.
146 K10 **Dundee** admin. div. Scotland U.K.
227 K8 **Dundee** MI U.S.A.
232 I6 **Dundee** NY U.S.A.
106 I4 **Dundgovĭ** prov. Mongolia
107 O5 **Dund Hot** Nei Mongol China
147 K3 **Dundonald** Northern Ireland U.K.
146 G11 **Dundonald** South Ayrshire, Scotland U.K.
85 J9 **Dundoo** Qld Austr.
146 G8 **Dundreggan** Highland, Scotland U.K.
146 I13 **Dundrennan** Dumfries and Galloway, Scotland U.K.
147 J6 **Dundrum** Dublin Ireland
147 F7 **Dundrum** Tipperary Ireland
147 K4 **Dundrum** Northern Ireland U.K.
147 K4 **Dundrum Bay** Northern Ireland U.K.
116 I6 **Dundwa Range** mts India/Nepal
224 F1 **Dune, Lac** l. Que. Can.
146 I11 **Duneaton Water** r. Scotland U.K.
146 L8 **Dunecht** Aberdeenshire, Scotland U.K.
81 E12 **Dunedin** South I. N.Z.
231 F11 **Dunedin** FL U.S.A.
83 L5 **Dunedoo** N.S.W. Austr.
121 S3 **Dunenbay** Kazakh.
163 F7 **Dunes** France
222 E3 **Dune Za Keyih Provincial Park** nat. park B.C. Can.
148 B3 **Dunfanaghy** Ireland
146 J10 **Dunfermline** Fife, Scotland U.K.
147 I3 **Dungannon** Northern Ireland U.K.
Dún Garbhán Ireland see **Dungarvan**
116 E5 **Dungargarh** Rajasthan India
116 D8 **Dungarpur** Rajasthan India
147 H7 **Dungarvan** Kilkenny Ireland
147 G8 **Dungarvan** Waterford Ireland
173 N4 **Dungau** reg. Ger.
111 J11 **Dung Co** l. Xizang China
151 N6 **Dungeness** hd England U.K.
259 C9 **Dungeness, Punta** pt Arg.
169 D10 **Düngenheim** Ger.
147 I3 **Dungiven** Northern Ireland U.K.
147 F3 **Dungloe** Ireland
83 M5 **Dungog** N.S.W. Austr.
147 F9 **Dungourney** Ireland
96 I7 **Dung Quât, Vung** b. Vietnam
208 F4 **Dungu** Dem. Rep. Congo
94 E2 **Dungun** Malaysia
203 H4 **Dungunab** Sudan
149 Q7 **Dunholme** Lincolnshire, England U.K.
Dunhou Jiangxi China see **Ji'an**
100 F7 **Dunhua** Jilin China
110 L6 **Dunhuang** Gansu China
161 E6 **Dunières** France
174 E1 **Duninowo** Pol.
85 L9 **Dunkeld** Qld Austr.
83 I7 **Dunkeld** Vic. Austr.
146 I9 **Dunkeld** Perth and Kinross, Scotland U.K.
147 E6 **Dunkellin** r. Ireland
179 L3 **Dunkelsteiner Wald** for. Austria
156 D1 **Dunkerque** France
147 G7 **Dunkerrin** Ireland
150 E5 **Dunkery Hill** England U.K.
147 F3 **Dunkineely** Ireland
Dunkirk France see **Dunkerque**
151 N5 **Dunkirk** Kent, England U.K.
232 F6 **Dunkirk** NY U.S.A.
232 B8 **Dunkirk** OH U.S.A.
85 K4 **Dunk Island** Qld Austr.
206 E5 **Dunkwa** Ghana
147 J6 **Dún Laoghaire** Ireland
236 H5 **Dunlap** IA U.S.A.
226 I8 **Dunlap** IN U.S.A.
231 E8 **Dunlap** TN U.S.A.
147 I6 **Dunlavin** Ireland
147 J5 **Dunleer** Ireland
162 H3 **Dun-le-Palestel** France
160 E2 **Dun-les-Places** France
148 A3 **Dunlewy** Ireland
146 G11 **Dunlop** East Ayrshire, Scotland U.K.
147 J2 **Dunloy** Northern Ireland U.K.
145 D4 **Dunluce** tourist site Northern Ireland U.K.
147 C9 **Dunmanus** Ireland
147 C10 **Dunmanus Bay** Ireland
147 D9 **Dunmanway** Ireland
84 D4 **Dunmarra** N.T. Austr.
147 G8 **Dunmoon** Ireland
147 E5 **Dunmore** Ireland
234 D2 **Dunmore** PA U.S.A.
232 F10 **Dunmore** WV U.S.A.
147 I8 **Dunmore East** Ireland
246 E1 **Dunmore Town** Eleuthera Bahamas
147 K3 **Dunmurry** Northern Ireland U.K.
231 H8 **Dunn** NC U.S.A.
147 H3 **Dunnamanagh** Northern Ireland U.K.
231 F11 **Dunnellon** FL U.S.A.
146 J5 **Dunnet** Highland, Scotland U.K.
146 J5 **Dunnet Bay** Scotland U.K.
146 J5 **Dunnet Head** Scotland U.K.
240 K3 **Dunnigan** CA U.S.A.
146 I10 **Dunning** Perth and Kinross, Scotland U.K.
236 E5 **Dunning** NE U.S.A.
172 F5 **Dunningen** Ger.
149 P6 **Dunnington** York, England U.K.
87 E12 **Dunn Rock Nature Reserve** W.A. Austr.
87 E8 **Dunns Range** hills W.A. Austr.
227 O7 **Dunnville** Ont. Can.
156 B8 **Dunois** reg. France
83 I7 **Dunolly** Vic. Austr.
146 G11 **Dunoon** Argyll and Bute, Scotland U.K.
147 B8 **Dunquin** Ireland
146 J11 **Dun Rig** hill Scotland U.K.
146 L11 **Duns** Scottish Borders, Scotland U.K.
81 G10 **Dunsandel** South I. N.Z.
87 C12 **Dunsborough** W.A. Austr.
146 I12 **Dunscore** Dumfries and Galloway, Scotland U.K.
236 E1 **Dunseith** ND U.S.A.
168 G5 **Dünsen** Ger.
147 I5 **Dunshaughlin** Ireland
238 C6 **Dunsmuir** CA U.S.A.
151 K4 **Dunstable** Bedfordshire, England U.K.
81 D12 **Dunstan Mountains** South I. N.Z.
150 F5 **Dunster** Somerset, England U.K.
160 B3 **Dun-sur-Auron** France
157 J5 **Dun-sur-Meuse** France
146 H8 **Duntelchaig, Loch** l. Scotland U.K.
81 E11 **Duntroon** South I. N.Z.
168 E3 **Dunum** Ger.
148 H3 **Dunure** South Ayrshire, Scotland U.K.
150 D4 **Dunvant** Swansea, Wales U.K.
146 C8 **Dunvegan** Highland, Scotland U.K.
146 C7 **Dunvegan, Loch** b. Scotland U.K.
146 C7 **Dunvegan Head** Scotland U.K.
223 J2 **Dunvegan Lake** N.W.T. Can.
151 P3 **Dunwich** Suffolk, England U.K.
123 N7 **Dunyapur** Pak.
107 S2 **Duobukur He** r. China
Duolun Nei Mongol China see **Dolonnur**
111 F9 **Duomula** Xizang China
97 G9 **Dương Đông** Vietnam
114 F5 **Dupadu** Andhra Prad. India
109 H6 **Dupang Ling** mts China
227 O1 **Duparquet** Que. Can.
227 O1 **Duparquet, Lac** l. Que. Can.
Duperré Alg. see **Aïn Defla**
179 K7 **Duplica** Slovenia
197 L8 **Dupnitsa** Bulg.
236 E3 **Dupree** SD U.S.A.
86 C6 **Dupuy, Cape** W.A. Austr.
124 F7 **Duqaylah** i. Saudi Arabia
Duque de Bragança Angola see **Calandula**
257 F5 **Duque de Caxias** Brazil
259 B8 **Duque de York, Isla** i. Chile
226 B3 **Duquette** MN U.S.A.
230 C6 **Du Quoin** IL U.S.A.
210 C2 **Dura** r. Eth.
128 D7 **Dūrā** West Bank
191 M2 **Dura, Cima** mt. Italy
173 I6 **Durach** Ger.
76 C3 **Durack** r. W.A. Austr.
86 I4 **Durack Range** hills W.A. Austr.
Dura Europos Syria see **Aş Şālihīyah**
126 G3 **Durağan** Turkey
116 F8 **Duraha** Madh. Prad. India
199 J3 **Durak** Turkey
183 O3 **Durana** Spain
163 E7 **Durance** France
161 F9 **Durance** r. France
227 K7 **Durand** MI U.S.A.
226 C5 **Durand** WI U.S.A.
78 □5 **Durand, Récif** rf New Caledonia
185 J3 **Duranes** hill Spain
241 Q9 **Durango** Baja California Mex.
244 C1 **Durango** Durango Mex.
244 C1 **Durango** state Mex.
183 O2 **Durango** Spain
239 K8 **Durango** CO U.S.A.
244 B2 **Durango, Sierra de** mts Mex.
123 L6 **Durani** reg. Afgh.
197 Q7 **Durankulak** Bulg.
191 M3 **Duranno, Monte** mt. Italy
261 G5 **Durañona** Arg.
237 K9 **Durant** MS U.S.A.
237 G8 **Durant** OK U.S.A.
163 E6 **Duras** France
183 L5 **Duratón** r. Spain
163 G6 **Duravel** France
128 E4 **Duraykīsh** Syria
258 C3 **Durazno** Arg.
261 I3 **Durazno** Uru.
261 I3 **Durazno** dept Uru.
Durazzo Albania see **Durrës**
172 E4 **Durbach** Ger.
163 G9 **Durban** France
215 P5 **Durban** S. Africa
161 B11 **Durban-Corbières** France
214 C9 **Durbanville** S. Africa
172 F5 **Dürbheim** Ger.
232 F10 **Durbin** WV U.S.A.
157 L7 **Durbion** r. France
123 K7 **Durbun** Pak.
165 H8 **Durbuy** Belgium
185 L7 **Dúrcal** Spain
185 M7 **Dúrcal** r. Spain
177 H2 **Ďurčiná** Slovakia
160 B4 **Durdat-Larequille** France
159 M2 **Durdent** r. France
188 F2 **Đurđevac** Croatia
210 F2 **Durdura, Raas** pt Somalia
110 I3 **Düre** Xinjiang China
169 B9 **Düren** Ger.
122 G5 **Düren** Iran
122 G5 **Duren, Kūh-e** mt. Iran
161 D9 **Durfort** France
116 H9 **Durg** Chhattisgarh India
117 M7 **Durgapur** Bangl.
117 K8 **Durgapur** W. Bengal India
227 N5 **Durham** Ont. Can.
149 N4 **Durham** Durham, England U.K.
149 M4 **Durham** admin. div. England U.K.
240 K2 **Durham** CA U.S.A.
235 J2 **Durham** CT U.S.A.
231 H8 **Durham** NC U.S.A.
233 □O5 **Durham** NH U.S.A.
80 □ **Durham, Point** Chatham Is S. Pacific Ocean
233 □S2 **Durham Bridge** N.B. Can.
85 H9 **Durham Downs** Qld Austr.
149 O4 **Durham Tees Valley** airport England U.K.
210 D3 **Durhi** well Eth.
94 D4 **Duri** Sumatera Indon.
95 H5 **Duriansebatang** Kalimantan Indon.
146 I12 **Durisdeer** Dumfries and Galloway, Scotland U.K.
Durlas Ireland see **Thurles**
136 H6 **Durleşti** Moldova
179 M7 **Durmanec** Croatia
156 G1 **Durme** r. Belgium
172 H5 **Dürmentingen** Ger.
172 E4 **Durmersheim** Ger.
196 H7 **Durmitor** mt. Montenegro
196 G7 **Durmitor** nat. park Montenegro
146 G5 **Durness** Highland, Scotland U.K.
146 G5 **Durness, Kyle of** inlet Scotland U.K.
179 O3 **Dürnkrut** Austria
Durocortorum France see **Reims**
85 M9 **Durong South** Qld Austr.
Durostorum Bulg. see **Silistra**
Durovernum Kent, England U.K. see **Canterbury**
196 H9 **Durrës** Albania
84 H8 **Durrie** Qld Austr.
173 I5 **Dürrlauingen** Ger.
171 J8 **Dürröhrsdorf-Dittersbach** Ger.
147 H7 **Durrow** Ireland
173 I3 **Dürrwangen** Ger.
147 B9 **Dursey Head** Ireland
147 B9 **Dursey Island** Ireland
150 H4 **Dursley** Gloucestershire, England U.K.
199 J3 **Dursunbey** Turkey
159 K6 **Durtal** France
Duru Guizhou China see **Wuchuan**
208 F4 **Duru** r. Dem. Rep. Congo
125 M4 **Duru** reg. Oman
128 F2 **Duruca** Turkey
183 O5 **Duruelo de la Sierra** Spain
122 I5 **Dūruḩ** Iran
210 E2 **Durukhsi** Somalia
199 J1 **Durusu Gölü** l. Turkey
128 E6 **Durūz, Jabal ad** mt. Syria
91 I7 **D'Urville, Tanjung** pt Papua Indon.
80 H7 **D'Urville Island** South I. N.Z.
234 D2 **Duryea** PA U.S.A.
146 □N2 **Dury Voe** inlet Scotland U.K.
123 K4 **Durzab** Afgh.
122 H3 **Duşak** Turkm.
138 I6 **Dusetos** Lith.
123 K7 **Dushai** Pak.
108 F6 **Dushan** Guizhou China
123 M2 **Dushanbe** Tajik.
110 G4 **Dushanzi** Xinjiang China
137 L1 **Dushatino** Rus. Fed.
129 F3 **Dushet'i** Georgia
107 N6 **Dushikou** Hebei China
227 R8 **Dushore** PA U.S.A.
138 G7 **Dusia** l. Lith.
81 A12 **Dusky Sound** inlet South I. N.Z.
175 M1 **Dusmenys** Lith.
177 H5 **Dusnok** Hungary
174 G2 **Dusocin** Pol.
100 I3 **Dusse-Alin', Khrebet** mts Rus. Fed.
86 J3 **Dussejour, Cape** W.A. Austr.
169 C8 **Düsseldorf** Ger.
169 B7 **Düsseldorf** admin. reg. Ger.
164 G5 **Dussen** Neth.
172 G5 **Dußlingen** Ger.
171 G7 **Düßnitz** Ger.
123 M3 **Dūstí** Tajik.
238 F3 **Dusty** WA U.S.A.
174 E3 **Duszniki** Pol.
174 E5 **Duszniki-Zdrój** Pol.
Dutch East Indies country Asia see **Indonesia**
234 H1 **Dutchess County** county NY U.S.A.
Dutch Guiana country S. America see **Suriname**
220 B4 **Dutch Harbor** AK U.S.A.
241 S1 **Dutch Mountain** UT U.S.A.
Dutch New Guinea prov. Indon. see **Papua**
Dutch West Indies terr. West Indies see **Netherlands Antilles**
179 I8 **Dutovlje** Slovenia
207 H4 **Dutsan-Wai** Nigeria
207 H4 **Dutse** Nigeria
207 G3 **Dutsin-Ma** Nigeria
85 I6 **Dutton** r. Qld Austr.
227 M7 **Dutton** Ont. Can.
238 I3 **Dutton** MT U.S.A.
82 F4 **Dutton, Lake** salt flat S.A. Austr.
241 T3 **Dutton, Mount** UT U.S.A.
223 J5 **Duval** Sask. Can.
134 L5 **Duvan** Rus. Fed.
137 R4 **Duvanka** r. Ukr.
134 I4 **Duvannoye** Rus. Fed.
Duvannyy Azer. see **Qobustan**
Duvannyy, Ostrov i. Azer. see **Zänbil Adası**
140 L5 **Duved** Sweden
246 H4 **Duvergé** Dom. Rep.
225 G1 **Duvert, Lac** l. Que. Can.
Duvno Bos.-Herz. see **Tomislavgrad**
111 D8 **Duwa** Xinjiang China
122 D9 **Duweihin** well Saudi Arabia
125 J3 **Duweihin, Khor** b. Saudi Arabia/U.A.E.
127 L5 **Duwin** Iraq
111 E8 **Düxanbibazar** Xinjiang China
129 G5 **Düyärli** Azer.
96 C6 **Duyinzeik** Myanmar
108 F5 **Duyun** Guizhou China
123 J8 **Duzab** Pak.
199 M2 **Düzce** Turkey
199 M1 **Düzce** prov. Turkey
129 G4 **Düz Cırdaxan** Azer.
Duzdab Iran see **Zāhedān**
129 A5 **Düzköy** Turkey
136 F1 **Dvarets** Belarus
197 N7 **Dve Mogili** Bulg.
138 J5 **Dviete** Latvia
Dvinsk Latvia see **Daugavpils**
134 G2 **Dvinskaya Guba** g. Rus. Fed.
139 O5 **Dvin'ye, Ozero** l. Rus. Fed.
136 F3 **Dvirets'** Ukr.
175 M5 **Dvirtsi** Ukr.
188 F3 **Dvor** Croatia
177 G2 **Dvorce** Czech Rep.
137 Q4 **Dvorichna** Ukr.
139 V5 **Dvoriki** Rus. Fed.
177 H4 **Dvory nad Žitavou** Slovakia
139 W6 **Dvoyni** Rus. Fed.
176 E1 **Dvůr Králové** Czech Rep.
211 B8 **Dwangwa** Malawi
116 B8 **Dwarka** Gujarat India
212 E5 **Dwarsberg** S. Africa
123 N5 **Dwatoi** Pak.
195 □ **Dwejra, Il-Ponta tad-** pt Gozo Malta
87 D12 **Dwellingup** W.A. Austr.
215 M8 **Dwesa Nature Reserve** S. Africa
215 O6 **Dweshula** S. Africa
226 F8 **Dwight** IL U.S.A.
175 J5 **Dwikozy** Pol.
164 J3 **Dwingelderveld, Nationaal Park** nat. park Neth.
164 J3 **Dwingeloo** Neth.
238 G3 **Dworshak Reservoir** ID U.S.A.
214 F9 **Dwyka** S. Africa
214 F9 **Dwyka** r. S. Africa
137 T4 **D'yachenkovo** Rus. Fed.
134 H4 **D'yakonovo** Kostromskaya Oblast' Rus. Fed.
137 O2 **D'yakonovo** Kurskaya Oblast' Rus. Fed.
137 S6 **Dyakove** Ukr.
148 D5 **Dyan** Northern Ireland U.K.
197 O7 **Dyankovo** Bulg.
139 R8 **Dyat'kovo** Rus. Fed.
234 E1 **Dyberry** PA U.S.A.
234 E1 **Dyberry Creek** r. PA U.S.A.
146 L8 **Dyce** Aberdeen, Scotland U.K.
174 D4 **Dychów** Pol.
175 K6 **Dydnia** Pol.
100 G4 **Dydy** Rus. Fed.
221 L3 **Dyer, Cape** Nunavut Can.
227 M4 **Dyer Bay** Ont. Can.
262 T2 **Dyer Plateau** Antarctica
237 K7 **Dyersburg** TN U.S.A.
81 J8 **Dyeville** North I. N.Z.
Dyffryn Isle of Anglesey, Wales U.K. see **Valley**
Dyfrdwy r. England/Wales U.K. see **Dee**
174 D1 **Dygowo** Pol.
167 H4 **Dyje** r. Austria/Czech Rep.
137 N4 **Dykan'ka** Ukr.
146 I7 **Dyke** Moray, Scotland U.K.
146 J9 **Dykehead** Angus, Scotland U.K.
129 E2 **Dykh-Tau, Gora** mt. Rus. Fed.
165 G7 **Dyle** r. Belgium
176 B2 **Dyleň** hill Czech Rep.
175 J2 **Dylewo** Pol.
175 H2 **Dylewska Góra** hill Pol.
129 H2 **Dylym** Rus. Fed.
151 N5 **Dymchurch** Kent, England U.K.
136 J3 **Dymer** Ukr.
139 Q2 **Dymi** Rus. Fed.
150 H4 **Dymock** Gloucestershire, England U.K.
138 M1 **Dymovka** r. Rus. Fed.
137 Q5 **Dymytrov** Ukr.
137 L5 **Dymytrove** Kirovohrads'ka Oblast' Ukr.
137 L5 **Dymytrove** Kirovohrads'ka Oblast' Ukr.
142 E1 **Dyna** mt. Norway
83 J3 **Dynevor Downs** Qld Austr.
175 K6 **Dynów** Pol.
160 E4 **Dyo** France
215 M7 **Dyoki** S. Africa
140 N2 **Dyrøyhamn** Norway
Dyrrhachium Albania see **Durrës**
85 L7 **Dysart** Qld Austr.
150 F1 **Dyserth** Denbighshire, Wales U.K.
173 P2 **Dýšina** Czech Rep.
138 J6 **Dysna** r. Lith.
138 J6 **Dysnų ežeras** l. Lith.
214 G9 **Dysselsdorp** S. Africa
198 B4 **Dytiki Ellada** admin. reg. Greece
198 C2 **Dytiki Makedonia** admin. reg. Greece
131 O3 **Dyuendyu** Rus. Fed.
197 P8 **Dyulino** Bulg.
129 H4 **Dyul'tydag, Gora** mt. Rus. Fed.
134 K5 **Dyurtyuli** Rus. Fed.
136 I8 **Dyviziya** Ukr.
175 I2 **Dywity** Pol.
106 G3 **Dzaanhushuu** Mongolia
106 F3 **Dzadgay** Mongolia
106 F3 **Dzag Gol** r. Mongolia
106 F4 **Dzalaa** Mongolia
107 L5 **Dzamïn Üüd** Mongolia
208 C4 **Dzanga-Ndoki, Parc National de** nat. park C.A.R.
208 C4 **Dzanga-Sangha, Réserve Spéciale de Forêt Dense de** nature res. C.A.R.
217 □3b **Dzaoudzi** Mayotte
Dzaudzhikau Rus. Fed. see **Vladikavkaz**
106 D2 **Dzavhan** prov. Mongolia
106 C2 **Dzavhan Gol** r. Mongolia
176 C1 **Džbán** mts Czech Rep.
106 H3 **Dzegstey** Mongolia
136 F4 **Dzelentsi** Ukr.
106 I1 **Dzelter** Mongolia
138 J4 **Dzeņi** Latvia
Dzerzhinsk Homyel'skaya Voblasts' Belarus see **Dzyarzhynsk**
Dzerzhinsk Minskaya Voblasts' Belarus see **Dzyarzhynsk**
134 H4 **Dzerzhinsk** Rus. Fed.
137 Q5 **Dzerzhyns'k** Donets'ka Oblast' Ukr.
136 G3 **Dzerzhyns'k** Zhytomyrs'ka Oblast' Ukr.
100 F2 **Dzhagdy, Khrebet** mts Rus. Fed.
100 I4 **Dzhaki-Unakhta Yakbyyana, Khrebet** mts Rus. Fed.
Dzhaksy Kazakh. see **Zhaksy**
120 K5 **Dzhalagash** Kazakh.
Dzhalalabad Azer. see **Cälilabad**
Dzhalal-Abad Kyrg. see **Jalal-Abad**
Dzhalal-Abadskaya Oblast' admin. div. Kyrg. see **Jalal-Abad**
134 K5 **Dzhalil'** Rus. Fed.
100 C2 **Dzhalinda** Rus. Fed.
Dzhaltyr Kazakh. see **Zhaltyr**
Dzhambeyty Kazakh. see **Zhympity**
Dzhambul Kazakh. see **Taraz**
Dzhambulskaya Oblast' admin. div. Kazakh. see **Zhambylskaya Oblast'**
Dzhandari Georgia see **Jandari**
120 D3 **Dzhangala** Kazakh.
Dzhangi-Dzhol Kyrg. see **Jangy-Jol**
Dzhankel'dy Uzbek. see **Jongeldi**
137 N8 **Dzhankoy** Ukr.
121 R5 **Dzhansugurov** Kazakh.
Dzhany-Bazar Kyrg. see **Jangy-Bazar**
Dzhany-Dzhol Kyrg. see **Jangy-Jol**
Dzhaparidze Georgia see **Jap'aridze**
Dzharkent Kazakh. see **Zharkent**
137 L7 **Dzharylhach, Ostriv** i. Ukr.
137 L7 **Dzharylhats'ka Zatoka** b. Ukr.
100 K3 **Dzhaur** r. Rus. Fed.
131 O3 **Dzhebariki-Khaya** Rus. Fed.
197 N9 **Dzhebel** Bulg.
130 G1 **Dzheksona, Ostrov** i. Zemlya Frantsa-Iosifa Rus. Fed.
Dzhelondi Tajik. see **Jelondí**
Dzhergalan Kyrg. see **Jyrgalang**
Dzhermuk Armenia see **Jermuk**
Dzheti-Oguz Kyrg. see **Jeti-Ögüz**
Dzhetygara Kazakh. see **Zhitikara**
120 K6 **Dzhetymtau, Gory** hills Uzbek.
Dzhetyoguz Kyrg. see **Jeti-Ögüz**
Dzhetysay Kazakh. see **Zhetysay**
Dzhezdy Kazakh. see **Zhezdy**
Dzhezkazgan Kazakh. see **Zhezkazgan**
106 J1 **Dzhida** Rus. Fed.
106 J1 **Dzhida** r. Rus. Fed.
106 H1 **Dzhidinskiy, Khrebet** mts Mongolia/Rus. Fed.
Dzhilandy Kŭhistoni Badakhshon Tajik. see **Jelondí**
Dzhingil'dy Uzbek. see **Jongeldi**
Dzhirgatal' Tajik. see **Jirgatol**
Dzhizak Jizzax Uzbek. see **Jizzax**
Dzhizak Oblast admin. div. Uzbek. see **Jizzax**
Dzhokhar Ghala Rus. Fed. see **Groznyy**
Dzhordzhiashvili Georgia see **Jorjiashvili**
135 G7 **Dzhubga** Rus. Fed.
131 O4 **Dzhugdzhur, Khrebet** mts Rus. Fed.
Dzhul'fa Azer. see **Culfa**
136 I5 **Dzhulynka** Ukr.
Dzhuma Uzbek. see **Juma**
121 R5 **Dzhungarskiy Alatau, Khrebet** mts China/Kazakh.
121 T5 **Dzhungarskiye Vorota** val. Kazakh.
129 H3 **Dzhurmut** r. Rus. Fed.
Dzhurun Kazakh. see **Zhuryn**
136 H5 **Dzhuryn** Ukr.
120 K5 **Dzhusaly** Kazakh.
175 K3 **Dziadkowice** Pol.
174 F4 **Dziadowa Kłoda** Pol.
175 H2 **Działdówka** r. Pol.
175 I2 **Działdowo** Pol.
175 I5 **Działoszyce** Pol.
174 G4 **Działoszyn** Pol.
175 H2 **Działyń** Pol.
243 O8 **Dzibalchén** Mex.
174 F1 **Dziemiany** Pol.
174 G5 **Dziergowice** Pol.
175 I3 **Dzierząźnia** Pol.
174 E3 **Dzierżążno Wielkie** Pol.
175 H2 **Dzierzgoń** Pol.
175 I2 **Dzierzgowo** Pol.
174 E5 **Dzierżoniów** Pol.
175 J1 **Dzietrzychowo** Pol.
174 F3 **Dziewierzewo** Pol.
243 O7 **Dzilam de Bravo** Mex.
205 G2 **Dzioua** Alg.
138 L6 **Dzisna** Belarus
243 O7 **Dzitás** Mex.
138 I8 **Dzitva** r. Belarus
136 D2 **Dzivin** Belarus
174 C2 **Dziwna** r. Pol.
174 C1 **Dziwnów** Pol.
175 L3 **Dzmitravichy** Belarus
207 F5 **Dzodze** Ghana
107 J3 **Dzogsool** Mongolia
106 F1 **Dzöölön** Mongolia
129 F5 **Dzoraget** r. Armenia
138 H7 **Dzūkija** nat. park Lith.
Dzungarian Basin China see **Junggar Pendi**
121 T5 **Dzungarian Gate** pass China/Kazakh.
106 D2 **Dzur** Mongolia
107 L4 **Dzüünbayan** Mongolia
106 J2 **Dzüünharaa** Mongolia
106 J3 **Dzuunmod** Mongolia
106 C3 **Dzüyl** Mongolia
175 I2 **Dźwierzuty** Pol.
170 L2 **Dźwirzyno** Pol.
175 K5 **Dzwola** Pol.
175 H5 **Dzwonowice** Pol.
138 J9 **Dzyaniskavichy** Belarus
139 O8 **Dzyarazhnya** Belarus
139 P8 **Dzyarazhnya** r. Belarus
138 H8 **Dzyarechyn** Belarus
136 G2 **Dzyarzhynsk** Homyel'skaya Voblasts' Belarus
138 K8 **Dzyarzhynsk** Minskaya Voblasts' Belarus
138 I8 **Dzyatlava** Belarus
136 F1 **Dzyatlavichy** Belarus
138 K6 **Dzyerkawshchyna** Belarus
136 I2 **Dzyornavichy** Belarus

E

224 C3 **Eabamet Lake** Ont. Can.
236 D6 **Eads** CO U.S.A.
241 W7 **Eagar** AZ U.S.A.
225 J2 **Eagle** r. Nfld and Lab. Can.
220 D3 **Eagle** AK U.S.A.
239 K7 **Eagle** CO U.S.A.
234 D4 **Eagle** PA U.S.A.
236 E3 **Eagle Butte** SD U.S.A.
238 F4 **Eagle Cap** mt. OR U.S.A.
240 O6 **Eagle Crags** mt. CA U.S.A.
223 J4 **Eagle Creek** r. Sask. Can.
223 M5 **Eagle Lake** l. Ont. Can.
233 □Q1 **Eagle Lake** ME U.S.A.
238 D6 **Eagle Lake** l. CA U.S.A.
233 □P2 **Eagle Lake** l. ME U.S.A.
233 □Q1 **Eagle Lake** l. ME U.S.A.
241 Q8 **Eagle Mountain** CA U.S.A.
226 D2 **Eagle Mountain** hill MN U.S.A.
237 G9 **Eagle Mountain Lake** TX U.S.A.
237 E11 **Eagle Pass** TX U.S.A.
259 F9 **Eagle Passage** Falkland Is
239 L11 **Eagle Peak** TX U.S.A.
220 E3 **Eagle Plain** Y.T. Can.
82 □3 **Eagle Point** S. Pacific Ocean
226 F2 **Eagle River** MI U.S.A.
226 E4 **Eagle River** WI U.S.A.
232 F11 **Eagle Rock** VA U.S.A.
149 O4 **Eaglescliffe** Stockton-on-Tees, England U.K.
146 J12 **Eaglesfield** Dumfries and Galloway, Scotland U.K.
222 G4 **Eaglesham** Alta Can.
146 H11 **Eaglesham** East Renfrewshire, Scotland U.K.
241 S8 **Eagle Tail Mountains** AZ U.S.A.
234 E4 **Eagleville** PA U.S.A.
151 L4 **Ealing** Greater London, England U.K.
Eap i. Micronesia see **Yap**
87 F8 **Earaheedy** W.A. Austr.
146 H9 **Earba, Lochan na h-** l. Scotland U.K.
149 M6 **Earby** Lancashire, England U.K.
150 F3 **Eardisley** Herefordshire, England U.K.
223 M5 **Ear Falls** Ont. Can.
151 M3 **Earith** Cambridgeshire, England U.K.
240 M6 **Earlimart** CA U.S.A.
81 B12 **Earl Mountains** South I. N.Z.
151 K3 **Earls Barton** Northamptonshire, England U.K.
151 N4 **Earls Colne** Essex, England U.K.
151 J2 **Earl Shilton** Leicestershire, England U.K.
146 H10 **Earl's Seat** hill Scotland U.K.
146 K11 **Earlston** Scottish Borders, Scotland U.K.
151 O3 **Earl Stonham** Suffolk, England U.K.
227 O2 **Earlton** Ont. Can.
146 J10 **Earn** r. Scotland U.K.
81 D12 **Earnscleugh** South I. N.Z.
81 C11 **Earnslaw, Mount** South I. N.Z.
241 R7 **Earp** CA U.S.A.
146 B9 **Earsairidh** Western Isles, Scotland U.K.
237 D8 **Earth** TX U.S.A.
146 E10 **Easdale** Argyll and Bute, Scotland U.K.
151 K6 **Easebourne** West Sussex, England U.K.
149 O4 **Easington** Durham, England U.K.
149 R6 **Easington** East Riding of Yorkshire, England U.K.
149 O5 **Easingwold** North Yorkshire, England U.K.
147 E4 **Easky** Ireland
231 F8 **Easley** SC U.S.A.
87 G10 **East, Mount** hill W.A. Austr.
84 D2 **East Alligator** r. N.T. Austr.
263 H1 **East Antarctica** reg. Antarctica
233 J7 **East Ararat** PA U.S.A.
232 G6 **East Aurora** NY U.S.A.
146 H12 **East Ayrshire** admin. div. Scotland U.K.
84 B3 **East Baines** r. N.T. Austr.
234 E3 **East Bangor** PA U.S.A.
237 K11 **East Bay** LA U.S.A.
235 H3 **East Bay** NY U.S.A.
231 E10 **East Bay** inlet FL U.S.A.
East Bengal country Asia see **Bangladesh**
151 O4 **East Bergholt** Suffolk, England U.K.
235 J1 **East Berlin** CT U.S.A.
234 B5 **East Berlin** PA U.S.A.
234 C2 **East Berwick** PA U.S.A.
81 I8 **Eastbourne** North I. N.Z.
151 M6 **Eastbourne** East Sussex, England U.K.
232 F8 **East Brady** PA U.S.A.
233 J7 **East Branch** NY U.S.A.
232 G7 **East Branch Clarion River Reservoir** PA U.S.A.
151 K2 **East Bridgford** Nottinghamshire, England U.K.
149 Q6 **Eastburn** East Riding of Yorkshire, England U.K.
246 H3 **East Caicos** i. Turks and Caicos Is
80 M4 **East Cape** North I. N.Z.
East Cape Rus. Fed. see **Dezhneva, Mys**
241 V2 **East Carbon City** UT U.S.A.
266 E5 **East Caroline Basin** sea feature N. Pacific Ocean
226 G8 **East Chicago** IN U.S.A.
99 M5 **East China Sea** N. Pacific Ocean
80 I3 **East Coast Bays** North I. N.Z.
150 G6 **East Coker** Somerset, England U.K.
223 H5 **East Coulee** Alta Can.
151 M6 **East Dean** East Sussex, England U.K.
East Dereham England U.K. see **Dereham**
146 H11 **East Dunbartonshire** admin. div. Scotland U.K.
223 I5 **Eastend** Sask. Can.
231 □2 **East End Point** New Prov. Bahamas
92 □ **East Entrance** sea chan. Palau
87 B10 **Easter Group** is W.A. Austr.
Easter Island S. Pacific Ocean see **Pascua, Isla de**
206 E5 **Eastern** admin. reg. Ghana
210 C5 **Eastern** prov. Kenya
206 C4 **Eastern** prov. Sierra Leone
211 A8 **Eastern** prov. Zambia
234 C7 **Eastern Bay** MD U.S.A.
185 □ **Eastern Beach** Gibraltar
215 K7 **Eastern Cape** prov. S. Africa
85 H6 **Eastern Creek** r. Qld Austr.
Eastern Desert Egypt see **Aş Şaḩrā' ash Sharqīyah**
210 B3 **Eastern Equatoria** state Sudan
114 E7 **Eastern Ghats** mts India
Eastern Lesser Sunda Islands prov. Indon. see **Nusa Tenggara Timur**
123 M8 **Eastern Nara** canal Pak.
234 C6 **Eastern Neck Island** MD U.S.A.
Eastern Samoa terr. S. Pacific Ocean see **American Samoa**
Eastern Sayan Mountains Rus. Fed. see **Vostochnyy Sayan**
Eastern Taurus plat. Turkey see **Güneydoğu Toroslar**
Eastern Transvaal prov. S. Africa see **Mpumalanga**
146 H7 **Easter Ross** reg. Scotland U.K.
Easter Skeld Scotland U.K. see **Skeld**
223 L4 **Easterville** Man. Can.
259 F9 **East Falkland** i. Falkland Is
233 O7 **East Falmouth** MA U.S.A.
149 R7 **East Fen** reg. England U.K.
149 Q5 **Eastfield** North Yorkshire, England U.K.
East Flanders prov. Belgium see **Oost-Vlaanderen**
East Frisian Islands Ger. see **Ostfriesische Inseln**
149 M4 **Eastgate** Durham, England U.K.
240 O2 **Eastgate** NV U.S.A.
236 G2 **East Grand Forks** MN U.S.A.
226 I7 **East Grand Rapids** MI U.S.A.
234 E4 **East Greenville** PA U.S.A.
151 L5 **East Grinstead** West Sussex, England U.K.
235 K2 **East Haddam** CT U.S.A.
235 J1 **East Hampton** CT U.S.A.
233 M6 **Easthampton** MA U.S.A.
235 K3 **East Hampton** NY U.S.A.
151 J4 **East Hanney** Oxfordshire, England U.K.
151 N3 **East Harling** Norfolk, England U.K.
235 J1 **East Hartford** CT U.S.A.
235 J2 **East Haven** CT U.S.A.
85 H4 **East Haydon** Qld Austr.
233 □Q4 **East Holden** ME U.S.A.
151 L5 **East Horsley** Surrey, England U.K.
150 G5 **East Huntspill** Somerset, England U.K.
265 K6 **East Indiaman Ridge** sea feature Indian Ocean
80 M4 **East Island** North I. N.Z.
233 M5 **East Jamaica** VT U.S.A.
226 I4 **East Jordan** MI U.S.A.
East Kazakhstan Oblast admin. div. Kazakh. see **Vostochnyy Kazakhstan**
149 R7 **East Keal** Lincolnshire, England U.K.
146 H11 **East Kilbride** South Lanarkshire, Scotland U.K.
226 H5 **East Lake** MI U.S.A.
East Lamma Channel H.K. China see **Tung Pok Liu Hoi Hap**
237 F9 **Eastland** TX U.S.A.
226 J7 **East Lansing** MI U.S.A.
151 J6 **Eastleigh** Hampshire, England U.K.
232 B8 **East Liberty** OH U.S.A.
146 K11 **East Linton** East Lothian, Scotland U.K.
235 I1 **East Litchfield** CT U.S.A.
232 E8 **East Liverpool** OH U.S.A.
146 C6 **East Loch Roag** inlet Scotland U.K.
146 C7 **East Loch Tarbert** inlet Scotland U.K.
215 L9 **East London** S. Africa
233 M6 **East Longmeadow** MA U.S.A.
150 D7 **East Looe** Cornwall, England U.K.
146 K11 **East Lothian** admin. div. Scotland U.K.
235 K2 **East Lyme** CT U.S.A.
224 E2 **Eastmain** Que. Can.
224 E2 **Eastmain** r. Que. Can.
151 M5 **East Malling** Kent, England U.K.
233 M3 **Eastman** Que. Can.
231 F9 **Eastman** GA U.S.A.
266 F5 **East Mariana Basin** sea feature Pacific Oce[an]
149 P7 **East Markham** Nottinghamshire, Engla[nd U.K.]
85 J7 **Eastmere** Qld Austr.
233 L5 **East Middlebury** VT U[.S.A.]
233 □Q3 **East Millinocket** ME U[.S.A.]
235 I1 **East Morris** CT U.S.A.
231 G12 **East Naples** FL U.S.A.
235 I3 **East Northport** NY U.S[.A.]
149 P6 **Eastoft** North Lincolnsh[ire,] England U.K.
150 H6 **Easton** Dorset, Englan[d U.K.]
240 M5 **Easton** CA U.S.A.
235 I2 **Easton** CT U.S.A.
233 I10 **Easton** MD U.S.A.
234 E3 **Easton** PA U.S.A.
150 G5 **Easton-in-Gordano** N[orth] Somerset, England U.K.
235 I2 **Easton Reservoir** CT [U.S.A.]
235 G3 **East Orange** NJ U.S.A.
267 L8 **East Pacific Ridge** S. Pacific Ocean
267 L4 **East Pacific Rise** sea [feature] N. Pacific Ocean
East Pakistan country [Asia] see **Bangladesh**
232 E8 **East Palestine** OH U.S[.A.]
240 J2 **East Park Reservoir** C[A U.S.A.]
226 E9 **East Peoria** IL U.S.A.
234 C4 **East Petersburg** PA U[.S.A.]
82 □2 **East Point** Lord Howe [I.]
225 I4 **East Point** P.E.I. Can.
216 □2c **East Point** Tristan da C[unha] S. Atlantic Ocean
233 □S4 **Eastport** ME U.S.A.
226 I4 **Eastport** MI U.S.A.
235 J3 **Eastport** NY U.S.A.
151 L6 **East Preston** West Su[ssex,] England U.K.
234 B5 **East Prospect** PA U.S[.A.]
235 J3 **East Quogue** NY U.S.A[.]
240 O1 **East Range** mts NV U[.S.A.]
146 H11 **East Renfrewshire** ad[min. div.] Scotland U.K.
East Retford England [U.K. see] **Retford**
East Retford Nottingha[mshire,] England U.K. see **Retfo[rd]**
231 E8 **East Ridge** TN U.S.A.
149 Q6 **East Riding of Yorksh[ire]** admin. div. England U.K.
146 J13 **Eastriggs** Dumfries an[d] Galloway, Scotland U.K.
151 O5 **Eastry** Kent, England U[.K.]
230 B6 **East St Louis** IL U.S.A[.]
East Sea N. Pacific Oc[ean see] **Japan, Sea of**
235 I3 **East Setauket** NY U.S[.A.]
223 L5 **East Shoal Lake** Man. [Can.]
East Siberian Sea Ru[s. Fed.] see **Vostochno-Sibirsko[ye More]**
234 D2 **East Side** PA U.S.A.
240 M6 **East Side Canal** r. CA [U.S.A.]
83 L8 **East Sister Island** Tas[.]
234 E2 **East Stroudsburg** PA [U.S.A.]
151 M6 **East Sussex** admin. d[iv.] England U.K.
241 W2 **East Tavaputs Platea[u]** UT U.S.A.
232 B4 **East Tawas** MI U.S.A.
93 D8 **East Timor** country As[ia]
117 J7 **East Tons** r. India
83 J4 **East Toorale** N.S.W. A[ustr.]
226 F7 **East Troy** WI U.S.A.
227 J5 **East Twin Lake** MI U.S[.A.]
241 U7 **East Verde** r. AZ U.S.A[.]
Eastview Ont. Can. se[e]
233 J11 **Eastville** VA U.S.A.
240 M3 **East Walker** r. NV U.S[.A.]
151 K6 **East Wittering** West S[ussex,] England U.K.
149 O7 **Eastwood** Nottinghams[hire,] England U.K.
151 J5 **East Woodhay** Hamps[hire,] England U.K.
227 O6 **East York** Ont. Can.
97 H8 **Ea Sup** Vietnam
82 D2 **Eateringinna Creek** watercourse S.A. Austr[.]
146 C9 **Eatharna, Loch** inlet Scotland U.K.
87 C12 **Eaton** W.A. Austr.
238 L6 **Eaton** CO U.S.A.
230 E6 **Eaton** OH U.S.A.
151 K4 **Eaton Bray** Bedfordsh[ire,] England U.K.
223 I5 **Eatonia** Sask. Can.
226 J7 **Eaton Rapids** MI U.S.A[.]
235 I3 **Eatons Neck** NY U.S.A[.]
235 I3 **Eatons Neck Point** NY [U.S.A.]
151 L3 **Eaton Socon** Cambrid[geshire,] England U.K.
231 F9 **Eatonton** GA U.S.A.
235 G4 **Eatontown** NJ U.S.A.
233 □P1 **Eatonville** Que. Can.
238 C3 **Eatonville** WA U.S.A.
226 C5 **Eau Claire** WI U.S.A.
226 C5 **Eau Claire** r. WI U.S.A.
224 F1 **Eau Claire, Lac à l'** l. Q[ue. Can.]
156 B4 **Eaulne** r. France
163 G9 **Eaunes** France
91 J5 **Eauripik** atoll Microne[sia]
266 E5 **Eauripik Rise-New Gui[nea Rise]** sea feature N. Pacific Oc[ean]
Eaurypyg atoll Microne[sia see] **Eauripik**
163 D10 **Eaux-Bonnes** France
163 E8 **Eauze** France
78 □3a **Ebadon** i. Kwajalein Ma[rshall Is]
85 I3 **Ebagoola** Qld Austr.
207 G4 **Eban** Nigeria
245 I3 **Ebano** Mex.
178 F4 **Ebbs** Austria
150 F4 **Ebbw Vale** Blaenau Gw[ent,] Wales U.K.
207 H6 **Ebebiyin** Equat. Guine[a]
169 K8 **Ebeleben** Ger.
142 G5 **Ebeltoft** Denmark
178 E5 **Eben am Achensee** A[ustria]
215 M8 **Ebende** S. Africa
212 C5 **Ebenerde** Namibia
179 I6 **Ebene Reichenau** Aus[tria]
179 N4 **Ebenfurth** Austria
179 H5 **Eben im Pongau** Aust[ria]
232 G8 **Ebensburg** PA U.S.A.
179 I4 **Ebensee** Austria
169 K10 **Ebensfeld** Ger.
179 J6 **Ebenthal** Austria
172 H6 **Ebenweiler** Ger.
179 N5 **Eberau** Austria
172 F3 **Eberbach** Ger.
199 M4 **Eber Gölü** l. Turkey
169 J7 **Ebergötzen** Ger.
172 H5 **Eberhardzell** Ger.
173 L3 **Ebermannsdorf** Ger.
173 K2 **Ebermannstadt** Ger.
169 K10 **Ebern** Ger.
179 K6 **Eberndorf** Austria
171 I8 **Ebersbach** Sachsen G[er.]
171 K8 **Ebersbach** Sachsen G[er.]
172 H4 **Ebersbach an der Fils** [Ger.]
173 L5 **Ebersberg** Ger.
179 I3 **Eberschwang** Austria
179 M5 **Ebersdorf** Austria
168 H3 **Ebersdorf** Niedersachs[en Ger.]
171 E10 **Ebersdorf** Thüringen G[er.]
157 O7 **Ebersmunster** France
179 K6 **Eberstein** Austria
170 I5 **Eberswalde-Finow** Ge[r.]
234 D3 **Ebervale** PA U.S.A.
177 K4 **Ebes** Hungary
102 S3 **Ebetsu** Japan
78 □3a **Ebeye** Kwajalein Marsh[all Is]
172 F4 **Ebhausen** Ger.
108 D4 **Ebian** Sichuan China
190 E1 **Ebikon** Switz.
105 J5 **Ebina** Japan
103 H14 **Ebino** Japan
Ebi Nor salt l. China se[e] **Ebinur Hu**
110 F4 **Ebinur Hu** salt l. China
128 E3 **Ebla** tourist site Syria
190 G1 **Ebnat-Kappel** Switz.
209 B7 **Ebo** Angola
208 D4 **Ebola** r. Dem. Rep. Co[ngo]
193 O6 **Eboli** Italy
207 H6 **Ebolowa** Cameroon
212 B4 **Ebony** Namibia
207 H5 **Ebonyi** state Nigeria

Ebrach Ger.
Ebrâhîm Ḥeṣâr Iran
Ebre r. Spain see Ebro
Ebreichsdorf Austria
Ébreuil France
Ebrillos r. Spain
Ebringen Ger.
Ebro r. Spain
Ebro, Embalse del resr Spain
Ebrón r. Spain
Ebsdorfergrund-Dreihausen Ger.
Ebsdorfergrund-Rauischholzhausen Ger.
Ebstorf Ger.
Eburacum York, England U.K. see York
Eburodunum France see Embrun
Ebusus i. Spain see Eivissa
Ecatepec Mex.
Écaussinnes-d'Enghien Belgium
Ecbatana Iran see Hamadān
Ecclefechan Dumfries and Galloway, Scotland U.K.
Eccles Greater Manchester, England U.K.
Eccles Scottish Borders, Scotland U.K.
Eccles WV U.S.A.
Ecclesfield South Yorkshire, England U.K.
Eccleshall Staffordshire, England U.K.
Eccleston Lancashire, England U.K.
Ecclesville Trin. and Tob.
Eceabat Turkey
Echague Luzon Phil.
Echallens Switz.
Echandi, Cerro mt. Costa Rica
Echaot'l Koe N.W.T. Can. see Fort Liard
Echarri Spain
Echarri-Aranaz Spain see Etxarri-Aranatz
Échauffour France
Echeda Rus. Fed.
Echeng Hubei China see Ezhou
Échenoz-la-Méline France
Echeverria, Pico mt. Mex.
Echigawa Japan
Echigo-Sanzan-Tadami Kokutei-kōen park Japan
Échillais France
Eching Bayern Ger.
Eching Bayern Ger.
Echinos Greece
Échiré France
Échirolles France
Echizen Japan
Echizen-dake mt. Japan
Echizen-Kaga-kaigan Kokutei-kōen park Japan
Echizen-misaki pt Japan
Echmiadzin Armenia see Ejmiatsin
Echo OR U.S.A.
Echo, Lake Tas. Austr.
Echo Bay N.W.T. Can.
Echo Bay Ont. Can.
Echo Cliffs esc. AZ U.S.A.
Echoing r. Man./Ont. Can.
Échouani, Lac l. Que. Can.
Échourgnac France
Echsenbach Austria
Echt Neth.
Echt Aberdeenshire, Scotland U.K.
Echte Ger.
Echternach Lux.
Echuca Vic. Austr.
Echzell Ger.
Écija Spain
Ecilda Paullier Uru.
Eck, Loch l. Scotland U.K.
Ečka Vojvodina Serbia
Eckartsberga Ger.
Eckbolsheim France
Eckental Ger.
Eckerman MI U.S.A.
Eckernförde Ger.
Eckernförder Bucht b. Ger.
Eckerö Åland Fin.
Eckerö i. Fin.
Eckersdorf Ger.
Eckford Scottish Borders, Scotland U.K.
Eckington Derbyshire, England U.K.
Eckington Worcestershire, England U.K.
Eckman WV U.S.A.
Eckville Alta Can.
Eckwarden (Butjadingen) Ger.
Éclaron-Braucourt-Ste-Livière France
Eclipse Sound sea chan. Nunavut Can.
Écommoy France
Ecoporanga Brazil
Écorce, Lac de l' l. Que. Can.
Écos France
Écouché France
Écouflant France
Écouis France
Écrins, Parc National des nat. park France
Écrouves France
Écs Hungary
Ecséd Hungary
Ecseg Hungary
Ecsegfalva Hungary
Ecser Hungary
Ecuador country S. America
Ecuandureo Mex.
Écueillé France
Écuisses France
Écury-sur-Coole France
Ed Eritrea
Ed Sweden
Edam Sask. Can.
Edam Neth.
Eday i. Scotland U.K.
Ed Da'ein Sudan
Ed Dair, Jebel mt. Sudan
Ed Damazin Sudan
Ed Damer Sudan
Ed Debba Sudan
Eddeki well Chad
Eddelak Ger.
Edderitz Ger.
Edderton Highland, Scotland U.K.
Eddies Cove Nfld and Lab. Can.
Eddrachillis Bay Scotland U.K.
Ed Dueim Sudan
Eddystone Point Tas. Austr.
Eddyville KY U.S.A.
Ede Neth.
Ede Nigeria
Edéa Cameroon
Edegem Belgium
Edehon Lake Nunavut Can.
Edéia Brazil
Edelény Hungary
Edelschrott Austria
Edemissen Ger.
Eden N.S.W. Austr.
Eden Northern Ireland U.K.
Eden r. England U.K.
Eden NC U.S.A.
Eden TX U.S.A.
Eden WY U.S.A.
Eden, Tanjung pt Maluku Indon.
Edenbridge Kent, England U.K.
Edenburg S. Africa
Edendale South I. N.Z.
Edendale S. Africa
Edenderry Ireland
Edenfield Lancashire, England U.K.
Edenhope Vic. Austr.
Edenkoben Ger.
Eden Prairie MN U.S.A.
Edenton NC U.S.A.
Edenvale S. Africa

215 L3 Edenville S. Africa
169 H8 Eder r. Ger.
169 H8 Edermünde Ger.
147 G3 Ederny Northern Ireland U.K.
169 G8 Eder-Stausee resr Ger.
198 D2 Edessa Greece
Edessa Turkey see Şanlıurfa
140 L5 Edevik Sweden
168 E4 Edewecht Ger.
168 E4 Edewechterdamm Ger.
Edfu Egypt see Idfū
236 G5 Edgar NE U.S.A.
86 F6 Edgar, Mount hill W.A. Austr.
86 G5 Edgar Ranges hills W.A. Austr.
233 O7 Edgartown MA U.S.A.
80 K4 Edgecumbe North I. N.Z.
80 K5 Edgecumbe, Mount hill North I. N.Z.
Edgecumbe Island Santa Cruz Is Solomon Is see Utupua
231 G9 Edgefield SC U.S.A.
Edge Island Svalbard see Edgeøya
236 F2 Edgeley ND U.S.A.
234 C6 Edgemere MD U.S.A.
236 D4 Edgemont SD U.S.A.
140 □ Edgeøya i. Svalbard
223 I4 Edgerton Alta Can.
232 A7 Edgerton OH U.S.A.
232 H12 Edgerton VA U.S.A.
226 E7 Edgerton WI U.S.A.
222 G5 Edgewood B.C. Can.
234 C6 Edgewood MD U.S.A.
234 B3 Edgewood PA U.S.A.
147 G5 Edgeworthstown Ireland
78 □3a Edgigen i. Kwajalein Marshall Is
150 H2 Edgmond Telford and Wrekin, England U.K.
Édhessa Greece see Edessa
81 D12 Edievale South I. N.Z.
169 D10 Ediger-Eller Ger.
207 G2 Édîkel well Niger
129 E4 Edik'ilisa Georgia
236 I5 Edina MO U.S.A.
232 E7 Edinboro PA U.S.A.
237 F12 Edinburg TX U.S.A.
232 G10 Edinburg VA U.S.A.
146 J11 Edinburgh Edinburgh, Scotland U.K.
146 J11 Edinburgh admin. div. Scotland U.K.
199 I2 Edincik Turkey
136 G5 Edineț Moldova
211 B8 Edingeni Malawi
172 F3 Edingen-Neckarhausen Ger.
126 C3 Edirne Turkey
199 H1 Edirne prov. Turkey
129 F3 Edisa Georgia
234 E4 Edison PA U.S.A.
129 F1 Edissiya Rus. Fed.
231 G9 Edisto r. SC U.S.A.
238 I3 Edith, Mount MT U.S.A.
82 F6 Edithburgh S.A. Austr.
222 G4 Edith Cavell, Mount Alta Can.
Edith Ronne Land ice feature Antarctica see Ronne Ice Shelf
87 F8 Edith Withnell, Lake salt flat W.A. Austr.
209 B9 Ediva Angola
205 H4 Edjeleh Libya
207 F2 Édjérir watercourse Mali
87 G10 Edjudina W.A. Austr.
173 M5 Edling Ger.
149 N3 Edlingham Northumberland, England U.K.
179 N4 Edlitz Austria
237 G8 Edmond OK U.S.A.
238 C3 Edmonds WA U.S.A.
147 E5 Edmondstown Ireland
85 J4 Edmonton Qld Austr.
222 H4 Edmonton Alta Can.
230 E7 Edmonton KY U.S.A.
226 I6 Edmore MI U.S.A.
236 F1 Edmore ND U.S.A.
149 N4 Edmundbyers Durham, England U.K.
223 M4 Edmund Lake Man. Can.
225 G4 Edmundston N.B. Can.
237 G11 Edna TX U.S.A.
222 C4 Edna Bay AK U.S.A.
Edo Japan see Tōkyō
207 G5 Edo state Nigeria
105 K4 Edo-gawa r. Japan
190 I3 Edolo Italy
128 D8 Edom reg. Israel/Jordan
105 L4 Edosaki Japan
199 I3 Edremit Turkey
199 H3 Edremit Körfezi b. Turkey
106 E4 Edrengiyn Nuruu mts Mongolia
182 G5 Edrosa Port.
182 G5 Edroso Port.
143 O2 Edsbro Sweden
143 M3 Edsbruk Sweden
141 M6 Edsbyn Sweden
140 N5 Edsele Sweden
222 G4 Edson Alta Can.
260 E4 Eduardo Castex Arg.
222 D1 Eduni, Mount N.W.T. Can.
83 J6 Edward r. N.S.W. Austr.
85 H3 Edward r. Qld Austr.
208 F5 Edward, Lake Dem. Rep. Congo/Uganda
262 T1 Edward, Mount Antarctica
86 K7 Edward, Mount N.T. Austr.
Edwardesabad Pak. see Bannu
84 E3 Edward Island N.T. Austr.
226 F1 Edward Island Ont. Can.
85 H3 Edward River Aboriginal Reserve Qld Austr.
233 J4 Edwards NY U.S.A.
81 A12 Edwardson Sound inlet South I. N.Z.
237 E10 Edwards Plateau TX U.S.A.
236 K6 Edwardsville IL U.S.A.
263 D2 Edward VIII Bay Antarctica
262 N1 Edward VII Peninsula Antarctica
235 G5 Edwin B. Forsythe National Wildlife Refuge nature res. NJ U.S.A.
149 O7 Edwinstowe Nottinghamshire, England U.K.
222 D3 Edziza, Mount B.C. Can.
Edzo N.W.T. Can. see Rae-Edzo
208 B5 Edzouga Congo
164 J4 Eefde Neth.
165 E6 Eeklo Belgium
240 H1 Eel r. CA U.S.A.
240 I1 Eel, South Fork r. CA U.S.A.
164 K2 Eelde-Paterswolde Neth.
164 H4 Eem r. Neth.
164 H4 Eemnes Neth.
164 K2 Eemshaven pt Neth.
164 K2 Eemskanaal canal Neth.
214 C8 Eendekuil S. Africa
164 J2 Eenrum Neth.
214 E3 Eenzamheid Pan salt pan S. Africa
164 J4 Eerbeek Neth.
165 D6 Eernegem Belgium
165 H6 Eersel Neth.
Eesti country Europe see Estonia
78 □5 Éfaté i. Vanuatu
179 J3 Eferding Austria
173 K2 Effeltrich Ger.
226 A2 Effie MN U.S.A.
151 L5 Effingham Surrey, England U.K.
236 K6 Effingham IL U.S.A.
234 E3 Effort PA U.S.A.
190 F1 Effretikon Switz.
126 F3 Eflâni Turkey
172 D6 Efringen-Kirchen Ger.
Efsus Turkey see Afşin
197 K6 Eftimie Murgu Romania
93 F4 Eftorobi i. Papua Indon.
107 L2 Eg Mongolia
183 Q4 Ega r. Spain
261 H5 Egana Arg.
241 R3 Egan Range mts NV U.S.A.
227 Q4 Eganville Ont. Can.
207 G4 Egbe Nigeria
187 D10 Egea hill Spain
Egedesminde Greenland see Aasiaat
171 D7 Egeln Ger.
173 K5 Egenhofen Ger.
223 K3 Egenolf Lake Man. Can.

Egentliga Finland reg. Fin. see Varsinais-Suomi
171 F10 Eger r. Ger.
173 J4 Eger r. Ger.
177 J4 Eger Hungary
177 J4 Egerbakta Hungary
177 J3 Egercsehi Hungary
86 □1 Egeria Point Christmas I.
168 I1 Egernsund Denmark
142 C3 Egersund Norway
87 D8 Egerton, Mount hill W.A. Austr.
176 F5 Egervár Hungary
168 J4 Egestorf Ger.
178 A5 Egg Austria
168 H1 Eggebek Ger.
142 F2 Eggedøla r. Norway
169 G7 Eggegebirge hills Ger.
179 M2 Eggenburg Austria
173 N5 Eggenfelden Ger.
172 E3 Eggenstein-Leopoldshafen Ger.
168 E5 Eggermühlen Ger.
171 E7 Eggersdorf Ger.
179 M5 Eggersdorf bei Graz Austria
170 I5 Eggersdorf bei Strausberg Ger.
170 J3 Eggesin Ger.
226 G4 Egg Harbor WI U.S.A.
234 F5 Egg Harbor City NJ U.S.A.
172 E6 Eggingen Ger.
216 □2b Egg Island St Helena
234 E6 Egg Island Point NJ U.S.A.
190 D2 Eggiwil Switz.
223 J4 Egg Lake Sask. Can.
173 O4 Egglham Ger.
173 K2 Eggolsheim Ger.
173 M6 Eggstätt Ger.
140 L2 Eggum Norway
151 K5 Egham Surrey, England U.K.
165 G7 Eghezée Belgium
183 Q3 Egiarreta Spain
146 K4 Egilsay i. Scotland U.K.
140 □F1 Egilsstaðir Iceland
Eğin Turkey see Kemaliye
86 E6 Eginbah W.A. Austr.
Egindibulaq Kazakh. see Yegindybulak
121 P2 Egindy Kazakh.
173 O4 Eging am See Ger.
199 L5 Eğirdir Turkey
199 L5 Eğirdir Gölü l. Turkey
106 H2 Egiyn Gol r. Mongolia
162 I5 Égletons France
173 L6 Egling Ger.
173 J5 Egling an der Paar Ger.
149 N3 Eglingham Northumberland, England U.K.
147 H2 Eglinton Northern Ireland U.K.
220 G2 Eglinton Island N.W.T. Can.
172 F6 Eglisau Switz.
148 D5 Eglish Northern Ireland U.K.
173 K2 Egloffstein Ger.
150 E2 Eglwys Fach Ceredigion, Wales U.K.
150 C3 Eglwyswrw Pembrokeshire, Wales U.K.
164 G3 Egmond aan Zee Neth.
164 G3 Egmond-Binnen Neth.
80 H6 Egmont, Cape North I. N.Z.
Egmont, Mount vol. North I. N.Z. see Taranaki, Mount
80 I6 Egmont National Park North I. N.Z.
80 I6 Egmont Village North I. N.Z.
191 K3 Egna Italy
149 J5 Egremont Cumbria, England U.K.
199 K3 Eğrigöz Dağı mts Turkey
156 F7 Égriselles-le-Bocage France
149 P5 Egton North Yorkshire, England U.K.
142 F6 Egtved Denmark
250 E3 Egua Col.
254 D5 Éguas r. Brazil
92 C8 Eguet Point Phil.
Eguiarreta Spain see Egiarreta
161 G9 Éguilles France
156 I7 Éguilly-sous-Bois France
157 N7 Eguisheim France
162 H3 Éguzon, Barrage d' dam France
162 H3 Éguzon-Chantôme France
131 T3 Egvekinot Rus. Fed.
177 J4 Egyek Hungary
179 O5 Egyházasfalu Hungary
177 H5 Egyházaskozár Hungary
176 F4 Egyházasrádóc Hungary
203 F2 Egypt country Africa
234 D3 Egypt PA U.S.A.
Ehcel well Mali see Agous-n-Ehsel
128 D4 Ehden Lebanon
173 J2 Ehebach r. Ger.
173 K4 Ehekirchen Ger.
106 G7 Ehen Hudag Nei Mongol China
103 J13 Ehime pref. Japan
173 J3 Ehingen Ger.
172 H5 Ehingen (Donau) Ger.
171 E6 Ehle r. Ger.
169 H8 Ehlen (Habichtswald) Ger.
172 F4 Ehningen Ger.
168 K5 Ehra-Lessien Ger.
241 R8 Ehrenberg AZ U.S.A.
84 C7 Ehrenberg Range hills N.T. Austr.
169 J10 Ehrenberg-Wüstensachsen Ger.
168 G5 Ehrenburg Ger.
179 M6 Ehrenhausen Austria
169 F9 Ehringshausen Ger.
178 C5 Ehrwald Austria
103 H15 Ei Japan
79 □9 Eiao i. Fr. Polynesia
183 P2 Eibar Spain
173 I2 Eibelstadt Ger.
171 G10 Eibenstock Ger.
164 K4 Eibergen Neth.
179 L6 Eibiswald Austria
173 K7 Eibsee l. Ger.
172 E2 Eich Ger.
173 K5 Eichenau Ger.
171 D6 Eichenbarleben Ger.
169 I10 Eichenberg hill Ger.
172 G2 Eichenbühl Ger.
173 N4 Eichendorf Ger.
169 I10 Eichenzell Ger.
179 M3 Eichgraben Austria
171 F10 Eichigt Ger.
169 J8 Eichsfeld reg. Ger.
173 K4 Eichstätt Ger.
172 D5 Eichstetten Ger.
171 I6 Eichwalde Ger.
171 E7 Eickendorf Ger.
168 J5 Eicklingen Ger.
140 I5 Eide Norway
168 G2 Eider r. Ger.
142 D1 Eidfjord Norway
144 D1 Eiði Faroe Is
140 J5 Eidsvåg Norway
85 M8 Eidsvold Qld Austr.
142 H1 Eidsvoll Norway
140 □ Eidsvollfjellet mt. Svalbard
169 C10 Eifel hills Ger.
172 F6 Eigeltingen Ger.
104 D5 Eigenji Japan
190 E2 Eiger mt. Switz.
142 B3 Eigerøya i. Norway
146 D9 Eigg i. Scotland U.K.
146 D9 Eigg, Sound of sea chan. Scotland U.K.
114 C9 Eight Degree Channel India/Maldives
262 R2 Eights Coast Antarctica
86 F5 Eighty Mile Beach W.A. Austr.
104 D3 Eiheiji Japan
165 I7 Eijsden Neth.
142 B1 Eikelandsosen Norway
142 D3 Eiken Norway
142 F2 Eikeren l. Norway
146 F9 Eil, Loch inlet Scotland U.K.
Eilat Israel see Elat
83 J7 Eildon Vic. Austr.
83 K7 Eildon, Lake Vic. Austr.
223 J2 Eileen Lake N.W.T. Can.
171 G8 Eilenburg Ger.
171 D7 Eilenstedt Ger.
251 G4 Eilerts de Haan, Natuurreservaat nature res. Suriname
251 G4 Eilerts de Haan Gebergte mts Suriname
92 □ Eil Malk i. Palau
171 D6 Eilsleben Ger.

169 I6 Eime Ger.
169 I7 Eimen Ger.
Eimeo i. Fr. Polynesia see Moorea
168 J5 Eimke Ger.
142 G1 Eina Norway
146 C6 Einacleit Western Isles, Scotland U.K.
85 J5 Einasleigh Qld Austr.
85 I4 Einasleigh r. Qld Austr.
142 G1 Einavatnet l. Norway
169 I7 Einbeck Ger.
165 H6 Eindhoven Neth.
214 D1 Eindpaal Namibia
171 E7 Eine r. Ger.
172 F2 Einhausen Ger.
146 G7 Einig r. Scotland U.K.
96 B6 Einme Myanmar
171 G9 Einsiedel Ger.
190 F1 Einsiedeln Switz.
157 L6 Einville-au-Jard France
128 D8 Ein Yahav Israel
216 □1c Eiras, Ponta das pt São Jorge Azores
264 G2 Eirik Ridge sea feature N. Atlantic Ocean
Eiriosgaigh i. Scotland U.K. see Eriskay
250 D6 Eiru r. Brazil
250 D6 Eirunepé Brazil
169 I8 Eisberg hill Ger.
165 J9 Eisch r. Lux.
165 I7 Eisden Belgium
169 J7 Eisdorf Ger.
212 D3 Eiseb watercourse Namibia
173 M5 Eiselfing Ger.
169 J9 Eisenach Ger.
172 E6 Eisenbach (Hochschwarzwald) Ger.
171 E9 Eisenberg Ger.
172 E2 Eisenberg (Pfalz) Ger.
179 K4 Eisenerz Austria
179 J4 Eisenerzer Alpen mts Austria
Eisenhower, Mount Alta Can. see Castle Mountain
179 I6 Eisenhut mt. Austria
171 K6 Eisenhüttenstadt Ger.
179 K7 Eisenkappel Austria
179 O4 Eisenstadt Austria
179 K4 Eisenwurzen reg. Austria
169 K10 Eisfeld Ger.
146 E8 Eishort, Loch inlet Scotland U.K.
138 H7 Eišiškės Lith.
144 J1 Eislandet Norway
171 E7 Eisleben Lutherstadt Ger.
172 H4 Eislingen (Fils) Ger.
80 J4 Eistow North I. N.Z.
Eitape P.N.G. see Aitape
173 K4 Eitensheim Ger.
169 I9 Eiterfeld Ger.
169 D9 Eitorf Ger.
169 I6 Eitzum (Despetal) Ger.
141 H6 Eivinvik Norway
187 H10 Eivissa Spain
187 I9 Eivissa i. Spain
182 F4 Eixe, Serra do mts Spain
182 C7 Eixo Port.
182 D6 Eja Port.
186 C3 Ejea de los Caballeros Spain
213 □J5 Ejeda Madag.
Ejin Horo Qi Nei Mongol China see Altan Shiret
Ejin Qi Nei Mongol China see Dalain Hob
204 B5 Ej Jill, Sebkhet salt flat Maur.
Ejmiadzin Armenia see Ejmiatsin
129 F5 Ejmiatsin Armenia
186 D6 Ejulve Spain
206 E5 Ejura Ghana
245 K9 Ejutla Mex.
238 L4 Ekalaka MT U.S.A.
207 H5 Ekang Nigeria
215 M1 Ekangala S. Africa
208 B4 Ékata Gabon
103 J13 Ekawasaki Japan
141 Q7 Ekenäs Fin.
142 J3 Ekenäs Sweden
141 Q7 Ekenäskärgårds nationalpark nat. park Fin.
122 F2 Ekerem Turkm.
165 F6 Ekeren Belgium
143 N2 Ekerö Sweden
207 G5 Eket Nigeria
80 J7 Eketahuna North I. N.Z.
Ekhínos Greece see Echinos
Ekhmîm Egypt see Akhmīm
121 P2 Ekibastuz Kazakh.
100 H2 Ekimchan Rus. Fed.
128 H2 Ekinyazı Turkey
207 G5 Ekiti state Nigeria
143 M4 Eknö i. Sweden
208 E5 Ekoli Dem. Rep. Congo
143 N2 Ekoln l. Sweden
131 L3 Ekonda Rus. Fed.
207 H5 Ekondo Titi Cameroon
140 V3 Ekostrovskaya Imandra, Ozero l. Rus. Fed.
208 C4 Ekouamou Congo
207 G5 Ekpoma Nigeria
165 E6 Eksaarde Belgium
165 H6 Eksel Belgium
Eksere Turkey see Gündoğmuş
142 J1 Ekshärad Sweden
199 L5 Ekşili Turkey
143 K4 Eksjö Sweden
100 C1 Ekskavatornyy Rus. Fed.
214 B4 Eksteenfontein S. Africa
262 X2 Ekström Ice Shelf Antarctica
140 O4 Ekträsk Sweden
208 D5 Ekuku Dem. Rep. Congo
224 D2 Ekwan r. Ont. Can.
224 D2 Ekwan Point Ont. Can.
96 C5 Ela Myanmar
El Aaiún Western Sahara see Laâyoune
260 B5 El Abanico Chile
203 F6 El Abbasiya Sudan
198 D6 Elafonisos i. Greece
198 D6 Elafonisou, Steno sea chan. Greece
206 D2 El Aghlâf well Maur.
244 E7 El Aguaje Mex.
128 C3 Elaia, Cape Cyprus
203 G5 El Aiadia well Sudan
198 F2 Elaiochori Greece
204 A5 El 'Aïouej well Maur.
El 'Alamein Egypt see Al 'Alamayn
245 H2 El Alamito Mex.
242 A2 El Alamo Mex.
244 C6 El Alcihuatl Mex.
187 D12 El Algar Spain
205 G2 El Alia Alg.
189 B7 El Alia Tunisia
184 G6 El Aljarafe reg. Spain
184 E5 El Almendro Spain
185 O7 El Alquián Spain
258 D3 El Alto Catamarca Arg.
260 D2 El Alto La Rioja Arg.
250 A6 El Alto Peru
156 C6 Élancourt France
184 E5 El Andévalo reg. Spain
215 O1 Elands r. S. Africa
213 F5 Elands r. S. Africa
215 K8 Elandsberg mt. S. Africa
215 N1 Elandsdoorn S. Africa
215 J8 Elandsdrif S. Africa
215 O4 Elandskraal S. Africa
215 N4 Elandslaagte S. Africa
215 K1 Elandsputte S. Africa
150 E3 Elan Village Powys, Wales U.K.
Elar Armenia see Abovyan
184 H6 El Arahal Spain
El Araïche Morocco see Larache
242 C3 El Arco Mex.
183 J8 El Arenal Castilla y León Spain
El Arenal Illes Balears Spain see S'Arenal
205 E2 El Aricha Alg.
85 K4 El Arish Qld Austr.
205 G1 El Arrouch Alg.
199 H7 Elasa i. Greece
El Asnam Alg. see Chlef
198 D3 Elassona Greece
183 M2 El Astillero Spain
128 C9 Elat Israel

183 N7 El Atazar, Embalse de resr Spain
204 B5 El 'Aţf reg. Western Sahara
91 K5 Elato atoll Micronesia
126 I4 Elazığ Turkey
129 A7 Elazığ prov. Turkey
231 D10 Elba AL U.S.A.
192 E2 Elba, Isola d' i. Italy
185 O3 El Ballestero Spain
100 J3 El'ban Rus. Fed.
250 C2 El Banco Col.
206 D2 El Bânoûn well Maur.
182 I8 El Barco de Ávila Spain
El Barco de Valdeorras Spain see O Barco
183 K8 El Barraco Spain
245 I1 El Barranco Tamaulipas Mex.
245 I3 El Barranco Tamaulipas Mex.
242 F2 El Barreal salt l. Mex.
244 E2 El Barril Mex.
210 B2 El Barun Sudan
196 I9 Elbasan Albania
126 G4 Elbaşı Turkey
203 G5 El Bauga Sudan
250 D2 El Baúl Venez.
205 F2 El Bayadh Alg.
168 H3 Elbe r. Ger. alt. Labe (Czech Rep.)
238 C3 Elbe WA U.S.A.
171 E6 Elbe-Havel-Kanal canal Ger.
206 C2 'Elb el Fçâl des. Maur.
260 B3 El Belloto airport Chile
168 K3 Elbe-Lübeck-Kanal canal Ger.
128 E4 El Béqaa val. Lebanon
169 D6 Elbergen Ger.
206 C2 El Berié well Maur.
183 M7 El Berrueco Spain
239 K7 Elbert, Mount CO U.S.A.
226 H5 Elberta MI U.S.A.
241 U2 Elberta UT U.S.A.
231 F8 Elberton GA U.S.A.
210 D4 El Beru Hagia Somalia
210 C4 El Bes well Kenya
156 B5 Elbeuf France
128 F2 Elbeyli Turkey
206 C2 El Beyyeḍ well Maur.
204 C5 El Beyyeḍ well Maur.
182 F4 El Bierzo reg. Spain
178 B5 Elbigenalp Austria
244 F7 El Billete, Cerro mt. Mex.
Elbing Pol. see Elbląg
169 K7 Elbingerode (Harz) Ger.
126 H4 Elbistan Turkey
184 I9 El-Biutz Morocco
143 P7 Elbląg Pol.
175 H1 Elbląski, Kanał canal Pol.
242 □R11 El Bluff Nic.
182 G8 El Bodón Spain
260 A4 El Boldo Chile
El Bollo Spain see O Bolo
259 C6 El Bolsón Arg.
185 N3 El Bonillo Spain
244 E3 El Bordo Mex.
184 H9 El-Borj Morocco
205 H3 El Borma Tunisia
185 I7 El Bosque Spain
El Boulaïda Alg. see Blida
223 J5 Elbow Sask. Can.
231 I12 Elbow Cay i. Bahamas
236 G2 Elbow Lake MN U.S.A.
244 F2 El Bozal Mex.
243 I4 El Brasil Mex.
129 D2 El'brus Rus. Fed.
129 D2 El'brus mt. Rus. Fed.
129 D2 El'brusskiy Rus. Fed.
171 J9 Elbsandstein Gebirge hills Ger.
208 F3 El Buheyrat state Sudan
185 P4 El Buitre mt. Spain
185 K2 El Bullaque Spain
164 I4 Elburg Neth.
185 J7 El Burgo Spain
183 O3 Elburgo Spain
186 D4 El Burgo de Ebro Spain
183 N5 El Burgo de Osma Spain
183 J4 El Burgo Ranero Spain
208 E2 El Burma well Sudan
244 E2 El Burrito Mex.
Elburz Mountains Iran see Alborz, Reshteh-ye
183 Q5 El Buste Spain
137 S7 El'buzd r. Rus. Fed.
182 H7 El Cabaco Spain
185 P6 El Cabildo y la Campana Spain
185 O7 El Cabo de Gata Spain
258 D2 El Cadillal, Embalse resr Arg.
259 C6 El Cain Arg.
240 P9 El Cajon CA U.S.A.
242 □P10 El Cajón, Represa dam Hond.
251 F3 El Callao Venez.
El Caló Spain see Es Caló
245 G8 El Camotal, Sierra mts Mex.
183 J9 El Campillo de la Jara Spain
El Campo Spain see Campo Lugar
237 G11 El Campo TX U.S.A.
183 J7 El Campo de Peñaranda Spain
183 P9 El Cañavate Spain
244 G1 El Canelo Mex.
261 I4 El Caño Uru.
250 D3 El Canton Venez.
237 E12 El Capulin r. Mex.
244 F1 El Cardito Mex.
250 D2 El Carmelo Venez.
258 D2 El Carmen Jujuy Arg.
260 C1 El Carmen San Juan Arg.
252 E3 El Carmen Beni Bol.
253 F4 El Carmen Santa Cruz Bol.
260 B5 El Carmen Chile
250 B5 El Carmen Ecuador
250 E4 El Carmen Venez.
245 N7 El Carmen, Laguna l. Mex.
187 D9 El Caroche mt. Spain
185 K5 El Carpio Spain
183 L9 El Carpio de Tajo Spain
244 G9 El Carrizal Mex.
183 N7 El Casar Spain
183 K8 El Casar de Escalona Spain
242 G5 El Casco Mex.
187 D7 El Castellar Spain
186 C4 El Castellar reg. Spain
184 G5 El Castillo de las Guardas Spain
243 M10 El Cebú, Cerro mt. Mex.
185 L4 El Centenillo Spain
241 Q9 El Centro CA U.S.A.
253 E4 El Cerro Bol.
184 F5 El Cerro de Andévalo Spain
260 E2 El Chacho Arg.
261 F6 El Chanco, Salina salt pan Arg.
251 E2 El Chaparro Venez.
245 H3 El Chapulín Mex.
261 F6 El Chara Arg.
187 D11 Elche, Embalse de resr Spain
185 O4 Elche de la Sierra Spain
187 D11 Elche-Elx Spain
245 M8 El Chichón Mex.
243 M9 El Chichónal vol. Mex.
245 I5 El Chico, Parque Nacional nat. park Mex.
242 G3 El Chilicote Mex.
173 I5 Elchingen Ger.
226 E4 Elcho WI U.S.A.
84 E1 Elcho Island N.T. Austr.
183 O3 Elciego Spain
244 G5 El Cimatario, Parque Nacional nat. park Mex.
El Coca Ecuador see Coca
250 C3 El Cocuy, Parque Nacional nat. park Col.
185 K3 El Collado hill Spain
244 C6 El Colomo Mex.
244 G8 El Conejo, Sierra mts Mex.
186 J5 El Congost r. Spain
185 O5 El Contador, Puerto de pass Spain
184 H6 El Coronil Spain
245 M8 El Corte r. Mex.
245 L10 El Coyol Mex.
245 L8 El Coyolito Mex.
182 H7 El Cubo de Don Sancho Spain
182 I6 El Cubo de Tierra del Vino Spain
184 G7 El Cuervo Spain
244 B4 El Custodio, Punta pt Mex.
259 C5 El Cuy Arg.
243 P7 El Cuyo Mex.
187 D11 Elda Spain

187 D10 Elda, Embalse de resr Spain
210 B4 Eldama Ravine Kenya
186 L3 El Daró r. Spain
242 C3 El Dátil Mex.
210 D3 El Debb well Eth.
227 O3 Eldee Ont. Can.
170 D4 Eldena Ger.
226 E8 Eldena IL U.S.A.
82 □3 Elder, Mount hill S. Pacific Ocean
226 E5 Elderon WI U.S.A.
239 H12 El Desemboque Mex.
140 □D2 Eldhraun lava field Iceland
242 H3 El Diamante Mex.
250 C2 El Difícil Col.
131 O3 El'dikan Rus. Fed.
168 J5 Eldingen Ger.
244 C6 El Divisadero Mex.
250 B4 El Diviso Col.
261 G6 El Divisorio Arg.
El Djezair Alg. see Alger
242 B2 El Doctor Mex.
236 I6 Eldon MO U.S.A.
236 I4 Eldora IA U.S.A.
234 F6 Eldora NJ U.S.A.
261 G4 El Dorado Arg.
258 G2 Eldorado Arg.
256 C6 Eldorado Brazil
250 D4 El Dorado Col.
242 F5 El Dorado Mex.
237 I9 El Dorado AR U.S.A.
237 G7 El Dorado KS U.S.A.
237 E10 Eldorado TX U.S.A.
251 F3 El Dorado Venez.
241 R6 Eldorado Mountains NV U.S.A.
210 B4 Eldoret Kenya
234 F1 Eldred NY U.S.A.
260 E5 El Durazno Arg.
Elea, Cape Cyprus see Elaia, Cape
232 D10 Eleanor WV U.S.A.
238 I4 Electric Peak MT U.S.A.
198 E4 Elefsina Greece
204 D4 El Eglab plat. Alg.
203 F5 El 'Ein well Sudan
138 G5 Eleja Latvia
185 N7 El Ejido Spain
177 K5 Elek Hungary
Elek r. Rus. Fed. see Ilek
121 V2 Elekmonar Rus. Fed.
138 H7 Elektrėnai Lith.
139 V6 Elektrogorsk Rus. Fed.
139 V6 Elektrostal' Rus. Fed.
139 V6 Elektrougli Rus. Fed.
207 G5 Elele Nigeria
210 B3 Elemi Triangle terr. Africa
197 N8 Elena Bulg.
186 E5 Elena, Planas de plain Spain
250 C5 El Encanto Col.
241 P9 El Encinal Baja California Mex.
245 I1 El Encinal Tamaulipas Mex.
245 H2 El Encino Mex.
169 K7 Elend Ger.
260 D3 Eleodoro Lobos Arg.
198 B3 Eleousa Greece
244 G3 El Epazote Mex.
114 C3 Elephanta Caves tourist site Mahar. India
239 K10 Elephant Butte Reservoir NM U.S.A.
262 U2 Elephant Island Antarctica
114 G8 Elephant Pass Sri Lanka
117 N9 Elephant Point Bangl.
183 L7 El Escorial Spain
197 L9 Eleshnitsa Bulg.
127 K4 Eleşkirt Turkey
184 G5 El Esparragal, Embalse resr Spain
183 L7 El Espinar Spain
243 O10 El Estor Guat.
187 D12 El Estrecho Spain
261 I2 El Eucaliptus Uru.
246 E1 Eleuthera i. Bahamas
226 C5 Eleva WI U.S.A.
237 J7 Eleven Point r. MO U.S.A.
183 O2 Elexalde Spain
189 B7 El Fahs Tunisia
El Faiyûm Egypt see Al Fayyūm
205 H2 El Faouar Tunisia
202 E6 El Fasher Sudan
180 D5 El Fendek Morocco
El Ferrol Spain see Ferrol
El Ferrol del Caudillo Spain see Ferrol
169 I10 Elfershausen Ger.
186 L3 El Fluvià r. Spain
186 H5 El Francolí r. Spain
206 B2 El Freïoua well Maur.
183 K7 El Fresno Spain
241 W10 Elfrida AZ U.S.A.
210 D3 El Fud Eth.
242 E4 El Fuerte Mex.
208 F2 El Fula Sudan
141 K5 Elgå Norway
205 F4 El Gaa Taatzebar basin Alg.
185 O5 El Gabar mt. Spain
186 H5 El Gaià r. Spain
210 C4 Elgal waterhole Kenya
244 G5 El Gallo Mex.
184 G5 El Garrobo Spain
185 I7 El Gastor Spain
245 I1 El Gavilán Mex.
204 D5 El Gçaib well Mali
118 C6 El Geili Sudan
202 D6 El Geneina Sudan
169 H8 Elgershausen (Schauenburg) Ger.
183 P2 Elgeta Spain
203 G6 El Geteina Sudan
203 G6 El Gezira state Sudan
203 F5 El Ghaba Sudan
204 C5 El Ghallâouîya well Maur.
206 C2 El Gheddiya Maur.
142 H2 Elgheia hill Norway
El Ghor plain Jordan/West Bank see Al Ghawr
146 J7 Elgin Moray, Scotland U.K.
226 F7 Elgin IL U.S.A.
236 E2 Elgin ND U.S.A.
241 R4 Elgin NV U.S.A.
238 F4 Elgin OR U.S.A.
237 G10 Elgin TX U.S.A.
85 K7 Elgin Down Qld Austr.
131 P3 El'ginskiy Rus. Fed.
203 F5 El Gir well Sudan
El Gîza Egypt see Al Jīzah
244 G4 El Gogorrón, Parque Nacional nat. park Mex.
183 P2 Elgoibar Spain
146 D8 Elgol Highland, Scotland U.K.
205 F3 El Goléa Alg.
216 □3c El Golfo Lanzarote Canary Is
216 □3e El Golfo b. El Hierro Canary Is
242 B2 El Golfo de Santa Clara Mex.
210 B4 Elgon, Mount Uganda
140 U2 Elgoras, Gora hill Rus. Fed.
141 K5 Elgpiggen mt. Norway
186 F3 El Grado Spain
186 F3 El Grado, Embalse de resr Spain
184 E5 El Granado Spain
187 E8 El Grau de Borriana Spain
244 C6 El Grullo Jalisco Mex.
243 J5 El Grullo Tamaulipas Mex.
245 N8 El Guanal Mex.
242 G2 El Guante Mex.
205 H2 El Guetar Tunisia
204 E5 El Gueṭṭâra well Mali
131 M3 El'gyay Rus. Fed.
189 A7 El Hadjar Alg.
205 G2 El Hadjira Alg.
205 H2 El Hamma Tunisia
204 C5 El Ḥammâmi reg. Maur.
204 D4 El Hank reg. Alg.
204 C5 El Ḥank esc. Mali/Maur.
189 C7 El Haouaria Tunisia
124 B9 El Hasira Sudan
242 □R13 El Hato del Volcán Panama
203 G6 El Hawata Sudan
El Hazim Jordan see Al Hazīm
216 □3e El Hierro i. Canary Is
245 I4 El Higo Mex.
202 E6 El Hilla Sudan
183 O9 El Hito Spain
205 F3 El Homr Alg.
203 F6 El Homra Sudan
206 C2 El Houeïtat well Maur.
183 L7 El Hoyo de Pinares Spain
260 B5 El Huecu Arg.
203 F5 El Husheim well Sudan

207 H3 Eli well Niger
93 G8 Eliase Maluku Indon.
209 D7 Elias Garcia Angola
246 H4 Elías Piña Dom. Rep.
193 L2 Elice Italy
Elichpur Mahar. India see Achalpur
232 A8 Elida OH U.S.A.
245 J4 El Idolo, Isla i. Mex.
146 K10 Elie Fife, Scotland U.K.
114 C7 Elikalpeni Bank sea feature India
198 D4 Elikonas mts Greece
208 E5 Elila Dem. Rep. Congo
209 E5 Elila r. Dem. Rep. Congo
214 D10 Elim S. Africa
220 B3 Elim AK U.S.A.
138 J1 Elimäki Fin.
Elimberrum France see Auch
234 A2 Elimsport PA U.S.A.
244 G6 El Infiernillo Mex.
Eling Guizhou China see Yinjiang
151 J6 Eling Hampshire, England U.K.
208 E5 Elingampangu Dem. Rep. Congo
197 L8 Elin Pelin Bulg.
129 F2 Elin-Yurt Rus. Fed.
193 P4 Elio, Monte d' hill Italy
225 I1 Eliot, Mount Nfld and Lab. Can.
208 E5 Elipa Dem. Rep. Congo
208 D4 Elisabetha Dem. Rep. Congo
Élisabethville Dem. Rep. Congo see Lubumbashi
254 E4 Eliseu Martins Brazil
El Iskandarîya Egypt see Al Iskandarīyah
135 I7 Elista Rus. Fed.
178 H4 Elixhausen Austria
110 C7 Elixku Xinjiang China
233 K8 Elizabeth NJ U.S.A.
232 D9 Elizabeth WV U.S.A.
86 I4 Elizabeth, Mount hill W.A. Austr.
233 □S1 Elizabeth, Mount hill N.B. Can.
231 I7 Elizabeth City NC U.S.A.
84 G5 Elizabeth Creek r. Qld Austr.
Elizabeth Island Pitcairn Is see Henderson Island
233 O7 Elizabeth Islands MA U.S.A.
212 B5 Elizabeth Point Namibia
77 F4 Elizabeth Reef Austr.
232 C12 Elizabethton TN U.S.A.
237 K7 Elizabethtown IL U.S.A.
230 E7 Elizabethtown KY U.S.A.
231 H8 Elizabethtown NC U.S.A.
233 L4 Elizabethtown NY U.S.A.
234 B4 Elizabethtown PA U.S.A.
227 R9 Elizabethville PA U.S.A.
186 B1 Elizondo Spain
244 B2 El Jacuixtle Mex.
204 C2 El Jadida Morocco
242 G4 El Jaralito Mex.
182 G8 Eljas Spain
245 H5 El Jazmin Mex.
203 G6 El Jebelein Sudan
205 H2 El Jem Tunisia
242 □P11 El Jicaro Nic.
244 G8 El Jilguero Mex.
245 M8 El Juile Mex.
216 □3e El Julán slope El Hierro Canary Is
222 H5 Elk r. B.C. Can.
175 K2 Ełk Pol.
175 K2 Ełk r. Pol.
234 D6 Elk r. MD U.S.A.
231 D8 Elk r. TN U.S.A.
El Kaa Lebanon see Qaa
203 G5 El Kab Sudan
236 J4 Elkader IA U.S.A.
205 H1 El Kala Alg.
118 C6 El Kamlin Sudan
203 G5 El Karabi Sudan
138 I4 Elkas kalns hill Latvia
232 B11 Elkatawa KY U.S.A.
203 G6 El Kawa Sudan
237 F8 Elk City OK U.S.A.
240 J2 Elk Creek CA U.S.A.
84 E6 Elkedra N.T. Austr.
84 F6 Elkedra watercourse N.T. Austr.
204 D2 El Kelaâ des Srarhna Morocco
169 E9 Elkenroth Ger.
210 D3 Ēl Kerē Eth.
222 H5 Elkford B.C. Can.
240 K3 Elk Grove CA U.S.A.
El Khalil West Bank see Hebron
203 F5 El Khandaq Sudan
El Khârga Egypt see Al Khārijah
230 E5 Elkhart IN U.S.A.
237 E7 Elkhart KS U.S.A.
El Khartûm Sudan see Khartoum
El Khenachich esc. Mali see El Khnâchîch
204 D5 El Khnâchîch esc. Mali
226 F7 Elkhorn WI U.S.A.
236 G5 Elkhorn r. NE U.S.A.
232 C11 Elkhorn City KY U.S.A.
129 F2 El'khotovo Rus. Fed.
197 O8 Elkhovo Bulg.
Elki Turkey see Beytüşşebap
231 G7 Elkin NC U.S.A.
232 F10 Elkins WV U.S.A.
234 E4 Elkins Park PA U.S.A.
223 H4 Elk Island National Park Y.T. Can.
224 D4 Elk Lake Ont. Can.
226 I5 Elk Lake l. MI U.S.A.
232 H7 Elkland PA U.S.A.
234 D5 Elk Mills MD U.S.A.
238 K6 Elk Mountain WY U.S.A.
234 D5 Elk Neck MD U.S.A.
222 H5 Elko B.C. Can.
238 G6 Elko NV U.S.A.
210 E3 Ēl K'oran Eth.
223 I4 Elk Point Alta Can.
236 G4 Elk Point SD U.S.A.
234 B6 Elkridge MD U.S.A.
226 A4 Elk River MN U.S.A.
El Ksaib Ounane well Mali see El Gçaib
241 X1 Elk Springs CO U.S.A.
230 D7 Elkton KY U.S.A.
234 D5 Elkton MD U.S.A.
232 G10 Elkton VA U.S.A.
232 D10 Elkview WV U.S.A.
245 K9 El Labrador, Cerro mt. Mex.
208 F2 El Lagowa Sudan
143 O1 Ellan Sweden
129 H4 Elläryoğu Dağı hill Azer.
Ellas country Europe see Greece
261 G2 El Laurel Arg.
87 C8 Ellavalla W.A. Austr.
231 E9 Ellaville GA U.S.A.
178 D5 Ellbögen Austria
158 D6 Ellé r. France
171 F10 Ellefeld Ger.
221 H2 Ellef Ringnes Island Nunavut Can.
210 C4 Ēl Lēh Eth.
210 D5 El Lein well Kenya
128 E1 Ellek Turkey
87 D13 Elleker W.A. Austr.
202 C5 Elléloyé well Chad
241 V3 Ellen, Mount UT U.S.A.
116 E5 Ellenabad Haryana India
173 I3 Ellenberg Ger.
232 D9 Ellenboro WV U.S.A.
233 L4 Ellenburg Depot NY U.S.A.
233 J10 Ellendale DE U.S.A.
236 F2 Ellendale ND U.S.A.
238 D3 Ellensburg WA U.S.A.
235 G1 Ellenville NY U.S.A.
244 B1 El León, Cerro mt. Mex.
244 G1 El Leoncito Mex.
78 □3a Eller i. Kwajalein Marshall Is
168 I3 Ellerau Ger.
168 I3 Ellerbek Ger.
168 I3 Ellerhoop Ger.
81 C11 Ellery, Lake South I. N.Z.
81 G10 Ellesmere South I. N.Z.
150 G2 Ellesmere Shropshire, England U.K.
81 G10 Ellesmere, Lake South I. N.Z.
221 J2 Ellesmere Island Nunavut Can.
149 L7 Ellesmere Port Cheshire, England U.K.
165 E7 Ellezelles Belgium

Ermelo S. Africa
Ermenek Turkey
Ermenek r. Turkey
Ermesinde Port.
Ermidas do Sado Port.
Ermil Sudan
Ermioni Greece
Ermita de los Correas Mex.
Ermont France
Ermoupoli Syros Greece
Erms r. Ger.
Ermsleben Ger.
Ermua Spain
Ernabella S.A. Austr.
Ernakulam Kerala India
Erndtebrück Ger.
Erne r. Ireland/U.K.
Ernée France
Ernée r. France
Ernest Giles Range hills W.A. Austr.
Ernest Sound sea chan. AK U.S.A.
Ernstbrunn Austria
Ernz Noire r. Lux.
Erode Tamil Nadu India
Eroj i. Majuro Marshall Is
Erolzheim Ger.
Eromanga Qld Austr.
Erongo admin. reg. Namibia
'Eroûg well Mali
Erp Neth.
Érpatak Hungary
Erpel Ger.
Erpeli Rus. Fed.
Erpu Xinjiang China
Erqu Shaanxi China see Zhouzhi
Erquelinnes Belgium
Erquy France
Errabiddy Hills W.A. Austr.
Er Rachidia Morocco
Er Rahad Sudan
Erraid i. Scotland U.K.
Erramala Hills India
Er Raoui des. Alg.
Erratzu Spain
Errego Moz.
Er Renk Sudan
Errenteria Spain
Errezil Spain
Erribera Spain
Errigal hill Ireland
Errill Ireland
Errindlev Denmark
Errinundra National Park Vic. Austr.
Erris Head Ireland
Erro r. Italy
Erro r. Spain
Errochty, Loch l. Scotland U.K.
Errochty Water r. Scotland U.K.
Er Rogel Sudan
Errogie Highland, Scotland U.K.
Errol NH U.S.A.
Erromango i. Vanuatu
Erronan i. Vanuatu see Futuna
Er Roseires Sudan
Er Rua'at Sudan
Érsekcsanád Hungary
Ersekë Albania
Érsekvadkert Hungary
Ershausen Ger.
Ershiyizhan Heilong. China
Ersis Turkey see Kılıçkaya
Erskine MN U.S.A.
Erstan b. Fin.
Erstein France
Erstfeld Switz.
Erta Ale vol. Eth.
Ertai Xinjiang China
Ertil' Rus. Fed.
Ertingen Ger.
Ertis Kazakh. see Irtyshsk
Ertis r. Kazakh./Rus. Fed. see Irtysh
Ertix He r. China/Kazakh.
Erto Italy
Eru i. Kwajalein Marshall Is
Erudina S.A. Austr.
Erufu Nigeria
Eruh Turkey
Erula Sardegna Italy
Eru laht b. Estonia
Eruwa Nigeria
Erval Brazil
Ervália Brazil
Erve r. France
Ervedosa do Douro Port.
Ervidel Port.
Ervillers France
Ervões Port.
Ervy-le-Châtel France
Erwin TN U.S.A.
Erwitte Ger.
Erxleben Sachsen-Anhalt Ger.
Erxleben Sachsen-Anhalt Ger.
Erymanthos mts Greece
Erymanthos r. Greece
Erythres Greece
Erythropotamos r. Greece
Eryuan Yunnan China
Erzen r. Albania
Erzerum Turkey see Erzurum
Erzgebirge mts Czech Rep./Ger.
Erzhan Heilong. China
Erzhausen Ger.
Erzin Rus. Fed.
Erzin Turkey
Erzincan Turkey
Erzincan prov. Turkey
Erzurum Turkey
Erzurum prov. Turkey
Eržvilkas Lith.
Esa-ala P.N.G.
Esanatoglia Italy
Esan-misaki pt Japan
Esaro r. Italy
Esaro r. Italy
Esashi Hokkaidō Japan
Esashi Hokkaidō Japan
Esashi Iwate Japan
Esbjerg Denmark
Esbjerg airport Denmark
Esbly France
Esbo Fin. see Espoo
Escada Brazil
Escairón Spain
Escalante Negros Phil.
Escalante Spain
Escalante UT U.S.A.
Escalante r. UT U.S.A.
Escalante Desert UT U.S.A.
Escalaplano Sardegna Italy
Escales, Embassament d' resr Spain
Escaleta, Punta de la pt Spain
Escalhão Port.
Escaliers, Pic des mt. France
Escaló Spain
Es Caló Spain
Escalón Mex.
Escalon CA U.S.A.
Escalona Spain
Escalona del Prado Spain
Escalos de Baixo Port.
Escalos de Cima Port.
Escalote r. Spain
Escambia r. FL U.S.A.
Escamilla Spain
Escanaba MI U.S.A.
Escandón, Puerto de pass Spain
Escandorgue ridge France
Escañuela Spain
Escape Reefs South I. N.Z.
Escárcega Mex.
Escariche Spain
Escarigo Port.
Escároz Spain
Escarpada Point Luzon Phil.
Es Castell Spain
Escatalens France
Escatrón Spain
Escaudain France
Escaut r. Belgium
Esch Neth.
Eschach r. Ger.
Eschau France
Eschau Ger.
169 G10 Eschborn Ger.
168 C5 Esche Ger.
168 J4 Escheburg Ger.
168 J5 Eschede Ger.
190 E1 Eschenbach Switz.
173 L2 Eschenbach in der Oberpfalz Ger.
169 F9 Eschenburg-Eibelshausen Ger.
169 I8 Eschenstruth (Helsa) Ger.
169 I7 Eschershausen Ger.
178 D6 Eschio r. Italy
173 N3 Eschlkam Ger.
190 D2 Escholzmatt Switz.
165 I10 Esch-sur-Alzette Lux.
165 I9 Esch-sur-Sûre Lux.
169 J8 Eschwege Ger.
169 B9 Eschweiler Ger.
247 I4 Escocesa, Bahía b. Dom. Rep.
252 C3 Escoma Bol.
187 D12 Escombreras Spain
237 E11 Escondido r. Mex.
242 □R11 Escondido r. Nic.
240 O8 Escondido CA U.S.A.
187 K8 Escorca Spain
186 D6 Escorihuela Spain
163 B9 Escos France
163 I10 Escouloubre France
163 B7 Escource France
163 B7 Escource r. France
161 J9 Escragnolles France
186 D6 Escucha Spain
241 W8 Escudilla mt. AZ U.S.A.
244 B3 Escuinapa Mex.
243 N10 Escuintla Guat.
243 M10 Escuintla Mex.
250 D2 Escuque Venez.
184 H2 Escurial Spain
186 D5 Escuriza r. Spain
160 C4 Escurolles France
256 D2 Escurso r. Brazil
183 K8 Escusa mt. Spain
185 L6 Escúzar Spain
207 H6 Eséka Cameroon
131 O3 Ese-Khayya Rus. Fed.
199 K6 Eşen Turkey
199 K6 Eşen r. Turkey
199 J2 Esence Turkey
129 A6 Esence Dağları mts Turkey
129 F6 Eşengöl Dağı mt. Iran/Turkey
122 E3 Esenguly Turkm.
122 E3 Esenguly Döwlet Gorugy nature res. Turkm.
199 J2 Esenköy Turkey
128 C2 Esenpınar Turkey
168 E3 Esens Ger.
129 B5 Esenyurt Erzurum Turkey
199 J1 Esenyurt İstanbul Turkey
186 F3 Ésera r. Spain
122 D5 Eşfahān Iran
122 E5 Eşfahān prov. Iran
123 J8 Esfandak Iran
122 E6 Esfandāran Iran
122 G3 Esfarayen, Reshteh-ye mts Iran
122 H5 Esfīdeh Iran
182 E4 Esgos Spain
183 K5 Esgueva r. Spain
183 L5 Esguevillas de Esgueva Spain
122 H8 Es'hak Iran
108 D6 Eshan Yunnan China
146 □M2 Esha Ness hd Scotland U.K.
151 L5 Esher Surrey, England U.K.
129 B2 Eshera Georgia
209 E6 Eshimba Dem. Rep. Congo
123 M3 Eshkamesh Afgh.
122 E8 Eshkanān Iran
215 P4 Eshowe S. Africa
122 D4 Eshtehārd Iran
213 F4 Esigodini Zimbabwe
215 Q4 Esikhawini S. Africa
Esil Kazakh. see Yesil'
Esil r. Kazakh./Rus. Fed. see Ishim
191 O8 Esino r. Italy
129 B5 Esirçölü Tepe mt. Turkey
215 O3 eSizameleni S. Africa
85 N9 Esk Qld Austr.
83 K9 Esk r. Tas. Austr.
149 K5 Esk r. Cumbria, England U.K.
149 K4 Esk r. England/Scotland U.K.
146 J11 Esk r. Midlothian/Scottish Borders, Scotland U.K.
80 K6 Eskdale North I. N.Z.
146 J12 Eskdale val. Scotland U.K.
146 J12 Eskdalemuir Dumfries and Galloway, Scotland U.K.
147 F3 Eske, Lough l. Ireland
Eskene Kazakh. see Iskininskiy
225 H2 Esker Nfld and Lab. Can.
137 P4 Eskhar Ukr.
140 □F1 Eskifjörður Iceland
199 K3 Eski Gediz Turkey
170 E1 Eskilstrup Denmark
143 M2 Eskilstuna Sweden
220 E3 Eskimo Lakes N.W.T. Can.
Eskimo Point Nunavut Can. see Arviat
121 O7 Eski-Nookat Kyrg.
126 F3 Eskipazar Turkey
199 L3 Eskişehir Turkey
199 M3 Eskişehir prov. Turkey
183 N2 Eskutxi mt. Spain
183 H6 Esla r. Spain
Esla, Embalse de resr Spain see Ricobayo, Embalse de
122 B4 Eslāmābād-e Gharb Iran
122 H4 Eslām Qal'eh Iran
173 N2 Eslarn Ger.
183 R3 Eslava Spain
199 K5 Esler Dağı mt. Turkey
169 F8 Eslohe (Sauerland) Ger.
142 J6 Eslöv Sweden
122 G7 Esmā'īlī-ye Soflá Iran
199 J4 Eşme Turkey
129 D5 Eşmeçayır Turkey
129 D6 Esmer Turkey
261 G2 Esmeralda Arg.
260 B3 Esmeralda Chile
246 D3 Esmeralda Cuba
259 B8 Esmeralda, Isla i. Chile
257 E3 Esmeraldas Brazil
250 B4 Esmeraldas Ecuador
250 B4 Esmeraldas prov. Ecuador
252 D3 Esmeraldo r. Bol.
186 □ Es Mercadal Spain
186 □ Es Migjorn Gran Spain
232 G11 Esmont VA U.S.A.
182 C7 Esmoriz Port.
224 C3 Esnagami Lake Ont. Can.
226 J1 Esnagi Lake Ont. Can.
156 F3 Esnes France
165 I7 Esneux Belgium
187 D8 Espada, Serra d' mts Spain
187 E8 Espadán, Pico de mt. Spain
182 H4 Espadañedo Spain
122 I8 Espakeh Iran
Espalha r. Brazil see São Francisco
161 B7 Espalion France
Espalmador, Isla i. Spain see S'Espalmador
161 D6 Espaly-St-Marcel France
España country Europe see Spain
227 M3 Espanola Ont. Can.
239 K8 Espanola NM U.S.A.
250 □ Española, Isla i. Islas Galápagos Ecuador
184 G3 Esparragalejo Spain
185 I3 Esparragosa Spain
186 I4 Esparreguera Spain
161 H9 Esparron France
242 □P10 Esparta Hond.
187 H10 Espartar, Illa s' i. Spain
261 F5 Espartillar Arg.
240 J3 Esparto CA U.S.A.
186 C2 Esparza de Salazar Spain
121 P6 Espe Kazakh.
182 G7 Espeja Spain
183 N5 Espeja de San Marcelino Spain
185 J5 Espejo Spain
183 N5 Espejón Spain
164 I3 Espel Neth.
163 B9 Espelette France
169 G6 Espelkamp Ger.
169 H8 Espenau Ger.
184 H7 Espera Spain
184 E2 Esperança Port.
256 B6 Esperança, Serra de mts Brazil
87 F12 Esperance W.A. Austr.
87 F13 Esperance Bay W.A. Austr.
254 D3 Esperantinópolis Brazil
262 U2 Esperanza research stn Antarctica
259 C8 Esperanza Santa Cruz Arg.
261 G2 Esperanza Santa Fé Arg.
245 J7 Esperanza Puebla Mex.
242 E4 Esperanza Sonora Mex.
252 C2 Esperanza Peru
92 E6 Esperanza Masbate Phil.
247 □1 Esperanza Puerto Rico
261 I3 Esperanza Uru.
242 □P10 Esperanza, Sierra de la mts Hond.
163 I10 Espéraza France
193 L5 Esperia Italy
163 I10 Espezel France
184 A4 Espichel, Cabo c. Port.
185 J4 Espiel Spain
255 C8 Espigão, Serra do mts Brazil
261 G5 Espigas Arg.
183 K3 Espigüete mt. Spain
161 E9 Espiguette, Pointe de l' pt France
245 J5 Espina Mex.
183 K2 Espinama Spain
161 I8 Espinasses France
243 I4 Espinazo Mex.
245 M8 Espinazo del Diablo, Sierra mts Mex.
260 B6 Espinazo del Zorro Arg.
257 F2 Espinhaço, Serra do mts Brazil
184 B6 Espinhaço de Cão, Serra do mts Port.
182 D8 Espinhal Port.
209 B9 Espinheira Angola
184 D4 Espinheira hill Port.
182 C6 Espinho Port.
255 B9 Espinilho, Serra do hills Brazil
183 L2 Espinilla Spain
251 E2 Espino Venez.
255 E5 Espinosa Brazil
183 M5 Espinosa de Cerrato Spain
183 N7 Espinosa de Henares Spain
183 M2 Espinosa de los Monteros Spain
183 K9 Espinoso del Rey Spain
161 B9 Espinouse, Monts de l' mts France
163 J10 Espira-de-l'Agly France
Espirito Santo Brazil see Vila Velha
257 G3 Espírito Santo state Brazil
184 D5 Espírito Santo Port.
92 C3 Espiritu Luzon Phil.
252 D4 Espíritu Santo Bol.
244 F3 Espíritu Santo Mex.
78 □5 Espíritu Santo i. Vanuatu
243 P8 Espíritu Santo, Bahía del b. Mex.
242 D5 Espíritu Santo, Isla i. Mex.
243 O7 Espita Mex.
182 C9 Espite Port.
254 F4 Esplanada Brazil
183 P7 Esplegares Spain
186 J5 Esplugues de Llobregat Spain
186 F4 Esplús Spain
186 L3 Espolla Spain
161 C10 Espondeilham France
186 K3 Esponellà Spain
141 R6 Espoo Fin.
187 K8 Esporles Spain
182 C5 Esposende Port.
186 H2 Espot Spain
160 I1 Esprels France
185 P5 Espuña mt. Spain
187 B12 Espuña, Sierra de mts Spain
213 G4 Espungabera Moz.
234 C2 Espy PA U.S.A.
242 E2 Esqueda Mex.
259 C6 Esquel Arg.
222 F5 Esquimalt B.C. Can.
261 H2 Esquina Arg.
243 O10 Esquipulas Guat.
183 M8 Esquivias Spain
140 P3 Esrange Sweden
142 I5 Esrum Sø l. Denmark
210 A1 Es Samalat Sudan
93 E1 Essang Sulawesi Indon.
204 C3 Essaouira Morocco
159 L4 Essay France
207 H5 Essé Cameroon
168 I5 Essel Ger.
204 C4 Es Semara Western Sahara
165 F6 Essen Belgium
169 D8 Essen Ger.
168 E5 Essen (Oldenburg) Ger.
173 M4 Essenbach Ger.
87 F8 Essendon, Mount hill W.A. Austr.
160 J1 Essert France
227 L7 Essex Ont. Can.
151 N4 Essex admin. div. England U.K.
241 Q7 Essex CA U.S.A.
235 K2 Essex CT U.S.A.
233 O6 Essex MA U.S.A.
234 C6 Essex MD U.S.A.
233 L4 Essex NY U.S.A.
235 G3 Essex County county NJ U.S.A.
233 L4 Essex Junction VT U.S.A.
Essexvale Zimbabwe see Esigodini
227 K6 Essexville MI U.S.A.
173 I4 Essingen Ger.
150 H2 Essington Staffordshire, England U.K.
172 G4 Esslingen am Neckar Ger.
131 Q4 Esso Rus. Fed.
156 F5 Essômes-sur-Marne France
156 D6 Essonne dept France
156 D6 Essonne r. France
156 I7 Essoyes France
207 H5 Essu Cameroon
138 J2 Essu Estonia
203 F5 Es Suaifi well Sudan
203 G6 Es Suki Sudan
207 I5 Est prov. Cameroon
157 L7 Est, Canal de l' France
225 I4 Est, Île de l' i. Que. Can.
233 □P1 Est, Lac de l' l. Que. Can.
225 I3 Est, Pointe de l' pt Que. Can.
182 E1 Estaca de Bares, Punta de pt Spain
261 H2 Estacas Arg.
244 G2 Estación Catorce Mex.
241 R9 Estación Coahuila Mex.
185 L4 Estación de Baeza Spain
244 G2 Estación Laguna Seca Mex.
186 F3 Estadilla Spain
259 D9 Estados, Isla de los i. Arg.
163 J10 Estagel France
92 D3 Estagno Point Luzon Phil.
122 F7 Eşţahbān Iran
161 B7 Estaing France
227 N3 Estaire Ont. Can.
156 E2 Estaires France
256 B2 Estância Goiás Brazil
254 F4 Estância Sergipe Brazil
239 K9 Estancia NM U.S.A.
259 C9 Estancia Camerón Chile
259 C9 Estancia Carmen Arg.
185 O5 Estancias, Sierra de las mts Spain
122 I6 Estand, Kūh-e mt. Iran
163 D8 Estang France
122 H7 Estārm Iran
182 C7 Estarreja Port.
186 D2 Estarrón r. Spain
186 H2 Estats, Pic d' mt. France/Spain
190 B2 Estavayer-le-Lac Switz.
215 N5 Estcourt S. Africa
168 I3 Este r. Ger.
191 L5 Este Italy
247 I4 Este, Parque Nacional del nat. park Dom. Rep.
247 □1 Este, Punta pt Puerto Rico
186 D4 Esteban hill Spain
261 F5 Esteban A. Gazcón Arg.
258 D1 Esteban de Urizar Arg.
Esteban Echeverria Arg. see Monte Grande
170 D5 Estedt Ger.
182 C6 Estela Port.
242 □P11 Estelí Nic.
183 P3 Estella Spain
234 F6 Estell Manor NJ U.S.A.
184 G2 Estena hill Spain
185 J2 Estena r. Spain
173 I2 Estenfeld Ger.
185 J6 Estepa Spain
183 M4 Estepar Spain
185 I8 Estepona Spain
185 J3 Esteras r. Spain
183 P6 Esteras de Medinaceli Spain
186 D6 Estercuel Spain
161 J9 Esterel reg. France
163 B9 Estérençuby France
173 K6 Estergebirge mts Ger.
223 K5 Esterhazy Sask. Can.
208 A4 Esterias, Cap c. Gabon
156 G6 Esternay France
179 I2 Esternberg Austria
245 J3 Estero Mex.
240 K6 Estero Bay CA U.S.A.
190 C8 Esteron r. Italy
245 I3 Esteros Mex.
253 E5 Esteros Para.
186 H2 Esterri d'Aneu Spain
168 E5 Esterwegen Ger.
238 L6 Estes Park CO U.S.A.
250 A1 Este Sudeste, Cayos del is Col.
223 K5 Estevan Sask. Can.
222 D4 Estevan Group is B.C. Can.
236 H4 Estherville IA U.S.A.
161 E6 Estiavreilles France
231 G9 Estill SC U.S.A.
163 F7 Estillac France
165 F8 Estinnes-au-Mont Belgium
156 G7 Estissac France
257 D5 Estiva Brazil
254 D3 Estiva r. Brazil
160 B4 Estivareilles France
187 E8 Estivella Spain
184 D6 Estói Port.
184 C6 Estômbar Port.
223 I5 Eston Sask. Can.
149 O4 Eston Redcar and Cleveland, England U.K.
138 I3 Estonia country Europe
Estonskaya S.S.R. country Europe see Estonia
168 H3 Estorf Niedersachsen Ger.
168 H5 Estorf Niedersachsen Ger.
184 A3 Estoril Port.
161 I9 Estoublon France
160 F5 Estrablin France
156 E5 Estrées-St-Denis France
258 H3 Estreito Brazil
182 E9 Estreito Port.
184 □ Estreito da Calheta Madeira
184 E4 Estrela Port.
182 E8 Estrela, Serra da mts Port.
257 E3 Estrela do Indaiá Brazil
256 D3 Estrela do Sul Brazil
185 L4 Estrella mt. Spain
242 B2 Estrella, Punta pt Mex.
241 T8 Estrella, Sierra mts AZ U.S.A.
78 □6 Estrella Bay Sta Isabel Solomon Is
252 D2 Estrema Brazil
182 B10 Estremadura reg. Port.
183 N8 Estremera Spain
183 N8 Estremera, Canal de Spain
183 O8 Estremera, Embalse de resr Spain
184 D3 Estremoz Port.
183 O6 Estriégala Spain
163 C8 Estrigon r. France
254 C4 Estrondo, Serra hills Brazil
208 A4 Estuaire prov. Gabon
184 B4 Estuário do Sado, Reserva Natural do nature res. Port.
184 B3 Estuário do Tejo, Reserva Natural do nature res. Port.
122 C4 Estūh Iran
Esu Cameroon see Essu
208 D4 Esumba, Île i. Dem. Rep. Congo
159 M7 Esvres France
177 K4 Esztár Hungary
177 H4 Esztergom Hungary
158 F4 Étables-sur-Mer France
82 G3 Etadunna S.A. Austr.
162 F4 Étagnac France
116 G6 Etah Uttar Prad. India
157 K5 Étain France
160 C1 Étais-la-Sauvin France
160 F1 Étalante France
165 I9 Étalle Belgium
225 J3 Étamamiou Que. Can.
156 D7 Étampes France
82 G2 Etamunbanie, Lake salt flat S.A. Austr.
217 □1c Étang-Salé Réunion
160 E3 Étang-sur-Arroux France
156 C2 Étaples France
162 B4 Étaules France
162 C5 Étauliers France
116 F7 Etawah Rajasthan India
116 G6 Etawah Uttar Prad. India
78 □3a Etcharai i. Kwajalein Marshall Is
242 E4 Etchojoa Mex.
208 A5 Étéké Gabon
158 E6 Étel France
141 S6 Etelä-Suomi prov. Fin.
161 I6 Étendard, Pic de l' mt. France
160 I2 Éternoz France
215 O2 Ethandakukhanya S. Africa
165 I9 Ethe Belgium
87 E8 Ethel watercourse W.A. Austr.
223 K5 Ethelbert Man. Can.
86 F7 Ethel Creek W.A. Austr.
85 I3 Ethel Creek r. Qld Austr.
214 G5 E'Thembini S. Africa
85 I4 Etheridge r. Qld Austr.
210 C3 Ethiopia country Africa
199 H3 Etili Turkey
126 F4 Etimesğut Turkey
160 H3 Étival France
157 M7 Étival-Clairefontaine France
146 F10 Etive, Loch inlet Scotland U.K.
156 H8 Étivey France
245 K8 Etla Mex.
141 K6 Etna r. Norway
195 I8 Etna, Monte vol. Sicilia Italy
Etna, Mount vol. Sicilia Italy see Etna, Monte
194 H8 Etna, Parco dell' park Italy
142 B2 Etne Norway
227 O6 Etobicoke Ont. Can.
156 G6 Étoges France
161 G10 Étoile, Chaîne de l' hills France
161 F7 Étoile-sur-Rhône France
208 D4 Etoka Dem. Rep. Congo
220 E4 Etolin Island AK U.S.A.
85 L6 Eton Qld Austr.
151 K5 Eton Windsor and Maidenhead, England U.K.
Etorofu-tō i. Kuril'skiye O-va Rus. Fed. see Iturup, Ostrov
212 B3 Etosha National Park Namibia
212 C3 Etosha Pan salt pan Namibia
208 B4 Etoumbi Congo
235 F4 Etra NJ U.S.A.
156 D7 Étréchy France
122 F3 Etrek Turkm.
156 C5 Étrépagny France
159 L2 Étretat France
156 G4 Étreux France
197 M8 Etropole Bulg.
190 C4 Etroubles Italy
163 C10 Etsaut France
212 D3 Etsha Botswana
165 J9 Ettelbruck Lux.
78 □4a Etten i. Chuuk Micronesia
172 D5 Ettenheim Ger.
164 G5 Etten-Leur Neth.
146 H8 Etteridge Highland, Scotland U.K.
171 D8 Ettersburg Ger.
206 A2 Et Tîdra i. Maur.
151 I3 Ettington Warwickshire, England U.K.
172 E4 Ettlingen Ger.
146 J12 Ettrick Scottish Borders, Scotland U.K.
149 L2 Ettrickbridge Scottish Borders, Scotland U.K.
146 J11 Ettrick Forest reg. Scotland U.K.
146 K11 Ettrick Water r. Scotland U.K.
169 D10 Ettringen Ger.
114 E8 Ettumanur Kerala India
208 E5 Etumba Dem. Rep. Congo
160 H2 Étuz France
151 I2 Etwall Derbyshire, England U.K.
186 B1 Etxalar Spain
Etxarri Spain see Echarri
183 P3 Etxarri-Aranatz Spain
244 C5 Etzatlán Mex.
223 I5 Etzicom Coulee r. Alta Can.
156 B3 Eu France
79 □8a 'Eua i. Tonga
83 K5 Euabalong N.S.W. Austr.
79 □8a 'Euaiki i. Tonga
Eubarca, Cabo c. Spain see Mossons, Cap des
172 H2 Eubigheim Ger.
Euboea i. Greece see Evvoia
87 J11 Eucla W.A. Austr.
232 D7 Euclid OH U.S.A.
254 F4 Euclides da Cunha Brazil
256 A5 Euclides da Cunha Paulista Brazil
83 L7 Eucumbene, Lake N.S.W. Austr.
225 H3 Eudistes, Lac des l. Que. Can.
237 J9 Eudora AR U.S.A.
82 G6 Eudunda S.A. Austr.
'Eueiki i. Tonga see 'Euaiki
169 J10 Euerbach Ger.
169 J10 Euerdorf Ger.
231 E10 Eufaula AL U.S.A.
237 H8 Eufaula OK U.S.A.
237 H8 Eufaula Lake resr OK U.S.A.
261 F1 Eufrasio Loza Arg.
178 H4 Eugendorf Austria
238 C4 Eugene OR U.S.A.
253 F2 Eugênia r. Brazil
242 B4 Eugenia, Punta pt Mex.
163 D8 Eugénie-les-Bains France
163 A10 Eugi, Embalse de resr Spain
83 L5 Eugowra N.S.W. Austr.
183 P3 Eulate Spain
83 J3 Eulo Qld Austr.
182 E2 Eume r. Spain
182 E2 Eume, Encoro do resr Spain
257 H2 Eunápolis Brazil
85 L6 Eungella Qld Austr.
85 L6 Eungella National Park Qld Austr.
237 I10 Eunice LA U.S.A.
237 D9 Eunice NM U.S.A.
165 J7 Eupen Belgium
171 G7 Euper Ger.
118 F3 Euphrates r. Asia alt. Al Furāt (Iraq/Syria), alt. Fırat (Turkey)
237 K9 Eupora MS U.S.A.
141 Q6 Eura Fin.
141 P6 Eurajoki Fin.
173 K5 Eurasburg Bayern Ger.
173 K6 Eurasburg Bayern Ger.
179 K3 Euratsfeld Austria
156 B5 Eure dept France
156 B5 Eure r. France
156 B7 Eure-et-Loir dept France
238 B6 Eureka CA U.S.A.
237 G7 Eureka KS U.S.A.
238 G2 Eureka MT U.S.A.
241 Q2 Eureka NV U.S.A.
232 C10 Eureka OH U.S.A.
236 F3 Eureka SD U.S.A.
241 T2 Eureka UT U.S.A.
221 J2 Eureka Sound sea chan. Nunavut Can.
237 I7 Eureka Springs AR U.S.A.
240 O4 Eureka Valley CA U.S.A.
82 H4 Eurinilla watercourse S.A. Austr.
83 H4 Euriowie N.S.W. Austr.
83 J7 Euroa Vic. Austr.
85 L8 Eurombah Qld Austr.
85 L8 Eurombah Creek r. Qld Austr.
201 H6 Europa, Île i. Indian Ocean
183 J2 Europa, Picos de mts Spain
Europa, Punta de pt Gibraltar see Europa Point
185 □ Europa Flats Gibraltar
185 □ Europa Point Gibraltar
132 Europe continent
164 F5 Europoort reg. Neth.
157 J6 Eurville-Bienville France
169 C9 Euskirchen Ger.
169 I10 Eußenheim Ger.
231 G11 Eustis FL U.S.A.
83 I6 Euston N.S.W. Austr.
231 D9 Eutaw AL U.S.A.
168 K2 Eutin Ger.
172 F5 Eutingen im Gäu Ger.
222 E4 Eutsuk Lake B.C. Can.
171 G7 Eutzsch Ger.
157 K6 Euville France
84 E4 Eva Downs N.T. Austr.
209 B9 Evale Angola
190 D4 Evançon r. Italy
215 N2 Evander S. Africa
224 E3 Evans, Lac l. Que. Can.
236 C6 Evans, Mount CO U.S.A.
222 H4 Evansburg Alta Can.
232 E8 Evans City PA U.S.A.
234 C2 Evans Falls PA U.S.A.
83 N3 Evans Head N.S.W. Austr.
262 S1 Evans Ice Stream Antarctica
221 J3 Evans Strait Nunavut Can.
226 G7 Evanston IL U.S.A.
238 I6 Evanston WY U.S.A.
224 D4 Evansville Ont. Can.
230 D7 Evansville IN U.S.A.
226 E7 Evansville WI U.S.A.
238 K5 Evansville WY U.S.A.
237 F10 Evant TX U.S.A.
146 H7 Evanton Highland, Scotland U.K.
Eva Perón Arg. see La Plata
Eva Perón prov. Arg. see La Pampa
226 I6 Evart MI U.S.A.
215 L2 Evaton S. Africa
160 A4 Évaux-les-Bains France
122 F8 Evaz Iran
129 F6 Evci Turkey
199 K4 Evciler Turkey
128 C1 Evcili Turkey
226 B2 Eveleth MN U.S.A.
237 J7 Evening Shade AR U.S.A.
151 J4 Evenlode r. England U.K.
131 Q3 Evensk Rus. Fed.
140 N2 Evenskjær Norway
82 E4 Everard, Lake salt flat S.A. Austr.
84 D7 Everard, Mount N.T. Austr.
82 D2 Everard, Mount S.A. Austr.
82 D2 Everard Range hills S.A. Austr.
150 G5 Evercreech Somerset, England U.K.
164 H5 Everdingen Neth.
Everek Turkey see Develi
117 K6 Everest, Mount China/Nepal
233 □R1 Everett N.B. Can.
232 G8 Everett PA U.S.A.
238 C3 Everett WA U.S.A.
165 E6 Evergem Belgium
231 G12 Everglades swamp FL U.S.A.
231 G13 Everglades City FL U.S.A.
231 G13 Everglades National Park FL U.S.A.
231 D10 Evergreen AL U.S.A.
228 D7 Everman, Volcán vol. Mex.
238 C2 Everson WA U.S.A.
251 G3 Everton Guyana
141 L6 Evertsberg Sweden
85 I7 Evesham Qld Austr.
151 I3 Evesham Worcestershire, England U.K.
151 I3 Evesham, Vale of val. England U.K.
169 K6 Evessen Ger.
160 J4 Évian-les-Bains France
140 Q5 Evijärvi Fin.
207 H6 Evinayong Equat. Guinea
232 F11 Evington VA U.S.A.
198 C4 Evinos r. Greece
192 B3 Evisa Corse France
142 D3 Evje Norway
190 D3 Evolène Switz.
184 D3 Évora Port.
184 D3 Évora admin. dist. Port.
184 D3 Évora-Monte Port.
100 J3 Evoron, Ozero l. Rus. Fed.
198 D2 Evosmos Greece
122 A2 Evowghlī Iran
158 H5 Évran France
159 I7 Èvre r. France
159 J3 Évrecy France
156 B5 Évreux France
159 K5 Évron France
126 C3 Evros r. Greece/Turkey
199 H2 Evros r. Greece alt. Meriç (Turkey), alt. Maritsa (Bulgaria)
198 D6 Evrotas r. Greece
156 D6 Évry France
128 A3 Evrychou Cyprus
Evrykhou Cyprus see Evrychou
100 J3 Evur r. Rus. Fed.
198 F4 Evvoia i. Greece
198 D1 Evzonoi Greece
240 □C12 'Ewa HI U.S.A.
240 □D12 'Ewa Beach HI U.S.A.
85 J5 Ewan Qld Austr.
246 □ Ewarton Jamaica
210 D4 Ewaso Ngiro r. Kenya
214 H2 Ewbank S. Africa
146 E7 Ewe, Loch b. Scotland U.K.
151 L5 Ewell Surrey, England U.K.
226 E3 Ewen MI U.S.A.
Ewenkizu Zizhiqi Nei Mongol China see Bayan Tohoi
151 L5 Ewhurst Surrey, England U.K.
234 F4 Ewing NJ U.S.A.
262 T2 Ewing Island Antarctica
110 H5 Ewirgol Xinjiang China
208 B5 Ewo Congo
252 D3 Exaltación Bol.
198 D5 Examilia Greece
215 L4 Excelsior S. Africa
240 M3 Excelsior Mountain CA U.S.A.
240 N3 Excelsior Mountains NV U.S.A.
236 H6 Excelsior Springs MO U.S.A.
234 B2 Exchange PA U.S.A.
162 G5 Excideuil France
150 F6 Exe r. England U.K.
150 E5 Exebridge Somerset, England U.K.
262 P1 Executive Committee Range mts Antarctica
226 C4 Exeland WI U.S.A.
83 M6 Exeter N.S.W. Austr.
227 M6 Exeter Ont. Can.
150 E6 Exeter Devon, England U.K.
240 M5 Exeter CA U.S.A.
233 □O6 Exeter NH U.S.A.
223 I1 Exeter Lake N.W.T. Can.
161 J6 Exilles Italy
164 K3 Exloo Neth.
159 L4 Exmes France
150 F6 Exminster Devon, England U.K.
150 E5 Exmoor hills England U.K.
150 E5 Exmoor National Park England U.K.
233 J11 Exmore VA U.S.A.
86 C6 Exmouth W.A. Austr.
150 F6 Exmouth Devon, England U.K.
83 L4 Exmouth, Mount N.S.W. Austr.
86 C7 Exmouth Gulf W.A. Austr.
222 H1 Exmouth Lake N.W.T. Can.
265 L6 Exmouth Plateau sea feature Indian Ocean
199 H6 Exo Vathy Notio Aigaio Greece
85 L8 Expedition National Park Qld Austr.
85 L8 Expedition Range mts Qld Austr.
225 K3 Exploits r. Nfld and Lab. Can.
222 H5 Exshaw Alta Can.
234 D4 Exton PA U.S.A.
245 H4 Extoraz r. Mex.
182 N10 Extremadura aut. comm. Spain
207 I4 Extrême-Nord prov. Cameroon
182 D5 Extremo Port.
246 E1 Exuma Cays is Bahamas
246 F1 Exuma Sound sea chan. Bahamas
135 G7 Eya r. Rus. Fed.
149 N7 Eyam Derbyshire, England U.K.
208 D5 Eyangu Dem. Rep. Congo
211 B5 Eyasi, Lake salt l. Tanz.
Eyawadi r. Myanmar see Irrawaddy
161 H6 Eybens France
162 H5 Eyburie France
163 G10 Eycheil France
142 E3 Eydehavn Norway
168 G5 Eydelstedt Ger.
151 L2 Eye Peterborough, England U.K.
151 O3 Eye Suffolk, England U.K.
223 J2 Eyeberry Lake N.W.T. Can.
134 M2 Eyelenoborsk Rus. Fed.
146 L11 Eyemouth Scottish Borders, Scotland U.K.
146 D6 Eye Peninsula Scotland U.K.
147 C9 Eyeries Ireland
161 G8 Eygues r. France
161 H8 Eyguians France
161 G9 Eyguières France
162 I4 Eygurande France
162 E5 Eygurande-et-Gardedeuil France
140 □D2 Eyjafjallajökull ice cap Iceland
140 □D1 Eyjafjörður inlet Iceland
210 F3 Eyl Somalia
Eylau Rus. Fed. see Bagrationovsk
163 E6 Eymet France
199 J5 Eymir Turkey
162 H4 Eymoutiers France
122 B5 'Eyn Gazān Iran
Eynihal Turkey see Kale
146 B8 Eynort, Loch inlet Scotland U.K.
151 M5 Eynsford Kent, England U.K.
151 J4 Eynsham Oxfordshire, England U.K.
161 F9 Eyragues France
162 C5 Eyrans France
163 B6 Eyre r. France
82 F3 Eyre (North), Lake salt flat S.A. Austr.
147 F6 Eyrecourt Ireland
84 G9 Eyre Creek watercourse Qld Austr.
162 H5 Eyrein France
81 C12 Eyre Mountains South I. N.Z.
81 C12 Eyre Peak South I. N.Z.
82 E5 Eyre Peninsula S.A. Austr.
161 F7 Eyrieux r. France
163 C6 Eysines France
168 H5 Eystrup Ger.
130 A3 Eysturoy i. Faroe Is
144 D1 Eysturoy i. Faroe Is
151 O5 Eythorne Kent, England U.K.
211 C5 Eyuku waterhole Kenya
207 H5 Eyumojok Cameroon
122 E4 Eyvānaki Iran
160 F6 Eyzin-Pinet France
215 O4 Ezakheni S. Africa
215 N2 eZamokuhle S. Africa
183 O4 Ezcaray Spain
161 K9 Èze France
232 B11 Ezel KY U.S.A.
215 M3 Ezenzeleni S. Africa
260 C6 Ezequiel Ramos Mexía, Embalse resr Arg.
138 K5 Ezernieki Latvia
138 K5 Ežezers l. Latvia
109 J3 Ezhou Hubei China
134 J3 Ezhva Rus. Fed.
199 J4 Eziler Turkey
199 H3 Ezine Turkey
126 H3 Ezinepazar Turkey
186 B1 Ezkurra Spain
Ezo i. Japan see Hokkaidō
128 A4 Ezousa r. Cyprus
127 M8 Ezra's Tomb tourist site Iraq
156 B6 Ézy-sur-Eure France

F

79 □9a Faaa Tahiti Fr. Polynesia
142 G6 Faaborg Denmark
114 C10 Faadhippolhu Atoll Maldives
113 D10 Faadhippolhu Atoll Maldives
210 D4 Faafxadhuun Somalia
179 I6 Faaker See l. Austria
79 □9a Faaone Tahiti Fr. Polynesia
Faarava atoll Arch. des Tuamotu Fr. Polynesia see Fakarava
79 □9a Faaupo, Pointe pt Moorea Fr. Polynesia
186 F5 Fabara Spain
163 G9 Fabas France
239 K11 Fabens TX U.S.A.
94 □ Faber, Mount hill Sing.
222 G2 Faber Lake N.W.T. Can.
182 G3 Fabero Spain
177 L4 Fábiánháza Hungary
175 H3 Fabianki Pol.
177 J5 Fábiánsebestyén Hungary
177 I3 Fabova hoľa mt. Slovakia
161 D9 Fabrègues France
191 N9 Fabriano Italy
193 I3 Fabrica di Roma Italy
185 O3 Fábricas de San Juan de Alcaraz Spain
195 K7 Fabrizia Italy
192 I2 Fabro Italy
216 □1c Faca, Ponta da pt Pico Azores
250 C3 Facatativá Col.
209 D6 Facauma Angola
182 C5 Facha Port.
207 H2 Fachi Niger
184 H8 Facinas Spain
85 M7 Facing Island Qld Austr.
78 □1 Facpi Point Guam
234 D1 Factoryville PA U.S.A.
259 C7 Facundo Arg.
202 D5 Fada Chad
184 E2 Fadagosa Port.
122 F7 Fadāmī Iran
207 F3 Fada-N'Gourma Burkina
177 H5 Fadd Hungary
127 J6 Fadghāmī Syria
125 J4 Faḑīlah well Saudi Arabia
124 G9 Faḑli reg. Yemen
205 H4 Fadnoun, Plateau du Alg.
206 C4 Fadugu Sierra Leone
191 O3 Faedis Italy
191 L7 Faenza Italy
Færingehavn Greenland see Kangerluarsoruseq
Færoerne terr. N. Atlantic Ocean see Faroe Islands
Faeroes terr. N. Atlantic Ocean see Faroe Islands
Faesulae Italy see Fiesole
192 G2 Faete, Monte hill Italy
208 C3 Fafa r. C.A.R.
79 □8a Fafa i. Tonga
93 G5 Fafanlap Papua Indon.
182 D6 Fafe Port.
210 E3 Fafen Shet' watercourse Eth.
210 D5 Fafi waterhole Kenya
207 F3 Faga watercourse Burkina
191 O3 Fagagna Italy
78 □2 Fagaloa Bay Samoa
78 □2 Fagamalo Samoa
197 M5 Făgăraş Romania
Fagatau atoll Arch. des Tuamotu Fr. Polynesia see Fangatau
78 □2 Fagatogo American Samoa
140 J5 Fagerhaug Norway
141 J6 Fagernes Norway
143 L2 Fagersta Sweden
197 K5 Făget Romania
93 G4 Fagita Papua Indon.
259 C9 Fagnano, Lago l. Arg./Chile
193 Q8 Fagnano Castello Italy
165 F8 Fagne reg. Belgium
156 H6 Fagnières France
207 G2 Fagochia well Niger
206 D2 Faguibine, Lac l. Mali
140 □E2 Fagurhólsmýri Iceland
210 A2 Fagwir Jonglei Sudan
208 F2 Fagwir Wahda Sudan
148 C3 Fahan Ireland
205 G3 Fahl, Oued el watercourse Alg.
122 D6 Fahlīān, Rūdkhāneh-ye watercourse Iran
122 F6 Fahraj Iran
168 I1 Fahrdorf Ger.
168 J3 Fahrenkrug Ger.
173 L5 Fahrenzhausen Ger.
171 H6 Fahrland Ger.
125 M4 Fahūd, Jabal hill Oman
216 □1c Faial i. Azores
184 □ Faial Madeira
216 □1c Faial, Canal do sea chan. Azores
193 M5 Faicchio Italy
78 □4a Faichuk is Chuuk Micronesia
203 G2 Fā'id Egypt
169 D10 Faid Ger.
190 F3 Faido Switz.
182 G5 Failde Port.
227 R1 Faillon, Lac l. Que. Can.
165 H7 Faimes Belgium
160 E1 Fain-lès-Montbard France
157 J6 Fains-Véel France
220 D3 Fairbanks AK U.S.A.
232 A9 Fairborn OH U.S.A.
236 G5 Fairbury NE U.S.A.
226 D5 Fairchild WI U.S.A.
81 C13 Fairfax South I. N.Z.
232 H10 Fairfax VA U.S.A.
233 L4 Fairfax VT U.S.A.
81 E12 Fairfield South I. N.Z.
240 J3 Fairfield CA U.S.A.
235 I2 Fairfield CT U.S.A.
236 J5 Fairfield IA U.S.A.
238 G5 Fairfield ID U.S.A.
236 K6 Fairfield IL U.S.A.
232 A9 Fairfield OH U.S.A.
237 G10 Fairfield TX U.S.A.
241 T1 Fairfield UT U.S.A.
232 F11 Fairfield VA U.S.A.
235 I2 Fairfield County county CT U.S.A.
151 I4 Fairford Gloucestershire, England U.K.
227 K6 Fairgrove MI U.S.A.
233 O7 Fairhaven MA U.S.A.
235 G4 Fair Haven NJ U.S.A.
233 L5 Fair Haven VT U.S.A.
147 J2 Fair Head Northern Ireland U.K.
234 D5 Fair Hill MD U.S.A.
92 A6 Fairie Queen sea feature Phil.
146 □M3 Fair Isle i. Scotland U.K.
235 G3 Fair Lawn NJ U.S.A.
234 C6 Fairlee MD U.S.A.
233 M5 Fairlee VT U.S.A.
234 F4 Fairless Hills PA U.S.A.
81 E11 Fairlie South I. N.Z.
146 G11 Fairlie North Ayrshire, Scotland U.K.
85 J3 Fairlight Qld Austr.
151 N6 Fairlight East Sussex, England U.K.
236 H4 Fairmont MN U.S.A.
232 E9 Fairmont WV U.S.A.
222 H5 Fairmont Hot Springs B.C. Can.
151 J6 Fair Oak Hampshire, England U.K.
237 J8 Fair Oaks AR U.S.A.
226 H7 Fair Plain MI U.S.A.
239 L7 Fairplay CO U.S.A.
226 H4 Fairport MI U.S.A.
234 E6 Fairton NJ U.S.A.
85 J3 Fairview Qld Austr.
222 G3 Fairview Alta Can.
226 D9 Fairview IL U.S.A.
232 B10 Fairview KY U.S.A.
227 J5 Fairview MI U.S.A.
235 G4 Fairview NJ U.S.A.
235 H1 Fairview NY U.S.A.
237 F7 Fairview OK U.S.A.
232 E6 Fairview PA U.S.A.
241 U2 Fairview UT U.S.A.
226 D6 Fairview WI U.S.A.
109 □J7 Fairview Park H.K. China
234 D5 Fairville PA U.S.A.
222 B3 Fairweather, Cape AK U.S.A.
222 B3 Fairweather, Mount Can./U.S.A.
148 C4 Fairy Water r. Northern Ireland U.K.
91 J5 Fais i. Micronesia
123 O6 Faisalabad Pak.
156 I4 Faissault France
236 D3 Faith SD U.S.A.
193 M6 Faito, Monte mt. Italy
Faizabad Badakhshān Afgh. see Feyzābād
123 K3 Faizabad Fāryāb Afgh.
116 I6 Faizabad Uttar Prad. India
184 □ Fajã da Ovelha Madeira
216 □1b Fajã de Cima São Miguel Azores
182 E8 Fajão Port.

184 B3 Fajarda Port.
247 □1 Fajardo Puerto Rico
126 I9 Fajr, Wādī watercourse Saudi Arabia
175 K4 Fajsławice Pol.
177 H5 Fajsz Hungary
81 □1 Fakaofo atoll Tokelau
Fakaofu atoll Tokelau see Fakaofo
79 □9 Fakarava atoll Arch. des Tuamotu Fr. Polynesia
134 K4 Fakel Rus. Fed.
151 N2 Fakenham Norfolk, England U.K.
140 M5 Fåker Sweden
120 C3 Fakeyevo Kazakh.
91 H7 Fakfak Papua Indon.
122 E6 Fakhrabad Iran
117 M6 Fakiragram Assam India
177 P8 Fakiyska Reka r. Bulg.
142 I6 Fakse Denmark
142 I6 Fakse Bugt b. Denmark
107 R5 Faku Liaoning China
150 C7 Fal r. England U.K.
206 C4 Falaba Sierra Leone
191 E2 Faladoira, Serra da mts Spain
207 F3 Falagountou Burkina
159 K4 Falaise France
222 G2 Falaise Lake N.W.T. Can.
117 L6 Falakata W. Bengal India
96 A3 Falam Myanmar
122 D5 Falavarjan Iran
191 L3 Falcade Italy
147 F2 Falcarragh Ireland
183 Q4 Falces Spain
197 Q4 Fălciu Romania
157 M5 Falck France
191 L8 Falco, Monte mt. Italy
182 B3 Falcoeira, Punta c. Spain
250 D2 Falcón state Venez.
194 G9 Falconara Sicilia Italy
193 Q9 Falconara Albanese Italy
191 O8 Falconara Marittima Italy
195 I7 Falcone Sicilia Italy
192 A6 Falcone, Capo del c. Sardegna Italy
192 C5 Falcone, Punta pt Sardegna Italy
216 □3a Falcones, Punta pt La Gomera Canary Is
223 M5 Falcon Lake Man. Can.
243 J4 Falcon Lake l. Mex./U.S.A.
260 E2 Falda del Carmen Arg.
81 □1 Fale Tokelau
78 □2 Falealupo Samoa
78 □2 Falefa Samoa
78 □2 Falelatai Samoa
78 □2 Falelima Samoa
206 B3 Falémé r. Mali/Senegal
134 J4 Falenki Rus. Fed.
193 I3 Faleria Italy
Falerii Italy see Civita Castellana
193 Q9 Falerna Italy
193 K1 Falerone Italy
Faleshty Moldova see Fălești
136 G6 Fălești Moldova
78 □2 Fale'ula Samoa
237 F12 Falfurrias TX U.S.A.
222 G4 Falher Alta Can.
124 D7 Falkat watercourse Eritrea
169 J8 Falken Ger.
173 M2 Falkenberg Bayern Ger.
173 N5 Falkenberg Bayern Ger.
170 I5 Falkenberg Brandenburg Ger.
171 M4 Falkenberg Brandenburg Ger.
142 I5 Falkenberg Sweden
170 F4 Falkenhagen Ger.
171 G8 Falkenhain Ger.
170 H5 Falkensee Ger.
173 M3 Falkenstein Bayern Ger.
171 F10 Falkenstein Sachsen Ger.
170 H5 Falkenthal Ger.
146 I11 Falkirk Falkirk, Scotland U.K.
146 I11 Falkirk admin. div. Scotland U.K.
146 J10 Falkland Fife, Scotland U.K.
264 F9 Falkland Escarpment sea feature S. Atlantic Ocean
259 F8 Falkland Islands terr. S. Atlantic Ocean
264 F9 Falkland Plateau sea feature S. Atlantic Ocean
259 E9 Falkland Sound sea chan. Falkland Is
259 D6 Falkner Arg.
198 E6 Falkonera i. Greece
142 J3 Falköping Sweden
175 I4 Falków Pol.
237 H7 Fall r. KS U.S.A.
232 C12 Fall Branch TN U.S.A.
240 O8 Fallbrook CA U.S.A.
226 C5 Fall Creek WI U.S.A.
190 C4 Fallère, Monte mt. Italy
158 H8 Falleron France
140 F4 Fallfors Sweden
262 T2 Fallières Coast Antarctica
146 I10 Fallin Stirling, Scotland U.K.
168 I5 Fallingbostel Ger.
147 B4 Fallmore Ireland
215 L9 Fallodon S. Africa
240 N2 Fallon NV U.S.A.
233 N7 Fall River MA U.S.A.
238 L6 Fall River Pass CO U.S.A.
234 D2 Falls PA U.S.A.
234 A7 Falls Church VA U.S.A.
236 H5 Falls City NE U.S.A.
232 G7 Falls Creek PA U.S.A.
234 F4 Fallsington PA U.S.A.
234 C5 Fallston MD U.S.A.
190 F3 Falmenta Italy
247 □2 Falmouth Antigua and Barbuda
246 □ Falmouth Jamaica
150 B7 Falmouth Cornwall, England U.K.
232 A10 Falmouth KY U.S.A.
233 O7 Falmouth MA U.S.A.
233 □O5 Falmouth ME U.S.A.
234 B4 Falmouth PA U.S.A.
232 H10 Falmouth VA U.S.A.
150 B7 Falmouth Bay England U.K.
247 □2 Falmouth Harbour Antigua and Barbuda
206 D3 Falo Mali
206 D3 Falou Mali
261 F6 Falsa, Bahía b. Arg.
252 C5 Falsa Chipana, Punta pt Chile
225 G1 False r. Que. Can.
214 C10 False Bay S. Africa
214 C10 False Bay Park S. Africa
220 B4 False Pass AK U.S.A.
117 K9 False Point India
186 G5 Falset Spain
246 H5 Falso, Cabo c. Dom. Rep.
242 □R10 Falso, Cabo c. Hond.
259 C9 Falso Cabo de Hornos c. Chile
142 H7 Falster i. Denmark
149 M3 Falstone Northumberland, England U.K.
197 O3 Fălticeni Romania
143 L1 Falun Sweden
191 M2 Falzarego, Passo di pass Italy
93 G4 Fam, Kepulauan is Papua Indon.
Famagusta Cyprus see Ammochostos
Famagusta Bay Cyprus see Ammochostos Bay
182 F8 Famalicão Port.
258 D3 Famatina Arg.
258 C3 Famatina, Sierra de mts Arg.
169 J9 Fambach Ger.
157 L5 Fameck France
122 C4 Famenin Iran
165 G8 Famenne val. Belgium
87 G8 Fame Range hills W.A. Austr.
223 M5 Family Lake Man. Can.
86 I7 Family Well W.A. Austr.
122 D7 Fāmūr, Daryācheh-ye l. Iran
206 D3 Fana Mali
147 G2 Fanad Head Ireland
78 □4a Fanaik i. Chuuk Micronesia
80 J2 Fanal Island North I. N.Z.
213 □K2 Fanambana Madag.
78 □4a Fanan i. Chuuk Micronesia
78 □4a Fananenei, Mochun sea chan. Chuuk Micronesia
213 □K3 Fanandrana Madag.
191 J7 Fanano Italy
78 □4a Fanapanges i. Chuuk Micronesia
199 H5 Fanari, Akrotirio pt Ikaria Greece
109 L3 Fanchang Anhui China
213 □J4 Fandriana Madag.
147 J5 Fane r. Ireland
191 M2 Fanes Sennes Braies, Parco Naturale nature res. Italy
78 □4a Fanew, Mochun sea chan. Chuuk Micronesia
96 D5 Fang Thai.
210 A2 Fangak Sudan
186 G6 Fangar, Punta del pt Spain
79 □9 Fangatau atoll Arch. des Tuamotu Fr. Polynesia
79 □9 Fangataufa atoll Arch. des Tuamotu Fr. Polynesia
79 □8a Fanga Uta inlet Tongatapu Tonga
Fangcheng Guangxi China see Fangchenggang
109 I2 Fangcheng Henan China
108 G8 Fangchenggang Guangxi China
108 G3 Fangdou Shan mts China
109 M7 Fangliao Taiwan
192 B3 Fango r. Corse France
143 M3 Fångö i. Sweden
109 M7 Fangshan Taiwan
108 H2 Fangxian Hubei China
100 F6 Fangzheng Heilong. China
196 H9 Fani i Vogël r. Albania
138 K8 Fanipal' Belarus
163 I9 Fanjeaux France
108 G3 Fankuai Sichuan China
Fankuaidian Sichuan China see Fankuai
109 □J7 Fanling H.K. China
186 E2 Fanlo Spain
146 F7 Fannich, Loch l. Scotland U.K.
Fanning Island atoll Kiribati see Tabuaeran
140 J5 Fannrem Norway
122 H8 Fannūj Iran
142 E6 Fanø i. Denmark
191 O8 Fano Italy
142 E6 Fanø Bugt b. Denmark
78 □4a Fanos i. Chuuk Micronesia
Fanoualie i. Tonga see Fonualei
109 K3 Fanshan Anhui China
109 M5 Fanshan Zhejiang China
107 M7 Fanshi Shanxi China
177 K5 Fântâna Rece hill Romania
177 K5 Fântânele Romania
Fanum Fortunae Italy see Fano
182 C5 Fão Port.
122 D7 Faqīh Aḥmadān Iran
Farab Turkm. see Farap
206 C3 Faraba Mali
Farab-Pristan' Turkm. see Jeýhun
208 F4 Faradje Dem. Rep. Congo
Faradofay Madag. see Tôlañaro
213 □J4 Farafangana Madag.
206 B3 Farafenni Gambia
193 M3 Fara Filiorum Petri Italy
202 F3 Farāfirah, Wāḩāt al oasis Egypt
Farafra Oasis Egypt see Farāfirah, Wāḩāt al
122 E6 Farāgheh Iran
123 J5 Farāh Afgh.
123 I5 Farāh prov. Afgh.
Faraḩābād Iran see Khezerābād
213 □K2 Farahalana Madag.
123 I6 Farah Rūd watercourse Afgh.
193 J3 Fara in Sabina Italy
123 M4 Farakhulm Afgh.
244 B6 Farallón, Punta pt Mex.
91 K3 Farallon de Medinilla i. N. Mariana Is
91 J2 Farallon de Pajaros vol. N. Mariana Is
250 B4 Farallones de Cali, Parque Nacional nat. park Col.
240 I4 Farallon National Wildlife Refuge nature res. CA U.S.A.
182 I5 Faramontanos de Tábara Spain
208 E2 Faramuti I. Sudan
206 C4 Faranah Guinea
123 P4 Faranshat Jammu and Kashmir
197 O4 Faraoani Romania
206 B2 Far'aoun well Maur.
123 J2 Farap Turkm.
125 L7 Fararah Oman
124 E7 Farasān Saudi Arabia
124 E7 Farasān, Jazā'ir is Saudi Arabia
193 M3 Fara San Martino Italy
186 C3 Farasdues Spain
213 □J3 Faratsiho Madag.
91 J5 Faraulep atoll Micronesia
197 M3 Farcău, Vârful mt. Romania
173 K6 Farchant Ger.
165 G8 Farciennes Belgium
177 L6 Fârdea Romania
185 N5 Fardes r. Spain
147 G6 Fardrum Ireland
157 M5 Farébersviller France
151 J6 Fareham Hampshire, England U.K.
156 F6 Faremoutiers France
Farewell, Cape Greenland see Nunap Isua
80 G7 Farewell, Cape South I. N.Z.
80 G7 Farewell Spit South I. N.Z.
193 J3 Farfa r. Italy
142 I3 Färgelanda Sweden
Farghona Uzbek. see Farg'ona
Farghona Wiloyati admin. div. Uzbek. see Farg'ona
231 F10 Fargo GA U.S.A.
236 G2 Fargo ND U.S.A.
121 N7 Farg'ona Uzbek.
121 N7 Farg'ona admin. div. Uzbek.
163 D6 Fargues-St-Hilaire France
163 E7 Fargues-sur-Ourbise France
168 H1 Fårhus Denmark
236 I3 Faribault MN U.S.A.
225 G1 Faribault, Lac l. Que. Can.
116 F5 Faridabad Haryana India
116 E4 Faridkot Punjab India
117 L8 Faridpur Bangl.
116 G5 Faridpur Uttar Prad. India
202 C2 Fārigh, Wādī al watercourse Libya
141 M6 Färila Sweden
182 A10 Farilhões i. Port.
206 B3 Farim Guinea-Bissau
122 H4 Farīmān Iran
151 I4 Faringdon Oxfordshire, England U.K.
149 L6 Farington Lancashire, England U.K.
254 D3 Farinha r. Brazil
190 H6 Farini Italy
125 J6 Fāris, Qalamat oasis Saudi Arabia
182 H6 Fariza de Sayago Spain
143 M5 Färjestaden Öland Sweden
198 D3 Farkadona Greece
Farkhar Afgh. see Farkhato
123 M3 Farkhato Afgh.
123 M3 Farkhor Tajik.
211 B6 Farkwa Tanz.
85 L6 Farleigh Qld Austr.
151 J5 Farleigh Wallop Hampshire, England U.K.
186 D4 Farlete Spain
192 G1 Farma r. Italy
122 C4 Farmahin Iran
199 I5 Farmakonisi i. Greece
150 H5 Farmborough Bath and North East Somerset, England U.K.
226 F9 Farmer City IL U.S.A.
224 D1 Farmer Island Nunavut Can.
237 I9 Farmerville LA U.S.A.
235 G4 Farmingdale NJ U.S.A.
222 F4 Farmington B.C. Can.
235 J1 Farmington CT U.S.A.
234 D7 Farmington DE U.S.A.
226 D9 Farmington IL U.S.A.
233 □O4 Farmington ME U.S.A.
237 J7 Farmington MO U.S.A.
233 □N5 Farmington NH U.S.A.
239 J8 Farmington NM U.S.A.
238 I6 Farmington UT U.S.A.
232 B6 Farmington Hills MI U.S.A.
235 I3 Farmingville NY U.S.A.
177 I4 Farmos Hungary
222 E4 Far Mountain B.C. Can.
232 G11 Farmville VA U.S.A.
177 H3 Farná Slovakia
151 K5 Farnborough Hampshire, England U.K.
149 L7 Farndon Cheshire, England U.K.
149 P7 Farndon Nottinghamshire, England U.K.
143 M1 Färnebofjärden l. Sweden
143 M1 Färnebofjärdens nationalpark nat. park Sweden
149 N2 Farne Islands England U.K.
192 H2 Farnese Italy
233 M3 Farnham Que. Can.
151 K5 Farnham Surrey, England U.K.
232 I11 Farnham VA U.S.A.
87 I8 Farnham, Lake salt flat W.A. Austr.
222 G5 Farnham, Mount B.C. Can.
151 K4 Farnham Royal Buckinghamshire, England U.K.
171 E8 Farnstädt Ger.
149 M6 Farnworth Greater Manchester, England U.K.
261 G6 Faro Arg.
251 G5 Faro Brazil
207 I4 Faro r. Cameroon
222 C2 Faro Y.T. Can.
184 D6 Faro Port.
184 C6 Faro admin. dist. Port.
182 E3 Faro mt. Spain
143 P4 Fårö Gotland Sweden
143 P4 Fårö i. Sweden
246 F8 Faro, Punta pt Col.
207 I4 Faro, Réserve du nature res. Cameroon
182 E4 Faro, Serra do mts Spain
144 D1 Faroe Islands terr. N. Atlantic Ocean
190 C4 Faroma, Monte mt. Italy
143 P4 Fårösund Gotland Sweden
217 □2 Farquhar Atoll Seychelles
217 □2 Farquhar Group is Seychelles
87 G9 Farquharson Tableland hills W.A. Austr.
146 H8 Farr Highland, Scotland U.K.
191 M3 Farra d'Alpago Italy
232 H7 Farrandsville PA U.S.A.
147 C8 Farranfore Ireland
146 G8 Farrar r. Scotland U.K.
85 H8 Farrars Creek watercourse Qld Austr.
124 F6 Farrāsh, Jabal al hill Saudi Arabia
122 E7 Farrāshband Iran
263 G2 Farr Bay Antarctica
227 S4 Farrellton Que. Can.
260 B3 Farrelones Chile
122 H5 Farrokhī Iran
Farruch, Cabo c. Spain see Ferrutx, Cap
Farrukhabad Uttar Prad. India see Fatehgarh
122 E7 Fārs prov. Iran
129 B1 Fars r. Rus. Fed.
122 F5 Farsakh Iran
198 D3 Farsala Greece
198 D3 Farsaliotis r. Greece
123 J5 Fārsī Afgh.
122 D8 Fārsi, Jazīreh-ye i. Būshehr Iran
127 O9 Fārsī, Jazīreh-ye i. Būshehr Iran
142 F5 Farsø Denmark
238 J5 Farson WY U.S.A.
142 C3 Farsund Norway
125 J8 Fartak, Jabal mts Yemen
125 K8 Fartak, Ra's c. Yemen
197 P5 Fărțănești Romania
256 B2 Fartura r. Brazil
255 B8 Fartura, Serra da mts Brazil
122 H3 Fārūj Iran
122 G3 Farūmād Iran
142 F5 Fårvang Denmark
Farvel, Kap c. Greenland see Nunap Isua
226 J6 Farwell MI U.S.A.
237 D8 Farwell TX U.S.A.
123 K3 Fāryāb prov. Afgh.
122 G8 Fāryāb Hormozgan Iran
122 G7 Fāryāb Kermān Iran
138 L6 Farynava Belarus
122 E7 Fasā Iran
195 M2 Fasano Italy
141 K5 Fåset Norway
137 R5 Fashchivka Ukr.
128 A2 Faşikan Geçidi pass Turkey
210 C1 Fasil Ghebbi and Gonder Monuments tourist site Eth.
216 □3a Fasnia Tenerife Canary Is
168 J5 Faßberg Ger.
123 I9 Fāsteh, Ra's-e pt Iran
136 I3 Fastiv Ukr.
Fastov Ukr. see Fastiv
208 F4 Fataki Dem. Rep. Congo
193 K5 Fate, Monte delle mt. Italy
116 E5 Fatehabad Haryana India
116 F7 Fatehgarh Madh. Prad. India
116 G6 Fatehgarh Uttar Prad. India
116 F4 Fatehgarh Sahib Punjab India
116 E7 Fatehnagar Rajasthan India
116 E6 Fatehpur Rajasthan India
116 H7 Fatehpur Uttar Prad. India
123 N6 Fatehpur Pak.
116 F6 Fatehpur Sikri Uttar Prad. India
182 F8 Fatela Port.
215 L4 Fateng-Tse-Ntsho S. Africa
137 N1 Fateyevka Rus. Fed.
137 O1 Fatezh Rus. Fed.
122 F7 Fatḩābād Iran
210 A2 Fathai Sudan
227 M4 Fathom Five National Marine Park Ont. Can.
206 A3 Fatick Senegal
182 C9 Fátima Port.
Fattoilep atoll Micronesia see Faraulep
Fatuhiva i. Fr. Polynesia see Fatu Hiva
79 □9 Fatu Hiva i. Fr. Polynesia
209 F6 Fatuma Dem. Rep. Congo
209 C6 Fatundu Dem. Rep. Congo
78 □6 Fauabu Malaita Solomon Is
160 I4 Faucille, Col de la pass France
157 M8 Faucogney-et-la-Mer France
161 C9 Faugères France
147 H2 Faughan r. Northern Ireland U.K.
190 J8 Fauglia Italy
163 E7 Fauguerolles France
172 G2 Faulbach Ger.
146 I11 Fauldhouse West Lothian, Scotland U.K.
170 G3 Faulenrost Ger.
236 F3 Faulkton SD U.S.A.
157 M5 Faulquemont France
156 D2 Fauquembergues France
222 G5 Fauquier B.C. Can.
187 E8 Faura Spain
87 B8 Faure Island W.A. Austr.
215 J5 Fauresmith S. Africa
78 □6 Fauro i. Solomon Is
140 M3 Fauske Norway
222 H4 Faust Alta Can.
261 H3 Faustino M. Parera Arg.
159 M2 Fauville-en-Caux France
163 F6 Faux France
162 H4 Faux-la-Montagne France
182 F6 Favaios Port.
190 G7 Favale di Malvaro Italy
191 M9 Favalto, Monte mt. Italy
194 F9 Favara Sicilia Italy
187 E9 Favara Spain
186 □ Favàritx, Cap de c. Spain
160 I5 Faverges France
157 L8 Faverney France
161 C7 Faverolles France
151 N5 Faversham Kent, England U.K.
157 K7 Favières France
194 C8 Favignana Sicilia Italy
194 C8 Favignana, Isola i. Sicilia Italy
222 H4 Fawcett Alta Can.
151 J6 Fawley Hampshire, England U.K.
224 B2 Fawn r. Ont. Can.
234 C5 Fawn Grove PA U.S.A.
215 O5 Fawnleas S. Africa
124 F2 Fawwārah Saudi Arabia
140 □B1 Faxaflói b. Iceland
140 N5 Faxälven r. Sweden
234 B2 Faxon PA U.S.A.
202 C5 Faya Chad
78 □5 Fayaoué Îles Loyauté New Caledonia
156 D8 Fay-aux-Loges France
163 H6 Faycelles France
124 F2 Fayd Saudi Arabia
158 H7 Fay-de-Bretagne France
161 J9 Fayence France
231 D9 Fayette AL U.S.A.
226 H4 Fayette MI U.S.A.
236 I6 Fayette MO U.S.A.
237 J10 Fayette MS U.S.A.
232 A7 Fayette OH U.S.A.
237 H7 Fayetteville AR U.S.A.
231 E9 Fayetteville GA U.S.A.
231 H8 Fayetteville NC U.S.A.
233 I5 Fayetteville NY U.S.A.
232 H9 Fayetteville PA U.S.A.
231 D8 Fayetteville TN U.S.A.
232 D10 Fayetteville WV U.S.A.
124 F7 Fayfā Saudi Arabia
127 N9 Faylakah i. Kuwait
157 K8 Fayl-la-Forêt France
157 M8 Faymont France
186 F5 Fayón Spain
128 B10 Fayrān well Egypt
128 B10 Fayrān, Wādī watercourse Egypt
128 C10 Fayranī, Jabal mt. Egypt
161 E7 Fay-sur-Lignon France
91 L5 Fayu i. Micronesia
128 E9 Fazair al Ghrazi watercourse Saudi Arabia
191 P6 Fažana Croatia
207 F4 Fazao Malfakassa, Parc National de nat. park Togo
207 H2 Fazeï well Niger
151 I2 Fazeley Staffordshire, England U.K.
116 E4 Fazilka Punjab India
123 N7 Fazilpur Pak.
125 I2 Fazrān, Jabal hill Saudi Arabia
204 B5 Fdérik Maur.
Fead Group is P.N.G. see Nuguria Islands
147 C8 Feale r. Ireland
231 I9 Fear, Cape NC U.S.A.
146 E7 Fearnmore Highland, Scotland U.K.
163 C9 Féas France
234 E4 Feasterville PA U.S.A.
240 K3 Feather r. CA U.S.A.
240 K2 Feather, North Fork r. CA U.S.A.
81 J8 Featherston North I. N.Z.
150 H2 Featherstone Staffordshire, England U.K.
149 O6 Featherstone West Yorkshire, England U.K.
213 F3 Featherstone Zimbabwe
159 L2 Fécamp France
192 G1 Feccia r. Italy
157 N7 Fecht r. France
188 G3 Federacija Bosna i Hercegovina aut. div. Bos.-Herz.
261 I2 Federación Arg.
261 I3 Federación Uru.
261 H2 Federal Arg.
207 G4 Federal Capital Territory admin. div. Nigeria
Federal District admin. dist. Brazil see Distrito Federal
Federal District admin. dist. Mex. see Distrito Federal
Federal District admin. dist. Venez. see Distrito Capital
233 J10 Federalsburg MD U.S.A.
172 H5 Federsee l. Ger.
144 J1 Fedje Norway
137 O7 Fedorivka Ukr.
Fedorov Kazakh. see Fedorovka
120 J1 Fedorovka Kostanayskaya Oblast' Kazakh.
121 Q1 Fedorovka Pavlodarskaya Oblast' Kazakh.
120 D2 Fedorovka Zapadnyy Kazakhstan Kazakh.
120 F1 Fedorovka Respublika Bashkortostan Rus. Fed.
137 R6 Fedorovka Rostovskaya Oblast' Rus. Fed.
120 C1 Fedorovka Samarskaya Oblast' Rus. Fed.
135 I6 Fedorovka Saratovskaya Oblast' Rus. Fed.
137 R8 Fedorovskaya Rus. Fed.
139 W5 Fedorovskoye Rus. Fed.
137 O7 Fedotova Kosa spit Ukr.
139 X6 Fedotovo Rus. Fed.
116 D6 Fedusar Rajasthan India
147 C5 Fee, Lough l. Ireland
147 C5 Feeagh, Lough l. Ireland
146 H8 Feehlin r. Scotland U.K.
147 H3 Feeny Northern Ireland U.K.
210 E3 Feerfeer Somalia
78 □4a Fefan i. Chuuk Micronesia
158 G6 Fégréac France
177 J4 Fegyvernek Hungary
177 L4 Fehérgyarmat Hungary
177 K5 Fehér-Körös r. Hungary
177 J5 Fehér-tó l. Hungary
177 J5 Fehér-tó l. Hungary
177 H4 Fehérvárcsurgó Hungary
223 M1 Fehet Lake Nunavut Can.
170 D2 Fehmarn i. Ger.
Fehmarn Belt str. Denmark/Ger. see Femer Bælt
168 K2 Fehmarnsund sea chan. Ger.
170 G5 Fehrbellin Ger.
179 N6 Fehring Austria
257 G4 Feia, Lagoa lag. Brazil
Feicheng Shandong China see Feixian
109 K3 Feidong Anhui China
156 G3 Feignies France
252 C2 Feijó Brazil
184 A3 Feijó Port.
172 D2 Feilbingert Ger.
80 J7 Feilding North I. N.Z.
171 E10 Feilitzsch Ger.
160 F4 Feillens France
138 J5 Feimaņu ezers l. Latvia
109 □J7 Fei Ngo Shan hill H.K. China
Feio r. Brazil see Aguapeí
Feira Zambia see Luangwa
254 F5 Feira de Santana Brazil
160 I5 Feissons-sur-Isère France
179 J6 Feistritz im Rosental Austria
179 K6 Feistritz ob Bleiburg Austria
184 D6 Feiteira Port.
109 K3 Feixi Anhui China
107 O9 Feixian Shandong China
107 N8 Feixiang Hebei China
205 H2 Fejaj, Chott el salt l. Tunisia
189 A7 Fejd-el-Abiod pass Alg.
177 H4 Fejér county Hungary
142 H7 Fejø i. Denmark
126 G5 Feke Turkey
177 K5 Fekete-Körös r. Hungary
187 L9 Felanitx Spain
205 G6 Felaou well Alg.
170 J4 Felchow Ger.
169 J9 Felda r. Ger.
173 K6 Feldafing Ger.
179 I6 Feld am See Austria
179 M6 Feldbach Austria
160 K1 Feldbach France
170 H4 Feldberg Ger.
172 E6 Feldberg mt. Ger.
168 I2 Felde Ger.
177 J4 Feldebrő Hungary
178 A5 Feldkirch Austria
172 H7 Feldkirch admin. reg. Austria
173 L5 Feldkirchen Ger.
179 L5 Feldkirchen bei Graz Austria
179 J6 Feldkirchen in Kärnten Austria
173 L6 Feldkirchen-Westerham Ger.
197 M3 Feldru Romania
182 G6 Felgar Port.
182 D6 Felgueiras Port.
177 J5 Felgyő Hungary
261 H2 Feliciano r. Arg.
217 □2a Félicité i. Inner Islands Seychelles
232 A10 Felicity OH U.S.A.
113 D11 Felidhu Atoll Maldives
113 □1 Felidhu Channel Maldives
150 F3 Felindre Powys, Wales U.K.
161 D6 Félines France
190 I6 Felino Italy
244 C1 Felipe Carrillo Puerto Durango Mex.
244 E6 Felipe Carrillo Puerto Michoacán Mex.
243 O8 Felipe C. Puerto Mex.
193 O7 Felitto Italy
185 N7 Félix Spain
179 N4 Felixdorf Austria
257 E3 Felixlândia Brazil
151 O4 Felixstowe Suffolk, England U.K.
215 P4 Felixton S. Africa
190 E6 Felizzano Italy
172 B2 Fell Ger.
146 J12 Fell, Loch hill Scotland U.K.
191 O3 Fella r. Italy
172 G4 Fellbach Ger.
162 I4 Felletin France
149 N4 Felling Tyne and Wear, England U.K.
246 □ Fellowship Jamaica
232 F9 Fellowsville WV U.S.A.
168 J2 Felm Ger.
177 K5 Felnac Romania
Fels Lux. see Larochette
169 H8 Felsberg Ger.
Felsina Italy see Bologna
177 K3 Felsődobsza Hungary
177 I4 Felsőlajos Hungary
177 H5 Felsőnyék Hungary
177 G6 Felsőszentmárton Hungary
177 J4 Felsőtárkány Hungary
179 O6 Felső-Válicka r. Hungary
177 J3 Felsőzsolca Hungary
168 H1 Felsted Denmark
151 M4 Felsted Essex, England U.K.
149 N3 Felton Northumberland, England U.K.
234 D6 Felton DE U.S.A.
234 B5 Felton PA U.S.A.
191 L3 Feltre Italy
151 N3 Feltwell Norfolk, England U.K.
193 K2 Fema, Monte mt. Italy
254 D5 Femeas r. Brazil
168 K1 Femer Bælt str. Denmark/Ger.
216 □3c Femés hill Lanzarote Canary Is
143 K5 Femlingen l. Sweden
195 L5 Femminamorta, Monte mt. Italy
194 H8 Femmina Morta, Portella pass Italy
142 H7 Femø i. Denmark
142 H2 Femsjøen l. Norway
141 K5 Femunden l. Norway
141 L5 Femundsmarka Nasjonalpark nat. park Norway
147 I7 Fenagh Carlow Ireland
148 B5 Fenagh Leitrim Ireland
192 F3 Fenaio, Punta del pt Italy
216 □1b Fenais da Ajuda São Miguel Azores
213 □J5 Fenambosy, Lohatanjona pt Madag.
78 □1 Fena Valley Reservoir Guam
160 G2 Fénay France
163 H9 Fendeille France
182 D2 Fene Spain
227 P5 Fenelon Falls Ont. Can.
78 □4a Feneppi i. Chuuk Micronesia
128 D2 Fener Burnu hd Turkey
Fénérive Madag. see Fenoarivo Atsinanana
129 A4 Fenerköyü Turkey
190 C5 Fenestrelle Italy
157 N6 Fénétrange France
159 J6 Feneu France
136 J3 Fenevychi Ukr.
199 G2 Fengari mt. Samothraki Greece
Fengcheng Fujian China see Yongding
Fengcheng Fujian China see Lianjiang
Fengcheng Fujian China see Anxi
Fengcheng Guangdong China see Xinfeng
Fengcheng Guangxi China see Fengshan
Fengcheng Guizhou China see Tianzhu
109 J4 Fengcheng Jiangxi China
101 D8 Fengcheng Liaoning China
Fengchuan Jiangxi China see Fengxin
108 F4 Fengdu Chongqing China
Fenggang Fujian China see Shaxian
108 F5 Fenggang Guizhou China
Fenggang Jiangxi China see Yihuang
106 J9 Fenggeling Gansu China
109 M4 Fenghua Zhejiang China
108 G5 Fenghuang Hunan China
Fengjiaba Sichuan China see Wangcang
108 G3 Fengjie Chongqing China
109 H7 Fengkai Guangdong China
109 M7 Fenglin Taiwan
Fengming Shaanxi China see Qishan
107 P7 Fengnan Hebei China
107 O6 Fengning Hebei China
Fengqi Shaanxi China see Luochuan
108 B6 Fengqing Yunnan China
107 N9 Fengqiu Henan China
107 P7 Fengrun Hebei China
Fengshan Fujian China see Luoyuan
108 F6 Fengshan Guangxi China
Fengshan Hubei China see Luotian
Fengshan Yunnan China see Fengqing
109 J6 Fengshuba Shuiku resr China
100 C2 Fengshui Shan mt. Heilong. China
109 K2 Fengtai Anhui China
108 D3 Fengtongzai Giant Panda Reserve nature res. China
108 B7 Fengwei Yunnan China
Fengweiba Yunnan China see Fengwei
107 O9 Fengxian Jiangsu China
108 F2 Fengxian Shaanxi China
109 M3 Fengxian Shanghai China
Fengxiang Heilong. China see Luobei
Fengxiang Yunnan China see Lincang
109 J4 Fengxin Jiangxi China
109 K2 Fengyang Anhui China
Fengyi Guizhou China see Zheng'an
Fengyi Sichuan China see Maoxian
107 K9 Fengyuan Shaanxi China
109 M6 Fengyüan Taiwan
107 M6 Fengzhen Nei Mongol China
107 L9 Fen He r. China
107 L7 Fenhe Shuiku resr China
117 M8 Feni Bangl.
91 L7 Feni Islands P.N.G.
162 D2 Fenioux France
190 C4 Fenis Italy
147 C8 Fenit Ireland
150 F6 Feniton Devon, England U.K.
117 M8 Fenny r. Bangl./India
192 B4 Feno, Capo di c. Corse France
192 C5 Feno, Capo di c. Corse France
213 □K3 Fenoarivo Atsinanana Madag.
213 □J3 Fenoarivo Be Madag.
163 G8 Fenouillet France
163 I10 Fenouillet reg. France
109 L4 Fenshui Zhejiang China
151 L3 Fenstanton Cambridgeshire, England U.K.
173 M3 Fensterbach r. Ger.
227 K7 Fenton MI U.S.A.
81 □1 Fenua Fale Tokelau
81 □1 Fenua Loa i. Tokelau
81 □1 Fenua Loa i. Tokelau
Fenua Ura atoll Arch. de la Société Fr. Polynesia see Manuae
146 H11 Fenwick East Ayrshire, Scotland U.K.
149 N2 Fenwick Northumberland, England U.K.
232 E10 Fenwick WV U.S.A.
108 F1 Fenxiang Shaanxi China
107 L8 Fenyang Shanxi China
177 L3 Fényeslitke Hungary
109 J5 Fenyi Jiangxi China
150 B7 Feock Cornwall, England U.K.
137 O8 Feodosiya Ukr.
137 O8 Feodosiys'ka Zatoka b. Ukr.
138 M3 Feofilova Pustyn' Rus. Fed.
146 D11 Feolin Ferry Argyll and Bute, Scotland U.K.
147 E8 Feonanagh Ireland
205 G1 Fer, Cap de c. Alg.
78 □6 Fera i. Solomon Is
160 H3 Fer-à-Cheval, Cirque du corrie France
Férai Greece see Feres
147 G6 Ferbane Ireland
171 F6 Ferchland Ger.
195 K6 Ferdinandea Italy
170 I3 Ferdinandshof Ger.
122 H5 Ferdows Iran
156 G6 Fère-Champenoise France
197 N3 Feredeului, Obcina ridge Romania
156 G5 Fère-en-Tardenois France
158 G7 Férel France
193 J2 Ferentillo Italy
193 K4 Ferentino Italy
199 H2 Feres Greece
185 P4 Férez Spain
Fergana Oblast admin. div. Uzbek. see Farg'ona
Fergana Range mts Kyrg. see Fergana Too Tizmegi
121 O7 Fergana Too Tizmegi mts Kyrg.
Ferganskiy Khrebet mts Kyrg. see Fergana Too Tizmegi
227 N6 Fergus Ont. Can.
147 E7 Fergus r. Ireland
236 G2 Fergus Falls MN U.S.A.
223 L2 Ferguson Lake Nunavut Can.
84 C3 Fergusson r. N.T. Austr.
91 L8 Fergusson Island P.N.G.
184 F3 Feria, Sierra de hills Spain
205 H2 Fériana Tunisia
199 L2 Ferizli Turkey
140 □C1 Ferjukot Iceland
206 D4 Ferkessédougou Côte d'Ivoire
194 H9 Ferla Sicilia Italy
179 J6 Ferlach Austria
206 B3 Ferlo, Vallée du watercourse Senegal
206 B3 Ferlo-Nord, Réserve de Faune du nature res. Senegal
206 B3 Ferlo-Sud, Réserve de Faune du nature res. Senegal
147 G4 Fermanagh county Northern Ireland U.K.
182 C7 Fermelã Port.
182 C7 Fermentelos Port.
191 N8 Fermignano Italy
193 L1 Fermo Italy
225 H2 Fermont Que. Can.
182 H6 Fermoselle Spain
147 F8 Fermoy Ireland
148 B3 Fern, Lough l. Ireland
185 L2 Fernáncaballero Spain
250 □ Fernandina, Isla i. Islas Galápagos Ecuador
231 G10 Fernandina Beach FL U.S.A.
259 B9 Fernando de Magallanes, Parque Nacional nat. park Chile
264 G6 Fernando de Noronha i. Brazil
256 B4 Fernandópolis Brazil
Fernando Poó i. Equat. Guinea see Bioco
185 J5 Fernán Núñez Spain
257 E2 Fernão Dias Brazil
213 I2 Fernão Veloso Moz.
213 I2 Fernão Veloso, Baía de b. Moz.
234 B6 Ferndale MD U.S.A.
234 F1 Ferndale NY U.S.A.
238 C2 Ferndale WA U.S.A.
179 I6 Ferndorf Austria
151 I6 Ferndown Dorset, England U.K.
146 I8 Ferness Highland, Scotland U.K.
160 I4 Ferney-Voltaire France
80 K6 Fernhill North I. N.Z.
150 H3 Fernhill Heath Worcestershire, England U.K.
151 K5 Fernhurst West Sussex, England U.K.
222 H5 Fernie B.C. Can.
179 M6 Fernitz Austria
83 K3 Fernlee Qld Austr.
240 M2 Fernley NV U.S.A.
178 C5 Fernpass pass Austria
234 D2 Ferndridge PA U.S.A.
147 I7 Ferns Ireland
238 F3 Fernwood ID U.S.A.
195 K6 Feroleto Antico Italy
Ferozepore Punjab India see Firozpur
161 B10 Ferrals-les-Corbières France
195 K3 Ferrandina Italy
191 L6 Ferrara Italy
191 L6 Ferrara prov. Italy
191 M6 Ferrarese r. Italy
192 D9 Ferrato, Capo c. Sardegna Italy
193 N4 Ferrazzano Italy
261 G4 Ferré Arg.
182 F1 Ferreira Spain
184 C4 Ferreira do Alentejo Port.
182 D9 Ferreira do Zêzere Port.
251 I4 Ferreira-Gomes Brazil
256 A4 Ferreiros Brazil
184 A2 Ferrel Port.
232 C10 Ferrellsburg WV U.S.A.
250 B6 Ferreñafe Peru
182 H5 Ferreras de Abajo Spain
182 H5 Ferreras de Arriba Spain
190 D6 Ferrere Italy
186 □ Ferreries Spain
186 C5 Ferreruela de Huerva Spain
182 H5 Ferreruela de Tábara Spain
160 K1 Ferrette France
261 E2 Ferreyra Arg.
237 J10 Ferriday LA U.S.A.
190 H6 Ferriere Italy
156 H3 Ferrière-la-Grande France
165 I8 Ferrières Belgium
156 E7 Ferrières France
161 C6 Ferrières-St-Mary France
163 H10 Ferrières-sur-Ariège France
194 H9 Ferro r. Sicilia Italy
195 L4 Ferro r. Italy
192 D5 Ferro, Capo c. Sardegna Italy
184 □ Ferro, Ilhéu de i. Madeira
192 A6 Ferro, Porto b. Sardegna Italy
182 D2 Ferrol Spain
182 D2 Ferrol, Ría de inlet Spain
241 U2 Ferron UT U.S.A.
257 F3 Ferros Brazil
192 D8 Ferru, Monte hill Sardegna Italy
193 M3 Ferruccio, Punta di pt Italy
232 E12 Ferrum VA U.S.A.
187 L8 Ferrutx, Cap c. Spain
147 I8 Ferrycarrig Ireland
146 L9 Ferryden Angus, Scotland U.K.
149 N4 Ferryhill Durham, England U.K.
225 K4 Ferryland Nfld and Lab. Can.
Ferryville Tunisia see Menzel Bourguiba
172 A2 Ferschweiler Ger.
120 H1 Fershampenuaz Rus. Fed.
192 A6 Fertilia Sardegna Italy
179 O4 Fertő l. Austria/Hungary
179 O4 Fertőd Hungary
176 F4 Fertőrákos Hungary
176 F4 Fertőszentmiklós Hungary
179 O4 Fertőszéplak Hungary
176 F4 Fertő-tavi nat. park Hungary
182 D6 Fervença Port.
182 C3 Fervenza, Encoro da resr Spain
164 I2 Ferwert Neth.
139 T7 Ferzikovo Rus. Fed.
204 D2 Fès Morocco
209 C6 Feshi Dem. Rep. Congo
146 I8 Feshiebridge Highland, Scotland U.K.
236 F2 Fessenden ND U.S.A.
157 O8 Fessenheim France
156 G4 Festieux France
161 H7 Festre, Col du pass France
93 F4 Fet Dom, Tanjung pt Indon.
206 B3 Fété Bowé Senegal
216 □1c Feteira Faial Azores
216 □1b Feteiras São Miguel A
197 P6 Fetești Romania
197 P6 Fetești-Gară Romania
146 □N1 Fethaland, Point of Scotland U.K.
147 G8 Fethard Tipperary Irela
147 I8 Fethard Wexford Irela
Fethiye Malatya Turkey see Yazıhan
199 K6 Fethiye Muğla Turkey
120 E6 Fetisovo Kazakh.
146 □O1 Fetlar i. Scotland U.K.
194 D8 Feto, Capo c. Sicilia It
146 K9 Fettercairn Aberdeens Scotland U.K.
173 K3 Feucht Ger.
173 I3 Feuchtwangen Ger.
163 E7 Feugarolles France
225 G1 Feuilles, Rivière aux Que. Can.
156 C4 Feuquières France
156 C3 Feuquières-en-Vime
160 E5 Feurs France
100 G2 Fevral'sk Rus. Fed.
126 H5 Fevzipaşa Turkey
162 G4 Feytiat France
123 N3 Feyzābād Afgh.
122 F6 Feyzābād Kermān Iran
122 H4 Feyzābād Khorāsān Ir
Fez Morocco see Fès
202 B3 Fezzan reg. Libya
150 E2 Ffestiniog Gwynedd, W
150 D3 Ffostrasol Ceredigion, Wales U.K.
Ffynnon Taf Wales U. Taff's Well
163 H8 Fiac France
258 D2 Fiambalá Arg.
258 D2 Fiambala r. Arg.
193 K3 Fiamignano Italy
206 E4 Fian Ghana
213 □J4 Fianarantsoa Madag.
213 □J4 Fianarantsoa prov. M
208 B2 Fianga Chad
190 D5 Fiano Italy
193 J3 Fiano Romano Italy
191 O9 Fiastra r. Italy
193 K1 Fiastra, Lago di l. Ital
191 J4 Fiavè Italy
184 E5 Ficalho hill Port.
194 E7 Ficarazzi Sicilia Italy
191 K6 Ficarolo Italy
210 C2 Fichē Eth.
173 L2 Fichtelberg Ger.
171 F10 Fichtelgebirge hills G
171 F10 Fichtelgebirge park G
173 M2 Fichtelnaab r. Ger.
172 H4 Fichtenberg Ger.
215 L4 Ficksburg S. Africa
192 I2 Ficulle Italy
194 G9 Ficuzza r. Sicilia Italy
125 M4 Fidā Oman
125 K6 Fidā oasis Saudi Arab
146 J8 Fiddich r. Scotland U.
147 H8 Fiddown Ireland
190 I6 Fidenza Italy
142 C3 Fidjeland Norway
176 G2 Fidlův Kopec hill Cze
206 C4 Fié r. Guinea
178 E6 Fiè allo Sciliar Italy
178 G5 Fieberbrunn Austria
193 K1 Fiegni, Monte mt. Ital
222 G5 Field B.C. Can.
227 N3 Field Ont. Can.
232 B12 Field KY U.S.A.
84 D2 Field Island N.T. Aust
138 J5 Fiemanka r. Latvia
197 N5 Fieni Romania
198 A2 Fier Albania
160 H5 Fier r. France
178 E7 Fiera di Primiero Italy
84 G5 Fiery Creek r. Qld Aus
196 I8 Fierzes, Liqeni i resr
190 E3 Fiesch Switz.
191 K8 Fiesole Italy
191 L6 Fiesso Umbertiano It
146 K10 Fife admin. div. Scotla
226 I5 Fife Lake MI U.S.A.
146 K10 Fife Ness pt Scotland
83 K5 Fifield N.S.W. Austr.
226 D4 Fifield WI U.S.A.
Fifth Cataract rapids see 5th Cataract
222 H3 Fifth Meridian Alta Ca
181 F5 Figalo, Cap c. Alg.
161 I9 Figanières France
192 B2 Figarella r. Corse Fran
192 C5 Figari Corse France
192 D6 Figari, Capo c. Sarde
163 I6 Figeac France
191 K8 Figline Valdarno Italy
247 □2 Fig Tree St Kitts and
184 C4 Figueira r. Port.
182 C8 Figueira da Foz Port.
182 G7 Figueira de Castelo Port.
184 C4 Figueira dos Cavalei
184 D2 Figueira e Barros Po
182 E7 Figueiredo de Alva P
184 D1 Figueiró r. Port.
182 F7 Figueiró da Granja P
182 D9 Figueiró dos Vinhos
Figueras Spain see Fi
186 K3 Figueres Spain
182 H5 Figueruela de Arriba
205 E2 Figuig Morocco
207 I4 Figuil Cameroon
128 E9 Fiha al 'Ināb reg. Sau
213 □J3 Fihaonana Madag.
79 □7 Fiji country S. Pacific
266 G7 Fiji Islands S. Pacific
164 F5 Fijnaart Neth.
210 D2 Fīk' Eth.
207 H4 Fika Nigeria
185 N6 Filabres, Sierra de lo Spain
213 F4 Filabusi Zimbabwe
242 □Q12 Filadelfia Costa Rica
195 K6 Filadelfia Italy
253 E5 Filadelfia Para.
177 I3 Fil'akovo Slovakia
206 D4 Filamana Mali
138 L4 Filatova-Gora Rus. Fe
190 H7 Filattiera Italy
262 V1 Filchner Ice Shelf An
193 K4 Filettino Italy
149 Q5 Filey North Yorkshire, England U.K.
129 I4 Filfili Azer.
195 □ Filfla i. Malta
193 P6 Filiano Italy
197 L6 Filiași Romania
198 B3 Filiates Greece
198 C5 Filiatra Greece
Filibe Bulg. see Plovdi
194 H6 Filicudi, Isola i. Isole Li
194 H6 Filicudi Porto Isole Lip
207 F3 Filingué Niger
Filipinas country Asia Philippines
175 K1 Filipów Pol.
100 J1 Filippa, Mys hd Rus. F
198 B3 Filippiada Greece
198 F1 Filippoi tourist site Gre
143 K2 Filipstad Sweden
190 H2 Filisur Switz.
140 J5 Fillan Norway
156 D3 Fillièvres France
160 I4 Fillinges France
Fillíra Greece see Filly
240 N7 Fillmore CA U.S.A.
241 T3 Fillmore UT U.S.A.
151 I3 Fillongley Warwickshir England U.K.
199 G1 Fillyra Greece
245 H8 Filo de los Caballos
245 J5 Filomeno Mata Mex.
199 G5 Filotio Naxos Greece
191 O9 Filottrano Italy
172 G4 Fils r. Ger.
168 E4 Filsum Ger.
150 G4 Filton South Glouceste England U.K.
210 D3 Filtu Eth.
179 I5 Filzmoos Austria
149 P5 Fimber East Riding of Yorkshire, England U.K.

161 F10 Fos, Golfe de b. France
190 I7 Fosdinovo Italy
109 I7 Foshan Guangdong China
109 □J7 Fo Shek Chau i. H.K. China
141 L6 Foskvallen Sweden
140 K5 Fosna pen. Norway
206 E5 Foso Ghana
140 □E2 Foss Iceland
193 M3 Fossacesia Italy
178 G8 Fossalta di Portogruaro Italy
190 D6 Fossano Italy
191 N9 Fossato di Vico Italy
162 F5 Fossemagne France
165 G8 Fosses-la-Ville Belgium
140 □E1 Fosshóll Iceland
160 G4 Fossiat France
238 D4 Fossil OR U.S.A.
86 H5 Fossil Downs W.A. Austr.
191 N8 Fossombrone Italy
161 F10 Fos-sur-Mer France
83 K8 Foster Vic. Austr.
232 A10 Foster KY U.S.A.
222 C3 Foster, Mount Can./U.S.A.
221 P2 Foster Bugt b. Greenland
234 F1 Fosterdale NY U.S.A.
223 J3 Foster Lakes Sask. Can.
233 □R3 Fosterville N.B. Can.
232 B7 Fostoria OH U.S.A.
177 I4 Fót Hungary
213 □J5 Fotadrevo Madag.
149 Q7 Fotherby Lincolnshire, England U.K.
137 N2 Fotovyzh Ukr.
79 □8 Fotuha'a atoll Tonga
Fotuna i. Vanuatu see Futuna
156 C4 Foucarmont France
160 G2 Foucherans France
158 C6 Fouesnant France
157 K6 Foug France
208 A5 Fougamou Gabon
158 I5 Fougères France
217 □1c Fougères, Plaine des hills Réunion
157 L8 Fougerolles France
159 J5 Fougerolles-du-Plessis France
156 E4 Fouilloy France
146 □L2 Foula i. Scotland U.K.
206 D4 Foulabala Mali
157 J7 Foulain France
206 B3 Foulamôri Guinea
163 F7 Foulayronnes France
203 G4 Foul Bay Egypt
146 L11 Foulden Scottish Borders, Scotland U.K.
208 A5 Foulenzem Gabon
96 B5 Foul Island Myanmar
147 I8 Foulkesmill Ireland
151 N4 Foulness Point England U.K.
208 C2 Foulounga Chad
114 G8 Foul Point Sri Lanka
Foulpointe Madag. see Mahavelona
149 M6 Foulridge Lancashire, England U.K.
81 F8 Foulwind, Cape South I. N.Z.
207 H5 Foumban Cameroon
207 H5 Foumbot Cameroon
217 □3a Foumbouni Njazidja Comoros
204 D3 Foum Zguid Morocco
262 T1 Foundation Ice Stream glacier Antarctica
206 A3 Foundiougne Senegal
207 F4 Founougo Benin
232 B12 Fount KY U.S.A.
226 B6 Fountain MN U.S.A.
147 D7 Fountain Cross Ireland
241 U2 Fountain Green UT U.S.A.
234 E3 Fountain Hill PA U.S.A.
149 N5 Fountains Abbey and Royal Water Garden (NT) tourist site England U.K.
184 E6 Foupana r. Port.
162 B4 Fouras France
163 E8 Fourcès France
160 C2 Fourchambault France
157 K7 Fourches, Mont des hill France
240 O7 Four Corners CA U.S.A.
151 M5 Four Elms Kent, England U.K.
215 M4 Fouriesburg S. Africa
151 J5 Four Marks Hampshire, England U.K.
156 H3 Fourmies France
220 B4 Four Mountains, Islands of the AK U.S.A.
161 C7 Fournels France
80 □ Fournier, Cape Chatham Is S. Pacific Ocean
225 H3 Fournier, Lac l. Que. Can.
199 H5 Fournoi Greece
199 H5 Fournoi i. Greece
151 N6 Four Oaks East Sussex, England U.K.
246 □ Four Paths Jamaica
161 F9 Fourques Languedoc-Roussillon France
163 J10 Fourques Languedoc-Roussillon France
163 E7 Fourques-sur-Garonne France
247 □7 Four Roads Trin. and Tob.
160 D3 Fours France
226 E3 Fourteen Mile Point MI U.S.A.
206 B4 Fouta Djallon reg. Guinea
81 B13 Foveaux Strait South I. N.Z.
234 B5 Fowbelsburg MD U.S.A.
150 C7 Fowey Cornwall, England U.K.
150 C7 Fowey r. England U.K.
231 I13 Fowl Cay i. Bahamas
240 M5 Fowler CA U.S.A.
239 L7 Fowler CO U.S.A.
230 D5 Fowler IN U.S.A.
226 J6 Fowler MI U.S.A.
262 S1 Fowler Ice Rise Antarctica
82 D4 Fowlers Bay S.A. Austr.
82 D5 Fowlers Bay b. S.A. Austr.
227 J7 Fowlerville MI U.S.A.
127 N5 Fowman Iran
150 G3 Fownhope Herefordshire, England U.K.
222 E3 Fox r. B.C. Can.
223 M3 Fox r. Man. Can.
226 F8 Fox r. IL U.S.A.
226 E6 Fox r. WI U.S.A.
85 K7 Fox Creek r. Qld Austr.
222 G4 Fox Creek Alta Can.
148 H5 Foxdale Isle of Man
221 K3 Foxe Basin g. Nunavut Can.
221 J3 Foxe Channel Nunavut Can.
142 H2 Foxen l. Sweden
221 K3 Foxe Peninsula Nunavut Can.
147 D5 Foxford Ireland
81 E10 Fox Glacier South I. N.Z.
220 B4 Fox Islands AK U.S.A.
222 H3 Fox Lake Alta Can.
226 F7 Fox Lake IL U.S.A.
222 C2 Fox Mountain Y.T. Can.
238 K6 Foxpark WY U.S.A.
80 J7 Foxton North I. N.Z.
80 J7 Foxton Beach North I. N.Z.
223 I5 Fox Valley Sask. Can.
146 H8 Foyers Highland, Scotland U.K.
148 B6 Foygh Ireland
147 H3 Foyle r. Ireland/U.K.
147 H2 Foyle, Lough b. Ireland/U.K.
147 D7 Foynes Ireland
184 C2 Foz Port.
182 F1 Foz Spain
255 C8 Foz de Areia, Represa de resr Brazil
250 D6 Foz de Gregório Brazil
184 A2 Foz do Arelho Port.
251 F5 Foz do Copeá Brazil
209 A9 Foz do Cunene Angola
255 B8 Foz do Iguaçu Brazil
252 E2 Foz do Jamari Brazil
252 C2 Foz do Jordão Brazil
250 E5 Foz do Jutaí Brazil
250 E5 Foz do Mamoriá Brazil
252 C1 Foz do Riosinho Brazil
182 E9 Foz Giraldo Port.
190 D7 Frabosa Soprana Italy
175 L2 Frącki Pol.
227 R9 Frackville PA U.S.A.
182 I7 Frades de la Sierra Spain
260 E3 Fraga Arg.
186 F4 Fraga Spain
195 M3 Fragagnano Italy
179 J3 Fraham Austria
258 G4 Fraile Muerto Uru.
185 L6 Frailes Spain
165 G8 Fraire Belgium
160 H2 Fraisans France
161 B9 Fraisse-sur-Agout France
157 N7 Fraize France
262 Q1 Frakes, Mount Antarctica
165 E8 Frameries Belgium
151 M6 Framfield East Sussex, England U.K.
233 N6 Framingham MA U.S.A.
151 O3 Framlingham Suffolk, England U.K.
143 M1 Främlingshem Sweden
169 H10 Frammersbach Ger.
263 E2 Framnes Mountains Antarctica
263 D2 Fram Peak Antarctica
175 K5 Frampol Pol.
151 L2 Frampton Lincolnshire, England U.K.
150 H4 Frampton on Severn Gloucestershire, England U.K.
256 D4 Franca Brazil
78 □5 Français, Récif des rf New Caledonia
193 M3 Francavilla al Mare Italy
195 I8 Francavilla di Sicilia Sicilia Italy
195 N2 Francavilla Fontana Italy
193 Q7 Francavilla in Sinni Italy
154 F3 France country Europe
221 Q2 France, Île de i. Greenland
82 H7 Frances S.A. Austr.
222 D2 Frances r. Y.T. Can.
246 B3 Francés, Punta pt Cuba
163 E7 Francescas France
216 □3d Franceses La Palma Canary Is
192 C5 Francesi, Punta di li pt Sardegna Italy
222 D2 Frances Lake Y.T. Can.
222 D2 Frances Lake l. Y.T. Can.
226 H9 Francesville IN U.S.A.
208 B5 Franceville Gabon
157 K8 Franche-Comté admin. reg. France
261 I3 Francia Uru.
182 H7 Francia, Peña de mt. Spain
223 K5 Francis Sask. Can.
Francis atoll Gilbert Is Kiribati see Beru
233 N3 Francis, Lake NH U.S.A.
Francisco de Orellana Ecuador see Coca
250 C5 Francisco de Orellana Peru
245 N9 Francisco I. Madero Chiapas Mex.
242 H5 Francisco I. Madero Coahuila Mex.
244 C1 Francisco I. Madero Durango Mex.
244 C4 Francisco I. Madero Nayarit Mex.
261 H5 Francisco Meeks Arg.
257 F2 Francisco Sá Brazil
242 A1 Francisco Zarco Mex.
213 E4 Francistown Botswana
182 F6 Franco Port.
256 D5 Franco da Rocha Brazil
194 H9 Francofonte Sicilia Italy
225 J4 Francois Nfld and Lab. Can.
222 E4 François Lake B.C. Can.
87 B8 Francois Peron National Park W.A. Austr.
234 A7 Franconia VA U.S.A.
165 I8 Francorchamps Belgium
163 G6 Francoulès France
238 J5 Francs Peak WY U.S.A.
164 I2 Franeker Neth.
160 H4 Frangy France
169 G8 Frankenau Ger.
171 H9 Frankenberg Ger.
169 G8 Frankenberg (Eder) Ger.
179 H3 Frankenburg am Hausruck Austria
179 L4 Frankenfels Austria
169 K9 Frankenhain Ger.
169 J9 Frankenheim Ger.
173 I3 Frankenhöhe park Ger.
179 H4 Frankenmarkt Austria
227 K6 Frankenmuth MI U.S.A.
172 E2 Frankenthal (Pfalz) Ger.
171 E10 Frankenwald mts Ger.
171 E10 Frankenwald park Ger.
246 □ Frankfield Jamaica
227 Q5 Frankford Ont. Can.
215 M3 Frankfort S. Africa
230 D5 Frankfort IN U.S.A.
230 E6 Frankfort KY U.S.A.
226 H5 Frankfort MI U.S.A.
232 B9 Frankfort OH U.S.A.
Frankfurt Ger. see Frankfurt am Main
169 G10 Frankfurt am Main Ger.
171 K6 Frankfurt an der Oder Ger.
87 F12 Frank Hann National Park W.A. Austr.
241 Q1 Frankin Lake NV U.S.A.
173 J4 Fränkische Alb hills Ger.
173 K3 Fränkische Rezat r. Ger.
169 I10 Fränkische Saale r. Ger.
173 K2 Fränkische Schweiz reg. Ger.
171 D10 Fränkische Schweiz Veldensteiner Forst park Ger.
87 D13 Frankland r. W.A. Austr.
83 K8 Frankland, Cape Tas. Austr.
150 H3 Frankley Worcestershire, England U.K.
215 N6 Franklin S. Africa
241 W9 Franklin AZ U.S.A.
231 E9 Franklin GA U.S.A.
230 D6 Franklin IN U.S.A.
230 D7 Franklin KY U.S.A.
237 J11 Franklin LA U.S.A.
233 N6 Franklin MA U.S.A.
233 □Q4 Franklin ME U.S.A.
231 F8 Franklin NC U.S.A.
236 F5 Franklin NE U.S.A.
233 N5 Franklin NH U.S.A.
234 F2 Franklin NJ U.S.A.
232 A9 Franklin OH U.S.A.
232 F7 Franklin PA U.S.A.
231 D8 Franklin TN U.S.A.
237 G10 Franklin TX U.S.A.
232 I12 Franklin VA U.S.A.
226 F7 Franklin WI U.S.A.
232 F10 Franklin WV U.S.A.
220 F3 Franklin Bay N.W.T. Can.
234 A4 Franklinburg PA U.S.A.
228 C1 Franklin D. Roosevelt Lake resr WA U.S.A.
232 C10 Franklin Furnace OH U.S.A.
83 J10 Franklin-Gordon National Park Tas. Austr.
226 E8 Franklin Grove IL U.S.A.
82 F5 Franklin Harbor b. S.A. Austr.
263 L1 Franklin Island Antarctica
222 F2 Franklin Mountains N.W.T. Can.
81 B11 Franklin Mountains South I. N.Z.
234 F4 Franklin Park NJ U.S.A.
83 K9 Franklin Sound sea chan. Tas. Austr.
235 H3 Franklin Square NY U.S.A.
221 I2 Franklin Strait Nunavut Can.
237 J10 Franklinton LA U.S.A.
234 E5 Franklinville NJ U.S.A.
232 G6 Franklinville NY U.S.A.
175 I1 Frankowo Pol.
140 L5 Frankrike Sweden
83 J8 Frankston Vic. Austr.
81 C12 Frankton South I. N.Z.
160 H2 Franois France
214 G5 Fransenhof S. Africa
212 B4 Fransfontein Namibia
221 Q2 Franske Øer is Greenland
141 N5 Fränsta Sweden
176 B1 Františkovy Lázně Czech Rep.
130 G2 Frantsa-Iosifa, Zemlya is Rus. Fed.
224 C3 Franz Ont. Can.
170 G2 Franzburg Ger.
81 E10 Franz Josef Glacier South I. N.Z.
Franz Josef Land is Rus. Fed. see Frantsa-Iosifa, Zemlya
173 L5 Franz Josef Strauss airport Ger.
192 A8 Frasca, Capo della c. Sardegna Italy
194 H9 Frasca, Monte hill Italy
193 J4 Frascati Italy
193 Q8 Frascineto Italy
173 M6 Frasdorf Ger.
86 G4 Fraser r. W.A. Austr.
222 F5 Fraser r. B.C. Can.
225 I1 Fraser r. Nfld and Lab. Can.
87 E8 Fraser, Mount hill W.A. Austr.
214 F7 Fraserburg S. Africa
146 L7 Fraserburgh Aberdeenshire, Scotland U.K.
224 D3 Fraserdale Ont. Can.
85 N8 Fraser Island Qld Austr.
87 B7 Fraser Island W.A. Austr.
85 N8 Fraser Island National Park Qld Austr.
222 E4 Fraser Lake B.C. Can.
83 J7 Fraser National Park Vic. Austr.
222 E4 Fraser Plateau B.C. Can.
87 G12 Fraser Range W.A. Austr.
87 G12 Fraser Range hills W.A. Austr.
80 L5 Frasertown North I. N.Z.
160 I3 Frasne France
160 I3 Frasne, Étang de lag. France
165 E7 Frasnes-lez-Buissenal Belgium
165 F7 Frasnes-lez-Gosselies Belgium
191 J7 Frassinoro Italy
193 N5 Frasso Telesino Italy
178 A5 Frastanz Austria
182 E9 Fratel Port.
194 H7 Fratello r. Sicilia Italy
226 J2 Frater Ont. Can.
197 N7 Frăteşti Romania
191 L5 Fratta r. Italy
191 L5 Fratta Polesine Italy
193 I2 Fratta Todina Italy
190 D1 Fraubrunnen Switz.
173 O4 Frauenau Ger.
190 F1 Frauenfeld Switz.
179 O4 Frauenkirchen Austria
171 I9 Frauenstein Ger.
179 L6 Frauental an der Laßnitz Austria
169 K9 Frauenwald Ger.
173 L5 Fraunberg Ger.
171 F9 Fraureuth Ger.
261 H3 Fray Bentos Uru.
260 E6 Fray Luis Beltrán Río Negro Arg.
261 G3 Fray Luis Beltrán Santa Fé Arg.
258 G4 Fray Marcos Uru.
163 G6 Frayssinet-le-Gélat France
234 D4 Frazer PA U.S.A.
232 C8 Frazeysburg OH U.S.A.
86 F5 Frazier Downs Aboriginal Reserve W.A. Austr.
240 N7 Frazier Park CA U.S.A.
182 D6 Freamunde Port.
197 Q6 Frecăţei Romania
161 C9 Frech, Mont mt. France
182 F6 Frechas Port.
169 C9 Frechen Ger.
183 K4 Frechilla Spain
149 L6 Freckleton Lancashire, England U.K.
169 I7 Freden (Leine) Ger.
168 H3 Fredenbeck Ger.
226 J5 Frederic MI U.S.A.
226 B4 Frederic WI U.S.A.
234 E6 Frederica DE U.S.A.
142 F6 Fredericia Denmark
87 D8 Frederick r. W.A. Austr.
232 H9 Frederick MD U.S.A.
237 F8 Frederick OK U.S.A.
221 O1 Frederick E. Hyde Fjord inlet Greenland
84 E2 Frederick Hills N.T. Austr.
224 D3 Frederick House Lake Ont. Can.
226 B7 Fredericksburg IA U.S.A.
234 C4 Fredericksburg PA U.S.A.
237 F10 Fredericksburg TX U.S.A.
232 H10 Fredericksburg VA U.S.A.
222 C3 Frederick Sound sea chan. AK U.S.A.
237 J7 Fredericktown MO U.S.A.
232 C8 Fredericktown OH U.S.A.
225 H4 Fredericton N.B. Can.
233 □S3 Fredericton Junction N.B. Can.
142 I6 Frederiksborg county Denmark
Frederikshåb Greenland see Paamiut
142 G4 Frederikshavn Denmark
142 I6 Frederikssund Denmark
247 K5 Frederiksted Virgin Is (U.S.A.)
142 I6 Frederiksværk Denmark
170 I5 Fredersdorf Ger.
241 T5 Fredonia AZ U.S.A.
237 H7 Fredonia KS U.S.A.
232 F6 Fredonia NY U.S.A.
232 E7 Fredonia PA U.S.A.
226 G6 Fredonia WI U.S.A.
140 O4 Fredrika Sweden
143 K1 Fredriksberg Sweden
Fredrikshamn Fin. see Hamina
142 G2 Fredrikstad Norway
Fredriksvern Norway see Stavern
175 K6 Fredropol Pol.
234 B3 Freeburg PA U.S.A.
233 K8 Freehold NJ U.S.A.
234 D2 Freeland PA U.S.A.
82 G6 Freeling S.A. Austr.
84 D7 Freeling, Mount hill N.T. Austr.
82 G4 Freeling Heights hill S.A. Austr.
240 M3 Freel Peak CA U.S.A.
225 K3 Freels, Cape Nfld and Lab. Can.
236 G4 Freeman SD U.S.A.
226 H9 Freeman, Lake IN U.S.A.
234 E3 Freemansburg PA U.S.A.
140 □ Freemansundet sea chan. Svalbard
231 D10 Freeport FL U.S.A.
226 E7 Freeport IL U.S.A.
233 □O5 Freeport ME U.S.A.
235 H3 Freeport NY U.S.A.
232 F8 Freeport PA U.S.A.
237 H11 Freeport TX U.S.A.
231 H12 Freeport City Gd Bahama Bahamas
237 F12 Freer TX U.S.A.
226 H5 Freesoil MI U.S.A.
215 K4 Free State prov. S. Africa
247 □2 Freetown Antigua and Barbuda
206 B4 Freetown Sierra Leone
235 K3 Freetown NY U.S.A.
235 G4 Freewood Acres NJ U.S.A.
217 □2a Frégate i. Inner Islands Seychelles
224 F2 Frégate, Lac de la l. Que. Can.
217 □2a Frégate, L'Îlot i. Inner Islands Seychelles
184 F4 Fregenal de la Sierra Spain
192 I4 Fregene Italy
186 G6 Freginals Spain
82 D2 Fregon S.A. Austr.
158 G4 Fréhel France
158 G4 Fréhel, Cap c. France
171 H9 Freiberg Ger.
171 G8 Freiberger Mulde r. Ger.
172 E6 Freiburg admin. reg. Ger.
Freiburg Switz. see Fribourg
168 H3 Freiburg (Elbe) Ger.
172 D5 Freiburg im Breisgau Ger.
169 H10 Freiensteinau Ger.
168 H1 Freienwill Ger.
257 G2 Frei Gonzaga Brazil
173 L2 Freihung Ger.
257 G3 Frei Inocêncio Brazil
185 N5 Freila Spain
173 N6 Freilassing Ger.
172 E2 Freinsheim Ger.
260 A6 Freire Chile
172 C2 Freisen Ger.
173 L5 Freising Ger.
161 J7 Freissinières France
179 K2 Freistadt Austria
157 L5 Freistroff France
171 I9 Freital Ger.
182 F7 Freixedas Port.
182 D9 Freixianda Port.
182 F6 Freixiel Port.
182 E7 Freixiosa Port.
182 C5 Freixo Port.
182 G6 Freixo de Espada à Cinta Port.
163 I8 Fréjairolles France
161 J10 Fréjus France
161 J10 Fréjus, Golfe de b. France
161 J6 Fréjus Tunnel France/Italy
142 B1 Frekhaug Norway
169 K6 Frellstedt Ger.
87 C12 Fremantle W.A. Austr.
173 I4 Fremdingen Ger.
150 D5 Fremington Devon, England U.K.
240 K4 Fremont CA U.S.A.
226 J8 Fremont IN U.S.A.
226 I6 Fremont MI U.S.A.
236 G5 Fremont NE U.S.A.
232 B7 Fremont OH U.S.A.
226 F5 Fremont WI U.S.A.
241 V3 Fremont r. UT U.S.A.
241 U3 Fremont Junction UT U.S.A.
232 B11 Frenchburg KY U.S.A.
246 G3 French Cay i. Turks and Caicos Is
French Congo country Africa see Congo
232 F7 French Creek r. PA U.S.A.
251 H4 French Guiana terr. S. America
French Guinea country Africa see Guinea
83 J8 French Island Vic. Austr.
238 K2 Frenchman r. MT U.S.A.
233 □Q4 Frenchman Bay ME U.S.A.
236 E5 Frenchman Creek r. NE U.S.A.
240 L2 Frenchman Lake CA U.S.A.
241 Q5 Frenchman Lake NV U.S.A.
81 H7 French Pass South I. N.Z.
79 □9 French Polynesia terr. S. Pacific Ocean
French Somaliland country Africa see Djibouti
73 G6 French Southern and Antarctic Lands terr. Indian Ocean
French Sudan country Africa see Mali
French Territory of the Afars and Issas country Africa see Djibouti
234 E3 Frenchtown NJ U.S.A.
233 □Q1 Frenchville ME U.S.A.
156 C2 Frencq France
205 F2 Frenda Alg.
156 C5 Freneuse France
173 J2 Frensdorf Ger.
151 K5 Frensham Surrey, England U.K.
177 H2 Frenštát pod Radhoštěm Czech Rep.
193 M4 Frentani, Monti dei mts Italy
215 N4 Frere S. Africa
169 E6 Freren Ger.
179 I6 Fresach Austria
193 N4 Fresagrandinaria Italy
251 I6 Fresco r. Brazil
206 D5 Fresco Côte d'Ivoire
263 K2 Freshfield, Cape Antarctica
147 H7 Freshford Ireland
151 J6 Freshwater Isle of Wight, England U.K.
150 C4 Freshwater East Pembrokeshire, Wales U.K.
156 C7 Fresnay-l'Évêque France
159 L5 Fresnay-sur-Sarthe France
185 L3 Fresnedas r. Spain
185 J4 Fresnedillas hill Spain
160 H1 Fresne-St-Mamès France
157 K5 Fresnes-en-Woëvre France
157 K8 Fresnes-sur-Apance France
156 G3 Fresnes-sur-Escaut France
244 E2 Fresnillo Mex.
244 G5 Fresno Mex.
240 M5 Fresno CA U.S.A.
240 L5 Fresno r. CA U.S.A.
182 I7 Fresno Alhándiga Spain
182 I5 Fresno de la Ribera Spain
182 I6 Fresno de Sayago Spain
183 J6 Fresno el Viejo Spain
156 B4 Fresnoy-Folny France
156 F4 Fresnoy-le-Grand France
224 F2 Fressel, Lac l. Que. Can.
156 C3 Fressenneville France
157 M8 Fresse-sur-Moselle France
151 O3 Fressingfield Suffolk, England U.K.
141 I6 Fresvikbreen glacier Norway
146 J5 Freswick Highland, Scotland U.K.
160 H2 Fretigney-et-Velloreille France
187 L8 Freu, Cap des c. Spain
172 G2 Freudenberg Baden-Württemberg Ger.
173 L3 Freudenberg Bayern Ger.
169 E9 Freudenberg Nordrhein-Westfalen Ger.
172 B2 Freudenburg Ger.
172 E5 Freudenstadt Ger.
156 D3 Frévent France
84 E6 Frew watercourse N.T. Austr.
232 F6 Frewsburg NY U.S.A.
171 E8 Freyburg (Unstrut) Ger.
87 B9 Freycinet Estuary inlet W.A. Austr.
83 L10 Freycinet Peninsula Tas. Austr.
170 F4 Freyenstein Ger.
157 M5 Freyming-Merlebach France
261 F2 Freyre Arg.
173 K3 Freystadt Ger.
173 P4 Freyung Ger.
206 B4 Fria Guinea
212 B3 Fria, Cape Namibia
244 E4 Fria, Sierra mts Mex.
240 M5 Friant CA U.S.A.
240 M6 Friant-Kern Canal CA U.S.A.
258 D3 Frías Arg.
183 N3 Frías Spain
190 C2 Fribourg Switz.
190 C2 Fribourg canton Switz.
190 E1 Frick Switz.
172 G6 Frickingen Ger.
238 C2 Friday Harbor WA U.S.A.
149 P5 Fridaythorpe East Riding of Yorkshire, England U.K.
172 F5 Fridingen an der Donau Ger.
173 N6 Fridolfing Ger.
262 M1 Fridtjof Nansen, Mount Antarctica
169 J8 Frieda (Meinhard) Ger.
179 N5 Friedberg Austria
173 J5 Friedberg Ger.
169 G10 Friedberg (Hessen) Ger.
168 E4 Friedeburg Ger.
171 E7 Friedeburg (Saale) Ger.
173 M2 Friedenfels Ger.
232 G8 Friedens PA U.S.A.
234 C3 Friedensburg PA U.S.A.
172 E6 Friedenweiler Ger.
171 I6 Friedersdorf Brandenburg Ger.
171 F7 Friedersdorf Sachsen-Anhalt Ger.
169 I9 Friedewald Hessen Ger.
169 E9 Friedewald Rheinland-Pfalz Ger.
171 J6 Friedland Brandenburg Ger.
170 I3 Friedland Mecklenburg-Vorpommern Ger.
169 I8 Friedland Niedersachsen Ger.
Friedland Rus. Fed. see Pravdinsk
169 K9 Friedrichroda Ger.
171 D7 Friedrichsbrunn Ger.
169 G10 Friedrichsdorf Ger.
172 H6 Friedrichshafen Ger.
171 K7 Friedrichshain Ger.
171 D6 Friedrichskanal canal Ger.
168 G2 Friedrichskoog Ger.
170 E3 Friedrichsruhe Ger.
168 H2 Friedrichstadt Ger.
170 H5 Friedrichsthal Ger.
170 I4 Friedrichswalde Ger.
169 H9 Frielendorf Ger.
169 K9 Friemar Ger.
236 G5 Friend NE U.S.A.
Friendly Islands country S. Pacific Ocean see Tonga
246 □ Friendship Jamaica
232 G6 Friendship NY U.S.A.
224 B5 Friendship WI U.S.A.
232 E12 Fries VA U.S.A.
179 J6 Friesach Austria
170 G5 Friesack Ger.
169 E9 Friesenhagen Ger.
172 D5 Friesenheim Ger.
173 J6 Friesenried Ger.
164 I2 Friese Wad tidal flat Neth.
164 I2 Friesland prov. Neth.
168 E4 Friesoythe Ger.
Frigate Island Inner Islands Seychelles see Frégate
141 N6 Friggesund Sweden
185 L7 Frigiliana Spain
191 J7 Frignano reg. Italy
156 I6 Frignicourt France
151 K5 Frimley Surrey, England U.K.
78 □6 Frindsbury Reef Solomon Is
151 O4 Frinton-on-Sea Essex, England U.K.
237 F11 Frio r. TX U.S.A.
237 F11 Frio r. TX U.S.A.
237 D8 Frio watercourse NM/TX U.S.A.
146 K9 Friockheim Angus, Scotland U.K.
182 E2 Friol Spain
146 D9 Frisa, Loch l. Scotland U.K.
165 J9 Frisange Lux.
239 K7 Frisco CO U.S.A.
241 S3 Frisco Mountain UT U.S.A.
149 R7 Friskney Lincolnshire, England U.K.
233 L6 Frissell, Mount hill CT U.S.A.
150 D6 Frithelstock Stone Devon, England U.K.
142 I4 Fritsla Sweden
178 E5 Fritzens Austria
169 H8 Fritzlar Ger.
191 O3 Friuli-Venezia Giulia admin. reg. Italy
156 C3 Friville-Escarbotin France
149 K4 Frizington Cumbria, England U.K.
234 A5 Frizzellburg MD U.S.A.
140 J4 Froan nature res. Norway
140 J5 Froan park Norway
Frobisher Bay Nunavut Can. see Iqaluit
221 L3 Frobisher Bay b. Nunavut Can.
223 I3 Frobisher Lake Sask. Can.
142 G6 Frøbjerg Bavnehøj hill Denmark
178 B7 Frodolfo r. Italy
149 L7 Frodsham Cheshire, England U.K.
157 O6 Frœschwiller France
161 H6 Froges France
151 K5 Frogmore Hampshire, England U.K.
140 J5 Frohavet b. Norway
171 G8 Frohburg Ger.
172 H2 Frohnberg hill Ger.
179 L5 Frohnleiten Austria
157 L8 Froideconche France
156 D4 Froissy France
135 H6 Frolovo Rus. Fed.
134 K3 Frolovskaya Rus. Fed.
143 P7 Frombork Pol.
82 F3 Frome watercourse S.A. Austr.
246 □ Frome Jamaica
150 H5 Frome Somerset, England U.K.
150 H6 Frome r. England U.K.
82 G4 Frome, Lake salt flat S.A. Austr.
82 G4 Frome Downs S.A. Austr.
157 I3 Fromelennes France
156 G6 Fromentières France
158 G8 Fromentine France
183 L4 Frómista Spain
158 A5 Fromveur, Passage du str. France
157 J7 Froncles France
169 E8 Fröndenberg Ger.
169 G9 Fronhausen Ger.
163 D6 Fronsac Aquitaine France
163 F10 Fronsac Midi-Pyrénées France
184 D2 Fronteira Port.
254 E3 Fronteiras Brazil
160 G3 Frontenard France
162 C3 Frontenay-Rohan-Rohan France
173 N4 Frontenhausen Ger.
216 □3e Frontera El Hierro Canary Is
243 I4 Frontera Coahuila Mex.
243 M8 Frontera Tabasco Mex.
243 M8 Frontera, Punta pt Mex.
242 E2 Fronteras Mex.
161 D10 Frontignan France
163 G8 Fronton France
247 □1 Frontón de la Brea pt Puerto Rico
232 G10 Front Royal VA U.S.A.
171 D7 Frose Ger.
193 K4 Frosinone Italy
193 K4 Frosinone prov. Italy
193 M4 Frosolone Italy
140 K5 Frosta Norway
232 G9 Frostburg MD U.S.A.
263 I2 Frost Glacier Antarctica
157 L6 Frouard France
182 D1 Frouxeira, Punta da pt Spain
143 L2 Frövi Sweden
140 J5 Frøya i. Norway
156 E5 Froyéres France
156 D2 Fruges France
241 X2 Fruita CO U.S.A.
233 J10 Fruitland MD U.S.A.
241 V1 Fruitland UT U.S.A.
81 D12 Fruitlands South I. N.Z.
226 H6 Fruitport MI U.S.A.
241 X2 Fruitvale CO U.S.A.
139 W7 Fruktovaya Rus. Fed.
183 L6 Frumales Spain
121 N7 Frunze Batken Kyrg.
Frunze Bishkek Kyrg. see Bishkek
137 N7 Frunze Khersons'ka Oblast' Ukr.
137 N7 Frunze Khersons'ka Oblast' Ukr.
137 N9 Frunzens'ke Ukr.
Frunzenskoye Kyrg. see Frunze
136 I6 Frunzivka Ukr.
Frusino Italy see Frosinone
196 H5 Fruška Gora hills Serbia
196 H5 Fruska Gora nat. park Serbia
256 C4 Frutal Brazil
190 D2 Frutigen Switz.
259 B6 Frutillar Chile
253 E3 Frutuoso Brazil
139 V5 Fryanovo Rus. Fed.
139 V6 Fryazino Rus. Fed.
177 H2 Frýdek-Místek Czech Rep.
176 E1 Frýdlant Czech Rep.
233 □O4 Fryeburg ME U.S.A.
151 M4 Fryerning Essex, England U.K.
175 I2 Frygnowo Pol.
176 D3 Frymburk Czech Rep.
177 G2 Fryšták Czech Rep.
175 J6 Frysztak Pol.
79 □8a Fua'amotu Tongatapu Tonga
109 L5 Fu'an Fujian China
146 F9 Fuar Bheinn hill Scotland U.K.
190 E6 Fubine Italy
191 J8 Fucecchio Italy
Fucheng Anhui China see Fengyang
Fucheng Shaanxi China see Fuxian
173 M2 Fuchsmühl Ger.
173 J6 Fuchstal Ger.
103 K12 Fuchū Hiroshima Japan
105 J4 Fuchu Japan
104 F2 Fuchū Toyama Japan
109 H6 Fuchuan Guangxi China
109 M3 Fuchun Jiang r. China
193 K2 Fucino r. Italy
102 S6 Fudai Japan
146 B8 Fuday i. Scotland U.K.
109 K6 Fude Fujian China
109 M5 Fuding Fujian China
211 C5 Fudua waterhole Kenya
125 H4 Fudul reg. Saudi Arabia
216 □3d Fuencaliente La Palma Canary Is
185 K4 Fuencaliente Spain
216 □3d Fuencaliente, Punta de pt La Palma Canary Is
183 R5 Fuendejalón Spain
185 J7 Fuengirola Spain
183 M8 Fuenlabrada Spain
185 J2 Fuenlabrada de los Montes Spain
183 O4 Fuenmayor Spain
183 L8 Fuensalida Spain
185 O2 Fuensanta Castilla-La Mancha Spain
185 P5 Fuensanta Murcia Spain
185 O4 Fuensanta, Embalse de la resr Spain
187 C10 Fuente-Álamo Spain
187 C12 Fuente Álamo Spain
185 P3 Fuente Albilla, Cerro de mt. Spain
183 N5 Fuentearmegil Spain
183 N5 Fuentecambrón Spain
183 M5 Fuentecén Spain
184 G4 Fuente de Cantos Spain
184 H4 Fuente del Arco Spain
184 G3 Fuente del Maestre Spain
183 N9 Fuente de Pedro Naharro Spain
185 J6 Fuente de Piedra Spain
185 J6 Fuente de Piedra, Laguna de l. Spain
185 L2 Fuente el Fresno Spain
183 K6 Fuente el Sol Spain
182 G8 Fuenteguinaldo Spain
Fuente la Higuera Spain see La Font de la Figuera
183 J6 Fuentelapeña Spain
183 M5 Fuentelcésped Spain
183 O9 Fuentelespino de Haro Spain
183 R9 Fuentelespino de Moya Spain
183 P6 Fuentelmonge Spain
185 I4 Fuente Obejuna Spain
185 I5 Fuente Palmera Spain
183 L6 Fuentepelayo Spain
183 O5 Fuentepinilla Spain
186 D5 Fuenterodos Spain
Fuenterrabía Spain see Hondarribia
183 M6 Fuenterrebollo Spain
182 I7 Fuenterroble de Salvatierra Spain
185 I1 Fuente Santa mt. Spain
183 J6 Fuentesaúco Spain
183 L6 Fuentesaúco de Fuentidueña Spain
186 C6 Fuentes-Claras Spain
185 I6 Fuentes de Andalucía Spain
186 D4 Fuentes de Ebro Spain
183 Q6 Fuentes de Jiloca Spain
184 F4 Fuentes de León Spain
183 K4 Fuentes de Nava Spain
182 G7 Fuentes de Oñoro Spain
183 L4 Fuentes de Valdepero Spain
186 F6 Fuentespalda Spain
183 Q4 Fuentestrún r. Spain
185 K5 Fuente-Tójar Spain
185 L6 Fuente Vaqueros Spain
183 M6 Fuentidueña Spain
100 F7 Fu'er He r. China
185 L5 Fuerte del Rey Spain
253 F5 Fuerte Olimpo Para.
183 P8 Fuertescusa Spain
216 □3b Fuerteventura i. Canary Is
92 C2 Fuga i. Phil.
178 E5 Fügen Austria
178 E5 Fügenberg Austria
144 D1 Fugloy i. Faroe Is
140 L4 Fuglstad Norway
108 B5 Fugong Yunnan China
109 J2 Fugou Henan China
107 L7 Fugu Shaanxi China
Fuguo Shandong China see Zhanhua
110 H3 Fuhai Xinjiang China
110 I3 Fuhai Linchang Xinjiang China
127 K6 Fuḩaymī Iraq
171 F7 Fuhne r. Ger.
168 I5 Fuhrberg (Burgwedel) Ger.
Fujairah U.A.E. see Al Fujayrah
Fujeira U.A.E. see Al Fujayrah
Fuji Sichuan China see Xiaoshi
Fuji Sichuan China see Luxian
105 I5 Fuji Japan
109 K6 Fujian prov. China
108 F4 Fu Jiang r. Sichuan China
105 H6 Fujieda Japan
105 K7 Fuji-Hakone-Izu Kokuritsu-kōen nat. park Japan
104 D4 Fujihashi Japan
104 C6 Fujiidera Japan
105 I5 Fujikawa Japan
105 I5 Fuji-kawa r. Japan
105 H4 Fujimi Nagano Japan
105 K4 Fujimi Saitama Japan
100 G5 Fujin Heilong. China
105 J4 Fujino Japan
105 I5 Fujinomiya Japan
104 F5 Fujioka Aichi Japan
105 J3 Fujioka Gunma Japan
105 K3 Fujioka Tochigi Japan
105 I5 Fuji-san vol. Japan
105 J5 Fujisawa Japan
105 L4 Fujishiro Japan
104 E5 Fujiwara Mie Japan
105 K2 Fujiwara Tochigi Japan
105 I5 Fujiyoshida Japan
102 T3 Fukagawa Japan
126 C8 Fūkah Egypt
110 H4 Fukang Xinjiang China
102 Q6 Fukaura Japan
79 □8a Fukave i. Tonga
105 J3 Fukaya Japan
100 B2 Fukeshan Heilong. China
105 J3 Fukiage Japan
Fukien prov. China see Fujian
104 B5 Fukuchiyama Japan
105 G6 Fukude Japan
103 F14 Fukue Japan
103 F14 Fukue-jima i. Japan
104 D3 Fukui Japan
104 D4 Fukui pref. Japan
104 E2 Fukumitsu Japan
104 E2 Fukuno Japan
103 H13 Fukuoka Fukuoka Japan
104 F4 Fukuoka Gifu Japan
104 E2 Fukuoka Toyama Japan
103 H13 Fukuoka pref. Japan
105 G6 Fukuroi Japan
104 A6 Fukusaki Japan
102 R9 Fukushima Fukushima Japan
102 R5 Fukushima Hokkaidō Japan
105 L1 Fukushima pref. Japan
103 H15 Fukuyama Japan
128 A9 Fūl, Jabal hill Egypt
206 B4 Fulacunda Guinea-Bissau
122 E3 Fūlād Maïalleh Iran
125 N4 Fulayj Oman
151 M3 Fulbourn Cambridgeshire, England U.K.
117 L7 Fulchhari Bangl.
169 I9 Fulda Ger.
169 I8 Fulda r. Ger.
108 E6 Fule Yunnan China
149 O6 Fulford York, England U.K.
151 L5 Fulham Greater London, England U.K.
Fuli Heilong. China see Jixian
109 K2 Fuliji Anhui China
Fulin Sichuan China see Hanyuan
108 F4 Fuling Chongqing China
Fulitun Heilong. China see Jixian
85 H6 Fullarton r. Qld Austr.
247 □7 Fullarton Trin. and Tob.
240 O8 Fullerton CA U.S.A.
236 G5 Fullerton NE U.S.A.
223 N2 Fullerton, Cape Nunavut Can.
177 G2 Fulnek Czech Rep.
177 L4 Fülöp Hungary
177 I5 Fülöpháza Hungary
177 I5 Fülöpszállás Hungary
178 D5 Fulpmes Austria
261 H5 Fulton Arg.
236 J5 Fulton IL U.S.A.
237 K7 Fulton KY U.S.A.
234 B6 Fulton MD U.S.A.
236 J6 Fulton MO U.S.A.
237 K8 Fulton MS U.S.A.
232 I5 Fulton NY U.S.A.
141 L6 Fulufjällets national park nature res. Sweden
141 L6 Fulunäs Sweden
213 G5 Fumane Moz.
156 I4 Fumay France
163 F7 Fumel France
108 D6 Fumin Yunnan China
193 K4 Fumone Italy
105 K4 Funabashi Chiba Japan
104 F2 Funabashi Toyama Japan
77 H2 Funafuti atoll Tuvalu
109 J2 Funan Anhui China
Funan Guangxi China see Fusui
101 C8 Funan Liaoning China
140 L5 Funäsdalen Sweden
184 □ Funchal Madeira
246 F8 Fundación Col.
182 D9 Fundada Port.
257 G3 Fundão Brazil
182 F8 Fundão Port.
Fundi Italy see Fondi
242 E4 Fundición Mex.
206 □ Fundo das Figuerias Cape Verde
197 O6 Fundulea Romania
178 C5 Fundusfeiler mt. Austr
225 H4 Fundy, Bay of g. N.B./N
Fünen i. Denmark see
240 P5 Funeral Peak CA U.S.A.
191 L2 Funes Italy
Fünfkirchen Hungary se
109 □I7 Fung Wong Shan hill H China
213 G4 Funhalouro Moz.
109 L2 Funing Jiangsu China
108 E7 Funing Yunnan China
109 H2 Funiu Shan mts China
85 L7 Funnel Creek r. Qld Au
206 E4 Funsi Ghana
222 C3 Funter AK U.S.A.
207 G4 Funtua Nigeria
146 □O1 Funzie Shetland, Scotla
107 N7 Fuping Hebei China
108 G1 Fuping Shaanxi China
109 L6 Fuqing Fujian China
108 F5 Fuquan Guizhou China
143 L5 Fur Sweden
182 C7 Furadouro Port.
213 G2 Furancungo Moz.
102 T3 Furano Japan
100 F4 Furao Heilong. China
193 N3 Furci Italy
189 E7 Furci Siculo Sicilia Ital
102 W3 Füren-gawa r. Japan
102 W3 Füren-ko l. Japan
142 I6 Furesø l. Denmark
122 G8 Fürgun, Kūh-e mt. Ira
192 C2 Furiani Corse France
190 E2 Furkapass pass Switz.
234 E4 Furlong PA U.S.A.
139 Y4 Furmanov Rus. Fed.
Furmanovka Kazakh. s Moyynkum
Furmanovo Kazakh. se Zhalpaktal
100 I7 Furmanovo Rus. Fed.
146 F10 Furnace Argyll and But Scotland U.K.
234 B6 Furnace Branch MD U
216 □1b Furnas São Miguel Azc
187 I9 Furnás hill Spain
257 D4 Furnas, Represa resr
Furneaux atoll Arch. de Tuamotu Fr. Polynesia s Marutea (Nord)
83 L9 Furneaux Group is Tas
Furnes Belgium see Ve
Furong Jiangxi China s Wan'an
128 F4 Furqlus Syria
168 E5 Fürstenau Ger.
170 H4 Fürstenberg Brandenb
169 H7 Fürstenberg Niedersach
169 G8 Fürstenberg (Lichtenfe
179 N5 Fürstenfeld Austria
173 K5 Fürstenfeldbruck Ger.
173 O4 Fürstenstein Ger.
171 J6 Fürstenwalde Ger.
170 I4 Fürstenwerder Ger.
173 O4 Fürstenzell Ger.
177 K4 Furta Hungary
192 B8 Furtei Sardegna Italy
173 J3 Fürth Bayern Ger.
173 M4 Furth Ger.
172 F2 Fürth Hessen Ger.
179 M3 Furth bei Göttweig Au
173 N3 Furth im Wald Ger.
172 E5 Furtwangen im Schwa Ger.
102 R3 Furubira Japan
141 M6 Furudal Sweden
105 M1 Furudono Japan
104 F3 Furukawa Gifu Japan
102 R8 Furukawa Miyagi Japa
221 J3 Fury and Hecla Strait Nunavut Can.
250 C3 Fusagasugá Col.
Fusan S. Korea see Pu
193 Q9 Fuscaldo Italy
178 H4 Fuschlsee l. Austria
108 G9 Fushan Hainan China
107 Q8 Fushan Shandong Chir
107 L9 Fushan Shanxi China
196 H9 Fushë-Krujë Albania
104 C6 Fushimi Japan
Fushun Liaoning China Funan
107 R6 Fushun Liaoning China
108 E4 Fushun Sichuan China
78 □2 Fusi Samoa
79 □8 Fusi, Hakau rf Vava'u Tonga
191 L7 Fusignano Italy
179 I6 Fusine in Valromana
104 E5 Fuso Japan
100 E7 Fusong Jilin China
105 J4 Fussa Japan
190 H1 Fußach Austria
173 J6 Füssen Ger.
159 P7 Fussy France
183 R4 Fustiñana Spain
108 F7 Fusui Guangxi China
105 H4 Futaba Japan
104 F6 Futagawa Japan
103 I13 Futago-san vol. Japan
105 I3 Futago-yama mt. Japa
259 C6 Futaleufú Chile
104 E6 Futami Japan
103 □3 Futatsu-ne i. Japan
109 □J7 Fu Tau Pun Chau i. H. China
157 J5 Futeau France
196 H5 Futog Vojvodina Serbia
105 K5 Futtsu Japan
105 K5 Futtsu-misaki pt Japa
78 □5 Futuna i. Vanuatu
77 I3 Futuna, Île i. Wallis and Futuna Is
Futuna Islands Wallis and Futuna Is see Hoorn, Îles de
109 K5 Futun Xi r. China
161 H10 Fuveau France
125 J2 Fuwayriṭ Qatar
Fuxian Liaoning China Wafangdian
107 K9 Fuxian Shaanxi China
108 D6 Fuxian Hu l. China
107 Q5 Fuxin Liaoning China
107 Q5 Fuxin Liaoning China
Fuxing Guizhou China s Wangmo
Fuxinzhen Liaoning Ch Fuxin
102 Q8 Fuya Japan
109 J2 Fuyang Anhui China
Fuyang Guangxi China Fuchuan
109 L3 Fuyang Zhejiang China
107 O7 Fuyang He r. China
109 M5 Fuying Dao i. China
Fuyu Anhui China see S
107 S3 Fuyu Heilong. China
Fuyu Jilin China see So
100 E6 Fuyu Jilin China
100 I4 Fuyuan Heilong. China
108 E6 Fuyuan Yunnan China
106 A3 Fuyun Xinjiang China
177 J4 Füzesabony Hungary
177 K4 Füzesgyarmat Hungary
184 D6 Fuzeta Port.
109 L5 Fuzhou Fujian China
109 K5 Fuzhou Jiangxi China
191 R5 Fužine Croatia
129 I6 Füzuli Azer.
209 D6 Fwamba Dem. Rep. Co
151 M4 Fyfield Essex, England
149 L6 Fylde lowland England
142 G6 Fyn county Denmark
142 G6 Fyn i. Denmark
146 G10 Fyne r. Scotland U.K.
146 F11 Fyne, Loch inlet Scotland U.K.
168 I1 Fynshav Denmark
142 G6 Fyns Hoved hd Denma
142 E2 Fyresdal Norway
142 E2 Fyresvatn l. Norway
143 N2 Fyrisån r. Sweden

F.Y.R.O.M. *country* Europe *see* **Macedonia**
Fyteies Greece
Fyvie *Aberdeenshire, Scotland* U.K.
Fyzabad Trin. and Tob.
Gaafaru *i. N. Male* Maldives
Gaafaru Atoll *N. Male* Maldives
Gaafaru Channel Maldives
Gaâfour Tunisia
Gaal Austria
Gaalkacyo Somalia
Gaat *r.* Malaysia
Gab *watercourse* Namibia
Gabakly Turkm.
Gabaldón Spain
Gabangab *well* Eth.
Gabarret France
Gabas *r.* France
Gabasumdo *Qinghai* China *see* Tongde
Gabbac, Raas *pt* Somalia
Gabbs *NV* U.S.A.
Gabbs Valley Range *mts NV* U.S.A.
Gabčíkovo Slovakia
Gabd Pak.
Gabela Angola
Gaberl *pass* Austria
Gaberones Botswana *see* Gaborone
Gabersdorf Austria
Gabès Tunisia
Gabès, Golfe de *g.* Tunisia
Gabgaba, Wadi *watercourse* Sudan
Gabia Dem. Rep. Congo
Gabia la Grande Spain
Gabian France
Gabicce Mare Italy
Gąbin Pol.
Gabino Barreda Mex.
Gable End Foreland *hd North I.* N.Z.
Gablingen Ger.
Gablitz Austria
Gabon *country* Africa
Gabon, Estuaire du *est.* Gabon
Gaborone Botswana
Gaboto Arg.
Gabou Senegal
Gabriac France
Gabriel Island Mauritius
Gabriel Vera Bol.
Gabriel y Galán, Embalse de *resr* Spain
Gabriel Zamora Mex.
Gābrīk Iran
Gābrīk *watercourse* Iran
Gabrnik Slovenia
Gabrovnitsa Bulg.
Gabrovo Bulg.
Gabu Dem. Rep. Congo
Gabú Guinea-Bissau
Gabuli *vol.* Eth.
Gaby Italy
Gać Pol.
Gacé France
Gachenbach Ger.
Gach Sār Iran
Gachsārān Iran
Gacko Bos.-Herz.
Gädäbäy Azer.
Gadabedji, Réserve Totale de Faune de *nature res.* Niger
Gadag *Karnataka* India
Gadchiroli *Mahar.* India
Gäddede Sweden
Gadê *Qinghai* China
Gadebusch Ger.
Gadenstedt (Lahstedt) Ger.
Gadera *r.* Italy
Gades Spain *see* **Cádiz**
Gadhada *Gujarat* India
Gadhada *Gujarat* India
Gadhap Pak.
Gadhka *Gujarat* India
Gadhra *Gujarat* India
Gädi Dağı *mt.* Azer.
Gadjou-Lamdjahala *depr. Njazidja* Comoros
Gadmen Switz.
Gadoni *Sardegna* Italy
Gádor Spain
Gádor, Sierra de *mts* Spain
Gádoros Hungary
Gadra *Balochistan* Pak.
Gadra *Sindh* Pak.
Gadsden *AL* U.S.A.
Gadsden *AZ* U.S.A.
Gadwal *Andhra Prad.* India
Gadyach Ukr. *see* **Hadyach**
Gadyn Turkm.
Gadzi C.A.R.
Gadžin Han Serbia
Gaeiras Port.
Gael Hamke Bugt *b.* Greenland
Gaer *Powys, Wales* U.K.
Găești Romania
Gaeta Italy
Gaeta, Golfo di *g.* Italy
Gafanha da Boa Hora Port.
Gafanha da Encarnação Port.
Gafanha da Nazaré Port.
Gafanha do Carmo Port.
Gafanhoeira Port.
Gafaru *i. N. Male* Maldives *see* Gaafaru
Gafaru Atoll *N. Male* Maldives *see* **Gaafaru Atoll**
Gafaru Channel Maldives *see* Gaafaru Channel
Gaferut *i.* Micronesia
Gáfete Port.
Gaffney *SC* U.S.A.
Gafsa Tunisia
Gag *i. Papua* Indon.
Gagal Chad
Gagaon *Madh. Prad.* India
Gagarin Rus. Fed.
Gagarin Uzbek.
Găgăuzia *reg.* Moldova
Gägelow Ger.
Gagere *watercourse* Nigeria
Gaggenau Ger.
Gaggi *Sicilia* Italy
Gaggio Montano Italy
Gaglianico Italy
Gagliano Castelferrato *Sicilia* Italy
Gagliano del Capo Italy
Gagnières France
Gagnoa Côte d'Ivoire
Gagnon *Que.* Can.
Gago Coutinho Angola *see* Lumbala N'guimbo
Gagra Georgia
Gagris K'edi *hills* Georgia
Gahai *Qinghai* China
Gaiab *watercourse* Namibia
Gaibandha Bangl.
Găiceana Romania
Gaïdouronisi *i.* Greece
Gaienhofen Ger.
Gail *r.* Austria
Gail *TX* U.S.A.
Gaildorf Ger.
Gailingen Ger.
Gaillac France
Gaillac-d'Aveyron France
Gaillard, Lake *CT* U.S.A.
Gaillimh Ireland *see* **Galway**
Gaillon France
Gailtaler Alpen *mts* Austria
Gaimersheim Ger.
Găina *mt.* Romania
Gaindainqoinkor *Xizang* China
Gainesboro *TN* U.S.A.
Gainestown Ireland
Gainesville *FL* U.S.A.
Gainesville *GA* U.S.A.
237 I7 **Gainesville** *MO* U.S.A.
237 G9 **Gainesville** *TX* U.S.A.
149 N4 **Gainford** *Durham, England* U.K.
149 P7 **Gainsborough** *Lincolnshire, England* U.K.
191 K9 **Gaiole in Chianti** Italy
87 E13 **Gairdner** *r. W.A.* Austr.
82 E4 **Gairdner, Lake** *salt flat S.A.* Austr.
146 E7 **Gairloch** *Highland, Scotland* U.K.
146 E7 **Gair Loch** *b. Scotland* U.K.
192 D8 **Gairo** *Sardegna* Italy
211 C6 **Gairo** Tanz.
146 K4 **Gairsay** *i. Scotland* U.K.
191 L2 **Gais** Italy
190 G1 **Gais** Switz.
179 K4 **Gaishorn** Austria
173 L6 **Gaißach** Ger.
172 H7 **Gaißau** Austria
232 H9 **Gaithersburg** *MD* U.S.A.
Gaixian *Liaoning* China *see* Gaizhou
107 R6 **Gaizhou** *Liaoning* China
138 I5 **Gaiziņkalns** *hill* Latvia
177 H4 **Gaja** *r.* Hungary
94 D1 **Gajah Hutan, Bukit** *hill* Malaysia
102 □G17 **Gaja-jima** *i. Nansei-shotō* Japan
183 O7 **Gajanejos** Spain
115 H3 **Gajapatinagaram** *Andhra Prad.* India
123 K8 **Gajar** Pak.
176 F3 **Gajary** Slovakia
207 H4 **Gaji** *r.* Nigeria
207 I3 **Gajiram** Nigeria
117 L7 **Gajol** *W. Bengal* India
214 H3 **Gakarosa** *mt.* S. Africa
207 H5 **Gakem** Nigeria
177 I6 **Gakovo** *Vojvodina* Serbia
116 D1 **Gakuch** Jammu and Kashmir
111 I12 **Gala** *Xizang* China
Galaasiya Uzbek. *see* Galaosiyo
111 I12 **Gala Co** *l.* China
175 L1 **Gaładuś, Jezioro** *l.* Pol.
176 G5 **Galambok** Hungary
163 E9 **Galan** France
258 D2 **Galán, Cerro** *mt.* Arg.
211 D5 **Galana** *r.* Kenya
122 F3 **Galand** Iran
197 N3 **Gălănești** Romania
94 F4 **Galang Besar** *i.* Indon.
209 C8 **Galangue** Angola
140 Q2 **Gálaniitu** Norway
177 G3 **Galanta** Slovakia
120 K8 **Galaosiyo** Uzbek.
183 M7 **Galapagar** Spain
250 □ **Galápagos, Islas** *is* Pacific Ocean
Galapagos Islands *is* Pacific Ocean *see* Galápagos, Islas
267 M6 **Galapagos Rise** *sea feature* Pacific Ocean
184 F5 **Galaroza** Spain
210 C4 **Galas** *well* Kenya
146 K11 **Galashiels** *Scottish Borders, Scotland* U.K.
197 P7 **Galata** Bulg.
80 K5 **Galatea** *North I.* N.Z.
197 Q5 **Galați** Romania
195 O3 **Galatina** Italy
198 C2 **Galatini** Greece
198 E2 **Galatista** Greece
195 O3 **Galatone** Italy
187 K8 **Galatzó, Puig de** *mt.* Spain
149 L2 **Gala Water** *r. Scotland* U.K.
232 E12 **Galax** *VA* U.S.A.
198 D4 **Galaxidi** Greece
Galaymor Turkm. *see* Galaýmor
123 J4 **Galaýmor** Turkm.
147 F8 **Galbally** Ireland
183 P3 **Galbarra** Spain
85 H4 **Galbraith** *Qld* Austr.
216 □3f **Gáldar** *Gran Canaria* Canary Is
141 J6 **Galdhøpiggen** *mt.* Norway
206 C3 **Galé** Mali
183 N2 **Galea, Punta** *pt* Spain
242 F2 **Galeana** *Chihuahua* Mex.
243 I5 **Galeana** *Nuevo León* Mex.
191 L8 **Galeata** Italy
203 G6 **Galegu** Sudan
122 E8 **Galeh Dār** Iran
93 E3 **Galela** *Halmahera* Indon.
220 C3 **Galena** *AK* U.S.A.
236 J4 **Galena** *IL* U.S.A.
237 H7 **Galena** *KS* U.S.A.
234 D6 **Galena** *MD* U.S.A.
237 I7 **Galena** *MO* U.S.A.
222 G5 **Galena Bay** *B.C.* Can.
170 I3 **Galenbecker See** *l.* Ger.
182 G4 **Galende** Spain
247 □7 **Galeota Point** Trin. and Tob.
185 N5 **Galera** Spain
185 N5 **Galera** *r.* Spain
259 B6 **Galera, Punta** *pt* Chile
250 A4 **Galera, Punta** *pt* Ecuador
245 J10 **Galera, Punta** *pt* Mex.
247 □7 **Galera Point** Trin. and Tob.
192 B3 **Galéria** *Corse* France
192 A3 **Galéria, Golfe de** *b. Corse* France
236 J5 **Galesburg** *IL* U.S.A.
226 I7 **Galesburg** *MI* U.S.A.
235 K2 **Gales Ferry** *CT* U.S.A.
215 I4 **Galeshewe** S. Africa
226 C5 **Galesville** *WI* U.S.A.
232 H7 **Galeton** *PA* U.S.A.
217 □1c **Galets, Pointe des** *pt* Réunion
217 □1c **Galets, Rivière des** *r.* Réunion
174 G4 **Galewice** Pol.
147 C8 **Galey** *r.* Ireland
177 I4 **Galga** *r.* Hungary
177 I4 **Galgagyörk** Hungary
177 I4 **Galgamácsa** Hungary
162 D6 **Galgon** France
210 E3 **Galguduud** *admin. reg.* Somalia
210 E3 **Gal Hareeri** Somalia
129 C3 **Gali** Georgia
256 C5 **Gália** Brazil
222 F5 **Galiano Island** *B.C.* Can.
161 I6 **Galibier, Col du** *pass* France
197 L6 **Galicea Mare** Romania
134 H4 **Galich** Rus. Fed.
134 H4 **Galichskaya Vozvyshennost'** *hills* Rus. Fed.
182 E3 **Galicia** *aut. comm.* Spain
196 I9 **Galičica** *nat. park* Macedonia
129 C3 **Galidzga** *r.* Georgia
85 J7 **Galilee, Lake** *salt flat Qld* Austr.
Galilee, Sea of *l.* Israel *see* **Kinneret, Yam**
257 G3 **Galiléia** Brazil
190 I8 **Galileo** *airport* Italy
207 I5 **Galim Tignère** Cameroon
178 A5 **Galinakopf** *mt.* Austria/Liechtenstein
246 □ **Galina Point** Jamaica
244 G5 **Galindo** Mex.
182 C4 **Galiñeiro** *hill* Spain
175 I1 **Galiny** Pol.
232 C8 **Galion** *OH* U.S.A.
247 □3 **Galion, Baie du** *b.* Martinique
198 F5 **Galissas** *Syros* Greece
182 H9 **Galisteo** Spain
205 H1 **Galite, Canal de la** *sea chan.* Tunisia
139 U8 **Galitsa** Rus. Fed.
241 V9 **Galiuro Mountains** *AZ* U.S.A.
84 E2 **Galiwinku** *N.T.* Austr.
123 J2 **Galkynyş** Turkm.
203 H6 **Gallabat** Sudan
121 L7 **G'allaorol** Uzbek.
190 F4 **Gallarate** Italy
156 C6 **Gallardon** France
161 E9 **Gallargues-le-Montueux** France
236 I6 **Gallatin** *MO* U.S.A.
231 D7 **Gallatin** *TN* U.S.A.
238 I4 **Gallatin** *r. MT* U.S.A.
114 G9 **Galle** Sri Lanka
186 D4 **Gállego** *r.* Spain
185 N6 **Gallegón** *r.* Spain
267 L6 **Gallego Rise** *sea feature* Pacific Ocean
259 C8 **Gallegos** *r.* Arg.
259 B7 **Gallegos, Cabo** *c.* Chile
182 G7 **Gallegos de Argañan** Spain
183 J7 **Gallegos de Solmirón** Spain
191 J8 **Galleno** Italy
193 I3 **Gallese** Italy
147 E9 **Galley Head** Ireland
Gallia *country* Europe *see* France
162 C5 **Gallian-en-Médoc** France
190 F5 **Galliate** Italy
193 J4 **Gallicano nel Lazio** Italy
170 F3 **Gallin** *Mecklenburg-Vorpommern* Ger.
168 K3 **Gallin** *Mecklenburg-Vorpommern* Ger.
250 D1 **Gallinas, Punta** *pt* Col.
191 L4 **Gallio** Italy
195 O3 **Gallipoli** Italy
Gallipoli Turkey *see* **Gelibolu**
232 C10 **Gallipolis** *OH* U.S.A.
186 E6 **Gallipuén, Embalse de** *resr* Spain
140 P3 **Gällivare** Sweden
179 K6 **Gallizien** Austria
179 J3 **Gallneukirchen** Austria
183 P7 **Gallo** *r.* Spain
140 M5 **Gällö** Sweden
194 E7 **Gallo, Capo** *c. Sicilia* Italy
190 I2 **Gallo, Lago di** *l.* Italy
183 Q7 **Gallocanta, Laguna de** *l.* Spain
232 I5 **Gallo Island** *NY* U.S.A.
193 L5 **Galluccio** Italy
232 C10 **Gallup** *KY* U.S.A.
239 J9 **Gallup** *NM* U.S.A.
183 R5 **Gallur** Spain
192 B6 **Gallura** *reg. Sardegna* Italy
207 G4 **Galma** *watercourse* Nigeria
146 D9 **Galmisdale** *Highland, Scotland* U.K.
148 B8 **Galmoy** Ireland
Galne *Chechenskaya Respublika* Rus. Fed. *see* **Ken'yurt**
Galne *Chechenskaya Respublika* Rus. Fed. *see* **Kalinovskaya**
83 L6 **Galong** *N.S.W.* Austr.
114 G8 **Galoya** Sri Lanka
114 G9 **Gal Oya National Park** Sri Lanka
147 G6 **Galros** Ireland
210 E2 **Gal Shiikh** Somalia
175 L1 **Galstas** *l.* Lith.
146 H11 **Galston** *East Ayrshire, Scotland* U.K.
240 K3 **Galt** *CA* U.S.A.
210 E4 **Gal Tardo** Somalia
204 B4 **Galtat Zemmour** Western Sahara
147 F8 **Galtee Mountains** *hills* Ireland
192 D7 **Galtelli** *Sardegna* Italy
143 M2 **Galten** *l.* Sweden
178 B6 **Galtür** Austria
147 F8 **Galtymore** *hill* Ireland
122 F7 **Galūgāh, Kūh-e** *mts* Iran
122 H4 **Galūgāh-e Āsīyeh** Iran
211 B7 **Galula** Tanz.
226 D8 **Galva** *IL* U.S.A.
260 A6 **Galvarino** Chile
186 D6 **Galve** Spain
183 N6 **Galve de Sorbe** Spain
184 D2 **Galveias** Port.
226 H9 **Galveston** *IN* U.S.A.
237 H11 **Galveston** *TX* U.S.A.
237 H11 **Galveston Bay** *TX* U.S.A.
261 G3 **Galvez** Arg.
183 L9 **Gálvez** Spain
116 H5 **Galwa** Nepal
147 D6 **Galway** Ireland
147 D6 **Galway** *county* Ireland
147 D6 **Galway Bay** Ireland
247 □2 **Galways Soufrière** *vol.* Montserrat
93 F4 **Gam** *i. Papua* Indon.
93 G4 **Gam** *i. Papua* Indon.
96 G4 **Gâm, Sông** *r.* Vietnam
256 C2 **Gamá** Brazil
259 E6 **Gama, Isla** *i.* Arg.
156 C4 **Gamaches** France
104 F6 **Gamagōri** Japan
215 O6 **Gamalakhe** S. Africa
93 E3 **Gamalama** *vol. Maluku* Indon.
163 C8 **Gamarde-les-Bains** France
250 C2 **Gamarra** Col.
Gámas Fin. *see* **Kaamanen**
177 G5 **Gamás** Hungary
207 H3 **Gamawa** Nigeria
260 E5 **Gamay** Arg.
92 E5 **Gamay Bay** *Samar* Phil.
209 C7 **Gamba** Angola
Gamba *Xizang* China *see* Gongbalou
208 A5 **Gamba** Gabon
206 E4 **Gambaga** Ghana
190 I5 **Gambara** Italy
195 J7 **Gambarie** Italy
191 J8 **Gambassi Terme** Italy
193 N4 **Gambatesa** Italy
210 B2 **Gambēla** Eth.
210 B3 **Gambēla Hizboch** *admin. reg.* Eth.
210 B3 **Gambēla National Park** Eth.
220 A3 **Gambell** *AK* U.S.A.
234 B6 **Gamber** *MD* U.S.A.
191 M7 **Gambettola** Italy
Gambia *country* Africa *see* **The Gambia**
206 A3 **Gambia** *r.* Gambia
206 B3 **Gambie** *r.* Senegal
84 C1 **Gambier, Cape** *N.T.* Austr.
Gambier, Île *i. Arch. des Tuamotu* Fr. Polynesia *see* **Mangareva**
79 □9 **Gambier, Îles** *is Arch. des Tuamotu* Fr. Polynesia
82 F6 **Gambier Islands** *S.A.* Austr.
Gambier Islands *Arch. des Tuamotu* Fr. Polynesia *see* Gambier, Îles
231 □2 **Gambier Village** *New Prov.* Bahamas
225 K3 **Gambo** *Nfld and Lab.* Can.
208 D3 **Gambo** C.A.R.
190 F5 **Gambolò** Italy
208 B5 **Gamboma** Congo
85 I4 **Gamboola** *Qld* Austr.
208 B3 **Gamboula** C.A.R.
234 B6 **Gambrills** *MD* U.S.A.
157 O6 **Gambsheim** France
Gamda *Sichuan* China *see* **Zamtang**
Gameti *N.W.T.* Can. *see* **Rae Lakes**
179 L4 **Gaming** Austria
129 H5 **Gamış Dağı** *mt.* Azer.
214 F9 **Gamka** *r.* S. Africa
93 E3 **Gamkunoro, Gunung** *vol. Halmahera* Indon.
Gamlakarleby Fin. *see* **Kokkola**
143 M4 **Gamleby** Sweden
151 L3 **Gamlingay** *Cambridgeshire, England* U.K.
179 M6 **Gamlitz** Austria
203 G5 **Gammams** *well* Sudan
173 L4 **Gammelsdorf** Ger.
140 Q4 **Gammelstaden** Sweden
172 G5 **Gammertingen** Ger.
82 G4 **Gammon Ranges National Park** *S.A.* Austr.
104 D5 **Gamō** Japan
214 C5 **Gamoep** S. Africa
182 I2 **Gamonal** *mt.* Spain
100 G7 **Gamova, Mys** *pt* Rus. Fed.
114 G9 **Gampaha** Sri Lanka
114 G9 **Gampola** Sri Lanka
190 G1 **Gams** Switz.
123 I7 **Gamshadzai Kūh** *mts* Iran
108 B3 **Gamtog** *Xizang* China
215 J9 **Gamtoos** *r.* S. Africa
210 C3 **Gamud** *mt.* Eth.
140 T1 **Gamvik** Norway
163 D9 **Gan** France
113 □2 **Gan** *Addu Atoll* Maldives
113 □2 **Gan** *i. Addu Atoll* Maldives
108 C2 **Gana** *Sichuan* China
241 W6 **Ganado** *AZ* U.S.A.
161 H8 **Ganagobie** France
203 G5 **Gananita** Sudan
224 E4 **Gananoque** *Ont.* Can.
129 H5 **Gäncä** Azer.
129 H5 **Gäncäçay** *r.* Azer.
110 I6 **Gancaohu** *Xinjiang* China
108 G9 **Gancheng** *Hainan* China
Gand Belgium *see* **Gent**
209 B8 **Ganda** Angola
111 L11 **Ganda** *Xizang* China
93 A5 **Gandadiwata, Bukit** *mt.* Indon.
116 H9 **Gandai** *Chhattisgarh* India
209 D6 **Gandajika** Dem. Rep. Congo
117 I6 **Gandak Barrage** *dam* Nepal
123 I5 **Gandalak** Afgh.
116 E2 **Gandarbal** Jammu and Kashmir
182 D6 **Gandarela** Port.
123 M7 **Gandari Mountain** Pak.
123 I5 **Gandarra** Afgh.
123 L7 **Gandava** Pak.
190 H4 **Gandellino** Italy
225 K3 **Gander** *Nfld and Lab.* Can.
221 M5 **Gander** *r. Nfld and Lab.* Can.
168 G4 **Ganderkesee** Ger.
225 K3 **Gander Lake** *Nfld and Lab.* Can.
186 F5 **Gandesa** Spain
116 D9 **Gandevi** *Gujarat* India
116 C8 **Gandhidham** *Gujarat* India
116 D8 **Gandhinagar** *Gujarat* India
116 E7 **Gandhi Sagar** *resr* India
208 E2 **Gandi, Wadi** *watercourse* Sudan
187 E10 **Gandía** Spain
190 H4 **Gandino** Italy
216 □3f **Gando, Punta de** *pt Gran Canaria* Canary Is
122 D6 **Gandomān** Iran
129 J4 **Gändov** Azer.
182 C4 **Gandra** *Viana do Castelo* Port.
182 D5 **Gandra** *Viana do Castelo* Port.
254 F5 **Gandu** Brazil
106 H9 **Gandu** *Qinghai* China
140 T1 **Gandvik** Norway
Gandzha Azer. *see* **Gäncä**
206 C2 **Gâneb** *well* Maur.
182 C4 **Ganfei** Port.
117 L7 **Ganga** *r.* India *alt.* **Padma (Bangladesh),** *conv.* **Ganges**
207 G4 **Ganga** Nigeria
114 G9 **Ganga** *r.* Sri Lanka
Ganga Cone *sea feature* Indian Ocean *see* **Ganges Cone**
114 E3 **Gangakher** *Mahar.* India
208 F4 **Gangala Na Bodia** Dem. Rep. Congo
259 C6 **Gangán** Arg.
259 C6 **Gangán, Pampa de** *plain* Arg.
116 D5 **Ganganagar** *Rajasthan* India
114 D3 **Gangapur** *Mahar.* India
116 E7 **Gangapur** *Rajasthan* India
116 F6 **Gangapur** *Rajasthan* India
207 H3 **Gangara** Niger
117 L9 **Ganga Sagar** *W. Bengal* India
116 C7 **Ganga Sera** *Rajasthan* India
114 D5 **Gangavali** *r.* India
96 B3 **Gangaw** Myanmar
114 E5 **Gangawati** *Karnataka* India
96 C3 **Gangaw Range** *mts* Myanmar
106 G8 **Gangca** *Qinghai* China
116 E8 **Gangdhar** *Rajasthan* India
111 F11 **Gangdisê Shan** *mts Xizang* China
117 L8 **Ganges** *r.* Bangl./India *alt.* **Ganga (India),** *alt.* **Padma (Bangladesh)**
161 D9 **Ganges** France
117 L9 **Ganges, Mouths of the** Bangl./India
265 J3 **Ganges Cone** *sea feature* Indian Ocean
194 G8 **Gangi** *Sicilia* Italy
194 G8 **Gangi** *r. Sicilia* Italy
173 N5 **Gangkofen** Ger.
206 C5 **Ganglota** Liberia
106 E7 **Gangou** *Qinghai* China
106 I9 **Gangouyi** *Gansu* China
Gangra Turkey *see* **Çankırı**
116 E7 **Gangrar** *Rajasthan* India
117 L6 **Gangtok** *Sikkim* India
106 I9 **Gangu** *Gansu* China
107 N8 **Gangziyao** *Hebei* China
107 S2 **Gan He** *r.* China
110 I4 **Ganhezi** *Xinjiang* China
93 F4 **Gani** *Halmahera* Indon.
206 C4 **Ganiakali** Guinea
115 I3 **Ganjam** *Orissa* India
122 D6 **Ganjgūn** Iran
109 K4 **Gan Jiang** *r.* China
107 R5 **Ganjig** *Nei Mongol* China
107 L9 **Ganjing** *Shaanxi* China
107 N4 **Ganjur Sum** *Nei Mongol* China
139 Q2 **Gankovo** Rus. Fed.
108 D4 **Ganluo** *Sichuan* China
107 R3 **Gannan** *Heilong.* China
160 C4 **Gannat** France
225 J2 **Gannet Islands Ecological Reserve** *nature res. Nfld and Lab.* Can.
238 J5 **Gannett Peak** *WY* U.S.A.
136 F3 **Gannopil'** Ukr.
236 F3 **Gannvalley** *SD* U.S.A.
111 K8 **Ganq** *Qinghai* China
107 K8 **Ganquan** *Shaanxi* China
214 D10 **Gansbaai** S. Africa
169 D10 **Gänsehals** *hill* Ger.
179 O3 **Gänserndorf** Austria
165 F7 **Ganshoren** Belgium
108 F4 **Ganshui** *Chongqing* China
106 E6 **Gansu** *prov.* China
210 D4 **Gantamaa** Somalia
106 I8 **Gantang** *Nei Mongol* China
117 I9 **Gantapara** *Orissa* India
86 G4 **Gantheaume Point** *W.A.* Austr.
129 B2 **Gant'iadi** *Ap'khazet'i* Georgia
129 F4 **Gant'iadi** Georgia
Ganting *Shaanxi* China *see* Huxian
190 C2 **Gantrisch** *mt.* Switz.
Gantsevichi Belarus *see* **Hantsavichy**
95 H6 **Gantung** Indon.
109 J6 **Ganxian** *Jiangxi* China
116 F8 **Ganyal** *r. Madh. Prad.* India
207 I4 **Ganye** Nigeria
214 I2 **Ganyesa** S. Africa
107 P9 **Ganyu** *Jiangsu* China
120 C4 **Ganyushkino** Kazakh.
Ganzhe *Fujian* China *see* **Minhou**
109 J6 **Ganzhou** *Jiangxi* China
210 A3 **Ganzi** Sudan
170 F4 **Ganzlin** Ger.
207 E2 **Gao** Mali
207 F2 **Gao** *admin. reg.* Mali
109 J4 **Gao'an** *Jiangxi* China
106 H8 **Gaoba** *Gansu* China
107 N7 **Gaocheng** *Hebei* China
Gaocheng *Sichuan* China *see* Litang
109 L3 **Gaochun** *Jiangsu* China
Gaocun *Hunan* China *see* Mayang
109 M4 **Gaojian** *Zhejiang* China
106 H8 **Gaolan** *Gansu* China
Gaoleshan *Hubei* China *see* Xianfeng
Gaoliangjian *Jiangsu* China *see* **Hongze**
108 B6 **Gaoligong Shan** *mts* China
107 K9 **Gaoling** *Shaanxi* China
107 P8 **Gaomi** *Shandong* China
109 H5 **Gaomutang** *Hunan* China
107 M9 **Gaoping** *Shanxi* China
107 O8 **Gaoqing** *Shandong* China
106 F7 **Gaotai** *Gansu* China
107 O8 **Gaotang** *Shandong* China
Gaotangling *Hunan* China *see* Wangcheng
Gaoting *Zhejiang* China *see* Daishan
107 K7 **Gaotouyao** *Nei Mongol* China
206 E4 **Gaoua** Burkina
206 B4 **Gaoual** Guinea
Gaoxian *Sichuan* China *see* Wenjiang
Gaoxiong Taiwan *see* **Kaohsiung**
107 N7 **Gaoyang** *Hebei* China
109 I7 **Gaoyao** *Guangdong* China
107 N8 **Gaoyi** *Hebei* China
109 L2 **Gaoyou** *Jiangsu* China
109 L2 **Gaoyou Hu** *l.* China
108 H8 **Gaozhou** *Guangdong* China
161 I7 **Gap** France
234 C5 **Gap** *PA* U.S.A.
80 □ **Gap, Point** *Chatham Is* S. Pacific Ocean
92 C4 **Gapan** *Luzon* Phil.
161 I10 **Gapeau** *r.* France
208 E3 **Gapi** Dem. Rep. Congo
84 E2 **Gapuwiyak** *N.T.* Austr.
111 F12 **Gaqoi** *Xizang* China
117 K5 **Gaqung** *Xizang* China
98 D5 **Gar** *Xizang* China
123 J8 **Gar** Pak.
100 F2 **Gar'** *r.* Rus. Fed.
177 I5 **Gara** Hungary
147 F5 **Gara, Lough** *l.* Ireland
205 H3 **Garaa Tebourt** *well* Tunisia
187 C8 **Garaballa** Spain
123 K2 **Garabekewül** Turkm.
123 J3 **Garabil Belentligi** *hills* Turkm.
208 B4 **Garabinzam** Congo
161 C7 **Garabit, Viaduc de** France
122 E1 **Garabogaz** Turkm.
122 E1 **Garabogazköl** Turkm.
122 E1 **Garabogazköl Aýlagy** *b.* Turkm.
Garabogazköl Aylagy *b.* Turkm. *see* **Garabogazköl Aýlagy**
122 E1 **Garabogazköl Bogazy** *sea chan.* Turkm.
210 F3 **Garacad** Somalia
216 □3a **Garachico** *Tenerife* Canary Is
242 □T13 **Garachiné** Panama
242 □T13 **Garachiné, Punta** *pt* Panama
210 E2 **Garadag** Somalia
148 D7 **Garadice** Ireland
147 G4 **Garadice Lough** *l.* Ireland
205 G6 **Gara Ekar** *hill* Alg.
216 □3d **Garafía** *La Palma* Canary Is
183 P2 **Garagarza** Spain
122 I6 **Garāgheh** Iran
250 C3 **Garagoa** Col.
122 E2 **Garagöl** Turkm.
Garagum *des.* Kazakh. *see* **Karakum, Peski**
122 I2 **Garagum** *des.* Turkm.
123 I3 **Garagum Kanaly** *canal* Turkm.
193 Q6 **Garaguso** Italy
83 L3 **Garah** *N.S.W.* Austr.
123 O4 **Garai** Pak.
216 □3a **Garajonay, Parque Nacional de** *nat. park La Gomera* Canary Is
206 D4 **Garalo** Mali
Garamätnyyaz Turkm. *see* Garamätnyýaz
123 K3 **Garamätnyýaz** Turkm.
208 F4 **Garamba** *r.* Dem. Rep. Congo
208 F3 **Garamba, Parc National de la** *nat. park* Dem. Rep. Congo
106 G8 **Garang** *Qinghai* China
254 F4 **Garanhuns** Brazil
215 L1 **Ga-Rankuwa** S. Africa
254 B5 **Garapu** Brazil
256 D2 **Garapuava** Brazil
208 D2 **Garar, Plaine de** *plain* Chad
116 G7 **Garautha** *Uttar Prad.* India
161 G8 **Garaux, Rocher** *mt.* France
84 F4 **Garawa Aboriginal Land** *res. N.T.* Austr.
208 D2 **Garba** C.A.R.
210 D4 **Garbahaarrey** Somalia
175 J4 **Garbatka-Letnisko** Pol.
210 C4 **Garba Tula** Kenya
185 J2 **Garbayuela** Spain
240 I1 **Garberville** *CA* U.S.A.
122 D5 **Garbosh, Kūh-e** *mt.* Iran
197 O5 **Gârbova, Vârful** *hill* Romania
175 K4 **Garbów** Pol.
169 I6 **Garbsen** Ger.
116 H4 **Garbyang** *Uttaranchal* India
256 C5 **Garça** Brazil
256 A1 **Garças, Rio das** *r.* Brazil
197 P4 **Gârceni** Romania
173 N5 **Garching an der Alz** Ger.
173 L5 **Garching bei München** Ger.
160 C2 **Garchizy** France
186 G5 **Garcia** Spain
244 D5 **García, Cerro** *mt.* Mex.
244 D4 **Garcia de la Cadena** Mex.
256 A4 **Garcias** Brazil
185 I2 **Garcia Sola, Embalse de** *resr* Spain
184 H2 **Garciaz** Spain
183 J7 **Garcihernández** Spain
183 L7 **Garcillán** Spain
197 O4 **Gârcina** Romania
183 O8 **Garcinarro** Spain
161 E8 **Gard** *dept* France
161 F9 **Gard** *r.* France
191 J4 **Garda** Italy
191 J5 **Garda, Lago di** *l.* Italy
129 G4 **Gardabani** Georgia
197 K4 **Gârda de Sus** Romania
161 G10 **Gardanne** France
189 A7 **Garde, Cap de** *c.* Alg.
174 G2 **Gardeja** Pol.
223 J2 **Garde Lake** *N.W.T.* Can.
170 D5 **Gardelegen** Ger.
191 L2 **Gardena** *r.* Italy
236 E7 **Garden City** *KS* U.S.A.
235 H3 **Garden City** *NY* U.S.A.
237 E10 **Garden City** *TX* U.S.A.
226 H4 **Garden Corners** *MI* U.S.A.
240 O8 **Garden Grove** *CA* U.S.A.
223 M4 **Garden Hill** *Man.* Can.
87 C12 **Garden Island** *W.A.* Austr.
226 I4 **Garden Island** *MI* U.S.A.
232 D11 **Garden Mountain** *VA* U.S.A.
234 A2 **Garden View** *PA* U.S.A.
164 I4 **Garderen** Neth.
142 G1 **Gardermoen** *airport* Norway
261 H5 **Gardey** Arg.
123 M5 **Gardēz** Afgh.
Gardinas Belarus *see* **Hrodna**
233 □P4 **Gardiner** *ME* U.S.A.
238 I4 **Gardiner** *MT* U.S.A.
84 D7 **Gardiner, Mount** *N.T.* Austr.
84 B5 **Gardiner Range** *hills N.T.* Austr.
235 K2 **Gardiners Bay** *NY* U.S.A.
235 K2 **Gardiners Island** *NY* U.S.A.
84 D7 **Gardiner's Range** *mts N.T.* Austr.
168 G2 **Garding** Ger.
Gardner *atoll* Micronesia *see* Faraulep
226 F8 **Gardner** *IL* U.S.A.
233 N6 **Gardner** *MA* U.S.A.
262 T1 **Gardner Inlet** Antarctica
Gardner Island *atoll Phoenix Is* Kiribati *see* **Nikumaroro**
235 K1 **Gardner Lake** *CT* U.S.A.
233 □R4 **Gardner Lake** *ME* U.S.A.
75 H2 **Gardner Pinnacles** *is HI* U.S.A.
240 M3 **Gardnerville** *NV* U.S.A.
143 N7 **Gardno, Jezioro** *lag.* Pol.
161 E8 **Gardon d'Alès** *r.* France
161 D8 **Gardon de St-Jean** *r.* France
191 J4 **Gardone Riviera** Italy
190 I4 **Gardone Val Trompia** Italy
163 E6 **Gardonne** France
177 H4 **Gárdony** Hungary
163 H9 **Gardouch** France
140 N4 **Gardsjönås** Sweden
143 M5 **Gärdslösa** *Öland* Sweden
Gáregasnjárga Fin. *see* Karigasniemi
163 C7 **Garein** France
148 H1 **Gare Loch** *inlet Scotland* U.K.
146 G10 **Garelochhead** *Argyll and Bute, Scotland* U.K.
Gares Spain *see* **Puente la Reina**
188 F3 **Garešnica** Croatia
190 E7 **Garessio** Italy
78 □5 **Garet, Mount** *vol.* Vanuatu
205 G4 **Garet El Djenoun** *mt.* Alg.
251 H3 **Gare Tigre** Fr. Guiana
239 K7 **Garfield** *CO* U.S.A.
235 G3 **Garfield** *NJ* U.S.A.
149 O6 **Garforth** *West Yorkshire, England* U.K.
193 Q8 **Garga** *r.* Italy
198 C5 **Gargalianoi** Greece
184 H2 **Gargáligas** Spain
185 H2 **Gargáligas** *r.* Spain
186 D6 **Gargallo** Spain
162 H4 **Gargan, Mont** *hill* France
193 P4 **Gargano, Parco Nazionale del** *nat. park* Italy
182 I8 **Garganta la Olla** Spain
224 C4 **Gargantua, Cape** *Ont.* Can.
127 N8 **Gargar** Iran
161 G9 **Gargas** France
191 K2 **Gargazzone** Italy
178 A6 **Gargellen** Austria
156 D6 **Garges-lès-Gonesse** France
162 H2 **Gargilesse-Dampierre** France
191 J4 **Gargnano** Italy
161 D8 **Gargo** *mt.* France
149 M6 **Gargrave** *North Yorkshire, England* U.K.
146 H10 **Gargunnock Hills** *Scotland* U.K.
Gargunsa *Xizang* China *see* **Gar**
138 E6 **Gargždai** Lith.
116 G8 **Garhakota** *Madh. Prad.* India
117 K8 **Garhbeta** *W. Bengal* India
116 G8 **Garhi** *Madh. Prad.* India
116 E8 **Garhi** *Rajasthan* India
123 L7 **Garhi Khairo** Pak.
116 G7 **Garhi Malehra** *Madh. Prad.* India
116 G5 **Garhmuktesar** *Uttar Prad.* India
116 F4 **Garhshankar** *Punjab* India
117 I7 **Garhwa** *Jharkhand* India
193 L5 **Gari** *r.* Italy
255 C9 **Garibaldi** Brazil
222 F5 **Garibaldi** *B.C.* Can.
222 F5 **Garibaldi, Mount** *B.C.* Can.
222 F5 **Garibaldi Provincial Park** *B.C.* Can.
215 J6 **Gariep Dam** *resr* S. Africa
215 J6 **Gariep Dam Nature Reserve** S. Africa
214 B6 **Garies** S. Africa
193 L5 **Garigliano** *r.* Italy
183 Q3 **Garínoain** Spain
210 C5 **Garissa** Kenya
138 H4 **Garkalne** Latvia
111 H10 **Garkung Caka** *l. Xizang* China
Gârla Mare *r.* Moldova *see* **Gîrla Mare**
237 G9 **Garland** *TX* U.S.A.
190 F5 **Garlasco** Italy
179 K4 **Garlenz** Austria
138 G7 **Garliava** Lith.
197 Q6 **Gârliciu** Romania
146 H13 **Garlieston** *Dumfries and Galloway, Scotland* U.K.
163 D8 **Garlin** France
185 I3 **Garlitos** Spain
147 I5 **Garlowcross** Ireland
168 J4 **Garlstorf** Ger.
Garm Tajik. *see* **Gharm**
123 K5 **Garmab** Afgh.
122 G4 **Garmab** Iran
122 H5 **Garm Ab, Chashmeh-ye** *spring* Iran
122 C6 **Garmdasht** Iran
122 F5 **Garmeh** *Eşfahān* Iran
122 G3 **Garmeh** *Khorāsān* Iran
122 C2 **Garmī** Iran
173 K7 **Garmisch-Partenkirchen** Ger.
146 E10 **Garmony** *Argyll and Bute, Scotland* U.K.
122 E7 **Garmosht** Iran
122 E4 **Garmsar** Iran
123 J6 **Garmsel** *reg.* Afgh.
123 J6 **Garmushki** Afgh.
236 I4 **Garner** *IA* U.S.A.
232 C11 **Garner** *KY* U.S.A.
236 H6 **Garnett** *KS* U.S.A.
147 B9 **Garnish** Ireland
122 H7 **Gārnow** Iran
83 I5 **Garnpung Lake** *imp. l. N.S.W.* Austr.
117 M7 **Garo Hills** *Meghalaya* India
186 G2 **Garona** *r.* Spain
163 C6 **Garonne** *r.* France
163 E7 **Garonne, Canal latéral à la** France
161 E9 **Garons** France
210 F2 **Garoowe** Somalia
255 C9 **Garopaba** Brazil
116 E7 **Garoth** *Madh. Prad.* India
206 E2 **Garou, Lac** *l.* Mali
207 I4 **Garoua** Cameroon
207 I5 **Garoua Boulai** Cameroon
143 K2 **Garphyttan** Sweden
143 K2 **Garphyttans nationalpark** *nat. park* Sweden
111 K10 **Gar Qu** *r. Qinghai* China
111 K10 **Garqu Yan** *Qinghai* China
182 I3 **Garrafe de Torio** Spain
163 B10 **Garralda** Spain
147 D9 **Garrane** Ireland
183 P5 **Garray** Spain
261 F5 **Garré** Arg.
168 F5 **Garrel** Ger.
92 □ **Garreru** *i.* Palau
226 I8 **Garrett** *IN* U.S.A.
161 D9 **Garrigues** *reg.* France
147 F4 **Garrison** *Northern Ireland* U.K.
232 B10 **Garrison** *KY* U.S.A.
236 I2 **Garrison** *MN* U.S.A.
236 E2 **Garrison** *ND* U.S.A.
235 H2 **Garrison** *NY* U.S.A.
147 J5 **Garristown** Ireland
129 E4 **Garrnarrich** Armenia
245 L7 **Garro** Mex.
147 K2 **Garron Point** *Northern Ireland* U.K.
182 G9 **Garrovillas** Spain
185 P6 **Garrucha** Spain
186 D6 **Garrucha, Sierra de la** *mts* Spain
123 K7 **Garruk** Pak.
146 G8 **Garry** *r. Scotland* U.K.
146 G8 **Garry, Loch** *l. Highland, Scotland* U.K.
122 I3 **Garryçyrla** Turkm.
221 H3 **Garry Lake** *Nunavut* Can.
146 C6 **Garrynahine** *Western Isles, Scotland* U.K.
215 L7 **Garryowen** S. Africa
147 F9 **Garryvoe** Ireland
173 M5 **Gars am Inn** Ger.
179 M2 **Gars am Kamp** Austria
149 M5 **Garsdale Head** *Cumbria, England* U.K.
211 D5 **Garsen** Kenya
Garshy Turkm. *see* **Garşy**
202 D6 **Garsila** Sudan
143 K6 **Gärsnäs** Sweden
149 L6 **Garstang** *Lancashire, England* U.K.
168 J4 **Garstedt** Ger.
179 J3 **Garsten** Austria
81 C12 **Garston** *South I.* N.Z.
122 E1 **Garşy** Turkm.
Gartar *Sichuan* China *see* Qianning
162 F2 **Gartempe** *r.* France
150 E3 **Garth** *Powys, Wales* U.K.
150 F2 **Garthmyl** *Powys, Wales* U.K.
146 G10 **Gartocharn** *West Dunbartonshire, Scotland* U.K.
Gartog *Xizang* China *see* Markam
Gartok *Xizang* China *see* Garyarsa
170 D4 **Gartow** Ger.
172 F4 **Gärtringen** Ger.
170 J4 **Gartz** Ger.
212 C5 **Garub** Namibia
92 □ **Garusuun** Palau
95 G8 **Garut** *Jawa* Indon.
147 G5 **Garvagh** Ireland
147 I3 **Garvagh** *Northern Ireland* U.K.
147 H4 **Garvaghy** *Northern Ireland* U.K.
146 K11 **Garvald** *East Lothian, Scotland* U.K.
146 H8 **Garvamore** *Highland, Scotland* U.K.
184 C5 **Garvão** Port.
146 D10 **Garvard** *Argyll and Bute, Scotland* U.K.
146 G7 **Garve** *Highland, Scotland* U.K.
81 C12 **Garvie Mountains** *South I.* N.Z.
175 J4 **Garwolin** Pol.
111 E10 **Gar Xincun** *Xizang* China
230 D5 **Gary** *IN* U.S.A.
232 D11 **Gary** *WV* U.S.A.
111 E11 **Garyarsa** *Xizang* China
108 B3 **Garyi** *Sichuan* China
103 J12 **Garyū-zan** *mt.* Japan
170 H2 **Garz** Ger.
258 E3 **Garza** Arg.
111 D10 **Gar Zangbo** *r.* China
245 H1 **Garza Valdez** Mex.
108 B3 **Garzê** *Sichuan* China
250 C4 **Garzón** Col.
Gasan-Kuli Turkm. *see* **Esenguly**
174 F3 **Gąsawa** Pol.
178 B6 **Gaschurn** Austria
171 F8 **Gaschwitz** Ger.
163 C8 **Gascogne** *reg.* France
154 C5 **Gascogne, Golfe de** *g.* France/Spain
236 J6 **Gasconade** *r. MO* U.S.A.
Gascony *reg.* France *see* Gascogne
Gascony, Gulf of France/Spain *see* **Gascogne, Golfe de**
87 C8 **Gascoyne** *r. W.A.* Austr.
87 D8 **Gascoyne, Mount** *hill W.A.* Austr.
87 C8 **Gascoyne Junction** *W.A.* Austr.
183 O8 **Gascueña** Spain
Gascuña, Golfo de *g.* France/Spain *see* Gascogne, Golfe de
111 H11 **Gase** *Xizang* China
113 □1 **Gasfinolhu** *i. N. Male* Maldives
124 C8 **Gash and Setit** *prov.* Eritrea
116 F2 **Gasherbrum I** *mt.* Jammu and Kashmir
123 Q4 **Gasherbrum II** *mt.* China/Jammu and Kashmir
203 H6 **Gash Setit Wildlife Reserve** *nature res.* Eritrea
123 I8 **Gasht** Iran
111 J7 **Gas Hu** *salt l.* China
207 H3 **Gashua** Nigeria
146 B7 **Gasker** *i. Scotland* U.K.
175 K2 **Gąski** Pol.
156 C5 **Gasny** France
175 I3 **Gąsocin** Pol.
246 D3 **Gaspar** Cuba
94 G6 **Gaspar, Selat** *sea chan.* Indon.
225 H3 **Gaspé** *Que.* Can.
225 H3 **Gaspé, Baie de** *b. Que.* Can.
225 H3 **Gaspé, Cap** *c. Que.* Can.
225 H3 **Gaspé, Péninsule de** *pen. Que.* Can.
195 L6 **Gasperina** Italy
179 I3 **Gaspoltshofen** Austria
206 E3 **Gassan** Burkina
102 R8 **Gassan** *vol.* Japan
206 B3 **Gassane** Senegal
232 E10 **Gassaway** *WV* U.S.A.
164 K3 **Gasselte** Neth.
164 K3 **Gasselternijveen** Neth.
185 L2 **Gasset, Embalse de** *resr* Spain
161 J10 **Gassin** France
207 H4 **Gassol** Nigeria
241 Q5 **Gass Peak** *NV* U.S.A.
178 H5 **Gasteiner Tal** *val.* Austria
Gasteiz Spain *see* **Vitoria-Gasteiz**
100 M4 **Gastello** *Sakhalin* Rus. Fed.
179 L2 **Gastern** Austria
163 B7 **Gastes** France
232 H12 **Gaston** *NC* U.S.A.
232 H12 **Gaston, Lake** *NC* U.S.A.
231 G8 **Gastonia** *NC* U.S.A.
198 C5 **Gastouni** Greece
259 C6 **Gastre** Arg.
182 G8 **Gata** Spain
185 O7 **Gata, Cabo de** *c.* Spain
128 B4 **Gata, Cape** Cyprus
182 G8 **Gata, Sierra de** *mts* Spain
187 F10 **Gata de Gorgos** Spain
222 E3 **Gataga** *r. B.C.* Can.
196 J5 **Gătaia** Romania
Gatas, Akra *c.* Cyprus *see* Gata, Cape
139 N2 **Gatchina** Rus. Fed.
232 C12 **Gate City** *VA* U.S.A.
146 H13 **Gatehouse of Fleet** *Dumfries and Galloway, Scotland* U.K.
177 I5 **Gátér** Hungary
171 D7 **Gatersleben** Ger.
149 N4 **Gateshead** *Tyne and Wear, England* U.K.
221 H2 **Gateshead Island** *Nunavut* Can.
220 C3 **Gates of the Arctic National Park and Preserve** *AK* U.S.A.
231 I7 **Gatesville** *NC* U.S.A.
237 G10 **Gatesville** *TX* U.S.A.
241 X3 **Gateway** *CO* U.S.A.
235 G4 **Gateway National Recreational Area** *park NJ* U.S.A.
252 C5 **Gatico** Chile
156 E7 **Gâtinais** *reg.* France
159 L7 **Gâtine** *reg.* France
224 F4 **Gatineau** *Que.* Can.
224 F4 **Gatineau** *r. Que.* Can.
185 J4 **Gato** *r.* Spain
Gatong *Xizang* China *see* Jomda
Gatooma Zimbabwe *see* Kadoma
187 D8 **Gátova** Spain
179 O3 **Gattendorf** Austria
191 M7 **Gatteo a Mare** Italy
161 K9 **Gattières** France
190 E4 **Gattinara** Italy
85 N9 **Gatton** *Qld* Austr.
250 B2 **Gatún** Panama
242 □S13 **Gatún, Lago** *l.* Panama
122 C5 **Gatvand** Iran
79 □7 **Gau** *i.* Fiji
172 E2 **Gau-Algesheim** Ger.
254 B5 **Gaúcha do Norte** Brazil
156 F4 **Gauchy** France
185 I7 **Gaucín** Spain
185 J7 **Gaudalteba, Embalse de** *resr* Spain
223 L3 **Gauer Lake** *Man.* Can.
Gauhati *Assam* India *see* Guwahati
138 H4 **Gauja** *r.* Latvia
138 I7 **Gauja** *r.* Lith.
138 I4 **Gaujas nacionālais parks** *nat. park* Latvia
172 H2 **Gaukönigshofen** Ger.
Gaul *country* Europe *see* France
184 □ **Gaula** Madeira
140 K5 **Gaula** *r.* Norway
232 D10 **Gauley Bridge** *WV* U.S.A.
165 I9 **Gaume** *reg.* Belgium
172 E2 **Gau-Odernheim** Ger.
141 I6 **Gaupne** Norway
Gaurdak Turkm. *see* Gowurdak
114 E6 **Gauribidanur** *Karnataka* India
117 M8 **Gaurnadi** Bangl.
142 E2 **Gausta** *mt.* Norway
215 M2 **Gauteng** *prov.* S. Africa
173 K5 **Gauting** Ger.
186 E4 **Gautizalema** *r.* Spain
123 K4 **Gauzan** Afgh.
186 J5 **Gavà** Spain
127 P9 **Gāvakān** Iran
190 I4 **Gavardo** Italy
122 H3 **Gavāreshg** Iran
163 D10 **Gavarnie** France
163 D10 **Gavarnie, Cirque de** *corrie* France/Spain
129 G5 **Gavarr** Armenia
123 I9 **Gavāter** Iran
177 K3 **Gávavencsellő** Hungary
122 E8 **Gāvbandī** Iran
122 E8 **Gāvbūs, Kūh-e** *mts* Iran
198 F8 **Gavdopoula** *i.* Greece
198 F8 **Gavdos** *i.* Greece
163 B8 **Gave** *r.* France
182 D4 **Gave** Port.
163 D9 **Gave d'Arrens** *r.* France
163 C9 **Gave d'Aspe** *r.* France
163 B8 **Gave d'Oloron** *r.* France
163 C9 **Gave d'Ossau** *r.* France
122 B4 **Gāveh Rūd** *r.* Iran
165 E7 **Gavere** Belgium
190 F6 **Gavi** Italy
193 K6 **Gavi, Isola di** *i.* Italy
255 E5 **Gavião** *r.* Brazil
184 D2 **Gavião** Port.
250 D6 **Gaviãozinho** Brazil
122 B4 **Gavīleh** Iran
261 F6 **Gaviotas** Arg.
190 F4 **Gavirate** Italy
122 E5 **Gav Khūnī** Iran
143 N1 **Gävle** Sweden
143 M1 **Gävleborg** *county* Sweden
143 N1 **Gävlebukten** *b.* Sweden
192 C7 **Gavoi** *Sardegna* Italy
192 F2 **Gavorrano** Italy
158 I4 **Gavray** France
135 H5 **Gavrilovka Vtoraya** Rus. Fed.
139 X5 **Gavrilov Posad** Rus. Fed.
139 W4 **Gavrilov-Yam** Rus. Fed.
198 F5 **Gavrio** *Andros* Greece
212 C5 **Gawachab** Namibia
96 C1 **Gawai** Myanmar
117 J7 **Gawan** *Jharkhand* India
202 B3 **Gawat** *well* Libya
179 O3 **Gaweinstal** Austria

122 H3 Gäwers Turkm.
116 F9 Gawilgarh Hills India
82 G6 Gawler S.A. Austr.
82 E5 Gawler Ranges hills S.A. Austr.
175 K1 Gawliki Wielkie Pol.
174 D4 Gaworzyce Pol.
149 M7 Gawsworth Cheshire, England U.K.
149 M5 Gawthrop Cumbria, England U.K.
207 G4 Gawu Nigeria
122 F2 Gäwür watercourse Turkm.
106 G5 Gaxun Nur salt l. Nei Mongol China
120 H2 Gay Rus. Fed.
226 F2 Gay MI U.S.A.
117 J7 Gaya Bihar India
95 L1 Gaya i. Malaysia
95 M2 Gaya i. Malaysia
207 F4 Gaya Niger
Gayá r. Spain see El Gaià
100 F7 Gaya He r. China
116 D2 Gayal Gah Jammu and Kashmir
95 K8 Gayam Jawa Indon.
210 A5 Gayaza Uganda
148 C7 Gaybrook Ireland
204 C4 G'Aydat al Jhoucha ridge Western Sahara
137 Q9 Gayduk Rus. Fed.
207 F3 Gayéri Burkina
226 J4 Gaylord MI U.S.A.
236 H3 Gaylord MN U.S.A.
85 M8 Gayndah Qld Austr.
139 T4 Gaynovo Rus. Fed.
134 K3 Gayny Rus. Fed.
Gaysin Ukr. see Haysyn
151 N2 Gayton Norfolk, England U.K.
134 G4 Gayutino Rus. Fed.
Gayvoron Ukr. see Hayvoron
122 D5 Gaz Eşfahān Iran
122 G8 Gaz Hormozgan Iran
128 C7 Gaza terr. Asia
128 C7 Gaza Gaza
213 G4 Gaza prov. Moz.
122 G6 Gazak Iran
121 M7 G'azalkent Uzbek.
123 L7 Gazan Pak.
207 I4 Gazawa Cameroon
78 □5 Gazelle, Récif de la rf New Caledonia
122 F5 Gazestān Iran
208 E4 Gazi Dem. Rep. Congo
126 H5 Gaziantep Turkey
128 F2 Gaziantep prov. Turkey
Gazibenli Turkey see Yahyalı
122 I5 Gazīk Iran
129 E5 Gaziler Turkey
Gazimağusa Cyprus see Ammochostos
100 B2 Gazimur r. Rus. Fed.
107 L2 Gazimuro-Ononskiy Khrebet mts Rus. Fed.
100 A3 Gazimurskiy Khrebet mts Rus. Fed.
126 F5 Gazipaşa Turkey
196 I8 Gazivode Jezero l. Serbia
120 J7 Gazli Uzbek.
122 H8 Gaz Māhū Iran
122 E3 Gaznāsarā Iran
123 I1 Gazojak Turkm.
Gazojak Turkm. see Gazojak
183 Q3 Gazolaz Spain
191 J5 Gazoldo degli Ippoliti Italy
191 K5 Gazzo Veronese Italy
191 J5 Gazzuolo Italy
206 D5 Gbaaka Liberia
208 D3 Gbadolite Dem. Rep. Congo
206 B5 Gbangbatok Sierra Leone
206 C5 Gbarnga Liberia
206 C5 Gbatala Liberia
177 H4 Gbelce Slovakia
176 G3 Gbely Slovakia
207 F4 Gbéroubouè Benin
207 H5 Gboko Nigeria
208 D4 Gbwado Dem. Rep. Congo
143 O7 Gdańsk Pol.
175 H1 Gdańsk, Gulf of Pol./Rus. Fed.
Gdańska, Zatoka g. Pol./Rus. Fed. see Gdańsk, Gulf of
Gdingen Pol. see Gdynia
138 K3 Gdov Rus. Fed.
175 I6 Gdów Pol.
143 O7 Gdynia Pol.
186 C7 Gea de Albarracín Spain
140 Q2 Geaidnovuohppi Norway
146 H8 Geal Charn hill Highland, Scotland U.K.
146 J8 Geal Charn hill Highland, Scotland U.K.
146 E4 Gealldruig Mhòr i. Scotland U.K.
163 I11 Géant, Pic du mt. France
78 □3a Gea Passage Kwajalein Marshall Is
238 D5 Gearhart Mountain OR U.S.A.
Gearraidh na h-Aibhne Scotland U.K. see Garrynahine
Gearraidh na h-Aibhne Western Isles, Scotland U.K. see Garrynahine
148 C7 Geashill Ireland
234 F6 Geat Sound b. NJ U.S.A.
163 D8 Geaune France
Geavvú Fin. see Kevo
93 F3 Gebe i. Maluku Indon.
203 H5 Gebeit Sudan
203 H4 Gebeit Mine Sudan
169 K8 Gebesee Ger.
169 E9 Gebhardshain Ger.
174 E3 Gębice Pol.
199 L5 Gebiz Turkey
210 C2 Gebre Guracha Eth.
199 K2 Gebze Turkey
210 B3 Gech'a Eth.
Gecheng Chongqing China see Chengkou
172 F4 Gechingen Ger.
129 C6 Geçit Turkey
Geçitkale Cyprus see Lefkonikon
94 D6 Gedang, Gunung mt. Indon.
138 H7 Gedanonių kalnas hill Lith.
203 G6 Gedaref Sudan
203 G6 Gedaref state Sudan
151 K3 Geddington Northamptonshire, England U.K.
177 H5 Géderlak Hungary
169 H10 Gedern Ger.
202 E6 Gedid Ras el Fil Sudan
165 G9 Gedinne Belgium
199 K4 Gediz Turkey
199 H4 Gediz r. Turkey
210 E3 Gedlegubē Eth.
151 M2 Gedney Drove End Lincolnshire, England U.K.
210 C2 Gēdo Eth.
210 D4 Gedo admin. reg. Somalia
95 I4 Gedong Sarawak Malaysia
94 □ Gedong, Tanjong pt Sing.
163 E10 Gèdre France
142 H7 Gedser Denmark
142 H7 Gedser Odde c. Denmark
142 F5 Gedsted Denmark
94 F7 Gedungpakuan Sumatera Indon.
Gedzheti Georgia see Gejet'i
165 H6 Geel Belgium
83 J8 Geelong Vic. Austr.
87 B10 Geelvink Channel W.A. Austr.
214 E5 Geel Vloer salt pan S. Africa
165 I7 Geer r. Belgium
164 G5 Geertruidenberg Neth.
168 D5 Geeste Ger.
168 G3 Geeste r. Ger.
164 K4 Geesteren Neth.
170 E5 Geestgottberg Ger.
168 J4 Geesthacht Ger.
165 H7 Geetbets Belgium
171 E10 Gefell Ger.
210 C2 Gefersa Eth.
164 H5 Geffen Neth.
171 E10 Gefrees Ger.
138 E6 Gėgė r. Lith.
Gegechkori Georgia see Martvili
177 K3 Gégény Hungary
129 F5 Geghadir Armenia
129 F5 Geghama Lerrnashght'a mts Armenia
129 G5 Geghamasar Armenia
138 H7 Gegužinė Lith.
111 E10 Gê'gyai Xizang China
78 □3a Gehh i. Kwajalein Marshall Is
168 F5 Gehrde Ger.
169 I6 Gehrden Ger.
171 D9 Gehren Ger.
109 L3 Ge Hu l. China
207 H3 Geidam Nigeria
172 G2 Geiersberg hill Ger.
173 N3 Geiersthal Ger.
234 D4 Geigertown PA U.S.A.
223 K3 Geikie r. Sask. Can.
224 B3 Geikie Island Ont. Can.
85 I2 Geikie Range hills Qld Austr.
169 B9 Geilenkirchen Ger.
142 E1 Geilo Norway
104 D6 Geinō Japan
141 I5 Geiranger Norway
169 I9 Geisa Ger.
169 H10 Geiselbach Ger.
173 M4 Geiselhöring Ger.
173 I2 Geiselwind Ger.
173 L4 Geisenfeld Ger.
173 M5 Geisenhausen Ger.
172 D2 Geisenheim Ger.
171 I9 Geising Ger.
172 F6 Geisingen Ger.
169 J8 Geisleden Ger.
172 F5 Geislingen Ger.
172 H4 Geislingen an der Steige Ger.
169 J8 Geismar Ger.
157 O6 Geispolsheim France
178 F5 Geißstein mt. Austria
179 L5 Geistthal Austria
Geisûm, Gezâ'ir is Egypt see Qaysūm, Juzur
211 B5 Geita Tanz.
171 G8 Geithain Ger.
140 L4 Geittind mt. Norway
129 D3 Gejet'i Georgia
108 D7 Gejiu Yunnan China
122 G2 Gëkdepe Turkm.
210 A3 Gel r. Sudan
208 F2 Gel watercourse Sudan
194 G9 Gela Sicilia Italy
194 G9 Gela r. Sicilia Italy
194 G9 Gela, Golfo di g. Sicilia Italy
111 J10 Gêladaindong mt. Qinghai China
210 E3 Geladī Eth.
211 C5 Gelai vol. Tanz.
95 I6 Gelam i. Indon.
161 K8 Gélas, Cime du mt. France/Italy
170 F2 Gelbensande Ger.
173 I2 Gelchsheim Ger.
164 J4 Gelderland prov. Neth.
164 H5 Geldermalsen Neth.
169 B7 Geldern Ger.
169 J10 Geldersheim Ger.
165 I6 Geldrop Neth.
165 I7 Geleen Neth.
199 I3 Gelembe Turkey
210 D2 Gelemso Eth.
171 G9 Gelenau Ger.
199 M4 Gelendost Turkey
135 G7 Gelendzhik Rus. Fed.
210 B2 Gelhak Sudan
199 H2 Gelibolu Turkey
199 H2 Gelibolu Yarımadası pen. Turkey
199 H2 Gelibolu Yarımadası Tarihi Milli Parkı nat. park Turkey
Gelidonya Burnu pt Turkey see Yardımcı Burnu
199 L4 Gelincik Dağı mt. Turkey
210 E3 Gelinsoor Somalia
163 E7 Gelise r. France
176 F5 Gellénháza Hungary
150 F4 Gelligaer Caerphilly, Wales U.K.
78 □3a Gellinam i. Kwajalein Marshall Is
122 G5 Gelmord Iran
169 H10 Gelnhausen Ger.
177 J3 Gelnica Slovakia
163 D9 Gelos France
163 C8 Geloux r. France
142 E6 Gels r. Denmark
186 E5 Gelsa Spain
176 F5 Gelse Hungary
169 D7 Gelsenkirchen Ger.
173 K5 Geltendorf Ger.
190 C3 Gelten-Iffigen nature res. Switz.
168 I1 Gelting Ger.
171 G6 Geltow Ger.
94 F6 Gelumbang Sumatera Indon.
94 E3 Gemas Malaysia
165 G7 Gembloux Belgium
207 H5 Gembu Nigeria
160 G2 Gemeaux France
208 C4 Gemena Dem. Rep. Congo
177 H5 Gemenci park Hungary
161 H10 Gémenos France
126 H4 Gemerek Turkey
177 J3 Gemerská Hôrka Slovakia
177 J3 Gemerská Poloma Slovakia
164 I5 Gemert Neth.
Geminokağı Cyprus see Karavostasi
199 K5 Gemiş Turkey
199 K2 Gemlik Turkey
199 J2 Gemlik Körfezi b. Turkey
140 □B1 Gemlufall Iceland
172 F3 Gemmingen Ger.
191 O3 Gemona del Friuli Italy
162 C4 Gémozac France
212 D5 Gemsbok National Park Botswana
214 E2 Gemsbokplein well S. Africa
214 I1 Gemsbokvlakte S. Africa
172 C2 Gemünden Ger.
169 G9 Gemünden (Wohra) Ger.
169 I10 Gemünden am Main Ger.
185 I8 Genal r. Spain
210 D3 Genalē Wenz r. Eth.
165 F7 Genappe Belgium
185 N4 Génave Spain
122 D7 Genāveh Iran
193 J4 Genazzano Italy
129 B7 Genç Turkey
162 E3 Gençay France
176 F4 Gencsapáti Hungary
124 C9 Gendoa r. Eth.
111 C14 Gendoli Rajasthan India
160 H2 Gendrey France
164 J5 Gendringen Neth.
164 I5 Gendt Neth.
160 E3 Génelard France
164 J3 Genemuiden Neth.
260 E5 General Acha Arg.
261 G5 General Alvear Buenos Aires Arg.
260 D4 General Alvear Mendoza Arg.
261 G4 General Arenales Arg.
253 F6 General Artigas Para.
261 H4 General Belgrano Arg.
General Belgrano II research stn Antarctica see Belgrano II
262 U2 General Bernardo O'Higgins research stn Antarctica
243 J5 General Bravo Mex.
261 F3 General Cabrera Arg.
261 H2 General Campos Arg.
256 A1 General Carneiro Brazil
259 B7 General Carrera, Lago l. Arg./Chile
261 I5 General Conesa Buenos Aires Arg.
259 D6 General Conesa Río Negro Arg.
261 F6 General Daniel Cerri Arg.
261 F3 General Deheza Arg.
167 H2 Generał Dezyderego Chłapowskiego, Park Krajobrazowy imieniu Pol.
243 I5 General Escobeda Mex.
General Freire Angola see Muxaluando
261 H3 General Galarza Arg.
261 I5 General Guido Arg.
260 C3 General Gutiérrez Arg.
187 C8 Generalísimo, Embalse del resr Spain
258 F2 General José de San Martín Arg.
261 I5 General Juan Madariaga Arg.
252 C4 General Lagos Chile
261 G5 General La Madrid Arg.
261 H4 General Las Heras Arg.
261 I5 General Lavalle Arg.
261 F4 General Levalle Arg.
92 F7 General Luna Phil.
92 E6 General MacArthur Samar Phil.
General Machado Angola see Camacupa
261 I4 General Mansilla Arg.
258 D2 General Martín Miguel de Güemes Arg.
261 G4 General O'Brien Arg.
258 F2 General Paz Arg.
261 F4 General Pico Arg.
261 G4 General Pinto Arg.
261 I5 General Pirán Arg.
260 D6 General Roca Arg.
261 H4 General Rodriguez Arg.
261 G3 General Rojo Arg.
253 E4 General Saavedra Bol.
256 B4 General Salgado Brazil
General San Martín research stn Antarctica see San Martín
261 H4 General San Martín Buenos Aires Arg.
261 F5 General San Martín La Pampa Arg.
92 E8 General Santos Mindanao Phil.
244 D1 General Simón Bolívar Mex.
243 J5 General Terán Mex.
197 Q7 General Toshevo Bulg.
242 F3 General Trías Mex.
261 G4 General Viamonte Arg.
261 F4 General Villegas Arg.
232 H7 Genesee PA U.S.A.
232 H5 Genesee r. NY U.S.A.
232 H6 Geneseo NY U.S.A.
182 H2 Genestoso Spain
210 C2 Genet Eth.
158 I4 Genêts France
215 L3 Geneva S. Africa
Geneva Switz. see Genève
231 E10 Geneva AL U.S.A.
226 F8 Geneva IL U.S.A.
236 G5 Geneva NE U.S.A.
232 H6 Geneva NY U.S.A.
232 E7 Geneva OH U.S.A.
Geneva, Lake France/Switz. see Léman, Lac
226 F7 Geneva, Lake WI U.S.A.
190 A3 Genève Switz.
160 I4 Genève canton Switz.
183 P3 Genevilla Spain
160 I4 Genevois mts France
Genf Switz. see Genève
191 N9 Genga Italy
Gengda Sichuan China see Gana
172 E5 Gengenbach Ger.
109 I7 Genglou Guangdong China
108 B7 Gengma Yunnan China
Gengqing Sichuan China see Dêgê
209 D5 Gengwa Dem. Rep. Congo
Gengxuan Yunnan China see Gengma
107 P1 Gen He r. China
210 B3 Geni r. Sudan
175 L1 Geniai Lith.
Genichesk Ukr. see Heniches'k
185 I5 Genil r. Spain
198 F1 Genisea Greece
163 D6 Génissac France
160 H4 Génissiat, Barrage de dam France
116 D8 Genji Rajasthan India
165 I7 Genk Belgium
103 H13 Genkai-nada b. Japan
160 G2 Genlis France
192 C8 Gennargentu, Monti del mts Sardegna Italy
192 C9 Genn'Argiolas, Monte hill Italy
164 I5 Gennep Neth.
162 D1 Gennes France
83 L7 Genoa Vic. Austr.
Genoa Italy see Genova
226 F7 Genoa IL U.S.A.
161 D8 Génolhac France
192 C8 Genoni Sardegna Italy
162 H3 Genouillac France
162 E3 Genouillé France
159 O7 Genouilly France
190 F7 Genova Italy
190 G7 Genova prov. Italy
190 F7 Genova, Golfo di g. Italy
187 E10 Genovés Spain
250 □ Genovesa, Isla i. Islas Galápagos Ecuador
163 E6 Gensac France
165 E6 Gent Belgium
94 G8 Genteng Jawa Indon.
95 J8 Genteng i. Indon.
171 F6 Genthin Ger.
94 D3 Genting Highlands Malaysia
254 E4 Gentio do Ouro Brazil
162 I4 Gentioux, Plateau de France
162 H4 Gentioux-Pigerolles France
Genua Italy see Genova
193 Q6 Genzano di Lucania Italy
193 J4 Genzano di Roma Italy
197 L4 Geoagiu r. Romania
146 D10 Geodha, Rubh' a' pt Scotland U.K.
87 C12 Geographe Bay W.A. Austr.
87 B8 Geographe Channel W.A. Austr.
221 P2 Geographical Society Ø i. Greenland
Geok-Tepe Turkm. see Gëkdepe
130 F1 Georga, Zemlya i. Zemlya Frantsa-Iosifa Rus. Fed.
86 D6 George r. W.A. Austr.
225 H1 George r. Que. Can.
214 G9 George S. Africa
225 I4 George, Cape N.S. Can.
83 L6 George, Lake N.S.W. Austr.
82 G7 George, Lake S.A. Austr.
86 G7 George, Lake salt flat W.A. Austr.
210 A4 George, Lake Uganda
231 G11 George, Lake FL U.S.A.
233 L5 George, Lake NY U.S.A.
84 C7 George Gills Range mts N.T. Austr.
150 D5 Georgeham Devon, England U.K.
216 □2b George Island St Helena
George Land i. Zemlya Frantsa-Iosifa Rus. Fed. see Georga, Zemlya
173 M2 Georgenberg Ger.
173 K3 Georgensgmünd Ger.
233 M5 Georges Mills NH U.S.A.
81 B11 George Sound inlet South I. N.Z.
85 I5 Georgetown Qld Austr.
83 K9 George Town Tas. Austr.
246 F2 George Town Gt Exuma Bahamas
224 E5 Georgetown Ont. Can.
246 C4 George Town Cayman Is
206 B3 Georgetown Gambia
251 G3 Georgetown Guyana
94 D2 George Town Malaysia
216 □2a Georgetown Ascension S. Atlantic Ocean
247 □3 Georgetown St Vincent
235 I2 Georgetown CT U.S.A.
233 J10 Georgetown DE U.S.A.
231 E10 Georgetown GA U.S.A.
230 E6 Georgetown KY U.S.A.
232 B10 Georgetown OH U.S.A.
231 H9 Georgetown SC U.S.A.
237 G10 Georgetown TX U.S.A.
262 T2 George VI Sound sea chan. Antarctica
263 K2 George V Land reg. Antarctica
237 F11 George West TX U.S.A.
129 E4 Georgia country Asia
231 F9 Georgia state U.S.A.
222 E5 Georgia, Strait of B.C. Can.
231 D10 Georgiana AL U.S.A.
224 D4 Georgian Bay Ont. Can.
227 O5 Georgian Bay Islands National Park Ont. Can.
Georgi Dimitrov, Yazovir resr Bulg. see Koprinka, Yazovir
84 G8 Georgina watercourse Qld Austr.
198 F7 Georgioupoli Kriti Greece
Georgi Traykov Bulg. see Dolni Chiflik
Georgiu-Dezh Rus. Fed. see Liski
120 G2 Georgiyevka Aktyubinskaya Oblast' Kazakh.
121 S3 Georgiyevka Vostochnyy Kazakhstan Kazakh.
Georgiyevka Zhambylskaya Oblast' Kazakh. see Korday
129 E1 Georgiyevsk Rus. Fed.
134 I4 Georgiyevskoye Kostromskaya Oblast' Rus. Fed.
129 A1 Georgiyevskoye Krasnodarskiy Kray Rus. Fed.
139 T2 Georgiyevskoye Vologodskaya Oblast' Rus. Fed.
168 D5 Georgsdorf Ger.
168 D4 Georgsheil Ger.
169 F6 Georgsmarienhütte Ger.
Georg von Neumayer research stn Antarctica see Neumayer
178 C6 Gepatsch, Stausee resr Austria
163 D9 Ger Aquitaine France
159 J4 Ger Basse-Normandie France
186 I3 Ger Spain
171 F9 Gera Ger.
165 E7 Geraardsbergen Belgium
169 K9 Geraberg Ger.
172 H3 Gerabronn Ger.
195 K7 Gerace Italy
195 K7 Gerace r. Italy
194 G8 Geraci Siculo Sicilia Italy
147 C9 Gerahies Ireland
198 E2 Gerakarou Greece
198 B5 Gerakas, Akrotirio pt Zakynthos Greece
198 E6 Gerakas, Akrotirio pt Greece
198 D6 Geraki Greece
256 B6 Geral, Serra mts Brazil
254 D4 Geral de Goiás, Serra hills Brazil
81 F11 Geraldine South I. N.Z.
254 D5 Geral do Paraná, Serra hills Brazil
87 C10 Geraldton W.A. Austr.
93 E1 Gerama i. Indon.
198 E5 Geraneia mts Greece
128 C7 Gerar watercourse Israel
157 M7 Gérardmer France
179 M2 Geras Austria
179 N3 Gerasdorf bei Wien Austria
122 F8 Gerāsh Iran
156 H7 Géraudot France
210 B2 Gerba Dima Eth.
240 J1 Gerber CA U.S.A.
157 M7 Gerbéviller France
161 E7 Gerbier de Jonc mt. France
171 E7 Gerbstedt Ger.
176 G4 Gérce Hungary
172 H2 Gerchsheim Ger.
127 J5 Gercüş Turkey
168 J5 Gerdau Ger.
215 K2 Gerdau S. Africa
Gerdauen Rus. Fed. see Zheleznodorozhnyy
177 H4 Gerecsei park Hungary
126 F3 Gerede Turkey
126 F3 Gerede r. Turkey
184 G5 Gerena Spain
177 J5 Gerendás Hungary
182 D5 Gerês, Serra do mts Port.
177 H5 Geresdlak Hungary
123 K6 Gereshk Afgh.
178 G3 Geretsberg Austria
173 K6 Geretsried Ger.
185 N6 Gérgal Spain
129 I3 Gergebil' Rus. Fed.
192 C8 Gergei Sardegna Italy
177 K3 Gergely-hegy hill Hungary
160 F3 Gergy France
173 J2 Gerhardshofen Ger.
94 D2 Gerik Malaysia
122 H5 Gerīmenj Iran
183 L9 Gerindote Spain
236 D5 Gering NE U.S.A.
171 G8 Geringswalde Ger.
177 J4 Gerje r. Hungary
177 H5 Gerjen Hungary
238 E6 Gerlach NV U.S.A.
177 J2 Gerlachovský štít mt. Slovakia
172 G4 Gerlingen Ger.
178 F5 Gerlos Austria
178 F5 Gerlospass pass Austria
225 H2 Germaine, Lac l. Que. Can.
261 F4 Germania Arg.
Germania country Europe see Germany
221 Q2 Germania Land reg. Greenland
Germanicea Turkey see Kahramanmaraş
222 E4 Germansen Landing B.C. Can.
German South-West Africa country Africa see Namibia
232 H9 Germantown MD U.S.A.
232 A9 Germantown OH U.S.A.
237 K8 Germantown TN U.S.A.
226 F6 Germantown WI U.S.A.
166 E3 Germany country Europe
173 J6 Germaringen Ger.
157 J7 Germay France
199 I5 Germencik Turkey
173 K5 Germering Ger.
172 E3 Germersheim Ger.
156 D8 Germigny-des-Prés France
215 M2 Germiston S. Africa
183 O2 Gernika-Lumo Spain
171 D7 Gernrode Sachsen-Anhalt Ger.
169 J8 Gernrode Thüringen Ger.
172 E4 Gernsbach Ger.
172 E2 Gernsheim Ger.
104 F4 Gero Japan
198 G6 Gero Angeli, Akrotirio pt Greece
190 H3 Gerola Alta Italy
171 E10 Geroldsgrün Ger.
173 K5 Gerolsbach Ger.
169 C10 Gerolstein Ger.
173 I2 Gerolzhofen Ger.
Gerona Spain see Girona
198 F7 Geropotamos r. Kriti Greece
191 R4 Gerovo Croatia
165 G8 Gerpinnes Belgium
192 C9 Gerrei reg. Sardegna Italy
Gerri Spain see Guerri de la Sal
Gerrit Denys is P.N.G. see Lihir Group
163 E8 Gers dept France
163 F7 Gers r. France
190 F2 Gersau Switz.
169 I10 Gersfeld (Rhön) Ger.
172 C3 Gersheim Ger.
114 D5 Gersoppa Karnataka India
168 E5 Gersten Ger.
173 I4 Gerstetten Ger.
157 O7 Gerstheim France
173 J5 Gersthofen Ger.
169 J9 Gerstungen Ger.
170 I4 Gerswalde Ger.
161 G7 Gervanne r. France
171 E6 Gerwisch Ger.
Géryville Alg. see El Bayadh
160 C5 Gerzat France
111 G10 Gêrzê Xizang China
126 G3 Gerze Turkey
173 M4 Gerzen Ger.
169 D7 Gescher Ger.
179 N5 Geschriebenstein hill Austria
169 K9 Geschwenda Ger.
169 G7 Geseke Ger.
192 C8 Gesico Sardegna Italy
Gesoriacum France see Boulogne-sur-Mer
157 I4 Gespunsart France
173 J5 Gessertshausen Ger.
261 G2 Gessler Arg.
190 D7 Gesso r. Italy
187 D8 Gestalgar Spain
159 I7 Gesté France
192 C8 Gesturi Sardegna Italy
193 O5 Gesualdo Italy
165 H8 Gesves Belgium
177 K5 Geszt Hungary
177 K4 Gesztered Hungary
141 O6 Geta Åland Fin.
183 M8 Getafe Spain
107 L9 Getai Shaanxi China
122 E4 Getcheh, Kūh-e hills Iran
165 H7 Gete r. Belgium
197 L6 Getic, Podişul plat. Romania
158 I7 Gétigné France
129 G5 Getik r. Armenia
168 I2 Gettorf Ger.
234 A5 Gettysburg PA U.S.A.
236 F3 Gettysburg SD U.S.A.
232 H9 Gettysburg National Military Park nat. park PA U.S.A.
108 F6 Getu He r. China
256 C4 Getulina Brazil
255 B8 Getúlio Vargas Brazil
262 P2 Getz Ice Shelf Antarctica
165 I7 Geul r. Neth.
94 B3 Geumapang r. Indon.
94 B2 Geumpang Sumatera Indon.
94 B2 Geureudong, Gunung vol. Indon.
83 L5 Geurie N.S.W. Austr.
122 H8 Gevān-e Ţāleb Khānī Iran
127 K4 Gevaş Turkey
161 C7 Gévaudan reg. France
169 D8 Gevelsberg Ger.
158 H5 Gévezé France
197 K9 Gevgelija Macedonia
184 E2 Gévora r. Spain
114 D3 Gevrai Mahar. India
160 F2 Gevrey-Chambertin France
210 D2 Gewanē Wildlife Reserve nature res. Eth.
160 I4 Gex France
Gexianzhuang Hebei China see Qinghe
Gey Iran see Nīkshahr
128 A2 Geydik Dağları mts Turkey
171 G9 Geyer Ger.
199 H3 Geyikli Turkey
94 □ Geylang Sing.
94 □ Geylang r. Sing.
117 M6 Geylegphug Bhutan
215 J2 Geysdorp S. Africa
240 J3 Geyserville CA U.S.A.
199 L2 Geyve Turkey
256 C2 Gezarina Brazil
198 B1 Gezavesh Albania
106 G7 Gezidong Qinghai China
122 F8 Gezīr Iran
179 L2 Gföhl Austria
195 □ Ġgantija Temples Gozo Malta
214 H3 Ghaap Plateau S. Africa
128 E5 Ghabāghib Syria
202 E6 Ghabeish Sudan
127 K7 Ghadaf, Wādī al watercourse Iraq
128 E7 Ghadaf, Wādī al watercourse Jordan
123 N4 Ghadai Pak.
Ghadamés Libya see Ghadāmis
202 A2 Ghadāmis Libya
202 B3 Ghaddūwah Libya
122 E3 Ghaem Shahr Iran
125 L5 Ghāfah, Ramlat al des. Saudi Arabia
123 O7 Ghaggar, Dry Bed of watercourse Pak.
117 J7 Ghaghara r. India
78 □6 Ghaghe i. Solomon Is
117 J8 Ghaghra Jharkhand India
195 □ Għaġin, Xrobb l- pt Malta
123 L8 Ghaibi Dero Pak.
195 □ Għajnsielem Gozo Malta
195 □ Għajn Tuffieħa, Ir-Ramla ta' b. Malta
123 I6 Ghalend Iran
120 J3 Ghalkarteniz, Solonchak salt marsh Kazakh.
208 E2 Ghalla, Wadi El watercourse Sudan
Ghallaorol Uzbek. see G'allaorol
195 □ Għallis, Ġebel ta' l- is Malta
206 E4 Ghana country Africa
125 L3 Ghanādah, Rās pt U.A.E.
125 M6 Ghānāh well Oman
125 K6 Ghanīm well Saudi Arabia
116 D6 Ghanliala Rajasthan India
116 C8 Ghantila Gujarat India
116 C9 Ghantwar Gujarat India
125 I2 Ghanwā Saudi Arabia
212 D4 Ghanzi Botswana
212 D4 Ghanzi admin. dist. Botswana
Ghap'an Armenia see Kapan
125 I2 Ghār, Ras al pt Saudi Arabia
Gharakach' Armenia see Lusashogh
124 F5 Gharāmīl, Jabal al hill Saudi Arabia
128 D8 Gharandal Jordan
128 A9 Gharandal, Wādī watercourse Egypt
195 □ Għarb Gozo Malta
205 F2 Ghardaïa Alg.
189 B7 Ghardimaou Tunisia
189 C7 Ghar el Melh Tunisia
123 K4 Ghargharib Afgh.
117 I8 Gharghoda Chhattisgarh India
195 □ Għarghur Malta
203 G2 Ghārib, Jabal mt. Egypt
128 B10 Ghārib, Ra's pt Egypt
123 N2 Gharm Tajik.
125 M6 Gharm, Wādī r. Oman
125 I3 Ghār Mihnān Saudi Arabia
123 L9 Gharo Pak.
122 C4 Gharq Ābād Iran
202 B1 Gharyān Libya
126 H7 Gharz, Wādī al watercourse Syria
125 M7 Gharzaut i. Oman
202 A3 Ghāt Libya
116 H6 Ghatampur Uttar Prad. India
78 □6 Ghatere Sta Isabel Solomon Is
117 J9 Ghatgan Orissa India
116 E8 Ghatol Rajasthan India
117 K8 Ghatsila Jharkhand India
123 M7 Ghauspur Pak.
Għawdex i. Malta see Gozo
124 G8 Ghaymān Yemen
202 C6 Ghazal, Bahr el watercourse Chad
208 F2 Ghazal, Bahr el r. Sudan
Ghazalkent Uzbek. see G'azalkent
204 E2 Ghazaouet Alg.
116 F5 Ghaziabad Uttar Prad. India
117 I7 Ghazipur Uttar Prad. India
125 M2 Ghazira, Ghubbat al inlet Oman
123 L6 Ghazluna Pak.
Ghazna Afgh. see Ghaznī
123 M5 Ghaznī Afgh.
123 L5 Ghaznī prov. Afgh.
123 L5 Ghazni r. Afgh.
123 L5 Ghazoor Afgh.
124 E2 Ghazzālah Saudi Arabia
122 G5 Ghebar Gumbad Iran
190 I5 Ghedi Italy
197 K5 Ghelari Romania
197 O5 Ghelinţa Romania
125 J3 Ghemeis, Ras pt U.A.E.
Ghent Belgium see Gent
232 D11 Ghent WV U.S.A.
Gheorghe Gheorghiu-Dej Romania see Oneşti
197 P6 Gheorghe Lazăr Romania
197 N4 Gheorgheni Romania
114 D4 Gherdi Mahar. India
197 L3 Gherla Romania
190 F4 Ghiffa Italy
Ghijduwon Uzbek. see G'ijduvon
192 B7 Ghilarza Sardegna Italy
123 L6 Ghilzai reg. Afgh.
126 I8 Ghīnah, Wādī al watercourse Saudi Arabia
177 K5 Ghioroc Romania
197 L6 Ghioroiu Romania
177 K6 Ghiroda Romania
165 E7 Ghislenghien Belgium
192 C3 Ghisonaccia Corse France
192 C3 Ghisoni Corse France
123 L5 Ghizao Afgh.
116 D1 Ghizar Jammu and Kashmir
177 K6 Ghizela Romania
123 L9 Ghizri Creek inlet Pak.
78 □6 Ghizunabeana Islands Solomon Is
114 C3 Ghod Mahar. India
114 D3 Ghod r. India
116 D9 Gholvad Mahar. India
123 L9 Ghorabari Pak.
117 L7 Ghoraghat Bangl.
123 K5 Ghorak Afgh.
123 M4 Ghorband r. Afgh.
222 H2 Ghost Lake N.W.T. Can.
116 C6 Ghotaru Rajasthan India
123 M8 Ghotki Pak.
123 K4 Ghowr prov. Afgh.
125 K9 Ghubbah Suquţrā Yemen
Ghudamis Libya see Ghadāmis
123 O2 Ghŭdara Tajik.
117 K7 Ghugri r. India
114 F3 Ghugus Mahar. India
Ghukasyan Armenia see Ashots'k'
123 M9 Ghulam Mohammed Barrage Pak.
128 F4 Ghunthur Syria
128 F7 Ghurayfah hill Saudi Arabia
122 F7 Ghūrī Iran
123 I4 Ghurian Afgh.
124 G3 Ghurrab, Jabal hill Saudi Arabia
124 F4 Ghurūb, Jabal hill Saudi Arabia
116 H8 Ghutipari Madh. Prad. India
128 G9 Ghuwayţah, Nafūd al des. Saudi Arabia
125 M4 Ghuzayn Oman
202 C2 Ghuzayyil, Sabkhat salt marsh Libya
Ghuzor Uzbek. see G'uzor
156 E1 Ghyvelde France
135 H7 Giaginskaya Rus. Fed.
128 B3 Gialias r. Cyprus
97 H8 Gia Nghia Vietnam
96 H6 Gianh, Sông r. Vietnam
199 H7 Gianisada i. Greece
198 D2 Giannitsa Greece
192 G3 Giannutri, Isola di i. Italy
193 J2 Giano dell'Umbria Italy
215 N5 Giant's Castle mt. S. Africa
147 I2 Giant's Causeway lava field Northern Ireland U.K.
235 K2 Giant's Neck CT U.S.A.
95 K9 Gianyar Bali Indon.
97 G10 Gia Rai Vietnam
195 I8 Giardini-Naxos Sicilia Italy
196 J5 Giarmata Romania
194 H9 Giarratana Sicilia Italy
195 I8 Giarre Sicilia Italy
162 I4 Giat France
192 B7 Giave Sardegna Italy
190 C5 Giaveno Italy
190 D4 Giavino, Monte mt. Italy
192 B9 Giba Sardegna Italy
184 H7 Gibalbín hill Spain
246 E3 Gibara Cuba
184 H5 Gibarrayo hill Spain
86 I3 Gibb r. W.A. Austr.
236 F5 Gibbon NE U.S.A.
238 H4 Gibbonsville ID U.S.A.
86 I4 Gibb River W.A. Austr.
86 I4 Gibb River Aboriginal Reserve W.A. Austr.
234 F5 Gibbsboro NJ U.S.A.
231 □1 Gibb's Hill Bermuda
234 E5 Gibbstown NJ U.S.A.
194 D8 Gibellina Nuova Sicilia Italy
212 C5 Gibeon Namibia
159 K3 Giberville France
140 O2 Gibostad Norway
162 A2 Giboule r. France
184 F6 Gibraleón Spain
185 I8 Gibraltar Europe
185 □ Gibraltar, Bay of Gibraltar/Spain
184 H8 Gibraltar, Campo de reg. Spain
204 D2 Gibraltar, Strait of Morocco/Spain
185 □ Gibraltar Harbour Gibraltar
149 R7 Gibraltar Point England U.K.
83 N3 Gibraltar Range National Park N.S.W. Austr.
87 F12 Gibson W.A. Austr.
231 F9 Gibson GA U.S.A.
226 F9 Gibson City IL U.S.A.
87 G8 Gibson Desert W.A. Austr.
87 H8 Gibson Desert Nature Reserve W.A. Austr.
234 C6 Gibson Island MD U.S.A.
222 F5 Gibsons B.C. Can.
175 L1 Giby Pol.
129 K5 Gicäki Dağı mt. Azer.
106 D4 Gichgeniyn Nuruu mts Mongolia
210 B2 Gīdamī Eth.
123 L7 Gidar Pak.
134 K4 Gidayevo Rus. Fed.
210 B2 Gidda Eth.
114 F5 Giddalur Andhra Prad. India
237 G10 Giddings TX U.S.A.
Giddi Pass hill Egypt see Jiddī, Jabal al
140 O5 Gideälven r. Sweden
175 H5 Gidle Pol.
210 C3 Gīdolē Eth.
172 H2 Giebelstadt Ger.
169 J7 Gieboldehausen Ger.
175 H4 Gieczno Pol.
168 K2 Giekau Ger.
167 K3 Giełczew r. Pol.
175 I4 Gielniów Pol.
170 G3 Gielow Ger.
156 E8 Gien France
173 I4 Giengen an der Brenz Ger.
161 I10 Giens, Golfe de b. France
161 I10 Giens, Presqu'île de pen. France
161 H6 Gières France
165 G6 Gierle Belgium
171 E7 Giersleben Ger.
169 K8 Gierstädt Ger.
175 I2 Gierzwałd Pol.
Giesecke Isfjord inlet Greenland see Kangerlussuaq
169 I7 Gieselwerder (Oberweser) Ger.
169 G9 Gießen Ger.
169 G9 Gießen admin. reg. Ger.
164 K2 Gieten Neth.
175 I2 Gietrzwałd Pol.
159 O7 Gièvres France
122 G3 Gīfan Iran
Gifatin Island Egypt see Jiftūn al Kabīr
149 L2 Gifford East Lothian, Scotland U.K.
163 I7 Giffou r. France
160 I4 Giffre r. France
169 K6 Gifhorn Ger.
222 H4 Gift Lake Alta Can.
104 E5 Gifu Japan
104 E4 Gifu pref. Japan
135 H7 Gigant Rus. Fed.
242 D4 Giganta, Cerro mt. Mex.
250 C4 Gigante Col.
185 P5 Gigante mt. Spain
161 D9 Gigean France
146 E11 Gigha i. Scotland U.K.
146 E11 Gigha, Sound of sea chan. Scotland U.K.
197 L7 Gighera Romania
192 F3 Giglio, Isola del i. Italy
192 F3 Giglio Castello Italy
161 D9 Gignac Languedoc-Roussillon France
161 H9 Gignac Provence-Alpes-Côte d'Azur France
190 C4 Gignod Italy
161 G8 Gigondas France
120 K7 G'ijduvon Uzbek.
182 I1 Gijón-Xixón Spain
163 I8 Gijou r. France
211 A5 Gikongoro Rwanda
241 R9 Gila r. AZ U.S.A.
93 F2 Gila, Tanjung pt Maluku Indon.
241 T9 Gila Bend AZ U.S.A.
241 S8 Gila Bend Mountains AZ U.S.A.
241 R9 Gila Mountains AZ U.S.A.
122 C3 Gīlān prov. Iran
122 A4 Gīlān-e Gharb Iran
241 U8 Gila River Indian Reservation res. AZ U.S.A.
197 L4 Gilău Romania
129 K5 Giläzi Azer.
149 P6 Gilberdyke East Riding of Yorkshire, England U.K.
261 H3 Gilbert Arg.
85 H4 Gilbert r. Qld Austr.
241 U8 Gilbert AZ U.S.A.
226 B2 Gilbert MN U.S.A.
232 D11 Gilbert WV U.S.A.
Gilbert Islands country Pacific Ocean see Kiriba
234 C3 Gilberton PA U.S.A.
85 I5 Gilbert Range mts Qld
266 G6 Gilbert Ridge sea featu Pacific Ocean
85 I5 Gilbert River Qld Austr.
234 D4 Gilbertsville PA U.S.A.
232 B7 Gilboa OH U.S.A.
254 D4 Gilbués Brazil
122 G4 Gil Chashmeh Iran
173 K5 Gilching Ger.
238 I2 Gildford MT U.S.A.
213 H3 Gilé Moz.
Gilead reg. Jordan see
185 J6 Gilena Spain
87 E10 Giles, Lake salt flat W.
84 C4 Giles Creek r. N.T. Aust
87 J8 Giles Meteorological S W.A. Austr.
84 D6 Giles Range mts N.T. A
161 K9 Gilette France
Gilf Kebir Plateau Egy Jilf al Kabīr, Haḑabat al
147 J4 Gilford Northern Ireland
83 M3 Gilgai N.S.W. Austr.
83 L4 Gilgandra N.S.W. Austr
129 K4 Gilgilçay Azer.
83 L3 Gil Gil Creek r. N.S.W.
116 E2 Gilgit Jammu and Kash
116 E2 Gilgit r. Jammu and Kas
83 K5 Gilgunnia N.S.W. Austr.
95 K8 Gili Iyang i. Indon.
95 K9 Gilimanuk Bali Indon.
Gilındire Turkey see Ay
222 D4 Gil Island B.C. Can.
147 F4 Gill, Lough l. Ireland
223 M3 Gillam Man. Can.
149 P5 Gillamoor North Yorksh England U.K.
142 I5 Gilleleje Denmark
84 E7 Gillen watercourse N.T.
87 H9 Gillen, Lake salt flat W.A. Austr.
169 C10 Gillenfeld Ger.
82 F5 Gilles, Lake salt flat S.A. Austr.
81 D10 Gillespies Point South
232 I7 Gillett PA U.S.A.
226 F5 Gillett WI U.S.A.
238 L4 Gillette WY U.S.A.
140 M5 Gillhov Sweden
85 H6 Gilliat Qld Austr.
85 H6 Gilliat r. Qld Austr.
150 H5 Gillingham Dorset, England U.K.
151 N5 Gillingham Medway, England U.K.
149 N5 Gilling West North York England U.K.
216 □2b Gill Point St Helena
146 J5 Gills Highland, Scotland
226 G4 Gills Rock WI U.S.A.
160 I5 Gilly-sur-Isère France
160 D3 Gilly-sur-Loire France
235 K1 Gilman CT U.S.A.
226 G9 Gilman IL U.S.A.
226 D4 Gilman WI U.S.A.
237 H9 Gilmer TX U.S.A.
146 I10 Gilmerton Perth and Ki Scotland U.K.
221 K4 Gilmour Island Nunavu
197 L6 Gilort r. Romania
240 K4 Gilroy CA U.S.A.
169 H9 Gilserberg Ger.
149 L4 Gilsland Northumberlan England U.K.
146 K11 Gilston Scottish Border Scotland U.K.
168 I5 Gilten Ger.
91 J8 Giluwe, Mount P.N.G.
150 F4 Gilwern Monmouthshire Wales U.K.
164 G5 Gilze Neth.
210 B2 Gīmbī Eth.
247 □3 Gimie, Mount vol. St L
195 L6 Gimigliano Italy
223 L5 Gimli Man. Can.
143 O1 Gimo Sweden
163 F9 Gimonde, Barrage de France
163 G8 Gimone r. France
163 F8 Gimont France
160 C3 Gimouille France
161 H9 Ginasservis France
203 H6 Ginda Eritrea
85 L7 Gindie Qld Austr.
252 D3 Ginebra, Laguna l. Bol
192 D7 Ginepro, Cala b. Sarde Italy
216 □3c Ginés, Punta pt Lanzar Canary Is
161 B10 Ginestas France
216 □1b Ginetes São Miguel Az
140 □ Ginevrabotnen str. Sva
114 G9 Gin Ganga r. Sri Lanka
114 F6 Gingee Tamil Nadu Indi
165 H7 Gingelom Belgium
172 H4 Gingen an der Fils Ge
246 □ Ginger Hill Jamaica
85 M8 Gin Gin Qld Austr.
87 C11 Gingin W.A. Austr.
215 P5 Gingindlovu S. Africa
92 E7 Gingoog Mindanao Phil.
170 H2 Gingst Ger.
210 D3 Gīnīr Eth.
138 G6 Ginkūnai Lith.
163 I10 Ginoles France
195 L2 Ginosa Italy
195 I6 Ginostra Isole Lipari Ital
102 □1 Ginowan Okinawa Japa
114 G9 Gintota Sri Lanka
Ginzo de Limia Galicia see Xinzo de Limia
184 D6 Giões Port.
198 G7 Giofyros r. Kriti Greece
193 O7 Gioi Italy
195 J6 Gioia, Golfo di b. Italy
193 L4 Gioia dei Marsi Italy
195 L2 Gioia del Colle Italy
193 M5 Gioia Sannitica Italy
195 J7 Gioia Tauro Italy
195 K7 Gioiosa Ionica Italy
194 H7 Gioiosa Marea Sicilia I
Gióna Óros mts Greece Gkiona
190 F3 Giornico Switz.
198 F3 Gioura i. Greece
193 L3 Giovenco r. Italy
191 J3 Gioveretto mt. Italy
178 C7 Gioveretto, Lago di l.
191 K8 Giovi, Monte hill Italy
193 R5 Giovinazzo Italy
224 F2 Gipouloux r. Que. Can.
83 J8 Gippsland reg. Vic. Aus
113 □1 Giraavaru i. N. Male Ma
116 C6 Girab Rajasthan India
192 C1 Giraglia, Île de la i. Co France
177 K2 Giraltovce Slovakia
122 H8 Gīrān Iran
157 L7 Girancourt France
122 H7 Gīrān Rīg mt. Iran
116 G9 Girar Mahar. India
237 H7 Girard KS U.S.A.
232 E7 Girard OH U.S.A.
232 E6 Girard PA U.S.A.
225 H1 Girardin, Lac l. Que. C
234 C3 Girardville PA U.S.A.
192 D8 Girasole Sardegna Italy
Giravaru i. N. Male Mal see Giraavaru
122 G4 Girdab Iran
123 M6 Girdao Pak.
123 K8 Girdar Dhor r. Pak.
123 I6 Girdi Iran
207 I4 Girei Nigeria
126 I3 Giresun Turkey
Girgenti Sicilia Italy see Agrigento
208 C4 Giri r. Dem. Rep. Congo
210 C4 Giribabor well Kenya
117 K7 Giridih Jharkhand India
195 K6 Girifalco Italy
83 K4 Girilambone N.S.W. Au
177 K4 Girişu de Criş Romani
136 G6 Gîrla Mare r. Moldova
116 E9 Girna r. India

Gir National Park India
Girne Cyprus see Keryneia
Giroc Romania
Girod Ger.
Girolata, Golfe de b. Corse France
Giromagny France
Girón Ecuador
Giron Sweden see Kiruna
Girona Spain
Girona prov. Spain
Gironde dept France
Gironde est. France
Gironde-sur-Dropt France
Girondo Arg.
Gironella Spain
Girot Pak.
Girou r. France
Giroussens France
Girton Cambridgeshire, England U.K.
Giruá Brazil
Girvan South Ayrshire, Scotland U.K.
Girvas Rus. Fed.
Girwan Uttar Prad. India
Gisborne North I. N.Z.
Gisborne admin. reg. North I. N.Z.
Gisburn Lancashire, England U.K.
Giscome B.C. Can.
Gisenyi Rwanda
Gislaved Sweden
Gisors France
Gisozi Burundi see Kisosi
Gissar Tajik. see Hisor
Gissar Range mts Tajik./Uzbek.
Gissarskiy Khrebet mts Tajik./Uzbek. see Gissar Range
Gissi Italy
Gistel Belgium
Gistredo, Sierra de mts Spain
Giswil Switz.
Gitarama Rwanda
Gitega Burundi
Gittelde Ger.
Giuba r. Somalia see Jubba
Giubega Romania
Giubiasco Switz.
Giudicarie, Valli val. Italy
Giugliano in Campania Italy
Giuliano di Roma Italy
Giulianova Italy
Giuncugnano Italy
Giurgeului, Munții mts Romania
Giurgiu Romania
Givar Iran
Give Denmark
Giverny France
Givet France
Givors France
Givry Belgium
Givry France
Givry-en-Argonne France
Giyani S. Africa
Giyon Eth.
Giza Al Jīzah Egypt see Al Jīzah
Gizałki Pol.
Gīzeh Rūd r. Iran
Gizel' Rus. Fed.
Gizeux France
Gizhiga Rus. Fed.
Gizio r. Italy
Gizo New Georgia Is Solomon Is
Gizo i. New Georgia Is Solomon Is
Giżycko Pol.
Gizzeria Italy
Gjalicë e Lumës, Mal mt. Albania
Gjerde Norway
Gjerstad Norway
Gjirokastër Albania
Gjoa Haven Nunavut Can.
Gjögur Iceland
Gjøra Norway
Gjøvik Norway
Gjuhëzës, Kepi i pt Albania
Gkinas, Akrotirio pt Rodos Greece
Gkiona mts Greece
Glace Bay N.S. Can.
Glacier, Monte mt. Italy
Glacier Bay AK U.S.A.
Glacier Bay National Park and Preserve AK U.S.A.
Glacier National Park B.C. Can.
Glacier National Park MT U.S.A.
Glacier Peak vol. WA U.S.A.
Gladbeck Ger.
Gladenbach Ger.
Glade Spring VA U.S.A.
Gladstad Norway
Gladstone Qld Austr.
Gladstone S.A. Austr.
Gladstone Tas. Austr.
Gladstone Man. Can.
Gladstone North I. N.Z.
Gladstone MI U.S.A.
Gladstone NJ U.S.A.
Gladstone VA U.S.A.
Gladwin MI U.S.A.
Gladys VA U.S.A.
Gladys Lake B.C. Can.
Glainans France
Glamis Angus, Scotland U.K.
Glamis CA U.S.A.
Glamoč Bos.-Herz.
Glan r. Austria
Glan r. Ger.
Glan Mindanao Phil.
Glan l. Sweden
Glanaman Carmarthenshire, Wales U.K.
Glanaruddery Mountains hills Ireland
Glandage France
Glandon France
Glandon r. France
Glandorf Ger.
Glane r. France
Glane r. Ger.
Glanegg Austria
Glanerbrug Neth.
Glanmire Ireland
Glanworth Ont. Can.
Glarner Alpen mts Switz.
Glärnisch mts Switz.
Glarryford Northern Ireland U.K.
Glarus Switz.
Glarus canton Switz.
Glas Bheinn hill Scotland U.K.
Glasbury Powys, Wales U.K.
Glascarnoch, Loch l. Scotland U.K.
Glasco KS U.S.A.
Glasfjorden l. Sweden
Glasford IL U.S.A.
Glasgow Jamaica
Glasgow Glasgow, Scotland U.K.
Glasgow admin. div. Scotland U.K.
Glasgow DE U.S.A.
Glasgow KY U.S.A.
Glasgow MT U.S.A.
Glasgow VA U.S.A.
Glashütte Ger.
Glashütten Ger.
Gläshütten Ger.
Glaskogens naturreservat nature res. Norway
Glaslough Ireland
Glaslyn Sask. Can.
Glas Maol mt. Scotland U.K.
Glass, Loch l. Scotland U.K.
Glassan Ireland
Glassboro NJ U.S.A.
Glassford South Lanarkshire, Scotland U.K.
Glass Mountain CA U.S.A.
Glasson Cumbria, England U.K.
Glass Peninsula AK U.S.A.

150 G5 Glastonbury Somerset, England U.K.
235 J1 Glastonbury CT U.S.A.
146 I9 Glas Tulaichean mt. Scotland U.K.
190 E1 Glatt r. Switz.
171 H8 Glaubitz Ger.
171 G9 Glauchau Ger.
197 N6 Glavacioc r. Romania
197 O8 Glavan Bulg.
197 P4 Glăvănești Romania
197 O7 Glavinitsa Bulg.
198 F1 Glavki Greece
196 J8 Glavnik Kosovo Serbia
129 I2 Glavnyy Kut Rus. Fed.
139 O6 Glazomichi Rus. Fed.
207 F5 Glazoué Benin
134 K4 Glazov Rus. Fed.
139 T9 Glazunovka Rus. Fed.
139 N6 Glazunovo Rus. Fed.
226 E4 Gleason WI U.S.A.
222 H5 Gleichen Alta Can.
171 E8 Gleina Ger.
179 K5 Gleinalpe mt. Austria
179 M5 Gleisdorf Austria
Gleiwitz Pol. see Gliwice
160 F5 Gleizé France
151 N3 Glemsford Suffolk, England U.K.
140 L5 Glen Sweden
233 □N4 Glen NH U.S.A.
148 F2 Glenacardoch Point Scotland U.K.
146 F8 Glen Affric val. Scotland U.K.
227 N3 Glen Afton Ont. Can.
80 J4 Glen Afton North I. N.Z.
232 H11 Glen Allen VA U.S.A.
147 E5 Glenamaddy Ireland
147 C4 Glenamoy Ireland
147 C4 Glenamoy r. Ireland
158 D6 Glénan, Îles de is France
226 I5 Glen Arbor MI U.S.A.
147 J2 Glenariff Northern Ireland U.K.
147 K3 Glenarm Northern Ireland U.K.
146 H10 Glen Artney val. Scotland U.K.
146 I8 Glen Avon val. Scotland U.K.
81 F11 Glenavy South I. N.Z.
147 J3 Glenavy Northern Ireland U.K.
146 E11 Glenbarr Argyll and Bute, Scotland U.K.
146 E9 Glenbeg Highland, Scotland U.K.
147 C9 Glenbeg Lough l. Ireland
147 C8 Glenbeigh Ireland
223 L5 Glenboro Man. Can.
146 J12 Glenbreck Scottish Borders, Scotland U.K.
146 D8 Glenbrittle Highland, Scotland U.K.
234 D1 Glenburn PA U.S.A.
234 B6 Glen Burnie MD U.S.A.
146 F8 Glen Cannich val. Scotland U.K.
241 U4 Glen Canyon gorge UT U.S.A.
241 U5 Glen Canyon Dam AZ U.S.A.
241 V4 Glen Canyon National Recreation Area park UT U.S.A.
146 I12 Glencaple Dumfries and Galloway, Scotland U.K.
146 J10 Glencarse Perth and Kinross, Scotland U.K.
146 G6 Glen Cassley val. Scotland U.K.
146 J9 Glen Clova val. Scotland U.K.
224 D5 Glencoe Ont. Can.
215 O4 Glencoe S. Africa
146 F9 Glencoe Highland, Scotland U.K.
146 F9 Glen Coe val. Scotland U.K.
236 H3 Glencoe MN U.S.A.
147 E3 Glencolumbkille Ireland
215 J9 Glenconnor S. Africa
235 H3 Glen Cove NY U.S.A.
147 J6 Glencullen Ireland
227 J3 Glendale Ont. Can.
241 T8 Glendale AZ U.S.A.
240 N7 Glendale CA U.S.A.
241 T4 Glendale UT U.S.A.
232 G8 Glendale Lake PA U.S.A.
82 E4 Glendambo S.A. Austr.
146 F10 Glendaruel val. Scotland U.K.
146 I8 Glen Dee val. Scotland U.K.
85 L6 Glenden Qld Austr.
238 L3 Glendive MT U.S.A.
223 I4 Glendon Alta Can.
234 E3 Glendon PA U.S.A.
238 L5 Glendo Reservoir WY U.S.A.
147 G3 Glendowan Ireland
147 F8 Glenduff Ireland
147 J2 Glendun r. Northern Ireland U.K.
146 I10 Gleneagles Perth and Kinross, Scotland U.K.
148 E8 Glenealy Ireland
146 D11 Glenegedale Argyll and Bute, Scotland U.K.
82 H8 Glenelg r. Vic. Austr.
146 E8 Glenelg Highland, Scotland U.K.
146 J10 Glenfarg Perth and Kinross, Scotland U.K.
147 G4 Glenfarne Ireland
146 I8 Glen Feshie val. Scotland U.K.
151 J2 Glenfield Leicester, England U.K.
233 J5 Glenfield NY U.S.A.
146 F9 Glenfinnan Highland, Scotland U.K.
147 H2 Glengad Head Ireland
234 F3 Glen Gardner NJ U.S.A.
147 C9 Glengarriff Ireland
146 F8 Glen Garry val. Highland, Scotland U.K.
146 H9 Glen Garry val. Perth and Kinross, Scotland U.K.
87 E9 Glengarry Range hills W.A. Austr.
148 B5 Glengavlen Ireland
246 □ Glengoffe Jamaica
84 G8 Glengyle Qld Austr.
81 C13 Glenham South I. N.Z.
147 H2 Glenhead Northern Ireland U.K.
84 D7 Glen Helen N.T. Austr.
86 J4 Glen Hill Aboriginal Reserve W.A. Austr.
83 M3 Glen Innes N.S.W. Austr.
146 K8 Glenkindie Aberdeenshire, Scotland U.K.
146 G13 Glenluce Dumfries and Galloway, Scotland U.K.
146 H9 Glen Lyon val. Scotland U.K.
234 C2 Glen Lyon PA U.S.A.
222 C2 Glenlyon Peak Y.T. Can.
80 I4 Glen Massey North I. N.Z.
234 D4 Glenmoore PA U.S.A.
146 G8 Glen More val. Scotland U.K.
85 L9 Glenmorgan Qld Austr.
146 J9 Glen Muick val. Scotland U.K.
80 I4 Glen Murray North I. N.Z.
240 J2 Glenn CA U.S.A.
241 V10 Glenn, Mount AZ U.S.A.
147 C5 Glennagevlagh Ireland
220 D3 Glennallen AK U.S.A.
146 F9 Glen Nevis val. Scotland U.K.
227 K5 Glennie MI U.S.A.
232 I11 Glenns VA U.S.A.
238 G5 Glenns Ferry ID U.S.A.
148 F4 Glenoe Northern Ireland U.K.
222 D3 Glenora B.C. Can.
85 H4 Glenore Qld Austr.
84 G7 Glenormiston Qld Austr.
87 F10 Glenorn Aboriginal Reserve W.A. Austr.
146 G6 Glen Oykel val. Scotland U.K.
83 N4 Glenreagh N.S.W. Austr.
233 K3 Glen Robertson Ont. Can.
234 B5 Glen Rock PA U.S.A.
232 D11 Glen Rogers WV U.S.A.
237 G9 Glen Rose TX U.S.A.
146 J10 Glenrothes Fife, Scotland U.K.
86 I4 Glenroy W.A. Austr.
233 L5 Glens Falls NY U.S.A.
148 D4 Glenshane Pass Northern Ireland U.K.
146 J9 Glen Shee val. Scotland U.K.
146 F8 Glen Shiel val. Scotland U.K.
234 E4 Glenside PA U.S.A.
146 G9 Glen Spean val. Scotland U.K.
234 F2 Glen Spey NY U.S.A.
147 F3 Glenties Ireland
147 H2 Glentogher Ireland

146 H8 Glen Tromie val. Scotland U.K.
81 F10 Glentunnel South I. N.Z.
147 G2 Glenveagh National Park Ireland
232 E10 Glenville WV U.S.A.
148 H5 Glen Vine Isle of Man
226 E1 Glenwater Ont. Can.
232 F11 Glen Wilton VA U.S.A.
237 I8 Glenwood AR U.S.A.
240 □F14 Glenwood HI U.S.A.
236 H5 Glenwood IA U.S.A.
236 H3 Glenwood MN U.S.A.
235 G2 Glenwood NJ U.S.A.
239 J10 Glenwood NM U.S.A.
241 U3 Glenwood UT U.S.A.
232 C10 Glenwood WV U.S.A.
226 B4 Glenwood City WI U.S.A.
239 K7 Glenwood Springs CO U.S.A.
160 J2 Glère France
171 F8 Glesien Ger.
146 □N2 Gletness Shetland, Scotland U.K.
190 E2 Gletsch Switz.
Glevum Gloucestershire, England U.K. see Gloucester
170 G2 Glewitz Ger.
226 D3 Glidden WI U.S.A.
171 J6 Glienicke Ger.
Glikí Greece see Glyki
147 D7 Glin Ireland
188 F3 Glina r. Bos.-Herz./Croatia
188 F3 Glina Croatia
168 J3 Glinde Ger.
171 G6 Glindow Ger.
139 R8 Glinishchevo Rus. Fed.
136 G6 Glinjeni Moldova
139 P7 Glinka Rus. Fed.
175 I3 Glinojeck Pol.
151 L2 Glinton Peterborough, England U.K.
141 J6 Glittertinden mt. Norway
174 G5 Gliwice Pol.
174 G5 Gliwicki, Kanał canal Pol.
179 K6 Globasnitz Austria
241 V8 Globe AZ U.S.A.
177 L6 Glodea, Vârful hill Romania
197 O6 Glodeanu-Sărat Romania
136 G6 Glodeni Moldova
197 M4 Glodeni Romania
179 J6 Glödnitz Austria
174 E2 Głodowa Pol.
Glodyany Moldova see Glodeni
Glogau Pol. see Głogów
179 M4 Gloggnitz Austria
190 G2 Glogn r. Switz.
196 I8 Glogovac Kosovo Serbia
174 E4 Głogów Pol.
174 F5 Głogówek Pol.
175 J5 Głogów Małopolski Pol.
174 G2 Głogowo Pol.
140 L3 Glomfjord Norway
140 O4 Glommersträsk Sweden
173 L6 Glonn Ger.
173 L5 Glonn r. Ger.
178 C6 Glorenza Italy
254 F4 Glória Brazil
184 B2 Glória do Ribatejo Port.
217 □2 Glorieuses, Îles is Indian Ocean
Glorioso Islands Indian Ocean see Glorieuses, Îles
159 M4 Glos-la-Ferrière France
198 E3 Glossa Greece
149 N7 Glossop Derbyshire, England U.K.
171 E7 Glöthe Ger.
135 I5 Glotovka Rus. Fed.
83 M4 Gloucester N.S.W. Austr.
91 K8 Gloucester New Britain P.N.G.
150 H4 Gloucester Gloucestershire, England U.K.
233 O6 Gloucester MA U.S.A.
232 I11 Gloucester VA U.S.A.
150 H4 Gloucester, Vale of val. England U.K.
234 E5 Gloucester City NJ U.S.A.
234 E5 Gloucester County county NJ U.S.A.
85 L6 Gloucester Island Qld Austr.
232 I11 Gloucester Point VA U.S.A.
150 H4 Gloucestershire admin. div. England U.K.
147 F9 Glounthaune Ireland
243 P9 Glover Reef Belize
233 K5 Gloversville NY U.S.A.
225 K3 Glovertown Nfld and Lab. Can.
175 J4 Głowaczów Pol.
174 F1 Główczyce Pol.
170 H1 Glowe Ger.
170 F5 Glöwen Ger.
175 H4 Głowno Pol.
174 F5 Głubczyce Pol.
100 I5 Glubinnoye Rus. Fed.
137 T5 Glubokaya r. Rus. Fed.
135 H6 Glubokiy Rostovskaya Oblast' Rus. Fed.
135 H7 Glubokiy Rostovskaya Oblast' Rus. Fed.
Glubokoye Belarus see Hlybokaye
121 T2 Glubokoye Kazakh.
138 M1 Glubokoye, Ozero l. Rus. Fed.
174 F5 Głuchołazy Pol.
175 I4 Głuchów Pol.
168 I1 Glücksburg (Ostsee) Ger.
168 H3 Glückstadt Ger.
144 D1 Gluggarnir hill Faroe Is
161 F7 Gluiras France
Glukhov Ukr. see Hlukhiv
94 A2 Glumpangminyeuk Sumatera Indon.
149 N6 Glusburn North Yorkshire, England U.K.
137 N2 Glushkovo Rus. Fed.
174 E5 Głuszyca Pol.
174 G3 Głuszyńskie, Jezioro l. Pol.
150 D1 Glyder Fawr hill Wales U.K.
198 B3 Glyki Greece
150 F2 Glyn Ceiriog Wrexham, Wales U.K.
150 E4 Glyncorrwg Neath Port Talbot, Wales U.K.
Glynebwy Wales U.K. see Ebbw Vale
142 E5 Glyngøre Denmark
147 K3 Glynn Northern Ireland U.K.
150 E4 Glynneath Neath Port Talbot, Wales U.K.
Glyn-Nedd Wales U.K. see Glynneath
120 B2 Gmelinka Rus. Fed.
179 I6 Gmünd Kärnten Austria
179 K2 Gmünd Niederösterreich Austria
173 L6 Gmund am Tegernsee Ger.
179 I4 Gmunden Austria
232 D8 Gnadenhutten OH U.S.A.
141 N5 Gnarp Sweden
168 H4 Gnarrenburg Ger.
179 M6 Gnas Austria
147 D8 Gneevgullia Ireland
171 G8 Gneisenaustadt Schildau Ger.
195 □ Ġnejna, Il-Bajja tal- b. Malta
179 I6 Gnesau Austria
Gnesen Pol. see Gniezno
143 N2 Gnesta Sweden
142 H5 Gniben pt Denmark
179 M6 Gniebing Austria
174 G2 Gniew Pol.
174 G1 Gniewino Pol.
174 G3 Gniewkowo Pol.
175 I5 Gnieździska Pol.
174 F3 Gniezno Pol.
143 O4 Gnisvärd Gotland Sweden
196 J8 Gnjilane Kosovo Serbia
191 M6 Gnocchetta Italy
170 G3 Gnoien Ger.
174 F5 Gnojna Pol.
175 I6 Gnojnik Pol.
175 I5 Gnojno Pol.
150 H2 Gnosall Staffordshire, England U.K.
173 J3 Gnotzheim Ger.
87 D12 Gnowangerup W.A. Austr.
87 D10 Gnows Nest Range hills W.A. Austr.
168 I2 Gnutz Ger.
114 C5 Goa Goa India
114 D5 Goa state India
212 C5 Goageb Namibia
83 M7 Goalen Head N.S.W. Austr.

117 M6 Goalpara Assam India
93 A8 Goang Flores Indon.
206 E5 Goaso Ghana
146 F11 Goat Fell hill Scotland U.K.
247 □2 Goat Point Antigua and Barbuda
210 D3 Goba Eth.
212 C4 Gobabis Namibia
Gobannium Monmouthshire, Wales U.K. see Abergavenny
212 C5 Gobas Namibia
260 C5 Gobernador Ayala Arg.
261 G2 Gobernador Crespo Arg.
260 D6 Gobernador Duval Arg.
259 C8 Gobernador Gregores Arg.
261 H3 Gobernador Mansilla Arg.
259 C8 Gobernador Mayer Arg.
261 G2 Gobernador Racedo Arg.
261 G4 Gobernador Ugarte Arg.
258 F3 Gobernador Virasoro Arg.
106 J4 Gobi Desert China/Mongolia
139 Q8 Gobiki Rus. Fed.
179 I3 Göblberg hill Austria
104 B8 Gobō Japan
150 F2 Gobowen Shropshire, England U.K.
Gobustan Azer. see Qobustan
199 J6 Göcek Turkey
169 B7 Goch Ger.
212 C5 Gochas Namibia
169 J10 Gochsheim Ger.
97 H9 Go Công Vietnam
179 O6 Göcsej hills Hungary
177 I4 Göd Hungary
171 J8 Göda Ger.
117 L7 Godagari Bangl.
142 F2 Godal Norway
151 K5 Godalming Surrey, England U.K.
114 G4 Godavari r. India
114 H4 Godavari, Cape India
114 H4 Godavari, Mouths of the India
225 H3 Godbout Que. Can.
225 H3 Godbout r. Que. Can.
117 K7 Godda Jharkhand India
222 C3 Goddard AK U.S.A.
240 N4 Goddard, Mount CA U.S.A.
172 F2 Goddelau Ger.
169 G8 Goddelsheim (Lichtenfels) Ger.
210 D3 Godē Eth.
184 C3 Godeal hill Port.
197 L7 Godech Bulg.
234 F2 Godeffroy NY U.S.A.
178 F8 Godega di Sant'Urbano Italy
129 F6 Gödekli Turkey
187 D9 Godelleta Spain
224 D5 Goderich Ont. Can.
159 L2 Goderville France
Godhavn Greenland see Qeqertarsuaq
116 D8 Godhra Gujarat India
116 B8 Godia Creek b. Gujarat India
190 G6 Godiasco Italy
182 E6 Godim Port.
210 E3 Godinlabe Somalia
175 H1 Godkowo Pol.
81 E10 Godley r. South I. N.Z.
151 L3 Godmanchester Cambridgeshire, England U.K.
104 E5 Gōdo Japan
93 D4 Godo, Gunung mt. Indon.
184 E4 Godolín r. Port./Spain
177 I4 Gödöllő Hungary
179 J8 Godovič Slovenia
261 G3 Godoy Arg.
260 C3 Godoy Cruz Arg.
177 G5 Gödre Hungary
223 M3 Gods r. Man. Can.
223 M4 Gods Lake Man. Can.
223 O2 God's Mercy, Bay of Nunavut Can.
151 L5 Godstone Surrey, England U.K.
Godthåb Greenland see Nuuk
140 O2 Godučohkka mt. Sweden
Godwin-Austen, Mount China/Jammu and Kashmir see K2
174 G4 Godziesze Wielkie Pol.
175 K5 Godziszów Pol.
215 K6 Goedemoed S. Africa
164 E5 Goedereede Neth.
Goedgegun Swaziland see Nhlangano
214 C5 Goegap Nature Reserve S. Africa
224 E3 Goéland, Lac au l. Que. Can.
225 I2 Goélands, Lac aux l. Que. Can.
164 E5 Goes Neth.
227 J3 Goetzville MI U.S.A.
233 N5 Goffstown NH U.S.A.
179 L2 Göfritz an der Wild Austria
224 D4 Gogama Ont. Can.
103 J12 Gō-gawa r. Japan
226 E3 Gogebic, Lake MI U.S.A.
226 E3 Gogebic Range hills MI U.S.A.
128 H2 Gögeç Turkey
172 H4 Göggingen Ger.
129 G6 Gogi Lerr mt. Armenia/Azer.
138 J1 Gogland, Ostrov i. Rus. Fed.
213 G4 Gogoi Moz.
139 O7 Gogolevka Rus. Fed.
174 G5 Gogolin Pol.
197 K6 Gogoșu Romania
207 F4 Gogounou Benin
Gogra Jharkhand India see Ghaghra
Gogra r. India see Ghaghara
208 F2 Gogrial Sudan
116 D7 Gogunda Rajasthan India
116 G6 Gohad Madh. Prad. India
116 F5 Gohana Haryana India
116 F8 Goharganj Madh. Prad. India
168 K2 Göhl Ger.
171 F7 Gohrau Ger.
168 K4 Göhrde Ger.
170 I2 Göhren, Ostseebad Ger.
170 G4 Göhren-Lebbin Ger.
254 G3 Goiana Brazil
256 C3 Goiandira Brazil
255 C5 Goianésia Brazil
256 C2 Goiânia Brazil
254 G3 Goianinha Brazil
256 C2 Goianira Brazil
256 B1 Goiás Brazil
256 B2 Goiás state Brazil
256 C3 Goiatuba Brazil
111 E10 Goicangmai Xizang China
92 □ Goikul Palau
146 G10 Goil, Loch inlet Scotland U.K.
108 C2 Goincang Qinghai China
142 J5 Göinge reg. Sweden
256 A6 Goio r. Brazil
256 A6 Goio-Erê Brazil
209 E6 Goi-Pula Dem. Rep. Congo
164 H5 Goirle Neth.
182 D8 Góis Port.
158 G8 Gois, Passage du France
191 J5 Goito Italy
186 B1 Goizueta Spain
210 C3 Gojeb Wenz r. Eth.
104 C7 Gojō Japan
102 R7 Gojōme Japan
123 O6 Gojra Pak.
175 H4 Gojść Pol.
105 K3 Goka Japan
114 D4 Gokak Karnataka India
114 D5 Gokarn Karnataka India
128 A1 Gök Çay r. Turkey
199 G2 Gökçeada i. Turkey
199 J3 Gökçedağ Turkey
129 A5 Gökçedere Turkey
199 L5 Gökçehüyük Turkey
199 M2 Gökçekaya Barajı resr Turkey
199 I4 Gökçen Turkey
199 J4 Gökçeören Turkey
129 B6 Gökçeşeyh Turkey
Gökdepe Turkm. see Gëkdepe
128 A2 Gökdere r. Turkey
168 H2 Gokels Ger.
126 G3 Gökirmak r. Turkey
122 G1 Goklenkuy, Solonchak salt l. Turkm.
129 C6 Gökoğlan Turkey
199 J5 Gökova Muğla Turkey
Gökova Muğla Turkey see Ula
199 I6 Gökova Körfezi b. Turkey
123 J9 Gokprosh Hills Pak.
129 D6 Göksu r. Turkey
126 H4 Göksun Turkey
126 G5 Göksu Nehri r. Turkey
128 B2 Goksu Parkı Turkey

96 C3 Gokteik Myanmar
128 A2 Göktepe Turkey
213 F3 Gokwe Zimbabwe
142 E1 Gol Norway
176 G5 Gola Croatia
117 J8 Gola Jharkhand India
116 H5 Gola Uttar Prad. India
175 J4 Gołąb Pol.
191 Q4 Golac Slovenia
Golada Spain see Agolada
117 N6 Golaghat Assam India
147 F2 Gola Island Ireland
179 I8 Golak mt. Slovenia
117 L6 Golakganj Assam India
128 D5 Golan hills Syria
174 F3 Gołańcz Pol.
175 K4 Gołaszyn Pol.
122 G7 Golbāf Iran
123 M4 Golbahār Afgh.
126 H5 Gölbaşı Turkey
199 K6 Gölbent Turkey
157 L7 Golbey France
114 F4 Golconda Andhra Prad. India
237 K7 Golconda IL U.S.A.
238 F6 Golconda NV U.S.A.
199 I3 Gölcük Balıkesir Turkey
Gölçük Turkey see Etili
199 K2 Gölcük Kocaeli Turkey
199 J3 Gölcük r. Turkey
176 E2 Golčův Jeníkov Czech Rep.
175 H5 Gołcza Pol.
174 C2 Golczewo Pol.
232 H7 Gold PA U.S.A.
172 G7 Goldach Switz.
175 K1 Gołdap Pol.
175 J1 Gołdapa r. Pol.
169 H10 Goldbach Ger.
238 B5 Gold Beach OR U.S.A.
170 E5 Goldbeck Ger.
170 F3 Goldberg Ger.
150 G4 Goldcliff Newport, Wales U.K.
Gold Coast country Africa see Ghana
83 N3 Gold Coast Qld Austr.
206 E5 Gold Coast coastal area Ghana
179 H6 Goldeck mt. Austria
178 H5 Goldegg Austria
168 H1 Goldelund Ger.
222 G5 Golden B.C. Can.
147 G8 Golden Ireland
80 G7 Golden Bay South I. N.Z.
238 D4 Goldendale WA U.S.A.
81 G8 Golden Downs South I. N.Z.
222 F5 Golden Ears Provincial Park B.C. Can.
169 K7 Goldene Aue reg. Ger.
215 M4 Golden Gate Highlands National Park S. Africa
240 J4 Golden Gate National Recreation Area park CA U.S.A.
246 □ Golden Grove Jamaica
222 E5 Golden Hinde mt. B.C. Can.
224 E4 Golden Lake Ont. Can.
237 J11 Golden Meadow LA U.S.A.
151 K5 Golden Pot Hampshire, England U.K.
223 I5 Golden Prairie Sask. Can.
247 □2 Golden Rock airport St Kitts and Nevis
168 F5 Goldenstedt Ger.
116 F2 Golden Throne mt. Jammu and Kashmir
147 F7 Golden Vale lowland Ireland
215 J8 Golden Valley S. Africa
150 G3 Golden Valley val. England U.K.
213 F3 Golden Valley Zimbabwe
240 O4 Goldfield NV U.S.A.
173 L1 Goldkronach Ger.
175 J1 Gołdopiwo, Jezioro l. Pol.
222 E5 Gold River B.C. Can.
223 K3 Goldsand Lake Man. Can.
234 D6 Goldsboro MD U.S.A.
231 I8 Goldsboro NC U.S.A.
240 P6 Goldstone Lake CA U.S.A.
86 E6 Goldsworthy W.A. Austr.
237 F10 Goldthwaite TX U.S.A.
129 E7 Göldüzü Turkey
232 H10 Goldvein VA U.S.A.
127 K3 Göle Turkey
184 C2 Golegã Port.
170 K5 Golenice Pol.
174 C2 Goleniów Pol.
123 J5 Golestān Afgh.
122 F3 Golestān prov. Iran
174 G6 Goleszów Pol.
240 M7 Goleta CA U.S.A.
242 □R13 Golfito Costa Rica
192 D6 Golfo Aranci Sardegna Italy
192 C7 Golfo di Orosei Gennargentu e Asinara, Parco Nazionale del nat. park Sardegna Italy
199 J6 Gölgeli Dağları mts Turkey
199 K5 Gölhisar Turkey
191 Q5 Goli hill Croatia
191 R6 Goli i. Croatia
237 G11 Goliad TX U.S.A.
196 I7 Golija nat. park Serbia
196 I7 Golija Planina mts Serbia
174 G3 Golina Pol.
107 Q4 Golin Baixing Nei Mongol China
161 B7 Golinhac France
139 U6 Golitsyno Rus. Fed.
126 H3 Gölköy Turkey
173 I2 Gollach r. Ger.
Gollel Swaziland see Lavumisa
179 N3 Göllersdorf Austria
172 E2 Göllheim Ger.
170 I4 Gollin Ger.
170 E3 Göllin Ger.
178 H4 Golling an der Salzach Austria
171 D8 Göllingen Ger.
170 I4 Gollmitz Ger.
171 G6 Golm Ger.
199 I4 Gölmarmara Turkey
169 I7 Golmbach Ger.
171 H6 Golmberg hill Ger.
186 G4 Golmes Spain
106 D8 Golmud Qinghai China
106 D8 Golmud He r. China
179 J7 Golnik Slovenia
192 D2 Golo r. Corse France
92 C5 Golo i. Phil.
139 X6 Golobino Rus. Fed.
121 L7 Golodnaya Step' plain Uzbek.
Gologory hills Ukr. see Holohory
258 E3 Golondrina Arg.
185 I2 Golondrinos, Sierra de los mts Spain
208 C2 Golongosso C.A.R.
139 X7 Golovanovo Rus. Fed.
128 D2 Gölovası Turkey
137 O3 Golovchino Rus. Fed.
129 A2 Golovinka Rus. Fed.
100 N7 Golovnino Kuril'skiye O-va Rus. Fed.
122 D5 Golpāyegān Iran
199 L2 Gölpazarı Turkey
182 I6 Golpejas Spain
179 O4 Gols Austria
179 M3 Gölsen r. Austria
146 I7 Golspie Highland, Scotland U.K.
171 I7 Golßen Ger.
179 K7 Golte mts Slovenia
171 F9 Göltzsch r. Ger.
175 H2 Golub-Dobrzyń Pol.
137 Q8 Golubitskaya Rus. Fed.
121 P1 Golubovka Kazakh.
174 F4 Gołuchów Pol.
139 U8 Golun' Rus. Fed.
209 B7 Golungo Alto Angola
122 I5 Gol Vardeh Iran
210 E4 Golweyn Somalia
197 M9 Golyama Syutkya mt. Bulg.
197 M8 Golyama Zhelyazna Bulg.
197 M9 Golyam Perelik mt. Bulg.
197 M9 Golyam Persenk mt. Bulg.
129 D7 Gölyanı Turkey
Golyashi Belarus see Sasnovy Bor
199 J2 Gölyazı Turkey
175 I3 Gołymin-Ośrodek Pol.
139 O7 Golynki Rus. Fed.
Golyshi Rus. Fed. see Vetluzhskiy

129 B5 Gölyurt Geçidi pass Turkey
170 J5 Golzow Brandenburg Ger.
171 G6 Golzow Brandenburg Ger.
208 F5 Goma Dem. Rep. Congo
211 A5 Goma Uganda
172 G5 Gomadingen Ger.
116 F2 Goma Hanu Jammu and Kashmir
111 I11 Gomang Co salt l. China
106 G9 Gomangxung Qinghai China
104 C7 Gomanodan-zan mt. Japan
183 P5 Gómara Spain
183 P5 Gómara, Campo de reg. Spain
172 G5 Gomaringen Ger.
116 I7 Gomati r. India
94 □ Gombak, Bukit hill Sing.
208 F4 Gombari Dem. Rep. Congo
207 H4 Gombe Nigeria
207 H4 Gombe state Nigeria
211 A6 Gombe r. Tanz.
199 K6 Gömbe Turkey
211 A6 Gombe Stream National Park Tanz.
207 I4 Gombi Nigeria
129 G4 Gombori Georgia
206 E4 Gomboussougou Burkina
217 □1a Gombrani Island Rodrigues I. Mauritius
Gombroon Iran see Bandar-e 'Abbās
199 H3 Gömeç Turkey
182 I6 Gomecello Spain
Gomel' Belarus see Homyel'
Gomel Oblast admin. div. Belarus see Homyel'skaya Voblasts'
Gomel'skaya Oblast' admin. div. Belarus see Homyel'skaya Voblasts'
184 C5 Gomes Aires Port.
146 D10 Gometra i. Scotland U.K.
245 H2 Gómez Farías Mex.
242 H5 Gómez Palacio Mex.
250 A5 Gómez Rendón Ecuador
122 E3 Gomīshān Iran
171 E6 Gommern Ger.
111 G10 Gomo Xizang China
111 G10 Gomo Co salt l. China
139 R1 Gomorovichi Rus. Fed.
190 E3 Goms reg. Switz.
93 E4 Gomumu i. Maluku Indon.
175 H4 Gomunice Pol.
Gonabad Iran see Jūymand
246 G4 Gonaïves Haiti
213 F4 Gonarezhou National Park Zimbabwe
246 G4 Gonâve, Île de la i. Haiti
122 E5 Gonbad, Chāh-e well Iran
122 F3 Gonbad-e Kavus Iran
177 K3 Gönc Hungary
182 F8 Gonçalo Port.
161 H6 Goncelin France
116 I6 Gonda Uttar Prad. India
116 C9 Gondal Gujarat India
210 E2 Gonda Libah well Eth.
250 C5 Gondar Col.
Gondar Eth. see Gonder
182 D6 Gondar Braga Port.
182 D6 Gondar Porto Port.
172 F3 Gondelsheim Ger.
210 C1 Gonder Eth.
129 E6 Gönderme Geçidi pass Turkey
169 D10 Gondershausen Ger.
182 G5 Gondesende Port.
208 C2 Gondey Chad
116 H9 Gondia Mahar. India
182 C6 Gondomar Port.
182 C4 Gondomar Spain
169 D10 Gondorf Ger.
182 D5 Gondoriz Port.
157 K6 Gondrecourt-le-Château France
157 K6 Gondreville France
157 M6 Gondrexange, Étang de l. France
163 E8 Gondrin France
199 I2 Gönen Balıkesir Turkey
199 L5 Gönen Isparta Turkey
199 I2 Gönen r. Turkey
161 I10 Gonfaron France
159 L2 Gonfreville-l'Orcher France
209 C8 Gonga Angola
109 I3 Gong'an Hubei China
111 I12 Gongbalou Xizang China
111 K12 Gongbo'gyamda Xizang China
106 E7 Gongchakou Gansu China
Gongchang Gansu China see Longxi
108 H6 Gongcheng Guangxi China
111 J12 Gonggar Xizang China
108 C4 Gongga Shan mt. Sichuan China
106 G8 Gonghe Qinghai China
Gonghe Yunnan China see Mouding
107 N6 Gonghui Hebei China
Gongjiang Jiangxi China see Yudu
110 F5 Gongliu Xinjiang China
207 I4 Gongola r. Nigeria
83 K4 Gongolgon N.S.W. Austr.
208 A5 Gongoué Gabon
106 E6 Gongpoquan Gansu China
108 E4 Gongquan Sichuan China
108 B5 Gongshan Yunnan China
108 D6 Gongwang Shan mts Yunnan China
Gongxian Henan China see Gongyi
Gongxian Sichuan China see Gongquan
107 M9 Gongyi Henan China
100 D7 Gongzhuling Jilin China
192 C8 Goni Sardegna Italy
261 I3 Goñi Uru.
175 K2 Goniądz Pol.
207 I4 Goniri Nigeria
Gonjo Xizang China see Kasha
108 B3 Gonjo Xizang China
192 A9 Gonnesa Sardegna Italy
192 A9 Gonnesa, Golfo di b. Sardegna Italy
198 D3 Gonnoi Greece
192 B9 Gonnosfanadiga Sardegna Italy
192 B8 Gonnosnò Sardegna Italy
102 S6 Gonohe Japan
103 G13 Gōnoura Japan
160 I2 Gonsans France
215 M8 Gonubie S. Africa
177 G4 Gönyű Hungary
191 J6 Gonzaga Italy
245 I3 Gonzáles Mex.
240 K5 Gonzales CA U.S.A.
237 G11 Gonzales TX U.S.A.
261 F4 González Moreno Arg.
244 D2 González Ortega Mex.
242 □T13 Gonzalo Vásquez Panama
100 D2 Gonzha Rus. Fed.
232 H11 Goochland VA U.S.A.
232 F11 Goode VA U.S.A.
263 I2 Goodenough, Cape Antarctica
91 L8 Goodenough Island P.N.G.
227 P5 Gooderham Ont. Can.
226 I4 Good Harbor Bay MI U.S.A.
226 I4 Good Hart MI U.S.A.
215 J1 Good Hope Botswana
226 D9 Good Hope IL U.S.A.
214 C10 Good Hope, Cape of S. Africa
222 E5 Good Hope Mountain B.C. Can.
238 G5 Gooding ID U.S.A.
236 E6 Goodland KS U.S.A.
217 □1b Goodlands Mauritius
226 F4 Goodman WI U.S.A.
83 K3 Goodooga N.S.W. Austr.
84 D2 Goodparla N.T. Austr.
226 D4 Goodrich WI U.S.A.
223 I4 Goodsoil Sask. Can.
263 E2 Goodspeed Nunataks nunataks Antarctica
150 C3 Goodwick Pembrokeshire, Wales U.K.
225 G2 Goodwood r. Que. Can.
81 E12 Goodwood South I. N.Z.
149 P6 Goole East Riding of Yorkshire, England U.K.
83 J6 Goolgowi N.S.W. Austr.
82 G6 Goolwa S.A. Austr.
84 D1 Goomadeer r. N.T. Austr.
87 D11 Goomalling W.A. Austr.

83 J3 Goombalie N.S.W. Austr.
85 N9 Goomeri Qld Austr.
213 G3 Goonda Moz.
83 M3 Goondiwindi Qld Austr.
87 F10 Goongarrie, Lake salt flat W.A. Austr.
87 F10 Goongarrie National Park W.A. Austr.
150 B7 Goonhavern Cornwall, England U.K.
85 K6 Goonyella Qld Austr.
164 K4 Goor Neth.
87 D11 Goorly, Lake salt flat W.A. Austr.
225 I2 Goose r. Nfld and Lab. Can.
236 G2 Goose r. ND U.S.A.
Goose Bay Nfld and Lab. Can. see Happy Valley-Goose Bay
81 H9 Goose Bay South I. N.Z.
231 G9 Goose Creek SC U.S.A.
238 H5 Goose Creek r. ID/NV U.S.A.
259 F8 Goose Green Falkland Is
238 D6 Goose Lake CA U.S.A.
240 M6 Goose Lake Canal r. CA U.S.A.
114 E5 Gooty Andhra Prad. India
115 J3 Gop Orissa India
117 L8 Gopalganj Bangl.
117 J6 Gopalganj Bihar India
115 I3 Gopalpur Orissa India
183 O3 Gopegi Spain
116 G4 Gopeshwar Uttaranchal India
114 E7 Gopichettipalayam Tamil Nadu India
116 I7 Gopiganj Uttar Prad. India
174 G3 Gopło, Jezioro l. Pol.
172 H4 Göppingen Ger.
108 A4 Goqên Xizang China
185 N6 Gor Spain
185 M5 Gor r. Spain
174 E4 Góra Dolnośląskie Pol.
175 I3 Góra Mazowieckie Pol.
Goradiz Azer. see Horadiz
185 M6 Gorafe Spain
129 G2 Goragorskiy Rus. Fed.
175 K5 Goraj Pol.
175 J4 Góra Kalwaria Pol.
117 I6 Gorakhpur Uttar Prad. India
129 H5 Goranboy Azer.
175 J4 Góra Puławska Pol.
177 H1 Góra Świętej Anny, Park Krajobrazowy Pol.
174 D2 Gorawino Pol.
188 G4 Goražde Bos.-Herz.
139 U8 Gorbachevo Rus. Fed.
260 A6 Gorbea Chile
177 K4 Görbeháza Hungary
183 O2 Gorbeia mt. Spain
100 A2 Gorbitsa Rus. Fed.
261 H4 Gorchs Arg.
134 H4 Gorchukha Rus. Fed.
177 H6 Görcsöny Hungary
175 I6 Gorczański Park Narodowy nat. park Pol.
246 B6 Gorda, Banco sea feature Hond.
216 □3d Gorda, Punta pt La Palma Canary Is
242 □R10 Gorda, Punta pt Nic.
240 H1 Gorda, Punta pt CA U.S.A.
185 K6 Gorda, Sierra mts Spain
246 E1 Gorda Cay i. Bahamas
141 L6 Gördalen Sweden
183 J4 Gordaliza del Pino Spain
190 H7 Gordana r. Italy
161 G9 Gordes France
199 J4 Gördes Turkey
139 O9 Gordeyevka Rus. Fed.
190 F3 Gordola Switz.
87 D13 Gordon r. W.A. Austr.
146 K11 Gordon Scottish Borders, Scotland U.K.
236 D4 Gordon NE U.S.A.
234 C3 Gordon PA U.S.A.
226 C3 Gordon WI U.S.A.
259 C9 Gordon, Isla i. Chile
83 K10 Gordon, Lake Tas. Austr.
190 G3 Gordona Italy
84 C1 Gordon Bay N.T. Austr.
84 C4 Gordon Creek r. N.T. Austr.
86 J5 Gordon Downs W.A. Austr.
223 I3 Gordon Lake Alta Can.
222 H2 Gordon Lake N.W.T. Can.
222 C2 Gordon Landing Y.T. Can.
214 C10 Gordon's Bay S. Africa
232 G10 Gordonsville VA U.S.A.
85 J4 Gordonvale Qld Austr.
234 C4 Gordonville PA U.S.A.
208 C3 Goré Chad
210 B2 Gorē Eth.
81 C13 Gore South I. N.Z.
232 G9 Gore VA U.S.A.
227 L4 Gore Bay Ont. Can.
146 J11 Gorebridge Midlothian, Scotland U.K.
199 I4 Görece Turkey
139 U7 Gorelki Rus. Fed.
129 E4 Gorelovka Georgia
135 H5 Goreloye Rus. Fed.
126 G4 Göreme Milli Parkı nat. park Turkey
179 L8 Gorenja Straža Slovenia
179 J7 Gorenja vas Slovenia
220 C4 Gore Point AK U.S.A.
147 I7 Goresbridge Ireland
139 S6 Goretovo Rus. Fed.
147 J7 Gorey Ireland
122 H7 Gorg Iran
122 F3 Gorgān Iran
122 E3 Gorgān, Khalīj-e b. Iran
122 E3 Gorgān, Rūd-e r. Iran
Gorgany mts Ukr. see Horhany
86 E6 Gorge Range hills W.A. Austr.
85 J5 Gorge Range mts Qld Austr.
81 C13 Gorge Road South I. N.Z.
214 B3 Gorges Namibia
176 G5 Gőrgeteg Hungary
193 Q7 Gorgoglione Italy
206 B2 Gorgol admin. reg. Maur.
190 H9 Gorgona, Isola di i. Italy
190 G4 Gorgonzola Italy
210 C1 Gorgora Eth.
207 H3 Gorgoram Nigeria
187 F10 Gorgos r. Spain
197 R5 Gorgova, Lacul l. Romania
129 C6 Görgü Turkey
233 N4 Gorham NH U.S.A.
129 F4 Gori Georgia
196 H8 Gorica Montenegro
179 O7 Goričan Croatia
179 N6 Goričko reg. Slovenia
164 G5 Gorinchem Neth.
151 J4 Goring Oxfordshire, England U.K.
191 M6 Gorino Italy
129 H6 Goris Armenia
173 J6 Görisried Ger.
197 P8 Goritsa Bulg.
139 T4 Goritsy Rus. Fed.
170 I4 Göritz Ger.
191 P4 Gorizia Italy
191 P4 Gorizia prov. Italy
179 L8 Gorjanci mts Slovenia
139 V5 Gorka Rus. Fed.
129 F1 Gor'kaya Balka r. Rus. Fed.
117 J6 Gorkha Nepal
Gorki Belarus see Horki
134 I4 Gorki Rus. Fed.
Gor'kiy Rus. Fed. see Nizhniy Novgorod
Gor'kovskaya Oblast' admin. div. Rus. Fed. see Nizhegorodskaya Oblast'
139 N4 Gor'kovskoye Vodokhranilishche resr Rus. Fed.
121 S1 Gor'koye, Ozero salt l. Rus. Fed.
121 S1 Gor'koye, Ozero salt l. Rus. Fed.
170 D4 Gorleben Ger.
142 H6 Gørlev Denmark
175 J6 Gorlice Pol.
171 K8 Görlitz Ger.
170 D4 Gorlosen Ger.
Gorlovka Ukr. see Horlivka
139 W8 Gorlovo Rus. Fed.
171 I7 Görlsdorf Ger.
146 D11 Gorm, Loch l. Scotland U.K.
147 J5 Gormanstown Ireland
183 O5 Gormaz Spain

Great Rhos hill Wales U.K.
Great Rift Valley Africa
Great Ruaha r. Tanz.
Great Sacandaga Lake NY U.S.A.
Great St Bernard Pass Italy/Switz.
Great Sale Cay i. Bahamas
Great Salkeld Cumbria, England U.K.
Great Salt Lake UT U.S.A.
Great Salt Lake Desert UT U.S.A.
Great Salt Pond l. St Kitts and Nevis
Great Sampford Essex, England U.K.
Great Sand Dunes National Park and Preserve CO U.S.A.
Great Sand Hills Sask. Can.
Great Sand Sea des. Egypt/Libya
Great Sandy Desert W.A. Austr.
Great Sandy Island Qld Austr. see Fraser Island
Great Sandy Island Nature Reserve W.A. Austr.
Great Sea Reef Fiji
Great Shelford Cambridgeshire, England U.K.
Great Slave Lake N.W.T. Can.
Great Smoky Mountains NC/TN U.S.A.
Great Smoky Mountains National Park NC/TN U.S.A.
Great Snow Mountain B.C. Can.
Great Sound b. Bermuda
Great South Bay NY U.S.A.
Great Stour r. England U.K.
Great Sugar Loaf hill Ireland
Great Torrington Devon, England U.K.
Great Usutu r. Africa see Usutu
Great Victoria Desert W.A. Austr.
Great Victoria Desert Conservation Park nature res. S.A. Austr.
Great Victoria Desert Nature Reserve W.A. Austr.
Great Wakering Essex, England U.K.
Great Wall research stn Antarctica
Great Wall tourist site China
Great Waltham Essex, England U.K.
Great Wass Island ME U.S.A.
Great Western Erg des. Alg. see Grand Erg Occidental
Great Western Tiers mts Tas. Austr.
Great West Torres Islands Myanmar
Great Whernside hill England U.K.
Great Winterhoek mt. S. Africa
Great Wyrley Staffordshire, England U.K.
Great Yarmouth Norfolk, England U.K.
Great Yeldham Essex, England U.K.
Great Zimbabwe National Monument tourist site Zimbabwe
Grebbestad Sweden
Grebenau Ger.
Grebendorf (Meinhard) Ger.
Grebenhain Ger.
Grebenkovskiy Ukr. see Hrebinka
Grebenskaya Rus. Fed.
Grebenski Rus. Fed. see Grebenskaya
Grebenstein Ger.
Grebin Ger.
Grębków Pol.
Grebnevo Rus. Fed.
Grębocice Pol.
Grębocin Pol.
Grębów Pol.
Grebyonka Ukr. see Hrebinka
Greccio Italy
Greci Italy
Greci, Vârful hill Romania
Greco, Cape Cyprus see Greko, Cape
Greco, Monte mt. Italy
Greding Ger.
Gredos, Sierra de mts Spain
Greec Chile
Greece country Europe
Greece NY U.S.A.
Greeley CO U.S.A.
Greeley PA U.S.A.
Greely Center NE U.S.A.
Greely Fiord inlet Nunavut Can.
Greem-Bell, Ostrov i. Zemlya Frantsa-Iosifa Rus. Fed.
Green r. N.B. Can.
Green r. KY U.S.A.
Green r. ND U.S.A.
Green r. WY U.S.A.
Green Bay WI U.S.A.
Green Bay b. WI U.S.A.
Greenbelt MD U.S.A.
Greenbrier r. WV U.S.A.
Greenbushes W.A. Austr.
Green Cape N.S.W. Austr.
Greencastle Bahamas
Greencastle Ireland
Greencastle Northern Ireland U.K.
Greencastle Northern Ireland U.K.
Greencastle IN U.S.A.
Greencastle PA U.S.A.
Green Cay i. Bahamas
Green Cove Springs FL U.S.A.
Green Creek NJ U.S.A.
Greene Ger.
Greene IA U.S.A.
Greene ME U.S.A.
Greene NY U.S.A.
Greeneville TN U.S.A.
Greenfield CA U.S.A.
Greenfield IA U.S.A.
Greenfield IN U.S.A.
Greenfield MA U.S.A.
Greenfield MO U.S.A.
Greenfield OH U.S.A.
Greenfield WI U.S.A.
Greenfield Park NY U.S.A.
Greengairs North Lanarkshire, Scotland U.K.
Greenham West Berkshire, England U.K.
Green Haven MD U.S.A.
Green Head W.A. Austr.
Green Head hd W.A. Austr.
Greenhead Northumberland, England U.K.
Greenhill Island N.T. Austr.
Greenhills South I. N.Z.
Green Island Jamaica
Greenisland Northern Ireland U.K.
Green Island Bay Palawan Phil.
Green Islands P.N.G.
Green Lake Sask. Can.
Green Lake l. B.C. Can.
Green Lake l. South I. N.Z.
Green Lake WI U.S.A.
Greenland terr. N. America
Greenland MI U.S.A.
Greenland Basin sea feature Arctic Ocean
Greenland Reservoir South I. N.Z.
Greenland Sea Greenland/Svalbard
Green Lane PA U.S.A.
Green Lane Reservoir PA U.S.A.
Greenlaw Scottish Borders, Scotland U.K.
Greenloaning Perth and Kinross, Scotland U.K.
Green Lowther hill Scotland U.K.

82 E6 Greenly Island S.A. Austr.
234 B5 Greenmount MD U.S.A.
233 M4 Green Mountains VT U.S.A.
146 G11 Greenock Inverclyde, Scotland U.K.
149 K5 Greenodd Cumbria, England U.K.
147 J4 Greenore Ireland
147 J8 Greenore Point Ireland
87 C10 Greenough W.A. Austr.
87 C10 Greenough r. W.A. Austr.
82 □3 Green Point S. Pacific Ocean
235 G2 Green Pond NJ U.S.A.
233 M7 Greenport NY U.S.A.
241 V3 Green River UT U.S.A.
238 J6 Green River WY U.S.A.
231 D9 Greensboro AL U.S.A.
231 F9 Greensboro GA U.S.A.
234 D7 Greensboro MD U.S.A.
231 H7 Greensboro NC U.S.A.
230 E6 Greensburg IN U.S.A.
237 F7 Greensburg KS U.S.A.
230 E7 Greensburg KY U.S.A.
237 J10 Greensburg LA U.S.A.
232 F8 Greensburg PA U.S.A.
241 W7 Greens Peak NM U.S.A.
146 E7 Greenstone Point Scotland U.K.
231 H8 Green Swamp NC U.S.A.
226 I9 Greentown IN U.S.A.
234 E2 Greentown PA U.S.A.
236 K6 Greenup IL U.S.A.
232 C10 Greenup KY U.S.A.
85 J5 Greenvale Qld Austr.
233 K3 Green Valley Ont. Can.
241 V10 Green Valley AZ U.S.A.
222 D4 Greenville B.C. Can.
206 C5 Greenville Liberia
231 D10 Greenville AL U.S.A.
240 L1 Greenville CA U.S.A.
231 F10 Greenville FL U.S.A.
231 E9 Greenville GA U.S.A.
236 K6 Greenville IL U.S.A.
230 D7 Greenville KY U.S.A.
233 □P3 Greenville ME U.S.A.
226 I6 Greenville MI U.S.A.
237 J7 Greenville MO U.S.A.
237 J9 Greenville MS U.S.A.
231 I8 Greenville NC U.S.A.
233 N6 Greenville NH U.S.A.
236 M5 Greenville OH U.S.A.
232 E7 Greenville PA U.S.A.
231 F8 Greenville SC U.S.A.
237 G9 Greenville TX U.S.A.
232 F10 Greenville VA U.S.A.
226 D1 Greenwater Lake Ont. Can.
223 K4 Greenwater Provincial Park Sask. Can.
150 C4 Greenway Pembrokeshire, Wales U.K.
Greenwich atoll Micronesia see Kapingamarangi
151 L5 Greenwich Greater London, England U.K.
235 H2 Greenwich CT U.S.A.
234 E6 Greenwich NJ U.S.A.
233 L5 Greenwich NY U.S.A.
232 C7 Greenwich OH U.S.A.
237 H8 Greenwood AR U.S.A.
234 D7 Greenwood DE U.S.A.
230 D6 Greenwood IN U.S.A.
237 J9 Greenwood MS U.S.A.
231 F8 Greenwood SC U.S.A.
226 D5 Greenwood WI U.S.A.
235 G2 Greenwood Lake NY U.S.A.
235 G2 Greenwood Lake l. NJ U.S.A.
231 F8 Greer SC U.S.A.
237 I8 Greers Ferry Lake AR U.S.A.
148 D8 Greese r. Ireland
168 D3 Greetsiel (Krummhörn) Ger.
250 D6 Gregório r. Brazil
84 G5 Gregory r. Qld Austr.
227 J7 Gregory MI U.S.A.
236 F4 Gregory SD U.S.A.
82 G3 Gregory, Lake salt flat S.A. Austr.
86 I6 Gregory, Lake salt flat W.A. Austr.
87 E8 Gregory, Lake salt flat W.A. Austr.
84 G5 Gregory Downs Qld Austr.
84 C4 Gregory National Park N.T. Austr.
85 I5 Gregory Range hills Qld Austr.
86 F6 Gregory Range hills W.A. Austr.
178 H6 Greifenburg Austria
171 H8 Greifendorf Ger.
190 F1 Greifensee l. Switz.
169 F9 Greifenstein Ger.
170 I4 Greiffenberg Ger.
170 H2 Greifswald Ger.
170 I2 Greifswalder Bodden b. Ger.
170 I2 Greifswalder Oie i. Ger.
179 K3 Grein Austria
171 F9 Greiz Ger.
128 C4 Greko, Cape Cyprus
168 K2 Gremersdorf Ger.
134 G1 Gremikha Rus. Fed.
139 V7 Gremyachev Rus. Fed.
134 L4 Gremyachinsk Permskaya Oblast' Rus. Fed.
98 I1 Gremyachinsk Respublika Buryatiya Rus. Fed.
137 S2 Gremyach'ye Rus. Fed.
142 G5 Grenå Denmark
237 K9 Grenada MS U.S.A.
247 □6 Grenada country West Indies
237 K9 Grenada Lake resr MS U.S.A.
163 G8 Grenade France
163 D8 Grenade-sur-l'Adour France
157 K8 Grenant France
190 C1 Grenchen Switz.
142 G4 Grenen spit Denmark
83 L5 Grenfell N.S.W. Austr.
223 K5 Grenfell Sask. Can.
161 H6 Grenoble France
140 U2 Grense-Jakobselv Norway
247 □6 Grenville Grenada
85 I1 Grenville, Cape Qld Austr.
Grenville Island Fiji see Rotuma
172 D6 Grenzach-Wyhlen Ger.
161 H9 Gréoux-les-Bains France
170 F2 Gresenhorst Ger.
123 K8 Greshag Pak.
123 L8 Greshak Pak.
238 C4 Gresham OR U.S.A.
163 H7 Grésigne, Forêt de la reg. France
95 J8 Gresik Jawa Indon.
146 D6 Gress Western Isles, Scotland U.K.
140 L4 Gressåmoen Nasjonalpark nat. park Norway
190 C4 Gressan Italy
161 H6 Gresse r. France
168 K4 Gresse Ger.
161 H7 Gresse-en-Vercors France
190 D4 Gressoney-la-Trinite Italy
179 L4 Gresten Austria
160 H5 Grésy-sur-Aix France
160 I5 Grésy-sur-Isère France
149 L5 Greta r. England U.K.
192 G2 Gretano r. Italy
146 J13 Gretna Dumfries and Galloway, Scotland U.K.
237 J11 Gretna LA U.S.A.
232 F12 Gretna VA U.S.A.
173 I2 Grettstadt Ger.
169 K8 Greußen Ger.
157 K7 Greux France
191 K8 Greve r. Italy
191 K8 Greve in Chianti Italy
164 E5 Grevelingen sea chan. Neth.
168 K4 Greven Mecklenburg-Vorpommern Ger.
169 E6 Greven Nordrhein-Westfalen Ger.
198 C2 Grevena Greece
165 I6 Grevenbicht Neth.
169 C8 Grevenbroich Ger.
165 J9 Grevenmacher Lux.
165 J9 Grevenmacher admin. dist. Lux.
170 D3 Grevesmühlen Ger.
225 J4 Grey r. Nfld and Lab. Can.
81 F9 Grey r. South I. N.Z.
84 F2 Grey, Cape N.T. Austr.
147 K3 Greyabbey Northern Ireland U.K.
238 J4 Greybull WY U.S.A.
238 J4 Greybull r. WY U.S.A.

222 C2 Grey Hunter Peak Y.T. Can.
225 K3 Grey Islands Nfld and Lab. Can.
215 M2 Greylingstad S. Africa
233 L6 Greylock, Mount MA U.S.A.
81 F9 Greymouth South I. N.Z.
148 F4 Grey Point Northern Ireland U.K.
83 I3 Grey Range hills Qld Austr.
87 C8 Grey's Plains W.A. Austr.
149 L4 Greystoke Cumbria, England U.K.
213 F4 Greystone Zimbabwe
147 J6 Greystones Ireland
214 D10 Greyton S. Africa
81 J8 Greytown North I. N.Z.
215 O5 Greytown S. Africa
165 G7 Grez-Doiceau Belgium
159 J6 Grez-en-Bouère France
191 K4 Grezzana Italy
179 I7 Grgar Slovenia
198 F5 Gria, Akrotirio pt Andros Greece
Griais Scotland U.K. see Gress
135 H6 Gribanovskiy Rus. Fed.
208 C2 Gribingui r. C.A.R.
208 C3 Gribingui-Bamingui, Réserve de Faune du nature res. C.A.R.
134 F2 Gridino Rus. Fed.
240 K2 Gridley CA U.S.A.
226 F9 Gridley IL U.S.A.
171 E6 Grieben Ger.
183 Q8 Griegos Spain
157 O6 Gries France
178 D5 Gries am Brenner Austria
172 E5 Griesbach Ger.
173 O5 Griesbach im Rottal Ger.
172 F2 Griesheim Ger.
179 I3 Grieskirchen Austria
171 K7 Grießen Ger.
173 M6 Griesstätt Ger.
179 K6 Griffen Austria
231 E9 Griffin GA U.S.A.
83 K6 Griffith N.S.W. Austr.
227 Q4 Griffith Ont. Can.
220 F2 Griffiths Point N.W.T. Can.
232 D10 Griffithsville WV U.S.A.
Grigan i. N. Mariana Is see Agrihan
192 B8 Grighini, Monte hill Italy
Grigioni canton Switz. see Graubünden
138 I7 Grigiškės Lith.
190 G4 Grigna mt. Italy
190 I4 Grigna r. Italy
161 F8 Grignan France
191 L3 Grigno Italy
191 L3 Grigno r. Italy
163 D7 Grignols France
160 F5 Grigny France
136 I6 Grigoriopol Moldova
183 K4 Grijota Spain
164 J2 Grijpskerk Neth.
Grik Malaysia see Gerik
161 F8 Grillon France
83 J9 Grim, Cape Tas. Austr.
193 Q9 Grimaldi Italy
208 D3 Grimari C.A.R.
161 J10 Grimaud France
146 A7 Griminis Point Scotland U.K.
171 G8 Grimma Ger.
170 H2 Grimmen Ger.
179 I4 Grimming mt. Austria
170 I5 Grimnitzsee l. Ger.
149 R7 Grimoldby Lincolnshire, England U.K.
146 B8 Grimsay i. Scotland U.K.
227 O6 Grimsby Ont. Can.
149 Q6 Grimsby North East Lincolnshire, England U.K.
190 E2 Grimsel nature res. Switz.
140 □E1 Grímsey i. Iceland
222 G3 Grimshaw Alta Can.
140 □E1 Grímsstaðir Iceland
142 E3 Grimstad Norway
151 N2 Grimston Norfolk, England U.K.
142 B2 Grindafjord Norway
141 J6 Grindaheim Norway
140 □B2 Grindavík Iceland
190 E2 Grindelwald Switz.
142 E6 Grindsted Denmark
227 L5 Grind Stone City MI U.S.A.
197 O6 Grindu Ialomița Romania
197 Q5 Grindu Tulcea Romania
197 Q6 Grindul Chituc spit Romania
197 O4 Grindușu, Vârful mt. Romania
139 Q9 Grinevo Rus. Fed.
149 P7 Gringley on the Hill Nottinghamshire, England U.K.
236 I5 Grinnell IA U.S.A.
221 I2 Grinnell Peninsula Nunavut Can.
183 M8 Griñón Spain
178 C5 Grins Austria
197 N3 Grințieș Romania
188 E2 Grintovec mt. Slovenia
178 D5 Grinzens Austria
183 R5 Grío r. Spain
Griomasaigh i. Scotland U.K. see Grimsay
215 N6 Griqualand East reg. S. Africa
214 H4 Griqualand West reg. S. Africa
214 H4 Griquatown S. Africa
Grischun canton Switz. see Graubünden
221 J2 Grise Fiord Nunavut Can.
186 C4 Grisén Spain
Grishino Ukr. see Krasnoarmiys'k
191 L5 Grisignano di Zocco Italy
94 E6 Grisik Sumatera Indon.
156 C2 Gris Nez, Cap c. France
193 P8 Grisolia Italy
163 G8 Grisolles France
Grisons canton Switz. see Graubünden
143 O1 Grisslehamn Sweden
146 K5 Gritley Orkney, Scotland U.K.
137 R8 Grivenskaya Rus. Fed.
149 K5 Grizebeck Cumbria, England U.K.
204 E4 Grizim well Alg.
222 F1 Grizzly Bear Mountain hill N.W.T. Can.
188 F3 Grmeč mts Bos.-Herz.
225 K3 Groais Island Nfld and Lab. Can.
165 G6 Grobbendonk Belgium
173 K5 Gröbenzell Ger.
171 F8 Gröbers Ger.
138 E5 Grobiņa Latvia
215 N1 Groblersdal S. Africa
214 G4 Groblershoop S. Africa
179 I5 Gröbming Austria
171 E7 Gröbzig Ger.
196 I6 Grocka Serbia
168 G1 Gröde-Appelland i. Ger.
175 K4 Gródek Lubelskie Pol.
175 L2 Gródek Podlaskie Pol.
171 I8 Gröden Ger.
178 H4 Grödig Austria
171 H8 Gröditz Ger.
175 I2 Gródki Pol.
174 F5 Grodków Pol.
Grodnenskaya Oblast' admin. div. Belarus see Hrodzyenskaya Voblasts'
Grodnenskaya Vozvyshennost' hills Belarus see Hrodnyendskaye Wzvyshsha
Grodno Belarus see Hrodna
Grodno Oblast admin. div. Belarus see Hrodzyenskaya Voblasts'
175 H2 Grodziczno Pol.
174 G3 Grodziec Pol.
175 K3 Grodzisk Pol.
175 I3 Grodzisk Mazowiecki Pol.
174 E3 Grodzisk Wielkopolski Pol.
214 H6 Groen watercourse Northern Cape S. Africa
214 B6 Groen watercourse S. Africa
164 K4 Groenlo Neth.
215 O3 Groenvlei S. Africa
237 G10 Groesbeck TX U.S.A.
164 I5 Groesbeek Neth.
140 □B1 Gröf Iceland
85 J4 Groganville Qld Austr.
169 H6 Grohnde (Emmerthal) Ger.
177 L6 Grohot, Vârful hill Romania
171 F8 Groitzsch Ger.
158 E6 Groix France
158 E6 Groix, Île de i. France
175 I4 Grójec Pol.

175 I2 Grom Pol.
174 D4 Gromadka Pol.
189 C7 Grombalia Tunisia
168 K2 Grömitz Ger.
175 I6 Gromnik Pol.
190 H4 Gromo Italy
168 G1 Grønå r. Denmark
169 I6 Gronau (Leine) Ger.
169 D6 Gronau (Westfalen) Ger.
193 Q8 Grondo r. Italy
173 I6 Grönenbach Ger.
140 L4 Grong Norway
171 D7 Gröningen Ger.
164 K2 Groningen Neth.
164 K2 Groningen prov. Neth.
251 H3 Groningen Suriname
164 J2 Groninger Wad tidal flat Neth.
Grønland terr. N. America see Greenland
Grønnedal Greenland see Kangilinnguit
175 H1 Gronowo Pol.
143 L4 Grönskåra Sweden
170 F1 Grønsund sea chan. Denmark
237 E8 Groom TX U.S.A.
241 Q4 Groom Lake NV U.S.A.
147 K3 Groomsport Northern Ireland U.K.
214 I9 Groot r. Eastern Cape S. Africa
214 D8 Groot r. Western Cape S. Africa
214 F9 Groot r. Western Cape S. Africa
214 E3 Groot-Aar Pan salt pan S. Africa
214 C8 Groot Berg r. S. Africa
215 J7 Groot Brak r. S. Africa
214 G10 Groot Brakrivier S. Africa
215 N2 Grootdraaidam dam S. Africa
214 F4 Grootdrink S. Africa
164 H3 Grootebroek Neth.
84 F2 Groote Eylandt i. N.T. Austr.
84 F3 Groote Eylandt Aboriginal Land res. N.T. Austr.
164 J2 Grootegast Neth.
212 C3 Grootfontein Namibia
215 J4 Groot-Grannapan salt pan S. Africa
212 C5 Groot Karas Berg plat. Namibia
212 D4 Groot Laagte watercourse Botswana/Namibia
213 F4 Groot Letaba r. S. Africa
215 K1 Groot Marico S. Africa
214 B5 Grootmis S. Africa
215 K1 Grootpan S. Africa
214 H9 Grootrivierhoogte mts S. Africa
214 F9 Groot Swartberge mts S. Africa
214 C2 Grootvaalgraspan salt pan Namibia
215 M2 Grootvlei S. Africa
214 E5 Grootvloer salt pan S. Africa
215 K8 Groot Winterberg mt. S. Africa
215 I9 Groot-Winterhoekberge mts S. Africa
190 F5 Gropello Cairoli Italy
197 P5 Gropeni Romania
187 D12 Grosa, Isla i. Spain
161 I9 Gros Bessillon hill France
160 F2 Grosbois-en-Montagne France
161 K6 Groscavallo Italy
190 I3 Grosio Italy
247 □3 Gros Islet St Lucia
247 □3 Gros-Morne Martinique
225 J3 Gros Morne National Park Nfld and Lab. Can.
160 F3 Grosne r. France
178 B7 Grosotto Italy
247 □3 Gros Piton mt. St Lucia
187 I9 Grossa, Punta pt Spain
173 J5 Großaitingen Ger.
169 I8 Großalmerode Ger.
171 E6 Groß Ammensleben Ger.
178 H5 Großarl Austria
212 C4 Gross Barmen Namibia
169 J8 Großbartloff Ger.
171 H6 Großbeeren Ger.
168 D5 Groß Berßen Ger.
172 F2 Groß-Bieberau Ger.
169 J8 Großbodungen Ger.
171 G8 Großbothen Ger.
172 G4 Großbottwar Ger.
171 D9 Großbreitenbach Ger.
169 I6 Großburgwedel (Burgwedel) Ger.
169 J8 Großburschla Ger.
170 I5 Groß Dölln Ger.
171 J8 Großdubrau Ger.
169 H5 Große Aue r. Ger.
172 F4 Große Enz r. Ger.
173 N4 Große Laaber r. Ger.
172 H5 Große Lauter r. Ger.
169 J6 Groß Elbe (Elbe) Ger.
172 F5 Grosselfingen Ger.
168 I3 Großenaspe Ger.
170 D2 Großenbrode Ger.
169 G9 Großen-Buseck Ger.
169 K8 Großenehrich Ger.
179 O3 Groß Engersdorf Austria
169 K8 Großengottern Ger.
171 I8 Großenhain Ger.
168 F5 Großenkneten Ger.
169 I9 Großenlüder Ger.
168 J3 Großensee Ger.
171 F9 Großenstein Ger.
168 H1 Großenwiehe Ger.
179 O3 Groß-Enzersdorf Austria
247 □2 Grosse Pointe Guadeloupe
173 O3 Großer Arber mt. Ger.
169 K9 Großer Beerberg hill Ger.
179 J5 Grosser Bösenstein mt. Austria
169 J10 Großer Breitenberg hill Ger.
179 K4 Grosser Buchstein mt. Austria
172 D3 Großer Eyberg hill Ger.
169 K10 Großer Gleichberg hill Ger.
170 H1 Großer Jasmunder Bodden b. Ger.
171 F10 Großer Kornberg hill Ger.
170 H3 Großer Landgraben r. Ger.
178 E5 Grosser Löffler mt. Austria
171 I6 Großer Müggelsee l. Ger.
171 H8 Große Röder r. Ger.
176 C2 Großer Osser mt. Czech Rep./Ger.
168 J2 Großer Plöner See l. Ger.
179 J4 Grosser Priel mt. Austria
173 O4 Großer Rachel mt. Ger.
171 I6 Großer Selchower See l. Ger.
179 I6 Grosser Speikkofel mt. Austria
179 K6 Grosser Speikkogel mt. Austria
171 E10 Großer Waldstein hill Ger.
168 D4 Großes Meer l. Ger.
178 G5 Großes Wiesbachhorn mt. Austria
158 H8 Grosse Terre, Pointe de pt France
192 G2 Grosseto Italy
192 G2 Grosseto prov. Italy
192 B4 Grosseto-Prugna Corse France
100 K5 Grossevichi Rus. Fed.
173 M4 Große Vils r. Ger.
170 I4 Groß Fredenwalde Ger.
169 K8 Großfurra Ger.
170 E5 Groß Garz Ger.
172 E2 Groß-Gerau Ger.
179 K2 Groß-Gerungs Austria
169 I6 Groß Giesen Ger.
171 H6 Groß Glienicke Ger.
178 G5 Großglockner mt. Austria
173 N6 Großgmain Ger.
170 E4 Groß Godems Ger.
179 L2 Großgöttfritz Austria
168 K3 Groß Grönau Ger.
173 J3 Großhabersdorf Ger.
168 J3 Großhansdorf Ger.
179 N2 Großharras Austria
169 J6 Groß Heere (Heere) Ger.
171 K9 Großhennersdorf Ger.
171 E8 Großheringen Ger.
168 D5 Groß-Hesepe Ger.
172 G2 Großheubach Ger.
168 G5 Groß Ippener Ger.
173 M6 Großkarolinenfeld Ger.
171 E8 Großkayna Ger.

170 H2 Groß Kiesow Ger.
179 L6 Großklein Austria
171 F8 Großkorbetha Ger.
171 I6 Groß Köris Ger.
171 J8 Großkoschen Ger.
171 G6 Groß Kreutz Ger.
179 O2 Großkrut Austria
168 J2 Groß Kummerfeld Ger.
170 E4 Groß Laasch Ger.
169 J6 Groß Lafferde (Lahstedt) Ger.
173 I2 Großlangheim Ger.
171 F8 Großlehna Ger.
171 J6 Groß Leine Ger.
171 J6 Groß Leuthen Ger.
171 K6 Groß Lindow Ger.
169 C10 Großlittgen Ger.
169 K8 Großlohra Ger.
171 I8 Großmehlen Ger.
173 L4 Großmehring Ger.
170 I3 Groß Miltzow Ger.
170 G2 Groß Mohrdorf Ger.
171 D8 Großmonra Ger.
171 E7 Groß Mühlingen Ger.
171 I8 Großnaundorf Ger.
171 G7 Groß Naundorf Ger.
170 H4 Groß Nemerow Ger.
168 J5 Groß Oesingen Ger.
171 H9 Großolbersdorf Ger.
171 D7 Großörner Ger.
171 J7 Groß Oßnig Ger.
172 G2 Großostheim Ger.
179 N5 Großpetersdorf Austria
170 G3 Groß Plasten Ger.
171 D7 Groß Quenstedt Ger.
179 K4 Großraming Austria
171 J7 Großräschen Ger.
172 H2 Großrinderfeld Ger.
172 E2 Groß-Rohrheim Ger.
171 J8 Großröhrsdorf Ger.
171 E7 Groß Rosenburg Ger.
172 B3 Großrosseln Ger.
171 D8 Großrudestedt Ger.
179 N3 Großrußbach Austria
179 L6 Groß Sankt Florian Austria
171 J8 Groß Särchen Ger.
171 K7 Groß Schacksdorf Ger.
171 H9 Großschirma Ger.
179 K2 Großschönau Austria
171 K9 Großschönau Ger.
170 I5 Groß Schönebeck Ger.
170 E5 Groß Schwechten Ger.
171 K8 Großschweidnitz Ger.
169 J6 Groß Schwülper (Schwülper) Ger.
179 L2 Groß-Siegharts Austria
168 I1 Großsolt Ger.
168 D5 Groß Stavern Ger.
171 G8 Großsteinberg Ger.
170 D3 Groß Stieten Ger.
171 G7 Großtreben Ger.
169 K6 Groß Twülpstedt Ger.
212 C4 Gross Ums Namibia
172 F2 Groß-Umstadt Ger.
178 F5 Großvenediger mt. Austria
172 G2 Großwallstadt Ger.
190 E1 Grosswangen Switz.
170 E4 Groß Warnow Ger.
169 K8 Großwechsungen Ger.
179 M3 Großweikersdorf Austria
170 F4 Groß Welle Ger.
168 I2 Groß Wittensee Ger.
170 F3 Groß Wokern Ger.
170 F5 Großwudicke Ger.
170 G3 Groß Wüstenfelde Ger.
170 I5 Groß Ziethen Ger.
172 F2 Groß-Zimmern Ger.
157 M6 Grostenquin France
188 E3 Grosuplje Slovenia
263 L1 Grosvenor Mountains Antarctica
238 I5 Gros Ventre Range mts WY U.S.A.
225 J2 Groswater Bay Nfld and Lab. Can.
165 F6 Grote Nete r. Belgium
235 K2 Groton CT U.S.A.
233 I6 Groton NY U.S.A.
236 F3 Groton SD U.S.A.
193 J4 Grottaferrata Italy
195 M2 Grottaglie Italy
193 L2 Grottammare Italy
193 L1 Grottazzolina Italy
194 F9 Grotte Sicilia Italy
192 H2 Grotte di Castro Italy
195 K7 Grotteria Italy
232 G10 Grottoes VA U.S.A.
195 K2 Grottole Italy
164 I2 Grou Neth.
222 G1 Grouard Lake N.W.T. Can.
222 G4 Grouard Mission Alta Can.
158 H4 Grouin, Pointe du pt France
206 E5 Groumania Côte d'Ivoire
224 D3 Groundhog r. Ont. Can.
237 H7 Grove OK U.S.A.
232 B9 Grove City OH U.S.A.
232 E7 Grove City PA U.S.A.
231 D10 Grove Hill AL U.S.A.
141 L5 Grövelsjön Sweden
263 F2 Grove Mountains Antarctica
234 B1 Grover PA U.S.A.
240 L6 Grover Beach CA U.S.A.
233 N4 Groveton NH U.S.A.
237 H10 Groveton TX U.S.A.
234 F4 Groveville NJ U.S.A.
140 N2 Grovfjord Norway
241 S9 Growler Mountains AZ U.S.A.
197 P7 Grozd'ovo Bulg.
129 G2 Groznyy Rus. Fed.
171 D10 Grub am Forst Ger.
142 C3 Grubbåfjellet mt. Norway
165 J6 Grubbenvorst Neth.
170 D2 Grube Ger.
188 F3 Grubišno Polje Croatia
174 G2 Gruczno Pol.
Grudovo Bulg. see Sredets
175 I2 Grudusk Pol.
174 G2 Grudziądz Pol.
190 F6 Grue r. Italy
157 L7 Gruey-lès-Surance France
190 D5 Grugliasco Italy
146 E7 Gruinard Bay Scotland U.K.
146 D11 Gruinart, Loch inlet Scotland U.K.
161 C10 Gruissan France
182 H2 Grullos Spain
140 □ Grumantbyen Svalbard
197 O3 Grumăzești Romania
171 I8 Grumbach Ger.
193 P7 Grumento Nova Italy
195 L1 Grumo Appula Italy
142 J2 Grums Sweden
171 G9 Grüna Ger.
179 M3 Grünau Niederösterreich Austria
179 I4 Grünau Oberösterreich Austria
212 C5 Grünau Namibia
171 I6 Grünau-Grünheider Wald und Seengebiet park Ger.
179 M4 Grünbach am Schneeberg Austria
169 G9 Grünberg Ger.
Grünberg Pol. see Zielona Góra
179 J4 Grünburg Austria
141 L5 Grundagssätern Sweden
140 □B1 Grundarfjörður Iceland
141 L6 Grundforsen Sweden
179 I4 Grundlsee l. Austria
179 I4 Grundlsee nature res. Austria
214 B1 Grundorner Namibia
140 O5 Grundsuna Sweden
232 C11 Grundy VA U.S.A.
236 I4 Grundy Center IA U.S.A.
170 H5 Grüneberg Ger.
168 I3 Grünendeich Ger.
171 I8 Grünewald Ger.
171 I7 Grünewalde Ger.
171 I6 Grünheide Ger.
244 F1 Gruñidora Mex.
172 H6 Grünkraut Ger.
171 J6 Grunow Ger.
172 H2 Grünsfeld Ger.
172 E2 Grünstadt Ger.
191 K2 Gruppo de Tessa, Parco Naturale nature res. Italy
160 D3 Grury France
174 G2 Gruta Pol.
146 □N3 Grutness Shetland, Scotland U.K.
237 E7 Gruver TX U.S.A.
190 C2 Gruyère, Lac de la l. Switz.

190 C2 Gruyères Switz.
138 G5 Gruzdžiai Lith.
Gruzinskaya S.S.R. country Asia see Georgia
139 W9 Gryazi Rus. Fed.
139 W7 Gryaznoye Rus. Fed.
134 H4 Gryazovets Rus. Fed.
175 I6 Grybów Pol.
143 M1 Grycken l. Sweden
174 D2 Gryfice Pol.
174 C2 Gryfino Pol.
174 D4 Gryfów Śląski Pol.
174 F3 Grylewo Pol.
140 N2 Gryllefjord Norway
142 B2 Grytenuten hill Norway
143 N1 Gryttjom Sweden
259 □ Grytviken S. Georgia
175 I2 Gryźliny Pol.
174 E3 Grzebienisko Pol.
174 G3 Grzegorzew Pol.
174 E2 Grzmiąca Pol.
174 C2 Grzybno Pol.
174 G3 Grzymiszew Pol.
174 G2 Grzywna Pol.
178 D5 Gschnitz Austria
179 I4 Gschwandt Austria
172 H4 Gschwend Ger.
190 C3 Gstaad Switz.
173 M6 Gstadt am Chiemsee Ger.
190 C3 Gsteig Switz.
117 J8 Gua Jharkhand India
191 L5 Guà r. Italy
242 □R13 Guabito Panama
244 C2 Guacamayita Mex.
246 E3 Guacanayabo, Golfo de b. Cuba
247 J8 Guacara Venez.
250 D3 Guacharía r. Col.
244 A1 Guachimetas de Arriba Mex.
258 D2 Guachipas Arg.
255 B7 Guaçu Brazil
257 G4 Guaçuí Brazil
185 M5 Guadahortuna Spain
185 N5 Guadahortuna r. Spain
184 G6 Guadaira r. Spain
184 H6 Guadairilla r. Spain
184 F3 Guadajira r. Spain
184 H5 Guadajoz Spain
185 J5 Guadajoz r. Spain
244 D5 Guadalajara Mex.
183 N7 Guadalajara Spain
183 P7 Guadalajara prov. Spain
187 C7 Guadalaviar r. Spain
184 I5 Guadalbacar r. Spain
185 L5 Guadalbullón r. Spain
184 H7 Guadalcacín, Embalse de resr Spain
78 □6 Guadalcanal i. Solomon Is
184 H4 Guadalcanal Spain
185 J5 Guadalcázar Spain
184 H3 Guadalefra r. Spain
185 L4 Guadalén r. Spain
185 M4 Guadalén, Embalse del resr Spain
185 N5 Guadalentín r. Spain
185 Q5 Guadalentín r. Spain
260 D4 Guadales Arg.
187 E10 Guadalest, Embalse de resr Spain
184 G7 Guadalete r. Spain
185 K7 Guadalhorce r. Spain
185 J7 Guadalhorce, Embalse de resr Spain
185 L5 Guadalimar r. Spain
185 I5 Guadalmazán r. Spain
185 J4 Guadalmellato, Embalse de resr Spain
185 N4 Guadalmena r. Spain
185 N4 Guadalmena, Embalse del resr Spain
185 J3 Guadalmez Spain
185 J3 Guadalmez r. Spain
186 E5 Guadalope r. Spain
185 G7 Guadalquivir r. Spain
254 E3 Guadalupe Brazil
243 I5 Guadalupe Nuevo León Mex.
245 J6 Guadalupe Puebla Mex.
245 H1 Guadalupe Tamaulipas Mex.
244 E3 Guadalupe Zacatecas Mex.
245 I9 Guadalupe Mex.
242 A3 Guadalupe i. Mex.
241 P9 Guadalupe watercourse Mex.
250 B6 Guadalupe Peru
185 I2 Guadalupe Spain
241 U8 Guadalupe AZ U.S.A.
240 L7 Guadalupe CA U.S.A.
237 G11 Guadalupe r. TX U.S.A.
237 G11 Guadalupe r. TX U.S.A.
184 H2 Guadalupe, Sierra de mts Spain
244 C1 Guadalupe Aguilera Mex.
239 K11 Guadalupe Bravos Mex.
244 A1 Guadalupe de los Reyes Mex.
239 L11 Guadalupe Mountains National Park TX U.S.A.
237 C10 Guadalupe Peak TX U.S.A.
241 Q9 Guadalupe Victoria Baja California Mex.
244 C1 Guadalupe Victoria Durango Mex.
242 F4 Guadalupe y Calvo Mex.
185 I5 Guadalvacarejo r. Spain
183 O8 Guadamajud r. Spain
185 I3 Guadamatilla r. Spain
184 H3 Guadamez r. Spain
183 L9 Guadamur Spain
183 L7 Guadarrama Spain
183 L9 Guadarrama r. Spain
250 D2 Guadarrama Venez.
183 L7 Guadarrama, Puerto de pass Spain
183 L7 Guadarrama, Sierra de mts Spain
183 Q9 Guadazaón r. Spain
247 □2 Guadeloupe terr. West Indies
247 □ Guadeloupe, Parc National de la nat. park Guadeloupe
247 □2 Guadeloupe Passage Caribbean Sea
184 G7 Guadiamar r. Spain
185 E6 Guadiana r. Port./Spain
246 A2 Guadiana, Bahía de b. Cuba
185 M2 Guadiana, Canal del Spain
185 M5 Guadiana Menor r. Spain
185 I8 Guadiaro r. Spain
185 I5 Guadiato r. Spain
183 P8 Guadiela r. Spain
183 J8 Guadiervas r. Spain
185 M6 Guadix Spain
259 B6 Guafo, Isla i. Chile
92 C4 Guagua Luzon Phil.
255 C9 Guaíba Brazil
247 □7 Guaico Trin. and Tob.
257 E2 Guaiçuí Brazil
253 F5 Guaicuras Brazil
250 B4 Guaillabamba r. Ecuador
246 E3 Guáimaro Cuba
251 F3 Guaina Venez.
250 D4 Guainía dept Col.
250 E4 Guainía r. Col./Venez.
251 F3 Guaiquinima, Cerro mt. Venez.
255 B8 Guaíra Brazil
256 C4 Guaíra Brazil
256 A5 Guairaçá Brazil
259 B6 Guaitecas, Islas is Chile
106 H6 Guaizihu Nei Mongol China
254 C2 Guajará Açu Brazil
252 D2 Guajará Mirim Brazil
251 F6 Guajaratuba Brazil
183 L9 Guajaraz r. Spain
185 L7 Guájar-Faraguit Spain
252 D1 Guajarraã Brazil
247 □1 Guajataca r. Puerto Rico
247 □1 Guajataca, Lago de l. Puerto Rico
242 H3 Guaje, Laguna de l. Mex.
242 H4 Guaje, Llano de plain Mex.
250 D2 Guajira, Península de la pen. Col.
250 B5 Gualaceo Ecuador
240 I3 Gualala CA U.S.A.
243 O10 Gualán Guat.
250 B5 Gualaquiza Ecuador
193 J2 Gualdo Cattaneo Italy
191 N9 Gualdo Tadino Italy
261 H3 Gualeguay Arg.
261 H3 Gualeguay r. Arg.
261 H3 Gualeguaychu Arg.
259 D6 Gualicho, Salina salt flat Arg.
259 C6 Gualjaina Arg.

252 C4 Guallatiri vol. Chile
260 B4 Gualleco Chile
260 B6 Gualletue, Lago de l. Chile
244 D2 Gualterio Mex.
191 J6 Gualtieri Italy
91 J4 Guam terr. N. Pacific Ocean
247 I8 Guama Venez.
259 B7 Guamblin, Isla i. Chile
261 F5 Guamini Arg.
246 E3 Guamo Cuba
251 E3 Guampí, Sierra de mts Venez.
242 E5 Guamúchil Mex.
94 D2 Gua Musang Malaysia
107 O7 Gu'an Hebei China
246 B2 Guanabacoa Cuba
252 C2 Guanabara Brazil
257 F5 Guanabara, Baía de b. Brazil
242 □Q12 Guanacaste, Cordillera de mts Costa Rica
242 □Q12 Guanacaste, Parque Nacional nat. park Costa Rica
242 G5 Guanacevi Mex.
261 F5 Guanaco, Cerro hill Arg.
246 A2 Guanahacabibes, Península de pen. Cuba
242 □Q9 Guanaja Hond.
246 B2 Guanajay Cuba
244 F4 Guanajuato Mex.
244 G4 Guanajuato state Mex.
244 F4 Guanajuato, Sierra de mts Mex.
254 E5 Guanambi Brazil
244 F3 Guaname Mex.
250 B7 Guañape, Islas de is Peru
247 □7 Guanapo Trin. and Tob.
260 B2 Guanaqueros Chile
250 D2 Guanare Venez.
250 E2 Guanare Viejo r. Venez.
250 D2 Guanarito Venez.
250 D2 Guanarito r. Venez.
216 □3f Guanarteme, Punta de pt Gran Canaria Canary Is
252 D3 Guanay Bol.
258 C3 Guandacol Arg.
107 L9 Guandaokou Henan China
107 L8 Guandi Shan mt. Shanxi China
257 G3 Guandu r. Brazil
109 I6 Guandu Guangdong China
246 A2 Guane Cuba
108 F3 Guang'an Sichuan China
109 K5 Guangchang Jiangxi China
109 L3 Guangde Anhui China
109 J7 Guangdong prov. China
109 L4 Guangfeng Jiangxi China
109 I8 Guanghai Guangdong China
108 E3 Guanghan Sichuan China
Guanghua Hubei China see Laohekou
107 N7 Guangling Shanxi China
108 C5 Guangmao Shan mt. Yunnan China
Guangming Sichuan China see Xide
109 L3 Guangming Ding mt. Anhui China
108 E6 Guangnan Yunnan China
109 I7 Guangning Guangdong China
Guangning Liaoning China see Beining
107 P8 Guangrao Shandong China
109 J3 Guangshan Henan China
109 I3 Guangshui Hubei China
Guangxi aut. reg. China see Guangxi Zhuangzu Zizhiqu
108 G7 Guangxi Zhuangzu Zizhiqu aut. reg. China
108 E2 Guangyuan Sichuan China
109 K5 Guangze Fujian China
109 I7 Guangzhou Guangdong China
107 N8 Guangzong Hebei China
257 F3 Guanhães Brazil
257 F3 Guanhães r. Brazil
107 P9 Guan He r. China
107 P9 Guanhe Kou r. mouth China
247 □1 Guánica Puerto Rico
246 A2 Guaniguanico, Cordillera de mts Cuba
251 F2 Guanipa r. Venez.
108 E6 Guanling Guizhou China
108 G3 Guanmian Shan mts China
251 F2 Guanoca Venez.
108 H2 Guanpo Henan China
101 D8 Guanshui Liaoning China
Guansuo Guizhou China see Guanling
260 B1 Guanta Chile
251 E2 Guanta Venez.
246 F3 Guantánamo Cuba
246 F4 Guantánamo Bay Naval Base military base Cuba
107 N8 Guantao Hebei China
108 E2 Guanting Gansu China
106 H9 Guanting Qinghai China
107 N6 Guanting Shuiku resr China
Guanxian Sichuan China see Dujiangyan
109 H6 Guanyang Guangxi China
108 C3 Guanyinqiao Sichuan China
107 P9 Guanyun Jiangsu China
Guapay r. Bol. see Grande
257 E4 Guapé Brazil
250 B4 Guapí Col.
256 C6 Guapiara Brazil
242 □R12 Guápiles Costa Rica
247 □7 Guapo Bay Trin. and Tob.
252 D3 Guaporé r. Bol./Brazil
255 C9 Guaporé Brazil
Guaporé state Brazil see Rondônia
252 C4 Guaqui Bol.
256 D4 Guará Brazil
254 D5 Guará r. Brazil
186 E3 Guara, Sierra de mts Spain
254 G3 Guarabira Brazil
257 F4 Guaraciaba Brazil
250 B5 Guaranda Ecuador
257 F4 Guarani Brazil
256 A6 Guaraniaçu Brazil
256 C4 Guarantã Brazil
257 G4 Guarapari Brazil
256 B6 Guarapuava Brazil
256 C6 Guaraqueçaba Brazil
256 B4 Guararapes Brazil
257 H2 Guaratinga Brazil
257 E5 Guaratinguetá Brazil
255 C8 Guaratuba Brazil
252 C3 Guarayos Bol.
216 □3e Guarazoca El Hierro Canary Is
193 K4 Guarcino Italy
182 F7 Guarda Port.
182 F7 Guarda admin. dist. Port.
Guardafui, Cape Somalia see Gwardafuy, Gees
185 N5 Guardal r. Spain
187 D11 Guardamar del Segura Spain
256 D2 Guarda Mor Brazil
250 E2 Guardatinajas Venez.
195 K6 Guardavalle Italy
258 E3 Guardia Escolta Arg.
193 M3 Guardiagrele Italy
193 N4 Guardialfiera, Lago di l. Italy
241 Q9 Guardianes de la Patria Mex.
193 Q7 Guardia Perticara Italy
193 Q9 Guardia Piemontese Italy
193 N5 Guardia Sanframondi Italy
185 N7 Guardias Viejas Spain
186 I3 Guardiola de Berguedà Spain
183 K3 Guardo Spain
182 H6 Guardramiro Spain
182 E9 Guardunha, Serra de mts Port.
184 G3 Guareña Spain
183 J6 Guareña r. Spain
186 E3 Guarga r. Spain
253 E1 Guariba r. Brazil
250 E2 Guárico state Venez.
246 F3 Guarico, Punta pt Cuba
185 J7 Guaro Spain
185 L4 Guarrizas r. Spain
250 D3 Guarrojo r. Col.
185 L4 Guarromán Spain
256 D5 Guarujá Brazil
256 D5 Guarulhos Brazil
256 D5 Guarulhos airport Brazil
246 H8 Guasare r. Venez.
242 E5 Guasave Mex.
250 D3 Guasdualito Venez.
192 C8 Guasila Sardegna Italy
251 F3 Guasipati Venez.
191 J6 Guastalla Italy
243 O10 Guastatoya Guat.
117 L9 Guasuba r. India

243 N10 Guatemala country Central America
243 N10 Guatemala Guat.
267 M5 Guatemala Basin sea feature Pacific Ocean
Guatemala City Guat. see Guatemala
261 F3 Guatimozin Arg.
216 □3c Guatiza Lanzarote Canary Is
261 F5 Guatrache Arg.
259 D6 Guatrochi Arg.
247 □7 Guatuaro Point Trin. and Tob.
250 D4 Guaviare dept Col.
250 E3 Guaviare r. Col.
256 D4 Guaxupé Brazil
250 D3 Guayabal Col.
246 E3 Guayabal Cuba
247 □1 Guayabal, Lago l. Puerto Rico
260 D2 Guayaguas, Sierra da mts Arg.
247 □7 Guayaguayare Trin. and Tob.
245 J3 Guayalejo r. Mex.
247 □1 Guayama Puerto Rico
247 □1 Guayanilla Puerto Rico
247 □1 Guayanilla, Punta pt Puerto Rico
250 E3 Guayapo, Serranía mts Venez.
250 B5 Guayaquil Ecuador
250 A5 Guayaquil, Golfo de g. Ecuador
252 D2 Guayaramerín Bol.
250 A5 Guayas prov. Ecuador
258 D1 Guayatayoc, Laguna de imp. l. Arg.
242 D4 Guaymas Mex.
247 □1 Guaynabo Puerto Rico
261 H2 Guayquirard Arg.
261 H2 Guayquiraró r. Arg.
243 N10 Guazacapán Guat.
106 D6 Guazhou Gansu China
210 B2 Guba Eth.
120 H6 Gubadag Turkm.
134 L4 Gubakha Rus. Fed.
Gûbâl Island Egypt see Jûbâl, Jazirat
210 E2 Guban plain Somalia
92 E5 Gubat Luzon Phil.
148 B5 Gubaveeny Ireland
114 F6 Gubbi Karnataka India
191 N9 Gubbio Italy
129 I3 Gubden Rus. Fed.
134 E3 Gubdor Rus. Fed.
210 F2 Gubed Binna b. Somalia
107 O6 Gubeikou Beijing China
171 K7 Guben Ger.
197 N8 Gübene Bulg.
175 J1 Guber r. Pol.
174 C4 Gubin Pol.
139 S6 Gubino Rus. Fed.
207 I3 Gubio Nigeria
135 G6 Gubkin Rus. Fed.
106 H8 Gucheng Gansu China
106 F6 Gucheng Gansu China
107 N8 Gucheng Hebei China
109 H2 Gucheng Hubei China
107 L9 Gucheng Shanxi China
114 E7 Gudalur Tamil Nadu India
129 F3 Gudamaqris K'edi hills Georgia
186 D7 Gudar Spain
187 D7 Gudar, Sierra de mts Spain
Gudara Tajik. see Ghŭdara
115 H3 Gudari Orissa India
129 B2 Gudaut'a Georgia
141 J6 Gudbrandsdalen val. Norway
113 G2 Guddu Barrage Pak.
142 G5 Gudenå r. Denmark
169 H8 Gudensberg Ger.
129 H2 Gudermes Rus. Fed.
168 I1 Guderup Denmark
143 K6 Gudhjem Bornholm Denmark
207 H4 Gudi Nigeria
114 G4 Gudivada Andhra Prad. India
114 F6 Gudiyattam Tamil Nadu India
195 □ Gudja Malta
142 G6 Gudme Denmark
157 J7 Gudmont-Villiers France
100 F7 Gudong He r. China
168 K3 Gudow Ger.
123 J8 Gudri r. Pak.
126 F3 Güdül Turkey
114 F5 Gudur Andhra Prad. India
114 F5 Gudur Andhra Prad. India
141 I6 Gudvangen Norway
100 H4 Gudzhal r. Rus. Fed.
138 G6 Gudžiūnai Lith.
225 G1 Gué, Rivière du r. Que. Can.
157 N8 Guebwiller France
Guecho Spain see Algorta
206 C4 Guéckédou Guinea
158 F6 Guégon France
227 Q1 Guéguen, Lac l. Que. Can.
185 M6 Güéjar-Sierra Spain
204 C5 Guelb er Rîchât hill Maur.
208 B2 Guéléngdeng Chad
205 G1 Guelma Alg.
189 A7 Guelma prov. Alg.
204 C3 Guelmine Morocco
224 D5 Guelph Ont. Can.
205 E5 Guem waterhole Mali
205 G2 Guémar Alg.
157 N7 Guémar France
158 H6 Guéméné-Penfao France
158 E5 Guéméné-sur-Scorff France
245 H2 Güémez Mex.
157 L5 Guénange France
206 C2 Guendour well Maur.
207 F4 Guéné Benin
183 N2 Güeñes Spain
158 H6 Guenrouet France
206 B3 Guent Paté Senegal
158 G6 Guer France
208 C3 Guéra pref. Chad
208 C2 Guéra, Massif du mts Chad
158 E4 Guérande France
205 G2 Guerara Alg.
225 H1 Guérard, Lac l. Que. Can.
204 E2 Guercif Morocco
202 C5 Guéré watercourse Chad
208 D2 Guéréda Chad
202 D4 Guerende Libya
162 H3 Guéret France
160 C2 Guérigny France
207 F4 Guérin-Kouka Togo
158 E5 Guerlédan, Lac de l. France
240 J3 Guerneville CA U.S.A.
Guernica Spain see Gernika-Lumo
158 F3 Guernsey terr. Channel Is
238 L5 Guernsey WY U.S.A.
206 C2 Guérou Maur.
164 E5 Guerreiros do Rio Port.
261 I4 Guerrero Arg.
237 E11 Guerrero Coahuila Mex.
243 J4 Guerrero Tamaulipas Mex.
244 G8 Guerrero state Mex.
184 F3 Guerrero r. Spain
245 H8 Guerrero, Parque Natural de nature res. Mex.
244 B4 Guerrero Negro Mex.
163 E10 Guerreys, Pic de mt. France
186 H3 Guerri de la Sal Spain
225 H1 Guers, Lac l. Que. Can.
204 E3 Guerzim Alg.
186 C2 Guesa Spain
204 D4 Guetâtîra well Mali
163 A9 Guéthary France
160 E3 Gueugnon France
206 D5 Guéyo Côte d'Ivoire
Gufeng Fujian China see Pingnan
Gufu Hubei China see Xingshan
129 F5 Gugark' Armenia
210 C3 Gugē mt. Eth.
78 □3a Gugegwe i. Kwajalein Marshall Is
123 O6 Gugera Pak.
122 E4 Gügerd, Küh-e mts Iran
150 □ Gugh i. England U.K.
261 F2 Guglieri Arg.
172 F3 Güglingen Ger.
193 N4 Guglionesi Italy
210 C2 Gugu mts Eth.
91 K3 Guguan i. N. Mariana Is
94 F8 Guhakolak, Tanjung pt Indon.
109 K3 Guhe Anhui China
122 H8 Güh Küh mt. Iran
170 G4 Gühlen-Glienicke Ger.
Guhuai Henan China see Pingyu
253 F3 Guia Brazil
182 C9 Guia Port.
216 □3a Guía de Isora Tenerife Canary Is
182 G4 Guiana mt. Spain
264 F5 Guiana Basin sea feature N. Atlantic Ocean
249 F2 Guiana Highlands reg. Guyana/Venez.
250 E3 Guiana Highlands mts S. America
206 D5 Guibéroua Côte d'Ivoire
156 B6 Guichainville France
158 H6 Guichen France
82 G7 Guichen Bay S.A. Austr.
Guichi Anhui China see Chizhou
245 L8 Guichicovi Mex.
261 I3 Guichón Uru.
158 D4 Guiclan France
207 G3 Guidan-Roumji Niger
208 C2 Guidari Chad
106 G9 Guide Qinghai China
158 E6 Guidel France
149 N3 Guide Post Northumberland, England U.K.
207 I4 Guider Cameroon
207 H3 Guidiguir Niger
207 I4 Guidiguis Cameroon
206 B3 Guidimaka admin. reg. Maur.
108 F5 Guiding Guizhou China
191 J5 Guidizzolo Italy
109 I6 Guidong Hunan China
193 J4 Guidonia-Montecelio Italy
257 F4 Guidoval Brazil
245 L9 Guienagati Mex.
206 B2 Guier, Lac de l. Senegal
160 H5 Guiers r. France
208 A5 Guietsou Gabon
108 G7 Guigang Guangxi China
191 J7 Guiglia Italy
206 D5 Guiglo Côte d'Ivoire
158 H6 Guignen France
156 E6 Guignes France
156 G5 Guignicourt France
247 J8 Güigüe Venez.
213 G5 Guija Moz.
108 H7 Gui Jiang r. China
109 M4 Guiji Shan mts China
182 H8 Guijo de Coria Spain
182 H8 Guijo de Galisteo Spain
182 H8 Guijo de Granadilla Spain
182 I7 Guijuelo Spain
161 J7 Guil r. France
151 K5 Guildford Surrey, England U.K.
233 N4 Guildhall VT U.S.A.
146 J10 Guildtown Perth and Kinross, Scotland U.K.
158 B5 Guilers France
235 J2 Guilford CT U.S.A.
233 □P3 Guilford ME U.S.A.
161 F7 Guilherand France
Guilherme Capelo Angola see Cacongo
182 D5 Guilhofrei Port.
108 H6 Guilin Guangxi China
221 K4 Guillaume-Delisle, Lac l. Que. Can.
161 J8 Guillaumes France
184 G5 Guillena Spain
161 J7 Guillestre France
158 G5 Guilliers France
160 E1 Guillon France
163 C6 Guillos France
158 C6 Guilvinec France
216 □3a Güímar Tenerife Canary Is
216 □3a Güímar, Punta de pt Tenerife Canary Is
254 D2 Guimarães Brazil
182 D6 Guimarães Port.
92 D6 Guimaras i. Phil.
92 D6 Guimaras Strait Phil.
107 O9 Guimeng Ding mt. Shandong China
207 F4 Guinagourou Benin
106 G9 Guinan Qinghai China
246 D2 Guinchos Cay i. Cuba
92 E7 Guindulman Bohol Phil.
206 C4 Guinea country Africa
207 G6 Guinea, Gulf of Africa
264 I5 Guinea Basin sea feature N. Atlantic Ocean
206 B4 Guinea-Bissau country Africa
Guinea-Conakry country Africa see Guinea
Guinea Ecuatorial country Africa see Equatorial Guinea
Guiné-Bissau country Africa see Guinea-Bissau
Guinée country Africa see Guinea
206 C4 Guinée-Forestière admin. reg. Guinea
206 B4 Guinée-Maritime admin. reg. Guinea
246 B2 Güines Cuba
156 C2 Guînes France
225 I2 Guînes, Lac l. Nfld and Lab. Can.
158 E4 Guingamp France
206 B3 Guinguinéo Senegal
242 □Q13 Guiones, Punta pt Costa Rica
158 C5 Guipavas France
108 H7 Guiping Guangxi China
158 H5 Guipry France
186 A1 Guipúzcoa prov. Spain
206 E2 Guîr well Mali
246 B2 Güira de Melena Cuba
255 B6 Guiratinga Brazil
251 F2 Güiria Venez.
251 I3 Guisanbourg Fr. Guiana
183 J8 Guisando Spain
161 J7 Guisane r. France
149 O4 Guisborough Redcar and Cleveland, England U.K.
156 F4 Guiscard France
158 D5 Guiscriff France
156 G4 Guise France
149 N6 Guiseley West Yorkshire, England U.K.
Guishan Yunnan China see Xinping
207 F2 Guissefa well Mali
158 C4 Guissény France
186 H4 Guissona Spain
151 N2 Guist Norfolk, England U.K.
182 E2 Guitiriz Spain
162 D5 Guîtres France
206 D5 Guitri Côte d'Ivoire
92 E6 Guiuan Samar Phil.
140 S2 Guivi hill Fin.
Guixi Chongqing China see Dianjiang
108 F5 Guiyang Guizhou China
109 I5 Guiyang Hunan China
109 I6 Guiyang Hunan China
108 F5 Guizhou prov. China
109 H7 Guizi Guangdong China
163 B6 Gujan-Mestras France
116 D8 Gujarat state India
129 E4 Gujaret'i Georgia
123 O5 Gujar Khan Pak.
207 H4 Gujba Nigeria
Gujerat state India see Gujarat
107 M8 Gujiao Shanxi China
123 P5 Gujranwala Pak.
123 P5 Gujrat Pak.
Gukasyan Armenia see Ashots'k'
135 G6 Gukovo Rus. Fed.
122 A3 Gük Tappeh Iran
116 F3 Gulabgarh Jammu and Kashmir
129 H6 Gulablı Azer.
106 H8 Gulang Gansu China
Gulân Islands Egypt see Qul'ân, Jazâ'ir
83 L4 Gulargambone N.S.W. Austr.
199 H4 Gülbahçe Turkey
121 M7 Gulbahor Uzbek.
114 E4 Gulbarga Karnataka India
94 □ Gul Basin dock Sing.
138 J4 Gulbene Latvia
Gul'cha Kyrg. see Gülchö
121 O7 Gülchö Kyrg.
128 D2 Gülcihan Turkey
129 C4 Gül dağı mt. Turkey
170 E1 Guldborg Denmark
170 E1 Guldborgsund str. Denmark
128 B1 Güldere Turkey
129 A6 Güleç Turkey
126 G5 Gülek Turkey
118 C2 Gülek Boğazı pass Turkey
Gulf of Chihli China see Bo Hai
237 K10 Gulfport MS U.S.A.
231 D10 Gulf Shores AL U.S.A.
83 L5 Gulgong N.S.W. Austr.
113 □1 Gulhi i. S. Male Maldives
100 C2 Gulian Heilong. China
108 E5 Gulin Sichuan China
123 L6 Gulistan Pak.
Gulistan Uzbek. see Guliston
121 M7 Guliston Uzbek.
92 □ Gulitel hill Palau
170 E4 Gülitz Ger.
107 R2 Guliya Shan mt. Nei Mongol China
Gulja Xinjiang China see Yining
123 M6 Gul Kach Pak.
135 H7 Gul'kevichi Rus. Fed.
224 B3 Gull r. Ont. Can.
148 D4 Gulladuff Northern Ireland U.K.
146 K10 Gullane East Lothian, Scotland U.K.
141 I6 Gullbrå Norway
226 I4 Gull Island MI U.S.A.
141 Q7 Gullkrona fjärd b. Fin.
223 I5 Gull Lake Sask. Can.
142 H3 Gullmarn inlet Sweden
223 M5 Gullrock Lake Ont. Can.
143 H3 Gullspång Sweden
126 D3 Güllü Erzurum Turkey
199 K4 Güllü Uşak Turkey
199 I5 Güllübahçe Turkey
129 H4 Güllük Azer.
199 I5 Güllük Turkey
199 I5 Güllük Körfezi b. Turkey
126 F5 Gülnar Turkey
165 I7 Gulpen Neth.
170 F5 Gülper See l. Ger.
199 H3 Gülpınar Turkey
123 I4 Gulran Afgh.
129 C3 Gulrip'shi Georgia
126 G4 Gülşehir Turkey
121 P4 Gul'shat Kazakh.
170 H3 Gültz Ger.
Gulu Henan China see Xincai
210 B4 Gulu Uganda
197 N8 Gŭlŭbovo Bulg.
85 M9 Guluguba Qld Austr.
207 I4 Gulumba Gana Nigeria
84 F1 Guluwuru Island N.T. Austr.
146 F9 Gulvain hill Scotland U.K.
211 C6 Gulwe Tanz.
197 M7 Gulyantsi Bulg.
134 K1 Gulyayevskiye Koshki, Ostrova is Rus. Fed.
170 F3 Gülzow Mecklenburg-Vorpommern Ger.
168 J4 Gülzow Schleswig-Holstein Ger.
Guma Xinjiang China see Pishan
123 N6 Gumal r. Pak.
212 D3 Gumare Botswana
123 M6 Gumbaz Pak.
Gumbinnen Rus. Fed. see Gusev
210 A3 Gumbiri mt. Sudan
122 F2 Gumdag Turkm.
207 H3 Gumel Nigeria
Gümgüm Turkey see Varto
183 M5 Gumiel de Hizán Spain
183 M4 Gumiel de Mercado Spain
129 C2 Gumist'is Nakrdzali nature res. Georgia
117 J8 Gumla Jharkhand India
Gumma Japan see Gunma
Gumma pref. Japan see Gunma
169 E8 Gummersbach Ger.
94 B2 Gumpang r. Indon.
169 J9 Gumpelstadt Ger.
207 H3 Gumsi Nigeria
170 D3 Gumtow Ger.
126 I3 Gümüşhane Turkey
129 A5 Gümüşhane prov. Turkey
199 I4 Gümüşsuyu Turkey
199 J1 Gümüşyaka Turkey
116 F7 Guna Madh. Prad. India
Gunan Chongqing China see Qijiang
177 I6 Gunaroš Vojvodina Serbia
210 C2 Guna Terara mt. Eth.
83 J6 Gunbar N.S.W. Austr.
Gund r. Tajik. see Gunt
83 J4 Gundabooka National Park N.S.W. Austr.
83 L6 Gundagai N.S.W. Austr.
116 H9 Gundardehi Chhattisgarh India
172 D5 Gundelfingen Ger.
173 I4 Gundelfingen an der Donau Ger.
172 G3 Gundelsheim Baden-Württemberg Ger.
173 J2 Gundelsheim Bayern Ger.
114 E6 Gunderi Karnataka India
157 O6 Gundershoffen France
208 D4 Gundji Dem. Rep. Congo
114 G5 Gundlakamma r. India
114 E7 Gundlupet Karnataka India
126 F5 Gündoğmuş Turkey
Gundorovka Rus. Fed. see Donetsk
199 L3 Gündüzler Turkey
129 D6 Gündüzü Turkey
199 J3 Güneşli Turkey
199 K4 Güney Denizli Turkey
199 J3 Güney Kütahya Turkey
126 J4 Güneydoğu Toroslar plat. Turkey
199 L4 Güneyköy Turkey
199 H2 Güneyli Turkey
129 B5 Güneysu Turkey
128 A2 Güneyyurt Turkey
96 D1 Gunglilap Myanmar
209 C6 Gungu Dem. Rep. Congo
209 B8 Gungue Angola
129 H3 Gunib Rus. Fed.
223 L4 Gunisao r. Man. Can.
223 L4 Gunisao Lake Man. Can.
188 G3 Gunja Croatia
206 A3 Gunjur Gambia
199 K3 Günlüce Turkey
105 J5 Gunma Japan
105 I2 Gunma pref. Japan
140 N4 Gunnarn Sweden
140 P3 Gunnarsbyn Sweden
85 J4 Gunnawarra Qld Austr.
221 P3 Gunnbjørn Fjeld nunatak Greenland
83 M4 Gunnedah N.S.W. Austr.
217 □1b Gunners Quoin Mauritius
149 P6 Gunness North Lincolnshire, England U.K.
83 L6 Gunning N.S.W. Austr.
150 D6 Gunnislake Cornwall, England U.K.
239 K7 Gunnison CO U.S.A.
241 O2 Gunnison UT U.S.A.
239 J7 Gunnison r. CO U.S.A.
241 O2 Gunnison Reservoir UT U.S.A.
84 C2 Gunn Point N.T. Austr.
Gunong Ayer Sarawak Malaysia see Gunung Ayer
247 □3 Gun Point Grenada
Gunpowder Creek r. Qld Austr.
234 G5 Gunpowder Falls r. MD U.S.A.
Güns Hungary see Kőszeg
114 E3 Gun Sangari Mahar. India
179 I3 Gunskirchen Austria
171 D8 Günstedt Ger.
123 N3 Gunt r. Tajik.
114 F3 Guntakal Andhra Prad. India
169 K7 Güntersberge Ger.
172 E2 Guntersblum Ger.
179 N2 Guntersdorf Austria
172 H2 Güntersleben Ger.
231 D8 Guntersville AL U.S.A.
182 E3 Guntín de Pallares Spain
179 N3 Guntramsdorf Austria
114 G4 Guntur Andhra Prad. India
84 G4 Gununa Qld Austr.
93 E7 Gunungapi i. Maluku Indon.
95 I3 Gunung Ayer Sarawak Malaysia
95 L6 Gunungbatubesar Kalimantan Indon.
95 H4 Gunung Gading National Park Malaysia
94 G8 Gunung Gede Pangrango, Taman Nasional nat. park Indon.
94 G8 Gunung Halimun, Taman Nasional nat. park Indon.
94 B3 Gunung Leuser, Taman Nasional nat. park Indon.
95 K2 Gunung Mulu National Park Malaysia
95 H4 Gunung Niyut, Suaka Margasatwa nature res. Indon.
95 I5 Gunung Palung, Taman Nasional nat. park Indon.
95 L9 Gunung Rinjani, Taman Nasional nat. park Lombok Indon.
94 B4 Gunungsitoli Indon.
94 F7 Gunungsugih Sumatera Indon.
94 C4 Gunungtua Sumatera Indon.
115 H3 Gunupur Orissa India
126 E4 Günyüzü Turkey
173 I5 Günz r. Ger.
Gunza Angola see Porto Amboim
173 I5 Günzburg Ger.
173 J3 Gunzenhausen Ger.
106 I8 Guochengyi Gansu China
109 J2 Guo He r. China
109 K2 Guo He r. China
106 I9 Guojia Gansu China
108 H3 Guojiaba Hubei China
107 O6 Guojiatun Hebei China
Guoluezhen Henan China see Lingbao
Guovdageaidnu Norway see Kautokeino
109 K2 Guoyang Anhui China
Guozhen Shaanxi China see Baoji
116 D1 Gupis Jammu and Kashmir
100 J3 Gur r. Rus. Fed.
197 O5 Gura Caliței Romania
Guradu i. S. Male Maldives see Guraidhu
136 H7 Gura Galbenei Moldova
177 L5 Gurahonț Romania
197 N3 Gura Humorului Romania
113 □1 Guraidhu i. S. Male Maldives
116 E2 Gurais Jammu and Kashmir
197 J3 Gura Portiței sea chan. Romania
207 G4 Gurara r. Nigeria
177 L6 Gurasada Romania
197 N6 Gura Șuții Romania
197 O5 Gura Teghii Romania
208 E4 Gurba r. Dem. Rep. Congo
107 M5 Gurban Obo Nei Mongol China
112 H1 Gurbansoltan Eje Turkm.
110 H4 Gurbantünggüt Shamo des. China
129 F6 Gürbulak Turkey
129 D5 Gürbüzler Turkey
116 E3 Gurdaspur Punjab India
122 I9 Gurdim Iran
237 I9 Gurdon AR U.S.A.
Gurdzhaani Georgia see Gurjaani
199 H3 Güre Balıkesir Turkey
199 K4 Güre Uşak Turkey
129 L5 Gürgän Azer.
Gurgan Iran see Gorgān
116 F5 Gurgaon Haryana India
202 E6 Gurgei, Jebel mt. Sudan
197 M3 Gurghiu r. Romania
197 M4 Gurghiului, Munții mts Romania
254 E3 Gurgueia r. Brazil
116 C7 Gurha Rajasthan India
251 F3 Guri, Embalse de resr Venez.
84 D1 Gurig National Park N.T. Austr.
256 G3 Gurinhatã Brazil
129 G4 Gurjaani Georgia
179 J6 Gurk Austria
179 K6 Gurk r. Austria
122 H7 Gur Khar Iran
179 J6 Gurktal val. Austria
179 I6 Gurktaler Alpen mts Austria
120 I7 Gurlan Uzbek.
Gurlen Uzbek. see Gurlan
114 E4 Gurmatkal Karnataka India
226 G7 Gurnee IL U.S.A.
150 E4 Gurnos Powys, Wales U.K.
213 G3 Guro Moz.
127 K4 Gürpınar Turkey
114 F6 Gurramkonda Andhra Prad. India
186 D3 Gurrea de Gállego Spain
199 J2 Gürsu Bursa Turkey
129 C2 Gürsu Rize Turkey
123 L3 Guruşmagdan Kärhanasy Turkm.
Gu-ru i. S. Male Maldives see Gulhi
Guru i. S. Male Maldives see Gulhi
213 H2 Gurué Moz.
126 H4 Gürün Turkey
251 I5 Gurupá Brazil
251 I5 Gurupa, Ilha Grande de i. Brazil
254 C4 Gurupi Brazil
254 D2 Gurupi, Cabo c. Brazil
254 C3 Gurupi, Serra do hills Brazil
116 D7 Guru Sikhar mt. Rajasthan India
213 F3 Guruve Zimbabwe
Guruwe Zimbabwe see Guruve
114 F4 Guruzala Andhra Prad. India
106 H5 Gurvan Sayan Uul mts Mongolia
Gur'yev Kazakh. see Atyrau
138 D7 Gur'yevsk Rus. Fed.
Gur'yevskaya Oblast' admin. div. Kazakh. see Atyrauskaya Oblast'
123 K5 Gurz Afgh.
139 Y7 Gus' r. Rus. Fed.
207 G3 Gusau Nigeria
170 D4 Gusborn Ger.
171 E6 Güsen Ger.
138 F7 Gusev Rus. Fed.
139 X6 Gusevskiy Rus. Fed.
123 J3 Guşgy r. Turkm.
101 L5 Gushan Liaoning China
137 Q2 Gushchino Rus. Fed.
109 J2 Gushi Henan China
207 E4 Gushiegu Ghana
102 □1 Gushikami Okinawa Japan
102 □D20 Gushikawa Nansei-shotō Japan
102 □1 Gushikawa Okinawa Japan
196 H8 Gusinje Montenegro
139 O7 Gusino Rus. Fed.
106 J1 Gusinoozersk Rus. Fed.
106 J1 Gusinoye, Ozero l. Rus. Fed.
117 K8 Guskara W. Bengal India
139 X6 Gus'-Khrustal'nyy Rus. Fed.
170 H2 Gusow Ger.
192 B8 Guspini Sardegna Italy
190 I4 Gussago Italy
179 N5 Güssing Austria
190 I5 Gussola Italy
179 L4 Gußwerk Austria
140 □ Gustav Adolf Land reg. Svalbard
Gustav Holm, Kap c. Greenland see Tasiilap Karra
247 L5 Gustavia St Barthélemy West Indies
237 F12 Gustavo Díaz Ordaz Mex.
245 M8 Gustavo Díaz Ordaz Mex.
242 C2 Gustavo Sotelo Mex.
143 O2 Gustavsberg Sweden
228 E3 Gustavus AK U.S.A.
140 □ Gustav V Land reg. Svalbard
171 E7 Güsten Ger.
172 B2 Gusterath Ger.
240 L4 Gustine CA U.S.A.
170 F3 Güstrow Ger.
102 □C22 Gusukube Nansei-shotō Japan
172 E5 Gutach (Schwarzwaldbahn) Ger.
197 L3 Gutâiului, Munții mts Romania
111 L12 Gutang Xizang China
179 N3 Gutau Austria
146 □N1 Gutcher Shetland, Scotland U.K.
179 M4 Gutenstein Austria
171 H6 Güterfelde Ger.
171 E7 Güterglück Ger.
169 F7 Gütersloh Ger.
241 W9 Guthrie AZ U.S.A.
230 D7 Guthrie KY U.S.A.
237 G8 Guthrie OK U.S.A.
237 E9 Guthrie TX U.S.A.
236 H5 Guthrie Center IA U.S.A.
234 D4 Guthriesville PA U.S.A.
109 K6 Gutian Fujian China
109 L5 Gutian Fujian China
109 L5 Gutian Shuiku resr China
252 E4 Gutiérrez Bol.
245 N7 Gutiérrez Gómez Mex.
245 J5 Gutiérrez Zamora Mex.
Guting Shandong China see Yutai
172 A2 Gutland reg. Ger./Lux.
165 J9 Gutland reg. Lux.
129 H4 Guton, Gora mt. Azer./Rus. Fed.
176 F5 Gutorfölde Hungary
170 F3 Gutow Ger.
190 E2 Guttannen Switz.
179 K6 Guttaring Austria
236 J4 Guttenberg IA U.S.A.
213 F3 Gutu Zimbabwe
170 F3 Gützkow Ger.
129 B7 Güveçli Turkey
140 N4 Guvertfjället mts Sweden
117 M6 Guwahati Assam India
127 K5 Guwêr Iraq
Guwlumayak Turkm. see Guwlumaýak
122 E1 Guwlumaýak Turkm.
169 H8 Guxhagen Ger.
109 J5 Guxian Jiangxi China
251 G3 Guyana country S. America
Guyane Française terr. S. America see French Guiana
Guyang Hunan China see Guzhang
107 L6 Guyang Nei Mongol China
160 F3 Guye r. France
163 C6 Guyenne reg. France
83 N4 Guy Fawkes River National Park N.S.W. Austr.
Guyi Guangxi China see Sanjiang
237 E7 Guymon OK U.S.A.
122 E7 Güyom Iran
Guyong Fujian China see Jiangle
83 M4 Guyra N.S.W. Austr.
223 O5 Guysborough N.S. Can.
213 F4 Guyu Zimbabwe
107 N6 Guyuan Hebei China
106 J9 Guyuan Ningxia China
129 C6 Güzelhisar Turkey
199 I4 Güzelhisar Barajı resr Turkey
129 C6 Güzelkent Turkey
128 C2 Güzeloluk Turkey
Güzelyurt Cyprus see Morfou
108 G4 Guzhang Hunan China
109 K2 Guzhen Anhui China
Guzhou Guizhou China see Rongjiang
242 F2 Guzmán Mex.
242 F2 Guzmán, Lago de l. Mex.
138 D7 Gvardeysk Rus. Fed.
Gvardeyskoye Rus. Fed. see Elin-Yurt
142 F2 Gvarv Norway
100 J5 Gvasyugi Rus. Fed.
137 T3 Gvazda Rus. Fed.
96 B6 Gwa Myanmar
83 L4 Gwabegar N.S.W. Austr.
207 G4 Gwada Nigeria
207 G3 Gwadabawa Nigeria
123 J9 Gwadar Pak.
123 J9 Gwadar West Bay Pak.
Gwador Pak. see Gwadar
222 D4 Gwaii Haanas National Park Reserve B.C. Can.
213 E3 Gwai River Zimbabwe
116 G4 Gwaldam Uttaranchal India
123 M4 Gwal Haidarzai Pak.
116 E7 Gwalior Madh. Prad. India
116 G6 Gwalior Madh. Prad. India
213 F4 Gwanda Zimbabwe
208 E3 Gwane Dem. Rep. Congo
210 F2 Gwardafuy, Gees c. Somalia
207 G4 Gwarzo Nigeria
123 K9 Gwash Pak.
123 I9 Gwatar Bay Pak.
150 E6 Gwaun-Cae-Gurwen Neath Port Talbot, Wales U.K.
208 F3 Gwawele Dem. Rep. Congo
213 E3 Gwayi Zimbabwe
213 E3 Gwayi r. Zimbabwe
174 E2 Gwda r. Pol.
174 E2 Gwda Wielka Pol.
96 B2 Gwedaukkon Myanmar
147 F3 Gweebarra Bay Ireland
147 F2 Gweedore Ireland
Gweelo Zimbabwe see Gweru
213 F3 Gweru Zimbabwe
212 E4 Gweta Botswana
222 F4 Gwillim Lake Provincial Park B.C. Can.
226 G3 Gwinn MI U.S.A.
236 G2 Gwinner ND U.S.A.
150 B7 Gwithian Cornwall, England U.K.
207 I4 Gwoza Nigeria
83 L3 Gwydir r. N.S.W. Austr.
150 D1 Gwynedd admin. div. Wales U.K.
150 E1 Gwytherin Conwy, Wales U.K.
160 H2 Gy France
111 K11 Gyablung Xizang China
111 K12 Gyaca Xizang China
111 F10 Gyaco Xizang China
Gyaijêpozhanggê Qinghai China see Zhidoi
111 L11 Gyai Qu r. Xizang China
108 A2 Gyairong Qinghai China
Gyaisi Sichuan China see Jiulong
177 I4 Gyál Hungary
199 I6 Gyali i. Greece
111 E10 Gyamug Xizang China
Gyandzha Azer. see Gäncä
111 H9 Gyangnyi Caka salt l. China
111 G11 Gyangrang Xizang China
Gyangtse Xizang China see Gyangzê
111 I12 Gyangzê Xizang China
111 E11 Gya'nyima Xizang China
116 G8 Gyaraspur Madh. Prad. India
106 E9 Gyaring Qinghai China
111 I11 Gyaring Co l. China
106 E9 Gyaring Hu l. Qinghai China
117 O5 Gyarishing Arun. Prad. India
176 G4 Gyarmat Hungary
198 F5 Gyaros Greece
Gyaros i. Greece
Gyaurs Turkm. see Gäwers
Gydan, Khrebet mts Rus. Fed. see Kolymskiy, Khrebet
130 I2 Gydanskiy Poluostrov pen. Rus. Fed.
214 D9 Gydopas pass S. Africa
Gyêgu Qinghai China see Yushu
176 G5 Gyékényes Hungary
111 K12 Gyêmdong Xizang China
177 H4 Gyermely Hungary
111 G11 Gyêsar Co l. Xizang China
156 H7 Gyé-sur-Seine France
Gyêwa Xizang China see Zabqung
168 H4 Gyhum Ger.
108 A4 Gyigang Xizang China
111 K11 Gyimda Xizang China
111 E9 Gyipug Xizang China
111 G12 Gyirong Xizang China
111 G12 Gyirong Xizang China
108 A3 Gyitang Xizang China
Gyixong Xizang China see Gonggar
111 L10 Gyiza Qinghai China
Gyldenløve Fjord inlet Greenland see Umiiviip Kangertiva
142 H6 Gyldenløveshøj hill Denmark
147 F9 Gyleen Ireland
140 Q3 Gyljen Sweden
85 N9 Gympie Qld Austr.
96 B5 Gyobingauk Myanmar
105 J3 Gyōda Japan
177 J5 Gyomaendrőd Hungary
177 G4 Gyömöre Hungary
177 I4 Gyömrő Hungary
177 I4 Gyöngyös Hungary
176 F4 Gyöngyös r. Hungary
177 G6 Gyöngyös r. Romania
177 I4 Gyöngyöshalász Hungary
177 I4 Gyöngyöspata Hungary
177 H5 Gyönk Hungary
176 G4 Győr Hungary
176 G4 Győr-Moson-Sopron county Hungary
177 G4 Győrság Hungary
Győrszentmárton Hungary see Pannonhalma
177 L4 Győrtelek Hungary
177 G4 Győrújbarát Hungary
177 G4 Győrújfalu Hungary
222 H2 Gypsum Point N.W.T. Can.
223 L5 Gypsumville Man. Can.
225 G1 Gyrfalcon Islands Que. Can.
198 D6 Gytheio Greece
164 I2 Gytsjerk Neth.
177 K5 Gyula Hungary
Gyulafehérvár Romania see Alba Iulia
177 L3 Gyulaháza Hungary
177 H5 Gyulaj Hungary
129 J4 Gyul'gerychay r. Rus. Fed.
Gyümai Qinghai China see Darlag
129 E5 Gyumri Armenia
111 D10 Gyungcang Xizang China
197 O9 Gyurgen Bair hill Turkey
123 K3 Gyzylaýak Turkm.
120 J9 Gyzylbaýdak Turkm.
Gyzylbaydak Turkm. see Gyzylbaýdak
122 E2 Gyzylsuw Turkm.
139 R6 Gzhat' r. Rus. Fed.
Gzhatsk Rus. Fed. see Gagarin
195 □ Gżira Malta
175 I3 Gzy Pol.

H

117 L6 Ha Bhutan
138 H2 Haabneeme Estonia
165 G7 Haacht Belgium
138 H3 Häädemeeste Estonia
179 K3 Haag Austria
179 I3 Haag am Hausruck Austria
173 L5 Haag an der Amper Ger.
173 M5 Haag in Oberbayern Ger.
140 □ Haakon VII Land reg. Svalbard
164 K4 Haaksbergen Neth.
165 F7 Haaltert Belgium
106 C2 Haanhöhiy Uul mts Mongolia
138 K4 Haanja Estonia
79 □8 Ha'ano i. Tonga
79 □8 Ha'apai Group is Tonga
134 D3 Haapajärvi Fin.
140 R4 Haapavesi Fin.
79 □9a Haapiti Moorea Fr. Polynesia
138 G3 Haapsalu Estonia
173 L5 Haar Ger.
173 O4 Haarbach Ger.
172 D3 Haardt hills Ger.
172 C2 Haardtkopf hill Ger.
164 G4 Haarlem Neth.
214 H9 Haarlem S. Africa
169 F7 Haarstrang ridge Ger.
81 D10 Haast South I. N.Z.
81 D10 Haast r. South I. N.Z.
84 C7 Haast Bluff N.T. Austr.
81 C11 Haast Range mts South I. N.Z.
164 G5 Haastrecht Neth.
84 C7 Haasts Bluff Aboriginal Land res. N.T. Austr.
210 D4 Haaway Somalia
123 L9 Hab r. Pak.
173 K6 Habach Ger.
110 H2 Habahe Xinjiang China
Habai Group is Tonga see Ha'apai Group
Habana Cuba see La Habana
114 G8 Habarane Sri Lanka
125 J4 Habarūt well Saudi Arabia
173 N1 Habartov Czech Rep.
125 K7 Habarūt Oman
163 C8 Habas France
210 C4 Habaswein Kenya
124 G7 Habawnāh, Wādī watercourse Saudi Arabia
222 G3 Habay Alta Can.
165 I9 Habay-la-Neuve Belgium
124 H8 Habbān Yemen
127 K6 Habbānīyah, Hawr al l. Iraq
123 L9 Hab Chauki Pak.
124 E6 Habbah ash Shaykh, Ḥarrat lava field Saudi Arabia
178 D5 Habicht mt. Austria
169 H8 Habichtswald park Ger.
117 M7 Habiganj Bangl.
104 C6 Habikino Japan
107 N4 Habirag Nei Mongol China
143 K4 Habo Sweden
102 S2 Haboro Japan
177 I2 Habovka Slovakia
117 L8 Habra W. Bengal India
176 E2 Habry Czech Rep.
157 N8 Habsheim France
125 J7 Habshiyah, Jabal mts Yemen
250 C5 Hacha Col.
260 B6 Hachado, Paso de pass Arg./Chile
169 E9 Hachenburg Ger.
105 H3 Hachibuse-yama mt. Japan
103 Q13 Hachijō-jima i. Japan
104 E5 Hachikai Japan
104 E4 Hachiman Japan
105 L5 Hachiman-misaki c. Japan
102 Q6 Hachimori Japan
104 G3 Hachimori-yama mt. Japan
102 S6 Hachinohe Japan
105 J4 Hachiōji Japan
102 Q6 Hachiryū Japan
129 H6 Hacıalılı Azer.
199 K3 Hacıbekir Turkey
126 G4 Hacıbektaş Turkey
245 H1 Hacienda de la Mesa Mex.
129 E6 Hacıhalit Turkey
Hacıköy Turkey see Çekerek
199 L5 Hacılar Turkey
183 N5 Hacinas Spain
127 J4 Hacıömer Turkey
128 E2 Hacıpaşa Turkey
129 J6 Hacıqabul Gölü l. Azer.
129 J6 Hacıqährämanlı Azer.
199 I2 Hacıvelioba Turkey
129 K5 Hacı Zeynalabdin Azer.
82 G4 Hack, Mount S.A. Austr.
241 Q4 Hackberry AZ U.S.A.
172 D2 Hackenheim Ger.
235 G3 Hackensack NJ U.S.A.
232 E10 Hacker Valley WV U.S.A.
147 I7 Hacketstown Ireland
233 F3 Hackettstown NJ U.S.A.
151 K3 Hackleton Northamptonshire, England U.K.
151 O5 Hacklinge Kent, England U.K.
149 P5 Hackness North Yorkshire, England U.K.
234 D6 Hack Point MD U.S.A.
209 B7 Haco Angola
213 G4 Hacufera Moz.
175 J6 Haczów Pol.
110 F6 Hadadong Xinjiang China
114 D5 Hadagalli Karnataka India
169 F10 Hadamar Ger.
123 L6 Hada Mountains Afgh.
124 E5 Hadan, Harrat lava field Saudi Arabia
105 J5 Hadano Japan
106 I9 Hadapu Gansu China
124 E6 Hadārah i. Saudi Arabia
203 H4 Hadarba, Ras pt Sudan
107 P2 Hadat Nei Mongol China
107 S2 Hadayang Nei Mongol China
125 N4 Hadd, Ra's al pt Oman
202 C6 Haddad, Ouadi watercourse Chad
151 K4 Haddenham Buckinghamshire, England U.K.
146 K11 Haddington East Lothian, Scotland U.K.
151 P2 Haddiscoe Norfolk, England U.K.
234 E5 Haddonfield NJ U.S.A.
217 □2a Haddon Point Inner Islands Seychelles
207 H3 Hadejia Nigeria
207 I3 Hadejia watercourse N
142 G1 Hadeland reg. Norway
128 C6 Hadera Israel
128 C6 Hadera r. Israel
142 F6 Haderslev Denmark
142 E5 Haderup Denmark
114 E3 Hadgaon Mahar. India
124 E4 Hādhah Saudi Arabia
125 I5 Hādh Banī Zaynān de Saudi Arabia
113 D11 Hadhdhunmathi Atoll Maldives
Hadhramaut reg. Yem Ḥaḍramawt
128 E8 Hādī, Jabal al mts Jo
125 K9 Hadiboh Suquṭrā Yem
111 H8 Hadilik Xinjiang China
126 F5 Hadım Turkey
202 D5 Hadjer Momou mt. Ch
151 N3 Hadleigh Suffolk, Engl
150 H2 Hadley Telford and Wre England U.K.
221 H2 Hadley Bay Nunavut C
235 K2 Hadlyme CT U.S.A.
171 D7 Hadmersleben Ger.
157 L7 Hadol France
108 E8 Ha Đông Vietnam
126 H8 Hadraj, Wādī watercourse Saudi Arabia
125 I7 Ḥaḍramawt governora Yemen
125 H8 Ḥaḍramawt reg. Yeme
125 I7 Ḥaḍramawt, Wādī watercourse Yemen
Hadranum Sicilia Italy Adrano
179 N2 Hadres Austria
Hadria Italy see Adria
149 M3 Hadrian's Wall tourist England U.K.
Hadrumetum Tunisia Sousse
129 I6 Hadrut Azer.
140 M2 Hadseløy i. Norway
142 G5 Hadsten Denmark
142 G5 Hadsund Denmark
137 M3 Hadyach Ukr.
139 N8 Hadzilavichy Belarus
102 □1 Haebaru Okinawa Japa
261 I3 Haedo, Cuchilla de h
101 D9 Haeju N. Korea
101 D10 Haeju-man b. N. Kore
165 I6 Haelen Neth.
240 □B11 Hā'ena HI U.S.A.
101 E11 Haenam S. Korea
124 H3 Hafar al 'Atk well Sau
124 G1 Hafar al Bāṭin Saudi A
122 H9 Haffah, Ra's pt Oman
170 J3 Haffküste park Ger.
223 J4 Hafford Sask. Can.
126 H4 Hafik Turkey
128 E7 Ḥafīrah, Qā' al salt pa Jordan
128 D7 Ḥafīrah, Wādī al wate Jordan
124 D2 Ḥafirat al 'Aydā Saud
124 H3 Ḥafirat Nasah Saudi A
125 L4 Ḥafit Oman
125 L3 Ḥafit, Jabal mt. U.A.E.
123 O5 Hafizabad Pak.
117 N7 Haflong Assam India
140 □C1 Hafnarfjörður Iceland
179 L3 Hafnerbach Austria
122 C3 Haft Gel Iran
129 J7 Haftoni Azer.
122 E8 Haftvān Iran
140 □B1 Hafursfjörður b. Icela
Haga Myanmar see Ha
203 G6 Hag Abdullah Sudan
105 I6 Hagachi-zaki pt Japa
215 M8 Haga-Haga S. Africa
179 O8 Haganj Croatia
227 N3 Hagar Ont. Can.
114 E5 Hagari r. India
203 H5 Hagar Nish Plateau E
78 □1 Hagåtña Guam
143 M5 Hagby Sweden
168 D3 Hage Ger.
165 G7 Hageland reg. Belgium
171 G6 Hagelberg hill Ger.
220 B4 Hagemeister Island A
169 D8 Hagen Ger.
169 E6 Hagen am Teutoburg Ger.
172 E3 Hagenbach Ger.
169 H6 Hagenburg Ger.
178 H5 Hagengebirge mts Au
168 G4 Hagen im Bremische
170 D4 Hagenow Ger.
222 E4 Hagensborg B.C. Can.
171 K8 Hagenwerder Ger.
210 C2 Hägere Hiywet Eth.
210 C3 Hägere Selam Eth.
232 C11 Hagerhill KY U.S.A.
232 H9 Hagerstown MD U.S.A.
163 C8 Hagetaubin France
163 C8 Hagetmau France
143 J1 Hagfors Sweden
143 L1 Häggen l. Sweden
140 M5 Häggenås Sweden
238 H3 Haggin, Mount MT U.
140 L5 Häggsjön Sweden
140 M5 Häggsjövik Sweden
103 I12 Hagi Japan
96 G3 Ha Giang Vietnam
104 F4 Hagiwara Japan
150 G3 Hagley Herefordshire, England U.K.
150 H3 Hagley Worcestershire, England U.K.
HaGolan hills Syria see
157 L5 Hagondange France
147 C8 Hag's Head Ireland
233 L5 Hague NY U.S.A.
158 H2 Hague, Cap de la c. F
157 O6 Haguenau France
217 □3a Hahaïa Njazidja Comor
103 □2 Hahajima-rettō is Ogas shotō Japan
169 J7 Hahausen Ger.
173 L2 Hahnbach Ger.
172 F2 Hähnlein Ger.
169 F10 Hahnstätten Ger.
176 F5 Hahót Hungary
211 C5 Hai Tanz.
94 C1 Hai, Ko i. Thai.
108 H8 Hai'an Guangdong Chi
109 M2 Hai'an Jiangsu China
Haian Shanmo mts Ta T'aitung Shan
212 C6 Haib watercourse Nam
172 H2 Haibach Bayern Ger.
173 N3 Haibach Bayern Ger.
104 C6 Haibara Nara Japan
105 H6 Haibara Shizuoka Japa
Haibowan Nei Mongol see Wuhai
Haicheng Guangdong see Haifeng
107 R6 Haicheng Liaoning Chi
Haicheng Ningxia Chi Haiyuan
116 H6 Haidargarh Uttar Prad.
173 M2 Haidenaab r. Ger.
179 J3 Haidershofen Austria
106 C9 Haiding Hu salt l. Qing
173 P4 Haidmühle Ger.
96 H4 Hai Dương Vietnam
Haifa Israel see Ḥefa
109 J7 Haifeng Guangdong C
87 I11 Haig W.A. Austr.
169 F9 Haiger Ger.
172 F5 Haigerloch Ger.
107 O7 Hai He r. China
106 G8 Haihu Qinghai China
Haikakan country Asia Armenia
Haikang Guangdong C Leizhou
103 G13 Haiki Japan
108 H8 Haikou Hainan China
124 E2 Ḥā'il Saudi Arabia
124 F2 Ḥā'il, Wādī watercours Saudi Arabia
117 N7 Hailakandi Assam Indi
Hailar Nei Mongol Chi Hulun Buir
107 O2 Hailar He r. China

173 M4 Hohenthann Ger.
171 F7 Hohenthurm Ger.
179 I6 Hohenthurn Austria
231 D8 Hohenwald TN U.S.A.
170 F3 Hohen Wangelin Ger.
173 K4 Hohenwart Ger.
171 E9 Hohenwartetalsperre resr Ger.
173 N3 Hohenwarth Ger.
168 I2 Hohenwestedt Ger.
170 E5 Hohenwulsch Ger.
179 I3 Hohenzell Austria
179 I5 Hoher Dachstein mt. Austria
Hoh Ereg Nei Mongol China see Wuchuan
178 H4 Hoher Göll mt. Austria/Ger.
169 I10 Hohe Rhön mts Ger.
178 B5 Hoher Ifen mt. Austria/Ger.
169 H10 Hoher Vogelsberg, Naturpark nature res. Ger.
178 F5 Hohe Salve mt. Austria
169 H8 Hohes Gras hill Ger.
169 J8 Hohes Kreuz Ger.
178 F5 Hohe Tauern mts Austria
178 G5 Hohe Tauern, Nationalpark nat. park Austria
165 J8 Hohe Venn moorland Belgium
179 M4 Hohe Wand nature res. Austria
190 D2 Hohgant mt. Switz.
107 L6 Hohhot Nei Mongol China
172 E4 Hohloh hill Ger.
169 E9 Höhn Ger.
168 I2 Hohn Ger.
168 J5 Hohne Ger.
157 N7 Hohneck mt. France
168 K4 Hohnstorf (Elbe) Ger.
207 F5 Hohoe Ghana
109 □J7 Ho Hok Shan H.K. China
103 H12 Hōhoku Japan
137 M4 Hoholeve Ukr.
137 K3 Hoholiv Ukr.
137 N7 Hoholivka Ukr.
106 C9 Hoh Sai Hu l. Qinghai China
168 K2 Hohwacht (Ostsee) Ger.
168 K2 Hohwachter Bucht b. Ger.
111 J9 Hoh Xil Hu salt l. China
111 I9 Hoh Xil Shan mts China
106 F8 Hoh Yanhu salt l. Qinghai China
96 I7 Hôi An Vietnam
106 F9 Hoika Qinghai China
210 A4 Hoima Uganda
168 J3 Hoisdorf Ger.
236 F6 Hoisington KS U.S.A.
106 E8 Hoit Taria Qinghai China
122 G2 Hojagala Turkm.
117 N7 Hojai Assam India
123 K2 Hojambaz Turkm.
168 G1 Højer Denmark
103 J13 Hōjo Japan
96 E4 Hok r. Myanmar
143 J4 Hökensås hills Sweden
143 K3 Hokensås naturreservat nature res. Sweden
80 H2 Hokianga Harbour North I. N.Z.
105 L2 Hōki-gawa r. Japan
80 J7 Hokio Beach North I. N.Z.
81 E9 Hokitika South I. N.Z.
100 M7 Hokkaidō i. Japan
102 T3 Hokkaidō pref. Japan
142 F2 Hokksund Norway
122 G3 Hokmābād Iran
81 C13 Hokonui South I. N.Z.
81 C12 Hokonui Hills South I. N.Z.
105 M3 Hokota Japan
104 A6 Hokudan Japan
104 E4 Hokunō Japan
105 H1 Hokura-gawa r. Japan
104 E5 Hokusei Japan
142 E1 Hol Buskerud Norway
140 N2 Hol Nordland Norway
211 C5 Hola Kenya
177 J3 Hoľa mt. Slovakia
114 E5 Holalkere Karnataka India
252 D3 Holanda Bol.
137 L7 Hola Prystan' Ukr.
174 F6 Holasovice Czech Rep.
142 H6 Holbæk Denmark
215 O2 Holbank S. Africa
151 M2 Holbeach Lincolnshire, England U.K.
151 M2 Holbeach Marsh England U.K.
222 D5 Holberg B.C. Can.
168 H1 Holbøl Denmark
85 L5 Holborne Island Qld Austr.
83 K6 Holbrook N.S.W. Austr.
151 O4 Holbrook Suffolk, England U.K.
241 V7 Holbrook AZ U.S.A.
235 I3 Holbrook NY U.S.A.
226 C4 Holcombe WI U.S.A.
226 C4 Holcombe Flowage resr WI U.S.A.
223 H4 Holden Alta Can.
149 M6 Holden Lancashire, England U.K.
241 T2 Holden UT U.S.A.
237 G8 Holdenville OK U.S.A.
149 Q6 Holderness pen. England U.K.
259 C7 Holdich Arg.
168 F5 Holdorf Ger.
236 F5 Holdrege NE U.S.A.
168 L1 Holeby Denmark
246 E1 Hole in the Wall pt Gt Abaco Bahamas
114 E6 Hole Narsipur Karnataka India
177 G2 Holešov Czech Rep.
247 □4 Holetown Barbados
214 A4 Holgat watercourse S. Africa
232 A7 Holgate OH U.S.A.
182 H9 Holguera Spain
246 E3 Holguín Cuba
176 G3 Holíč Slovakia
176 E1 Holice Czech Rep.
137 M2 Holinka Ukr.
141 L6 Höljes Sweden
179 N2 Hollabrunn Austria
169 E6 Hollage (Wallenhorst) Ger.
Holland country Europe see Netherlands
226 H7 Holland MI U.S.A.
232 G6 Holland NY U.S.A.
232 B7 Holland OH U.S.A.
237 J9 Hollandale MS U.S.A.
246 □ Holland Bay Jamaica
151 L2 Holland Fen reg. England U.K.
Hollandia Papua Indon. see Jayapura
151 O4 Holland-on-Sea Essex, England U.K.
164 K3 Hollandscheveld Neth.
164 F5 Hollands Diep est. Neth.
146 L4 Hollandstoun Scotland U.K.
165 I9 Hollange Belgium
169 J6 Holle Ger.
171 E8 Holleben Ger.
173 K5 Hollenbach Ger.
168 K3 Hollenbek Ger.
179 L6 Hollenegg Austria
179 I4 Höllengebirge hills Austria
168 I4 Hollenstedt Ger.
179 K4 Hollenstein an der Ybbs Austria
151 O3 Hollesley Bay England U.K.
232 G5 Holley NY U.S.A.
173 K2 Hollfeld Ger.
262 T2 Hollick-Kenyon Peninsula Antarctica
262 Q1 Hollick-Kenyon Plateau Antarctica
232 G8 Hollidaysburg PA U.S.A.
168 H2 Hollingstedt Ger.
151 N6 Hollington East Sussex, England U.K.
149 N7 Hollingworth Greater Manchester, England U.K.
222 C4 Hollis AK U.S.A.
237 F8 Hollis OK U.S.A.
240 K5 Hollister CA U.S.A.
190 F2 Holloch Karst nature res. Switz.
177 K3 Hollóháza Hungary
177 I3 Hollókő Hungary
141 R6 Hollola Fin.
164 I2 Hollum Neth.
227 K7 Holly MI U.S.A.
148 H3 Hollybush East Ayrshire, Scotland U.K.
150 H3 Hollybush Worcestershire, England U.K.
81 B11 Hollyford r. South I. N.Z.
235 G5 Holly Park NJ U.S.A.
237 K8 Holly Springs MS U.S.A.
147 I6 Hollywood Ireland
240 N7 Hollywood CA U.S.A.
231 G13 Hollywood FL U.S.A.
168 I3 Holm Ger.
140 L4 Holm Norway
136 I6 Hol'ma Ukr.
220 G2 Holman N.W.T. Can.
235 G4 Holmdel NJ U.S.A.
215 N2 Holmdene S. Africa
149 P6 Holme-on-Spalding-Moor East Riding of Yorkshire, England U.K.
235 H1 Holmes NY U.S.A.
149 M7 Holmes Chapel Cheshire, England U.K.
149 N7 Holmesfield Derbyshire, England U.K.
85 K4 Holmes Reef Coral Sea Is Terr. Austr.
142 G2 Holmestrand Norway
232 D8 Holmesville OH U.S.A.
149 N6 Holmfirth West Yorkshire, England U.K.
Holmgard Rus. Fed. see Velikiy Novgorod
Holm Ø i. Greenland see Kiatassuaq
140 P5 Holmöarna naturreservat nature res. Sweden
134 C3 Holmön i. Sweden
140 P5 Holmsund Sweden
141 N6 Holmsveden Sweden
143 P3 Holmudden pt Gotland Sweden
136 E2 Holoby Ukr.
177 L5 Holod Romania
197 K4 Holod r. Romania
175 L5 Hołodowska Pol.
136 D4 Holohory hills Ukr.
128 C6 Holon Israel
212 C5 Holoog Namibia
86 H2 Holothuria Banks rf W.A. Austr.
173 P2 Holoubkov Czech Rep.
137 N9 Holovanivka Ukr.
136 J5 Holovanivs'k Ukr.
136 B4 Holovets'ko Ukr.
137 L4 Holovkivka Ukr.
175 M4 Holovne Ukr.
136 H3 Holovyne Ukr.
85 H3 Holroyd r. Qld Austr.
87 G9 Holroyd Bluff hills W.A. Austr.
142 I4 Holsljunga Sweden
215 M3 Holspruit r. S. Africa
168 G4 Holste Ger.
142 E5 Holstebro Denmark
142 E6 Holsted Denmark
190 D1 Hölstein Switz.
236 H4 Holstein IA U.S.A.
Holsteinsborg Greenland see Sisimiut
232 B12 Holston r. TN U.S.A.
232 D12 Holston Lake TN U.S.A.
150 D6 Holsworthy Devon, England U.K.
151 O2 Holt Norfolk, England U.K.
150 H5 Holt Wiltshire, England U.K.
150 G1 Holt Wrexham, Wales U.K.
226 J7 Holt MI U.S.A.
164 J4 Holten Neth.
168 E3 Holtgast Ger.
170 D3 Holthusen Ger.
168 E4 Holtland Ger.
236 H6 Holton KS U.S.A.
226 H6 Holton MI U.S.A.
149 Q6 Holton le Clay Lincolnshire, England U.K.
168 E4 Holtrop (Großefehn) Ger.
168 I2 Holtsee Ger.
241 Q9 Holtville CA U.S.A.
234 C5 Holtwood PA U.S.A.
240 □F14 Hōlualoa HI U.S.A.
137 O5 Holubivka Ukr.
137 M9 Holubynka Ukr.
164 I2 Holwerd Neth.
164 K2 Holwierde Neth.
147 G7 Holycross Ireland
220 C3 Holy Cross AK U.S.A.
239 K7 Holy Cross, Mount of the CO U.S.A.
150 C1 Holyhead Isle of Anglesey, Wales U.K.
150 C1 Holyhead Bay Wales U.K.
149 N2 Holy Island England U.K.
146 F11 Holy Island Scotland U.K.
150 C1 Holy Island Wales U.K.
236 D5 Holyoke CO U.S.A.
233 M6 Holyoke MA U.S.A.
Holy See Europe see Vatican City
150 F1 Holywell Flintshire, Wales U.K.
147 G4 Holywell Northern Ireland U.K.
146 I12 Holywood Dumfries and Galloway, Scotland U.K.
147 K3 Holywood Northern Ireland U.K.
169 E10 Holzappel Ger.
171 H7 Holzdorf Ger.
169 I7 Holzen Ger.
172 G4 Holzgerlingen Ger.
171 F8 Holzhausen Ger.
169 E10 Holzhausen an der Haide Ger.
173 I5 Holzheim Bayern Ger.
173 J4 Holzheim Bayern Ger.
173 J4 Holzheim Bayern Ger.
169 G10 Holzheim Hessen Ger.
173 L6 Holzkirchen Ger.
169 H7 Holzminden Ger.
169 K8 Holzthaleben Ger.
171 F7 Holzweißig Ger.
169 E7 Holzwickede Ger.
214 C4 Hom watercourse Namibia
122 C5 Homā Iran
210 B5 Homa Bay Kenya
96 B2 Homalin Myanmar
222 E5 Homathko r. B.C. Can.
Homāyūnshahr Iran see Khomeynīshahr
169 H8 Homberg (Efze) Ger.
169 G9 Homberg (Ohm) Ger.
Hombetsu Japan see Honbetsu
156 E4 Hombleux France
206 E3 Hombori Mali
157 L5 Hombourg-Budange France
157 M5 Hombourg-Haut France
258 D2 Hombre Muerto, Salar del salt flat Arg.
172 C3 Homburg Ger.
182 C4 Home, Cabo de pt Spain
221 L3 Home Bay Nunavut Can.
157 K5 Homécourt France
85 K5 Home Hill Qld Austr.
86 □2 Home Island Cocos Is
182 D5 Homem r. Port.
80 I2 Home Point North I. N.Z.
220 C4 Homer AK U.S.A.
231 F8 Homer GA U.S.A.
237 I9 Homer LA U.S.A.
226 J7 Homer MI U.S.A.
233 I6 Homer NY U.S.A.
232 F8 Homer City PA U.S.A.
151 O3 Homersfield Suffolk, England U.K.
231 F10 Homerville GA U.S.A.
85 J6 Homestead Qld Austr.
231 G13 Homestead FL U.S.A.
234 D3 Hometown PA U.S.A.
234 D5 Homeville PA U.S.A.
81 J8 Homewood North I. N.Z.
231 D9 Homewood AL U.S.A.
140 L4 Hommelstø Norway
140 K5 Hommelvik Norway
114 E4 Homnabad Karnataka India
197 P4 Homocea Romania
207 I2 Homodji well Niger
213 G4 Homoine Moz.
177 I5 Homokmégy Hungary
177 G5 Homokszentgyörgy Hungary
177 M4 Homoroade Romania
177 L3 Homorod r. Romania
Homs Libya see Al Khums
Homs Syria see Ḥimş
137 K1 Homyel' Belarus
Homyel Oblast admin. div. Belarus see Homyel'skaya Voblasts'
139 M9 Homyel'skaya Voblasts' admin. div. Belarus
232 D11 Honaker VA U.S.A.
Honan prov. China see Henan
240 □F14 Hōnaunau HI U.S.A.
114 E6 Honavalli Karnataka India
114 D5 Honavar Karnataka India
199 K5 Honaz Turkey
102 U3 Honbetsu Japan
136 J2 Honcharivs'ke Ukr.
137 M9 Honcharne Ukr.
97 G9 Hon Chông Vietnam
250 C3 Honda Col.
117 J9 Honda Orissa India
250 C1 Honda, Bahía b. Col.
92 B7 Honda Bay Palawan Phil.
117 J9 Hondapa Orissa India
186 B1 Hondarribia Spain
213 G3 Honde Moz.
214 I6 Hondeblaf r. S. Africa
214 B6 Hondeklipbaai S. Africa
243 O8 Hondo r. Belize/Mex.
103 H14 Hondo Japan
239 L10 Hondo NM U.S.A.
237 F11 Hondo TX U.S.A.
239 L10 Hondo r. NM U.S.A.
187 D11 Hondón de las Nieves Spain
187 D11 Hondón de los Frailes Spain
156 E2 Hondschoote France
164 K2 Hondsrug reg. Neth.
246 A6 Honduras country Central America
242 □P9 Honduras, Gulf of Belize/Hond.
190 D4 Hône Italy
142 G1 Hønefoss Norway
232 H6 Honeoye Falls NY U.S.A.
234 E1 Honesdale PA U.S.A.
245 I5 Honey Mex.
234 D4 Honey Brook PA U.S.A.
240 L1 Honey Lake salt l. CA U.S.A.
159 L3 Honfleur France
96 H4 Hong, Mouths of the Vietnam
96 H4 Hông, Sông r. Vietnam
109 J3 Hong'an Hubei China
106 H8 Hongchengzi Gansu China
101 E10 Hongch'ŏn S. Korea
107 J8 Hongde Gansu China
110 J7 Honggouzi Qinghai China
106 H8 Honggu Gansu China
109 J7 Honghai Wan b. China
108 D7 Honghe Yunnan China
109 J2 Hong He r. China
109 I4 Honghu Hubei China
109 I4 Hong Hu l. China
Hongjialou Shandong China see Licheng
108 G5 Hongjiang Hunan China
108 G5 Hongjiang Hunan China
Hongjiang Sichuan China see Wangcang
109 □J7 Hong Kong H.K. China
109 J7 Hong Kong special admin. reg. China
109 □J7 Hong Kong Harbour sea chan. H.K. China
109 □J7 Hong Kong Island H.K. China
106 F6 Hongliu Daquan well Nei Mongol China
106 D6 Hongliuhe Gansu China
107 K7 Hongliu He r. China
110 J7 Hongliuquan Qinghai China
Hongliuwan Gansu China see Aksay
106 H7 Hongliuyuan Gansu China
110 L6 Hongliuyuan Gansu China
97 G9 Hông Ngư Vietnam
107 M4 Hongor Nei Mongol China
107 M4 Hongor Mongolia
Hongqiao Hunan China see Qidong
Hongqiao Hunan China see Qidong
109 M3 Hongqiao airport China
106 C5 Hongqicun Xinjiang China
Hongqizhen Hainan China see Wuzhishan
108 B4 Hongshan Yunnan China
106 I7 Hongshansi Nei Mongol China
100 E7 Hongshi Jilin China
108 H7 Hongshui He r. China
107 L8 Hongtong Shanxi China
104 C8 Hongū Japan
225 H3 Honguedo, Détroit d' sea chan. Que. Can.
Hongwansi Gansu China see Sunan
101 E8 Hongwŏn N. Korea
107 R4 Hongxing Jilin China
106 H7 Hongyashan Shuiku resr Gansu China
108 D2 Hongyuan Sichuan China
109 L2 Hongze Jiangsu China
109 L2 Hongze Hu l. China
78 □6 Honiara Guadalcanal Solomon Is
150 F6 Honiton Devon, England U.K.
102 R7 Honjō Akita Japan
105 G3 Honjo Japan
105 J3 Honjō Saitama Japan
141 Q6 Honkajoki Fin.
105 H5 Honkawane Japan
149 N6 Honley West Yorkshire, England U.K.
114 D5 Honnali Karnataka India
140 R1 Honningsvåg Norway
240 □F13 Honoka'a HI U.S.A.
240 □E13 Honokahua HI U.S.A.
80 L4 Honokawa mt. North I. N.Z.
240 □D12 Honolulu HI U.S.A.
240 □ Honolulu County county HI U.S.A.
240 □F14 Honomū HI U.S.A.
226 H5 Honor MI U.S.A.
174 G3 Honoratka Pol.
240 □C12 Honouliuli HI U.S.A.
174 B3 Hönow Ger.
183 P9 Honrubia Spain
183 M6 Honrubia de la Cuesta Spain
103 K11 Honshū i. Japan
183 P9 Hontacillas Spain
183 L6 Hontalbilla Spain
183 O9 Hontanaya Spain
163 D8 Hontanx France
177 H3 Hontianske Nemce Slovakia
183 M4 Hontoria de la Cantera Spain
183 N5 Hontoria del Pinar Spain
183 M5 Hontoria de Valdearados Spain
240 □F14 Honu'apo HI U.S.A.
114 D4 Honwad Karnataka India
151 N5 Hoo Medway, England U.K.
238 D4 Hood, Mount vol. OR U.S.A.
222 C3 Hood Bay AK U.S.A.
Hood Island Islas Galápagos Ecuador see Española, Isla
87 E13 Hood Point W.A. Austr.
238 D4 Hood River OR U.S.A.
164 G4 Hoofddorp Neth.
168 G1 Hooge Ger.
168 G1 Hooge i. Ger.
165 F6 Hoogerheide Neth.
164 J3 Hoogersmilde Neth.
164 J3 Hoogeveen Neth.
164 K2 Hoogezand-Sappemeer Neth.
164 G5 Hooge Zwaluwe Neth.
164 K3 Hooghalen Neth.
Hooghly r. mouth India see Hugli
164 H3 Hoogkarspel Neth.
164 J5 Hoog-Keppel Neth.
164 J2 Hoogkerk Neth.
164 H4 Hoogland Neth.
168 C5 Hoogstede Ger.
165 G6 Hoogstraten Belgium
164 F5 Hoogvliet Neth.
149 P6 Hook East Riding of Yorkshire, England U.K.
151 K5 Hook Hampshire, England U.K.
237 E7 Hooker OK U.S.A.
84 C5 Hooker Creek watercourse N.T. Austr.
84 C4 Hooker Creek Aboriginal Land res. N.T. Austr.
147 I8 Hook Head Ireland
151 J4 Hook Norton Oxfordshire, England U.K.
Hook of Holland Neth. see Hoek van Holland
85 N8 Hook Point Qld Austr.
85 L5 Hook Reef Qld Austr.
168 F3 Hooksiel Ger.
240 □D12 Ho'olehua HI U.S.A.
106 H4 Hoolt Mongolia
220 E4 Hoonah AK U.S.A.
238 C6 Hoopa Valley Indian Reservation res. CA U.S.A.
220 B3 Hooper Bay AK U.S.A.
233 I10 Hooper Island MD U.S.A.
226 G9 Hoopeston IL U.S.A.
215 J3 Hoopstad S. Africa
142 J6 Höör Sweden
164 H3 Hoorn Neth.
77 I3 Hoorn, Îles de is Wallis and Futuna Is
164 G5 Hoornaar Neth.
105 H4 Hōō-san mt. Japan
233 L6 Hoosick NY U.S.A.
241 R5 Hoover Dam AZ/NV U.S.A.
232 C8 Hoover Memorial Reservoir OH U.S.A.
106 G4 Höövör Mongolia
140 □C1 Hóp lag. Iceland
127 J3 Hopa Turkey
234 F3 Hopatcong NJ U.S.A.
234 F3 Hopatcong, Lake NJ U.S.A.
234 D1 Hop Bottom PA U.S.A.
222 F5 Hope B.C. Can.
81 H8 Hope South I. N.Z.
81 G9 Hope r. South I. N.Z.
150 F1 Hope Flintshire, Wales U.K.
237 I9 Hope AR U.S.A.
234 F3 Hope NJ U.S.A.
82 G3 Hope, Lake salt flat S.A. Austr.
87 F12 Hope, Lake salt flat W.A. Austr.
146 G6 Hope, Loch l. Scotland U.K.
220 B3 Hope, Point AK U.S.A.
246 □ Hope Bay Jamaica
225 I2 Hopedale Nfld and Lab. Can.
237 K11 Hopedale LA U.S.A.
214 C9 Hopefield S. Africa
Hopei prov. China see Hebei
243 O8 Hopelchén Mex.
146 J7 Hopeman Moray, Scotland U.K.
225 I2 Hope Mountains Nfld and Lab. Can.
140 □ Hopen i. Svalbard
225 G1 Hopes Advance, Baie b. Que. Can.
221 L3 Hopes Advance, Cap c. Que. Can.
Hopes Advance Bay Que. Can. see Aupaluk
83 I6 Hopetoun Vic. Austr.
87 F12 Hopetoun W.A. Austr.
214 I5 Hopetown S. Africa
85 J3 Hope Vale Qld Austr.
85 J3 Hope Vale Aboriginal Reserve Qld Austr.
233 N7 Hope Valley RI U.S.A.
234 F4 Hopewell NJ U.S.A.
232 H11 Hopewell VA U.S.A.
224 E1 Hopewell Islands Nunavut Can.
235 H1 Hopewell Junction NY U.S.A.
178 F5 Hopfgarten im Brixental Austria
178 G6 Hopfgarten in Defereggen Austria
241 V6 Hopi Indian Reservation res. AZ U.S.A.
96 C2 Hopin Myanmar
83 I8 Hopkins r. Vic. Austr.
87 J8 Hopkins, Lake salt flat W.A. Austr.
230 D7 Hopkinsville KY U.S.A.
235 L2 Hopkinton RI U.S.A.
240 I3 Hopland CA U.S.A.
79 □8a Hopohoponga, Mui pt Tongatapu Tonga
96 C4 Hopong Myanmar
172 C2 Hoppstädten Ger.
140 S1 Hopseidet Norway
169 E6 Hopsten Ger.
151 P2 Hopton Norfolk, England U.K.
151 N3 Hopton Suffolk, England U.K.
150 G3 Hoptonheath Shropshire, England U.K.
209 B8 Hoque Angola
238 C3 Hoquiam WA U.S.A.
106 G9 Hor Qinghai China
111 E11 Hor Xizang China
136 J3 Hora Ukr.
210 D2 Hora Califo Eth.
129 I6 Horadiz Azer.
104 E4 Horado Japan
104 G6 Hōrai Japan
104 G6 Hōraiji-san hill Japan
151 M6 Horam East Sussex, England U.K.
127 K3 Horasan Turkey
176 C2 Horažďovice Czech Rep.
172 F5 Horb am Neckar Ger.
170 F1 Horbelev Denmark
151 L2 Horbling Lincolnshire, England U.K.
157 N7 Horbourg-Wihr France
178 A4 Hörbranz Austria
143 J6 Hörby Sweden
183 J6 Horcajo de las Torres Spain
185 J2 Horcajo de los Montes Spain
183 O9 Horcajo de Santiago Spain
183 J7 Horcajo Medianero Spain
242 G3 Horcasitas Mex.
183 N7 Horche Spain
260 B3 Horcón Chile
185 J3 Horcón hill Spain
245 J4 Horconcitos Mex.
258 D2 Horcones r. Arg.
142 C2 Horda Norway
142 C1 Hordaland county Norway
169 J7 Hörden Ger.
151 I6 Hordle Hampshire, England U.K.
150 D3 Horeb Ceredigion, Wales U.K.
80 H2 Horeke North I. N.Z.
197 L5 Horezu Romania
173 J5 Horgau Ger.
190 F1 Horgen Switz.
172 H6 Horgenzell Ger.
106 F2 Horgo Mongolia
196 H4 Horgoš Vojvodina Serbia
136 C5 Horhany mts Ukr.
106 I5 Hörh Uul mts Mongolia
197 Q5 Horia Romania
176 E1 Hořice Czech Rep.
226 F6 Horicon WI U.S.A.
105 G3 Horigane Japan
107 L6 Horinger Nei Mongol China
105 I1 Horinouchi Japan
179 O4 Horitschon Austria
106 G4 Horiult Mongolia
266 H7 Horizon Deep sea feature S. Pacific Ocean
179 J7 Horjul Slovenia
171 K8 Horka Ger.
139 N7 Horki Belarus
151 L5 Horley Surrey, England U.K.
262 Q1 Horlick Mountains Antarctica
171 I7 Hörlitz Ger.
137 R5 Horlivka Ukr.
122 I7 Hormak Iran
247 □1 Hormigueros Puerto Rico
183 O4 Hormilla Spain
122 G8 Hormoz i. Iran
122 F8 Hormoz, Kūh-e mt. Iran
122 G8 Hormozgān prov. Iran
122 F8 Hormūd-e Bāgh Iran
122 F8 Hormūd-e Mīr Khūnd Iran
122 G8 Hormuz, Strait of Iran/Oman
179 M2 Horn Austria
222 G2 Horn r. N.W.T. Can.
140 □B1 Horn c. Iceland
Horn, Cape Chile see Hornos, Cabo de
184 G3 Hornachos Spain
185 I5 Hornachuelos Spain
167 J4 Hornád r. Slovakia
177 I2 Horna Orava park Slovakia
176 G3 Horná Potôň Slovakia
177 H3 Horná Štubňa Slovakia
140 N3 Hornavan l. Sweden
172 C3 Hornbach Ger.
169 G7 Horn-Bad Meinberg Ger.
237 I10 Hornbeck LA U.S.A.
172 E5 Hornberg Ger.
142 J3 Hornborgasjöns naturreservat nature res. Sweden
238 C6 Hornbrook CA U.S.A.
169 K6 Hornburg Ger.
149 L5 Hornby Lancashire, England U.K.
149 Q7 Horncastle Lincolnshire, England U.K.
143 M1 Horndal Sweden
151 J6 Horndean Hampshire, England U.K.
Horne, Îles de is Wallis and Futuna Is see Hoorn, Îles de
168 I3 Horneburg Ger.
140 O5 Hörnefors Sweden
232 H6 Hornell NY U.S.A.
224 C3 Hornepayne Ont. Can.
235 F4 Hornerstown NJ U.S.A.
177 G3 Horné Saliby Slovakia
177 H2 Horné Srnie Slovakia
147 F2 Horn Head Ireland
177 H2 Horní Bečva Czech Rep.
177 G2 Horní Benešov Czech Rep.
171 J10 Horní Beřkovice Czech Rep.
176 C2 Horní Bříza Czech Rep.
176 E2 Horní Cerekev Czech Rep.
176 C1 Horní Jiřetín Czech Rep.
242 E4 Hornillos Mex.
176 G2 Horní Moštěnice Czech Rep.
141 I6 Hornindal Norway
151 O2 Horning Norfolk, England U.K.
176 D3 Horní Planá Czech Rep.
171 J10 Horní Počaply Czech Rep.
172 E4 Hornisgrinde mt. Ger.
85 I1 Horn Island Qld Austr.
237 K10 Horn Island MS U.S.A.
176 B1 Horní Slavkov Czech Rep.
176 D3 Horní Stropnice Czech Rep.
212 C4 Hornkranz Namibia
222 F2 Horn Mountains N.W.T. Can.
185 N4 Hornos Spain
259 D9 Hornos, Cabo de c. Chile
259 D9 Hornos, Parque Nacional de nat. park Chile
137 K1 Hornostayivka Chernihivs'ka Oblast' Ukr.
137 M6 Hornostayivka Khersons'ka Oblast' Ukr.
137 P8 Hornostayivka Respublika Krym Ukr.
171 K7 Hornow Ger.
156 C4 Hornoy-le-Bourg France
222 D2 Horn Peak Y.T. Can.
83 M5 Hornsby N.S.W. Austr.
149 Q6 Hornsea East Riding of Yorkshire, England U.K.
141 N6 Hornslandet pen. Sweden
142 G5 Hornslet Denmark
170 E3 Hornstorf Ger.
140 □B1 Hornstrandir reg. Iceland
140 □ Hornsund inlet Svalbard
168 F1 Hörnum Ger.
177 I3 Horný Tisovník Slovakia
177 L4 Horoatu Crasnei Romania
136 E5 Horodenka Ukr.
136 F2 Horodets' Ukr.
175 M5 Horodło Pol.
137 K2 Horodnya Ukr.
136 G3 Horodnytsya Ukr.
136 F4 Horodok Khmel'nyts'ka Oblast' Ukr.
136 C4 Horodok L'vivs'ka Oblast' Ukr.
137 K4 Horodyshche Cherkas'ka Oblast' Ukr.
137 K2 Horodyshche Chernihivs'ka Oblast' Ukr.
137 S4 Horodyshche Luhans'ka Oblast' Ukr.
136 E4 Horodyshche Ternopils'ka Oblast' Ukr.
102 T2 Horokanai Japan
136 D3 Horokhiv Ukr.
137 Q4 Horokhuvatka Ukr.
171 J10 Horoměřice Czech Rep.
177 L3 Horonda Ukr.
102 S1 Horonobe Japan
110 F5 Horo Shan mts China
102 T4 Horoshiri-dake mt. Japan
102 T1 Horoshiri-yama hill Japan
176 C2 Hořovice Czech Rep.
107 Q5 Horqin Shadi reg. China
Horqin Youyi Qianqi Nei Mongol China see Ulanhot
Horqin Zuoyi Houqi Nei Mongol China see Ganjig
Horqin Zuoyi Zhongqi Nei Mongol China see Baokang
253 F5 Horqueta Para.
150 D6 Horrabridge Devon, England U.K.
156 I7 Horre, Étang de la l. France
170 E1 Horreby Denmark
142 I4 Horred Sweden
151 N3 Horringer Suffolk, England U.K.
87 C10 Horrocks W.A. Austr.
111 J11 Horru Xizang China
86 □2 Horsburgh Island Cocos Is
179 J3 Hörsching Austria
238 L6 Horse Creek r. WY U.S.A.
222 F4 Horsefly B.C. Can.
227 R7 Horseheads NY U.S.A.
149 N5 Horsehouse North Yorkshire, England U.K.
225 K3 Horse Islands Nfld and Lab. Can.
169 J8 Hörsel r. Ger.
147 E6 Horseleap Galway Ireland
147 G6 Horseleap Westmeath Ireland
142 F6 Horsens Denmark
84 E8 Horseshoe Bend N.T. Austr.
238 F5 Horseshoe Bend ID U.S.A.
241 U7 Horseshoe Reservoir AZ U.S.A.
264 H3 Horseshoe Seamounts sea feature N. Atlantic Ocean
151 O2 Horsford Norfolk, England U.K.
149 N6 Horsforth West Yorkshire, England U.K.
83 I7 Horsham Vic. Austr.
151 L5 Horsham West Sussex, England U.K.
234 E4 Horsham PA U.S.A.
136 H3 Horshchyk Ukr.
171 D6 Hörsingen Ger.
168 L1 Horslunde Denmark
151 M5 Horsmonden Kent, England U.K.
176 B2 Horšovský Týn Czech Rep.
169 H10 Horst hill Ger.
165 J6 Horst Neth.
168 I3 Horst (Holstein) Ger.
151 O2 Horstead Norfolk, England U.K.
168 H4 Horstedt Ger.
169 E6 Hörstel Ger.
169 D6 Horstmar Ger.
199 J5 Horsunlu Turkey
177 I4 Hort Hungary
216 □1c Horta Faial Azores
142 G2 Horten Norway
261 G4 Hortensia Arg.
183 O6 Hortezuela Spain
183 N4 Hortigüela Spain
177 K4 Hortobágy Hungary
177 J4 Hortobágy-Berettyó canal Hungary
177 K4 Hortobágyi nat. park Hungary
220 F3 Horton r. N.W.T. Can.
151 J6 Horton Heath Hampshire, England U.K.
149 M5 Horton in Ribblesdale North Yorkshire, England U.K.
168 I1 Høruphav Denmark
139 N9 Horval' Belarus
190 E1 Horw Switz.
149 L6 Horwich Greater Manchester, England U.K.
224 D3 Horwood Lake Ont. Can.
139 O8 Hory Belarus
136 F2 Horyn' r. Ukr.
175 L5 Horyniec-Zdrój Pol.
175 L5 Horyszów Pol.
104 C6 Hōryūji tourist site Japan
210 C3 Hosa'ina Eth.
169 H10 Hösbach Ger.
114 E6 Hosdurga Karnataka India
95 J3 Hose, Pegunungan mts Malaysia
171 J8 Hosena Ger.
169 H9 Hosenfeld Ger.
202 D4 Hosenofu well Libya
122 B4 Ḩoseynābād Iran
122 F4 Ḩoseynān, Band-e mts Iran
122 C6 Ḩoseynīyeh Iran
123 J8 Hoshab Pak.
116 F8 Hoshangabad Madh. Prad. India
136 F3 Hoshcha Ukr.
116 E4 Hoshiarpur Punjab India
106 H2 Höshööt Arhangay Mongolia
106 A2 Höshööt Bayan-Ölgiy Mongolia
165 J8 Hosingen Lux.
91 L8 Hoskins New Britain P.N.G.
199 I2 Hoşköy Turkey
104 G6 Hosoe Japan
114 E5 Hospet Karnataka India
163 F10 Hospice de France France
Hospitalet Cataluña Spain see L'Hospitalet de l'Infant
Hospitalet Cataluña Spain see L'Hospitalet de Llobregat
140 T4 Hossa Fin.
163 B8 Hosseger France
207 I4 Hosséré Vokre mt. Cameroon
198 D4 Hossios Luckas tourist site Greece
172 G6 Hoßkirch Ger.
177 K4 Hosszúpályi Hungary
176 G4 Hosszúpereszteg Hungary
186 K4 Hostalríc Spain
Hostalrich Spain see Hostalríc
259 C9 Hoste, Isla i. Chile
163 C7 Hostens France
176 F3 Hostěradice Czech Rep.
177 H3 Hostie Slovakia
176 E1 Hostinné Czech Rep.
176 D1 Hostivice Czech Rep.
171 J10 Hoštka Czech Rep.
176 C1 Hostomice Czech Rep.
173 N2 Hostouň Czech Rep.
168 H1 Hostrupskov Denmark
114 E6 Hosur Tamil Nadu India
140 M5 Hotagen r. Sweden
Hotahudo East Timor see Hatudo
105 G3 Hotaka Japan
104 G3 Hotaka-dake mt. Japan
105 J2 Hotaka-yama mt. Japan
111 E8 Hotan Xinjiang China
110 E6 Hotan He watercourse China
214 G3 Hotazel S. Africa
235 I1 Hotchkissville CT U.S.A.
241 P3 Hot Creek r. NV U.S.A.
241 P3 Hot Creek Range mts NV U.S.A.
171 D6 Hötensleben Ger.
87 D12 Hotham r. W.A. Austr.
84 C2 Hotham, Cape N.T. Austr.
93 G5 Hoti Seram Indon.
140 N4 Hoting Sweden
179 M7 Hotinja vas Slovenia
79 □9a Hotopuu Tahiti Fr. Polynesia
237 I8 Hot Springs AR U.S.A.
Hot Springs NM U.S.A. see Truth or Consequences
236 D4 Hot Springs SD U.S.A.
238 K6 Hot Sulphur Springs CO U.S.A.
222 G1 Hottah Lake N.W.T. Can.
246 F4 Hotte, Massif de la mts Haiti
212 B5 Hottentots Bay Namibia
214 C9 Hottentots-Holland Nature Reserve S. Africa
212 B5 Hottentots Point Namibia
165 H8 Hotton Belgium
172 E6 Hotzenwald reg. Ger.
78 □5 Houaïlu New Caledonia
158 F7 Houat, Île d' i. France
156 E3 Houdain France
156 C6 Houdan France
157 J6 Houdelaincourt France
157 K7 Houécourt France
163 E7 Houeillès France
163 E9 Houeydets France
165 I8 Houffalize Belgium
94 □ Hougang Sing.
85 K5 Houghton r. Qld Austr.
149 L4 Houghton Cumbria, England U.K.
226 F2 Houghton MI U.S.A.
232 G6 Houghton NY U.S.A.
226 J5 Houghton Lake MI U.S.A.
226 J5 Houghton Lake l. MI U.S.A.
149 O4 Houghton le Spring Tyne and Wear, England U.K.
151 K4 Houghton Regis Bedfordshire, England U.K.
96 F4 Houie Moc, Phou mt. Laos
157 M6 Houillères de la Sarve, Canal des France
159 K3 Houlgate France
233 □R2 Houlton ME U.S.A.
107 L9 Houma Shanxi China
79 □8a Houma Tongatapu Tonga
79 □8a Houma Tonga
237 J11 Houma LA U.S.A.
109 J7 Houmen Guangdong China
205 H2 Houmt Souk Tunisia
206 E4 Houndé Burkina
146 K11 Houndslow Scottish Borders, Scotland U.K.
156 E2 Houplines France
156 C3 Hourdel, Pointe du pt France
106 F8 Houri Qinghai China
146 E8 Hourn, Loch inlet Scotland U.K.
162 B5 Hourtin France
162 B5 Hourtin et de Carcans, Étang d' l. France
162 B5 Hourtin-Plage France
233 L6 Housatonic MA U.S.A.
235 I2 Housatonic r. CT U.S.A.
241 S2 House Range mts UT U.S.A.
149 M3 Housesteads tourist site England U.K.
222 E4 Houston B.C. Can.
234 E7 Houston DE U.S.A.
226 C6 Houston MN U.S.A.
237 J7 Houston MO U.S.A.
237 K9 Houston MS U.S.A.
237 H11 Houston TX U.S.A.
214 C10 Hout Bay S. Africa
214 C10 Hout Bay b. S. Africa
164 H4 Houten Neth.
165 H6 Houthalen Belgium
165 C7 Houthulst Belgium
214 I6 Houtkraal S. Africa
87 B10 Houtman Abrolhos is W.A. Austr.
146 J5 Houton Orkney, Scotland U.K.
141 P6 Houtskär Fin.
214 H6 Houwater S. Africa
110 H5 Houxia Xinjiang China
165 H8 Houyet Belgium
106 G8 Houzihe Qinghai China
142 G6 Hov Denmark
142 G1 Hov Norway
143 K3 Hova Sweden
106 B3 Hovd Hovd Mongolia
106 H4 Hovd Övörhangay Mongolia
106 C3 Hovd prov. Mongolia
142 E3 Hovdefjell hill Norway
142 D2 Hovden park Norway
106 C2 Hovd Gol r. Mongolia
151 L6 Hove Brighton and Hove, England U.K.
169 G7 Hövelhof Ger.
136 D5 Hoverla, Hora mt. Ukr.
151 O2 Hoveton Norfolk, England U.K.
122 C6 Hoveyzeh Iran
143 L1 Hovfjället naturreservat nature res. Sweden
149 P5 Hovingham North Yorkshire, England U.K.
226 E2 Hovland MN U.S.A.
143 L5 Hovmantorp Sweden
129 L5 Hövsan Azer.
107 K5 Hövsgöl Mongolia
106 G1 Hövsgöl prov. Mongolia
106 G1 Hövsgöl Nuur l. Mongolia
137 M4 Hovtva Ukr.
137 M4 Hovtva r. Ukr.
106 H5 Hövüün Mongolia
202 D6 Howa, Ouadi watercourse Chad/Sudan
202 E5 Howar, Wadi watercourse Sudan
85 N8 Howard Qld Austr.
237 G7 Howard KS U.S.A.
236 G3 Howard SD U.S.A.
226 F5 Howard WI U.S.A.
226 I6 Howard City MI U.S.A.
234 B6 Howard County county MD U.S.A.
149 O5 Howardian Hills England U.K.
84 E2 Howard Island N.T. Austr.
223 J2 Howard Lake N.W.T. Can.
84 C2 Howard Springs N.T. Austr.
149 P6 Howden East Riding of Yorkshire, England U.K.
226 I8 Howe IN U.S.A.
83 L7 Howe, Cape Vic. Austr.
262 O1 Howe, Mount Antarcti
227 K7 Howell MI U.S.A.
146 K9 Howe of the Mearns Scotland U.K.
236 D3 Howes SD U.S.A.
233 L3 Howick Que. Can.
215 O5 Howick S. Africa
82 G2 Howitt, Lake salt flat S.A. Austr.
233 □Q3 Howland ME U.S.A.
77 I1 Howland Island N. Pacific Ocean
83 K6 Howlong N.S.W. Austr.
Howrah W. Bengal Indi Haora
147 J6 Howth Ireland
122 H5 Ḩowz well Iran
122 F5 Ḩowz-e Gīvar Iran
122 G5 Ḩowz-e Khān well Iran
122 G6 Ḩowz-e Panj Iran
122 F5 Ḩowz-e Panj waterhol
122 F5 Ḩowz i-Mian i-Tak Iran
96 H6 Hô Xa Vietnam
236 E6 Hoxie KS U.S.A.
169 H7 Höxter Ger.
110 H3 Hoxtolgay Xinjiang Chi
110 H5 Hoxud Xinjiang China
146 J5 Hoy i. Scotland U.K.
168 H5 Hoya Ger.
105 K4 Hōya Japan
185 P3 Hoya Gonzalo Spain
141 I6 Høyanger Norway
171 J8 Hoyerswerda Ger.
149 K7 Hoylake Merseyside, England U.K.
149 O7 Hoyland South Yorkshi England U.K.
140 L4 Høylandet Norway
227 M1 Hoyle Ont. Can.
171 D7 Hoym Ger.
183 M7 Hoyo de Manzanares
106 I6 Hoyor Amt Nei Mongol
182 G8 Hoyos Spain
183 J8 Hoyos del Espino Spa
140 T5 Höytiäinen l. Fin.
126 I4 Hozat Turkey
185 I8 Hozgarganta r. Spain
138 G8 Hozha Belarus
104 C5 Hozu-gawa r. Japan
104 E5 Hozumi Japan
96 C6 Hpa-an Myanmar
96 C5 Hpapun Myanmar
136 I5 Hrabove Ukr.
137 Q3 Hrachivka Ukr.
173 O2 Hracholusky, Vodní n resr Czech Rep.
176 E1 Hradec Králové Czech
177 G2 Hradec nad Moravicí Czech Rep.
176 F2 Hradec nad Svitavou Czech Rep.
173 P2 Hrádek Czech Rep.
176 D1 Hrádek nad Nisou Czech Rep.
176 C2 Hradešice Czech Rep.
176 C1 Hradiště hill Czech Re
177 H3 Hradište Slovakia
137 M4 Hradyz'k Ukr.
138 L8 Hradzyanka Belarus
175 L2 Hrandzichy Belarus
176 B1 Hranice Karlovarský kra Czech Rep.
177 G2 Hranice Olomoucký kra Czech Rep.
137 Q6 Hranitne Donets'ka Oblast' Ukr.
136 I3 Hranitne Zhytomyrs'ka Oblast' Uk
177 J3 Hranovnica Slovakia
188 G4 Hrasnica Bos.-Herz.
179 L7 Hrastnik Slovenia
140 □C1 Hraun Iceland
140 □F1 Hraun slope Iceland
138 I7 Hrawzhyshki Belarus
129 F5 Hrazdan Armenia
171 J9 Hrazený hill Czech Rep
137 L3 Hrebinka Ukr.
136 J4 Hrebinky Ukr.
191 R5 Hreljin Croatia
137 M1 Hrem"yach Ukr.
137 L6 Hreyhove Ukr.
177 J3 Hrhov Slovakia
175 L6 Hrimne Ukr.
177 I3 Hriňová Slovakia
Hristós Ikaria Greece se Raches
136 H5 Hristovaia Moldova
171 I9 Hrob Czech Rep.
177 I3 Hrochoť Slovakia
176 E2 Hrochův Týnec Czech
138 G8 Hrodna Belarus
Hrodna Oblast admin. Belarus see Hrodzyenskaya Voblas
175 L2 Hrodnyendskaye Wzvy hills Belarus
138 I8 Hrodzyenskaya Voblas admin. div. Belarus
137 N7 Hromivka Ukr.
173 O2 Hromnice Czech Rep.
177 H4 Hron r. Slovakia
177 I3 Hronec Slovakia
176 F1 Hronov Czech Rep.
177 H3 Hronský Beňadik Slov
176 F2 Hrotovice Czech Rep.
171 G10 Hroznětín Czech Rep.
175 L5 Hrubieszów Pol.
175 M4 Hrudky Ukr.
137 N3 Hrun' Ukr.
137 N3 Hrun' r. Ukr.
137 P4 Hrushuvakha Ukr.
179 J8 Hrušica mts Slovenia
176 F3 Hrušky Czech Rep.
177 I3 Hrusov Slovakia
176 F3 Hrušovany nad Jevišo Czech Rep.
179 O1 Hrušovany u Brna Cze
177 I2 Hruštín Slovakia
175 K3 Hruszniew Pol.
Hrvatska country Europ Croatia
188 F3 Hrvatska Kostajnica C
Hrvatsko Grahovo Bos see Bosansko Grahovo
137 L2 Hryhorivka Chernihivs'k Oblast' Ukr.
137 P5 Hryhorivka Dnipropetro Oblast' Ukr.
137 M7 Hryhorivka Khersons'ka Oblast' Ukr.
136 F4 Hrymayliv Ukr.
136 D6 Hrynyava Ukr.
136 H4 Hryshkivtsi Ukr.
137 M8 Hryshyne Ukr.
136 G4 Hrytsiv Ukr.
96 C3 Hsenwi Myanmar
Hsiang Chang i. H.K. C see Hong Kong Island
Hsiang Kang H.K. China Hong Kong
96 C4 Hsi-hseng Myanmar
96 D4 Hsin, Nam r. Myanmar
Hsin-chia-p'o country A Singapore
Hsin-chia-p'o Sing. see Singapore
109 M6 Hsinchu Taiwan
Hsinking Jilin China see Changchun
109 M7 Hsinying Taiwan
96 C3 Hsipaw Myanmar
Hsi-sha Ch'un-tao is S. China Sea see Paracel Islands
109 L7 Hsiyüp'ing Yü i. Taiwan
109 M6 Hsüeh Shan mt. Taiwan
109 K6 Hua'an Fujian China
212 B4 Huab watercourse Nami
107 N8 Huabei Pingyuan plain
252 A2 Huacaibamba Peru
252 E3 Huacaraje Bol.
252 E5 Huacaya Bol.
109 J6 Huacheng Guangdong C
252 E3 Huachi Bol.
107 K8 Huachi Gansu China
242 E2 Huachinera Mex.
252 A2 Huacho Peru
252 B2 Huachón Peru
100 G5 Huachuan Heilong. Chin
241 V10 Huachuca City AZ U.S.
260 C2 Huaco Arg.

I

244 D2 Ignacio Zaragoza *Zacatecas* Mex.
138 J6 Ignalina Lith.
100 C2 Ignashino Rus. Fed.
126 C3 İğneada Turkey
126 D3 İğneada Burnu *pt* Turkey
177 L5 Ignești Romania
157 L7 Igney France
115 M7 Ignoitijala *Andaman & Nicobar Is* India
160 G1 Igon *r.* France
134 H4 Igodovo Rus. Fed.
93 G4 Igom *Papua* Indon.
211 B6 Igoma Tanz.
211 A6 Igombe *r.* Tanz.
139 Q6 Igorevskaya Rus. Fed.
160 E2 Igornay France
198 B3 Igoumenitsa Greece
134 K4 Igra Rus. Fed.
186 E3 Igriés Spain
130 H3 Igrim Rus. Fed.
255 B8 Iguaçu *r.* Brazil
256 A6 Iguaçu, Parque Nacional do *nat. park* Brazil
Iguaçu, Saltos do *waterfall* Arg./Brazil *see* Iguaçu Falls
258 G2 Iguaçu Falls Arg./Brazil
255 E5 Iguaí Brazil
250 C4 Iguaje, Mesa de *hills* Col.
245 H7 Iguala Mex.
186 I4 Igualada Spain
185 I7 Igualeja Spain
245 I8 Igualtepec Mex.
256 D6 Iguape Brazil
256 B5 Iguaraçu Brazil
257 E4 Iguarapé Brazil
257 E4 Iguatama Brazil
255 B7 Iguatemi Brazil
255 B7 Iguatemi *r.* Brazil
254 F3 Iguatu Brazil
Iguazú, Cataratas do *waterfall* Arg./Brazil *see* Iguaçu Falls
258 G2 Iguazú, Parque Nacional del *nat. park* Arg.
208 A5 Iguéla Gabon
188 F3 Iguêña Spain
160 E4 Iguerande France
204 C4 Iguetti, Sebkhet *salt flat* Maur.
204 D4 Iguidi, Erg *des.* Alg./Maur.
211 B6 Igunga Tanz.
207 G5 Iguobazuwa Nigeria
213 F3 Igusi Zimbabwe
211 B5 Igusule Tanz.
Iguvium Italy *see* Gubbio
213 □K2 Iharaña Madag.
176 G5 Iharosberény Hungary
114 C9 Ihavandhippolhu Atoll Maldives
85 J7 Ihbulag Mongolia
102 □E19 Iheya-jima *i. Nansei-shotō* Japan
106 I3 Ihhayrhan Mongolia
207 G5 Ihiala Nigeria
205 G5 Ihirène, Oued *watercourse* Alg.
177 J2 Iňany Slovakia
168 E4 Ihlowerhörn (Ihlow) Ger.
176 G2 Ihnatpil' Ukr.
163 B9 Iholdy France
213 □J4 Ihosy Madag.
168 D4 Ihrhove Ger.
172 D5 Ihringen Ger.
173 L4 Ihrlerstein Ger.
126 E5 Ihsaniye Turkey
106 J2 Ihsuuj Mongolia
107 R5 Ih Tal *Nei Mongol* China
105 G4 Iida Japan
102 Q9 Iide-san *mt.* Japan
105 G2 Iijima Japan
140 I4 Iijoki *r.* Fin.
104 D7 Iinan Japan
105 M4 Iioka Japan
140 H5 Iisalmi Fin.
104 D7 Iitaka Japan
138 J1 Iitti Fin.
105 H2 Iiyama Japan
103 H13 Iizuka Japan
204 C5 Ijâfene *des.* Maur.
211 D5 Ijara Kenya
207 F5 Ijebu-Ode Nigeria
95 K9 Ijen-Merapi-Maelang, Cagar Alam *nature res. Jawa* Indon.
129 G5 Ijevan Armenia
164 I2 IJlst Neth.
164 I3 IJmuiden Neth.
206 B2 Ijnâouene *well* Maur.
205 D3 Ijoubbâne *des.* Mali
164 I3 IJssel *r.* Neth.
164 H3 IJsselmeer *l.* Neth.
164 I3 IJsselmuiden Neth.
164 H4 IJsselstein Neth.
255 B9 Ijuí Brazil
253 G6 Ijuí *r.* Brazil
164 E2 IJzendijke Neth.
165 C7 IJzer *r.* Belgium *alt.* Yser (France)
Ikaahuk *N.W.T.* Can. *see* Sachs Harbour
141 Q6 Ikaalinen Fin.
215 K1 Ikageleng S. Africa
215 L2 Ikageng S. Africa
213 □J3 Ikahavo *hill* Madag.
105 I3 Ikaho Japan
213 □J4 Ikalamavony Madag.
Ikaluktutiak *Nunavut* Can. *see* Cambridge Bay
81 F9 Ikamatua *South I.* N.Z.
209 D5 Ikanda-Nord Dem. Rep. Congo
207 H5 Ikang Nigeria
207 G4 Ikara Nigeria
207 G5 Ikare Nigeria
208 C5 Ikari Dem. Rep. Congo
199 H5 Ikaria *i.* Greece
104 C6 Ikaruga Japan
142 F5 Ikast Denmark
208 C4 Ikau Dem. Rep. Congo
105 H5 Ikawa Japan
81 E11 Ikawai *South I.* N.Z.
80 K5 Ikawhenua Range *mts North I.* N.Z.
104 D4 Ikeda *Fukui* Japan
104 E5 Ikeda *Gifu* Japan
102 U4 Ikeda *Hokkaidō* Japan
105 G3 Ikeda *Nagano* Japan
104 C5 Ikeda *Ōsaka* Japan
103 K12 Ikeda *Tokushima* Japan
103 K13 Ikegawa Japan
104 D7 Ikegoya-yama *mt.* Japan
102 □1 Ikei-jima *i. Okinawa* Japan
207 F5 Ikeja Nigeria
208 D5 Ikela Dem. Rep. Congo
208 C4 Ikelemba *r.* Dem. Rep. Congo
209 E7 Ikelenge Zambia
207 G5 Ikem Nigeria
208 C5 Ikengo Dem. Rep. Congo
208 A5 Ikéngue Gabon
207 G5 Ikere Nigeria
Ikerre Nigeria *see* Ikere
176 F4 Ikervár Hungary
129 I4 Ikhrek Rus. Fed.
197 L8 Ikhtiman Bulg.
215 I4 Ikhutseng S. Africa
128 H1 Ikiağiz Turkey
135 I7 Iki-Burul Rus. Fed.
211 A5 Ikimba, Lake Tanz.
207 G5 Ikire Nigeria
103 G13 Iki-shima *i.* Japan
103 G13 Iki-suidō *sea chan.* Japan
129 B5 İkizdere Turkey
138 H4 Ikla Estonia
211 C6 Ikola Tanz.
207 H5 Ikom Nigeria
104 C6 Ikoma Japan
211 B5 Ikoma Tanz.
213 □J4 Ikongo Madag.
217 □3a Ikoni *Njazidja* Comoros
129 C1 Ikon-Khalk Rus. Fed.
213 □J3 Ikopa *r.* Madag.
137 S3 Ikorets *r.* Rus. Fed.
207 F5 Ikorodu Nigeria
208 E5 Ikosi Dem. Rep. Congo
207 G5 Ikot Ekpene Nigeria
205 H4 Ikouhaouene, Adrar *mt.* Alg.
Ikpiarjuk *Nunavut* Can. *see* Arctic Bay
177 G4 Ikrény Hungary
101 E11 Iksan S. Korea
104 F2 Ikuji-hana *pt* Japan
211 B6 Ikungi Tanz.
211 B6 Ikungu Tanz.
104 A5 Ikuno Japan
105 G3 Ikusaka Japan
136 E3 Ikva *r.* Ukr.
205 F5 Ilaferh, Oued *watercourse* Alg.
211 A6 Ilagala Tanz.
92 C3 Ilagan *Luzon* Phil.
210 C4 Ilaisamis Kenya
114 F8 Ilaiyankudi *Tamil Nadu* India
213 □K3 Ilaka Atsinanana Madag.
122 B5 Īlām Iran
122 B5 Īlām *prov.* Iran
118 F5 Ilam Nepal
107 M6 Ilan Taiwan
174 C3 Ilanka *r.* Pol.
190 G2 Ilanz Switz.
207 G4 Ila Orangun Nigeria
137 O5 Ilarionove Ukr.
207 F5 Ilaro Nigeria
252 C4 Ilave Peru
175 H2 Iława Pol.
207 G5 Ilawe-Ekiti Nigeria
175 H2 Iławskie, Pojezierze *reg.* Pol.
122 G7 Ilazārān, Kūh-e *mt.* Iran
195 □ Il-Barkja, Ras *pt Gozo* Malta
106 F4 Il Bogd Uul *mts* Mongolia
192 D8 Ilbono *Sardegna* Italy
150 G6 Ilchester *Somerset, England* U.K.
199 H4 Ildır Turkey
121 O5 Ile *r.* China/Kazakh.
223 J4 Île-à-la-Crosse *Sask.* Can.
223 J4 Île-à-la-Crosse, Lac *l. Sask.* Can.
246 G4 Île-à-Vache *i.* Haiti
209 D6 Ilebo Dem. Rep. Congo
225 I3 Île d'Anticosti, Réserve Faunique de l' *nature res. Que.* Can.
156 E6 Île-de-France *admin. reg.* France
211 B7 Ileje Tanz.
120 E2 Ilek Kazakh.
120 E2 Ilek *r.* Rus. Fed.
137 O3 Ilek-Pen'kovka Rus. Fed.
147 D9 Ilen *r.* Ireland
Ilerda *prov.* Spain *see* Lleida
210 C3 Ileret Kenya
Île Royale *i. N.S.* Can. *see* Cape Breton Island
Ilesa Nigeria *see* Ilesha
207 G5 Ilesha Nigeria
207 F4 Ilesha Ibariba Nigeria
134 J5 Ilet' *r.* Rus. Fed.
134 H3 Ileza Rus. Fed.
169 K7 Ilfeld Ger.
223 M3 Ilford *Man.* Can.
151 M4 Ilford *Greater London, England* U.K.
85 J7 Ilfracombe *Qld* Austr.
150 D5 Ilfracombe *Devon, England* U.K.
126 F3 Ilgaz Turkey
126 F3 Ilgaz Dağları *mts* Turkey
126 E4 Ilgın Turkey
175 M1 Ilgis *l.* Lith.
195 □ Il-Griebeġ, Ras *pt* Malta
216 □1c Ilha, Ponta da *pt Pico* Azores
257 E5 Ilhabela Brazil
251 E5 Ilha Grande Brazil
257 E5 Ilha Grande, Baía da *b.* Brazil
255 B7 Ilha Grande, Parque Nacional da *nat. park* Brazil
255 B7 Ilha Grande, Represa *resr* Brazil
195 □ Il-Hamrija, Ras *pt* Malta
256 B4 Ilha Solteira, Represa *resr* Brazil
182 C7 Ílhavo Port.
255 F5 Ilhéus Brazil
Ili *r.* China/Kazakh. *see* Ile
Ili Kazakh. *see* Kapchagay
197 K5 Ilia Romania
220 C4 Iliamna Lake *AK* U.S.A.
126 I4 İliç Turkey
129 B6 Ilica *Bingöl* Turkey
129 C6 Ilica *Erzurum* Turkey
129 C1 Il'ich Rus. Fed.
Il'ichevsk Azer. *see* Şärur
Il'ichevsk Ukr. *see* Illichivs'k
Ilici Spain *see* Elche-Elx
210 F3 Ilig, Raas *pt* Somalia
92 E7 Iligan *Mindanao* Phil.
92 E7 Iligan Bay *Mindanao* Phil.
92 D2 Iligan Point *Luzon* Phil.
Ili He *r.* China/Kazakh. *see* Ile
188 G4 Ilijaš Bos.-Herz.
221 P2 Ilimananngip Nunaa *i.* Greenland
131 L3 Ilimpeya *r.* Rus. Fed.
120 G3 Il'inka Kazakh.
139 T7 Il'inka *Kaluzhskaya Oblast'* Rus. Fed.
121 U2 Il'inka *Respublika Altay* Rus. Fed.
106 D1 Il'inka *Respublika Tyva* Rus. Fed.
139 O6 Il'ino Rus. Fed.
134 K4 Il'inskiy *Permskaya Oblast'* Rus. Fed.
139 P1 Il'inskiy *Respublika Kareliya* Rus. Fed.
100 M5 Il'inskiy *Sakhalin* Rus. Fed.
134 I3 Il'insko-Podomskoye Rus. Fed.
137 S8 Il'inskoye *Krasnodarskiy Kray* Rus. Fed.
139 S8 Il'inskoye *Orlovskaya Oblast'* Rus. Fed.
139 U5 Il'inskoye *Tverskaya Oblast'* Rus. Fed.
139 V4 Il'inskoye *Yaroslavskaya Oblast'* Rus. Fed.
139 W5 Il'inskoye-Khovanskoye Rus. Fed.
92 C5 Ilin Strait Phil.
Il'intsy Ukr. *see* Illintsi
93 E8 Iliomar East Timor
233 J5 Ilion *NY* U.S.A.
240 □D12 'Īlio Point *HI* U.S.A.
188 E3 Ilirska Bistrica Slovenia
129 H4 İlisu Qoruğu *nature res.* Azer.
Ilium *tourist site* Turkey *see* Truva
138 K7 Iliya *r.* Belarus
Iliysk Kazakh. *see* Kapchagay
177 L3 Ilk Hungary
114 E5 Ilkal *Karnataka* India
151 J2 Ilkeston *Derbyshire, England* U.K.
149 N6 Ilkley *West Yorkshire, England* U.K.
195 □ Il-Kullana *pt* Malta
157 O6 Ill *r.* France
183 O8 Illana Spain
92 D8 Illana Bay *Mindanao* Phil.
260 B2 Illapel Chile
260 B2 Illapel *r.* Chile
185 N7 Illar Spain
191 K5 Illasi *r.* Italy
163 D6 Illats France
82 D2 Illbillee, Mount *hill S.A.* Austr.
158 H5 Ille *r.* France
158 H5 Ille-et-Rance, Canal d' France
158 H5 Ille-et-Vilaine *dept* France
207 G3 Illéla Niger
207 G3 Illela Nigeria
173 H5 Iller *r.* Ger.
173 I5 Illerrieden Ger.
173 I5 Illertissen Ger.
181 G3 Illes Balears *aut. comm.* Spain
183 M8 Illescas Spain
258 G4 Illescas Uru.
163 J10 Ille-sur-Têt France
137 O8 Illicheve Ukr.
136 J7 Illichivs'k Ukr.
156 B7 Illiers-Combray France
252 D4 Illimani, Nevado de *mt.* Bol.
172 F4 Illingen *Baden-Württemberg* Ger.
172 C3 Illingen *Saarland* Ger.
136 J7 Illinka *Odes'ka Oblast'* Ukr.
137 M8 Illinka *Respublika Krym* Ukr.
226 D9 Illinois *r. IL* U.S.A.
236 K6 Illinois *state* U.S.A.
226 E8 Illinois and Mississippi Canal *IL* U.S.A.
136 I4 Illintsi Ukr.
205 H4 Illizi Alg.
157 O6 Illkirch-Graffenstaden France
172 G6 Illmensee Ger.
179 O4 Illmitz Austria
84 E8 Illogwa *watercourse N.T.* Austr.
185 L6 Íllora Spain
192 B7 Illorai *Sardegna* Italy
173 L3 Illschwang Ger.
183 Q5 Illueca Spain
157 N8 Illzach France
171 E8 Ilm *r.* Ger.
173 L4 Ilm *r.* Ger.
87 I10 Ilma, Lake *salt flat W.A.* Austr.
124 G6 'Ilmān, Jabal al *hill* Saudi Arabia
139 O3 Il'men', Ozero *l.* Rus. Fed.
169 K9 Ilmenau Ger.
168 J4 Ilmenau *r.* Ger.
195 □ Il-Minkba *pt* Malta
150 G6 Ilminster *Somerset, England* U.K.
178 F8 Il Montello *mt.* Italy
171 D9 Ilmtal *park* Ger.
136 C5 Il'nytsya Ukr.
252 C4 Ilo Peru
207 G5 Ilobu Nigeria
92 B6 Iloc *i.* Phil.
260 A4 Iloca Chile
92 D6 Iloilo *Panay* Phil.
92 D6 Iloilo Strait Phil.
140 U5 Ilomantsi Fin.
211 B6 Ilongero Tanz.
207 G4 Ilorin Nigeria
188 F3 Ilova *r.* Croatia
135 I6 Ilovatka Rus. Fed.
137 R6 Ilovays'k Ukr.
197 K9 Ilovica Macedonia
191 R7 Ilovik Croatia
188 E3 Ilovik *i.* Croatia
137 R3 Ilovka Rus. Fed.
135 H6 Ilovlya Rus. Fed.
135 H6 Ilovlya *r.* Rus. Fed.
175 I3 Iłów Pol.
174 D4 Iłowa Pol.
175 I2 Iłowo Osada Pol.
164 G4 Ilpendam Neth.
131 R3 Il'pyrskoye Rus. Fed.
195 □ Il-Qala, Ras *pt Gozo* Malta
141 N6 Ilsbo Sweden
169 K6 Ilse *r.* Ger.
169 J6 Ilsede Ger.
169 K7 Ilsenburg (Harz) Ger.
172 G3 Ilsfeld Ger.
172 H3 Ilshofen Ger.
150 E6 Ilsington *Devon, England* U.K.
137 R9 Il'skiy Rus. Fed.
192 A10 Il Toro, Isola *i. Sardegna* Italy
138 J6 Ilūkste Latvia
221 M3 Ilulissat Greenland
211 B6 Ilunde Tanz.
211 B6 Ilungu Tanz.
Ilva *i.* Italy *see* Elba, Isola d'
195 □ Il-Wahx, Ras *pt* Malta
138 K7 Il'ya Belarus
Il'yaly Turkm. *see* Gurbansoltan Eje
134 L3 Ilych *r.* Rus. Fed.
175 K1 Ilyushino Rus. Fed.
179 M5 Ilz Austria
173 O4 Ilz *r.* Ger.
175 J4 Iłża Pol.
175 J4 Iłżanka *r.* Pol.
103 J12 Imabari Japan
102 R5 Imabetsu Japan
251 G5 Imabú *r.* Brazil
104 D4 Imadate Japan
102 R4 Imagane Japan
105 K2 Imaichi Japan
104 D4 Imajō Japan
213 H2 Imala Moz.
127 L8 Imām al Ḩamzah Iraq
123 J3 Imam-baba Turkm.
126 G5 İmamoğlu Turkey
Iman Rus. Fed. *see* Dal'nerechensk
100 H6 Iman *r.* Rus. Fed.
134 F2 Imandra Rus. Fed.
121 M1 Imantau, Ozero *l.* Kazakh.
103 G13 Imari Japan
206 E3 Imasgo Burkina
Imassogo Burkina *see* Imasgo
252 C3 Imata Peru
251 F3 Imataca, Serranía de *mts* Venez.
141 T6 Imatra Fin.
138 I3 Imavere Estonia
104 D5 Imazu Japan
250 B4 Imbabura *prov.* Ecuador
251 F3 Imbaimadai Guyana
Imba-numa *l.* Japan *see* Inba-numa
255 C9 Imbituba Brazil
256 B6 Imbituva Brazil
199 L6 İmecik Turkey
177 H4 Imeľ Slovakia
imeni 26 Bakinskikh Komissarov Azer. *see* Uzboy
134 H4 imeni Babushkina Rus. Fed.
imeni Chapayevka Turkm. *see* S. A. Nyýazow Adyndaky
131 P3 imeni Gastello Rus. Fed.
imeni G. I. Petrovskogo Ukr. *see* Horodyshche
139 X5 imeni Gor'kogo Rus. Fed.
imeni G. Ya. Sedova Ukr. *see* Syedove
imeni Kalinina Tajik. *see* Cheshtebe
137 O2 imeni Karla Libknekhta Rus. Fed.
imeni Khamzy Khakikmzade Uzbek. *see* Hamza
imeni Kirova Kazakh. *see* Kopbirlik
imeni Kirova *Donets'ka Oblast'* Ukr. *see* Kirovs'k
imeni Kirova *Donets'ka Oblast'* Ukr. *see* Kirove
imeni L. M. Kaganovicha Ukr. *see* Popasna
134 I4 imeni M. I. Kalinina Rus. Fed.
imeni Petra Stuchki Latvia *see* Aizkraukle
100 J2 imeni Poliny Osipenko Rus. Fed.
imeni Voroshilova Kyrg. *see* Tash-Bashat
139 T3 imeni Zhelyabova Rus. Fed.
137 O5 Imeny Lenina, Ozero *l.* Ukr.
191 L3 Imèr Italy
194 G8 Imera *r. Sicilia* Italy
251 E4 Imeri, Serra *mts* Brazil
208 C4 Imese Dem. Rep. Congo
210 D3 Īmī Eth.
204 D2 Imilchil Morocco
204 C3 Imi-n-Tanoute Morocco
204 B4 Imirikliy Labyad *reg.* Western Sahara
Imishli Azer. *see* İmişli
129 J6 İmişli Azer.
116 D1 Imit Jammu and Kashmir
101 E11 Imja-do *i.* S. Korea
101 E10 Imjin-gang *r.* N. Korea/S. Korea
227 K6 Imlay City *MI* U.S.A.
204 B5 Imlili Western Sahara
169 J9 Immelborn Ger.
143 K5 Immeln *l.* Sweden
172 F6 Immendingen Ger.
169 H8 Immenhausen Ger.
173 L2 Immenreuth Ger.
172 G6 Immenstaad am Bodensee Ger.
173 I6 Immenstadt im Allgäu Ger.
149 Q6 Immingham *North East Lincolnshire, England* U.K.
231 G12 Immokalee *FL* U.S.A.
207 G5 Imo *state* Nigeria
191 L7 Imola Italy
188 F4 Imotski Croatia
215 N5 Impendle S. Africa
250 E6 Imperatriz *Amazonas* Brazil
254 D3 Imperatriz *Maranhão* Brazil
190 E8 Imperia Italy
190 D7 Imperia *prov.* Italy
260 A6 Imperial *r.* Chile
252 A3 Imperial Peru
241 Q9 Imperial *CA* U.S.A.
236 E5 Imperial *NE* U.S.A.
240 O9 Imperial Beach *CA* U.S.A.
241 R9 Imperial Dam *AZ/CA* U.S.A.
241 Q9 Imperial Valley *plain CA* U.S.A.
86 E4 Imperieuse Reef *W.A.* Austr.
208 C4 Impfondo Congo
117 N7 Imphal *Manipur* India
160 C3 Imphy France
151 M3 Impington *Cambridgeshire, England* U.K.
191 K8 Impruneta Italy
199 J2 İmralı Adası *i.* Turkey
124 G9 Imrān Yemen
177 I5 Imrehegy Hungary
199 G2 İmroz *Gökeada* Turkey
İmroz *i.* Turkey *see* Gökçeada
ımrun Turkey *see* Pütürge
101 E11 Imsil S. Korea
178 C5 Imst Austria
128 E6 Imtān Syria
242 D2 Imuris Mex.
92 B6 Imuruan Bay *Palawan* Phil.
175 M3 Imyanin Belarus
180 E5 Imzouren Morocco
100 H4 In *r.* Rus. Fed.
105 K1 Ina *Fukushima* Japan
105 L4 Ina *Ibaraki* Japan
105 G4 Ina *Nagano* Japan
174 C2 Ina *r.* Pol.
207 F2 I-n-Âbâlene *well* Mali
207 G2 I-n-Abangharit *well* Niger
104 E5 Inabe Japan
104 G5 Inabu Japan
216 □2c Inaccessible Island *Tristan da Cunha* S. Atlantic Ocean
104 D5 Inae Japan
205 H5 In Afaleleh *well* Alg.
92 B7 Inagauan *Palawan* Phil.
104 B6 Inagawa Japan
104 B6 Ina-gawa *r.* Japan
105 L4 Inage Japan
147 D7 Inagh Ireland
105 K4 Inagi Japan
213 H2 Inago Moz.
252 B1 Inahuaya Peru
254 F4 Inajá Brazil
253 H2 Inaja *r.* Brazil
253 H2 Inaja, Serra do *hills* Brazil
206 E2 I-n-Akhmed *well* Mali
205 E5 I-n-Akli *well* Mali
78 □6 Inakona *Guadalcanal* Solomon Is
Inalahan Guam *see* Inarajan
207 F2 I-n-Alakam *well* Mali
206 E2 I-n-Alchi *well* Mali
207 F2 I-n-Alchig *well* Mali
206 E2 I-n-Aleï *well* Mali
206 C2 I-n-'Amar *well* Maur.
Inamba-jima *i.* Japan *see* Inanba-jima
252 C3 Inambari Peru
252 C3 Inambari *r.* Peru
206 D2 I-n-Ameddé *well* Mali
205 H3 In Aménas Alg.
205 G5 In Amguel Alg.
104 A6 Inami *Hyōgo* Japan
104 E2 Inami *Toyama* Japan
104 B8 Inami *Wakayama* Japan
95 L1 Inanam *Sabah* Malaysia
103 Q13 Inanba-jima *i.* Japan
177 K3 Ináncs Hungary
215 O5 Inanda S. Africa
81 F8 Inangahua Junction *South I.* N.Z.
91 H7 Inanwatan *Papua* Indon.
252 C2 Iñapari Peru
78 □1 Inarajan Guam
207 F2 I-n-Areï *well* Mali
140 U5 Inari *Itä-Suomi* Fin.
140 S2 Inari *Lappi* Fin.
131 L3 Inarigda Rus. Fed.
140 S2 Inarijärvi *l.* Fin.
140 R2 Inarijoki *r.* Fin./Norway
207 G2 I-n-Arouinat *well* Niger
104 G6 Inasa Japan
207 F2 I-n-Atankarer *well* Mali
252 D2 Inauini *r.* Brazil
103 R9 Inawashiro-ko *l.* Japan
205 G4 I-n Azaoua *well* Alg.
205 G5 In-Azaoua *well* Alg.
207 G1 I-n-Azaoua *watercourse* Niger
202 A2 In Azar *well* Libya
104 E5 Inazawa Japan
202 A3 In Azāwah *well* Libya
207 F2 I-n-Azerraf *well* Mali
105 L4 Inba Japan
105 L4 Inba-numa *l.* Japan
205 F4 In Belbel Alg.
187 K8 Inca Spain
258 C2 Inca de Oro Chile
199 I2 İnce Burnu *pt* Turkey
126 G2 İnce Burun *pt* Turkey
199 K5 İnceler Turkey
147 C8 Inch *Kerry* Ireland
147 J7 Inch *Wexford* Ireland
146 K9 Inchbare *Angus, Scotland* U.K.
81 F9 Inchbonnie *South I.* N.Z.
122 G3 Īncheh Iran
173 K4 Inchenhofen Ger.
156 B3 Incheville France
147 D9 Inchigeelagh Ireland
210 C3 Inch'īnī Terara *mt.* Eth.
146 H11 Inchinnan *Renfrewshire, Scotland* U.K.
204 B5 Inchiri *admin. reg.* Maur.
147 H2 Inch Island Ireland
149 K1 Inchkeith *i. Scotland* U.K.
101 E10 Inch'ŏn S. Korea
213 G3 Inchope Moz.
207 F2 I-n-Choumaguene *well* Mali
146 J10 Inchture *Perth and Kinross, Scotland* U.K.
183 M3 Incinillas Spain
Incio Spain *see* A Cruz do Incio
128 D2 Incirli *Adana* Turkey
Incirli *Sakarya* Turkey *see* Karasu
213 G5 Incomati *r.* Moz.
165 G7 Incourt Belgium
192 C4 Incudine, Monte *mt.* France
138 H4 Inčukalns Latvia
146 D11 Indaal, Loch *b. Scotland* U.K.
204 E5 I-n-Dagouber *well* Mali
257 E3 Indaiá *r.* Brazil
256 A3 Indaiá Grande *r.* Brazil
256 D5 Indaiatuba Brazil
140 N5 Indalsälven *r.* Sweden
141 H6 Indalstø Norway
244 G6 Indaparapeo Mex.
116 G7 Indargarh *Madh. Prad.* India
116 F7 Indargarh *Rajasthan* India
210 C1 Inda Silasē Eth.
96 B3 Indaw *Sagaing* Myanmar
96 C4 Indaw *Shan* Myanmar
96 C2 Indawgyi, Lake Myanmar
242 G5 Indé Mex.
Indefatigable Island *Islas Galápagos* Ecuador *see* Santa Cruz, Isla
207 F3 I-n-Délimane *well* Mali
240 N5 Independence *CA* U.S.A.
236 J4 Independence *IA* U.S.A.
237 H7 Independence *KS* U.S.A.
230 E6 Independence *KY* U.S.A.
226 B3 Independence *MN* U.S.A.
236 H6 Independence *MO* U.S.A.
232 D12 Independence *VA* U.S.A.
226 C5 Independence *WI* U.S.A.
221 P1 Independence Fjord *inlet* Greenland
238 F6 Independence Mountains *NV* U.S.A.
252 D4 Independencia Bol.
254 E3 Independência Brazil
245 K5 Independencia Mex.
197 P6 Independența *Călărași* Romania
197 Q7 Independența *Constanța* Romania
197 P5 Independența *Galați* Romania
107 R3 Inder *Nei Mongol* China
120 D3 Inder, Ozero *salt l.* Kazakh.
210 B3 Inderacha Eth.
120 D3 Inderborskiy Kazakh.
114 E4 Indi *Karnataka* India
113 H6 India *country* Asia
226 H3 Indian *r. MI* U.S.A.
232 F8 Indiana *PA* U.S.A.
230 D5 Indiana *state* U.S.A.
265 L8 Indian-Antarctic Ridge *sea feature* Southern Ocean
230 D6 Indianapolis *IN* U.S.A.
222 G3 Indian Cabins *Alta* Can.
Indian Desert India/Pak. *see* Thar Desert
232 B11 Indian Fields *KY* U.S.A.
225 J2 Indian Harbour *Nfld and Lab.* Can.
223 K5 Indian Head *Sask.* Can.
233 K5 Indian Lake *NY* U.S.A.
226 H4 Indian Lake *l. MI* U.S.A.
233 K5 Indian Lake *l. NY* U.S.A.
232 B8 Indian Lake *l. OH* U.S.A.
232 G8 Indian Lake *l. PA* U.S.A.
235 J2 Indian Neck *CT* U.S.A.
213 □G5 Indian Ocean *OCEAN*
236 I5 Indianola *IA* U.S.A.
237 J9 Indianola *MS* U.S.A.
256 D3 Indianópolis Brazil
241 S3 Indian Peak *UT* U.S.A.
226 J4 Indian River *MI* U.S.A.
241 Q5 Indian Springs *NV* U.S.A.
241 V6 Indian Wells *AZ* U.S.A.
256 B2 Indiara Brazil
254 F4 Indiaroba Brazil
210 C2 Indibir Eth.
247 □1 Indiera Alta Puerto Rico
134 J2 Indiga Rus. Fed.
131 P2 Indigirka *r.* Rus. Fed.
134 J2 Indigskaya Guba *b.* Rus. Fed.
196 I5 Inđija *Vojvodina* Serbia
96 B3 Indin Myanmar
222 H1 Indin Lake *N.W.T.* Can.
242 □R12 Indio *r.* Nic.
241 P8 Indio *CA* U.S.A.
261 G6 Indio Rico Arg.
116 G9 Indira Priyadarshini Pench National Park India
77 G3 Indispensable Reefs Solomon Is
78 □6 Indispensable Strait Solomon Is
90 C3 Indo-China *reg.* Asia
137 O8 Indol *r.* Ukr.
139 U1 Indomanka *r.* Rus. Fed.
90 D7 Indonesia *country* Asia
116 E8 Indore *Madh. Prad.* India
94 E5 Indragiri *r.* Indon.
95 H8 Indramayu *Jawa* Indon.
95 H8 Indramayu, Tanjung *pt* Indon.
94 D6 Indrapura *Sumatera* Indon.
Indrapura, Gunung *vol.* Indon. *see* Kerinci, Gunung
94 D6 Indrapura, Tanjung *pt* Indon.
115 G3 Indravati *r.* India
159 O8 Indre *dept* France
162 E1 Indre *r.* France
159 M7 Indre-et-Loire *dept* France
140 U1 Indre Kiberg Norway
142 C1 Indre Samlen *b.* Norway
82 D2 Indulkana *S.A.* Austr.
209 C8 Indungo Angola
Indur *Andhra Prad.* India *see* Nizamabad
138 G8 Indura Belarus
114 F4 Indurti *Andhra Prad.* India
123 L10 Indus *r.* China/Pak. *alt.* Shiquan He (China)
123 L9 Indus, Mouths of the Pak.
265 I3 Indus Cone *sea feature* Indian Ocean
215 L7 Indwe S. Africa
215 L8 Indwe *r.* S. Africa
197 P8 Indzhe Voyvoda Bulg.
104 B4 Ine Japan
205 G5 In Ebeggi *well* Alg.
126 F3 İnebolu Turkey
204 E5 I-n-Échaï *well* Mali
199 K2 İnegöl Turkey
205 G4 In Ekker Alg.
93 B8 Inerie *vol. Flores* Indon.
261 G4 Inés Indart Arg.
197 J4 Ineu *Arad* Romania
177 L4 Ineu *Bihor* Romania
Inevi Turkey *see* Cihanbeyli
232 C11 Inez *KY* U.S.A.
204 C3 Inezgane Morocco
205 H5 In Ezzane *well* Alg.
214 E10 Infanta, Cape S. Africa
250 C3 Infantas Col.
Infantes Spain *see* Villanueva de los Infantes
245 M9 Inferior, Laguna *lag.* Mex.
253 E2 Infernao, Cachoeira *waterfall* Brazil
258 C2 Infielés, Punta *pt* Chile
244 F7 Infiernillo, Presa *resr* Mex.
183 J2 Infiesto Spain
193 O8 Infreschi, Punta degli *pt* Italy
96 E4 Ing, Nam Mae *r.* Thai.
209 B6 Inga Dem. Rep. Congo
141 R6 Ingå Fin.
134 F2 Inga Rus. Fed.
96 B6 Ingabu Myanmar
207 G2 Ingal Niger
84 D6 Ingallanna *watercourse N.T.* Austr.
240 L2 Ingalls, Mount *CA* U.S.A.
223 J2 Ingalls Lake *N.W.T.* Can.
208 D5 Inganda Dem. Rep. Congo
151 M4 Ingatestone *Essex, England* U.K.
172 H3 Ingelfingen Ger.
172 E2 Ingelheim am Rhein Ger.
165 D7 Ingelmunster Belgium
143 K5 Ingelstad Sweden
208 C5 Ingende Dem. Rep. Congo
260 D4 Ingeniero Balloffet Arg.
258 E1 Ingeniero Guillermo Nueva Juárez Arg.
260 D6 Ingeniero Huergo Arg.
259 C6 Ingeniero Jacobacci Arg.
260 E4 Ingeniero Luiggi Arg.
261 H4 Ingeniero Maschwitz Arg.
261 H4 Ingeniero Otamendi Arg.
222 E3 Ingenika *r. B.C.* Can.
216 □3f Ingenio *Gran Canaria* Canary Is
252 B3 Ingenio *r.* Peru
224 D5 Ingersoll *Ont.* Can.
210 B2 Ingessana Hills Sudan
106 H2 Ingettolgoy Mongolia
Ingezi Zimbabwe *see* Ngezi
93 F3 Inggelang *i. Maluku* Indon.
85 K5 Ingham *Qld* Austr.
205 F4 In Ghar Alg.
120 L8 Ingichka Uzbek.
183 O3 Inglares *r.* Spain
149 M5 Ingleborough *hill England* U.K.
221 K2 Inglefield Land *reg.* Greenland
149 N4 Ingleton *Durham, England* U.K.
149 M5 Ingleton *North Yorkshire, England* U.K.
149 L6 Inglewhite *Lancashire, England* U.K.
83 M3 Inglewood *Qld* Austr.
83 I7 Inglewood *Vic.* Austr.
80 I6 Inglewood *North I.* N.Z.
240 N8 Inglewood *CA* U.S.A.
149 L4 Inglewood Forest *England* U.K.
84 F2 Inglis Island *N.T.* Austr.
107 N1 Ingoda *r.* Rus. Fed.
96 C2 Ingoka Pum *mt.* Myanmar
172 H5 Ingoldingen Ger.
149 R7 Ingoldmells *Lincolnshire, England* U.K.
221 Q1 Ingolf Fjord *inlet* Greenland
173 K4 Ingolstadt Ger.
82 E3 Ingomar *S.A.* Austr.
238 K3 Ingomar *MT* U.S.A.
225 I4 Ingonish *N.S.* Can.
117 L7 Ingraj Bazar *W. Bengal* India
146 M12 Ingram *Northumberland, England* U.K.
232 F12 Ingram *VA* U.S.A.
226 D4 Ingram *WI* U.S.A.
159 J7 Ingrandes *Pays de la Loire* France
159 M8 Ingrandes *Poitou-Charentes* France
222 G1 Ingray Lake *N.W.T.* Can.
252 E5 Ingre Bol.
156 C8 Ingré France
263 F2 Ingrid Christensen Coast Antarctica
205 G6 I-n-Guezzam Alg.
158 E6 Inguiniel France
207 F3 I-n-Guita *well* Mali
Ingul *r.* Ukr. *see* Inhul
Ingulets Ukr. *see* Inhulets'
140 L4 Ingulsvatn Norway
Ingushetia *aut. rep.* Rus. Fed. *see* Ingushetiya, Respublika
129 G3 Ingushetiya, Respublika *aut. rep.* Rus. Fed.
215 Q3 Ingwavuma S. Africa
Ingwavuma *r.* Swaziland *see* Ngwavuma
209 E8 Ingwe Zambia
157 N6 Ingwiller France
215 Q1 Inhaca Moz.
213 G5 Inhaca, Península *pen.* Moz.
215 Q1 Inhaca e dos Portugueses, Ilhas da *nature res.* Moz.
213 G4 Inhafenga Moz.
213 G4 Inhambane Moz.
213 G4 Inhambane *prov.* Moz.
254 F4 Inhambupe Brazil
213 G3 Inhaminga Moz.
213 G3 Inhamitanga Moz.
257 F3 Inhapim Brazil
213 G5 Inharrime Moz.
213 G4 Inhassoro Moz.
254 D5 Inhaúmas Brazil
205 F5 I-n-Hihaou, Adrar *hills* Alg.
199 L2 İnhisar Turkey
137 K7 Inhul *r.* Ukr.
137 M6 Inhulets' Ukr.
137 L7 Inhulets' *r.* Ukr.
256 C2 Inhumas Brazil
93 B8 Inielika *vol. Flores* Indon.
185 P2 Iniesta Spain
257 E3 Inimutaba Brazil
138 E1 Iniö Fin.
250 E4 Inírida *r.* Col.
Inis Ireland *see* Ennis
Inis Córthaidh Ireland *see* Enniscorthy
147 B5 Inishark *i.* Ireland
147 B5 Inishbofin *i.* Ireland
147 F2 Inishbofin *i.* Ireland
147 C6 Inisheer *i.* Ireland
147 B4 Inishkea North *i.* Ireland
147 B4 Inishkea South *i.* Ireland
147 C6 Inishmaan *i.* Ireland
147 C6 Inishmore *i.* Ireland
147 E4 Inishmurray *i.* Ireland
147 H2 Inishowen *pen.* Ireland
147 I2 Inishowen Head Ireland
147 H2 Inishtrahull *i.* Ireland
147 H2 Inishtrahull Sound *sea chan.* Ireland
147 B5 Inishturk *i.* Ireland
107 P4 Injgan Sum *Nei Mongol* China
210 C2 Injibara Eth.
85 L8 Injune *Qld* Austr.
120 K5 Inkardar'ya Kazakh.
151 I3 Inkberrow *Worcestershire, England* U.K.
176 G5 Inke Hungary
206 D2 I-n-Kerchef *well* Mali
85 H4 Inkerman *Qld* Austr.
137 M9 Inkerman Ukr.
222 C3 Inklin *B.C.* Can.
222 C3 Inklin *r. B.C.* Can.
123 I3 Inkylap Turkm.
81 H9 Inland Kaikoura Range *mts South I.* N.Z.
Inland Sea Japan *see* Seto-naikai
233 K5 Inlet *NY* U.S.A.
206 E2 I-n-Milach *well* Mali
173 I8 Inn *r.* Europe
221 L2 Innaanganeq *c.* Greenland
103 I13 Innai Japan
82 H2 Innamincka *S.A.* Austr.
82 H2 Innamincka Regional Reserve *nature res. S.A.* Austr.
140 M3 Inndyr Norway
146 G11 Innellan *Argyll and Bute, Scotland* U.K.
178 A5 Innerbraz Austria
217 □2a Inner Islands Seychelles
146 J11 Innerleithen *Scottish Borders, Scotland* U.K.
Inner Mongolia *aut. reg.* China *see* Nei Mongol Zizhiqu
173 O4 Innernzell Ger.
Inner Port Shelter *b. H.K.* China *see* Sai Kung Hoi
146 E8 Inner Sound *sea chan. Scotland* U.K.
190 E2 Innertkirchen Switz.
178 F6 Innervillgraten Austria
82 F6 Innes National Park *S.A.* Austr.
140 M3 Innhavet Norway
195 □ In-Niexfa, Ras *pt* Malta
173 K5 Inning am Ammersee Ger.
85 K4 Innisfail *Qld* Austr.
222 H4 Innisfail *Alta* Can.
147 E9 Innishannon Ireland
147 I4 Inniskeen Ireland
100 F4 Innokent'yevka Rus. Fed.
103 K12 Innoshima Japan
178 D5 Innsbruck Austria
191 K1 Innsbruck *airport* Austria
224 E1 Innuksuak *r. Que.* Can.
179 H3 Innviertel *reg.* Austria
147 G5 Inny *r.* Ireland
147 B9 Inny *r.* Ireland
103 K13 Ino Japan
93 D3 Inobonto *Sulawesi* Indon.
256 B3 Inocência Brazil
104 E2 Inokuchi Japan
208 C5 Inongo Dem. Rep. Congo
209 B5 Inoni Congo
250 C5 Inonias Peru
199 L3 İnönü Turkey
250 D1 Inosu Col.
Inoucdjouac *Que.* Can. *see* Inukjuak
206 E2 I-n-Ouchef *well* Mali
205 F5 I-n-Ouzzal, Oued *watercourse* Alg.
177 H3 Inovec *mt.* Slovakia
175 I4 Inowłódz Pol.
174 G3 Inowrocław Pol.
129 E1 Inozemtsevo Rus. Fed.
252 D4 Inquisivi Bol.
190 C1 Ins Switz.
205 F4 In Salah Alg.
135 I5 Insar Rus. Fed.
146 K8 Insch *Aberdeenshire, Scotland* U.K.
87 B8 Inscription, Cape *W.A.* Austr.
96 C6 Insein Myanmar
170 J3 Insel Usedom *park* Ger.
170 M4 Iński Park Krajobrazowy Pol.
174 D2 Ińsko Pol.
174 D2 Ińsko, Jezioro *l.* Pol.
157 M6 Insming France
205 F3 In Sokki, Oued *watercourse* Alg.
Insterburg Rus. Fed. *see* Chernyakhovsk
129 H5 İnstitut Azer.
138 E7 Instruch *r.* Rus. Fed.
197 P6 Însurăţei Romania
244 G6 Insurgente José María Morelos y Pavón, Parque Nacional *nat. park* Mex.
213 E3 Insuza *r.* Zimbabwe
134 M2 Inta Rus. Fed.
207 G2 I-n-Tabakat *well* Niger
207 H1 I-n-Tadéra *well* Niger
207 H2 I-n-Tadrof *well* Niger
205 G4 In Takoufi, Oued *watercourse* Alg.
207 F2 I-n-Talak *well* Mali
207 F2 I-n-Tassit *well* Mali
207 F2 I-n-Tebezas Mali
207 F2 I-n-Tefiniti *well* Mali
207 F2 I-n-Téguift *well* Mali
207 F3 I-n-Tékélit *well* Mali
207 F3 I-n-Tekoret *well* Mali
207 F2 I-n-Telli *well* Mali
207 F2 I-n-Témegui *well* Mali
261 F4 Intendente Alvear Arg.
199 H2 İntepe Turkey
Interamna Italy *see* Teramo
190 D2 Interlaken Switz.
226 A1 International Falls *MN* U.S.A.
236 E1 International Peace Garden *tourist site* Can./U.S.A.
115 M6 Interview Island *Andaman & Nicobar Is* India
124 D8 Intich'o Eth.
206 E3 I-n-Tillit Mali
197 O5 Întorsura Buzăului Romania
207 F2 I-n-Touft *well* Mali
237 H11 Intracoastal Waterway *canal TX* U.S.A.
190 G4 Introbio Italy
134 H2 Intsy Rus. Fed.
213 E3 Intundhla Zimbabwe
250 C5 Intutu Peru
105 M4 Inubō-zaki *pt* Japan
103 I13 Inukai Japan
224 E1 Inukjuak *Que.* Can.
259 C9 Inútil, Bahía *b.* Chile
220 E3 Inuvik *N.W.T.* Can.
252 B2 Inuya *r.* Peru
104 E5 Inuyama Japan
134 L4 In'va *r.* Rus. Fed.
147 F3 Inver Ireland
146 E7 Inveralligin *Highland, Scotland* U.K.
146 M7 Inverallochy *Aberdeensh Scotland* U.K.
147 D6 Inveran Ireland
146 F10 Inveraray *Argyll and Bute Scotland* U.K.
146 K9 Inverarity *Angus, Scotlanc*
146 G10 Inverarnan *Argyll and Bu Scotland* U.K.
147 F3 Inver Bay Ireland
146 L9 Inverbervie *Aberdeenshi Scotland* U.K.
81 C13 Invercargill *South I.* N.Z.
146 G7 Invercassley *Highland, Scotland* U.K.
146 G11 Inverclyde *admin. div. Scotland* U.K.
83 M3 Inverell *N.S.W.* Austr.
146 I9 Inverey *Aberdeenshire, Scotland* U.K.
146 G8 Invergarry *Highland, Scotland* U.K.
146 H7 Invergordon *Highland, Scotland* U.K.
146 F10 Inverinan *Argyll and Bute Scotland* U.K.
146 K9 Inverkeilor *Angus, Scotla* U.K.
146 J10 Inverkeithing *Fife, Scotland* U.K.
146 F6 Inverkirkaig *Highland, Scotland* U.K.
146 F7 Inverlael *Highland, Scotland* U.K.
85 H5 Inverleigh *Qld* Austr.
223 K5 Invermay *Sask.* Can.
146 G8 Invermoriston *Highland, Scotland* U.K.
225 I4 Inverness *N.S.* Can.
146 H8 Inverness *Highland, Scotland* U.K.
240 J3 Inverness *CA* U.S.A.
231 F11 Inverness *FL* U.S.A.
146 F10 Invernoaden *Argyll and Scotland* U.K.
146 G10 Inversnaid *Stirling, Scotland* U.K.
146 L8 Inverurie *Aberdeenshire, Scotland* U.K.
84 B4 Inverway *N.T.* Austr.
97 C8 Investigator Channel Myanmar
82 E5 Investigator Group *is S.A.* Austr.
265 K5 Investigator Ridge *sea feature* Indian Ocean
82 F6 Investigator Strait *S.A.*
115 M7 Invisible Bank *sea featu Andaman & Nicobar Is* Inc
232 G9 Inwood *WV* U.S.A.
215 M7 Inxu *r.* S. Africa
110 H1 Inya Rus. Fed.
Inyanga Zimbabwe *see* Nyanga
213 G3 Inyanga Mountains Zimbabwe
Inyanga National Park Zimbabwe *see* Nyanga National Park
213 G3 Inyangani *mt.* Zimbabwe
Inyati Zimbabwe *see* Nya
Inyazura Zimbabwe *see* Nyazura
240 O6 Inyokern *CA* U.S.A.
240 N4 Inyo Mountains *CA* U.S.
211 B6 Inyonga Tanz.
135 I5 Inza Rus. Fed.
105 L4 Inzai Japan
173 N6 Inzell Ger.
120 G1 Inzer Rus. Fed.
134 L5 Inzer *r.* Rus. Fed.
135 H5 Inzhavino Rus. Fed.
178 D5 Inzing Austria
158 E6 Inzinzac-Lochrist Franc
198 B3 Ioannina Greece
191 O3 Iôf di Montasio *mt.* Italy
103 □2 Iō-jima *i. Kazan-rettō* Jap
102 □H16 Iō-jima *i.* Japan
134 G2 Iokanga *r.* Rus. Fed.
237 H7 Iola *KS* U.S.A.
234 B2 Iola *PA* U.S.A.
226 E5 Iola *WI* U.S.A.
Iolotan' Turkm. *see* Ýolöt
209 B9 Iona Angola
225 I4 Iona *N.S.* Can.
146 D10 Iona *i. Scotland* U.K.
209 B9 Iona, Parque Nacional *nat. park* Angola
146 D10 Iona, Sound of *sea char Scotland* U.K.
146 D10 Iona Abbey *tourist site Scotland* U.K.
240 O3 Ione *NV* U.S.A.
238 F2 Ione *WA* U.S.A.
197 M6 Ionești Romania
226 I7 Ionia *MI* U.S.A.
198 A3 Ionia Nisia *is* Greece
Ionian Islands Greece *se* Ionia Nisia
198 A5 Ionian Sea Greece/Italy
Ionio *prov.* Italy *see* Tara
105 L2 Iōno Japan
131 P4 Iony, Ostrov *i.* Rus. Fed.
Iordān Uzbek. *see* Yordo
129 H4 Iori *r.* Georgia
199 G6 Ios *i.* Greece
Iō-shima *i.* Japan *see* Iō
102 □F19 Iō-Tori-jima *i. Nansei-sh* Japan
206 A2 Iouîk Maur.
198 F5 Ioulis *Kea* Greece
236 J5 Iowa *r. IA* U.S.A.
236 I4 Iowa *state* U.S.A.
236 J5 Iowa City *IA* U.S.A.
236 I4 Iowa Falls *IA* U.S.A.
104 E2 Iō-zan *hill* Japan
136 I1 Ipa *r.* Belarus
244 B5 Ipala Mex.
211 B6 Ipala Tanz.
256 C2 Ipameri Brazil
257 G3 Ipanema Brazil
254 F4 Ipanema *r.* Brazil
252 B2 Iparía Peru
257 F3 Ipatinga Brazil
135 H7 Ipatovo Rus. Fed.
256 C5 Ipauçu Brazil
226 D9 Ipava *IL* U.S.A.
198 B3 Ipeiros *admin. reg.* Gree
129 E6 İpek Geçidi *pass* Turkey
177 H4 Ipeľ *r.* Slovakia
215 J3 Ipelegeng S. Africa
177 H4 Ipeľská pahorkatina *mt* Slovakia
173 I2 Iphofen Ger.
256 C3 Ipiaçu Brazil
250 B4 Ipiales Col.
254 F5 Ipiaú Brazil
254 F5 Ipirá Brazil
250 D5 Ipiranga *Amazonas* Braz
251 F6 Ipiranga *Amazonas* Braz
256 B6 Ipiranga *Paraná* Brazil
Ípiros *admin. reg.* Greec Ipeiros
78 □4a Ipis *i. Chuuk* Micronesia
252 B1 Ipixuna Brazil
252 B1 Ipixuna *r.* Brazil
251 F6 Ipixuna *r.* Brazil
94 D2 Ipoh Malaysia
211 B6 Ipole Tanz.
177 H4 Ipoly *r.* Hungary
215 J5 Ipopeng S. Africa
256 B2 Iporá Brazil
256 C6 Iporanga Brazil
194 G10 Ippari *r. Sicilia* Italy
173 I2 Ippesheim Ger.
150 E7 Ipplepen *Devon, Englanc*
208 D3 Ippy C.A.R.
199 H2 İpsala Turkey
173 I2 Ipsheim Ger.
149 N7 Ipstones *Staffordshire, England* U.K.
85 N9 Ipswich *Qld* Austr.
246 □ Ipswich Jamaica
151 O3 Ipswich *Suffolk, England*
236 F3 Ipswich *SD* U.S.A.

Ipu Brazil
Ipuã Brazil
Ipueiras Brazil
Ipuh Sumatera Indon.
Ipuiúna Brazil
Ipupiara Brazil
Iput' r. Rus. Fed.
Iputs' r. Belarus
Iqaluit Nunavut Can.
Iqe Qinghai China
Iqe He r. China
Iquê r. Brazil
Iquique Chile
Iquiri r. Brazil see Ituxi
Iquitos Peru
Ira Banda C.A.R.
Irabu-jima i. Nansei-shotō Japan
Iracoubo Fr. Guiana
Irafshān Iran
Irafshān reg. Iran
Irago-misaki pt Japan
Irago-suidō str. Japan
Irai Brazil
Irai Island P.N.G.
Irakleia Greece
Irakleia i. Greece
Irakleio Kriti Greece
Irakleiou, Kolpos b. Kriti Greece
Iráklia i. Greece see Irakleia
Iraklion Kriti Greece see Irakleio
Irala Arg.
Irala Para.
Iramaia Brazil
Iran country Asia
Iran, Pegunungan mts Indon.
Irānābād Iran
Iranamadu Tank resr Sri Lanka
Irancy France
Īrānshāh Iran
Īrānshahr Iran
Irapa Venez.
Irapuato Mex.
Iraq country Asia
Irarrarene reg. Alg.
Irasville VT U.S.A.
Iratapuru r. Brazil
Irati Brazil
Irati r. Spain
Iratoşu Romania
Irayel' Rus. Fed.
Irazú, Volcán vol. Costa Rica
Irbe r. Latvia
Irbes šaurums sea chan. Estonia/Latvia see Irbe Strait
Irbe Strait Estonia/Latvia
Irbe väin sea chan. Estonia/Latvia see Irbe Strait
Irbid Jordan
Irbil Iraq see Arbīl
Irbit Rus. Fed.
Irchester Northamptonshire, England U.K.
Irdning Austria
Irdyn' Ukr.
Irebu Dem. Rep. Congo
Irecê Brazil
Iregszemcse Hungary
Iregua r. Spain
Ireko Dem. Rep. Congo
Ireland country Europe
Ireland Corners NY U.S.A.
Ireland Island Bermuda
Ireland's Eye i. Ireland
Iren' r. Rus. Fed.
Irene Arg.
Irene, Mount South I. N.Z.
Ireng r. Guyana/Venez.
Iretama Brazil
Irgakly Rus. Fed.
Irganch'ai Georgia
Irgıllı Turkey
Irgiz Kazakh.
Irgiz r. Kazakh.
Irgoli Sardegna Italy
Irharhar, Oued watercourse Illizi/Tamanrasset Alg.
Irharhar, Oued watercourse Illizi/Tamanrasset Alg.
Irherm Morocco
Irhil M'Goun mt. Morocco
Iri S. Korea see Iksan
Irian, Teluk b. Papua Indon. see Cenderawasih, Teluk
Irian Barat prov. Indon. see Papua
Irian Jaya prov. Indon. see Papua
Irian Jaya reg. Indon.
Iriba Chad
Iricoumé, Serra hills Brazil
Īrī Dāgh mt. Iran
Irig Vojvodina Serbia
Iriga Luzon Phil.
Irigny France
Iriklinskiy Rus. Fed.
Iriklinskoye Vodokhranilishche resr Rus. Fed.
Iringa Tanz.
Iringa admin. reg. Tanz.
Irinjalakuda Kerala India
Iriomote-jima i. Nansei-shotō Japan
Iriomote Kokuritsu-kōen nat. park Nansei-shotō Japan
Iriri r. Brazil
Iriri Novo r. Brazil
Irish Sea Ireland/U.K.
Irissarry France
Irituia Brazil
'Irj well Saudi Arabia
Irkeshtam Kyrg. see Erkech-Tam
Irkliyevskaya Rus. Fed.
Irkliyiv Ukr.
Irkutsk Rus. Fed.
Irkutskaya Oblast' admin. div. Rus. Fed.
Irkutsk Oblast admin. div. Rus. Fed. see Irkutskaya Oblast'
Irlbach Ger.
Irma Alta Can.
Irma WI U.S.A.
Irmak Turkey
Irminger Basin sea feature N. Atlantic Ocean
Irminio r. Sicilia Italy
Irmo SC U.S.A.
Irnijärvi l. Fin.
Iro, Lac l. Chad
Irodouër France
Iroise, Mer d' g. France
Iron Baron S.A. Austr.
Iron Bottom Sound sea chan. Solomon Is
Iron Bridge Ont. Can.
Ironbridge Telford and Wrekin, England U.K.
Irondequoit NY U.S.A.
Iron Junction MN U.S.A.
Iron Knob S.A. Austr.
Iron Mountain MI U.S.A.
Iron Mountain mt. UT U.S.A.
Iron Mountains hills Ireland
Iron Range National Park Qld Austr.
Iron River MI U.S.A.
Iron River WI U.S.A.
Ironton MO U.S.A.
Ironton OH U.S.A.
Ironwood MI U.S.A.
Ironwood Forest National Monument nat. park AZ U.S.A.
Iroquois Ont. Can.
Iroquois r. IN U.S.A.
Iroquois Falls Ont. Can.
Irosin Luzon Phil.
Irō-zaki pt Japan
Irpen' Ukr. see Irpin'
Irpin' Ukr.
Irpin' r. Ukr.
Īrqah Yemen
Irqieqa, Ras i- pt Malta
Ir-Raheb, Ras pt Malta
Irramarne Aboriginal Land res. N.T. Austr.
195 □ Ir-Ramla b. Gozo Malta
96 B6 Irrawaddy admin. div. Myanmar
96 B7 Irrawaddy r. Myanmar
96 B7 Irrawaddy, Mouths of the Myanmar
172 A2 Irrel Ger.
172 B2 Irsch Ger.
178 H6 Irschen Austria
173 L6 Irschenberg Ger.
173 J6 Irsee Ger.
136 I3 Irsha r. Ukr.
123 P3 Irshad Pass Afgh./Pak.
136 H3 Irshans'k Ukr.
136 C5 Irshava Ukr.
193 Q6 Irsina Italy
143 M2 Irsta Sweden
134 J3 Irta Rus. Fed.
149 L4 Irthing r. England U.K.
151 K3 Irthlingborough Northamptonshire, England U.K.
121 M1 Irtysh r. Kazakh./Rus. Fed.
121 P1 Irtyshsk Kazakh.
Irtyshskoye Kazakh. see Irtyshsk
183 O7 Iruest Spain
105 J4 Iruma Japan
105 K4 Iruma-gawa r. Japan
208 F4 Irumu Dem. Rep. Congo
186 B1 Irun Spain
Iruña Spain see Pamplona
252 D4 Irupana Bol.
186 B1 Irurita Spain
183 R3 Irurozqui Spain
183 Q3 Irurtzun Spain
Irurzun Spain see Irurtzun
146 G11 Irvine North Ayrshire, Scotland U.K.
240 O8 Irvine CA U.S.A.
232 B11 Irvine KY U.S.A.
85 J4 Irvinebank Qld Austr.
146 G11 Irvine Bay Scotland U.K.
262 T2 Irvine Glacier Antarctica
147 G4 Irvinestown Northern Ireland U.K.
237 Q9 Irving TX U.S.A.
87 C10 Irwin r. W.A. Austr.
231 F9 Irwinton GA U.S.A.
171 D6 Irxleben Ger.
207 G3 Isa Nigeria
124 F8 'Īsā, Ra's pt Yemen
85 L7 Isaac r. Qld Austr.
222 F4 Isaac Lake B.C. Can.
186 D2 Isaba Spain
236 E3 Isabel SD U.S.A.
92 D6 Isabela Negros Phil.
92 C8 Isabela Phil.
247 □1 Isabela Puerto Rico
246 H4 Isabela, Cabo c. Dom. Rep.
250 □ Isabela, Isla i. Islas Galápagos Ecuador
244 B4 Isabela, Isla i. Mex.
242 □Q11 Isabelia, Cordillera mts Nic.
226 C2 Isabella MN U.S.A.
86 I6 Isabella, Lake salt flat W.A. Austr.
226 J6 Isabella Indian Reservation res. MI U.S.A.
240 N6 Isabella Lake CA U.S.A.
226 G2 Isabelle, Point MI U.S.A.
247 □1 Isabel Segunda Puerto Rico
186 F3 Isábena r. Spain
199 K5 İsabey Turkey
129 E7 İsabey Dağı mt. Turkey
158 G6 Isac r. France
197 Q5 Isaccea Romania
130 J2 Isachenko, Ostrov i. Rus. Fed.
221 H2 Isachsen, Cape Nunavut Can.
140 □B1 Ísafjarðardjúp est. Iceland
140 □B1 Ísafjörður Iceland
116 F7 Isagarh Madh. Prad. India
103 H14 Isahaya Japan
123 K8 Isai Kalat Pak.
208 C5 Isaka Dem. Rep. Congo
123 N5 Isa Khel Pak.
134 H2 Isakogorka Rus. Fed.
139 Q1 Isakovo Leningradskaya Oblast' Rus. Fed.
139 R6 Isakovo Smolenskaya Oblast' Rus. Fed.
192 D7 Isalle r. Italy
197 L6 Işalniţa Romania
213 □J4 Isalo, Massif de l' mts Madag.
213 □J4 Isalo, Parc National de l' nat. park Madag.
250 D4 Isana r. Col.
208 D5 Isanga Dem. Rep. Congo
211 A7 Isangano National Park Zambia
207 G4 Isanlu Nigeria
205 G4 Isaouane-n-Tifernine des. Alg.
173 N4 Isar r. Ger.
191 K3 Isarco r. Italy
92 D5 Isarog, Mount Phil.
177 I4 Isaszeg Hungary
105 I4 Isawa Japan
156 D2 Isbergues France
146 □N1 Isbister Shetland, Scotland U.K.
146 □O2 Isbister Shetland, Scotland U.K.
Isca Newport, Wales U.K. see Caerleon
183 K6 Íscar Spain
252 D5 Iscayachi Bol.
199 L4 İscehisar Turkey
157 K7 Isches France
178 B5 Ischgl Austria
193 L6 Ischia Italy
193 L6 Ischia, Isola d' i. Italy
260 C2 Ischigualasto, Parque Provincial nat. park Arg.
193 P4 Ischitella Italy
86 H4 Isdell r. W.A. Austr.
156 D8 Isdes France
104 E7 Ise Japan
142 H6 Isefjord b. Denmark
105 J5 Isehara Japan
211 B6 Iseke Tanz.
178 G6 Isel r. Austria
178 G6 Iseltal val. Austria
173 M5 Isen Ger.
173 N5 Isen r. Ger.
157 J7 Is-en-Bassigny France
134 K4 Isenbayevo Rus. Fed.
169 K6 Isenbüttel Ger.
208 E4 Isengi Dem. Rep. Congo
102 □F19 Isen-zaki hd Nansei-shotō Japan
190 I4 Iseo Italy
190 I4 Iseo, Lago d' l. Italy
161 K6 Iseran, Col de l' pass France
161 H6 Isère dept France
161 F7 Isère r. France
251 H3 Isère, Pointe pt Fr. Guiana
169 E8 Iserlohn Ger.
169 I6 Isernhagen Ger.
193 M4 Isernia Italy
193 M4 Isernia prov. Italy
105 J3 Isesaki Japan
104 E7 Ise-shima Kokuritsu-kōen nat. park Japan
104 E6 Ise-wan b. Japan
207 F5 Iseyin Nigeria
Isfahan Iran see Eşfahān
121 M8 Isfana Kyrg.
Isfandaqeh Iran see Sangū'īyeh
123 N1 Isfara Tajik.
140 □ Isfjorden inlet Svalbard
140 □ Isfjord Radio Svalbard
129 G2 Ishcherskaya Rus. Fed.
134 L3 Isherim, Gora mt. Rus. Fed.
251 G4 Isherton Guyana
135 J5 Isheyevka Rus. Fed.
105 K3 Ishibashi Japan
104 D5 Ishibe Japan
102 S7 Ishidoriya Japan
102 □B22 Ishigaki Nansei-shotō Japan
102 □B22 Ishigaki-jima i. Nansei-shotō Japan
105 K3 Ishige Japan
102 S3 Ishikari Japan
102 S3 Ishikari-gawa r. Japan
102 R3 Ishikari-wan b. Japan
105 L1 Ishikawa Fukushima Japan
102 □1 Ishikawa Okinawa Japan
104 D3 Ishikawa pref. Japan
121 N1 Ishim r. Kazakh./Rus. Fed.
130 H4 Ishim Rus. Fed.
104 A8 I-shima i. Japan
120 G1 Ishimbay Rus. Fed.
102 S8 Ishinomaki Japan
105 L3 Ishioka Japan
103 K13 Ishizuchi-san mt. Japan
123 N3 Ishkoshim Tajik.
116 D1 Ishkuman Jammu and Kashmir
139 W4 Ishnya Rus. Fed.
226 G3 Ishpeming MI U.S.A.
Ishtikhon Uzbek. see Ishtixon
121 L8 Ishtixon Uzbek.
123 N3 Ishtragh Afgh.
117 L7 Ishurdi Bangl.
252 D3 Isiboro r. Bol.
252 D4 Isiboro Sécure, Parque Nacional nat. park Bol.
159 I4 Isigny-le-Buat France
159 I3 Isigny-sur-Mer France
199 L4 Işıklar Turkey
199 K4 Işıklı Turkey
199 K4 Işıklı Barajı resr Turkey
192 C8 Isili Sardegna Italy
130 I4 Isil'kul' Rus. Fed.
211 B6 Isimbira Tanz.
250 B5 Isinliví Ecuador
210 C4 Isiolo Kenya
215 O5 Isipingo S. Africa
208 E4 Isiro Dem. Rep. Congo
85 J8 Isisford Qld Austr.
140 □ Isispynten pt Svalbard
179 J8 Iška r. Slovenia
123 L3 Iskabad Canal Afgh.
123 N3 Iskan Afgh.
134 K2 Iskateley Rus. Fed.
İskele Cyprus see Trikomon
126 H5 İskenderun Turkey
126 G5 İskenderun Körfezi b. Turkey
126 G3 İskilip Turkey
Iski-Naukat Kyrg. see Eski-Nookat
120 E4 Iskine Kazakh.
120 E4 Iskininskiy Kazakh.
130 J4 Iskitim Rus. Fed.
139 W7 Iskra Rus. Fed.
137 M5 Iskrivka Kirovohrads'ka Oblast' Ukr.
137 O4 Iskrivka Poltavs'ka Oblast' Ukr.
197 M7 Iskŭr r. Bulg.
197 L8 Iskŭr, Yazovir resr Bulg.
210 F2 Iskushuban Somalia
222 D3 Iskut r. B.C. Can.
245 L7 Isla Mex.
146 J9 Isla r. Angus/Perth and Kinross, Scotland U.K.
258 C2 Isla, Salar de la salt flat Chile
261 I2 Isla Cabellos Uru.
184 E6 Isla Canela Spain
184 E6 Isla Cristina Spain
250 C2 Isla de Salamanca, Parque Nacional nat. park Col.
85 L8 Isla Gorge National Park Qld Austr.
126 H5 İslahiye Turkey
129 B5 İslâhiye Turkey
Islamabad Jammu and Kashmir see Anantnag
123 O5 Islamabad Pak.
259 B7 Isla Magdalena, Parque Nacional nat. park Chile
184 G6 Isla Mayor marsh Spain
184 G6 Isla Menor marsh Spain
123 N8 Islamgarh Pak.
123 N9 Islamkot Pak.
231 G13 Islamorada FL U.S.A.
117 J7 Islampur Bihar India
222 F2 Island r. N.W.T. Can.
Ísland country Europe see Iceland
92 B7 Island Bay Palawan Phil.
233 □Q2 Island Falls ME U.S.A.
82 F4 Island Lagoon salt flat S.A. Austr.
223 M4 Island Lake Man. Can.
223 M4 Island Lake l. Man. Can.
226 B2 Island Lake l. MN U.S.A.
147 K3 Island Magee pen. Northern Ireland U.K.
238 I4 Island Park ID U.S.A.
233 N4 Island Pond VT U.S.A.
80 I2 Islands, Bay of North I. N.Z.
182 C4 Islas Atlánticas de Galicia, Parque Nacional de las nature res. Spain
242 □Q9 Islas de Bahá, Parque Nacional nat. park Hond.
261 F3 Isla Verde Arg.
146 D11 Islay i. Scotland U.K.
146 D11 Islay, Sound of sea chan. Scotland U.K.
197 M7 Islaz Romania
162 G4 Isle France
162 D6 Isle r. France
151 M3 Isleham Cambridgeshire, England U.K.
150 D1 Isle of Anglesey admin. div. Wales U.K.
148 H5 Isle of Man i. Irish Sea
146 H13 Isle of Whithorn Dumfries and Galloway, Scotland U.K.
151 J6 Isle of Wight admin. div. England U.K.
232 I12 Isle of Wight VA U.S.A.
226 F2 Isle Royale National Park MI U.S.A.
156 H5 Isles-sur-Suippe France
260 B1 Islón Chile
247 □7 Islote Point Trin. and Tob.
252 C4 Isluga, Parque Nacional nat. park Chile
261 I3 Ismael Cortinas Uru.
Ismail Ukr. see Izmayil
Ismâ'ilîya Egypt see Al Ismā'īlīyah
Ismailly Azer. see İsmayıllı
173 L5 Ismaning Ger.
129 J5 İsmayıllı Azer.
129 J5 İsmayıllı Qoruğu nature res. Azer.
123 N2 Ismoili Somoní, Qullai mt. Tajik.
203 G3 Isnā Egypt
182 E9 Isna Port.
194 G8 Isnello Sicilia Italy
173 I6 Isny im Allgäu Ger.
213 □J4 Isoanala Madag.
104 E7 Isobe Japan
105 K5 Isogo Japan
141 P5 Isojoki Fin.
211 B7 Isoka Zambia
140 S3 Isokylä Fin.
140 Q5 Isokyrö Fin.
161 K8 Isola France
161 K8 Isola 2000 France
192 C3 Isolaccio-di-Fiumorbo Corse France
193 L2 Isola del Gran Sasso d'Italia Italy
191 K5 Isola della Scala Italy
194 E7 Isola delle Femmine Sicilia Italy
193 L4 Isola del Liri Italy
195 M6 Isola di Capo Rizzuto Italy
158 D6 Isole r. France
190 F6 Isole del Cantone Italy
186 H3 Isona Spain
191 P4 Isonzo r. Italy
211 A7 Isopa Tanz.
216 □3e Isora El Hierro Canary Is
213 □J4 Isorana Madag.
190 I5 Isorella Italy
140 S4 Iso-Syöte hill Fin.
161 D8 Ispagnac France
Ispahan Iran see Eşfahān
199 L5 Isparta Turkey
199 L5 Isparta prov. Turkey
197 O7 Isperikh Bulg.
194 H10 Ispica Sicilia Italy
194 H10 Ispica r. Sicilia Italy
123 J8 Ispikan Pak.
127 J3 İspir Turkey
Ispisar Tajik. see Khŭjand
123 L7 Isplinji Pak.
163 B9 Ispoure France
190 F4 Ispra Italy
129 C1 Ispravnaya Rus. Fed.
172 F4 Ispringen Ger.
128 C6 Israel country Asia
256 B2 Israelândia Brazil
87 G12 Israelite Bay W.A. Austr.
Isra'īl country Asia see Israel
Issa Croatia see Vis
135 I5 Issa Rus. Fed.
138 L5 Issa r. Rus. Fed.
161 J10 Issambres, Pointe des pt France
207 H5 Issanguele Cameroon
251 G3 Issano Guyana
205 G4 Issaouane, Erg des. Alg.
161 E7 Issarlès France
202 B6 Isséirom Chad
169 B7 Isselburg Ger.
157 N8 Issenheim France
104 F6 Isshiki Japan
206 D5 Issia Côte d'Ivoire
163 F6 Issigeac France
190 D4 Issime Italy
93 C3 Issimu Sulawesi Indon.
127 L8 Issin tourist site Iraq
185 P4 Isso Spain
190 D4 Issogne Italy
160 C5 Issoire France
161 I10 Issole r. France
207 F2 Issouanka well Mali
162 H2 Issoudun France
205 F5 Issoulane Erareine slope Alg.
169 B7 Issum Ger.
211 B6 Issuna Tanz.
160 G1 Is-sur-Tille France
Issyk-Ata Kyrg. see Ysyk-Ata
Issyk-Kul' Kyrg. see Balykchy
Issyk-Kul', Ozero salt l. Kyrg. see Ysyk-Köl
Issyk-Kul Oblast admin. div. Kyrg. see Ysyk-Köl
Issyk-Kul'skaya Oblast' admin. div. Kyrg. see Ysyk-Köl
160 D3 Issy-l'Évêque France
191 R7 Ist Croatia
191 R7 Ist i. Croatia
139 T8 Ista r. Rus. Fed.
124 D3 Iştabl 'Antar Saudi Arabia
127 K6 Iştablāt tourist site Iraq
123 M5 Īstādeh-ye Moqor, Āb-e l. Afgh.
177 J3 Istállós-kő hill Hungary
185 J7 Istán Spain
199 J1 İstanbul Turkey
199 J1 İstanbul prov. Turkey
199 K1 İstanbul Boğazı str. Turkey
151 M5 Istead Rise Kent, England U.K.
174 G6 Istebna Pol.
177 I2 Istebné Slovakia
176 F5 Isten dombja hill Hungary
122 C5 Īstgāh-e Eznā Iran
258 F3 Isthilart Arg.
198 E4 Istiaia Greece
123 P3 Istik r. Tajik.
129 G6 İstisu Azer.
250 B3 Istmina Col.
137 R2 Istobnoye Rus. Fed.
196 I8 Istok Kosovo Serbia
231 G12 Istokpoga, Lake FL U.S.A.
188 D3 Istra pen. Croatia
139 T6 Istra Rus. Fed.
161 F9 Istres France
Istria pen. Croatia see Istra
197 Q6 Istria Romania
197 O5 Istriţa, Dealul hill Romania
163 B9 Isturits France
139 X7 Ist'ya r. Rus. Fed.
186 E3 Isuela r. Aragón Spain
183 R5 Isuela r. Spain
163 B11 Isuerre Spain
105 L5 Isumi Japan
105 L5 Isumi-gawa r. Japan
117 L8 Iswaripur Bangl.
215 O2 Iswepe S. Africa
120 G1 Isyangulovo Rus. Fed.
254 F4 Itabaianinha Brazil
257 G4 Itabapoana Brazil
257 G4 Itabapoana r. Brazil
256 C5 Itaberá Brazil
254 E5 Itaberaba Brazil
256 C2 Itaberaí Brazil
257 F3 Itabira Brazil
257 F4 Itabirito Brazil
251 F6 Itaboca Brazil
257 F5 Itaboraí Brazil
255 F5 Itabuna Brazil
254 C3 Itacaiuna r. Brazil
254 D4 Itacajá Brazil
257 F2 Itacambira Brazil
255 D5 Itacarambi Brazil
254 F5 Itacaré Brazil
253 H1 Itacayunas, Serra hills Brazil
251 G5 Itacoatiara Brazil
250 D6 Itacuaí r. Brazil
253 F6 Itacurubí del Rosario Para.
104 E4 Itadori Japan
254 E5 Itaetê Brazil
211 B6 Itaga Tanz.
Itagmatana Iran see Hamadān
257 H2 Itagmirim Brazil
257 G3 Itaguaçu Brazil
257 F5 Itaguaí Brazil
256 B5 Itaguajé Brazil
257 E4 Itaguara Brazil
252 C3 Itahuania Peru
256 C5 Itaí Brazil
254 E3 Itaim r. Brazil
255 C8 Itaiópolis Brazil
255 B8 Itaipu, Represa de resr Brazil
141 S6 Itäisen Suomenlahden kansallispuisto nat. park Fin.
251 G6 Itaituba Brazil
256 B3 Itajá Brazil
255 C8 Itajaí Brazil
256 C4 Itajobi Brazil
257 E5 Itajubá Brazil
255 F5 Itajuipe Brazil
100 A2 Itaka Rus. Fed.
117 J8 Itaki Jharkhand India
105 M4 Itako Japan
105 K3 Itakura Gunma Japan
105 H1 Itakura Niigata Japan
215 P3 Itala Game Reserve nature res. S. Africa
Italia country Europe see Italy
261 F4 Italó Arg.
188 E5 Italy country Europe
254 G3 Itamaracá, Ilha de i. Brazil
257 H2 Itamaraju Brazil
257 F2 Itamarandiba Brazil
254 D2 Itamataré Brazil
257 G3 Itambacuri Brazil
257 G3 Itambacuri r. Brazil
255 E5 Itambé Brazil
257 F3 Itambé, Pico de mt. Brazil
104 B6 Itami Japan
104 B6 Itami airport Japan
213 □I5 Itampolo Madag.
112 H6 Itanagar Arun. Prad. India
254 D5 Itanguari r. Brazil
256 D6 Itanhaém Brazil
257 E5 Itanhandu Brazil
251 F6 Itanhauã r. Brazil
257 G2 Itanhém Brazil
257 H2 Itanhém r. Brazil
257 G3 Itanhomi Brazil
251 H4 Itany r. Fr. Guiana/Suriname
257 G2 Itaobím Brazil
257 F4 Itaocara Brazil
254 C5 Itapaci Brazil
254 F2 Itapagé Brazil
256 C3 Itapajipe Brazil
251 F6 Itaparaná r. Brazil
254 F4 Itaparica, Represa de resr Brazil
257 H1 Itapebi Brazil
261 I2 Itapebí Uru.
257 E4 Itapecerica Brazil
257 G4 Itapemirim Brazil
257 G4 Itaperuna Brazil
255 E5 Itapetinga Brazil
256 C5 Itapetininga Brazil
256 C5 Itapeva Brazil
255 C9 Itapeva, Lago l. Brazil
251 G5 Itapi r. Brazil
254 E4 Itapicuru Brazil
254 F4 Itapicuru r. Brazil
254 D3 Itapicuru, Serra de hills Brazil
254 D2 Itapicuru Mirim Brazil
254 F4 Itapicuru Mirim r. Brazil
251 F6 Itapinima Brazil
254 F2 Itapipoca Brazil
256 D5 Itapira Brazil
251 G5 Itapiranga Brazil
256 B1 Itapirapuã Brazil
261 I1 Itapitocai Brazil
254 F3 Itapiúna Brazil
256 C4 Itápolis Brazil
254 F3 Itaporanga Paraíba Brazil
256 C5 Itaporanga São Paulo Brazil
255 C9 Itapuã Brazil
255 C5 Itapuranga Brazil
256 D5 Itaquaquecetuba Brazil
255 A9 Itaqui Brazil
257 G3 Itarana Brazil
257 G1 Itarantim Brazil
256 C6 Itararé Brazil
256 C5 Itararé r. Brazil
116 F8 Itarsi Madh. Prad. India
256 B3 Itarumã Brazil
140 T5 Itä-Suomi prov. Fin.
260 A5 Itata r. Chile
253 F7 Itati, Laguna l. Arg.
256 D5 Itatiba Brazil
256 C5 Itatinga Brazil
251 F6 Itatuba Brazil
251 I5 Itatupã Brazil
256 C2 Itauçu Brazil
254 E3 Itaueira r. Brazil
251 E5 Itaúna Amazonas Brazil
257 E4 Itaúna Minas Gerais Brazil
257 H3 Itaúnas Brazil
257 H3 Itaúnas r. Brazil
92 C1 Itbayat i. Phil.
222 E4 Itcha Ilgachuz Provincial Park B.C. Can.
222 H1 Itchen Lake N.W.T. Can.
252 C4 Ite Peru
198 D4 Itea Greece
208 F5 Itebero Dem. Rep. Congo
121 N1 Itemgen, Ozero l. Kazakh.
211 B6 Itende Tanz.
183 L4 Itero de la Vega Spain
211 C7 Itete Tanz.
162 E3 Iteuil France
209 E8 Itezhi-Tezhi Dam Zambia
Ithaca Greece see Ithaki
Ithaca i. Greece see Ithaki
226 J6 Ithaca MI U.S.A.
232 I6 Ithaca NY U.S.A.
198 B4 Ithaki Greece
198 B4 Ithaki i. Greece
198 B4 Ithakis, Steno sea chan. Greece
169 H6 Ith Hils ridge Ger.
128 F7 Ithrah Saudi Arabia
211 B6 Itigi Tanz.
221 M3 Itilleq Greenland
208 D4 Itimbiri r. Dem. Rep. Congo
257 G2 Itinga Brazil
255 B6 Itiquira Brazil
253 F4 Itiquira r. Brazil
256 D5 Itirapina Brazil
256 D4 Itirapuã Brazil
254 F4 Itiúba Brazil
254 F4 Itiúba, Serra de hills Brazil
258 E1 Itiyura r. Arg.
117 J7 Itkhari Jharkhand India
120 E3 Itmurinkol', Ozero l. Kazakh.
105 J6 Itō Japan
213 I2 Itoculo Moz.
105 G1 Itoigawa Japan
208 D5 Itoko Dem. Rep. Congo
102 □1 Itoman Okinawa Japan
156 B5 Iton r. France
213 □J4 Itongafeno mt. Madag.
Iton-Qälla Rus. Fed. see Itum-Kale
104 E5 Itonuki Japan
185 L7 Itrabo Spain
193 L5 Itri Italy
217 □3a Itsandzéni Njazidja Comoros
217 □3a Itsikoudi Njazidja Comoros
103 H14 Itsuki Japan
103 J12 Itsukushima i. Japan
205 G2 Ittel, Oued watercourse Alg.
192 B6 Ittireddu Sardegna Italy
192 B6 Ittiri Sardegna Italy
221 P2 Ittoqqortoormiit Greenland
165 F7 Ittre Belgium
256 D5 Itu Brazil
207 G5 Itu Nigeria
90 D4 Itu Abu Island S. China Sea
254 E5 Ituaçu Brazil
254 F5 Ituberá Brazil
252 C1 Itucumã r. Brazil
182 G8 Ituero de Azaba Spain
250 D6 Ituí r. Brazil
256 C3 Ituiutaba Brazil
209 E5 Itula Dem. Rep. Congo
211 B6 Itumba Tanz.
256 C3 Itumbiara Brazil
256 C3 Itumbiara, Barragem resr Brazil
129 G3 Itum-Kale Rus. Fed.
211 B7 Itungi Port Malawi
251 G3 Ituni Guyana
254 C3 Itupiranga Brazil
256 B3 Iturama Brazil
253 F6 Iturbe Para.
243 O8 Iturbide Campeche Mex.
245 H1 Iturbide Nuevo León Mex.
208 E4 Ituri r. Dem. Rep. Congo
99 Q3 Iturup, Ostrov i. Kuril'skiye O-va Rus. Fed.
257 E4 Itutinga Brazil
256 D4 Ituverava Brazil
252 D1 Ituxi r. Brazil
258 F2 Ituzaingo Arg.
Ityopia country Africa see Ethiopia
169 K11 Itz r. Ger.
168 I3 Itzehoe Ger.
168 J3 Itzstedt Ger.
250 D4 Iuaretê Brazil
194 H8 Iudica, Monte hill Sicilia Italy
237 K8 Iuka MS U.S.A.
131 T3 Iul'tin Rus. Fed.
213 H2 Iuluti Moz.
257 G4 Iúna Brazil
250 D4 Iutica Brazil
256 B6 Ivaí Brazil
256 A5 Ivaí r. Brazil
256 B6 Ivaiporã Brazil
213 □J4 Ivakoany mt. Madag.
140 S2 Ivalo Fin.
140 S2 Ivalojoki r. Fin.
176 F4 Iván Hungary
175 L6 Ivana Franka Ukr.
136 E1 Ivanava Belarus
176 F2 Ivančice Czech Rep.
188 F2 Ivanec Croatia
138 L2 Ivangorod Rus. Fed.
Ivangrad Montenegro see Berane
83 J5 Ivanhoe N.S.W. Austr.
86 J3 Ivanhoe W.A. Austr.
224 D3 Ivanhoe r. Ont. Can.
240 M5 Ivanhoe CA U.S.A.
236 G3 Ivanhoe MN U.S.A.
232 E12 Ivanhoe VA U.S.A.
223 J2 Ivanhoe Lake N.W.T. Can.
227 L1 Ivanhoe Lake Ont. Can.
188 F3 Ivanić-Grad Croatia
137 O2 Ivanino Rus. Fed.
139 X6 Ivanishchi Rus. Fed.
137 Q3 Ivanivka Kharkivs'ka Oblast' Ukr.
137 L7 Ivanivka Khersons'ka Oblast' Ukr.
137 N7 Ivanivka Khersons'ka Oblast' Ukr.
137 K4 Ivanivka Kyivs'ka Oblast' Ukr.
137 R5 Ivanivka Luhans'ka Oblast' Ukr.
136 J7 Ivanivka Odes'ka Oblast' Ukr.
137 M8 Ivanivka Respublika Krym Ukr.
177 L3 Ivanivka Zakarpats'ka Oblast' Ukr.
136 G5 Ivanivtsi Ukr.
196 I7 Ivanjica Serbia
176 G3 Ivanka pri Dunaji Slovakia
136 I3 Ivankiv Ukr.
188 G3 Ivankovo Croatia
139 U7 Ivan'kovo Rus. Fed.
139 X5 Ivan'kovskiy Rus. Fed.
139 T5 Ivan'kovskoye Vodokhranilishche resr Rus. Fed.
100 I4 Ivankovtsy Rus. Fed.
136 D5 Ivano-Frankivs'k Ukr.
136 D5 Ivano-Frankivs'ka Oblast' admin. div. Ukr.
Ivano-Frankivs'k Oblast admin. div. Ukr. see Ivano-Frankivs'ka Oblast'
136 C4 Ivano-Frankove Ukr.
Ivano-Frankovsk Ukr. see Ivano-Frankivs'k
Ivano-Frankovskaya Oblast' admin. div. Ukr. see Ivano-Frankivs'ka Oblast'
Ivano-Frankovsk Oblast admin. div. Ukr. see Ivano-Frankivs'ka Oblast'
136 H4 Ivanopil' Ukr.
137 O3 Ivano-Shyychyne Ukr.
Ivanovka Kazakh. see Kokzhayyk
100 E3 Ivanovka Amurskaya Oblast' Rus. Fed.
120 E1 Ivanovka Orenburgskaya Oblast' Rus. Fed.
Ivanovo Belarus see Ivanava
197 N7 Ivanovo tourist site Bulg.
139 X5 Ivanovo Ivanovskaya Oblast' Rus. Fed.
139 N5 Ivanovo Pskovskaya Oblast' Rus. Fed.
139 U3 Ivanovo Tverskaya Oblast' Rus. Fed.
Ivanovo Oblast admin. div. Rus. Fed. see Ivanovskaya Oblast'
137 R8 Ivanovskaya Rus. Fed.
139 Y4 Ivanovskaya Oblast' admin. div. Rus. Fed.
121 T2 Ivanovskiy Khrebet mts Kazakh.
137 N2 Ivanovskoye Kurskaya Oblast' Rus. Fed.
139 T8 Ivanovskoye Orlovskaya Oblast' Rus. Fed.
139 W5 Ivanovskoye Yaroslavskaya Oblast' Rus. Fed.
241 Q6 Ivanpah Lake CA U.S.A.
188 E2 Ivanšćica mts Croatia
179 O8 Ivanska Croatia
197 P7 Ivanski Bulg.
120 C1 Ivanteyevka Rus. Fed.
Ivantsevichi Belarus see Ivatsevichy
136 D3 Ivanychi Ukr.
137 L3 Ivanytsya Ukr.
213 □J4 Ivato Madag.
138 I9 Ivatsevichy Belarus
197 O9 Ivaylovgrad Bulg.
197 N9 Ivaylovgrad, Yazovir resr Bulg.
134 M3 Ivdel' Rus. Fed.
217 □3a Ivembeni Njazidja Comoros
151 K4 Iver Buckinghamshire, England U.K.
147 C9 Iveragh reg. Ireland
140 □ Iversenfjellet hill Svalbard
197 P5 Iveşti Galaţi Romania
197 P4 Iveşti Vaslui Romania
208 B5 Ivindo r. Gabon
151 K4 Ivinghoe Buckinghamshire, England U.K.
255 B7 Ivinheima Brazil
256 A5 Ivinheima r. Brazil
139 R1 Ivinskiy Razliv resr Rus. Fed.
253 H1 Iviti Brazil
221 N3 Ivittuut Greenland
Iviza i. Spain see Eivissa
137 P2 Ivnya Rus. Fed.
213 □J4 Ivohibe Madag.
256 B2 Ivolândia Brazil
252 D2 Ivón Bol.
232 I12 Ivor VA U.S.A.
Ivory Coast country Africa see Côte d'Ivoire
143 K5 Ivösjön l. Sweden
139 R8 Ivot Rus. Fed.
137 M2 Ivot Ukr.
137 M2 Ivotka r. Ukr.
190 D5 Ivrea Italy
199 I3 İvrindi Turkey
129 F3 Ivris Ugheltekhili pass Georgia
129 G4 Ivris Zegani plat. Georgia
156 B6 Ivry-la-Bataille France
156 D6 Ivry-sur-Seine France
Ivugivik Que. Can. see Ivujivik
221 K3 Ivujivik Que. Can.
211 B7 Ivuna Tanz.
220 E3 Ivvavik National Park Y.T. Can.
138 J8 Ivyanyets Belarus
150 E7 Ivybridge Devon, England U.K.
232 D10 Ivydale WV U.S.A.
104 B7 Iwade Japan
151 N5 Iwade Kent, England U.K.
105 K3 Iwafune Japan
105 K3 Iwai Japan
103 I13 Iwai-shima i. Japan
102 S7 Iwaizumi Japan
105 M1 Iwaki Japan
102 R6 Iwaki-san vol. Japan
103 J12 Iwakuni Japan
104 E5 Iwakura Japan
105 L3 Iwama Japan
103 J13 Iwamatsu Japan
102 S3 Iwamizawa Japan
104 F5 Iwamura Japan
105 H3 Iwamurada Japan
95 K4 Iwan r. Indon.
102 R4 Iwanai Japan
211 B7 Iwanda Tanz.
175 J5 Iwaniska Pol.
102 R8 Iwanuma Japan
102 Q6 Iwasaki Japan
105 L3 Iwase Japan
104 F2 Iwasehama Japan
105 I2 Iwasuge-yama vol. Japan
105 G6 Iwata Japan
104 B4 Iwataki Japan
102 S7 Iwate Japan
102 S7 Iwate pref. Japan
102 R7 Iwate-san vol. Japan
105 K4 Iwatsuki Japan
175 I6 Iwkowa Pol.
207 G5 Iwo Nigeria
84 D7 Iwupataka Aboriginal Land res. N.T. Austr.
138 I8 Iwye Belarus
245 L9 Ixaltepec Mex.
245 I7 Ixcamilpa Mex.
245 H7 Ixcateopan Mex.
245 M9 Ixhuatán Mex.
245 I5 Ixhuatlán Veracruz Mex.
245 K6 Ixhuatlán Veracruz Mex.
252 C3 Ixiamas Bol.
245 H5 Ixmiquilpán Mex.
215 O6 Ixopo S. Africa
245 J6 Ixtacamaxtitlán Mex.
243 M9 Ixtacomitán Mex.
244 F8 Ixtapa Guerrero Mex.
244 B5 Ixtapa Jalisco Mex.
244 F8 Ixtapa, Punta pt Mex.
245 H7 Ixtapan de la Sal Mex.
245 H6 Ixtlahuaca Mex.
244 D6 Ixtlahuacán Mex.
244 E5 Ixtlán Michoacán Mex.
244 C4 Ixtlán Nayarit Mex.
245 K8 Ixtlán Oaxaca Mex.
151 N3 Ixworth Suffolk, England U.K.
93 B8 Iya i. Indon.
98 G1 Iya r. Rus. Fed.
203 F6 Iyal Bakhit Sudan
211 B7 Iyayi Tanz.
129 B4 İyidere Turkey
İyirmi Altı Bakı Komissarı Azer. see Uzboy
103 J13 Iyo Japan
103 K13 Iyomishima Japan
103 J13 Iyo-nada b. Japan
197 L3 Iza r. Romania
177 H4 Iža Slovakia
242 □O10 Izabal Guat.
243 O10 Izabal, Lago de l. Guat.
183 R3 Izaga, Peña de mt. Spain
183 N2 Izalde r. Spain
243 O7 Izamal Mex.
243 M10 Izapa tourist site Mex.
102 S4 Izari-dake mt. Japan
183 O3 Izarra Spain
211 B6 Izazi Tanz.
134 H2 Izba Bol'shaya Bab'ya Rus. Fed.
197 M5 Izbăşeşti hill Romania
129 I3 Izberbash Rus. Fed.
175 L5 Izbica Pol.
174 G3 Izbica Kujawska Pol.
183 Q3 Izco, Sierra de mts Spain
139 Q6 Izdeshkovo Rus. Fed.
161 G6 Izeaux France
182 G5 Izeda Port.
165 D7 Izegem Belgium
122 C6 Īzeh Iran
102 □E20 Izena-jima i. Nansei-shotō Japan
160 H4 Izernore France
161 G6 Izeron France
207 H2 Izgagane well Niger
123 O4 Izgal Pak.
134 K4 Izhevsk Rus. Fed.
139 X7 Izhevskoye Rus. Fed.
134 K2 Izhma Respublika Komi Rus. Fed.
Izhma Respublika Komi Rus. Fed. see Sosnogorsk
134 K2 Izhma r. Rus. Fed.
125 M4 Izkī Oman
Izmail Ukr. see Izmayil
139 U9 Izmalkovo Rus. Fed.
136 H8 Izmayil Ukr.
Izmeny, Proliv sea chan. Japan/Rus. Fed. see Notsuke-suidō
199 I4 İzmir Turkey
199 I4 İzmir prov. Turkey
199 H4 İzmir Körfezi g. Turkey
199 K2 İzmit Turkey
199 K2 İzmit Körfezi b. Turkey
180 E5 Izmorene Morocco
185 K6 Iznájar Spain
185 K6 Iznajar, Embalse de resr Spain
185 L6 Iznalloz Spain
199 K2 İznik Turkey
199 K2 İznik Gölü l. Turkey
139 S7 Iznoski Rus. Fed.
137 O2 Iznoskovo Rus. Fed.
161 J7 Izoard, Col d' pass France
Izobil'noye Rus. Fed. see Izobil'nyy
135 H7 Izobil'nyy Rus. Fed.
188 D3 Izola Slovenia
139 T5 Izoplit Rus. Fed.
253 E4 Izozog Bol.
253 E4 Izozog Bajo Bol.
128 E6 Izra' Syria
177 I5 Izsák Hungary
245 I6 Iztaccíhuatl, Volcán vol. Mex.
245 I6 Iztaccíhuatl-Popocatépetl, Parque Nacional nat. park Mex.
197 N9 Iztochni Rodopi mts Bulg.
245 I7 Izúcar de Matamoros Mex.
105 I6 Izu-hantō pen. Japan
103 G12 Izuhara Japan
104 E4 Izumi Fukui Japan
105 M2 Izumi Fukushima Japan
103 H14 Izumi Kagoshima Japan
105 J5 Izumi Kanagawa Japan
102 R8 Izumi Miyagi Japan
104 B7 Izumi Ōsaka Japan
104 B6 Izumiōtsu Japan
104 B7 Izumisano Japan
105 L1 Izumizaki Japan
103 J11 Izumo Japan
103 P9 Izumozaki Japan
105 I5 Izunagaoka Japan
266 E3 Izu-Ogasawara Trench sea feature N. Pacific Ocean
104 A5 Izushi Japan
105 J7 Izu-shotō is Japan
Izu-tobu vol. Japan see Amagi-san
130 J2 Izvestiy Tsentral'nogo Ispolnitel'nogo Komiteta, Ostrova Rus. Fed.
100 G4 Izvestkovyy Rus. Fed.
197 N6 Izvoarele Giurgiu Romania
197 M6 Izvoarele Olt Romania
197 O5 Izvoarele Prahova Romania
197 N6 Izvoru Romania
136 F3 Izyaslav Ukr.
134 L2 Iz"yayu Rus. Fed.
120 H5 Izyndy Kazakh.
137 Q4 Izyum Ukr.

J

141 S6 Jaala Fin.
138 K2 Jaama Estonia
124 G9 Ja'ar Yemen
140 R3 Jaatila Fin.
122 G4 Jaba watercourse Iran
183 P8 Jabaga Spain
191 R6 Jabalanac Croatia
123 M4 Jabal as Sirāj Afgh.
185 N5 Jabalcón mt. Spain
125 I4 Jabal Dab Saudi Arabia
185 K3 Jabalón r. Spain
187 C7 Jabaloyas Spain
116 G8 Jabalpur Madh. Prad. India
185 L4 Jabalquinto Spain
184 F2 Jabarriega hill Spain
124 E6 Jabbārah Fara Islands Saudi Arabia
165 D6 Jabbeke Belgium
128 F2 Jabbūl Syria
128 F3 Jabbūl, Sabkhat al salt flat Syria
170 G3 Jabel Ger.
84 D2 Jabiluka Aboriginal Land res. N.T. Austr.
125 N4 Jabir reg. Oman
84 D2 Jabiru N.T. Austr.
128 D3 Jablah Syria
191 Q5 Jablanac, Rt pt Croatia
188 F4 Jablanica Bos.-Herz.
197 J7 Jablanica r. Serbia
175 L4 Jabłoń Pol.
176 E1 Jablonec nad Nisou Czech Rep.
176 G3 Jablonica Slovakia
175 H6 Jabłonka Pol.
175 K3 Jabłonka Kościelna Pol.
175 I3 Jabłonna Pol.
175 K3 Jabłonna Lacka Pol.
175 K4 Jabłonna Pierwsza Pol.
176 D1 Jablonné v Podještědí Czech Rep.
175 H2 Jabłonowo Pomorskie Pol.
177 G2 Jablůnka Czech Rep.
177 H2 Jablunkov Czech Rep.
254 G4 Jaboatão Pernambuco Brazil
254 G4 Jaboatão Brazil
256 C4 Jaboticabal Brazil
257 F3 Jaboticatubas Brazil
161 F7 Jabron r. France
184 F5 Jabugo Spain
188 E4 Jabuka i. Croatia
196 I6 Jabuka Vojvodina Serbia
94 F5 Jabung, Tanjung pt Indon.
251 E6 Jaburu Brazil
251 G6 Jabuti Brazil
186 D2 Jaca Spain
245 H4 Jacala Mex.
243 N10 Jacaltenango Guat.
254 B5 Jacaré Mato Grosso Brazil
252 D2 Jacaré Rondônia Brazil
254 E4 Jacaré r. Brazil
251 F6 Jacaré r. Brazil
251 G6 Jacareacanga Brazil
257 D5 Jacareí Brazil
253 F2 Jacaretinga Brazil
256 C5 Jacarézinho Brazil
257 F4 Jaceaba Brazil
260 D2 Jáchal r. Arg.
173 L6 Jachen r. Ger.
173 K6 Jachenau Ger.
176 B1 Jáchymov Czech Rep.
255 B5 Jaciara Brazil
257 G2 Jacinto Brazil
261 F6 Jacinto Arauz Arg.
255 C9 Jacinto Machado Brazil
252 D2 Jaciparaná Brazil
252 D2 Jaciparaná r. Brazil
85 J3 Jack r. Qld Austr.
226 H1 Jackfish Ont. Can.
223 I4 Jackfish Lake Sask. Can.
227 P5 Jack Lake Ont. Can.
237 I9 Jack Lee, Lake resr AR U.S.A.
233 □O3 Jackman ME U.S.A.
232 A12 Jacksboro TN U.S.A.
237 F9 Jacksboro TX U.S.A.
85 L9 Jackson Qld Austr.
231 D10 Jackson AL U.S.A.
240 L3 Jackson CA U.S.A.
231 F9 Jackson GA U.S.A.
232 B11 Jackson KY U.S.A.
226 J7 Jackson MI U.S.A.
236 H4 Jackson MN U.S.A.
237 K7 Jackson MO U.S.A.
237 J9 Jackson MS U.S.A.
231 I7 Jackson NC U.S.A.
232 C9 Jackson OH U.S.A.
237 K8 Jackson TN U.S.A.
226 F6 Jackson WI U.S.A.
238 I5 Jackson WY U.S.A.
81 I7 Jackson, Cape South I. N.Z.

Jieyang Guangdong China
Jieznas Lith.
Jiftūn al Kabīr i. Egypt
Jigalong Aboriginal Reserve W.A. Austr.
Jigawa state Nigeria
Jigerbent Turkm.
Jiggalong W.A. Austr.
Jiggs NV U.S.A.
Jiguaní Cuba
Jigzhi Qinghai China
Jiḩār, Wādī al watercourse Syria
Jihlava Czech Rep.
Jihlava r. Czech Rep.
Jihočeský kraj admin. reg. Czech Rep.
Jihomoravský kraj admin. reg. Czech Rep.
Jija Sarai Afgh.
Jijel Alg.
Jijia r. Romania
Jijiga Eth.
Jījīrud Iran
Jijitai Gansu China
Jijona-Xixona Spain
Jijü Sichuan China
Jil'ād reg. Jordan
Jilava Romania
Jilbadji Nature Reserve W.A. Austr.
Jilemnice Czech Rep.
Jilf al Kabīr, Haḑabat al plat. Egypt
Jilga r. Afgh.
Jilh al 'Ishār plain Saudi Arabia
Jilib Somalia
Jili Hu l. China
Jilin Jilin China
Jilin prov. China
Jiling Gansu China
Jilin Hada Ling mts China
Jiliu He r. China
Jilo Rajasthan India
Jiloca r. Spain
Jilong Taiwan see Chilung
Jilotepec Mex.
Jilotlán de los Dolores Mex.
Jílové Czech Rep.
Jílové u Prahy Czech Rep.
Jīma Eth.
Jima Ali well Eth.
Jimaní Haiti
Jimbo Tanz.
Jimbolia Romania
Jimda Sichuan China see Zindo
Jimena Spain
Jimena de la Frontera Spain
Jiménez Chihuahua Mex.
Jiménez Coahuila Mex.
Jiménez Tamaulipas Mex.
Jiménez del Téul Mex.
Jimeng Qinghai China
Jimeta Nigeria
Jimi r. P.N.G.
Jim Jim Creek r. N.T. Austr.
Jimo Shandong China
Jimokuji Japan
Jimramov Czech Rep.
Jimsar Xinjiang China
Jim Thorpe PA U.S.A.
Jina Romania
Jinan Shandong China
Jin'an Sichuan China see Songpan
Jinbi Yunnan China see Dayao
Jince Czech Rep.
Jinchang Gansu China
Jincheng Shanxi China
Jincheng Sichuan China see Leibo
Jincheng Sichuan China see Yilong
Jincheng Yunnan China see Wuding
Jinchengjiang Guangxi China see Hechi
Jinchuan Gansu China see Jinchang
Jinchuan Jiangxi China see Xingan
Jinchuan Sichuan China
Jind Haryana India
Jindabyne N.S.W. Austr.
Jinding Yunnan China see Lanping
Jindřichov Czech Rep.
Jindřichův Hradec Czech Rep.
Jin'e Sichuan China see Longchang
Jinfosi Gansu China
Jing Xinjiang China see Jinghe
Jing'an Guangdong China see Doumen
Jingbian Shaanxi China
Jingchuan Gansu China
Jingde Anhui China
Jingdezhen Jiangxi China
Jingdong Yunnan China
Jinggangshan Jiangxi China
Jinggang Shan hill Jiangxi China
Jinggongqiao Jiangxi China
Jinggu Gansu China
Jinggu Yunnan China
Jinghai Tianjin China
Jinghe Xinjiang China
Jing He r. China
Jinghong Yunnan China
Jingjiang Jiangsu China
Jingle Shanxi China
Jingmen Hubei China
Jingning Gansu China
Jingpeng Nei Mongol China
Jingpo Heilong. China
Jingpo Hu l. China
Jingsha Hubei China see Jingzhou
Jingshan Hubei China
Jingtai Gansu China
Jingtieshan Gansu China
Jingxi Guangxi China
Jingxian Anhui China
Jingxian Hunan China see Jingzhou
Jingxin Yunnan China see Yongshan
Jingyan Sichuan China
Jingyang Anhui China see Jingde
Jingyu Jilin China
Jingyuan Gansu China
Jingzhou Hubei China
Jingzhou Hubei China
Jingzhou Hunan China
Jinhe Nei Mongol China
Jinhe Yunnan China see Jinping
Jinhua Yunnan China see Jianchuan
Jinhua Zhejiang China
Jining Nei Mongol China
Jining Shandong China
Jinja Uganda
Jinjiang Fujian China
Jinjiang Hainan China see Chengmai
Jinjiang Yunnan China
Jin Jiang r. China
Jin Jiang r. China
Jinka Eth.
Jinkouhe Sichuan China
Jinmen Taiwan see Chinmen
Jinmu Jiao pt China
Jinning Yunnan China
Jinotega Nic.
Jinotepe Nic.
Jinping Guizhou China
Jinping Yunnan China see Jingdong
Jinping Yunnan China
Jinping Yunnan China see Qiubei
Jinping Shan mts Sichuan China
Jinsen S. Korea see Inch'ŏn
108 F5 Jinsha Guizhou China
112 J6 Jinsha Jiang r. China alt. Chang Jiang, alt. Tongtian He, conv. Yangtze, long Yangtze Kiang
107 P6 Jinshan Nei Mongol China
Jinshan Nei Mongol China see Guyang
Jinshan Shanghai China see Zhujing
Jinshan Yunnan China see Lufeng
Jinshi Hunan China see Xinning
109 H4 Jinshi Hunan China
106 F7 Jinta Gansu China
109 L3 Jintan Jiangsu China
108 E3 Jintang Sichuan China
108 H7 Jintiancun Guangxi China
92 D6 Jintotolo i. Phil.
92 D6 Jintotolo Channel Phil.
114 E3 Jintur Mahar. India
Jinxi Anhui China see Taihu
109 K5 Jinxi Jiangxi China
Jinxi Liaoning China see Lianshan
109 L5 Jin Xi r. China
109 K4 Jinxian Jiangxi China
Jinxian Liaoning China see Linghai
107 O9 Jinxiang Shandong China
109 M5 Jinxiang Zhejiang China
108 H6 Jinxiu Guangxi China
108 D5 Jinyang Sichuan China
Jinyuan Sichuan China see Dayi
109 M4 Jinyun Zhejiang China
128 E8 Jinz, Qā' al salt flat Jordan
109 J3 Jinzhai Anhui China
107 M8 Jinzhong Shanxi China
107 Q6 Jinzhou Liaoning China
107 Q7 Jinzhou Liaoning China
107 Q7 Jinzhou Wan b. China
Jinzhu Sichuan China see Daocheng
104 F2 Jinzū-gawa r. Japan
253 E2 Ji-Paraná Brazil
253 E2 Jiparaná r. Brazil
250 A5 Jipijapa Ecuador
111 M11 Ji Qu r. Qinghai China
242 □O11 Jiquilisco El Salvador
244 E6 Jiquilpan de Juárez Mex.
245 N9 Jiquipilas Mex.
257 H2 Jiquitaia Brazil
128 B9 Jirā', Wādī watercourse Egypt
128 G7 Jirānīyāt, Shi'bān al watercourse Saudi Arabia
252 D2 Jirau Brazil
123 N2 Jirgatol Tajik.
117 N7 Jiri r. India
107 O4 Jirin Gol Nei Mongol China
203 F3 Jirjā Egypt
176 C1 Jirkov Czech Rep.
164 I2 Jirnsum Neth.
171 K10 Jirny Czech Rep.
122 G7 Jīroft Iran
210 F3 Jirriiban Somalia
125 J4 Jirwān Saudi Arabia
125 J4 Jirwan well Saudi Arabia
107 L9 Jishan Shanxi China
Jishi Qinghai China see Xunhua
106 H9 Jishishan Gansu China
108 G4 Jishou Hunan China
Jishui Jiangxi China see Yongfeng
128 E3 Jisr ash Shughūr Syria
176 D2 Jistebnice Czech Rep.
Jitian Guangdong China see Lianshan
243 M9 Jitotol Mex.
94 D1 Jitra Malaysia
197 L7 Jiu r. Romania
Jiuchenggong Shaanxi China see Linyou
106 J7 Jiudengkou Nei Mongol China
108 D3 Jiuding Shan mt. Sichuan China
109 J4 Jiugong Shan mt. Hubei China
109 J4 Jiujiang Jiangxi China
109 K4 Jiujiang Jiangxi China
Jiulian Yunnan China see Mojiang
109 J4 Jiuling Shan mts China
Jiulong H.K. China see Kowloon
108 C4 Jiulong Sichuan China
Jiulong Sichuan China see Yuechi
107 Q5 Jiumiao Liaoning China
108 G6 Jiuqian Guizhou China
106 F7 Jiuquan Gansu China
107 R8 Jiurongcheng Shandong China
100 D6 Jiutai Jilin China
107 L7 Jiuxian Shanxi China
108 F6 Jiuxu Guangxi China
108 E2 Jiuzhaigou Sichuan China
109 K6 Jiuzhen Fujian China
123 I9 Jiwani Pak.
107 R1 Jiwen Nei Mongol China
109 L3 Jixi Anhui China
100 G6 Jixi Heilong. China
Jixian Hebei China see Jizhou
100 G5 Jixian Heilong. China
Jixian Henan China see Weihui
107 L8 Jixian Shanxi China
107 M9 Jiyuan Henan China
125 K7 Jiz, Wādī al r. Yemen
124 F7 Jīzān Saudi Arabia
124 F7 Jīzān prov. Saudi Arabia
176 D1 Jizera r. Czech Rep.
176 E1 Jizerské hory mts Czech Rep.
176 E1 Jizerské hory park Czech Rep.
107 N8 Jizhou Hebei China
124 D3 Jizl watercourse Saudi Arabia
105 J2 Jizō-dake mt. Japan
103 K11 Jizō-zaki pt Japan
Jizzakh Uzbek. see Jizzax
Jizzakh Wiloyati admin. div. Uzbek. see Jizzax
121 L7 Jizzax Jizzax Uzbek.
121 L7 Jizzax admin. div. Uzbek.
255 C8 Joaçaba Brazil
170 I5 Joachimsthal Ger.
245 K7 Joachín Mex.
257 G2 Joaíma Brazil
206 A3 Joal-Fadiout Senegal
251 I5 Joana Peres Brazil
182 D6 Joane Port.
João Belo Moz. see Xai-Xai
João de Almeida Angola see Chibia
257 F3 João Monlevade Brazil
254 G3 João Pessoa Brazil
256 D2 João Pinheiro Brazil
257 E2 Joaquim Felício Brazil
258 D2 Joaquin V. González Arg.
160 D5 Job France
246 E3 Jobabo Cuba
105 M2 Jōban Japan
116 E8 Jobat Madh. Prad. India
177 I4 Jobbágyi Hungary
92 F7 Jobo Point Mindanao Phil.
247 □1 Jobos Puerto Rico
240 N2 Job Peak NV U.S.A.
178 F5 Jochberg Austria
171 F9 Jocketa Ger.
140 Q3 Jockfall Sweden
172 E3 Jockgrim Ger.
260 C3 Jocoli Arg.
243 O10 Jocotán Guat.
244 D5 Jocotepec Mex.
245 H6 Jocotitlán, Volcán vol. Mex.
117 J8 Joda Orissa India
185 M5 Jódar Spain
116 D6 Jodhpur Rajasthan India
116 C8 Jodiya Gujarat India
165 G7 Jodoigne Belgium
225 K3 Joe Batt's Arm Nfld and Lab. Can.
140 T5 Joensuu Fin.
140 M4 Joesjö Sweden
241 U2 Joe's Valley Reservoir UT U.S.A.
105 H1 Jōetsu Japan
157 L5 Jœuf France
213 G4 Jofane Moz.
222 H5 Joffre, Mount Alta/B.C. Can.
104 F2 Jōganji-gawa r. Japan
105 K5 Jōga-shima i. Japan
117 K6 Jogbani Bihar India
116 H5 Jogbura Nepal
138 J3 Jõgeva Estonia
122 G3 Joghatāy Iran
122 G3 Joghatay, Kūh-ye hill Iran
122 G8 Joghdān Iran
117 M6 Jogighopa Assam India
116 F4 Jogindarnagar Hima. Prad. India
Jogjakarta Indon. see Yogyakarta
138 K2 Jõgua Estonia
104 E2 Jōhana Japan
215 L2 Johannesburg S. Africa
240 O6 Johannesburg CA U.S.A.
171 G10 Johanngeorgenstadt Ger.
173 N4 Johanniskirchen Ger.
221 K2 Johan Peninsula Nunavut Can.
103 J14 Jōhen Japan
116 H8 Johilla r. Madh. Prad. India
86 J4 John, Mount hill W.A. Austr.
246 □ John Crow Mountains hills Jamaica
238 E4 John Day OR U.S.A.
238 D4 John Day r. OR U.S.A.
238 E4 John Day, Middle Fork r. OR U.S.A.
238 E4 John Day, North Fork r. OR U.S.A.
222 H3 John D'Or Prairie Alta Can.
233 L8 John F. Kennedy airport NY U.S.A.
232 G12 John H. Kerr Reservoir VA U.S.A.
222 D3 John Jay, Mount Can./U.S.A.
222 F1 Johnny Hoe r. N.W.T. Can.
146 J5 John o'Groats Highland, Scotland U.K.
237 E7 Johnson KS U.S.A.
233 M4 Johnson VT U.S.A.
232 G7 Johnsonburg PA U.S.A.
227 S7 Johnson City NY U.S.A.
231 F7 Johnson City TN U.S.A.
237 F10 Johnson City TX U.S.A.
240 N6 Johnsondale CA U.S.A.
237 E10 Johnson Draw watercourse TX U.S.A.
247 □3 Johnson Point St Vincent
222 C2 Johnson's Crossing Y.T. Can.
247 □2 Johnsons Point Antigua and Barbuda
231 H9 Johnsonville SC U.S.A.
150 C4 Johnston Pembrokeshire, Wales U.K.
231 G9 Johnston SC U.S.A.
87 F12 Johnston, Lake salt flat W.A. Austr.
Johnston and Sand Islands atoll N. Pacific Ocean see Johnston Atoll
75 H2 Johnston Atoll N. Pacific Ocean
146 G11 Johnstone Renfrewshire, Scotland U.K.
146 J12 Johnstonebridge Dumfries and Galloway, Scotland U.K.
Johnstone Lake Sask. Can. see Old Wives Lake
222 E5 Johnstone Strait B.C. Can.
87 E10 Johnston Range hills W.A. Austr.
147 G7 Johnstown Ireland
233 K5 Johnstown NY U.S.A.
232 C8 Johnstown OH U.S.A.
232 G8 Johnstown PA U.S.A.
147 I6 Johnstown Bridge Ireland
105 L3 Jōhoku Japan
94 E4 Johor state Malaysia
94 □ Johor, Selat str. Malaysia/Sing.
94 □ Johor, Sungai Malaysia
94 □ Johor Bahru Malaysia
171 H9 Jöhstadt Ger.
138 K2 Jõhvi Estonia
156 F8 Joigny France
255 C8 Joinville Brazil
157 J7 Joinville France
262 U2 Joinville Island Antarctica
245 H7 Jojutla Mex.
138 H1 Jokela Fin.
221 P2 Jøkelbugten b. Greenland
141 Q6 Jokioinen Fin.
140 Q5 Jokiperä Fin.
140 O3 Jokkmokk Sweden
140 □B1 Jökulbunga hill Iceland
140 □B1 Jökulfirðir inlet Iceland
140 □F1 Jökulsá á Dál r. Iceland
140 □E1 Jökulsá á Fjöllum r. Iceland
245 I7 Jolalpan Mex.
191 L6 Jolanda di Savoia Italy
114 F6 Jolarpettai Tamil Nadu India
127 L4 Jolfa Iran
226 F8 Joliet IL U.S.A.
234 C3 Joliet PA U.S.A.
224 E3 Joliet, Lac l. Que. Can.
224 F4 Joliette Que. Can.
223 H1 Jolly Lake N.W.T. Can.
92 C8 Jolo Phil.
92 C9 Jolo i. Phil.
160 J5 Joly, Mont mt. France
138 C1 Jomala Åland Fin.
92 D4 Jomalig i. Phil.
85 M1 Jomard Entrance sea chan. P.N.G.
95 J8 Jombang Jawa Indon.
108 B3 Jomda Xizang China
142 F3 Jomfruland i. Norway
105 J3 Jōmine-san mt. Japan
141 K6 Jømna Norway
117 I5 Jomsom Nepal
190 F1 Jona Switz.
122 F8 Jonāḩ Iran
232 C11 Jonancy KY U.S.A.
243 O9 Jonathan Point Belize
138 H6 Jonava Lith.
156 G5 Jonchery-sur-Vesle France
160 F3 Joncy France
142 C1 Jondal Norway
120 K8 Jondor Uzbek.
106 H9 Jonê Gansu China
104 G3 Jōnen-dake mt. Japan
237 J8 Jonesboro AR U.S.A.
237 K7 Jonesboro IL U.S.A.
226 I9 Jonesboro IN U.S.A.
237 I9 Jonesboro LA U.S.A.
233 □R4 Jonesboro ME U.S.A.
232 C12 Jonesboro TN U.S.A.
148 E5 Jonesborough Northern Ireland U.K.
232 F8 Jones Mills PA U.S.A.
262 R2 Jones Mountains Antarctica
86 □1 Jones Point Christmas I.
233 □R4 Jonesport ME U.S.A.
221 J2 Jones Sound sea chan. Nunavut Can.
234 C4 Jonestown PA U.S.A.
237 J10 Jonesville LA U.S.A.
232 B12 Jonesville VA U.S.A.
120 J7 Jongeldi Uzbek.
210 A3 Jonglei Sudan
210 B3 Jonglei state Sudan
210 A3 Jonglei Canal Sudan
175 I3 Joniec Pol.
138 H5 Joniškėlis Lith.
138 G5 Joniškis Lith.
117 I9 Jonk r. India
143 K4 Jönköping Sweden
143 K4 Jönköping county Sweden
175 I2 Jonkowo Pol.
225 G3 Jonquière Que. Can.
161 F8 Jonquières France
243 M8 Jonuta Mex.
162 D5 Jonzac France
210 F2 Joog-Joogto, Raas pt Somalia
237 H7 Joplin MO U.S.A.
245 I3 Jopoy Mex.
Joppa Israel see Tel Aviv-Yafo
234 C6 Joppatowne MD U.S.A.
195 J6 Joppolo Italy
116 F6 Jora Madh. Prad. India
186 D6 Jorcas Spain
128 E7 Jordan country Asia
128 D7 Jordan r. Asia
238 K3 Jordan MT U.S.A.
232 I5 Jordan NY U.S.A.
238 F5 Jordan r. OR U.S.A.
241 T1 Jordan r. UT U.S.A.
85 J7 Jordan Creek watercourse Qld Austr.
257 G1 Jordânia Brazil
161 A7 Jordanne r. France
175 H6 Jordanów Pol.
174 E5 Jordanów Śląski Pol.
238 F5 Jordan Valley OR U.S.A.
170 G3 Jördenstorf Ger.
141 L6 Jordet Norway
142 G6 Jordløse Denmark
259 B8 Jorge Montt, Isla i. Chile
117 O6 Jorhat Assam India
110 D7 Jor Hu l. China
129 F4 Jorjiashvili Georgia
252 C5 Jorjino, Punta pt Chile
168 I3 Jork Ger.
142 H4 Jörlanda Sweden
123 N3 Jorm Afgh.
140 M4 Jormvattnet Sweden
140 P4 Jörn Sweden
141 S5 Joroinen Fin.
95 K6 Jorong Kalimantan Indon.
142 C2 Jørpeland Norway
185 P2 Jorquera Spain
207 H4 Jos Nigeria
92 E9 Jose Abad Santos Mindanao Phil.
254 B4 José Bispo r. Brazil
253 E3 José Bonifácio Rondônia Brazil
256 C4 José Bonifácio São Paulo Brazil
245 K6 José Cardel Mex.
254 E3 José de Freitas Brazil
259 C7 José de San Martin Arg.
261 I3 José Enrique Rodó Uru.
261 F2 Josefina Arg.
171 L9 Josefův Důl Czech Rep.
253 F4 Joselândia Brazil
244 A1 José López Portillo, Presa resr Mex.
244 E3 José María Morelos Mex.
92 D4 Jose Pañganiban Luzon Phil.
258 G4 José Pedro Varela Uru.
225 H2 Joseph, Lac l. Nfld and Lab. Can.
86 J3 Joseph Bonaparte Gulf W.A. Austr.
241 V7 Joseph City AZ U.S.A.
185 I5 José Torán, Embalse de resr Spain
116 G4 Joshimath Uttaranchal India
105 H2 Jōshinetsu-kōgen Kokuritsu-kōen nat. park Japan
117 K9 Joshipur Orissa India
235 J2 Joshua Point CT U.S.A.
241 P7 Joshua Tree CA U.S.A.
241 Q8 Joshua Tree National Park CA U.S.A.
156 C8 Josnes France
207 H4 Jos Plateau Nigeria
158 F6 Josselin France
171 F9 Jößnitz Ger.
140 K4 Jossund Norway
141 I6 Jostedalsbreen glacier Norway
141 I6 Jostedalsbreen Nasjonalpark nat. park Norway
138 G6 Josvainiai Lith.
141 J6 Jotunheimen mts Norway
141 J6 Jotunheimen Nasjonalpark nat. park Norway
182 F6 Jou Port.
128 D5 Jouaiya Lebanon
159 J5 Jouanne r. France
156 F6 Jouarre France
214 H9 Joubertina S. Africa
215 K2 Jouberton S. Africa
162 F1 Joué-lès-Tours France
158 I6 Joué-sur-Erdre France
160 B2 Jouet-sur-l'Aubois France
160 I3 Jougne France
140 S4 Joukokylä Fin.
128 D5 Joûnié Lebanon
161 H9 Jouques France
237 F11 Jourdanton TX U.S.A.
164 I3 Joure Neth.
162 F6 Journiac France
222 H4 Joussard Alta Can.
141 S6 Joutsa Fin.
141 T6 Joutseno Fin.
140 S3 Joutsijärvi Fin.
160 H3 Joux, Forêt de la for. France
160 I3 Joux, Lac de l. Switz.
190 A2 Joux, Vallée de val. Switz.
160 D1 Joux-la-Ville France
156 C6 Jouy France
157 L5 Jouy-aux-Arches France
156 D5 Jouy-le-Moutier France
156 C8 Jouy-le-Potier France
156 G5 Jouy-lès-Reims France
246 C2 Jovellanos Cuba
117 N7 Jowai Meghalaya India
122 D3 Jowr Deh Iran
122 I6 Jowzak Iran
122 C4 Jowzān Iran
123 K3 Jowzjān prov. Afgh.
222 C2 Joy, Mount Y.T. Can.
243 O11 Joya de Cerén tourist site El Salvador
147 C5 Joyce's Country reg. Ireland
161 E8 Joyeuse France
104 C6 Jōyō Japan
117 L7 Joypurhat Bangl.
160 C5 Joze France
175 J4 Józefów Lubelskie Pol.
175 L5 Józefów Lubelskie Pol.
175 J3 Józefów Mazowieckie Pol.
215 Q3 Jozini S. Africa
204 B4 Jrayfiya well Western Sahara
206 A2 Jreïda Maur.
250 E5 Juami r. Brazil
247 □1 Juana Díaz Puerto Rico
244 D1 Juan Aldama Mex.
261 F6 Juan A. Pradere Arg.
261 G4 Juan Bautista Alberdi Arg.
107 N9 Juancheng Shandong China
261 I5 Juancho Arg.
246 □ Juan de Bolas hill Jamaica
222 E5 Juan de Fuca Strait Can./U.S.A.
260 E6 Juan de Garay Arg.
213 □I3 Juan de Nova i. Indian Ocean
245 L7 Juan Díaz Covarrubias Mex.
261 G5 Juan E. Barra Arg.
244 C4 Juan Escutia Mex.
252 □ Juan Fernández, Archipiélago is S. Pacific Ocean
Juan Fernández Islands S. Pacific Ocean see Juan Fernández, Archipiélago
251 F2 Juangriego Venez.
245 L8 Juanita Mex.
260 E3 Juan Jorba Arg.
261 H2 Juan Jorge Arg.
261 F4 Juan José Paso Arg.
252 A1 Juanjuí Peru
140 T5 Juankoski Fin.
161 K9 Juan-les-Pins France
261 I4 Juan L. Lacaze Uru.
260 E3 Juan Llerena Arg.
242 E2 Juan Mata Ortíz Mex.
261 H6 Juan N. Fernández Arg.
245 J4 Juan Ramírez, Isla i. Mex.
245 L7 Juan Rodriguez Clara Mex.
Juanshui Hubei China see Tongcheng
261 I4 Juan Soler Uru.
259 B7 Juan Stuven, Isla i. Chile
207 F5 Juapon Ghana
253 F2 Juara Brazil
243 I4 Juaréz Mex.
245 K8 Juárez, Sierra mts Mex.
242 A1 Juárez, Sierra de mts Mex.
257 E5 Juatinga, Ponta da pt Brazil
254 E4 Juàzeiro Brazil
254 F3 Juàzeiro do Norte Brazil
206 C5 Juazohn Liberia
Juba r. Somalia see Jubba
210 A3 Juba Sudan
124 A2 Jūbāl, Jazīrat i. Egypt
124 G8 Juban Yemen
262 U2 Jubany research stn Antarctica
210 D5 Jubba r. Somalia
210 D4 Jubbada Dhexe admin. reg. Somalia
210 D4 Jubbada Hoose admin. reg. Somalia
124 E1 Jubbah Saudi Arabia
Jubbulpore Madh. Prad. India see Jabalpur
168 H1 Jübek Ger.
87 I10 Jubilee Lake salt flat W.A. Austr.
225 K3 Jubilee Lake Nfld and Lab. Can.
261 H2 Jubileo Arg.
117 K6 Jubing Nepal
159 K5 Jublains France
204 B4 Juby, Cap c. Morocco
183 P8 Júcar r. Spain
187 E9 Jucar-Turia, Canal r. Spain
254 F3 Jucas Brazil
245 J9 Juchatengo Mex.
169 B8 Jüchen Ger.
244 D4 Juchipila Mex.
244 D4 Juchipila r. Mex.
245 L9 Juchitán Mex.
244 C5 Juchitlán Mex.
175 L2 Juchnowiec Kościelne Pol.
174 E2 Juchowo Pol.
169 K10 Jüchsen Ger.
257 H2 Jucuruçu Brazil
257 H2 Jucuruçu r. Brazil
142 B2 Judaberg Norway
128 C7 Judaea reg. Israel
127 J8 Judaidat al Hamir Iraq
126 I6 Judaydah Syria
128 E5 Judaydat al Wādī Syria
127 J8 Judayyidat 'Ar'ar well Iraq
171 D10 Judenbach Ger.
179 K5 Judenburg Austria
183 P6 Judes mt. Spain
108 B5 Judian Yunnan China
187 C11 Judio, Embalse del resr Spain
187 C11 Judío, Rambla del r. Spain
238 J3 Judith r. MT U.S.A.
238 J3 Judith Gap MT U.S.A.
Juegang Jiangsu China see Rudong
185 M3 Juego de Bolos mt. Spain
142 G6 Juelsminde Denmark
257 H2 Juerana Brazil
183 Q7 Juez mt. Spain
251 F5 Jufari r. Brazil
158 G5 Jugon-les-Lacs France
Jugoslavija country Europe see Serbia and Montenegro
107 K8 Juh Nei Mongol China
124 F7 Juḩā Saudi Arabia
124 D3 Juhaynah reg. Saudi Arabia
125 J5 Juḩaysh, Qalamat al oasis Saudi Arabia
169 I8 Jühnde Ger.
106 E8 Juhongtu Qinghai China
178 E4 Juifen mt. Austria
242 □Q11 Juigalpa Nic.
159 K7 Juigné-sur-Loire France
162 G5 Juillac France
163 E9 Juillan France
225 I2 Juillet, Lac l. Que. Can.
156 E5 Juilly France
253 F2 Juína Brazil
253 F3 Juina r. Brazil
156 D6 Juine r. France
168 C3 Juist Ger.
168 D3 Juist i. Ger.
257 F4 Juiz de Fora Brazil
94 D5 Jujuhan r. Indon.
122 I3 Ju Ju Klu Turkm.
160 G4 Jujurieux France
258 D1 Jujuy prov. Arg.
140 P3 Jukkasjärvi Sweden
105 I3 Jukkoku-tōge pass Japan
252 D5 Julaca Bol.
179 I2 Julbach Austria
173 N5 Julbach Ger.
236 D5 Julesburg CO U.S.A.
252 C4 Juli Peru
250 E5 Julia Brazil
252 C3 Juliaca Peru
85 H6 Julia Creek Qld Austr.
85 H6 Julia Creek r. Qld Austr.
240 P8 Julian CA U.S.A.
224 E2 Julian, Lac l. Que. Can.
164 G3 Julianadorp Neth.
247 □10 Julianadorp Curaçao Neth. Antilles
165 I6 Juliana Kanaal canal Neth.
Julian Alps mts Slovenia see Julijske Alpe
Julianatop mt. Papua Indon. see Mandala, Puncak
251 G4 Juliana Top mt. Suriname
Julianehåb Greenland see Qaqortoq
147 J5 Julianstown Ireland
169 B9 Jülich Ger.
160 E3 Julien, Mont hill France
160 F4 Juliénas France
188 D2 Julijske Alpe mts Slovenia
242 G3 Julimes Mex.
255 B9 Júlio de Castilhos Brazil
Juliomagus France see Angers
256 C5 Júlio Mesquita Brazil
84 G6 Julius, Lake Qld Austr.
234 F4 Juliustown NJ U.S.A.
158 H4 Jullouville France
Jullundur Punjab India see Jalandhar
244 D6 Juluapan Mex.
251 E6 Juma r. Brazil
121 L8 Juma Uzbek.
107 N7 Juma He r. China
108 B2 Jumanggoin Sichuan China
210 D5 Jumba Somalia
250 B6 Jumbilla Peru
161 C6 Jumeaux France
162 G5 Jumilhac-le-Grand France
187 C11 Jumilla Spain
116 I5 Jumla Nepal
168 E4 Jümme r. Ger.
Jumna r. India see Yamuna
226 C4 Jump r. WI U.S.A.
138 H5 Jumprava Latvia
116 C9 Junagadh Gujarat India
115 H3 Junagarh Orissa India
107 P9 Junan Shandong China
128 A8 Junayfah Egypt
128 B9 Junaynah, Ra's al mt. Egypt
122 H5 Junbuk Iran
107 P4 Jun Bulen Nei Mongol China
260 B3 Juncal mt. Chile
182 C9 Juncal Port.
247 □1 Juncos Puerto Rico
186 G5 Juncosa Spain
237 F10 Junction TX U.S.A.
241 T3 Junction UT U.S.A.
84 D1 Junction Bay N.T. Austr.
236 G6 Junction City KS U.S.A.
238 C4 Junction City OR U.S.A.
85 I8 Jundah Qld Austr.
256 D5 Jundiaí Brazil
220 E4 Juneau AK U.S.A.
222 C3 Juneau Icefield B.C. Can.
186 G4 Juneda Spain
83 K6 Junee N.S.W. Austr.
128 D5 Jûn el Khudr b. Lebanon
244 G6 Jungapeo Mex.
Jungar Qi Nei Mongol China see Xuejiawan
190 D2 Jungfrau mt. Switz.
110 H4 Junggar Pendi basin China
172 G5 Jungingen Ger.
165 J9 Junglinster Lux.
123 L9 Jungshahi Pak.
111 J10 Jungsi Xizang China
210 B2 Junguls Sudan
227 Q9 Juniata r. PA U.S.A.
234 A3 Juniata County county PA U.S.A.
196 I8 Junik Kosovo Serbia
261 G4 Junín Arg.
260 C3 Junin Arg.
252 A2 Junín Peru
252 B2 Junín dept Peru
232 F10 Junior WV U.S.A.
233 □R2 Juniper N.B. Can.
241 S6 Juniper Mountains AZ U.S.A.
240 K5 Junipero Serro Peak CA U.S.A.
156 H5 Juniville France
169 C10 Jünkerath Ger.
140 M3 Junkerdalen Balvatnet nature res. Norway
108 E4 Junlian Sichuan China
109 J6 Junmenling Jiangxi China
128 C10 Junnah, Jabal mts Egypt
114 C3 Junnar Mahar. India
237 E10 Juno TX U.S.A.
140 Q3 Junosuando Sweden
256 B4 Junqueirópolis Brazil
140 N5 Junsele Sweden
109 K4 Junshan Hu l. China
238 E5 Juntura OR U.S.A.
140 T4 Juntusranta Fin.
Junxi Fujian China see Datian
Junxian Hubei China see Danjiangkou
108 B2 Ju'nyung Sichuan China
Ju'nyunggoin Sichuan China see Ju'nyung
105 M2 Jūō Japan
138 E6 Juodkrantė Lith.
138 I7 Juodšiliai Lith.
138 I5 Juodupė Lith.
140 Q3 Juoksengi Sweden
138 H6 Juosta r. Lith.
138 H6 Juostinikai Lith.
138 I7 Juozapinės kalnas hill Lith.
122 G6 Jūpār Iran
257 G3 Juparanã, Lagoa l. Brazil
256 B4 Jupiá Brazil
256 B4 Jupía, Represa resr Brazil
159 L6 Jupilles France
231 G12 Jupiter FL U.S.A.
165 I7 Juprelle Belgium
256 D6 Juquiá Brazil
256 D6 Juquiá r. Brazil
256 D5 Juquitiba Brazil
208 F2 Jur r. Sudan
160 H3 Jura dept France
160 G5 Jura mts France/Switz.
138 F6 Jūra r. Lith.
190 C1 Jura canton Switz.
146 E10 Jura i. Scotland U.K.
124 G2 Jur'ā, Nafūd al des. Saudi Arabia
146 E11 Jura, Sound of sea chan. Scotland U.K.
250 B3 Juradó Col.
257 F2 Juramento Brazil
163 D9 Jurançon France
256 A6 Juranda Brazil
138 F6 Jurbarkas Lith.
165 E7 Jurbise Belgium
254 E4 Juremal Brazil
128 D8 Jurf ad Darāwīsh Jordan
170 E3 Jürgenshagen Ger.
170 G3 Jürgenstorf Ger.
86 G5 Jurgurra r. W.A. Austr.
107 Q4 Jurh Nei Mongol China
107 Q4 Jurh Nei Mongol China
138 H2 Jüri Estonia
87 C11 Jurien W.A. Austr.
87 C11 Jurien Bay W.A. Austr.
162 D4 Jurignac France
197 Q6 Jurilovca Romania
251 G5 Juriti Velho Brazil
191 R6 Jurjevo Croatia
179 L7 Jurklošter Slovenia
138 G5 Jūrmala Latvia
141 P7 Jurmo Fin.
140 S4 Jurmu Fin.
184 E3 Juromenha Port.
109 L3 Jurong Jiangsu China
94 □ Jurong Sing.
94 □ Jurong, Sungai r. Sing.
94 □ Jurong Island reg. Sing.
Jur pri Bratislave Slovakia see Svätý Jur
251 E5 Juruá Brazil
250 E5 Juruá r. Brazil
253 F3 Juruena Brazil
253 F1 Juruena r. Brazil
256 C5 Jurumirim, Represa de resr Brazil
253 G2 Juruna r. Brazil
252 C1 Jurupari r. Brazil
251 G5 Juruti Brazil
140 P5 Jurva Fin.
102 R5 Jūsan-ko l. Japan
251 F2 Jusepín Venez.
104 E5 Jūshiyama Japan
122 G3 Jūshqān Iran
128 E4 Jūsīyah Syria
162 I6 Jussac France
256 B1 Jussara Brazil
138 G2 Jussarö i. Fin.
157 K8 Jussey France
232 D11 Justice WV U.S.A.
261 F3 Justiniano Posse Arg.
260 E3 Justo Daract Arg.
177 G5 Juta Hungary
250 D6 Jutaí Brazil
250 E5 Jutaí r. Brazil
171 H7 Jüterbog Ger.
255 B7 Juti Brazil
243 O10 Jutiapa Guat.
242 □P10 Jutiapa Hond.
242 □P10 Juticalpa Hond.
Jutland pen. Denmark see Jylland
174 F4 Jutrosin Pol.
140 T5 Juuka Fin.
141 R6 Juupajoki Fin.
138 J1 Juurikorpi Fin.
141 S6 Juva Fin.
244 G5 Juventino Rosas Mex.
246 B3 Juventud, Isla de la i. Cuba
159 I5 Juvigné France
159 I4 Juvigny-le-Tertre France
159 J4 Juvigny-sous-Andaine France
123 I6 Juwain Afgh.
95 I8 Juwana Jawa Indon.
107 P9 Juxian Shandong China
107 O9 Juye Shandong China
122 H4 Jūymand Iran
122 E7 Jūyom Iran
157 I7 Juzennecourt France
163 F10 Juzet-d'Izaut France
Južnoukrajinsk Ukr. see Yuzhnoukrayinsk
212 E5 Jwaneng Botswana
142 H6 Jyderup Denmark
142 F5 Jylland pen. Denmark
121 R6 Jyrgalang Kyrg.
141 R5 Jyväskylä Fin.

K

116 F2 K2 mt. China/Jammu and Kashmir
207 G4 Ka r. Nigeria
240 □D12 Ka'a'awa HI U.S.A.
210 B4 Kaabong Uganda
253 E4 Kaa-Iya del Gran Chaco, Parque Nacional nat. park Bol.
Kaakhka Turkm. see Kaka
240 □C12 Ka'ala mt. HI U.S.A.
78 □5 Kaala-Gomen New Caledonia
214 I5 Kaalpan salt pan S. Africa
215 P1 Kaalrug S. Africa
140 S2 Kaamanen Fin.
138 K4 Kääpa Estonia
215 P1 Kaapamuiden S. Africa
Kaapstad S. Africa see Cape Town
141 Q6 Kaarina Fin.
170 D4 Kaarßen Ger.
169 C8 Kaarst Ger.
206 C3 Kaarta reg. Mali
164 H5 Kaatsheuvel Neth.
140 T5 Kaavi Fin.
Kaba Xinjiang China see Habahe
121 V4 Kaba r. China/Kazakh.
177 K4 Kaba Hungary
93 B6 Kabaena i. Indon.
129 D5 Kabak Tepe mt. Turkey
206 C4 Kabala Sierra Leone
211 A5 Kabale Uganda
Kabalega Falls National Park Uganda see Murchison Falls National Park
209 E6 Kabalo Dem. Rep. Congo
209 E6 Kabambare Dem. Rep. Congo
121 L1 Kaban' Kazakh.
121 L1 Kabanbay Severnyy Kazakhstan Kazakh.
209 C6 Kabanga Dem. Rep. Congo
211 A5 Kabanga Tanz.
209 D7 Kabangu Dem. Rep. Congo
94 C3 Kabanjahe Sumatera Indon.
120 D1 Kabanovka Rus. Fed.
Kabanye Ukr. see Krasnorichens'ke
79 □7 Kabara i. Fiji
93 G4 Kabarai Papua Indon.
137 Q9 Kabardinka Rus. Fed.
Kabardino-Balkarskaya A.S.S.R. aut. rep. Rus. Fed. see Kabardino-Balkarskaya Respublika
129 E2 Kabardino-Balkarskaya Respublika aut. rep. Rus. Fed.
129 E2 Kabardino-Balkarskiy Zapovednik nature res. Rus. Fed.
208 F5 Kabare Dem. Rep. Congo
Kabarega National Park Uganda see Murchison Falls National Park
92 D8 Kabasalan Mindanao Phil.
105 L3 Kaba-san hill Japan
103 G14 Kaba-shima i. Japan
96 C5 Kabaung r. Myanmar
96 B3 Kabaw Valley Myanmar
129 B6 Kabayel Turkey
207 G5 Kabba Nigeria
114 E6 Kabbani r. India
140 P3 Kåbdalis Sweden
207 I3 Kabélawa Niger
226 J1 Kabenung Lake Ont. Can.
138 I2 Kaberneeme Estonia
205 F3 Kabertene Alg.
93 B3 Kabetan i. Indon.
226 B1 Kabetogama Lake MN U.S.A.
209 E6 Kabeya Dem. Rep. Congo
177 G4 Kab-hegy hill Hungary
224 C3 Kabinakagami r. Ont. Can.
224 C3 Kabinakagami Lake Ont. Can.
209 E6 Kabinda Dem. Rep. Congo
93 D8 Kabir Indon.
128 D3 Kabīr r. Syria
102 □B22 Kabira Nansei-shotō Japan
122 B5 Kabīrkūh mts Iran
129 I6 Käbirli Azer.
123 N6 Kabirwala Pak.
138 H3 Kabli Estonia
116 G9 Kabneshwar Mahar. India
208 C3 Kabo C.A.R.
Kabodiyon Tajik. see Kabutiyon
209 E8 Kabompo Zambia
209 D8 Kabompo r. Zambia
209 E7 Kabondo-Dianda Dem. Rep. Congo
95 I4 Kabong Sarawak Malaysia
209 E6 Kabongo Dem. Rep. Congo
97 C8 Kabosa Island Myanmar
208 D3 Kabou C.A.R.
207 F4 Kabou Togo
139 S3 Kabozha Rus. Fed.
206 A3 Kabrousse Senegal
124 F3 Kabshah, Jabal hills Saudi Arabia
122 I5 Kabūdeh Iran
122 H3 Kabūd Gonbad Iran
122 C4 Kabūd Rāhang Iran
92 C3 Kabugao Luzon Phil.
123 M4 Kābul Afgh.
123 M4 Kābul prov. Afgh.
123 O5 Kābul r. Afgh.
209 F8 Kabunda Dem. Rep. Congo
211 A7 Kabunda Zambia
93 A8 Kabunduk Sumba Indon.
105 J3 Kabura-gawa r. Japan
93 E2 Kaburuang i. Indon.
203 G5 Kabushiya Sudan
122 G6 Kabūtar Khān Iran
123 M3 Kabutiyon Tajik.
209 F8 Kabwe Zambia
120 J3 Kabyrga r. Kazakh.
196 J8 Kačanik Kosovo Serbia
93 F4 Kacepi Maluku Indon.
137 M9 Kacha r. Ukr.
123 K8 Kacha Daman Pak.
210 B4 Kachagalau mt. Kenya
Kachagani Georgia see Qach'aghani
123 I7 Kacha Kuh mts Iran/Pak.
135 I6 Kachalinskaya Rus. Fed.
123 K9 Kachari, Ras pt Pak.
116 B8 Kachchh, Gulf of Gujarat India
116 C7 Kachchh, Rann of marsh India
123 L6 Kachh Pak.
116 E7 Kachhola Rajasthan India
117 I7 Kachhwa Uttar Prad. India
207 G4 Kachia Nigeria
212 E3 Kachikau Botswana
96 C1 Kachin state Myanmar
121 Q1 Kachiry Kazakh.
210 C2 Kachīsī Eth.
211 A8 Kacholola Zambia
98 I1 Kachug Rus. Fed.
210 B4 Kachung Uganda
171 I10 Kačice Czech Rep.
127 J3 Kaçkar Dağı mt. Turkey
129 E6 Kaçmaz Turkey
167 H3 Kaczawa r. Pol.
174 E2 Kaczory Pol.
104 B7 Kada Japan
96 C6 Kadaingti Myanmar
114 E8 Kadaiyanallur Tamil Nadu India
210 B4 Kadam mt. Uganda
176 C1 Kadaň Czech Rep.
202 D6 Kadana Chad
123 K6 Kadanai r. Afgh./Pak.
97 D8 Kadan Kyun i. Myanmar
95 K7 Kadapongan i. Indon.
177 G5 Kadarkút Hungary
93 C6 Kadatuang i. Indon.
116 G6 Kadaura Uttar Prad. India
79 □7 Kadavu i. Fiji
79 □7a Kadavu Passage Fiji
107 P1 Kadaya Rus. Fed.
114 F3 Kaddam l. India
206 E5 Kade Ghana
102 □1 Kadena Okinawa Japan
87 I9 Kadgo, Lake salt flat W.A. Austr.
203 F4 Kadhdhāb, Sinn al esc. Egypt
Kādhimain Iraq see Al Kāẓimīyah
116 D8 Kadi Gujarat India
206 D4 Kadiana Mali
114 E8 Kadiapattanam Tamil Nadu India
Kadijica mt. Bulg. see Kadiytsa
199 H2 Kadıköy Çanakkale Turkey
199 K2 Kadıköy İstanbul Turkey
82 F5 Kadina S.A. Austr.
96 F5 Kading r. Laos
126 F4 Kadınhanı Turkey
206 D4 Kadiolo Mali
206 C4 Kadiondola, Mont mt. Guinea
114 F5 Kadiri Andhra Prad. India
126 H5 Kadirli Turkey
123 O6 Kadirpur Pak.
Kadiyevka Ukr. see Stakhanov
197 K9 Kadiytsa mt. Bulg.
207 F5 Kadjebi Ghana
114 C7 Kadmat atoll India
134 H4 Kadnikov Rus. Fed.
207 H5 Kado Nigeria
101 D9 Ka-do i. N. Korea
103 I14 Kadogawa Japan
94 E2 Kadok Malaysia
236 E4 Kadoka SD U.S.A.
135 H5 Kadom Rus. Fed.
213 F3 Kadoma Zimbabwe
96 B7 Kadonkani Myanmar
138 J2 Kadrina Estonia
208 F2 Kadugli Sudan
207 G4 Kaduna Nigeria
207 G4 Kaduna r. Nigeria
207 G4 Kaduna state Nigeria
114 E6 Kadur Karnataka India
108 A4 Kadusam mt. China/India
139 U2 Kaduy Rus. Fed.
134 H4 Kadyy Rus. Fed.
Kadzharan Armenia see K'ajaran
134 K2 Kadzherom Rus. Fed.
Kadzhi-Say Kyrg. see Kajy-Say
175 J2 Kadzidło Pol.
101 D9 Kaechon N. Korea
206 B2 Kaédi Maur.
225 K3 Kaegudeck Lake Nfld and Lab. Can.
207 I4 Kaélé Cameroon
240 □E13 Ka'elekū HI U.S.A.
240 □C12 Ka'ena Point HI U.S.A.

97 D8 Kaeng Krachan National Park Thai.
80 H2 Kaeo North I. N.Z.
168 I1 Kær Denmark
101 E10 Kaesŏng N. Korea
126 H8 Kāf Saudi Arabia
Kafa Ukr. see Feodosiya
209 D7 Kafakumba Dem. Rep. Congo
Kafan Armenia see Kapan
207 H4 Kafanchan Nigeria
Kāfar Qal'eh Iran see Eslām Qal'eh
215 K5 Kafferrivier S. Africa
207 H3 Kaffin-Hausa Nigeria
215 J5 Kaffir r. S. Africa
206 B3 Kaffrine Senegal
208 E2 Kafia Kingi Sudan
93 F4 Kafiau i. Papua Indon.
198 F5 Kafireos, Steno sea chan. Greece
123 N4 Kafiristan reg. Pak.
Kafirnigan Tajik. see Kofarnihon
206 D4 Kafolo Côte d'Ivoire
203 F2 Kafr ash Shaykh Egypt
126 E8 Kafr ash Shaykh governorate Egypt
128 E3 Kafr Buhum Syria
202 E2 Kafret Rihama Egypt
128 E4 Kafrūn Bashūr Syria
210 B4 Kafu r. Uganda
209 F8 Kafue Zambia
209 F8 Kafue r. Zambia
209 E8 Kafue Flats marsh Zambia
209 E8 Kafue National Park Zambia
104 D3 Kaga Japan
120 G1 Kaga Rus. Fed.
208 C3 Kaga Bandoro C.A.R.
137 S6 Kagal'nik Rus. Fed.
137 S6 Kagal'nik r. Rus. Fed.
135 H7 Kagal'nitskaya Rus. Fed.
105 L1 Kagamiishi Japan
123 O4 Kagan Pak.
Kagan Uzbek. see Kogon
106 G9 Kagang Qinghai China
Kaganovich Rus. Fed. see Tovarkovskiy
Kaganovichabad Tajik. see Kolkhozobod
Kaganovichi Pervyye Ukr. see Polis'ke
Kagarlyk Ukr. see Kaharlyk
103 L12 Kagawa pref. Japan
227 L4 Kagawong Ont. Can.
140 P4 Kåge Sweden
211 A5 Kagera admin. reg. Tanz.
215 L2 Kagiso S. Africa
127 K3 Kağızman Turkey
203 F6 Kagmar Sudan
94 C5 Kagologolo Indon.
208 C2 Kagopal Chad
105 I5 Kagosaka-tōge pass Japan
103 H15 Kagoshima Japan
102 □H15 Kagoshima pref. Japan
103 H15 Kagoshima-wan b. Japan
Kagul Moldova see Cahul
122 G3 Kāhak Iran
122 C3 Kahak Qazvin Iran
240 □E13 Kahakuloa HI U.S.A.
240 □B11 Kahala Point HI U.S.A.
240 □D12 Kahalu'u HI U.S.A.
211 B5 Kahama Tanz.
123 M7 Kahan Pak.
240 □D12 Kahana HI U.S.A.
136 J4 Kaharlyk Ukr.
93 E3 Kahatola i. Maluku Indon.
212 B4 Kahawero waterhole Namibia
95 K6 Kahayan r. Indon.
209 C6 Kahemba Dem. Rep. Congo
240 □C12 Kahe Point HI U.S.A.
81 B12 Kaherekoau Mountains South I. N.Z.
169 G10 Kahl r. Ger.
171 E9 Kahla Ger.
169 H10 Kahl am Main Ger.
222 F3 Kahntah B.C. Can.
Kahnu Iran see Kahnūj
122 G8 Kahnūj Kermān Iran
122 H6 Kahnūj Kermān Iran
206 C5 Kahnwia Liberia
80 H2 Kahoe North I. N.Z.
236 J5 Kahoka MO U.S.A.
104 E2 Kahoku-gata l. Japan
240 □E13 Kaho'olawe i. HI U.S.A.
130 D3 Kahperusvaarat mts Fin.
123 I8 Kahrād Iran
126 H5 Kahramanmaraş Turkey
123 N7 Kahror Pak.
126 I5 Kâhta Turkey
240 □F13 Kahuā HI U.S.A.
122 G4 Kahugish well Iran
80 □ Kahuitara Point Chatham Is S. Pacific Ocean
240 □D12 Kahuku HI U.S.A.
240 □C12 Kahuku Point HI U.S.A.
136 H8 Kahul, Ozero l. Ukr.
Kahulaui i. HI U.S.A. see Kaho'olawe
240 □E13 Kahului HI U.S.A.
122 H7 Kahūrak Iran
81 G8 Kahurangi National Park South I. N.Z.
80 G7 Kahurangi Point South I. N.Z.
123 O5 Kahuta Pak.
208 E5 Kahuzi-Biega, Parc National du nat. park Dem. Rep. Congo
91 H8 Kai, Kepulauan is Indon.
210 A3 Kaia r. Sudan
80 H2 Kaiaka North I. N.Z.
207 F4 Kaiama Nigeria
91 K8 Kaiapit P.N.G.
81 G10 Kaiapoi South I. N.Z.
241 T5 Kaibab AZ U.S.A.
241 T5 Kaibab Plateau AZ U.S.A.
106 E7 Kaibamardang Qinghai China
104 B5 Kaibara Japan
91 H8 Kai Besar i. Indon.
241 U5 Kaibito Plateau AZ U.S.A.
78 □6 Kaichui, Mount Guadalcanal Solomon Is
104 G4 Kaida Japan
110 H6 Kaidu He r. China
251 G3 Kaieteur Falls Guyana
107 N9 Kaifeng Henan China
107 N9 Kaifeng Henan China
80 H2 Kaihu North I. N.Z.
Kaihua Yunnan China see Wenshan
109 L4 Kaihua Zhejiang China
214 F5 Kaiingveld reg. S. Africa
108 F3 Kaijiang Sichuan China
91 H8 Kai Kecil i. Indon.
109 □J7 Kai Keung Leng H.K. China
80 H2 Kaikohe North I. N.Z.
81 H9 Kaikoura South I. N.Z.
81 H9 Kaikoura Peninsula South I. N.Z.
206 C4 Kailahun Sierra Leone
116 H5 Kailali Nepal
Kailas mt. Xizang China see Kangrinboqê Feng
117 N7 Kailashahar Tripura India
Kailas Range mts Xizang China see Gangdisê Shan
108 F5 Kaili Guizhou China
210 B3 Kailongong waterhole Kenya
107 Q5 Kailu Nei Mongol China
240 □D12 Kailua HI U.S.A.
240 □F14 Kailua-Kona HI U.S.A.
80 J4 Kaimai North I. N.Z.
80 J4 Kaimai-Mamaku Forest Park nature res. North I. N.Z.
80 J4 Kaimai Range hills North I. N.Z.
91 H7 Kaimana Papua Indon.
80 K5 Kaimanawa Forest Park nature res. North I. N.Z.
80 J6 Kaimanawa Mountains North I. N.Z.
108 A2 Kaimar Qinghai China
81 F9 Kaimata South I. N.Z.
116 G6 Kaimganj Uttar Prad. India
103 H15 Kaimon-dake hill Japan
116 H7 Kaimur Range hills India
138 F3 Käina Estonia
103 L13 Kainan Tokushima Japan
104 B7 Kainan Wakayama Japan
Kainda Kyrg. see Kayyngdy
96 B4 Kaing Myanmar
80 K5 Kaingaroa Forest North I. N.Z.
80 □ Kaingaroa Harbour b. Chatham Is S. Pacific Ocean
207 F3 Kaingiwa Nigeria
207 G4 Kainji Lake National Park Nigeria
207 G4 Kainji Lake National Park Nigeria
207 G4 Kainji Reservoir Nigeria
117 J9 Kaintaragarh Orissa India
140 Q3 Kainulasjärvi Sweden
80 I3 Kaipara Flats North I. N.Z.
80 I3 Kaipara Harbour North I. N.Z.
241 U4 Kaiparowits Plateau UT U.S.A.
109 I7 Kaiping Guangdong China
Kaiping Yunnan China see Dêqên
225 J2 Kaipokok Bay Nfld and Lab. Can.
Kaira Gujarat India see Kheda
80 K6 Kairakau Beach North I. N.Z.
140 S3 Kairala Fin.
116 F5 Kairana Uttar Prad. India
93 F5 Kairatu Seram Indon.
205 H2 Kairouan Tunisia
140 O2 Kaisepakte Sweden
178 F4 Kaisergebirge mts Austria
178 F4 Kaisergebirge nature res. Austria
172 D3 Kaiserslautern Ger.
263 F2 Kaiser Wilhelm II Land reg. Antarctica
100 F7 Kaishantun Jilin China
173 J4 Kaisheim Ger.
138 H7 Kaišiadorys Lith.
94 G6 Kait, Tanjung pt Indon.
103 J12 Kaita Japan
80 H2 Kaitaia North I. N.Z.
81 D13 Kaitangata South I. N.Z.
80 L5 Kaitawa North I. N.Z.
116 F8 Kaitha Madh. Prad. India
116 F5 Kaithal Haryana India
Kaitong Jilin China see Tongyu
140 P3 Kaitum Sweden
140 P3 Kaitumälven r. Sweden
93 E8 Kaiwatu Maluku Indon.
240 □D13 Kaiwi Channel HI U.S.A.
108 G3 Kaixian Chongqing China
108 F5 Kaiyang Guizhou China
107 S5 Kaiyuan Liaoning China
108 D7 Kaiyuan Yunnan China
Kaiyun Hunan China see Hengshan
104 E5 Kaizu Japan
104 B7 Kaizuka Japan
140 S4 Kajaani Fin.
84 H6 Kajabbi Qld Austr.
123 K5 Kajaki Afgh.
94 D3 Kajang Malaysia
123 N7 Kajanpur Pak.
85 L9 Kajarabie, Lake resr Qld Austr.
129 H6 K'ajaran Armenia
177 H5 Kajdacs Hungary
123 I8 Kajdar Iran
211 C5 Kajiado Kenya
105 H4 Kajikazawa Japan
103 H15 Kajiki Japan
208 E2 Kajok Sudan
210 A4 Kajo Kaji Sudan
176 D3 Kájov Czech Rep.
123 K5 Kajrān Afgh.
122 B3 Kaju Iran
83 J5 Kajuligah Nature Reserve N.S.W. Austr.
207 G4 Kajuru Nigeria
121 Q6 Kajy-Say Kyrg.
121 L1 Kak, Ozero salt l. Kazakh.
210 B2 Kaka Sudan
122 H3 Kaka Turkm.
95 M3 Kakaban i. Indon.
224 B3 Kakabeka Falls Ont. Can.
129 G4 Kakabet'i Georgia
93 C7 Kakabia i. Indon.
84 D2 Kakadu Aboriginal Land res. N.T. Austr.
84 D2 Kakadu National Park N.T. Austr.
223 M5 Kakagi Lake Ont. Can.
92 E8 Kakal r. Mindanao Phil.
93 A4 Kakali Sulawesi Barat Indon.
214 E4 Kakamas S. Africa
210 B4 Kakamega Kenya
104 E5 Kakamigahara Japan
209 A6 Kakamoéka Congo
115 M8 Kakana Andaman & Nicobar Is India
188 G3 Kakanj Bos.-Herz.
81 E12 Kakanui Mountains South I. N.Z.
123 L8 Kakar Pak.
207 H3 Kakarahil well Niger
80 I6 Kakaramea North I. N.Z.
80 J5 Kakaramea vol. North I. N.Z.
177 H5 Kakasd Hungary
206 C5 Kakata Liberia
80 J6 Kakatahi North I. N.Z.
117 O7 Kakching Manipur India
103 J12 Kake Japan
222 C3 Kake AK U.S.A.
105 H6 Kakegawa Japan
209 D6 Kakenge Dem. Rep. Congo
168 I4 Kakenstorf Ger.
170 D5 Kakerbeck Ger.
102 □G18 Kakeroma-jima i. Nansei-shotō Japan
211 B5 Kakesio Tanz.
129 C3 Kakhat'i Georgia
129 G3 Kakhet'is K'edi hills Georgia
Kakhi Azer. see Qax
129 H3 Kakhib Rus. Fed.
137 M7 Kakhovka Ukr.
137 M7 Kakhovs'ke Vodoskhovyshche resr Ukr.
122 H4 Kakht Iran
Kakhul Moldova see Cahul
122 D7 Kākī Iran
114 H4 Kakinada Andhra Prad. India
196 H8 Kakinjës, Maja e mt. Albania
222 G2 Kakisa N.W.T. Can.
222 G2 Kakisa r. N.W.T. Can.
222 G2 Kakisa Lake N.W.T. Can.
138 E5 Kākišķe Latvia
105 H1 Kakizaki Japan
209 C6 Kakobola Dem. Rep. Congo
104 A6 Kakogawa Japan
104 A6 Kako-gawa r. Japan
175 K4 Kąkolewnica Wschodnia Pol.
174 E4 Kąkolewo Pol.
211 A5 Kakonko Tanz.
106 B4 Kakpak Kuduk well Xinjiang China
206 E4 Kakpin Côte d'Ivoire
116 G6 Kakrala Uttar Prad. India
206 B4 Kakrima r. Guinea
119 L1 Kakshaal-Too mts China/Kyrg.
220 D2 Kaktovik AK U.S.A.
177 I4 Kakucs Hungary
102 R9 Kakuda Japan
210 B4 Kakuma Kenya
122 D6 Kakun Iran
95 J3 Kakus r. Malaysia
222 G4 Kakwa r. Alta Can.
222 F4 Kakwa Provincial Park B.C. Can.
222 G4 Kakwa Wildland Provincial Park Alta Can.
188 E3 Kal hill Croatia
177 J4 Kál Hungary
207 I3 Kala Nigeria
123 N6 Kala Pak.
211 A7 Kala Tanz.
205 H2 Kalaâ Kebira Tunisia
Kalaallit Nunaat terr. N. America see Greenland
123 N5 Kalabagh Pak.
93 D8 Kalabahi Indon.
Kalabak mt. Bulg./Greece see Radomir
Kalabáka Greece see Kalampaka
95 L2 Kalabakan Sabah Malaysia
Kalabákion Greece see Kalampaki
210 E2 Kalabaydh Togdheer Somalia
210 D2 Kalabaydh Woqooyi Galbeed Somalia
114 F4 Kalabgur Andhra Prad. India
82 H4 Kalabity S.A. Austr.
209 D8 Kalabo Zambia
135 H6 Kalach Rus. Fed.
123 L4 Kalacha Afgh.
210 C4 Kalacha Dida Kenya
135 H6 Kalach-na-Donu Rus. Fed.
96 A4 Kaladan r. India/Myanmar
224 E4 Kaladar Ont. Can.
114 D4 Kaladgi Karnataka India
93 B5 Kalaena r. Indon.
96 C3 Kalagwe Myanmar
212 D4 Kalahari Desert Africa
214 E1 Kalahari Gemsbok National Park S. Africa
240 □B12 Kalaheo HI U.S.A.
Kalaikhum Tajik. see Qal'aikhum
Kalai-Khumb Tajik. see Qal'aikhum
117 J6 Kalaiya Nepal
140 Q4 Kalajoki Fin.
140 Q4 Kalajoki r. Fin.
140 S1 Kalak Norway
197 O7 Kalakoch hill Bulg.
207 F4 Kalalé Benin
93 B4 Kalaliok Sulawesi Indon.
93 D1 Kalalusu i. Indon.
116 G9 Kalam Mahar. India
123 O4 Kalam Pak.
Kalámai Greece see Kalamata
198 D3 Kalamaki Greece
212 E4 Kalamare Botswana
198 D2 Kalamaria Greece
198 B3 Kalamas r. Greece
198 D5 Kalamata Greece
226 I7 Kalamazoo MI U.S.A.
226 H7 Kalamazoo r. MI U.S.A.
95 K7 Kalambau i. Indon.
114 E3 Kalamnuri Mahar. India
198 B4 Kalamos i. Greece
199 G6 Kalamos, Akrotirio pt Greece
198 C3 Kalampaka Greece
198 F1 Kalampaki Greece
137 M8 Kalamyts'ka Zatoka b. Ukr.
138 F3 Kalana Estonia
206 C4 Kalana Mali
111 C12 Kalanaur Haryana India
116 E4 Kalanaur Punjab India
137 M7 Kalanchak Ukr.
123 J7 Kalandi Pak.
Kalandula Angola see Calandula
210 B5 Kalangala Uganda
211 B6 Kalangali Tanz.
107 O1 Kalanguy Rus. Fed.
87 D11 Kalannie W.A. Austr.
202 D2 Kalanshiyū ar Ramlī al Kabīr, Sarīr des. Libya
116 E5 Kalanwali Haryana India
122 H8 Kālān Zīād Iran
93 B7 Kalao i. Indon.
240 □F14 Kalaoa HI U.S.A.
92 E8 Kalaong Mindanao Phil.
93 B7 Kalaotoa i. Indon.
114 F8 Kala Oya r. Sri Lanka
94 F5 Kalapa Indon.
240 □G14 Kalapana HI U.S.A.
122 I9 Kalar watercourse Iran
127 L6 Kalār Iraq
Kalarash Moldova see Călărași
139 S4 Kalashnikovo Rus. Fed.
96 F6 Kalasin Thai.
123 L5 Kalāt Afgh.
Kalāt Khorāsān Iran see Kabūd Gonbad
122 H9 Kalāt Sīstān va Balūchestān Iran
123 K9 Kalat Balochistan Pak.
123 L7 Kalat Balochistan Pak.
122 H4 Kalat, Kūh-e mt. Iran
123 I5 Kalata Barangak Afgh.
122 F3 Kalāteh-ye Molla Iran
240 □E12 Kalaupapa HI U.S.A.
135 I7 Kalaus r. Rus. Fed.
116 C8 Kalavad Gujarat India
198 D4 Kalavryta Greece
174 D3 Kaława Pol.
125 I8 Kalb, Ra's al c. Yemen
125 M3 Kalbā U.A.E.
129 H5 Kälbäcär Azer.
87 C9 Kalbarri W.A. Austr.
87 C9 Kalbarri National Park W.A. Austr.
214 C9 Kalbaskraal S. Africa
170 D5 Kalbe (Milde) Ger.
121 T3 Kalbinskiy Khrebet mts Kazakh.
122 H4 Kalbū Iran
179 J8 Kalce Slovenia
173 K2 Kalchreuth Ger.
137 Q6 Kal'chyk Ukr.
137 Q6 Kal'chyk r. Ukr.
176 G4 Káld Hungary
128 D2 Kaldırım Turkey
120 E3 Kaldygayty r. Kazakh.
199 K6 Kale Antalya Turkey
199 J5 Kale Denizli Turkey
129 A5 Kale Gümüşhane Turkey
129 A4 Kale r. Turkey
126 F3 Kalecik Turkey
93 C6 Kaledupa i. Indon.
169 J7 Kalefeld Ger.
96 C7 Kalegauk Island Myanmar
122 C3 Kaleh Sarai Iran
96 B5 Kaleindaung inlet Myanmar
210 B4 Kalekol Kenya
209 E6 Kalema Dem. Rep. Congo
209 F6 Kalemie Dem. Rep. Congo
96 B3 Kalemyo Myanmar
122 F4 Kāl-e Namak Iran
120 D3 Kalenoye Kazakh.
198 B3 Kalentzi Greece
188 G3 Kalesija Bos.-Herz.
174 G5 Kalety Pol.
140 U4 Kalevala Rus. Fed.
96 B3 Kalewa Myanmar
146 L11 Kale Water r. Scotland U.K.
122 B2 Kaleybar Iran
107 P1 Kalga Rus. Fed.
87 D13 Kalgan r. W.A. Austr.
Kalgan Hebei China see Zhangjiakou
114 D5 Kalghatgi Karnataka India
87 F11 Kalgoorlie W.A. Austr.
207 H3 Kalguéri Niger
122 H6 Kāl Gūsheh Iran
188 E3 Kali Croatia
116 H5 Kali r. India/Nepal
197 Q7 Kaliakra, Nos pt Bulg.
94 F7 Kalianda Sumatera Indon.
92 D6 Kalibo Panay Phil.
232 A8 Kalida OH U.S.A.
94 C6 Kaliet Indon.
123 M3 Kalifgan Afgh.
117 J6 Kali Gandaki r. Nepal
114 F5 Kaligiri Andhra Prad. India
Kalikata W. Bengal India see Kolkata
139 W9 Kalikino Rus. Fed.
208 E5 Kalima Dem. Rep. Congo
95 I6 Kalimantan reg. Indon.
95 I4 Kalimantan Barat prov. Indon.
95 K6 Kalimantan Selatan prov. Indon.
95 J5 Kalimantan Tengah prov. Indon.
95 L3 Kalimantan Timur prov. Indon.
177 G5 Kali-medence park Hungary
Kálimnos i. Greece see Kalymnos
117 L6 Kalimpang W. Bengal India
114 D5 Kalinadi r. India
116 H6 Kali Nadi r. India
211 B7 Kalinda Zambia
115 I3 Kalingapatnam Andhra Prad. India
Kalinin Kyrg. see Tash-Bashat
Kalinin Rus. Fed. see Tver'
Kalinin Turkm. see Boldumsaz
Kalininabad Tajik. see Kalininobod
Kalinin Adyndaky Tajik. see Cheshtebe
137 M8 Kalinine Ukr.
138 D7 Kaliningrad Rus. Fed.
Kaliningrad Oblast admin. div. Rus. Fed. see Kaliningradskaya Oblast'
138 E7 Kaliningradskaya Oblast' admin. div. Rus. Fed.
138 C7 Kaliningradskiy Zaliv b. Rus. Fed.
129 G4 Kalininkänd Azer.
Kalinino Armenia see Tashir
175 K1 Kalinino Kaliningradskaya Oblast' Rus. Fed.
134 H4 Kalinino Kostromskaya Oblast' Rus. Fed.
137 S8 Kalinino Krasnodarskiy Kray Rus. Fed.
121 O1 Kalinino Omskaya Oblast' Rus. Fed.
134 L4 Kalinino Permskaya Oblast' Rus. Fed.
123 M3 Kalininobod Tajik.
Kalininsk Moldova see Cupcina
135 I6 Kalininsk Rus. Fed.
135 G7 Kalininskaya Rus. Fed.
Kalininskaya Oblast' admin. div. Rus. Fed. see Tverskaya Oblast'
137 L6 Kalinins'ke Ukr.
116 E8 Kalinjara Rajasthan India
136 I1 Kalinkavichy Belarus
Kalinkovichi Belarus see Kalinkavichy
129 J6 Kalinovka Azer.
120 F3 Kalinovka Kazakh.
137 N2 Kalinovka Rus. Fed.
Kalinovka Ukr. see Kalynivka
129 G2 Kalinovskaya Rus. Fed.
129 H2 Kalinovskiy Rus. Fed.
174 G4 Kalinowa Pol.
175 K2 Kalinowo Pol.
210 B4 Kaliro Uganda
210 F2 Kalis Somalia
95 J9 Kalisat Jawa Indon.
Kalisch Pol. see Kalisz
114 E1 Kali Sindh r. India
174 G2 Kaliska Pol.
238 G2 Kalispell MT U.S.A.
176 D3 Kaliště hill Czech Rep.
174 G4 Kalisz Pol.
174 D2 Kalisz Pomorski Pol.
122 G7 Kalituyeh Iran
135 H6 Kalitva r. Rus. Fed.
211 A6 Kaliua Tanz.
116 H7 Kaliujar Uttar Prad. India
140 Q4 Kalix Sweden
140 Q4 Kalixälven r. Sweden
116 F4 Kalka Haryana India
137 Q6 Kalka r. Ukr.
179 J4 Kalkalpen, Nationalpark nat. park Austria
199 K6 Kalkan Turkey
129 B5 Kalkandere Turkey
169 B7 Kalkar Ger.
84 C4 Kalkaringi N.T. Austr.
226 I5 Kalkaska MI U.S.A.
212 C4 Kalkfeld Namibia
215 J5 Kalkfonteindam dam S. Africa
215 J5 Kalkfontein Dam Nature Reserve S. Africa
170 D3 Kalkhorst Ger.
114 G9 Kalkudah Sri Lanka
251 G3 Kalkuni Guyana
214 F4 Kalkwerf S. Africa
169 C9 Kall Ger.
114 F7 Kallakkurichchi Tamil Nadu India
82 F2 Kallakoopah Creek watercourse S.A. Austr.
140 N3 Kallaktjåkkå mt. Sweden
114 E3 Kallam Mahar. India
142 J3 Kållandsö i. Sweden
94 □ Kallang Sing.
94 □ Kallang r. Sing.
138 K3 Kallaste Estonia
140 S5 Kallavesi l. Fin.
140 L5 Kållberget Sweden
140 Q4 Kallfjärden b. Sweden
179 I3 Kallham Austria
198 D4 Kallidromo mts Greece
198 C3 Kallifoni Greece
143 L5 Kallinge Sweden
196 H9 Kallmet i Madh Albania
173 L3 Kallmünz Ger.
198 G5 Kalloni Tinos Greece
199 H3 Kallonis, Kolpos b. Lesvos Greece
177 K4 Kállósemjén Hungary
140 L5 Kallsjön l. Sweden
114 E4 Kallur Karnataka India
120 K4 Kalmakkyrgan watercourse Kazakh.
177 K4 Kálmánháza Hungary
121 T1 Kalmanka Rus. Fed.
143 M5 Kalmar Sweden
143 M4 Kalmar county Sweden
143 M4 Kalmarsund sea chan. Sweden
172 E3 Kalmit hill Ger.
137 Q6 Kal'mius r. Ukr.
165 F6 Kalmthout Belgium
165 F6 Kalmthoutse Heide Natuurreservaat nature res. Belgium
122 G3 Kalmūkh Qal'eh Iran
114 G9 Kalmunai Sri Lanka
Kalmykia aut. rep. Rus. Fed. see Kalmykiya-Khalm'g-Tangch, Respublika
135 I7 Kalmykiya-Khalm'g-Tangch, Respublika aut. rep. Rus. Fed.
Kalmykovo Kazakh. see Taypak
Kalmytskaya Avtonomnaya Oblast' aut. rep. Rus. Fed. see Kalmykiya-Khalm'g-Tangch, Respublika
117 I8 Kalnai Chhattisgarh India
177 H3 Kalná nad Hronom Slovakia
138 G5 Kalnciems Latvia
117 M7 Kalni r. Bangl.
188 F2 Kalnik mts Croatia
177 H5 Kalocsa Hungary
136 F2 Kalodnaye Belarus
240 □D13 Kalohi Channel HI U.S.A.
128 A3 Kalokhorio Cyprus
209 E6 Kaloko Dem. Rep. Congo
116 D8 Kalol Gujarat India
116 D8 Kalol Gujarat India
93 D2 Kaloma i. Indon.
209 E9 Kalomo Zambia
96 C3 Kalon Myanmar
222 E4 Kalone Peak B.C. Can.
93 E1 Kalongan Sulawesi Indon.
128 A4 Kalopanagiotis Cyprus
78 □6 Kalourat, Mount Malaita Solomon Is
122 B2 Kalow r. Iran
177 H5 Káloz Hungary
140 U3 Kalozhnoye, Ozero l. Rus. Fed.
116 G4 Kalpa Hima. Prad. India
198 B3 Kalpaki Greece
114 C7 Kalpeni atoll India
114 E7 Kalpetta Kerala India
116 G6 Kalpi Uttar Prad. India
110 D6 Kalpin Xinjiang China
114 F8 Kalpitiya Sri Lanka
Kalquduq Uzbek. see Ko'lquduq
127 M6 Kal Safīd Iran
178 G5 Kals am Großglockner Austria
179 L6 Kalsdorf bei Graz Austria
122 G3 Kāl-Shūr, Rūd-e r. Iran
116 F4 Kalsi Uttaranchal India
220 C3 Kaltag AK U.S.A.
138 I6 Kaltanėnai Lith.
134 K5 Kaltasy Rus. Fed.
190 G1 Kaltbrunn Switz.
178 E5 Kaltenbach Austria
168 I3 Kaltenkirchen Ger.
169 J9 Kaltennordheim Ger.
169 J9 Kaltensundheim Ger.
169 J9 Kaltenwestheim Ger.
138 F6 Kaltinėnai Lith.
84 B8 Kaltukatjara N.T. Austr.
207 H4 Kaltungo Nigeria
116 D5 Kalu Rajasthan India
114 C3 Kalu r. India
240 □E12 Kalua'aha HI U.S.A.
196 I6 Kaluđerica Serbia
139 T7 Kaluga Rus. Fed.
Kaluga Oblast admin. div. Rus. Fed. see Kaluzhskaya Oblast'
137 L6 Kaluha Ukr.
95 L7 Kalukalukuang i. Indon.
93 A5 Kaluku Sulawesi Barat Indon.
95 K3 Kalulong, Bukit mt. Malaysia
209 F8 Kalulushi Zambia
86 I3 Kalumburu W.A. Austr.
86 I3 Kalumburu Aboriginal Reserve W.A. Austr.
142 H6 Kalundborg Denmark
209 E7 Kalundwe Dem. Rep. Congo
95 L1 Kalupis Falls Malaysia
123 N5 Kalur Kot Pak.
136 D4 Kalush Ukr.
175 J3 Kałuszyn Pol.
114 F9 Kalutara Sri Lanka
139 S7 Kaluzhskaya Oblast' admin. div. Rus. Fed.
141 H6 Kalvåg Norway
116 E9 Kalvan Mahar. India
138 G7 Kalvarija Lith.
138 I7 Kalveliai Lith.
134 C3 Kälviä Fin.
141 S6 Kalvitsa Fin.
141 R6 Kalvola Fin.
175 I2 Kalwa, Jezioro l. Pol.
114 F4 Kalwakurti Andhra Prad. India
179 K5 Kalwang Austria
175 H6 Kalwaria Zebrzydowska Pol.
134 L3 Kal'ya Rus. Fed.
114 C3 Kalyan Mahar. India
114 E5 Kalyandurg Andhra Prad. India
114 E4 Kalyani Karnataka India
115 H3 Kalyansingapuram Orissa India
139 U4 Kalyazin Rus. Fed.
136 E2 Kalyena Belarus
199 H6 Kalymnos Greece
199 H5 Kalymnos i. Greece
136 J3 Kalynivka Kyivs'ka Oblast' Ukr.
137 O8 Kalynivka Respublika Krym Ukr.
136 H4 Kalynivka Vinnyts'ka Oblast' Ukr.
139 N6 Kalyshki Belarus
137 K3 Kalyta Ukr.
199 J6 Kalythies Rodos Greece
198 C4 Kalyvia Greece
207 H4 Kam Nigeria
209 E5 Kama Dem. Rep. Congo
96 B5 Kama Myanmar
134 K4 Kama Rus. Fed.
134 K4 Kama r. Rus. Fed.
105 K4 Kamagaya Japan
102 S7 Kamaishi Japan
103 □3 Kama-iwa i. Japan
105 K5 Kamakura Japan
251 G3 Kamakusa Guyana
206 B4 Kamakwie Sierra Leone
202 C4 Kamal Chad
114 F5 Kamalapuram Andhra Prad. India
123 O6 Kamalia Pak.
240 □E12 Kamalō HI U.S.A.
96 C6 Kamamaung Myanmar
116 F6 Kaman Rajasthan India
126 F4 Kaman Turkey
105 I4 Kamanashi-gawa r. Japan
105 H4 Kamanashi-yama mt. Japan
214 G9 Kamanassie r. S. Africa
214 G9 Kamanassieberg mts S. Africa
227 Q4 Kamaniskeg Lake Ont. Can.
212 B3 Kamanjab Namibia
78 □6 Kamaosi Sta Isabel Solomon Is
124 F8 Kamaran Yemen
124 F8 Kamarān i. Yemen
251 F3 Kamarang Guyana
Kamaran Island Yemen see Kamarān
123 L4 Kamard reg. Afgh.
138 H5 Kamarde Latvia
114 F3 Kamareddi Andhra Prad. India
198 C4 Kamares Dytiki Ellas Greece
198 F6 Kamares Sifnos Greece
251 G3 Kamaria Falls Guyana
129 G4 Kämärli Azer.
Kamarlu Armenia see Artashat
136 J2 Kamaryn Belarus
Kamashi Uzbek. see Qamashi
116 H7 Kamasin Uttar Prad. India
213 E3 Kamativi Zimbabwe
207 F4 Kamba Nigeria
96 D2 Kambaiti Myanmar
208 C3 Kamba Kota C.A.R.
87 F11 Kambalda W.A. Austr.
134 I1 Kambal'nitskiye Koshki, Ostrova is Rus. Fed.
114 E8 Kambam Tamil Nadu India
94 D5 Kambang Sumatera Indon.
95 H9 Kambangan i. Indon.
209 C6 Kamba-Poko Dem. Rep. Congo
Kambara i. Fiji see Kabara
Kambara Japan see Kanbara
110 E6 Kambardi Xinjiang China
134 K4 Kambarka Rus. Fed.
206 B4 Kambia Sierra Leone
Kambing, Pulau i. East Timor see Ataúro, Ilha de
86 □2 Kambling Island Cocos Is
Kambo-san mt. N. Korea see Kwanmo-bong
209 E7 Kambove Dem. Rep. Congo
93 B5 Kambuno, Bukit mt. Indon.
197 O7 Kamburovo Bulg.
202 E2 Kambūt Libya
131 R4 Kamchatka r. Rus. Fed.
131 Q4 Kamchatka, Poluostrov pen. Rus. Fed.
266 G2 Kamchatka Basin sea feature Bering Sea
Kamchatka Peninsula Rus. Fed. see Kamchatka, Poluostrov
131 R4 Kamchatskiy Proliv str. Rus. Fed.
131 R4 Kamchatskiy Zaliv b. Rus. Fed.
197 P7 Kamchiya r. Bulg.
197 P8 Kamchiyska Planina hills Bulg.
214 H3 Kamden S. Africa
123 N4 Kamdesh Afgh.
Kameia, Parque Nacional de nat. park Angola see Cameia, Parque Nacional da
120 C1 Kamelik r. Rus. Fed.
197 N7 Kamen Bulg.
169 E7 Kamen Ger.
131 K3 Kamen', Gory mts Rus. Fed.
209 E6 Kamende Dem. Rep. Congo
176 D3 Kamenec mt. Czech Rep.
Kamenets-Podol'skiy Ukr. see Kam"yanets'-Podil's'kyy
197 K7 Kamenica Serbia
177 J2 Kamenica Slovakia
176 E2 Kamenice nad Lipou Czech Rep.
171 J9 Kamenický Šenov Czech Rep.
177 H4 Kameničná Slovakia
177 H4 Kamenín Slovakia
126 A3 Kamenitsa mt. Bulg.
197 M7 Kamenitsa r. Bulg.
177 H6 Kamenjak hill Croatia
188 D3 Kamenjak, Rt pt Croatia
120 D2 Kamenka Kazakh.
Kamenka Moldova see Camenca
134 I2 Kamenka Arkhangel'skaya Oblast' Rus. Fed.
139 S7 Kamenka Kaluzhskaya Oblast' Rus. Fed.
138 M1 Kamenka Leningradskaya Oblast' Rus. Fed.
135 I5 Kamenka Penzenskaya Oblast' Rus. Fed.
100 J6 Kamenka Primorskiy Kray Rus. Fed.
139 P6 Kamenka Smolenskaya Oblast' Rus. Fed.
135 G6 Kamenka Voronezhskaya Oblast' Rus. Fed.
Kamenka Ukr. see Kam"yanka
Kamenka-Bugskaya Ukr. see Kam"yanka-Buz'ka
Kamenka-Shevchenkovskaya Ukr. see Kam"yanka
Kamen'-Kashirskiy Ukr. see Kamin'-Kashyrs'kyy
Kamenka-Strumilovskaya Ukr. see Kam"yanka-Buz'ka
139 U5 Kamenki Rus. Fed.
130 J4 Kamen'-na-Obi Rus. Fed.
134 G4 Kamenniki Rus. Fed.
138 M1 Kamennogorsk Rus. Fed.
129 B1 Kamennomostskiy Rus. Fed.
140 U4 Kamennoye, Ozero l. Rus. Fed.
176 D2 Kamenný Přívoz Czech Rep.
176 D3 Kamenný Újezd Czech Rep.
197 P8 Kameno Bulg.
137 T6 Kamenolomni Rus. Fed.
Kamenongue Angola see Camanongue
100 H6 Kamen'-Rybolov Rus. Fed.
135 I6 Kamenskiy Rus. Fed.
131 R3 Kamenskoye Koryakskiy Avtonomnyy Okrug Rus. Fed.
139 V9 Kamenskoye Lipetskaya Oblast' Rus. Fed.
Kamenskoye Ukr. see Dniprodzerzhyns'k
135 H6 Kamensk-Shakhtinskiy Rus. Fed.
130 H4 Kamensk-Ural'skiy Rus. Fed.
171 J8 Kamenz Ger.
104 C5 Kameoka Japan
210 B4 Kameramaido Uganda
170 F5 Kamern Ger.
146 F11 Kames Argyll and Bute, Scotland U.K.
139 X5 Kameshkovo Rus. Fed.
111 D11 Kamet mt. Xizang China
104 D6 Kameyama Japan
196 H9 Kamëz Albania
104 A5 Kami Hyōgo Japan
105 G5 Kami Nagano Japan
103 G12 Kamiagata Japan
238 F3 Kamiah ID U.S.A.
104 F2 Kamichi Japan
175 L4 Kamień Lubelskie Pol.
175 K5 Kamień Podkarpackie Pol.
175 I6 Kamienica Pol.
174 E3 Kamieniec Pol.
174 E5 Kamieniec Ząbkowicki Pol.
174 F2 Kamień Krajeński Pol.
175 J4 Kamienna r. Pol.
174 E5 Kamienna Gora Pol.
174 F5 Kamiennik Pol.
174 C2 Kamień Pomorski Pol.
175 H4 Kamieńsk Pol.
170 K5 Kamień Wielkie Pol.
214 C6 Kamiesberg S. Africa
214 C6 Kamiesberge mts S. Africa
214 B6 Kamieskroon S. Africa
105 K4 Kamifukuoka Japan
102 T3 Kamifurano Japan
104 D5 Kami-ishizu Japan
209 D6 Kamiji Dem. Rep. Congo
104 E6 Kami-jima i. Japan
102 T3 Kamikawa Hokkaidō Japan
105 J3 Kamikawa Saitama Japan
105 K2 Kamikawachi Japan
104 C7 Kamikitayama Japan
103 G15 Kami-Koshiki-jima i. Japan
105 I4 Kamikuishiki Japan
84 H5 Kamileroi Qld Austr.
223 K2 Kamilukuak Lake Nunavut Can.
209 E7 Kamina Dem. Rep. Congo
209 E7 Kamina Base Dem. Rep. Congo
104 C5 Kaminaka Japan
223 M2 Kaminak Lake Nunavut Can.
136 D2 Kamin'-Kashyrs'kyy Ukr.
104 F4 Kaminoho Japan
105 K3 Kaminokawa Japan
102 R5 Kaminokuni Japan
102 □G18 Kaminone-jima i. Nansei-shotō Japan
102 R8 Kaminoyama Japan
188 E2 Kaminške in Savinjske Alpe mts Slovenia
139 Y4 Kaminskiy Rus. Fed.
Kaminuriak Lake Nunavut Can. see Qamanirjuaq Lake
104 F3 Kamioka Japan
175 I3 Kamion Mazowieckie Pol.
175 I4 Kamion Mazowieckie Pol.
175 K4 Kamionka Pol.
199 I6 Kamiros Rodos Greece
104 D3 Kamishihi Japan
102 U3 Kamishihoro Japan
105 M4 Kamisu Japan
104 E3 Kami-taira Japan
104 F3 Kami-takara Japan
103 G12 Kamitsushima Japan
209 F5 Kamituga Dem. Rep. Congo
104 F5 Kami-yahagi Japan
102 □H16 Kamiyaku Japan
105 H3 Kamiyamada Japan
102 U2 Kamiyūbetsu Japan
117 O7 Kamjong Manipur India
121 N5 Kamkaly Kazakh.
117 K6 Kamla r. India
117 N6 Kamla r. India
121 U2 Kamlak Rus. Fed.
222 F5 Kamloops B.C. Can.
222 F5 Kamloops Lake B.C. Can.
173 I5 Kammel r. Ger.
214 I9 Kammiebos S. Africa
173 I5 Kammlach Ger.
Kammuri-jima i. Japan see Kanmuri-jima
Kammuri-yama mt. Japan see Kanmuri-yama
188 E2 Kamnik Slovenia
179 I7 Kamno Slovenia
Kamo Armenia see Gavarr
104 C6 Kamo Kyōto Japan
105 I6 Kamo Yamanashi Japan
80 I2 Kamo North I. N.Z.
203 H5 Kamob Sanha Sudan
104 A8 Kamoda-misaki pt Japan
102 R3 Kamoenai Japan
105 L5 Kamogawa Japan
103 L12 Kamojima Japan
123 P6 Kamoke Pak.
209 E6 Kamola Dem. Rep. Congo
211 A6 Kamonanira Tanz.
179 M3 Kamp r. Austria
169 E10 Kamp Ger.
94 F5 Kampa Indon.
210 B4 Kampala Uganda
198 F4 Kampanos, Akrotirio pt Andros Greece
94 E4 Kampar r. Indon.
94 D2 Kampar Malaysia
117 I8 Kampara Chhattisgarh India
138 F4 Kamparkalns hill Latvia
94 D4 Kamparkiri r. Indon.
168 F1 Kampen Ger.
164 I3 Kampen Neth.
209 E5 Kampene Dem. Rep. Congo
172 F4 Kämpfelbach Ger.
96 D6 Kamphaeng Phet Thai.
211 B6 Kampi Katoto Tanz.
175 I3 Kampinos Pol.
175 I3 Kampinoski Park Narodowy nat. park Pol.
114 E5 Kampli Karnataka India
169 C8 Kamp-Lintfort Ger.
103 G11 Kamp'o S. Korea
209 F7 Kampolombo, Lake Zambia
97 G9 Kâmpóng Cham Cambodia
97 G8 Kâmpóng Chhnăng Cambodia
97 G8 Kâmpóng Khleăng Cambodia
Kâmpóng Saôm Cambodia see Sihanoukville
97 G9 Kâmpóng Spœ Cambodia
97 G8 Kâmpóng Thum Cambodia
97 G9 Kâmpóng Trâbêk Cambodia
97 G9 Kâmpóng Tranch Cambodia
97 G9 Kâmpôt Cambodia
206 E4 Kampti Burkina
Kampuchea country Asia see Cambodia
91 H7 Kamrau, Teluk b. Papua Indon.
223 K5 Kamsack Sask. Can.
206 B4 Kamsar Guinea
171 D9 Kamsdorf Ger.
134 K3 Kamskiy Rus. Fed.
135 J5 Kamskoye Ust'ye Rus. Fed.
134 L4 Kamskoye Vodokhranilishche resr Rus. Fed.
210 D4 Kamsuuma Somalia
116 H9 Kamtha Mahar. India
223 K3 Kamuchawie Lake Man./Sask. Can.
102 T4 Kamui-dake mt. Japan
210 B4 Kamuli Uganda
209 E6 Kamungu Dem. Rep. Congo
177 J5 Kamut Hungary
210 A4 Kamwenge Uganda
136 G2 Kam"yane Rivnens'ka Oblast' Ukr.
137 N3 Kam"yane Sums'ka Oblast' Ukr.
136 F5 Kam"yanets'-Podil's'kyy Ukr.
137 L4 Kam"yanka Cherkas'ka Oblast' Ukr.
137 Q4 Kam"yanka Kharkivs'ka Oblast' Ukr.
137 L5 Kam"yanka r. Ukr.
136 D3 Kam"yanka-Buz'ka U
137 N6 Kam"yanka-Dniprovs
136 I8 Kam"yans'ke Odes'ka Oblast' Ukr.
137 O6 Kam"yans'ke Zaporiz' Oblast' Ukr.
138 G9 Kamyanyets Belarus
138 G9 Kamyanyuki Belarus
122 B4 Kāmyārān Iran
138 L6 Kamyen' Belarus
138 H8 Kamyenka Belarus
135 G7 Kamyshevatskaya Ru
135 I6 Kamyshin Rus. Fed.
135 K5 Kamyshla Rus. Fed.
120 I4 Kamyshlybash Kazak
Kamyshnaya r. Rus. F see Komyshna
120 C3 Kamysh-Samarskiye lakes Kazakh.
Kamyslybas Kazakh. s Kamyshlybash
120 I4 Kamyslybas, Ozero l.
120 I2 Kamysty Kazakh.
120 C4 Kamyzyak Rus. Fed.
125 M2 Kamzar Oman
131 K4 Kan r. Rus. Fed.
210 A2 Kan Sudan
208 F4 Kana Dem. Rep. Cong
213 E3 Kana r. Zimbabwe
224 E2 Kanaaupscow r. Que.
241 T4 Kanab UT U.S.A.
241 T5 Kanab Creek r. AZ U.
79 □7 Kanacea Taveuni Fiji
105 G5 Kanae Japan
220 A4 Kanaga Island AK U.S
105 J5 Kanagawa pref. Japa
102 R6 Kanagi Japan
251 F3 Kanaima Falls Guyan
225 J2 Kanairiktok r. Nfld and
123 L7 Kanak Pak.
114 E6 Kanakapura Karnatak
179 I7 Kanal Slovenia
198 F5 Kanala Kythnos Greec
198 B3 Kanali Greece
198 B3 Kanallaki Greece
127 L7 Kan'ān Iraq
140 M4 Kanan Sweden
215 K2 Kanana S. Africa
209 D6 Kananga Dem. Rep. C
83 M5 Kanangra-Boyd Natio Park N.S.W. Austr.
Kanarak Orissa India s Konarka
241 S4 Kanarraville UT U.S.A
214 B3 Kanas watercourse N
105 L2 Kanasagō Japan
134 I5 Kanash Rus. Fed.
110 H2 Kanas Köl l. China
Kanathea Taveuni Fiji Kanacea
134 K3 Kanava Rus. Fed.
95 K3 Kanawang, Bukit mt. Malaysia
232 C10 Kanawha r. WV U.S.A
105 H6 Kanaya Shizuoka Japa
104 B7 Kanaya Wakayama Ja
104 F4 Kanayama Japan
121 S3 Kanayka Kazakh.
104 E2 Kanazawa Ishikawa Ja
105 K5 Kanazawa Kanagawa
104 D3 Kanazu Japan
96 B3 Kanbalu Myanmar
105 I5 Kanbara Japan
97 D8 Kanchanaburi Thai.
Kanchanjanga mt. In see Kangchenjunga
117 L6 Kanchenjunga Conse Area nature res. Nepa
114 F6 Kanchipuram Tamil N
175 K6 Kańczuga Pol.
123 L6 Kand mt. Pak.
123 L7 Kanda Pak.
123 K6 Kandahār Afgh.
123 K6 Kandahār prov. Afgh.
114 E3 Kandahar Mahar. Indi
140 V3 Kandalaksha Rus. Fe
134 F2 Kandalakshskiy Zaliv Rus. Fed.
209 C6 Kandale Dem. Rep. C
94 B3 Kandang Sumatera In
95 K6 Kandangan Kalimanta
138 F4 Kandava Latvia
Kandavu i. Fiji see Ka
Kandavu Passage Fij Kadavu Passage
207 F4 Kandé Togo
172 E3 Kandel Ger.
172 E5 Kandel mt. Ger.
170 H2 Kandelin Ger.
190 D2 Kander r. Switz.
172 D6 Kandern Ger.
190 D3 Kandersteg Switz.
123 M7 Kandhkot Pak.
123 N4 Kandhura Pak.
207 F4 Kandi Benin
123 L7 Kandi Pak.
93 B3 Kandi, Tanjung pt Inc
123 M8 Kandiaro Pak.
198 B4 Kandila Dytiki Ellas Gr
198 D5 Kandila Peloponnisos
207 H3 Kandil Bouzou well N
129 E6 Kandil Dağı mt. Turke
129 B6 Kandilli Turkey
199 L1 Kandıra Turkey
208 D3 Kandja C.A.R.
116 C8 Kandla Gujarat India
113 □1 Kandooma Fushi i. S Maldives
83 L5 Kandos N.S.W. Austr.
115 J1 Kandra Jharkhand Ind
213 □J3 Kandreho Madag.
117 I8 Kandri Chhattisgarh In
91 K8 Kandrian New Britain
114 F5 Kandukur Andhra Pra
114 G9 Kandy Sri Lanka
120 G3 Kandyagash Kazakh.
232 G7 Kane PA U.S.A.
221 L2 Kane Bassin b. Green
122 E8 Kaneh watercourse Ir
202 B6 Kanem pref. Chad
240 □D12 Kāne'ohe HI U.S.A.
240 □D12 Kāne'ohe Bay HI U.S
116 E7 Kanera Rajasthan Indi
123 L7 Kaneti Pak.
Kanev Ukr. see Kaniv
134 G2 Kanevka Rus. Fed.
135 G7 Kanevskaya Rus. Fed
104 F5 Kaneyama Gifu Japan
103 R8 Kaneyama Yamagata
191 P5 Kanfanar Croatia
206 B4 Kanfarande Guinea
123 I6 Kang Afgh.
212 D4 Kang Botswana
117 L9 Kanga r. Bangl.
221 M3 Kangaamiut Greenlan
221 K2 Kangaarsussuaq c. G
221 M3 Kangaatsiaq Greenla
206 C4 Kangaba Mali
126 H4 Kangal Turkey
131 N3 Kangalassy Rus. Fed.
122 E8 Kangān Būshehr Iran
122 G9 Kangān Hormozgan Ir
86 E6 Kangan Aboriginal R W.A. Austr.
Kangandala, Parque Nacional de nat. park see Cangandala, Parq Nacional de
94 D1 Kangar Malaysia
206 C4 Kangaré Mali
82 F6 Kangaroo Island S.A.
84 G4 Kangaroo Point Qld A
251 G3 Kangaruma Guyana
141 R6 Kangasala Fin.
140 T5 Kangaslampi Fin.
141 S6 Kangasniemi Fin.
122 B4 Kangāvar Iran
114 E7 Kangayam Tamil Nadu
107 N6 Kangbao Hebei China
117 L6 Kangchenjunga mt. India/Nepal
108 C3 Kangding Sichuan Ch
95 K8 Kangean, Kepulauan Indon.
221 L3 Kangeeak Point Nuna
210 B3 Kangen r. Sudan
221 N3 Kangeq c. Greenland
221 M3 Kangerluarsoruseq Greenland
221 M3 Kangerlussuaq Greer

Kangerlussuaq *inlet* Greenland
Kangerlussuaq *inlet* Greenland
Kangerlussuaq *inlet* Greenland
Kangerlussuatsiaq *inlet* Greenland
Kangersuatsiaq Greenland
Kangertittivaq *sea chan.* Greenland
Kangertittivatsiaq *inlet* Greenland
Kangetet Kenya
Kanggye N. Korea
Kangikajik *c.* Greenland
Kangilinnguit Greenland
Kangiqcliniq *Nunavut* Can. *see* **Rankin Inlet**
Kangiqsualujjuaq *Que.* Can.
Kangiqsujuaq *Que.* Can.
Kangiqtugaapik *Nunavut* Can. *see* **Clyde River**
Kangirsuk *Que.* Can.
Kang Krung National Park Thai.
Kangle *Gansu* China
Kangle *Jiangxi* China *see* **Wanzai**
Kangmar *Xizang* China
Kangnŭng S. Korea
Kango Gabon
Kangoku-iwa *i.* Japan
Kangos Sweden
Kangping *Liaoning* China
Kangra *Hima. Prad.* India
Kangri Karpo Pass China/India
Kangrinboqê Feng *mt.* *Xizang* China
Kangro *Xizang* China
Kangsangdobdê *Xizang* China *see* **Xainza**
Kang Tipayan Dakula *i.* Phil.
Kangto *mt.* China/India
Kangtog *Xizang* China
Kangxian *Gansu* China
Kangxiwar *Xinjiang* China
Kangyidaung Myanmar
Kanhan *r.* India
Kanhar *r.* *Jharkhand* India
Kanhargaon *Mahar.* India
Kanholmsfjärden *b.* Sweden
Kani Côte d'Ivoire
Kānī Iran
Kani Japan
Kani Myanmar
Kaniama Dem. Rep. Congo
Kaniama, Réserve des Éléphants de *nature res.* Dem. Rep. Congo
Kanibadam Tajik. *see* **Konibodom**
Kanibongan *Sabah* Malaysia
Kanie Japan
Kaniere *South I.* N.Z.
Kaniere, Lake *South I.* N.Z.
Kanifing Gambia
Kanifinolhu *i.* *N. Male* Maldives
Kanigiri *Andhra Prad.* India
Kaniguram Pak.
Kani-Kéli Mayotte
Kanin, Poluostrov *pen.* Rus. Fed.
Kanin Nos Rus. Fed.
Kanin Nos, Mys *c.* Rus. Fed.
Kaninskiy Bereg *coastal area* Rus. Fed.
Kānī Rash Iraq
Kanisfluh *mt.* Austria
Kanita Japan
Kaniv Ukr.
Kaniva *Vic.* Austr.
Kanivs'ke Vodoskhovyshche *resr* Ukr.
Kaniwara *Madh. Prad.* India
Kanjiroba *mt.* Nepal
Kanjiža *Vojvodina* Serbia
Kankaanpää Fin.
Kankakee *IL* U.S.A.
Kankakee *r.* *IL* U.S.A.
Kankan Guinea
Kankan, Réserve Naturelle de *nature res.* Guinea
Kanker *Chhattisgarh* India
Kankesanturai Sri Lanka
Kankiya Nigeria
Kankossa Maur.
Kanlaon, Mount *vol.* Phil.
Kanmaw Kyun *i.* Myanmar
Kanmuri-jima *i.* Japan
Kanmuri-yama *mt.* Japan
Kanmuri-yama *mt.* Japan
Kannad *Mahar.* India
Kanna-gawa *r.* Japan
Kannami Japan
Kannapolis *NC* U.S.A.
Kannauj *Uttar Prad.* India
Kannawurf Ger.
Kanniyakumari *Tamil Nadu* India
Kanniya Kumari *c.* India *see* **Comorin, Cape**
Kannod *Madh. Prad.* India
Kannonkoski Fin.
Kannon-zaki *pt* Japan
Kannur *Kerala* India *see* **Cannanore**
Kannus Fin.
Kannuskoski Fin.
Kano *i.* Indon.
Kano Nigeria
Kano *r.* Nigeria
Kano *state* Nigeria
Kano-gawa *r.* Japan
Kanon, Punt *pt* *Curaçao* Neth. Antilles
Kanona Zambia
Kanonerka Kazakh.
Kan'onji Japan
Kanonpunt *pt* S. Africa
Kanor *Rajasthan* India
Kanorado *KS* U.S.A.
Kanosh *UT* U.S.A.
Kanovlei Namibia
Kanowit *Sarawak* Malaysia
Kanoya Japan
Kanpantxua Spain
Kanpur *Uttar Prad.* India
Kanpur Pak.
Kanra Japan
Kanrach *reg.* Pak.
Kansai *airport* Japan
Kansanshi Zambia
Kansas *r.* *KS* U.S.A.
Kansas *state* U.S.A.
Kansas City *KS* U.S.A.
Kansas City *MO* U.S.A.
Kansenia Dem. Rep. Congo
Kansk Rus. Fed.
Kansu *Xinjiang* China
Kansu *prov.* China *see* **Gansu**
Kanta *mt.* Eth.
Kantala Fin.
Kantang Thai.
Kantara *hill* Cyprus
Kantaralak Thai.
Kantarkaya Turkey
Kantarlı Turkey
Kantauri Mendilerroa *mts* Spain
Kantavu *i.* Fiji *see* **Kadavu**
Kantchari Burkina
Kantemirovka Rus. Fed.
Kantens Neth.
Kanth *Uttar Prad.* India
Kanthi *W. Bengal* India
Kanti *Bihar* India
Kantilo *Orissa* India
Kantishna *r.* *AK* U.S.A.
Kantli *r.* India
Kantō-heiya *plain* Japan
Kanton *atoll* *Phoenix Is* Kiribati
Kan-Too, Pik *mt.* Kazakh./Kyrg. *see* **Khan-Tengri, Pik**
Kanto-sanchi *mts* Japan
Kanttaji Aboriginal Land *res.* *N.T.* Austr.
Kantulong Myanmar
147 E8 **Kanturk** Ireland
84 E5 **Kanturrpa Aboriginal Land** *res.* *N.T.* Austr.
122 F5 **Kanūgar** Iran
251 G4 **Kanuku Mountains** Guyana
105 K2 **Kanuma** Japan
211 A5 **Kanungu** Uganda
114 E5 **Kanur** *Andhra Prad.* India
212 C5 **Kanus** Namibia
91 J8 **Kanuwe** *r.* P.N.G.
Kanyakubja *Uttar Prad.* India *see* **Kannauj**
215 P1 **Kanyamazane** S. Africa
212 E5 **Kanye** Botswana
213 F2 **Kanyemba** Zimbabwe
139 Q6 **Kanyutino** Rus. Fed.
104 A5 **Kanzaki** Japan
93 E3 **Kao** *Halmahera* Indon.
207 G3 **Kao** Niger
79 □8 **Kao** *i.* Tonga
93 E3 **Kao, Teluk** *b.* *Halmahera* Indon.
109 M7 **Kaohsiung** Taiwan
97 F9 **Kaôh Tang** *i.* Cambodia
212 B3 **Kaokoveld** *plat.* Namibia
206 A3 **Kaolack** Senegal
78 □6 **Kaolo** *Sta Isabel* Solomon Is
209 F7 **Kaoma** *Northern* Zambia
209 E8 **Kaoma** *Western* Zambia
202 C5 **Kaortchi** *well* Chad
208 D3 **Kaouadja** C.A.R.
79 □8 **Kapa** *i.* *Vava'u Gp* Tonga
240 □B11 **Kapa'a** *HI* U.S.A.
240 □F13 **Kapa'au** *HI* U.S.A.
121 R5 **Kapal** Kazakh.
93 E4 **Kapalabuaya** *Maluku* Indon.
196 H8 **Kapa Moračka** *mt.* Montenegro
129 H6 **Kapan** Armenia
209 D7 **Kapanga** Dem. Rep. Congo
209 F6 **Kapangolo** Dem. Rep. Congo
Kapara Te Hau *l.* *South I.* N.Z. *see* **Grassmere, Lake**
198 E4 **Kaparelli** Greece
122 C6 **Kaparhā** Iran
136 H1 **Kapatkyevichy** Belarus
211 A7 **Kapatu** Zambia
121 Q6 **Kapchagay** Kazakh.
121 Q6 **Kapchagayskoye Vodokhranilishche** *resr* Kazakh.
210 B4 **Kapchorwa** Uganda
138 G8 **Kapčiamiestis** Lith.
Kap Dan Greenland *see* **Kulusuk**
164 E6 **Kapelle** Neth.
165 F6 **Kapellen** Belgium
198 E6 **Kapello, Akrotirio** *pt* *Kythira* Greece
143 P2 **Kapellskär** Sweden
Kapelskär Sweden *see* **Kapellskär**
210 B4 **Kapenguria** Kenya
179 L5 **Kapfenberg** Austria
179 M6 **Kapfenstein** Austria
199 I2 **Kapıdağı Yarımadası** *pen.* Turkey
117 M6 **Kapili** *r.* India
77 F1 **Kapingamarangi** *atoll* Micronesia
266 F5 **Kapingamarangi Rise** *sea feature* N. Pacific Ocean
199 L2 **Kapıorman Dağları** *mts* Turkey
123 M6 **Kapip** Pak.
209 F8 **Kapiri Mposhi** Zambia
123 M4 **Kāpīsā** *prov.* Afgh.
221 M3 **Kapisillit** Greenland
224 D2 **Kapiskau** *r.* *Ont.* Can.
227 M2 **Kapiskong Lake** *Ont.* Can.
95 J3 **Kapit** *Sarawak* Malaysia
137 K5 **Kapitanivka** Ukr.
81 I7 **Kapiti Island** *North I.* N.Z.
251 H4 **Kapiting** Brazil
202 D5 **Kapka** *well* Chad
202 D6 **Kapka, Massif du** *mts* Chad
93 E5 **Kaplamada, Gunung** *mt.* *Buru* Indon.
122 F1 **Kaplankyr, Chink** *esc.* Turkm./Uzbek.
122 G1 **Kaplankyr Döwlet Gorugy** *nature res.* Turkm.
176 D3 **Kaplice** Czech Rep.
97 D10 **Kapoe** Thai.
210 B3 **Kapoeta** Sudan
177 J4 **Kápolna** Hungary
93 C8 **Kapondai, Tanjung** *pt* *Flores* Indon.
80 I6 **Kaponga** *North I.* N.Z.
211 B7 **Kaporo** Malawi
196 G4 **Kapos** *r.* Romania
177 G5 **Kaposfő** Hungary
177 H5 **Kaposszekcső** Hungary
177 G5 **Kaposvár** Hungary
123 J9 **Kappar** Pak.
172 C2 **Kappel** Ger.
179 J6 **Kappel am Krappfeld** Austria
172 D5 **Kappel-Grafenhausen** Ger.
168 I1 **Kappeln** Ger.
172 E4 **Kappelrodeck** Ger.
178 B5 **Kappl** Austria
116 F7 **Kapran** *Rajasthan* India
178 G5 **Kaprun** Austria
210 B4 **Kapsabet** Kenya
123 J8 **Kap Salt Swamp** Pak.
101 F8 **Kapsan** N. Korea
139 Q2 **Kapsha** *r.* Rus. Fed.
198 D5 **Kapsia** Greece
Kapsukas Lith. *see* **Marijampolė**
117 N8 **Kaptai** Bangl.
107 P2 **Kaptsegaytuy** Rus. Fed.
136 H1 **Kaptsevichy** Belarus
175 L2 **Kaptsyowka** Belarus
95 H5 **Kapuas** *r.* Indon.
95 K6 **Kapuas** *r.* Indon.
95 J4 **Kapuas Hulu, Pegunungan** *mts* Indon./Malaysia
82 G6 **Kapunda** *S.A.* Austr.
116 D6 **Kapuriya** *Rajasthan* India
116 E4 **Kapurthala** *Punjab* India
177 K2 **Kapušany** Slovakia
224 D3 **Kapuskasing** *Ont.* Can.
224 D3 **Kapuskasing** *r.* *Ont.* Can.
135 I6 **Kapustin Yar** Rus. Fed.
137 K3 **Kapustyntsi** *Kyivs'ka Oblast'* Ukr.
137 N3 **Kapustyntsi** *Sums'ka Oblast'* Ukr.
209 F7 **Kaputa** Zambia
122 H9 **Kapūtānī** Iran
83 M4 **Kaputar** *mt.* *N.S.W.* Austr.
210 B4 **Kaputir** Kenya
176 G4 **Kapuvár** Hungary
Kapydzhik, Gora *mt.* Armenia/Azer. *see* **Qazangödağ**
138 K8 **Kapyl'** Belarus
101 E10 **Kap'yŏng** S. Korea
139 P6 **Kapyrevshchina** Rus. Fed.
111 L11 **Ka Qu** *r.* *Xizang* China
116 H7 **Kara** *Uttar Prad.* India
134 N1 **Kara** *r.* Rus. Fed.
207 F4 **Kara** Togo
127 J4 **Kara** *r.* Turkey
199 K2 **Kara** *r.* Turkey
199 H4 **Kara Ada** *i.* Turkey
199 I6 **Kara Ada** *i.* Turkey
199 H3 **Karaağaç** Turkey
126 F4 **Karaali** Turkey
110 A7 **Kara Art Pass** *Xinjiang* China
Karaaul Kazakh. *see* **Karaul**
121 O6 **Kara-Balta** Kyrg.
120 J1 **Karabalyk** Kazakh.
139 V5 **Karabanovo** Rus. Fed.
121 O3 **Karabas** Kazakh.
120 E3 **Karabau** Kazakh.
120 F6 **Karabaur, Uval** *hills* Uzbek.
Karabekaul Turkm. *see* **Garabekewül**
129 C7 **Karabey** Turkey
199 I2 **Karabiga** Turkey
129 B6 **Karaboğa Dağları** *mts* Turkey
Kara-Bogaz-Gol Turkm. *see* **Garabogazköl**
Karaboynak Turkm. *see* **Ataýap**
129 I3 **Karabudakhkent** Rus. Fed.
126 F3 **Karabük** Turkey
121 R5 **Karabulak** *Almatinskaya Oblast'* Kazakh.
121 U4 **Karabulak** *Vostochnyy Kazakhstan* Kazakh.
129 F2 **Karabulak** Rus. Fed.
121 P3 **Karabulakskaya** Kazakh.
Karabura *Xinjiang* China *see* **Yumin**
199 J4 **Karaburç** Turkey
199 H4 **Karaburun** Turkey
120 I3 **Karabutak** Kazakh.
199 J2 **Karacabey** Turkey
126 F5 **Karacadağ** *mts* Turkey
199 I1 **Karacakılavuz** Turkey
126 D3 **Karacaköy** Turkey
127 I5 **Karacalı Dağ** *mt.* Turkey
128 A2 **Karaçal Tepe** *mt.* Turkey
199 L5 **Karacaören Barajı** *resr* Turkey
199 J5 **Karacasu** Turkey
199 L6 **Karaca Yarımadası** *pen.* Turkey
Karachay-Cherkess Republic *aut. rep.* Rus. Fed. *see* **Karachayevo-Cherkesskaya Respublika**
Karachayevo-Cherkesskaya A.S.S.R. *aut. rep.* Rus. Fed. *see* **Karachayevo-Cherkesskaya Respublika**
129 C2 **Karachayevo-Cherkesskaya Respublika** *aut. rep.* Rus. Fed.
129 C2 **Karachayevsk** Rus. Fed.
139 R8 **Karachev** Rus. Fed.
123 L9 **Karachi** Pak.
137 M6 **Karachunivs'ke Vodoskhovyshche** *resr* Ukr.
127 K4 **Karaçoban** Turkey
199 K6 **Karaçulha** Turkey
Karacurun Turkey *see* **Hilvan**
177 G5 **Karád** Hungary
114 D4 **Karad** *Mahar.* India
128 G2 **Kara Dağ** *hill* Turkey
199 H2 **Kara Dağ** *hill* Turkey
199 J2 **Kara Dağ** *hills* Turkey
126 F5 **Kara Dağ** *mt.* Turkey
121 O7 **Kara-Darya** *r.* Kyrg.
Kara-Dar'ya Uzbek. *see* **Payshanba**
Kara Deniz *sea* Asia/Europe *see* **Black Sea**
206 E4 **Karaga** Ghana
100 B2 **Karagan** Rus. Fed.
121 O3 **Karaganda** Kazakh.
121 O3 **Karagandinskaya Oblast'** *admin. div.* Kazakh.
129 G1 **Karagas** Rus. Fed.
121 Q5 **Karagash** Kazakh.
120 D2 **Karagay** Kazakh.
134 K4 **Karagay** Rus. Fed.
121 P3 **Karagayly** Kazakh.
121 U3 **Karagaylybulak** Kazakh.
122 F2 **Karagez** Turkm.
131 R4 **Karaginskiy, Ostrov** *i.* Rus. Fed.
120 D6 **Karagiye, Vpadina** *depr.* Kazakh.
117 K7 **Karagola** *Bihar* India
129 B6 **Karagöl Dağları** *mts* Turkey
121 T2 **Karaguzhikha** Kazakh.
211 A5 **Karagwe** Tanz.
197 P9 **Karahalil** Turkey
199 K4 **Karahallı** Turkey
126 G4 **Karahasanlı** Turkey
199 J5 **Karahisar** Turkey
134 L5 **Karaidel'** Rus. Fed.
114 F7 **Karaikal** *Pondicherry* India
114 F7 **Karaikkudi** *Tamil Nadu* India
121 U4 **Kara Irtysh** *r.* Kazakh.
126 G5 **Karaisalı** Turkey
95 L4 **Karaitan** *Kalimantan* Indon.
122 D4 **Karaj** Iran
Karak Jordan *see* **Al Karak**
Kara-Kala Turkm. *see* **Magtymguly**
Karakalli Turkey *see* **Özalp**
Karakalpakistan, Respublika *aut. rep.* Uzbek. *see* **Qoraqalpog'iston Respublikasi**
Karakalpakskaya Respublika *aut. rep.* Uzbek. *see* **Qoraqalpog'iston Respublikasi**
Karakalpakstan *aut. rep.* Uzbek. *see* **Qoraqalpog'iston Respublikasi**
129 C5 **Karakamış** Turkey
83 I7 **Kara Kara State Park** *nature res.* *Vic.* Austr.
Karakax *Xinjiang* China *see* **Moyu**
111 E7 **Karakax He** *r.* China
111 E9 **Karakax Shan** *mts* *Xinjiang* China
129 C5 **Karakaya** Turkey
129 D6 **Karakaya** *r.* Turkey
129 C6 **Karakaya Tepe** *mt.* Turkey
126 I5 **Karakeçi** Turkey
126 F4 **Karakeçili** Turkey
93 E1 **Karakelong** *i.* Indon.
111 E8 **Karaki** *Xinjiang* China
93 D2 **Karakitang** *i.* Indon.
Karaklis Armenia *see* **Vanadzor**
127 J4 **Karakoçan** Turkey
121 N1 **Karakoga** Kazakh.
Karakoin *salt l.* Kazakh. *see* **Karakoyyn, Ozero**
120 E3 **Karakol'** Kazakh.
121 O7 **Kara-Köl** Kyrg.
121 Q7 **Karakol** *Ysyk-Köl* Kyrg.
121 R6 **Karakol** *Ysyk-Köl* Kyrg.
Karakolka Kyrg. *see* **Karakol**
Karaköprü Turkey *see* **Karaçoban**
116 F2 **Karakoram Pass** China/Jammu and Kashmir
123 P3 **Karakoram Range** *mts* Asia
210 C2 **Kara K'orē** Eth.
206 B3 **Karakoro** *r.* Mali/Maur.
Karaköse *Ağrı* Turkey *see* **Ağrı**
128 D2 **Karaköse** *Hatay* Turkey
199 H3 **Karaköy** Turkey
129 I3 **Karakoysu** *r.* Rus. Fed.
129 F6 **Karakoyunlu** Turkey
121 M4 **Karakoyyn, Ozero** *salt l.* Kazakh.
Karakubbud Ukr. *see* **Komsomol's'ke**
Kara-Kuga Kazakh. *see* **Karakoga**
Kara Kul' Kyrg. *see* **Kara-Köl**
Karakul', Ozero *l.* Tajik. *see* **Qarokŭl**
Kara-Kul'dzha Kyrg. *see* **Kara-Kulja**
134 K4 **Karakulino** Rus. Fed.
121 O7 **Kara-Kulja** Kyrg.
120 J1 **Karakul'skoye** Rus. Fed.
121 R4 **Karakum** Kazakh.
120 E5 **Karakum, Peski** *des.* Kazakh.
Karakum Desert Kazakh. *see* **Karakum, Peski**
Karakum Desert Turkm. *see* **Garagum**
127 K3 **Karakurt** *Kars* Turkey
199 I3 **Karakurt** *Manisa* Turkey
199 L4 **Karakuş Dağı** *ridge* Turkey
212 C3 **Karakuwisa** Namibia
208 B1 **Karal** Chad
138 E3 **Karala** Estonia
87 E8 **Karalundi** *W.A.* Austr.
93 A5 **Karama** *r.* Indon.
Karamagay *Xinjiang* China *see* **Haramgai**
199 J3 **Karaman** *Balıkesir* Turkey
126 F5 **Karaman** *Karaman* Turkey
128 B1 **Karaman** *prov.* Turkey
199 L6 **Karamanbeyli Geçidi** *pass* Turkey
199 K5 **Karamanlı** Turkey
110 G4 **Karamay** *Xinjiang* China
123 O3 **Karambar Pass** Afgh./Pak.
95 L6 **Karambu** *Kalimantan* Indon.
81 G8 **Karamea** *South I.* N.Z.
81 G8 **Karamea** *r.* *South I.* N.Z.
81 F8 **Karamea Bight** *b.* *South I.* N.Z.
120 K2 **Karamendy** Kazakh.
95 K7 **Karamian** *i.* Indon.
199 L4 **Karamıkkaracaören** Turkey
111 G8 **Karamiran** *Xinjiang* China
111 G8 **Karamiran He** *r.* China
111 H8 **Karamiran Shankou** *pass* *Xinjiang* China
131 Q3 **Karamken** Rus. Fed.
199 K2 **Karamürsel** Turkey
175 K1 **Karamyshevo** *Kaliningradskaya Oblast'* Rus. Fed.
138 L4 **Karamyshevo** *Pskovskaya Oblast'* Rus. Fed.
123 N3 **Karan** *r.* Afgh.
Karan *state* Myanmar *see* **Kayin**
125 I2 **Karān** *i.* Saudi Arabia
251 G4 **Karanambo** Guyana
177 I3 **Karancsalja** Hungary
177 I3 **Karancskeszi** Hungary
177 I3 **Karancsság** Hungary
206 A3 **Karang** Senegal
93 A4 **Karang, Tanjung** *pt* Indon.
94 F6 **Karangagung** *Sumatera* Indon.
94 F7 **Karangan** *Sumatera* Indon.
81 D10 **Karangarua** *South I.* N.Z.
95 K9 **Karangasem** *Bali* Indon.
95 H9 **Karangbolong, Tanjung** *pt* Indon.
93 D2 **Karangetang** *vol.* Indon.
208 B4 **Karangoua** *r.* Congo
116 F9 **Karanja** *Mahar.* India
114 E3 **Karanja** *r.* India
116 H8 **Karanjia** *Madh. Prad.* India
117 J9 **Karanjia** *Orissa* India
116 D5 **Karanpura** *Rajasthan* India
121 Q1 **Karaoba** Kazakh.
199 I5 **Karaova** Turkey
199 K6 **Karaovabeli Geçidi** *pass* Turkey
121 P5 **Karaoy** *Almatinskaya Oblast'* Kazakh.
121 P5 **Karaoy** *Almatinskaya Oblast'* Kazakh.
197 P7 **Karapelit** Bulg.
128 E2 **Karapınar** *Gaziantep* Turkey
126 F5 **Karapınar** *Konya* Turkey
199 J3 **Karapürçek** *Balıkesir* Turkey
199 L2 **Karapürçek** *Sakarya* Turkey
110 C6 **Karaqi** *Xinjiang* China
212 C5 **Karas** *admin. reg.* Namibia
214 B3 **Karas** *mts* Namibia
129 A6 **Karasakal Dağları** *mts* Turkey
126 E3 **Karaşar** Turkey
111 F8 **Karasay** *Xinjiang* China
121 Q7 **Kara-Say** Kyrg.
212 C6 **Karasburg** Namibia
Kara Sea Rus. Fed. *see* **Karskoye More**
139 W5 **Karash** Rus. Fed.
121 P2 **Karashoky** Kazakh.
188 G3 **Karašica** *r.* Croatia
177 H6 **Karasica** *r.* Hungary/Romania
137 N8 **Karasivka** *r.* Ukr.
Kárášjohka *Finnmark* Norway *see* **Karasjok**
140 R2 **Kárášjohka** *r.* Norway
140 R2 **Karasjok** *Finnmark* Norway
Karasjokka *r.* Norway *see* **Kárášjohka**
121 P2 **Karasor** Kazakh.
121 M1 **Karasor, Ozero** *l.* Kazakh.
121 P2 **Karasor, Ozero** *salt l.* Kazakh.
121 P3 **Karasor, Ozero** *salt l.* Kazakh.
Kara Strait Rus. Fed. *see* **Karskiye Vorota, Proliv**
104 E6 **Karasu** Japan
121 P4 **Karasu** *Karagandinskaya Oblast'* Kazakh.
120 J2 **Karasu** *Kostanayskaya Oblast'* Kazakh.
120 K1 **Karasu** *Kostanayskaya Oblast'* Kazakh.
121 P1 **Karasu** *r.* Kazakh.
128 E2 **Karasu** *r.* Syria/Turkey
Karasu *Bitlis* Turkey *see* **Hizan**
199 L1 **Karasu** *Sakarya* Turkey
127 K4 **Karasu** *r.* Turkey
Karasubazar Ukr. *see* **Bilohirs'k**
105 J3 **Karasu-gawa** *r.* Japan
121 R1 **Karasuk** Rus. Fed.
136 H8 **Karasulak** *r.* Ukr.
121 O7 **Kara-Suu** Kyrg.
105 L2 **Karasuyama** Japan
136 E2 **Karasyn** Ukr.
122 I4 **Karāt** Iran
129 H3 **Karata** Rus. Fed.
121 U4 **Karatal** Kazakh.
126 G5 **Karataş** *Adana* Turkey
128 E2 **Karataş** *Hatay* Turkey
199 J4 **Karatas** Turkey
Karataş Burnu *hd* Turkey *see* **Fener Burnu**
121 N6 **Karatau** Kazakh.
121 L5 **Karatau, Khrebet** *mts* Kazakh.
134 M1 **Karatayka** Rus. Fed.
128 A2 **Karatepe** Turkey
97 D9 **Karathuri** Myanmar
114 F8 **Karativu** *i.* Sri Lanka
140 O3 **Karatj** *l.* Sweden
120 E3 **Karatobe** Kazakh.
120 H4 **Karatobe, Mys** *pt* Kazakh.
120 H3 **Karatogay** Kazakh.
121 Q4 **Karatol** *r.* Kazakh.
120 J1 **Karatomarskoye Vodokhranilishche** *resr* Kazakh.
120 E4 **Karaton** Kazakh.
140 O3 **Karats** Sweden
103 G13 **Karatsu** Japan
93 E1 **Karatung** *i.* Indon.
106 A3 **Karatüngü** *Xinjiang* China
120 H4 **Karatup, Poluostrov** *pen.* Kazakh.
120 K2 **Kara-Turgay** *r.* Kazakh.
121 R3 **Karaul** Kazakh.
116 F6 **Karauli** *Rajasthan* India
Karaulkel'dy Kazakh. *see* **Bayganin**
127 K3 **Karaurgan** Turkey
Karavan Kyrg. *see* **Kerben**
198 D6 **Karavas** *Kythira* Greece
196 H10 **Karavastasë, Gjiri i** *b.* Albania
196 H10 **Karavastasë, Laguna e** *lag.* Albania
136 J1 **Karavatsichy** Belarus
139 Y4 **Karavayevo** Rus. Fed.
198 E6 **Karavia** *i.* Greece
199 H7 **Karavonisia** *i.* Greece
128 A3 **Karavostasi** Cyprus
198 E7 **Karavoutas, Akra** *pt* *Kriti* Greece
208 D4 **Karawa** Dem. Rep. Congo
94 G8 **Karawang** *Jawa* Indon.
179 J6 **Karawanken** *mts* Austria
Karaxahar *r.* China *see* **Kaidu He**
129 D6 **Karayazı** Turkey
128 E2 **Karayılan** Turkey
110 E6 **Karayulgan** *Xinjiang* China
121 N3 **Karazhal** Kazakh.
120 D5 **Karazhanbas** Kazakh.
121 O4 **Karazhingil** Kazakh.
127 L7 **Karbalā'** Iraq
127 K7 **Karbalā'** *governorate* Iraq
169 G10 **Karben** Ger.
170 F4 **Karbow-Vietlübbe** Ger.
121 P3 **Karbushevka** Kazakh.
168 I1 **Karby** Ger.
177 J4 **Karcag** Hungary
177 K3 **Karcsa** Hungary
175 J3 **Karczew** Pol.
175 K4 **Karczmiska** Pol.
197 Q7 **Kardam** Bulg.
199 I6 **Kardamaina** *Kos* Greece
198 D6 **Kardamyli** Greece
179 K1 **Kardašova Řečice** Czech Rep.
Kardeljevo Croatia *see* **Ploče**
169 D10 **Karden** Ger.
Kardhaámaina *Kos* Greece *see* **Kardamaina**
Kardhítsa Greece *see* **Karditsa**
198 G6 **Kardiotissa** *i.* Greece
140 Q3 **Kardis** Sweden
198 C3 **Karditsa** Greece
138 F3 **Kärdla** Estonia
177 J5 **Kardos** Hungary
179 O4 **Kardos-ér** *r.* Hungary
177 J5 **Kardoskút** Hungary
139 P7 **Kardymovo** Rus. Fed.
129 F2 **Kardzhin** Rus. Fed.
215 K4 **Karee** S. Africa
214 F6 **Kareeberge** *mts* S. Africa
214 G6 **Kareebospoort** *pass* S. Africa
214 I9 **Kareedouw** S. Africa
180 D5 **Kareha, Jebel** *mt.* Morocco
203 F5 **Kareima** Sudan
129 E4 **K'areli** Georgia
116 G8 **Kareli** *Madh. Prad.* India
Karelia *aut. rep.* Rus. Fed. *see* **Kareliya, Respublika**
138 J8 **Karelichy** Belarus
134 F3 **Kareliya, Respublika** *aut. rep.* Rus. Fed.
Karel'skaya A.S.S.R. *aut. rep.* Rus. Fed. *see* **Kareliya, Respublika**
134 F2 **Karel'skiy Bereg** *coastal area* Rus. Fed.
211 A6 **Karema** *Rukwa* Tanz.
Karen *state* Myanmar *see* **Kayin**
99 K1 **Karenga** *r.* Rus. Fed.
116 G7 **Karera** *Madh. Prad.* India
140 Q2 **Karesuando** Sweden
122 I8 **Kārevāndar** Iran
80 I4 **Karewa** *i.* *North I.* N.Z.
80 K4 **Karewa Island** *North I.* N.Z.
123 I5 **Karez Dasht** Afgh.
120 F2 **Kargala** Rus. Fed.
129 H2 **Kargalinskaya** Rus. Fed.
Kargalinski Rus. Fed. *see* **Kargalinskaya**
120 G2 **Kargalinskoye** Kazakh.
121 P3 **Kargaly** Kazakh.
127 J4 **Kargapazarı Dağları** *mts* Turkey
Karghalik *Xinjiang* China *see* **Yecheng**
126 G3 **Kargı** Turkey
116 F3 **Kargiakh** Jammu and Kashmir
116 F2 **Kargil** Jammu and Kashmir
Kargilik *Xinjiang* China *see* **Yecheng**
128 C2 **Kargıpınarı** Turkey
134 G3 **Kargopol'** Rus. Fed.
174 D3 **Kargowa** Pol.
122 G8 **Kargūshkī** Iran
116 G6 **Karhal** *Uttar Prad.* India
207 H4 **Kari** Nigeria
204 D2 **Karia Ba Mohammed** Morocco
122 G8 **Karīān** Iran
137 U1 **Karian** Rus. Fed.
198 E2 **Kariani** Greece
181 E5 **Kariat-Arkmane** Morocco
213 F3 **Kariba** Zimbabwe
209 E9 **Kariba, Lake** *resr* Zambia/Zimbabwe
209 F9 **Kariba Dam** Zambia/Zimbabwe
102 Q4 **Kariba-yama** *vol.* Japan
212 B4 **Karibib** Namibia
214 H9 **Kariega** *r.* S. Africa
125 I7 **Karīf Salāsil** *well* Yemen
140 R2 **Karigasniemi** Fin.
138 J1 **Karijärvi** *l.* Fin.
87 E7 **Karijini National Park** *W.A.* Austr.
80 H1 **Karikari, Cape** *North I.* N.Z.
122 F5 **Karīmābād** Iran
95 H5 **Karimata** *i.* Indon.
95 H5 **Karimata, Pulau-pulau** *is* Indon.
95 H5 **Karimata, Selat** *str.* Indon.
117 N7 **Karimganj** *Assam* India
122 D4 **Karim Khanch** Iran
114 F3 **Karimnagar** *Andhra Prad.* India
94 E4 **Karimun Besar** *i.* Indon.
95 I7 **Karimunjawa** *i.* Indon.
95 I7 **Karimunjawa, Pulau-pulau** *is* Indon.
210 E2 **Karin** Somalia
141 Q6 **Karinainen** Fin.
199 J5 **Karınçalı Dağı** *mts* Turkey
141 L5 **Käringsjön** Sweden
215 P1 **Karino** S. Africa
80 I4 **Karioi** *hill* *North I.* N.Z.
141 Q6 **Karis** Fin.
211 A5 **Karisimbi, Mont** *vol.* Rwanda
Káristos Greece *see* **Karystos**
122 G5 **Karit** Iran
198 D2 **Karitsa** Greece
104 E6 **Kariya** Japan
213 E3 **Kariyangwe** Zimbabwe
Karjaa Fin. *see* **Karis**
138 G1 **Karjalohja** Fin.
116 D8 **Karjan** *Gujarat* India
114 D3 **Karjat** *Mahar.* India
117 K8 **Karkai** *r.* *Jharkhand* India
114 D6 **Karkal** *Karnataka* India
114 D4 **Karkamb** *Mahar.* India
214 B6 **Karkams** S. Africa
121 P3 **Karkaralinsk** Kazakh.
92 E9 **Karkaralong, Kepulauan** *is* Indon.
91 K7 **Karkar Island** P.N.G.
122 D5 **Karkas, Kūh-e** *mts* Iran
123 L8 **Karkh** Pak.
122 B6 **Karkheh, Rūdkhāneh-ye** *r.* Iran
137 L8 **Karkinits'ka Zatoka** *g.* Ukr.
141 R6 **Karkkila** Fin.
141 R6 **Kärkölä** Fin.
Karkonoski Park Narodowy *nat. park* Czech Rep./Pol. *see* **Krkonošský narodní park**
174 D5 **Karkonoski Park Narodowy** *nat. park* Pol.
138 I3 **Karksi-Nuia** Estonia
124 C3 **Karkūmā, Ra's** *hd* Saudi Arabia
123 N5 **Karlachi** Pak.
84 D5 **Karlantijpa North Aboriginal Land** *res.* *N.T.* Austr.
84 D6 **Karlantijpa South Aboriginal Land** *res.* *N.T.* Austr.
138 D2 **Karlby** *Åland* Fin.
143 N1 **Karlholmsbruk** Sweden
129 C5 **Karlı** Turkey
117 I8 **Karlidi** *Chhattisgarh* India
106 D5 **Karlik Shan** *mts* *Xinjiang* China
174 D1 **Karlino** Pol.
127 J4 **Karlıova** Turkey
137 O4 **Karlivka** Ukr.
129 E6 **Karlıyayla** Turkey
123 O3 **Karl Marks, Qullai** *mt.* Tajik.
Karl-Marx-Stadt Ger. *see* **Chemnitz**
Karlo-Libknekhtovsk Ukr. *see* **Soledar**
188 E3 **Karlovac** Croatia
176 B1 **Karlovarský kraj** *admin. reg.* Czech Rep.
199 H5 **Karlovasi** *Samos* Greece
176 G1 **Karlovice** Czech Rep.
Karlovka Ukr. *see* **Karlivka**
197 M8 **Karlovo** Bulg.
176 B1 **Karlovy Vary** Czech Rep.
172 F4 **Karlsbad** Ger.
141 M6 **Karlsberg** Sweden
143 K3 **Karlsborg** Sweden
170 I3 **Karlsburg** Ger.
Karlsburg Romania *see* **Alba Iulia**
172 F3 **Karlsdorf-Neuthard** Ger.
173 K5 **Karlsfeld** Ger.
170 I2 **Karlshagen** Ger.
143 K5 **Karlshamn** Sweden
168 H4 **Karlshöfen** Ger.
173 K4 **Karlshuld** Ger.
143 K2 **Karlskoga** Sweden
173 K4 **Karlskron** Ger.
143 L5 **Karlskrona** Sweden
143 N4 **Karlsöarna** *i.* Sweden
172 E3 **Karlsruhe** Ger.
172 F4 **Karlsruhe** *admin. reg.* Ger.
142 J2 **Karlstad** Sweden
236 G1 **Karlstad** *MN* U.S.A.
172 H2 **Karlstadt** Ger.
169 H10 **Karlstein am Main** Ger.
179 L2 **Karlstein an der Thaya** Austria
179 M3 **Karlstetten** Austria
220 C4 **Karluk** *AK* U.S.A.
140 □ **Karl XII Øyane** *i.* Svalbard
123 L3 **Karlyk** Turkm.
139 N8 **Karma** Belarus
207 F3 **Karma** Niger
202 C6 **Karma, Ouadi** *watercourse* Chad
129 F3 **Karmadon** Rus. Fed.
114 D3 **Karmala** *Mahar.* India
139 R6 **Karmanovo** Rus. Fed.
140 O3 **Karmas** Sweden
128 D6 **Karmel, Har** *hill* Israel
Karmir Armenia *see* **Chambarak**
Karmona Spain *see* **Córdoba**
142 B2 **Karmøy** *i.* Norway
123 O7 **Karmpur** Pak.
117 N8 **Karnafuli Reservoir** Bangl.
116 F5 **Karnal** *Haryana* India
116 H5 **Karnali** *r.* Nepal
136 J7 **Karnaliyivka** Ukr.
117 M8 **Karnaphuli** *r.* Bangl.
116 G4 **Karnaprayag** *Uttaranchal* India
114 D5 **Karnataka** *state* India
137 N5 **Karnaukhivka** Ukr.
237 G11 **Karnes City** *TX* U.S.A.
174 D1 **Karnice** Pol.
175 I3 **Karniewo** Pol.
178 G6 **Karnische Alpen** *mts* Austria
197 O8 **Karnobat** Bulg.
179 I6 **Kärnten** *land* Austria
123 K8 **Karodi** Pak.
213 F3 **Karoi** Zimbabwe
191 P5 **Karojba** Croatia
96 C7 **Karokpi** Myanmar
111 J12 **Karo La** *pass* *Xizang* China
177 H2 **Karolinka** Czech Rep.
93 B7 **Karompalompo** *i.* Indon.
117 O7 **Karong** *Manipur* India
211 B7 **Karonga** Malawi
87 G11 **Karonie** *W.A.* Austr.
121 Q7 **Karool-Döbö** Kyrg.
Karool-Tëbë Kyrg. *see* **Karool-Döbö**
214 G8 **Karoo National Park** S. Africa
82 G6 **Karoonda** *S.A.* Austr.
123 N6 **Karor** Pak.
203 H5 **Karora** Eritrea
Káros *i.* Greece *see* **Keros**
93 A4 **Karossa** *Sulawesi Barat* Indon.
95 M9 **Karossa, Tanjung** *pt* *Sumba* Indon.
199 H1 **Karoti** Greece
206 E2 **Karouassa** *well* Mali
202 D6 **Karoub** Chad
198 A3 **Karousades** *Kerkyra* Greece
170 F3 **Karow** *Mecklenburg-Vorpommern* Ger.
171 F6 **Karow** *Sachsen-Anhalt* Ger.
174 D5 **Karpacz** Pol.
128 C3 **Karpasia** *pen.* Cyprus
Karpas Peninsula Cyprus *see* **Karpasia**
199 I7 **Karpathos** *Karpathos* Greece
199 I7 **Karpathos** *i.* Greece
199 I6 **Karpathou, Steno** *sea chan.* Greece
136 D5 **Karpats'kiy** *nat. park* Ukr.
Karpaty *mts* Europe *see* **Carpathian Mountains**
198 C4 **Karpenisi** Greece
Karpilovka Belarus *see* **Aktsyabrski**
134 M4 **Karpinsk** Rus. Fed.
134 I2 **Karpogory** Rus. Fed.
137 L1 **Karpovychi** Ukr.
199 I5 **Karpuzlu** *Aydın* Turkey
199 H2 **Karpuzlu** *Edirne* Turkey
136 J3 **Karpylivka** *Chernihivs'ka Oblast'* Ukr.
137 M3 **Karpylivka** *Chernihivs'ka Oblast'* Ukr.
136 G2 **Karpylivka** *Rivnens'ka Oblast'* Ukr.
86 D6 **Karratha** *W.A.* Austr.
Karrats Fjord *inlet* Greenland *see* **Nuugaatsiaap Imaa**
170 E4 **Karrenzin** Ger.
122 D7 **Karrī** Iran
215 L6 **Karringmelkspruit** S. Africa
Karroo *plat.* S. Africa *see* **Great Karoo**
87 E10 **Karroun Hill Nature Reserve** *W.A.* Austr.
123 J4 **Karrukh** Afgh.
Karrychirla Turkm. *see* **Garryçyrla**
127 K3 **Kars** Turkey
129 E5 **Kars** *prov.* Turkey
129 E5 **Kars** *r.* Turkey
121 L4 **Karsakpay** Kazakh.
140 R5 **Kärsämäki** Fin.
138 K5 **Kārsava** Latvia
171 E8 **Karsdorf** Ger.
Karshi *Qashqadaryo* Uzbek. *see* **Qarshi**
129 C4 **Karşıköy** Turkey
174 F2 **Karsin** Pol.
199 J2 **Karşıyaka** *Balıkesir* Turkey
199 I4 **Karşıyaka** *İzmir* Turkey
117 L6 **Karsiyang** *W. Bengal* India
130 G3 **Karskiye Vorota, Proliv** *str.* Rus. Fed.
170 L5 **Karsko** Pol.
130 I2 **Karskoye More** *sea* Rus. Fed.
170 E4 **Karstädt** *Brandenburg* Ger.
170 D4 **Karstädt** *Mecklenburg-Vorpommern* Ger.
134 D3 **Karstula** Fin.
135 I5 **Karsun** Rus. Fed.
177 I4 **Kartal** Hungary
199 K2 **Kartal** Turkey
217 □3a **Kartala** *vol.* *Njazidja* Comoros
217 □3a **Kartala, Forêt du** *for.* *Njazidja* Comoros
120 I1 **Kartaly** Rus. Fed.
116 E4 **Kartarpur** *Punjab* India
139 O6 **Kartashevichi** Rus. Fed.
139 O6 **Kartavshchina** Rus. Fed.
134 K2 **Kartayel'** Rus. Fed.
138 E6 **Kartena** Lith.
232 G7 **Karthaus** *PA* U.S.A.
178 G6 **Kartitsch** Austria
178 G6 **Kartitscher Sattel** *pass* Austria
129 F3 **K'art'lis K'edi** *hills* Georgia
Kartsa Rus. Fed. *see* **Oktyabr'skoye**
139 N5 **Kartsevo** Rus. Fed.
198 F4 **Kartsino, Akrotirio** *pt* *Skyros* Greece
140 S5 **Karttula** Fin.
251 G3 **Kartuni** Guyana
143 O7 **Kartuzy** Pol.
209 F8 **Karubwe** Zambia
105 I3 **Karuizawa** Japan
122 H7 **Karūk** Iran
102 S6 **Karumai** Japan
85 H4 **Karumba** *Qld* Austr.
122 D6 **Karun, Kūh-e** *hill* Iran
122 C6 **Kārūn, Rūd-e** *r.* Iran
114 E8 **Karunagapalli** *Kerala* India
140 Q3 **Karungi** Sweden
210 B5 **Karungu** Kenya
93 A8 **Karuni** *Sumba* Indon.
86 I4 **Karunjie** *W.A.* Austr.
142 F5 **Karup** Denmark
142 F5 **Karup** *r.* Denmark
114 F7 **Karur** *Tamil Nadu* India
211 A5 **Karuzi** Burundi
114 F6 **Karvetnagar** *Andhra Prad.* India
141 Q5 **Karvia** Fin.
177 H2 **Karviná** Czech Rep.
136 H3 **Karvynivka** Ukr.
114 D5 **Karwar** *Karnataka* India
178 D5 **Karwendelgebirge** *mts* Austria
178 D5 **Karwendelgebirge** *nature res.* Austria
116 H7 **Karwi** *Uttar Prad.* India
175 J2 **Karwica** Pol.
170 D4 **Karwitz** Ger.
198 B4 **Karya** *Lefkada* Greece
Karyagino Azer. *see* **Füzuli**
198 F2 **Karyes** Greece
99 J1 **Karymskoye** Rus. Fed.
120 E6 **Karynzharyk, Peski** *des.* Kazakh.
198 F4 **Karystos** Greece
137 N2 **Karyzh** Rus. Fed.
202 E6 **Kas** Sudan
199 K6 **Kaş** Turkey
114 C3 **Kasa** *Mahar.* India
Kasaba Turkey *see* **Turgutlu**
211 A7 **Kasaba Lodge** Zambia
224 B2 **Kasabonika** *Ont.* Can.
224 B2 **Kasabonika Lake** *Ont.* Can.
211 A6 **Kasacasia** Tanz.
104 G3 **Kasaga-dake** *mt.* Japan
104 C6 **Kasagi** Japan
104 F4 **Kasagi-yama** *mt.* Japan
104 F5 **Kasahara** Japan
209 C5 **Kasaï** *r.* Dem. Rep. Congo
104 A6 **Kasai** Japan
209 D6 **Kasaï, Plateau du** Dem. Rep. Congo
209 D6 **Kasaï-Occidental** *prov.* Dem. Rep. Congo
209 E6 **Kasaï-Oriental** *prov.* Dem. Rep. Congo
209 D7 **Kasaji** Dem. Rep. Congo
105 J3 **Kasakake** Japan
105 L3 **Kasama** Japan
211 A7 **Kasama** Zambia
104 E5 **Kasamatsu** Japan
Kasan Uzbek. *see* **Koson**
211 A5 **Kasana** Tanz.
212 E3 **Kasane** Botswana
211 A7 **Kasanga** Tanz.
209 B6 **Kasangulu** Dem. Rep. Congo
209 F8 **Kasanka National Park** Zambia
104 D3 **Kasano-misaki** *pt* Japan
Kasansay Uzbek. *see* **Kosonsoy**
209 C6 **Kasanza** Dem. Rep. Congo
203 H5 **Kasar, Ras** *pt* Sudan
114 D6 **Kasaragod** *Kerala* India
102 □G18 **Kasarai-zaki** *hd* *Nansei-shotō* Japan
138 G3 **Kasari** *r.* Estonia
138 L6 **Kasary** Belarus
100 G4 **Kasatkino** Rus. Fed.
104 D6 **Kasatori-yama** *hill* Japan
223 K2 **Kasba Lake** Can.
204 D2 **Kasba Tadla** Morocco
142 E5 **Kås Bredning** *b.* Denmark
103 H15 **Kaseda** Japan
176 C2 **Kasejovice** Czech Rep.
209 E8 **Kasempa** Zambia
171 D10 **Kasendorf** Ger.
209 D7 **Kasenga** *Katanga* Dem. Rep. Congo
209 F7 **Kasenga** *Katanga* Dem. Rep. Congo
208 F4 **Kasenye** Dem. Rep. Congo
208 E5 **Kasese** Dem. Rep. Congo
210 A4 **Kasese** Uganda
Kasevo Rus. Fed. *see* **Neftekamsk**
116 G6 **Kasganj** *Uttar Prad.* India
108 B3 **Kasha** *Xizang* China
210 D5 **Kasha** *waterhole* Kenya
224 B3 **Kashabowie** *Ont.* Can.
239 K9 **Kasha-Katuwe Tent Rocks National Monument** *nat. park* *NM* U.S.A.
122 D5 **Kāshān** Iran
135 H6 **Kashary** Rus. Fed.
224 D2 **Kashechewan** *Ont.* Can.
Kashgar *Xinjiang* China *see* **Kashi**
110 C7 **Kashi** *Xinjiang* China
104 C6 **Kashiba** Japan
104 C7 **Kashihara** Japan
105 M4 **Kashima** *Ibaraki* Japan
104 E2 **Kashima** *Ishikawa* Japan
103 H13 **Kashima** *Saga* Japan
105 M3 **Kashima-nada** *b.* Japan
104 G2 **Kashimayaria-dake** *mt.* Japan
104 F4 **Kashimo** Japan
139 U4 **Kashin** Rus. Fed.
139 U4 **Kashinka** *r.* Rus. Fed.
209 F7 **Kashiobwe** Dem. Rep. Congo
116 G5 **Kashipur** *Uttaranchal* India
139 V7 **Kashira** Rus. Fed.
139 V7 **Kashirka** *r.* Rus. Fed.
137 S2 **Kashirskoye** Rus. Fed.
209 F8 **Kashitu** Zambia
105 K4 **Kashiwa** Japan
104 C6 **Kashiwara** Japan
103 P9 **Kashiwazaki** Japan
Kashkadar'ya *r.* Uzbek. *see* **Qashqadaryo**
Kashkadarya Oblast *admin. div.* Uzbek. *see* **Qashqadaryo**
121 O5 **Kashkanteniz** Kazakh.
134 G2 **Kashkarantsy** Rus. Fed.
Kashken-Teniz Kazakh. *see* **Kashkanteniz**
129 E2 **Kashkhatau** Rus. Fed.
122 F6 **Kashku'iyeh** Iran
139 O6 **Kashkurino** Rus. Fed.
137 P6 **Kashlahach** *r.* Ukr.
122 H4 **Kāshmar** Iran
Kashmir *terr.* Asia *see* **Jammu and Kashmir**
116 E2 **Kashmir, Vale of** *reg.* India
123 M7 **Kashmor** Pak.
123 N4 **Kashmund** *reg.* Afgh.
137 M9 **Kashtany** Ukr.
209 E6 **Kashyukulu** Dem. Rep. Congo
Kasi *Uttar Prad.* India *see* **Varanasi**
117 I6 **Kasia** *Uttar Prad.* India
123 N4 **Kasigar** Afgh.
139 Q8 **Kasilovo** Rus. Fed.
93 A4 **Kasimbar** *Sulawesi* Indon.
199 M5 **Kasımlar** Turkey
135 H5 **Kasimov** Rus. Fed.
179 N8 **Kašina** Croatia
208 F4 **Kasingi** Dem. Rep. Congo
93 E4 **Kasiruta** *i.* *Maluku* Indon.
177 I5 **Kaskantyú** Hungary
236 K7 **Kaskaskia** *r.* *IL* U.S.A.
223 N3 **Kaskattama** *r.* *Man.* Can.
121 Q6 **Kaskelen** Kazakh.
141 P5 **Kaskinen** Fin.
Kas Klong *i.* Cambodia *see* **Kŏng, Kaôh**
Kaskö Fin. *see* **Kaskinen**
122 E1 **Kaskyrbulak Yuzhnyy, Gora** *hill* Turkm.
222 G5 **Kaslo** *B.C.* Can.
223 K3 **Kasmere Lake** *Man.* Can.
139 R6 **Kasnya** *r.* Rus. Fed.
209 F7 **Kasomeno** Dem. Rep. Congo
95 J5 **Kasongan** *Kalimantan* Indon.
209 E6 **Kasongo** Dem. Rep. Congo
209 C6 **Kasongo-Lunda** Dem. Rep. Congo
209 C6 **Kasongo Lunda Falls** Angola/Dem. Rep. Congo
209 E6 **Kasonguele** Dem. Rep. Congo
199 H7 **Kasos** *i.* Greece
199 I7 **Kasou, Steno** *sea chan.* Greece
176 C2 **Kašperské Hory** Czech Rep.
129 F4 **Kaspi** Georgia
Kaspīy Mangy Oypaty *lowland* Kazakh./Rus. Fed. *see* **Prikaspiyskaya Nizmennost'**
129 I3 **Kaspiysk** Rus. Fed.
Kaspiyskiy Rus. Fed. *see* **Lagan'**
Kaspiyskoye More *l.* Asia/Europe *see* **Caspian Sea**
139 O7 **Kasplya** Rus. Fed.
139 N6 **Kasplya** *r.* Rus. Fed.
116 E8 **Kasrawad** *Madh. Prad.* India
Kasrik Turkey *see* **Gürpınar**
129 H4 **Kasristsqali** Georgia
Kassa Slovakia *see* **Košice**
138 F3 **Kassaare laht** *b.* Estonia
203 H6 **Kassala** Sudan
203 G6 **Kassala** *state* Sudan
198 E3 **Kassandras, Akrotirio** *pt* Greece
198 E2 **Kassandras, Kolpos** *b.* Greece
198 E2 **Kassandras Chersonisos** *pen.* Greece
198 E2 **Kassandreia** Greece
168 K2 **Kasseedorf** Ger.
169 I8 **Kassel** Ger.
169 H8 **Kassel** *admin. reg.* Ger.
205 H2 **Kasserine** Tunisia
Kassinga Angola *see* **Cassinga**
226 B5 **Kasson** *MN* U.S.A.
207 H3 **Kassouloua** *well* Niger
123 I9 **Kastag** Pak.
126 F3 **Kastamonu** Turkey
169 D10 **Kastellaun** Ger.
199 G7 **Kastelli** *Kriti* Greece
Kastéllion *Kriti* Greece *see* **Kissamos**
Kastellorizon *i.* Greece *see* **Megisti**
199 I7 **Kastelo, Akrotirio** *pt* *Karpathos* Greece
165 G6 **Kasterlee** Belgium
173 L3 **Kastl** *Bayern* Ger.
173 N5 **Kastl** *Bayern* Ger.

168 K3 Kastorf Ger.
198 C2 Kastoria Greece
198 C2 Kastorias, Limni l. Greece
135 G6 Kastornoye Rus. Fed.
198 B4 Kastos i. Greece
198 C4 Kastrakiou, Techniti Limni resr Greece
138 K3 Kastre Estonia
139 P8 Kastsyukovichy Belarus
139 N9 Kastsyukowka Belarus
104 E5 Kasuga Gifu Japan
104 B5 Kasuga Hyōgo Japan
104 E5 Kasugai Japan
105 K4 Kasukabe Japan
215 K9 Kasuka Road S. Africa
105 J3 Kasukawa Japan
208 E5 Kasuku Dem. Rep. Congo
211 A6 Kasulu Tanz.
101 I11 Kasumi Japan
105 L3 Kasumigaura Japan
105 L3 Kasumiga-ura l. Japan
129 J4 Kasumkent Rus. Fed.
211 B8 Kasungu Malawi
211 B8 Kasungu National Park Malawi
123 P6 Kasur Pak.
177 J5 Kaszaper Hungary
174 E4 Kaszczor Pol.
174 G1 Kaszubskie, Pojezierze reg. Pol.
143 O7 Kaszubski Park Krajobrazowy Pol.
209 E9 Kataba Zambia
207 H3 Katagum Nigeria
233 □Q3 Katahdin, Mount ME U.S.A.
116 G2 Katak Jammu and Kashmir
209 E5 Katako-Kombe Dem. Rep. Congo
198 C5 Katakolo Greece
198 C5 Katakolo, Akrotirio pt Greece
210 B4 Katakwi Uganda
207 I3 Katalui Chad
208 F5 Katana Dem. Rep. Congo
209 D6 Katanda Dem. Rep. Congo
209 E7 Katanga prov. Dem. Rep. Congo
116 G8 Katangi Madh. Prad. India
116 G9 Katangi Madh. Prad. India
100 M3 Katangli Sakhalin Rus. Fed.
87 D12 Katanning W.A. Austr.
104 C6 Katano Japan
208 E5 Katanti Dem. Rep. Congo
122 D3 Kata Pusht Iran
139 P9 Katashin Rus. Fed.
105 J2 Katashina Japan
105 J2 Katashina-gawa r. Japan
198 B5 Katastari Zakynthos Greece
104 C5 Katata Japan
211 A6 Katavi National Park Tanz.
123 M5 Katawaz Afgh.
123 L5 Katawaz reg. Afgh.
115 M9 Katchall i. Andaman & Nicobar Is India
207 F4 Katchamba Togo
209 C8 Katchiungo Angola
209 E6 Katea Dem. Rep. Congo
209 D6 Katende Dem. Rep. Congo
198 D2 Katerini Greece
136 J5 Katerynopil' Ukr.
147 J4 Katesbridge Northern Ireland U.K.
211 B6 Katesh Tanz.
220 E4 Kate's Needle mt. Can./U.S.A.
211 B8 Katete Zambia
129 H4 Katex Azer.
117 I8 Katghora Chhattisgarh India
96 C2 Katha Myanmar
84 D3 Katherine N.T. Austr.
84 C3 Katherine r. N.T. Austr.
85 I7 Katherine Creek watercourse Qld Austr.
Katherine Gorge National Park N.T. Austr. see Nitmiluk National Park
116 E9 Kathi Mahar. India
116 C8 Kathiawar pen. Gujarat India
124 F8 Kathīb, Ra's al pt Yemen
114 G8 Kathiraveli Sri Lanka
84 C3 Kathleen Falls N.T. Austr.
171 J7 Kathlow Ger.
117 J6 Kathmandu Nepal
214 H3 Kathu S. Africa
116 E3 Kathua Jammu and Kashmir
211 C5 Kathua watercourse Kenya
206 C3 Kati Mali
95 J3 Katibas r. Malaysia
177 K4 Kati-ér r. Hungary
117 K7 Katihar Bihar India
80 J4 Katikati North I. N.Z.
215 L8 Katikati S. Africa
80 J4 Katikati Entrance sea chan. North I. N.Z.
212 E3 Katima Mulilo Namibia
223 L4 Katimik Lake Man. Can.
139 W8 Katino Rus. Fed.
206 D4 Katiola Côte d'Ivoire
Kā Tiritiri o te Moana mts South I. N.Z. see Southern Alps
84 C8 Katiti Aboriginal Land res. N.T. Austr.
214 E6 Katkop Hills S. Africa
136 H8 Katlabukh, Ozero l. Ukr.
215 M2 Katlehong S. Africa
169 J7 Katlenburg-Lindau Ger.
177 G3 Kátlovce Slovakia
111 G7 Katma Xinjiang China
220 C4 Katmai National Park and Preserve AK U.S.A.
Katmandu Nepal see Kathmandu
198 C4 Kato Achaïa Greece
109 □J7 Kat O Chau i. H.K. China
198 C4 Katochi Greece
199 G7 Kato Chorio Kriti Greece
198 D5 Kato Doliana Greece
198 D6 Kato Glykovrysi Greece
109 □J7 Kat O Hoi b. H.K. China
116 G9 Katol Mahar. India
140 O5 Katölandet i. Fin.
208 D6 Katombe Dem. Rep. Congo
199 G6 Katomeri, Akrotirio pt Naxos Greece
209 E6 Katompi Dem. Rep. Congo
235 H2 Katonah NY U.S.A.
209 F8 Katondwe Zambia
198 F1 Kato Nevrokopi Greece
94 □ Katong Sing.
210 A4 Katonga r. Uganda
121 U3 Katon-Karagay Kazakh.
Katonqaraghay Kazakh. see Katon-Karagay
83 M5 Katoomba N.S.W. Austr.
93 B4 Katoposa, Gunung mt. Indon.
116 D8 Katosan Gujarat India
198 D4 Kato Tithorea Greece
Kåtotjåkka mt. Sweden see Godučohkka
176 C2 Katovice Czech Rep.
175 H5 Katowice Pol.
117 L8 Katoya W. Bengal India
116 D9 Katpur Gujarat India
199 K5 Katrancık Dağı mts Turkey
203 G2 Kātrīnā, Jabal mt. Egypt
146 G10 Katrine, Loch l. Scotland U.K.
141 M3 Katrineholm Sweden
179 I5 Katschberghöhe pass Austria
179 J3 Katsdorf Austria
215 M5 Katse Dam Lesotho
213 □J2 Katsepy Madag.
198 B3 Katsikas Greece
207 G3 Katsina Nigeria
207 G4 Katsina state Nigeria
207 H5 Katsina-Ala Nigeria
103 G13 Katsumoto Japan
105 I4 Katsunuma Japan
105 J4 Katsura-gawa r. Japan
104 C7 Katsuragi Japan
104 C7 Katsuragi-san hill Japan
102 □1 Katsuren-zaki c. Okinawa Japan
105 L5 Katsuura Japan
104 E3 Katsuyama Fukui Japan
104 A3 Katsuyama Okayama Japan
225 H1 Kattaktoc, Cap c. Que. Can.
86 I6 Kattamudda Well W.A. Austr.
125 K9 Kattānahan, Ra's pt Suquṭrā Yemen
121 L8 Kattaqo'rg'on Uzbek.
Kattaqŭrghon Uzbek. see Kattaqo'rg'on
123 L5 Kattasang Hills Afgh.
199 I7 Kattavia Rodos Greece
142 H5 Kattegat str. Denmark/Sweden
140 O4 Kattisavan Sweden
Kattowitz Pol. see Katowice
114 F7 Kattuputtur Tamil Nadu India
209 E6 Katumba Dem. Rep. Congo
211 B7 Katumbi Malawi
110 G1 Katun' r. Rus. Fed.
134 I4 Katunino Rus. Fed.
110 G1 Katunskiy Khrebet mts Rus. Fed.
123 M7 Katur Pak.
Katwa W. Bengal India see Katoya
164 F4 Katwijk aan Zee Neth.
175 J2 Katy Pol.
Katyk Ukr. see Shakhtars'k
177 I5 Katymár Hungary
139 O7 Katyn' Rus. Fed.
174 E4 Katy Wrocławskie Pol.
173 M3 Katzbach r. Ger.
179 N4 Katzelsdorf Austria
172 G3 Katzenbuckel hill Ger.
169 E10 Katzenelnbogen Ger.
171 D9 Katzhütte Ger.
172 D2 Katzweiler Ger.
240 □B11 Kaua'i i. HI U.S.A.
240 □B12 Kaua'i Channel HI U.S.A.
169 E10 Kaub Ger.
212 D3 Kaudom Game Park nature res. Namibia
173 J6 Kaufbeuren Ger.
173 J5 Kaufering Ger.
237 G9 Kaufman TX U.S.A.
169 I8 Kaufungen Ger.
141 Q5 Kauhajoki Fin.
141 Q5 Kauhanevan-Pohjankankaan kansallispuisto nat. park Fin.
140 Q5 Kauhava Fin.
226 F5 Kaukauna WI U.S.A.
96 C2 Kaukkwè Hills Myanmar
140 R3 Kaukonen Fin.
138 K2 Kauksi Estonia
240 □B12 Kaulakahi Channel HI U.S.A.
165 I6 Kaulille Belgium
140 Q3 Kaulinranta Fin.
171 D9 Kaulsdorf Ger.
80 J7 Kaumai North I. N.Z.
225 I1 Kaumajet Mountains Nfld and Lab. Can.
240 □B12 Kaumakani HI U.S.A.
240 □D13 Kaumalapau HI U.S.A.
240 □E13 Kaunakakai HI U.S.A.
138 G7 Kaunas Lith.
138 K5 Kaunata Latvia
120 E6 Kaundy, Vpadina depr. Kazakh.
234 F1 Kauneonga Lake NY U.S.A.
178 C6 Kaunertal val. Austria
117 L7 Kaunia Bangl.
140 Q3 Kaunisvaara Sweden
138 H7 Kauno marios l. Lith.
81 F9 Kaupiri South I. N.Z.
175 K1 Kaupiškiai Lith.
240 □E13 Kaupō HI U.S.A.
207 G3 Kaura-Namoda Nigeria
109 □J7 Kau Sai Chau i. H.K. China
Kaushany Moldova see Căușeni
140 Q5 Kaustinen Fin.
165 J9 Kautenbach Lux.
140 Q2 Kautokeino Norway
179 L2 Kautzen Austria
97 D9 Kau-ye Kyun i. Myanmar
131 R3 Kavacha Rus. Fed.
197 K9 Kavadarci Macedonia
196 H9 Kavajë Albania
199 H2 Kavak Çanakkale Turkey
126 H3 Kavak Samsun Turkey
199 H3 Kavak Dağı hill Turkey
199 J4 Kavaklıdere Manisa Turkey
199 J5 Kavaklıdere Muğla Turkey
198 F2 Kavala Greece
198 F2 Kavalas, Kolpos b. Greece
100 I6 Kavalerovo Rus. Fed.
114 G5 Kavali Andhra Prad. India
139 N6 Kavalyova Belarus
251 F3 Kavanayen Venez.
122 E7 Kavār Iran
114 C7 Kavaratti Lakshadweep India
114 C7 Kavaratti atoll India
197 Q7 Kavarna Bulg.
138 H6 Kavarskas Lith.
139 Q6 Kavel'shchino Rus. Fed.
170 F3 Kavelstorf Ger.
206 B4 Kavendou, Mont mt. Guinea
114 F7 Kaveri r. India
114 F6 Kaveripatnam Tamil Nadu India
116 D8 Kavi Gujarat India
91 L7 Kavieng New Ireland P.N.G.
122 F4 Kavir Iran
122 G4 Kavīr, Chāh-e well Iran
122 F4 Kavīr, Dasht-e des. Iran
122 G4 Kavīr Kūshk well Iran
Kavirondo Gulf Kenya see Winam Gulf
129 D1 Kavkazskiy Rus. Fed.
129 B2 Kavkazskiy Zapovednik nature res. Rus. Fed.
175 L6 Kavs'ke Ukr.
251 H3 Kaw Fr. Guiana
93 F5 Kawa Seram Indon.
102 R7 Kawabe Akita Japan
104 F5 Kawabe Gifu Japan
104 B8 Kawabe Wakayama Japan
105 L4 Kawachi Ibaraki Japan
104 E3 Kawachi Ishikawa Japan
105 K2 Kawachi Tochigi Japan
104 E1 Kawachi-dake hill Japan
104 C7 Kawachi-Nagano Japan
224 E4 Kawagama Lake Ont. Can.
104 E6 Kawage Japan
105 J4 Kawagoe Japan
105 I1 Kawaguchi Niigata Japan
105 K4 Kawaguchi Saitama Japan
105 I4 Kawaguchiko Japan
105 I4 Kawaguchi-ko l. Japan
104 B5 Kawahara Japan
105 I4 Kawai Gifu Japan
102 S7 Kawai Iwate Japan
240 □F13 Kawaihae HI U.S.A.
240 □A12 Kawaihoa Point HI U.S.A.
240 □B11 Kawaikini mt. HI U.S.A.
240 □C12 Kawailoa Beach HI U.S.A.
103 J12 Kawajiri Japan
105 I4 Kawakami Nagano Japan
104 C7 Kawakami Nara Japan
80 I2 Kawakawa North I. N.Z.
104 E3 Kawakita Japan
102 R9 Kawamata Japan
103 I14 Kawaminami Japan
105 J3 Kawamoto Japan
209 E8 Kawana Zambia
105 H2 Kawanakajima Japan
105 J6 Kawana-zaki pt Japan
105 H6 Kawane Japan
93 D3 Kawangkoan Sulawesi Indon.
104 C5 Kawanishi Hyōgo Japan
105 I1 Kawanishi Niigata Japan
102 R9 Kawanishi Yamagata Japan
103 J3 Kawarazawa-gawa r. Japan
116 H8 Kawardha Chhattisgarh India
224 E4 Kawartha Lakes Ont. Can.
209 F7 Kawasa Dem. Rep. Congo
105 K4 Kawasaki Japan
104 E5 Kawashima Japan
103 I12 Kawashiri-misaki pt Japan
93 C4 Kawato Sulawesi Indon.
105 K2 Kawauchi Japan
104 G4 Kawaue Japan
80 I3 Kawau Island North I. N.Z.
103 H14 Kawaura Japan
225 H2 Kawawachikamach Que. Can.
105 I6 Kawazu Japan
96 C7 Kawdut Myanmar
93 G3 Kawe i. Papua Indon.
240 N5 Kaweah, Lake CA U.S.A.
Kawega i. Tonga see 'Euaiki
80 K6 Kaweka Forest Park nature res. North I. N.Z.
80 K6 Kaweka Range mts North I. N.Z.
240 □C12 Kawela Bay HI U.S.A.
226 C1 Kawene Ont. Can.
80 K5 Kawerau North I. N.Z.
80 I5 Kawhia North I. N.Z.
80 I5 Kawhia Harbour North I. N.Z.
241 P4 Kawich Peak NV U.S.A.
241 P4 Kawich Range mts NV U.S.A.
223 L4 Kawinaw Lake Man. Can.
95 M9 Kawinda Sumbawa Indon.
93 D1 Kawio i. Indon.
124 F8 Kawkabān Yemen
96 D6 Kawkareik Myanmar
237 G7 Kaw Lake OK U.S.A.
96 B3 Kawlin Myanmar
96 C5 Kawludo Myanmar
97 D8 Kawmapyin Myanmar
203 G3 Kawm Umbū Egypt
96 D3 Kawngmeum Myanmar
97 D9 Kawthaung Myanmar
Kawthoolei state Myanmar see Kayin
Kawthule state Myanmar see Kayin
Kaxgar Xinjiang China see Kashi
110 C7 Kaxgar He r. China
110 E5 Kax He r. China
111 F8 Kaxtax Shan mts China
134 K4 Kay Rus. Fed.
206 E3 Kaya Burkina
129 D5 Kayaaltı Turkey
199 J5 Kayabaşı Turkey
121 H3 Kayacı Dağı hill Turkey
126 H4 Kayadibi Turkey
105 I4 Kayaga-take mt. Japan
96 C5 Kayah state Myanmar
129 I3 Kayakent Rus. Fed.
114 F8 Kayalpatnam Tamil Nadu India
211 A7 Kayambi Zambia
95 I5 Kayan r. Indon.
95 L3 Kayan r. Indon.
96 C6 Kayan Myanmar
211 A5 Kayanaza Burundi
92 □ Kayangel Atoll Palau
92 □ Kayangel Passage Palau
114 E8 Kayankulam Kerala India
95 K3 Kayan Mentarang, Taman Nasional nat. park Indon.
114 F3 Kayar Mahar. India
93 E3 Kayasa Halmahera Indon.
129 G1 Kayasula Rus. Fed.
Kaybagar, Ozero l. Kazakh. see Koybagar, Ozero
238 K5 Kaycee WY U.S.A.
120 E5 Kaydak, Sor dry lake Kazakh.
Kaydanovo Belarus see Dzyarzhynsk
209 D7 Kayembe-Mukulu Dem. Rep. Congo
241 V5 Kayenta AZ U.S.A.
209 B6 Kayes Congo
206 C3 Kayes Mali
206 C3 Kayes admin. reg. Mali
120 K2 Kayga Kazakh.
Kaygy Kazakh. see Kayga
206 C4 Kayima Sierra Leone
96 C5 Kayin state Myanmar
165 J10 Kayl Lux.
199 J4 Kaymakçı Turkey
121 P1 Kaymanachikha Kazakh.
199 M3 Kaymaz Turkey
171 F9 Kayna Ger.
129 B6 Kaynakdüzü Turkey
121 Q3 Kaynar Kazakh.
121 P6 Kaynar Zhambylskaya Oblast' Kazakh.
126 H4 Kaynar Turkey
199 L1 Kaynarca Turkey
197 P9 Kaynarlı r. Turkey
199 M2 Kaynaşlı Turkey
104 B4 Kayo Japan
102 □1 Kayō Okinawa Japan
93 E3 Kayoa i. Maluku Indon.
Kayrakkum Tajik. see Qayroqqum
Kayrakkumskoye Vodokhranilishche resr Tajik. see Qayroqqum, Obanbori
120 B3 Kaysatskoye Rus. Fed.
126 G4 Kayseri Turkey
157 N7 Kaysersberg France
93 B7 Kayuadi i. Indon.
94 F6 Kayuagung Sumatera Indon.
210 B4 Kayunga Uganda
209 E5 Kayuyu Dem. Rep. Congo
130 J3 Kayyerkan Rus. Fed.
121 O6 Kayyngdy Kyrg.
139 V8 Kazachka Rus. Fed.
131 O2 Kazach'ye Rus. Fed.
Kazakh Azer. see Qazax
Kazakhdar'ya Uzbek. see Qozoqdaryo
Kazakhskaya S.S.R. country Asia see Kazakhstan
121 N2 Kazakhskiy Melkosopochnik plain Kazakh.
120 E6 Kazakhskiy Zaliv b. Kazakh.
120 T3 Kazakhstan country Asia
Kazakhstan Kazakh. see Aksay
139 V9 Kazaki Rus. Fed.
Kazakstan country Asia see Kazakhstan
120 J5 Kazalinsk Kazakh.
223 M2 Kazan r. Nunavut Can.
134 J5 Kazan' Rus. Fed.
129 D6 Kazan Turkey
121 S3 Kazanchunkur Kazakh.
126 F5 Kazancı Turkey
Kazandzhik Turkm. see Bereket
198 B3 Kazanje, Mal mt. Albania
134 J5 Kazanka r. Rus. Fed.
137 L6 Kazanka Ukr.
Kazanketken Uzbek. see Qozonketkan
128 C2 Kazanlı Turkey
197 N8 Kazanlŭk Bulg.
139 V8 Kazanovka Rus. Fed.
175 J4 Kazanów Pol.
103 □2 Kazan-rettō is N. Pacific Ocean
135 H6 Kazanskaya Rus. Fed.
137 O8 Kazantip, Mys pt Ukr.
137 O8 Kazantips'ka Zatoka b. Ukr.
Kazatin Ukr. see Kozyatyn
120 H3 Kazatskiy Kazakh.
207 H3 Kazaure Nigeria
210 C1 Kaza Wenz r. Eth.
Kazbegi Georgia see Qazbegi
129 F3 Kazbek mt. Georgia/Rus. Fed.
199 H3 Kaz Dağı mts Turkey
122 D7 Kāzerūn Iran
121 N1 Kazgorodok Kazakh.
134 J3 Kazhim Rus. Fed.
123 J8 Kazhmak r. Pak.
137 N7 Kazhovs'kyy Mahistral'nyy Kanal canal Ukr.
Kazidi Kŭhistoni Badakhshon Tajik. see Qozideh
199 K5 Kazıkbeli Geçidi pass Turkey
Kazi Magomed Azer. see Qazımämmäd
136 B2 Kazimierski Park Krajobrazowy Pol.
175 I5 Kazimierza Wielka Pol.
174 G3 Kazimierz Biskupi Pol.
175 J4 Kazimierz Dolne Pol.
Kāzimīyah Iraq see Al Kāẓimīyah
177 J3 Kazincbarcika Hungary
137 Q3 Kazinka Belgorodskaya Oblast' Rus. Fed.
139 W9 Kazinka Lipetskaya Oblast' Rus. Fed.
139 W8 Kazinka Ryazanskaya Oblast' Rus. Fed.
137 T3 Kazinka Voronezhskaya Oblast' Rus. Fed.
117 N6 Kaziranga National Park India
138 I8 Kazlowshchyna Hrodzyenskaya Voblasts' Belarus
138 L6 Kazlowshchyna Vitsyebskaya Voblasts' Belarus
138 G7 Kazlų Rūda Lith.
174 E3 Kaźmierz Pol.
176 E2 Kaznějov Czech Rep.
105 K3 Kazo Japan
120 C3 Kaztalovka Kazakh.
212 E3 Kazuma Pan National Park Zimbabwe
209 D6 Kazumba Dem. Rep. Congo
209 E9 Kazungula Zambia
102 R6 Kazuno Japan
105 L5 Kazusa Japan
122 G2 Kazy Turkm.
138 M6 Kazyany Belarus
121 M7 Kazygurt Kazakh.
130 H3 Kazym r. Rus. Fed.
130 H3 Kazymskiy Mys Rus. Fed.
196 H8 Kçirë Albania
174 F3 Kcynia Pol.
176 C2 Kdyně Czech Rep.
240 □F14 Kea'au HI U.S.A.
78 □6 Kea'auloa Reef Solomon Is
147 I4 Keady Northern Ireland U.K.
240 □E14 Keahole Point HI U.S.A.
146 D10 Keal, Loch na b. Scotland U.K.
240 □D13 Kealaikahiki Channel HI U.S.A.
240 □F14 Kealakekua HI U.S.A.
240 □F14 Kealakekua Bay HI U.S.A.
240 □F14 Kealia HI U.S.A.
147 D9 Kealkill Ireland
241 V6 Keams Canyon AZ U.S.A.
Kéamu i. Vanuatu see Anatom
235 G4 Keansburg NJ U.S.A.
147 L4 Kearney Northern Ireland U.K.
236 F5 Kearney NE U.S.A.
232 H9 Kearneysville WV U.S.A.
241 V8 Kearny AZ U.S.A.
235 G3 Kearny NJ U.S.A.
198 F5 Keas, Steno sea chan. Greece
215 O4 Keate's Drift S. Africa
240 □F14 Keauhou HI U.S.A.
240 □E13 Keawakapu HI U.S.A.
126 I4 Keban Turkey
126 I4 Keban Barajı resr Turkey
208 B5 Kébara Congo
95 H6 Kebatu i. Indon.
207 F3 Kebbi state Nigeria
206 A3 Kébémèr Senegal
207 I4 Kébi r. Cameroon
206 D4 Kébi Côte d'Ivoire
205 H2 Kebili Tunisia
128 D4 Kebīr, Nahr al r. Lebanon/Syria
202 E6 Kebkabiya Sudan
140 O3 Kebnekaise mt. Sweden
146 D6 Kebock Head Scotland U.K.
210 E3 K'ebrī Dehar Eth.
95 H8 Kebumen Jawa Indon.
94 E6 Kebur Sumatera Indon.
177 I5 Kecel Hungary
123 J8 Kech reg. Pak.
210 C3 K'ech'a Terara mt. Eth.
208 D2 Kéché C.A.R.
106 E8 Kecheng Qinghai China
222 E3 Kechika r. B.C. Can.
123 M7 Kechi Kalat Pak.
199 G4 Kechros Greece
199 L5 Keçiborlu Turkey
177 I5 Kecskemét Hungary
94 D1 Kedah state Malaysia
138 G6 Kėdainiai Lith.
Kedairu Passage Fiji see Kadavu Passage
111 D11 Kedarnath Peak Uttaranchal India
208 C2 Kédédéssé Chad
225 H4 Kedgwick N.B. Can.
109 I3 Kedian Hubei China
151 K3 Kedington Suffolk, England U.K.
95 J8 Kediri Jawa Indon.
100 E5 Kedong Heilong. China
206 B3 Kédougou Senegal
95 I4 Kedukul Kalimantan Indon.
134 K2 Kedva r. Rus. Fed.
174 G5 Kędzierzyn-Koźle Pol.
149 Q6 Keelby Lincolnshire, England U.K.
222 E1 Keele r. Y.T. Can.
149 M7 Keele Staffordshire, England U.K.
222 D2 Keele Peak Y.T. Can.
240 O5 Keeler CA U.S.A.
223 I4 Keeley Lake Sask. Can.
Keeling Islands terr. Indian Ocean see Cocos Islands
Keelung Taiwan see Chilung
146 K9 Keen, Mount hill Scotland U.K.
147 G5 Keenagh Ireland
92 B8 Keenapusan i. Phil.
240 N6 Keene CA U.S.A.
233 M6 Keene NH U.S.A.
235 H1 Keene NY U.S.A.
226 D3 Keene OH U.S.A.
84 B3 Keep r. N.T. Austr.
83 M4 Keepit, Lake resr N.S.W. Austr.
84 B3 Keep River National Park N.T. Austr.
165 G7 Keerbergen Belgium
215 K4 Keeromsberg mt. Free State S. Africa
214 D9 Keeromsberg mt. Western Cape S. Africa
85 H2 Keer-weer, Cape Qld Austr.
212 C5 Keetmanshoop Namibia
223 M5 Keewatin Ont. Can.
226 A2 Keewatin MN U.S.A.
Kefallinia i. Greece see Kefallonia
198 B4 Kefallonia i. Greece
199 H6 Kefalos Kos Greece
198 F5 Kefalos, Akrotirio pt Kythnos Greece
93 D8 Kefamenanu Timor Indon.
Kefe Ukr. see Feodosiya
169 H10 Kefenrod Ger.
179 K3 Kefermarkt Austria
207 G4 Keffi Nigeria
199 L1 Kefken Turkey
140 □B1 Keflavík Iceland
97 I9 Kê Gà, Mui pt Vietnam
114 G9 Kegalla Sri Lanka
Kegayli Uzbek. see Kegeyli
121 R6 Kegen Kazakh.
121 P6 Kegeti Kyrg.
120 H6 Kegeyli Uzbek.
225 H1 Keglo, Baie de b. Que. Can.
222 G3 Keg River Alta Can.
135 I7 Kegul'ta Rus. Fed.
138 I5 Kegums Latvia
151 J2 Kegworth Leicestershire, England U.K.
203 G5 Keheili Sudan
122 E3 Kehl Iran
172 D4 Kehl Ger.
206 D2 Kehoula well Maur.
138 I2 Kehra Estonia
169 D10 Kehrig Ger.
96 C4 Kehsi Mansam Myanmar
138 H3 Kehtna Estonia
137 O4 Kehychivka Ukr.
149 N6 Keighley West Yorkshire, England U.K.
104 C5 Keihoku Japan
138 H2 Keila Estonia
138 H2 Keila r. Estonia
208 F2 Keilak Sudan
210 B2 Keili Sudan
109 □J7 Kei Ling Ha Hoi b. H.K. China
83 J7 Keilor Vic. Austr.
214 E4 Keimoes S. Africa
215 M8 Kei Mouth S. Africa
215 L8 Kei Road S. Africa
215 L9 Keiskama r. S. Africa
215 L8 Keiskammahoek S. Africa
146 J5 Keiss Highland, Scotland U.K.
207 G3 Keïta Niger
208 C2 Kéita, Bahr r. Chad
140 S5 Keitele Fin.
140 S5 Keitele l. Fin.
82 H7 Keith S.A. Austr.
146 K7 Keith Moray, Scotland U.K.
84 C1 Keith, Cape N.T. Austr.
222 F1 Keith Arm b. N.W.T. Can.
222 F4 Keithley Creek B.C. Can.
79 □7a Keiyasi Viti Levu Fiji
225 H4 Kejimkujik National Park N.S. Can.
104 G2 Kekachi-yama mt. Japan
240 □B12 Kekaha HI U.S.A.
Këk-Art Kyrg. see Kök-Art
138 H5 Kekava Latvia
Këkaygyr Kyrg. see Kök-Aygyr
177 L3 Kékcse Hungary
81 H9 Kekerengu South I. N.Z.
177 J4 Kékes mt. Hungary
93 F4 Kekik i. Maluku Indon.
114 G8 Kekirawa Sri Lanka
92 □ Keklau Palau
199 K6 Kekova Adası i. Turkey
131 P4 Kekra Rus. Fed.
116 E7 Kekri Rajasthan India
Këk-Tash Kyrg. see Kök-Tash
210 E3 K'elafo Eth.
114 C9 Kelai i. Maldives
107 L7 Kelan Shanxi China
93 E5 Kelang i. Maluku Indon.
Kelang Malaysia see Klang
94 E1 Kelantan r. Malaysia
94 D2 Kelantan state Malaysia
93 F8 Kelapa i. Maluku Indon.
93 A6 Kelara r. Indon.
122 D3 Kelārdasht Iran
95 H5 Kelawar i. Indon.
169 C10 Kelberg Ger.
171 D8 Kelbra (Kyffhäuser) Ger.
177 G2 Kelč Czech Rep.
198 B2 Këlcyrë Albania
129 E4 Kel Dağı mt. Turkey
210 B4 Kele Uganda
177 I5 Kelebia Hungary
199 K5 Kelekçi Turkey
211 B6 Kelema Dodoma Tanz.
199 K3 Keles Turkey
121 M7 Keles Uzbek.
177 K4 Keleti-főcsatorna canal Hungary
177 H5 Kelet-Mecsek park Hungary
173 I5 Kelheim Ger.
205 H1 Kelibia Tunisia
123 L3 Kelif Turkm.
123 J2 Kelif Uzboýy marsh Turkm.
122 H9 Kelīri Iran
169 F10 Kelkheim (Taunus) Ger.
126 I3 Kelkit Turkey
126 H3 Kelkit r. Turkey
172 B2 Kell Ger.
81 A12 Kelland, Mount South I. N.Z.
146 J7 Kellas Moray, Scotland U.K.
138 J2 Kellavere hill Estonia
208 B5 Kéllé Congo
170 D2 Kellenhusen Ger.
87 D11 Kellerberrin W.A. Austr.
222 F2 Keller Lake N.W.T. Can.
121 M1 Kellerovka Kazakh.
220 F2 Kellett, Cape N.W.T. Can.
232 C7 Kelleys Island OH U.S.A.
223 K5 Kelliher Sask. Can.
168 I3 Kellinghusen Ger.
173 I5 Kellmünz an der Iller Ger.
238 F3 Kellogg ID U.S.A.
140 T3 Kelloselkä Fin.
147 B9 Kells Kerry Ireland
147 H7 Kells Kilkenny Ireland
147 I5 Kells Meath Ireland
147 J3 Kells Northern Ireland U.K.
147 J3 Kells r. Northern Ireland U.K.
84 G7 Kelly Creek watercourse Qld Austr.
87 F8 Kelly Range hills W.A. Austr.
147 F6 Kellysgrove Ireland
138 F6 Kelmė Lith.
136 F5 Kel'mentsi Ukr.
165 J7 Kelmis Belgium
208 C3 Kélo Chad
78 □6 Keloma i. Solomon Is
222 G5 Kelowna B.C. Can.
222 E5 Kelp Head B.C. Can.
149 L7 Kelsall Cheshire, England U.K.
226 B2 Kelsey MN U.S.A.
240 J3 Kelseyville CA U.S.A.
81 D12 Kelso South I. N.Z.
146 L11 Kelso Scottish Borders, Scotland U.K.
241 Q6 Kelso CA U.S.A.
238 C3 Kelso WA U.S.A.
169 G10 Kelsterbach Ger.
180 D5 Kelti, Jebel mt. Morocco
146 J10 Kelty Fife, Scotland U.K.
94 E4 Keluang Malaysia
140 S3 Kelujärvi Fin.
151 N4 Kelvedon Essex, England U.K.
151 M4 Kelvedon Hatch Essex, England U.K.
223 K4 Kelvington Sask. Can.
224 B3 Kelvin Island Ont. Can.
123 O9 Kelwara Rajasthan India
134 F2 Kem' Rus. Fed.
134 F2 Kem' r. Rus. Fed.
139 U1 Kema r. Rus. Fed.
95 K2 Kemabung Sabah Malaysia
Ke Macina Mali see Massina
126 I4 Kemah Turkey
197 O9 Kemal Turkey
126 I4 Kemaliye Turkey
129 C4 Kemalpaşa Artvin Turkey
199 I4 Kemalpaşa İzmir Turkey
78 □6 Kemalu i. Solomon Is
222 E4 Kemano B.C. Can.
94 E2 Kemasik Malaysia
178 D5 Kematen in Tirol Austria
208 D3 Kemba C.A.R.
95 I4 Kembayan Kalimantan Indon.
208 D3 Kembé C.A.R.
171 G7 Kemberg Ger.
234 D5 Kemblesville PA U.S.A.
210 D3 Kembolcha Eth.
157 N8 Kembs France
176 G4 Kemeneshát hills Hungary
176 G4 Kemenesmagasi Hungary
176 G4 Kemenesszömjén Hungary
199 K6 Kemer Antalya Turkey
199 L6 Kemer Antalya Turkey
199 L5 Kemer Burdur Turkey
199 K6 Kemer Muğla Turkey
199 J5 Kemer Barajı resr Turkey
130 J4 Kemerovo Rus. Fed.
Kemerovo Oblast admin. div. Rus. Fed. see Kemerovskaya Oblast'
98 E1 Kemerovskaya Oblast' admin. div. Rus. Fed.
177 H6 Kémes Hungary
179 N5 Kemeten Austria
140 R4 Kemi Fin.
140 T3 Kemihaara Fin.
140 S3 Kemijärvi Fin.
140 S3 Kemijärvi l. Fin.
140 R4 Kemijoki r. Fin.
121 P6 Kemin Kyrg.
140 R4 Keminmaa Fin.
Kemiö Fin. see Kimito
135 I5 Kemlya Rus. Fed.
165 C7 Kemmel Belgium
165 C7 Kemmelberg hill Belgium
238 I6 Kemmerer WY U.S.A.
173 J2 Kemmern Ger.
195 □ Kemmuna i. Malta
195 □ Kemmunett i. Malta
173 L2 Kemnath Ger.
146 L8 Kemnay Aberdeenshire, Scotland U.K.
170 I2 Kemnitz Mecklenburg-Vorpommern Ger.
171 K8 Kemnitz Sachsen Ger.
208 C3 Kémo pref. C.A.R.
237 F9 Kemp, Lake TX U.S.A.
134 M2 Kempazh r. Rus. Fed.
140 R4 Kempele Fin.
169 B8 Kempen Ger.
131 M3 Kempendyay Rus. Fed.
165 D10 Kempenich Ger.
165 H6 Kempisch Kanaal canal Belgium
263 D2 Kemp Land reg. Antarctica
262 U2 Kemp Peninsula Antarctica
246 E1 Kemp's Bay Andros Bahamas
83 N4 Kempsey N.S.W. Austr.
150 H3 Kempsey Worcestershire, England U.K.
151 L3 Kempston Bedfordshire, England U.K.
224 F4 Kempt, Lac l. Que. Can.
173 I6 Kempten (Allgäu) Ger.
83 K10 Kempton Tas. Austr.
215 M2 Kempton Park S. Africa
227 S4 Kemptville Ont. Can.
151 M5 Kemsing Kent, England U.K.
95 I7 Kemujan i. Indon.
Kemulta Georgia see Qemult'a
116 H7 Ken r. India
146 H13 Ken, Loch l. Scotland U.K.
227 O2 Kenabeek Ont. Can.
220 C3 Kenai AK U.S.A.
220 C4 Kenai Fiords National Park AK U.S.A.
220 C4 Kenai Mountains AK U.S.A.
94 F7 Kenam, Tanjung pt Indon.
225 J2 Kenamu r. Nfld and Lab. Can.
210 B3 Kenamuke Swamp Sudan
231 I8 Kenansville NC U.S.A.
122 I4 Kenar-e Kapeh Afgh.
220 H4 Kenaston Sask. Can.
232 G12 Kenbridge VA U.S.A.
95 I8 Kencong Jawa Indon.
116 I8 Kenda Chhattisgarh India
95 I8 Kendal Jawa Indon.
246 □ Kendal Jamaica
215 M2 Kendal S. Africa
149 L5 Kendal Cumbria, England U.K.
83 N3 Kendall N.S.W. Austr.
85 H3 Kendall r. Qld Austr.
231 G13 Kendall FL U.S.A.
223 O2 Kendall, Cape Nunavut Can.
81 G8 Kendall, Mount South I. N.Z.
230 E5 Kendallville IN U.S.A.
93 C5 Kendari Sulawesi Indon.
95 I6 Kendawangan Kalimantan Indon.
95 I6 Kendawangan r. Indon.
208 C2 Kendégué Chad
177 J4 Kenderes Hungary
Kendrikí Makedhonía admin. reg. Greece see Kentriki Makedonia
177 K3 Kendice Slovakia
117 K9 Kendrapara Orissa India
214 I8 Kendrew S. Africa
238 F3 Kendrick ID U.S.A.
241 U6 Kendrick Peak AZ U.S.A.
117 L7 Kendua Bangl.
121 P6 Kendyktas mts Kazakh.
120 E6 Kendyrli-Kayasanskoye, Plato plat. Kazakh.
120 F6 Kendyrlisor, Solonchak salt l. Kazakh.
83 L4 Kenebri N.S.W. Austr.
237 G11 Kenedy TX U.S.A.
215 N6 Kenega r. S. Africa
206 C5 Kenema Sierra Leone
95 I4 Kenepai, Gunung mt. Indon.
177 J3 Kenézlő Hungary
150 E4 Kenfig Bridgend, Wales U.K.
209 C6 Kenge Dem. Rep. Congo
209 E7 Kengere Dem. Rep. Congo
96 D4 Keng Hkam Myanmar
140 Q3 Kengis Sweden
117 M6 Kengkhar Bhutan
96 E4 Keng Lap Myanmar
96 D4 Keng Lon Myanmar
96 D4 Keng Tawng Myanmar
96 D4 Kengtung Myanmar
209 B5 Kengué Congo
177 J4 Kengyel Hungary
Kengzharyq Kazakh. see Kenzharyk
214 F5 Kenhardt S. Africa
234 D4 Kenhorst PA U.S.A.
206 C3 Kéniéba Mali
206 C3 Kéniébaoulé, Réserve de nature res. Mali
151 I3 Kenilworth Warwickshire, England U.K.
234 D4 Kenilworth PA U.S.A.
204 D2 Kénitra Morocco
129 G3 Kenkhi Rus. Fed.
107 P8 Kenli Shandong China
147 C9 Kenmare Ireland
236 E1 Kenmare ND U.S.A.
147 B9 Kenmare River inlet Ireland
213 F3 Kenmaur Zimbabwe
146 I9 Kenmore Perth and Kinross, Scotland U.K.
232 G6 Kenmore NY U.S.A.
172 B2 Kenn Ger.
237 D9 Kenna NM U.S.A.
146 F11 Kennacraig Argyll and Bute, Scotland U.K.
236 F4 Kennebec SD U.S.A.
233 □P4 Kennebec r. ME U.S.A.
233 □O5 Kennebunk ME U.S.A.
233 □O5 Kennebunkport ME U.S.A.
85 J5 Kennedy Qld Austr.
85 J3 Kennedy r. Qld Austr.
Kennedy, Cape FL U.S.A. see Canaveral, Cape
87 C8 Kennedy Range hills W.A. Austr.
87 C8 Kennedy Range National Park W.A. Austr.
109 □J7 Kennedy Town H.K. China
234 D6 Kennedyville MD U.S.A.
237 J11 Kenner LA U.S.A.
151 K5 Kennet r. England U.K.
146 K8 Kennethmont Aberdeenshire, Scotland U.K.
87 D7 Kenneth Range hills W.A. Austr.
237 J7 Kennett MO U.S.A.
234 D5 Kennett Square PA U.S.A.
238 E3 Kennewick WA U.S.A.
151 J4 Kennington Oxfordshire, England U.K.
146 J10 Kennoway Fife, Scotland U.K.
224 C3 Kenogami r. Ont. Can.
227 N1 Kenogami Lake Ont. Can.
227 N1 Kenogamisis Lake Ont. Can.
222 C2 Keno Hill Y.T. Can.
223 M5 Kenora Ont. Can.
226 G7 Kenosha WI U.S.A.
232 C10 Kenova WV U.S.A.
134 G3 Kenozero, Ozero l. Rus. Fed.
146 D8 Kensaleyre Highland, Scotland U.K.
235 H2 Kensico Reservoir NY U.S.A.
225 I4 Kensington P.E.I. Can.
235 J1 Kensington CT U.S.A.
151 L4 Kensworth Bedfordshire, England U.K.
151 N5 Kent admin. div. England U.K.
149 L5 Kent r. England U.K.
235 I1 Kent CT U.S.A.
232 D7 Kent OH U.S.A.
237 L11 Kent TX U.S.A.
232 G12 Kent VA U.S.A.
238 C3 Kent WA U.S.A.
151 M5 Kent, Vale of val. England U.K.
234 D6 Kent Acres DE U.S.A.
215 M8 Kentani S. Africa
121 M6 Kentau Kazakh.
234 D6 Kent County county DE U.S.A.
234 C6 Kent County county MD U.S.A.
83 K8 Kent Group is Tas. Austr.
234 C7 Kent Island MD U.S.A.
230 C7 Kentland IN U.S.A.
150 F6 Kenton Devon, England U.K.
234 D6 Kenton DE U.S.A.
226 F3 Kenton MI U.S.A.
232 B8 Kenton OH U.S.A.
215 K9 Kenton-on-Sea S. Africa
220 H3 Kent Peninsula Nunavut Can.
234 C7 Kent Point MD U.S.A.
198 E2 Kentriki Makedonia admin. reg. Greece
232 B11 Kentucky r. KY U.S.A.
232 A11 Kentucky state U.S.A.
237 K7 Kentucky Lake KY U.S.A.
237 J10 Kentwood LA U.S.A.
226 I7 Kentwood MI U.S.A.
Kenxa Rus. Fed. see Kenkhi
210 C4 Kenya country Africa
Kenya, Mount Kenya see Kirinyaga
176 G4 Kenyeri Hungary
94 E2 Kenyir, Tasik resr Malaysia
226 B5 Kenyon MN U.S.A.
129 G2 Ken'yurt Rus. Fed.
105 K5 Ken-zaki pt Japan
121 N3 Kenzharyk Kazakh.
129 E2 Kenzhe Rus. Fed.
172 D5 Kenzingen Ger.
240 □E13 Kēōkea HI U.S.A.
226 C9 Keokuk IA U.S.A.
116 F6 Keoladeo National Park India
240 □D12 Keolu Hills HI U.S.A.
117 J9 Keonjhar Orissa India
236 J5 Keosauqua IA U.S.A.
146 D6 Keose Western Isles, Scotland U.K.
231 F8 Keowee, Lake resr SC U.S.A.
94 E6 Kepahiang Sumatera Indon.
143 M7 Kępice Pol.
78 □4b Kepidau en Pohnahtik sea chan. Pohnpei Micronesia
134 H2 Kepina Rus. Fed.
134 H2 Kepina r. Rus. Fed.
81 B12 Kepler Mountains South I. N.Z.
174 F4 Kępno Pol.
85 M7 Keppel Bay Qld Austr.
94 □ Keppel Harbour sea chan. Sing.
Keppel Island Tonga see Tafahi
199 J3 Kepsut Turkey
Kepulauan Bangka-Be[lilitung] prov. Indon. see Bangka-Belitung
114 D7 Kerala state India
102 □E20 Kerama-rettō is Nanse[i-shotō] Japan
198 F2 Keramoti Greece
207 F4 Kéran, Parc National nat. park Togo
83 I6 Kerang Vic. Austr.
198 B3 Kerasona Greece
198 E5 Keratea Greece
86 E5 Keraudren, Cape W.A. [Austr.]
141 R6 Kerava Fin.
94 E6 Kerbau, Tanjung pt In[don.]
Kerbela Iraq see Karba[la']
121 N7 Kerben Kyrg.
100 J2 Kerbi r. Rus. Fed.
225 H2 Kerbodot, Lac l. Que. [Can.]
195 □ Kercem Gozo Malta
137 P8 Kerch Ukr.
134 K3 Kerchem'ya Rus. Fed.
Kerchens'ka Protoka str. Rus. Fed./Ukr. see Ker[ch Strait]
Kerchenskiy Proliv str. Rus. Fed./Ukr. see Ker[ch Strait]
137 O8 Kerchens'kyy Pivostriv pen. Ukr.
134 L4 Kerchevskiy Rus. Fed.
Kerch Peninsula Ukr. see Kerchens'kyy Pivostriv
137 P8 Kerch Strait Rus. Fed./Ukr.
208 E3 Kéré C.A.R.
210 C3 Kere Eth.
177 J4 Kerecsend Hungary
127 P9 Kereft Iran
208 E2 Kereidila l. Sudan
177 I5 Kerekegyháza Hunga[ry]
91 K8 Kerema P.N.G.
222 G5 Keremeos B.C. Can.
126 F2 Kerempe Burun pt Tu[rkey]
203 H6 Keren Eritrea
122 B4 Kerend Iran
80 J4 Kerepehi North I. N.Z.
177 I4 Kerepestarcsa Hunga[ry]
139 O2 Kerest' r. Rus. Fed.
136 C5 Kerets'ky Ukr.
206 A3 Kerewan Gambia
121 M2 Kerey watercourse Ka[zakh.]
121 M2 Kerey, Ozero salt l. K[azakh.]
122 G2 Kergeli Turkm.
265 I8 Kerguélen, Îles is Indian Ocean
Kerguelen Islands Indian Ocean see Kerguélen, Îles
265 I8 Kerguelen Plateau sea feature Indian Oce[an]
210 B5 Kericho Kenya
95 J4 Kerihun mt. Indon.
80 I2 Kerikeri North I. N.Z.
141 T6 Kerimäki Fin.
94 D6 Kerinci, Danau l. Indo[n.]
94 D5 Kerinci, Gunung vol. [Indon.]
94 D6 Kerinci Seblat, Tama[n] Nasional nat. park Ind[on.]
Kerintji vol. Indon. see Kerinci, Gunung
210 C4 Kerio watercourse Ken[ya]
Keriya Xinjiang China s[ee] Yutian
111 F7 Keriya He watercourse [China]
111 E9 Keriya Shankou pass China
196 E4 Kerka r. Romania
164 H5 Kerkdriel Neth.
203 H5 Kerkebet Eritrea
169 B8 Kerken Ger.
205 H2 Kerkenah, Îles is Tuni[sia]
123 K3 Kerkiçi Turkm.
198 E1 Kerkini, Limni l. Gree[ce]
Kerkini Oros mts Bulg./Macedonia see B[elasitsa]
Kerkini Oros mts Euro[pe] Belasitsa
Kérkira i. Greece see K[erkyra]
205 H1 Kerkouane tourist site [Tunisia]
165 J7 Kerkrade Neth.
164 H5 Kerkwijk Neth.
198 A3 Kerkyra Kerkyra Greec[e]
198 A3 Kerkyra i. Greece
158 C4 Kerlouan France
203 F5 Kerma Sudan
77 I5 Kermadec Islands S. Pacific Ocean
266 H8 Kermadec Trench se[a feature] S. Pacific Ocean
122 G6 Kermān Iran
122 G7 Kermān prov. Iran
240 L5 Kerman CA U.S.A.
122 H7 Kermān, Bīābān-e d[es.] Iran
122 B4 Kermānshāh Iran
122 B4 Kermānshāh prov. Ira[n]
122 F6 Kermānshāhān Iran
Kermānshāhān prov. Iran see Kermānshāh
Kermine Uzbek. see N[avoiy]
237 D10 Kermit TX U.S.A.
240 M6 Kern r. CA U.S.A.
240 N6 Kern, South Fork r. C[A U.S.A.]
158 E5 Kernascléden France
225 H1 Kernertut, Cap c. Qu[e. Can.]
179 M4 Kernhof Austria
84 D8 Kernot Range hills N.[T. Austr.]
190 E2 Kerns Switz.
240 N6 Kernville CA U.S.A.
Keroh Malaysia see Pengkalan Hulu
199 G6 Keros i. Greece
134 K3 Keros Rus. Fed.
207 F4 Kérou Benin
206 C4 Kérouané Guinea
169 C9 Kerpen Ger.
263 K1 Kerr, Cape Antarctica
146 E10 Kerrera i. Scotland U.[K.]
223 I5 Kerrobert Sask. Can.
237 F10 Kerrville TX U.S.A.
147 D8 Kerry county Ireland
147 C8 Kerry Head Ireland
147 G2 Kerrykeel Ireland
210 C3 Kersa Dek Eth.
231 G8 Kershaw SC U.S.A.
149 L3 Kershopefoot Cumbri[a,] England U.K.
171 D8 Kerspleben Ger.
143 M1 Kerstinbo Sweden
180 E5 Kert, Oued r. Morocco
94 E2 Kerteh Malaysia
142 G6 Kerteminde Denmark
177 K4 Kertészsziget Hungar[y]
95 J8 Kertosono Jawa Indo[n.]
95 K1 Keruak Lombok Indon[.]
Kerulen r. China/Mong[olia] Herlen Gol
94 E5 Kerumutan, Suaka Margasatwa nature re[s.]
114 D4 Kerur Karnataka India
139 W6 Kerva Rus. Fed.
158 E6 Kervignac France
128 B3 Keryneia Cyprus
205 E3 Kerzaz Alg.
190 C2 Kerzers Switz.
134 I4 Kerzhenets r. Rus. Fe[d.]
224 E3 Kesagami r. Ont. Can[.]
224 D3 Kesagami Lake Ont. [Can.]
141 T6 Kesälahti Fin.
199 H2 Keşan Turkey
126 I3 Keşap Turkey
197 N7 Kesarevo Bulg.
117 J6 Kesariya Bihar India
209 C5 Kese Dem. Rep. Cong[o]
102 S8 Kesennuma Japan
151 O3 Kesgrave Suffolk, Eng[land U.K.]
147 F4 Kesh Ireland
147 G3 Kesh Northern Ireland [U.K.]
100 D4 Keshan Heilong. Chin[a]
129 E3 K'eshelt'a Georgia
123 N3 Keshem Afgh.
226 F5 Keshena WI U.S.A.
123 L3 Keshendeh-ye Bala [Afgh.]
122 H7 Keshīt Iran
116 C9 Keshod Gujarat India
116 F7 Keshorai Patan Rajas[than] India
127 N7 Keshvar Iran
126 F4 Keskin Turkey
134 F3 Keskozero Rus. Fed.
139 U3 Kes'ma Rus. Fed.
199 M5 Kesme Turkey
139 U4 Kesova Gora Rus. Fe[d.]

Kęsowo Pol.
Kessel Belgium
Kessel r. Ger.
Kessel Neth.
Kessingland Suffolk, England U.K.
Kestel Bursa Turkey
Kestel Bursa Turkey see Gürsu
Kestel Gölü l. Turkey
Kestell S. Africa
Kesten'ga Rus. Fed.
Kestilä Fin.
Keswick Ont. Can.
Keswick Cumbria, England U.K.
Keszthely Hungary
Keszthelyihegység park Hungary
Ket' r. Rus. Fed.
Keta Ghana
Ketahun Sumatera Indon.
Ketam, Pulau i. Sing.
Ketapang Jawa Indon.
Ketapang Kalimantan Indon.
Ketchikan AK U.S.A.
Ketchum ID U.S.A.
Ketchum Glacier Antarctica
Kétegyháza Hungary
Kete Krachi Ghana
Ketelmeer l. Neth.
Kéthely Hungary
Ketian Qinghai China
Keti Bandar Pak.
Ketmen', Khrebet mts China/Kazakh.
Kétou Benin
Ketrysanivka Ukr.
Kętrzyn Pol.
Kétsoprony Hungary
Ketta Congo
Kétté Cameroon
Kettenkamp Ger.
Kettering Northamptonshire, England U.K.
Kettering OH U.S.A.
Kettershausen Ger.
Kettinge Denmark
Kettle r. B.C. Can.
Kettle r. MN U.S.A.
Kettle Creek r. PA U.S.A.
Kettle Falls WA U.S.A.
Kettleman City CA U.S.A.
Kettle River MN U.S.A.
Kettle River Range mts WA U.S.A.
Kettletoft Orkney, Scotland U.K.
Kettlewell North Yorkshire, England U.K.
Ketungau r. Indon.
Kęty Pol.
Ketzerbach r. Ger.
Ketzin Ger.
Keuka NY U.S.A.
Keuka Lake NY U.S.A.
Keula Ger.
Keumgang, Mount N. Korea see Kumgang-san
Keumsang, Mount N. Korea see Kumgang-san
Keur Massène Maur.
Keurusselkä l. Fin.
Keuruu Fin.
Keutschach am See Austria
Keutscharcher See l. Austria
Kevelaer Ger.
Kevermes Hungary
Kevo Fin.
Kevon luonnonpuisto nature res. Fin.
Kew Turks and Caicos Is
Kewanee IL U.S.A.
Kewapante Flores Indon.
Kewaskum WI U.S.A.
Kewaunee WI U.S.A.
Keweenaw Bay MI U.S.A.
Keweenaw Bay b. MI U.S.A.
Keweenaw Peninsula MI U.S.A.
Keweenaw Point MI U.S.A.
Kewstoke North Somerset, England U.K.
Key, Lough l. Ireland
Keyala Sudan
Keya Paha r. NE U.S.A.
Key Harbour Ont. Can.
Keyi Xinjiang China
Keyihe Nei Mongol China
Keyingham East Riding of Yorkshire, England U.K.
Key Largo FL U.S.A.
Key Largo National Marine Sanctuary nature res. FL U.S.A.
Keyling Inlet N.T. Austr.
Keymir Turkm.
Keymir Turkm. see Keymir
Keynsham Bath and North East Somerset, England U.K.
Keyser WV U.S.A.
Keysers Ridge MD U.S.A.
Keystone Lake OK U.S.A.
Keystone Lake PA U.S.A.
Keystone Peak AZ U.S.A.
Keysville VA U.S.A.
Keytesville MO U.S.A.
Keytū Iran
Keyvy, Vozvyshennost' hills Rus. Fed.
Key West FL U.S.A.
Keyworth Nottinghamshire, England U.K.
Kez Rus. Fed.
Kezar Falls ME U.S.A.
Kezi Zimbabwe
Kežmarok Slovakia
Kgakala S. Africa
Kgalagadi admin. dist. Botswana
Kgalagadi Transfrontier Park nat. park Botswana/S. Africa
Kgatleng admin. dist. Botswana
Kgotsong S. Africa
Kgubetswana S. Africa
Khabab Syria
Khabar Iran
Khabarikha Rus. Fed.
Khabarovsk Rus. Fed.
Khabarovskiy Kray admin. div. Rus. Fed.
Khabarovsk Kray admin. div. Rus. Fed. see Khabarovskiy Kray
Khabary Rus. Fed.
Khabb, Wādī watercourse Yemen
Khabbah, Ra's al pt Oman
Khabez Rus. Fed.
Khabis Iran see Shahdād
Khabody Pass Afgh.
Khabovichy Belarus
Khabr Iran
Khabrā al'Arn salt pan Saudi Arabia
Khabrah Sāfiyah hill Saudi Arabia
Khābūr, Nahr al r. Syria
Khachmas Azer. see Xaçmaz
Khachrod Madh. Prad. India
Khadar, Jabal mt. Oman
Khaḑāran Saudi Arabia
Khadari watercourse Sudan
Khadd, Wādī al watercourse Saudi Arabia
Khādeyn Iran
Khadun' Belarus
Khadyzhensk Rus. Fed.
Khadzhalmakhi Rus. Fed.
Khadzhidimovo Bulg.
Khadzhiolen Turkm.
Khadzhybeys'kyy Lyman l. Ukr.
Khadziloni Belarus
Khafs Banbān well Saudi Arabia
Khafs Daghrah Saudi Arabia
Khāftar Iran
Khaga Uttar Prad. India
Khagaria Bihar India
Khagaul Bihar India
117 M8 Khagrachari Bangl.
Khagrachchari Bangl. see Khagrachari
116 H9 Khairagarh Chhattisgarh India
111 C13 Khairagarh Uttar Prad. India
123 N7 Khairgarh Pak.
116 H5 Khairigarh Uttar Prad. India
123 O7 Khairpur Pak.
123 M8 Khairpur Pak.
116 D8 Khairwara Rajasthan India
129 D3 Khaishi Georgia
122 D6 Khāīz, Kūh-e mt. Iran
123 K3 Khaja Du Koh hill Afgh.
123 M5 Khajuri Kach Pak.
98 F1 Khakasiya, Respublika aut. rep. Rus. Fed.
Khakassia aut. rep. Rus. Fed. see Khakasiya, Respublika
Khakasskaya A.S.S.R. aut. rep. Rus. Fed. see Khakasiya, Respublika
123 M4 Khāk-e Jabbar Afgh.
129 G3 Khakhalgi, Gora mt. Rus. Fed.
212 D5 Khakhea Botswana
123 K6 Khak-rēz Afgh.
123 K6 Khakriz reg. Afgh.
129 I3 Khalagork r. Rus. Fed.
122 D4 Khalajestan reg. Iran
129 H4 Khalakhurkats, Pereval pass Rus. Fed.
138 M6 Khalamyer"ye Belarus
129 E3 Khalatsa, Mt'a Georgia/Rus. Fed.
116 F2 Khalatse Jammu and Kashmir
122 E5 Khalidabad Iran
123 L6 Khalifat mt. Pak.
117 I6 Khalilabad Uttar Prad. India
122 H4 Khalilabad Iran
122 E8 Khalīlī Iran
120 H2 Khalilovo Rus. Fed.
123 J1 Khalkabad Turkm.
122 C3 Khalkhāl Iran
Khálki i. Greece see Chalki
129 G3 Khal-Kiloy Rus. Fed.
Khalkís Greece see Chalkida
115 I3 Khallikot Orissa India
134 N2 Khal'mer-Yu Rus. Fed.
138 L7 Khalopyenichy Belarus
Khalqobod Uzbek. see Xalqobod
117 J6 Khalte Nepal
Khalturin Rus. Fed. see Orlov
129 H2 Khamamatyurt Rus. Fed.
106 H1 Khamar-Daban, Khrebet mts Rus. Fed.
116 H8 Khamaria Madh. Prad. India
116 B8 Khambhaliya Gujarat India
116 D8 Khambhat Gujarat India
114 B3 Khambhat, Gulf of India
116 F9 Khamgaon Mahar. India
122 F8 Khamīr Iran
124 F7 Khamir Yemen
213 F4 Khami Ruins National Monument tourist site Zimbabwe
124 F6 Khamis Mushayţ Saudi Arabia
120 D4 Khamit Yergaliyev Kazakh.
96 G5 Khamkkeut Laos
124 H2 Khamma well Saudi Arabia
114 G4 Khammam Andhra Prad. India
131 N3 Khampa Rus. Fed.
96 B3 Khampat Myanmar
131 M3 Khamra Rus. Fed.
128 A8 Khamsah Egypt
122 C4 Khamseh reg. Iran
129 B1 Khamyshki Rus. Fed.
Khamza Uzbek. see Hamza
123 M5 Khan Afgh.
96 F5 Khan, Nam r. Laos
123 M3 Khānābād Afgh.
127 K7 Khān al Baghdādī Iraq
127 L7 Khān al Maḩāwīl Iraq
127 L7 Khān al Mashāhidah Iraq
127 L7 Khān al Muşallá Iraq
114 D5 Khanapur Karnataka India
114 D4 Khanapur Mahar. India
122 A3 Khānaqāh Iran
127 L8 Khān ar Raḩbah Iraq
127 L4 Khanasur Pass Iran/Turkey
122 F3 Khān Bāgh Iran
Khanbalik Beijing China see Beijing
122 A3 Khānch Iran
83 L7 Khancoban N.S.W. Austr.
106 C1 Khandagayty Rus. Fed.
114 D4 Khandala Mahar. India
116 E6 Khandela Rajasthan India
123 O3 Khandud Afgh.
116 F9 Khandwa Madh. Prad. India
131 O3 Khandyga Rus. Fed.
122 E6 Khāneh Khowreh Iran
123 N6 Khanewal Pak.
123 N7 Khangarh Pak.
Khan Hung Vietnam see Soc Trăng
131 N4 Khani Rus. Fed.
Khaniá Kriti Greece see Chania
116 G7 Khaniadhana Madh. Prad. India
139 T7 Khanino Rus. Fed.
122 E7 Khānī Yek Iran
127 L7 Khān Jadwal Iraq
100 H6 Khanka, Lake China/Rus. Fed.
Khanka, Ozero l. China/Rus. Fed. see Khanka, Lake
Khankendi Azer. see Xankändi
Khanki Uzbek. see Xonqa
116 F4 Khanna Punjab India
128 E6 Khannā, Qā' salt pan Jordan
205 G4 Khannfoussa hill Alg.
134 M2 Khanovey Rus. Fed.
123 N7 Khanpur Pak.
Khān Ruḩābah Iraq see Khān ar Raḩbah
128 E3 Khān Shaykhūn Syria
210 E2 Khansiir, Raas pt Somalia
129 A1 Khanskaya Rus. Fed.
137 R7 Khanskoye, Ozero salt l. Rus. Fed.
121 O5 Khantau Kazakh.
131 K3 Khantayskoye, Ozero l. Rus. Fed.
130 J3 Khantayskoye Vodokhranilishche resr Rus. Fed.
121 S6 Khan-Tengri, Pik mt. Kazakh./Kyrg.
130 H3 Khanty-Mansiysk Rus. Fed.
134 M3 Khanty-Mansiyskiy Avtonomnyy Okrug-Yugra admin. div. Rus. Fed.
128 C7 Khān Yūnis Gaza
97 E8 Khao Ang Rua Nai Wildlife Reserve nature res. Thai.
97 D11 Khao Banthat Wildlife Reserve nature res. Thai.
97 D10 Khao Chum Thong Thai.
97 D7 Khaoen Si Nakarin National Park Thai.
97 D7 Khao Laem National Park Thai.
96 D7 Khao Laem Reservoir Thai.
97 D10 Khao Luang National Park Thai.
97 D11 Khao Pu-Khao Ya National Park Thai.
97 F8 Khao Soi Dao Wildlife Reserve nature res. Thai.
97 D10 Khao Sok National Park Thai.
97 E7 Khao Yai National Park Thai.
116 G9 Khapa Mahar. India
116 F2 Khapalu Jammu and Kashmir
107 M2 Khapcheranga Rus. Fed.
116 H5 Khaptad National Park Nepal
120 B4 Kharabali Rus. Fed.
129 E3 Kharagauli Georgia
117 K7 Kharagdiha Jharkhand India
116 C8 Kharaghoda Gujarat India
117 K7 Kharagpur Bihar India
117 K8 Kharagpur W. Bengal India
122 G3 Kharakī Iran
122 H8 Khārān r. Iran
123 K7 Kharan Pak.
107 O2 Kharanor Rus. Fed.
Kharari Rajasthan India see Abu Road
175 M3 Kharava Belarus
114 D3 Kharda Mahar. India
114 C3 Khardi Mahar. India
116 F2 Khardung La pass Jammu and Kashmir
123 I4 Kharez Ilias Afgh.
127 M8 Kharfiyah Iraq
100 H2 Kharga r. Rus. Fed.
Kharga Oasis Egypt see Khārijah, Wāḩāt al
116 G7 Khargapur Madh. Prad. India
Khārg Island Iran see Khārk
122 D7 Khārg Islands Iran
116 E9 Khargon Madh. Prad. India
116 E7 Khari r. Rajasthan India
123 O9 Khari r. Rajasthan India
123 O5 Kharian Pak.
117 I9 Khariar Orissa India
203 F3 Khārijah, Wāḩāt al oasis Egypt
128 B8 Kharīm, Jabal hill Egypt
129 E3 Kharist'vala Georgia
122 D7 Khārk i. Iran
116 H9 Kharkhara r. India
116 F5 Kharkhauda Haryana India
Kharkiv r. Rus. Fed./Ukr. see Khar'kov
137 P4 Kharkiv Ukr.
Kharkiv Oblast admin. div. Ukr. see Kharkivs'ka Oblast'
137 P4 Kharkivs'ka Oblast' admin. div. Ukr.
137 P3 Khar'kov r. Rus. Fed./Ukr.
Khar'kov Ukr. see Kharkiv
Kharkov Oblast admin. div. Ukr. see Kharkivs'ka Oblast'
Khar'kovskaya Oblast' admin. div. Ukr. see Kharkivs'ka Oblast'
122 E6 Khār Kūh mt. Iran
134 G1 Kharlovka Rus. Fed.
134 E3 Kharlu Rus. Fed.
125 K9 Kharmah, Ghubbat b. Suquţrā Yemen
116 F2 Kharmang Jammu and Kashmir
197 N9 Kharmanli Bulg.
116 H9 Kharora Chhattisgarh India
123 M5 Kharoti reg. Afgh.
134 H4 Kharovsk Rus. Fed.
100 J3 Kharpin r. Rus. Fed.
122 D4 Khar Rūd r. Iran
117 J8 Kharsawan Jharkhand India
117 I8 Kharsia Chhattisgarh India
117 M6 Kharteng Arun. Prad. India
203 G6 Khartoum Sudan
203 G6 Khartoum state Sudan
203 G6 Khartoum North Sudan
137 R5 Khartsyz'k Ukr.
Kharuf, Ra's mt. Israel see Ḩarif, Har
134 L2 Kharutoyuvom Rus. Fed.
123 M5 Kharwar reg. Afgh.
125 L2 Khasab, Khor b. Oman
129 E2 Khasan'ya Rus. Fed.
129 D2 Khasaut Rus. Fed.
129 H2 Khasavyurt Rus. Fed.
123 J6 Khash Afgh.
123 I7 Khāsh Iran
123 J6 Khāsh, Dasht-e des. Afgh.
130 H3 Khashgort Rus. Fed.
203 G6 Khashm el Girba Sudan
210 B1 Khashm el Girba Dam Sudan
124 C2 Khashm Şana' Saudi Arabia
123 I6 Khash Rūd r. Afgh.
129 B2 Khashup'sa Georgia
129 E4 Khashuri Georgia
117 M7 Khasi Hills Meghalaya India
197 N9 Khaskovo Bulg.
124 D2 Khatam, Jabal al hill Saudi Arabia
131 L2 Khatanga Rus. Fed.
131 L2 Khatanga r. Rus. Fed.
Khatanga, Gulf of Rus. Fed. see Khatangskiy Zaliv
131 L2 Khatangskiy Zaliv b. Rus. Fed.
134 L2 Khatayakha Rus. Fed.
116 F8 Khategaon Madh. Prad. India
123 N3 Khatinza Pass Pak.
123 M3 Khatlon admin. div. Tajik.
Khatlon Oblast admin. div. Tajik. see Khatlon
124 G6 Khaţmah, Banī reg. Saudi Arabia
125 M3 Khatmat al Malāha Oman
129 F2 Khatuley Rus. Fed.
122 F6 Khātūnābād Iran
131 S3 Khatyrka Rus. Fed.
137 S2 Khava r. Rus. Fed.
123 M4 Khāvāk, Khowtal-e pass Afgh.
116 B8 Khavda Gujarat India
129 E4 Khavet'i Georgia
125 L9 Khawlaf, Ra's pt Suquţrā Yemen
125 M3 Khawr Fakkan U.A.E.
125 K6 Khawr Shiban well Saudi Arabia
96 C7 Khawsa Myanmar
124 E6 Khawsh Saudi Arabia
215 J7 Khayamnandi S. Africa
124 D3 Khaybar Al Madīnah Saudi Arabia
124 F6 Khaybar 'Asīr Saudi Arabia
121 N8 Khaydarken Kyrg.
214 C10 Khayelitsha S. Africa
134 L1 Khaypudyrskaya Guba b. Rus. Fed.
Khazarasp Uzbek. see Hazorasp
129 H3 Khebda Rus. Fed.
114 C3 Khed Mahar. India
114 C4 Khed Mahar. India
116 D8 Kheda Gujarat India
116 D7 Khedbrahma Gujarat India
122 H4 Khedrī Iran
Khefa Israel see Ḩefa
213 G4 Khehuene, Ponta pt Moz.
96 B1 Khela Arun. Prad. India
116 H5 Khela Uttaranchal India
117 J8 Khelari Jharkhand India
141 U6 Khelyulya Rus. Fed.
180 D5 Khemis Beni Arous Morocco
205 F1 Khemis Miliana Alg.
204 D2 Khemisset Morocco
204 C2 Khemis Zemamra Morocco
96 G6 Khemmarat Thai.
205 G2 Khenchela Alg.
204 D2 Khenifra Morocco
123 M4 Khenjan Afgh.
116 D8 Kheralu Gujarat India
122 E7 Kherāmeh Iran
122 E8 Kherreh Iran
122 D6 Khersan r. Iran
137 L7 Kherson Ukr.
137 M9 Khersones, Mys pt Ukr.
Kherson Oblast admin. div. Ukr. see Khersons'ka Oblast'
137 M7 Khersons'ka Oblast' admin. div. Ukr.
Khersonskaya Oblast' admin. div. Ukr. see Khersons'ka Oblast'
96 H6 Khe Sanh Vietnam
123 M4 Khesh Afgh.
122 D7 Khesht Iran
131 L2 Kheta r. Rus. Fed.
139 N1 Kheynyasensari, Ostrov i. Rus. Fed.
122 F7 Kheyrābād Iran
122 E3 Khezerābād Iran
97 E7 Khiaw, Khao mt. Thai.
117 J9 Khiching Orissa India
124 G5 Khidā, Jabal hill Saudi Arabia
129 F4 Khidist'avi Georgia
116 F7 Khilchipur Madh. Prad. India
Khiliomódhion Greece see Chiliomodi
107 L1 Khilok Rus. Fed.
107 J1 Khilok r. Rus. Fed.
Khimadhítis, Límni l. Greece see Cheimaditida, Limni
139 U6 Khimki Rus. Fed.
100 G4 Khingansk Rus. Fed.
100 F4 Khinganskiy Zapovednik nature res. Rus. Fed.
123 N9 Khinsar Pak.
116 C6 Khinyan Rajasthan India
Khíos i. Greece see Chios
Khios Strait Greece see Chios Strait
128 F3 Khirbat Isrīyah Syria
116 F8 Khirkiya Madh. Prad. India
197 M8 Khisarya Bulg.
139 P7 Khislavichi Rus. Fed.
111 D9 Khitai Dawan pass Aksai Chin
129 I4 Khiv Rus. Fed.
Khiwa Uzbek. see Xiva
122 B2 Khīyāv Iran
138 M1 Khiytola Rus. Fed.
139 R6 Khlepen' Rus. Fed.
139 W9 Khlevnoye Rus. Fed.
175 L5 Khlivchany Ukr.
97 E8 Khlong, Mae r. Thai.
97 D10 Khlong Saeng Wildlife Reserve nature res. Thai.
96 D6 Khlong Wang Chao National Park Thai.
97 F8 Khlung Thai.
139 R1 Khmelezero Rus. Fed.
139 V9 Khmelinets Rus. Fed.
139 Q6 Khmelita Rus. Fed.
137 M3 Khmeliv Ukr.
Khmel'nik Ukr. see Khmil'nyk
Khmel'nitskaya Oblast' admin. div. Ukr. see Khmel'nyts'ka Oblast'
Khmel'nitskiy Ukr. see Khmel'nyts'kyy
Khmelnitskiy Oblast admin. div. Ukr. see Khmel'nyts'ka Oblast'
136 G4 Khmel'nyts'ka Oblast' admin. div. Ukr.
136 F4 Khmel'nyts'kyy Ukr.
Khmelnytskyy Oblast admin. div. Ukr. see Khmel'nyts'ka Oblast'
137 K5 Khmel'ove Ukr.
Khmer Republic country Asia see Cambodia
180 D5 Khmes, Jebel mt. Morocco
136 G4 Khmil'nyk Ukr.
175 L3 Khmyelyeva Belarus
129 G6 Khndzorut Armenia
97 G10 Khoai, Hon i. Vietnam
120 F2 Khobda Kazakh.
129 C3 Khobi r. Georgia
139 X8 Khobotovo Rus. Fed.
175 M5 Khobultova Ukr.
122 G5 Khodā Āfarīd spring Iran
129 H6 Khodā Āfarīn Iran
138 I8 Khodarawtsy Belarus
139 O8 Khodasy Belarus
136 D4 Khodoriv Ukr.
136 I3 Khodorkiv Ukr.
129 B1 Khodz' Rus. Fed.
Khodzhal, Gora mt. Georgia see Khojali, Mt'a
Khodzhavend Azer. see Xocavänd
Khodzhent Tajik. see Khŭjand
Khodzheyli Qoraqalpog'iston Respublikasi Uzbek. see Xo'jayli
Khodzhorni Georgia see Khojorni
136 I8 Khodzhyder r. Ukr.
208 E3 Khogali Sudan
129 C3 Khojali, Mt'a Georgia
Khojand Tajik. see Khŭjand
129 F4 Khojorni Georgia
139 U2 Khokhlovo Rus. Fed.
135 G6 Khokhol'skiy Rus. Fed.
123 N9 Khokhropar Pak.
116 F3 Koksar Hima. Prad. India
116 F9 Kholapur Mahar. India
137 R3 Kholkhol-Trostyanka Rus. Fed.
123 L3 Kholm Afgh.
Kholm Pol. see Chełm
139 O4 Kholm Novgorodskaya Oblast' Rus. Fed.
139 O6 Kholm Smolenskaya Oblast' Rus. Fed.
139 O6 Kholm Smolenskaya Oblast' Rus. Fed.
139 R9 Kholmechi Rus. Fed.
177 L3 Kholmets' Ukr.
134 H2 Kholmogory Rus. Fed.
100 L5 Kholmsk Sakhalin Rus. Fed.
137 R9 Kholmskiy Rus. Fed.
137 L2 Kholmy Ukr.
136 J1 Kholmyech Belarus
139 Q6 Kholm-Zhirkovskiy Rus. Fed.
Kholon Israel see Ḩolon
139 P3 Kholova r. Rus. Fed.
106 H1 Kholtoson Rus. Fed.
121 U2 Kholzun, Khrebet mts Kazakh./Rus. Fed.
122 C3 Khoman Iran
129 I6 Khomārlū Iran
212 C4 Khomas admin. reg. Namibia
212 B4 Khomas Highland hills Namibia
122 D5 Khomeyn Iran
122 D5 Khomeynīshahr Iran
136 G3 Khomora r. Ukr.
175 N3 Khomsk Belarus
137 M3 Khomutets' Ukr.
137 R6 Khomutove Ukr.
137 N2 Khomutovka Rus. Fed.
139 U9 Khomutovo Rus. Fed.
Khong, Mae Nam r. Myanmar see Salween
129 D3 Khoni Georgia
122 E8 Khonj Iran
122 E8 Khonj, Kūh-e mts Iran
96 F6 Khon Kaen Thai.
Khon Kriel Cambodia see Phumĭ Kon Kriel
Khonobod Uzbek. see Xonobod
Khonqa Uzbek. see Xonqa
117 O6 Khonsa Arun. Prad. India
131 P3 Khonuu Rus. Fed.
135 H6 Khoper r. Rus. Fed.
129 D3 Khop'uri Georgia
100 I5 Khor Rus. Fed.
100 I5 Khor r. Rus. Fed.
Khóra Greece see Chora
122 F4 Khorāsān, Chāh-e well Iran
122 H5 Khorāsān-e Janūbī prov. Iran
122 G4 Khorāsān-e Razavī prov. Iran
122 G3 Khorāsān-e Shemālī prov. Iran
96 F6 Khorat Plateau Thai.
Khorazm Wiloyati admin. div. Uzbek. see Xorazm
134 L2 Khoreyver Rus. Fed.
Khorezm Oblast admin. div. Uzbek. see Xorazm
99 I1 Khorinsk Rus. Fed.
212 B4 Khorixas Namibia
137 M7 Khorly Ukr.
122 D7 Khormūj, Kūh-e mt. Iran
Khorog Tajik. see Khorugh
100 H6 Khorol Rus. Fed.
137 M4 Khorol Ukr.
137 M4 Khorol r. Ukr.
137 P5 Khoroshe Ukr.
121 R1 Khorosheye Rus. Fed.
122 B2 Khoroslū Dāgh hills Iran
136 E4 Khorostkiv Ukr.
122 C5 Khorramābād Iran
122 C3 Khorram Darreh Iran
122 C6 Khorramshahr Iran
123 N3 Khorugh Tajik.
137 M3 Khoruzhivka Ukr.
134 L2 Khosedayu r. Rus. Fed.
122 H5 Khosf Iran
135 I7 Khosheutovo Rus. Fed.
122 C6 Khosravī Iran
129 F5 Khosrovi Argelanots' nature res. Armenia
122 C6 Khosrowābād Iran
127 L6 Khosrowvī Iran
Khost prov. Afgh. see Khowst
123 L6 Khost Pak.
129 A2 Khosta Rus. Fed.
122 F7 Khosūyeh Iran
116 F5 Khot Haryana India
Khotan Xinjiang China see Hotan
117 K6 Khotang Nepal
175 M4 Khoteshiv Ukr.
139 T9 Khotetovo Rus. Fed.
137 P4 Khotimlya r. Ukr.
137 N2 Khotin' Ukr.
139 S8 Khot'kovo Kaluzhskaya Oblast' Rus. Fed.
139 U5 Khot'kovo Moskovskaya Oblast' Rus. Fed.
137 O3 Khotmyzhsk Rus. Fed.
139 Q8 Khotsimsk Belarus
137 K4 Khots'ky Ukr.
136 F5 Khotyn Ukr.
139 S8 Khotynets Rus. Fed.
204 D2 Khouribga Morocco
123 M2 Khovaling Tajik.
117 M7 Khowai Tripura India
Khowos Uzbek. see Xovos
122 E6 Khowrjān Iran
122 F5 Khowrnag, Kūh-e mt. Iran
123 M5 Khowst Afgh.
123 M5 Khowst prov. Afgh.
123 M5 Khowst reg. Afgh./Pak.
116 B2 Khowt-e Ashrow Afgh.
100 M3 Khoye Rus. Fed.
136 I2 Khoyniki Belarus
127 K3 Khozap'ini, Tba l. Georgia
124 F9 Khozor Anghar Djibouti
97 E8 Khram, Ko i. Thai.
137 T2 Khrenovoye Rus. Fed.
137 L4 Khrestyteleve Ukr.
96 A4 Khreum Myanmar
117 M6 Khri r. India
Khrisoúpolis Greece see Chrysoupoli
134 I3 Khristoforovo Rus. Fed.
131 P2 Khroma r. Rus. Fed.
120 H2 Khromtau Kazakh.
117 O6 Khru r. India
Khrushchev Ukr. see Svitlovods'k
139 X7 Khrushchevo Rus. Fed.
100 I6 Khrustalnyy Rus. Fed.
Khrysokhou Bay Cyprus see Chrysochou Bay
137 M6 Khrystoforivka Dnipropetrovs'ka Oblast' Ukr.
137 L6 Khrystoforivka Mykolayivs'ka Oblast' Ukr.
136 I5 Khrystynivka Ukr.
123 O5 Khuar Pak.
215 M5 Khubelu r. Lesotho
129 I4 Khuchni Rus. Fed.
Khudat Azer. see Xudat
122 F2 Khudayberdy Turkm.
123 L8 Khude Hills Pak.
123 P6 Khudian Pak.
125 I7 Khuḑrah, Wādī r. Yemen
212 E4 Khudumelapye Botswana
Khudzhand Tajik. see Khŭjand
124 H4 Khufaysah, Khashm al hill Saudi Arabia
124 G3 Khuff Saudi Arabia
Khugiana Afgh. see Pirzada
123 L6 Khugiani Afgh.
122 I9 Khūh Lab, Ra's pt Iran
214 F2 Khuis Botswana
123 M1 Khŭjand Tajik.
Khŭjand admin. div. Tajik. see Soghd
Khŭjayli Uzbek. see Xo'jayli
97 G7 Khu Khan Thai.
137 N3 Khukhra Ukr.
124 D4 Khulays Saudi Arabia
116 E9 Khuldabad Mahar. India
134 M2 Khulga r. Rus. Fed.
134 M3 Khulimsunt Rus. Fed.
123 L3 Khulm r. Afgh.
117 L8 Khulna Bangl.
117 L8 Khulna admin. div. Bangl.
215 K2 Khuma S. Africa
129 F2 Khumalag Rus. Fed.
97 G9 Khŭm Batheay Cambodia
128 F4 Khunayzīr, Jabal al mts Syria
203 F6 Khuneiqa watercourse Sudan
122 H5 Khūnīk Bālā Iran
Khūnīnshahr Iran see Khorramshahr
116 E1 Khunjerab National Park Jammu and Kashmir
116 E1 Khunjerab Pass China/Jammu and Kashmir
122 D5 Khunsar Iran
117 J8 Khunti Jharkhand India
96 C5 Khun Yuam Thai.
129 H3 Khunzakh Rus. Fed.
139 X8 Khupta r. Rus. Fed.
122 H4 Khūr Iran
122 H5 Khur Iran
116 G7 Khurai Madh. Prad. India
122 F8 Khūran sea chan. Iran
125 I3 Khurayş Saudi Arabia
124 G6 Khurb, Banī hills Saudi Arabia
117 J9 Khurda Orissa India
202 E6 Khureit Sudan
Khuria Tank resr Chhattisgarh India see Maniari Tank
116 F5 Khurja Uttar Prad. India
123 J5 Khurmalik Afgh.
100 J3 Khurmuli Rus. Fed.
127 K8 Khurr, Wādī al watercourse Saudi Arabia
122 E7 Khūrrāb Iran
122 F4 Khurz Iran
129 D2 Khurzuk Rus. Fed.
123 O5 Khushab Pak.
123 N5 Khushalgarh Pak.
122 C3 Khūshāvar Iran
122 H6 Khushk Rud Iran
128 E9 Khushshah, Wādī al watercourse Jordan/Saudi Arabia
122 F3 Khush Yailaq hill Iran
123 J5 Khuspas Afgh.
136 C5 Khust Ukr.
138 L8 Khutar Belarus
116 H9 Khutgaon Mahar. India
128 A8 Khutmīyah, Mamarr al pass Egypt
135 H7 Khutorskoy Rus. Fed.
212 E4 Khutse Game Reserve nature res. Botswana
215 L2 Khutsong S. Africa
100 K4 Khutu r. Rus. Fed.
203 F6 Khuwei Sudan
123 L8 Khuzdar Pak.
122 C6 Khūzestān prov. Iran
122 I4 Khvāf reg. Iran
122 B2 Khvājeh Iran
122 I6 Khvājeh Dow Chāhī Iran
123 M3 Khvājeh Ghār Afgh.
120 C1 Khvalynsk Rus. Fed.
129 E3 Khvanchkara Georgia
122 F7 Khvānsār Iran
139 S6 Khvashchevka Rus. Fed.
139 S8 Khvastovichi Rus. Fed.
122 F6 Khvodrān Iran
122 F5 Khvor Iran
122 G4 Khvord Nārvan Iran
122 D7 Khvormūj Iran
139 X9 Khvorostyanka Lipetskaya Oblast' Rus. Fed.
120 C1 Khvorostyanka Samarskaya Oblast' Rus. Fed.
122 B3 Khvosh Maqām Iran
139 N6 Khvoshna Belarus
122 A2 Khvoy Iran
139 R3 Khvoynaya Rus. Fed.
100 E1 Khvoynyy Rus. Fed.
97 D8 Khwae Noi r. Thai.
123 N3 Khwahan Afgh.
123 J6 Khwaja Ali Afgh.
123 L6 Khwaja Amran mt. Pak.
123 N3 Khwaja Muhammad Range mts Afgh.
123 N4 Khyber Pass Afgh./Pak.
Khynchest' Moldova see Hînceşti
Khynchesty Moldova see Hînceşti
175 K6 Khyriv Ukr.
Khyrov Ukr. see Khyriv
Khyzy Azer. see Xızı
129 H3 Khzanor r. Rus. Fed.
78 □6 Kia Sta Isabel Solomon Is
122 H9 Kīā'ī Iran
83 M6 Kiama N.S.W. Austr.
92 E8 Kiamba Mindanao Phil.
209 F6 Kiambi Dem. Rep. Congo
234 F1 Kiamesha Lake NY U.S.A.
237 H9 Kiamichi r. OK U.S.A.
Kiangsi prov. China see Jiangxi
Kiangsu prov. China see Jiangsu
206 B3 Kiang West National Park Gambia
Kianly Turkm. see Tarta
140 T4 Kiantajärvi l. Fin.
116 G3 Kiari Jammu and Kashmir
122 E3 Kīāseh Iran
221 M2 Kiatassuaq i. Greenland
198 D4 Kiato Greece
142 E5 Kibæk Denmark
211 C6 Kibaha Tanz.
209 B6 Kibala Angola
210 A4 Kibale Uganda
208 F4 Kibali r. Dem. Rep. Congo
209 B6 Kibambi Dem. Rep. Congo
209 B5 Kibangou Congo
211 B5 Kibara Tanz.
209 E7 Kibara, Monts mts Dem. Rep. Congo
211 B7 Kibau Tanz.
92 E8 Kibawe Mindanao Phil.
211 C6 Kibaya Tanz.
211 C6 Kiberashi Tanz.
211 C6 Kiberege Tanz.
104 B7 Kibi Japan
209 C6 Kibinga Dem. Rep. Congo
210 A4 Kiboga Uganda
209 E5 Kibombo Dem. Rep. Congo
211 A5 Kibondo Tanz.
Kibray Uzbek. see Qibray
210 C3 Kibre Mengist Eth.
Kibris country Asia see Cyprus
211 A5 Kibungo Rwanda
211 A5 Kibuye Rwanda
211 A6 Kibwesa Tanz.
151 K2 Kibworth Harcourt Leicestershire, England U.K.
196 I9 Kičevo Macedonia
202 C5 Kichi-Kichi well Chad
134 I4 Kichmengskiy Gorodok Rus. Fed.
210 A5 Kichwamba Uganda
122 F2 Kiçi Balkan Daglary hill Turkm.
129 I5 Kiçik Dähnä Azer.
222 G5 Kicking Horse Pass Alta/B.C. Can.
207 F2 Kidal Mali
207 F2 Kidal admin. reg. Mali
211 C6 Kidatu Tanz.
211 C6 Kidayi Tanz.
150 H3 Kidderminster Worcestershire, England U.K.
215 L9 Kidd's Beach S. Africa
210 B4 Kidepo Valley National Park Uganda
211 C6 Kidete Tanz.
206 B3 Kidira Senegal
151 J4 Kidlington Oxfordshire, England U.K.
116 G3 Kidmang Jammu and Kashmir
80 L6 Kidnappers, Cape North I. N.Z.
179 M7 Kidričevo Slovenia
149 M7 Kidsgrove Staffordshire, England U.K.
211 C6 Kidugallo Tanz.
95 J3 Kidurong, Tanjung pt Malaysia
124 E6 Kidwat at A'waj Saudi Arabia
150 D4 Kidwelly Carmarthenshire, Wales U.K.
169 F10 Kiedrich Ger.
173 M6 Kiefersfelden Ger.
174 E3 Kiekrz Pol.
168 J2 Kiel Ger.
226 F6 Kiel WI U.S.A.
Kiel Canal Ger. see Nord-Ostsee-Kanal
175 I5 Kielce Pol.
175 J3 Kiełczew Pol.
174 G4 Kiełczygłów Pol.
149 L3 Kielder Water resr England U.K.
165 F6 Kieldrecht Belgium
168 K2 Kieler Bucht b. Ger.
168 J2 Kieler Förde g. Ger.
206 E3 Kiembara Burkina
175 H3 Kiemozia Pol.
173 M5 Kienberg Ger.
209 E7 Kienge Dem. Rep. Congo
169 E8 Kierspe Ger.
169 J9 Kieselbach Ger.
78 □6 Kieta P.N.G.
174 G5 Kietrz Pol.
170 K5 Kietz Ger.
Kīev Kazakh. see Kiyevka
Kiev Ukr. see Kyiv
Kiev Oblast admin. div. Ukr. see Kyivs'ka Oblast'
206 C2 Kiffa Maur.
198 E4 Kifisia Greece
198 E4 Kifisos r. Greece
127 L6 Kifrī Iraq
209 C6 Kifwanzondo Dem. Rep. Congo
211 A5 Kigali Rwanda
127 J4 Kiğı Turkey
225 I1 Kiglapait Mountains Nfld and Lab. Can.
206 D4 Kignan Mali
211 A6 Kigoma Tanz.
211 A6 Kigoma admin. reg. Tanz.
211 A6 Kigosi r. Tanz.
211 B6 Kigwe Tanz.
95 J5 Kihambatang Kalimantan Indon.
240 □E13 Kīhei HI U.S.A.
80 J5 Kihikihi North I. N.Z.
140 Q3 Kihlanki Fin.
141 Q5 Kihniö Fin.
138 G3 Kihnu i. Estonia
240 □F14 Kīholo HI U.S.A.
104 C8 Kii-hantō pen. Japan
140 U5 Kiihtelysvaara Fin.
121 O4 Kiik Kazakh.
138 G1 Kiikala Fin.
141 Q6 Kiikoinen Fin.
140 R4 Kiiminki Fin.
104 D7 Kii-Nagashima Japan
103 H15 Kiire Japan
104 C8 Kii-sanchi mts Japan
140 R3 Kiistala Fin.
104 A8 Kii-suidō sea chan. Japan
191 Q6 Kijac, Rt pt Croatia
175 I5 Kije Pol.
174 G2 Kijewo Królewskie Pol.
105 H2 Kijimadaira Japan
103 I14 Kijo Japan
211 C6 Kijungu Well Tanz.
102 □G18 Kikai Nansei-shotō Japan
102 □H18 Kikai-jima i. Nansei-shotō Japan
138 M2 Kikerino Rus. Fed.
196 I5 Kikinda Vojvodina Serbia
123 J9 Kikki Pak.
Kikládhes is Greece see Kyklades
134 I4 Kiknur Rus. Fed.
175 H3 Kikół Pol.
102 R5 Kikonai Japan
209 E7 Kikondja Dem. Rep. Congo
209 C6 Kikongo Dem. Rep. Congo
91 J8 Kikori P.N.G.
91 J8 Kikori r. P.N.G.
174 D2 Kikorze Pol.
103 H14 Kikuchi Japan
105 H6 Kikugawa Japan
135 H6 Kikvidze Rus. Fed.
209 C6 Kikwit Dem. Rep. Congo
142 F3 Kil Norway
142 J2 Kil Sweden
143 N3 Kilaån r. Sweden
141 N6 Kilafors Sweden
114 F8 Kilakkarai Tamil Nadu India
122 E4 Kīlan Iran
116 F3 Kilar Hima. Prad. India
240 □B11 Kilauea HI U.S.A.
240 □F14 Kilauea Crater HI U.S.A.
179 L3 Kilb Austria
147 C7 Kilbaha Ireland
147 H6 Kilbeggan Ireland
147 F8 Kilbeheny Ireland
147 H6 Kilberry Kildare Ireland
147 I5 Kilberry Meath Ireland
146 E11 Kilberry Argyll and Bute, Scotland U.K.
148 H2 Kilbirnie North Ayrshire, Scotland U.K.
140 L3 Kilboghamn Norway
93 G5 Kilbon Seram Indon.
140 N2 Kilbotn Norway
146 F12 Kilbrannan Sound sea chan. Scotland U.K.
147 J6 Kilbride Meath Ireland
148 E7 Kilbride Wicklow Ireland
147 J7 Kilbride Wicklow Ireland
146 F10 Kilbride Argyll and Bute, Scotland U.K.
147 E9 Kilbrittain Ireland
147 E3 Kilcar Ireland
147 H6 Kilcavan Ireland
172 F7 Kilchberg Switz.
137 O5 Kil'chen' r. Ukr.
146 E12 Kilchenzie Argyll and Bute, Scotland U.K.
146 D9 Kilchoan Highland, Scotland U.K.
146 F10 Kilchrenan Argyll and Bute, Scotland U.K.
101 F8 Kilchu N. Korea
147 I6 Kilcock Ireland
147 E6 Kilcolgan Ireland
147 E9 Kilcolman Ireland
147 G8 Kilcommon Ireland
147 F6 Kilconnell Ireland
147 H4 Kilconney Ireland
147 J6 Kilcoole Ireland
147 G6 Kilcormac Ireland
85 N9 Kilcoy Qld Austr.
146 G11 Kilcreggan Argyll and Bute, Scotland U.K.
147 F6 Kilcrow r. Ireland
147 I6 Kilcullen Ireland
147 I5 Kildalkey Ireland
147 I6 Kildare Ireland
147 I6 Kildare county Ireland
140 V2 Kil'dinstroy Rus. Fed.
146 F12 Kildonan North Ayrshire, Scotland U.K.
213 F3 Kildonan Zimbabwe
147 F8 Kildorrery Ireland
147 I3 Kildress Northern Ireland U.K.
134 I4 Kilemary Rus. Fed.
209 C6 Kilembe Dem. Rep. Congo
209 E6 Kileo Dem. Rep. Congo
147 D7 Kilfenora Ireland
146 F11 Kilfinan Argyll and Bute, Scotland U.K.
147 F8 Kilfinnane Ireland
150 C4 Kilgetty Pembrokeshire, Wales U.K.
147 F6 Kilglass Galway Ireland
147 F5 Kilglass Roscommon Ireland
147 F5 Kilglass Lough l. Ireland
147 C8 Kilgobnet Ireland
237 H9 Kilgore TX U.S.A.
84 E4 Kilgour r. N.T. Austr.
149 Q5 Kilham East Riding of Yorkshire, England U.K.
149 M2 Kilham Northumberland, England U.K.
Kilia Ukr. see Kiliya
205 H5 Kilian, Erg des. Alg.
209 F5 Kiliba Dem. Rep. Congo
207 F4 Kilibo Benin
199 L5 Kılıç Turkey
129 C5 Kılıçkaya Turkey
129 A5 Kılıçlı Turkey
211 C5 Kilifi Kenya
111 B8 Kilik Pass Xinjiang China
211 C5 Kilimanjaro admin. reg. Tanz.
211 C5 Kilimanjaro vol. Tanz.
211 C5 Kilimanjaro National Park Tanz.
211 B6 Kilimatinde Tanz.
77 F2 Kilinailau Islands P.N.G.
211 C6 Kilindoni Tanz.
138 H3 Kilingi-Nõmme Estonia
126 H5 Kilis Turkey
128 F2 Kilis prov. Turkey
136 I8 Kiliya Ukr.
148 D8 Kilkea Ireland
147 C7 Kilkee Ireland
147 K4 Kilkeel Northern Ireland U.K.
147 E5 Kilkelly Ireland
147 H7 Kilkenny Ireland
147 H7 Kilkenny county Ireland
147 E5 Kilkerrin Ireland
150 D6 Kilkhampton Cornwall, England U.K.
147 D8 Kilkinlea Ireland
198 D2 Kilkis Greece
85 N9 Kilkivan Qld Austr.
147 I6 Kill Kildare Ireland
147 H8 Kill Waterford Ireland
147 C9 Killabunane Ireland
148 B5 Killadeas Northern Ireland U.K.
147 D7 Killadysert Ireland
148 E3 Killagan Bridge Northern Ireland U.K.
147 D4 Killala Ireland
147 D4 Killala Bay Ireland
226 H1 Killala Lake Ont. Can.
147 F7 Killaloe Ireland
227 Q4 Killaloe Station Ont. Can.
223 I4 Killam Alta Can.
147 H8 Killamerry Ireland
147 I7 Killann Ireland
147 C7 Killard Ireland
84 C4 Killarney N.T. Austr.
83 N3 Killarney Qld Austr.
224 D4 Killarney Ont. Can.
147 D8 Killarney Ireland
231 □2 Killarney, Lake New Prov. Bahamas
147 C9 Killarney National Park Ireland
227 M3 Killarney Provincial Park Ont. Can.
147 D6 Killarone Ireland
147 C5 Killary Harbour b. Ireland
148 C7 Killaskillen Ireland
147 E8 Killavullen Ireland
147 G9 Killeagh Cork Ireland
146 E11 Killean Argyll and Bute, Scotland U.K.
147 C6 Killeany Ireland
146 H10 Killearn Stirling, Scotland U.K.
237 G10 Killeen TX U.S.A.
147 H6 Killeigh Ireland
147 G3 Killen Northern Ireland U.K.
147 I7 Killerrig Ireland
147 G4 Killeshandra Ireland
129 D5 Kıllı Dağ mt. Turkey
146 I9 Killiecrankie Perth and Kinross, Scotland U.K.
199 J4 Killik Turkey
147 D7 Killimer Ireland
147 F6 Killimor Ireland
146 H10 Killin Stirling, Scotland U.K.
147 D7 Killinaboy Ireland
147 K4 Killinchy Northern Ireland U.K.
Killinek Island Nfld and Lab./Nunavut Can. see Killiniq Island
140 P3 Killinge Sweden
149 N3 Killingworth Tyne and Wear, England U.K.
235 J2 Killingworth CT U.S.A.
Killíni mt. Greece see Kyllini
225 H1 Killiniq Que. Can.
225 H1 Killiniq Island Nfld and Lab./Nunavut Can.
141 Q5 Killinkoski Fin.
147 C8 Killorglin Ireland
147 J6 Killough Ireland
147 K4 Killough Northern Ireland U.K.
148 C6 Killucan Ireland
146 E9 Killundine Highland, Scotland U.K.
147 I8 Killurin Ireland
147 F3 Killybegs Ireland
147 H3 Killyclogher Northern Ireland U.K.
147 H5 Killyconnan Ireland
147 G3 Killygordon Ireland
147 I4 Killylea Northern Ireland U.K.
148 E7 Kilmacanogue Ireland
148 H2 Kilmacolm Inverclyde, Scotland U.K.
147 G2 Kilmacrenan Ireland
147 H8 Kilmacthomas Ireland
147 H8 Kilmaganny Ireland
147 D5 Kilmaine Ireland
147 D7 Kilmaley Ireland
146 F9 Kilmalieu Highland, Scotland U.K.
147 E8 Kilmallock Ireland
146 D7 Kilmaluag Highland, Scotland U.K.
147 H7 Kilmanagh Ireland
146 H11 Kilmarnock East Ayrshire, Scotland U.K.
233 I11 Kilmarnock VA U.S.A.
146 F10 Kilmartin Argyll and Bute, Scotland U.K.
148 H2 Kilmaurs East Ayrshire, Scotland U.K.

148 D7 Kilmeague Ireland
147 C5 Kilmeena Ireland
146 F10 Kilmelford Argyll and Bute, Scotland U.K.
134 J4 Kil'mez' Rus. Fed.
134 J4 Kil'mez' r. Rus. Fed.
147 J7 Kilmichael Point Ireland
150 F6 Kilmington Devon, England U.K.
147 E9 Kilmona Ireland
83 J7 Kilmore Vic. Austr.
147 E7 Kilmore Clare Ireland
147 I8 Kilmore Wexford Ireland
147 I8 Kilmore Quay Ireland
147 D8 Kilmorna Ireland
146 E11 Kilmory Argyll and Bute, Scotland U.K.
146 D8 Kilmory Highland, Scotland U.K.
147 E7 Kilmurry Ireland
148 D8 Kilmyshall Ireland
147 H5 Kilnaleck Ireland
147 J7 Kilnamanagh Ireland
146 D9 Kilninian Argyll and Bute, Scotland U.K.
146 E10 Kilninver Argyll and Bute, Scotland U.K.
147 E5 Kilnock Ireland
146 D10 Kiloran Argyll and Bute, Scotland U.K.
211 C6 Kilosa Tanz.
140 P2 Kilpisjärvi Fin.
140 R4 Kilpua Fin.
147 I7 Kilquiggin Ireland
147 I3 Kilrea Northern Ireland U.K.
147 F3 Kilrean Ireland
147 F6 Kilreekill Ireland
147 C6 Kilronan Ireland
147 G3 Kilross Donegal Ireland
147 F8 Kilross Tipperary Ireland
147 D7 Kilrush Ireland
147 E5 Kilsallagh Ireland
148 E6 Kilsaran Ireland
147 I5 Kilskeer Ireland
148 B5 Kilskeery Northern Ireland U.K.
146 H11 Kilsyth North Lanarkshire, Scotland U.K.
114 C7 Kiltan atoll India
147 E6 Kiltartan Ireland
147 I7 Kiltealy Ireland
148 D7 Kilteel Ireland
147 E5 Kiltimagh Ireland
147 I7 Kiltogan Ireland
147 F6 Kiltoom Ireland
147 E6 Kiltullagh Ireland
137 P7 Kil'tychchya r. Ukr.
148 A5 Kiltyclogher Ireland
209 F7 Kilwa Dem. Rep. Congo
211 C7 Kilwa Kivinje Tanz.
211 C7 Kilwa Masoko Tanz.
147 K3 Kilwaughter Northern Ireland U.K.
146 G11 Kilwinning North Ayrshire, Scotland U.K.
147 F8 Kilworth Ireland
Kilyazi Azer. see Giläzi
208 B2 Kim Chad
116 D9 Kim r. India
237 D7 Kim CO U.S.A.
211 C7 Kimambi Tanz.
95 K2 Kimanis, Teluk b. Malaysia
82 F5 Kimba S.A. Austr.
209 B5 Kimba Congo
236 D5 Kimball NE U.S.A.
232 C7 Kimball OH U.S.A.
91 L8 Kimbe New Britain P.N.G.
222 H5 Kimberley B.C. Can.
215 I4 Kimberley S. Africa
151 O2 Kimberley Norfolk, England U.K.
86 H4 Kimberley Downs W.A. Austr.
86 I4 Kimberley Plateau W.A. Austr.
87 E9 Kimberley Range hills W.A. Austr.
234 D4 Kimberton PA U.S.A.
206 D4 Kimbirila-Sud Côte d'Ivoire
151 L3 Kimbolton Cambridgeshire, England U.K.
101 F8 Kimch'aek N. Korea
101 F10 Kimch'ŏn S. Korea
101 F11 Kimhae S. Korea
Kími Greece see Kymi
141 Q6 Kimito Fin.
105 K5 Kimitsu Japan
101 E11 Kimje S. Korea
221 L3 Kimmirut Nunavut Can.
102 R4 Kimobetsu Japan
198 F6 Kimolos i. Greece
198 F6 Kimolou-Sifnou, Steno sea chan. Greece
209 B6 Kimongo Congo
139 V8 Kimovsk Rus. Fed.
209 E6 Kimpanga Dem. Rep. Congo
209 B6 Kimpangu Dem. Rep. Congo
206 D3 Kimparana Mali
232 C11 Kimper KY U.S.A.
209 B6 Kimpese Dem. Rep. Congo
209 B6 Kimpila Congo
209 B6 Kimpoko Dem. Rep. Congo
Kimpoku-san mt. Japan see Kinpoku-san
151 L4 Kimpton Hertfordshire, England U.K.
139 U5 Kimry Rus. Fed.
222 E4 Kimsquit B.C. Can.
143 L3 Kimstad Sweden
209 B6 Kimvula Dem. Rep. Congo
134 I2 Kimzha Rus. Fed.
102 □1 Kin Okinawa Japan
102 □1 Kina Okinawa Japan
95 L1 Kinabalu, Gunung mt. Sabah Malaysia
95 L1 Kinabalu National Park Malaysia
95 L2 Kinabatangan r. Malaysia
95 M2 Kinabatangan, Kuala r. mouth Malaysia
199 K2 Kınalıada i. Turkey
211 C6 Kinango Kenya
199 H6 Kinaros i. Greece
95 L2 Kinarut Sabah Malaysia
105 H2 Kinasa Japan
175 M6 Kinashiv Ukr.
222 D3 Kinaskan Lake B.C. Can.
222 G4 Kinbasket Lake B.C. Can.
Kinbirila Côte d'Ivoire see Kimbirila-Sud
146 I6 Kinbrace Highland, Scotland U.K.
137 K7 Kinburns'ka Kosa spit Ukr.
223 J5 Kincaid Sask. Can.
224 D4 Kincardine Ont. Can.
149 J1 Kincardine Fife, Scotland U.K.
146 K8 Kincardine O'Neil Aberdeenshire, Scotland U.K.
96 D1 Kinchang Myanmar
83 I5 Kinchega National Park N.S.W. Austr.
222 D4 Kincolith B.C. Can.
146 I8 Kincraig Highland, Scotland U.K.
177 H4 Kincses Hungary
209 E7 Kinda Dem. Rep. Congo
209 B5 Kindamba Congo
96 B3 Kindat Myanmar
179 L4 Kindberg Austria
227 L6 Kinde MI U.S.A.
209 B6 Kindeje Angola
171 D8 Kindelbrück Ger.
209 E7 Kindele Dem. Rep. Congo
209 C6 Kindembe Dem. Rep. Congo
237 I10 Kinder LA U.S.A.
169 D10 Kinderbeuern Ger.
164 G5 Kinderdijk Neth.
149 N7 Kinder Scout hill England U.K.
223 I5 Kindersley Sask. Can.
206 B4 Kindia Guinea
173 K4 Kinding Ger.
209 C5 Kindongo-Mbe Dem. Rep. Congo
137 N2 Kindrativka Ukr.
172 D3 Kindsbach Ger.
209 E5 Kindu Dem. Rep. Congo
135 J5 Kinel' Rus. Fed.
120 D1 Kinel'-Cherkasy Rus. Fed.
134 H4 Kineshma Rus. Fed.
151 I4 Kineton Gloucestershire, England U.K.
84 D1 King r. N.T. Austr.
84 D3 King r. N.T. Austr.
86 J3 King r. W.A. Austr.
259 B7 King, Canal sea chan. Chile
87 F8 King, Lake salt flat W.A. Austr.
232 I11 King and Queen Courthouse VA U.S.A.
209 B6 Kinganga Dem. Rep. Congo
85 M9 Kingaroy Qld Austr.
147 F3 Kingarrow Ireland
146 F11 Kingarth Argyll and Bute, Scotland U.K.
221 H2 King Christian Island Nunavut Can.
240 K5 King City CA U.S.A.
222 E5 Kingcome r. B.C. Can.
84 G8 King Creek watercourse Qld Austr.
86 I3 King Edward r. W.A. Austr.
157 N8 Kingersheim France
233 □O4 Kingfield ME U.S.A.
237 G8 Kingfisher OK U.S.A.
232 H10 King George VA U.S.A.
259 E8 King George Bay Falkland Is
262 U2 King George Island Antarctica
224 E1 King George Islands Nunavut Can.
King George Islands Arch. des Tuamotu Fr. Polynesia see Roi Georges, Îles du
87 E13 King George Sound b. W.A. Austr.
251 F3 King George VI Falls Guyana
263 A2 King Haakon VII Sea Southern Ocean
86 G7 King Hill W.A. Austr.
146 J10 Kinghorn Fife, Scotland U.K.
146 F8 Kingie r. Scotland U.K.
209 B6 Kingimbi Dem. Rep. Congo
138 L2 Kingisepp Rus. Fed.
83 I8 King Island Tas. Austr.
222 E4 King Island B.C. Can.
King Island Myanmar see Kadan Kyun
Kingisseppa Estonia see Kuressaare
227 O1 King Kirkland Ont. Can.
83 J7 Kinglake National Park Vic. Austr.
263 F2 King Leopold and Queen Astrid Coast Antarctica
86 H4 King Leopold Range National Park W.A. Austr.
86 H4 King Leopold Ranges hills W.A. Austr.
241 R6 Kingman AZ U.S.A.
237 F7 Kingman KS U.S.A.
233 □Q3 Kingman ME U.S.A.
75 I3 Kingman Reef N. Pacific Ocean
222 D3 King Mountain B.C. Can.
237 D10 King Mountain hill TX U.S.A.
Kingnait Nunavut Can. see Cape Dorset
234 E4 King of Prussia PA U.S.A.
209 E5 Kingombe Mbali Dem. Rep. Congo
209 C6 Kingondji Dem. Rep. Congo
82 E4 Kingoonya S.A. Austr.
262 S1 King Peak Antarctica
262 R2 King Peninsula Antarctica
82 □2 King Point Lord Howe I. Austr.
123 M6 Kingri Pak.
147 H7 Kings r. Ireland
240 L5 Kings r. CA U.S.A.
238 E6 Kings r. NV U.S.A.
146 K10 Kingsbarns Fife, Scotland U.K.
150 E7 Kingsbridge Devon, England U.K.
240 M5 Kingsburg CA U.S.A.
151 I2 Kingsbury Warwickshire, England U.K.
150 G6 Kingsbury Episcopi Somerset, England U.K.
84 C8 Kings Canyon N.T. Austr.
240 N5 Kings Canyon National Park CA U.S.A.
151 J5 Kingsclere Hampshire, England U.K.
82 F6 Kingscote S.A. Austr.
235 H3 Kings County county NY U.S.A.
147 I5 Kingscourt Ireland
151 O5 Kingsdown Kent, England U.K.
80 I4 Kingseat North I. N.Z.
262 U2 King Sejong research stn Antarctica
226 F4 Kingsford MI U.S.A.
146 H10 Kingshouse Stirling, Scotland U.K.
150 E7 Kingskerswell Devon, England U.K.
231 G10 Kingsland GA U.S.A.
226 I9 Kingsland IN U.S.A.
151 L4 Kings Langley Hertfordshire, England U.K.
215 O3 Kingsley S. Africa
149 N7 Kingsley Staffordshire, England U.K.
226 I5 Kingsley MI U.S.A.
151 M2 King's Lynn Norfolk, England U.K.
77 H2 Kingsmill Group is Gilbert Is Kiribati
151 N5 Kingsnorth Kent, England U.K.
86 G4 King Sound b. W.A. Austr.
235 I3 Kings Park NY U.S.A.
238 I6 Kings Peak UT U.S.A.
232 C12 Kingsport TN U.S.A.
151 J3 King's Sutton Northamptonshire, England U.K.
150 E6 Kingsteignton Devon, England U.K.
150 G4 Kingsthorne Herefordshire, England U.K.
83 K10 Kingston Tas. Austr.
224 E4 Kingston Ont. Can.
246 □ Kingston Jamaica
82 □1 Kingston Norfolk I.
81 C12 Kingston South I. N.Z.
146 J7 Kingston Moray, Scotland U.K.
233 O7 Kingston MA U.S.A.
236 H6 Kingston MO U.S.A.
233 K7 Kingston NY U.S.A.
232 C9 Kingston OH U.S.A.
234 D2 Kingston PA U.S.A.
231 E8 Kingston TN U.S.A.
232 D11 Kingston WV U.S.A.
151 J4 Kingston Bagpuize Oxfordshire, England U.K.
150 G3 Kingstone Herefordshire, England U.K.
241 Q6 Kingston Peak CA U.S.A.
150 G5 Kingston Seymour North Somerset, England U.K.
82 G7 Kingston South East S.A. Austr.
149 Q6 Kingston upon Hull Kingston upon Hull, England U.K.
149 Q6 Kingston upon Hull admin. div. England U.K.
151 L5 Kingston upon Thames Greater London, England U.K.
247 □3 Kingstown St Vincent
231 H9 Kingstree SC U.S.A.
234 C6 Kingsville MD U.S.A.
237 G12 Kingsville TX U.S.A.
150 E7 Kingswear Devon, England U.K.
150 G5 Kingswood South Gloucestershire, England U.K.
151 L5 Kingswood Surrey, England U.K.
151 J5 Kings Worthy Hampshire, England U.K.
150 F3 Kington Herefordshire, England U.K.
209 C6 Kingungi Dem. Rep. Congo
225 I1 Kingurutik r. Nfld and Lab. Can.
146 H8 Kingussie Highland, Scotland U.K.
232 H11 King William VA U.S.A.
221 I3 King William Island Nunavut Can.
206 C5 King William's Town Liberia
Kingwilliamstown Ireland see Ballydesmond
215 L8 King William's Town S. Africa
237 H11 Kingwood TX U.S.A.
232 F9 Kingwood WV U.S.A.
209 F7 Kiniama Dem. Rep. Congo
199 K6 Kınık Antalya Turkey
199 I3 Kınık İzmir Turkey
215 M6 Kinirapoort S. Africa
223 J4 Kinistino Sask. Can.
137 O6 Kinka r. Ukr.
209 B6 Kinkala Congo
102 S8 Kinka-san i. Japan
80 J5 Kinleith North I. N.Z.
81 C11 Kinloch South I. N.Z.
146 D8 Kinloch Highland, Scotland U.K.
146 F6 Kinlochbervie Highland, Scotland U.K.
146 F9 Kinlocheil Highland, Scotland U.K.
146 F7 Kinlochewe Highland, Scotland U.K.
146 F8 Kinloch Hourn Highland, Scotland U.K.
146 G9 Kinlochleven Highland, Scotland U.K.
146 H9 Kinloch Rannoch Perth and Kinross, Scotland U.K.
146 I7 Kinloss Moray, Scotland U.K.
147 F4 Kinlough Ireland
96 B5 Kinmaw Myanmar
150 E1 Kinmel Bay Conwy, Wales U.K.
Kinmen Taiwan see Chinmen
102 □1 Kin-misaki pt Okinawa Japan
227 P5 Kinmount Ont. Can.
142 I4 Kinna Sweden
147 C5 Kinnadoohy Ireland
81 D10 Kinnaird, Mount South I. N.Z.
114 G4 Kinnarasani r. India
140 S1 Kinnarodden pt Norway
147 H6 Kinnegad Ireland
235 G2 Kinnelon NJ U.S.A.
128 D6 Kinneret, Yam l. Israel
142 J3 Kinneviken b. Sweden
147 G6 Kinnitty Ireland
114 G8 Kinniyai Sri Lanka
140 R5 Kinnula Fin.
224 D2 Kinoje r. Ont. Can.
104 B7 Kino-kawa r. Japan
104 D5 Kinomoto Japan
223 K3 Kinoosao Sask. Can.
104 A4 Kinosaki Japan
102 P8 Kinpoku-san mt. Japan
165 I6 Kinrooi Belgium
215 N2 Kinross S. Africa
146 J10 Kinross Perth and Kinross, Scotland U.K.
147 E9 Kinsale Ireland
232 I10 Kinsale VA U.S.A.
142 C1 Kinsarvik Norway
209 C6 Kinsele Dem. Rep. Congo
209 B6 Kinshasa Dem. Rep. Congo
209 C6 Kinshasa mun. Dem. Rep. Congo
137 P6 Kins'ki Rozdory Ukr.
237 F7 Kinsley KS U.S.A.
232 E7 Kinsman OH U.S.A.
231 I8 Kinston NC U.S.A.
138 E6 Kintai Lith.
206 E4 Kintampo Ghana
209 B6 Kintata Dem. Rep. Congo
151 J5 Kintbury West Berkshire, England U.K.
234 E3 Kintersville PA U.S.A.
206 C4 Kintinian Guinea
93 C4 Kintom Sulawesi Indon.
95 K6 Kintop Kalimantan Indon.
84 B7 Kintore N.T. Austr.
146 L8 Kintore Aberdeenshire, Scotland U.K.
82 C2 Kintore, Mount S.A. Austr.
86 J7 Kintore Range hills N.T. Austr.
146 D11 Kintour Argyll and Bute, Scotland U.K.
129 D4 Kintrishis Nakrdzali nature res. Georgia
146 E11 Kintyre pen. Scotland U.K.
96 B3 Kin-U Myanmar
105 L4 Kinu-gawa r. Japan
105 J2 Kinunuma-yama mt. Japan
224 D2 Kinushseo r. Ont. Can.
222 H4 Kinuso Alta Can.
147 E6 Kinvara Ireland
147 C6 Kinvarra Ireland
150 H3 Kinver Staffordshire, England U.K.
102 □1 Kin-wan b. Okinawa Japan
114 F3 Kinwat Mahar. India
211 B6 Kinyangiri Tanz.
210 B4 Kinyeti mt. Sudan
120 G3 Kinzhaly Kazakh.
172 D4 Kinzig r. Ger.
169 G10 Kinzig r. Ger.
211 B6 Kiomboi Tanz.
129 E3 Kion-Khokh, Gora mt. Rus. Fed.
227 P3 Kiosk Ont. Can.
239 L7 Kiowa CO U.S.A.
237 F7 Kiowa KS U.S.A.
238 L6 Kiowa Creek r. CO U.S.A.
223 K4 Kipahigan Lake Man./Sask. Can.
240 □E13 Kīpahulu HI U.S.A.
Kiparissía Greece see Kyparissia
224 E4 Kipawa, Lac l. Que. Can.
110 C6 Kipchak Pass Xinjiang China
134 G4 Kipelovo Rus. Fed.
211 B6 Kipembawe Tanz.
138 M2 Kipen' Rus. Fed.
211 B7 Kipengere Range mts Tanz.
173 K4 Kipfenberg Ger.
211 A6 Kipili Tanz.
211 D5 Kipini Kenya
223 K5 Kipling Sask. Can.
Kipling Station Sask. Can. see Kipling
149 O6 Kippax West Yorkshire, England U.K.
190 D3 Kippel Switz.
146 H10 Kippen Stirling, Scotland U.K.
172 D5 Kippenheim Ger.
147 J6 Kippure hill Ireland
121 T1 Kiprino Rus. Fed.
134 I4 Kipshenga Rus. Fed.
137 K2 Kipti Ukr.
233 J11 Kiptopeke VA U.S.A.
Kipungo Angola see Quipungo
209 E7 Kipushi Dem. Rep. Congo
209 F8 Kipushia Dem. Rep. Congo
104 F6 Kira Japan
129 B6 Kıraçtepe Turkey
117 I7 Kirakat Uttar Prad. India
78 □6 Kirakira San Cristobal Solomon Is
140 T2 Kirakkajärvi Fin.
177 J3 Király Hungary
177 G5 Királyegyháza Hungary
177 J5 Királyhegyes Hungary
199 H4 Kiran Dağları hills Turkey
114 G3 Kirandul Chhattisgarh India
206 C3 Kirané Mali
213 □J3 Kiranomena Madag.
128 B2 Kıravga Turkey
138 M8 Kirawsk Belarus
199 J4 Kiraz Turkey
138 G3 Kirbla Estonia
237 I10 Kirbyville TX U.S.A.
173 N6 Kirchanschöring Ger.
172 F3 Kirchardt Ger.
178 H6 Kirchbach Austria
179 M6 Kirchbach in Steiermark Austria
173 O4 Kirchberg Bayern Ger.
171 G9 Kirchberg Sachsen Ger.
190 D1 Kirchberg Bern Switz.
190 G1 Kirchberg St Gallen Switz.
172 C2 Kirchberg (Hunsrück) Ger.
179 M3 Kirchberg am Wagram Austria
179 L2 Kirchberg am Walde Austria
179 M4 Kirchberg am Wechsel Austria
173 I5 Kirchberg an der Iller Ger.
172 H3 Kirchberg an der Jagst Ger.
179 L3 Kirchberg an der Pielach Austria
179 M6 Kirchberg an der Raab Austria
178 F5 Kirchberg in Tirol Austria
178 F4 Kirchbichl Austria
169 I7 Kirchbrak Ger.
170 D3 Kirchdorf Mecklenburg-Vorpommern Ger.
168 G5 Kirchdorf Niedersachsen Ger.
173 N5 Kirchdorf am Inn Ger.
173 L5 Kirchdorf an der Amper Ger.
179 J4 Kirchdorf an der Krems Austria
173 O4 Kirchdorf im Wald Ger.
178 F4 Kirchdorf in Tirol Austria
173 K2 Kirchehrenbach Ger.
169 E9 Kirchen (Sieg) Ger.
171 E10 Kirchenlamitz Ger.
173 L2 Kirchenpingarten Ger.
173 K2 Kirchensittenbach Ger.
172 G4 Kirchentellinsfurt Ger.
173 L2 Kirchenthumbach Ger.
169 G9 Kirchhain Ger.
169 K8 Kirchheilingen Ger.
172 H2 Kirchheim Bayern Ger.
169 I9 Kirchheim Hessen Ger.
172 G3 Kirchheim am Neckar Ger.
173 L5 Kirchheim bei München Ger.
172 E2 Kirchheim-Bolanden Ger.
173 I5 Kirchheim in Schwaben Ger.
172 G4 Kirchheim unter Teck Ger.
169 F8 Kirchhundem Ger.
170 D4 Kirch Jesar Ger.
169 K10 Kirchlauter Ger.
168 H5 Kirchlinteln Ger.
170 E3 Kirch Mulsow Ger.
169 H6 Kirchohsen (Emmerthal) Ger.
173 N4 Kirchroth Ger.
179 N4 Kirchschlag in der Buckligen Welt Austria
168 G5 Kirchseelte Ger.
168 H4 Kirchtimke Ger.
168 H4 Kirchwalsede Ger.
173 N5 Kirchweidach Ger.
168 G4 Kirchwistedt Ger.
169 J8 Kirchworbis Ger.
172 D6 Kirchzarten Ger.
172 G2 Kirchzell Ger.
147 K4 Kircubbin Northern Ireland U.K.
129 E5 Kırdamı Turkey
202 C5 Kirdimi Chad
129 C5 Kireçli Geçidi pass Turkey
Kirehesjävri Fin. see Kirakkajärvi
131 L4 Kirensk Rus. Fed.
Kirey watercourse Kazakh. see Kerey
Kirey, Ozero salt l. Kazakh. see Kerey, Ozero
139 U8 Kireyevsk Rus. Fed.
139 S8 Kireykovo Rus. Fed.
Kirghizia country Asia see Kyrgyzstan
121 O6 Kirghiz Range mts Asia
120 F1 Kirgiz-Miyaki Rus. Fed.
Kirgizskaya S.S.R. country Asia see Kyrgyzstan
Kirgizskiy Khrebet mts Asia see Kirghiz Range
Kirgizstan country Asia see Kyrgyzstan
208 C5 Kiri Dem. Rep. Congo
Kíria Greece see Kyrgia
Kiriákion Greece see Kyriaki
77 J2 Kiribati country Pacific Ocean
210 E2 Kiridh Somalia
105 H3 Kiriga-mine mt. Japan
127 J3 Kırık Turkey
126 H5 Kırıkhan Turkey
126 F4 Kırıkkale Turkey
106 B4 Kirikkuduk Xinjiang China
80 I2 Kirikopuni North I. N.Z.
139 V2 Kirillov Rus. Fed.
100 M5 Kirillovo Sakhalin Rus. Fed.
138 M1 Kirillovskoye Rus. Fed.
Kirin Jilin China see Jilin
Kirin prov. China see Jilin
114 G9 Kirinda Sri Lanka
210 C5 Kirinyaga mt. Kenya
123 N6 Kiri Shamozai Pak.
139 P2 Kirishi Rus. Fed.
102 □H15 Kirishima-Yaku Kokuritsu-kōen nat. park Japan
103 H15 Kirishima-yama vol. Japan
267 I5 Kiritimati atoll Kiribati
Kiriwina Islands P.N.G. see Trobriand Islands
199 L3 Kırka Turkey
199 I3 Kırkağaç Turkey
146 I13 Kirkbean Dumfries and Galloway, Scotland U.K.
149 K4 Kirkbride Cumbria, England U.K.
122 B3 Kirk Bulāg Dāgi mt. Iran
149 N6 Kirkburton West Yorkshire, England U.K.
149 L7 Kirkby Merseyside, England U.K.
149 O7 Kirkby in Ashfield Nottinghamshire, England U.K.
149 L5 Kirkby Lonsdale Cumbria, England U.K.
149 N5 Kirkby Malzeard North Yorkshire, England U.K.
149 P5 Kirkbymoorside North Yorkshire, England U.K.
149 M5 Kirkby Stephen Cumbria, England U.K.
149 L4 Kirkby Thore Cumbria, England U.K.
146 J10 Kirkcaldy Fife, Scotland U.K.
146 F13 Kirkcolm Dumfries and Galloway, Scotland U.K.
146 I12 Kirkconnel Dumfries and Galloway, Scotland U.K.
146 G13 Kirkcowan Dumfries and Galloway, Scotland U.K.
146 H13 Kirkcudbright Dumfries and Galloway, Scotland U.K.
148 I4 Kirkcudbright Bay Scotland U.K.
172 C3 Kirkel-Neuhäusel Ger.
142 I1 Kirkenær Norway
140 U2 Kirkenes Norway
227 P5 Kirkfield Ont. Can.
149 L6 Kirkham Lancashire, England U.K.
146 H13 Kirkinner Dumfries and Galloway, Scotland U.K.
146 H11 Kirkintilloch East Dunbartonshire, Scotland U.K.
141 R6 Kirkkonummi Fin.
241 T7 Kirkland AZ U.S.A.
226 F7 Kirkland IL U.S.A.
224 D3 Kirkland Lake Ont. Can.
129 A6 Kırklar Dağı mt. Turkey
129 B5 Kırklar Dağı mt. Turkey
126 C3 Kırklareli Turkey
199 I1 Kırklareli prov. Turkey
197 P9 Kırklareli Barajı resr Turkey
149 O5 Kirklevington Stockton-on-Tees, England U.K.
146 J11 Kirkliston Edinburgh, Scotland U.K.
81 E11 Kirkliston Range mts South I. N.Z.
148 H5 Kirk Michael Isle of Man
146 I9 Kirkmichael Perth and Kinross, Scotland U.K.
146 G12 Kirkmichael South Ayrshire, Scotland U.K.
146 I11 Kirkmuirhill South Lanarkshire, Scotland U.K.
138 K1 Kirkonmaanselkä b. Fin.
195 □ Kirkop Malta
149 L4 Kirkoswald Cumbria, England U.K.
146 G12 Kirkoswald South Ayrshire, Scotland U.K.
197 N9 Kirkovo Bulg.
129 C7 Kırköy Turkey
263 L1 Kirkpatrick, Mount Antarctica
146 J12 Kirkpatrick-Fleming Dumfries and Galloway, Scotland U.K.
149 O6 Kirk Sandall South Yorkshire, England U.K.
236 I5 Kirksville MO U.S.A.
148 F1 Kirkton Argyll and Bute, Scotland U.K.
146 L8 Kirkton of Durris Aberdeenshire, Scotland U.K.
146 K9 Kirkton of Menmuir Angus, Scotland U.K.
146 L8 Kirktown of Auchterless Aberdeenshire, Scotland U.K.
146 K7 Kirktown of Deskford Moray, Scotland U.K.
127 L6 Kirkūk Iraq
146 K5 Kirkwall Orkney, Scotland U.K.
215 J9 Kirkwood S. Africa
234 D5 Kirkwood DE U.S.A.
234 C5 Kirkwood PA U.S.A.
149 M2 Kirk Yetholm Scottish Borders, Scotland U.K.
Kirman Iran see Kermān
126 E3 Kırmır r. Turkey
129 A6 Kırmızıköprü Turkey
172 C2 Kirn Ger.
Kırobası Turkey see Mağara
Kīrov Kazakh. see Balpyk Bi
Kirov Kyrg. see Kyzyl-Adyr
139 R7 Kirov Kaluzhskaya Oblast' Rus. Fed.
134 J4 Kirov Kirovskaya Oblast' Rus. Fed.
Kirova, Zaliv b. Azer. see Qızılağac Körfäzi
Kirovabad Azer. see Gäncä
Kirovabad Tajik. see Panj
Kirovakan Armenia see Vanadzor
137 Q5 Kirove Donets'ka Oblast' Ukr.
137 M5 Kirove Kirovohrads'ka Oblast' Ukr.
137 O6 Kirove Zaporiz'ka Oblast' Ukr.
120 E2 Kirovo Kazakh.
Kirovo Donets'ka Oblast' Ukr. see Kirove
Kirovo Kirovohrads'ka Oblast' Ukr. see Kirovohrad
Kirovo Uzbek. see Beshariq
Kirov Oblast admin. div. Rus. Fed. see Kirovskaya Oblast'
134 J4 Kirovo-Chepetsk Rus. Fed.
Kirovo-Chepetskiy Rus. Fed. see Kirovo-Chepetsk
Kirovograd Ukr. see Kirovohrad
Kirovograd Oblast admin. div. Ukr. see Kirovohrads'ka Oblast'
Kirovogradskaya Oblast' admin. div. Ukr. see Kirovohrads'ka Oblast'
137 L5 Kirovohrad Ukr.
Kirovohrad Oblast admin. div. Ukr. see Kirovohrads'ka Oblast'
136 L5 Kirovohrads'ka Oblast' admin. div. Ukr.
129 J7 Kirovsk Azer.
139 N2 Kirovsk Leningradskaya Oblast' Rus. Fed.
134 F2 Kirovsk Murmanskaya Oblast' Rus. Fed.
Kirovsk Turkm. see Badabaýhan
137 Q4 Kirovs'k Donets'ka Oblast' Ukr.
137 R5 Kirovs'k Luhans'ka Oblast' Ukr.
137 T7 Kirovskaya Rus. Fed.
134 J4 Kirovskaya Oblast' admin. div. Rus. Fed.
137 N5 Kirovs'ke Dnipropetrovs'ka Oblast' Ukr.
137 R5 Kirovs'ke Donets'ka Oblast' Ukr.
137 M8 Kirovs'ke Respublika Krym Ukr.
137 O8 Kirovs'ke Respublika Krym Ukr.
Kirovskiy Kazakh. see Balpyk Bi
120 C5 Kirovskiy Astrakhanskaya Oblast' Rus. Fed.
137 P2 Kirovskiy Kurskaya Oblast' Rus. Fed.
100 H6 Kirovskiy Primorskiy Kray Rus. Fed.
Kirovskoye Kyrg. see Kyzyl-Adyr
Kirovskoye Dnipropetrovs'ka Oblast' Ukr. see Kirovs'ke
Kirovskoye Donets'ka Oblast' Ukr. see Kirovs'ke
Kirovskoye Respublika Krym Ukr. see Kirovs'ke
Kırpaşa pen. Cyprus see Karpasia
137 R8 Kirpili r. Rus. Fed.
122 G2 Kirpili Turkm.
137 S8 Kirpil'skaya Rus. Fed.
137 R8 Kirpil'skiy Liman marsh Rus. Fed.
146 J9 Kirriemuir Angus, Scotland U.K.
134 K4 Kirs Rus. Fed.
135 H5 Kirsanov Rus. Fed.
120 E2 Kirsanovo Kazakh.
172 C2 Kirschweiler Ger.
126 G4 Kırşehir Turkey
175 L1 Kirsna r. Lith.
207 F3 Kirtachi Niger
123 L9 Kirthar National Park Pak.
123 L8 Kirthar Range mts Pak.
151 J4 Kirtlington Oxfordshire, England U.K.
151 L2 Kirton Lincolnshire, England U.K.
151 O3 Kirton Suffolk, England U.K.
149 P7 Kirton in Lindsey North Lincolnshire, England U.K.
169 H9 Kirtorf Ger.
129 D3 Kirts'khi Georgia
140 P3 Kiruna Sweden
211 A5 Kirundo Burundi
208 E5 Kirundu Dem. Rep. Congo
262 X2 Kirwan Escarpment Antarctica
135 I5 Kirya Rus. Fed.
105 J3 Kiryū Japan
139 V5 Kirzhach Rus. Fed.
143 L4 Kisa Sweden
102 Q7 Kisakata Japan
211 C6 Kisaki Tanz.
Kisama, Parque Nacional de nat. park Angola see Quiçama, Parque Nacional do
208 E4 Kisangani Dem. Rep. Congo
211 C6 Kisangire Tanz.
209 C6 Kisantete Dem. Rep. Congo
177 L3 Kisar Hungary
93 E8 Kisar i. Maluku Indon.
94 C3 Kisaran Sumatera Indon.
211 C6 Kisarawe Tanz.
105 K5 Kisarazu Japan
128 G1 Kısas Turkey
176 G5 Kis-Balaton park Hungary
177 H4 Kisbér Hungary
104 D7 Kisei Japan
98 E1 Kiselevsk Rus. Fed.
188 G4 Kiseljak Bos.-Herz.
139 P1 Kisel'nya Rus. Fed.
100 K3 Kisel'ovka Rus. Fed.
211 B6 Kisere Tanz.
177 J3 Kisgyőr Hungary
122 F8 Kish i. Iran
117 K6 Kishanganj Bihar India
116 G7 Kishangarh Madh. Prad. India
116 C6 Kishangarh Rajasthan India
116 E6 Kishangarh Rajasthan India
116 D2 Kishen Ganga r. India/Pak.
207 F4 Kishi Nigeria
104 B7 Kishigawa Japan
104 B7 Kishi-gawa r. Japan
121 N1 Kishi-Karoy, Ozero salt l. Kazakh.
102 □I16 Kishika-zaki pt Japan
Kishinev Moldova see Chişinău
Kishiözen r. Kazakh./Rus. Fed. see Malyy Uzen'
104 B7 Kishiwada Japan
121 O1 Kishkenekol' Kazakh.
117 M7 Kishoreganj Bangl.
146 E8 Kishorn, Loch inlet Scotland U.K.
116 E3 Kishtwar Jammu and Kashmir
211 A6 Kisi Tanz.
175 H2 Kisielice Pol.
175 K2 Kisielnica Pol.
211 B6 Kisigo r. Tanz.
211 A5 Kisiguru Rwanda
210 B5 Kisii Kenya
211 C6 Kisiju Tanz.
129 E5 Kısır Dağı mt. Turkey
220 A4 Kiska Island AK U.S.A.
223 L4 Kiskittogisu Lake Man. Can.
223 L4 Kiskitto Lake Man. Can.
141 Q6 Kisko Fin.
177 J4 Kisköre Hungary
177 J4 Kiskörei-Víztároló resr Hungary
177 I5 Kiskőrös Hungary
177 I5 Kiskunfélegyháza Hungary
177 I5 Kiskunhalas Hungary
177 I4 Kiskunlacháza Hungary
177 I5 Kiskunmajsa Hungary
177 I4 Kiskunság reg. Hungary
177 I4 Kiskunsági nat. park Hungary
177 H5 Kisláng Hungary
177 K4 Kisléta Hungary
177 G4 Kislőd Hungary
129 D2 Kislovodsk Rus. Fed.
137 S7 Kislyakovskaya Rus. Fed.
210 D5 Kismaayo Somalia
177 K4 Kismarja Hungary
Kismayu Somalia see Kismaayo
105 G4 Kiso Japan
104 G4 Kisofukushima Japan
104 E5 Kisogawa Japan
104 E5 Kiso-gawa r. Japan
105 I5 Kiso-gawa r. Japan
211 A5 Kisoro Uganda
104 E5 Kisosaki Japan
105 F5 Kiso-sanmyaku mts Japan
209 F5 Kisosi Burundi
179 K7 Kisovec Slovenia
222 E4 Kispiox B.C. Can.
222 E4 Kispiox r. B.C. Can.
198 E7 Kissamos Kriti Greece
198 E7 Kissamou, Kolpos b. Kriti Greece
Kisseraing Island Myanmar see Kanmaw Kyun
206 C4 Kissidougou Guinea
231 G11 Kissimmee FL U.S.A.
231 G12 Kissimmee r. FL U.S.A.
231 G12 Kissimmee, Lake FL U.S.A.
173 J5 Kissing Ger.
223 K4 Kississing Lake Man. Can.
172 H6 Kißlegg Ger.
202 E4 Kissu, Jebel mt. Sudan
177 I5 Kisszállás Hungary
172 H2 Kist Ger.
188 E4 Kistanje Croatia
177 I5 Kistelek Hungary
135 H5 Kistendey Rus. Fed.
223 M4 Kistigan Lake Man. Can.
Kistna r. India see Krishna
177 J3 Kistokaj Hungary
140 R1 Kistrand Norway
177 J4 Kisújszállás Hungary
103 J11 Kisuki Japan
210 B5 Kisumu Kenya
177 L3 Kisvárda Hungary
Kisykkamys Kazakh. see Dzhangala
174 F3 Kiszkowo Pol.
177 J5 Kiszombor Hungary
210 A3 Kit r. Sudan
104 B6 Kita Hyōgo Japan
104 C5 Kita Kyōto Japan
206 C3 Kita Mali
Kitab Uzbek. see Kitob
99 N6 Kita-Daitō-jima i. Japan
104 E5 Kitagata Japan
103 I14 Kitagawa Japan
102 Q4 Kitahiyama Japan
105 M2 Kitaibaraki Japan
103 □2 Kita-Iō-jima vol. Kazan-rettō Japan
104 A7 Kitajima Japan
102 S7 Kitakami Japan
102 S7 Kitakami-gawa r. Japan
102 Q9 Kitakata Fukushima Japan
103 I14 Kitakata Miyazaki Japan
103 H13 Kita-Kyūshū Japan
210 B4 Kitale Kenya
102 U3 Kitami Japan
105 H3 Kitamimaki Japan
102 T2 Kitami-sanchi mts Japan
105 K3 Kitamoto Japan
209 E6 Kitanda Dem. Rep. Congo
103 □3 Kitano-hana c. Iō-jima Japan
105 J3 Kitatachibana Japan
105 M3 Kitaura Ibaraki Japan
103 I14 Kitaura Miyazaki Japan
105 M4 Kita-ura l. Japan
104 C8 Kitayama Japan
104 C8 Kitayama-gawa r. Japan
236 D6 Kit Carson CO U.S.A.
224 D5 Kitchener Ont. Can.
224 E3 Kitchigama r. Que. Can.
209 E6 Kiteba Dem. Rep. Congo
140 U5 Kitee Fin.
209 F6 Kitendwe Dem. Rep. Congo
210 B4 Kitgum Uganda
Kíthira i. Greece see Kythira
Kíthnos i. Greece see Kythnos
Kíthnou, Stenón sea chan. Greece see Kythnou, Steno
Kiti, Cape Cyprus see Kition, Cape
222 D4 Kitimat B.C. Can.
140 S3 Kitinen r. Fin.
128 B4 Kition, Cape Cyprus
Kitiou, Akra c. Cyprus see Kition, Cape
222 D4 Kitkatla B.C. Can.
222 E4 Kitlope Heritage Conservancy Provincial Park B.C. Can.
121 L8 Kitob Uzbek.
139 Y5 Kitovo Rus. Fed.
198 F6 Kitriani i. Greece
140 V2 Kitsa Rus. Fed.
222 D4 Kitsault B.C. Can.
223 I4 Kitscoty Alta Can.
136 E5 Kitsman' Ukr.
103 I13 Kitsuki Japan
105 L2 Kitsuregawa Japan
232 F8 Kittanning PA U.S.A.
234 F3 Kittatinny Mountains hills NJ U.S.A.
233 □O5 Kittery ME U.S.A.
140 R3 Kittilä Fin.
105 M1 Kittoya-yama hill Japan
179 P3 Kittsee Austria
114 D5 Kittur Karnataka India
231 J7 Kitty Hawk NC U.S.A.
211 C5 Kitui Kenya
211 C5 Kitumbeine vol. Tanz.
211 C7 Kitumbini Tanz.
211 B6 Kitunda Tanz.
222 D4 Kitwanga B.C. Can.
209 F8 Kitwe Zambia
178 F5 Kitzbühel Austria
178 F5 Kitzbüheler Alpen mts Austria
178 F5 Kitzbüheler Horn mt. Austria
179 L6 Kitzeck im Sausal Austria
171 F8 Kitzen Ger.
173 I2 Kitzingen Ger.
171 G8 Kitzscher Ger.
178 G5 Kitzsteinhorn mt. Austria
211 C5 Kiu Kenya
175 H5 Kiucze Pol.
141 Q6 Kiukainen Fin.
96 D5 Kiu Lom Reservoir Thai.
91 J8 Kiunga P.N.G.
211 D5 Kiunga Marine National Reserve nature res. Kenya
140 S5 Kiuruvesi Fin.
140 R4 Kivalo ridge Fin.
198 D5 Kiveri Greece
139 T4 Kiverichi Rus. Fed.
136 E3 Kivertsi Ukr.
140 R5 Kivijärvi Fin.
138 K1 Kivijärvi l. Fin.
140 R5 Kivijärvi l. Fin.
143 K6 Kivik Sweden
140 Q2 Kivilompolo Norway
138 J2 Kiviõli Estonia
140 U5 Kivivaara Fin.
138 H3 Kivi-Vigala Estonia
137 Q4 Kivsharivka Ukr.
208 F5 Kivu, Lake Dem. Rep. Congo/Rwanda
104 C8 Kiwa Japan
209 C7 Kiwaba N'zogi Angola
91 J8 Kiwai Island P.N.G.
211 C7 Kiwawa Tanz.
86 I7 Kiwirrkurra Aboriginal Reserve W.A. Austr.
175 I1 Kiwity Pol.
121 M3 Kiyakty, Ozero salt l. Kazakh.
102 □1 Kiyan Okinawa Japan
102 □1 Kiyan-zaki c. Okinawa Japan
124 E6 Kiyāt Saudi Arabia
Kiyev Ukr. see Kyiv
121 N2 Kiyevka Kazakh.
Kiyevskaya Oblast' admin. div. Ukr. see Kyivs'ka Oblast'
139 T6 Kiyevskiy Rus. Fed.
Kiyevskoye Vodokhranilishche resr Ukr. see Kyyivs'ke Vodoskhovyshche
197 Q9 Kıyıköy Turkey
121 L2 Kiyma Kazakh.
104 F3 Kiyomi Japan
105 L5 Kiyosumi-yama hill Ja
105 I1 Kiyotsu-gawa r. Japan
134 L4 Kizel Rus. Fed.
134 I3 Kizema Rus. Fed.
107 K1 Kizha Rus. Fed.
134 F3 Kizhi, Ostrov i. Rus. F
209 E7 Kiziba-Baluba, Réser nature res. Dem. Rep.
211 B6 Kizigo Game Reserve nature res. Tanz.
199 L4 Kızık Turkey
110 F6 Kizil Xinjiang China
128 B2 Kızılalan Turkey
110 C7 Kizilawat Xinjiang Chir
128 B2 Kızılca Turkey
199 K5 Kızılcadağ Turkey
199 K6 Kızılca Dağ mt. Turkey
126 F3 Kızılcahamam Turkey
199 L3 Kızılcaören Turkey
199 K4 Kızılcasöğüt Turkey
129 E6 Kızılcaziyaret Dağı m
129 A7 Kızılcık Turkey
129 B6 Kızılçubuk Turkey
128 C1 Kızıldağ mt. Turkey
128 B2 Kızıldağ mt. Turkey
126 I4 Kızıl Dağı mt. Turkey
126 F3 Kızılırmak Turkey
126 G3 Kızılırmak r. Turkey
199 L5 Kızılkaya Turkey
199 L4 Kızılören Afyon Turkey
126 F5 Kızılören Konya Turkey
120 H1 Kizil'skoye Rus. Fed.
137 Q8 Kiziltashskiy Liman la Rus. Fed.
127 J5 Kızıltepe Turkey
128 A1 Kızılyaka Karaman Tur
199 J5 Kızılyaka Muğla Turkey
129 H2 Kizilyurt Rus. Fed.
211 C6 Kizimkazi, Ras pt Tan
128 C2 Kızkalesi Turkey
129 H2 Kizlyar Respublika Dag Rus. Fed.
129 F2 Kizlyar Respublika Sev Osetiya-Alaniya Rus. Fe
129 H1 Kizlyarskiy Zaliv b. R
134 J4 Kizner Rus. Fed.
104 C6 Kizu Japan
104 C6 Kizu-gawa r. Japan
Kizyl-Arbat Turkm. see
Kizyl-Atrek Turkm. see
111 D9 Kizyl Jilga Aksai Chin
142 F5 Kjellerup Denmark
141 K6 Kjemmoen Norway
140 M3 Kjerringøy Norway
140 S1 Kjøllefjord Norway
140 N2 Kjøpsvik Norway
214 G9 Klaarstroom S. Africa
164 F5 Klaaswaal Neth.
176 C2 Klabava r. Czech Rep
143 J1 Klacken hill Sweden
177 H3 Kľačno Slovakia
188 G3 Kladanj Bos.-Herz.
170 E5 Kläden Ger.
176 D1 Kladno Czech Rep.
197 K6 Kladovo Serbia
176 B2 Kladruby Czech Rep.
95 L2 Klagan Sabah Malaysi
179 J6 Klagenfurt Austria
191 Q2 Klagenfurt airport Aus
241 W6 Klagetoh AZ U.S.A.
138 E6 Klaipėda Lith.
175 I6 Kłaj Pol.
177 H3 Kľak mt. Slovakia
177 I2 Kľak mt. Slovakia
Klaksvig Faroe Is see
144 D1 Klaksvík Faroe Is
238 B6 Klamath CA U.S.A.
238 B6 Klamath r. CA U.S.A.
238 D5 Klamath Falls OR U.S
238 C6 Klamath Mountains CA U.S.A.
143 N2 Klämmingen l. Swede
95 L4 Klampo Kalimantan In
191 Q5 Klana Croatia
94 D3 Klang Malaysia
174 E1 Kłanino Pol.
179 M7 Klanjec Croatia
168 G1 Klanxbüll Ger.
222 D3 Klappan r. B.C. Can.
142 J2 Klarälven r. Sweden
140 N5 Klärke Sweden
177 H3 Klasov Slovakia
142 I2 Klässbol Sweden
176 C1 Klášterec nad Ohří Czech Rep.
95 I8 Klaten Jawa Indon.
176 C2 Klatovy Czech Rep.
179 J4 Klaus an der Pyhrnb Austria
171 H6 Klausdorf Brandenbu
170 H2 Klausdorf Mecklenbu Vorpommern Ger.
168 J2 Klausdorf Schleswig-Holstein Ger.
172 B2 Klausen Ger.
179 N3 Klausen Leopoldsdo
136 J3 Klavdiyevo-Tarasove
142 H4 Klåverön naturreser nature res. Sweden
214 C7 Klawer S. Africa
220 E4 Klawock AK U.S.A.
164 K3 Klazienaveen Neth.
206 C5 Kle Liberia
179 H6 Kleblach-Lind Austria
174 E2 Klębowiec Pol.
234 E3 Klecknersville PA U.S
174 F3 Kłecko Pol.
174 G3 Kleczew Pol.
222 E5 Kleena Kleene B.C.
128 C3 Kleides Islands Cypr
179 H5 Kleinarl Austria
214 F4 Kleinbegin S. Africa
168 D5 Klein Berßen Ger.
172 C3 Kleinblittersdorf Ger.
247 □8 Klein Bonaire i. Neth.
170 I3 Klein Bünzow Ger.
247 □10 Klein Curaçao i. Neth
214 D7 Klein Doring r. S. Afri
171 H7 Kleine Elster r. Ger.
140 J5 Kleinegga mt. Norway
173 N4 Kleine Laaber r. Ger.
173 K4 Kleine Paar r. Ger.
170 I2 Kleiner Jasmunder b. Ger.
178 D5 Kleiner Solstein mt.
171 J7 Kleine Spree r. Ger.
173 M4 Kleine Vils r. Ger.
234 C4 Kleinfeltersville PA U
172 G2 Kleinheubach Ger.
171 E8 Kleinjena Ger.
212 C5 Klein Karas Namibia
171 G6 Klein Kreutz Ger.
179 K5 Kleinlobming Austria
171 H6 Kleinmachnow Ger.
214 D10 Kleinmond S. Africa
168 I3 Klein Nordende Ger.
172 G1 Kleinostheim Ger.
171 E7 Kleinpaschleben Ge
215 I9 Kleinpoort S. Africa
179 K4 Kleinreifling Austria
172 H2 Kleinrinderfeld Ger.
214 E9 Klein Roggeveldberg S. Africa
168 J3 Klein Rönnau Ger.
179 K6 Klein Sankt Paul Aus
214 B5 Kleinsee S. Africa
170 G4 Kleinseenplatte Neu park Ger.
214 F9 Klein Swartberg mt.
215 K4 Klein-Vet r. S. Africa
172 G2 Kleinwallstadt Ger.
171 D6 Klein Wanzleben Ge
169 K6 Kleinwinnigstedt (Winnigstedt) Ger.
179 M4 Kleinzell Austria
198 D5 Kleitoria Greece
175 L3 Klejniki Pol.
188 F3 Klekovača mt. Bos.-
136 H5 Klembivka Ukr.
222 D4 Klemtu B.C. Can.
176 B2 Klenčí pod Čerchove Czech Rep.
174 D4 Klenica Pol.
177 I3 Klenovec Slovakia
176 G2 Klenovice na Hané Czech Rep.
177 I3 Klenovský Vepor mt.
175 L2 Kleosin Pol.
175 L2 Klepacze Pol.

Klepovka Rus. Fed.
Kleppe Norway
Kleppestø Norway
Klępsk Pol.
Klepynine Ukr.
Klerksdorp S. Africa
Klerkskraal S. Africa
Klesiv Ukr.
Kleszczele Pol.
Kleszczewo Pol.
Kleszczów Pol.
Kletnya Rus. Fed.
Kletsk Belarus *see* **Klyetsk**
Kletskaya Rus. Fed.
Kletskiy Rus. Fed. *see* Kletskaya
Klettgau *reg.* Ger./Switz.
Klettwitz Ger.
Klevan' Ukr.
Kleve Ger.
Kleven' *r.* Rus. Fed.
Klichaw Belarus
Klichka Rus. Fed.
Klidhes Islands Cyprus *see* Kleides Islands
Klieken Ger.
Klietz Ger.
Klimatino Rus. Fed.
Klimavichy Belarus
Klimawka Belarus
Kliment Bulg.
Klimkovice Czech Rep.
Klimkovka Rus. Fed.
Klimontów *Małopolskie* Pol.
Klimontów *Świętokrzyskie* Pol.
Klimovichi Belarus *see* Klimavichy
Klimovo Rus. Fed.
Klimovsk Rus. Fed.
Klimovskaya Rus. Fed.
Klimov Zavod Rus. Fed.
Klimpfjäll Sweden
Klin Rus. Fed.
Klin Slovakia
Klina *Kosovo* Serbia
Klinaklini *r. B.C.* Can.
Kling *Mindanao* Phil.
Klingenberg Ger.
Klingenberg am Main Ger.
Klingenthal Ger.
Klingerstown *PA* U.S.A.
Klingkang, Banjaran *mts* Indon./Malaysia
Klink Ger.
Klínovec *mt.* Czech Rep.
Klinsko-Dmitrovskaya Gryada *ridge* Rus. Fed.
Klintehamn *Gotland* Sweden
Klintsovka Rus. Fed.
Klintsy Rus. Fed.
Klip *r.* S. Africa
Klipdale S. Africa
Klipfontein S. Africa
Kliplev Denmark
Klippan Sweden
Klipplaat S. Africa
Kliprand S. Africa
Klipskool S. Africa
Klis Croatia
Klishino *Moskovskaya Oblast'* Rus. Fed.
Klishino *Novgorodskaya Oblast'* Rus. Fed.
Klisura Serbia
Klitmøller Denmark
Klitória Greece *see* **Kleitoria**
Klitten Ger.
Klixbüll Ger.
Kljajićevo *Vojvodina* Serbia
Ključ Bos.-Herz.
Klobouky Czech Rep.
Kłobuck Pol.
Klöch Austria
Kłoczew Pol.
Kłodawa *Lubuskie* Pol.
Kłodawa *Wielkopolskie* Pol.
Kłodzko Pol.
Kløfta Norway
Kłomnice Pol.
Klondike Gold Rush National Historical Park *nat. park AK* U.S.A.
Klonowa Pol.
Klooga Estonia
Kloosterhaar Neth.
Kloosterzande Neth.
Kloptaň *mt.* Slovakia
Klos Albania
Kloštar Ivanić Croatia
Kloštar Podravski Croatia
Klosterfelde Ger.
Klosterhäseler Ger.
Klösterle Austria
Klosterlechfeld Ger.
Klostermansfeld Ger.
Klosterneuburg Austria
Klosters Switz.
Klosterwasser *r.* Ger.
Kloster Zinna Ger.
Kloten Switz.
Klotten Ger.
Klötze (Altmark) Ger.
Kluane *r. Y.T.* Can.
Kluane Game Sanctuary *nature res. Y.T.* Can.
Kluane Lake *Y.T.* Can.
Kluane National Park *Y.T.* Can.
Kluang Malaysia *see* **Keluang**
Kluang, Tanjung *pt* Indon.
Kluczbork Pol.
Kluczewsko Pol.
Klukhori Rus. Fed. *see* Karachayevsk
Klukhoris Ugheltekhili *pass* Georgia/Rus. Fed.
Klukhorskiy, Pereval *pass* Rus. Fed.
Kluki Pol.
Klukowo Pol.
Klukwan *AK* U.S.A.
Klumpang, Teluk *b.* Indon.
Klundert Neth.
Klungkung *Bali* Indon.
Klupro Pak.
Kluse Ger.
Kľušov Slovakia
Klusy Pol.
Klütz Ger.
Klwów Pol.
Klyastsitsy Belarus
Klyava *r.* Belarus
Klyavlino Rus. Fed.
Klyaz'ma *r.* Rus. Fed.
Klyetsk Belarus
Klymivka Ukr.
Klyosato Japan
Klyshky Ukr.
Klyuchevskaya, Sopka *vol.* Rus. Fed.
Klyuchi *Altayskiy Kray* Rus. Fed.
Klyuchi *Amurskaya Oblast'* Rus. Fed.
Klyuchi *Kamchatskaya Oblast'* Rus. Fed.
Kmagha *Sta Isabel* Solomon Is
Knaben Norway
Knapdaar S. Africa
Knapdale *South I.* N.Z.
Knapdale *reg. Scotland* U.K.
Knapp Mound *hill WI* U.S.A.
Knäred Sweden
Knaresborough *North Yorkshire, England* U.K.
Knästen *hill* Sweden
Knayton *North Yorkshire, England* U.K.
Knebworth *Hertfordshire, England* U.K.
Knee Lake *Man.* Can.
Knee Lake *Sask.* Can.
Knesebeck Ger.
Knesselare Belgium
Knetzgau Ger.
Knežak Slovenia
Kneževi Vinogradi Croatia
Kneževo Croatia
Knezha Bulg.
Kněžmost Czech Rep.
Knić Serbia
236 E2 **Knife** *r. ND* U.S.A.
226 C3 **Knife River** *MN* U.S.A.
222 E5 **Knight Inlet** *B.C.* Can.
150 F3 **Knighton** *Powys, Wales* U.K.
240 K3 **Knights Landing** *CA* U.S.A.
188 F3 **Knin** Croatia
143 K5 **Knislinge** Sweden
179 K5 **Knittelfeld** Austria
172 F3 **Knittlingen** Ger.
143 N2 **Knivsta** Sweden
176 D3 **Knížecí stolec** *mt.* Czech Rep.
197 N9 **Knizhovnik** Bulg.
197 K7 **Knjaževac** Serbia
87 C10 **Knobby Head** *W.A.* Austr.
Knob Lake *Nfld and Lab.* Can. *see* **Schefferville**
86 J3 **Knob Peak** *hill W.A.* Austr.
147 D7 **Knock** *Clare* Ireland
147 E5 **Knock** *Mayo* Ireland
146 E10 **Knock** *Argyll and Bute, Scotland* U.K.
147 D9 **Knockaboy** *hill* Ireland
147 D8 **Knockacummer** *hill* Ireland
147 G9 **Knockadoon Head** Ireland
147 E4 **Knockalongy** *hill* Ireland
147 D7 **Knockalough** Ireland
148 E8 **Knockananna** Ireland
148 D8 **Knockanarrigan** Ireland
146 J8 **Knockandhu** *Moray, Scotland* U.K.
147 D8 **Knockanefune** *hill* Ireland
146 G7 **Knockban** *Highland, Scotland* U.K.
147 J7 **Knockbrandon** Ireland
147 J5 **Knockbridge** Ireland
147 G7 **Knockbrit** Ireland
147 F5 **Knockcroghery** Ireland
146 K7 **Knock Hill** *Scotland* U.K.
147 E5 **Knock International** *airport* Ireland
147 J2 **Knocklayd** *hill Northern Ireland* U.K.
147 F8 **Knocklong** Ireland
147 F8 **Knockmealdown Mountains** *hills* Ireland
147 D4 **Knockmore** Ireland
147 F6 **Knockmoyle** Ireland
147 D8 **Knocknaboul** Ireland
148 E3 **Knocknacarry** *Northern Ireland* U.K.
147 D8 **Knocknagree** Ireland
147 F8 **Knocknaskagh** *hill* Ireland
147 F9 **Knockraha** Ireland
147 E9 **Knocks** Ireland
165 D6 **Knokke-Heist** Belgium
170 H3 **Knorrendorf** Ger.
198 G7 **Knosos** *tourist site* Greece
Knossós *tourist site* Greece *see* **Knosos**
149 O6 **Knottingley** *West Yorkshire, England* U.K.
151 I3 **Knowle** *West Midlands, England* U.K.
262 T2 **Knowles, Cape** Antarctica
233 □Q2 **Knowles Corner** *ME* U.S.A.
233 M3 **Knowlton** *Que.* Can.
230 D5 **Knox** *IN* U.S.A.
232 F7 **Knox** *PA* U.S.A.
222 C4 **Knox, Cape** *B.C.* Can.
Knox Atoll Kiribati *see* **Tarawa**
226 B9 **Knox City** *MO* U.S.A.
263 G2 **Knox Coast** Antarctica
231 F9 **Knoxville** *GA* U.S.A.
236 I5 **Knoxville** *IA* U.S.A.
231 F8 **Knoxville** *TN* U.S.A.
146 E8 **Knoydart** *mts Scotland* U.K.
150 F3 **Knucklas** *Powys, Wales* U.K.
221 L2 **Knud Rasmussen Land** *reg.* Greenland
169 H9 **Knüllgebirge** *hills* Ger.
169 H8 **Knüllwald-Remsfeld** Ger.
174 G5 **Knurów** Pol.
149 M7 **Knutsford** *Cheshire, England* U.K.
134 I5 **Knyaginino** Rus. Fed.
138 K7 **Knyahinin** Belarus
100 I4 **Knyaze-Bolkonskaye** Rus. Fed.
137 M6 **Knyaze-Hryhorivka** Ukr.
138 L5 **Knyazevo** Rus. Fed.
175 M5 **Knyazhe** Ukr.
139 T4 **Knyazhikha** Rus. Fed.
138 L3 **Knyazhitsy** Rus. Fed.
139 N7 **Knyazhytsy** Belarus
214 H10 **Knysna** S. Africa
175 K2 **Knyszyn** Pol.
100 J5 **Ko, Gora** *mt.* Rus. Fed.
208 F2 **Koalib, Jebel** *mt.* Sudan
81 I8 **Koamaru, Cape** *South I.* N.Z.
211 C6 **Koani** Tanz.
Koartac *Que.* Can. *see* Quaqtaq
214 D5 **Koa Valley** *watercourse* S. Africa
94 G6 **Koba** Indon.
179 L6 **Kobansko** *mts* Slovenia
179 I7 **Kobarid** Slovenia
103 H15 **Kobayashi** Japan
140 T2 **Kobbfoss** Norway
93 E3 **Kobe** *Halmahera* Indon.
104 B6 **Kōbe** Japan
137 N4 **Kobelyaky** Ukr.
142 I6 **København** Denmark
142 I6 **København** *mun.* Denmark
206 C3 **Kobenni** Maur.
179 K5 **Kobenz** Austria
178 H3 **Kobernaußer Wald** *for.* Austria
179 N4 **Kobersdorf** Austria
93 F5 **Kobi** *Seram* Indon.
207 I4 **Kobi** Nigeria
175 H4 **Kobiele Wielkie** Pol.
174 E5 **Kobierzyce** Pol.
174 G5 **Kobiór** Pol.
102 □A21 **Kōbi-sho** *i. Nansei-shotō* Japan
208 C2 **Koblagué** Chad
169 E10 **Koblenz** Ger.
137 K7 **Kobleve** Ukr.
210 C1 **K'obo** Eth.
117 O6 **Kobo** *Assam* India
210 A4 **Koboko** Uganda
100 H2 **Koboldo** Rus. Fed.
139 T3 **Kobozha** *r.* Rus. Fed.
134 J4 **Kobra** Rus. Fed.
Kobrin Belarus *see* **Kobryn**
91 H8 **Kobroör** *i.* Indon.
170 E3 **Kobrow** Ger.
136 D1 **Kobryn** Belarus
105 H4 **Kobuchizawa** Japan
220 C3 **Kobuk Valley National Park** *AK* U.S.A.
129 C4 **K'obulet'i** Georgia
105 I4 **Kobushiga-take** *mt.* Japan
131 N3 **Kobyay** Rus. Fed.
174 F4 **Kobyla Góra** Pol.
174 C2 **Kobylanka** Pol.
136 D5 **Kobylets'ka Polyana** Ukr.
176 F3 **Kobylí** Czech Rep.
174 F4 **Kobylin** Pol.
175 K2 **Kobylin-Borzymy** Pol.
175 J3 **Kobyłka** Pol.
174 F1 **Kobylnica** Pol.
175 I3 **Kobylniki** Pol.
199 J2 **Kocaafşar** *r.* Turkey
199 L1 **Kocaali** Turkey
199 L5 **Kocaaliler** Turkey
199 I3 **Kocaavşar** Turkey
199 K5 **Kocabaş** Turkey
199 K4 **Koca Dag** *mt.* Turkey
Kocaeli Turkey *see* **İzmit**
199 K2 **Kocaeli** *prov.* Turkey
199 K1 **Kocaeli Yarımadası** *pen.* Turkey
129 E5 **Kocaköy** Turkey
197 K9 **Kočani** Macedonia
129 E6 **Kocapınar** Turkey
199 I5 **Koçarlı** Turkey
129 D6 **Kocasu** *r.* Turkey
199 J2 **Kocasu** *r.* Turkey
128 F1 **Kocatepe** Turkey
129 E6 **Koçbaşı Tepe** *mt.* Turkey
106 H9 **Kocê** *Gansu* China
196 H6 **Koceljevo** Serbia
188 E3 **Kočevje** Slovenia
191 R4 **Kočevska Reka** Slovenia
101 E11 **Koch'ang** S. Korea
174 G5 **Kochanowice** Pol.
117 L6 **Koch Bihar** *W. Bengal* India
173 K6 **Kochel am See** Ger.
173 K6 **Kochelsee** *l.* Ger.
172 G3 **Kocher** *r.* Ger.
137 O5 **Kocherezhky** Ukr.
197 L8 **Kocherinovo** Bulg.
136 I3 **Kocheriv** Ukr.
137 P2 **Kochetovka** Rus. Fed.
134 K4 **Kochevo** Rus. Fed.
Kochi *Kerala* India *see* **Cochin**
103 K13 **Kōchi** Japan
103 K13 **Kōchi** *pref.* Japan
245 I8 **Kochihuehuetlán** Mex.
102 □1 **Kochinda** *Okinawa* Japan
Koçhisar Turkey *see* **Kızıltepe**
120 I1 **Kochkar'** Rus. Fed.
121 P6 **Kochkor** Kyrg.
Kochkorka Kyrg. *see* **Kochkor**
135 I5 **Kochkurovo** Rus. Fed.
134 M2 **Kochmes** Rus. Fed.
129 H1 **Kochubey** Rus. Fed.
129 C1 **Kochubeyevskoye** Rus. Fed.
198 F4 **Kochylas** *hill Skyros* Greece
175 K4 **Kock** Pol.
129 C5 **Koçkaya** Turkey
128 F1 **Köçke** Turkey
129 F5 **Koçkıran** Turkey
129 E5 **Koçköyü** Turkey
170 D5 **Köckte** Ger.
177 G3 **Kočovce** Slovakia
177 H4 **Kocs** Hungary
177 I4 **Kocsér** Hungary
177 H5 **Kocsola** Hungary
174 F2 **Koczała** Pol.
114 D5 **Kod** *Karnataka* India
134 K3 **Kodachdikost** Rus. Fed.
114 E7 **Kodaikanal** *Tamil Nadu* India
105 J4 **Kodaira** Japan
102 □G17 **Kodakara-jima** *i. Nansei-shotō* Japan
136 J3 **Kodaky** Ukr.
115 I3 **Kodala** *Orissa* India
105 J3 **Kodama** Japan
117 J6 **Kodari** Nepal
117 J7 **Kodarma** *Jharkhand* India
138 K3 **Kodavere** Estonia
175 L4 **Kodeń** Pol.
137 S3 **Kodentsovo** Rus. Fed.
104 A6 **Kōdera** Japan
171 K8 **Kodersdorf** Ger.
220 C4 **Kodiak** *AK* U.S.A.
220 C4 **Kodiak Island** *AK* U.S.A.
116 C9 **Kodinar** *Gujarat* India
134 G3 **Kodino** Rus. Fed.
138 E1 **Kodisjoki** Fin.
171 E10 **Köditz** Ger.
114 F7 **Kodiyakkarai** *Tamil Nadu* India
176 G4 **Kodó** *r.* Hungary
210 B2 **Kodok** Sudan
102 R5 **Kodomari** Japan
102 R5 **Kodomari-misaki** *pt* Japan
129 C3 **Kodori** *r.* Georgia
129 C3 **Kodoris K'edi** *hills* Georgia
136 I3 **Kodra** Ukr.
175 H4 **Kodrąb** Pol.
114 E5 **Kodumuru** *Andhra Prad.* India
136 I5 **Kodyma** Ukr.
136 J5 **Kodyma** *r.* Ukr.
197 N9 **Kodzhaele** *mt.* Bulg./Greece
Kodzhori Georgia *see* **Kojori**
214 E8 **Koedoesberg** *mts* S. Africa
214 G5 **Koegas** S. Africa
214 F5 **Koegrabie** S. Africa
164 J3 **Koekange** Neth.
165 C6 **Koekelare** Belgium
214 C7 **Koekenaap** S. Africa
212 C5 **Koës** Namibia
165 E6 **Koewacht** Neth.
241 S8 **Kofa Mountains** *AZ* U.S.A.
241 R8 **Kofa National Wildlife Refuge** *nature res. AZ* U.S.A.
123 M2 **Kofarnihon** Tajik.
123 M3 **Kofarnihon** *r.* Tajik.
197 P9 **Kofçaz** Turkey
173 M4 **Köfering** Ger.
215 J5 **Koffiefontein** S. Africa
198 G8 **Kofinas** *mt. Kriti* Greece
179 L5 **Köflach** Austria
206 E5 **Koforidua** Ghana
103 K11 **Kōfu** *Tottori* Japan
105 I4 **Kōfu** *Yamanashi* Japan
179 N7 **Kog** Slovenia
105 K3 **Koga** Japan
197 Q6 **Kogălniceanu** *airport* Romania
224 E1 **Kogaluc** *r. Que.* Can.
224 E1 **Kogaluc, Baie de** *b. Que.* Can.
225 I1 **Kogaluk** *r. Nfld and Lab.* Can.
85 M9 **Kogan** *Qld* Austr.
105 K4 **Koganei** Japan
Kögart Kyrg. *see* **Kök-Art**
142 I6 **Køge** Denmark
142 I6 **Køge Bugt** *b.* Denmark
134 L3 **Kogel'** *r.* Rus. Fed.
207 G4 **Kogi** *state* Nigeria
179 M5 **Koglhof** Austria
120 K8 **Kogon** Uzbek.
206 D3 **Kogoni** Mali
103 H12 **Kogushi** Japan
Kogyl'nicheny Moldova *see* **Cogîlniceni**
Kōhaihai *pt South I.* N.Z. *see* **Gillespies Point**
123 K9 **Kohaliuen** Pak.
123 L8 **Kohan** Pak.
123 N5 **Kohat** Pak.
123 K4 **Kohestānāt** Afgh.
122 D6 **Kohgīlūyeh va Būyer Aḥmad** *prov.* Iran
138 H2 **Kohila** Estonia
117 O7 **Kohima** *Nagaland* India
78 □6 **Kohinggo** *i. New Georgia Is* Solomon Is
123 O4 **Kohistan** *reg.* Pak.
173 M2 **Kohlberg** Ger.
168 G3 **Köhlen** Ger.
262 Q2 **Kohler Range** *mts* Antarctica
241 U7 **Kohls Ranch** *AZ* U.S.A.
123 M7 **Kohlu** Pak.
122 F4 **Kohneh 'Omar** Iran
202 D5 **Kohouro** *well* Chad
171 G8 **Kohrener Land** *park* Ger.
123 I4 **Kohsan** Afgh.
138 K2 **Kohtla-Järve** Estonia
80 J4 **Kohukohunui** *hill North I.* N.Z.
101 E11 **Kohŭng** S. Korea
81 E11 **Kohurau** *mt. South I.* N.Z.
136 I8 **Kohyl'nyk** *r.* Ukr.
105 I1 **Koide** Japan
222 A2 **Koidern** *Y.T.* Can.
222 A2 **Koidern Mountain** *Y.T.* Can.
Koidu Sierra Leone *see* **Sefadu**
138 I3 **Koigi** Estonia
115 M8 **Koihoa** *Andaman & Nicobar Is* India
111 L9 **Koikyim Qu** *r. Qinghai* China
198 B5 **Koiliomeno** *Zakynthos* Greece
114 E4 **Koilkonda** *Andhra Prad.* India
114 F5 **Koilkuntla** *Andhra Prad.* India
217 □3a **Koimbani** *Njazidja* Comoros
101 E8 **Koin** N. Korea
134 J3 **Koin** *r.* Rus. Fed.
214 B6 **Koingnaas** S. Africa
127 L5 **Koi Sanjaq** Iraq
140 U5 **Koitere** *l.* Fin.
105 K5 **Koito-gawa** *r.* Japan
140 R3 **Koivu** Fin.
122 I9 **Koja, Kowr-e** *watercourse* Iran
101 F11 **Kŏje-do** *i.* S. Korea
176 G2 **Kojetín** Czech Rep.
102 Q5 **Ko-jima** *i.* Japan
103 Q13 **Ko-jima** *i.* Japan
87 D12 **Kojonup** *W.A.* Austr.
129 F4 **Kojori** Georgia
122 D3 **Kojūr** Iran
96 E4 **Kok, Nam Mae** *r.* Thai.
177 I4 **Kóka** Hungary
104 D6 **Kōka** Japan
233 □P3 **Kokadjo** *ME* U.S.A.
105 L4 **Kokai-gawa** *r.* Japan
120 K3 **Kokalat** Kazakh.
Kokand *Farg'ona* Uzbek. *see* **Qo'qon**
Kokankishlak Uzbek. *see* **Paxtaobod**
141 P7 **Kökar** *Åland* Fin.
138 D2 **Kökar** *i. Åland* Fin.
120 I4 **Kokaral** Kazakh.
138 D2 **Kökarsfjärden** *b.* Fin.
121 P7 **Kök-Art** *Osh* Kyrg.
81 F9 **Kokatahi** *South I.* N.Z.
104 A8 **Kokatsu-shima** *i.* Japan
177 I3 **Kokava nad Rimavicou** Slovakia
104 B7 **Kokawa** Japan
121 P7 **Kök-Aygyr** Kyrg.
123 M3 **Kokcha** *r.* Afgh.
Kokchetav Kazakh. *see* Kokshetau
141 Q6 **Kokemäki** Fin.
212 C6 **Kokerboom** Namibia
96 D5 **Ko Kha** Thai.
138 M7 **Kokhanava** Belarus
139 Y5 **Kokhma** Rus. Fed.
206 B3 **Koki** Senegal
121 O7 **Kök-Janggak** Kyrg.
114 G8 **Kokkilai** Sri Lanka
128 A3 **Kokkina** Cyprus
198 D3 **Kokkino Nero** Greece
140 Q5 **Kokkola** Fin.
110 H4 **Kok Kuduk** *well Xinjiang* China
138 I5 **Koknese** Latvia
207 G5 **Koko** *Edo* Nigeria
207 G4 **Koko** *Kebbi* Nigeria
206 C3 **Kokofata** Mali
240 □D12 **Koko Head** *HI* U.S.A.
206 D5 **Kokolo-Pozo** Côte d'Ivoire
230 D5 **Kokomo** *IN* U.S.A.
212 D5 **Kokong** Botswana
103 I13 **Kokonoe** Japan
138 K3 **Kokora** Estonia
139 R9 **Kokorevka** Rus. Fed.
138 M4 **Kokorevo** Rus. Fed.
207 F4 **Kokoro** Benin
210 C3 **Kokosa** Eth.
139 U6 **Kokoshkino** Rus. Fed.
215 L2 **Kokosi** S. Africa
206 B4 **Kokou** *mt.* Guinea
121 T3 **Kokpekti** Kazakh.
179 J7 **Kokra** *r.* Slovenia
179 J7 **Kokrica** Slovenia
101 E9 **Koksan** N. Korea
121 M6 **Koksaray** Kazakh.
Kokshaal-Tau, Khrebet *mts* China/Kyrg. *see* **Kakshaal-Too**
134 I4 **Koksharka** Rus. Fed.
121 M1 **Kokshetau** Kazakh.
165 C6 **Koksijde** Belgium
225 G1 **Koksoak** *r. Que.* Can.
215 N6 **Kokstad** S. Africa
121 Q5 **Koksu** *Almatinskaya Oblast'* Kazakh.
121 R5 **Koksu** Kazakh.
121 M7 **Koksu** *Yuzhnyy Kazakhstan* Kazakh.
121 R5 **Koktal** Kazakh.
121 O7 **Kök-Tash** Kyrg.
121 R4 **Kokterek** *Almatinskaya Oblast'* Kazakh.
120 C3 **Kokterek** *Zapadnyy Kazakhstan* Kazakh.
121 Q2 **Koktobe** Kazakh.
106 A3 **Koktokay** *Xinjiang* China
Koktokay *Xinjiang* China *see* Fuyun
120 G3 **Koktubek** Kazakh.
121 S5 **Koktuma** Kazakh.
93 B6 **Koku, Tanjung** *pt* Indon.
103 H15 **Kokubu** Japan
105 K3 **Kokubunji** Japan
104 F3 **Kokufu** Japan
105 I4 **Kokushiga-take** *mt.* Japan
106 B3 **Koküy** *Xinjiang* China
Kok-Yangak Kyrg. *see* Kök-Janggak
111 C8 **Kokyar** *Xinjiang* China
121 T3 **Kokzhayyk** Kazakh.
140 V2 **Kola** Rus. Fed.
140 V2 **Kola** *r.* Rus. Fed.
Kolab *r.* India *see* **Sabari**
117 J9 **Kolabira** *Orissa* India
123 L8 **Kolachi** *r.* Pak.
175 H4 **Kołacin** Pol.
174 E2 **Kołacz** Pol.
175 L4 **Kołacze** Pol.
174 F3 **Kołaczkowo** Pol.
175 J6 **Kołaczyce** Pol.
124 C9 **Kola Diba** Eth.
117 K8 **Kolaghat** *W. Bengal* India
116 E2 **Kolahoi** *mt.* Jammu and Kashmir
206 C4 **Kolahun** Liberia
93 B6 **Kolaka** *Sulawesi* Indon.
175 K2 **Kołaki Kościelne** Pol.
92 D7 **Kolambugan** *Mindanao* Phil.
93 D8 **Kolana** Indon.
138 I9 **Kolansk** Belarus
97 D11 **Ko Lanta** Thai.
Kola Peninsula Rus. Fed. *see* **Kol'skiy Poluostrov**
114 G3 **Kolar** *Chhattisgarh* India
114 F6 **Kolar** *Karnataka* India
116 F7 **Kolaras** *Madh. Prad.* India
177 I3 **Koláre** Slovakia
114 F6 **Kolar Gold Fields** *Karnataka* India
140 Q3 **Kolari** Fin.
Kolarovgrad Bulg. *see* Shumen
177 G4 **Kolárovo** Slovakia
140 L5 **Kolåsen** Sweden
117 N7 **Kolasib** *Mizoram* India
196 H8 **Kolašin** Montenegro
116 D6 **Kolayat** *Rajasthan* India
143 M2 **Kolbäck** Sweden
170 K4 **Kołbacz** Pol.
93 D9 **Kolbano** *Timor* Indon.
174 C2 **Kołbaskowo** Pol.
Kolberg Pol. *see* **Kołobrzeg**
173 M6 **Kolbermoor** Ger.
175 J3 **Kołbiel** Pol.
211 D5 **Kolbio** Kenya
142 G2 **Kolbotn** Norway
174 G1 **Kolbudy Górne** Pol.
175 J5 **Kolbuszowa** Pol.
139 P1 **Kolchanovo** Rus. Fed.
139 W5 **Kol'chugino** Rus. Fed.
137 M9 **Kol'chuhyne** Ukr.
136 B5 **Kol'chyne** Ukr.
177 L3 **Kölcse** Hungary
174 F1 **Kołczygłowy** Pol.
174 D3 **Kołczyn** Pol.
206 B3 **Kolda** Senegal
208 C3 **Koldaga** Chad
199 I4 **Koldere** Turkey
142 F6 **Kolding** Denmark
209 D5 **Kole** *Kasaï-Oriental* Dem. Rep. Congo
208 E4 **Kole** *Orientale* Dem. Rep. Congo
240 □E13 **Kolekole** *mt. HI* U.S.A.
100 M1 **Kolendo** *Sakhalin* Rus. Fed.
140 P4 **Koler** Sweden
177 H5 **Kölesd** Hungary
138 I3 **Kolga-Jaani** Estonia
134 J1 **Kolguyev, Ostrov** *i.* Rus. Fed.
117 J8 **Kolhan** *reg. Jharkhand* India
114 D4 **Kolhapur** *Mahar.* India
141 R5 **Kolho** Fin.
113 D11 **Kolhumadulu Atoll** Maldives
206 B3 **Koliba** *r.* Guinea/Guinea-Bissau
Kolikata *W. Bengal* India *see* Kolkata
140 R5 **Kolima** *l.* Fin.
176 E1 **Kolín** Czech Rep.
176 C2 **Kolinec** Czech Rep.
140 T5 **Kolin kansallispuisto** *nat. park* Fin.
210 C3 **K'olīto** Eth.
173 I2 **Kolitzheim** Ger.
138 F3 **Kõljala** Estonia
138 F4 **Kolkasrags** *pt* Latvia
117 L8 **Kolkata** *W. Bengal* India
177 H6 **Kölked** Hungary
129 C3 **Kolkhet'is Nakrdzali** *nature res.* Georgia
Kolkhozabad Tajik. *see* Kolkhozobod
123 M3 **Kolkhozobod** Tajik.
171 J7 **Kolkwitz** Ger.
136 E2 **Kolky** Ukr.
Kollam *Kerala* India *see* **Quilon**
173 O4 **Kollbach** *r.* Ger.
171 D8 **Kölleda** Ger.
114 E6 **Kollegal** *Karnataka* India
114 G4 **Kolleru Lake** India
173 N3 **Kollnburg** Ger.
168 I3 **Kölln-Reisiek** Ger.
207 F3 **Kollo** Niger
164 J2 **Kollum** Neth.
168 H1 **Kollund** Denmark
169 C9 **Köln** Ger.
169 B9 **Köln** *admin. reg.* Ger.
169 D9 **Köln-Bonn** *airport* Ger.
175 L2 **Kolnica** Pol.
175 J2 **Kolno** *Podlaskie* Pol.
175 I2 **Kolno** *Warmińsko-Mazurskie* Pol.
209 B6 **Kolo** Dem. Rep. Congo
174 G3 **Koło** Pol.
211 B6 **Kolo** Tanz.
240 □B12 **Kōloa** *HI* U.S.A.
139 Y5 **Kolobovo** Rus. Fed.
143 L7 **Kołobrzeg** Pol.
171 H7 **Kolochau** Ger.
136 C5 **Kolochava** Ukr.
139 U2 **Kolodenskoye, Ozero** *l.* Rus. Fed.
137 S2 **Kolodeznyy** Rus. Fed.
136 E4 **Kolodne** Ukr.
137 Q3 **Kolodyazne** Ukr.
118 C7 **Kologi** Sudan
134 I4 **Kologriv** Rus. Fed.
206 C3 **Kolokani** Mali
134 K1 **Kolokolkova, Guba** *b.* Rus. Fed.
139 X5 **Koloksha** *r.* Rus. Fed.
137 O4 **Kolomak** Ukr.
137 N4 **Kolomak** *r.* Ukr.
78 □6 **Kolombangara** *i. New Georgia Is* Solomon Is
Kolomea Ukr. *see* **Kolomyya**
139 V6 **Kolomna** Rus. Fed.
209 D6 **Kolomonyi** Dem. Rep. Congo
Kołomyja Ukr. *see* **Kolomyya**
136 E5 **Kolomyya** Ukr.
206 D4 **Kolondiéba** Mali
93 B5 **Kolonedale** *Sulawesi* Indon.
79 □8a **Kolonga** *Tongatapu* Tonga
128 A4 **Koloni** Cyprus
78 □4b **Kolonia** *Pohnpei* Micronesia
196 H10 **Kolonjë** Albania
212 D5 **Kolonkwaneng** Botswana
93 C6 **Kolono** *Sulawesi* Indon.
174 G5 **Kolonowskie** Pol.
137 O2 **Kolontayevka** Rus. Fed.
137 N4 **Kolontayiv** Ukr.
139 S1 **Koloshma** *r.* Rus. Fed.
79 □8a **Kolovai** *Tongatapu* Tonga
120 D2 **Kolovertnoye** Kazakh.
93 C6 **Kolowana Watobo, Teluk** *b.* Indon.
140 V2 **Kolozero, Ozero** *l.* Rus. Fed.
Kolozsvár Romania *see* Cluj-Napoca
139 T2 **Kolp'** *r.* Rus. Fed.
139 Y6 **Kolp'** *r.* Rus. Fed.
130 J4 **Kolpashevo** Rus. Fed.
139 N2 **Kolpino** Rus. Fed.
135 G5 **Kolpny** Rus. Fed.
120 J6 **Ko'lquduq** Uzbek.
178 E5 **Kolsass** Austria
139 Y4 **Kolshevo** Rus. Fed.
134 F2 **Kol'skiy Poluostrov** *pen.* Rus. Fed.
174 D4 **Kolsko** Pol.
143 M2 **Kolsnaren** *l.* Sweden
143 L2 **Kolsva** Sweden
141 M6 **Kölsvallen** Sweden
177 H3 **Kolta** Slovakia
137 M8 **Kol'tsove** Ukr.
120 D1 **Koltubanovskiy** Rus. Fed.
196 I6 **Kolubara** *r.* Serbia
Kölük Turkey *see* **Kâhta**
203 I6 **Koluli** Eritrea
175 H4 **Koluszki** Pol.
121 M2 **Koluton** Kazakh.
134 L2 **Kolva** *r.* Rus. Fed.
134 L3 **Kolva** *r.* Rus. Fed.
114 C3 **Kolvan** *Mahar.* India
140 K4 **Kolvereid** Norway
140 R1 **Kolvik** Norway
134 F2 **Kolvitskoye, Ozero** *l.* Rus. Fed.
123 K8 **Kolwa** *reg.* Pak.
209 E7 **Kolwezi** Dem. Rep. Congo
114 D4 **Kolya** *r.* India
139 W8 **Kolybel'skoye** Rus. Fed.
131 R3 **Kolyma** *r.* Rus. Fed.
Kolyma Lowland Rus. Fed. *see* **Kolymskaya Nizmennost'**
Kolyma Range *mts* Rus. Fed. *see* **Kolymskiy, Khrebet**
131 Q3 **Kolymskaya Nizmennost'** *lowland* Rus. Fed.
131 R3 **Kolymskiy, Khrebet** *mts* Rus. Fed.
131 P3 **Kolymskoye Vodokhranilishche** *resr* Rus. Fed.
135 I5 **Kolyshley** Rus. Fed.
131 T3 **Kolyuchinskaya Guba** *b.* Rus. Fed.
139 O8 **Kolyudy** Rus. Fed.
121 T2 **Kolyvan'** Rus. Fed.
121 S6 **Kol'zhat** Kazakh.
197 L7 **Kom** *mt.* Bulg.
110 H2 **Kom** *Xinjiang* China
96 D7 **Koma** Myanmar
177 K4 **Komádi** Hungary
207 I3 **Komadugu-gana** *watercourse* Nigeria
105 K4 **Komae** Japan
105 G4 **Komaga-dake** *mt.* Japan
105 G4 **Komagane** Japan
105 J1 **Komaga-take** *mt.* Japan
102 R4 **Komaga-take** *vol.* Japan
140 Q1 **Komagfjord** Norway
214 B5 **Komaggas** S. Africa
214 B5 **Komaggas Mountains** S. Africa
140 U1 **Komagvær** Norway
104 E5 **Komaki** Japan
175 K6 **Komańcza** Pol.
100 K3 **Komandnaya, Gora** *mt.* Rus. Fed.
131 R4 **Komandorskiye Ostrova** *is* Rus. Fed.
139 R9 **Komarichi** Rus. Fed.
196 G7 **Komarnica** *r.* Montenegro
177 H4 **Komárno** Slovakia
136 C4 **Komarno** Ukr.
177 H4 **Komárom** Hungary
177 H4 **Komárom-Esztergom** *county* Hungary
176 C2 **Komárov** Czech Rep.
136 E2 **Komarove** Ukr.
138 M1 **Komarovo** *Leningradskaya Oblast'* Rus. Fed.
139 Q3 **Komarovo** *Novgorodskaya Oblast'* Rus. Fed.
175 K4 **Komarówka Podlaska** Pol.
175 L5 **Komarów Osada** Pol.
139 Q6 **Komary** Rus. Fed.
215 P1 **Komati** *r.* Swaziland
215 P1 **Komatipoort** S. Africa
104 D3 **Komatsu** Japan
104 A7 **Komatsushima** Japan
208 E4 **Komba** Dem. Rep. Congo
93 C7 **Komba** *i.* Indon.
93 C4 **Kombakomba** *Sulawesi* Indon.
212 C3 **Kombat** Namibia
209 E6 **Kombe** Dem. Rep. Congo
211 A6 **Kombe** Tanz.
206 E3 **Kombissiri** Burkina
Kombótion Greece *see* Kompoti
92 □ **Komebail Lagoon** Palau
179 I8 **Komen** Slovenia
94 F6 **Komering** *r.* Indon.
215 L8 **Komga** S. Africa
134 J3 **Komi, Respublika** *aut. rep.* Rus. Fed.
Komi A.S.S.R. *aut. rep.* Rus. Fed. *see* Komi, Respublika
179 N7 **Komin** Croatia
102 R6 **Kominato** Japan
Komintern Ukr. *see* **Marhanets'**
136 J7 **Kominternivs'ke** Ukr.
188 F4 **Komiža** Croatia
177 H3 **Komjatice** Slovakia
177 I2 **Komjatná** Slovakia
214 C7 **Komkans** S. Africa
177 H5 **Komló** Hungary
177 J4 **Kömlő** Hungary
214 G9 **Kommandokraal** S. Africa
214 C10 **Kommetjie** S. Africa
215 L5 **Kommissiepoort** S. Africa
Kommuna Turkm. *see* Badabaýhan
134 H4 **Kommunar** *Kostromskaya Oblast'* Rus. Fed.
139 N2 **Kommunar** *Leningradskaya Oblast'* Rus. Fed.
139 X5 **Kommunar** *Vladimirskaya Oblast'* Rus. Fed.
Kommunarsk Ukr. *see* Alchevs'k
Kommunizm, Qullai *mt.* Tajik. *see* **Ismoili Somoní, Qullai**
Kommunizma, Pik *mt.* Tajik. *see* **Ismoili Somoní, Qullai**
179 I7 **Komna** *slope* Slovenia
93 A8 **Komodo** *i.* Indon.
93 A8 **Komodo, Taman Nasional** *nat. park* Indon.
206 C4 **Komodou** Guinea
206 E5 **Komoé** *r.* Côte d'Ivoire
209 B5 **Komono** Congo
104 E5 **Komono** Japan
91 I8 **Komoran** *i. Papua* Indon.
174 E3 **Komorniki** Pol.
177 L3 **Komoró** Hungary
105 H3 **Komoro** Japan
175 J3 **Komorowo** Pol.
174 E2 **Komorze, Jezioro** *l.* Pol.
174 G4 **Komorzno** Pol.
143 J4 **Komosse SNF-reservat** *nature res.* Sweden
199 G1 **Komotini** Greece
137 L5 **Kompaniyivka** Ukr.
177 I5 **Kömpöc** Hungary
Kompong Cham Cambodia *see* **Kâmpóng Cham**
Kompong Chhnang Cambodia *see* Kâmpóng Chhnăng
Kompong Kleang Cambodia *see* **Kâmpóng Khleăng**
Kompong Som Cambodia *see* Sihanoukville
Kompong Som Bay Cambodia *see* **Sihanoukville, Chhâk**
Kompong Speu Cambodia *see* Kâmpóng Spœ
Kompong Thom Cambodia *see* **Kâmpóng Thum**
Kompong Trach Cambodia *see* **Kâmpóng Tranch**
198 C3 **Kompoti** Greece
174 F5 **Komprachcice** Pol.
198 G1 **Kompsatos** *r.* Greece
Komrat Moldova *see* **Comrat**
214 F8 **Komsberg** *mt.* S. Africa
214 E8 **Komsberg** *mts* S. Africa
Komsomol *Atyrauskaya Oblast'* Kazakh. *see* **Komsomol'skiy**
Komsomol *Kostanayskaya Oblast'* Kazakh. *see* **Karabalyk**
120 J8 **Komsomol** Turkm.
Komsomol Turkm. *see* Komsomol
131 K1 **Komsomolets, Ostrov** *i. Severnaya Zemlya* Rus. Fed.
120 E5 **Komsomolets, Zaliv** *b.* Kazakh.
139 X4 **Komsomol'sk** *Ivanovskaya Oblast'* Rus. Fed.
175 I1 **Komsomol'sk** Rus. Fed.
138 D7 **Komsomol'sk** *Kaliningradskaya Oblast'* Rus. Fed.
137 M4 **Komsomol's'k** Ukr.
137 R6 **Komsomol's'ke** *Donets'ka Oblast'* Ukr.
137 P4 **Komsomol's'ke** *Kharkivs'ka Oblast'* Ukr.
120 E4 **Komsomol'skiy** Kazakh.
131 S3 **Komsomol'skiy** *Chukotskiy Avtonomnyy Okrug* Rus. Fed.
Komsomol'skiy *Khanty-Mansiyskiy Avtonomnyy Okrug* Rus. Fed. *see* **Yugorsk**
129 H2 **Komsomol'skiy** *Respublika Dagestan* Rus. Fed.
135 I7 **Komsomol'skiy** *Respublika Kalmykiya-Khalm'g-Tangch* Rus. Fed.
135 I5 **Komsomol'skiy** *Respublika Mordoviya* Rus. Fed.
100 J3 **Komsomol'sk-na-Amure** Rus. Fed.
120 I2 **Komsomol'skoye** Kazakh.
120 B2 **Komsomol'skoye** Rus. Fed.
197 N9 **Komuniga** Bulg.
128 E2 **Kömürçukuru** Turkey
127 K3 **Kömürlü** Turkey
137 L7 **Komyshany** Ukr.
137 S5 **Komyshna** *r.* Rus. Fed./Ukr.
137 M3 **Komyshnya** Ukr.
137 O6 **Komyshuvakha** Ukr.
137 K5 **Komyshuvate** Ukr.
137 P6 **Komysh-Zorya** Ukr.
117 I7 **Kon** *Uttar Prad.* India
128 D2 **Konacık** Turkey
115 H3 **Konada** *Andhra Prad.* India
129 D6 **Konakkuran** Turkey
139 T5 **Konakovo** Rus. Fed.
104 E5 **Kōnan** *Aichi* Japan
104 D6 **Kōnan** *Shiga* Japan
Konarak *Orissa* India *see* Konarka
115 J3 **Konarka** *Orissa* India
175 K2 **Konarzyce** Pol.
174 F2 **Konarzyny** Pol.
116 G7 **Konch** *Uttar Prad.* India
139 R3 **Konchanskoye-Suvorovskoye** Rus. Fed.
134 F3 **Konchezero** Rus. Fed.
136 E1 **Konchytsy** Belarus
104 B5 **Konda** Japan
114 G3 **Kondagaon** *Chhattisgarh* India
129 I6 **Köndäläncay** *r.* Azer.
114 G4 **Kondapalle** *Andhra Prad.* India
85 J4 **Kondaparinga Aboriginal Holding** *res. Qld* Austr.
114 G4 **Kondavid** *Andhra Prad.* India
227 R3 **Kondiaronk, Lac** *l. Que.* Can.
87 E12 **Kondinin** *W.A.* Austr.
130 H3 **Kondinskoye** *Khanty-Mansiyskiy Avtonomnyy Okrug* Rus. Fed.
Kondinskoye *Khanty-Mansiyskiy Avtonomnyy Okrug* Rus. Fed. *see* **Oktyabr'skoye**
211 B6 **Kondoa** Tanz.
135 I5 **Kondol'** Rus. Fed.
129 G4 **Kondoli** Georgia
134 F3 **Kondopoga** Rus. Fed.
177 J5 **Kondoros** Hungary
174 E5 **Kondratowice** Pol.
138 L1 **Kondrat'yevo** Rus. Fed.
139 S7 **Kondrovo** Rus. Fed.
Kondūz Afgh. *see* **Kunduz**
78 □5 **Kone** New Caledonia
197 K9 **Konečka Planina** *mts* Macedonia
134 L2 **Konetsbor** Rus. Fed.
122 H1 **Köneürgenç** Turkm.
Köneürgench Turkm. *see* Köneürgenç
139 N1 **Konevits, Ostrov** *i.* Rus. Fed.
207 I5 **Kong** Cameroon
206 D4 **Kong** Côte d'Ivoire
97 F9 **Kŏng, Kaôh** *i.* Cambodia
97 H8 **Kông, Tônlé** *r.* Cambodia
96 H7 **Kong, Xé** *r.* Laos
206 C3 **Kongassambougou, Réserve de** *nature res.* Mali
92 □ **Kongauru** *i.* Palau
208 D3 **Kongbo** C.A.R.
221 O3 **Kong Christian IX Land** *reg.* Greenland
221 P2 **Kong Christian X Land** *reg.* Greenland
142 E6 **Kongeå** *r.* Denmark
Kongelab *atoll* Marshall Is *see* Rongelap
142 I6 **Kongens Lyngby** Denmark
210 B3 **Kongettit** Sudan
221 M3 **Kong Frederik IX Land** *reg.* Greenland
221 P2 **Kong Frederik VIII Land** *reg.* Greenland
221 N3 **Kong Frederik VI Kyst** *coastal area* Greenland
140 □ **Kong Karls Land** *is* Svalbard
95 L4 **Kong Kat** *hill* Indon.
95 L4 **Kongkemul** *mt.* Indon.
104 F3 **Kongōdo-san** *mt.* Japan
104 C6 **Kongō-Ikoma Kokutei-kōen** *park* Japan
212 D3 **Kongola** Namibia
209 E6 **Kongolo** Dem. Rep. Congo
210 A3 **Kongor** Sudan
221 P2 **Kong Oscars Fjord** *inlet* Greenland
206 E3 **Kongoussi** Burkina
142 F2 **Kongsberg** Norway
140 T1 **Kongsfjord** Norway
140 □ **Kongsøya** *i.* Svalbard
142 I1 **Kongsvinger** Norway
110 B7 **Kongur Shan** *mt. Xinjiang* China
211 C6 **Kongwa** Tanz.
221 P2 **Kong Wilhelm Land** *reg.* Greenland
123 N1 **Konibodom** Tajik.
176 F2 **Konice** Czech Rep.
175 H5 **Koniecpol** Pol.
172 H2 **Königheim** Ger.
Königsberg Rus. Fed. *see* Kaliningrad
169 K10 **Königsberg in Bayern** Ger.
171 E6 **Königsborn** Ger.
173 I4 **Königsbronn** Ger.
171 I8 **Königsbrück** Ger.
173 J5 **Königsbrunn** Ger.
173 K6 **Königsdorf** Ger.
171 D9 **Königsee** Ger.
173 K2 **Königsfeld** Ger.
172 E5 **Königsfeld im Schwarzwald** Ger.
171 H6 **Königsgraben** *r.* Ger.
171 K8 **Königshain** Ger.
171 E8 **Königshofen** Ger.
Königshütte Pol. *see* **Chorzów**
169 K6 **Königslutter am Elm** Ger.
173 K4 **Königsmoos** Ger.
173 N6 **Königssee** Ger.
173 N6 **Königssee** *l.* Ger.
173 L2 **Königstein** *Bayern* Ger.
171 J9 **Königstein** *Sachsen* Ger.
172 F3 **Königstuhl** *hill* Ger.
171 H9 **Königswalde** Ger.
171 J8 **Königswartha** Ger.
179 K3 **Königswiesen** Austria
169 D9 **Königswinter** Ger.
171 I6 **Königs Wusterhausen** Ger.
Konimekh Uzbek. *see* Konimex
120 K7 **Konimex** Uzbek.
174 G3 **Konin** Pol.
100 J2 **Konin** *r.* Rus. Fed.
198 B2 **Konitsa** Greece
171 E9 **Könitz** Ger.
190 C2 **Köniz** Switz.
188 F4 **Konj** *mt.* Bos.-Herz.
188 F4 **Konjic** Bos.-Herz.
188 G3 **Konjuh** *mts* Bos.-Herz.
140 Q2 **Könkämäeno** *r.* Fin./Sweden
212 C6 **Konkiep** *watercourse* Namibia
139 W9 **Kon'-Kolodez'** Rus. Fed.
207 G4 **Konkwesso** Nigeria
206 E3 **Konna** Mali
232 D12 **Konnarock** *VA* U.S.A.
171 E7 **Könnern** Ger.
171 F10 **Konnersreuth** Ger.
140 S5 **Konnevesi** Fin.
141 S6 **Konnivesi** *l.* Fin.
104 D4 **Kōno** Japan
137 K4 **Kononcha** Ukr.
206 E5 **Konongo** Ghana
137 L3 **Kononivka** Ukr.
177 I1 **Konopiska** Pol.
175 I2 **Konopki** Pol.
136 J6 **Konoplyane** Ukr.
134 H3 **Konosha** Rus. Fed.
105 K3 **Kōnosu** Japan
174 D4 **Konotop** Pol.
137 M2 **Konotop** Ukr.
117 I8 **Konpara** *Chhattisgarh* India
97 I7 **Kon Plông** Vietnam
110 I6 **Konqi He** *r.* China
171 E10 **Konradsreuth** Ger.
92 □ **Konrei** Palau
105 J2 **Konsei-tōge** *pass* Japan
175 I4 **Końskie** Pol.
167 K3 **Końskowola** Pol.
210 C3 **Konso** Eth.
175 J3 **Konstancin-Jeziorna** Pol.
Konstantinograd Ukr. *see* Krasnohrad
100 E4 **Konstantinovka** Rus. Fed.
Konstantinovka *Donets'ka Oblast'* Ukr. *see* Kostyantynivka
Konstantinovka *Kharkivs'ka Oblast'* Ukr. *see* Kostyantynivka
Konstantinovka *Khersons'ka Oblast'* Ukr. *see* Kostyantynivka
Konstantinovka *Zaporiz'ka Oblast'* Ukr. *see* Kostyantynivka
139 V5 **Konstantinovo** Rus. Fed.
135 H7 **Konstantinovsk** Rus. Fed.
139 W4 **Konstantinovskiy** Rus. Fed.
176 B2 **Konstantinovy Lázně** Czech Rep.
175 L3 **Konstantynów** Pol.
175 H4 **Konstantynów Łódzki** Pol.
172 G6 **Konstanz** Ger.
123 I8 **Kont** Iran
207 G4 **Kontagora** Nigeria
207 I5 **Kontcha** Cameroon
96 C4 **Kontha** Myanmar
140 T5 **Kontiolahti** Fin.
140 T4 **Kontiomäki** Fin.
140 S4 **Konttila** Fin.
97 H7 **Kon Tum** Vietnam
97 I8 **Kon Tum, Cao Nguyên** *plat.* Vietnam
Könugard Ukr. *see* **Kyiv**
199 M2 **Konuralp** Turkey
134 H2 **Konushin, Mys** *pt* Rus. Fed.
126 F5 **Konya** Turkey
177 K4 **Konyár** Hungary
121 P4 **Konyrat** Kazakh.
121 R5 **Konyrolen** Kazakh.
137 O2 **Konyshevka** Rus. Fed.
120 E3 **Konystanu** Kazakh.
121 N1 **Konyukhovo** Kazakh.
172 B2 **Konz** Ger.
173 N3 **Konzell** Ger.
134 L4 **Konzhakovskiy Kamen', Gora** *mt.* Rus. Fed.
222 H5 **Koocanusa, Lake** *resr* Can./U.S.A.
87 F10 **Kookynie** *W.A.* Austr.
86 G3 **Koolan Island** *W.A.* Austr.
240 □D12 **Ko'olau Range** *mts HI* U.S.A.
87 D7 **Kooline** *W.A.* Austr.
84 G8 **Koolivoo, Lake** *salt flat Qld* Austr.
82 F3 **Koolkootinnie, Lake** *salt flat S.A.* Austr.
82 G5 **Koolunga** *S.A.* Austr.
87 E11 **Koolyanobbing** *W.A.* Austr.
83 J6 **Koondrook** *Vic.* Austr.
138 H3 **Koonga** Estonia
86 I5 **Koongie Park Aboriginal Reserve** *W.A.* Austr.
82 D4 **Koonibba** *S.A.* Austr.
232 G9 **Koon Lake** *PA* U.S.A.
214 E3 **Koopan-Suid** S. Africa
83 L6 **Koorawatha** *N.S.W.* Austr.
87 D11 **Koorda** *W.A.* Austr.
86 C7 **Koordarrie** *W.A.* Austr.
138 I4 **Koorküla** Estonia
170 H2 **Koos** *i.* Ger.
138 K3 **Koosa** Estonia
241 U3 **Koosharem** *UT* U.S.A.
238 F3 **Kooskia** *ID* U.S.A.
222 G5 **Kootenay** *r. B.C.* Can.
222 G5 **Kootenay Bay** *B.C.* Can.
222 G5 **Kootenay Lake** *B.C.* Can.
222 G5 **Kootenay National Park** *B.C.* Can.
83 M4 **Kootingal** *N.S.W.* Austr.
214 E7 **Kootjieskolk** S. Africa
164 I4 **Kootwijkerbroek** Neth.
121 P6 **Kopa** *Almatinskaya Oblast'* Kazakh.
121 R4 **Kopa** *Vostochnyy Kazakhstan* Kazakh.
177 I2 **Kopa** *mt.* Slovakia
211 A7 **Kopa** Zambia
129 D6 **Kopal** Turkey
174 E1 **Kopań, Jezioro** *lag.* Pol.
137 O6 **Kopani** Ukr.
174 D3 **Kopanica** Pol.
135 I7 **Kopanovka** Rus. Fed.
137 R7 **Kopanskaya** Rus. Fed.
196 I7 **Kopaonik** *mts* Serbia
196 I7 **Kopaonik** *nat. park* Serbia
114 D3 **Kopargaon** *Mahar.* India
140 □E1 **Kópasker** Iceland

136 G5 Kopayhorod Ukr.
121 Q4 Kopbirlik Kazakh.
176 G3 Kopčany Slovakia
188 D3 Koper Slovenia
142 B2 Kopervik Norway
122 G2 Kopet Dag mts Iran/Turkm.
Kopet-Dag, Khrebet mts Iran/Turkm. see Kopet Dag
129 B5 Kop Geçidi pass Turkey
176 F4 Kópháza Hungary
174 F5 Kopice Pol.
176 E1 Kopidlno Czech Rep.
143 M2 Köping Sweden
196 H8 Koplik Albania
140 O5 Köpmanholmen Sweden
139 R6 Koporikha Rus. Fed.
114 D6 Koppa Karnataka India
114 E5 Koppal Karnataka India
141 K6 Koppang Norway
196 G4 Koppány r. Romania
143 L2 Kopparberg Sweden
Kopparberg county Sweden see Dalarna
Koppeh Dāgh mts Iran/Turkm. see Kopet Dag
169 E10 Köppel hill Ger.
100 L4 Koppi r. Rus. Fed.
215 L3 Koppies S. Africa
215 L3 Koppies Dam Nature Reserve S. Africa
214 E3 Koppieskraal Pan salt pan S. Africa
178 H4 Koppl Austria
197 N8 Koprinka, Yazovir resr Bulg.
188 F2 Koprivnica Croatia
126 E5 Köprü r. Turkey
199 J4 Köprübaşı Manisa Turkey
129 B5 Köprübaşı Trabzon Turkey
129 C6 Köprüköy Turkey
126 F5 Köprülü Turkey
199 M5 Köprülü Kanyon Milli Parkı nat. park Turkey
175 J5 Koprzywianka r. Pol.
175 J5 Koprzywnica Pol.
215 L7 Kopshorn mt. S. Africa
165 J9 Kopstal Lux.
139 N6 Koptsi Belarus
138 I3 Kõpu Estonia
138 I3 Kõpu r. Estonia
80 J4 Kopu North I. N.Z.
80 L6 Kopuawhara North I. N.Z.
136 E4 Kopychyntsi Ukr.
Kopyl' Belarus see Kapyl'
137 U2 Kopyl Rus. Fed.
122 E7 Kor, Rūd-e watercourse Iran
116 H6 Kora Uttar Prad. India
104 D5 Kōra Japan
196 I9 Korab mts Albania/Macedonia
139 X8 Korablino Rus. Fed.
116 H9 Koracha Chhattisgarh India
210 E3 Koraf well Eth.
210 E3 K'orahē Eth.
123 K8 Korak Pak.
92 □ Korak i. Palau
199 H3 Korakas, Akrotirio pt Lesvos Greece
179 K6 Koralpe mts Austria
111 G8 Koramlik Xinjiang China
188 E3 Korana r. Bos.-Herz./Croatia
114 E4 Korangal Andhra Prad. India
123 L9 Korangi Pak.
123 N3 Korān va Monjan Afgh.
115 H3 Koraput Orissa India
Korat Thai. see Nakhon Ratchasima
114 F3 Koratla Andhra Prad. India
117 I8 Korba Chhattisgarh India
205 H1 Korba Tunisia
169 G8 Korbach Ger.
139 R1 Korbenichi Rus. Fed.
208 C2 Korbol Chad
129 E3 Korbouli Georgia
189 C7 Korbous Tunisia
94 D2 Korbu, Gunung mt. Malaysia
198 B2 Korçë Albania
121 S1 Korchino Rus. Fed.
175 L5 Korchiv Ukr.
136 F4 Korchivka Ukr.
170 D4 Körchow Ger.
136 G3 Korchyk r. Ukr.
188 F4 Korčula Croatia
188 F4 Korčula i. Croatia
188 F4 Korčulanski Kanal sea chan. Croatia
175 K3 Korczew Pol.
175 J6 Korczyna Pol.
121 P6 Korday Kazakh.
172 B2 Kordel Ger.
136 H4 Kordelivka Ukr.
122 B4 Kordestān prov. Iran
202 D5 Kordi, Ouadi watercourse Chad
127 N6 Kord Khvord Iran
122 F3 Kord Kūy Iran
134 L4 Kordon Rus. Fed.
122 I8 Kords reg. Iran
101 D9 Korea Bay g. China/N. Korea
103 F12 Korea Strait Japan/S. Korea
114 D4 Koregaon Mahar. India
136 D4 Korelychi Ukr.
210 C1 Korem Eth.
137 P3 Koren' r. Rus. Fed.
137 N2 Korenevo Rus. Fed.
176 E1 Kořenov Czech Rep.
135 G7 Korenovsk Rus. Fed.
Korenovskaya Rus. Fed. see Korenovsk
134 L3 Korepino Rus. Fed.
206 C3 Koréra-Koré Mali
136 G3 Korets' Ukr.
131 R3 Korf Rus. Fed.
174 F5 Korfantów Pol.
199 K2 Körfez Turkey
262 T1 Korff Ice Rise Antarctica
100 I4 Korfovskiy Rus. Fed.
121 N2 Korgalzhyn Kazakh.
110 E4 Korgas Xinjiang China
121 L3 Korgasyn Kazakh.
140 L3 Korgen Norway
129 K5 Korgöz Azer.
199 M3 Körhasan Turkey
206 D4 Korhogo Côte d'Ivoire
102 R9 Kōri Japan
251 G3 Koriabo Guyana
206 C5 Koribundu Sierra Leone
116 B8 Kori Creek inlet Gujarat India
214 C9 Koringberg S. Africa
214 E8 Koringplaas S. Africa
80 J6 Koriniti North I. N.Z.
198 D2 Korinos Greece
142 G6 Korinth Denmark
198 D4 Korinthiakos Kolpos sea chan. Greece
198 D5 Korinthos Greece
198 E5 Korinthou, Dioryga b. Greece
177 G4 Kőris-hegy hill Hungary
198 F5 Korisia Kea Greece
198 B5 Korithi Zakynthos Greece
196 I8 Koritnik mt. Albania
Koritsa Albania see Korçë
103 R9 Kōriyama Japan
140 U4 Korkana Fin.
122 G3 Korkī Iran
123 K8 Korkian Pak.
130 H4 Korkino Rus. Fed.
131 Q3 Korkodon r. Rus. Fed.
199 M4 Körküler Turkey
199 L5 Korkuteli Turkey
138 G3 Kõrkvere Estonia
120 J5 Korkyt Kazakh.
110 H6 Korla Xinjiang China
169 I8 Körle Ger.
128 A3 Kormakitis, Cape Cyprus
196 H7 Korman mt. Montenegro
176 F4 Körmend Hungary
137 M8 Kormove Ukr.
175 L6 Kornalovychi Ukr.
188 E4 Kornat i. Croatia
188 E4 Kornat nat. park Croatia
169 K8 Körner Ger.
Korneshty Moldova see Corneşti
179 N3 Korneuburg Austria
175 I1 Kornevo Rus. Fed.
121 P2 Korneyevka Karagandinskaya Oblast' Kazakh.
121 M1 Korneyevka Severnyy Kazakhstan Kazakh.
120 C2 Korneyevka Rus. Fed.
174 F3 Kórnik Pol.
121 S1 Kornilovo Rus. Fed.
Kornisi Georgia see Qornisi
142 H3 Kornsjø Norway
172 G4 Kornwestheim Ger.
177 H4 Környe Hungary
136 I3 Kornyn Ukr.
206 D4 Koro Côte d'Ivoire
79 □7 Koro i. Fiji
93 B4 Koro r. Indon.
206 E3 Koro Mali
79 □7a Koroba mt. Viti Levu Fiji
139 Q7 Korobets Rus. Fed.
225 H1 Koroc r. Que. Can.
135 G6 Korocha Rus. Fed.
137 P3 Korocha r. Rus. Fed.
126 F3 Köroğlu Dağları mts Turkey
126 F3 Köroğlu Tepesi mt. Turkey
210 D3 Korogo well Eth.
211 C6 Korogwe Tanz.
136 C5 Korolevé Ukr.
79 □7a Korolevu Viti Levu Fiji
79 □7a Korolevu Viti Levu Fiji
208 C2 Korom, Bahr watercourse Chad
191 Q6 Koromačno Croatia
Koromba mt. Viti Levu Fiji see Koroba
81 □3 Koromiri i. Rarotonga Cook Is
198 E2 Koroneia, Limni l. Greece
198 C6 Koroni Greece
198 B3 Koronisia Greece
174 F2 Koronowo Pol.
174 F2 Koronowskie, Jezioro l. Pol.
137 L2 Korop Ukr.
198 E5 Koropi Greece
92 □ Koror Palau
92 □ Koror i. Palau
196 I4 Körös r. Romania
79 □7 Koro Sea b. Fiji
177 I5 Körös-ér r. Hungary
177 K5 Körösladány Hungary
177 K4 Körösszakál Hungary
177 K5 Köröstarcsa Hungary
139 T6 Korostelevo Rus. Fed.
136 H3 Korosten' Ukr.
136 I3 Korostyshiv Ukr.
177 K5 Körös-vidék reg. Hungary
134 M1 Korotaikha r. Rus. Fed.
202 C5 Koro Toro Chad
135 G6 Korotoyak Rus. Fed.
Korovino Kurskaya Oblast' Rus. Fed. see Solntsevo
120 E1 Korovino Orenburgskaya Oblast' Rus. Fed.
220 A4 Korovin Volcano AK U.S.A.
79 □7a Korovou Viti Levu Fiji
78 □6 Korovou Solomon Is
137 M3 Korovyntsi Ukr.
79 □7a Koroyanitu Viti Levu Fiji
139 V4 Korozhechna r. Rus. Fed.
172 A2 Körperich Ger.
138 K1 Korpijärvi l. Fin.
141 R5 Korpilahti Fin.
140 Q3 Korpilombolo Sweden
140 U5 Korpisel'kya Rus. Fed.
140 T5 Korpivaara Fin.
141 P6 Korpo Fin.
Korppoo Fin. see Korpo
108 A3 Korra Xizang China
129 H6 Korrnidzor Armenia
120 E4 Korsak Kazakh.
137 O7 Korsak r. Ukr.
100 M5 Korsakov Sakhalin Rus. Fed.
139 U8 Korsakovo Rus. Fed.
143 L4 Korsberga Sweden
137 T2 Korshevo Rus. Fed.
139 P8 Korsiki Rus. Fed.
141 M6 Korskrogen Sweden
140 P5 Korsnäs Fin.
138 I1 Korso Fin.
142 H6 Korsør Denmark
129 C6 Körsu Turkey
137 K4 Korsun'-Shevchenkivs'kyy Ukr.
Korsun'-Shevchenkovskiy Ukr. see Korsun'-Shevchenkivs'kyy
143 R7 Korsze Pol.
203 F6 Kortala Sudan
136 D2 Kortelisy Ukr.
165 D6 Kortemark Belgium
140 Q5 Kortesjärvi Fin.
165 H7 Kortessem Belgium
164 E5 Kortgene Neth.
203 F5 Korti Sudan
134 J3 Kortkeros Rus. Fed.
165 D7 Kortrijk Belgium
134 H4 Kortsovo Rus. Fed.
128 A1 Korualan Turkey
199 I3 Korucu Turkey
83 J8 Korumburra Vic. Austr.
207 H5 Korup, Parc National de nat. park Cameroon
140 S3 Korvala Fin.
116 G7 Korwai Madh. Prad. India
131 Q4 Koryakskaya, Sopka vol. Rus. Fed.
131 S3 Koryakskiy Khrebet mts Rus. Fed.
134 I3 Koryazhma Rus. Fed.
176 G2 Koryčany Czech Rep.
175 L2 Korycin Pol.
104 C6 Kōryō Japan
103 J11 Koryō Japan
101 F11 Koryŏng S. Korea
175 J3 Korytnica Pol.
137 L2 Koryukivka Ukr.
175 I6 Korzenna Pol.
174 E4 Korzeńsko Pol.
139 P9 Korzhovka Golubovka Rus. Fed.
120 E3 Korzhyn Kazakh.
174 E1 Korzybie Pol.
199 I6 Kos Kos Greece
199 I6 Kos i. Greece
134 K4 Kosa Rus. Fed.
134 K3 Kosa r. Rus. Fed.
137 O7 Kosa Biryuchyy Ostriv i. Ukr.
136 J2 Kosachivka Ukr.
120 J2 Kosagal Kazakh.
121 P1 Kosagash Kazakh.
104 G6 Kosai Japan
102 R6 Kosaka Japan
174 G1 Kosakowo Pol.
116 H7 Kosam Uttar Prad. India
101 E9 Kosan N. Korea
129 B6 Koşan Dağı mts Turkey
138 I9 Kosava Belarus
121 L3 Kosay Kazakh.
139 U7 Kosaya Gora Rus. Fed.
120 E4 Koschagyl Kazakh.
173 L4 Kösching Ger.
179 J7 Koschutnikturm mt. Austria/Slovenia
174 E3 Kościan Pol.
174 G3 Kościelec Pol.
174 G4 Kościelna Wieś Pol.
174 E1 Kościernica Pol.
143 N7 Kościerzyna Pol.
237 K9 Kosciusko MS U.S.A.
Kosciusko, Mount N.S.W. Austr. see Kosciuszko, Mount
222 C3 Kosciusko Island AK U.S.A.
83 L7 Kosciuszko, Mount N.S.W. Austr.
83 L7 Kosciuszko National Park N.S.W. Austr.
138 I2 Kose Estonia
129 A5 Köse Turkey
177 H2 Košeca Slovakia
128 B2 Köseçobanlı Turkey
129 D6 Köse Dağı mt. Turkey
126 H3 Köse Dağı mt. Turkey
129 A5 Kösedağı Geçidi pass Turkey
199 H3 Kösedere Turkey
104 D5 Kōsei Japan
168 I1 Kosel Ger.
177 K4 Kösély r. Hungary
143 J5 Kösen l. Sweden
170 J2 Koserow Ger.
114 E4 Kosgi Andhra Prad. India
203 F4 Kosha Sudan
106 A2 Kosh-Agach Rus. Fed.
120 C3 Koshankol' Kazakh.
123 I1 Koshbulakskoye Vodokhranilishche resr Turkm.
121 P7 Kosh-Döbö Kyrg.
105 K4 Koshigaya Japan
103 G15 Koshikijima-rettō is Japan
103 G15 Koshiki-kaikyō sea chan. Japan
102 V3 Koshimizu Japan
104 D3 Koshino Japan
123 J4 Koshk Afgh.
122 I4 Koshkak Iran
120 E4 Koshkar Kazakh.
129 M2 Koshkar-Ata, Ozero l. Kazakh.
121 S4 Koshkarkol', Ozero l. Kazakh.
123 J4 Koshk-e Kohneh Afgh.
135 J5 Koshki Rus. Fed.
226 F7 Koshkonong, Lake WI U.S.A.
136 F4 Koshlyaky Ukr.
137 N4 Koshmanivka Ukr.
105 H2 Kōshoku Japan
Koshtëbë Kyrg. see Kosh-Döbö
116 F6 Kosi Uttar Prad. India
116 G5 Kosi r. India
215 Q2 Kosi Bay S. Africa
215 Q3 Kosi Bay Nature Reserve S. Africa
177 K3 Košice Slovakia
177 K3 Košický kraj admin. reg. Slovakia
114 E5 Kosigi Andhra Prad. India
117 K6 Kosi Reservoir Nepal
120 G2 Kos-Istek Kazakh.
136 E5 Kosiv Ukr.
137 M5 Kosivka Ukr.
196 H7 Kosjerić Serbia
199 J5 Köşk Turkey
141 Q6 Koski Länsi-Suomi Fin.
139 Q7 Koski Rus. Fed.
121 L3 Koskol' Kazakh.
177 K2 Koškovce Slovakia
139 Q1 Kos'kovo Rus. Fed.
121 Q5 Koskuduk Kazakh.
140 P3 Koskullskulle Sweden
134 J3 Koslan Rus. Fed.
Köslin Pol. see Koszalin
134 J2 Kosma r. Rus. Fed.
171 K10 Kosmonosy Czech Rep.
139 X4 Kosmynino Rus. Fed.
188 G3 Košnica r. Croatia
174 F2 Kosobudy Pol.
120 K8 Koson Uzbek.
101 F8 Kosŏng Hamgyŏng-namdo N. Korea
101 F9 Kosŏng Kangwŏn-do N. Korea
121 N7 Kosonsoy Uzbek.
137 P1 Kosorzha Rus. Fed.
Kosova prov. Serbia see Kosovo
196 I8 Kosovo prov. Serbia
Kosovo-Metohija prov. Serbia see Kosovo
196 J8 Kosovo Polje Kosovo Serbia
196 I8 Kosovo Polje plain Serbia
197 J8 Kosovska Kamenica Kosovo Serbia
196 I8 Kosovska Mitrovica Kosovo Serbia
175 K3 Kosów Lacki Pol.
266 F5 Kosrae atoll Micronesia
111 C8 Kosrap Xinjiang China
128 D1 Kösreli Turkey
206 D3 Kossa well Maur.
207 I3 Kossatori well Niger
171 H8 Koßdorf Ger.
173 L2 Kösseine hill Ger.
178 F4 Kössen Austria
173 O5 Kößlar r. Ger.
92 □ Kossol Passage Palau
92 □ Kossol Reef Palau
206 D5 Kossou, Lac de l. Côte d'Ivoire
Kosta-Khetagurovo Rus. Fed. see Nazran'
120 J1 Kostanay Kazakh.
120 J1 Kostanayskaya Oblast' admin. div. Kazakh.
179 L8 Kostanjevica Krško Slovenia
179 I8 Kostanjevica Nova Gorica Slovenia
191 R4 Kostel Slovenia
176 D2 Kostelec nad Černými Lesy Czech Rep.
171 K10 Kostelec nad Labem Czech Rep.
176 F1 Kostelec nad Orlicí Czech Rep.
197 L8 Kostenets Bulg.
215 K1 Koster S. Africa
139 W6 Kosterevo Rus. Fed.
142 H3 Kosteroarna naturreservat nature res. Sweden
203 G6 Kosti Sudan
179 O2 Kostice Czech Rep.
197 L8 Kostinbrod Bulg.
130 J3 Kostino Rus. Fed.
137 L1 Kostobobriv Ukr.
196 J6 Kostolac Serbia
174 E4 Kostomłoty Pol.
140 U4 Kostomuksha Rus. Fed.
140 U4 Kostomukshskiy Zapovednik nature res. Rus. Fed.
136 F3 Kostopil' Ukr.
Kostopol' Ukr. see Kostopil'
139 X4 Kostroma Rus. Fed.
134 H4 Kostroma r. Rus. Fed.
Kostroma Oblast admin. div. Rus. Fed. see Kostromskaya Oblast'
134 H4 Kostromskaya Oblast' admin. div. Rus. Fed.
174 C3 Kostrzyn Lubuskie Pol.
174 F3 Kostrzyn Wielkopolskie Pol.
175 K3 Kostrzyń r. Pol.
137 Q5 Kostyantynivka Donets'ka Oblast' Ukr.
137 O4 Kostyantynivka Kharkivs'ka Oblast' Ukr.
137 M7 Kostyantynivka Khersons'ka Oblast' Ukr.
137 O7 Kostyantynivka Zaporiz'ka Oblast' Ukr.
139 Q7 Kostyri Rus. Fed.
Kostyukovichi Belarus see Kastsyukovichy
138 M4 Kostyzhitsy Rus. Fed.
207 F4 Kosubosu Nigeria
105 I4 Kosuge Japan
104 F2 Kosugi Japan
177 L3 Kosyny Ukr.
134 L2 Kos'yu Rus. Fed.
134 L2 Kos'yu r. Rus. Fed.
134 L2 Kos'yuvom Rus. Fed.
143 M7 Koszalin Pol.
174 G5 Koszęcin Pol.
176 F4 Kőszeg Hungary
176 F4 Kőszegi park Hungary
179 N5 Kőszegi-hegység hill Hungary
175 I5 Koszyce Pol.
114 G5 Kota Andhra Prad. India
116 I8 Kota Chhattisgarh India
116 E7 Kota Rajasthan India
104 F6 Kōta Japan
94 F7 Kotaagung Sumatera Indon.
Kota Baharu Malaysia see Kota Bharu
95 I5 Kotabaru Kalimantan Indon.
95 L6 Kotabaru Kalimantan Indon.
94 B3 Kotabaru Sumatera Indon.
95 L1 Kota Belud Sabah Malaysia
95 J6 Kotabesi Kalimantan Indon.
94 E1 Kota Bharu Malaysia
94 F7 Kotabumi Sumatera Indon.
93 D3 Kotabunan Sulawesi Indon.
123 N6 Kot Addu Pak.
95 L2 Kota Kinabalu Sabah Malaysia
140 T3 Kotala Fin.
93 D3 Kotamobagu Sulawesi Indon.
222 E2 Kotaneelee Range mts N.W.T./Y.T. Can.
121 Q4 Kotanemel', Gora mt. Kazakh.
114 H3 Kotaparh Orissa India
94 D4 Kotapinang Sumatera Indon.
116 H7 Kotar Madh. Prad. India
116 E7 Kotari r. India
95 I4 Kota Samarahan Sarawak Malaysia
94 D4 Kotatengah Sumatera Indon.
94 E4 Kota Tinggi Malaysia
95 I6 Kotawaringin Kalimantan Indon.
117 L8 Kotchandpur Bangl.
222 F3 Kotcho r. B.C. Can.
222 F3 Kotcho Lake B.C. Can.
123 M8 Kot Diji Pak.
116 G5 Kotdwara Uttaranchal India
177 K5 Kötegyán Hungary
197 O8 Kotel Bulg.
177 J4 Kötelek Hungary
134 J4 Kotel'nich Rus. Fed.
135 H7 Kotel'nikovo Rus. Fed.
131 O2 Kotel'nyy, Ostrov i. Novosibirskiye O-va Rus. Fed.
170 I3 Kotelow Ger.
137 N3 Kotel'va Ukr.
80 L6 Kotemaori North I. N.Z.
123 O4 Kotgala Pak.
115 H3 Kotgar Orissa India
116 F4 Kotgarh Hima. Prad. India
Kothagudem Andhra Prad. India see Kottagudem
171 E7 Köthen (Anhalt) Ger.
116 H7 Kothi Madh. Prad. India
206 B3 Kotiari Naoude Senegal
210 B4 Kotido Uganda
100 I5 Kotikovo Rus. Fed.
123 M8 Kot Imamgarh Pak.
141 S6 Kotka Fin.
116 E4 Kot Kapura Punjab India
134 J2 Kotkino Rus. Fed.
174 E4 Kotla Pol.
134 I3 Kotlas Rus. Fed.
123 O5 Kotli Pak.
220 B3 Kotlik AK U.S.A.
174 F4 Kotlin Pol.
139 R3 Kotlovan Rus. Fed.
140 □D2 Kötlutangi pt Iceland
138 L2 Kotly Rus. Fed.
104 D5 Kotō Japan
207 G4 Koton-Karifi Nigeria
102 R6 Kotooka Japan
196 G8 Kotor Montenegro
179 O7 Kotoriba Croatia
207 G3 Kotorkoshi Nigeria
139 W4 Kotorosl' r. Rus. Fed.
188 G3 Kotorsko Bos.-Herz.
188 F3 Kotor Varoš Bos.-Herz.
206 E4 Kotouba Côte d'Ivoire
137 N4 Kotovka Ukr.
135 I6 Kotovo Rus. Fed.
Kotovsk Moldova see Hînceşti
135 H5 Kotovsk Rus. Fed.
136 I6 Kotovs'k Ukr.
116 F6 Kot Putli Rajasthan India
138 H8 Kotra r. Belarus
116 D7 Kotra Rajasthan India
123 L7 Kotra Pak.
114 G3 Kotri r. India
123 M9 Kotri Pak.
123 L9 Kotri Allahrakhio Shah Pak.
198 D6 Kotronas Greece
120 H3 Kotrtas Kazakh.
123 L10 Kot Sarae Pak.
178 H6 Kötschach Austria
114 G4 Kottagudem Andhra Prad. India
114 E8 Kottayam Kerala India
114 D7 Kottayam Pondicherry India
Kotte Sri Lanka see Sri Jayewardenepura Kotte
169 D10 Kottenheim Ger.
179 L3 Kottes Austria
179 J6 Köttmannsdorf Austria
208 D3 Kotto r. C.A.R.
114 E5 Kotturu Karnataka India
79 □8 Kotu Group is Tonga
175 K3 Kotuń Pol.
131 L2 Kotuy r. Rus. Fed.
117 I8 Kotwar Peak Chhattisgarh India
Kotyuzhany Moldova see Cotiujeni
173 I5 Kötz Ger.
220 B3 Kotzebue AK U.S.A.
220 B3 Kotzebue Sound sea chan. AK U.S.A.
214 B4 Kotzehoop S. Africa
214 B6 Kotzesrus S. Africa
173 N3 Kötzting Ger.
208 D3 Kouango C.A.R.
202 C6 Kouba Olanga Chad
206 C4 Koubia Guinea
225 H4 Kouchibouguac National Park N.B. Can.
166 A3 Koudekerke Neth.
206 E3 Koudougou Burkina
164 H3 Koudum Neth.
214 D8 Kouebokkeveld mts S. Africa
206 E4 Kouéré Burkina
214 H8 Koueveldberge mts S. Africa
198 D2 Koufalia Greece
207 I3 Koufey Niger
199 H8 Koufonisi i. Kriti Greece
199 G6 Koufonisi i. Greece
214 I9 Kouga r. S. Africa
214 H9 Kougaberge mts S. Africa
208 B3 Koui C.A.R.
206 D5 Kouibli Côte d'Ivoire
209 A6 Kouilou admin. reg. Congo
206 D4 Kouka Burkina
221 K3 Koukdjuak, Great Plain of the Nunavut Can.
208 C3 Kouki C.A.R.
208 D3 Koukourou C.A.R.
208 C3 Koukourou r. C.A.R.
208 C3 Koukourou-Bamingui, Réserve de Faune du nature res. C.A.R.
208 B5 Koulamoutou Gabon
202 D6 Koulbo Chad
Koulen Cambodia see Kulen
206 D3 Koulikoro Mali
206 D3 Koulikoro admin. reg. Mali
207 F3 Koulou Niger
202 B6 Kouloudia Chad
207 I4 Koum Cameroon
208 C3 Kouma r. C.A.R.
78 □5 Koumac New Caledonia
85 I6 Koumala Qld Austr.
208 A4 Koumameyong Gabon
208 D2 Koumbala C.A.R.
206 E4 Koumbia Burkina
206 B4 Koumbia Guinea
106 C5 Koumenzi Xinjiang China
105 H3 Koumi Japan
208 C2 Koumra Chad
206 B3 Koundâra Guinea
206 C3 Koundian Mali
206 D4 Koundougou Burkina
206 B3 Koungheul Senegal
217 □3b Koungou Mayotte
206 B3 Kounkané Senegal
199 H6 Kounoupoi i. Greece
121 P4 Kounradskiy Karagandinskaya Oblast' Kazakh.
Kounradskiy Karagandinskaya Oblast' Kazakh. see Konyrat
206 B4 Kounsitél Guinea
207 H3 Kountchi well Niger
237 H10 Kountze TX U.S.A.
214 F9 Koup S. Africa
206 E3 Koupéla Burkina
Kouqian Jilin China see Yongji
217 □3a Kourani Njazidja Comoros
208 B2 Kourayadjé Chad
207 I3 Kouridinga well Niger
102 □1 Kouri-jima i. Okinawa Japan
176 D2 Kouřim Czech Rep.
198 F7 Kournas Kriti Greece
251 H3 Kourou Fr. Guiana
206 C2 Koûroudjél Maur.
206 C4 Kouroussa Guinea
206 B3 Koussanar Senegal
206 C3 Koussané Mali
207 I3 Kousséri Cameroon
207 F4 Koussountou Togo
206 D3 Koutiala Mali
173 N3 Kout na Šumavě Czech Rep.
206 D4 Kouto Côte d'Ivoire
78 □5 Koutouma i. New Caledonia
198 D5 Koutsopodi Greece
80 M5 Koutunui Head North I. N.Z.
141 S6 Kouvola Fin.
208 C5 Kouyou r. Congo
196 I5 Kovačica Vojvodina Serbia
199 L5 Kovada Gölü Milli Parkı nat. park Turkey
177 H5 Kővágószőlős Hungary
136 J4 Kovalivka Ukr.
134 B2 Kovallberget Sweden
177 H3 Kovarce Slovakia
176 C1 Kovářská Czech Rep.
137 K2 Kovchyn Ukr.
140 U3 Kovdor Rus. Fed.
140 U3 Kovdozero Rus. Fed.
140 V3 Kovdozero, Ozero l. Rus. Fed.
136 D2 Kovel' Ukr.
134 H4 Kovernino Rus. Fed.
196 I5 Kovilj Vojvodina Serbia
114 E8 Kovilpatti Tamil Nadu India
196 I6 Kovin Vojvodina Serbia
Kovno Lith. see Kaunas
134 J2 Kovriga, Gora hill Rus. Fed.
139 Y5 Kovrov Rus. Fed.
137 S5 Kovsuh r. Ukr.
137 O4 Kov"yahy Ukr.
135 H5 Kovylkino Rus. Fed.
137 M8 Kovyl'ne Ukr.
139 U1 Kovzha canal Rus. Fed.
139 U1 Kovzhskoye, Ozero l. Rus. Fed.
175 H3 Kowal Pol.
174 G4 Kowale Pol.
175 K1 Kowale Oleckie Pol.
174 G4 Kowale-Pańskie Pol.
174 G2 Kowalewo Pomorskie Pol.
174 C3 Kowalów Pol.
95 M9 Kowangge Sumbawa Indon.
85 H3 Kowanyama Qld Austr.
85 H3 Kowanyama Aboriginal Reserve Qld Austr.
212 B3 Kowares waterhole Namibia
174 D5 Kowary Pol.
138 M8 Kowbcha Belarus
208 E5 Kowe Dem. Rep. Congo
81 F9 Kowhitirangi South I. N.Z.
175 I4 Kowiesy Pol.
122 E6 Kowlī Kosh, Gardaneh-ye pass Iran
109 □J7 Kowloon H.K. China
Kowloon Peak hill H.K. China see Fei Ngo Shan
109 □ Kowloon Peninsula H.K. China
109 □J7 Kowloon Peninsula pen. H.K. China
109 □J7 Kowloon Reservoirs H.K. China
101 E9 Kowŏn N. Korea
106 C6 Kox Kuduk well Xinjiang China
111 E7 Koxlax Xinjiang China
111 D8 Koxtag Xinjiang China
104 C7 Kōya Japan
104 C7 Kōyaguchi Japan
206 C5 Koyama Guinea
103 I12 Kōyama-misaki pt Japan
104 C7 Kōya-Ryūjin Kokutei-kōen park Japan
120 K1 Koybagar, Ozero l. Kazakh.
199 J6 Köyceğiz Turkey
199 J6 Köyceğiz Gölü l. Turkey
134 H2 Koyda Rus. Fed.
134 J3 Koygorodok Rus. Fed.
197 M7 Koynare Bulg.
114 C4 Koyna Reservoir India
134 L3 Koyp, Gora mt. Rus. Fed.
123 K3 Köytendag Turkm.
220 C3 Koyukuk r. AK U.S.A.
126 H3 Koyulhisar Turkey
129 C5 Koyunören Turkey
207 I4 Koza Cameroon
134 G4 Koza Rus. Fed.
137 P3 Kozacha Lopan' Ukr.
137 N7 Kozachi Laheri Ukr.
Kozağacı Turkey see Günyüzü
104 F6 Kozakai Japan
105 L4 Kōzaki Japan
103 G12 Kō-zaki pt Japan
126 G5 Kozan Turkey
198 C2 Kozani Greece
124 E8 Kozar, Ras pt Eritrea
188 F3 Kozara mts Bos.-Herz.
188 F3 Kozara nat. park Bos.-Herz.
177 H5 Kozármisleny Hungary
137 K3 Kozarn Ukr.
177 H3 Kozárovce Slovakia
Kozarska Dubica Bos.-Herz. see Bosanska Dubica
137 M7 Kozats'ke Khersons'ka Oblast' Ukr.
137 M2 Kozats'ke Sums'ka Oblast' Ukr.
137 K3 Kozelets' Ukr.
137 M4 Kozel'shchyna Ukr.
139 S7 Kozel'sk Rus. Fed.
202 C4 Kozen well Chad
177 J4 Közép-tiszai park Hungary
120 I5 Kozhabakhy Kazakh.
121 M2 Kozhakol', Ozero l. Kazakh.
136 I4 Kozhanka Ukr.
131 M2 Kozhevnikovo Rus. Fed.
Kozhikode Kerala India see Calicut
134 L3 Kozhim-Iz, Gora mt. Rus. Fed.
136 G4 Kozhukliv Ukr.
134 L2 Kozhva Rus. Fed.
134 L2 Kozhva r. Rus. Fed.
134 L2 Kozhym r. Rus. Fed.
175 H5 Koziegłowy Pol.
174 C2 Kozielice Pol.
175 J4 Kozienice Pol.
136 A2 Kozienicki Park Krajobrazowy Pol.
188 D3 Kozina Slovenia
137 O3 Koziyivka Ukr.
176 C2 Kožlany Czech Rep.
197 L7 Kozloduy Bulg.
177 H2 Kozlovice Czech Rep.
134 J5 Kozlovka Chuvashskaya Respublika Rus. Fed.
135 I5 Kozlovka Respublika Mordoviya Rus. Fed.
135 H6 Kozlovka Voronezhskaya Oblast' Rus. Fed.
137 T3 Kozlovka Voronezhskaya Oblast' Rus. Fed.
139 T5 Kozlovo Rus. Fed.
175 I5 Kozłów Pol.
175 I3 Kozłów Biskupi Pol.
175 I2 Kozłowo Pol.
126 E3 Kozlu Turkey
199 L5 Kozluca Turkey
188 G3 Kozluk Bos.-Herz.
175 J3 Kozły Pol.
129 H2 Koz'maul Rus. Fed.
174 G4 Koźminek Pol.
174 F4 Koźmin Wielkopowski Pol.
134 I4 Koz'modem'yansk Rus. Fed.
121 M6 Kozmoldak Kazakh.
197 L8 Koznitsa mt. Bulg.
136 E4 Kozova Ukr.
177 J1 Kozubowski Park Krajobrazowy Pol.
175 K4 Kozubszczyzna Pol.
174 D4 Kożuchów Pol.
197 K9 Kožuf mts Greece/Macedonia
105 J7 Kōzu-shima i. Japan
136 H4 Kozyatyn Ukr.
137 L2 Kozylivka Ukr.
136 J3 Kozyn Kyivs'ka Oblast' Ukr.
137 K4 Kozyn Kyivs'ka Oblast' Ukr.
199 H1 Kozyörük Turkey
137 K7 Kozyrka Ukr.
207 F5 Kpalimé Togo
207 E4 Kpandae Ghana
207 F5 Kpandu Ghana
207 F5 Kpedze Ghana
207 F4 Kpèssi Togo
96 C1 Kpungan Pass India/Myanmar
97 D9 Kra, Isthmus of Thai.
215 K6 Kraai r. S. Africa
214 I5 Kraankuil S. Africa
261 G5 Krabbé Arg.
165 F6 Krabbendijke Neth.
138 J4 Krabi Estonia
97 D10 Krabi Thai.
97 D9 Kra Buri Thai.
97 H8 Krâchéh Cambodia
141 M6 Kräckelbäcken Sweden
170 J4 Krackow Ger.
139 R4 Kraftino, Ozero l. Rus. Fed.
171 E9 Kraftsdorf Ger.
174 E1 Krąg Pol.
95 I8 Kragan Jawa Indon.
142 F3 Kragerø Norway
164 I3 Kraggenburg Neth.
174 E2 Krągi Pol.
196 I6 Kragujevac Serbia
173 M5 Kraiburg am Inn Ger.
172 E3 Kraichbach r. Ger.
172 F3 Kraichgau reg. Ger.
173 K5 Krailling Ger.
174 F2 Krajenka Pol.
174 F2 Krajeńskie, Pojezierze reg. Pol.
174 C2 Krajnik Dolny Pol.
94 F8 Krakatau i. Indon.
94 F8 Krakatau, Taman Nasional nat. park Indon.
Krakau Pol. see Kraków
140 K5 Kråklivollen Norway
97 G8 Krâkôr Cambodia
136 C4 Krakovets' Ukr.
175 H5 Kraków Pol.
226 F5 Krakow WI U.S.A.
170 F3 Krakow am See Ger.
170 F3 Krakower See l. Ger.
175 G4 Krakowsko-Częstochowska, Wyżyna plat. Pol.
97 F8 Krâlănh Cambodia
247 □8 Kralendijk Bonaire Neth. Antilles
97 D9 Kra Lenya r. Myanmar
176 F1 Králíky Czech Rep.
188 E3 Kraljevica Croatia
196 I7 Kraljevo Serbia
177 G3 Kráľová, Vodná nádrž resr Slovakia
177 J3 Kráľova hoľa mt. Slovakia
177 G3 Kráľová nad Váhom Slovakia
177 G3 Kráľov Brod Slovakia
176 E1 Královéhradecký kraj admin. reg. Czech Rep.
176 C2 Kralovice Czech Rep.
177 K3 Kráľovský Chlmec Slovakia
176 D1 Kralupy nad Vltavou Czech Rep.
176 D2 Králův Dvůr Czech Rep.
174 F1 Kramarzyny Pol.
137 Q5 Kramators'k Ukr.
140 N5 Kramfors Sweden
164 F5 Krammer est. Neth.
140 U1 Krampenes Norway
178 E5 Kramsach Austria
174 G3 Kramsk Pol.
169 B7 Kranenburg Ger.
198 C3 Krania Greece
198 E5 Kranidi Greece
188 E2 Kranj Slovenia
94 □ Kranji Reservoir Sing.
179 I7 Kranjska Gora Slovenia
137 L7 Kranoznam"yans'kyy Kanal canal Ukr.
215 M4 Kransfontein S. Africa
215 O4 Kranskop S. Africa
215 N3 Kranskop mt. S. Africa
173 L5 Kranzberg Ger.
188 E4 Krapanj Croatia
174 D2 Krąpiel Pol.
188 E2 Krapina Croatia
188 E2 Krapinske Toplice Croatia
139 S8 Krapivna Kaluzhskaya Oblast' Rus. Fed.
139 Q7 Krapivna Smolenskaya Oblast' Rus. Fed.
174 F5 Krapkowice Pol.
179 I8 Kras plat. Slovenia
134 I3 Krasavino Rus. Fed.
137 L4 Krasenivka Ukr.
175 K6 Krasiczyn Pol.
Krasilov Ukr. see Krasyliv
Krasilovka Chernihivs'ka Oblast' Ukr. see Krasylivka
Krasilovka Zhytomyrs'ka Oblast' Ukr. see Krasylivka
130 G2 Krasino Novaya Zemlya Rus. Fed.
175 L6 Krasiv Ukr.
136 E4 Krasiyiv Ukr.
100 G7 Kraskino Rus. Fed.
138 K6 Krāslava Latvia
176 B1 Kraslice Czech Rep.
137 R4 Krasna r. Ukr.
171 K9 Krásná Lípa Czech Rep.
139 O8 Krasnapollye Mahilyowskaya Voblasts' Belarus
138 M6 Krasnapollye Vitsyebskaya Voblasts' Belarus
137 Q6 Krasna Polyana Donets'ka Oblast' Ukr.
137 L8 Krasna Polyana Respublika Krym Ukr.
136 J4 Krasna Slobidka Ukr.
138 H8 Krasnasyel'ski Belarus
139 O8 Krasnaya Gora Rus. Fed.
134 H5 Krasnaya Gorbatka Rus. Fed.
121 O3 Krasnaya Polyana Kazakh.
129 B2 Krasnaya Polyana Rus. Fed.
137 O3 Krasnaya Yaruga Rus. Fed.
139 U9 Krasnaya Zarya Rus. Fed.
175 I3 Krasne Mazowieckie Pol.
175 K5 Krasne Podkarpackie Pol.
137 K2 Krasne Chernihivs'ka Oblast' Ukr.
137 L2 Krasne Chernihivs'ka Oblast' Ukr.
136 D5 Krasne Ivano-Frankivs'ka Oblast' Ukr.
137 L7 Krasne Khersons'ka Oblast' Ukr.
136 D4 Krasne L'vivs'ka Oblast' Ukr.
136 F4 Krasne Ternopils'ka Oblast' Ukr.
136 H5 Krasne Vinnyts'ka Oblast' Ukr.
175 L5 Kraśniczyn Pol.
175 K5 Kraśnik Pol.
136 I6 Krasni Okny Ukr.
Krasnoarmeysk Kazakh. see Tayynsha
139 V5 Krasnoarmeysk Moskovskaya Oblast' Rus. Fed.
135 I6 Krasnoarmeysk Saratovskaya Oblast' Rus. Fed.
Krasnoarmeysk Ukr. see Krasnoarmiys'k
Krasnoarmeyskaya Rus. Fed. see Poltavskaya
131 S3 Krasnoarmeyskiy Chukotskiy Avtonomnyy Okrug Rus. Fed.
135 H7 Krasnoarmeyskiy Rostovskaya Oblast' Rus. Fed.
Krasnoarmeyskoye Rus. Fed. see Urus-Martan
137 Q5 Krasnoarmiys'k Ukr.
137 Q6 Krasnoarmiys'ke Ukr.
139 S2 Krasnobarskiy Rus. Fed.
134 I3 Krasnoborsk Rus. Fed.
175 L5 Krasnobród Pol.
177 M1 Krasnobrodzki Park Krajobrazowy Pol.
135 G7 Krasnodar Rus. Fed.
Krasnodar Kray admin. div. Rus. Fed. see Krasnodarskiy Kray
129 B1 Krasnodarskiy Kray admin. div. Rus. Fed.
137 S5 Krasnodon Luhans'ka Oblast' Ukr.
137 S5 Krasnodon Luhans'ka Oblast' Ukr.
139 O2 Krasnofarfornyy Rus. Fed.
137 N8 Krasnoflots'ke Ukr.
Krasnogorka Kazakh. see Ul'ken Sulutor
138 L5 Krasnogorodskoye Rus. Fed.
139 U6 Krasnogorsk Moskovskaya Oblast' Rus. Fed.
100 M4 Krasnogorsk Sakhalin Rus. Fed.
121 V1 Krasnogorskoye Altayskiy Kray Rus. Fed.
134 K4 Krasnogorskoye Udmurtskaya Respublika Rus. Fed.
Krasnograd Ukr. see Krasnohrad
Krasnogvardeysk Uzbek. see Bulung'ur
139 X5 Krasnogvardeyskiy Rus. Fed.
137 R3 Krasnogvardeyskoye Belgorodskaya Oblast' Rus. Fed.
137 S8 Krasnogvardeyskoye Respublika Adygeya Rus. Fed.
135 H7 Krasnogvardeyskoye Stavropol'skiy Kray Rus. Fed.
137 O8 Krasnohirka Ukr.
137 Q5 Krasnohorivka Ukr.
137 O4 Krasnohrad Ukr.
137 N8 Krasnohvardiys'ke Ukr.
107 P2 Krasnokamensk Rus. Fed.
134 K4 Krasnokamsk Rus. Fed.
120 F2 Krasnokholm Rus. Fed.
Krasnokutsk Kazakh. see Aktogay
137 O3 Krasnokuts'k Ukr.
Krasnokutskoye Kazakh. see Aktogay
135 G6 Krasnolesnyy Rus. Fed.
138 F7 Krasnoles'ye Rus. Fed.
137 R2 Krasnolip'ye Rus. Fed.
137 N9 Krasnolissya Ukr.
139 R4 Krasnomayskiy Rus. Fed.
177 H2 Krásno nad Kysucou Slovakia
138 L1 Krasnoostrovskiy Rus. Fed.
137 P4 Krasnopavivs'ke Vodoskhovyshche l. U
137 P4 Krasnopavlivka Ukr.
137 M8 Krasnoperekops'k Uk
136 H4 Krasnopil' Ukr.
136 J5 Krasnopilka Ukr.
137 O3 Krasnopillya Ukr.
175 L1 Krasnopol Pol.
100 M4 Krasnopol'ye Sakhalin Rus. Fed.
100 I6 Krasnorechenskiy Rus
Krasnorechenskoye U
Krasnorichens'ke
137 R4 Krasnorichens'ke Ukr.
130 J3 Krasnosel'kup Rus. Fe
Krasnoselsk Armenia s
Chambarak
138 M1 Krasnosel'skoye Rus.
121 T2 Krasnoshchekovo Rus
134 G2 Krasnoshchel'ye Rus.
175 J2 Krasnosielc Pol.
136 I5 Krasnosilka Vinnyts'ka Oblast' Ukr.
136 G4 Krasnosilka Zhytomyrs Oblast' Ukr.
137 L5 Krasnosillya Ukr.
135 H5 Krasnoslobodsk Rus.
137 U1 Krasnosvobodnoye R
130 H4 Krasnotur'insk Rus. F
134 L4 Krasnoufimsk Rus. Fe
120 G1 Krasnousol'skiy Rus.
134 L3 Krasnovishersk Rus.
Krasnovodsk Turkm. s
Türkmenbaşy
122 E2 Krasnovodsk, Mys pt
Krasnovodskaya Obla
admin. div. Turkm. see
122 E1 Krasnovodskoye Plat
Turkm.
100 F3 Krasnoyarovo Rus. Fe
131 K4 Krasnoyarsk Rus. Fed
120 H2 Krasnoyarskiy Rus. Fe
98 F1 Krasnoyarskiy Kray admin. div. Rus. Fed.
Krasnoyarsk Kray adr
Rus. Fed. see Krasnoyarskiy Kray
135 G6 Krasnoye Belgorodska Oblast' Rus. Fed.
137 R3 Krasnoye Belgorodska Oblast' Rus. Fed.
139 Q8 Krasnoye Bryanskaya Rus. Fed.
134 I4 Krasnoye Kirovskaya O Rus. Fed.
137 S7 Krasnoye Krasnodarsk Rus. Fed.
139 V9 Krasnoye Lipetskaya O Rus. Fed.
138 M5 Krasnoye Pskovskaya Rus. Fed.
Krasnoye Respublika Kalmykiya-Khalm'g-Tan Rus. Fed. see Ulan Erg
139 O7 Krasnoye Smolenskaya Rus. Fed.
131 S3 Krasnoye, Ozero l. Ru
139 X6 Krasnoye Ekho Rus.
139 Y4 Krasnoye-na-Volge R
139 V5 Krasnoye Plamya Ru
139 S4 Krasnoye Znamya Ru
136 E5 Krasnoyil's'k Ukr.
134 J3 Krasnozatonskiy Rus.
139 V5 Krasnozavodsk Rus.
138 F7 Krasnoznamensk Rus.
Krasnoznamenskiy K
see Yegindykol'
137 L7 Krasnoznam"yanka U
175 L5 Krasnystaw Pol.
139 O7 Krasnyy Rus. Fed.
107 K1 Krasnyy Chikoy Rus.
134 I4 Krasnyy Baki Rus. F
135 I7 Krasnyy Barrikady
139 W4 Krasnyy Tkachi Rus
139 Q4 Krasnyy Gorodok Rus
Krasnyy Kamyshanik
Rus. Fed. see Komson
139 U3 Krasnyy Kholm Rus.
120 B2 Krasnyy Kut Rus. Fed
137 S2 Krasnyy Liman Rus.
139 N4 Krasnyy Luch Rus. Fe
137 R5 Krasnyy Luch Ukr.
137 Q5 Krasnyy Lyman Ukr.
137 M9 Krasnyy Mak Ukr.
121 Q4 Krasnyy Oktyabr' Kaz
139 V5 Krasnyy Oktyabr' Rus
139 X4 Krasnyy Profintern R
139 Q8 Krasnyy Rog Bryansk Oblast' Rus. Fed.
139 Q9 Krasnyy Rog Bryansk Oblast' Rus. Fed.
137 T6 Krasnyy Sulin Rus. Fe
135 I6 Krasnyy Tekstil'shch Rus. Fed.
121 M1 Krasnyy Yar Kazakh.
120 C4 Krasnyy Yar Astrakhan Oblast' Rus. Fed.
120 D1 Krasnyy Yar Samarsk Oblast' Rus. Fed.
135 I6 Krasnyy Yar Volgogra Oblast' Rus. Fed.
175 I5 Krasocin Pol.
136 I2 Krasyatychi Ukr.
136 F4 Krasyliv Ukr.
137 K2 Krasylivka Chernihivs' Oblast' Ukr.
136 H2 Krasylivka Zhytomyrs' Oblast' Ukr.
174 G4 Kraszewice Pol.
175 I1 Kraszewo Pol.
Kratie Cambodia see
197 K8 Kratovo Macedonia
172 G5 Krauchenwies Ger.
138 J6 Krauja Latvia
262 X2 Kraul Mountains Anta
Kraulshavn Greenland
Nuussuaq
171 K7 Krauschwitz Ger.
179 K4 Kräuterin mts Austria
172 H3 Krautheim Ger.
Krâvanh, Chuŏr Phn
Cambodia see Cardamom Range
177 H2 Kravaře Czech Rep.
137 K1 Krawtsowka Belarus
129 I2 Kraynovka Rus. Fed.
171 K8 Kreba-Neudorf Ger.
169 J7 Krebeck Ger.
205 E4 Krebs, Erg el des. Alg
139 O3 Krechevitsy Rus. Fed.
169 C8 Krefeld Ger.
169 I7 Kreiensen Ger.
164 H3 Kreileroord Neth.
171 I9 Kreischa Ger.
138 H6 Krekenava Lith.
198 C4 Kremaston, Techniti resr Greece
188 E3 Kremen mt. Croatia
Kremenchug Ukr. see
Kremenchuk
137 M4 Kremenchuk Ukr.
137 L4 Kremenchuts'ka Vodoskhovyshche re
136 E3 Kremenets' Ukr.
139 U7 Kremenki Rus. Fed.
135 H6 Kremenskaya Rus. Fe
139 S6 Kremenskoye Rus. Fe
176 E2 Křemešník hill Czech
Kremges Ukr. see Svit
137 R4 Kreminna Ukr.
136 D5 Kremintsi Ukr.
Kreml' Rus. Fed. see
Solovetskiy
170 H5 Kremmen Ger.
238 K6 Kremmling CO U.S.A.
198 E6 Kremmydi, Akrotirio Greece
177 H3 Kremnica Slovakia
168 I3 Krempe Ger.
175 J6 Krempna Pol.
179 L3 Krems r. Austria
179 M3 Krems an der Donau
179 I6 Kremsbrücke Austria
179 J3 Kremsmünster Austri
176 D3 Křemže Czech Rep.
220 B4 Krenitzin Islands AK
179 O2 Křepice Czech Rep.
137 S6 Krepkaya r. Rus. Fed.
197 J6 Krepoljin Serbia
234 E3 Kresgeville PA U.S.A.
171 J9 Křešice Czech Rep.

Kresna Bulg.
Kresnice Slovenia
Kressbronn am Bodensee Ger.
Kresta, Zaliv g. Rus. Fed.
Krestena Greece
Krest-Khal'dzhayy Rus. Fed.
Krestovka Rus. Fed.
Kresttsy Rus. Fed.
Kresty Moskovskaya Oblast' Rus. Fed.
Kresty Pskovskaya Oblast' Rus. Fed.
Kresty Tul'skaya Oblast' Rus. Fed.
Krestyakh Rus. Fed.
Kretinga Lith.
Kretzschau Ger.
Kreuth Ger.
Kreuzau Ger.
Kreuzeck mt. Austria
Kreuzeck Gruppe mts Austria
Kreuzjoch mt. Austria
Kreuzlingen Switz.
Kreuztal Ger.
Kreuzwertheim Ger.
Kreva Belarus
Kribi Cameroon
Krichev Belarus see Krychaw
Krichim Bulg.
Krieglach Austria
Kriegstetten Switz.
Kriel S. Africa
Krien Ger.
Kriens Switz.
Krievukalns hill Latvia
Krieza Greece
Krikellos Greece
Krikovo Moldova see Cricova
Kril'on, Mys c. Sakhalin Rus. Fed.
Krim mt. Slovenia
Krim-Krim Chad
Krimmler Wasserfälle waterfall Austria
Krimpen aan de IJssel Neth.
Křinec Czech Rep.
Krinides Greece
Krios, Akrotirio pt Kriti Greece
Kripka r. Rus. Fed./Ukr. see Krepkaya
Krippenstein mt. Austria
Krishna Andhra Prad. India
Krishna r. India
Krishna, Mouths of the India
Krishnagiri Tamil Nadu India
Krishnai r. India
Krishnanagar W. Bengal India
Krishnaraja Sagara l. India
Krishnarajpet Karnataka India
Kristdala Sweden
Kristiania Norway see Oslo
Kristiansand Norway
Kristianstad Sweden
Kristiansund Norway
Kristiinankaupunki Länsi-Suomi Fin. see Kristinestad
Kristinehamn Sweden
Kristinestad Fin.
Kristinopol' Ukr. see Chervonohrad
Kriti admin. reg. Greece
Kriti i. Kriti Greece
Kritiko Pelagos sea Greece
Kritzmow Ger.
Kriūkai Lith.
Kriulyany Moldova see Criuleni
Kriusha Rus. Fed.
Kriushi Kazakh. see Arshaly
Krivača mt. Serbia
Krivaja r. Bos.-Herz.
Krivaja r. Serbia
Krivandino Rus. Fed.
Kriva Palanka Macedonia
Kriva Reka r. Macedonia
Krivaya Polyana Rus. Fed.
Krivets Rus. Fed.
Krivi Put Croatia
Krivogaštani Macedonia
Křivoklátská vrchovina hills Czech Rep.
Krivoles Rus. Fed.
Krivopolyan'ye Rus. Fed.
Krivorozh'ye Rus. Fed.
Krivoy Porog Rus. Fed.
Krivoy Rog Ukr. see Kryvyy Rih
Križ, Rt pt Croatia
Křižanov Czech Rep.
Križevci Croatia
Krk mt. Bos.-Herz.
Krk Croatia
Krk i. Croatia
Krka r. Croatia
Krka Slovenia
Krka r. Slovenia
Krkonoše mts Czech Rep.
Krkonošský narodní park nat. park Czech Rep./Pol.
Krn mt. Slovenia
Krnica Croatia
Krnjača Serbia
Krnov Czech Rep.
Krobia Pol.
Kroczyce Pol.
Krøderen Norway
Krøderen l. Norway
Krögis Ger.
Krohnwodoke Liberia
Krokeaí Greece see Krokees
Krokees Greece
Krokek Sweden
Kroknes Norway
Krokom Sweden
Krokong Sarawak Malaysia
Krokowa Pol.
Króksfjarðarnes Iceland
Krokstadøra Norway
Krokstranda Norway
Krolevets' Ukr.
Królewska Huta Pol. see Chorzów
Królowy Most Pol.
Krölpa Ger.
Krom r. S. Africa
Kroma r. Rus. Fed.
Kromdraai S. Africa
Kroměříž Czech Rep.
Krommenie Neth.
Krompachy Slovakia
Kromsdorf Ger.
Kromy Rus. Fed.
Kronach Ger.
Kronau Ger.
Kronberg im Taunus Ger.
Kronfjell hill Norway
Krŏng Kaôh Kŏng Cambodia
Kronli Arun. Prad. India
Kronoberg county Sweden
Kronoby Fin.
Kronotskiy Poluostrov pen. Rus. Fed.
Kronotskiy Zaliv b. Rus. Fed.
Kronotskoye Ozero l. Rus. Fed.
Kronprins Christian Land reg. Greenland
Kronprins Frederik Bjerge nunataks Greenland
Kronprinzenkoog Ger.
Kronshagen Ger.
Kronshtadt Rus. Fed.
Kronstadt Romania see Braşov
Kronstadt Rus. Fed. see Kronshtadt
Kronstorf Austria
Kronwa Myanmar
Kroonstad S. Africa
Kropa Slovenia
Kröpelin Ger.
Kropotkin Rus. Fed.
Kropp Ger.
Kroppefjäll hills Sweden
Kroppenstedt Ger.
Kropstädt Ger.
Kropyvnya Ukr.
Krościenko nad Dunajcem Pol.
Kröslin Ger.
175 L1 Krosna Lith.
174 F4 Krośnice Pol.
175 H3 Krośniewice Pol.
175 J6 Krosno Pol.
174 D3 Krosno Odrzańskie Pol.
171 E9 Krossen Ger.
142 E2 Krossen Norway
171 F8 Krostitz Ger.
174 E4 Krotoszyce Pol.
174 F4 Krotoszyn Pol.
179 M5 Krottendorf Austria
237 J10 Krotz Springs LA U.S.A.
176 F2 Krouna Czech Rep.
198 F7 Krousonas Kriti Greece
172 C2 Kröv Ger.
95 H8 Kroya Jawa Indon.
191 Q5 Kršan Croatia
188 E3 Krško Slovenia
196 I8 Krstača mt. Montenegro
174 F3 Kruchowo Pol.
170 E5 Krüden Ger.
169 D10 Kruft Ger.
215 K4 Krugerdrifdam resr S. Africa
215 P1 Kruger National Park S. Africa
215 L2 Krugersdorp S. Africa
100 I4 Kruglikovo Rus. Fed.
129 D1 Kruglolesskoye Rus. Fed.
Kruglyakov Rus. Fed. see Oktyabr'skiy
138 M7 Kruhlaye Belarus
94 E7 Krui Sumatera Indon.
214 F8 Kruidfontein S. Africa
165 F6 Kruiningen Neth.
215 I10 Kruisfontein S. Africa
165 E7 Kruishoutem Belgium
196 H9 Krujë Albania
175 L6 Krukenychi Ukr.
175 J1 Kruklanki Pol.
175 J2 Krukowo Pol.
179 N4 Krumbach Austria
173 I5 Krumbach (Schwaben) Ger.
196 I8 Krumë Albania
168 K3 Krummesse Ger.
197 N9 Krumovgrad Bulg.
171 E8 Krumpa (Geiseltal) Ger.
179 J6 Krumpendorf am Wörther See Austria
173 K6 Krün Ger.
Krungkao Thai. see Ayutthaya
Krung Thep Thai. see Bangkok
138 G5 Kruoja r. Lith.
Krupa Bos.-Herz. see Bosanska Krupa
Krupa na Uni Bos.-Herz. see Bosanska Krupa
196 H6 Krupanj Serbia
175 N2 Krupava Belarus
175 L4 Krupe Pol.
137 N2 Krupets Rus. Fed.
177 I3 Krupina Slovakia
177 H3 Krupinica r. Slovakia
177 I3 Krupinská planina plat. Slovakia
176 C1 Krupka Czech Rep.
138 M7 Krupki Belarus
137 L4 Krupodernytsi Ukr.
137 L5 Krups'ke Ukr.
174 G5 Krupski Młyn Pol.
168 H1 Kruså Denmark
196 J7 Kruševac Serbia
196 J9 Kruševo Macedonia
176 B1 Krušné hory mts Czech Rep.
177 H3 Krušovce Slovakia
138 J5 Krustkalnu rezervāts nature res. Latvia
174 E3 Kruszewo Pol.
174 G3 Kruszwica Pol.
174 F1 Kruszyna Pomorskie Pol.
175 H5 Kruszyna Śląskie Pol.
174 F2 Kruszyńskie, Jezioro l. Pol.
137 S2 Krutchenskaya Baygora Rus. Fed.
137 K7 Krutoyarka Ukr.
139 U9 Krutoye Orlovskaya Oblast' Rus. Fed.
139 O6 Krutoye Smolenskaya Oblast' Rus. Fed.
137 L2 Kruty Ukr.
177 K2 Kružlov Slovakia
220 E4 Kruzof Island AK U.S.A.
138 M6 Krybinka r. Belarus
139 O8 Krychaw Belarus
196 I8 Kryezi Albania
199 H6 Krykello, Akrotirio pt Greece
136 F3 Kryliv Ukr.
264 H4 Krylov Seamount sea feature N. Atlantic Ocean
137 S7 Krylovskaya Krasnodarskiy Kray Rus. Fed.
137 S7 Krylovskaya Krasnodarskiy Kray Rus. Fed.
175 M5 Kryłów Pol.
Krym' aut. rep. Ukr. see Krym, Respublika
Krym' pen. Ukr. see Kryms'kyy Pivostriv
137 N8 Krym, Respublika aut. rep. Ukr.
129 D1 Krymgireyevskoye Rus. Fed.
175 M4 Krymne Ukr.
135 G7 Krymsk Rus. Fed.
Krymskaya Rus. Fed. see Krymsk
137 R5 Kryms'ke Ukr.
137 N9 Kryms'ki Hori mts Ukr.
137 N8 Kryms'kyy Pivostriv pen. Ukr.
137 N9 Kryms'kyy Zapovidnyk nature res. Ukr.
175 I6 Krynica Pol.
143 P7 Krynica Morska Pol.
174 F5 Krynka r. Pol.
137 R6 Krynka r. Ukr.
139 N6 Krynki Belarus
175 L2 Krynki Pol.
137 N5 Krynychky Dnipropetrovs'ka Oblast' Ukr.
137 K6 Krynychky Mykolayivs'ka Oblast' Ukr.
137 R5 Krynychna Ukr.
137 N6 Krynychuvate Ukr.
175 K2 Krypno Kościelne Pol.
121 P5 Krypsalo Kazakh.
171 H10 Kryry Czech Rep.
137 L2 Krysky Ukr.
Krystynopol Ukr. see Chervonohrad
137 R9 Kryukovskoye Vodokhranilishche resr Rus. Fed.
137 R6 Kryva Kosa spit Ukr.
137 L4 Kryva Ruda Ukr.
136 I4 Kryvchunka Ukr.
136 J6 Kryve Ozero Ukr.
138 K7 Kryvichy Belarus
137 M6 Kryvyy Rih Ukr.
136 H5 Kryzhopil' Ukr.
174 G5 Krzanowice Pol.
175 K4 Krzczonów-Wójtostwo Pol.
174 D2 Krzęcin Pol.
174 E4 Krzelów Pol.
174 G5 Krzepice Pol.
174 E4 Krzepielów Pol.
175 K3 Krzesk-Królowa Niwa Pol.
175 K5 Krzeszów Pol.
175 H5 Krzeszowice Pol.
174 D3 Krzeszyce Pol.
175 H5 Krzętów Pol.
175 L3 Krzna r. Pol.
175 K4 Krzna Południowa r. Pol.
174 G3 Krzymów Wielkopolskie Pol.
170 J5 Krzymów Zachodniopomorskie Pol.
175 I2 Krzynowłoga Mała Pol.
174 D4 Krzystkowice Pol.
175 K6 Krzywcza Pol.
175 K4 Krzywda Pol.
174 E4 Krzywiń Pol.
170 J4 Krzywin Pol.
175 L4 Krzywowierzba Pol.
175 H3 Krzyżanów Pol.
174 G6 Krzyżanowice Pol.
174 E3 Krzyż Wielkopolski Pol.
205 E3 Ksabi Alg.
129 F4 Ksani r. Georgia
205 F2 Ksar Chellala Alg.
205 F2 Ksar el Boukhari Alg.
205 F2 Ksar el Hirane Alg.
204 D2 Ksar el Kebir Morocco
Ksar-es-Souk Morocco see Er Rachidia
180 D5 Ksar Sghir Morocco
136 J3 Ksaverivka Ukr.
134 K3 Ksenofontova Rus. Fed.
139 U9 Kshen' r. Rus. Fed.
135 G6 Kshenskiy Rus. Fed.
176 F1 Książański Park Krajobrazowy Pol.
175 H2 Książki Pol.
175 I5 Książ Wielki Pol.
174 F3 Książ Wielkopolski Pol.
175 K5 Księżpol Pol.
205 E2 Ksour, Monts des mts Alg.
205 H2 Ksour, Monts des mts Tunisia
205 H2 Ksour Essaf Tunisia
134 I4 Kstovo Rus. Fed.
139 S8 Ktsyn' Rus. Fed.
125 H2 Kū', Jabal al hill Saudi Arabia
202 E6 Ku, Wadi el watercourse Sudan
94 C1 Kuah Malaysia
Kuaidamao Jilin China see Tonghua
95 K2 Kuala Belait Brunei
Kuala Dungun Malaysia see Dungun
95 I6 Kualajelai Kalimantan Indon.
94 D2 Kuala Kangsar Malaysia
95 K6 Kualakapuas Kalimantan Indon.
94 E2 Kuala Kerai Malaysia
95 J5 Kualakuayan Kalimantan Indon.
94 D3 Kuala Kubu Baharu Malaysia
95 J5 Kualakurun Kalimantan Indon.
94 B2 Kualalangsa Sumatera Indon.
94 D2 Kuala Lipis Malaysia
94 D3 Kuala Lumpur Malaysia
94 D1 Kuala Nerang Malaysia
95 J6 Kualapembuang Kalimantan Indon.
95 K2 Kuala Penyu Sabah Malaysia
94 E3 Kuala Pilah Malaysia
240 □D12 Kualapu'u HI U.S.A.
94 E3 Kuala Rompin Malaysia
95 J6 Kualasampit Indon.
94 D3 Kuala Selangor Malaysia
94 D2 Kuala Sepetang Malaysia
94 C2 Kualasimpang Sumatera Indon.
94 E2 Kuala Terengganu Malaysia
94 E5 Kualatungal Sumatera Indon.
95 L2 Kuamut Sabah Malaysia
95 L2 Kuamut r. Malaysia
107 P6 Kuancheng Hebei China
101 D8 Kuandian Liaoning China
Kuangyuan Yunnan China see Yiliang
109 M7 Kuanshan Taiwan
94 E3 Kuantan Malaysia
80 J3 Kuaotunu North I. N.Z.
Kuba Azer. see Quba
129 E2 Kuba Rus. Fed.
129 I3 Kubachi Rus. Fed.
129 C2 Kuban' r. Rus. Fed.
129 A1 Kubanskaya Rus. Fed.
129 D1 Kubanskoye Vodokhranilishche resr Rus. Fed.
127 I6 Kubār Dayr az Zawr Syria
127 I6 Kubār Dayr az Zawr Syria
125 M4 Kubārah Oman
138 G3 Kübassaare poolsaar pen. Estonia
128 F3 Kubaybāt Syria
127 K7 Kubaysah Iraq
140 O5 Kubbe Sweden
208 D2 Kubbum Sudan
177 J5 Kübekháza Hungary
134 G4 Kubenskoye, Ozero l. Rus. Fed.
Kuberle Rus. Fed. see Krasnoarmeyskiy
105 H1 Kubiki Japan
139 T6 Kubinka Rus. Fed.
170 H2 Kubitzer Bodden b. Ger.
190 H2 Küblis Switz.
136 I5 Kublych r. Ukr.
134 J5 Kubnya r. Rus. Fed.
103 K13 Kubokawa Japan
197 O7 Kubrat Bulg.
139 V5 Kubrinsk Rus. Fed.
95 K9 Kubu Bali Indon.
95 H5 Kubu Kalimantan Indon.
95 K3 Kubuang Kalimantan Indon.
107 N1 Kubukhay Rus. Fed.
95 K4 Kubumesaäi Kalimantan Indon.
102 □22 Kubura Nansei-shotō Japan
197 J6 Kučevo Serbia
116 E6 Kuchaman Rajasthan India
134 H2 Kuchema Rus. Fed.
172 H4 Kuchen Ger.
116 E6 Kuchera Rajasthan India
137 N2 Kucherivka Ukr.
95 I4 Kuching Sarawak Malaysia
102 □H16 Kuchino-Erabu-shima i. Japan
102 □G17 Kuchino-shima i. Nansei-shotō Japan
103 H14 Kuchinotsu Japan
178 H4 Kuchl Austria
121 R1 Kuchukskoye, Ozero salt l. Rus. Fed.
136 I7 Kuchurhan r. Ukr.
Kucing Sarawak Malaysia see Kuching
175 H4 Kuciny Pol.
175 L1 Kučiūnai Lith.
170 J3 Kückelsberg hill Ger.
198 A2 Kuçovë Albania
129 F6 Küçük Ağrı Dağı mt. Turkey
128 E2 Küçükdalyan Turkey
199 L5 Küçükköy Antalya Turkey
199 H3 Küçükköy Balıkesir Turkey
199 H3 Küçükkuyu Turkey
199 H2 Küçükmenderes r. Turkey
199 I5 Küçükmenderes r. Turkey
175 I2 Kuczbork-Osada Pol.
116 C8 Kuda Gujarat India
114 D4 Kudachi Karnataka India
113 □1 Kuda Finolhu i. S. Male Maldives
102 □1 Kudaka-jima i. Okinawa Japan
114 C5 Kudal Mahar. India
113 □1 Kudalhi i. N. Male Maldives
103 I13 Kudamatsu Japan
95 I5 Kudangan Kalimantan Indon.
94 E4 Kudap Sumatera Indon.
107 J1 Kudara-Somon Rus. Fed.
Kudarebe pt Aruba see Cudarebe
95 L1 Kudat Sabah Malaysia
124 E6 Kudayd Saudi Arabia
168 J3 Kuddewörde Ger.
138 L4 Kudev r. Rus. Fed.
138 M5 Kudever' Rus. Fed.
138 F7 Kudirkos Naumiestis Lith.
114 E5 Kudligi Karnataka India
174 E5 Kudowa-Zdrój Pol.
104 C7 Kudoyama Japan
114 D6 Kudremukh mt. Karnataka India
139 S7 Kudrinskaya Rus. Fed.
139 S8 Kudryavets Rus. Fed.
137 K6 Kudryavtsivka Ukr.
207 G4 Kudu Nigeria
95 I8 Kudus Jawa Indon.
134 K4 Kudymkar Rus. Fed.
109 N6 Kueishan Tao i. Taiwan
Kūfah Iraq see Al Kūfah
93 G5 Kufar Seram Indon.
178 F4 Kufstein Austria
221 J3 Kugaaruk Nunavut Can.
121 R5 Kugaly Kazakh.
134 I4 Kugesi Rus. Fed.
137 S7 Kugey Rus. Fed.
111 I11 Kugka Lhai Xizang China
220 G3 Kugluktuk Nunavut Can.
220 E3 Kugmallit Bay N.W.T. Can.
137 S7 Kugo-Eya r. Rus. Fed.
106 F9 Kugri Qinghai China
135 H7 Kugul'ta Rus. Fed.
104 F3 Kuguno Japan
122 G9 Kūh, Ra's-al- pt Iran
123 J8 Kūhak Iran
173 K5 Kühbach Ger.
170 F4 Kuhbier Ger.
122 G6 Kūhbonān Iran
122 B5 Kūhdasht Iran
122 G8 Kūhestak Iran
170 D5 Kuhfelde Ger.
122 C3 Kūhīn Iran
122 I8 Kūhīrī Iran
123 O3 Kŭhistoni Badakhshon aut. rep. Tajik.
170 E3 Kuhlen Ger.
170 E2 Kühlung park Ger.
170 E2 Kühlungsborn, Ostseebad Ger.
140 T4 Kuhmo Fin.
141 R6 Kuhmoinen Fin.
169 J9 Kühndorf Ger.
122 E5 Kūhpāyeh Iran
122 G6 Kūhpāyeh mt. Iran
122 H8 Kūhrān, Kūh-e mt. Iran
122 D6 Kūhrang r. Iran
171 G8 Kühren Ger.
168 G3 Kührstedt Ger.
170 F3 Kuhs Ger.
168 G4 Kuhstedt Ger.
97 D8 Kui Buri Thai.
127 P5 Kuidzhuk Turkm.
107 S2 Kuile He r. China
138 I2 Kuimetsa Estonia
164 I3 Kuinre Neth.
212 C5 Kuis Namibia
212 B4 Kuiseb watercourse Namibia
109 J7 Kuitan Guangdong China
209 C8 Kuito Angola
Kuitun Xinjiang China see Kuytun
222 C3 Kuiu Island AK U.S.A.
140 R4 Kuivaniemi Fin.
138 G3 Kuivastu Estonia
138 J5 Kuja r. Latvia
174 G4 Kujakowice Dolne Pol.
117 K9 Kujang Orissa India
101 E9 Kujang N. Korea
174 G2 Kujawsko-Pomorskie prov. Pol.
102 S6 Kuji Japan
105 M3 Kuji-gawa r. Japan
105 L4 Kujikuri Japan
102 S6 Kuji-wan b. Japan
105 L5 Kujūkuri-hama coastal area Japan
103 I13 Kujū-san vol. Japan
122 D6 Kukālār, Kūh-e hill Iran
100 H4 Kukan Rus. Fed.
100 H4 Kukan r. Rus. Fed.
227 L1 Kukatush Ont. Can.
207 I3 Kukawa Nigeria
87 E12 Kukerin W.A. Austr.
196 I8 Kukës Albania
136 E2 Kukhits'ka Volya Ukr.
105 K3 Kuki Japan
105 L4 Kukizaki Japan
104 D7 Kuki-zaki pt Japan
140 R4 Kukkola Fin.
175 I2 Kuklin Pol.
174 F4 Kuklinów Pol.
179 N5 Kukmirn Austria
134 J4 Kukmor Rus. Fed.
134 G4 Kukoboy Rus. Fed.
138 K2 Kukruse Estonia
116 E8 Kukshi Madh. Prad. India
78 □6 Kukudu New Georgia Is Solomon Is
240 □F13 Kukuihaele HI U.S.A.
206 B4 Kukuna Sierra Leone
114 G4 Kukunuru Andhra Prad. India
94 E4 Kukup Malaysia
122 H2 Kükürtli Turkm.
95 K6 Kukusan, Gunung hill Indon.
134 L4 Kukushtan Rus. Fed.
122 F8 Kūl r. Iran
197 K7 Kula Bulg.
Kula r. Moldova see Cula
207 G5 Kula Nigeria
196 H5 Kula Vojvodina Serbia
196 H8 Kula mt. Montenegro
199 J4 Kula Turkey
94 C4 Kulabu, Gunung mt. Indon.
123 N6 Kulachi Pak.
139 P9 Kulagi Rus. Fed.
120 D3 Kulagino Kazakh.
117 M5 Kula Kangri mt. Bhutan
124 E5 Kulākh Saudi Arabia
210 C4 Kulal, Mount Kenya
120 D5 Kulaly, Ostrov i. Kazakh.
121 O6 Kulan Kazakh.
121 P7 Kulanak Kyrg.
120 H4 Kulandy Kazakh.
123 J9 Kulaneh reg. Pak.
121 M2 Kulanotpes watercourse Kazakh.
123 K7 Kulao r. Pak.
131 O2 Kular Rus. Fed.
92 C8 Kulassein i. Phil.
95 L4 Kulat, Gunung mt. Indon.
138 G7 Kulautuva Lith.
93 A4 Kulawi Sulawesi Indon.
203 F4 Kulb Sudan
137 N2 Kul'baki Rus. Fed.
138 E5 Kuldīga Latvia
Kuldja Xinjiang China see Yining
100 G4 Kul'dur Rus. Fed.
212 D4 Kule Botswana
135 H5 Kulebaki Rus. Fed.
97 G8 Kulen Cambodia
199 L5 Kuleönü Turkey
139 U9 Kuleshi Rus. Fed.
137 S6 Kuleshovka Rus. Fed.
175 K2 Kulesze Pol.
175 K2 Kulesze Kościelne Pol.
120 I1 Kulevchinskoye Rus. Fed.
Kulevi Georgia see Qulevi
84 D8 Kulgera N.T. Austr.
120 G1 Kulgunino Rus. Fed.
129 I3 Kuli Rus. Fed.
138 E6 Kuliai Lith.
134 K4 Kuligi Rus. Fed.
121 R6 Kulikovka Kazakh.
134 I3 Kulikovo Arkhangel'skaya Oblast' Rus. Fed.
139 W9 Kulikovo Lipetskaya Oblast' Rus. Fed.
94 D2 Kulim Malaysia
87 E12 Kulin W.A. Austr.
114 F7 Kulittalai Tamil Nadu India
87 D11 Kulja W.A. Austr.
83 J4 Kulkyne watercourse N.S.W. Austr.
141 Q6 Kullaa Fin.
138 H3 Kullamaa Estonia
142 I5 Kullen pt Sweden
169 J8 Küllstedt Ger.
116 F4 Kullu Hima. Prad. India
173 L2 Kulmain Ger.
171 D10 Kulmbach Ger.
123 M3 Kŭlob Tajik.
139 Q3 Kulotino Rus. Fed.
134 H3 Kuloy Rus. Fed.
134 H2 Kuloy r. Rus. Fed.
127 J4 Kulp Turkey
82 F6 Kulpara S.A. Austr.
234 C3 Kulpmont PA U.S.A.
120 F4 Kul'sary Kazakh.
208 F2 Kulshabi Sudan
172 H2 Külsheim Ger.
177 G5 Külső-Somogy reg. Hungary
126 F4 Kulu Turkey
199 L5 Kulübe Tepe mt. Turkey
121 R1 Kulunda Rus. Fed.
121 R1 Kulunda r. Rus. Fed.
121 P1 Kulundinskaya Step' plain Kazakh./Rus. Fed.
121 R1 Kulundinskoye, Ozero salt l. Rus. Fed.
221 O3 Kulusuk Greenland
107 N1 Kulusutay Rus. Fed.
122 F6 Kūlvand Iran
83 I6 Kulwin Vic. Austr.
Kulyab Tajik. see Kŭlob
136 D4 Kulykiv Ukr.
137 K2 Kulykivka Ukr.
103 J13 Kuma Japan
129 H1 Kuma r. Rus. Fed.
140 U3 Kuma r. Rus. Fed.
175 I1 Kumachevo Rus. Fed.
137 R6 Kumachove Ukr.
105 J3 Kumagaya Japan
95 I6 Kumai Kalimantan Indon.
95 I6 Kumai, Teluk b. Indon.
102 Q4 Kumaishi Japan
120 I2 Kumak Rus. Fed.
120 H2 Kumak r. Rus. Fed.
251 G4 Kumaka Guyana
107 M1 Kumakhta Rus. Fed.
199 L4 Kumalar Dağı mts Turkey
103 H14 Kumamoto Japan
103 H14 Kumamoto pref. Japan
104 D8 Kumano Japan
104 C8 Kumanogawa Japan
197 J8 Kumanovo Macedonia
81 F9 Kumara South I. N.Z.
100 E3 Kumara Rus. Fed.
81 F9 Kumara Junction South I. N.Z.
117 L8 Kumarkhali Bangl.
206 E5 Kumasi Ghana
215 M7 Ku-Mayima S. Africa
Kumayri Armenia see Gyumri
207 H5 Kumba Cameroon
199 I2 Kumbağ Turkey
114 F7 Kumbakonam Tamil Nadu India
179 M5 Kumberg Austria
199 L3 Kümbet Turkey
114 C4 Kumbharli Ghat mt. Mahar. India
116 H5 Kumbher Nepal
114 D6 Kumbla Kerala India
207 H5 Kumbo Cameroon
138 F5 Kumbri Latvia
212 D4 Kumchuru Botswana
Kum-Dag Turkm. see Gumdag
124 G5 Kumdah Saudi Arabia
199 L4 Kumdanlı Turkey
103 K11 Kume Japan
102 □D20 Kume-jima i. Nansei-shotō Japan
122 E4 Kumel well Iran
134 J4 Kumeny Rus. Fed.
120 F1 Kumertau Rus. Fed.
101 E11 Kŭm-gang r. S. Korea
101 F9 Kumgang-san mt. N. Korea
117 M6 Kumguri Assam India
111 C11 Kumharsain Hima. Prad. India
173 M4 Kumhausen Ger.
116 F6 Kumher Rajasthan India
101 F11 Kŭmho-gang r. S. Korea
101 F10 Kumi S. Korea
210 B4 Kumi Uganda
104 A4 Kumihama Japan
104 A4 Kumihama-wan l. Japan
207 I4 Kumishe Nigeria
104 C6 Kumiyama Japan
199 H3 Kumkale Turkey
110 J6 Kum Kuduk well Xinjiang China
143 L2 Kumla Sweden
141 P6 Kumlinge Åland Fin.
128 E2 Kumlu Turkey
199 L6 Kumluca Turkey
170 D4 Kummer Ger.
170 G3 Kummerow Ger.
170 G3 Kummerower See l. Ger.
173 L3 Kümmersbruck Ger.
171 H6 Kummersdorf-Alexanderdorf Ger.
171 H6 Kummersdorf Gut Ger.
207 H4 Kumo Nigeria
101 E11 Kŭmŏ-do i. S. Korea
121 L4 Kumola watercourse Kazakh.
96 C2 Kumon Range mts Myanmar
105 I4 Kumotori-yama mt. Japan
104 E6 Kumozu-gawa r. Japan
191 P6 Kumpare, Rt pt Croatia
96 F6 Kumphawapi Thai.
140 R3 Kumputunturi hill Fin.
179 M7 Kumrovec Croatia
214 D4 Kums Namibia
114 D5 Kumta Karnataka India
129 I2 Kumtorkala Rus. Fed.
208 E4 Kumu Dem. Rep. Congo
240 □G14 Kumukahi, Cape HI U.S.A.
129 I3 Kumukh Rus. Fed.
Kumul Xinjiang China see Hami
117 I9 Kumund Orissa India
129 E4 Kumurdo Georgia
110 I5 Kümüx Xinjiang China
Kumylzhenskaya Rus. Fed. see Kumylzhenskiy
135 H6 Kumylzhenskiy Rus. Fed.
121 N6 Kumyshtag, Pik mt. Kyrg.
96 C5 Kun r. Myanmar
177 I5 Kunadacs Hungary
177 K5 Kunágota Hungary
87 G7 Kunanaggi Well W.A. Austr.
123 N4 Kunar prov. Afgh.
123 N4 Kunar r. Afgh.
100 O6 Kunashir, Ostrov i. Kuril'skiye O-va Rus. Fed.
Kunashirskiy Proliv sea chan. Japan/Rus. Fed. see Nemuro-kaikyō
177 I5 Kunbaja Hungary
177 I5 Kunbaracs Hungary
129 G1 Kun'bator Rus. Fed.
96 C3 Kunchaung Myanmar
209 E5 Kunda Dem. Rep. Congo
138 J2 Kunda Estonia
138 J2 Kunda r. Estonia
116 H7 Kunda Uttar Prad. India
209 C7 Kunda-dia-Baze Angola
138 J2 Kunda laht b. Estonia
114 D6 Kundapura Karnataka India
123 M5 Kundar r. Afgh./Pak.
209 E7 Kundelungu, Parc National de nat. park Dem. Rep. Congo
209 E7 Kundelungu Ouest, Parc National de nat. park Dem. Rep. Congo
114 D5 Kundgol Karnataka India
123 N5 Kundian Pak.
178 E5 Kundl Austria
116 C9 Kundla Gujarat India
137 T6 Kundryuch'ya r. Rus. Fed./Ukr.
94 E4 Kundur i. Indon.
123 M3 Kunduz Afgh.
123 M3 Kunduz prov. Afgh.
209 A9 Kunene r. Angola/Namibia alt. Cunene
212 B3 Kunene admin. reg. Namibia
Künes Xinjiang China see Xinyuan
110 F5 Künes Chang Xinjiang China
110 E5 Künes He r. China
110 G5 Künes Linchang Xinjiang China
177 I5 Kunfehértó Hungary
142 H4 Kungälv Sweden
106 E1 Kungar-Tuk Rus. Fed.
121 Q6 Kungei Alatau mts Kazakh./Kyrg.
Kunggar Xizang China see Maizhokunggar
222 D4 Kunghit Island B.C. Can.
Küngöy Ala-Too mts Kazakh./Kyrg. see Kungei Alatau
143 N2 Kungsängen Sweden
142 I4 Kungsbacka Sweden
142 H3 Kungshamn Sweden
143 M2 Kungsör Sweden
208 C4 Kungu Dem. Rep. Congo
Kungur mt. Xinjiang China see Kongur Shan
134 L4 Kungur Rus. Fed.
96 B6 Kungyangon Myanmar
177 J4 Kunhegyes Hungary
157 O7 Kunheim France
108 B8 Kunhing Myanmar
114 F3 Kuni r. India
105 I2 Kuni Japan
174 E4 Kunice Pol.
122 H8 Kūnīch Iran
Kunicha Moldova see Cunicea
Kunié i. New Caledonia see Pins, Île des
114 E6 Kunigai Karnataka India
104 D3 Kunimi-dake hill Japan
103 I14 Kunimi-dake mt. Japan
177 G2 Kunín Czech Rep.
138 K2 Kuningaküla Estonia
95 H8 Kuningan Jawa Indon.
174 G5 Kuniów Pol.
103 I13 Kunisaki Japan
117 J9 Kunjabar Orissa India
234 E3 Kunkletown PA U.S.A.
116 C9 Kunlavav Gujarat India
96 D3 Kunlong Myanmar
117 L7 Kunlui r. India/Nepal
106 C9 Kunlun Shan mts China
106 D9 Kunlun Shankou pass Qinghai China
177 J4 Kunmadaras Hungary
108 D6 Kunming Yunnan China
86 H3 Kunmunya Aboriginal Reserve W.A. Austr.
116 F6 Kuno r. India
176 G2 Kunovice Czech Rep.
175 J5 Kunów Pol.
171 K6 Kunowice Pol.
174 F4 Kunowo Pol.
144 D1 Kunoy i. Faroe Is
177 I4 Kunpeszér Hungary
170 D5 Kunrau Ger.
101 E11 Kunsan S. Korea
109 M3 Kunshan Jiangsu China
176 F2 Kunštát Czech Rep.
177 I5 Kunszállás Hungary
177 J5 Kunszentmárton Hungary
177 I4 Kunszentmiklós Hungary
209 D5 Kuntshankoie Dem. Rep. Congo
86 J3 Kununurra W.A. Austr.
223 L2 Kunwak r. Nunavut Can.
116 G6 Kunwari r. India
139 N5 Kun'ya Rus. Fed.
139 O4 Kun'ya r. Rus. Fed.
Kunyang Henan China see Yexian
Kunyang Yunnan China see Jinning
Kunyang Zhejiang China see Pingyang
Kunya-Urgench Turkm. see Köneürgenç
137 Q4 Kun'ye Ukr.
107 Q8 Kunyu Shan mts China
176 E2 Kunžak Czech Rep.
169 I9 Künzell Ger.
172 H3 Künzelsau Ger.
171 D8 Künzels-Berg hill Ger.
173 O4 Künzing Ger.
209 C5 Kunzulu Dem. Rep. Congo
109 M4 Kuocang Shan mts China
140 T3 Kuolayarvi Rus. Fed.
141 S6 Kuolimo l. Fin.
140 S5 Kuopio Fin.
141 R6 Kuorevesi Fin.
140 T3 Kuosku Fin.
174 F5 Kup Pol.
188 F3 Kupa r. Croatia/Slovenia
93 C9 Kupang Timor Indon.
93 C9 Kupang, Teluk b. Timor Indon.
139 V5 Kupanskoye Rus. Fed.
117 K9 Kupari Orissa India
Kupchino Moldova see Cupcina
171 E10 Kupferberg Ger.
172 H3 Kupferzell Ger.
137 Q3 Kupino Rus. Fed.
138 H6 Kupiškis Lith.
191 R5 Kupjak Croatia
199 K2 Küplü Turkey
172 E4 Kuppenheim Ger.
138 K4 Kuprava Latvia
222 C3 Kupreanof AK U.S.A.
220 E4 Kupreanof Island AK U.S.A.
220 C4 Kupreanof Point AK U.S.A.
139 Y6 Kupreyevo Rus. Fed.
171 D10 Küps Ger.
139 N5 Kupuy Rus. Fed.
116 E2 Kupwara Jammu and Kashmir
137 Q4 Kup"yans'k Ukr.
137 Q4 Kup"yans'k-Vuzlovyy Ukr.
136 D3 Kupychiv Ukr.
110 F6 Kuqa Xinjiang China
129 H5 Kür Azer.
129 K6 Kür r. Azer.
100 I4 Kur r. Rus. Fed.
129 G4 Kura r. Turkey/Georgia
129 G1 Kura r. Rus. Fed.
87 D8 Kurabuka r. W.A. Austr.
121 O6 Kuragaty Kazakh.
207 H4 Kuragwi Nigeria
103 J12 Kurahashi-jima i. Japan
104 F3 Kurai-yama mt. Japan
129 H5 Küräkçay r. Azer.
129 I4 Kurakh Rus. Fed.
137 Q6 Kurakhove Ukr.
Kurakhovo Ukr. see Kurakhove
Kurakhovstroy Ukr. see Kurakhove
Kura kurk sea chan. Estonia/Latvia see Irbe Strait
124 E3 Kuramā, Ḩarrat lava field Saudi Arabia
104 C5 Kurama-yama hill Japan
85 J4 Kuranda Qld Austr.
122 H8 Kūrān Dap Iran
120 G2 Kurashasayskiy Kazakh.
103 K12 Kurashiki Japan
116 I8 Kurasia Chhattisgarh India
86 I5 Kura Soak well W.A. Austr.
125 I2 Kurayn i. Saudi Arabia
103 K11 Kurayoshi Japan
106 A1 Kurayskiy Khrebet mts Rus. Fed.
139 W4 Kurba Rus. Fed.
199 K2 Kurban Dağı mt. Turkey
137 R2 Kurbatovo Rus. Fed.
100 F4 Kurbin He r. China
196 I4 Kurca r. Romania
129 H2 Kurchaloy Rus. Fed.
137 Q8 Kurchanskiy Liman salt l. Rus. Fed.
135 F6 Kurchatov Rus. Fed.
121 T3 Kurchum Kazakh.
121 T3 Kurchum r. Kazakh.
129 I5 Kürd Azer.
177 H5 Kurd Hungary
129 J5 Kürdämir Azer.
121 P6 Kurday Kazakh.
122 E7 Kūr Deh Iran
122 F8 Kūrdeh Iran
129 K7 Kür Dili pt Azer.
114 D3 Kurduvadi Mahar. India
197 N9 Kŭrdzhali Bulg.
129 B2 Kurdzhinovo Rus. Fed.
103 J12 Kure Japan
126 F3 Küre Turkey
75 G1 Kure Atoll HI U.S.A.
138 F3 Kuressaare Estonia
138 M3 Kureya r. Rus. Fed.
130 J3 Kureyskoye Vodokhranilishche resr Rus. Fed.
Kurgal'dzhino Kazakh. see Korgalzhyn
130 H4 Kurgan Rus. Fed.
135 H7 Kurganinsk Rus. Fed.
Kurgannaya Rus. Fed. see Kurganinsk
Kurgantyube Tajik. see Qŭrghonteppa
Kurgasyn Kazakh. see Korgasyn
116 G9 Kurhad Mahar. India
123 N3 Kuri Afgh.
116 C6 Kuri Rajasthan India
77 H1 Kuria is Gilbert Is Kiribati
Kuria Muria Bay Oman see Ḩalāniyāt, Khalīj al
Kuria Muria Islands Oman see Ḩalāniyāt, Juzur al
84 H6 Kuridala Qld Austr.
117 L7 Kurigram Bangl.
105 K5 Kurihama Japan
105 K3 Kurihashi Japan
140 Q5 Kurikka Fin.
102 R8 Kurikoma-yama vol. Japan
266 E2 Kuril Basin sea feature Sea of Okhotsk
196 H8 Kurile, Mal mt. Albania
Kuril Islands Rus. Fed. see Kuril'skiye Ostrova
120 C2 Kurilovka Rus. Fed.
99 Q2 Kuril'sk Kuril'skiye O-va Rus. Fed.
99 Q2 Kuril'skiye Ostrova is Rus. Fed.
266 E3 Kuril Trench sea feature N. Pacific Ocean
176 F2 Kuřim Czech Rep.
177 K2 Kurima Slovakia
105 L4 Kurimoto Japan
103 H15 Kurino Japan
129 A1 Kurinskaya Rus. Fed.
102 S3 Kuriyama Hokkaidō Japan
105 K2 Kuriyama Tochigi Japan
Kurkçü Turkey see Sarıkavak
139 V8 Kurkino Rus. Fed.
87 I7 Kurlkuta Aboriginal Reserve W.A. Austr.
139 X6 Kurlovskiy Rus. Fed.
120 D1 Kurmanayevka Rus. Fed.
Kurmashkino Kazakh. see Kurchum
138 H5 Kurmene Latvia
210 B2 Kurmuk Sudan
173 I2 Kürnach Ger.
172 F3 Kürnbach Ger.
136 H3 Kurne Ukr.
114 E5 Kurnool Andhra Prad. India
105 L2 Kurobane Japan
104 F2 Kurobe Japan
104 F2 Kurobe-gawa r. Japan
104 G2 Kurobe-ko resr Japan
104 B5 Kurodashō Japan
105 G2 Kurohime-yama mt. Japan
105 J3 Kurohone Japan
105 I1 Kurohume-yama hill Japan
102 R6 Kuroishi Japan
105 L2 Kuroiso Japan
102 R4 Kuromatsunai Japan
203 F4 Kuror, Jebel mt. Sudan
171 I9 Kurort Bad Gottleuba Ger.
171 I9 Kurort-Berggießhübel Ger.
169 J9 Kurort Brotterode Ger.
137 P8 Kurortne Ukr.
171 G10 Kurort Oberwiesenthal Ger.
169 J9 Kurort Schmalkalden Ger.
169 K9 Kurort Steinbach-Hallenberg Ger.
137 O6 Kuroshany r. Ukr.
102 □B22 Kuro-shima i. Nansei-shotō Japan
104 B7 Kuro-shima i. Japan
102 □G16 Kuro-shima i. Japan
104 D6 Kuroso-yama mt. Japan
100 E1 Kurovskiy Rus. Fed.
139 T7 Kurovskoy Rus. Fed.
139 V6 Kurovskoye Rus. Fed.
175 M6 Kurovychi Ukr.
81 E11 Kurow South I. N.Z.
175 K4 Kurów Pol.
175 H4 Kurowice Pol.
123 N5 Kurram r. Afgh./Pak.
123 N5 Kurram Pak.
83 M5 Kurri Kurri N.S.W. Austr.
129 D1 Kursavka Rus. Fed.
117 K7 Kursela Bihar India
138 F5 Kuršėnai Lith.
124 F4 Kursh, Jabal hill Saudi Arabia
Kürshim Kazakh. see Kurchum
Kurshskiy Zaliv b. Lith./Rus. Fed. see Courland Lagoon
138 J9 Kurshynavichy Belarus
138 F5 Kursīši Latvia
Kuršių marios b. Lith./Rus. Fed. see Courland Lagoon
138 D6 Kuršių neringos nacionalinis parkas nat. park Lith.
135 G6 Kursk Rus. Fed.
129 F1 Kurskaya Rus. Fed.
135 G6 Kurskaya Oblast' admin. div. Rus. Fed.
Kurskiy Zaliv b. Lith./Rus. Fed. see Courland Lagoon
Kursk Oblast admin. div. Rus. Fed. see Kurskaya Oblast'
137 O2 Kurskoye Vodokhranilishche resr Rus. Fed.
196 J7 Kuršumlija Serbia
126 F3 Kurşunlu Turkey
127 J5 Kurtalan Turkey
199 H1 Kurtbey Turkey
Kürti r. Kazakh. see Kurtty
240 □F14 Kurtistown HI U.S.A.
129 F4 K'urt'lari Georgia
199 J6 Kurtoğlu Burnu pt Turkey
128 D2 Kurtpınar Turkey
128 D1 Kurttepe Turkey
121 Q5 Kurtty r. Kazakh.
Kurty r. Kazakh. see Kurtty
183 O2 Kurtzea Spain
141 Q6 Kuru Fin.
Kurú r. Greece see Kompsatos
117 J8 Kuru Jharkhand India
208 E2 Kuru watercourse Sudan
206 C4 Kurubonla Sierra Leone
126 F3 Kurucaşile Turkey
129 B7 Kurucu Geçidi pass Turkey
116 H9 Kurud Chhattisgarh India
199 L2 Kurudere Turkey
116 F5 Kurukshetra Haryana India
110 H6 Kuruktag mts China
214 H3 Kuruman S. Africa
214 E2 Kuruman watercourse S. Africa
214 H3 Kuruman Hills S. Africa
103 H13 Kurume Japan
99 J1 Kurumkan Rus. Fed.
210 B3 Kurun r. Sudan
84 E6 Kurundi watercourse N.T. Austr.
114 D4 Kurundvad Mahar. India
114 G9 Kurunegala Sri Lanka
107 O1 Kurunzulay Rus. Fed.
115 H3 Kurupam Andhra Prad. India
251 G3 Kurupukari Guyana
203 F4 Kurush, Jebel hills Sudan
121 T2 Kur'ya Altayskiy Kray Rus. Fed.
134 L3 Kur'ya Respublika Komi Rus. Fed.
137 R4 Kuryachivka Ukr.
120 D6 Kuryk Kazakh.
175 M2 Kurylavichy Belarus
137 N5 Kurylivka Ukr.
175 K5 Kuryłówka Pol.
103 G11 Kuryongp'o S. Korea
175 H5 Kurzelów Pol.
175 I4 Kurzeszyn Pol.
175 H2 Kurzętnik Pol.
199 I5 Kuşadası Turkey
199 I5 Kuşadası Körfezi b. Turkey
Kusaie atoll Micronesia see Kosrae
128 E2 Kuşalanı Turkey
Kusary Azer. see Qusar
105 I2 Kusatsu Gunma Japan
104 C5 Kusatsu Shiga Japan
222 B2 Kusawa Lake Y.T. Can.
128 D2 Kuşcenneti nature res. Turkey
199 I2 Kuşcenneti Milli Parkı nat. park Turkey
103 K11 Kuse Japan
172 C2 Kusel Ger.
170 D5 Kusey Ger.
199 I2 Kuş Gölü l. Turkey
116 E8 Kushalgarh Rajasthan India
139 T4 Kushalino Rus. Fed.
122 G4 Kūshank Iran
135 G7 Kushchevskaya Rus. Fed.
207 G4 Kusheriki Nigeria
102 □1 Kushi Okinawa Japan
104 E6 Kushida-gawa r. Japan
105 H4 Kushigata Japan
104 F5 Kushihara Japan
103 H15 Kushikino Japan
103 I15 Kushima Japan
103 M13 Kushimoto Japan
102 V4 Kushiro Japan
102 V3 Kushiro-Shitsugen Kokuritsu-kōen nat. park Japan
Kushka Turkm. see Serhetabat
122 B5 Kūshkī Iran
134 I3 Kushkopola Rus. Fed.
120 K1 Kushmurun Kazakh.
120 K1 Kushmurun, Ozero salt l. Kazakh.
134 K5 Kushnarenkovo Rus. Fed.
114 E5 Kushtagi Karnataka India
117 L8 Kushtia Bangl.
122 H7 Kushtih Iran
139 T1 Kushtozero, Ozero l. Rus. Fed.
137 O6 Kushuhum Ukr.
106 J7 Kushui He r. China
120 D2 Kushum Kazakh.
120 D3 Kushum r. Kazakh.
128 B2 Kuskan Turkey
220 B3 Kuskokwim r. AK U.S.A.
220 B4 Kuskokwim Bay AK U.S.A.
220 C3 Kuskokwim Mountains AK U.S.A.
139 S6 Kuskovo Rus. Fed.
Kuşluyan Turkey see Gölköy
190 F1 Küsnacht Switz.
101 D9 Kusŏng N. Korea
129 E2 Kusparty Rus. Fed.
102 V3 Kussharo-ko l. Japan
190 E1 Küssnacht Switz.
Kustanay Kazakh. see Kostanay

L

222 C2 Lansing r. Y.T. Can.
226 C6 Lansing IA U.S.A.
226 J7 Lansing MI U.S.A.
226 B6 Lansing MN U.S.A.
140 Q5 Länsi-Suomi prov. Fin.
140 Q3 Lansjärv Sweden
175 I2 Łańskie, Jezioro l. Pol.
176 F2 Lanškroun Czech Rep.
161 J6 Lanslebourg-Mont-Cenis France
163 H8 Lanta France
97 D11 Lanta, Ko i. Thai.
183 L4 Lantadilla Spain
109 □I7 Lantau Island H.K. China
Lantau Peak hill H.K. China see Fung Wong Shan
157 L8 Lanterne r. France
Lantian Hunan China see Lianyuan
107 K9 Lantian Shaanxi China
163 B6 Lanton France
161 K9 Lantosque France
137 R4 Lantratívka Ukr.
161 E6 Lantriac France
160 D3 Lanty France
187 E10 La Nucía Spain
161 C8 Lanuéjols France
163 I7 Lanuéjouls France
192 A6 La Nurra reg. Sardegna Italy
261 H4 Lanús Arg.
192 D8 Lanusei Sardegna Italy
92 F7 Lanuza Mindanao Phil.
92 F7 Lanuza Bay Mindanao Phil.
158 G5 Lanvallay France
158 C5 Lanvéoc France
158 F4 Lanvollon France
100 E5 Lanxi Heilong. China
109 L4 Lanxi Zhejiang China
107 L7 Lanxian Shanxi China
171 I10 Lány Czech Rep.
174 G5 Łany Pol.
210 A3 Lanya Sudan
107 L7 Lanyi He r. China
109 M7 Lan Yü i. Taiwan
170 E4 Lanz Ger.
208 C4 Lanza Congo
183 K8 Lanzahita Spain
216 □3c Lanzarote i. Canary Is
179 N4 Lanzenkirchen Austria
176 F3 Lanžhot Czech Rep.
106 H8 Lanzhou Gansu China
107 R4 Lanzijing Jilin China
190 C5 Lanzo Torinese Italy
193 P8 Lao r. Italy
96 D5 Lao, Nam Mae r. Thai.
92 C2 Laoag Luzon Phil.
92 E5 Laoang Phil.
108 B7 Laobie Shan mts Yunnan China
183 O9 La Obispalía reg. Spain
108 G6 Laobukou Guangxi China
96 F3 Lao Cai Vietnam
100 E3 Laodaodian Heilong. China
Laodicea Syria see Al Lādhiqīyah
Laodicea Turkey see Denizli
Laodicea ad Lycum Turkey see Denizli
Laodicea ad Mare Syria see Al Lādhiqīyah
110 F3 Laofengkou Xinjiang China
107 Q5 Laoha He r. China
100 G7 Laoheishan Heilong. China
109 H2 Laohekou Hubei China
107 Q7 Laohutun Liaoning China
147 H7 Laois county Ireland
Laojie Yunnan China see Yongping
Laojunmiao Gansu China see Yumen
101 E8 Laoling Jilin China
101 E8 Lao Ling mts China
216 □3b La Oliva Fuerteventura Canary Is
Laolong Guangdong China see Longchuan
156 G4 Laon France
226 F4 Laona WI U.S.A.
156 G4 Laonnois reg. France
156 B6 Laons France
106 A5 Laoqitai Xinjiang China
216 □3a La Orotava Tenerife Canary Is
252 B2 La Oroya Peru
96 F5 Laos country Asia
107 Q8 Laoshan Shandong China
110 G4 Laoshawan Xinjiang China
Laotieshan Shuidao sea chan. China see Bohai Haixia
100 F7 Laotougou Jilin China
101 D8 Laotuding Shan hill Liaoning China
180 D5 Laou, Oued r. Morocco
206 E4 Laoudi-Ba Côte d'Ivoire
205 G5 Laouni, Oued watercourse Alg.
161 B9 Laouzas, Lac de l. France
Laowohi pass Jammu and Kashmir see Khardung La
106 G6 Laoximiao Nei Mongol China
106 H8 Laoyacheng Qinghai China
100 E7 Laoye Ling mts China
100 F7 Laoye Ling mts China
106 D4 Laoyemiao Xinjiang China
255 C8 Lapa Brazil
92 C9 Lapac i. Phil.
185 P5 La Paca Spain
160 D4 La Pacaudière France
258 F2 Lapachito Arg.
207 G4 Lapai Nigeria
160 D4 Lapalisse France
162 B3 La Pallice France
216 □3d La Palma i. Canary Is
260 B4 La Palma Chile
250 C3 La Palma Col.
243 O9 La Palma Guat.
242 □T13 La Palma Panama
187 D12 La Palma Spain
241 U9 La Palma AZ U.S.A.
184 F6 La Palma del Condado Spain
161 B11 La Palme France
161 C11 Lapalme, Étang de lag. France
258 G4 La Paloma Uru.
250 C2 La Paloma Venez.
161 F8 Lapalud France
161 I9 La Palud-sur-Verdon France
260 E5 La Pampa prov. Arg.
175 I6 Łapanów Pol.
240 L6 La Panza Range mts CA U.S.A.
261 F2 La Para Arg.
251 F3 La Paragua Venez.
92 B9 Laparan i. Phil.
244 F1 La Pardita Mex.
216 □3b La Pared Fuerteventura Canary Is
261 G3 La Parejas Arg.
244 C2 La Parilla Mex.
184 F3 La Parra Spain
183 P9 La Parra de Las Vegas Spain
184 G2 La Parrilla hill Spain
198 C4 Lapas Greece
182 C9 Lapas Port.
250 C4 La Paya, Parque Nacional nat. park Col.
260 E3 La Paz Córdoba Arg.
261 H2 La Paz Entre Ríos Arg.
260 D3 La Paz Mendoza Arg.
252 C4 La Paz Bol.
252 C3 La Paz dept Bol.
242 □P10 La Paz Hond.
242 D5 La Paz Mex.
242 □P11 La Paz Nic.
261 I4 La Paz Uru.
226 H8 Lapaz IN U.S.A.
250 C2 La Paz Venez.
242 D5 La Paz, Bahía b. Mex.
250 D5 La Pedrera Col.
227 K6 Lapeer MI U.S.A.
184 □ Lapeiras Madeira
261 G2 La Pelada Arg.
159 I5 La Pellerine France
245 I2 La Peña Tamaulipas Mex.
245 L8 La Peña Veracruz Mex.
242 □S13 La Peña Panama
161 J9 La Penne France
161 H10 La Penne-sur-Huveaune France
183 O8 La Peraleja Spain
242 G3 La Perla Mex.
102 S1 La Pérouse Strait Japan/Rus. Fed.
245 J2 La Pesca Mex.
182 H8 La Pesga Spain
157 N6 La Petite-Pierre France
185 M6 La Peza Spain
150 E6 Lapford Devon, England U.K.
261 G2 La Picada Arg.
244 E5 La Piedad Mex.
238 D5 La Pine OR U.S.A.
92 E5 Lapinig Samar Phil.
187 C12 La Pinilla Spain
141 S6 Lapinjärvi Fin.
140 S5 Lapinlahti Fin.
242 □S13 La Pintada Panama
128 B3 Lapithos Cyprus
194 E8 La Pizzuta mt. Sicilia Italy
237 J10 Laplace LA U.S.A.
96 E6 Lap Lae Thai.
160 J5 La Plagne France
217 □1c La Plaine-des-Cafres Réunion
217 □1c La Plaine-des-Palmistes Réunion
158 G7 La-Plaine-sur-Mer France
140 V3 Laplandskiy Zapovednik nature res. Rus. Fed.
236 E3 La Plant SD U.S.A.
261 I4 La Plata Arg.
232 I10 La Plata MD U.S.A.
236 I5 La Plata MO U.S.A.
261 I4 La Plata, Río de sea chan. Arg./Uru.
260 E2 La Playa Arg.
216 □3f La Playa de Mogán Gran Canaria Canary Is
261 F3 La Playosa Arg.
182 H2 La Plaza Spain
244 B1 La Plazuela Mex.
162 I5 Lapleau France
223 J4 La Plonge, Lac l. Sask. Can.
163 F7 Laplume France
138 G4 Lapmežciems Latvia
186 F6 La Pobla de Benifassá Spain
186 I3 La Pobla de Lillet Spain
186 G3 La Pobla de Segur Spain
182 I3 La Pola de Gordón Spain
258 D2 La Poma Arg.
134 H2 Lapominka Rus. Fed.
159 J7 La Pommeraye France
192 C3 La Porta Corse France
230 D5 La Porte IN U.S.A.
227 R8 Laporte PA U.S.A.
222 E2 Laporte, Mount Y.T. Can.
186 F6 La Portellada Spain
187 C9 La Portera Spain
93 A6 Laposo, Bukit mt. Indon.
217 □1c La Possession Réunion
261 F2 La Posta Arg.
225 F1 La Potherie, Lac l. Que. Can.
159 J6 La Pouëze France
157 N7 Lapoutroie France
250 C3 La Poyata Col.
242 C5 La Poza Grande Mex.
140 Q5 Lappajärvi l. Fin.
143 L2 Lappe Sweden
141 T6 Lappeenranta Fin.
173 M3 Lappersdorf Ger.
141 P6 Lappi Fin.
140 S3 Lappi prov. Fin.
140 O3 Lappland reg. Europe
138 E1 Lappo Åland Fin.
138 G2 Lappohja Fin.
140 Q3 Lappträsk Sweden
233 L3 La Prairie Que. Can.
245 H2 La Presa Mex.
244 G1 La Presas Mex.
163 I11 La Preste France
261 G5 Laprida Arg.
261 G5 La Primavera Arg.
183 P4 La Proveda de Soria Spain
237 F11 La Pryor TX U.S.A.
199 H2 Lâpseki Turkey
161 E6 Lapte France
138 L5 Laptevo Pskovskaya Oblast' Rus. Fed.
Laptevo Tul'skaya Oblast' Rus. Fed. see Yasnogorsk
Laptev Sea Rus. Fed. see Laptevykh, More
131 N2 Laptevykh, More sea Rus. Fed.
140 Q5 Lapua Fin.
140 Q5 Lapuanjoki r. Fin.
La Puebla Spain see Sa Pobla
183 N9 La Puebla de Almoradiel Spain
183 O3 La Puebla de Arganzón Spain
185 I6 La Puebla de Cazalla Spain
186 E5 La Puebla de Híjar Spain
185 I5 La Puebla de los Infantes Spain
184 G6 La Puebla del Río Spain
183 L9 La Puebla de Montalbán Spain
183 K3 La Puebla de Valdavia Spain
187 D7 La Puebla de Valverde Spain
183 K9 La Pueblanueva Spain
258 D3 La Puerta Catamarca Arg.
261 F2 La Puerta Córdoba Arg.
250 D2 La Puerta Venez.
185 N4 La Puerta de Segura Spain
177 L6 Lăpugiu de Jos Romania
93 C6 Lapuko Sulawesi Indon.
92 D6 Lapu-Lapu Phil.
260 E3 La Punilla Arg.
190 H2 La Punt Switz.
258 D3 La Punta Arg.
Lapurdum France see Bayonne
242 C4 La Purísima Mex.
197 M3 Lăpuș Romania
197 L3 Lăpuș r. Romania
197 J6 Lăpușnicu Mare Romania
196 I8 Lapušnik Kosovo Serbia
151 I3 Lapworth Warwickshire, England U.K.
175 K3 Łapy Pol.
202 F4 Laqiya Arbain well Sudan
202 F5 Laqiya 'Umran well Sudan
258 D1 La Quiaca Arg.
193 K3 L'Aquila Italy
193 L3 L'Aquila prov. Italy
241 P8 La Quinta CA U.S.A.
122 F8 Lār Iran
83 J8 Lara Vic. Austr.
250 D2 Lara state Venez.
182 C2 Laracha Spain
204 D2 Larache Morocco
180 C5 Larache prov. Morocco
148 D6 Laracor Ireland
148 E7 Laragh Ireland
161 H8 Laragne-Montéglin France
216 □3a La Rajita La Gomera Canary Is
122 G8 Lārak i. Iran
208 B2 Laramanay Chad
185 J5 La Rambla Spain
238 L6 Laramie WY U.S.A.
238 L5 Laramie r. WY U.S.A.
238 L5 Laramie Mountains WY U.S.A.
Laranda Turkey see Karaman
251 G6 Laranjal Brazil
256 D5 Laranjal Paulista Brazil
254 F4 Laranjeiras Brazil
256 C6 Laranjeiras, Baía das b. Brazil
256 A6 Laranjeiras do Sul Brazil
180 B3 Laranjeiro Port.
256 B5 Laranjinha r. Brazil
93 C8 Larantuka Flores Indon.
183 O7 Laranueva Spain
183 N5 La Rasa Spain
91 H8 Larat i. Indon.
160 H5 La Ravoire France
161 G7 La Raye mt. France
204 B5 La Raygat reg. Western Sahara
146 I10 Larbert Falkirk, Scotland U.K.
186 I5 L'Arboç Spain
160 F5 L'Arbresle France
143 O4 Lärbro Gotland Sweden
163 B9 Larceveau-Arros-Cibits France
159 I5 Larchamp France
156 E7 Larchant France
162 G5 Larche Limousin France
161 J8 Larche Provence-Alpes-Côte d'Azur France
190 B7 Larche, Col de pass Italy
235 H3 Larchmont NY U.S.A.
227 M3 Larchwood Ont. Can.
191 J4 Lardaro Italy
191 J9 Larderello Italy
227 O1 Larder Lake Ont. Can.
227 O1 Larder Lake l. Ont. Can.
182 F9 Lardosa Port.
183 N2 Laredo Spain
237 F12 Laredo TX U.S.A.
161 B10 La Redorte France
260 D5 La Reforma Arg.
245 J9 La Reforma Oaxaca Mex.
239 I12 La Reforma Sonora Mex.
245 J5 La Reforma Veracruz Mex.
227 O1 La Reine Que. Can.
164 J4 Laren Gelderland Neth.
164 H4 Laren Noord-Holland Neth.
163 D6 La Réole France
247 □1 Lares Puerto Rico
122 F4 Lārestān Iran
216 □3e La Restinga El Hierro Canary Is
147 E4 Largan Ireland
Largeau Chad see Faya
161 E7 Largentière France
161 J7 L'Argentière-la-Bessée France
231 F12 Largo FL U.S.A.
246 C3 Largo, Cayo i. Cuba
146 K10 Largo Bay Scotland U.K.
146 K10 Largoward Fife, Scotland U.K.
146 G11 Largs North Ayrshire, Scotland U.K.
186 B1 La Rhune hill Spain
122 B2 Lārī Iran
191 J8 Lari Italy
205 H1 L'Ariana Tunisia
189 C7 L'Ariana admin. div. Tunisia
93 A4 Lariang Sulawesi Barat Indon.
93 A4 Lariang r. Indon.
183 O6 La Riba de Escalote Spain
261 H4 La Rica Arg.
161 E6 La Ricamarie France
122 B2 Lārījān Iran
236 G1 Larimore ND U.S.A.
261 F2 La Rinconada Arg.
184 H6 La Rinconada Spain
193 N4 Larino Italy
258 D3 La Rioja Arg.
260 D1 La Rioja prov. Arg.
183 P4 La Rioja aut. comm. Spain
139 N1 Larionovo Rus. Fed.
198 D3 Larisa Greece
Larissa Greece see Larisa
122 G8 Laristan reg. Iran
217 □1c La Rivière Réunion
123 M8 Larkana Pak.
146 I11 Larkhall South Lanarkshire, Scotland U.K.
225 J3 Lark Harbour Nfld and Lab. Can.
151 I5 Larkhill Wiltshire, England U.K.
123 J5 Lar Koh mt. Afgh.
85 J3 Lark Passage Qld Austr.
151 N3 Larling Norfolk, England U.K.
160 I3 Larmont mt. France/Switz.
158 E6 Larmor-Plage France
Larnaca Cyprus see Larnaka
128 B4 Larnaka Cyprus
147 K3 Larne Northern Ireland U.K.
236 F6 Larned KS U.S.A.
147 K3 Larne Lough inlet Northern Ireland U.K.
207 I4 Laro Cameroon
182 I3 La Robla Spain
184 F2 La Roca de la Sierra Spain
190 C2 La Roche Switz.
162 E5 La Rochebeaucourt-et-Argentine France
158 G6 La Roche-Bernard France
162 H5 La Roche-Canillac France
162 E5 La Roche-Chalais France
161 J7 La Roche-de-Rame France
158 E4 La Roche-Derrien France
161 H7 La Roche-des-Arnauds France
165 I8 La Roche-en-Ardenne Belgium
162 E4 La Rochefoucauld France
156 C5 La Roche-Guyon France
162 B3 La Rochelle France
160 E3 Larochemillay France
159 M8 La Roche-Posay France
160 F3 La Rochepot France
156 F8 Laroche-St-Cydroine France
160 I4 La Roche-sur-Foron France
158 I8 La Roche-sur-Yon France
161 I6 La Rochette France
165 J9 Larochette Lux.
185 O2 La Roda Spain
185 J6 La Roda de Andalucía Spain
159 I6 La Roë France
185 N6 Laroles Spain
247 I4 La Romana Dom. Rep.
187 D11 La Romana Spain
163 E8 La Romieu France
223 J4 La Ronge Sask. Can.
223 J4 La Ronge, Lac l. Sask. Can.
162 I6 Laroquebrou France
161 H10 La Roquebrussanne France
161 G9 La Roque-d'Anthéron France
163 H10 Laroque-d'Olmes France
161 C8 La Roque-Ste-Marguerite France
163 F7 Laroque-Timbaut France
243 I5 La Rosa Mex.
241 P9 La Rosa de Castilla Mex.
243 I3 La Rosita Mex.
182 E5 Larouco, Serra do mts Spain
163 H7 La Rouquette France
183 Q3 Larraga Spain
186 B2 Larrainzar Spain
183 Q3 Larrasoaina Spain
163 C9 Larrau France
163 G8 Larrazet France
163 E8 Larressingle France
163 B9 Larressore France
86 E5 Larrey Point W.A. Austr.
84 D3 Larrimah N.T. Austr.
84 D3 Larrimah Aboriginal Land res. N.T. Austr.
183 P3 Larrión Spain
261 H3 Larroque Arg.
263 E2 Lars Christensen Coast Antarctica
262 T2 Larsen Ice Shelf Antarctica
140 Q5 Larsmo Fin.
Larsmo Fin. see Larsmo
140 H5 Larsnes Norway
195 □ L-Artal, Ras pt Malta
La Rúa Spain see A Rúa
261 G2 La Rubia Arg.
163 D10 Laruns France
162 D5 Laruscade France
185 M5 Larva Spain
142 G2 Larvik Norway
130 J3 Lar'yak Rus. Fed.
137 Q6 Laryne Ukr.
161 C8 Larzac, Causse du plat. France
191 J2 Lasà Italy
258 F2 La Sabana Arg.
250 D4 La Sabana Col.
183 M8 La Sagra reg. Spain
216 □3c Las Agujas hill Canary Is
93 C6 Lasahau Sulawesi Indon.
241 W3 La Sal UT U.S.A.
261 I5 La Salada Grande, Laguna l. Arg.
244 G2 Las Albercas Mex.
260 C2 La Salina salt pan Arg.
217 □1c La Saline Réunion
241 W3 La Sal Junction UT U.S.A.
224 F4 La Salle Que. Can.
161 D8 Lasalle France
190 C4 La Salle Italy
226 E8 La Salle IL U.S.A.
161 J7 La Salle les Alpes France
163 I7 La Salvetat-Peyralès France
163 G8 La Salvetat-St-Gilles France
161 B9 La Salvetat-sur-Agout France
186 F7 La Salzadella Spain
95 K4 Lasan Kalimantan Indon.
236 D6 Las Animas CO U.S.A.
242 C3 Las Ánimas, Punta pt Mex.
Las Anod Somalia see Laascaanood
216 □3c La Santa Lanzarote Canary Is
183 K2 Las Arenas Spain
190 C2 La Sarine r. Switz.
261 I5 Las Armas Arg.
224 E3 La Sarre Que. Can.
261 E3 Las Asequias Arg.
244 G4 La Sauceda Mex.
163 F8 La Sauvetat France
163 E6 La Sauvetat-du-Dropt France
161 I10 La Sauvette hill France
247 J8 Las Aves, Islas is West Indies
187 H10 La Savina Spain
261 G1 Las Avispas Arg.
242 D3 Las Avispas Mex.
225 F2 La Savonnière, Lac l. Que. Can.
261 G3 Las Bandurrias Arg.
179 K3 Lasberg Austria
183 K7 Las Berlanas Spain
251 E3 Las Bonitas Venez.
258 E2 Las Breñas Arg.
142 F5 Låsby Denmark
184 H7 Las Cabezas de San Juan Spain
260 B4 Las Cabras Chile
244 B3 Las Cabras Mex.
185 O4 Las Cabras mt. Spain
216 □3d Las Caletas La Palma Canary Is
216 □3a Las Cañadas vol. crater Tenerife Canary Is
260 A4 Las Cañas Chile
261 H3 Las Cañas Uru.
194 F8 Lascari Sicilia Italy
187 E8 Las Casas Spain
260 C2 Las Casuarinas Arg.
260 C3 Las Catitas Arg.
244 B1 Las Cebollas Mex.
260 E3 Las Chacras Arg.
259 D6 Las Chapas Arg.
245 M8 Las Choapas Mex.
225 K3 La Scie Nfld and Lab. Can.
253 F4 Las Conchas Bol.
242 F3 Las Cruces Mex.
240 L7 Las Cruces CA U.S.A.
239 K10 Las Cruces NM U.S.A.
245 H2 Las Crucitas Mex.
186 G3 Lascuarre Spain
183 K6 La Seca Spain
159 J7 La Séguinière France
246 H4 La Selle, Pic mt. Haiti
186 H5 La Selva del Camp Spain
163 J7 La Selve France
186 F6 La Sènia Spain
260 B1 La Serena Chile
184 H3 La Serena reg. Spain
243 I4 Las Esperanças Mex.
161 H10 La Seyne-sur-Mer France
261 H5 Las Flores Buenos Aires Arg.
258 E2 Las Flores Salta Arg.
260 C2 Las Flores San Juan Arg.
245 J3 Las Flores Mex.
260 B2 Las Galenas Chile
260 B4 Las Garzas Chile
261 H3 Las Golas Arg.
239 J11 Las Guacamatas, Cerro resr Mex.
244 E7 Las Guacamayas Mex.
123 I8 Lāshār r. Iran
223 I4 Lashburn Sask. Can.
260 C3 Las Heras Arg.
183 K9 Las Herencias Spain
250 C4 Las Hermosas, Parque Nacional nat. park Col.
242 G5 Las Herreras Mex.
261 E3 Las Higueras Arg.
96 C3 Lashio Myanmar
123 K6 Lashkar Gāh Afgh.
259 C8 Las Horquetas Arg.
260 A6 Las Hortensias Chile
244 F1 Las Huertas Mex.
182 H8 Las Hurdes reg. Spain
195 L5 La Sila reg. Italy
175 H2 Łasin Pol.
216 □3d Las Indias La Palma Canary Is
245 K9 La Sirena, Cerro mt. Mex.
260 E3 Las Isletas Arg.
136 F2 Lasitsk Belarus
122 E4 Lāsjerd Iran
244 F5 Las Jicamas Mex.
260 C4 Las Juntas Arg.
258 C3 Las Juntas Chile
244 G6 Las Juntas Mex.
261 F2 Las Junturas Arg.
175 H4 Łask Pol.
127 O6 Laskarak Iran
175 J4 Łaskarzew Pol.
136 E4 Laskivtsi Ukr.
179 L7 Laško Slovenia
175 I6 Laskowa Pol.
174 G2 Laskowice Pol.
185 L2 Las Labores Spain
260 B6 Las Lajas Arg.
251 E3 Las Lajitas Venez.
245 I2 Las Lavaderos Mex.
260 B4 Las Leñas Arg.
250 A6 Las Lomas Peru
258 E2 Las Lomitas Arg.
183 P8 Las Majadas Spain
260 C4 Las Malvinas Arg.
184 F6 Las Marismas marsh Spain
259 D7 Las Martinetas Arg.
182 G4 Las Médulas tourist site Spain
185 O6 Las Menas Spain
250 E2 Las Mercedes Venez.
185 N2 Las Mesas Spain
242 G3 Las Mesteñas Mex.
175 K2 Łaśmiady, Jezioro l. Pol.
251 E2 Las Minas Venez.
243 O10 Las Minas, Cerro de mt. Hond.
260 C4 Las Molles Arg.
Las Mulatas is Panama see San Blas, Archipiélago de
245 H6 Las Navajas, Cerro mt. Mex.
185 I5 Las Navas de la Concepción Spain
183 L7 Las Navas del Marqués Spain
165 F7 Lasne Belgium
185 P7 Las Negras Spain
242 G4 Las Nieves Mex.
242 H5 Las Nopaleras, Cerro mt. Mex.
185 M3 La Solana Spain
93 C5 Lasolo, Teluk b. Indon.
182 H3 Las Omañas reg. Spain
244 G8 La Sombra Mex.
250 B3 Las Orquideas, Parque Nacional nat. park Col.
162 G3 La Souterraine France
260 B5 Las Ovejas Arg.
174 G5 Lasowice Małe Pol.
258 F2 Las Palmas Arg.
244 E2 Las Palmas Mex.
241 O9 Las Palmas watercourse Mex.
242 □S13 Las Palmas Panama
216 □3f Las Palmas de Gran Canaria Gran Canaria Canary Is
260 C4 Las Paredes Arg.
244 G7 Las Parotas r. Mex.
185 N2 Las Pedroñeras Spain
261 F2 Las Peñas Arg.
244 B5 Las Peñitas, Punta pt Mex.
261 F3 Las Perdices Arg.
253 F4 Las Petas Bol.
190 H7 La Spezia Italy
190 H7 La Spezia prov. Italy
261 I4 Las Piedras Uru.
193 P7 La Spina, Monte mt. Italy
261 I4 Las Pipinas Arg.
242 □Q10 Las Planchas Hond.
192 B8 Las Plassas Sardegna Italy
259 D6 Las Plumas Arg.
186 F2 Laspuña Spain
123 O3 Laspur Pak.
261 G3 Las Rosas Arg.
187 F10 Las Rotas Spain
183 M7 Las Rozas de Madrid Spain
168 K3 Lassahn Ger.
216 □3b Las Salinas Fuerteventura Canary Is
170 I3 Lassan Ger.
257 E2 Lassance Brazil
159 K5 Lassay-les-Châteaux France
240 K1 Lassen Peak vol. CA U.S.A.
240 K1 Lassen Volcanic National Park CA U.S.A.
163 D9 Lasseube France
156 E4 Lassigny France
179 K4 Lassing Niederösterreich Austria
179 J4 Lassing Steiermark Austria
179 M5 Laßnitzhöhe Austria
260 B3 Las Tablas Chile
245 H3 Las Tablas Mex.
242 □S14 Las Tablas Panama
259 B7 Lastarria, Parque Nacional de nat. park Chile
236 D6 Last Chance CO U.S.A.
191 K4 Lastebasse Italy
191 L3 Lastè delle Sute mt. Italy
258 D2 Las Termas Arg.
185 P5 Las Terreras Spain
223 J5 Last Mountain Lake Sask. Can.
187 C11 Las Torres de Cotillas Spain
260 C1 Las Tórtolas, Cerro mt. Chile
163 I9 Lastours France
208 B5 Lastoursville Gabon
188 F4 Lastovo i. Croatia
188 F4 Lastovski Kanal sea chan. Croatia
261 G5 Lastra Arg.
186 D6 Lastra, Sierra de mts Spain
191 K8 Lastra a Signa Italy
183 L6 Lastras de Cuéllar Spain
183 J1 Lastres, Cabo c. Spain
242 C4 Las Tres Vírgenes, Volcán vol. Mex.
251 E3 Las Trincheras Venez.
168 E5 Lastrup Ger.
246 E3 Las Tunas Cuba
261 F4 Las Tunas Grandes, Laguna l. Arg.
159 L6 La Suze-sur-Sarthe France
138 K4 Lasva Estonia
260 B2 Las Vacas Chile
250 D3 Las Varas Col.
242 F3 Las Varas Chihuahua Mex.
244 B4 Las Varas Nayarit Mex.
250 D3 Las Varas Venez.
261 F2 Las Varillas Arg.
244 B1 Las Vegas Mex.
239 L9 Las Vegas NM U.S.A.
241 Q5 Las Vegas NV U.S.A.
182 I7 Las Veguillas Spain
183 L9 Las Ventas con Peña Aguilera Spain
183 J8 Las Ventas de San Julián Spain
260 E3 Las Vertientes Arg.
245 J6 Las Vigas de Ramirez Mex.
185 I2 Las Villuercas mt. Spain
252 C4 Las Yaras Peru
177 L1 Lasy Janowskie, Park Krajobrazowy Pol.
175 L5 Łaszczów Pol.
175 K5 Laszki Pol.
Lászláfalva Hungary see Szentkirály
78 □6 Lata Santa Cruz Is Solomon Is
225 J3 La Tabatière Que. Can.
250 B5 Latacunga Ecuador
262 S2 Latady Island Antarctica
160 E3 La Tagnière France
250 C5 La Tagua Col.
Latakia Syria see Al Lādhiqīyah
93 E4 Latalata i. Maluku Indon.
161 E6 La Talaudière France
159 J5 La Tannière France
244 G3 La Tapona Mex.
227 O2 Latchford Ont. Can.
151 N4 Latchingdon Essex, England U.K.
79 □8 Late i. Vava'u Gp Tonga
117 J8 Latehar Jharkhand India
191 L3 Latemar mt. Italy
195 L2 Laterza Italy
163 B6 La Teste-de-Buch France
244 C5 La Tetilla, Cerro mt. Mex.
138 K5 Latgales augstiene hills Latvia
87 D10 Latham W.A. Austr.
168 D5 Lathen Ger.
146 J6 Latheron Highland, Scotland U.K.
116 C9 Lathi Gujarat India
116 C6 Lathi Rajasthan India
116 F3 Latho Jammu and Kashmir
240 K4 Lathrop CA U.S.A.
190 B4 La Thuile Italy
162 F3 Lathus France
195 N2 Latiano Italy
122 F8 Lātīdān Iran
140 N4 Latikberg Sweden
193 J5 Latina Italy
193 K5 Latina prov. Italy
245 K7 La Tinaja Mex.
191 O4 Latisana Italy
137 R2 Latnaya Rus. Fed.
195 L3 Lato r. Italy
260 E3 La Toma Arg.
177 K3 Latorica r. Slovakia
190 C3 La Tornette mt. Switz.
186 G3 La Torre de Cabdella Spain
251 E2 La Tortuga, Isla i. Venez.
136 B5 Latorytsya r. Ukr.
86 F5 Latouche Treville, Cape W.A. Austr.
202 B4 Latouma well Niger
162 E5 La Tour-Blanche France
161 H9 La Tour-d'Aigues France
160 B5 La Tour-d'Auvergne France
163 H11 Latour-de-Carol France
163 J10 Latour-de-France France
163 H9 La Tour-du-Crieu France
160 G5 La Tour-du-Pin France
160 I5 La Tournette mt. France
161 C9 La Tour-sur-Orb France
161 I6 La Toussuire France
175 J3 Latowicz Pol.
260 D3 La Tranca Arg.
162 B3 La Tranche-sur-Mer France
163 G9 Latrape France
157 I8 Latrecey-Ormoy-sur-Aube France
162 B4 La Tremblade France
162 G3 La Trimouille France
242 □P11 La Trinidad Nic.
92 C3 La Trinidad Luzon Phil.
243 M9 La Trinitaria Mex.
161 K9 La Trinité France
247 □3 La Trinité Martinique
159 M4 La Trinité-de-Réville France
158 F5 La Trinité-Porhoët France
158 E6 La Trinité-sur-Mer France
83 K9 Latrobe Tas. Austr.
232 F8 Latrobe PA U.S.A.
161 H6 La Tronche France
193 Q7 Latronico Italy
163 I6 Latronquière France
258 C3 La Troya r. Arg.
128 C7 Latrun West Bank
139 V3 Latskoye Rus. Fed.
Lattaquié Syria see Al Lādhiqīyah
193 Q9 Lattarico Italy
Latte Island Vava'u Gp Tonga see Late
161 D9 Lattes France
164 K4 Lattrop Neth.
227 O2 Latulipe Que. Can.
225 F4 La Tuque Que. Can.
114 E3 Latur Mahar. India
158 G7 La Turballe France
138 G5 Latvia country Europe
Latvija country Europe see Latvia
Latviyskaya S.S.R. country Europe see Latvia
207 H4 Lau Nigeria
210 A3 Lau r. Sudan
117 J8 Laua r. Chhattisgarh India
169 G9 Laubach Hessen Ger.
169 D10 Laubach Rheinland-Pfalz Ger.
212 D3 Lauban waterhole Namibia
173 I5 Lauben Bayern Ger.
173 I6 Lauben Bayern Ger.
171 J8 Laubusch Ger.
252 C4 Lauca, Parque Nacional nat. park Chile
171 E8 Laucha (Unstrut) Ger.
172 G5 Lauchert r. Ger.
171 I8 Lauchhammer Ger.
173 I4 Lauchheim Ger.
172 E6 Lauchringen Ger.
172 H2 Lauda-Königshofen Ger.
172 F2 Laudenbach Ger.
146 K11 Lauder Scottish Borders, Scotland U.K.
234 F5 Lauderdale NJ U.S.A.
Laudio Spain see Llodio
161 F8 Laudun France
169 H6 Lauenau Ger.
168 I4 Lauenbrück Ger.
168 K4 Lauenburg (Elbe) Ger.
169 H7 Lauenförde Ger.
169 J10 Lauer r. Ger.
172 E4 Lauf Ger.
169 H10 Laufach Ger.
173 K2 Lauf an der Pegnitz Ger.
173 N6 Laufen Ger.
190 D1 Laufen Switz.
190 E1 Laufenberg Switz.
172 E6 Laufenburg (Baden) Ger.
140 □C1 Laugarbakki Iceland
221 L2 Lauge Koch Kyst reg. Greenland
150 D4 Laugharne Carmarthenshire, Wales U.K.
84 E7 Laughlen, Mount N.T. Austr.
239 L8 Laughlin Peak NM U.S.A.
163 F7 Laugnac France
141 Q5 Lauhanvuoren kansallispuisto nat. park Fin.
173 I4 Lauingen (Donau) Ger.
185 N7 Laujar de Andarax Spain
138 F3 Lauka Estonia
140 R5 Laukaa Fin.
138 F6 Laukuva Lith.
78 □2 Lauli'i Samoa
97 D9 Laun Thai.
163 G8 Launac France
227 P1 Launay Que. Can.
83 K9 Launceston Tas. Austr.
150 D6 Launceston Cornwall, England U.K.
147 C8 Laune r. Ireland
96 D2 Launggyaung Myanmar
97 D8 Launglon Myanmar
97 C8 Launglon Bok Islands Myanmar
243 M10 La Unidad Mex.
253 E3 La Unión Bol.
259 B6 La Unión Chile
250 B4 La Unión Col.
242 □P11 La Unión El Salvador
242 □P10 La Unión Hond.
244 F8 La Unión Mex.
252 A2 La Unión Huánuco Peru
250 A6 La Unión Piura Peru
187 D12 La Unión Spain
156 I4 Launois-sur-Vence France
190 C2 Laupen Switz.
172 H5 Laupheim Ger.
92 C4 Laur Luzon Phil.
85 J3 Laura Qld Austr.
82 G5 Laura S.A. Austr.
163 H9 Lauragais reg. France
163 I9 Lauraguel France
250 E3 La Urbana Venez.
195 K7 Laureana di Borrello Italy
233 J10 Laurel DE U.S.A.
237 K10 Laurel MS U.S.A.
238 J4 Laurel MT U.S.A.
236 G4 Laurel NE U.S.A.
234 D4 Laureldale PA U.S.A.
253 F6 Laureles Para.
232 F9 Laurel Hill hills PA U.S.A.
234 E5 Laurel Springs NJ U.S.A.
234 A3 Laurelton PA U.S.A.
146 L9 Laurencekirk Aberdeenshire, Scotland U.K.
147 F6 Laurencetown Ireland
161 C9 Laurens France
236 H4 Laurens IA U.S.A.
231 G8 Laurens SC U.S.A.
225 G4 Laurentides, Réserve Faunique des nature res. Que. Can.
193 P7 Laurenzana Italy
163 B9 Laurhibar r. France
116 H7 Lauri Madh. Prad. India
193 P7 Lauria Italy
262 V2 Laurie Island S. Orkney Is Antarctica
162 G3 Laurière France
146 H13 Laurieston Dumfries and Galloway, Scotland U.K.
83 N4 Laurieton N.S.W. Austr.
231 H8 Laurinburg NC U.S.A.
193 O7 Laurino Italy
161 G9 Lauris France
81 F10 Lauriston South I. N.Z.
226 F2 Laurium MI U.S.A.
194 H2 Lauro Italy
Lauru i. Solomon Is see Choiseul
190 B2 Lausanne Switz.
171 D7 Lausehügel hill Ger.
171 K8 Lausitzer Gebirge hills Ger.
171 I7 Lausitzer Grenzwall park Ger.
171 G7 Laußig Ger.
171 I8 Laußnitz Ger.
161 E7 Laussonne France
163 F6 Laussou France
95 H2 Laut i. Indon.
95 H5 Laut i. Indon.
95 L6 Laut i. Indon.
95 K6 Laut, Selat sea chan. Indon.
171 J8 Lauta Ger.
161 I6 Lautaret, Col du pass France
260 A6 Lautaro Chile
259 B8 Lautaro, Volcán vol. Chile
93 E8 Lautem East Timor
172 E4 Lautenbach Ger.
157 P6 Lauter r. France/Ger.
171 G9 Lauter Ger.
178 A5 Lauterach Austria
173 L3 Lauterach r. Ger.
157 P6 Lauterbourg France
190 D2 Lauterbrunnen Switz.
172 D2 Lauterecken Ger.
173 L3 Lauterhofen Ger.
169 H9 Lautersbach (Hessen) Ger.
172 H4 Lauterstein Ger.
169 K10 Lautertal Ger.
95 K7 Laut Kecil, Kepulauan is Indon.
79 □7a Lautoka Viti Levu Fiji
163 I8 Lautrec France
94 B2 Lauttawar, Danau l. Indon.
140 K4 Lauvsnes Norway
140 T5 Lauvuskylä Fin.
164 J2 Lauwersmeer l. Neth.
163 G7 Lauzerte France
163 H6 Lauzès France
175 J1 Lava r. Rus. Fed.
234 E1 Lava NY U.S.A.
238 D6 Lava Beds National Monument nat. park CA U.S.A.
237 G11 Lavaca r. TX U.S.A.
192 A10 La Vacca, Isola i. Sardegna Italy
182 D1 Lavadoiro, Punta pt Spain
190 G7 Lavagna Italy
190 G7 Lavagne r. Italy
224 F4 Laval Que. Can.
159 J5 Laval France
163 I9 Lavalette France
232 C10 Lavalette WV U.S.A.
161 H10 La Valette-du-Var France
187 E8 La Vall d'Uixó Spain
260 C3 Lavalle Arg.
191 L2 La Valle Italy
179 K6 Lavamünd Austria
122 E8 Lāvān Iran
122 E8 Lāvān i. Iran
78 □6 Lavanggu Rennell Solomon Is
186 H3 Lavansa r. Spain
160 H4 Lavans-lès-St-Claude France
179 K6 Lavant r. Austria/Slovenia
179 K5 Lavanttal val. Austria
258 B5 Lavapié, Punta pt Chile
122 D7 Lāvar Iran
199 H1 Lavara Greece
213 □J4 Lavaraty Madag.
163 E7 Lavardac France
163 F8 Lavardens France
122 F6 Lāvar Meydān salt marsh Iran
161 C6 Lavaudieu France
163 H8 Lavaur France
162 I3 Lavaveix-les-Mines France
240 K5 Laveaga Peak CA U.S.A.
183 J3 La Vecilla Spain
163 D10 Lavedan reg. France
246 H4 La Vega Dom. Rep.
244 D5 La Vega Mex.
182 I2 La Vega Spain
182 I2 La Vega Spain
183 K2 La Vega Cantabria Spain
La Vega Galicia Spain see A Veiga
250 D2 La Vela Venez.
163 H10 Lavelanet France
182 I6 La Vellés Spain
193 P5 Lavello Italy
237 D11 La Venada r. Mex.
190 F4 Lavena Ponte Tresa Italy
151 N3 Lavenham Suffolk, England U.K.
190 F4 Laveno Italy
242 □P10 La Venta Hond.
245 N8 La Venta r. Mex.
156 E2 Laventie France
183 P8 La Ventosa Spain
250 D3 La Venturosa Col.
182 I9 La Vera reg. Spain
260 E4 La Verde Arg.
195 K7 La Verde r. Italy
161 H9 La Verdière France
161 D8 La Vernarède France
237 F7 Laverne OK U.S.A.
150 F5 Lavernock Point Wales
160 G5 La Verpillière France
159 J8 La Verrie France
87 G10 Laverton W.A. Austr.
156 H5 La Veuve France
192 C5 Lavezzi, Îles i. Corse Fra
192 C5 Lavezzi, Réserve Naturel Îles nature res. Corse Fran
141 Q6 Lavia Fin.
193 O6 Laviano Italy
242 H4 La Víbora Mex.
244 G1 La Victoria Mex.
185 J5 La Victoria Spain
247 J8 La Victoria Venez.
181 □ La Victoria de Acentejo Tenerife Canary Is
183 N5 La Vid Spain
227 P4 Lavieille, Lake Ont. Can
227 N3 Lavigne Ont. Can.
192 E3 La Villa Italy
183 N9 La Villa de Don Fadriqu Spain
156 B8 La Ville-aux-Clercs Fra
161 D7 La Villedieu France
161 E7 Lavilledieu France
162 E3 La Villedieu-du-Clain F
157 L8 La Villedieu-en-Fonten France
245 I2 Lavin Mex.
258 D2 La Viña Arg.
250 B6 La Viña Peru
238 J3 Lavina MT U.S.A.
193 J5 Lavinio-Lido di Enea Ita
261 G3 La Violeta Arg.
160 J2 Laviron France
191 K3 Lavìs Italy
163 F8 Lavit France
261 F6 La Vitícola Arg.
157 L7 La Vôge reg. France
Lavongal i. P.N.G. see New Hanover
138 I7 Lavoriškės Lith.
182 C8 Lavos Port.
161 F7 La Voulte-sur-Rhône F
161 C6 Lavoûte-Chilhac France
161 D6 Lavoûte-sur-Loire Fran
257 E4 Lavras Brazil
255 B9 Lavras do Sul Brazil
184 C3 Lavre Port.
184 B3 Lavre r. Port.
120 K1 Lavrent'yevka Kazakh.
198 F5 Lavrio Greece
139 T9 Lavrovo Orlovskaya Obla Rus. Fed.
139 U2 Lavrovo Vologodskaya O Rus. Fed.
215 P3 Lavumisa Swaziland
211 A8 Lavushi-Manda Nation Park Zambia
206 C5 Lawa r. Liberia
96 C2 Lawa Myanmar
123 N5 Lawa Pak.
224 E3 Lawagamau r. Ont. Can
116 I9 Lawan Chhattisgarh Indi
95 L9 Lawang i. Indon.
157 O6 La Wantzenau France
95 K2 Lawas Sarawak Malaysia
224 D2 Lawashi r. Ont. Can.
124 G9 Lawdar Yemen
263 H2 Law Dome ice feature Antarctica
93 C6 Lawele Sulawesi Indon.
146 H9 Lawers Perth and Kinros Scotland U.K.
151 O4 Lawford Essex, England
93 F4 Lawin i. Maluku Indon.
95 J4 Lawit, Gunung mt. Indon./Malaysia
94 E2 Lawit, Gunung mt. Mala
96 C4 Lawksawk Myanmar
226 B6 Lawler IA U.S.A.
86 H3 Lawley r. W.A. Austr.
234 B4 Lawn PA U.S.A.
117 N8 Lawngtlai Mizoram India
84 G5 Lawn Hill Qld Austr.
84 G5 Lawn Hill Creek r. Qld
84 G5 Lawn Hill National Par Qld Austr.
127 K9 Lawqah Saudi Arabia
206 E4 Lawra Ghana
81 D12 Lawrence South I. N.Z.
81 E10 Lawrence r. South I. N.Z
236 H6 Lawrence KS U.S.A.
233 N6 Lawrence MA U.S.A.
231 D8 Lawrenceburg TN U.S.
233 □R3 Lawrence Station N.B.
147 J4 Lawrencetown Norther Ireland U.K.
230 D6 Lawrenceville IL U.S.A.
234 F4 Lawrenceville NJ U.S.A
232 H7 Lawrenceville PA U.S.A
232 H12 Lawrenceville VA U.S.A
87 F9 Lawrence Wells, Moun W.A. Austr.
175 K2 Ławsk Pol.
237 F8 Lawton OK U.S.A.
95 I8 Lawu, Gunung vol. Indo
170 K5 Ławy Pol.
124 B1 Lawz, Jabal al mt. Saudi Arabia
143 K3 Laxå Sweden
182 C2 Laxe Spain
182 C2 Laxe, Cabo de c. Spain
148 I5 Laxey Isle of Man
214 H2 Laxey S. Africa
148 I5 Laxey Bay Isle of Man
146 F6 Laxford, Loch inlet Scotland U.K.
146 F6 Laxford Bridge Highlan Scotland U.K.
222 D4 Lax Kw'alaams B.C. Ca
146 □N2 Laxo Shetland, Scotland
111 G9 Laxong Co l. Xizang Chi
157 L6 Laxou France
140 M5 Laxsjö Sweden
143 K3 Laxsjön l. Sweden
162 B3 Lay r. France
134 L2 Laya r. Rus. Fed.
186 C3 Layana Spain
95 L7 Layar, Tanjung pt Indor
252 C4 La Yarada Peru
134 I1 Laydennyy, Mys c. Rus
93 F7 Layeni Maluku Indon.
244 C4 La Yesca Mex.
124 H4 Laylá Saudi Arabia
128 G7 Layla salt pan Saudi Ara
162 C1 Layon r. France
183 L9 Layos Spain
247 □3 Layou St Vincent
163 F7 Layrac France
75 H2 Laysan Island HI U.S.A
110 F5 Laysu Xinjiang China
234 F2 Layton NJ U.S.A.
240 I2 Laytonville CA U.S.A.
Layturi Georgia see Lai
179 N8 Laz Croatia
108 A5 Laza Myanmar
182 F4 Laza Spain
242 E6 La Zacatosa, Picacho Mex.
183 P4 Lazagurría Spain
261 F5 La Zanja Arg.
217 □2b Lazare, Pointe pt Mahé Seychelles
177 L5 Lăzăreni Romania
100 L2 Lazarev Rus. Fed.
196 I6 Lazarevac Serbia
139 U8 Lazarevo Rus. Fed.
129 A2 Lazarevskoye Rus. Fed
242 B2 Lázaro Cárdenas Baja California Mex.
242 B2 Lázaro Cárdenas Baja California Mex.
245 N9 Lázaro Cárdenas Chiapa
244 E8 Lázaro Cárdenas Michoacán Mex.
177 J3 Lazberci park Hungary
258 G4 Lazcano Uru.
138 G7 Lazdijai Lith.
111 E9 Lazhuglung Xizang Chir
139 R7 Lazinki Rus. Fed.
193 J3 Lazio admin. reg. Italy

Lazise Italy
Łaziska Pol.
Lázně Bělohrad Czech Rep.
Lázně Bohdaneč Czech Rep.
Lázně Kynžvart Czech Rep.
Lazo Arg.
Lazo *Primorskiy Kray* Rus. Fed.
Lazo *Respublika Sakha (Yakutiya)* Rus. Fed.
Lazonby *Cumbria, England* U.K.
La Zorra *watercourse* Mex.
Lazovsk Moldova *see* Sîngerei
Lazuri Romania
Lazuri de Beiuș Romania
Lazurne Ukr.
Łazy Pol.
Lazzarino Arg.
Lazzaro, Monte *hill* Italy
Leacan, Rubha nan *pt Scotland* U.K.
Leach Cambodia
Leach Island *Ont.* Can.
Leacock *PA* U.S.A.
Lead *SD* U.S.A.
Leadburn *Midlothian, Scotland* U.K.
Leadenham *Lincolnshire, England* U.K.
Leader *Sask.* Can.
Leader Heights *PA* U.S.A.
Leader Water *r. Scotland* U.K.
Leadgate *Durham, England* U.K.
Leadhills *South Lanarkshire, Scotland* U.K.
Leadville *N.S.W.* Austr.
Leadville *CO* U.S.A.
Leaf *r. MS* U.S.A.
Leaf Bay *Que.* Can. *see* Tasiujaq
Leaf Rapids *Man.* Can.
Leahy, Cape Antarctica
Leake, Mount *hill W.A.* Austr.
Leakesville *MS* U.S.A.
Leakey *TX* U.S.A.
Leaksville *NC* U.S.A. *see* Eden
Leal, Mount *hill W.A.* Austr.
Leales Arg.
Leamington *Ont.* Can.
Leamington Spa, Royal *Warwickshire, England* U.K.
Le'an *Jiangxi* China
Leandra S. Africa
Leandro N. Alem *Buenos Aires* Arg.
Leandro N. Alem *Misiones* Arg.
Leane, Lough *l.* Ireland
Leanja Madag.
Leányfalu Hungary
Leap Ireland
Learmonth *W.A.* Austr.
Leasingham *Lincolnshire, England* U.K.
Leatherhead *Surrey, England* U.K.
L'Eau d'Heure *l.* Belgium
L'Eau d'Heure *r.* Belgium
Leava Wallis and Futuna Is *see* Sigave
Leavening *North Yorkshire, England* U.K.
Leavenworth *KS* U.S.A.
Leavenworth *WA* U.S.A.
Leavitt Peak *CA* U.S.A.
Leavvajohka Norway
Łeba Pol.
Łeba *r.* Pol.
Łeba *r.* Pol.
Lebach Ger.
Lebak *Mindanao* Phil.
Lebaleng S. Africa
Lébamba Gabon
Lebane Serbia
Lebanon *country* Asia
Lebanon *IN* U.S.A.
Lebanon *KS* U.S.A.
Lebanon *KY* U.S.A.
Lebanon *MO* U.S.A.
Lebanon *NH* U.S.A.
Lebanon *NJ* U.S.A.
Lebanon *OH* U.S.A.
Lebanon *OR* U.S.A.
Lebanon *PA* U.S.A.
Lebanon *TN* U.S.A.
Lebanon *VA* U.S.A.
Lebanon County *county PA* U.S.A.
Le Ban-St-Martin France
Lebap Turkm.
Lebap *admin. div.* Turkm.
Lebap Oblast *admin. div.* Turkm. *see* Lebap
Le Barcarès France
Le Barp France
Lebbeke Belgium
Lebda *tourist site* Libya *see* Leptis Magna
Le Béage France
Le Beausset France
Lebec *CA* U.S.A.
Le Bec-Hellouin France
Lebedin Ukr. *see* Lebedyn
Lebedyan' Rus. Fed.
Lebedyn Ukr.
Lebel-sur-Quévillon *Que.* Can.
Lebendorf Ger.
Le Bény-Bocage France
Lébénymiklós Hungary
Le Bez France
Lebiez France
Lebiolali *well* Eth.
Le Biot France
Le Blanc France
Le Bleymard France
Łebno Pol.
Lebo Dem. Rep. Congo
Lebo *Sulawesi* Indon.
Lebohang S. Africa
Le Bois-d'Oingt France
Le Bois-Plage-en-Ré France
Lebomboberge *hills* Moz. *see* Lebombo Mountains
Lebombo Mountains *hills* Moz.
Lebong *W. Bengal* India
Le Boréon France
Lębork Pol.
Le Boulou France
Le Boupère France
Le Bourg France
Le Bourg-d'Oisans France
Le Bourget-du-Lac France
Le Bourgneuf-la-Forêt France
Le Bouscat France
Le Bousquet-d'Orb France
Lebowakgomo S. Africa
Lebrade Ger.
Le Breuil *Bourgogne* France
Le Breuil *Champagne-Ardenne* France
Le Brévent *mt.* France
Lebrija Spain
Lebring-Sankt Margarethen Austria
Le Brouilh-Monbert France
Le Brûlé Réunion
Le Brusquet France
Łebsko, Jezioro *lag.* Pol.
Lebu Chile
Lebução Port.
Le Bugue France
Le Buisson France
Le Buisson-de-Cadouin France
Lebus Ger.
Lebusa Ger.
Le Busseau France
Leb"yazhe Ukr.
Lebyazhiy, Liman *l.* Rus. Fed.
Lebyazh'ye Kazakh. *see* Akku
Lebyazh'ye *Kirovskaya Oblast'* Rus. Fed.
Lebyazh'ye *Leningradskaya Oblast'* Rus. Fed.
Lebyazh'ye *Lipetskaya Oblast'* Rus. Fed.
Leça da Palmeira Port.
Leça do Bailio Port.
Le Caire Egypt *see* Al Qāhirah
Lecamp, Plateau de France
Le Cannet France
Le Cannet-des-Maures France
158 B5 Le Cap *c.* France
247 □3 Le Carbet Martinique
147 F5 Lecarrow Ireland
161 H10 Le Castellet France
156 G3 Le Cateau-Cambrésis France
156 F3 Le Catelet France
161 C9 Le Caylar France
161 B7 Le Cayrol France
195 O3 Lecce Italy
195 O3 Lecce *prov.* Italy
190 G4 Lecco Italy
190 G4 Lecco *prov.* Italy
190 G4 Lecco, Lago di *l.* Italy
236 I3 Le Center *MN* U.S.A.
186 D5 Lécera Spain
178 B5 Lech Austria
178 C4 Lech *r.* Austria/Ger.
198 C5 Lechaina Greece
161 E6 Le Chambon-Feugerolles France
161 E6 Le Chambon-sur-Lignon France
109 I6 Lechang *Guangdong* China
178 C5 Lechaschau Austria
190 B2 Le Chasseron *mt.* Switz.
162 B4 Le Château-d'Oléron France
160 I5 Le Châtelard France
159 P8 Le Châtelet France
156 E6 Le Châtelet-en-Brie France
173 J6 Lechbruck Ger.
156 H6 Le Chêne France
156 I4 Le Chesne France
160 J4 Le Cheval Blanc *mt.* France
161 I6 Le Cheval Noir *mt.* France
161 E7 Le Cheylard France
161 H6 Le Cheylas France
197 M3 Lechința Romania
197 M4 Lechința *r.* Romania
129 D3 Lech'khumis K'edi *hills* Georgia
151 I4 Lechlade *Gloucestershire, England* U.K.
178 B5 Lechtal *val.* Austria
178 B5 Lechtaler Alpen *mts* Austria
169 F6 Lechtingen (Wallenhorst) Ger.
186 D4 Leciñena Spain
168 G1 Leck Ger.
147 F4 Leckaun Ireland
146 F7 Leckmelm *Highland, Scotland* U.K.
161 C9 Le Clapier France
161 D8 Le Collet-de-Dèze France
237 I10 Lecompte *LA* U.S.A.
158 B5 Le Conquet France
161 I6 Le Corbier France
160 E4 Le Coteau France
156 C5 Le Coudray-St-Germer France
158 I5 Lécousse France
161 D9 Le Crès France
160 E3 Le Creusot France
185 L7 Lecrín Spain
158 F7 Le Croisic France
156 C3 Le Crotoy France
163 F8 Lectoure France
175 K4 Łęczna Pol.
175 H3 Łęczyca Pol.
174 F1 Łęczyce Pol.
168 D4 Leda *r.* Ger.
146 F10 Ledaig *Argyll and Bute, Scotland* U.K.
185 P2 Ledaña Spain
183 O7 Ledanca Spain
94 E3 Ledang, Gunung *mt.* Malaysia
188 F2 Ledava *r.* Slovenia
151 K4 Ledburn *Buckinghamshire, England* U.K.
150 H3 Ledbury *Herefordshire, England* U.K.
165 E7 Lede Belgium
163 F7 Lède *r.* France
176 E2 Ledeč nad Sázavou Czech Rep.
165 D7 Ledegem Belgium
134 I4 Ledengskoye Rus. Fed.
176 D3 Ledenice Czech Rep.
163 I7 Lédergues France
182 I6 Ledesma Spain
163 C9 Ledeuix France
161 D7 Le Devès *mt.* France
247 □3 Le Diamant Martinique
209 C5 Lediba Dem. Rep. Congo
161 E9 Lédignan France
183 K4 Ledigos Spain
134 J2 Ledkovo Rus. Fed.
146 G6 Ledmore *Highland, Scotland* U.K.
134 F2 Ledmozero Rus. Fed.
177 H2 Lednica Slovakia
176 F3 Lednice Czech Rep.
95 H4 Ledo *Kalimantan* Indon.
108 G9 Ledong *Hainan* China
96 I5 Ledong *Hainan* China
160 D4 Le Donjon France
162 G3 Le Dorat France
Ledosus France *see* Lezoux
182 I8 Ledrada Spain
178 C8 Ledro, Lago di *l.* Italy
106 H8 Ledu *Qinghai* China
222 H4 Leduc *Alta* Can.
161 H8 Le Duffre *mt.* France
131 S3 Ledyanaya, Gora *mt.* Rus. Fed.
174 E2 Lędyczek Pol.
174 D1 Lędzin Pol.
175 H5 Lędziny Pol.
147 F9 Lee *r.* Ireland
149 L6 Lee *Lancashire, England* U.K.
233 L6 Lee *MA* U.S.A.
233 □Q3 Lee *ME* U.S.A.
232 F8 Leechburg *PA* U.S.A.
236 H2 Leech Lake *MN* U.S.A.
236 H2 Leech Lake Indian Reservation *res. MN* U.S.A.
149 N6 Leeds *West Yorkshire, England* U.K.
149 N6 Leeds Bradford International *airport England* U.K.
150 B7 Leedstown *Cornwall, England* U.K.
164 J2 Leek Neth.
149 M7 Leek *Staffordshire, England* U.K.
87 C10 Leeman *W.A.* Austr.
149 N5 Leeming *North Yorkshire, England* U.K.
150 D7 Lee Moor *Devon, England* U.K.
147 C5 Leenane Ireland
165 I6 Leende Neth.
164 J2 Leens Neth.
151 J6 Lee-on-the-Solent *Hampshire, England* U.K.
232 F7 Leeper *PA* U.S.A.
168 D4 Leer (Ostfriesland) Ger.
164 H5 Leerdam Neth.
164 H4 Leersum Neth.
163 C10 Lées-Athas France
231 G11 Leesburg *FL* U.S.A.
231 E10 Leesburg *GA* U.S.A.
232 A10 Leesburg *KY* U.S.A.
234 F6 Leesburg *NJ* U.S.A.
232 B9 Leesburg *OH* U.S.A.
232 H9 Leesburg *VA* U.S.A.
169 H5 Leese Ger.
234 D4 Leesport *PA* U.S.A.
236 H6 Lees Summit *MO* U.S.A.
87 F8 Lee Steere Range *hills W.A.* Austr.
81 G10 Leeston *South I.* N.Z.
237 I10 Leesville *LA* U.S.A.
232 F11 Leesville Lake *VA* U.S.A.
83 K6 Leeton *N.S.W.* Austr.
215 K3 Leeudoringstad S. Africa
214 F8 Leeu-Gamka S. Africa
215 J4 Leeukop *mt.* S. Africa
215 L5 Leeurivierdam *l.* S. Africa
214 F8 Leeuw *r.* S. Africa
164 I2 Leeuwarden Neth.
87 C13 Leeuwin, Cape *W.A.* Austr.
87 C12 Leeuwin-Naturaliste National Park *W.A.* Austr.
240 M4 Lee Vining *CA* U.S.A.
247 K4 Leeward Islands Caribbean Sea
Leeward Islands *Arch. de la Société* Fr. Polynesia *see* Sous le Vent, Îles
170 D3 Leezen *Mecklenburg-Vorpommern* Ger.
168 J3 Leezen *Schleswig-Holstein* Ger.
158 C5 Le Faou France
158 E5 Le Faouët France
163 G9 Le Fauga France
197 N7 Lefedzha *r.* Bulg.
158 H8 Le Fenouiller France
156 D1 Leffrinckoucke France
208 B5 Léfini, Réserve de Chasse de la *nature res.* Congo
128 A3 Lefka Cyprus
198 B4 Lefkada *Lefkada* Greece
198 B4 Lefkada *i.* Greece
198 E7 Lefka Ori *mts Kriti* Greece
Lefkás *Lefkada* Greece *see* Lefkada
Lefke Cyprus *see* Lefka
198 B3 Lefkimmi *Kerkyra* Greece
Lefkoniko Cyprus *see* Lefkonikon
128 B3 Lefkonikon Cyprus
198 E4 Lefkonisia *i.* Greece
Lefkoșa Cyprus *see* Lefkosia
128 B3 Lefkosia Cyprus
163 E6 Le Fleix France
158 C4 Le Folgoët France
156 F3 Leforest France
163 G9 Le Fossat France
163 G9 Le Fousseret France
247 □3 Le François Martinique
225 G1 Lefroy *r. Que.* Can.
87 G11 Lefroy, Lake *salt flat W.A.* Austr.
161 J8 Le Fugeret France
159 I7 Le Fuilet France
175 J5 Łęg *r.* Pol.
78 □3a Legan *i. Kwajalein* Marshall Is
183 M8 Leganés Spain
183 O8 Leganiel Spain
224 C3 Legarde *r. Ont.* Can.
92 D5 Legaspi *Luzon* Phil.
173 I6 Legau Ger.
156 B7 Le Gault-St-Denis France
156 G6 Le Gault-Soigny France
186 A1 Legazpi Spain
170 E5 Legde Ger.
169 D6 Legden Ger.
158 H8 Legé France
163 B6 Lège-Cap-Ferret France
86 D6 Legendre Island *W.A.* Austr.
159 J5 Le Genest-St-Isle France
83 K9 Legges Tor *mt. Tas.* Austr.
240 I2 Leggett *CA* U.S.A.
147 G3 Leggs *Northern Ireland* U.K.
Leghorn Italy *see* Livorno
175 I3 Legionowo Pol.
165 I9 Léglise Belgium
191 K5 Legnago Italy
190 F4 Legnano Italy
174 E4 Legnica Pol.
174 E4 Legnickie Pole Pol.
190 G3 Legnone, Monte *mt.* Italy
Legohli *N.W.T.* Can. *see* Norman Wells
162 E4 Le Gond-Pontouvre France
247 □2 Le Gosier Guadeloupe
174 G1 Łęgowo Pol.
179 O7 Legrad Croatia
240 L4 Le Grand *CA* U.S.A.
87 F13 Le Grand, Cape *W.A.* Austr.
217 □1c Le Grand Bénare *mt.* Réunion
160 I5 Le Grand-Bornand France
162 H3 Le Grand-Bourg France
161 J8 Le Grand Coyer *mt.* France
160 H4 Le Grand Crêt d'Eau *mt.* France
161 G6 Le Grand-Lemps France
159 L6 Le Grand-Lucé France
160 J5 Le Grand Mont *mt.* France
159 M8 Le Grand-Pressigny France
156 B5 Le Grand-Quevilly France
161 G6 Le Grand-Serre France
160 I3 Le Grand Taureau *mt.* France
161 H7 Le Grand Veymont *mt.* France
161 E9 Le Grau-du-Roi France
217 □1c Le Gros Morne *mt.* Réunion
159 M3 Le Gros Theil France
161 H6 Le Gua France
252 C5 Leguena Chile
158 E4 Léguer *r.* France
163 G8 Léguevin France
208 E4 Leguga Dem. Rep. Congo
261 H2 Leguizamón Arg.
84 B3 Legune *N.T.* Austr.
183 O3 Legutiano Spain
208 E4 Legwe *r.* Dem. Rep. Congo
96 C4 Le-gya Myanmar
116 F2 Leh Jammu and Kashmir
157 J8 Le Haut du Sec *hill* France
159 L2 Le Havre France
168 H2 Lehe Ger.
171 D10 Lehesten Ger.
241 U1 Lehi *UT* U.S.A.
234 E3 Lehigh *r. PA* U.S.A.
234 D3 Lehigh County *county PA* U.S.A.
234 D3 Lehighton *PA* U.S.A.
197 O6 Lehliu-Gară Romania
215 M6 Lehlohonolo S. Africa
261 G2 Lehmann Arg.
169 D10 Lehmen Ger.
168 J2 Lehmkuhlen Ger.
171 F9 Lehndorf Ger.
176 G3 Lehnice Slovakia
171 G6 Lehnin Ger.
170 H5 Lehnitz Ger.
157 N7 Le Hohwald France
158 G5 Léhon France
159 K5 Le Horps France
177 G3 Lehota Slovakia
163 D8 Le Houga France
173 J3 Lehrberg Ger.
169 K6 Lehre Ger.
169 I6 Lehrte Ger.
170 D4 Lehsen Ger.
140 Q5 Lehtimäki Fin.
240 □A11 Lehua *i. HI* U.S.A.
212 D4 Lehututu Botswana
192 B7 Lei *Sardegna* Italy
123 N6 Leiah Pak.
198 D4 Leianokladi Greece
172 G5 Leibertingen Ger.
173 M4 Leiblfing Ger.
179 M6 Leibnitz Austria
108 D4 Leibo *Sichuan* China
171 I6 Leibsch Ger.
151 J2 Leicester *Leicester, England* U.K.
151 J2 Leicester *admin. div. England* U.K.
151 K2 Leicestershire *admin. div. England* U.K.
84 G4 Leichhardt *r. Qld* Austr.
84 G5 Leichhardt Falls *Qld* Austr.
85 K6 Leichhardt Range *mts Qld* Austr.
169 D8 Leichlingen (Rheinland) Ger.
164 G4 Leiden Neth.
164 G4 Leiderdorp Neth.
164 F4 Leidschendam Neth.
165 E6 Leie *r.* Belgium
138 J3 Leie Estonia
169 J6 Leiferde Ger.
82 G3 Leigh *watercourse S.A.* Austr.
80 I3 Leigh *North I.* N.Z.
149 L7 Leigh *Greater Manchester, England* U.K.
150 H3 Leigh *Worcestershire, England* U.K.
82 G4 Leigh Creek *S.A.* Austr.
147 I7 Leighlinbridge Ireland
151 K4 Leighton Buzzard *Bedfordshire, England* U.K.
141 I6 Leikanger Norway
96 C5 Leiktho Myanmar
172 F3 Leimen Ger.
164 G4 Leimuiden Neth.
173 K3 Leinburg Ger.
169 I5 Leine *r.* Ger.
169 J8 Leinefelde Ger.
172 G4 Leinfelden-Echterdingen Ger.
190 D5 Leinì Italy
87 F10 Leinster *W.A.* Austr.
147 I6 Leinster *reg.* Ireland
147 I7 Leinster, Mount *hill* Ireland
172 H4 Leinzell Ger.
183 O2 Leioa Spain
138 G7 Leipalingis Lith.
173 I5 Leipheim Ger.
140 P3 Leipojärvi Sweden
234 D6 Leipsic *DE* U.S.A.
232 B7 Leipsic *OH* U.S.A.
234 E6 Leipsic *r. DE* U.S.A.
199 H5 Leipsoi *i.* Greece
171 F8 Leipzig Ger.
171 G8 Leipzig *admin. reg.* Ger.
171 F8 Leipzig-Halle *airport* Ger.
140 J5 Leira *Møre og Romsdal* Norway
141 J6 Leira *Oppland* Norway
182 D4 Leirado Spain
140 M3 Leiranger Norway
160 C6 Leiranoux *mt.* France
140 Q1 Leirbotn Norway
182 C9 Leiria Port.
182 C9 Leiria *admin. dist.* Port.
182 D4 Leiro Spain
182 C8 Leirosa Port.
142 B2 Leirvik Norway
178 G6 Leisach Austria
179 N2 Leiser Berge *park* Austria
108 G5 Leishan *Guizhou* China
109 I5 Lei Shui *r.* China
138 F3 Leisi Estonia
84 B7 Leisler, Mount *hill N.T.* Austr.
82 C3 Leisler Hills *S.A.* Austr.
171 G8 Leisnig Ger.
151 P3 Leiston *Suffolk, England* U.K.
182 H3 Leitariegos, Puerto de *pass* Spain
230 D7 Leitchfield *KY* U.S.A.
149 K2 Leith *Edinburgh, Scotland* U.K.
179 O4 Leithagebirge *hills* Austria
81 G10 Leithfield *South I.* N.Z.
151 L5 Leith Hill *England* U.K.
147 F4 Leitrim *county* Ireland
186 B1 Leitza Spain
173 L6 Leitzach *r.* Ger.
171 E6 Leitzkau Ger.
141 S6 Leivonmäki Fin.
172 B2 Leiwen Ger.
147 J6 Leixlip Ireland
Leiyang *Anhui* China *see* Wangjiang
109 I5 Leiyang *Hunan* China
108 H8 Leizhou *Guangdong* China
108 G8 Leizhou Bandao *pen.* China
108 H8 Leizhou Wan *b.* China
143 K1 Lejberget *hill* Sweden
164 G5 Lek *r.* Neth.
140 K4 Leka Norway
140 K4 Leka *i.* Norway
208 B5 Lékana Congo
177 L3 Lekárovce Slovakia
208 D5 Lekatero Dem. Rep. Congo
175 H6 Łękawica Pol.
205 H1 Le Kef Tunisia
189 B8 Le Kef *admin. div.* Tunisia
183 P2 Lekeitio Spain
208 B5 Lékéti *r.* Congo
215 K9 Lekfontein S. Africa
Lekhainá Greece *see* Lechaina
206 C2 Lekhcheb Maur.
139 N6 Lekhovo Rus. Fed.
208 B5 Lékila Gabon
93 D4 Lekitobi *Maluku* Indon.
214 B5 Lekkersing S. Africa
174 C4 Łęknica Pol.
206 C3 Léko Mali
140 L2 Lekoes Norway
207 I6 Lékoli-Pandaka, Réserve de Faune de la *nature res.* Congo
208 B5 Lékoni Gabon
209 B5 Lékoumou *admin. reg.* Congo
174 D2 Lekowo Pol.
143 L1 Leksand Sweden
Lek'suiri Georgia *see* Lentekhi
93 E5 Leksula *Buru* Indon.
Leksura Georgia *see* Lentekhi
140 K5 Leksvik Norway
186 B1 Lekunberri Spain
93 F3 Lelai, Tanjung *pt Halmahera* Indon.
247 □3 Le Lamentin Martinique
140 L3 Leland Norway
226 F8 Leland *IL* U.S.A.
226 I4 Leland *MI* U.S.A.
237 J9 Leland *MS* U.S.A.
142 I2 Lelång *l.* Sweden
162 C3 Le Langon France
162 G5 Le Lardin-St-Lazare France
161 I8 Le Lauzet-Ubaye France
161 I10 Le Lavandou France
259 C6 Leleque Arg.
177 L3 Leles Slovakia
177 L6 Lelese Romania
136 H2 Leleta Ukr.
163 C8 Le Leuy France
Leli *Guangxi* China *see* Tianlin
78 □6 Leli *i.* Solomon Is
175 H3 Lelice Pol.
188 G4 Lelija *mt.* Bos.-Herz.
107 O8 Leling *Shandong* China
93 G5 Lelinta *Papua* Indon.
159 J6 Le Lion-d'Angers France
175 J2 Lelis Pol.
175 I1 Lelkowo Pol.
190 B1 Le Locle Switz.
93 C8 Lelogama *Timor* Indon.
158 I7 Le Loroux-Bottereau France
247 □3 Le Lorrain Martinique
206 B4 Lélouma Guinea
159 J6 Le Louroux-Béconnais France
175 H5 Lelów Pol.
161 I10 Le Luc France
159 L6 Le Lude France
161 B6 Le Luguet *mt.* France
251 H3 Lelydorp Suriname
164 H3 Lelystad Neth.
259 D9 Le Maire, Estrecho de *sea chan.* Arg.
161 C7 Le Malzieu-Ville France
190 A3 Léman, Lac *l.* France/Switz.
159 L5 Le Mans France
247 □3 Le Marin Martinique
157 N8 Le Markstein France
236 G4 Le Mars *IA* U.S.A.
161 E8 Le Martinet France
163 E7 Le Mas-d'Agenais France
163 G9 Le Mas-d'Azil France
210 D3 Lema Shilindi Eth.
163 J8 Le Masnau-Massuguiès France
161 C8 Le Massegros France
160 D4 Le Mayet-de-Montagne France
262 T2 LeMay Range *mts* Antarctica
159 J7 Le May-sur-Èvre France
179 I2 Lembach im Mühlkreis Austria
211 C6 Lembai *well* Tanz.
95 L9 Lembar *Lombok* Indon.
93 D3 Lembeh *i.* Indon.
165 E6 Lembeke Belgium
157 N5 Lemberg France
172 D3 Lemberg Ger.
172 F5 Lemberg *mt.* Ger.
Lemberg Ukr. *see* L'viv
163 D9 Lembeye France
163 G7 Lemboulas *r.* France
163 F6 Lembras France
168 F5 Lembruch Ger.
95 L3 Lembu *Kalimantan* Indon.
94 B2 Lembu, Gunung *mt.* Indon.
95 L2 Lembubut *Kalimantan* Indon.
Lemdiyya Alg. *see* Médéa
256 D5 Leme Brazil
164 J4 Lemele Neth.
164 J4 Lemelerveld Neth.
159 L4 Le Mêle-sur-Sarthe France
210 E3 Lemem Bar YeWha Gudgwad *well* Eth.
159 L4 Le Merlerault France
161 G7 Le Merlu Rocher *mt.* France
177 K3 Lemešany Slovakia
139 O6 Lemeshi Rus. Fed.
137 K1 Lemeshivka Ukr.
156 H6 Le Mesnil-sur-Oger France
128 B4 Lemesos Cyprus
169 F6 Lemförde Ger.
169 G6 Lemgo Ger.
238 H4 Lemhi *r. ID* U.S.A.
238 H4 Lemhi Range *mts ID* U.S.A.
141 S6 Lemi Fin.
174 C3 Lemierzyce Pol.
221 L3 Lemieux Islands *Nunavut* Can.
141 P6 Lemland *Åland* Fin.
140 R2 Lemmenjoen kansallispuisto *nat. park* Fin.
164 I3 Lemmer Neth.
236 D3 Lemmon *SD* U.S.A.
241 V9 Lemmon, Mount *AZ* U.S.A.
Lemnos *i.* Greece *see* Limnos
214 E9 Lemoenshoek S. Africa
159 J3 Le Molay-Littry France
160 I4 Le Môle *mt.* France
190 C2 Le Moleson *mt.* Switz.
246 G4 Le Môle St-Nicolas Haiti
161 C7 Le Monastier France
161 D7 Le Monastier-sur-Gazeille France
240 M5 Lemoncove *CA* U.S.A.
161 J7 Le Monêtier-les-Bains France
240 O9 Lemon Grove *CA* U.S.A.
226 F8 Lemont *IL* U.S.A.
78 □5 Le Mont-Dore New Caledonia
160 C4 Le Montet France
158 H4 Le Mont-St-Michel *tourist site* France
240 M5 Lemoore *CA* U.S.A.
217 □1b Le Morne Brabant *pen.* Mauritius
247 □3 Le Morne-Rouge Martinique
78 □4a Lemotol Bay *Chuuk* Micronesia
247 □2 Le Moule Guadeloupe
161 D7 Le Moure de la Gardille *mt.* France
161 I7 Le Mourre Froid *mt.* France
225 G1 Le Moyne, Lac *l. Que.* Can.
141 Q6 Lempäälä Fin.
160 C5 Lempdes *Auvergne* France
161 C6 Lempdes *Auvergne* France
96 A4 Lemro *r.* Myanmar
134 L3 Lemtybozh Rus. Fed.
95 H4 Lemukutan *i.* Indon.
193 Q5 Le Murge *hills* Italy
161 J10 Le Muy France
134 M2 Lemva *r.* Rus. Fed.
142 E5 Lemvig Denmark
168 G4 Lemwerder Ger.
147 G8 Lemybrien Ireland
96 B6 Lemyethna Myanmar
134 L3 Lem'yu *r.* Rus. Fed.
142 G1 Lena Norway
182 C9 Lena *r.* Port.
131 N3 Lena *r.* Rus. Fed.
226 E7 Lena *IL* U.S.A.
226 F5 Lena *WI* U.S.A.
147 D4 Lenadoon Point Ireland
78 □5 Lénakel Vanuatu
95 L9 Lenangguar *Sumbawa* Indon.
179 M6 Lenart Slovenia
138 E5 Lēnas Latvia
177 J6 Lenauheim Romania
162 E2 Lencloître France
254 E2 Lençóis Maranhenses, Parque Nacional dos *nat. park* Brazil
256 C5 Lençóis Paulista Brazil
163 D7 Lencouacq France
178 H5 Lend Austria
208 F4 Lenda *r.* Dem. Rep. Congo
177 J2 Lendak Slovakia
188 F2 Lendava Slovenia
122 D6 Lendeh Iran
165 D7 Lendelede Belgium
134 E3 Lendery Rus. Fed.
191 L5 Lendinara Italy
179 H6 Lendorf Austria
148 C6 Lene, Lough *l.* Ireland
176 C1 Lenešice Czech Rep.
159 M3 Le Neubourg France
178 H3 Lengau *Oberösterreich* Austria
178 G5 Lengau *Salzburg* Austria
122 H7 Lengbarūt Iran
173 M5 Lengdorf Ger.
169 J6 Lengede Ger.
171 H9 Lengefeld Ger.
171 F9 Lengenfeld Ger.
169 J8 Lengenfeld unterm Stein Ger.
173 J6 Lengenwang Ger.
121 M6 Lenger Kazakh.
168 E5 Lengerich *Niedersachsen* Ger.
169 E6 Lengerich *Nordrhein-Westfalen* Ger.
173 L6 Lenggries Ger.
110 K7 Lenghuzhen *Qinghai* China
106 G7 Lenglong Ling *mts* China
190 C1 Lengnau Switz.
208 C5 Lengoué *r.* Congo
109 H5 Lengshuijiang *Hunan* China
109 H5 Lengshuitan *Hunan* China
260 B2 Lengua de Vaca, Punta *pt* Chile
211 B8 Lengwe National Park Malawi
177 G5 Lengyeltóti Hungary
151 N5 Lenham *Kent, England* U.K.
234 D3 Lenhartsville *PA* U.S.A.
143 L5 Lenhovda Sweden
192 B9 Leni *r.* Italy
129 H5 Lenin Azer.
Lenīn Kazakh. *see* Kazygurt
123 M2 Lenin Tajik.
Lenin, Qullai *mt.* Kyrg./Tajik. *see* Lenin Peak
129 F2 Lenina, Kanal *canal* Rus. Fed.
Lenina, Pik *mt.* Kyrg./Tajik. *see* Lenin Peak
Leninabad Tajik. *see* Khŭjand
Leninabad Oblast *admin. div.* Tajik. *see* Soghd
Leninakan Armenia *see* Gyumri
Lenin Atyndagy Choku *mt.* Kyrg./Tajik. *see* Lenin Peak
137 L6 Lenine *Mykolayivs'ka Oblast'* Ukr.
137 O8 Lenine *Respublika Krym* Ukr.
157 M6 Léning France
Leningori Georgia *see* Akhalgori
Leningrad Rus. Fed. *see* Sankt-Peterburg
123 N2 Leningrad Tajik.
Leningrad Oblast *admin. div.* Rus. Fed. *see* Leningradskaya Oblast'
135 G7 Leningradskaya Rus. Fed.
139 P2 Leningradskaya Oblast' *admin. div.* Rus. Fed.
131 S3 Leningradskiy Rus. Fed.
Leningradskiy Tajik. *see* Leningrad
137 K2 Leninivka Ukr.
129 I3 Leninkent Rus. Fed.
100 I6 Lenino Rus. Fed.
Lenino Ukr. *see* Lenine
Leninobod Tajik. *see* Khŭjand
Leninobod Uzbek. *see* Qanliko'l
Leninogor Kazakh. *see* Leninogorsk
121 T2 Leninogorsk Kazakh.
135 K5 Leninogorsk Rus. Fed.
121 O8 Lenin Peak Kyrg./Tajik.
121 N6 Leninpol' Kyrg.
Leninsk Kazakh. *see* Baykonyr
135 I6 Leninsk Rus. Fed.
Leninsk Turkm. *see* Akdepe
Leninsk Uzbek. *see* Asaka
137 N6 Lenins'ke *Dnipropetrovs'ka Oblast'* Ukr.
137 N8 Lenins'ke *Respublika Krym* Ukr.
137 O8 Lenins'ke *Respublika Krym* Ukr.
120 G3 Leninskiy Kazakh.
139 U7 Leninskiy Rus. Fed.
130 J4 Leninsk-Kuznetskiy Rus. Fed.
Leninskoye *Yuzhnyy Kazakhstan* Kazakh. *see* Kazygurt
120 C3 Leninskoye *Zapadnyy Kazakhstan* Kazakh.
134 I4 Leninskoye *Kirovskaya Oblast'* Rus. Fed.
100 H5 Leninskoye *Yevreyskaya Avtonomnaya Oblast'* Rus. Fed.
163 D7 Le Nizan France
190 C3 Lenk Switz.
136 G4 Lenkivtsi Ukr.
Lenkoran' Azer. *see* Länkäran
86 H4 Lennard *r. W.A.* Austr.
169 I7 Lenne Ger.
169 D8 Lenne *r.* Ger.
169 F8 Lennestadt Ger.
172 G4 Lenningen Ger.
259 D9 Lennox, Isla *i.* Chile
263 L1 Lennox-King Glacier Antarctica
146 H11 Lennoxtown *East Dunbartonshire, Scotland* U.K.
190 I5 Leno Italy
231 G8 Lenoir *NC* U.S.A.
231 E8 Lenoir City *TN* U.S.A.
190 B1 Le Noirmont Switz.
193 K5 Lenola Italy
232 C11 Lenore *WV* U.S.A.
223 J4 Lenore Lake *Sask.* Can.
156 G3 Le Nouvion-en-Thiérache France
233 L6 Lenox *MA* U.S.A.
165 E7 Lens Belgium
156 E3 Lens France
168 K2 Lensahn Ger.
131 M3 Lensk Rus. Fed.
160 G4 Lent France
164 I5 Lent Neth.
129 D3 Lentekhi Georgia
168 I3 Lentföhrden Ger.
176 F5 Lenti Hungary
191 M3 Lentiai Italy
173 K4 Lenting Ger.
195 I9 Lentini *Sicilia* Italy
195 I9 Lentini *r. Sicilia* Italy
140 T4 Lentua *l.* Fin.
Lentvaravas Lith. *see* Lentvaris
138 I7 Lentvaris Lith.
139 T3 Lent'yevo Rus. Fed.
240 O7 Lenwood *CA* U.S.A.
97 D9 Lenya Myanmar
190 E1 Lenzburg Switz.
170 D4 Lenzen Ger.
179 I4 Lenzing Austria
172 E6 Lenzkirch Ger.
206 E4 Léo Burkina
191 J7 Leo *r.* Italy
179 I6 Leoben *Kärnten* Austria
179 L5 Leoben *Steiermark* Austria
179 N3 Leobendorf Austria
179 N4 Leobersdorf Austria
Leodhais, Eilean *i. Scotland* U.K. *see* Lewis, Isle of
246 G4 Léogane Haiti
178 G5 Leogang Austria
178 G5 Leoganger Steinberge *mts* Austria
163 C6 Léognan France
93 B3 Leok *Sulawesi* Indon.
236 F3 Leola *SD* U.S.A.
150 G3 Leominster *Herefordshire, England* U.K.
233 N6 Leominster *MA* U.S.A.
163 B8 Léon France
244 F4 León Mex.
242 □P11 León Nic.
182 I3 León Spain
182 I3 León *prov.* Spain
236 I5 Leon *IA* U.S.A.
237 G10 Leon *r. TX* U.S.A.
163 B8 Léon, Étang de *l.* France
184 G8 León, Isla de *i.* Spain
182 G4 León, Montes de *mts* Spain
237 G9 Leonard *TX* U.S.A.
193 I4 Leonardo da Vinci *airport* Italy
232 I10 Leonardtown *MD* U.S.A.
212 C4 Leonardville Namibia
Leonarisso Cyprus *see* Leonarisson
128 C3 Leonarisson Cyprus
243 P7 Leona Vicario Mex.
172 G4 Leonberg Ger.
161 G7 Léoncel France
Leondárion Greece *see* Leontari
179 J3 Leonding Austria
78 □2 Leone American Samoa
190 E3 Leone, Monte *mt.* Italy/Switz.
261 F3 Leones Arg.
193 J2 Leonessa Italy
194 G8 Leonforte *Sicilia* Italy
83 J8 Leongatha *Vic.* Austr.
192 G2 Leoni, Monte *hill* Italy
198 D5 Leonidio Greece
100 M4 Leonidovo *Sakhalin* Rus. Fed.
87 F10 Leonora *W.A.* Austr.
198 D3 Leontari Greece
117 M6 Leopani Bhutan
86 I5 Leopold *r. W.A.* Austr.
232 E9 Leopold *WV* U.S.A.
86 H5 Leopold Downs *W.A.* Austr.
86 H4 Leopold Downs Aboriginal Reserve *W.A.* Austr.
Léopold II, Lac *l.* Dem. Rep. Congo *see* Mai-Ndombe, Lac
257 F4 Leopoldina Brazil
256 C2 Leopoldo de Bulhões Brazil
165 H6 Leopoldsburg Belgium
179 O3 Leopoldsdorf im Marchfelde Austria
170 I3 Leopoldshagen Ger.
169 G6 Leopoldshöhe Ger.
172 D5 Leopoldskanal *canal* Ger.
Léopoldville Dem. Rep. Congo *see* Kinshasa
236 E6 Leoti *KS* U.S.A.
136 H7 Leova Moldova
223 J4 Leoville *Sask.* Can.
Leovo Moldova *see* Leova
158 E7 Le Palais France
162 G4 Le Palais-sur-Vienne France
158 I7 Le Pallet France
94 G6 Lepar *i.* Indon.
156 D3 Le Parcq France
163 F7 Le Passage France
156 G7 Le Pavillon-Ste-Julie France
260 B3 Lepe Chile
184 E6 Lepe Spain
161 F6 Le Péage-de-Roussillon France
162 H2 Le Pêchereau France
Lepel' Belarus *see* Lyepyel'
158 H7 Le Pellerin France
198 C4 Lepenou Greece
161 H7 Le Périer France
163 J11 Le Perthus France
159 I5 Le Pertre France
156 B5 Le Petit-Quevilly France
213 E4 Lephalale S. Africa
212 E4 Lephepe Botswana
215 J6 Lephoi S. Africa
162 C6 Le Pian-Médoc France
159 L4 Le Pin-au-Haras France
156 H6 L'Épine *Champagne-Ardenne* France
161 H8 L'Épine *Provence-Alpes-Côte d'Azur* France
109 K4 Leping *Jiangxi* China
159 M5 Le Pin-la-Garenne France
217 □1c Le Piton Réunion
162 E5 Le Pizou France
163 G9 Le Plan France
156 E5 Le Plessis-Belleville France
134 M3 Lep'lya *r.* Rus. Fed.
161 H8 Le Poët France
188 F2 Lepoglava Croatia
159 O8 Le Poinçonnet France
158 H8 Le Poiré-sur-Vie France
160 H5 Le Pont-de-Beauvoisin France
161 H6 Le Pont-de-Claix France
161 D8 Le Pont-de-Monvert France
161 F9 Le Pontet France
190 E3 Lepontine, Alpi *mts* Italy/Switz.
195 M3 Leporano Italy
163 B6 Le Porge France
163 B6 Le Porge-Océan France
217 □1c Le Port Réunion
156 C2 Le Portel France
196 I7 Leposavić *Kosovo* Serbia
217 □1b Le Pouce *hill* Mauritius
161 D9 Le Pouget France
158 D6 Le Pouldu France
158 G7 Le Pouliguen France
161 F7 Le Pouzin France
140 R5 Leppävesi Fin.
140 S5 Leppävirta Fin.
161 I10 Le Pradet France
225 H4 Lepreau, Point *N.B.* Can.
247 □3 Le Prêcheur Martinique
Lepsa Kazakh. *see* Lepsy
Lepsa *r.* Kazakh. *see* Lepsy
177 H4 Lepsény Hungary
Lepsi Kazakh. *see* Lepsinsk
121 S5 Lepsinsk Kazakh.
121 R4 Lepsy Kazakh.
121 R4 Lepsy *r.* Kazakh.
202 B1 Leptis Magna *tourist site* Libya
198 D2 Leptokarya Greece
156 C7 Le Puiset France
161 D6 Le Puy-en-Velay France
159 K7 Le Puy-Notre-Dame France
161 G9 Le Puy-Ste-Réparade France
206 B2 Leqçeïba Maur.
156 G3 Le Quesnoy France
206 D4 Léraba *r.* Burkina/Côte d'Ivoire
156 E6 Le Raincy France
213 E4 Lerala Botswana
163 H10 Léran France
215 L4 Leratswana S. Africa
194 F8 Lercara Friddi *Sicilia* Italy
83 J7 Lerderderg State Park *nature res. Vic.* Austr.
245 L7 Lerdo Mex.
208 B2 Léré Chad
160 B2 Léré France
206 D3 Léré Mali
207 H4 Lere Nigeria
93 A4 Lereh, Tanjung *pt* Indon.
158 C5 Le Relecq-Kerhuon France
182 C4 Lérez *r.* Spain
158 H5 Le Rheu France
190 H7 Lerici Italy
250 D5 Lérida Col.
Lérida Spain *see* Lleida
Lérida *prov. Cataluña* Spain *see* Lleida
129 J7 Lerik Azer.
183 Q4 Lerín Spain
161 K9 Lérins, Îles de *is* France
243 N8 Lerma Mex.
244 E5 Lerma *r.* Mex.
183 M4 Lerma Spain
245 H6 Lerma de Vilada Mex.
163 D7 Lerm-et Musset France
129 D1 Lermontov Rus. Fed.
100 I5 Lermontovka Rus. Fed.
Lermontovskiy Rus. Fed. *see* Lermontov
178 C5 Lermoos Austria
192 C6 Lerno, Monte *mt.* Italy
247 □3 Le Robert Martinique
160 J5 Le Roignais *mt.* France
199 H5 Leros *i.* Greece
163 I6 Le Rouget France
157 K6 Lérouville France
226 F9 Le Roy *IL* U.S.A.
226 B6 Le Roy *MN* U.S.A.
232 H6 Le Roy *NY* U.S.A.
234 B1 Leroy *PA* U.S.A.
224 F1 Le Roy, Lac *l. Que.* Can.
161 C8 Le Rozier France
157 L7 Lerrain France
190 E7 Lerrone *r.* Italy
142 I4 Lerum Sweden
160 J2 Le Russey France
146 □N2 Lerwick *Shetland, Scotland* U.K.
208 E2 Ler Zerai *well* Sudan
163 F10 Lés Spain
190 F4 Lesa Italy
160 H5 Les Abrets France
247 □2 Les Abymes Guadeloupe
178 G6 Lesachtal *val.* Austria
161 J9 Les Adrets-de-l'Estérel France
186 J4 Les Agudes *mt.* Spain
160 B2 Les Aix-d'Angillon France
186 B1 Lesaka Spain
163 J11 Les Albères *reg.* France
160 B5 Les Ancizes-Comps France
156 B5 Les Andelys France
161 F9 Les Angles *Languedoc-Roussillon* France
163 I10 Les Angles *Languedoc-Roussillon* France
247 □3 Les Anses-d'Arlets Martinique
159 L4 Le Sap France
161 I10 Les Arcs *Provence-Alpes-Côte d'Azur* France
160 J5 Les Arcs *Rhône-Alpes* France
159 J8 Les Aubiers France
161 J8 Le Sauze-Super-Sauze France
186 G4 Les Avellanes Spain
160 H5 Les Avenières France
217 □1c Les Avirons Réunion
161 D8 Les Bondons France
156 D8 Les Bordes France
163 G9 Les Bordes-sur-Arize France
186 G4 Les Borges Blanques Spain
186 H5 Les Borges del Camp Spain
Lesbos *i.* Greece *see* Lesvos
160 H4 Les Bouchoux France
190 B1 Les Brenets Switz.
149 N3 Lesbury *Northumberland, England* U.K.
163 H10 Les Cabannes France
186 L3 L'Escala Spain
161 I8 L'Escale France
217 □1b L'Escalier Mauritius
163 I9 Les Cammazes France
163 D9 Lescar France
161 K9 L'Escarène France
160 J4 Les Carroz-d'Arâches France
186 G6 Les Cases d'Alcanar Spain
246 G4 Les Cayes Haiti
179 J7 Lesce Slovenia
159 K5 Les Coëvrons *hills* France
158 C6 Lesconil France
160 J5 Les Contamines-Montjoie France
160 J4 Les Cornettes de Bise *mts* France/Switz.
187 F7 Les Coves de Vinromà Spain
163 I8 Lescure-d'Albigeois France
161 I6 Les Deux-Alpes France
190 C3 Les Diablerets Switz.
190 C3 Les Diablerets *mts* Switz.
208 D4 Lese *r.* Dem. Rep. Congo
195 L5 Lese *r.* Italy
161 H6 Les Échelles France
158 H3 Les Écréhou *is* Channel Is
162 D5 Les Églisottes-et-Chalaures France
161 J8 Le Seignus-d'Allos France
158 H6 Le Sel-de-Bretagne France
163 C7 Le Sen France
176 G5 Lesencetomaj Hungary
190 A2 Le Sentier Switz.
157 K5 Les Éparges France
159 J8 Les Epesses France
186 I2 Les Escaldes Andorra
225 G3 Les Escoumins *Que.* Can.
160 G3 Les Essards-Taignevaux France
158 I8 Les Essarts France
233 □Q1 Les Étroits *Que.* Can.
186 H3 Le Seu d'Urgell Spain
163 G6 Les Eyzies-de-Tayac-Sireuil France
160 J2 Les Fins France
157 L7 Les Forges France
160 I3 Les Fourgs France
160 J4 Les Gets France
108 D4 Leshan *Sichuan* China
157 I4 Les Hautes-Rivières France
137 P2 Leshchinka *r.* Rus. Fed.
162 B2 Les Herbiers France
Leshou *Hebei* China *see* Xianxian
160 J5 Les Houches France
134 I2 Leshukonskoye Rus. Fed.
129 D3 Lesichine Georgia
179 M7 Lesično Slovenia
156 E6 Lésigny France
190 G6 Lesima, Monte *mt.* Italy
193 O4 Lesina Italy
193 O4 Lesina, Lago di *lag.* Italy
161 J10 Les Issambres France
141 J5 Lesja Norway
143 K2 Lesjöfors Sweden
163 G6 Les Junies France
161 I6 Les Karellis France
129 E2 Lesken Rus. Fed.
Leskhimstroy Ukr. *see* Syeverodonets'k
175 K6 Lesko Pol.
197 J8 Leskovac Serbia
198 B2 Leskovik Albania
263 F2 Leskov Island Antarctica
137 L4 Les'ky Ukr.
159 I8 Les Landes-Genusson France
162 E5 Les Lèches France
161 H10 Les Lecques France
146 J10 Leslie *Fife, Scotland* U.K.
226 J7 Leslie *MI* U.S.A.
158 I8 Les Lucs-sur-Boulogne France
146 I11 Lesmahagow *South Lanarkshire, Scotland* U.K.

160 G2 Les Maillys France
247 □2 Les Mangles Guadeloupe
160 I6 Les Marches France
160 C5 Les Martres-de-Veyre France
161 D9 Les Matelles France
159 J7 Les Mauges reg. France
156 I4 Les Mazures France
225 H3 Les Méchins Que. Can.
186 L3 Les Medes is Spain
161 H8 Les Mées France
161 J6 Les Menuires France
158 G4 Les Minquiers is Channel Is
161 I8 Les Monges mt. France
156 H7 Lesmont France
156 C6 Les Mureaux France
177 G2 Lešná Czech Rep.
174 D4 Leśna Pol.
175 L3 Leśna r. Pol.
158 C4 Lesneven France
174 G5 Leśnica Pol.
174 D4 Leśniów Wielki Pol.
156 H7 Les Noës-près-Troyes France
134 K4 Lesnoy Kirovskaya Oblast' Rus. Fed.
Lesnoy Murmanskaya Oblast' Rus. Fed. see Umba
139 X7 Lesnoy Ryazanskaya Oblast' Rus. Fed.
139 O6 Lesnoy Smolenskaya Oblast' Rus. Fed.
138 L1 Lesnoy, Ostrov i. Rus. Fed.
139 S3 Lesnoye Rus. Fed.
134 K4 Lesnyye Polyany Rus. Fed.
100 M4 Lesogorsk Sakhalin Rus. Fed.
138 L1 Lesogorskiy Rus. Fed.
161 F7 Les Ollières-sur-Eyrieux France
100 I5 Lesopil'noye Rus. Fed.
161 J7 Les Orres France
131 K4 Lesosibirsk Rus. Fed.
215 M5 Lesotho country Africa
215 M5 Lesotho Highlands Water Project Lesotho
100 H6 Lesozavodsk Rus. Fed.
162 C5 Lesparre-Médoc France
162 D5 Les Peintures France
161 G10 Les Pennes-Mirabeau France
217 □2b L'Espérance Mahé Seychelles
77 I5 L'Espérance Rock i. N.Z.
163 B8 Lesperon France
156 H5 Les Petites-Loges France
197 L3 Lespezi hill Romania
158 H2 Les Pieux France
161 C10 Lespignan France
186 F6 L'Espina mt. Spain
163 J9 Lespinassière France
160 I3 Les Planches-en-Montagne France
186 H5 L'Espluga Calba Spain
186 H5 L'Espluga de Francolí Spain
162 C1 Les Ponts-de-Cé France
190 B1 Les Ponts-de-Martel Switz.
186 J3 Les Preses Spain
163 F9 Lespugue France
156 H8 Les Riceys France
159 K7 Les Rosiers-sur-Loire France
160 I4 Les Rousses France
162 A3 Les Sables-d'Olonne France
179 I5 Lessach Austria
161 E8 Les Salles-du-Gardon France
158 H3 Lessay France
165 G8 Lesse r. Belgium
165 H8 Lesse et Lomme, Parc Naturel de nature res. Belgium
158 E4 Les Sept-Îles is France
247 J7 Lesser Antilles is Caribbean Sea
129 D4 Lesser Caucasus mts Asia
116 F4 Lesser Himalaya mts India/Nepal
Lesser Khingan Mountains China see Xiao Hinggan Ling
222 H4 Lesser Slave Lake Alta Can.
222 H4 Lesser Slave Lake Provincial Park Alta Can.
90 E8 Lesser Sunda Islands Indon.
125 L2 Lesser Tunb i. The Gulf
156 G7 Les Sièges France
165 E7 Lessines Belgium
215 K5 Lessingskop mt. S. Africa
191 J4 Lessini, Monti mts Italy
217 □2a Les Sœurs is Inner Islands Seychelles
158 H7 Les Sorinières France
163 D9 Lestelle-Bétharram France
232 D11 Lester WV U.S.A.
161 C6 Les Ternes France
156 C5 Les Thilliers-en-Vexin France
161 J8 Les Thuiles France
140 R5 Lestijärvi Fin.
140 Q4 Lestijoki r. Fin.
161 B8 Lestrade France
158 D4 Les Triagoz is France
217 □1c Les Trois Bassins Réunion
247 □3 Les Trois-Îlets Martinique
159 L7 Les Trois-Moutiers France
208 E3 Les Trois Rivieres C.A.R.
161 B7 Les Trucs d'Aubrac mt. France
177 L5 Leșu, Lacul l. Romania
86 I2 Lesueur Island W.A. Austr.
156 D6 Les Ulis France
95 K4 Lesung, Bukit mt. Indon.
161 E8 Les Vans France
161 C8 Les Vignes France
199 G3 Lesvos i. Greece
174 D2 Leszczyn Pol.
175 K4 Leszkowice Pol.
175 I3 Leszno Mazowieckie Pol.
174 E4 Leszno Wielkopolskie Pol.
174 D4 Leszno Górne Pol.
161 H6 Le Taillefer mt. France
186 E2 Le Taillon mt. Spain
159 K8 Le Tallud France
143 K2 Letälven r. Sweden
217 □1c Le Tampon Réunion
161 E7 Le Tanargue mt. France
177 K4 Létavértes Hungary
151 L4 Letchworth Garden City Hertfordshire, England U.K.
163 B6 Le Teich France
161 F7 Le Teil France
159 J4 Le Teilleul France
160 E2 Le Télégraphe hill France
163 C6 Le Temple France
176 F5 Letenye Hungary
116 F7 Leteri Madh. Prad. India
96 A3 Letha Range mts Myanmar
222 H5 Lethbridge Alta Can.
225 K3 Lethbridge Nfld and Lab. Can.
168 F4 Lethe r. Ger.
159 M5 Le Theil France
158 I6 Le-Theil-de-Bretagne France
251 G4 Lethem Guyana
151 O2 Letheringsett Norfolk, England U.K.
157 M8 Le Thillot France
157 M7 Le Tholy France
161 I10 Le Thoronet France
93 E8 Leti i. Maluku Indon.
93 E8 Leti, Kepulauan is Maluku Indon.
250 D6 Leticia Col.
107 P7 Leting Hebei China
193 M5 Letino Italy
214 G8 Letjiesbos S. Africa
177 H4 Letkés Hungary
215 L1 Letlhabile S. Africa
212 E4 Letlhakane Botswana
212 E5 Letlhakeng Botswana
134 F2 Letnerechenskiy Rus. Fed.
134 G2 Letniy Navolok Rus. Fed.
93 F8 Letoda Maluku Indon.
191 M2 Le Tofane mt. Italy
195 I8 Letoianni Sicilia Italy
179 O1 Letonice Czech Rep.
156 C2 Le Touquet-Paris-Plage France
161 C9 Le Tour d'Arre hill France
161 H6 Le Touvet France
176 F2 Letovice Czech Rep.
96 B6 Letpadan Myanmar
156 B3 Le Tréport France
161 B8 Le Truel France
141 M6 Letsbo Sweden
170 J5 Letschin Ger.
97 D9 Letsok-aw Kyun i. Myanmar
215 J2 Letsopa S. Africa
207 I5 Letta Cameroon
Lette Island Vava'u Gp Tonga see Late
142 I1 Letten l. Sweden
148 B5 Letterbreen Northern Ireland U.K.
147 C6 Lettercallow Ireland
147 C9 Letterfinish Ireland
147 C5 Letterfrack Ireland
147 G3 Letterkenny Ireland
150 C4 Letterston Pembrokeshire, Wales U.K.
94 F3 Letung Indon.
185 O4 Letur Spain
163 C7 Le Tuzan France
93 F7 Letwurung Maluku Indon.
135 H6 Letyazhevka Rus. Fed.
136 G4 Letychiv Ukr.
Lëtzebuerg country Europe see Luxembourg
171 D6 Letzlingen Ger.
197 M6 Leu Romania
209 D7 Léua Angola
171 H8 Leuben Ger.
171 D8 Leubingen Ger.
163 I9 Leuc France
Leucas Lefkada Greece see Lefkada
163 K10 Leucate France
163 K10 Leucate, Cap c. France
163 K10 Leucate, Étang de l. France
146 K10 Leuchars Fife, Scotland U.K.
173 M2 Leuchtenberg Ger.
170 I5 Leuenberg Ger.
157 I8 Leuglay France
190 D3 Leuk Switz.
Leukas Lefkada Greece see Lefkada
190 D3 Leukerbad Switz.
146 D6 Leumrabhagh Western Isles, Scotland U.K.
169 F9 Leun Ger.
109 □J7 Leung Shuen Wan Chau i. H.K. China
134 H2 Leunovo Rus. Fed.
241 V6 Leupp AZ U.S.A.
85 L7 Leura Qld Austr.
164 H4 Leusden Neth.
94 B3 Leuser, Gunung mt. Indon.
178 D5 Leutasch Austria
173 K7 Leutascher Dreitorspitze mt. Ger.
171 D9 Leutenberg Ger.
173 I3 Leutershausen Ger.
169 D10 Leutesdorf Ger.
173 I6 Leutkirch im Allgäu Ger.
179 L6 Leutschach Austria
165 G7 Leuven Belgium
165 E7 Leuze-en-Hainaut Belgium
161 I10 Le Val France
157 L8 Le Val-d'Ajol France
157 J8 Le Vallinot-Longeau-Percey France
158 I4 Le Val-St-Père France
198 A2 Levan Albania
241 U2 Levan UT U.S.A.
140 K5 Levanger Norway
161 I10 Levant, Île du i. France
190 F7 Levante, Riviera di coastal area Italy
190 H7 Levanto Italy
194 C8 Levanzo Sicilia Italy
194 C7 Levanzo, Isola di i. Sicilia Italy
129 I3 Levashi Rus. Fed.
247 □3 Le Vauclin Martinique
137 S2 Levaya Rossosh' Rus. Fed.
176 G4 Levél Hungary
237 D9 Levelland TX U.S.A.
81 F11 Levels South I. N.Z.
149 Q6 Leven East Riding of Yorkshire, England U.K.
146 K10 Leven Fife, Scotland U.K.
146 F9 Leven, Loch inlet Scotland U.K.
146 J10 Leven, Loch l. Scotland U.K.
161 K9 Levens France
149 L5 Levens Cumbria, England U.K.
190 F3 Leventina, Valle val. Switz.
146 □N3 Levenwick Shetland, Scotland U.K.
86 G4 Lévêque, Cape W.A. Austr.
80 □ L'Eveque, Cape Chatham Is S. Pacific Ocean
195 O3 Leverano Italy
146 B7 Leverburgh Western Isles, Scotland U.K.
162 B4 Le-Verdon-sur-Mer France
226 J4 Levering MI U.S.A.
169 C8 Leverkusen Ger.
222 G1 Lever Lake N.W.T. Can.
163 H9 Le Vernet France
Leverville Dem. Rep. Congo see Lusanga
156 B7 Lèves France
159 P8 Levet France
161 B8 Lévézou mts France
177 H3 Levice Slovakia
191 K3 Levico Terme Italy
198 D5 Levidi Greece
192 C4 Levie Corse France
160 I3 Levier France
161 D9 Le Vigan France
163 G8 Lévignac France
163 E6 Lévignac-de-Guyenne France
163 B7 Lévignacq France
191 M9 Le Ville Italy
80 J7 Levin North I. N.Z.
225 G4 Lévis Que. Can.
199 H6 Levitha i. Greece
Levittown NJ U.S.A. see Willingboro
235 H3 Levittown NY U.S.A.
234 F4 Levittown PA U.S.A.
158 H4 Le-Vivier-sur-Mer France
197 O9 Levka Bulg.
Levkás i. Greece see Lefkada
Levkímmi Kerkyra Greece see Lefkimmi
177 J2 Levoča Slovakia
177 J2 Levočské vrchy mts Slovakia
162 H2 Levroux France
197 N7 Levski Bulg.
Levskigrad Bulg. see Karlovo
139 W8 Lev Tolstoy Rus. Fed.
79 □7a Levuka Ovalau Fiji
138 H6 Lėvuo r. Lith.
158 I2 Lévy, Cap c. France
93 A8 Lewa Sumba Indon.
96 C5 Lewe Myanmar
151 M6 Lewes East Sussex, England U.K.
233 J10 Lewes DE U.S.A.
174 F5 Lewin Brzeski Pol.
241 X4 Lewis CO U.S.A.
237 F7 Lewis KS U.S.A.
238 C4 Lewis r. WA U.S.A.
146 C6 Lewis, Isle of i. Scotland U.K.
84 D7 Lewis, Lake salt flat N.T. Austr.
234 B4 Lewisberry PA U.S.A.
232 A9 Lewisburg OH U.S.A.
227 R9 Lewisburg PA U.S.A.
231 D8 Lewisburg TN U.S.A.
232 E11 Lewisburg WV U.S.A.
222 D3 Lewis Cass, Mount Can./U.S.A.
225 J3 Lewis Hills Nfld and Lab. Can.
115 M6 Lewis Inlet Andaman & Nicobar Is India
81 G9 Lewis Pass South I. N.Z.
81 G9 Lewis Pass National Reserve nature res. South I. N.Z.
225 K3 Lewisporte Nfld and Lab. Can.
86 J6 Lewis Range hills W.A. Austr.
238 G2 Lewis Range mts MT U.S.A.
231 D8 Lewis Smith, Lake AL U.S.A.
238 F3 Lewiston ID U.S.A.
233 □O4 Lewiston ME U.S.A.
227 J5 Lewiston MI U.S.A.
226 C6 Lewiston MN U.S.A.
232 F5 Lewiston NY U.S.A.
226 D9 Lewistown IL U.S.A.
226 C9 Lewistown MO U.S.A.
238 J3 Lewistown MT U.S.A.
232 H8 Lewistown PA U.S.A.
237 I9 Lewisville AR U.S.A.
232 D9 Lewisville OH U.S.A.
170 E4 Lewitz park Ger.
93 C8 Lewoleba Indon.
93 C8 Lewotobi, Gunung vol. Flores Indon.
231 F9 Lexington GA U.S.A.
226 F9 Lexington IL U.S.A.
230 E6 Lexington KY U.S.A.
227 L6 Lexington MI U.S.A.
236 I6 Lexington MO U.S.A.
237 J9 Lexington MS U.S.A.
231 G8 Lexington NC U.S.A.
236 F5 Lexington NE U.S.A.
232 C8 Lexington OH U.S.A.
231 G9 Lexington SC U.S.A.
237 K8 Lexington TN U.S.A.
232 F11 Lexington VA U.S.A.
232 I10 Lexington Park MD U.S.A.
149 N5 Leyburn North Yorkshire, England U.K.
Leyden Neth. see Leiden
108 F6 Leye Guangxi China
122 B3 Leyla Dāgh mt. Iran
149 L6 Leyland Lancashire, England U.K.
163 H6 Leyme France
151 N5 Leysdown-on-Sea Kent, England U.K.
190 C3 Leysin Switz.
92 E6 Leyte i. Phil.
92 E6 Leyte Gulf Phil.
190 C3 Leytron Switz.
163 G10 Lez r. France
183 P4 Leza r. Spain
175 K5 Leżajsk Pol.
250 E2 Lezama Venez.
161 E8 Lézan France
158 E4 Lézardrieux France
163 G9 Lézat-sur-Lèze France
162 D3 Lezay France
163 G9 Lèze r. France
196 H9 Lezhë Albania
108 E3 Lezhi Sichuan China
139 X5 Lezhnevo Rus. Fed.
161 B10 Lézignan-Corbières France
175 H2 Leźno Pol.
160 C5 Lezoux France
185 O3 Lezuza Spain
185 O2 Lezuza r. Spain
175 H4 Lgota Wielka Pol.
135 F6 L'gov Rus. Fed.
111 H12 Lhagoi Kangri mt. Xizang China
146 J7 Lhanbryde Moray, Scotland U.K.
Lhari Xizang China see Si'erdingka
111 K11 Lhari Xizang China
87 B8 Lharidon Bight b. W.A. Austr.
111 J10 Lharigarbo Xizang China
111 J12 Lhasa Xizang China
111 J12 Lhasa He r. China
111 K12 Lhasoi Xizang China
108 A3 Lhatog Xizang China
156 D6 L'Hay-les-Roses France
111 H12 Lhazê Xizang China
111 L11 Lhazê Xizang China
179 J1 Lhenice Czech Rep.
163 G9 Lherm France
162 C2 L'Hermenault France
158 H5 L'Hermitage France
113 □1 Lhohifushi i. N. Male Maldives
94 A2 Lhokkruet Sumatera Indon.
94 B2 Lhokseumawe Sumatera Indon.
94 B2 Lhoksukon Sumatera Indon.
111 J11 Lhomar Xizang China
163 G7 L'Honor-de-Cos France
111 L11 Lhorong Xizang China
163 G7 L'Hospitalet France
186 G6 L'Hospitalet de l'Infant Spain
186 J5 L'Hospitalet de Llobregat Spain
161 C9 L'Hospitalet-du-Larzac France
163 H10 L'Hospitalet-près-l'Andorre France
186 G6 L'Hostal del Alls Spain
162 B3 L'Houmeau France
137 N8 L'hovs'ke Ukr.
111 J12 Lhozhag Xizang China
160 H5 Lhuis France
159 J5 L'Huisserie France
156 H6 Lhuître France
117 M6 Lhuntshi Bhutan
Lhünzê Xizang China see Xingba
111 K12 Lhünzê Xizang China
96 D5 Li, Mae r. Thai.
199 H6 Liadi i. Greece
129 F3 Liakhvis Nakrdzali nature res. Georgia
198 D4 Liakoura mt. Greece
192 B3 Liamone r. Corse France
247 □2 Liamuiga, Mount vol. St Kitts and Nevis
109 K6 Liancheng Fujian China
Liancheng Guizhou China see Qinglong
Liancheng Yunnan China see Guangnan
156 D5 Liancourt France
101 G10 Liancourt Rocks i. N. Pacific Ocean
156 C2 Liane r. France
Lianfeng Fujian China see Liancheng
93 C4 Liang Sulawesi Indon.
92 F7 Liangā Mindanao Phil.
92 F7 Liangā Bay Mindanao Phil.
107 M6 Liangcheng Nei Mongol China
108 F2 Liangdang Gansu China
111 J11 Liangdaohe Xizang China
108 H6 Liangfeng Guangxi China
108 G5 Lianghe Chongqing China
108 B6 Lianghe Yunnan China
Lianghekou Chongqing China see Lianghe
108 E2 Lianghekou Gansu China
108 D3 Lianghekou Sichuan China
Liangjiayoufang Shanxi China see Youyu
108 F3 Liangping Chongqing China
95 K4 Liangpran, Bukit mt. Indon.
Liangshan Chongqing China see Liangping
96 D2 Liang Shan mt. Myanmar
Liangshi Hunan China see Shaodong
108 H8 Liangtian Guangxi China
94 D3 Liang Timur, Gunung mt. Malaysia
108 D6 Liangwang Shan mts Yunnan China
107 K8 Liangzhen Shaanxi China
Liangzhou Gansu China see Wuwei
109 J3 Liangzi Hu l. China
Lianhe Chongqing China see Qianjiang
109 I5 Lianhua Jiangxi China
109 J7 Lianhua Shan mts China
109 L5 Lianjiang Fujian China
108 H8 Lianjiang Guangdong China
Lianjiang Jiangxi China see Xingguo
108 F6 Lian Jiang r. China
109 I6 Lianjiangkou Guangdong China
109 I6 Liannan Guangdong China
109 J6 Lianping Guangdong China
Lianran Yunnan China see Anning
109 I6 Lianshan Guangdong China
107 Q6 Lianshan Liaoning China
Liant, Cape i. Thai. see Samae San, Laem
Liantang Jiangxi China see Nanchang
109 H3 Liantuo Hubei China
Lianxian Guangdong China see Lianzhou
100 C2 Lianyin Heilong. China
109 H5 Lianyuan Hunan China
107 P9 Lianyungang Jiangsu China
109 I6 Lianzhou Guangdong China
Lianzhou Guangxi China see Hepu
100 G6 Lianzhushan Heilong. China
107 N8 Liaocheng Shandong China
107 P6 Liaodong Bandao pen. China
107 Q6 Liaodong Wan b. China
106 C5 Liaodun Xinjiang China
106 C5 Liaodunzhan Xinjiang China
Liaogao Guizhou China see Songtao
107 R6 Liao He r. China
107 R6 Liaoning prov. China
107 R6 Liaoyang Liaoning China
100 D7 Liaoyuan Jilin China
107 R6 Liaozhong Liaoning China
198 A3 Liapades Kerkyra Greece
123 N5 Liaqatabad Pak.
222 F2 Liard r. Can.
222 F2 Liard Highway N.W.T. Can.
222 E2 Liard Plateau Y.T. Can.
222 E3 Liard River B.C. Can.
123 L9 Liari Pak.
156 H4 Liart France
94 G6 Liat i. Indon.
146 F7 Liathach mt. Scotland U.K.
143 K5 Liatorp Sweden
Liban country Asia see Lebanon
176 E1 Libáň Czech Rep.
128 E4 Liban, Jebel mts Lebanon
261 G5 Líbano Arg.
250 C3 Líbano Col.
185 I7 Líbar, Sierra de mts Spain
Libau Latvia see Liepāja
146 I11 Libberton South Lanarkshire, Scotland U.K.
238 G2 Libby MT U.S.A.
176 C1 Libčeves Czech Rep.
171 J10 Libčice nad Vltavou Czech Rep.
208 C4 Libenge Dem. Rep. Congo
175 I2 Liberadz Pol.
237 E7 Liberal KS U.S.A.
257 E5 Liberdade Brazil
254 B4 Liberdade r. Brazil
252 C1 Liberdade r. Brazil
176 E1 Liberec Czech Rep.
176 E1 Liberecký kraj admin. reg. Czech Rep.
206 C5 Liberia country Africa
242 □Q12 Liberia Costa Rica
247 □2 Liberta Antigua and Barbuda
261 I2 Libertad Arg.
261 I4 Libertad Uru.
250 D2 Libertad Venez.
258 D1 Libertador General San Martin Arg.
260 E3 Libertador General San Martín Arg.
215 L4 Libertase S. Africa
230 E6 Liberty IN U.S.A.
230 E7 Liberty KY U.S.A.
233 □P4 Liberty ME U.S.A.
236 H6 Liberty MO U.S.A.
233 K7 Liberty NY U.S.A.
234 A1 Liberty PA U.S.A.
237 H10 Liberty TX U.S.A.
232 A7 Liberty Center OH U.S.A.
234 B6 Liberty Lake MD U.S.A.
226 G7 Libertyville IL U.S.A.
171 J9 Liběšice Czech Rep.
175 H5 Libiąż Pol.
176 E1 Libice nad Cidlinou Czech Rep.
165 H9 Libin Belgium
176 D3 Libín mt. Czech Rep.
176 G2 Libina Czech Rep.
92 D5 Libmanan Luzon Phil.
128 B8 Libnī, Jabal hill Egypt
108 F6 Libo Guizhou China
93 F4 Libobo, Tanjung pt Halmahera Indon.
171 J10 Libochovice Czech Rep.
215 N7 Libode S. Africa
198 B2 Libohovë Albania
210 D4 Liboi Kenya
209 D8 Libonda Zambia
97 D11 Libong, Ko i. Thai.
215 M4 Libono Lesotho
260 E3 Liborio Luna Arg.
171 J9 Libouchec Czech Rep.
163 D6 Libourne France
86 H7 Libral Well W.A. Austr.
165 H9 Libramont Belgium
196 I9 Librazhd Albania
242 D3 Libre, Sierra mts Mex.
245 J6 Libres Mex.
208 A4 Libreville Gabon
187 C12 Librilla Spain
187 C7 Libros Spain
92 E8 Libuganon r. Mindanao Phil.
202 C3 Libya country Africa
202 E3 Libyan Desert Egypt/Libya
202 E2 Libyan Plateau Egypt
260 A4 Licantén Chile
194 F9 Licata Sicilia Italy
190 I7 Licciana Nardi Italy
127 J4 Lice Turkey
193 J3 Licenza Italy
183 N6 Liceras Spain
169 G9 Lich Ger.
198 D4 Lichas pen. Greece
Licheng Fujian China see Xianyou
Licheng Guangxi China see Lipu
107 O8 Licheng Shandong China
107 M8 Licheng Shanxi China
80 J5 Lichfield North I. N.Z.
151 I2 Lichfield Staffordshire, England U.K.
211 B8 Lichinga Moz.
177 G1 Lichnov Czech Rep.
174 G1 Lichnowy Pol.
171 D9 Lichte Ger.
172 E4 Lichtenau Baden-Württemberg Ger.
173 J3 Lichtenau Bayern Ger.
169 G7 Lichtenau Nordrhein-Westfalen Ger.
179 L2 Lichtenau im Waldviertel Austria
171 E10 Lichtenberg Bayern Ger.
171 H9 Lichtenberg Sachsen Ger.
215 K2 Lichtenburg S. Africa
171 D10 Lichtenfels Ger.
171 G9 Lichtenstein Ger.
164 K5 Lichtenvoorde Neth.
179 N4 Lichtenwörth Austria
170 I5 Lichterfelde Ger.
165 D6 Lichtervelde Belgium
108 G3 Lichuan Hubei China
109 K5 Lichuan Jiangxi China
213 H3 Liciro Moz.
232 A9 Licking r. KY U.S.A.
188 E3 Lički Osik Croatia
194 D8 Licodia Eubea Sicilia Italy
193 N7 Licosa, Isola i. Italy
163 C9 Licq-Athérey France
156 C2 Licques France
Licun Shandong China see Laoshan
139 S2 Lid' r. Rus. Fed.
138 I8 Lida Belarus
142 J3 Lidan r. Sweden
149 L3 Liddel Water r. England/Scotland U.K.
146 K12 Liddesdale val. Scotland U.K.
215 K8 Liddleton S. Africa
177 H2 Lidečko Czech Rep.
142 J5 Lidhult Sweden
143 O2 Lidingö Sweden
208 C4 Lidjombo C.A.R.
142 J3 Lidköping Sweden
191 M5 Lido Italy
191 M7 Lido Adriano Italy
191 M7 Lido di Classe Italy
193 J5 Lido di Foce Verde Italy
191 N4 Lido di Jesolo Italy
195 L3 Lido di Metaponto Italy
193 I4 Lido di Ostia Italy
193 P4 Lido di Siponto Italy
191 M6 Lido di Spina Italy
140 M4 Lidsjöberg Sweden
138 K5 Lidumnieki Latvia
175 H2 Lidzbark Pol.
143 Q7 Lidzbark Warmiński Pol.
179 K2 Liebenau Austria
169 H8 Liebenau Hessen Ger.
168 H5 Liebenau Niedersachsen Ger.
215 M3 Liebenbergs Vlei r. S. Africa
169 J6 Liebenburg Ger.
179 J6 Liebenfels Austria
170 H5 Liebenwalde Ger.
171 J7 Lieberose Ger.
171 F8 Liebertwolkwitz Ger.
84 C7 Liebig, Mount N.T. Austr.
196 J5 Liebling Romania
179 L6 Lieboch Austria
171 I9 Liebstadt Ger.
172 H7 Liechtenstein country Europe
183 R3 Liédena Spain
165 I7 Liège Belgium
165 I8 Liège prov. Belgium
Liegnitz Pol. see Legnica
140 U5 Lieksa Fin.
138 K5 Lielais Ludzas l. Latvia
138 H4 Lielupe r. Latvia
138 H5 Lielvārde Latvia
164 H5 Liempde Neth.
140 N5 Lien Sweden
164 I5 Lienden Neth.
169 E6 Lienen Ger.
97 I9 Liên Nghia Vietnam
97 I8 Liên Sơn Vietnam
178 G6 Lienz Austria
138 E5 Liepāja Latvia
Liepaya Latvia see Liepāja
170 I5 Liepe Ger.
170 H3 Liepen Ger.
170 J3 Liepgarten Ger.
138 K4 Liepna Latvia
175 M1 Lieponys Lith.
165 G6 Lier Belgium
160 E2 Liernais France
165 I8 Lierneux Belgium
Lierre Belgium see Lier
177 I2 Liesek Slovakia
172 C2 Lieser Ger.
164 I5 Lieshout Neth.
178 L5 Liesing r. Austria
138 G1 Liesjärven kansallispuisto nat. park Fin.
165 I6 Liessel Neth.
156 G4 Liesse-Notre-Dame France
190 C1 Liestal Switz.
177 H3 Lieštany Slovakia
138 F1 Lieto Fin.
185 P3 Liétor Spain
Lietuva country Europe see Lithuania
141 S6 Lietvesi l. Fin.
159 M3 Lieurey France
159 L3 Lieuvin reg. France
141 S5 Lievestuore Fin.
156 E3 Liévin France
224 F4 Lièvre r. Que. Can.
179 J4 Liezen Austria
93 E4 Lifamatola i. Indon.
208 D4 Lifanga Dem. Rep. Congo
148 E7 Liffey r. Ireland
157 K7 Liffol-le-Grand France
147 H3 Lifford Ireland
158 H5 Liffré France
259 C6 Lifi Mahuida mt. Arg.
78 □5 Lifou i. Îles Loyauté New Caledonia
150 D6 Lifton Devon, England U.K.
Lifu i. Îles Loyauté New Caledonia see Lifou
Lifudzin Rus. Fed. see Rudnyy
79 □8 Lifuka i. Tonga
92 D5 Ligao Luzon Phil.
163 E7 Ligardes France
208 D4 Ligasa Dem. Rep. Congo
138 I4 Līgatne Latvia
87 G10 Lightfoot Lake salt flat W.A. Austr.
243 P9 Lighthouse Reef Belize
83 K3 Lightning Ridge N.S.W. Austr.
234 C2 Lightstreet PA U.S.A.
179 L6 Ligist Austria
191 O4 Lignano Pineta Italy
191 O4 Lignano Sabbiadoro Italy
158 I7 Ligné France
158 H8 Ligneron r. France
165 J8 Ligneuville Belgium
159 P8 Lignières France
160 D5 Lignon r. France
161 E6 Lignon r. France
157 J6 Ligny-en-Barrois France
156 G8 Ligny-le-Châtel France
156 C8 Ligny-le-Ribault France
190 I7 Ligonchio Italy
213 H3 Ligonha r. Moz.
226 I8 Ligonier IN U.S.A.
232 F8 Ligonier PA U.S.A.
Ligoúrion Greece see Asklipieio
175 H3 Ligowo Pol.
260 B3 Ligua, Bahía de la b. Chile
82 E6 Liguanea Island S.A. Austr.
159 M7 Ligueil France
162 E2 Ligugé France
242 D5 Ligui Mex.
Ligure, Mar sea France/Italy see Ligurian Sea
190 F7 Liguria admin. reg. Italy
188 B4 Ligurian Sea France/Italy
Ligurienne, Mer sea France/Italy see Ligurian Sea
241 R9 Ligurta AZ U.S.A.
81 □4 Liha Point Niue
91 L7 Lihir Group is P.N.G.
142 E5 Lihme Denmark
85 M4 Lihou Reef and Cays Coral Sea Is Terr. Austr.
240 □B11 Līhu'e HI U.S.A.
260 E5 Lihuel Calel, Parque Nacional nat. park Arg.
138 G3 Lihula Estonia
Liidli Kue N.W.T. Can. see Fort Simpson
Liivi laht b. Estonia/Latvia see Riga, Gulf of
195 □ Lija Malta
185 O6 Lijar Spain
185 I7 Líjar, Sierra de mts Spain
108 C5 Lijiang Yunnan China
Lijiang Yunnan China see Yuanjiang
96 J2 Li Jiang r. China
109 J3 Lijiazhai Henan China
96 F5 Lik, Nam r. Laos
188 E3 Lika reg. Croatia
122 D6 Līkak Iran
208 C4 Likala Dem. Rep. Congo
209 E7 Likasi Dem. Rep. Congo
208 D4 Likati Dem. Rep. Congo
208 E4 Likati r. Dem. Rep. Congo
222 F4 Likely B.C. Can.
Likhachevo Ukr. see Pervomays'kyy
Likhachyovo Ukr. see Pervomays'kyy
Likhás pen. Greece see Lichas
139 S4 Likhoslavl' Rus. Fed.
137 T5 Likhovskoy Rus. Fed.
208 D4 Likimi Dem. Rep. Congo
139 V6 Likino-Dulevo Rus. Fed.
Likisia East Timor see Liquiçá
116 I9 Likma Chhattisgarh India
208 D5 Likolia Dem. Rep. Congo
208 C4 Likouala admin. reg. Congo
208 C5 Likouala r. Congo
208 C5 Likouala aux Herbes r. Congo
143 N3 Likstammen l. Sweden
95 H4 Liku Kalimantan Indon.
95 K2 Liku Sarawak Malaysia
81 □4 Liku Niue
93 D3 Likupang Sulawesi Indon.
134 H4 Likurga Rus. Fed.
79 □7a Likuri Harbour b. Viti Levu Fiji
159 L7 L'Île-Bouchard France
192 B2 L'Île-Rousse Corse France
179 M3 Lilienfeld Austria
168 G4 Lilienthal Ger.
109 I5 Liling Hunan China
138 J1 Liljendal Fin.
123 O5 Lilla Pak.
142 I3 Lilla Edet Sweden
140 P3 Lilla Luleälven r. Sweden
140 N4 Lillblaiken hill Sweden
165 G6 Lille Belgium
156 F2 Lille France
142 F6 Lille Bælt sea chan. Denmark
159 M2 Lillebonne France
141 K6 Lillehammer Norway
156 D2 Lillers France
142 E3 Lillesand Norway
150 H2 Lilleshall Telford and Wrekin, England U.K.
142 H2 Lillestrøm Norway
226 I6 Lilley MI U.S.A.
87 I9 Lillian, Point hill W.A. Austr.
263 L2 Lillie Glacier Antarctica
146 K11 Lilliesleaf Scottish Borders, Scotland U.K.
231 H8 Lillington NC U.S.A.
183 N9 Lillo Spain
222 F5 Lillooet B.C. Can.
222 F5 Lillooet r. B.C. Can.
222 F5 Lillooet Range mts B.C. Can.
208 E5 Lilo r. Dem. Rep. Congo
117 N7 Lilong Manipur India
211 B8 Lilongwe Malawi
258 E2 Lilo Viejo Arg.
92 D7 Liloy Mindanao Phil.
226 F4 Lily WI U.S.A.
82 G5 Lilydale S.A. Austr.
83 K9 Lilydale Tas. Austr.
196 H7 Lim r. Montenegro/Serbia
261 H4 Lima Arg.
191 J7 Lima r. Italy
253 F5 Lima Para.
252 A3 Lima Peru
252 A2 Lima dept Peru
226 C9 Lima IL U.S.A.
238 H4 Lima MT U.S.A.
232 H6 Lima NY U.S.A.
232 A8 Lima OH U.S.A.
251 F4 Limaão Brazil
260 B3 Limache Chile
257 F4 Lima Duarte Brazil
160 C5 Limagne reg. France
125 M3 Līmah Oman
Lima Islands Guangdong China see Wanshan Qundao
120 B5 Liman Rus. Fed.
178 F7 Limana Italy
175 I6 Limanowa Pol.
93 E7 Limar Maluku Indon.
260 B2 Limarí r. Chile
94 F4 Limas Indon.
92 E7 Limasawa i. Phil.
Limassol Cyprus see Lemesos
147 I2 Limavady Northern Ireland U.K.
260 D6 Limay r. Arg.
156 C5 Limay France
260 D5 Limay Mahuida Arg.
172 G3 Limbach Baden-Württemberg Ger.
172 B3 Limbach Saarland Ger.
171 F9 Limbach Sachsen Ger.
171 G9 Limbach-Oberfrohna Ger.
195 J6 Limbadi Italy
95 K2 Limbang Sarawak Malaysia
95 K2 Limbang r. Sarawak Malaysia
252 C3 Limbani Peru
192 C6 Limbara, Monte mts Sardegna Italy
138 H4 Limbaži Latvia
116 C8 Limbdi Gujarat India
207 H5 Limbe Cameroon
211 B8 Limbe Malawi
93 C3 Limboto Sulawesi Indon.
93 C3 Limboto, Danau l. Indon.
165 I7 Limbourg Belgium
213 H3 Limbuè Moz.
93 A6 Limbung Sulawesi Indon.
95 K6 Limbungan Kalimantan Indon.
84 B4 Limbunya N.T. Austr.
165 H6 Limburg prov. Belgium
165 I6 Limburg prov. Neth.
169 F10 Limburg an der Lahn Ger.
172 E3 Limburgerhof Ger.
94 □ Lim Chu Kang Sing.
94 □ Lim Chu Kang hill Sing.
214 H4 Lime Acres S. Africa
141 L6 Limedsforsen Sweden
81 C13 Limehills South I. N.Z.
256 D5 Limeira Brazil
149 K1 Limekilns Fife, Scotland U.K.
198 F2 Limenaria Thasos Greece
199 G7 Limenas Chersonisou Kriti Greece
147 E7 Limerick Ireland
147 E8 Limerick county Ireland
226 B6 Lime Springs IA U.S.A.
233 □R2 Limestone ME U.S.A.
223 L4 Limestone Point Man. Can.
142 E5 Limfjorden sea chan. Denmark
182 D5 Limia r. Spain
140 L4 Limingen Norway
140 L4 Limingen l. Norway
233 □O5 Limington ME U.S.A.
140 R4 Liminka Fin.
142 J4 Limmared Sweden
164 G3 Limmen Neth.
84 F3 Limmen Bight b. N.T. Austr.
84 E3 Limmen Bight River r. N.T. Austr.
198 E4 Limni Greece
199 G3 Limnos i. Greece
254 G3 Limoeiro Brazil
233 J3 Limoges Ont. Can.
162 G4 Limoges France
163 H7 Limogne, Causse de hills France
163 H7 Limogne-en-Quercy France
242 □Q10 Limón Hond.
236 D6 Limon CO U.S.A.
217 □1a Limon, Mount hill Rodrigues I. Mauritius
190 D7 Limone Piemonte Italy
250 B4 Limones Ecuador
160 F5 Limonest France
191 J4 Limone sul Garda Italy
184 F3 Limonetes r. Spain
126 G5 Limonlu Turkey
Limonum France see Poitiers
252 D3 Limoquije Bol.
193 N4 Limosano Italy
162 H4 Limousin admin. reg. France
162 H4 Limousin, Monts du hills France
162 G4 Limousin, Plateaux du France
163 I9 Limoux France
213 F4 Limpopo prov. S. Africa
213 G5 Limpopo r. S. Africa/Zimbabwe
213 F4 Limpopo National Park S. Africa
108 H6 Limu Guangxi China
79 □8 Limu atoll Tonga
81 □4 Limufuafua Point Niue
209 D8 Limulunga Zambia
140 Q3 Linaälven r. Sweden
124 F1 Līnah Saudi Arabia
215 M5 Linakeng Lesotho
140 U2 Linakhamari Rus. Fed.
Lin'an Yunnan China see Jianshui
109 L3 Lin'an Zhejiang China
92 E8 Linao Bay Mindanao Phil.
92 B6 Linapacan i. Phil.
92 B6 Linapacan Strait Phil.
162 H4 Linards France
260 B4 Linares Chile
243 J5 Linares Mex.
185 L4 Linares Spain
183 M5 Linares, Embalse de resr Spain
187 D7 Linares de Mora Spain
182 I7 Linares de Riofrío Spain
192 B9 Linas, Monte mt. Sardegna Italy
190 G5 Linate airport Italy
95 K3 Linau Balui plat. Malaysia
108 C7 Lincang Yunnan China
165 H7 Lincent Belgium
Lincheng Hainan China see Lingao
Lincheng Hunan China see Huitong
Linchuan Jiangxi China see Fuzhou
262 R1 Linck Nunataks nunataks Antarctica
261 G4 Lincoln Arg.
81 G10 Lincoln South I. N.Z.
149 P7 Lincoln Lincolnshire, England U.K.
240 K3 Lincoln CA U.S.A.
234 E7 Lincoln DE U.S.A.
230 C5 Lincoln IL U.S.A.
236 F6 Lincoln KS U.S.A.
233 □Q3 Lincoln ME U.S.A.
227 K5 Lincoln MI U.S.A.
236 G5 Lincoln NE U.S.A.
233 N4 Lincoln NH U.S.A.
234 C4 Lincoln PA U.S.A.
238 B4 Lincoln City OR U.S.A.
90 D3 Lincoln Island Paracel Is
82 E6 Lincoln National Park S.A. Austr.
232 B6 Lincoln Park MI U.S.A.
221 N1 Lincoln Sea Can./Greenland
149 Q7 Lincolnshire admin. div. England U.K.
149 Q7 Lincolnshire Wolds hills England U.K.
231 F9 Lincolnton GA U.S.A.
234 D5 Lincoln University PA U.S.A.
235 G4 Lincroft NJ U.S.A.
254 E5 Linda, Serra hills Brazil
84 G7 Linda Creek watercourse Qld Austr.
144 J1 Lindas Norway
171 F6 Lindau Sachsen-Anhalt
168 I1 Lindau Schleswig-Holste
172 H6 Lindau (Bodensee) Ger
164 I3 Linde r. Neth.
168 K1 Lindelse Denmark
85 L6 Lindeman Group is Qlo
222 H5 Linden Alta Can.
169 G9 Linden Hessen Ger.
168 H2 Linden Schleswig-Holste
251 G3 Linden Guyana
231 D9 Linden AL U.S.A.
240 K3 Linden CA U.S.A.
232 B6 Linden MI U.S.A.
235 G3 Linden NJ U.S.A.
231 D8 Linden TN U.S.A.
237 H9 Linden TX U.S.A.
170 F4 Lindenberg Brandenbur
170 I5 Lindenberg Brandenbur
171 J6 Lindenberg Brandenbur
172 H6 Lindenberg im Allgäu
172 F2 Lindenfels Ger.
226 B2 Linden Grove MN U.S.A
Lindenow Fjord inlet Greenland see Kangerlussuatsiaq
234 F5 Lindenwold NJ U.S.A.
168 E5 Lindern (Oldenburg) G
143 L2 Lindesberg Sweden
142 D3 Lindesnes c. Norway
168 H1 Lindewitt Ger.
151 L5 Lindfield West Sussex, England U.K.
169 H6 Lindhorst Ger.
Líndhos Rodos Greece Lindos
208 E4 Lindi r. Dem. Rep. Cong
211 C7 Lindi Tanz.
211 C7 Lindi admin. reg. Tanz.
107 S3 Lindian Heilong. China
Lindisfarne i. England U Holy Island
81 D11 Lindis Peak South I. N.
169 D8 Lindlar Ger.
215 L3 Lindley S. Africa
256 D5 Lindóia Brazil
142 I4 Lindome Sweden
107 P5 Lindong Nei Mongol Ch
199 J6 Lindos Rodos Greece
182 D5 Lindoso Port.
170 G5 Lindow Ger.
157 M6 Lindre, Étang de l. Fra
233 □R2 Lindsay N.B. Can.
224 E4 Lindsay Ont. Can.
240 M5 Lindsay CA U.S.A.
238 L3 Lindsay MT U.S.A.
87 F9 Lindsay Gordon Lagoo salt flat W.A. Austr.
236 G6 Lindsborg KS U.S.A.
143 M5 Lindsdal Sweden
232 E11 Lindside WV U.S.A.
170 E5 Lindstedt Ger.
Lindum Lincolnshire, En U.K. see Lincoln
168 I5 Lindwedel Ger.
176 C2 Líně Czech Rep.
234 B5 Lineboro MD U.S.A.
266 I5 Line Islands S. Pacific
234 E4 Line Lexington PA U.S.
137 O1 Linets Rus. Fed.
107 L8 Linfen Shanxi China
234 D4 Linfield PA U.S.A.
151 M5 Linford Thurrock, Englar
146 F8 Ling r. Scotland U.K.
114 H4 Lingamparti Andhra Pra India
114 D6 Linganamakki Reservo India
108 G9 Lingao Hainan China
161 D8 Lingas, Montagne du r France
92 C3 Lingayen Luzon Phil.
92 C3 Lingayen Gulf Luzon Ph
107 L9 Lingbao Henan China
109 K2 Lingbi Anhui China
Lingcheng Anhui China Lingbi
Lingcheng Guangxi Chi Lingshan
Lingcheng Hainan China Lingshui
Lingcheng Shandong C see Lingxian
108 H6 Lingchuan Guangxi Chi
107 M9 Lingchuan Shanxi China
215 K8 Lingelethu S. Africa
215 J8 Lingelihle S. Africa
168 D5 Lingen (Ems) Ger.
178 A5 Lingenau Austria
172 E3 Lingenfeld Ger.
151 L5 Lingfield Surrey, Englan
94 F5 Lingga i. Indon.
95 I4 Lingga Sarawak Malaysi
94 F5 Lingga, Kepulauan is In
111 I10 Linggo Co l. Xizang Chi
107 Q6 Linghai Liaoning China
92 F8 Lingig Mindanao Phil.
95 L1 Lingkabau Sabah Malay
95 L3 Lingkas Kalimantan Ind
238 L5 Lingle WY U.S.A.
234 B4 Linglestown PA U.S.A.
84 G4 Lingnoonganee Island Qld Austr.
157 O6 Lingolsheim France
208 D4 Lingomo Dem. Rep. Co
107 N7 Lingqiu Shanxi China
108 G7 Lingshan Guangxi China
107 Q9 Lingshan Wan b. China
117 L6 Lingshi Bhutan
107 L8 Lingshi Shanxi China
108 G9 Lingshui Hainan China
108 G9 Lingshui Wan b. China
114 E4 Lingsugur Karnataka Inc
107 J9 Lingtai Gansu China
195 I8 Linguaglossa Sicilia Ital
206 B3 Linguère Senegal
108 H6 Lingui Guangxi China
192 C3 Linguizzetta Corse Frar
151 O2 Lingwood Norfolk, England U.K.
Lingxi Hunan China see Yongshun
Lingxian Hunan China s Yanling
107 O8 Lingxian Shandong Chir
109 J3 Lingxiang Hubei China
Lingyang Hunan China s
107 P6 Lingyuan Liaoning China
108 F6 Lingyun Guangxi China
108 A4 Lingza Xizang China
Lingzhi Bhutan see Ling
111 D9 Lingzi Tang reg. Aksai
109 M4 Linhai Zhejiang China
257 G3 Linhares Brazil
182 F7 Linhares Port.
107 J6 Linhe Nei Mongol China
96 B2 Linhpa Myanmar
174 F1 Linia Pol.
81 D11 Linidis Valley South I. N
233 □O2 Linière Que. Can.
174 G1 Liniewo Pol.
Linjiang Fujian China se Shanghang
108 E2 Linjiang Gansu China
101 E8 Linjiang Jilin China
Linjiang Sichuan China s Cangxi
172 E3 Linkenheim-Hochstett
143 L3 Linköping Sweden
100 G6 Linkou Heilong. China
146 J5 Linksness Orkney, Scotland U.K.
138 G5 Linkuva Lith.
109 H4 Linli Hunan China
146 I11 Linlithgow West Lothian Scotland U.K.
107 M8 Linlü Shan mt. Henan C
Linmingguan Hebei Chi Yongnian
236 J6 Linn MO U.S.A.
237 F12 Linn TX U.S.A.
240 J1 Linn, Mount CA U.S.A.
141 T5 Linnansaaren kansallis to nat. park Fin.
142 H2 Linnekleppen hill Norw
233 □R2 Linneus ME U.S.A.
150 B4 Linney Head Wales U.K.
146 E9 Linnhe, Loch inlet Scotland U.K.
169 B9 Linnich Ger.
189 D8 Linosa, Isola di i. Sicilia

Linova Belarus
Linovo Rus. Fed.
Linow Ger.
Linpo Myanmar
Linqing Shandong China
Linru Henan China see Ruzhou
Linruzhen Henan China
Lins Brazil
Linsan Guinea
Linsburg Ger.
Linshui Sichuan China
Linstead Jamaica
Linta r. Madag.
Lintah, Selat sea chan. Indon.
Lintan Gansu China
Lintao Gansu China
Linth r. Switz.
Linthal Switz.
Linthe Ger.
Linthicum Heights MD U.S.A.
Lintig Ger.
Linton North I. N.Z.
Linton Cambridgeshire, England U.K.
Linton ND U.S.A.
Lintong Shaanxi China
Lintzoain Spain
Linum Ger.
Linwood NJ U.S.A.
Linwu Hunan China
Linxe France
Linxi Nei Mongol China
Linxia Gansu China
Linxia Gansu China
Linxian Henan China see Linzhou
Linxian Shanxi China
Linxiang Hunan China
Linyanti r. Botswana/Namibia
Linyanti Swamp Namibia
Linyi Shandong China
Linyi Shandong China
Linyi Shanxi China
Linying Henan China
Linyola Spain
Linyou Shaanxi China
Linz Austria
Linz am Rhein Ger.
Linze Gansu China
Linzgau reg. Ger.
Linzhou Henan China
Lioboml' Ukr.
Lioma Moz.
Lio Matoh Sarawak Malaysia
Lion, Golfe du g. France
Lionel Town Jamaica
Lioni Italy
Lions, Gulf of France see Lion, Golfe du
Lions Bay B.C. Can.
Lions Den Zimbabwe
Lion's Head Ont. Can.
Lion-sur-Mer France
Lioppa Maluku Indon.
Liorac-sur-Louyre France
Lioua Chad
Liouesso Congo
Lipa Luzon Phil.
Lipa Pol.
Lipang i. Indon.
Lipany Slovakia
Lipari Isole Lipari Italy
Lipari, Isola i. Isole Lipari Italy
Lipari, Isole is Italy
Lipatkain Sumatera Indon.
Lipawki Belarus
Lipcani Moldova
Lipce Reymontowskie Pol.
Liperi Fin.
Lipetsk Rus. Fed.
Lipetskaya Oblast' admin. div. Rus. Fed.
Lipetsk Oblast admin. div. Rus. Fed. see Lipetskaya Oblast'
Lipez, Cordillera de mts Bol.
Liphook Hampshire, England U.K.
Lipiany Pol.
Lipin Bor Rus. Fed.
Liping Guizhou China
Lipinki Pol.
Lipinki Łużyckie Pol.
Lipitsy Rus. Fed.
Lipka Pol.
Lipkany Moldova see Lipcani
Lipki Rus. Fed.
Lipki Wielkie Pol.
Lipljan Kosovo Serbia
Lipnaya Gorka Rus. Fed.
Lipnica Kujawsko-Pomorskie Pol.
Lipnica Pomorskie Pol.
Lipnica Murowana Pol.
Lipnik Pol.
Lipnika Wielka Pol.
Lipník nad Bečvou Czech Rep.
Lipno Kujawsko-Pomorskie Pol.
Lipno Wielkopolskie Pol.
Lipno, Vodní nádrž resr Czech Rep.
Liposthey France
Lipova Romania
Lipovei, Dealurile hills Romania
Lipovka Volgogradskaya Oblast' Rus. Fed.
Lipovka Voronezhskaya Oblast' Rus. Fed.
Lipovu Romania
Lipowiec Pol.
Lippe r. Ger.
Lippenhuizen Neth.
Lippoldsberg (Wahlsburg) Ger.
Lippstadt Ger.
Lipscomb TX U.S.A.
Lipsk Pol.
Lipsko Pol.
Lipsoí i. Greece see Leipsoi
Liptál Czech Rep.
Lipti Lekh pass Nepal
Liptougou Burkina
Liptovská Kokava Slovakia
Liptovská Mara, Vodná nádrž resr Slovakia
Liptovská Osada Slovakia
Liptovská Teplička Slovakia
Liptovský Hrádok Slovakia
Liptovský Mikuláš Slovakia
Liptrap, Cape Vic. Austr.
Liptsy Rus. Fed.
Lipu Guangxi China
Lipuda r. Italy
Lipusz Pol.
Liquiçá East Timor
Liquissa East Timor see Liquiçá
Lira Uganda
Liran i. Maluku Indon.
Liranga Congo
Liré France
Lires, Ría de b. Spain
Liri r. Italy
Liri, Jebel el mt. Sudan
Liro r. Italy
Lirung Sulawesi Indon.
Lis Albania
Lisa Romania
Lisacul Ireland
Lisakovsk Kazakh.
Lisala Dem. Rep. Congo
Lisas Bay Trin. and Tob.
Lisbane Northern Ireland U.K.
Lisbellaw Northern Ireland U.K.
Lisboa Port.
Lisboa admin. dist. Port.
Lisbon Port. see Lisboa
Lisbon IL U.S.A.
Lisbon MD U.S.A.
Lisbon ME U.S.A.
Lisbon ND U.S.A.
Lisbon NH U.S.A.
Lisbon OH U.S.A.
Lisbon Falls ME U.S.A.
Lisburn Northern Ireland U.K.
Lisca Blanca, Isola i. Isole Lipari Italy
Liscannor Ireland
Liscannor Bay Ireland
Liscarney Ireland
Liscarroll Ireland

192 C5 Liscia r. Sardegna Italy
192 C5 Liscia, Lago di l. Sardegna Italy
192 C7 Liscoi r. Italy
225 I4 Liscomb Game Sanctuary nature res. N.S. Can.
147 D6 Lisdoonvarna Ireland
147 H5 Lisduff Ireland
197 K9 Lisec mt. Macedonia
142 H5 Liseleje Denmark
147 F7 Lisgarode Ireland
147 F9 Lisgoold Ireland
Lishan Shaanxi China see Lintong
109 M6 Lishan Taiwan
136 H3 Lishchyn Ukr.
108 C6 Lishe Jiang r. Yunnan China
Lishi Jiangxi China see Dingnan
107 L8 Lishi Shanxi China
122 D6 Līshtar-e Bālā Iran
100 D7 Lishu Jilin China
109 L3 Lishui Jiangsu China
109 L4 Lishui Zhejiang China
108 H4 Li Shui r. China
175 J5 Lisia Góra Pol.
75 H2 Lisianski Island HI U.S.A.
Lisichansk Ukr. see Lysychans'k
174 F5 Lisięcice Pol.
159 L3 Lisieux France
139 N1 Lisiy Nos Rus. Fed.
143 K1 Lisjön l. Sweden
150 D7 Liskeard Cornwall, England U.K.
135 G6 Liski Rus. Fed.
177 I2 Lisková Slovakia
162 F5 Lisle France
147 I3 Lislea Northern Ireland U.K.
156 D5 L'Isle-Adam France
160 G5 L'Isle-d'Abeau France
163 E8 L'Isle-de-Noé France
162 E4 L'Isle-d'Espagnac France
163 F9 L'Isle-en-Dodon France
163 G8 L'Isle-Jourdain Midi-Pyrénées France
162 F3 L'Isle-Jourdain Poitou-Charentes France
161 G9 L'Isle-sur-la-Sorgue France
160 J2 L'Isle-sur-le-Doubs France
160 E1 L'Isle-sur-Serein France
163 H8 Lisle-sur-Tarn France
83 N3 Lismore N.S.W. Austr.
81 F10 Lismore South I. N.Z.
147 G8 Lismore Ireland
146 E10 Lismore i. Scotland U.K.
147 E7 Lisnagry Ireland
147 H8 Lisnakill Ireland
147 I3 Lisnamuck Northern Ireland U.K.
147 G4 Lisnarrick Northern Ireland U.K.
147 H4 Lisnaskea Northern Ireland U.K.
136 I7 Lisne Ukr.
192 G3 L'Isolotto i. Italy
160 H2 Lison r. France
176 D2 Lišov Czech Rep.
147 E9 Lispatrick Ireland
147 B8 Lispole Ireland
147 G8 Lisronagh Ireland
148 C6 Lisryan Ireland
128 G7 Liss mt. Saudi Arabia
151 K5 Liss Hampshire, England U.K.
Lissa Croatia see Vis
Lissa Pol. see Leszno
163 H6 Lissac-et-Mouret France
148 D4 Lissan Northern Ireland U.K.
164 G4 Lisse Neth.
147 C8 Lisselton Ireland
169 C10 Lissendorf Ger.
205 H2 Lisseri, Oued watercourse Tunisia
142 J1 Lisskogsbrändan Sweden
190 G4 Lissone Italy
199 G2 Lissos r. Greece
147 D7 Lissycasey Ireland
168 F1 List Ger.
142 C3 Lista pen. Norway
142 C3 Listafjorden b. Norway
143 L6 Listed Bornholm Denmark
263 K1 Lister, Mount Antarctica
147 H8 Listerlin Ireland
148 F5 Listooder Northern Ireland U.K.
84 G8 Listore watercourse Qld Austr.
224 D5 Listowel Ont. Can.
147 D8 Listowel Ireland
85 J8 Listowel Downs Qld Austr.
162 C5 Listrac-Médoc France
121 U3 Listvyaga, Khrebet mts Kazakh./Rus. Fed.
174 H4 Liswarta r. Pol.
150 G4 Liswerry Newport, Wales U.K.
175 H5 Liszki Pol.
174 F2 Liszkowo Pol.
140 M5 Lit Sweden
108 G7 Litang Guangxi China
108 C3 Litang Sichuan China
108 C4 Litang Qu r. Sichuan China
251 H4 Litani r. Fr. Guiana/Suriname
128 D5 Lītâni, Nahr el r. Lebanon
177 I3 Litava Slovakia
176 D2 Litavka r. Czech Rep.
240 L1 Litchfield CA U.S.A.
235 I1 Litchfield CT U.S.A.
236 K6 Litchfield IL U.S.A.
226 J7 Litchfield MI U.S.A.
236 H3 Litchfield MN U.S.A.
232 C7 Litchfield OH U.S.A.
234 I1 Litchfield County county CT U.S.A.
211 D7 Litembe Tanz.
138 K4 Litene Latvia
177 G4 Litér Hungary
163 B7 Lit-et-Mixe France
164 H5 Lith Neth.
124 E5 Līth, Wādī al watercourse Saudi Arabia
149 L7 Litherland Merseyside, England U.K.
83 M5 Lithgow N.S.W. Austr.
198 F8 Lithino, Akrotirio pt Kriti Greece
138 G6 Lithuania country Europe
188 E2 Litija Slovenia
227 R9 Lititz PA U.S.A.
177 I3 Litke Hungary
131 T2 Litke, Mys c. Rus. Fed.
198 D2 Litochoro Greece
176 D1 Litoměřice Czech Rep.
176 F2 Litomyšl Czech Rep.
184 B1 Litoral reg. Port.
176 G2 Litovel Czech Rep.
100 I4 Litovko Rus. Fed.
Litovskaya S.S.R. country Europe see Lithuania
179 L2 Litschau Austria
190 E1 Littau Switz.
237 I10 Little r. LA U.S.A.
237 I9 Little r. OK U.S.A.
237 G10 Little r. TX U.S.A.
231 I12 Little Abaco i. Bahamas
224 D3 Little Abitibi r. Ont. Can.
224 D3 Little Abitibi Lake Ont. Can.
Little Aden Yemen see 'Adan aş Şughrá
115 M7 Little Andaman i. Andaman & Nicobar Is India
Little Ararat mt. Turkey see Küçük Ağrı Dağı
236 G7 Little Arkansas r. KS U.S.A.
231 H12 Little Bahama Bank sea feature Bahamas
80 J3 Little Barrier i. North I. N.Z.
185 □ Little Bay Gibraltar
226 G4 Little Bay de Noc MI U.S.A.
Little Belt sea chan. Denmark see Lille Bælt
238 I3 Little Belt Mountains MT U.S.A.
238 K4 Little Bighorn r. MT U.S.A.
Little Bitter Lake Egypt see Murrah aş Şughrá, Al Buḩayrah al
236 G6 Little Blue r. KS U.S.A.
149 M6 Littleborough Greater Manchester, England U.K.
222 H5 Little Bow r. Alta Can.
222 H2 Little Buffalo r. N.W.T. Can.
246 C4 Little Cayman i. Cayman Is
223 M3 Little Churchill r. Man. Can.
151 O4 Little Clacton Essex, England U.K.
97 A8 Little Coco Island Cocos Is

146 D10 Little Colonsay i. Scotland U.K.
241 U5 Little Colorado r. AZ U.S.A.
151 M6 Little Common East Sussex, England U.K.
234 E6 Little Creek DE U.S.A.
241 T4 Little Creek Peak UT U.S.A.
148 H2 Little Cumbrae i. Scotland U.K.
224 D4 Little Current Ont. Can.
224 C3 Little Current r. Ont. Can.
150 E6 Little Dart r. England U.K.
150 H4 Littledean Gloucestershire, England U.K.
82 H7 Little Desert National Park Vic. Austr.
151 M3 Little Downham Cambridgeshire, England U.K.
235 G5 Little Egg Harbor inlet NJ U.S.A.
246 F2 Little Exuma i. Bahamas
236 H3 Little Falls MN U.S.A.
233 K5 Little Falls NY U.S.A.
146 H7 Littleferry Highland, Scotland U.K.
241 S5 Littlefield AZ U.S.A.
237 D9 Littlefield TX U.S.A.
215 K9 Little Fish r. S. Africa
226 A1 Little Fork MN U.S.A.
226 A1 Little Fork r. MN U.S.A.
222 F5 Little Fort B.C. Can.
Little Ganges atoll Cook Is see Rakahanga
234 D3 Little Gap PA U.S.A.
223 M4 Little Grand Rapids Man. Can.
240 K2 Little Grass Valley Reservoir CA U.S.A.
151 K6 Littlehampton West Sussex, England U.K.
246 G3 Little Inagua Island Bahamas
232 D9 Little Kanawha r. WV U.S.A.
214 C3 Little Karas Berg plat. Namibia
214 E9 Little Karoo plat. S. Africa
240 O6 Little Lake CA U.S.A.
146 F7 Little Loch Broom inlet Scotland U.K.
Little Mecatina r. Nfld and Lab./Que. Can. see Petit Mécatina
Little Mecatina Island Que. Can. see Petit Mécatina, Île du
232 A9 Little Miami r. OH U.S.A.
146 I7 Littlemill Highland, Scotland U.K.
146 B7 Little Minch sea chan. Scotland U.K.
151 K4 Little Missenden Buckinghamshire, England U.K.
236 D2 Little Missouri r. ND U.S.A.
151 J4 Littlemore Oxfordshire, England U.K.
232 D9 Little Muskingum r. OH U.S.A.
115 M9 Little Nicobar i. Andaman & Nicobar Is India
151 O4 Little Oakley Essex, England U.K.
215 N1 Little Olifants r. S. Africa
151 M3 Little Ouse r. England U.K.
123 P3 Little Pamir mts Afgh.
235 K2 Little Peconic Bay NY U.S.A.
226 H1 Little Pic r. Ont. Can.
234 A2 Little Pine Creek r. PA U.S.A.
234 A5 Little Pipe Creek r. MD U.S.A.
151 M3 Littleport Cambridgeshire, England U.K.
238 L4 Little Powder r. MT U.S.A.
222 D2 Little Rancheria r. B.C. Can.
116 C8 Little Rann marsh Gujarat India
237 J8 Little Red r. AR U.S.A.
222 H3 Little Red River Alta Can.
81 G10 Little River South I. N.Z.
231 H9 Little River SC U.S.A.
237 I8 Little Rock AR U.S.A.
240 O7 Littlerock CA U.S.A.
226 H6 Little Sable Point MI U.S.A.
223 M4 Little Sachigo Lake Ont. Can.
222 C2 Little Salmon Lake Y.T. Can.
241 T4 Little Salt Lake UT U.S.A.
87 E7 Little Sandy Desert W.A. Austr.
246 F1 Little San Salvador i. Bahamas
236 G5 Little Sioux r. IA U.S.A.
220 A4 Little Sitkin Island AK U.S.A.
222 G4 Little Smoky Alta Can.
222 G4 Little Smoky r. Alta Can.
238 J6 Little Snake r. CO U.S.A.
231 □1 Little Sound b. Bermuda
151 N6 Littlestone-on-Sea Kent, England U.K.
234 A5 Littlestown PA U.S.A.
Little Tibet reg. Jammu and Kashmir see Ladakh
247 □5 Little Tobago i. Trin. and Tob.
148 B8 Littleton Ireland
151 J5 Littleton Hampshire, England U.K.
226 D9 Littleton IL U.S.A.
233 N4 Littleton NH U.S.A.
232 E9 Littleton WV U.S.A.
226 I4 Little Traverse Bay MI U.S.A.
233 K4 Little Tupper Lake NY U.S.A.
226 B1 Little Turtle Lake Ont. Can.
232 G6 Little Valley NY U.S.A.
236 K7 Little Wabash r. IL U.S.A.
81 G8 Little Wanganui South I. N.Z.
236 E4 Little White r. SD U.S.A.
237 G9 Little Wichita r. TX U.S.A.
238 J5 Little Wind r. WY U.S.A.
238 G5 Little Wood r. ID U.S.A.
Little Zab r. Iraq see Zāb aş Şaghīr, Nahr az
143 S1 Littoinen Fin.
207 H5 Littoral prov. Cameroon
260 B4 Litueche Chile
211 B8 Litunde Moz.
222 B3 Lituya Bay AK U.S.A.
176 C1 Litvínov Czech Rep.
136 H4 Lityn Ukr.
173 K2 Litzendorf Ger.
138 H3 Liu Estonia
Liu'an Anhui China see Lu'an
108 F2 Liuba Shaanxi China
175 L1 Liubavas Lith.
96 I2 Liucheng Guangxi China
109 L4 Liucheng Zhejiang China
109 M7 Liuchiu Yü i. Taiwan
108 F5 Liuchong He r. Guizhou China
Liuchow Guangxi China see Liuzhou
Liudu Guangdong China see Yun'an
175 L1 Liudvinavas Lith.
107 R8 Liugong Dao i. China
107 Q6 Liugu He r. China
100 D7 Liuhe Jilin China
107 P6 Liu He r. China
107 R6 Liu He r. China
109 N4 Liuheng Dao i. China
109 H3 Liujiachang Hubei China
108 G6 Liujiang Guangxi China
Liujiaxia Gansu China see Yongjing
106 H9 Liujiaxia Shuiku resr Gansu China
100 E5 Liukesong Heilong. China
108 B6 Liuku Yunnan China
Liulin Gansu China see Jonê
107 L8 Liulin Shanxi China
Liupai Guangxi China see Tian'e
106 J9 Liupan Shan mts China
Liupanshui Guizhou China see Lupanshui
213 H2 Liupo Moz.
107 O9 Liuquan Jiangsu China
242 □P11 Liure Hond.
106 C5 Liushuquan Xinjiang China
209 D8 Liuwa Plain Zambia
209 D8 Liuwa Plain National Park Zambia
109 I4 Liuyang Hunan China
109 I4 Liuyang He r. China
110 L6 Liuyuan Gansu China
107 S1 Liuzhan Heilong. China
Liuzhangzhen Shanxi China see Yuanqu
108 G6 Liuzhou Guangxi China
177 K5 Livada Arad Romania

197 L3 Livada Satu Mare Romania
199 G5 Livada, Akrotirio pt Tinos Greece
198 D4 Livadeia Greece
198 C2 Livadero Greece
198 D2 Livadi Greece
198 E1 Livadia Greece
100 H7 Livadiya Rus. Fed.
198 E4 Livanates Greece
138 J5 Līvāni Latvia
188 F3 Livanjsko Polje plain Bos.-Herz.
159 L3 Livarot France
138 G5 Livbērze Latvia
137 R3 Livenka Rus. Fed.
191 M4 Livenza r. Italy
240 K2 Live Oak CA U.S.A.
231 F10 Live Oak FL U.S.A.
157 L6 Liverdun France
86 H5 Liveringa W.A. Austr.
240 K4 Livermore CA U.S.A.
239 L11 Livermore, Mount TX U.S.A.
233 □O4 Livermore Falls ME U.S.A.
163 H6 Livernon France
83 M5 Liverpool N.S.W. Austr.
84 E2 Liverpool r. N.T. Austr.
225 H4 Liverpool N.S. Can.
149 L7 Liverpool Merseyside, England U.K.
233 I5 Liverpool NY U.S.A.
234 B3 Liverpool PA U.S.A.
221 K2 Liverpool, Cape Nunavut Can.
220 E3 Liverpool Bay N.W.T. Can.
149 K7 Liverpool Bay England U.K.
83 M4 Liverpool Plains N.S.W. Austr.
83 L4 Liverpool Range mts N.S.W. Austr.
149 N6 Liversedge West Yorkshire, England U.K.
192 G3 Lividonia, Punta pt Italy
190 I2 Livigno Italy
243 O10 Livingston Guat.
146 I11 Livingston West Lothian, Scotland U.K.
237 K9 Livingston AL U.S.A.
240 L4 Livingston CA U.S.A.
232 A11 Livingston KY U.S.A.
237 J10 Livingston LA U.S.A.
238 I4 Livingston MT U.S.A.
235 G3 Livingston NJ U.S.A.
237 H10 Livingston TX U.S.A.
237 H10 Livingston, Lake TX U.S.A.
209 E9 Livingstone Zambia
211 B7 Livingstone Mountains Tanz.
211 B7 Livingstonia Malawi
262 T2 Livingston Island Antarctica
233 K7 Livingston Manor NY U.S.A.
81 C11 Livingston Mountains South I. N.Z.
188 F4 Livno Bos.-Herz.
139 U9 Livny Rus. Fed.
140 U4 Livo r. Rus. Fed.
191 R4 Livold Slovenia
227 K7 Livonia MI U.S.A.
232 H6 Livonia NY U.S.A.
190 I8 Livorno Italy
190 J9 Livorno prov. Italy
190 E5 Livorno Ferraris Italy
160 D6 Livradois, Monts du mts France
160 D5 Livradois Forez, Parc Naturel Régional du nature res. France
216 □1b Livramento São Miguel Azores
254 E5 Livramento do Brumado Brazil
161 F7 Livron-sur-Drôme France
175 J3 Liw Pol.
125 M3 Liwā Oman
128 E6 Liwā', Wādī al watercourse Syria
211 C7 Liwale Tanz.
211 C7 Liwale Juu Tanz.
175 J3 Liwiec r. Pol.
211 B8 Liwonde Malawi
211 B8 Liwonde National Park Malawi
Liwu Hebei China see Lixian
106 I9 Lixian Gansu China
107 N7 Lixian Hebei China
109 H4 Lixian Hunan China
108 D3 Lixian Sichuan China
109 K2 Lixin Anhui China
157 M5 Lixing-lès-St-Avold France
198 B4 Lixouri Kefallonia Greece
Lixus Morocco see Larache
Liyang Anhui China see Hexian
Liyang Hunan China see Lixian
109 L3 Liyang Jiangsu China
Liyuan Hunan China see Sangzhi
182 C9 Liz r. Port.
150 B8 Lizard Cornwall, England U.K.
254 D4 Lizarda Brazil
85 J3 Lizard Island Qld Austr.
150 B8 Lizard Point England U.K.
Lizarra Spain see Estella
183 P3 Lizarraga Spain
232 D10 Lizemores WV U.S.A.
137 S3 Lizinovka Rus. Fed.
108 D4 Liziping Sichuan China
162 E5 Lizonne r. France
156 F5 Lizy-sur-Ourcq France
195 O3 Lizzanello Italy
195 M3 Lizzano Italy
196 I6 Ljig Serbia
142 D2 Ljomsnuten mt. Norway
188 F3 Ljubija Bos.-Herz.
196 H7 Ljubišnja mts Bos.-Herz./Montenergo
188 E2 Ljubljana Slovenia
179 J7 Ljubljana airport Slovenia
179 K7 Ljubljanica r. Slovenia
196 H6 Ljubovija Serbia
188 F4 Ljubuški Bos.-Herz.
143 O4 Ljugarn Gotland Sweden
140 N5 Ljungå Sweden
141 N5 Ljungan r. Sweden
141 N5 Ljungaverk Sweden
143 J5 Ljungby Sweden
143 M5 Ljungbyån r. Sweden
140 L5 Ljungdalen Sweden
143 L3 Ljungsbro Sweden
142 H3 Ljungskile Sweden
141 N6 Ljusdal Sweden
143 L3 Ljusfallshammar Sweden
142 J1 Ljusnan r. Sweden
141 N6 Ljusnan r. Sweden
141 N6 Ljusne Sweden
188 F2 Ljutomer Slovenia
186 K4 Llagostera Spain
260 B6 Llaima, Volcán vol. Chile
261 G2 Llambí Campbell Arg.
150 D2 Llanaelhaearn Gwynedd, Wales U.K.
Llanandras Wales U.K. see Presteigne
150 F2 Llanarmon Dyffryn Ceiriog Wrexham, Wales U.K.
150 D3 Llanarth Ceredigion, Wales U.K.
150 D4 Llanarthney Carmarthenshire, Wales U.K.
150 F1 Llanasa Flintshire, Wales U.K.
150 D3 Llanbadarn Fawr Ceredigion, Wales U.K.
150 D1 Llanbadrig Isle of Anglesey, Wales U.K.
Llanbedr Ceredigion, Wales U.K. see Lampeter
150 D2 Llanbedr Gwynedd, Wales U.K.
150 D2 Llanbedrog Gwynedd, Wales U.K.
Llanbedr Pont Steffan Wales U.K. see Lampeter
150 D1 Llanberis Gwynedd, Wales U.K.
150 F3 Llanbister Powys, Wales U.K.
150 E2 Llanbryn-mair Powys, Wales U.K.
186 L3 Llançà Spain
260 C4 Llancanelo, Laguna l. Arg.
260 C4 Llancanelo, Salina salt flat Arg.
150 D2 Llandanwg Gwynedd, Wales U.K.
150 D4 Llanddarog Carmarthenshire, Wales U.K.
150 D1 Llanddeiniolen Gwynedd, Wales U.K.
150 E2 Llandderfel Gwynedd, Wales U.K.
150 C4 Llanddowror Carmarthenshire, Wales U.K.

150 E4 Llandeilo Carmarthenshire, Wales U.K.
150 G4 Llandinabo Herefordshire, England U.K.
150 F3 Llandinam Powys, Wales U.K.
150 C4 Llandissilio Pembrokeshire, Wales U.K.
150 E4 Llandovery Carmarthenshire, Wales U.K.
150 F2 Llandrillo Denbighshire, Wales U.K.
150 F3 Llandrindod Wells Powys, Wales U.K.
150 E1 Llandudno Conwy, Wales U.K.
Llandudoch Wales U.K. see St Dogmaels
150 D1 Llandwrog Gwynedd, Wales U.K.
150 D4 Llandybie Carmarthenshire, Wales U.K.
150 D3 Llandysul Ceredigion, Wales U.K.
150 D4 Llanegwad Carmarthenshire, Wales U.K.
150 D1 Llaneilian Isle of Anglesey, Wales U.K.
150 D4 Llanelli Carmarthenshire, Wales U.K.
150 E2 Llanelltyd Gwynedd, Wales U.K.
150 F4 Llanelly Monmouthshire, Wales U.K.
Llanelwy Denbighshire, Wales U.K. see St Asaph
Llanelwy Wales U.K. see St Asaph
183 K2 Llanes Spain
150 D1 Llanfaelog Isle of Anglesey, Wales U.K.
150 F2 Llanfair Caereinion Powys, Wales U.K.
150 E1 Llanfairfechan Conwy, Wales U.K.
150 D1 Llanfairpwllgwyngyll Isle of Anglesey, Wales U.K.
150 E1 Llanfair Talhaiarn Conwy, Wales U.K.
Llanfair-ym-Muallt Wales U.K. see Builth Wells
150 C1 Llanfair-yn-neubwll Isle of Anglesey, Wales U.K.
150 D3 Llanfarian Ceredigion, Wales U.K.
150 D3 Llanfihangel-ar-arth Carmarthenshire, Wales U.K.
150 F2 Llanfyllin Powys, Wales U.K.
150 F1 Llanfynydd Flintshire, Wales U.K.
150 F2 Llangadfan Powys, Wales U.K.
150 E4 Llangadog Carmarthenshire, Wales U.K.
150 D1 Llangefni Isle of Anglesey, Wales U.K.
150 D3 Llangeler Carmarthenshire, Wales U.K.
150 D2 Llangelynin Gwynedd, Wales U.K.
150 D4 Llangendeirne Carmarthenshire, Wales U.K.
150 E1 Llangernyw Conwy, Wales U.K.
150 D1 Llangoed Isle of Anglesey, Wales U.K.
150 F2 Llangollen Denbighshire, Wales U.K.
150 D3 Llangrannog Ceredigion, Wales U.K.
150 D1 Llangristiolus Isle of Anglesey, Wales U.K.
150 D4 Llangunnor Carmarthenshire, Wales U.K.
150 E3 Llangurig Powys, Wales U.K.
150 C4 Llangwm Pembrokeshire, Wales U.K.
150 F4 Llangynidr Powys, Wales U.K.
150 F4 Llanharan Rhondda Cynon Taff, Wales U.K.
150 E3 Llanidloes Powys, Wales U.K.
150 D3 Llanilar Ceredigion, Wales U.K.
150 F4 Llanishen Cardiff, Wales U.K.
150 F2 Llanllwchaiarn Powys, Wales U.K.
150 D1 Llanllyfni Gwynedd, Wales U.K.
150 D1 Llannerch-y-medd Isle of Anglesey, Wales U.K.
150 D4 Llannon Carmarthenshire, Wales U.K.
150 D3 Llan-non Ceredigion, Wales U.K.
150 D2 Llannor Gwynedd, Wales U.K.
242 D2 Llano Mex.
237 F10 Llano TX U.S.A.
237 F10 Llano r. TX U.S.A.
237 D9 Llano Estacado plain NM/TX U.S.A.
244 B2 Llano Grande Durango Mex.
244 B3 Llano Grande Nayarit Mex.
250 D3 Llanos plain Col./Venez.
260 D2 Llanos, Sierra de los mts Arg.
259 B6 Llanquihue, Lago l. Chile
150 F2 Llanrhaeadr-ym-Mochnant Powys, Wales U.K.
150 D4 Llanrhidian Swansea, Wales U.K.
150 D3 Llanrhystud Ceredigion, Wales U.K.
150 D1 Llanrug Gwynedd, Wales U.K.
150 F4 Llanrumney Cardiff, Wales U.K.
150 E1 Llanrwst Conwy, Wales U.K.
Llansá Spain see Llançà
150 E1 Llansanffraid Glan Conwy Conwy, Wales U.K.
150 E1 Llansannan Conwy, Wales U.K.
150 D3 Llansawel Carmarthenshire, Wales U.K.
150 D4 Llansteffan Carmarthenshire, Wales U.K.
Llanstephan Carmarthenshire, Wales U.K. see Llansteffan
150 F4 Llanthony Monmouthshire, Wales U.K.
150 F4 Llantilio Pertholey Monmouthshire, Wales U.K.
150 G4 Llantrisant Monmouthshire, Wales U.K.
150 F4 Llantrisant Rhondda Cynon Taff, Wales U.K.
150 F5 Llantwit Major Vale of Glamorgan, Wales U.K.
150 E2 Llanuwchllyn Gwynedd, Wales U.K.
150 F2 Llanwddyn Powys, Wales U.K.
150 D3 Llanwenog Ceredigion, Wales U.K.
150 D1 Llanwnda Gwynedd, Wales U.K.
150 F2 Llanwnog Powys, Wales U.K.
150 E4 Llanwrda Carmarthenshire, Wales U.K.
150 E3 Llanwrtyd Wells Powys, Wales U.K.
150 D3 Llanybydder Carmarthenshire, Wales U.K.
Llanymddyfri Carmarthenshire, Wales U.K. see Llandovery
150 C1 Llanynghenedl Isle of Anglesey, Wales U.K.
150 D2 Llanystumdwy Gwynedd, Wales U.K.
186 G5 Llardecans Spain
252 A2 Llata Peru
187 E9 Llaurí Spain
186 H2 Llavorsí Spain
150 F1 Llay Wrexham, Wales U.K.
260 B3 Llay-Llay Chile
187 K9 Llebeig, Es Cap des c. Spain
150 E3 Lledrod Ceredigion, Wales U.K.
186 G4 Lleida Spain
186 H3 Lleida prov. Cataluña Spain
187 H10 Llentrisca, Cap c. Spain
184 G4 Llera Spain
245 H2 Llera de Canales Mex.
184 G4 Llerena Spain
150 C2 Lleyn Peninsula Wales U.K.
252 C4 Llica Bol.
187 D8 Lliria Spain
186 I3 Llívia Spain
186 H4 Llobregós r. Spain
183 O2 Llodio Spain
260 B3 Llolleo Chile
186 I5 Llorenç del Penedès Spain

186 K4 Lloret de Mar Spain
198 A2 Llorgara nat. park Albania
187 D9 Llosa de Ranes Spain
187 K8 Lloseta Spain
85 I2 Lloyd Bay Qld Austr.
222 E3 Lloyd George, Mount B.C. Can.
235 I3 Lloyd Harbor NY U.S.A.
223 I3 Lloyd Lake Sask. Can.
223 I4 Lloydminster Alta Can.
187 L8 Llubí Spain
Lluchmayor Spain see Llucmajor
187 K9 Llucmajor Spain
246 □ Lluidas Vale Jamaica
252 C6 Llullaillaco, Parque Nacional nat. park Chile
252 C6 Llullaillaco, Volcán vol. Chile
Llyn Tegid l. Wales U.K. see Bala Lake
150 F3 Llyswen Powys, Wales U.K.
174 G2 Lniano Pol.
165 C7 Lo Belgium
Lo i. Vanuatu see Loh
96 G4 Lô, Sông r. China/Vietnam
252 C5 Loa r. Chile
241 U3 Loa UT U.S.A.
95 K3 Loagan Bunut National Park Malaysia
95 L5 Loakulu Kalimantan Indon.
256 A5 Loanda Brazil
146 J11 Loanhead Midlothian, Scotland U.K.
190 E7 Loano Italy
146 G11 Loans South Ayrshire, Scotland U.K.
186 D3 Loarre Spain
92 E7 Loay Bohol Phil.
139 S5 Lob' r. Rus. Fed.
175 M5 Lobachivka Ukr.
215 P2 Lobamba Swaziland
134 J4 Loban' r. Rus. Fed.
139 V8 Lobanovo Rus. Fed.
93 C5 Lobata Sulawesi Indon.
185 K6 Lobatejo mt. Spain
212 E5 Lobatse Botswana
171 K8 Löbau Ger.
208 C3 Lobaye pref. C.A.R.
208 C4 Lobaye r. C.A.R.
161 K7 Lobbie, Cima delle mt. Italy
171 E7 Löbejün Ger.
171 G8 Löbenberg hill Ger.
186 C3 Lobera de Onsella Spain
261 H6 Loberia Arg.
174 D2 Łobez Pol.
92 E6 Lobi, Mount vol. Phil.
78 □3b Lobikaere i. Majuro Marshall Is
164 J5 Lobith Neth.
209 B8 Lobito Angola
250 A6 Lobitos Peru
170 G2 Löbnitz Mecklenburg-Vorpommern Ger.
171 F7 Löbnitz Sachsen Ger.
139 U5 Lobnya Rus. Fed.
208 C5 Loboko Congo
180 C3 Lobón Spain
261 H4 Lobos Arg.
216 □3b Lobos i. Canary Is
185 O5 Lobos mt. Spain
242 C3 Lobos, Cabo c. Mex.
242 D4 Lobos, Isla i. Mex.
245 J4 Lobos, Isla de i. Mex.
260 A4 Lobos, Punta de pt Chile
246 E2 Lobos Cay i. Cuba
250 A6 Lobos de Afuera, Islas is Peru
250 A6 Lobos de Tierra, Isla i. Peru
Lobositz Czech Rep. see Lovosice
137 N5 Loboykivka Ukr.
171 F8 Lobstädt Ger.
171 F6 Loburg Ger.
81 G10 Loburn South I. N.Z.
174 F2 Łobżenica Pol.
190 C5 Locana Italy
190 F3 Locarno Switz.
96 H4 Lôc Binh Vietnam
169 H6 Loccum (Rehburg-Loccum) Ger.
192 D8 Loceri Sardegna Italy
146 G9 Lochaber reg. Scotland U.K.
146 E9 Lochailort Highland, Scotland U.K.
146 E9 Lochaline Highland, Scotland U.K.
227 J1 Lochalsh Ont. Can.
146 F13 Lochans Dumfries and Galloway, Scotland U.K.
146 I12 Locharbriggs Dumfries and Galloway, Scotland U.K.
178 A4 Lochau Austria
109 □J7 Lo Chau i. H.K. China
146 F10 Lochawe Argyll and Bute, Scotland U.K.
146 H10 Lochay r. Scotland U.K.
Loch Baghasdail Western Isles, Scotland U.K. see Lochboisdale
146 B8 Lochboisdale Western Isles, Scotland U.K.
146 E10 Lochbuie Argyll and Bute, Scotland U.K.
146 E8 Lochcarron Highland, Scotland U.K.
146 E10 Lochdon Argyll and Bute, Scotland U.K.
146 H10 Lochearnhead Stirling, Scotland U.K.
164 J4 Lochem Neth.
178 H3 Lochen Austria
146 H8 Lochend Highland, Scotland U.K.
85 I8 Lochern National Park Qld Austr.
162 F1 Loches France
Loch Garman Ireland see Wexford
146 J10 Lochgelly Fife, Scotland U.K.
146 F10 Lochgilphead Argyll and Bute, Scotland U.K.
146 G10 Lochgoilhead Argyll and Bute, Scotland U.K.
81 C13 Lochiel South I. N.Z.
215 O2 Lochiel S. Africa
209 E8 Lochinvar National Park Zambia
146 F6 Lochinver Highland, Scotland U.K.
146 G10 Loch Lomond 1 Trossachs National Park Scotland U.K.
146 J12 Lochmaben Dumfries and Galloway, Scotland U.K.
146 B7 Lochmaddy Western Isles, Scotland U.K.
81 C11 Lochnagar l. South I. N.Z.
146 J9 Lochnagar mt. Scotland U.K.
Loch na Madadh Western Isles, Scotland U.K. see Lochmaddy
176 C2 Lochovice Czech Rep.
175 J3 Łochów Pol.
146 F11 Lochranza North Ayrshire, Scotland U.K.
234 B6 Loch Raven Reservoir MD U.S.A.
165 E6 Lochristi Belgium
238 G3 Lochsa r. ID U.S.A.
146 B8 Loch Sgioport Western Isles, Scotland U.K.
146 G11 Lochwinnoch Renfrewshire, Scotland U.K.
146 G9 Lochy, Loch l. Scotland U.K.
82 E5 Lock S.A. Austr.
232 C9 Lockbourne OH U.S.A.
232 I6 Locke NY U.S.A.
240 K3 Lockeford CA U.S.A.
179 N5 Lockenhaus Austria
146 J12 Lockerbie Dumfries and Galloway, Scotland U.K.
86 C6 Locker Point W.A. Austr.
83 K6 Lockhart N.S.W. Austr.
237 G11 Lockhart TX U.S.A.
85 I2 Lockhart River Qld Austr.
85 I2 Lockhart River Aboriginal Reserve Qld Austr.
232 H7 Lock Haven PA U.S.A.
150 G5 Locking North Somerset, England U.K.
170 J4 Löcknitz Ger.
170 D4 Löcknitz r. Ger.
232 G5 Lockport NY U.S.A.
151 J6 Locks Heath Hampshire, England U.K.

149 P5 Lockton North Yorkshire, England U.K.
158 E7 Locmaria France
158 B5 Locmaria-Plouzané France
158 F6 Locmariaquer France
158 F6 Locminé France
158 E6 Locmiquélic France
97 H9 Lôc Ninh Vietnam
158 E6 Locoal-Mendon France
193 P5 Locone r. Italy
195 M2 Locorotondo Italy
158 D4 Locquirec France
195 K7 Locri Italy
158 C5 Locronan France
158 C6 Loctudy France
192 D7 Loculi Sardegna Italy
252 C4 Locumba r. Peru
235 G4 Locust NJ U.S.A.
235 H3 Locust Valley NY U.S.A.
128 C7 Lod Israel
171 E7 Lödderitz Ger.
170 J2 Loddin Ger.
150 E7 Loddiswell Devon, England U.K.
83 I6 Loddon r. Vic. Austr.
151 O2 Loddon Norfolk, England U.K.
192 D6 Lodè Sardegna Italy
138 I4 Lode Latvia
244 B5 Lo de Marcos Mex.
176 D1 Loděnice Czech Rep.
171 E8 Lodersleben Ger.
161 C9 Lodève France
139 Q1 Lodeynoye Pole Rus. Fed.
222 B3 Lodge, Mount Can./U.S.A.
223 I5 Lodge Creek r. Can./U.S.A.
238 K4 Lodge Grass MT U.S.A.
236 D5 Lodgepole Creek r. WY U.S.A.
116 G9 Lodhikheda Madh. Prad. India
123 N7 Lodhran Pak.
190 H5 Lodi Italy
190 H5 Lodi prov. Italy
240 K3 Lodi CA U.S.A.
235 G3 Lodi NJ U.S.A.
232 C7 Lodi OH U.S.A.
226 E6 Lodi WI U.S.A.
140 M3 Løding Norway
140 M2 Lødingen Norway
190 G5 Lodi Vecchio Italy
209 D5 Lodja Dem. Rep. Congo
Lodomeria Rus. Fed. see Vladimir
79 □7a Lodoni Viti Levu Fiji
183 P4 Lodosa Spain
183 Q5 Lodosa, Canal de Spain
116 C8 Lodrani Gujarat India
210 B4 Lodwar Kenya
175 H6 Łodygowice Pol.
175 H4 Łódź Pol.
175 H4 Łódzkie prov. Pol.
183 N8 Loeches Spain
96 E6 Loei Thai.
164 J4 Loenen Gelderland Neth.
164 H4 Loenen Utrecht Neth.
215 J9 Loerie S. Africa
214 D6 Loeriesfontein S. Africa
169 D10 Löf Ger.
178 G4 Lofer Austria
172 E6 Löffingen Ger.
140 L2 Lofoten is Norway
141 L5 Lofsdalen Sweden
215 J6 Lofter S. Africa
149 P4 Loftus Redcar and Cleveland, England U.K.
87 E8 Lofty Range hills W.A. Austr.
210 B4 Lofusa Sudan
135 H6 Log Rus. Fed.
179 I7 Log Slovenia
207 F3 Loga Niger
214 I1 Logageng S. Africa
146 H12 Logan East Ayrshire, Scotland U.K.
236 H5 Logan IA U.S.A.
237 D8 Logan NM U.S.A.
232 C9 Logan OH U.S.A.
238 I6 Logan UT U.S.A.
232 D11 Logan WV U.S.A.
222 A2 Logan, Mount Y.T. Can.
238 D2 Logan, Mount WA U.S.A.
85 K6 Logan Creek r. Qld Austr.
236 G5 Logan Creek r. NE U.S.A.
241 R5 Logandale NV U.S.A.
222 F5 Logan Lake B.C. Can.
222 D2 Logan Mountains N.W.T./Y.T. Can.
230 D5 Logansport IN U.S.A.
237 I10 Logansport LA U.S.A.
234 B5 Loganville PA U.S.A.
188 E3 Logatec Slovenia
140 O4 Lögda Sweden
140 O5 Lögdeälven r. Sweden
209 B6 Loge r. Angola
150 H2 Loggerheads Staffordshire, England U.K.
142 D3 Logna r. Norway
158 H7 Logne r. France
208 B1 Logone r. Africa
207 I4 Logone Birni Cameroon
208 B2 Logone Occidental pref. Chad
208 C2 Logone Oriental pref. Chad
206 D5 Logoualé Côte d'Ivoire
106 G9 Logpung Qinghai China
197 L6 Logreşti Romania
156 B7 Logron France
183 P4 Logroño Spain
185 I2 Logrosán Spain
142 F5 Løgstør Denmark
117 N7 Logtak Lake India
192 B6 Logudoro reg. Sardegna Italy
142 E6 Løgumkloster Denmark
78 □5 Loh i. Vanuatu
142 G6 Lohals Denmark
117 J8 Lohardaga Jharkhand India
116 E5 Loharu Haryana India
214 H4 Lohatlha S. Africa
116 D6 Lohawat Rajasthan India
173 O3 Lohberg Ger.
158 H6 Lohéac France
168 H2 Lohe-Rickelshof Ger.
169 I8 Lohfelden Ger.
Lohifushi i. N. Male Maldives see Lhohifushi
Lohil r. China/India see Zayü Qu
141 T6 Lohilahti Fin.
140 R3 Lohiniva Fin.
141 R6 Lohja Fin.
138 G1 Lohjanjärvi l. Fin.
169 D9 Lohmar Ger.
170 I1 Lohme Ger.
170 F3 Lohmen Mecklenburg-Vorpommern Ger.
171 J9 Lohmen Sachsen Ger.
169 F9 Löhnberg Ger.
169 G6 Löhne Ger.
168 F5 Lohne (Oldenburg) Ger.
179 H3 Lohnsburg am Kobernaußerwald Austria
172 H2 Lohr r. Ger.
169 G9 Lohra Ger.
172 H2 Lohr am Main Ger.
171 J8 Lohsa Ger.
140 Q4 Lohtaja Fin.
138 K3 Lohusuu Estonia
96 E4 Loi, Nam r. Myanmar alt. Nanlei He (China)
191 K7 Loiano Italy
173 M4 Loiching Ger.
159 J6 Loigné-sur-Mayenne France
156 C7 Loigny-la-Bataille France
96 C5 Loikaw Myanmar
96 C5 Loi Lan mt. Myanmar/Thai.
208 D5 Loile r. Dem. Rep. Congo
96 C4 Loi-lem Myanmar
96 D3 Loi Lun Myanmar
141 Q6 Loimaa Fin.
138 F1 Loimaan kunta Fin.
138 F1 Loimijoki r. Fin.
156 E7 Loing r. France
96 C2 Loipyet Hills Myanmar
156 B7 Loir r. France
159 L6 Loir, Les Vaux du val. France
159 J6 Loiré France
160 E5 Loire dept France
159 G7 Loire r. France
160 C3 Loire, Canal latéral à la France
160 E5 Loire, Gorges de la France
156 C8 Loire, Val de val. France
158 G7 Loire-Atlantique dept France
160 C3 Loire et de l'Allier, Plaines de la plain France

Loire-Inférieure *dept* France *see* Loire-Atlantique
160 F5 **Loire-sur-Rhône** France
156 D8 **Loiret** *dept* France
156 C8 **Loiret** *r.* France
156 B8 **Loir-et-Cher** *dept* France
192 C6 **Loiri-Porto San Paolo** *Sardegna* Italy
159 J5 **Loiron** France
173 K6 **Loisach** *r.* Ger.
96 C4 **Loi Sang** *mt.* Myanmar
160 E5 **Loise** *r.* France
157 J5 **Loison** *r.* France
96 C3 **Loi Song** *mt.* Myanmar
156 I6 **Loisy-sur-Marne** France
211 B5 **Loita Plains** Kenya
170 H3 **Loitz** Ger.
182 F5 **Loivos** Port.
182 E6 **Loivos do Monte** Port.
247 □1 **Loiza Aldea** Puerto Rico
250 B6 **Loja** Ecuador
250 B6 **Loja** *prov.* Ecuador
185 K6 **Loja** Spain
177 H3 **Lok** Slovakia
136 D3 **Lokachi** Ukr.
95 L2 **Lokan** *r.* Malaysia
208 E5 **Lokandu** Dem. Rep. Congo
140 S3 **Lokan tekojärvi** *l.* Fin.
179 I8 **Lokavec** Slovenia
129 K5 **Lökbatan** Azer.
177 I2 **Lokca** Slovakia
134 J3 **Lokchim** *r.* Rus. Fed.
142 H2 **Løken** Norway
165 F6 **Lokeren** Belgium
176 B1 **Loket** Czech Rep.
179 I8 **Lokev** Slovenia
212 D5 **Lokgwabe** Botswana
137 M3 **Lokhvytsya** Ukr.
210 B4 **Lokichar** Kenya
210 B3 **Lokichokio** Kenya
93 B4 **Lokilalaki, Gunung** *mt.* Indon.
210 B3 **Lokitaung** Kenya
140 S3 **Lokka** Fin.
142 F4 **Løkken** Denmark
140 J5 **Løkken** Norway
139 N5 **Loknya** Rus. Fed.
136 E2 **Loknytsya** Ukr.
207 G4 **Loko** Nigeria
208 D5 **Lokofe** Dem. Rep. Congo
207 G5 **Lokoja** Nigeria
208 C5 **Lokolama** Dem. Rep. Congo
208 C5 **Lokolo** *r.* Dem. Rep. Congo
207 I6 **Lokomo** Cameroon
208 D5 **Lokona** Dem. Rep. Congo
208 C5 **Lokoro** *r.* Dem. Rep. Congo
208 C4 **Lokosafa** C.A.R.
177 K5 **Lőkösháza** Hungary
207 F5 **Lokossa** Benin
139 R9 **Lokot'** Rus. Fed.
138 I2 **Loksa** Estonia
140 N2 **Løksebotn** Norway
221 L3 **Loks Land** *i. Nunavut* Can.
78 □6 **Lokuru** *New Georgia Is* Solomon Is
Lokutu Dem. Rep. Congo *see* **Elisabetha**
191 R5 **Lokve** Croatia
179 I7 **Lokve** Slovenia
208 F3 **Lol** Sudan
208 F2 **Lol** *watercourse* Sudan
209 B8 **Lola** Angola
206 C5 **Lola** Guinea
240 L2 **Lola, Mount** *CA* U.S.A.
136 E5 **Lolishniy Shepit** Ukr.
142 H7 **Lolland** *i.* Denmark
169 G9 **Lollar** Ger.
210 A2 **Lolle** *watercourse* Sudan
187 D10 **L'Olleria** Spain
211 B5 **Lollondo** Tanz.
208 D4 **Lolo** Dem. Rep. Congo
238 G3 **Lolo** *MT* U.S.A.
93 F3 **Lolobata** *Halmahera* Indon.
93 E3 **Loloda** *Halmahera* Indon.
93 E2 **Loloda Utara, Kepulauan** *is Maluku* Indon.
207 H6 **Lolodorf** Cameroon
260 B4 **Lolol** Chile
238 G3 **Lolo Pass** *MT* U.S.A.
93 D8 **Lolotoi** East Timor
94 B4 **Lolowau** Indon.
78 □5 **Lolvavana, Passage** Vanuatu
214 H2 **Lolwane** S. Africa
197 L7 **Lom** Bulg.
197 L7 **Lom** *r.* Bulg.
171 I9 **Lom** Czech Rep.
141 J6 **Lom** Norway
139 W4 **Lom** Rus. Fed.
241 X2 **Loma** *CO* U.S.A.
252 D2 **Loma Alta** Bol.
245 L7 **Loma Bonita** Mex.
185 M4 **Loma de Chiclana** *reg.* Spain
260 C5 **Loma del Jaguel Moro** *mt.* Arg.
185 M5 **Loma de Úbeda** *reg.* Spain
163 F8 **Lomagne** *reg.* France
208 D4 **Lomako** *r.* Dem. Rep. Congo
240 O7 **Loma Linda** *CA* U.S.A.
77 I3 **Lomaloma** Fiji
209 E4 **Lomami** *r.* Dem. Rep. Congo
206 C4 **Loma Mountains** Sierra Leone
261 G5 **Loma Negra** Arg.
260 E5 **Loma Negra, Planicie de la** *plain* Arg.
123 L5 **Lomar Pass** Afgh.
252 B3 **Lomas** Peru
262 T3 **Lomas, Bahía de** *b.* Chile
259 D6 **Lomas Coloradas** *hills* Arg.
261 H4 **Lomas de Zamora** Arg.
Lomati *r.* S. Africa *see* **Mlumati**
261 H4 **Loma Verde** Arg.
79 □7a **Lomawai** *Viti Levu* Fiji
175 L4 **Łomazy** Pol.
209 D8 **Lomba** *r.* Angola
216 □1b **Lomba da Fazenda** *São Miguel* Azores
216 □1b **Lomba da Maia** *São Miguel* Azores
251 H4 **Lombarda, Serra** *hills* Brazil
190 H5 **Lombardia** *admin. reg.* Italy
86 G4 **Lombardina** *W.A.* Austr.
163 I8 **Lombers** France
163 F9 **Lombez** France
93 C8 **Lomblen** *i.* Indon.
95 L9 **Lombok** *Lombok* Indon.
95 L9 **Lombok** *i.* Indon.
95 K9 **Lombok, Selat** *sea chan.* Indon.
159 L5 **Lombron** France
207 F5 **Lomé** Togo
208 D5 **Lomela** Dem. Rep. Congo
208 D5 **Lomela** *r.* Dem. Rep. Congo
190 F5 **Lomello** Italy
175 I3 **Łomianki** Pol.
207 I6 **Lomié** Cameroon
226 F6 **Lomira** *WI* U.S.A.
171 H8 **Lommatzsch** Ger.
156 E2 **Lomme** France
165 H6 **Lommel** Belgium
174 D3 **Łomnica** Pol.
176 F2 **Lomnice** Czech Rep.
176 D2 **Lomnice** *r.* Czech Rep.
179 K1 **Lomnice nad Lužnicí** Czech Rep.
176 E1 **Lomnice nad Popelkou** Czech Rep.
177 I2 **Lomno** *mt.* Slovakia
225 J3 **Lomond** *Nfld and Lab.* Can.
146 G10 **Lomond, Loch** *l. Scotland* U.K.
138 M2 **Lomonosov** Rus. Fed.
268 M1 **Lomonosov Ridge** *sea feature* Arctic Ocean
160 J2 **Lomont** *hills* France
134 H2 **Lomovoye** Rus. Fed.
Lomphat Cambodia *see* **Lumphăt**
95 M7 **Lompobatang, Hutan Lindung** *nature res. Sulawesi* Indon.
93 A6 **Lompobattang, Gunung** *mt.* Indon.
240 L7 **Lompoc** *CA* U.S.A.
96 E6 **Lom Sak** Thai.
140 N4 **Lomsjö** Sweden
175 K2 **Łomża** Pol.
97 I8 **Lon, Hon** *i.* Vietnam
114 E3 **Lonar** *Mahar.* India
190 I5 **Lonato** Italy
114 C3 **Lonavale** *Mahar.* India
176 G6 **Lončarica** Croatia
100 I5 **Lonchakovo** Rus. Fed.
260 A6 **Loncoche** Chile
260 B5 **Loncopangue** Chile
260 B6 **Loncopue** Arg.
117 M8 **Londa** Bangl.
114 D5 **Londa** *Karnataka* India
191 L8 **Londa** Italy
209 B6 **Londéla-Kayes** Congo
165 F7 **Londerzeel** Belgium
156 B4 **Londinières** France
Londinium *Greater London, England* U.K. *see* **London**
207 H6 **Londji** Cameroon
100 H4 **Londoko** Rus. Fed.
224 D5 **London** *Ont.* Can.
151 L4 **London** *Greater London, England* U.K.
232 A11 **London** *KY* U.S.A.
232 B9 **London** *OH* U.S.A.
152 **London area map** U.K.
247 □6 **London Bridge** *i.* Grenada
151 M4 **London City** *airport England* U.K.
147 H3 **Londonderry** *Northern Ireland* U.K.
147 I3 **Londonderry** *county Northern Ireland* U.K.
233 M5 **Londonderry** *VT* U.S.A.
86 I2 **Londonderry, Cape** *W.A.* Austr.
259 C9 **Londonderry, Isla** *i.* Chile
151 L5 **London Gatwick** *airport England* U.K.
151 L5 **London Heathrow** *airport England* U.K.
Londoni Fiji *see* **Lodoni**
151 M4 **London Stansted** *airport England* U.K.
258 D2 **Londres** Arg.
256 B5 **Londrina** Brazil
209 B8 **Londuimbali** Angola
227 M4 **Lonely Island** *Ont.* Can.
213 F3 **Lonely Mine** Zimbabwe
235 I3 **Lonelyville** *NY* U.S.A.
240 N5 **Lone Pine** *CA* U.S.A.
156 C3 **Long** France
96 D5 **Long** Thai.
247 □3 **Long, Îlet** *i.* Martinique
146 G10 **Long, Loch** *inlet Argyll and Bute, Scotland* U.K.
163 E10 **Long, Pic** *mt.* France
209 C8 **Longa** Angola
209 C9 **Longa** *r. Cuando Cubango* Angola
209 B7 **Longa** *r.* Angola
198 C6 **Longa** Greece
131 S2 **Longa, Proliv** *sea chan.* Rus. Fed.
163 G9 **Longages** France
95 K3 **Longagung** *Kalimantan* Indon.
210 B3 **Longairo** Sudan
95 K3 **Long Akah** *Sarawak* Malaysia
209 D9 **Longa-Mavinga, Coutada Pública do** *nature res.* Angola
108 F7 **Long'an** *Guangxi* China
Long'an *Sichuan* China *see* **Pingwu**
217 □3b **Longani, Baie de** *b.* Mayotte
100 D5 **Long'anqiao** *Heilong.* China
191 L5 **Longare** Italy
186 C5 **Longares** Spain
191 M3 **Longarone** Italy
150 G5 **Long Ashton** *North Somerset, England* U.K.
260 B4 **Longaví** Chile
260 B4 **Longaví** *r.* Chile
260 B5 **Longaví, Nevado de** *mt.* Chile
95 K3 **Longbawan** *Kalimantan* Indon.
246 □ **Long Bay** Jamaica
246 □ **Long Bay** *b.* Jamaica
246 □ **Long Bay** *b.* Jamaica
231 H9 **Long Bay** *b. NC* U.S.A.
81 F11 **Longbeach** *South I.* N.Z.
240 N8 **Long Beach** *CA* U.S.A.
235 H3 **Long Beach** *NY* U.S.A.
238 B3 **Long Beach** *WA* U.S.A.
235 G5 **Long Beach** *coastal area NJ* U.S.A.
151 K2 **Long Bennington** *Lincolnshire, England* U.K.
149 N3 **Longbenton** *Tyne and Wear, England* U.K.
95 K3 **Longberini** *Kalimantan* Indon.
95 L3 **Longbia** *Kalimantan* Indon.
Longbo *Hunan* China *see* **Shuangpai**
95 K4 **Longboh** *Kalimantan* Indon.
233 L8 **Long Branch** *NJ* U.S.A.
150 H5 **Longbridge Deverill** *Wiltshire, England* U.K.
109 J6 **Longbu** *Jiangxi* China
151 J3 **Long Buckby** *Northamptonshire, England* U.K.
80 J7 **Longburn** *North I.* N.Z.
246 F2 **Long Cay** *i.* Bahamas
108 E4 **Longchang** *Sichuan* China
160 H4 **Longchaumois** France
Longcheng *Anhui* China *see* **Xiaoxian**
Longcheng *Guangdong* China *see* **Longmen**
Longcheng *Jiangxi* China *see* **Pengze**
Longcheng *Yunnan* China *see* **Chenggong**
109 J6 **Longchuan** *Guangdong* China
Longchuan *Yunnan* China *see* **Chengzi**
Longchuan *Yunnan* China *see* **Nanhua**
108 A6 **Longchuan** *Yunnan* China
108 A7 **Longchuan Jiang** *r.* China
151 I4 **Long Compton** *Warwickshire, England* U.K.
82 E3 **Long Creek** *watercourse S.A.* Austr.
223 K5 **Long Creek** *r. Sask.* Can.
238 E4 **Long Creek** *OR* U.S.A.
151 J4 **Long Crendon** *Buckinghamshire, England* U.K.
106 J9 **Longde** *Ningxia* China
151 I2 **Longdon** *Staffordshire, England* U.K.
151 J2 **Long Eaton** *Derbyshire, England* U.K.
160 G2 **Longecourt-en-Plaine** France
157 J6 **Longeville-en-Barrois** France
157 M5 **Longeville-lès-St-Avold** France
162 B3 **Longeville-sur-Mer** France
81 G9 **Longfellow, Mount** *South I.* N.Z.
147 G5 **Longford** Ireland
147 G5 **Longford** *county* Ireland
146 J10 **Longforgan** *Perth and Kinross, Scotland* U.K.
149 N3 **Longframlington** *Northumberland, England* U.K.
Longgang *Chongqing* China *see* **Dazu**
109 J7 **Longgang** *Guangdong* China
95 L3 **Longgi** *r.* Indon.
151 J4 **Long Hanborough** *Oxfordshire, England* U.K.
Long Harbour *H.K.* China *see* **Tai Tan Hoi Hap**
150 H4 **Longhope** *Gloucestershire, England* U.K.
146 J5 **Longhope** *Orkney, Scotland* U.K.
149 N3 **Longhorsley** *Northumberland, England* U.K.
149 N3 **Longhoughton** *Northumberland, England* U.K.
107 O6 **Longhua** *Hebei* China
109 H5 **Longhui** *Hunan* China
263 K1 **Longhurst, Mount** Antarctica
194 H7 **Longi** *Sicilia* Italy
95 L3 **Longibau** *Kalimantan* Indon.
211 C5 **Longido** Tanz.
95 L5 **Longikis** *Kalimantan* Indon.
262 U2 **Longing, Cape** Antarctica
95 K5 **Longiram** *Kalimantan* Indon.
85 L7 **Long Island** *Qld* Austr.
246 F2 **Long Island** Bahamas
225 H4 **Long Island** *N.S.* Can.
224 E2 **Long Island** *Nunavut* Can.
115 M6 **Long Island** *Andaman & Nicobar Is* India
81 A12 **Long Island** *South I.* N.Z.
91 K8 **Long Island** P.N.G.
Long Island *Inner Islands* Seychelles *see* **Longue, Île**
233 M8 **Long Island** *NY* U.S.A.
233 L7 **Long Island Sound** *sea chan. CT/NY* U.S.A.
151 J3 **Long Itchington** *Warwickshire, England* U.K.
107 R3 **Longjiang** *Heilong.* China
108 G6 **Long Jiang** *r.* China
Longjin *Fujian* China *see* **Qingliu**
Longjin *Jiangxi* China *see* **Anyi**
Longjuzhai *Shaanxi* China *see* **Danfeng**
107 Q8 **Longkou** *Shandong* China
107 Q8 **Longkou Gang** *b.* China
224 C3 **Longlac** *Ont.* Can.
233 □S1 **Long Lake** *l. N.B.* Can.
224 C3 **Long Lake** *l. Ont.* Can.
233 K5 **Long Lake** *NY* U.S.A.
233 □Q1 **Long Lake** *l. ME* U.S.A.
226 I5 **Long Lake** *l. MI* U.S.A.
227 K4 **Long Lake** *l. MI* U.S.A.
233 K4 **Long Lake** *l. NY* U.S.A.
95 K3 **Long Lama** *Sarawak* Malaysia
214 I4 **Longlands** S. Africa
151 J3 **Long Lawford** *Warwickshire, England* U.K.
108 F5 **Longli** *Guizhou* China
165 H9 **Longlier** Belgium
108 E6 **Longlin** *Guangxi* China
108 B6 **Longling** *Yunnan* China
146 L7 **Longmanhill** *Aberdeenshire, Scotland* U.K.
108 E4 **Longmatan** *Sichuan* China
233 M6 **Longmeadow** *MA* U.S.A.
151 N3 **Long Melford** *Suffolk, England* U.K.
109 J7 **Longmen** *Guangdong* China
100 E4 **Longmen** *Heilong.* China
108 E2 **Longmen Shan** *mts Sichuan* China
108 F7 **Longming** *Guangxi* China
238 L6 **Longmont** *CO* U.S.A.
146 J7 **Longmorn** *Moray, Scotland* U.K.
95 K3 **Long Murum** *Sarawak* Malaysia
108 E2 **Longnan** *Gansu* China
109 J6 **Longnan** *Jiangxi* China
95 K4 **Longnawan** *Kalimantan* Indon.
146 K11 **Longniddry** *East Lothian, Scotland* U.K.
159 M4 **Longny-au-Perche** France
193 Q9 **Longobardi** Italy
195 L5 **Longobucco** Italy
184 D2 **Longomel** Port.
209 B8 **Longonjo** Angola
182 D4 **Longos Vales** Port.
260 B3 **Longotoma** Chile
95 K4 **Longpahangai** *Kalimantan* Indon.
97 H10 **Long Phu** Vietnam
Longping *Guizhou* China *see* **Luodian**
231 □2 **Long Point** *pt New Prov.* Bahamas
224 D5 **Long Point** *Ont.* Can.
223 L4 **Long Point** *pt Man.* Can.
224 D5 **Long Point** *pt Ont.* Can.
80 L6 **Long Point** *pt North I.* N.Z.
81 B13 **Long Point** *pt South I.* N.Z.
81 D13 **Long Point** *pt South I.* N.Z.
227 N7 **Long Point Bay** *Ont.* Can.
234 F6 **Longport** *NJ* U.S.A.
236 H3 **Long Prairie** *MN* U.S.A.
156 C3 **Longpré-les-Corps-Saints** France
149 M5 **Long Preston** *North Yorkshire, England* U.K.
95 K3 **Longpujungan** *Kalimantan* Indon.
Longquan *Guizhou* China *see* **Fenggang**
Longquan *Guizhou* China *see* **Danzhai**
Longquan *Hunan* China *see* **Xintian**
Longquan *Yunnan* China *see* **Yimen**
109 L4 **Longquan** *Zhejiang* China
109 M4 **Longquan Xi** *r.* China
225 J3 **Long Range Mountains** *Nfld and Lab.* Can.
225 J4 **Long Range Mountains** *Nfld and Lab.* Can.
162 D3 **Longré** France
85 J7 **Longreach** *Qld* Austr.
86 H2 **Long Reef** *W.A.* Austr.
85 M1 **Long Reef** P.N.G.
108 D2 **Longriba** *Sichuan* China
149 L6 **Longridge** *Lancashire, England* U.K.
182 F7 **Longroiva** Port.
Longshan *Guizhou* China *see* **Longli**
108 G4 **Longshan** *Hunan* China
Longshan *Yunnan* China *see* **Longling**
106 J9 **Long Shan** *mts* China
108 H6 **Longsheng** *Guangxi* China
150 □ **Longships** *is England* U.K.
106 G7 **Longshou Shan** *mts* China
81 A13 **Long Sound** *inlet South I.* N.Z.
238 L6 **Longs Peak** *CO* U.S.A.
151 O3 **Long Stratton** *Norfolk, England* U.K.
151 M2 **Long Sutton** *Lincolnshire, England* U.K.
150 G5 **Long Sutton** *Somerset, England* U.K.
95 K3 **Long Teru** *Sarawak* Malaysia
109 H4 **Longtian** *Hunan* China
222 G1 **Longtom Lake** *N.W.T.* Can.
215 O1 **Long Tompas** *pass* S. Africa
85 J6 **Longton** *Qld* Austr.
149 L6 **Longton** *Lancashire, England* U.K.
150 H2 **Longton** *Stoke-on-Trent, England* U.K.
107 R2 **Longtou** *Nei Mongol* China
149 L3 **Longtown** *Cumbria, England* U.K.
217 □2b **Longue, Île** *i. Inner Islands* Seychelles
156 D4 **Longueau** France
162 D1 **Longué-Jumelles** France
156 D2 **Longuenesse** France
225 H3 **Longue-Pointe** *Que.* Can.
233 L3 **Longueuil** *Que.* Can.
156 F6 **Longueville** France
156 B4 **Longueville-sur-Scie** France
157 K5 **Longuyon** France
240 I2 **Longvale** *CA* U.S.A.
241 U7 **Long Valley** *AZ* U.S.A.
234 F3 **Long Valley** *NJ* U.S.A.
160 G2 **Longvic** France
160 G2 **Longvic** *airport* France
222 H5 **Longview** *Alta* Can.
237 H9 **Longview** *TX* U.S.A.
238 C3 **Longview** *WA* U.S.A.
95 L4 **Longwai** *Kalimantan* Indon.
100 H6 **Longwangmiao** *Heilong.* China
111 I10 **Longwei Co** *l. Xizang* China
148 D7 **Longwood** Ireland
216 □2b **Longwood** St Helena
157 K4 **Longwy** France
106 I9 **Longxi** *Gansu* China
Longxian *Guangdong* China *see* **Wengyuan**
106 J9 **Longxian** *Shaanxi* China
Longxingchang *Nei Mongol* China *see* **Wuyuan**
109 K5 **Longxi Shan** *mt. Fujian* China
Longxun *Fujian* China *see* **Dehua**
97 G9 **Long Xuyên** Vietnam
109 K6 **Longyan** *Fujian* China
107 N8 **Longyao** *Hebei* China
140 □ **Longyearbyen** Svalbard
100 E4 **Longzhen** *Heilong.* China
108 F7 **Longzhou** *Guangxi* China
Longzhouping *Hubei* China *see* **Changyang**
191 K5 **Lonigo** Italy
168 E5 **Löningen** Ger.
188 F3 **Lonja** *r.* Croatia
179 N8 **Lonjica** Croatia
188 F3 **Lonjsko Polje** *plain* Croatia
213 □K3 **Lonkintsy** Madag.
159 J4 **Lonlay-l'Abbaye** France
164 K4 **Lonneker** Neth.
156 I4 **Lonny** France
237 J8 **Lonoke** *AR* U.S.A.
261 F5 **Lonquimay** Arg.
260 B6 **Lonquimay** Chile
260 B6 **Lonquimay, Volcán** *vol.* Chile
163 D9 **Lons** France
143 K5 **Lönsboda** Sweden
140 M3 **Lønsdalen** *val.* Norway
160 H3 **Lons-le-Saunier** France
142 F4 **Lønstrup** Denmark
93 F6 **Lontar** *i. Maluku* Indon.
96 C2 **Lonton** Myanmar
251 I6 **Lontra** Brazil
255 B7 **Lontra** *r.* Brazil
254 C3 **Lontra** *r.* Brazil
260 B4 **Lontué** Chile
165 J7 **Lontzen** Belgium
177 L3 **Lónya** Hungary
138 H2 **Loo** Estonia
129 A2 **Loo** Rus. Fed.
92 D5 **Looc** Phil.
Loochoo Islands Japan *see* **Nansei-shotō**
226 J7 **Looking Glass** *r. MI* U.S.A.
224 D2 **Lookout, Cape** *Ont.* Can.
231 I8 **Lookout, Cape** *NC* U.S.A.
227 K5 **Lookout, Point** *MI* U.S.A.
240 N5 **Lookout Mountain** *CA* U.S.A.
85 J3 **Lookout Point** *Qld* Austr.
87 E13 **Lookout Point** *W.A.* Austr.
211 B5 **Loolmalasin** *vol. crater* Tanz.
86 H5 **Looma** *W.A.* Austr.
224 B3 **Loon** *Ont.* Can.
222 H3 **Loon** *r. Alta* Can.
87 I11 **Loongana** *W.A.* Austr.
223 I4 **Loon Lake** *Sask.* Can.
233 □P2 **Loon Lake** *l. ME* U.S.A.
164 H5 **Loon op Zand** Neth.
156 D2 **Loon-Plage** France
164 H5 **Loonse en Drunense Duinen** *nature res.* Neth.
147 C7 **Loop Head** Ireland
156 F2 **Loos** France
179 L3 **Loosdorf** Austria
151 N5 **Loose** *Kent, England* U.K.
215 I7 **Lootsberg Pass** S. Africa
111 E8 **Lop** *Xinjiang* China
137 P4 **Lopan** *r.* Ukr.
139 R9 **Lopandino** Rus. Fed.
191 R6 **Lopar** Croatia
213 □J4 **Lopary** Madag.
Lopasnya Rus. Fed. *see* **Chekhov**
139 U7 **Lopasnya** *r.* Rus. Fed.
129 I2 **Lopatin** Rus. Fed.
100 M3 **Lopatina, Gora** *mt. Sakhalin* Rus. Fed.
120 A1 **Lopatino** Rus. Fed.
139 V6 **Lopatinskiy** Rus. Fed.
Lopatka, Cape Rus. Fed. *see* **Lopatka, Mys**
131 Q2 **Lopatka, Mys** *c.* Rus. Fed.
131 Q4 **Lopatka, Mys** *c.* Rus. Fed.
139 P9 **Lopatni** Rus. Fed.
136 G5 **Lopatnic** Moldova
138 L4 **Lopatovo** Rus. Fed.
136 D3 **Lopatyn** Ukr.
139 P8 **Lopazna** Rus. Fed.
97 E7 **Lop Buri** Thai.
151 I5 **Lopcombe Corner** *Wiltshire, England* U.K.
208 A5 **Lopé-Okanda, Réserve de** *nature res.* Gabon
158 C5 **Loperhet** France
78 □5 **Lopévi** *i.* Vanuatu
261 H5 **López** *Buenos Aires* Arg.
261 G2 **López** *Santa Fé* Arg.
92 D5 **Lopez** *Luzon* Phil.
234 C2 **Lopez** *PA* U.S.A.
208 A5 **Lopez, Cap** *c.* Gabon
261 F6 **López Lecube** Arg.
175 L4 **Łopiennik Górny** Pol.
192 B3 **Lopigna** *Corse* France
164 G5 **Lopik** Neth.
Lopnur *Xinjiang* China *see* **Yuli**
110 J6 **Lop Nur** *salt flat* China
208 C4 **Lopori** *r.* Dem. Rep. Congo
164 K2 **Loppersum** Neth.
140 P1 **Lopphavet** *b.* Norway
141 R6 **Loppi** Fin.
134 J3 **Loptyuga** Rus. Fed.
175 I5 **Łopuszno** Pol.
183 P3 **Lóquiz, Sierra de** *mts* Spain
182 F4 **Lor** *r.* Spain
123 L6 **Lora** *r.* Afgh.
82 E3 **Lora** *watercourse S.A.* Austr.
141 J5 **Lora** Norway
123 K8 **Lora** Pak.
123 K7 **Lora, Hamun-i-** *dry lake* Pak.
260 A4 **Lora, Punta** *pt* Chile
184 H5 **Lora del Río** Spain
232 C7 **Lorain** *OH* U.S.A.
226 C9 **Loraine** *IL* U.S.A.
123 M6 **Loralai** Pak.
123 M6 **Loralai** *r.* Pak.
93 B5 **Lorana** *Sulawesi* Indon.
183 N8 **Loranca de Tajuña** Spain
234 D4 **Lorane** *PA* U.S.A.
185 P5 **Lorca** Spain
172 H4 **Lorch** *Baden-Württemberg* Ger.
169 E10 **Lorch** *Hessen* Ger.
187 E10 **Lorcha** Spain
92 A6 **Lord Auckland** *sea feature* Phil.
182 D6 **Lordelo** Port.
Lord Hood *atoll Arch. des Tuamotu* Fr. Polynesia *see* **Marutea (Sud)**
Lord Howe Atoll Solomon Is *see* **Ontong Java Atoll**
82 □2 **Lord Howe Island** Austr.
266 F7 **Lord Howe Rise** *sea feature* S. Pacific Ocean
97 C9 **Lord Loughborough Island** Myanmar
182 E7 **Lordosa** Port.
239 J10 **Lordsburg** *NM* U.S.A.
234 E2 **Lords Valley** *PA* U.S.A.
93 E8 **Lore** East Timor
93 B4 **Lore Lindu, Taman Nasional** *nat. park* Indon.
257 E5 **Lorena** Brazil
91 K7 **Lorengau** *Admiralty Is* P.N.G.
91 I8 **Lorentz** *r. Papua* Indon.
91 I7 **Lorentz, Taman Nasional** *nat. park Papua* Indon.
245 J3 **Lorenzo del Real** Mex.
261 I3 **Lorenzo Geyres** Uru.
191 M5 **Loreo** Italy
122 C5 **Lorestān** *prov.* Iran
258 F2 **Loreto** Arg.
254 D3 **Loreto** Brazil
191 P9 **Loreto** Italy
242 D4 **Loreto** *Baja California Sur* Mex.
244 E3 **Loreto** *Zacatecas* Mex.
253 F5 **Loreto** Para.
250 C5 **Loreto** *dept* Peru
92 E6 **Loreto** Phil.
193 L3 **Loreto Aprutino** Italy
226 D4 **Loretta** *WI* U.S.A.
161 I9 **Lorgues** France
210 C4 **Lorian Swamp** Kenya
250 C2 **Lorica** Col.
158 E6 **Lorient** France
182 E8 **Loriga** Port.
162 C5 **Lorignac** France
233 K3 **L'Orignal** *Ont.* Can.
187 D8 **Loriguilla** Spain
187 D8 **Loriguilla, Embalse de** *resr* Spain
123 J8 **Lorikand** Pak.
221 I3 **Lorillard** *r. Nunavut* Can.
177 I4 **Lőrinci** Hungary
238 K2 **Loring** *MT* U.S.A.
161 F7 **Loriol-sur-Drôme** France
160 D2 **Lormes** France
116 H8 **Lormi** *Chhattisgarh* India
163 C6 **Lormont** France
146 E10 **Lorn, Firth of** *est. Scotland* U.K.
85 J8 **Lorne** *Qld* Austr.
83 I8 **Lorne** *Vic.* Austr.
84 F5 **Lorne** *watercourse N.T.* Austr.
111 K12 **Loro** *r.* China
191 L8 **Loro Ciuffenna** Italy
206 E4 **Loropéni** Burkina
193 K1 **Loro Piceno** Italy
163 G9 **Lorp-Sentaraille** France
157 M6 **Lorquin** France
172 D6 **Lörrach** Ger.
157 M6 **Lorrain, Plateau** France
84 G5 **Lorraine** *Qld* Austr.
157 L6 **Lorraine** *admin. reg.* France
157 J5 **Lorraine** *reg.* France
165 I11 **Lorraine, Parc Naturel Régional de** *nature res.* France
157 K7 **Lorraine, Plaine** *plain* France
156 E7 **Lorrez-le-Bocage-Préaux** France
156 E8 **Lorris** France
172 F2 **Lorsch** Ger.
87 F12 **Lort** *r. W.A.* Austr.
141 N5 **Lörudden** Sweden
168 E5 **Lorup** Ger.
205 H3 **Lorzot** Tunisia
206 B4 **Los, Îles de** *is* Guinea
Los', Ostrov *i.* Azer. *see* **Qarasu Adası**
245 J4 **Losa** Mex.
183 N3 **Losa** *r.* Spain
182 H5 **Losacino** Spain
187 D8 **Losa del Obispo** Spain
210 C4 **Losai National Reserve** *nature res.* Kenya
116 E6 **Losal** *Rajasthan* India
240 L7 **Los Alamos** *CA* U.S.A.
239 K9 **Los Alamos** *NM* U.S.A.
187 D12 **Los Alcázares** Spain
243 J4 **Los Aldamas** Mex.
259 C6 **Los Alerces, Parque Nacional** *nat. park* Arg.
187 C12 **Los Algezares** Spain
245 J6 **Los Altos** Mex.
244 G3 **Los Amoles** Mex.
258 F3 **Los Amores** Arg.
260 B3 **Los Andes** Chile
260 A5 **Los Ángeles** Chile
240 N7 **Los Angeles** *CA* U.S.A.
240 N6 **Los Angeles Aqueduct** *canal CA* U.S.A.
259 C7 **Los Antiguos** Arg.
246 C2 **Los Arabos** Cuba
260 C3 **Los Árboles** Arg.
183 P3 **Los Arcos** Spain
187 E11 **Los Arenales del Sol** Spain
183 P8 **Losares** *mt.* Spain
245 H8 **Los Arroyos** Mex.
244 B4 **Los Ayala** Mex.
244 G6 **Los Azufres, Parque Natural** *nature res.* Mex.
242 F4 **Los Baños** Mex.
240 L4 **Los Banos** *CA* U.S.A.
185 O3 **Los Barreros** *mt.* Spain
184 I8 **Los Barrios** Spain
182 I3 **Los Barrios de Luna** Spain
187 D12 **Los Belones** Spain
258 E1 **Los Blancos** Arg.
187 C12 **Los Cantareros** Spain
261 G3 **Los Cardos** Arg.
260 E2 **Los Cerrillos** Arg.
261 H2 **Los Charrúas** Arg.
261 F5 **Los Chilenos, Laguna** *l.* Arg.
242 □Q12 **Los Chiles** Costa Rica
260 D1 **Los Colorados** Arg.
260 E3 **Los Condores** Arg.
261 H2 **Los Conquistadores** Arg.
250 C2 **Los Corales del Rosario, Parque Nacional** *nat. park* Col.
240 O9 **Los Coronados, Islas** *is* Mex.
183 L2 **Los Corrales de Buelna** Spain
186 C5 **Loscos** Spain
216 □3a **Los Cristianos** *Tenerife* Canary Is
252 D3 **Los Cusis** *Beni* Bol.
252 D3 **Los Cusis** *Beni* Bol.
Los Difuntios, Lago de *l.* Uru. *see* **Negra, Lago**
187 C12 **Los Dolores** Spain
135 H6 **Losevo** Rus. Fed.
211 C6 **Loseya** *well* Tanz.
185 P6 **Los Gallardos** Spain
245 I4 **Los Gatos** *r.* Mex.
240 K4 **Los Gatos** *CA* U.S.A.
216 □3a **Los Gigantes** *Tenerife* Canary Is
260 E2 **Los Gigantes, Cerro** *mt.* Arg.
259 B8 **Los Glaciares, Parque Nacional** *nat. park* Arg.
247 I4 **Los Haitises** *nat. park* Dom. Rep.
172 B2 **Losheim** Ger.
183 O9 **Los Hinojosos** Spain
242 E2 **Los Hoyos** Mex.
259 B7 **Los Huemules, Parque Nacional** *nat. park* Chile
175 K3 **Łosice** Pol.
243 M8 **Los Idolos** Mex.
188 E3 **Lošinj** *i.* Croatia
175 L3 **Łosinka** Pol.
258 E3 **Los Juríes** Arg.
250 B3 **Los Katios, Parque Nacional** *nat. park* Col.
215 N4 **Loskop** S. Africa
215 N1 **Loskop Dam Nature Reserve** S. Africa
259 B5 **Los Lagos** Chile
259 B6 **Los Lagos** *admin. reg.* Chile
Loslau Pol. *see* **Wodzisław Śląski**
260 A6 **Los Laureles** Chile
242 G3 **Los Leones** Mex.
216 □3d **Los Llanos de Aridane** *La Palma* Canary Is
239 K9 **Los Lunas** *NM* U.S.A.
260 B3 **Los Maitenes** *Santiago* Chile
260 B3 **Los Maitenes** *Valparaíso* Chile
187 C12 **Los Maldonados** Spain
260 E5 **Los Manatiales** Arg.
245 H5 **Los Mármoles, Parque Nacional** *nat. park* Mex.
187 C12 **Los Martinez** Spain
259 C6 **Los Menucos** Arg.
139 R6 **Los'mino** Rus. Fed.
242 E5 **Los Mochis** Mex.
184 H6 **Los Molares** Spain
216 □3b **Los Molinos** *Fuerteventura* Canary Is
183 L7 **Los Molinos** Spain
240 J1 **Los Molinos** *CA* U.S.A.
260 B2 **Los Molles** *r.* Chile
186 D4 **Los Monegros** *reg.* Spain
245 I1 **Los Morales** Mex.
245 K7 **Los Naranjos** Mex.
183 K9 **Los Navalmorales** Spain
183 K9 **Los Navalucillos** Spain
250 C3 **Los Nevados, Parque Nacional** *nat. park* Col.
245 I3 **Los Olímpicos** Mex.
190 F3 **Losone** Switz.
175 I6 **Łososina Dolna** Pol.
246 B2 **Los Palacios** Cuba
184 H6 **Los Palacios y Villafranca** Spain
183 M2 **Los Pandos** Spain
93 E8 **Lospatos** East Timor
185 I3 **Los Pedroches** *plat.* Spain
187 C9 **Los Pedrones** Spain
260 B2 **Los Peladeros** Chile
245 J2 **Los Pericos** Mex.
244 G7 **Los Placeres del Oro** Mex.
185 L3 **Los Pozuelos de Calatrava** Spain
183 P5 **Los Rábanos** Spain
258 D2 **Los Ralos** Arg.
216 □3a **Los Realejos** *Tenerife* Canary Is
244 A1 **Los Remedios** *r.* Mex.
244 E6 **Los Reyes** Mex.
250 B5 **Los Ríos** *prov.* Ecuador
244 G4 **Los Rodriquez** Mex.
250 E2 **Los Roques, Islas** *is* Venez.
185 O5 **Los Royos** Spain
171 D8 **Lossa** *r.* Ger.
171 D8 **Lossa (Finne)** Ger.
182 I7 **Los Santos** Spain
184 G4 **Los Santos de Maimona** Spain
216 □3d **Los Sauces** *La Palma* Canary Is
260 A5 **Los Sauces** Chile
244 F4 **Los Sauces** Mex.
172 E5 **Loßburg** Ger.
163 D7 **Losse** France
164 K4 **Losser** Neth.
146 J7 **Lossie** *r. Scotland* U.K.
146 J7 **Lossiemouth** *Moray, Scotland* U.K.
216 □3a **Los Silos** *Tenerife* Canary Is
171 G9 **Lößnitz** Ger.
190 G3 **Lostallo** Switz.
250 D2 **Los Taques** Venez.
171 E6 **Lostau** Ger.
232 B11 **Lost Creek** *KY* U.S.A.
258 E3 **Los Telares** Arg.
244 D6 **Los Tepames** Mex.
250 E2 **Los Teques** Venez.
251 F2 **Los Testigos** *is* Venez.
240 M6 **Lost Hills** *CA* U.S.A.
258 E2 **Los Tigres** Arg.
245 L8 **Los Tigres** Mex.
149 M7 **Lostock Gralam** *Cheshire, England* U.K.
183 L2 **Los Tojos** Spain
238 H4 **Lost Trail Pass** *ID* U.S.A.
150 C7 **Lostwithiel** *Cornwall, England* U.K.
139 N6 **Losvida, Vozyera** *l.* Belarus
241 S10 **Los Vidrios** Mex.
252 C6 **Los Vientos** Chile
185 L5 **Los Villares** Spain
260 B2 **Los Vilos** Chile
244 C5 **Los Volcanes** Mex.
183 M9 **Los Yébenes** Spain
137 K3 **Losynivka** Ukr.
163 H6 **Lot** *dept* France
161 C8 **Lot** *r.* France
258 B5 **Lota** Chile
210 B3 **Lotagipi Swamp** Kenya
141 I6 **Lote** Norway
141 K6 **Løten** Norway
163 F7 **Lot-et-Garonne** *dept* France
122 H3 **Lotfābād** Turkm.
146 K4 **Loth** *Orkney, Scotland* U.K.
210 B3 **Lothagum Hills** Sudan
215 O2 **Lothair** S. Africa
146 I6 **Lothmore** *Highland, Scotland* U.K.
Lothringen *reg.* France *see* **Lorraine**
210 B3 **Lotikipi Plain** Kenya
208 D5 **Loto** Dem. Rep. Congo
208 C5 **Lotoi** *r.* Dem. Rep. Congo
139 S5 **Lotoshino** Rus. Fed.
137 L6 **Lotskyne** Ukr.
Lot's Wife *i.* Japan *see* **Sōfu-gan**
140 U2 **Lotta** *r.* Fin./Rus. Fed. *alt.* **Lutto**
169 E6 **Lotte** Ger.
80 M4 **Lottin Point** *North I.* N.Z.
172 F6 **Lottstetten** Ger.
210 B3 **Lotuke** *mt.* Sudan
174 E2 **Lotyń** Pol.
192 D8 **Lotzorai** *Sardegna* Italy
159 K6 **Louailles** France
96 E4 **Louangnamtha** Laos
96 F5 **Louangphabang** Laos
156 E8 **L'Ouanne** *r.* France
158 E4 **Louannec** France
158 E4 **Louargat** France
209 B6 **Loubomo** Congo
171 L10 **Loučeň** Czech Rep.
176 C1 **Loučná** *hill* Czech Rep.
176 D3 **Loučovice** Czech Rep.
158 F5 **Loudéac** France
161 D6 **Loudes** France
109 H5 **Loudi** *Hunan* China
209 B6 **Loudima** Congo
231 E8 **Loudon** *TN* U.S.A.
232 C8 **Loudonville** *OH* U.S.A.
162 E1 **Loudun** France
159 K6 **Loué** France
160 G2 **Loue** *r.* France
209 B5 **Louéssé** *r.* Congo
107 L7 **Loufan** *Shanxi* China
206 A3 **Louga** Senegal
261 G5 **Louge** Arg.
163 G9 **Louge** *r.* France
147 F2 **Loughanure** Ireland
151 J2 **Loughborough** *Leicestershire, England* U.K.
147 J4 **Loughbrickland** *Northern Ireland* U.K.
221 H2 **Lougheed Island** *Nunavut* Can.
147 C8 **Lougher** Ireland
147 I4 **Loughgall** *Northern Ireland* U.K.
147 G5 **Lough Gowna** Ireland
147 K4 **Loughinisland** *Northern Ireland* U.K.
147 G7 **Loughmoe** Ireland
150 D4 **Loughor** *Swansea, Wales* U.K.
150 D4 **Loughor** *r. Wales* U.K.
147 E6 **Loughrea** Ireland
147 E3 **Loughros More Bay** Ireland
151 M4 **Loughton** *Essex, England* U.K.
163 F6 **Lougratte** France
160 G3 **Louhans** France
232 C10 **Louisa** *KY* U.S.A.
232 H10 **Louisa** *VA* U.S.A.
86 I5 **Louisa Downs Aboriginal Reserve** *W.A.* Austr.
225 J4 **Louisbourg** *N.S.* Can.
Louisburg *N.S.* Can. *see* **Louisbourg**
231 H7 **Louisburg** *NC* U.S.A.
222 G2 **Louise Falls** *N.W.T.* Can.
Louis-Gentil Morocco *see* **Youssoufia**
91 L9 **Louisiade Archipelago** *is* P.N.G.
236 J6 **Louisiana** *MO* U.S.A.
237 J10 **Louisiana** *state* U.S.A.
214 F4 **Louisvale** S. Africa
231 F9 **Louisville** *GA* U.S.A.
236 K6 **Louisville** *IL* U.S.A.
230 E6 **Louisville** *KY* U.S.A.
237 K9 **Louisville** *MS* U.S.A.
232 D8 **Louisville** *OH* U.S.A.
266 H8 **Louisville Ridge** *sea feature* S. Pacific Ocean
224 E2 **Louis-XIV, Pointe** *pt Que.* Can.
134 F2 **Loukhi** Rus. Fed.
208 C5 **Loukoléla** Congo
209 B5 **Loukouo** Congo
160 I2 **Loulans** France
162 C3 **Loulay** France
184 C6 **Loulé** Port.
206 D4 **Loulouni** Mali
207 H5 **Loum** Cameroon
176 C1 **Louny** Czech Rep.
161 K9 **Loup** *r.* France
236 G5 **Loup** *r. NE* U.S.A.
236 F5 **Loup City** *NE* U.S.A.
225 F1 **Loups Marins, Lacs des** *lakes Que.* Can.
225 F1 **Loups Marins, Petit lac des** *l. Que.* Can.
225 J3 **Lourdes** *Nfld and Lab.* Can.
163 D9 **Lourdes** France
226 B6 **Lourdes** *IA* U.S.A.
162 H3 **Lourdoueix-St-Pierre** France
251 I4 **Lourenço** Brazil
Lourenço Marques Moz. *see* **Maputo**
184 A3 **Loures** Port.
182 C8 **Louriçal** Port.
184 A2 **Lourinhã** Port.
161 G9 **Lourmarin** France
198 B3 **Louros** Greece
182 C7 **Lourosa** Port.
156 D8 **Loury** France
182 D8 **Lousã** Port.
184 A3 **Lousa** Port.
182 D8 **Lousã, Serra da** *mts* Port.
182 D6 **Lousada** Port.
Loushanguan *Guizhou* China *see* **Tongzi**
214 H9 **Louterwater** S. Africa
83 J4 **Louth** *N.S.W.* Austr.
147 I5 **Louth** Ireland
147 I5 **Louth** *county* Ireland
149 Q7 **Louth** *Lincolnshire, England* U.K.
198 F5 **Loutra** *Kythnos* Greece
198 E4 **Loutra Aidipsou** Greece
198 D5 **Loutraki** Greece
198 D2 **Loutro** Greece
Louvain Belgium *see* **Leuven**
165 I7 **Louveigné** Belgium
159 J5 **Louverné** France
163 D9 **Louvie-Juzon** France
156 B5 **Louviers** France
158 I5 **Louvigné-de-Bais** France
159 I5 **Louvigné-du-Désert** France
156 E5 **Louvres** France
156 G3 **Louvroil** France
214 I2 **Louwna** S. Africa
215 P3 **Louwsburg** S. Africa
156 I7 **Louze** France
140 P4 **Lövånger** Sweden
177 H4 **Lovasberény** Hungary
176 F5 **Lovászi** Hungary
177 G4 **Lovászpatona** Hungary
139 O3 **Lovat'** *r.* Rus. Fed.
140 M5 **Lövberga** Sweden
196 G8 **Lovćen** *nat. park* Mont
196 H5 **Lovćenac** *Vojvodina* Se
197 M7 **Lovech** Bulg.
238 L6 **Loveland** *CO* U.S.A.
233 □O4 **Lovell** *ME* U.S.A.
238 J4 **Lovell** *WY* U.S.A.
Lovello, Monte *mt.* Au **Grosser Löffler**
81 D13 **Lovells Flat** *South I.* N.
247 □3 **Lovell Village** St Vince
240 N1 **Lovelock** *NV* U.S.A.
234 C1 **Lovelton** *PA* U.S.A.
165 E6 **Lovendegem** Belgium
190 I4 **Lovere** Italy
190 I3 **Lovero** Italy
232 E12 **Lovers' Leap** *mt. VA* U
226 E7 **Loves Park** *IL* U.S.A.
141 S6 **Loviisa** Fin.
140 Q3 **Lovikka** Sweden
232 G11 **Lovingston** *VA* U.S.A.
237 D9 **Lovington** *NM* U.S.A.
177 I3 **Lovinobaňa** Slovakia
141 L6 **Lövnäsvallen** Sweden
142 F5 **Lovns Bredning** *b.* Der
176 F4 **Lövő** Hungary
171 J9 **Lovosice** Czech Rep.
134 F1 **Lovozero** Rus. Fed.
188 E3 **Lovran** Croatia
191 P5 **Lovreč** Croatia
179 L6 **Lovrenc** Slovenia
196 I5 **Lovrin** Romania
143 K1 **Lövsjön** Sweden
143 N1 **Lövstabukten** *b.* Swed
139 W6 **Lovtsy** Rus. Fed.
209 D6 **Lóvua** Angola
209 D7 **Lôvua** Angola
227 S4 **Low** *Que.* Can.
223 O2 **Low, Cape** *Nunavut* Ca
208 E5 **Lowa** Dem. Rep. Congo
208 E5 **Lowa** *r.* Dem. Rep. Con
123 N4 **Lowarai Pass** Pak.
175 L4 **Łowcza** Pol.
149 O7 **Lowdham** *Nottinghams England* U.K.
226 G8 **Lowell** *IN* U.S.A.
233 N6 **Lowell** *MA* U.S.A.
226 I7 **Lowell** *MI* U.S.A.
238 C5 **Lowell** *OR* U.S.A.
233 M4 **Lowell** *VT* U.S.A.
210 B3 **Lowelli** Sudan
233 □O3 **Lowelltown** *ME* U.S.A.
214 B3 **Löwen** *watercourse* Na
170 H5 **Löwenberg** Ger.
172 G3 **Löwenstein** Ger.
222 G5 **Lower Arrow Lake** *B.C*
Lower Austria *land* Au *see* **Niederösterreich**
147 J3 **Lower Ballinderry** *Nor Ireland* U.K.
151 L5 **Lower Beeding** *West S England* U.K.
236 F3 **Lower Brule Indian Reservation** *res. SD* U.
Lower California *pen. see* **Baja California**
150 H4 **Lower Cam** *Gloucester England* U.K.
146 E7 **Lower Diabaig** *Highlan Scotland* U.K.
82 H8 **Lower Glenelg Nation** *Vic.* Austr.
241 S6 **Lower Granite Gorge** *AZ* U.S.A.
81 I8 **Lower Hutt** *North I.* N.Z
146 D10 **Lower Kilchattan** *Argyl Bute, Scotland* U.K.
146 D11 **Lower Killeyan** *Argyll a Bute, Scotland* U.K.
238 D5 **Lower Klamath Nation Wildlife Refuge** *nature OR* U.S.A.
222 C2 **Lower Laberge** *Y.T.* Ca
240 J3 **Lower Lake** *CA* U.S.A.
215 N5 **Lower Loteni** S. Africa
147 G4 **Lower Lough Erne** *l. N Ireland* U.K.
224 A3 **Lower Manitou Lake** *Ont.* Can.
235 G3 **Lower New York Bay** *NY* U.S.A.
94 □ **Lower Peirce Reservoi**
215 M6 **Lower Pitseng** S. Africa
222 D3 **Lower Post** *B.C.* Can.
236 H2 **Lower Red Lake** *MN* U
215 P1 **Lower Sabie** S. Africa
Lower Saxony *land* Ger **Niedersachsen**
Lower Tunguska *r.* Rus *see* **Nizhnyaya Tungusk**
209 F8 **Lower Zambezi Nation Park** Zambia
151 P3 **Lowestoft** *Suffolk, England* U.K.
123 M4 **Lowgar** *prov.* Afgh.
149 N2 **Lowick** *Northumberland, England* U.K.
175 H3 **Łowicz** Pol.
Low Island Kiribati *see* **Starbuck Island**
123 J6 **Lowkhi** Afgh.
232 F11 **Lowmoor** *VA* U.S.A.
86 □1 **Low Point** Christmas I.
83 J10 **Low Rocky Point** *Tas.* A
151 O2 **Low Street** *Norfolk, England* U.K.
232 E9 **Lowsville** *WV* U.S.A.
146 I12 **Lowther Hills** *Scotland*
221 I2 **Lowther Island** *Nunavu*
233 J5 **Lowville** *NY* U.S.A.
174 D3 **Łowyń** Pol.
245 K9 **Loxicha** Mex.
168 G4 **Loxstedt** Ger.
82 H6 **Loxton** *S.A.* Austr.
214 G7 **Loxton** S. Africa
146 H6 **Loyal, Loch** *l. Scotland*
227 R8 **Loyalsock Creek** *r. PA*
240 L2 **Loyalton** *CA* U.S.A.
234 B3 **Loyalton** *PA* U.S.A.
Loyalty Islands New Caledonia *see* **Loyauté, Îles**
Loyang *Henan* China *see* **Luoyang**
78 □5 **Loyauté, Îles** *is* New Caledonia
226 D6 **Loyd** *WI* U.S.A.
215 P2 **Loyengo** Swaziland
160 G5 **Loyettes** France
Loyev Belarus *see* **Loyew**
136 J2 **Loyew** Belarus
146 F8 **Loyne, Loch** *l. Scotland*
134 K4 **Loyno** Rus. Fed.
259 C8 **Loyola, Punta** *pt* Arg.
140 L4 **Løypskardtinden** *mt.* No
161 D7 **Lozère** *dept* France
161 D8 **Lozère, Mont** *mt.* Franc
196 H6 **Loznica** Serbia
197 O7 **Loznitsa** Bulg.
137 R4 **Lozno-Oleksandrivka** U
137 Q3 **Loznoye** Rus. Fed.
176 G3 **Lozorno** Slovakia
137 O4 **Lozova** *Kharkivs'ka Oblas*
137 P5 **Lozova** *Kharkivs'ka Oblas*
Lozovaya Kazakh. *see* **Lozovoye**
Lozovaya Ukr. *see* **Lozov**
136 G4 **Lozove** Ukr.
137 P4 **Lozoven'ka** Ukr.
196 J6 **Lozovik** Serbia
121 Q1 **Lozovoye** Kazakh.
137 T3 **Lozovoye** Rus. Fed.
183 M7 **Lozoya** Spain
183 N7 **Lozoya** *r.* Spain
183 M7 **Lozoya, Canal de** Spain
183 M7 **Lozoyuela** Spain
137 O7 **Lozuvatka** *r.* Ukr.
134 M3 **Loz'va** *r.* Rus. Fed.
191 M3 **Lozzo di Cadore** Italy
84 E8 **Ltyentye Apurte Aborig Land** *res. N.T.* Austr.
209 E7 **Luabo** Dem. Rep. Congo
213 H3 **Luabo** Moz.
209 D7 **Luacano** Angola
209 D7 **Luachimo** Angola
209 D6 **Luachimo** *r.* Angola/Dem. Rep. Congo
209 D6 **Luaco** Angola
208 C4 **Lua Dekere** *r.* Dem. Rep. Congo
209 E6 **Luakila** Dem. Rep. Cong

Luala r. Moz.
Luali Dem. Rep. Congo
C12 Lualualei HI U.S.A.
Luambe National Park Zambia
Luampa Zambia
Luampa r. Zambia
Lu'an Anhui China
Luana Point Jamaica
Luân Châu Vietnam
Luanchuan Henan China
Luanco Spain
Luanda Angola
Luanda prov. Angola
Luando Angola
Luando r. Angola
Luando, Reserva Natural Integral do nature res. Angola
Luang i. Maluku Indon.
Luang, Huai r. Thai.
0 Luang, Khao mt. Thai.
1 Luang, Thale lag. Thai.
Luanginga r. Zambia
Luangiua i. Solomon Is
Luang Nam Tha Laos see Louangnamtha
Luang Phrabang, Thiu Khao mts Laos/Thai. see Luang Prabang Range
Luang Prabang Laos see Louangphabang
0 Luang Prabang Range mts Laos/Thai.
Luangue Angola
Luanguinga r. Angola
Luangwa Zambia
Luangwa r. Zambia
Luanhaizi Qinghai China
Luan He r. China
Luannan Hebei China
Lua Nova Brazil
Luanping Hebei China
Luanshya Zambia
Luan Toro Arg.
Luanxian Hebei China
Luanza Dem. Rep. Congo
Luanzhou Hebei China see Luanxian
Luao Angola see Luau
Luapula r. Dem. Rep. Congo/Zambia
Luapula prov. Zambia
Luar i. Cocos Is see Horsburgh Island
Luar, Danau l. Indon.
Luarca Spain
Luashi Dem. Rep. Congo
Luatamba Angola
Luatize r. Moz.
Luau Angola
Luba Equat. Guinea
Lubaczów Pol.
Lubaczówka r. Pol.
Lubalo Angola
Lubań Pol.
Lubāna Latvia
Lubānas ezers l. Latvia
Lubang Phil.
Lubang i. Phil.
Lubang Islands Phil.
Lubango Angola
Lubanowo Pol.
Lubao Dem. Rep. Congo
Lübars Ger.
Lubartów Pol.
Lubasz Pol.
Lubawa Pol.
Lubawka Pol.
Lübbecke Ger.
Lubbeek Belgium
Lübben Ger.
Lübbenau Ger.
Lubbeskolk salt pan S. Africa
Lubbock TX U.S.A.
Lübbow Ger.
Lubczyna Pol.
4 Lubec ME U.S.A.
Lübeck Ger.
Lubeck WV U.S.A.
Lübecker Bucht b. Ger.
Lubefu Dem. Rep. Congo
Lubei Nei Mongol China
Ľubeľa Slovakia
Lubelska, Wyżyna hills Pol.
Lubelskie prov. Pol.
Lüben Pol. see Lubin
Lubenec Czech Rep.
Lubenia Pol.
Lubeník Slovakia
Lubenka Kazakh.
Lubero Dem. Rep. Congo
Lubéron, Montagne du ridge France
Lubéron, Parc Naturel Régional du nature res. France
Lubersac France
Lübesse Ger.
Lubián Spain
Łubianka Pol.
Lubiąż Pol.
Lubic i. Phil.
Ľubica r. Slovakia
Lubichowo Pol.
Lubicz Dolny Pol.
Lubie, Jezioro l. Pol.
Lubięcin Pol.
Lubień Pol.
Lubienka r. Pol.
Lubień Kujawski Pol.
Lubieszewo Pol.
Lubiewo Pol.
Lubin Pol.
Lubiń Pol.
Lubirizi Dem. Rep. Congo
Lubisi Dam resr S. Africa
Lubiszyn Pol.
Lublin Pol.
Lubliniec Pol.
Lubmin Ger.
Lubnān country Asia see Lebanon
Lubnia Pol.
Łubniany Pol.
Łubnice Łódzkie Pol.
Łubnice Świętokrzyskie Pol.
Lubniewice Pol.
Łubno Łódzkie Pol.
Łubno Pomorskie Pol.
Lubno Pol.
Lubny Ukr.
Lubok Antu Sarawak Malaysia
Lubombo admin. dist. Swaziland
Lubomino Pol.
Luboń Pol.
Lubosalma Rus. Fed.
Ľubotice Slovakia
Ľubotín Slovakia
Lübow Ger.
Lubowidz Pol.
Łubowo Wielkopolskie Pol.
Łubowo Zachodniopomorskie Pol.
Lubraniec Pol.
Lubrín Spain
Lubrza Lubuskie Pol.
Lubrza Opolskie Pol.
Lubsko Pol.
Lübstorf Ger.
Lubstów Pol.
Lubsza Pol.
Lubsza r. Pol.
Lübtheen Ger.
Lubuagan Luzon Phil.
Lububu Dem. Rep. Congo
Lubudi Dem. Rep. Congo
Lubudi r. Dem. Rep. Congo
Lubukbalang Sumatera Indon.
Lubuklinggau Sumatera Indon.
Lubukpakam Sumatera Indon.
Lubuksikaping Sumatera Indon.
Lubumbashi Dem. Rep. Congo
Lubunda Dem. Rep. Congo
Lubungu Zambia
Lubuskie prov. Pol.
Lubuskie, Pojezierze reg. Pol.
Lubuta Zambia
Lubutu Dem. Rep. Congo
Lubutu r. Dem. Rep. Congo
209 F7 Lubwe Zambia
176 B1 Luby Czech Rep.
139 S9 Lubyanki Rus. Fed.
175 L5 Lubycza Królewska Pol.
170 F4 Lübz Ger.
161 D7 Luc Languedoc-Roussillon France
163 J7 Luc Midi-Pyrénées France
185 O6 Lucainena de las Torres Spain
209 B7 Lucala Angola
227 M6 Lucan Ont. Can.
147 J6 Lucan Ireland
252 B3 Lucanas Peru
177 L5 Lucani Romania
196 I7 Lučani Serbia
222 A2 Lucania, Mount Y.T. Can.
111 L8 Lücaoshan Qinghai China
209 D7 Lucapa Angola
185 O6 Lúcar Spain
185 O6 Lúcar mt. Spain
185 N6 Lúcar, Sierra de mts Spain
261 H2 Lucas r. Arg.
253 G3 Lucas Brazil
261 H3 Lucas González Arg.
261 H2 Lucas Sur Arg.
232 C10 Lucasville OH U.S.A.
231 H12 Lucaya Gd Bahama Bahamas
159 N7 Luçay-le-Mâle France
190 J8 Lucca Italy
190 J8 Lucca prov. Italy
236 G2 Lucca ND U.S.A.
194 E8 Lucca Sicula Sicilia Italy
192 C2 Lucciana Corse France
156 B7 Lucé France
179 K7 Luče Slovenia
246 □ Lucea Jamaica
146 G13 Luce Bay Scotland U.K.
237 K10 Lucedale MS U.S.A.
256 B4 Lucélia Brazil
92 C5 Lucena Luzon Phil.
185 K6 Lucena Spain
187 E7 Lucena, Riu r. Spain
185 L5 Lucena, Sierra de mts Spain
186 C4 Lucena de Jalón Spain
187 E7 Lucena del Cid Spain
160 C3 Lucenay-lès-Aix France
160 E2 Lucenay-l'Évêque France
161 G7 Luc-en-Diois France
177 I3 Lučenec Slovakia
186 C4 Luceni Spain
193 O4 Lucera Italy
161 K9 Lucéram France
252 C3 Lucerna Peru
Lucerne Switz. see Luzern
240 J2 Lucerne CA U.S.A.
240 P7 Lucerne Valley CA U.S.A.
242 F2 Lucero Mex.
157 K6 Lucey France
177 I3 Lucfalva Hungary
136 H2 Luchanky Ukr.
138 K6 Luchay Belarus
100 I5 Luchegorsk Rus. Fed.
129 I4 Luchek Rus. Fed.
Lucheng Guangxi China see Luchuan
107 M8 Lucheng Shanxi China
Lucheng Sichuan China see Kangding
159 L6 Luché-Pringé France
211 C7 Lucheringo r. Moz.
156 D3 Lucheux France
139 W5 Luchki Rus. Fed.
139 N7 Luchosa r. Belarus
170 D5 Lüchow Ger.
108 H7 Luchuan Guangxi China
108 D7 Lüchun Yunnan China
156 D4 Luchy France
185 K3 Luciana Spain
175 H4 Luciąża r. Pol.
175 H3 Lucień Pol.
191 L9 Lucignano Italy
188 D3 Lucija Slovenia
182 H4 Lucillo de Somoza Spain
85 K5 Lucinda Qld Austr.
82 H7 Lucindale S.A. Austr.
179 J7 Lučine Slovenia
245 H3 Lucio Vázquez Mex.
93 E6 Lucipara, Kepulauan is Maluku Indon.
209 B8 Lucira Angola
193 N4 Lucito Italy
197 P6 Luciu Romania
Łuck Ukr. see Luts'k
226 B4 Luck WI U.S.A.
171 F8 Lucka Ger.
171 I7 Luckau Ger.
Luckeesarai Bihar India see Lakhisarai
171 H6 Luckenwalde Ger.
215 I5 Luckhoff S. Africa
227 M6 Lucknow Ont. Can.
116 H6 Lucknow Uttar Prad. India
170 E5 Lückstedt Ger.
191 K2 Luco, Monte mt. Italy
193 K4 Luco dei Marsi Italy
162 B3 Luçon France
108 H3 Lücongpo Hubei China
163 C9 Lucq-de-Béarn France
246 F3 Lucrecia, Cabo c. Cuba
159 K3 Luc-sur-Mer France
209 B6 Lucunga Angola
209 D8 Lucusse Angola
84 F7 Lucy Creek N.T. Austr.
160 D1 Lucy-le-Bois France
Lüda Liaoning China see Dalian
134 G2 Luda Rus. Fed.
146 B8 Ludag Western Isles, Scotland U.K.
197 P7 Luda Kamchiya r. Bulg.
188 F2 Ludbreg Croatia
169 E8 Lüdenscheid Ger.
168 K5 Lüder Ger.
171 E5 Lüderitz Ger.
212 B5 Lüderitz Namibia
168 K3 Lüdersdorf Ger.
178 A5 Ludesch Austria
211 B7 Ludewa Tanz.
151 I5 Ludgershall Wiltshire, England U.K.
150 A7 Ludgvan Cornwall, England U.K.
116 E4 Ludhiana Punjab India
108 D5 Ludian Yunnan China
108 D4 Luding Sichuan China
169 D7 Lüdinghausen Ger.
226 H6 Ludington MI U.S.A.
235 H1 Ludingtonville NY U.S.A.
234 F6 Ludlam Bay NJ U.S.A.
150 G3 Ludlow Shropshire, England U.K.
241 P7 Ludlow CA U.S.A.
233 M5 Ludlow VT U.S.A.
179 J6 Ludmannsdorf Austria
197 O7 Ludogorie reg. Bulg.
197 O7 Ludogorsko Plato plat. Bulg.
138 M3 Ludoni Rus. Fed.
162 C6 Ludon-Médoc France
231 G10 Ludowici GA U.S.A.
157 L6 Ludres France
197 M4 Luduş Romania
143 L1 Ludvika Sweden
173 K3 Ludwig-Donau-Main-Kanal canal Ger.
169 I9 Ludwigsau-Friedlos Ger.
172 G4 Ludwigsburg Ger.
171 L8 Ludwigsdorf Ger.
171 H6 Ludwigsfelde Ger.
172 G6 Ludwigshafen Ger.
172 E3 Ludwigshafen am Rhein Ger.
170 D4 Ludwigslust Ger.
170 D4 Ludwigsluster Kanal canal Ger.
Ludwigsort Rus. Fed. see Ladushkin
171 D10 Ludwigsstadt Ger.
175 K4 Ludwin Pol.
138 K5 Ludza Latvia
163 C7 Lüe France
209 D6 Luebo Dem. Rep. Congo
209 E5 Lueki Dem. Rep. Congo
209 E5 Lueki r. Dem. Rep. Congo
182 H6 Luelmo Spain
209 F5 Luemba Dem. Rep. Congo
209 F8 Luembe Zambia
209 C7 Luena Angola
209 E7 Luena Dem. Rep. Congo
209 F7 Luena Zambia
209 D8 Luena r. Zambia
209 D8 Luena Flats plain Zambia
209 D9 Luengé, Coutada Pública do nature res. Angola
209 D9 Luengue r. Angola
213 G3 Luenha r. Moz./Zimbabwe
251 F3 Luepa Venez.
169 I7 Lüerdissen Ger.
186 C3 Luesia Spain
108 F2 Lüeyang Shaanxi China
109 J7 Lufeng Guangdong China
Lufeng Hunan China see Xupu
108 D6 Lufeng Yunnan China
209 B6 Lufico Angola
209 E7 Lufira r. Dem. Rep. Congo
209 E7 Lufira, Lac de retenue de la resr Dem. Rep. Congo
237 H10 Lufkin TX U.S.A.
Lufu Yunnan China see Shilin
211 A7 Lufubu r. Zambia
196 J6 Lug r. Serbia
138 M3 Luga Rus. Fed.
138 L2 Luga r. Rus. Fed.
190 F3 Lugano Switz.
190 F4 Lugano, Lago di l. Italy/Switz.
Lugano, Lake Italy/Switz. see Lugano, Lago di
Lugansk Ukr. see Luhans'k
Luganskaya Oblast' admin. div. Ukr. see Luhans'ka Oblast'
Lugansk Oblast admin. div. Ukr. see Luhans'ka Oblast'
78 □5 Luganville Vanuatu
177 L4 Lugaşu de Jos Romania
171 G9 Lugau Ger.
169 H7 Lügde Ger.
Lugdunum France see Lyon
213 H3 Lugela Moz.
213 H3 Lugela r. Moz.
213 H1 Lugenda r. Moz.
150 G3 Lugg r. Wales U.K.
81 D11 Luggate South I. N.Z.
111 J11 Luggudontsen mt. Xizang China
210 D2 Lughaye Somalia
163 C7 Luglon France
193 I2 Lugnano in Teverina Italy
147 J7 Lugnaquilla hill Ireland
160 F4 Lugny France
160 E4 Lugny-lès-Charolles France
191 L7 Lugo Italy
182 E2 Lugo Spain
182 F3 Lugo prov. Spain
192 C3 Lugo-di-Nazza Corse France
197 J5 Lugoj Romania
182 I2 Lugones Spain
162 D6 Lugon-et-l'Île-du-Carnay France
163 C7 Lugos France
139 U5 Lugovaya Rus. Fed.
Lugovaya Proleyka Rus. Fed. see Primorsk
121 O6 Lugovoy Kazakh.
160 J4 Lugrin France
185 M6 Lugros Spain
108 D4 Lugu Sichuan China
111 G10 Lugu Xizang China
92 C9 Lugus i. Phil.
136 D3 Luha r. Ukr.
177 G2 Luhačovice Czech Rep.
137 S5 Luhan' r. Ukr.
137 S5 Luhanchyk r. Ukr.
141 R6 Luhanka Fin.
137 S5 Luhans'k Ukr.
137 S4 Luhans'ka Oblast' admin. div. Ukr.
137 N8 Luhans'ke Ukr.
Luhansk Oblast admin. div. Ukr. see Luhans'ka Oblast'
139 N6 Luhawskiya Belarus
169 H6 Luhden Ger.
109 J7 Luhe Guangdong China
109 L2 Luhe Jiangsu China
107 K8 Lu He r. China
168 J4 Luhe r. Ger.
173 M2 Luhe-Wildenau Ger.
128 E6 Luḩfī, Wādī watercourse Jordan
107 P3 Luhin Sum Nei Mongol China
Luhit r. China/India see Zayü Qu
96 B1 Luhit r. India
170 I2 Lühmannsdorf Ger.
211 C7 Luhombero Tanz.
137 O8 Luhove Ukr.
140 U5 Luhtapohja Fin.
Luhua Sichuan China see Heishui
108 C3 Luhuo Sichuan China
136 H2 Luhyny Ukr.
209 D7 Luia Angola
209 D6 Luia r. Angola
213 G3 Luia r. Moz.
209 D9 Luiana Angola
209 D9 Luiana r. Angola
209 D9 Luiana, Coutada Pública do nature res. Angola
197 O6 Luica Romania
146 G7 Luichart, Loch l. Scotland U.K.
Luichow Peninsula China see Leizhou Bandao
213 G4 Luido Moz.
Luik Belgium see Liège
208 D5 Luilaka r. Dem. Rep. Congo
Luimbale Angola see Londuimbali
Luimneach Ireland see Limerick
146 E10 Luing i. Scotland U.K.
146 E10 Luing, Sound of sea chan. Scotland U.K.
190 F4 Luino Italy
182 E4 Luintra Spain
209 D8 Luio r. Angola
140 S3 Luiro r. Fin.
156 B7 Luisant France
254 E2 Luís Correia Brazil
241 P9 Luis Echeverría Álvarez Mex.
254 F3 Luís Gomes Brazil
209 E7 Luishia Dem. Rep. Congo
242 G3 Luis L. León, Presa resr Mex.
244 D1 Luis Moya Durango Mex.
244 E3 Luis Moya Zacatecas Mex.
247 □1 Luis Peña, Cayo de i. Puerto Rico
262 V1 Luitpold Coast Antarctica
244 G7 Luivanos Mex.
209 D6 Luiza Dem. Rep. Congo
209 E6 Luizi Dem. Rep. Congo
261 H4 Luján Buenos Aires Arg.
260 E3 Luján San Luis Arg.
261 H4 Lujan r. Arg.
260 C3 Luján de Cuyo Arg.
109 K3 Lujiang Anhui China
106 I9 Lüjing Gansu China
137 M3 Luka Ukr.
100 H2 Lukachek Rus. Fed.
177 G3 Lukáčovce Slovakia
176 F4 Lukácsháza Hungary
209 B6 Lukala Dem. Rep. Congo
209 C6 Lukanga Dem. Rep. Congo
209 E8 Lukanga Swamps Zambia
Lukapa Angola see Lucapa
137 N6 Lukasheve Ukr.
188 G3 Lukavac Bos.-Herz.
175 L5 Łukawiec Pol.
87 D9 Luke, Mount hill W.A. Austr.
209 E7 Lukenga, Lac l. Dem. Rep. Congo
209 C5 Lukenie r. Dem. Rep. Congo
147 H8 Lukeswell Ireland
241 T10 Lukeville AZ U.S.A.
134 H4 Lukh Rus. Fed.
134 H4 Lukh r. Rus. Fed.
139 W7 Lukhovitsy Rus. Fed.
197 M9 Lŭki Bulg.
139 R1 Lukinskaya Rus. Fed.
136 D2 Lukiv Ukr.
109 □J7 Luk Keng H.K. China
208 C5 Lukolela Équateur Dem. Rep. Congo
209 E6 Lukolela Kasaï-Oriental Dem. Rep. Congo
138 M7 Lukomskaye, Vozyera l. Belarus
Lukou Hunan China see Zhuzhou
188 G3 Lukovac r. Bos.-Herz.
198 A3 Lukovë Albania
197 M7 Lukovit Bulg.
139 R5 Lukovnikovo Rus. Fed.
191 R6 Lukovo Croatia
175 K4 Łuków Pol.
175 K3 Łukowisko Pol.
135 I5 Lukoyanov Rus. Fed.
110 I5 Lükqün Xinjiang China
93 C4 Luksagu Sulawesi Indon.
138 G7 Lukšiai Lith.
209 E6 Lukuga r. Dem. Rep. Congo
209 B6 Lukula Dem. Rep. Congo
211 C7 Lukuledi Tanz.
209 D8 Lukulu Zambia
211 B7 Lukumburu Tanz.
209 C6 Lukuni Dem. Rep. Congo
209 F8 Lukusashi r. Zambia
211 B8 Lukusuzi National Park Zambia
136 C4 Luky Ukr.
209 D5 Lula r. Dem. Rep. Congo
192 C7 Lula Sardegna Italy
140 Q4 Luleå Sweden
140 Q4 Luleälven r. Sweden
199 I1 Lüleburgaz Turkey
258 D2 Lules Arg.
108 D6 Luliang Yunnan China
107 L8 Lüliang Shan mts China
209 F6 Lulimba Dem. Rep. Congo
237 G11 Luling TX U.S.A.
147 I6 Lullymore Ireland
107 P7 Lulong Hebei China
208 C4 Lulonga Dem. Rep. Congo
208 C4 Lulonga r. Dem. Rep. Congo
208 D4 Lulu r. Dem. Rep. Congo
Luluabourg Dem. Rep. Congo see Kananga
111 G12 Lülung Xizang China
87 D9 Lulworth, Mount hill W.A. Austr.
78 □2 Luma American Samoa
209 C7 Luma Cassai Angola
111 H11 Lumachomo Xizang China
260 A6 Lumaco Chile
209 D8 Lumai Angola
95 J9 Lumajang Jawa Indon.
111 E9 Lumajangdong Co salt l. China
209 E5 Lumana Dem. Rep. Congo
138 F3 Lümanda Estonia
127 M7 Lūmār Iran
Lumbala Moxico Angola see Lumbala Kaquengue
Lumbala Moxico Angola see Lumbala N'guimbo
209 D8 Lumbala Kaquengue Angola
209 D8 Lumbala N'guimbo Angola
211 A6 Lumbe Tanz.
209 D9 Lumbe r. Zambia
231 H8 Lumber r. SC U.S.A.
231 H8 Lumberton NC U.S.A.
209 C6 Lumbi Dem. Rep. Congo
183 R3 Lumbier Spain
95 L2 Lumbis Kalimantan Indon.
213 I2 Lumbo Moz.
182 G7 Lumbrales Spain
183 O4 Lumbreras Spain
156 D2 Lumbres France
117 N7 Lumding Assam India
211 B7 Lumecha Tanz.
190 I4 Lumezzane Italy
91 J7 Lumi P.N.G.
140 R4 Lumijoki Fin.
197 Q6 Lumina Romania
257 E4 Luminárias Brazil
192 B2 Lumio Corse France
143 O4 Lummelunda Gotland Sweden
165 H7 Lummen Belgium
96 D5 Lum-nan-pai Wildlife Reserve nature res. Thai.
141 P6 Lumparland Åland Fin.
138 D1 Lumparn b. Fin.
146 K8 Lumphanan Aberdeenshire, Scotland U.K.
97 H8 Lumphăt Cambodia
186 C4 Lumpiaque Spain
231 E9 Lumpkin GA U.S.A.
223 J5 Lumsden Sask. Can.
81 C12 Lumsden South I. N.Z.
94 D2 Lumut Malaysia
95 K5 Lumut, Gunung mt. Indon.
94 F6 Lumut, Tanjung pt Indon.
209 E7 Lumwana Zambia
191 R6 Lun Croatia
106 I3 Lün Mongolia
191 R6 Lun, Rt pt Croatia
92 C3 Luna Luzon Phil.
186 D3 Luna Spain
184 H8 Luna hill Spain
182 I4 Luna r. Spain
241 X8 Luna NM U.S.A.
209 D8 Lunache Angola
156 E7 Lunain r. France
192 B8 Lunamatrona Sardegna Italy
146 L9 Lunan Bay Scotland U.K.
108 D5 Lunan Shan mts Sichuan China
227 K8 Luna Pier MI U.S.A.
161 C9 Lunas France
116 D8 Lunavada Gujarat India
124 C3 Lunayyir, Ḩarrat lava field Saudi Arabia
177 L5 Lunca Bihor Romania
197 M7 Lunca Teleorman Romania
197 N4 Lunca Bradului Romania
177 L6 Lunca Cernii de Jos Romania
197 M3 Lunca Ilvei Romania
146 J10 Luncarty Perth and Kinross, Scotland U.K.
197 M6 Luncavăţ r. Romania
177 L5 Luncoiu de Jos Romania
123 M8 Lund Pak.
142 J6 Lund Sweden
241 Q3 Lund NV U.S.A.
241 S3 Lund UT U.S.A.
209 C7 Lunda Norte prov. Angola
223 L5 Lundar Man. Can.
209 D7 Lunda Sul prov. Angola
211 B8 Lundazi Zambia
222 H5 Lundbreck Alta Can.
168 K1 Lundby Denmark
142 E6 Lunde Denmark
168 H2 Lunden Ger.
142 C3 Lundevatn l. Norway
Lundi r. Zimbabwe see Runde
146 K10 Lundin Links Fife, Scotland U.K.
226 F5 Lunds WI U.S.A.
143 K2 Lundsfjärden l. Sweden
95 H4 Lundu Sarawak Malaysia
211 B7 Lundu Tanz.
150 C5 Lundy i. England U.K.
168 G3 Lune r. Ger.
149 L5 Lune r. England U.K.
169 B10 Lünebach Ger.
215 O3 Luneberg S. Africa
168 J4 Lüneburg Ger.
168 J4 Lüneburger Heide reg. Ger.
168 I4 Lüneburger Heide, Naturpark nature res. Ger.
161 E9 Lunel France
161 K6 Lunella, Punta mt. Italy
161 E9 Lunel-Viel France
169 E7 Lünen Ger.
232 G12 Lunenburg VA U.S.A.
178 A5 Lünersee l. Austria
159 P8 Lunery France
168 G4 Lunestedt Ger.
157 L6 Lunéville France
213 I2 Lunga Moz.
209 E8 Lunga r. Zambia
179 H5 Lungau r. source Austria
190 E2 Lungern Switz.
78 □6 Lungga Guadalcanal Solomon Is
111 F11 Lunggar Xizang China
111 F11 Lunggar Shan mts Xizang China
206 B4 Lungi Sierra Leone
109 □I7 Lung Kwu Chau i. H.K. China
Lungleh Mizoram India see Lunglei
117 N8 Lunglei Mizoram India
111 H11 Lungmari mt. Xizang China
111 E9 Lungmu Co salt l. China
193 J3 Lungo, Lago l. Italy
193 Q8 Lungro Italy
209 D8 Lungué-Bungo r. Angola
209 D8 Lungwebungu r. Zambia
117 I5 Lunh Nepal
116 D6 Luni Rajasthan India
116 C7 Luni r. India
123 N6 Luni r. Pak.
Luninets Belarus see Luninyets
240 N3 Luning NV U.S.A.
135 I5 Lunino Rus. Fed.
136 F1 Luninyets Belarus
163 G8 L'Union France
116 D5 Lunkaransar Rajasthan India
116 D5 Lunkha Rajasthan India
123 O3 Lunkho mt. Afgh./Pak.
140 S3 Lunkkaus Fin.
138 H8 Lunna Belarus
146 □N2 Lunna Ness hd Scotland U.K.
169 D6 Lünne Ger.
85 M1 Lunn Island P.N.G.
170 J5 Lunow Ger.
206 B4 Lunsar Sierra Leone
209 F8 Lunsemfwa r. Zambia
213 F5 Lunsklip S. Africa
110 G6 Luntai Xinjiang China
164 I4 Lunteren Neth.
198 B2 Lunxhërisë, Mali i ridge Albania
95 L9 Lunyuk Sumbawa Indon.
171 G9 Lunzenau Ger.
211 A7 Lunzua Zambia
100 G5 Luobei Heilong. China
110 I7 Luobuzhuang Xinjiang China
Luocheng Fujian China see Hui'an
106 F7 Luocheng Gansu China
108 G6 Luocheng Guangxi China
107 K9 Luochuan Shaanxi China
108 F6 Luodian Guizhou China
109 H7 Luoding Guangdong China
140 R4 Luodonselkä sea chan. Fin.
108 H8 Luodou Sha i. China
192 C5 Luogosanto Sardegna Italy
109 J2 Luohe Henan China
107 M9 Luo He r. Henan China
107 L9 Luo He r. Shaanxi China
108 E3 Luojiang Sichuan China
108 H8 Luo Jiang r. China
107 P9 Luoma Hu l. China
107 L9 Luonan Shaanxi China
107 L9 Luoning Henan China
141 S6 Luonteri l. Fin.
108 E6 Luoping Yunnan China
141 R6 Luopioinen Fin.
109 J2 Luoshan Henan China
109 J3 Luotian Hubei China
106 E6 Luotuoquan Gansu China
140 T1 Luovttejohka Norway
109 I5 Luoxiao Shan mts China
Luoxiong Yunnan China see Luoping
Luoyang Guangdong China see Boluo
107 M9 Luoyang Henan China
Luoyang Zhejiang China see Taishun
109 L5 Luoyuan Fujian China
209 B6 Luozi Dem. Rep. Congo
100 G7 Luozigou Jilin China
211 B7 Lupa Market Tanz.
213 E3 Lupane Zimbabwe
108 E5 Lupanshui Guizhou China
95 I4 Lupar r. Malaysia
143 N7 Łupawa r. Pol.
173 L3 Lupburg Ger.
184 D2 Lupe r. Port.
197 N4 Lupeni Harghita Romania
197 L5 Lupeni Hunedoara Romania
246 H4 Luperón Dom. Rep.
172 F5 Lupfen hill Ger.
163 E8 Lupiac France
211 B7 Lupilichi Moz.
186 D3 Lupiñén Spain
185 L5 Lupión Spain
209 C8 Lupire Angola
211 C7 Lupiro Tanz.
175 K6 Łupków Pol.
191 Q5 Lupoglav Croatia
92 F8 Lupon Mindanao Phil.
170 L5 Łupowo Pol.
171 G8 Luppa Ger.
157 L6 Luppy France
241 W6 Lupton AZ U.S.A.
134 K3 Lup'ya r. Rus. Fed.
Luqiao Sichuan China see Luding
106 H9 Luqu Gansu China
Lu Qu r. China see Tao He
107 N7 Luquan Hebei China
108 D6 Luquan Yunnan China
185 K5 Luque Spain
209 C7 Luquembo Angola
247 □1 Luquillo Puerto Rico
247 □1 Luquillo, Sierra de mts Puerto Rico
192 C6 Luras Sardegna Italy
122 A3 Lūrā Shīrīn Iran
226 C9 Luray MO U.S.A.
232 G10 Luray VA U.S.A.
163 C9 Lurbe-St-Christau France
160 B3 Lurcy-Lévis France
157 L8 Lure France
161 H8 Lure, Montagne de mt. France
161 H8 Lure, Sommet de mt. France
211 C8 Lureco r. Moz.
209 C7 Luremo Angola
146 F6 Lurgainn, Loch l. Scotland U.K.
147 J4 Lurgan Northern Ireland U.K.
122 H5 Lūrg-e Shotorān salt pan Iran
192 C2 Luri Corse France
210 A3 Luri r. Sudan
252 D4 Luribay Bol.
252 A3 Lurín Peru
213 I2 Lúrio Moz.
213 I2 Lurio r. Moz.
213 I2 Lúrio, Baía do b. Moz.
140 L3 Lurøy Norway
161 H9 Lurs France
159 P7 Lury-sur-Arnon France
142 C2 Lusaheia park Norway
211 A5 Lusahunga Tanz.
209 F6 Lusaka Dem. Rep. Congo
209 F8 Lusaka Zambia
209 F8 Lusaka prov. Zambia
209 D6 Lusambo Dem. Rep. Congo
91 L8 Lusancay Islands and Reefs P.N.G.
209 C6 Lusanga Dem. Rep. Congo
209 E6 Lusangi Dem. Rep. Congo
129 F6 Lusashogh Armenia
194 G2 Lusciano Italy
223 I4 Luseland Sask. Can.
209 F7 Lusenga Plain National Park Zambia
190 C6 Luserna San Giovanni Italy
211 C7 Lusewa Tanz.
86 I4 Lush, Mount hill W.A. Austr.
108 D3 Lushan Sichuan China
Lushar Qinghai China see Huangzhong
107 L9 Lushi Henan China
196 H10 Lushnjë Albania
211 C6 Lushoto Tanz.
100 E7 Lushuihe Jilin China
107 Q7 Lüshun Liaoning China
109 M2 Lüsi Jiangsu China
95 I8 Lusi r. Indon.
162 E3 Lusignan France
160 C3 Lusigny France
156 H7 Lusigny-sur-Barse France
215 N7 Lusikisiki S. Africa
82 □3 Lusitania Bay S. Pacific Ocean
211 A8 Lusiwasi Zambia
147 J5 Lusk Ireland
238 L5 Lusk WY U.S.A.
161 H7 Lus-la-Croix-Haute France
Luso Angola see Luena
182 D8 Luso Port.
146 G10 Luss Argyll and Bute, Scotland U.K.
162 D6 Lussac France
162 F3 Lussac-les-Châteaux France
162 G3 Lussac-les-Églises France
148 F2 Lussa Loch l. Scotland U.K.
161 E8 Lussan France
256 B4 Lussanvira Brazil
168 J5 Lüßberg hill Ger.
170 F3 Lüssow Ger.
209 B7 Lussusso Angola
146 C7 Lusta Highland, Scotland U.K.
172 E3 Lustadt Ger.
190 H1 Lustenau Austria
215 P2 Lusushwana r. Swaziland
Lusutufu r. Africa see Usutu
175 H3 Luszyn Pol.
Lut, Bahrat salt l. Asia see Dead Sea
122 H6 Lut, Dasht-e des. Iran
191 L2 Lutago Italy
Lutai Tianjin China see Ninghe
109 M7 Lü Tao i. Taiwan
168 K4 Lütau Ger.
256 B5 Lutécia Brazil
209 D8 Lutembo Angola
143 Q8 Luterskie, Jezioro l. Pol.
Lutetia France see Paris
122 H7 Lūt-e Zangī Aḩmad des. Iran
226 I5 Luther MI U.S.A.
227 N6 Luther Lake Ont. Can.
232 G7 Luthersburg PA U.S.A.
171 G7 Lutherstadt Wittenberg Ger.
208 F5 Lutiba Dem. Rep. Congo
176 G2 Lutín Czech Rep.
168 K2 Lütjenburg Ger.
168 J3 Lütjensee Ger.
175 H3 Lutocin Pol.
175 H4 Lutomiersk Pol.
151 L4 Luton Luton, England U.K.
151 L4 Luton admin. div. England U.K.
95 K2 Lutong Sarawak Malaysia
213 F3 Lutope r. Zimbabwe
175 K6 Lutowiska Pol.
175 I1 Lutry Pol.
223 I2 Łutselk'e N.W.T. Can.
209 E6 Lutshi Dem. Rep. Congo
136 E3 Luts'k Ukr.
169 J7 Lutter am Barenberge Ger.
157 N8 Lutterbach France
151 J3 Lutterworth Leicestershire, England U.K.
214 G8 Luttig S. Africa
Lutto r. Fin./Rus. Fed. see Lotta
209 D8 Lutuai Angola
137 S5 Lutuhyne Ukr.
174 G4 Lututów Pol.
174 F3 Lutynia r. Pol.
231 F11 Lutz FL U.S.A.
171 F8 Lützen Ger.
169 D10 Lutzerath Ger.
173 J4 Lutzingen Ger.
179 O5 Lutzmannsburg Austria
170 D3 Lützow Ger.
263 C2 Lützow-Holm Bay Antarctica
214 E4 Lutzputs S. Africa
171 F8 Lützschena Ger.
214 C7 Lutzville S. Africa
92 C9 Luuk Phil.
141 S6 Luumäki Fin.
210 D4 Luuq Somalia
140 S3 Luusua Fin.
209 B6 Luvaka Dem. Rep. Congo
215 P2 Luve Swaziland
231 D10 Luverne AL U.S.A.
236 G4 Luverne MN U.S.A.
141 P6 Luvia Fin.
209 B6 Luvo Angola
140 U4 Luvozero Rus. Fed.
209 E6 Luvua r. Dem. Rep. Congo
209 D8 Luvuei Angola
213 F4 Luvuvhu r. S. Africa
211 B8 Luwawa Malawi
211 C7 Luwegu r. Tanz.
210 B4 Luwero Uganda
209 F7 Luwingu Zambia
93 F3 Luwo i. Maluku Indon.
95 I5 Luwuhuyu Kalimantan Indon.
93 C4 Luwuk Sulawesi Indon.
160 G2 Lux France
165 H8 Luxembourg prov. Belgium
165 J9 Luxembourg country Europe
165 J9 Luxembourg Lux.
165 J9 Luxembourg admin. dist. Lux.
Luxemburg country Europe see Luxembourg
226 G5 Luxemburg WI U.S.A.
163 B9 Luxe-Sumberraute France
157 L8 Luxeuil-les-Bains France
163 C7 Luxey France
109 J5 Luxi Jiangxi China
108 B6 Luxi Yunnan China
108 D6 Luxi Yunnan China
108 E4 Luxian Sichuan China
215 J7 Luxolweni S. Africa
Luxor Egypt see Al Uqşur
150 C7 Luxulyan Cornwall, England U.K.
163 B8 Luy r. France
Luyang Sichuan China see Lushan
107 L7 Luya Shan mts China
163 C8 Luy de Béarn r. France
163 C8 Luy de France r. France
182 H4 Luyego de Somoza Spain
109 J2 Luyi Henan China
165 H6 Luyksgestel Neth.
159 M7 Luynes France
Luyuan Shaanxi China see Gaoling
257 E3 Luz Brazil
184 E4 Luz Évora Port.
184 B6 Luz Faro Port.
184 D6 Luz Faro Port.
182 H5 Luz hill Port.
134 I3 Luza Rus. Fed.
134 I3 Luza r. Rus. Fed.
134 L2 Luza r. Rus. Fed.
183 P7 Luzaga Spain
156 D5 Luzarches France
163 D10 Luz-Ardiden France
176 F2 Luže Czech Rep.
163 G7 Luzech France
176 D1 Lužec nad Vltavou Czech Rep.
190 E1 Luzern Switz.
190 E1 Luzern canton Switz.
234 D2 Luzerne PA U.S.A.
234 C2 Luzerne County county PA U.S.A.
139 T7 Luzha r. Rus. Fed.
108 G6 Luzhai Guangxi China
108 B6 Luzhang Yunnan China
108 E5 Luzhi Guizhou China
108 E4 Luzhou Sichuan China
184 C5 Luzianes Port.
256 D2 Luziânia Brazil
176 D1 Lužické hory mts Czech Rep.
254 E2 Luzilândia Brazil
174 G1 Luzino Pol.
183 L2 Luzmela Spain
176 C1 Lužná Czech Rep.
175 J6 Łużna Pol.
138 E4 Lūžņas Latvia
176 D2 Lužnice r. Czech Rep.
92 D4 Luzon i. Phil.
183 P6 Luzón Spain
92 C1 Luzon Strait Phil.
163 E10 Luz-St-Sauveur France
160 D3 Luzy France
174 G4 Łużyca r. Pol.
191 J6 Luzzara Italy
193 Q9 Luzzi Italy
136 G1 L'va r. Ukr.
136 D4 L'viv Ukr.
Lviv Oblast admin. div. Ukr. see L'vivs'ka Oblast'
136 D3 L'vivs'ka Oblast' admin. div. Ukr.
L'vov Ukr. see L'viv
Lvov Oblast admin. div. Ukr. see L'vivs'ka Oblast'
L'vovskaya Oblast' admin. div. Ukr. see L'vivs'ka Oblast'
139 U6 L'vovskiy Rus. Fed.
129 I2 L'vovskiy Pervyy Rus. Fed.
Lwów Ukr. see L'viv
174 E3 Lwówek Pol.
174 D4 Lwówek Śląski Pol.
136 G5 Lyadova r. Ukr.
139 O7 Lyady Belarus
138 L3 Lyady Rus. Fed.
138 J8 Lyakhavichy Belarus
Lyakhovichi Belarus see Lyakhavichy
131 P2 Lyakhovskiye Ostrova is Novosibirskiye O-va Rus. Fed.
137 L1 Lyalichi Rus. Fed.
81 B12 Lyall, Mount South I. N.Z.
Lyallpur Pak. see Faisalabad
Lyal'mikar Uzbek. see Lalmikor
135 I5 Lyambir' Rus. Fed.
134 L4 Lyamino Rus. Fed.
134 G2 Lyamtsa Rus. Fed.
Lyangar Navoiy Uzbek. see Langar
Lyangar Qashqadaryo Uzbek. see Langar
134 M3 Lyapin r. Rus. Fed.
137 L4 Lyashivka Ukr.
141 U6 Lyaskelya Rus. Fed.
197 N7 Lyaskovets Bulg.
138 I9 Lyasnaya Belarus
138 G9 Lyasnaya r. Belarus
175 L3 Lyasnaya Lyevaya r. Belarus
177 L3 Lybokhora Ukr.
146 J6 Lybster Highland, Scotland U.K.
175 M4 Lybytiv Ukr.
170 H4 Lychen Ger.
170 H4 Lychen-Boitzenberg park Ger.
137 O4 Lychkove Ukr.
139 P4 Lychkovo Rus. Fed.
Lyck Pol. see Ełk
140 O4 Lycksele Sweden
234 A2 Lycoming County county PA U.S.A.
234 A2 Lycoming Creek r. PA U.S.A.
Lycopolis Egypt see Asyūţ
151 N6 Lydd Kent, England U.K.
Lydda Israel see Lod
262 W2 Lyddan Island Antarctica
213 F5 Lydenburg S. Africa
150 D6 Lydford Devon, England U.K.
199 I4 Lydia reg. Turkey
150 G4 Lydney Gloucestershire, England U.K.
175 I3 Łydynia r. Pol.
138 I8 Lyebyada r. Belarus
136 H2 Lyel'chytsy Belarus
240 M4 Lyell, Mount CA U.S.A.
84 C7 Lyell Brown, Mount hill N.T. Austr.
222 D4 Lyell Island B.C. Can.
81 G8 Lyell Range mts South I. N.Z.
137 K1 Lyenina Belarus
175 M3 Lyeninski Belarus
138 L7 Lyepyel' Belarus
231 □2 Lyford Cay New Prov. Bahamas
142 I4 Lygnern l. Sweden
138 G5 Lygumai Lith.
137 P4 Lyhivka Ukr.
227 R9 Lykens PA U.S.A.
137 K2 Lykhachiv Ukr.
137 M5 Lykhivka Ukr.
139 Q3 Lykoshino Rus. Fed.
214 I3 Lykso S. Africa
226 B6 Lyle MN U.S.A.
136 I8 Lyman Ukr.
238 I6 Lyman WY U.S.A.
137 P4 Lyman, Ozero l. Ukr.
136 I7 Lymans'ke Ukr.
150 G6 Lyme Bay England U.K.
150 G6 Lyme Regis Dorset, England U.K.
151 O5 Lyminge Kent, England U.K.
151 I6 Lymington Hampshire, England U.K.
149 M7 Lymm Warrington, England U.K.
151 O5 Lympne Kent, England U.K.
150 F6 Lympstone Devon, England U.K.
143 R7 Łyna r. Pol.
232 C12 Lynch KY U.S.A.
231 D8 Lynchburg TN U.S.A.
232 F11 Lynchburg VA U.S.A.
231 H9 Lynches r. SC U.S.A.
232 F11 Lynch Station VA U.S.A.
233 □O4 Lynchville ME U.S.A.
85 I4 Lynd r. Qld Austr.
238 C2 Lynden WA U.S.A.
85 J5 Lyndhurst Qld Austr.
82 G4 Lyndhurst S.A. Austr.
151 I6 Lyndhurst Hampshire, England U.K.
87 C7 Lyndon W.A. Austr.
87 B7 Lyndon r. W.A. Austr.
236 H6 Lyndon KS U.S.A.
226 E6 Lyndon Station WI U.S.A.
232 G5 Lyndonville NY U.S.A.
233 M4 Lyndonville VT U.S.A.
149 K4 Lyne r. England U.K.
151 I4 Lyneham Wiltshire, England U.K.
149 N3 Lynemouth Northumberland, England U.K.
146 J5 Lyness Orkney, Scotland U.K.
142 E5 Lyngby nature res. Denmark
142 D3 Lyngdal Norway
140 P2 Lyngen sea chan. Norway
140 P2 Lyngseidet Norway
150 D7 Lynher r. England U.K.
86 F3 Lynher Reef W.A. Austr.
150 E5 Lynmouth Devon, England U.K.
Lynn Norfolk, England U.K. see King's Lynn
233 O6 Lynn MA U.S.A.
222 C3 Lynn Canal sea chan. AK U.S.A.
241 T2 Lynndyl UT U.S.A.
231 E10 Lynn Haven FL U.S.A.
223 K3 Lynn Lake Man. Can.
137 N2 Lynove Ukr.
137 L3 Lynovytsya Ukr.
87 C10 Lynton W.A. Austr.
150 E5 Lynton Devon, England U.K.
138 J6 Lyntupy Belarus
223 J2 Lynx Lake N.W.T. Can.
226 C6 Lynxville WI U.S.A.
160 F5 Lyon France
Lyon airport France see Satolas
146 I9 Lyon r. Scotland U.K.
146 G9 Lyon, Loch l. Scotland U.K.
233 L4 Lyon Mountain NY U.S.A.
160 F5 Lyonnais, Monts du hills France
82 D4 Lyons S.A. Austr.
87 C8 Lyons r. W.A. Austr.
Lyons France see Lyon
231 F9 Lyons GA U.S.A.
236 F6 Lyons KS U.S.A.
232 I5 Lyons NY U.S.A.
233 J5 Lyons Falls NY U.S.A.
156 B5 Lyons-la-Forêt France
235 I2 Lyons Plain CT U.S.A.
234 D4 Lyon Station PA U.S.A.
139 N6 Lyozna Belarus
136 E3 Lypa r. Ukr.
136 H2 Lypnyky Ukr.
137 M3 Lypova Dolyna Ukr.
136 I4 Lypovets' Ukr.
137 P3 Lyptsi Ukr.
77 F2 Lyra Reef P.N.G.
156 F2 Lys r. France
190 D4 Lys r. Italy
168 J1 Lysabild Denmark
177 H2 Lysá hora mt. Czech Rep.
137 K5 Lysa Hora Ukr.
171 K10 Lysá nad Labem Czech Rep.
177 H2 Lysá pod Makytou Slovakia
175 J2 Łyse Pol.
142 C2 Lysefjorden inlet Norway
142 C2 Lysekammen mt. Norway
142 H3 Lysekil Sweden
139 P9 Lyshchichi Rus. Fed.
175 L3 Lyshchytsy Belarus
128 B3 Lysi Cyprus
175 I5 Łysica hill Pol.
176 F2 Lysice Czech Rep.
198 C4 Lysimacheia, Limni l. Greece
175 M3 Lyskava Belarus
139 N6 Lys'kava Belarus
174 G5 Lyski Pol.
134 I4 Lyskovo Rus. Fed.
137 S6 Lysogorka Rus. Fed.
174 G2 Łysomice Pol.
96 I7 Ly Sơn, Đao i. Vietnam
190 C1 Lyss Switz.
142 G5 Lystrup Denmark
134 L4 Lys'va Rus. Fed.
142 J1 Lysvik Sweden
136 J4 Lysyanka Ukr.
137 R5 Lysychans'k Ukr.
135 I6 Lysyye Gory Rus. Fed.
175 H4 Łyszkowice Pol.
150 H6 Lytchett Matravers Dorset, England U.K.
150 H6 Lytchett Minster Dorset, England U.K.
146 J5 Lyth Highland, Scotland U.K.
149 K6 Lytham St Anne's Lancashire, England U.K.
139 U6 Lytkarino Rus. Fed.
175 M5 Lytovezh Ukr.
81 G10 Lyttelton South I. N.Z.
81 G10 Lyttelton Harbour South I. N.Z.
222 F5 Lytton B.C. Can.
138 L9 Lyuban' Belarus
139 O2 Lyuban' Rus. Fed.

138 L9 Lyubanskaye Vodaskhovishcha resr Belarus
136 G4 Lyubar Ukr.
136 J6 Lyubashivka Ukr.
139 N7 Lyubavichi Rus. Fed.
137 O1 Lyubazh Rus. Fed.
138 J8 Lyubcha Belarus
136 J2 Lyubech Ukr.
139 U6 Lyubertsy Rus. Fed.
136 E2 Lyubeshiv Ukr.
134 H4 Lyubim Rus. Fed.
197 O9 Lyubimets Bulg.
137 O2 Lyubimovka Kurskaya Oblast' Rus. Fed.
139 V8 Lyubimovka Tul'skaya Oblast' Rus. Fed.
138 I9 Lyubishchytsy Belarus
139 R3 Lyubitovo Rus. Fed.
175 I1 Lyublino Rus. Fed.
175 M4 Lyublynets' Ukr.
139 R8 Lyubokhna Rus. Fed.
175 M4 Lyubokhyny Ukr.
137 L6 Lyubomyrivka Ukr.
137 O2 Lyubostan' Rus. Fed.
Lyubotin Ukr. see Lyubotyn
137 O4 Lyubotyn Ukr.
138 K8 Lyubyacha Belarus
137 P6 Lyubymivka Ukr.
175 L6 Lyubyntsi Ukr.
139 Q3 Lyubytino Rus. Fed.
139 R8 Lyudinovo Rus. Fed.
139 Q1 Lyugovichi Rus. Fed.
197 P8 Lyulyakovo Bulg.
134 I4 Lyunda r. Rus. Fed.
138 J9 Lyusina Belarus
137 O3 Lyutivka Ukr.
134 L2 Lyzha r. Rus. Fed.
137 R4 Lyzyne Ukr.
138 L4 Lzha r. Rus. Fed.

M

96 D3 Ma r. Myanmar
96 E4 Ma, Nam r. Laos
96 G5 Ma, Sông r. Vietnam
113 □1 Maabadi i. N. Male Maldives
Maafushi i. S. Male Maldives see Mafushi
240 □E13 Ma'alaea HI U.S.A.
114 C10 Maalhosmadulu Atoll Maldives
147 C5 Maam Ireland
Maamakundhoo i. N. Male Maldives see Makunudhoo
209 E9 Maamba Zambia
147 C6 Maam Cross Ireland
207 H6 Ma'an Cameroon
128 D8 Ma'ān Jordan
Maan Turkey see Nusratiye
140 S5 Maaninka Fin.
140 T3 Maaninkavaara Fin.
140 T5 Maanselkä Fin.
109 L3 Ma'anshan Anhui China
106 H2 Maanyt Bulgan Mongolia
107 J3 Maanyt Töv Mongolia
138 I2 Maardu Estonia
165 I6 Maarheeze Neth.
Maarianhamina Åland Fin. see Mariehamn
124 G6 Ma'āriḍ, Banī des. Saudi Arabia
164 H4 Maarn Neth.
128 E2 Ma'arrat al Ikhwān Syria
128 E3 Ma'arrat an Nu'mān Syria
164 H4 Maarssen Neth.
164 H4 Maarssenbroek Neth.
164 H4 Maartensdijk Neth.
164 G5 Maas r. Neth. alt. Meuse (Belgium/France)
147 F3 Maas Ireland
165 I6 Maasbracht Neth.
165 J6 Maasbree Neth.
164 G5 Maasdam Neth.
165 I6 Maaseik Belgium
92 E6 Maasin Leyte Phil.
164 F5 Maasland Neth.
165 I7 Maasmechelen Belgium
169 A8 Maas-Schwalm-Nette nat. park Ger./Neth.
164 F5 Maassluis Neth.
165 I7 Maastricht Neth.
83 K10 Maatsuyker Group is Tas. Austr.
Maba Guangdong China see Qujiang
109 L2 Maba Jiangsu China
93 F3 Maba Halmahera Indon.
202 D6 Maba, Ouadi watercourse Chad
215 K1 Mabaalstad North West S. Africa
215 K1 Mabaalstad North West S. Africa
212 E3 Mababe Depression Botswana
92 C4 Mabalacat Luzon Phil.
213 G4 Mabalane Moz.
208 F4 Mabana Dem. Rep. Congo
208 A5 Mabanda Gabon
124 G8 Ma'bar Yemen
251 G2 Mabaruma Guyana
Mabating Yunnan China see Hongshan
96 C3 Mabein Myanmar
82 E3 Mabel Creek S.A. Austr.
86 I4 Mabel Downs W.A. Austr.
224 B3 Mabella Ont. Can.
222 G5 Mabel Lake B.C. Can.
227 R5 Maberly Ont. Can.
108 D4 Mabian Sichuan China
111 H12 Mabja Xizang China
149 R7 Mablethorpe Lincolnshire, England U.K.
160 E4 Mably France
215 M1 Mabopane S. Africa
213 G4 Mabote Moz.
225 I4 Mabou N.S. Can.
128 D8 Mabrak, Jabal mt. Jordan
206 E2 Mabroûk well Mali
202 B4 Mabrous well Niger
212 D5 Mabuasehube Game Reserve nature res. Botswana
92 C1 Mabudis i. Phil.
214 I1 Mabule Botswana
102 □1 Mabuni Okinawa Japan
202 D3 Ma'būs Yūsuf oasis Libya
212 D5 Mabutsane Botswana
259 B7 Macá, Monte mt. Chile
261 F5 Macachín Arg.
87 D8 Macadam Plains W.A. Austr.
84 B3 Macadam Range hills N.T. Austr.
257 G5 Macaé Brazil
185 O6 Macael Spain
129 C4 Maçahel Geçidi pass Turkey
254 G3 Macaíba Brazil
92 E7 Macajalar Bay Mindanao Phil.
254 E5 Macajuba Brazil
211 B8 Macaloge Moz.
221 H3 MacAlpine Lake Nunavut Can.
224 E3 Macamic Que. Can.
Macan, Kepulauan atolls Indon. see Taka'Bonerate, Kepulauan
213 G4 Macandze Moz.
215 Q1 Macaneta, Ponta de pt Moz.
186 K3 Maçanet de Cabrenys Spain
109 I7 Macao Macao China
182 E9 Mação Port.
251 I4 Macapá Amapá Brazil
252 D2 Macapá Amazonas Brazil
Macar Turkey see Gebiz
250 B6 Macará Ecuador
242 □S14 Macaracas Panama
255 E5 Macarani Brazil
250 C4 Macarena, Cordillera mts Col.
251 F2 Macareo, Caño r. Venez.
83 I8 Macarthur Vic. Austr.
250 B5 Macas Ecuador
182 G6 Maçãs r. Port./Spain
Macassar Sulawesi Indon. see Makassar
Macassar Strait Indon. see Makassar, Selat
187 D9 Macastre Spain
213 H3 Macatanja Moz.
254 F3 Macau Brazil
162 C5 Macau France
252 C2 Macauã r. Brazil
254 C4 Macaúba Brazil
254 E5 Macaúbas Brazil
77 I5 Macauley Island N.Z.
250 C4 Macayari Col.
210 F2 Macbar, Raas pt Somalia
259 F8 Macbride Head Falkland Is
190 F3 Maccagno Italy
213 G5 Maccaretane Moz.
195 I8 Macchia r. Sicilia Italy
193 M4 Macchiagodena Italy
231 F10 Macclenny FL U.S.A.
149 M7 Macclesfield Cheshire, England U.K.
90 D3 Macclesfield Bank sea feature S. China Sea
224 B3 Macdiarmid Ont. Can.
86 J7 Macdonald, Lake salt flat W.A. Austr.
84 C7 Macdonnell Ranges mts N.T. Austr.
223 M4 MacDowell Lake Ont. Can.
146 L7 Macduff Aberdeenshire, Scotland U.K.
177 K5 Macea Romania
182 E4 Maceda Spain
261 I5 Macedo Arg.
182 G5 Macedo de Cavaleiros Port.
Macedon country Europe see Macedonia
197 J9 Macedonia country Europe
235 I1 Macedonia CT U.S.A.
254 G4 Maceió Brazil
254 F3 Maceio, Ponta da pt Brazil
182 F7 Maceira Guarda Port.
182 C9 Maceira Leiria Port.
179 M7 Macelj Croatia
206 C4 Macenta Guinea
191 O9 Macerata Italy
191 O9 Macerata prov. Italy
191 M8 Macerata Feltria Italy
82 F5 Macfarlane, Lake salt flat S.A. Austr.
147 C9 Macgillycuddy's Reeks mts Ireland
148 E4 MacGregor's Corner Northern Ireland U.K.
123 L7 Mach Pak.
131 M3 Macha Rus. Fed.
257 G2 Machacalis Brazil
252 D4 Machacamarca Bol.
250 B5 Machachi Ecuador
253 E2 Machadinho r. Brazil
257 E4 Machado Brazil
215 O1 Machadodorp S. Africa
184 E4 Machados Port.
209 E8 Machai Zambia
213 G4 Machaila Moz.
211 C5 Machakos Kenya
250 B5 Machala Ecuador
260 B4 Machali Chile
Machali Qinghai China see Madoi
95 J4 Machan Sarawak Malaysia
78 □1 Machanao, Mount hill Guam
213 G4 Machanga Moz.
253 E5 Macharetí Bol.
210 B2 Machar Marshes Sudan
84 G8 Machattie, Lake salt flat Qld Austr.
215 Q1 Machatuine Moz.
156 I5 Machault France
Machaze Moz. see Chitobe
158 H8 Machecoul France
165 F7 Machelen Belgium
150 F4 Machen Caerphilly, Wales U.K.
109 J3 Macheng Hubei China
157 M5 Macheren France
114 F4 Macherla Andhra Prad. India
171 G8 Machern Ger.
185 K2 Machero mt. Spain
226 E7 Machesney Park IL U.S.A.
117 K9 Machhagan Orissa India
116 F4 Machhiwara Punjab India
116 I7 Machhlishahr Uttar Prad. India
233 □R4 Machias ME U.S.A.
232 G6 Machias NY U.S.A.
233 □Q2 Machias r. ME U.S.A.
233 □R4 Machias Bay ME U.S.A.
184 □ Machico Madeira
105 J4 Machida Japan
114 G4 Machilipatnam Andhra Prad. India
211 B8 Machinga Malawi
250 C2 Machiques Venez.
146 D11 Machir Bay Scotland U.K.
Machiwara Punjab India see Machhiwara
123 I9 Māch Kowr Iran
239 L10 Macho, Arroyo del watercourse NM U.S.A.
245 N7 Machona, Laguna lag. Mex.
146 E12 Machrihanish Argyll and Bute, Scotland U.K.
137 N4 Machukhy Ukr.
252 B3 Machu Picchu tourist site Peru
252 D3 Machupo r. Bol.
150 E2 Machynlleth Powys, Wales U.K.
213 G5 Macia Moz.
Macias Nguema i. Equat. Guinea see Bioco
175 J4 Maciejowice Pol.
261 G3 Maciel Arg.
197 Q5 Măcin Romania
192 C2 Macinaggio Corse France
83 M3 Macintyre r. N.S.W. Austr.
83 M3 Macintyre Brook r. Qld Austr.
252 B3 Macizo de Tocate mts Peru
241 X2 Mack CO U.S.A.
129 A5 Maçka Turkey
85 L6 Mackay Qld Austr.
223 I3 MacKay r. Alta Can.
238 H4 Mackay ID U.S.A.
86 J7 Mackay, Lake salt flat W.A. Austr.
223 I2 MacKay Lake N.W.T. Can.
262 O1 Mackay Mountains Antarctica
172 D3 Mackenbach Ger.
169 K7 Mackenrode Ger.
85 L7 Mackenzie r. Qld Austr.
222 F4 Mackenzie B.C. Can.
226 F1 Mackenzie Ont. Can.
222 E1 Mackenzie r. N.W.T. Can.
Mackenzie Guyana see Linden
Mackenzie atoll Micronesia see Ulithi
263 E2 Mackenzie Bay Antarctica
220 E3 Mackenzie Bay Y.T. Can.
222 G2 Mackenzie Bison Sanctuary nature res. N.W.T. Can.
222 G2 Mackenzie Highway N.W.T. Can.
221 G2 Mackenzie King Island N.W.T. Can.
222 C1 Mackenzie Mountains N.W.T./Y.T. Can.
Mackillop, Lake salt flat Qld Austr. see Yamma Yamma, Lake
226 I4 Mackinac, Straits of lake channel MI U.S.A.
226 J4 Mackinac Island MI U.S.A.
226 E9 Mackinaw r. IL U.S.A.
226 J4 Mackinaw City MI U.S.A.
223 I4 Macklin Sask. Can.
179 N6 Mačkovci Slovenia
83 N4 Macksville N.S.W. Austr.
85 H7 Mackunda Creek watercourse Qld Austr.
83 N3 Maclean N.S.W. Austr.
215 L8 Macleantown S. Africa
215 M7 Maclear S. Africa
83 N4 Macleay r. N.S.W. Austr.
MacLeod Alta Can. see Fort Macleod
87 B8 MacLeod, Lake imp. l. W.A. Austr.
Macleod's Table South hill Scotland U.K. see Healabhal Bheag
222 C2 Macmillan r. Y.T. Can.
222 D2 Macmillan Pass Y.T. Can.
147 G4 Macnean Lower, Lough l. Northern Ireland U.K.
147 G4 Macnean Upper, Lough l. Ireland/U.K.
213 G4 Maçobere Moz.
209 C6 Macocola Angola
226 D9 Macomb IL U.S.A.
192 B7 Macomer Sardegna Italy
211 D8 Macomia Moz.
160 F4 Mâcon France
231 F9 Macon GA U.S.A.
236 I6 Macon MO U.S.A.
237 K9 Macon MS U.S.A.
232 B10 Macon OH U.S.A.
237 J10 Macon, Bayou r. LA U.S.A.
209 D8 Macondo Angola
160 F4 Mâconnais reg. France
235 G2 Macopin NJ U.S.A.
213 G3 Macossa Moz.
183 J7 Macotera Spain
223 K3 Macoun Lake Sask. Can.
213 G4 Macovane Moz.
Macpherson Robertson Land reg. Antarctica see Mac. Robertson Land
83 K4 Macquarie r. N.S.W. Austr.
83 K9 Macquarie r. Tas. Austr.
83 M5 Macquarie, Lake b. N.S.W. Austr.
83 J10 Macquarie Harbour Tas. Austr.
82 □3 Macquarie Island S. Pacific Ocean
83 K4 Macquarie Marshes N.S.W. Austr.
83 L5 Macquarie Mountain N.S.W. Austr.
266 F9 Macquarie Ridge sea feature S. Pacific Ocean
81 E12 Macraes Flat South I. N.Z.
94 □ MacRitchie Reservoir Sing.
263 E2 Mac. Robertson Land reg. Antarctica
147 E9 Macroom Ireland
243 N9 Mactún Mex.
250 D4 Macú Brazil
190 D4 Macugnaga Italy
245 K8 Macuiltianguis Mex.
250 D1 Macuira, Parque Nacional nat. park Col.
250 C4 Macuje Col.
196 I9 Macukull Albania
82 E2 Macumba S.A. Austr.
82 F2 Macumba watercourse S.A. Austr.
234 D3 Macungie PA U.S.A.
254 F4 Macururé Brazil
252 C3 Macusani Peru
243 M9 Macuspana Mex.
242 E4 Macuzari, Presa resr Mex.
213 H3 Macuze Moz.
233 □Q3 Macwahoc ME U.S.A.
177 K3 Mád Hungary
128 D7 Mādabā Jordan
215 O3 Madadeni S. Africa
123 K7 Madagan Pak.
213 □ Madagascar i. Africa
265 H6 Madagascar Basin sea feature Indian Ocean
265 G7 Madagascar Ridge sea feature Indian Ocean
129 H5 Madagiz Azer.
207 I4 Madagli Nigeria
124 C2 Madā'in Ṣāliḥ Saudi Arabia
114 E6 Madakasira Andhra Prad. India
92 □ Madalai Palau
216 □1c Madalena Pico Azores
254 F3 Madalena Brazil
202 B4 Madama Niger
197 M9 Madan Bulg.
122 H3 Ma'dan Iran
208 C2 Madana Chad
202 C5 Madana well Chad
114 F6 Madanapalle Andhra Prad. India
91 K8 Madang P.N.G.
116 G7 Madaora Uttar Prad. India
207 G3 Madaoua Niger
197 P7 Madara Bulg.
177 I5 Madaras Hungary
197 J4 Mădăraş Romania
117 M8 Madaripur Bangl.
207 G3 Madarounfa Niger
Madaw Turkm. see Madaw
122 F2 Madaw Turkm.
227 Q4 Madawaska Ont. Can.
224 E4 Madawaska r. Ont. Can.
233 □Q1 Madawaska ME U.S.A.
96 C3 Madaya Myanmar
192 C5 Maddalena, Isola i. Sardegna Italy
195 I9 Maddalena, Penisola della pen. Sicilia Italy
192 C9 Maddalena Spiaggia Sardegna Italy
193 M5 Maddaloni Italy
114 G3 Madded Chhattisgarh India
114 E6 Maddur Karnataka India
164 G5 Made Neth.
208 F3 Madeir Sudan
251 G5 Madeira r. Brazil
184 □ Madeira terr. N. Atlantic Ocean
184 □ Madeira, Arquipélago da is N. Atlantic Ocean
Madeira, Arquipélago da terr. N. Atlantic Ocean see Madeira
184 □ Madeira, Ilha da i. Madeira
184 □ Madeira, Parque Natural de nature res. Madeira
Madeira Islands N. Atlantic Ocean see Madeira, Arquipélago da
253 E2 Madeirinha r. Brazil
225 I4 Madeleine, Îles de la is Que. Can.
160 D4 Madeleine, Monts de la mts France
150 H2 Madeley Staffordshire, England U.K.
150 H2 Madeley Telford and Wrekin, England U.K.
236 H3 Madelia MN U.S.A.
226 D3 Madeline Island WI U.S.A.
208 C2 Madel Ouèï Chad
126 I4 Maden Turkey
121 R4 Madeniyet Kazakh.
188 B2 Mäder Austria
242 E3 Madera Mex.
185 N4 Madera r. Spain
240 L5 Madera CA U.S.A.
183 K5 Maderano r. Spain
178 B5 Madererspitze mt. Austria
183 M6 Maderuelo Spain
140 S3 Madetkoski Fin.
114 C5 Madgaon Goa India
217 □2a Madge Rocks is Inner Islands Seychelles
210 D1 Madgoul Djibouti
116 C9 Madhavpur Gujarat India
117 K7 Madhepura Bihar India
111 E13 Madhoganj Uttar Prad. India
117 K6 Madhubani Bihar India
114 E6 Madhugiri Karnataka India
117 K7 Madhupur Jharkhand India
116 G8 Madhya Pradesh state India
95 J4 Madi, Dataran Tinggi plat. Indon.
211 B7 Madibira Tanz.
215 J2 Madibogo S. Africa
252 D3 Madidi r. Bol.
82 F3 Madigan Gulf salt flat S.A. Austr.
114 D6 Madikeri Karnataka India
237 G8 Madill OK U.S.A.
209 B6 Madimba Angola
209 B6 Madimba Dem. Rep. Congo
206 D4 Madinani Côte d'Ivoire
124 F8 Madīnat al 'Abīd Yemen
124 G9 Madīnat ash Sha'b Yemen
128 G3 Madīnat ath Thawrah Syria
157 K6 Madine, Lac de l. France
209 A6 Madingo-Kayes Congo
209 B6 Madingou Congo
207 I4 Madingrin Cameroon
163 D8 Madiran France
213 □J3 Madirovalo Madag.
231 D8 Madison AL U.S.A.
235 J2 Madison CT U.S.A.
231 F10 Madison FL U.S.A.
231 F9 Madison GA U.S.A.
230 E6 Madison IN U.S.A.
233 □P4 Madison ME U.S.A.
236 G3 Madison MN U.S.A.
236 G5 Madison NE U.S.A.
235 G3 Madison NJ U.S.A.
232 D7 Madison OH U.S.A.
236 G3 Madison SD U.S.A.
232 G10 Madison VA U.S.A.
226 E6 Madison WI U.S.A.
232 D10 Madison WV U.S.A.
238 I4 Madison r. MT U.S.A.
232 F11 Madison Heights VA U.S.A.
230 D7 Madisonville KY U.S.A.
231 E8 Madisonville TN U.S.A.
237 H10 Madisonville TX U.S.A.
93 B9 Madita Sumba Indon.
95 I8 Madiun Jawa Indon.
208 B4 Madjingo Gabon
205 I4 Madjūl Libya
150 G3 Madley Herefordshire, England U.K.
87 G8 Madley, Mount hill W.A. Austr.
138 I5 Madliena Latvia
Madnishkevi Rus. Fed. see Uchkulan
208 F4 Mado Dem. Rep. Congo
224 E4 Madoc Ont. Can.
177 H5 Madocsa Hungary
210 C4 Mado Gashi Kenya
106 F9 Madoi Qinghai China
157 L6 Madon r. France
138 J5 Madona Latvia
212 D4 Madongo Pan salt pan Botswana
194 F8 Madonie mts Sicilia Italy
234 B5 Madonna MD U.S.A.
191 J3 Madonna di Campiglio Italy
116 C7 Madpura Rajasthan India
199 H3 Madra Dağı mts Turkey
124 D5 Madrakah Saudi Arabia
125 M6 Madrakah, Ra's c. Oman
Madras Tamil Nadu India see Chennai
Madras state India see Tamil Nadu
238 D4 Madras OR U.S.A.
129 J5 Mädräsä Azer.
245 J1 Madre, Laguna lag. Mex.
237 G12 Madre, Laguna lag. TX U.S.A.
Madre, Sierra mts Mex. see Madre de Chiapas, Sierra
92 C3 Madre, Sierra mt. Luzon Phil.
245 N9 Madre de Chiapas, Sierra mts Mex.
257 E4 Madre de Deus de Minas Brazil
252 C2 Madre de Dios dept Peru
259 B8 Madre de Dios, Isla i. Chile
244 F7 Madre del Sur, Sierra mts Mex.
208 F3 Madreggi Sudan
244 B1 Madre Occidental, Sierra mts Mex.
244 F1 Madre Oriental, Sierra mts Mex.
163 I10 Madrès, Pic de mt. France
92 E7 Madrid Mindanao Phil.
183 M8 Madrid Spain
183 M7 Madrid aut. comm. Spain
92 D6 Madridejos Phil.
185 L2 Madridejos Spain
183 K6 Madrigal de las Altas Torres Spain
183 J8 Madrigal de la Vera Spain
183 M4 Madrigal del Monte Spain
184 H2 Madrigalejo Spain
185 P2 Madrigueras Spain
178 A6 Madrisahorn mt. Austria/Switz.
143 L4 Madroken l. Sweden
150 □ Madron Cornwall, England U.K.
185 K4 Madrona, Sierra mts Spain
184 H2 Madroñera Spain
185 P3 Madroño mt. Spain
246 C2 Madruga Cuba
202 B3 Madrūsah Libya
93 B7 Madu i. Indon.
113 □1 Madu i. S. Male Maldives
209 B6 Maduda Dem. Rep. Congo
115 H4 Madugula Andhra Prad. India
87 I11 Madura W.A. Austr.
95 J8 Madura i. Indon.
95 J8 Madura, Selat sea chan. Indon.
114 F8 Madurai Tamil Nadu India
114 F6 Madurantakam Tamil Nadu India
122 F6 Madvār, Kūh-e mt. Iran
116 H7 Madwas Madh. Prad. India
123 O4 Madyan Pak.
211 B6 Madyo Tanz.
129 I3 Madzhalis Rus. Fed.
197 N9 Madzharovo Bulg.
213 F3 Madziwadzido Zimbabwe
213 F3 Madziwa Mine Zimbabwe
191 M3 Maè r. Italy
Maé i. Vanuatu see Émaé
105 J3 Maebashi Japan
96 D5 Mae Chang Reservoir Thai.
96 C5 Mae Hong Son Thai.
102 □1 Mae-jima i. Okinawa Japan
93 C3 Maelang Sulawesi Indon.
158 E5 Maël-Carhaix France
142 E2 Mælefjell mt. Norway
186 F5 Maella Spain
183 K7 Maello Spain
150 C4 Maenclochog Pembrokeshire, Wales U.K.
96 D5 Mae Ngat Reservoir Thai.
150 E2 Maentwrog Gwynedd, Wales U.K.
193 K4 Maenza Italy
96 D6 Mae Ping National Park Thai.
96 D6 Mae Ramat Thai.
96 D5 Mae Rim Thai.
197 K3 Măerişte Romania
96 D4 Mae Sai Thai.
96 C5 Mae Sariang Thai.
96 D6 Mae Sot Thai.
150 E4 Maesteg Bridgend, Wales U.K.
246 E4 Maestra, Sierra mts Cuba
185 I6 Maestre hill Spain
92 C5 Maestre de Campo i. Phil.
191 L9 Maestro, Canale canal Italy
96 D5 Mae Suai Thai.
96 D6 Mae Tuen Wildlife Reserve nature res. Thai.
213 □J3 Maevatanana Madag.
78 □5 Maéwo i. Vanuatu
96 D7 Mae Wong National Park Thai.
96 E5 Mae Yom National Park Thai.
183 P3 Maeztu Spain
93 E3 Mafa Halmahera Indon.
217 □1c Mafaté, Cirque de vol. crater Réunion
223 K4 Mafeking Man. Can.
Mafeking S. Africa see Mafikeng
215 L5 Mafeteng Lesotho
83 K7 Maffra Vic. Austr.
211 C7 Mafia Channel Tanz.
211 C6 Mafia Island Tanz.
215 J1 Mafikeng S. Africa
211 B7 Mafinga Tanz.
255 C8 Mafra Brazil
184 A3 Mafra Port.
Mafraq Jordan see Al Mafraq
254 E4 Mafrense Brazil
213 F3 Mafungabusi Plateau Zimbabwe
113 □1 Mafushi i. S. Male Maldives
215 O6 Magabeni S. Africa
184 H3 Magacela hill Spain
131 Q4 Magadan Rus. Fed.
211 C5 Magadi Kenya
213 G4 Magaiza Moz.
161 C10 Magalas France
215 L1 Magaliesberg mts S. Africa
215 L1 Magaliesburg S. Africa
Magallanes Chile see Punta Arenas
92 D5 Magallanes Luzon Phil.
259 C9 Magallanes, Estrecho de sea chan. Chile
246 E2 Magallanes Bank sea feature Bahamas
259 B9 Magallanes y Antártica Chilena admin. reg. Chile
183 R5 Magallón Spain
187 K8 Magalluf Spain
183 P5 Magaña Spain
147 I7 Maganey Ireland
250 C2 Magangue Col.
126 F5 Mağara Turkey
129 E5 Mağara tourist site Turkey
128 A2 Mağara Dağı mt. Turkey
128 G2 Mağarali Turkey
129 J4 Magaramkent Rus. Fed.
207 H3 Magaria Niger
102 □1 Magari-zaki pt Okinawa Japan
Magas Iran see Zābolī
129 F2 Magas Rus. Fed.
92 C3 Magat r. Luzon Phil.
183 L5 Magaz Spain
237 I8 Magazine Mountain hill AR U.S.A.
194 E9 Magazzolo r. Sicilia Italy
208 D4 Magbakele Dem. Rep. Congo
206 C4 Magburaka Sierra Leone
100 D2 Magdagachi Rus. Fed.
171 D9 Magdala Ger.
261 I4 Magdalena Arg.
252 D3 Magdalena Bol.
250 C2 Magdalena dept Col.
250 C2 Magdalena r. Col.
242 C4 Magdalena Baja California Sur Mex.
242 D2 Magdalena Sonora Mex.
242 D2 Magdalena r. Mex.
239 K9 Magdalena NM U.S.A.
250 B3 Magdalena, Bahía b. Col.
242 D5 Magdalena, Bahía b. Mex.
259 B7 Magdalena, Isla i. Chile
242 C5 Magdalena, Isla i. Mex.
187 C10 Magdalena, Sierra de la mts Spain
245 J7 Magdalena Cuayucatepec Mex.
Magdalena Island Fr. Polynesia see Fatu Hiva
95 L2 Magdaline, Gunung mt. Malaysia
171 E6 Magdeburg Ger.
171 F6 Magdeburgerforth Ger.
85 M4 Magdelaine Cays atoll Coral Sea Is Terr. Austr.
237 K10 Magee MS U.S.A.
95 I8 Magelang Jawa Indon.
Magellan, Strait of Chile see Magallanes, Estrecho de
266 E4 Magellan Seamounts sea feature N. Pacific Ocean
190 F5 Magenta Italy
87 E12 Magenta, Lake salt flat W.A. Austr.
140 R1 Magerøya i. Norway
163 B8 Magescq France
102 □H16 Mage-shima i. Japan
177 L4 Măgeşti Romania
190 F3 Maggia Switz.
190 F3 Maggia r. Switz.
261 F3 Maggiolo Arg.
190 G6 Maggiorasca, Monte mt. Italy
192 I1 Maggiore, Isola i. Italy
190 F4 Maggiore, Lago l. Italy
Maggiore, Lake Italy see Maggiore, Lago
192 D6 Maggiore, Monte hill Sardegna Italy
193 M5 Maggiore, Monte mt. Italy
246 □ Maggotty Jamaica
203 F2 Maghāghah Egypt
128 C10 Maghā'ir Shu'ayb tourist site Saudi Arabia
206 B3 Maghama Maur.
147 C9 Maghanlawaun Ireland
128 B8 Maghārah, Jabal hill Egypt
Magharee Islands Ireland see The Seven Hogs
147 E3 Maghera Ireland
147 I3 Maghera Northern Ireland U.K.
147 I3 Magherafelt Northern Ireland U.K.
148 E5 Magheralin Northern Ireland U.K.
147 H3 Magheramason Northern Ireland U.K.
147 I3 Maghery Northern Ireland U.K.
204 E2 Maghnia Alg.
123 J4 Maghor Afgh.
149 L6 Maghull Merseyside, England U.K.
148 D3 Magilligan Northern Ireland U.K.
147 I2 Magilligan Point Northern Ireland U.K.
185 M5 Mágina mt. Spain
185 L5 Mágina, Sierra mts Spain
211 B7 Magingo Tanz.
192 I1 Magione Italy
195 L5 Magisano Italy
245 I3 Magiscatzín Mex.
Magitang Qinghai China see Jainca
Magiyan Tajik. see Moghiyon
188 G3 Maglaj Bos.-Herz.
160 J4 Magland France
197 L6 Maglavit Romania
193 K3 Magliano de'Marsi Italy
192 G2 Magliano in Toscana Italy
193 I3 Magliano Sabina Italy
195 O3 Maglie Italy
177 I4 Maglód Hungary
241 U8 Magma AZ U.S.A.
162 G3 Magnac-Laval France
162 E4 Magnac-sur-Touvre France
194 C10 Magna Grande hill Italy
195 I8 Magna Grande mt. Sicilia Italy
162 C3 Magné France
263 D2 Magnet Bay Antarctica
85 K5 Magnetic Island Qld Austr.
85 K5 Magnetic Passage Qld Austr.
134 F1 Magnetity Rus. Fed.
157 M7 Magnières France
195 I9 Magnisi, Penisola pen. Sicilia Italy
139 S9 Magnitnyy Rus. Fed.
120 H1 Magnitogorsk Rus. Fed.
237 I9 Magnolia AR U.S.A.
234 E6 Magnolia DE U.S.A.
234 C6 Magnolia MD U.S.A.
237 J10 Magnolia MS U.S.A.
142 I2 Magnor Norway
175 J4 Magnuszew Pol.
160 C3 Magny-Cours France
156 C5 Magny-en-Vexin France
100 L2 Mago Rus. Fed.
177 H5 Mágocs Hungary
177 J5 Mágocs-ér r. Hungary
213 F2 Màgoé Moz.
225 F4 Magog Que. Can.
211 C6 Magole Tanz.
192 B7 Magomadas Sardegna Italy
210 C3 Mago National Park Eth.
Magosa Cyprus see Ammochostos
209 E8 Magoye Zambia
245 J4 Magozal Mex.
225 H3 Magpie Que. Can.
224 C4 Magpie r. Ont. Can.
225 H3 Magpie r. Que. Can.
225 H3 Magpie, Lac l. Que. Can.
225 H3 Magpie-Ouest r. Que. Can.
190 H7 Magra r. Italy
222 H5 Magrath Alta Can.
187 E9 Magre r. Spain
240 O4 Magruder Mountain NV U.S.A.
203 F6 Magrur Sudan
202 E5 Magrur, Wadi watercourse Sudan
206 B2 Magṭa' Laḥjar Maur.
122 G2 Magtymguly Turkm.
211 B5 Magu Tanz.
122 G5 Magu, Chashmeh-ye well Iran
100 J2 Magu, Khrebet mts Rus. Fed.
108 E7 Maguan Yunnan China
254 C2 Maguarinho, Cabo c. Brazil
213 G5 Magude Moz.
215 P3 Magudu S. Africa
182 E6 Magueija Port.
242 H4 Magueyal Mex.
216 □3c Máguez Lanzarote Canary Is
184 H4 Maguilla Spain
147 H4 Maguiresbridge Northern Ireland U.K.
207 I3 Magumeri Nigeria
233 □R3 Magundy N.B. Can.
213 F3 Magunge Zimbabwe
117 L8 Magura Bangl.
177 H3 Magura mt. Slovakia
136 G6 Măgura, Dealul hill Moldova
197 K3 Măgura Mare, Vârful hill Romania
197 K5 Măgurii, Vârful mt. Romania
223 M2 Maguse Lake Nunavut Can.
215 L8 Magwali S. Africa
Magway Myanmar see Magwe
Magway admin. div. Myanmar see Magwe
96 B4 Magwe Myanmar
96 B4 Magwe admin. div. Myanmar
210 B3 Magwe Sudan
212 D3 Magwegqana watercourse Botswana
177 K4 Magy Hungary
177 G5 Magyaratád Hungary
177 H6 Magyarbóly Hungary
Magyarkanizsa Vojvodina Serbia see Kanjiža
Magyar Köztársaság country Europe see Hungary
177 H5 Magyarszék Hungary
96 A4 Magyichaung Myanmar
122 A3 Mahābād Iran
114 C4 Mahabaleshwar Mahar. India
213 □J3 Mahabe Madag.
116 J6 Mahabharat Range mts Nepal
213 □J4 Mahabo Toliara Madag.
213 □J4 Mahabo Toliara Madag.
213 □J4 Mahaboboka Madag.
114 C3 Mahad Mahar. India
210 E4 Mahaddayweyne Somalia
116 F8 Mahadeo Hills Madh. Prad. India
114 G3 Mahadeopur Andhra Prad. India
79 □9a Mahaena Tahiti Fr. Polynesia
232 G8 Mahaffey PA U.S.A.
208 F4 Mahagi Dem. Rep. Congo
208 F4 Mahagi Port Dem. Rep. Congo
111 L7 Mahai Qinghai China
251 G3 Mahaicony Guyana
213 □J2 Mahajamba r. Madag.
116 D5 Mahajan Rajasthan India
213 □J2 Mahajanga Madag.
213 □J3 Mahajanga prov. Madag.
95 L5 Mahakam r. Indon.
213 E4 Mahalapye Botswana
211 A6 Mahale Mountains National Park Tanz.
213 □K2 Mahalevona Madag.
122 D5 Mahallāt Iran
116 F5 Maham Haryana India
122 G6 Māhān Iran
117 K9 Mahanadi r. India
213 □K3 Mahanoro Madag.
234 C3 Mahanoy City PA U.S.A.
234 B3 Mahanoy Creek r. PA U.S.A.
234 B3 Mahantango Creek r. PA U.S.A.
114 G9 Maha Oya Sri Lanka
117 J6 Maharajganj Bihar India
116 H6 Maharajganj Uttar Prad. India
117 I6 Maharajganj Uttar Prad. India
116 G7 Maharajpur Madh. Prad. India
114 D3 Maharashtra state India
124 B2 Mahārish, Ra's pt Saudi Arabia
122 E7 Mahārlū, Daryācheh-ye salt l. Iran
116 I9 Mahasamund Chhattisgarh India
96 F6 Maha Sarakham Thai.
213 □J5 Mahatalaky Madag.
128 E7 Maḥaṭṭat Ḍab'ah Jordan
247 □2 Mahaut Dominica
213 □J2 Mahavavy r. Madag.
213 □K3 Mahavelona Madag.
114 G8 Mahaweli Ganga r. Sri Lanka
213 □J3 Mahazoma Madag.
203 F6 Mahbub Sudan
114 G4 Mahbubabad Andhra Prad. India
114 E4 Mahbubnagar Andhra Prad. India
124 E4 Mahd adh Dhahab Saudi Arabia
125 L3 Maḥḍah Oman
137 N5 Mahdalynivka Dnipropetrovs'ka Oblast' Ukr.
137 M7 Mahdalynivka Khersons'ka Oblast' Ukr.
205 F2 Mahdia Alg.
251 G3 Mahdia Guyana
205 H2 Mahdia Tunisia
106 I9 Mahe Gansu China
114 D7 Mahe Pondicherry India
217 □2b Mahé i. Inner Islands Seychelles
217 □1b Mahébourg Mauritius
148 F5 Mahee Island Northern Ireland U.K.
117 L7 Mahendraganj Meghalaya India
116 F5 Mahendragarh Haryana India
115 I3 Mahendragiri mt. Orissa India
211 C7 Mahenge Tanz.
81 E12 Maheno South I. N.Z.
175 L5 Maheriv Ukr.
116 D8 Mahesana Gujarat India
116 E8 Maheshwar Madh. Prad. India
125 L9 Maḥfirhīn Suquṭrā Yemen
116 G6 Mahgawan Madh. Prad. India
116 D8 Mahi r. Rajasthan India
122 H7 Māhī watercourse Iran
80 L6 Mahia North I. N.Z.
80 L6 Mahia Peninsula North I. N.Z.
182 H5 Mahíde Spain
78 □6 Mahige Island Solomon Is
139 N8 Mahilyow Belarus
Mahilyow Oblast admin. div. Belarus see Mahilyowskaya Voblasts'
139 N8 Mahilyowskaya Voblasts' admin. div. Belarus
114 C3 Mahim Mahar. India
207 G5 Mahin Nigeria
79 □9a Mahina Tahiti Fr. Polynesia
206 C3 Mahina Mali
81 E9 Mahinapua, Lake South I. N.Z.
81 D12 Mahinerangi, Lake South I. N.Z.
116 G3 Mahiya Jammu and Kashmir
114 G9 Mahiyangana Sri Lanka
122 E6 Mah Jān Iran
140 L4 Mahkene mt. Sweden
215 P4 Mahlabatini S. Africa
96 B4 Mahlaing Myanmar
215 P3 Mahlangasi S. Africa
215 L4 Mahlatswetsa S. Africa
172 D5 Mahlberg Ger.
171 H6 Mahlow Ger.
170 D5 Mahlsdorf Ger.
171 E6 Mahlwinkel Ger.
116 H6 Mahmudabad Uttar Prad. India
122 E3 Mahmudabad Iran
123 M4 Maḥmūd-e Rāqī Afgh.
197 R5 Mahmudia Romania
199 H3 Mahmudiye Çanakkale Turkey
199 L3 Mahmudiye Eskişehir Turkey
128 A2 Mahmutlar Turkey
199 K1 Mahmutşevketpaşa Turkey
122 C4 Mahniān Iran
236 G2 Mahnomen MN U.S.A.
114 G9 Maho Sri Lanka
116 G7 Mahoba Uttar Prad. India
80 I5 Mahoenui North I. N.Z.
116 H6 Maholi Uttar Prad. India
186 □ Mahón Spain
225 H4 Mahone Bay N.S. Can.
212 D3 Mahongo Game Park nature res. Namibia
222 E1 Mahony Lake N.W.T. Can.
235 H2 Mahopac NY U.S.A.
235 H2 Mahopac Lake NY U.S.A.
185 P2 Mahora Spain
206 D3 Mahou Mali
208 C2 Mahoua Chad
125 J7 Mahrāt, Jabal mt. Yemen
125 J7 Mahrāt, Wādī r. Yemen
116 G7 Mahrauni Uttar Prad. India
Mähren reg. Czech Rep. see Morava
205 H2 Mahrès Tunisia
173 N2 Mähring Ger.
122 I5 Māhrūd Iran
Mahsana Gujarat India see Mahesana
111 L8 Mahuanggou Qinghai China
117 O8 Mahudaung mts Myanmar
240 □F13 Māhukona HI U.S.A.
117 N7 Mahur Assam India
114 E3 Mahur Mahar. India
207 G4 Mahuta Nigeria
211 C7 Mahuta Tanz.
116 C9 Mahuva Gujarat India
116 F6 Mahwa Rajasthan India
197 P9 Mahya Dağı mt. Turkey
122 D5 Mahyār Iran
93 E6 Mai i. Maluku Indon.
Mai i. Vanuatu see Émaé
78 □2 Maia American Samoa
216 □1b Maia São Miguel Azores
182 C6 Maia Port.
Maiaia Moz. see Nacala
186 G5 Maials Spain
77 H1 Maiana atoll Gilbert Is Kiribati
117 N7 Maibang Assam India
250 C2 Maicao Col.
224 E3 Maicasagi r. Que. Can.
224 E3 Maicasagi, Lac l. Que. C
160 J2 Maîche France
108 G8 Maichen Guangdong Ch
251 F6 Maici r. Brazil
251 H5 Maicuru r. Brazil
195 K6 Maida Italy
150 H5 Maiden Bradley Wiltshi England U.K.
234 D4 Maiden Creek r. PA U.S
151 K4 Maidenhead Windsor a Maidenhead, England U.
150 G6 Maiden Newton Dorset, England U.K.
226 B5 Maiden Rock WI U.S.A.
146 G12 Maidens South Ayrshire Scotland U.K.
93 E3 Maidi Halmahera Indon.
223 I4 Maidstone Sask. Can.
151 N5 Maidstone Kent, Englan
207 I4 Maiduguri Nigeria
193 M3 Maiella, Parco Naziona della nat. park Italy
190 H1 Maienfeld Switz.
195 K6 Maierato Italy
173 I6 Maierhöfen Ger.
197 M3 Maieru Romania
187 D10 Maigmó mt. Spain
156 E4 Maignelay-Montigny F
210 C3 Mai Gudo mt. Eth.
147 E7 Maigue r. Ireland
116 H7 Maihar Madh. Prad. Ind
104 D5 Maihara Japan
80 J5 Maihiihi North I. N.Z.
117 M8 Maijdi Bangl.
108 E1 Maiji Gansu China
108 F2 Maiji Shan mt. Gansu C
116 H8 Maikala Range hills Ma Prad. India
172 E3 Maikammer Ger.
208 E4 Maiko r. Dem. Rep. Cor
208 E5 Maiko, Parc National e nat. park Dem. Rep. Co
117 I8 Mailan Hill mt. Chhattis India
116 H5 Mailani Uttar Prad. India
208 B2 Maïlao Chad
94 C6 Maileppe Indon.
240 □C12 Mā'ili HI U.S.A.
163 D7 Maillas France
156 B6 Maillebois France
162 C3 Maillezais France
156 H6 Mailly-le-Camp France
160 D1 Mailly-le-Château Fra
156 E3 Mailly-Maillet France
123 O7 Mailsi Pak.
108 D2 Maima Gansu China
169 F10 Main r. Ger.
124 G7 Ma'īn tourist site Yeme
117 L6 Mainaguri W. Bengal In
198 D5 Mainalo mts Greece
172 G2 Mainaschaff Ger.
173 I2 Mainbernheim Ger.
225 K3 Main Brook Nfld and La
173 L4 Mainburg Ger.
224 D4 Main Channel lake cha Ont. Can.
114 E4 Maindargi Mahar. India
208 C5 Mai-Ndombe, Lac l. Dem. Rep. Congo
173 J2 Main-Donau-Kanal ca
227 R6 Main Duck Island Ont.
159 J7 Maine r. France
159 K5 Maine reg. France
233 □P3 Maine state U.S.A.
233 □P5 Maine, Gulf of U.S.A.
159 K7 Maine-et-Loire dept F
250 C5 Mainé Hanari, Cerro h
207 I3 Maïné-Soroa Niger
96 C1 Maingkwan Myanmar
97 D8 Maingy Island Myanma
147 I6 Mainham Ireland
172 H3 Mainhardt Ger.
92 E7 Mainit Mindanao Phil.
92 E7 Mainit, Lake Mindanao
108 B4 Mainkung Xizang China
146 J4 Mainland i. Orkney, Scotland U.K.
146 □N2 Mainland i. Shetland, Scotland U.K.
171 D10 Mainleus Ger.
111 L12 Mainling Xizang China
84 E3 Mainoru N.T. Austr.
84 E3 Mainoru r. N.T. Austr.
117 I8 Mainpat reg. Chhattisg India
116 G6 Mainpuri Uttar Prad. In
83 N3 Main Range National Qld Austr.
162 I3 Mainsat France
156 C6 Maintenon France
213 □J3 Maintirano Madag.
140 S4 Mainua Fin.
156 B7 Mainvilliers France
96 B3 Mainyaung Myanmar
169 F10 Mainz Ger.
206 □ Maio i. Cape Verde
191 O9 Maiolati Spontini Italy
184 B2 Maior r. Port.
182 C8 Maiorca Port.
182 C9 Maiorga Port.
194 H2 Maiori Italy
260 B3 Maipó r. Chile
260 C4 Maipó, Volcán vol. Ch
261 I5 Maipú Buenos Aires Ar
260 C3 Maipú Mendoza Arg.
260 B3 Maipú Chile
250 E3 Maipures Col.
251 G3 Maipuri Landing Guya
250 E2 Maiquetía Venez.
111 H12 Maiqu Zangbo r. Xizan
190 D6 Maira r. Italy
184 H6 Mairena del Alcor Spa
254 E4 Mairi Brazil
256 D5 Mairiporã Brazil
256 C2 Mairipotaba Brazil
182 F5 Mairos mt. Spain
173 K5 Maisach Ger.
173 K5 Maisach r. Ger.
104 G6 Maisaka Japan
178 G5 Maishofen Austria
246 F3 Maisí Cuba
138 I7 Maišiagala Lith.
117 M9 Maiskhal Channel inle
117 M9 Maiskhal Island Bangl
156 D6 Maisons-Laffitte Fran
179 M2 Maissau Austria
156 D7 Maisse France
165 H9 Maissin Belgium
Maitea i. Arch. de la So Fr. Polynesia see Mehe
173 M5 Maitenbeth Ger.
258 C3 Maitencillo Chile
213 E4 Maitengwe Botswana
117 K8 Maithon W. Bengal Ind
83 M5 Maitland N.S.W. Austr.
82 F6 Maitland S.A. Austr.
86 D6 Maitland r. W.A. Austr.
95 L2 Maitland, Banjaran m Malaysia
87 F9 Maitland, Lake salt fla W.A. Austr.
263 A2 Maitri research stn An
Maiwo i. Vanuatu see M
84 E3 Maiwok r. N.T. Austr.
84 B4 Maiyu, Mount hill N.T.
242 □R11 Maíz, Islas del is Nic.
111 J12 Maizhokunggar Xizang
156 G6 Maizières-la-Grande-Paroisse France
157 L5 Maizières-lès-Metz F
104 B5 Maizuru Japan
184 H7 Majaceite r. Spain
183 M8 Majadahonda Spain
182 I9 Majadas de Tiétar Sp
196 H8 Maja Jezercë mt. Alba
114 E3 Majalgaon Mahar. Indi
251 F4 Majari r. Brazil
125 I8 Majḍahah Yemen
175 J5 Majdan Królewski Po
175 L5 Majdan Niepryski Pol
197 J6 Majdanpek Serbia
128 D5 Majdel Aanjar tourist Lebanon
257 F5 Majé Brazil
93 A5 Majene Sulawesi Barat
188 G3 Majevica mts Bos.-He
116 H7 Majhgawan Madh. Pra
116 G8 Majholi Madh. Prad. In

198 D6 Mani pen. Greece
207 G3 Mani Nigeria
116 F6 Mania Rajasthan India
213 □J3 Mania r. Madag.
194 H8 Maniace Sicilia Italy
191 N3 Maniago Italy
198 C2 Maniakoi Greece
209 D7 Mania-Muna Dem. Rep. Congo
116 H8 Maniari Tank resr Chhattisgarh India
213 G3 Manica Moz.
213 G3 Manica prov. Moz.
213 G3 Manicaland prov. Zimbabwe
251 F6 Manicoré Brazil
251 F6 Manicoré r. Brazil
225 G3 Manicouagan Que. Can.
225 G3 Manicouagan r. Que. Can.
225 H2 Manicouagan, Petit Lac l. Que. Can.
225 G3 Manicouagan, Réservoir resr Que. Can.
225 G3 Manic Trois, Réservoir resr Que. Can.
208 E5 Maniema prov. Dem. Rep. Congo
125 I2 Manīfah Saudi Arabia
85 M7 Manifold, Cape Qld Austr.
108 B3 Maniganggo Sichuan China
223 L5 Manigotagan Man. Can.
117 K7 Manihari Bihar India
79 □9 Manihi atoll Arch. des Tuamotu Fr. Polynesia
81 □2 Manihiki atoll Cook Is
221 M3 Maniitsoq Greenland
123 K9 Maniji r. Pak.
209 E7 Manika Dem. Rep. Congo
209 E7 Manika, Plateau de la Dem. Rep. Congo
117 N8 Manikchhari Bangl.
117 M8 Manikganj Bangl.
Manikgarh Mahar. India see Rajura
116 H7 Manikpur Uttar Prad. India
92 C4 Manila Luzon Phil.
238 J6 Manila UT U.S.A.
92 C4 Manila Bay Luzon Phil.
138 H3 Manilaid i. Estonia
83 L5 Manildra N.S.W. Austr.
83 M4 Manilla N.S.W. Austr.
185 I8 Manilva Spain
131 R3 Manily Rus. Fed.
93 A4 Manimbaya, Tanjung pt Indon.
84 E2 Maningrida N.T. Austr.
94 D5 Maninjau, Danau l. Indon.
93 E5 Manipa i. Maluku Indon.
93 E5 Manipa, Selat sea chan. Maluku Indon.
Manipur Manipur India see Imphal
117 N7 Manipur state India
96 B3 Manipur r. India/Myanmar
199 I4 Manisa Turkey
199 J4 Manisa prov. Turkey
187 E8 Manises Spain
95 I6 Manismata Kalimantan Indon.
254 B4 Manissauá Missu r. Brazil
226 H5 Manistee MI U.S.A.
226 H5 Manistee r. MI U.S.A.
226 H4 Manistique MI U.S.A.
226 I3 Manistique Lake MI U.S.A.
223 L4 Manitoba prov. Can.
223 L5 Manitoba, Lake Man. Can.
223 I4 Manito Lake Sask. Can.
223 L5 Manitou Man. Can.
225 H3 Manitou r. Que. Can.
224 D4 Manitou, Lake Ont. Can.
232 H5 Manitou Beach NY U.S.A.
223 M5 Manitou Falls Ont. Can.
226 G2 Manitou Island MI U.S.A.
226 H4 Manitou Islands MI U.S.A.
224 D4 Manitoulin Island Ont. Can.
224 C3 Manitouwadge Ont. Can.
227 M4 Manitowaning Ont. Can.
226 J1 Manitowik Lake Ont. Can.
226 E3 Manitowish Waters WI U.S.A.
226 G5 Manitowoc WI U.S.A.
224 F4 Maniwaki Que. Can.
113 □1 Maniyafushi i. S. Male Maldives
250 C3 Manizales Col.
213 □J4 Manja Madag.
213 G5 Manjacaze Moz.
213 □J3 Manjak Madag.
124 A4 Manjam Umm Qurayyāt waterhole Egypt
114 D6 Manjarabad Karnataka India
114 E7 Manjeri Kerala India
123 M9 Manjhand Pak.
101 E7 Man Jiang r. China
122 C3 Manjil Iran
87 D13 Manjimup W.A. Austr.
207 H5 Manjo Cameroon
114 E3 Manjra r. India
179 L3 Mank Austria
96 C1 Man Kabat Myanmar
117 L7 Mankachar Assam India
Mankanza Dem. Rep. Congo see Makanza
236 F6 Mankato KS U.S.A.
236 H3 Mankato MN U.S.A.
123 N6 Mankera Pak.
207 I5 Mankim Cameroon
136 J5 Man'kivka Cherkas'ka Oblast' Ukr.
137 R4 Man'kivka Luhans'ka Oblast' Ukr.
136 I5 Man'kivka Vinnyts'ka Oblast' Ukr.
206 D4 Mankono Côte d'Ivoire
223 J5 Mankota Sask. Can.
114 G8 Mankulam Sri Lanka
160 E2 Manlay France
186 J4 Manlleu Spain
236 I4 Manly IA U.S.A.
116 E9 Manmad Mahar. India
84 E2 Mann r. N.T. Austr.
78 □3a Mann i. Kwajalein Marshall Is
84 B8 Mann, Mount N.T. Austr.
94 E7 Manna Sumatera Indon.
96 C3 Man Na Myanmar
82 G5 Mannahill S.A. Austr.
114 F8 Mannar Sri Lanka
114 F8 Mannar, Gulf of India/Sri Lanka
114 F7 Mannargudi Tamil Nadu India
172 F7 Männedorf Switz.
84 F7 Manners watercourse N.T. Austr.
179 O4 Mannersdorf am Leithagebirge Austria
179 O5 Mannersdorf an der Rabnitz Austria
114 G5 Manneru r. India
225 G2 Mannessier, Lac l. Que. Can.
172 E3 Mannheim Ger.
Mannicolo Islands Santa Cruz Is Solomon Is see Vanikoro Islands
138 H3 Männikuste Estonia
222 G3 Manning Alta Can.
236 D2 Manning ND U.S.A.
231 G9 Manning SC U.S.A.
222 F5 Manning Provincial Park B.C. Can.
78 □6 Manning Strait Solomon Is
232 E9 Mannington WV U.S.A.
151 O4 Manningtree Essex, England U.K.
147 E5 Mannin Lake Ireland
190 D2 Männlifluh mt. Switz.
84 B8 Mann Ranges mts S.A. Austr.
233 I5 Mannsville NY U.S.A.
192 A6 Mannu r. Sardegna Italy
192 B8 Mannu r. Sardegna Italy
192 C9 Mannu r. Sardegna Italy
192 D6 Mannu r. Sardegna Italy
192 A6 Mannu, Capo c. Sardegna Italy
192 A7 Mannu, Capo c. Sardegna Italy
192 A7 Mannu, Monte hill Italy
223 I4 Mannville Alta Can.
206 C5 Mano r. Liberia/Sierra Leone
206 B5 Mano Sierra Leone
252 D2 Manoa Bol.
247 □5 Man of War Bay Trin. and Tob.
Man-of-War Rocks is HI U.S.A. see Gardner Pinnacles
111 C13 Manoharpur Rajasthan India
116 F7 Manohar Thana Rajasthan India
220 C4 Manokotak AK U.S.A.
91 H7 Manokwari Papua Indon.
186 L3 Manol r. Spain
197 P3 Manoleasa Romania
213 □I4 Manombo Atsimo Madag.
213 □K3 Manompana Madag.
209 E6 Manono Dem. Rep. Congo
123 L9 Manora Head Pak.
150 C4 Manorbier Pembrokeshire, Wales U.K.
235 H3 Manorhaven NY U.S.A.
206 C5 Mano River Liberia
97 D9 Manoron Myanmar
235 J3 Manorville NY U.S.A.
259 C7 Manos, Cueva de las cave Arg.
161 H9 Manosque France
225 G3 Manouane, Lac l. Que. Can.
103 P9 Mano-wan b. Japan
174 E1 Manowo Pol.
96 C3 Man Pan Myanmar
101 E8 Manp'o N. Korea
116 E8 Manpur Madh. Prad. India
77 I2 Manra i. Phoenix Is Kiribati
186 I4 Manresa Spain
116 D8 Mansa Gujarat India
116 E5 Mansa Punjab India
209 F7 Mansa Zambia
206 B3 Mansabá Guinea-Bissau
206 B3 Mansa Konko Gambia
92 C5 Mansalay Bay Mindoro Phil.
93 C4 Mansalean Sulawesi Indon.
96 C3 Man Sam Myanmar
170 K5 Manschnow Ger.
123 O4 Mansehra Pak.
221 K3 Mansel Island Nunavut Can.
140 T3 Mansel'kya ridge Fin./Rus. Fed.
171 D7 Mansfeld Ger.
83 K7 Mansfield Vic. Austr.
149 O7 Mansfield Nottinghamshire, England U.K.
237 H8 Mansfield AR U.S.A.
237 I9 Mansfield LA U.S.A.
233 N6 Mansfield MA U.S.A.
232 C8 Mansfield OH U.S.A.
232 H7 Mansfield PA U.S.A.
233 M4 Mansfield, Mount VT U.S.A.
235 K1 Mansfield Center CT U.S.A.
149 O7 Mansfield Woodhouse Nottinghamshire, England U.K.
96 C2 Man Si Myanmar
96 B2 Mansi Myanmar
254 E4 Mansidão Brazil
183 O4 Mansilla Spain
183 O4 Mansilla, Embalse de resr Spain
183 J4 Mansilla de las Mulas Spain
162 E4 Mansle France
Manso r. Brazil see Mortes, Rio das
192 B3 Manso Corse France
206 E5 Manso-Nkwanta Ghana
163 F7 Mansonville France
182 D7 Mansores Port.
150 H6 Manston Dorset, England U.K.
93 F5 Mansuela Seram Indon.
127 N8 Manşūrī Iran
126 G5 Mansurlu Turkey
250 A5 Manta Ecuador
92 A7 Mantalingajan, Mount Palawan Phil.
208 D5 Mantantale Dem. Rep. Congo
93 D4 Mantarara Maluku Indon.
252 B3 Mantaro r. Peru
240 K4 Manteca CA U.S.A.
250 D3 Mantecal Venez.
93 D3 Mantehage i. Indon.
182 E8 Manteigas Port.
173 M2 Mantel Ger.
257 G3 Mantena Brazil
226 G8 Manteno IL U.S.A.
231 J8 Manteo NC U.S.A.
165 J9 Manternach Lux.
156 C6 Mantes-la-Jolie France
156 C6 Mantes-la-Ville France
163 I11 Mantet, Réserve Naturelle de nature res. France
114 F3 Manthani Andhra Prad. India
159 M7 Manthelan France
241 U2 Manti UT U.S.A.
257 D5 Mantiqueira, Serra da mts Brazil
242 □P10 Manto Hond.
160 H2 Mantoche France
235 G4 Mantoloking NJ U.S.A.
226 I5 Manton MI U.S.A.
252 C5 Mantos Blancos Chile
198 E4 Mantoudi Greece
191 J5 Mantova Italy
191 J5 Mantova prov. Italy
141 R6 Mäntsälä Fin.
215 M5 Mantsonyane Lesotho
141 R5 Mänttä Fin.
246 A2 Mantua Cuba
Mantua Italy see Mantova
234 E5 Mantua NJ U.S.A.
232 D7 Mantua OH U.S.A.
85 K8 Mantuan Downs Qld Austr.
134 I4 Manturovo Kostromskaya Oblast' Rus. Fed.
137 Q2 Manturovo Kurskaya Oblast' Rus. Fed.
141 S6 Mäntyharju Fin.
140 S3 Mäntyjärvi Fin.
Manu r. Bol. see Mapiri
252 C3 Manú r. Peru
252 B3 Manu, Parque Nacional nat. park Peru
81 □2 Manuae atoll Cook Is
79 □9 Manuae atoll Arch. de la Société Fr. Polynesia
78 □2 Manu'a Islands American Samoa
215 M8 Manubi S. Africa
245 I3 Manuel Mex.
187 E9 Manuel Spain
254 C4 Manuel Alves r. Brazil
245 I7 Manuel Ávila Camacho, Presa resr Mex.
261 I4 Manuel J. Cobo Arg.
244 E6 Manuel M. Diéguez Mex.
261 G3 Manuel Ocampo Arg.
256 B6 Manuel Ribas Brazil
259 B9 Manuel Rodriguez, Isla i. Chile
252 C2 Manuel Urbano Brazil
254 E5 Manuel Vitorino Brazil
254 B3 Manuelzinho Brazil
93 C5 Manui i. Indon.
122 G8 Manūjān Iran
93 G6 Manuk i. Maluku Indon.
92 D7 Manukan Mindanao Phil.
80 I3 Manukau North I. N.Z.
80 I4 Manukau Harbour North I. N.Z.
80 □ Manukau Point Chatham Is S. Pacific Ocean
92 B9 Manuk Manka i. Phil.
147 D5 Manulla Ireland
82 G5 Manunda watercourse S.A. Austr.
252 D2 Manupari r. Bol.
252 D2 Manurimi r. Bol.
252 D2 Manuripi r. Bol.
93 F5 Manusela, Taman Nasional nat. park Seram Indon.
91 K7 Manus Island Admiralty Is P.N.G.
80 L5 Manutuke North I. N.Z.
114 E5 Manvi Karnataka India
234 F3 Manville NJ U.S.A.
114 E3 Manwat Mahar. India
237 I10 Many LA U.S.A.
84 D3 Manyallaluk Aboriginal Reserve N.T. Austr.
213 F2 Manyame r. Moz./Zimbabwe
211 B5 Manyara, Lake salt l. Tanz.
199 I2 Manyas Turkey
Manyas Gölü l. Turkey see Kuş Gölü
197 L7 Manyashki Vrŭkh hill Bulg.
215 L5 Manyatseng S. Africa
223 I5 Manyberries Alta Can.
135 H7 Manych-Gudilo, Ozero l. Rus. Fed.
137 T6 Manychskaya Rus. Fed.
241 W5 Many Farms AZ U.S.A.
209 E8 Manyinga Zambia
223 I5 Many Island Lake Alta/Sask. Can.
136 G4 Manykivtsi Ukr.
211 B6 Manyoni Tanz.
85 M8 Many Peaks Qld Austr.
87 E13 Many Peaks, Mount hill W.A. Austr.
162 F5 Manzac-sur-Vern France
123 N5 Manzai Pak.
Manzala, Lake lag. Egypt see Manzilah, Buḩayrat al
182 H3 Manzanal, Puerto del pass Spain
182 H5 Manzanal de Arriba Spain
182 H3 Manzanal del Puerto Spain
185 M2 Manzanares Spain
183 M8 Manzanares r. Spain
183 M7 Manzanares el Real Spain
182 F4 Manzaneda Spain
182 F4 Manzaneda, Cabeza de mt. Spain
183 M3 Manzanedo Spain
183 M9 Manzaneque Spain
187 D7 Manzanera Spain
247 □7 Manzanilla Bay Trin. and Tob.
247 □7 Manzanilla Point Trin. and Tob.
246 E3 Manzanillo Cuba
244 C6 Manzanillo Mex.
242 □T13 Manzanillo, Punta pt Panama
191 O4 Manzano Italy
244 F4 Manzano Mex.
209 F6 Manzanza Dem. Rep. Congo
122 D4 Manzariyeh Iran
160 B5 Manzat France
209 C6 Manzengele Dem. Rep. Congo
137 M4 Manzheliya Ukr.
107 O2 Manzhouli Nei Mongol China
192 I3 Manziana Italy
160 F4 Manziat France
128 A7 Manzilah, Buḩayrat al lag. Egypt
215 P2 Manzini Swaziland
215 P2 Manzini admin. dist. Swaziland
Manzovka Rus. Fed. see Sibirtsevo
202 B6 Mao Chad
246 H4 Mao Dom. Rep.
Maó Spain see Mahón
Mao, Nam r. Myanmar see Shweli
108 F5 Maoba Guizhou China
108 G3 Maoba Hubei China
109 I3 Maocifan Hubei China
108 D2 Mao'ergai Sichuan China
106 J8 Maojiachuan Gansu China
106 J8 Maojing Gansu China
91 I7 Maoke, Pegunungan mts Papua Indon.
215 L3 Maokeng S. Africa
101 C8 Maokui Shan mt. Liaoning China
107 R5 Maolin Jilin China
106 H8 Maomao Shan mt. Gansu China
108 H8 Maoming Guangdong China
111 H9 Maoniupo Xizang China
106 E8 Maoniushan Qinghai China
109 □J7 Ma On Shan hill H.K. China
Maoping Hubei China see Zigui
109 M8 Maopi T'ou c. Taiwan
93 E7 Maopora i. Maluku Indon.
108 C6 Maotou Shan mt. Yunnan China
Maowen Sichuan China see Maoxian
108 D3 Maoxian Sichuan China
213 F4 Mapai Moz.
111 E11 Mapam Yumco l. China
93 B4 Mapane Sulawesi Indon.
209 E9 Mapanza Zambia
250 D2 Maparari Venez.
243 M10 Mapastepec Mex.
215 Q4 Mapelane Nature Reserve S. Africa
215 J6 Maphodi S. Africa
91 I8 Mapi r. Papua Indon.
250 E3 Mapiche, Serranía mts Venez.
242 H5 Mapimí Mex.
213 G4 Mapinhane Moz.
251 E3 Mapire Venez.
251 H4 Mapireme Brazil
252 C3 Mapiri Bol.
252 D2 Mapiri r. Bol.
250 C4 Mapirpán Col.
80 J5 Mapiu North I. N.Z.
236 H5 Maple r. IA U.S.A.
226 J7 Maple r. MI U.S.A.
236 F3 Maple r. ND U.S.A.
236 G2 Maple r. ND U.S.A.
223 I5 Maple Creek Sask. Can.
241 W8 Maple Peak AZ U.S.A.
236 H4 Mapleton IA U.S.A.
241 U1 Mapleton UT U.S.A.
226 G5 Maplewood WI U.S.A.
266 G4 Mapmakers Seamounts sea feature N. Pacific Ocean
85 H1 Mapoon Qld Austr.
85 I2 Mapoon Aboriginal Reserve Qld Austr.
94 F4 Mapor i. Indon.
215 L5 Mapoteng Lesotho
81 E10 Mapourika, Lake South I. N.Z.
91 J7 Maprik P.N.G.
114 C5 Mapuca Goa India
251 G5 Mapuera r. Brazil
213 G5 Mapulanguene Moz.
215 P5 Mapumulo S. Africa
209 E7 Mapunda Dem. Rep. Congo
213 G5 Maputo Moz.
213 G5 Maputo prov. Moz.
213 G5 Maputo r. Moz./S. Africa
215 Q2 Maputo, Baía de b. Moz.
215 Q2 Maputo, Reserva de Elefantes de nature res. Moz.
215 L4 Maputsoe Lesotho
Maqanshy Kazakh. see Makanchi
127 J8 Maqar an Na'am well Iraq
Maqat Kazakh. see Makat
106 G9 Maqên Qinghai China
111 J11 Maqên Xizang China
106 F9 Maqên Kangri mt. Qinghai China
110 H4 Maqiao Xinjiang China
128 D10 Maqla, Jabal al mt. Saudi Arabia
124 B1 Maqnā Saudi Arabia
125 J8 Maqrat Yemen
129 I6 Maqşūdlū Iran
204 C5 Maqţeïr reg. Maur.
108 D2 Maqu Gansu China
Ma Qu r. China see Huang He
111 G12 Maquan He r. Xizang China
183 L8 Maqueda Spain
92 D5 Maqueda Channel Phil.
209 B6 Maquela do Zombo Angola
259 C6 Maquinchao Arg.
260 D3 Maquinista Levet Arg.
236 J4 Maquoketa IA U.S.A.
236 J4 Maquoketa r. IA U.S.A.
142 E1 Mår l. Norway
142 E2 Mår r. Norway
123 K9 Mar r. Pak.
182 C5 Mar Port.
256 C6 Mar, Serra do mts Brazil
257 E5 Mar, Serra do mts Brazil
257 F5 Mar, Serra do mts Brazil
255 C9 Mar, Serra do mts Brazil
251 G3 Mara Guyana
117 O5 Mara Arun. Prad. India
117 I8 Mara Madh. Prad. India
192 B7 Mara Sardegna Italy
211 B5 Mara admin. reg. Tanz.
251 E5 Maraã Brazil
79 □9a Maraa Tahiti Fr. Polynesia
254 C3 Marabá Brazil
95 K6 Marabahan Kalimantan Indon.
256 B5 Marabá Paulista Brazil
95 K7 Marabatua i. Indon.
250 E4 Marabitanas Brazil
85 L7 Maraboon, Lake resr Qld Austr.
157 J8 Marac France
251 I5 Maracá r. Brazil
251 F4 Maracá, Ilha reg. Brazil
251 I4 Maracá, Ilha de i. Brazil
256 B5 Maracaí Brazil
250 D2 Maracaibo Venez.
250 D2 Maracaibo, Lago de l. Venez.
Maracaibo, Lake Venez. see Maracaibo, Lago de
253 G5 Maracaju Brazil
253 G5 Maracaju, Serra de hills Brazil
192 C9 Maracalagonis Sardegna Italy
254 D2 Maracanã Brazil
251 H5 Maracanaquará, Planalto plat. Brazil
Maracanda Uzbek. see Samarqand
254 E5 Maracás Brazil
254 E5 Maracás, Chapada de hills Brazil
247 □7 Maracas Bay Trin. and Tob.
250 E2 Maracay Venez.
202 C2 Marādah Libya
Maradhoo i. Addu Atoll Maldives see Maradu
207 G3 Maradi Niger
207 G3 Maradi dept Niger
123 M5 Maradin Pak.
113 □2 Maradu i. Addu Atoll Maldives
79 □9a Maraetiria, Pointe pt Tahiti Fr. Polynesia
129 J4 Maraga Rus. Fed.
182 H4 Maragatería reg. Spain
122 F8 Marāgh Iran
122 B3 Marāgheh Iran
254 G4 Maragogi Brazil
92 C4 Maragondon Luzon Phil.
124 G3 Marah Saudi Arabia
206 D5 Marahoué r. Côte d'Ivoire
251 E4 Marahuaca, Cerro mt. Venez.
158 G8 Marais breton marsh France
236 H6 Marais des Cygnes r. KS U.S.A.
158 I3 Marais du Cotentin et du Bessin, Parc Naturel Régional des nature res. France
162 C3 Marais Poitevin, Val de Sèvre et Vendée, Parc Naturel Régional nature res. France
254 C2 Marajó, Baía de est. Brazil
251 I5 Marajó, Ilha de i. Brazil
215 M5 Marakabeis Lesotho
77 H1 Marakei atoll Gilbert Is Kiribati
122 H8 Marākī Iran
Maraki atoll Gilbert Is Kiribati see Marakei
114 F6 Marakkanam Tamil Nadu India
Maralaba i. Vanuatu see Mere Lava
210 C4 Maralal Kenya
Maralbashi Xinjiang China see Bachu
121 Q1 Maraldy Kazakh.
121 Q1 Maraldy, Ozero salt l. Kazakh.
208 C3 Marali C.A.R.
129 E5 Maralik Armenia
82 C4 Maralinga S.A. Austr.
82 C3 Maralinga-Tjarutja Aboriginal Lands res. S.A. Austr.
Maralwexi Xinjiang China see Bachu
78 □6 Maramasike i. Solomon Is
Maramba Zambia see Livingstone
262 U2 Marambio research stn Antarctica
93 E1 Marampit i. Indon.
197 M3 Maramureşului, Munţii mts Romania
94 E3 Maran Malaysia
123 K7 Maran mt. Pak.
122 A4 Marāna Iraq
241 U9 Marana AZ U.S.A.
183 P6 Maranchón Spain
183 P6 Maranchóon, Puerto de pass Spain
122 A2 Marand Iran
Marandellas Zimbabwe see Marondera
191 J6 Maranello Italy
94 E2 Marang Malaysia
97 D9 Marang Myanmar
157 L5 Marange-Silvange France
254 F2 Maranguape Brazil
254 C5 Maranhão r. Brazil
254 D3 Maranhão state Brazil
184 D2 Maranhão Port.
184 D2 Maranhão, Barragem do resr Port.
191 K7 Marano Italy
191 O4 Marano, Laguna di lag. Italy
85 L9 Maranoa r. Qld Austr.
194 G2 Marano di Napoli Italy
250 C6 Marañón r. Peru
191 J7 Marano sul Panaro Italy
162 C3 Marans France
157 I7 Maranville France
213 G5 Marão Moz.
182 E6 Marão mt. Port.
182 D6 Marão, Serra do mts Port.
206 D5 Maraoué, Parc National de la nat. park Côte d'Ivoire
78 □6 Marapa i. Solomon Is
254 D2 Marapanim Brazil
253 F3 Marape Brazil
94 D5 Marapi, Gunung vol. Sumatera Indon.
192 A7 Marargiu, Capo c. Sardegna Italy
250 E6 Marari Brazil
81 B12 Mararoa r. South I. N.Z.
254 C5 Mara Rosa Brazil
Maraş Cyprus see Varosia
Maraş Turkey see Kahramanmaraş
95 M7 Marasende i. Indon.
197 P5 Mărăşeşti Romania
197 P6 Mărașu Romania
193 P8 Maratea Italy
184 B3 Marateca Port.
198 B5 Marathia, Akrotirio pt Zakynthos Greece
198 D4 Marathias Greece
199 H5 Marathokampos Samos Greece
224 C3 Marathon Ont. Can.
Marathón Greece see Marathonas
231 G13 Marathon FL U.S.A.
233 I6 Marathon NY U.S.A.
237 D10 Marathon TX U.S.A.
226 E5 Marathon WI U.S.A.
198 E4 Marathonas Greece
95 M3 Maratua i. Indon.
95 I6 Marau Kalimantan Indon.
250 E5 Marauá Brazil
251 E5 Marauiá r. Brazil
161 C10 Maraussan France
247 □7 Maraval Trin. and Tob.
244 G6 Maravatío Mex.
237 D11 Maravillas Creek watercourse TX U.S.A.
78 □6 Maravovo Guadalcanal Solomon Is
202 D1 Marāwah Libya
92 E7 Marawi Mindanao Phil.
125 K3 Marawwaḩ, Jazīrat i. U.A.E.
156 G7 Maraye-en-Othe France
260 D2 Marayes Arg.
123 M7 Maray Lake Pak.
125 J7 Mar'ayt Yemen
129 J5 Märäzä Azer.
150 B7 Marazion Cornwall, England U.K.
171 H8 Marbach Ger.
190 D2 Marbach Switz.
172 G4 Marbach am Neckar Ger.
185 J7 Marbella Spain
185 J8 Marbella, Ensenada de b. Spain
86 E6 Marble Bar W.A. Austr.
241 U5 Marble Canyon AZ U.S.A.
241 U5 Marble Canyon gorge AZ U.S.A.
213 F5 Marble Hall S. Africa
237 K7 Marble Hill MO U.S.A.
223 N2 Marble Island Nunavut Can.
160 G4 Marboz France
116 E3 Marbul Pass Jammu and Kashmir
215 O6 Marburg S. Africa
Marburg Slovenia see Maribor
234 B5 Marburg, Lake PA U.S.A.
169 G9 Marburg an der Lahn Ger.
252 A2 Marca Peru
177 L4 Marca Romania
209 A9 Marca, Ponta do pt Angola
176 G4 Marcal r. Hungary
242 □O10 Marcala Hond.
176 G5 Marcali Hungary
176 G4 Marcaltő Hungary
191 P6 Marčana Croatia
194 C8 Marcanzotta r. Sicilia Italy
252 C3 Marcapata Peru
191 J5 Marcaria Italy
250 E5 Marcelino Brazil
261 G2 Marcelino Escalada Arg.
193 J3 Marcellina Italy
226 I7 Marcellus MI U.S.A.
233 I6 Marcellus NY U.S.A.
251 I5 Marcelo Brazil
177 H4 Marcelová Slovakia
162 D5 Marcenais France
161 B6 Marcenat France
179 O2 March r. Austria alt. Morava
151 M2 March Cambridgeshire, England U.K.
116 H4 Marcha Uttaranchal India
214 E4 Marchand S. Africa
81 B12 Marchant, Lake South I. N.Z.
82 G5 Marchant Hill S.A. Austr.
162 G3 Marche reg. France
191 N8 Marche admin. reg. Italy
162 H3 Marche, Plateaux de la France
165 H8 Marche-en-Famenne Belgium
179 O3 Marchegg Austria
185 I6 Marchena Spain
250 □ Marchena, Isla i. Islas Galápagos Ecuador
156 B8 Marchenoir France
163 C6 Marcheprime France
192 E2 Marchese, Punta del pt Italy
179 O3 Marchfeld reg. Austria
156 F3 Marchiennes France
260 B4 Marchihue Chile
165 H8 Marchin Belgium
84 F1 Marchinbar Island N.T. Austr.
151 I2 Marchington Staffordshire, England U.K.
261 I5 Mar Chiquita Arg.
261 F2 Mar Chiquita, Laguna l. Arg.
261 I5 Mar Chiquita, Laguna l. Arg.
179 J3 Marchtrenk Austria
150 G1 Marchwiel Wrexham, Wales U.K.
137 N2 Marchykhyna Buda Ukr.
163 E8 Marciac France
192 E2 Marciana Italy
192 E2 Marciana Marina Italy
193 M5 Marcianise Italy
191 L9 Marciano della Chiana Italy
138 J5 Mārciena Latvia
160 E4 Marcigny France
163 H6 Marcilhac-sur-Célé France
162 C5 Marcillac France
162 I5 Marcillac-la-Croisille France
163 I7 Marcillac-Vallon France
160 B4 Marcillat-en-Combraille France
159 O7 Marcilly-en-Gault France
156 D8 Marcilly-en-Villette France
156 G7 Marcilly-le-Hayer France
156 B6 Marcilly-sur-Eure France
175 M1 Marcinkonys Lith.
175 I6 Marcinkowice Małopolskie Pol.
174 E2 Marcinkowice Zachodniopomorskie Pol.
174 E5 Marciszów Pol.
156 C2 Marck France
157 O7 Marckolsheim France
182 D6 Marco de Canaveses Port.
156 F3 Marcoing France
253 F2 Marcolino r. Brazil
191 M4 Marcòn Italy
252 B3 Marcona Peru
224 E1 Marcopeet Islands Que. Can.
191 M5 Marco Polo airport Italy
261 F3 Marcos Juárez Arg.
261 H4 Marcos Paz Arg.
161 I8 Marcoux France
156 F2 Marcq-en-Barœul France
233 L4 Marcy, Mount NY U.S.A.
129 L5 Mărdăkan Azer.
123 O4 Mardan Pak.
136 I6 Mardarivka Ukr.
261 I5 Mar de Ajó Arg.
261 I5 Mar del Plata Arg.
150 G3 Marden Herefordshire, England U.K.
151 M5 Marden Kent, England U.K.
156 G5 Mardeuil France
123 L3 Mardīān Afgh.
86 C6 Mardie W.A. Austr.
127 J5 Mardın Turkey
140 O4 Mårdsele Sweden
140 P3 Mårdudden Sweden
106 H4 Mardzad Mongolia
160 E5 Mare r. France
93 E3 Mare i. Maluku Indon.
78 □5 Maré i. Îles Loyauté New Caledonia
217 □1b Mare aux Vacoas Reservoir Mauritius
191 L2 Marebbe Italy
191 N7 Marecchia r. Italy
186 □ Mare de Déu del Toro hill Spain
146 F7 Maree, Loch l. Scotland U.K.
85 J4 Mareeba Qld Austr.
162 I5 Marèges, Barrage de dam France
122 H8 Mareh Iran
149 Q7 Mareham le Fen Lincolnshire, England U.K.
192 G2 Maremma, Parco Naturale della nature res. Italy
206 C3 Maréna Mali
207 G2 Marendet Niger
236 I5 Marengo IA U.S.A.
226 F7 Marengo IL U.S.A.
226 D3 Marengo WI U.S.A.
226 E3 Marenisco MI U.S.A.
162 B4 Marennes France
163 B8 Marensin reg. France
195 M3 Mare Piccolo b. Italy
195 K6 Marepotamo r. Italy
213 □J4 Marerano Madag.
151 M6 Maresfield East Sussex, England U.K.
86 H3 Maret Islands W.A. Austr.
194 C8 Marettimo Sicilia Italy
194 C8 Marettimo, Isola i. Sicilia Italy
162 E5 Mareuil France
159 P8 Mareuil-sur-Arnon France
156 H5 Mareuil-sur-Ay France
162 B2 Mareuil-sur-Lay-Dissais France
139 P4 Marevo Rus. Fed.
160 G1 Marey-sur-Tille France
239 L11 Marfa TX U.S.A.
Marfa Point Malta see Cirkewwa, Il-Ponta tac-
195 □ Marfa Ridge Malta
111 H9 Margai Caka l. Xizang China
150 E4 Margam Neath Port Talbot, Wales U.K.
111 G10 Margam Ri mts Xizang China
Marganets Kazakh. see Zhezdy
Marganets Ukr. see Marhanets'
Margao Goa India see Madgaon
86 H5 Margaret r. W.A. Austr.
82 F3 Margaret watercourse S.A. Austr.
86 D7 Margaret, Mount hill W.A. Austr.
222 E5 Margaret Bay B.C. Can.
222 H3 Margaret Lake Alta Can.
222 G1 Margaret Lake N.W.T. Can.
87 C12 Margaret River W.A. Austr.
233 K6 Margaretville NY U.S.A.
258 E3 Margarita Arg.
251 F2 Margarita, Isla de i. Venez.
100 I7 Margaritovo Primorskiy Kray Rus. Fed.
137 R7 Margaritovo Rostovskaya Oblast' Rus. Fed.
215 O6 Margate S. Africa
151 O5 Margate Kent, England U.K.
235 F6 Margate City NJ U.S.A.
197 K4 Mărgău Romania
162 C5 Margaux France
177 K3 Margecany Slovakia
161 C6 Margeride, Monts de la mts France
156 I6 Margerie-Hancourt France
149 N7 Margery Hill England U.K.
172 H2 Margetshöchheim Ger.
117 O6 Margherita Assam India
Margherita, Lake Eth. see Ābaya Hāyk'
193 Q5 Margherita di Savoia Italy
208 F4 Margherita Peak Dem. Rep. Congo/Uganda
Marghilon Uzbek. see Marg'ilon
197 K3 Marghita Romania
121 N7 Marg'ilon Uzbek.
177 L6 Margina Romania
197 N3 Marginea Romania
138 H8 Margionys Lith.
156 E5 Margny-lès-Compiègne France
111 H10 Margog Caka l. Xizang China
190 C5 Margone Italy
174 F3 Margonin Pol.
252 A2 Margos Peru
92 D8 Margosatubig Mindanao Phil.
123 J6 Mārgow, Dasht-e des. Afgh.
165 I7 Margraten Neth.
222 F4 Marguerite B.C. Can.
Marguerite, Pic mt. Dem. Rep. Congo/Uganda see Margherita Peak
262 T2 Marguerite Bay Antarctica
161 E9 Marguerittes France
157 J4 Margut France
111 J12 Margyang Xizang China
127 M7 Marhaj Khalīl Iraq
151 N2 Marham Norfolk, England U.K.
121 O7 Marhamat Uzbek.
177 K2 Marhaň Slovakia
127 K5 Marhan Dāgh hill Iraq
137 N6 Marhanets' Ukr.
205 E2 Marhoum Alg.
252 D1 Mari r. Brazil
96 D1 Mari Myanmar
91 J8 Mari P.N.G.
255 B7 Maria r. Brazil
79 □9 Maria atoll Arch. des Tuamotu Fr. Polynesia
79 □9 Maria atoll Îs Australes Fr. Polynesia
185 O5 María Spain
185 O5 María, Sierra de mts Spain
179 M3 Maria Anzbach Austria
161 E7 Mariac France
244 A4 María Cleofas, Isla i. Mex.
187 E7 María Cristina, Embalse de resr Spain
252 C5 María Elena Chile
261 G2 Mariá Eugenia Arg.
142 F5 Mariager Denmark
261 H5 María Ignacia Arg.
84 E3 Maria Island N.T. Austr.
83 L10 Maria Island Tas. Austr.
85 J8 Mariala National Park Qld Austr.
179 L5 Maria Lankowitz Austria
245 L8 María Lombardo de Casso Mex.
178 G6 Maria Luggau Austria
261 G2 María Luisa Arg.
182 F7 Marialva Port.
244 A4 María Madre, Isla i. Mex.
244 A4 María Magdelena, Isla i. Mex.
85 L6 Marian Qld Austr.
257 F4 Mariana Brazil
183 P8 Mariana Spain
246 B2 Marianao Cuba
266 E4 Mariana Ridge sea feature N. Pacific Ocean
266 E5 Mariana Trench sea feature N. Pacific Ocean
117 O6 Mariani Assam India
Mariánica, Cordillera mts Spain see Morena, Sierra
222 G2 Marian Lake N.W.T. Can.
237 J8 Marianna AR U.S.A.
231 E10 Marianna FL U.S.A.
217 □2a Marianne i. Inner Islands Seychelles
143 L4 Mariannelund Sweden
190 G4 Mariano Comense Italy
258 F3 Mariano Loza Arg.
Mariano Machado Angola see Ganda
260 B6 Mariano Moreno Arg.
194 F8 Marianopoli Sicilia Italy
261 G5 Mariano Unzué Arg.
174 D2 Marianowo Pol.
176 B2 Mariánské Lázně Czech Rep.
179 I5 Mariapfarr Austria
250 D4 Mariapirí, Mesa de hills Col.
256 B4 Mariápolis Brazil
179 J6 Maria Rain Austria
238 I3 Marias r. MT U.S.A.
244 A4 Marías, Islas is Mex.
179 J6 Maria Saal Austria
261 G4 María Teresa Arg.
242 □S14 Mariato, Punta pt Panama
80 G1 Maria van Diemen, Cape North I. N.Z.
179 J6 Maria Wörth Austria
179 L4 Mariazell Austria
124 G8 Ma'rib Yemen
124 G8 Ma'rib governorate Yemen
226 G5 Maribel WI U.S.A.
142 H7 Maribo Denmark
188 E2 Maribor Slovenia
257 F5 Maricá Brazil
Marica r. Bulg. see Maritsa
247 □1 Maricao Puerto Rico
114 F8 Marichchukkaddi Sri Lanka
215 K1 Marico Bosveld Nature Reserve S. Africa
241 T8 Maricopa AZ U.S.A.
240 M6 Maricopa CA U.S.A.
241 T8 Maricopa Mountains AZ U.S.A.
Maricourt Que. Can. see Kangiqsujuaq
208 F3 Maridi Sudan
208 F3 Maridi watercourse Sudan
250 E5 Marié r. Brazil
Marie Anne Island Inner Islands Seychelles see Marianne
262 P1 Marie Byrd Land reg. Antarctica
143 N2 Mariefred Sweden
247 □2 Marie-Galante i. Guadeloupe
141 O6 Mariehamn Åland Fin.
Mari El aut. rep. Rus. Fed. see Mariy El, Respublika
254 C5 Mariembero r. Brazil
165 G8 Mariembourg Belgium
Marienbad Czech Rep. see Mariánské Lázně
171 H9 Marienberg Ger.
Marienburg Pol. see Malbork
168 D3 Marienhafe Ger.
169 I6 Marienhagen Ger.
169 E8 Marienheide Ger.
169 K6 Mariental Ger.
212 C5 Mariental Namibia
232 F7 Marienville PA U.S.A.
Marienwerder Pol. see Kwidzyn
143 J3 Mariestad Sweden
224 E1 Mariet r. Que. Can.
231 E9 Marietta GA U.S.A.
232 D9 Marietta OH U.S.A.
237 G9 Marietta OK U.S.A.
234 B4 Marietta PA U.S.A.
233 L3 Marieville Que. Can.
207 G4 Mariga r. Nigeria
193 M6 Marigliano Italy
192 B3 Marignana Corse France
161 G10 Marignane France
159 L6 Marigné-Laillé France
160 J4 Marignier France
158 I3 Marigny France
156 G7 Marigny-le-Châtel France
160 D2 Marigny-l'Église France
247 □2 Marigot Dominica
247 L4 Marigot West Indies
100 M1 Marii, Mys pt Sakhalin Rus. Fed.
120 I1 Mariinskoye Rus. Fed.
138 G7 Marijampolė Lith.
215 L1 Marikana S. Africa
197 L9 Marikostinovo Bulg.
256 C5 Marília Brazil
86 E7 Marillana W.A. Austr.
256 A6 Mariluz Brazil
209 C7 Marimba Angola
95 K5 Marimun Kalimantan Indon.
243 I5 Marín Mex.
182 C4 Marín Spain
240 K5 Marina CA U.S.A.
192 G2 Marina di Alberese Italy
195 L4 Marina di Amendolara
192 A8 Marina di Arbus Sardeg Italy
193 O7 Marina di Camerota Ita
192 E2 Marina di Campo Italy
192 F1 Marina di Castagneto Donoratico Italy
190 I9 Marina di Cecina Italy
193 O4 Marina di Chieuti Italy
195 L3 Marina di Ginosa Italy
195 K7 Marina di Gioiosa Ionic
192 F2 Marina di Grosseto Italy
195 O4 Marina di Leuca Italy
190 I7 Marina di Massa Italy
194 F9 Marina di Palma Sicilia
195 M3 Marina di Pulsano Italy
194 H10 Marina di Ragusa Sicilia
191 M6 Marina di Ravenna Italy
Mar'ina Gorka Belarus s Mar"ina Horka
138 L8 Mar"ina Horka Belarus
185 J6 Marinaleda Spain
193 L1 Marina Palmense Italy
191 M6 Marina Romea Italy
195 L4 Marina Schiavonea Italy
92 C5 Marinduque i. Phil.
227 L7 Marine City MI U.S.A.
194 D8 Marinella Sicilia Italy
192 D5 Marinella, Golfo di b. Sardegna Italy
194 E8 Marineo Sicilia Italy
263 L2 Mariner Glacier Antarct
156 C5 Marines France
187 D8 Marines Spain
226 G4 Marinette WI U.S.A.
256 B5 Maringá Brazil
208 C4 Maringa r. Dem. Rep. Co
232 C8 Maringo OH U.S.A.
213 G3 Maringué Moz.
160 C5 Maringues France
182 C8 Marinha das Ondas Po
182 C9 Marinha Grande Port.
184 B2 Marinhais Port.
182 C5 Marinhas Port.
191 Q5 Marinići Croatia
122 D4 Marinjab Iran
129 E1 Mar'in Kolodtsy Rus. Fe
193 J4 Marino Italy
129 A2 Marino Rus. Fed.
Marino Alejandro Selki Isla i. S. Pacific Ocean s Alejandro Selkirk, Isla
138 L3 Mar'insko Rus. Fed.
231 D9 Marion AL U.S.A.
237 J8 Marion AR U.S.A.
235 J1 Marion CT U.S.A.
237 K7 Marion IL U.S.A.
230 E5 Marion IN U.S.A.
236 G6 Marion KS U.S.A.
237 K7 Marion KY U.S.A.
226 I5 Marion MI U.S.A.
231 F8 Marion NC U.S.A.
232 B8 Marion OH U.S.A.
231 H8 Marion SC U.S.A.
232 D12 Marion VA U.S.A.
226 F5 Marion WI U.S.A.
231 G9 Marion, Lake SC U.S.A.
82 F6 Marion Bay S.A. Austr.
84 G7 Marion Downs Qld Aus
236 G6 Marion Lake KS U.S.A.
85 N5 Marion Reef Coral Sea Austr.
193 R5 Mariotto Italy
205 H5 Mariou, Adrar mt. Alg.
251 E3 Maripa Venez.
251 H4 Maripasoula Fr. Guiana
92 E6 Maripipi i. Phil.
240 M4 Mariposa CA U.S.A.
240 L4 Mariposa r. CA U.S.A.
250 C3 Mariquita Col.
93 B3 Marisa Sulawesi Indon.
245 I8 Mariscala Mex.
253 E5 Mariscal José Félix Estigarribia Para.
197 L4 Mărişel Romania
197 M3 Mărişelu Romania
161 J8 Maritime Alps mts France/Italy
Maritime Kray admin. d Rus. Fed. see Primorski
Maritsa Bulg. see Simeonovgrad
197 O9 Maritsa r. Bulg. alt. Evros (Greece), alt. Meriç (Turkey)
199 H2 Maritsa r. Turkey alt. Evros (Greece), alt. Maritsa (Bulgaria)
134 J4 Mari-Turek Rus. Fed.
137 Q6 Mariupol' Ukr.
251 F2 Mariusa nat. park Venez
251 F2 Mariusa, Isla i. Venez.
127 M6 Marīvān Iran
134 J4 Mariy El, Respublika a Rus. Fed.
Mariyskaya A.S.S.R. au Rus. Fed. see Mariy El, Respublika
160 E3 Marizy France
183 M9 Marjaliza Spain
138 H3 Märjamaa Estonia
Marjan Afgh. see Wazi
122 E7 Marjān Iran
128 D5 Marjayoûn Lebanon
123 L2 Marjonbuloq Uzbek.
223 L1 Marjorie Lake Nunavut
150 G5 Mark Somerset, Englanc
128 E7 Mārkā Jordan
124 E6 Markā i. Saudi Arabia
210 E4 Marka Somalia
121 U3 Markakol', Ozero l. Ka
206 D3 Markala Mali
134 L3 Markalasta Rus. Fed.
108 B4 Markam Xizang China
108 B4 Markam Shan mts Xiza China
129 G7 Mārkān Iran
114 F5 Markapur Andhra Prad.
143 J5 Markaryd Sweden
210 E3 Markawene well Eth.
125 M6 Markaz, Ra's c. Oman
122 D4 Markazī prov. Iran
227 N5 Markdale Ont. Can.
172 G6 Markdorf Ger.
164 K4 Markelo Neth.
170 D1 Markelsdorfer Huk pt
164 H4 Marken i. Neth.
213 F4 Marken S. Africa
164 H3 Markermeer l. Neth.
171 G9 Markersdorf bei Burgst
151 J2 Market Bosworth Leicestershire, England
151 L2 Market Deeping Lincol England U.K.
150 H2 Market Drayton Shrop England U.K.
151 K3 Market Harborough Leicestershire, England
147 I4 Markethill Northern Irela
151 I5 Market Lavington Wilts England U.K.
149 Q7 Market Rasen Lincolns England U.K.
149 O7 Market Warsop Nottinghamshire, Englan
149 P6 Market Weighton East of Yorkshire, England U.
151 J2 Markfield Leicestershire England U.K.
172 G4 Markgröningen Ger.
131 M3 Markha r. Rus. Fed.
224 E5 Markham Ont. Can.
263 K1 Markham, Mount Anta
223 K2 Markham Lake N.W.T.
175 J3 Marki Pol.
137 S3 Marki Rus. Fed.
183 P2 Markina-Xemein Spair
146 J10 Markinch Fife, Scotlanc
171 I6 Märkisch Buchholz Ge
110 C7 Markit Xinjiang China
140 P3 Markitta Sweden
137 S4 Markivka Ukr.
136 H5 Markivka r. Ukr.
171 F8 Markkleeberg Ger.
240 M3 Markleeville CA U.S.A.
232 F9 Markleysburg PA U.S.
173 N4 Marklkofen Ger.
168 H5 Marklohe Ger.

Marknesse Neth.
Markneukirchen Ger.
Márkó Hungary
Markog Qu r. Sichuan China
Markopoulo Greece
Markounda C.A.R.
Markovac Trojstveni Croatia
Markovo Chukotskiy Avtonomnyy Okrug Rus. Fed.
Markovo Ivanovskaya Oblast' Rus. Fed.
Markovo Kurskaya Oblast' Rus. Fed.
Markoye Burkina
Markranstädt Ger.
Marks Rus. Fed.
Marks MS U.S.A.
Marksboro NJ U.S.A.
Marks Tey Essex, England U.K.
Marksuhl Ger.
Marksville LA U.S.A.
Markt Allhau Austria
Marktbergel Ger.
Markt Berolzheim Ger.
Markt Bibart Ger.
Marktbreit Ger.
Markt Erlbach Ger.
Markt Hartmannsdorf Austria
Marktheidenfeld Ger.
Markt Indersdorf Ger.
Marktl Ger.
Marktleugast Ger.
Marktleuthen Ger.
Marktoberdorf Ger.
Marktoffingen Ger.
Marktosis B.C. Can.
Markt Piesting Austria
Marktredwitz Ger.
Markt Rettenbach Ger.
Marktrodach Ger.
Markt Sankt Florian Austria
Markt Sankt Martin Austria
Marktschellenberg Ger.
Markt Schwaben Ger.
Marktseft Ger.
Markt Wald Ger.
Markusevec Croatia
Markuszów Pol.
Markyate Hertfordshire, England U.K.
Marl Ger.
Marla S.A. Austr.
Marlandy Hill W.A. Austr.
Marlboro NJ U.S.A.
Marlboro NJ U.S.A.
Marlboro NY U.S.A.
Marlborough Qld Austr.
Marlborough admin. reg. South I. N.Z.
Marlborough Wiltshire, England U.K.
Marlborough CT U.S.A.
Marlborough MA U.S.A.
Marlborough NH U.S.A.
Marlborough Downs hills England U.K.
Marldon Devon, England U.K.
Marle France
Marlengo Italy
Marlenheim France
Marlera, Rt pt Croatia
Marlette MI U.S.A.
Marlhes France
Marlieux France
Marlin TX U.S.A.
Marlinton WV U.S.A.
Marlishausen Ger.
Marlo Vic. Austr.
Marloth Nature Reserve S. Africa
Marlow Ger.
Marlow Buckinghamshire, England U.K.
Marlton NJ U.S.A.
Marly Lorraine France
Marly Nord-Pas-de-Calais France
Marly Switz.
Marly-la-Ville France
Marmagao Goa India
Marmagne Bourgogne France
Marmagne Centre France
Marmande France
Marmara Turkey
Marmara, Sea of g. Turkey see Marmara Denizi
Marmara Adası i. Turkey
Marmara Denizi g. Turkey
Marmaraereğlisi Turkey
Marmara Gölü l. Turkey
Marmarica reg. Libya
Marmaris Turkey
Marmaro Chios Greece
Marmarth ND U.S.A.
Marmê Xizang China
Marmelar Port.
Marmeleira Port.
Marmelete Port.
Marmelos r. Brazil
Marmet WV U.S.A.
Marmion, Lake salt l. W.A. Austr.
Marmion Lake Ont. Can.
Marmirolo Italy
Mármol Mex.
Marmolada mt. Italy
Marmolejo Spain
Marmore r. Italy
Marmoutier France
Marnay France
Marnaz France
Marne dept France
Marne r. France
Marne Ger.
Marne, Source de la France
Marne à la Saône, Canal de la France
Marne au Rhin, Canal de la France
Marne-la-Vallée France
Marneuli Georgia
Marnheim Ger.
Marnhull Dorset, England U.K.
Marnitz Ger.
Marniu Arun. Prad. India
Marnoo Vic. Austr.
Maro Chad
Maroambihy Madag.
Maroantsetra Madag.
Maroba r. Brazil
Marofandilia Madag.
Maroglio r. Sicilia Italy
Marokau atoll Arch. des Tuamotu Fr. Polynesia
Marokopa North I. N.Z.
Marol Jammu and Kashmir
Marol Pak.
Marolambo Madag.
Maroldsweisach Ger.
Marolles-les-Braults France
Maromandia Madag.
Maromme France
Maromokotro mt. Madag.
Marondera Zimbabwe
Maroni r. Fr. Guiana
Maronne r. France
Maroochydore Qld Austr.
Maroonah W.A. Austr.
Maroon Peak CO U.S.A.
Maroon Town Jamaica
Maros Sulawesi Indon.
Maros r. Indon.
Maros r. Hungary
Maroseranana Madag.
Maros-Körös Köze plain Hungary
Maroslele Hungary
Marostica Italy
Marosvásárhely Romania see Târgu Mureș
Marotandrano Madag.
Marotiri is Îs Australes Fr. Polynesia
Marotiri Islands North I. N.Z.
Marotolana Madag.
Maroua Cameroon
Maroué France
Marova Brazil
Marovato Antsirañana Madag.
Marovato Toliara Madag.
Marovoay Mahajanga Madag.
Marovoay Toamasina Madag.
213 □J3 Marovoay Atsimo Madag.
93 B4 Marowali Sulawesi Indon.
251 H3 Marowijne r. Suriname
175 I2 Maróz, Jezioro l. Pol.
172 C3 Marpingen Ger.
149 M7 Marple Greater Manchester, England U.K.
127 J6 Marqādah Syria
Marqakōl l. Kazakh. see Markakol', Ozero
215 L4 Marquard S. Africa
173 M6 Marquartstein Ger.
245 I9 Marquelia Mex.
156 C3 Marquenterre reg. France
183 O6 Marquesado de Berlanga reg. Spain
Marquesas Islands Fr. Polynesia see Marquises, Îles
231 F13 Marquesas Keys is FL U.S.A.
257 F5 Marquês de Valença Brazil
226 G3 Marquette MI U.S.A.
237 G10 Marquez TX U.S.A.
256 A6 Marquinho Brazil
156 F3 Marquion France
247 □3 Marquis, Cap c. St Lucia
156 C2 Marquise France
79 □9 Marquises, Îles is Fr. Polynesia
163 I10 Marquixanes France
83 I4 Marra N.S.W. Austr.
83 K4 Marra r. N.S.W. Austr.
202 E6 Marra, Jebel mt. Sudan
202 E6 Marra, Jebel plat. Sudan
84 E3 Marra Aboriginal Land res. N.T. Austr.
213 H3 Marracua Moz.
213 G5 Marracuene Moz.
191 L7 Marradi Italy
124 E7 Marrāk i. Saudi Arabia
204 D3 Marrakech Morocco
Marrakesh Morocco see Marrakech
124 E6 Marrān Saudi Arabia
140 R3 Marraskoski Fin.
83 J9 Marrawah Tas. Austr.
82 G3 Marree S.A. Austr.
237 J11 Marrero LA U.S.A.
213 G3 Marromeu Moz.
213 G3 Marromeu, Reserva de nature res. Moz.
245 H1 Marroquin Mex.
192 B8 Marrubiu Sardegna Italy
164 I2 Marrum Neth.
211 C8 Marrupa Moz.
82 D2 Marryat S.A. Austr.
161 A6 Mars r. France
232 E8 Mars PA U.S.A.
203 G3 Marsá al 'Alam Egypt
202 C2 Marsa al Burayqah Libya
181 E5 Marsa-Ben-Mehidi Alg.
210 C4 Marsabit Kenya
210 C4 Marsabit National Reserve nature res. Kenya
160 D6 Marsac-en-Livradois France
158 H6 Marsac-sur-Don France
203 H5 Marsa Darur Sudan
203 H4 Marsa Delwein Sudan
190 G6 Marsaglia Italy
124 B3 Marsá Ijlī Egypt
157 M6 Marsal France
194 C8 Marsala Sicilia Italy
195 □ Marsalforn Gozo Malta
124 C5 Marsa Mar'ob Sudan
202 E2 Marsá Maṭrūḥ Egypt
160 F2 Marsannay-la-Côte France
161 F7 Marsanne France
203 H4 Marsa Oseif Sudan
124 C5 Marsa Salak Sudan
124 C5 Marsa Shin'ab Sudan
Marsaskala Malta see Wied Il-Għajn
206 B3 Marsassoum Senegal
124 B3 Marsá Ṭunḍubah Egypt
195 □ Marsaxlokk Malta
195 □ Marsaxlokk, Il-Bajja ta' b. Malta
246 E2 Mars Bay Andros Bahamas
216 □2a Mars Bay b. Ascension S. Atlantic Ocean
169 G8 Marsberg Ger.
168 J4 Marschacht Ger.
193 I2 Marsciano Italy
83 K5 Marsden N.S.W. Austr.
223 I4 Marsden Sask. Can.
149 N6 Marsden West Yorkshire, England U.K.
80 I2 Marsden Point N.Z.
164 G3 Marsdiep sea chan. Neth.
161 D10 Marseillan France
161 G10 Marseille France
Marseille airport France see Provence
161 F9 Marseille au Rhône, Canal de France
156 C4 Marseille-en-Beauvaisis France
Marseilles France see Marseille
226 F8 Marseilles IL U.S.A.
252 D3 Marsella Bol.
140 M4 Marsfjället mt. Sweden
128 C10 Marshah, Jabal mt. Saudi Arabia
84 F7 Marshall watercourse N.T. Austr.
223 I4 Marshall Sask. Can.
237 I8 Marshall AR U.S.A.
230 D6 Marshall IL U.S.A.
226 J7 Marshall MI U.S.A.
236 H3 Marshall MN U.S.A.
236 I6 Marshall MO U.S.A.
231 F8 Marshall NC U.S.A.
237 H9 Marshall TX U.S.A.
232 H10 Marshall VA U.S.A.
266 F5 Marshall Islands country N. Pacific Ocean
234 E2 Marshalls Creek PA U.S.A.
234 D5 Marshallton DE U.S.A.
236 I4 Marshalltown IA U.S.A.
234 D4 Marsh Creek Lake PA U.S.A.
150 H5 Marshfield South Gloucestershire, England U.K.
237 I7 Marshfield MO U.S.A.
226 D5 Marshfield WI U.S.A.
231 I12 Marsh Harbour Bahamas
233 □R2 Mars Hill ME U.S.A.
237 J11 Marsh Island LA U.S.A.
222 C2 Marsh Lake Y.T. Can.
222 C2 Marsh Lake l. Y.T. Can.
223 M3 Marsh Point Man. Can.
122 C3 Marshūn Iran
161 E9 Marsillargues France
238 F5 Marsing ID U.S.A.
149 O4 Marske-by-the-Sea Redcar and Cleveland, England U.K.
157 K5 Mars-la-Tour France
156 I6 Marson France
163 I8 Marssac-sur-Tarn France
143 N2 Märsta Sweden
142 G7 Marstal Denmark
168 K1 Marstal Bugt b. Denmark
190 G1 Märstetten Switz.
151 J4 Marston Oxfordshire, England U.K.
150 G6 Marston Magna Somerset, England U.K.
151 K3 Marston Moretaine Bedfordshire, England U.K.
78 □3a Marsugalt i. Kwajalein Marshall Is
117 J6 Marsyangdi r. Nepal
234 D7 Marsyhope r. MD U.S.A.
192 H2 Marta Italy
192 H3 Marta r. Italy
Martaban, Gulf of Myanmar see Mottama, Gulf of
192 H2 Martana, Isola i. Italy
95 L1 Martanai Besar i. Malaysia
195 O3 Martano Italy
193 J2 Martano, Monte mt. Italy
207 I5 Martap Cameroon
95 K6 Martapura Kalimantan Indon.
94 F7 Martapura Sumatera Indon.
207 I3 Marte Nigeria
162 H6 Martel France
232 C8 Martel OH U.S.A.
162 G6 Martel, Causse de hills France
165 I9 Martelange Belgium
191 M4 Martellago Italy
191 J2 Martello Italy
177 J5 Mártély Hungary
177 J5 Mártélyi park Hungary
224 E4 Marten River Ont. Can.
223 J4 Martensville Sask. Can.
243 J4 Marte R. Gómez, Presa resr Mex.
187 D9 Martés mt. Spain
187 C9 Martés, Serra mts Spain
168 H5 Martfeld Ger.
177 J4 Martfű Hungary
151 P2 Martham Norfolk, England U.K.
233 O7 Martha's Vineyard i. MA U.S.A.
162 E4 Marthon France
246 E3 Martí Cuba
182 H8 Martiago Spain
191 O3 Martignacco Italy
193 I3 Martignano, Lago di l. Italy
163 C6 Martignas-sur-Jalle France
159 K7 Martigné-Briand France
158 I6 Martigné-Ferchaud France
159 J5 Martigné-sur-Mayenne France
190 C3 Martigny Switz.
160 E3 Martigny-le-Comte France
157 K7 Martigny-les-Bains France
157 K7 Martigny-les-Gerbonvaux France
161 G10 Martigues France
183 K7 Martiherrero Spain
185 I9 Martil Morocco
163 C6 Martillac France
184 D6 Martim Longo Port.
Martim Vaz, Ilhas is S. Atlantic Ocean see Martin Vaz, Ilhas
222 F2 Martin r. N.W.T. Can.
177 H2 Martin Slovakia
186 E5 Martín r. Spain
236 E4 Martin SD U.S.A.
146 F7 Martin, Isle i. Scotland U.K.
231 E9 Martin, Lake AL U.S.A.
195 M2 Martina Franca Italy
81 J8 Martinborough North I. N.Z.
182 D9 Martinchel Port.
261 H4 Martín Chico Uru.
261 H5 Martín Colman Arg.
185 J6 Martín de la Jara Spain
260 D4 Martín de Loyola Arg.
182 H7 Martín de Yeltes Spain
190 H4 Martinengo Italy
186 I3 Martinet Spain
245 J5 Martínez Mex.
240 J3 Martinez CA U.S.A.
231 F9 Martinez GA U.S.A.
241 R9 Martinez Lake AZ U.S.A.
169 J8 Martinfeld Ger.
182 C9 Martingança Port.
261 H4 Martín García, Isla i. Arg.
185 K4 Martín Gonzalo, Embalse de resr Spain
257 E3 Martinho Campos Brazil
247 □3 Martinique terr. West Indies
247 □2 Martinique Passage Dominica/Martinique
183 K6 Martín Muñoz de las Posadas Spain
198 E4 Martino Greece
256 B5 Martinópolis Brazil
262 Q2 Martin Peninsula Antarctica
182 I2 Martinporra Spain
81 B11 Martins Bay South I. N.Z.
179 L3 Martinsberg Austria
232 C8 Martinsburg OH U.S.A.
232 G8 Martinsburg PA U.S.A.
232 H9 Martinsburg WV U.S.A.
191 Q6 Martinšćica Croatia
234 E3 Martins Creek PA U.S.A.
234 D1 Martins Creek r. PA U.S.A.
232 E8 Martins Ferry OH U.S.A.
193 L2 Martinsicuro Italy
147 F8 Martinstown Ireland
230 D6 Martinsville IN U.S.A.
232 F12 Martinsville VA U.S.A.
264 H7 Martin Vaz, Ilhas is S. Atlantic Ocean
Martin Vaz Islands S. Atlantic Ocean see Martin Vaz, Ilhas
192 B6 Martis Sardegna Italy
159 N8 Martizay France
151 O3 Martlesham Suffolk, England U.K.
150 H3 Martley Worcestershire, England U.K.
150 G6 Martock Somerset, England U.K.
Martök Kazakh. see Martuk
111 E11 Martoli Uttaranchal India
80 J7 Marton North I. N.Z.
177 H4 Martonvásar Hungary
186 I5 Martorell Spain
185 L5 Martos Spain
163 G9 Martres-Tolosane France
140 T3 Martti Fin.
141 Q6 Marttila Fin.
120 G2 Martuk Kazakh.
129 G5 Martuni Armenia
129 D3 Martvili Georgia
137 L3 Martynivka Ukr.
136 I2 Martynovychi Ukr.
106 H9 Maru Gansu China
207 G3 Maru Nigeria
123 J4 Maruchak Afgh.
95 K2 Marudi Sarawak Malaysia
95 L1 Marudu, Teluk b. Malaysia
123 L6 Maruf Afgh.
103 K12 Marugame Japan
183 L7 Marugán Spain
195 N3 Maruggio Italy
81 G8 Maruia r. South I. N.Z.
254 F4 Maruim Brazil
129 C2 Marukhis Ugheltekhili pass Georgia/Rus. Fed.
105 H3 Maruko Japan
83 L6 Marulan N.S.W. Austr.
261 F2 Marull Arg.
164 J2 Marum Neth.
78 □5 Marum, Mount vol. Vanuatu
122 C6 Mārūn r. Iran
209 D9 Marunga Angola
104 D3 Maruoka Japan
121 U1 Marushka Rus. Fed.
116 C6 Marusthali reg. India
175 J4 Maruszów Mazowieckie Pol.
175 J5 Maruszów Świętokrzyskie Pol.
79 □9 Marutea (Nord) atoll Arch. des Tuamotu Fr. Polynesia
79 □9 Marutea (Sud) atoll Arch. des Tuamotu Fr. Polynesia
86 I7 Maruwa Aboriginal Reserve W.A. Austr.
210 B3 Maruwa Hills Sudan
105 K5 Maruyama Japan
104 A4 Maruyama-gawa r. Japan
184 E2 Marvão Port.
122 F6 Marvast Iran
122 E7 Marv Dasht Iran
161 C7 Marvejols France
87 E11 Marvel Loch W.A. Austr.
157 J5 Marville France
241 U3 Marvine, Mount UT U.S.A.
116 D7 Marwar Junction Rajasthan India
223 I4 Marwayne Alta Can.
173 J4 Marxheim Ger.
Marxwalde Ger. see Neuhardenberg
172 E4 Marxzell Ger.
84 C2 Mary r. N.T. Austr.
85 N8 Mary r. Qld Austr.
86 I5 Mary r. W.A. Austr.
123 I3 Mary Turkm.
122 J3 Mary admin. div. Turkm.
208 E2 Maryal Bai Sudan
137 N8 Mar"yanivka Respublika Krym Ukr.
175 M5 Mar"yanivka Volyns'ka Oblast' Ukr.
137 P6 Mar"yanivka Zaporiz'ka Oblast' Ukr.
136 G3 Mar"yanivka Zhytomyrs'ka Oblast' Ukr.
137 R8 Mar'yanskaya Rus. Fed.
Mary A.S.S.R. aut. rep. Rus. Fed. see Mariy El, Respublika
146 G7 Marybank Highland, Scotland U.K.
85 N8 Maryborough Qld Austr.
83 I7 Maryborough Vic. Austr.
214 G5 Marydale S. Africa
234 D6 Marydel MD U.S.A.
120 C1 Mar'yevka Rus. Fed.
146 □N2 Maryfield Shetland, Scotland U.K.
223 J2 Mary Frances Lake N.W.T. Can.
137 Q6 Mar"yinka Ukr.
Maryino Rus. Fed. see Pristen'
137 P8 Mar"yivka Respublika Krym Ukr.
137 N6 Mar"yivka Zaporiz'ka Oblast' Ukr.
146 K9 Marykirk Aberdeenshire, Scotland U.K.
223 K2 Mary Lake N.W.T. Can.
234 B7 Maryland state U.S.A.
234 B5 Maryland Line MD U.S.A.
136 E5 Marynychi Ukr.
Mary Oblast admin. div. Turkm. see Mary
146 J8 Marypark Moray, Scotland U.K.
149 K4 Maryport Cumbria, England U.K.
225 K2 Mary's Harbour Nfld and Lab. Can.
225 K4 Marystown Nfld and Lab. Can.
241 T3 Marysvale UT U.S.A.
83 J7 Marysville Vic. Austr.
225 H4 Marysville N.B. Can.
240 K2 Marysville CA U.S.A.
236 G6 Marysville KS U.S.A.
227 L7 Marysville MI U.S.A.
232 B8 Marysville OH U.S.A.
234 B4 Marysville PA U.S.A.
238 C2 Marysville WA U.S.A.
84 E8 Maryvale N.T. Austr.
85 J5 Maryvale Qld Austr.
236 H5 Maryville MO U.S.A.
231 F8 Maryville TN U.S.A.
146 K8 Marywell Aberdeenshire, Scotland U.K.
191 K7 Marzabotto Italy
256 C2 Marzagão Brazil
171 G6 Marzahna Ger.
171 G5 Marzahne Ger.
195 I10 Marzamemi Sicilia Italy
158 G6 Marzan France
191 L7 Marzeno r. Italy
173 L5 Marzling Ger.
250 B3 Marzo, Cabo c. Col.
160 C3 Marzy France
183 M3 Masa Spain
242 □P12 Masachapa Nic.
128 D7 Masada tourist site Israel
Más Afuera i. S. Pacific Ocean see Alejandro Selkirk, Isla
210 E4 Masagaweyn Somalia
243 N10 Masagua Guat.
211 C7 Masaguro Tanz.
122 F6 Masāhūn, Kūh-e mt. Iran
211 B5 Masai Mara National Reserve nature res. Kenya
192 B9 Masainas Sardegna Italy
211 C6 Masai Steppe plain Tanz.
210 A5 Masaka Uganda
215 K7 Masakhane S. Africa
211 C6 Masaki Tanz.
212 D4 Masalanyane Pan salt pan Botswana
187 D9 Masalavés Spain
95 K7 Masalembu Besar i. Indon.
95 K7 Masalembu Kecil i. Indon.
129 J6 Masallı Azer.
93 B5 Masamba Sulawesi Indon.
93 B5 Masamba mt. Indon.
101 F11 Masan S. Korea
137 N9 Masandra Ukr.
93 E7 Masapun Maluku Indon.
124 F7 Masāqif i. Saudi Arabia
211 C7 Masasi Tanz.
242 □P12 Masatepe Nic.
Más á Tierra i. S. Pacific Ocean see Robinson Crusoe, Isla
253 E4 Masavi Bol.
242 □P12 Masaya Nic.
242 □P12 Masaya, Volcán vol. Nic.
92 D5 Masbate Masbate Phil.
92 D5 Masbate i. Phil.
163 I9 Mas-Cabardès France
195 I8 Mascali Sicilia Italy
195 I8 Mascalucia Sicilia Italy
205 F2 Mascara Alg.
183 M9 Mascaraque Spain
265 H6 Mascarene Basin sea feature Indian Ocean
265 H6 Mascarene Plain sea feature Indian Ocean
265 H5 Mascarene Ridge sea feature Indian Ocean
182 F5 Mascarenhas Port.
245 J4 Mascareõs Mex.
260 D2 Mascasín Arg.
260 D2 Mascasín, Salinas de salt pan Arg.
193 P6 Maschito Italy
163 G6 Masclat France
244 C5 Mascota Mex.
244 B5 Mascota r. Mex.
230 K3 Mascouche Que. Can.
186 E3 Mascún r. Spain
186 F6 Mas de Barberans Spain
186 E6 Mas de las Matas Spain
183 P7 Masegosa Spain
185 O3 Masegoso Spain
183 O7 Masegoso de Tajuña Spain
96 B3 Masein Myanmar
95 L3 Ma Sekatok b. Indon.
93 F8 Masela Maluku Indon.
93 F8 Masela i. Maluku Indon.
172 H5 Maselheim Ger.
210 B4 Maseno Kenya
93 C5 Masepe i. Indon.
190 E3 Masera Italy
178 F8 Maserada sul Piave Italy
227 R1 Masères, Lac l. Que. Can.
215 L5 Maseru Lesotho
157 M8 Masevaux France
141 H6 Masfjorden Norway
163 G8 Mas-Grenier France
Mashaba Zimbabwe see Mashava
124 C3 Mashābih i. Saudi Arabia
215 M5 Mashai Lesotho
209 D6 Mashala Dem. Rep. Congo
149 N5 Masham North Yorkshire, England U.K.
108 G7 Mashan Guangxi China
213 F4 Mashava Zimbabwe
116 F2 Masherbrum mt. Jammu and Kashmir
137 L1 Masheve Ukr.
122 H3 Mashhad Iran
116 E6 Mashi r. India
102 S3 Mashike Japan
105 L3 Mashiko Japan
122 B2 Mashīrān Iran
137 N4 Mashivka Ukr.
123 J7 Mashkel, Hamun-i- salt flat Pak.
123 J8 Mashket r. Pak.
123 J7 Mashki Chah Pak.
123 J8 Māshkīd r. Iran
213 F3 Mashonaland Central prov. Zimbabwe
213 F3 Mashonaland East prov. Zimbabwe
213 F3 Mashonaland West prov. Zimbabwe
Mashtagi Azer. see Maştağa
140 Q2 Masi Norway
242 E4 Masiáca Mex.
209 C5 Masia-Mbia Dem. Rep. Congo
215 L7 Masibambane S. Africa
182 D4 Maside Spain
125 J8 Masīlah, Wādī al watercourse Yemen
215 K4 Masilo S. Africa
209 C6 Masi-Manimba Dem. Rep. Congo
93 A4 Masimbu Sulawesi Barat Indon.
210 A4 Masindi Uganda
92 B4 Masinloc Luzon Phil.
190 H3 Masino r. Italy
214 H7 Masinyusane S. Africa
Masira, Gulf of Oman see Maşīrah, Khalīj
Masira Channel Oman see Maşīrah, Tur'at
125 N5 Maşīrah, Jazīrat i. Oman
125 N6 Maşīrah, Khalīj b. Oman
125 N5 Maşīrah, Tur'at sea chan. Oman
Masira Island Oman see Maşīrah, Jazīrat
129 F5 Masis Armenia
252 B2 Masisea Peru
208 F5 Masisi Dem. Rep. Congo
191 L6 Masi Torello Italy
93 G5 Masiwang r. Seram Indon.
215 M4 Masjaing S. Africa
122 C6 Masjed Soleymān Iran
147 D5 Mask, Lough l. Ireland
125 I1 Maskān i. Kuwait
118 E7 Maskan, Raas pt Somalia
128 G2 Maskanah Syria
122 H8 Maskūtān Iran
163 C9 Maslacq France
177 K5 Maşloc Romania
137 P3 Maslova Pristan' Rus. Fed.
137 S2 Maslovka Rus. Fed.
175 H4 Masłowice Pol.
123 K7 Maslti Pak.
182 F1 Masma r. Spain
125 I8 Maşna'ah Yemen
191 L3 Maso r. Italy
213 □K2 Masoala, Parc National de nat. park Madag.
213 □K2 Masoala, Saikanosy pen. Madag.
213 □K2 Masoala, Tanjona c. Madag.
93 F5 Masohi Seram Indon.
226 J7 Mason MI U.S.A.
232 A9 Mason OH U.S.A.
237 F10 Mason TX U.S.A.
226 C3 Mason WI U.S.A.
232 C9 Mason WV U.S.A.
87 E9 Mason, Lake salt flat W.A. Austr.
81 B13 Mason Bay Stewart I. N.Z.
236 I4 Mason City IA U.S.A.
226 E9 Mason City IL U.S.A.
190 F6 Masone Italy
247 □5 Mason Hall Trin. and Tob.
93 D4 Masoni i. Indon.
81 G9 Masons Flat South I. N.Z.
232 F9 Masontown PA U.S.A.
232 F9 Masontown WV U.S.A.
216 □3f Maspalomas Gran Canaria Canary Is
216 □3f Maspalomas, Punta de pt Gran Canaria Canary Is
125 N4 Masqaţ Oman
125 N4 Masqaţ governorate Oman
125 M3 Masqaţ reg. Oman
209 B5 Massa Congo
190 I7 Massa Italy
233 M6 Massachusetts state U.S.A.
233 O6 Massachusetts Bay MA U.S.A.
190 I8 Massaciuccoli, Lago di l. Italy
241 X1 Massadona CO U.S.A.
190 H7 Massa e Carrara prov. Italy
191 M6 Massa Fiscaglia Italy
195 M2 Massafra Italy
202 B6 Massaguet Chad
161 C8 Mas-St-Chély France
202 B6 Massakory Chad
208 C2 Massalassef Chad
191 L7 Massa Lombarda Italy
193 M6 Massa Lubrense Italy
187 E8 Massamagrell Spain
192 F1 Massa Marittimo Italy
193 J2 Massa Martana Italy
213 G2 Massamba Moz.
255 B9 Massambará Brazil
208 A5 Massana Gabon
213 G4 Massangena Moz.
209 C7 Massango Angola
213 G2 Massangulo Moz.
235 I3 Massapequa NY U.S.A.
254 E4 Massaroca Brazil
190 I8 Massarosa Italy
163 G10 Massat France
209 C6 Massau Angola
203 H6 Massawa Eritrea
203 H5 Massawa Channel Eritrea
159 O7 Massay France
169 J10 Maßbach Ger.
171 I7 Massen Ger.
233 K4 Massena NY U.S.A.
208 C2 Massenya Chad
162 H4 Masseret France
195 M2 Masseria Risana hill Italy
222 C4 Masset B.C. Can.
222 C4 Masset Inlet B.C. Can.
163 F9 Masseube France
224 D4 Massey Ont. Can.
234 D6 Massey MD U.S.A.
161 C6 Massiac France
209 D7 Massibi Angola
193 L5 Massico, Monte hill Italy
232 C9 Massieville OH U.S.A.
161 C6 Massif Central mts France
206 D4 Massigui Mali
Massilia France see Marseille
232 D8 Massillon OH U.S.A.
190 E7 Massimino Italy
206 D3 Massina Mali
173 N5 Massing Ger.
213 G4 Massinga Moz.
213 G4 Massingir Moz.
227 S4 Masson Que. Can.
192 F2 Massoncello, Monte hill Italy
263 G2 Masson Island Antarctica
156 D6 Massy France
129 K5 Maştağa Azer.
190 E4 Mastallone, Parco Naturale nature res. Italy
123 M2 Mastchoh Tajik.
169 D10 Mastershausen Ger.
81 J7 Masterton North I. N.Z.
235 J3 Mastic NY U.S.A.
235 J3 Mastic Beach NY U.S.A.
246 E1 Mastic Point Andros Bahamas
224 F4 Mastigouche, Réserve Faunique de nature res. Que. Can.
192 D8 Mastixi, Punta su pt Sardegna Italy
144 J1 Mastrevik Norway
123 O3 Mastuj Pak.
123 L7 Mastung Pak.
124 D4 Mastūrah Saudi Arabia
138 H8 Masty Belarus
192 A9 Masua Sardegna Italy
103 I12 Masuda Japan
105 H4 Masuho Japan
209 D6 Masuika Dem. Rep. Congo
Masuku Gabon see Franceville
122 C3 Masuleh Iran
Masulipatam Andhra Prad. India see Machilipatnam
192 B8 Masullas Sardegna Italy
Masuna i. American Samoa see Tutuila
94 D6 Masurai, Bukit mt. Indon.
213 F4 Masvingo Zimbabwe
213 F4 Masvingo prov. Zimbabwe
211 B5 Maswa Tanz.
211 B5 Maswe Game Reserve nature res. Tanz.
128 E3 Maşyāf Syria
136 C2 Masyevichy Belarus
174 C3 Maszewo Lubuskie Pol.
174 F1 Maszewo Pomorskie Pol.
174 D2 Maszewo Zachodniopomorskie Pol.
196 H9 Mat r. Albania
96 G5 Mat, Nam r. Laos
217 □1c Mât, Rivière du r. Réunion
96 C1 Mata Myanmar
80 M4 Mata r. North I. N.Z.
251 E3 Mata, Serranía de mts Venez.
259 C8 Mata Amarilla Arg.
209 D8 Mataba Zambia
210 E3 Matabaan Somalia
213 E3 Matabeleland North prov. Zimbabwe
213 F4 Matabeleland South prov. Zimbabwe
117 L6 Matabhanga W. Bengal India
183 M6 Matabuena Spain
184 G3 Matachel r. Spain
224 D4 Matachewan Ont. Can.
242 F3 Matachic Mex.
209 B6 Matadi Dem. Rep. Congo
237 E8 Matador TX U.S.A.
186 J4 Matagalls mt. Spain
242 □Q11 Matagalpa Nic.
224 E3 Matagami Que. Can.
224 E3 Matagami, Lac l. Que. Can.
237 G11 Matagorda TX U.S.A.
237 G11 Matagorda Island TX U.S.A.
254 F4 Mata Grande Brazil
80 J6 Matahiwi North I. N.Z.
79 □9a Mataiea Tahiti Fr. Polynesia
Mataigou Ningxia China see Taole
94 G3 Matak i. Indon.
121 P3 Matak Kazakh.
80 K4 Matakana Island North I. N.Z.
80 M4 Matakaoa Point North I. N.Z.
81 G8 Matakitaki South I. N.Z.
209 B8 Matala Angola
184 F6 Matalascañas Spain
114 G9 Matale Sri Lanka
183 P5 Matalebreras Spain
214 I4 Mataleng S. Africa
124 E2 Maţāli', Jabal hill Saudi Arabia
183 J4 Matallana de Valmadrigal Spain
206 B3 Matam Senegal
183 O5 Matamala de Almazán Spain
80 J4 Matamata North I. N.Z.
214 E1 Mata-Mata S. Africa
80 K7 Matamau North I. N.Z.
207 H3 Matamey Niger
234 F2 Matamoras PA U.S.A.
243 N8 Matamoros Campeche Mex.
237 C12 Matamoros Chihuahua Mex.
242 H5 Matamoros Coahuila Mex.
245 L8 Matamoros Oaxaca Mex.
243 K5 Matamoros Tamaulipas Mex.
183 L3 Matamorosa Spain
206 B2 Ma'ta Moûlana well Maur.
182 C9 Mata Mourisca Port.
93 B5 Matana, Danau l. Indon.
92 D8 Matanal Point Phil.
202 D4 Ma'ţan as Sārah well Libya
202 D4 Ma'ţan Bishrah well Libya
260 B2 Matancilla Chile
211 C7 Matandu r. Tanz.
225 H3 Matane Que. Can.
225 H3 Matane, Réserve Faunique de nature res. Que. Can.
251 F2 Mata Negra Venez.
213 □J4 Matanga Madag.
80 J4 Matangi North I. N.Z.
207 G3 Matankari Niger
123 N5 Matanui Pak.
246 C2 Matanzas Cuba
260 C5 Matanzilla, Pampa de la plain Arg.
256 C4 Matão Brazil
254 C4 Matão, Serra do hills Brazil
261 I2 Mataojo Uru.
242 □R13 Matapalo, Cabo c. Costa Rica
Matapan, Cape pt Greece see Tainaro, Akrotirio
174 G5 Mata Panew r. Pol.
225 H3 Matapédia, Lac l. Que. Can.
81 □4 Mata Point Niue
183 L3 Mataporquera Spain
183 K6 Matapozuelos Spain
260 A4 Mataquito r. Chile
125 H2 Maţār well Saudi Arabia
258 E3 Matará Arg.
114 G10 Matara Sri Lanka
198 C4 Mataragka Greece
95 L9 Mataram Lombok Indon.
Matarânga Greece see Mataragka
252 B4 Matarani Peru
84 D3 Mataranka N.T. Austr.
93 C5 Matarape, Teluk b. Indon.
128 A9 Matārimah, Ra's pt Egypt
92 E6 Matarinao Bay Samar Phil.
204 E2 Matarka Morocco
186 J4 Mataró Spain
80 J6 Mataroa North I. N.Z.
93 C5 Matarombea r. Indon.
196 I7 Mataruška Banja Serbia
216 □3b Matas Blancas Fuerteventura Canary Is
95 K7 Matasiri i. Indon.
203 F5 Matassi well Sudan
211 C6 Matassi Tanz.
215 M6 Matatiele S. Africa
116 G7 Matatila Dam India
78 □2 Matatula, Cape American Samoa
80 I6 Matau North I. N.Z.
81 C13 Mataura South I. N.Z.
81 C13 Mataura r. South I. N.Z.
78 □2 Matautu Samoa
77 I3 Matā'utu Wallis and Futuna Is
79 □9a Matavai, Baie de b. Tahiti Fr. Polynesia
78 □2 Matavanu, Mount vol. crater Samoa
81 □3 Matavera Rarotonga Cook Is
80 L5 Matawai North I. N.Z.
80 H2 Matawaia North I. N.Z.
235 G4 Matawan NJ U.S.A.
230 K2 Matawin r. Que. Can.
121 R5 Matay Kazakh.
125 J3 Maţbakh, Ra's al pt Qatar
Matcha Tajik. see Mastchoh
227 Q1 Matchi-Manitou, Lac l. Que. Can.
96 G5 Mat Con, Hon i. Vietnam
253 E3 Mategua Bol.
244 G2 Matehuala Mex.
197 M4 Matei Romania
208 C2 Matékaga Chad
213 F4 Mateke Hills Zimbabwe
191 O9 Matelica Italy
247 □7 Matelot Trin. and Tob.
211 C7 Matemanga Tanz.
80 I6 Matemateaonga Range hills North I. N.Z.
209 C9 Matende Angola
213 G2 Matenge Moz.
195 L2 Matera Italy
193 R7 Matera prov. Italy
191 Q4 Materija Slovenia
193 M5 Matese, Lago del l. Italy
193 M5 Matese, Monti del mts Italy
177 L4 Mátészalka Hungary
212 E3 Matetsi Zimbabwe
205 H1 Mateur Tunisia
257 E3 Mateus Leme Brazil
232 C11 Matewan WV U.S.A.
162 D4 Matha France
116 C6 Mathaji Rajasthan India
160 J2 Mathay France
224 D3 Matheson Ont. Can.
233 I11 Mathews VA U.S.A.
190 D5 Mathi Italy
232 G10 Mathias WV U.S.A.
113 □1 Mathidahura i. N. Male Maldives
237 G11 Mathis TX U.S.A.
83 J6 Mathoura N.S.W. Austr.
198 A3 Mathraki i. Greece
116 F6 Mathura Uttar Prad. India
217 □1a Mathurin Bay Rodrigues I. Mauritius
116 E8 Mathwar Madh. Prad. India
92 F8 Mati Mindanao Phil.
207 F3 Matiacoali Burkina
117 L6 Matiali W. Bengal India
109 I5 Matianxu Hunan China
123 M9 Matiari Pak.
257 F4 Matias Barbosa Brazil
254 E5 Matias Cardoso Brazil
245 L9 Matías Romero Mex.
213 I2 Matibane Moz.
158 G4 Matignon France
156 F4 Matigny France
225 H2 Matimekosh Que. Can.
116 I8 Matin Chhattisgarh India
242 □R12 Matina Costa Rica
224 D4 Matinenda Lake Ont. Can.
233 □Q5 Matinicus Island ME U.S.A.
195 O3 Matino Italy
79 □9a Matiti Tahiti Fr. Polynesia
108 D2 Matizi Sichuan China
214 E9 Matjiesfontein S. Africa
129 D3 Mat'khoji Georgia
117 L9 Matla r. India
123 M9 Matli Pak.
149 N7 Matlock Derbyshire, England U.K.
149 N7 Matlock Bath Derbyshire, England U.K.
215 L3 Matlwangtlwang S. Africa
203 G6 Matna Sudan
251 E3 Mato r. Venez.
251 E3 Mato, Cerro mt. Venez.
232 D11 Matoaka WV U.S.A.
213 F4 Matobo Hills Zimbabwe
213 F4 Matobo National Park Zimbabwe
253 F3 Mato Grosso Brazil
256 A2 Mato Grosso state Brazil
254 B5 Mato Grosso, Planalto do plat. Brazil
256 A4 Mato Grosso do Sul state Brazil
213 G5 Matola Moz.
213 G3 Matondo Moz.
211 B8 Matope Malawi
Matopo Hills Zimbabwe see Matobo Hills
Matoriki i. Fiji see Moturiki
216 □3b Matorral, Punta del pt Fuerteventura Canary Is
252 D3 Matos r. Bol.
182 C6 Matosinhos Port.
Matou Guangxi China see Pingguo
160 E4 Matour France
257 E3 Matozinhos Brazil
177 I4 Mátra mts Hungary
177 J4 Mátraballa Hungary
125 N4 Maţrah Oman
177 J4 Matrai park Hungary
142 I1 Matrand Norway
177 I3 Mátraterenye Hungary
177 I4 Mátraverebély Hungary
178 D5 Matrei am Brenner Austria
178 G5 Matrei in Osttirol Austria
214 D9 Matroosberg S. Africa
214 D9 Matroosberg mt. S. Africa
215 K1 Matrooster S. Africa
206 B5 Matru Sierra Leone
126 C8 Maţrūḥ governorate Egypt
147 I5 Matry Ireland
138 G3 Matsalu laht b. Estonia
138 G3 Matsalu riiklik looduskaitseala nature res. Estonia
214 G4 Matsap S. Africa
129 A2 Matsesta Rus. Fed.
213 □J4 Matsiatra r. Madag.
215 L5 Matsieng Lesotho
212 E4 Matsitama Botswana
211 F8 Matsoandakana Madag.
104 C6 Matsubara Japan
105 J5 Matsuda Japan
105 I1 Matsudai Japan
105 K4 Matsudo Japan
103 K11 Matsue Japan
105 I3 Matsuida Japan
105 G3 Matsukawa Nagano Japan
105 G4 Matsukawa Nagano Japan
102 R5 Matsumae Japan
105 G3 Matsumoto Japan
103 J13 Matsuno Japan
105 I1 Matsunoyama Japan
105 L4 Matsuo Japan
104 D3 Matsuoka Japan
104 E6 Matsusaka Japan
105 H2 Matsushiro Japan
109 M5 Matsu Tao i. Taiwan
103 G13 Matsuura Japan
103 J13 Matsuyama Japan
105 I6 Matsuzaki Japan
190 G2 Matt Switz.
224 D3 Mattagami r. Ont. Can.
157 L7 Mattaincourt France
261 E4 Mattaldi Arg.
231 I8 Mattamuskeet, Lake NC U.S.A.
224 E4 Mattawa Ont. Can.
233 □Q3 Mattawamkeag ME U.S.A.
190 D4 Matterhorn mt. Italy/Switz.
238 G6 Matterhorn mt. NV U.S.A.
179 N4 Mattersburg Austria
190 D3 Mattertal val. Switz.
Matthew atoll Gilbert Is Kiribati see Marakei
77 H4 Matthew Island S. Pacific Ocean
231 G8 Matthews NC U.S.A.
210 C4 Matthews Peak Kenya
251 F3 Matthews Ridge Guyana
246 G3 Matthew Town Gt Inagua Bahamas
125 K4 Maţţī, Sabkhat salt pan Saudi Arabia
178 H3 Mattighofen Austria
193 Q4 Mattinata Italy
151 O2 Mattishall Norfolk, England U.K.
235 J3 Mattituck NY U.S.A.
140 L5 Mattmar Sweden
104 E2 Mattō Japan
236 K6 Mattoon IL U.S.A.
178 H4 Mattsee Austria
178 H4 Mattsee l. Austria
141 M6 Mattsmyra Sweden
140 P4 Måttsund Sweden
Matturai Sri Lanka see Matara
95 I3 Matu Sarawak Malaysia
252 A2 Matucana Peru
114 G9 Matugama Sri Lanka
175 M1 Matuizos Lith.
79 □7 Matuku i. Fiji
191 Q5 Matulji Croatia
209 C8 Matumbo Angola
Matun Afgh. see Khowst
247 □7 Matura Trin. and Tob.
247 □7 Matura Bay Trin. and Tob.
251 F2 Maturín Venez.
251 F3 Maturuca Brazil
213 F3 Matusadona National Park Zimbabwe
183 P5 Matute mt. Spain
257 E3 Matutina Brazil
93 D1 Matutuang i. Indon.
92 E8 Matutum, Mount vol. Phil.
134 L1 Matveyev, Ostrov i. Rus. Fed.
120 E1 Matveyevka Rus. Fed.
137 R6 Matveyev Kurgan Rus. Fed.
137 K6 Matviyivka Mykolayivs'ka Oblast' Ukr.
137 O6 Matviyivka Zaporiz'ka Oblast' Ukr.
215 L4 Matwabeng S. Africa
183 O2 Matxitxako, Cabo c. Spain
Maty Island P.N.G. see Wuvulu Island
137 S1 Matyra r. Rus. Fed.
139 W9 Matyrskiy Rus. Fed.
139 W9 Matyrskoye Vodokhranilishche resr Rus. Fed.
138 L6 Matyryna Belarus
135 I6 Matyshevo Rus. Fed.
116 G6 Mau Madh. Prad. India
116 H7 Mau Uttar Prad. India
213 H2 Maúa Moz.
116 H7 Mau Aimma Uttar Prad. India
186 G2 Maubermé, Pic de mt. France/Spain
156 H4 Maubert-Fontaine France
156 G3 Maubeuge France
115 N4 Maubin Myanmar
96 C2 Ma-ubin Myanmar
163 E9 Maubourguet France
162 B5 Maubuisson France
146 H11 Mauchline East Ayrshire, Scotland U.K.
146 L7 Maud Aberdeenshire, Scotland U.K.
87 B7 Maud, Point W.A. Austr.
116 H7 Maudaha Uttar Prad. India
83 J6 Maude N.S.W. Austr.
264 J10 Maud Seamount sea feature S. Atlantic Ocean
Mau-é-ele Moz. see Marão
179 N3 Mauerbach Austria
178 H3 Mauerkirchen Austria
173 L4 Mauern Ger.
173 J6 Mauerstetten Ger.
251 G5 Maués Brazil
251 G5 Maués r. Brazil
Mauga Afi mt. Samoa see Afi, Mount
116 H7 Mauganj Madh. Prad. India
148 I5 Maughold Isle of Man
148 I5 Maughold Head Isle of Man
91 K2 Maug Islands N. Mariana Is
161 E9 Mauguio France
240 □E13 Maui i. HI U.S.A.
81 □2 Mauke i. Cook Is
96 B3 Maukkadaw Myanmar
172 F4 Maulbronn Ger.
157 O8 Maulburg Ger.
162 H4 Maulde r. France
151 L3 Maulden Bedfordshire, England U.K.
260 B4 Maule Chile
260 A4 Maule admin. reg. Chile

260 A4 **Maule** *r.* Chile
260 B5 **Maule, Lago del** *l.* Chile
162 C2 **Mauléon** France
163 F10 **Mauléon-Barousse** France
163 D8 **Mauléon-d'Armagnac** France
163 C9 **Mauléon-Licharre** France
159 J7 **Maulévrier** France
259 B6 **Maullín** Chile
147 D4 **Maumakeogh** *hill* Ireland
80 J4 **Maumaupaki** *hill North I.* N.Z.
232 B7 **Maumee** *OH* U.S.A.
232 B7 **Maumee** *r. OH* U.S.A.
232 B7 **Maumee Bay** *MI/OH* U.S.A.
93 C8 **Maumere** *Flores* Indon.
147 C5 **Maumturk Mountains** *hills* Ireland
212 D3 **Maun** Botswana
247 □1 **Maunabo** Puerto Rico
240 □F14 **Mauna Kea** *vol. HI* U.S.A.
240 □D12 **Mauna Loa** *HI* U.S.A.
240 □F14 **Mauna Loa** *vol. HI* U.S.A.
240 □D12 **Maunalua Bay** *HI* U.S.A.
117 I7 **Maunath Bhanjan** *Uttar Prad.* India
213 E4 **Maunatlala** Botswana
116 G9 **Maunda** *Mahar.* India
80 K6 **Maungaharuru Range** *mts North I.* N.Z.
80 L5 **Maungahaumi** *mt. North I.* N.Z.
80 L5 **Maungapohatu** *mt. North I.* N.Z.
80 I6 **Maungarau** *hill North I.* N.Z.
80 K5 **Maungataniwha** *mt. North I.* N.Z.
80 I2 **Maungatapere** *North I.* N.Z.
80 I3 **Maungaturoto** *North I.* N.Z.
96 A4 **Maungdaw** Myanmar
97 C7 **Maungmagan Islands** Myanmar
97 D7 **Maungmagon** Myanmar
220 F3 **Maunoir, Lac** *l. N.W.T.* Can.
79 □9 **Maupihaa** *atoll Arch. de la Société* Fr. Polynesia
238 D4 **Maupin** *OR* U.S.A.
142 G1 **Maura** Norway
116 G7 **Mau Ranipur** *Uttar Prad.* India
116 H6 **Maurawan** *Uttar Prad.* India
161 I8 **Maure, Col de** *pass* France
158 H6 **Maure-de-Bretagne** France
163 J11 **Maureillas-las-Illas** France
162 E6 **Maurens** France
237 J10 **Maurepas, Lake** *LA* U.S.A.
161 I10 **Maures, Massif des** *hills* France
252 C4 **Mauri** *r.* Bol.
163 D6 **Mauriac** *Aquitaine* France
162 I5 **Mauriac** *Auvergne* France
Maurice *country* Indian Ocean *see* **Mauritius**
234 E6 **Maurice** *r. NJ* U.S.A.
82 C3 **Maurice, Lake** *salt flat S.A.* Austr.
234 F6 **Mauricetown** *NJ* U.S.A.
161 I6 **Maurienne** *reg.* France
164 H5 **Maurik** Neth.
204 C6 **Mauritania** *country* Africa
Mauritanie *country* Africa *see* Mauritania
217 □1b **Mauritius** *country* Indian Ocean
193 N4 **Mauro, Monte** *mt.* Italy
158 G5 **Mauron** France
163 G7 **Mauroux** France
163 I6 **Maurs** France
163 J10 **Maury** France
234 B3 **Mausdale** *PA* U.S.A.
161 F9 **Maussanne-les-Alpilles** France
226 D6 **Mauston** *WI* U.S.A.
174 F1 **Mausz, Jezioro** *l.* Pol.
179 M3 **Mautern an der Donau** Austria
179 I5 **Mauterndorf** Austria
179 K5 **Mautern in Steiermark** Austria
173 P4 **Mauth** Ger.
179 K3 **Mauthausen** Austria
178 H6 **Mauthen** Austria
Mauti *i.* Cook Is *see* **Mauke**
157 K6 **Mauvages** France
161 F6 **Mauves** France
163 F8 **Mauvezin** France
190 C3 **Mauvoisin** Switz.
162 C3 **Mauzé-sur-le-Mignon** France
208 E4 **Mava** Dem. Rep. Congo
251 E4 **Mavaca** *r.* Venez.
211 C8 **Mavago** Moz.
77 I3 **Mavana** Fiji
213 G4 **Mavanza** Moz.
140 N3 **Mavasjaure** *l.* Sweden
209 C9 **Mavengue** Angola
199 L6 **Mavikent** Turkey
209 D8 **Mavinga** Angola
246 □ **Mavis Bank** Jamaica
232 C11 **Mavisdale** *VA* U.S.A.
146 □N2 **Mavis Grind** *isth. Scotland* U.K.
213 G3 **Mavita** Moz.
193 L2 **Mavone** *r.* Italy
199 H6 **Mavria** *i.* Greece
198 C2 **Mavrodendri** Greece
199 G6 **Mavropetra, Akrotirio** *pt* Greece
198 E2 **Mavrothalassa** Greece
196 I9 **Mavrovo** *nat. park* Macedonia
213 G4 **Mavume** Moz.
215 L7 **Mavuya** S. Africa
95 J4 **Mawa, Bukit** *mt.* Indon.
109 □J7 **Ma Wan** *i. H.K.* China
124 H4 **Māwān, Khashm** *hill* Saudi Arabia
116 F5 **Mawana** *Uttar Prad.* India
209 C6 **Mawanga** Dem. Rep. Congo
93 C6 **Mawasangka** *Sulawesi* Indon.
96 C5 **Mawchi** Myanmar
97 D9 **Mawdaung Pass** Myanmar/Thai.
109 L5 **Mawei** *Fujian* China
80 M5 **Mawhai Point** *North I.* N.Z.
81 F9 **Mawheraiti** *South I.* N.Z.
Māwheranui *r. South I.* N.Z. *see* **Grey**
96 C2 **Mawhun** Myanmar
124 G9 **Māwiyah** Yemen
128 D7 **Mawjib, Wādī al** *r.* Jordan
96 D6 **Mawkhi** Myanmar
96 C4 **Mawkmai** Myanmar
96 B3 **Mawlaik** Myanmar
96 C6 **Mawlamyaing** Myanmar
96 B6 **Mawlamyainggyun** Myanmar
Mawlamyine Myanmar *see* Mawlamyaing
150 B7 **Mawnan** *Cornwall, England* U.K.
117 M7 **Mawphlang** *Meghalaya* India
124 E2 **Mawqaq** Saudi Arabia
203 I6 **Mawshij** Yemen
263 E2 **Mawson** *research stn* Antarctica
263 E2 **Mawson Coast** Antarctica
263 E2 **Mawson Escarpment** Antarctica
263 K2 **Mawson Peninsula** Antarctica
97 D9 **Maw Taung** *mt.* Myanmar
124 F9 **Mawza** Yemen
236 E2 **Max** *ND* U.S.A.
210 E3 **Maxaas** Somalia
258 D3 **Maxán** Arg.
234 D3 **Maxatawny** *PA* U.S.A.
243 O7 **Maxcanú** Mex.
158 G6 **Maxent** France
222 F3 **Maxhamish Lake** *B.C.* Can.
173 M3 **Maxhütte-Haidhof** Ger.
192 B9 **Maxia, Punta** *mt. Sardegna* Italy
182 E9 **Maxieira** Port.
261 G3 **Máximo Paz** Arg.
197 P5 **Măxineni** Romania
213 G4 **Maxixe** Moz.
140 Q5 **Maxmo** Fin.
169 E9 **Maxsain** Ger.
233 K3 **Maxville** *Ont.* Can.
80 I6 **Maxwell** *North I.* N.Z.
85 I6 **Maxwelton** *Qld* Austr.
86 G4 **May** *r. W.A.* Austr.
146 K10 **May, Isle of** *i. Scotland* U.K.
208 C3 **Maya** Chad
108 D2 **Maya** *Gansu* China
95 H5 **Maya** *i.* Indon.
131 O3 **Maya** *r.* Rus. Fed.
137 N4 **Mayachka** Ukr.
135 K5 **Mayachnyy** Rus. Fed.
246 G2 **Mayaguana** *i.* Bahamas
246 G2 **Mayaguana Passage** Bahamas
247 □1 **Mayagüez** Puerto Rico
247 □1 **Mayagüez, Bahía de** *b.* Puerto Rico
207 G3 **Mayahi** Niger
100 J4 **Mayak** Rus. Fed.
120 F2 **Mayak** Rus. Fed.
Mayakovskiy Georgia *see* Baghdat'i
123 N3 **Mayakovskiy, Qullai** *mt.* Tajik.
Mayakovskogo, Pik *mt.* Tajik. *see* **Mayakovskiy, Qullai**
175 K1 **Mayakovskoye** Rus. Fed.
121 M6 **Mayakum** Kazakh.
136 H5 **Mayaky** Ukr.
209 C6 **Mayala** Dem. Rep. Congo
93 G4 **Mayalibit, Teluk** *b. Papua* Indon.
Mayals Spain *see* **Maials**
209 B5 **Mayama** Congo
209 C6 **Mayamba** Dem. Rep. Congo
122 F3 **Mayamey** Iran
243 O9 **Maya Mountains** Belize/Guat.
Mayan *Gansu* China *see* Mayanhe
108 G5 **Mayang** *Hunan* China
106 I9 **Mayanhe** *Gansu* China
Mayaqum Kazakh. *see* Mayakum
146 J9 **Mayar** *hill Scotland* U.K.
246 F3 **Mayarí** Cuba
247 □7 **Mayaro** *county* Trin. and Tob.
247 □7 **Mayaro Bay** Trin. and Tob.
104 B6 **Maya-san** *hill* Japan
102 Q8 **Maya-san** *mt.* Japan
238 J6 **Maybell** *CO* U.S.A.
232 D11 **Maybeury** *WV* U.S.A.
146 G12 **Maybole** *South Ayrshire, Scotland* U.K.
235 G2 **Maybrook** *NY* U.S.A.
210 C1 **Maych'ew** Eth.
246 □ **May Day Mountains** *hills* Jamaica
83 K10 **Maydena** *Tas.* Austr.
210 E2 **Maydh** Somalia
Maydos Turkey *see* **Eceabat**
169 D10 **Mayen** Ger.
159 J5 **Mayenne** France
159 J5 **Mayenne** *dept* France
159 J7 **Mayenne** *r.* France
241 T7 **Mayer** *AZ* U.S.A.
111 H10 **Mayêr Kangri** *mt. Xizang* China
237 J9 **Mayersville** *MS* U.S.A.
222 H4 **Mayerthorpe** *Alta* Can.
159 L6 **Mayet** France
125 H8 **Mayfa'ah** Yemen
81 F10 **Mayfield** *South I.* N.Z.
149 N7 **Mayfield** *Staffordshire, England* U.K.
237 K7 **Mayfield** *KY* U.S.A.
234 D1 **Mayfield** *PA* U.S.A.
241 U2 **Mayfield** *UT* U.S.A.
106 H3 **Mayhan** Mongolia
239 L10 **Mayhill** *NM* U.S.A.
100 F6 **Mayi He** *r.* China
121 P2 **Maykain** Kazakh.
121 Q4 **Maykamys** Kazakh.
123 M2 **Maykhura** Tajik.
129 B1 **Maykop** Rus. Fed.
134 K4 **Maykor** Rus. Fed.
Maylibash Kazakh. *see* Maylybas
121 O7 **Mayluu-Suu** Kyrg.
120 J5 **Maylybas** Kazakh.
Mayly-Say Kyrg. *see* Mayluu-Suu
121 U1 **Mayma** Rus. Fed.
121 N6 **Maymak** Kazakh.
244 B1 **Maymorita** Mex.
98 F1 **Mayna** *Respublika Khakasiya* Rus. Fed.
135 I5 **Mayna** *Ul'yanovskaya Oblast'* Rus. Fed.
231 F7 **Maynardville** *TN* U.S.A.
85 H7 **Mayne** *watercourse Qld* Austr.
114 D4 **Mayni** *Mahar.* India
227 Q4 **Maynooth** *Ont.* Can.
147 I6 **Maynooth** Ireland
222 C2 **Mayo** *Y.T.* Can.
239 J13 **Mayo** *r.* Mex.
252 A1 **Mayo** *r.* Peru
147 D5 **Mayo** Ireland
147 D5 **Mayo** *county* Ireland
231 F10 **Mayo** *FL* U.S.A.
234 B7 **Mayo** *MD* U.S.A.
207 I4 **Mayo Alim** Cameroon
207 I4 **Mayo-Belwa** Nigeria
147 J4 **Mayobridge** *Northern Ireland* U.K.
207 H5 **Mayo Darlé** Cameroon
208 B2 **Mayo-Kebbi** *pref.* Chad
208 B5 **Mayoko** Congo
208 D5 **Mayoko** Dem. Rep. Congo
222 C2 **Mayo Lake** *Y.T.* Can.
Mayo Landing *Y.T.* Can. *see* Mayo
208 B3 **Mayo Lara** C.A.R.
92 D5 **Mayon** *vol. Luzon* Phil.
183 O8 **Mayor** *r.* Spain
183 Q4 **Mayor** *r.* Spain
183 M2 **Mayor, Cabo** *c.* Spain
Mayor, Puig *mt.* Spain *see* Major, Puig
261 F6 **Mayor Buratovich** Arg.
183 J4 **Mayorga** Spain
80 K4 **Mayor Island** *North I.* N.Z.
253 E4 **Mayor Pablo Lagerenza** Para.
217 □3b **Mayotte** *terr.* Africa
246 □ **May Pen** Jamaica
Mayqayyng Kazakh. *see* Maykain
92 C2 **Mayraira Point** *Luzon* Phil.
247 □3 **Mayreau** *i.* St Vincent
161 E7 **Mayres** France
163 H9 **Mayreville** France
178 E5 **Mayrhofen** Austria
128 D7 **Maysah, Tall al** *mt.* Jordan
127 M8 **Maysān** *governorate* Iraq
169 D9 **Mayschoss** Ger.
175 I1 **Mayskaya** *r.* Rus. Fed.
137 N8 **Mays'ke** Ukr.
100 F2 **Mayskiy** *Amurskaya Oblast'* Rus. Fed.
137 P3 **Mayskiy** *Belgorodskaya Oblast'* Rus. Fed.
129 F2 **Mayskiy** *Kabardino-Balkarskaya Respublika* Rus. Fed.
134 K4 **Mayskiy** *Permskaya Oblast'* Rus. Fed.
137 T6 **Mayskiy** *Rostovskaya Oblast'* Rus. Fed.
121 R2 **Mayskoye** Kazakh.
234 F6 **Mays Landing** *NJ* U.S.A.
223 J3 **Mayson Lake** *Sask.* Can.
232 B10 **Maysville** *KY* U.S.A.
236 H6 **Maysville** *MO* U.S.A.
Maytag *Xinjiang* China *see* **Dushanzi**
93 E3 **Mayu** *i. Maluku* Indon.
96 A4 **Mayu** *r.* Myanmar
210 B4 **Mayuge** Uganda
209 A5 **Mayumba** Gabon
111 F11 **Mayum La** *pass Xizang* China
114 F7 **Mayuram** *Tamil Nadu* India
227 K6 **Mayville** *MI* U.S.A.
236 G2 **Mayville** *ND* U.S.A.
232 F6 **Mayville** *NY* U.S.A.
236 E5 **Maywood** *NE* U.S.A.
131 O3 **Mayya** Rus. Fed.
261 F5 **Maza** Arg.
139 T2 **Maza** Rus. Fed.
209 E8 **Mazabuka** Zambia
Mazaca Turkey *see* **Kayseri**
Mazagan Morocco *see* El Jadida
251 I5 **Mazagão** Brazil
251 I5 **Mazagão Velho** Brazil
184 F6 **Mazagón** Spain
156 I5 **Mazagran** France
138 H5 **Maza Jugla** *r.* Latvia
186 F5 **Mazaleón** Spain
163 I9 **Mazamet** France
244 D6 **Mazamitla** Mex.
161 G8 **Mazan** France
250 C5 **Mazán** Peru
122 D3 **Māzandarān** *prov.* Iran
161 E7 **Mazan-l'Abbaye** France
209 D7 **Mazao** Dem. Rep. Congo
244 F1 **Mazapil** Mex.
111 C8 **Mazar** *Xinjiang* China
128 D7 **Mazār** Jordan
125 N4 **Mazāra** Oman
194 D8 **Mazara, Val di** *reg. Sicilia* Italy
194 D8 **Mazara del Vallo** *Sicilia* Italy
183 L9 **Mazarambroz** Spain
123 L3 **Mazār-e Sharīf** Afgh.
183 P7 **Mazarete** Spain
194 D8 **Mazaro** *r. Sicilia* Italy
259 D7 **Mazarredo** Arg.
187 C12 **Mazarrón** Spain
187 C13 **Mazarrón, Golfo de** *b.* Spain
110 E7 **Mazartag** *Xinjiang* China
110 D7 **Mazartag** *mt. Xinjiang* China
251 G3 **Mazaruni** *r.* Guyana
242 D3 **Mazatán** Mex.
245 K7 **Mazateca, Sierra** *mts* Mex.
243 N10 **Mazatenango** Guat.
244 A2 **Mazatlán** Mex.
241 U7 **Mazatzal Peak** *AZ* U.S.A.
122 G8 **Mazāvī** *watercourse* Iran
159 K7 **Mazé** France
104 F4 **Maze** Japan
104 F4 **Maze-gawa** *r.* Japan
138 F5 **Mažeikiai** Lith.
207 H2 **Mazelet** *well* Niger
234 B3 **Mazeppa** *PA* U.S.A.
215 M8 **Mazeppa Bay** S. Africa
211 C5 **Mazeras** Kenya
163 H9 **Mazères** France
163 D9 **Mazerolles** France
161 E6 **Mazet-St-Voy** France
163 G6 **Mazeyrolles** France
129 A6 **Mazgirt** Turkey
124 F2 **Maẕhūr, 'Irq al** *des.* Saudi Arabia
199 I5 **Mazı** Turkey
138 K5 **Mazīča** *r.* Latvia
232 C10 **Mazie** *KY* U.S.A.
162 D2 **Mazières-en-Gâtine** France
125 M4 **Mazīm** Oman
209 C6 **Mazinda** Dem. Rep. Congo
138 F4 **Mazirbe** Latvia
216 □3d **Mazo** *La Palma* Canary Is
242 D3 **Mazocahui** Mex.
252 C4 **Mazocruz** Peru
Mazoe Zimbabwe *see* **Mazowe**
226 E6 **Mazomanie** *WI* U.S.A.
209 E6 **Mazomeno** Dem. Rep. Congo
211 C6 **Mazomora** Tanz.
106 E6 **Mazong Shan** *mt. Gansu* China
106 D6 **Mazong Shan** *mts* China
183 M3 **Mazorra, Puerto de la** *pass* Spain
213 F3 **Mazowe** Zimbabwe
213 G3 **Mazowe** *r.* Zimbabwe
175 I3 **Mazowiecka, Nizina** *reg.* Pol.
175 I4 **Mazowiecka, Nizina** *reg.* Pol.
175 J3 **Mazowieckie** *prov.* Pol.
136 A1 **Mazowiecki Park Krajobrazowy** Pol.
122 C3 **Mazr'eh** Iran
203 F6 **Mazrub** *well* Sudan
138 I4 **Mazsalaca** Latvia
122 C5 **Māzū** Iran
213 F4 **Mazunga** Zimbabwe
175 I2 **Mazurskie, Pojezierze** *reg.* Pol.
167 J2 **Mazurski Park Krajobrazowy** Pol.
175 J1 **Mazurskiy Kanal** *canal* Pol./Rus. Fed.
136 I1 **Mazyr** Belarus
136 I1 **Mazyrskaye Hrada** *ridge* Belarus
190 I4 **Mazzano** Italy
193 I3 **Mazzano Romano** Italy
194 G9 **Mazzarino** *Sicilia* Italy
194 H9 **Mazzarrone** *Sicilia* Italy
178 B7 **Mazzo di Valtellina** Italy
205 H2 **Mazzouna** Tunisia
207 H5 **Mba** Cameroon
Mba *Viti Levu* Fiji *see* **Ba**
215 P2 **Mbabane** Swaziland
206 B3 **Mbacké** Senegal
208 C4 **Mbaéré** *r.* C.A.R.
206 B2 **Mbagne** Maur.
206 D5 **Mbahiakro** Côte d'Ivoire
208 C4 **Mbaïki** C.A.R.
207 I5 **Mbakaou** Cameroon
207 I5 **Mbakaou, Lac de** *l.* Cameroon
209 C5 **Mbala** Dem. Rep. Congo
211 A7 **Mbala** Zambia
213 F4 **Mbalabala** Zimbabwe
207 I6 **Mbalam** Cameroon
210 B4 **Mbale** Uganda
207 H6 **Mbalmayo** Cameroon
78 □6 **Mbalo** *Guadalcanal* Solomon Is
207 H5 **Mbam** *r.* Cameroon
207 I7 **Mbama** Congo
211 B7 **Mbamba Bay** Tanz.
208 C5 **Mbandaka** Dem. Rep. Congo
207 H5 **Mbandjok** Cameroon
208 B4 **Mbandza** Congo
207 I5 **Mbang** *Adamaoua* Cameroon
207 I6 **Mbang** *Est* Cameroon
207 H5 **Mbanga** Cameroon
78 □6 **Mbanika** *i.* Solomon Is
209 B6 **M'banza Congo** Angola
209 B6 **Mbanza-Ngungu** Dem. Rep. Congo
206 B3 **Mbar** Senegal
211 C7 **Mbarangandu** Tanz.
210 A5 **Mbarara** Uganda
208 D3 **Mbari** *r.* C.A.R.
211 C7 **Mbarika Mountains** Tanz.
215 Q3 **Mbaswana** S. Africa
208 C4 **Mbata** C.A.R.
211 A7 **Mbati** Zambia
Mbatiki *i.* Fiji *see* **Batiki**
Mbau *i.* Fiji *see* **Bau**
78 □6 **Mbava** *i. New Georgia Is* Solomon Is
207 I5 **Mbé** Cameroon
209 B5 **Mbé** Congo
211 B8 **Mbemba** Moz.
213 F3 **Mbembesi** Zimbabwe
211 C7 **Mbemkuru** *r.* Tanz.
Mbengga *i.* Fiji *see* **Beqa**
207 H5 **Mbengwi** Cameroon
217 □3a **Mbéni** *Njazidja* Comoros
206 D4 **Mbenqué** Côte d'Ivoire
213 F4 **Mberengwa** Zimbabwe
209 F7 **Mbereshi** Zambia
211 B7 **Mbeya** Tanz.
211 B7 **Mbeya** *admin. reg.* Tanz.
207 I5 **Mbi** *r.* Cameroon
208 C3 **Mbi** *r.* C.A.R.
208 A5 **Mbigou** Gabon
208 A5 **Mbilapé** Gabon
208 F3 **Mbili** Sudan
196 H8 **Mbilqethit, Maja e** *mt.* Albania
208 B5 **Mbinda** Congo
211 B7 **Mbinga** Tanz.
207 H6 **Mbini** Equat. Guinea
207 H6 **Mbini** *r.* Equat. Guinea
78 □6 **Mbita'ama** *Malaita* Solomon Is
208 D3 **Mbiyi** C.A.R.
213 F4 **Mbizi** Zimbabwe
211 A7 **Mbizi Mountains** Tanz.
208 C2 **Mbo** C.A.R.
208 E3 **Mboki** C.A.R.
208 D3 **Mboli** Dem. Rep. Congo
Mbolompo Point S. Africa *see* **Mncwasa Point**
208 B4 **Mbomo** Congo
208 D3 **Mbomou** *pref.* C.A.R.
208 D3 **Mbomou** *r.* C.A.R./Dem. Rep. Congo
208 B5 **Mbon** Congo
206 A3 **Mboro** Senegal
78 □6 **Mborokua** *i.* Solomon Is
207 H5 **Mbouda** Cameroon
206 B3 **Mboun** Senegal
206 A3 **Mbour** Senegal
206 B2 **Mbout** Maur.
209 E8 **Mbowela** Zambia
211 B7 **Mbozi** Tanz.
208 C3 **Mbrès** C.A.R.
198 A2 **Mbrostar** Albania
Mbua *Vanua Levu* Fiji *see* **Bua**
209 D6 **Mbuji-Mayi** Dem. Rep. Congo
78 □6 **Mbulo** *i. New Georgia Is* Solomon Is
211 B5 **Mbulu** Tanz.
215 P2 **Mbuluzana** *r.* Swaziland
215 Q2 **Mbuluzi** *r.* Swaziland
211 B7 **Mbura** Tanz.
258 F3 **Mburucuyá** Arg.
78 □6 **Mburuku** *New Georgia Is* Solomon Is
Mbutha *Vanua Levu* Fiji *see* Buca
215 P2 **Mbutini Hills** Swaziland
211 C6 **Mbuyuni** Tanz.
211 C6 **Mbwewe** Tanz.
225 H4 **McAdam** *N.B.* Can.
234 D3 **McAdoo** *PA* U.S.A.
234 F2 **McAfee** *NJ* U.S.A.
237 H8 **McAlester** *OK* U.S.A.
234 A3 **McAlisterville** *PA* U.S.A.
237 F12 **McAllen** *TX* U.S.A.
226 G4 **McAllister** *WI* U.S.A.
84 F3 **McArthur** *r. N.T.* Austr.
232 C9 **McArthur** *OH* U.S.A.
227 Q4 **McArthur Mills** *Ont.* Can.
222 C2 **McArthur Wildlife Sanctuary** *nature res. Y.T.* Can.
226 I5 **McBain** *MI* U.S.A.
222 F4 **McBride** *B.C.* Can.
238 F4 **McCall** *ID* U.S.A.
237 D10 **McCamey** *TX* U.S.A.
238 H5 **McCammon** *ID* U.S.A.
223 J2 **McCann Lake** *N.W.T.* Can.
226 F4 **McCaslin Mountain** *hill WI* U.S.A.
222 D4 **McCauley Island** *B.C.* Can.
263 K1 **McClintock, Mount** Antarctica
221 H2 **McClintock Channel** *Nunavut* Can.
86 I5 **McClintock Range** *hills W.A.* Austr.
84 D1 **McCluer Island** *N.T.* Austr.
232 B7 **McClure** *OH* U.S.A.
232 H8 **McClure** *PA* U.S.A.
240 L4 **McClure, Lake** *CA* U.S.A.
220 G2 **McClure Strait** *N.W.T.* Can.
236 E2 **McClusky** *ND* U.S.A.
237 J10 **McComb** *MS* U.S.A.
232 B7 **McComb** *OH* U.S.A.
236 E5 **McConaughy, Lake** *NE* U.S.A.
232 H9 **McConnellsburg** *PA* U.S.A.
232 D9 **McConnelsville** *OH* U.S.A.
236 E5 **McCook** *NE* U.S.A.
231 F9 **McCormick** *SC* U.S.A.
232 E11 **McCoy** *VA* U.S.A.
222 H2 **McCrea** *r. N.W.T.* Can.
223 L5 **McCreary** *Man.* Can.
241 Q6 **McCullough Range** *mts NV* U.S.A.
232 B8 **McCutchenville** *OH* U.S.A.
222 D3 **McDame** *B.C.* Can.
238 F6 **McDermitt** *NV* U.S.A.
232 B10 **McDermott** *OH* U.S.A.
265 I8 **McDonald Islands** Indian Ocean
238 H3 **McDonald Peak** *MT* U.S.A.
82 G3 **McDonnell Creek** *watercourse S.A.* Austr.
231 E9 **McDonough** *GA* U.S.A.
84 E5 **McDouall Range** *hills N.T.* Austr.
214 A5 **McDougall's Bay** S. Africa
241 U8 **McDowell Peak** *AZ* U.S.A.
234 B2 **McEwensville** *PA* U.S.A.
240 M6 **McFarland** *CA* U.S.A.
226 E6 **McFarland** *WI* U.S.A.
223 J3 **McFarlane** *r. Sask.* Can.
81 D10 **McFarlane, Mount** *South I.* N.Z.
241 R2 **McGill** *NV* U.S.A.
225 H4 **McGivney** *N.B.* Can.
220 C3 **McGrath** *AK* U.S.A.
226 A3 **McGrath** *MN* U.S.A.
222 F4 **McGregor** *r. B.C.* Can.
214 D9 **McGregor** S. Africa
226 A3 **McGregor** *MN* U.S.A.
222 H5 **McGregor, Lake** *Alta* Can.
227 M3 **McGregor Bay** *Ont.* Can.
85 I9 **McGregor Range** *hills Qld* Austr.
238 G4 **McGuire, Mount** *ID* U.S.A.
129 F3 **Mchadijvari** Georgia
204 D4 **Mcherrah** *reg.* Alg.
211 C7 **Mchinga** Tanz.
211 B8 **Mchinji** Malawi
85 I3 **McIlwraith Range** *hills Qld* Austr.
223 M4 **McInnes Lake** *Ont.* Can.
236 E3 **McIntosh** *SD* U.S.A.
86 G7 **McKay Range** *hills W.A.* Austr.
77 I2 **McKean** *i. Phoenix Is* Kiribati
232 A11 **McKee** *KY* U.S.A.
234 F6 **McKee** *NJ* U.S.A.
232 F8 **McKeesport** *PA* U.S.A.
232 E8 **McKees Rocks** *PA* U.S.A.
232 H12 **McKenney** *VA* U.S.A.
237 K7 **McKenzie** *TN* U.S.A.
238 C4 **McKenzie** *r. OR* U.S.A.
81 C11 **McKerrow, Lake** *South I.* N.Z.
85 H6 **McKinlay** *Qld* Austr.
85 H6 **McKinlay** *r. Qld* Austr.
220 C3 **McKinley, Mount** *AK* U.S.A.
237 G9 **McKinney** *TX* U.S.A.
240 M6 **McKittrick** *CA* U.S.A.
236 E3 **McLaughlin** *SD* U.S.A.
226 E9 **McLean** *IL* U.S.A.
234 A7 **McLean** *VA* U.S.A.
236 K6 **McLeansboro** *IL* U.S.A.
222 G4 **McLennan** *Alta* Can.
222 H4 **McLeod** *r. Alta* Can.
223 I2 **McLeod Bay** *N.W.T.* Can.
222 F4 **McLeod Lake** *B.C.* Can.
97 D9 **McLeod's Island** Myanmar
86 □1 **McMicken Point** Christmas I.
84 D8 **McMinns Creek** *watercourse N.T.* Austr.
238 C4 **McMinnville** *OR* U.S.A.
231 E8 **McMinnville** *TN* U.S.A.
263 L1 **McMurdo** *research stn* Antarctica
263 L1 **McMurdo Sound** *b.* Antarctica
241 W7 **McNary** *AZ* U.S.A.
226 E4 **McNaughton** *WI* U.S.A.
McNaughton Lake *B.C.* Can. *see* **Kinbasket Lake**
241 W10 **McNeal** *AZ* U.S.A.
225 H2 **McPhadyen** *r. Nfld and Lab.* Can.
236 G6 **McPherson** *KS* U.S.A.
83 N3 **McPherson Range** *mts N.S.W.* Austr.
222 B2 **McQuesten** *r. Y.T.* Can.
231 F9 **McRae** *GA* U.S.A.
232 C11 **McRoberts** *KY* U.S.A.
234 A5 **McSherrystown** *PA* U.S.A.
147 E3 **McSwynes Bay** Ireland
220 G3 **McTavish Arm** *b. N.W.T.* Can.
232 H8 **McVeytown** *PA* U.S.A.
222 F1 **McVicar Arm** *b. N.W.T.* Can.
232 E9 **McWhorter** *WV* U.S.A.
139 P3 **Mda** *r.* Rus. Fed.
215 L8 **Mdantsane** S. Africa
205 G1 **M'Daourouch** Alg.
217 □3a **Mde** *Njazidja* Comoros
195 □ **Mdina** Malta
180 D5 **Mdiq** Morocco
97 I8 **M'Đrak** Vietnam
96 G5 **Mê, Hon** *i.* Vietnam
241 R5 **Mead, Lake** *resr NV* U.S.A.
235 H2 **Mead Corners** *NY* U.S.A.
237 E7 **Meade** *KS* U.S.A.
220 C2 **Meade** *r. AK* U.S.A.
87 C9 **Meadow** *W.A.* Austr.
236 D3 **Meadow** *SD* U.S.A.
241 T3 **Meadow** *UT* U.S.A.
232 E11 **Meadow Bridge** *WV* U.S.A.
223 I4 **Meadow Lake** *Sask.* Can.
223 I4 **Meadow Lake Provincial Park** *Sask.* Can.
241 R5 **Meadow Valley Wash** *r. NV* U.S.A.
232 D12 **Meadowview** *VA* U.S.A.
237 J10 **Meadville** *MS* U.S.A.
232 E7 **Meadville** *PA* U.S.A.
227 N5 **Meaford** *Ont.* Can.
102 V3 **Meaken-dake** *vol.* Japan
146 B6 **Mealasta Island** *Scotland* U.K.
146 G8 **Meal Fuar-mhonaidh** *hill Scotland* U.K.
182 D8 **Mealhada** Port.
146 B6 **Mealisval** *hill Scotland* U.K.
146 H9 **Meall Chuaich** *hill Scotland* U.K.
146 G8 **Meall Dubh** *hill Scotland* U.K.
149 K4 **Mealsgate** *Cumbria, England* U.K.
225 J2 **Mealy Mountains** *Nfld and Lab.* Can.
192 C8 **Meana Sardo** *Sardegna* Italy
85 L9 **Meandarra** *Qld* Austr.
222 G3 **Meander River** *Alta* Can.
150 G5 **Meare** *Somerset, England* U.K.
93 D1 **Meares** *i.* Indon.
151 I2 **Mease** *r. England* U.K.
151 I2 **Measham** *Leicestershire, England* U.K.
147 I5 **Meath** *county* Ireland
161 H6 **Méaudre, Roche de** *mt.* France
160 B3 **Meaulne** France
156 E4 **Méaulte** France
156 E6 **Meaux** France
163 G7 **Meauzac** France
209 B6 **Mebridege** *r.* Angola
117 O5 **Mebu** *Arun. Prad.* India
95 K9 **Mebulu, Tanjung** *pt* Indon.
213 G2 **Mecanhelas** Moz.
244 B4 **Mecatán** Mex.
Mecca Saudi Arabia *see* Makkah
241 P8 **Mecca** *CA* U.S.A.
232 E7 **Mecca** *OH* U.S.A.
233 □O4 **Mechanic Falls** *ME* U.S.A.
232 B8 **Mechanicsburg** *OH* U.S.A.
234 A4 **Mechanicsburg** *PA* U.S.A.
232 E11 **Mechanicsburg** *VA* U.S.A.
232 H11 **Mechanicsville** *VA* U.S.A.
233 L6 **Mechanicville** *NY* U.S.A.
210 D2 **Mechāra** Eth.
165 F6 **Mechelen** Belgium
165 I7 **Mechelen** Neth.
Mecherchar *i.* Palau *see* **Eil Malk**
205 E2 **Mecheria** Alg.
169 C9 **Mechernich** Ger.
135 H7 **Mechetinskaya** Rus. Fed.
202 B6 **Mechiméré** Chad
261 G4 **Mechita** Arg.
197 N8 **Mechka** *r.* Bulg.
261 H6 **Mechongue** Arg.
174 D2 **Mechowo** Pol.
168 J4 **Mechtersen** Ger.
169 K9 **Mechterstädt** Ger.
199 H2 **Mecidiye** *Edirne* Turkey
199 I4 **Mecidiye** *Manisa* Turkey
176 C2 **Měčín** Czech Rep.
185 M7 **Mecina-Bombarón** Spain
174 E4 **Męcinka** Pol.
126 G3 **Mecitözü** Turkey
172 H6 **Meckenbeuren** Ger.
169 D9 **Meckenheim** Ger.
172 F3 **Meckesheim** Ger.
170 D2 **Mecklenburger Bucht** *b.* Ger.
170 D3 **Mecklenburgische Seenplatte** *reg.* Ger.
170 G3 **Mecklenburg-Vorpommern** *land* Ger.
Mecklenburg - West Pomerania *land* Ger. *see* Mecklenburg-Vorpommern
183 N7 **Meco** Spain
213 H2 **Meconta** Moz.
235 K3 **Mecox Bay** *NY* U.S.A.
177 H5 **Mecsek** *mts* Hungary
177 H5 **Mecseknádasd** Hungary
213 H2 **Mecubúri** Moz.
213 I2 **Mecubúri** *r.* Moz.
213 I2 **Mecúfi** Moz.
211 C8 **Mecula** Moz.
86 G4 **Meda** *r. W.A.* Austr.
182 F7 **Meda** Port.
182 E4 **Meda** *mt.* Spain
114 F3 **Medak** *Andhra Prad.* India
94 C3 **Medan** *Sumatera* Indon.
95 L9 **Medang** *i.* Indon.
260 E2 **Medano** Arg.
261 F6 **Médanos** *Buenos Aires* Arg.
261 H3 **Médanos** *Entre Ríos* Arg.
259 D8 **Medanosa, Punta** *pt* Arg.
250 D2 **Médanos de Coro, Parque Nacional** *nat. park* Venez.
226 H8 **Medaryville** *IN* U.S.A.
182 D6 **Medas** Port.
114 G8 **Medawachchiya** Sri Lanka
114 F4 **Medchal** *Andhra Prad.* India
172 D2 **Meddersheim** Ger.
164 K4 **Meddo** Neth.
233 □R3 **Meddybemps Lake** *ME* U.S.A.
190 F5 **Mede** Italy
205 F1 **Médéa** Alg.
169 G8 **Medebach** Ger.
257 G2 **Medeiros Neto** Brazil
182 F8 **Medelim** Port.
250 C3 **Medellín** Col.
184 H3 **Medellín** Spain
168 G3 **Medem** *r.* Ger.
164 H3 **Medemblik** Neth.
149 P7 **Meden** *r. England* U.K.
205 H2 **Medenine** Tunisia
Medenitsa Ukr. *see* Medenychi
136 C4 **Medenychi** Ukr.
124 E8 **Meder** Eritrea
206 B2 **Mederdra** Maur.
190 I6 **Medesano** Italy
233 M8 **Medford** *NY* U.S.A.
237 G7 **Medford** *OK* U.S.A.
238 C5 **Medford** *OR* U.S.A.
226 D4 **Medford** *WI* U.S.A.
234 F5 **Medford Lakes** *NJ* U.S.A.
197 Q6 **Medgidia** Romania
177 J5 **Medgyesbodzás** Hungary
177 K5 **Medgyesegyháza** Hungary
113 □1 **Medhufinolhu** *i. N. Male* Maldives
234 E5 **Media** *PA* U.S.A.
206 E2 **Mediadilet** *well* Mali
260 D4 **Media Luna** Arg.
242 □R10 **Media Luna, Arrecife de la** *rf* Hond.
186 D5 **Mediana** Spain
185 P7 **Media Naranja, Punta de la** *pt* Spain
186 F3 **Mediano, Embalse de** *resr* Spain
197 M4 **Mediaș** Romania
238 F3 **Medical Lake** *WA* U.S.A.
191 L7 **Medicina** Italy
238 K6 **Medicine Bow** *WY* U.S.A.
238 K6 **Medicine Bow** *r. WY* U.S.A.
238 K6 **Medicine Bow Mountains** *WY* U.S.A.
238 K6 **Medicine Bow Peak** *WY* U.S.A.
223 I5 **Medicine Hat** *Alta* Can.
238 L2 **Medicine Lake** *MT* U.S.A.
237 F7 **Medicine Lodge** *KS* U.S.A.
257 G2 **Medina** Brazil
250 C3 **Medina** Col.
Medina *Al Madīnah* Saudi Arabia *see* **Al Madīnah**
236 F2 **Medina** *ND* U.S.A.
232 G5 **Medina** *NY* U.S.A.
232 D7 **Medina** *OH* U.S.A.
237 G11 **Medina** *r. TX* U.S.A.
183 P6 **Medinaceli** Spain
184 G4 **Medina de las Torres** Spain
183 K6 **Medina del Campo** Spain
183 N3 **Medina de Pomar** Spain
183 J5 **Medina de Rioseco** Spain
206 B3 **Medina Gounas** Senegal
237 F11 **Medina Lake** *TX* U.S.A.
184 H8 **Medina-Sidonia** Spain
217 □1b **Medine** Mauritius
117 K8 **Medinipur** *W. Bengal* India
192 B8 **Medio-Campidano** *prov.* Italy
Mediolanum Italy *see* **Milano**
162 C4 **Médis** France
132 F7 **Mediterranean Sea**
161 D9 **Méditerranée** *airport* France
208 E4 **Medje** Dem. Rep. Congo
205 F2 **Medjedel** Alg.
189 A7 **Medjerda, Monts de la** *mts* Alg.
176 G2 **Medlov** Czech Rep.
120 G2 **Mednogorsk** Rus. Fed.
139 S5 **Mednoye** Rus. Fed.
131 R4 **Mednyy, Ostrov** *i.* Rus. Fed.
162 B5 **Médoc** *reg.* France
111 L12 **Mêdog** *Xizang* China
191 K6 **Medolla** Italy
236 D2 **Medora** *ND* U.S.A.
208 A4 **Médouneu** Gabon
175 I1 **Medovoye** Rus. Fed.
260 C3 **Medrano** Arg.
175 I5 **Mędrzechów** Pol.
223 I4 **Medstead** *Sask.* Can.
151 J5 **Medstead** *Hampshire, England* U.K.
Medu Kongkar *Xizang* China *see* **Maizhokunggar**
191 P6 **Medulin** Croatia
179 N7 **Međumurje** *reg.* Croatia
191 N4 **Meduna** *r.* Italy
191 N3 **Meduno** Italy
Meduro *atoll* Marshall Is *see* Majuro
197 J8 **Medveđa** Serbia
137 M8 **Medvedeve** Ukr.
134 I4 **Medvedevo** Rus. Fed.
135 H6 **Medveditsa** *r.* Rus. Fed.
137 N8 **Medvedivka** Ukr.
188 E3 **Medvednica** *mts* Croatia
134 J4 **Medvedok** Rus. Fed.
137 S8 **Medvedovskaya** Rus. Fed.
138 F6 **Medvėgalio kalnis** *hill* Lith.
137 P2 **Medvenka** Rus. Fed.
131 R2 **Medvezh'i, Ostrova** *is* Rus. Fed.
134 F3 **Medvezh'yegorsk** Rus. Fed.
179 J7 **Medvode** Slovenia
151 N5 **Medway** *admin. div. England* U.K.
151 M5 **Medway** *r. England* U.K.
86 □1 **Medwin Point** Christmas I.
175 K6 **Medyka** Pol.
139 S7 **Medyn'** Rus. Fed.
136 G4 **Medzhybizh** Ukr.
177 K2 **Medzilaborce** Slovakia
87 C9 **Meeberrie** *W.A.* Austr.
164 K2 **Meeden** Neth.
169 K10 **Meeder** Ger.
87 E9 **Meekatharra** *W.A.* Austr.
238 K6 **Meeker** *CO* U.S.A.
232 B8 **Meeker** *OH* U.S.A.
240 L2 **Meeks Bay** *CA* U.S.A.
210 F2 **Meeladeen** Somalia
214 I8 **Meelberg** *mt.* S. Africa
147 F6 **Meelick** Ireland
225 J3 **Meelpaeg Reservoir** *Nfld and Lab.* Can.
147 F3 **Meenacross** Ireland
147 F3 **Meenanarwa** Ireland
147 F3 **Meentullynagarn** Ireland
165 G6 **Meer** Belgium
171 F9 **Meerane** Ger.
138 K3 **Meerapalu** Estonia
169 H6 **Meerbeck** Ger.
169 C8 **Meerbusch** Ger.
165 H6 **Meerhout** Belgium
164 G5 **Meerkerk** Neth.
165 G6 **Meerle** Belgium
164 J5 **Meerlo** Neth.
172 G6 **Meersburg** Ger.
165 I7 **Meerssen** Neth.
113 □1 **Meerufenfushi** *i. N. Male* Maldives
116 F5 **Meerut** *Uttar Prad.* India
163 B8 **Mées** France
238 J4 **Meeteetse** *WY* U.S.A.
Me'etia *i. Arch. de la Société* Fr. Polynesia *see* **Mehetia**
165 D6 **Meetkerke** Belgium
165 I6 **Meeuwen** Belgium
140 N2 **Mefjordvær** Norway
210 C3 **Mēga** Eth.
94 D6 **Mega** *i.* Indon.
210 C3 **Mega Escarpment** Eth./Kenya
198 C3 **Megala Kalyvia** Greece
198 E2 **Megali Panagia** Greece
210 D3 **Megalo** Eth.
199 I6 **Megalo Chorio** Greece
198 D5 **Megalopoli** Greece
199 H5 **Megalos Anthropofagos** *i.* Greece
198 B4 **Meganisi** *i.* Greece
225 G4 **Mégantic, Lac** *l. Que.* Can.
198 E4 **Megara** Greece
164 I5 **Megen** Neth.
160 J5 **Megève** France
210 C2 **Megezez** *mt.* Eth.
117 M7 **Meghalaya** *state* India
117 K9 **Meghasani** *mt. Orissa* India
117 M8 **Meghna** *r.* Bangl.
129 H7 **Meghri** Armenia
Meghrut Armenia *see* **Gugark'**
122 G2 **Megin** Turkm.
130 I3 **Megion** Rus. Fed.
227 S1 **Mégiscane, Lac** *l. Que.* Can.
199 K6 **Megisti** *i.* Greece
139 R3 **Megletsy** Rus. Fed.
139 S3 **Meglino, Ozero** *l.* Rus. Fed.
139 S1 **Megra** *r.* Rus. Fed.
139 Q1 **Megrega** Rus. Fed.
Megri Armenia *see* **Meghri**
139 Q1 **Megrozero** Rus. Fed.
Megrut Armenia *see* **Gugark'**
197 K5 **Mehadica** Romania
165 H7 **Mehaigne** *r.* Belgium
205 F2 **Mehaïguène, Oued** *watercourse* Alg.
140 S1 **Mehamn** Norway
137 O9 **Mehanom, Mys** *pt* Ukr.
123 L8 **Mehar** Pak.
87 E7 **Meharry, Mount** *W.A.* Austr.
Mehdia Tunisia *see* **Mahdia**
122 B4 **Mehdīkhān** Iran
122 E4 **Mehdīshahr** Iran
168 H3 **Mehe** *r.* Ger.
143 N1 **Mehedeby** Sweden
205 F4 **Mehedjibat, Erg** *des.* Alg.
116 F9 **Mehekar** *Mahar.* India
117 L8 **Meherpur** Bangl.
232 G11 **Meherrin** *VA* U.S.A.
232 I12 **Meherrin** *r. VA* U.S.A.
79 □9 **Mehetia** *i. Arch. de la Société* Fr. Polynesia
116 E8 **Mehidpur** *Madh. Prad.* India
167 J5 **Méhkerék** Hungary
171 F9 **Mehltheuer** Ger.
236 J6 **Mehlville** *MO* U.S.A.
116 D8 **Mehmadabad** *Gujarat* India
117 I6 **Mehndawal** *Uttar Prad.* India
234 C1 **Mehoopany** *PA* U.S.A.
122 B2 **Mehrābān** Iran
122 F8 **Mehrān** Iran
122 F8 **Mehrān** *watercourse* Iran
127 M7 **Mehrān** Iraq
169 C10 **Mehren** Ger.
172 B2 **Mehring** Ger.
171 E7 **Mehringen** Ger.
179 H3 **Mehrnbach** Austria
172 H5 **Mehrstetten** Ger.
123 N4 **Mehtar Lām** Afgh.
162 I1 **Mehun-sur-Yèvre** France
256 C3 **Meia Ponte** *r.* Brazil
Meicheng *Anhui* China *see* Qianshan
Meicheng *Fujian* China *see* Minqing
109 H4 **Meichengzhen** *Hunan* China
108 E1 **Meichuan** *Gansu* China
207 I5 **Meidougou** Cameroon
150 D4 **Meidrim** *Carmarthenshire, Wales* U.K.
207 I5 **Meiganga** Cameroon
148 E5 **Meigh** *Northern Ireland* U.K.
221 I2 **Meighen Island** *Nunavut* Can.
146 J9 **Meigle** *Perth and Kinross, Scotland* U.K.
108 D4 **Meigu** *Sichuan* China
100 D7 **Meihekou** *Jilin* China
104 F4 **Meihō** Japan
165 I6 **Meijel** Neth.
164 F4 **Meijendel** *nature res.* Neth.
Meijiang *Jiangxi* China *see* Ningdu
109 J6 **Mei Jiang** *r.* China
109 J6 **Meikeng** *Guangdong* China
222 G3 **Meikle** *r. Alta* Can.
148 I1 **Meikle Bin** *hill Scotland* U.K.
148 G2 **Meikle Kilmory** *Argyll and Bute, Scotland* U.K.
146 J9 **Meikleour** *Perth and Kinross, Scotland* U.K.
146 K11 **Meikle Says Law** *hill Scotland* U.K.
96 B4 **Meiktila** Myanmar
190 F1 **Meilen** Switz.
163 C8 **Meilhan** France
163 E6 **Meilhan-sur-Garonne** France
Meilin *Jiangxi* China *see* Ganxian
158 H5 **Meillac** France
160 A3 **Meillant** France
160 J4 **Meillerie** France
222 E2 **Meilleur** *r. N.W.T.* Can.
108 H8 **Meilu** *Guangdong* China
182 F8 **Meimoa** Port.
190 F4 **Meina** Italy
169 K6 **Meine** Ger.
169 J6 **Meinersen** Ger.
169 E8 **Meinerzhagen** Ger.
178 A5 **Meiningen** Austria
169 J9 **Meiningen** Ger.
182 F2 **Meira** Spain
182 F2 **Meira, Serra de** *mts* S
190 E2 **Meiringen** Switz.
214 G9 **Meiringspoort** *pass* S.
146 D9 **Meirleach, Rubha nan** *Scotland* U.K.
171 D7 **Meisdorf** Ger.
172 D2 **Meisenheim** Ger.
Meishan *Anhui* China *s* Jinzhai
108 D3 **Meishan** *Sichuan* China
171 H8 **Meißen** Ger.
168 I5 **Meißendorf** Ger.
172 D5 **Meißenheim** Ger.
169 I8 **Meißner** *hill* Ger.
169 I8 **Meißner-Kaufunger W** Naturpark *nature res.*
222 D2 **Meister** *r. Y.T.* Can.
108 F5 **Meitan** *Guizhou* China
173 J4 **Meitingen** Ger.
105 K3 **Meiwa** *Gunma* Japan
104 E6 **Meiwa** *Mie* Japan
165 H9 **Meix-devant-Virton** Be
100 F5 **Meixi** *Heilong.* China
Meixian *Guangdong* Ch Meizhou
109 J6 **Meixian** *Guangdong* Ch
107 J9 **Meixian** *Shaanxi* China
Meixing *Sichuan* China Xiaojin
109 K6 **Meizhou** *Guangdong* C
116 F7 **Mej** *r.* India
116 I7 **Meja** *Uttar Prad.* India
161 E7 **Méjan, Sommet de** *mt* France
204 D5 **Mejaouda** *well* Maur.
78 □3a **Mejatto** *i. Kwajalein* Ma
161 C8 **Méjean, Causse** *plat.*
189 B7 **Mejez el Bab** Tunisia
258 D3 **Mejicana** *mt.* Arg.
252 C5 **Mejillones** Chile
252 C5 **Mejillones del Sur, Ba** *b.* Chile
183 K8 **Mejorada** Spain
183 N8 **Mejorada del Campo**
203 G5 **Mekadio** *well* Sudan
208 B4 **Mékambo** Gabon
199 L2 **Mekece** Turkey
210 C1 **Mek'elē** Eth.
129 G2 **Meken-Yurt** Rus. Fed.
205 F4 **Mekerrhane, Sebkha** *salt pan* Alg.
139 Q1 **Mekhbaza** Rus. Fed.
206 A3 **Mékhé** Senegal
129 H3 **Mekhel'ta** Rus. Fed.
123 M6 **Mekhtar** Pak.
210 C2 **Mekī** Eth.
179 K7 **Mekinje** Slovenia
207 F5 **Mekkaw** Nigeria
204 D2 **Meknès** Morocco
97 G9 **Mekong** *r.* Asia
alt. **Lancang Jiang** (C
alt. **Mènam Khong** (La
97 H10 **Mekong, Mouths of th** Vietnam
129 D3 **Mek'vena** Georgia
191 M3 **Mel** Italy
208 D2 **Méla, Mont** *hill* C.A.R.
260 B4 **Melado** *r.* Chile
205 G3 **Melah, Oued el** *waterco*
94 E3 **Melaka** Malaysia
94 E3 **Melaka** *state* Malaysia
95 K2 **Melalap** *Sabah* Malays
94 F5 **Melalo, Tanjung** *pt* Inc
193 O6 **Melandro** *r.* Italy
266 F6 **Melanesia** *is* Oceania
266 F5 **Melanesian Basin** *sea* Pacific Ocean
140 □B1 **Melar** Iceland
191 K5 **Melara** Italy
95 I4 **Melawi** *r.* Indon.
160 E4 **Melay** *Bourgogne* Fran
157 K8 **Melay** *Champagne-Ard* France
159 J7 **Melay** *Pays de la Loire*
190 E6 **Melazzo** Italy
168 J4 **Melbeck** Ger.
151 M3 **Melbourn** *Cambridgesh England* U.K.
83 J7 **Melbourne** *Vic.* Austr.
151 J2 **Melbourne** *Derbyshire, England* U.K.
237 J7 **Melbourne** *AR* U.S.A.
231 G11 **Melbourne** *FL* U.S.A.
140 M2 **Melbu** Norway
146 □M2 **Melby** *Shetland, Scotla*
140 □ **Melchers, Kapp** *c.* Sv
259 B7 **Melchor, Isla** *i.* Chile
243 O9 **Melchor de Mencos** G
243 I5 **Melchor Ocampo** Mex
170 I5 **Melchow** Ger.
140 J5 **Meldal** Norway
191 M7 **Meldola** Italy
168 H2 **Meldorf** Ger.
232 B12 **Meldrum** *KY* U.S.A.
224 D4 **Meldrum Bay** *Ont.* Car
190 F7 **Mele** Italy
190 E8 **Mele, Capo** *c.* Italy
139 T4 **Melech** *r.* Rus. Fed.
190 G5 **Melegnano** Italy
176 G4 **Meleg-víz** *r.* Hungary
92 □ **Melekeiok** Palau
Melekess Rus. Fed. *se* Dimitrovgrad
134 K4 **Melekhina** Rus. Fed.
139 Y5 **Melekhovo** Rus. Fed.
137 Q7 **Melekyne** Ukr.
216 □3f **Melenara** *Gran Canaria* Canary Is
196 I5 **Melenci** *Vojvodina* Sert
126 G4 **Melendiz Dağı** *mt.* Tur
195 O3 **Melendugno** Italy
135 H5 **Melenki** Rus. Fed.
158 H5 **Melesse** France
Melet Turkey *see* **Mesu**
120 F1 **Meleuz** Rus. Fed.
225 G1 **Mélèzes, Rivière aux** *Que.* Can.
193 L4 **Melfa** *r.* Italy
233 J11 **Melfa** *VA* U.S.A.
208 C2 **Melfi** Chad
193 P6 **Melfi** Italy
223 J4 **Melfort** *Sask.* Can.
251 I5 **Melgaço** Brazil
182 D4 **Melgaço** Port.
183 M9 **Melgar** *r.* Spain
183 J4 **Melgar de Arriba** Spa
183 L4 **Melgar de Fernament** Spain
182 H5 **Melgar de Tera** Spain
158 D6 **Melgven** France
140 K5 **Melhus** Norway
223 M2 **Meliadine Lake** *Nunav*
95 I5 **Meliau** *Kalimantan* Indo
165 J6 **Melick** Neth.
195 K7 **Melicucco** Italy
182 E3 **Melide** Spain
184 B4 **Melides** Port.
198 C5 **Meligalas** Greece
129 E5 **Melikköyü** Turkey
93 C4 **Melilis** *i.* Indon.
181 E5 **Melilla** N. Africa
195 I9 **Melilli** *Sicilia* Italy
259 B7 **Melimoyu, Monte** *mt.*
81 D11 **Melina, Mount** *South*
261 G3 **Melincué** Arg.
261 G3 **Melincué, Laguna** *l.* A
95 L5 **Melintang, Danau** *l.* Ir
137 O5 **Melioratyvne** Ukr.
260 B6 **Melipeuco** Chile
260 B3 **Melipilla** Chile
157 M8 **Mélisey** France
164 E5 **Meliskerke** Neth.
195 M5 **Melissa** Italy
223 K5 **Melita** *Man.* Can.
Melitene Turkey *see* **M**
198 C2 **Meliti** Greece
195 J8 **Melito** *r.* Italy
195 J8 **Melito di Porto Salvo**
137 O7 **Melitopol'** Ukr.
179 L3 **Melk** Austria
179 L3 **Melk** *r.* Austria
215 I8 **Melk** *r.* S. Africa
210 C3 **Melka Guba** Eth.
214 B5 **Melkbospunt** *pt* S. Afr
214 C9 **Melkbosstrand** S. Afri
150 H5 **Melksham** *Wiltshire, England* U.K.
190 I5 **Mella** *r.* Italy

232 H11 Midlothian VA U.S.A.
168 G3 Midlum Ger.
215 O5 Midmar Nature Reserve S. Africa
227 M5 Midmay Ont. Can.
Midnapore W. Bengal India see Medinipur
213 □J4 Midongy Atsimo Madag.
105 K4 Midori Japan
103 H14 Midori-gawa r. Japan
163 C8 Midou r. France
163 C8 Midouze r. France
266 F4 Mid-Pacific Mountains sea feature N. Pacific Ocean
215 M1 Midrand S. Africa
92 E8 Midsayap Mindanao Phil.
150 H5 Midsomer Norton Bath and North East Somerset, England U.K.
140 I5 Midsund Norway
108 C6 Midu Yunnan China
113 □2 Midu i. Addu Atoll Maldives
238 F4 Midvale ID U.S.A.
Midway Oman see Thamarīt
241 U1 Midway UT U.S.A.
75 H2 Midway Islands N. Pacific Ocean
87 G7 Midway Well W.A. Austr.
238 K5 Midwest WY U.S.A.
237 G8 Midwest City OK U.S.A.
164 L2 Midwolda Neth.
124 B2 Midyan reg. Saudi Arabia
127 J5 Midyat Turkey
Midye Turkey see Kıyıköy
146 □N1 Mid Yell Shetland, Scotland U.K.
197 K7 Midzhur mt. Bulg./Yugo.
103 I14 Mie Japan
104 D7 Mie pref. Japan
175 I5 Miechów Pol.
177 L1 Miecзka r. Pol.
178 D5 Mieders Austria
183 R6 Miedes Spain
174 C2 Miedwie, Jezioro l. Pol.
175 I5 Miedziana Góra Pol.
174 D3 Miedzichowo Pol.
175 K3 Miedzna Pol.
175 H6 Miedźna Pol.
174 G5 Miedźno Pol.
175 K2 Międzybórz Pol.
174 D3 Międzychód Pol.
174 E5 Międzylesie Pol.
175 K4 Międzyrzec Podlaski Pol.
174 D3 Międzyrzecz Pol.
167 I3 Międzyrzecza Warty i Widawki, Park Krajobrazowy Pol.
174 C2 Międzyzdroje Pol.
141 S6 Miehikkälä Fin.
169 E10 Miehlen Ger.
175 J6 Miejsce Piastowe Pol.
174 E4 Miejska Górka Pol.
174 E4 Miękinia Pol.
163 E9 Miélan France
161 G8 Miélandre, Montagne de mt. France
175 J5 Mielec Pol.
170 K4 Mielęcin Pol.
174 F3 Mieleszyn Pol.
168 J2 Mielkendorf Ger.
175 L3 Mielnik Pol.
174 E1 Mielno Pol.
211 C7 Miembwe Tanz.
178 D5 Mieming Austria
178 C5 Mieminger Gebirge mts Austria
175 G3 Mień r. Pol.
143 K5 Mien l. Sweden
83 K9 Miena Tas. Austr.
209 C9 Mienga Angola
209 F8 Miengwe Zambia
109 N6 Mienhua Yü i. Taiwan
183 M2 Miera r. Spain
140 S2 Mieraslompolo Fin.
Mierašluoppal Fin. see Mieraslompolo
197 N4 Miercurea-Ciuc Romania
182 I2 Mieres Spain
Mieres del Camín Spain see Mieres
Mieres del Camino Spain see Mieres
165 I6 Mierlo Neth.
140 Q2 Mierojávri Norway
174 E5 Mieroszów Pol.
163 H6 Miers France
244 G2 Mier y Noriega Mex.
175 I5 Mierzawa r. Pol.
170 J4 Mierzyn Pol.
172 C3 Miesau Ger.
173 L6 Miesbach Ger.
174 F5 Mieścisko Pol.
172 D3 Miesenbach Ger.
210 D2 Mī'eso Eth.
171 D6 Mieste Ger.
171 D6 Miesterhorst Ger.
174 F3 Mieszków Pol.
174 C3 Mieszkowice Pol.
172 H5 Mietingen Ger.
141 P6 Mietoinen Fin.
160 J4 Meussy France
182 G6 Mieza Spain
124 E6 Mīfah Saudi Arabia
232 C8 Mifflin OH U.S.A.
227 Q9 Mifflinburg PA U.S.A.
232 H8 Mifflintown PA U.S.A.
234 C2 Mifflinville PA U.S.A.
104 F1 Mifune-zaki pt Japan
106 J9 Migang Shan mt. Gansu/Ningxia China
215 J2 Migdol S. Africa
163 G8 Migennes France
122 H6 Mighān Iran
117 O5 Miging Arun. Prad. India
191 G6 Migliarino Italy
190 I8 Migliarino-San Rossore-Massaciuccoli, Parco Naturale di nature res. Italy
191 L6 Migliaro Italy
195 K2 Miglionica Italy
162 E2 Mignaloux-Beauvoir France
193 L5 Mignano Monte Lungo Italy
192 H3 Mignone r. Italy
160 I3 Mignovillard France
111 J10 Migriggyangzham Co l. Qinghai China
225 H3 Miguasha, Parc de nature res. N.B. Can.
245 K7 Miguel Alemán Mex.
245 K7 Miguel Alemán, Presa resr Mex.
254 E3 Miguel Alves Brazil
244 D1 Miguel Auza Mex.
254 E4 Miguel Calmon Brazil
242 □S13 Miguel de la Borda Panama
245 K8 Miguel de la Madrid, Presa resr Mex.
183 N9 Miguel Esteban Spain
261 I4 Miguelete Uru.
245 H3 Miguel Hidalgo Mex.
242 E4 Miguel Hidalgo, Presa resr Mex.
257 F5 Miguel Pereira Brazil
182 E3 Miguel Riglos Arg.
185 L3 Miguelturra Spain
138 M6 Migushino Rus. Fed.
96 B5 Migyaunye Myanmar
197 N6 Mihăileşti Romania
176 G5 Miháld Hungary
199 L2 Mihalgazi Turkey
199 E4 Mihalıççık Turkey
176 G4 Mihályi Hungary
104 E6 Mihama Aichi Japan
104 C4 Mihama Fukui Japan
104 D8 Mihama Mie Japan
104 B8 Mihama Wakayama Japan
103 K12 Mihara Hiroshima Japan
104 A7 Mihara Hyōgo Japan
105 J6 Mihara-yama vol. Japan
107 P8 Mi He r. China
Mihidjan W. Bengal India see Chittaranjan
117 K8 Mihijam Jharkhand India
114 G8 Mihintale Sri Lanka
169 J8 Mihla Ger.
105 L4 Mihō Japan
103 K11 Miho-wan b. Japan
211 C7 Mihumo Chini Tanz.
183 K8 Mijares Spain
187 D7 Mijares r. Spain
185 J7 Mijas Spain
185 J7 Mijas mt. Spain
164 G4 Mijdrecht Neth.
105 J1 Mijōga-take mt. Japan
160 I4 Mijoux France
102 S3 Mikasa Japan
136 G1 Mikashevichy Belarus
104 C4 Mikata Japan
104 C4 Mikata-ko l. Japan
104 D3 Mikawa Japan
104 F6 Mikawa-wan b. Japan
104 F6 Mikawa-wan Kokutei-kōen park Japan
177 K4 Mikepércs Hungary
Mikhailovo Rus. Fed. see Paneyevo
139 W6 Mikhali Rus. Fed.
138 J7 Mikhalishki Belarus
138 K8 Mikhanavichy Belarus
Mikha Tskhakaia Georgia see Senaki
Mikhaylovkskiy Rus. Fed. see Prozorovo
139 W7 Mikhaylov Rus. Fed.
Mikhaylovgrad Bulg. see Montana
121 Q1 Mikhaylovka Pavlodarskaya Oblast' Kazakh.
Mikhaylovka Zhambylskaya Oblast' Kazakh. see Sarykemer
100 F4 Mikhaylovka Amurskaya Oblast' Rus. Fed.
100 A3 Mikhaylovka Chitinskaya Oblast' Rus. Fed.
137 O1 Mikhaylovka Kurskaya Oblast' Rus. Fed.
100 H7 Mikhaylovka Primorskiy Kray Rus. Fed.
Mikhaylovka Tul'skaya Oblast' Rus. Fed. see Kimovsk
135 H6 Mikhaylovka Volgogradskaya Oblast' Rus. Fed.
197 L7 Mikhaylovo Bulg.
137 T4 Mikhaylovo-Aleksandrovskiy Rus. Fed.
Mikhaylovskiy Altayskiy Kray Rus. Fed. see Malinovoye Ozero
121 R2 Mikhaylovskiy Altayskiy Kray Rus. Fed.
Mikhaylovskoye Rus. Fed. see Shpakovskoye
263 F2 Mikhaytov Island Antarctica
139 U6 Mikhnevo Rus. Fed.
128 C9 Mikhrot Timna Israel
124 E6 Mikhwa Saudi Arabia
104 A6 Miki Japan
Míkines tourist site Greece see Mycenae
117 N6 Mikir Hills India
104 D8 Miki-zaki pt Japan
106 G6 Mikkabi Japan
141 S6 Mikkeli Fin.
141 S6 Mikkelin mlk Fin.
222 H3 Mikkwa r. Alta Can.
179 M6 Miklavž Slovenia
175 J2 Mikołajki Pol.
175 H2 Mikołajki Pomorskie Pol.
174 G5 Mikołów Pol.
Mikonos i. Greece see Mykonos
174 G1 Mikoszewo Pol.
Mikoyan Armenia see Yeghegnadzor
Mikoyanovka Rus. Fed. see Oktyabr'skiy
198 E1 Mikropoli Greece
174 F4 Mikstat Pol.
171 J9 Mikulášovice Czech Rep.
176 G3 Mikulčice Czech Rep.
134 I2 Mikulkin, Mys c. Rus. Fed.
176 F3 Mikulov Czech Rep.
176 G1 Mikulovice Czech Rep.
211 C6 Mikumi Tanz.
211 C6 Mikumi National Park Tanz.
104 E6 Mikumo Japan
134 J3 Mikun' Rus. Fed.
104 D3 Mikuni Japan
105 I2 Mikuni-sanmyaku mts Japan
105 I4 Mikuni-yama mt. Japan
105 K8 Mikura-jima i. Japan
205 G1 Mila Alg.
236 I3 Milaca MN U.S.A.
114 C9 Miladhunmadulu Atoll Maldives
254 F3 Milagres Brazil
260 E2 Milagro Arg.
250 B5 Milagro Ecuador
183 Q4 Milagro Spain
183 M5 Milagros Spain
175 I1 Milakowo Pol.
116 H4 Milam Uttaranchal India
Milan Italy see Milano
227 K7 Milan MI U.S.A.
236 I5 Milan MO U.S.A.
232 C7 Milan OH U.S.A.
209 C7 Milando Angola
209 C7 Milando, Reserva Especial do nature res. Angola
82 G6 Milang S.A. Austr.
213 G3 Milange Moz.
190 G5 Milano Italy
190 G5 Milano prov. Italy
190 F4 Milano (Malpensa) airport Italy
213 □K2 Milanoa Madag.
191 M7 Milano Marittima Italy
Milanovice Slovakia see Veľký Kýr
175 K4 Milanów Pol.
175 I3 Milanówek Pol.
234 E1 Milanville PA U.S.A.
197 M4 Milaş Romania
199 I5 Milas Turkey
136 G2 Milashavichy Belarus
137 M2 Milashevichi Rus. Fed.
138 I9 Milavidy Belarus
195 I7 Milazzo Sicilia Italy
195 I7 Milazzo, Capo di c. Sicilia Italy
195 I7 Milazzo, Golfo di b. Sicilia Italy
236 G3 Milbank SD U.S.A.
150 H6 Milborne Port Somerset, England U.K.
150 H6 Milborne St Andrew Dorset, England U.K.
233 □R4 Milbridge ME U.S.A.
170 E5 Milde r. Ger.
151 N3 Mildenhall Suffolk, England U.K.
227 R8 Mildred PA U.S.A.
168 H2 Mildstedt Ger.
83 I6 Mildura Vic. Austr.
129 I5 Mil Düzü lowland Azer.
108 D6 Mile Yunnan China
210 D2 Milē Eth.
148 F4 Milebush Northern Ireland U.K.
151 N4 Mile End Essex, England U.K.
246 □ Mile Gully Jamaica
175 L3 Milejczyce Pol.
175 H1 Milejewo Pol.
175 K4 Milejów Pol.
174 F9 Milena Sicilia Italy
85 M9 Miles Qld Austr.
232 H8 Milesburg PA U.S.A.
238 L3 Miles City MT U.S.A.
210 D2 Milē Serdo Reserve nature res. Eth.
176 C1 Milešovka hill Czech Rep.
147 F7 Milestone Ireland
197 P3 Miletin r. Romania
195 K6 Mileto Italy
193 M5 Miletto, Monte mt. Italy
87 D9 Mileura W.A. Austr.
176 D2 Milevsko Czech Rep.
139 S8 Mileyevo Rus. Fed.
149 M2 Milfield Northumberland, England U.K.
184 B5 Milfontes Port.
147 E8 Milford Cork Ireland
147 G2 Milford Donegal Ireland
151 K5 Milford Surrey, England U.K.
235 I2 Milford CT U.S.A.
234 E7 Milford DE U.S.A.
226 G9 Milford IL U.S.A.
233 N6 Milford MA U.S.A.
234 B6 Milford MD U.S.A.
233 □Q4 Milford ME U.S.A.
232 B6 Milford MI U.S.A.
236 G5 Milford NE U.S.A.
233 N6 Milford NH U.S.A.
235 H2 Milford NJ U.S.A.
234 E6 Milford PA U.S.A.
241 S3 Milford UT U.S.A.
232 H10 Milford VA U.S.A.
150 B4 Milford Haven Pembrokeshire, Wales U.K.
236 G6 Milford Lake KS U.S.A.
151 I6 Milford on Sea Hampshire, England U.K.
81 B11 Milford Sound South I. N.Z.
81 B11 Milford Sound inlet South I. N.Z.
234 E4 Milford Square PA U.S.A.
85 H5 Milgarra Qld Austr.
87 E8 Milgun W.A. Austr.
Milḥ, Baḥr al l. Iraq see Razāzah, Buḥayrat ar
182 G5 Milhão Port.
161 E9 Milhaud France
174 F4 Milicz Pol.
Milid Turkey see Malatya
182 F1 Milikapiti N.T. Austr.
84 C1 Milikapiti N.T. Austr.
87 D11 Miling W.A. Austr.
84 E2 Milingimbi N.T. Austr.
78 □5 Milip Vanuatu
192 B7 Milis Sardegna Italy
194 H9 Militello in Val di Catania Sicilia Italy
158 B5 Milizac France
179 M7 Miljana Croatia
238 K2 Milk r. MT U.S.A.
203 F5 Milk, Wadi el watercourse Sudan
171 J8 Milkel Ger.
175 J2 Miłki Pol.
131 Q4 Mil'kovo Rus. Fed.
171 K6 Milkowice Pol.
223 H5 Milk River Alta Can.
164 I5 Mill Neth.
85 J4 Millaa Millaa Qld Austr.
234 B9 Millard MO U.S.A.
187 D9 Millares Spain
231 □2 Millars New Prov. Bahamas
161 C8 Millau France
160 E3 Millay France
231 E11 Millboro VA U.S.A.
227 P5 Millbrook Ont. Can.
150 D7 Millbrook Cornwall, England U.K.
231 D9 Millbrook AL U.S.A.
233 L7 Millbrook NY U.S.A.
146 I7 Mill Buie hill Scotland U.K.
238 C4 Mill City OR U.S.A.
232 F10 Mill Creek WV U.S.A.
240 J1 Mill Creek r. CA U.S.A.
234 C5 Mill Creek r. PA U.S.A.
235 J1 Milldale CT U.S.A.
231 F9 Milledgeville GA U.S.A.
226 E8 Milledgeville IL U.S.A.
236 I2 Mille Lacs lakes MN U.S.A.
224 B3 Mille Lacs, Lac des l. Ont. Can.
231 G9 Millen GA U.S.A.
Millennium Island atoll Kiribati see Caroline Island
82 E4 Miller watercourse S.A. Austr.
214 H9 Miller S. Africa
236 F3 Miller SD U.S.A.
226 D4 Miller Dam Flowage resr WI U.S.A.
227 M4 Miller Lake Ont. Can.
135 H6 Millerovo Rus. Fed.
241 V10 Miller Peak AZ U.S.A.
241 S6 Millers Creek S.A. Austr.
232 D8 Millersburg MI U.S.A.
232 D8 Millersburg OH U.S.A.
227 R9 Millersburg PA U.S.A.
82 F4 Millers Creek S.A. Austr.
232 B11 Millers Creek KY U.S.A.
233 M6 Millers Falls MA U.S.A.
81 D12 Millers Flat South I. N.Z.
232 C9 Millersport OH U.S.A.
234 A3 Millerstown PA U.S.A.
234 B6 Millersville MD U.S.A.
234 C5 Millersville PA U.S.A.
233 L7 Millerton NY U.S.A.
240 N4 Millerton Lake CA U.S.A.
146 F12 Millerur Point Scotland U.K.
162 I4 Millevaches France
162 H4 Millevaches, Plateau de France
147 I4 Millford Northern Ireland U.K.
263 L1 Mill Glacier Antarctica
234 B4 Mill Hall PA U.S.A.
235 G4 Millhurst NJ U.S.A.
82 H7 Millicent S.A. Austr.
157 J7 Millières France
86 H5 Milligidie Aboriginal Reserve W.A. Austr.
164 J5 Millingen aan de Rijn Neth.
234 D6 Millington MD U.S.A.
227 K6 Millington MI U.S.A.
237 K8 Millington TN U.S.A.
262 T2 Mill Inlet Antarctica
233 □Q3 Millinocket ME U.S.A.
255 C5 Millirí, Cerro mt. Bol.
263 G2 Mill Island Antarctica
221 K3 Mill Island Nunavut Can.
147 K3 Millisle Northern Ireland U.K.
85 M9 Millmerran Qld Austr.
234 A3 Millmont PA U.S.A.
149 K5 Millom Cumbria, England U.K.
146 G11 Millport North Ayrshire, Scotland U.K.
234 F2 Millrift PA U.S.A.
233 J10 Millsboro DE U.S.A.
85 I7 Mills Creek watercourse Qld Austr.
222 G2 Mills Lake N.W.T. Can.
179 I6 Millstatt Austria
179 I6 Millstätter See l. Austria
226 D5 Millston WI U.S.A.
232 D11 Millstone KY U.S.A.
232 E10 Millstone WV U.S.A.
234 F3 Millstone r. NJ U.S.A.
86 D6 Millstream W.A. Austr.
86 D6 Millstream-Chichester National Park W.A. Austr.
147 D8 Millstreet Ireland
225 H4 Milltown N.B. Can.
148 C5 Milltown Cavan Ireland
147 E5 Milltown Galway Ireland
147 C8 Milltown Kerry Ireland
148 D7 Milltown Kildare Ireland
147 J4 Milltown Northern Ireland U.K.
238 H3 Milltown MT U.S.A.
226 B4 Milltown WI U.S.A.
147 D7 Milltown Malbay Ireland
146 K8 Milltown of Kildrummy Aberdeenshire, Scotland U.K.
146 K7 Milltown of Rothiemay Moray, Scotland U.K.
85 H5 Millungera Qld Austr.
215 K1 Millvale S. Africa
240 J4 Mill Valley CA U.S.A.
233 □R2 Millville N.B. Can.
234 E7 Millville NJ U.S.A.
234 B2 Millville PA U.S.A.
235 H2 Millwood NY U.S.A.
237 I9 Millwood Lake AR U.S.A.
156 D7 Milly-la-Forêt France
160 F4 Milly-Lamartine France
87 D9 Milly Milly W.A. Austr.
183 O6 Milmarcos Spain
170 I4 Milmersdorf Ger.
165 I7 Milmort Belgium
146 J10 Milnathort Perth and Kinross, Scotland U.K.
Milne Land i. Greenland see Ilimananngip Nunaa
146 H11 Milngavie East Dunbartonshire, Scotland U.K.
149 M6 Milnrow Greater Manchester, England U.K.
149 L5 Milnthorpe Cumbria, England U.K.
206 C4 Milo r. Guinea
195 I8 Milo Sicilia Italy
233 □Q3 Milo ME U.S.A.
174 E2 Miłocice Pol.
100 I7 Milogradovo Rus. Fed.
191 O5 Milohnić Croatia
240 □F14 Miloli'i HI U.S.A.
171 M5 Miłomłyn Pol.
174 G1 Miłoradz Pol.
198 F6 Milos i. Greece
139 W8 Miloslavskoye Rus. Fed.
174 F3 Miłosław Pol.
204 D4 Miloud well Alg.
146 C8 Milovaig Highland, Scotland U.K.
137 Q3 Milove Kharkivs'ka Oblast' Ukr.
137 T4 Milove Luhans'ka Oblast' Ukr.
171 K10 Milovice Czech Rep.
171 F5 Milow Brandenburg Ger.
170 E4 Milow Mecklenburg-Vorpommern Ger.
175 H6 Milówka Pol.
83 H3 Milparinka N.S.W. Austr.
240 K4 Milpitas CA U.S.A.
232 H8 Milroy PA U.S.A.
173 N3 Miltach Ger.
172 G2 Miltenberg Ger.
83 M6 Milton N.S.W. Austr.
227 O6 Milton Ont. Can.
81 D13 Milton South I. N.Z.
146 G8 Milton Highland, Scotland U.K.
Milton Perth and Kinross, Scotland U.K.
233 J10 Milton DE U.S.A.
231 D10 Milton FL U.S.A.
233 □O5 Milton NH U.S.A.
235 H1 Milton NY U.S.A.
234 B2 Milton PA U.S.A.
233 L4 Milton VT U.S.A.
232 C10 Milton WV U.S.A.
150 D6 Milton Abbot Devon, England U.K.
238 E4 Milton-Freewater OR U.S.A.
151 K3 Milton Keynes Milton Keynes, England U.K.
151 K3 Milton Keynes admin. div. England U.K.
170 H2 Miltzow Ger.
109 I4 Miluo Hunan China
227 N6 Milverton Ont. Can.
150 F5 Milverton Somerset, England U.K.
226 G6 Milwaukee WI U.S.A.
264 E4 Milwaukee Deep sea feature Caribbean Sea
120 I3 Mily Kazakh.
121 P3 Milybulabk Kazakh.
135 H6 Milyutinskaya Rus. Fed.
169 K10 Milz Ger.
163 C8 Mimbaste France
208 C4 Mimbelly Congo
239 K10 Mimbres watercourse NM U.S.A.
183 N2 Mimetiz Spain
82 D2 Mimili S.A. Austr.
114 F8 Mimisal Tamil Nadu India
103 I14 Mimitsu Japan
163 B7 Mimizan France
163 B7 Mimizan-Plage France
176 D1 Mimoň Czech Rep.
208 A5 Mimongo Gabon
257 G4 Mimoso do Sul Brazil
103 L11 Mimuro-yama mt. Japan
243 I4 Mina Mex.
240 N3 Mina NV U.S.A.
252 C3 Mina, Nevado mt. Peru
125 H1 Mīnā' 'Abd Allāh Kuwait
122 G8 Mināb Iran
122 G8 Mīnāb r. Iran
123 M6 Mina Bazar Pak.
104 B8 Minabe Japan
104 B8 Minabegawa Japan
260 E2 Mina Clavero Arg.
254 C5 Minaçu Brazil
184 E5 Mina de São Domingos Port.
223 L4 Minago r. Man. Can.
93 B3 Minahasa, Semenanjung pen. Indon.
Minahassa Peninsula Indon. see Minahasa, Semenanjung
125 L3 Mina Jebel Ali U.A.E.
105 I2 Minakami Japan
Minaker B.C. Can. see Prophet River
128 F2 Minakh Syria
223 M5 Minaki Ont. Can.
104 D6 Minakuchi Japan
103 H14 Minamata Japan
104 E4 Minami Japan
84 E3 Minamia N.T. Austr.
105 H4 Minami-arupusu Kokuritsu-kōen nat. park Japan
105 J5 Minamiashigara Japan
105 K6 Minami-Bōsō Kokutei-kōen park Japan
104 E6 Minamichita Japan
99 N6 Minami-Daitō-jima i. Japan
104 C4 Minami-gawa r. Japan
103 □2 Minami-Iō-jima vol. Kazan-rettō Japan
105 I6 Minamiizu Japan
105 J3 Minami-kawara Japan
105 H3 Minamimaki Japan
105 K3 Minamiminowa Japan
105 L2 Minaminasu Japan
105 G5 Minamishinano Japan
Min'an Hunan China see Longshan
105 J3 Minano Japan
146 F10 Minard Argyll and Bute, Scotland U.K.
81 D11 Minaret Peaks South I. N.Z.
246 E3 Minas Cuba
94 D4 Minas Sumatera Indon.
258 G4 Minas Uru.
243 O10 Minas, Sierra de las mts Guat.
127 N9 Minā' Sa'ūd Kuwait
225 H4 Minas Basin b. N.S. Can.
225 H4 Minas Channel N.S. Can.
258 G3 Minas de Corrales Uru.
246 B2 Minas de Matahambre Cuba
184 F5 Minas de Riotinto Spain
256 D3 Minas Gerais state Brazil
250 D2 Minas Novas Brazil
245 H4 Minateda Spain
245 P4 Minatitlán Colima Mex.
185 M7 Minatitlán Veracruz Mex.
96 A4 Minbu Myanmar
123 O6 Minchinabad Pak.
259 B6 Minchinmávida vol. Chile
146 J11 Minch Moor hill Scotland U.K.
191 J5 Mincio r. Italy
129 H6 Mincivan Azer.
92 E8 Mindanao i. Phil.
92 E8 Mindanao r. Mindanao Phil.
82 H6 Mindarie S.A. Austr.
96 A4 Mindat Sakan Myanmar
182 C9 Minde Port.
173 I4 Mindel r. Ger.
173 I4 Mindelheim Ger.
206 □ Mindelo Cape Verde
182 C6 Mindelo Port.
173 L4 Mindelstetten Ger.
224 E4 Minden Ont. Can.
169 G6 Minden Ger.
237 I9 Minden LA U.S.A.
236 F5 Minden NE U.S.A.
240 M3 Minden NV U.S.A.
227 L6 Minden City MI U.S.A.
165 G6 Mindenhout Belgium
86 C6 Minderoo W.A. Austr.
96 B5 Mindon Myanmar
83 I5 Mindona Lake imp. l. N.S.W. Austr.
92 C5 Mindoro i. Phil.
92 B5 Mindoro Strait Phil.
209 B6 Mindouli Congo
177 J5 Mindszent Hungary
177 J5 Mindszentgodisa Hungary
255 J3 Minduri Brazil
177 F5 Mindyak Rus. Fed.
120 H1 Mindzhivan Azer. see Mincivan
103 I12 Mine Japan
227 B1 Mine Centre Ont. Can.
147 G9 Mine Head hd Ireland
150 F5 Minehead Somerset, England U.K.
256 A2 Mineiros Brazil
194 H9 Mineo Sicilia Italy
235 H3 Mineola NY U.S.A.
237 H9 Mineola TX U.S.A.
150 F1 Minera Wrexham, Wales U.K.
232 H10 Mineral VA U.S.A.
245 I5 Mineral del Monte Mex.
245 G4 Mineral del Refugio Mex.
260 E6 Minerales de la Pampa Arg.
129 E1 Mineral'nyye Vody Rus. Fed.
226 D7 Mineral Point WI U.S.A.
237 F9 Mineral Wells TX U.S.A.
232 E10 Mineralwells WV U.S.A.
192 C3 Minerbio Italy
234 C3 Minersville PA U.S.A.
241 T3 Minersville UT U.S.A.
Minerva atoll Arch. des Tuamotu Fr. Polynesia see Reao
232 D8 Minerva OH U.S.A.
77 I4 Minerva Reefs Fiji
193 Q5 Minervino Murge Italy
161 B10 Minervois reg. France
161 B10 Minervois, Monts du hills France
104 B4 Mineyama Japan
172 E3 Minfeld Ger.
111 F8 Minfeng Xinjiang China
209 E7 Minga Dem. Rep. Congo
211 A8 Minga Zambia
129 I5 Mingäçevir Azer.
129 H5 Mingäçevir Su Anbarı resr Azer.
208 D3 Mingala C.A.R.
225 H3 Mingan Que. Can.
225 I3 Mingan, Îles de is Que. Can.
193 O7 Mingardo r. Italy
82 H5 Mingary S.A. Austr.
120 J6 Mingbuloq Uzbek.
Mingechaur Azer. see Mingäçevir
Mingechaurskoye Vodokhranilishche resr Azer. see Mingäçevir Su Anbarı
85 K5 Mingela Qld Austr.
87 C10 Minginew W.A. Austr.
84 F6 Mingera Creek watercourse Qld Austr.
Mingfeng Hubei China see Yuan'an
109 J2 Minggang Henan China
109 L2 Mingguang Anhui China
96 B3 Mingin Myanmar
96 B3 Mingin Range mts Myanmar
121 P7 Ming-Kush Kyrg.
183 Q9 Minglanilla Spain
232 E8 Mingo Junction OH U.S.A.
183 K7 Mingorría Spain
211 C7 Mingoyo Tanz.
Mingshan Chongqing China see Fengdu
108 D3 Mingshan Sichuan China
106 E5 Mingshui Gansu China
100 D5 Mingshui Heilong. China
111 B8 Mingteke Xinjiang China
186 C6 Minguez, Puerto de pass Spain
146 A9 Mingulay i. Scotland U.K.
96 A3 Mingun Myanmar
213 I2 Mingüri Moz.
109 K5 Mingxi Fujian China
Mingzhou Hebei China see Weixian
Mingzhou Shaanxi China see Suide
Minhe Jiangxi China see Jinxian
112 J4 Minhe Qinghai China
96 B5 Minhla Magwe Myanmar
96 B6 Minhla Pegu Myanmar
182 D5 Minho reg. Port.
109 L5 Minhou Fujian China
158 H4 Miniac-Morvan France
191 F2 Minico, Parco del park Italy
114 C8 Minicoy atoll India
238 G5 Minidoka Internment National Monument nat. park ID U.S.A.
87 G10 Minigwal, Lake salt flat W.A. Austr.
179 N6 Minihof-Liebau Austria
138 E6 Minija r. Lith.
184 G5 Minilla, Embalse de la resr Spain
87 C7 Minilya W.A. Austr.
87 B7 Minilya r. W.A. Austr.
252 C4 Miñimiñe Chile
260 A5 Mininco Chile
206 D4 Mininian Côte d'Ivoire
225 I2 Minipi Lake Nfld and Lab. Can.
224 B3 Miniss Lake Ont. Can.
183 D6 Ministra mt. Spain
183 O6 Ministra, Sierra mts Spain
223 K4 Minitonas Man. Can.
139 R1 Minitskaya Rus. Fed.
Minjian Sichuan China see Mabian
108 E4 Min Jiang r. Sichuan China
109 L5 Min Jiang r. China
84 D1 Minjilang N.T. Austr.
129 H6 Minkänd Azer.
Min-Kush Kyrg. see Ming-Kush
182 F6 Minlaton S.A. Austr.
106 G7 Minle Gansu China
207 G4 Minna Nigeria
263 L1 Minna Bluff pt Antarctica
102 □1 Minna-jima i. Okinawa Japan
102 □B22 Minna-shima i. Okinawa Japan
141 M5 Minne Sweden
236 G6 Minneapolis KS U.S.A.
226 A5 Minneapolis MN U.S.A.
223 L5 Minnedosa Man. Can.
237 F10 Minnehaha Springs WV U.S.A.
236 G4 Minneola KS U.S.A.
236 H2 Minnesota r. MN U.S.A.
236 I2 Minnesota state U.S.A.
226 C5 Minnesota City MN U.S.A.
236 F1 Minnewaukan ND U.S.A.
97 D8 Min-ngaw Myanmar
87 C7 Minnie Creek W.A. Austr.
146 H13 Minnigaff Dumfries and Galloway, Scotland U.K.
82 F5 Minnipa S.A. Austr.
224 B3 Minnitaki Lake Ont. Can.
104 E4 Mino Japan
182 C5 Miño r. Port./Spain
105 H5 Minobu Japan
105 H5 Minobu-san mt. Japan
105 H6 Minobu-sanchi mts Japan
104 F5 Minokamo Japan
104 F5 Mino-Mikawa-kōgen reg. Japan
261 H2 Miñones Arg.
226 C3 Minong WI U.S.A.
226 D7 Minonk IL U.S.A.
104 B6 Minoo Japan
Minorca i. Spain see Menorca
192 I1 Minore, Isola i. Italy
105 L3 Minori Japan
160 F1 Minot France
236 E1 Minot ND U.S.A.
105 G4 Minowa Japan
128 F6 Minqār, Ghadīr imp. l. Syria
106 H7 Minqin Gansu China
109 L5 Minqing Fujian China
106 G4 Minqiao Hebei China
107 N9 Minquan Henan China
168 E3 Minsen Ger.
108 D2 Min Shan mts Sichuan China
96 B2 Minsin Myanmar
138 K8 Minsk Belarus
Minskaya Oblast' admin. div. Belarus see Minskaya Voblasts'
138 K8 Minskaya Voblasts' admin. div. Belarus
175 J3 Mińsk Mazowiecki Pol.
Minsk Oblast admin. div. Belarus see Minskaya Voblasts'
151 N5 Minster Kent, England U.K.
151 O5 Minster Kent, England U.K.
232 A8 Minster OH U.S.A.
150 G2 Minsterley Shropshire, England U.K.
207 I5 Minta Cameroon
121 P9 Mintaka Pass China/Jammu and Kashmir
108 C2 Mintang Qinghai China
146 M7 Mintlaw Aberdeenshire, Scotland U.K.
225 H4 Minto N.B. Can.
Minto atoll Arch. des Tuamotu Fr. Polynesia see Tenarunga
224 F1 Minto, Lac l. Que. Can.
263 L2 Minto, Mount Antarctica
220 G2 Minto Inlet N.W.T. Can.
207 I6 Minton Cameroon
223 J5 Minton Sask. Can.
173 M4 Mintraching Ger.
239 K7 Minturn CO U.S.A.
Minturnae Italy see Minturno
193 L5 Minturno Italy
190 I7 Minucciano Italy
122 F3 Minudasht Iran
203 F2 Minūf Egypt
126 E8 Minūfiyah governorate Egypt
98 F1 Minusinsk Rus. Fed.
190 F3 Minusio Switz.
117 N6 Minutang Arun. Prad. India
183 C3 Minutos, Barragem dos resr Port.
208 B4 Minvoul Gabon
106 I9 Minxian Gansu China
Minya Konka mt. Sichuan China see Gongga Shan
134 L5 Minyar Rus. Fed.
83 I7 Minyip Vic. Austr.
96 B3 Minywa Myanmar
117 P6 Minzong Arun. Prad. India
207 H2 Mio well Niger
227 J5 Mio MI U.S.A.
196 I6 Mionica Serbia
160 F5 Mionnay France
160 F5 Mions France
163 C6 Mios France
84 G8 Mipia, Lake salt flat Qld Austr.
110 H5 Miquan Xinjiang China
224 E3 Miquelon Que. Can.
225 J4 Miquelon i. St Pierre and Miquelon
245 H2 Miquihuana Mex.
138 J8 Mir Belarus
250 B4 Mira r. Col.
191 M5 Mira Italy
182 C8 Mira Port.
184 B5 Mira r. Port.
183 Q9 Mira Spain
183 I3 Mira r. Spain
182 H5 Mira, Peña mt. Spain
187 C8 Mira, Sierra de mts Spain
161 H9 Mirabeau France
233 K3 Mirabel Que. Can.
163 G7 Mirabel France
182 H9 Mirabel Spain
257 E2 Mirabela Brazil
161 G8 Mirabel-aux-Baronnies France
194 G9 Mirabella Imbaccari Sicilia Italy
257 F4 Miracema Brazil
Miracema do Norte Brazil see Miracema do Tocantins
254 C4 Miracema do Tocantins Brazil
Miracema Hills CA U.S.A. see La Mirada
182 C9 Mira de Aire Port.
256 A5 Mirador Brazil
243 O9 Mirador-Dos Lagunos-Río Azul, Parque Nacional nat. park Guat.
257 F4 Miradouro Brazil
163 F8 Miradoux France
250 C3 Miraflores Boyaca Col.
250 C4 Miraflores Guaviare Col.
242 E6 Miraflores Mex.
183 M7 Miraflores de la Sierra Spain
127 J7 Mirah, Wādī al watercourse Iraq/Saudi Arabia
257 F4 Miraí Brazil
114 D4 Miraj Mahar. India
257 F2 Miralta Brazil
261 I6 Miramar Buenos Aires Arg.
261 F2 Miramar Córdoba Arg.
259 B8 Miramar, Canal sea chan. Chile
243 N9 Miramar, Lago l. Mex.
191 N7 Miramare Italy
161 G9 Miramas France
162 C5 Mirambeau France
186 E6 Mirambel Spain
225 H4 Miramichi N.B. Can.
225 H4 Miramichi Bay N.B. Can.
163 E6 Miramont-de-Guyenne France
163 D8 Miramont-Sensacq France
123 N5 Miram Shah Pak.
110 I7 Miran Xinjiang China
250 D5 Miraña Col.
261 H5 Miranda Arg.
253 F5 Miranda Brazil
253 F4 Miranda r. Brazil
Miranda Moz. see Macaloge
240 I1 Miranda CA U.S.A.
250 E2 Miranda state Venez.
87 F9 Miranda, Lake salt flat W.A. Austr.
183 O4 Miranda de Arga Spain
183 O3 Miranda de Ebro Spain
182 I8 Miranda del Castañar Spain
182 D8 Miranda do Corvo Port.
182 H5 Miranda do Douro Port.
163 E8 Mirande France
182 F6 Mirandela Port.
184 G2 Mirandiba Brazil
244 E5 Mirandillas Mex.
191 K6 Mirandola Italy
163 I7 Mirandol-Bourgnounac France
256 B4 Mirandópolis Brazil
191 M5 Mirano Italy
256 B5 Mirante, Serra do hills Brazil
256 B5 Mirante do Paranapanema Brazil
261 F4 Mira Pampa Arg.
251 F5 Mirapinima Brazil
198 B2 Miras Albania
103 J12 Mirasaka Japan
256 C4 Mirassol Brazil
182 G3 Miravalles mt. Spain
182 I9 Miravete, Puerto de pass Spain
123 M4 Mir Bacheh Kowt Afgh.
Mir-Bashir Azer. see Tärtär
125 L7 Mirbāṭ Oman
125 L7 Mirbāṭ, Ra's c. Oman
129 J6 Mircälal Azer.
175 L5 Mircze Pol.
Mirear Island Egypt see Murayr, Jazirat
246 G4 Mirebalais Haiti
160 G2 Mirebeau Bourgogne France
162 E2 Mirebeau Poitou-Charentes France
157 J7 Mirecourt France
202 B6 Miréméné Chad
163 G9 Miremont France
179 I8 Miren Slovenia
163 H9 Mirepoix France
161 D9 Mireval France
117 J6 Mirganj Bihar India
Mirgorod Ukr. see Myrhorod
95 K2 Miri Sarawak Malaysia
123 J7 Miri mt. Pak.
207 H3 Miria Niger
114 F4 Mirialguda Andhra Prad. India
85 M7 Miriam Vale Qld Austr.
117 O6 Miri Hills India
258 G4 Mirim, Lagoa l. Brazil/Uru.
255 C9 Mirim, Lagoa do l. Brazil
250 D2 Mirimire Venez.
Mirina Limnos Greece see Myrina
83 I3 Mirintu watercourse Qld Austr.
114 D5 Mirjan Karnataka India
123 I7 Mīrjāveh Iran
197 M8 Mirkovo Bulg.
188 D3 Mirna r. Croatia
179 L8 Mirna Slovenia
179 L8 Mirna r. Slovenia
179 L8 Mirna Peč Slovenia
263 G2 Mirny research stn Antarctica
134 H3 Mirnyy Arkhangel'skaya Oblast' Rus. Fed.
139 O9 Mirnyy Bryanskaya Oblast' Rus. Fed.
131 M3 Mirnyy Respublika Sakha (Yakutiya) Rus. Fed.
129 F1 Mirnyy Stavropol'skiy Kray Rus. Fed.
197 K6 Miroč hills Serbia
174 D4 Mirocin Górny Pol.
81 E10 Miromiro mt. South I. N.Z.
223 K4 Mirond Lake Sask. Can.
Mironovka Kharkivs'ka Oblast' Ukr. see Myronivka
Mironovka Kyivs'ka Oblast' Ukr. see Myronivka
179 N2 Mirošov Czech Rep.
174 E2 Mirosławiec Pol.
176 C2 Mirošov Czech Rep.
171 L7 Mirostowice Dolne Pol.
176 D2 Mirovice Czech Rep.
170 G4 Mirow Ger.
123 O5 Mirpur Pak.
123 M9 Mirpur Batoro Pak.
123 M9 Mirpur Khas Pak.
123 L9 Mirpur Sakro Pak.
222 H4 Mirror Alta Can.
210 E3 Mirsale Somalia
110 G6 Mirsali Xinjiang China
Mirs Bay Guangdong/H.K. China see Dapeng Wan
174 D5 Mirsk Pol.
85 K6 Mirtna Qld Austr.
Mirtoan Sea Greece see Myrtoo Pelagos
195 L4 Mirto Crosia Italy
183 J7 Mirueña de los Infanz...
Spain
213 F2 Miruro Moz.
Miryalaguda Andhra Pr...
India see Mirialguda
101 F11 Miryang S. Korea
122 E5 Mīrzā, Chāh-e well Iran
Mirzachirla Turkm. see Murzechirla
Mirzachul Uzbek. see ...
117 I7 Mirzapur Uttar Prad. In...
175 J4 Mirzec Pol.
191 M3 Mis, Lago del l. Italy
191 O8 Misa r. Italy
105 I4 Misaka Japan
105 L5 Misaki Chiba Japan
103 J13 Misaki Ehime Japan
104 B7 Misaki Ōsaka Japan
105 G5 Misakubo Japan
111 E7 Misalay Xinjiang China
191 N8 Misano Adriatico Italy
245 K6 Misantla Mex.
105 I3 Misato Gunma Japan
104 D6 Misato Mie Japan
105 G3 Misato Nagano Japan
102 □1 Misato Okinawa Japan
105 J3 Misato Saitama Japan
105 K4 Misato Saitama Japan
104 B7 Misato Wakayama Japa...
207 H4 Misau Nigeria
102 S6 Misawa Japan
223 K5 Misaw Lake Sask. Can
177 K5 Mişca Romania
193 N5 Miscano r. Italy
190 D3 Mischabel mt. Switz.
179 N5 Mischendorf Austria
225 H4 Miscou Island N.B. Ca...
224 B3 Misehkow r. Ont. Can.
193 M6 Miseno, Capo c. Italy
160 H2 Miserey-Salines Franc...
185 □ Misery, Mount hill Gib...
116 E1 Misgar Jammu and Ka...
214 H9 Misgund S. Africa
122 G4 Mish, Kūh-e hill Iran
115 M9 Misha Andaman & Nico...
India
122 G2 Mishamattawa r. Ont. ...
211 A6 Mishamo Tanz.
100 G6 Mishan Heilong. China
125 I3 Mishāsh al Ashāwī we...
Saudi Arabia
125 I2 Mishāsh al Hādī well
Saudi Arabia
125 I3 Mishāsh az Zuayyinī ...
Saudi Arabia
125 I3 Mishāsh 'Uwayr well
Saudi Arabia
226 H8 Mishawaka IN U.S.A.
139 W6 Misheronskiy Rus. Fe...
226 I1 Mishibishu Lake Ont.
226 G5 Mishicot WI U.S.A.
105 I5 Mishima Japan
103 I12 Mi-shima i. Japan
134 L5 Mishkino Rus. Fed.
124 G5 Mishlah, Khashm hill
Saudi Arabia
129 I4 Mishlesh Rus. Fed.
117 O5 Mishmi Hills India
139 N6 Mishnëvichi Rus. Fed.
134 K2 Mishvan' Rus. Fed.
194 E7 Misilmeri Sicilia Italy
85 N1 Misima Island P.N.G.
258 G2 Misiones prov. Arg.
129 D4 Mısırlı Turkey
128 D2 Misis Dağ hills Turkey
124 F3 Miskah Saudi Arabia
177 I5 Miske Hungary
125 M4 Miskin Oman
242 □R10 Miskitos, Cayos is Nic...
Miskitos, Costa de coastal area Nic. see Costa de Mosquitos
177 J3 Miskolc Hungary
179 L7 Mislinja Slovenia
188 E2 Mislinja r. Slovenia
124 E2 Mismā, Jibāl al mts Saudi Arabia
128 F6 Mismā, Tall al hill Jor...
252 C3 Mismi, Nevado mt. Pe...
161 H8 Mison France
93 G4 Misoöl i. Papua Indon.
234 E7 Mispillion r. DE U.S.A.
226 C2 Misquah Hills MN U.S...
233 □Q3 Misquamicut RI U.S.A.
235 L2 Misr country Africa see...
Misraç Turkey see Kur...
202 B1 Misrātah Libya
116 H6 Misrikh Uttar Prad. Ind...
227 J1 Missanabie Ont. Can.
193 Q7 Missanello Italy
158 G7 Missillac France
224 D3 Missinaibi r. Ont. Can.
227 K1 Missinaibi Lake Ont.
223 J4 Missinipe Sask. Can.
85 H2 Mission r. Qld Austr.
85 I8 Mission SD U.S.A.
237 F12 Mission TX U.S.A.
223 K3 Mission Beach Qld Au...
240 O8 Mission Viejo CA U.S.
206 B3 Missira Senegal
224 C2 Missisa r. Ont. Can.
224 C2 Missisa Lake Ont. Ca...
224 F3 Missisicabi r. Que. Ca...
224 D4 Mississagi r. Ont. Can
224 E5 Mississauga Ont. Can
226 I9 Mississinewa Lake IN...
224 E4 Mississippi r. Ont. Ca...
237 K11 Mississippi r. U.S.A.
237 K9 Mississippi state U.S.A.
237 K11 Mississippi Delta LA ...
227 R4 Mississippi Lake Ont.
237 K10 Mississippi Sound se...
MS U.S.A.
Missolonghi Greece se...
Mesolongi
238 H3 Missoula MT U.S.A.
204 E2 Missour Morocco
236 J6 Missouri r. U.S.A.
236 I6 Missouri state U.S.A.
236 H5 Missouri Valley IA U.S...
84 B4 Mistake Creek N.T. A...
85 K6 Mistake Creek r. Qld ...
225 I3 Mistanipisipou r. Que...
225 F3 Mistassibi r. Que. Can
225 F3 Mistassini Que. Can.
225 F3 Mistassini r. Que. Can
224 F3 Mistassini, Lac l. Que...
225 I2 Mistastin Lake Nfld a...
Lab. Can.
179 O2 Mistelbach Austria
173 K2 Mistelgau Ger.
195 I8 Misterbianco Sicilia It...
143 M4 Mistershults nature re...
Sweden
246 B4 Misteriosa Bank sea ...
Caribbean Sea
149 P7 Misterton Nottingham...
England U.K.
225 I1 Mistinibi, Lac l. Que. ...
224 F3 Mistissini Que. Can.
137 R4 Mistky Ukr.
261 F2 Mistolar, Laguna del ...
198 D5 Mistras tourist site Gr...
194 G8 Mistretta Sicilia Italy
220 E4 Misty Fiords National Monument Wildernes...
nat. park AK U.S.A.
223 K3 Misty Lake Man. Can.
104 D6 Misugi Japan
103 I12 Misumi Japan
Misurata Libya see M...
191 M2 Misurina Italy
140 M3 Misvær Norway
244 B5 Mita, Punta de pt Me...
105 K4 Mitaka Japan
104 F5 Mitake Gifu Japan
104 G4 Mitake Nagano Japan
84 C2 Mitake Moz.
251 H4 Mitaraca hill Suriname
250 D2 Mitare Venez.
203 H6 Mitatib Sudan
150 H4 Mitcheldean Gloucest...
England U.K.
85 K9 Mitchell Qld Austr.
83 N3 Mitchell r. N.S.W. Aust...
85 H3 Mitchell r. Qld Austr.
83 K7 Mitchell r. Vic. Austr.
227 M6 Mitchell Ont. Can.
238 D4 Mitchell OR U.S.A.
236 F4 Mitchell SD U.S.A.
85 J4 Mitchell, Lake Qld Au...

Mitchell, Lake MI U.S.A.
Mitchell, Mount NC U.S.A.
Mitchell and Alice Rivers National Park Qld Austr.
Mitchell Island Cook Is see Nassau
Mitchell Island atoll Tuvalu see Nukulaelae
Mitchell Point N.T. Austr.
Mitchell Range hills N.T. Austr.
Mitchell River National Park Vic. Austr.
Mitchells Pass S. Africa
Mitchelltown VA U.S.A.
Mitchelstown Ireland
Mīt Ghamr Egypt
Mithapur Gujarat India
Mitha Tiwano Pak.
Mithi Pak.
Míthimna Greece see Mithymna
Mithrani Can canal Pak.
Mithrau Pak.
Mithymna Greece
Miti i. Maluku Indon.
Mitiaro i. Cook Is
Mitiero i. Cook Is see Mitiaro
Mitilíni Lesvos Greece see Mytilini
Mitishkino Rus. Fed.
Mititai North I. N.Z.
Mitkof Island AK U.S.A.
Mitla Mex.
Mito Aichi Japan
Mito Ibaraki Japan
Mitō Japan
Mitole Tanz.
Mitomi Japan
Mitomoni Tanz.
Mitra, Kapp c. Svalbard
Mitre mt. North I. N.Z.
Mitre, Península pen. Arg.
Mitre Island Solomon Is
Mitre Peak South I. N.Z.
Mitrofanovka Rus. Fed.
Mitrovica Kosovo Serbia see Kosovska Mitrovica
Mitry-Mory France
Mitsamiouli Njazidja Comoros
Mitsikeli mt. Greece
Mitsinjo Madag.
Mits'iwa Eritrea see Massawa
Mitsoudjé Njazidja Comoros
Mitsue Japan
Mitsuishi Japan
Mitsukaidō Japan
Mitsuke Japan
Mitsumatarenge-dake mt. Japan
Mitsushima Japan
Mitsutōge-yama mt. Japan
Mittagong N.S.W. Austr.
Mitta Mitta Vic. Austr.
Mittelberg Tirol Austria
Mittelberg Vorarlberg Austria
Mittelberg hill Ger.
Mittelbiberach Ger.
Mittelelbe park Ger.
Mittelfranken admin. reg. Ger.
Mittelhausen Ger.
Mittelkalbach Ger.
Mittelland reg. Switz.
Mittellandkanal canal Ger.
Mittelsinn Ger.
Mittelspitze mt. Ger.
Mittenwald Ger.
Mittenwalde Brandenburg Ger.
Mittenwalde Brandenburg Ger.
Mitterbach am Erlaufsee Austria
Mitterding Austria
Mitterdorf im Mürztal Austria
Mitterfels Ger.
Mittersheim France
Mittersill Austria
Mitterskirchen Ger.
Mitterteich Ger.
Mittet Norway
Mittimatalik Nunavut Can. see Pond Inlet
Mittlands skogen reg. Öland Sweden
Mittleres Saaletal park Ger.
Mittweida Ger.
Mitú Col.
Mituas Col.
Mitumba, Chaîne des mts Dem. Rep. Congo
Mitumba, Monts mts Dem. Rep. Congo
Mitwaba Dem. Rep. Congo
Mitwitz Ger.
Mitzic Gabon
Miughalaigh i. Scotland U.K. see Mingulay
Miura Japan
Miura-hantō pen. Japan
Mius r. Rus. Fed.
Miusskiy Liman est. Rus. Fed.
Miusyns'k Ukr.
Miwa Fukushima Japan
Miwa Ibaraki Japan
Miwa Kyōto Japan
Mixian Henan China see Xinmi
Mixteco r. Mex.
Mixtlán Mex.
Miya Japan
Miyada Japan
Miyagase-ko resr Japan
Miyagawa Gifu Japan
Miyagawa Mie Japan
Miya-gawa r. Japan
Miya-gawa r. Japan
Miyagi Okinawa Japan
Miyagi pref. Japan
Miyagusuku-jima i. Okinawa Japan
Miyah, Wādī al watercourse Saudi Arabia
Miyāh, Wādī al watercourse Syria
Miyajima Japan
Miyake-jima i. Japan
Miyako Japan
Miyakoji Japan
Miyako-jima i. Nansei-shotō Japan
Miyakonojō Japan
Miyako-rettō is Japan
Miyako-wan b. Japan
Miyaly Kazakh.
Miyama Fukui Japan
Miyama Gifu Japan
Miyama Kyōto Japan
Miyama Mie Japan
Miyama Wakayama Japan
Miyamae Japan
Miyang Yunnan China see Mile
Miyani Gujarat India
Miyanojō Japan
Miyanoura-dake mt. Japan
Miyazaki Fukui Japan
Miyazaki Miyazaki Japan
Miyazaki pref. Japan
Miyazu Japan
Miyazu-wan b. Japan
Miyi Sichuan China
Miyoshi Aichi Japan
Miyoshi Chiba Japan
Miyoshi Hiroshima Japan
Miyota Japan
Miyun Beijing China
Miyun Shuiku resr China
Mīzāni Afgh.
Mīzan Teferī Eth.
Mizar Turkey see Karakeçi
Mizdah Libya
Mizen Head Ireland
Mizen Head Ireland
Mizhevichy Belarus
Mizhhir"ya Ukr.
Mizhi Shaanxi China
Mizil Romania
Miziya Bulg.
Mizoch Ukr.
Mizofato r. Italy
Mizo Hills state India see Mizoram
Mizoram state India
Mizpah NJ U.S.A.
Mizpe Ramon Israel
252 D4 Mizque Bol.
252 D4 Mizque r. Bol.
105 I4 Mizugaki-yama mt. Japan
104 F2 Mizuhashi Japan
104 B5 Mizuho Kyōto Japan
105 J4 Mizuho Tōkyō Japan
104 F5 Mizunami Japan
105 K3 Mizuno-gawa r. Japan
102 S7 Mizusawa Japan
140 M3 Mjelde Norway
143 L3 Mjölby Sweden
141 I6 Mjølfell Norway
142 G2 Mjøndalen Norway
142 I4 Mjörn l. Sweden
142 G1 Mjøsa l. Norway
215 N7 Mkambati S. Africa
215 O7 Mkambati Nature Reserve S. Africa
211 C6 Mkata Tanz.
211 C6 Mkata Plain Tanz.
215 P2 Mkhaya Game Reserve nature res. Swaziland
215 P2 Mkhondvo r. Swaziland
211 C6 Mkoani Tanz.
211 C6 Mkokotoni Tanz.
211 C6 Mkomazi Tanz.
211 C5 Mkomazi Game Reserve nature res. Tanz.
211 C6 Mkujani Tanz.
211 C6 Mkumbi, Ras pt Tanz.
Mkumvura Zimbabwe see Mukumbura
211 C7 Mkunja Tanz.
211 C6 Mkuranga Tanz.
211 B6 Mkurusi Tanz.
209 F8 Mkushi Zambia
215 Q3 Mkuze S. Africa
215 Q3 Mkuze r. S. Africa
215 Q3 Mkuzi Game Reserve nature res. S. Africa
176 D1 Mladá Boleslav Czech Rep.
176 D2 Mladá Vožice Czech Rep.
176 E1 Mladé Buky Czech Rep.
196 I6 Mladenovac Serbia
197 J8 Mlado Nagoričane Macedonia
211 A6 Mlala Hills Tanz.
211 C6 Mlandizi Tanz.
211 B7 Mlangali Tanz.
215 Q2 Mlaula r. Swaziland
196 J6 Mlava r. Serbia
175 I2 Mława Pol.
175 I3 Mławka r. Pol.
215 Q2 Mlawula Nature Reserve Swaziland
215 P2 Mlilwane Nature Reserve Swaziland
217 □3b Mlima Bénara hill Mayotte
217 □3b Mlima Choungui hill Mayotte
188 F4 Mljet i. Croatia
188 F4 Mljet nat. park Croatia
188 F4 Mljetski Kanal sea chan. Croatia
137 P2 Mlodat' r. Rus. Fed.
175 I3 Młodzieszyn Pol.
211 C7 Mlowoka Tanz.
215 P1 Mlumati r. S. Africa
215 K7 Mlungisi S. Africa
175 H1 Młynary Pol.
175 J3 Młynarze Pol.
136 E3 Mlyniv Ukr.
175 M6 Mlynys'ka Ukr.
215 J1 Mmabatho S. Africa
213 E4 Mmadinare Botswana
212 E4 Mmamabula Botswana
212 E4 Mmashoro Botswana
212 E5 Mmathethe Botswana
215 N8 Mncwasa Point S. Africa
176 D2 Mnichovice Czech Rep.
176 D1 Mnichovo Hradiště Czech Rep.
175 I5 Mnichów Pol.
198 B4 Mnimati mt. Lefkada Greece
175 I4 Mniów Pol.
177 J3 Mníšek nad Hnilcom Slovakia
175 J4 Mniszew Pol.
175 I4 Mniszków Pol.
215 P2 Mnjoli Dam Swaziland
100 K1 Mnogovershinnyy Rus. Fed.
141 H6 Mo Norway
252 B1 Moa r. Brazil
246 F3 Moa Cuba
93 F8 Moa i. Maluku Indon.
128 D7 Moab reg. Jordan
241 W3 Moab UT U.S.A.
208 A5 Moabi Gabon
252 C1 Moaco r. Brazil
91 J9 Moa Island Qld Austr.
79 □7 Moala i. Fiji
122 F4 Mo'allemān Iran
213 G5 Moamba Moz.
81 F9 Moana South I. N.Z.
182 C4 Moaña Spain
208 B5 Moanda Gabon
241 R5 Moapa NV U.S.A.
147 G6 Moate Ireland
213 G3 Moatize Moz.
209 F6 Moba Dem. Rep. Congo
105 L5 Mobara Japan
122 E7 Mobārakābād Iran
122 D5 Mobārakeh Eşfahān Iran
122 F7 Mobārakeh Yazd Iran
208 D3 Mobaye C.A.R.
Mobayembongo Dem. Rep. Congo see Mobayi-Mbongo
208 D3 Mobayi-Mbongo Dem. Rep. Congo
149 M7 Mobberley Cheshire, England U.K.
208 C4 Mobeka Dem. Rep. Congo
236 I6 Moberly MO U.S.A.
222 F4 Moberly Lake B.C. Can.
226 I1 Mobert Ont. Can.
231 C10 Mobile AL U.S.A.
241 T8 Mobile AZ U.S.A.
237 K10 Mobile Bay AL U.S.A.
231 D10 Mobile Point AL U.S.A.
85 J9 Moble watercourse Qld Austr.
92 D5 Mobo Masbate Phil.
236 E3 Mobridge SD U.S.A.
Mobutu, Lake Dem. Rep. Congo/Uganda see Albert, Lake
Mobutu Sese Seko, Lake Dem. Rep. Congo/Uganda see Albert, Lake
246 H4 Moca Dom. Rep.
128 B2 Moca Geçidi pass Turkey
254 C2 Mocajuba Brazil
213 H2 Moçambicano, Planalto plat. Moz.
Moçambique country Africa see Mozambique
213 I2 Moçambique Moz.
213 I2 Mocambo, Porto b. Moz.
Moçâmedes Angola see Namibe
216 □3e Mocanal El Hierro Canary Is
234 C2 Mocanaqua PA U.S.A.
184 B2 Moçarria Port.
240 L4 Moccasin CA U.S.A.
232 C12 Moccasin Gap VA U.S.A.
96 G4 Môc Châu Vietnam
183 M9 Mocejón Spain
177 G3 Močenok Slovakia
139 U6 Mocha r. Rus. Fed.
Mocha Yemen see Al Mukhā
258 B5 Mocha, Isla i. Chile
183 Q6 Mochales Spain
78 □4a Mochenap sea chan. Chuuk Micronesia
242 E5 Mochicahui Mex.
139 V7 Mochily Rus. Fed.
251 E2 Mochirma, Parque Nacional nat. park Venez.
105 H3 Mochizuki Japan
246 □ Mocho Mountains Jamaica
78 □4a Mochonap sea chan. Chuuk Micronesia
175 H3 Mochowo Pol.
212 E5 Mochudi Botswana
174 E3 Mochy Pol.
211 D7 Mocimboa da Praia Moz.
211 C7 Mocimboa do Rovuma Moz.
197 M4 Mociu Romania
143 K2 Möckeln l. Sweden
143 K5 Möckeln l. Sweden
171 E6 Möckern Ger.
171 F6 Möckern-Magdeburger Forst park Ger.
172 G3 Möckmühl Ger.
171 G7 Mockrehna Ger.
231 G8 Mocksville NC U.S.A.
185 L6 Moclín Spain
185 K7 Moclinejo Spain
250 E5 Mocó r. Brazil
250 B4 Mocoa Col.
256 D4 Mococa Brazil
213 G4 Mocoduene Moz.
261 I2 Mocoretá r. Arg.
242 F5 Mocorito Mex.
242 F2 Moctezuma Chihuahua Mex.
244 F3 Moctezuma San Luis Potosí Mex.
242 E3 Moctezuma Sonora Mex.
245 I4 Moctezuma r. Mex.
239 J12 Moctezuma r. Mex.
213 H3 Mocuba Moz.
109 I7 Mocun Guangdong China
161 J6 Modane France
116 D8 Modasa Gujarat India
165 H8 Modave Belgium
150 E7 Modbury Devon, England U.K.
215 I5 Modder r. S. Africa
214 I5 Modderivier S. Africa
123 P6 Model Town Pak.
191 J6 Modena Italy
191 J7 Modena prov. Italy
235 G1 Modena NY U.S.A.
234 D5 Modena PA U.S.A.
241 S4 Modena UT U.S.A.
157 O6 Moder r. France
260 E4 Modestino Pizarro Arg.
240 L4 Modesto CA U.S.A.
194 H10 Modica Sicilia Italy
191 L7 Modigliana Italy
213 F5 Modimolle S. Africa
194 D8 Modione r. Sicilia Italy
175 K5 Modliborzyce Pol.
179 N3 Mödling Austria
175 I4 Modliszewice Pol.
192 B7 Modolo Sardegna Italy
107 K3 Modot Mongolia
176 G3 Modra Slovakia
179 L6 Modriach Austria
188 G3 Modriča Bos.-Herz.
176 F2 Modřice Czech Rep.
179 J6 Mödringberg mt. Austria
177 I3 Modrý Kameň Slovakia
195 L1 Modugno Italy
83 K8 Moe Vic. Austr.
213 H3 Moebase Moz.
80 J3 Moehau hill North I. N.Z.
158 D6 Moëlan-sur-Mer France
150 F1 Moel Famau hill Wales U.K.
150 D1 Moelfre Isle of Anglesey, Wales U.K.
150 F2 Moel Sych hill Wales U.K.
141 K6 Moelv Norway
215 L4 Moemaneng S. Africa
209 D6 Moembe Dem. Rep. Congo
Moen i. Chuuk Micronesia see Weno
140 O2 Moen Norway
191 L3 Moena Italy
251 H3 Moengo Suriname
241 U5 Moenkopi AZ U.S.A.
241 U6 Moenkopi Wash r. AZ U.S.A.
81 E12 Moeraki Point South I. N.Z.
165 E6 Moerbeke Belgium
80 I2 Moerewa North I. N.Z.
164 H5 Moergestel Neth.
165 D6 Moerkerke Belgium
Moero, Lake Dem. Rep. Congo/Zambia see Mweru, Lake
169 C8 Moers Ger.
190 G3 Moesa r. Switz.
214 G3 Moeswal S. Africa
78 □6 Moetambe, Mount Choiseul Solomon Is
146 J12 Moffat Dumfries and Galloway, Scotland U.K.
182 G5 Mofreita Port.
177 L4 Moftin Romania
116 E4 Moga Punjab India
Mogadishu Somalia see Muqdisho
Mogador Morocco see Essaouira
182 G6 Mogadouro Port.
182 G6 Mogadouro, Serra de mts Port.
213 F4 Mogalakwena r. S. Africa
208 C4 Mogalo Dem. Rep. Congo
114 G4 Mogalturra Andhra Prad. India
102 Q8 Mogami-gawa r. Japan
216 □3f Mogán Gran Canaria Canary Is
208 E4 Mogandjo Dem. Rep. Congo
213 F5 Moganyaka S. Africa
110 L7 Mogao Ku Gansu China
124 C8 Mogareb watercourse Eritrea
96 C2 Mogaung Myanmar
100 H3 Mogdy Rus. Fed.
147 F9 Mogeely Ireland
170 F5 Mögelin Ger.
168 G1 Møgeltønder Denmark
179 N6 Mogersdorf Austria
205 G2 Moggar Alg.
191 O3 Moggio Udinese Italy
172 H4 Mögglingen Ger.
123 L2 Moghiyon Tajik.
205 E2 Moghrar-Foukani Alg.
175 I4 Mogielnica Pol.
175 I6 Mogielnica mt. Pol.
256 D5 Mogi-Guaçu Brazil
196 J9 Mogila Macedonia
175 H6 Mogilany Pol.
Mogilev Belarus see Mahilyow
Mogilev Oblast admin. div. Belarus see Mahilyowskaya Voblasts'
Mogilev Podol'skiy Ukr. see Mohyliv Podil's'kyy
Mogilevskaya Oblast' admin. div. Belarus see Mahilyowskaya Voblasts'
174 E3 Mogilnica r. Pol.
174 F3 Mogilno Pol.
256 D5 Mogi-Mirim Brazil
213 I2 Mogincual Moz.
257 H2 Mogiquiçaba Brazil
191 J6 Moglia Italy
191 O9 Mogliano Italy
191 M4 Mogliano Veneto Italy
172 G4 Möglingen Ger.
260 C2 Mogna Arg.
100 A2 Mogocha Rus. Fed.
139 T4 Mogocha r. Rus. Fed.
205 H1 Mogod mts Tunisia
212 E5 Mogoditshane Botswana
182 D8 Mogofores Port.
210 A2 Mogogh Sudan
96 C3 Mogok Myanmar
241 U7 Mogollon Plateau AZ U.S.A.
185 M4 Mogón Spain
Mogontiacum Ger. see Mainz
210 D3 Mogor Eth.
192 B8 Mogorella Sardegna Italy
192 B8 Mogoro Sardegna Italy
192 B8 Mogoro r. Sardegna Italy
197 P3 Mogoşeşti Romania
261 I6 Mogotes, Punta pt Arg.
175 I3 Mogowo Pol.
107 N1 Mogoytuy Rus. Fed.
208 B2 Mogroum Chad
184 F6 Moguer Spain
107 R3 Moguqi Nei Mongol China
213 F4 Mogwadi S. Africa
215 L1 Mogwase S. Africa
177 I4 Mogyoród Hungary
177 H6 Mohács Hungary
80 L6 Mohaka r. North I. N.Z.
116 H9 Mohala Chhattisgarh India
215 M5 Mohale Dam Lesotho
215 L6 Mohale's Hoek Lesotho
236 E1 Mohall ND U.S.A.
122 H4 Mohammad Iran
Moḩammadābād Iran see Darreh Gaz
205 F2 Mohammadia Alg.
Mohammad Reza Shah Pahlavi Dam resr Iran see Dez, Sadd-e
116 H5 Mohan r. India/Nepal
116 F7 Mohana Madh. Prad. India
117 M7 Mohanganj Bangl.
116 G9 Mohari Mahar. India
185 P4 Moharque Spain
241 R6 Mohave, Lake NV U.S.A.
241 R7 Mohave Mountains AZ U.S.A.
226 F2 Mohawk MI U.S.A.
233 L6 Mohawk r. NY U.S.A.
241 S9 Mohawk Mountains AZ U.S.A.
116 H7 Mohdra Madh. Prad. India
100 C2 Mohe Heilong. China
141 N6 Mohed Sweden
143 K4 Moheda Sweden
182 H8 Mohedas de Granadilla Spain
235 K2 Mohegan CT U.S.A.
235 H2 Mohegan Lake NY U.S.A.
Mohéli i. Comoros see Mwali
176 F2 Mohelnice Czech Rep.
176 F2 Mohelno Czech Rep.
212 D3 Mohembo Botswana
123 M8 Mohenjo Daro tourist site Pak.
147 D7 Moher, Cliffs of Ireland
183 N7 Mohernando Spain
147 H7 Mohil Ireland
137 P6 Mohila Bel'mak, Hora hill Ukr.
147 G5 Mohill Ireland
140 U5 Möhkö Fin.
215 L2 Mohlakeng S. Africa
171 F7 Möhlau Ger.
140 □ Mohn, Kapp c. Svalbard
169 E8 Möhne r. Ger.
169 F8 Möhnetalsperre resr Ger.
234 C4 Mohnton PA U.S.A.
96 C2 Mohnyin Myanmar
252 C3 Moho Peru
114 D4 Mohol Mahar. India
241 S7 Mohon Peak AZ U.S.A.
177 I4 Mohora Hungary
171 H9 Mohorn Ger.
217 □3a Mohoro Njazidja Comoros
211 C7 Mohoro Tanz.
116 G8 Mohpani Madh. Prad. India
173 J2 Möhrendorf Ger.
168 I1 Mohrkirch Ger.
234 D4 Mohrsville PA U.S.A.
136 G5 Mohyliv Podil's'kyy Ukr.
136 F3 Mohylyany Ukr.
142 C3 Moi Rogaland Norway
142 D3 Moi Vest-Agder Norway
186 J4 Moià Spain
194 H1 Moiano Italy
146 E9 Moidart reg. Scotland U.K.
212 E4 Moijabana Botswana
182 E7 Moimenta da Beira Port.
111 E11 Moincêr Xizang China
111 J12 Moinda Xizang China
117 M6 Moindawang Arun. Prad. India
78 □5 Moindou New Caledonia
159 I7 Moine r. France
213 G5 Moine Moz.
197 O4 Moineşti Romania
160 E5 Moingt France
Moinkum des. Kazakh. see Moyynkum, Peski
Mointy Kazakh. see Moyynty
147 J4 Moira Northern Ireland U.K.
251 I5 Moiraba Brazil
Moírai Kriti Greece see Moires
140 M3 Mo i Rana Norway
117 N7 Moirang Manipur India
160 H4 Moirans-en-Montagne France
163 F7 Moirax France
198 F7 Moires Kriti Greece
138 I3 Mõisaküla Estonia
168 I4 Moisburg Ger.
158 I6 Moisdon-la-Rivière France
197 M3 Moisei Romania
261 G2 Moisés Ville Arg.
225 H3 Moisie Que. Can.
225 H3 Moisie r. Que. Can.
156 E4 Moislains France
163 G7 Moissac France
161 I9 Moissac-Bellevue France
208 C2 Moïssala Chad
160 H2 Moissey France
192 C3 Moïta Corse France
182 D8 Moita Aveiro Port.
184 B3 Moita Setúbal Port.
251 E3 Moitaco Venez.
187 D10 Moixent-Mogente Spain
143 O2 Möja i. Sweden
185 P6 Mojácar Spain
183 K6 Mojados Spain
240 N6 Mojave CA U.S.A.
240 O7 Mojave r. CA U.S.A.
240 O6 Mojave Desert CA U.S.A.
108 C7 Mojiang Yunnan China
256 D5 Moji das Cruzes Brazil
256 C4 Moji-Guaçu r. Brazil
103 H13 Mojikō Japan
185 L3 Mojina mt. Spain
196 H8 Mojkovac Montenegro
252 D5 Mojo Bol.
210 C2 Mojo Eth.
95 J8 Mojokerto Jawa Indon.
185 M6 Mojón Alto mt. Spain
183 P9 Mojón Alto mt. Spain
258 D2 Mojones, Cerro mt. Arg.
252 D3 Mojos, Llanos de plain Bol.
210 D3 Mojo Shet' r. Eth.
252 D4 Mojotoro Bol.
179 I7 Mojstrana Slovenia
254 C2 Moju Brazil
105 L3 Mōka Japan
217 □1b Moka Mauritius
80 J5 Mokai North I. N.Z.
117 J7 Mokama Bihar India
209 F8 Mokambo Dem. Rep. Congo
240 □D12 Mōkapu Peninsula HI U.S.A.
208 D4 Mokaria Dem. Rep. Congo
80 I5 Mokau North I. N.Z.
80 I5 Mokau r. North I. N.Z.
208 B4 Mokéko Congo
240 K3 Mokelumne r. CA U.S.A.
240 K3 Mokelumne Aqueduct canal CA U.S.A.
122 F7 Mokh, Gowd-e l. Iran
215 M5 Mokhoabong Pass Lesotho
215 N5 Mokhotlong Lesotho
139 T9 Mokhovoye Rus. Fed.
131 N3 Mokhsogollokh Rus. Fed.
122 H5 Mokhtārān Iran
209 F6 Mokimbo Dem. Rep. Congo
81 B14 Mokinui Island Stewart I. N.Z.
136 G3 Mokiyivtsi Ukr.
205 H2 Moknine Tunisia
175 K3 Mokobody Pol.
Mokogai i. Fiji see Makogai
80 J2 Mokohinau Islands North I. N.Z.
117 O6 Mokokchung Nagaland India
207 I4 Mokolo Cameroon
213 E4 Mokolo r. S. Africa
213 F5 Mokopane S. Africa
81 D13 Mokoreta South I. N.Z.
81 D13 Mokoreta hill South I. N.Z.
81 C13 Mokotua South I. N.Z.
101 E11 Mokp'o S. Korea
196 I8 Mokra Gora mts Montenegro/Serbia
137 K5 Mokra Kalyhirka Ukr.
177 K3 Mokrance Slovakia
175 J2 Mokre, Jezioro l. Pol.
196 I5 Mokrin Vojvodina Serbia
137 P6 Mokri Yaly r. Ukr.
179 L8 Mokronog Slovenia
120 B2 Mokrous Rus. Fed.
139 S6 Mokroye Moskovskaya Oblast' Rus. Fed.
139 T8 Mokroye Tul'skaya Oblast' Rus. Fed.
135 H5 Moksha r. Rus. Fed.
135 I5 Mokshan Rus. Fed.
Môktama Myanmar see Mottama
240 □D12 Moku 'Āuia i. HI U.S.A.
240 □C12 Mokulē'ia HI U.S.A.
240 □D12 Moku Lua is HI U.S.A.
Mokundurra Rajasthan India see Mukandwara
Mokvin Pershotravnevoye Ukr. see Mokvyn
136 F3 Mokvyn Ukr.
207 G4 Mokwa Nigeria
215 L3 Mokwallo S. Africa
165 H6 Mol Belgium
177 J6 Mol Vojvodina Serbia
187 J8 Mola, Cap de sa c. Spain
186 E7 Mola de Ares mt. Spain
195 M1 Mola di Bari Italy
Molaly Kazakh. see Mulaly
163 H9 Molandier France
245 I5 Molango Mex.
198 D6 Molaoi Greece
192 D6 Molara, Isola i. Sardegna Italy
190 F6 Molare Italy
191 R7 Molat Croatia
188 E3 Molat i. Croatia
187 C10 Molatón mt. Spain
168 E5 Molbergen Ger.
179 J6 Mölbling Austria
150 F1 Mold Flintshire, Wales U.K.
121 R2 Moldary Kazakh.
177 J3 Moldava nad Bodvou Slovakia
Moldavia country Europe see Moldova
Moldavskaya S.S.R. country Europe see Moldova
140 I5 Molde Norway
140 I5 Moldefjorden inlet Norway
140 M3 Moldjord Norway
136 H7 Moldova country Europe
197 O4 Moldova r. Romania
197 J6 Moldova Nouă Romania
197 M5 Moldoveanu, Vârful mt. Romania
197 M2 Moldovei, Podişul plat. Romania
136 G6 Moldovei Centrale, Podişul plat. Moldova
136 G6 Moldovei de Nord, Cîmpia lowland Moldova
136 G5 Moldovei de Nord, Podişul plat. Moldova
136 H7 Moldovei de Sud, Cîmpia plain Moldova
197 N3 Moldoviţa Romania
129 A2 Moldovka Rus. Fed.
211 B7 Mole Tanz.
150 E6 Mole r. England U.K.
108 A6 Mole Chaung r. Myanmar
182 C5 Moledo Viana do Castelo Port.
182 E7 Moledo Viseu Port.
225 H4 Molega Lake N.S. Can.
208 D3 Molegbe Dem. Rep. Congo
182 D7 Molelos Port.
215 M3 Molen r. S. Africa
206 E4 Mole National Park Ghana
165 F7 Molenbeek-St-Jean Belgium
158 B5 Molène, Île de i. France
212 E5 Molepolole Botswana
149 Q6 Molescroft East Riding of Yorkshire, England U.K.
156 H8 Molesmes France
138 I6 Molėtai Lith.
193 R5 Molfetta Italy
168 J2 Molfsee Ger.
140 O5 Moliden Sweden
163 G7 Molières Midi-Pyrénées France
163 H6 Molières Midi-Pyrénées France
161 E8 Molières-sur-Cèze France
163 B8 Moliets-et-Maa France
260 C3 Molina Arg.
260 B4 Molina Chile
193 L3 Molina Aterno Italy
183 Q7 Molina de Aragón Spain
187 C11 Molina de Segura Spain
191 J4 Molina di Ledro Italy
193 N5 Molinara Italy
182 H3 Molinaseca Spain
236 J5 Moline IL U.S.A.
237 G7 Moline KS U.S.A.
191 L6 Molinella Italy
161 J7 Molines-en-Queyras France
160 D4 Molinet France
160 H4 Molinges France
185 O4 Molinicos Spain
191 L2 Molini di Tures Italy
231 D10 Molino FL U.S.A.
234 C3 Molino PA U.S.A.
186 E3 Molino de Villobas Spain
261 G3 Molino Doll Arg.
258 D2 Molinos Arg.
186 E6 Molinos Spain
184 G3 Molinos de Matachel, Embalse de los resr Spain
186 J5 Molins de Rei Spain
209 F7 Moliro Dem. Rep. Congo
193 N4 Molise admin. reg. Italy
193 P7 Moliterno Italy
163 I10 Molitg-les-Bains France
177 L5 Moliviş mt. Romania
171 F8 Mölkau Ger.
143 J2 Molkom Sweden
178 H6 Möll r. Austria
192 A5 Molla, Capo c. Sardegna Italy
122 C4 Mollā Bodāgh Iran
120 F8 Mollagara Turkm.
129 J5 Mollakänd Azer.
129 B6 Mollaömer Turkey
142 F6 Møllebjerg hill Denmark
183 L2 Molledo Spain
140 Q2 Mollejos hill Norway
117 O7 Mol Len mt. Nagaland India
170 H4 Möllenbeck Ger.
252 C4 Mollendo Peru
170 G3 Möllenhagen Ger.
87 D11 Mollerin, Lake salt flat W.A. Austr.
186 G4 Mollerussa Spain
160 D4 Molles France
186 J4 Mollet del Vallès Spain
156 D4 Molliens-Dreuil France
185 J6 Mollina Spain
190 G1 Mollis Switz.
179 J4 Molln Austria
170 H3 Mölln Mecklenburg-Vorpommern Ger.
168 K3 Mölln Schleswig-Holstein Ger.
186 J3 Molló Spain
178 G5 Mölltal val. Austria
143 K3 Mölltorp Sweden
142 I4 Mölnlycke Sweden
240 □B11 Moloa'a HI U.S.A.
137 O6 Molochans'k Ukr.
137 O7 Molochna r. Ukr.
137 M8 Molochne Ukr.
134 G4 Molochnoye Rus. Fed.
134 F1 Molochnyy Rus. Fed.
137 O7 Molochnyy Lyman inlet Ukr.
Molodechno Belarus see Maladzyechna
137 L5 Molodizhne Kirovohrads'ka Oblast' Ukr.
137 N9 Molodizhne Respublika Krym Ukr.
139 P8 Molod'kovo Rus. Fed.
206 D3 Molodo Mali
121 N1 Molodogvardeyskoye Kazakh.
139 Q5 Molodoy Tud Rus. Fed.
139 U3 Mologa r. Rus. Fed.
240 □D12 Moloka'i i. HI U.S.A.
139 T3 Molokovo Rus. Fed.
134 J4 Moloma r. Rus. Fed.
161 C6 Molompize France
83 L5 Molong N.S.W. Austr.
212 D6 Molopo watercourse Botswana/S. Africa
214 I1 Moloporivier Botswana
198 D4 Molos Greece
Molotov Rus. Fed. see Perm'
Molotovo Rus. Fed. see Oktyabr'skoye
Molotovsk Kyrg. see Kayyngdy
Molotovsk Arkhangel'skaya Oblast' Rus. Fed. see Severodvinsk
Molotovsk Kirovskaya Oblast' Rus. Fed. see Nolinsk
207 I6 Moloundou Cameroon
136 I6 Molovata Moldova
209 D6 Molowaie Dem. Rep. Congo
160 F1 Moloy France
169 K8 Molschleben Ger.
157 N6 Molsheim France
223 L5 Molson Man. Can.
223 L4 Molson Lake Man. Can.
215 K7 Molteno S. Africa
214 G8 Moltenopass pass S. Africa
192 C3 Moltifao Corse France
91 H8 Molu i. Indon.
Moluccas is Indon. see Maluku
Molucca Sea Indon. see Maluku, Laut
183 R10 Moluengo mt. Spain
213 H2 Molumbo Moz.
191 J3 Molveno Italy
191 J3 Molveno, Lago di l. Italy
139 P4 Molvotitsy Rus. Fed.
209 E7 Molwe Dem. Rep. Congo
208 D5 Moma Dem. Rep. Congo
213 H3 Moma Moz.
244 D4 Momax Mex.
83 I4 Momba N.S.W. Austr.
254 F3 Mombaça Brazil
190 E6 Mombaldone Italy
211 C5 Mombasa Kenya
184 C4 Mombeja Port.
183 J8 Mombeltrán Spain
208 C4 Mombenzélé Dem. Rep. Congo
190 E6 Mombercelli Italy
Mombetsu Hokkaidō Japan see Monbetsu
117 N7 Mombi New Manipur India
208 C5 Momboyo r. Dem. Rep. Congo
169 H10 Mömbris Ger.
256 A3 Mombuca, Serra da hills Brazil
182 H4 Mombuey Spain
197 N9 Momchilgrad Bulg.
124 E7 Momed i. Saudi Arabia
Momeik Myanmar see Mong Mit
226 G8 Momence IL U.S.A.
125 L9 Momi, Ra's pt Suquṭrā Yemen
184 H8 Momia, Sierra mts Spain
165 F8 Momignies Belgium
242 □P11 Momotombo, Volcán vol. Nic.
104 B7 Momoyama Japan
92 D5 Mompog Passage Phil.
208 D4 Mompono Dem. Rep. Congo
250 C2 Mompós Col.
131 P3 Momskiy Khrebet mts Rus. Fed.
163 C8 Momuy France
142 I6 Møn i. Denmark
117 O6 Mon Nagaland India
96 C6 Mon state Myanmar
241 U2 Mona UT U.S.A.
247 J4 Mona, Isla i. Puerto Rico
185 L7 Mona, Punta de la pt Spain
232 E8 Monaca PA U.S.A.
146 A7 Monach, Sound of sea chan. Scotland U.K.
185 L6 Monachil Spain
185 L6 Monachil r. Spain
146 A7 Monach Islands Scotland U.K.
192 C4 Monacia-d'Aullène Corse France
161 K9 Monaco country Europe
264 H4 Monaco Basin sea feature N. Atlantic Ocean
146 G8 Monadhliath Mountains Scotland U.K.
251 F2 Monagas state Venez.
147 I4 Monaghan Ireland
147 I4 Monaghan county Ireland
237 D10 Monahans TX U.S.A.
147 J7 Monamolin Ireland
247 I4 Mona Passage Dom. Rep./Puerto Rico
213 I2 Monapo Moz.
209 C7 Mona Quimbundo Angola
146 F8 Monar, Loch l. Scotland U.K.
222 E5 Monarch Mountain B.C. Can.
239 K7 Monarch Pass CO U.S.A.
241 U2 Mona Reservoir UT U.S.A.
222 G5 Monashee Mountains B.C. Can.
195 L7 Monasterace Italy
147 H6 Monasterevin Ireland
192 C9 Monastir Sardegna Italy
Monastir Macedonia see Bitola
205 H2 Monastir Tunisia
175 M6 Monastyrets' Ukr.
Monastyrishche Ukr. see Monastyryshche
139 O7 Monastyrshchina Rus. Fed.
136 I5 Monastyryshche Ukr.
136 E4 Monastyrys'ka Ukr.
207 H5 Monatélé Cameroon
81 E11 Monavale South I. N.Z.
79 □7a Monavatu mt. Viti Levu Fiji
147 G8 Monavullagh Mountains hills Ireland
163 F6 Monbahus France
163 E6 Monbazillac France
163 G8 Monbéqui France
102 T4 Monbetsu Hokkaidō Japan
102 U2 Monbetsu Hokkaidō Japan
207 I4 Monboré Cameroon
163 G8 Monbrun France
187 E8 Moncada Spain
190 D5 Moncalieri Italy
190 E5 Moncalvo Italy
182 G4 Moncalvo mt. Spain
182 D4 Monção Port.
184 D6 Moncarapacho Port.
163 E7 Moncaut France
183 Q5 Moncayo, Sierra del mts Spain
159 L6 Moncé-en-Belin France
157 L6 Moncel-sur-Seille France
190 E2 Mönch mt. Switz.
140 V3 Monchegorsk Rus. Fed.
169 B8 Mönchengladbach Ger.
179 O4 Mönchhof Austria
190 I7 Monchio delle Corti Italy
184 B6 Monchique Port.
184 B6 Monchique, Serra de mts Port.
173 J4 Mönchsdeggingen Ger.
247 □3 Monchy St Lucia
231 G9 Moncks Corner SC U.S.A.
163 F7 Monclar France
163 H8 Monclar-de-Quercy France
243 I4 Monclova Mex.
187 E8 Moncofa Spain
158 F5 Moncontour Bretagne France
159 K8 Moncontour Poitou-Charentes France
225 G3 Moncouche, Lac l. Que. Can.
159 J8 Moncoutant France
163 E7 Moncrabeau France
225 H4 Moncton N.B. Can.
185 J7 Monda Spain
255 B8 Mondai Brazil
182 D4 Mondariz Spain
182 D4 Mondariz-Balneario Spain
163 G9 Mondavezan France
191 N8 Mondavio Italy
182 C8 Mondego r. Port.
182 C8 Mondego, Cabo c. Port.
183 N8 Mondéjar Spain
194 E7 Mondello Sicilia Italy
159 K3 Mondeville France
208 D4 Mondimbi Dem. Rep. Congo
182 E6 Mondim de Basto Port.
208 D4 Mondjamboli Dem. Rep. Congo
215 O3 Mondlo S. Africa
202 B6 Mondo Chad
191 O8 Mondolfo Italy
182 F2 Mondoñedo Spain
165 J9 Mondorf-les-Bains Lux.
159 M6 Mondoubleau France
190 D7 Mondovì Italy
226 C5 Mondovi WI U.S.A.
161 F8 Mondragon France
193 L5 Mondragone Italy
179 H4 Mondsee Austria
179 H4 Mondsee l. Austria
211 C5 Monduli Tanz.
187 E9 Mondúver hill Spain
246 □ Moneague Jamaica
177 L5 Moneasa Romania
162 H4 Monédières, Massif des hills France
226 G8 Monee IL U.S.A.
147 E6 Moneen Ireland
190 G7 Moneglia Italy
186 E4 Monegrillo Spain
186 D4 Monegros, Canal de Spain
163 C9 Monein France
198 E6 Monemvasia Greece
100 L5 Moneron, Ostrov i. Rus. Fed.
232 F8 Monessen PA U.S.A.
184 G4 Monesterio Spain
161 H7 Monestier-de-Clermont France
163 I7 Monestiés France
227 S1 Monet Que. Can.
232 F11 Moneta VA U.S.A.
238 K5 Moneta WY U.S.A.
156 G8 Monéteau France
237 I7 Monett MO U.S.A.
186 D5 Moneva, Embalse de resr Spain
147 G7 Moneygall Ireland
146 D13 Moneyglass Northern Ireland U.K.
147 I3 Moneymore Northern Ireland U.K.
148 D4 Moneyneany Northern Ireland U.K.
148 F4 Moneyreagh Northern Ireland U.K.
191 P4 Monfalcone Italy
193 N6 Monfecorvino Rovella Italy
163 F6 Monflanquin France
250 D4 Monfort Col.
163 F8 Monfort France
184 E2 Monforte Port.
182 F9 Monforte da Beira Port.
190 D6 Monforte d'Alba Italy
187 D11 Monforte del Cid Spain
182 E3 Monforte de Lemos Spain
186 D5 Monforte de Moyuela Spain
182 G8 Monfortinho Port.
184 C3 Monfurado hill Port.
184 C3 Monfurado, Serra de mts Port.
209 E7 Monga Katanga Dem. Rep. Congo
208 D3 Monga Orientale Dem. Rep. Congo
256 D6 Mongaguá Brazil
208 C4 Mongala r. Dem. Rep. Congo
210 A3 Mongalla Sudan
117 M6 Mongar Bhutan
234 F2 Mongaup r. NY U.S.A.
234 F1 Mongaup Valley NY U.S.A.
208 F4 Mongbwalu Dem. Rep. Congo
96 H4 Mông Cai Vietnam
209 D5 Mongemputu Dem. Rep. Congo
87 D10 Mongers Lake salt flat W.A. Austr.
78 □6 Mongga New Georgia Is Solomon Is
107 P2 Monggon Qulu Nei Mongol China
96 D4 Mong Hai Myanmar
96 D4 Mong Hang Myanmar
191 K7 Monghidoro Italy
108 C8 Mong Hkan Myanmar
96 D4 Mong Hkok Myanmar
96 D4 Mong Hpayak Myanmar
96 D4 Mong Hsat Myanmar
96 C4 Mong Hsawk Myanmar
96 D4 Mong Hsu Myanmar
Monghyr Bihar India see Munger
96 C4 Mong Kung Myanmar
96 D5 Mong Kyawt Myanmar
117 L8 Mongla Bangl.
96 E4 Mong La Myanmar
96 C4 Mong Lang Myanmar
96 E4 Mong Lin Myanmar
96 E4 Mong Loi Myanmar
96 C3 Mong Long Myanmar
96 D4 Mong Ma Myanmar
96 C5 Mong Mau Myanmar
96 C3 Mong Mit Myanmar
96 C4 Mong Nai Myanmar
96 D4 Mong Nawng Myanmar
202 C6 Mongo Chad
Mongó hill Spain see Montgó
106 H3 Mongolia country Asia
Mongolküre Xinjiang China see Zhaosu
Mongol Uls country Asia see Mongolia
207 H6 Mongomo Equat. Guinea
86 I3 Mongona, Mount hill W.A. Austr.
207 I3 Mongonu Nigeria
123 O4 Mongora Pak.
202 D6 Mongororo Chad
208 C4 Mongoumba C.A.R.
146 L9 Mongour hill Scotland U.K.
96 D4 Mong Pan Myanmar
96 D3 Mong Pat Myanmar
96 D3 Mong Pawk Myanmar
96 D4 Mong Ping Myanmar
96 D4 Mong Pu Myanmar
96 D4 Mong Pu-awn Myanmar
190 E4 Mongrando Italy
244 E8 Mongrove, Punta pt Mex.
96 D3 Mong Si Myanmar
108 B8 Mong Ton Myanmar
96 D4 Mong Tum Myanmar
108 A7 Mong Tung Myanmar
209 D8 Mongu Zambia
209 B9 Mongua Angola
206 B2 Mônguel Maur.
191 M2 Monguelfo Italy
96 E4 Mong Un Myanmar
96 D3 Mong Yai Myanmar
96 D4 Mong Yang Myanmar
96 D4 Mong Yawn Myanmar
96 E4 Mong Yawng Myanmar
96 C3 Mong Yu Myanmar
106 H3 Mönhbulag Mongolia
233 □P5 Monhegan Island ME U.S.A.
173 J4 Monheim Ger.
106 B3 Mönh Hayrhan Uul mt. Mongolia
146 I12 Moniaive Dumfries and Galloway, Scotland U.K.
226 E4 Monico WI U.S.A.
161 G8 Monieux France
146 K10 Monifieth Angus, Scotland U.K.
261 G2 Monigotes Arg.
148 C6 Monilea Ireland
250 C3 Moniquirá Col.
161 D7 Monistrol-d'Allier France
186 I4 Monistrol de Montserrat Spain
161 E6 Monistrol-sur-Loire France
240 P3 Monitor Mountain NV U.S.A.
240 P3 Monitor Range mts NV U.S.A.
250 B2 Moñitos Col.
122 E6 Monj Iran
183 P9 Monje, Sierra del mts Spain
257 E3 Monjolos Brazil
122 F2 Monjukly Turkm.
168 J2 Mönkeberg Ger.
211 B8 Monkey Bay Malawi
87 B8 Monkey Mia W.A. Austr.
175 K2 Mońki Pol.
84 H8 Monkira Qld Austr.
222 F4 Monkman Provincial Park B.C. Can.
150 D6 Monkokehampton Devon, England U.K.
208 D5 Monkoto Dem. Rep. Congo
151 N3 Monks Eleigh Suffolk, England U.K.
227 M6 Monkton Ont. Can.
234 B5 Monkton MD U.S.A.
163 F9 Monléon-Magnoac France
187 E7 Monlleó, Riu r. Spain
150 G4 Monmouth Monmouthshire, Wales U.K.
240 M5 Monmouth CA U.S.A.
236 J5 Monmouth IL U.S.A.
235 G4 Monmouth County county NJ U.S.A.
234 F4 Monmouth Junction NJ U.S.A.
222 F5 Monmouth Mountain B.C. Can.
150 G4 Monmouthshire admin. div. Wales U.K.
159 M6 Monnaie France
232 B8 Monnett OH U.S.A.
164 H4 Monnickendam Neth.
150 G4 Monnow r. England/Wales U.K.
207 F5 Mono r. Togo
242 □R12 Mono, Punta del pt Nic.
78 □6 Mono Island Solomon Is
177 K3 Monok Hungary
240 N3 Mono Lake CA U.S.A.
199 I6 Monolithos Rodos Greece
233 P7 Monomoy Island MA U.S.A.
226 H9 Monon IN U.S.A.
226 C6 Monona IA U.S.A.
232 F8 Monongahela r. PA U.S.A.
195 M2 Monopoli Italy
177 I4 Monor Hungary
247 □7 Monos Island Trin. and Tob.
177 K4 Monostorpályi Hungary
202 D5 Monou Chad
187 D11 Monóvar Spain
Monover Spain see Monóvar
81 B12 Monowai, Lake South I. N.Z.
163 F6 Monpazier France
183 R3 Monreal Spain
185 N2 Monreal r. Spain
186 C6 Monreal del Campo Spain
194 E7 Monreale Sicilia Italy
146 G13 Monreith Dumfries and Galloway, Scotland U.K.
231 F9 Monroe GA U.S.A.
236 I5 Monroe IA U.S.A.
237 I9 Monroe LA U.S.A.
227 K8 Monroe MI U.S.A.
231 G8 Monroe NC U.S.A.
234 F2 Monroe NJ U.S.A.
235 G2 Monroe NY U.S.A.
241 T3 Monroe UT U.S.A.
232 F11 Monroe VA U.S.A.

238 D3 Monroe WA U.S.A.
226 E7 Monroe WI U.S.A.
226 E5 Monroe Center WI U.S.A.
236 J6 Monroe City MO U.S.A.
234 E2 Monroe County county PA U.S.A.
230 D6 Monroe Lake IN U.S.A.
227 R8 Monroeton PA U.S.A.
231 D10 Monroeville AL U.S.A.
226 J9 Monroeville IN U.S.A.
234 E5 Monroeville NJ U.S.A.
232 C7 Monroeville OH U.S.A.
206 C5 Monrovia Liberia
182 H9 Monroy Spain
186 E6 Monroyo Spain
165 E8 Mons Belgium
161 B9 Mons Languedoc-Roussillon France
161 J9 Mons Provence-Alpes-Côte d'Azur France
261 I5 Monsalvo Arg.
193 L2 Monsampolo del Tronto Italy
182 F8 Monsanto Port.
257 H3 Monsarás, Ponta de pt Brazil
184 E4 Monsaraz Port.
169 B9 Monschau Ger.
162 F5 Monsec France
163 D9 Monségur Aquitaine France
163 E6 Monségur Aquitaine France
191 L5 Monselice Italy
163 F7 Monsempron-Libos France
156 F2 Mons-en-Barœul France
235 G2 Monsey NY U.S.A.
172 F4 Mönsheim Ger.
172 E2 Mönsheim Ger.
142 I7 Møns Klint cliff Denmark
160 F4 Monsols France
233 □P3 Monson ME U.S.A.
164 F4 Monster Neth.
143 M4 Mönsterås Sweden
191 J8 Monsummano Terme Italy
190 D6 Monta Italy
169 E10 Montabaur Ger.
187 E10 Montaberner Spain
163 K9 Montady France
178 A5 Montafon val. Austria
161 C10 Montagnac France
191 K5 Montagnana Italy
162 D6 Montagne France
213 □K2 Montagne d'Ambre, Parc National de la nat. park Madag.
156 G5 Montagne de Reims, Parc Naturel Régional de la nature res. France
160 H2 Montagney France
161 C9 Montagnol France
160 E4 Montagny France
162 E5 Montagrier France
214 E9 Montagu S. Africa
225 I4 Montague P.E.I. Can.
234 F2 Montague NJ U.S.A.
237 G9 Montague TX U.S.A.
220 D3 Montague Island AK U.S.A.
87 E9 Montague Range hills W.A. Austr.
86 H3 Montague Sound b. W.A. Austr.
249 G7 Montagu Island S. Sandwich Is
Montagu Island Vanuatu see Nguna
158 I8 Montaigu France
163 G7 Montaigu-de-Quercy France
160 B4 Montaigut France
163 G8 Montaigut-sur-Save France
191 J8 Montaione Italy
95 K5 Montalat r. Indon.
186 D6 Montalbán Spain
185 J5 Montalbán de Córdoba Spain
195 I7 Montalbano Elicona Sicilia Italy
195 L3 Montalbano Jonico Italy
183 O9 Montalbo Spain
192 G1 Montalcino Italy
191 K8 Montale Italy
182 E5 Montalegre Port.
160 G5 Montalieu-Vercieu France
162 B5 Montalivet-les-Bains France
194 E9 Montallegro Sicilia Italy
195 J7 Montalto mt. Italy
193 L2 Montalto delle Marche Italy
192 H3 Montalto di Castro Italy
192 H3 Montalto Marina Italy
193 Q9 Montalto Uffugo Italy
182 E9 Montalvão Port.
250 B5 Montalvo Ecuador
240 M7 Montalvo CA U.S.A.
182 I5 Montamarta Spain
197 L7 Montana Bulg.
190 C3 Montana Switz.
238 J3 Montana state U.S.A.
216 □3c Montaña Clara i. Canary Is
242 □P10 Montaña de Comayagua, Parque Nacional nat. park Hond.
243 O10 Montaña de Cusuco, Parque Nacional nat. park Hond.
242 □P10 Montaña de Yoro nat. park Hond.
Montañana Spain see Puente de Montañana
242 □Q10 Montañas de Colón mts Hond.
184 G2 Montánchez hill Spain
184 G2 Montánchez, Sierra de mts Spain
234 B3 Montandon PA U.S.A.
187 D7 Montanejos Spain
163 D9 Montaner France
257 G3 Montanha Brazil
251 H4 Montanhas do Tumucumaque, Parque Nacional nat. park Brazil
193 O7 Montano Antilia Italy
163 H8 Montans France
193 M4 Montaquila Italy
184 C2 Montargil Port.
184 C2 Montargil, Barragem de resr Port.
156 E8 Montargis France
163 H8 Montastruc-la-Conseillère France
156 D5 Montataire France
163 G7 Montauban France
158 G5 Montauban-de-Bretagne France
163 I9 Montaud, Pic de mt. France
159 J5 Montaudin France
233 N7 Montauk NY U.S.A.
235 L2 Montauk, Lake b. NY U.S.A.
233 N7 Montauk Point NY U.S.A.
163 F6 Montauriol France
161 J9 Montauroux France
163 C8 Montaut Aquitaine France
163 D9 Montaut Aquitaine France
163 H9 Montaut Midi-Pyrénées France
163 F8 Montaut-les-Crénaux France
215 M4 Mont-aux-Sources mt. Lesotho
163 F7 Montayral France
193 M4 Montazzoli Italy
160 E1 Montbard France
160 H2 Montbarrey France
163 G8 Montbartier France
163 I7 Montbazens France
161 D9 Montbazin France
159 M7 Montbazon France
160 J1 Montbéliard France
160 I3 Montbenoît France
163 F9 Montbernard France
163 G7 Montbeton France
161 C10 Montblanc France
186 H5 Montblanc Spain
Montblanch Spain see Montblanc
217 □1b Mont Blanche Mauritius
160 J5 Mont Blanc Tunnel France/Italy
161 F7 Montboucher-sur-Jabron France
160 I2 Montbozon France
186 H5 Montbrió del Camp Spain
160 E5 Montbrison France
162 F4 Montbron France
163 H6 Montbrun France
161 G8 Montbrun-les-Bains France
232 D11 Montcalm WV U.S.A.
163 E6 Montcaret France
156 C2 Montcavrel France
160 E3 Montceau-les-Mines France
160 E3 Montcenis France
161 J6 Mont Cenis, Lac du l. France
160 E3 Montchanin France
235 G3 Montclair NJ U.S.A.
156 H4 Montcornet France
156 E8 Montcresson France
163 G7 Montcuq France
156 I4 Montcy-Notre-Dame France
161 D9 Montdardier France
161 J7 Mont-Dauphin France
163 D8 Mont-de-Marsan France
156 E4 Montdidier France
160 B5 Mont-Dore France
261 F5 Monte, Laguna del l. Arg.
193 P8 Montea mt. Italy
252 D4 Monteagudo Bol.
183 Q5 Monteagudo Spain
183 Q9 Monteagudo de las Salinas Spain
183 P6 Monteagudo de las Vicarías Spain
260 A5 Monte Águila Chile
245 K8 Monte Alban tourist site Mex.
251 H5 Monte Alegre Brazil
256 B2 Monte Alegre r. Brazil
254 D5 Monte Alegre de Goiás Brazil
187 C10 Montealegre del Castillo Spain
256 C3 Monte Alegre de Minas Brazil
256 C4 Monte Alto Brazil
256 C4 Monte Aprazível Brazil
255 E5 Monte Azul Brazil
256 C4 Monte Azul Paulista Brazil
224 F4 Montebello Que. Can.
250 C6 Monte Bello Peru
195 J8 Montebello Ionico Italy
86 C6 Montebello Islands W.A. Austr.
191 K5 Montebello Vicentino Italy
191 M4 Montebelluna Italy
158 I3 Montebourg France
190 G6 Montebruno Italy
261 F3 Monte Buey Arg.
191 N8 Montecalvo in Foglia Italy
258 G2 Montecarlo Arg.
161 K9 Monte-Carlo Monaco
256 D3 Monte Carmelo Brazil
261 I2 Monte Caseros Arg.
191 O9 Montecassiano Italy
193 I2 Monte Castello di Vibio Italy
193 I2 Montecastrilli Italy
191 J8 Montecatini Terme Italy
191 J9 Montecatini Val di Cecina Italy
191 N8 Montecchio Italy
190 I6 Montecchio Emilia Italy
191 K4 Montecchio Maggiore Italy
163 G8 Montech France
190 E5 Montechiaro d'Asti Italy
184 C6 Montechoro Port.
193 N4 Montecilfone Italy
240 M7 Montecito CA U.S.A.
182 E9 Monte Claro Port.
260 D4 Monte Comán Arg.
182 D6 Monte Córdova Port.
193 N7 Montecorice Italy
191 K3 Monte Corno, Parco Naturale nature res. Italy
193 Q7 Monte Cotugna, Lago di l. Italy
191 N3 Montecreale Valcellina Italy
191 J7 Montecreto Italy
246 H4 Monte Cristi Dom. Rep.
246 H4 Monte Cristi nat. park Dom. Rep.
250 A5 Montecristi Ecuador
261 F2 Monte Cristo Arg.
253 E3 Monte Cristo Bol.
213 E4 Monte Cristo S. Africa
192 E3 Montecristo, Isola di i. Italy
191 N9 Monte Cucco, Parco Naturale Regionale del park Italy
184 D2 Monte da Pedra Port.
184 C5 Monte da Rocha, Barragem do resr Port.
182 F4 Montederramo Spain
259 C9 Monte Dinero Arg.
193 M6 Monte di Procida Italy
191 M8 Montedoglio, Lago di l. Italy
184 D4 Monte do Trigo Port.
251 H5 Monte Dourado Brazil
244 D3 Monte Escobedo Mex.
193 N6 Montefalcione Italy
193 J2 Montefalco Italy
193 N4 Montefalcone Italy
193 O5 Montefalcone di Val Fortore Italy
191 L8 Monte Falterona, Campigna e delle Foreste Casentinesi, Parco Nazionale del nat. park Italy
191 O9 Montefano Italy
191 N8 Montefelcino Italy
191 M8 Montefeltro reg. Italy
192 I2 Montefiascone Italy
184 C6 Monte Figo, Serra de mts Port.
193 L1 Montefiore dell'Aso Italy
191 J7 Montefiorino Italy
193 N6 Monteforte Irpino Italy
193 K2 Montefortino Italy
193 J2 Montefranco Italy
185 K6 Montefrío Spain
195 L3 Montegiordano Italy
193 L1 Montegiorgio Italy
246 □ Montego Bay Jamaica
246 □ Montego Bay b. Jamaica
184 E6 Monte Gordo Port.
191 P9 Montegranaro Italy
261 H4 Monte Grande Arg.
163 E9 Montégut-Arros France
261 G6 Monte Hermoso Arg.
182 H8 Montehermoso Spain
195 M3 Monteiasi Italy
163 H7 Monteils France
254 F3 Monteiro Brazil
216 □1c Monteiros, Ponta dos pt São Jorge Azores
185 I7 Montejaque Spain
185 M5 Montejícar Spain
84 C4 Montejinnie N.T. Austr.
183 M6 Montejo de la Sierra Spain
184 A2 Montejunto, Serra de hill Port.
191 N8 Montelabbate Italy
193 K4 Montelanico Italy
184 A3 Montelavar Port.
160 B5 Montel-de-Gelat France
259 C8 Monte León Arg.
193 O5 Monteleone di Puglia Italy
193 J2 Monteleone di Spoleto Italy
192 I2 Monteleone d'Orvieto Italy
192 B7 Monteleone Rocca Doria Sardegna Italy
193 J3 Monteleone Sabino Italy
194 E7 Montelepre Sicilia Italy
250 C2 Monte Líbano Col.
193 J3 Montelibretti Italy
161 G7 Montélier France
161 F7 Montélimar France
253 F5 Monte Lindo r. Para.
193 O6 Montella Italy
184 H6 Montellano Spain
226 E6 Montello WI U.S.A.
163 G9 Montels France
191 K8 Montelupo Fiorentino Italy
191 P9 Montelupone Italy
194 F8 Montemaggiore Belsito Sicilia Italy
261 F3 Monte Maíz Arg.
193 O6 Montemarano Italy
191 O8 Montemarciano Italy
185 O3 Montemayon r. Spain
185 J5 Montemayor Spain
259 D7 Montemayor, Meseta de plat. Arg.
183 L5 Montemayor de Pililla Spain
162 F4 Montemboeuf France
195 M2 Montemesola Italy
193 P5 Montemilone Italy
184 G4 Montemolín Spain
193 K2 Montemonaco Italy
243 J5 Montemorelos Mex.
184 C3 Montemor-o-Novo Port.
182 C8 Montemor-o-Velho Port.
191 K8 Montemurlo Italy
182 D6 Montemuro, Serra de mts Port.
193 P7 Montemurro Italy
159 J5 Montenay France
162 D5 Montendre France
196 H8 Montenegro country Europe
183 O4 Montenegro de Cameros Spain
193 N4 Montenero di Bisaccia Italy
193 M3 Montenerodomo Italy
195 M3 Monteparano Italy
257 H2 Monte Pascoal, Parque Nacional de nat. park Brazil
260 B2 Monte Patria Chile
247 I4 Monte Plata Dom. Rep.
191 O8 Monte Porzio Italy
193 L2 Monteprandone Italy
211 C8 Montepuez Moz.
211 D8 Montepuez r. Moz.
192 H1 Montepulciano Italy
192 H1 Montepulciano, Lago di l. Italy
258 E2 Monte Quemado Arg.
158 F6 Monterblanc France
191 M9 Monterchi Italy
182 C9 Monte Real Port.
193 K2 Montereale Italy
156 E7 Montereau-fault-Yonne France
182 C9 Monte Redondo Port.
191 K7 Monterenzio Italy
Monterey Mex. see Monterrey
240 K5 Monterey CA U.S.A.
232 F10 Monterey VA U.S.A.
240 J5 Monterey Bay CA U.S.A.
240 J5 Monterey Bay National Marine Sanctuary nature res. CA U.S.A.
250 C2 Montería Col.
191 K9 Monteriggioni Italy
253 E4 Montero Bol.
193 M4 Monteroduni Italy
192 H3 Monte Romano Italy
191 K9 Monteroni d'Arbia Italy
195 O3 Monteroni di Lecce Italy
251 F3 Monte Roraima, Parque Nacional do nat. park Brazil
258 D2 Monteros Arg.
193 I3 Monterosi Italy
190 H7 Monterosso al Mare Italy
194 H9 Monterosso Almo Sicilia Italy
195 K6 Monterosso Calabro Italy
193 J3 Monterotondo Italy
192 F1 Monterotondo Marittimo Italy
182 F5 Monterrei Spain
241 Q9 Monterrey Baja California Mex.
243 I5 Monterrey Nuevo León Mex.
182 E3 Monterroso Spain
185 I3 Monterrubio de la Serena Spain
193 L1 Monterubbiano Italy
187 D10 Montesa Spain
254 D3 Montes Altos Brazil
193 K5 Monte San Biagio Italy
193 L4 Monte San Giovanni Campano Italy
238 C3 Montesano WA U.S.A.
195 O4 Montesano Salentino Italy
193 P7 Montesano sulla Marcellana Italy
191 L9 Monte San Savino Italy
191 M9 Monte Santa Maria Tiberina Italy
193 P4 Monte Sant'Angelo Italy
254 F4 Monte Santo Brazil
256 D4 Monte Santo de Minas Brazil
192 D7 Monte Santu, Capo di c. Sardegna Italy
193 N5 Montesarchio Italy
195 L2 Montescaglioso Italy
257 F2 Montes Claros Brazil
183 K8 Montesclaros Spain
191 J9 Montescudaio Italy
261 F6 Montes de Oca Arg.
191 J7 Montese Italy
193 M2 Montesilvano Italy
163 G7 Montesquieu France
163 G9 Montesquieu-Volvestre France
163 E8 Montesquiou France
163 F8 Montestruc-sur-Gers France
193 J1 Monte Subasio, Parco Naturale Regionale del park Italy
184 C5 Montes Velhos Port.
161 F8 Monteux France
194 D8 Montevago Sicilia Italy
191 L8 Montevarchi Italy
192 B8 Montevecchia Sardegna Italy
261 G2 Monte Vera Arg.
193 P5 Monteverde Italy
261 I4 Montevideo Uru.
261 I4 Montevideo dept Uru.
236 H3 Montevideo MN U.S.A.
184 B4 Montevil Port.
239 K8 Monte Vista CO U.S.A.
182 G5 Montezinho, Parque Natural de nature res. Port.
236 I5 Montezuma IA U.S.A.
237 E7 Montezuma KS U.S.A.
241 W4 Montezuma Creek UT U.S.A.
241 W4 Montezuma Creek r. CO U.S.A.
240 O4 Montezuma Peak NV U.S.A.
163 H6 Montfaucon Midi-Pyrénées France
159 I7 Montfaucon Pays de la Loire France
157 J5 Montfaucon-d'Argonne France
161 E6 Montfaucon-en-Velay France
163 F8 Montferran-Savès France
161 I9 Montferrat France
163 H10 Montferrier France
164 G4 Montfoort Neth.
163 C9 Montfort Aquitaine France
158 H5 Montfort Bretagne France
163 C8 Montfort-en-Chalosse France
156 C6 Montfort-l'Amaury France
159 L5 Montfort-le-Gesnois France
159 M3 Montfort-sur-Risle France
182 I9 Montfragüe, Parque Natural de nature res. Spain
186 G4 Montgai Spain
163 E9 Montgaillard Midi-Pyrénées France
163 F8 Montgaillard Midi-Pyrénées France
163 H10 Montgaillard Midi-Pyrénées France
161 J7 Montgenèvre France
161 J7 Montgenèvre, Col de pass France
156 D6 Montgeron France
163 H9 Montgiscard France
159 O8 Montgivray France
187 F10 Montgó hill Spain
186 L3 Montgó, Cala b. Spain
150 F2 Montgomery Powys, Wales U.K.
231 D9 Montgomery AL U.S.A.
235 G1 Montgomery NY U.S.A.
232 A9 Montgomery OH U.S.A.
227 R8 Montgomery PA U.S.A.
232 D10 Montgomery WV U.S.A.
236 J6 Montgomery City MO U.S.A.
234 A6 Montgomery County county MD U.S.A.
234 E4 Montgomery County county PA U.S.A.
86 G3 Montgomery Islands W.A. Austr.
162 D5 Montguyon France
156 I4 Monthermé France
190 B3 Monthey Switz.
156 I5 Monthois France
157 K7 Monthureux-sur-Saône France
192 C6 Monti Sardegna Italy
191 N4 Monticano r. Italy
190 H5 Monticelli d'Ongina Italy
192 B2 Monticello Corse France
237 J9 Monticello AR U.S.A.
231 F10 Monticello FL U.S.A.
231 F9 Monticello GA U.S.A.
236 K5 Monticello IL U.S.A.
230 D5 Monticello IN U.S.A.
230 E7 Monticello KY U.S.A.
233 □R2 Monticello ME U.S.A.
236 I3 Monticello MN U.S.A.
236 J5 Monticello MO U.S.A.
237 J10 Monticello MS U.S.A.
234 F1 Monticello NY U.S.A.
241 W4 Monticello UT U.S.A.
226 E7 Monticello WI U.S.A.
190 I5 Montichiari Italy
192 G1 Monticiano Italy
185 N3 Montiel Spain
261 H2 Montiel, Cuchilla de hills Arg.
159 O8 Montierchaume France
156 I7 Montier-en-Der France
192 G1 Montieri Italy
157 J6 Montiers-sur-Saulx France
162 G5 Montignac France
165 F8 Montignies-le-Tilleul Belgium
190 I7 Montignoso Italy
157 M6 Montigny France
227 Q1 Montigny, Lac de l. Que. Can.
156 G8 Montigny-la-Resie France
157 J7 Montigny-le-Roi France
157 L5 Montigny-lès-Metz France
160 G1 Montigny-Mornay-Villeneuve-sur-Vingeanne France
157 I8 Montigny-sur-Aube France
184 B3 Montijo Port.
184 F3 Montijo Spain
185 J5 Montilla Spain
185 L5 Montillana Spain
209 B8 Montipa Angola
163 I7 Montirat France
193 K2 Monti Sibillini, Parco Nazionale dei nat. park Italy
193 K4 Monti Simbruini, Parco Naturale Regionale dei nature res. Italy
256 B2 Montividiu Brazil
159 L2 Montivilliers France
185 M4 Montizón Spain
185 M4 Montizón r. Spain
161 B8 Montjaux France
159 J5 Montjean France
159 J7 Montjean-sur-Loire France
225 G3 Mont-Joli Que. Can.
190 D4 Montjovet Italy
163 J9 Montlaur France
224 F4 Mont-Laurier Que. Can.
156 D6 Montlhéry France
162 D5 Montlieu-la-Garde France
225 H3 Mont Louis Que. Can.
163 I10 Mont-Louis France
159 M7 Montlouis-sur-Loire France
160 B4 Montluçon France
160 G5 Montluel France
221 K5 Montmagny Que. Can.
160 B4 Montmarault France
158 H4 Montmartin-sur-Mer France
157 J4 Montmédy France
160 I5 Montmélian France
160 F4 Montmerle-sur-Saône France
161 F7 Montmeyran France
161 I9 Montmeyan France
156 G6 Montmirail Champagne-Ardenne France
159 M5 Montmirail Pays de la Loire France
160 H2 Montmirey-le-Château France
162 E5 Montmoreau-St-Cybard France
226 G9 Montmorenci IN U.S.A.
230 L2 Montmorency Que. Can.
162 F3 Montmorillon France
161 H8 Montmorin France
160 H3 Montmorot France
156 G6 Montmort-Lucy France
186 K4 Montnegre de Llevant hill Spain
85 M8 Monto Qld Austr.
158 G7 Montoir-de-Bretagne France
159 M6 Montoire-sur-le-Loir France
156 F6 Montois slope France
161 F7 Montoison France
184 D3 Montoito Port.
163 I9 Montolieu France
183 R6 Montón Spain
191 M9 Montone Italy
191 M7 Montone r. Italy
193 J3 Montopoli di Sabina Italy
193 L2 Montorio al Vomano Italy
185 K4 Montoro Spain
185 L4 Montoro r. Spain
185 K3 Montoro, Embalse de resr Spain
163 C9 Montory France
234 B2 Montour County county PA U.S.A.
232 I6 Montour Falls NY U.S.A.
159 J8 Montournais France
227 R8 Montoursville PA U.S.A.
206 D5 Mont Peko, Parc National du nat. park Côte d'Ivoire
246 □ Montpelier Jamaica
238 I5 Montpelier ID U.S.A.
226 I9 Montpelier IN U.S.A.
232 A7 Montpelier OH U.S.A.
233 M4 Montpelier VT U.S.A.
161 D9 Montpellier France
161 B7 Montpeyroux France
163 F7 Montpezat France
163 F9 Montpézat France
163 G7 Montpezat-de-Quercy France
161 E7 Montpezat-sous-Bauzon France
162 E5 Montpon-Ménestérol France
160 G3 Montpont-en-Bresse France
159 N6 Mont-près-Chambord France
Montreal Que. Can. see Montréal
224 F4 Montréal Que. Can.
224 C4 Montreal r. Ont. Can.
224 E4 Montreal r. Ont. Can.
160 E1 Montréal Bourgogne France
163 I9 Montréal Languedoc-Roussillon France
163 E8 Montréal Midi-Pyrénées France
226 D3 Montreal WI U.S.A.
226 J2 Montreal Island Ont. Can.
160 H4 Montréal-la-Cluse France
223 J4 Montreal Lake Sask. Can.
223 J4 Montreal Lake l. Sask. Can.
224 F4 Montréal-Mirabel airport Que. Can.
224 C4 Montreal River Ont. Can.
224 F4 Montréal-Trudeau airport Que. Can.
163 I8 Montredon-Labessonnié France
161 E6 Montregard France
163 F9 Montréjeau France
159 N7 Montrésor France
192 B7 Montresta Sardegna Italy
160 G3 Montret France
156 D6 Montreuil Île-de-France France
156 C3 Montreuil Nord-Pas-de-Calais France
159 K7 Montreuil-Bellay France
159 J6 Montreuil-Juigné France
190 B3 Montreux Switz.
159 I7 Montrevault France
160 G4 Montrevel-en-Bresse France
159 N7 Montrichard France
163 H7 Montricoux France
160 J4 Montriond France
161 C7 Montrodat France
161 B9 Montrodre mt. France
186 G5 Mont-roig del Camp Spain
160 H3 Montrond France
160 E5 Montrond-les-Bains France
214 E2 Montrose well S. Africa
146 L9 Montrose Angus, Scotland U.K.
239 K7 Montrose CO U.S.A.
227 K6 Montrose MI U.S.A.
235 H2 Montrose NY U.S.A.
233 J7 Montrose PA U.S.A.
232 F9 Montrose WV U.S.A.
232 I10 Montross VA U.S.A.
187 D9 Montroy Spain
161 B8 Montrozier France
162 F1 Monts France
156 B5 Mont-St-Aignan France
160 E2 Mont-St-Jean France
157 K4 Mont-St-Martin France
158 H4 Mont-St-Michel, Baie du b. France
156 G8 Mont-St-Sulpice France
160 E3 Mont-St-Vincent France
163 I6 Montsalvy France
206 D5 Mont Sangbé, Parc National du nat. park Côte d'Ivoire
186 G5 Montsant r. Spain
160 E2 Montsauche-les-Settons France
163 F9 Montsaunès France
186 G3 Montsec, Serra del mts Spain
163 H10 Montségur France
186 J4 Montseny Spain
186 J4 Montseny, Parc Natural de nature res. Spain
247 □2 Montserrat terr. West Indies
159 L7 Montsoreau France
163 C8 Montsoué France
160 H3 Mont-sous-Vaudrey France
159 L8 Monts-sur-Guesnes France
Mont St-Michel tourist site France see Le Mont-St-Michel
159 J5 Montsûrs France
156 H7 Montsuzain France
187 K8 Montuïri Spain
242 □R14 Montuosa, Isla i. Panama
185 J6 Monturque Spain
232 F11 Montvale VA U.S.A.
163 H6 Montvalent France
225 G2 Montviel, Lac l. Que. Can.
156 B4 Montville France
235 K2 Montville CT U.S.A.
165 I7 Montzen Belgium
157 J5 Montzéville France
237 D9 Monument Draw watercourse NM/TX U.S.A.
241 V5 Monument Valley reg. AZ U.S.A.
208 D4 Monveda Dem. Rep. Congo
215 K3 Monyakeng S. Africa
96 B3 Monywa Myanmar
190 G4 Monza Italy
209 E9 Monze Zambia
Monze, Cape pt Pak. see Muari, Ras
172 C2 Monzelfeld Ger.
104 E1 Monzen Japan
172 D2 Monzingen Ger.
252 A2 Monzón Peru
186 F4 Monzón Spain
183 L4 Monzón de Campos Spain
235 K1 Moodus CT U.S.A.
235 K1 Moodus Reservoir CT U.S.A.
215 O4 Mooi r. KwaZulu-Natal S. Africa
215 K2 Mooi r. North West S. Africa
215 O5 Mooirivier S. Africa
164 I5 Mook Neth.
212 E4 Mookane Botswana
82 G3 Moolawatana S.A. Austr.
82 H3 Moomba S.A. Austr.
83 L3 Moomin Creek r. N.S.W. Austr.
84 G7 Moonah Creek watercourse Qld Austr.
82 E4 Moonaree S.A. Austr.
83 M4 Moonbi Range mts N.S.W. Austr.
147 H8 Mooncoin Ireland
84 H8 Moonda Lake salt flat Qld Austr.
147 I7 Moone Ireland
85 M9 Moonie Qld Austr.
83 L3 Moonie r. N.S.W./Qld Austr.
82 F6 Moonta S.A. Austr.
87 D11 Moora W.A. Austr.
85 H8 Mooraberree Qld Austr.
171 E10 Moorbad Lobenstein Ger.
238 L4 Moorcroft WY U.S.A.
215 M6 Moordenaarsnek pass S. Africa
168 D4 Moordorf (Südbrookmerland) Ger.
164 G5 Moordrecht Neth.
87 C11 Moore r. W.A. Austr.
238 J3 Moore MT U.S.A.
87 D10 Moore, Lake salt flat W.A. Austr.
79 □9a Moorea i. Fr. Polynesia
263 K1 Moore Embayment b. Antarctica
232 G9 Moorefield WV U.S.A.
231 G12 Moore Haven FL U.S.A.
149 P6 Moorends South Yorkshire, England U.K.
173 K5 Moorenweis Ger.
85 L4 Moore Reef Coral Sea Is Terr. Austr.
233 N4 Moore Reservoir NH/VT U.S.A.
87 C11 Moore River National Park W.A. Austr.
261 F4 Moores Arg.
234 B3 Mooresburg PA U.S.A.
246 E1 Moores Island Bahamas
233 □R3 Moores Mills N.B. Can.
234 F5 Moorestown NJ U.S.A.
246 □ Moore Town Jamaica
148 E4 Moorfields Northern Ireland U.K.
146 J11 Moorfoot Hills Scotland U.K.
236 G2 Moorhead MN U.S.A.
83 I5 Moornanyah Lake imp. l. N.S.W. Austr.
82 H6 Moorook S.A. Austr.
84 E1 Mooroongga Island N.T. Austr.
83 J7 Mooroopna Vic. Austr.
240 N7 Moorpark CA U.S.A.
214 C9 Moorreesburg S. Africa
85 J6 Moorrinya National Park Qld Austr.
165 D7 Moorslede Belgium
168 E3 Moorweg Ger.
172 F6 Moos Baden-Württemberg Ger.
173 N4 Moos Bayern Ger.
173 M2 Moosbach Ger.
179 J6 Moosburg Austria
173 L5 Moosburg an der Isar Ger.
224 D3 Moose r. Ont. Can.
224 D3 Moose Factory Ont. Can.
233 □P3 Moosehead Lake ME U.S.A.
223 J5 Moose Jaw Sask. Can.
223 J5 Moose Jaw r. Sask. Can.
226 B3 Moose Lake MN U.S.A.
233 □O4 Mooselookmeguntic Lake ME U.S.A.
223 K5 Moose Mountain Creek r. Sask. Can.
178 G5 Mooserboden, Stausee resr Austria
224 D3 Moose River Ont. Can.
233 N4 Moosilauke, Mount NH U.S.A.
173 L5 Moosinning Ger.
179 L6 Mooskirchen Austria
223 K5 Moosomin Sask. Can.
224 D3 Moosonee Ont. Can.
173 N4 Moosthenning Ger.
83 I4 Mootwingee National Park N.S.W. Austr.
213 F4 Mopane S. Africa
213 G3 Mopeia Moz.
Mopelia atoll Arch. de la Société Fr. Polynesia see Maupihaa
212 E4 Mopipi Botswana
206 D3 Mopti Mali
206 E3 Mopti admin. reg. Mali
210 B1 Moqatta Sudan
123 L5 Moqor Afgh.
252 C4 Moquegua Peru
252 C4 Moquegua dept Peru
261 H4 Moquehuá Arg.
177 H4 Mór Hungary
207 I4 Mora Cameroon
184 C3 Mora Port.
183 M9 Mora Spain
141 M6 Mora Sweden
226 A4 Mora MN U.S.A.
239 L9 Mora NM U.S.A.
239 L9 Mora r. NM U.S.A.
260 B4 Mora, Cerro mt. Arg./Chile
196 H8 Morača r. Montenegro
138 K9 Morach r. Belarus
123 L7 Morad r. Pak.
116 G5 Moradabad Uttar Prad. India
252 C1 Morada Nova Amazonas Brazil
254 F3 Morada Nova Ceará Brazil
257 E3 Morada Nova de Minas Brazil
186 G5 Móra d'Ebre Spain
187 D7 Mora de Rubielos Spain
183 M5 Moradillo de Roa Spain
129 J6 Morādlū Iran
213 □J3 Morafenobe Madag.
175 H2 Morąg Pol.
177 I5 Mórahalom Hungary
223 J1 Moraine Lake N.W.T. Can.
187 F10 Moraira, Punta de pt Spain
182 G5 Morais Port.
186 G5 Móra la Nova Spain
185 L3 Moral de Calatrava Spain
259 B7 Moraleda, Canal sea chan. Chile
185 L6 Moraleda de Zafayona Spain
182 G8 Moraleja Spain
182 I6 Moraleja del Vino Spain
182 I6 Moraleja de Sayago Spain
242 □O10 Morales Guat.
185 O7 Morales r. Spain
182 I6 Morales del Vino Spain
183 J5 Morales de Toro Spain
182 I5 Morales de Valverde Spain
182 H6 Moralina Spain
114 E4 Moram Mahar. India
213 □K3 Moramanga Madag.
226 J4 Moran MI U.S.A.
238 I5 Moran WY U.S.A.
85 L6 Moranbah Qld Austr.
116 G4 Morang Hima. Prad. India
Morang Nepal see Biratnagar
256 A3 Morangas Brazil
117 O6 Moranhat Assam India
129 J6 Moranlı Azer.
193 Q8 Morano Calabro Italy
190 E5 Morano sul Po Italy
246 □ Morant Bay Jamaica
246 F5 Morant Cays is Jamaica
246 □ Morant Point Jamaica
114 F6 Morappur Tamil Nadu India
146 E9 Morar Highland, Scotland U.K.
146 E9 Morar hills Scotland U.K.
146 E9 Morar, Loch l. Scotland U.K.
116 G3 Morari, Tso l. Jammu and Kashmir
142 I5 Mörarp Sweden
182 F1 Morás, Punta de pt Spain
182 H7 Morasverdes Spain
183 R6 Morata de Jalón Spain
183 N8 Morata de Tajuña Spain
185 P4 Moratalla Spain
114 F9 Moratuwa Sri Lanka
176 F2 Morava reg. Czech Rep.
179 O3 Morava r. Europe
alt. March (Austria)
191 R4 Morava Slovenia
179 O1 Moravany Czech Rep.
177 K3 Moravany Slovakia
213 □K2 Moravato Madag.
179 K8 Moravče Slovenia
122 F3 Moraveh Tappeh Iran
Moravia reg. Czech Rep. see Morava
232 I6 Moravia NY U.S.A.
196 I7 Moravica r. Serbia
197 J7 Moravica r. Serbia
177 G2 Moravice r. Czech Rep.
177 H2 Morávka Czech Rep.
176 E3 Moravská Dyje r. Czech Rep.
179 P2 Moravská Nová Ves Czech Rep.
176 F2 Moravská Třebová Czech Rep.
176 E2 Moravské Budějovice Czech Rep.
177 H2 Moravskoslezské Beskydy mts Czech Rep.
177 H2 Moravskoslezský kraj admin. reg. Czech Rep.
176 G2 Moravský Beroun Czech Rep.
Moravský Ján Slovakia see Moravský Svätý Ján
176 F2 Moravský Kras park Czech Rep.
179 N1 Moravský Krumlov Czech Rep.
176 G3 Moravský Písek Czech Rep.
176 G3 Moravský Svätý Ján Slovakia
87 C10 Morawa W.A. Austr.
251 G2 Morawhanna Guyana
175 I5 Morawica Pol.
146 J7 Moray admin. div. Scotland U.K.
85 K6 Moray Downs Qld Austr.
146 H7 Moray Firth b. Scotland U.K.
84 C3 Moray Range hills N.T. Austr.
172 C2 Morbach Ger.
190 H3 Morbegno Italy
116 C8 Morbi Gujarat India
160 I3 Morbier France
158 F6 Morbihan dept France
179 O4 Mörbisch am See Austria
143 M5 Mörbylånga Öland Sweden
163 C7 Morcenx France
195 O4 Morciano di Leuca Italy
191 N8 Morciano di Romagna Italy
244 C1 Morcillo Mex.
193 N5 Morcone Italy
100 B3 Mordaga Nei Mongol China
127 L5 Mor Dağı mt. Turkey
158 H5 Mordelles France
223 L5 Morden Man. Can.
199 H4 Mordoğan Turkey
Mordovia aut. rep. Rus. Fed. see Mordoviya, Respublika
135 I5 Mordoviya, Respublika aut. rep. Rus. Fed.
135 H5 Mordoviya Zapovednik nature res. Rus. Fed.
135 H5 Mordovo Rus. Fed.
Mordovskaya A.S.S.R. aut. rep. Rus. Fed. see Mordoviya, Respublika
139 V7 Mordves Rus. Fed.
Mordvinia aut. rep. Rus. Fed. see Mordoviya, Respublika
137 O7 Mordvynivka Ukr.
175 K3 Mordy Pol.
146 G6 More, Loch l. Highland, Scotland U.K.
146 I6 More, Loch l. Highland, Scotland U.K.
158 F6 Moréac France
184 D5 Moreanes Port.
236 E3 Moreau r. SD U.S.A.
236 D3 Moreau, South Fork r. SD U.S.A.
146 L11 Morebattle Scottish Borders, Scotland U.K.
149 L5 Morecambe Lancashire, England U.K.
149 K5 Morecambe Bay England U.K.
182 I2 Moreda Spain
183 P3 Moreda Spain
83 L3 Moree N.S.W. Austr.
156 B8 Morée France
91 J8 Morehead P.N.G.
232 B10 Morehead KY U.S.A.
231 I8 Morehead City NC U.S.A.
251 F5 Moreira Brazil
182 D6 Moreira do Rei Port.
116 F6 Morel r. India
190 E3 Mörel Switz.
250 C4 Morelia Col.
244 F6 Morelia Mex.
85 I7 Morella Qld Austr.
186 E6 Morella Spain
194 G9 Morello r. Sicilia Italy
244 E3 Morelos Mex.
245 I7 Morelos state Mex.
245 J7 Morelos Cañada Mex.
212 D3 Moremi Wildlife Reserve nature res. Botswana
116 G6 Morena Madh. Prad. India
184 G5 Morena, Sierra mts Spain
241 W8 Morenci AZ U.S.A.
227 J8 Morenci MI U.S.A.
197 N6 Moreni Romania
261 H4 Moreno Arg.
242 D3 Moreno Mex.
240 O8 Moreno Valley CA U.S.A.
183 P3 Morentín Spain
140 I5 Møre og Romsdal county Norway
253 F2 Morerú r. Brazil
182 I5 Moreruela de Tábara Spain
192 B6 Mores Sardegna Italy
220 E4 Moresby, Mount B.C. Can.
222 C4 Moresby Island B.C. Can.
149 J4 Moresby Parks Cumbria, England U.K.
160 G5 Morestel France
85 N9 Moreton Bay Qld Austr.
150 E6 Moretonhampstead Devon, England U.K.
151 I4 Moreton-in-Marsh Gloucestershire, England U.K.
85 N9 Moreton Island Qld Austr.
150 G2 Moreton Say Shropshire, England U.K.
156 E7 Moret-sur-Loing France
190 D6 Moretta Italy
156 D4 Moreuil France
134 L1 Moreyu r. Rus. Fed.
160 I3 Morez France
150 C2 Morfa Nefyn Gwynedd, Wales U.K.
190 H6 Morfasso Italy
172 F2 Mörfelden Ger.
198 C2 Morfi Greece
128 A3 Morfou Cyprus
128 A3 Morfou Bay Cyprus
140 R2 Morgam-Viibus hill Fin.
82 G6 Morgan S.A. Austr.
231 E10 Morgan GA U.S.A.
232 A10 Morgan KY U.S.A.
240 N4 Morgan, Mount CA U.S…
237 J11 Morgan City LA U.S.A.
230 D7 Morganfield KY U.S.A.
240 K4 Morgan Hill CA U.S.A.
231 G8 Morganton NC U.S.A.
230 D7 Morgantown KY U.S.A.
234 D4 Morgantown PA U.S.A.
232 F9 Morgantown WV U.S.A.
235 G4 Morganville NJ U.S.A.
158 B5 Morgat France
184 B5 Morgavel, Barragem d… Port.
215 N2 Morgenzon S. Africa
190 B2 Morges Switz.
190 C4 Morgex Italy
123 M4 Morgh, Kowtal-e pass
122 E6 Morghāb Iran
157 M6 Morhange France
117 J7 Morhar r. India
106 B5 Mori Xinjiang China
191 J4 Mori Italy
102 R4 Mori Hokkaidō Japan
105 G6 Mori Shizuoka Japan
247 □5 Moriah Trin. and Tob.
241 R2 Moriah, Mount NV U.S…
239 L9 Moriarty NM U.S.A.
83 J3 Moriarty's Range hills Qld Austr.
206 C4 Moribaya Guinea
149 K4 Moricambe b. England
222 E4 Morice Lake B.C. Can.
222 E4 Moricetown B.C. Can.
123 O3 Morich Pak.
250 D4 Morichal Col.
235 J3 Moriches Bay NY U.S.…
193 J3 Moricone Italy
138 F4 Moricsalas rezervāts nature res. Latvia
156 E5 Morienval France
117 N6 Morigaon Assam India
104 C6 Moriguchi Japan
215 L5 Morija Lesotho
207 G3 Moriki Nigeria
185 J6 Moriles Spain
Morin Dawa Nei Mong… see Nirji
188 G4 Morine pass Bos.-Herz…
169 I7 Moringen Ger.
193 K4 Morino Italy
139 N4 Morino Rus. Fed.
102 S7 Morioka Japan
213 G3 Morire Moz.
242 E3 Moris Mex.
197 O3 Morișca r. Romania
83 M5 Morisset N.S.W. Austr.
146 G8 Moriston r. Scotland U…
245 H3 Morita Mex.
171 I8 Moritzburg Ger.
105 K4 Moriya Japan
104 D5 Moriyama Japan
102 R6 Moriyoshi Japan
102 R7 Moriyoshi-zan vol. Jap…
140 Q3 Morjärv Sweden
123 J7 Morjen r. Pak.
134 J4 Morki Rus. Fed.
139 T4 Morkiny Gory Rus. Fe…
163 D9 Morlaàs France
158 D4 Morlaix France
158 D4 Morlaix, Baie de b. Fr…
163 C8 Morlanne France
165 F8 Morlanwelz Belgium
172 F2 Mörlenbach Ger.
222 H5 Morley Alta Can.
157 J6 Morley France
149 N6 Morley West Yorkshire, England U.K.
138 M9 Mormal' Belarus
193 Q8 Mormanno Italy
156 E6 Mormant France
161 G8 Mormoiron France
241 U7 Mormon Lake AZ U.S…
Mormugao Goa India s… Marmagao
160 E5 Mornand France
160 F5 Mornant France
161 F8 Mornas France
247 □2 Morne-à-l'Eau Guadel…
247 □2 Morne Constant hill Guadeloupe
247 □ Morne Diablotin Natio… Park Dominica
247 □2 Morne Diablotins vol. Dominica
247 □2 Morne Macaque vol. Dominica
190 F6 Mornese Italy
217 □2b Morne Seychellois hill… Seychelles
247 □2 Morne Trois Pitons N… Park Dominica
85 H8 Morney Qld Austr.
85 H8 Morney watercourse Q…
259 B8 Mornington, Isla i. Ch…
264 D9 Mornington Abyssal P… sea feature S. Atlantic…
84 G4 Mornington Island Qld…
83 J8 Mornington Peninsula National Park Vic. Aus…
198 C4 Mornos r. Greece
173 K4 Mörnsheim Ger.
123 L8 Moro Pak.
238 D4 Moro OR U.S.A.
183 P9 Moro, Cerro mts Spain
187 C11 Moro, Rambla del r. S…
91 K8 Morobe P.N.G.
204 D3 Morocco country Afric…
226 G9 Morocco IN U.S.A.
136 E2 Morochne Ukr.
237 I9 Moro Creek r. AR U.S.…
211 C6 Morogoro Tanz.
211 C7 Morogoro admin. reg.…
92 D8 Moro Gulf Phil.
215 K5 Morojaneng S. Africa
214 H2 Morokweng S. Africa
244 F5 Moroleón Mex.
193 K4 Morolo Italy
93 D7 Moromaho i. Indon.
213 □I4 Morombe Madag.
252 D4 Moromoro Bol.
259 E6 Morón Arg.
246 D2 Morón Cuba
245 J3 Morón Mex.
106 G2 Mörön Mongolia
190 C1 Moron mt. Switz.
247 I8 Morón Venez.
250 B5 Morona Ecuador
250 B6 Morona r. Peru
250 B5 Morona-Santiago prov… Ecuador
213 □J4 Morondava Madag.
183 P6 Morón de Almazán Sp…
185 I6 Morón de la Frontera…
206 D4 Morondo Côte d'Ivoire
244 D4 Morone, Sierra mts M…
240 P7 Morongo Valley CA U.…
217 □3a Moroni Njazidja Comor…
241 U2 Moroni UT U.S.A.
Moron Us He r. Qingha… see Tongtian He
183 Q6 Moros Spain
183 L6 Moros r. Spain
192 C3 Morosaglia Corse Fran…
93 F2 Morotai i. Maluku Indo…
93 E2 Morotai, Selat sea cha… Maluku Indon.
210 B4 Moroto Uganda
210 B4 Moroto, Mount Ugand…
103 I14 Morotsuka Japan
196 H5 Morović Vojvodina Serb…
247 □1 Morovis Puerto Rico
81 B12 Morowai South I. N.Z.
93 B4 Morowali, Cagar Alam… nature res. Indon.
139 N2 Morozova Rus. Fed.
137 S3 Morozovka Rus. Fed.
139 X5 Morozovo Rus. Fed.
135 H6 Morozovsk Rus. Fed.
190 D7 Morozzo Italy
254 E4 Morpara Brazil
227 M7 Morpeth Ont. Can.
149 N3 Morpeth Northumberla… England U.K.
Morphou Cyprus see M…
172 G2 Morre r. Ger.
186 I3 Morreres, Puig de les… Spain
256 C6 Morretes Brazil
232 A11 Morrill KY U.S.A.
236 D4 Morrill NE U.S.A.

Morrilton AR U.S.A.
Morrin Alta Can.
Morrinhos Brazil
Morrinsville North I. N.Z.
Morris Man. Can.
Morris IL U.S.A.
Morris MN U.S.A.
Morris PA U.S.A.
Morrisburg Ont. Can.
Morris County county NJ U.S.A.
Morris Jesup, Kap c. Greenland
Morrison Arg.
Morrison IL U.S.A.
Morrisons South I. N.Z.
Morris Plains NJ U.S.A.
Morris Run PA U.S.A.
Morriston Swansea, Wales U.K.
Morristown AZ U.S.A.
Morristown NJ U.S.A.
Morristown NY U.S.A.
Morristown TN U.S.A.
Morrisville NY U.S.A.
Morrisville PA U.S.A.
Morrisville VT U.S.A.
Morr Morr Aboriginal Holding res. Qld Austr.
Morro Brazil
Morro, Monte hill Italy
Morro, Punta pt Chile
Morro Agudo Brazil
Morro Bay CA U.S.A.
Morro d'Anta Brazil
Morro del Águila hill Spain
Morro de Papanoa hd Mex.
Morro de Petatlán hd Mex.
Morro do Chapéu Brazil
Morro do Coco Brazil
Morro do Sinal hills Brazil
Morro Mazatán Mex.
Morrone, Monte mt. Italy
Morros Brazil
Morrosquillo, Golfo de b. Col.
Morrovalle Italy
Morrumbala Moz.
Morrumbene Moz.
Mors reg. Denmark
Morsbach Ger.
Morsberg hill Ger.
Morschen Ger.
Morse Sask. Can.
Morse TX U.S.A.
Morse WI U.S.A.
Morse, Cape Antarctica
Morshanka Rus. Fed.
Morshansk Rus. Fed. see Morshanka
Morshyn Ukr.
Morsi Mahar. India
Morskaya Chapura, Ostrov i. Rus. Fed.
Morskaya Masel'ga Rus. Fed.
Mors'ke Ukr.
Morsleben Ger.
Morsum Ger.
Mørsvikbotn Norway
Mort watercourse Qld Austr.
Mort, Lac du l. N.W.T. Can.
Mortagne r. France
Mortagne-au-Perche France
Mortagne-sur-Gironde France
Mortagne-sur-Sèvre France
Mortágua Port.
Mortain France
Mortara Italy
Morte r. France
Morteau France
Morteaux-Coulibœuf France
Morte Bay England U.K.
Mortefontaine France
Mortegliano Italy
Mortehoe Devon, England U.K.
Mortelle Sicilia Italy
Morteros Arg.
Morteros Mex.
Mortes, Rio das r. Brazil
Mortes, Rio das r. Brazil
Mortimer S. Africa
Mortimer West Berkshire, England U.K.
Mortimer's Long I. Bahamas
Mortimer's Cross Herefordshire, England U.K.
Mortlach Sask. Can.
Mortlake Vic. Austr.
Mortlock Islands Micronesia
Mortlock Islands P.N.G. see Takuu Islands
Morton Lincolnshire, England U.K.
Morton Lincolnshire, England U.K.
Morton IL U.S.A.
Morton TX U.S.A.
Morton WA U.S.A.
Morton National Park N.S.W. Austr.
Mortorio, Isola i. Sardegna Italy
Mortrée France
Mörtschach Austria
Mortsel Belgium
Moruga Trin. and Tob.
Moruga Point Trin. and Tob.
Morundah N.S.W. Austr.
Morungole mt. Uganda
Morupule Botswana
Moruroa atoll Arch. des Tuamotu Fr. Polynesia see Mururoa
Moruya N.S.W. Austr.
Morvan hills France
Morvan, Parc Naturel Régional du nature res. France
Morven Qld Austr.
Morven South I. N.Z.
Morven hill Aberdeenshire, Scotland U.K.
Morven hill Highland, Scotland U.K.
Morvern reg. Scotland U.K.
Morvi Gujarat India see Morbi
Morville Shropshire, England U.K.
Morwara Gujarat India
Morwell Vic. Austr.
Morwenstow Cornwall, England U.K.
Mor'ye Rus. Fed.
Moryń Pol.
Morzeszczyn Pol.
Morzhovets, Ostrov i. Rus. Fed.
Morzine France
Mosal'sk Rus. Fed.
Moşana Moldova
Mosbach Ger.
Mosborough South Yorkshire, England U.K.
Mosby MT U.S.A.
Moscarter, Punta des pt Spain
Moscavide Port.
Mošćenička Draga Croatia
Moscia r. Italy
Mosciano Sant'Angelo Italy
Moscow Rus. Fed. see Moskva
Moscow ID U.S.A.
Moscow PA U.S.A.
Moscow Oblast admin. div. Rus. Fed. see Moskovskaya Oblast'
Moscow University Ice Shelf Antarctica
Mosel Ger.
Mosel r. Ger.
Moselebe watercourse Botswana
Moseley VA U.S.A.
Moselle dept France
Moselle r. France
Möser Ger.
Moses, Mount NV U.S.A.
Moses Lake WA U.S.A.
Mosetse Botswana
Moseyevo Rus. Fed.
Mosgiel South I. N.Z.
232 G7 Moshannon PA U.S.A.
214 G2 Moshaweng watercourse S. Africa
138 K2 Moshchnyy, Ostrov i. Rus. Fed.
139 R3 Moshenskoye Rus. Fed.
227 J1 Mosher Ont. Can.
122 F7 Moshgān Iran
207 G4 Moshi r. Nigeria
211 C5 Moshi Tanz.
137 K4 Moshny Ukr.
134 K2 Mosh'yuga Rus. Fed.
174 E3 Mosina Pol.
226 E5 Mosinee WI U.S.A.
Mosi-oa-Tunya National Park Zimbabwe see Victoria Falls National Park
215 I2 Mosita S. Africa
140 L4 Mosjøen Norway
100 M2 Moskal'vo Sakhalin Rus. Fed.
140 P2 Moskángáisi mt. Norway
140 L3 Moskenesøy i. Norway
140 L3 Moskenestraumen sea chan. Norway
175 H5 Moskorzew Pol.
140 O4 Moskosel Sweden
139 V6 Moskovskaya Oblast' admin. div. Rus. Fed.
Moskovskiy Uzbek. see Shahrihon
137 S2 Moskovskoye Rus. Fed.
139 U6 Moskva Rus. Fed.
139 V6 Moskva r. Rus. Fed.
123 M3 Moskva Tajik.
139 U5 Moskvy, Kanal imeni canal Rus. Fed.
177 G6 Moslavna Podravska Croatia
260 D3 Mosmota Arg.
197 P4 Moşna Romania
177 K6 Moşniţa Nouă Romania
78 □5 Moso i. Vanuatu
191 K2 Moso in Passiria Italy
176 G4 Mosonmagyaróvár Hungary
188 F4 Mosor mts Croatia
177 H3 Mošovce Slovakia
137 P4 Mos'panove Ukr.
137 R6 Mospyne Ukr.
250 B4 Mosquera Col.
239 L9 Mosquero NM U.S.A.
187 E7 Mosqueruela Spain
242 □R10 Mosquitia reg. Hond.
247 □1 Mosquito Puerto Rico
232 E7 Mosquito Creek Lake OH U.S.A.
223 K2 Mosquito Lake N.W.T. Can.
242 □S13 Mosquitos, Golfo de los b. Panama
142 G2 Moss Norway
208 C5 Mossaka Congo
Mossâmedes Angola see Namibe
256 B2 Mossâmedes Brazil
146 K8 Mossat Aberdeenshire, Scotland U.K.
81 C12 Mossburn South I. N.Z.
Mosselbaai S. Africa see Mossel Bay
214 G10 Mossel Bay S. Africa
214 G10 Mossel Bay b. S. Africa
209 B5 Mossendjo Congo
163 I10 Mosset France
83 J5 Mossgiel N.S.W. Austr.
215 N1 Mossiesdal S. Africa
172 G5 Mössingen Ger.
148 F4 Mossley Northern Ireland U.K.
85 J4 Mossman Qld Austr.
142 F5 Mossø l. Denmark
187 H9 Mossons, Cap des c. Spain
254 F3 Mossoró Brazil
147 J2 Moss-side Northern Ireland U.K.
146 J7 Mosstodloch Moray, Scotland U.K.
213 I2 Mossuril Moz.
83 M6 Moss Vale N.S.W. Austr.
223 K4 Mossy r. Sask. Can.
197 N9 Most Bulg.
176 C1 Most Czech Rep.
195 □ Mosta Malta
122 F5 Moşţafaabad Iran
205 F2 Mostaganem Alg.
188 F4 Mostar Bos.-Herz.
255 C9 Mostardas Brazil
184 D5 Mosteiro Beja Port.
182 E9 Mosteiro Castelo Branco Port.
182 F2 Mosteiro Galicia Spain
216 □1b Mosteiros São Miguel Azores
197 N6 Moşteni Romania
197 O6 Mostiştea r. Romania
175 I2 Mostkowo Warmińsko-Mazurskie Pol.
174 D3 Mostkowo Zachodniopomorskie Pol.
179 I7 Most na Soči Slovenia
183 M8 Móstoles Spain
223 I4 Mostoos Hills Sask. Can.
136 J6 Mostove Ukr.
129 B1 Mostovskoy Rus. Fed.
175 J3 Mostówka Pol.
Mosty Belarus see Masty
175 L4 Mosty Pol.
95 M2 Mostyn Sabah Malaysia
136 C4 Mostys'ka Ukr.
175 L6 Mostys'ka Druha Ukr.
212 E4 Mosu Botswana
Mosul Iraq see Al Mawşil
110 H4 Mosuowan Xinjiang China
142 E2 Møsvatn Austfjell park Norway
142 E2 Møsvatnet l. Norway
140 K5 Mosvik Norway
175 M4 Mosyr Ukr.
175 H4 Moszczenica Pol.
210 C2 Mot'a Eth.
78 □5 Mota i. Vanuatu
208 C4 Motaba r. Congo
185 N2 Mota del Cuervo Spain
183 J5 Mota del Marqués Spain
243 O10 Motagua r. Guat.
108 B6 Motai Myanmar
136 E1 Motal' Belarus
143 L3 Motala Sweden
78 □5 Mota Lava i. Vanuatu
174 F1 Motarzyno Pol.
213 G5 Motaze Moz.
197 O3 Moţca Romania
105 L2 Motegi Japan
208 C4 Motenge-Boma Dem. Rep. Congo
215 M4 Moteng Pass Lesotho
213 F5 Motetema S. Africa
116 G7 Moth Uttar Prad. India
146 I11 Motherwell North Lanarkshire, Scotland U.K.
214 H3 Mothibistad S. Africa
198 E6 Mothonaio, Akrotirio pt Kythira Greece
93 E3 Moti i. Maluku Indon.
101 C8 Motian Ling hill Liaoning China
190 B2 Môtiers Switz.
117 J6 Motihari Bihar India
185 I3 Motilla hill Spain
183 Q9 Motilla del Palancar Spain
80 K4 Motiti Island North I. N.Z.
143 J2 Motjärnshyttan Sweden
213 F4 Motloutse r. Botswana
102 □1 Motobu Okinawa Japan
102 □1 Motobu-hantō pen. Okinawa Japan
251 E3 Motocurunya Venez.
212 D5 Motokwe Botswana
105 L4 Motono Japan
183 Q7 Motos Spain
104 E5 Motosu Japan
105 I5 Motosu-ko l. Japan
140 V2 Motovskiy Zaliv sea chan. Rus. Fed.
191 P5 Motovun Croatia
103 □3 Moto-yama hill Iō-jima Japan
102 S8 Motoyoshi Japan
243 M10 Motozintla Mex.
185 L7 Motril Spain
197 K6 Motru Romania
197 L6 Motru r. Romania
215 L1 Motshikiri S. Africa
214 I5 Motswedimosa S. Africa
236 D2 Mott ND U.S.A.
96 C6 Mottama Myanmar
96 C6 Mottama, Gulf of Myanmar
193 O4 Motta Montecorvino Italy
195 J7 Motta San Giovanni Italy
190 F5 Motta Visconti Italy
169 I10 Motten Ger.
173 J4 Möttingen Ger.
252 D7 Motto Botello Arg.
195 M2 Mottola Italy
81 H8 Motueka South I. N.Z.
81 □1 Motu Fakataga i. Tokelau
Motuhora Island North I. N.Z. see Moutohora Island
Motu Ihupuku i. N.Z. see Campbell Island
79 □9 Motu Iti i. Fr. Polynesia
Motuiti i. Fr. Polynesia see Motu Iti
81 G10 Motukarara South I. N.Z.
243 O7 Motul Mex.
81 H10 Motunau Island South I. N.Z.
79 □9 Motu One atoll Arch. de la Société Fr. Polynesia
79 □9 Motu One i. Fr. Polynesia
81 G8 Motupiko South I. N.Z.
80 G7 Motupipi South I. N.Z.
79 □7a Moturiki i. Fiji
80 H1 Motutangi North I. N.Z.
81 □3 Motutapu i. Rarotonga Cook Is
178 C5 Mötz Austria
142 G5 Mou Denmark
208 C4 Mouali Gbangba Congo
96 G5 Mouan, Nam r. Laos
207 H6 Mouanko Cameroon
161 J9 Mouans-Sartoux France
Mouaskar Alg. see Mascara
263 L2 Moubray Bay Antarctica
225 G3 Mouchalagane r. Que. Can.
159 I8 Mouchamps France
163 E8 Mouchan France
160 H3 Mouchard France
161 C7 Mouchet, Mont mt. France
246 H3 Mouchoir Bank sea feature Turks and Caicos Is
246 H3 Mouchoir Passage Turks and Caicos Is
182 E6 Mouçós Port.
108 C6 Mouding Yunnan China
206 B2 Moudjéria Maur.
190 B2 Moudon Switz.
198 G3 Moudros Limnos Greece
208 C2 Moufa Chad
208 A5 Mougalaba, Réserve de la nature res. Gabon
161 K9 Mougins France
206 B2 Mougri well Maur.
141 Q6 Mouhijärvi Fin.
206 E4 Mouhoun r. Africa alt. Volta Noire, conv. Black Volta
208 A5 Mouila Gabon
205 E4 Mouilah well Alg.
159 J8 Mouilleron-en-Pareds France
208 D3 Mouka C.A.R.
207 I3 Moul well Niger
83 J6 Moulamein N.S.W. Austr.
83 I6 Moulamein Creek r. N.S.W. Austr.
163 I7 Moularès France
Moulavibazar Bangl. see Moulvibazar
159 J5 Moulay France
247 □3 Moule à Chique, Cape St Lucia
209 A5 Moulèngui Binza Gabon
206 D2 Moulentâr well Mali
163 F6 Mouleydier France
210 D1 Moulhoulê Djibouti
159 L7 Mouliherne France
163 H9 Moulin-Neuf France
160 C3 Moulins France
160 D3 Moulins-Engilbert France
159 L4 Moulins-la-Marche France
163 G10 Moulis France
162 C5 Moulis-en-Médoc France
162 F3 Moulismes France
163 D9 Moulle de Jaut, Pic du mt. France
Moulmein Myanmar see Mawlamyaing
204 E2 Moulouya, Oued r. Morocco
151 L6 Moulsecoomb Brighton and Hove, England U.K.
159 K3 Moult France
151 L2 Moulton Lincolnshire, England U.K.
151 K3 Moulton Northamptonshire, England U.K.
151 M3 Moulton Suffolk, England U.K.
231 D8 Moulton AL U.S.A.
262 P1 Moulton, Mount Antarctica
233 N5 Moultonborough NH U.S.A.
231 F10 Moultrie GA U.S.A.
231 H9 Moultrie, Lake SC U.S.A.
117 M7 Moulvibazar Bangl.
Moumolu-Naunitu i. Solomon Is see San Jorge
208 B5 Mounana Gabon
237 K7 Mound City IL U.S.A.
236 H6 Mound City KS U.S.A.
236 H5 Mound City MO U.S.A.
236 E3 Mound City SD U.S.A.
208 C2 Moundou Chad
232 E9 Moundsville WV U.S.A.
231 D9 Moundville AL U.S.A.
208 B5 Moungoundou-Sud Congo
161 J8 Mounier, Mont mt. France
198 B4 Mounta, Akrotirio pt Kefallonia Greece
198 B4 Mounta, Akrotirio pt Greece
116 D7 Mount Abu Rajasthan India
234 C4 Mount Aetna PA U.S.A.
239 K9 Mountainair NM U.S.A.
150 F4 Mountain Ash Rhondda Cynon Taff, Wales U.K.
231 D9 Mountain Brook AL U.S.A.
232 D12 Mountain City TN U.S.A.
237 I7 Mountain Grove MO U.S.A.
237 I7 Mountain Home AR U.S.A.
238 G5 Mountain Home ID U.S.A.
234 E2 Mountainhome PA U.S.A.
241 V1 Mountain Home UT U.S.A.
226 B2 Mountain Iron MN U.S.A.
232 F9 Mountain Lake Park MD U.S.A.
235 G3 Mountain Lakes NJ U.S.A.
241 Q6 Mountain Pass CA U.S.A.
234 D2 Mountain Top PA U.S.A.
237 I8 Mountain View AR U.S.A.
240 J4 Mountain View CA U.S.A.
240 □F14 Mountain View HI U.S.A.
220 B3 Mountain Village AK U.S.A.
215 J8 Mountain Zebra National Park S. Africa
234 A6 Mount Airy MD U.S.A.
232 E12 Mount Airy NC U.S.A.
86 G4 Mount Anderson Aboriginal Reserve W.A. Austr.
82 H7 Mount Arapiles-Tooan State Park nature res. Vic. Austr.
234 F3 Mount Arlington NJ U.S.A.
81 C11 Mount Aspiring National Park South I. N.Z.
222 H5 Mount Assiniboine Provincial Park B.C. Can.
87 D8 Mount Augustus W.A. Austr.
215 N6 Mount Ayliff S. Africa
236 H5 Mount Ayr IA U.S.A.
240 O7 Mount Baldy CA U.S.A.
82 G6 Mount Barker S.A. Austr.
87 D13 Mount Barker W.A. Austr.
86 H4 Mount Barnett W.A. Austr.
86 I4 Mount Barnett Aboriginal Reserve W.A. Austr.
83 K7 Mount Beauty Vic. Austr.
147 F6 Mount Bellew Ireland
146 J11 Mountbenger Scottish Borders, Scotland U.K.
80 J7 Mount Bruce North I. N.Z.
227 M7 Mount Brydges Ont. Can.
83 K7 Mount Buffalo National Park Vic. Austr.
85 J4 Mount Carbine Qld Austr.
233 □S1 Mount Carleton Provincial Park N.B. Can.
230 D6 Mount Carmel IL U.S.A.
234 C3 Mount Carmel PA U.S.A.
232 C12 Mount Carmel TN U.S.A.
241 T4 Mount Carmel Junction UT U.S.A.
226 E7 Mount Carroll IL U.S.A.
84 D8 Mount Cavenagh N.T. Austr.
147 F3 Mountcharles Ireland
87 D8 Mount Clere W.A. Austr.
147 D8 Mountcollins Ireland
Mount Cook South I. N.Z. see Aoraki
85 K6 Mount Coolon Qld Austr.
215 N6 Mount Currie Nature Reserve S. Africa
213 F3 Mount Darwin Zimbabwe
84 D7 Mount Denison N.T. Austr.
233 □Q4 Mount Desert Island ME U.S.A.
82 E4 Mount Eba S.A. Austr.
84 D8 Mount Ebenezer N.T. Austr.
82 H8 Mount Eccles National Park Vic. Austr.
222 C3 Mount Edgecumbe AK U.S.A.
222 D3 Mount Edziza Provincial Park B.C. Can.
237 H10 Mount Enterprise TX U.S.A.
226 I9 Mount Etna IN U.S.A.
148 C4 Mountfield Northern Ireland U.K.
83 K10 Mount Field National Park Tas. Austr.
215 M6 Mount Fletcher S. Africa
224 D5 Mount Forest Ont. Can.
87 D13 Mount Frankland National Park W.A. Austr.
215 M6 Mount Frere S. Africa
82 H7 Mount Gambier S.A. Austr.
85 J4 Mount Garnet Qld Austr.
232 C11 Mount Gay WV U.S.A.
232 C8 Mount Gilead OH U.S.A.
91 J8 Mount Hagen P.N.G.
148 C4 Mount Hamilton Northern Ireland U.K.
234 F5 Mount Holly NJ U.S.A.
234 A4 Mount Holly Springs PA U.S.A.
83 J5 Mount Hope N.S.W. Austr.
82 E6 Mount Hope S.A. Austr.
232 D11 Mount Hope WV U.S.A.
226 E6 Mount Horeb WI U.S.A.
86 H4 Mount House W.A. Austr.
85 I9 Mount Howitt Qld Austr.
81 F10 Mount Hutt South I. N.Z.
237 I8 Mount Ida AR U.S.A.
84 G6 Mount Isa Qld Austr.
232 G10 Mount Jackson VA U.S.A.
87 D8 Mount James Aboriginal Reserve W.A. Austr.
232 G7 Mount Jewett PA U.S.A.
147 H3 Mountjoy Northern Ireland U.K.
147 I3 Mountjoy Northern Ireland U.K.
234 B4 Mount Joy PA U.S.A.
83 M4 Mount Kaputar National Park N.S.W. Austr.
87 F9 Mount Keith W.A. Austr.
210 C5 Mount Kenya National Park Kenya
235 H2 Mount Kisco NY U.S.A.
85 M7 Mount Larcom Qld Austr.
232 E8 Mount Lebanon PA U.S.A.
82 G6 Mount Lofty Range mts S.A. Austr.
227 N2 Mount MacDonald Ont. Can.
87 D10 Mount Magnet W.A. Austr.
83 I5 Mount Manara N.S.W. Austr.
87 E10 Mount Manning Nature Reserve W.A. Austr.
80 K4 Mount Maunganui North I. N.Z.
Mount McKinley National Park AK U.S.A. see Denali National Park and Preserve
240 L1 Mount Meadows Reservoir CA U.S.A.
147 H6 Mountmellick Ireland
85 J4 Mount Molloy Qld Austr.
215 L6 Mount Moorosi Lesotho
85 M7 Mount Morgan Qld Austr.
226 E7 Mount Morris IL U.S.A.
227 K6 Mount Morris MI U.S.A.
232 H6 Mount Morris NY U.S.A.
83 I4 Mount Murchison N.S.W. Austr.
232 E10 Mount Nebo WV U.S.A.
147 J4 Mount Norris Northern Ireland U.K.
147 H5 Mount Nugent Ireland
232 A10 Mount Olivet KY U.S.A.
232 B9 Mount Orab OH U.S.A.
225 K4 Mount Pearl Nfld and Lab. Can.
234 D4 Mount Penn PA U.S.A.
85 M8 Mount Perry Qld Austr.
86 I5 Mount Pierre Aboriginal Reserve W.A. Austr.
81 D11 Mount Pisa South I. N.Z.
82 G6 Mount Pleasant S.A. Austr.
231 □2 Mount Pleasant New Prov. Bahamas
225 H4 Mount Pleasant P.E.I. Can.
236 J5 Mount Pleasant IA U.S.A.
226 J6 Mount Pleasant MI U.S.A.
232 F8 Mount Pleasant PA U.S.A.
231 H9 Mount Pleasant SC U.S.A.
237 H9 Mount Pleasant TX U.S.A.
241 U2 Mount Pleasant UT U.S.A.
234 A3 Mount Pleasant Mills PA U.S.A.
234 E2 Mount Pocono PA U.S.A.
234 B7 Mount Rainier MD U.S.A.
238 D3 Mount Rainier National Park WA U.S.A.
147 H6 Mountrath Ireland
82 G5 Mount Remarkable National Park S.A. Austr.
222 G5 Mount Revelstoke National Park B.C. Can.
81 H8 Mount Richmond Forest Park nature res. South I. N.Z.
222 G4 Mount Robson Provincial Park B.C. Can.
232 D12 Mount Rogers National Recreation Area park VA U.S.A.
214 I4 Mount Rupert S. Africa
238 C3 Mount St Helens National Volcanic Monument nat. park WA U.S.A.
234 F3 Mount Salem NJ U.S.A.
84 C4 Mount Sanford N.T. Austr.
150 B7 Mount's Bay England U.K.
147 F7 Mountshannon Ireland
238 C6 Mount Shasta CA U.S.A.
81 F10 Mount Somers South I. N.Z.
151 J2 Mountsorrel Leicestershire, England U.K.
236 J6 Mount Sterling IL U.S.A.
232 B10 Mount Sterling KY U.S.A.
232 B9 Mount Sterling OH U.S.A.
214 I9 Mount Stewart S. Africa
232 F9 Mount Storm WV U.S.A.
85 J5 Mount Surprise Qld Austr.
84 E7 Mount Swan N.T. Austr.
147 F5 Mount Talbot Ireland
232 H8 Mount Union PA U.S.A.
233 J6 Mount Upton NY U.S.A.
87 E8 Mount Vernon W.A. Austr.
237 K10 Mount Vernon AL U.S.A.
231 F9 Mount Vernon GA U.S.A.
236 K6 Mount Vernon IL U.S.A.
230 D7 Mount Vernon IN U.S.A.
232 A11 Mount Vernon KY U.S.A.
237 I7 Mount Vernon MO U.S.A.
235 H3 Mount Vernon NY U.S.A.
232 C8 Mount Vernon OH U.S.A.
237 H9 Mount Vernon TX U.S.A.
238 C2 Mount Vernon WA U.S.A.
234 C4 Mountville PA U.S.A.
84 D7 Mount Wedge N.T. Austr.
82 E5 Mount Wedge S.A. Austr.
86 D6 Mount Welcome Aboriginal Reserve W.A. Austr.
83 L9 Mount William National Park Tas. Austr.
82 E2 Mount Willoughby S.A. Austr.
234 B4 Mount Wolf PA U.S.A.
234 B7 Mount Zion MD U.S.A.
85 L8 Moura Qld Austr.
251 F5 Moura Brazil
252 B1 Moura r. Brazil
184 E4 Moura Port.
184 E4 Mourão Port.
208 D2 Mouraya Chad
202 D5 Mourdi, Dépression du depr. Chad
206 D3 Mourdiah Mali
182 D5 Moure Port.
163 C9 Mourenx France
161 F9 Mouriès France
182 D7 Mourisca do Vouga Port.
182 D9 Mouriscas Port.
156 H5 Mourmelon-le-Grand France
148 C4 Mourne r. Northern Ireland U.K.
147 J4 Mourne Mountains hills Northern Ireland U.K.
217 □1c Mourouvin, Forêt reg. Réunion
161 I9 Mourre de Chanier mt. France
161 G9 Mourre Nègre mt. France
198 G3 Mourtzeflos, Akrotirio pt Limnos Greece
146 □N2 Mousa i. Scotland U.K.
165 D7 Mouscron Belgium
165 D7 Mouscron dept Belgium
208 C2 Mousgougou Chad
232 C11 Mousie KY U.S.A.
161 E9 Moussac France
208 C2 Moussafoyo Chad
161 B10 Moussan France
157 N7 Moussey France
202 C5 Mousso well Chad
202 C6 Moussoro Chad
163 I9 Moussoulens France
160 C2 Moussy France
158 E4 Moustéru France
163 C7 Moustey France
161 I9 Moustiers-Ste-Marie France
209 B5 Moutamba Congo
160 I3 Mouthe France
160 G3 Mouthier-en-Bresse France
160 I2 Mouthier-Haute-Pierre France
162 E4 Mouthiers-sur-Boëme France
232 D12 Mouth of Wilson VA U.S.A.
163 J10 Mouthoumet France
190 C1 Moutier Switz.
162 I3 Moutier-d'Ahun France
160 J6 Moûtiers France
162 B3 Moutiers-les-Mauxfaits France
179 O1 Moutnice Czech Rep.
80 K4 Moutohora Island North I. N.Z.
93 B3 Moutong Sulawesi Indon.
207 I4 Moutourwa Cameroon
161 B10 Moux France
160 E2 Moux-en-Morvan France
156 D5 Mouy France
205 F4 Mouydir, Monts du plat. Alg.
209 B5 Mouyondzi Congo
198 C3 Mouzaki Greece
202 B6 Mouzarak Chad
157 J5 Mouzay France
157 J4 Mouzon France
157 K7 Mouzon r. France
242 E3 Movas Mex.
122 C6 Moveyleh Iran
197 P5 Movila Miresii Romania
197 M6 Movileni Romania
147 H2 Moville Ireland
86 G4 Mowanjum Aboriginal Reserve W.A. Austr.
85 M9 Mowbullan, Mount Qld Austr.
138 I8 Mowchadz' Belarus
146 L9 Mowtie Aberdeenshire, Scotland U.K.
232 C9 Moxahala OH U.S.A.
246 E1 Moxey Town Andros Bahamas
209 C8 Moxico prov. Angola
233 □P3 Moxie, Lake ME U.S.A.
147 D4 Moy r. Ireland
146 H8 Moy Highland, Scotland U.K.
147 I4 Moy Northern Ireland U.K.
216 □3f Moya Gran Canaria Canary Is
217 □3 Moya Nzwani Comoros
187 C8 Moya Castilla-La Mancha Spain
Moya Cataluña Spain see Moià
244 D4 Moyahua Mex.
210 C4 Moyale Eth.
206 B4 Moyamba Sierra Leone
147 B5 Moyard Ireland
147 D6 Moycullen Ireland
156 F4 Moy-de-l'Aisne France
204 D2 Moyen Atlas mts Morocco
208 C2 Moyen-Chari pref. Chad
Moyen Congo country Africa see Congo
215 L6 Moyeni Lesotho
157 M7 Moyenmoutier France
217 □2b Moyenne, Île i. Inner Islands Seychelles
206 B4 Moyenne-Guinée admin. reg. Guinea
156 C3 Moyenneville France
208 A5 Moyen-Ogooué prov. Gabon
147 I5 Moyer hill Ireland
157 L5 Moyeuvre-Grande France
147 I4 Moygashel Northern Ireland U.K.
147 D4 Moylaw Ireland
148 C6 Moylett Ireland
147 E6 Moylough Ireland
139 S8 Moylovo Rus. Fed.
147 I5 Moynalty Ireland
Moynaq Uzbek. see Mo'ynoq
147 G5 Moyne Ireland
120 H6 Mo'ynoq Uzbek.
209 E5 Moyo Dem. Rep. Congo
95 L9 Moyo i. Indon.
210 A4 Moyo Uganda
250 B6 Moyobamba Peru
148 D4 Moyola r. Northern Ireland U.K.
211 A6 Moyowosi r. Tanz.
140 M2 Møysalen mt. Norway
202 C6 Moyto Chad
111 D8 Moyu Xinjiang China
210 C4 Moyum waterhole Kenya
147 I6 Moyvalley Ireland
147 D7 Moyvane Ireland
148 B6 Moyvore Ireland
148 B7 Moyvoughly Ireland
121 O5 Moyynkum Kazakh.
121 O6 Moyynkum Kazakh.
121 L4 Moyynkum, Peski des. Kazakh.
121 M5 Moyynkum, Peski des. Kazakh.
121 O4 Moyynty Kazakh.
160 C5 Mozac France
213 G4 Mozambique country Africa
213 I4 Mozambique Channel Africa
265 G6 Mozambique Ridge sea feature Indian Ocean
182 I7 Mozárbez Spain
129 F2 Mozdok Rus. Fed.
122 I3 Mozdūrān Iran
232 B11 Mozelle KY U.S.A.
182 E7 Mozelos Port.
137 P4 Mozh r. Ukr.
138 M7 Mozha r. Belarus
137 S5 Mozhayevka Rus. Fed.
139 T6 Mozhaysk Rus. Fed.
134 K4 Mozhga Rus. Fed.
122 I4 Mozhnābād Iran
108 A2 Mozhong Qinghai China
179 K7 Mozirje Slovenia
179 K7 Mozirske planine mts Slovenia
96 B3 Mozo Myanmar
137 L4 Mozoliyivka Ukr.
183 L6 Mozoncillo Spain
177 G5 Mozsgó Hungary
Mozyr' Belarus see Mazyr
175 J1 Mozyr' Rus. Fed.
206 A3 Mpal Senegal
211 A6 Mpanda Tanz.
212 E3 Mpandamatenga Botswana
211 A7 Mpande Zambia
208 B5 Mpé Congo
215 O3 Mpemvana S. Africa
206 D3 Mpessoba Mali
215 M8 Mpetu S. Africa
210 B4 Mpigi Uganda
211 A7 Mpika Zambia
215 K8 Mpofu Game Reserve nature res. S. Africa
208 C3 Mpoko r. C.A.R.
215 O5 Mpolweni S. Africa
209 F8 Mpongwe Zambia
209 F7 Mporokoso Zambia
215 Q4 Mposa S. Africa
208 C5 Mpouya Congo
211 A7 Mpui Tanz.
211 A7 Mpulungu Zambia
215 O5 Mpumalanga S. Africa
215 N2 Mpumalanga prov. S. Africa
211 C6 Mpwapwa Tanz.
195 □ Mqabba Malta
215 M7 Mqanduli S. Africa
Mqinvartsveri mt. Georgia/Rus. Fed. see Kazbek
175 J2 Mrągowo Pol.
173 N3 Mrákov Czech Rep.
135 L5 Mrakovo Rus. Fed.
96 A4 Mrauk-U Myanmar
Mrewa Zimbabwe see Murehwa
188 E3 Mrežnica r. Croatia
188 F3 Mrkonjić-Grad Bos.-Herz.
191 R5 Mrkopalj Croatia
174 F2 Mrocza Pol.
174 F4 Mroczeń Pol.
175 I4 Mroczków Pol.
175 H2 Mroczno Pol.
175 H3 Mroga r. Pol.
175 J3 Mrozy Pol.
137 K2 Mryn Ukr.
205 H2 M'Saken Tunisia
211 C6 Msambweni Kenya
211 C6 Msata Tanz.
174 E1 Mścice Pol.
176 D1 Mšeno Czech Rep.
138 M2 Mshinskaya Rus. Fed.
205 G2 M'Sila Alg.
139 R4 Msta Rus. Fed.
139 O3 Msta r. Rus. Fed.
139 P3 Mstinskiy Most Rus. Fed.
Mstislavl' Belarus see Mstsislaw
175 H5 Mstów Pol.
139 O7 Mstsislaw Belarus
215 Q3 Msunduze r. S. Africa
175 I6 Mszana Dolna Pol.
175 I4 Mszczonów Pol.
211 A6 Mtakuja Tanz.
211 C7 Mtama Tanz.
129 G3 Mt'at'ushet'is Nakrdzali nature res. Georgia
210 B4 Mtelo Kenya
211 B6 Mtera Reservoir Tanz.
Mtoko Zimbabwe see Mutoko
215 P4 Mtonjaneni S. Africa
Mtorashanga Zimbabwe see Mutorashanga
217 □3b Mtsamboro Mayotte
217 □3b Mtsangamouji Mayotte
139 T8 Mtsensk Rus. Fed.
129 F4 Mts'khet'a Georgia
213 G6 Mtubatuba S. Africa
211 C7 Mtukula Tanz.
215 P4 Mtunzini S. Africa
211 D7 Mtwara Tanz.
211 C7 Mtwara admin. reg. Tanz.
96 B4 Mu r. Myanmar
184 C6 Mu hill Port.
79 □8a Mu'a Tongatapu Tonga
Mu'āb, Jibāl reg. Jordan see Moab
211 C8 Muaguide Moz.
213 G2 Mualadzi Moz.
213 H3 Mualama Moz.
254 C2 Muana Brazil
209 B6 Muanda Dem. Rep. Congo
96 G4 Muang Ham Laos
96 F4 Muang Hiam Laos
96 G6 Muang Hinboun Laos
96 E5 Muang Hôngsa Laos
108 D8 Muang Hounxianghoung Laos
96 F5 Muang Kao Laos
96 E5 Muang Khi Laos
97 G7 Muang Không Laos
96 G7 Muang Khôngxédôn Laos
96 F4 Muang Khoua Laos
96 G5 Muang Mok Laos
96 F4 Muang Ngoy Laos
96 H6 Muang Nong Laos
96 E3 Muang Ou Nua Laos
96 E5 Muang Pakbeng Laos
96 E4 Muang Paktha Laos
96 G6 Muang Phalan Laos
96 E5 Muang Phiang Laos
96 H6 Muang Phin Laos
96 F5 Muang Phôn-Hông Laos
96 G7 Muang Sam Sip Thai.
96 E4 Muang Sing Laos
96 G6 Muang Songkhon Laos
96 F5 Muang Soum Laos
96 F5 Muang Souy Laos
96 E5 Muang Thadua Laos
Muang Thai country Asia see Thailand
96 F4 Muang Va Laos
96 F5 Muang Vangviang Laos
96 F4 Muang Xon Laos
213 G3 Muanza Moz.
94 E3 Muar Malaysia
94 E3 Muar r. Malaysia
95 K2 Muara Brunei
95 L4 Muaraancalong Kalimantan Indon.
95 L4 Muaraatap Kalimantan Indon.
94 E6 Muarabeliti Sumatera Indon.
94 E5 Muarabulian Sumatera Indon.
94 E5 Muarabungo Sumatera Indon.
94 F7 Muaradua Sumatera Indon.
94 E6 Muaraenim Sumatera Indon.
95 K5 Muarainu Kalimantan Indon.
95 L5 Muarajawa Kalimantan Indon.
95 L5 Muarakaman Kalimantan Indon.
95 L4 Muara Kaman Sedulang, Cagar Alam nature res. Kalimantan Indon.
94 D5 Muaralabuh Sumatera Indon.
94 E6 Muaralakitan Sumatera Indon.
95 K5 Muaralaung Kalimantan Indon.
95 L4 Muaralesan Kalimantan Indon.
95 L4 Muaramayang Kalimantan Indon.
95 L4 Muaranawai Kalimantan Indon.
94 E6 Muararupit Sumatera Indon.
94 E5 Muarasabak Sumatera Indon.
94 C5 Muarasiberut Indon.
94 C4 Muarasipongi Sumatera Indon.
94 C4 Muarasoma Sumatera Indon.
95 M4 Muaras Reef Indon.
94 E5 Muaratebo Sumatera Indon.
94 E5 Muaratembesi Sumatera Indon.
95 K5 Muarateweh Kalimantan Indon.
Muara Tuang Sarawak Malaysia see Kota Samarahan
95 L4 Muarawahau Kalimantan Indon.
93 E4 Muari i. Maluku Indon.
123 L9 Muari, Ras pt Pak.
213 H2 Muatua Moz.
125 I2 Mu'ayqil, Khashm al hill Saudi Arabia
116 E4 Muazzam Punjab India
128 D9 Mubārak, Jabal mt. Jordan/Saudi Arabia
117 I6 Mubarakpur Uttar Prad. India
Mubarek Uzbek. see Muborak
127 J9 Mubarraz well Saudi Arabia
210 A4 Mubende Uganda
207 I4 Mubi Nigeria
120 K8 Muborak Uzbek.
94 G3 Mubur i. Indon.
209 B6 Mucaba Angola
209 B6 Mucaba, Serra mts Angola
251 G5 Mucajá Brazil
251 F4 Mucajaí r. Brazil
251 F4 Mucajaí, Serra do mts Brazil
225 H1 Mucalic r. Que. Can.
213 F2 Mucanha r. Moz.
196 I7 Mučanj mt. Serbia
86 F6 Muccan W.A. Austr.
193 K1 Muccia Italy
169 D9 Much Ger.
175 H6 Mucharz Pol.
87 C11 Muchea W.A. Austr.
171 E8 Mücheln (Geiseltal) Ger.
Mucheng Henan China see Wuzhi
100 B2 Muchikan Rus. Fed.
211 A8 Muchinga Escarpment Zambia
253 E4 Muchiri Bol.
135 H6 Muchkapskiy Rus. Fed.
134 J2 Muchkas Rus. Fed.
170 E4 Muchow Ger.
175 I6 Muchówka Pol.
108 D4 Muchuan Sichuan China
150 G2 Much Wenlock Shropshire, England U.K.
183 K5 Mucientes Spain
146 D9 Muck i. Scotland U.K.
171 K8 Mücka Ger.
85 L9 Muckadilla Qld Austr.
84 D5 Muckaty Aboriginal Land res. N.T. Austr.
169 H9 Mücke Große-Eichen Ger.
169 H9 Mücke-Nieder-Ohmen Ger.
147 F2 Muckish Mountain hill Ireland
146 □O1 Muckle Flugga i. Scotland U.K.
146 □N2 Muckle Roe i. Scotland U.K.
148 D5 Muckno Lake Ireland
250 D3 Muco r. Col.
211 D8 Mucojo Moz.
209 D7 Muconda Angola
195 K5 Mucone r. Italy
209 B9 Mucope Angola
177 H5 Mucsi-hegy hill Hungary
177 J3 Múcsony Hungary
213 H3 Mucubela Moz.
213 H3 Mucúbi Moz.
251 F5 Mucucuaú r. Brazil
251 E6 Mucuim r. Brazil
213 F3 Mucumbura Moz.
209 C9 Mucundi Angola
209 C8 Mucunha Angola
213 H3 Mucupia Moz.
126 G4 Mucur Turkey
251 F5 Mucura Brazil
257 H3 Mucuri Brazil
257 H3 Mucuri r. Brazil
257 G3 Mucurici Brazil
250 D5 Mucuripe Brazil
254 F2 Mucuripe, Ponta de pt Brazil
209 D9 Mucusso, Coutada Pública do nature res. Angola
209 D7 Mucussueje Angola
216 □3b Muda hill Fuerteventura Canary Is
94 D2 Muda r. Malaysia
114 D6 Mudabidri Karnataka India
Mudan Shandong China see Heze
100 F6 Mudanjiang Heilong. China
100 F5 Mudan Jiang r. China
100 E7 Mudan Ling mts China
199 J2 Mudanya Turkey
172 G2 Mudau Ger.
127 M9 Mudayrah Kuwait
128 E7 Mudaysīsāt, Jabal al hill Jordan
114 E4 Muddebihal Karnataka India
140 O3 Muddus nationalpark nat. park Sweden
241 R5 Muddy r. NV U.S.A.
237 H9 Muddy Boggy Creek r. OK U.S.A.
234 C5 Muddy Creek r. PA U.S.A.
241 V3 Muddy Creek r. UT U.S.A.
238 K5 Muddy Gap pass WY U.S.A.
241 R5 Muddy Peak NV U.S.A.
234 C5 Muddy Run Reservoir PA U.S.A.
122 H5 Mūd-e Dahanāb Iran
215 O4 Muden S. Africa
168 J5 Müden (Aller) Ger.
168 J5 Müden (Örtze) Ger.
169 E9 Mudersbach Ger.
114 E5 Mudgal Karnataka India
83 L5 Mudgee N.S.W. Austr.
114 D4 Mudhol Karnataka India
114 D6 Mudigere Karnataka India
223 J3 Mudjatik r. Sask. Can.
114 E3 Mudkhed Mahar. India
116 E4 Mudki Punjab India
240 O4 Mud Lake NV U.S.A.
96 C6 Mudon Myanmar
Mudraya country Africa see Egypt
210 E3 Mudug admin. reg. Somalia
211 B5 Mudukani Tanz.
212 D3 Mudumu National Park Namibia
199 M2 Mudurnu Turkey
199 L2 Mudurnu r. Turkey
134 G3 Mud'yuga Rus. Fed.
213 H2 Muecate Moz.
211 C7 Mueda Moz.
186 C5 Muel Spain
183 M4 Muela de Quintanilla hill Spain
182 I5 Muelas del Pan Spain
86 I5 Mueller Range hills W.A. Austr.
213 G2 Muende Moz.
245 M9 Muerto, Mar lag. Mex.
246 C1 Muertos Cays is Bahamas
125 I1 Mufattah, Khawr b. Saudi Arabia
147 H2 Muff Ireland
203 G4 Muftah well Sudan
134 I2 Muftyuga Rus. Fed.
209 F8 Mufulira Zambia
209 E8 Mufumbwe Zambia
109 J4 Mufu Shan mts China
182 H6 Muga de Sayago Spain
225 H4 Mugaguadavic Lake N.B. Can.
129 J5 Muğan Azer.
129 J6 Muğan Düzü lowland Azer.
129 H4 Muğanlı Azer.
182 D2 Mugardos Spain
184 B2 Muge Port.
184 B2 Muge r. Port.
213 H3 Mugeba Moz.
104 E4 Mugegawa Japan
171 H8 Mügeln Sachsen Ger.
171 H7 Mügeln Sachsen-Anhalt Ger.
172 E4 Muggensturm Ger.
191 P4 Muggia Italy
Mughalbhin Pak. see Jati
117 I7 Mughal Sarai Uttar Prad. India
122 E5 Mūghār Iran
126 H9 Mughayrā' Saudi Arabia
124 G3 Mughayrā' well Saudi Arabia
125 L6 Mughshin Oman
123 N2 Mughsu r. Tajik.
104 F4 Mugi Gifu Japan
103 L13 Mugi Tokushima Japan
Mugia Spain see Muxía
209 F6 Mugila, Monts mts Dem. Rep. Congo
199 J5 Muğla Turkey
199 J5 Muğla prov. Turkey
120 H3 Mugodzharskoye Kazakh.
120 H4 Mugodzhary, Gory mts Kazakh.
106 C9 Mug Qu r. Qinghai China
163 C8 Mugron France
211 C8 Muguia Moz.
116 H5 Mugu Karnali r. Nepal
211 B5 Mugumu Tanz.
106 B1 Mugur-Aksy Rus. Fed.
111 L10 Mugxung Qinghai China
128 G4 Mūḩ, Sabkhat imp. l. Syria
208 E2 Muhagiriya Sudan
Muhala Xinjiang China see Yutian
209 F6 Muhala Dem. Rep. Congo
203 G3 Muḩammad, Ra's pt Egypt
117 I7 Muhammadabad Uttar Prad. India
123 M8 Muhammad Ashraf Pak.
203 H4 Muhammad Qol Sudan
Muhammarah Iran see Khorramshahr
106 F8 Muhar Qinghai China
128 C8 Muhashsham, Wādī al watercourse Egypt
124 G4 Muḩayriqah Saudi Arabia
128 E9 Muḩaysh, Wādī al watercourse Jordan
128 H2 Muhaysin Syria
211 C6 Muheza Tanz.
172 F4 Mühlacker Ger.
171 G7 Mühlanger Ger.
170 I3 Mühlbach r. Ger.
171 H8 Mühlberg Brandenburg Ger.
169 K9 Mühlberg Thüringen Ger.
179 H6 Mühldorf Austria
173 N5 Mühldorf am Inn Ger.
179 K5 Mühlen Austria
170 G2 Mühlen hill Ger.
170 H5 Mühlenbeck Ger.
170 D3 Mühlen-Eichsen Ger.
172 F3 Mühlhausen Baden-Württemberg Ger.
173 K3 Mühlhausen Bayern Ger.
169 J8 Mühlhausen (Thüringen) Ger.
169 G10 Mühlheim am Main Ger.
172 F5 Mühlheim an der Donau Ger.
263 A2 Mühlig-Hofmann Mountains Antarctica
172 G6 Mühlingen Ger.
171 E9 Mühltroff Ger.
179 J2 Mühlviertel reg. Austria
140 R4 Muhos Fin.

128 E3 Muḩradah Syria
173 J3 Muhr am See Ger.
123 L7 Muhri Pak.
138 G3 Muhu i. Estonia
211 B7 Muhukuru Tanz.
213 H2 Muhula Moz.
208 E5 Muhulu Dem. Rep. Congo
210 B3 Mui Eth.
Mui Bai Bung c. Vietnam see Ca Mau, Mui
164 H4 Muiden Neth.
156 B5 Muids France
211 C7 Muidumbe Moz.
209 D8 Muié Angola
105 I1 Muika Japan
93 F4 Muiliyk i. Maluku Indon.
Muineachán Ireland see Monaghan
147 I7 Muine Bheag Ireland
182 E5 Muiños Spain
226 J7 Muir MI U.S.A.
234 B3 Muir PA U.S.A.
146 K9 Muirdrum Angus, Scotland U.K.
222 B3 Muir Glacier Can./U.S.A.
146 J10 Muirhead Angus, Scotland U.K.
146 H11 Muirkirk East Ayrshire, Scotland U.K.
146 D6 Muirneag hill Scotland U.K.
146 K8 Muir of Fowlis Aberdeenshire, Scotland U.K.
146 H7 Muir of Ord Highland, Scotland U.K.
250 B4 Muisne Ecuador
213 H2 Muite Moz.
156 G5 Muizon France
122 F4 Mūjān, Chāh-e well Iran
243 P7 Mujeres, Isla i. Mex.
111 D8 Muji Xinjiang China
95 J3 Mujong r. Malaysia
101 E10 Muju S. Korea
251 H5 Mujuí Joboti Brazil
122 B2 Mujūmbar Iran
Mukačevo Ukr. see Mukacheve
136 B5 Mukacheve Ukr.
Mukachevo Ukr. see Mukacheve
95 J3 Mukah Sarawak Malaysia
95 J3 Mukah r. Malaysia
Mukalla Yemen see Al Mukallā
116 E6 Mukandgarh Rajasthan India
116 F7 Mukandwara Rajasthan India
209 D6 Mukanga Dem. Rep. Congo
125 I5 Mukassir, Banī des. Saudi Arabia
102 S4 Mukawa Hokkaidō Japan
105 H4 Mukawa Yamanashi Japan
102 S4 Mu-kawa r. Japan
203 H4 Mukawwar, Gezirat i. Sudan
96 G6 Mukdahan Thai.
Mukden Liaoning China see Shenyang
116 E4 Mukerian Punjab India
92 □ Mukeru Palau
224 C2 Muketei r. Ont. Can.
210 C2 Muke T'urī Eth.
175 L3 Mukhavyets Belarus
175 M3 Mukhavyets r. Belarus
100 J4 Mukhen Rus. Fed.
100 E2 Mukhino Rus. Fed.
107 K1 Mukhorshibir' Rus. Fed.
Mukhtuya Rus. Fed. see Lensk
129 F6 Mūkhvor Iran
122 G5 Mūkīk, Chashmeh-ye spring Iran
87 E11 Mukinbudin W.A. Austr.
104 C6 Mukō Japan
97 F9 Mu Ko Chang Marine National Park Thai.
103 □2 Muko-jima i. Japan
103 □2 Mukojima-rettō is Japan
94 D6 Mukomuko Sumatera Indon.
210 B4 Mukono Uganda
209 F7 Mukoshi Zambia
123 K3 Mukry Turkm.
Muksu r. Tajik. see Mughsu
117 I5 Muktinath Nepal
116 E4 Muktsar Punjab India
209 F8 Mukuku Zambia
213 F3 Mukumbura Zimbabwe
209 F7 Mukunsa Zambia
120 F4 Mukur Atyrauskaya Oblast' Kazakh.
121 S2 Mukur Vostochnyy Kazakhstan Kazakh.
223 L4 Mukutawa r. Man. Can.
226 F7 Mukwonago WI U.S.A.
116 G9 Mul Mahar. India
114 D3 Mula r. India
123 L7 Mula r. Pak.
187 C11 Mula Spain
185 Q4 Mula r. Spain
Mulaku atoll Maldives see Mulaku Atoll
113 D11 Mulaku Atoll Maldives
121 R5 Mulaly Kazakh.
100 F6 Mulan Heilong. China
92 D5 Mulanay Luzon Phil.
211 B8 Mulanje Malawi
213 G2 Mulanje, Mount Malawi
82 F3 Mulapula, Lake salt flat S.A. Austr.
192 C8 Mulargia, Lago l. Sardegna Italy
242 E3 Mulatos Mex.
242 □U13 Mula-tupo Panama
124 G2 Mulayḩ Saudi Arabia
128 G9 Mulayḩ salt pan Saudi Arabia
125 I2 Mulayjah Saudi Arabia
128 B8 Mulayz, Wādī al watercourse Egypt
190 H7 Mulazzo Italy
114 F6 Mulbagal Karnataka India
151 O2 Mulbarton Norfolk, England U.K.
116 F2 Mulbekh Jammu and Kashmir
146 J7 Mulben Moray, Scotland U.K.
237 H8 Mulberry AR U.S.A.
220 C3 Mulchatna r. AK U.S.A.
260 A5 Mulchén Chile
171 H9 Mulda Ger.
171 F7 Mulde r. Ger.
171 F7 Muldenstein Ger.
211 A5 Muleba Tanz.
238 L5 Mule Creek WY U.S.A.
242 C4 Mulegé Mex.
211 B7 Mulekatembo Zambia
93 B8 Mules i. Indon.
237 D8 Muleshoe TX U.S.A.
213 H3 Mulevala Moz.
172 H3 Mulfingen Ger.
86 E7 Mulga Downs W.A. Austr.
84 C8 Mulga Park N.T. Austr.
82 E4 Mulgathing S.A. Austr.
185 M6 Mulhacén mt. Spain
Mülhausen France see Mulhouse
169 C8 Mülheim an der Ruhr Ger.
169 D10 Mülheim-Kärlich Ger.
157 N8 Mulhouse France
108 C5 Muli Sichuan China
Muli Rus. Fed. see Vysokogorniy
78 □2 Mulifanua Samoa
113 □2 Mulikadu i. Addu Atoll Maldives
116 C8 Mulila Gujarat India
211 B7 Mulilansolo Zambia
100 G6 Muling Heilong. China
100 G6 Muling Heilong. China
100 H6 Muling He r. China
78 □2 Mulitapu'ili, Cape Samoa
179 K8 Muljava Slovenia
146 E10 Mull i. Scotland U.K.
146 D9 Mull, Sound of sea chan. Scotland U.K.
122 C3 Mulla Ali Iran
210 E2 Mullaaxe Beyle Somalia
148 D6 Mullagh Cavan Ireland
147 D7 Mullagh Clare Ireland
147 C5 Mullagh Mayo Ireland
147 I6 Mullagh Meath Ireland
147 D8 Mullaghareirk hill Ireland
147 D8 Mullaghareirk Mountains hills Ireland
147 H3 Mullaghcarn hill Northern Ireland U.K.
147 J6 Mullaghcleevaun hill Ireland
147 H3 Mullaghcloga hill Northern Ireland U.K.
147 F4 Mullaghmore Ireland
114 G8 Mullaittivu Sri Lanka
83 L4 Mullaley N.S.W. Austr.
147 I4 Mullan Ireland
147 G4 Mullan Northern Ireland U.K.
146 F8 Mullardoch, Loch l. Scotland U.K.
147 K4 Mullartown Northern Ireland U.K.
236 E4 Mullen NE U.S.A.
83 K4 Mullengudgery N.S.W. Austr.
232 D11 Mullens WV U.S.A.
84 E7 Muller watercourse N.T. Austr.
95 J4 Muller, Pegunungan mts Indon.
226 J4 Mullett Lake MI U.S.A.
87 C10 Mullewa W.A. Austr.
146 K5 Mull Head Orkney, Scotland U.K.
172 D6 Müllheim Ger.
234 G5 Mullica r. NJ U.S.A.
234 E5 Mullica Hill NJ U.S.A.
84 G8 Mulligan watercourse Qld Austr.
147 H8 Mullinavat Ireland
147 H5 Mullingar Ireland
231 H8 Mullins SC U.S.A.
150 B7 Mullion Cornwall, England U.K.
83 L5 Mullion Creek N.S.W. Austr.
145 E4 Mull of Galloway c. Scotland U.K.
146 E12 Mull of Kintyre hd Scotland U.K.
146 D11 Mull of Oa hd Scotland U.K.
135 J5 Mullovka Rus. Fed.
171 J6 Müllrose Ger.
143 J4 Mullsjö Sweden
138 F3 Mullutu laht l. Estonia
209 E9 Mulobezi Zambia
209 B8 Mulondo Angola
209 D9 Mulonga Plain Zambia
209 E6 Mulongo Dem. Rep. Congo
147 C5 Mulrany Ireland
147 G2 Mulroy Bay Ireland
159 L6 Mulsanne France
114 C3 Mulshi Lake India
116 G9 Multai Madh. Prad. India
123 I8 Mūltān Iran
123 N6 Multan Pak.
140 R5 Multia Fin.
156 E6 Multien reg. France
95 K2 Mulu, Gunung mt. Malaysia
114 F3 Mulug Andhra Prad. India
209 E7 Mulumbe, Monts mts Dem. Rep. Congo
83 I5 Mulurulu Lake N.S.W. Austr.
208 D4 Muma Dem. Rep. Congo
208 E2 Mumallah Sudan
122 I9 Mūmān Iran
114 C3 Mumbai Mahar. India
209 D8 Mumbeji Zambia
83 L5 Mumbil N.S.W. Austr.
150 E4 Mumbles Head Wales U.K.
209 B7 Mumbondo Angola
209 C8 Mumbué Angola
209 E8 Mumbwa Zambia
211 C6 Mumbwi Tanz.
209 E7 Mume Dem. Rep. Congo
Muminabad Tajik. see Leningrad
Mŭ'minobod Tajik. see Leningrad
190 D1 Mümliswil Switz.
97 D11 Mum Nok, Laem pt Thai.
209 D6 Mumoma Dem. Rep. Congo
120 B5 Mumra Rus. Fed.
192 A9 Mumullonis, Punta hill Italy
96 G7 Mun, Mae Nam r. Thai.
93 C6 Muna i. Indon.
243 O7 Muna Mex.
131 N3 Muna r. Rus. Fed.
123 N9 Munabao Pak.
140 □C1 Munaðarnes Iceland
114 F4 Munagala Andhra Prad. India
103 H13 Munakata Japan
183 J7 Muñana Spain
124 B4 Munayjah, Jabal mts Egypt/Sudan
120 F4 Munayly Kazakh.
120 E6 Munayshy Kazakh.
171 E10 Münchberg Ger.
171 J5 Müncheberg Ger.
173 L5 München Ger.
München airport Ger. see Franz Josef Strauss
171 E9 Münchenbernsdorf Ger.
190 C1 Münchenbuchsee Switz.
München-Gladbach Ger. see Mönchengladbach
169 G9 Münchhausen Ger.
250 B4 Munchique, Parque Nacional nat. park Col.
222 E3 Muncho Lake B.C. Can.
222 E3 Muncho Lake Provincial Park B.C. Can.
101 E9 Munch'ŏn N. Korea
173 L4 Münchsmünster Ger.
173 J2 Münchsteinach Ger.
172 D3 Münchweiler an der Rodalb Ger.
190 G1 Münchwilen Switz.
230 E5 Muncie IN U.S.A.
84 G8 Muncoonie West, Lake salt flat Qld Austr.
227 R8 Muncy PA U.S.A.
234 B2 Muncy Creek r. PA U.S.A.
234 B2 Muncy Valley PA U.S.A.
209 B9 Munda Angola
208 D4 Munda Dem. Rep. Congo
123 N6 Munda Pak.
78 □6 Munda New Georgia Is Solomon Is
183 O2 Mundaka Spain
114 F9 Mundel Lake Sri Lanka
207 H5 Mundemba Cameroon
178 H3 Munderfing Austria
172 H5 Munderkingen Ger.
151 O2 Mundesley Norfolk, England U.K.
151 N2 Mundford Norfolk, England U.K.
87 F7 Mundiwindi W.A. Austr.
85 H5 Mundjura Creek r. Qld Austr.
185 P4 Mundo r. Spain
157 O6 Mundolsheim France
254 E4 Mundo Novo Brazil
116 B8 Mundra Gujarat India
87 I11 Mundrabilla W.A. Austr.
241 U7 Munds Park AZ U.S.A.
85 M8 Mundubbera Qld Austr.
116 D6 Mundwa Rajasthan India
183 Q6 Munebrega Spain
185 O2 Munera Spain
114 G4 Muneru r. India
230 E7 Munfordville KY U.S.A.
85 K9 Mungallala Qld Austr.
83 K3 Mungallala Creek r. Qld Austr.
85 J4 Mungana Qld Austr.
116 G7 Mungaoli Madh. Prad. India
213 G3 Mungári Moz.
86 E6 Mungaroona Range Nature Reserve W.A. Austr.
208 F4 Mungbere Dem. Rep. Congo
116 H8 Mungeli Chhattisgarh India
117 K7 Munger Bihar India
227 K6 Munger MI U.S.A.
82 G3 Mungeranie S.A. Austr.
Mu Nggava i. Solomon Is see Rennell
95 H4 Munggresak, Tanjung pt Indon.
183 O2 Mungia Spain
Mu Ngiki i. Solomon Is see Bellona
87 H8 Mungilli Aboriginal Reserve W.A. Austr.
83 L3 Mungindi N.S.W. Austr.
84 E6 Mungkarta Aboriginal Land res. N.T. Austr.
209 C7 Mungo Angola
83 I5 Mungo, Lake N.S.W. Austr.
83 I5 Mungo National Park N.S.W. Austr.
147 E7 Mungret Ireland
Munguía Spain see Mungia
211 A7 Mungwi Zambia
101 E10 Mun'gyŏng S. Korea
209 C8 Munhango Angola
209 B8 Munhino Angola
256 D5 Munhoz Brazil
Munich Ger. see München
183 J7 Muñico Spain
182 G2 Muniellos, Reserva Natural Integral de nature res. Spain
186 D5 Muniesa Spain
183 P4 Munilla Spain
226 H3 Munising MI U.S.A.
257 G4 Muniz Freire Brazil
116 C8 Munjpur Gujarat India
Munkács Ukr. see Mukacheve
134 E1 Munkebakken Norway
142 H3 Munkedal Sweden
140 M5 Munkflohögen Sweden
142 J2 Munkfors Sweden
106 G1 Munku-Sardyk, Gora mt. Mongolia/Rus. Fed.
165 E7 Munkzwalm Belgium
146 H7 Munlochy Highland, Scotland U.K.
169 J10 Münnerstadt Ger.
173 J4 Munningen Ger.
80 □ Munning Point Chatham Is S. Pacific Ocean
183 K7 Muñogalindo Spain
83 L9 Munro, Mount Tas. Austr.
223 L3 Munroe Lake Man. Can.
93 C6 Munse Sulawesi Indon.
117 M8 Munshiganj Bangl.
173 K6 Münsing Ger.
172 G5 Münsingen Ger.
190 D2 Münsingen Switz.
178 E5 Münster Austria
157 N7 Munster France
172 F2 Münster Hessen Ger.
168 J5 Münster Niedersachsen Ger.
169 E7 Münster Nordrhein-Westfalen Ger.
169 E7 Münster admin. reg. Ger.
147 E8 Munster reg. Ireland
190 E3 Münster Switz.
168 I3 Münsterdorf Ger.
173 I5 Münsterhausen Ger.
169 E7 Münsterland reg. Ger.
169 D10 Münstermaifeld Ger.
169 E6 Münster-Osnabrück airport Ger.
87 E11 Muntadgin W.A. Austr.
178 G5 Muntanitz mt. Austria
93 A3 Munte Sulawesi Indon.
197 L4 Muntele Mare, Vârful mt. Romania
164 K2 Muntendam Neth.
197 P5 Munteni Romania
210 B4 Muntu Uganda
209 F7 Mununga Zambia
195 □ Munxar Gozo Malta
Munyal-Par sea feature India see Bassas de Pedro Padua Bank
213 F3 Munyati r. Zimbabwe
215 M7 Munyu S. Africa
169 G10 Münzenberg Ger.
179 I3 Münzkirchen Austria
126 I4 Munzur Vadisi Milli Parkı nat. park Turkey
140 Q3 Muodoslompolo Sweden
140 T4 Muojärvi l. Fin.
96 F3 Mường Nhe Vietnam
Muong Sai Laos see Xay
96 F3 Mường Te Vietnam
140 Q3 Muonio Fin.
140 Q3 Muonioälven r. Fin./Sweden
140 Q3 Muonionalusta Sweden
Muonionjoki r. Fin./Sweden see Muonioälven
93 F3 Muor i. Maluku Indon.
190 F2 Muotathal Switz.
209 B9 Mupa Angola
209 B8 Mupa, Parque Nacional da nat. park Angola
213 F3 Mupfure r. Zimbabwe
107 Q8 Muping Shandong China
203 F5 Muqaddam watercourse Sudan
210 E3 Muqakoori Somalia
124 H9 Muqaybirah Yemen
125 I4 Muqaynimah well Saudi Arabia
210 E4 Muqdisho Somalia
125 K6 Muqhshin, Wādī r. Oman
125 M4 Muqnīyāt Oman
129 J4 Müqtädir Azer.
254 C5 Muquem Brazil
257 G4 Muqui Brazil
Muqyr Kazakh. see Mukur
179 L5 Mur r. Austria alt. Mura (Croatia/Slovenia)
128 B10 Mu'r, Wādī watercourse Egypt
179 O7 Mura r. Croatia/Slovenia alt. Mur (Austria)
173 M3 Murach r. Ger.
182 E9 Muradal, Serra do mts Port.
199 I4 Muradiye Manisa Turkey
127 K4 Muradiye Van Turkey
136 H5 Murafa r. Ukr.
94 □ Murai, Tanjong pt Sing.
94 □ Murai Reservoir Sing.
102 Q8 Murakami Japan
176 F5 Murakeresztúr Hungary
259 B8 Murallón, Cerro mt. Chile
211 A5 Muramvya Burundi
177 J3 Muráň Slovakia
177 J3 Muráň r. Slovakia
210 C5 Murang'a Kenya
191 M5 Murano Italy
177 I3 Muránska planina park Slovakia
103 L11 Muraoka Japan
182 E2 Muras Spain
134 J4 Murashi Rus. Fed.
161 B9 Murasson France
176 F5 Muraszemenye Hungary
161 B6 Murat France
129 C7 Murat r. Turkey
127 I4 Murat r. Turkey
129 C7 Muratgören Turkey
199 I1 Muratlı Turkey
192 C2 Murato Corse France
161 B9 Murat-sur-Vèbre France
179 J5 Murau Austria
175 M3 Murava Belarus
192 D9 Muravera Sardegna Italy
102 R8 Murayama Japan
124 E3 Murayr, Jabal hill Saudi Arabia
203 G4 Murayr, Jazīrat i. Egypt
202 E2 Muraysah, Ra's al pt Libya
190 E7 Murazzano Italy
157 N8 Murbach France
182 F6 Murça Port.
183 Q4 Murchante Spain
122 D5 Murcheh Khvort Iran
170 I3 Murchin Ger.
83 J7 Murchison Vic. Austr.
87 C9 Murchison watercourse W.A. Austr.
81 G8 Murchison South I. N.Z.
263 L2 Murchison, Mount Antarctica
87 D9 Murchison, Mount hill W.A. Austr.
81 F10 Murchison, Mount South I. N.Z.
210 A4 Murchison Falls National Park Uganda
224 B3 Murchison Island Ont. Can.
81 B12 Murchison Mountains South I. N.Z.
84 E6 Murchison Range hills N.T. Austr.
187 C12 Murcia Spain
185 Q5 Murcia aut. comm. Spain
92 D7 Murcielagos Bay Mindanao Phil.
174 F3 Murczyn Pol.
161 B7 Mur-de-Barrez France
158 F5 Mûr-de-Bretagne France
234 E6 Murderkill r. DE U.S.A.
159 O7 Mur-de-Sologne France
236 E4 Murdo SD U.S.A.
225 H3 Murdochville Que. Can.
105 H2 Mure Japan
179 M6 Mureck Austria
199 I2 Mürefte Turkey
207 G4 Muregi Nigeria
213 F3 Murehwa Zimbabwe
184 E3 Mures r. Port.
196 I4 Mureşul r. Romania
163 G9 Muret France
Murewa Zimbabwe see Murehwa
140 M4 Murfjället mt. Norway
237 I8 Murfreesboro AR U.S.A.
231 I7 Murfreesboro NC U.S.A.
231 D8 Murfreesboro TN U.S.A.
172 E6 Murg Ger.
172 E4 Murg r. Ger.
Murgab Tajik. see Murghob
Murgab Turkm. see Murgap
Murgab r. Turkm. see Murgap
123 J3 Murgap Turkm.
123 J3 Murgap r. Turkm.
84 D1 Murgenella Creek r. N.T. Austr.
197 Q4 Murgeni Romania
190 D1 Murgenthal Switz.
195 M3 Murge Tarantine hills Italy
123 J4 Murghab r. Afgh.
123 J4 Murghab reg. Afgh.
123 M6 Murgha Kibzai Pak.
123 L6 Murgha Mehterzai Pak.
123 P2 Murghob Tajik.
123 O2 Murghob r. Tajik.
129 G5 Murghuz Lerr mt. Armenia
183 O3 Murgia Spain
193 R6 Murgia Sant'Elia hill Italy
85 M9 Murgon Qld Austr.
87 D9 Murgoo W.A. Austr.
129 C4 Murgul Turkey
106 F8 Muri Qinghai China
106 G8 Muri Qinghai China
117 J8 Muri Jharkhand India
122 G3 Mūrī Iran
190 E1 Muri Aargau Switz.
190 C2 Muri Bern Switz.
95 I8 Muria, Gunung mt. Indon.
257 F4 Muriaé Brazil
182 H3 Murias de Paredes Spain
123 L7 Murid Pak.
183 M2 Muriedas Spain
209 D7 Muriege Angola
95 H4 Murih, Pulau i. Indon.
102 U3 Murii-dake mt. Japan
226 E1 Murillo Ont. Can.
183 R4 Murillo el Fruto Spain
190 E5 Murisengo Italy
170 G4 Müritz l. Ger.
170 H4 Müritz, Nationalpark nat. park Ger.
170 D4 Müritz-Elde-Wasserstraße r. Ger.
170 G4 Müritz Seenpark nature res. Ger.
80 L5 Muriwai North I. N.Z.
140 P3 Murjek Sweden
117 O6 Murkong Selek Assam India
148 C5 Murley Northern Ireland U.K.
192 G1 Murlo Italy
140 V2 Murmansk Rus. Fed.
140 W2 Murmanskaya Oblast' admin. div. Rus. Fed.
134 F1 Murmanskiy Bereg coastal area Rus. Fed.
Murmansk Oblast admin. div. Rus. Fed. see Murmanskaya Oblast'
140 V2 Murmashi Rus. Fed.
139 X7 Murmino Rus. Fed.
173 M6 Murn r. Ger.
173 K6 Murnau am Staffelsee Ger.
147 I8 Murntown Ireland
104 D6 Muro Japan
182 C6 Muro Port.
187 L8 Muro Spain
187 L8 Muro r. Spain
192 B4 Muro, Capo di c. Corse France
104 D6 Murō-Akame-Aoyama Kokutei-kōen park Japan
187 E10 Muro de Alcoy Spain
160 B5 Murol France
195 O3 Muro Leccese Italy
193 O6 Muro Lucano Italy
134 H5 Murom Rus. Fed.
104 F2 Muromagi-gawa r. Japan
162 C3 Muron France
211 A5 Murongo Tanz.
177 K5 Murony Hungary
102 R4 Muroran Japan
192 B6 Muros Sardegna Italy
182 H1 Muros Asturias Spain
182 B3 Muros Galicia Spain
182 B3 Muros e Noia, Ría de est. Spain
103 L13 Muroto Japan
104 A8 Muroto-Anan-kaigan Kokutei-kōen park Japan
103 L13 Muroto-zaki pt Japan
175 M5 Murovane Ukr.
136 G5 Murovani Kurylivtsi Ukr.
129 H5 Murovdağ Silsiläsi hills Azer.
174 F5 Murów Pol.
174 F3 Murowana Goślina Pol.
238 F5 Murphy ID U.S.A.
231 F8 Murphy NC U.S.A.
240 L3 Murphys CA U.S.A.
125 I4 Murrah reg. Saudi Arabia
128 C10 Murrah, Wādī watercourse Egypt
203 G2 Murrah al Kubrá, Al Buḩayrah al l. Egypt
128 A8 Murrah aş Şughrá, Al Buḩayrah al l. Egypt
83 K3 Murra Murra Qld Austr.
84 D4 Murranji Aboriginal Land res. N.T. Austr.
82 G6 Murray r. S.A. Austr.
87 C12 Murray r. W.A. Austr.
222 F3 Murray r. B.C. Can.
237 K7 Murray KY U.S.A.
91 J8 Murray, Lake P.N.G.
231 G8 Murray, Lake SC U.S.A.
222 D2 Murray, Mount Y.T. Can.
82 G6 Murray Bridge S.A. Austr.
232 C9 Murray City OH U.S.A.
84 E6 Murray Downs N.T. Austr.
225 I4 Murray Harbour P.E.I. Can.
86 □1 Murray Hill Christmas I.
87 J8 Murray Range hills W.A. Austr.
214 H7 Murraysburg S. Africa
82 H6 Murray Sunset National Park Vic. Austr.
82 H6 Murrayville Vic. Austr.
123 O5 Murree Pak.
190 D2 Mürren Switz.
172 H4 Murrhardt Ger.
240 O8 Murrieta CA U.S.A.
83 L6 Murringo N.S.W. Austr.
147 C5 Murrisk reg. Ireland
213 H3 Murroa Moz.
147 D6 Murroogh Ireland
83 L6 Murrumbateman N.S.W. Austr.
83 I6 Murrumbidgee r. N.S.W. Austr.
213 H2 Murrupula Moz.
83 M4 Murrurundi N.S.W. Austr.
159 J7 Mûrs-Erigné France
117 L7 Murshidabad W. Bengal India
188 F2 Murska Sobota Slovenia
179 N6 Mursko Središće Croatia
116 F9 Murtajapur Mahar. India
185 M7 Murtas Spain
182 D8 Murtede Port.
190 C2 Murten Switz.
190 C2 Murtensee l. Switz.
188 E4 Murter Croatia
188 E4 Murter i. Croatia
83 I7 Murtoa Vic. Austr.
182 C7 Murtosa Port.
140 T4 Murtovaara Fin.
252 C2 Muru r. Brazil
Murua i. P.N.G. see Woodlark Island
210 B4 Murua Ngithigerr mts Kenya
114 C3 Murud Mahar. India
95 K3 Murud, Gunung mt. Indon.
95 K5 Murui r. Indon.
107 Q5 Muruin Sum Shuiku resr China
95 K5 Murung r. Indon.
95 K6 Murung r. Indon.
114 G8 Murunkan Sri Lanka
120 K7 Muruntov Uzbek.
80 K5 Murupara North I. N.Z.
79 □9 Mururoa atoll Arch. des Tuamotu Fr. Polynesia
251 I5 Muruti, Ilha i. Brazil
251 G5 Murutinga Brazil
Murviedro Spain see Sagunto
161 C10 Murviel-lès-Béziers France
124 D4 Murwānī, Wādī watercourse Saudi Arabia
116 H8 Murwara Madh. Prad. India
83 N3 Murwillumbah N.S.W. Austr.
134 J4 Murygino Kirovskaya Oblast' Rus. Fed.
139 P7 Murygino Smolenskaya Oblast' Rus. Fed.
179 L5 Mürz r. Austria
122 I2 Murzechirla Turkm.
179 M4 Mürzsteg Austria
202 B3 Murzūq Libya
202 B3 Murzuq, Ḩamādat plat. Libya
202 B3 Murzūq, Idhān des. Libya
174 D3 Murzynowo Pol.
179 M4 Mürzzuschlag Austria
127 J4 Muş Turkey
129 C7 Muş prov. Turkey
208 C4 Musa Dem. Rep. Congo
138 H5 Mūša r. Lith. alt. Mūsa (Latvia)
141 R8 Mūsa r. Latvia alt. Mūša (Lith.)
124 A1 Mūsá, Jabal mt. Egypt
122 C6 Mūsā, Khowr-e b. Iran
124 F9 Musa Āli Terara vol. Africa
117 K8 Musabani Jharkhand India
128 E2 Musabeyli Turkey
124 E6 Muşabih Saudi Arabia
123 M6 Musa Khel Bazar Pak.
197 L8 Musala mt. Bulg.
94 C4 Musala i. Indon.
128 C2 Musalı Turkey
101 F7 Musan N. Korea
125 M3 Musandam admin. reg. Oman
125 M2 Musandam Peninsula Oman/U.A.E.
123 K5 Musa Qala Afgh.
123 K5 Mūsá Qal'eh, Rūd-e r. Afgh.
105 K4 Musashino Japan
Musay'īd Qatar see Umm Sa'id
124 G9 Musaymir Yemen
202 E6 Musbat well Sudan
150 F6 Musbury Devon, England U.K.
Muscat Oman see Masqaţ
Muscat reg. Oman see Masqaţ
Muscat and Oman country Asia see Oman
236 J5 Muscatine IA U.S.A.
171 F8 Muschwitz Ger.
226 D6 Muscoda WI U.S.A.
234 E3 Musconetcong r. NJ U.S.A.
233 □P5 Muscongus Bay ME U.S.A.
138 H7 Musė r. Lith.
192 B9 Musei Sardegna Italy
85 I3 Musgrave Qld Austr.
81 E10 Musgrave, Mount South I. N.Z.
225 K3 Musgrave Harbour Nfld and Lab. Can.
82 C2 Musgrave Ranges mts S.A. Austr.
123 M5 Mūshakī Afgh.
128 E9 Mushāsh al Kabid well Jordan
128 E10 Mushash Dabl well Saudi Arabia
128 E7 Mushāsh Ḩadraj Jordan
128 G10 Mushāsh Mudayyān well Saudi Arabia
124 G7 Mushaynīqah well Yemen
128 E8 Mushayyish, Wādī al watercourse Jordan
209 D6 Mushenge Dem. Rep. Congo
209 C5 Mushie Dem. Rep. Congo
207 F5 Mushin Nigeria
137 M5 Mushuryn Rig Ukr.
114 F4 Musi r. India
94 F6 Musi r. Indon.
196 J9 Musica mt. Macedonia
241 S6 Music Mountain AZ U.S.A.
117 I5 Musikot Nepal
191 N4 Musile di Piave Italy
213 F4 Musina S. Africa
241 U2 Musinia Peak UT U.S.A.
137 L4 Musiyivka Ukr.
222 F2 Muskeg r. N.W.T. Can.
233 O7 Muskeget Channel MA U.S.A.
226 H6 Muskegon MI U.S.A.
226 H6 Muskegon r. MI U.S.A.
226 H6 Muskegon Heights MI U.S.A.
222 G4 Muskeg River Alta Can.
232 D9 Muskingum r. OH U.S.A.
237 H8 Muskogee OK U.S.A.
227 O5 Muskoka Ont. Can.
224 E4 Muskoka, Lake Ont. Can.
223 N4 Muskrat Dam Lake Ont. Can.
222 F3 Muskwa r. B.C. Can.
123 L6 Muslimbagh Pak.
Muslim-Croat Federation aut. div. Bos.-Herz. see Federacija Bosna i Hercegovina
128 F2 Muslimīyah Syria
134 K5 Muslyumovo Rus. Fed.
203 G5 Musmar Sudan
209 F8 Musofu Zambia
211 B5 Musoma Tanz.
211 B6 Musombe Tanz.
191 P9 Musone r. Italy
198 D1 Mušov Grob pass Macedonia
225 I3 Musquanousse, Lac l. Que. Can.
225 I3 Musquaro Que. Can.
225 I3 Musquaro, Lac l. Que. Can.
209 D8 Mussaca Angola
91 K7 Mussau Island P.N.G.
146 J11 Musselburgh East Lothian, Scotland U.K.
164 L3 Musselkanaal Neth.
238 K3 Musselshell r. MT U.S.A.
209 C7 Mussende Angola
129 B2 Mussera Georgia
209 B6 Musserra Angola
162 E5 Mussidan France
209 C7 Mussolo Angola
194 F8 Mussomeli Sicilia Italy
165 I9 Musson Belgium
116 G4 Mussoorie Uttaranchal India
209 D8 Mussuma Angola
209 D8 Mussuma r. Angola
156 I8 Mussy-sur-Seine France
116 G6 Mustafabad Uttar Prad. India
116 H7 Mustafabad Uttar Prad. India
199 J2 Mustafakemalpaşa Turkey
210 E3 Mustahīl Eth.
190 I2 Müstair Switz.
138 K1 Mustamaa i. Fin.
237 E10 Mustang Draw watercourse TX U.S.A.
110 G3 Mustau, Gora mt. Xinjiang China
120 E2 Mustayevo Rus. Fed.
259 C7 Musters, Lago l. Arg.
247 □3 Mustique i. St Vincent
138 F3 Mustjala Estonia
138 J4 Mustjõgi r. Estonia
138 I3 Mustla Estonia
140 T2 Mustola Fin.
138 J3 Mustvee Estonia
101 F8 Musu-dan pt N. Korea
129 I5 Müsüslü Azer.
83 M5 Muswellbrook N.S.W. Austr.
175 I2 Muszaki Pol.
175 I6 Muszyna Pol.
203 F3 Mūţ Egypt
126 F5 Mut Turkey
179 L6 Muta Slovenia
178 C6 Muta, Lago di l. Italy
254 F5 Mutá, Ponta do pt Brazil
81 □4 Mutalau Niue
209 E8 Mutanda Zambia
213 G3 Mutare Zimbabwe
124 G5 Mutarjim, Khashm hill Saudi Arabia
124 H2 Mutayr reg. Saudi Arabia
209 E6 Mutengwa Dem. Rep. Congo
179 P2 Mutěnice Czech Rep.
209 F7 Muteta Dem. Rep. Congo
146 I10 Muthill Perth and Kinross, Scotland U.K.
125 M4 Mutī Oman
183 Q3 Mutilva Baja Spain
Mutina Italy see Modena
124 A2 Mu'tiq, Jabal mts Egypt
250 B3 Mutis Col.
93 D8 Mutis, Gunung mt. Timor Indon.
134 K2 Mutnyy Materik Rus. Fed.
213 G3 Mutoko Zimbabwe
209 D6 Mutombo Dem. Rep. Congo
82 H5 Mutooroo S.A. Austr.
213 F3 Mutorashanga Zimbabwe
209 D6 Mutoto Dem. Rep. Congo
193 N5 Mutria, Monte mt. Italy
217 □3 Mutsamudu Nzwani Comoros
209 E7 Mutshatsha Dem. Rep. Congo
102 S5 Mutsu Japan
102 S5 Mutsu-wan b. Japan
105 L5 Mutsuzawa Japan
85 J7 Muttaburra Qld Austr.
199 L3 Muttalip Turkey
178 C5 Muttekopf mt. Austria
190 D1 Muttenz Switz.
178 D5 Mutters Austria
172 E3 Mutterstadt Ger.
82 □2 Mutton Bird Island Lord Howe I. Austr.
81 C13 Muttonbird Islands Stewart I. N.Z.
Muttonbird Islands N.Z. see Titi Islands
147 C7 Mutton Island Ireland
114 G5 Muttukuru Andhra Prad. India
114 F7 Muttupet Tamil Nadu India
213 H2 Mutuali Moz.
257 G3 Mutum Brazil
250 D6 Mutum r. Brazil
211 A5 Mutumba Burundi
207 H4 Mutum Biyu Nigeria
252 D2 Mutumparaná Brazil
209 C6 Mutungu-Tari Dem. Rep. Congo
254 C5 Mutunópolis Brazil
114 G8 Mutur Sri Lanka
187 E11 Mutxamel Spain
137 M2 Mutyn Ukr.
157 N6 Mutzig France
171 G8 Mutzschen Ger.
138 J2 Muuga Estonia
141 R5 Muurame Fin.
141 Q6 Muurla Fin.
140 R3 Muurola Fin.
107 K7 Mu Us Shamo des. China
209 B7 Muxaluando Angola
129 H4 Muxax Azer.
Muxi Sichuan China see Muchuan
182 B2 Muxía Spain
209 B7 Muxima Angola
207 H4 Muya Nigeria
134 F3 Muyezerskiy Rus. Fed.
211 A5 Muyinga Burundi
Muynoq Uzbek. see Mo'ynoq
211 B7 Muyombe Zambia
207 H5 Muyuka Cameroon
209 E6 Muyumba Dem. Rep. Congo
108 H3 Muyuping Hubei China
123 O4 Muzaffarabad Pak.
123 N6 Muzaffargarh Pak.
116 F5 Muzaffarnagar Uttar Prad. India
117 J6 Muzaffarpur Bihar India
213 G4 Muzamane Moz.
256 D4 Muzambinho Brazil
110 F6 Muzat He r. China
120 F6 Muzbel', Uval hills Kazakh.
213 F2 Muze Moz.
129 F2 Muzhichi Rus. Fed.
158 G6 Muzillac France
123 I8 Mūzīn Iran
250 C3 Muzo Col.
222 C4 Muzon, Cape AK U.S.A.
243 I4 Múzquiz Mex.
111 E9 Muztag mt. Xinjiang China
111 H8 Muz Tag mt. Xinjiang China
110 B7 Muztagata mt. Xinjiang China
Muztor Kyrg. see Toktogul
190 G5 Muzza, Canale canal Italy
191 O4 Muzzana del Turgnano Italy
208 B4 Mvadi Gabon
207 H6 Mvangan Cameroon
208 F3 Mvolo Sudan
211 C6 Mvomero Tanz.
208 B4 Mvoung r. Gabon
217 □3a Mvouni Njazidja Comoros
209 B6 Mvouti Congo
213 F3 Mvuma Zimbabwe
213 F3 Mvurwi Zimbabwe
217 □3 Mwali i. Comoros
213 F3 Mwami Zimbabwe
209 E9 Mwandi Zambia
211 C5 Mwanga Tanz.
211 B6 Mwanisenga Tanz.
78 □6 Mwaniwowo San Cristobal Solomon Is
211 B8 Mwanjawira Zambia
211 B8 Mwanya Zambia
211 B8 Mwanza Malawi
211 B5 Mwanza Tanz.
211 B5 Mwanza admin. reg. Tanz.
211 A8 Mwape Zambia
211 A5 Mwaro Burundi
209 E6 Mweho Dem. Rep. Congo
209 D6 Mweka Dem. Rep. Congo
211 C6 Mwele Tanz.
209 F7 Mwenda Zambia
209 D7 Mwene-Biji Dem. Rep. Congo
209 D6 Mwene-Ditu Dem. Rep. Congo
213 F4 Mwenezi Zimbabwe
213 F4 Mwenezi r. Zimbabwe
209 F5 Mwenga Dem. Rep. Congo
209 F7 Mwense Zambia
211 C6 Mwereni Kenya
209 F7 Mweru, Lake Dem. Rep. Congo/Zambia
211 C7 Mweru Plateau Tanz.
209 F7 Mweru Wantipa, Lake Zambia
209 F7 Mweru Wantipa National Park Zambia
211 A7 Mwewa Zambia
209 D7 Mwimba Dem. Rep. Congo
211 C5 Mwingi Kenya
209 E7 Mwinilunga Zambia
205 G3 Mya, Oued watercourse Alg.
96 C3 Myadaung Myanmar
138 J7 Myadzyel Belarus
138 J7 Myadzyel, Vozyera l. Belarus
108 D3 Myaglo Sichuan China
96 B4 Myaing Myanmar
116 C6 Myajlar Rajasthan India
138 L5 Myakishevo Rus. Fed.
131 Q3 Myakit Rus. Fed.
136 F3 M"yakoty Ukr.
83 N5 Myall Lakes National Park N.S.W. Austr.
96 B5 Myanaung Myanmar
96 B3 Myanmar country Asia
138 K6 Myaretskiya Belarus
139 S7 Myatlevo Rus. Fed.
131 P3 Myaundzha Rus. Fed.
96 B6 Myaungmya Myanmar
96 D6 Myawadi Thai.
146 J6 Mybster Highland, Scotland U.K.
198 D5 Mycenae tourist site Greece
143 L4 Mycklaflon l. Sweden
96 A4 Myebon Myanmar
136 C2 Myedna Belarus
97 D8 Myeik Myanmar
97 C9 Myeik Kyunzu is Myanmar
139 N9 Myerkulavichy Belarus
232 B10 Myers KY U.S.A.
234 C4 Myerstown PA U.S.A.
96 B4 Myingyan Myanmar
97 D8 Myinmoletkat mt. Myanmar
96 B4 Myinmu Myanmar
96 C2 Myitkyina Myanmar
96 C3 Myitson Myanmar
97 D7 Myitta Myanmar
96 C4 Myittha Myanmar
115 N1 Myittha r. Myanmar
177 G3 Myjava Slovakia
176 F3 Myjava r. Slovakia
137 L4 Mykhaylivka Cherkas'ka Oblast' Ukr.
137 O5 Mykhaylivka Dnipropetrovs'ka Oblast' Ukr.
137 R6 Mykhaylivka Donets'ka Oblast' Ukr.
137 P4 Mykhaylivka Kharkivs'ka Oblast' Ukr.
137 N4 Mykhaylivka Poltavs'ka Oblast' Ukr.
137 O6 Mykhaylivka Zaporiz'ka Oblast' Ukr.
137 O6 Mykhaylivka Zaporiz'ka Oblast' Ukr.
137 K2 Mykhaylo-Kotsyubyns'ke Ukr.
136 G3 Mykhaylyuchka Ukr.
144 D1 Mykines i. Faroe Is
140 M3 Myklebostad Norway
136 C4 Mykolayiv L'vivs'ka Oblast' Ukr.
175 M5 Mykolayiv L'vivs'ka Oblast' Ukr.
137 L7 Mykolayiv Mykolayivs'ka Oblast' Ukr.
137 L1 Mykolayivka Chernihivs'ka Oblast' Ukr.
137 N6 Mykolayivka Dnipropetrovs'ka Oblast' Ukr.
137 P5 Mykolayivka Dnipropetrovs'ka Oblast' Ukr.
137 Q5 Mykolayivka Donets'ka Oblast' Ukr.
137 P5 Mykolayivka Kharkivs'ka Oblast' Ukr.
137 N6 Mykolayivka Khersons'ka Oblast' Ukr.
136 J6 Mykolayivka Odes'ka Oblast' Ukr.
136 J8 Mykolayivka Odes'ka Oblast' Ukr.
137 P6 Mykolayivka Zaporiz'ka Oblast' Ukr.
136 I7 Mykolayivka-Novorosiys'[...]
Mykolayiv Oblast admin[...] Ukr. see Mykolayivs'ka O[...]
137 L6 Mykolayivs'ka Oblast' admin. div. Ukr.
137 L6 Mykolo-Hulak Ukr.
199 G5 Mykonos Mykonos Greece
199 G5 Mykonos i. Greece
136 E4 Mykulyntsi Ukr.
175 M5 Mykytychi Ukr.
134 J2 Myla Rus. Fed.
134 J2 Myla r. Rus. Fed.
Mylae Sicilia Italy see Mi[...]
Mylasa Turkey see Milas
171 F9 Mylau Ger.
138 J1 Myllykoski Fin.
150 B7 Mylor Cornwall, England [...]
Mymensing Bangl. see Mymensingh
117 M7 Mymensingh Bangl.
138 E1 Mynäjoki r. Fin.
141 Q6 Mynämäki Fin.
121 O5 Mynaral Kazakh.
214 H6 Mynfontein S. Africa
Myngaral Kazakh. see M[...]
105 I3 Myōgi Japan
105 I3 Myōgi-Arafune-Saku-kō[...] Kokutei-kōen park Japa[...]
105 I3 Myōgi-san mt. Japan
104 A6 Myōken-yama hill Japan
105 H2 Myōkō Japan
105 H2 Myōkō-kōgen Japan
160 H2 Myon France
101 F8 Myŏnggan N. Korea
138 K6 Myory Belarus
96 B4 Myotha Myanmar
96 B4 Myothit Myanmar
103 Q15 Myozin-sho i. Japan
103 R15 Myozin-sho i. Japan
97 H9 My Phươc Vietnam
140 □D2 Mýrdalsjökull ice cap Iceland
140 □D2 Mýrdalssandur sand are[...] Iceland
140 M2 Myre Nordland Norway
140 M2 Myre Nordland Norway
140 P4 Myrheden Sweden
137 M4 Myrhorod Ukr.
198 G3 Myrina Limnos Greece
137 M5 Myrivs'ke Ukr.
140 N2 Myrlandshaugen Norwa[...]
223 I4 Myrnam Alta Can.
137 Q6 Myrne Donets'ka Oblast' [...]
137 M7 Myrne Khersons'ka Oblas[...]
137 K3 Myrne Kyivs'ka Oblast' U[...]
175 M5 Myrne Volyns'ka Oblast' [...]
137 O7 Myrne Zaporiz'ka Oblast' [...]
136 I7 Myrnopillya Ukr.
137 M8 Myrnyy Ukr.
137 P4 Myronivka Kharkivs'ka Oblast' Ukr.
136 J4 Myronivka Kyivs'ka Obla[...]
136 G3 Myropil' Ukr.
137 O2 Myropillya Ukr.
137 N6 Myrove Ukr.
141 R6 Myrskylä Fin.
231 H9 Myrtle Beach SC U.S.A.
238 C5 Myrtle Creek OR U.S.A.
83 K7 Myrtleford Vic. Austr.
238 B5 Myrtle Point OR U.S.A.
198 E6 Myrtoo Pelagos sea Gre[...]
121 M7 Myrzakent Kazakh.
142 H2 Mysen Norway
148 D8 Myshall Ireland
138 I9 Myshanka r. Belarus
139 V4 Myshkin Rus. Fed.
Myshkino Rus. Fed. see Myshkin
137 Q9 Myskhako Rus. Fed.
174 C3 Myśla r. Pol.
Mys Lazareva Rus. Fed. see Lazarev
175 H6 Myślenice Pol.
174 C3 Myśliborskie, Jezioro l.
174 C3 Myślibórz Pol.
175 H2 Myślice Pol.
175 H5 Mysłowice Pol.
Myslowitz Pol. see Mysł[...]
96 I7 My Son tourist site Vietn[...]
114 E6 Mysore Karnataka India
Mysore state India see Karnataka
137 N8 Mysove Ukr.
Mysovsk Rus. Fed. see Babushkin
131 T3 Mys Shmidta Rus. Fed.
235 L2 Mystic CT U.S.A.
235 G5 Mystic Islands NJ U.S.A.
134 K3 Mysy Rus. Fed.
175 H1 Myszewo Pol.
175 H5 Myszków Pol.
175 J2 Myszyniec Pol.
134 H4 Myt Rus. Fed.
97 H9 My Tho Vietnam
198 D2 Mytikas mt. Greece
Mytilene i. Greece see L[...]
199 H3 Mytilini Lesvos Greece
199 H5 Mytilinioi Samos Greece
126 C4 Mytilini Strait Greece/Tu[...]
139 U6 Mytishchi Rus. Fed.
177 I3 Mýtna Slovakia
176 C2 Mýto Czech Rep.
241 V1 Myton UT U.S.A.
137 L5 Mytrofanivka Ukr.
129 I3 Myuregi Rus. Fed.
140 □E1 Mývatn l. Iceland
140 □E1 Mývatn-Laxá nature res. Iceland
140 □E1 Mývatnsöræfi lava field Iceland
134 K3 Myyeldino Rus. Fed.
Myylybulak Kazakh. see Milybulabk
136 D2 Myzove Ukr.
205 F2 M'Zab, Vallée du tourist s[...]
215 K7 Mzamomhle S. Africa
176 B2 Mže r. Czech Rep.
211 C6 Mziha Tanz.
211 B7 Mzimba Malawi
213 F4 Mzingwani r. Zimbabwe
211 B7 Mzuzu Malawi
129 A2 Mzymta r. Rus. Fed.

N

96 F3 Na, Nam r. China/Vietnam
173 M3 Naab r. Ger.
164 F5 Naaldwijk Neth.
240 □F14 Nā'ālehu HI U.S.A.
208 F2 Naam Sudan
205 E2 Naama Alg.
141 Q6 Naantali Fin.
164 H4 Naarden Neth.
179 K3 Naarn im Machlande A[...]
147 I6 Naas Ireland
140 T2 Näätämö Fin.
140 T5 Näätänmaa Fin.
96 C2 Naba Myanmar
214 B5 Nababeep S. Africa
Nabadwip W. Bengal Ind[...] see Navadwip
129 C3 Nabakevi Georgia
182 D9 Nabão r. Port.
115 H3 Nabarangapur Orissa In[...]
104 D6 Nabari Japan
104 D6 Nabari-gawa r. Japan
92 D6 Nabas Panay Phil.
128 D5 Nabatîyé et Tahta Leba[...]
87 F8 Nabberu, Lake salt flat W.A. Austr.
173 M3 Nabburg Ger.
206 E4 Nabéré, Réserve Partie[...] nature res. Burkina
211 C6 Naberera Tanz.
137 R2 Naberezhnoye Rus. Fed.

188 G3 Našice Croatia
175 I3 Nasielsk Pol.
141 Q6 Näsijärvi l. Fin.
Nasik Mahar. India see Nashik
79 □7a Nasilai Reef Fiji
95 I4 Nasilat Kalimantan Indon.
123 M7 Nasir Pak.
210 B2 Nasir Sudan
203 G4 Nāşir, Buḩayrat resr Egypt
Nasirabad Bangl. see Mymensingh
116 E6 Nasirabad Rajasthan India
123 M7 Nasirabad Pak.
Nāşirīyah Iraq see An Nāşirīyah
225 I2 Naskaupi r. Nfld and Lab. Can.
202 B2 Nasmah Libya
117 J7 Nasmganj Bihar India
143 M3 Näsnaren l. Sweden
194 H7 Naso Sicilia Italy
194 H7 Naso r. Sicilia Italy
209 E7 Nasondoye Dem. Rep. Congo
226 D5 Nasonville WI U.S.A.
79 □7 Nasorolevu mt. Vanua Levu Fiji
Nasosnyy Azer. see Hacı Zeynalabdin
122 G5 Nasqenj Iran
203 F2 Naşr Egypt
122 D4 Naşrābād Eşfahān Iran
122 H4 Naşrābād Khorāsān Iran
Nasratabad Iran see Zābol
122 H8 Naşrī Iran
122 B5 Naşrīān-e Pā'īn Iran
222 D4 Nass r. B.C. Can.
207 G4 Nassarawa Nigeria
207 H4 Nassarawa state Nigeria
85 H3 Nassau r. Qld Austr.
246 E1 Nassau New Prov. Bahamas
81 □2 Nassau i. Cook Is
169 E10 Nassau Rheinland-Pfalz Ger.
171 I9 Nassau Sachsen Ger.
233 L6 Nassau NY U.S.A.
169 E10 Nassau, Naturpark nature res. Ger.
235 H3 Nassau County county NY U.S.A.
233 J11 Nassawadox VA U.S.A.
170 H5 Nassenheide Ger.
Nasser, Lake resr Egypt see Nāşir, Buḩayrat
178 C5 Nassereith Austria
206 E4 Nassian Côte d'Ivoire
143 K4 Nässjö Sweden
165 H8 Nassogne Belgium
221 M3 Nassuttooq inlet Greenland
224 E1 Nastapoca r. Que. Can.
224 E1 Nastapoka Islands Nunavut Can.
169 E10 Nastätten Ger.
138 I1 Nastola Fin.
105 L1 Nasu Japan
105 K1 Nasu-dake vol. Japan
92 C4 Nasugbu Luzon Phil.
175 K4 Nasutów Pol.
139 N5 Nasva Rus. Fed.
139 N5 Nasva r. Rus. Fed.
141 N6 Näsviken Sweden
177 H4 Naszály Hungary
212 E4 Nata Botswana
212 E4 Nata watercourse Botswana/Zimbabwe
93 E5 Nataboti Buru Indon.
253 E1 Natal Amazonas Brazil
254 G3 Natal Rio Grande do Norte Brazil
94 C4 Natal Sumatera Indon.
Natal prov. S. Africa see KwaZulu-Natal
265 G7 Natal Basin sea feature Indian Ocean
234 C3 Natalie PA U.S.A.
122 D5 Naţanz Iran
104 C5 Natashō Japan
225 I3 Natashquan Que. Can.
225 I3 Natashquan r. Nfld and Lab./Que. Can.
81 □1 Na Taulaga i. Tokelau
237 J10 Natchez MS U.S.A.
237 I10 Natchitoches LA U.S.A.
149 M5 Nateby Cumbria, England U.K.
174 D3 Natecka, Puszcza for. Pol.
190 D3 Naters Switz.
79 □7 Natewa Bay Vanua Levu Fiji
83 J7 Nathalia Vic. Austr.
116 E4 Nathana Punjab India
84 E3 Nathan River N.T. Austr.
116 D7 Nathdwara Rajasthan India
Nathilau Point Viti Levu Fiji see Nacilau Point
140 □ Nathorst Land reg. Svalbard
186 □ Nati, Punta pt Spain
207 F4 Natiaboani Burkina
243 I5 Natillas Mex.
240 O9 National City CA U.S.A.
80 J6 National Park North I. N.Z.
212 B4 National West Coast Tourist Recreation Area park Namibia
191 O4 Natisone r. Italy
207 F4 Natitingou Benin
242 B4 Natividad, Isla i. Mex.
257 G4 Natividade Rio de Janeiro Brazil
254 D4 Natividade Tocantins Brazil
97 C7 Natkyizin Myanmar
222 D2 Natla r. N.W.T. Can.
96 B4 Natmauk Myanmar
96 B4 Natogyi Myanmar
239 J12 Nátora Mex.
117 L7 Natore Bangl.
102 R8 Natori Japan
211 C5 Natron, Lake salt l. Tanz.
105 M1 Natsui-gawa r. Japan
138 G9 Natsyyanal'ny Park Byelavyezhskaya Pushcha Belarus
136 G2 Natsyyanal'ny Park Prypyatski nature res. Belarus
83 M6 Nattai National Park N.S.W. Austr.
96 B5 Nattalin Myanmar
114 F7 Nattam Tamil Nadu India
143 O3 Nåttarö i. Sweden
96 C5 Nattaung mt. Myanmar
140 P3 Nattavaara Sweden
140 P3 Nattavaara by Sweden
179 I3 Natternback Austria
173 I4 Nattheim Ger.
122 I4 Na'tū Iran
79 □7 Natua Vanua Levu Fiji
225 I2 Natuashish Nfld and Lab. Can.
137 Q9 Natukhayevskaya Rus. Fed.
95 G2 Natuna, Kepulauan is Indon.
95 H2 Natuna Besar i. Indon.
232 F11 Natural Bridge VA U.S.A.
241 V4 Natural Bridges National Monument nat. park UT U.S.A.
87 C12 Naturaliste, Cape W.A. Austr.
87 A8 Naturaliste Channel W.A. Austr.
265 L7 Naturaliste Plateau sea feature Indian Ocean
214 H9 Nature's Valley S. Africa
241 X3 Naturita CO U.S.A.
191 J2 Naturno Italy
Nau Tajik. see Nov
226 I3 Naubinway MI U.S.A.
163 I7 Naucelle France
162 I6 Naucelles France
212 C4 Nauchas Namibia
111 F10 Nau Co l. Xizang China
178 C6 Nauders Austria
214 I8 Naudesberg Pass S. Africa
213 H2 Nauela Moz.
170 G5 Nauen Ger.
171 E7 Nauendorf Ger.
235 I2 Naugatuck CT U.S.A.
235 I2 Naugatuck r. CT U.S.A.
172 E2 Nauheim Ger.
123 L6 Nau Hissar Pak.
Naujaat Nunavut Can. see Repulse Bay
162 B5 Naujac-sur-Mer France
92 C5 Naujan Mindoro Phil.
138 F5 Naujoji Akmenė Lith.
116 D6 Naukh Rajasthan India
147 J5 Naul Ireland
209 B9 Naulila Angola
169 H8 Naumburg (Hessen) Ger.
171 E8 Naumburg (Saale) Ger.
171 H8 Naundorf Sachsen Ger.
171 H9 Naundorf Sachsen Ger.
96 C6 Naunglon Myanmar
96 C5 Naungpale Myanmar
128 D7 Na'ūr Jordan
169 E9 Nauroth Ger.
123 K7 Nauroz Kalat Pak.
129 G2 Naurskaya Rus. Fed.
77 G2 Nauru i. Nauru
77 G2 Nauru country S. Pacific Ocean
123 M8 Naushahro Firoz Pak.
123 M8 Naushara Pak.
106 J1 Naushki Rus. Fed.
79 □7a Nausori Viti Levu Fiji
161 D7 Naussac, Barrage de dam France
141 H6 Naustdal Norway
250 C6 Nauta Peru
Nautaca Uzbek. see Qarshi
117 I6 Nautanwa Uttar Prad. India
214 B2 Naute Dam Namibia
245 K5 Nautla Mex.
140 T2 Nautsi Rus. Fed.
226 C9 Nauvoo IL U.S.A.
123 K5 Nauzad Afgh.
208 E4 Nava r. Dem. Rep. Congo
243 I3 Nava Mex.
183 J2 Nava Spain
Navabad Tajik. see Novobod
183 J8 Navacepeda de Tormes Spain
183 M7 Navacerrada, Puerto de pass Spain
183 L7 Navacerreda Spain
185 L7 Navachica mt. Spain
182 I8 Navaconcejo Spain
183 K7 Nava de Arévalo Spain
183 L6 Nava de la Asunción Spain
183 J6 Nava del Rey Spain
183 J7 Nava de Sotrobal Spain
138 K6 Navadrutsk Belarus
117 L8 Navadwip W. Bengal India
183 M6 Navafría Spain
183 L9 Navahermosa Spain
129 K5 Navahı Azer.
138 I8 Navahrudak Belarus
138 I8 Navahrudskaye Wzvyshsha hills Belarus
187 E8 Navajas Spain
239 K8 Navajo r. CO U.S.A.
241 W6 Navajo Indian Reservation res. AZ U.S.A.
239 K8 Navajo Lake NM U.S.A.
241 V4 Navajo Mountain UT U.S.A.
183 J4 Navajos hill Spain
92 E6 Naval Phil.
186 F3 Naval Spain
183 L8 Navalagamella Spain
183 O5 Navalcaballo Spain
183 J8 Navalcán Spain
183 J8 Navalcán, Embalse de resr Spain
183 L8 Navalcarnero Spain
183 O5 Navalero Spain
183 L6 Navalmanzano Spain
183 K8 Navalmoral Spain
183 K7 Navalmoral, Puerto de pass Spain
182 I9 Navalmoral de la Mata Spain
183 J8 Navalonguilla Spain
183 K8 Navalosa Spain
183 L7 Navalperal de Pinares Spain
185 J2 Navalpino Spain
183 K8 Navaluenga Spain
183 J9 Navalvillar de Ibor Spain
185 I2 Navalvillar de Pela Spain
183 K8 Navamorcuende Spain
147 I5 Navan Ireland
Navangar Gujarat India see Jamnagar
138 L6 Navapolatsk Belarus
123 L5 Nāvar, Dasht-e depr. Afgh.
186 I4 Navarcles Spain
186 C2 Navardún Spain
131 S3 Navarin, Mys c. Rus. Fed.
259 D9 Navarino, Isla i. Chile
183 Q3 Navarra aut. comm. Spain
83 I7 Navarre Vic. Austr.
Navarre aut. comm. Spain see Navarra
182 H7 Navarredonda de la Rinconada Spain
163 C9 Navarrenx France
187 D9 Navarrés Spain
183 O4 Navarrete Spain
261 H4 Navarro Arg.
250 C6 Navarro Peru
240 I2 Navarro r. CA U.S.A.
186 I4 Navàs Spain
163 D10 Navasa Spain
186 C2 Navascués Spain
185 J1 Navas de Estrena Spain
182 G9 Navas del Madroño Spain
183 L8 Navas del Rey Spain
183 L6 Navas de Oro Spain
185 M4 Navas de San Juan Spain
182 G8 Navasfrías Spain
134 H5 Navashino Rus. Fed.
237 G10 Navasota TX U.S.A.
237 G10 Navasota r. TX U.S.A.
246 F4 Navassa Island terr. West Indies
136 H1 Navasyolki Belarus
186 K3 Navata Spain
183 K8 Navatalgordo Spain
138 I8 Navayel'nya Belarus
190 I4 Nave Italy
184 B6 Nave Port.
182 B3 Nave, Cabo da c. Spain
182 F4 Navea r. Spain
182 G7 Nave de Haver Port.
148 E2 Nave Island Scotland U.K.
193 L3 Navelli Italy
160 I1 Navenne France
146 H5 Naver r. Scotland U.K.
146 H6 Naver, Loch l. Scotland U.K.
184 C6 Nave Redonda Port.
142 H3 Naverstad Sweden
162 H5 Naves France
186 I4 Navès Spain
139 U9 Navesnoye Rus. Fed.
138 H3 Navesti r. Estonia
247 □7 Navet Trin. and Tob.
185 I1 Navezuelas Spain
260 D4 Navia Arg.
182 G1 Navia Spain
182 G1 Navia r. Spain
182 G1 Navia, Ría de inlet Spain
116 B9 Navibandar Gujarat India
260 B3 Navidad Chile
237 G11 Navidad r. TX U.S.A.
247 I3 Navidad Bank sea feature Caribbean Sea
190 G5 Naviglio di Pavia canal Italy
190 G5 Naviglio Grande canal Italy
160 G3 Navilly France
114 C3 Navi Mumbai Mahar. India
255 B7 Naviraí Brazil
79 □7 Naviti i. Fiji
136 E2 Naviz Ukr.
116 C8 Navlakhi Gujarat India
139 R9 Navlya Rus. Fed.
139 R9 Navlya r. Rus. Fed.
197 Q6 Năvodari Romania
120 K7 Navoiy Uzbek.
120 J7 Navoiy admin. div. Uzbek.
242 E4 Navojoa Mex.
242 F5 Navolato Mex.
79 □7 Navotuvotu hill Vanua Levu Fiji
Navoy Oblast admin. div. Uzbek. see Navoiy
Návpaktos Greece see Nafpaktos
Návplion Greece see Nafplio
143 L5 Nävragöl Sweden
142 C3 Navrestad hill Norway
206 E4 Navrongo Ghana
Navşar Turkey see Şemdinli
116 D9 Navsari Gujarat India
79 □7a Navua Viti Levu Fiji
79 □7a Navua r. Viti Levu Fiji
79 □7a Navula rf Fiji
116 E6 Nawa Rajasthan India
128 E6 Nawá Syria
117 L7 Nawabganj Bangl.
98 D6 Nawabganj Uttar Prad. India
111 F13 Nawabganj Uttar Prad. India
123 M8 Nawabshah Pak.
117 J7 Nawada Bihar India
117 I9 Nawagaon Chhattisgarh India
123 L5 Nāwah Afgh.
117 J6 Nawakot Nepal
123 N7 Nawakot Pak.
116 E6 Nawalgarh Rajasthan India
123 N6 Nawan Kot Pak.
111 C11 Nawanshahr Punjab India
124 F5 Nawāşīf, Ḩarrat lava field Saudi Arabia
96 C3 Nawnghkio Myanmar
96 D3 Nawngleng Myanmar
Nawoiy Uzbek. see Navoiy
Nawoiy Wiloyati admin. div. Uzbek. see Navoiy
175 I6 Nawojowa Pol.
125 L7 Naws, Ra's c. Oman
129 G6 Naxçıvan Azer.
129 G6 Naxçıvan aut. reg. Azer.
129 G6 Naxçıvançay r. Azer.
108 E4 Naxi Sichuan China
199 G5 Naxos Naxos Greece
199 G5 Naxos i. Greece
250 B4 Naya Col.
111 K10 Nayag Xizang China
117 J9 Nayagarh Orissa India
123 L4 Nayak Afgh.
244 C3 Nayar Mex.
244 C3 Nayarit state Mex.
122 G5 Nāy Band, Kūh-e mt. Iran
163 D9 Nay-Bourdettes France
137 N8 Nayd'onivka Ukr.
125 J6 Nayfah oasis Saudi Arabia
108 E5 Nayong Guizhou China
102 T2 Nayoro Japan
96 C5 Naypyidaw Myanmar
125 K9 Nayt Suquţrā Yemen
211 B8 Nayuchi Malawi
114 F6 Nayudupeta Andhra Prad. India
124 D1 Nayyāl, Wādī watercourse Saudi Arabia
116 F8 Nazarabad Madh. Prad. India
250 E4 Nazare Amazonas Brazil
251 H6 Nazaré Brazil
254 E3 Nazare Piauí Brazil
182 B9 Nazaré Port.
242 H5 Nazareno Mex.
114 E8 Nazareth Tamil Nadu India
Nazareth Israel see Nazerat
234 E3 Nazareth PA U.S.A.
256 C2 Nazário Brazil
242 G5 Nazas Mex.
242 G5 Nazas r. Mex.
252 B3 Nazca Peru
267 N7 Nazca Ridge sea feature S. Pacific Ocean
102 □G18 Naze Nansei-shotō Japan
151 M4 Nazeing Essex, England U.K.
159 M7 Nazelles-Négron France
128 D6 Nazerat Israel
122 C5 Nazian Iran
122 A2 Nāzīk Iran
122 I7 Nāzīl Iran
199 J5 Nazilli Turkey
123 L9 Nazimabad Pak.
127 I4 Nazımiye Turkey
206 E4 Nazinon r. Burkina conv. Red Volta
117 O6 Nazira Assam India
117 M8 Nazir Hat Bangl.
129 I5 Näzirli Azer.
139 O2 Naziya Rus. Fed.
222 F4 Nazko B.C. Can.
222 F4 Nazko r. B.C. Can.
122 A3 Nāzlū r. Iran
129 F2 Nazran' Rus. Fed.
210 C2 Nazrēt Eth.
125 M4 Nazwá Oman
130 I4 Nazyvayevsk Rus. Fed.
206 B2 Nbâk Maur.
206 D2 Nbeïket Ḑlîm well Maur.
215 J9 Ncanaha S. Africa
209 F7 Nchelenge Zambia
Ncheu Malawi see Ntcheu
212 D4 Ncojane Botswana
215 L7 Ncora S. Africa
207 H6 Ncue Equat. Guinea
206 C2 Ndaghma Barké well Maur.
211 B6 Ndala Tanz.
209 B7 N'dalatando Angola
207 F4 Ndali Benin
208 D3 Ndanda C.A.R.
213 F4 Ndanga Zimbabwe
93 C9 Ndao i. Indon.
211 B6 Ndareda Tanz.
208 B5 Ndekabalandji Gabon
208 D2 Ndélé C.A.R.
207 I5 Ndélélé Cameroon
208 A5 Ndendé Gabon
Ndende i. Santa Cruz Is Solomon Is see Ndeni
78 □6 Ndeni i. Santa Cruz Is Solomon Is
207 H5 Ndikiniméki Cameroon
208 B3 Ndim C.A.R.
209 A5 Ndindi Gabon
206 B3 Ndioum Guènt Senegal
N'Djamena Chad see Ndjamena
202 B6 Ndjamena Chad
208 D3 Ndji r. C.A.R.
207 H5 Ndjim r. Cameroon
208 A5 Ndjolé Gabon
Ndjouani i. Comoros see Nzwani
208 B5 Ndjounou Gabon
206 B3 Ndofane Senegal
208 A5 Ndogo, Lagune lag. Gabon
Ndoi i. Fiji see Doi
207 I5 Ndok Cameroon
209 F8 Ndola Zambia
206 D4 Ndorola Burkina
210 C4 Ndoto mt. Kenya
208 A5 Ndougou Gabon
208 D3 Ndoukou C.A.R.
208 C3 Ndoumbou C.A.R.
78 □6 Ndovele New Georgia Is Solomon Is
78 □6 Nduindui Solomon Is
Nduke i. New Georgia Is Solomon Is see Kolombangara
211 C7 Ndumbwe Tanz.
215 Q2 Ndumu S. Africa
215 Q2 Ndumu Game Reserve nature res. Moz.
208 F4 Nduye Dem. Rep. Congo
215 O5 Ndwedwe S. Africa
162 D4 Né r. France
96 G5 Ne, Hon i. Vietnam
163 E10 Né, Mont mt. France
198 G7 Nea Alikarnassos Kriti Greece
198 D3 Nea Anchialos Greece
198 E2 Nea Apollonia Greece
198 E4 Nea Artaki Greece
85 K9 Neabul Creek r. Qld Austr.
198 E5 Nea Epidavros Greece
198 C5 Nea Figaleia Greece
104 D3 Neagari Japan
147 J3 Neagh, Lough l. Northern Ireland U.K.
238 B2 Neah Bay WA U.S.A.
197 N6 Neajlov r. Romania
198 E2 Nea Kallikrateia Greece
198 F2 Nea Karvali Greece
147 D5 Neale Ireland
84 C8 Neale, Lake salt flat N.T. Austr.
87 H10 Neale Junction Nature Reserve W.A. Austr.
82 F3 Neales watercourse S.A. Austr.
198 E4 Nea Liosia Greece
198 E4 Nea Makri Greece
199 H4 Nea Monu tourist site Greece
198 E2 Nea Moudania Greece
197 O3 Neamţ r. Romania
198 F2 Nea Peramos Greece
198 C2 Neapoli Dytiki Makedonia Greece
199 G7 Neapoli Kriti Greece
198 E6 Neapoli Peloponnisos Greece
Neapolis Italy see Napoli
198 E2 Nea Roda Greece
149 L5 Near Sawrey Cumbria, England U.K.
198 D2 Nea Santa Greece
Néa Stíra Greece see Nea Styra
198 F4 Nea Styra Greece
150 E4 Neath Neath Port Talbot, Wales U.K.
150 E4 Neath r. Wales U.K.
150 E4 Neath Port Talbot admin. div. Wales U.K.
198 E1 Nea Zichni Greece
104 G5 Neba Japan
210 A4 Nebbi Uganda
192 C2 Nebbio reg. Corse France
206 E4 Nebbou Burkina
168 F1 Nebel Ger.
173 I7 Nebelhorn mt. Ger.
110 E5 Nebesnaya, Gora mt. Xinjiang China
163 I10 Nébias France
83 K3 Nebine Creek r. Qld Austr.
85 L6 Nebo Qld Austr.
241 U2 Nebo, Mount UT U.S.A.
139 Q2 Nebolchi Rus. Fed.
163 F9 Nébouzan reg. France
171 E8 Nebra (Unstrut) Ger.
236 E5 Nebraska state U.S.A.
236 H5 Nebraska City NE U.S.A.
183 M5 Nebreda Spain
194 G8 Nebrodi, Monti mts Sicilia Italy
139 W5 Nebyloye Rus. Fed.
245 J5 Necaxa r. Mex.
226 D5 Necedah WI U.S.A.
226 D5 Necedah National Wildlife Refuge nature res. WI U.S.A.
176 E1 Nechanice Czech Rep.
137 K7 Nechayane Ukr.
139 X6 Nechayevskaya Rus. Fed.
137 L5 Nechayivka Ukr.
237 I11 Neches r. TX U.S.A.
250 C2 Nechí r. Col.
210 C3 Nechisar National Park Eth.
185 M7 Nechite r. Spain
171 H10 Nechranice, Vodní nádrž resr Czech Rep.
172 E2 Neckar r. Ger.
172 F3 Neckarbischofsheim Ger.
172 F3 Neckargemünd Ger.
172 F3 Neckarsteinach Ger.
172 G3 Neckarsulm Ger.
172 G3 Neckartal-Odenwald, Naturpark nature res. Ger.
75 H2 Necker Island HI U.S.A.
261 H6 Necochea Arg.
250 B2 Necoclí Col.
151 N2 Necton Norfolk, England U.K.
198 C5 Neda r. Greece
182 D2 Neda Spain
136 J2 Nedanchychi Ukr.
177 H2 Nedašov Czech Rep.
170 H3 Neddemin Ger.
202 C6 Nédéley Chad
197 N9 Nedelino Bulg.
188 F2 Nedelišće Croatia
139 T7 Nedel'noye Rus. Fed.
Nederland country Europe see Netherlands
Nederlandse Antillen terr. West Indies see Netherlands Antilles
164 H4 Nederlangbroek Neth.
164 H5 Neder Rijn r. Neth.
170 E1 Neder Vindinge Denmark
165 I6 Nederweert Neth.
Nédha r. Greece see Neda
175 M1 Nedingis l. Lith.
171 F6 Nedlitz Ger.
225 F1 Nedlouc, Lac l. Que. Can.
Nedluk Lake Que. Can. see Nedlouc, Lac
136 F5 Nedoboyivtsi Ukr.
111 J12 Nêdong Xizang China
140 P2 Nedre Soppero Sweden
142 F2 Nedre Tokke l. Norway
137 M3 Nedryhayliv Ukr.
142 B2 Nedstrand Norway
142 B2 Nedstrandsfjorden sea chan. Norway
208 F4 Neduka r. Dem. Rep. Congo
176 F2 Nedvědice Czech Rep.
174 G5 Nędza Pol.
105 I2 Neeba-san mt. Japan
164 K4 Neede Neth.
233 N6 Needham MA U.S.A.
151 O3 Needham Market Suffolk, England U.K.
151 L3 Needingworth Cambridgeshire, England U.K.
241 R7 Needles CA U.S.A.
232 G9 Needmore PA U.S.A.
116 E7 Neemuch Madh. Prad. India
226 F5 Neenah WI U.S.A.
223 L5 Neepawa Man. Can.
165 J6 Neer Neth.
221 J2 Neergaard Lake Nunavut Can.
164 H5 Neerijnen Neth.
168 D4 Neermoor Ger.
165 I6 Neeroeteren Belgium
165 H6 Neerpelt Belgium
142 E5 Nees Sund sea chan. Denmark
168 K4 Neetze Ger.
210 C2 Nefas Mewch'a Eth.
234 D3 Neffs PA U.S.A.
234 C4 Neffsville PA U.S.A.
205 G2 Nefta Tunisia
129 K6 Neftçala Azer.
129 L5 Neft Daşları Azer.
Neftechala Azer. see Uzboy
Neftechala Azer. see Neftçala
129 A1 Neftegorsk Krasnodarskiy Kray Rus. Fed.
100 M2 Neftegorsk Sakhalin Rus. Fed.
120 D1 Neftegorsk Samarskaya Oblast' Rus. Fed.
134 K4 Neftekamsk Rus. Fed.
129 F1 Neftekumsk Rus. Fed.
190 F1 Neftenbach Switz.
130 I3 Nefteyugansk Rus. Fed.
Neftezavodsk Turkm. see Seýdi
Neftyanyye Kamni Azer. see Neft Daşları
150 C2 Nefyn Gwynedd, Wales U.K.
189 B7 Nefza Tunisia
210 E3 Negada Weyn well Eth.
209 B6 Negage Angola
206 C3 Négala Mali
122 G7 Negār Iran
95 K9 Negara Bali Indon.
95 K6 Negara Kalimantan Indon.
95 K6 Negara r. Indon.
226 G3 Negaunee MI U.S.A.
210 C3 Negēlē Oromīya Eth.
210 C3 Negēlē Oromīya Eth.
94 E3 Negeri Sembilan state Malaysia
128 D8 Negev des. Israel
209 B8 Negola Angola
211 C7 Negomane Moz.
114 F9 Negombo Sri Lanka
197 K6 Negotin Serbia
196 I9 Negotino Macedonia
197 K9 Negotino Macedonia
252 A2 Negra, Cordillera mts Peru
258 G4 Negra, Lago l. Uru.
182 H4 Negra, Peña mt. Spain
250 A6 Negra, Punta pt Peru
257 F3 Negra, Serra mts Brazil
253 E3 Negra, Serranía de mts Bol.
96 B7 Negrais, Cape Myanmar
191 J4 Negrar Italy
185 N5 Negratín, Embalse de resr Spain
163 H11 Negre, Pic mt. Andorra
183 O6 Negredo Spain
182 C3 Negreira Spain
252 C4 Negreiros Chile
163 H7 Nègrepelisse France
197 P4 Negreşti Romania
197 L3 Negreşti-Oaş Romania
260 A5 Negrete Chile
187 D12 Negrete, Cabo c. Spain
84 B4 Negri r. N.T. Austr.
197 O4 Negri Romania
140 □ Negribreen glacier Svalbard
246 □ Negril Jamaica
205 G2 Négrine Alg.
Negri Sembilan state Malaysia see Negeri Sembilan
250 A6 Negritos Peru
260 D6 Negro r. Arg.
253 F4 Negro r. Brazil
253 F6 Negro r. Para.
251 G5 Negro r. S. America
182 H4 Negro r. Spain
261 H3 Negro r. Uru.
261 I3 Negro r. Uru.
180 D5 Negro, Cabo c. Morocco
Negroponte i. Greece see Evvoia
92 D7 Negros i. Phil.
197 Q7 Negru Vodă Romania
238 C4 Nehalem r. OR U.S.A.
122 C4 Nehavand Iran
122 I6 Nehbandān Iran
107 S2 Nehe Heilong. China
197 O5 Nehoiu Romania
209 C9 Nehone Angola
79 □8 Neiafu Vava'u Gp Tonga
246 H4 Neiba Dom. Rep.
157 L5 Neid Française r. France
106 I9 Neiguanying Gansu China
108 E4 Neijiang Sichuan China
183 N4 Neila, Sierra de mts Spain
223 I4 Neilburg Sask. Can.
214 E4 Neilersdrif S. Africa
115 M7 Neill Island Andaman & Nicobar Is India
226 D5 Neillsville WI U.S.A.
107 H6 Nei Mongol Zizhiqu aut. reg. China
171 D7 Neinstedt Ger.
107 N8 Neiqiu Hebei China
171 K6 Neiße r. Ger./Pol.
250 C4 Neiva Col.
182 C5 Neiva r. Port.
190 E6 Neive Italy
109 H2 Neixiang Henan China
244 E7 Neixpa r. Mex.
223 L3 Nejanilini Lake Man. Can.
245 L9 Nejapa Mex.
Nejd reg. Saudi Arabia see Najd
176 B1 Nejdek Czech Rep.
122 E3 Neka Iran
122 E3 Neka r. Iran
210 C2 Nek'emtē Eth.
135 H6 Nekhayevskaya Rus. Fed.
Nekhayevskiy Rus. Fed. see Nekhayevskaya
137 L2 Nekhayivka Ukr.
174 F3 Nekla Pol.
139 X6 Neklyudovo Rus. Fed.
117 L7 Nekmarad Bangl.
104 A4 Neko-zaki pt Japan
136 H4 Nekrasove Ukr.
135 I6 Nekrasovo Rus. Fed.
139 U5 Nekrasovskiy Rus. Fed.
139 X4 Nekrasovskoye Rus. Fed.
142 H6 Nekselø i. Denmark
143 L6 Neksø Bornholm Denmark
183 N3 Nela r. Spain
114 E6 Nelamangala Karnataka India
116 G4 Nelang Hima. Prad. India
182 E7 Nelas Port.
142 E3 Nelaug l. Norway
139 U2 Nelazskoye Rus. Fed.
85 I6 Nelia Qld Austr.
139 P5 Nelidovo Rus. Fed.
236 G4 Neligh NE U.S.A.
131 O4 Nel'kan Khabarovskiy Kray Rus. Fed.
131 P3 Nel'kan Respublika Sakha (Yakutiya) Rus. Fed.
78 □3a Nell i. Kwajalein Marshall Is
227 N1 Nellie Lake Ont. Can.
140 T2 Nellim Fin.
172 H4 Nellingen Ger.
114 F5 Nellore Andhra Prad. India
78 □3a Nell Passage Kwajalein Marshall Is
128 H2 Nelluz watercourse Turkey
100 K5 Nel'ma Rus. Fed.
215 O1 Nelshoogte pass S. Africa
261 G2 Nelson Arg.
222 G5 Nelson B.C. Can.
223 M3 Nelson r. Man. Can.
81 H8 Nelson South I. N.Z.
81 H8 Nelson admin. reg. South I. N.Z.
149 M6 Nelson Lancashire, England U.K.
241 S6 Nelson AZ U.S.A.
236 F5 Nelson NE U.S.A.
241 R6 Nelson NV U.S.A.
226 B5 Nelson WI U.S.A.
82 H8 Nelson, Cape Vic. Austr.
259 B8 Nelson, Estrecho str. Chile
83 N5 Nelson Bay N.S.W. Austr.
81 F9 Nelson Creek South I. N.Z.
222 F3 Nelson Forks B.C. Can.
223 L4 Nelson House Man. Can.
233 J11 Nelsonia VA U.S.A.
81 G9 Nelson Lakes National Park South I. N.Z.
235 H2 Nelsonville NY U.S.A.
214 H8 Nelspoort S. Africa
215 O1 Nelspruit S. Africa
134 K3 Nem r. Rus. Fed.
206 D2 Néma Maur.
134 J4 Nema Rus. Fed.
226 B3 Nemadji r. MN U.S.A.
Neman r. Belarus/Lith. see Nyoman
138 F6 Neman Rus. Fed.
alt. Nemunas (Lith.)
alt. Nyoman (Belarus)
138 F6 Neman r. Rus. Fed.
122 H7 Ne'matābād Iran
Nemausus France see Nîmes
78 □6 Nembao Santa Cruz Is Solomon Is
207 G5 Nembe Nigeria
190 H4 Nembro Italy
177 I3 Nemce Slovakia
134 H4 Nemda r. Rus. Fed.
198 D5 Nemea Greece
134 K3 Nemed Rus. Fed.
227 K2 Nemegos Ont. Can.
227 K1 Nemegosenda Lake Ont. Can.
138 I7 Nemenčine Lith.
205 G2 Nementcha, Monts des mts Alg.
198 B2 Nëmerçkë, Mal ridge Albania
176 G4 Nemesszalók Hungary
176 G5 Nemesvid Hungary
177 H5 Németkér Hungary
Nemetocenna France see Arras
140 U2 Nemetskiy, Mys c. Rus. Fed.
Nemirov Ukr. see Nemyriv
224 E3 Nemiscau r. Que. Can.
224 E3 Nemiscau, Lac l. Que. Can.
136 J3 Nemishayeve Ukr.
107 S2 Nemor He r. China
Nemours Alg. see Ghazaouet
156 E7 Nemours France
127 K4 Nemrut Dağı mt. Turkey
171 E8 Nemsdorf-Göhrendorf Ger.
177 H3 Nemšová Slovakia
100 I4 Nemta r. Rus. Fed.
175 M1 Nemunaitis Lith.
138 E6 Nemunas r. Lith.
alt. Neman (Rus. Fed.)
alt. Nyoman (Belarus)
138 H5 Nemunėlio Radviliškis Lith.
138 I5 Nemunėlis r. Lith.
102 W3 Nemuro Japan
102 W3 Nemuro-hantō pen. Japan
102 W3 Nemuro-kaikyō sea chan. Japan/Rus. Fed.
102 W3 Nemuro-wan b. Japan
136 C3 Nemyriv L'vivs'ka Oblast' Ukr.
136 H5 Nemyriv Vinnyts'ka Oblast' Ukr.
136 G4 Nemyryntsi Ukr.
147 F7 Nenagh Ireland
100 D4 Nenan Heilong. China
220 D3 Nenana AK U.S.A.
139 U7 Nenashevo Rus. Fed.
190 C3 Nendaz Switz.
151 M2 Nene r. England U.K.
Nenets Autonomous Okrug admin. div. Rus. Fed. see Nenetskiy Avtonomnyy Okrug
134 K2 Nenetskiy Avtonomnyy Okrug admin. div. Rus. Fed.
177 I3 Nenince Slovakia
107 S2 Nenjiang Heilong. China
107 S4 Nen Jiang r. China
168 D3 Nenndorf Ger.
170 G5 Nennhausen Ger.
173 K3 Nennslingen Ger.
134 G2 Nenoksa Rus. Fed.
169 I8 Nentershausen Hessen Ger.
169 E10 Nentershausen Rheinland-Pfalz Ger.
149 M4 Nenthead Cumbria, England U.K.
178 A5 Nenzing Austria
104 E4 Neo Japan
198 D2 Neo Agioneri Greece
78 □4a Neoch atoll Chuuk Micronesia
198 F2 Neo Erasmio Greece
104 E5 Neo-gawa r. Japan
Neokhórion Greece see Oichalia
241 V1 Neola UT U.S.A.
146 J4 Neolithic Orkney tourist site Scotland U.K.
198 D3 Neo Monastiri Greece
192 B7 Neoneli Sardegna Italy
Néon Karlovásion Samos Greece see Karlovasi
226 F5 Neopit WI U.S.A.
237 H7 Neosho MO U.S.A.
237 H7 Neosho r. KS U.S.A.
198 E2 Neos Marmaras Greece
161 I10 Néoules France
186 F2 Néouvielle, Pic de mt. France
163 E10 Néouvielle, Réserve Naturelle de nature res. France
116 I5 Nepal country Asia
116 H5 Nepalganj Nepal
116 H6 Nepalganj Road Uttar Prad. India
116 F9 Nepanagar Madh. Prad. India
224 F4 Nepean Ont. Can.
82 □1 Nepean Island Norfolk I.
241 U2 Nephi UT U.S.A.
147 D4 Nephin hill Ireland
147 C4 Nephin Beg Range hills Ireland
193 I3 Nepi Italy
221 L5 Nepisiguit r. N.B. Can.
176 C2 Nepomuk Czech Rep.
139 V8 Nepryadva r. Rus. Fed.
235 G4 Neptune City NJ U.S.A.
82 F6 Neptune Islands S.A. Austr.
175 G3 Ner r. Pol.
193 I3 Nera r. Italy
163 E7 Nérac France
114 C3 Neral Mahar. India
85 N9 Nerang Qld Austr.
176 D1 Neratovice Czech Rep.
177 J6 Nerău Romania
138 H7 Neravai Lith.
171 G8 Nerchau Ger.
99 K1 Nerchinsk Rus. Fed.
100 A3 Nerchinskiy Zavod Rus. Fed.
162 D4 Nercillac France
192 D7 Nercone, Monte su mt. Italy
134 K4 Nerdva Rus. Fed.
162 D4 Néré France
197 O5 Nereju Romania
139 X4 Nerekhta Rus. Fed.
173 I4 Neresheim Ger.
225 G2 Néret, Lac l. Que. Can.
138 I5 Nereta Latvia
193 L2 Nereto Italy
188 F4 Neretva r. Bos.-Herz./Croatia
175 L4 Neretva r. Ukr.
188 F4 Neretvanski Kanal sea chan. Croatia
191 Q6 Nerezine Croatia
116 G9 Neri Mahar. India
111 J11 Nêri Pünco l. Xizang China
209 D8 Neriquinha Angola
138 G7 Neris r. Lith.
160 B4 Néris-les-Bains France
185 L7 Nerja Spain
220 C4 Nerka, Lake AK U.S.A.
139 X5 Nerl' Ivanovskaya Oblast' Rus. Fed.
139 V4 Nerl' Tverskaya Oblast' Rus. Fed.
139 U4 Nerl' r. Rus. Fed.
139 W4 Nero, Ozero l. Rus. Fed.
134 M3 Nerokhi Rus. Fed.
160 E5 Néronde France
160 B3 Nérondes France
256 C2 Nerópolis Brazil
169 C10 Neroth Ger.
137 S3 Nerovnovka Rus. Fed.
134 L2 Neroyka, Gora mt. Rus. Fed.
116 F9 Ner Pinglai Mahar. India
185 O4 Nerpio Spain
162 E4 Nersac France
173 I5 Nersingen Ger.
136 J7 Nerubays'ke Ukr.
139 T9 Neruch' r. Rus. Fed.
139 Q9 Nerussa r. Rus. Fed.
184 F5 Nerva Spain
191 M4 Nervesa della Battaglia Italy
160 E5 Nervieux France
183 O2 Nervión r. Spain
190 D4 Nery, Monte mt. Italy
131 N4 Neryungri Rus. Fed.
164 I2 Nes Neth.
142 F1 Nes Norway
134 I2 Nes' Rus. Fed.
134 I2 Nes' r. Rus. Fed.
122 G7 Nesā' Iran
122 D3 Nesa' Iran
142 F1 Nesbyen Norway
171 J8 Neschwitz Ger.
234 F5 Nesco NJ U.S.A.
234 C2 Nescopeck PA U.S.A.
234 C2 Nescopeck Creek r. PA U.S.A.
197 P8 Nesebŭr Bulg.
247 □4 Nesfield Barbados
142 C2 Nes Flaten Norway
234 F4 Neshaminy Creek r. PA U.S.A.
140 □G1 Neskaupstaður Iceland
156 E4 Nesle France
177 H2 Nesluša Slovakia
140 L3 Nesna Norway
136 G3 Nesolon' Ukr.
176 G2 Nesovice Czech Rep.
161 F8 Nesque r. France
234 D3 Nesquehoning PA U.S.A.
114 D4 Nesri Mahar. India
146 H8 Ness r. Scotland U.K.
146 G8 Ness, Loch l. Scotland U.K.
192 B2 Nessa Corse France
236 F6 Ness City KS U.S.A.
168 D3 Nesse Ger.
169 J9 Nesse r. Ger.
222 C3 Nesselrode, Mount Can./U.S.A.
173 J6 Nesselwang Ger.
190 G1 Nesslau Switz.
163 F9 Neste r. France
138 F7 Nesterov Rus. Fed.
Nesterov Ukr. see Zhovkva
139 Q7 Nestery Rus. Fed.
149 K7 Neston Cheshire, England U.K.
247 □7 Nestor Trin. and Tob.
193 I2 Nestore r. Italy
191 M9 Nestore r. Italy
223 M5 Nestor Falls Ont. Can.
226 F3 Nestoria MI U.S.A.
198 F2 Nestos r. Greece
142 E2 Nesvatn l. Norway
Nesvizh Belarus see Nyasvizh
128 C6 Netanya Israel
117 J8 Netarhat Jharkhand India
234 F3 Netcong NJ U.S.A.
169 H7 Nethe r. Ger.
164 I3 Netherlands country Europe
247 I7 Netherlands Antilles terr. West Indies
146 L8 Netherley Aberdeenshire, Scotland U.K.
150 F5 Nether Stowey Somerset, England U.K.
149 M3 Netherton Northumberland, England U.K.
146 I8 Nethy Bridge Highland, Scotland U.K.
213 H2 Netia Moz.
136 F3 Netishyn Ukr.
195 M5 Neto r. Italy
176 D2 Netolice Czech Rep.
169 F9 Netphen Ger.
169 J8 Netra (Ringgau) Ger.
117 M7 Netrakona Bangl.
116 D9 Netrang Gujarat India
190 G1 Netstal Switz.
157 I6 Nettancourt France
169 C10 Nettersheim Ger.
169 B8 Nettetal Ger.
221 K3 Nettilling Lake Nunavut Can.
226 A1 Nett Lake MN U.S.A.
149 Q7 Nettleham Lincolnshire, England U.K.
193 J5 Nettuno Italy
171 F9 Netzschkau Ger.
173 M2 Neualbenreuth Ger.
169 G10 Neu-Anspach Ger.
210 B3 Neubari r. Sudan
168 I1 Neuberend Ger.
179 M4 Neuberg an der Mürz Austria
173 M6 Neubeuern Ger.
173 L5 Neubiberg Ger.
168 D5 Neubörger Ger.
159 M3 Neubourg, Campagne … France
170 H3 Neubrandenburg Ger.
168 G5 Neubruchhausen Ger.
172 H2 Neubrunn Ger.
170 E2 Neubukow Ger.
172 F4 Neubulach Ger.
173 O4 Neuburg am Inn Ger.
172 E4 Neuburg am Rhein Ger.
173 K4 Neuburg an der Donau …
173 I5 Neuburg an der Kamm…
170 E3 Neuburg-Steinhausen …
171 H8 Neuburxdorf Ger.
190 B2 Neuchâtel Switz.
190 B1 Neuchâtel canton Switz
190 B2 Neuchâtel, Lac de l. Sw…
168 K4 Neu Darchau Ger.
169 K9 Neudietendorf Ger.
179 N4 Neudorf Austria
171 G10 Neudorf Ger.
171 E10 Neudrossenfeld Ger.
172 F4 Neuenbürg Ger.
172 D6 Neuenburg am Rhein G…
173 J3 Neuendettelsau Ger.
171 I6 Neuendorfer See l. Ger.
170 J5 Neuenhagen Ger.
170 I5 Neuenhagen Berlin Ge…
169 C6 Neuenhaus Ger.
172 E7 Neuenhof Switz.
190 E1 Neuenkirch Switz.
170 H1 Neuenkirchen Mecklenb… Vorpommern Ger.
170 H2 Neuenkirchen Mecklenb… Vorpommern Ger.
168 G3 Neuenkirchen Niedersachsen Ger.
168 G4 Neuenkirchen Niedersachsen Ger.
168 G5 Neuenkirchen Niedersachsen Ger.
168 I4 Neuenkirchen Niedersachsen Ger.
169 E6 Neuenkirchen Niedersachsen Ger.
169 D6 Neuenkirchen Nordrhei… Westfalen Ger.
168 H2 Neuenkirchen Schleswi… Holstein Ger.
169 F5 Neuenkirchen (Oldenbur…
169 D9 Neuenkirchen-Seelschei…
169 E8 Neuenrade Ger.
172 G3 Neuenstadt am Kocher…
172 H3 Neuenstein Ger.
168 G3 Neuenwalde Ger.
169 B10 Neuerburg Ger.
173 L5 Neufahrn bei Freising …
173 M4 Neufahrn in Niederbaye…
157 O7 Neuf-Brisach France
165 H9 Neufchâteau Belgium
157 K7 Neufchâteau France
156 B4 Neufchâtel-en-Bray Fra…
159 L5 Neufchâtel-en-Saosnoi… France
156 C2 Neufchâtel-Hardelot Fr…
156 H5 Neufchâtel-sur-Aisne F…
168 H3 Neufeld Ger.
179 N4 Neufeld an der Leitha …
179 J3 Neufelden Austria
172 G4 Neuffen Ger.
157 I4 Neufmanil France
172 G5 Neufra Ger.
171 E7 Neugattersleben Ger.
171 K9 Neugersdorf Ger.
170 H4 Neuglobsow Ger.
170 J5 Neuhardenberg Ger.
168 E3 Neuharlingersiel Ger.
179 K6 Neuhaus Kärnten Austri…
179 L4 Neuhaus Niederösterreic… Austria
168 K4 Neuhaus (Elbe) Ger.
168 H3 Neuhaus (Oste) Ger.
173 O5 Neuhaus am Inn Ger.
179 N6 Neuhaus am Klausenb… Austria
171 D9 Neuhaus am Rennweg …
173 L2 Neuhaus an der Pegni…
172 F4 Neuhausen Baden-Württemberg Ger.
171 H9 Neuhausen Sachsen Ge…
Neuhausen Rus. Fed. se… Gur'yevsk
190 F1 Neuhausen Switz.
172 F6 Neuhausen ob Eck Ger…
171 D10 Neuhaus-Schierschnitz…
169 I10 Neuhof Ger.
173 J3 Neuhof an der Zenn Ge…
179 J3 Neuhofen an der Krem… Austria
179 K3 Neuhofen an der Ybbs Austria
159 M6 Neuillé-Pont-Pierre Fra…
160 D2 Neuilly France
156 D5 Neuilly-en-Thelle Franc…
160 C4 Neuilly-le-Réal France
157 J8 Neuilly-l'Évêque France
156 F5 Neuilly-St-Front France
156 D6 Neuilly-sur-Seine Franc…
169 G10 Neu-Isenburg Ger.
170 G3 Neukalen Ger.
170 D4 Neu Kaliß Ger.
168 E4 Neukamperfehn Ger.
171 F8 Neukieritzsch Ger.
172 H6 Neukirch Baden-Württemberg Ger.
171 J8 Neukirch Sachsen Ger.
169 H9 Neukirchen Hessen Ger.
171 F9 Neukirchen Sachsen Ge…
171 G9 Neukirchen Sachsen Ge…
170 D2 Neukirchen Schleswig-Holstein Ger.
168 G1 Neukirchen Schleswig-Holstein Ger.
178 F5 Neukirchen am Großvenediger Austria
178 H3 Neukirchen an der Enk… Austria
179 I3 Neukirchen an der Vöc… Austria
173 M3 Neukirchen-Balbini Ge…
173 L2 Neukirchen bei Sulzba… Rosenberg Ger.
173 O4 Neukirchen vorm Wald…
170 E3 Neukloster Ger.
Neukuhren Rus. Fed. se… Pionerskiy
168 D4 Neulehe Ger.
179 M3 Neulengbach Austria
173 I4 Neuler Ger.
170 J5 Neulewin Ger.
160 E5 Neulise France
186 K3 Neulós, Puig mt. Spain
171 I6 Neu Lübbenau Ger.
172 B2 Neumagen Ger.
171 F9 Neumark Sachsen Ger.
171 D8 Neumark Thüringen Ger.
178 H4 Neumarkt am Wallerse… Austria
179 J3 Neumarkt im Mühlkreis… Austria
173 K3 Neumarkt in der Oberpfa…
179 J5 Neumarkt in Steiermar… Austria
173 N5 Neumarkt-Sankt Veit G…
262 X2 Neumayer research stn Antarctica
168 I2 Neumünster Ger.
96 G5 Neun, Nam r. Laos
173 M3 Neunburg vorm Wald G…
171 F9 Neundorf Ger.
159 O6 Neung-sur-Beuvron Fra…
190 F1 Neunkirch Switz.
179 N4 Neunkirchen Austria
169 F9 Neunkirchen Nordrhein-Westfalen Ger.
172 C3 Neunkirchen Saarland G…
173 K2 Neunkirchen am Sand …
173 N5 Neuötting Ger.
171 J7 Neupetershain Ger.
179 L2 Neupölla Austria
260 C6 Neuquén Arg.
260 C6 Neuquén prov. Arg.
260 D6 Neuquén r. Arg.
173 P4 Neureichenau Ger.
173 K5 Neuried Ger.
170 G5 Neuruppin Ger.
171 K8 Neusalza-Spremberg G…
Neu Sandez Pol. see Nowy Sącz
173 J5 Neusäß Ger.
173 O4 Neuschönau Ger.
231 I8 Neuse r. NC U.S.A.

Neuseddin Ger.
Neusiedl am See Austria
Neusiedler See *l.* Austria/Hungary
Neusiedler See Seewinkel, Nationalpark *nat. park* Austria
Neusorg Ger.
Neuss Ger.
Neussargues-Moissac France
Neustadt *Baden-Württemberg* Ger.
Neustadt *Brandenburg* Ger.
Neustadt *Thüringen* Ger.
Neustadt (Harz) Ger.
Neustadt (Hessen) Ger.
Neustadt (Wied) Ger.
Neustadt am Kulm Ger.
Neustadt am Rennsteig Ger.
Neustadt am Rübenberge Ger.
Neustadt an der Aisch Ger.
Neustadt an der Donau Ger.
Neustadt an der Hardt Ger. *see* **Neustadt an der Weinstraße**
Neustadt an der Waldnaab Ger.
Neustadt an der Weinstraße Ger.
Neustadt bei Coburg Ger.
Neustadt-Glewe Ger.
Neustadt in Holstein Ger.
Neustadt in Sachsen Ger.
Neustift im Stubaital Austria
Neustrelitz Ger.
Neutraubling Ger.
Neutrebbin Ger.
Neu-Ulm Ger.
Neuvéglise France
Neuves-Maisons France
Neuvic *Aquitaine* France
Neuvic *Limousin* France
Neuvic, Barrage de *dam* France
Neuville-aux-Bois France
Neuville-de-Poitou France
Neuville-les-Dames France
Neuville-lès-Dieppe France
Neuville-sur-Saône France
Neuville-sur-Sarthe France
Neuvilly-en-Argonne France
Neuvy-Grandchamp France
Neuvy-le-Roi France
Neuvy-Pailloux France
Neuvy-St-Sépulchre France
Neuvy-Sautour France
Neuvy-sur-Barangeon France
Neuwegersleben Ger.
Neuweiler Ger.
Neuwerk *i.* Ger.
Neuwied Ger.
Neuwittenbek Ger.
Neu Wulmstorf Ger.
Neuwürschnitz Ger.
Neu Zauche Ger.
Neuzelle Ger.
Neu Zittau Ger.
Neva *r.* Rus. Fed.
Névache France
Nevada *IA* U.S.A.
Nevada *MO* U.S.A.
Nevada *state* U.S.A.
Nevada, Sierra *mt.* Arg.
Nevada, Sierra *mts* Spain
Nevada, Sierra *nature res.* Spain
Nevada, Sierra *mts CA* U.S.A.
Nevada City *CA* U.S.A.
Nevado, Cerro *mt.* Arg.
Nevado, Sierra del *mts* Arg.
Nevado de Colima, Parque Nacional *nat. park* Mex.
Nevado de Tolúca, Parque Nacional *nat. park* Mex.
Nevado de Toluca, Volcán *vol.* Mex.
Névalo *r.* Spain
Nevasa *Mahar.* India
Nevatim Israel
Nevdol'sk Rus. Fed.
Nevdubstroy Rus. Fed. *see* **Kirovsk**
Neve, Serra da *mts* Angola
Neveklov Czech Rep.
Nevel' Rus. Fed.
Nevel', Ozero *l.* Rus. Fed.
Nevele Belgium
Nevel'sk *Sakhalin* Rus. Fed.
Nevera *mt.* Spain
Neverkino Rus. Fed.
Nevern *Pembrokeshire, Wales* U.K.
Neveronys Lith.
Nevers France
Neversink *r. NY* U.S.A.
Nevertire *N.S.W.* Austr.
Neves Brazil
Neves, Lago di *l.* Italy
Nevesinje Bos.-Herz.
Névez France
Nevėžis *r.* Lith.
Névian France
Neviano Italy
Néville France
Nevinnomyssk Rus. Fed.
Nevis *i.* St Kitts and Nevis
Nevis, Loch *inlet Scotland* U.K.
Nevis Peak *hill* St Kitts and Nevis
Nevşehir Turkey
Nevskoye Rus. Fed.
New *r. CA* U.S.A.
New *r. WV* U.S.A.
New Abbey *Dumfries and Galloway, Scotland* U.K.
New Aberdour *Aberdeenshire, Scotland* U.K.
New Addington *Greater London, England* U.K.
New Aiyansh *B.C.* Can.
Newala Tanz.
New Albany *IN* U.S.A.
New Albany *MS* U.S.A.
New Albany *PA* U.S.A.
Newald *WI* U.S.A.
New Alresford *Hampshire, England* U.K.
New Amsterdam Guyana
New Angledool *N.S.W.* Austr.
Newark S. Africa
Newark *CA* U.S.A.
Newark *DE* U.S.A.
Newark *NJ* U.S.A.
Newark *NY* U.S.A.
Newark *OH* U.S.A.
Newark *airport NJ* U.S.A.
Newark Lake *NV* U.S.A.
Newark-on-Trent *Nottinghamshire, England* U.K.
Newark Valley *NY* U.S.A.
New Ash Green *Kent, England* U.K.
New Augusta *MS* U.S.A.
Newaygo *MI* U.S.A.
New Bedford *MA* U.S.A.
Newberg *OR* U.S.A.
New Berlin *NY* U.S.A.
New Berlin *PA* U.S.A.
New Berlinville *PA* U.S.A.
New Bern *NC* U.S.A.
Newberry *MI* U.S.A.
Newberry *SC* U.S.A.
Newberry National Volcanic Monument *nat. park OR* U.S.A.
Newberry Springs *CA* U.S.A.
Newberrytown *PA* U.S.A.
New Bethlehem *PA* U.S.A.
Newbiggin-by-the-Sea *Northumberland, England* U.K.
Newbigging *South Lanarkshire, Scotland* U.K.
New Bight *Cat I.* Bahamas
Newbliss Ireland
New Bloomfield *PA* U.S.A.
Newboro *Ont.* Can.
New Boston *OH* U.S.A.
New Boston *TX* U.S.A.
New Braunfels *TX* U.S.A.
Newbridge *Galway* Ireland
Newbridge *Kildare* Ireland
Newbridge *Limerick* Ireland
Newbridge *Caerphilly, Wales* U.K.
150 F3 **Newbridge on Wye** *Powys, Wales* U.K.
232 E8 **New Brighton** *PA* U.S.A.
91 K8 **New Britain** *i.* P.N.G.
235 J1 **New Britain** *CT* U.S.A.
234 E4 **New Britain** *PA* U.S.A.
266 F6 **New Britain Trench** *sea feature* Pacific Ocean
246 □ **New Broughton** Jamaica
225 H4 **New Brunswick** *prov.* Can.
233 K8 **New Brunswick** *NJ* U.S.A.
226 H8 **New Buffalo** *MI* U.S.A.
234 B4 **New Buffalo** *PA* U.S.A.
147 H3 **New Buildings** *Northern Ireland* U.K.
232 H8 **Newburg** *PA* U.S.A.
227 R5 **Newburgh** *Ont.* Can.
146 L8 **Newburgh** *Aberdeenshire, Scotland* U.K.
146 J10 **Newburgh** *Fife, Scotland* U.K.
146 J12 **Newburgh** *Scottish Borders, Scotland* U.K.
233 K7 **Newburgh** *NY* U.S.A.
151 J5 **Newbury** *West Berkshire, England* U.K.
Newbury *admin. div. England* U.K. *see* **West Berkshire**
233 O6 **Newburyport** *MA* U.S.A.
207 G4 **New Bussa** Nigeria
149 L5 **Newby Bridge** *Cumbria, England* U.K.
146 L7 **New Byth** *Aberdeenshire, Scotland* U.K.
New Caledonia *i.* S. Pacific Ocean *see* **Nouvelle Calédonie**
78 □5 **New Caledonia** *terr.* S. Pacific Ocean
266 F7 **New Caledonia Trough** *sea feature* Tasman Sea
235 I2 **New Canaan** *CT* U.S.A.
225 H3 **New Carlisle** *Que.* Can.
232 A9 **New Carlisle** *OH* U.S.A.
234 B7 **New Carrollton** *MD* U.S.A.
83 M5 **Newcastle** *N.S.W.* Austr.
224 E5 **Newcastle** *Ont.* Can.
246 □ **Newcastle** Jamaica
147 J6 **Newcastle** *Dublin* Ireland
147 E6 **Newcastle** *Galway* Ireland
147 G8 **Newcastle** *Tipperary* Ireland
147 J6 **Newcastle** *Wicklow* Ireland
215 N3 **Newcastle** S. Africa
247 □2 **Newcastle** St Kitts and Nevis
147 K4 **Newcastle** *Northern Ireland* U.K.
150 F3 **Newcastle** *Shropshire, England* U.K.
240 K3 **Newcastle** *CA* U.S.A.
234 D5 **New Castle** *DE* U.S.A.
230 E6 **New Castle** *IN* U.S.A.
230 E6 **New Castle** *KY* U.S.A.
233 □P4 **Newcastle** *ME* U.S.A.
232 E7 **New Castle** *PA* U.S.A.
241 S4 **Newcastle** *UT* U.S.A.
232 E11 **New Castle** *VA* U.S.A.
238 L5 **Newcastle** *WY* U.S.A.
234 D5 **New Castle County** *county DE* U.S.A.
84 D4 **Newcastle Creek** *r. N.T.* Austr.
150 D3 **Newcastle Emlyn** *Ceredigion, Wales* U.K.
85 I5 **Newcastle Range** *hills Qld* Austr.
146 K12 **Newcastleton** *Scottish Borders, Scotland* U.K.
149 M7 **Newcastle-under-Lyme** *Staffordshire, England* U.K.
149 N4 **Newcastle upon Tyne** *Tyne and Wear, England* U.K.
84 D4 **Newcastle Waters** *N.T.* Austr.
147 D8 **Newcastle West** Ireland
147 E9 **Newcestown** Ireland
233 J11 **New Church** *VA* U.S.A.
Newchwang *Liaoning* China *see* **Yingkou**
235 H2 **New City** *NY* U.S.A.
234 B2 **New Columbia** *PA* U.S.A.
234 C2 **New Columbus** *PA* U.S.A.
241 X5 **Newcomb** *NM* U.S.A.
232 D8 **Newcomerstown** *OH* U.S.A.
232 D9 **New Concord** *OH* U.S.A.
235 H2 **New Croton Reservoir** *NY* U.S.A.
234 B4 **New Cumberland** *PA* U.S.A.
146 H12 **New Cumnock** *East Ayrshire, Scotland* U.K.
146 L7 **New Deer** *Aberdeenshire, Scotland* U.K.
87 E12 **Newdegate** *W.A.* Austr.
116 F5 **New Delhi** *Delhi* India
233 □R1 **New Denmark** *N.B.* Can.
240 L4 **New Don Pedro Reservoir** *CA* U.S.A.
149 O6 **New Earswick** *York, England* U.K.
234 F4 **New Egypt** *NJ* U.S.A.
172 B2 **Newel** Ger.
85 J4 **Newell** *Qld* Austr.
236 D3 **Newell** *SD* U.S.A.
232 E8 **Newell** *WV* U.S.A.
87 I8 **Newell, Lake** *salt flat W.A.* Austr.
223 I5 **Newell, Lake** *Alta* Can.
83 M4 **New England Range** *mts N.S.W.* Austr.
264 F3 **New England Seamounts** *sea feature* N. Atlantic Ocean
220 B4 **Newenham, Cape** *AK* U.S.A.
150 H4 **Newent** *Gloucestershire, England* U.K.
226 H6 **New Era** *MI* U.S.A.
232 G5 **Newfane** *NY* U.S.A.
233 M6 **Newfane** *VT* U.S.A.
234 E5 **Newfield** *NJ* U.S.A.
151 I6 **New Forest National Park** *England* U.K.
233 N5 **Newfound Lake** *NH* U.S.A.
225 J3 **Newfoundland** *i. Nfld and Lab.* Can.
235 G2 **Newfoundland** *NJ* U.S.A.
234 E2 **Newfoundland** *PA* U.S.A.
225 J2 **Newfoundland and Labrador** *prov.* Can.
238 H6 **Newfoundland Evaporation Basin** *salt l. UT* U.S.A.
234 B5 **New Freedom** *PA* U.S.A.
146 H12 **New Galloway** *Dumfries and Galloway, Scotland* U.K.
78 □6 **New Georgia** *i. New Georgia Is* Solomon Is
78 □6 **New Georgia Islands** Solomon Is
78 □6 **New Georgia Sound** *sea chan.* Solomon Is
226 E7 **New Glarus** *WI* U.S.A.
225 I4 **New Glasgow** *N.S.* Can.
147 J5 **Newgrange** Ireland
145 D5 **Newgrange Tomb** *tourist site* Ireland
247 □7 **New Grant** Trin. and Tob.
235 G5 **New Gretna** *NJ* U.S.A.
91 J8 **New Guinea** *i.* Indon./P.N.G.
203 G6 **New Halfa** Sudan
240 N7 **Newhall** *CA* U.S.A.
235 H1 **New Hamburg** *NY* U.S.A.
233 N4 **New Hampshire** *state* U.S.A.
226 B6 **New Hampton** *IA* U.S.A.
235 G2 **New Hampton** *NY* U.S.A.
91 L7 **New Hanover** *i.* P.N.G.
215 O5 **New Hanover** S. Africa
233 J5 **New Hartford** *NY* U.S.A.
151 M6 **Newhaven** *East Sussex, England* U.K.
233 M7 **New Haven** *CT* U.S.A.
226 B6 **New Haven** *IA* U.S.A.
226 I8 **New Haven** *IN* U.S.A.
227 L7 **New Haven** *MI* U.S.A.
232 D10 **New Haven** *WV* U.S.A.
235 J2 **New Haven County** *county CT* U.S.A.
222 E4 **New Hazelton** *B.C.* Can.
New Hebrides *country* S. Pacific Ocean *see* **Vanuatu**
266 G7 **New Hebrides Trench** *sea feature* Pacific Ocean
240 L3 **New Hogan Reservoir** *CA* U.S.A.
New Holland *country* Oceania *see* **Australia**
234 C4 **New Holland** *PA* U.S.A.
226 F6 **New Holstein** *WI* U.S.A.
234 F4 **New Hope** *PA* U.S.A.
237 J10 **New Iberia** *LA* U.S.A.
151 M6 **Newick** *East Sussex, England* U.K.
151 N5 **Newington** *Kent, England* U.K.
235 J1 **Newington** *CT* U.S.A.
148 C6 **New Inn** *Cavan* Ireland
147 H6 **New Inn** *Laois* Ireland
147 G8 **Newinn** Ireland
91 L7 **New Ireland** *i.* P.N.G.
234 G5 **New Jersey** *state* U.S.A.
116 C8 **New Kandla** *Gujarat* India
232 F8 **New Kensington** *PA* U.S.A.
232 H11 **New Kent** *VA* U.S.A.
147 E7 **New Kildimo** Ireland
239 L9 **Newkirk** *NM* U.S.A.
237 G7 **Newkirk** *OK* U.S.A.
146 I11 **New Lanark** *Scotland* U.K.
146 I11 **New Lanark World Heritage Site** *tourist site Scotland* U.K.
231 G7 **Newland** *NC* U.S.A.
87 G10 **Newland Range** *hills W.A.* Austr.
146 L7 **New Leeds** *Aberdeenshire, Scotland* U.K.
232 C9 **New Lexington** *OH* U.S.A.
226 D6 **New Lisbon** *WI* U.S.A.
224 E4 **New Liskeard** *Ont.* Can.
233 M7 **New London** *CT* U.S.A.
232 C7 **New London** *OH* U.S.A.
226 F5 **New London** *WI* U.S.A.
235 K1 **New London County** *county CT* U.S.A.
146 G13 **New Luce** *Dumfries and Galloway, Scotland* U.K.
150 □ **Newlyn** *Cornwall, England* U.K.
146 L8 **Newmachar** *Aberdeenshire, Scotland* U.K.
237 K7 **New Madrid** *MO* U.S.A.
87 E7 **Newman** *W.A.* Austr.
80 J7 **Newman** *North I.* N.Z.
240 K4 **Newman** *CA* U.S.A.
87 E7 **Newman, Mount** *W.A.* Austr.
262 O1 **Newman Island** Antarctica
234 C4 **Newmanstown** *PA* U.S.A.
224 E4 **Newmarket** *Ont.* Can.
246 □ **Newmarket** Jamaica
147 D8 **Newmarket** *Cork* Ireland
147 H8 **Newmarket** *Kilkenny* Ireland
151 M3 **Newmarket** *Suffolk, England* U.K.
146 D6 **Newmarket** *Western Isles, Scotland* U.K.
233 □O5 **Newmarket** *NH* U.S.A.
232 G10 **New Market** *VA* U.S.A.
147 E7 **Newmarket-on-Fergus** Ireland
232 E9 **New Martinsville** *WV* U.S.A.
238 F4 **New Meadows** *ID* U.S.A.
239 L9 **New Mexico** *state* U.S.A.
232 A9 **New Miami** *OH* U.S.A.
235 I1 **New Milford** *CT* U.S.A.
233 J7 **New Milford** *PA* U.S.A.
146 K7 **Newmill** *Moray, Scotland* U.K.
149 M7 **New Mills** *Derbyshire, England* U.K.
146 H11 **Newmilns** *East Ayrshire, Scotland* U.K.
151 I6 **New Milton** *Hampshire, England* U.K.
151 O4 **New Mistley** *Essex, England* U.K.
232 B9 **New Moorefield** *OH* U.S.A.
231 E9 **Newnan** *GA* U.S.A.
150 H4 **Newnham** *Gloucestershire, England* U.K.
87 D11 **New Norcia** *W.A.* Austr.
83 K10 **New Norfolk** *Tas.* Austr.
237 J11 **New Orleans** *LA* U.S.A.
234 A5 **New Oxford** *PA* U.S.A.
233 K7 **New Paltz** *NY* U.S.A.
226 I8 **New Paris** *IN* U.S.A.
232 A9 **New Paris** *OH* U.S.A.
232 D8 **New Philadelphia** *OH* U.S.A.
234 C3 **New Philadelphia** *PA* U.S.A.
146 L7 **New Pitsligo** *Aberdeenshire, Scotland* U.K.
80 I6 **New Plymouth** *North I.* N.Z.
150 C6 **New Polzeath** *Cornwall, England* U.K.
246 □ **Newport** Jamaica
147 C5 **Newport** *Mayo* Ireland
147 F7 **Newport** *Tipperary* Ireland
151 M4 **Newport** *Essex, England* U.K.
146 J6 **Newport** *Highland, Scotland* U.K.
151 J6 **Newport** *Isle of Wight, England* U.K.
150 F4 **Newport** *Newport, Wales* U.K.
150 C3 **Newport** *Pembrokeshire, Wales* U.K.
150 H2 **Newport** *Telford and Wrekin, England* U.K.
150 G4 **Newport** *admin. div. Wales* U.K.
237 J8 **Newport** *AR* U.S.A.
234 D5 **Newport** *DE* U.S.A.
230 D6 **Newport** *IN* U.S.A.
233 □P4 **Newport** *ME* U.S.A.
227 K8 **Newport** *MI* U.S.A.
233 M5 **Newport** *NH* U.S.A.
234 E6 **Newport** *NJ* U.S.A.
238 B4 **Newport** *OR* U.S.A.
234 A4 **Newport** *PA* U.S.A.
233 N7 **Newport** *RI* U.S.A.
231 F8 **Newport** *TN* U.S.A.
233 M4 **Newport** *VT* U.S.A.
238 F2 **Newport** *WA* U.S.A.
150 C3 **Newport Bay** *Wales* U.K.
240 O8 **Newport Beach** *CA* U.S.A.
232 I11 **Newport News** *VA* U.S.A.
146 K10 **Newport-on-Tay** *Fife, Scotland* U.K.
151 K3 **Newport Pagnell** *Milton Keynes, England* U.K.
231 F11 **New Port Richey** *FL* U.S.A.
147 I3 **Newport Trench** *Northern Ireland* U.K.
235 I1 **New Preston** *CT* U.S.A.
246 E1 **New Providence** *i.* Bahamas
235 G3 **New Providence** *NJ* U.S.A.
234 C5 **New Providence** *PA* U.S.A.
150 D3 **New Quay** *Ceredigion, Wales* U.K.
150 B7 **Newquay** *Cornwall, England* U.K.
150 F3 **New Radnor** *Powys, Wales* U.K.
225 H3 **New Richmond** *Que.* Can.
232 A10 **New Richmond** *OH* U.S.A.
226 B4 **New Richmond** *WI* U.S.A.
234 D3 **New Ringgold** *PA* U.S.A.
241 T8 **New River** *AZ* U.S.A.
81 C13 **New River Estuary** *South I.* N.Z.
237 J10 **New Roads** *LA* U.S.A.
235 H3 **New Rochelle** *NY* U.S.A.
236 F2 **New Rockford** *ND* U.S.A.
151 N6 **New Romney** *Kent, England* U.K.
225 H4 **New Ross** *N.S.* Can.
147 I8 **New Ross** Ireland
84 B4 **Newry** *N.T.* Austr.
147 J4 **Newry** *Northern Ireland* U.K.
226 D6 **Newry** *WI* U.S.A.
147 J4 **Newry Canal** *Northern Ireland* U.K.
New Siberia Islands Rus. Fed. *see* **Novosibirskiye Ostrova**
231 G11 **New Smyrna Beach** *FL* U.S.A.
83 K5 **New South Wales** *state* Austr.
232 F8 **New Stanton** *PA* U.S.A.
235 K3 **New Suffolk** *NY* U.S.A.
232 B12 **New Tazewell** *TN* U.S.A.
261 H4 **Newton** Arg.
146 F10 **Newton** *Argyll and Bute, Scotland* U.K.
149 M6 **Newton** *Lancashire, England* U.K.
231 E10 **Newton** *GA* U.S.A.
236 I5 **Newton** *IA* U.S.A.
236 K6 **Newton** *IL* U.S.A.
236 G6 **Newton** *KS* U.S.A.
233 N6 **Newton** *MA* U.S.A.
237 K9 **Newton** *MS* U.S.A.
231 G8 **Newton** *NC* U.S.A.
234 F2 **Newton** *NJ* U.S.A.
237 I10 **Newton** *TX* U.S.A.
150 E6 **Newton Abbot** *Devon, England* U.K.
149 N4 **Newton Aycliffe** *Durham, England* U.K.
233 K4 **Newton Falls** *NY* U.S.A.
150 D7 **Newton Ferrers** *Devon, England* U.K.
146 L8 **Newtonhill** *Aberdeenshire, Scotland* U.K.
149 L7 **Newton-le-Willows** *Merseyside, England* U.K.
151 K4 **Newton Longville** *Buckinghamshire, England* U.K.
146 H11 **Newton Mearns** *East Renfrewshire, Scotland* U.K.
146 H8 **Newtonmore** *Highland, Scotland* U.K.
150 F6 **Newton Poppleford** *Devon, England* U.K.
150 E6 **Newton St Cyres** *Devon, England* U.K.
146 H13 **Newton Stewart** *Dumfries and Galloway, Scotland* U.K.
140 □ **Newtontoppen** *mt.* Svalbard
147 E8 **Newtown** *Cork* Ireland
147 H7 **Newtown** *Laois* Ireland
147 F6 **Newtown** *Roscommon* Ireland
147 F8 **Newtown** *Tipperary* Ireland
147 H8 **Newtown** *Waterford* Ireland
150 G3 **Newtown** *Herefordshire, England* U.K.
150 F2 **Newtown** *Powys, Wales* U.K.
235 I2 **Newtown** *CT* U.S.A.
236 D1 **New Town** *ND* U.S.A.
234 C3 **Newtown** *PA* U.S.A.
234 F4 **Newtown** *PA* U.S.A.
147 K3 **Newtownabbey** *Northern Ireland* U.K.
147 K3 **Newtownards** *Northern Ireland* U.K.
Newtownbarry Ireland *see* **Bunclody**
147 H4 **Newtownbutler** *Northern Ireland* U.K.
148 E4 **Newtown Crommelin** *Northern Ireland* U.K.
147 G3 **Newtowncunningham** Ireland
147 G5 **Newtown Forbes** Ireland
147 G4 **Newtown Gore** Ireland
147 I4 **Newtownhamilton** *Northern Ireland* U.K.
147 H6 **Newtownlow** Ireland
147 J6 **Newtownmountkennedy** Ireland
146 K11 **Newtown St Boswells** *Scottish Borders, Scotland* U.K.
234 E5 **Newtown Square** *PA* U.S.A.
147 H3 **Newtownstewart** *Northern Ireland* U.K.
150 F4 **New Tredegar** *Caerphilly, Wales* U.K.
234 D3 **New Tripoli** *PA* U.S.A.
146 J9 **Newtyle** *Angus, Scotland* U.K.
236 H3 **New Ulm** *MN* U.S.A.
232 B9 **New Vienna** *OH* U.S.A.
232 H8 **Newville** *PA* U.S.A.
233 □O4 **New Vineyard** *ME* U.S.A.
149 Q6 **New Waltham** *North East Lincolnshire, England* U.K.
234 A5 **New Windsor** *MD* U.S.A.
235 G2 **New Windsor** *NY* U.S.A.
233 J6 **New Woodstock** *NY* U.S.A.
233 L8 **New York** *NY* U.S.A.
233 J6 **New York** *state* U.S.A.
235 H3 **New York County** *county NY* U.S.A.
241 Q6 **New York Mountains** *CA* U.S.A.
80 I9 **New Zealand** *country* Oceania
245 I7 **Nexapa** *r.* Mex.
162 G4 **Nexon** France
134 H4 **Neya** Rus. Fed.
134 H4 **Neya** *r.* Rus. Fed.
104 C6 **Neyagawa** Japan
122 I5 **Neybasteh** Afgh.
122 G7 **Ney Bīd** Iran
122 E5 **Neyestānak** Iran
150 C4 **Neyland** *Pembrokeshire, Wales* U.K.
122 F7 **Neyrīz** Iran
122 H3 **Neyshābūr** Iran
114 E8 **Neyyattinkara** *Kerala* India
245 H6 **Nezahualcóyotl** Mex.
245 N8 **Nezahualcóyotl, Presa** *resr* Mex.
176 G2 **Nezamyslice** Czech Rep.
176 D2 **Nežárka** *r.* Czech Rep.
217 □1c **Nez de Bœuf** *mt.* Réunion
137 P3 **Nezhegol'** *r.* Rus. Fed.
Nezhin Ukr. *see* **Nizhyn**
129 E1 **Nezlobnaya** Rus. Fed.
238 F3 **Nezperce** *ID* U.S.A.
238 F3 **Nez Perce Indian Reservation** *res. ID* U.S.A.
177 I4 **Nézsa** Hungary
176 C2 **Nezvěstice** Czech Rep.
136 E5 **Nezvys'ko** Ukr.
95 H4 **Ngabang** *Kalimantan* Indon.
209 C5 **Ngabé** Congo
97 D7 **Nga Chong, Khao** *mt.* Myanmar/Thai.
207 I3 **Ngadda** *watercourse* Nigeria
93 A8 **Ngadubolu** *Sumba* Indon.
96 C2 **Ngagahtawng** Myanmar
80 I2 **Ngaiotonga** *North I.* N.Z.
92 □ **Ngajangel** *i.* Palau
211 B6 **Ngajira** Tanz.
208 D4 **Ngala** Dem. Rep. Congo
207 I3 **Ngala** Nigeria
93 D2 **Ngalipaëng** *Sulawesi* Indon.
93 B9 **Ngalu** *Sumba* Indon.
208 C2 **Ngam** Chad
208 C2 **Ngama** Chad
212 D3 **Ngamaseri** *watercourse* Botswana
80 I6 **Ngamatapouri** *North I.* N.Z.
207 H5 **Ngambé** Cameroon
108 A3 **Ngamda** *Xizang* China
92 □ **Ngamegei Passage** Palau
212 D3 **Ngamiland** *admin. dist.* Botswana
111 H12 **Ngamring** *Xizang* China
210 A3 **Ngangala** Sudan
111 F11 **Ngangla Ringco** *salt l.* China
111 E10 **Nganglong Kangri** *mt. Xizang* China
111 E10 **Nganglong Kangri** *mts Xizang* China
209 B7 **N'gangula** Angola
111 H11 **Ngangzê Co** *salt l.* China
111 H11 **Ngangzê Shan** *mts Xizang* China
109 □J7 **Ngan Hei Shui Tong** *resr H.K.* China
95 I8 **Nganjuk** *Jawa* Indon.
108 E9 **Ngan Sâu, Sông** *r.* Vietnam
96 G3 **Ngân Sơn** Vietnam
96 D5 **Ngao** Thai.
207 I5 **Ngaoundal** Cameroon
207 I5 **Ngaoundéré** Cameroon
80 J5 **Ngapuke** *North I.* N.Z.
211 B7 **Ngara** Malawi
211 A5 **Ngara** Tanz.
94 F7 **Ngaras** *Sumatera* Indon.
92 □ **Ngardmau** Palau
92 □ **Ngardmau Bay** Palau
92 □ **Ngaregur** *i.* Palau
211 C7 **Ngarimbi** Tanz.
92 □ **Ngariungs** *i.* Palau
82 H6 **Ngarkat Conservation Park** *nature res. S.A.* Austr.
80 J4 **Ngaruawahia** *North I.* N.Z.
80 K6 **Ngaruroro** *r. North I.* N.Z.
80 H1 **Ngataki** *North I.* N.Z.
81 □3 **Ngatangiia** *Rarotonga* Cook Is
80 L5 **Ngatapa** *North I.* N.Z.
80 J4 **Ngatea** *North I.* N.Z.
92 □ **Ngateguil, Point** Palau
96 B6 **Ngathainggyaung** Myanmar
207 I6 **Ngato** Cameroon
Ngau *i.* Fiji *see* **Gau**
109 □J7 **Ngau Mei Hoi** *b. H.K.* China
Ngawa *Sichuan* China *see* **Aba**
97 D8 **Ngawan Chaung** *r.* Myanmar
95 I8 **Ngawi** *Jawa* Indon.
96 B6 **Ngayok Bay** Myanmar
208 B4 **Ngbala** Congo
Ngcheangel *atoll* Palau *see* **Kayangel Atoll**
Ngeaur *i.* Palau *see* **Angaur**
211 A6 **Ngegera** Tanz.
Ngemelachel Palau *see* **Malakal**
92 □ **Ngemelis Islands** Palau
92 □ **Ngergoi** *i.* Palau
91 H5 **Ngeruangel** *i.* Palau
92 □ **Ngesebus** *i.* Palau
213 F4 **Ngezi** Zimbabwe
Nggamea *i.* Fiji *see* **Qamea**
78 □6 **Nggatokae** *i. New Georgia Is* Solomon Is
78 □6 **Nggela Sule** *i.* Solomon Is
212 D4 **Nghabe** *r.* Botswana
97 G9 **Nghê, Hon** *i.* Vietnam
96 F5 **Ngiap** *r.* Laos
93 D8 **Ngilmina** *Timor* Indon.
95 J8 **Ngimbang** *Jawa* Indon.
Ngiva Angola *see* **Ondjiva**
208 B5 **Ngo** Congo
92 □ **Ngobasangel** *i.* Palau
93 E3 **Ngofakiaha** *Maluku* Indon.
111 L11 **Ngoichogê** *Xizang* China
207 I6 **Ngoïla** Cameroon
111 I11 **Ngoin, Co** *salt l.* China
96 H7 **Ngok Linh** *mt.* Vietnam
207 6 **Ngoko** *r.* Cameroon/Congo
208 B5 **Ngoko** Congo
106 F8 **Ngola Shan** *mts Qinghai* China
106 F9 **Ngola Shankou** *pass Qinghai* China
207 H4 **Ngol Bembo** Nigeria
209 E8 **Ngoma** Zambia
212 E3 **Ngoma Bridge** Botswana
209 B6 **Ngoma Tsé-Tsé** Congo
211 B7 **Ngomba** Tanz.
215 P3 **Ngome** S. Africa
111 M11 **Ngom Qu** *r. Xizang* China
207 I4 **Ngong** Cameroon
209 C8 **Ngongola** Angola
80 K5 **Ngongotaha** *North I.* N.Z.
109 □J7 **Ngong Shuen Chau** *pen. H.K.* China
111 H10 **Ngoqumaima** *Xizang* China
106 E9 **Ngoring** *Qinghai* China
106 E9 **Ngoring Hu** *l. Qinghai* China
211 B5 **Ngorongoro Conservation Area** *nature res.* Tanz.
211 B5 **Ngorongoro Crater** Tanz.
208 C3 **Ngoto** C.A.R.
207 H6 **Ngoulémakong** Cameroon
207 H6 **Ngoumou** *Centre* Cameroon
207 I5 **Ngoumou** *Est* Cameroon
208 A5 **Ngounié** *prov.* Gabon
208 A5 **Ngounié** *r.* Gabon
208 B5 **Ngouoni** Gabon
202 C6 **Ngoura** Chad
202 B6 **Ngouri** Chad
207 I3 **Ngourti** Niger
202 C5 **Ngoutchey** *well* Chad
208 E3 **Ngouyo** C.A.R.
211 A5 **Ngozi** Burundi
215 N7 **Ngqeleni** S. Africa
215 M7 **Ngqungqu** S. Africa
208 B3 **Nguia Bouar** C.A.R.
207 I3 **Nguigmi** Niger
207 H3 **Nguini** *well* Niger
84 C1 **Nguiu** *N.T.* Austr.
111 K11 **Ngükang** *Xizang* China
84 E3 **Ngukurr** *N.T.* Austr.
91 I5 **Ngulu** *atoll* Micronesia
96 F5 **Ngum, Nam** *r.* Laos
78 □5 **Nguna** *i.* Vanuatu
213 F4 **Ngundu** Zimbabwe
209 B7 **N'gungo** Angola
80 I2 **Ngunguru Bay** *North I.* N.Z.
93 B9 **Ngunju, Tanjung** *pt Sumba* Indon.
Ngunza Angola *see* **Sumbe**
Ngunza-Kabolu Angola *see* **Sumbe**
108 C1 **Ngura** *Gansu* China
207 H3 **Nguru** Nigeria
211 C6 **Nguru Mountains** Tanz.
212 D4 **Ngwako Pan** *salt pan* Botswana
Ngwane *country* Africa *see* **Swaziland**
215 L3 **Ngwathe** S. Africa
215 Q2 **Ngwavuma** *r.* Swaziland
215 P4 **Ngwelezana** S. Africa
215 P2 **Ngwempisi** *r.* S. Africa
209 E9 **Ngwezi** *r.* Zambia
213 G4 **Nhachengue** Moz.
213 G3 **Nhamassonge** Moz.
213 G3 **Nhamatanda** Moz.
251 G5 **Nhamundá** Brazil
251 G5 **Nhamundá** *r.* Brazil
256 B4 **Nhandeara** Brazil
209 C7 **N'harea** Angola
97 I8 **Nha Trang** Vietnam
253 F4 **Nhecolândia** Brazil
82 H7 **Nhill** *Vic.* Austr.
215 P3 **Nhlangano** Swaziland
215 P4 **Nhlazatshe** S. Africa
212 D3 **Nhoma** Namibia
96 G4 **Nho Quan** Vietnam
Nhow *i.* Fiji *see* **Gau**
84 F2 **Nhulunbuy** *N.T.* Austr.
253 G7 **Nhu Pora** Brazil
208 E5 **Niabembe** Dem. Rep. Congo
206 E5 **Niablé** Ghana
223 J4 **Niacam** *Sask.* Can.
206 E3 **Niafounké** Mali
226 G4 **Niagara** *WI* U.S.A.
224 E5 **Niagara Falls** *Ont.* Can.
232 F5 **Niagara Falls** *NY* U.S.A.
227 O6 **Niagara-on-the-Lake** *Ont.* Can.
206 C3 **Niagassola** Guinea
206 C4 **Niagouelé, Mont du** *hill* Guinea
111 D9 **Niagzu** Aksai Chin
95 J3 **Niah** *Sarawak* Malaysia
117 J5 **Niak** Nepal
206 D4 **Niakaramandougou** Côte d'Ivoire
207 F3 **Niamey** Niger
206 D3 **Niamina** Mali
122 H8 **Nīām Kand** Iran
207 F4 **Niamtougou** Togo
Nianbai *Qinghai* China *see* **Ledu**
206 C4 **Niandan** *r.* Guinea
206 C4 **Niandankoro** Guinea
211 C6 **Niangandu** Tanz.
208 E4 **Niangara** Dem. Rep. Congo
206 E3 **Niangay, Lac** *l.* Mali
206 D4 **Niangoloko** Burkina
237 I7 **Niangua** *r. MO* U.S.A.
Niangxi *Hunan* China *see* **Xinshao**
208 E4 **Nia-Nia** Dem. Rep. Congo
206 D4 **Niankorodougou** Burkina
235 K2 **Niantic** *CT* U.S.A.
Nianyuwan *Liaoning* China *see* **Xingangzhen**
107 R3 **Nianzishan** *Heilong.* China
208 E4 **Niapu** Dem. Rep. Congo
209 B5 **Niari** *admin. reg.* Congo
94 B4 **Nias** *i.* Indon.
213 H2 **Niassa** *prov.* Moz.
Niassa, Lago *l.* Africa *see* **Nyasa, Lake**
211 C8 **Niassa, Reserva do** *nature res.* Moz.
198 D6 **Niata** Greece
Niaur *i.* Palau *see* **Angaur**
163 H10 **Niaux** France
122 I4 **Nīāzābād** Iran
190 G6 **Nibbiano** Italy
86 H7 **Nibil Well** *W.A.* Austr.
129 I5 **Nic** Azer.
195 M5 **Nicà** *r.* Italy
138 E5 **Nīca** Latvia
Nicaea Turkey *see* **İznik**
246 A7 **Nicaragua** *country* Central America
242 □Q12 **Nicaragua, Lago de** *l.* Nic.
Nicaragua, Lake Nic. *see* **Nicaragua, Lago de**
246 F3 **Nicaro** Cuba
195 K6 **Nicastro** Italy
161 K9 **Nice** France
Nice *airport* France *see* **Côte d'Azur**
240 J2 **Nice** *CA* U.S.A.
Nicephorium Syria *see* **Ar Raqqah**
231 D10 **Niceville** *FL* U.S.A.
190 D5 **Nichelino** Italy
123 L7 **Nichera** Pak.
225 G2 **Nichicun, Lac** *l. Que.* Can.
103 I12 **Nichihara** Japan
103 I15 **Nichinan** Japan
117 I6 **Nichlaul** *Uttar Prad.* India
246 C2 **Nicholas Channel** Bahamas/Cuba
230 E7 **Nicholasville** *KY* U.S.A.
246 D1 **Nicholl's Town** *Andros* Bahamas
233 I6 **Nichols** *NY* U.S.A.
86 J5 **Nicholson** *W.A.* Austr.
84 G4 **Nicholson** *r. Qld* Austr.
227 K2 **Nicholson** *Ont.* Can.
234 D1 **Nicholson** *PA* U.S.A.
223 K2 **Nicholson Lake** *N.W.T.* Can.
87 D9 **Nicholson Range** *hills W.A.* Austr.
233 K4 **Nicholville** *NY* U.S.A.
179 P4 **Nickelsdorf** Austria
232 C12 **Nickelsville** *VA* U.S.A.
86 D6 **Nickol Bay** *W.A.* Austr.
115 M8 **Nicobar Islands** *Andaman & Nicobar Is* India
197 Q6 **Nicolae Bălcescu** Romania
243 O8 **Nicolás Bravo** Mex.
260 E4 **Nicolás Bruzzone** Arg.
261 F6 **Nicolás Levalle** Arg.
245 H6 **Nicolás Romero** Mex.
240 K3 **Nicolaus** *CA* U.S.A.
194 G8 **Nicoletti, Lago** *l. Sicilia* Italy
217 □1b **Nicolière, Lac** *l.* Mauritius
195 I8 **Nicolosi** *Sicilia* Italy
Nicomedia Turkey *see* **İzmit**
258 G4 **Nico Pérez** Uru.
Nicopolis Bulg. *see* **Nikopol**
Nicosia Cyprus *see* **Lefkosia**
194 G8 **Nicosia** *Sicilia* Italy
195 J6 **Nicotera** Italy
242 □Q12 **Nicoya** Costa Rica
242 □Q13 **Nicoya, Golfo de** *b.* Costa Rica
242 □Q13 **Nicoya, Península de** *pen.* Costa Rica
233 □R1 **Nictau** *N.B.* Can.
213 H3 **Nicuadala** Moz.
197 Q5 **Niculițel** Romania
138 D6 **Nida** Lith.
175 I2 **Nida** *r.* Pol.
175 I5 **Nida** *r.* Pol.
114 G4 **Nidadavole** *Andhra Prad.* India
114 F4 **Nidagunda** *Andhra Prad.* India
190 C1 **Nidau** Switz.
149 O5 **Nidd** *r. England* U.K.
169 H10 **Nidda** Ger.
169 G10 **Nidda** *r.* Ger.
169 G10 **Nidder** *r.* Ger.
149 N5 **Nidderdale** *val. England* U.K.
142 E3 **Nidelva** *r.* Norway
190 E2 **Nidwalden** *canton* Switz.
131 K3 **Nidym** Rus. Fed.
197 J10 **Nidže** *mt.* Greece/Macedonia
175 I2 **Nidzica** Pol.
175 I5 **Nidzica** *r.* Pol.
175 J2 **Nidzkie, Jezioro** *l.* Pol.
164 J2 **Niebert** Neth.
184 F6 **Niebla** Spain
175 I3 **Nieborów** Pol.
168 G1 **Niebüll** Ger.
175 J6 **Niebylec** Pol.
174 F3 **Niechanowo** Pol.
175 H4 **Niechcice** Pol.
175 I2 **Niechłonin** Pol.
174 E4 **Niechlów** Pol.
174 D1 **Niechorze** Pol.
157 M5 **Nied** *r.* France
157 L5 **Nied Allemande** *r.* France
169 H8 **Niedenstein** Ger.
173 M4 **Niederaichbach** Ger.
165 J9 **Niederanven** Lux.
169 I9 **Niederaula** Ger.
173 N4 **Niederbayern** *admin. reg.* Ger.
190 D1 **Niederbipp** Switz.
169 F10 **Niederbrechen** Ger.
157 O6 **Niederbronn-les-Bains** France
171 F6 **Niederer Fläming** *park* Ger.
172 F5 **Niedereschach** Ger.
179 I5 **Niedere Tauern** *mts* Austria
170 I5 **Niederfinow** Ger.
169 E9 **Niederfischbach** Ger.
169 H9 **Nieder-Gemünden** Ger.
171 G7 **Niedergörsdorf** Ger.
169 D9 **Niederkassel** Ger.
172 D2 **Niederkirchen** Ger.
169 B8 **Niederkrüchten** Ger.
168 D5 **Niederlangen** Ger.
171 I7 **Niederlausitz** *reg.* Ger.
171 I6 **Niederlehme** Ger.
171 D6 **Niederndodeleben** Ger.
178 F4 **Niederndorf** Austria
169 F10 **Niederneisen** Ger.
172 H3 **Niedernhall** Ger.
169 F10 **Niedernhausen** Ger.
178 G5 **Niedernsill** Austria
169 H6 **Niedernwöhren** Ger.
172 E2 **Nieder-Olm** Ger.
169 J8 **Niederorschel** Ger.
179 M3 **Niederösterreich** *land* Austria
169 H10 **Nieder-Rodenbach** Ger.
171 D8 **Niederroßla** Ger.
168 G5 **Niedersachsen** *land* Ger.
165 K1 **Niedersächsisches Wattenmeer, Nationalpark** *nat. park* Ger.
169 K7 **Niedersachswerfen** Ger.
169 F10 **Niederselters** Ger.
172 H3 **Niederstetten** Ger.
173 I4 **Niederstotzingen** Ger.
171 E8 **Niedertrebra** Ger.
190 G1 **Niederurnen** Switz.
173 M4 **Niederviehbach** Ger.
169 J10 **Niederwerrn** Ger.
171 H9 **Niederwiesa** Ger.
173 N4 **Niederwinkling** Ger.
172 C2 **Niederwörresbach** Ger.
169 D10 **Niederzissen** Ger.
175 K4 **Niedrzwica Duża** Pol.
175 K2 **Niedźwiadna** Pol.
175 I6 **Niedźwiedź** Pol.
207 H6 **Niefang** Equat. Guinea
172 F4 **Niefern-Öschelbronn** Ger.
175 J1 **Niegocin, Jezioro** *l.* Pol.
174 D3 **Niegosław** Pol.
174 D4 **Niegosławice** Pol.
175 H5 **Niegowa** Pol.
171 E6 **Niegripp** Ger.
169 H7 **Nieheim** Ger.
164 J2 **Niekerk** Neth.
214 G5 **Niekerkshoop** S. Africa
175 I4 **Niekłań Wielki** Pol.
174 E2 **Niekursko** Pol.
165 F6 **Niel** Belgium
175 L5 **Nielisz** Pol.
206 D4 **Niellé** Côte d'Ivoire
208 B3 **Niem** C.A.R.
209 F6 **Niemba** Dem. Rep. Congo
171 F7 **Niemberg** Ger.
175 K4 **Niemce** Pol.
174 E5 **Niemcza** Pol.
171 G6 **Niemegk** Ger.
140 P3 **Niemisel** Sweden
174 F5 **Niemodlin** Pol.
174 G4 **Niemysłów** Pol.
206 D4 **Niéna** Mali
175 K5 **Nienadówka** Pol.
168 I2 **Nienborstel** Ger.
171 E7 **Nienburg (Saale)** Ger.
168 H5 **Nienburg (Weser)** Ger.
168 J5 **Nienhagen** Ger.
170 E2 **Nienhagen, Ostseebad** Ger.
169 H6 **Nienstädt** Ger.
170 G2 **Niepars** Ger.
175 I5 **Niepołomice** Pol.
175 J3 **Nieporęt** Pol.
156 E2 **Nieppe** France
206 B3 **Niéri Ko** *watercourse* Senegal
169 A7 **Niers** *r.* Ger.
172 E2 **Nierstein** Ger.
171 K8 **Niesky** Ger.
169 I8 **Nieste** Ger.
175 I4 **Nieświń** Pol.
174 G3 **Nieszawa** Pol.
175 J5 **Nietulisko Duże** Pol.
162 G4 **Nieul** France
162 A2 **Nieul-le-Dolent** France
162 B3 **Nieul-sur-Mer** France
251 H3 **Nieuw Amsterdam** Suriname
164 J5 **Nieuw-Bergen** Neth.
164 H4 **Nieuwegein** Neth.
164 G3 **Nieuwe-Niedorp** Neth.
164 K2 **Nieuwe Pekela** Neth.
164 F5 **Nieuwerkerk** Neth.
164 G5 **Nieuwerkerk aan de IJssel** Neth.
165 H7 **Nieuwerkerken** Belgium
164 L2 **Nieuweschans** Neth.
164 F5 **Nieuwe-Tonge** Neth.
164 J4 **Nieuw-Heeten** Neth.
251 H3 **Nieuw-Jacobkondre** Suriname
164 G4 **Nieuwkoop** Neth.
164 K3 **Nieuwlande** Neth.
164 J3 **Nieuwleusen** Neth.
164 H4 **Nieuw-Loosdrecht** Neth.
164 I4 **Nieuw-Milligen** Neth.
165 F6 **Nieuw-Namen** Neth.
251 G3 **Nieuw Nickerie** Suriname
164 K2 **Nieuwolda** Neth.
214 D7 **Nieuwoudtville** S. Africa
165 C6 **Nieuwpoort** Belgium
247 □10 **Nieuwpoort** *Curaçao* Neth. Antilles
164 G4 **Nieuwveen** Neth.
164 G4 **Nieuw-Vennep** Neth.
164 F5 **Nieuw-Vossemeer** Neth.
164 K3 **Nieuw-Weerdinge** Neth.
169 E10 **Nievern** Ger.
244 D2 **Nieves** Mex.
Nieves Spain *see* **As Neves**
216 □3f **Nieves, Pico de las** *mt. Gran Canaria* Canary Is
160 D2 **Nièvre** *dept* France
160 C2 **Nièvre** *r.* France
160 C3 **Nièvre de Champlemy** *r.* France
175 K4 **Niewęgłosz** Pol.
93 G5 **Nif** *Seram* Indon.
126 G5 **Niğde** Turkey
215 M2 **Nigel** S. Africa
207 H2 **Niger** *country* Africa
207 G5 **Niger** *r.* Africa
207 G4 **Niger** *state* Nigeria
207 G5 **Niger, Mouths of the** Nigeria
206 C4 **Niger, Source of the** Guinea
264 J5 **Niger Cone** *sea feature* S. Atlantic Ocean
207 G4 **Nigeria** *country* Africa
146 H7 **Nigg Bay** *Scotland* U.K.
116 H5 **Nighasan** *Uttar Prad.* India
81 C12 **Nightcaps** *South I.* N.Z.
224 D3 **Nighthawk Lake** *Ont.* Can.
216 □2c **Nightingale Island** *Tristan da Cunha* S. Atlantic Ocean
85 I2 **Night Island** *Qld* Austr.
182 C4 **Nigrán** Spain
138 F5 **Nīgrande** Latvia
198 E2 **Nigrita** Greece
244 F3 **Nigromante** Mex.
185 L7 **Nigüelas** Spain
138 H3 **Nigula looduskaitseala** *nature res.* Estonia
159 O8 **Niherne** France
123 K7 **Nihing** Pak.
Nihommatsu Japan *see* **Nihonmatsu**
Nihon *country* Asia *see* **Japan**
102 R9 **Nihonmatsu** Japan
260 C4 **Nihuil, Embalse del** *resr* Arg.
102 Q9 **Niigata** Japan
105 H1 **Niigata** *pref.* Japan
105 H2 **Niigata-yake-yama** *vol.* Japan
103 K13 **Niihama** Japan
105 I2 **Niihari** Japan
240 □A12 **Ni'ihau** *i. HI* U.S.A.
105 J7 **Nii-jima** *i.* Japan
102 T4 **Niikappu** Japan
103 K12 **Niimi** Japan
102 Q9 **Niitsu** Japan
185 O7 **Níjar** Spain
206 C2 **Nijerâne** *well* Maur.
164 J3 **Nijeveen** Neth.
128 D8 **Nijil** Jordan
128 D8 **Nijil, Wādī** *watercourse* Jordan
164 H4 **Nijkerk** Neth.
165 G6 **Nijlen** Belgium
164 I5 **Nijmegen** Neth.
164 J4 **Nijverdal** Neth.
198 D3 **Nikaia** Greece
81 □3 **Nikao** *Rarotonga* Cook Is
140 U2 **Nikel'** Rus. Fed.
120 H2 **Nikel'tau** Kazakh.
124 E5 **Nikhb** Saudi Arabia
93 D8 **Nikiniki** *Timor* Indon.
137 R3 **Nikitovka** Rus. Fed.
140 O3 **Nikkaluokta** Sweden
207 F4 **Nikki** Benin
105 K2 **Nikkō** Japan
105 K2 **Nikkō Kokuritsu-kōen** *nat. park* Japan
179 L5 **Niklasdorf** Austria
134 I4 **Nikola** Rus. Fed.
197 N8 **Nikolaevo** Bulg.
Nikolayev Ukr. *see* **Mykolayiv**
121 L1 **Nikolayevka** Kazakh.
139 O8 **Nikolayevka** *Bryanskaya Oblast'* Rus. Fed.
120 J1 **Nikolayevka** *Chelyabinskaya Oblast'* Rus. Fed.
100 I4 **Nikolayevka** *Khabarovskiy Kray* Rus. Fed.
137 R6 **Nikolayevka** *Rostovskaya Oblast'* Rus. Fed.
135 I5 **Nikolayevka** *Ul'yanovskaya Oblast'* Rus. Fed.
Nikolayev Oblast *admin. div.* Ukr. *see* **Mykolayivs'ka Oblast'**
135 I6 **Nikolayevsk** Rus. Fed.
Nikolayevskaya Oblast' *admin. div.* Ukr. *see* **Mykolayivs'ka Oblast'**
Nikolayevskiy Rus. Fed. *see* **Nikolayevsk**
100 L2 **Nikolayevsk-na-Amure** Rus. Fed.
Nikolayevskoye Rus. Fed. *see* **Krasnogvardeyskoye**
139 U5 **Nikolo-Kropotki** Rus. Fed.
178 G6 **Nikolsdorf** Austria
135 I5 **Nikol'sk** *Penzenskaya Oblast'* Rus. Fed.
134 I4 **Nikol'sk** *Vologodskaya Oblast'* Rus. Fed.
Nikol'skaya Pestravka Rus. Fed. *see* **Nikol'sk**
Nikol'skiy Kazakh. *see* **Satpayev**
139 R1 **Nikol'skiy** Rus. Fed.
131 R4 **Nikol'skoye** *Kamchatskaya Oblast'* Rus. Fed.
139 Y4 **Nikol'skoye** *Kostromskaya Oblast'* Rus. Fed.
139 W9 **Nikol'skoye** *Lipetskaya Oblast'* Rus. Fed.
120 F1 **Nikol'skoye** *Orenburgskaya Oblast'* Rus. Fed.
139 T9 **Nikol'skoye** *Orlovskaya Oblast'* Rus. Fed.
129 F1 **Nikol'skoye** *Stavropol'skiy Kray* Rus. Fed.
Nikol'skoye *Vologodskaya Oblast'* Rus. Fed. *see* **Sheksna**
139 U2 **Nikol'skoye** *Vologodskaya Oblast'* Rus. Fed.
197 M7 **Nikopol** Bulg.
137 N6 **Nikopol'** Ukr.
198 B3 **Nikopoli** Greece
122 C3 **Nīk Pey** Iran
126 H3 **Niksar** Turkey
122 I8 **Nīkshahr** Iran
196 G8 **Nikšić** Montenegro
122 I8 **Nīkū Jahān** Iran
139 X6 **Nikulino** Rus. Fed.
77 I2 **Nikumaroro** *atoll Phoenix Is* Kiribati
77 H2 **Nikunau** *i. Gilbert Is* Kiribati
Nīl, Nahr an *r.* Africa *see* **Nile**
93 F7 **Nila** *vol. Maluku* Indon.
123 O5 **Nila** Pak.
117 K9 **Nilagiri** *Orissa* India
140 S5 **Nilakka** *l.* Fin.
114 E7 **Nilakkottai** *Tamil Nadu* India
114 E7 **Nilambur** *Kerala* India
241 Q8 **Niland** *CA* U.S.A.
113 D11 **Nilandhoo Atoll** Maldives
Nilang *Hima. Prad.* India *see* **Nelang**
114 E3 **Nilanga** *Mahar.* India
114 G8 **Nilaveli** Sri Lanka
203 F2 **Nile** *r.* Africa
203 G5 **Nile** *state* Sudan
122 F6 **Nīleh** Iran
226 H8 **Niles** *MI* U.S.A.
232 E7 **Niles** *OH* U.S.A.
114 D6 **Nileswaram** *Kerala* India
114 E7 **Nilgiri Hills** India
123 L5 **Nīlī** Afgh.
124 D9 **Nili** *r.* Eth.
140 P3 **Nilivaara** Sweden
110 F5 **Nilka** *Xinjiang* China

123 L4 Nil Kowtal pass Afgh.
257 F5 Nilópolis Brazil
117 L7 Nilphamari Bangl.
17 T5 Nilsiä Fin.
245 M9 Niltepec Mex.
199 J2 Nilüfer r. Turkey
157 L5 Nilvange France
142 F6 Nim Denmark
103 J11 Nima Japan
Nimach Madh. Prad. India see Neemuch
116 E6 Nimaj Rajasthan India
100 H3 Niman r. Rus. Fed.
Nimba, Monts mts Africa see Nimba, Mount
206 C5 Nimba, Mount mts Africa
117 E6 Nimbahera Rajasthan India
114 D4 Nimbal Karnataka India
86 G7 Nimberra Well W.A. Austr.
Nimbhera Rajasthan India see Nimbahera
100 J2 Nimelen r. Rus. Fed.
161 E9 Nimes France
191 O3 Nimis Italy
116 E6 Nimka Thana Rajasthan India
83 L7 Nimmitabel N.S.W. Austr.
199 I6 Nimos i. Greece
222 E5 Nimpkish r. B.C. Can.
263 K1 Nimrod Glacier Antarctica
123 J6 Nimruz prov. Afgh.
116 F2 Nimu Jammu and Kashmir
210 B4 Nimule Sudan
210 B4 Nimule National Park Sudan
Nimwegen Neth. see Nijmegen
138 K3 Nina Estonia
78 □3a Ninai i. Kwajalein Marshall Is
127 K6 Ninawá governorate Iraq
127 K5 Ninawá tourist site Iraq
209 D8 Ninda Angola
211 B7 Nindai Tanz.
83 L3 Nindigully Qld Austr.
168 H2 Nindorf Ger.
114 C8 Nine Degree Channel India
Nine Islands P.N.G. see Kilinailau Islands
Ninemile Bar Dumfries and Galloway, Scotland U.K. see Crocketford
83 I4 Nine Mile Lake salt flat N.S.W. Austr.
241 P2 Ninemile Peak NV U.S.A.
Ninepin Group is H.K. China see Kwo Chau Kwan To
265 J7 Ninetyeast Ridge sea feature Indian Ocean
83 K8 Ninety Mile Beach Vic. Austr.
80 G1 Ninety Mile Beach North I. N.Z.
Nineveh tourist site Iraq see Ninawá
259 D6 Ninfas, Punta pt Arg.
151 M6 Ninfield East Sussex, England U.K.
87 B7 Ningaloo Marine Park nature res. W.A. Austr.
109 F6 Ning'an Heilong. China
109 M4 Ningbo Zhejiang China
107 P6 Ningcheng Nei Mongol China
109 L5 Ningde Fujian China
109 J5 Ningdu Jiangxi China
Ning'er Yunnan China see Pu'er
109 L3 Ningguo Anhui China
109 M4 Ninghai Zhejiang China
107 O7 Ninghe Tianjin China
Ninghsia Hui Autonomous Region aut. reg. China see Ningxia Huizu Zizhiqu
109 K5 Ninghua Fujian China
207 H4 Ningi Nigeria
117 O5 Ningjing Arun. Prad. India
108 B3 Ningjing Shan mts Xizang China
108 C5 Ninglang Yunnan China
107 N9 Ningling Henan China
108 F7 Ningming Guangxi China
108 D5 Ningnan Sichuan China
108 F2 Ningqiang Shaanxi China
108 G2 Ningshan Shaanxi China
107 M7 Ningwu Shanxi China
Ningxia aut. reg. China see Ningxia Huizu Zizhiqu
106 I8 Ningxia Huizu Zizhiqu aut. reg. China
107 J9 Ningxian Gansu China
109 I4 Ningxiang Hunan China
107 O9 Ningyang Shandong China
109 H6 Ningyuan Hunan China
Ningzhou Yunnan China see Huaning
96 H4 Ninh Binh Vietnam
97 I8 Ninh Hoa Vietnam
97 I9 Ninh Son Vietnam
260 A5 Ninhue Chile
91 J7 Ninigo Group atolls P.N.G.
263 J2 Ninnis Glacier Antarctica
263 K2 Ninnis Glacier Tongue Antarctica
184 H8 Niño, Sierra del mts Spain
102 S6 Ninohe Japan
105 J5 Ninomiya Kanagawa Japan
105 K3 Ninomiya Tochigi Japan
129 E4 Ninotsminda Georgia
165 F7 Ninove Belgium
259 B7 Ninualac, Canal sea chan. Chile
129 E1 Niny Rus. Fed.
253 G5 Nioaque Brazil
236 F4 Niobrara r. NE U.S.A.
221 Q2 Nioghalvfjerdsfjorden inlet Greenland
208 F4 Nioka Dem. Rep. Congo
208 C5 Nioki Dem. Rep. Congo
117 O6 Niokio Arun. Prad. India
206 B3 Niokolo Koba, Parc National du nat. park Senegal
206 D3 Niono Mali
206 C3 Nioro Mali
206 B3 Nioro du Rip Senegal
162 D3 Niort France
206 D3 Niou well Maur.
91 J8 Nipa P.N.G.
114 D4 Nipani Karnataka India
93 C5 Nipanipa, Tanjung pt Indon.
260 A5 Ñipas Chile
223 J4 Nipawin Sask. Can.
116 E9 Niphad Mahar. India
224 B3 Nipigon Ont. Can.
236 K1 Nipigon r. Ont. Can.
224 B3 Nipigon, Lake Ont. Can.
224 C3 Nipigon Bay Ont. Can.
213 H3 Nipiodi Moz.
225 I2 Nipishish Lake Nfld and Lab. Can.
227 O3 Nipissing Ont. Can.
224 E4 Nipissing, Lake Ont. Can.
240 L6 Nipomo CA U.S.A.
Nippon country Asia see Japan
Nippon Hai sea N. Pacific Ocean see Japan, Sea of
127 L7 Nippur tourist site Iraq
241 Q6 Nipton CA U.S.A.
254 C5 Niquelândia Brazil
260 B5 Niquen Chile
246 E3 Niquero Cuba
260 C2 Niquivil Arg.
122 B2 Nir Ardabil Iran
122 F6 Nir Yazd Iran
114 D4 Nira r. India
105 H4 Nirasaki Japan
105 I5 Nirayama Japan
260 A4 Nirivilo Chile
107 S2 Nirji Nei Mongol China
114 F3 Nirmal Andhra Prad. India
117 K6 Nirmali Bihar India
114 E3 Nirmal Range hills India
138 K5 Nīrzas l. Latvia
197 J7 Niš Serbia
182 E9 Nisa Port.
182 E9 Nisa r. Port.
124 H8 Nisāb Yemen
124 H3 Nisah, Wādī watercourse Saudi Arabia
197 J7 Nišava r. Serbia
146 K11 Nisbet Scottish Borders, Scotland U.K.
194 G9 Niscemi Sicilia Italy
102 R4 Niseko Japan
111 G10 Nishan Xizang China
Nishāpūr Iran see Neyshābūr
138 L6 Nishcha r. Belarus
108 H4 Nishi Hunan China
104 D5 Nishiazai Japan
102 W3 Nishibetsu-gawa r. Japan
105 L1 Nishigō Japan
105 I6 Nishiizu Japan
103 H15 Nishikata Kagoshima Japan
105 K3 Nishikata Tochigi Japan
105 I4 Nishikatsura Japan
102 R8 Nishikawa Japan
104 B5 Nishi-maizuru Japan
105 K2 Nishinasuno Japan
104 B6 Nishinomiya Japan
102 □H16 Nishino-omote Japan
103 K10 Nishino-shima i. Japan
104 F6 Nishino-shima vol. Japan
104 F6 Nishio Japan
103 G14 Nishi-Sonogi-hantō pen. Japan
103 G12 Nishi-suidō sea chan. Japan/S. Korea
104 A6 Nishiwaki Japan
104 C7 Nishiyoshino Japan
254 G3 Nísia Floresta Brazil
Nisibis Turkey see Nusaybin
104 E5 Nisiharu Japan
103 I14 Nisi-mera Japan
Nisiros i. Greece see Nisyros
140 S4 Niskanselkä l. Fin.
233 L6 Niskayuna NY U.S.A.
224 B1 Niskibi r. Ont. Can.
175 K5 Nisko Pol.
222 B2 Nisling r. Y.T. Can.
165 G8 Nismes Belgium
165 G8 Nismes, Forêt de for. Belgium
136 H6 Nisporeni Moldova
142 I5 Nissan r. Sweden
161 C10 Nissan-lez-Enserune France
142 E2 Nisser l. Norway
104 F5 Nisshin Japan
194 G8 Nissoria Sicilia Italy
142 E5 Nissum Bredning b. Denmark
164 I5 Nistelrode Neth.
136 J7 Nistru r. Moldova
alt. Dnister (Ukraine), conv. Dniester
136 I6 Nistrului Inferior, Cîmpia lowland Moldova
222 C2 Nisutlin r. Y.T. Can.
199 I6 Nisyros i. Greece
103 K11 Nita Japan
125 I2 Niṭā Saudi Arabia
103 G12 Nitchequon Que. Can.
225 G2 Nitchequon Que. Can.
Nitendi i. Santa Cruz Is Solomon Is see Ndeni
257 F5 Niterói Brazil
146 I12 Nith r. Scotland U.K.
146 I12 Nithsdale val. Scotland U.K.
93 D8 Nitibe East Timor
119 L3 Niti Pass Xizang China
84 D3 Nitmiluk National Park N.T. Austr.
177 H3 Nitra Slovakia
177 H3 Nitra r. Slovakia
177 H3 Nitriansko Pravno Slovakia
177 H3 Nitriansky kraj admin. reg. Slovakia
232 D10 Nitro WV U.S.A.
156 G8 Nitry France
103 J3 Nitta Japan
142 G1 Nittedal Norway
172 A2 Nittel Ger.
173 M3 Nittenau Ger.
173 L3 Nittendorf Ger.
Niua i. Vanuatu see Aniwa
77 I3 Niuafo'ou i. Tonga
Niuafu'ou i. Tonga see Niuafo'ou
77 I3 Niuatoputapu i. Tonga
79 □8a Niu 'Aunofo cliff Tongatapu Tonga
110 K7 Niubiziliang Qinghai China
81 □4 Niue terr. S. Pacific Ocean
Niujing Yunnan China see Binchuan
77 H3 Niulakita i. Tuvalu
108 D5 Niulan Jiang r. Yunnan China
240 □F13 Niuli'i HI U.S.A.
94 E5 Niur, Pulau i. Indon.
Niushan Jiangsu China see Donghai
77 H2 Niutao i. Tuvalu
109 L3 Niutoushan Anhui China
107 R6 Niuzhuang Liaoning China
140 R5 Nivala Fin.
140 V5 Nivastroy Rus. Fed.
85 K8 Nive watercourse Qld Austr.
163 B9 Nive r. France
85 K8 Nive Downs Qld Austr.
165 F7 Nivelles Belgium
175 I1 Nivenskoye Rus. Fed.
156 C2 Nivernais reg. France
160 D2 Nivernais, Canal du France
158 G6 Nivillac France
156 D5 Nivillers France
139 P8 Nivnoye Rus. Fed.
160 G5 Nivolas-Vermelle France
134 K3 Nivshera Rus. Fed.
140 V3 Nivskiy Rus. Fed.
116 E6 Niwai Rajasthan India
116 G7 Niwari Madh. Prad. India
116 H8 Niwas Madh. Prad. India
175 J5 Niwiska Pol.
157 J5 Nixéville-Blercourt France
Nixia Sichuan China see Sêrxü
240 M2 Nixon NV U.S.A.
Niya Xinjiang China see Minfeng
111 F8 Niya He r. China
129 J4 Niyazoba Azer.
95 H4 Niyut, Gunung mt. Indon.
139 S2 Niz Rus. Fed.
105 K4 Niza Japan
114 F3 Nizamabad Andhra Prad. India
114 G5 Nizampatnam Andhra Prad. India
114 E3 Nizam Sagar l. India
176 D2 Nižbor Czech Rep.
122 G2 Nizh Aydere Turkm.
134 I4 Nizhegorodskaya Oblast' admin. div. Rus. Fed.
131 L4 Nizhneangarsk Rus. Fed.
137 Q9 Nizhnebakanskiy Rus. Fed.
135 G6 Nizhnedevitsk Rus. Fed.
121 U1 Nizhnekamenka Rus. Fed.
134 J5 Nizhnekamsk Rus. Fed.
134 K5 Nizhnekamskoye Vodokhranilishche resr Rus. Fed.
131 R3 Nizhnekolymsk Rus. Fed.
139 Q1 Nizhne-Svirskiy Zapovednik nature res. Rus. Fed.
100 K3 Nizhnetambovskoye Rus. Fed.
98 G1 Nizhneudinsk Rus. Fed.
130 I3 Nizhnevartovsk Rus. Fed.
Nizhnevolzhsk Rus. Fed. see Narimanov
131 O2 Nizhneyansk Rus. Fed.
139 P9 Nizhneye Rus. Fed.
107 O1 Nizhneye Giryunino Rus. Fed.
134 L4 Nizhni Irginski Rus. Fed.
135 I6 Nizhniy Baskunchak Rus. Fed.
134 K2 Nizhniy Bugayevo Rus. Fed.
129 E2 Nizhniy Chegem Rus. Fed.
135 H6 Nizhniy Chir Rus. Fed.
129 I3 Nizhniy Dzhengutay Rus. Fed.
121 O3 Nizhniye Kayrakty Kazakh.
Nizhniye Kresty Rus. Fed. see Cherskiy
Nizhniye Ustriki Pol. see Ustrzyki Dolne
137 S3 Nizhniy Karabut Rus. Fed.
137 T3 Nizhniy Kislyay Rus. Fed.
129 F2 Nizhniy Kurp Rus. Fed.
135 H5 Nizhniy Lomov Rus. Fed.
137 T3 Nizhniy Mamon Rus. Fed.
134 H4 Nizhniy Novgorod Rus. Fed.
Nizhniy Novgorod Oblast admin. div. Rus. Fed. see Nizhegorodskaya Oblast'
134 K3 Nizhniy Odes Rus. Fed.
137 R3 Nizhniy Ol'shan Rus. Fed.
Nizhniy Pyandzh Tajik. see Panji Poyon
130 G4 Nizhniy Tagil Rus. Fed.
107 N1 Nizhniy Tsasuchey Rus. Fed.
134 I4 Nizhniy Yenangsk Rus. Fed.
134 J2 Nizhnyaya Kamenka Rus. Fed.
134 I2 Nizhnyaya Mola Rus. Fed.
134 K3 Nizhnyaya Omra Rus. Fed.
134 I2 Nizhnyaya Pesha Rus. Fed.
140 V3 Nizhnyaya Pirenga, Ozero l. Rus. Fed.
131 K4 Nizhnyaya Poyma Rus. Fed.
121 R1 Nizhnyaya Suyetka Rus. Fed.
129 C2 Nizhnyaya Teberda Rus. Fed.
131 J3 Nizhnyaya Tunguska r. Rus. Fed.
130 G4 Nizhnyaya Tura Rus. Fed.
137 R2 Nizhnyaya Veduga Rus. Fed.
134 H2 Nizhnyaya Zolotitsa Rus. Fed.
137 K2 Nizhyn Ukr.
126 H5 Nizip Turkey
139 N6 Nizkabor"ye Belarus
177 K2 Nízke Beskydy hills Slovakia
177 I3 Nízke Tatry mts Slovakia
177 I3 Nízke Tatry nat. park Slovakia
100 I7 Nizmennyy, Mys pt Rus. Fed.
177 J3 Nižná Slaná Slovakia
177 K3 Nižný Hrušov Slovakia
177 K3 Nižný Žipov Slovakia
Nizwá Oman see Nazwá
Nizza France see Nice
195 I8 Nizza di Sicilia Sicilia Italy
190 E6 Nizza Monferrato Italy
217 □3a Njazidja i. Comoros
196 G8 Njegoš mts Montenegro
Njellim Fin. see Nellim
213 F4 Njesuthi mt. Lesotho/S. Africa
211 C7 Njinjo Tanz.
191 R5 Njivice Croatia
209 E9 Njoko r. Zambia
211 B7 Njombe Tanz.
211 B6 Njombe r. Tanz.
78 □6 Njoroveto New Georgia Is Solomon Is
141 N5 Njurundabommen Sweden
141 N6 Njutånger Sweden
Nkai Zimbabwe see Nkayi
207 H5 Nkambe Cameroon
215 P4 Nkandla S. Africa
211 A6 Nkasi Tanz.
206 E5 Nkawkaw Ghana
213 F3 Nkayi Zimbabwe
207 D2 Nkhaïlé well Maur.
211 B7 Nkhata Bay Malawi
211 B8 Nkhotakota Malawi
211 B8 Nkhotakota Game Reserve nature res. Malawi
208 A4 Nkolabona Gabon
207 H5 Nkomfap Nigeria
208 A5 Nkomi, Lagune lag. Gabon
211 A6 Nkondwe Tanz.
207 H5 Nkongsamba Cameroon
206 E5 Nkoranza Ghana
207 I5 Nkoteng Cameroon
215 L6 Nkululeko S. Africa
211 A6 Nkundi Tanz.
211 A6 Nkungwi Tanz.
212 C3 Nkurenkuru Namibia
210 A4 Nkusi r. Uganda
215 P4 Nkwalini S. Africa
207 F4 Nkwanta Ghana
215 K9 Nkwenkwezi S. Africa
96 C2 Nmai Hka r. Myanmar
117 P6 Noa Dihing r. India
163 D7 Noaillan France
156 D5 Noailles France
163 A10 Noain Spain
117 M8 Noakhali Bangl.
191 M4 Noale Italy
185 L5 Noalejo Spain
117 J8 Noamundi Jharkhand India
164 G2 Noardburgum Neth.
190 C5 Noasca Italy
220 B3 Noatak r. AK U.S.A.
220 C3 Noatak National Preserve nature res. AK U.S.A.
148 D6 Nobber Ireland
103 I14 Nobeoka Japan
172 G1 Nobitz Ger.
183 N9 Noblejas Spain
230 D5 Noblesville IN U.S.A.
215 L7 Nobokwe S. Africa
102 S4 Noboribetsu Japan
253 F3 Nobres Brazil
85 I9 Noccundra Qld Austr.
159 M5 Nocé France
191 K3 Noce r. Italy
193 P8 Noce r. Italy
182 H3 Noceda Spain
193 N6 Nocera Inferiore Italy
193 Q9 Nocera Terinese Italy
193 J1 Nocera Umbra Italy
190 I6 Noceto Italy
244 E4 Nochistlán Mex.
245 J8 Nochixtlán Mex.
179 K3 Nöchling Austria
195 M2 Noci Italy
175 M1 Noćia r. Belarus/Lith.
195 O3 Nociglia Italy
234 E4 Nockamixon Lake PA U.S.A.
85 I9 Nockatunga Qld Austr.
83 J3 Nocoleche Nature Reserve N.S.W. Austr.
237 G9 Nocona TX U.S.A.
105 K4 Noda Japan
104 B4 Nodagawa Japan
259 D8 Nodales, Bahía de los b. Arg.
236 H6 Nodaway r. MO U.S.A.
142 D3 Nodeland Norway
160 I2 Nods France
163 G9 Noé France
163 B9 Noé France
253 E3 Noel Kempff Mercado, Parque Nacional nat. park Bol.
224 D4 Noelville Ont. Can.
214 E3 Noenieput S. Africa
193 Q7 Noepoli Italy
168 J2 Noer Ger.
261 F3 Noetinger Arg.
156 I3 Noeux-les-Mines France
183 L9 Noez Spain
163 L9 Noez, Pico de mt. Spain
183 N3 Nofuentes Spain
242 D2 Nogales Mex.
184 F3 Nogales Spain
239 I11 Nogales AZ U.S.A.
129 F2 Nogamirzin-Yurt Rus. Fed.
191 K5 Nogara Italy
163 D8 Nogaro France
174 H1 Nogat r. Pol.
103 H13 Nōgata Japan
Nogayk Ukr. see Prymors'ke
129 H1 Nogayskaya Step' reg. Rus. Fed.
120 F3 Nogayty Kazakh.
157 J7 Nogent France
159 L5 Nogent-le-Bernard France
156 C6 Nogent-le-Roi France
159 M5 Nogent-le-Rotrou France
157 J6 Nogent-sur-Aube France
156 D6 Nogent-sur-Marne France
156 D5 Nogent-sur-Oise France
156 G7 Nogent-sur-Seine France
156 F6 Nogent-sur-Vernisson France
105 K3 Nogi Japan
131 K3 Noginsk Evenkiyskiy Avtonomnyy Okrug Rus. Fed.
139 V6 Noginsk Moskovskaya Oblast' Rus. Fed.
100 M3 Nogliki Sakhalin Rus. Fed.
85 M8 Nogo r. Qld Austr.
85 L7 Nogoa r. Qld Austr.
104 E4 Nōgōhaku-san mt. Japan
106 I7 Nogon Toli Nei Mongol China
261 H3 Nogoyá Arg.
183 Q3 Nogoyá r. Arg.
177 I3 Nógrád Hungary
177 I3 Nógrád county Hungary
183 M6 Nograles Spain
104 G3 Noguchigorō-dake mt. Japan
182 G5 Nogueira, Serra de mts Port.
186 G4 Noguera reg. Spain
183 Q8 Noguera de Albarracín Spain
163 C9 Noguères France
183 Q3 Nogueruelas Spain
160 B2 Nohain r. France
243 O8 Nohalal Mex.
159 O8 Nohant-Vic France
116 E5 Nohar Rajasthan India
163 I10 Nohèdes, Réserve Naturelle de nature res. France
205 K5 Noheji Japan
172 C2 Nohfelden Ger.
163 G8 Nohic France
240 □B11 Nohili Point HI U.S.A.
106 D7 Nohoit Qinghai China
122 G2 Nohur Turkm.
182 C3 Noia Spain
195 L1 Noicattaro Italy
116 F5 Noida Uttar Prad. India
160 I1 Noidans-lès-Vesoul France
163 F8 Noilhan France
161 C8 Noir, Causse plat. France
227 R4 Noire r. Que. Can.
163 I9 Noire, Montagne mts France
180 E5 Noires, Pointe pt Morocco
158 D5 Noires, Montagnes hills France
160 D5 Noirétable France
158 G8 Noirmoutier, Île de i. France
158 G7 Noirmoutier-en-l'Île France
157 L5 Noisseville France
183 M2 Noja Spain
105 K6 Nojima-zaki c. Japan
105 H2 Nojiri-ko l. Japan
104 B7 Nokami Japan
232 H10 Nokesville VA U.S.A.
116 D6 Nokha Rajasthan India
123 J9 Nokhbur Pak.
122 I8 Nokhowch, Kūh-e mt. Iran
141 Q6 Nokia Fin.
Nökis Uzbek. see Nukus
123 J8 Nok Kundi Pak.
223 J5 Nokomis Sask. Can.
223 K3 Nokomis Lake Sask. Can.
202 B6 Nokou Chad
117 M7 Nokrek Peak Meghalaya India
142 I4 Nol Sweden
208 C4 Nola C.A.R.
194 H2 Nola Italy
160 F3 Nolay France
190 E7 Noli Italy
190 E7 Noli, Capo di c. Italy
231 F7 Nolichuky r. TN U.S.A.
134 J4 Nolinsk Rus. Fed.
214 G9 Noll S. Africa
142 D1 Nolsøy i. Faroe Is
103 H15 Noma-misaki pt Japan
233 O7 No Mans Land i. MA U.S.A.
183 L8 Nombela Spain
244 C2 Nombre de Dios Mex.
220 B3 Nome AK U.S.A.
215 O4 Nomgoma S. Africa
179 J7 Nomenj Slovenia
157 L6 Nomeny France
157 L7 Nomexy France
106 I5 Nomgon Mongolia
106 E8 Nomhon Qinghai China
106 D8 Nomhon He r. Qinghai China
108 G1 Nomin Gol r. China
107 S2 Nonoi Islands Micronesia see Mortlock Islands
215 K7 Nomonde S. Africa
78 □4a Nomoneas is Chuuk Micronesia
103 G14 Nomo-zaki pt Japan
106 I1 Nomto Rus. Fed.
104 G3 Nomugi-tōge pass Japan
77 I4 Nomuka Tonga
79 □8 Nomuka i. Tonga
79 □8 Nomuka Group is Tonga
79 □8 Nomuka Iki i. Tonga
91 L5 Nomwin atoll Micronesia
134 H4 Nomzha Rus. Fed.
223 I2 Nonacho Lake N.W.T. Can.
156 B6 Nonancourt France
159 L4 Nonant-le-Pin France
191 K6 Nonantola Italy
186 F5 Nonaspe Spain
215 O4 Nondweni S. Africa
156 D5 Nonette r. France
100 D6 Nong'an Jilin China
96 G5 Nông Hêt Laos
97 F7 Nong Hong Thai.
Nonghui Sichuan China see Guang'an
117 M7 Nongkha Meghalaya India
96 F6 Nong Khai Thai.
215 P3 Nongoma S. Africa
117 M7 Nongpoh Meghalaya India
117 M7 Nongstoin Meghalaya India
161 E7 Nonières France
172 D5 Nonnenweier Ger.
Nonni r. China see Nen Jiang
82 F5 Nonning S.A. Austr.
172 B2 Nonnweiler Ger.
250 B5 Nono Ecuador
255 B8 Nonoai Brazil
242 F4 Nonoava Mex.
104 E2 Nonoichi Japan
77 H2 Nonouti atoll Gilbert Is Kiribati
260 A5 Nonquén Chile
101 E10 Nonsan S. Korea
231 □1 Nonsuch Island Bermuda
97 E7 Nonthaburi Thai.
162 F4 Nontron France
192 C2 Nonza Corse France
214 I6 Nonzwakazi S. Africa
138 J3 Nõo Estonia
87 D9 Nookawarra W.A. Austr.
82 F2 Noolyeanna Lake salt flat S.A. Austr.
84 C2 Noonamah N.T. Austr.
87 E10 Noondie, Lake salt flat W.A. Austr.
86 H5 Noonkanbah W.A. Austr.
86 H5 Noonkanbah Aboriginal Reserve W.A. Austr.
83 H4 Noonthorangee Range hills N.S.W. Austr.
85 J9 Noorama Creek watercourse Qld Austr.
164 E5 Noordbeveland i. Neth.
164 H5 Noord-Brabant prov. Neth.
164 K2 Noordbroek-Uiterburen Neth.
164 G3 Noorderhaaks i. Neth.
164 G3 Noord-Holland prov. Neth.
164 G3 Noordhollands Duinreservaat nature res. Neth.
215 P1 Noordkaap S. Africa
214 C8 Noordoewer S. Africa
214 B4 Noordoewer Namibia
164 I3 Noordoost Polder Neth.
247 □10 Noordpunt pt Curaçao Neth. Antilles
164 F4 Noordwijk aan Zee Neth.
164 F4 Noordwijk-Binnen Neth.
164 F4 Noordwijkerhout Neth.
164 J3 Noordwolde Neth.
141 P6 Noormarkku Fin.
220 B3 Noorvik AK U.S.A.
85 N9 Noosa Heads Qld Austr.
164 F4 Nootdorp Neth.
222 E5 Nootka Island B.C. Can.
245 K9 Nopala Mex.
245 J7 Nopaltepec Mex.
223 M5 Nopiming Provincial Park Man. Can.
260 D2 Noqueves Arg.
209 B6 Nóqui Angola
193 H8 Nora r. Italy
180 F3 Nora r. Rus. Fed.
143 L2 Nora Sweden
192 B7 Noragugume Sardegna Italy
122 H1 Norak Tajik.
123 M2 Norak, Obanbori resr Tajik.
Norakert Armenia see Bagharyan
92 E8 Norala Mindanao Phil.
224 E3 Noranda Que. Can.
Nor-Bayazet Armenia see Gavarr
143 L1 Norberg Sweden
261 H4 Norberto de la Riestra Arg.
111 G11 Norcang Xizang China
193 K2 Norcia Italy
233 □Q3 Norcross ME U.S.A.
207 I4 Nord prov. Cameroon
156 F3 Nord dept France
Nord Greenland see Station Nord
156 F3 Nord, Canal du France
217 □3a Nord, Pointe pt Njazidja Comoros
217 □3b Nord, Récif du rf Mayotte
140 □ Nordaustlandet i. Svalbard
142 F6 Nordborg Denmark
143 K6 Nord-Bornholm nature res. Bornholm Denmark
140 Q2 Nordbotn Norway
142 G6 Nordby Denmark
168 D3 Norddeich Ger.
168 F1 Norddorf Ger.
222 G4 Nordegg Alta Can.
168 D3 Norden Ger.
168 F2 Nordendorf Ger.
168 F4 Nordenham Ger.
131 K2 Nordenshel'da, Arkhipelag is Rus. Fed.
222 B2 Nordenskiold r. Y.T. Can.
140 □ Nordenskiöld Land reg. Svalbard
Nordenskjold Archipelago is Rus. Fed. see Nordenshel'da, Arkhipelag
168 G2 Norder Hever sea chan. Ger.
168 D3 Norderland reg. Ger.
168 D3 Norderney Ger.
168 D3 Norderney i. Ger.
168 F1 Norderoogsand i. Ger.
168 J3 Norderstedt Ger.
216 □1b Nordeste São Miguel Azores
216 □1b Nordestinho São Miguel Azores
140 U1 Nordfjord Norway
141 H6 Nordfjord reg. Norway
141 H6 Nordfjordeid Norway
140 □ Nordfjorden inlet Svalbard
140 M3 Nordfold Norway
168 F1 Nordfriesische Inseln is Ger.
168 G1 Nordfriesland reg. Ger.
171 D6 Nordgermersleben Ger.
171 E10 Nordhalben Ger.
168 F2 Nordhastedt Ger.
169 K8 Nordhausen Ger.
172 G3 Nordheim Ger.
168 G3 Nordholz Ger.
169 D6 Nordhorn Ger.
142 B2 Nordhuglo Norway
140 O5 Nordingrå naturreservat nature res. Sweden
142 F5 Nordjylland county Denmark
Nordkapp c. Iceland see Horn
140 R1 Nordkapp c. Norway
140 S1 Nordkinnhalvøya i. Norway
169 E7 Nordkirchen Ger.
208 F5 Nord-Kivu prov. Dem. Rep. Congo
140 O1 Nordkvaløy i. Norway
140 M3 Nordland county Norway
168 G3 Nordleda Ger.
140 L4 Nordli Norway
173 M2 Nördlicher Oberpfälzer Wald park Ger.
169 K7 Nördliches Harzvorland park Ger.
173 I4 Nördlingen Ger.
140 O3 Nordmaling Sweden
142 D1 Nordmannslågen l. Norway
140 P2 Nordmannvik Norway
168 G1 Nordmarsch-Langeness i. Ger.
221 O2 Nord-og Østgrønland, Nationalparken i nat. park Greenland
168 H2 Nord-Ostsee-Kanal canal Ger.
207 H5 Nord-Ouest prov. Cameroon
130 A3 Nordøyar i. Faroe Is
156 E3 Nord-Pas-de-Calais admin. reg. France
156 F3 Nord-Pas-de-Calais, Parc Naturel Régional du nature res. France
172 D2 Nordpfälzer Bergland reg. Ger.
Nordre Strømfjord inlet Greenland see Nassuttooq
169 D8 Nordrhein-Westfalen land Ger.
169 I6 Nordstemmen Ger.
168 G1 Nordstrand pen. Ger.
168 G1 Nordstrandischmoor i. Ger.
140 L4 Nord-Trøndelag county Norway
140 □D1 Norðurland eystra constituency Iceland
140 □C1 Norðurland vestra constituency Iceland
131 M2 Nordvik Rus. Fed.
140 J5 Nordvika Norway
169 D6 Nordwalde Ger.
147 I8 Nore r. Ireland
163 I9 Nore, Pic de mt. France
Noreg country Europe see Norway
138 G7 Noreikiškės Lith.
182 I3 Noreña Spain
142 F1 Noresund Norway
186 L3 Norfeu, Cap de c. Spain
151 N2 Norfolk admin. div. England U.K.
236 G4 Norfolk NE U.S.A.
233 K4 Norfolk NY U.S.A.
233 I12 Norfolk VA U.S.A.
82 □1 Norfolk Island terr. S. Pacific Ocean
266 G7 Norfolk Island Ridge sea feature Tasman Sea
237 I7 Norfork Lake AR U.S.A.
164 J2 Norg Neth.
Norge country Europe see Norway
149 M2 Norham Northumberland, England U.K.
Norheimsund Norway
142 C1 Noria Chile
252 C5 Noria de Ángeles Mex.
244 F3 Norias Mex.
244 E1 Norikura-dake vol. Japan
104 G3 Noril'sk Rus. Fed.
130 J3 Norino Rus. Fed.
137 M1 Norkyung Xizang China
111 I12 Norland Ont. Can.
227 P5 Norma Italy
193 J4 Norma NJ U.S.A.
234 E6 Norma Co l. Xizang China
111 I10 Normal IL U.S.A.
226 F9 Norman r. Qld Austr.
85 H4 Norman OK U.S.A.
237 G8 Norman, Lake resr NC U.S.A.
231 G8 Norman r. Qld Austr.
85 J3 Normanby r. Qld Austr.
80 I6 Normanby North I. N.Z.
91 L8 Normanby Island P.N.G.
85 M7 Normanby Range hills Qld Austr.
Normandes, Îles is English Chan. see Channel Islands
251 G4 Normandia Brazil
159 J4 Normandie reg. France
159 J4 Normandie, Collines de hills France
159 K5 Normandie-Maine, Parc Naturel Régional nature res. France
215 N3 Normandien S. Africa
Normandy reg. France see Normandie
85 H4 Normanton Qld Austr.
149 O6 Normanton West Yorkshire, England U.K.
82 G6 Normanville S.A. Austr.
222 E1 Norman Wells N.W.T. Can.
227 O1 Normétal Que. Can.
87 D13 Normalup W.A. Austr.
78 □6 Noro New Georgia Is Solomon Is
242 E4 Norogachic Mex.
160 I1 Noroy-le-Bourg France
223 K5 Norquay Sask. Can.
260 B5 Norquín Arg.
259 C6 Norquinco Arg.
143 L1 Norra Barken l. Sweden
143 N2 Norra Björkfjärden b. Sweden
140 P4 Norra Bredåker Sweden
140 P5 Norra gloppet b. Fin.
140 M4 Norråker Sweden
140 P5 Norra Kvarken str. Fin./Sweden
143 O2 Norra Ljusterö i. Sweden
140 O3 Norrbotten county Sweden
142 F5 Norreå r. Denmark
142 H7 Nørre Alslev Denmark
168 I1 Nørreballe Denmark
142 E5 Nørre Lyndelse Denmark
142 E6 Nørre Nebel Denmark
156 D2 Norrent-Fontes France
142 F6 Nørre Snede Denmark
140 P4 Norrfjärden Sweden
143 K1 Norr Hörken l. Sweden
140 N2 Norrhult-Klavreström Sweden
232 B12 Norris Lake TN U.S.A.
234 E4 Norristown PA U.S.A.
143 M3 Norrköping Sweden
141 N6 Norrsundet Sweden
143 O2 Norrtälje Sweden
87 F12 Norseman W.A. Austr.
80 K7 Norsewood North I. N.Z.
142 F2 Norsjø l. Norway
140 O4 Norsjö Sweden
100 F2 Norsk Rus. Fed.
221 Q2 Norske Øer is Greenland
78 □5 Norsup Vanuatu
251 I4 Norte, Cabo c. Brazil
251 I4 Norte, Canal do sea chan. Brazil
247 □1 Norte, Cayo i. Puerto Rico
261 I5 Norte, Punta pt Arg.
259 C8 Norte, Punta pt Arg.
259 E8 Norte, Punta pt Arg.
216 □3e Norte, Punta pt El Hierro Canary Is
253 F2 Norte, Serra do hills Brazil
261 E2 Norte, Sierra de mts Arg.
250 C2 Norte de Santander dept Col.
216 □1c Norte Grande São Jorge Azores
253 F3 Nortelândia Brazil
169 I7 Nörten-Hardenberg Ger.
216 □1c Norte Pequeno São Jorge Azores
263 L2 North, Cape Antarctica
225 I4 North, Cape N.S. Can.
233 L6 North Adams MA U.S.A.
149 O5 Northallerton North Yorkshire, England U.K.
87 D11 Northam W.A. Austr.
150 D5 Northam Devon, England U.K.
218 North America continent
233 □R3 North Amity ME U.S.A.
87 C10 Northampton W.A. Austr.
151 K3 Northampton Northamptonshire, England U.K.
233 M6 Northampton MA U.S.A.
234 E3 Northampton PA U.S.A.
234 E3 Northampton County county PA U.S.A.
85 J8 Northampton Downs Qld Austr.
151 K3 Northamptonshire admin. div. England U.K.
115 M6 North Andaman i. Andaman & Nicobar Is India
232 H11 North Anna r. VA U.S.A.
233 □P4 North Anson ME U.S.A.
222 H2 North Arm b. N.W.T. Can.
225 I1 North Aulatsivik Island Nfld and Lab. Can.
265 L5 North Australian Basin sea feature Indian Ocean
146 G11 North Ayrshire admin. div. Scotland U.K.
151 J6 North Baddesley Hampshire, England U.K.
92 E5 North Balabac Strait Phil.
232 B7 North Baltimore OH U.S.A.
223 I4 North Battleford Sask. Can.
224 E4 North Bay Ont. Can.
224 E1 North Belcher Islands Nunavut Can.
238 B5 North Bend OR U.S.A.
232 H7 North Bend PA U.S.A.
233 L5 North Bennington VT U.S.A.
235 G3 North Bergen NJ U.S.A.
146 K10 North Berwick East Lothian, Scotland U.K.
233 □O5 North Berwick ME U.S.A.
North Borneo state Malaysia see Sabah
237 G10 North Bosque r. TX U.S.A.
83 J6 North Bourke N.S.W. Austr.
227 K6 North Branch MI U.S.A.
226 B4 North Branch MN U.S.A.
234 F3 North Branch NJ U.S.A.
235 J2 North Branford CT U.S.A.
246 I3 North Caicos i. Turks and Caicos Is
237 H8 North Canadian r. OK U.S.A.
225 H4 North Cape c. P.E.I. Can.
North Cape c. Norway see Nordkapp
80 H1 North Cape c. North I. N.Z.
259 □ North Cape c. S. Georgia
226 F7 North Cape WI U.S.A.
220 A4 North Cape c. AK U.S.A.
234 F7 North Cape May NJ U.S.A.
224 B2 North Caribou Lake Ont. Can.
231 H7 North Carolina state U.S.A.
238 D2 North Cascades National Park WA U.S.A.
234 E3 North Catasauqua PA U.S.A.
149 P6 North Cave East Riding of Yorkshire, England U.K.
231 □2 North Cay i. New Prov. Bahamas
86 I7 North Central Aboriginal Reserve W.A. Austr.
224 D4 North Channel lake channel Ont. Can.
146 D12 North Channel Northern Ireland/Scotland U.K.
231 H9 North Charleston SC U.S.A.
150 H5 North Cheriton Somerset, England U.K.
238 K4 North Cheyenne Indian Reservation res. MT U.S.A.
87 D13 Northcliffe W.A. Austr.
263 G2 Northcliffe Glacier Antarctica
232 G6 North Collins NY U.S.A.
237 E10 North Concho r. TX U.S.A.
233 □N4 North Conway NH U.S.A.
North Cousin Islet i. Inner Islands Seychelles see Cousin
225 F2 North Cowichan B.C. Can.
149 N5 North Cowton North Yorkshire, England U.K.
233 L5 North Creek NY U.S.A.
236 E2 North Dakota state U.S.A.
146 D6 North Dell Western Isles, Scotland U.K.
150 G6 North Dorset Downs hills England U.K.
151 K5 North Downs hills England U.K.
149 P6 North Duffield North Yorkshire, England U.K.
213 E4 North-East admin. dist. Botswana
234 D5 North East MD U.S.A.
232 F6 North East PA U.S.A.
216 □2a North East Bay Ascension S. Atlantic Ocean
85 N6 North East Cay rf Coral Sea Is Terr. Austr.
210 D4 North Eastern prov. Kenya
North-East Frontier Agency state India see Arunachal Pradesh
149 Q6 North East Lincolnshire admin. div. England U.K.
267 I4 Northeast Pacific Basin sea feature Pacific Ocean
246 G2 Northeast Point Acklins I. Bahamas
246 G2 Northeast Point Gt Inagua Bahamas
86 □1 North East Point Christmas I.
246 □ Northeast Point Jamaica
246 E1 Northeast Providence Channel Bahamas
240 O6 North Edwards CA U.S.A.
169 I7 Northeim Ger.
151 N2 North Elmham Norfolk, England U.K.
North Rhine - Westphalia land Ger. see Nordrhein-Westfalen
231 J13 North End Point Bahamas
92 □ North Entrance sea chan. Palau
206 E4 Northern admin. reg. Ghana
211 B7 Northern admin. reg. Malawi
206 C4 Northern prov. Sierra Leone
203 F4 Northern state Sudan
209 F7 Northern prov. Zambia
Northern Aegean admin. reg. Greece see Voreio Aigaio
123 O3 Northern Areas admin. div. Pak.
208 E2 Northern Bahr el Ghazal state Sudan
214 D5 Northern Cape prov. S. Africa
81 □2 Northern Cook Islands Cook Is
202 E5 Northern Darfur state Sudan
Northern Donets r. Rus. Fed. see Severskiy Donets
Northern Dvina r. Rus. Fed. see Severnaya Dvina
223 L3 Northern Indian Lake Man. Can.
147 I3 Northern Ireland prov. U.K.
203 F6 Northern Kordofan state Sudan
77 I3 Northern Lau Group is Fiji
224 B3 Northern Light Lake Ont. Can.
91 J3 Northern Mariana Islands terr. N. Pacific Ocean
Northern Pindus Mountains Greece see Voreia Pindos
86 □1 Northern Plateau Christmas I.
247 □7 Northern Range hills Trin. and Tob.
Northern Rhodesia country Africa see Zambia
222 E3 Northern Rocky Mountains Provincial Park nat. park B.C. Can.
Northern Sporades is Greece see Voreies Sporades
84 D4 Northern Territory admin. div. Austr.
Northern Transvaal prov. S. Africa see Limpopo
146 L9 North Esk r. Angus, Scotland U.K.
236 J6 North Fabius r. MO U.S.A.
149 P6 North Ferriby East Riding of Yorkshire, England U.K.
233 M6 Northfield MA U.S.A.
226 A5 Northfield MN U.S.A.
234 F6 Northfield NJ U.S.A.
233 M4 Northfield VT U.S.A.
226 C5 Northfield WI U.S.A.
151 M5 Northfleet Kent, England U.K.
235 J2 Northford CT U.S.A.
151 O5 North Foreland c. England U.K.
240 M4 North Fork CA U.S.A.
241 J7 North Fox Island MI U.S.A.
235 K1 North Franklin CT U.S.A.
224 D3 North French r. Ont. Can.
247 □2 North Friar's Bay St Kitts and Nevis
North Frisian Islands Ger. see Nordfriesische Inseln
221 K2 North Geomagnetic Pole Nunavut Can.
149 P5 North Grimston North Yorkshire, England U.K.
235 J2 North Haven CT U.S.A.
233 □S4 North Head N.B. Can.
80 I3 North Head hd North I. N.Z.
82 □3 North Head hd S. Pacific Ocean
223 L2 North Henik Lake Nunavut Can.
233 L4 North Hero VT U.S.A.
240 K3 North Highlands CA U.S.A.
210 C4 North Horr Kenya
233 L5 North Hudson NY U.S.A.
149 P7 North Hykeham Lincolnshire, England U.K.
151 L3 Northill Bedfordshire, England U.K.
84 F3 North Island N.T. Austr.
87 B10 North Island W.A. Austr.
114 C7 North Island India
80 H5 North Island N.Z.
92 C1 North Island Phil.
217 □2a North Island Inner Islands Seychelles
92 C7 North Islet rf Phil.
241 V6 North Jadito Canyon gorge AZ U.S.A.
226 H8 North Judson IN U.S.A.
North Kazakhstan Oblast admin. div. Kazakh. see Severnyy Kazakhstan
86 □2 North Keeling Island Cocos Is
85 J3 North Kennedy r. Qld Austr.
146 H7 North Kessock Highland, Scotland U.K.
232 E7 North Kingsville OH U.S.A.
223 M3 North Knife r. Man. Can.
223 M3 North Knife Lake Man. Can.
117 I7 North Koel r. Jharkhand India
241 U9 North Komelik AZ U.S.A.
101 E8 North Korea country Asia
117 O6 North Lakhimpur Assam India
146 I11 North Lanarkshire admin. div. Scotland U.K.
80 I2 Northland admin. reg. North I. N.Z.
North Land is Rus. Fed. see Severnaya Zemlya
80 H2 Northland Forest Park nature res. North I. N.Z.
241 Q5 North Las Vegas NV U.S.A.
151 I4 Northleach Gloucestershire, England U.K.
226 H8 North Liberty IN U.S.A.
232 E8 North Lima OH U.S.A.
149 P6 North Lincolnshire admin. div. England U.K.
237 I8 North Little Rock AR U.S.A.
235 F5 North Loup r. NE U.S.A.
211 B7 North Luangwa National Park Zambia
222 C2 North Macmillan r. Y.T. Can.
235 J2 North Madison CT U.S.A.
221 F1 North Magnetic Pole Arctic Ocean
113 □1 North Male Atoll Maldives
239 K7 North Mam Peak CO U.S.A.
226 I9 North Manchester IN U.S.A.
226 H4 North Manitou Island MI U.S.A.
232 A10 North Middletown KY U.S.A.
150 E5 North Molton Devon, England U.K.
223 K4 North Moose Lake Man. Can.
234 C2 North Mountain mts PA U.S.A.
86 C6 North Muiron Island W.A. Austr.
222 F2 North Nahanni r. N.W.T. Can.
246 □ North Negril Point Jamaica
227 M8 North Olmsted OH U.S.A.
236 H2 Northome MN U.S.A.
North Ossetia aut. rep. Rus. Fed. see Severnaya Osetiya-Alaniya, Respublika
240 N4 North Palisade mt. CA U.S.A.
236 E5 North Platte NE U.S.A.
236 E5 North Platte r. NE U.S.A.
87 C11 North Point W.A. Austr.
247 □4 North Point H.K. China see Tsat Tsze Mui
216 □2a North Point Ascension S. Atlantic Ocean
216 □2c North Point Tristan da Cunha S. Atlantic Ocean
217 □2b North Point Mahé Seychelles
268 A1 North Pole POLE Arctic Ocean
231 D9 Northport AL U.S.A.
231 F12 North Port FL U.S.A.
226 I3 Northport MI U.S.A.
149 K1 North Queensferry Fife, Scotland U.K.
115 M6 North Reef Island Andaman & Nicobar Is India
North Rhine - Westphalia land Ger. see Nordrhein-Westfalen
241 T5 North Rim AZ U.S.A.
225 I4 North River Bridge N.S. Can.
82 □2 North Rock i. Lord Howe I. Austr.
146 □N1 North Roe Shetland, Scotland U.K.
North Rona i. Western Isles, Scotland U.K. see Rona
146 L4 North Ronaldsay i. Scotland U.K.
146 L4 North Ronaldsay Firth sea chan. Scotland U.K.
238 C4 North Santiam r. OR U.S.A.
223 J4 North Saskatchewan r. Alta/Sask. Can.
241 R2 North Schell Peak NV U.S.A.
144 H3 North Sea sea Europe
235 K3 North Sea NY U.S.A.
223 L3 North Seal r. Man. Can.
115 M7 North Sentinel Island Andaman & Nicobar Is India
149 O3 North Shields Tyne and Wear, England U.K.
223 L5 North Shoal Lake Man. Can.
240 O2 North Shoshone Peak NV U.S.A.
North Siberian Lowland Rus. Fed. see Severo-Sibirskaya Nizmennost'

North Simlipal National Park India
North Sinai governorate Egypt see Shamāl Sīnā'
North Slope plain AK U.S.A.
North Somercotes Lincolnshire, England U.K.
North Somerset admin. div. England U.K.
North Sound sea chan. Ireland
North Spirit Lake Ont. Can.
North Stradbroke Island Qld Austr.
North Stratford NH U.S.A.
North Sunderland Northumberland, England U.K.
North Taranaki Bight b. North I. N.Z.
North Thompson r. B.C. Can.
North Thoresby Lincolnshire, England U.K.
Northton Western Isles, Scotland U.K.
North Tonawanda NY U.S.A.
North Trap rf South I. N.Z.
North Troy VT U.S.A.
North Truro MA U.S.A.
North Tuas Basin dock Sing.
North Twin Island Nunavut Can.
North Twin Lake Nfld and Lab. Can.
North Tyne r. England U.K.
North Ubian i. Phil.
North Ugie r. Scotland U.K.
North Uist i. Scotland U.K.
Northumberland admin. div. England U.K.
Northumberland PA U.S.A.
Northumberland County county PA U.S.A.
Northumberland Isles Qld Austr.
Northumberland National Park England U.K.
Northumberland Strait Can.
North Umpqua r. OR U.S.A.
North Vancouver B.C. Can.
North Verde i. Phil.
Northville NY U.S.A.
North Wabasca Lake Alta Can.
North Wales PA U.S.A.
North Walsham Norfolk, England U.K.
North Waterford ME U.S.A.
North Weald Bassett Essex, England U.K.
North West prov. S. Africa
Northwest Atlantic Mid-Ocean Channel N. Atlantic Ocean
North West Bay Mahé Seychelles see Beau Vallon, Baie
North West Bluff c. Montserrat
North West Cape W.A. Austr.
North Westchester CT U.S.A.
North-Western prov. Zambia
North West Frontier prov. Pak.
North West Nelson Forest Park nat. park South I. N.Z. see Kahurangi National Park
Northwest Pacific Basin sea feature N. Pacific Ocean
North West Point Christmas I.
Northwest Providence Channel Bahamas
North West River Nfld and Lab. Can.
Northwest Territories admin. div. Can.
Northwich Cheshire, England U.K.
North Wichita r. TX U.S.A.
North Wildwood NJ U.S.A.
North Windham CT U.S.A.
North Windham ME U.S.A.
Northwind Ridge sea feature Arctic Ocean
North Wingfield Derbyshire, England U.K.
Northwood Isle of Wight, England U.K.
Northwood IA U.S.A.
Northwood ND U.S.A.
Northwood NH U.S.A.
Northwoods Beach WI U.S.A.
North York Ont. Can.
North York Moors moorland England U.K.
North York Moors National Park England U.K.
North Yorkshire admin. div. England U.K.
Nortmoor Ger.
Norton N.B. Can.
Norton North Yorkshire, England U.K.
Norton Suffolk, England U.K.
Norton KS U.S.A.
Norton VA U.S.A.
Norton VT U.S.A.
Norton Zimbabwe
Norton Canes Staffordshire, England U.K.
Norton de Matos Angola see Balombo
Norton Fitzwarren Somerset, England U.K.
Norton Shores MI U.S.A.
Norton Sound sea chan. AK U.S.A.
Nortorf Ger.
Nortrup Ger.
Nort-sur-Erdre France
Norumbega Arg.
Norvegia, Cape Antarctica
Norwalk CT U.S.A.
Norwalk OH U.S.A.
Norwalk WI U.S.A.
Norwalk r. CT U.S.A.
Norway country Europe
Norway ME U.S.A.
Norway Bay Que. Can.
Norway House Man. Can.
Norwegian Basin sea feature N. Atlantic Ocean
Norwegian Bay Nunavut Can.
Norwegian Sea N. Atlantic Ocean
Norwich Ont. Can.
Norwich Norfolk, England U.K.
Norwich CT U.S.A.
Norwich NY U.S.A.
Norwick Shetland, Scotland U.K.
Norwood MA U.S.A.
Norwood NC U.S.A.
Norwood NY U.S.A.
Norwood OH U.S.A.
Norzagaray Luzon Phil.
Nosaka Japan
Nosapu-misaki pt Japan
Nose Japan
Nosegawa Japan
Nose Lake Nunavut Can.
Noshappu-misaki hd Japan
Noshiro Japan
Noshul' Rus. Fed.
Nosivka Ukr.
Noskivtsi Ukr.
Noskovo Rus. Fed.
Nosop watercourse Botswana alt. Nossob (Namibia/S. Africa)
Nosovaya Rus. Fed.
Nosovka Ukr. see Nosivka
Noşratābād Iran
Noss, Isle of i. Scotland U.K.
Nossan r. Sweden
Nossa Senhora da Boa Fé Port.
Nossa Senhora da Glória Brazil
Nossa Senhora da Graça de Póvoa e Meadas Port.
Nossa Senhora da Graça do Divor Port.
Nossa Senhora das Neves Port.
Nossa Senhora da Torega Port.
Nossa Senhora de Machede Port.
253 F3 Nossa Senhora do Livramento Brazil
216 □1b Nossa Senhora dos Remédios São Miguel Azores
142 I3 Nossebro Sweden
171 H8 Nossen Ger.
170 G3 Nossendorf Ger.
170 F3 Nossentiner Hütte Ger.
146 J6 Noss Head Scotland U.K.
214 E2 Nossob watercourse Namibia/S. Africa alt. Nosop (Botswana)
214 E1 Nossob Camp S. Africa
206 D3 Nossombougou Mali
213 □K4 Nosy Varika Madag.
176 G4 Noszlop Hungary
177 J4 Noszvaj Hungary
140 U2 Nota r. Fin./Rus. Fed.
Notabile Malta see Mdina
225 I1 Notakwanon r. Nfld and Lab. Can.
193 L2 Notaresco Italy
241 S2 Notch Peak UT U.S.A.
174 D3 Noteć r. Pol.
174 F2 Notecki, Kanał canal Pol.
198 C3 Notia Pindos mts Greece
222 G3 Notikewin r. Alta Can.
177 I4 Nőtincs Hungary
198 H6 Notio Aigaio admin. reg. Greece
Nótion Aiyaíon admin. reg. Greece see Notio Aigaio
198 E4 Notios Evvoïkos Kolpos sea chan. Greece
198 B3 Notio Steno Kerkyras sea chan. Greece
138 E2 Nötö Fin.
195 I10 Noto Sicilia Italy
104 F1 Noto Japan
195 I10 Noto, Golfo di g. Sicilia Italy
142 F2 Notodden Norway
104 D5 Notogawa Japan
104 E1 Noto-hantō pen. Japan
104 E1 Noto-hantō Kokutei-kōen park Japan
104 F1 Notojima Japan
104 F1 Noto-jima i. Japan
102 V2 Notoro-ko l. Japan
179 J8 Notranje Gorice Slovenia
225 G4 Notre Dame, Monts mts Que. Can.
225 K3 Notre Dame Bay Nfld and Lab. Can.
159 M3 Notre-Dame-de-Gravenchon France
Notre-Dame-de-Koartac Que. Can. see Quaqtaq
227 S4 Notre-Dame-de-la-Salette Que. Can.
158 G8 Notre-Dame-de-Monts France
158 H8 Notre-Dame-de-Riez France
162 F5 Notre-Dame-de-Sanilhac France
233 □N3 Notre-Dame-des-Bois Que. Can.
159 M7 Notre-Dame-d'Oé France
227 S3 Notre-Dame-du-Laus Que. Can.
227 O2 Notre-Dame-du-Nord Que. Can.
179 I6 Nötsch im Gailtal Austria
207 F5 Notsé Togo
103 I13 Notsu Japan
102 W3 Notsuke-saki pt Japan
102 W3 Notsuke-suidō sea chan. Japan/Rus. Fed.
227 N5 Nottawasaga Bay Ont. Can.
224 E3 Nottaway r. Que. Can.
168 I4 Nottensdorf Ger.
151 J2 Nottingham Nottingham, England U.K.
151 J2 Nottingham admin. div. England U.K.
234 C5 Nottingham PA U.S.A.
151 J2 Nottingham East Midlands airport England U.K.
221 K3 Nottingham Island Nunavut Can.
215 O5 Nottingham Road S. Africa
149 P7 Nottinghamshire admin. div. England U.K.
232 G11 Nottoway VA U.S.A.
232 I12 Nottoway r. VA U.S.A.
169 D7 Nottuln Ger.
223 J5 Notukeu Creek r. Sask. Can.
105 G1 Nou Japan
208 C4 Nouabalé-Ndoki, Parc National nat. park Congo
204 A5 Nouâdhibou Maur.
204 A5 Nouâdhibou, Râs c. Maur.
206 B2 Nouakchott Maur.
206 D2 Noual well Maur.
206 A2 Nouâmghâr Maur.
159 P6 Nouan-le-Fuzelier France
159 N7 Nouans-les-Fontaines France
157 J5 Nouart France
96 H7 Nouei Vietnam
206 B2 Noueïch well Maur.
78 □5 Nouméa New Caledonia
207 H5 Noun r. Cameroon
206 E3 Nouna Burkina
146 J4 Noup Head Scotland U.K.
215 I7 Noupoort S. Africa
215 M4 Noupoortsnek pass S. Africa
140 T3 Nousu Fin.
Nouveau-Comptoir Que. Can. see Wemindji
Nouvelle Anvers Dem. Rep. Congo see Makanza
78 □5 Nouvelle Calédonie i. S. Pacific Ocean
Nouvelle Calédonie terr. S. Pacific Ocean see New Caledonia
Nouvelles Hébrides country S. Pacific Ocean see Vanuatu
156 C3 Nouvion France
158 H5 Nouvoitou France
159 M6 Nouzilly France
156 I4 Nouzonville France
123 M1 Nov Tajik.
138 G2 Nõva Estonia
176 F5 Nova Hungary
257 G4 Nova Almeida Brazil
254 C5 Nova América Brazil
256 A5 Nova Andradina Brazil
137 R4 Nova Astrakhan' Ukr.
256 C3 Nova Aurora Brazil
Novabad Tajik. see Novobod
177 H3 Nová Baňa Slovakia
136 H3 Nova Borova Ukr.
176 E2 Nová Bystřice Czech Rep.
209 B6 Nova Caipemba Angola
256 A6 Nova Cantu Brazil
Nova Chaves Angola see Muconda
197 L5 Novaci Romania
196 I5 Nova Crnja Vojvodina Serbia
254 G3 Nova Cruz Brazil
177 H3 Nová Dubnica Slovakia
257 F3 Nova Era Brazil
Nova Esperança Angola see Buengas
256 A5 Nova Esperança Brazil
191 M8 Novafeltria Italy
Nova Freixa Moz. see Cuamba
257 F5 Nova Friburgo Brazil
Nova Gaia Angola see Cambundi-Catembo
Nova Goa Goa India see Panaji
213 G4 Nova Golegã Moz.
188 D3 Nova Gorica Slovenia
188 F3 Nova Gradiška Croatia
256 C4 Nova Granada Brazil
137 M4 Nova Haleshchyna Ukr.
257 F5 Nova Iguaçu Brazil
137 M7 Nova Kakhovka Ukr.
137 M6 Nova Kam"yanka Ukr.
177 H3 Nováky Slovakia
160 H5 Novalaise France
186 E3 Novales Spain
191 L3 Nova Levante Italy
257 F3 Nova Lima Brazil
Nova Lisboa Angola see Huambo
191 R6 Novalja Croatia
256 A5 Nova Londrina Brazil
177 J2 Nová Ľubovňa Slovakia
138 M7 Novalukoml' Belarus
213 G4 Nova Mambone Moz.
137 M7 Nova Mayachka Ukr.
213 H3 Nova Nabúri Moz.
137 K6 Nova Odesa Ukr.
176 E1 Nová Paka Czech Rep.
137 O4 Nova Parafiyivka Ukr.
251 F4 Nova Paraiso Brazil
196 I6 Nova Pazova Vojvodina Serbia
254 E4 Nova Pilão Arcado Brazil
256 D3 Nova Ponte Brazil
256 D3 Nova Ponte, Represa resr Minas Gerais Brazil
255 D6 Nova Ponte, Represa resr Brazil
137 L5 Nova Praha Ukr.
190 F5 Novara Italy
190 E3 Novara prov. Italy
195 I7 Novara di Sicilia Sicilia Italy
254 E4 Nova Remanso Brazil
256 D4 Nova Resende Brazil
171 G10 Nová Role Czech Rep.
254 D5 Nova Roma Brazil
254 E3 Nova Russas Brazil
225 H5 Nova Scotia prov. Can.
254 E4 Nova Sento Sé Brazil
257 E3 Nova Serrana Brazil
Nova Sintra Angola see Catabola
195 L3 Nova Siri Italy
137 N2 Nova Sloboda Ukr.
254 F4 Nova Soure Brazil
190 G3 Novate Mezzola Italy
240 J3 Novato CA U.S.A.
188 F3 Nova Topola Bos.-Herz.
134 I3 Novator Rus. Fed.
136 G5 Nova Ushytsya Ukr.
213 G3 Nova Vandúzi Moz.
196 H7 Nova Varoš Serbia
179 J8 Nova Vas Slovenia
179 L1 Nová Včelnice Czech Rep.
257 G3 Nova Venécia Brazil
171 L10 Nová Ves Czech Rep.
257 H2 Nova Viçosa Brazil
250 E5 Nova Vida Amazonas Brazil
253 E2 Nova Vida Rondônia Brazil
137 O4 Nova Vodolaha Ukr.
254 B5 Nova Xavantino Brazil
137 T2 Novaya Chigla Rus. Fed.
Novaya Kakhovka Ukr. see Nova Kakhovka
137 T3 Novaya Kalitva Rus. Fed.
120 C3 Novaya Kazanka Kazakh.
139 P1 Novaya Ladoga Rus. Fed.
Novaya Odessa Ukr. see Nova Odesa
Novaya Pismyanka Rus. Fed. see Leninogorsk
131 P2 Novaya Sibir', Ostrov i. Novosibirskiye O-va Rus. Fed.
137 S2 Novaya Usman' Rus. Fed.
100 J4 Novaya Ussura Rus. Fed.
Novaya Volodaga Ukr. see Nova Vodolaha
136 J2 Novaya Yolcha Belarus
130 G2 Novaya Zemlya is Rus. Fed.
Novaya Zhizn Rus. Fed. see Kazinka
197 O8 Nova Zagora Bulg.
137 L7 Nova Zbur"yivka Ukr.
137 L5 Nove Ukr.
176 D3 Nové Hrady Czech Rep.
187 D11 Novelda Spain
191 J6 Novellara Italy
176 F1 Nové Město nad Metuj Czech Rep.
177 G3 Nové Mesto nad Váhom Slovakia
176 F2 Nové Město na Moravé Czech Rep.
175 K6 Nove Misto Ukr.
176 F3 Nové Mlýny, Vodní nádrž resr Czech Rep.
176 B6 Noventa di Piave Italy
191 L5 Noventa Vicentina Italy
161 F9 Noves France
183 L8 Novés Spain
171 G10 Nové Sedlo Czech Rep.
171 I10 Nové Strašecí Czech Rep.
177 H4 Nové Zámky Slovakia
Novgorod Rus. Fed. see Velikiy Novgorod
138 L4 Novgorodka Rus. Fed.
Novgorod Oblast admin. div. Rus. Fed. see Novgorodskaya Oblast'
Novgorod-Severskiy Ukr. see Novhorod-Sivers'kyy
139 P3 Novgorodskaya Oblast' admin. div. Rus. Fed.
Novgorod-Volynskiy Ukr. see Novohrad-Volyns'kyy
Novgradets Bulg. see Suvorovo
137 L5 Novhorodka Ukr.
137 O7 Novhorodkivka Ukr.
137 M2 Novhorod-Sivers'kyy Ukr.
137 Q5 Novhorods'ke Ukr.
227 K7 Novi MI U.S.A.
196 I5 Novi Bečej Vojvodina Serbia
136 H2 Novi Bilokorovychi Ukr.
137 K2 Novi Borovychi Ukr.
136 E2 Novi Chervyshcha Ukr.
121 S1 Novichikha Rus. Fed.
191 J6 Novi di Modena Italy
183 P5 Noviergas Spain
Novi Grad Bos.-Herz. see Bosanski Novi
191 P5 Novigrad Croatia
176 F5 Novigrad Podravski Croatia
197 L8 Novi Iskŭr Bulg.
177 J5 Novi Kneževac Vojvodina Serbia
100 M5 Novikovo Sakhalin Rus. Fed.
196 I5 Novi Kozarci Vojvodina Serbia
Novi Kritsim Bulg. see Stamboliyski
190 F6 Novi Ligure Italy
160 I2 Novillars France
165 G7 Noville Belgium
244 B3 Novillero Mex.
188 F2 Novi Marof Croatia
137 L2 Novi Mlyny Ukr.
156 H4 Novion-Porcien France
197 P7 Novi Pazar Bulg.
196 I7 Novi Pazar Serbia
196 H5 Novi Sad Vojvodina Serbia
137 N4 Novi Sanzhary Ukr.
175 M6 Novi Strilyshcha Ukr.
188 F3 Novi Travnik Bos.-Herz.
188 E3 Novi Vinodolski Croatia
139 Y5 Novki Rus. Fed.
251 I4 Novo, Lago l. Brazil
100 M5 Novoaleksandropov Sakhalin Rus. Fed.
137 R3 Novoaleksandrovka Rus. Fed.
135 H7 Novoaleksandrovsk Rus. Fed.
139 R7 Novoaleksandrovskiy Rus. Fed.
Novoalekseyevka Kazakh. see Khobda
98 D1 Novoaltaysk Rus. Fed.
137 R6 Novoamvrosiyivs'ke Ukr.
137 N8 Novoandriyivka Ukr.
135 H6 Novoanninskiy Rus. Fed.
251 F6 Novo Aripuanã Brazil
136 J5 Novoarkhanhel's'k Ukr.
137 S5 Novoaydar Ukr.
137 R6 Novoazovs'k Ukr.
137 S7 Novobataysk Rus. Fed.
137 S4 Novobelaya Rus. Fed.
196 I6 Novo Beograd Serbia
137 S8 Novobeysugskaya Rus. Fed.
137 S4 Novobila Ukr.
129 I2 Novobiryuzyak Rus. Fed.
123 M2 Novobod Tajik.
123 N2 Novobod Tajik.
Novobogatinsk Kazakh. see Khamit Yergaliyev
137 O6 Novobohdanivka Ukr.
137 R4 Novoborove Ukr.
100 F4 Novobureyskiy Rus. Fed.
134 I4 Novocheboksarsk Rus. Fed.
135 J5 Novocheremshansk Rus. Fed.
135 H7 Novocherkassk Rus. Fed.
100 H6 Novochuguyevka Rus. Fed.
257 G2 Novo Cruzeiro Brazil
137 N7 Novodanylivka Ukr.
137 R7 Novoderevyankovskaya Rus. Fed.
136 G5 Novodnistrovs'k Ukr.
121 O2 Novodolinka Kazakh.
137 Q5 Novodonets'ke Ukr.
107 M1 Novodoroninskoye Rus. Fed.
137 R5 Novodruzhes'k Ukr.
139 R6 Novodugino Rus. Fed.
134 H2 Novodvinsk Rus. Fed.
Novoekonomicheskoye Ukr. see Dymytrov
136 I4 Novofastiv Ukr.
137 K7 Novofedorivka Ukr.
100 E3 Novogeorgiyevka Rus. Fed.
139 S9 Novognezdilovo Rus. Fed.
Novogroznenskiy Rus. Fed. see Oyskhara
Novogrudok Belarus see Navahrudak
139 U7 Novogurovskiy Rus. Fed.
255 C9 Novo Hamburgo Brazil
137 O6 Novohorivka Ukr.
256 C4 Novo Horizonte Brazil
137 L6 Novohradivka Ukr.
176 D3 Novohradské hory mts Czech Rep.
136 G3 Novohrad-Volyns'kyy Ukr.
137 Q5 Novohrodivka Ukr.
137 N7 Novohryhorivka Ukr.
121 L1 Novoishimskiy Kazakh.
137 N6 Novoivanivka Dnipropetrovs'ka Oblast' Ukr.
137 R6 Novoivanivka Donets'ka Oblast' Ukr.
137 M8 Novoivanivka Respublika Krym Ukr.
137 O5 Novoivankivka Ukr.
129 G5 Novoivanovka Azer.
120 H1 Novokaolinovyy Rus. Fed.
129 I3 Novokayakent Rus. Fed.
Novokazalinsk Kazakh. see Ayteke Bi
135 H6 Novokhopersk Rus. Fed.
138 M6 Novokhovansk Rus. Fed.
100 F3 Novokiyevskiy Uval Rus. Fed.
137 K6 Novokostyantynivka Mykolayivs'ka Oblast' Ukr.
137 O7 Novokostyantynivka Zaporiz'ka Oblast' Ukr.
137 K5 Novokrasne Ukr.
137 R4 Novokrasnyanka Ukr.
137 N8 Novokryms'ke Ukr.
135 H7 Novokubansk Rus. Fed.
Novokubanskiy Rus. Fed. see Novokubansk
120 C1 Novokuybyshevsk Rus. Fed.
130 J4 Novokuznetsk Rus. Fed.
137 M7 Novokyyivka Ukr.
129 H2 Novolakskoye Rus. Fed.
263 A2 Novolazarevskaya research stn Antarctica
137 S8 Novoleushkovskaya Rus. Fed.
Novolukoml' Belarus see Novalukoml'
139 V8 Novol'vovsk Rus. Fed.
137 S8 Novomalorossiyskaya Rus. Fed.
251 E5 Novo Marapi Brazil
121 O2 Novomarkovka Kazakh.
137 N5 Novomar"yivka Ukr.
137 T3 Novomelovatka Rus. Fed.
188 E3 Novo Mesto Slovenia
139 W7 Novomichurinsk Rus. Fed.
135 G7 Novomikhaylovskiy Rus. Fed.
196 I5 Novo Miloševo Vojvodina Serbia
137 R7 Novominskaya Rus. Fed.
Novomirgorod Ukr. see Novomyrhorod
139 V7 Novomoskovsk Rus. Fed.
137 O5 Novomoskovs'k Ukr.
175 I1 Novomoskovskiy Rus. Fed.
252 C1 Novo Mundo Brazil
137 N7 Novomykhaylivka Ukr.
137 R4 Novomykil's'ke Ukr.
137 N5 Novomykolayivka Dnipropetrovs'ka Oblast' Ukr.
137 L7 Novomykolayivka Khersons'ka Oblast' Ukr.
137 N7 Novomykolayivka Khersons'ka Oblast' Ukr.
136 I8 Novomykolayivka Odes'ka Oblast' Ukr.
137 O6 Novomykolayivka Zaporiz'ka Oblast' Ukr.
137 K5 Novomyrhorod Ukr.
137 M7 Novonatalivka Ukr.
Novonazyvayevka Rus. Fed. see Nazyvayevsk
121 N6 Novonikolayevka Kazakh.
Novonikolayevsk Rus. Fed. see Novosibirsk
137 R8 Novonikolayevskaya Rus. Fed.
135 H6 Novonikolayevskiy Rus. Fed.
135 I6 Novonikol'skoye Rus. Fed.
137 N7 Novooleksandrivka Ukr.
137 N7 Novooleksiyivka Ukr.
251 G5 Novo Olinda do Norte Brazil
177 I6 Novo Orahovo Vojvodina Serbia
254 E3 Novo Oriente Brazil
120 H2 Novoorsk Rus. Fed.
137 L3 Novoorzhyts'ke Ukr.
137 M8 Novoozerne Ukr.
136 H2 Novoozeryanka Ukr.
254 E3 Novo Parnarama Brazil
Novopashiyskiy Rus. Fed. see Gornozavodsk
137 P5 Novopavlivka Dnipropetrovs'ka Oblast' Ukr.
136 J6 Novopavlivka Mykolayivs'ka Oblast' Ukr.
107 K1 Novopavlovka Rus. Fed.
129 E2 Novopavlovsk Rus. Fed.
Novopavlovskaya Rus. Fed. see Novopavlovsk
137 N4 Novopetrivka Ukr.
137 N5 Novopidkryazh Ukr.
120 K1 Novopokrovka Kostanayskaya Oblast' Kazakh.
121 L1 Novopokrovka Severnyy Kazakhstan Kazakh.
121 S2 Novopokrovka Vostochnyy Kazakhstan Kazakh.
100 I6 Novopokrovka Primorskiy Kray Rus. Fed.
137 T1 Novopokrovka Tambovskaya Oblast' Rus. Fed.
137 N5 Novopokrovka Ukr.
135 H7 Novopokrovskaya Rus. Fed.
Novopolotsk Belarus see Navapolatsk
137 L6 Novopoltavka Mykolayivs'ka Oblast' Ukr.
137 P6 Novopoltavka Zaporiz'ka Oblast' Ukr.
139 W8 Novopolyan'ye Rus. Fed.
137 S4 Novopskov Ukr.
Novo Redondo Angola see Sumbe
120 C2 Novorepnoye Rus. Fed.
100 F2 Novorossiyka Rus. Fed.
135 G7 Novorossiysk Rus. Fed.
Novorossiyskiy Kazakh. see Akzhar
137 S8 Novorozhdestvenskaya Rus. Fed.
121 N2 Novorybinka Akmolinskaya Oblast' Kazakh.
121 L1 Novorybinka Severnyy Kazakhstan Kazakh.
131 L2 Novorybnaya Rus. Fed.
138 M4 Novorzhev Rus. Fed.
136 I6 Novosamarka Ukr.
129 G5 Novosaratovka Azer.
171 I9 Novosedlice Czech Rep.
176 F3 Novosedly Czech Rep.
106 J1 Novoselenginsk Rus. Fed.
129 E1 Novoselitskoye Rus. Fed.
136 I6 Novoselivka Ukr.
137 M8 Novoselivs'ke Ukr.
139 V7 Novoselki Moskovskaya Oblast' Rus. Fed.
139 O6 Novoselki Tverskaya Oblast' Rus. Fed.
197 K9 Novo Selo Macedonia
175 I1 Novoselovo Kaliningradskaya Oblast' Rus. Fed.
139 W5 Novoselovo Vladimirskaya Oblast' Rus. Fed.
Novoselskoye Rus. Fed. see Achkhoy-Martan
138 L3 Novosel'ye Rus. Fed.
136 F5 Novoselytsya Ukr.
120 E1 Novosergiyevka Rus. Fed.
135 G7 Novoshakhtinsk Rus. Fed.
100 H6 Novoshakhtinskiy Rus. Fed.
137 R7 Novoshcherbinovskaya Rus. Fed.
135 J5 Novosheshminsk Rus. Fed.
130 J4 Novosibirsk Rus. Fed.
131 P2 Novosibirskiye Ostrova is Rus. Fed.
139 U9 Novosil' Rus. Fed.
137 L8 Novosil's'ke Ukr.
137 R2 Novosil'skoye Rus. Fed.
137 L7 Novosofiyivka Ukr.
139 N5 Novosokol'niki Rus. Fed.
137 P7 Novospas'ke Ukr.
120 B1 Novospasskoye Rus. Fed.
175 J1 Novostroyevo Rus. Fed.
137 S5 Novosvitlivka Ukr.
177 I2 Novoť Slovakia
129 I1 Novoterechnoye Rus. Fed.
137 R8 Novotitarovskaya Rus. Fed.
100 G4 Novotroichkoye Rus. Fed.
120 H2 Novotroitsk Rus. Fed.
Novotroitskoye Kazakh. see Tole Bi
139 Q8 Novotroitskoye Rus. Fed.
137 Q5 Novotroyits'ke Donets'ka Oblast' Ukr.
137 Q6 Novotroyits'ke Donets'ka Oblast' Ukr.
137 N7 Novotroyits'ke Khersons'ka Oblast' Ukr.
137 O6 Novotroyits'ke Zaporiz'ka Oblast' Ukr.
Novoukrainka Kirovohrads'ka Oblast' Ukr. see Novoukrayinka
Novoukrainka Rivnens'ka Oblast' Ukr. see Novoukrayinka
137 K5 Novoukrayinka Kirovohrads'ka Oblast' Ukr.
136 E3 Novoukrayinka Rivnens'ka Oblast' Ukr.
120 G2 Novoural'sk Rus. Fed.
120 C2 Novouzensk Rus. Fed.
121 P1 Novovarshavka Rus. Fed.
137 O7 Novovasylivka Zaporiz'ka Oblast' Ukr.
137 P7 Novovasylivka Zaporiz'ka Oblast' Ukr.
188 F2 Novo Virje Croatia
136 D3 Novovolyns'k Ukr.
135 G6 Novovoronezh Rus. Fed.
Novovoronezhskiy Rus. Fed. see Novovoronezh
137 M6 Novovorontsovka Ukr.
100 E2 Novo-Voskresenovka Rus. Fed.
137 M6 Novovoskresens'ke Ukr.
121 R6 Novovoznesenovka Kyrg.
137 O5 Novov"yazivs'ke Ukr.
137 N1 Novoyamskoye Rus. Fed.
136 C4 Novoyavorivs'ke Ukr.
139 W9 Novoye Dubovoye Rus. Fed.
121 S2 Novoyegor'yevskoye Rus. Fed.
139 X5 Novoye Leushino Rus. Fed.
139 T5 Novozavidovskiy Rus. Fed.
134 J2 Novozhilovskaya Rus. Fed.
136 I4 Novozhyvotiv Ukr.
139 O9 Novozybkov Rus. Fed.
188 F3 Novska Croatia
136 J1 Novy Barsuk Belarus
139 N6 Novy Boletsk Belarus
176 D1 Nový Bor Czech Rep.
176 E1 Nový Bydžov Czech Rep.
139 N8 Novy Bykhaw Belarus
156 H4 Novy-Chevrières France
175 M2 Novy Dvor Hrodzyenskaya Voblasts' Belarus
138 H9 Novy Dvor Hrodzyenskaya Voblasts' Belarus
Novyj Cholmogory Rus. Fed. see Arkhangel'sk
Novyj Holmogory Rus. Fed. see Arkhangel'sk
177 G2 Nový Jičín Czech Rep.
176 G2 Nový Malín Czech Rep.
Novyy Afon Georgia see Akhali Ap'oni
138 K6 Novyya Kruki Belarus
138 L7 Novyya Valosavichy Belarus
139 N8 Novyya Zhuravichy Belarus
134 K2 Novyy Bor Rus. Fed.
Novyy Bug Ukr. see Novyy Buh
137 L6 Novyy Buh Ukr.
137 K3 Novyy Bykiv Ukr.
Novyy Donbass Ukr. see Dymytrov
175 M5 Novyy Dvir Ukr.
Novyye Aneny Moldova see Anenii Noi
Novyye Belokorovichi Ukr. see Novi Bilokorovychi
120 B1 Novyye Burasy Rus. Fed.
139 Q9 Novyye Ivaytenki Rus. Fed.
Novyye Petushki Rus. Fed. see Petushki
138 K4 Novyy Izborsk Rus. Fed.
Novyy Kholmogory Rus. Fed. see Arkhangel'sk
Novyy Margelan Uzbek. see Farg'ona
137 O4 Novyy Merchyk Ukr.
139 V4 Novyy Nekouz Rus. Fed.
135 G6 Novyy Oskol Rus. Fed.
130 I3 Novyy Port Rus. Fed.
137 L1 Novyy Ropsk Rus. Fed.
136 D4 Novyy Rozdil Ukr.
139 T8 Novyy Sinets Rus. Fed.
137 M5 Novyystarodub Ukr.
137 R6 Novyy Svit Donets'ka Oblast' Ukr.
137 N9 Novyy Svit Respublika Krym Ukr.
129 I2 Novyy Terek r. Rus. Fed.
134 J4 Novyy Tor'yal Rus. Fed.
130 I3 Novyy Urengoy Rus. Fed.
100 H3 Novyy Urgal Rus. Fed.
Novyy Uzen' Kazakh. see Zhanaozen
175 M5 Novyy Vytkiv Ukr.
175 M6 Novyy Yarychiv Ukr.
134 K5 Novyy Zay Rus. Fed.
176 G3 Nový Život Slovakia
122 F6 Now Iran
175 H4 Nowa Brzeźnica Pol.
175 L2 Nowa Chodorówka Pol.
175 J5 Nowa Dęba Pol.
174 G1 Nowa Karczma Pol.
174 E5 Nowa Ruda Pol.
175 K5 Nowa Sarzyna Pol.
175 J5 Nowa Słupia Pol.
174 D4 Nowa Sól Pol.
237 H7 Nowata OK U.S.A.
171 L6 Nowa Wieś Pol.
175 K2 Nowa Wieś Ełcka Pol.
174 F1 Nowa Wieś Lęborskie Pol.
174 G3 Nowa Wieś Wielka Pol.
175 L2 Nowa Wola Pol.
175 J4 Nowa Wola Gołębiowska Pol.
122 C4 Nowbarān Iran
122 H5 Now Deh Iran
122 D4 Now Dezh Iran
122 C3 Nowdī Iran
174 G2 Nowe Pol.
175 I5 Nowe Brzesko Pol.
174 C2 Nowe Czarnowo Pol.
174 D4 Nowe Miasteczko Pol.
175 I3 Nowe Miasto Pol.
175 H2 Nowe Miasto Lubawskie Pol.
175 I4 Nowe Miasto nad Pilicą Pol.
147 D9 Nowen Hill Ireland
175 H3 Nowe Ostrowy Pol.
175 K3 Nowe Piekuty Pol.
174 F4 Nowe Skalmierzyce Pol.
174 C2 Nowe Warpno Pol.
122 D4 Nowfel low Shātow Qom Iran
122 E5 Now Gombad Iran
Nowgong Assam India see Nagaon
116 G7 Nowgong Madh. Prad. India
175 K2 Nowinka Pol.
127 N4 Nowjeh Deh Iran
122 F3 Now Kharegan Iran
223 K2 Nowleye Lake Nunavut Can.
175 K4 Nowodwór Pol.
174 D2 Nowogard Pol.
175 J2 Nowogród Pol.
174 D4 Nowogród Bobrzański Pol.
174 D3 Nowogródek Pomorski Pol.
174 D4 Nowogrodziec Pol.
238 K4 Nowood r. WY U.S.A.
Noworadomsk Pol. see Radomsko
175 L3 Nowosady Pol.
175 K6 Nowosielce Pol.
175 K5 Nowosielec Pol.
175 H4 Nowosolna Pol.
83 M6 Nowra N.S.W. Austr.
122 C2 Nowshahr Iran
122 D3 Nowshahr Iran
123 O4 Nowshera Pak.
122 B4 Nowsūd Iran
223 L2 Nowyak Lake Nunavut Can.
175 K3 Nowy Bartków Pol.
175 H3 Nowy Duninów Pol.
174 F2 Nowy Dwór Kujawsko-Pomorskie Pol.
175 L2 Nowy Dwór Podlaskie Pol.
143 P7 Nowy Dwór Gdański Pol.
175 I3 Nowy Dwór Mazowiecki Pol.
175 I5 Nowy Korczyn Pol.
175 L5 Nowy Lubliniec Pol.
175 I6 Nowy Sącz Pol.
143 P7 Nowy Staw Pol.
175 I6 Nowy Targ Pol.
174 E3 Nowy Tomyśl Pol.
175 J6 Nowy Żmigród Pol.
227 R8 Noxen PA U.S.A.
237 K9 Noxubee National Wildlife Refuge nature res. MS U.S.A.
96 G6 Noy, Xé r. Laos
Noya Cataluña Spain see Sant Sadurní d'Anoia
Noya Galicia Spain see Noia
130 I3 Noyabr'sk Rus. Fed.
158 G6 Noyal-Muzillac France
158 F6 Noyalo France
158 F5 Noyal-Pontivy France
159 L6 Noyant France
159 K7 Noyant-la-Plaine France
161 H6 Noyarey France
127 Q5 Noyek Iran
129 G4 Noyemberyan Armenia
159 K6 Noyen-sur-Sarthe France
156 G8 Noyers France
159 N7 Noyers-sur-Cher France
161 H8 Noyers-sur-Jabron France
222 C4 Noyes Island AK U.S.A.
114 E7 Noyil r. India
156 E4 Noyon France
105 H2 Nozawaonsen-mura Japan
158 H6 Nozay France
175 K6 Nozdrzec Pol.
160 I3 Nozeroy France
129 H2 Nozhay-Yurt Rus. Fed.
215 J6 Nozizwe S. Africa
178 B8 Nozza r. Italy
210 B4 Npitamaiong mt. Kenya
215 O6 Nqabeni S. Africa
215 L8 Nqamakwe S. Africa
215 O4 Nqutu S. Africa
129 H7 Nrnadzor Armenia
208 B5 Nsa Congo
211 A8 Nsalamu Zambia
208 C5 Nsambi Dem. Rep. Congo
211 B8 Nsanje Malawi
206 E5 Nsawam Ghana
211 A7 Nseluka Zambia
207 H6 Nsoc Equat. Guinea
215 P3 Nsoko Swaziland
209 F7 Nsombo Zambia
208 C5 Nsondia Dem. Rep. Congo
207 G5 Nsukka Nigeria
Nsumbu National Park Zambia see Sumbu National Park
204 B5 Ntalfa well Maur.
209 E8 Ntambu Zambia
208 C5 Ntandembele Dem. Rep. Congo
211 B8 Ntcheu Malawi
211 B8 Ntchisi Malawi
207 H6 Ntem r. Cameroon
215 L3 Ntha S. Africa
215 M2 Nthorwane S. Africa
215 M7 Ntibane S. Africa
202 B6 Ntiona Chad
198 F4 Ntoro, Kavo pt Greece
210 A4 Ntoroko Uganda
208 A4 Ntoum Gabon
217 □3a Ntsamouéni Njazidja Comoros
215 N3 Ntshingwayo Dam S. Africa
217 □3a Ntsoudjini Njazidja Comoros
207 H5 Ntui Cameroon
211 A5 Ntungamo Uganda
212 E4 Ntwetwe Pan salt pan Botswana
215 M7 Ntywenka S. Africa
159 J7 Nuaillé France
162 C3 Nuaillé-d'Aunis France
Nuanetsi r. Zimbabwe see Mwenezi
93 D3 Nuangan Sulawesi Indon.
234 D2 Nuangola PA U.S.A.
117 I9 Nuapara Orissa India
125 L4 Nu'aym reg. Oman
203 F4 Nuba, Lake resr Sudan
210 A2 Nuba Mountains Sudan
168 I2 Nübbel Ger.
245 K9 Nube Flan, Cerro mt. Mex.
168 I1 Nübel Ger.
203 G4 Nubian Desert Sudan
140 Q2 Nubivarri hill Norway
260 A5 Ñuble r. Chile
182 I1 Nubledo Spain
116 F2 Nubra r. India
79 □7 Nubu Vanua Levu Fiji
197 K4 Nucet Romania
241 X3 Nucla CO U.S.A.
107 L5 Nüden Mongolia
171 G7 Nudersdorf Ger.
169 J10 Nüdlingen Ger.
139 T5 Nudol' Rus. Fed.
175 M4 Nudyzhe Ukr.
237 G12 Nueces r. TX U.S.A.
159 J8 Nueil-sur-Argent France
223 L2 Nueltin Lake Man./Nunavut Can.
165 I6 Nuenen Neth.
186 E3 Nueno Spain
183 K2 Nueva Spain
259 D9 Nueva, Isla i. Chile
250 C6 Nueva Alejandría Peru
242 □O10 Nueva Arcadia Hond.
260 C3 Nueva California Arg.
185 K5 Nueva-Carteya Spain
237 F12 Nueva Ciudad Guerrero Mex.
260 D4 Nueva Constitución Arg.
260 E3 Nueva Escocia Arg.
251 E2 Nueva Esparta state Venez.
250 D2 Nueva Florida Venez.
260 E4 Nueva Galia Arg.
253 F5 Nueva Germania Para.
246 B3 Nueva Gerona Cuba
259 D9 Nueva Harberton Arg.
261 I4 Nueva Helvecia Uru.
260 A6 Nueva Imperial Chile
244 E6 Nueva Italia de Ruiz Mex.
184 G7 Nueva Jarilla Spain
259 C7 Nueva Lubecka Arg.
242 □O10 Nueva Ocotepeque Hond.
261 H3 Nueva Palmira Uru.
258 E2 Nueva Población Arg.
245 I3 Nueva Polonia Mex.
243 I4 Nueva Rosita Mex.
243 O11 Nueva San Salvador El Salvador
Nueva Tabarca i. Spain see Plana, Isla
245 I1 Nueva Villa de Padilla Mex.
Nueve de Julio Arg. see 9 de Julio
246 E3 Nuevitas Cuba
243 N7 Nuevo, Cayo i. Mex.
259 D6 Nuevo, Golfo g. Arg.
261 I3 Nuevo Berlín Uru.
242 F2 Nuevo Casas Grandes Mex.
242 G5 Nuevo Ideal Mex.
243 J4 Nuevo Laredo Mex.
241 Q9 Nuevo León Mex.
244 G1 Nuevo León state Mex.
251 F2 Nuevo Mamo Venez.
245 H3 Nuevo-Morelos Mex.
244 C2 Nuevo Pilares Mex.
250 C5 Nuevo Rocatuerte Ecuador
244 F4 Nuevo Valle de Moreno Mex.
124 G4 Nufayyid Şabḩah des. Saudi Arabia
106 D2 Nuga Mongolia
210 F2 Nugaal admin. reg. Somalia
210 F3 Nugaal watercourse Somalia
85 L8 Nuga Nuga, Lake Qld Austr.
81 D13 Nugget Point South I. N.Z.
82 □3 Nuggetts Point S. Pacific Ocean
192 C6 Nughedu di San Nicolò Sardegna Italy
139 T8 Nugr' r. Rus. Fed.
114 E6 Nugu r. India
77 F2 Nuguria Islands P.N.G.
123 J9 Nuh, Ras pt Pak.
80 L6 Nuhaka North I. N.Z.
199 L4 Nuhköy Turkey
77 H2 Nui atoll Tuvalu
Nui Con Voi r. Vietnam see Hông, Sông
138 L1 Nuijamaa Fin.
159 J6 Nuillé-sur-Vicoin France
96 I7 Nui Thanh Vietnam
96 H7 Nui Ti On mt. Vietnam
156 H8 Nuits France
160 F2 Nuits-St-Georges France
Nu Jiang r. Myanmar see Salween
104 F6 Nukata Japan
82 E5 Nukey Bluff hill S.A. Austr.
Nukha Azer. see Şäki
78 □6 Nukiki Choiseul Solomon Is
122 E5 Nūklok, Chāh-e well Iran
79 □8a Nuku i. Tonga
79 □8a Nuku'alofa Tongatapu Tonga
77 H2 Nukufetau atoll Tuvalu
79 □9 Nuku Hiva i. Fr. Polynesia
Nukuhiva i. Fr. Polynesia see Nuku Hiva
77 H2 Nukulaelae atoll Tuvalu
Nukulailai atoll Tuvalu see Nukulaelae
77 F2 Nukumanu Islands P.N.G.
Nukunau i. Gilbert Is Kiribati see Nikunau
Nukunono atoll Tokelau see Nukunonu
81 □1 Nukunonu Tokelau
81 □1 Nukunonu atoll Tokelau
120 H6 Nukus Uzbek.
164 H5 Nuland Neth.
220 C3 Nulato AK U.S.A.
192 C7 Nule Sardegna Italy
187 E8 Nules Spain
86 F6 Nullagine W.A. Austr.
86 F6 Nullagine r. W.A. Austr.
82 C4 Nullarbor S.A. Austr.
82 C4 Nullarbor National Park S.A. Austr.
82 B4 Nullarbor Plain S.A. Austr.
82 C4 Nullarbor Regional Reserve park S.A. Austr.
224 E1 Nuluarniavik, Lac l. Que. Can.
107 P6 Nulu'erhu Shan mts China
192 B6 Nulvi Sardegna Italy
91 I7 Num i. Papua Indon.
117 K6 Num Nepal
83 J3 Numalla, Lake salt flat Qld Austr.
207 I4 Numan Nigeria
124 B2 Nu'mān i. Saudi Arabia
191 P8 Numana Italy
92 E7 Numancia Phil.
164 F5 Numansdorp Neth.
105 J2 Numata Gunma Japan
102 S3 Numata Hokkaidō Japan
208 E3 Numatinna watercourse Sudan
105 I5 Numazu Japan
215 P1 Numbi Gate S. Africa
Numbu Vanua Levu Fiji see Nubu
84 E3 Numbulwar N.T. Austr.
142 F1 Numedal val. Norway
91 H7 Numfoor i. Papua Indon.
100 E5 Numin He r. China
212 C3 Numkaub Namibia
141 Q6 Nummi Fin.
83 J7 Numurkah Vic. Austr.
225 I2 Nunaksaluk Island Nfld and Lab. Can.
221 N3 Nunakuluut i. Greenland
221 N3 Nunap Isua c. Greenland
Nunarsuit i. Greenland see Nunakuluut
224 E1 Nunavik reg. Que. Can.
223 L2 Nunavut admin. div. Can.
250 C3 Nunchía Col.
171 H8 Nünchritz Ger.
209 F5 Nunda Dem. Rep. Congo
232 H6 Nunda NY U.S.A.
83 M4 Nundle N.S.W. Austr.
151 J2 Nuneaton Warwickshire, England U.K.
87 E11 Nungarin W.A. Austr.
117 N7 Nungba Manipur India
223 M5 Nungesser Lake Ont. Can.
107 P4 Nungnain Sum Nei Mongol China
213 H2 Nungo Moz.
211 C6 Nungwi, Ras pt Tanz.
220 B4 Nunivak Island AK U.S.A.
117 J9 Nunkapasi Orissa India
172 B3 Nunkirchen Ger.
116 F3 Nunkun mt. Jammu and Kashmir
131 T3 Nunligran Rus. Fed.
187 H9 Nunó, Cap c. Spain
252 C3 Nuñoa Peru
182 H8 Nuñomoral Spain
171 H6 Nunsdorf Ger.
164 I4 Nunspeet Neth.
95 L3 Nunukan i. Indon.
Nuojiang Sichuan China see Tongjiang
192 C7 Nuoro Sardegna Italy
192 C7 Nuoro prov. Sardegna Italy
Nuorttijoki r. Rus. Fed. see Nota
78 □6 Nupani i. Santa Cruz Is Solomon Is
122 F6 Nūq Iran
202 C4 Nuqayy, Jabal mts Libya
124 E3 Nuqrah Saudi Arabia
203 G3 Nuquş, Jabal mt. Egypt
250 B3 Nuquí Col.
111 E8 Nur Xinjiang China
122 E3 Nur r. Iran
175 K3 Nur Pol.
121 Q6 Nura Almatinskaya Oblast' Kazakh.
121 P3 Nura Kazakh.
121 M2 Nura r. Kazakh.
122 D6 Nūrābād Iran
122 C4 Nūrābād Iran
192 C8 Nuragus Sardegna Italy
Nurakita i. Tuvalu see Niulakita
192 C8 Nurallao Sardegna Italy
192 C9 Nuraminis Sardegna Italy
Nurata Uzbek. see Nurota
128 E1 Nurdağı Turkey
126 G5 Nur Dağları mts Turkey
190 H5 Nure r. Italy
192 B8 Nureci Sardegna Italy
Nurek Tajik. see Norak
Nurek Reservoir Tajik. see Norak, Obanbori
Nurekskoye Vodokhranilishche resr Tajik. see Norak, Obanbori
Nuremberg Ger. see Nürnberg
234 C3 Nuremberg PA U.S.A.
123 N4 Nūrestān prov. Afgh.
123 N4 Nūrestān reg. Afgh.
123 N4 Nūr Gal Afgh.
242 E3 Nuri Mex.
203 G5 Nuri Sudan
95 H5 Nuri, Teluk b. Indon.
193 K3 Nuria, Monte mt. Italy
Nuristan prov. Afgh. see Nūrestān
116 F2 Nurla Jammu and Kashmir
135 J5 Nurlat Rus. Fed.
134 J5 Nurlaty Rus. Fed.
140 T5 Nurmes Fin.
141 R6 Nurmijärvi Fin.
140 Q5 Nurmo Fin.
173 K3 Nürnberg Ger.
148 D8 Nurney Carlow Ireland
148 D7 Nurney Kildare Ireland
121 L8 Nurobad Uzbek.
120 K7 Nurota Uzbek.
121 L7 Nurota tizmasi mts Uzbek.
123 N6 Nurpur Pak.
82 C3 Nurrai Lakes salt flat S.A. Austr.

192 C8 Nurri Sardegna Italy
83 K4 Nurri, Mount hill N.S.W. Austr.
140 L4 Nursfjellet mt. Norway
Nursia Italy see Norcia
138 F3 Nurste Estonia
172 G4 Nürtingen Ger.
111 K8 Nur Turu Qinghai China
175 K3 Nurzec r. Pol.
175 L3 Nurzec-Stacja Pol.
190 C4 Nus Italy
95 H8 Nusa Kambaran, Cagar Alam nature res. Jawa Indon.
93 F5 Nusa Laut i. Maluku Indon.
95 L9 Nusa Tenggara Barat prov. Indon.
93 B8 Nusa Tenggara Timur prov. Indon.
127 J5 Nusaybin Turkey
193 O6 Nusco Italy
93 G4 Nusela, Kepulauan is Papua Indon.
197 K3 Nuşfalău Romania
108 B5 Nu Shan mts China
104 A7 Nu-shima i. Japan
123 L7 Nushki Pak.
172 F5 Nusplingen Ger.
128 G2 Nusratiye Turkey
179 J4 Nußbach Austria
173 N6 Nußdorf Ger.
173 M6 Nußdorf am Inn Ger.
178 G6 Nußdorf-Debant Austria
168 K3 Nusse Ger.
225 I1 Nutak Nfld and Lab. Can.
223 L2 Nutarawit Lake Nunavut Can.
165 I7 Nuth Neth.
171 H6 Nuthe r. Ger.
151 L5 Nuthurst West Sussex, England U.K.
235 G3 Nutley NJ U.S.A.
241 W8 Nutrioso AZ U.S.A.
123 M7 Nuttal Pak.
147 J3 Nutt's Corner Northern Ireland U.K.
84 E3 Nutwood Downs N.T. Austr.
221 M2 Nuugaatsiaap Imaa inlet Greenland
221 M2 Nuugaatsiaq Greenland
221 M3 Nuuk Greenland
138 H1 Nuuksion kansallispuisto nat. park Fin.
140 S3 Nuupas Fin.
79 □9a Nuupere, Pointe pt Moorea Fr. Polynesia
221 M2 Nuussuaq Greenland
221 M2 Nuussuaq pen. Greenland
78 □2 Nu'uuli American Samoa
117 I5 Nuwakot Nepal
125 L3 Nuway Oman
203 G2 Nuwaybi' al Muzayyinah Egypt
214 H9 Nuwekloof pass S. Africa
214 C7 Nuwerus S. Africa
214 F8 Nuweveldberge mts S. Africa
244 G8 Nuxco Mex.
192 B9 Nuxis Sardegna Italy
175 M4 Nuyno Ukr.
87 D13 Nuyts, Point W.A. Austr.
82 D5 Nuyts Archipelago is S.A. Austr.
82 D5 Nuyts Archipelago Conservation Park nature res. S.A. Austr.
87 H12 Nuytsland Nature Reserve W.A. Austr.
128 H3 Nuzayzah reg. Syria
178 A5 Nüziders Austria
114 G4 Nuzvid Andhra Prad. India
207 H5 Nwa Cameroon
212 E3 Nxai Pan National Park Botswana
212 D3 Nxaunxau Botswana
95 K4 Nyaän, Bukit hill Indon.
207 H6 Nyabessan Cameroon
87 E12 Nyabing W.A. Austr.
233 L7 Nyack NY U.S.A.
130 H3 Nyagan' Rus. Fed.
Nyagquka Sichuan China see Yajiang
Nyagrong Sichuan China see Xinlong
211 B6 Nyahua Tanz.
210 C4 Nyahururu Kenya
83 I6 Nyah West Vic. Austr.
111 K12 Nyaimai Xizang China
111 J11 Nyainqêntanglha Feng mt. Xizang China
111 J12 Nyainqêntanglha Shan mts Xizang China
111 K10 Nyainrong Xizang China
211 A5 Nyakahanga Tanz.
211 A5 Nyakahura Kagera Tanz.
211 A6 Nyaka Kangaga Tanz.
211 B5 Nyakaliro Tanz.
215 K3 Nyakallong S. Africa
211 A5 Nyakanazi Tanz.
140 O5 Nyåker Sweden
Nyakh Rus. Fed. see Nyagan'
138 I9 Nyakhachava Belarus
206 E5 Nyakrom Ghana
134 M3 Nyaksimvol' Rus. Fed.
202 E6 Nyala Sudan
Nyalam Xizang China see Congdü
140 □ Ny-Ålesund Svalbard
209 F8 Nyama Zambia
213 F3 Nyamandhlovu Zimbabwe
213 G3 Nyamapanda Zimbabwe
211 B5 Nyambiti Tanz.
211 A5 Nyamirembe Kagera Tanz.
208 E2 Nyamlell Sudan
211 C7 Nyamtumbo Tanz.
175 N3 Nyamyerzha Belarus
Nyande Zimbabwe see Masvingo
134 H3 Nyandoma Rus. Fed.
134 G3 Nyandomskiy Vozvyshennost' hills Rus. Fed.
208 A5 Nyanga Congo
209 A5 Nyanga Gabon
209 A5 Nyanga prov. Gabon
213 G3 Nyanga Zimbabwe
213 G3 Nyanga National Park Zimbabwe
111 K11 Nyangbo Xizang China
111 I12 Nyang Qu r. China
111 L12 Nyang Qu r. China
206 E4 Nyankpala Ghana
211 A5 Nyanza Rwanda
211 A6 Nyanza-Lac Burundi
95 L4 Nyapa, Gunung mt. Indon.
210 B3 Nyapongeth Sudan
116 G4 Nyar r. India
176 G4 Nyárád Hungary
222 H2 Nyarling r. N.W.T. Can.
177 I5 Nyárlőrinc Hungary
177 I4 Nyársapát Hungary
211 A5 Nyarugumba Rwanda
211 B7 Nyasa, Lake Africa
Nyasaland country Africa see Malawi
134 K2 Nyashabozh Rus. Fed.
138 J8 Nyasvizh Belarus
213 F3 Nyathi Zimbabwe
96 C6 Nyaunglebin Myanmar
96 B4 Nyaungu Myanmar
134 M3 Nyays r. Rus. Fed.
213 G3 Nyazura Zimbabwe
168 I1 Nybøl Nor b. Denmark
142 G6 Nyborg Denmark
140 T1 Nyborg Norway
140 Q4 Nyborg Sweden
143 L5 Nybro Sweden
177 H2 Nýdek Czech Rep.
221 M1 Nyeboe Land reg. Greenland
138 K8 Nyeharelaye Belarus
111 J12 Nyêmo Xizang China
Nyenchen Tanglha Range mts Xizang China see Nyainqêntanglha Shan
210 C5 Nyeri Kenya
210 B2 Nyerol Sudan
138 M6 Nyeshcharda, Vozyera l. Belarus
140 □ Ny-Friesland reg. Svalbard
143 K1 Nyhammar Sweden
111 H9 Nyi, Co l. Xizang China
211 B7 Nyika National Park Zambia
211 B7 Nyika Plateau Malawi
111 H11 Nyima Xizang China
111 K11 Nyima Xizang China
211 A8 Nyimba Zambia
111 L12 Nyingchi Xizang China
111 J11 Nyingzhong Xizang China
Nyinma Gansu China see Maqu
177 L4 Nyírábrány Hungary
177 K4 Nyíracsád Hungary
176 G4 Nyirád Hungary
177 K4 Nyíradony Hungary
211 A5 Nyiragongo vol. Dem. Rep. Congo
177 L4 Nyírbátor Hungary
177 L4 Nyírbéltek Hungary
177 L4 Nyírbogát Hungary
177 K3 Nyírbogdány Hungary
177 L4 Nyírcsászári Hungary
177 K4 Nyíregyháza Hungary
177 K4 Nyírgelse Hungary
211 C5 Nyiri Desert Kenya
177 L4 Nyírlugos Hungary
177 K4 Nyírmártonfalva Hungary
177 K4 Nyírmihálydi Hungary
177 K3 Nyírtelek Hungary
177 K3 Nyírtét Hungary
177 K3 Nyírtura Hungary
210 C4 Nyiru, Mount Kenya
177 L4 Nyírvasvári Hungary
140 Q5 Nykarleby Fin.
142 H7 Nykøbing Denmark
142 E5 Nykøbing Mors Denmark
142 H6 Nykøbing Sjælland Denmark
143 N3 Nyköping Sweden
143 K2 Nykroppa Sweden
143 N2 Nykvarn Sweden
134 B3 Nyland Sweden
83 K5 Nymagee N.S.W. Austr.
83 N3 Nymboida N.S.W. Austr.
83 N3 Nymboida National Park N.S.W. Austr.
176 E1 Nymburk Czech Rep.
142 E6 Nymindegab Denmark
143 N3 Nynäshamn Sweden
83 K4 Nyngan N.S.W. Austr.
111 F11 Nyogzê Xizang China
105 K2 Nyohō-san mt. Japan
159 J6 Nyoiseau France
215 M8 Nyokana S. Africa
138 G8 Nyoman r. Belarus
alt. Neman (Rus. Fed.)
alt. Nemunas (Lith.)
138 I8 Nyomanskaya Nizina lowland Belarus
190 A3 Nyon Switz.
207 H6 Nyong r. Cameroon
161 G8 Nyons France
170 F1 Nyord i. Denmark
170 E1 Nyråd Denmark
176 C2 Nýřany Czech Rep.
134 L3 Nyrob Rus. Fed.
176 C2 Nýrsko Czech Rep.
140 T2 Nyrud Norway
174 F5 Nysa Pol.
174 F5 Nysa Kłodzka r. Pol.
142 I2 Nysäter Sweden
140 L5 Nysätern Sweden
100 M3 Nysh Sakhalin Rus. Fed.
142 I2 Nysockensjön l. Sweden
238 F5 Nyssa OR U.S.A.
Nystad Fin. see Uusikaupunki
142 H7 Nysted Denmark
134 J3 Nyuchpas Rus. Fed.
102 Q7 Nyūdō-zaki pt Japan
105 H4 Nyūgasa-yama mt. Japan
177 K4 Nyugati-főcsatorna canal Hungary
104 F3 Nyūkawa Japan
134 I3 Nyukhcha Rus. Fed.
134 I3 Nyuksenitsa Rus. Fed.
177 G4 Nyúl Hungary
209 F6 Nyunzu Dem. Rep. Congo
131 M3 Nyurba Rus. Fed.
134 J3 Nyuvchim Rus. Fed.
131 M3 Nyuya Rus. Fed.
131 M3 Nyuya r. Rus. Fed.
104 G2 Nyūzen Japan
137 M8 Nyva Ukr.
100 M1 Nyvrovo Rus. Fed.
175 M5 Nyvytsi Ukr.
100 M2 Nyyskiy Zaliv lag. Sakhalin Rus. Fed.
136 B4 Nyzhankovychi Ukr.
137 N7 Nyzhni Sirohozy Ukr.
137 N7 Nyzhni Torhayi Ukr.
136 C5 Nyzhni Vorota Ukr.
136 C5 Nyzhniy Bystryy Ukr.
137 S5 Nyzhniy Nahol'chyk Ukr.
137 N8 Nyzhn'ohirs'kyy Ukr.
137 R4 Nyzhnya Dubanka Ukr.
137 N3 Nyzhnya Syrovatka Ukr.
137 O5 Nyzhnya Tersa r. Ukr.
177 M2 Nyzhnya Vysots'ke Ukr.
177 L2 Nyzhnya Yablun'ka Ukr.
137 N3 Nyzy Ukr.
208 D3 Nzako C.A.R.
209 A5 Nzambi Congo
208 F3 Nzara Sudan
206 C4 Nzébéla Guinea
211 B6 Nzega Tanz.
206 C5 Nzérékoré Guinea
209 B6 N'zeto Angola
206 D5 Nzi r. Côte d'Ivoire
209 E7 Nzilo, Lac l. Dem. Rep. Congo
209 E5 Nzingu Dem. Rep. Congo
206 D5 Nzo r. Côte d'Ivoire
206 D5 N'Zo, Réserve de Faune du nature res. Côte d'Ivoire
209 B6 Nzobe Dem. Rep. Congo
210 B4 Nzoia r. Kenya
208 F4 Nzoro r. Dem. Rep. Congo
217 □3 Nzwani i. Comoros

O

236 F4 Oacoma SD U.S.A.
151 J2 Oadby Leicestershire, England U.K.
236 E3 Oahe, Lake SD U.S.A.
240 □D12 O'ahu i. HI U.S.A.
Oaitupu i. Tuvalu see Vaitupu
82 H5 Oakbank S.A. Austr.
233 O7 Oak Bluffs MA U.S.A.
241 T2 Oak City UT U.S.A.
226 G7 Oak Creek WI U.S.A.
240 L4 Oakdale CA U.S.A.
235 K2 Oakdale CT U.S.A.
237 I10 Oakdale LA U.S.A.
235 I3 Oakdale NY U.S.A.
150 H2 Oakengates Telford and Wrekin, England U.K.
236 F2 Oakes ND U.S.A.
85 M9 Oakey Qld Austr.
232 G5 Oakfield NY U.S.A.
234 F4 Oakford PA U.S.A.
237 J9 Oak Grove LA U.S.A.
226 J5 Oak Grove MI U.S.A.
151 K2 Oakham Rutland, England U.K.
232 B7 Oak Harbor OH U.S.A.
238 C2 Oak Harbor WA U.S.A.
232 C10 Oak Hill OH U.S.A.
232 D11 Oak Hill WV U.S.A.
240 M4 Oakhurst CA U.S.A.
235 G4 Oakhurst NJ U.S.A.
226 D3 Oak Island WI U.S.A.
240 L7 Oak Knolls CA U.S.A.
223 K5 Oak Lake Man. Can.
240 J4 Oakland CA U.S.A.
232 F9 Oakland MD U.S.A.
233 □P4 Oakland ME U.S.A.
236 G5 Oakland NE U.S.A.
235 G2 Oakland NJ U.S.A.
238 C5 Oakland OR U.S.A.
240 J4 Oakland airport CA U.S.A.
230 D6 Oakland City IN U.S.A.
83 K6 Oaklands N.S.W. Austr.
226 G8 Oak Lawn IL U.S.A.
151 K3 Oakley Bedfordshire, England U.K.
151 J4 Oakley Buckinghamshire, England U.K.
146 I10 Oakley Fife, Scotland U.K.
151 J5 Oakley Hampshire, England U.K.
236 E6 Oakley KS U.S.A.
227 J6 Oakley MI U.S.A.
232 F8 Oakmont PA U.S.A.
86 F6 Oakover r. W.A. Austr.
226 G8 Oak Park IL U.S.A.
235 G2 Oak Ridge NJ U.S.A.
238 C5 Oakridge OR U.S.A.
231 E7 Oak Ridge TN U.S.A.
234 E4 Oaks PA U.S.A.
234 F5 Oak Shade NJ U.S.A.
80 H6 Oakura North I. N.Z.
82 H5 Oakvale S.A. Austr.
240 M7 Oak View CA U.S.A.
224 E5 Oakville Ont. Can.
235 I1 Oakville CT U.S.A.
232 A7 Oakwood OH U.S.A.
232 A9 Oakwood OH U.S.A.
234 D5 Oakwood Beach NJ U.S.A.
81 E12 Oamaru South I. N.Z.
105 L4 Ōamishirasato Japan
80 H6 Oaonui North I. N.Z.
105 M3 Ōarai Japan
81 H9 Oaro South I. N.Z.
182 C4 O Arrabal Spain
103 J12 Ōasa Japan
105 K3 Ōashi-gawa r. Japan
240 O4 Oasis CA U.S.A.
238 G6 Oasis NV U.S.A.
197 L2 Oaşului, Munţii mts Romania
Oates Coast reg. Antarctica see Oates Land
263 K2 Oates Land reg. Antarctica
83 K10 Oatlands Tas. Austr.
214 I8 Oatlands S. Africa
245 K8 Oaxaca Mex.
245 K8 Oaxaca state Mex.
121 M1 Ob' r. Rus. Fed.
Ob, Gulf of sea chan. Rus. Fed. see Obskaya Guba
224 C3 Oba Ont. Can.
Oba i. Vanuatu see Aoba
Obaghan r. Kazakh. see Ubagan
104 C7 Obako-dake mt. Japan
128 A2 Obaköy Turkey
138 M6 Obal' Vitsyebskaya Voblasts' Belarus
138 M6 Obal' Vitsyebskaya Voblasts' Belarus
138 M6 Obal' canal Belarus
207 H5 Obala Cameroon
227 J1 Oba Lake Ont. Can.
104 C5 Obama Japan
104 C4 Obama-wan b. Japan
207 H5 Oban Nigeria
146 F10 Oban Argyll and Bute, Scotland U.K.
102 R8 Obanazawa Japan
207 H5 Oban Hills mt. Nigeria
104 F5 Obara Japan
182 G4 O Barco Spain
183 N3 Obarenes, Montes mts Spain
197 P4 Obârşeni, Dealul hill Romania
104 E6 Obata Japan
129 D5 Obayayla Turkey
Obbia Somalia see Hobyo
140 P5 Obbola Sweden
197 N3 Obcina Mare ridge Romania
179 K5 Obdach Austria
164 G3 Obdam Neth.
Obdorsk Rus. Fed. see Salekhard
176 C2 Obecnice Czech Rep.
Óbecse Vojvodina Serbia see Bečej
222 G4 Obed Alta Can.
185 J4 Obejo Spain
129 A5 Öbektaş Turkey
138 I6 Obeliai Lith.
175 L1 Obelija l. Lith.
81 D12 Obelisk mt. South I. N.Z.
258 G2 Oberá Arg.
179 L5 Oberaich Austria
178 H4 Oberalm Austria
190 F2 Oberalpstock mt. Switz.
173 K6 Oberammergau Ger.
173 J3 Oberasbach Ger.
173 K6 Oberau Ger.
173 M6 Oberaudorf Ger.
169 H9 Oberaula Ger.
173 L6 Oberbayern admin. reg. Ger.
172 F3 Oberderdingen Ger.
173 L5 Oberding Ger.
169 J8 Oberdorla Ger.
178 G6 Oberdrauburg Austria
172 F5 Obere Donau park Ger.
190 H1 Oberegg Switz.
169 J10 Oberelsbach Ger.
190 H2 Ober Engadin reg. Switz.
190 E1 Oberentfelden Switz.
173 N3 Oberer Bayerischer Wald park Ger.
171 E9 Obere Saale park Ger.
172 H6 Oberessendorf Ger.
171 G10 Oberes Westerzgebirge park Ger.
169 D10 Oberfell Ger.
171 D11 Oberfranken admin. reg. Ger.
169 J6 Oberg (Lahstedt) Ger.
190 D1 Obergösgen Switz.
179 M3 Ober-Grafendorf Austria
173 K5 Obergriesbach Ger.
173 I6 Obergünzburg Ger.
178 D6 Obergurgl Austria
171 J8 Obergurig Ger.
179 L6 Oberhaag Austria
173 L5 Oberhaching Ger.
173 J2 Oberhaid Ger.
172 E5 Oberharmersbach Ger.
173 K4 Oberhausen Bayern Ger.
169 C8 Oberhausen Nordrhein-Westfalen Ger.
169 K9 Oberhof Ger.
190 D2 Oberhofen Switz.
178 D5 Oberhofen im Inntal Austria
157 O6 Oberhoffen-sur-Moder France
178 B4 Oberjochpass pass Austria/Ger.
172 E4 Oberkirch Ger.
173 I4 Oberkochen Ger.
171 E10 Oberkotzau Ger.
168 D5 Oberlangen Ger.
171 J8 Oberlausitz reg. Ger.
171 J8 Oberlausitzer Bergland park Ger.
171 J8 Oberlichtenau Ger.
178 G6 Oberlienz Austria
236 E6 Oberlin KS U.S.A.
237 I10 Oberlin LA U.S.A.
232 C7 Oberlin OH U.S.A.
172 H5 Obermarchtal Ger.
169 J9 Obermaßfeld-Grimmenthal Ger.
172 D2 Obermoschel Ger.
157 N7 Obernai France
179 H3 Obernberg am Inn Austria
172 G2 Obernburg am Main Ger.
173 J4 Oberndorf am Lech Ger.
172 F5 Oberndorf am Neckar Ger.
179 L3 Oberndorf an der Melk Austria
178 G4 Oberndorf bei Salzburg Austria
179 J3 Oberneukirchen Austria
169 J7 Obernfeld Ger.
172 F5 Obernheim Ger.
172 D3 Obernheim-Kirchenarnbach Ger.
169 H6 Obernkirchen Ger.
173 P4 Obernzell Ger.
173 I3 Obernzenn Ger.
171 K9 Oberoderwitz Ger.
172 E2 Ober-Olm Ger.
83 L5 Oberon N.S.W. Austr.
173 J6 Oberostendorf Ger.
179 I3 Oberösterreich land Austria
173 L2 Oberpfalz admin. reg. Ger.
173 M2 Oberpfälzer Wald mts Ger.
176 B2 Oberpfälzer Wald park Ger.
173 L5 Oberpframmern Ger.
179 O4 Oberpullendorf Austria
172 F2 Ober-Ramstadt Ger.
172 H6 Oberreute Ger.
172 D6 Oberried Ger.
173 I5 Oberrieden Ger.
190 H1 Oberriet Switz.
171 D8 Oberröblingen Ger.
172 F2 Ober-Roden Ger.
171 D8 Oberroßla Ger.
172 H3 Oberrot Ger.
172 D5 Oberrotweil Ger.
173 L5 Oberschleißheim Ger.
173 N4 Oberschneiding Ger.
171 H9 Oberschöna Ger.
179 N5 Oberschützen Austria
179 O3 Obersiebenbrunn Austria
190 E1 Obersiggenthal Switz.
169 I10 Obersinn Ger.
172 H3 Obersontheim Ger.
169 K8 Oberspier Ger.
172 H5 Oberstadion Ger.
173 I6 Oberstaufen Ger.
173 I7 Oberstdorf Ger.
172 G3 Oberstenfeld Ger.
173 M5 Obertaufkirchen Ger.
172 G6 Oberteuringen Ger.
172 C2 Oberthal Ger.
169 I10 Oberthulba Ger.
178 G6 Obertilliach Austria
173 M4 Obertraubling Ger.
173 K2 Obertrubach Ger.
178 H4 Obertrum am See Austria
178 H4 Obertrumer See l. Austria
169 G10 Obertshausen Ger.
136 E5 Obertyn Ukr.
170 I4 Oberueckersee l. Ger.
169 G10 Oberursel (Taunus) Ger.
178 H6 Obervellach Austria
173 M3 Oberviechtach Ger.
190 E2 Oberwald Switz.
169 H7 Oberwälder Land reg. Ger.
179 N4 Oberwaltersdorf Austria
179 N5 Oberwart Austria
169 E10 Oberwesel Ger.
179 M3 Oberwölbling Austria
172 E5 Oberwolfach Ger.
179 J5 Oberwölz Austria
137 N2 Obesta r. Rus. Fed.
171 E8 Obhausen Ger.
93 E4 Obi i. Maluku Indon.
207 H4 Obi Nigeria
93 E4 Obi, Kepulauan is Maluku Indon.
93 E4 Obi, Selat sea chan. Maluku Indon.
251 H5 Óbidos Brazil
184 A2 Óbidos Port.
184 A2 Óbidos, Lagoa de lag. Port.
123 M2 Obigarm Tajik.
102 U4 Obihiro Japan
93 E4 Obilatu i. Maluku Indon.
196 J8 Obilić Kosovo Serbia
135 I7 Obil'noye Rus. Fed.
173 M5 Obing Ger.
237 K7 Obion r. TN U.S.A.
102 S2 Obira Japan
250 D2 Obispos Venez.
261 F2 Obispo Trejo Arg.
Obitochnaya Kosa spit Ukr. see Obytichna Kosa
105 K5 Obitsu-gawa r. Japan
162 G5 Objat France
174 F1 Objazda Pol.
175 M4 Oblapy Ukr.
179 I5 Öblarn Austria
135 H6 Oblivskaya Rus. Fed.
100 G4 Obluch'ye Rus. Fed.
139 T6 Obninsk Rus. Fed.
208 E3 Obo C.A.R.
106 G8 Obo Qinghai China
214 E3 Obobogorap S. Africa
210 D2 Obock Djibouti
136 I5 Obodivka Ukr.
101 F8 Ŏbŏk N. Korea
208 E5 Obokote Dem. Rep. Congo
110 K7 Obo Liang Qinghai China
207 G5 Obolo Nigeria
182 F4 O Bolo Spain
137 L4 Obolon' Ukr.
186 D6 Obón Spain
95 K2 Obong, Gunung mt. Malaysia
177 K3 Oborín Slovakia
174 E3 Oborniki Pol.
174 E4 Oborniki Śląskie Pol.
208 B5 Obouya Congo
135 G6 Oboyan' Rus. Fed.
134 H3 Obozerskiy Rus. Fed.
117 I7 Obra Uttar Prad. India
174 D3 Obra r. Pol.
258 F3 Obrage Arg.
242 E4 Obregón, Presa resr Mex.
223 K2 Obre Lake N.W.T. Can.
196 I6 Obrenovac Serbia
238 C5 O'Brien OR U.S.A.
172 G3 Obrigheim Ger.
172 E2 Obrigheim (Pfalz) Ger.
Obringa r. Switz. see Aare
176 C1 Obrnice Czech Rep.
197 Q7 Obrochishte Bulg.
191 Q4 Obrov Slovenia
174 G3 Obrowo Pol.
126 F4 Obruk Turkey
174 E4 Obry, Kanał canal Pol.
175 J3 Obryte Pol.
174 E3 Obrzycko Pol.
82 D3 Observatory Hill S.A. Austr.
222 D4 Observatory Inlet B.C. Can.
82 □2 Observatory Rock i. Lord Howe I. Austr.
139 P6 Obsha r. Rus. Fed.
120 D2 Obshchiy Syrt hills Rus. Fed.
130 I3 Obskaya Guba sea chan. Rus. Fed.
175 K5 Obsza Pol.
137 M2 Obtove Ukr.
104 E5 Ōbu Japan
206 E5 Obuasi Ghana
207 H5 Obubra Nigeria
188 G3 Obudovac Bos.-Herz.
207 H5 Obudu Nigeria
136 J3 Obukhiv Ukr.
Obukhov Ukr. see Obukhiv
139 V6 Obukhovo Rus. Fed.
105 H2 Obuse Japan
134 K4 Obva r. Rus. Fed.
190 E2 Obwalden canton Switz.
134 J3 Ob"yachevo Rus. Fed.
137 P7 Obytichna Kosa spit Ukr.
137 O7 Obytichna Zakota b. Ukr.
182 F2 O Cádavo Spain
231 F11 Ocala FL U.S.A.
182 C5 O Calvario Spain
242 E3 Ocampo Chihuahua Mex.
242 H4 Ocampo Coahuila Mex.
244 F4 Ocampo Guanajuato Mex.
245 H3 Ocampo Tamaulipas Mex.
182 D2 O Campo da Feira Spain
250 C2 Ocaña Col.
192 B4 Ocana Corse France
252 B3 Ocaña Peru
183 N9 Ocaña Spain
183 N9 Ocaña, Mesa de plat. Spain
182 D4 O Carballiño Spain
182 D4 O Castelo Spain
182 D3 O Castro Spain
182 E3 O Castro de Ferreira Spain
191 L6 Occhiobello Italy
193 N4 Occhito, Lago di l. Italy
252 C4 Occidental, Cordillera mts Chile
250 B4 Occidental, Cordillera mts Col.
252 C4 Occidental, Cordillera mts Peru
190 F5 Occimiano Italy
232 H10 Occoquan VA U.S.A.
232 D11 Oceana WV U.S.A.
235 I3 Ocean Beach NY U.S.A.
222 B3 Ocean Cape AK U.S.A.
246 D1 Ocean Cay i. Bahamas
233 J10 Ocean City MD U.S.A.
234 F6 Ocean City NJ U.S.A.
235 G5 Ocean County county NJ U.S.A.
222 E4 Ocean Falls B.C. Can.
235 G5 Ocean Gate NJ U.S.A.
235 G4 Ocean Grove NJ U.S.A.
74 Oceania continent
Ocean Island Kiribati see Banaba
Ocean Island atoll HI U.S.A. see Kure Atoll
240 L6 Oceano CA U.S.A.
240 O8 Oceanside CA U.S.A.
237 K10 Ocean Springs MS U.S.A.
234 F6 Ocean View NJ U.S.A.
235 G6 Oceanville NJ U.S.A.
183 N6 Ocejón mt. Spain
78 □4a Ocha i. Chuuk Micronesia
78 □4a Ocha, Mochun sea chan. Chuuk Micronesia
186 C2 Ochagavía Spain
137 K7 Ochakiv Ukr.
129 C3 Och'amch'ire Georgia
182 E2 O Chao Spain
134 K4 Ocher Rus. Fed.
136 I4 Ocheretnya Ukr.
137 O6 Ocheretuvate Ukr.
157 K6 Ochey France
198 F4 Ochi mt. Greece
103 J11 Ōchi Japan
102 W3 Ochiishi-misaki pt Japan
146 I10 Ochil Hills Scotland U.K.
146 H12 Ochiltree East Ayrshire, Scotland U.K.
137 M1 Ochkyne Ukr.
231 E11 Ochlockonee r. GA U.S.A.
175 H3 Ochnia r. Pol.
168 E4 Ocholt Ger.
246 □ Ocho Rios Jamaica
Ochrida, Lake Albania/Macedonia see Ohrid, Lake
173 I2 Ochsenfurt Ger.
172 H5 Ochsenhausen Ger.
169 D10 Ochtendung Ger.
171 D6 Ochtmersleben Ger.
169 D6 Ochtrup Ger.
231 F10 Ocilla GA U.S.A.
141 N6 Ockelbo Sweden
168 G1 Ockholm Ger.
146 E9 Ockle Highland, Scotland U.K.
197 N4 Ocland Romania
231 F10 Ocmulgee r. GA U.S.A.
197 L4 Ocna Mureş Romania
197 M5 Ocna Sibiului Romania
136 G5 Ocniţa Moldova
197 N4 Ocolaşul Mare, Vârful mt. Romania
252 B4 Ocoña Peru
231 F9 Oconee, Lake resr GA U.S.A.
85 I6 O'Connell Creek r. Qld Austr.
226 F6 Oconomowoc WI U.S.A.
226 G5 Oconto WI U.S.A.
226 F5 Oconto Falls WI U.S.A.
182 C4 O Convento Spain
182 F3 O Corgo Spain
242 E5 Ocoroni Mex.
252 C3 Ocoruro Peru
243 M10 Ocos Guat.
243 M9 Ocosingo Mex.
242 □P11 Ocotal Nic.
245 K9 Ocotepec Mex.
244 E5 Ocotlán Jalisco Mex.
245 K9 Ocotlán Oaxaca Mex.
177 I3 Očová Slovakia
243 M9 Ocozocoautla Mex.
182 E9 Ocreza r. Port.
177 I4 Ócsa Hungary
177 I4 Ocsai park Hungary
177 H5 Őcsény Hungary
177 J5 Öcsöd Hungary
158 H2 Octeville France
159 L2 Octeville-sur-Mer France
October Revolution Island Severnaya Zemlya Rus. Fed. see Oktyabr'skoy Revolyutsii, Ostrov
234 C5 Octoraro Creek r. MD U.S.A.
234 C5 Octoraro Lake PA U.S.A.
242 □S14 Ocú Panama
213 H2 Ocua Moz.
245 H7 Ocuilan de Arteaga Mex.
247 J8 Ocumare del Tuy Venez.
252 D4 Ocurí Bol.
174 G2 Ocypel Pol.
206 E5 Oda Ghana
103 J11 Ōda Japan
203 H4 Oda, Jebel mt. Sudan
128 E2 Odabaşı Turkey
140 □E1 Ódáðahraun lava field Iceland
101 F8 Ŏdaejin N. Korea
101 F10 Odae-san National Park S. Korea
104 D7 Ōdai Japan
104 D7 Ōdaigahara-zan mt. Japan
104 G4 Odaira-tōge pass Japan
102 R9 Odaka Japan
226 D3 Odanah WI U.S.A.
102 R6 Ōdate Japan
105 J5 Odawara Japan
142 C1 Odda Norway
142 G6 Odder Denmark
146 □O1 Oddsta Shetland, Scotland U.K.
184 D4 Odearce r. Port.
184 B6 Odeceixe Port.
223 L3 Odei r. Man. Can.
184 E6 Odeleite Port.
184 E6 Odeleite r. Port.
226 F8 Odell IL U.S.A.
184 C6 Odelouca r. Port.
173 K5 Odelzhausen Ger.
237 G12 Odem TX U.S.A.
184 B5 Odemira Port.
199 I4 Ödemiş Turkey
186 I4 Òdena Spain
Ödenburg Hungary see Sopron
215 K3 Odendaalsrus S. Africa
143 L2 Odensbacken Sweden
142 G6 Odense Denmark
142 G6 Odense Fjord b. Denmark
234 B6 Odenton MD U.S.A.
172 F2 Odenwald reg. Ger.
174 C2 Oder r. Ger.
alt. Odra (Poland)
169 I7 Oder r. Ger.
170 J5 Oderberg Ger.
170 J5 Oderbruch reg. Ger.
170 J2 Oderbucht b. Ger.
170 J3 Oderhaff b. Ger.
170 H5 Oder-Havel-Kanal canal Ger.
171 I6 Oderin Ger.
172 D2 Odernheim am Glan Ger.
191 M4 Oderzo Italy
136 J7 Odesa Ukr.
134 K3 Odesdino Rus. Fed.
143 K3 Ödeshog Sweden
136 I6 Odes'ka Oblast' admin. div. Ukr.
Odessa Ukr. see Odesa
234 D6 Odessa DE U.S.A.
237 D10 Odessa TX U.S.A.
238 E3 Odessa WA U.S.A.
Odessa Oblast admin. div. Ukr. see Odes'ka Oblast'
Odesskaya Oblast' admin. div. Ukr. see Odes'ka Oblast'
121 O1 Odesskoye Rus. Fed.
Odessus Bulg. see Varna
158 C6 Odet r. France
203 H5 Odi watercourse Sudan
184 B6 Odiáxere Port.
184 F6 Odiel r. Spain
206 D4 Odienné Côte d'Ivoire
151 K5 Odiham Hampshire, England U.K.
164 H4 Odijk Neth.
208 A5 Odimba Gabon
139 U6 Odintsovo Rus. Fed.
184 C4 Odivelas Beja Port.
184 A3 Odivelas Lisboa Port.
184 C4 Odivelas r. Port.
184 C4 Odivelas, Barragem de resr Port.
197 P5 Odobeşti Romania
197 O5 Odobeştilor, Măgura hill Romania
174 F4 Odolanów Pol.
171 J10 Odolena Voda Czech Rep.
262 T2 Odom Inlet Antarctica
159 K3 Odon r. France
183 Q7 Odón Spain
97 G9 Ŏdôngk Cambodia
164 K3 Odoorn Neth.
197 N4 Odorheiu Secuiesc Romania
139 T8 Odoyev Rus. Fed.
174 C2 Odra r. Pol.
alt. Oder (Germany)
183 L4 Odra r. Spain
137 N7 Odradivka Ukr.
177 G2 Odry Czech Rep.
175 I4 Odrzywół Pol.
196 H5 Odžaci Vojvodina Serbia
208 B4 Odzala, Parc National d' nat. park Congo
213 G3 Odzi Zimbabwe
213 G3 Odzi r. Zimbabwe
104 B5 Ōe Japan
Oea Libya see Ţarābulus
169 K6 Oebisfelde Ger.
169 I7 Oedelsheim (Oberweser) Ger.
171 H9 Oederan Ger.
168 H3 Oederquart Ger.
103 G11 Oedong S. Korea
164 I5 Oeffelt Neth.
164 G4 Oegstgeest Neth.
254 E3 Oeiras Brazil
184 A3 Oeiras Port.
184 D5 Oeiras r. Port.
169 F7 Oelde Ger.
168 I3 Oelixdorf Ger.
236 D4 Oelrichs SD U.S.A.
171 F10 Oelsnitz Sachsen Ger.
171 G9 Oelsnitz Sachsen Ger.
236 J4 Oelwein IA U.S.A.
164 J4 Oene Neth.
84 D2 Oenpelli N.T. Austr.
190 D1 Oensingen Switz.
168 H4 Oerel Ger.
168 J3 Oering Ger.
169 J10 Oerlenbach Ger.
169 G7 Oerlinghausen Ger.
Oesel i. Estonia see Hiiumaa
165 I9 Oesling hills Lux.
165 F6 Oesterdam barrage Neth.
258 E2 Oetling Arg.
171 E9 Oettersdorf Ger.
173 J4 Oettingen in Bayern Ger.
178 C5 Oetz Austria
168 K4 Oetzen Ger.
225 F2 Oeufs, Lac des l. Que. Can.
168 H1 Oeversee Ger.
104 B5 Ōe-yama hill Japan
163 B8 Œyreluy France
127 J3 Of Turkey
238 L3 O'Fallon r. MT U.S.A.
193 Q5 Ofanto r. Italy
128 C7 Ofaqim Israel
193 L3 Ofena Italy
207 G4 Offa Nigeria
147 G6 Offaly county Ireland
190 H5 Offanengo Italy
157 M8 Offemont France
169 G10 Offenbach am Main Ger.
172 E3 Offenbach an der Queich Ger.
173 N4 Offenberg Ger.
172 D5 Offenburg Ger.
179 I4 Offensee l. Austria
140 M5 Offerdal Sweden
193 L2 Offida Italy
173 I5 Offingen Ger.
156 B4 Offranville France
199 H6 Ofidoussa i. Greece
79 □8 Ofolanga atoll Tonga
182 D3 O Forte Spain
140 N2 Ofotfjorden sea chan. Norway
172 G5 Ofterdingen Ger.
78 □2 Ofu i. American Samoa
102 S7 Ōfunato Japan
95 K4 Oga r. Indon.
102 Q7 Oga Japan
102 R7 Ogachi Japan
105 K1 Oga-dake mt. Japan
210 E3 Ogadēn reg. Eth.
102 Q7 Oga-hantō pen. Japan
104 E5 Ōgaki Japan
236 E5 Ogallala NE U.S.A.
94 F6 Ogan r. Indon.
105 J3 Ogano Japan
105 H6 Ogasa Japan
103 □2 Ogasawara-shotō is N. Pacific Ocean
227 P2 Ogascanane, Lac l. Que. Can.
105 H1 Ōgata Japan
105 H3 Ōga-tō mt. Japan
105 M1 Ogawa Fukushima Japan
105 L3 Ogawa Ibaraki Japan
105 L2 Ogawa Ibaraki Japan
105 G2 Ogawa Nagano Japan
105 J3 Ogawa Saitama Japan
105 L2 Ōgawa Japan
102 R8 Ōgawara Japan
102 S6 Ogawara-ko l. Japan
207 G4 Ogbomosho Nigeria
Ogbomoso Nigeria see Ogbomosho
236 H4 Ogden IA U.S.A.
238 I6 Ogden UT U.S.A.
222 C3 Ogden, Mount B.C. Can.
234 F2 Ogdensburg NJ U.S.A.
233 J4 Ogdensburg NY U.S.A.
231 G10 Ogeechee r. GA U.S.A.
226 D4 Ogema WI U.S.A.
168 E3 Ogenbargen Ger.
156 H6 Oger France
163 C9 Ogeu-les-Bains France
157 M6 Ogéviller France
190 G4 Oggiono Italy
116 D7 Oghna Rajasthan India
78 □6 Ogho Choiseul Solomon Is
103 P9 Ogi Japan
224 C4 Ogidaki Ont. Can.
220 E3 Ogilvie r. Y.T. Can.
220 D3 Ogilvie Mountains Y.T. Can.
102 □1 Ogimi Okinawa Japan
129 D6 Oğlaksuyu Turkey
122 F2 Oglanly Turkm.
204 E5 'Oglât el Khnâchîch well Mali
204 D4 Oglat Sbot well Alg.
192 D8 Ogliastra prov. Sardegna Italy
192 D8 Ogliastra reg. Sardegna Italy
192 D8 Ogliastra, Isola dell' i. Sardegna Italy
192 C2 Ogliastro Corse France
194 H9 Ogliastro, Lago di l. Sicilia Italy
190 J5 Oglio r. Italy
100 K2 Oglongi Rus. Fed.
85 L7 Ogmore Qld Austr.
150 E5 Ogmore Vale of Glamorgan, Wales U.K.
150 E4 Ogmore Vale Bridgend, Wales U.K.
160 G2 Ognon r. France
Oğnut Turkey see Göynük
105 J3 Ōgo Japan
93 B3 Ogoamas, Gunung mt. Indon.
105 J4 Ogōchi-damu dam Japan
100 H2 Ogodzha Rus. Fed.
207 H5 Ogoja Nigeria
224 C3 Ogoki r. Ont. Can.
224 C3 Ogoki Lake Ont. Can.
224 B3 Ogoki Reservoir Ont. Can.
100 M5 Ogon'ki Rus. Fed.
183 O2 Ogoño, Cabo c. Spain
208 A5 Ogooué r. Gabon
208 B5 Ogooué-Ivindo prov. Gabon
208 B5 Ogooué-Lolo prov. Gabon
208 A5 Ogooué-Maritime prov. Gabon
103 I12 Ogōri Japan
100 F1 Ogoron Rus. Fed.
105 J4 Ogose Japan
197 L7 Ogosta r. Bulg.
207 F5 Ogou r. Togo
87 D11 O'Grady, Lake salt flat W.A. Austr.
197 K9 Ogražden mts Bulg./Macedonia
Ograzhden mts Bulg./Macedonia see Ogražden
138 H5 Ogre Latvia
138 H5 Ogre r. Latvia
175 J3 Ogrodniki Pol.
175 H5 Ogrodzieniec Pol.
171 J7 Ogrosen Ger.
182 C4 O Grove Spain
104 E5 Ōguchi Japan
139 V5 Ogudnevo Rus. Fed.
204 E4 Oguîlet Merzoug well Mali
188 E3 Ogulin Croatia
207 F5 Ogun state Nigeria
105 I1 Oguni Japan
233 □O5 Ogunquit ME U.S.A.
122 E2 Ogurjaly Adasy i. Turkm.
129 I4 Oğuz Azer.
129 I1 Oguzer Rus. Fed.
177 K6 Ohaba Lungă Romania
207 G5 Ohafia Nigeria
81 B12 Ohai South I. N.Z.
80 J6 Ohakune North I. N.Z.
210 E3 Ohale well Somalia
185 N6 Ohanes Spain
205 H3 Ohanet Alg.
212 C3 Ohangwena admin. reg. Namibia
105 L5 Ōhara Japan
102 S5 Ōhata Japan
80 J7 Ohau North I. N.Z.
81 E11 Ohau r. South I. N.Z.
81 D11 Ohau, Lake South I. N.Z.
80 J4 Ohaupo North I. N.Z.
Ohcejohka Fin. see Utsjoki
168 E4 Ohe r. Ger.
173 O4 Ohe r. Ger.
Ohétéroah i. Îs Australes Fr. Polynesia see Rurutu
165 H8 Ohey Belgium
252 C5 O'Higgins Chile
260 B4 O'Higgins admin. reg.
259 B8 O'Higgins, Lago l. Chil
80 J4 Ohinewai North I. N.Z.
226 E8 Ohio IL U.S.A.
236 K7 Ohio r. OH/WV U.S.A.
232 C8 Ohio state U.S.A.
232 A8 Ohio City OH U.S.A.
262 Q1 Ohio Range mts Antarc
235 G1 Ohioville NY U.S.A.
105 K3 Ōhira Japan
105 I5 Ōhito Japan
80 L4 Ohiwa Harbour North I.
137 O4 Ohiyivka Ukr.
172 D5 Ohlsbach Ger.
179 I4 Ohlsdorf Austria
173 K6 Ohlstadt Ger.
169 G9 Ohm r. Ger.
138 J3 Õhne r. Estonia
169 D6 Ohne Ger.
172 F6 Öhningen Ger.
79 □8 'Ohonua Tonga
80 L4 Ohope North I. N.Z.
177 G3 Ohrady Slovakia
169 K9 Ohrdruf Ger.
176 D1 Ohře r. Czech Rep.
171 E6 Ohre r. Ger.
196 I9 Ohrid Macedonia
196 I9 Ohrid, Lake Albania/Macedonia
Ohridsko Ezero l. Albania/Macedonia see Ohrid, Lake
213 F5 Ohrigstad S. Africa
172 G3 Öhringen Ger.
Ohrit, Liqeni i l. Albania/Macedonia see Ohrid, Lake
169 K6 Ohrum Ger.
80 I5 Ohura North I. N.Z.
104 C5 Ōi Fukui Japan
105 J5 Ōi Kanagawa Japan
182 C7 Oiã Port.
251 I4 Oiapoque Brazil
186 B1 Oiartzun Spain
250 C3 Oiba Col.
146 G8 Oich r. Scotland U.K.
146 G8 Oich, Loch l. Scotland
198 C3 Oichalia Greece
113 □1 Oidhuni i. S. Male Mald
111 K12 Oiga Xizang China
105 H6 Ōigawa Japan
104 C5 Ōi-gawa r. Japan
105 H6 Ōi-gawa r. Japan
146 C9 Oigh-sgeir is Scotland
156 E3 Oignies France
160 H4 Oignin r. France
182 D4 O Igrexario Spain
140 R4 Oijärvi Fin.
164 H5 Oijen Neth.
Oik Kazakh. see Uyuk
232 F7 Oil City PA U.S.A.
240 M6 Oildale CA U.S.A.
108 C4 Oilê Sichuan China
147 I8 Oilgate Ireland
147 F3 Oily r. Ireland
182 F5 Oímbra Spain
183 P3 Oion Spain
108 B4 Oi Qu r. Xizang China
102 S6 Oirase-gawa r. Japan
182 D3 O Irixo Spain
159 K8 Oiron France
164 H5 Oirschot Neth.
161 H6 Oisans reg. France
156 D5 Oise dept France
156 D6 Oise r. France
156 F5 Oise à l'Aisne, Canal France
163 B6 Oiseaux, Île aux i. Fra
206 A2 Oiseaux du Djoudj, Pa National des nat. park Senegal
160 H2 Oiselay-et-Grachaux
156 C4 Oisemont France
105 J5 Ōiso Japan
159 J5 Oisseau France
156 B5 Oissel France
164 H5 Oisterwijk Neth.
247 □4 Oistins Barbados
103 I13 Ōita Japan
103 I13 Ōita pref. Japan
182 C4 Oitavén r. Spain
198 D4 Oiti mt. Greece
198 D4 Oitis, Ethnikos Drymo nat. park Greece
197 O4 Oituz r. Romania
198 D6 Oitylo Greece
202 C4 Oiuru well Libya
102 S4 Oiwake Japan
159 Q7 Oizon France
105 J3 Ōizumi Gunma Japan
105 H4 Ōizumi Yamanashi Jap
104 E3 Oizuruga-dake mt. Ja
143 N3 Öja i. Sweden
240 M7 Ojai CA U.S.A.
185 L3 Ojailén r. Spain
Ojalava i. Samoa see
138 K2 Ojamaa r. Estonia
143 M1 Öjaren l. Sweden
175 H5 Ojcowski Park Narod nat. park Pol.
141 L6 Öje Sweden
261 E4 Ojeda Arg.
185 J7 Ojén Spain
104 C6 Ōji Japan
103 F13 Ojika-jima i. Japan
242 G3 Ojinaga Mex.
245 K7 Ojitlán Mex.
105 I1 Ojiya Japan
207 G5 Ojobo Nigeria
244 E3 Ojocaliente Mex.
239 K8 Ojo Caliente NM U.S.A.
260 E2 Ojo de Agua Arg.
244 G5 Ojo de Agua Mex.
242 F3 Ojo de Laguna Mex.
242 B4 Ojo de Liebre, Lago b
185 L2 Ojos del Guadiana lak Spain
258 C2 Ojos del Salado, Neva Arg./Chile
183 R7 Ojos Negros Spain
175 I3 Ojrzeń Pol.
207 H5 Oju Nigeria
244 F4 Ojuelos de Jalisco Me
141 M6 Öjung Sweden
207 G5 Oka Nigeria
139 W7 Oka r. Rus. Fed.
105 J3 Okabe Saitama Japan
105 H6 Okabe Shizuoka Japan
212 C4 Okahandja Namibia
Okahu b. South I. N.Z. Jackson Bay
80 J5 Okahukura North I. N.
80 H2 Okaihau North I. N.Z.
81 H10 Okains Bay South I. N.
81 H10 Okains Bay b. South I.
207 F4 Okaka Nigeria
212 C4 Okakarara Namibia
225 I1 Okak Islands Nfld and L
175 H2 Okalewo Pol.
222 G5 Okanagan Falls B.C.
222 G5 Okanagan Lake B.C.
114 G9 Okanda Sri Lanka
238 E2 Okanogan WA U.S.A.
238 E2 Okanogan r. WA U.S.A
238 D2 Okanogan Range mts WA U.S.A.
177 K5 Okány Hungary
208 E4 Okapi, Parc National nat. park Dem. Rep. C
212 C4 Okaputa Namibia
123 O6 Okara Pak.
81 E10 Okarito Lagoon South
80 H6 Okato North I. N.Z.
212 B3 Okaukuejo Namibia
212 D3 Okavango r. Botswana/Namibia
212 C3 Okavango admin. reg.
212 D3 Okavango Delta swam Botswana
103 H13 Ōkawa Japan
104 A5 Ōkawachi Japan
80 □ Okawa Point Chatham S. Pacific Ocean
105 H3 Okaya Japan
103 K12 Okayama Japan
103 K12 Okayama pref. Japan
104 F6 Okazaki Japan
129 B5 Okçular Dağı mt. Turk
231 G12 Okeechobee FL U.S.A.
231 G12 Okeechobee, Lake FL
237 F7 Okeene OK U.S.A.

Okefenokee National Wildlife Refuge and Wilderness nature res. GA U.S.A.
Okefenokee Swamp GA U.S.A.
Okegawa Japan
Okehampton Devon, England U.K.
Oke-Iho Nigeria
Okemah OK U.S.A.
Okement r. England U.K.
Okene Nigeria
Oker r. Ger.
Oketo Japan
Okha Gujarat India
Okha Sakhalin Rus. Fed.
Okhadunga Nepal see Okhaldhunga
Okhaldhunga Nepal
Okhansk Rus. Fed.
Okhimath Uttaranchal India
Okhinskiy Peresheyek isth. Rus. Fed.
Ókhi Óros mt. Greece see Ochi
Okhochevka Rus. Fed.
Okhotino Rus. Fed.
Okhotka r. Rus. Fed.
Okhotnykove Ukr.
Okhotsk Rus. Fed.
Okhotsk, Sea of Japan/Rus. Fed.
Okhotskoye More sea Japan/Rus. Fed. see Okhotsk, Sea of
Okhrimivka Ukr.
Okhthoniá Greece see Oktonia
Okhtyrka Ukr.
Okhvat Rus. Fed.
Okiep S. Africa
Okinawa Okinawa Japan
Okinawa i. Japan
Okinawa pref. Japan
Okinawa-guntō is Japan see Okinawa-shotō
Okinawa-shotō is Japan
Okino-Daitō-jima i. Japan
Okinoerabu-jima i. Nansei-shotō Japan
Okino-shima i. Japan
Okino-shima i. Japan
Okino-shima i. Japan
Okino-Tori-shima i. Japan
Oki-shotō is Japan
Oki-shotō is Japan
Okitipupa Nigeria
Okkan Myanmar
Oklahoma state U.S.A.
Oklahoma City OK U.S.A.
Oklawaha r. FL U.S.A.
Okmulgee OK U.S.A.
Okna r. Slovakia
Oknitsa Moldova see Ocnița
Oko, Wadi watercourse Sudan
Okoč Slovakia
Okola Cameroon
Okolona MS U.S.A.
Okolona OH U.S.A.
Okombache Namibia
Okondja Gabon
Okonek Pol.
Okopy Pol.
Okor r. Hungary
Okotoks Alta Can.
Okotusu well Namibia
Okovskiy Les for. Rus. Fed.
Okoyo Congo
Okpety, Gora mt. Kazakh.
Okříšky Czech Rep.
Okrouhlice Czech Rep.
Okrzeja Pol.
Oksa Pol.
Oksbøl Denmark
Øksfjord Norway
Okskiy Zapovednik nature res. Rus. Fed.
Oksovskiy Rus. Fed.
Oksskolten mt. Norway
Oktemberyan Armenia see Armavir
Oktonia Greece
Oktumgum des. Turkm.
Oktwin Myanmar
Oktyabr' Aktyubinskaya Oblast' Kazakh. see Kandyagash
Oktyabr' Rus. Fed.
Oktyabr'sk Kazakh. see Kandyagash
Oktyabr'sk Rus. Fed.
Oktyabr'skaya Belarus see Aktsyabrskaya
Oktyabr'skaya Rus. Fed.
Oktyabr'skiy Homyel'skaya Voblasts' Belarus see Aktsyabrski
Oktyabr'skiy Vitsyebskaya Voblasts' Belarus see Aktsyabrski
Oktyabr'skiy Kazakh.
Oktyabr'skiy Amurskaya Oblast' Rus. Fed.
Oktyabr'skiy Amurskaya Oblast' Rus. Fed.
Oktyabr'skiy Arkhangel'skaya Oblast' Rus. Fed.
Oktyabr'skiy Belgorodskaya Oblast' Rus. Fed.
Oktyabr'skiy Ivanovskaya Oblast' Rus. Fed.
Oktyabr'skiy Kaluzhskaya Oblast' Rus. Fed.
Oktyabr'skiy Kamchatskaya Oblast' Rus. Fed.
Oktyabr'skiy Krasnodarskiy Kray Rus. Fed.
Oktyabr'skiy Murmanskaya Oblast' Rus. Fed.
Oktyabr'skiy Respublika Adygeya Rus. Fed. see Takhtamukay
Oktyabr'skiy Respublika Bashkortostan Rus. Fed.
Oktyabr'skiy Rostovskaya Oblast' Rus. Fed.
Oktyabr'skiy Ryazanskaya Oblast' Rus. Fed.
Oktyabr'skiy Ryazanskaya Oblast' Rus. Fed.
Oktyabr'skiy Sverdlovskaya Oblast' Rus. Fed.
Oktyabr'skiy Volgogradskaya Oblast' Rus. Fed.
Oktyabr'skoye Kazakh.
Oktyabr'skoye Chelyabinskaya Oblast' Rus. Fed.
Oktyabr'skoye Khanty-Mansiyskiy Avtonomnyy Okrug Rus. Fed.
Oktyabr'skoye Lipetskaya Oblast' Rus. Fed.
Oktyabr'skoye Orenburgskaya Oblast' Rus. Fed.
Oktyabr'skoye Respublika Severnaya Osetiya-Alaniya Rus. Fed.
Oktyabr'skoye Yevreyskaya Avtonomnaya Oblast' Rus. Fed.
Oktyabr'skoy Revolyutsii, Ostrov i. Severnaya Zemlya Rus. Fed.
Oku Okinawa Japan
Okučani Croatia
Okuchi Japan
Ōkuchi Japan
Okulovka Rus. Fed.
Ok'umi Georgia
Okureshi Georgia see Oqureshi
Okuru South I. N.Z.
Oku-sangai-dake mt. Japan
Okushiri-kaikyō sea chan. Japan
Okushiri-tō i. Japan
Okuta Nigeria
Okutadami-ko resr Japan
Okutama Japan
Okutama-ko l. Japan
Okutango-hantō pen. Japan
Okutone-ko resr Japan
Ōkuwa Japan
Okwa watercourse Botswana
Ola Rus. Fed.
237 I8 Ola AR U.S.A.
261 F3 Olaeta Arg.
140 □B1 Ólafsvík Iceland
186 B2 Olague Spain
113 □1 Olahali i. N. Male Maldives
138 G5 Olaine Latvia
114 F6 Olakkur Tamil Nadu India
182 D9 Olalhas Port.
161 I7 Olan, Pic d' mt. France
240 N5 Olancha CA U.S.A.
240 N5 Olancha Peak CA U.S.A.
242 □P10 Olanchito Hond.
143 N5 Öland i. Sweden
143 N4 Ölands norra udde pt Öland Sweden
143 M5 Ölands sodra udde pt Öland Sweden
140 U3 Olanga Rus. Fed.
161 B9 Olargues France
177 K5 Olari Romania
82 H5 Olary S.A. Austr.
82 H5 Olary watercourse S.A. Austr.
261 G4 Olascoaga Arg.
177 K3 Olaszliszka Hungary
236 H6 Olathe KS U.S.A.
114 E7 Olavakod Kerala India
261 G5 Olavarría Arg.
183 Q3 Olave Spain
140 □ Olav V Land reg. Svalbard
174 F5 Oława Pol.
183 P3 Olazti Spain
187 D7 Olba Spain
179 N5 Olbendorf Austria
171 H9 Olbernhau Ger.
171 K9 Olbersdorf Ger.
171 D8 Olbersleben Ger.
192 C6 Olbia Sardegna Italy
192 D6 Olbia, Golfo di b. Sardegna Italy
192 C6 Olbia-Tempio prov. Sardegna Italy
175K5 Olbięcin Pol.
176 D2 Olbramovice Czech Rep.
177 K5 Olcea Romania
129 D4 Ölçek Turkey
129 C6 Ölçekli Turkey
131 P3 Ol'chan Rus. Fed.
173 K5 Olching Ger.
232 G5 Olcott NY U.S.A.
129 E5 Ölçülü Turkey
246 D2 Old Bahama Channel Bahamas/Cuba
151 J5 Old Basing Hampshire, England U.K.
114 G3 Old Bastar Chhattisgarh India
235 G4 Old Bridge NJ U.S.A.
150 H2 Oldbury West Midlands, England U.K.
147 H5 Oldcastle Ireland
86 H5 Old Cherrabun W.A. Austr.
150 E1 Old Colwyn Conwy, Wales U.K.
85 H7 Old Cork Qld Austr.
220 E3 Old Crow Y.T. Can.
146 G12 Old Dailly South Ayrshire, Scotland U.K.
203 F5 Old Dongola Sudan
164 J3 Oldeberkoop Neth.
164 I4 Oldebroek Neth.
164 J2 Oldehove Neth.
141 H6 Oldeide Norway
164 I3 Oldemarkt Neth.
168 F4 Oldenbrok Ger.
168 F4 Oldenburg Ger.
168 K2 Oldenburg in Holstein Ger.
168 H3 Oldendorf Ger.
168 K4 Oldendorf (Luhe) Ger.
168 G2 Oldenswort Ger.
164 K4 Oldenzaal Neth.
140 P2 Olderdalen Norway
151 O4 Old Felixstowe Suffolk, England U.K.
87 F12 Oldfield r. W.A. Austr.
233 K5 Old Forge NY U.S.A.
234 D2 Old Forge PA U.S.A.
232 B7 Old Fort OH U.S.A.
231 □2 Old Fort Point New Prov. Bahamas
247 □2 Old Fort Point Montserrat
87 E9 Old Gidgee W.A. Austr.
149 M6 Oldham Greater Manchester, England U.K.
246 □ Old Harbour Jamaica
246 □ Old Harbour Bay Jamaica
147 E9 Old Head of Kinsale Ireland
171 D8 Oldisleben Ger.
150 H5 Oldland South Gloucestershire, England U.K.
149 R7 Old Leake Lincolnshire, England U.K.
235 K2 Old Lyme CT U.S.A.
220 G5 Oldman r. Alta Can.
234 E5 Oldman's Creek r. NJ U.S.A.
146 L8 Oldmeldrum Aberdeenshire, Scotland U.K.
209 F8 Old Mkushi Zambia
215 N7 Old Morley S. Africa
235 L2 Old Mystic CT U.S.A.
233 □O5 Old Orchard Beach ME U.S.A.
225 K4 Old Perlican Nfld and Lab. Can.
240 M6 Old River CA U.S.A.
247 □2 Old Road Antigua and Barbuda
147 I8 Old Ross Ireland
222 H5 Olds Alta Can.
235 K2 Old Saybrook CT U.S.A.
233 □O4 Old Speck Mountain ME U.S.A.
168 F1 Oldsum Ger.
147 J5 Oldtown Ireland
149 L5 Old Town Cumbria, England U.K.
232 C10 Oldtown KY U.S.A.
233 □Q4 Old Town ME U.S.A.
211 B5 Olduvai Gorge tourist site Tanz.
232 D8 Old Washington OH U.S.A.
234 F3 Oldwick NJ U.S.A.
223 J5 Old Wives Lake Sask. Can.
241 Q7 Old Woman Mountains CA U.S.A.
106 G2 Öldziyt Arhangay Mongolia
107 K4 Öldziyt Dornogovĭ Mongolia
232 G6 Olean NY U.S.A.
175 K1 Olecko Pol.
182 F9 Oledo Port.
190 F4 Oleggio Italy
182 E9 Oleiros Port.
131 N3 Olekma r. Rus. Fed.
131 N3 Olekminsk Rus. Fed.
137 L2 Oleksandrivka Chernihivs'ka Oblast' Ukr.
137 P6 Oleksandrivka Dnipropetrovs'ka Oblast' Ukr.
137 P5 Oleksandrivka Donets'ka Oblast' Ukr.
137 O3 Oleksandrivka Kharkivs'ka Oblast' Ukr.
137 K5 Oleksandrivka Kirovohrads'ka Oblast' Ukr.
137 L5 Oleksandrivka Kirovohrads'ka Oblast' Ukr.
137 K6 Oleksandrivka Mykolayivs'ka Oblast' Ukr.
137 L7 Oleksandrivka Mykolayivs'ka Oblast' Ukr.
137 N8 Oleksandrivka Respublika Krym Ukr.
137 O7 Oleksandrivka Zaporiz'ka Oblast' Ukr.
Oleksandrivs'k Ukr. see Zaporizhzhya
137 M5 Oleksandriya Kirovohrads'ka Oblast' Ukr.
136 F3 Oleksandriya Rivnens'ka Oblast' Ukr.
137 Q5 Oleksiyevo-Druzhkivka Ukr.
137 M7 Oleksiyivka Khersons'ka Oblast' Ukr.
137 R4 Oleksiyivka Luhans'ka Oblast' Ukr.
137 M8 Oleksiyivka Respublika Krym Ukr.
134 I2 Olema Rus. Fed.
165 G6 Olen Belgium
142 B2 Ølen Norway
134 F1 Olenegorsk Rus. Fed.
131 M3 Olenek Rus. Fed.
131 M2 Olenek r. Rus. Fed.
Olenek Bay Rus. Fed. see Olenekskiy Zaliv
131 N2 Olenekskiy Zaliv b. Rus. Fed.
Ölengti r. Kazakh. see Olenti
139 Q5 Olenino Rus. Fed.
134 F2 Olenitsa Rus. Fed.
137 Q6 Olenivka Ukr.
Olenivs'ki Kar"yery Ukr. see Dokuchayevs'k
130 I2 Oleniy, Ostrov i. Rus. Fed.
120 E3 Olenti r. Kazakh.
121 P1 Olenti r. Kazakh.
107 N1 Olentuy Rus. Fed.
Olenya Rus. Fed. see Olenegorsk
162 B4 Oléron, Île d' i. France
186 I4 Olesa de Montserrat Spain
Oleshky Ukr. see Tsyurupyns'k
137 K2 Oleshnya Chernihivs'ka Oblast' Ukr.
137 N3 Oleshnya Sums'ka Oblast' Ukr.
136 D4 Oles'ko Ukr.
174 F4 Oleśnica Dolnośląskie Pol.
175 J5 Oleśnica Świętokrzyskie Pol.
175 I5 Olesno Małopolskie Pol.
174 G5 Olesno Opolskie Pol.
175 L5 Oleszyce Pol.
192 C2 Oletta Corse France
163 I10 Olette France
95 L9 Olet Tongo mt. Sumbawa Indon.
136 G2 Olevs'k Ukr.
234 D4 Oley PA U.S.A.
169 D7 Olfen Ger.
140 M3 Ølfjellet mt. Norway
100 I7 Ol'ga Rus. Fed.
224 E3 Olga, Lac l. Que. Can.
84 C8 Olga, Mount N.T. Austr.
140 □ Olgastretet str. Svalbard
190 G4 Olginate Italy
137 R9 Ol'ginka Rus. Fed.
100 H2 Ol'ginsk Rus. Fed.
137 R8 Ol'ginskaya Krasnodarskiy Kray Rus. Fed.
137 S6 Ol'ginskaya Rostovskaya Oblast' Rus. Fed.
Olginskoye Rus. Fed. see Kochubeyevskoye
106 A2 Ölgiy Mongolia
146 I6 Olgrinmore Highland, Scotland U.K.
184 A2 Olhalvo Port.
184 D6 Olhão Port.
140 R4 Olhava Fin.
184 A2 Olho Marinho Port.
257 F2 Olhos d'Agua Brazil
113 □1 Olhuveli i. S. Male Maldives
84 C8 Olia Chain mts N.T. Austr.
186 H3 Oliana Spain
186 H3 Oliana, Embassament d' resr Spain
183 M9 Olías del Rey Spain
191 R7 Olib Croatia
188 E3 Olib i. Croatia
192 C7 Oliena Sardegna Italy
192 C7 Oliena r. Sardegna Italy
186 D5 Oliete Spain
212 C5 Olifants watercourse Namibia
214 C7 Olifants r. Western Cape S. Africa
214 F9 Olifants r. Western Cape S. Africa
213 F4 Olifants r. S. Africa
214 G3 Olifantshoek S. Africa
214 C8 Olifantsrivierberge mts S. Africa
193 N7 Oligastro Marina Italy
91 K5 Olimarao atoll Micronesia
Olimbos hill Cyprus see Olympos
Olimbos mt. Greece see Mytikas
256 C4 Olímpia Brazil
199 L6 Olimpos Beydağları Milli Parkı nat. park Turkey
245 I8 Olinalá Mex.
254 G3 Olinda Brazil
213 H3 Olinda, Ponta pt Moz.
85 J1 Olinda Entrance sea chan. Qld Austr.
213 H3 Olinga Moz.
141 M6 Olingsjövallen Sweden
85 I6 Olio Qld Austr.
186 H4 Oliola Spain
Öli Qoltyq Sory dry lake Kazakh. see Mertvyy Kultuk, Sor
Olisipo Port. see Lisboa
183 Q4 Olite Spain
261 F3 Oliva Arg.
193 Q9 Oliva r. Italy
187 E10 Oliva Spain
184 G3 Oliva hill Spain
258 C3 Oliva, Cordillera de mts Arg./Chile
184 F4 Oliva de la Frontera Spain
184 G3 Oliva de Mérida Spain
182 C6 Olival Port.
260 C2 Olivares, Cerro de mt. Arg./Chile
183 P9 Olivares de Júcar Spain
232 B10 Olive Hill KY U.S.A.
240 K2 Olivehurst CA U.S.A.
257 E4 Oliveira Brazil
182 D7 Oliveira de Azeméis Port.
182 D7 Oliveira de Frades Port.
182 D7 Oliveira do Bairro Port.
182 E8 Oliveira do Conde Port.
182 C6 Oliveira do Douro Port.
182 E8 Oliveira do Hospital Port.
254 E5 Oliveira dos Brejinhos Brazil
Olivença Moz. see Lupilichi
Olivença-a-Nova Angola see Capunda Cavilongo
193 P5 Olivento r. Italy
184 E3 Olivenza r. Port./Spain
184 E3 Olivenza Spain
184 E3 Olivenza, Llanos de plain Spain
222 G5 Oliver B.C. Can.
195 I7 Oliveri Sicilia Italy
223 K3 Oliver Lake Sask. Can.
261 G3 Oliveros Arg.
156 C8 Olivet France
226 J7 Olivet MI U.S.A.
236 G4 Olivet SD U.S.A.
193 O6 Oliveto Citra Italy
193 Q6 Oliveto Lucano Italy
236 H3 Olivia MN U.S.A.
81 C11 Olivine Range mts South I. N.Z.
190 F2 Olivone Switz.
136 E4 Oliyiv Ukr.
107 J7 Oljoq Nei Mongol China
211 C6 Oljoro Wells Tanz.
141 I6 Øljuvatnet l. Norway
177 K2 Olka Slovakia
177 K3 Olka r. Slovakia
210 C5 Ol Kalou Kenya
Ölkeyek r. Kazakh. see Ul'kayak
135 H5 Ol'khi Rus. Fed.
135 G6 Ol'khovatka Rus. Fed.
139 W8 Ol'khovets Rus. Fed.
135 I6 Ol'khovka Rus. Fed.
175 H5 Olkusz Pol.
146 □N1 Ollaberry Shetland, Scotland U.K.
252 C3 Ollachea Peru
252 C5 Ollagüe Chile
252 C5 Ollagüe, Volcán vol. Bol.
192 C9 Ollastu r. Italy
149 O7 Ollerton Nottinghamshire, England U.K.
160 D5 Olliergues France
161 H10 Ollioules France
260 B2 Ollita, Cordillera de mts Arg./Chile
260 B2 Ollitas mt. Arg.
183 Q3 Ollo Spain
140 U5 Öllölä Fin.
192 C7 Ollolai Sardegna Italy
208 B5 Ollombo Congo
190 B3 Ollon Switz.
121 M7 Olmaliq Uzbek.
183 M5 Olmedilla de Roa Spain
192 A6 Olmedo Sardegna Italy
183 K6 Olmedo Spain
192 C2 Olmeta-di-Tuda Corse France
192 B4 Olmeto Corse France
261 F3 Olmos Arg.
250 B6 Olmos Peru
183 L3 Olmos de Ojeda Spain
Olmütz Czech Rep. see Olomouc
151 K3 Olney Milton Keynes, England U.K.
236 K6 Olney IL U.S.A.
234 A6 Olney MD U.S.A.
237 F9 Olney TX U.S.A.
187 D8 Olocau Spain
186 E6 Olocau del Rey Spain
100 A3 Olochi Rus. Fed.
143 K5 Olofström Sweden
121 L1 Ol'oinka Kazakh.
225 I3 Olomane r. Que. Can.
78 □6 Olomburi Malaita Solomon Is
176 G2 Olomouc Czech Rep.
176 G2 Olomoucký kraj admin. reg. Czech Rep.
190 G5 Olona r. Italy
139 P1 Olonets Rus. Fed.
139 Q1 Olonetskaya Vozvyshennost' hills Rus. Fed.
92 C4 Olongapo Luzon Phil.
95 K5 Olongliko Kalimantan Indon.
139 P1 Olonka r. Rus. Fed.
162 A2 Olonne-sur-Mer France
161 B10 Olonzac France
163 C9 Oloron-Ste-Marie France
78 □2 Olosega i. American Samoa
Olosenga atoll American Samoa see Swains Island
186 J3 Olot Spain
120 J8 Olot Uzbek.
171 G10 Oloví Czech Rep.
188 G3 Olovo Bos.-Herz.
107 N1 Olovyannaya Rus. Fed.
240 □E13 Olowalu HI U.S.A.
Oloy, Qatorkŭhi mts Asia see Alai Range
116 D9 Olpad Gujarat India
260 D2 Olpas Arg.
169 E8 Olpe Ger.
178 E5 Olperer mt. Austria
138 M8 Ol'sa r. Belarus
176 F2 Olšany Czech Rep.
176 G2 Olšany u Prostějova Czech Rep.
142 J2 Olsätter Sweden
177 G2 Olšava r. Czech Rep.
177 K3 Olšava r. Slovakia
169 F8 Olsberg Ger.
177 H2 Olše r. Czech Rep.
139 O7 Ol'sha Rus. Fed.
137 Q2 Ol'shanka Rus. Fed.
137 K6 Ol'shans'ke Ukr.
164 J4 Olst Neth.
175 K3 Olszanka Mazowieckie Pol.
174 F5 Olszanka Opolskie Pol.
175 K6 Olszany Pol.
175 J2 Olszewka Pol.
175 J2 Olszewo-Borki Pol.
174 G3 Olszówka Pol.
175 H5 Olsztyn Śląskie Pol.
175 I2 Olsztyn Warmińsko-Mazurskie Pol.
175 I2 Olsztynek Pol.
175 L3 Olszyn Pol.
174 D4 Olszyna Pol.
197 M7 Olt r. Romania
260 D2 Olta Arg.
259 C6 Olte, Sierra de mts Arg.
142 C3 Oltedal Norway
190 D1 Olten Switz.
197 O6 Oltenița Romania
197 M6 Olteț r. Romania
197 P6 Oltina Romania
120 H6 Oltinko'l Uzbek.
Oltinkŭl Uzbek. see Oltinko'l
123 M1 Oltintopkan Tajik.
127 J3 Oltu Turkey
129 C5 Oltu r. Turkey
109 M8 Oluan Pi c. Taiwan
113 □1 Olugiri i. N. Male Maldives
129 D5 Oluklu Turkey
185 O6 Olula del Río Spain
129 D5 Olur Turkey
92 D8 Olutanga i. Phil.
183 Q5 Ólvega Spain
186 F3 Olvena Spain
185 I7 Olvera Spain
150 G4 Olveston South Gloucestershire, England U.K.
Ol'viopol' Ukr. see Pervomays'k
136 E3 Olyka Ukr.
139 V9 Olym r. Rus. Fed.
Olymbos hill Cyprus see Olympos
198 C5 Olympia tourist site Greece
238 C3 Olympia WA U.S.A.
198 E2 Olympiada Greece
238 C3 Olympic National Park WA U.S.A.
128 B3 Olympos hill Cyprus
199 L6 Olympos tourist site Turkey
198 D2 Olympou, Ethnikos Drymos nat. park Greece
Olympus, Mount Greece see Mytikas
238 C3 Olympus, Mount WA U.S.A.
137 R2 Olymskiy Rus. Fed.
234 D2 Olyphant PA U.S.A.
137 K2 Olyshivka Ukr.
131 R3 Olyutorskiy Rus. Fed.
131 S4 Olyutorskiy, Mys c. Rus. Fed.
131 R4 Olyutorskiy Zaliv b. Rus. Fed.
192 C7 Olzai Sardegna Italy
Olzheras Rus. Fed. see Mezhdurechensk
111 F10 Oma Xizang China
102 R5 Ōma Japan
134 I2 Oma r. Rus. Fed.
105 G3 Ōmachi Japan
105 H6 Omaezaki Japan
105 H6 Omae-zaki pt Japan
102 R7 Ōmagari Japan
147 H3 Omagh Northern Ireland U.K.
250 C6 Omaguas Peru
236 H5 Omaha NE U.S.A.
236 G4 Omaha Indian Reservation res. NE U.S.A.
212 C4 Omaheke admin. reg. Namibia
80 K7 Omakere North I. N.Z.
129 G3 Omalo Georgia
129 G3 Omalo Georgia
100 J2 Omal'skiy Khrebet mts Rus. Fed.
114 F7 Omalur Tamil Nadu India
105 J3 Ōmama Japan
125 K6 Oman country Asia
125 M3 Oman, Gulf of Asia
212 B4 Omangambo Namibia
80 H2 Omapere, Lake North I. N.Z.
81 D11 Omarama South I. N.Z.
197 O8 Omarchevo Bulg.
123 N7 Omarkot Pak.
188 F3 Omarska Bos.-Herz.
212 B4 Omaruru Namibia
252 A3 Omas Peru
212 D3 Omatako watercourse Namibia
252 C4 Omate Peru
212 B4 Omatjette Namibia
214 G1 Omaweneno Botswana
102 R5 Ōma-zaki c. Japan
Omba i. Vanuatu see Aoba
93 D8 Ombai, Selat sea chan. Indon.
Ombalantu Namibia see Uutapi
208 C3 Ombella-Mpoko pref. C.A.R.
150 H3 Ombersley Worcestershire, England U.K.
207 H5 Ombessa Cameroon
Ombetsu Japan see Onbetsu
212 B3 Ombika waterhole Namibia
94 B4 Ombolata Indon.
208 A5 Omboué Gabon
192 G2 Ombrone r. Italy
111 H11 Ombu Xizang China
261 I3 Ombúes de Lavalle Uru.
129 C6 Omcalı Turkey
214 H6 Omdraaisvlei S. Africa
203 G6 Omdurman Sudan
105 J4 Ōme Japan
245 K7 Omealca Mex.
147 J4 Omeath Ireland
138 K3 Omedu Estonia
190 E4 Omegna Italy
137 M4 Omel'nyk Poltavs'ka Oblast' Ukr.
137 O6 Omel'nyk Zaporiz'ka Oblast' Ukr.
137 N8 Omelyanivka Ukr.
202 D5 Omena well Chad
83 K7 Omeo Vic. Austr.
232 B4 Omer MI U.S.A.
199 K3 Ömerler Turkey
182 D2 O Mesón do Vento Spain
192 C3 Omessa Corse France
242 □Q12 Ometepe, Isla de i. Nic.
245 I9 Ometepec Mex.
147 B5 Omey Island Ireland
96 D6 Omgoy Wildlife Reserve nature res. Thai.
203 H6 Om Hajēr Eritrea
105 H3 Omi Japan
105 G1 Ōmi Niigata Japan
104 D5 Ōmi Shiga Japan
122 C6 Omīdīyeh Iran
105 M4 Omigawa Japan
104 D5 Ōmihachiman Japan
81 G10 Omihi South I. N.Z.
Omilo Georgia see Omalo
222 E3 Omineca Mountains B.C. Can.
222 E4 Omineca Provincial Park B.C. Can.
188 F4 Omiš Croatia
191 R5 Omišalj Croatia
103 I12 Ōmi-shima i. Japan
212 C4 Omitara Namibia
245 H8 Omitlán r. Mex.
105 L2 Ōmiya Ibaraki Japan
104 B4 Ōmiya Kyōto Japan
104 D7 Ōmiya Mie Japan
105 K4 Ōmiya Saitama Japan
222 C3 Ommaney, Cape AK U.S.A.
142 E6 Omme r. Denmark
168 J1 Ommel Denmark
164 J3 Ommen Neth.
106 I5 Ömnögovĭ prov. Mongolia
192 C7 Omodeo, Lago l. Sardegna Italy
105 K3 Omōi-gawa r. Japan
207 G5 Omoku Nigeria
198 D3 Omolio Greece
131 R3 Omolon Rus. Fed.
131 Q3 Omolon r. Rus. Fed.
210 B3 Omo National Park Eth.
102 R7 Omono-gawa r. Japan
156 I4 Omont France
102 R7 Ōmori Japan
182 C3 O Mosteiro Galicia Spain
105 L1 Omotegō Japan
210 C3 Omo Wenz r. Eth.
209 B9 Ompupa Angola
226 F5 Omro WI U.S.A.
130 I4 Omsk Rus. Fed.
131 Q3 Omsukchan Rus. Fed.
102 T2 Ōmū Japan
96 D3 O-mu Myanmar
197 N5 Omu, Vârful mt. Romania
207 G4 Omu-Aran Nigeria
175 J2 Omulew r. Pol.
175 I2 Omulew, Jezioro l. Pol.
207 G5 Omuo-Ekiti Nigeria
103 G14 Ōmura Japan
103 G14 Ōmura-wan b. Japan
105 J6 Ōmuro-yama hill Japan
105 I5 Ōmuro-yama mt. Japan
105 J4 Ōmuro-yama mt. Japan
197 O7 Omurtag Bulg.
212 B3 Omusati admin. reg. Namibia
103 H13 Ōmuta Japan
134 K4 Omutninsk Rus. Fed.
183 N3 Oña Spain
102 S8 Onagawa Japan
147 C6 Onaght Ireland
80 K5 Onakuri, Lake North I. N.Z.
226 C6 Onalaska WI U.S.A.
224 C3 Onaman Lake Ont. Can.
236 I2 Onamia MN U.S.A.
78 □4a Onamue i. Chuuk Micronesia
233 J11 Onancock VA U.S.A.
93 A5 Onang Sulawesi Barat Indon.
208 A5 Onangué, Lac l. Gabon
192 C7 Onani Sardegna Italy
192 H2 Onano Italy
224 D4 Onaping Lake Ont. Can.
226 F9 Onarga IL U.S.A.
225 G3 Onatchiway, Lac l. Que. Can.
183 P2 Oñati Spain
242 E3 Onavas Mex.
236 G4 Onawa IA U.S.A.
227 J4 Onaway MI U.S.A.
102 U4 Onbetsu Japan
97 C7 Onbingwin Myanmar
183 P5 Oncala Spain
183 P5 Oncala, Puerto de pass Spain
261 F2 Oncativo Arg.
148 I5 Onchan Isle of Man
209 B9 Oncócua Angola
128 H2 Öncül Turkey
187 E8 Onda Spain
Ondal W. Bengal India see Andal
212 B3 Ondangwa Namibia
187 F10 Ondara Spain
183 P2 Ondarroa Spain
177 K3 Ondava r. Slovakia
214 E6 Onderstedorings S. Africa
209 B9 Ondjiva Angola
207 G5 Ondo Nigeria
207 G5 Ondo state Nigeria
107 L3 Öndörhaan Mongolia
107 Q4 Ondor Had Nei Mongol China
107 M2 Öndörhushuu Mongolia
106 A3 Ondorkara Xinjiang China
106 I6 Ondor Mod Nei Mongol China
107 M5 Ondor Sum Nei Mongol China
134 F3 Ondozero Rus. Fed.
163 B8 Ondres France
212 D4 One Botswana
113 D11 One and a Half Degree Channel Maldives
85 J3 One and a Half Mile Opening sea chan. Qld Austr.
One Arm Point W.A. Austr. see Bardi
235 L1 Oneco CT U.S.A.
134 G3 Onega Rus. Fed.
134 G3 Onega r. Rus. Fed.
Onega, Lake Rus. Fed. see Onezhskoye Ozero
Onega Bay g. Rus. Fed. see Onezhskaya Guba
190 E8 Oneglia Italy
One Hundred and Fifty Mile House B.C. Can. see 150 Mile House
One Hundred Mile House B.C. Can. see 100 Mile House
233 J5 Oneida NY U.S.A.
234 C3 Oneida PA U.S.A.
233 J5 Oneida Lake NY U.S.A.
236 F4 O'Neill NE U.S.A.
80 G7 Onekaka South I. N.Z.
226 H5 Onekama MI U.S.A.
131 Q5 Onekotan, Ostrov i. Kuril'skiye O-va Rus. Fed.
78 □3a Onemak i. Kwajalein Marshall Is
231 D9 Oneonta AL U.S.A.
233 J6 Oneonta NY U.S.A.
78 □6 Onepusu Malaita Solomon Is
81 □3 Oneroa i. Rarotonga Cook Is
80 J3 Oneroa North I. N.Z.
163 B7 Onesse-et-Laharie France
197 O4 Onești Romania
161 B8 Onet-le-Château France
79 □8a Onevai i. Tonga
134 F2 Onezhskaya Guba g. Rus. Fed.
139 S1 Onezhskiy Kanal canal Rus. Fed.
130 E3 Onezhskoye Ozero l. Rus. Fed.
134 F3 Onezhskoye Ozero l. Rus. Fed.
117 I9 Ong r. India
208 B5 Onga Gabon
212 B3 Ongandjera Namibia
80 K6 Ongaonga North I. N.Z.
97 G10 Ông Đôc, Sông r. Vietnam
209 E6 Ongeri Dem. Rep. Congo
214 H5 Ongers watercourse S. Africa
87 E12 Ongerup W.A. Austr.
106 H4 Ongi Dundgovĭ Mongolia
106 H3 Ongi Övörhangay Mongolia
106 H4 Ongiyn Gol r. Mongolia
101 D10 Ongjin N. Korea
161 H8 Ongles France
Ongniud Qi Nei Mongol China see Wudan
114 G5 Ongole Andhra Prad. India
106 H3 Ongon Mongolia
208 C5 Ongonyi Congo
Ongtüstik Qazaqstan Oblysy admin. div. Kazakh. see Yuzhnyy Kazakhstan
110 H1 Onguday Rus. Fed.
129 E3 Oni Georgia
146 F9 Onich Highland, Scotland U.K.
236 E3 Onida SD U.S.A.
192 D7 Onifai Sardegna Italy
192 C7 Oniferi Sardegna Italy
105 J3 Oniishi Japan
187 D10 Onil Spain
213 □I4 Onilahy r. Madag.
225 G3 Onistagane, Lac l. Que. Can.
207 G5 Onitsha Nigeria
212 C4 Onjati Mountain Namibia
Onjiva Angola see Ondjiva
105 L5 Onjuku Japan
140 U5 Onkamo Fin.
140 S5 Onkivesi l. Fin.
102 □1 Onna Okinawa Japan
102 □1 Onna-dake hill Okinawa Japan
156 G3 Onnaing France
78 □4a Onnang i. Chuuk Micronesia
131 O3 Onnes Rus. Fed.
79 □7 Ono i. Fiji
104 D4 Ōno Fukui Japan
105 M1 Ono Fukushima Japan
104 E5 Ōno Gifu Japan
102 R5 Ōno Hokkaidō Japan
104 A6 Ono Hyōgo Japan
234 B4 Ono PA U.S.A.
103 I13 Onoda Japan
105 J7 Ōnohara-jima i. Japan
103 Q12 Ōnohara-jima i. Japan
77 I4 Ono-i-Lau i. Fiji
103 H13 Ōnojō Japan
103 K12 Onomichi Japan
Onon atoll Micronesia see Namonuito
107 L2 Onon Mongolia
107 N1 Onon r. Rus. Fed.
107 M2 Onon Gol r. Mongolia
100 M3 Onor Rus. Fed.
100 M3 Onor, Gora mt. Sakhalin Rus. Fed.
77 H2 Onotoa atoll Gilbert Is Kiribati
182 C4 Ons, Illa de i. Spain
103 G11 Onsan S. Korea
214 D4 Onseepkans S. Africa
186 C2 Onsella r. Spain
170 E1 Ønslev Denmark
86 C6 Onslow W.A. Austr.
81 D12 Onslow, Lake South I. N.Z.
231 I8 Onslow Bay NC U.S.A.
100 F7 Onsŏng N. Korea
172 F5 Onstmettingen Ger.
164 L2 Onstwedde Neth.
104 F4 Ontake-san vol. Japan
185 P3 Ontalafia, Laguna de l. Spain
223 N5 Ontario prov. Can.
240 O7 Ontario CA U.S.A.
238 F4 Ontario OR U.S.A.
226 D6 Ontario WI U.S.A.
227 Q6 Ontario, Lake Can./U.S.A.
234 D4 Ontelaunee, Lake PA U.S.A.
Onteniente Spain see Ontinyent
186 F4 Ontiñena Spain
187 D10 Ontinyent Spain
140 T4 Ontojärvi l. Fin.
226 E3 Ontonagon MI U.S.A.
78 □6 Ontong Java Atoll Solomon Is
187 C10 Ontur Spain
137 M5 Onufriyivka Ukr.
175 M1 Onuškis Lith.
Onutu atoll Gilbert Is Kiribati see Onotoa
251 H3 Onverwacht Suriname
240 N6 Onyx CA U.S.A.
159 N6 Onzain France
182 I3 Onzonilla Spain
163 E10 Oô, Lac d' l. France
82 E2 Oodnadatta S.A. Austr.
210 E2 Oodweyne Somalia
105 G2 Ōoka Japan
240 □F13 'Ō'ōkala HI U.S.A.
147 F7 Oola Ireland
82 C4 Ooldea S.A. Austr.
82 C4 Ooldea Range hills S.A. Austr.
237 H7 Oologah Lake resr OK U.S.A.
164 F5 Ooltgensplaat Neth.
86 I3 Oombulg Aboriginal Reserve W.A. Austr.
86 I3 Oombulgurri W.A. Austr.
84 F6 Ooratippra r. N.T. Austr.
85 H6 Oorindi Qld Austr.
Oos-Londen S. Africa see East London
165 E6 Oostakker Belgium
231 E8 Oostanaula r. GA U.S.A.
165 D6 Oostburg Neth.
165 C6 Oostende Belgium
164 I4 Oostendorp Neth.
164 I5 Oosterbeek Neth.
164 G2 Oosterend Neth.
164 K3 Oosterhesselen Neth.
164 G5 Oosterhout Neth.
164 F5 Oosterland Neth.
164 E5 Oosterschelde est. Neth.
164 E5 Oosterscheldekering barrage Neth.
164 J3 Oosterwolde Neth.
165 E7 Oosterzele Belgium
157 J1 Oostham Belgium
164 G3 Oosthuizen Neth.
165 D6 Oostkamp Belgium
165 G6 Oostmalle Belgium
165 E6 Oost-Souburg Neth.
164 H4 Oostvaardersplassen nature res. Neth.
165 E7 Oost-Vlaanderen prov. Belgium
165 C7 Oostvleteren Belgium
164 H2 Oost-Vlieland Neth.
164 F5 Oostvoorne Neth.
164 G4 Oostzaan Neth.
Ootacamund Tamil Nadu India see Udagamandalam
164 K4 Ootmarsum Neth.
222 E4 Ootsa Lake B.C. Can.
222 E4 Ootsa Lake l. B.C. Can.
240 □C12 'Ōpae'ula r. HI U.S.A.
244 E1 Opal Mex.
208 E5 Opala Dem. Rep. Congo
174 E3 Opalenica Pol.
174 G2 Opalenie Pol.
177 L4 Ópályi Hungary
80 I5 Oparau North I. N.Z.
81 J7 Opari North I. N.Z.
210 B4 Opari Sudan
134 J4 Oparino Rus. Fed.
Oparo i. Îs Australes Fr. Polynesia see Rapa
224 D3 Opasatika r. Ont. Can.
224 D3 Opasatika Lake Ont. Can.
223 M4 Opasquia Ont. Can.
223 M4 Opasquia Provincial Park Ont. Can.
224 F3 Opataca, Lac l. Que. Can.
188 E3 Opatija Croatia
176 F2 Opatov Czech Rep.
176 E1 Opatovice nad Labem Czech Rep.
174 G5 Opatów Śląskie Pol.
175 J5 Opatów Świętokrzyskie Pol.
174 G4 Opatów Wielkopolskie Pol.
174 G4 Opatówek Pol.
175 I5 Opatowiec Pol.
175 J5 Opatówka r. Pol.
177 G2 Opava Czech Rep.
177 G1 Opava r. Czech Rep.
182 D4 O Pazo Spain
182 D2 O Pazo de Irixoa Spain
139 R3 Opechenskiy Posad Rus. Fed.
182 D3 O Pedrouzo Spain
164 J2 Opeinde Neth.
172 D2 Opel hill Ger.
231 E9 Opelika AL U.S.A.
237 I10 Opelousas LA U.S.A.
164 J2 Opende Neth.
261 H4 Open Door Arg.
224 E4 Opeongo Lake Ont. Can.
172 H6 Opfenbach Ger.
172 F7 Opfikon Switz.
165 I6 Opglabbeek Belgium
238 K2 Opheim MT U.S.A.
164 I5 Opheusden Neth.
227 K3 Ophir Ont. Can.
81 D12 Ophir South I. N.Z.
94 D4 Ophir, Gunung vol. Indon.
193 L4 Opi Italy
208 E4 Opienge Dem. Rep. Congo
81 F11 Opihi r. South I. N.Z.
240 □G14 Opihikao HI U.S.A.
80 J7 Opiki North I. N.Z.
93 F5 Opin Seram Indon.
224 E2 Opinaca r. Que. Can.
224 E2 Opinaca, Réservoir resr Que. Can.
224 D2 Opinnagau r. Ont. Can.
161 J9 Opio France
127 L7 Opis tourist site Iraq
225 G2 Opiscotéo, Lac l. Que. Can.
137 N4 Opishnya Ukr.
164 I5 Oploo Neth.
179 L7 Oplotnica Slovenia
179 L7 Oplotnica r. Slovenia
96 D5 Op Luang National Park Thai.
164 G3 Opmeer Neth.
207 G5 Opobo Nigeria
138 L5 Opochka Rus. Fed.
176 F1 Opočno Czech Rep.
252 D4 Opoco Bol.
225 H2 Opocopa, Lac l. Que. Can.
175 I4 Opoczno Pol.
242 D3 Opodepe Mex.
165 I6 Opoeteren Belgium
174 F5 Opole Pol.
175 J4 Opole Lubelskie Pol.
174 F5 Opolskie prov. Pol.
80 H2 Opononi North I. N.Z.
136 C5 Oporets' Ukr.
182 C4 O Porriño Spain
Oporto Port. see Porto
80 L5 Opotiki North I. N.Z.
163 J10 Opoul-Périllos France
196 I5 Opovo Vojvodina Serbia
231 D10 Opp AL U.S.A.
171 K8 Oppach Ger.
102 S8 Oppa-wan b. Japan
140 J5 Oppdal Norway
191 K5 Oppeano Italy
141 H6 Oppedal Norway
Oppeln Pol. see Opole
172 E5 Oppenau Ger.
172 E2 Oppenheim Ger.
172 G4 Oppenweiler Ger.
193 P6 Oppido Lucano Italy
195 J7 Oppido Mamertina Italy
171 F7 Oppin Ger.
142 G1 Oppkuven hill Norway
141 J6 Oppland county Norway
179 K4 Opponitz Austria
238 F3 Opportunity WA U.S.A.
171 E9 Oppurg Ger.
197 L6 Oprișor Romania
191 P5 Oprtalj Croatia
197 M6 Optași-Măgura Romania
237 E7 Optima Lake OK U.S.A.
80 I2 Opua North I. N.Z.
80 I4 Opuatia North I. N.Z.
80 H6 Opunake North I. N.Z.
79 □9a Opunoho, Baie d' b. Moorea Fr. Polynesia
177 J5 Ópusztaszer Hungary
212 B3 Opuwo Namibia
165 F7 Opwijk Belgium
120 D4 Opytnoye Kazakh.
120 K6 Oqbaytal Uzbek.
120 H6 Oqqal'a Uzbek.
Oqqal"a Uzbek. see Oqqal'a
123 P2 Oqsu r. Tajik.
120 K8 Oqtosh Uzbek.
236 J5 Oquawka IL U.S.A.
242 D2 Oquitoa Mex.
233 □O4 Oquossoc ME U.S.A.
129 D3 Oqureshi Georgia
177 L4 Ŏr Hungary
120 H2 Or' r. Rus. Fed.
160 I3 Or, Le Mont d' mt. France
191 K3 Ora Italy
105 J3 Ōra Japan
140 P1 Øra Norway
142 G2 Øra nature res. Norway
163 C9 Oraàs France
246 □ Oracabessa Jamaica
241 V9 Oracle AZ U.S.A.
184 E3 Orada Port.
197 J3 Oradea Romania
162 G4 Oradour-sur-Glane France
162 F4 Oradour-sur-Vayres France
196 I8 Orahovac Kosovo Serbia
188 F3 Orahovica Croatia
116 G7 Orai Uttar Prad. India
241 V6 Oraibi AZ U.S.A.
241 V6 Oraibi Wash watercourse AZ U.S.A.
160 G3 Orain r. France
161 H9 Oraison France
140 R3 Orajärvi Fin.
Oral Kazakh. see Ural'sk
205 E2 Oran Alg.
258 D1 Orán Arg.
136 J2 Orane Ukr.
97 H8 O Rang Cambodia
117 N6 Orang Assam India
101 F8 Ŏrang N. Korea
83 L5 Orange N.S.W. Austr.
161 F8 Orange France
212 C6 Orange r. Namibia/S. Africa
240 O8 Orange CA U.S.A.
235 I2 Orange CT U.S.A.
237 I10 Orange TX U.S.A.
232 G10 Orange VA U.S.A.
251 I3 Orange, Cabo c. Brazil
235 H2 Orangeburg NY U.S.A.
231 G9 Orangeburg SC U.S.A.
246 D1 Orange Cay i. Bahamas
236 G4 Orange City IA U.S.A.
264 J8 Orange Cone sea feature S. Atlantic Ocean
235 G2 Orange County county NY U.S.A.
240 M5 Orange Cove CA U.S.A.
Orange Free State prov. S. Africa see Free State
235 G1 Orange Lake NY U.S.A.
231 G10 Orange Park FL U.S.A.
240 K3 Orangevale CA U.S.A.
224 D5 Orangeville Ont. Can.
234 C2 Orangeville PA U.S.A.
241 U2 Orangeville UT U.S.A.
243 O8 Orange Walk Belize
206 A4 Orango, Ilha de i. Guinea-Bissau
192 C7 Orani Sardegna Italy
92 C4 Orani Luzon Phil.
171 F7 Oranienbaum Ger.
170 H5 Oranienburg Ger.
Oranje r. Namibia/S. Africa see Orange
251 H4 Oranje Gebergte hills Suriname
164 K3 Oranjekanaal canal Neth.
212 C6 Oranjemund Namibia
214 I5 Oranjerivier S. Africa
247 □9 Oranjestad Aruba
247 □2 Oranjestad St Eustatius Neth. Antilles
215 M2 Oranjeville S. Africa
147 E6 Oranmore Ireland
87 J7 Orantjugurr, Lake salt flat W.A. Austr.
135 I7 Oranzherei Rus. Fed.
212 E4 Orapa Botswana
184 F6 Oraque r. Spain
81 F11 Orari r. South I. N.Z.
92 E5 Oras Samar Phil.
188 F3 Orašac Bos.-Herz.
92 E5 Oras Bay Samar Phil.
197 L5 Orăștie Romania
197 L5 Orăștioara de Sus Romania
Orașul Stalin Romania see Brașov
136 I4 Orativ Ukr.
78 □6 Orava P.N.G.
177 I2 Orava r. Slovakia
177 I2 Orava, Vodná nádrž resr Slovakia
140 Q5 Oravais Fin.
197 J5 Oravița Romania
177 I2 Oravská Lesná Slovakia
177 I2 Oravská Magura mts Slovakia
177 I2 Oravská Polhora Slovakia
81 B13 Orawia South I. N.Z.
161 B9 Orb r. France
190 F6 Orba r. Italy
187 E10 Orba Spain
182 C5 Orbacém Port.
111 E9 Orba Co l. China
142 G6 Ørbæk Denmark
156 G6 Orbais-l'Abbaye France

186 C2 **Orbara** Spain
190 D5 **Orbassano** Italy
190 B2 **Orbe** Switz.
190 B2 **Orbe** *r.* Switz.
197 N6 **Orbeasca** Romania
159 L3 **Orbec** France
192 G3 **Orbetello** Italy
192 G3 **Orbetello, Laguna di** *lag.* Italy
157 N7 **Orbey** France
163 J9 **Orbieu** *r.* France
182 I5 **Orbigo** *r.* Spain
232 H8 **Orbisonia** *PA* U.S.A.
83 L7 **Orbost** *Vic.* Austr.
143 N1 **Örbyhus** Sweden
182 F8 **Orca** Port.
262 V2 **Orcadas** *research stn S. Orkney Is* Antarctica
185 O5 **Orce** Spain
185 N4 **Orcera** Spain
160 J2 **Orchamps-Vennes** France
234 B6 **Orchard Beach** *MD* U.S.A.
241 X2 **Orchard Mesa** *CO* U.S.A.
116 G7 **Orchha** *Madh. Prad.* India
156 F3 **Orchies** France
251 E2 **Orchila, Isla** *i.* Venez.
216 □3e **Orchilla, Punta** *pt El Hierro* Canary Is
198 D4 **Orchomenos** Greece
175 H4 **Orchów** Pol.
174 G3 **Orchowo** Pol.
146 F10 **Orchy** *r. Scotland* U.K.
192 G2 **Orcia** *r.* Italy
191 N8 **Orciano di Pesaro** Italy
161 I7 **Orcières** France
160 B5 **Orcival** France
190 D5 **Orco** *r.* Italy
129 I5 **Orconikidze** Azer.
129 I6 **Orconikidze** Azer.
252 B2 **Orcotuna** Peru
240 L7 **Orcutt** *CA* U.S.A.
86 J3 **Ord** *r. W.A.* Austr.
236 F5 **Ord** *NE* U.S.A.
86 H4 **Ord, Mount** *hill W.A.* Austr.
Orda Kazakh. *see* **Urda**
134 L4 **Orda** Rus. Fed.
163 E8 **Ordan-Larroque** France
Órdenes Spain *see* **Ordes**
241 T4 **Orderville** *UT* U.S.A.
182 D2 **Ordes** Spain
186 F2 **Ordesa-Monte Perdido, Parque Nacional** *nat. park* Spain
186 I2 **Ordino** Andorra
240 P7 **Ord Mountain** *CA* U.S.A.
193 P5 **Ordona** Italy
183 P3 **Ordoñana** Spain
261 F3 **Ordoñez** Arg.
107 L7 **Ordos** *Nei Mongol* China
86 J4 **Ord River Dam** *W.A.* Austr.
86 J3 **Ord River Nature Reserve** *W.A.* Austr.
Ordu *Hatay* Turkey *see* **Yayladağı**
126 H3 **Ordu** *Ordu* Turkey
129 H7 **Ordubad** Azer.
185 L6 **Orduña** *mt.* Spain
183 N2 **Ordunte, Montes de** *mts* Spain
236 D6 **Ordway** *CO* U.S.A.
Ordzhonikidze Georgia *see* **Kharagauli**
Ordzhonikidze Kazakh. *see* **Denisovka**
Ordzhonikidze Rus. Fed. *see* **Vladikavkaz**
137 M5 **Ordzhonikidze** *Dnipropetrovs'ka Oblast'* Ukr.
137 N6 **Ordzhonikidze** *Dnipropetrovs'ka Oblast'* Ukr.
Ordzhonikidzeabad Tajik. *see* **Kofarnihon**
Ordzhonikidzevskaya Rus. Fed. *see* **Sleptsovskaya**
129 C2 **Ordzhonikidzevskiy** Rus. Fed.
207 G5 **Ore** Nigeria
183 Q7 **Orea** Spain
182 D2 **O Real** Spain
251 G3 **Orealla** Guyana
141 M6 **Oreälven** *r.* Sweden
140 O5 **Öreälven** *r.* Sweden
240 N1 **Oreana** *NV* U.S.A.
78 □3a **Oreba** *i. Kwajalein* Marshall Is
141 L6 **Örebäcken** Sweden
143 L2 **Örebro** Sweden
143 K2 **Örebro** *county* Sweden
176 F2 **Ořechov** Czech Rep.
139 M3 **Oredezh** *r.* Rus. Fed.
234 D3 **Orefield** *PA* U.S.A.
177 H4 **Öreg-Futóné** *hill* Hungary
177 G5 **Öreglak** Hungary
226 E7 **Oregon** *IL* U.S.A.
236 H6 **Oregon** *MO* U.S.A.
232 B7 **Oregon** *OH* U.S.A.
226 E7 **Oregon** *WI* U.S.A.
238 D5 **Oregon** *state* U.S.A.
238 C4 **Oregon City** *OR* U.S.A.
143 O1 **Öregrund** Sweden
143 O1 **Öregrundsgrepen** *b.* Sweden
170 E1 **Orehoved** Denmark
Orekhi-Vydritsa Belarus *see* **Arekhawsk**
Orekhov Ukr. *see* **Orikhiv**
Orekhova Belarus *see* **Arekhava**
139 V6 **Orekhovo-Zuyevo** Rus. Fed.
Orekhovsk Belarus *see* **Arekhawsk**
139 T9 **Orel** *Orlovskaya Oblast'* Rus. Fed.
134 L4 **Orel** *Permskaya Oblast'* Rus. Fed.
137 N5 **Orel'** *r.* Ukr.
100 K1 **Orel, Gora** *mt.* Rus. Fed.
100 K2 **Orel', Ozero** *l.* Rus. Fed.
197 L9 **Orelek** *mt.* Bulg.
250 B5 **Orellana** *prov.* Ecuador
250 C6 **Orellana** Peru
185 I2 **Orellana, Embalse de** *resr* Spain
184 H2 **Orellana la Vieja** Spain
Orel Oblast *admin. div.* Rus. Fed. *see* **Orlovskaya Oblast'**
241 U1 **Orem** *UT* U.S.A.
Ore Mountains Czech Rep./Ger. *see* **Erzgebirge**
199 I5 **Ören** *Muğla* Turkey
199 K6 **Ören** *Muğla* Turkey
120 F2 **Orenburg** Rus. Fed.
Orenburg Oblast *admin. div.* Rus. Fed. *see* **Orenburgskaya Oblast'**
120 D2 **Orenburgskaya Oblast'** *admin. div.* Rus. Fed.
129 B5 **Örence** Turkey
199 K3 **Örencik** Turkey
172 B2 **Orenhofen** Ger.
261 H6 **Orense** Arg.
Orense Spain *see* **Ourense**
Orense *prov. Galicia* Spain *see* **Ourense**
Oreón, Dhíavlos *sea chan.* Greece *see* **Oreon, Diavlos**
198 D4 **Oreon, Diavlos** *sea chan.* Greece
Oreor Palau *see* **Koror**
Oreor *i.* Palau *see* **Koror**
81 B13 **Orepuki** *South I.* N.Z.
136 G3 **Orepy** Ukr.
186 C3 **Orés** Spain
197 N7 **Oresh** Bulg.
142 I4 **Öresjön** *l.* Sweden
142 H3 **Öreskilsälven** *r.* Sweden
199 H1 **Orestiada** Greece
Orestiás Greece *see* **Orestiada**
142 I6 **Öresund** *str.* Denmark/Sweden
Oretana, Cordillera *mts* Spain *see* **Toledo, Montes de**
81 C13 **Oreti** *r. South I.* N.Z.
80 I3 **Orewa** *North I.* N.Z.
165 H7 **Oreye** Belgium
207 G2 **Orfane** *well* Niger
198 E2 **Orfanou, Kolpos** *b.* Greece
83 K10 **Orford** *Tas.* Austr.
151 P3 **Orford** *Suffolk, England* U.K.
85 I1 **Orford Bay** *Qld* Austr.
151 P3 **Orford Ness** *hd England* U.K.
Orgañá Spain *see* **Organyà**
251 H3 **Organabo** Fr. Guiana
216 □3a **Órganos, Punta de los** *pt La Gomera* Canary Is
241 T9 **Organ Pipe Cactus National Monument** *nat. park AZ* U.S.A.
186 H3 **Organyà** Spain
183 M9 **Orgaz** Spain
156 D6 **Orge** *r.* France
160 H3 **Orgelet** France
156 C7 **Orgères-en-Beauce** France
Orgeyev Moldova *see* **Orhei**
191 K5 **Orgiano** Italy
106 F2 **Orgil** Mongolia
185 M7 **Orgiva** Spain
161 G9 **Orgon** France
107 M5 **Orgon Tal** *Nei Mongol* China
192 C7 **Orgosolo** *Sardegna* Italy
177 I5 **Orgovány** Hungary
177 I5 **Orgoványi** *park* Hungary
139 X5 **Orgtrud** Rus. Fed.
123 M5 **Orgūn** Afgh.
177 I3 **Őrhalom** Hungary
199 J3 **Orhaneli** Turkey
199 K2 **Orhangazi** Turkey
199 J6 **Orhaniye** Turkey
199 I3 **Orhanlar** Turkey
136 H6 **Orhei** Moldova
106 J1 **Orhon Gol** *r.* Mongolia
106 I2 **Orhontuul** Mongolia
186 C2 **Orhy, Pic d'** *mt.* France/Spain
195 N3 **Oria** Italy
185 O6 **Oria** Spain
186 A1 **Oria** *r.* Spain
182 C4 **O Rial** Spain
182 D4 **O Ribeiro** *reg.* Spain
215 O6 **Oribi Gorge Nature Reserve** S. Africa
134 J4 **Orichi** Rus. Fed.
233 □R3 **Orient** *ME* U.S.A.
235 K2 **Orient** *NY* U.S.A.
156 H7 **Orient, Lac d'** *resr* France
245 J6 **Oriental** Mex.
181 E5 **Oriental** *prov.* Morocco
252 D4 **Oriental, Cordillera** *mts* Bol.
250 C3 **Oriental, Cordillera** *mts* Col.
252 C3 **Oriental, Cordillera** *mts* Peru
208 E4 **Orientale** *prov.* Dem. Rep. Congo
261 G6 **Oriente** Arg.
252 D2 **Oriente** *Rondônia* Brazil
256 B5 **Oriente** *São Paulo* Brazil
235 K2 **Orient Island** *NY* U.S.A.
156 H4 **Origny-en-Thiérache** France
156 G7 **Origny-le-Sec** France
156 F4 **Origny-Ste-Benoîte** France
187 D11 **Orihuela** Spain
137 O6 **Orikhiv** Ukr.
198 A2 **Orikum** Albania
137 O4 **Oril'** *r.* Ukr.
137 P5 **Oril'ka** Ukr.
137 O5 **Oril'ka** *r.* Ukr.
224 E4 **Orillia** *Ont.* Can.
141 R6 **Orimattila** Fin.
238 L5 **Orin** *WY* U.S.A.
251 F3 **Orinduik Falls** Brazil/Guyana
251 F2 **Orinoco** *r.* Col./Venez.
251 F2 **Orinoco Delta** Venez.
186 A1 **Orio** Spain
184 D4 **Oriola** Port.
234 A2 **Oriole** *PA* U.S.A.
195 K3 **Oriolo** Italy
192 I3 **Oriolo Romano** Italy
141 Q6 **Oripää** Fin.
233 J5 **Oriskany** *NY* U.S.A.
117 J9 **Orissa** *state* India
138 G3 **Orissaare** Estonia
186 J4 **Oristà** Spain
192 B8 **Oristano** *Sardegna* Italy
192 B8 **Oristano** *prov. Sardegna* Italy
192 B8 **Oristano, Golfo di** *b. Sardegna* Italy
147 I5 **Oristown** Ireland
176 F5 **Őriszentpéter** Hungary
175 L6 **Oriv** Ukr.
141 R6 **Orivesi** Fin.
140 T5 **Orivesi** *l.* Fin.
251 H5 **Oriximiná** Brazil
245 J7 **Orizaba** Mex.
245 J6 **Orizaba, Pico de** *vol.* Mex.
245 I4 **Orizatlán** Mex.
256 C2 **Orizona** Brazil
Orjonikidze Georgia *see* **Kharagauli**
Orjonikidzeobod Tajik. *see* **Kofarnihon**
142 J5 **Örkelljunga** Sweden
177 I4 **Örkény** Hungary
Orkhey Moldova *see* **Orhei**
Orkhomenós Greece *see* **Orchomenos**
106 H3 **Orkhon Valley** *tourist site* Mongolia
215 K2 **Orkney** S. Africa
146 K5 **Orkney** *admin. div. Scotland* U.K.
144 F2 **Orkney Islands** *Scotland* U.K.
175 L3 **Orla** Pol.
174 E4 **Orla** *r.* Pol.
174 F2 **Orla** *r.* Pol.
237 D10 **Orla** *TX* U.S.A.
171 E9 **Orlamünde** Ger.
240 J2 **Orland** *CA* U.S.A.
256 D4 **Orlândia** Brazil
231 G11 **Orlando** *FL* U.S.A.
175 L3 **Orlanka** *r.* Pol.
255 C9 **Orleaes** Brazil
156 C7 **Orléanais** *reg.* France
156 C8 **Orléans** France
233 P7 **Orleans** *MA* U.S.A.
233 M4 **Orleans** *VT* U.S.A.
156 E7 **Orléans, Canal d'** France
225 G4 **Orléans, Île d'** *i. Que.* Can.
156 D8 **Orléans, Val d'** *val.* France
Orléansville Alg. *see* **Chlef**
163 E9 **Orleix** France
143 K3 **Orlen** *l.* Sweden
176 E1 **Orlice** *r.* Czech Rep.
177 I1 **Orlich Gniazd, Park Krajobrazowy** Pol.
176 F1 **Orlické hory** *mts* Czech Rep.
176 F1 **Orlické hory** *park* Czech Rep.
99 G1 **Orlik** Rus. Fed.
176 D2 **Orlik, Vodní nádrž** *resr* Czech Rep.
137 L2 **Orlivka** *Chernihivs'ka Oblast'* Ukr.
137 P7 **Orlivka** *Zaporiz'ka Oblast'* Ukr.
137 M8 **Orlivs'ke** Ukr.
188 F3 **Orljava** *r.* Croatia
134 J4 **Orlov** Rus. Fed.
177 H2 **Orlová** Czech Rep.
120 C2 **Orlov Gay** Rus. Fed.
137 T2 **Orlovka** Rus. Fed.
135 G6 **Orlovo** Rus. Fed.
139 T9 **Orlovskaya Oblast'** *admin. div.* Rus. Fed.
135 H7 **Orlovskiy** Rus. Fed.
137 O6 **Orlyans'ke** Ukr.
137 N5 **Orlyk** Ukr.
137 M9 **Orlyne** Ukr.
138 I5 **Ormaņkalns** *hill* Latvia
177 G6 **Ormánság** *reg.* Hungary
123 K9 **Ormara** Pak.
123 K9 **Ormara, Ras** *hd* Pak.
190 D7 **Ormea** Italy
177 J5 **Örménykút** Hungary
151 P2 **Ormesby St Margaret** *Norfolk, England* U.K.
Ormília Greece *see* **Ormylia**
223 J5 **Ormiston** *Sask.* Can.
149 L2 **Ormiston** *East Lothian, Scotland* U.K.
92 E6 **Ormoc** *Leyte* Phil.
80 L5 **Ormond** *North I.* N.Z.
231 G11 **Ormond Beach** *FL* U.S.A.
179 N7 **Ormož** Slovenia
149 L6 **Ormskirk** *Lancashire, England* U.K.
233 L3 **Ormstown** *Que.* Can.
198 E2 **Ormylia** Greece
123 L8 **Ornach** Pak.
186 E3 **Orna de Gállego** Spain
157 I6 **Ornain** *r.* France
161 B10 **Ornaisons** France
160 I2 **Ornans** France
190 E4 **Ornavasso** Italy
173 J3 **Ornbau** Ger.
159 L4 **Orne** *dept* France
159 K3 **Orne** *r.* France
159 L5 **Orne** *r.* France
140 L3 **Ørnes** Norway
143 Q7 **Orneta** Pol.
143 O2 **Ornö** *i.* Sweden
163 H10 **Ornolac-Ussat-les-Bains** France
140 O5 **Örnsköldsvik** Sweden
138 F2 **Örö** *i.* Fin.
101 E8 **Oro** N. Korea
Oro *r.* Spain *see* **Ouro**
192 C3 **Oro, Monte d'** *mt. Corse* France
252 E3 **Orobayaya** Bol.
190 H3 **Orobie, Alpi** *mts* Italy
254 F4 **Orocó** Brazil
250 D3 **Orocué** Col.
206 D4 **Orodara** Burkina
Orodzholari Georgia *see* **Orojolari**
186 D2 **Oroel, Peña de** *mt.* Spain
238 F3 **Orofino** *ID* U.S.A.
106 G4 **Orog Nuur** *salt l.* Mongolia
240 O7 **Oro Grande** *CA* U.S.A.
239 K10 **Orogrande** *NM* U.S.A.
79 □9a **Orohena** *mt. Tahiti* Fr. Polynesia
129 E4 **Orojolari** Georgia
Orol Dengizi *salt l.* Kazakh./Uzbek. *see* **Aral Sea**
191 L5 **Orolo** *r.* Italy
196 H5 **Orom** *Vojvodina* Serbia
210 C2 **Oromīya** *admin. reg.* Eth.
225 H4 **Oromocto** *N.B.* Can.
225 H4 **Oromocto Lake** *N.B.* Can.
128 D8 **Oron** Israel
207 H5 **Oron** Nigeria
77 I2 **Orona** *atoll Phoenix Is* Kiribati
190 B2 **Oron-la-Ville** Switz.
233 □Q4 **Orono** *ME* U.S.A.
251 G4 **Oronoque** Guyana
251 G4 **Oronoque** *r.* Guyana
186 B1 **Oronoz** Spain
146 D10 **Oronsay** *i. Scotland* U.K.
175 I4 **Orońsko** Pol.
128 E4 **Orontes** *r.* Asia *alt.* **'Āṣī (Lebanon),** *alt.* **Asi (Turkey),** *alt.* **'Āṣī, Nahr al (Syria)**
190 D4 **Oropa** Italy
250 C2 **Orope** Venez.
244 F7 **Oropeo** Mex.
183 J9 **Oropesa** *Castilla-La Mancha* Spain
187 F7 **Oropesa, Cabo de** *c.* Spain
187 F7 **Oropesa del Mar** *Valencia* Spain
247 □7 **Oropuche** *r.* Trin. and Tob.
Oroqen Zizhiqi *Nei Mongol* China *see* **Alihe**
92 D7 **Oroquieta** *Mindanao* Phil.
183 Q3 **Ororbia** Spain
254 F3 **Orós** Brazil
254 F3 **Orós, Açude** *resr* Brazil
192 D7 **Orosei** *Sardegna* Italy
192 D7 **Orosei, Golfo di** *b. Sardegna* Italy
177 J5 **Orosháza** Hungary
179 M8 **Oroslavje** Croatia
177 H4 **Oroszlány** Hungary
192 C7 **Orotelli** *Sardegna* Italy
78 □1 **Orote Peninsula** Guam
131 Q3 **Orotukan** Rus. Fed.
241 V9 **Oro Valley** *AZ* U.S.A.
240 K2 **Oroville** *CA* U.S.A.
238 E2 **Oroville** *WA* U.S.A.
240 K2 **Oroville, Lake** *resr CA* U.S.A.
161 H8 **Orpierre** France
107 Q2 **Orqohan** *Nei Mongol* China
226 B1 **Orr** *MN* U.S.A.
186 C1 **Orreaga** *Navarra* Spain
149 L6 **Orrell** *Greater Manchester, England* U.K.
192 B9 **Orri, Monte** *hill* Italy
186 H3 **Orri, Tossal de l'** *mt.* Spain
146 H7 **Orrin** *r. Scotland* U.K.
146 G7 **Orrin Reservoir** *Scotland* U.K.
186 D6 **Orrios** Spain
142 H1 **Orrkjølen** *hill* Norway
192 C8 **Orroli** *Sardegna* Italy
82 G5 **Orroroo** *S.A.* Austr.
232 D8 **Orrville** *OH* U.S.A.
141 M6 **Orsa** Sweden
193 O5 **Orsara di Puglia** Italy
156 D6 **Orsay** France
176 F5 **Őrség** *reg.* Hungary
176 F5 **Őrségi Tájvédelmi Körzet** *nature res.* Hungary
162 H3 **Orsennes** France
139 N7 **Orsha** Belarus
139 T5 **Orsha** Rus. Fed.
134 I4 **Orshanka** Rus. Fed.
190 C5 **Orsiera-Rocciavrè, Parco Naturale** *nature res.* Italy
190 C3 **Orsières** Switz.
141 N6 **Orsjön** *l.* Sweden
120 H2 **Orsk** Rus. Fed.
170 E1 **Ørslev** Denmark
193 M3 **Orsogna** Italy
193 P8 **Orsomarso** Italy
197 K6 **Orşova** Romania
140 I5 **Ørsta** Norway
143 N2 **Örsundaän** *r.* Sweden
143 N2 **Örsundsbro** Sweden
190 E4 **Orta, Lago d'** *l.* Italy
199 J6 **Ortaca** Turkey
129 B4 **Ortaköy** Turkey
193 P5 **Orta Nova** Italy
128 B2 **Orta Toroslar** *plat.* Turkey
129 G1 **Orta-Tyube** Rus. Fed.
193 I3 **Orte** Italy
182 E1 **Ortegal, Cabo** *c.* Spain
250 C4 **Orteguaza** *r.* Col.
172 D5 **Ortenau** *reg.* Ger.
172 D5 **Ortenberg** *Baden-Württemberg* Ger.
169 H10 **Ortenberg** *Hessen* Ger.
173 O4 **Ortenburg** Ger.
179 O3 **Orth an der Donau** Austria
163 C9 **Orthez** France
141 L5 **Ortholmen** Sweden
184 H3 **Ortiga** *r.* Spain
183 O4 **Ortigosa** Spain
256 B6 **Ortigueira** Brazil
182 E1 **Ortigueira** Spain
182 E1 **Ortigueira, Ría de** *inlet* Spain
191 L2 **Ortisei** Italy
196 J5 **Ortişoara** Romania
242 D3 **Ortíz** Mex.
250 E2 **Ortíz** Venez.
191 J2 **Ortles** *mt.* Italy
247 □7 **Ortoire** *r.* Trin. and Tob.
192 B4 **Ortolo** *r. Corse* France
149 L5 **Orton** *Cumbria, England* U.K.
193 M3 **Ortona** Italy
151 L2 **Orton Longueville** *Peterborough, England* U.K.
227 K7 **Ortonville** *MI* U.S.A.
236 G3 **Ortonville** *MN* U.S.A.
Ortospana Afgh. *see* **Kābul**
121 P6 **Orto-Tokoy** Kyrg.
190 E7 **Ortovera** Italy
171 I8 **Ortrand** Ger.
140 O4 **Örträsk** Sweden
193 L4 **Ortucchio** Italy
192 B7 **Ortueri** *Sardegna* Italy
Örtülü Turkey *see* **Şenkaya**
168 I5 **Örtze** *r.* Ger.
138 K2 **Oru** Estonia
92 □ **Orukuizu** *i.* Palau
131 N3 **Orulgan, Khrebet** *mts* Rus. Fed.
212 C4 **Orumbo** Namibia
206 D5 **Orumbo Boka** *hill* Côte d'Ivoire
122 A3 **Orūmīyeh** Iran
122 A3 **Orūmīyeh, Daryācheh-ye** *salt l.* Iran
192 C7 **Orune** *Sardegna* Italy
252 D4 **Oruro** Bol.
252 D4 **Oruro** *dept* Bol.
183 N8 **Orusco** Spain
142 H3 **Orust** *i.* Sweden
123 L5 **Orūzgān** Afgh.
159 P8 **Orval** France
182 E8 **Orvalho** Port.
158 H7 **Orvault** France
192 I2 **Orvieto** Italy
262 T1 **Orville Coast** Antarctica
198 E1 **Orvilos** *mts* Greece
193 J3 **Orvinio** Italy
140 □ **Orvin Land** *reg.* Svalbard
151 O3 **Orwell** *l. England* U.K.
232 E7 **Orwell** *OH* U.S.A.
233 L5 **Orwell** *VT* U.S.A.
234 C3 **Orwigsburg** *PA* U.S.A.
107 O2 **Orxon Gol** *r.* China
197 L7 **Oryakhovo** Bulg.
136 F5 **Orynyn** Ukr.
Oryol Rus. Fed. *see* **Orel**
175 J3 **Orz** *r.* Pol.
174 F3 **Orzechowo** Pol.
174 G5 **Orzesze** Pol.
175 L3 **Orzeszkowo** Pol.
136 F3 **Orzhiv** Ukr.
137 L4 **Orzhytsya** Ukr.
137 L4 **Orzhytsya** *r.* Ukr.
190 H5 **Orzinuovi** Italy
216 □3c **Orzola** *Lanzarote* Canary Is
175 J3 **Orzyc** *r.* Pol.
175 J2 **Orzyny** Pol.
175 J2 **Orzysz** Pol.
175 K2 **Orzysz, Jezioro** *l.* Pol.
140 K5 **Os** Norway
138 J5 **Oša** *r.* Latvia
175 G2 **Osa** *r.* Pol.
134 K4 **Osa** Rus. Fed.
242 □R13 **Osa, Península de** *pen.* Costa Rica
183 O9 **Osa de Vega** Spain
226 B6 **Osage** *IA* U.S.A.
232 E9 **Osage** *WV* U.S.A.
238 L4 **Osage** *WY* U.S.A.
236 I6 **Osage** *r. MO* U.S.A.
236 H6 **Osage City** *KS* U.S.A.
104 F4 **Osaka** Japan
104 B6 **Ōsaka** Japan
104 B6 **Ōsaka** *pref.* Japan
121 O2 **Osakarovka** Kazakh.
104 C7 **Ōsakasayama** Japan
104 B7 **Ōsaka-wan** *b.* Japan
190 H7 **Osaro, Monte** *mt.* Italy
256 D5 **Osasco** Brazil
104 F2 **Ōsawano** Japan
236 H6 **Osawatomie** *KS* U.S.A.
236 M1 **Osawin** *r. Ont.* Can.
149 O6 **Osbaldwick** *York, England* U.K.
182 E4 **Os Blancos** Spain
215 P4 **Osborn** S. Africa
236 F6 **Osborne** *KS* U.S.A.
172 B2 **Osburg** Ger.
172 B2 **Osburger Hochwald** *mts* Ger.
142 F6 **Øsby** Denmark
143 J5 **Osby** Sweden
177 H2 **Oščadnica** Slovakia
251 H4 **Oscar** Fr. Guiana
140 □ **Oscar II Land** *reg.* Svalbard
86 H4 **Oscar Range** *hills W.A.* Austr.
235 H2 **Oscawana Corners** *NY* U.S.A.
237 J8 **Osceola** *AR* U.S.A.
236 I5 **Osceola** *IA* U.S.A.
236 I6 **Osceola** *MO* U.S.A.
236 G5 **Osceola** *NE* U.S.A.
226 B4 **Osceola** *WI* U.S.A.
171 H8 **Oschatz** Ger.
171 D6 **Oschersleben (Bode)** Ger.
192 C6 **Oschiri** *Sardegna* Italy
227 K5 **Oscoda** *MI* U.S.A.
182 C3 **Os Dices** Spain
168 J2 **Osdorf** Ger.
196 H6 **Osečina** Serbia
182 C5 **O Seixo** Spain
183 J2 **Oseja de Sajambre** Spain
173 P2 **Osek** *Plzeňský kraj* Czech Rep.
171 I9 **Osek** *Ústecký kraj* Czech Rep.
Ösel *i.* Estonia *see* **Hiiumaa**
141 K6 **Osensjøen** *l.* Norway
186 D4 **Osera** Spain
137 T3 **Osered'** *r.* Rus. Fed.
174 E4 **Osetno** Pol.
103 G14 **Ōseto** Japan
139 V7 **Osetr** *r.* Rus. Fed.
103 F14 **Ōse-zaki** *pt* Japan
105 I5 **Ōse-zaki** *pt* Japan
224 F4 **Osgoode** *Ont.* Can.
238 F6 **Osgood Mountains** *NV* U.S.A.
121 O7 **Osh** Kyrg.
121 O7 **Osh** *admin. div.* Kyrg.
212 B3 **Oshakati** Namibia
Oshamambe Japan *see* **Oshamanbe**
102 R4 **Oshamanbe** Japan
212 B3 **Oshana** *admin. reg.* Namibia
224 E5 **Oshawa** *Ont.* Can.
102 S8 **Oshika** Japan
105 H4 **Ōshika** Japan
102 S8 **Oshika-hantō** *pen.* Japan
212 B3 **Oshikango** Namibia
212 C3 **Oshikoto** *admin. reg.* Namibia
212 B3 **Oshikuku** Namibia
105 I1 **Ōshima** *Niigata* Japan
105 J6 **Ōshima** *Tōkyō* Japan
104 F2 **Ōshima** *Toyama* Japan
104 D3 **Ō-shima** *i.* Japan
102 Q5 **Ō-shima** *i.* Japan
105 J6 **Ō-shima** *i.* Japan
103 M13 **Ō-shima** *i.* Japan
102 Q4 **Oshima-hantō** *pen.* Japan
104 E2 **Oshimizu** Japan
207 G4 **Oshin** *r.* Nigeria
105 I5 **Oshino** Japan
212 C3 **Oshivelo** Namibia
236 D5 **Oshkosh** *NE* U.S.A.
226 F5 **Oshkosh** *WI* U.S.A.
134 L2 **Oshkur'ya** Rus. Fed.
Oshmyany Belarus *see* **Ashmyany**
122 A3 **Oshnovīyeh** Iran
Osh Oblast *admin. div.* Kyrg. *see* **Osh**
207 G5 **Oshogbo** Nigeria
134 M2 **Oshper** Rus. Fed.
Oshskaya Oblast' *admin. div.* Kyrg. *see* **Osh**
122 C5 **Oshtorān Kūh** *mt.* Iran
127 N7 **Oshtorīnān** Iran
207 G5 **Oshun** *state* Nigeria
134 M2 **Oshvor** Rus. Fed.
209 C5 **Oshwe** Dem. Rep. Congo
177 H4 **Ősi** Hungary
197 M6 **Osica de Sus** Romania
192 C6 **Osidda** *Sardegna* Italy
174 G2 **Osie** Pol.
174 G3 **Osięciny** Pol.
174 G2 **Osieczna** *Pomorskie* Pol.
174 E4 **Osieczna** *Wielkopolskie* Pol.
174 D4 **Osiecznica** Pol.
175 H2 **Osiek** *Kujawsko-Pomorskie* Pol.
174 G2 **Osiek** *Pomorskie* Pol.
175 J5 **Osiek** *Świętokrzyskie* Pol.
175 J6 **Osiek Jasielski** Pol.
190 E7 **Osiglia** Italy
188 G3 **Osijek** Croatia
197 M8 **Osikovitsa** Bulg.
222 E3 **Osilinka** *r. B.C.* Can.
192 B6 **Osilo** *Sardegna* Italy
191 O9 **Osimo** Italy
174 D2 **Osina** Pol.
192 C8 **Osini** *Sardegna* Italy
107 K1 **Osinovka** Rus. Fed.
175 K4 **Osiny** Pol.
196 J6 **Osipaonica** Serbia
Osipenko Ukr. *see* **Berdyans'k**
Osipovichi Belarus *see* **Asipovichy**
212 C4 **Osire** Namibia
116 D6 **Osiyan** *Rajasthan* India
215 O3 **Osizweni** S. Africa
174 G4 **Osjaków** Pol.
188 F3 **Osječenica** *mts* Bos.-Herz.
134 A3 **Ösjön** *l.* Sweden
236 I5 **Oskaloosa** *IA* U.S.A.
236 H6 **Oskaloosa** *KS* U.S.A.
143 M4 **Oskarshamn** Sweden
142 I5 **Oskarström** Sweden
227 S1 **Oskélanéo** *Que.* Can.
Öskemen Kazakh. *see* **Ust'-Kamenogorsk**
137 Q4 **Oskil** *r.* Ukr. *alt.* **Oskol (Rus. Fed.)**
135 G6 **Oskol** *r.* Rus. Fed. *alt.* **Oskil (Ukraine)**
171 L10 **Oskořínek** Czech Rep.
177 H4 **Öskü** Hungary
139 O2 **Oskuya** *r.* Rus. Fed.
177 H3 **Osľany** Slovakia
176 F2 **Oslava** *r.* Czech Rep.
176 F2 **Oslavany** Czech Rep.
175 K6 **Osława** *r.* Pol.
176 G4 **Osli** Hungary
142 G2 **Oslo** Norway
Oslo *airport* Norway *see* **Gardermoen**
142 G2 **Oslo** *county* Norway
92 D7 **Oslob** *Cebu* Phil.
142 G2 **Oslofjorden** *sea chan.* Norway
169 K6 **Osloß** Ger.
183 N3 **Osma** Spain
114 E3 **Osmanabad** *Mahar.* India
126 G3 **Osmancık** Turkey
199 K2 **Osmaneli** Turkey
126 H5 **Osmaniye** Turkey
128 E1 **Osmaniye** *prov.* Turkey
114 F3 **Osmannagar** *Andhra Prad.* India
138 M2 **Os'mino** Rus. Fed.
143 N3 **Ösmo** Sweden
175 H3 **Osmolin** Pol.
138 G2 **Osmussaar** *i.* Estonia
169 F6 **Osnabrück** Ger.
Osnaburg *atoll Arch. des Tuamotu* Fr. Polynesia *see* **Mururoa**
Osnaburgh *Fife, Scotland* U.K. *see* **Dairsie**
174 C3 **Osno Lubuskie** Pol.
156 D5 **Osny** France
208 E5 **Oso** *r.* Dem. Rep. Congo
183 L7 **Oso** *mt.* Spain
177 G1 **Osoblaha** Czech Rep.
Osogbo Nigeria *see* **Oshogbo**
190 F3 **Osogna** Switz.
197 K8 **Osogovska Planina** *mts* Bulg./Macedonia
137 M6 **Osokorivka** Ukr.
191 O3 **Osoppo** Italy
191 Q6 **Osor** Croatia
188 E3 **Osor** *hill* Croatia
191 Q6 **Osor, Rt** *pt* Croatia
177 L4 **Oşorhei** Romania
255 C9 **Osório** Brazil
259 B6 **Osorno** Chile
183 L4 **Osorno** Spain
137 M2 **Osota** *r.* Ukr.
175 K1 **Osowa** Pol.
175 J3 **Osownica** *r.* Pol.
222 G5 **Osoyoos** *B.C.* Can.
142 B1 **Osøyri** Norway
192 C4 **Ospédale, Forêt de l'** *for. Corse* France
250 D2 **Ospino** Venez.
85 K2 **Osprey Reef** *Coral Sea Is Terr.* Austr.
164 I5 **Oss** Neth.
180 C3 **Ossa** *hill* Port.
83 K9 **Ossa, Mount** *Tas.* Austr.
184 D3 **Ossa, Serra de** *hills* Port.
185 N3 **Ossa de Montiel** Spain
191 J3 **Ossana** Italy
163 D10 **Ossau, Vallée d'** *val.* France
163 E7 **Osse** *r.* France
207 G5 **Osse** *r.* Nigeria
163 C9 **Osse-en-Aspe** France
163 H11 **Osséja** France
165 F6 **Ossendrecht** Neth.
226 C5 **Osseo** *WI* U.S.A.
163 B9 **Ossès** France
149 N6 **Ossett** *West Yorkshire, England* U.K.
192 B6 **Ossi** *Sardegna* Italy
179 I6 **Ossiach** Austria
179 I6 **Ossiacher See** *l.* Austria
226 C6 **Ossian** *IA* U.S.A.
227 K5 **Ossineke** *MI* U.S.A.
235 H2 **Ossining** *NY* U.S.A.
233 □N5 **Ossipee** *NH* U.S.A.
233 □N5 **Ossipee Lake** *NH* U.S.A.
225 H2 **Ossokmanuan Lake** *Nfld and Lab.* Can.
131 R4 **Ossora** Rus. Fed.
93 E8 **Ossu** East Timor
163 D9 **Ossun** France
137 M4 **Ostap"ye** Ukr.
139 S6 **Ostashevo** Rus. Fed.
139 Q4 **Ostashkov** Rus. Fed.
174 G1 **Ostaszewo** Pol.
169 E6 **Ostbevern** Ger.
141 L6 **Østby** Norway
168 H3 **Oste** *r.* Ger.
168 D3 **Osteel** Ger.
191 L6 **Ostellato** Italy
168 H3 **Osten** Ger.
Ostend Belgium *see* **Oostende**
261 I5 **Ostende** Arg.
Ostende Belgium *see* **Oostende**
168 H2 **Ostenfeld (Husum)** Ger.
139 P7 **Oster** Rus. Fed.
139 P8 **Oster** *r.* Rus. Fed.
136 J3 **Oster** Ukr.
142 E5 **Øster Agger** Denmark
173 O4 **Osterbach** *r.* Ger.
170 E5 **Osterburg (Altmark)** Ger.
172 G3 **Osterburken** Ger.
168 I2 **Osterby** Ger.
143 N1 **Österbybruk** Sweden
143 L4 **Österbymo** Sweden
169 F6 **Ostercappeln** Ger.
141 L6 **Österdalälven** *l.* Sweden
143 M1 **Österfärnebo** Sweden
171 E8 **Osterfeld** Ger.
143 L3 **Östergotland** *county* Sweden
171 E8 **Osterhausen** Ger.
168 G2 **Osterhever** Ger.
173 O4 **Osterhofen** Ger.
168 H1 **Øster Højst** Denmark
168 G4 **Osterholz-Scharmbeck** Ger.
142 G5 **Øster Hurup** Denmark
178 G3 **Ostermiething** Austria
190 C2 **Ostermundigen** Switz.
171 F7 **Osternienburg** Ger.
179 I6 **Osternig** *mt.* Austria/Italy
169 J7 **Osterode am Harz** Ger.
Österreich *country* Europe *see* **Austria**
168 I2 **Osterrönfeld** Ger.
140 M5 **Östersund** Sweden
170 E1 **Øster Ulslev** Denmark
143 N1 **Östervåla** Sweden
142 G4 **Østervrå** Denmark
168 D5 **Osterwald** Ger.
171 E6 **Osterweddingen** Ger.
169 K7 **Osterwieck** Ger.
171 I9 **Osterzgebirge** *park* Ger.
142 C1 **Østese** Norway
172 G4 **Ostfildern** Ger.
142 H2 **Østfold** *county* Norway
168 D3 **Ostfriesische Inseln** *is* Ger.
168 E4 **Ostfriesland** *reg.* Ger.
168 E4 **Ostgroßefehn (Großefehn)** Ger.
143 O1 **Östhammar** Sweden
169 J10 **Ostheim vor der Rhön** Ger.
172 E2 **Osthofen** Ger.
193 I4 **Ostia** Italy
190 I5 **Ostiano** Italy
191 K5 **Ostiglia** Italy
183 Q3 **Ostiz** Spain
136 G2 **Ostky** Ukr.
173 N6 **Östliche Chiemgauer Alpen** *nature res.* Ger.
178 D5 **Östliche Karwendelspitze** *mt.* Austria/Ger.
142 I1 **Östmark** Sweden
177 J6 **Ostojićevo** *Vojvodina* Serbia
179 O1 **Ostopovice** Czech Rep.
172 G6 **Ostrach** Ger.
172 G5 **Ostrach** *r.* Ger.
140 P5 **Östra gloppet** *b.* Fin.
140 P5 **Östra Kvarken** *str.* Fin./Sweden
143 L4 **Östra Lägern** *l.* Sweden
142 I4 **Östra Nedsjön** *l.* Sweden
142 J6 **Östra Ringsjön** *l.* Sweden
142 I2 **Östra Silen** *l.* Sweden
171 H8 **Ostrau** *Sachsen* Ger.
171 F7 **Ostrau** *Sachsen-Anhalt* Ger.
177 H2 **Ostrava** Czech Rep.
177 H2 **Ostravice** Czech Rep.
177 I3 **Ostredok** *mt.* Slovakia
168 E4 **Ostrhauderfehn** Ger.
172 F3 **Östringen** Ger.
171 K8 **Ostritz** Ger.
175 H2 **Ostróda** Pol.
135 G6 **Ostrogozhsk** Rus. Fed.
136 F3 **Ostroh** Ukr.
196 J7 **Oštro Koplje** *mt.* Serbia
175 J2 **Ostrołęka** Pol.
174 G2 **Ostromecko** Pol.
176 E1 **Ostroměř** Czech Rep.
174 E3 **Ostroróg** Pol.
176 B1 **Ostrov** Czech Rep.
197 P6 **Ostrov** *Constanța* Romania
197 Q6 **Ostrov** *Tulcea* Romania
138 L4 **Ostrov** Rus. Fed.
Ostrovets Pol. *see* **Ostrowiec Świętokrzyski**
137 N8 **Ostrovs'ke** Ukr.
134 H4 **Ostrovskoye** Rus. Fed.
175 J5 **Ostrów** Pol.
Ostrow Pol. *see* **Ostrów Wielkopolski**
174 G4 **Ostrówek** *Łódzkie* Pol.
175 K4 **Ostrówek** *Lubelskie* Pol.
174 D2 **Ostrowice** Pol.
Ostrowiec *Świętokrzyskie* Pol. *see* **Ostrowiec Świętokrzyski**
174 E1 **Ostrowiec** *Zachodniopomorskie* Pol.
175 J5 **Ostrowiec Świętokrzyski** Pol.
175 H2 **Ostrowite** *Kujawsko-Pomorskie* Pol.
174 G3 **Ostrowite** *Wielkopolskie* Pol.
175 K4 **Ostrów Lubelski** Pol.
175 J3 **Ostrów Mazowiecka** Pol.
174 G3 **Ostrowo** *Kujawsko-Pomorskie* Pol.
Ostrowo *Wielkopolskie* Pol. *see* **Ostrów Wielkopolski**
174 F4 **Ostrów Wielkopolski** Pol.
175 H5 **Ostrowy nad Okszą** Pol.
175 J4 **Ostrożeń** Pol.
174 F4 **Ostrzeszów** Pol.
168 J3 **Oststeinbek** Ger.
178 F6 **Osttirol** *reg.* Austria
244 D7 **Ostula** Mex.
195 N2 **Ostuni** Italy
157 O6 **Ostwald** France
139 R4 **Osuga** *r.* Rus. Fed.
139 R5 **Osuga** *r.* Rus. Fed.
105 G6 **Ōsuka** Japan
227 S2 **O'Sullivan, Lac** *l. Que.* Can.
224 C3 **O'Sullivan Lake** *Ont.* Can.
198 A2 **Osum** *r.* Albania
197 M7 **Osŭm** *r.* Bulg.
103 H16 **Ōsumi-hantō** *pen.* Japan
103 H16 **Ōsumi-kaikyō** *sea chan.* Japan
102 □H16 **Ōsumi-shotō** *is* Japan
Osun *state* Nigeria *see* **Oshun**
185 I6 **Osuna** Spain
256 B4 **Osvaldo Cruz** Brazil
149 O5 **Oswaldkirk** *North Yorkshire, England* U.K.
149 M6 **Oswaldtwistle** *Lancashire, England* U.K.
226 F8 **Oswego** *IL* U.S.A.
237 H7 **Oswego** *KS* U.S.A.
232 I5 **Oswego** *NY* U.S.A.
235 F5 **Oswego** *r. NJ* U.S.A.
232 I5 **Oswego** *r. NY* U.S.A.
150 F2 **Oswestry** *Shropshire, England* U.K.
175 H5 **Oświęcim** Pol.
138 L5 **Osyno** Rus. Fed.
137 P7 **Osypenko** Ukr.
192 B3 **Ota** *Corse* France
104 D4 **Ota** Japan
105 J3 **Ōta** Japan
184 B2 **Ota** Port.
184 B2 **Ota** *r.* Port.
81 D12 **Otago** *admin. reg. South I.* N.Z.
81 E12 **Otago Peninsula** *South I.* N.Z.
Otahiti *i.* Fr. Polynesia *see* **Tahiti**
80 J6 **Otairi** *North I.* N.Z.
104 G4 **Ōtake** Japan
102 □G17 **O-take** *vol. Nansei-shotō* Japan
102 □G17 **O-take** *vol. Nansei-shotō* Japan
105 J4 **Ōtake-san** *mt.* Japan
105 L5 **Ōtaki** *Chiba* Japan
105 I4 **Ōtaki** *Saitama* Japan
80 J7 **Otaki** *North I.* N.Z.
81 C12 **Otama** *South I.* N.Z.
80 K6 **Otamauri** *North I.* N.Z.
120 K6 **O'tamurot** Uzbek.
121 P6 **Otar** Kazakh.
105 G2 **Otari** Japan
102 R3 **Otaru** Japan
176 G2 **Otaslavice** Czech Rep.
81 C13 **Otatara** *South I.* N.Z.
245 K7 **Otatitlán** Mex.
81 B13 **Otautau** *South I.* N.Z.
176 D2 **Otava** *r.* Czech Rep.
141 S6 **Otava** Fin.
250 B4 **Otavalo** Ecuador
212 C3 **Otavi** Namibia
105 L2 **Ōtawara** Japan
209 B9 **Otchinjau** Angola
Otdia *atoll* Marshall Is *see* **Wotje**
121 Q6 **Otegen Batyr** Kazakh.
183 Q3 **Oteiza** Spain
81 E11 **Otekaieke** *South I.* N.Z.
225 G1 **Otelnuc, Lac** *l. Que.* Can.
197 K5 **Oţelu Roşu** Romania
81 E11 **Otematata** *South I.* N.Z.
128 E2 **Ötençay** Turkey
138 J3 **Otepää** Estonia
138 J3 **Otepää kõrgustik** *hills* Estonia
140 O2 **Oteren** Norway
182 H5 **Otero de Bodas** Spain
183 L7 **Otero de Herreros** Spain
239 J13 **Oteros** *r.* Mex.
198 B2 **Oteševo** Macedonia
175 I5 **Otfinów** Pol.
151 M5 **Otford** *Kent, England* U.K.
106 E3 **Otgon Tenger Uul** *mt.* Mongolia
157 J4 **Othain** *r.* France
156 F7 **Othe, Forêt d'** *for.* France
238 E3 **Othello** *WA* U.S.A.
198 A3 **Othonoi** *i.* Greece
198 D3 **Othrys** *mt.* Greece
207 F4 **Oti** *r.* Ghana/Togo
93 A4 **Oti** *Sulawesi* Indon.
207 F4 **Oti, Réserve de Faune de l'** *nature res.* Togo
177 G2 **Otice** Czech Rep.
172 E4 **Ötigheim** Ger.
215 P5 **Otimati** S. Africa
244 B1 **Otinapa** Mex.
81 F9 **Otira** *South I.* N.Z.
236 D5 **Otis** *CO* U.S.A.
233 I6 **Otisco Lake** *NY* U.S.A.
225 G3 **Otish, Monts** *hills Que.* Can.
172 F4 **Ötisheim** Ger.
234 F2 **Otisville** *NY* U.S.A.
185 L7 **Otívar** Spain
212 C4 **Otjinene** Namibia
212 B3 **Otjitambi** Namibia
212 C4 **Otjiwarongo** Namibia
212 C4 **Otjosondu** Namibia
212 B3 **Otjovasandu** *waterhole* Namibia
212 C4 **Otjozondjupa** *admin. reg.* Namibia
151 O3 **Otley** *Suffolk, England* U.K.
149 N6 **Otley** *West Yorkshire, England* U.K.
129 A6 **Otlukbeli** Turkey
129 A6 **Otlukbeli Dağları** *mts* Turkey
174 F5 **Otmuchów** Pol.
141 K6 **Otnes** Norway
179 O1 **Otnice** Czech Rep.
104 C7 **Ōto** Japan
102 R5 **Otobe** Japan
102 R4 **Otobe-dake** *mt.* Japan
188 E3 **Otočac** Croatia
102 U4 **Otofuke** Japan
Otog Qi *Nei Mongol* China *see* **Ulan**
102 T2 **Otoineppu** Japan
188 G3 **Otok** Croatia
188 F3 **Otoka** Bos.-Herz.
80 L5 **Otoko** *North I.* N.Z.
207 F4 **Otola** Benin
80 I2 **Otonga** *North I.* N.Z.
210 A2 **Otoro, Jebel** *mt.* Sudan
80 J5 **Otorohanga** *North I.* N.Z.
174 E3 **Otorowo** Pol.
224 B3 **Otoskwin** *r. Ont.* Can.
103 □2 **Otōto-jima** *i. Ogasawara-shotō* Japan
182 C4 **O Toural** Spain
104 F6 **Otowa** Japan
103 K13 **Ōtoyo** Japan
120 D5 **Otpan, Gora** *hill* Kazakh.
Otpor Rus. Fed. *see* **Zabaykal'sk**
142 E3 **Otra** *r.* Norway
247 □10 **Otrabanda** *Curaçao* Neth. Antilles
139 T8 **Otradinskiy** Rus. Fed.
129 C1 **Otradnaya** Rus. Fed.
139 N2 **Otradnoye** *Leningradskaya Oblast'* Rus. Fed.
Otradnoye *Samarskaya Oblast'* Rus. Fed. *see* **Otradnyy**
139 N1 **Otradnoye, Ozero** *l.* Rus. Fed.
120 D1 **Otradnyy** Rus. Fed.
195 O3 **Otranto** Italy
195 P2 **Otranto, Strait of** Albar
193 I3 **Otricoli** Italy
Otrogovo Rus. Fed. *see* **Stepnoye**
177 G2 **Otrokovice** Czech Rep.
131 S3 **Otrozhnyy** Rus. Fed.
179 L4 **Ötscher-Tormäuer** *natu* Austria
226 I7 **Otsego** *MI* U.S.A.
233 K6 **Otsego Lake** *NY* U.S.A.
105 M2 **Ōtsu** *Ibaraki* Japan
104 C5 **Ōtsu** *Shiga* Japan
102 S7 **Ōtsuchi** Japan
105 I4 **Ōtsuki** Japan
141 J6 **Otta** Norway
192 C7 **Ottana** *Sardegna* Italy
157 L5 **Ottange** France
224 F4 **Ottawa** *Ont.* Can.
224 F4 **Ottawa** *r. Ont./Que.* Can
226 F8 **Ottawa** *IL* U.S.A.
236 H6 **Ottawa** *KS* U.S.A.
232 A7 **Ottawa** *OH* U.S.A.
224 D1 **Ottawa Islands** *Nunavu*
171 I8 **Ottendorf-Okrilla** Ger.
172 D5 **Ottenheim** Ger.
172 E4 **Ottenhöfen im Schwar** Ger.
179 L3 **Ottenschlag** Austria
179 J3 **Ottensheim** Austria
169 H7 **Ottenstein** Ger.
179 L2 **Ottenstein Stausee** *res* Austria
168 I4 **Otter** Ger.
150 F6 **Otter** *r. England* U.K.
172 D3 **Otterbach** Ger.
172 D2 **Otterberg** Ger.
149 M3 **Otterburn** *Northumberla England* U.K.
146 F10 **Otter Ferry** *Argyll and B Scotland* U.K.
173 L6 **Otterfing** Ger.
226 H1 **Otter Island** *Ont.* Can.
223 J4 **Otter Lake** *Sask.* Can.
164 I4 **Otterlo** Neth.
168 G3 **Otterndorf** Ger.
224 D3 **Otter Rapids** *Ont.* Can.
168 H4 **Ottersberg** Ger.
142 J3 **Otterstad** Sweden
172 E4 **Ottersweier** Ger.
146 □N1 **Otterswick** *Shetland, Scotland* U.K.
142 G6 **Otterup** Denmark
171 G8 **Otterwisch** Ger.
150 D6 **Ottery** *r. England* U.K.
150 F6 **Ottery St Mary** *Devon, England* U.K.
177 G4 **Öttevény** Hungary
165 G7 **Ottignies** Belgium
192 D6 **Ottiolo, Punta d'** *pt Sar* Italy
157 O8 **Ottmarsheim** France
179 I3 **Ottnang am Hausruck**
143 M1 **Ottnaren** *l.* Sweden
173 I6 **Ottobeuren** Ger.
173 L5 **Ottobrunn** Ger.
221 J1 **Otto Fiord** *inlet Nunavu*
177 I5 **Öttömös** Hungary
190 G6 **Ottone** Italy
215 J2 **Ottosdal** S. Africa
215 J1 **Ottoshoop** S. Africa
169 H9 **Ottrau** Ger.
121 P7 **Ottuk** Kyrg.
236 I5 **Ottumwa** *IA* U.S.A.
172 C3 **Ottweiler** Ger.
207 G5 **Otukpa** Nigeria
207 H5 **Otukpo** Nigeria
245 I6 **Otumba** Mex.
252 D4 **Otuyo** Bol.
250 B6 **Otuzco** Peru
Otvazhniy Rus. Fed. *se* **Zhigulevsk**
232 B10 **Otway** *OH* U.S.A.
259 B9 **Otway, Bahía** *b.* Chile
83 I8 **Otway, Cape** *Vic.* Austr.
259 C9 **Otway, Seno** *b.* Chile
83 I8 **Otway National Park** *V* Austr.
83 I8 **Otway Range** *mts Vic.*
175 J3 **Otwock** Pol.
183 O2 **Otxandio** Spain
174 D4 **Otyń** Pol.
136 D5 **Otyniya** Ukr.
173 N4 **Otzing** Ger.
178 C5 **Ötztal** *val.* Austria
178 C6 **Ötztaler Alpen** *mts* Aus
96 F4 **Ou, Nam** *r.* Laos
207 H3 **Ouacha** Niger
237 J10 **Ouachita** *r. AR* U.S.A.
237 I8 **Ouachita, Lake** *AR* U.S
228 H4 **Ouachita Mountains** *AR/OK* U.S.A.
237 H8 **Ouachita Mountains** *AR/OK* U.S.A.
204 C5 **Ouadâne** Maur.
208 D2 **Ouadda** C.A.R.
202 D6 **Ouaddaï** *pref.* Chad
207 G1 **Ouadjinkarem** *well* Nig
206 B2 **Ouâd Nâga** Maur.
206 C3 **Ouadou** *watercourse* M
206 E3 **Ouagadougou** Burkina
206 E3 **Ouahigouya** Burkina
Ouahran Alg. *see* **Oran**
208 D3 **Ouaka** *pref.* C.A.R.
208 C3 **Ouaka** *r.* C.A.R.
206 D2 **Oualâta** Maur.
207 F4 **Oualé** *r.* Burkina
206 C3 **Oualia** Mali
207 F3 **Ouallam** Niger
205 F4 **Ouallene** Alg.
251 I3 **Ouanary** Fr. Guiana
202 C5 **Ouanazein** *well* Chad
208 D2 **Ouanda-Djailé** C.A.R.
208 C3 **Ouandago** C.A.R.
208 D2 **Ouandja** *Haute-Kotto* C
208 D2 **Ouandja** *Vakaga* C.A.R.
208 D2 **Ouandja-Vakaga, Rése Faune de la** *nature res.*
208 E3 **Ouando** C.A.R.
208 D3 **Ouango** C.A.R.
206 D4 **Ouangolodougou** Côte d'Ivoire
207 G3 **Ouani Kalaoua** *well* Nig
160 C1 **Ouanne** France
251 H4 **Ouaqui** Fr. Guiana
208 E3 **Ouara** *r.* C.A.R.
207 F4 **Ouargaye** Burkina
205 G3 **Ouargla** Alg.
207 F2 **Ouarissibitil** *well* Mali
207 F2 **Ouaritoufoulout** *well* M
204 C3 **Ouarkziz, Jbel** *ridge* Alg./Morocco
Ouarogou Burkina *see* **Ouargaye**
156 C7 **Ouarville** France
204 D3 **Ouarzazate** Morocco
207 F3 **Ouatagouna** Mali
Oubangui *r.* C.A.R./Der Congo *see* **Ubangi**
212 E7 **Oubergpas** *pass* S. Afr
182 C7 **Ouca** Port.
160 G2 **Ouche** *r.* France
104 D7 **Ōuchiyama** Japan
156 B8 **Oucques** France
104 C7 **Ouda** Japan
164 F5 **Oud-Beijerland** Neth.
164 E5 **Ouddorp** Neth.
164 J2 **Oudega** Neth.
164 I3 **Oudehaske** Neth.
206 E2 **Oudeïka** *well* Mali
164 I3 **Oudemirdum** Neth.
165 E7 **Oudenaarde** Belgium
164 G5 **Oudenbosch** Neth.
165 D6 **Oudenburg** Belgium
164 L2 **Oude Pekela** Neth.
164 G4 **Oude Rijn** *r.* Neth.
164 G4 **Ouderkerk aan de Ar** Neth.
164 G2 **Oudeschild** Neth.
164 F5 **Oude-Tonge** Neth.
164 G4 **Oudewater** Neth.
164 F5 **Oud-Gastel** Neth.
158 I7 **Oudon** France
159 J6 **Oudon** *r.* France
214 G9 **Oudtshoorn** S. Africa
165 G6 **Oud-Turnhout** Belgium
165 D6 **Oudzele** Belgium
180 D5 **Oued Laou** Morocco
204 D2 **Oued Zem** Morocco
78 □5 **Ouegoa** New Caledonia

Ouela Njazidja Comoros
Ouéléssébougou Mali
Ouella Niger
Ouémé r. Benin
Ouen i. New Caledonia
Ouessa Burkina
Ouessant, Île d' i. France
Ouèssè Benin
Ouesso Congo
Ouest prov. Cameroon
Ouest, Pointe de l' pt Que. Can.
Ouezzane Morocco
Ouffet Belgium
Oughter, Lough l. Ireland
Oughterard Ireland
Ougnat, Jbel mt. Morocco
Ougney France
Ougo-gawa r. Japan
Ouguela Port.
Ougura-yama mt. Japan
Ouham pref. C.A.R.
Ouham r. C.A.R./Chad
Ouham-Pendé pref. C.A.R.
Ouidah Benin
Ouinardene Mali
Ouiriego Mex.
Ouistreham France
Oujâf well Maur.
Oujda Morocco
Oujeft Maur.
Oulad Teïma Morocco
Oulainen Fin.
Oulangan kansallispuisto nat. park Fin.
Oulchy-le-Château France
Oulder Belgium
Ould Yenjé Maur.
Ouled Djellal Alg.
Ouled Naïl, Monts des mts Alg.
Ouled Saïd well Alg.
Ouli Cameroon
Oullins France
Oulmès Morocco
Oulton Suffolk, England U.K.
Oulu Fin.
Oulu prov. Fin.
Oulujärvi l. Fin.
Oulujoki r. Fin.
Oulunsalo Fin.
Oulx Italy
Oum-Chalouba Chad
Oumé Côte d'Ivoire
Oum el Bouaghi Alg.
Oum-Hadjer Chad
Oumm eḍ Ḍroûs Guebli, Sebkhet salt flat Maur.
Oumm eḍ Ḍroûs Telli, Sebkha salt flat Maur.
Oumm el A'sel well Mali
Ounane, Djebel mt. Alg.
Ounara Morocco
Ounasjoki r. Fin.
Oundle Northamptonshire, England U.K.
Oungre Sask. Can.
Ounianga Kébir Chad
Ounianga Sérir Chad
Ounissoui well Niger
Ouogo C.A.R.
Oupeye Belgium
Our r. Lux.
Oura, Akrotirio pt Chios Greece
Ouranoupoli Greece
Ōura-wan b. Okinawa Japan
Ouray CO U.S.A.
Ouray UT U.S.A.
Ource r. France
Ourcq r. France
Ouré Kaba Guinea
Ourém Brazil
Ourense Spain
Ourense prov. Galicia Spain
Ouricurí Brazil
Ourinhos Brazil
Ourini Chad
Ourique Port.
Ouro Brazil
Ouro r. Brazil
Ouro r. Spain
Ouro, Ponta do pt Moz.
Ouro Branco Brazil
Ouro Fino Brazil
Ourol Spain
Ouro Preto Brazil
Ouroux-en-Morvan France
Ouroux-sur-Saône France
Ourthe r. Belgium
Ourville-en-Caux France
Ouse r. East Sussex, England U.K.
Ouse r. England U.K.
Oust France
Oust r. France
Outamba Kilimi National Park Sierra Leone
Outão Port.
Outardes r. Que. Can.
Outardes Quatre, Réservoir resr Que. Can.
Outarville France
Outat Oulad el Haj Morocco
Outeïd Arkâs well Mali
Outeiro Bragança Port.
Outeiro Viana do Castelo Port.
Outeiro de Rei Spain
Outeiro Seco Port.
Outeniekwaberge mts S. Africa
Outer Hebrides is Scotland U.K.
Outer Island WI U.S.A.
Outer Mongolia country Asia see Mongolia
Outer Santa Barbara Channel CA U.S.A.
Ouṭfene well Maur.
Outjo Namibia
Outlook Sask. Can.
Outokumpu Fin.
Outomuro Spain
Outoul Alg.
Outram South I. N.Z.
Outreau France
Out Skerries is Scotland U.K.
Outwell Norfolk, England U.K.
Ouvéa atoll Îles Loyauté New Caledonia
Ouveillan France
Ouvèze r. France
Ouyanghai Shuiku resr China
Ouyen Vic. Austr.
Ouzel r. England U.K.
Ouzouer-le-Marché France
Ouzouer-sur-Loire France
Ova r. Turkey
Ovace, Punta d' mt. Corse France
Ovacık İçel Turkey
Ovacık Tunceli Turkey
Ovacık Dağı mt. Turkey
Ovada Italy
Ovaeymiri Turkey
Ova Gölü l. Turkey
Ovakent Turkey
Ovakışla Turkey
Ovakışlacık Turkey
Ovaköy Turkey
Oval PA U.S.A.
Ovalau i. Fiji
Ovalle Chile
Ovamboland reg. Namibia
Ovan Gabon
Ovar Port.
Ovaro Italy
Ovau i. Solomon Is
Oveja mt. Arg.
Ovejas Col.
Ovejería Arg.
Ovelgönne Ger.
Oveng Cameroon
Oveng Equat. Guinea
Ovens r. Vic. Austr.
Ovens Ireland
Overath Ger.
Overbister Orkney, Scotland U.K.
Overdinkel Neth.
Øvergard Norway
Overhalla Norway
165 G7 Overijse Belgium
164 K4 Overijssel prov. Neth.
164 J4 Overijssels Kanaal canal Neth.
140 Q3 Överkalix Sweden
87 C9 Overlander Roadhouse W.A. Austr.
236 H6 Overland Park KS U.S.A.
234 B6 Overlea MD U.S.A.
164 I5 Overloon Neth.
140 P5 Övermark Fin.
260 B4 Overo, Volcán vol. Arg.
165 H6 Overpelt Belgium
151 I2 Overseal Derbyshire, England U.K.
151 J5 Overton Hampshire, England U.K.
150 G2 Overton Wrexham, Wales U.K.
241 R5 Overton NV U.S.A.
237 H9 Overton TX U.S.A.
140 Q3 Övertorneå Sweden
146 I11 Overtown North Lanarkshire, Scotland U.K.
143 M4 Överum Sweden
140 M3 Överuman l. Sweden
164 G4 Overveen Neth.
151 I5 Over Wallop Hampshire, England U.K.
190 E3 Ovesca r. Italy
165 E6 Ovezande Neth.
182 E1 O Vicedo Spain
236 D5 Ovid CO U.S.A.
226 J6 Ovid MI U.S.A.
232 I6 Ovid NY U.S.A.
136 J7 Ovidiopol' Ukr.
197 Q6 Ovidiu Romania
182 I2 Oviedo Spain
182 H2 Oviedo prov. Spain
190 E6 Oviglio Italy
193 L3 Ovindoli Italy
139 T3 Ovinishchenskaya Vozvyshennost' hills Rus. Fed.
138 E4 Ovišrags hd Latvia
215 J6 Oviston Nature Reserve S. Africa
120 J7 Ovminzatov tog'lari hills Uzbek.
195 N3 Ovo, Punta dell' pt Italy
192 C7 Ovodda Sardegna Italy
106 E2 Övögdiy Mongolia
Ovolau i. Fiji see Ovalau
107 M4 Ovoot Mongolia
106 H4 Övörhangay prov. Mongolia
140 R2 Øvre Anárjohka Nasjonalpark nat. park Norway
141 I6 Øvre Årdal Norway
140 O2 Øvre Dividal Nasjonalpark nat. park Norway
140 K5 Øvre Forra nature res. Norway
142 J2 Övre Fryken l. Sweden
142 I2 Övre Gla l. Sweden
142 D1 Øvre Hein l. Norway
140 T2 Øvre Pasvik Nasjonalpark nat. park Norway
141 K6 Øvre Rendal Norway
140 P2 Övre Soppero Sweden
136 H2 Ovruch Ukr.
100 E2 Ovsyanka Rus. Fed.
106 H3 Övt Mongolia
80 K7 Owahanga North I. N.Z.
81 D13 Owaka South I. N.Z.
226 D1 Owakonze Ont. Can.
208 B5 Owando Congo
102 R6 Ōwani Japan
Owa Rafa i. Solomon Is see Santa Ana
104 F5 Owariasahi Japan
Owa Riki i. Solomon Is see Santa Catalina
232 I6 Owasco Lake NY U.S.A.
104 D7 Owase Japan
104 D7 Owase-wan b. Japan
237 H7 Owasso OK U.S.A.
236 I3 Owatonna MN U.S.A.
123 J4 Owbeh Afgh.
175 J4 Owczarnia Pol.
233 I6 Owego NY U.S.A.
147 H5 Owel, Lough l. Ireland
172 G4 Owen Ger.
81 G8 Owen, Mount South I. N.Z.
207 G5 Owena Nigeria
147 E4 Owenbeg Ireland
214 H4 Owendale S. Africa
147 C4 Owenduff r. Ireland
80 □ Owenga Chatham Is S. Pacific Ocean
147 C4 Oweniny r. Ireland
97 D9 Owen Island Myanmar
147 C4 Owenmore r. Ireland
147 H3 Owenreagh r. Northern Ireland U.K.
81 G8 Owen River South I. N.Z.
240 O5 Owens r. CA U.S.A.
230 D7 Owensboro KY U.S.A.
240 O5 Owens Lake CA U.S.A.
224 D4 Owen Sound Ont. Can.
227 N5 Owen Sound inlet Ont. Can.
84 D7 Owen Springs N.T. Austr.
91 K8 Owen Stanley Range mts P.N.G.
236 J6 Owensville MO U.S.A.
232 A9 Owensville OH U.S.A.
230 E6 Owenton KY U.S.A.
207 G5 Owerri Nigeria
147 F2 Owey Island Ireland
80 J6 Owhango North I. N.Z.
222 E5 Owikeno Lake B.C. Can.
172 G6 Owingen Ger.
232 I10 Owings MD U.S.A.
234 B6 Owings Mills MD U.S.A.
232 B10 Owingsville KY U.S.A.
223 M3 Owl r. Man. Can.
238 J5 Owl Creek r. WY U.S.A.
233 □P4 Owls Head ME U.S.A.
Owminzatow Toghi hills Uzbek. see Ovminzatov tog'lari
207 G5 Owo Nigeria
227 J7 Owosso MI U.S.A.
Owrtyn Wales U.K. see Overton
168 I2 Owschlag Ger.
238 F6 Owyhee NV U.S.A.
238 F5 Owyhee r. OR U.S.A.
238 F5 Owyhee Mountains ID U.S.A.
238 F5 Owyhee North Fork r. ID U.S.A.
238 F5 Owyhee South Fork r. ID U.S.A.
252 B2 Oxapampa Peru
140 □E1 Öxarfjörður b. Iceland
223 K5 Oxbow Sask. Can.
236 E1 Ox Creek r. ND U.S.A.
143 N3 Oxelösund Sweden
149 N6 Oxenhope West Yorkshire, England U.K.
81 G10 Oxford South I. N.Z.
151 J4 Oxford Oxfordshire, England U.K.
235 I2 Oxford CT U.S.A.
233 N6 Oxford MA U.S.A.
233 □O4 Oxford ME U.S.A.
227 K7 Oxford MI U.S.A.
237 K8 Oxford MS U.S.A.
231 H7 Oxford NC U.S.A.
234 F3 Oxford NJ U.S.A.
233 J6 Oxford NY U.S.A.
232 A9 Oxford OH U.S.A.
234 D5 Oxford PA U.S.A.
226 E6 Oxford WI U.S.A.
85 L6 Oxford Downs Qld Austr.
223 M4 Oxford House Man. Can.
223 M4 Oxford Lake Man. Can.
151 J4 Oxfordshire admin. div. England U.K.
142 J6 Oxie Sweden
243 O7 Oxkutzcab Mex.
83 J6 Oxley N.S.W. Austr.
83 M4 Oxleys Peak N.S.W. Austr.
83 N4 Oxley Wild Rivers National Park N.S.W. Austr.
Ox Mountains hills Ireland see Slieve Gamph
240 M7 Oxnard CA U.S.A.
151 L5 Oxshott Surrey, England U.K.
151 M5 Oxted Surrey, England U.K.
146 K11 Oxton Scottish Borders, Scotland U.K.
227 P4 Oxtongue Lake Ont. Can.
Oxus r. Asia see Amudar'ya
198 F4 Oxylithos Greece
95 I3 Oya Sarawak Malaysia
95 I3 Oya r. Malaysia
140 L3 Øya Norway
104 E2 Oyabe Japan
104 F2 Oyabe-gawa r. Japan
105 I5 Oyama Shizuoka Japan
105 K3 Oyama Tochigi Japan
104 F2 Ōyama Japan
105 J5 Ō-yama mt. Japan
105 K7 Ō-yama vol. Japan
104 D6 Ōyamada Japan
104 C6 Ōyamazaki Japan
183 L2 Oyambre, Cabo de c. Spain
251 I3 Oyapock r. Brazil/Fr. Guiana
251 I3 Oyapock, Baie d' b. Fr. Guiana
121 T4 Oychilik Kazakh.
208 A4 Oyem Gabon
223 I5 Oyen Alta Can.
156 D2 Oye-Plage France
142 H2 Øyeren l. Norway
106 E2 Oygon Mongolia
146 H7 Oykel r. Scotland U.K.
146 G7 Oykel Bridge Highland, Scotland U.K.
173 I6 Oy-Mittelberg Ger.
131 P3 Oymyakon Rus. Fed.
208 B5 Oyo Congo
207 F5 Oyo Nigeria
207 F4 Oyo state Nigeria
203 H4 Oyo Sudan
104 C7 Ōyodo Japan
252 A2 Oyón Peru
160 H4 Oyonnax France
120 K7 Oyoqog'itma botig'i depr. Uzbek.
120 K7 Oyoqquduq Uzbek.
Oysangur Rus. Fed. see Oyskhara
Oyshilik Kazakh. see Oychilik
129 H2 Oyskhara Rus. Fed.
214 I10 Oyster Bay S. Africa
235 H3 Oyster Bay NY U.S.A.
235 G6 Oyster Creek NJ U.S.A.
96 A4 Oyster Island Myanmar
114 D5 Oyster Rocks is India
121 O6 Oytal Kazakh.
121 P7 Oy-Tal Kyrg.
168 H4 Oyten Ger.
111 E8 Oytograk Xinjiang China
128 A2 Oyukludağı mt. Turkey
Oyyl Kazakh. see Uil
Oyyq Kazakh. see Uyuk
182 D2 Oza Spain
183 P3 Ozaeta Spain
102 T7 Ō-zaki pt Japan
127 L4 Özalp Turkey
92 D7 Ozamiz Mindanao Phil.
156 B7 Ozanne r. France
231 E10 Ozark AL U.S.A.
237 I8 Ozark AR U.S.A.
237 I7 Ozark MO U.S.A.
237 I7 Ozark Plateau MO U.S.A.
236 I6 Ozarks, Lake of the MO U.S.A.
175 J5 Ożarów Pol.
175 H5 Ożarowice Pol.
175 I3 Ożarów Mazowiecki Pol.
122 G4 Ozbagū Iran
179 L6 Ožbalt Slovenia
199 I5 Özbaşı Turkey
Ozbekiston country Asia see Uzbekistan
177 J3 Ózd Hungary
177 I3 Ožďany Slovakia
129 C5 Özdere Erzurum Turkey
199 I5 Özdere İzmir Turkey
129 C7 Özdilek Turkey
Özen Kazakh. see Kyzylsay
175 J6 Ożenna Pol.
139 R2 Ozerevo Rus. Fed.
139 Q7 Ozerishche Rus. Fed.
136 H8 Ozerne Odes'ka Oblast' Ukr.
136 E2 Ozerne Volyns'ka Oblast' Ukr.
136 H3 Ozerne Zhytomyrs'ka Oblast' Ukr.
139 T6 Ozerninskoye Vodokhranilishche resr Rus. Fed.
131 Q4 Ozernovskiy Rus. Fed.
120 J1 Ozernoye Kazakh.
120 D2 Ozernoye Rus. Fed.
Ozernyy Karagandinskaya Oblast' Kazakh. see Shashubay
Ozernyy Kostanayskaya Oblast' Kazakh. see Ozernoye
139 X4 Ozernyy Ivanovskaya Oblast' Rus. Fed.
120 I2 Ozernyy Orenburgskaya Oblast' Rus. Fed.
139 P6 Ozernyy Smolenskaya Oblast' Rus. Fed.
121 U1 Ozero Petrovskoye Rus. Fed.
198 C4 Ozeros, Limni l. Greece
100 L2 Ozerpakh Rus. Fed.
138 F7 Ozersk Rus. Fed.
100 M5 Ozerskiy Sakhalin Rus. Fed.
139 V7 Ozery Rus. Fed.
100 F3 Ozeryane Rus. Fed.
137 L3 Ozeryany Ukr.
121 O7 Özgön Kyrg.
139 V7 Ozherel'ye Rus. Fed.
131 Q3 Ozhogina r. Rus. Fed.
192 C6 Ozieri Sardegna Italy
174 G5 Ozimek Pol.
120 C2 Ozinki Rus. Fed.
129 B6 Özlüce Barajı resr Turkey
156 E6 Ozoir-la-Ferrière France
138 G5 Ozolnieki Latvia
237 E10 Ozona TX U.S.A.
177 H5 Ozora Hungary
175 H4 Ozorków Pol.
207 G5 Ozoro Nigeria
103 J13 Ōzu Ehime Japan
103 H14 Ōzu Kumamoto Japan
103 I12 Ozuki Japan
245 J4 Ozuluama Mex.
245 I6 Ozumba de Alzate Mex.
129 D4 Ozurget'i Georgia
128 A1 Özyurt Dağı mts Turkey
175 M5 Ozyutychi Ukr.
191 K7 Ozzano dell'Emilia Italy
190 E5 Ozzano Monferrato Italy

P

206 E4 Pâ Burkina
140 R4 Paakkola Fin.
165 H6 Paal Belgium
78 □5 Paama i. Vanuatu
221 N3 Paamiut Greenland
Pa-an Myanmar see Hpa-an
Paanopa i. Kiribati see Banaba
214 C9 Paarl S. Africa
138 J2 Paasvere Estonia
78 □4a Paata i. Chuuk Micronesia
Paatsjoki r. Europe see Patsoyoki
240 □F13 Pa'auilo HI U.S.A.
Pabaigh i. Western Isles, Scotland U.K. see Pabbay
Pabail Uarach Scotland U.K. see Upper Bayble
214 F4 Paballelo S. Africa
101 F8 P'abal-li N. Korea
146 B7 Pabbay i. Western Isles, Scotland U.K.
146 A9 Pabbay i. Western Isles, Scotland U.K.
244 E3 Pabeilón de Arteaga Mex.
260 B2 Pabellón Chile
175 H4 Pabianice Pol.
Pabianitz Pol. see Pabianice
192 B8 Pabillonis Sardegna Italy
245 H1 Pablillo r. Mex.
261 H5 Pablo Acosta Arg.
117 L7 Pabna Bangl.
179 K3 Pabneukirchen Austria
138 I7 Pabradė Lith.
123 L8 Pab Range mts Pak.
158 E4 Pabu France
252 D2 Pacaás, Serra dos hills Brazil
253 E2 Pacaás Novos, Parque Nacional nat. park Brazil
256 B4 Pacaembu Brazil
252 D2 Pacahuaras r. Bol.
254 F3 Pacajus Brazil
214 G10 Pacaltsdorp S. Africa
175 J5 Pacanów Pol.
252 B3 Pacapausa Peru
Pacaraimã, Serra mts S. America see Pakaraima Mountains
252 B3 Pacarán Peru
250 B6 Pacasmayo Peru
254 F2 Pacatuba Brazil
250 C6 Pacaya r. Peru
243 N10 Pacaya, Volcán de vol. Guat.
250 C6 Pacaya Samiria, Reserva Nacional nature res. Peru
158 H5 Pacé France
194 D8 Paceco Sicilia Italy
260 C2 Pachaco Arg.
114 F7 Pachaimalai Hills India
235 L1 Pachaug Pond l. CT U.S.A.
242 E2 Pacheco Chihuahua Mex.
244 E1 Pacheco Zacatecas Mex.
199 G6 Pacheia i. Greece
135 H5 Pachelma Rus. Fed.
252 C4 Pachía Peru
134 I3 Pachikha Rus. Fed.
195 I10 Pachino Sicilia Italy
252 B2 Pachitea r. Peru
252 A1 Pachiza Peru
116 G8 Pachmarhi Madh. Prad. India
198 F1 Pachni Greece
116 F8 Pachor Madh. Prad. India
116 E9 Pachora Mahar. India
116 D7 Pachpadra Rajasthan India
116 D7 Pachpadra Salt Depot Rajasthan India
245 I5 Pachuca Mex.
192 I1 Paciano Italy
240 J4 Pacifica CA U.S.A.
267 I9 Pacific-Antarctic Ridge sea feature Pacific Ocean
240 K5 Pacific Grove CA U.S.A.
266 Pacific Ocean
222 E5 Pacific Rim National Park B.C. Can.
92 E6 Pacijan i. Phil.
177 K3 Pácin Hungary
95 K8 Pacinan, Tanjung pt Indon.
196 H5 Pačir Vojvodina Serbia
95 I9 Pacitan Jawa Indon.
179 K6 Pack Austria
83 H4 Packsaddle N.S.W. Austr.
179 K6 Packsattel pass Austria
182 D6 Pacos de Ferreira Port.
176 E2 Pacov Czech Rep.
251 H5 Pacoval Brazil
176 G5 Pacsa Hungary
257 E2 Pacuí r. Brazil
177 K2 Pacutová hill Slovakia
175 H3 Pacyna Pol.
156 B5 Pacy-sur-Eure France
174 F5 Paczków Pol.
92 E8 Padada Mindanao Phil.
93 C5 Padalere Sulawesi Indon.
Padali Rus. Fed. see Amursk
93 B6 Padamarang i. Indon.
116 D5 Padampur Rajasthan India
116 B8 Padana Gujarat India
95 H5 Padang Kalimantan Indon.
93 B7 Padang Sulawesi Indon.
94 D5 Padang Sumatera Indon.
94 E4 Padang i. Indon.
94 E3 Padang Endau Malaysia
95 L5 Padang Luwai, Cagar Alam nature res. Kalimantan Indon.
94 D5 Padangpanjang Sumatera Indon.
94 C4 Padangsidimpuan Sumatera Indon.
95 H5 Padangtikar Kalimantan Indon.
95 H5 Padangtikar i. Indon.
134 F3 Padany Rus. Fed.
138 H9 Padarosk Belarus
129 J5 Padarqışlaq Azer.
95 K2 Padas r. Malaysia
141 R6 Padasjoki Fin.
122 C5 Padatha, Kūh-e mt. Iran
251 E5 Padauiri r. Brazil
96 B5 Padaung Myanmar
168 H1 Padborg Denmark
151 K4 Padbury Buckinghamshire, England U.K.
252 D5 Padcaya Bol.
83 J5 Paddington N.S.W. Austr.
215 O6 Paddock S. Africa
151 M5 Paddock Wood Kent, England U.K.
93 C5 Padeabesar i. Indon.
177 J6 Padej Vojvodina Serbia
232 E9 Paden City WV U.S.A.
169 G7 Paderborn Ger.
184 C6 Paderne Faro Port.
182 D4 Paderne Viana do Castelo Port.
182 E4 Paderne de Allariz Spain
210 B4 Pader Palwo Uganda
197 K5 Padeşu, Vârful mt. Romania
175 J5 Padew Narodowa Pol.
96 C3 Padibyu Myanmar
149 M6 Padiham Lancashire, England U.K.
252 D4 Padilla Bol.
197 P6 Padina Romania
196 I5 Padina Vojvodina Serbia
196 I6 Padinska Skela Serbia
163 H6 Padirac France
140 N3 Padjelanta nationalpark nat. park Sweden
139 O8 Padluzhzha Belarus
117 L8 Padma r. Bangl. alt. Ganga, conv. Ganges
114 E8 Padmanabhapuram Tamil Nadu India
116 H9 Padmapur Mahar. India
182 G4 Padornelo, Portilla del pass Spain
157 M7 Padoux France
191 L5 Padova Italy
191 L5 Padova prov. Italy
116 D8 Padra Gujarat India
117 J6 Padrauna Uttar Prad. India
184 F5 Padre Caro hill Spain
237 G12 Padre Island TX U.S.A.
237 G12 Padre Island National Seashore nature res. TX U.S.A.
257 G2 Padre Paraíso Brazil
192 B7 Padria Sardegna Italy
192 B3 Padro, Monte mt. Corse France
182 C3 Padrón Spain
215 K9 Padrone, Cape S. Africa
192 D6 Padru Sardegna Italy
150 C6 Padstow Cornwall, England U.K.
138 K6 Padsvillye Belarus
82 H7 Padthaway S.A. Austr.
115 H3 Padua Orissa India
Padua Italy see Padova
237 K7 Paducah KY U.S.A.
237 E8 Paducah TX U.S.A.
185 L6 Padul Spain
193 P7 Padula Italy
193 N5 Paduli Italy
116 F3 Padum Jammu and Kashmir
197 K4 Pădurea Craiului, Munții mts Romania
79 □9a Paea Tahiti Fr. Polynesia
101 F8 Paegam N. Korea
81 I7 Paekakariki North I. N.Z.
Paektu-san mt. China/N. Korea see Baotou Shan
101 D10 Paengnyŏng-do i. S. Korea
81 D12 Paerau South I. N.Z.
80 J4 Paeroa North I. N.Z.
80 K5 Paeroa hill North I. N.Z.
190 C6 Paesana Italy
191 M4 Paese Italy
195 H3 Paestum tourist site Italy
92 C4 Paete Luzon Phil.
128 A4 Pafos Cyprus
128 A4 Pafos airport Cyprus
213 F4 Pafuri Moz.
188 E3 Pag Croatia
188 E3 Pag i. Croatia
93 C8 Paga Flores Indon.
134 M2 Paga r. Rus. Fed.
251 H6 Paga Conta Brazil
95 G8 Pagadenbaru Jawa Indon.
92 D8 Pagadian Mindanao Phil.
94 D6 Pagai Selatan i. Indon.
94 D6 Pagai Utara i. Indon.
Pagalu i. Equat. Guinea see Annobón
91 K3 Pagan i. N. Mariana Is
191 K3 Paganella mt. Italy
193 K3 Paganica Italy
192 G2 Paganico Italy
260 D2 Paganzo Arg.
94 E6 Pagaralam Sumatera Indon.
198 D3 Pagasitikos Kolpos b. Greece
95 J6 Pagatan Kalimantan Indon.
95 K6 Pagatan Kalimantan Indon.
241 U5 Page AZ U.S.A.
86 H4 Page, Mount hill W.A. Austr.
138 E6 Pagėgiai Lith.
94 F6 Pagerdewa Sumatera Indon.
259 □ Paget, Mount S. Georgia
85 N5 Paget Cay rf Coral Sea Is Terr. Austr.
151 K6 Pagham West Sussex, England U.K.
123 M4 Paghman mt. Afgh.
138 H6 Pagiriai Kaunas Lith.
138 I7 Pagiriai Vilnius Lith.
192 I2 Paglia r. Italy
193 M3 Paglieta Italy
157 L6 Pagny-sur-Moselle France
78 □1 Pago Bay Guam
261 H1 Pago Largo Arg.
Pagon i. N. Mariana Is see Pagan
78 □2 Pago Pago American Samoa
239 K8 Pagosa Springs CO U.S.A.
207 F4 Pagouda Togo
Pagqên Qinghai China see Gadê
111 I13 Pagri Xizang China
247 □2 Pagua Bay Dominica
224 C3 Pagwachuan r. Ont. Can.
224 C3 Pagwa River Ont. Can.
240 □F14 Pāhala HI U.S.A.
94 E3 Pahang r. Malaysia
94 E3 Pahang state Malaysia
116 F6 Pahari Rajasthan India
117 L7 Paharpur tourist site Bangl.
123 N5 Paharpur Pak.
95 H4 Pahauman Kalimantan Indon.
81 B13 Pahia Point South I. N.Z.
80 J7 Pahiatua North I. N.Z.
173 K6 Pähl Ger.
Pahlavī Dezh Iran see Āq Qal'eh
168 H2 Pahlen Ger.
116 E2 Pahlgam Jammu and Kashmir
240 □G14 Pāhoa HI U.S.A.
231 G12 Pahokee FL U.S.A.
136 F1 Pahost Vodaskhovishcha resr Belarus
116 H7 Pahra Uttar Prad. India
123 I4 Pahra Kariz Afgh.
241 Q4 Pahranagat Range mts NV U.S.A.
138 G8 Pahranichny Belarus
241 Q5 Pahrump NV U.S.A.
116 G6 Pahuj r. India
240 P4 Pahute Mesa plat. NV U.S.A.
96 D5 Pai Thai.
240 □E13 Paia HI U.S.A.
253 F4 Paiaguás Brazil
182 C8 Paião Port.
240 K5 Paicines CA U.S.A.
138 I3 Paide Estonia
150 E7 Paignton Torbay, England U.K.
80 I2 Paihia North I. N.Z.
260 B2 Paihuano Chile
250 B6 Paiján Peru
141 R6 Päijänne l. Fin.
207 G4 Paiko Nigeria
111 G12 Paikü Co l. China
252 D4 Paila r. Bol.
260 A6 Pailahueque Chile
116 H7 Pailani Uttar Prad. India
163 G9 Pailhès France
97 F8 Pailin Cambodia
259 B6 Paillaco Chile
240 □E13 Pailolo Channel HI U.S.A.
158 G7 Paimbœuf France
141 Q6 Paimio Fin.
138 F1 Paimionselkä b. Fin.
158 E4 Paimpol France
158 G5 Paimpont France
158 G6 Paimpont, Forêt de for. France
94 D5 Painan Sumatera Indon.
114 E8 Painavu Kerala India
260 B3 Paine Chile
259 B8 Paine, Cerro mt. Chile
257 E3 Paineiras Brazil
255 C8 Painel Brazil
226 F2 Painesdale MI U.S.A.
232 D7 Painesville OH U.S.A.
257 E4 Pains Brazil
150 H4 Painswick Gloucestershire, England U.K.
241 U5 Painted Desert AZ U.S.A.
241 S8 Painted Rock Dam AZ U.S.A.
173 L4 Painten Ger.
Paint Hills Que. Can. see Wemindji
223 L4 Paint Lake Man. Can.
223 L4 Paint Lake Provincial Recreation Park Man. Can.
237 F10 Paint Rock TX U.S.A.
232 C11 Paintsville KY U.S.A.
250 C3 Paipa Col.
116 H9 Pairi r. India
227 M5 Paisley Ont. Can.
146 H11 Paisley Renfrewshire, Scotland U.K.
183 P2 País Vasco aut. comm. Spain
78 □5 Paita New Caledonia
250 A6 Paita Peru
95 L1 Paitan, Teluk b. Malaysia
114 D3 Paithan Mahar. India
109 M4 Paitou Zhejiang China
182 D6 Paiva r. Port.
Paiva Couceiro Angola see Quipungo
243 N9 Paixban Mex.
109 I3 Paizhou Hubei China
140 Q3 Pajala Sweden
250 A5 Paján Ecuador
245 M7 Pajapán Mex.
216 □3b Pájara Fuerteventura Canary Is
182 I2 Pajares, Puerto de pass Spain
250 C3 Pajarito Col.
183 Q9 Pajarón Spain
183 Q9 Pajaroncillo Spain
258 C3 Pájaros, Islotes Chile
174 G4 Pajęczno Pol.
176 F5 Páka Hungary
94 E2 Paka Malaysia
93 F3 Pakal i. Maluku Indon.
114 F6 Pakala Andhra Prad. India
Pakanbaru Sumatera Indon. see Pekanbaru
115 N2 Pakangyi Myanmar
138 G6 Pakapė Lith.
251 F4 Pakaraima Mountains S. America
224 B3 Pakashkan Lake Ont. Can.
117 K7 Pakaur Jharkhand India
80 G7 Pakawau South I. N.Z.
101 D9 Pakch'ŏn N. Korea
224 D4 Pakesley Ont. Can.
131 R3 Pakhachi Rus. Fed.
120 G3 Pakhar' Kazakh.
Pakhiá i. Greece see Pacheia
Pákhni Greece see Pachni
Pakhoi Guangxi China see Beihai
139 U7 Pakhomovo Rus. Fed.
123 K7 Pakistan country Asia
109 □J7 Pak Ka Shan hill H.K. China
94 C3 Pakkat Sumatera Indon.
188 E3 Paklenica nat. park Croatia
193 Q1 Pakleni Otoci is Croatia
Paknampho Thai. see Nakhon Sawan
176 G5 Pakod Hungary
96 B4 Pakokku Myanmar
174 G3 Pakość Pol.
174 G3 Pakoskie, Jezioro l. Pol.
174 F4 Pakosław Pol.
188 E4 Pakoštane Croatia
80 H2 Pakotai North I. N.Z.
223 I5 Pakowki Lake imp. l. Alta Can.
177 H4 Pákozd Hungary
123 O6 Pakpattan Pak.
97 E10 Pak Phanang Thai.
97 E11 Pak Phayun Thai.
188 F3 Pakra r. Croatia
188 F3 Pakrac Croatia
138 G6 Pakruojis Lith.
177 H5 Paks Hungary
Pakse Laos see Pakxé
109 □J7 Pak Tai To Yan mt. H.K. China
109 □J7 Pak Tam Chung H.K. China
97 F7 Pak Thong Chai Thai.
123 M5 Paktīā prov. Afgh.
123 M5 Paktīkā prov. Afgh.
95 J3 Paku r. Malaysia
94 G6 Paku, Tanjung pt Indon.
93 B5 Pakue Sulawesi Indon.
136 J2 Pakul' Ukr.
223 M5 Pakwash Lake Ont. Can.
96 F5 Pakxan Laos
96 G7 Pakxé Laos
96 F4 Pakxeng Laos
Pal Senegal see Mpal
208 B2 Pala Chad
97 D8 Pala Myanmar
94 G8 Palabuhanratu Jawa Indon.
94 F8 Palabuhanratu, Teluk b. Indon.
261 G2 Palacios Arg.
252 D3 Palacios Bol.
183 K6 Palacios de Goda Spain
183 N5 Palacios de la Sierra Spain
182 H3 Palacios del Sil Spain
182 G4 Palacios de Sanabria Spain
178 E7 Pala di San Martino mt. Italy
161 H6 Paladru, Lac de l. France
Palaestinia reg. Asia see Palestine
186 L4 Palafrugell Spain
195 L2 Palagianello Italy
195 M2 Palagiano Italy
194 H9 Palagonia Sicilia Italy
188 F4 Palagruža i. Croatia
191 J8 Palaia Italy
198 E5 Palaia Fokaia Greece
128 B4 Palaichori Cyprus
199 H7 Palaikastro Kriti Greece
198 E7 Palaiochora Kriti Greece
Palaiókastron Kriti Greece see Palaikastro
198 B4 Palairos Greece
156 D6 Palaiseau France
Palakkat Kerala India see Palghat
117 J9 Pala Laharha Orissa India
115 M7 Palalankwe Andaman & Nicobar Is India
212 D4 Palamakoloi Botswana
198 D3 Palamas Greece
93 E4 Palamea Maluku Indon.
186 L4 Palamós Spain
116 F3 Palam Pur Hima. Prad. India
117 J8 Palamu Jharkhand India
116 D6 Palana Rajasthan India
131 Q4 Palana Rus. Fed.
92 D3 Palanan Luzon Phil.
92 D3 Palanan Point Luzon Phil.
187 E8 Palancia, Riu r. Spain
129 B6 Palandöken Dağları mts Turkey
116 H9 Palandur Mahar. India
138 E6 Palanga Lith.
127 M6 Palangān Iran
122 I6 Palangān, Kūh-e mts Iran
161 B8 Palanges, Montagne des mts France
95 J6 Palangkaraya Kalimantan Indon.
114 E7 Palani Tamil Nadu India
116 D7 Palanpur Gujarat India
93 A6 Palanro Sulawesi Indon.
123 K8 Palantak Pak.
190 I7 Palanzano Italy
92 E5 Palapag Samar Phil.
213 E4 Palapye Botswana
114 G6 Palar r. India
123 O4 Palas Pak.
93 B3 Palasa Sulawesi Indon.
117 M6 Palasbari Assam India
182 E3 Palas de Rei Spain
138 L6 Palata r. Belarus
193 N4 Palata Italy
131 Q3 Palatka Rus. Fed.
231 G11 Palatka FL U.S.A.
192 C5 Palau Sardegna Italy
92 □ Palau country N. Pacific Ocean
93 G6 Palau Hatta i. Maluku Indon.
92 D2 Palaui i. Phil.
92 B4 Palauig Luzon Phil.
91 H5 Palau Islands Palau
97 D8 Palauk Myanmar
78 □2 Palauli Bay Samoa
94 F7 Palausekopong, Tanjung pt Indon.
266 D5 Palau Trench sea feature N. Pacific Ocean
176 F3 Pálava park Czech Rep.
161 D9 Palavas-les-Flots France
97 D8 Palaw Myanmar
92 A7 Palawan i. Phil.
92 A7 Palawan Passage str. Phil.
266 C5 Palawan Trough sea feature N. Pacific Ocean
92 C4 Palayan Luzon Phil.
114 E8 Palayankottai Tamil Nadu India
183 L7 Palazuelos de Eresma Spain
192 B3 Palazzo, Punta pt Corse France
194 E8 Palazzo Adriano Sicilia Italy
194 H9 Palazzolo Acreide Sicilia Italy
190 H4 Palazzolo sull'Oglio Italy
193 Q6 Palazzo San Gervasio Italy
114 G4 Palchal Lake India
179 M6 Paldau Austria
138 H2 Paldiski Estonia
188 G4 Pale Bos.-Herz.
96 B4 Pale Myanmar
134 H4 Palekh Rus. Fed.
Palekhori Cyprus see Palaichori
93 B3 Paleleh Sulawesi Indon.
94 F6 Palembang Sumatera Indon.
261 G4 Palemón Huergo Arg.
259 B6 Palena Aisén Chile
259 C6 Palena Los Lagos Chile
193 M4 Palena Italy
183 K4 Palencia Spain
183 K4 Palencia prov. Spain
185 J6 Palenciana Spain
243 M9 Palenque Mex.
183 L4 Palenzuela Spain
258 D2 Palermo Arg.
194 E7 Palermo Sicilia Italy
194 F8 Palermo prov. Sicilia Italy
194 E7 Palermo, Golfo di b. Sicilia Italy
128 D6 Palestine reg. Asia
237 H10 Palestine TX U.S.A.
193 J4 Palestrina Italy
96 A4 Paletwa Myanmar
100 M3 Palevo Rus. Fed.
123 M6 Palezgir Chauki Pak.
177 H5 Pálfa Hungary
114 C3 Palghar Mahar. India
114 E7 Palghat Kerala India
87 C7 Palgrave, Mount hill W.A. Austr.
212 B4 Palgrave Point Namibia
182 C7 Palhaça Port.
177 K3 Pálháza Hungary
255 C8 Palhoca Brazil
116 H8 Pali Madh. Prad. India
114 C3 Pali Mahar. India
116 D7 Pali Rajasthan India
193 K4 Paliano Italy
95 K8 Paliat i. Indon.
177 I5 Palić Vojvodina Serbia
196 H4 Palićko Jezero l. Serbia
138 L7 Palik Belarus
78 □4b Palikir Pohnpei Micronesia
78 □4b Palikir Passage Pohnpei Micronesia
92 E8 Palimbang Mindanao Phil.
160 E3 Palinges France
193 O7 Palinuro Italy
193 O7 Palinuro, Capo c. Italy
198 E3 Paliouri Greece
198 E3 Paliouri, Akrotirio pt Greece
156 G7 Palis France
239 J7 Palisade CO U.S.A.
165 H9 Paliseul Belgium
116 C9 Palitana Gujarat India
138 G3 Palivere Estonia
195 K8 Palizzi Italy
140 O3 Palja hill Sweden
140 T4 Paljakka hill Fin.
141 R6 Pälkäne Fin.
114 F8 Palk Bay Sri Lanka
138 L4 Palkino Rus. Fed.
140 S2 Palkisoja Fin.
115 H3 Palkohda Andhra Prad. India
114 F6 Palkonda Range mts India
117 J8 Palkot Jharkhand India
177 H2 Palkovice Czech Rep.
114 F8 Palk Strait India/Sri Lanka
Palla Bianca mt. Austria/Italy see Weißkugel
114 E7 Palladani Tamil Nadu India
195 L5 Pallagorio Italy
252 B3 Pallapalla mt. Peru
184 G4 Pallarés Spain
186 H3 Pallaresa r. Spain
186 G3 Pallaresa, Noguera r. Spain
147 F7 Pallas Green Ireland
140 Q2 Pallas ja Ounastunturin kansallispuisto nat. park Fin.
147 E7 Pallaskenry Ireland
120 B2 Pallasovka Rus. Fed.
114 G6 Pallavaram Tamil Nadu India
114 G4 Palleru r. India
196 H9 Pallës, Bishti i pt Albania
173 N5 Palling Ger.
87 E13 Pallinup r. W.A. Austr.
210 B4 Pallisa Uganda
81 J8 Palliser, Cape North I. N.Z.
79 □9 Palliser, Îles is Arch. des Tuamotu Fr. Polynesia
81 J8 Palliser Bay North I. N.Z.
192 A7 Pallosu, Cala su b. Sardegna Italy
116 E5 Pallu Rajasthan India
158 H8 Palluau France
159 N8 Palluau-sur-Indre France
254 D5 Palma r. Brazil
117 K8 Palma W. Bengal India
211 D7 Palma Moz.
184 B4 Palma Port.
187 K8 Palma, Badia de b. Spain
192 A8 Palma, Porto b. Sardegna Italy
193 N6 Palma Campania Italy
183 O6 Pálmaces, Embalse de resr Spain
185 I5 Palma del Río Spain
187 K8 Palma de Mallorca Spain
194 F9 Palma di Montechiaro Sicilia Italy
192 A6 Palmadula Sardegna Italy
114 F6 Palmaner Andhra Prad. India
191 O4 Palmanova Italy
187 K8 Palmanova Spain
244 F3 Palma Pegada Mex.
258 G4 Palmar, Punta del pt Uru.
244 G7 Palmar Chico Mex.
252 D2 Palmares Acre Brazil
254 G4 Palmares Pernambuco Brazil
255 C9 Palmares do Sul Brazil
190 H7 Palmaria, Isola i. Italy
250 D3 Palmarito Venez.
193 J6 Palmarola, Isola i. Italy
227 O1 Palmarolle Que. Can.
242 □R13 Palmar Sur Costa Rica
255 C8 Palmas Paraná Brazil
254 C4 Palmas Tocantins Brazil
206 D5 Palmas, Cape Liberia
192 B10 Palmas, Golfo di b. Sardegna Italy
245 K6 Palma Sola Mex.
247 I8 Palma Sola Venez.
246 F3 Palma Soriano Cuba
182 D7 Palmaz Port.
231 G12 Palm Bay FL U.S.A.
231 G11 Palm Coast FL U.S.A.
240 N7 Palmdale CA U.S.A.
241 P8 Palm Desert CA U.S.A.
256 C6 Palmeira Brazil
182 D5 Palmeira Port.
255 B8 Palmeira das Missões Brazil
254 F4 Palmeira dos Índios Brazil
254 E3 Palmeirais Brazil
254 D5 Palmeiras r. Brazil
256 C2 Palmeiras de Goiás Brazil
209 B7 Palmeirinhas, Ponta das pt Angola
184 B3 Palmela Port.
262 T2 Palmer research stn Antarctica
85 I4 Palmer r. Qld Austr.
84 D8 Palmer watercourse N.T. Austr.
220 D3 Palmer AK U.S.A.
262 T2 Palmer Land reg. Antarctica
234 B7 Palmer Park MD U.S.A.
Palmerston N.T. Austr. see Darwin
84 C2 Palmerston N.T. Austr.
227 N6 Palmerston Ont. Can.
81 □2 Palmerston atoll Cook Is
81 E12 Palmerston South I. N.Z.
147 J6 Palmerston Ireland
85 L6 Palmerston, Cape Qld Austr.
80 J7 Palmerston North North I. N.Z.
234 D3 Palmerton PA U.S.A.
85 J3 Palmerville Qld Austr.
231 F12 Palmetto FL U.S.A.
247 □2 Palmetto Point Antigua and Barbuda
231 I13 Palmetto Point Bahamas
195 J7 Palmi Italy
245 H2 Palmillas Mex.
260 C3 Palmira Arg.
250 B4 Palmira Col.
246 C2 Palmira Cuba
125 L3 Palm Islands tourist site U.A.E.
256 A6 Palmital Paraná Brazil
256 B5 Palmital São Paulo Brazil
261 I3 Palmitas Uru.
Palmnicken Rus. Fed. see Yantarnyy
184 I8 Palmones r. Spain
177 I5 Pálmonostora Hungary
240 P8 Palm Springs CA U.S.A.
85 L8 Palm Tree Creek r. Qld Austr.
84 D8 Palm Valley N.T. Austr.
Palmyra Syria see Tadmur
236 J6 Palmyra MO U.S.A.
234 E4 Palmyra NJ U.S.A.
232 H5 Palmyra NY U.S.A.
227 R9 Palmyra PA U.S.A.
232 G11 Palmyra VA U.S.A.
75 I3 Palmyra Atoll N. Pacific Ocean
117 K9 Palmyras Point India
146 I13 Palnackie Dumfries and Galloway, Scotland U.K.
192 C4 Palneca Corse France
114 E7 Palni Hills India
134 K3 Pal'niki Rus. Fed.
92 E6 Palo Leyte Phil.
192 C4 Palo, Étang de lag. Corse France
182 G2 Palo, Puerto del pass Spain
244 E4 Palo Alto Aguascalientes Mex.
245 H1 Palo Alto Tamaulipas Mex.
240 J4 Palo Alto CA U.S.A.
258 D2 Palo Blanco Arg.
243 I4 Palo Blanco Mex.
250 B3 Palo de las Letras Col.
195 L1 Palo del Colle Italy
237 E8 Palo Duro watercourse TX U.S.A.
95 I3 Paloh Sarawak Malaysia
210 B2 Paloich Sudan
140 Q2 Palojärvi Fin.
140 Q2 Palojoensuu Fin.
140 S2 Palomaa Fin.
252 C3 Palomani mt. Peru
186 D6 Palomar de Arroyos Spain
245 L8 Palomares Mex.
184 G6 Palomares del Río Spain
240 P8 Palomar Mountain CA U.S.A.
184 G3 Palomas Spain
184 H8 Palomas, Punta pt Spain
193 M3 Palombaro Italy
183 L2 Palombera, Embalse de mts Spain
183 L2 Palombera, Puerto de pass Spain
194 I10 Palombieri r. Sicilia Italy
183 P8 Palomera Spain
186 C6 Palomera, Sierra mts Spain
183 O9 Palomeras del Campo Spain
184 G3 Palomilas r. Spain
250 C2 Palomino Col.
258 D2 Palomitas Arg.
193 O6 Palomonte Italy
191 K4 Palòn, Cima mt. Italy
114 G4 Paloncha Andhra Prad. India
237 F9 Palo Pinto TX U.S.A.
93 B5 Palopo Sulawesi Indon.
187 D12 Palos, Cabo de c. Spain

Pati r. Brazil
Pati Madh. Prad. India
Pati Jawa Indon.
Patía r. Col.
Patiala Punjab India
Patillas Puerto Rico
Patillas, Puerto b. Puerto Rico
Patinti, Selat sea chan. Maluku Indon.
Pati Point Guam
Patiro, Tanjung pt Indon.
Patitiri Greece
Pativilca r. Peru
Patkai Bum mts India/Myanmar
Patkaklik Xinjiang China
Patlangıç Turkey
Patmos i. Greece
Patna Bihar India
2 Patna East Ayrshire, Scotland U.K.
Patnagarh Orissa India
Patnanongan i. Phil.
Patnos Turkey
Pątnów Pol.
Pato, Cerro mt. Chile
Pato Branco Brazil
Patoda Mahar. India
Patoka r. IN U.S.A.
Patomskoye Nagor'ye mts Rus. Fed.
Paton Uttaranchal India
Patoniva Fin.
Patos Albania
Patos Paraíba Brazil
Patos Piauí Brazil
Patos, Isla i. Venez.
Patos, Lagoa dos l. Brazil
Patos, Laguna de los l. Arg.
Patos, Río de los r. Arg.
Patos de Minas Brazil
Patquía Arg.
Patra Greece
Patrae Greece see Patra
Pátrai Greece see Patra
Patraïkos Kolpos b. Greece
Patrakeyevka Rus. Fed.
Patras Greece see Patra
Patrasaer W. Bengal India
Patratu Jharkhand India
1 Patreksfjörður Iceland
Patri Gujarat India
Patri r. Sicilia Italy
Patriarch, Mount South I. N.Z.
Patrica Italy
Patricia, Mount hill N.T. Austr.
Patricio Lynch, Isla i. Chile
Patrick Isle of Man
Patrick Creek watercourse Qld Austr.
2 Patrick Springs VA U.S.A.
Patrickswell Ireland
Patrimônio Brazil
Patrimonio Corse France
Patrington East Riding of Yorkshire, England U.K.
Patrocínio Brazil
Pátroha Hungary
Paţrū Iran
Patscherkofel mt. Austria
Patsoyoki r. Europe
Pattada Sardegna Italy
Pattadakal tourist site Karnataka India
Pattanapuram Kerala India
1 Pattani Thai.
1 Pattani, Mae Nam r. Thai.
Pattaya Thai.
3 Patten ME U.S.A.
Pattenburg NJ U.S.A.
Pattensen Ger.
Patterdale Cumbria, England U.K.
Patterson CA U.S.A.
Patterson LA U.S.A.
Patterson NY U.S.A.
Patterson r. WV U.S.A.
Patterson, Mount Y.T. Can.
Patterson, Point MI U.S.A.
Patterson Mountain CA U.S.A.
Patteson Passage Vanuatu see Lolvavana, Passage
Patti Uttar Prad. India
Patti Maluku Indon.
Patti Sicilia Italy
Pattijoki Fin.
Pättikkä Fin.
Pattikonda Andhra Prad. India
Pattingham Staffordshire, England U.K.
Pattisson, Cape Chatham Is S. Pacific Ocean
Pattukkottai Tamil Nadu India
Pattullo, Mount B.C. Can.
Patu Brazil
Patuakhali Bangl.
Patuanak Sask. Can.
10 Patuca r. Hond.
10 Patuca, Punta pt Hond.
10 Patucas, Parque Nacional nat. park Hond.
Pătulele Romania
Patur Mahar. India
Pâturages Belgium
Patutu mt. North I. N.Z.
Patuxent r. MD U.S.A.
Patuxent Range mts Antarctica
Patvinsuon kansallispuisto nat. park Fin.
Páty Hungary
Pátzcuaro Mex.
Pátzcuaro, Laguna de l. Mex.
Pau France
Pau airport France see Pyrénées
Pau Brasil, Parque Nacional do nat. park Brazil
Paucarbamba Peru
Paucartambo Peru
Paucartambo r. Peru see Yavero
Pau d'Arco Brazil
Pau d'Arco r. Brazil
Paudorf Austria
Pauhunri mt. China/India
Pauilhac France
Pauillac France
Pauini Brazil
Pauiní r. Brazil
Pauini r. Brazil
Pauk Myanmar
Paukkaung Myanmar
Pauktaw Myanmar
Paul Port.
Paularo Italy
Paulatuk N.W.T. Can.
Paulden AZ U.S.A.
Paulding MS U.S.A.
Paulding OH U.S.A.
Paulding Bay Antarctica
Paulhac France
Paulhac-en-Margeride France
Paulhaguet France
Paulhan France
Paulicéia Brazil
Paulilatino Sardegna Italy
Paulinenaue Ger.
Paulinet France
Paulins Kill r. NJ U.S.A.
Paulis Dem. Rep. Congo see Isiro
Păuliş Romania
Paul Island Nfld and Lab. Can.
Paulista Brazil
Paulistana Brazil
Paullina IA U.S.A.
Paulo Afonso Brazil
Paulo de Faria Brazil
Paulpietersburg S. Africa
Paüls Spain
Pauls Valley OK U.S.A.
Paulton Bath and North East Somerset, England U.K.
Paulx France
Paum i. Vanuatu see Paama
Paumotu, Îles is Fr. Polynesia see Tuamotu, Archipel des
260 E3 Paunero Arg.
197 P4 Păuneşti Romania
96 C6 Paung Myanmar
96 B2 Paungbyin Myanmar
96 B5 Paungde Myanmar
116 G9 Pauni Mahar. India
234 E2 Paupack PA U.S.A.
116 G4 Pauri Uttaranchal India
171 F9 Pausa Ger.
252 B3 Pausa Peru
250 D3 Pauto r. Col.
140 N4 Pauträsk Sweden
156 I5 Pauvres France
240 □E13 Pa'uwela HI U.S.A.
114 E5 Pavagada Karnataka India
257 G2 Pavão Brazil
250 B3 Pavarandocito Col.
134 L4 Pavda Rus. Fed.
122 B4 Päveh Iran
139 W8 Pavelets Rus. Fed.
190 G5 Pavia Italy
190 G5 Pavia prov. Italy
184 C3 Pavia Port.
182 D8 Pavia r. Port.
191 O4 Pavia di Udine Italy
187 E8 Pavías Spain
163 F8 Pavie France
232 G6 Pavilion NY U.S.A.
156 A4 Pavilly France
138 E5 Pāvilosta Latvia
134 I4 Pavino Rus. Fed.
138 F7 Pavištyčio kalnas hill Lith.
175 M4 Pavitstsye Belarus
197 N7 Pavlikeni Bulg.
139 Q7 Pavlinovo Rus. Fed.
136 I6 Pavlivka Odes'ka Oblast' Ukr.
137 N2 Pavlivka Sums'ka Oblast' Ukr.
136 D3 Pavlivka Volyns'ka Oblast' Ukr.
121 Q1 Pavlodar Kazakh.
Pavlodar Oblast admin. div. Kazakh. see Pavlodarskaya Oblast'
Pavlodar Oblysy admin. div. Kazakh. see Pavlodarskaya Oblast'
121 Q1 Pavlodarskaya Oblast' admin. div. Kazakh.
220 B4 Pavlof Volcano AK U.S.A.
Pavlograd Ukr. see Pavlohrad
121 O1 Pavlogradka Rus. Fed.
137 O5 Pavlohrad Ukr.
137 N6 Pavlopillya Ukr.
177 L3 Pavlovce nad Uhom Slovakia
121 O2 Pavlovka Akmolinskaya Oblast' Kazakh.
120 J1 Pavlovka Kostanayskaya Oblast' Kazakh.
134 L5 Pavlovka Respublika Bashkortostan Rus. Fed.
120 B1 Pavlovka Ul'yanovskaya Oblast' Rus. Fed.
134 H5 Pavlovo Rus. Fed.
121 T1 Pavlovsk Altayskiy Kray Rus. Fed.
139 N2 Pavlovsk Leningradskaya Oblast' Rus. Fed.
135 H6 Pavlovsk Voronezhskaya Oblast' Rus. Fed.
135 G7 Pavlovskaya Rus. Fed.
120 J1 Pavlovskiy Kazakh.
139 V6 Pavlovskiy Posad Rus. Fed.
139 X5 Pavlovskoye Rus. Fed.
134 L5 Pavlovskoye Vodokhranilishche resr Rus. Fed.
137 M5 Pavlysh Ukr.
191 J7 Pavullo nel Frignano Italy
78 □6 Pavuvu i. Solomon Is
138 M3 Pavy Rus. Fed.
78 □6 Pawa Solomon Is
108 B5 Pawahku Myanmar
116 H7 Pawai Madh. Prad. India
95 H5 Pawan r. Indon.
80 H2 Pawarenga North I. N.Z.
116 H5 Pawayan Uttar Prad. India
235 L2 Pawcatuck CT U.S.A.
171 G5 Päwesin Ger.
237 G7 Pawhuska OK U.S.A.
139 P8 Pawlavichy Belarus
235 H1 Pawling NY U.S.A.
174 F2 Pawłówek Pol.
174 G6 Pawłowice Śląskie Pol.
174 E4 Pawłowice Wielkopolskie Pol.
174 G5 Pawłowiczki Pol.
96 C5 Pawn r. Myanmar
237 G7 Pawnee OK U.S.A.
236 F6 Pawnee r. KS U.S.A.
236 G5 Pawnee City NE U.S.A.
174 G5 Pawonków Pol.
226 I7 Paw Paw MI U.S.A.
232 G9 Paw Paw WV U.S.A.
233 N7 Pawtucket RI U.S.A.
84 D6 Pawu Aboriginal Land res. N.T. Austr.
97 D8 Pawut Myanmar
182 F3 Paxaro mt. Spain
199 H7 Paximada i. Greece
198 F7 Paximadia i. Greece
234 B3 Paxinos PA U.S.A.
198 B3 Paxoi i. Greece
220 D3 Paxson AK U.S.A.
121 O7 Paxtaobod Uzbek.
146 L11 Paxton Scottish Borders, Scotland U.K.
226 F9 Paxton IL U.S.A.
236 E5 Paxton NE U.S.A.
234 B4 Paxtonia PA U.S.A.
234 A3 Paxtonville PA U.S.A.
93 E3 Payahe Halmahera Indon.
94 D5 Payakumbuh Sumatera Indon.
94 □ Paya Lebar Sing.
114 D6 Payaswani r. India
140 □ Payer, Kapp c. Svalbard
179 M4 Payerbach Austria
190 B2 Payerne Switz.
238 F4 Payette ID U.S.A.
238 F4 Payette r. ID U.S.A.
134 M1 Pay-Khoy, Khrebet hills Rus. Fed.
184 E5 Paymogo Spain
Payne Que. Can. see Kangirsuk
232 A7 Payne OH U.S.A.
224 F1 Payne, Lac l. Que. Can.
240 K1 Paynes Creek CA U.S.A.
87 D10 Payne's Find W.A. Austr.
83 K7 Paynesville Vic. Austr.
236 H3 Paynesville MN U.S.A.
184 F4 Payo, Sierra hills Spain
163 G6 Payrac France
163 I8 Payrin-Augmontel France
261 H3 Paysandú Uru.
261 I3 Paysandú dept Uru.
163 A9 Pays Basque reg. France
159 L3 Pays d'Auge reg. France
163 B7 Pays de Born reg. France
156 B4 Pays de Bray reg. France
159 M2 Pays de Caux reg. France
162 B1 Pays de la Loire admin. reg. France
158 B5 Pays de Léon reg. France
158 G7 Pays de Retz reg. France
163 I10 Pays de Sault reg. France
156 G7 Pays d'Othe reg. France
159 M4 Pays d'Ouche reg. France
121 L7 Payshanba Uzbek.
241 U7 Payson AZ U.S.A.
260 C5 Payún, Cerro vol. Arg.
95 J3 Payung, Tanjung pt Malaysia
260 C5 Payún Matrú, Altiplanicie del plat. Arg.
258 C5 Payún Matrú, Volcán vol. Arg.
134 N2 Payyer, Gora mt. Rus. Fed.
162 G5 Payzac France
Payzawat Xinjiang China see Jiashi
254 C4 Paz, Rio da r. Brazil
127 J3 Pazar Turkey
126 H5 Pazarcık Turkey
197 M8 Pazardzhik Bulg.
199 I3 Pazarköy Turkey
199 K4 Pazarlar Turkey
199 K3 Pazaryeri Turkey
129 B5 Pazaryolu Turkey
250 D3 Paz de Ariporo Col.
250 C3 Paz de Rio Col.
188 D3 Pazin Croatia
163 J10 Paziols France
252 D4 Pazña Bol.
178 B6 Paznauntal val. Austria
182 C4 Pazos Spain
122 G4 Pazūk Iran
139 O2 Pchevzha r. Rus. Fed.
175 H6 Pcim Pol.
197 J9 Pčinja r. Macedonia
97 D8 Pe Myanmar
79 □8a Pea Tongatapu Tonga
256 A5 Peabiru Brazil
236 G6 Peabody KS U.S.A.
233 O6 Peabody MA U.S.A.
222 I3 Peace r. Alta/B.C. Can.
231 F12 Peace r. FL U.S.A.
151 L6 Peacehaven East Sussex, England U.K.
223 H3 Peace Point Alta Can.
222 G3 Peace River Alta Can.
232 D11 Peach Creek WV U.S.A.
222 G5 Peachland B.C. Can.
241 S6 Peach Springs AZ U.S.A.
223 I1 Peacock Hills Nunavut Can.
251 F3 Peaima Falls Guyana
231 J8 Pea Island National Wildlife Refuge nature res. NC U.S.A.
87 F12 Peak Charles hill W.A. Austr.
87 F12 Peak Charles National Park W.A. Austr.
149 N7 Peak District National Park England U.K.
82 F3 Peake watercourse S.A. Austr.
233 □Q2 Peaked Mountain hill ME U.S.A.
83 L5 Peak Hill N.S.W. Austr.
87 E8 Peak Hill W.A. Austr.
240 M7 Peak Mountain CA U.S.A.
85 L7 Peak Range hills Qld Austr.
185 M5 Peal de Becerro Spain
241 W3 Peale, Mount UT U.S.A.
241 W10 Pearce AZ U.S.A.
84 B3 Pearce Point N.T. Austr.
182 E3 Peares, Encoro dos resr Spain
232 E11 Pearisburg VA U.S.A.
226 F1 Pearl Ont. Can.
237 K10 Pearl r. MS U.S.A.
75 H1 Pearl and Hermes Atoll HI U.S.A.
240 □D12 Pearl City HI U.S.A.
240 □C13 Pearl Harbor inlet HI U.S.A.
Pearl River r. Guangdong China see Zhu Jiang
235 G2 Pearl River NY U.S.A.
237 F11 Pearsall TX U.S.A.
261 G3 Pearson Arg.
231 F10 Pearson GA U.S.A.
226 E4 Pearson WI U.S.A.
82 E5 Pearson Islands S.A. Austr.
215 J8 Pearston S. Africa
221 I2 Peary Channel Nunavut Can.
221 O1 Peary Land reg. Greenland
237 F8 Pease r. TX U.S.A.
150 H5 Peasedown St John Bath and North East Somerset, England U.K.
158 G6 Péaule France
226 F3 Peavy Falls Reservoir MI U.S.A.
86 D6 Peawah r. W.A. Austr.
224 C2 Peawanuck Ont. Can.
213 H3 Pebane Moz.
250 D5 Pebas Peru
259 F8 Pebble Island Falkland Is
209 D6 Pebeangu Dem. Rep. Congo
93 B4 Pebengko Sulawesi Indon.
161 D6 Pébrac France
196 I8 Peć Kosovo Serbia
237 F10 Pecan Bayou r. TX U.S.A.
257 F3 Peçanha Brazil
237 I11 Pecan Island LA U.S.A.
256 C6 Peças, Ilha das i. Brazil
226 E7 Pecatonica IL U.S.A.
190 F3 Peccia Switz.
191 J8 Peccioli Italy
177 I4 Pécel Hungary
140 U2 Pecha r. Rus. Fed.
140 U2 Pechenga Rus. Fed.
140 U2 Pechenga r. Rus. Fed.
137 P4 Pechenihy Ukr.
139 R1 Pechenitsy Rus. Fed.
137 P4 Pecheniz'ke Vodoskhovyshche resr Ukr.
139 W7 Pecherniki Rus. Fed.
139 P7 Pechersk Rus. Fed.
216 □3c Pechiguera, Punta pt Lanzarote Canary Is
185 O7 Pechina Spain
134 L2 Pechora Rus. Fed.
134 K1 Pechora r. Rus. Fed.
Pechora Sea Rus. Fed. see Pechorskoye More
134 L3 Pechoro-Ilyiskiy Zapovednik nature res. Rus. Fed.
134 K1 Pechorskaya Guba b. Rus. Fed.
134 K1 Pechorskoye More sea Rus. Fed.
138 K4 Pechory Rus. Fed.
140 □ Pechuel Løsche, Kapp c. Svalbard
196 J4 Pecica Romania
197 Q7 Pecineaga Romania
206 A4 Pecixe, Ilha de i. Guinea-Bissau
227 L6 Peck MI U.S.A.
222 E3 Peck, Mount B.C. Can.
234 E2 Pecks Pond PA U.S.A.
176 E1 Pečky Czech Rep.
174 E4 Pęcław Pol.
97 H8 Pe Cô, Krông r. Vietnam
192 F2 Pecora r. Italy
192 A9 Pecora, Capo c. Sardegna Italy
237 D10 Pecos TX U.S.A.
237 E11 Pecos r. NM/TX U.S.A.
165 D7 Pecq Belgium
177 H5 Pécs Hungary
177 H5 Pécsvárad Hungary
174 G4 Pęczniew Pol.
242 □S14 Pedasí Panama
193 L1 Pedaso Italy
114 F3 Pedda Vagu r. India
114 F4 Peddavagu r. India
83 K10 Pedder, Lake Tas. Austr.
215 L9 Peddie S. Africa
138 K4 Pededze Latvia
138 J5 Pededze r. Latvia
250 A4 Pedernales Ecuador
246 H4 Pedernales Haiti
239 K12 Pedernales Mex.
237 F10 Pedernales r. TX U.S.A.
251 F2 Pedernales Venez.
258 C2 Pedernales, Salar de salt flat Chile
256 C5 Pederneiras Brazil
191 L4 Pederobba Italy
140 Q5 Pedersöre Fin.
209 B9 Pediva Angola
93 E3 Pediwang Halmahera Indon.
138 J3 Pedja r. Estonia
257 G1 Pedra Azul Brazil
206 □ Pedra Badejo Santiago Cape Verde
182 D5 Pedrada mt. Port.
182 F3 Pedrafita do Cebreiro Spain
182 C6 Pedra Furada Port.
183 K6 Pedrajas de San Esteban Spain
187 D8 Pedralba Spain
182 G4 Pedralba de la Pradería Spain
206 □ Pedra Lume Cape Verde
254 C5 Pedra Preta, Serra da mts Brazil
254 B3 Pedras r. Brazil
254 D5 Pedras r. Brazil
182 E8 Pedras Lavradas pass Port.
253 E3 Pedras Negras Brazil
242 □R13 Pedregal Panama
250 D2 Pedregal Venez.
187 F10 Pedreguer Spain
256 D4 Pedregulho Brazil
254 D3 Pedreiras Maranhão Brazil
256 D5 Pedreiras São Paulo Brazil
185 J6 Pedrera Spain
187 D11 Pedrera, Embalse de la resr Spain
186 J4 Pedres, Serrat de les hill Spain
242 H5 Pedriceña Mex.
234 E5 Pedricktown NJ U.S.A.
183 N5 Pedro r. Spain
114 G8 Pedro, Point Sri Lanka
185 K5 Pedro Abad Spain
254 C4 Pedro Afonso Brazil
245 I4 Pedro Antonio de los Santos Mex.
254 F3 Pedro Avelino Brazil
246 D5 Pedro Bank sea feature Jamaica
256 D6 Pedro Barros Brazil
183 K8 Pedro Bernardo Spain
246 E5 Pedro Cays is Jamaica
185 J4 Pedroche Spain
250 D4 Pedro Chico Col.
251 I4 Pedro de Freitas Brazil
252 C5 Pedro de Valdivia Chile
261 H2 Pedro Díaz Colodrero Arg.
244 G5 Pedro Escobedo Mex.
184 D4 Pedrógão Beja Port.
182 F8 Pedrógão Castelo Branco Port.
182 C9 Pedrógão Leiria Port.
182 D9 Pedrógão Grande Port.
182 D9 Pedrógão Pequeno Port.
255 B6 Pedro Gomes Brazil
184 H2 Pedro Gómez mt. Spain
254 E3 Pedro II Brazil
250 E4 Pedro II, Ilha reg. Brazil/Venez.
253 G5 Pedro Juan Caballero Para.
257 E3 Pedro Leopoldo Brazil
261 F6 Pedro Luro Arg.
185 M5 Pedro-Martínez Spain
185 N2 Pedro Muñoz Spain
258 G3 Pedro Osório Brazil
246 □ Pedro Point Jamaica
186 I3 Pedrós, Puig mt. Spain
183 M2 Pedrosa Spain
183 L4 Pedrosa del Príncipe Spain
182 I7 Pedrosillo de los Aires Spain
182 C6 Pedroso Port.
183 O4 Pedroso Spain
256 D6 Pedro Toledo Brazil
163 H10 Pédrous, Pic mt. France
182 C3 Pedrouzos Spain
192 B6 Pedruso, Monte hill Italy
82 H6 Peebinga S.A. Austr.
146 J11 Peebles Scottish Borders, Scotland U.K.
232 B10 Peebles OH U.S.A.
86 C6 Peedamulla W.A. Austr.
86 C6 Peedamulla Aboriginal Reserve W.A. Austr.
231 H9 Pee Dee r. SC U.S.A.
233 L7 Peekskill NY U.S.A.
220 E3 Peel r. Y.T. Can.
148 H5 Peel Isle of Man
81 F10 Peel, Mount South I. N.Z.
87 C12 Peel Inlet W.A. Austr.
170 I3 Peene r. Ger.
170 I2 Peenemünde Ger.
170 I3 Peenestrom sea chan. Ger.
165 H6 Peer Belgium
140 P2 Peera Fin.
82 G2 Peera Peera Poolanna Lake salt flat S.A. Austr.
222 H3 Peerless Lake Alta Can.
222 H3 Peerless Lake l. Alta Can.
222 G4 Peers Alta Can.
182 F8 Pega Port.
161 C9 Pégairolles-de-l'Escalette France
81 G10 Pegasus Bay South I. N.Z.
171 F8 Pegau Ger.
179 L5 Peggau Austria
190 F7 Pegli Italy
193 P7 Peglio r. Italy
173 L2 Pegnitz Ger.
173 J3 Pegnitz r. Ger.
184 C2 Pego Port.
187 E10 Pego Spain
184 C4 Pego do Altar, Barragem do resr Port.
184 B3 Pegões Port.
174 E4 Pęgów Pol.
96 C6 Pegu Myanmar
96 B5 Pegu admin. div. Myanmar
187 J8 Peguera Spain
93 B5 Pegunungan Latimojong nature res. Indon.
93 B5 Pegunungan Peruhumpenai nature res. Indon.
96 B5 Pegu Yoma mts Myanmar
151 O5 Pegwell Bay England U.K.
134 J3 Pegysh Rus. Fed.
199 H1 Pehlivanköy Turkey
207 F4 Péhonko Benin
116 F5 Pehowa Haryana India
261 G4 Pehuajó Arg.
261 G6 Pehuén-Có Arg.
109 M7 Peikang Taiwan
158 G6 Peillac France
161 K9 Peille France
146 D8 Peinchorran Highland, Scotland U.K.
252 C5 Peine Chile
169 J6 Peine Ger.
259 B8 Peineta, Cerro mt. Arg.
116 D9 Peint Mahar. India
191 J3 Peio Italy
161 H8 Peipin France
Peipsi järv l. Estonia/Rus. Fed. see Peipus, Lake
138 K3 Peipus, Lake Estonia/Rus. Fed.
161 K9 Peïra-Cava France
198 E5 Peiraias Greece
160 J5 Peisey-Nancroix France
Pei Shan mts China see Bei Shan
171 E7 Peißen Sachsen-Anhalt Ger.
171 F7 Peißen Sachsen-Anhalt Ger.
173 K6 Peißenberg Ger.
173 J6 Peiting Ger.
171 J7 Peitz Ger.
254 C5 Peixe Brazil
256 B4 Peixe r. Brazil
256 C2 Peixe r. Brazil
254 C5 Peixe r. Brazil
256 A2 Peixe, Rio do r. Brazil
257 F5 Peixes r. Brazil
253 F2 Peixes r. Brazil
107 O9 Peixian Jiangsu China
Peixian Jiangsu China see Pizhou
256 D4 Peixoto, Represa resr Brazil
254 B4 Peixoto de Azevedo Brazil
253 G2 Peixoto de Azevedo r. Brazil
164 K2 Peize Neth.
94 G4 Pejantan i. Indon.
Peje Kosovo Serbia see Peć
197 J6 Pek r. Serbia
215 L4 Peka Lesotho
93 A5 Pekabata Sulawesi Indon.
95 H8 Pekalongan Jawa Indon.
94 E3 Pekan Malaysia
94 D4 Pekanbaru Sumatera Indon.
225 H2 Pékans, Rivière aux r. Que. Can.
139 X8 Pekhlets Rus. Fed.
207 F5 Peki Ghana
226 E9 Pekin IL U.S.A.
Peking Beijing China see Beijing
139 Q8 Peklino Rus. Fed.
183 N6 Pela, Sierra de mts Spain
94 D3 Pelabuhan Klang Malaysia
259 C7 Pelada, Pampa hills Arg.
187 C8 Pelado mt. Spain
189 D8 Pelagie, Isole is Sicilia Italy
191 L8 Pelago Italy
196 J9 Pelagonija plain Macedonia
183 K8 Pelahustán Spain
95 K6 Pelaihari Kalimantan Indon.
94 E4 Pelalawan Sumatera Indon.
95 H5 Pelapis i. Indon.
260 B4 Pelarco Chile
182 C9 Pelariga Port.
182 H7 Pelarrodríguez Spain
198 D4 Pelasgia Greece
Pelasyía Greece see Pelasgia
161 J8 Pelat, Mont mt. France
215 M4 Pelatsoeu mt. Lesotho
78 □6 Pelau i. Solomon Is
95 L4 Pelawanbesar Kalimantan Indon.
174 D2 Pełczyce Pol.
197 K5 Peleaga, Vârful mt. Romania
183 J6 Peleagonzalo Spain
252 C3 Pelechuco Bol.
138 J5 Pelēči Latvia
247 □3 Pelée, Montagne vol. Martinique
224 D5 Pelee Island Ont. Can.
224 D5 Pelee Point Ont. Can.
193 Q1 Pelegrin, Rt pt Croatia
92 □ Peleliu i. Palau
93 C4 Peleng i. Indon.
93 C4 Peleng, Selat sea chan. Indon.
93 C4 Peleng, Teluk b. Indon.
134 J3 Peles Rus. Fed.
176 E2 Pelhřimov Czech Rep.
220 E4 Pelican AK U.S.A.
85 I4 Pelican Creek r. Qld Austr.
223 K4 Pelican Lake l. Man. Can.
226 E4 Pelican Lake WI U.S.A.
226 B1 Pelican Lake l. MN U.S.A.
223 K4 Pelican Narrows Sask. Can.
216 □3a Peligro, Punta del pt La Gomera Canary Is
185 L6 Peligros Spain
136 G6 Pelinia Moldova
161 G9 Pélissanne France
196 J10 Pelister mt. Macedonia
196 J10 Pelister nat. park Macedonia
188 F4 Pelješac pen. Croatia
140 S3 Pelkosenniemi Fin.
214 D5 Pella S. Africa
226 A1 Pelland MN U.S.A.
195 J7 Pellaro Italy
223 I1 Pellatt Lake N.W.T. Can.
231 D9 Pell City AL U.S.A.
261 F5 Pellegrini Arg.
260 D6 Pellegrini, Lago l. Arg.
190 H6 Pellegrino Parmense Italy
163 E6 Pellegrue France
91 J7 Pelleluhu Islands P.N.G.
177 H5 Pellérd Hungary
191 M5 Pellestrina Italy
159 N8 Pellevoisin France
190 D6 Pellice r. Italy
178 C7 Pellizzano Italy
140 Q3 Pello Fin.
226 J4 Pellston MI U.S.A.
260 A4 Pelluhue Chile
168 G1 Pellworm i. Ger.
222 B2 Pelly r. Y.T. Can.
Pelly Bay Nunavut Can. see Kugaaruk
222 B2 Pelly Crossing Y.T. Can.
222 C2 Pelly Mountains Y.T. Can.
169 C10 Pelm Ger.
178 F7 Pelmo, Monte mt. Italy
185 I2 Peloche Spain
95 M8 Pelokang is Indon.
Peloponnese admin. reg. Greece see Peloponnisos
Peloponnesus admin. reg. Greece see Peloponnisos
198 D5 Peloponnisos admin. reg. Greece
198 D5 Peloponnisos pen. Greece
195 H8 Peloritani, Monti mts Sicilia Italy
195 J7 Peloro, Capo c. Sicilia Italy
81 H8 Pelorus Sound sea chan. South I. N.Z.
258 G3 Pelotas Brazil
255 C8 Pelotas, Rio das r. Brazil
197 M7 Pelovo Bulg.
174 G2 Pelplin Pol.
151 I2 Pelsall West Midlands, England U.K.
87 B10 Pelsart Group is W.A. Austr.
170 I3 Pelsin Ger.
140 R2 Peltovuoma Fin.
128 A7 Pelusium tourist site Egypt
Pelusium, Bay of Egypt see Ţīnah, Khalīj aţ
161 F6 Pélussin France
161 I7 Pelvoux France
161 I7 Pelvoux, Massif du mts France
161 I7 Pelvoux, Mont mt. France
177 J4 Pély Hungary
150 C7 Pelynt Cornwall, England U.K.
227 K2 Pemache r. Ont. Can.
233 □Q3 Pemadumcook Lake ME U.S.A.
95 H8 Pemalang Jawa Indon.
95 H4 Pemangkat Kalimantan Indon.
95 L5 Pemarung, Pulau i. Indon.
94 C3 Pematangsiantar Sumatera Indon.
213 I2 Pemba Moz.
209 E9 Pemba Zambia
211 D8 Pemba, Baía de b. Moz.
211 C6 Pemba Channel Tanz.
211 C6 Pemba Island Tanz.
211 C6 Pemba North admin. reg. Tanz.
211 C6 Pemba South admin. reg. Tanz.
87 C13 Pemberton W.A. Austr.
222 F5 Pemberton B.C. Can.
234 F5 Pemberton NJ U.S.A.
222 H4 Pembina r. Alta Can.
236 G1 Pembina ND U.S.A.
236 G1 Pembina r. ND U.S.A.
226 G4 Pembine WI U.S.A.
150 D4 Pembrey Carmarthenshire, Wales U.K.
150 G3 Pembridge Herefordshire, England U.K.
224 E4 Pembroke Ont. Can.
150 C4 Pembroke Pembrokeshire, Wales U.K.
231 G9 Pembroke GA U.S.A.
233 □R4 Pembroke ME U.S.A.
259 F8 Pembroke, Cape Falkland Is
81 B11 Pembroke, Mount South I. N.Z.
150 C4 Pembroke Dock Pembrokeshire, Wales U.K.
231 G12 Pembroke Pines FL U.S.A.
150 C4 Pembrokeshire admin. div. Wales U.K.
150 B4 Pembrokeshire Coast National Park Wales U.K.
95 J6 Pembuanghulu Kalimantan Indon.
151 M5 Pembury Kent, England U.K.
260 B5 Pemehue, Cordillera de mts Chile
173 N3 Pemfling Ger.
95 I5 Pemuar Kalimantan Indon.
260 A5 Pemuco Chile
114 C3 Pen Mahar. India
96 A4 Pen r. Myanmar
137 O2 Pena r. Rus. Fed.
186 D3 Peña, Embalse de la resr Spain
252 D5 Pena Barrosa Bol.
260 B2 Peña Blanca Chile
183 O3 Peñacerrada Spain
182 D8 Penacova Port.
182 H8 Peña de Francia, Sierra de la mts Spain
184 F2 Peña del Águila, Embalse de la resr Spain
182 D6 Penafiel Port.
183 L5 Peñafiel Spain
185 I5 Peñaflor Spain
183 K5 Peñaflor de Hornija Spain
183 M2 Penagos Spain
247 □7 Penal Trin. and Tob.
183 K2 Peña Labra, Sierra de mts Spain
183 M7 Peñalara mt. Spain
186 E5 Peñalba Spain
182 G4 Peñalba de Santiago tourist site Spain
183 P7 Peñalén Spain
150 C4 Penally Pembrokeshire, Wales U.K.
185 I3 Peñalsordo Spain
182 E7 Penalva do Castelo Port.
182 F8 Penamacor Port.
Penambo Range mts Malaysia see Tama Abu, Banjaran
245 H4 Peñamiller Mex.
95 L2 Penampang Sabah Malaysia
245 H2 Peña Nevada, Cerro mt. Mex.
Penang state Malaysia see Pinang
256 B4 Penápolis Brazil
183 J7 Peñaranda de Bracamonte Spain
183 N5 Peñaranda de Duero Spain
234 E3 Pen Argyl PA U.S.A.
83 I6 Penarie N.S.W. Austr.
Penarlâg Wales U.K. see Hawarden
186 D7 Peñarroya mt. Spain
185 M2 Peñarroya, Embalse de resr Spain
185 I4 Peñarroya-Pueblonuevo Spain
185 O4 Peñarrubia Spain
150 F5 Penarth Vale of Glamorgan, Wales U.K.
182 I1 Peñas, Cabo de c. Spain
259 B7 Penas, Golfo de g. Chile
247 □7 Peñas, Punta pt Venez.
183 L2 Peña Sagra, Sierra mts Spain
260 D5 Peñas Blancas Arg.
242 □Q12 Peñas Blancas Nic.
239 L10 Peñasco watercourse NM U.S.A.
185 O3 Peñascosa Spain
183 M5 Peñas de Cervera hills Spain
185 P3 Peñas de San Pedro Spain
94 A2 Penasi, Pulau i. Indon.
182 I6 Peñausende Spain
150 D3 Penbryn Ceredigion, Wales U.K.
177 I4 Penc Hungary
150 D3 Pencader Carmarthenshire, Wales U.K.
146 K11 Pencaitland East Lothian, Scotland U.K.
116 G9 Pench r. India
Pencheng Jiangxi China see Ruichang
263 F2 Penck, Cape Antarctica
150 F4 Pencoed Bridgend, Wales U.K.
208 C3 Pendé r. C.A.R.
150 □ Pendeen Cornwall, England U.K.
206 C4 Pendembu Eastern Sierra Leone
206 B4 Pendembu Northern Sierra Leone
236 G4 Pender NE U.S.A.
86 G4 Pender Bay W.A. Austr.
86 G4 Pender Bay Aboriginal Reserve W.A. Austr.
199 K2 Pendik Turkey
182 E7 Pendilhe Port.
150 C4 Pendine Carmarthenshire, Wales U.K.
207 F4 Pendjari, Parc National de la nat. park Benin
149 M6 Pendle Hill England U.K.
238 E4 Pendleton OR U.S.A.
222 E4 Pendleton Bay B.C. Can.
94 E6 Pendopo Sumatera Indon.
238 F2 Pend Oreille r. WA U.S.A.
238 F2 Pend Oreille Lake ID U.S.A.
116 H8 Pendra Chhattisgarh India
116 H8 Pendra Road Chhattisgarh India
114 C4 Penduv Mahar. India
Pendzhikent Tajik. see Panjakent
95 H5 Penebangan i. Indon.
182 D5 Peneda, Serra da mts Port.
182 D5 Peneda Gerês, Parque Nacional da nat. park Port.
184 D5 Penedo Gordo Port.
182 F7 Penedono Port.
182 D8 Penela Port.
209 F6 Pene-Mende Dem. Rep. Congo
207 F4 Pénessoulou Benin
158 G7 Pénestin France
177 L4 Penészlek Hungary
227 O5 Penetanguishene Ont. Can.
232 G7 Penfield PA U.S.A.
Penfro Pembrokeshire, Wales U.K. see Pembroke
108 F3 Peng'an Sichuan China
114 F3 Penganga r. India
109 □J7 Peng Chau i. H.K. China
109 N6 P'engchia Yü i. Taiwan
209 E6 Penge Dem. Rep. Congo
109 L7 P'enghu Ch'üntao is Taiwan
P'enghu Liehtao is Taiwan see P'enghu Ch'üntao
109 L7 P'enghu Tao i. Taiwan
95 H4 Pengiki i. Indon.
226 A2 Pengilly MN U.S.A.
94 D2 Pengkalan Hulu Malaysia
94 □ Peng Kang hill Sing.
107 Q8 Penglai Shandong China
108 D3 Pengshan Sichuan China
108 G4 Pengshui Chongqing China
94 □ Peng Siang, Sungai r. Sing.
96 A4 Pengwa Myanmar
108 E3 Pengxi Sichuan China
Pengxian Sichuan China see Pengzhou
109 K4 Pengze Jiangxi China
108 D3 Pengzhou Sichuan China
255 C8 Penha Brazil
182 F8 Penha Garcia Port.
213 G3 Penhalonga Zimbabwe
182 D9 Penhascoso Port.
158 B5 Penhir, Pointe de pt France
215 K7 Penhoek Pass S. Africa
232 F12 Penhook VA U.S.A.
184 A2 Peniche Port.
146 J11 Penicuik Midlothian, Scotland U.K.
95 K9 Penida i. Indon.
171 G9 Penig Ger.
134 F3 Peninga Rus. Fed.
Peninsular Malaysia Malaysia see Malaysia, Semenanjung
146 E12 Peninver Argyll and Bute, Scotland U.K.
187 F7 Peñíscola Spain
149 N6 Penistone South Yorkshire, England U.K.
254 D4 Penitente, Serra do hills Brazil
207 H5 Penja Cameroon
244 F5 Penjamo Mex.
127 L6 Pēnjwīn Iraq
149 L7 Penketh Warrington, England U.K.
139 X5 Penkino Rus. Fed.
150 H2 Penkridge Staffordshire, England U.K.
170 J4 Penkun Ger.
150 G2 Penley Wrexham, Wales U.K.
156 B4 Penly France
158 C6 Penmarch France
158 C6 Penmarch, Pointe de pt France
Penn PA U.S.A. see Penn Hills
193 N3 Penna, Punta della pt Italy
193 I3 Penna in Teverina Italy
163 I9 Pennautier France
163 H7 Penne France
193 L3 Penne Italy
195 N2 Penne, Punta pt Italy
163 F7 Penne-d'Agenais France
263 L2 Pennell Coast Antarctica
114 G5 Penner r. India
82 F6 Penneshaw S.A. Austr.
233 □S3 Pennfield N.B. Can.
234 D3 Penn Forest Reservoir PA U.S.A.
232 F8 Penn Hills PA U.S.A.
160 K5 Pennine, Alpi mts Italy/Switz.
Pennine Alps mts Italy/Switz. see Pennine, Alpi
149 M5 Pennines hills England U.K.
215 O6 Pennington S. Africa
234 F4 Pennington NJ U.S.A.
232 B12 Pennington Gap VA U.S.A.
193 J1 Pennino, Monte mt. Italy
232 E9 Pennsboro WV U.S.A.
234 E4 Pennsburg PA U.S.A.
234 A3 Penns Creek PA U.S.A.
234 B3 Penns Creek r. PA U.S.A.
234 E5 Penns Grove NJ U.S.A.
234 D5 Pennsville NJ U.S.A.
227 P8 Pennsylvania state U.S.A.
247 □2 Pennville Dominica
232 H6 Penn Yan NY U.S.A.
146 D10 Pennyghael Argyll and Bute, Scotland U.K.
221 L3 Penny Icecap Nunavut Can.
263 K1 Penny Point Antarctica
234 F5 Penny Pot NJ U.S.A.
139 P5 Peno Rus. Fed.
233 □Q4 Penobscot r. ME U.S.A.
233 □Q4 Penobscot Bay ME U.S.A.
82 H7 Penola S.A. Austr.
242 G5 Peñón Blanco Mex.
187 F10 Peñón de Ifach pt Spain
82 D4 Penong S.A. Austr.
242 □S13 Penonomé Panama
150 D3 Penrhiw-pâl Ceredigion, Wales U.K.
81 □2 Penrhyn atoll Cook Is
267 I6 Penrhyn Basin sea feature Pacific Ocean
150 E1 Penrhyn Bay Conwy, Wales U.K.
150 D2 Penrhyndeudraeth Gwynedd, Wales U.K.
150 C2 Penrhyn Mawr pt Wales U.K.
83 M5 Penrith N.S.W. Austr.
149 L4 Penrith Cumbria, England U.K.
150 B7 Penryn Cornwall, England U.K.
231 D10 Pensacola FL U.S.A.
231 D10 Pensacola Bay FL U.S.A.
262 T1 Pensacola Mountains Antarctica
253 E3 Pensamiento Bol.
122 C2 Pensär Azer.
226 G5 Pensaukee WI U.S.A.
83 I7 Penshurst Vic. Austr.
95 L2 Pensiangan Sabah Malaysia
116 F3 Pensi La pass Jammu and Kashmir
150 D6 Pensilva Cornwall, England U.K.
128 B3 Pentadaktylos Range mts Cyprus
192 C3 Penta-di-Casinca Corse France
115 H4 Pentakota Andhra Prad. India
198 C2 Pentalofos Greece
86 I3 Pentecost r. W.A. Austr.
78 □5 Pentecost Island Vanuatu
225 H3 Pentecôte r. Que. Can.
Pentecôte, Île i. Vanuatu see Pentecost Island
197 O5 Penteleu, Vârful mt. Romania
158 F5 Penthièvre reg. France
222 G5 Penticton B.C. Can.
186 □ Pentinat, Punta pt Spain
150 D1 Pentir Gwynedd, Wales U.K.
150 B6 Pentire Point England U.K.
85 J6 Pentland Qld Austr.
146 J5 Pentland Firth sea chan. Scotland U.K.
146 I11 Pentland Hills Scotland U.K.
173 M4 Pentling Ger.
150 D1 Pentraeth Isle of Anglesey, Wales U.K.
150 E1 Pentrefoelas Conwy, Wales U.K.
226 H6 Pentwater MI U.S.A.
94 F5 Penuba Indon.
94 F6 Penuguan Sumatera Indon.
114 E5 Penukonda Andhra Prad. India
94 E2 Penunjuk, Tanjung pt Malaysia
158 E4 Penvénan France
96 C5 Penwegon Myanmar
149 L6 Penwortham Lancashire, England U.K.
137 O2 Peny Rus. Fed.
187 E7 Penyagolosa mt. Spain
150 F3 Penybont Powys, Wales U.K.
Pen-y-Bont ar Ogwr Bridgend, Wales U.K. see Bridgend
Pen-y-bont ar Ogwr Wales U.K. see Bridgend
150 F2 Penybontfawr Powys, Wales U.K.
150 E4 Pen-y-fai Bridgend, Wales U.K.
150 E2 Penygadair hill Wales U.K.
149 M5 Pen-y-Ghent hill England U.K.
150 D1 Penygroes Gwynedd, Wales U.K.
223 J2 Penylan Lake N.W.T. Can.
93 E6 Penyu, Kepulauan is Maluku Indon.
150 F4 Penywaun Rhondda Cynon Taff, Wales U.K.
135 I5 Penza Rus. Fed.
150 □ Penzance Cornwall, England U.K.
Penza Oblast admin. div. Rus. Fed. see Penzenskaya Oblast'
173 K6 Penzberg Ger.
135 I5 Penzenskaya Oblast' admin. div. Rus. Fed.
131 R3 Penzhinskaya Guba b. Rus. Fed.
173 J5 Penzing Ger.
170 H4 Penzlin Ger.
161 J8 Péone France
238 J2 Peoples Creek r. MT U.S.A.
241 T8 Peoria AZ U.S.A.
226 E9 Peoria IL U.S.A.
226 E9 Peoria Heights IL U.S.A.
240 □F14 Pepe'ekeo HI U.S.A.
206 B4 Pepel Sierra Leone
170 E2 Pepelow Ger.
261 I2 Pepe Nuñéz Uru.
210 B3 Peper Sudan
Peper, Teluk b. Indon. see Lada, Teluk
161 B10 Pépieux France
165 F7 Pepingen Belgium
165 I7 Pepinster Belgium
174 F4 Pępowo Pol.
215 N4 Pepworth S. Africa
196 H9 Pëqin Albania
235 G3 Pequannock NJ U.S.A.
182 H4 Peque Spain
234 C5 Pequea PA U.S.A.
234 C5 Pequea Creek r. PA U.S.A.
242 C4 Pequeña, Punta pt Mex.
234 E3 Pequest r. NJ U.S.A.
257 E3 Pequi Brazil
177 G4 Pér Hungary
184 C6 Pêra Port.
198 D4 Perachora Greece
114 G9 Peradeniya Sri Lanka
85 H2 Pera Head Qld Austr.
97 E12 Perai Malaysia
182 E9 Perais Port.
251 F3 Peraitepuy Venez.
94 C2 Perak i. Malaysia
94 D2 Perak r. Malaysia
94 D2 Perak state Malaysia
186 L3 Peralada Spain
183 J9 Peraleda de la Mata Spain
184 H4 Peraleda del Zaucejo Spain
186 C7 Peralejos Spain
186 D6 Perales del Alfambra Spain
182 G8 Perales del Puerto Spain
261 G6 Peralta Arg.
183 Q4 Peralta Spain
186 E4 Peralta de Alcofea Spain
186 F4 Peralta de la Sal Spain
186 E3 Peraltilla Spain
184 D6 Peralva Port.
183 P7 Peralveche Spain
198 F7 Perama Kriti Greece
114 F7 Perambalur Tamil Nadu India
140 R4 Perämeren kansallispuisto nat. park Fin.
211 B7 Peramiho Tanz.
186 H3 Peramola Spain
184 E5 Peramora r. Spain
94 E5 Peranap Sumatera Indon.
140 S3 Perä-Posio Fin.
178 F7 Perarolo di Cadore Italy
225 H3 Percé Que. Can.
159 L4 Perche, Collines du hills France
179 N3 Perchtoldsdorf Austria
86 H6 Percival Lakes salt flat W.A. Austr.
158 I4 Percy France
233 N4 Percy NH U.S.A.
85 M6 Percy Isles Qld Austr.
227 Q5 Percy Reach l. Ont. Can.
192 C8 Perdasdefogu Sardegna Italy
192 B9 Perdaxius Sardegna Italy
215 N3 Perdekop S. Africa
214 H9 Perdepoort pass S. Africa
261 H3 Perdices Arg.
183 P5 Perdices, Sierra de mts Spain
254 D4 Perdida r. Brazil
261 H5 Perdido r. Arg.
253 F5 Perdido r. Brazil
186 F2 Perdido, Monte mt. Spain
193 O7 Perdifumo Italy
186 D4 Perdiguera Spain
186 G2 Perdiguère, Pic mt. France/Spain
198 B3 Perdika Greece
234 B4 Perdix PA U.S.A.
256 D3 Perdizes Brazil
257 E4 Perdões Brazil
225 G3 Perdu, Lac l. Que. Can.
185 O5 Perea mt. Spain
136 F2 Perebrody Ukr.
136 B5 Perechyn Ukr.

139 S6 Peredel Kaluzhskaya Oblast' Rus. Fed.
139 X6 Peredel Vladimirskaya Oblast' Rus. Fed.
182 G6 Peredo Port.
130 H3 Peregrebnoye Rus. Fed.
177 J5 Peregu Mare Romania
136 D5 Perehins'ke Ukr.
250 C3 Pereira Col.
256 B4 Pereira Barreto Brazil
Pereira de Eça Angola see Ondjiva
184 C6 Pereiras Port.
254 F3 Pereiro Brazil
180 C4 Pereiro Port.
182 E1 Pereiro Spain
182 E4 Pereiro de Aguiar Spain
183 Q6 Perejiles r. Spain
139 O3 Perekhoda r. Rus. Fed.
137 M3 Perekopivka Ukr.
137 M8 Perekops'ka Zatoka b. Ukr.
135 H6 Perelazovskiy Rus. Fed.
139 O8 Perelazy Rus. Fed.
137 T2 Pereleshinskiy Rus. Fed.
120 D2 Perelyub Rus. Fed.
226 H6 Pere Marquette r. MI U.S.A.
120 D2 Peremetnoye Kazakh.
137 P4 Peremoha Kharkivs'ka Oblast' Ukr.
137 K3 Peremoha Kyivs'ka Oblast' Ukr.
114 C7 Peremul Par rf India
139 T7 Peremyshl' Rus. Fed.
136 D4 Peremyshlyany Ukr.
252 B2 Perené r. Peru
87 D10 Perenjori W.A. Austr.
182 I6 Pereruela Spain
136 H6 Peresecina Moldova
137 O4 Pereshchepyne Ukr.
139 V5 Pereslavl'-Zalesskiy Rus. Fed.
139 V5 Pereslavskiy Natsional'nyy Park nat. park Rus. Fed.
175 M5 Perespa Ukr.
179 O4 Pereszteg Hungary
191 K8 Peretola airport Italy
197 N6 Peretu Romania
137 R5 Pereval's'k Ukr.
137 L3 Perevid r. Ukr.
120 F2 Perevolotskiy Rus. Fed.
134 I5 Perevoz Rus. Fed.
100 I5 Pereyaslavka Rus. Fed.
Pereyaslav-Khmel'nitskiy Ukr. see Pereyaslav-Khmel'nyts'kyy
137 K3 Pereyaslav-Khmel'nyts'kyy Ukr.
261 G3 Pérez Arg.
258 C2 Pérez Chile
192 B6 Perfugas Sardegna Italy
179 K3 Perg Austria
261 G3 Pergamino Arg.
199 L6 Perge tourist site Turkey
191 L9 Pergine Valdarno Italy
191 K3 Pergine Valsugana Italy
191 N8 Pergola Italy
136 G2 Perha Ukr.
94 E2 Perhentian Besar, Pulau i. Malaysia
140 R5 Perho Fin.
196 I4 Periam Romania
185 K7 Periana Spain
244 E6 Peribán de Ramos Mex.
225 F3 Péribonka r. Que. Can.
225 G3 Péribonka, Lac l. Que. Can.
258 D2 Perico Arg.
244 B3 Pericos Nayarit Mex.
242 F5 Pericos Sinaloa Mex.
241 V8 Peridot AZ U.S.A.
197 P4 Perieni Romania
158 I3 Périers France
162 B3 Périgny France
162 F6 Périgord reg. France
162 F5 Périgord Blanc reg. France
163 F6 Périgord Noir reg. France
251 I5 Perigoso, Canal sea chan. Brazil
162 F5 Périgueux France
250 C2 Perijá, Parque Nacional nat. park Venez.
250 C2 Perija, Sierra de mts Venez.
182 I5 Perilla de Castro Spain
Perim Island Yemen see Barīm
177 K3 Perín-Chym Slovakia
94 E1 Peringat Malaysia
197 R5 Periprava Romania
197 P6 Perişoru Romania
198 E3 Peristera i. Greece
198 E4 Peristeri Greece
129 A7 Peri Suyu r. Turkey
197 R6 Periteasca-Gura Portiței nature res. Romania
259 C7 Perito Moreno Arg.
259 B7 Perito Moreno, Parque Nacional nat. park Arg.
114 E7 Perivar r. India
198 B3 Perivoli Kerkyra Greece
198 F7 Perivolia Kriti Greece
177 J4 Perje r. Hungary
234 E4 Perkasie PA U.S.A.
94 F5 Perkat, Tanjung pt Indon.
177 H4 Perkáta Hungary
234 E4 Perkiomen Creek r. PA U.S.A.
172 A3 Perl Ger.
242 □T13 Perlas, Archipiélago de las is Panama
242 □R11 Perlas, Laguna de lag. Nic.
242 □R11 Perlas, Punta de pt Nic.
173 M3 Perlbach r. Ger.
170 E4 Perleberg Ger.
175 K3 Perlejewo Pol.
173 O4 Perlesreut Ger.
137 R2 Perlevka Rus. Fed.
94 D1 Perlis state Malaysia
175 M1 Perloja Lith.
175 J1 Perły Pol.
134 L4 Perm' Rus. Fed.
191 Q5 Permani Croatia
134 I4 Permas Rus. Fed.
198 B2 Përmet Albania
134 K4 Permskiy Kray admin. div. Rus. Fed.
191 R7 Permuda Croatia
188 E3 Permuda i. Croatia
138 J1 Pernå Fin.
Pernambuco Brazil see Recife
254 F4 Pernambuco state Brazil
264 H6 Pernambuco Plain sea feature S. Atlantic Ocean
160 F2 Pernand-Vergelesses France
176 C2 Pernarec Czech Rep.
184 C5 Perna Seca, Barragem da resr Port.
191 Q6 Pernat, Rt pt Croatia
82 F4 Pernatty Lagoon salt flat S.A. Austr.
179 L5 Pernegg an der Mur Austria
114 C5 Pernem Goa India
179 N2 Pernersdorf Austria
184 B2 Pernes Port.
161 G9 Pernes-les-Fontaines France
198 F1 Perni Greece
197 L8 Pernik Bulg.
141 Q6 Perniö Fin.
179 M4 Pernitz Austria
Pernov Estonia see Pärnu
190 G4 Pero Italy
184 C4 Peroguarda Port.
256 A2 Perolândia Brazil
161 D9 Pérols France
160 H4 Péron France
87 B8 Peron, Cape W.A. Austr.
87 C12 Peron, Point W.A. Austr.
84 C2 Peron Islands N.T. Austr.
160 G4 Péronnas France
156 E4 Péronne France
87 B8 Peron Peninsula W.A. Austr.
190 C6 Perosa Argentina Italy
245 J6 Perote Mex.
160 G5 Pérouges France
182 F8 Pero Viseu Port.
83 M6 Perpendicular, Point N.S.W. Austr.
163 J10 Perpignan France
260 A6 Perquenco Chile
260 B4 Perquilauquén r. Chile
260 D5 Perra, Salitral de la salt pan Arg.
150 B7 Perranporth Cornwall, England U.K.
150 B7 Perranzabuloe Cornwall, England U.K.
160 E3 Perrecy-les-Forges France
Perrégaux Alg. see Mohammadia
160 E4 Perreux France
160 H3 Perrigny France
240 O8 Perris CA U.S.A.
184 G7 Perro, Punta del pt Spain
157 J8 Perrogney-les-Fontaines France
154 C2 Perros-Guirec France
233 L3 Perrot, Île i. Que. Can.
140 S2 Perrum-Äbmir Fin.
226 J2 Perry Ont. Can.
231 F10 Perry FL U.S.A.
231 F9 Perry GA U.S.A.
236 H5 Perry IA U.S.A.
233 □R4 Perry ME U.S.A.
227 J7 Perry MI U.S.A.
237 G7 Perry OK U.S.A.
234 A4 Perry County county PA U.S.A.
234 C6 Perry Hall MD U.S.A.
234 C6 Perryman MD U.S.A.
263 G2 Perrymennyy, Cape Antarctica
232 B7 Perrysburg OH U.S.A.
237 E7 Perryton TX U.S.A.
237 I8 Perryville AR U.S.A.
234 C5 Perryville MD U.S.A.
163 I6 Pers France
129 E4 P'ersa Georgia
156 D5 Persan France
129 D3 P'ersat'i Georgia
179 L3 Persenbeug Austria
122 E7 Persepolis tourist site Iran
253 E3 Perseverancia Bol.
143 N2 Pershagen Sweden
137 M5 Pershe Travnya Dnipropetrovs'ka Oblast' Ukr.
137 O5 Pershe Travnya Dnipropetrovs'ka Oblast' Ukr.
Pershnotravnevoye Ukr. see Pershotravens'k
150 H3 Pershore Worcestershire, England U.K.
137 P5 Pershotravens'k Ukr.
137 Q6 Pershotravneve Donets'ka Oblast' Ukr.
137 Q4 Pershotravneve Kharkivs'ka Oblast' Ukr.
137 L7 Pershotravneve Mykolayivs'ka Oblast' Ukr.
136 H2 Pershotravneve Zhytomyrs'ka Oblast' Ukr.
Pershotravnevoye Ukr. see Mokvyn
Persia country Asia see Iran
Persian Gulf Asia see The Gulf
Persis prov. Iran see Fārs
143 M4 Persnäs Öland Sweden
143 N3 Persö naturreservat nature res. Sweden
142 J5 Perstorp Sweden
126 I4 Pertek Turkey
83 K9 Perth Tas. Austr.
87 C11 Perth W.A. Austr.
224 E4 Perth Ont. Can.
146 J10 Perth Perth and Kinross, Scotland U.K.
235 G3 Perth Amboy NJ U.S.A.
146 H9 Perth and Kinross admin. div. Scotland U.K.
225 H4 Perth-Andover N.B. Can.
265 L6 Perth Basin sea feature Indian Ocean
156 H5 Perthes Champagne-Ardenne France
156 E7 Perthes Île-de-France France
156 I6 Perthois reg. France
163 J11 Perthus, Col du pass France/Spain
134 G2 Pertominsk Rus. Fed.
141 Q6 Pertteli Fin.
161 H9 Pertuis France
162 A3 Pertuis Breton sea chan. France
162 A3 Pertuis d'Antioche sea chan. France
141 S6 Pertunmaa Fin.
186 E3 Pertusa Spain
192 C5 Pertusato, Capo c. Corse France
261 E5 Perú Arg.
252 D3 Perú Bol.
Peru atoll Gilbert Is Kiribati see Beru
252 B2 Peru country S. America
226 E8 Peru IL U.S.A.
230 D5 Peru IN U.S.A.
233 L4 Peru NY U.S.A.
267 M7 Peru Basin sea feature S. Pacific Ocean
171 I10 Peruc Czech Rep.
267 N6 Peru-Chile Trench sea feature S. Pacific Ocean
188 F4 Perućko Jezero l. Croatia
193 I1 Perugia Italy
191 M9 Perugia prov. Italy
258 F3 Perugorría Arg.
256 D6 Peruíbe Brazil
114 E5 Peruru Andhra Prad. India
197 M8 Perushtitsa Bulg.
Perusia Italy see Perugia
165 E7 Péruwelz Belgium
129 C1 Pervaya Sinyukha Rus. Fed.
159 L5 Pervenchères France
165 C6 Pervijze Belgium
137 O1 Pervoavgustovskiy Rus. Fed.
136 I7 Pervomaisc Moldova
121 P6 Pervomay Kyrg.
121 N2 Pervomayka Kazakh.
135 H5 Pervomaysk Rus. Fed.
137 R5 Pervomays'k Luhans'ka Oblast' Ukr.
136 J5 Pervomays'k Mykolayivs'ka Oblast' Ukr.
138 L3 Pervomayskaya Rus. Fed.
137 L6 Pervomays'ke Mykolayivs'ka Oblast' Ukr.
137 M8 Pervomays'ke Respublika Krym Ukr.
121 T2 Pervomayskiy Kazakh.
Pervomayskiy Kyrg. see Pervomay
Pervomayskiy Arkhangel'skaya Oblast' Rus. Fed. see Novodvinsk
120 F2 Pervomayskiy Orenburgskaya Oblast' Rus. Fed.
139 P7 Pervomayskiy Smolenskaya Oblast' Rus. Fed.
139 X8 Pervomayskiy Tambovskaya Oblast' Rus. Fed.
139 U7 Pervomayskiy Tul'skaya Oblast' Rus. Fed.
Pervomayskoye Kyrg. see Pervomay
138 M1 Pervomayskoye Leningradskaya Oblast' Rus. Fed.
129 I3 Pervomayskoye Respublika Dagestan Rus. Fed.
100 M4 Pervomayskoye Sakhalinskaya Oblast' Rus. Fed.
137 P4 Pervomays'kyy Ukr.
131 R3 Pervorechenskiy Rus. Fed.
165 G7 Perwez Belgium
139 R3 Pes' Rus. Fed.
139 S2 Pes' r. Rus. Fed.
191 K8 Pesa r. Italy
183 M3 Pesadas de Burgos Spain
95 I5 Pesaguan Kalimantan Indon.
95 I6 Pesaguan r. Indon.
191 N8 Pesaro Italy
191 N8 Pesaro e Urbino prov. Italy
240 J4 Pescadero CA U.S.A.
Pescadores is Taiwan see P'enghu Ch'üntao
252 B4 Pescadores, Punta pt Peru
190 I8 Pescaglia Italy
191 J5 Pescantina Italy
193 M3 Pescara Italy
193 L3 Pescara prov. Italy
193 M3 Pescara r. Italy
197 J6 Pescari Romania
193 L4 Pescasseroli Italy
160 C5 Peschadoires France
135 H7 Peschanokopskoye Rus. Fed.
Peschanoye Rus. Fed. see Yashkul'
120 D6 Peschanyy, Mys pt Kazakh.
193 Q4 Peschici Italy
191 J8 Pescia Italy
193 L3 Pescina Italy
193 M4 Pescocostanzo Italy
193 M4 Pescolanciano Italy
193 O6 Pescopagano Italy
193 M4 Pescopennataro Italy
193 K3 Pescorocchiano Italy
193 N5 Pesco Sannita Italy
242 □S14 Pesé Panama
216 □3b Pesebre, Punta pt Fuerteventura Canary Is
94 □ Pesek, Pulau i. Sing.
94 □ Pesek Kechil, Pulau i. Sing.
190 B2 Peseux Switz.
134 I2 Pesha r. Rus. Fed.
123 I5 Peshanjan Afgh.
123 N4 Peshawar Pak.
196 I9 Peshkopi Albania
137 S7 Peshkovo Rus. Fed.
Peshnyye, Ostrova is Kazakh. see Bol'shiye Peshnyye, Ostrova
197 M8 Peshtera Bulg.
226 G4 Peshtigo WI U.S.A.
226 G5 Peshtigo r. WI U.S.A.
190 D7 Pesio r. Italy
121 L1 Peski Kazakh.
139 V6 Peski Moskovskaya Oblast' Rus. Fed.
135 H6 Peski Voronezhskaya Oblast' Rus. Fed.
123 J2 Peski Turkm.
134 K4 Peskovka Rus. Fed.
160 H2 Pesmes France
188 E2 Pesnica Slovenia
139 W3 Pesochnoye Rus. Fed.
139 Q8 Pesochnya Rus. Fed.
182 E6 Peso da Régua Port.
242 □P11 Pespire Hond.
254 F4 Pesqueira Brazil
242 D3 Pesqueira Mex.
183 L5 Pesquera de Duero Spain
163 C6 Pessac France
163 F8 Pessan France
164 J3 Pesse Neth.
170 G5 Pessin Ger.
177 I4 Pest county Hungary
139 S3 Pestovo Rus. Fed.
120 C1 Pestravka Rus. Fed.
134 H4 Pestyaki Rus. Fed.
183 L2 Pesués Spain
134 L1 Pesyakov, Ostrov i. Rus. Fed.
244 E8 Petacalco, Bahía de b. Mex.
193 N3 Petacciato Italy
128 C6 Petah Tiqwa Israel
141 R5 Petäjävesi Fin.
93 F3 Petak, Tanjung pt Halmahera Indon.
198 C6 Petalidi Greece
198 F4 Petalioi i. Greece
198 F4 Petalion, Kolpos sea chan. Greece
240 J3 Petaluma CA U.S.A.
165 I9 Pétange Lux.
95 K5 Petangis Kalimantan Indon.
250 E2 Petare Venez.
198 C3 Petas Greece
244 F8 Petatlán Mex.
211 A8 Petauke Zambia
227 S3 Petawaga, Lac l. Que. Can.
227 Q4 Petawawa Ont. Can.
243 O9 Petén Itzá, Lago l. Guat.
226 E5 Petenwell Lake WI U.S.A.
179 O7 Peteranec Croatia
224 D3 Peterbell Ont. Can.
82 G5 Peterborough S.A. Austr.
83 I8 Peterborough Vic. Austr.
224 E4 Peterborough Ont. Can.
151 L2 Peterborough Peterborough, England U.K.
151 L2 Peterborough admin. div. England U.K.
233 N6 Peterborough NH U.S.A.
146 L8 Peterculter Aberdeen, Scotland U.K.
146 M7 Peterhead Aberdeenshire, Scotland U.K.
177 I4 Péteri Hungary
262 R2 Peter I Island Antarctica
Peter I Øy i. Antarctica see Peter I Island
177 I5 Péteri-tó l. Hungary
223 M2 Peter Lake Nunavut Can.
149 O4 Peterlee Durham, England U.K.
222 H5 Peter Lougheed Provincial Park B.C. Can.
84 C8 Petermann Aboriginal Land res. N.T./W.A. Austr.
221 P2 Petermann Bjerg nunatak Greenland
84 B8 Petermann Ranges mts N.T. Austr.
260 B4 Peteroa, Volcán vol. Chile
223 I4 Peter Pond Lake Sask. Can.
225 G1 Peters, Lac l. Que. Can.
173 J3 Petersaurach Ger.
169 I9 Petersberg Ger.
215 I8 Petersburg S. Africa
220 E4 Petersburg AK U.S.A.
236 K6 Petersburg IL U.S.A.
230 D6 Petersburg IN U.S.A.
234 F6 Petersburg NJ U.S.A.
233 L6 Petersburg NY U.S.A.
232 E8 Petersburg OH U.S.A.
232 H11 Petersburg VA U.S.A.
232 F10 Petersburg WV U.S.A.
173 K4 Petersdorf Ger.
170 D2 Petersdorf auf Fehmarn Ger.
151 K5 Petersfield Hampshire, England U.K.
171 J6 Petershagen Brandenburg Ger.
169 G6 Petershagen Nordrhein-Westfalen Ger.
173 K5 Petershausen Ger.
251 G3 Peters Mine Guyana
232 E11 Peterstown WV U.S.A.
220 C3 Petersville AK U.S.A.
147 E6 Peterswell Ireland
Peter the Great Bay Rus. Fed. see Petra Velikogo, Zaliv
Pétervárad Vojvodina Serbia see Petrovaradin
177 J3 Pétervására Hungary
Peterwardein Vojvodina Serbia see Petrovaradin
114 D4 Peth Mahar. India
195 L5 Petilia Policastro Italy
186 C3 Petilla de Aragón Spain
182 F4 Petín Spain
Petit Atlas mts Morocco see Anti Atlas
247 □2 Petit-Bourg Guadeloupe
247 □2 Petit-Canal Guadeloupe
225 H4 Petitcodiac N.B. Can.
159 N3 Petit-Couronne France
247 □2 Petit Cul de Sac Marin b. Guadeloupe
161 E10 Petite Camargue reg. France
162 H3 Petite Creuse r. France
217 □1c Petite-Île Réunion
163 C7 Petite Leyre r. France
247 □3 Petite Martinique i. Grenada
157 M5 Petite-Rosselle France
159 P7 Petite Sauldre r. France
165 J9 Petite Suisse Luxembourgeoise reg. Lux.
217 □3b Petite Terre i. Mayotte
246 G4 Petit-Goâve Haiti
Petitjean Morocco see Sidi Kacem
159 I8 Petit Lay r. France
208 A5 Petit-Loango, Réserve de nature res. Gabon
158 I7 Petit Maine r. France
233 □R4 Petit Manan Point ME U.S.A.
158 I7 Petit-Mars France
225 I3 Petit Mécatina r. Nfld and Lab./Que. Can.
221 M4 Petit Mécatina r. Que. Can.
225 J3 Petit Mécatina, Île du i. Que. Can.
157 M6 Petitmont France
156 F6 Petit Morin r. France
160 G3 Petit-Noir France
222 F2 Petitot r. Alta/B.C. Can.
161 E10 Petit Rhône r. France
160 J5 Petit St-Bernard, Col du pass France
139 W7 Petkino Rus. Fed.
140 S3 Petkula Fin.
171 H7 Petkus Ger.
116 D8 Petlad Gujarat India
245 J7 Petlalcingo Mex.
116 E8 Petlawad Madh. Prad. India
177 L3 Petneháza Hungary
243 O7 Peto Mex.
177 I4 Petőfibánya Hungary
177 I5 Petőfiszállás Hungary
260 B3 Petorca Chile
226 J4 Petoskey MI U.S.A.
128 D8 Petra tourist site Jordan
187 L8 Petra Spain
195 J7 Petrace r. Italy
194 G8 Petralia-Soprana Sicilia Italy
194 G8 Petralia-Sottana Sicilia Italy
262 P1 Petras, Mount Antarctica
100 G7 Petra Velikogo, Zaliv b. Rus. Fed.
227 Q6 Petre, Point Ont. Can.
80 □ Petre Bay Chatham Is S. Pacific Ocean
Petrel Valencia Spain see Petrer
193 L5 Petrella, Monte mt. Italy
193 K3 Petrella Salto Italy
193 N4 Petrella Tifernina Italy
187 D11 Petrer Spain
177 L4 Petreşti Romania
192 B4 Petreto-Bicchisano Corse France
191 N8 Petriano Italy
197 L9 Petrich Bulg.
78 □5 Petrie, Récif rf New Caledonia
241 W6 Petrified Forest National Park AZ U.S.A.
188 G3 Petrijevci Croatia
Petrikau Pol. see Piotrków Trybunalski
Petrikov Belarus see Pyetrykaw
197 L5 Petrila Romania
188 F3 Petrinja Croatia
177 L5 Petriş Romania
193 L1 Petritoli Italy
137 N7 Petrivka Khersons'ka Oblast' Ukr.
136 J7 Petrivka Odes'ka Oblast' Ukr.
137 Q6 Petrivs'ke Ukr.
137 M4 Petrivtsi Ukr.
258 C3 Petro, Cerro de mt. Chile
Petroaleksandrovsk Uzbek. see To'rtko'l
138 M2 Petrodvorets Rus. Fed.
Petrograd Rus. Fed. see Sankt-Peterburg
Petrokov Pol. see Piotrków Trybunalski
Petrokrepost' Rus. Fed. see Shlissel'burg
139 O1 Petrokrepost', Bukhta b. Rus. Fed.
185 P3 Pétrola Spain
254 F4 Petrolândia Brazil
250 C2 Petrólea Col.
227 L7 Petrolia Ont. Can.
240 H1 Petrolia CA U.S.A.
250 E5 Petrolina Amazonas Brazil
254 E4 Petrolina Pernambuco Brazil
256 C2 Petrolina de Goiás Brazil
Petromaryevka Ukr. see Pervomays'k
198 C2 Petron, Limni l. Greece
195 L5 Petronà Italy
Petropavl Kazakh. see Petropavlovsk
137 P5 Petropavlivka Ukr.
121 S5 Petropavlovka Kazakh.
100 E2 Petropavlovka Amurskaya Oblast' Rus. Fed.
106 I1 Petropavlovka Respublika Buryatiya Rus. Fed.
135 H6 Petropavlovka Voronezhskaya Oblast' Rus. Fed.
121 M1 Petropavlovsk Kazakh.
Petropavlovsk Rus. Fed. see Petropavlovsk-Kamchatskiy
131 Q4 Petropavlovsk-Kamchatskiy Rus. Fed.
121 U1 Petropavlovskoye Rus. Fed.
257 F5 Petrópolis Brazil
197 L5 Petroşani Romania
194 D8 Petrosino Sicilia Italy
176 G3 Petrov Czech Rep.
Petrovac Bos.-Herz. see Bosanski Petrovac
196 J6 Petrovac Serbia
177 K3 Petrovany Slovakia
196 H5 Petrovaradin Vojvodina Serbia
137 M5 Petrove Ukr.
176 D2 Petrovice Czech Rep.
139 P8 Petrovichi Rus. Fed.
121 M1 Petrovka Kazakh.
120 A1 Petrovsk Rus. Fed.
135 G7 Petrovskaya Rus. Fed.
137 R5 Petrovs'ke Ukr.
139 X5 Petrovskiy Rus. Fed.
139 T5 Petrovskoye Moskovskaya Oblast' Rus. Fed.
120 G1 Petrovskoye Respublika Bashkortostan Rus. Fed.
Petrovskoye Stavropol'skiy Kray Rus. Fed. see Svetlograd
139 X9 Petrovskoye Tambovskaya Oblast' Rus. Fed.
139 W4 Petrovskoye Yaroslavskaya Oblast' Rus. Fed.
107 K1 Petrovsk-Zabaykal'skiy Rus. Fed.
135 I6 Petrov Val Rus. Fed.
134 F3 Petrozavodsk Rus. Fed.
197 M3 Petru Rareş Romania
215 J5 Petrusburg S. Africa
136 G6 Petruşeni Moldova
215 M3 Petrus Steyn S. Africa
214 I6 Petrusville S. Africa
177 H2 Petřvald Czech Rep.
137 N5 Petrykivka Ukr.
Petsamo Rus. Fed. see Pechenga
215 M3 Petsana S. Africa
Pettau Slovenia see Ptuj
164 G3 Petten Neth.
173 M3 Pettendorf Ger.
147 G3 Pettigo Northern Ireland U.K.
195 L5 Pettinascura, Monte mt. Italy
194 G8 Pettineo Sicilia Italy
173 N6 Petting Ger.
178 B5 Pettneu am Arlberg Austria
193 L4 Pettorano sul Gizio Italy
191 L3 Pettorina r. Italy
130 H4 Petukhovo Rus. Fed.
139 W6 Petushki Rus. Fed.
151 K6 Petworth West Sussex, England U.K.
178 G6 Petzeck mt. Austria
179 I3 Peuerbach Austria
94 B2 Peuetsagu, Gunung vol. Indon.
162 D5 Peujard France
260 B4 Peumo Chile
140 S3 Peurasuvanto Fin.
94 B2 Peureula Sumatera Indon.
131 S3 Pevek Rus. Fed.
151 M6 Pevensey East Sussex, England U.K.
151 M6 Pevensey Levels lowland England U.K.
190 D7 Peveragno Italy
151 I5 Pewsey Wiltshire, England U.K.
151 I5 Pewsey, Vale of val. England U.K.
168 D4 Pewsum (Krummhörn) Ger.
157 M7 Pexonne France
111 K10 Pêxung Xizang China
122 H9 Pey Beshk Iran
161 J9 Peymeinade France
161 C10 Peyne r. France
161 H10 Peynier France
122 G4 Pey Ostān Iran
161 H10 Peypin France
261 G3 Peyrano Arg.
162 H4 Peyrat-le-Château France
163 B8 Peyrehorade France
161 C8 Peyreleau France
162 I4 Peyrelevade France
163 E10 Peyresourde, Col de pass France
190 D8 Peyrevieille, Mont mt. Italy
161 B10 Peyriac-de-Mer France
163 J9 Peyriac-Minervois France
160 H5 Peyrieu France
161 G6 Peyrins France
161 H9 Peyrolles-en-Provence France
161 H8 Peyruis France
163 E8 Peyrusse-Grande France
163 I6 Peyrusse-le-Roc France
134 I2 Peza r. Rus. Fed.
161 C10 Pézenas France
174 D2 Pęzino Pol.
176 G3 Pezinok Slovakia
123 N5 Pezu Pak.
163 F6 Pezuls France
173 M4 Pfaffenberg Ger.
171 J6 Pfaffendorf Ger.
173 I5 Pfaffenhausen Ger.
173 L4 Pfaffenhofen an der Ilm Ger.
173 I5 Pfaffenhofen an der Roth Ger.
157 O6 Pfaffenhoffen France
179 M4 Pfaffensattel pass Austria
172 D6 Pfaffenweiler Ger.
190 F1 Pfäffikon Schwyz Switz.
190 F1 Pfäffikon Zürich Switz.
173 M5 Pfaffing Ger.
172 D3 Pfälzer Wald hills Ger.
172 D3 Pfälzer Wald park Ger.
169 E10 Pfalzfeld Ger.
172 F4 Pfalzgrafenweiler Ger.
173 N5 Pfarrkirchen Ger.
169 K10 Pfarrweisach Ger.
178 H5 Pfarrwerfen Austria
173 M4 Pfatter Ger.
172 G3 Pfedelbach Ger.
173 L4 Pfeffenhausen Ger.
178 C4 Pflach Austria
178 D5 Pfons Austria
173 L4 Pförring Ger.
173 J6 Pforzen Ger.
172 F4 Pforzheim Ger.
173 M3 Pfreimd Ger.
173 M2 Pfreimd r. Ger.
172 G5 Pfronstetten Ger.
173 J6 Pfronten Ger.
172 G6 Pfullendorf Ger.
172 G5 Pfullingen Ger.
178 C6 Pfunds Austria
172 F2 Pfungstadt Ger.
190 F1 Pfyn Switz.
96 F4 Phac Mo, Phu mt. Vietnam
213 F5 Phagameng Limpopo S. Africa
116 E4 Phagwara Punjab India
215 K4 Phahameng Free State S. Africa
213 F4 Phalaborwa S. Africa
123 O5 Phalia Pak.
116 D6 Phalodi Rajasthan India
157 N6 Phalsbourg France
116 C6 Phalsund Rajasthan India
114 D4 Phaltan Mahar. India
117 L6 Phalut Peak India/Nepal
97 E10 Phangan, Ko i. Thai.
96 E6 Phang Hoei, San Khao mts Thai.
97 D10 Phangnga Thai.
96 F3 Phăng Xi Păng mt. Vietnam
97 G7 Phanom Dong Rak, Thiu Khao mts Cambodia/Thai.
97 I9 Phan Rang-Thap Cham Vietnam
97 I9 Phan Ri Cưa Vietnam
97 I9 Phan Thiêt Vietnam
97 I9 Phan Thiêt, Vinh b. Vietnam
116 G6 Phaphund Uttar Prad. India
117 K6 Phaplu Nepal
148 E3 Pharis Northern Ireland U.K.
96 H4 Phat Diêm Vietnam
97 E11 Phatthalung Thai.
96 D5 Phayao Thai.
96 E7 Phayuhakhiri Thai.
117 O7 Phek Nagaland India
84 E3 Phelp r. N.T. Austr.
232 H6 Phelps NY U.S.A.
226 E3 Phelps WI U.S.A.
223 K3 Phelps Lake Sask. Can.
96 F6 Phen Thai.
232 G11 Phenix VA U.S.A.
231 E9 Phenix City AL U.S.A.
214 G1 Phephane watercourse S. Africa
97 D8 Phet Buri Thai.
96 E6 Phetchabun Thai.
97 G7 Phiafai Laos
96 E6 Phichai Thai.
96 E6 Phichit Thai.
Philadelphia Jordan see 'Ammān
214 C9 Philadelphia S. Africa
Philadelphia Turkey see Alaşehir
237 K9 Philadelphia MS U.S.A.
233 J4 Philadelphia NY U.S.A.
234 E5 Philadelphia PA U.S.A.
234 E5 Philadelphia County county PA U.S.A.
203 G4 Philae tourist site Egypt
Philip atoll Arch. des Tuamotu Fr. Polynesia see Makemo
236 E3 Philip SD U.S.A.
Philip Atoll Micronesia see Sorol
82 □1 Philip Island Norfolk I.
Philippeville Alg. see Skikda
165 G8 Philippeville Belgium
232 E9 Philippi WV U.S.A.
84 G8 Philippi, Lake salt flat Qld Austr.
165 E6 Philippine Neth.
266 D4 Philippine Basin sea feature N. Pacific Ocean
92 D4 Philippines country Asia
90 F3 Philippine Sea N. Pacific Ocean
266 D4 Philippine Trench sea feature N. Pacific Ocean
215 J6 Philippolis S. Africa
215 J6 Philippolis Road S. Africa
Philippopolis Bulg. see Plovdiv
172 E3 Philippsburg Ger.
173 P4 Philippsreut Ger.
169 J9 Philippsthal (Werra) Ger.
247 L4 Philipsburg St Maarten Neth. Antilles
238 H3 Philipsburg MT U.S.A.
232 G8 Philipsburg PA U.S.A.
164 F5 Philipsdam barrage Neth.
220 D3 Philip Smith Mountains AK U.S.A.
214 I6 Philipstown S. Africa
83 J8 Phillip Island Vic. Austr.
82 □2 Phillip Point Lord Howe I. Austr.
87 F12 Phillips r. W.A. Austr.
233 □O4 Phillips ME U.S.A.
226 D4 Phillips WI U.S.A.
222 E5 Phillips Arm B.C. Can.
236 F6 Phillipsburg KS U.S.A.
234 E3 Phillipsburg NJ U.S.A.
221 J1 Phillips Inlet Nunavut Can.
82 E3 Phillipson, Lake salt flat S.A. Austr.
86 H4 Phillips Range hills W.A. Austr.
232 F8 Phillipston PA U.S.A.
233 L6 Philmont NY U.S.A.
Philomelium Turkey see Akşehir
232 E12 Philpott Reservoir VA U.S.A.
96 G7 Phimun Mangsahan Thai.
215 L3 Phiritona S. Africa
96 E6 Phitsanulok Thai.
226 E4 Phlox WI U.S.A.
Phnom Penh Cambodia see Phnum Pénh
97 G9 Phnum Pénh Cambodia
97 E11 Pho, Laem pt Thai.
96 G5 Phô Châu Vietnam
233 K6 Phoenicia NY U.S.A.
217 □1b Phoenix Mauritius
241 T8 Phoenix AZ U.S.A.
233 I5 Phoenix NY U.S.A.
Phoenix Island Phoenix Is Kiribati see Rawaki
77 I2 Phoenix Islands Kiribati
234 D4 Phoenixville PA U.S.A.
215 N2 Phola S. Africa
96 G3 Phô Lu Vietnam
215 L3 Phomolong S. Africa
96 F7 Phon Thai.
96 H6 Phong Nha Vietnam
96 F4 Phôngsali Laos
Phong Saly Laos see Phôngsali
96 F3 Phong Thô Vietnam
96 F5 Phon Phisai Thai.
96 F6 Phon Thong Thai.
83 I8 Phoques Bay Tas. Austr.
84 H6 Phosphate Hill Qld Austr.
116 F2 Photaksur Jammu and Kashmir
96 E5 Phrae Thai.
Phra Nakhon Si Ayutthaya Thai. see Ayutthaya
96 D5 Phrao Thai.
97 D10 Phra Saeng Thai.
97 D10 Phra Thong, Ko i. Thai.
96 E6 Phrom Phiram Thai.
97 F9 Phsar Ream Cambodia
96 H6 Phu Bai Vietnam
97 G7 Phuchong-Nayoi National Park Thai.
Phu Cuong Vietnam see Thu Dâu Môt
96 G4 Phuc Yên Vietnam
212 E4 Phuduhudu Botswana
117 L6 Phuentsholing Bhutan
97 D11 Phuket Thai.
97 D11 Phuket, Ko i. Thai.
96 E6 Phu-khieo Wildlife Reserve nature res. Thai.
117 J9 Phulbani Orissa India
123 L8 Phulji Pak.
96 H6 Phu Lôc Vietnam
97 G10 Phu Lôc Vietnam
116 I7 Phulpur Uttar Prad. India
96 E6 Phu Luang National Park Thai.
96 G4 Phu Ly Vietnam
97 F8 Phumĭ Bânhchok Kon Cambodia
97 G8 Phumĭ Chhlong Cambodia
97 G9 Phumĭ Chhuk Cambodia
97 G7 Phumĭ Kâmpóng Srâlau Cambodia
97 G8 Phumĭ Kâmpóng Trâlach Cambodia
97 F9 Phumĭ Kaôh Kŏng Cambodia
97 F8 Phumĭ Kiliĕk Cambodia
97 F7 Phumĭ Kon Kriel Cambodia
97 F8 Phumĭ Koŭk Kduŏch Cambodia
97 G8 Phumĭ Mlu Prey Cambodia
97 F8 Phumĭ Prâmaôy Cambodia
97 G8 Phumĭ Prêk Kak Cambodia
97 F7 Phumĭ Sâmraông Cambodia
97 G8 Phumĭ Thalabârĭvăt Cambodia
97 G8 Phumĭ Toêng Cambodia
97 G9 Phumĭ Trâm Kak Cambodia
97 F7 Phumĭ Trom Cambodia
97 F9 Phumĭ Veal Renh Cambodia
97 I7 Phu My Vietnam
97 G10 Phung Hiêp Vietnam
Phuntsholing Bhutan see Phuentsholing
97 H9 Phươc Bưu Vietnam
97 H9 Phươc Hai Vietnam
97 G10 Phươc Long Vietnam
96 F6 Phu Phan National Park Thai.
97 F9 Phu Quôc, Đao i. Vietnam
97 I9 Phu Quy, Đao i. Vietnam
215 M4 Phuthaditjhaba S. Africa
96 G4 Phu Tho Vietnam
Phu Vinh Vietnam see Tra Vinh
96 F6 Phu Wiang Thai.
96 G4 Phu Yên Vietnam
96 C5 Phyu Myanmar
163 J10 Pia France
87 D9 Pia Aboriginal Reserve W.A. Austr.
95 J4 Piabung, Gunung mt. Indon.
254 D3 Piaca Brazil
256 B4 Piacatu Brazil
190 H5 Piacenza Italy
190 H6 Piacenza prov. Italy
225 G3 Piacouadie, Lac l. Que. Can.
190 I5 Piadena Italy
224 E2 Piagochioui r. Que. Can.
94 E4 Piai, Tanjung pt Malaysia
261 G3 Piamonte Arg.
83 L4 Pian r. N.S.W. Austr.
192 B3 Piana Corse France
192 A6 Piana, Isola i. Sardegna Italy
192 A9 Piana, Isola i. Sardegna Italy
190 E7 Piana Crixia Italy
194 E8 Piana degli Albanesi Sicilia Italy
193 K3 Piana del Fucino plain Italy
194 H9 Piana di Catania plain Sicilia Italy
192 H2 Piancastagnaio Italy
191 M8 Piandimeleto Italy
193 M3 Pianella Italy
190 G6 Pianello Val Tidone Italy
83 I6 Piangil Vic. Austr.
107 L7 Pianguan Shanxi China
96 D1 Pianma Yunnan China
191 K7 Piano del Voglio Italy
191 K7 Pianoro Italy
192 E2 Pianosa Italy
192 E2 Pianosa, Isola i. Italy
193 P3 Pianosa, Isole is Italy
192 C5 Pianotolli-Caldarello Corse France
192 H2 Piansano Italy
247 □7 Piarco airport Trin. and Tob.
184 E4 Pias Port.
182 G4 Pias, Embalse de resr Spain
175 J3 Piaseczno Mazowieckie Pol.
174 C2 Piaseczno Zachodniopomorskie Pol.
174 C3 Piasek Pol.
175 K4 Piaski Lubelskie Pol.
174 F4 Piaski Wielkopolskie Pol.
254 F4 Piassabussu Brazil
175 I3 Piastów Pol.
254 E5 Piatã Brazil
175 H3 Piątek Pol.
175 K2 Piątnica Poduchowna Pol.
197 N7 Piatra Romania
197 O4 Piatra Neamţ Romania
197 M6 Piatra Olt Romania
197 O4 Piatra Şoimului Romania
163 E10 Piau-Engaly France
254 E3 Piauí r. Brazil
254 E3 Piauí state Brazil
254 E4 Piauí, Serra de hills Brazil
191 N4 Piave r. Italy
244 A2 Piaxtla r. Mex.
190 I7 Piazza al Serchio Italy
194 G9 Piazza Armerina Sicilia Italy
190 H4 Piazza Brembana Italy
190 H4 Piazzatorre Italy
190 I3 Piazzi, Cima de' mt. Italy
259 B8 Piazzi, Isla i. Chile
191 L4 Piazzola sul Brenta Italy
210 B2 Pibor r. Sudan
210 B3 Pibor Post Sudan
163 G8 Pibrac France
224 C3 Pic r. Ont. Can.
252 C5 Pica Chile
241 U9 Picacho AZ U.S.A.
244 B3 Picachos Mex.
242 B3 Picachos, Cerro dos mt. Mex.
191 Q5 Pićan Croatia
187 C8 Picaracho mt. Spain
156 E4 Picardie admin. reg. France
156 C4 Picardie reg. France
Picardy reg. France see Picardie
187 E9 Picassent Spain
158 I3 Picauville France
237 K10 Picayune MS U.S.A.
191 L2 Picco della Croce mt. Italy
161 K6 Piccolo, Lago l. Italy
243 N8 Pich Mex.
260 B5 Pichachén, Paso pass Arg./Chile
242 F3 Picháchic Mex.
258 D1 Pichanal Arg.
260 B2 Pichasca Chile
170 D4 Picher Ger.
260 C3 Pichi Ciego Arg.
260 B3 Pichidanguí Chile
260 A4 Pichilemu Chile
242 D5 Pichilingue Mex.
260 E6 Pichi Mahuida Arg.
250 B5 Pichincha prov. Ecuador
179 I3 Pichl bei Wels Austria
116 G7 Pichor Madh. Prad. India
243 M9 Pichucalco Mex.
226 H1 Pic Island Ont. Can.
232 E10 Pickens WV U.S.A.
226 C1 Pickerel Lake Ont. Can.
227 O6 Pickering Ont. Can.
149 P5 Pickering North Yorkshi[re,] England U.K.
149 P5 Pickering, Vale of val. England U.K.
251 G3 Pickersgill Guyana
227 J3 Pickford MI U.S.A.
246 C3 Pickle Bank sea feature Caribbean Sea
224 B3 Pickle Lake Ont. Can.
216 □1c Pico i. Azores
216 □1c Pico mt. Pico Azores
193 L5 Pico Italy
183 J8 Pico, Puerto del pass S[pain]
242 □P10 Pico Bonito, Parque Nacional nat. park Hon[d.]
192 D9 Picocca r. Italy
251 E4 Pico da Neblina, Parqu[e] Nacional do nat. park B[razil]
245 J6 Pico de Orizaba, Parq[ue] Nacional nat. park Mex.
244 E6 Pico de Tancítaro, Par[que] Nacional nat. park Mex.
216 □1c Pico Gorda vol. Faial Az[ores]
185 K2 Picón Spain
254 E3 Picos Brazil
182 C5 Picos, Punta dos pt Sp[ain]
183 K2 Picos de Europa, Parq[ue] Nacional de los nat. pa[rk] Spain
250 B6 Picota Peru
182 C6 Picoto Port.
259 D7 Pico Truncado Arg.
156 D4 Picquigny France
226 H1 Pic River Ont. Can.
83 M6 Picton N.S.W. Austr.
224 E5 Picton Ont. Can.
81 I8 Picton South I. N.Z.
83 K10 Picton, Mount Tas. Aus[tr.]
225 I4 Pictou N.S. Can.
222 H5 Picture Butte Alta Can.
226 H3 Pictured Rocks Nationa[l] Lakeshore nature res. MI [U.S.A.]
234 B2 Picture Rocks PA U.S.A.
247 □1 Picua, Punta pt Puerto [Rico]
254 F3 Picuí Brazil
260 C6 Picún Leufú Arg.
260 C6 Picún Leufú r. Arg.
123 J9 Pidarak Pak.
175 M5 Pidberezzya Ukr.
175 L6 Pidbuzh Ukr.
150 H6 Piddle r. England U.K.
150 H6 Piddletrenthide Dorset, England U.K.
136 E4 Pidhaytsi Ukr.
136 J5 Pidhorodna Ukr.
137 O5 Pidhorodne Ukr.
175 L6 Pidhorodtsi Ukr.
173 N6 Piding Ger.
217 □3a Pidjani Njazidja Comoro[s]
136 E4 Pidkamin' Ukr.
137 L5 Pidlisne Ukr.
139 R1 Pid'ma Rus. Fed.
114 G9 Pidurutalagala mt. Sri [Lanka]
136 F4 Pidvolochys'k Ukr.
136 J5 Pidvysoke Ukr.
174 G3 Piechcin Pol.
174 D5 Piechowice Pol.
175 J2 Piecki Pol.
174 E2 Piecnik Pol.
216 □1c Piedade Pico Azores
256 D5 Piedade Brazil
184 B6 Piedade, Ponta da pt P[ort.]
260 C2 Pie de Palo, Sierra mts [Arg.]
192 C3 Piedicorte-di-Gaggio C[orse] France
192 C3 Piedicroce Corse Franc[e]
193 J2 Piediluco, Lago di l. Ita[ly]
195 I8 Piedimonte Etneo Sici[lia Italy]
193 M5 Piedimonte Matese Ita[ly]
190 E3 Piedimulera Italy
Piedmont admin. reg. It[aly see] Piemonte
231 E9 Piedmont AL U.S.A.
237 J7 Piedmont MO U.S.A.
232 D8 Piedmont OH U.S.A.
232 D8 Piedmont Lake OH U.S[.A.]
183 Q6 Piedra r. Spain
184 F3 Piedra Aguda, Embals[e de] resr Spain
185 K2 Piedrabuena Spain
259 C6 Piedra de Águila Arg.
245 J8 Piedra de Olla, Cerro m[t.]
Piedrafita Spain see Pedrafita do Cebreiro
182 F3 Piedrafita, Porto de pa[ss] Spain
182 H3 Piedrafita de Babia Sp[ain]
183 J8 Piedrahita Spain
183 K8 Piedralaves Spain
184 E6 Piedras, Embalse de r[esr] Spain
261 I4 Piedras, Punta pt Arg.
252 C3 Piedras, Río de las r. P[eru]
182 G9 Piedras Albas Spain
182 I1 Piedras Blancas Spain
240 K6 Piedras Blancas Point CA U.S.A.
183 L2 Piedrasluengas, Puert[o de] pass Spain
243 N9 Piedras Negras Guat.
243 I3 Piedras Negras Coahu[ila]
245 K7 Piedras Negras Veracru[z]
261 I3 Piedra Sola Uru.
261 F4 Piedritas Arg.
192 I2 Piegaro Italy
162 F4 Piégut-Pluviers France
226 E1 Pie Island Ont. Can.
174 G5 Piekary Śląskie Pol.
170 I1 Piekberg hill Ger.
175 I5 Piekoszów Pol.
140 S5 Pieksämäki Fin.
207 E3 Piéla Burkina
179 L3 Pielach r. Austria
140 S5 Pielavesi Fin.
140 S5 Pielavesi l. Fin.
174 D4 Pielgrzymka Pol.
140 T5 Pielinen l. Fin.
140 N3 Pieljekaise nationalpa[rk] nat. park Sweden
161 F10 Piémanson, Plage de coastal area France
190 D6 Piemonte admin. reg. It[aly]
215 M1 Pienaarsrivier S. Africa
174 E2 Pieniężnica Pol.
143 Q7 Pieniężno Pol.
175 I6 Pieniński Park Narodo[wy] nat. park Pol.
177 J2 Pieninský nat. park Slo[vakia]
174 E1 Pieńkowo Pol.
157 K5 Piennes France
174 D4 Pieńsk Pol.
192 H1 Pienza Italy
186 I4 Piera Spain
236 G4 Pierce NE U.S.A.
223 M4 Pierce Lake Man./Ont.
223 I4 Pierceland Sask. Can.
226 I8 Pierceton IN U.S.A.
261 H6 Pieres Arg.
198 D2 Pieria mts Greece
146 K4 Pierowall Orkney, Scotla[nd U.K.]
236 E3 Pierre SD U.S.A.
237 J10 Pierre, Bayou r. MS U.[S.A.]
237 I10 Pierre Bayou r. LA U.S[.A.]
162 G4 Pierre-Buffière France
161 H7 Pierre-Châtel France
160 G3 Pierre-de-Bresse Fran[ce]
161 I10 Pierrefeu-du-Var Fran[ce]
163 D10 Pierrefitte-Nestalas F[rance]
157 J6 Pierrefitte-sur-Aire Fr[ance]
160 D4 Pierrefitte-sur-Loire F[rance]
156 E5 Pierrefonds France
160 J2 Pierrefontaine-les-Va[rans] France
161 B7 Pierrefort France
161 F8 Pierrelatte France
157 K5 Pierrepont France
156 C6 Pierres France
160 D5 Pierre-sur-Haute mt. F[rance]
161 H9 Pierrevert France
247 □7 Pierreville Trin. and To[b.]
217 □1a Pierrot Island Rodrigu[es] Mauritius
156 G5 Pierry France
164 F5 Piershil Neth.
175 I5 Pierzchnica Pol.
171 D9 Piesau Ger.
178 G5 Piesendorf Austria
140 N3 Pieskehaure l. Sweden
174 D3 Pieski Pol.
172 B2 Piesport Ger.

Pieštany Slovakia
Pieszkowo Pol.
Pieszyce Pol.
Pieter Both *hill* Mauritius
Pietermaritzburg S. Africa
Pietersaari Fin. *see* **Jakobstad**
Pietersburg *Limpopo* S. Africa *see* **Polokwane**
Piet Plessis S. Africa
Pietrabbondante Italy
Pietracatella Italy
Pietracorbara *Corse* France
Pietra-di-Verde *Corse* France
Pietragalla Italy
Pietralba *Corse* France
Pietra Ligure Italy
Pietralunga Italy
Pietramelara Italy
Pietramontecorvino Italy
Pietraperzia *Sicilia* Italy
Pietraporzio Italy
Pietrasanta Italy
Pietra Spada, Passo di *pass* Italy
Pietrastornina Italy
Pietravairano Italy
Pietrelcina Italy
Piet Retief S. Africa
Pietroasa *Bihor* Romania
Pietroasa *Timiș* Romania
Pietrosella *Corse* France
Pietrosu, Vârful *mt.* Romania
Pietrosu, Vârful *mt.* Romania
Pietrosul Mare *nature res.* Romania
Pietrowice Wielkie Pol.
Pieve d'Alpago Italy
Pieve del Cairo Italy
Pieve di Bono Italy
Pieve di Cadore Italy
Pieve di Cadore, Lago di *l.* Italy
Pieve di Cento Italy
Pieve di Soligo Italy
Pieve di Teco Italy
Pievefavera, Lago di *l.* Italy
Pievepelago Italy
Pieve Santo Stefano Italy
Pieve Torina Italy
Pieve Vergonte Italy
Piffonds France
Pigeon *r.* Can./U.S.A.
Pigeon *MI* U.S.A.
Pigeon Bay *Ont.* Can.
Pigeon Bay *South I.* N.Z.
Pigeon Island Jamaica
Pigeon Lake *Alta* Can.
Pigeon Point St Lucia
Pigeon Point Trin. and Tob.
Pigeon River *MN* U.S.A.
Pigg *r. VA* U.S.A.
Piggott *AR* U.S.A.
Pigg's Peak Swaziland
Piglio Italy
Pigna Italy
Pignan France
Pignans France
Pignataro Interamna Italy
Pignataro Maggiore Italy
Pignola Italy
Pigon Aoou, Limni *l.* Greece
Pigs, Bay of Cuba *see* Cochinos, Bahía de
Pigüé Arg.
Piguicas *mt.* Mex.
Piha *North I.* N.Z.
Pihama *North I.* N.Z.
Pihani *Uttar Prad.* India
Piha Passage Tonga
Pi He *r.* China
Pihkva järv *l.* Estonia/Rus. Fed. *see* Pskov, Lake
Pihlajavesi *l.* Fin.
Pihlava Fin.
Pihtipudas Fin.
Pihuamo Mex.
Piikkiö Fin.
Piippola Fin.
Piirissaar *i.* Estonia
Piirsalu Estonia
Piispajärvi Fin.
Piis-Panewu *i. Chuuk* Micronesia
Piji *Sichuan* China *see* **Puge**
Pijijiapan Mex.
Pijnacker Neth.
Pikalevo Rus. Fed.
Pikasilla Estonia
Pike *NY* U.S.A.
Pike *WV* U.S.A.
Pike Bay *Ont.* Can.
Pike County *county PA* U.S.A.
Pikelot *i.* Micronesia
Pikes Creek Reservoir *PA* U.S.A.
Pikes Peak *CO* U.S.A.
Pikesville *MD* U.S.A.
Piketberg S. Africa
Piketon *OH* U.S.A.
Pikeville *KY* U.S.A.
Pikeville *TN* U.S.A.
Pikihatiti *b. Stewart I.* N.Z. *see* Port Pegasus
Pikirakatahi *mt. South I.* N.Z. *see* **Earnslaw, Mount**
Pikmeer *l.* Neth.
Pikou *Liaoning* China
Pikounda Congo
Pila Arg.
Pila Italy
Piła Pol.
Pila *mt.* Spain
Pila, Kyun *i.* Myanmar
Pila, Laguna de *l.* Arg.
Pila, Sierra de la *mts* Spain
Pilagá *r.* Arg.
Pilanesberg National Park S. Africa
Pilani *Rajasthan* India
Pilar *Buenos Aires* Arg.
Pilar *Córdoba* Arg.
Pilar *Santa Fé* Arg.
Pilar Para.
Pilar Phil.
Pilar, Cabo *c.* Chile
Pilar de Goiás Brazil
Pilar de la Horadada Spain
Pilar de la Mola Spain
Pilar do Sul Brazil
Pilas *i.* Phil.
Pilas Spain
Pilas Channel Phil.
Pilat, Mont *mt.* France
Pilat, Parc Naturel Régional du *nature res.* France
Pilatus *mt.* Switz.
Pilawa Pol.
Piława *r.* Pol.
Piława Górna Pol.
Pilaya *r.* Bol.
Pilcaniyeu Arg.
Pilchowicie, Jezioro *l.* Pol.
Pilchowo Pol.
Pilcomayo *r.* Bol./Para.
Pile, Jezioro *l.* Pol.
Pilenkovo Georgia *see* Gant'iadi
Piler *Andhra Prad.* India
Piles Spain
Píli *Kos* Greece *see* **Pyli**
Pili *Luzon* Phil.
Pili, Cerro *mt.* Chile
Piliakalnis *hill* Lith.
Pilibangan *Rajasthan* India
Pilibhit *Uttar Prad.* India
Pilica Pol.
Pilica *r.* Pol.
Pilipinas *country* Asia *see* Philippines
Pilis Hungary
Pilis *hill* Hungary
Piliscsév Hungary
Pilisi *park* Hungary
Pilisszentiván Hungary
Pilisszentkereszt Hungary
Pilisvörösvár Hungary
Pill Austria
Pillar *hill England* U.K.
Pillar Bay *Ascension* S. Atlantic Ocean

Pillau Rus. Fed. *see* **Baltiysk**
252 C3 **Pillcopata** Peru
178 G4 **Pillersee** *l.* Austria
83 L4 **Pilliga** *N.S.W.* Austr.
149 L6 **Pilling** *Lancashire, England* U.K.
261 G3 **Pillo, Isla del** *i.* Arg.
234 B3 **Pillow** *PA* U.S.A.
240 J2 **Pillsbury, Lake** *CA* U.S.A.
134 I5 **Pil'na** Rus. Fed.
137 P3 **Pil'na** Ukr.
137 P3 **Pil'na** *r.* Ukr.
150 G4 **Pilning** *South Gloucestershire, England* U.K.
134 L1 **Pil'nya, Ozero** *l.* Rus. Fed.
256 D2 **Pilões, Serra dos** *mts* Brazil
246 E4 **Pilón** Cuba
183 J2 **Piloña** *r.* Spain
Pílos Greece *see* **Pylos**
223 I2 **Pilot Lake** *N.W.T.* Can.
244 B5 **Piloto** Mex.
261 H2 **Piloto Ávila** Arg.
Piloto Juan Fernández *i.* S. Pacific Ocean *see* **Alejandro Selkirk, Isla**
240 O3 **Pilot Peak** *NV* U.S.A.
220 C4 **Pilot Point** *AK* U.S.A.
238 E4 **Pilot Rock** *OR* U.S.A.
220 B3 **Pilot Station** *AK* U.S.A.
237 K11 **Pilottown** *LA* U.S.A.
173 L3 **Pilsach** Ger.
Pilsen Czech Rep. *see* **Plzeň**
226 G5 **Pilsen** *WI* U.S.A.
175 H6 **Pilsko** *mt.* Pol.
173 N4 **Pilsting** Ger.
138 E4 **Piltene** Latvia
123 N9 **Pilu** Pak.
177 K5 **Pilu** Romania
96 C5 **Pilu, Nam** *r.* Myanmar
138 G7 **Pilvė** *r.* Lith.
138 G7 **Pilviškiai** Lith.
100 M3 **Pil'vo** Rus. Fed.
175 J6 **Pilzno** Pol.
241 W9 **Pima** *AZ* U.S.A.
253 E2 **Pimenta Bueno** Brazil
192 C9 **Pimentel** *Sardegna* Italy
116 E9 **Pimpalner** *Mahar.* India
150 H6 **Pimperne** *Dorset, England* U.K.
116 D9 **Pimpri** *Gujarat* India
208 D4 **Pimu** Dem. Rep. Congo
116 G3 **Pin** *r.* India
96 B4 **Pin** *r.* Myanmar
136 F1 **Pina** *r.* Belarus
186 D5 **Pina** Spain
187 D7 **Pina** *mt.* Spain
186 D4 **Pina, Embalse de** *resr* Spain
241 S10 **Pinacate, Cerro del** *mt.* Mex.
183 L5 **Piña de Esgueva** Spain
116 G6 **Pinahat** *Uttar Prad.* India
241 V9 **Pinaleno Mountains** *AZ* U.S.A.
92 C5 **Pinamalayan** *Mindoro* Phil.
261 I5 **Pinamar** Arg.
Pinang Malaysia *see* **George Town**
94 D2 **Pinang** *i.* Malaysia
94 D2 **Pinang** *state* Malaysia
95 L2 **Pinangah** *Sabah* Malaysia
185 I7 **Pinar** *mt.* Spain
187 L8 **Pinar, Cap des** *c.* Spain
185 O4 **Pinar, Puerto del** *pass* Spain
126 H4 **Pınarbaşı** Turkey
246 B2 **Pinar del Río** Cuba
126 C3 **Pınarhisar** Turkey
199 I5 **Pınarköy** Turkey
129 A7 **Pınarlar** Turkey
129 E6 **Pınarlı** Turkey
250 B5 **Piñas** Ecuador
190 C6 **Pinasca** Italy
90 F3 **Pinatubo, Mount** *vol.* Phil.
177 H5 **Pincehely** Hungary
151 L2 **Pinchbeck** *Lincolnshire, England* U.K.
222 H5 **Pincher Creek** *Alta* Can.
236 K6 **Pinckneyville** *IL* U.S.A.
159 J4 **Pinçon, Mont** *hill* France
227 K6 **Pinconning** *MI* U.S.A.
Pîncota Romania *see* **Pâncota**
175 I5 **Pińczów** Pol.
254 B5 **Pindaíba** Brazil
257 E5 **Pindamonhangaba** Brazil
87 C10 **Pindar** *W.A.* Austr.
116 G4 **Pindar** *r.* India
254 D2 **Pindaré** *r.* Brazil
254 D2 **Pindaré Mirim** Brazil
123 O5 **Pind Dadan Khay** Pak.
Píndhos Óros *mts* Greece *see* Pindos
123 O6 **Pindi Bhattian** Pak.
123 O5 **Pindi Gheb** Pak.
254 C2 **Pindobal** Brazil
198 B3 **Pindos** *mts* Greece
198 C3 **Pindou, Ethnikos Drymos** *nat. park* Greece
116 H8 **Pindrei** *Madh. Prad.* India
Pindus Mountains Greece *see* Pindos
116 D7 **Pindwara** *Rajasthan* India
82 H5 **Pine** *watercourse N.S.W.* Austr.
226 I5 **Pine** *r. MI* U.S.A.
226 J6 **Pine** *r. MI* U.S.A.
226 D6 **Pine** *r. WI* U.S.A.
226 F4 **Pine** *r. WI* U.S.A.
225 K4 **Pine, Cape** *Nfld and Lab.* Can.
237 I8 **Pine Bluff** *AR* U.S.A.
238 L6 **Pine Bluffs** *WY* U.S.A.
235 G1 **Pine Bush** *NY* U.S.A.
226 B4 **Pine City** *MN* U.S.A.
84 C2 **Pine Creek** *N.T.* Austr.
232 H7 **Pine Creek** *r. PA* U.S.A.
241 P1 **Pine Creek** *watercourse NV* U.S.A.
240 L3 **Pinecrest** *CA* U.S.A.
183 O8 **Pineda de Cigüela** Spain
183 N4 **Pineda de la Sierra** Spain
186 K4 **Pineda de Mar** Spain
238 J5 **Pinedale** *WY* U.S.A.
223 L5 **Pine Dock** *Man.* Can.
223 L5 **Pine Falls** *Man.* Can.
239 E8 **Pine Flat Lake** *CA* U.S.A.
134 H2 **Pinega** Rus. Fed.
134 H2 **Pinega** *r.* Rus. Fed.
87 C9 **Pinegrove** *W.A.* Austr.
232 A10 **Pine Grove** *KY* U.S.A.
227 R9 **Pine Grove** *PA* U.S.A.
232 E9 **Pine Grove** *WV* U.S.A.
84 D7 **Pine Hill** *N.T.* Austr.
234 F5 **Pine Hill** *NJ* U.S.A.
231 G11 **Pine Hills** *FL* U.S.A.
223 J4 **Pinehouse Lake** *Sask.* Can.
223 J4 **Pinehouse Lake** *l. Sask.* Can.
234 C6 **Pinehurst** *MD* U.S.A.
224 B2 **Pineimuta** *r. Ont.* Can.
198 D3 **Pineios** *r.* Greece
198 C5 **Pineiou, Techniti Limni** *resr* Greece
226 B5 **Pine Island** *MN* U.S.A.
235 G2 **Pine Island** *NY* U.S.A.
262 R2 **Pine Island Bay** Antarctica
262 R1 **Pine Island Glacier** Antarctica
231 F12 **Pine Islands** *FL* U.S.A.
231 G13 **Pine Islands** *FL* U.S.A.
182 G5 **Pinela** Port.
237 I10 **Pineland** *TX* U.S.A.
183 L5 **Piñel de Abajo** Spain
222 F4 **Pine Le Moray Provincial Park** *B.C.* Can.
81 D12 **Pinelheugh** *mt. South I.* N.Z.
231 F12 **Pinellas Park** *FL* U.S.A.
240 K6 **Pine Mountain** *CA* U.S.A.
241 S7 **Pine Peak** *AZ* U.S.A.
222 H2 **Pine Point** *N.W.T.* Can.
222 H2 **Pine Point** *pt N.W.T.* Can.
261 I3 **Piñera** Uru.
240 M4 **Pineridge** *CA* U.S.A.
236 D4 **Pine Ridge** *SD* U.S.A.
236 D4 **Pine Ridge Indian Reservation** *res. SD* U.S.A.
190 C6 **Pinerolo** Italy
198 F2 **Pines, Akrotirio** *pt* Greece
Pines, Isle of *i.* Cuba *see* **Juventud, Isla de la**
Pines, Isle of *i.* New Caledonia *see* Pins, Île des
237 H9 **Pines, Lake o' the** *TX* U.S.A.
190 F4 **Pinet di Appiano Tradate, Parco del** *park* Italy
193 M2 **Pineto** Italy
241 W7 **Pinetop** *AZ* U.S.A.
215 O5 **Pinetown** S. Africa
163 E6 **Pineuilh** France

227 R7 **Pine Valley** *NY* U.S.A.
232 B12 **Pineville** *KY* U.S.A.
237 I10 **Pineville** *LA* U.S.A.
234 E4 **Pineville** *PA* U.S.A.
232 D11 **Pineville** *WV* U.S.A.
156 H7 **Piney** France
96 E7 **Ping, Mae Nam** *r.* Thai.
116 D1 **Pingal** Jammu and Kashmir
106 H8 **Ping'an** *Qinghai* China
Ping'anyi *Qinghai* China *see* Ping'an
87 E12 **Pingaring** *W.A.* Austr.
108 F5 **Pingba** *Guizhou* China
108 D7 **Pingbian** *Yunnan* China
108 F3 **Pingchang** *Sichuan* China
108 C5 **Pingchuan** *Sichuan* China
107 P9 **Ping Dao** *i.* China
107 M8 **Pingding** *Shanxi* China
Pingdingbu *Hebei* China *see* Guyuan
109 I2 **Pingdingshan** *Henan* China
Pingdong Taiwan *see* P'ingtung
Pingdu *Jiangxi* China *see* **Anfu**
107 P8 **Pingdu** *Shandong* China
87 D12 **Pingelly** *W.A.* Austr.
100 D7 **Pinggang** *Liaoning* China
179 N5 **Pinggau** Austria
107 O6 **Pinggu** *Beijing* China
108 F7 **Pingguo** *Guangxi* China
109 J7 **Pinghai** *Guangdong* China
109 K6 **Pinghe** *Fujian* China
Pinghu *Guizhou* China *see* Pingtang
109 M3 **Pinghu** *Zhejiang* China
109 I4 **Pingjiang** *Hunan* China
108 H6 **Pingle** *Guangxi* China
108 G2 **Pingli** *Shaanxi* China
106 J9 **Pingliang** *Gansu* China
107 L9 **Pinglu** *Shanxi* China
106 J7 **Pingluo** *Ningxia* China
106 J7 **Pingluozhan** *Ningxia* China
Pingma *Guangxi* China *see* Tiandong
109 L5 **Pingnan** *Fujian* China
108 H7 **Pingnan** *Guangxi* China
107 J9 **Pingquan** *Gansu* China
107 P6 **Pingquan** *Hebei* China
87 E12 **Pingrup** *W.A.* Austr.
Pingshan *Guangdong* China *see* **Huidong**
107 N7 **Pingshan** *Hebei* China
108 E4 **Pingshan** *Sichuan* China
Pingshan *Yunnan* China *see* Luquan
109 I6 **Pingshi** *Guangdong* China
Pingshu *Hebei* China *see* Daicheng
109 L6 **Pingtan** *Fujian* China
Pingtan Dao *i.* China *see* **Haitan Dao**
108 F6 **Pingtang** *Guizhou* China
109 M7 **P'ingtung** Taiwan
108 E2 **Pingwu** *Sichuan* China
Pingxi *Guizhou* China *see* Yuping
Pingxiang *Gansu* China *see* Tongwei
108 F7 **Pingxiang** *Guangxi* China
109 I5 **Pingxiang** *Jiangxi* China
107 S2 **Pingyang** *Heilong.* China
109 M5 **Pingyang** *Zhejiang* China
107 M8 **Pingyao** *Shanxi* China
107 O9 **Pingyi** *Shandong* China
107 O8 **Pingyin** *Shandong* China
109 J2 **Pingyu** *Henan* China
109 J6 **Pingyuan** *Guangdong* China
107 O8 **Pingyuan** *Shandong* China
Pingyuan *Yunnan* China *see* Yingjiang
108 D7 **Pingyuanjie** *Yunnan* China
108 G6 **Pingzhai** *Guizhou* China
256 D5 **Pinhal** Brazil
184 B3 **Pinhal Novo** Port.
182 E6 **Pinhão** Port.
254 D2 **Pinheiro** Brazil
182 D6 **Pinheiro** *Porto* Port.
184 B4 **Pinheiro** *Setúbal* Port.
258 G3 **Pinheiro Machado** Brazil
257 G3 **Pinheiros** Brazil
182 F7 **Pinhel** Port.
150 F6 **Pinhoe** *Devon, England* U.K.
251 E6 **Pinhuã** *r.* Brazil
94 C4 **Pini** *i.* Indon.
185 N3 **Pinilla** *r.* Spain
183 M7 **Pinilla, Embalse de** *resr* Spain
183 Q7 **Pinilla de Molina** Spain
183 J5 **Pinilla de Toro** Spain
Piniós *r.* Greece *see* **Pineios**
87 C12 **Pinjarra** *W.A.* Austr.
87 G11 **Pinjin** *W.A.* Austr.
87 G11 **Pinjin Aboriginal Reserve** *W.A.* Austr.
179 N5 **Pinkafeld** Austria
82 E5 **Pinkawilinie Conservation Park** *nature res. S.A.* Austr.
84 B3 **Pinkerton Range** *hills N.T.* Austr.
222 F3 **Pink Mountain** *B.C.* Can.
96 C4 **Pinlaung** Myanmar
96 B2 **Pinlebu** Myanmar
81 H8 **Pinnacle** *mt. South I.* N.Z.
232 G9 **Pinnacle** *hill VA/WV* U.S.A.
240 K5 **Pinnacles National Monument** *nat. park CA* U.S.A.
82 H6 **Pinnaroo** *S.A.* Austr.
168 I3 **Pinnau** *r.* Ger.
168 I3 **Pinneberg** Ger.
171 K7 **Pinnow** Ger.
192 C2 **Pino** *Corse* France
182 H5 **Pino** Spain
183 K3 **Pino del Río** Spain
182 H8 **Pinofranqueado** Spain
95 I5 **Pinoh** *r.* Indon.
161 C6 **Pinols** France
240 O7 **Pinon Hills** *CA* U.S.A.
182 D3 **Piñor** Spain
244 F3 **Pinos** Mex.
186 I4 **Pinós** *hill* Spain
Pinos, Isla de *i.* Cuba *see* **Juventud, Isla de la**
240 M7 **Pinos, Mount** *CA* U.S.A.
187 C11 **Pinoso** Spain
183 O7 **Pinoso** *mt.* Spain
185 L6 **Pinos-Puente** Spain
245 I9 **Pinotepa Nacional** Mex.
93 A5 **Pinrang** *Sulawesi* Indon.
93 B5 **Pinrang** *Sulawesi* Indon.
217 □2b **Pins, Anse aux** *b. Mahé* Seychelles
78 □5 **Pins, Île des** *i.* New Caledonia
227 M7 **Pins, Pointe aux** *pt Ont.* Can.
163 H6 **Pinsac** France
179 I4 **Pinsdorf** Austria
136 F1 **Pinsk** Belarus
183 R4 **Pinsoro** Spain
250 □ **Pinta, Isla** *i. Islas Galápagos* Ecuador
241 S9 **Pinta, Sierra** *hill AZ* U.S.A.
239 L9 **Pintada Creek** *watercourse NM* U.S.A.
261 I2 **Pintado Grande** Uru.
252 C5 **Pintados** Chile
186 C2 **Pintano** Spain
95 L2 **Pintasan** *Sabah* Malaysia
183 M8 **Pinto** Spain
241 S4 **Pintura** *UT* U.S.A.
192 C6 **Pinu, Monte** *hill* Italy
146 G12 **Pinwherry** *South Ayrshire, Scotland* U.K.
191 N3 **Pinzano al Tagliamento** Italy
178 F5 **Pinzgau** *val.* Austria
182 F7 **Pinzio** Port.
191 J3 **Pinzolo** Italy
191 N8 **Piobbico** Italy
241 R4 **Pioche** *NV* U.S.A.
209 E6 **Piodi** Dem. Rep. Congo
78 □6 **Pio Island** Solomon Is
254 E3 **Pio IX** Brazil
161 F8 **Piolenc** France
190 G5 **Pioltello** Italy
193 M2 **Piomba** *r.* Italy
192 F2 **Piombino** Italy
192 E2 **Piombino, Canale di** *sea chan.* Italy
191 L4 **Piombino Dese** Italy
232 A7 **Pioneer** *OH* U.S.A.
238 H4 **Pioneer Mountains** *MT* U.S.A.
131 K2 **Pioner, Ostrov** *i. Severnaya Zemlya* Rus. Fed.

138 D7 **Pionerskiy** *Kaliningradskaya Oblast'* Rus. Fed.
130 H3 **Pionerskiy** *Khanty-Mansiyskiy Avtonomnyy Okrug* Rus. Fed.
175 J4 **Pionki** Pol.
160 B4 **Pionsat** France
80 J5 **Piopio** *North I.* N.Z.
Piopiotahi *inlet South I.* N.Z. *see* **Milford Sound**
193 J1 **Pioraco** Italy
251 F5 **Piorini** *r.* Brazil
251 F5 **Piorini, Lago** *l.* Brazil
190 C6 **Piossasco** Italy
174 E4 **Piotrkowice** Pol.
174 G3 **Piotrków Kujawski** Pol.
175 H4 **Piotrków Trybunalski** Pol.
191 M5 **Piove di Sacco** Italy
191 K4 **Piovene Rocchette** Italy
190 G3 **Pioverna** *r.* Italy
122 I8 **Pīp** Iran
100 F7 **Pipa Dingzi** *mt.* China
258 D3 **Pipanaco, Salar de** *salt flat* Arg.
116 D6 **Pipar** *Rajasthan* India
116 D6 **Pipar Road** *Rajasthan* India
198 F3 **Piperi** *i.* Greece
240 O4 **Piper Peak** *NV* U.S.A.
234 E4 **Pipersville** *PA* U.S.A.
223 K5 **Pipestone** *Man.* Can.
224 B2 **Pipestone** *r. Ont.* Can.
236 G4 **Pipestone** *MN* U.S.A.
197 O3 **Pipirig** Romania
80 J6 **Pipiriki** *North I.* N.Z.
116 E5 **Pipli** *Haryana* India
225 G3 **Pipmuacan, Réservoir** *resr Que.* Can.
86 E6 **Pippingarra Aboriginal Reserve** *W.A.* Austr.
116 H9 **Pipraud** *Chhattisgarh* India
158 H6 **Pipriac** France
Piqan *Xinjiang* China *see* **Shanshan**
110 E6 **Piqanlik** *Xinjiang* China
232 A8 **Piqua** *OH* U.S.A.
163 F9 **Pique** *r.* France
183 O4 **Piqueras, Puerto de** *pass* Spain
254 F3 **Piquet Carneiro** Brazil
257 E5 **Piquete** Brazil
256 A6 **Piquiri** *r.* Brazil
253 G4 **Piquiri** *r.* Brazil
177 L4 **Pir** Romania
256 D5 **Piracaia** Brazil
256 C2 **Piracanjuba** Brazil
256 C3 **Piracanjuba** *r.* Brazil
256 D5 **Piracicaba** Brazil
256 C5 **Piracicaba** *r.* Brazil
257 F3 **Piracicaba** *r.* Brazil
256 D4 **Piraçununga** Brazil
254 E2 **Piracuruca** Brazil
79 □9a **Pirae** *Tahiti* Fr. Polynesia
Piraeus Greece *see* **Peiraias**
256 C6 **Piraí do Sul** Brazil
Piráievs Greece *see* **Peiraias**
194 H7 **Piraino** *Sicilia* Italy
256 C5 **Piraju** Brazil
256 C3 **Pirajuba** Brazil
256 C4 **Pirajuí** Brazil
129 L5 **Pirallahı Adası** Azer.
191 P4 **Piran** Slovenia
258 F2 **Pirané** Arg.
257 F4 **Piranga** Brazil
257 F4 **Piranga** *r.* Brazil
257 E5 **Piranguinho** Brazil
254 F4 **Piranhas** *Alagoas* Brazil
251 F6 **Piranhas** *Amazonas* Brazil
256 B2 **Piranhas** *Goiás* Brazil
256 B2 **Piranhas** *r.* Brazil
254 F3 **Piranhas** *r.* Brazil
254 D2 **Pirapemas** Brazil
253 E1 **Pirapetinga** *Amazonas* Brazil
257 F4 **Pirapetinga** *Minas Gerais* Brazil
256 A5 **Pirapó** *r.* Brazil
257 E2 **Pirapora** Brazil
256 B5 **Pirapozinho** Brazil
253 F4 **Piraputangas** Brazil
256 C6 **Piraquara** Brazil
251 G4 **Pirara** Guyana
258 G4 **Pirarajá** Uru.
117 J6 **Pirari** Nepal
258 G3 **Piratini** Brazil
256 C5 **Piratininga** Brazil
225 G3 **Piraube, Lac** *l. Que.* Can.
116 F7 **Pirawa** *Rajasthan* India
129 I5 **Pirăză** Azer.
151 K5 **Pirbright** *Surrey, England* U.K.
Pirchevan Azer. *see* **Zängilan**
175 M1 **Pirčiupiai** Lith.
259 C6 **Pire Mahuida, Sierra** *mts* Arg.
256 C1 **Pirenópolis** Brazil
256 C2 **Pires do Rio** Brazil
117 L7 **Pirganj** Bangl.
Pírgos Greece *see* **Pyrgos**
197 N7 **Pirgovo** Bulg.
158 F7 **Piriac-sur-Mer** France
80 J5 **Piriaka** *North I.* N.Z.
258 G4 **Piriápolis** Uru.
177 L4 **Piricse** Hungary
197 L9 **Pirin** *mts* Bulg.
197 L9 **Pirin** *nat. park* Bulg.
254 E3 **Piripiri** Brazil
138 H2 **Pirita** *r.* Estonia
250 D2 **Píritu** *Falcón* Venez.
250 D2 **Píritu** *Portuguesa* Venez.
253 F4 **Pirizal** Brazil
179 L5 **Pirka** Austria
141 Q6 **Pirkkala** Fin.
123 I6 **Pir Kundil** Afgh.
Pirlerkondu Turkey *see* **Taşkent**
172 D3 **Pirmasens** Ger.
114 E8 **Pirmed** *Kerala* India
122 G5 **Pīr Morāl** *spring* Iran
171 I9 **Pirna** Ger.
146 F11 **Pirnmill** *North Ayrshire, Scotland* U.K.
117 L8 **Pirojpur** Bangl.
183 K6 **Pirón** *r.* Spain
80 J4 **Pirongia** *North I.* N.Z.
80 J4 **Pirongia** *vol. North I.* N.Z.
80 J4 **Pirongia Forest Park** *nature res. North I.* N.Z.
139 Q3 **Piros, Ozero** *l.* Rus. Fed.
197 K7 **Pirot** Serbia
261 G5 **Pirovano** Arg.
117 K7 **Pirpainti** *Bihar* India
116 E3 **Pir Panjal Pass** Jammu and Kashmir
116 D2 **Pir Panjal Range** *mts* India/Pak.
127 K4 **Pirrasit Dağ** *hill* Turkey
129 K6 **Pirsaat** Azer.
129 J5 **Pirsaatçay** *r.* Azer.
177 I5 **Pirtó** Hungary
140 O3 **Pirttivuopio** Sweden
93 F5 **Piru** *Seram* Indon.
93 F5 **Piru, Teluk** *b. Seram* Indon.
Pir'yakh, Gora *mt.* Tajik. *see* **Piryakh, Kŭhi**
123 M2 **Piryakh, Kŭhi** *mt.* Tajik.
Piryatin Ukr. *see* **Pyryatyn**
Piryetós Greece *see* **Pyrgetos**
Piryíon *Chios* Greece *see* **Pyrgi**
123 K6 **Pirzada** Afgh.
190 I8 **Pisa** Italy
191 J9 **Pisa** *prov.* Italy
175 J2 **Pisa** *r.* Pol.
252 C3 **Pisac** Peru
Pisae Italy *see* **Pisa**
252 C4 **Pisagua** Chile
78 □4a **Pisamwe** *i. Chuuk* Micronesia
93 F4 **Pisang** *i. Maluku* Indon.
162 C4 **Pisany** France
78 □4a **Pisar** *i. Chuuk* Micronesia
81 D11 **Pisa Range** *mts South I.* N.Z.
95 M1 **Pisau, Tanjung** *pt* Malaysia
Pisaurum Italy *see* **Pesaro**
250 C3 **Pisba, Parque Nacional** *nat. park* Col.
235 F3 **Piscataway** *NJ* U.S.A.
179 M5 **Pischelsdorf in der Steiermark** Austria
177 K6 **Pişchia** Romania
193 O7 **Pisciotta** Italy
252 A3 **Pisco** Peru
252 A3 **Pisco** *r.* Peru
260 B2 **Pisco Elqui** Chile
177 L4 **Pişcolt** Romania
179 M7 **Pišece** Slovenia
233 K5 **Piseco Lake** *NY* U.S.A.

176 D2 **Písek** Czech Rep.
81 B12 **Pisgah, Mount** *South I.* N.Z.
81 E12 **Pisgah, Mount** *South I.* N.Z.
122 F5 **Pish** Iran
Pisha *Sichuan* China *see* Ningnan
111 D8 **Pishan** *Xinjiang* China
136 C2 **Pishcha** Ukr.
136 I5 **Pishchana** Ukr.
137 K4 **Pishchane** Ukr.
136 H5 **Pishchanka** Ukr.
137 M8 **Pishchanyy, Mys** *pt* Ukr.
123 I8 **Pīshīn** Iran
123 L6 **Pishin** Pak.
123 K7 **Pishin Lora** *r.* Pak.
123 I9 **Pishkan, Ras** *pt* Pak.
Pishpek Kyrg. *see* **Bishkek**
120 G9 **Pīsh Qal'eh** Iran
175 I3 **Pisia** *r.* Pol.
126 E5 **Pisidia** *reg.* Turkey
93 B6 **Pising** *Sulawesi* Indon.
241 T9 **Pisinimo** *AZ* U.S.A.
78 □4a **Pisininin** *i. Chuuk* Micronesia
121 M7 **Piskent** Uzbek.
136 I3 **Piskivka** Ukr.
137 Q4 **Pisky** *Kharkivs'ka Oblast'* Ukr.
137 S4 **Pisky** *Luhans'ka Oblast'* Ukr.
240 L6 **Pismo Beach** *CA* U.S.A.
253 E3 **Piso Firme** Bol.
190 I4 **Pisogne** Italy
138 E7 **Pissa** *r.* Rus. Fed.
258 C2 **Pissis, Cerro** *mt.* Arg.
163 C7 **Pissos** France
140 U4 **Pista** *r.* Rus. Fed.
243 O7 **Pisté** Mex.
195 L3 **Pisticci** Italy
191 J8 **Pistoia** Italy
191 J8 **Pistoia** *prov.* Italy
Pistoriae Italy *see* **Pistoia**
139 X4 **Pistsovo** Rus. Fed.
183 K5 **Pisuerga** *r.* Spain
175 J2 **Pisz** Pol.
175 L4 **Piszczac** Pol.
238 C6 **Pit** *r. CA* U.S.A.
206 B4 **Pita** Guinea
225 H2 **Pitaga** *Nfld and Lab.* Can.
243 N8 **Pital** Mex.
250 B4 **Pitalito** Col.
256 B6 **Pitanga** Brazil
256 C4 **Pitangueiras** Brazil
257 E3 **Pitangui** Brazil
116 C8 **Pitar** *Gujarat* India
83 I6 **Pitarpunga Lake** *imp. l. N.S.W.* Austr.
186 D6 **Pitarque** Spain
267 K7 **Pitcairn Island** S. Pacific Ocean
206 B3 **Pitche** Guinea-Bissau
247 □7 **Pitch Lake** Trin. and Tob.
140 P4 **Piteå** Sweden
140 P4 **Piteälven** *r.* Sweden
191 J7 **Piteglio** Italy
135 H5 **Pitelino** Rus. Fed.
120 B2 **Piterka** Rus. Fed.
197 M6 **Pitești** Romania
87 D11 **Pithara** *W.A.* Austr.
156 D7 **Pithiviers** France
116 H5 **Pithoragarh** *Uttaranchal* India
78 □1 **Piti** Guam
123 L9 **Pitiani Creek** *inlet* Pak.
192 H2 **Pitigliano** Italy
116 G8 **Pitihra** *Madh. Prad.* India
183 Q4 **Pitillas** Spain
163 A11 **Pitillas, Laguna de** *l.* Spain
242 C2 **Pitiquito** Mex.
134 E3 **Pitkyaranta** Rus. Fed.
146 I9 **Pitlochry** *Perth and Kinross, Scotland* U.K.
234 E5 **Pitman** *NJ* U.S.A.
146 L8 **Pitmedden** *Aberdeenshire, Scotland* U.K.
150 F6 **Pitminster** *Somerset, England* U.K.
207 I4 **Pitoa** Cameroon
188 F3 **Pitomača** Croatia
217 □1c **Piton de la Fournaise** *vol.* Réunion
217 □1b **Piton de la Petite Rivière Noire** *hill* Mauritius
217 □1c **Piton des Neiges** *mt.* Réunion
Pitong *Sichuan* China *see* Pixian
156 B5 **Pîtres** France
185 M7 **Pitres** Spain
260 A6 **Pitrufquén** Chile
215 J1 **Pitsane Siding** Botswana
179 L6 **Pitschgau** Austria
215 M5 **Pitseng** Lesotho
151 K3 **Pitsford Reservoir** *England* U.K.
151 K4 **Pitstone** *Buckinghamshire, England* U.K.
Pitsunda Georgia *see* Bichvint'a
151 J5 **Pitt** *Hampshire, England* U.K.
165 D7 **Pittem** Belgium
179 N4 **Pitten** Austria
146 H7 **Pittentrail** *Highland, Scotland* U.K.
146 K10 **Pittenweem** *Fife, Scotland* U.K.
114 C7 **Pitti** *i.* India
114 C7 **Pitti Sand Bank** *sea feature* India
222 D4 **Pitt Island** *B.C.* Can.
80 □ **Pitt Island** *Chatham Is* S. Pacific Ocean
Pitt Islands *Santa Cruz Is* Solomon Is *see* Vanikoro Islands
237 K9 **Pittsboro** *MS* U.S.A.
231 H8 **Pittsboro** *NC* U.S.A.
240 K3 **Pittsburg** *CA* U.S.A.
237 H7 **Pittsburg** *KS* U.S.A.
233 N3 **Pittsburg** *NH* U.S.A.
237 H9 **Pittsburg** *TX* U.S.A.
232 F8 **Pittsburgh** *PA* U.S.A.
236 J6 **Pittsfield** *IL* U.S.A.
233 L6 **Pittsfield** *MA* U.S.A.
233 □P4 **Pittsfield** *ME* U.S.A.
233 N5 **Pittsfield** *NH* U.S.A.
233 M5 **Pittsfield** *VT* U.S.A.
234 D2 **Pittston** *PA* U.S.A.
233 □P3 **Pittston Farm** *ME* U.S.A.
80 □ **Pitt Strait** *Chatham Is* S. Pacific Ocean
226 D5 **Pittsville** *WI* U.S.A.
85 M9 **Pittsworth** *Qld* Austr.
84 G7 **Pituri Creek** *watercourse Qld* Austr.
177 J5 **Pitvaros** Hungary
223 L2 **Pitz Lake** *Nunavut* Can.
178 C5 **Pitztal** *val.* Austria
254 C4 **Pium** Brazil
257 E4 **Piumhí** Brazil
250 A6 **Piura** Peru
250 A6 **Piura** *dept* Peru
138 K4 **Piusa** *r.* Estonia
241 Q7 **Piute Mountains** *CA* U.S.A.
240 N6 **Piute Peak** *CA* U.S.A.
117 I5 **Piuthan** Nepal
224 D3 **Pivabiska** *r. Ont.* Can.
175 M1 **Pivašiūnai** Lith.
136 K7 **Pivdennyy Buh** *r.* Ukr.
250 C2 **Pivijay** Col.
188 E3 **Pivka** Slovenia
191 Q4 **Pivka** *r.* Slovenia
137 N8 **Pivnichno-Kryms'kyy Kanal** *canal* Ukr.
175 I6 **Piwniczna-Zdrój** Pol.
111 D8 **Pixa** *Xinjiang* China
Pixariá *mt.* Greece *see* **Pyxaria**
108 D3 **Pixian** *Sichuan* China
240 M6 **Pixley** *CA* U.S.A.
243 N8 **Pixoyal** Mex.
252 C4 **Pizacoma** Peru
185 J7 **Pizarra** Spain
190 H3 **Piz Bernina** *mt.* Italy/Switz.
178 E6 **Piz Boè** *mt.* Italy
178 B6 **Piz Buin** *mt.* Austria/Switz.
190 G2 **Piz d'Anarosa** *mt.* Switz.
190 H3 **Piz Duan** *mt.* Switz.
190 H2 **Piz Ela** *mt.* Switz.
134 J4 **Pizhanka** Rus. Fed.
207 G4 **Pizhi** Nigeria
134 I4 **Pizhma** Rus. Fed.
134 J4 **Pizhma** *r.* Rus. Fed.
134 K2 **Pizhma** *r.* Rus. Fed.
107 P9 **Pizhou** *Jiangsu* China
190 H2 **Piz Kesch** *mt.* Switz.
190 F2 **Piz Medel** *mt.* Switz.
190 G2 **Pizol** *mt.* Switz.

190 I2 **Piz Pisoc** *mt.* Switz.
190 H3 **Piz Platta** *mt.* Switz.
190 H3 **Piz Varuna** *mt.* Italy/Switz.
190 H5 **Pizzighettone** Italy
195 K6 **Pizzo** Italy
193 M4 **Pizzoferrato** Italy
193 K3 **Pizzoli** Italy
193 J3 **Pizzuto, Monte** *mt.* Italy
92 □ **Pkulagalid Point** Palau
92 □ **Pkulagasemieg** *pt* Palau
92 □ **Pkulngril** *pt* Palau
92 □ **Pkurengei** *pt* Palau
170 F3 **Plaaz** Ger.
158 C4 **Plabennec** France
160 L5 **Place Moulin, Lago di** *l.* Italy
225 K4 **Placentia** *Nfld and Lab.* Can.
Placentia Italy *see* **Piacenza**
225 K4 **Placentia Bay** *Nfld and Lab.* Can.
92 D6 **Placer** *Masbate* Phil.
92 E7 **Placer** *Mindanao* Phil.
240 L3 **Placerville** *CA* U.S.A.
239 J7 **Placerville** *CO* U.S.A.
246 D2 **Placetas** Cuba
252 D2 **Plácido de Castro** Brazil
260 B3 **Placilla** Chile
190 C2 **Plaffeien** Switz.
169 D10 **Plaidt** Ger.
97 F7 **Plai Mat, Lam** *r.* Thai.
159 P7 **Plaimpied-Givaudins** France
237 I9 **Plain Dealing** *LA* U.S.A.
209 A5 **Plaine Ouanga, Réserve de la** *nature res.* Gabon
157 N7 **Plainfaing** France
235 L1 **Plainfield** *CT* U.S.A.
230 D6 **Plainfield** *IN* U.S.A.
235 G3 **Plainfield** *NJ* U.S.A.
233 M4 **Plainfield** *VT* U.S.A.
226 E5 **Plainfield** *WI* U.S.A.
237 E7 **Plains** *KS* U.S.A.
237 D9 **Plains** *TX* U.S.A.
234 F4 **Plainsboro** *NJ* U.S.A.
158 F5 **Plaintel** France
226 B5 **Plainview** *MN* U.S.A.
236 G4 **Plainview** *NE* U.S.A.
235 I3 **Plainview** *NY* U.S.A.
237 E8 **Plainview** *TX* U.S.A.
235 J1 **Plainville** *CT* U.S.A.
236 F6 **Plainville** *KS* U.S.A.
226 I7 **Plainwell** *MI* U.S.A.
163 E8 **Plaisance** France
246 G4 **Plaisance** Haiti
163 G8 **Plaisance-du-Touch** France
156 C6 **Plaisir** France
233 N6 **Plaistow** *NH* U.S.A.
94 F6 **Plaju** *Sumatera* Indon.
199 G2 **Plaka** *Limnos* Greece
199 H7 **Plaka, Akrotirio** *pt Kriti* Greece
128 C3 **Plakoti, Cape** Cyprus
95 L9 **Plampang** *Sumbawa* Indon.
176 B2 **Planá** Czech Rep.
187 E11 **Plana, Isla** *i.* Spain
187 K9 **Plana, Sa Punta** *pt* Spain
246 G2 **Plana Cays** *is* Bahamas
240 L4 **Planada** *CA* U.S.A.
256 D1 **Planaltina** Brazil
171 L10 **Plaňany** Czech Rep.
157 M8 **Plancher-Bas** France
157 M8 **Plancher-les-Mines** France
260 **Planchón, Paso del** *pass* Arg.
Planchón, Portezuelo del *pass* Arg. *see* Planchón, Paso del
158 G4 **Plancoët** France
156 G6 **Plancy-l'Abbaye** France
245 J6 **Plan de Arroyos** Mex.
244 F4 **Plan de Ayala** Mex.
244 C4 **Plan de Barrancas** Mex.
161 G7 **Plan-de-Baux** France
161 G10 **Plan-de-Cuques** France
245 K6 **Plan de las Hayas** Mex.
161 J10 **Plan-de-la-Tour** France
196 J5 **Plandište** *Vojvodina* Serbia
161 F9 **Plan-d'Orgon** France
171 F6 **Plane** *r.* Ger.
217 □2b **Planeau, Montagne** *plat. Mahé* Seychelles
173 K5 **Planegg** Ger.
163 I11 **Planès** France
161 B7 **Planèze** *reg.* France
176 C2 **Plánice** Czech Rep.
161 G10 **Planier, Île de** *i.* France
191 Q5 **Planik** *mt.* Croatia
179 J8 **Planina** *Postojna* Slovenia
179 L7 **Planina** *Šentjur pri Celju* Slovenia
173 K2 **Plankenfels** Ger.
236 F4 **Plankinton** *SD* U.S.A.
226 F8 **Plano** *IL* U.S.A.
237 G9 **Plano** *TX* U.S.A.
261 I1 **Plano Alto** Brazil
178 C5 **Plansee** *l.* Austria
246 □ **Plantain Garden** *r.* Jamaica
260 B3 **Planta Los Queltehues** Chile
216 □2b **Plantation House** St Helena
163 G9 **Plantaurel, Montagnes du** *hills* France
231 F12 **Plant City** *FL* U.S.A.
235 J1 **Plantsville** *CT* U.S.A.
256 C4 **Planura** Brazil
237 J10 **Plaquemine** *LA* U.S.A.
182 H8 **Plasencia** Spain
186 C4 **Plasencia, Llano de** *plain* Spain
186 D3 **Plasencia del Monte** Spain
175 L2 **Płaska** Pol.
188 E3 **Plaški** Croatia
196 J9 **Plasnica** Macedonia
120 I1 **Plast** Rus. Fed.
241 Q9 **Plaster City** *CA* U.S.A.
225 H4 **Plaster Rock** *N.B.* Can.
215 P1 **Plaston** S. Africa
177 H3 **Plášťovce** Slovakia
100 J6 **Plastun** Rus. Fed.
129 A2 **Plastunka** Rus. Fed.
137 S8 **Plastunovskaya** Rus. Fed.
176 C2 **Plasy** Czech Rep.
196 G8 **Platamon, Rt** *pt* Montenegro
192 A6 **Platamona Lido** *Sardegna* Italy
198 D3 **Platamonas** Greece
252 C4 **Platanal** Peru
194 E9 **Platani** *r. Sicilia* Italy
195 K5 **Platania** Italy
198 E3 **Platanias** Greece
245 L9 **Platanillo** Mex.
198 F4 **Platanistos** Greece
198 C5 **Platanos** Greece
214 C6 **Platbakkies** S. Africa
215 N4 **Platberg** *mt.* S. Africa
170 E3 **Plate** Ger.
207 G4 **Plateau** *state* Nigeria
165 I8 **Plateau des Tailles, Réserves Domaniales du** *nature res.* Belgium
208 B5 **Plateaux** *admin. reg.* Congo
138 E5 **Plateliai** Lith.
140 □ **Platen, Kapp** *c.* Svalbard
168 K5 **Platendorf (Sassenburg)** Ger.
244 E2 **Plateros** Mex.
214 E9 **Plathuis** S. Africa
195 K7 **Platì** Italy
196 H6 **Platičevo** *Vojvodina* Serbia
Platíkambos Greece *see* Platykampos
240 J1 **Platina** *CA* U.S.A.
220 B4 **Platinum** *AK* U.S.A.
186 L4 **Platja d'Aro** Spain
137 S8 **Platnirovskaya** Rus. Fed.
250 C2 **Plato** Col.
258 C2 **Plato de Sopa** Chile
245 I4 **Platón Sánchez** Mex.
215 N3 **Platrand** S. Africa
236 H6 **Platte** *r. MO* U.S.A.
236 H5 **Platte** *r. NE* U.S.A.
236 H6 **Platte City** *MO* U.S.A.
217 □2 **Platte Island** Seychelles
235 G1 **Plattekill** *NY* U.S.A.
179 K3 **Plattenberg** *hill* Austria
238 L6 **Platteville** *CO* U.S.A.
236 J4 **Platteville** *WI* U.S.A.
173 N4 **Plattling** Ger.
233 L4 **Plattsburgh** *NY* U.S.A.
236 H5 **Plattsmouth** *NE* U.S.A.
198 D2 **Platy** Greece
198 D3 **Platykampos** Greece
170 F4 **Plau** Ger.
169 K9 **Plaue** Ger.
171 F9 **Plauen** Ger.
170 F4 **Plauer See** *l.* Ger.
196 H8 **Plav** Montenegro

136 G2 **Plav** *r.* Ukr.
139 U8 **Plava** *r.* Rus. Fed.
176 G3 **Plavecký Mikuláš** Slovakia
179 P3 **Plavecký Štvrtok** Slovakia
138 I5 **Pļaviņas** Latvia
137 T1 **Plavitsa** *r.* Rus. Fed.
188 E3 **Plavnik** *i.* Croatia
139 U8 **Plavsk** Rus. Fed.
244 E8 **Playa Azul** Mex.
216 □3c **Playa Blanca** *Lanzarote* Canary Is
216 □3b **Playa Blanca** *coastal area Fuerteventura* Canary Is
261 I6 **Playa Chapadmalal** Arg.
244 D7 **Playa Corrida de San Juan, Punta** *pt* Mex.
216 □3b **Playa de Barlovento** *coastal area Fuerteventura* Canary Is
184 F6 **Playa de Castilla** *coastal area* Spain
247 □1 **Playa de Fajardo** Puerto Rico
216 □3a **Playa de las Americas** *Tenerife* Canary Is
243 P7 **Playa del Carmen** Mex.
181 □ **Playa del Inglés** *Gran Canaria* Canary Is
216 □3b **Playa de Sotavento** *coastal area Fuerteventura* Canary Is
245 L7 **Playa Hermosa** Mex.
261 I4 **Playa Pascaul** Uru.
250 A5 **Playas** Ecuador
245 N8 **Playas** *r.* Mex.
216 □3b **Playas de Corralejo** *coastal area Fuerteventura* Canary Is
245 L8 **Playa Vicente** Mex.
84 F5 **Playford** *watercourse N.T.* Austr.
223 L4 **Playgreen Lake** *Man.* Can.
97 I8 **Plây Ku** Vietnam
242 E5 **Playón** Mex.
250 C2 **Playones de Santa Ana** *l.* Col.
183 O2 **Plaza** Spain
162 G5 **Plazac** France
185 J3 **Plaza del Judío** *mt.* Spain
260 C6 **Plaza Huincul** Arg.
175 L5 **Płazów** Pol.
241 T8 **Pleasant, Lake** *AZ* U.S.A.
233 □S3 **Pleasant, Mount** *hill N.B.* Can.
233 P7 **Pleasant Bay** *MA* U.S.A.
234 D3 **Pleasant Corners** *PA* U.S.A.
235 G4 **Pleasant Grove** *NJ* U.S.A.
241 U1 **Pleasant Grove** *UT* U.S.A.
240 J4 **Pleasant Hill** *CA* U.S.A.
232 A8 **Pleasant Hill** *OH* U.S.A.
240 K4 **Pleasanton** *CA* U.S.A.
237 F11 **Pleasanton** *TX* U.S.A.
81 F11 **Pleasant Point** *South I.* N.Z.
235 H1 **Pleasant Valley** *NY* U.S.A.
234 D5 **Pleasantville** *DE* U.S.A.
234 F6 **Pleasantville** *NJ* U.S.A.
235 H2 **Pleasantville** *NY* U.S.A.
234 B5 **Pleaseant Hill** *PA* U.S.A.
149 O7 **Pleasley** *Derbyshire, England* U.K.
235 K2 **Pleasure Beach** *CT* U.S.A.
234 B5 **Pleasureville** *PA* U.S.A.
162 I5 **Pleaux** France
173 K2 **Plech** Ger.
176 C3 **Plechý** *mt.* Czech Rep.
175 H3 **Plecka Dąbrowa** Pol.
158 F5 **Plédran** France
158 E4 **Pléhédel** France
97 H7 **Plei Doch** Vietnam
95 K6 **Pleihari Martapura, Suaka Margasatwa** *nature res.* Indon.
95 K7 **Pleihari Tanah, Suaka Margasatwa** *nature res. Kalimantan* Indon.
97 H7 **Plei Kân** Vietnam
158 H4 **Pleine-Fougères** France
173 J3 **Pleinfeld** Ger.
173 N5 **Pleiskirchen** Ger.
171 G9 **Pleiße** Ger.
171 F8 **Pleiße** *r.* Ger.
137 S1 **Plekhanovo** Rus. Fed.
158 G5 **Plélan-le-Grand** France
158 G5 **Plélan-le-Petit** France
158 F4 **Plélo** France
158 F5 **Plémet** France
158 G5 **Plénée-Jugon** France
158 F4 **Pléneuf-Val-André** France
84 F8 **Plenty** *watercourse N.T.* Austr.
80 K4 **Plenty, Bay of** *g. North I.* N.Z.
238 L2 **Plentywood** *MT* U.S.A.
183 O2 **Plentzia** Spain
158 F4 **Plérin** France
139 Y4 **Ples** Rus. Fed.
179 L5 **Pleschkogel** *mt.* Austria
158 F6 **Plescop** France
177 L5 **Pleșcuța** Romania
134 H3 **Plesetsk** Rus. Fed.
120 E1 **Pleshanovo** Rus. Fed.
Pleshchentsy Belarus *see* Plyeshchanitsy
139 V5 **Pleshcheyevo, Ozero** *l.* Rus. Fed.
177 J3 **Plešivec** Slovakia
179 K7 **Plešivec** *mt.* Slovenia
158 G4 **Pleslin-Trigavou** France
176 B1 **Plesná** Czech Rep.
139 S2 **Pleso** Rus. Fed.
169 J9 **Pleß** *hill* Ger.
171 I8 **Plessa** Ger.
158 H6 **Plessé** France
158 D4 **Plestin-les-Grèves** France
174 F4 **Pleszew** Pol.
137 K5 **Pletenyy Tashlyk** Ukr.
188 F3 **Pleternica** Croatia
225 G3 **Plétipi, Lac** *l. Que.* Can.
169 E8 **Plettenberg** Ger.
214 H10 **Plettenberg Bay** S. Africa
179 K5 **Pletzen** *mt.* Austria
158 E4 **Pleubian** France
158 H4 **Pleudihen-sur-Rance** France
159 M8 **Pleumartin** France
158 D4 **Pleumeur-Bodou** France
156 G6 **Pleurs** France
158 G4 **Pleurtuit** France
158 C6 **Pleuven** France
197 M7 **Pleven** Bulg.
Plevna Bulg. *see* **Pleven**
177 H2 **Plevník-Drienové** Slovakia
158 D5 **Pleyben** France
158 D4 **Pleyber-Christ** France
173 M2 **Pleystein** Ger.
187 C12 **Pliego** Spain
173 L5 **Pliening** Ger.
95 K3 **Plieran** *r.* Malaysia
177 I3 **Pliešovce** Slovakia
163 F8 **Plieux** France
191 J2 **Plima** *r.* Italy
138 F5 **Plinkšių ežeras** *l.* Lith.
174 C3 **Pliszka** *r.* Pol.
196 D6 **Plitvička Jezera** *nat. park* Croatia
188 E3 **Plješevica** *mts* Croatia
196 H7 **Pljevlja** Montenegro
192 B6 **Ploaghe** *Sardegna* Italy
158 C6 **Plobannalec** France
157 O7 **Plobsheim** France
188 F4 **Ploče** Croatia
172 G4 **Plochingen** Ger.
175 K1 **Płociczno** Pol.
175 H3 **Płock** Pol.
178 G6 **Plöckenpass** *pass* Austria/Italy
146 E8 **Plockton** *Highland, Scotland* U.K.
188 F4 **Pločno** *mt.* Bos.-Herz.
139 N1 **Plodovoye** Rus. Fed.
158 E6 **Ploemeur** France
158 F6 **Ploeren** France
158 G6 **Ploërmel** France
Ploești Romania *see* **Ploiești**
158 F5 **Plœuc-sur-Lié** France
158 C6 **Plogastel-St-Germain** France
158 C5 **Plogonnec** France
170 H1 **Plogshagen** Ger.
197 O6 **Ploiești** Romania
199 H4 **Plomari** *Lesvos* Greece
161 B6 **Plomb du Cantal** *mt.* France
157 L8 **Plombières-les-Bains** France
158 C6 **Plomelin** France
158 C6 **Plomeur** France
191 Q5 **Plomin** Croatia
158 C5 **Plomodiern** France
244 B2 **Plomosas** Mex.

Porech'ye Moskovskaya Oblast' Rus. Fed.
Porech'ye Pskovskaya Oblast' Rus. Fed.
Porech'ye Tverskaya Oblast' Rus. Fed.
Porech'ye-Rybnoye Rus. Fed.
Poretskoye Rus. Fed.
Poretta airport Corse France
Porezen mt. Slovenia
Pórfido, Punta pt Arg.
Porga Benin
Porgyang Xizang China
Pori Fin.
Pořičany Czech Rep.
Porirua North I. N.Z.
Porjus Sweden
Porkhov Rus. Fed.
Porkkalafjärden b. Fin.
Porlamar Venez.
Porlezza Italy
Porlock Somerset, England U.K.
Porma r. Spain
Porma, Embalse de resr Spain
Pormpuraaw Qld Austr.
Pornainen Fin.
Pornassio Italy
Pörnbach Ger.
Pornic France
Pornichet France
Poro i. Phil.
Poro Sta Isabel Solomon Is
Poro, Monte hill Italy
Porog Rus. Fed.
Poronaysk Sakhalin Rus. Fed.
Porong Xizang China
Pôrông, Stœng r. Cambodia
Porongo, Cerro mt. Arg.
Poros Greece
Poros i. Greece
Poroshkove Ukr.
Porosozero Rus. Fed.
Poroszló Hungary
Porozhsk Rus. Fed.
Porozina Croatia
Porpoise Bay Antarctica
Porpoise Point Ascension S. Atlantic Ocean
Porqueres Spain
Porquerolles, Île de i. France
Porquis Junction Ont. Can.
Porrara, Monte mt. Italy
Porrentruy Switz.
Porreres Spain
Porretta Terme Italy
Porrón hill Spain
Porsangerfjorden sea chan. Norway
Porsangerhalvøya pen. Norway
Porsgrunn Norway
Porspoder France
Porsuk r. Turkey
Port Ireland
Port, Pic du mt. France/Spain
Porta France
Portacloy Ireland
Portada Covunco Arg.
Port Adelaide S.A. Austr.
Portadown Northern Ireland U.K.
Port Adventure b. Stewart I. N.Z.
Portaferry Northern Ireland U.K.
Portage IN U.S.A.
Portage MI U.S.A.
Portage PA U.S.A.
Portage WI U.S.A.
Portage Lakes OH U.S.A.
Portage la Prairie Man. Can.
Portaje Spain
Portal ND U.S.A.
Port Alberni B.C. Can.
Port Albert Vic. Austr.
Portalegre Port.
Portalegre admin. dist. Port.
Portales NM U.S.A.
Port Alexander AK U.S.A.
Port-Alfred Que. Can. see La Baie
Port Alfred S. Africa
Port Alice B.C. Can.
Port Allegany PA U.S.A.
Port Alma Qld Austr.
Portals Vells Spain
Port Angeles WA U.S.A.
Port Antonio Jamaica
Port-à-Piment Haiti
Port Appin Argyll and Bute, Scotland U.K.
Portaria Greece
Portarlington Ireland
Port Arthur Tas. Austr.
Port Arthur Liaoning China see Lüshun
Port Arthur TX U.S.A.
Portas, Embalse das resr Spain
Port Askaig Argyll and Bute, Scotland U.K.
Port Augusta S.A. Austr.
Port-au-Port Bay Nfld and Lab. Can.
Port-au-Prince Haiti
Port Austin MI U.S.A.
Port aux Choix Nfld and Lab. Can.
Portavogie Northern Ireland U.K.
Portbail France
Portballintrae Northern Ireland U.K.
Port Bannatyne Argyll and Bute, Scotland U.K.
Port-Barcarès France
Port Barton b. Palawan Phil.
Port Beaufort S. Africa
Port Bell Uganda
Port Blair Andaman & Nicobar Is India
Port Bolster Ont. Can.
Portbou Spain
Port Bradshaw b. N.T. Austr.
Port Brillet France
Port Broughton S.A. Austr.
Port Burwell Ont. Can.
Port Campbell Vic. Austr.
Port Campbell National Park Vic. Austr.
Port Canning W. Bengal India
Port Carbon PA U.S.A.
Port Carling Ont. Can.
Port-Cartier Que. Can.
Port Chalmers South I. N.Z.
Port Charles North I. N.Z.
Port Charlotte FL U.S.A.
Portchester Hampshire, England U.K.
Port Chester NY U.S.A.
Port Clements B.C. Can.
Port Clinton OH U.S.A.
Port Clinton PA U.S.A.
Port Clyde ME U.S.A.
Port Colborne Ont. Can.
Port Colden NJ U.S.A.
Port Credit Ont. Can.
Port-Cros, Île de i. France
Port-Cros, Parc National de nat. park France
Port d'Addaia Spain
Port d'Andratx Spain
Port Darwin b. N.T. Austr.
Port Davey b. Tas. Austr.
Port-de-Bouc France
Port-d'Envaux France
Port de Pailhères pass France
Port-de-Paix Haiti
Port-de-Piles France
Port de Pollença Spain
Port Deposit MD U.S.A.
Port-des-Barques France
Port de Sóller Spain
Port de Venasque pass France/Spain
Port Dickson Malaysia
Port Douglas Qld Austr.
227 N7 Port Dover Ont. Can.
84 C1 Port Easington inlet N.T. Austr.
226 H4 Porte des Morts lake channel WI U.S.A.
222 D4 Port Edward B.C. Can.
215 O7 Port Edward S. Africa
226 E5 Port Edwards WI U.S.A.
251 G5 Porteira Brazil
257 F1 Porteirinha Brazil
251 I5 Portel Brazil
184 D4 Portel Port.
257 G4 Portela Brazil
256 A2 Portelândia Brazil
161 B10 Portel-des-Corbières France
225 H4 Port Elgin N.B. Can.
224 D4 Port Elgin Ont. Can.
215 J9 Port Elizabeth S. Africa
247 □3 Port Elizabeth St Vincent
186 E6 Portell de Morella Spain
146 D11 Port Ellen Argyll and Bute, Scotland U.K.
261 F2 Portena Arg.
159 J3 Port-en-Bessin-Huppain France
148 H5 Port Erin Isle of Man
223 J2 Porter Lake N.W.T. Can.
223 J3 Porter Lake Sask. Can.
222 D3 Porter Landing B.C. Can.
247 □3 Porter Point St Vincent
234 E2 Porters Lake PA U.S.A.
214 C9 Porterville S. Africa
240 M5 Porterville CA U.S.A.
150 G6 Portesham Dorset, England U.K.
161 F7 Portes-lès-Valence France
246 □ Port Esquivel Jamaica
163 F10 Portet d'Aspet, Col de pass France
Port Étienne Maur. see Nouâdhibou
Port Everglades FL U.S.A. see Fort Lauderdale
150 D4 Port Eynon Swansea, Wales U.K.
83 I8 Port Fairy Vic. Austr.
80 J3 Port Fitzroy North I. N.Z.
Port Francqui Dem. Rep. Congo see Ilebo
Port Fuad Egypt see Būr Fu'ād
208 A5 Port-Gentil Gabon
82 G5 Port Germein S.A. Austr.
237 J10 Port Gibson MS U.S.A.
146 G11 Port Glasgow Inverclyde, Scotland U.K.
147 J3 Portglenone Northern Ireland U.K.
81 I8 Port Gore b. South I. N.Z.
161 J10 Port Grimaud France
215 N7 Port Grosvenor S. Africa
150 F4 Porth Rhondda Cynon Taff, Wales U.K.
Porthaethwy Isle of Anglesey, Wales U.K. see Menai Bridge
207 G5 Port Harcourt Nigeria
222 E5 Port Hardy B.C. Can.
Port Harrison Que. Can. see Inukjuak
225 I4 Port Hawkesbury N.S. Can.
150 E5 Porthcawl Bridgend, Wales U.K.
86 E6 Port Hedland W.A. Austr.
246 □ Port Henderson Jamaica
146 E7 Port Henderson Highland, Scotland U.K.
233 L4 Port Henry NY U.S.A.
Port Herald Malawi see Nsanje
150 B7 Porthleven Cornwall, England U.K.
150 D2 Porthmadog Gwynedd, Wales U.K.
150 C2 Porth Neigwl b. Wales U.K.
227 P6 Port Hope Ont. Can.
227 L6 Port Hope MI U.S.A.
225 K2 Port Hope Simpson Nfld and Lab. Can.
240 M7 Port Hueneme CA U.S.A.
227 L7 Port Huron MI U.S.A.
192 B4 Porticcio Corse France
193 M6 Portici Italy
157 L7 Portieux France
129 J7 Port-İliç Azer.
183 P8 Portilla Spain
183 K2 Portilla de la Reina Spain
260 B3 Portillo Chile
246 E4 Portillo Cuba
183 K6 Portillo Spain
183 M2 Portillo de la Sía mt. Spain
183 L8 Portillo de Toledo Spain
163 F10 Portillon, Col du pass France
184 B6 Portimão Port.
140 S3 Portimo Fin.
187 I9 Portinatx Spain
150 C6 Port Isaac Bay England U.K.
150 G5 Portishead North Somerset, England U.K.
Port Island H.K. China see Chek Chau
Port Jackson N.S.W. Austr. see Sydney
83 M5 Port Jackson inlet N.S.W. Austr.
235 I3 Port Jefferson NY U.S.A.
235 I3 Port Jefferson Station NY U.S.A.
234 F2 Port Jervis NY U.S.A.
158 G8 Port-Joinville France
246 □ Port Kaiser Jamaica
251 G3 Port Kaituma Guyana
Port Keats N.T. Austr. see Wadeye
83 M6 Port Kembla N.S.W. Austr.
233 L4 Port Kent NY U.S.A.
Port-Khorly Ukr. see Khorly
Port Klang Malaysia see Pelabuhan Klang
146 K7 Portknockie Moray, Scotland U.K.
Port Láirge Ireland see Waterford
83 L5 Portland N.S.W. Austr.
82 H8 Portland Vic. Austr.
246 □ Portland parish Jamaica
80 I2 Portland North I. N.Z.
147 F6 Portland Ireland
235 J1 Portland CT U.S.A.
230 E5 Portland IN U.S.A.
233 □O5 Portland ME U.S.A.
226 J7 Portland MI U.S.A.
238 C4 Portland OR U.S.A.
150 H6 Portland, Isle of pen. England U.K.
82 H8 Portland Bay Vic. Austr.
246 □ Portland Bight inlet Jamaica
Portland Bill hd England U.K. see Bill of Portland
222 D4 Portland Canal inlet B.C. Can.
225 J3 Portland Creek Pond l. Nfld and Lab. Can.
150 H6 Portland Harbour England U.K.
222 D4 Portland Inlet B.C. Can.
80 L6 Portland Island North I. N.Z.
246 □ Portland Point Jamaica
216 □2a Portland Point Ascension S. Atlantic Ocean
246 □ Portland Ridge hill Jamaica
85 I2 Portland Roads Qld Austr.
246 E5 Portland Rock i. Jamaica
161 C10 Port-la-Nouvelle France
147 H6 Portlaoise Ireland
237 G11 Port Lavaca TX U.S.A.
147 H8 Portlaw Ireland
146 L8 Portlethen Aberdeenshire, Scotland U.K.
163 K10 Port-Leucate France
82 E6 Port Lincoln S.A. Austr.
146 G13 Port Logan Dumfries and Galloway, Scotland U.K.
206 B4 Port Loko Sierra Leone
158 E6 Port-Louis France
247 □2 Port-Louis Guadeloupe
217 □1b Port Louis Mauritius
Port-Lyautrey Morocco see Kénitra
82 H8 Port MacDonnell S.A. Austr.
83 N4 Port Macquarie N.S.W. Austr.
Portmadoc Gwynedd, Wales U.K. see Porthmadog
147 B9 Portmagee Ireland
146 I7 Portmahomack Highland, Scotland U.K.
234 E6 Port Mahon DE U.S.A.
187 D12 Portman Spain
158 D6 Port-Manec'h France
225 I1 Port Manvers inlet Nfld and Lab. Can.
246 □ Port Maria Jamaica
147 J6 Portmarnock Ireland
217 □1a Port Mathurin Rodrigues I. Mauritius
84 F3 Port McArthur b. N.T. Austr.
222 E5 Port McNeill B.C. Can.
225 H3 Port-Menier Que. Can.
220 B4 Port Moller b. AK U.S.A.
246 □ Port Morant Jamaica
246 □ Portmore Jamaica
91 K8 Port Moresby P.N.G.
156 B5 Port-Mort France
147 K3 Portmuck Northern Ireland U.K.
85 H1 Port Musgrave b. Qld Austr.
146 F9 Portnacroish Argyll and Bute, Scotland U.K.
146 D6 Portnaguran Western Isles, Scotland U.K.
146 C11 Portnahaven Argyll and Bute, Scotland U.K.
146 D8 Portnalong Highland, Scotland U.K.
Port nan Giúran Western Isles, Scotland U.K. see Portnaguran
146 B7 Port nan Long Western Isles, Scotland U.K.
158 F6 Port-Navalo France
237 I11 Port Neches TX U.S.A.
82 F6 Port Neill S.A. Austr.
246 F2 Port Nelson Rum Cay Bahamas
225 G3 Portneuf r. Que. Can.
238 H5 Portneuf r. ID U.S.A.
225 F4 Portneuf, Réserve Faunique de nature res. Que. Can.
Port Nis Scotland U.K. see Port of Ness
82 G6 Port Noarlunga S.A. Austr.
214 A5 Port Nolloth S. Africa
147 F3 Portnoo Ireland
234 E6 Port Norris NJ U.S.A.
Port-Nouveau-Québec Que. Can. see Kangiqsualujjuaq
254 E2 Porto Brazil
192 B3 Porto Corse France
182 C6 Porto Port.
182 D6 Porto admin. dist. Port.
182 G4 Porto Spain
192 B3 Porto, Golfe de b. Corse France
252 D2 Porto Acre Brazil
252 D2 Porto Alegre Amazonas Brazil
255 B7 Porto Alegre Mato Grosso do Sul Brazil
251 H6 Porto Alegre Pará Brazil
255 C9 Porto Alegre Rio Grande do Sul Brazil
256 B3 Porto Alencastro Brazil
Porto Alexandre Angola see Tombua
184 B3 Porto Alto Port.
253 E3 Porto Amarante Brazil
209 B7 Porto Amboim Angola
Porto Amélia Moz. see Pemba
253 G3 Porto Artur Brazil
192 E2 Porto Azzurro Italy
81 E12 Portobello South I. N.Z.
255 C8 Porto Belo Brazil
242 □T13 Portobelo Panama
242 □T13 Portobelo, Parque Nacional nat. park Panama
192 B9 Porto Botte Sardegna Italy
182 C3 Portobravo Spain
255 B7 Porto Camargo Brazil
254 G4 Porto Cavlo Brazil
192 D5 Porto Cervo Sardegna Italy
195 N3 Porto Cesareo Italy
187 L9 Portocolom Spain
184 B5 Porto Covo da Bandeira Port.
187 L8 Porto Cristo Spain
184 □ Porto da Cruz Madeira
254 F4 Porto da Fôlha Brazil
251 H6 Porto da Lontra Brazil
254 B5 Porto de Meinacos Brazil
182 C9 Porto de Mós Port.
182 D3 Portodemouros, Encoro de resr Spain
251 H5 Porto de Moz Brazil
251 H6 Porto do Barka Brazil
182 E1 Porto do Barqueiro Spain
253 E3 Porto do Massacas Brazil
253 F2 Porto dos Gaúchos Óbidos Brazil
182 B3 Porto do Son Spain
194 F9 Porto Empedocle Sicilia Italy
192 G3 Porto Ercole Italy
253 F4 Porto Esperança Brazil
253 F3 Porto Esperidião Brazil
253 F3 Porto Estrêla Brazil
256 D5 Porto Feliz Brazil
192 E2 Portoferraio Italy
256 D4 Porto Ferreira Brazil
190 G7 Portofino Italy
257 F4 Porto Firme Brazil
146 H10 Port of Menteith Stirling, Scotland U.K.
146 D6 Port of Ness Western Isles, Scotland U.K.
254 D3 Porto Franco Brazil
247 □7 Port of Spain Trin. and Tob.
191 M6 Porto Garibaldi Italy
251 I4 Porto Grande Brazil
191 N4 Portogruaro Italy
255 B7 Porto Guareí Brazil
206 □ Porto Inglês Cape Verde
253 F4 Porto Jofre Brazil
216 □1a Porto Judeu Terceira Azores
198 E3 Porto Koufo Greece
240 L2 Portola CA U.S.A.
194 H7 Porto Levante Isole Lipari Italy
191 M5 Porto Levante Veneto Italy
255 B8 Porto Luceno Brazil
191 L6 Portomaggiore Italy
182 E3 Portomarín Spain
255 B8 Porto Mauá Brazil
184 □ Porto Moniz Madeira
253 F5 Porto Murtinho Brazil
254 C4 Porto Nacional Brazil
207 F5 Porto-Novo Benin
206 □ Porto Novo Cape Verde
Porto Novo Tamil Nadu India see Parangipettai
194 D8 Porto Palo Sicilia Italy
189 E7 Portopalo di Capo Passero Sicilia Italy
187 L9 Porto Petro Spain
192 B10 Porto Pino Sardegna Italy
256 A5 Porto Primavera Brazil
256 A4 Porto Primavera, Represa resr Brazil
231 G11 Port Orange FL U.S.A.
238 C3 Port Orchard WA U.S.A.
191 P9 Porto Recanati Italy
238 B5 Port Orford OR U.S.A.
209 B6 Porto Rico Angola
206 □ Porto Rincão Santiago Cape Verde
192 D5 Porto Rotondo Sardegna Italy
191 P4 Portorož Slovenia
191 P9 Porto San Giorgio Italy
192 D6 Porto San Paolo Sardegna Italy
251 I5 Porto Santana Brazil
191 P9 Porto Sant'Elpidio Italy
184 □ Porto Santo, Ilha de i. Madeira
192 G3 Porto Santo Stefano Italy
256 A5 Porto São José Brazil
192 A9 Portoscuso Sardegna Italy
257 H2 Porto Seguro Brazil
191 M6 Porto Tolle Italy
192 A6 Porto Torres Sardegna Italy
253 E3 Porto Triunfo Brazil
255 C8 Porto União Brazil
192 C4 Porto-Vecchio Corse France
192 C4 Porto-Vecchio, Golfe de b. Corse France
252 E2 Porto Velho Brazil
190 H7 Portovenere Italy
250 A5 Portoviejo Ecuador
252 B2 Porto Wálter Brazil
146 F13 Portpatrick Dumfries and Galloway, Scotland U.K.
81 B14 Port Pegasus b. Stewart I. N.Z.
234 D5 Port Penn DE U.S.A.
227 P5 Port Perry Ont. Can.
83 J8 Port Phillip Bay Vic. Austr.
82 G5 Port Pirie S.A. Austr.
Port Radium N.W.T. Can. see Echo Bay
147 J6 Portrane Ireland
150 B7 Portreath Cornwall, England U.K.
146 D8 Portree Highland, Scotland U.K.
222 E5 Port Renfrew B.C. Can.
225 K3 Port Rexton Nfld and Lab. Can.
147 F7 Portroe Ireland
84 E3 Port Roper b. N.T. Austr.
227 N7 Port Rowan Ont. Can.
246 □ Port Royal Jamaica
232 H10 Port Royal VA U.S.A.
231 G9 Port Royal Sound inlet SC U.S.A.
147 I2 Portrush Northern Ireland U.K.
Port Said Egypt see Būr Sa'īd
163 E6 Port-Ste-Foy-et-Ponchapt France
163 E7 Port-Ste-Marie France
231 E11 Port St Joe FL U.S.A.
215 N7 Port St Johns S. Africa
Port St-Louis Madag. see Antsohimbondrona
161 F10 Port-St-Louis-du-Rhône France
231 G12 Port St Lucie City FL U.S.A.
148 H5 Port St Mary Isle of Man
158 H7 Port-St-Père France
158 B4 Portsall France
147 G2 Portsalon Ireland
259 F8 Port Salvador Falkland Is
227 L6 Port Sanilac MI U.S.A.
179 J6 Pörtschach am Wörther See Austria
186 F6 Ports de Beseit mts Spain
227 O5 Port Severn Ont. Can.
Port Shelter b. H.K. China see Ngau Mei Hoi
215 O6 Port Shepstone S. Africa
Port Simpson B.C. Can. see Lax Kw'alaams
247 □2 Portsmouth Dominica
151 J6 Portsmouth Portsmouth, England U.K.
151 J6 Portsmouth admin. div. England U.K.
233 □O5 Portsmouth NH U.S.A.
232 C10 Portsmouth OH U.S.A.
233 I12 Portsmouth VA U.S.A.
146 K7 Portsoy Aberdeenshire, Scotland U.K.
Port Stanley Falkland Is see Stanley
83 N5 Port Stephens b. N.S.W. Austr.
259 E9 Port Stephens Falkland Is
147 I2 Portstewart Northern Ireland U.K.
203 H5 Port Sudan Sudan
237 K11 Port Sulphur LA U.S.A.
157 L8 Port-sur-Saône France
Port Swettenham Malaysia see Pelabuhan Klang
150 E4 Port Talbot Neath Port Talbot, Wales U.K.
92 D5 Port Tambang b. Luzon Phil.
Port Taufiq Egypt see Būr Tawfīq
140 S2 Porttipahdan tekojärvi l. Fin.
238 C2 Port Townsend WA U.S.A.
234 B3 Port Trevorton PA U.S.A.
180 C3 Portugal country Europe
183 N2 Portugalete Spain
Portugália Angola see Chitato
250 D2 Portuguesa state Venez.
Portuguese East Africa country Africa see Mozambique
Portuguese Guinea country Africa see Guinea-Bissau
Portuguese Timor country Asia see East Timor
Portuguese West Africa country Africa see Angola
147 F6 Portumna Ireland
Portus Herculis Monoeci country Europe see Monaco
182 C5 Portuzelo Port.
163 K10 Port-Vendres France
82 F6 Port Victoria S.A. Austr.
78 □5 Port Vila Vanuatu
232 G6 Portville NY U.S.A.
82 F6 Port Vincent S.A. Austr.
140 V2 Port Vladimir Rus. Fed.
80 I4 Port Waikato North I. N.Z.
82 G6 Port Wakefield S.A. Austr.
86 H3 Port Warrender W.A. Austr.
235 H3 Port Washington NY U.S.A.
226 G6 Port Washington WI U.S.A.
Port Weld Malaysia see Kuala Sepetang
146 G13 Port William Dumfries and Galloway, Scotland U.K.
226 C3 Port Wing WI U.S.A.
114 F5 Porumamilla Andhra Prad. India
246 □ Porus Jamaica
139 O4 Porus'ya r. Rus. Fed.
261 F4 Porvenir Arg.
252 C2 Porvenir Pando Bol.
253 E3 Porvenir Santa Cruz Bol.
259 C9 Porvenir Chile
261 I3 Porvenir Uru.
141 R6 Porvoo Fin.
138 I1 Porvoonjoki r. Fin.
101 E10 Poryŏng S. Korea
175 J3 Porządzie Pol.
185 K2 Porzuna Spain
139 R1 Posad Rus. Fed.
192 D6 Posada Sardegna Italy
192 D6 Posada r. Sardegna Italy
182 I2 Posada Spain
183 K2 Posada de Valdeón Spain
258 G2 Posadas Arg.
185 I5 Posadas Spain
263 G2 Posadowsky Bay Antarctica
137 L7 Posad-Pokrovs'ke Ukr.
188 F3 Posavina reg. Bos.-Herz./Croatia
179 K7 Posavsko Hribovje reg. Slovenia
190 I3 Poschiavo Switz.
198 F5 Poseidonia Syros Greece
Poseidonia tourist site Italy see Paestum
Posen Pol. see Poznań
227 K4 Posen MI U.S.A.
170 H2 Poseritz Ger.
186 F2 Posets mt. Spain
134 G4 Poshekhon'ye Rus. Fed.
Poshekon'ye-Volodarsk Rus. Fed. see Poshekhon'ye
122 H7 Posht watercourse Iran
122 G4 Posht-e Āsemān spring Iran
122 F5 Posht-e Badam Iran
122 H6 Poshteh-ye Chaqvīr hill Iran
122 B5 Posht-e Kūh mts Iran
122 C3 Posht Kūh hill Iran
137 M9 Poshtove Ukr.
178 D8 Posina r. Italy
173 N3 Pösing Ger.
140 T3 Posio Fin.
193 M6 Positano Italy
Poskam Xinjiang China see Zepu
235 J2 Posnet CT U.S.A.
93 B4 Poso Sulawesi Indon.
93 B4 Poso r. Indon.
93 B4 Poso, Danau l. Indon.
93 B4 Poso, Teluk b. Indon.
127 K3 Posof Turkey
129 D4 Posof r. Turkey
101 E11 Posŏng S. Korea
250 A5 Posorja Ecuador
121 S1 Pospelikha Rus. Fed.
178 E8 Possagno Italy
254 D5 Posse Brazil
208 C3 Possel C.A.R.
171 I9 Possendorf Ger.
157 I6 Possesse France
212 B5 Possession Island Namibia
263 L2 Possession Islands Antarctica
171 E9 Pößneck Ger.
243 J1 Possum Kingdom Lake TX U.S.A.
237 E9 Post TX U.S.A.
193 K2 Posta Italy
197 O5 Poşta Câlnău Romania
Poşta Cîlnău Romania see Poşta Câlnău
191 K2 Postal Italy
193 P5 Posta Piana Italy
173 M4 Postau Ger.
Postavy Belarus see Pastavy
173 K3 Postbauer-Heng Ger.
215 J8 Post Chalmers S. Africa
217 □1b Poste de Flacq Mauritius
217 □1b Poste de Flacq, Rivière du r. Mauritius
Poste-de-la-Baleine Que. Can. see Kuujjuarapik
165 J6 Posterholt Neth.
214 H4 Postmasburg S. Africa
Post-Mawr Wales U.K. see Synod Inn
173 N5 Postmünster Ger.
188 E3 Postojna Slovenia
175 J3 Postoliska Pol.
176 C1 Postoloprty Czech Rep.
174 C3 Postomia r. Pol.
174 E1 Postomino Pol.
241 R7 Poston AZ U.S.A.
225 J2 Postville Nfld and Lab. Can.
226 C6 Postville IA U.S.A.
205 F4 Post Weygand Alg.
Postysheve Ukr. see Krasnoarmiys'k
188 F4 Posušje Bos.-Herz.
175 I4 Poświętne Łódzkie Pol.
175 J3 Poświętne Pol.
175 K3 Poświętne Podlaskie Pol.
100 G7 Pos'yet Rus. Fed.
93 B8 Pota Flores Indon.
242 D4 Pótam Mex.
198 F2 Potamia Thasos Greece
198 D6 Potamos Kythira Greece
139 P1 Potanino Rus. Fed.
236 E4 Potato Creek SD U.S.A.
215 L2 Potchefstroom S. Africa
197 M6 Potcoava Romania
257 G2 Poté Brazil
237 H8 Poteau OK U.S.A.
114 G3 Potegaon Mahar. India
174 F1 Potęgowo Pol.
135 I6 Potemkino Rus. Fed.
Potentia Italy see Potenza
193 P6 Potenza Italy
193 P6 Potenza prov. Italy
191 P9 Potenza r. Italy
191 P9 Potenza Picena Italy
81 B13 Poteriteri, Lake South I. N.Z.
183 K2 Potes Spain
214 I6 Potfontein S. Africa
254 E3 Poti r. Brazil
129 C3 P'ot'i Georgia
159 K4 Potigny France
114 G3 Potikal Chhattisgarh India
255 F5 Potiraguá Brazil
207 H4 Potiskum Nigeria
136 H3 Potiyivka Ukr.
238 F3 Potlatch ID U.S.A.
78 □5 Potnarvin Vanuatu
252 C3 Poto Peru
109 □J7 Po Toi i. H.K. China
175 K5 Potok Górny Pol.
175 H5 Potok Złoty Pol.
232 H9 Potomac MD U.S.A.
232 I10 Potomac r. MD/VA U.S.A.
232 G9 Potomac, South Branch r. WV U.S.A.
232 F10 Potomac, South Fork South Branch r. WV U.S.A.
93 D8 Potomana, Gunung mt. Indon.
206 C5 Potoru Sierra Leone
252 D4 Potosí Bol.
252 D5 Potosí dept Bol.
230 B7 Potosi MO U.S.A.
241 Q6 Potosi Mountain NV U.S.A.
92 D6 Pototan Panay Phil.
258 C2 Potrerillos Chile
242 □P10 Potrerillos Hond.
260 C3 Potrerilos Arg.
242 G3 Potrero del Llano Chihuahua Mex.
245 J4 Potrero del Llano Veracruz Mex.
245 M8 Potrero Largo Mex.
250 B6 Potro r. Peru
171 H6 Potsdam Ger.
233 K4 Potsdam NY U.S.A.
171 G6 Potsdamer Havelseengebiet park Ger.
177 G2 Potštát Czech Rep.
78 □5 Pott, Île i. New Caledonia
115 H3 Pottangi Orissa India
179 N4 Pottendorf Austria
179 N4 Pottenstein Austria
173 K2 Pottenstein Ger.
236 D5 Potter NE U.S.A.
150 H5 Potterne Wiltshire, England U.K.
151 L4 Potters Bar Hertfordshire, England U.K.
240 I2 Potter Valley CA U.S.A.
232 A6 Potterville MI U.S.A.
173 K4 Pöttmes Ger.
151 L3 Potton Bedfordshire, England U.K.
179 N4 Pöttsching Austria
234 B2 Potts Grove PA U.S.A.
234 D4 Pottstown PA U.S.A.
234 C3 Pottsville PA U.S.A.
114 G9 Pottuvil Sri Lanka
137 S2 Potudan' r. Rus. Fed.
123 O5 Potwar reg. Pak.
175 I4 Potworów Pol.
172 C2 Potzberg hill Ger.
158 I6 Pouancé France
222 F4 Pouce Coupe B.C. Can.
225 K4 Pouch Cove Nfld and Lab. Can.
78 □5 Pouébo New Caledonia
78 □5 Pouembout New Caledonia
233 L7 Poughkeepsie NY U.S.A.
235 H1 Poughquag NY U.S.A.
160 C2 Pougny France
160 C2 Pougues-les-Eaux France
156 H7 Pougy France
160 H2 Pouilley-les-Vignes France
163 C8 Pouillon France
160 F2 Pouilly-en-Auxois France
160 E4 Pouilly-sous-Charlieu France
160 B2 Pouilly-sur-Loire France
160 G2 Pouilly-sur-Saône France
159 O7 Poulaines France
158 C6 Pouldreuzic France
158 D6 Pouldu, Anse de b. France
160 E4 Poule-les-Écharmeaux France
147 D9 Poulgorm Bridge Ireland
159 N8 Pouligny-St-Pierre France
225 G3 Poulin de Courval, Lac l. Que. Can.
158 D5 Poullaouen France
147 G8 Poulnamucky Ireland
233 L5 Poultney VT U.S.A.
149 L6 Poulton-le-Fylde Lancashire, England U.K.
78 □5 Poum New Caledonia
207 H6 Pouma Cameroon
232 C11 Pound VA U.S.A.
198 F4 Pountas, Akrotirio pt Greece
214 I6 Poupan S. Africa
163 F8 Poupas France
160 H3 Poupet, Mont hill France
161 H10 Pourcieux France
80 K7 Pourerere North I. N.Z.
198 C3 Pournariou, Techniti Limni resr Greece
156 F8 Pourrain France
160 J5 Pourri, Mont mt. France
161 H9 Pourrières France
261 G5 Pourtalé Arg.
163 D10 Pourtalet, Col du pass France
182 F7 Pousada Port.
257 E5 Pouso Alegre Brazil
256 A2 Pouso Alto Brazil
182 C9 Pousos Port.
161 D10 Poussan France
157 L7 Poussay France
140 T4 Poussu Fin.
78 □2 Poutasi Samoa
97 F8 Poŭthĭsăt Cambodia
80 I3 Pouto North I. N.Z.
157 M7 Pouxeux France
96 E5 Pouy, Nam r. Laos
163 E9 Pouyastruc France
163 D8 Pouydesseaux France
163 G9 Pouy-de-Touges France
162 C2 Pouzauges France
159 M7 Pouzay France
139 U5 Povarovo Rus. Fed.
177 H2 Považská Bystrica Slovakia
177 G3 Považský Inovec mts Slovakia
139 R4 Poved' r. Rus. Fed.
185 N3 Povedilla Spain
134 F3 Povenets Rus. Fed.
80 L5 Poverty Bay North I. N.Z.
191 J6 Poviglio Italy
196 H6 Povlen mt. Serbia
184 D2 Póvoa, Barragem da resr Port.
216 □1b Povoação São Miguel Azores
257 H3 Povoação Brazil
182 D5 Póvoa de Lanhoso Port.
184 E4 Póvoa de São Miguel Port.
182 C6 Póvoa de Varzim Port.
182 F7 Póvoa do Concelho Port.
191 O3 Povoletto Italy
135 H6 Povorino Rus. Fed.
100 H7 Povorotnyy, Mys hd Rus. Fed.
136 E2 Povors'k Ukr.
171 J9 Povrly Czech Rep.
240 O9 Poway CA U.S.A.
149 N3 Powburn Northumberland, England U.K.
238 L3 Powder r. MT U.S.A.
238 F4 Powder r. OR U.S.A.
238 K5 Powder, South Fork r. WY U.S.A.
238 K5 Powder River WY U.S.A.
234 B1 Powell PA U.S.A.
238 J4 Powell WY U.S.A.
232 B12 Powell r. TN/VA U.S.A.
241 V4 Powell, Lake resr UT U.S.A.
85 I8 Powell Creek watercourse Qld Austr.
240 N3 Powell Mountain NV U.S.A.
246 E1 Powell Point Eleuthera Bahamas
222 E5 Powell River B.C. Can.
147 F9 Power Head Ireland
226 G4 Powers MI U.S.A.
147 F6 Power's Cross Ireland
237 J7 Powhatan AR U.S.A.
232 H11 Powhatan VA U.S.A.
232 E9 Powhatan Point OH U.S.A.
150 H3 Powick Worcestershire, England U.K.
174 F3 Powidz Pol.
174 F3 Powidzkie, Jezioro l. Pol.
146 I10 Powmill Perth and Kinross, Scotland U.K.
108 B2 Powo Sichuan China
Pöwrize Turkm. see Pöwrize
122 H3 Pöwrize Turkm.
150 F3 Powys admin. div. Wales U.K.
255 B5 Poxoréu Brazil
78 □5 Poya New Caledonia
183 J8 Poyales del Hoyo Spain
94 □ Poyan, Sungai r. Sing.
Poyang Jiangxi China see Boyang
109 K4 Poyang Hu l. China
94 □ Poyan Reservoir Sing.
100 F4 Poyarkovo Rus. Fed.
183 P8 Poyatos Spain
226 F5 Poygan, Lake WI U.S.A.
129 H4 Poylu Azer.
226 E6 Poynette WI U.S.A.
149 M7 Poynton Cheshire, England U.K.
147 J4 Poyntz Pass Northern Ireland U.K.
185 O5 Poyo, Cerro mt. Spain
199 I3 Poyrazcık Turkey
179 O2 Poysdorf Austria
141 Q6 Pöytyä Fin.
183 N3 Poza de la Sal Spain
183 K6 Pozaldez Spain
126 G5 Pozantı Turkey
196 J6 Požarevac Serbia
245 J5 Poza Rica Mex.
177 K3 Pozdišovce Slovakia
188 F3 Požega Croatia
196 I7 Požega Serbia
175 J1 Pozezdrze Pol.
139 O5 Pozhnya Rus. Fed.
137 O3 Pozhnya Ukr.
134 L4 Pozhva Rus. Fed.
177 G2 Pozlovice Czech Rep.
174 E3 Poznań Pol.
185 N5 Pozo, Sierra del mts Spain
185 N5 Pozo Alcón Spain
183 J5 Pozoantiguo Spain
258 D2 Pozo Betbeder Arg.
185 J4 Pozoblanco Spain
185 P3 Pozo Cañada Spain
253 F5 Pozo Colorado Para.
183 N8 Pozo de Guadalajara Spain
261 F3 Pozo del Molle Arg.
258 E2 Pozo del Tigre Arg.
258 D2 Pozo Hondo Arg.
185 P3 Pozohondo Spain
185 Q2 Pozo-Lorente Spain
183 R7 Pozondón Spain
183 R7 Pozondón, Puerto de pass Spain
216 □3b Pozo Negro Fuerteventura Canary Is
242 D3 Pozo Nuevo Mex.
179 O1 Pozořice Czech Rep.
183 O9 Pozorrubio Spain
259 D7 Pozos, Punta pt Arg.
258 E2 Pozo San Martin Arg.
174 D2 Poźrzadło Wielkie Pol.
Pozsony Slovakia see Bratislava
185 O3 Pozuelo Spain
183 M8 Pozuelo de Alarcón Spain
183 R5 Pozuelo de Aragón Spain
182 I4 Pozuelo del Páramo Spain
183 N8 Pozuelo del Rey Spain
182 H8 Pozuelo de Zarzón Spain
185 K3 Pozuelos de Calatrava Spain
252 B2 Pozuzo Peru
191 L3 Pozza di Fassa Italy
194 H10 Pozzallo Sicilia Italy
194 H8 Pozzillo, Lago di l. Sicilia Italy
190 F6 Pozzolo Formigaro Italy
192 B7 Pozzomaggiore Sardegna Italy
193 M6 Pozzuoli Italy
178 H8 Pozzuolo del Friuli Italy
206 E5 Pra r. Ghana
139 Y7 Pra r. Rus. Fed.
94 F6 Prabumulih Sumatera Indon.
175 H2 Prabuty Pol.
182 E9 Pracana, Barragem de resr Port.
176 D2 Prachatice Czech Rep.
115 J3 Prachi r. India
97 E7 Prachin Buri Thai.
169 E9 Pracht Ger.
97 D9 Prachuap Khiri Khan Thai.
173 N3 Prackenbach Ger.
182 G4 Prada, Embalse de resr Spain
182 F2 Pradairo mt. Spain
183 L3 Prádanos de Ojeda Spain
176 G1 Praděd mt. Czech Rep.
183 P4 Pradejón Spain
161 D7 Pradelles France
163 J9 Pradelles-en-Val France
183 M6 Prádena Spain
250 B4 Pradera Col.
163 I10 Prades Languedoc-Roussillon France
163 H10 Prades Midi-Pyrénées France
161 B7 Prades-d'Aubrac France
183 O4 Pradillo Spain
163 G7 Pradines France
257 H2 Prado Brazil
182 D5 Prado Port.
183 J3 Prado de la Guzpeña Spain
184 H7 Prado del Rey Spain
183 N4 Pradoluengo Spain
256 C4 Pradópolis Brazil
161 I8 Prads-Haute-Bléone France
Praeneste Italy see Palestrina
142 I6 Præstø Denmark
190 B5 Pragelato Italy
179 M7 Pragersko Slovenia
178 F5 Prägraten Austria
Prague Czech Rep. see Praha
176 D1 Praha Czech Rep.
171 J10 Praha admin. reg. Czech Rep.
176 C2 Praha hill Czech Rep.
162 D3 Prahecq France
197 O6 Prahova r. Romania
Prai Malaysia see Perai
206 □ Praia Santiago Cape Verde
216 □1c Praia, Ilhéu da i. Azores
193 P8 Praia a Mare Italy
182 C7 Praia da Barra Port.
184 B6 Praia da Rocha Port.
182 C8 Praia da Tocha Port.
182 C7 Praia de Esmoriz Port.
182 C8 Praia de Mira Port.
216 □1c Praia do Almoxarife Faial Azores
213 G5 Praia do Bilene Moz.
216 □1c Praia do Norte Faial Azores
256 D6 Praia Grande Brazil
194 H2 Praiano Italy
253 G3 Praia Rica Brazil
184 B3 Praias do Sado Port.
216 □1c Prainha Pico Azores
253 E1 Prainha Amazonas Brazil
251 H5 Prainha Pará Brazil
85 J6 Prairie Qld Austr.
226 A2 Prairie r. MN U.S.A.
238 E4 Prairie City OR U.S.A.
237 E8 Prairie Dog Town Fork r. TX U.S.A.
226 C6 Prairie du Chien WI U.S.A.
223 K4 Prairie River Sask. Can.
95 J8 Prajekan Jawa Indon.
97 F7 Prakhon Chai Thai.
177 J3 Prakovce Slovakia
161 J6 Pralognan-la-Vanoise France
161 J8 Pra-Loup France
139 P8 Pralyetarskaye Belarus
179 H3 Pram r. Austria
198 C3 Pramanta Greece
179 I3 Prambachkirchen Austria
207 F5 Prampram Ghana
97 E8 Pran r. Thai.
97 D8 Pran Buri Thai.
206 E5 Prang Ghana
138 I2 Prangli i. Estonia
114 F3 Pranhita r. India
179 J5 Prankerhöhe mt. Austria
94 C3 Prapat Sumatera Indon.
177 H3 Prašice Slovakia
129 F1 Praskoveya Rus. Fed.
176 G2 Přáslavice Czech Rep.
157 J8 Praslay France
217 □2a Praslin i. Inner Islands Seychelles
247 □3 Praslin Bay St Lucia
199 I7 Prasonisi, Akrotirio pt Rodos Greece
143 N2 Prästfjärden b. Sweden
174 G4 Praszka Pol.
259 B8 Prat i. Chile
256 C3 Prata Brazil
256 A3 Prata r. Brazil
256 C3 Prata r. Brazil
256 D2 Prata r. Brazil
191 N4 Prata di Pordenone Italy
116 E7 Pratapgarh Rajasthan India
171 G7 Pratau Ger.
186 F6 Prat de Comte Spain
Prat de Llobregat Spain see El Prat de Llobregat
186 G5 Pratdip Spain
193 M5 Pratella Italy
Prathes Thai country Asia see Thailand
256 D3 Pratinha Brazil
191 K8 Prato Italy
191 K8 Prato prov. Italy
191 J2 Prato allo Stelvio Italy
193 L3 Pratola Peligna Italy
194 H2 Pratola Serra Italy
191 L8 Pratovecchio Italy
186 J3 Prats de Lluçanès Spain
163 I11 Prats-de-Mollo-la-Preste France
237 F7 Pratt KS U.S.A.
190 D1 Pratteln Switz.
190 H2 Prättigau reg. Switz.
231 D9 Prattville AL U.S.A.
157 J8 Prauthoy France
114 D3 Pravara r. India
197 P7 Pravda Bulg.
138 E7 Pravdinsk Rus. Fed.
137 L7 Pravdyne Ukr.
182 H2 Pravia Spain
175 M2 Pravyya Masty Belarus
150 E7 Prawle Point England U.K.
95 L9 Praya Lombok Indon.
163 G6 Prayssac France
163 F7 Prayssas France
160 J5 Praz-sur-Arly France
97 H8 Preah, Prêk r. Cambodia
97 G8 Preăh Vihéar Cambodia
179 I5 Prebersee l. Austria
233 I6 Preble NY U.S.A.
179 L7 Prebold Slovenia
163 D7 Préchac France
163 C8 Préchacq-les-Bains France
139 P6 Prechistoye Smolenskaya Oblast' Rus. Fed.
134 H4 Prechistoye Yaroslavskaya Oblast' Rus. Fed.
193 K2 Preci Italy
159 K6 Précigné France
177 H2 Prečín Slovakia
85 M8 Precipice National Park Qld Austr.
160 E2 Précy-sous-Thil France
191 L7 Predappio Italy
191 L3 Predazzo Italy
197 N5 Predeal Romania
179 L6 Preding Austria
179 I5 Predlitz Austria
179 I8 Predmeja Slovenia
190 F6 Predosa Italy
223 K5 Preeceville Sask. Can.
159 K5 Pré-en-Pail France
150 G2 Prees Shropshire, England U.K.
149 L6 Preesall Lancashire, England U.K.
168 J2 Preetz Ger.
158 G7 Préfailles France
191 M4 Preganziòl Italy
179 K3 Pregarten Austria
138 D7 Pregolya r. Rus. Fed.
186 □ Pregonda, Cala b. Spain
179 M7 Pregrada Croatia
129 C2 Pregradnaya Rus. Fed.
163 D6 Preignac France
163 F8 Preignan France
138 J5 Preiļi Latvia
227 P1 Preissac, Lac l. Que. Can.
179 K6 Preitenegg Austria
163 I9 Preixan France
197 N5 Prejmer Romania
196 H8 Prekornica mts Montenegro
223 I5 Prelate Sask. Can.
179 O3 Prellenkirchen Austria
179 O7 Prelog Croatia
176 E1 Přelouč Czech Rep.
191 Q4 Prem Slovenia
188 D3 Premantura Croatia
83 L4 Premer N.S.W. Austr.
160 C2 Prémery France
190 E3 Premia Italy
186 J5 Premià de Mar Spain
191 L8 Premilcuore Italy
160 B4 Prémilhat France
170 F5 Premnitz Ger.
156 F4 Prémontré France
190 E3 Premosello Chiovenda Italy
136 H6 Prenistrului, Dealurile hills Moldova
188 F4 Prenj mts Bos.-Herz.
226 D4 Prentice WI U.S.A.
237 K10 Prentiss MS U.S.A.
170 I4 Prenzlau Ger.
100 H7 Preobrazheniye Rus. Fed.
137 N6 Preobrazhenka Ukr.
129 E1 Preobrazhenskoye Rus. Fed.
97 A7 Preparis Island Cocos Is
96 A7 Preparis North Channel Cocos Is
97 A7 Preparis South Channel Cocos Is
160 D3 Préporché France
176 G2 Přerov Czech Rep.
170 G2 Prerow am Darß, Ostseebad Ger.

182 D9 Presa Port.
244 G3 Presa de Guadalupe Mex.
243 I3 Presa de la Amistad, Parque Natural nature res. Mex.
161 E7 Présailles France
160 J5 Pre-St-Didier Italy
191 J3 Presanella, Cima mt. Italy
243 I5 Presa San Antonio Mex.
Prescelly Mts hills Wales U.K. see Preseli, Mynydd
149 L7 Prescot Merseyside, England U.K.
224 F4 Prescott Ont. Can.
237 I9 Prescott AR U.S.A.
241 T7 Prescott AZ U.S.A.
226 B5 Prescott WI U.S.A.
241 T7 Prescott Valley AZ U.S.A.
150 C4 Preseli, Mynydd hills Wales U.K.
81 A13 Preservation Inlet South I. N.Z.
197 J8 Preševo Serbia
236 E4 Presho SD U.S.A.
195 O4 Presicce Italy
258 F2 Presidencia Roca Arg.
258 E2 Presidencia Roque Sáenz Peña Arg.
256 C5 Presidente Alves Brazil
256 B5 Presidente Bernardes Brazil
258 F2 Presidente de la Plaza Arg.
254 D3 Presidente Dutra Brazil
262 U2 Presidente Eduardo Frei research stn Antarctica
256 A4 Presidente Epitácio Brazil
253 E2 Presidente Hermes Brazil
Presidente Juan Perón prov. Arg. see Chaco
257 E3 Presidente Juscelino Brazil
256 D3 Presidente Olegário Brazil
256 B5 Presidente Prudente Brazil
256 B4 Presidente Venceslau Brazil
244 A2 Presidio r. Mex.
239 L12 Presidio TX U.S.A.
Preslav Bulg. see Veliki Preslav
121 L1 Presnovka Kazakh.
190 I4 Presolana, Pizzo della mt. Italy
177 K3 Prešov Slovakia
177 K2 Prešovský kraj admin. reg. Slovakia
198 C2 Prespa, Lake Europe
Prespansko Ezero l. Europe see Prespa, Lake
198 C2 Prespes nat. park Greece
Prespës, Liqeni i l. Europe see Prespa, Lake
233 □Q2 Presque Isle ME U.S.A.
227 K4 Presque Isle MI U.S.A.
226 E3 Presque Isle WI U.S.A.
226 G3 Presque Isle Point MI U.S.A.
162 F3 Pressac France
173 L2 Pressath Ger.
179 N3 Pressbaum Austria
Pressburg Slovakia see Bratislava
171 E10 Presseck Ger.
179 H6 Pressegger See l. Austria
171 G7 Pressel Ger.
171 D10 Pressig Ger.
150 F1 Prestatyn Denbighshire, Wales U.K.
149 M7 Prestbury Cheshire, England U.K.
150 H4 Prestbury Gloucestershire, England U.K.
206 E5 Prestea Ghana
142 H3 Prestebakke Norway
150 F3 Presteigne Powys, Wales U.K.
176 C2 Přeštice Czech Rep.
150 H6 Preston Dorset, England U.K.
149 Q6 Preston East Riding of Yorkshire, England U.K.
149 L6 Preston Lancashire, England U.K.
146 L11 Preston Scottish Borders, Scotland U.K.
231 E9 Preston GA U.S.A.
238 I5 Preston ID U.S.A.
233 J10 Preston MD U.S.A.
226 B6 Preston MN U.S.A.
237 I7 Preston MO U.S.A.
86 D6 Preston, Cape W.A. Austr.
149 L2 Prestonpans East Lothian, Scotland U.K.
232 C11 Prestonsburg KY U.S.A.
262 N1 Prestrud Inlet Antarctica
149 M6 Prestwich Greater Manchester, England U.K.
146 G12 Prestwick South Ayrshire, Scotland U.K.
256 B3 Preto r. Brazil
256 C4 Preto r. Brazil
256 D2 Preto r. Brazil
253 E2 Preto r. Brazil
254 E4 Preto r. Brazil
251 E5 Preto r. Brazil
251 F5 Preto r. Brazil
215 M1 Pretoria S. Africa
Pretoria-Witwatersrand-Vereeniging prov. S. Africa see Gauteng
171 G7 Prettin Ger.
234 B5 Prettyboy Lake MD U.S.A.
173 K2 Pretzfeld Ger.
170 D5 Pretzier Ger.
171 G7 Pretzsch Ger.
171 I9 Pretzschendorf Ger.
159 M8 Preuilly-sur-Claise France
Preussisch-Eylau Rus. Fed. see Bagrationovsk
169 G6 Preußisch Oldendorf Ger.
Preußisch Stargard Pol. see Starogard Gdański
179 K6 Prevalje Slovenia
161 D7 Prévenchères France
162 I3 Préveranges France
198 B4 Preveza Greece
97 G9 Prey Vêng Cambodia
179 K7 Prežganje Slovenia
191 R4 Prezid Croatia
157 J7 Prez-sous-Lafauche France
178 D8 Priaforà, Monte mt. Italy
100 I4 Priamurskiy Rus. Fed.
120 J4 Priaral'skiye Karakumy, Peski des. Kazakh.
182 G3 Priaranza del Bierzo Spain
107 P1 Priargunsk Rus. Fed.
137 R8 Priazovskaya Rus. Fed.
177 H4 Pribeta Slovakia
176 F3 Přibice Czech Rep.
220 A4 Pribilof Islands AK U.S.A.
188 F3 Pribinić Bos.-Herz.
179 N7 Pribislavec Croatia
196 H7 Priboj Serbia
177 H2 Příbor Czech Rep.
170 G4 Priborn Ger.
176 D2 Příbram Czech Rep.
175 I1 Pribrezhnoye Rus. Fed.
176 E2 Přibyslav Czech Rep.
84 C3 Price r. N.T. Austr.
225 G3 Price Que. Can.
232 F12 Price NC U.S.A.
241 V2 Price UT U.S.A.
241 V2 Price r. UT U.S.A.
222 D4 Price Island B.C. Can.
138 E6 Prichaly Rus. Fed.
237 K10 Prichard AL U.S.A.
232 C10 Prichard WV U.S.A.
173 I2 Prichsenstadt Ger.
247 □6 Prickly Point Grenada
183 P8 Priego Spain
185 K6 Priego de Córdoba Spain
138 E5 Priekule Latvia
138 E6 Priekulė Lith.
138 I4 Priekuļi Latvia
138 G7 Prienai Kaunas Lith.
138 I7 Prienai Vilnius Lith.
173 M6 Prien am Chiemsee Ger.
171 I6 Prieros Ger.
214 G5 Prieska S. Africa
214 G5 Prieskapoort pass S. Africa
171 G8 Prießnitz Sachsen Ger.
171 E8 Prießnitz Sachsen-Anhalt Ger.
171 I8 Priestewitz Ger.
Priestholm i. Wales U.K. see Puffin Island
238 F2 Priest Lake ID U.S.A.
246 □ Priestman's River Jamaica
183 K2 Prieta, Peña mt. Spain
185 J7 Prieta, Sierra mt. Spain
185 M3 Prieto hill Spain
176 G3 Prievaly Slovakia
177 H3 Prievidza Slovakia
170 F4 Prignitz reg. Ger.
139 Q8 Prigor'ye Rus. Fed.
188 F3 Prijedor Bos.-Herz.
196 H7 Prijepolje Serbia
120 A5 Prikaspiyskaya Nizmennost' lowland Kazakh./Rus. Fed.
206 E5 Prikro Côte d'Ivoire
137 R8 Prikubanskaya Nizmennost' lowland Rus. Fed.
197 J9 Prilep Macedonia
Priluki Ukr. see Pryluky
187 H10 Prima, Punta pt Spain
252 D2 Primavera Bol.
254 B5 Primavera do Leste Brazil
176 B2 Přimda Czech Rep.
254 E2 Primeira Cruz Brazil
158 D4 Primel, Pointe de pt France
261 F2 Primero r. Arg.
246 D3 Primero de Enero Cuba
236 H4 Primghar IA U.S.A.
191 L4 Primolano Italy
175 I1 Primorsk Kaliningradskaya Oblast' Rus. Fed.
138 L1 Primorsk Leningradskaya Oblast' Rus. Fed.
135 I6 Primorsk Volgogradskaya Oblast' Rus. Fed.
Primorsk Ukr. see Prymors'k
100 G7 Primorskiy Rus. Fed.
100 I6 Primorskiy Kray admin. div. Rus. Fed.
135 G7 Primorsko-Akhtarsk Rus. Fed.
Primorskoye Ukr. see Prymors'ke
242 A1 Primo Tapia Mex.
222 B2 Primrose r. Y.T. Can.
223 I4 Primrose Lake Alta/Sask. Can.
172 B3 Prims r. Ger.
223 J4 Prince Albert Sask. Can.
214 G9 Prince Albert S. Africa
263 K1 Prince Albert Mountains Antarctica
223 J4 Prince Albert National Park Sask. Can.
220 G2 Prince Albert Peninsula N.W.T. Can.
214 F8 Prince Albert Road S. Africa
220 G2 Prince Albert Sound sea chan. N.W.T. Can.
220 F2 Prince Alfred, Cape N.W.T. Can.
214 D9 Prince Alfred Hamlet S. Africa
221 K3 Prince Charles Island Nunavut Can.
263 E2 Prince Charles Mountains Antarctica
225 I4 Prince Edward Island prov. Can.
265 G8 Prince Edward Islands Indian Ocean
227 R6 Prince Edward Point Ont. Can.
232 I10 Prince Frederick MD U.S.A.
86 H3 Prince Frederick Harbour W.A. Austr.
222 F4 Prince George B.C. Can.
234 B7 Prince George's County county MD U.S.A.
221 H2 Prince Gustaf Adolf Sea Nunavut Can.
263 C2 Prince Harald Coast Antarctica
220 B3 Prince of Wales, Cape AK U.S.A.
85 I1 Prince of Wales Island Qld Austr.
221 I2 Prince of Wales Island Nunavut Can.
220 E4 Prince of Wales Island AK U.S.A.
220 G2 Prince of Wales Strait N.W.T. Can.
220 G2 Prince Patrick Island N.W.T. Can.
86 H3 Prince Regent r. W.A. Austr.
221 I2 Prince Regent Inlet sea chan. Nunavut Can.
86 H3 Prince Regent Nature Reserve W.A. Austr.
222 D4 Prince Rupert B.C. Can.
247 □2 Prince Rupert Bay Dominica
151 K4 Princes Risborough Buckinghamshire, England U.K.
233 J10 Princess Anne MD U.S.A.
263 A2 Princess Astrid Coast Antarctica
85 I3 Princess Charlotte Bay Qld Austr.
263 F2 Princess Elizabeth Land reg. Antarctica
223 L1 Princess Mary Lake Nunavut Can.
86 H3 Princess May Range hills W.A. Austr.
81 B12 Princess Mountains South I. N.Z.
263 B2 Princess Ragnhild Coast Antarctica
87 F8 Princess Range hills W.A. Austr.
222 D4 Princess Royal Island B.C. Can.
247 □7 Prince's Town Trin. and Tob.
151 J3 Princethorpe Warwickshire, England U.K.
222 F5 Princeton B.C. Can.
240 J2 Princeton CA U.S.A.
226 E8 Princeton IL U.S.A.
230 D6 Princeton IN U.S.A.
230 D7 Princeton KY U.S.A.
233 □R3 Princeton ME U.S.A.
236 I5 Princeton MO U.S.A.
234 F4 Princeton NJ U.S.A.
226 E6 Princeton WI U.S.A.
232 D11 Princeton WV U.S.A.
234 F4 Princeton Junction NJ U.S.A.
150 E6 Princetown Devon, England U.K.
233 □R3 Prince William N.B. Can.
82 □2 Prince William Henry Bay Lord Howe I. Austr.
220 D3 Prince William Sound b. AK U.S.A.
207 G6 Príncipe i. São Tomé and Príncipe
238 D4 Prineville OR U.S.A.
198 F2 Prinos Thasos Greece
164 G5 Prinsenbeek Neth.
Prins Harald Kyst coastal area Antarctica see Prince Harald Coast
140 □ Prins Karls Forland i. Svalbard
137 Q3 Printsevka Rus. Fed.
242 □R11 Prinzapolca Nic.
168 G5 Prinzhöfte Ger.
195 I9 Priolo Gargallo Sicilia Italy
82 □3 Prion Lake S. Pacific Ocean
182 D1 Prior, Cabo c. Spain
182 D2 Prioriño Grande, Cabo c. Spain
183 K3 Prioro Spain
Priozernyy Kazakh. see Tugyl
139 N1 Priozersk Rus. Fed.
Priozyorsk Rus. Fed. see Priozersk
136 J2 Pripet r. Belarus/Ukr. alt. Pryp"yat' (Ukraine), alt. Prypyats' (Belarus)
136 D2 Pripet Marshes Belarus/Ukr.
111 K14 Priphema Nagaland India
134 L2 Pripolyarnyy Ural mts Rus. Fed.
197 P4 Priponeşti Romania
140 U2 Prirechnyy Rus. Fed.
197 P3 Prisăcani Romania
188 F3 Priseka hill Croatia
197 M3 Prislop, Pasul pass Romania
176 E1 Příšovice Czech Rep.
162 G2 Prissac France
160 F4 Prissé France
Pristan' Przheval'sk Kyrg. see Przheval'sk Pristany
137 P2 Pristen' Rus. Fed.
196 J8 Priština Kosovo Serbia
116 G7 Prithvipur Madh. Prad. India
173 J5 Prittriching Ger.
171 F6 Pritzerbe Ger.
170 D4 Pritzier Ger.
170 F4 Pritzwalk Ger.
161 F7 Privas France
193 K5 Priverno Italy
188 E3 Privlaka Croatia
139 S6 Privokzal'nyy Rus. Fed.
137 R7 Privol'naya Rus. Fed.
139 Y4 Privolzhsk Rus. Fed.
135 I6 Privolzhskaya Vozvyshennost' hills Rus. Fed.
135 I6 Privolzhskiy Rus. Fed.
120 A2 Privolzhskoye Rus. Fed.
120 C1 Privolzh'ye Rus. Fed.
135 H7 Priyutnoye Rus. Fed.
196 I8 Prizren Kosovo Serbia
194 E8 Prizzi Sicilia Italy
188 F3 Prnjavor Bos.-Herz.
182 H2 Proaza Spain
197 K8 Probištip Macedonia
95 J8 Probolinggo Jawa Indon.
168 J2 Probsteierhagen Ger.
171 D9 Probstzella Ger.
150 C7 Probus Cornwall, England U.K.
192 H2 Proceno Italy
174 E4 Prochowice Pol.
193 M6 Procida Italy
193 M6 Procida, Isola di i. Italy
226 B3 Proctor MN U.S.A.
233 L5 Proctor VT U.S.A.
232 C10 Proctorville OH U.S.A.
114 F5 Proddatur Andhra Prad. India
182 E9 Proença-a-Nova Port.
182 F8 Proença-a-Velha Port.
171 F8 Profen Ger.
251 H3 Professor van Blommestein Meer resr Suriname
165 G8 Profondeville Belgium
191 J5 Progno r. Italy
261 G2 Progreso Arg.
243 I4 Progreso Coahuila Mex.
245 H5 Progreso Hidalgo Mex.
245 K9 Progreso Oaxaca Mex.
243 O7 Progreso Yucatán Mex.
244 D2 Progreso Zacatecas Mex.
262 F2 Progress research stn Antarctica
100 F4 Progress Rus. Fed.
252 C2 Progresso Brazil
170 H2 Prohn Ger.
238 C6 Project City CA U.S.A.
175 I1 Prokhladnaya r. Rus. Fed.
129 F2 Prokhladnyy Rus. Fed.
137 P2 Prokhorovka Rus. Fed.
137 L2 Prokhory Ukr.
196 H8 Prokletije mts Albania/Yugo.
198 E4 Prokopi Greece
130 J4 Prokop'yevsk Rus. Fed.
197 J7 Prokuplje Serbia
139 O3 Proletariy Rus. Fed.
135 H7 Proletarsk Rus. Fed.
Proletarskaya Rus. Fed. see Proletarsk
137 O3 Proletarskiy Rus. Fed.
Prome Myanmar see Pyè
234 E2 Promised Land Lake PA U.S.A.
253 G4 Promissão Mato Grosso do Sul Brazil
256 C4 Promissão São Paulo Brazil
256 C4 Promissão, Represa resr Brazil
175 I4 Promna Pol.
193 P4 Promontorio del Gargano plat. Italy
234 E1 Prompton PA U.S.A.
234 E1 Prompton Lake PA U.S.A.
134 H4 Pronino Rus. Fed.
169 B10 Pronsfeld Ger.
139 W7 Pronsk Rus. Fed.
168 J3 Pronstorf Ger.
139 O8 Pronya r. Belarus
222 F3 Prophet r. B.C. Can.
222 F3 Prophet River B.C. Can.
226 E8 Prophetstown IL U.S.A.
254 F4 Propriá Brazil
192 B4 Propriano Corse France
170 I2 Prorer Wiek b. Ger.
129 H1 Prorva r. Rus. Fed.
120 K1 Proryvnoye Rus. Fed.
176 F2 Proseč Czech Rep.
171 I8 Prösen Ger.
179 N6 Prosenjakovci Slovenia
146 K9 Prosen Water r. Scotland U.K.
85 L6 Proserpine Qld Austr.
138 L6 Proshkava Belarus
Proskurov Ukr. see Khmel'nyts'kyy
199 G2 Proskynites Greece
174 F3 Prosna r. Pol.
198 E1 Prosotsani Greece
235 J1 Prospect CT U.S.A.
233 J5 Prospect NY U.S.A.
232 B8 Prospect OH U.S.A.
238 C5 Prospect OR U.S.A.
232 E8 Prospect PA U.S.A.
235 G4 Prospect Plains NJ U.S.A.
246 □ Prospect Point Jamaica
92 E7 Prosperidad Mindanao Phil.
148 D7 Prosperous Ireland
216 □2b Prosperous Bay St Helena
238 E3 Prosser WA U.S.A.
176 G2 Prostějov Czech Rep.
175 K2 Prostki Pol.
85 M9 Proston Qld Austr.
137 N8 Prostorne Ukr.
121 O3 Prostornoye Kazakh.
134 K2 Prosunduy Rus. Fed.
137 O4 Prosyane Ukr.
174 F5 Prószków Pol.
175 I5 Proszowice Pol.
175 I5 Proszówki Pol.
214 E10 Protem S. Africa
198 C5 Proti i. Greece
176 F2 Protivanov Czech Rep.
176 D2 Protivín Czech Rep.
137 Q8 Protoka r. Rus. Fed.
137 P4 Protopopivka Ukr.
136 J3 Protsiv Ukr.
139 T6 Protva Rus. Fed.
139 U7 Protva r. Rus. Fed.
139 U7 Protvino Rus. Fed.
170 I5 Prötzel Ger.
197 P7 Provadiya Bulg.
Prøven Greenland see Kangersuatsiaq
184 B5 Provença Port.
161 G10 Provence airport France
161 I9 Provence-Alpes-Côte d'Azur admin. reg. France
157 N7 Provenchères-sur-Fave France
Providence MD U.S.A. see Annapolis
233 N7 Providence RI U.S.A.
81 A13 Providence, Cape South I. N.Z.
217 □2 Providence Atoll Seychelles
227 L4 Providence Bay Ont. Can.
250 B5 Providencia Ecuador
246 C7 Providencia, Isla de i. Caribbean Sea
253 E2 Providência, Serra de hills Brazil
246 G3 Providenciales Island Turks and Caicos Is
131 T3 Provideniya Rus. Fed.
85 I2 Providential Channel Qld Austr.
233 O6 Provincetown MA U.S.A.
250 C3 Provincia Col.
156 F6 Provins France
241 U1 Provo UT U.S.A.
223 I4 Provost Alta Can.
188 F4 Prozor Bos.-Herz.
139 U3 Prozorovo Rus. Fed.
196 I9 Prrenjas Albania
206 E4 Pru r. Ghana
134 K3 Prub r. Rus. Fed.
137 L8 Prubiynyy, Mys pt Ukr.
175 K6 Pruchnik Pol.
256 B6 Prudentópolis Brazil
149 N4 Prudhoe Northumberland, England U.K.
220 D2 Prudhoe Bay AK U.S.A.
85 L6 Prudhoe Island Qld Austr.
137 N8 Prudi Ukr.
139 P7 Prudki Rus. Fed.
174 F5 Prudnik Pol.
137 P3 Prudyanka Ukr.
138 L6 Prudzinki Belarus
177 K3 Prügy Hungary
171 K10 Průhonice Czech Rep.
169 B10 Prüm Ger.
169 B11 Prüm r. Ger.
185 I7 Pruna Spain
197 M6 Prundeni Romania
197 O6 Prundu Romania
197 M3 Prundu Bârgăului Romania
Prundu Bîrgăului Romania see Prundu Bârgăului
192 C3 Prunelli-di-Fiumorbo Corse France
163 I6 Prunet France
161 I7 Prunières France
159 O7 Pruniers-en-Sologne France
232 E9 Pruntytown WV U.S.A.
Prusa Turkey see Bursa
179 O2 Prušánky Czech Rep.
Prushkov Pol. see Pruszków
174 E4 Prusice Pol.
177 G2 Prusinovice Czech Rep.
174 G2 Pruszcz Pol.
143 O7 Pruszcz Gdański Pol.
175 I3 Pruszków Pol.
136 H8 Prut r. Europe
173 M6 Prutting Ger.
178 C5 Prutz Austria
138 H9 Pruzhany Belarus
139 W9 Pruzhinki Rus. Fed.
177 H2 Pružina Slovakia
179 I8 Prvačina Slovenia
188 E3 Prvić i. Croatia
137 O2 Pryamitsyno Rus. Fed.
137 O6 Pryazovs'ka Vysochyna hills Ukr.
137 O7 Pryazovs'ke Ukr.
137 L6 Prychornomors'ka Nyzovyna lowland Ukr.
263 F2 Prydz Bay Antarctica
129 D2 Pryelbrussky Natsional'nyy Park nat. park Rus. Fed.
137 Q3 Prykolotne Ukr.
137 L3 Pryluky Ukr.
137 P7 Prymors'k Ukr.
Prymors'ke Donets'ka Oblast' Ukr. see Sartana
137 M7 Prymors'ke Khersons'ka Oblast' Ukr.
136 I8 Prymors'ke Odes'ka Oblast' Ukr.
137 O6 Prymors'ke Zaporiz'ka Oblast' Ukr.
137 O8 Prymors'kyy Ukr.
237 H7 Pryor OK U.S.A.
136 J2 Pryp"yat' Ukr.
136 J2 Pryp"yat' r. Ukr. alt. Prypyats' (Belarus), conv. Pripet
136 H1 Prypyats' r. Belarus alt. Pryp"yat' (Ukraine), conv. Pripet
138 K6 Prypyernaye Belarus
137 R4 Pryvillya Ukr.
137 L6 Pryvil'ne Ukr.
137 O8 Pryvitne Respublika Krym Ukr.
136 D3 Pryvitne Volyns'ka Oblast' Ukr.
137 M5 Pryyutivka Ukr.
175 I2 Przasnysz Pol.
174 F2 Przechlewo Pol.
175 H5 Przeciszów Pol.
175 J5 Przecław Pol.
177 I1 Przedborski Park Krajobrazowy Pol.
175 H4 Przedbórz Pol.
174 G3 Przedecz Pol.
174 D2 Przelewice Pol.
167 H3 Przemęcki Park Krajobrazowy Pol.
174 D4 Przemków Pol.
177 I1 Przemsza r. Pol.
175 K6 Przemyśl Pol.
175 K1 Przerośl Pol.
175 K3 Przesmyki Pol.
175 L5 Przewale Pol.
175 L4 Przewłoka Pol.
174 F5 Przeworno Pol.
175 K5 Przeworsk Pol.
174 C4 Przewóz Pol.
175 K3 Przeździatka Pol.
175 I2 Przezdzięk Wielki Pol.
175 H2 Przezmark Pol.
Przheval'sk Kyrg. see Karakol
100 H7 Przheval'skogo, Gory mts Rus. Fed.
139 O6 Przheval'skoye Rus. Fed.
121 R6 Przheval'sk Pristany Kyrg.
174 G1 Przodkowo Pol.
174 C2 Przybiernów Pol.
175 I3 Przyborowice Pol.
174 G3 Przybranowo Pol.
174 F4 Przygodzice Pol.
174 G4 Przykona Pol.
175 H5 Przyrów Pol.
175 J5 Przyrwa r. Pol.
174 G5 Przystajń Pol.
175 I4 Przysucha Pol.
174 D3 Przytoczna Pol.
175 K4 Przytoczno Pol.
175 K2 Przytuły Pol.
175 I4 Przytyk Pol.
174 G1 Przywidz Pol.
198 E4 Psachna Greece
Psakhná Greece see Psachna
198 F6 Psalidi, Akrotirio pt Milos Greece
199 G4 Psara Greece
199 G4 Psara i. Greece
198 F3 Psathoura i. Greece
129 B1 Psebay Rus. Fed.
129 F2 Psedakh Rus. Fed.
129 A1 Psekups r. Rus. Fed.
Psel r. Rus. Fed./Ukr. see Ps'ol
137 P2 Pselets Rus. Fed.
199 I6 Pserimos i. Greece
137 R9 Pshada Rus. Fed.
129 A1 Pshekha r. Rus. Fed.
137 N8 Pshenychne Ukr.
129 A1 Pshish r. Rus. Fed.
Pskent Uzbek. see Piskent
129 B2 P'skhu Georgia
129 C2 P'skhus Nakrdzali nature res. Georgia
138 L4 Pskov Rus. Fed.
138 K3 Pskov, Lake Estonia/Rus. Fed.
138 L4 Pskova r. Rus. Fed.
Pskov Oblast admin. div. Rus. Fed. see Pskovskaya Oblast'
138 M4 Pskovskaya Oblast' admin. div. Rus. Fed.
Pskovskoye Ozero l. Estonia/Rus. Fed. see Pskov, Lake
137 O2 Ps'ol r. Rus. Fed./Ukr.
188 F3 Psunj mts Croatia
129 E2 Psynodakh Rus. Fed.
174 D3 Pszczew Pol.
167 G2 Pszczewski Park Krajobrazowy Pol.
174 G1 Pszczółki Pol.
175 H4 Pszczonów Pol.
174 G6 Pszczyna Pol.
139 V8 Ptan' r. Rus. Fed.
198 D3 Pteleos Greece
Ptich' Belarus see Ptsich
198 C2 Ptolemaïda Greece
Ptolemais Israel see 'Akko
136 H1 Ptsich Belarus
138 L9 Ptsich r. Belarus
188 E2 Ptuj Slovenia
179 M7 Ptujsko jezero l. Slovenia
136 E3 Ptycha Ukr.
94 E6 Pu r. Indon.
260 A6 Púa Chile
96 E5 Pua Thai.
94 □ Puaka hill Sing.
240 □F14 Puakō HI U.S.A.
261 F5 Puán Arg.
108 E6 Pu'an Guizhou China
108 E3 Pu'an Sichuan China
78 □2 Pu'apu'a Samoa
78 □2 Puava, Cape Samoa
96 I3 Pubei Guangxi China
160 J4 Publier France
250 B6 Pucacaca Peru
250 C5 Pucacuro Peru
250 C5 Pucacuro r. Peru
250 B6 Pucalá Peru
252 B2 Pucallpa Peru
252 D4 Pucará Bol.
252 C3 Pucara Peru
252 C4 Pucarani Bol.
Pucarevo Bos.-Herz. see Novi Travnik
250 D5 Puca Urco Peru
178 H4 Puch bei Hallein Austria
179 M4 Puchberg am Schneeberg Austria
109 L5 Pucheng Fujian China
107 K9 Pucheng Shaanxi China
134 H4 Puchezh Rus. Fed.
173 K5 Puchheim Ger.
101 E10 Puch'ŏn S. Korea
177 H2 Púchov Slovakia
260 C2 Puchuzúh Arg.
197 N5 Pucioasa Romania
92 C6 Pucio Point Panay Phil.
143 O7 Puck Pol.
143 O7 Pucka, Zatoka b. Pol.
147 F7 Puckaun Ireland
87 D8 Puckford, Mount hill W.A. Austr.
187 E8 Puçol Spain
260 B6 Pucón Chile
Pudai watercourse Afgh. see Dor
122 F5 Pūdanū Iran
140 S4 Pudasjärvi Fin.
150 H6 Puddletown Dorset, England U.K.
169 E9 Puderbach Ger.
95 L6 Pudi Kalimantan Indon.
215 I3 Pudimoe S. Africa
108 E5 Puding Guizhou China
109 M3 Pudong Shanghai China
99 L5 Pudong airport Shanghai China
109 M3 Pudong airport China
134 G3 Pudozh Rus. Fed.
149 N6 Pudsey West Yorkshire, England U.K.
Pudu Hubei China see Suizhou
Puduchcheri Pondicherry India see Pondicherry
114 F7 Pudukkottai Tamil Nadu India
245 J5 Puebillo Mex.
241 Q9 Puebla Baja California Mex.
245 I6 Puebla Puebla Mex.
245 I7 Puebla state Mex.
261 G2 Puebla Brugo Arg.
186 D5 Puebla de Albortón Spain
185 I3 Puebla de Alcocer Spain
186 D4 Puebla de Alfindén Spain
183 O9 Puebla de Almenara Spain
183 N7 Puebla de Beleña Spain
185 O5 Puebla de Don Fadrique Spain
185 J2 Puebla de Don Rodrigo Spain
184 E5 Puebla de Guzmán Spain
184 F3 Puebla de la Calzada Spain
184 G3 Puebla de la Reina Spain
183 J2 Puebla de Lillo Spain
184 G4 Puebla del Maestre Spain
185 N3 Puebla del Príncipe Spain
184 G3 Puebla del Prior Spain
184 F2 Puebla de Obando Spain
182 G4 Puebla de Sanabria Spain
184 G4 Puebla de Sancho Pérez Spain
Puebla de San Julián Spain see A Pobra de San Xiao
187 C7 Puebla de San Miguel Spain
182 H7 Puebla de Yeltes Spain
Puebla de Zaragoza Mex. see Puebla
246 F8 Pueblito Col.
239 L7 Pueblo CO U.S.A.
261 H2 Pueblo Arrúa Arg.
258 C2 Pueblo Hundido Chile
261 F3 Pueblo Italiano Arg.
261 H2 Pueblo Libertador Arg.
261 G2 Pueblo Marini Arg.
244 B2 Pueblo Nuevo Mex.
242 □P11 Pueblo Nuevo Nic.
250 E4 Pueblo Viejo Col.
245 J3 Pueblo Viejo, Laguna de lag. Mex.
242 D4 Pueblo Yaqui Mex.
161 B8 Puech del Pal mt. France
163 I7 Puech de Rouet hill France
260 E6 Puelches Arg.
260 D5 Puelén Arg.
260 B3 Puente Alto Chile
Puenteareas Spain see Ponteareas
Puente Caldelas Spain see Ponte Caldelas
244 D4 Puente de Camotlán Mex.
182 G4 Puente de Domingo Flórez Spain
185 N4 Puente de Génave Spain
245 H7 Puente de Ixtla Mex.
182 I8 Puente del Congosto Spain
260 C3 Puente del Inca Arg.
186 G3 Puente de Montañana Spain
183 L2 Puente de San Miguel Spain
185 J6 Puente-Genil Spain
183 Q3 Puente la Reina Spain
183 L2 Puentenansa Spain
185 J4 Puente Nuevo, Embalse de resr Spain
185 P5 Puentes, Embalse de resr Spain
Puentes de García Rodríguez Spain see As Pontes de García Rodríguez
183 M6 Puentes Viejas, Embalse de resr Spain
250 D2 Puente Torres Venez.
183 M2 Puente Viesgo Spain
108 C7 Pu'er Yunnan China
247 □1 Puerca, Punta pt Puerto Rico
241 V7 Puerco watercourse AZ U.S.A.
239 K9 Puerco watercourse NM U.S.A.
252 C3 Puerto Acosta Bol.
259 B7 Puerto Aisén Chile
253 E3 Puerto Alegre Bol.
252 D3 Puerto Alejandría Bol.
250 D5 Puerto Alfonso Col.
250 B6 Puerto America Peru
243 K10 Puerto Ángel Mex.
245 K10 Puerto Angel Mex.
253 F6 Puerto Antequera Para.
245 N10 Puerto Arista Mex.
242 □R13 Puerto Armuelles Panama
250 B4 Puerto Asís Col.
250 E3 Puerto Ayacucho Venez.
250 □ Puerto Ayora Islas Galápagos Ecuador
259 B7 Puerto Bajo Pisagua Chile
250 □ Puerto Baquerizo Moreno Islas Galápagos Ecuador
242 □O10 Puerto Barrios Guat.
261 F6 Puerto Belgrano Arg.
258 F2 Puerto Bermejo Arg.
250 C3 Puerto Berrío Col.
250 C3 Puerto Boyacá Col.
250 D2 Puerto Cabello Venez.
242 □R10 Puerto Cabezas Nic.
242 □R10 Puerto Cabo Gracias á Dios Nic.
250 E3 Puerto Carreño Col.
253 F5 Puerto Casado Para.
252 D3 Puerto Cavinas Bol.
250 C5 Puerto Cerpera Peru
252 C2 Puerto Ceticayo Peru
259 B7 Puerto Chacabuco Chile
250 B6 Puerto Chicama Peru
259 B7 Puerto Cisnes Chile
259 C8 Puerto Coig Arg.
246 F8 Puerto Colombia Col.
261 H3 Puerto Constanza Arg.
250 D5 Puerto Córdoba Col.
242 □R13 Puerto Cortés Costa Rica
242 □P10 Puerto Cortés Hond.
242 D5 Puerto Cortés Mex.
250 C4 Puerto Cuemaní Col.
250 D2 Puerto Cumarebo Venez.
182 I8 Puerto de Béjar Spain
Puerto de Cabras Fuerteventura Canary Is see Puerto del Rosario
250 A5 Puerto de Cayo Ecuador
252 C3 Puerto Definitivo Peru
247 L8 Puerto de Hierro Venez.
216 □3b Puerto de la Cruz Fuerteventura Canary Is
216 □3a Puerto de la Cruz Tenerife Canary Is
216 □3e Puerto de la Estaca El Hierro Canary Is
244 G2 Puerto del Aire Mex.
216 □3b Puerto de la Peña Fuerteventura Canary Is
Puerto de la Selva Spain see El Port de la Selva
216 □3c Puerto del Carmen Lanzarote Canary Is
244 G8 Puerto del Gallo Mex.
245 H3 Puerto del Higuerón Mex.
242 C2 Puerto de Lobos Mex.
244 B2 Puerto de Los Ángeles, Parque Natural nature res. Mex.
245 I1 Puerto de los Ébanos Mex.
216 □3b Puerto del Rosario Fuerteventura Canary Is
Puerto del Son Galicia Spain see Porto do Son
Puerto del Son Galicia Spain see Porto do Son
187 C12 Puerto de Mazarrón Spain
243 P7 Puerto de Morelos Mex.
250 D2 Puerto de Nutrias Venez.
244 G4 Puerto de Palmas Mex.
244 G1 Puerto de Pastores Mex.
Puerto de Pollensa Spain see Port de Pollença
185 I1 Puerto de San Vicente Spain
Puerto de Sóller Spain see Port de Sóller
245 J10 Puerto Escondido Mex.
250 D1 Puerto Estrella Col.
250 B6 Puerto Eten Peru
258 C2 Puerto Flamenco Chile
Puerto Francisco de Orellana Orellana Ecuador see Coca
253 E3 Puerto Frey Bol.
261 F6 Puerto Galván Arg.
252 D3 Puerto Génova Bol.
252 D4 Puerto Grether Bol.
253 F5 Puerto Guarani Para.
259 D9 Puerto Harberton Arg.
252 C3 Puerto Heath Bol.
250 C4 Puerto Huitoto Col.
261 H3 Puerto Ibicuy Arg.
252 B2 Puerto Inca Peru
259 B7 Puerto Ingeniero Ibáñez Chile
261 F6 Puerto Ingeniero White Arg.
250 E4 Puerto Inírida Col.
258 E1 Puerto Irigoyen Arg.
253 F4 Puerto Isabel Bol.
242 □Q12 Puerto Jesús Costa Rica
243 P7 Puerto Juáres Mex.
247 K8 Puerto La Cruz Venez.
258 E1 Puerto La Paz Arg.
185 M2 Puerto Lápice Spain
186 F2 Puértolas Spain
250 C5 Puerto Leguizamo Col.
242 □R10 Puerto Lempira Hond.
242 C3 Puerto Libertad Mex.
242 □R12 Puerto Limón Costa Rica
185 K3 Puertollano Spain
259 D6 Puerto Lobos Arg.
250 D2 Puerto Lopez Col.
250 C3 Puerto Lopéz Col.
250 A5 Puerto López Ecuador
185 P5 Puerto Lumbreras Spain
243 M10 Puerto Madero Mex.
259 D6 Puerto Madryn Arg.
242 C5 Puerto Magdalena Mex.
252 C3 Puerto Maldonado Peru
252 D4 Puerto Mamoré Bol.
246 E3 Puerto Manatí Cuba
250 A6 Puerto Máncora Peru
253 F5 Puerto María Auxiliadora Para.
Puertomarín Spain see Portomarín
252 D3 Puerto Marquez Bol.
259 B6 Puerto Melinka Chile
250 C4 Puerto Mercedes Col.
Puerto México Mex. see Coatzacoalcos
253 F5 Puerto Mihanovich Para.
187 E7 Puertomingalvo Spain
250 E3 Puerto Miranda Venez.
259 B6 Puerto Montt Chile
242 □P11 Puerto Morazán Nic.
250 B7 Puerto Morín Peru
216 □3d Puerto Naos La Palma Canary Is
259 B8 Puerto Natales Chile
250 D3 Puerto Nuevo Col.
250 C3 Puerto Olaya Col.
251 F2 Puerto Ordaz Venez.
250 C4 Puerto Ospina Col.
246 E3 Puerto Padre Cuba
250 E3 Puerto Páez Venez.
252 D3 Puerto Pando Bol.
250 B5 Puerto Pardo Peru
252 C3 Puerto Pariamanu Peru
242 C2 Puerto Peñasco Mex.
253 F5 Puerto Pinasco Para.
259 D6 Puerto Pirámides Arg.
251 E2 Puerto Píritu Venez.
250 C5 Puerto Pizarro Col.
246 H4 Puerto Plata Dom. Rep.
252 B2 Puerto Portillo Peru
252 B2 Puerto Prado Peru
Puerto Presidente Stroessner Para. see Ciudad del Este
92 B7 Puerto Princesa Palawan Phil.
242 □Q13 Puerto Quepos Costa Rica
242 N11 Puerto Quetzal Guat.
243 N8 Puerto Real Mex.
184 G7 Puerto Real Spain
258 G2 Puerto Rico Arg.
252 D2 Puerto Rico Bol.
216 □3f Puerto Rico Gran Canaria Canary Is
250 C4 Puerto Rico Col.
247 □1 Puerto Rico terr. West Indies
264 E4 Puerto Rico Trench sea feature Caribbean Sea
261 H3 Puerto Ruiz Arg.
259 B5 Puerto Saavedra Chile
250 C3 Puerto Salgar Col.
Puerto Sama Cuba see Samá
250 D5 Puerto San Agustin Peru
259 B7 Puerto San Carlos Chile
242 □P11 Puerto Sandino Nic.
243 N11 Puerto San José Guat.
259 C8 Puerto Santa Cruz Arg.
253 F5 Puerto Sastre Para.
253 E3 Puerto Saucedo Bol.
Puertos de Beceite mts Spain see Ports de Beseit
182 G7 Puerto Seguro Spain
184 H7 Puerto Serrano Spain
252 D3 Puerto Siles Bol.
250 D5 Puerto Socorro Peru
Puerto Somoza Nic. see Puerto Sandino
253 F4 Puerto Suárez Bol.
252 A2 Puerto Supe Peru
252 C3 Puerto Tahuantisuyo Peru
250 B4 Puerto Tejado Col.
250 B5 Puerto Tunigrama Peru
250 B4 Puerto Umbría Col.
259 E6 Puerto Valdés Arg.
244 B5 Puerto Vallarta Mex.
259 B6 Puerto Varas Chile
250 □ Puerto Velasco Ibarra Islas Galápagos Ecuador
252 B2 Puerto Victoria Peru
250 □ Puerto Villamil Islas Galápagos Ecuador
253 E3 Puerto Villazon Bol.
259 D7 Puerto Visser Arg.
250 C3 Puerto Wilches Col.
259 C9 Puerto Yartou Chile
261 H2 Puerto Yerua Arg.
250 C5 Puesto Arturo Peru
260 D6 Puesto Sánchez Arg.
79 □9a Pueu Tahiti Fr. Polynesia
183 Q3 Pueyo Spain
191 L2 Puez-Odle, Parco Naturale nature res. Italy
150 D1 Puffin Island Wales U.K.
253 F4 Puga Brazil
120 C1 Pugachev Rus. Fed.
134 K4 Pugachevo Rus. Fed.
116 D5 Pugal Rajasthan India
211 C8 Puga Puga, Ilha i. Moz.
108 D5 Puge Sichuan China
95 J9 Puger Jawa Indon.
161 J10 Puget-sur-Argens Franc[e]
161 J9 Puget-Théniers France
161 I10 Puget-Ville France
234 D4 Pughtown PA U.S.A.
193 P5 Puglia admin. reg. Italy
193 I2 Puglia r. Italy
162 C5 Pugnac France
193 Q4 Pugnochiuso Italy
225 I4 Pugwash N.S. Can.
80 L5 Puha North I. N.Z.
122 F8 Pūhāl-e Khamīr, Kūh-e mts Iran
107 J9 Pu He r. China
Puhiwaero c. Stewart I. [N.Z.] see South West Cape
138 J3 Puhja Estonia
197 L5 Pui Romania
161 B10 Puichéric France
197 P5 Puieşti Romania
187 E8 Puig Spain
186 I3 Puigcerdà Spain
186 J3 Puigmal mt. France/Spa[in]
186 I4 Puig-reig Spain
186 G4 Puigverd de Lleida Spa[in]
161 I9 Puimoisson France
109 □I7 Pui O Wan b. H.K. China
160 B2 Puisaye reg. France
156 D7 Puiseaux France
156 E3 Puisieux France
163 D6 Puisseguin France
161 C10 Puisserguier France
156 H6 Puits r. France
202 C6 Puits 29 well Chad
202 C6 Puits 30 well Chad
163 I10 Puivert France
92 F8 Pujada Bay Mindanao Ph[il.]
161 F8 Pujaut France
206 C5 Pujehun Sierra Leone
Puji Shaanxi China see Wugong
109 L4 Pujiang Zhejiang China
163 E9 Pujo France
163 D6 Pujols Aquitaine France
163 F7 Pujols Aquitaine France
81 E11 Pukaki, Lake South I. N.[Z.]
177 H3 Pukanec Slovakia
101 E10 Puk'an-san National Pa[rk] S. Korea
81 □2 Pukapuka atoll Cook Is
79 □9 Pukapuka atoll Arch. des Tuamotu Fr. Polynesia
79 □9 Pukarua atoll Arch. des Tuamotu Fr. Polynesia
226 I1 Pukaskwa r. Ont. Can.
224 C3 Pukaskwa National Par[k] Ont. Can.
223 K4 Pukatawagan Man. Can[.]
101 D8 Pukchin N. Korea
101 F8 Pukch'ŏng N. Korea
196 H8 Pukë Albania
80 M4 Pukeamaru hill North I. [N.Z.]
80 I5 Pukearuhe North I. N.Z.
80 K6 Pukehoi North I. N.Z.
80 I4 Pukekohe North I. N.Z.
80 H1 Pukenui North I. N.Z.
80 J6 Pukeokahu North I. N.Z.
81 E12 Pukerangi South I. N.Z.
81 D13 Pukerau South I. N.Z.
80 J6 Pukeroa North I. N.Z.
81 I8 Pukerua Bay North I. N.[Z.]
81 G10 Puketeraki Range mts South I. N.Z.
80 K6 Puketitiri North I. N.Z.
80 L4 Puketoetoe mt. North I. [N.Z.]
80 K7 Puketoi Range hills North I. N.Z.
80 J5 Puketutu North I. N.Z.
81 F12 Pukeuri Junction South [I. N.Z.]
139 O6 Pukhnovo Rus. Fed.
137 S3 Pukhovo Rus. Fed.
141 R6 Pukkila Fin.
134 K4 Puksib Rus. Fed.
134 H3 Puksoozero Rus. Fed.
101 E8 Puksubaek-san mt. N. K[orea]
188 D3 Pula Croatia
191 P6 Pula airport Croatia
192 C9 Pula Sardegna Italy
192 C10 Pula, Capo di c. Sardeg[na] Italy
252 D5 Pulacayo Bol.
107 R7 Pulandian Liaoning Chin[a]
107 Q7 Pulandian Wan b. China
92 E8 Pulangi r. Mindanao Phil
95 K6 Pulangpisau Kalimantan [Indon.]
91 K5 Pulap atoll Micronesia
252 C6 Pular, Cerro mt. Chile
93 B7 Pulasi i. Indon.
233 I5 Pulaski NY U.S.A.
231 D8 Pulaski TN U.S.A.
232 E11 Pulaski VA U.S.A.
226 F5 Pulaski WI U.S.A.
91 I8 Pulau r. Papua Indon.
94 E5 Pulaukijang Sumatera In[don.]
95 J4 Pulaumajang Kalimantan Indon.
Pulau Pinang state Mala[ysia] see Pinang
175 J4 Puławy Pol.
151 K6 Pulborough West Sussex[,] England U.K.
191 O3 Pulfero Italy
116 G9 Pulgaon Mahar. India
183 L9 Pulgar Spain
169 C8 Pulheim Ger.
114 G6 Pulicat Tamil Nadu India
114 G6 Pulicat Lake inlet India
160 F3 Puligny-Montrachet Fra[nce]
114 F5 Pulivendla Andhra Prad. [India]
140 R2 Pulju Fin.
179 M2 Pulkau Austria
179 N2 Pulkau r. Austria
140 R4 Pulkkila Fin.
173 L5 Pullach in Isartal Ger.
238 F3 Pullman WA U.S.A.
252 B3 Pullo Peru
92 C3 Pulog, Mount Luzon Phi[l.]
140 V2 Pulozero Rus. Fed.
185 P6 Pulpí Spain
242 D4 Púlpito, Punta pt Mex.
195 M3 Pulsano Italy
171 H8 Pulsen Ger.
171 J8 Pulsnitz Ger.
171 I8 Pulsnitz r. Ger.
175 J3 Pułtusk Pol.
111 E8 Pulu Xinjiang China
127 I4 Pülümür Turkey
91 K5 Pulusuk atoll Micronesia
93 E1 Pulutan Sulawesi Indon.
91 K5 Puluwat atoll Micronesia
157 N8 Pulversheim France
116 E3 Pulwama Jammu and Ka[shmir]
211 B6 Puma Tanz.
259 B6 Pumalin, Parque nat. pa[rk] Chile
260 B4 Pumanque Chile
111 J12 Puma Yumco l. China
Pumiao Guangxi China s[ee] Yongning
238 L3 Pumpkin Creek r. MT U.[S.A.]
150 E3 Pumsaint Carmarthensh[ire,] Wales U.K.
258 E2 Puna Arg.
250 A5 Puná, Isla i. Ecuador
79 □9a Punaauia Tahiti Fr. Polyn[esia]
79 □9a Punaauia, Pointe pt Tah[iti] Fr. Polynesia
81 F9 Punakaiki South I. N.Z.
117 L6 Punakha Bhutan
240 □F14 Punalu'u HI U.S.A.
79 □9a Punaruu r. Tahiti Fr. Poly[nesia]
191 R5 Punat Croatia
252 D4 Punata Bol.
123 P5 Punch Pak.
222 F4 Punchaw B.C. Can.
213 F4 Punda Maria S. Africa
116 F5 Pundri Haryana India
114 C3 Pune Mahar. India
114 F6 Punganuru Andhra Prad. [India]
94 □ Punggol Sing.
94 □ Punggol, Sungai r. Sing.
209 B7 Pungo Andango Angola
101 F8 P'ungsan N. Korea
213 G3 Púnguè r. Moz.
191 J2 Puni r. Italy
208 E5 Punia Dem. Rep. Congo
175 M1 Punia Lith.
258 C3 Punilla, Cordillera de la Chile
109 K7 Puning Guangdong China
260 B2 Punitaqui Chile
116 E4 Punjab state India

Q

156 I5 Quatre-Champs France
217 □1b Quatre Cocos, Pointe pt Mauritius
187 E10 Quatretonda Spain
216 □1a Quatro Ribeiras Terceira Azores
129 J4 Quba Azer.
129 H6 Qubadlı Azer.
129 K5 Qubalıbalaoğlan Azer.
122 H3 Quchan Iran
128 G3 Qudaym Syria
125 M6 Qudaysah well Oman
215 O4 Qudeni S. Africa
129 J4 Qudıyalçay r. Azer.
212 B2 Qué Angola
83 L6 Queanbeyan A.C.T. Austr.
225 G4 Québec Que. Can.
225 F2 Québec prov. Can.
256 D3 Quebra Anzol r. Brazil
261 I3 Quebracho Uru.
258 E3 Quebrachos Arg.
260 E2 Quebrada del Condorito, Parque Nacional nat. park Arg.
247 □1 Quebradillas Puerto Rico
245 H8 Quechultenango Mex.
259 B6 Quedal, Cabo c. Chile
213 G3 Quedas Moz.
150 H4 Quedgeley Gloucestershire, England U.K.
171 D7 Quedlinburg Ger.
Queen Adelaide Islands Chile see Reina Adelaida, Archipiélago de la
128 D7 Queen Alia airport Jordan
234 D7 Queen Anne MD U.S.A.
234 C6 Queen Anne's County county MD U.S.A.
222 E5 Queen Bess, Mount B.C. Can.
151 N5 Queenborough Kent, England U.K.
222 C4 Queen Charlotte B.C. Can.
259 E8 Queen Charlotte Bay Falkland Is
222 C4 Queen Charlotte Islands B.C. Can.
222 D5 Queen Charlotte Sound sea chan. B.C. Can.
81 H8 Queen Charlotte Sound sea chan. South I. N.Z.
222 E5 Queen Charlotte Strait B.C. Can.
226 B9 Queen City MO U.S.A.
241 U8 Queen Creek AZ U.S.A.
221 H2 Queen Elizabeth Islands N.W.T./Nunavut Can.
210 A5 Queen Elizabeth National Park Uganda
263 K1 Queen Elizabeth Range mts Antarctica
263 C2 Queen Fabiola Mountains Antarctica
222 B2 Queen Mary, Mount Y.T. Can.
263 G2 Queen Mary Land reg. Antarctica
216 □2c Queen Mary's Peak Tristan da Cunha S. Atlantic Ocean
221 H3 Queen Maud Gulf Nunavut Can.
263 A2 Queen Maud Land reg. Antarctica
262 O1 Queen Maud Mountains Antarctica
215 O5 Queensburgh S. Africa
149 N6 Queensbury West Yorkshire, England U.K.
84 B3 Queens Channel N.T. Austr.
221 I2 Queens Channel Nunavut Can.
83 J8 Queenscliff Vic. Austr.
235 H3 Queens County county NY U.S.A.
85 J7 Queensland state Austr.
83 J10 Queenstown Tas. Austr.
81 C12 Queenstown South I. N.Z.
Queenstown Ireland see Cobh
215 K7 Queenstown S. Africa
94 □ Queenstown Sing.
234 C7 Queenstown MD U.S.A.
87 G11 Queen Victoria Spring Nature Reserve W.A. Austr.
238 B3 Queets WA U.S.A.
261 H3 Queguay Grande r. Uru.
252 D4 Quehua Bol.
260 E5 Quehué Arg.
202 D5 Queiba well Chad
160 I5 Queige France
183 M1 Queijo, Cabo c. Spain
253 E2 Queimada Brazil
251 I5 Queimada, Ilha i. Brazil
216 □1c Queimada, Ponta da pt Pico Azores
254 F4 Queimadas Brazil
216 □1a Queimado, Ponta do pt Terceira Azores
182 E7 Queiriga Port.
256 B4 Queiroz Brazil
183 P4 Quel Spain
209 C7 Quela Angola
159 J6 Quelaines-St-Gault France
213 H3 Quelimane Moz.
244 A2 Quelite Mex.
260 A5 Quella Chile
171 F7 Quellendorf Ger.
259 B6 Quellón Chile
209 B6 Quelo Angola
Quelpart Island S. Korea see Cheju-do
257 E5 Queluz Brazil
184 A3 Queluz Port.
183 M5 Quemada Spain
256 D6 Quemada Grande, Ilha i. Brazil
239 J9 Quemado NM U.S.A.
209 D8 Quembo r. Angola
259 B6 Quemchi Chile
Quemoy i. Taiwan see Chinmen Tao
261 F5 Quemú-Quemú Arg.
156 C3 Quend France
169 D6 Quendorf Ger.
171 D7 Quenstedt Ger.
185 M6 Quéntar Spain
234 C4 Quentin PA U.S.A.
114 D5 Quepem Goa India
Que Que Zimbabwe see Kwekwe
261 H6 Quequén Arg.
261 H6 Quequén Grande r. Arg.
186 J3 Queralbs Spain
190 I9 Quercianella Italy
163 G7 Quercy reg. France
184 D6 Querença Port.
254 B5 Querência Brazil
256 A5 Querência do Norte Brazil
244 G6 Queréndaro Mex.
169 K6 Querenhorst Ger.
244 G5 Querétaro Mex.
245 H5 Querétaro state Mex.
171 E8 Querfurt Ger.
163 I10 Quérigut France
168 I1 Quern Ger.
169 F6 Quernheim Ger.
149 L5 Quernmore Lancashire, England U.K.
191 L4 Quero Italy
183 N9 Quero Spain
242 D2 Querobabi Mex.
186 H5 Querol Spain
250 B6 Querpon Peru
158 H2 Querqueville France
156 D4 Querrieu France
157 L8 Quers France
187 D9 Quesa Spain
185 M5 Quesada Spain
185 M5 Quesada r. Spain
204 C4 Quesat watercourse Western Sahara
109 J2 Queshan Henan China
222 F4 Quesnel B.C. Can.
222 F4 Quesnel r. B.C. Can.
222 F4 Quesnel Lake B.C. Can.
156 F2 Quesnoy-sur-Deûle France
158 F5 Quessoy France
156 F4 Quessy France
158 G6 Questembert France
252 D5 Quetena de Lipez r. Bol.
226 C1 Quetico Provincial Park Ont. Can.
160 G2 Quetigny France
123 L6 Quetta Pak.
158 I2 Quettehou France
158 I4 Quettreville-sur-Sienne France
245 I9 Quetzala r. Mex.
245 H7 Quetzalapa Guerrero Mex.
245 H5 Quetzalapa Hidalgo Mex.
243 N10 Quetzaltenango Guat.
260 B5 Queuco Chile
259 B7 Queulat, Parque Nacional nat. park Chile
259 B5 Queule Chile
259 D6 Queupán Arg.
156 D4 Quevauvillers France
158 E6 Quéven France
158 G5 Quévert France
162 C5 Queyrac France
161 J7 Queyras, Parc Naturel Régional du nature res. France
163 I6 Quézac France
243 O11 Quezaltepeque El Salvador
92 D6 Quezon Negros Phil.
92 B7 Quezon Palawan Phil.
92 C4 Quezon City Luzon Phil.
124 E2 Qufār Saudi Arabia
107 O9 Qufu Shandong China
182 C8 Quiaios Port.
209 B7 Quibala Angola
209 B7 Quibaxe Angola
250 B3 Quibdó Col.
158 E7 Quiberon France
158 E6 Quiberon, Baie de b. France
158 E6 Quiberon, Presqu'île de pen. France
250 D2 Quíbor Venez.
209 B7 Quicabo Angola
209 B7 Quiçama, Parque Nacional do nat. park Angola
96 G5 Qui Châu Vietnam
168 I3 Quickborn Ger.
209 B7 Quiculungo Angola
157 N5 Quierschied Ger.
156 F4 Quierzy France
222 C2 Quiet Lake Y.T. Can.
156 G3 Quiévrechain France
209 B8 Quihita Angola
209 C6 Quihuhu Angola
253 F6 Quiindy Para.
242 F5 Quilá Mex.
260 A5 Quilaco Chile
242 □P11 Quilalí Nic.
259 B6 Quilán, Cabo c. Chile
114 D7 Quilandi Kerala India
252 B4 Quilca Peru
261 G5 Quilco Arg.
209 B7 Quilenda Angola
209 B8 Quilengues Angola
190 E7 Quiliano Italy
260 B3 Quilimarí Chile
260 E2 Quilino Arg.
252 D4 Quillacollo Bol.
260 B2 Quillaicillo Chile
163 I10 Quillan France
223 J5 Quill Lakes Sask. Can.
260 A5 Quillón Chile
260 B3 Quillota Chile
261 H4 Quilmes Arg.
209 B7 Quilombo dos Dembos Angola
114 E8 Quilon Kerala India
85 J9 Quilpie Qld Austr.
260 B3 Quilpué Chile
213 H3 Quilua Moz.
209 C7 Quimbango Angola
209 C6 Quimbele Angola
209 C7 Quimbonge Angola
252 D4 Quime Bol.
244 B3 Quimichis Mex.
258 E2 Quimilí Arg.
253 E4 Quimome Bol.
158 C6 Quimper France
158 D6 Quimperlé France
147 E7 Quin Ireland
146 F6 Quinag hill Scotland U.K.
92 D5 Quinalasag i. Phil.
238 B3 Quinault r. WA U.S.A.
238 B3 Quinault Indian Reservation res. WA U.S.A.
252 C3 Quince Mil Peru
190 D4 Quincinetto Italy
240 L2 Quincy CA U.S.A.
231 E10 Quincy FL U.S.A.
230 B6 Quincy IL U.S.A.
233 N6 Quincy MA U.S.A.
226 J8 Quincy MI U.S.A.
232 B8 Quincy OH U.S.A.
156 E6 Quincy-Voisins France
250 C3 Quindío dept Col.
260 E3 Quines Arg.
158 I2 Quinéville France
213 I2 Quinga Moz.
160 H2 Quingey France
110 I6 Quinggir Xinjiang China
220 B4 Quinhagak AK U.S.A.
206 B4 Quinhámel Guinea-Bissau
251 E3 Quinigua, Cerro mts Venez.
261 G5 Quiñihual Arg.
92 C6 Quiniluban i. Phil.
250 B4 Quinindé Ecuador
85 J3 Quinkan Aboriginal Holding res. Qld Austr.
238 E6 Quinn r. NV U.S.A.
241 Q4 Quinn Canyon Range mts NV U.S.A.
232 D11 Quinnimont WV U.S.A.
252 D2 Quiñones Bol.
161 I9 Quinson France
160 B4 Quinssaines France
184 D6 Quintã hill Port.
184 B3 Quinta do Anjo Port.
256 B5 Quintana Brazil
184 H3 Quintana de la Serena Spain
182 H3 Quintana del Castillo Spain
183 M3 Quintana del Pino Spain
183 L4 Quintana del Puente Spain
183 J3 Quintana de Rueda Spain
183 M4 Quintanapalla Spain
183 N9 Quintanar de la Orden Spain
183 N5 Quintanar de la Sierra Spain
185 P2 Quintanar del Rey Spain
183 O5 Quintana Redonda Spain
243 O8 Quintana Roo state Mex.
182 G5 Quintanilha Port.
Quintanilla de Abajo Spain see Quintanilla de Onésimo
183 L5 Quintanilla de Onésimo Spain
182 C7 Quintãs Port.
260 B3 Quintay Chile
161 F6 Quintenas France
236 E6 Quinter KS U.S.A.
260 B3 Quintero Chile
158 F5 Quintin France
260 E4 Quinto r. Arg.
186 E5 Quinto Spain
190 F2 Quinto Switz.
234 E5 Quinton NJ U.S.A.
182 D5 Quinxo, Monte do mts Port.
209 B6 Quinzau Angola
227 O2 Quinze, Lac des l. Que. Can.
211 D7 Quionga Moz.
245 K8 Quiotepec Mex.
254 G4 Quipapá Brazil
185 P4 Quipar r. Spain
209 B8 Quipungo Angola
252 D3 Quiquive r. Bol.
242 □O10 Quiriguá tourist site Guat.
260 A5 Quirihue Chile
209 C7 Quirima Angola
211 D8 Quirimbas, Parque Nacional das nat. park Moz.
83 M4 Quirindi N.S.W. Austr.
256 B3 Quirinópolis Brazil
247 L9 Quiriquire Venez.
227 L3 Quirke Lake Ont. Can.
261 G4 Quiroga Arg.
252 D4 Quiroga Bol.
244 F6 Quiroga Mex.
182 F4 Quiroga Spain
192 D8 Quirra, Isola di i. Sardegna Italy
182 I4 Quiruelas de Vidriales Spain
250 D2 Quisiro Venez.
183 L8 Quismondo Spain
161 E9 Quissac France
257 G5 Quissamã Brazil
211 D8 Quissanga Moz.
213 G5 Quissico Moz.
209 C7 Quitapa Angola
246 C6 Quita Sueño Bank sea feature Caribbean Sea
211 D7 Quiterajo Moz.
256 B4 Quitéria r. Brazil
209 B9 Quiteve Angola
Quitexe Angola see Dange
258 E2 Quitilipi Arg.
231 F10 Quitman GA U.S.A.
237 K9 Quitman MS U.S.A.
237 H9 Quitman TX U.S.A.
250 B5 Quito Ecuador
242 C2 Quitovac Mex.
259 B7 Quitralco, Parque Nacional nat. park Chile
156 A5 Quittebeuf France
254 F3 Quixadá Brazil
213 I2 Quixaxe Moz.
254 F3 Quixeramobim Brazil
209 B7 Quixinge Angola
109 I6 Qujiang Guangdong China
Qujiang Sichuan China see Quxian
108 F3 Qu Jiang r. China
108 H8 Qujie Guangdong China
108 D6 Qujing Yunnan China
215 M8 Quko S. Africa
Qulaly Araly i. Kazakh. see Kulaly, Ostrov
203 G3 Qul'ān, Jazā'ir i. Egypt
Qulandy Kazakh. see Kulandy
Qulanōtpes watercourse Kazakh. see Kulanotpes
127 M9 Qulbān Layyah well Iraq
129 C3 Qulevi Georgia
111 G11 Qulho Xizang China
107 R3 Qulin Gol r. China
120 J7 Quljuqtov tog'lari hills Uzbek.
Quljuqtow Toghi hills Uzbek. see Quljuqtov tog'lari
Qulsary Kazakh. see Kul'sary
126 E9 Qulūṣanā Egypt
128 A9 Qulzum, Baḥr al b. Egypt
106 D9 Qumar He r. China
106 C9 Qumarheyan Qinghai China
111 L10 Qumarlêb Qinghai China
215 M7 Qumbu S. Africa
111 L11 Qumdo Xizang China
111 H11 Qumigxung Xizang China
Qumola watercourse Kazakh. see Kumola
215 L8 Qumrha S. Africa
129 G4 Qūnäşli Azer.
124 G3 Qunayfidhah, Nafūd des. Saudi Arabia
124 G4 Qunayy well Saudi Arabia
202 D2 Qunayyin, Sabkhat al salt marsh Libya
125 I7 Qunfudh Yemen
Qŭnghirot Uzbek. see Qo'ng'irot
106 G9 Qu'ngoin r. Qinghai China
111 J10 Quntamari Xizang China
108 A3 Qu'nyido Xizang China
223 M1 Quoich r. Nunavut Can.
146 F8 Quoich, Loch l. Scotland U.K.
147 K4 Quoile r. Northern Ireland U.K.
217 □1b Quoin Channel Mauritius
84 B3 Quoin Island N.T. Austr.
214 D10 Quoin Point S. Africa
82 G5 Quorn S.A. Austr.
212 E4 Quoxo r. Botswana
122 E5 Qūptān Iran
Quqên Sichuan China see Jinchuan
Qŭqon Uzbek. see Qo'qon
118 C7 Quraid Sudan
125 N4 Qurayat Oman
128 E10 Qurayyah tourist site Saudi Arabia
128 C8 Qurayyah, Wādī watercourse Egypt
128 F7 Qurayyat al Milḥ l. Jordan
123 M3 Qŭrghonteppa Tajik.
129 H4 Qurmuxçay r. Azer.
129 F7 Qūrū Gol pass Iran
203 G3 Qūş Egypt
129 J4 Qusar Azer.
129 J4 Qusarçay r. Azer.
125 J8 Quşay'ir Saudi Arabia
Qushan Sichuan China see Beichuan
122 A3 Qūshchī Iran
122 B2 Qūsheh Dāgh mts Iran
Qŭshkŭpir Uzbek. see Qo'shko'pir
Qŭshrabot Uzbek. see Qo'shrabot
Qusmuryn Kazakh. see Kushmurun
Qusmuryn Kōli salt l. Kazakh. see Kushmurun, Ozero
111 D10 Qusum Xizang China
111 K12 Qusum Xizang China
Quthing Lesotho see Moyeni
215 L6 Quthing r. Lesotho
122 C4 Qūṭīābād Iran
124 F2 Quṭn, Jabal hill Saudi Arabia
221 K1 Quttinirpaaq National Park Nunavut Can.
124 E6 Qutū' i. Saudi Arabia
128 F3 Quwayq, Nahr r. Syria/Turkey
125 L6 Qū' Wishām reg. Oman
107 L9 Quwo Shanxi China
106 I8 Quwu Shan mts China
Quxi Guangdong China see Jiedong
108 F3 Quxian Sichuan China
Quxian Zhejiang China see Quzhou
111 J12 Qūxü Xizang China
Quyang Hunan China see Jingzhou
Quyghan Kazakh. see Kuygan
96 F4 Quynh Nhai Vietnam
97 I8 Quy Nhơn Vietnam
227 R4 Quyon Que. Can.
122 A3 Qūyūn Eshek i. Iran
124 E6 Qūz Saudi Arabia
129 I5 Quzanlı Azer.
107 N8 Quzhou Hebei China
109 L4 Quzhou Zhejiang China
107 J8 Quzi Gansu China
129 G4 Qvareli Georgia
129 E3 Qvirila r. Georgia
Qypshaq Kōli salt l. Kazakh. see Kypshak, Ozero
Qyteti Stalin Albania see Kuçovë
Qyzan Kazakh. see Kyzan
Qyzylaghash Kazakh. see Kyzylagash
Qyzylkesek Kazakh. see Kyzylkesek
Qyzylköl l. Kazakh. see Kyzylkol', Ozero
Qyzylorda Kazakh. see Kyzylorda
Qyzylorda Oblysy admin. div. Kazakh. see Kyzylordinskaya Oblast'
Qyzyltas Kazakh. see Kyzyltas
Qyzyltaū Kazakh. see Kyzyltau
Qyzyltū Kazakh. see Kishkenekol'
Qyzylzhar Kazakh. see Kyzylzhar

R

179 I3 Raab Austria
179 N6 Raab r. Austria
Raab Hungary see Győr
179 L2 Raabs an der Thaya Austria
140 R4 Raahe Fin.
140 T5 Rääkkylä Fin.
164 J4 Raalte Neth.
164 G5 Raamsdonksveer Neth.
124 F2 Ra'an, Khashm ar hill Saudi Arabia
140 R3 Raanujärvi Fin.
95 K8 Raas i. Indon.
146 D8 Raasay i. Scotland U.K.
146 D8 Raasay, Sound of sea chan. Scotland U.K.
138 I2 Raasiku Estonia
140 T4 Raate Fin.
191 R6 Rab Croatia
188 E3 Rab i. Croatia
176 G4 Rába r. Hungary
95 M9 Raba Sumbawa Indon.
175 I5 Raba r. Pol.
210 F2 Rabaale Somalia
191 Q5 Rabac Croatia
182 D8 Rabaçal Coimbra Port.
182 F7 Rabaçal Guarda Port.
182 F5 Rabaçal r. Port./Spain
182 E2 Rábade Spain
177 L5 Răbăgani Romania
176 F4 Rábahidvég Hungary
203 G6 Rabak Sudan
176 G4 Rábakecöl Hungary
182 H5 Rabanales Spain
111 E10 Rabang Xizang China
176 F4 Rábapaty Hungary
176 G4 Rábapordány Hungary
163 H8 Rabastens France
163 E9 Rabastens-de-Bigorre France
Rabat Gozo Malta see Victoria
195 □ Rabat Malta
204 D2 Rabat Morocco
Rabatakbaytal Tajik. see Rabotoqbaytal
122 H4 Rabāt-e Kamah Iran
91 L7 Rabaul New Britain P.N.G.
175 H6 Raba Wyżna Pol.
Rabbath Ammon Jordan see 'Ammān
191 M7 Rabbi r. Italy
191 J3 Rabbies r. Italy
222 E3 Rabbit r. B.C. Can.
84 C6 Rabbit Flat N.T. Austr.
222 F2 Rabbitskin r. N.W.T. Can.
177 G4 Rábca r. Hungary
177 I2 Rabča Slovakia
177 I2 Rabčice Slovakia
177 J5 Rabe Vojvodina Serbia
171 I9 Rabenau Ger.
179 L3 Rabenstein an der Pielach Austria
170 E3 Raben Steinfeld Ger.
139 Q4 Rabezha Rus. Fed.
79 □7 Rabi i. Fiji
93 G4 Rabia Papua Indon.
207 G3 Rabidine well Niger
124 D4 Rābigh Saudi Arabia
243 N10 Rabinal Guat.
174 D2 Rąbino Pol.
216 □3d Rabisca, Punta de pt La Palma Canary Is
190 G2 Rabiusa r. Switz.
142 G4 Rabjerg nature res. Denmark
175 H6 Rabka Pol.
169 K6 Räbke Ger.
Rabkob Chhattisgarh India see Dharmjaygarh
117 M9 Rabnabad Islands Bangl.
Râbnița Moldova see Rîbnița
216 □1b Rabo de Peixe São Miguel Azores
122 G7 Rābor Iran
191 M4 Raboso r. Italy
123 O2 Rabotoqbaytal Kūhistoni Badakhshon Tajik.
139 R1 Rabovichi Rus. Fed.
204 B5 Rabt Sbayta des. Western Sahara
202 D3 Rabyānah oasis Libya
202 D3 Rabyānah, Ramlat des. Libya
196 I6 Rača Serbia
112 I5 Racaka Xizang China
195 O4 Racale Italy
177 H4 Rácalmás Hungary
194 F9 Racalmuto Sicilia Italy
193 Q7 Racanello r. Italy
191 O3 Raccolana r. Italy
190 D6 Racconigi Italy
246 F2 Raccoon Cay i. Bahamas
234 E5 Raccoon Creek r. NJ U.S.A.
232 C10 Raccoon Creek r. OH U.S.A.
194 H7 Raccuia Sicilia Italy
179 M7 Rače Slovenia
225 K4 Race, Cape Nfld and Lab. Can.
237 J11 Raceland LA U.S.A.
233 O6 Race Point MA U.S.A.
128 D5 Rachaïya Lebanon
237 F12 Rachal TX U.S.A.
175 L5 Rachanie Pol.
94 C1 Racha Noi, Ko i. Thai.
94 C1 Racha Yai, Ko i. Thai.
157 J6 Rachecourt-sur-Marne France
241 Q4 Rachel NV U.S.A.
199 H5 Raches Ikaria Greece
139 U3 Rachevo Rus. Fed.
97 G10 Rach Gia Vietnam
97 G10 Rach Gia, Vinh b. Vietnam
129 E3 Rachis K'edi hills Georgia
174 F2 Raciąż Kujawsko-Pomorskie Pol.
175 I3 Raciąż Mazowieckie Pol.
175 I3 Raciążnica r. Pol.
174 G5 Racibórz Pol.
175 I6 Raciechowice Pol.
174 C2 Racimierz Pol.
226 G7 Racine WI U.S.A.
232 D10 Racine WV U.S.A.
227 K1 Racine Lake Ont. Can.
197 M4 Râciu Romania
177 H4 Ráckeve Hungary
146 J5 Rackwick Orkney, Scotland U.K.
171 F8 Rackwitz Ger.
175 I5 Racławice Pol.
197 N4 Racoș Romania
197 P5 Racovița Brăila Romania
177 K6 Racovița Timiș Romania
175 K2 Raczki Pol.
175 I2 Rączki Pol.
124 G8 Radā' Yemen
260 A6 Radal Chile
138 K7 Radashkovichy Belarus
197 N3 Rădăuți Romania
176 C2 Radbuza r. Czech Rep.
139 T5 Radchenko Rus. Fed.
137 T4 Radchenskoye Rus. Fed.
230 E7 Radcliff KY U.S.A.
149 M6 Radcliffe Greater Manchester, England U.K.
151 J2 Radcliffe on Trent Nottinghamshire, England U.K.
100 G4 Radde Rus. Fed.
194 H9 Raddusa Sicilia Italy
142 G2 Rade Norway
171 I8 Radeberg Ger.
171 I8 Radebeul Ger.
171 I8 Radeburg Ger.
179 L7 Radeče Slovenia
171 F8 Radefeld Ger.
171 F7 Radegast Ger.
136 D3 Radekhiv Ukr.
179 N6 Radenci Slovenia
137 L7 Radens'k Ukr.
170 G5 Radensleben Ger.
179 I6 Radenthein Austria
169 D8 Radevormwald Ger.
174 D1 Radew r. Pol.
178 E5 Radfeld Austria
232 E11 Radford VA U.S.A.
84 C1 Radford Point N.T. Austr.
151 J3 Radford Semele Warwickshire, England U.K.
116 C8 Radhanpur Gujarat India
171 J8 Radibor Ger.
192 H2 Radicofani Italy
191 K9 Radicondoli Italy
193 O4 Radicosa r. Italy
Radili Ko N.W.T. Can. see Fort Good Hope
171 G7 Radis Ger.
120 B1 Radishchevo Rus. Fed.
224 E2 Radisson Que. Can.
223 J4 Radisson Sask. Can.
226 C4 Radisson WI U.S.A.
139 R8 Raditsa-Krylovka Rus. Fed.
222 G5 Radium Hot Springs B.C. Can.
179 M7 Radizelj Slovenia
137 P2 Rad'kovka Rus. Fed.
174 E5 Radków Dolnośląskie Pol.
175 H5 Radków Świętokrzyskie Pol.
151 L4 Radlett Hertfordshire, England U.K.
262 R1 Radlinski, Mount Antarctica
179 L6 Radlje ob Dravi Slovenia
175 I5 Radłów Małopolskie Pol.
174 G5 Radłów Opolskie Pol.
197 N8 Radnevo Bulg.
176 C2 Radnice Czech Rep.
250 B4 Rado de Tumaco inlet Col.
139 R2 Radogoshcha Rus. Fed.
177 J6 Radojevo Vojvodina Serbia
172 F6 Radolfzell am Bodensee Ger.
175 J4 Radom Pol.
208 E2 Radom Sudan
175 H2 Radomin Pol.
197 K8 Radomir Bulg.
197 L9 Radomir mt. Bulg./Greece
175 J4 Radomka r. Pol.
177 K2 Radomka r. Slovakia
137 L2 Radomka Ukr.
208 D2 Radom National Park Sudan
175 J4 Radomska, Równina plain Pol.
175 H4 Radomsko Pol.
136 I3 Radomyshl' Ukr.
175 J5 Radomyśl nad Sanem Pol.
175 J5 Radomyśl Wielki Pol.
176 C1 Radonice Czech Rep.
Radoshkovichi Belarus see Radashkovichy
177 G3 Radošina Slovakia
176 G3 Radošovce Slovakia
175 I4 Radoszyce Pol.
174 D3 Radoszyn Pol.
197 O9 Radovets Bulg.
197 K9 Radoviš Macedonia
139 W6 Radovitskiy Rus. Fed.
188 E2 Radovljica Slovenia
174 D2 Radowo Małe Pol.
144 J1 Radøy i. Norway
179 H5 Radstadt Austria
179 H5 Radstädter Tauern mts Austria
179 I5 Radstädter Tauern pass Austria
150 H5 Radstock Bath and North East Somerset, England U.K.
82 E5 Radstock, Cape S.A. Austr.
197 P4 Răducăneni Romania
136 J2 Radul' Ukr.
138 H7 Radun' Belarus
143 O7 Radunia r. Pol.
137 M6 Radushne Ukr.
177 K2 Radvaň nad Laborcom Slovakia
138 G6 Radviliškis Lith.
124 D3 Raḍwá, Jabal mt. Saudi Arabia
174 D4 Radwanice Pol.
175 K6 Radymno Pol.
137 M4 Radyvonivka Ukr.
136 E3 Radyvyliv Ukr.
175 I3 Radzanów Pol.
175 I4 Radzice Duże Pol.
174 F2 Radzicz Pol.
175 J1 Radzieje Pol.
174 G3 Radziejów Pol.
175 I6 Radziejowa mt. Pol.
175 I3 Radziejowice Pol.
175 I5 Radziemice Pol.
174 C3 Radzików Pol.
175 K2 Radziłów Pol.
Radzivilovichi Belarus see Dzyarzhynsk
177 I3 Radzovce Slovakia
175 J3 Radzymin Pol.
174 G2 Radzyń Chełminski Pol.
175 K4 Radzyń Podlaski Pol.
116 H6 Rae Bareli Uttar Prad. India
222 G2 Rae-Edzo N.W.T. Can.
231 H8 Raeford NC U.S.A.
222 G1 Rae Lakes N.W.T. Can.
165 J7 Raeren Belgium
169 C7 Raesfeld Ger.
87 F10 Raeside, Lake salt flat W.A. Austr.
80 H2 Raetea hill North I. N.Z.
80 J6 Raetihi North I. N.Z.
127 I9 Rāf hill Saudi Arabia
260 A5 Rafael Chile
261 G2 Rafaela Arg.
246 F3 Rafael Freyre Cuba
245 J6 Rafael J. Garcia Mex.
261 G4 Rafael Obligado Arg.
Rafaḥ Gaza see Rafiah
208 D3 Rafaï C.A.R.
136 F2 Rafalivka Ukr.
187 E8 Rafelbunyol Spain
194 F9 Raffadali Sicilia Italy
222 K5 Rafferty Reservoir Can.
146 I7 Rafford Moray, Scotland U.K.
147 K4 Raffrey Northern Ireland U.K.
127 K9 Rafḥā' Saudi Arabia
128 C7 Rafiah Gaza
208 E3 Rafili Sudan
198 F4 Rafina Greece
147 E6 Raford r. Ireland
122 F6 Rafsanjān Iran
238 H5 Raft r. ID/NV U.S.A.
208 E2 Raga Sudan
208 E2 Ragag Sudan
183 J7 Rágama Spain
138 H4 Ragana Latvia
195 K4 Raganello r. Italy
92 E8 Ragang, Mount vol. Mindanao Phil.
92 D5 Ragay Gulf Luzon Phil.
170 G4 Rägelin Ger.
87 G12 Ragged, Mount hill W.A. Austr.
246 F2 Ragged Island Bahamas
233 □Q5 Ragged Island ME U.S.A.
247 □4 Ragged Point Barbados
123 N3 Rāgh Afgh.
116 F7 Raghogarh Madh. Prad. India
124 G1 Raghwah Saudi Arabia
124 G8 Raghwān, Wādī watercourse Yemen
80 I4 Raglan North I. N.Z.
150 G4 Raglan Monmouthshire, Wales U.K.
80 I4 Raglan Harbour North I. N.Z.
179 M6 Ragnitz Austria
140 N3 Rago Nasjonalpark nat. park Norway
171 G6 Ragösen Ger.
185 M6 Ragua, Puerto de la pass Spain
225 G3 Ragueneau Que. Can.
171 F7 Raguhn Ger.
Ragusa Croatia see Dubrovnik
194 H10 Ragusa Sicilia Italy
194 H10 Ragusa prov. Sicilia Italy
111 K11 Ragxi Xizang China
106 G9 Ra'gyagoinba Qinghai China
96 A1 Raha Assam India
93 C6 Raha Sulawesi Indon.
139 N8 Rahachow Belarus
203 G6 Rahad r. Sudan
203 G6 Rahad Canal Sudan
208 D2 Rahad el Berdi Sudan
202 E6 Rahad Wahal well Sudan
Rahaeng Thai. see Tak
124 E4 Rahaṭ, Ḥarrat lava field Saudi Arabia
116 F8 Rahatgaon Madh. Prad. India
169 G6 Rahden Ger.
114 D4 Rahimatpur Mahar. India
123 N7 Rahimyar Khan Pak.
157 L8 Rahin r. France
122 D4 Rāhjerd Iran
122 H6 Raḥmān, Chāh-e well Iran
80 H6 Rahotu North I. N.Z.
260 B6 Rahué Arg.
260 B6 Rahue mt. Chile
138 K3 Rahumäe Estonia
114 D3 Rahuri Mahar. India
123 I4 Rahzanak Afgh.
97 G10 Rai, Hon i. Vietnam
193 L3 Raiano Italy
79 □9 Raiatea i. Arch. de la Société Fr. Polynesia
Raibu i. Indon. see Air
261 H2 Raices Arg.
114 E4 Raichur Karnataka India
117 L7 Raiganj W. Bengal India
117 I9 Raigarh Chhattisgarh India
114 H3 Raigarh Orissa India
93 B9 Raijua i. Indon.
116 E4 Raikot Punjab India
241 Q3 Railroad Valley NV U.S.A.
117 L9 Raimangal r. Bangl.
225 G2 Raimbault, Lac l. Que. Can.
173 J4 Rain Bayern Ger.
173 M4 Rain Bayern Ger.
179 J2 Rainbach im Mühlkreis Austria
83 I6 Rainbow Vic. Austr.
85 N8 Rainbow Beach Qld Austr.
222 G3 Rainbow Lake Alta Can.
85 J1 Raine Entrance sea chan. Qld Austr.
85 J1 Raine Island Qld Austr.
232 E11 Rainelle WV U.S.A.
149 L6 Rainford Merseyside, England U.K.
123 M7 Raini r. Pak.
238 D3 Rainier, Mount vol. WA U.S.A.
93 E1 Rainis Sulawesi Indon.
149 M7 Rainow Cheshire, England U.K.
149 O7 Rainworth Nottinghamshire, England U.K.
236 H1 Rainy r. MN U.S.A.
223 M5 Rainy Lake Ont. Can.
223 M5 Rainy River Ont. Can.
140 P5 Raippaluoto i. Fin.
117 M8 Raipur Bangl.
116 H9 Raipur Chhattisgarh India
116 E6 Raipur Rajasthan India
117 K8 Raipur W. Bengal India
117 K8 Rairangpur Orissa India
78 □3b Rairik i. Majuro Marshall Is
182 E4 Rairiz de Veiga Spain
Rairoa atoll Arch. des Tuamotu Fr. Polynesia see Rangiroa
168 J2 Raisdorf Ger.
116 F8 Raisen Madh. Prad. India
194 E7 Raisi, Punta pt Sicilia Italy
116 D5 Raisinghnagar Rajasthan India
141 Q6 Raisio Fin.
156 F3 Raismes France
140 T3 Raistakka Fin.
116 F9 Raitalai Madh. Prad. India
173 K3 Raitenbuch Ger.
226 E1 Raith Ont. Can.
81 H8 Rai Valley South I. N.Z.
79 □9 Raivavae i. Îs Australes Fr. Polynesia
123 P6 Raiwind Pak.
138 J3 Raja Estonia
95 J8 Raja i. Indon.
94 B3 Raja, Ujung pt Indon.
93 F4 Rajaampat, Kepulauan is Papua Indon.
94 F7 Rajabasa, Gunung vol. Indon.
186 I4 Rajadell, Riera de r. Spain
117 J8 Rajagangapur Orissa India
114 G4 Rajahmundry Andhra Prad. India
140 T2 Raja-Jooseppi Fin.
116 E5 Rajaldesar Rajasthan India
138 H1 Rajamäki Fin.
114 F5 Rajampet Andhra Prad. India
95 I3 Rajang Sarawak Malaysia
95 I3 Rajang r. Malaysia
123 N7 Rajanpur Pak.
114 E8 Rajapalaiyam Tamil Nadu India
114 C4 Rajapur Mahar. India
116 D6 Rajasthan state India
116 D5 Rajasthan Canal India
117 J7 Rajauli Bihar India
117 L8 Rajbari Bangl.
176 F2 Rájec Czech Rep.
177 H2 Rajec Slovakia
177 H2 Rajecká Lesná Slovakia
116 F7 Rajgarh Madh. Prad. India
114 C3 Rajgarh Mahar. India
116 E5 Rajgarh Rajasthan India
116 F6 Rajgarh Rajasthan India
117 J7 Rajgir Bihar India
175 K2 Rajgród Pol.
175 K2 Rajgrodzkie, Jezioro l. Pol.
117 J7 Rajhara Jharkhand India
179 O1 Rajhrad Czech Rep.
176 F2 Rajhradice Czech Rep.
Rájijovsset Fin. see Raja-Jooseppi
94 F6 Rajik Indon.
116 H9 Rajim Chhattisgarh India
197 J8 Rajince Serbia
176 G3 Rajka Hungary
116 C8 Rajkot Gujarat India
117 K7 Rajmahal Jharkhand India
116 E7 Raj Mahal Rajasthan India
117 J7 Rajmahal Hills India
117 K8 Rajnagar W. Bengal India
116 H9 Raj Nandgaon Chhattisgarh India
116 E3 Rajouri Jammu and Kashmir
116 D9 Rajpipla Gujarat India
116 E9 Rajpur Madh. Prad. India
116 F4 Rajpura Punjab India
Rajputana Agency state India see Rajasthan
116 D7 Rajsamand Rajasthan India
117 L7 Rajshahi Bangl.
117 L7 Rajshahi admin. div. Bangl.
128 E2 Rājū Syria
116 C9 Rajula Gujarat India
116 G9 Rajur Mahar. India
Rajura Mahar. India see Ahmadpur
114 F3 Rajura Mahar. India
111 G12 Raka Xizang China
179 L8 Raka Slovenia
125 K5 Rakabah, Qalamat ar oasis Saudi Arabia
177 J3 Rakaca r. Hungary
81 □2 Rakahanga atoll Cook Is
Rakahuri r. South I. N.Z. see Ashley
210 A5 Rakai Uganda
81 G10 Rakaia South I. N.Z.
81 G10 Rakaia r. South I. N.Z.
177 K3 Rakamaz Hungary
125 J2 Rakan, Ra's pt Qatar
116 E1 Rakaposhi mt. Jammu and Kashmir
Raka Zangbo r. Xizang China see Dogxung Zangbo
81 B13 Rakeahua, Mount hill Stewart I. N.Z.
179 J8 Rakek Slovenia
Rakhaing state Myanmar see Arakan
Rakhine state Myanmar see Arakan
136 D5 Rakhiv Ukr.
137 M6 Rakhmanivka Ukr.
123 M6 Rakhni Pak.
123 J8 Rakhshan r. Pak.
79 □7a Rakiraki Viti Levu Fiji
95 H7 Rakit i. Indon.
95 L9 Rakit i. Indon.
179 J8 Rakitna Slovenia
197 N8 Rakitnitsa r. Bulg.
135 F6 Rakitnoye Belgorodskaya Oblast' Rus. Fed.
100 I6 Rakitnoye Primorskiy Kray Rus. Fed.
191 P5 Rakitovec Slovenia
80 J3 Rakitu Island North I. N.Z.
Rakiura i. N.Z. see Stewart Island
138 J3 Rakke Estonia
142 H2 Rakkestad Norway
110 H2 Rakmanovskie Klyuchi Kazakh.
123 N6 Rakni r. Pak.
177 J4 Rákóczifalva Hungary
177 J4 Rákócziújfalu Hungary
174 E3 Rakoniewice Pol.
212 E4 Rakops Botswana
177 L3 Rakoshyn Ukr.
177 H2 Raková Slovakia
197 K7 Rakovitsa Bulg.
176 C1 Rakovnická pahorkatina hills Czech Rep.
176 C1 Rakovník Czech Rep.
197 M8 Rakovski Bulg.
170 H2 Rakow Ger.
175 J5 Raków Pol.
175 K5 Rakszawa Pol.
135 K7 Rakusha Kazakh.
120 D6 Rakushechnyy, Mys pt Kazakh.
138 J2 Rakvere Estonia
176 F3 Rakvice Czech Rep.
215 M6 Ralebona Lesotho
237 K9 Raleigh MS U.S.A.
231 H8 Raleigh NC U.S.A.
251 G3 Raleighvallen Voltsberg, Natuurreservaat nature res. Suriname
172 B2 Ralingen Ger.
93 A6 Ralla Sulawesi Indon.
226 G3 Ralph MI U.S.A.
223 I5 Ralston Alta Can.
227 R8 Ralston PA U.S.A.
113 □1 Raluara Giri i. N. Male Maldives
222 F2 Ram r. N.W.T. Can.
128 D6 Rama Israel
242 □Q11 Rama Nic.
136 D3 Rama r. Ukr.
194 H9 Ramacca Sicilia Italy
260 B3 Ramada, Cerro de la mt.
Rāmadī Iraq see Ar Rāma
252 C5 Ramaditas Chile
115 I3 Ramagiri Orissa India
225 I1 Ramah Nfld and Lab. Can
183 N2 Ramales de la Victoria S
184 A2 Ramalhal Port.
254 D5 Ramalho, Serra do hills
128 D7 Ramallah West Bank
261 G3 Ramallo Arg.
114 E6 Ramanagaram Karnataka
114 F8 Ramanathapuram Tamil India
117 I8 Ramanuj Ganj Chhattisga India
235 G3 Ramapo r. NJ U.S.A.
266 E3 Ramapo Deep sea featur N. Pacific Ocean
117 I9 Ramapur Orissa India
114 C5 Ramas, Cape India
139 Q9 Ramasukha Rus. Fed.
215 J1 Ramatlabama watercour Botswana/S. Africa
215 J1 Ramatlabama S. Africa
161 J10 Ramatuelle France
114 F3 Ramayampet Andhra Pra India
140 L2 Ramberg Norway
157 M7 Rambervillers France
116 E8 Rambhapur Madh. Prad.
Rambi i. Fiji see Rabi
170 H2 Rambin Ger.
156 C6 Rambouillet France
156 C6 Rambouillet, Forêt de fo France
165 I9 Rambrouch Lux.
157 K6 Rambucourt France
91 K7 Rambutyo Island Admira P.N.G.
114 D5 Ramdurg Karnataka India
150 D7 Rame Cornwall, England
117 K6 Ramechhap Nepal
215 N7 Rame Head S. Africa
150 D7 Rame Head England U.K.
147 G2 Ramelton Ireland
143 L1 Rämen l. Sweden
213 □K2 Ramena Madag.
139 V6 Ramenskoye Rus. Fed.
156 H6 Ramerupt France
81 F9 Rameses, Mount South I
139 T4 Rameshki Rus. Fed.
114 F8 Rameswaram Tamil Nadu India
122 I9 Ramezān Kalak Iran
111 D13 Ramganga r. India
117 M8 Ramgarh Bangl.
117 J8 Ramgarh Jharkhand India
116 C6 Ramgarh Rajasthan India
116 E6 Ramgarh Rajasthan India
116 F6 Ramgarh Rajasthan India
123 N4 Ramgul reg. Afgh.
122 C6 Rāmhormoz Iran
165 G7 Ramillies Belgium
84 E2 Ramingining N.T. Austr.
179 I5 Ramingstein Austria
216 □1a Raminho Terceira Azores
182 E4 Ramirás Spain
Ramit Tajik. see Romit
Ramitan Uzbek. see Rom
117 I8 Ramkola Chhattisgarh Ind
128 C7 Ramla Israel
128 D9 Ramm Jordan
128 D9 Ramm, Jabal mts Jordar
172 C2 Rammelsbach Ger.
171 J8 Rammenau Ger.
173 I4 Rammingen Ger.
215 K3 Rammulotsi S. Africa
Ramnad Tamil Nadu India Ramanathapuram
116 H7 Ramnagar Madh. Prad. Ir
116 H8 Ramnagar Madh. Prad. Ir
116 G5 Ramnagar Uttaranchal In
116 E3 Ramnagar Jammu and Kashmir
143 M2 Ramnäs Sweden
142 G2 Ramnes Norway
139 N6 Ramni Belarus
197 P5 Râmnicul Sărat r. Romar
197 P5 Râmnicu Sărat Romania
197 M5 Râmnicu Vâlcea Romani
210 D3 Ramo Eth.
213 E4 Ramokgwebane Botswa
137 S2 Ramon' Rus. Fed.
240 P8 Ramona CA U.S.A.
157 M8 Ramonchamp France
244 D1 Ramón Corona Mex.
259 D7 Ramón Lista Arg.
260 C6 Ramón M. Castro Arg.
261 H6 Ramón Santamarina Arg
163 G8 Ramonville-St-Agne Fra
147 H5 Ramor, Lough l. Ireland
227 N1 Ramore Ont. Can.
258 D1 Ramos Arg.
242 G5 Ramos Mex.
237 C13 Ramos r. Mex.
243 I5 Ramos Arizpe Mex.
190 I2 Ramosch Switz.
212 E5 Ramotswa Botswana
107 M2 Rampart of Genghis Kh tourist site Asia
149 K5 Rampside Cumbria, England U.K.
111 C11 Rampur Hima. Prad. India
116 F5 Rampur Uttar Prad. India
116 G5 Rampur Uttar Prad. India
116 E7 Rampura Madh. Prad. Inc
Rampur Boalia Bangl. se Rajshahi
117 K7 Rampur Hat W. Bengal Ir
96 A5 Ramree Myanmar
96 A5 Ramree Island Myanmar
122 D3 Rāmsar Iran
179 I5 Ramsau am Dachstein Austria
173 N6 Ramsau bei Berchtesga Ger.
178 E5 Ramsau im Zillertal Aus
143 L2 Ramsberg Sweden
149 M6 Ramsbottom Greater Manchester, England U.K.
151 I5 Ramsbury Wiltshire, England U.K.
140 N5 Ramsele Sweden
172 F6 Ramsen Switz.
227 L2 Ramsey Ont. Can.
148 I5 Ramsey Isle of Man
151 L3 Ramsey Cambridgeshire, England U.K.
235 G2 Ramsey NJ U.S.A.
148 I5 Ramsey Bay Isle of Man
150 B4 Ramsey Island Wales U.
224 D4 Ramsey Lake Ont. Can.
151 L3 Ramsey St Mary's Cambridgeshire, England
215 O6 Ramsgate S. Africa
151 O5 Ramsgate Kent, England U.K.
117 L6 Ramshai Hat W. Bengal India
122 C6 Rāmshir Iran
117 O5 Ramsing Arun. Prad. Indi
117 O5 Ramsing mt. Arun. Prad. India
141 M5 Ramsjö Sweden
168 E4 Ramsloh (Saterland) Ge
172 D3 Ramstein Ger.
116 G9 Ramtek Mahar. India
117 N9 Ramu Bangl.
91 J7 Ramu r. P.N.G.
140 L5 Ramundberget Sweden
225 I2 Ramusio, Lac l. Que. Ca
140 N5 Ramvik Sweden
247 □3 Ramville, Îlet i. Martiniqu
138 H6 Ramygala Lith.
250 D4 Rana, Cerro hill Col.
182 G3 Rañadoiro, Puerto de p Spain
182 G2 Rañadoiro, Sierra de m Spain
117 L8 Ranaghat W. Bengal Indi
Ranai i. HI U.S.A. see Lā
116 E7 Rana Pratap Sagar resr
116 E8 Ranapur Madh. Prad. Ind
116 C7 Ranasar Rajasthan India
142 H1 Rånåsfoss Norway
95 L2 Ranau Sabah Malaysia
94 E7 Ranau, Danau l. Indon.
260 B4 Rancagua Chile
165 F8 Rance Belgium

Rance r. France
Rance r. France
Rancharia Brazil
Rancheria Y.T. Can.
Rancheria r. Y.T. Can.
Ranchester WY U.S.A.
Ranchi Jharkhand India
Rancho Cordova CA U.S.A.
Rancho de Caçados Tapiúnas Brazil
Rancho Grande Mex.
Rancho Nuevo Mex.
Ranchos Arg.
Ranchos de Taos NM U.S.A.
Ranco, Lago l. Chile
Rancocas Creek, North Branch r. NJ U.S.A.
Rancocas Woods NJ U.S.A.
Rand N.S.W. Austr.
Rand WV U.S.A.
Randalhurst S. Africa
Randallstown MD U.S.A.
Randalstown Northern Ireland U.K.
Randan France
Randazzo Sicilia Italy
Randburg S. Africa
Randegg Austria
Randers Denmark
Randersacker Ger.
Randfontein S. Africa
Randijaure l. Sweden
Randolph MA U.S.A.
Randolph ME U.S.A.
Randolph NY U.S.A.
Randolph UT U.S.A.
Randolph VT U.S.A.
Randonnai France
Randow r. Ger.
Randsburg CA U.S.A.
Randsfjorden l. Norway
Randsjö Sweden
Randsverk Norway
Randvaal S. Africa
Råneå Sweden
Ranérou Senegal
Rânes France
Ranfurly South I. N.Z.
Ranga r. India
Rangae Thai.
Rangamati Bangl.
Rangapara Assam India
Rangas, Tanjung pt Indon.
Rangasa, Tanjung pt Indon.
Rangatira Island Chatham Is S. Pacific Ocean
Rangaunu Bay North I. N.Z.
Rangeley ME U.S.A.
Rangeley Lake ME U.S.A.
Rangely CO U.S.A.
Rangendingen Ger.
Ranger Lake Ont. Can.
Ranger Lake l. Ont. Can.
Rangersdorf Austria
Rangi Mahar. India
Rangia Assam India
Rangiauria i. Chatham Is S. Pacific Ocean see Pitt Island
Rangiora South I. N.Z.
Rangipoua mt. North I. N.Z.
Rangiroa atoll Arch. des Tuamotu Fr. Polynesia
Rangitaiki North I. N.Z.
Rangitaiki r. North I. N.Z.
Rangitata South I. N.Z.
Rangitata r. South I. N.Z.
Rangitikei r. North I. N.Z.
Rangitoto Islands South I. N.Z.
Rangiwaea Junction North I. N.Z.
Rangiwahia North I. N.Z.
Rangkasbitung Jawa Indon.
Rangku Arun. Prad. India
Rangkŭl Tajik.
Rangôn Myanmar see Yangôn
Rangôn admin. div. Myanmar see Yangôn
Rangoon Myanmar see Yangôn
Rangoon admin. div. Myanmar see Yangôn
Rangoon r. Myanmar
Rangpur Bangl.
Rangpur Pak.
Rangsang i. Indon.
Rangsdorf Ger.
Rangse Myanmar
Rangtag Gansu China
Ranhados Port.
Rani Rajasthan India
Rania Haryana India
Ranibennur Karnataka India
Ranier City MN U.S.A.
Raniganj W. Bengal India
Ranijula Peak Chhattisgarh India
Ranikhet Uttaranchal India
Ranipur Pak.
Ranis Ger.
Raniwara Rajasthan India
Ranizów Pol.
Ranka Jharkhand India
Ranken watercourse N.T. Austr.
Rankin TX U.S.A.
Rankin Inlet Nunavut Can.
Rankin Inlet inlet Nunavut Can.
Rankin's Springs N.S.W. Austr.
Rankovićevo Serbia see Kraljevo
Rankweil Austria
Ranna Estonia
Rannes Qld Austr.
Ranneye Rus. Fed.
Rannoch, Loch l. Scotland U.K.
Rannoch Moor moorland Scotland U.K.
Rannoch Station Perth and Kinross, Scotland U.K.
Rannu Estonia
Rano Nigeria
Ränö i. Sweden
Rano, Mount New Georgia Is Solomon Is
Ranobe r. Madag.
Ranohira Madag.
Ranomafana Madag.
Ranomatana Madag.
Ranomena Madag.
Ranon Vanuatu
Ranong Thai.
Ranongga i. New Georgia Is Solomon Is
Ranopiso Madag.
Ranot Thai.
Ranotsara Avaratra Madag.
Ranova r. Rus. Fed.
Ranpur Gujarat India
Ranquilcó, Salitral salt pan Arg.
Ranquil del Norte Arg.
Ranrkan Pak.
Rānsa Iran
Ransbach-Baumbach Ger.
Ransby Sweden
Ransiki Papua Indon.
Ranskill Nottinghamshire, England U.K.
Ransom IL U.S.A.
Ransom PA U.S.A.
Ranst Belgium
Ranta Fin.
Rantabe Madag.
Rantasalmi Fin.
Rantau Kalimantan Indon.
Rantau i. Indon.
Rantaukampar Sumatera Indon.
Rantaupanjang Kalimantan Indon.
Rantaupanjang Kalimantan Indon.
Rantauprapat Sumatera Indon.
Rantaupulut Kalimantan Indon.
Rantemario, Gunung mt. Indon.
Ranten Austria
Rantepao Sulawesi Indon.
Rantoul IL U.S.A.
168 H2 Rantrum Ger.
139 R5 Rantsevo Rus. Fed.
140 R4 Rantsila Fin.
168 F1 Rantum Ger.
140 S4 Ranua Fin.
142 F5 Ranum Denmark
196 H9 Ranxë Albania
127 L5 Rānya Iraq
124 F5 Ranyah, Wādī watercourse Saudi Arabia
96 G5 Rao Go mt. Laos/Vietnam
100 H5 Raohe Heilong. China
157 M7 Raon-l'Étape France
191 K4 Raossi Italy
77 I4 Raoul Island N.Z.
79 □9 Rapa i. Îs Australes Fr. Polynesia
140 O3 Rapaälven r. Sweden
Rapa-iti i. Îs Australes Fr. Polynesia see Rapa
190 G7 Rapallo Italy
Rapa Nui i. S. Pacific Ocean see Pascua, Isla de
116 C8 Rapar Gujarat India
122 H9 Rapch watercourse Iran
260 B3 Rapel Chile
260 B3 Rapel r. Chile
260 B4 Rapel, Embalse resr Chile
148 B7 Rapemills Ireland
221 L3 Raper, Cape Nunavut Can.
147 G3 Raphoe Ireland
171 K6 Rapice Pol.
232 H10 Rapidan r. VA U.S.A.
82 G6 Rapid Bay S.A. Austr.
236 D3 Rapid City SD U.S.A.
227 P2 Rapide-Deux Que. Can.
227 P2 Rapide-Sept Que. Can.
193 L4 Rapido r. Italy
226 H4 Rapid River MI U.S.A.
138 K3 Räpina Estonia
252 D2 Rapirrān r. Brazil
138 H3 Rapla Estonia
191 L9 Rapolano Terme Italy
193 P6 Rapolla Italy
184 B2 Raposa Port.
176 G1 Rapotín Czech Rep.
182 F8 Rapoula do Côa Port.
232 I11 Rappahannock r. VA U.S.A.
93 A5 Rappang Sulawesi Indon.
169 K7 Rappbodetalstausee resr Ger.
172 F7 Rapperswil Switz.
179 L2 Rappottenstein Austria
116 I6 Rapti r. India
81 □3 Rapua Passage Rarotonga Cook Is
252 D3 Rapulo r. Bol.
114 F5 Rapur Andhra Prad. India
116 B8 Rapur Gujarat India
92 E5 Rapurapu i. Phil.
Raqqa Syria see Ar Raqqah
233 K4 Raquette r. NY U.S.A.
233 K5 Raquette Lake NY U.S.A.
84 F1 Raragala Island N.T. Austr.
116 I5 Rara National Park Nepal
156 E5 Raray France
234 F3 Raritan, South Branch r. NJ U.S.A.
235 G4 Raritan Bay NJ U.S.A.
79 □9 Raroia atoll Arch. des Tuamotu Fr. Polynesia
190 D3 Raron Switz.
81 □3 Rarotonga i. Cook Is
116 E6 Ras Rajasthan India
191 Q5 Raša Croatia
188 E3 Raša r. Croatia
92 B7 Rasa i. Phil.
259 E6 Rasa, Punta pt Arg.
125 M6 Ra's ad Daqm Oman
125 N4 Ra's al Ḩadd Oman
202 E2 Ra's al Ḩikmah Egypt
Ras al Khaimah U.A.E. see Ra's al Khaymah
125 L3 Ra's al Khaymah U.A.E.
125 I1 Ra's al Mish āb Saudi Arabia
124 F4 Raşan, Jabal hill Saudi Arabia
128 D8 Ra's an Naqb Jordan
128 E4 Ras Ba'albek Lebanon
216 □3a Rasca, Punta de la pt Tenerife Canary Is
183 M7 Rascafría Spain
Râşcani Moldova see Rîşcani
171 G9 Raschau Ger.
210 C1 Ras Dejen mt. Eth.
169 I9 Rasdorf Ger.
138 G6 Raseiniai Lith.
205 E2 Râs el Ma Alg.
206 D2 Râs el Mâ Mali
113 □1 Rasfaree i. N. Male Maldives
203 G2 Ra's Ghārib Egypt
106 B3 Rashaant Bayan-Ölgiy Mongolia
106 J4 Rashaant Dundgovĭ Mongolia
210 A2 Rashad Sudan
147 J3 Rasharkin Northern Ireland U.K.
147 G3 Rashedoge Ireland
203 F2 Rashīd Egypt
125 K4 Rāshid reg. Saudi Arabia
123 L6 Rashid Qala Afgh.
137 M3 Rashivka Ukr.
122 F4 Rashm Iran
215 L1 Rashoop S. Africa
125 H8 Rashshah Yemen
122 C3 Rasht Iran
179 K8 Rašica Slovenia
138 K3 Rasina Estonia
196 J7 Rasina r. Serbia
183 N2 Rasines Spain
179 O7 Rasinja Croatia
141 M5 Råsjö Sweden
123 I8 Räsk Iran
196 I7 Raška Serbia
111 B8 Raskam mts China
181 E5 Ras Kebdana Morocco
123 K7 Ras Koh mt. Pak.
123 K7 Raskoh mts Pak.
177 H2 Raškovice Czech Rep.
177 K2 Raslavice Slovakia
128 A9 Ra's Matārimah Egypt
124 B2 Ra's Muḩammad National Park Egypt
221 I3 Rasmussen Basin sea feature Nunavut Can.
139 O7 Rasna Mahilyowskaya Voblasts' Belarus
138 M7 Rasna Vitsyebskaya Voblasts' Belarus
197 N5 Râşnov Romania
206 □ Raso i. Cape Verde
259 D7 Raso, Cabo c. Arg.
254 F4 Raso da Catarina hills Brazil
87 H10 Rason Lake salt flat W.A. Austr.
138 L6 Rasony Belarus
197 P6 Rasova Romania
197 L7 Rasovo Bulg.
171 L9 Raspenava Czech Rep.
186 G5 Rasquera Spain
117 I7 Rasra Uttar Prad. India
124 C2 Ra's Sāq, Jabal hill Saudi Arabia
125 J8 Ra's Sharwayn c. Yemen
217 □3b Rassi Douamounyo c. Mayotte
125 M5 Ra's Şirāb Oman
189 C7 Rass Jebel Tunisia
135 H5 Rasskazovo Rus. Fed.
197 L7 Rast Romania
139 N8 Rasta r. Belarus
125 J2 Ras Tannūrah Saudi Arabia
172 E4 Rastatt Ger.
168 E5 Rastdorf Ger.
142 F5 Råsted Denmark
168 F4 Rastede Ger.
171 D8 Rastenberg Ger.
179 L2 Rastenfeld Austria
178 E5 Rastkogel mt. Austria
Rastorguyevo Rus. Fed. see Vidnoye
170 D4 Rastow Ger.
183 J6 Rasueros Spain
123 O5 Rasul Pak.
142 C3 Rasvåg Norway
143 L2 Råsvalen l. Sweden
174 F4 Raszków Pol.
137 P2 Rat' r. Rus. Fed.
80 J6 Rata North I. N.Z.
Ratae Leicester, England U.K. see Leicester
94 F7 Ratai, Gunung mt. Indon.
138 K8 Ratamka Belarus
215 M2 Ratanda S. Africa
116 E7 Ratangarh Madh. Prad. India
116 E5 Ratangarh Rajasthan India
116 I8 Ratanpur Chhattisgarh India
116 D9 Ratanpur Gujarat India
141 M5 Rätansbyn Sweden
175 L3 Rataychytsy Belarus
97 D8 Rat Buri Thai.
139 W8 Ratchino Lipetskaya Oblast' Rus. Fed.
120 F1 Ratchino Orenburgskaya Oblast' Rus. Fed.
179 I6 Rateče Slovenia
168 K3 Ratekau Ger.
214 C7 Ratelfontein S. Africa
182 C6 Rates Port.
116 G7 Rath Uttar Prad. India
148 B7 Rath Ireland
147 I6 Rathangan Ireland
236 I5 Rathbun Lake IA U.S.A.
147 F6 Rathcabban Ireland
147 G5 Rathconrath Ireland
147 E8 Rathcool Ireland
147 J6 Rathcoole Ireland
147 F8 Rathcormac Ireland
148 D8 Rathdangan Ireland
147 G7 Rathdowney Ireland
147 J7 Rathdrum Ireland
96 A4 Rathedaung Myanmar
170 F5 Rathenow Ger.
170 F5 Rathenower Wald- und Seengebiet park Ger.
150 A1 Rathfarnham Ireland
147 J4 Rathfriland Northern Ireland U.K.
146 J10 Rathillet Fife, Scotland U.K.
147 E7 Rathkeale Ireland
147 G8 Rathkeevin Ireland
147 D4 Rathlackan Ireland
147 D4 Rathlee Ireland
147 J2 Rathlin Island Northern Ireland U.K.
147 E3 Rathlin O'Birne Island Ireland
147 E8 Rathluirc Ireland
147 I6 Rathmolyon Ireland
147 D8 Rathmore Ireland
147 G2 Rathmullan Ireland
123 L9 Rath Nath Pak.
147 J7 Rathnew Ireland
146 J11 Ratho Edinburgh, Scotland U.K.
147 G5 Rathowen Ireland
Ratibor Pol. see Racibórz
169 C8 Ratingen Ger.
Ratisbon Ger. see Regensburg
188 E2 Ratitovec mt. Slovenia
116 E5 Ratiya Haryana India
128 E9 Raţīyah, Wādī watercourse Jordan
177 K3 Rátka Hungary
223 L3 Rat Lake Man. Can.
116 E8 Ratlam Madh. Prad. India
114 C4 Ratnagiri Mahar. India
114 G9 Ratnapura Sri Lanka
136 D2 Ratne Ukr.
Ratno Ukr. see Ratne
148 E6 Ratoath Ireland
123 M8 Rato Dero Pak.
239 L8 Raton NM U.S.A.
161 G10 Ratonneau, Île i. France
169 K10 Rattelsdorf Ger.
179 M5 Ratten Austria
140 R3 Rattosjärvi Fin.
146 J9 Rattray Perth and Kinross, Scotland U.K.
146 M7 Rattray Head Scotland U.K.
141 M6 Rättvik Sweden
222 C3 Ratz, Mount B.C. Can.
168 K3 Ratzeburg Ger.
168 K3 Ratzeburger See l. Ger.
171 D6 Rätzlingen Ger.
93 F2 Rau i. Maluku Indon.
94 D3 Raub Malaysia
169 E9 Raubach Ger.
173 M6 Raubling Ger.
261 H5 Rauch Arg.
234 A2 Rauchtown PA U.S.A.
260 B4 Rauco Chile
157 I4 Raucourt-et-Flaba France
245 N8 Raudales de Malpaso Mex.
140 □B1 Rauðamýri Iceland
140 S3 Raudanjoki r. Fin.
197 K5 Râu de Mori Romania
127 M9 Raudhatain Kuwait
138 I3 Raudna r. Estonia
138 G7 Raudondvaris Lith.
171 J6 Rauen Ger.
172 F3 Rauenberg Ger.
171 D10 Rauenstein Ger.
140 □F1 Raufarhöfn Iceland
138 L1 Rauha Fin.
173 J2 Rauhe Ebrach r. Ger.
80 L4 Raukokore North I. N.Z.
80 M4 Raukumara mt. North I. N.Z.
80 L4 Raukumara Forest Park nature res. North I. N.Z.
80 L5 Raukumara Range mts North I. N.Z.
117 I9 Raul r. India
161 B7 Raulhac France
257 F4 Raul Soares Brazil
141 P6 Rauma Fin.
81 I7 Raumati North I. N.Z.
138 I4 Rauna Latvia
151 K3 Raunds Northamptonshire, England U.K.
80 J6 Raurimu North I. N.Z.
178 G5 Rauris Austria
117 J8 Raurkela Orissa India
Rauschen Rus. Fed. see Svetlogorsk
169 G9 Rauschenberg Ger.
102 W2 Rausu Japan
102 W2 Rausu-dake mt. Japan
136 I6 Răut r. Moldova
191 N3 Raut, Monte mt. Italy
140 S5 Rautalampi Fin.
140 T5 Rautavaara Fin.
171 F10 Rautenkranz Ger.
141 T6 Rautjärvi Fin.
Rauza Mahar. India see Khuldabad
163 D6 Rauzan France
79 □9 Ravahere atoll Arch. des Tuamotu Fr. Polynesia
122 I8 Rāvak Iran
238 G3 Ravalli MT U.S.A.
122 G8 Rāvang Iran
122 B4 Ravānsar Iran
194 F9 Ravanusa Sicilia Italy
122 G6 Rāvar Iran
136 C3 Rava-Rus'ka Ukr.
121 N8 Ravat Kyrg.
193 N6 Ravello Italy
165 G6 Ravels Belgium
179 M2 Ravelsbach Austria
143 L5 Rävemåla Sweden
233 L6 Ravena NY U.S.A.
149 K5 Ravenglass Cumbria, England U.K.
191 M7 Ravenna Italy
191 M7 Ravenna prov. Italy
236 F5 Ravenna NE U.S.A.
232 D7 Ravenna OH U.S.A.
234 E4 Raven Rock NJ U.S.A.
85 J8 Ravensbourne Creek watercourse Qld Austr.
172 H6 Ravensburg Ger.
148 E5 Ravensdale Ireland
85 J4 Ravenshoe Qld Austr.
164 I5 Ravenstein Neth.
87 F12 Ravensthorpe W.A. Austr.
149 M5 Ravenstonedale Cumbria, England U.K.
85 K6 Ravenswood Qld Austr.
232 D10 Ravenswood WV U.S.A.
116 F9 Raver Mahar. India
123 N6 Ravi r. Pak.
161 B9 Raviège, Lac de la l. France
156 H8 Ravières France
234 C3 Ravine PA U.S.A.
188 E3 Ravna Gora Croatia
188 F3 Ravna Gora hill Croatia
179 L7 Ravne Slovenia
179 K6 Ravne na Koroškem Slovenia
120 H6 Ravshan Uzbek.
168 H1 Ravsted Denmark
93 B6 Rawa Aopa Watumohai, Taman Nasional nat. park Indon.
127 J6 Rāwah Iraq
128 A10 Rawāhimī, Ra's pt Egypt
203 G5 Rawai well Sudan
77 I2 Rawaki i. Phoenix Is Kiribati
123 O5 Rawala Kot Pak.
123 O5 Rawalpindi Pak.
222 H1 Rawalpindi Lake N.W.T. Can.
175 I4 Rawa Mazowiecka Pol.
127 L5 Rawāndiz Iraq
94 E6 Rawas r. Indon.
116 E5 Rawatsar Rajasthan India
149 P6 Rawcliffe East Riding of Yorkshire, England U.K.
149 O6 Rawcliffe York, England U.K.
124 G8 Rawḑah Yemen
128 F10 Rawghah watercourse Saudi Arabia
227 L3 Rawhide Lake Ont. Can.
94 C1 Rawi, Ko i. Thai.
174 E4 Rawicz Pol.
175 I3 Rawka r. Pol.
87 H11 Rawlinna W.A. Austr.
238 K6 Rawlins WY U.S.A.
87 I8 Rawlinson, Mount hill W.A. Austr.
87 J8 Rawlinson Range hills W.A. Austr.
149 O7 Rawmarsh South Yorkshire, England U.K.
123 J2 Rawnina Turkm.
Rawnina Turkm. see Rawnina
261 G4 Rawson Buenos Aires Arg.
259 D6 Rawson Chubut Arg.
262 N1 Rawson Mountains Antarctica
214 D9 Rawsonville S. Africa
149 M6 Rawtenstall Lancashire, England U.K.
108 A4 Rawu Xizang China
179 M4 Raxalpe mts Austria
117 J6 Raxaul Bihar India
226 A1 Ray MN U.S.A.
225 J4 Ray, Cape Nfld and Lab. Can.
95 I5 Raya, Bukit mt. Kalimantan Indon.
95 J5 Raya, Bukit mt. Kalimantan Indon.
114 F5 Rayachoti Andhra Prad. India
114 E5 Rayadurg Andhra Prad. India
115 H3 Rayagada Orissa India
128 E5 Rayak Lebanon
123 O3 Rayan Pak.
100 F4 Raychikhinsk Rus. Fed.
139 T3 Rayda Rus. Fed.
124 G8 Raydah Yemen
125 I7 Raydah, Wādīar r. Yemen
122 G7 Rāyen Iran
240 M7 Rayes Peak CA U.S.A.
120 F1 Rayevskiy Rus. Fed.
137 K4 Rayhorod Ukr.
137 S5 Rayhorodka Ukr.
137 Q5 Rayhorodok Ukr.
151 N4 Rayleigh Essex, England U.K.
222 H5 Raymond Alta Can.
233 N5 Raymond NH U.S.A.
238 C3 Raymond WA U.S.A.
83 M5 Raymond Terrace N.S.W. Austr.
237 G12 Raymondville TX U.S.A.
223 J5 Raymore Sask. Can.
117 K8 Rayna W. Bengal India
151 N4 Rayne Essex, England U.K.
263 D2 Rayner Glacier Antarctica
161 I10 Rayol-Canadel-sur-Mer France
245 H4 Rayón Mex.
244 G6 Rayón, Parque Nacional nat. park Mex.
243 I5 Rayones Mex.
97 E8 Rayong Thai.
137 L4 Rayozero Ukr.
237 G9 Ray Roberts, Lake TX U.S.A.
232 G8 Raystown Lake PA U.S.A.
125 K7 Raysūt Oman
128 F10 Rayth al Khayl watercourse Saudi Arabia
215 M1 Rayton S. Africa
111 L11 Rayü Xizang China
237 J9 Rayville LA U.S.A.
124 D4 Rayyis Saudi Arabia
158 B5 Raz, Pointe du pt France
162 F5 Razac-sur-l'Isle France
115 H3 Razam Andhra Prad. India
122 C4 Razan Iran
122 C5 Rāzān Iran
123 N5 Razani Pak.
197 J7 Ražanj Serbia
127 K7 Razāzah, Buḩayrat ar l. Iraq
Razdan Armenia see Hrazdan
Razdel'naya Ukr. see Rozdil'na
100 G7 Razdol'noye Rus. Fed.
129 H1 Razdol'ye Rus. Fed.
179 J8 Razdrto Slovenia
138 J9 Razdzyalavichy Belarus
122 C5 Razeh Iran
162 G3 Razès France
163 I9 Razès reg. France
197 O7 Razgrad Bulg.
175 M2 Razhanka Belarus
111 J11 Razhêng Zangbo r. Xizang China
197 Q6 Razim, Lacul lag. Romania
197 L9 Razlog Bulg.
138 K5 Rāznas l. Latvia
177 H3 Ráztočno Slovakia
137 P3 Razumnoye Rus. Fed.
Raz"yezd 3km Rus. Fed. see Novyy Urgal
192 C5 Razzoli, Isola i. Sardegna Italy
232 D11 R. D. Bailey Lake WV U.S.A.
162 B3 Ré, Île de i. France
147 E6 Rea, Lough l. Ireland
150 G3 Rea Brook r. England U.K.
246 □ Reading Jamaica
151 K5 Reading Reading, England U.K.
151 K5 Reading admin. div. England U.K.
226 J8 Reading MI U.S.A.
232 A9 Reading OH U.S.A.
234 D4 Reading PA U.S.A.
234 F3 Readington NJ U.S.A.
233 M6 Readsboro VT U.S.A.
226 D6 Readstown WI U.S.A.
147 I5 Reaghstown Ireland
215 K1 Reagile S. Africa
254 F4 Real r. Brazil
261 H5 Real Audiencia Arg.
260 D4 Real de Padre Arg.
195 N2 Reale, Canale r. Italy
192 A5 Reale, Rada della b. Sardegna Italy
185 I8 Reales mt. Spain
261 E4 Realicó Arg.
163 I8 Réalmont France
194 E9 Realmonte Sicilia Italy
163 G7 Réalville France
234 C4 Reamstown PA U.S.A.
97 F8 Reăng Kesei Cambodia
79 □9 Reao atoll Arch. des Tuamotu Fr. Polynesia
243 I4 Reata Mex.
Reate Italy see Rieti
163 E7 Réaup France
234 F4 Reaville NJ U.S.A.
146 I5 Reay Highland, Scotland U.K.
205 H3 Rebaa Alg.
156 F6 Rebais France
140 O1 Rebbenesøya i. Norway
87 G10 Rebecca, Lake salt flat W.A. Austr.
165 F7 Rebecq Belgium
163 D9 Rébénacq France
163 I10 Rébenty r. France
222 G1 Rebesca Lake N.W.T. Can.
Rebiana Sand Sea des. Libya see Rabyānah, Ramlat
185 K4 Rebollera mt. Spain
183 M6 Rebollo Spain
183 O6 Rebollosa de Jadraque Spain
140 U5 Reboly Rus. Fed.
182 F5 Rebordelo Port.
182 D2 Rebordelo Spain
210 E3 Rebrebti Dhubo well Eth.
121 T1 Rebrikha Rus. Fed.
102 R1 Rebun-suidō sea chan. Japan
102 R1 Rebun-tō i. Japan
261 G5 Recalde Arg.
194 G1 Recale Italy
191 P9 Recanati Italy
197 J5 Recaş Romania
183 M8 Recas Spain
190 G7 Recco Italy
136 H6 Recea Moldova
147 C6 Recess Ireland
157 I8 Recey-sur-Ource France
139 O5 Rechane Rus. Fed.
87 G13 Recherche, Archipelago of the is W.A. Austr.
87 G13 Recherche Archipelago Nature Reserve W.A. Austr.
157 M6 Réchicourt-le-Château France
Rechitsa Belarus see Rechytsa
170 G4 Rechlin Ger.
123 O6 Rechna Doab lowland Pak.
179 N5 Rechnitz Austria
165 J8 Recht Belgium
172 H2 Rechtenbach Ger.
168 D3 Rechtsupweg Ger.
136 F2 Rechytsa Brestskaya Voblasts' Belarus
136 J1 Rechytsa Homyel'skaya Voblasts' Belarus
179 L7 Rečica Slovenia
254 G4 Recife Brazil
215 J10 Recife, Cape S. Africa
217 □2a Récifs, Île aux i. Inner Islands Seychelles
260 B5 Recinto Chile
169 E6 Recke Ger.
190 E3 Reckingen Switz.
169 D7 Recklinghausen Ger.
170 F2 Recknitz r. Ger.
191 K4 Recoaro Terme Italy
258 F3 Reconquista Arg.
161 G7 Recoubeau-Jansac France
161 B8 Recoules-Prévinquières France
262 V1 Recovery Glacier Antarctica
253 F2 Recreio Mato Grosso Brazil
257 F4 Recreio Minas Gerais Brazil
258 D3 Recreo Catamarca Arg.
261 G2 Recreo Santa Fé Arg.
177 J4 Recsk Hungary
232 B10 Rectorville KY U.S.A.
183 O6 Recuerda Spain
174 D2 Recz Pol.
175 H4 Ręczno Pol.
85 I4 Red r. Qld Austr.
222 E3 Red r. B.C. Can.
223 L5 Red r. Can./U.S.A.
237 J10 Red r. U.S.A.
237 F8 Red, North Fork r. OK U.S.A.
174 G1 Reda Pol.
174 G1 Reda r. Pol.
94 E2 Redang i. Malaysia
165 I9 Redange Lux.
235 G4 Red Bank NJ U.S.A.
231 E8 Red Bank TN U.S.A.
Red Basin Sichuan China see Sichuan Pendi
225 J3 Red Bay Nfld and Lab. Can.
223 J4 Redberry Lake Sask. Can.
87 E8 Red Bluff hill W.A. Austr.
240 J1 Red Bluff CA U.S.A.
237 D10 Red Bluff Lake TX U.S.A.
151 L4 Redbourn Hertfordshire, England U.K.
241 T6 Red Butte mt. AZ U.S.A.
149 O4 Redcar Redcar and Cleveland, England U.K.
149 O4 Redcar and Cleveland admin. div. England U.K.
148 C3 Redcastle Ireland
223 I5 Redcliff Alta Can.
226 D3 Red Cliff WI U.S.A.
213 F3 Redcliff Zimbabwe
150 G5 Redcliff Bay North Somerset, England U.K.
85 N9 Redcliffe Qld Austr.
87 F10 Redcliffe, Mount hill W.A. Austr.
83 I6 Red Cliffs Vic. Austr.
236 F5 Red Cloud NE U.S.A.
147 J7 Redcross Ireland
222 H4 Red Deer Alta Can.
222 I5 Red Deer r. Alta/Sask. Can.
223 K4 Red Deer r. Man./Sask. Can.
223 K4 Red Deer Lake Man. Can.
170 E2 Reddelich Ger.
215 K5 Reddersburg S. Africa
238 C6 Redding CA U.S.A.
235 I2 Redding CT U.S.A.
235 I2 Redding Ridge CT U.S.A.
151 I3 Redditch Worcestershire, England U.K.
149 M3 Rede r. England U.K.
222 H3 Red Earth Creek Alta Can.
170 D4 Redefin Ger.
214 C8 Redelinghuys S. Africa
254 C3 Redenção Pará Brazil
254 D4 Redenção Piauí Brazil
158 E6 Rédené France
161 E9 Redessan France
205 H2 Redeyef Tunisia
236 F3 Redfield SD U.S.A.
146 K9 Redford Angus, Scotland U.K.
222 B2 Red Granite Mountain Y.T. Can.
247 □7 Redhead Trin. and Tob.
82 G5 Redhill S.A. Austr.
151 L5 Redhill Surrey, England U.K.
234 E4 Red Hill PA U.S.A.
147 H4 Redhills Ireland
237 F7 Red Hills KS U.S.A.
233 L7 Red Hook NY U.S.A.
176 F5 Rédics Hungary
111 I12 Red Idol Gorge China
225 J3 Red Indian Lake Nfld and Lab. Can.
157 N6 Réding France
Redingen Lux. see Redange
182 C8 Redinha Port.
230 E5 Redkey IN U.S.A.
139 T5 Redkino Rus. Fed.
222 G2 Redknife r. N.W.T. Can.
223 M5 Red Lake Ont. Can.
223 M5 Red Lake l. Ont. Can.
241 T6 Red Lake AZ U.S.A.
236 H2 Red Lake MN U.S.A.
236 G2 Red Lake r. MN U.S.A.
236 G2 Red Lake Falls MN U.S.A.
236 H1 Red Lake Indian Reservation res. MN U.S.A.
236 H1 Red Lakes MN U.S.A.
240 O7 Redlands CA U.S.A.
234 F5 Red Lion NJ U.S.A.
234 B5 Red Lion PA U.S.A.
238 J4 Red Lodge MT U.S.A.
151 I6 Redlynch Wiltshire, England U.K.
80 J3 Red Mercury Island North I. N.Z.
238 D4 Redmond OR U.S.A.
241 U2 Redmond UT U.S.A.
173 J2 Rednitz r. Ger.
173 K3 Rednitzhembach Ger.
236 H5 Red Oak IA U.S.A.
235 H1 Red Oaks Mill NY U.S.A.
210 C5 Redojari waterhole Kenya
158 G6 Redon France
247 □2 Redonda i. Antigua and Barbuda
182 C4 Redondela Spain
182 E5 Redondelo Port.
184 D3 Redondo Port.
240 N8 Redondo Beach CA U.S.A.
238 H3 Red Peak MT U.S.A.
146 E7 Red Point Highland, Scotland U.K.
Red River r. Vietnam see Hông, Sông
Red River, Mouths of the Vietnam see Hong, Mouths of the
224 B3 Red Rock Ont. Can.
241 U9 Red Rock AZ U.S.A.
227 R8 Red Rock PA U.S.A.
238 H4 Red Rock r. MT U.S.A.
222 H1 Redrock Lake N.W.T. Can.
87 I12 Red Rocks Point W.A. Austr.
150 C4 Red Roses Carmarthenshire, Wales U.K.
150 B7 Redruth Cornwall, England U.K.
124 B2 Red Sea Africa/Asia
203 G5 Red Sea state Sudan
222 F4 Redstone B.C. Can.
222 E1 Redstone r. N.W.T. Can.
227 M1 Redstone r. Ont. Can.
223 M4 Red Sucker Lake Man. Can.
164 I2 Reduzum Neth.
206 E4 Red Volta r. Burkina/Ghana alt. Nazinon (Burkina)
238 L2 Redwater r. MT U.S.A.
240 I1 Redway CA U.S.A.
150 D1 Red Wharf Bay Wales U.K.
236 E5 Red Willow Creek r. NE U.S.A.
225 J2 Red Wine r. Nfld and Lab. Can.
226 B5 Red Wing MN U.S.A.
171 D10 Redwitz an der Rodach Ger.
240 J4 Redwood City CA U.S.A.
236 H3 Redwood Falls MN U.S.A.
238 B6 Redwood National Park CA U.S.A.
240 I2 Redwood Valley CA U.S.A.
175 H5 Rędziny Pol.
147 G5 Ree, Lough l. Ireland
226 I6 Reed City MI U.S.A.
223 K4 Reed Lake Man. Can.
240 M5 Reedley CA U.S.A.
235 G6 Reeds Bay NJ U.S.A.
226 E6 Reedsburg WI U.S.A.
238 B5 Reedsport OR U.S.A.
232 D9 Reedsville OH U.S.A.
232 H8 Reedsville PA U.S.A.
233 I11 Reedville VA U.S.A.
232 D10 Reedy WV U.S.A.
85 J7 Reedy Creek watercourse Qld Austr.
262 P1 Reedy Glacier Antarctica
Reef Islands Vanuatu see Rowa
81 F9 Reefton South I. N.Z.
147 E7 Reens Ireland
151 O2 Reepham Norfolk, England U.K.
169 B7 Rees Ger.
227 K6 Reese MI U.S.A.
240 P1 Reese r. NV U.S.A.
168 H4 Reeßum Ger.
170 E4 Reetz Brandenburg Ger.
171 F6 Reetz Brandenburg Ger.
164 G4 Reeuwijksebrug Neth.
126 I4 Refahiye Turkey
182 C5 Refóios do Lima Port.
237 K9 Reform AL U.S.A.
243 M9 Reforma Chiapas Mex.
245 M9 Reforma Oaxaca Mex.
234 C5 Refton PA U.S.A.
237 G11 Refugio TX U.S.A.
174 D1 Rega r. Pol.
182 D6 Regadas Port.
244 F8 Regaditos Mex.
187 E8 Regajo, Embalse del resr Spain
194 H8 Regalbuto Sicilia Italy
186 E5 Regallo r. Spain
179 I4 Regau Austria
173 O4 Regen Ger.
173 M3 Regen r. Ger.
257 H3 Regência Brazil
173 M3 Regensburg Ger.
190 E1 Regensdorf Switz.
173 M3 Regenstauf Ger.
256 B5 Regente Feijó Brazil
205 F4 Reggane Alg.
164 J3 Regge r. Neth.
191 L8 Reggello Italy
Reggio Calabria Italy see Reggio di Calabria
Reggio Emilia-Romagna Italy see Reggio nell'Emilia
195 J7 Reggio di Calabria Italy
195 K7 Reggio di Calabria prov. Italy
Reggio Emilia Italy see Reggio nell'Emilia
191 J6 Reggio nell'Emilia Italy
191 J6 Reggio nell'Emilia prov. Italy
197 M4 Reghin Romania
123 K5 Regi Afgh.
193 L6 Regi Lagni canal Italy
175 I3 Regimin Pol.
223 J5 Regina Sask. Can.
251 H3 Régina Fr. Guiana
123 K6 Registān reg. Afgh.
256 D6 Registro Brazil
256 B1 Registro do Araguaia Brazil
Regium Lepidum Italy see Reggio nell'Emilia
171 F10 Regnitzlosau Ger.
160 E5 Régny France
117 O5 Regong Arun. Prad. India
140 U4 Regozero Rus. Fed.
182 C4 Reguengo Spain
184 D4 Reguengos de Monsaraz Port.
158 F6 Réguiny France
171 F10 Rehau Ger.
169 H6 Rehburg (Rehburg-Loccum) Ger.
168 F5 Rehden Ger.
116 G8 Rehli Madh. Prad. India
173 J5 Rehling Ger.
172 B3 Rehlingen-Siersburg Ger.
171 I9 Řehlovice Czech Rep.
170 D3 Rehna Ger.
212 C4 Rehoboth Namibia
233 J10 Rehoboth Bay DE U.S.A.
233 J10 Rehoboth Beach DE U.S.A.
157 K4 Réhon France
128 C7 Rehovot Israel
Reïbell Alg. see Ksar Chellala
171 F7 Reibitz Ger.
173 J2 Reiche Ebrach r. Ger.
172 F2 Reichelsheim (Odenwald) Ger.
169 G10 Reichelsheim (Wetterau) Ger.
172 G6 Reichenau Ger.
179 M4 Reichenau an der Rax Austria
172 F2 Reichenbach Hessen Ger.
171 F9 Reichenbach Sachsen Ger.
190 D2 Reichenbach Switz.
171 K8 Reichenbach (Oberlausitz) Ger.
172 H2 Reichenberg Ger.
179 K5 Reichenfels Austria
169 J8 Reichensachsen (Wehretal) Ger.
173 K2 Reichenschwand Ger.
178 F5 Reichenspitze mt. Austria
179 J2 Reichenthal Austria
173 L5 Reichertshausen Ger.
173 M5 Reichertsheim Ger.
173 K4 Reichertshofen Ger.
173 J6 Reichling Ger.
171 D9 Reichmannsdorf Ger.
172 H2 Reicholzheim Ger.
179 J4 Reichraming Austria
157 O6 Reichshoffen France
157 O6 Reichstett France
87 J11 Reid W.A. Austr.
190 D1 Reiden Switz.
146 E7 Reidh, Rubha pt Scotland U.K.
231 F9 Reidsville GA U.S.A.
231 H7 Reidsville NC U.S.A.
182 G7 Reigada Port.
151 L5 Reigate Surrey, England U.K.
162 C5 Reignac France
160 I4 Reignier France
169 D10 Reil Ger.
241 V9 Reiley Peak AZ U.S.A.
163 G6 Reilhaguet France
172 F3 Reilingen Ger.
161 H9 Reillanne France
183 Q9 Reillo Spain
156 H5 Reims France
184 H4 Reina Spain
259 B9 Reina Adelaida, Archipiélago de la is Chile
190 E1 Reinach Aargau Switz.
190 D1 Reinach Basellandschaft Switz.
142 C2 Reinaknuten hill Norway
168 J3 Reinbek Ger.
170 H2 Reinberg Ger.
223 K4 Reindeer r. Sask. Can.
223 L4 Reindeer Island Man. Can.
223 K3 Reindeer Lake Man./Sask. Can.
140 L3 Reine Norway
232 D9 Reinersville OH U.S.A.
141 J6 Reineskarvet mt. Norway
168 J3 Reinfeld (Holstein) Ger.
80 G1 Reinga, Cape North I. N.Z.
169 H7 Reinhardswald mts Ger.
172 F2 Reinheim Ger.
234 C4 Reinholds PA U.S.A.
183 L3 Reinosa Spain
160 E4 Reins r. France
171 G7 Reinsdorf Sachsen-Anhalt Ger.
171 D8 Reinsdorf Thüringen Ger.
172 B2 Reinsfeld Ger.
142 C2 Reinsnosi mt. Norway
140 □B1 Reiphólsfjöll hill Iceland
Reirson Island atoll Cook Is see Rakahanga
140 Q2 Reisa Nasjonalpark nat. park Norway
173 N4 Reisbach Ger.
173 N5 Reischach Ger.
140 R5 Reisjärvi Fin.
169 G9 Reiskirchen Ger.
234 B6 Reisterstown MD U.S.A.
194 G8 Reitano Sicilia Italy
164 J2 Reitdiep r. Neth.
173 M6 Reit im Winkl Ger.
215 M3 Reitz S. Africa
215 L3 Reitzburg S. Africa
138 H3 Reiu r. Estonia
214 I3 Reivilo S. Africa
210 A3 Rejaf Sudan
143 L3 Rejmyre Sweden
175 L4 Rejowiec Pol.
175 L4 Rejowiec Fabryczny Pol.
179 O7 Reka Croatia
191 Q5 Reka r. Slovenia
114 G4 Rekapalle Andhra Prad. India
169 D7 Reken Ger.
123 L7 Rekgwash Pak.
164 K4 Rekken Neth.
175 M5 Reklynets' Ukr.
Rekohua i. Chatham Is S. Pacific Ocean see Chatham Island
196 J7 Rekovac Serbia
175 M6 Rekshyn Ukr.
142 E1 Reksjåeggi mt. Norway
138 G6 Rėkyvos ežeras l. Lith.
223 I2 Reliance N.W.T. Can.
194 H10 Religione, Punta pt Sicilia Italy
184 C5 Relíquias Port.
205 F2 Relizane Alg.
242 G4 Rellano Mex.
187 E10 Relleu Spain
115 H4 Relli Andhra Prad. India
168 I3 Rellingen Ger.
216 □1b Relva São Miguel Azores
177 I5 Rém Hungary
205 H2 Remada Tunisia
169 D9 Remagen Ger.
159 M5 Rémalard France
82 G5 Remarkable, Mount hill S.A. Austr.
95 I8 Rembang Jawa Indon.
157 J6 Rembercourt-Sommaisne France
171 D9 Remda Ger.
261 F5 Remecó Arg.
216 □1b Remédios São Miguel Azores
250 C3 Remedios Col.
246 D2 Remedios Cuba
244 A1 Remedios Mex.
243 O11 Remedios, Punta pt El Salvador
182 B3 Remedios, Punta dos pt Spain
205 H3 Remel el Abiod des. Tunisia
168 E4 Remels (Uplengen) Ger.
138 L5 Remennikovo Rus. Fed.
236 I2 Remer MN U.S.A.
122 H8 Remeshk Iran
140 S5 Remeskylä Fin.
177 L5 Remetea Romania
177 K6 Remetea Mare Romania
197 L3 Remeți Romania
179 N7 Remetinec Croatia
Remi France see Reims
165 J9 Remich Lux.
165 H7 Remicourt Belgium
157 I4 Remilly-Aillicourt France
232 H10 Remington VA U.S.A.
251 H3 Rémire Fr. Guiana
217 □2 Rémire i. Seychelles
157 M7 Remiremont France
169 K6 Remlingen Ger.
238 D2 Remmel Mountain WA U.S.A.
186 C4 Remolinos Spain
157 L7 Remoncourt France
135 H7 Remontnoye Rus. Fed.
165 I8 Remouchamps Belgium
161 F9 Remoulins France
94 F4 Rempang i. Indon.
217 □1c Remparts, Rivière des r. Réunion
170 G3 Remplin Ger.
171 E9 Remptendorf Ger.
172 G4 Rems r. Ger.
169 D8 Remscheid Ger.
178 B7 Remulo r. Italy
158 F6 Remungol France
226 I6 Remus MI U.S.A.
161 G8 Rémuzat France
141 K6 Rena Norway
141 K6 Rena r. Norway
184 H2 Rena Spain
227 K1 Renabie Ont. Can.
161 G6 Renage France
260 A5 Renaico Chile
160 D4 Renaison France
Renaix Belgium see Ronse
96 D1 Renam Myanmar
114 E3 Renapur Mahar. India
159 I6 Renazé France
260 E3 Renca Arg.
172 E4 Renchen Ger.
213 F4 Renco Zimbabwe
Rende Yunnan China see Xundian
193 Q9 Rende Italy
236 K6 Rend Lake IL U.S.A.
78 □6 Rendova i. New Georgia Is Solomon Is
168 I2 Rendsburg Ger.
183 M2 Renedo Cantabria Spain
183 K5 Renedo Castilla y León Spain
183 K4 Renedo de la Vega Spain
225 G3 René-Levasseur, Île i. Que. Can.
190 B2 Renens Switz.
164 E5 Renesse Neth.
225 K4 Renews Nfld and Lab. Can.
224 E4 Renfrew Ont. Can.
146 H11 Renfrew Renfrewshire, Scotland U.K.
146 G11 Renfrewshire admin. div. Scotland U.K.
117 J9 Rengali Reservoir Orissa India
94 E5 Rengat Sumatera Indon.
260 B4 Rengo Chile
169 D9 Rengsdorf Ger.
169 I8 Rengshausen (Knüllwald) Ger.
108 G2 Ren He r. China
109 J3 Renheji Henan China
Renhou Hebei China see Tangxian
109 I6 Renhua Guangdong China
108 F5 Renhuai Guizhou China
136 H8 Reni Ukr.
232 E11 Renick WV U.S.A.
114 F6 Renigunta Andhra Prad. India
146 C7 Renish Point Scotland U.K.
168 D5 Renkenberge Ger.
138 H1 Renko Fin.
164 I5 Renkum Neth.
Renland reg. Greenland see Tuttut Nunaat
82 H6 Renmark S.A. Austr.
194 H10 Renna r. Sicilia Italy
169 K6 Rennau Ger.
78 □6 Rennell i. Solomon Is
259 B8 Rennell, Islas is Chile
169 F9 Rennerod Ger.
84 D5 Renner Springs N.T. Austr.
173 K4 Rennertshofen Ger.
158 H5 Rennes France
158 H5 Rennes, Bassin de basin France
163 I10 Rennes-les-Bains France
142 B2 Rennesøy i. Norway
263 K2 Rennick Glacier Antarctica
223 M5 Rennie Man. Can.
223 J2 Rennie Lake N.W.T. Can.
172 F4 Renningen Ger.
149 N3 Rennington Northumberland, England U.K.
179 I5 Rennweg Austria
191 M6 Reno r. Italy
226 C6 Reno MN U.S.A.
240 M2 Reno NV U.S.A.
191 K2 Renòn Italy
192 C3 Rénoso, Monte mt. Corse France
215 K2 Renoster r. S. Africa
214 E7 Renoster watercourse S. Africa

214 G8 Renosterkop S. Africa
215 K2 Renostersruit S. Africa
232 H7 Renovo PA U.S.A.
107 O7 Renqiu Hebei China
168 H1 Rens Denmark
108 E4 Renshou Sichuan China
174 F5 Reńska Wieś Opolskie Pol.
174 G5 Reńska Wieś Opolskie Pol.
230 D5 Rensselaer IN U.S.A.
233 L6 Rensselaer NY U.S.A.
164 I4 Renswoude Neth.
Rentería Spain see Errenteria
198 C3 Rentina Greece
140 O4 Rentjärn Sweden
238 C3 Renton WA U.S.A.
169 K10 Rentweinsdorf Ger.
117 I7 Renukut Uttar Prad. India
156 I4 Renwez France
81 H8 Renwick South I. N.Z.
139 U3 Renya r. Rus. Fed.
170 D3 Renzow Ger.
206 E3 Réo Burkina
93 B8 Reo Flores Indon.
251 G5 Repartimento Brazil
176 F4 Répce r. Hungary
176 G4 Répcelak Hungary
213 G4 Repembe r. Moz.
123 J2 Repetek Turkm.
123 J2 Repetek Döwlet Gorugy nature res. Turkm.
139 P6 Repino Rus. Fed.
175 K3 Repki Pol.
160 F4 Replonges France
140 R2 Repokaira reg. Fin.
138 M2 Repolka Rus. Fed.
80 K5 Reporoa North I. N.Z.
141 P6 Reposaari Fin.
170 F2 Reppelin Ger.
168 J4 Reppenstedt Ger.
232 B7 Republic OH U.S.A.
238 E2 Republic WA U.S.A.
236 G6 Republican r. NE U.S.A.
236 E5 Republican, South Fork r. NE U.S.A.
188 F3 Republika Srpska aut. div. Bos.-Herz.
161 E6 République, Col de la pass France
85 L6 Repulse Bay b. Qld Austr.
221 J3 Repulse Bay Nunavut Can.
140 R1 Repvåg Norway
135 G6 Rep'yevka Rus. Fed.
195 □ Reqqa, Il-Ponta ta' pt Gozo Malta
183 L3 Requejada, Embalse de resr Spain
182 G4 Requejo Spain
250 C6 Requena Peru
187 C9 Requena Spain
260 B4 Requinoa Chile
163 J7 Réquista France
78 □6 Rere Guadalcanal Solomon Is
170 E2 Rerik, Ostseebad Ger.
254 E3 Reriutaba Brazil
127 K4 Reşadiye Turkey
Reşadiye Bolu Turkey see Yeniçağa
126 H3 Reşadiye Tokat Turkey
199 I6 Reşadiye Yarımadası pen. Turkey
94 F7 Resag, Gunung mt. Indon.
191 L4 Resana Italy
197 J6 Resava r. Serbia
197 J6 Resavica Serbia
146 K9 Rescobie Angus, Scotland U.K.
196 J9 Resen Macedonia
257 E5 Resende Brazil
182 E2 Resende Port.
256 B6 Reserva Brazil
239 J10 Reserve NM U.S.A.
139 T5 Reshetnikovo Rus. Fed.
137 N4 Reshetylivka Ukr.
109 H4 Reshi Hunan China
106 G8 Reshui Qinghai China
191 J2 Resia, Lago di l. Italy
178 C6 Resia, Passo di pass Austria/Italy
234 E2 Resica Falls PA U.S.A.
258 F2 Resistencia Arg.
197 J5 Reşiţa Romania
174 D2 Resko Pol.
174 D1 Resko Przymorskie, Jezioro lag. Pol.
221 I2 Resolute Nunavut Can.
221 L3 Resolution Island Nunavut Can.
81 A12 Resolution Island South I. N.Z.
150 E4 Resolven Neath Port Talbot, Wales U.K.
146 B6 Resort, Loch inlet Scotland U.K.
183 K3 Respenda de la Peña Spain
257 G3 Resplendor Brazil
139 S7 Ressa r. Rus. Fed.
251 G5 Ressaca Brazil
215 P1 Ressango Garcia S. Africa
139 S8 Resseta r. Rus. Fed.
156 E4 Ressons-sur-Matz France
252 B2 Restauração Brazil
161 J8 Restefond, Col de pass France
196 I9 Restelica Kosovo Serbia
233 □S1 Restigouche r. N.B. Can.
180 D5 Restinga Morocco
216 □3e Restinga, Punta de la pt El Hierro Canary Is
257 E5 Restinga de Marambaia coastal area Brazil
255 B9 Restinga Seca Brazil
250 C3 Restrepo Col.
Resülayn Turkey see Ceylanpınar
194 G8 Resuttano Sicilia Italy
137 M2 Ret' r. Ukr.
243 N10 Retalhuleu Guat.
183 M7 Retamal Spain
260 C3 Retamito Arg.
94 □ Retan Laut, Pulau i. Sing.
182 E9 Retaxo Port.
205 G2 Retem, Oued er watercourse Alg.
260 B3 Retén Atalaya Chile
260 A4 Retén Llico Chile
197 K5 Retezat, Parcul Naţional nat. park Romania
149 P7 Retford Nottinghamshire, England U.K.
156 H4 Rethel France
168 H5 Rethem (Aller) Ger.
Réthimnon Kriti Greece see Rethymno
156 E5 Rethondes France
198 F7 Rethymno Kriti Greece
165 H6 Retie Belgium
183 N7 Retiendas Spain
158 I6 Retiers France
184 G3 Retín r. Spain
260 B5 Retiro Chile
191 R4 Retje Slovenia
177 K3 Rétköz reg. Hungary
182 H7 Retortillo Spain
183 L3 Retortillo tourist site Spain
185 I5 Retortillo, Embalse de resr Spain
183 O6 Retortillo de Soria Spain
161 E6 Retournac France
85 I8 Retreat Qld Austr.
177 I4 Rétság Hungary
173 I6 Rettenberg Ger.
186 C6 Retuerta mt. Spain
185 K2 Retuerta del Bullaque Spain
179 M2 Retz Austria
171 F6 Reuden Sachsen-Anhalt Ger.
171 F8 Reuden Sachsen-Anhalt Ger.
159 P7 Reuilly France
260 A5 Reunión Chile
217 □1c Réunion terr. Indian Ocean
169 K10 Reurieth Ger.
185 H5 Reus Spain
94 B3 Reusam, Pulau i. Indon.
165 H6 Reusel Neth.
165 H5 Reusel r. Neth.
190 E1 Reuss r. Switz.
173 N5 Reut Ger.
Reut r. Moldova see Răut
137 O2 Reut r. Rus. Fed.
172 D5 Reute Ger.
136 G6 Reutel Moldova
170 G3 Reuterstadt Stavenhagen Ger.
173 M2 Reuth bei Erbendorf Ger.
172 G5 Reutlingen Ger.
139 U6 Reutov Rus. Fed.
178 C5 Reutte Austria
165 J6 Reuver Neth.
123 N3 Revak Afgh.
Reval Estonia see Tallinn
134 F2 Revda Rus. Fed.
241 P4 Reveille Peak NV U.S.A.
Revel Estonia see Tallinn
163 I9 Revel France
117 J7 Revelganj Bihar India
192 B2 Revellata, Pointe de la pt Corse France
190 C6 Revello Italy
222 G5 Revelstoke B.C. Can.
245 I3 Reventadero Mex.
250 A6 Reventazón Peru
234 E3 Revere PA U.S.A.
160 G5 Revermont reg. France
161 H8 Revest-du-Bion France
177 G5 Révfülöp Hungary
213 H2 Révia Moz.
197 P6 Reviga Romania
197 P6 Reviga r. Romania
157 I6 Revigny-sur-Ornain France
183 L3 Revilla de Collazos Spain
183 M4 Revilla del Campo Spain
228 D7 Revillagigedo, Islas is Mex.
220 E4 Revillagigedo Island AK U.S.A.
156 I4 Revin France
191 M4 Revine-Lago Italy
128 C7 Revivim Israel
139 R9 Revna r. Rus. Fed.
176 D2 Řevnice Czech Rep.
176 C1 Řevničov Czech Rep.
191 K3 Revò Italy
185 O4 Revolcadores mt. Spain
Revolyutsii, Pik mt. Tajik. see Revolyutsiya, Qullai
123 O2 Revolyutsiya, Qullai mt. Tajik.
140 N2 Revsnes Norway
177 J3 Revúca Slovakia
213 G3 Revuè r. Moz.
139 U7 Revyakino Rus. Fed.
79 □7a Rewa r. Viti Levu Fiji
117 H7 Rewa Madh. Prad. India
81 J8 Rewa hill North I. N.Z.
174 D1 Rewal Pol.
116 F5 Rewari Haryana India
262 S2 Rex, Mount Antarctica
238 I5 Rexburg ID U.S.A.
225 H4 Rexton N.B. Can.
242 □T13 Rey, Isla del i. Panama
136 H3 Reya Ukr.
207 I4 Rey Bouba Cameroon
151 P3 Reydon Suffolk, England U.K.
252 D3 Reyes Bol.
216 □3e Reyes, Bahía de los b. El Hierro Canary Is
240 I3 Reyes, Point CA U.S.A.
250 B4 Reyes, Punta pt Col.
128 E1 Reyhanlı Turkey
140 □C1 Reykir Iceland
140 □B2 Reykjanes constituency Iceland
264 G2 Reykjanes Ridge sea feature N. Atlantic Ocean
140 □B2 Reykjanestá pt Iceland
140 □C1 Reykjavík Iceland
84 C2 Reynolds r. N.T. Austr.
232 C9 Reynoldsburg OH U.S.A.
84 D7 Reynolds Range mts N.T. Austr.
243 J4 Reynosa Mex.
160 F5 Reyrieux France
160 F4 Reyssouze r. France
122 E5 Rezā Iran
122 D5 Rezā, Kūh-e hill Iran
Rezā'ābād Iran
122 E6 Rezā'īyeh Iran see Orūmīyeh
Rezā'īyeh, Daryācheh-ye salt l. Iran see Orūmīyeh, Daryācheh-ye
158 H7 Rezé France
138 K5 Rēzekne Latvia
138 K5 Rēzekne r. Latvia
176 G5 Rezi Hungary
136 H6 Rezina Moldova
188 E3 Rezinjski vrh mt. Slovenia
197 Q9 Rezovska Reka r. Bulg./Turkey
123 I7 Rezvān Iran
Rezvāndeh Iran see Rezvānshahr
122 C3 Rezvānshahr Iran
190 I4 Rezzato Italy
190 D7 Rezzo Italy
190 G6 Rezzoaglio Italy
R. F. Magón Mex. see Ricardo Flores Magón
197 K6 Rgotina Serbia
168 H4 Rhade Ger.
Rhaeadr Gwy Wales U.K. see Rhayader
205 F3 Rharbi, Oued el watercourse Alg.
190 H1 Rhätikon mts Switz.
172 C2 Rhaunen Ger.
150 E3 Rhayader Powys, Wales U.K.
169 F7 Rheda-Wiedenbrück Ger.
169 C7 Rhede Ger.
168 D4 Rhede (Ems) Ger.
169 I6 Rheden Ger.
234 B4 Rheems PA U.S.A.
Rhegium Italy see Reggio di Calabria
150 D3 Rheidol r. Wales U.K.
Rheims France see Reims
168 B7 Rhein r. Ger.
alt. Rhin (France), conv. Rhine
172 D4 Rheinau Ger.
169 C9 Rheinbach Ger.
169 C7 Rheinberg Ger.
172 D2 Rheinböllen Ger.
172 D2 Rheinbreitbach Ger.
169 D10 Rheinbrohl Ger.
169 D6 Rheine Ger.
190 H1 Rheineck Switz.
190 D1 Rheinfelden Switz.
172 D8 Rheinfelden (Baden) Ger.
169 E10 Rheingaugebirge hills Ger.
169 B10 Rheinisches Schiefergebirge hills Ger.
169 D11 Rheinland-Pfalz land Ger.
169 C8 Rhein-Ruhr airport Ger.
170 G4 Rheinsberg Ger.
172 D3 Rheinstetten Ger.
169 F10 Rhein-Taunus, Naturpark nature res. Ger.
190 G2 Rheinwaldhorn mt. Switz.
190 D9 Rhein-Westerwald, Naturpark nature res. Ger.
172 E3 Rheinzabern Ger.
190 C4 Rhêmes-Notre-Dame Italy
190 C4 Rhêmes-St-Georges Italy
204 D3 Rhemilès well Alg.
164 I5 Rhenen Neth.
169 E10 Rhens Ger.
204 D3 Rheris, Oued watercourse Morocco
146 G6 Rhiconich Highland, Scotland U.K.
157 P6 Rhin r. France
alt. Rhein (Germany), conv. Rhine
170 G4 Rhin r. Ger.
157 O7 Rhinau France
168 B7 Rhine r. Europe
alt. Rhein (Germany), alt. Rhin (France)
233 L7 Rhinebeck NY U.S.A.
226 E4 Rhinelander WI U.S.A.
Rhineland-Palatinate land Ger. see Rheinland-Pfalz
170 G5 Rhinkanal canal Ger.
170 G5 Rhinluch marsh Ger.
146 H12 Rhinns of Kells hills Scotland U.K.
210 A4 Rhino Camp Uganda
170 F5 Rhinow Ger.
170 F5 Rhinowes Berge hills Ger.
204 C3 Rhir, Cap c. Morocco
165 G7 Rhisnes Belgium
Rhiwabon Wales U.K. see Ruabon
190 G4 Rho Italy
246 □ Rhoades, Point Jamaica
147 H6 Rhode Ireland
233 N7 Rhode Island state U.S.A.
169 H8 Rhoden (Diemelstadt) Ger.
Rhodes Rodos Greece see Rodos
Rhodes i. Greece see Rodos
Rhodesia country Africa see Zimbabwe
Rhodes Inyanga National Park Zimbabwe see Nyanga National Park
Rhodes Matopos National Park Zimbabwe see Matobo National Park
238 G3 Rhodes Peak ID U.S.A.
197 L9 Rhodope Mountains Bulg./Greece
Rhodus i. Greece see Rodos
169 I10 Rhön mts Ger.
150 F4 Rhondda reg. Wales U.K.
150 F4 Rhondda Cynon Taff admin. div. Wales U.K.
160 F5 Rhône dept France
161 F9 Rhône r. France/Switz.
161 F9 Rhône-Alpes admin. reg. France
161 E9 Rhône à Sète, Canal du France
157 N8 Rhône au Rhin, Canal du France
150 F5 Rhoose Vale of Glamorgan, Wales U.K.
173 M6 Rhordorf Ger.
150 E4 Rhos Neath Port Talbot, Wales U.K.
150 F1 Rhosllanerchrugog Wrexham, Wales U.K.
150 E1 Rhôs-on-Sea Conwy, Wales U.K.
150 D4 Rhossili Swansea, Wales U.K.
205 G2 Rhoufi Alg.
148 H1 Rhu Argyll and Bute, Scotland U.K.
Rhube, Oasis of Syria see Ruḩbah
150 F1 Rhuddlan Denbighshire, Wales U.K.
161 A6 Rhue r. France
Rhum i. Scotland U.K. see Rum
169 J7 Rhumspringe Ger.
Rhuthun Denbighshire, Wales U.K. see Ruthin
158 F6 Rhuys, Presqu'île de pen. France
Rhydaman Carmarthenshire, Wales U.K. see Ammanford
150 F1 Rhyl Denbighshire, Wales U.K.
150 F4 Rhymney Caerphilly, Wales U.K.
146 K8 Rhynie Aberdeenshire, Scotland U.K.
207 H6 Riaba Equat. Guinea
195 K7 Riace Italy
255 C6 Riachão Brazil
254 D4 Riachão das Neves Brazil
257 G3 Riacho Brazil
254 E5 Riacho de Santana Brazil
257 F1 Riacho dos Machados Brazil
259 E6 Riachos, Islas de los is Arg.
184 D6 Ria Formosa, Parque Natural da nature res. Port.
183 N6 Riaguas r. Spain
158 I6 Riaillé France
Rialb de Noguera Spain see Rialp
255 C5 Rialma Brazil
186 H3 Rialp Spain
186 H4 Rialp, Pantà de resr Spain
240 O7 Rialto CA U.S.A.
95 I5 Riam Kalimantan Indon.
117 N6 Riang Arun. Prad. India
208 F2 Riangnom Sudan
Rianjo Galicia Spain see Rianxo
193 J3 Riano Italy
183 K3 Riaño Spain
183 J3 Riaño, Embalse de resr Spain
253 H3 Rianópolis Brazil
161 H9 Rians France
183 N9 Riansáres r. Spain
158 E6 Riantec France
182 C3 Rianxo Spain
116 E3 Riasi Jammu and Kashmir
94 C2 Riau prov. Indon.
94 E4 Riau, Kepulauan is Indon.
190 E3 Riaz Switz.
183 N6 Riaza Spain
183 M5 Riaza r. Spain
183 M5 Riba Spain
182 D4 Ribadavia Spain
182 D4 Ribadelago Spain
182 F1 Ribadeo Spain
182 F1 Ribadeo, Ría del inlet Spain
183 P7 Ribadeo de Saelices Spain
183 J2 Ribadesella Spain
183 Q4 Ribaforada Spain
183 H8 Ribagorza Spain
186 G4 Ribagorçana, Noguera r. Spain
186 F5 Riba-roja, Pantà de resr Spain
186 F5 Riba-roja d'Ebre Spain
Ribas de Fresser Spain see Ribes de Freser
255 B7 Ribas do Rio Pardo Brazil
123 M3 Ribat Afgh.
184 C2 Ribatejo reg. Port.
213 H2 Ribáuè Moz.
169 K6 Ribbesbüttel Ger.
149 L6 Ribble r. England U.K.
149 M5 Ribblesdale val. England U.K.
142 E6 Ribe Denmark
142 E6 Ribe county Denmark
157 N7 Ribeauvillé France
156 E4 Ribécourt-Dreslincourt France
256 C6 Ribeira Brazil
256 D6 Ribeira r. Brazil
182 E2 Ribeira, Encoro da resr Spain
184 □ Ribeira Brava Madeira
184 □ Ribeira da Janela Madeira
182 E5 Ribeira de Pena Port.
216 □1b Ribeira Grande São Miguel Azores
252 D2 Ribeirão Brazil
256 B6 Ribeirão r. Brazil
256 C6 Ribeirão Branco Brazil
257 E3 Ribeirão das Neves Brazil
256 B5 Ribeirão do Pinhal Brazil
256 D4 Ribeirão Preto Brazil
256 D3 Ribeirão Vermelho Brazil
216 □1c Ribeiras Pico Azores
216 □1c Ribeira Seca São Jorge Azores
216 □1b Ribeira Seca São Miguel Azores
216 □1c Ribeirinha Faial Azores
216 □1c Ribeirinha Pico Azores
216 □1a Ribeirinha Terceira Azores
156 F4 Ribemont France
194 E8 Ribera Sicilia Italy
162 E5 Ribérac France
184 G3 Ribera del Fresno Spain
252 D2 Riberalta Bol.
183 Q4 Ribera Navarra reg. Spain
186 H5 Ribesalbes Spain
186 J3 Ribes de Freser Spain
161 H8 Ribiers France
177 L5 Ribita Romania
176 G9 Ribnica Radlje Ob Dravi Slovenia
188 E3 Ribnica Ribnica Slovenia
136 I5 Rîbnița Moldova
170 F2 Ribnitz-Damgarten Ger.
197 L9 Ribnovo Bulg.
139 Q4 Ribnovsk Rus. Fed.
183 L8 Ribota Spain
252 C5 Rica Aventura Chile
195 J6 Ricadi Italy
179 N1 Říčany Jihomoravský kraj Czech Rep.
176 D2 Říčany Středočeský kraj Czech Rep.
242 F3 Ricardo Flores Magón Mex.
149 P5 Riccal r. England U.K.
193 N5 Riccia Italy
191 M9 Riccione Italy
191 N7 Riccione Italy
190 H7 Riccò del Golfo di Spezia Italy
241 R7 Rice CA U.S.A.
232 G11 Rice VA U.S.A.
227 L2 Rice Lake l. Ont. Can.
224 E4 Rice Lake l. Ont. Can.
226 C4 Rice Lake WI U.S.A.
226 A3 Rice Lake l. MN U.S.A.
226 B6 Riceville IA U.S.A.
232 C11 Riceville KY U.S.A.
157 L6 Richardménil France
215 Q4 Richards Bay S. Africa
263 L1 Richards Inlet Antarctica
220 E3 Richards Island N.W.T. Can.
223 I3 Richardson r. Alta Can.
222 G1 Richardson Island N.W.T. Can.
233 □O4 Richardson Lakes ME U.S.A.
220 E3 Richardson Mountains N.W.T. Can.
81 C11 Richardson Mountains South I. N.Z.
206 B2 Richard Toll Senegal
234 E4 Richboro PA U.S.A.
217 □1b Riche en Eau Mauritius
164 H2 Richel i. Neth.
233 L3 Richelieu Que. Can.
162 E1 Richelieu France
234 A3 Richfield PA U.S.A.
241 T3 Richfield UT U.S.A.
233 K6 Richfield Springs NY U.S.A.
233 I6 Richford NY U.S.A.
234 F6 Richford VT U.S.A.
233 M4 Richgrove CA U.S.A.
240 M6 Richhill Northern Ireland U.K.
147 I4 Richibucto N.B. Can.
225 H4 Rich Lake Alta Can.
223 I4 Richland NJ U.S.A.
234 F6 Richland PA U.S.A.
234 C4 Richland WA U.S.A.
238 E3 Richland Center WI U.S.A.
226 D6 Richlands VA U.S.A.
232 D11 Richlandtown PA U.S.A.
234 E4 Richmond N.S.W. Austr.
83 M5 Richmond Qld Austr.
85 I6 Richmond Ont. Can.
227 S4 Richmond Que. Can.
225 F4 Richmond Jamaica
246 □ Richmond South I. N.Z.
81 H8 Richmond KwaZulu-Natal S. Africa
215 O5 Richmond Northern Cape S. Africa
214 H7 Richmond North Yorkshire, England U.K.
149 N5 Richmond CA U.S.A.
240 J4 Richmond IL U.S.A.
226 F7 Richmond IN U.S.A.
230 E6 Richmond KY U.S.A.
232 A11 Richmond ME U.S.A.
233 □P4 Richmond MI U.S.A.
227 L7 Richmond TX U.S.A.
237 H11 Richmond VA U.S.A.
232 H11 Richmond VT U.S.A.
233 M4 Richmond, Mount South I. N.Z.
81 H8 Richmond County county NY U.S.A.
235 G3 Richmond Dale OH U.S.A.
232 C9 Richmond Hill Ont. Can.
224 E5 Richmond Hill GA U.S.A.
231 G10 Richmond Peak St Vincent
247 □3 Richmond Range hills N.S.W. Austr.
83 N3 Richmond Range mts South I. N.Z.
81 H8 Richmondville NY U.S.A.
233 K6 Richoi Xizang China
111 H11 Richtenberg Ger.
170 G2 Richtersveld National Park S. Africa
214 B4 Richterswil Switz.
172 F7 Richton MS U.S.A.
237 K10 Richvald Slovakia
177 K2 Richvale CA U.S.A.
240 K2 Richwood OH U.S.A.
232 B8 Richwood WV U.S.A.
232 E10 Ricigliano Italy
193 O6 Rickenbach Ger.
172 D6 Rickinghall Suffolk, England U.K.
151 N3 Ricklean r. Sweden
140 P4 Rickling Ger.
168 J2 Rickmansworth Hertfordshire, England U.K.
151 L4 Ricla Spain
183 R5 Ricobayo, Embalse de resr Spain
182 I5 Ricomagus France see Riom
Ricse Hungary
177 K3 Riddell Nunataks nunataks Antarctica
263 E2 Ridder Kazakh. see Leninogorsk
164 G5 Ridderkerk Neth.
190 C3 Riddes Switz.
232 G8 Riddlesburg PA U.S.A.
227 S4 Rideau r. Ont. Can.
224 E4 Rideau Lakes Ont. Can.
234 B6 Riderwood MD U.S.A.
233 I2 Ridge r. Ont. Can.
235 J3 Ridge NY U.S.A.
240 O6 Ridgecrest CA U.S.A.
235 I2 Ridgefield CT U.S.A.
235 G3 Ridgefield NJ U.S.A.
237 J9 Ridgeland MS U.S.A.
231 G9 Ridgeland SC U.S.A.
226 C4 Ridgeland WI U.S.A.
234 D7 Ridgely MD U.S.A.
227 M7 Ridgetown Ont. Can.
226 C6 Ridgeway IA U.S.A.
235 G4 Ridgeway NJ U.S.A.
232 F12 Ridgeway VA U.S.A.
235 G3 Ridgewood NJ U.S.A.
232 G7 Ridgway PA U.S.A.
177 I6 Riđica Vojvodina Serbia
146 M13 Riding Mill Northumberland, England U.K.
223 K5 Riding Mountain National Park Man. Can.
86 E6 Ridley r. W.A. Austr.
215 K3 Riebeeckstad S. Africa
214 C9 Riebeek-Kasteel S. Africa
214 C9 Riebeek-Oos S. Africa
214 C9 Riebeek-Wes S. Africa
140 N3 Riebnes l. Sweden
250 D2 Riecito Venez.
158 D6 Riec-sur-Belon France
173 K5 Ried Ger.
190 E3 Ried Switz.
173 I7 Riedbergerhorn mt. Ger.
168 G5 Riede Ger.
173 L3 Rieden Ger.
168 G4 Riedenburg Ger.
173 M6 Riedering Ger.
179 H3 Ried im Innkreis Austria
173 O5 Ried im Oberinntal Austria
178 E5 Ried im Zillertal Austria
179 K3 Ried in der Riedmark Austria
157 N8 Riedisheim France
172 G5 Riedlingen Ger.
172 B3 Riegelsberg Ger.
179 M5 Riegersburg Austria
173 J3 Riegsee Ger.
184 H7 Riego, Canal de Spain
182 I4 Riego de la Vega Spain
190 D1 Riehen Switz.
215 K1 Riekertsdam S. Africa
172 F6 Rielasingen-Worblingen Ger.
182 I3 Riello Spain
183 L9 Rielves Spain
165 I7 Riemst Belgium
169 I10 Rieneck Ger.
177 L5 Rieni Romania
191 L2 Rienza r. Italy
140 P2 Riepposgai'sa mt. Norway
168 K2 Riepsdorf Ger.
171 H8 Riesa Ger.
259 B9 Riesco, Isla i. Chile
168 I1 Rieseby Ger.
194 G9 Riesi Sicilia Italy
169 F6 Rieste Ger.
171 D8 Riestedt Ger.
214 H5 Riet r. S. Africa
214 E7 Riet watercourse S. Africa
138 E6 Rietavas Lith.
169 F7 Rietberg Ger.
214 H8 Rietbron S. Africa
214 E2 Rietfontein S. Africa
170 J3 Rieth Ger.
165 H6 Riethoven Neth.
214 F10 Rietkuil S. Africa
193 J3 Rieti Italy
193 J3 Rieti prov. Italy
215 N3 Rietkuil S. Africa
214 C6 Rietpoort S. Africa
171 K8 Rietschen Ger.
214 E6 Riet se Vloer salt pan S. Africa
215 O5 Rietvlei S. Africa
215 M1 Rietvlei Nature Reserve S. Africa
178 D5 Rietz Austria
163 G9 Rieumes France
163 I7 Rieupeyroux France
161 C7 Rieutort-de-Randon France
158 G6 Rieux Bretagne France
163 G9 Rieux Midi-Pyrénées France
163 J9 Rieux-Minervois France
161 I9 Riez France
128 E6 Rīfā'ī, Tall mt. Jordan/Syria
256 D4 Rifaina Brazil
Rifeng Jiangxi China see Lichuan
178 H4 Riffelkopf mt. Austria
191 K2 Rifiano Italy
239 K7 Rifle CO U.S.A.
210 B4 Rift Valley prov. Kenya
Rift Valley Lakes National Park Eth. see Abijatta-Shalla National Park
111 L12 Riga Arun. Prad. India
138 H5 Rīga Latvia
138 G4 Riga, Gulf of Estonia/Latvia
207 G4 Rigacikun Nigeria
111 H10 Rigain Pünco l. Xizang China
198 D3 Rigaio Greece
122 H7 Rīgān Iran
Rigas jūras līcis b. Estonia/Latvia see Riga, Gulf of
233 K3 Rigaud Que. Can.
161 J9 Rigaud France
238 I5 Rigby ID U.S.A.
238 F4 Riggins ID U.S.A.
160 K3 Riggisberg Switz.
146 E11 Righ Mòr, Loch l. Scotland U.K.
190 F1 Rigi mts Switz.
190 H5 Riglio r. Italy
129 K7 Rig Matī Iran
163 H8 Rignac France
183 J3 Rignano Flaminio Italy
193 P4 Rignano Garganico Italy
191 K8 Rignano sull'Arno Italy
156 G7 Rigny-le-Ferron France
160 E3 Rigny-sur-Arroux France
159 L7 Rigny-Ussé France
225 J2 Rigolet Nfld and Lab. Can.
202 B6 Rig-Rig Chad
146 I11 Rigside South Lanarkshire, Scotland U.K.
183 R4 Riguel r. Spain
124 D6 Rīḩ, Gezirat er i. Sudan
124 D6 Rīḩ, Gezirat er i. Sudan
113 □1 Rihiveli i. S. Male Maldives
Riia laht b. Estonia/Latvia see Riga, Gulf of
141 R6 Riihimäki Fin.
140 S3 Riipi Fin.
262 W2 Riiser-Larsen Ice Shelf Antarctica
138 H2 Riisipere Estonia
140 T3 Riisitunturin kansallispuisto nat. park Fin.
242 B1 Riito Mex.
207 G4 Rijau Nigeria
188 E3 Riječki Zaliv b. Croatia
188 E3 Rijeka Croatia
191 R5 Rijeka airport Croatia
164 G5 Rijen Neth.
165 G6 Rijkevorsel Belgium
164 G4 Rijnsaterwoude Neth.
164 F4 Rijnsburg Neth.
140 □ Rijpfjorden inlet Svalbard
164 G5 Rijsbergen Neth.
164 K4 Rijssen Neth.
164 F4 Rijswijk Neth.
136 C5 Rika r. Ukr.
124 G4 Rikā, Wādī ar watercourse Saudi Arabia
94 B2 Rikitgaib Sumatera Indon.
117 O5 Riksar Arun. Prad. India
140 O2 Riksgränsen Sweden
140 Q2 Rikubetsu Japan
103 J3 Rikuchū-kaigan
102 T7 Kokuritsu-kōen nat. park Japan
102 S7 Rikuzen-takata Japan
197 L8 Rila Bulg.
197 L8 Rila mts Bulg.
111 G12 Rila Xizang China
238 E5 Riley OR U.S.A.
232 G10 Rileyville VA U.S.A.
162 G4 Rilhac-Rancon France
165 F6 Rilland Neth.
159 L7 Rillé France
160 F5 Rillieux-la-Pape France
241 U9 Rillito AZ U.S.A.
186 D6 Rillo Spain
183 Q7 Rillo de Gallo Spain
156 H5 Rilly-la-Montagne France
207 G3 Rima watercourse Niger/Nigeria
124 F2 Rimah, Wādī al watercourse Saudi Arabia
79 □9 Rimatara i. Îs Australes Fr. Polynesia
Rimatara i. Îs Australes Fr. Polynesia see Rimatara
94 F6 Rimau, Pulau i. Indon.
157 J7 Rimaucourt France
177 J3 Rimava r. Slovakia
177 I3 Rimavská Baňa Slovakia
177 J3 Rimavská Seč Slovakia
177 J3 Rimavská Sobota Slovakia
173 N3 Rimbach Bayern Ger.
172 F2 Rimbach Hessen Ger.
222 H4 Rimbey Alta Can.
143 O2 Rimbo Sweden
232 F7 Rimersburg PA U.S.A.
197 L4 Rimetea Romania
143 L3 Rimforsa Sweden
191 N7 Rimini Italy
191 M7 Rimini prov. Italy
Rîmnicu Sărat Romania see Râmnicu Sărat
Rîmnicu Vîlcea Romania see Râmnicu Vâlcea
116 F2 Rimo Glacier Jammu and Kashmir
156 I4 Rimogne France
163 G10 Rimont France
225 G3 Rimouski Que. Can.
225 G3 Rimouski, Réserve Faunique de nature res. Que. Can.
172 H2 Rimpar Ger.
179 I7 Rimske Toplice Slovenia
173 M6 Rimsting Ger.
81 J8 Rimutaka Forest Park nature res. North I. N.Z.
111 I12 Rinbung Xizang China
93 A8 Rinca i. Indon.
256 C4 Rincão Brazil
173 O4 Rinchnach Ger.
258 D2 Rincón Arg.
Rincon Morocco see Mdiq
247 □8 Rincón Bonaire Neth. Antilles
247 □1 Rincón Puerto Rico
247 □1 Rincón, Bahía de b. Puerto Rico
252 D6 Rincón, Cerro del mt. Chile
258 D1 Rinconada Arg.
245 K6 Rinconada Mex.
185 J2 Rinconada, Sierra de la mts Spain
187 C7 Rincón de Ademuz reg. Spain
261 I3 Rincón de Cololó Uru.
260 C4 Rincón del Atuel Arg.
185 K7 Rincón de la Victoria Spain
261 I3 Rincón del Bonete, Lago Artificial de resr Uru.
260 C5 Rincón de los Sauces Arg.
261 I4 Rincón del Pino Uru.
261 I3 Rincón de Ramírez Uru.
244 E3 Rincón de Romos Mex.
183 Q4 Rincón de Soto Spain
116 H7 Rind r. India
138 E4 Rinda r. Latvia
140 J5 Rindal Norway
117 L5 Rindü Xizang China
198 G5 Rineia i. Greece
194 H6 Rinella Isole Lipari Italy
232 E11 Riner VA U.S.A.
83 K9 Ringarooma Bay Tas. Austr.
143 M3 Ringarum Sweden
116 E6 Ringas Rajasthan India
147 F9 Ringaskiddy Ireland
142 G6 Ringe Denmark
168 C5 Ringe Ger.
141 K6 Ringebu Norway
190 G2 Ringelspitz mt. Switz.
170 I4 Ringenwalde Ger.
231 E8 Ringgold GA U.S.A.
96 D1 Ringhkung Myanmar
207 H3 Ringim Nigeria
142 E5 Ringkøbing Denmark
142 E5 Ringkøbing county Denmark
142 E6 Ringkøbing Fjord lag. Denmark
151 O2 Ringland Norfolk, England U.K.
171 D8 Ringleben Ger.
151 M6 Ringmer East Sussex, England U.K.
234 F4 Ringoes NJ U.S.A.
148 D3 Ringsend Northern Ireland U.K.
142 H6 Ringsted Denmark
111 F11 Ringtor Xizang China
140 O2 Ringvassøya i. Norway
147 G8 Ringville Ireland
151 I6 Ringwood Hampshire, England U.K.
233 K7 Ringwood NJ U.S.A.
Rinia i. Greece see Rineia
168 I1 Rinkenæs Denmark
146 J8 Rinloan Aberdeenshire, Scotland U.K.
178 E5 Rinn Austria
146 D11 Rinns of Islay pen. Scotland U.K.
146 D11 Rinns Point Scotland U.K.
256 B4 Rinópolis Brazil
169 H6 Rinteln Ger.
196 F5 Rinya r. Romania
226 E6 Rio WI U.S.A.
252 A1 Río Abiseo, Parque Nacional nat. park Peru
253 F4 Rio Alegre Brazil
255 C8 Rio Azul Brazil
250 B5 Riobamba Ecuador
257 G3 Rio Bananal Brazil
260 B3 Río Blanco Chile
239 K7 Rio Blanco CO U.S.A.
257 F5 Rio Bonito Brazil
252 D2 Rio Branco Brazil
Rio Branco state Brazil see Roraima
251 F4 Rio Branco, Parque Nacional do nat. park Brazil
256 C6 Rio Branco do Sul Brazil
242 H3 Río Bravo, Parque Internacional del nat. park Mex.
255 B7 Rio Brilhante Brazil
259 B6 Río Bueno Chile
246 □ Rio Bueno Jamaica
182 D5 Rio Caldo Port.
251 F2 Río Caribe Venez.
257 F4 Rio Casca Brazil
260 E2 Río Ceballos Arg.
259 C8 Río Chico Arg.
251 E2 Río Chico Venez.
257 E5 Rio Claro Rio de Janeiro Brazil
256 D5 Rio Claro São Paulo Brazil
247 □7 Rio Claro Trin. and Tob.
247 I9 Río Claro Venez.
246 □ Rio Cobre r. Jamaica
261 E6 Río Colorado Arg.
250 B5 Río Corrientes Ecuador
260 E3 Río Cuarto Arg.
213 G4 Rio das Pedras Moz.
257 F5 Rio de Janeiro Brazil
257 F4 Rio de Janeiro state Brazil
242 □S14 Río de Jesús Panama
238 B6 Rio Dell CA U.S.A.
258 E3 Río de los Sauces Arg.
182 F7 Rio de Mel Port.
184 C5 Rio de Moinhos Beja Port.
184 D3 Rio de Moinhos Évora Port.
184 C4 Rio de Moinhos Setúbal Port.
182 G5 Rio de Onor Port.
204 A5 Río de Oro, Bahía de b. Western Sahara
187 C7 Riodeva r. Spain
191 L2 Rio di Pusteria Italy
257 F4 Rio Doce Brazil
255 C8 Rio do Sul Brazil
182 E5 Rio Douro Port.
254 G4 Rio Formoso Brazil
242 □R12 Río Frío Costa Rica
183 K7 Riofrío Spain
182 H5 Riofrío de Aliste Spain
183 N6 Riofrío de Riaza Spain
259 C8 Río Gallegos Arg.
185 K7 Riogordo Spain
259 D9 Río Grande Arg.
252 D5 Río Grande Bol.
258 G4 Rio Grande Brazil
246 □ Rio Grande r. Jamaica
245 J10 Río Grande Oaxaca Mex.
244 D2 Río Grande Zacatecas Mex.
243 K5 Rio Grande r. Mex./U.S.A.
alt. Bravo del Norte, Río
247 □1 Río Grande Puerto Rico
234 F6 Rio Grande NJ U.S.A.
258 C2 Río Grande, Salar de salt flat Arg.
237 F12 Rio Grande City TX U.S.A.
247 □1 Río Grande de Loíza, Embalse resr Puerto Rico
254 F3 Rio Grande do Norte state Brazil
255 B9 Rio Grande do Sul state Brazil
264 G8 Rio Grande Rise sea feature S. Atlantic Ocean
250 C2 Riohacha Col.
242 □S13 Río Hato Panama
258 D2 Río Hondo, Embalse resr Arg.
250 B6 Rioja Peru
185 O7 Rioja Spain
243 O7 Río Lagartos Mex.
254 G4 Rio Largo Brazil
192 B8 Riola Sardo Sardegna Italy
182 H9 Riolobos Spain
245 K7 Río Lodo Mex.
161 L7 Riolo Terme Italy
161 B9 Riols France
160 C5 Riom France
191 K5 Riomaggiore Italy
184 B2 Rio Maior Port.
260 B4 Río Malo Chile
253 G3 Rio Manso, Represa do resr Brazil
192 E2 Rio Marina Italy
182 C6 Rio Mau Port.
161 B6 Riom-ès-Montagnes France
246 □ Rio Minho r. Jamaica
258 E2 Río Muerto Arg.
252 D4 Rio Mulatos Bol.
207 H6 Rio Muni reg. Equat. Guinea
163 G8 Rion-des-Landes France
260 D6 Río Negro prov. Arg.
255 C8 Rio Negro Brazil
259 B6 Río Negro Chile
261 I3 Río Negro dept Uru.
182 H4 Rionegro del Puente Spain
192 H7 Rionero in Vulture Italy
193 M4 Rionero Sannitico Italy
129 C3 Rioni r. Georgia
257 F4 Rio Novo Brazil
257 G4 Rio Novo do Sul Brazil
163 D6 Rions France
181 E3 Riópar Spain
256 B7 Rio Paranacito Arg.
256 B4 Río Pardo de Minas Brazil
257 F1 Rio Pedro r. Jamaica
246 □ Río Plátano, Reserva Biosfera del nature res. Hond.
242 □Q10 Rio Pomba Brazil
257 F4 Rio Preto Brazil
257 F5 Rio Preto, Serra do hills Brazil
256 D2 Río Primero Arg.
261 F2 Río Rancho NM U.S.A.
239 K9 Riorges France
160 E4 Rio Rico AZ U.S.A.
241 V10 Rioscuro Spain
182 F5 Rioseco de Tapia Spain
182 I3 Río Segundo Arg.
261 F2 Riosequillo, Embalse de resr Spain
183 M7 Riosucio Col.
250 B3 Rio Tala Arg.
261 H3 Río Tercero Arg.
261 E3 Rio Tercero, Embalse resr Arg.
250 B5 Rio Tigre Ecuador
254 G3 Rio Tinto Brazil
251 E2 Río Tocuyo Venez.
182 F5 Rio Torto Port.
92 A7 Rio Tuba Palawan Phil.
161 G10 Riou, Île de i. France
223 J3 Riou Lake Sask. Can.
256 B2 Rio Verde Brazil
259 C9 Río Verde Chile
250 B4 Rioverde Ecuador
190 D6 Rioverde r. Italy
243 O8 Río Verde Quintana Roo Mex.
245 H4 Río Verde San Luis Potosí Mex.
255 B6 Rio Verde de Mato Grosso Brazil
257 F3 Rio Vermelho Brazil
240 K3 Rio Vista CA U.S.A.
160 I2 Rioz France
252 D2 Riozinho Amazonas Brazil
253 E2 Riozinho Rondônia Brazil
255 E5 Riozinho r. Brazil
253 F4 Riozinho r. Brazil
190 B5 Ripa r. Italy
192 E2 Ripalti, Punta dei pt Italy
196 I6 Ripanj Serbia
191 J9 Riparbella Italy
193 J3 Ripa Sottile, Lago di l. Italy
193 L2 Ripatransone Italy
140 P3 Ripats Sweden
191 O8 Ripe Italy
193 K4 Ripi Italy
193 O7 Ripiti r. Italy
137 K2 Ripky Ukr.
150 I2 Ripley Derbyshire, England U.K.
149 N5 Ripley North Yorkshire, England U.K.
237 K8 Ripley MS U.S.A.
232 F6 Ripley NY U.S.A.
232 B10 Ripley OH U.S.A.
237 K8 Ripley TN U.S.A.
232 D10 Ripley WV U.S.A.
186 J3 Ripoll Spain
186 J3 Ripolles reg. Spain
149 N5 Ripon North Yorkshire, England U.K.
240 K4 Ripon CA U.S.A.
226 F6 Ripon WI U.S.A.
195 J8 Riposto Sicilia Italy
150 H3 Ripple Worcestershire, England U.K.
149 N6 Ripponden West Yorkshire, England U.K.
164 I5 Rips Neth.
117 M6 Ripu Assam India
157 N7 Riquewihr France
123 O4 Risalpur Pak.
128 B8 Rīsān 'Unayzah hill Egypt
250 C3 Risaralda dept Col.
141 M6 Risarven Sweden
208 E5 Risasi Dem. Rep. Congo
140 M4 Risbäck Sweden
150 F4 Risca Caerphilly, Wales U.K.
136 G6 Rîşcani Moldova
163 D8 Riscle France
260 C4 Risco Plateado mt. Arg.
140 M4 Risede Sweden
142 F5 Risgårde Bredning b. Denmark
124 G3 Rishā, Wādī ar watercourse Saudi Arabia
116 G4 Rishikesh Uttaranchal India
102 R1 Rishiri-Rebun-Sarobetsu Kokuritsu-kōen nat. park Japan
102 S1 Rishiri-tō i. Japan
100 L6 Rishiri-zan vol. Japan
128 C7 Rishon Le Ziyyon Israel
123 J8 Rish Pish Iran
149 M6 Rishton Lancashire, England U.K.
230 E6 Rising Sun IN U.S.A.
234 C5 Rising Sun MD U.S.A.
159 L3 Risle r. France
188 E3 Risnjak nat. park Croatia
Rîşnov Romania see Râşnov
237 I8 Rison AR U.S.A.
142 F3 Risør Norway
156 D6 Ris-Orangis France
116 E1 Risoux, Mont mt. France
140 M2 Risøyhamn Norway
169 E6 Riß r. Ger.
140 J5 Rissa Norway
162 I4 Risse r. France
80 K6 Rissington North I. N.Z.
141 S6 Ristiina Fin.
140 T4 Ristijärvi Fin.
140 U2 Ristikent Rus. Fed.
111 D10 Risum Xizang China
168 G1 Risum-Lindholm Ger.
95 K4 Ritan r. Indon.
111 K12 Ritang Xizang China
138 H5 Ritausma Latvia
214 I5 Ritchie S. Africa
115 M6 Ritchie's Archipelago is Andaman & Nicobar Is India
78 □1 Ritidian Point Guam
209 C9 Rito Angola
129 B2 Ritsa Georgia
262 X2 Ritscher Upland mts Antarctica
140 N3 Ritsem Sweden
129 B2 Ritsis Nakrdzali nature res. Georgia
240 M4 Ritter, Mount CA U.S.A.
168 G4 Ritterhude Ger.
169 B10 Rittersdorf Ger.
171 G10 Rittersgrün Ger.
104 C5 Rittō Japan
183 P5 Rituerto r. Spain
138 K5 Ritupe r. Latvia
238 E3 Ritzville WA U.S.A.
186 H5 Riudoms Spain
136 H4 Riv r. Ukr.
138 E5 Rīva r. Latvia
159 K3 Riva Bella France
261 F4 Rivadavia Buenos Aires Arg.
260 C3 Rivadavia Mendoza Arg.
258 E2 Rivadavia Salta Arg.
260 B1 Rivadavia Chile
191 J4 Riva del Garda Italy
178 B8 Riva di Solto Italy
190 I4 Riva di Tures Italy
140 □ Rivalensundet str. Svalbard
190 D8 Riva Ligure Italy
190 G6 Rivanazzano Italy
239 K12 Riva Palacio Mex.
190 F7 Rivarolo Ligure Italy
190 F5 Rivarolo Canavese Italy
190 I5 Rivarolo Mantovano Italy
261 H4 Rivas Arg.
242 □Q12 Rivas Nic.
261 I2 Rivas Uru.
122 F4 Rīvash Iran
183 N8 Rivas-Vaciamadrid Spain
162 F5 Rive-de-Gier France
160 F5 Rivedoux-Plage France
193 P7 Rivello Italy
261 F5 Rivera Arg.
255 B9 Rivera Uru.
209 C5 River Cess Liberia
240 M5 Riverdale CA U.S.A.
226 B5 River Falls WI U.S.A.
233 M8 Riverhead NY U.S.A.
223 J5 Riverhurst Sask. Can.
87 F10 Riverina W.A. Austr.
83 J6 Riverina reg. N.S.W. Austr.
259 B7 Rivero, Isla i. Chile
207 G5 Rivers state Nigeria
81 C12 Riversdale South I. N.Z.
214 F10 Riversdale S. Africa
81 K8 Riverside Beach North I. N.Z.
81 F11 Riverside South I. N.Z.
215 N6 Riverside S. Africa
240 O8 Riverside CA U.S.A.
234 F4 Riverside NJ U.S.A.
234 B3 Riverside PA U.S.A.
222 E5 Rivers Inlet B.C. Can.
84 G5 Riversleigh Qld Austr.
147 F4 Riverstown Sligo Ireland
147 F4 Riverstown Tipperary Ireland
223 L5 Riverton Man. Can.
81 C13 Riverton South I. N.Z.
214 I4 Riverton S. Africa
234 E4 Riverton NJ U.S.A.
241 U1 Riverton UT U.S.A.
232 G10 Riverton VA U.S.A.
238 J5 Riverton WY U.S.A.
225 H4 Riverview N.B. Can.
235 G4 River View S. Africa
235 G4 Riverwood NJ U.S.A.
156 D4 Rivery France
161 H6 Rives France
163 J10 Rivesaltes France
232 E9 Rivesville WV U.S.A.
234 C4 Riviera Beach MD U.S.A.
235 G4 Riviera Beach NJ U.S.A.
225 H3 Rivière-au-Renard Que. Can.

215 L7 Rossouw S. Africa
170 G4 Rossow Ger.
226 G1 Rossport Ont. Can.
84 E7 Ross River N.T. Austr.
222 C2 Ross River Y.T. Can.
263 L1 Ross Sea Antarctica
173 J3 Roßtal Ger.
164 H5 Rossum Neth.
140 M4 Røssvatnet l. Norway
226 C6 Rossville IA U.S.A.
226 G9 Rossville IL U.S.A.
226 H9 Rossville IN U.S.A.
234 B4 Rossville PA U.S.A.
171 H8 Roßwein Ger.
222 D4 Rosswood B.C. Can.
127 L5 Rōst Iraq
140 L3 Røst Norway
136 J4 Rostabytsya r. Ukr.
123 M3 Rostāq Afgh.
122 F7 Rostāq Fārs Iran
122 E8 Rostāq Hormozgan Iran
174 E3 Rostarzewo Pol.
140 L3 Røsthavet sea chan. Norway
223 J4 Rosthern Sask. Can.
170 F2 Rostock Ger.
140 P2 Rostonsölkä ridge Sweden
137 T2 Rostoshi Rus. Fed.
139 W4 Rostov Rus. Fed.
135 G7 Rostov-na-Donu Rus. Fed.
Rostov Oblast admin. div. Rus. Fed. see Rostovskaya Oblast'
Rostov-on-Don Rus. Fed. see Rostov-na-Donu
135 H7 Rostovskaya Oblast' admin. div. Rus. Fed.
215 J2 Rostrataville S. Africa
158 E5 Rostrenen France
147 J4 Rostrevor Northern Ireland U.K.
140 P2 Rostujávri l. Sweden
147 C5 Rosturk Ireland
140 M3 Røsvik Norway
140 P4 Rosvik Sweden
231 E9 Roswell GA U.S.A.
239 L10 Roswell NM U.S.A.
149 K1 Rosyth Fife, Scotland U.K.
177 J5 Röszke Hungary
172 H5 Rot r. Ger.
91 K4 Rota i. N. Mariana Is
184 G7 Rota Spain
172 H6 Rotach r. Ger.
193 Q9 Rota Greca Italy
173 I3 Rot am See Ger.
173 I5 Rot an der Rot Ger.
171 G10 Rotava Czech Rep.
Rotch Island Gilbert Is Kiribati see Tamana
93 C9 Rote i. Indon.
193 N4 Rotello Italy
168 H4 Rotenburg (Wümme) Ger.
169 I8 Rotenburg an der Fulda Ger.
171 D10 Roter Main r. Ger.
178 A5 Rote Wand mt. Austria
Rot-Front Ukr. see Dobropillya
179 H5 Rotgülden Austria
173 K3 Roth Ger.
173 I5 Roth r. Ger.
173 K3 Roth r. Ger.
171 F8 Rötha Ger.
169 F9 Rothaargebirge hills Ger.
149 N3 Rothbury Northumberland, England U.K.
149 N3 Rothbury Forest England U.K.
173 K3 Röthenbach an der Pegnitz Ger.
172 F2 Rothenberg Ger.
172 G2 Rothenbuch Ger.
171 E7 Rothenburg Ger.
171 K8 Rothenburg (Oberlausitz) Ger.
173 I3 Rothenburg ob der Tauber Ger.
158 H4 Rothéneuf France
172 H2 Rothenfels Ger.
171 E9 Rothenstein Ger.
151 K6 Rother r. England U.K.
262 T2 Rothera research stn Antarctica
151 M5 Rotherfield East Sussex, England U.K.
81 G9 Rotherham South I. N.Z.
149 O7 Rotherham South Yorkshire, England U.K.
146 J7 Rothes Moray, Scotland U.K.
146 F11 Rothesay Argyll and Bute, Scotland U.K.
165 H7 Rotheux-Rimière Belgium
146 K4 Rothiesholm Orkney, Scotland U.K.
173 I2 Röthlein Ger.
172 D7 Rothrist Switz.
226 E5 Rothschild WI U.S.A.
262 T2 Rothschild Island Antarctica
234 C4 Rothsville PA U.S.A.
151 K3 Rothwell Northamptonshire, England U.K.
149 O6 Rothwell West Yorkshire, England U.K.
169 I8 Rothwesten (Fuldatal) Ger.
93 C9 Roti Indon.
Roti i. Indon. see Rote
93 C9 Roti, Selat sea chan. Indon.
Rotja, Punta pt Spain see Roja, Punta
83 J5 Roto N.S.W. Austr.
80 J6 Rotoaira, Lake North I. N.Z.
80 K5 Rotoehu, Lake North I. N.Z.
80 K5 Rotoiti, Lake North I. N.Z.
81 G8 Rotoiti, Lake South I. N.Z.
80 K5 Rotoma, Lake North I. N.Z.
Rotomagus France see Rouen
80 K5 Rotomahana, Lake North I. N.Z.
81 F9 Rotomanu South I. N.Z.
193 Q8 Rotonda Italy
195 L3 Rotondella Italy
192 C3 Rotondo, Monte mt. Corse France
190 E2 Rotondo, Pizzo mt. Switz.
81 G8 Rotoroa, Lake South I. N.Z.
80 K5 Rotorua North I. N.Z.
80 K5 Rotorua, Lake North I. N.Z.
165 G7 Rotselaar Belgium
178 G6 Rotsteinberg mt. Austria
173 J6 Rott Ger.
173 O5 Rott r. Ger.
171 G7 Rotta Ger.
173 L6 Rottach-Egern Ger.
173 M6 Rott am Inn Ger.
157 L6 Rotte r. France
172 H5 Rottenacker Ger.
173 J2 Röttenbach Bayern Ger.
173 K3 Röttenbach Bayern Ger.
171 D9 Rottenbach Ger.
173 J6 Rottenbuch Ger.
172 F5 Rottenburg am Neckar Ger.
173 M4 Rottenburg an der Laaber Ger.
173 I2 Rottendorf Ger.
179 J4 Rottenmann Austria
179 J5 Rottenmanner Tauern mts Austria
164 G5 Rotterdam Neth.
233 L6 Rotterdam NY U.S.A.
164 J2 Rottevalle Neth.
173 O5 Rotthalmünster Ger.
151 L6 Rottingdean Brighton and Hove, England U.K.
172 H2 Röttingham Ger.
169 K7 Rottleberode Ger.
142 I2 Rottnan r. Sweden
143 L5 Rottnen l. Sweden
87 C12 Rottnest Island W.A. Austr.
190 H5 Rottofreno Italy
164 K1 Rottumeroog i. Neth.
164 J1 Rottumerplaat i. Neth.
172 F5 Rottweil Ger.
77 H3 Rotuma i. Fiji
197 M7 Rotunda Romania
140 M5 Rötviken Sweden
173 L6 Rotwand mt. Ger.
173 N3 Rötz Ger.
158 H7 Rouans France
156 F2 Roubaix France
161 F7 Roubion r. France
186 H2 Rouch, Mont mt. France/Spain
160 D4 Rouchain, Barrage du dam France
176 F2 Rouchovany Czech Rep.
176 D1 Roudnice nad Labem Czech Rep.
156 B5 Rouen France
163 I7 Rouergue reg. France
157 N8 Rouffach France
162 I5 Rouffiac France
162 F5 Rouffignac France
138 J4 Rõuge Estonia
158 I6 Rougé France
247 □7 Rouge, Point Trin. and Tob.
224 F4 Rouge-Matawin, Réserve Faunique nature res. Que. Can.
160 I2 Rougemont France
157 M8 Rougemont-le-Château France
81 D12 Rough Ridge South I. N.Z.
151 O2 Roughton Norfolk, England U.K.
147 C9 Roughty r. Ireland
162 E4 Rougnac France
202 A4 Roui, Oued er watercourse Niger
162 D4 Rouillac France
162 E3 Rouillé France
161 C9 Roujan France
160 I2 Roulans France
Roulers Belgium see Roeselare
232 G7 Roulette PA U.S.A.
84 D7 Roulpmaulpma Aboriginal Land res. N.T. Austr.
Roumania country Europe see Romania
162 F4 Roumazières-Loubert France
159 M3 Roumois reg. France
161 I9 Roumoules France
225 G2 Roundeyed Lake Que. Can.
232 B8 Roundhead OH U.S.A.
149 O5 Round Hill England U.K.
83 K5 Round Hill Nature Reserve N.S.W. Austr.
217 □1b Round Island Mauritius
224 E4 Round Lake Ont. Can.
83 N4 Round Mountain mt. N.S.W. Austr.
240 O3 Round Mountain NV U.S.A.
241 W5 Round Rock AZ U.S.A.
237 G10 Round Rock TX U.S.A.
147 C6 Roundstone Ireland
234 B3 Round Top hill PA U.S.A.
238 J3 Roundup MT U.S.A.
234 F3 Round Valley Reservoir NJ U.S.A.
151 I5 Roundway Wiltshire, England U.K.
148 E7 Roundwood Ireland
251 H3 Roura Fr. Guiana
190 C5 Roure Italy
146 J4 Rousay i. Scotland U.K.
233 L4 Rouses Point NY U.S.A.
176 F2 Rousínov Czech Rep.
148 C4 Rousky Northern Ireland U.K.
161 H10 Rousset France
161 G7 Rousset, Col de pass France
161 G9 Roussillon Provence-Alpes-Côte d'Azur France
155 G4 Roussillon Rhône-Alpes France
163 J10 Roussillon reg. France
161 E8 Rousson France
Routh Bank sea feature Phil. see Seahorse Bank
159 M3 Routot France
164 J3 Rouveen Neth.
159 K4 Rouvre r. France
156 E3 Rouvroy France
156 I4 Rouvroy-sur-Audry France
161 J10 Roux, Cap c. France
215 K6 Rouxville S. Africa
160 D2 Rouy France
224 E3 Rouyn-Noranda Que. Can.
Rouyuan Gansu China see Huachi
Rouyuanchengzi Gansu China see Huachi
140 R3 Rovaniemi Fin.
190 E5 Rovasenda r. Italy
190 I4 Rovato Italy
190 G6 Rovegno Italy
135 G6 Roven'ki Rus. Fed.
Rovenki Ukr. see Roven'ky
137 S5 Roven'ky Ukr.
Rovenskaya Oblast' admin. div. Ukr. see Rivnens'ka Oblast'
191 J5 Roverbella Italy
190 G3 Roveredo Switz.
191 K4 Rovereto Italy
170 F2 Rövershagen Ger.
258 E2 Roversi Arg.
193 J3 Roviano Italy
97 G8 Rôviĕng Tbong Cambodia
191 L5 Rovigo Italy
191 L5 Rovigo prov. Italy
197 L6 Rovinari Romania
188 D3 Rovinj Croatia
176 G3 Rovinka Slovakia
179 O8 Rovišće Croatia
Rovno Ukr. see Rivne
Rovno Oblast admin. div. Ukr. see Rivnens'ka Oblast'
138 L3 Rovnoye Pskovskaya Oblast' Rus. Fed.
120 B2 Rovnoye Saratovskaya Oblast' Rus. Fed.
174 C3 Rów Pol.
78 □5 Rowa Vanuatu
150 H5 Rowde Wiltshire, England U.K.
83 L3 Rowena N.S.W. Austr.
234 F2 Rowland PA U.S.A.
232 F9 Rowlesburg WV U.S.A.
221 K3 Rowley Island Nunavut Can.
86 E4 Rowley Shoals sea feature W.A. Austr.
138 M6 Rownaye Belarus
Równe Ukr. see Rivne
174 E4 Rów Polski r. Pol.
232 C8 Rowsburg OH U.S.A.
92 C3 Roxas Luzon Phil.
92 D7 Roxas Mindanao Phil.
92 C5 Roxas Mindoro Phil.
92 B6 Roxas Palawan Phil.
92 D6 Roxas Panay Phil.
231 H7 Roxboro NC U.S.A.
247 □5 Roxborough Trin. and Tob.
84 G7 Roxborough Downs Qld Austr.
81 D12 Roxburgh South I. N.Z.
Roxburgh Island Cook Is see Rarotonga
235 I1 Roxbury CT U.S.A.
235 I1 Roxbury Falls CT U.S.A.
82 F4 Roxby Downs S.A. Austr.
143 L3 Roxen l. Sweden
184 C5 Roxo r. Port.
184 C5 Roxo, Barragem do resr Port.
151 L3 Roxton Bedfordshire, England U.K.
146 G9 Roy r. Scotland U.K.
238 J3 Roy MT U.S.A.
239 L8 Roy NM U.S.A.
161 L9 Roya r. France/Italy
147 H6 Royal Canal Ireland
226 H9 Royal Center IN U.S.A.
117 J6 Royal Chitwan National Park Nepal
226 F1 Royale, Isle i. MI U.S.A.
215 M4 Royal Natal National Park S. Africa
227 K7 Royal Oak MI U.S.A.
263 K1 Royal Society Range mts Antarctica
116 H5 Royal Sukla Phanta Wildlife Reserve nature res. Nepal
234 B4 Royalton PA U.S.A.
226 F5 Royalton WI U.S.A.
162 B4 Royan France
160 C5 Royat France
161 G6 Roybon France
151 N2 Roydon Norfolk, England U.K.
151 O3 Roydon Norfolk, England U.K.
156 E4 Roye France
162 H4 Royère-de-Vassivière France
234 D4 Royersford PA U.S.A.
86 E7 Roy Hill W.A. Austr.
137 K2 Royishche Ukr.
151 L3 Royston Hertfordshire, England U.K.
149 O6 Royston South Yorkshire, England U.K.
149 M6 Royton Greater Manchester, England U.K.
140 R4 Röyttä Fin.
183 R8 Royuela Spain
196 I8 Rožaje Montenegro
183 O9 Rozalén del Monte Spain
175 J3 Różan Pol.
196 H6 Rožanj hill Serbia
174 D3 Różanki Pol.
182 H3 Rozas, Embalse de las resr Spain
156 E6 Rozay-en-Brie France
176 E1 Rožďalovice Czech Rep.
175 M6 Rozdil Ukr.
136 J7 Rozdil'na Ukr.
137 R6 Rozdol'ne Donets'ka Oblast' Ukr.
137 M8 Rozdol'ne Respublika Krym Ukr.
137 O5 Rozdory Ukr.
174 F4 Rozdrażew Pol.
164 F5 Rozenburg Neth.
164 I4 Rozendaal Neth.
121 N2 Rozhdestvenka Kazakh.
139 T5 Rozhdestveno Tverskaya Oblast' Rus. Fed.
139 U4 Rozhdestveno Yaroslavskaya Oblast' Rus. Fed.
134 I4 Rozhdestvenskoye Rus. Fed.
139 Q4 Rozhdestvo Rus. Fed.
129 B2 Rozhkao Rus. Fed.
137 N1 Rozhkovychi Rus. Fed.
137 L3 Rozhnivka Ukr.
136 J3 Rozhny Ukr.
136 D5 Rozhnyativ Ukr.
136 E3 Rozhyshche Ukr.
197 M8 Rozino Bulg.
137 Q6 Rozivka Ukr.
176 C2 Rožmitál pod Třemšínem Czech Rep.
177 J3 Rožňava Slovakia
174 G3 Rożniatów Pol.
177 H2 Rožnov pod Radhoštěm Czech Rep.
175 I6 Rożnów Pol.
174 E3 Roznowo Pol.
175 J2 Rozoga r. Pol.
175 J2 Rozogi Pol.
156 H4 Rozoy-sur-Serre France
175 H4 Rozprza Pol.
137 R4 Rozsypne Ukr.
175 L5 Roztoczański Park Narodowy nat. park Pol.
175 I6 Roztoka Wielka Pol.
171 I10 Roztoky Středočeský kraj Czech Rep.
171 J10 Roztoky Středočeský kraj Czech Rep.
122 D5 Rozveh Iran
190 G5 Rozzano Italy
196 H9 Rrëshen Albania
196 H9 Rrogozhinë Albania
135 H5 Rtishchevo Rus. Fed.
182 D2 Ru Spain
182 E7 Rua Port.
93 A8 Rua, Tanjung pt Sumba Indon.
150 F2 Ruabon Wrexham, Wales U.K.
212 B3 Ruacana Namibia
211 B6 Ruaha National Park Tanz.
80 K6 Ruahine Forest Park nature res. North I. N.Z.
80 K7 Ruahine Range mts North I. N.Z.
80 I2 Ruakaka North I. N.Z.
147 E7 Ruan Ireland
Ruanda country Africa see Rwanda
93 D2 Ruang i. Indon.
80 J6 Ruapehu, Mount vol. North I. N.Z.
81 C13 Ruapuke Island South I. N.Z.
150 G4 Ruardean Gloucestershire, England U.K.
211 B7 Ruarwe Malawi
80 I2 Ruatangata North I. N.Z.
81 E9 Ruatapu South I. N.Z.
80 M4 Ruatoria North I. N.Z.
159 L6 Ruaudin France
78 □6 Ruavatu Guadalcanal Solomon Is
139 N6 Ruba Belarus
124 H6 Rub' al Khālī des. Saudi Arabia
177 H4 Rúbaň Slovakia
148 G5 Rubane Northern Ireland U.K.
137 N7 Rubanivka Ukr.
191 L5 Rubano Italy
138 K6 Rubashki Belarus
125 I3 Rubaydā reg. Saudi Arabia
183 M2 Rubayo Spain
211 C6 Rubeho Mountains Tanz.
169 K7 Rübeland Ger.
257 F2 Rubelita Brazil
183 M4 Rubena Spain
171 H9 Rübenau Ger.
244 G8 Rubén Figueroa Mex.
102 U3 Rubeshibe Japan
Rubezhnoye Ukr. see Rubizhne
Rubha an t-Siumpain hd Scotland U.K. see Tiumpan Head
Rubha Robhanais hd Scotland U.K. see Butt of Lewis
208 E4 Rubi r. Dem. Rep. Congo
186 J5 Rubí Spain
182 G4 Rubiá Spain
256 B4 Rubiácea Brazil
187 C8 Rubial, Serra de mts Spain
240 K3 Rubicon r. CA U.S.A.
191 M7 Rubicone r. Italy
183 K6 Rubí de Bracamonte Spain
186 C6 Rubielos de la Cérida Spain
187 D7 Rubielos de Mora Spain
191 J6 Rubiera Italy
257 G2 Rubim Brazil
256 B4 Rubinéia Brazil
183 M6 Rubio mt. Spain
137 R4 Rubizhne Ukr.
170 I3 Rubkow Ger.
183 N3 Rublacedo de Abajo Spain
211 A5 Rubondo National Park Tanz.
137 Q4 Rubtsi Ukr.
121 S2 Rubtsovsk Rus. Fed.
211 B6 Rubuga Tanz.
124 F6 Rubūţ, Jabal ar hill Saudi Arabia
220 C3 Ruby AK U.S.A.
81 H8 Ruby Bay South I. N.Z.
238 G6 Ruby Dome mt. NV U.S.A.
136 G2 Rubyel' Belarus
139 N6 Rubyezhnitsa Belarus
241 Q1 Ruby Lake NV U.S.A.
241 Q1 Ruby Lake National Wildlife Refuge nature res. NV U.S.A.
241 Q1 Ruby Mountains NV U.S.A.
222 E4 Rubyrock Lake Provincial Park nat. park B.C. Can.
241 T4 Rubys Inn UT U.S.A.
85 K7 Rubyvale Qld Austr.
241 Q1 Ruby Valley NV U.S.A.
260 E5 Rucanelo Arg.
197 N5 Rucăr Romania
138 K6 Ruchay Belarus
Rucheng Guangdong China see Ruyuan
109 I6 Rucheng Hunan China
137 M3 Ruchky Ukr.
137 M8 Ruch"yi Ukr.
175 J2 Ruciane-Nida Pol.
171 I7 Rückersdorf Ger.
232 G10 Ruckersville VA U.S.A.
164 G5 Rucphen Neth.
174 G4 Ruda Pol.
177 J3 Rudabánya Hungary
175 L4 Ruda-Huta Pol.
86 G7 Rudall watercourse W.A. Austr.
86 G7 Rudall River National Park W.A. Austr.
87 L7 Rudalls watercourse N.T. Austr.
175 I4 Ruda Maleniecka Pol.
175 L1 Rudamina Lith.
175 L5 Ruda Różaniecka Pol.
117 I6 Rudarpur Uttar Prad. India
174 G5 Ruda Śląska Pol.
116 H6 Rudauli Uttar Prad. India
176 E1 Rudawski Park Krajobrazowy Pol.
123 J6 Rudbar Afgh.
127 P9 Rūdbār Fārs Iran
122 C3 Rūdbār Gīlān Iran
165 D6 Ruddervoorde Belgium
151 J2 Ruddington Nottinghamshire, England U.K.
173 L4 Rudelzhausen Ger.
179 K6 Ruden Austria
170 I2 Ruden i. Ger.
172 H4 Rudersberg Ger.
179 N5 Rudersdorf Austria
171 I6 Rüdersdorf Berlin Ger.
169 J7 Rüdershausen Ger.
173 O4 Ruderting Ger.
136 I4 Rude Selo Ukr.
172 D2 Rüdesheim Ger.
172 D2 Rüdesheim am Rhein Ger.
151 L5 Rudgwick West Sussex, England U.K.
196 H7 Rudina pass Montenegro
138 H7 Rūdiškės Lith.
169 K9 Rudisleben Ger.
137 L3 Rudivka Chernihivs'ka Oblast' Ukr.
137 R4 Rudivka Luhans'ka Oblast' Ukr.
175 K3 Rudka Pol.
175 L3 Rudka r. Pol.
142 G7 Rudkøbing Denmark
175 L6 Rudky Ukr.
171 J10 Rudná Czech Rep.
174 E4 Rudna Pol.
197 K6 Rudna Glava Serbia
174 E4 Rudna Wielka Pol.
100 I6 Rudnaya Pristan' Primorskiy Kray Rus. Fed.
100 I7 Rudnaya Pristan' Primorskiy Kray Rus. Fed.
136 C4 Rudne Ukr.
177 I1 Rudniański, Park Krajobrazowy Pol.
170 L5 Rudnica Pol.
134 K4 Rudnichnyy Rus. Fed.
174 G5 Rudnik Śląskie Pol.
174 G4 Rudniki Pol.
Rudnik Ingichka Uzbek. see Ingichka
175 K5 Rudnik nad Sadem Podkarpackie Pol.
170 I5 Rüdnitz Ger.
175 M3 Rudnya Belarus
139 O7 Rudnya Smolenskaya Oblast' Rus. Fed.
139 O5 Rudnya Tverskaya Oblast' Rus. Fed.
135 I6 Rudnya Volgogradskaya Oblast' Rus. Fed.
136 G3 Rudnya-Ivanivs'ka Ukr.
175 L6 Rudnyky Ukr.
136 H5 Rudnytsya Ukr.
120 J1 Rudnyy Kazakh.
100 I6 Rudnyy Rus. Fed.
Rudolf, Lake salt l. Eth./Kenya see Turkana, Lake
130 G1 Rudol'fa, Ostrov i. Zemlya Frantsa-Iosifa Rus. Fed.
260 C4 Rudolfo Iselin Arg.
179 K2 Rudolfov Czech Rep.
Rudolph Island Zemlya Frantsa-Iosifa Rus. Fed. see Rudol'fa, Ostrov
171 D9 Rudolstadt Ger.
109 M2 Rudong Jiangsu China
197 M9 Rudozem Bulg.
183 M3 Rudrón resr Spain
122 D3 Rūdsar Iran
142 E2 Rudsgrendi Norway
149 Q5 Rudston East Riding of Yorkshire, England U.K.
226 J3 Rudyard MI U.S.A.
174 F5 Rudziczka Pol.
138 K8 Rudzyensk Belarus
156 C3 Rue France
184 H2 Ruecas r. Spain
183 K6 Rueda Spain
156 D6 Rueil-Malmaison France
227 M2 Ruel Ont. Can.
Ruen mt. Macedonia see Rujen
183 L2 Ruente Spain
213 G3 Ruenya r. Zimbabwe
178 D5 Ruetz r. Austria
203 G6 Rufa'a Sudan
195 O4 Ruffano Italy
159 N8 Ruffec Centre France
162 E3 Ruffec Poitou-Charentes France
160 G2 Ruffey-lès-Echirey France
160 G3 Ruffey-sur-Seille France
158 G6 Ruffiac France
160 H4 Ruffieu France
160 H5 Ruffieux France
149 L6 Rufford Lancashire, England U.K.
211 C7 Rufiji r. Tanz.
191 K8 Rufina Italy
261 F4 Rufino Arg.
206 A3 Rufisque Senegal
209 F8 Rufunsa Zambia
138 K4 Rugāji Latvia
109 M2 Rugao Jiangsu China
170 E3 Rugberg hill Ger.
151 J3 Rugby Warwickshire, England U.K.
236 E1 Rugby ND U.S.A.
151 I2 Rugeley Staffordshire, England U.K.
170 H2 Rügen i. Ger.
170 H1 Rügen, Naturpark nature res. Ger.
222 E5 Rugged Mountain B.C. Can.
203 F5 Rugheiwa well Sudan
173 J3 Rügland Ger.
159 M4 Rugles France
179 N8 Rugvica Croatia
211 C7 Ruhangino Tanz.
125 H3 Ruḩayyat al Ḩamr'ā' waterhole Saudi Arabia
126 H7 Ruḩbah oasis Syria
169 K6 Rühen Ger.
211 A5 Ruhengeri Rwanda
169 J9 Ruhla Ger.
171 I8 Ruhland Ger.
173 N4 Ruhmannsfelden Ger.
170 E3 Rühn Ger.
138 G4 Ruhnu i. Estonia
173 N6 Ruhpolding Ger.
169 C8 Ruhr r. Ger.
173 O5 Ruhstorf an der Rott Ger.
211 B7 Ruhudji r. Tanz.
114 G9 Ruhuna National Park Sri Lanka
122 H6 Ru'ī, Chāh well Iran
109 M5 Rui'an Zhejiang China
109 J4 Ruichang Jiangxi China
185 N3 Ruidera Spain
239 L12 Ruidosa TX U.S.A.
239 L10 Ruidoso NM U.S.A.
109 J6 Ruijin Jiangxi China
108 A6 Ruili Yunnan China
192 B8 Ruinas Sardegna Italy
164 J3 Ruinen Neth.
164 J3 Ruinerwold Neth.
211 C7 Ruipa Tanz.
165 D6 Ruiselede Belgium
182 D5 Ruivães Port.
184 □ Ruivo, Pico mt. Madeira
244 B4 Ruiz Mex.
245 I3 Ruiz Cortines Mex.
197 K8 Ruj mt. Bulg.
138 I4 Rūja r. Latvia
174 E4 Ruja Pol.
128 F6 Rujaylah, Ḩarrat ar lava field Jordan
197 K8 Rujen mt. Macedonia
138 I4 Rūjiena Latvia
129 J4 Rük Azer.
Ruk is Micronesia see Chuuk
123 M8 Ruk Pak.
123 O7 Rukanpur Pak.
125 I2 Rukbah well Saudi Arabia
129 J3 Rukel' Rus. Fed.
129 C3 Rukhi Georgia
208 C4 Ruki r. Dem. Rep. Congo
117 I5 Rukumkot Nepal
210 A5 Rukungiri Uganda
93 D6 Rukuwa Sulawesi Indon.
211 A6 Rukwa admin. reg. Tanz.
211 B7 Rukwa, Lake Tanz.
141 M6 Rulbo Sweden
125 M3 Rūl Ḑadnah U.A.E.
237 J9 Ruleville MS U.S.A.
86 I2 Rulhieres, Cape W.A. Austr.
Rulin Hunan China see Chengbu
169 F6 Rulle (Wallenhorst) Ger.
168 K4 Rullstorf Ger.
160 F3 Rully France
Rulong Sichuan China see Xinlong
172 E3 Rülzheim Ger.
178 D5 Rum Austria
176 F4 Rum Hungary
122 H5 Rūm Iran
Rum Jordan see Ramm
146 D9 Rum i. Scotland U.K.
236 I3 Rum r. MN U.S.A.
Rum, Jebel mts Jordan see Ramm, Jabal
146 D9 Rum, Sound of sea chan. Scotland U.K.
207 G3 Ruma Nigeria
196 H5 Ruma Vojvodina Serbia
124 F9 Rumādah Yemen
125 H3 Rumāh Saudi Arabia
210 B5 Ruma National Park Kenya
Rumania country Europe see Romania
124 F7 Rumayn i. Saudi Arabia
93 D3 Rumbai Sulawesi Indon.
208 F3 Rumbek Sudan
185 L4 Rumblar r. Spain
185 L4 Rumblar, Embalse del resr Spain
176 D1 Rumburk Czech Rep.
246 F2 Rum Cay i. Bahamas
165 J10 Rumelange Lux.
165 D7 Rumes Belgium
233 □O4 Rumford ME U.S.A.
143 O7 Rumia Pol.
156 H4 Rumigny France
160 H5 Rumilly France
84 C2 Rum Jungle N.T. Austr.
124 E2 Rummān, Jabal ar mts Saudi Arabia
128 G5 Rummānā hill Syria
150 F4 Rumney Cardiff, Wales U.K.
102 S3 Rumoi Japan
211 A5 Rumonge Burundi
157 J6 Rumont France
211 B7 Rumphi Malawi
235 H4 Rumson NJ U.S.A.
165 F6 Rumst Belgium
85 J4 Rumula Qld Austr.
210 C4 Rumuruti Kenya
93 F6 Run i. Maluku Indon.
184 A2 Runa Port.
147 J2 Runabay Head Northern Ireland U.K.
109 J2 Runan Henan China
81 F9 Runanga South I. N.Z.
80 L4 Runaway, Cape North I. N.Z.
246 □ Runaway Bay Jamaica
149 L7 Runcorn Halton, England U.K.
197 L5 Runcu Romania
177 L6 Runcu r. Romania
213 G4 Runde r. Zimbabwe
212 C3 Rundu Namibia
93 D6 Runduma i. Indon.
140 O5 Rundvik Sweden
97 F9 Rŭng, Kaôh i. Cambodia
95 J6 Rungan r. Indon.
208 E4 Rungu Dem. Rep. Congo
211 A6 Rungwa Rukwa Tanz.
211 B6 Rungwa Singida Tanz.
211 A6 Rungwa r. Tanz.
211 B6 Rungwa Game Reserve nature res. Tanz.
109 K2 Runheji Anhui China
Runing Henan China see Runan
122 E7 Rūnīz-e Bālā Iran
169 F10 Runkel Ger.
143 O2 Runmarö i. Sweden
143 L1 Runn l. Sweden
240 O7 Running Springs CA U.S.A.
237 E9 Running Water watercourse NM/TX U.S.A.
143 M4 Runnö i. Sweden
87 G7 Runton Range hills W.A. Austr.
151 N4 Runwell Essex, England U.K.
78 □4a Ruo i. Chuuk Micronesia
141 T6 Ruokolahti Fin.
161 E8 Ruoms France
110 I7 Ruoqiang Xinjiang China
110 I7 Ruoqiang He r. China
106 G6 Ruo Shui watercourse China
193 P6 Ruoti Italy
141 S6 Ruotsinpyhtää Fin.
141 R6 Ruovesi Fin.
191 Q5 Rupa Croatia
117 N6 Rupa Arun. Prad. India
94 D4 Rupat i. Indon.
197 N4 Rupea Romania
224 E3 Rupert r. Que. Can.
238 H5 Rupert ID U.S.A.
232 E11 Rupert WV U.S.A.
224 E3 Rupert Bay Que. Can.
262 O1 Rupert Coast Antarctica
85 I6 Rupert Creek r. Qld Austr.
116 F4 Rupnagar Punjab India
116 E6 Rupnagar Rajasthan India
211 C7 Ruponda Tanz.
170 G5 Ruppiner See l. Ger.
179 L3 Ruprechtshofen Austria
116 F3 Rupshu reg. Jammu and Kashmir
157 M8 Rupt-sur-Moselle France
124 F5 Ruqayṭah Saudi Arabia
128 D6 Ruqqād, Wādī ar watercourse Israel
232 D12 Rural Retreat VA U.S.A.
252 D3 Rurrenabaque Bol.
169 B9 Rurstausee resr Ger.
79 □9 Rurutu i. Îs Australes Fr. Polynesia
197 L3 Rus Romania
185 M4 Rus Spain
185 N2 Rus r. Spain
Rusaddir N. Africa see Melilla
137 N8 Rusakivka Ukr.
137 M3 Rusanivka Ukr.
213 G3 Rusape Zimbabwe
197 K5 Rusca Montană Romania
Ruschuk Bulg. see Ruse
197 M3 Ruscova Romania
197 N7 Ruse Bulg.
179 M6 Ruše Slovenia
197 O7 Rusenski Lom nat. park Bulg.
117 K7 Rusera Bihar India
197 P6 Ruşeţu Romania
147 J5 Rush Ireland
151 I2 Rushall West Midlands, England U.K.
107 Q8 Rushan Shandong China
Rushan Tajik. see Rushon
Rushanskiy Khrebet mts Tajik. see Rushon, Qatorkŭhi
236 D6 Rush Creek r. CO U.S.A.
151 K3 Rushden Northamptonshire, England U.K.
226 C6 Rushford MN U.S.A.
213 G3 Rushinga Zimbabwe
226 F6 Rush Lake WI U.S.A.
232 I11 Rushmere VA U.S.A.
151 O3 Rushmere St Andrew Suffolk, England U.K.
117 O5 Rushon Arun. Prad. India
123 N2 Rushon Tajik.
123 N3 Rushon, Qatorkŭhi mts Tajik.
106 J9 Rushui He r. China
236 J5 Rushville IL U.S.A.
230 E6 Rushville IN U.S.A.
236 D4 Rushville NE U.S.A.
232 C9 Rushville OH U.S.A.
83 J7 Rushworth Vic. Austr.
174 G4 Rusiec Pol.
175 I4 Rusinów Pol.
174 E2 Rusinowo Pol.
237 H10 Rusk TX U.S.A.
140 O4 Ruskele Sweden
143 K4 Rusken l. Sweden
196 H5 Ruski Krstur Vojvodina Serbia
231 F12 Ruskin FL U.S.A.
149 Q7 Ruskington Lincolnshire, England U.K.
137 P3 Rus'ki Tyshky Ukr.
177 J6 Rusko Selo Vojvodina Serbia
177 K3 Ruskov Slovakia
138 E6 Rusnė Lith.
197 P8 Rusokastro Bulg.
138 J5 Rušona Latvia
138 J5 Rušonu ezers l. Latvia
136 H5 Rusova r. Ukr.
150 G4 Ruspidge Gloucestershire, England U.K.
138 F2 Russarö i. Fin.
254 F3 Russas Brazil
223 K5 Russell Man. Can.
233 J3 Russell Ont. Can.
80 I2 Russell North I. N.Z.
236 F6 Russell KS U.S.A.
232 F7 Russell PA U.S.A.
262 P2 Russell Bay Antarctica
221 I2 Russell Island Nunavut Can.
78 □6 Russell Islands Solomon Is
223 K3 Russell Lake Man. Can.
222 H2 Russell Lake N.W.T. Can.
223 J3 Russell Lake Sask. Can.
231 D8 Russellville AL U.S.A.
237 I8 Russellville AR U.S.A.
230 D7 Russellville KY U.S.A.
232 B10 Russellville OH U.S.A.
234 D5 Russellville PA U.S.A.
172 E1 Rüsselsheim Ger.
191 M7 Russi Italy
Russia country Asia/Europe see Russian Federation
130 F4 Russian Federation country Asia/Europe
Russian Soviet Federal Socialist Republic country Asia/Europe see Russian Federation
121 O1 Russkaya-Polyana Rus. Fed.
135 H6 Russkaya Zhuravka Rus. Fed.
139 U9 Russkiy Brod Rus. Fed.
120 B1 Russkiy Kameshkir Rus. Fed.
134 K1 Russkiy Zavorot, Poluostrov pen. Rus. Fed.
139 P8 Russkoye Smolenskaya Oblast' Rus. Fed.
129 F2 Russkoye Stavropol'skiy Kray Rus. Fed.
131 P2 Russkoye Ust'ye Rus. Fed.
179 O4 Rust Austria
129 G5 Rüstäm Äliyev Azer.
129 G4 Rust'avi Georgia
232 F11 Rustburg VA U.S.A.
215 M1 Rust de Winter S. Africa
215 M1 Rust de Winter Nature Reserve S. Africa
129 D6 Rüstemgedik Turkey
215 L1 Rustenburg S. Africa
215 L1 Rustenburg Nature Reserve S. Africa
142 D3 Rustfjellheii mt. Norway
215 K5 Rustfontein Dam l. S. Africa
215 L3 Rustig S. Africa
151 K6 Rustington West Sussex, England U.K.
237 I9 Ruston LA U.S.A.
129 J4 Rustov Azer.
161 G9 Rustrel France
190 E1 Ruswil Switz.
174 D4 Ruszów Pol.
139 T6 Rut' r. Rus. Fed.
93 E4 Ruta Maluku Indon.
81 □3 Rutaki Passage Rarotonga Cook Is
192 C2 Rutali Corse France
211 A5 Rutana Burundi
Rutanzige, Lake Dem. Rep. Congo/Uganda see Edward, Lake
185 K6 Rute Spain
93 B8 Ruteng Flores Indon.
213 F4 Rutenga Zimbabwe
172 F4 Rutesheim Ger.
241 Q2 Ruth NV U.S.A.
169 F8 Rüthen Ger.
Ruthenia admin. div. Ukr. see Zakarpats'ka Oblast'
235 G3 Rutherford NJ U.S.A.
231 G8 Rutherfordton NC U.S.A.
83 K7 Rutherglen Vic. Austr.
227 O3 Rutherglen Ont. Can.
146 H11 Rutherglen South Lanarkshire, Scotland U.K.
232 H11 Ruther Glen VA U.S.A.
150 F1 Ruthin Denbighshire, Wales U.K.
116 F7 Ruthiyai Madh. Prad. India
190 F1 Rüti Switz.
195 M1 Rutigliano Italy
193 O7 Rutino Italy
134 I4 Rutka r. Rus. Fed.
175 K1 Rutka-Tartak Pol.
175 K2 Rutki-Kossaki Pol.
151 K2 Rutland admin. div. England U.K.
233 M5 Rutland VT U.S.A.
115 M7 Rutland Island Andaman & Nicobar Is India
85 H3 Rutland Plains Qld Austr.
151 K2 Rutland Water resr England U.K.
232 B12 Rutledge TN U.S.A.
223 I2 Rutledge Lake N.W.T. Can.
111 H12 Rutog Xizang China
111 K12 Rutog Xizang China
111 D10 Rutog Xizang China
208 F5 Rutshuru Dem. Rep. Congo
164 I3 Rutten Neth.
227 N3 Rutter Ont. Can.
129 I4 Rutul Rus. Fed.
140 R4 Ruukki Fin.
164 J4 Ruurlo Neth.
138 K3 Ruusa Estonia
140 T5 Ruvaslahti Fin.
193 P6 Ruvo del Monte Italy
193 Q5 Ruvo di Puglia Italy
140 U3 Ruvozero Rus. Fed.
140 U3 Ruvozero, Ozero l. Rus. Fed.
Ruvu Tanz. see Pangani
211 D7 Ruvuma r. Moz./Tanz.
211 C7 Ruvuma admin. reg. Tanz.
124 G3 Ruwaydah Saudi Arabia
125 N5 Ruways, Ra's ar c. Oman
128 F6 Ruwayshid, Wādī watercourse Jordan
128 E9 Ruwayṭah, Wādī watercourse Jordan
128 C9 Ruweijil pt Saudi Arabia
125 K3 Ruweis U.A.E.
Ruwenzori National Park Uganda see Queen Elizabeth National Park
160 G5 Ruy France
213 G3 Ruya r. Zimbabwe
127 Q5 Ruyan Iran
211 A5 Ruyigi Burundi
161 C6 Ruynes-en-Margeride France
150 G2 Ruyton-XI-Towns Shropshire, England U.K.
109 I6 Ruyuan Guangdong China
139 T6 Ruza Rus. Fed.
121 L1 Ruzayevka Kazakh.
135 I5 Ruzayevka Rus. Fed.
138 H9 Ruzhany Belarus
139 R9 Ruzhnoye Rus. Fed.
107 M9 Ruzhou Henan China
136 I4 Ruzhyn Ukr.
177 I2 Ružomberok Slovakia
177 I5 Ruzsa Hungary
211 A5 Rwanda country Africa
208 F5 Rwenzori mts Dem. Rep. Congo/Uganda
210 A4 Rwenzori Mountains National Park Uganda
142 F5 Ry Denmark
142 F4 Ryå r. Denmark
122 F3 Ryābād Iran
138 L1 Ryabovo Rus. Fed.
137 O3 Ryabyna Ukr.
81 C13 Ryal Bush South I. N.Z.
81 F9 Ryall, Mount South I. N.Z.
146 F12 Ryan, Loch b. Scotland U.K.
137 N4 Ryas'ke Ukr.
137 O3 Ryasne Ukr.
137 K6 Ryasnopil' Ukr.
139 W7 Ryazan' Rus. Fed.
Ryazan Oblast admin. div. Rus. Fed. see Ryazanskaya Oblast'
139 W6 Ryazanovskiy Rus. Fed.
137 S9 Ryazanskaya Rus. Fed.
139 X7 Ryazanskaya Oblast' admin. div. Rus. Fed.
139 W5 Ryazantsevo Rus. Fed.
139 X8 Ryazhsk Rus. Fed.
140 V2 Rybachiy, Poluostrov pen. Rus. Fed.
121 S4 Rybach'ye Kazakh.
Rybach'ye Kyrg. see Balykchy
177 H3 Rybany Slovakia
139 V3 Rybinsk Rus. Fed.
139 V3 Rybinskoye Vodokhranilishche resr Rus. Fed.
176 E1 Rybitví Czech Rep.
174 G5 Rybnik Pol.
Rybnitsa Moldova see Rîbniţa
175 I3 Rybno Mazowieckie Pol.
175 H2 Rybno Warmińsko-Mazurskie Pol.
175 J2 Rybno Warmińsko-Mazurskie Pol.
139 W7 Rybnoye Rus. Fed.
175 L3 Ryboły Pol.
134 F3 Rybreka Rus. Fed.
175 H2 Rychliki Pol.
176 F1 Rychnov nad Kněžnou Czech Rep.
171 L9 Rychnov u Jablonce n Nisou Czech Rep.
175 I2 Rychnowo Pol.
174 F4 Rychtal Pol.
174 G3 Rychwał Pol.
170 H2 Ryck r. Ger.
222 G4 Rycroft Alta Can.
175 J4 Ryczywół Mazowieckie
174 E3 Ryczywół Wielkopolskie
143 K5 Ryd Sweden
262 S2 Rydberg Peninsula Antarctica
151 J6 Ryde Isle of Wight, England U.K.
136 E4 Rydomyl' Ukr.
174 G5 Rydułtowy Pol.
174 E4 Rydzyna Pol.
151 N6 Rye East Sussex, England U.K.
149 P5 Rye r. England U.K.
235 H3 Rye NY U.S.A.
151 N6 Rye Bay England U.K.
233 □O6 Rye Beach NH U.S.A.
238 J3 Ryegate MT U.S.A.
240 N1 Rye Patch Dam NV U.S
240 N1 Rye Patch Reservoir NV U.S.A.
159 J3 Ryes France
175 J6 Ryglice Pol.
151 L2 Ryhall Rutland, England
174 G2 Ryjewo Pol.
136 G3 Rykhal's'ke Ukr.
175 J4 Ryki Pol.
Rykovo Ukr. see Yenak
175 M5 Rykovychi Ukr.
175 M1 Ryliškiai Lith.
135 F6 Ryl'sk Rus. Fed.
83 L5 Rylstone N.S.W. Austr.
175 J6 Rymanów Pol.
176 G2 Rýmařov Czech Rep.
141 P6 Rymättylä Fin.
143 R8 Ryn Pol.
174 F2 Rynarzewo Pol.
134 G1 Rynda Rus. Fed.
120 C4 Ryn-Peski des. Kazakh
174 G2 Ryńsk Pol.
175 J2 Ryńskie, Jezioro l. Pol
105 I3 Ryōgami-san mt. Japa
104 E4 Ryōhaku-sanchi mts
Ryojun Liaoning China Lüshun
105 I3 Ryōkami Japan
102 S7 Ryōri-zaki pt Japan
102 P8 Ryōtsu Japan
104 D5 Ryōzen-zan mt. Japan
175 H2 Rypin Pol.
Ryshkany Moldova see Rîşcani
137 O1 Ryshkovo Rus. Fed.
141 H6 Rysjedal Norway
168 D4 Rysum (Krummhörn)
177 J2 Rysy mt. Pol.
174 F2 Rytel Pol.
143 K6 Rytterknægten hill Bo Denmark
138 H1 Ryttylä Fin.
175 J5 Rytwiany Pol.
104 D5 Ryūga-dake mt. Japan
105 L4 Ryūgasaki Japan
104 B8 Ryūjin Japan
139 P9 Ryukhovo Rus. Fed.
Ryukyu Islands Japan Nansei-shotō
Ryūkyū-rettō is Japan Nansei-shotō
266 D4 Ryukyu Trench sea fe N. Pacific Ocean
104 D5 Ryūō Shiga Japan
105 I4 Ryūō Yamanashi Japan
105 H5 Ryūsō-san mt. Japan
105 G6 Ryūyō Japan
139 O7 Ryzhikovo Rus. Fed.
139 N8 Ryzhkawka Belarus
136 J4 Ryzyne Ukr.
175 J3 Rządza r. Pol.
175 H4 Rząśnia Pol.
175 J3 Rząśnik Pol.
188 G4 Rzav r. Bos.-Herz.
174 F2 Rzeczenica Pol.
174 G4 Rzeczyca Łódzkie Pol.
175 I4 Rzeczyca Łódzkie Pol.
175 I2 Rzęgnowo Pol.
175 H4 Rzejowice Pol.
175 J2 Rzekuń Pol.
175 J6 Rzepiennik Strzyżews
174 C3 Rzepin Pol.
175 H5 Rzerzęczyce Pol.
174 D2 Rzesznikowo Pol.
175 K5 Rzeszów Pol.
175 H4 Rzgów Pol.
174 G3 Rzgów Pierwszy Pol.
135 H5 Rzhaksa Rus. Fed.
139 Q8 Rzhanitsa Rus. Fed.
138 M6 Rzhawka Belarus
139 N9 Rzhawka r. Belarus
139 R5 Rzhev Rus. Fed.
137 K4 Rzhyshchiv Ukr.
175 I4 Rzuców Pol.

S

122 G4 Sa'ābād Iran
210 D4 Saacow Somalia
128 E9 Sa'ādah al Barṣā' pas Saudi Arabia
122 E6 Sa'ādatābād Fārs Iran
122 F7 Sa'ādatābād Hormozg
214 F7 Saaifontein S. Africa
170 F2 Saal Ger.
173 O6 Saalach r. Ger.
173 L4 Saal an der Donau Ge
169 J10 Saal an der Saale Ger
172 E3 Saalbach r. Ger.
178 G5 Saalbach-Hinterglem Austria
171 E10 Saalburg Ger.
173 N6 Saaldorf Ger.
171 E8 Saale park Ger.
171 E7 Saale r. Ger.
170 F2 Saaler Bodden inlet G
157 N7 Saales France
171 D9 Saalfeld Ger.
178 G5 Saalfelden am Steine Meer Austria
Saamba K'e N.W.T. Ca Trout Lake
156 A4 Saâne r. France
190 C2 Saane r. Switz.
190 C3 Saanen Switz.
222 F5 Saanich B.C. Can.
Saar land Ger. see Saa
172 B2 Saar r. Ger.
172 B3 Saarbrücken Ger.
172 B2 Saarburg Ger.
138 J3 Saare Estonia
138 F4 Sääre Estonia
138 F3 Saaremaa i. Estonia
140 R3 Saarenkylä Fin.
172 A3 Saargau reg. Ger.
172 B2 Saar-Hunsrück, Natu nature res. Ger.
141 T6 Saari Fin.
140 R5 Saarijärvi Fin.
140 S3 Saari-Kämä Fin.
140 P2 Saarikoski Fin.
140 S2 Saariselkä Fin.
Saaristomeren Kansallispuisto nat. p see Skärgårdshavets nationalpark
172 B3 Saarland land Ger.
172 B3 Saarlouis Ger.
172 B3 Saarwellingen Ger.
190 H2 Saas Switz.
190 D3 Saas Fee Switz.
190 D3 Saas Grund Switz.
190 D3 Saastal val. Switz.
203 F6 Sa'ata Sudan
129 J6 Saatlı Azer.
Saatly Azer. see Saatlı
138 K4 Saatse Estonia
261 F5 Saavedra Buenos Aires
261 G2 Saavedra Santa Fé Arg

Saba i. Neth. Antilles
Saba, Wādī watercourse Saudi Arabia
Saba'ah Egypt
Sab' Ābār Syria
Sababurg Ger.
Šabac Serbia
Sabadell Spain
Sabadou Baranama Guinea
Sabae Japan
Sabagusi Tanz.
Sabah state Malaysia
Sabak Malaysia
Sabaki r. Kenya
Sabalan, Kūhhā-ye mts Iran
Sabalana i. Indon.
Sabalana, Kepulauan is Indon.
Sabalgarh Madh. Prad. India
Saban Venez.
Sabana, Archipiélago de is Cuba
Sabana de la Mar Dom. Rep.
Sabanagrande Hond.
Sabana Grande Puerto Rico
Sabanalarga Col.
Sabaneta Aruba see Savaneta
Sabaneta Dom. Rep.
Sabaneta Venez.
Sabang Aceh Indon.
Sabang Sulawesi Indon.
Sabang Sulawesi Indon.
Sabano Col.
Şabanözü Turkey
Săbăoani Romania
Sabará Brazil
Sabarat France
Sabari r. India
Sabarmati r. Gujarat India
Sabaru i. Indon.
Sabastiya West Bank
Sab'atayn, Ramlat as des. Yemen
Sabato r. Italy
Sabaudia Italy
Sabaudia, Lago di lag. Italy
Sabaya Bol.
Şabāyā i. Saudi Arabia
Sabazho Georgia
Sabbionetta Italy
Sabelo S. Africa
Sabena Desert Kenya
Sāberi, Hāmuūn-e marsh Afgh.
Sabero Spain
Şabḩā Jordan
Sabhā Libya
Şabḩā' Saudi Arabia
Sabhrai Gujarat India
Sabi r. India
Sabi r. Moz./Zimbabwe see Save
Sabie Moz.
Sabie r. Moz./S. Africa
Sabie S. Africa
Sabiha Gökçen airport Turkey
Sabile Latvia
Sabina OH U.S.A.
Sabinal Mex.
Sabinal, Cayo i. Cuba
Sabiñánigo Spain
Sabinar, Punta pt Spain
Sabinar, Punta del mt. Spain
Sabinas Mex.
Sabinas r. Mex.
Sabinas r. Mex.
Sabinas Hidalgo Mex.
Sabine r. LA/TX U.S.A.
Sabine Lake LA/TX U.S.A.
Sabine Land reg. Svalbard
Sabine National Wildlife Refuge nature res. LA U.S.A.
Sabine Pass TX U.S.A.
Sabini, Monti mts Italy
Sabinópolis Brazil
Sabinosa El Hierro Canary Is
Sabinov Slovakia
Sabiote Spain
Sabir Azer.
Sabirabad Azer.
Sablayan Mindoro Phil.
Sable, Cape N.S. Can.
Sable, Cape FL U.S.A.
Sable, Île de i. New Caledonia
Sable, Lac du l. Que. Can.
Sable, Rivière du r. Que. Can.
Sable Blanc, Récif du rf Mayotte
Sable Island N.S. Can.
Sables, Île aux i. Rodrigues I. Mauritius
Sables, River aux r. Ont. Can.
Sables-d'Or-les-Pins France
Sablé-sur-Sarthe France
Sablet France
Sablières France
Sablinskoye Rus. Fed.
Sablon, Pointe du pt France
Sablons France
Sablū'īyeh Iran
Saboeiro Brazil
Sabóia Port.
Sabon Kafi Niger
Sabor r. Port.
Sabou Burkina
Sabourin, Lac l. Que. Can.
Sabrātah Libya
Sabres France
Sabrina Coast Antarctica
Sabrosa Port.
Sabtang i. Phil.
Sabue Georgia
Sabugal Port.
Sabugueiro Évora Port.
Sabugueiro Guarda Port.
Sabulu Sulawesi Indon.
Sabunçu Azer.
Sabuncu Turkey
Sabunten i. Indon.
Saburyū-yama mt. Japan
Şabyā Saudi Arabia
Sabzawar Afgh. see Shīndand
Sabzevār Iran
Sabzvārān Iran see Jīroft
Saca, Vârful mt. Romania
Sacaba Bol.
Sacaca Bol.
Săcădat Romania
Săcălaz Romania
Sacalinul Mare, Insula i. Romania
Sacanana, Pampa plain Arg.
Sacandaga r. NY U.S.A.
Sacandica Angola
Sacañet Spain
Sacanta Arg.
Săcășeni Romania
Sacaton AZ U.S.A.
Şacavém Port.
Saccarel, Mont mt. France/Italy
Sac City IA U.S.A.
Sacco r. Italy
Sacecorbo Spain
Sacedón Spain
Săcele Brașov Romania
Săcele Constanța Romania
Săceni Romania
Saceruela Spain
Saç Geçidi pass Turkey
Sachanga Angola
Sachigo r. Ont. Can.
Sachigo Lake Ont. Can.
Sachin Gujarat India
Sach'khere Georgia
Sach'on S. Korea
Sach Pass Hima. Prad. India
Sachseln Switz.
Sachsen land Ger.
Sachsen-Anhalt land Ger.
Sachsen bei Ansbach Ger.
Sachsenberg (Lichtenfels) Ger.
Sachsenbrunn Ger.
Sachsenburg Austria
Sachsenhagen Ger.
Sachsenhausen (Waldeck) Ger.
Sachsenheim Ger.
Sachs Harbour N.W.T. Can.
Sächsische Schweiz park Ger.
Sächsische Schweiz, Nationalpark nat. park Ger.

191 M4 Sacile Italy
Sacirsuyu r. Syria/Turkey see Sājūr, Nahr
233 I5 Sackets Harbor NY U.S.A.
169 G9 Sackpfeife hill Ger.
225 H4 Sackville N.B. Can.
233 □O5 Saco ME U.S.A.
238 K2 Saco MT U.S.A.
92 D8 Sacol i. Phil.
177 K6 Sacoșu Turcesc Romania
160 G1 Sacquenay France
183 M5 Sacramenia Spain
256 D3 Sacramento Brazil
240 K3 Sacramento CA U.S.A.
240 K3 Sacramento r. CA U.S.A.
252 A1 Sacramento, Pampa del plain Peru
239 K9 Sacramento Mountains NM U.S.A.
240 J1 Sacramento Valley CA U.S.A.
185 M7 Sacratif, Cabo c. Spain
253 F3 Sacre r. Brazil
187 I10 Sa Creu, Punta de pt Spain
149 N4 Sacriston Durham, England U.K.
193 I3 Sacrofano Italy
197 K3 Săcueni Romania
177 L5 Săcuieu Romania
253 F3 Sacuriuiná r. Brazil
243 O8 Sacxán Mex.
217 □3b Sada Mayotte
215 K8 Sada S. Africa
182 D2 Sada Spain
163 B10 Sada Spain
183 R4 Sádaba Spain
116 G6 Sadabad Uttar Prad. India
122 D7 Sa'dābād Iran
Sá da Bandeira Angola see Lubango
128 E4 Şadad Syria
124 F7 Şa'dah Yemen
124 F7 Şa'dah governorate Yemen
192 C8 Sadali Sardegna Italy
103 J13 Sada-misaki pt Japan
93 A5 Sadang r. Indon.
211 C6 Sadani Tanz.
97 E11 Sadao Thai.
125 I8 Şadārah Yemen
129 F6 Sädäräk Azer.
114 E4 Sadaseopet Andhra Prad. India
123 N5 Sadda Pak.
128 E7 Sadd as Sultānī Jordan
127 L7 Saddat al Hindīyah Iraq
146 E11 Saddell Argyll and Bute, Scotland U.K.
215 P1 Saddleback pass S. Africa
Saddleback hill England U.K. see Blencathra
237 D8 Saddleback Mesa mt. NM U.S.A.
85 J3 Saddle Hill Qld Austr.
81 H8 Saddle Hill mt. South I. N.Z.
Saddle Island Vanuatu see Mota Lava
115 M6 Saddle Peak hill Andaman & Nicobar Is India
97 G9 Sa Đec Vietnam
125 L7 Sadḩ Oman
116 F4 Sadhaura Haryana India
247 □7 Sadhoowa Trin. and Tob.
210 B2 Sadi Eth.
122 H9 Sadīj watercourse Iran
123 N7 Sadiqabad Pak.
129 G4 Sadıqlı Azer.
117 O6 Sadiya Assam India
124 D5 Sa'diya Saudi Arabia
127 M7 Sa'dīyah, Hawr as imp. l. Iraq
125 L3 Sa'diyyat i. U.A.E.
213 □K2 Sadjoavato Madag.
122 G3 Sad-Kharv Iran
174 F2 Sadki Pol.
175 I4 Sadkowice Pol.
174 E2 Sadkowo Pol.
174 G2 Sadlinki Pol.
184 B4 Sado r. Port.
102 P9 Sadoga-shima i. Japan
184 B5 Sado Morgavel, Canal do Port.
127 L2 Sadon Rus. Fed.
95 I4 Sadong r. Malaysia
192 C6 Sa Donna, Pico mt. Italy
137 N8 Sadove Ukr.
175 J1 Sadovoye Kaliningradskaya Oblast' Rus. Fed.
135 I7 Sadovoye Respublika Kalmykiya-Khalm'g-Tangch Rus. Fed.
137 T2 Sadovoye Voronezhskaya Oblast' Rus. Fed.
175 J5 Sadowie Pol.
175 J3 Sadowne Pol.
187 J8 Sa Dragonera i. Spain
114 G6 Sadras Tamil Nadu India
116 D7 Sadri Rajasthan India
234 D5 Sadsburyville PA U.S.A.
171 K10 Sadská Czech Rep.
116 E5 Sadulshahar Rajasthan India
124 H3 Sādūs Saudi Arabia
128 C7 Sadūt Egypt
142 G4 Sæby Denmark
168 G1 Sæd Denmark
232 E7 Saegertown PA U.S.A.
183 O9 Saelices Spain
183 P7 Saelices de la Sal Spain
183 J3 Saelices del Rio Spain
183 J4 Saelices de Mayorga Spain
Saena Julia Italy see Siena
169 E6 Saerbeck Ger.
165 I9 Saeul Lux.
Safad Israel see Zefat
Safâga Island Egypt see Safājah, Jazīrat
Safājah, Jazīrat i. Egypt
203 G3 Safané Burkina
206 E3 Safara Port.
184 E4 Šafárikovo Slovakia see Tornaľa
Şafarlū Iran
129 I6 Şafāshahr Iran
122 E6 Safata Bay Samoa
78 □2 Safayal Maqūf well Iraq
127 M8 Safed Khirs mts Afgh.
123 N2 Safed Koh mts Afgh.
123 K4 Safed Koh mts Afgh./Pak.
123 N4 Saffānīyah, Ra's as pt Saudi Arabia
125 I1 Säffle Sweden
142 I2 Safford AZ U.S.A.
241 W9 Saffré France
158 H6 Saffron Walden Essex, England U.K.
151 M3 Safi Jordan see Aş Şāfī
Safi Morocco
204 C2 Safiabad Iran
122 G3 Safīd r. Iran
122 D3 Safīd, Chashmeh-ye spring Iran
122 G5 Safīd, Daryā-ye r. Afgh.
123 K3 Safid Ab Iran
122 E4 Safidabeh Iran
122 I6 Safīdār, Kūh-e mt. Iran
122 E7 Safid Dasht Iran
122 C5 Safid Kūh mts Afgh. see Paropamisus
Safīd Sagak Iran
122 I4 Sāfir Yemen
124 H8 Safiras, Serra das mts Brazil
257 G3 Şāfītā Syria
128 E4 Safonovo Arkhangel'skaya Oblast' Rus. Fed.
134 J2 Safonovo Murmanskaya Oblast' Rus. Fed.
134 F1 Safonovo Smolenskaya Oblast' Rus. Fed.
139 Q6 Safotu Samoa
78 □2 Safrā' al Asyāḩ esc. Saudi Arabia
124 F2 Safrā' as Sark esc. Saudi Arabia
124 G2 Safranbolu Turkey
126 F3 Safune Samoa
78 □2 Şafwa Saudi Arabia
125 I2 Safwān Iraq
127 M8 Sâg Romania
177 L4 Şag Romania
196 J5 Saga Xizang China
111 G12 Saga Kōchi Japan
103 K13 Saga Saga Japan
103 H13 Saga pref. Japan
103 H13

120 J3 Saga Kostanayskaya Oblast' Kazakh.
120 K2 Saga Kostanayskaya Oblast' Kazakh.
102 R8 Sagae Japan
96 B4 Sagaing Myanmar
96 B3 Sagaing admin. div. Myanmar
Sagala Mali see Séguéla
192 B7 Sagama Sardegna Italy
105 J4 Sagamihara Japan
105 J4 Sagamiko Japan
105 J6 Sagami-nada g. Japan
105 J5 Sagami-wan b. Japan
232 F8 Sagamore PA U.S.A.
Sagamu Nigeria see Shagamu
227 L1 Saganash Lake Ont. Can.
103 I13 Saganoseki Japan
97 D8 Saganthit Kyun i. Myanmar
114 D5 Sagar Karnataka India
114 E4 Sagar Karnataka India
116 G8 Sagar Madh. Prad. India
105 H6 Sagara Japan
170 I1 Sagard Ger.
Sagaredzho Georgia see Sagarejo
129 G4 Sagarejo Georgia
117 M8 Sagaria Bangl.
117 L9 Sagar Island India
Sagarmatha mt. China/Nepal see Everest, Mount
117 K6 Sagarmatha National Park Nepal
131 N2 Sagastyr Rus. Fed.
117 J6 Sagauli Bihar India
220 D2 Sagavanirktok r. AK U.S.A.
168 F5 Sage Ger.
238 I6 Sage WY U.S.A.
238 I2 Sage Creek r. MT U.S.A.
143 K1 Sågen Sweden
147 J6 Saggart Ireland
140 N3 Saggat l. Sweden
128 C8 Saggi, Har mt. Israel
122 F5 Saghand Iran
123 J5 Saghar Afgh.
235 K3 Sag Harbor NY U.S.A.
Saghyz Kazakh. see Sagiz
114 F5 Sagileru r. India
227 K6 Saginaw MI U.S.A.
226 B3 Saginaw MN U.S.A.
227 K6 Saginaw Bay MI U.S.A.
199 J3 Sağırlar Turkey
193 L3 Sagittario r. Italy
120 E4 Sagiz Atyrauskaya Oblast' Kazakh.
120 F3 Sagiz Atyrauskaya Oblast' Kazakh.
Sagiz r. Kazakh. see Sagyz
199 I2 Sağlamtaş Turkey
129 J7 Şağlasär Azer.
206 C5 Sagleipie Liberia
225 I1 Saglek Bay Nfld and Lab. Can.
Saglouc Que. Can. see Salluit
106 B1 Sagly Rus. Fed.
192 B3 Sagone Corse France
192 B3 Sagone, Golfe de b. Corse France
185 N5 Sagra mt. Spain
260 B4 Sagrada Familia Chile
184 B6 Sagres Port.
184 B7 Sagres, Ponta de pt Port.
106 E4 Sagsay watercourse Mongolia
116 E8 Sagthale Rajasthan India
93 C8 Sagu Indon.
96 B4 Sagu Myanmar
177 K5 Şagu Romania
239 K7 Saguache CO U.S.A.
239 L8 Saguache Creek r. CO U.S.A.
246 F3 Sagua de Tánamo Cuba
246 C2 Sagua la Grande Cuba
241 V9 Saguaro National Park AZ U.S.A.
225 G3 Saguenay r. Que. Can.
94 G8 Saguling, Waduk resr Jawa Indon.
Sagunt Spain see Sagunto
187 E8 Sagunto Spain
Saguntum Spain see Sagunto
137 S3 Saguny Rus. Fed.
142 B2 Sagvåg Norway
116 E8 Sagwara Rajasthan India
160 G3 Sagy France
120 D5 Sagyndyk, Mys pt Kazakh.
120 E4 Sagyz r. Kazakh.
128 E7 Saḩāb Jordan
116 G5 Sahabab Uttar Prad. India
122 C2 Şahağac Azer.
245 I6 Sahagún Mex.
183 J4 Sahagún Spain
141 R6 Sahalahti Fin.
151 N2 Saham Toney Norfolk, England U.K.
122 B3 Sahand, Kūh-e mt. Iran
129 D5 Sahandöken Turkey
204 G6 Sahara des. Africa
Saharan Atlas mts Alg. see Atlas Saharien
116 F5 Saharanpur Uttar Prad. India
86 G6 Sahara Well W.A. Austr.
117 K7 Saharsa Bihar India
116 G5 Sahaswan Uttar Prad. India
122 F4 Sahat, Kūh-e hill Iran
117 J7 Sahatwar Uttar Prad. India
213 □K4 Sahavato Madag.
125 I4 Sahbā', Wādī as watercourse Saudi Arabia
129 G6 Şahbuz Azer.
129 G5 Şahdağ Silsiläsi hills Armenia/Azer.
206 C3 Sahel reg. Africa
124 D7 Sahel prov. Eritrea
206 E3 Sahel, Réserve Partielle du nature res. Burkina
117 K7 Sahibganj Jharkhand India
123 O6 Sahiwal Punjab Pak.
123 O6 Sahiwal Punjab Pak.
122 H5 Sahlābād Iran
124 D2 Sahl al Maţrān Saudi Arabia
124 E5 Sahl Rakbah plain Saudi Arabia
125 M3 Şaḩm Oman
122 B4 Şaḩneh Iran
127 L8 Şaḩrā al Ḩijārah reg. Iraq
Sahu Qinghai China see Zadoi
93 E3 Sahu Halmahera Indon.
242 E3 Sahuaripa Mex.
241 V10 Sahuarita AZ U.S.A.
244 E5 Sahuayo Mex.
186 F2 Sahun Spain
161 G8 Sahune France
137 L4 Sahunivka Ukr.
124 E3 Şāḩūq reg. Saudi Arabia
124 F3 Şāḩūq, Wādī watercourse Saudi Arabia
97 I7 Sa Huynh Vietnam
129 C6 Şahvelet Dağları mts Turkey
177 H3 Šahy Slovakia
Sahyadri mts India see Western Ghats
116 E9 Sahyadriparvat Range hills India
128 E3 Şahyūn tourist site Syria
116 I7 Sai r. India
91 J8 Saibai Island Qld Austr.
97 E11 Sai Buri Thai.
97 E11 Sai Buri, Mae Nam r. Thai.
205 F2 Saïda Alg.
128 D5 Saïda Lebanon
97 F8 Sai Dao Tai, Khao mt. Thai.
125 M4 Sa'id Bin Sahrān Oman
123 J8 Sa'īdī Iran
181 E5 Saïdia Morocco
Sa'īdīyeh Iran see Solţānīyeh
117 L7 Saidpur Bangl.
117 I7 Saidpur Uttar Prad. India
123 O4 Saidu Pak.
104 E2 Sai-gawa r. Japan
105 H2 Sai-gawa r. Japan
146 B7 Saighdinis Western Isles, Scotland U.K.
162 I5 Saignes France
161 G9 Saignon France
103 K10 Saigō Japan
Saigon Vietnam see Hô Chi Minh
117 N8 Saiha Mizoram India
107 M5 Saihan Tal Nei Mongol China
106 G6 Saihan Toroi Nei Mongol China
140 T3 Saija Fin.
103 K13 Saijō Japan

103 G13 Saikai Kokuritsu-kōen nat. park Japan
103 I14 Saiki Japan
103 I14 Saiki-wan b. Japan
109 □J7 Sai Kung H.K. China
109 □J7 Sai Kung Hoi b. H.K. China
116 E8 Sailana Madh. Prad. India
163 I11 Saillagouse-Llo France
161 G7 Saillans France
162 F4 Saillat-sur-Vienne France
93 G4 Sailolof Papua Indon.
160 D5 Sail-sous-Couzan France
141 T6 Saimaa l. Fin.
141 T6 Saimaankanava r. Fin.
126 H4 Saimbeyli Turkey
244 D2 Sain Alto Mex.
160 C3 Saincaize-Meauce France
123 I7 Saindak Pak.
122 B3 Sa'īndezh Iran
Sa'īn Qal'eh Iran see Sa'īndezh
206 C3 Saïnsoubou Senegal
156 G4 Sains-Richaumont France
236 K7 Saint r. IL U.S.A.
146 L11 St Abbs Scottish Borders, Scotland U.K.
185 □ St Abb's Head Gibraltar
146 L11 St Abb's Head Scotland U.K.
156 D3 St-Acheul France
161 B9 St-Affrique France
161 B8 St-Affrique, Causse de plat. France
160 D3 St-Agnan Bourgogne France
160 E2 St-Agnan Bourgogne France
161 G7 St-Agnan-en-Vercors France
162 C4 St-Agnant France
162 H3 St-Agnant-de-Versillat France
150 B7 St Agnes Cornwall, England U.K.
150 □ St Agnes i. England U.K.
161 E6 St-Agrève France
162 G1 St-Aignan France
159 I6 St-Aignan-sur-Roë France
162 D5 St-Aigulin France
160 F4 St-Albain France
158 F4 St-Alban France
161 F6 St-Alban-d'Ay France
160 H5 St-Alban-Leysse France
225 K4 St Alban's Nfld and Lab. Can.
151 L4 St Albans Hertfordshire, England U.K.
233 L4 St Albans VT U.S.A.
232 D10 St Albans WV U.S.A.
St Alban's Head England U.K. see St Aldhelm's Head
161 C7 St-Alban-sur-Limagnole France
222 H4 St Albert Alta Can.
150 H6 St Aldhelm's Head England U.K.
159 J3 St-Amand France
160 C1 St-Amand-en-Puisaye France
156 F3 St-Amand-les-Eaux France
159 N6 St-Amand-Longpré France
160 B3 St-Amand-Montrond France
156 I6 St-Amand-sur-Fion France
161 C7 St-Amans France
161 B7 St-Amans-des-Cots France
163 I9 St-Amans-Soult France
162 E4 St-Amant-de-Boixe France
160 D5 St-Amant-Roche-Savine France
160 C5 St-Amant-Tallende France
157 N8 St-Amarin France
225 G3 St-Ambroise Que. Can.
161 E8 St-Ambroix France
160 G4 St-Amour France
161 F9 St-Andiol France
163 J10 St-André Languedoc-Roussillon France
161 K9 St-André Provence-Alpes-Côte d'Azur France
217 □1b St-André Mauritius
217 □1c St-André Réunion
St-André, Cap pt Madag. see Vilanandro, Tanjona
156 B6 St-André, Plaine de plain France
160 F5 St-André-de-Corcy France
161 E8 St-André-de-Cruzières France
162 D6 St-André-de-Cubzac France
156 B6 St-André-de-l'Eure France
161 J7 St-André-d'Embrun France
161 D9 St-André-de-Sangonis France
163 B8 St-André-de-Seignanx France
161 D8 St-André-de-Valborgne France
160 D2 St-André-en-Morvan France
160 H5 St-André-le-Gaz France
161 J9 St-André-les-Alpes France
156 H7 St-André-les-Vergers France
246 □ St Andrew parish Jamaica
247 □7 St Andrew county Trin. and Tob.
233 □R3 St Andrews N.B. Can.
81 F11 St Andrews South I. N.Z.
146 K10 St Andrews Fife, Scotland U.K.
231 G10 St Andrew Sound inlet GA U.S.A.
162 I4 St-Angel France
246 □ St Ann parish Jamaica
158 G2 St Anne Channel Is
226 G8 St Anne IL U.S.A.
246 □ St Ann's Bay Jamaica
150 B4 St Ann's Head Wales U.K.
226 B6 St Ansgar IA U.S.A.
160 D5 St-Anthème France
225 K3 St Anthony Nfld and Lab. Can.
238 I5 St Anthony ID U.S.A.
128 A10 St Anthony, Monastery of tourist site Egypt
163 H7 St-Antonin-Noble-Val France
159 O8 St-Août France
160 G2 St-Apollinaire France
161 D6 St-Arcons-d'Allier France
83 I7 St Arnaud Vic. Austr.
81 G8 St Arnaud South I. N.Z.
81 G9 St Arnaud Range mts South I. N.Z.
156 C6 St-Arnoult-en-Yvelines France
150 F1 St Asaph Denbighshire, Wales U.K.
84 C1 St Asaph Bay N.T. Austr.
162 F5 St-Astier Aquitaine France
163 E6 St-Astier Aquitaine France
150 F5 St Athan Vale of Glamorgan, Wales U.K.
161 J9 St-Auban France
161 G8 St-Auban-sur-l'Ouvèze France
160 G2 St-Aubin France
156 F8 St-Aubin-Château-Neuf France
158 H5 St-Aubin-d'Aubigné France
158 I5 St-Aubin-du-Cormier France
156 B5 St-Aubin-lès-Elbeuf France
159 K3 St-Aubin-sur-Mer France
225 J3 St-Augustin Que. Can.
225 J3 St Augustin r. Nfld and Lab./Que. Can.
231 G11 St Augustine FL U.S.A.
162 E5 St-Aulaye France
150 C7 St Austell Cornwall, England U.K.
150 C7 St Austell Bay England U.K.
158 F6 St-Avé France
159 M7 St-Avertin France
157 M5 St-Avold France
156 C8 St-Ay France
161 J10 St-Aygulf France
160 H5 St-Baldoph France
225 J3 St Barbe Nfld and Lab. Can.
225 F4 St-Barthélemy Que. Can.
247 L5 St-Barthélemy i. West Indies
163 H10 St-Barthélemy, Pic de mt. France
163 E6 St-Barthélemy-d'Agenais France
159 K7 St-Barthélemy-d'Anjou France
162 E5 St-Barthélemy-de-Bellegarde France
161 F6 St-Barthélemy-de-Vals France
81 D11 St Bathans South I. N.Z.
81 D11 St Bathans, Mount South I. N.Z.
161 D9 St-Bauzille-de-Putois France
163 F10 St-Béat France
161 B8 St-Beauzély France
149 J5 St Bees Cumbria, England U.K.

149 J4 St Bees Head England U.K.
160 C2 St-Benin-d'Azy France
163 I9 St-Benoît Languedoc-Roussillon France
162 E2 St-Benoît Poitou-Charentes France
217 □1c St-Benoît Réunion
163 I7 St-Benoît-de-Carmaux France
162 G3 St-Benoît-du-Sault France
156 D8 St-Benoît-sur-Loire France
81 H9 St Bernard mt. South I. N.Z.
160 H5 St-Béron France
159 J5 St-Berthevin France
163 F9 St-Bertrand-de-Comminges France
190 B1 St-Blaise Switz.
157 N7 St-Blaise-la-Roche France
157 J7 St-Blin-Semilly France
160 F3 St-Boil France
162 F3 St-Bonnet-de-Bellac France
160 E4 St-Bonnet-de-Joux France
160 E4 St-Bonnet-des-Bruyères France
161 I7 St-Bonnet-en-Champsaur France
161 E6 St-Bonnet-le-Château France
161 E6 St-Bonnet-le-Froid France
162 C5 St-Bonnet-sur-Gironde France
160 E2 St-Brancher France
159 M7 St-Branchs France
158 G3 St Brelade Channel Is
158 G7 St-Brevin-les-Pins France
158 G4 St-Briac-sur-Mer France
150 G4 St Briavels Gloucestershire, England U.K.
156 H5 St-Brice-Courcelles France
158 I5 St-Brice-en-Coglès France
150 B4 St Brides Pembrokeshire, Wales U.K.
150 B4 St Bride's Bay Wales U.K.
150 E5 St Brides Major Vale of Glamorgan, Wales U.K.
158 F4 St-Brieuc France
158 F4 St-Brieuc, Baie de b. France
156 G8 St-Bris-le-Vineux France
160 E2 St-Brisson France
157 I8 St-Broing-les-Moines France
158 H4 St-Broladre France
150 □ St Buryan Cornwall, England U.K.
159 M6 St-Calais France
161 G9 St-Cannat France
158 G4 St-Cast-le-Guildo France
224 E5 St Catharines Ont. Can.
246 □ St Catherine parish Jamaica
128 B10 St Catherine, Monastery of tourist site Egypt
247 □6 St Catherine, Mount hill Grenada
225 K4 St Catherine's Nfld and Lab. Can.
231 G10 St Catherines Island GA U.S.A.
231 □1 St Catherine's Point Bermuda
151 J6 St Catherine's Point England U.K.
163 H6 St-Céré France
190 A3 St-Cergue Switz.
160 I4 St-Cergues France
162 I5 St-Cernin France
233 L3 St-Césaire Que. Can.
161 J7 St-Chaffrey France
163 G6 St-Chamarand France
161 G9 St-Chamas France
161 F6 St-Chamond France
161 E9 St-Chaptes France
227 N3 St Charles Ont. Can.
238 I5 St Charles ID U.S.A.
232 I10 St Charles MD U.S.A.
227 J6 St Charles MI U.S.A.
226 B6 St Charles MN U.S.A.
236 J6 St Charles MO U.S.A.
160 G5 St-Chef France
161 C7 St-Chély-d'Apcher France
161 B7 St-Chély-d'Aubrac France
161 B10 St-Chinian France
161 G8 St-Christol France
161 E8 St-Christol-lès-Alès France
162 C5 St-Christoly-de-Blaye France
162 C5 St-Christoly-Médoc France
160 K5 St-Christophe Italy
158 H8 St-Christophe-du-Ligneron France
159 O7 St-Christophe-en-Bazelle France
160 E4 St-Christophe-en-Brionnais France
162 C5 St-Ciers-sur-Gironde France
161 E7 St-Cirgues-en-Montagne France
163 H7 St-Cirq-Lapopie France
224 D5 St Clair r. Can./U.S.A.
227 L7 St Clair MI U.S.A.
234 C3 St Clair PA U.S.A.
227 L7 St Clair, Lake Can./U.S.A.
161 F6 St-Clair-du-Rhône France
156 C5 St-Clair-sur-Epte France
159 I3 St-Clair-sur-l'Elle France
232 E8 St Clairsville OH U.S.A.
163 F8 St-Clar France
162 E4 St-Claud France
160 H4 St-Claude France
247 □2 St-Claude Guadeloupe
150 D4 St Clears Carmarthenshire, Wales U.K.
158 G3 St Clement Channel Is
156 F7 St-Clément Bourgogne France
162 H5 St-Clément Limousin France
157 M6 St-Clément Lorraine France
161 D9 St-Clément de-Rivière France
231 G11 St Cloud FL U.S.A.
236 H3 St Cloud MN U.S.A.
225 G3 St-Coeur-de-Marie Que. Can.
150 C7 St Columb Major Cornwall, England U.K.
146 M7 St Combs Aberdeenshire, Scotland U.K.
163 I6 St-Constant France
159 L5 St-Cosme-en-Vairais France
162 F5 St-Crépin-de-Richemont France
163 C8 St-Cricq-Chalosse France
221 L5 St Croix r. Can./U.S.A.
226 B4 St Croix r. WI U.S.A.
247 K5 St Croix i. Virgin Is (U.S.A.)
226 B4 St Croix Falls WI U.S.A.
163 G6 St-Cyprien Aquitaine France
163 K10 St-Cyprien Languedoc-Roussillon France
163 G7 St-Cyprien Midi-Pyrénées France
156 D6 St-Cyr-l'École France
162 F1 St-Cyr-sur-Loire France
161 H10 St-Cyr-sur-Mer France
156 F6 St-Cyr-sur-Morin France
161 J8 St-Dalmas-le-Selvage France
225 G4 St-Damien-de-Buckland Que. Can.
247 □7 St David county Trin. and Tob.
241 V10 St David AZ U.S.A.
226 D9 St David IL U.S.A.
150 B4 St David's Pembrokeshire, Wales U.K.
150 B4 St David's Head Wales U.K.
231 □1 St David's Island Bermuda
150 B7 St Day Cornwall, England U.K.
156 D6 St-Denis Île-de-France France
163 I9 St-Denis Languedoc-Roussillon France
217 □1c St-Denis Réunion
159 K6 St-Denis-d'Anjou France
159 J5 St-Denis-de-Gastines France
162 H2 St-Denis-de-Jouhet France
162 B3 St-Denis-d'Oléron France
159 K5 St-Denis-d'Orques France
St-Denis-du-Sig Alg. see Sig
160 G5 St-Denis-en-Bugey France
160 G4 St-Denis-lès-Bourg France
150 C7 St Dennis Cornwall, England U.K.
158 G4 St-Denoual France
160 F3 St-Désert France
161 E6 St-Didier-en-Velay France
160 F4 St-Didier-sur-Chalaronne France
160 D5 St-Didier-sur-Rochefort France
157 M7 St-Dié France
160 C5 St-Dier-d'Auvergne France
157 I6 St-Dizier France

162 H3 St-Dizier-Leyrenne France
150 C3 St Dogmaels Pembrokeshire, Wales U.K.
158 G6 St-Dolay France
158 H5 St-Domineuc France
St-Domingue country West Indies see Haiti
161 F6 St-Donat-sur-l'Herbasse France
159 P7 St-Doulchard France
159 L2 Ste-Adresse France
162 F6 Ste-Alvère France
223 L5 Sainte Anne Man. Can.
247 □2 Ste-Anne Guadeloupe
247 □3 Ste-Anne Martinique
217 □1c Ste-Anne Réunion
217 □2b Ste-Anne i. Seychelles
222 H4 Sainte Anne, Lac l. Alta Can.
225 H3 Ste-Anne, Lac l. Que. Can.
158 F6 Ste-Anne-d'Auray France
225 G4 Ste-Anne-de-Beaupré Que. Can.
233 □Q1 Ste-Anne-de-Madawaska N.B. Can.
225 G3 Ste-Anne-de-Portneuf Que. Can.
225 H3 Ste-Anne-des-Monts Que. Can.
227 S3 Ste-Anne-du-Lac Que. Can.
161 H10 Ste-Baume, Chaîne de la mts France
163 E6 Ste-Bazeille France
233 □O2 Ste-Camille-de-Lellis Que. Can.
208 A5 Ste-Catherine, Pointe pt Gabon
161 F8 Ste-Cécile-les-Vignes France
160 G3 Ste-Croix Bourgogne France
161 G7 Ste-Croix Rhône-Alpes France
190 B2 Ste-Croix Switz.
161 I9 Ste-Croix, Barrage de dam France
161 I9 Ste-Croix, Lac de l. France
163 G9 Ste-Croix-Volvestre France
224 F4 Ste-Émélie-de-l'Énergie Que. Can.
163 C9 Ste-Engrâce France
161 C8 Ste-Énimie France
161 B8 Ste-Eulalie d'Olt France
163 B7 Ste-Eulalie-en-Born France
162 H3 Ste-Feyre France
161 C6 Ste-Florine France
162 H5 Ste-Fortunade France
163 G9 Ste-Foy-de-Peyrolières France
163 E6 Ste-Foy-la-Grande France
160 E5 Ste-Foy-l'Argentière France
160 F5 Ste-Foy-lès-Lyon France
160 J5 Ste-Foy-Tarentaise France
159 L4 Ste-Gauburge-Ste-Colombe France
162 B3 Ste-Gemme-la-Plaine France
156 D5 Ste-Geneviève France
236 J7 Sainte Genevieve MO U.S.A.
161 B7 Ste-Geneviève-sur-Argence France
161 H6 St-Égrève France
162 C6 Ste-Hélène France
162 B2 Ste-Hermine France
233 □O2 Ste-Justine Que. Can.
233 □P1 St-Éleuthère Que. Can.
220 D4 St Elias, Cape AK U.S.A.
222 A2 St Elias, Mount AK U.S.A.
222 A2 St Elias Mountains Y.T. Can.
251 H3 St-Élie Fr. Guiana
163 F7 Ste-Livrade-sur-Lot France
163 G9 St-Élix-le-Château France
163 E9 St-Élix-Theux France
246 □ St Elizabeth parish Jamaica
159 P7 Ste-Lizaigne France
160 B4 St-Éloy-les-Mines France
247 □3 Ste-Luce Martinique
192 C4 Ste-Lucie-de-Tallano Corse France
225 H3 Ste-Marguerite r. Que. Can.
225 H3 Sainte-Marguerite 3 resr Que. Can.
157 M7 Ste-Marguerite France
225 G4 Ste-Marie Que. Can.
161 B7 Ste-Marie Auvergne France
163 K10 Ste-Marie Languedoc-Roussillon France
247 □3 Ste-Marie Martinique
217 □1c Ste-Marie Réunion
Ste-Marie, Cap c. Madag. see Vohimena, Tanjona
Sainte-Marie, Île i. Madag. see Boraha, Nosy
157 N7 Ste-Marie-aux-Mines France
159 M7 Ste-Maure, Plateau de France
163 E7 Ste-Maure-de-Peyriac France
162 F1 Ste-Maure-de-Touraine France
161 J10 Ste-Maxime France
157 I5 Ste-Menehould France
158 I3 Ste-Mère-Église France
160 E3 St-Émiland France
163 D6 St-Émilion France
150 C6 St Endellion Cornwall, England U.K.
150 C7 St Enoder Cornwall, England U.K.
162 G5 Ste-Orse France
158 H7 Ste-Pazanne France
159 K8 Ste-Radegonde France
156 G4 St-Erme-Outre-et-Ramecourt France
247 □2 Ste-Rose Guadeloupe
217 □1c Ste-Rose Réunion
Ste-Rose-du-Dégelé Que. Can. see Dégelis
223 L5 Sainte Rose du Lac Man. Can.
150 B7 St Erth Cornwall, England U.K.
162 C4 Saintes France
247 □2 Saintes, Îles des is Guadeloupe
160 F2 Ste-Sabine France
156 H7 Ste-Savine France
Ste-Scholastique Que. Can. see Mirabel
162 I3 Ste-Sévère-sur-Indre France
161 E6 Ste-Sigolène France
247 □3 St-Esprit Martinique
163 B9 St-Esteben France
162 C5 St-Estèphe France
163 J10 St-Estève France
159 K5 Ste-Suzanne France
217 □1c Ste-Suzanne Réunion
233 L3 Ste-Thérèse Que. Can.
222 F1 Sainte Thérèse, Lac l. N.W.T. Can.
161 E6 St-Étienne France
162 I6 St-Étienne-Cantalès France
163 B9 St-Étienne-de-Baïgorry France
161 H6 St-Étienne-de-Crossey France
161 E7 St-Étienne-de-Fontbellon France
162 H3 St-Étienne-de-Fursac France
161 D7 St-Étienne-de-Lugdarès France
158 H7 St-Étienne-de-Montluc France
161 G6 St-Étienne-de-St-Geoirs France
161 J8 St-Étienne-de-Tinée France
163 G7 St-Étienne-de-Tulmont France
160 G4 St-Étienne-du-Bois France
156 B5 St-Étienne-du-Rouvray France
161 H7 St-Étienne-en-Dévoluy France
161 H8 St-Étienne-les-Orgues France
157 M7 St-Étienne-lès-Remiremont France
161 D8 St-Étienne-Vallée-Française France
161 H9 Ste-Tulle France
233 K3 St Eugene Ont. Can.
233 □Q1 St-Eusèbe Que. Can.
233 L3 St-Eustache Que. Can.
158 C6 St-Évarzec France
156 G8 Ste-Vertu France
161 H9 Ste-Victoire, Montagne mt. France
225 G3 St-Fabien Que. Can.
215 O6 St Faith's S. Africa

160 C1 St-Fargeau France
225 F3 St-Félicien Que. Can.
161 F6 St-Félicien France
227 P1 St-Félix-de-Dalquier Que. Can.
163 H9 St-Félix-Lauragais France
146 M7 St Fergus Aberdeenshire, Scotland U.K.
163 E6 St-Ferme France
147 K4 Saintfield Northern Ireland U.K.
146 H10 St Fillans Perth and Kinross, Scotland U.K.
157 L7 St-Firmin Lorraine France
161 I7 St-Firmin Provence-Alpes-Côte d'Azur France
156 G7 St-Flavy France
192 C2 St-Florent Corse France
192 C2 St-Florent, Golfe de b. Corse France
162 B2 St-Florent-des-Bois France
156 G7 St-Florentin France
159 I7 St-Florent-le-Vieil France
162 I2 St-Florent-sur-Cher France
208 D2 St Floris, Parc National nat. park C.A.R.
161 C6 St-Flour France
159 N8 St-Flovier France
160 F5 St-Fons France
162 C5 St-Fort-sur-Gironde France
163 F9 St-Frajou France
237 J10 St Francesville LA U.S.A.
233 □Q1 St Francis r. Can./U.S.A.
236 E6 St Francis KS U.S.A.
233 □Q1 St Francis ME U.S.A.
237 J8 St Francis r. AR/MO U.S.A.
215 I10 St Francis, Cape S. Africa
215 J10 St Francis Bay S. Africa
82 D5 St Francis Isles S.A. Austr.
225 F4 St-François r. Que. Can.
247 □2 St-François Guadeloupe
217 □2 St François i. Seychelles
225 G4 St-François, Lac l. Que. Can.
161 I6 St-François-Longchamp France
233 □Q2 St Froid Lake ME U.S.A.
161 E7 St-Front France
162 E5 St-Front-de-Pradoux France
159 I8 St-Fulgent France
160 E5 St-Galmier France
159 L3 St-Gatien-des-Bois France
163 F9 St-Gaudens France
162 G2 St-Gaultier France
233 □O3 St-Gédéon Que. Can.
163 D8 St-Gein France
161 D9 St-Gély-du-Fesc France
161 E6 St-Genest-Malifaux France
160 F3 St-Gengoux-le-National France
161 E9 St-Geniès-de-Malgoirès France
161 I8 St-Geniez France
161 B8 St-Geniez-d'Olt France
162 C5 St-Genis-de-Saintonge France
163 J10 St-Génis-des-Fontaines France
160 F5 St-Genis-Laval France
160 I4 St-Genis-Pouilly France
160 H5 St-Genix-sur-Guiers France
150 C6 St Gennys Cornwall, England U.K.
159 N8 St-Genou France
161 H6 St-Geoire-en-Valdaine France
83 L3 St George Qld Austr.
85 J4 St George r. Qld Austr.
231 □1 St George Bermuda
225 H4 St George N.B. Can.
247 □7 St George county Trin. and Tob.
220 B4 St George AK U.S.A.
231 G9 St George SC U.S.A.
241 S4 St George UT U.S.A.
91 L7 St George, Cape New Ireland P.N.G.
238 B6 St George, Point CA U.S.A.
83 M6 St George Head A.C.T. Austr.
220 B4 St George Island AK U.S.A.
231 E11 St George Island FL U.S.A.
86 H5 St George Range hills W.A. Austr.
225 J3 St George's Nfld and Lab. Can.
225 G4 St-Georges Que. Can.
251 I4 St-Georges Fr. Guiana
247 □6 St George's Grenada
234 D5 St Georges DE U.S.A.
225 J3 St George's Bay Nfld and Lab. Can.
225 I4 St George's Bay N.S. Can.
159 J5 St-Georges-Buttavent France
243 P9 St George's Cay i. Belize
115 M9 St George's Channel Andaman & Nicobar Is India
91 L7 St George's Channel P.N.G.
147 J9 St George's Channel Ireland/U.K.
161 D6 St-Georges-d'Aurac France
161 H6 St-Georges-de-Commiers France
162 C4 St-Georges-de-Didonne France
161 B8 St-Georges-de-Luzençon France
160 B5 St-Georges-de-Mons France
158 I8 St-Georges-de-Montaigu France
160 F4 St-Georges-de-Reneins France
159 J4 St-Georges-des-Groseillers France
160 G5 St-Georges-d'Espéranche France
162 B4 St-Georges-d'Oléron France
159 M3 St-Georges-du-Vièvre France
160 D5 St-Georges-en-Couzan France
231 □1 St George's Harbour b. Bermuda
231 □1 St George's Island Bermuda
159 L8 St-Georges-lès-Baillargeaux France
156 G8 St-Georges-sur-Baulche France
159 N7 St-Georges-sur-Cher France
156 B7 St-Georges-sur-Eure France
159 J7 St-Georges-sur-Loire France
163 B8 St-Geours-de-Maremne France
160 D4 St-Gérand-le-Puy France
226 E4 St Germain WI U.S.A.
160 C3 St-Germain-Chassenay France
161 D8 St-Germain-de-Calberte France
159 M5 St-Germain-de-la-Coudre France
160 C4 St-Germain-des-Fossés France
162 C5 St-Germain-d'Esteuil France
163 G6 St-Germain-du-Bel-Air France
160 G3 St-Germain-du-Bois France
159 L5 St-Germain-du-Corbéis France
160 F3 St-Germain-du-Plain France
162 I1 St-Germain-du-Puy France
161 C8 St-Germain-du-Teil France
156 D6 St-Germain-en-Laye France
160 E5 St-Germain-Laval France
161 C6 St-Germain-Lembron France
162 G4 St-Germain-les-Belles France
160 D4 St-Germain-Lespinasse France
162 H5 St-Germain-les-Vergnes France
161 D6 St-Germain-l'Herm France
150 D7 St Germans Cornwall, England U.K.
163 D8 St-Germé France
156 C5 St-Germer-de-Fly France
158 G8 St-Gervais Pays de la Loire France
161 G6 St-Gervais Rhône-Alpes France
160 B4 St-Gervais-d'Auvergne France
159 N6 St-Gervais-la-Forêt France
160 J5 St-Gervais-les-Bains France
159 L8 St-Gervais-les-Trois-Clochers France
161 C9 St-Gervais-sur-Mare France
163 H7 St-Géry France
165 E8 St-Ghislain Belgium

158 G7 St-Gildas, Pointe de pt France
158 F6 St-Gildas-de-Rhuys France
158 G6 St-Gildas-des-Bois France
247 □5 St Giles Islands Trin. and Tob.
161 E9 St-Gilles France
158 H8 St-Gilles-Croix-de-Vie France
217 □1c St-Gilles-les-Bains Réunion
160 J4 St-Gingolph France
163 G10 St-Girons France
163 B8 St-Girons-Plage France
156 F4 St-Gobain France
St Gotthard Pass pass Switz. see San Gottardo, Passo del
150 C4 St Govan's Head Wales U.K.
158 H5 St-Grégoire France
158 C6 St-Guénolé France
161 D9 St-Guilhem-le-Désert France
160 D4 St-Haon-le-Châtel France
160 E5 St-Héand France
226 J5 St Helen MI U.S.A.
216 □2b St Helena terr. S. Atlantic Ocean
240 J3 St Helena CA U.S.A.
214 C8 St Helena Bay S. Africa
214 C8 St Helena Bay b. S. Africa
231 G9 St Helena Sound inlet SC U.S.A.
83 L9 St Helens Tas. Austr.
149 L7 St Helens Merseyside, England U.K.
238 C4 St Helens OR U.S.A.
238 C3 St Helens, Mount vol. WA U.S.A.
83 L9 St Helens Point Tas. Austr.
158 G3 St Helier Channel Is
158 H7 St-Herblain France
163 I9 St-Hilaire France
156 H5 St-Hilaire-au-Temple France
161 E8 St-Hilaire-de-Brethmas France
158 I7 St-Hilaire-de-Loulay France
163 F7 St-Hilaire-de-Lusignan France
158 H8 St-Hilaire-de-Riez France
162 C3 St-Hilaire-des-Loges France
162 C4 St-Hilaire-de-Villefranche France
159 I4 St-Hilaire-du-Harcouët France
161 G6 St-Hilaire-du-Rosier France
160 D3 St-Hilaire-Fontaine France
156 H5 St-Hilaire-le-Grand France
159 K7 St-Hilaire-St-Florent France
157 N7 St-Hippolyte Alsace France
160 J2 St-Hippolyte Franche-Comté France
161 D9 St-Hippolyte-du-Fort France
117 K8 Sainthiya W. Bengal India
161 J8 St-Honorat, Mont mt. France
160 D3 St-Honoré-les-Bains France
161 E6 St-Hostien France
165 H8 St-Hubert Belgium
225 F4 St-Hyacinthe Que. Can.
226 J4 St Ignace MI U.S.A.
224 C3 St Ignace Island Ont. Can.
251 G4 St Ignatius Guyana
190 B1 St-Imier Switz.
190 B1 St-Imier, Vallon de val. Switz.
150 D4 St Ishmael Carmarthenshire, Wales U.K.
161 H6 St-Ismier France
150 D7 St Ive Cornwall, England U.K.
151 L3 St Ives Cambridgeshire, England U.K.
150 □ St Ives Cornwall, England U.K.
150 B7 St Ives Bay England U.K.
161 B9 St-Izaire France
233 □Q1 St-Jacques N.B. Can.
St Jacques, Cap Vietnam see Vung Tau
224 E3 St-Jacques-de-Dupuy Que. Can.
158 H5 St-Jacques-de-la-Lande France
158 G4 St-Jacut-de-la-Mer France
158 I4 St-James France
246 □ St James parish Jamaica
226 I4 St James MI U.S.A.
236 H4 St James MN U.S.A.
236 J6 St James MO U.S.A.
235 I3 St James NY U.S.A.
222 D5 St James, Cape B.C. Can.
225 H3 St-Jean r. Que. Can.
225 H3 St-Jean r. Que. Can.
163 G8 St-Jean France
251 H3 St-Jean Fr. Guiana
225 F3 St-Jean, Lac l. Que. Can.
158 F6 St-Jean-Brévelay France
161 K9 St-Jean-Cap-Ferrat France
St-Jean-d'Acre Israel see 'Akko
162 C4 St-Jean-d'Angély France
159 L5 St-Jean-d'Assé France
160 G5 St-Jean-de-Bournay France
156 C8 St-Jean-de-Braye France
159 I3 St-Jean-de-Daye France
156 C8 St-Jean-de-la-Ruelle France
160 G2 St-Jean-de-Losne France
163 A9 St-Jean-de-Luz France
161 E8 St-Jean-de-Mauréjols-et-Avéjan France
161 I6 St-Jean-de-Maurienne France
158 G8 St-Jean-de-Monts France
161 F6 St-Jean-de-Muzols France
225 G4 St-Jean-de-Port-Joli Que. Can.
159 L8 St-Jean-de-Sauves France
160 I5 St-Jean-de-Sixt France
161 D9 St-Jean-de-Védas France
163 C6 St-Jean-d'Illac France
161 C8 St-Jean-du-Bruel France
163 H9 St-Jean-du-Falga France
161 D8 St-Jean-du-Gard France
161 G6 St-Jean-en-Royans France
163 B9 St-Jean-Pied-de-Port France
163 E8 St-Jean-Poutge France
160 E6 St-Jean-Soleymieux France
159 K5 St-Jean-sur-Erve France
160 G4 St-Jean-sur-Reyssouze France
225 F4 St-Jean-sur-Richelieu Que. Can.
160 I4 St-Jeoire France
224 F4 St-Jérôme Que. Can.
161 F6 St-Jeure-d'Ay France
161 E6 St-Jeures France
158 G7 St-Joachim France
238 F3 St Joe r. ID U.S.A.
225 H4 Saint John N.B. Can.
158 G3 St John Channel Is
206 C5 St John r. Liberia
236 F6 St John KS U.S.A.
233 □S3 St John r. ME U.S.A.
247 K4 St John i. Virgin Is (U.S.A.)
225 K3 St John, Cape Nfld and Lab. Can.
225 J3 St John Bay Nfld and Lab. Can.
225 J3 St John Island Nfld and Lab. Can.
247 □2 St John's Antigua and Barbuda
225 K4 St John's Nfld and Lab. Can.
241 W7 St Johns AZ U.S.A.
226 J6 St Johns MI U.S.A.
232 A8 St Johns OH U.S.A.
231 G10 St Johns r. FL U.S.A.
233 M4 St Johnsbury VT U.S.A.
147 K4 St John's Point Northern Ireland U.K.
148 C4 St Johnstown Ireland
146 H12 St John's Town of Dalry Dumfries and Galloway, Scotland U.K.
233 K6 St Johnsville NY U.S.A.
158 I3 St-Jores France
160 I5 St-Jorioz France
163 G8 St-Jory France
162 F4 St-Jory-de-Chalais France
247 □2 St Joseph Dominica
247 □3 St-Joseph Martinique
217 □1c St-Joseph Réunion
237 J10 St Joseph LA U.S.A.
226 H7 St Joseph MI U.S.A.
236 H6 St Joseph MO U.S.A.
226 H7 St Joseph r. MI U.S.A.
226 I8 St Joseph r. MI U.S.A.
224 B3 St Joseph, Lake Ont. Can.
St-Joseph-d'Alma Que. Can. see Alma
224 D4 St Joseph Island Ont. Can.
237 G12 St Joseph Island TX U.S.A.
158 H4 St-Jouan-des-Guérets France
159 L2 St-Jouin-Bruneval France
159 K8 St-Jouin-de-Marnes France
224 F4 St-Jovité Que. Can.
163 I8 St-Juéry France
St Julian's Malta see San Ġiljan
St Julian's Bay Malta see Spinola, Ix-Xatt ta'
160 G4 St-Julien Franche-Comté France
163 G9 St-Julien Midi-Pyrénées France
162 C5 St-Julien-Beychevelle France
161 E7 St-Julien-Boutières France
160 E4 St-Julien-de-Civry France
154 D3 St-Julien-de-Concelles France
158 I6 St-Julien-de-Vouvantes France
156 F7 St-Julien-du-Sault France
161 J9 St-Julien-du-Verdon France
161 H7 St-Julien-en-Beauchêne France
163 B7 St-Julien-en-Born France
160 I4 St-Julien-en-Genevois France
161 G7 St-Julien-en-Quint France
162 F2 St-Julien-l'Ars France
161 E8 St-Julien-les-Rosiers France
156 H7 St-Julien-les-Villas France
160 G4 St-Julien-sur-Reyssouze France
162 F4 St-Junien France
161 F8 St-Just France
150 □ St Just Cornwall, England U.K.
156 D4 St-Just-en-Chaussée France
160 D5 St-Just-en-Chevalet France
163 B9 St-Just-Ibarre France
163 D8 St-Justin France
150 B7 St Just in Roseland Cornwall, England U.K.
160 E5 St-Just-la-Pendue France
162 B4 St-Just-Luzac France
156 G6 St-Just-Sauvage France
160 E6 St-Just-St-Rambert France
150 B7 St Keverne Cornwall, England U.K.
146 □1 St Kilda i. Western Isles, Scotland U.K.
146 □1 St Kilda is Scotland U.K.
247 □2 St Kitts i. St Kitts and Nevis
247 □2 St Kitts and Nevis country West Indies
159 K7 St-Lambert-des-Levées France
159 J7 St-Lambert-du-Lattay France
163 E8 St-Lary France
163 E10 St-Lary-Soulan France
161 J8 St-Laurent France
St-Laurent, Golfe du g. Que. Can. see St Lawrence, Gulf of
156 E3 St-Laurent-Blangy France
163 D9 St-Laurent-Bretagne France
161 E9 St-Laurent-d'Aigouze France
161 F8 St-Laurent-de-Carnols France
186 K3 St-Laurent-de-Cerdans France
160 E5 St-Laurent-de-Chamousset France
161 B10 St-Laurent-de-la-Cabrerisse France
163 J10 St-Laurent-de-la-Salanque France
163 E9 St-Laurent-de-Neste France
251 H3 St-Laurent-du-Maroni Fr. Guiana
161 H6 St-Laurent-du-Pont France
161 K9 St-Laurent-du-Var France
159 M2 St-Laurent-en-Caux France
160 H3 St-Laurent-en-Grandvaux France
161 D7 St-Laurent-les-Bains France
162 C5 St-Laurent-Médoc France
156 C8 St-Laurent-Nouan France
162 F4 St-Laurent-sur-Gorre France
157 K5 St-Laurent-sur-Othain France
159 J8 St-Laurent-sur-Sèvre France
85 L7 St Lawrence Qld Austr.
225 K4 St Lawrence Nfld and Lab. Can.
225 G3 St Lawrence inlet Que. Can.
234 D4 St Lawrence PA U.S.A.
225 I4 St Lawrence, Cape N.S. Can.
225 I3 St Lawrence, Gulf of Que. Can.
220 B3 St Lawrence Island AK U.S.A.
227 S5 St Lawrence Islands National Park Ont. Can.
224 F4 St Lawrence Seaway sea chan. Can./U.S.A.
223 K5 St Lazare Man. Can.
165 I9 St-Léger Belgium
160 D2 St-Léger-de-Fougeret France
160 C3 St-Léger-des-Vignes France
156 C6 St-Léger-en-Yvelines France
160 E3 St-Léger-sous-Beuvray France
160 F3 St-Léger-sur-Dheune France
225 H4 St-Léonard N.B. Can.
225 F4 St-Léonard Que. Can.
157 M7 St-Léonard France
232 I10 St Leonard MD U.S.A.
162 G4 St-Léonard-de-Noblat France
151 I6 St Leonards Dorset, England U.K.
162 F5 St-Léon-sur-l'Isle France
217 □1c St-Leu Réunion
156 D5 St-Leu-d'Esserent France
225 K2 St Lewis Nfld and Lab. Can.
225 J2 St Lewis r. Nfld and Lab. Can.
163 G9 St-Lizier France
159 I3 St-Lô France
163 B8 St-Lon-les-Mines France
160 H3 St-Lothian France
163 D6 St-Loubès France
160 L1 St-Louis France
247 □2 St-Louis Guadeloupe
217 □1c St-Louis Réunion
206 A2 St-Louis Senegal
226 J6 St Louis MI U.S.A.
236 J6 St Louis MO U.S.A.
226 B3 St Louis r. MN U.S.A.
233 L3 St-Louis, Lac l. Que. Can.
246 G4 St-Louis du Nord Haiti
157 N6 St-Louis-lès-Bitche France
161 D9 St-Loup, Pic hill France
160 F3 St-Loup-de-la-Salle France
156 F6 St-Loup-de-Naud France
159 K8 St-Loup-Lamairé France
157 L8 St-Loup-sur-Semouse France
156 B6 St-Lubin-des-Joncherets France
158 I7 St-Luce-sur-Loire France
247 □3 St Lucia country West Indies
215 Q4 St Lucia, Lake S. Africa
247 □3 St Lucia Channel Martinique/St Lucia
215 Q4 St Lucia Estuary S. Africa
215 Q4 St Lucia Game Reserve nature res. S. Africa
215 Q4 St Lucia Park nature res. S. Africa
St Luke's Island Myanmar see Zadetkale Kyun
158 G4 St-Lunaire France
160 H4 St-Lupicin France
156 H7 St-Lyé France
163 G8 St-Lys France
163 D6 St-Macaire France
162 C1 St-Macaire-en-Mauges France
163 C6 St-Magne France
163 D6 St-Magne-de-Castillon France
146 □M2 St Magnus Bay Scotland U.K.
161 H9 St-Maime France
162 D3 St-Maixent-l'École France
158 G4 St-Malo France
158 G4 St-Malo, Golfe de g. France
158 H3 St-Malo-de-la-Lande France
161 E9 St-Mamert-du-Gard France
163 I6 St-Mamet-la-Salvetat France
161 H10 St-Mandrier-sur-Mer France
246 G4 St-Marc Haiti
246 G4 St-Marc, Canal de sea chan. Haiti
160 F3 St-Marcel Bourgogne France
162 H2 St-Marcel Centre France
156 B5 St-Marcel Haute-Normandie France
161 F8 St-Marcel-d'Ardèche France
161 F6 St-Marcel-lès-Annonay France
161 F7 St-Marcel-lès-Sauzet France
161 F7 St-Marcel-lès-Valence France
161 G6 St-Marcellin France
163 F9 St-Marcet France
159 I3 St-Marcouf, Îles is France
156 I8 St-Marc-sur-Seine France
156 G7 St-Mards-en-Othe France
151 O5 St Margaret's at Cliffe Kent, England U.K.
246 □ St Margaret's Bay Jamaica
146 K5 St Margaret's Hope Orkney, Scotland U.K.
238 F3 St Maries ID U.S.A.
St Mark's S. Africa see Cofimvaba
215 L8 St Marks S. Africa
231 E10 St Marks National Wildlife Refuge nature res. FL U.S.A.
163 J10 St-Marsal France
159 L6 St-Mars-d'Outillé France
158 I7 St-Mars-du-Désert France
159 L5 St-Mars-la-Brière France
158 I6 St-Mars-la-Jaille France
161 D8 St-Martial France
163 G6 St-Martial-de-Nabirat France
162 F4 St-Martial-de-Valette France
158 F3 St Martin Guernsey Channel Is
158 G3 St Martin Jersey Channel Is
161 H9 St-Martin France
247 L4 St-Martin i. West Indies
247 □3 St-Martin, Cap c. Martinique
214 B8 St Martin, Cape S. Africa
223 L5 St Martin, Lake Man. Can.
156 C2 St-Martin-Boulogne France
156 G5 St-Martin-d'Ablois France
163 B9 St-Martin-d'Arrossa France
159 P7 St-Martin-d'Auxigny France
161 J6 St-Martin-de-Belleville France
161 H9 St-Martin-de-Castillon France
161 F9 St-Martin-de-Crau France
161 D7 St-Martin-de-Fugères France
158 I4 St-Martin-de-Landelles France
161 D9 St-Martin-de-Londres France
161 J8 St-Martin-d'Entraunes France
162 B3 St-Martin-de-Ré France
159 J3 St-Martin-des-Besaces France
158 I4 St-Martin-des-Champs Basse-Normandie France
158 D4 St-Martin-des-Champs Bretagne France
163 B8 St-Martin-de-Seignanx France
161 E7 St-Martin-de-Valamas France
161 E8 St-Martin-de-Valgalgues France
161 H6 St-Martin-d'Hères France
163 C8 St-Martin-d'Oney France
160 H4 St-Martin-du-Frêne France
160 G4 St-Martin-du-Mont France
161 K9 St-Martin-du-Var France
160 G3 St-Martin-en-Bresse France
160 F5 St-Martin-en-Haut France
226 H4 St Martin Island MI U.S.A.
160 F5 St-Martin-la-Plaine France
159 M7 St-Martin-le-Beau France
150 F2 St Martin's Shropshire, England U.K.
150 □ St Martin's i. England U.K.
117 N9 St Martin's Island Bangl.
156 F8 St-Martin-sur-Ouanne France
162 I5 St-Martin-Valmeroux France
161 K8 St-Martin-Vésubie France
163 F9 St-Martory France
222 H5 St Mary r. B.C. Can.
246 □ St Mary parish Jamaica
81 D11 St Mary, Mount South I. N.Z.
151 J5 St Mary Bourne Hampshire, England U.K.
151 N5 St Mary in the Marsh Kent, England U.K.
82 G4 St Mary Peak S.A. Austr.
83 L9 St Marys Tas. Austr.
227 M6 St Mary's Ont. Can.
247 □7 St Mary's Trin. and Tob.
146 K5 St Mary's Orkney, Scotland U.K.
150 □ St Mary's i. England U.K.
236 G6 St Marys KS U.S.A.
232 A8 St Marys OH U.S.A.
232 G7 St Marys PA U.S.A.
232 D9 St Marys WV U.S.A.
236 M5 St Marys r. OH U.S.A.
225 K4 St Mary's, Cape Nfld and Lab. Can.
225 K4 St Mary's Bay b. Nfld and Lab. Can.
151 N5 St Mary's Bay Kent, England U.K.
232 I10 St Marys City MD U.S.A.
146 J12 St Mary's Loch l. Scotland U.K.
227 P1 St-Mathieu Que. Can.
162 F4 St-Mathieu France
158 B5 St-Mathieu, Pointe de pt France
162 A2 St-Mathurin France
220 A3 St Matthew Island AK U.S.A.
231 G9 St Matthews SC U.S.A.
St Matthew's Island Myanmar see Zadetkyi Kyun
91 K7 St Matthias Group is P.N.G.
159 O8 St-Maur France
156 E6 St-Maur-des-Fossés France
224 F4 St-Maurice r. Que. Can.
190 B3 St-Maurice Switz.
224 F4 St-Maurice, Réserve Faunique du nature res. Que. Can.
160 F5 St-Maurice-de-Beynost France
161 E6 St-Maurice-de-Lignon France
162 F4 St-Maurice-des-Lions France
162 G3 St-Maurice-la-Souterraine France
161 F6 St-Maurice-l'Exil France
161 D9 St-Maurice-Navacelles France
163 F7 St-Maurin France
150 B7 St Mawes Cornwall, England U.K.
157 L6 St-Max France
156 C3 St-Maxent France
156 D5 St-Maximin France
161 H10 St-Maximin-la-Ste-Baume France
162 E5 St-Méard-de-Drône France
162 D5 St-Médard-de-Guizières France
163 C6 St-Médard-en-Jalles France
158 G5 St-Méen-le-Grand France
158 H4 St-Méloir-des-Ondes France
162 D4 St-Même-les-Carrières France
156 H6 St-Memmie France
157 I4 St-Menges France
160 C3 St-Menoux France
150 C6 St Merryn Cornwall, England U.K.
162 G5 St-Mesmin Aquitaine France
156 G7 St-Mesmin Champagne-Ardenne France
159 J8 St-Mesmin Pays de la Loire France
163 F7 St-Mézard France
233 I10 St Michaels MD U.S.A.
225 K2 St Michael's Bay Nfld and Lab. Can.
150 □ St Michael's Mount tourist site England U.K.
163 E9 St-Michel Midi-Pyrénées France
156 H4 St-Michel Picardie France
162 E4 St-Michel Poitou-Charentes France
158 D5 St-Michel, Montagne hill France
158 D5 St-Michel, Réservoir de resr France
158 G7 St-Michel-Chef-Chef France
163 D7 St-Michel-de-Castelnau France
161 I6 St-Michel-de-Maurienne France
224 F4 St-Michel-des-Saints Que. Can.
158 D4 St-Michel-en-Grève France
162 B3 St-Michel-en-l'Herm France
159 J8 St-Michel-Mont-Mercure France
157 M7 St-Michel-sur-Meurthe France
157 K6 St-Mihiel France
146 K10 St Monans Fife, Scotland U.K.
163 D8 St-Mont France
161 F8 St-Montant France
157 M7 St-Nabord France
163 G8 St-Nauphary France
158 G7 St-Nazaire France
St-Nazaire, Étang de lag. France see Canet, Étang de
161 G6 St-Nazaire-en-Royans France
161 G7 St-Nazaire-le-Désert France
160 B5 St-Nectaire France
151 L3 St Neots Cambridgeshire, England U.K.
St Nicolas Belgium see Sint-Niklaas
156 E3 St-Nicolas France
165 J9 St-Nicolas, Mont hill Lux.
156 B4 St-Nicolas-d'Aliermont France
163 G7 St-Nicolas-de-la-Grave France
157 L6 St-Nicolas-de-Port France
158 G6 St-Nicolas-de-Redon France
158 E5 St-Nicolas-du-Pélem France
146 □N3 St Ninian's Isle i. Scotland U.K.
158 F6 St-Nolff France
164 H5 St-Oedenrode Neth.
156 D2 St-Omer France
162 C4 Saintonge reg. France
163 H8 St-Orens-de-Gameville France
163 E9 St-Ost France
151 O4 St Osyth Essex, England U.K.
158 G3 St Ouen Channel Is
156 B8 St-Ouen Centre France
156 D3 St-Ouen Picardie France
159 J5 St-Ouen-des-Toits France
156 H6 St-Ouen-Domprot France
150 G4 St Owen's Cross Herefordshire, England U.K.
225 G4 St-Pacôme Que. Can.
158 H4 St-Pair-sur-Mer France
163 B9 St-Palais France
162 B4 St-Palais-sur-Mer France
161 D6 St-Pal-de-Chalancon France
161 E6 St-Pal-de-Mons France
233 □P2 St-Pamphile Que. Can.
160 E3 St-Pantaléon Bourgogne France
163 G7 St-Pantaléon Midi-Pyrénées France
162 G5 St-Pantaléon-de-Larche France
163 I9 St-Papoul France
162 G3 St-Pardoux, Lac de l. France
163 E6 St-Pardoux-Isaac France
162 F5 St-Pardoux-la-Rivière France
232 B8 St Paris OH U.S.A.
160 C3 St-Parize-le-Châtel France
156 H7 St-Parres-lès-Vaudes France
225 G4 St-Pascal Que. Can.
159 L5 St-Paterne France
159 L6 St-Paterne-Racan France
227 Q3 St-Patrice, Lac l. Que. Can.
247 □7 St Patrick county Trin. and Tob.
223 I4 St Paul Alta Can.
225 J3 St Paul r. Nfld and Lab./Que. Can.
161 J7 St-Paul France
St-Paul atoll Arch. des Tuamotu Fr. Polynesia see Héréhérétué
206 C5 St Paul r. Liberia
217 □1c St-Paul Réunion
226 A5 St Paul MN U.S.A.
236 F5 St Paul NE U.S.A.
232 C12 St Paul VA U.S.A.
217 □1c St-Paul, Baie de b. Réunion
207 F5 St Paul, Cape Ghana
265 J7 St-Paul, Île i. Indian Ocean
128 A10 St Paul, Monastery of tourist site Egypt
163 H8 St-Paul-Cap-de-Joux France
163 J10 St-Paul-de-Fenouillet France
163 H10 St-Paul-de-Jarrat France
162 I6 St-Paul-des-Landes France
163 F7 St-Paul-d'Espis France
163 B7 St-Paul-en-Born France
161 J9 St-Paul-en-Forêt France
161 D9 St-Paul-et-Valmalle France
161 D6 St-Paulien France
225 I4 St Paul Island N.S. Can.
220 A4 St Paul Island AK U.S.A.
161 E8 St-Paul-le-Jeune France
163 B8 St-Paul-lès-Dax France
161 H9 St-Paul-lès-Durance France
161 G6 St-Paul-lès-Romans France
247 □2 St Paul's St Kitts and Nevis
St Paul's Bay Malta see San Pawl il-Baħar
St Paul's Bay b. Malta see San Pawl il-Baħar, Il-Bajja ta'
St Paul's Islands Malta see San Pawl, Gżejjer ta'
92 B6 St Paul Subterranean River National Park Phil.
161 F8 St-Paul-Trois-Châteaux France
163 D9 St-Pé-de-Bigorre France
163 A9 St-Pée-sur-Nivelle France
161 F7 St-Péray France
160 D2 St-Père France
158 G7 St-Père-en-Retz France
236 I3 St Peter MN U.S.A.
St Peter and St Paul Rocks is N. Atlantic Ocean see São Pedro e São Paulo
158 F3 St Peter in the Wood Channel Is
158 F3 St Peter Port Channel Is
225 I4 St Peter's N.S. Can.
225 I4 St Peters P.E.I. Can.
151 O5 St Peter's Kent, England U.K.
St Petersburg Rus. Fed. see Sankt-Peterburg
231 F12 St Petersburg FL U.S.A.
156 G7 St-Phal France
158 H8 St-Philbert-de-Bouaine France
158 H7 St-Philbert-de-Grand-Lieu France
217 □1c St-Philippe Réunion
161 G9 St-Pierre mt. France
160 K5 St-Pierre Italy
247 □3 St-Pierre Martinique
217 □1b St-Pierre Mauritius
217 □1c St-Pierre Réunion
217 □2 St Pierre i. Seychelles
225 K4 St-Pierre St Pierre and Miquelon
225 F4 St-Pierre, Lac l. Que. Can.
225 J4 St Pierre and Miquelon terr. N. America
160 I5 St-Pierre-d'Albigny France
161 I6 St-Pierre-d'Allevard France
163 D6 St-Pierre-d'Aurillac France
161 H6 St-Pierre-de-Chartreuse France
162 F5 St-Pierre-de-Chignac France
162 F5 St-Pierre-de-Côle France
161 C9 St-Pierre-de-la-Fage France
159 M8 St-Pierre-de-Maillé France
158 H5 St-Pierre-de-Plesguen France
162 F1 St-Pierre-des-Corps France
159 J7 St-Pierre-des-Échaubrognes France
159 I5 St-Pierre-des-Landes France
159 K5 St-Pierre-des-Nids France
163 I8 St-Pierre-de-Trivisy France
163 B9 St-Pierre-d'Irube France
162 B4 St-Pierre-d'Oléron France
159 J8 St-Pierre-du-Chemin France
163 C8 St-Pierre-du-Mont France
158 I2 St-Pierre-Église France
160 I4 St-Pierre-en-Faucigny France
159 L2 St-Pierre-en-Port France
159 I5 St-Pierre-la-Cour France
160 C3 St-Pierre-le-Moûtier France
156 B5 St-Pierre-lès-Elbeuf France
156 E7 St-Pierre-lès-Nemours France
158 E6 St-Pierre-Quiberon France
159 K3 St-Pierre-sur-Dives France
161 E7 St-Pierreville France
163 F9 St-Plancard France
160 I3 St-Point, Lac de l. France
159 I4 St-Pois France
159 I6 St-Poix France
158 D4 St-Pol-de-Léon France
156 D1 St-Pol-sur-Mer France
156 D3 St-Pol-sur-Ternoise France
163 G6 St-Pompont France
161 J8 St-Pons France
161 B10 St-Pons-de-Thomières France
162 C4 St-Porchaire France
163 G7 St-Porquier France
160 C4 St-Pourçain-sur-Sioule France
190 A3 St-Prex Switz.
160 F5 St-Priest France
160 B5 St-Priest-de-Champs France
160 D5 St-Priest-Laprugne France
162 G4 St-Priest-Taurion France
162 I5 St-Privat France
161 D7 St-Privat-d'Allier France
161 E8 St-Privat-des-Vieux France
160 D4 St-Prix Auvergne France
161 F7 St-Prix Rhône-Alpes France
163 H7 St-Projet France
233 □O2 St-Prosper Que. Can.
163 E8 St-Puy France
225 H4 St Quentin N.B. Can.
156 F4 St-Quentin France
156 F4 St-Quentin, Canal de France
161 E8 St-Quentin-la-Poterie France
161 H6 St-Quentin-sur-Isère France
157 N6 St-Quirin France
161 F6 St-Rambert-d'Albon France
160 G5 St-Rambert-en-Bugey France
161 J10 St-Raphaël France
238 G3 St Regis MT U.S.A.
233 K4 St Regis r. NY U.S.A.
233 K4 St Regis Falls NY U.S.A.
161 E8 St-Remèze France
233 L3 St-Rémi Que. Can.
160 F3 St-Rémy France
161 F9 St-Rémy-de-Provence France
156 I6 St-Remy-en-Bouzemont-St-Genest-et-Isson France
156 B6 St-Rémy-sur-Avre France
160 D5 St-Rémy-sur-Durolle France
158 B5 St-Renan France
160 D2 St-Révérien France
190 C4 St-Rhemy Italy
160 E4 St-Rigaud, Mont mt. France
156 C3 St-Riquier France
159 L2 St-Romain-de-Colbosc France
160 G5 St-Romain-de-Jalionas France
160 F5 St-Romain-en-Gal France
160 E5 St-Romain-le-Puy France
160 E3 St-Romain-sous-Versigny France
159 N7 St-Romain-sur-Cher France
161 G6 St-Romans France
161 B8 St-Rome-de-Cernon France
161 B8 St-Rome-de-Tarn France
156 B4 St-Saëns France
158 F3 St Sampson Channel Is
163 I6 St-Santin France
162 I2 St-Saturnin France
161 G9 St-Saturnin-lès-Apt France
162 F4 St-Saud-Lacoussière France
160 D2 St-Saulge France
160 B5 St-Sauves-d'Auvergne France
158 C5 St-Sauveur Bretagne France
157 L8 St-Sauveur Franche-Comté France
161 F7 St-Sauveur-de-Montagut France
224 F4 St-Sauveur-des-Monts Que. Can.
160 C1 St-Sauveur-en-Puisaye France
161 G8 St-Sauveur-Gouvernet France
158 I3 St-Sauveur-Lendelin France
158 H3 St-Sauveur-le-Vicomte France
161 K8 St-Sauveur-sur-Tinée France
163 F8 St-Sauvy France
162 D5 St-Savin Aquitaine France
162 F2 St-Savin Poitou-Charentes France
162 C4 St-Savinien France
158 G3 St Saviour Channel Is
214 E10 St Sebastian Bay S. Africa
233 □O3 St-Sébastien Que. Can.
156 B5 St-Sébastien-de-Morsent France
158 H7 St-Sébastien-sur-Loire France
160 F2 St-Seine-l'Abbaye France
163 D6 St-Selve France
161 E7 St-Semin France
161 B9 St-Sernin-sur-Rance France
156 F7 St-Sérotin France
163 C8 St-Sever France
159 I4 St-Sever-Calvados France
225 G4 St-Siméon Que. Can.
161 G6 St-Siméon-de-Bressieux France
162 J6 St-Simon Auvergne France
156 F4 St-Simon Picardie France
231 G10 St Simons Island GA U.S.A.
160 I3 St-Sorlin, Mont de mt. France
161 I6 St-Sorlin-d'Arves France
156 E5 St-Soupplets France
233 □R3 St Stephen N.B. Can.
150 C7 St Stephen Cornwall, England U.K.
231 H9 St Stephen SC U.S.A.
163 H8 St-Sulpice France
162 B4 St-Sulpice-de-Royan France
158 H6 St-Sulpice-des-Landes France
162 G3 St-Sulpice-Laurière France
162 H3 St-Sulpice-le-Guérétois France
162 I4 St-Sulpice-les-Champs France
162 G3 St-Sulpice-les-Feuilles France
163 G9 St-Sulpice-sur-Lèze France
159 M4 St-Sulpice-sur-Risle France
159 K3 St-Sylvain France
159 K6 St-Sylvain-d'Anjou France
163 F7 St-Sylvestre-sur-Lot France
163 D7 St-Symphorien France
160 E5 St-Symphorien-de-Lay France
160 F5 St-Symphorien-d'Ozon France
160 E5 St-Symphorien-sur-Coise France
150 C6 St Teath Cornwall, England U.K.
222 C3 St Terese AK U.S.A.
158 D4 St-Thégonnec France
233 □O3 St-Théophile Que. Can.
223 M4 St Theresa Point Man. Can.
161 C10 St-Thibéry France
157 K7 St-Thiébault France
224 D5 St Thomas Ont. Can.
246 □ St Thomas parish Jamaica
247 K4 St Thomas i. Virgin Is (U.S.A.)
St Thomas Bay Malta see San Tumas, Il-Bajja ta'
158 D6 St-Thurien France
225 G4 St-Tite-des-Caps Que. Can.
160 G4 St-Trivier-de-Courtes France
160 F4 St-Trivier-sur-Moignans France
162 B4 St-Trojan-les-Bains France
St Trond Belgium see Sint-Truiden
161 J10 St-Tropez France
161 J10 St-Tropez, Cap de c. France
161 J10 St-Tropez, Golfe de b. France
150 D2 St Tudwal's Road b. Wales U.K.
163 H8 St-Urcisse France
161 C7 St-Urcize France
161 F6 St-Uze France
158 I2 St-Vaast-la-Hougue France
156 F7 St-Valérien France
159 M2 St-Valery-en-Caux France
155 C3 St-Valery-sur-Somme France
160 E3 St-Vallier Bourgogne France
160 F6 St-Vallier Rhône-Alpes France
161 J9 St-Vallier-de-Thiey France
159 K8 St-Varent France
162 H3 St-Vaury France
161 J7 St-Véran France
161 F6 St-Victor France
161 G10 St-Victoret France
161 F8 St-Victor-la-Coste France
159 J3 St-Vigor-le-Grand France
190 D4 St-Vincent Italy
236 G1 St Vincent MN U.S.A.
247 □3 St Vincent i. West Indies
St-Vincent, Cap pt Madag. see Ankaboa, Tanjona
83 J10 St Vincent, Cape Tas. Austr.
St Vincent, Cape Port. see São Vicente, Cabo de
82 F6 St Vincent, Gulf S.A. Austr.
247 □3 St Vincent and the Grenadines country West Indies
162 E5 St-Vincent-de-Connezac France
163 C8 St-Vincent-de-Paul France
163 B8 St-Vincent-de-Tyrosse France
231 E11 St Vincent Island FL U.S.A.
161 I8 St-Vincent-les-Forts France
247 □3 St Vincent Passage St Lucia/St Vincent
160 H2 St-Vit France
163 F7 St-Vite France
165 J8 St-Vith Belgium
162 B5 St-Vivien-de-Médoc France
223 I4 St Walburg Sask. Can.
227 N7 St Williams Ont. Can.
162 B3 St-Xandre France
160 E4 St-Yan France
163 G9 St-Ybars France
160 C4 St-Yorre France
162 G4 St-Yrieix-la-Perche France
162 E4 St-Yrieix-sur-Charente France
158 D6 St-Yvy France
161 H10 St-Zacharie France
107 J6 Sain Us Nei Mongol China
156 C7 Sainville France
186 B1 Saioa mt. Spain
116 H5 Saipal mt. Nepal
91 K3 Saipan i. N. Mariana Is
92 □ Saipan Palau
109 □J7 Sai Pok Liu Hoi Hap sea chan. H.K. China
261 F3 Saira Arg.
158 I2 Saire r. France
163 C9 Saison r. France
163 I9 Saissac France
105 I4 Saitama pref. Japan
Saiteli Turkey see Kadınhanı
96 A3 Saitlai Myanmar
103 I14 Saito Japan
140 Q2 Saivomuotka Sweden
163 I8 Saïx France
97 D7 Sai Yok National Park Thai.
252 C4 Sajama, Nevado mt. Bol.
124 E7 Sajïd Saudi Arabia
197 K8 Šajince Serbia
124 G3 Sājir Saudi Arabia
125 K7 Sājir, Ra's c. Oman
175 J1 Sajna r. Pol.
175 L2 Sajno, Jezioro l. Pol.
177 J4 Sajó r. Hungary
177 J3 Sajóhidvég Hungary
177 J3 Sajókaza Hungary
177 J3 Sajópetri Hungary
177 J3 Sajószentpéter Hungary
177 K4 Sajószöged Hungary
177 J3 Sajóvámos Hungary
128 G2 Sājūr, Nahr r. Syria/Turkey
122 E5 Sajzī Iran
214 F5 Sak watercourse S. Africa
210 C2 Saka Eth.
204 E2 Saka Morocco
105 J4 Sakado Japan
105 L4 Sakae Chiba Japan
105 I2 Sakae Nagano Japan
104 E5 Sakahogi Japan
104 D3 Sakai Fukui Japan
105 J3 Sakai Gunma Japan
105 K3 Sakai Ibaraki Japan
105 H3 Sakai Nagano Japan
104 B6 Sakai Ōsaka Japan
103 K12 Sakaide Japan
105 I4 Sakaigawa Japan
103 K11 Sakaiminato Japan
127 J9 Sakākah Saudi Arabia
123 K8 Saka Kalat Pak.
236 D2 Sakakawea, Lake ND U.S.A.
105 H3 Sakaki Japan
105 H3 Sakakita Japan
95 L8 Sakala i. Indon.
211 A7 Sakalile Tanz.
224 F2 Sakami Que. Can.
224 E2 Sakami r. Que. Can.
105 J5 Sakami-gawa r. Japan
224 E2 Sakami Lake Que. Can.
123 K9 Sakani, Ras pt Pak.
209 F8 Sakania Dem. Rep. Congo
209 F8 Sakania, Réserve de Hippopotames de nature res. Dem. Rep. Congo
209 F7 Sakania, Réserve Partielle aux, Éléphants de nature res. Dem. Rep. Congo
197 O9 Sakar mts Bulg.
123 J2 Sakar Turkm.
213 □J4 Sakaraha Madag.
123 I3 Sakarçäge Turkm.
Sakartvelo country Asia see Georgia
Sakarya Turkey see Adapazarı
199 L2 Sakarya prov. Turkey
199 L1 Sakarya r. Turkey
104 G4 Sakashita Japan
206 D5 Sakassou Côte d'Ivoire
102 Q8 Sakata Japan
104 D4 Sakauchi Japan
103 K13 Sakawa Japan
101 D8 Sakchu N. Korea
121 O3 Saken Seyfullin Kazakh.
97 E8 Sa Keo r. Thai.
207 F5 Sakété Benin
100 M4 Sakhalin i. Rus. Fed.
Sakhalin Oblast admin. div. Rus. Fed. see Sakhalinskaya Oblast'
100 M3 Sakhalinskaya Oblast' admin. div. Rus. Fed.
100 L2 Sakhalinskiy Zaliv b. Sakhalin Rus. Fed.
139 T5 Sakharovo Rus. Fed.
215 O1 Sakhelwe S. Africa
116 D5 Sakhi Rajasthan India
215 N2 Sakhile S. Africa
123 N7 Sakhi Sarwar Pak.
136 F4 Sakhnivtsi Ukr.
137 O4 Sakhnovshchyna Ukr.
129 I4 Şäki Azer.
Saki Nigeria see Shaki
Saki Ukr. see Saky
138 G7 Šakiai Lith.
189 B7 Sakiet Sidi Youssef Tunisia
123 L6 Sakir mt. Pak.
102 □A22 Sakishima-shotō is Japan
114 D6 Sakleshpur Karnataka India
120 F2 Sakmara Rus. Fed.
96 C5 Sa-koi Myanmar
116 G9 Sakoli Mahar. India
96 G6 Sakon Nakhon Thai.
233 N7 Sakonnet r. RI U.S.A.
94 □ Sakra, Pulau reg. Sing.
123 M8 Sakrand Pak.
214 E6 Sakrivier S. Africa
120 I4 Saksaul'skiy Kazakh.
Saksaul'skoye Kazakh. see Saksaul'skiy
140 K5 Sakshaug Norway
170 E1 Sakskøbing Denmark
117 I8 Sakti Chhattisgarh India
117 I7 Saktisgarh Uttar Prad. India
138 H2 Saku Estonia
105 H3 Saku Nagano Japan
105 H3 Saku Nagano Japan
Sakulia Georgia see Saqulia
105 G5 Sakuma Japan
105 L4 Sakura Japan
105 L4 Sakuragawa Japan
105 L3 Sakura-gawa r. Japan
104 C6 Sakurai Japan
103 H15 Sakura-jima vol. Japan
104 F6 Saku-shima i. Japan
137 M8 Saky Ukr.
141 O6 Säkylä Fin.
206 □ Sal i. Cape Verde
135 H7 Sal r. Rus. Fed.
252 B2 Sal, Cerros de la mts Peru
242 □P10 Sal, Punta pt Hond.
138 I5 Sala Jēkabpils Latvia
138 G5 Sala Rīga Latvia
177 G3 Šaľa Slovakia
143 M2 Sala Sweden
93 C5 Salabangka, Kepulauar[...]
Indon.
224 F4 Salaberry-de-Valleyfiel[...] Que. Can.
138 H4 Salaca r. Latvia
197 K3 Sălacea Romania
177 L4 Sălacea, Lacul l. Romar[...]
138 H4 Salacgrīva Latvia
193 P7 Sala Consilina Italy
258 C2 Salada, Bahía b. Chile
242 B1 Salada, Laguna salt l. M[...]
186 H3 Salada, Ribera r. Spain
187 D11 Salada de la Mata, Lag[...] Spain
187 D11 Salada de Torrevieja, L[...] l. Spain
258 F3 Saladas Arg.
128 D9 Salādīḩ, Wādī watercou[...] Jordan
261 H4 Saladillo Buenos Aires A[...]
260 E3 Saladillo San Luis Arg.
261 F3 Saladillo r. Arg.
261 G2 Saladillo r. Arg.
261 H4 Saladillo r. Arg.
258 E3 Saladillo r. Arg.
260 D5 Salado r. Arg.
260 E6 Salado r. Arg.
261 G3 Salado r. Arg.
261 I4 Salado r. Arg.
258 C3 Salado r. Arg.
259 D6 Salado r. Arg.
258 F2 Salado r. Arg.
246 E3 Salado r. Cuba
250 B5 Salado Ecuador
244 F2 Salado Mex.
245 H5 Salado r. Hidalgo/Méxic[...]
245 K8 Salado r. Oaxaca/Puebla
243 J4 Salado r. Mex.
184 G8 Salado r. Andalucía Spai[...]
184 H7 Salado r. Andalucía Spai[...]
185 K5 Salado r. Andalucía Spai[...]
185 K5 Salado r. Andalucía Spai[...]
239 K9 Salado watercourse NM[...]
206 C4 Saladou Guinea
206 E4 Salaga Ghana
162 G5 Salagnac France
161 C9 Salagou, Lac du l. Fran[...]
124 E5 Şalāḩ Saudi Arabia
128 G5 Şalāḩ, Tall hill Jordan
127 K6 Şalāḩ ad Dīn governora[...]
127 L5 Salahuddin Iraq
78 □2 Sala'ilua Samoa
161 F6 Salaise-sur-Sanne Fra[...]
177 M4 Sălaj county Romania
212 E4 Salajwe Botswana
125 M4 Salakh, Jabal mt. Omar[...]
202 C6 Salal Chad
203 H4 Salâla Sudan
125 L7 Şalālah Oman
207 I3 Salalé well Niger
243 N10 Salamá Guat.
242 □P10 Salamá Hond.
140 R5 Salamajärven kansallis[...] nat. park Fin.
260 B2 Salamanca Chile
244 F5 Salamanca Mex.
182 I7 Salamanca Spain
182 H7 Salamanca prov. Spain
232 G6 Salamanca NY U.S.A.
213 G5 Salamanga Moz.
Salamantica Spain see Salamanca
208 D2 Salamat pref. Chad
208 C2 Salamat, Bahr r. Chad
122 B4 Salamatābād Iran
95 K6 Salamban Kalimantan In[...]
122 H4 Salāmī Iran
198 E5 Salamina Greece
198 E5 Salamina i. Greece
128 B3 Salamis tourist site Cyp[...]
Salamis i. Greece see Salamina
128 F3 Salamīyah Syria
226 I9 Salamonie r. IN U.S.A.
226 I9 Salamonie Lake IN U.S[...]
117 K9 Salandi r. India
193 Q6 Salandra Italy
78 □2 Salani Samoa
138 E5 Salantai Lith.
216 □1c Salão Faial Azores
194 D8 Salaparuta Sicilia Italy
107 L6 Salaqi Nei Mongol China
185 K6 Salar Spain
197 K3 Sălard Romania
258 D2 Salar de Pocitos Arg.
186 G2 Salardu Spain
123 K8 Salari Pak.
250 B6 Salas Peru
197 K6 Salaš Serbia
182 H2 Salas Spain
182 E5 Salas, Embalse de resr[...]
183 N4 Salas de los Infantes [...]
138 H5 Salaspils Latvia
163 F9 Salat r. France
95 I8 Salatiga Jawa Indon.
177 I3 Salatín nature res. Slova[...]
162 C6 Salaunes France
134 K4 Salaush Rus. Fed.
197 M3 Sălăuța r. Romania
96 H7 Salavan Laos
120 F1 Salavat Rus. Fed.
252 A2 Salaverry Peru
93 G4 Salawati i. Papua Indon[...]
Salawin, Mae Nam r. China/Myanmar see Salw[...]
96 C5 Salawin Wildlife Rese[...] nature res. Thai.
92 E7 Salay Mindanao Phil.
116 B8 Salaya Gujarat India
93 B7 Salayar i. Indon.
93 B6 Salayar, Selat sea chan. [...]
267 L7 Sala y Gómez, Isla i. S. Pacific Ocean
Salazar Angola see N'dalatando
261 F5 Salazar Arg.
186 C2 Salazar r. Spain
217 □1c Salazie Réunion
217 □1c Salazie, Cirque de vol. Réunion
190 B5 Salbertrand Italy
162 I1 Salbris France
252 B3 Salccantay, Cerro mt. [...]
246 H4 Salcedo Dom. Rep.
173 N4 Salching Ger.
138 H7 Šalčia r. Lith.
197 O6 Sălciile Romania
138 I7 Šalčininkai Lith.
175 N1 Šalčininkėliai Lith.
197 O6 Sălcioara Romania
150 E7 Salcombe Devon, England U.K.
Saldae Alg. see Bejaïa
199 K5 Salda Gölü l. Turkey
250 C4 Saldaña Col.
183 K3 Saldaña Spain
214 B9 Saldanha S. Africa
214 B9 Saldanha Bay S. Africa
173 O4 Saldenburg Ger.
183 R8 Saldón Spain
183 O5 Salduero Spain
261 G6 Saldungaray Arg.
191 J2 Saldura r. Italy
138 F5 Saldus Latvia
83 K8 Sale Vic. Austr.
86 H4 Sale r. W.A. Austr.
190 F6 Sale Italy
96 B4 Sale Myanmar
149 M7 Sale Greater Mancheste[...] England U.K.
93 B4 Salea Sulawesi Indon.
163 F10 Saléchan France
247 □2 Salée sea chan. Guadel[...]
95 L9 Saleh, Teluk b. Sumbav[...] Indon.
122 C4 Şāleḩābād Hamadān Ira[...]
122 B5 Şāleḩābād Īlām Iran
122 I4 Şāleḩābād Khorāsān Ira[...]
151 M6 Salehurst East Sussex, England U.K.
130 H3 Salekhard Rus. Fed.
78 □2 Salelologa Samoa
172 G6 Salem Baden-Württembe[...]
168 K3 Salem Schleswig-Holste[...]
114 F7 Salem Tamil Nadu India
215 K9 Salem S. Africa
237 J7 Salem AR U.S.A.

Salem IL U.S.A.
Salem IN U.S.A.
Salem MA U.S.A.
Salem MO U.S.A.
Salem NJ U.S.A.
Salem NY U.S.A.
Salem OH U.S.A.
Salem OR U.S.A.
Salem SD U.S.A.
Salem UT U.S.A.
Salem VA U.S.A.
Salem WV U.S.A.
Salem r. NJ U.S.A.
Salem County county NJ U.S.A.
Salemi Sicilia Italy
Sälen Sweden
Salen l. Sweden
Salen Argyll and Bute, Scotland U.K.
Salen Highland, Scotland U.K.
Salernes France
Salerno Italy
Salerno prov. Italy
Salerno, Golfo di g. Italy
Salernum Italy see Salerno
Salers France
Sales Oliveira Brazil
Salesópolis Brazil
Sales Point England U.K.
Salettes France
Saleux France
Salève mt. France
Salford Greater Manchester, England U.K.
Salfords Surrey, England U.K.
Salgada Brazil
Salgado Brazil
Salgado r. Brazil
Salgótarján Hungary
Salgueiro Brazil
Salgueiro Port.
Salgueiros Port.
Salguero Arg.
Salhouse Norfolk, England U.K.
Salhus Norway
Salhyr r. Ukr.
Sali Alg.
Salian Afgh.
Salibabu i. Indon.
Salibea Trin. and Tob. see Salybia
Salice Salentino Italy
Saliceto Italy
Salici, Monte mt. Sicilia Italy
Salida CO U.S.A.
Saliena Latvia
Salies-de-Béarn France
Salies-du-Salat France
Salignac-Eyvignes France
Salihli Turkey
Salihorsk Belarus
Salihorskaye Vodaskhovishcha resr Belarus
Salikénié Senegal
Salillas de Jalón Spain
Salima Malawi
Salimbatu Kalimantan Indon.
Salime, Encoro de resr Spain
Salimi Dem. Rep. Congo
Salimo Moz.
Salin Myanmar
Salina KS U.S.A.
Salina UT U.S.A.
Salina, Il-Bajja tas- b. Malta
Salina, Isola i. Isole Lipari Italy
Salina Cruz Mex.
Salina Point Acklins I. Bahamas
Salinas Brazil
Salinas Ecuador
Salinas San Luis Potosí Mex.
Salinas Veracruz Mex.
Salinas r. Mex.
Salinas Puerto Rico
Salinas Asturias Spain
Salinas Valencia Spain
Salinas CA U.S.A.
Salinas r. CA U.S.A.
Salinas, Cabo de c. Spain see Salines, Cap de ses
Salinas, Pampa de las salt pan Arg.
Salinas, Ponta das pt Angola
Salinas, Punta pt La Palma Canary Is
Salinas, Punta pt Dom. Rep.
Salinas de Garci Mendoza Bol.
Salinas del Manzano Spain
Salinas de Pamplona Spain
Salinas de Pisuerga Spain
Salinas de Sín Spain
Salinas Peak NM U.S.A.
Salin-de-Giraud France
Salindres France
Saline r. Italy
Saline salt marsh Italy
Saline Fife, Scotland U.K.
Saline MI U.S.A.
Saline r. AR U.S.A.
Saline r. KS U.S.A.
Saline Bay Trin. and Tob.
Saline di Volterra Italy
Salinello r. Italy
Salines, Cap de ses c. Spain
Salines, Point Grenada
Saline Valley depr. CA U.S.A.
Salineville OH U.S.A.
Salingyi Myanmar
Salinópolis Brazil
Salinosó Lachay, Punta pt Peru
Salins France
Salins-les-Bains France
Salir Port.
Salisbury Wiltshire, England U.K.
Salisbury MD U.S.A.
Salisbury NC U.S.A.
Salisbury PA U.S.A.
Salisbury Zimbabwe see Harare
Salisbury Island Nunavut Can.
Salisbury Mills NY U.S.A.
Salisbury Plain England U.K.
Săliște Romania
Săliștea de Sus Romania
Salito r. Sicilia Italy
Salitral de Carrera Mex.
Salitre r. Brazil
Salka Slovakia
Şalkhad Syria
Salki r. India
Salkım Turkey
Sal'kove Ukr.
Salla Fin.
Salladasburg PA U.S.A.
Sallanches France
Sallatouk, Pointe pt Guinea
Sallent Spain
Sallent de Gállego Spain
Salles France
Salles-Curan France
Salles-d'Angles France
Salles-d'Aude France
Salles-la-Source France
Salles-sur-l'Hers France
Sallgast Ger.
Salling reg. Denmark
Sallingberg Austria
Sallins Ireland
Salliq Nunavut Can. see Coral Harbour
Salliqueló Arg.
Sallisaw OK U.S.A.
Sallom Sudan
Salluit Que. Can.
Sallum, Khalīj as b. Egypt
Sallyana Nepal
Sallypark Ireland
Salm r. Belgium
Salmá Syria
Salmankas Geçidi pass Turkey
Salmās Iran
Salmerón Spain
Salmeroncillos de Abajo Spain
Salmi Rus. Fed.
Salmivaara Fin.
Salmo B.C. Can.
238 H4 Salmon ID U.S.A.
235 K2 Salmon r. CT U.S.A.
238 F4 Salmon r. ID U.S.A.
238 G4 Salmon, Middle Fork r. ID U.S.A.
222 G5 Salmon Arm B.C. Can.
238 G5 Salmon Falls Creek r. ID/NV U.S.A.
87 F12 Salmon Gums W.A. Austr.
Salmonhurst N.B. Can. see New Denmark
233 J5 Salmon Reservoir NY U.S.A.
238 G4 Salmon River Mountains ID U.S.A.
214 D10 Salmonsdam Nature Reserve S. Africa
183 J7 Salmoral Spain
172 B2 Salmtal Ger.
140 U2 Sal'nyye Tundry, Khrebet mts Rus. Fed.
208 C4 Salo C.A.R.
141 Q6 Salo Fin.
191 J4 Salò Italy
134 J4 Salobelyak Rus. Fed.
185 N3 Salobre Spain
185 L7 Salobreña Spain
140 R4 Saloinen Fin.
241 S8 Salome AZ U.S.A.
247 □3 Salomon, Cap c. Martinique
156 H6 Salon France
160 H1 Salon r. France
116 H6 Salon Uttar Prad. India
161 G9 Salon-de-Provence France
208 D5 Salonga r. Dem. Rep. Congo
208 D5 Salonga Nord, Parc National de la nat. park Dem. Rep. Congo
208 D5 Salonga Sud, Parc National de la nat. park Dem. Rep. Congo
Salonica Greece see Thessaloniki
Salonika Greece see Thessaloniki
197 J4 Salonta Romania
Salop admin. div. England U.K. see Shropshire
182 F9 Salor r. Spain
184 G2 Salor, Embalse de resr Spain
186 H2 Salòria, Pic de mt. Spain
184 E2 Salorino Spain
160 F3 Salornay-sur-Guye France
191 K3 Salorno Italy
186 H5 Salou Spain
186 H5 Salou, Cap de c. Spain
156 D4 Salouël France
206 A3 Saloum watercourse Senegal
179 N6 Šalovci Slovenia
141 R6 Salpausselkä reg. Fin.
140 □ Salpynten pt Svalbard
128 E2 Salqīn Syria
206 □ Sal Rei Cape Verde
147 C5 Salruck Ireland
260 E2 Salsacate Arg.
140 K4 Salsbruket Norway
Salses, Étang de l. France see Leucate, Étang de
163 J10 Salses-le-Château France
135 H7 Sal'sk Rus. Fed.
194 F9 Salso r. Sicilia Italy
194 H8 Salso r. Sicilia Italy
193 P4 Salsola r. Italy
190 H6 Salsomaggiore Terme Italy
Salt Jordan see As Salţ
214 H9 Salt watercourse S. Africa
186 K4 Salt Spain
241 T8 Salt r. AZ U.S.A.
236 J6 Salt r. MO U.S.A.
238 I5 Salt r. WY U.S.A.
258 D2 Salta Arg.
258 D2 Salta prov. Arg.
149 N6 Saltaire West Yorkshire, England U.K.
235 I3 Saltaire NY U.S.A.
139 R9 Saltanovka Rus. Fed.
191 N8 Saltara Italy
150 D7 Saltash Cornwall, England U.K.
149 P4 Saltburn-by-the-Sea Redcar and Cleveland, England U.K.
231 □2 Salt Cay i. New Prov. Bahamas
146 G11 Saltcoats North Ayrshire, Scotland U.K.
232 C9 Salt Creek r. OH U.S.A.
151 L6 Saltdean Brighton and Hove, England U.K.
147 I8 Saltee Islands Ireland
184 G6 Salteras Spain
222 E5 Saltery Bay B.C. Can.
140 M3 Saltfjellet Svartisen Nasjonalpark nat. park Norway
140 L3 Saltfjorden sea chan. Norway
239 L11 Salt Flat TX U.S.A.
150 H5 Saltford Bath and North East Somerset, England U.K.
237 F7 Salt Fork r. KS U.S.A.
237 G7 Salt Fork Arkansas r. KS U.S.A.
237 E9 Salt Fork Brazos r. TX U.S.A.
232 D8 Salt Fork Lake OH U.S.A.
237 F8 Salt Fork Red r. OK U.S.A.
147 D6 Salthill Ireland
243 I5 Saltillo Mex.
Salt Island Vanuatu see Loh
116 E6 Salt Lake salt l. India
214 I5 Salt Lake S. Africa
238 I6 Salt Lake City UT U.S.A.
232 B10 Salt Lick KY U.S.A.
241 S2 Salt Marsh Lake salt l. UT U.S.A.
150 G1 Saltney Flintshire, Wales U.K.
261 G4 Salto Arg.
256 D5 Salto Brazil
193 J3 Salto r. Italy
182 E5 Salto Port.
261 I2 Salto Uru.
261 I2 Salto dept Uru.
193 K3 Salto, Lago del l. Italy
257 H2 Salto da Divisa Brazil
243 M9 Salto de Agua Chiapas Mex.
245 H3 Salto de Agua San Luis Potosí Mex.
260 C4 Saltode Las Rosas Arg.
253 G6 Salto del Guairá Para.
192 C8 Salto di Quirra reg. Sardegna Italy
261 G3 Salto Grande Arg.
256 C5 Salto Grande Brazil
244 A1 Salto Grande Mex.
261 I2 Salto Grande, Embalse de resr Uru.
241 P8 Salton City CA U.S.A.
241 Q8 Salton Sea salt l. CA U.S.A.
206 E5 Saltpond Ghana
223 H2 Salt River N.W.T. Can.
Saltrou Haiti see Belle-Anse
143 O2 Saltsjöbaden Sweden
141 P6 Saltvik Åland Fin.
232 D12 Saltville VA U.S.A.
81 E10 Saltwater Lagoon South I. N.Z.
139 W8 Saltyki Rus. Fed.
78 □2 Saluafata Samoa
231 G8 Saluda SC U.S.A.
232 I11 Saluda VA U.S.A.
231 F8 Saluda r. SC U.S.A.
191 N8 Saludecio Italy
93 C4 Saluebesar i. Indon.
93 C5 Saluekecil i. Indon.
93 C4 Salue Timpaus, Selat sea chan. Indon.
190 E5 Saluggia Italy
116 E7 Salumbar Rajasthan India
122 G3 Saluq, Kūh-e mt. Iran
115 H3 Salur Andhra Prad. India
190 E5 Salussola Italy
190 C6 Saluzzo Italy
129 H6 Şälvä Azer.
183 R8 Salvacañete Spain
184 D5 Salvada Port.
183 N3 Sálvada, Sierra mts Spain
260 E2 Salvador Arg.
254 F5 Salvador Brazil
182 F8 Salvador Port.
237 J11 Salvador, Lake LA U.S.A.
258 E1 Salvador Mazza Arg.
163 H8 Salvagnac France
184 F3 Salvaleón Spain
254 C2 Salvaterra Brazil
184 B2 Salvaterra de Magos Port.
182 G9 Salvaterra do Extremo Port.
244 G5 Salvatierra Mex.
183 P3 Salvatierra Spain
184 F4 Salvatierra de los Barros Spain
184 G2 Salvatierra de Santiago Spain
241 V3 Salvation Creek r. UT U.S.A.
195 O4 Salve Italy
163 G6 Salviac France
182 B4 Sálvora, Illa de i. Spain
125 J3 Salwah Saudi Arabia
125 J3 Salwah, Dawḩat b. Qatar/Saudi Arabia
108 B6 Salween r. China
96 C6 Salween r. Myanmar
129 D6 Salyamaç Turkey
129 J6 Salyan Azer.
Sal'yany Azer. see Salyan
247 □7 Salybia Trin. and Tob.
232 B11 Salyersville KY U.S.A.
179 K4 Salza r. Austria
178 G3 Salzach r. Austria/Ger.
179 I4 Salza-Stausee resr Austria
169 D6 Salzbergen Ger.
212 C5 Salzbrunn Namibia
178 H4 Salzburg Austria
178 H5 Salzburg land Austria
169 J6 Salzgitter Ger.
168 J4 Salzhausen Ger.
169 I6 Salzhemmendorf Ger.
179 I4 Salzkammergut reg. Austria
169 G7 Salzkotten Ger.
171 E7 Salzmünde Ger.
170 D5 Salzwedel Ger.
168 K5 Salzwedel-Diesdorf park Ger.
173 O4 Salzweg Ger.
208 A4 Sam Gabon
116 C6 Sam Rajasthan India
96 G5 Sam, Nam r. Laos/Vietnam
246 F3 Samá Cuba
174 E3 Sama r. Pol.
Šamac Bos.-Herz. see Bosanski Šamac
125 N4 Şamad Oman
163 D8 Samadet France
97 E8 Samae San, Laem i. Thai.
106 D1 Samagaltay Rus. Fed.
124 G1 Samāh well Saudi Arabia
Samaida Iran see Someydeh
252 E4 Samaipata Bol.
111 F10 Samaixung Xizang China
94 F5 Samak, Tanjung pt Indon.
206 C3 Samakoulou Mali
92 E8 Samal i. Phil.
78 □2 Samalae'ulu Samoa
94 B2 Samalanga Sumatera Indon.
95 H4 Samalantan Kalimantan Indon.
242 F2 Samalayuca Mex.
92 C9 Samales Group is Phil.
114 H4 Samalkot Andhra Prad. India
203 F2 Samālūţ Egypt
247 I4 Samaná Dom. Rep.
116 F4 Samana Punjab India
247 I4 Samaná, Cabo c. Dom. Rep.
246 G2 Samana Cay i. Bahamas
Samanala mt. Sri Lanka see Sri Pada
126 G5 Samandağı Turkey
123 L3 Samangān prov. Afgh.
122 I4 Samangān Iran
102 T4 Samani Japan
250 B4 Samaniego Col.
199 J2 Samanlı Dağları mts Turkey
203 F2 Samannūd Egypt
225 F3 Samaqua r. Que. Can.
Samar Kazakh. see Samarskoye
92 E6 Samar i. Phil.
120 D1 Samara Rus. Fed.
120 D1 Samara r. Rus. Fed.
137 O5 Samara r. Ukr.
Samarahan Sarawak Malaysia see Sri Aman
91 L9 Samarai P.N.G.
Samara Oblast admin. div. Rus. Fed. see Samarskaya Oblast'
190 F4 Samarate Italy
100 K5 Samarga Rus. Fed.
250 E3 Samariapo Venez.
198 E7 Samarias, Ethnikos Drymos nat. park Greece
179 O8 Samarica Croatia
95 L5 Samarinda Kalimantan Indon.
121 O3 Samarka Karagandinskaya Oblast' Kazakh.
100 I6 Samarka Rus. Fed.
Samarkand Uzbek. see Samarqand
Samarkand, Pik mt. Tajik. see Samarqand, Qullai
Samarkand Oblast admin. div. Uzbek. see Samarqand
Samarobriva France see Amiens
121 L8 Samarqand Uzbek.
121 L8 Samarqand admin. div. Uzbek.
123 M2 Samarqand, Qullai mt. Tajik.
Samarqand Wiloyati admin. div. Uzbek. see Samarqand
127 K6 Sāmarrā' Iraq
92 E6 Samar Sea g. Phil.
120 C1 Samarskaya Oblast' admin. div. Rus. Fed.
121 T3 Samarskoye Vostochnyy Kazakhstan Kazakh.
137 S7 Samarskoye Rus. Fed.
136 D2 Samary Ukr.
107 N4 Samarz Nei Mongol China
123 N7 Samasata Pak.
192 B9 Samassi Sardegna Italy
117 J7 Samastipur Bihar India
163 F9 Samatan France
93 G4 Samate Papua Indon.
192 C9 Samatzai Sardegna Italy
251 F6 Samaúma Brazil
129 J5 Şamaxı Azer.
208 D4 Samba Équateur Dem. Rep. Congo
209 E6 Samba Maniema Dem. Rep. Congo
95 J5 Samba r. Indon.
116 E3 Samba Jammu and Kashmir
209 B7 Samba Cajú Angola
182 G6 Sambade Port.
254 D3 Sambaiba Brazil
206 B3 Sambaïlo Guinea
95 L4 Sambaliung mts Indon.
117 I9 Sambalpur Orissa India
95 I6 Sambar, Tanjung pt Indon.
95 H4 Sambas Kalimantan Indon.
Sambat Ukr. see Kyiv
177 L5 Sâmbăta Romania
213 □K2 Sambava Madag.
137 S6 Sambek Rostovskaya Oblast' Rus. Fed.
137 S6 Sambek Rostovskaya Oblast' Rus. Fed.
Sambe-san vol. Japan see Sanbe-san
117 M6 Sambha Arun. Prad. India
116 G5 Sambhal Uttar Prad. India
116 E6 Sambhar Rajasthan India
116 E6 Sambhar Lake India
193 Q10 Sambiase Italy
93 C4 Sambiat Sulawesi Indon.
136 C4 Sambir Ukr.
95 M4 Sambit i. Indon.
209 C8 Sambo Angola
93 A5 Sambo Sulawesi Barat Indon.
183 L6 Samboal Spain
95 L5 Samboja Kalimantan Indon.
97 H8 Sâmbor Cambodia
Sambor Ukr. see Sambir
97 H8 Sâmbor Dam Cambodia
261 I4 Samborombón r. Arg.
261 I4 Samborombón, Bahía b. Arg.
175 J5 Samborzec Pol.
165 F8 Sambre r. Belgium/France
Sambu Japan see Sanbu
194 E8 Sambuca di Sicilia Sicilia Italy
191 K7 Sambuca Pistoiese Italy
161 K8 Sambuco Italy
194 G8 Sambughetti, Monte mt. Sicilia Italy
101 F10 Samch'ŏk S. Korea
Samch'ŏnp'o S. Korea see Sach'on
118 E2 Samdi Dag mt. Turkey
190 H2 Samedan Switz.
105 M1 Samegawa Japan
96 B4 Sameikkon Myanmar
182 F8 Sameiro Port.
156 C2 Samer France
169 D6 Samern Ger.
129 E3 Samerts'khle, Mt'a Georgia
183 J2 Sames Spain
139 X4 Samet' Rus. Fed.
97 E8 Samet, Ko i. Thai.
209 F7 Samfya Zambia
125 K9 Samḩah i. Yemen
125 L7 Samḩān, Jabal mts Oman
136 I4 Samhorodok Kyivs'ka Oblast' Ukr.
136 H4 Samhorodok Vinnyts'ka Oblast' Ukr.
198 B4 Sami Kefallonia Greece
116 C8 Sami Gujarat India
123 J8 Sami Pak.
93 C3 Samia, Tanjung pt Indon.
182 G5 Samil Port.
124 F2 Samīrah Saudi Arabia
182 H5 Samir de los Caños Spain
250 C6 Samiria r. Peru
Samirum Iran see Yazd-e Khvāst
124 F7 Sāmitah Saudi Arabia
137 N6 Samiylivka Ukr.
105 H2 Samizu Japan
101 F8 Samjiyŏn N. Korea
108 A3 Samka Xizang China
129 E3 Samkhret' Oset'i reg. Georgia
129 H5 Şämkir Azer.
129 H5 Şämkirçay r. Azer.
128 F1 Samköy Turkey
199 I3 Şamlı Turkey
195 L2 Sammichele di Bari Italy
124 C3 Samnah oasis Saudi Arabia
190 I2 Samnaun Switz.
178 B5 Samnaungruppe mts Austria
Sam Neua Laos see Xam Nua
202 B3 Samnū Libya
182 D3 Samo r. Spain
78 □2 Samoa country S. Pacific Ocean
266 H7 Samoa Basin sea feature Pacific Ocean
Samoa i Sisifo country S. Pacific Ocean see Samoa
260 B2 Samo Alto Chile
188 E3 Samobor Croatia
179 M8 Samoborska Gora hills Croatia
134 H3 Samoded Rus. Fed.
160 J4 Samoëns France
191 K6 Samoggia r. Italy
197 L8 Samokov Bulg.
190 G3 Samolaco Italy
136 F4 Samoluskivtsi Ukr.
138 K3 Samolva Rus. Fed.
184 B3 Samora Correia Port.
176 G3 Šamorín Slovakia
199 H5 Samos Samos Greece
199 H5 Samos i. Greece
182 F3 Samos Spain
94 C3 Samosir i. Indon.
Samothrace i. Greece see Samothraki
199 G2 Samothraki Samothraki Greece
199 G2 Samothraki i. Greece
197 N7 Samovodene Bulg.
135 H6 Samoylovka Rus. Fed.
206 E5 Sampa Côte d'Ivoire
260 E3 Sampacho Arg.
93 A5 Sampaga Sulawesi Barat Indon.
95 J8 Sampang Jawa Indon.
186 E5 Samper de Calanda Spain
190 C6 Sampeyre Italy
194 H10 Sampieri Sicilia Italy
157 K6 Sampigny France
95 J6 Sampit Kalimantan Indon.
95 J6 Sampit r. Indon.
95 J6 Sampit, Teluk b. Indon.
93 C6 Sampolawa Sulawesi Indon.
135 H5 Sampur Rus. Fed.
209 E7 Sampwe Dem. Rep. Congo
97 G7 Samran, Huai r. Thai.
237 H10 Sam Rayburn Reservoir TX U.S.A.
206 E5 Samreboe Ghana
138 L3 Samro, Ozero l. Rus. Fed.
Samrong Cambodia see Phumĭ Sâmraông
111 F11 Samsang Xizang China
96 F4 Sam Sao, Phou mts Laos/Vietnam
142 J4 Sämsjön l. Sweden
142 G6 Samsø i. Denmark
142 G6 Samsø Bælt sea chan. Denmark
96 G5 Sâm Sơn Vietnam
177 L4 Şamşud Romania
126 H3 Samsun Turkey
171 E6 Samswegen Ger.
121 Q6 Samsy Kazakh.
170 H2 Samtens Ger.
116 G7 Samthar Uttar Prad. India
129 D3 Samtredia Georgia
84 E5 Samuel, Mount hill N.T. Austr.
192 B8 Samugheo Sardegna Italy
97 E10 Samui, Ko i. Thai.
105 J5 Samukawa Japan
94 □ Samulun, Pulau i. Sing.
123 O6 Samundri Pak.
129 J4 Samur Azer.
129 J4 Samur r. Azer./Rus. Fed.
129 J4 Samur-Abşeron Kanalı canal Azer.
Samutlu Turkey see Temelli
97 E8 Samut Prakan Thai.
97 E8 Samut Sakhon Thai.
97 E8 Samut Songkhram Thai.
111 J12 Samyai Xizang China
206 D3 San Mali
175 J5 San r. Pol.
96 F5 San, Phou mt. Laos
97 H8 San, Tônlé r. Cambodia
188 F3 Sana r. Bos.-Herz.
124 G8 Şan'ā' Yemen
124 G8 Şan'ā' governorate Yemen
210 E2 Sanaag admin. reg. Somalia
182 H4 Sanabria reg. Spain
105 H3 Sanada Japan
183 Q4 San Adrián Spain
182 C2 San Adrián, Cabo c. Spain
262 X2 Sanae IV research stn Antarctica
207 H6 Sanaga r. Cameroon
104 F5 Sanage Japan
116 G7 Sanagir Madh. Prad. India
San Agostín FL U.S.A. see St Augustine
260 E2 San Agustín Arg.
216 □3f San Agustín Gran Canaria Canary Is
250 B4 San Agustín Col.
92 F8 San Agustin, Cape Mindanao Phil.
250 B4 San Agustín, Parque Arqueológico tourist site Col.
183 M7 San Agustín de Guadalix Spain
146 D11 Sanaigmore Argyll and Bute, Scotland U.K.
220 B4 Sanak Island AK U.S.A.
124 G4 Sanām Saudi Arabia
182 D4 San Amaro Spain
252 A6 San Ambrosio, Isla i. Islas de los Desventurados S. Pacific Ocean
93 D5 Sanana Maluku Indon.
122 B4 Sanandaj Iran
206 D3 Sanando Mali
240 L3 San Andreas CA U.S.A.
177 K6 Sânandrei Romania
252 D3 San Andrés Bol.
250 C3 San Andrés Col.
243 O9 San Andrés Guat.
92 E5 San Andres Phil.
246 C7 San Andrés, Isla de i. Caribbean Sea
185 L4 San Andrés, Sierra de mts Spain
261 H4 San Andrés de Giles Arg.
182 I3 San Andrés del Rabanedo Spain
244 D6 San Andrés Ixtlán Mex.
239 K10 San Andres Mountains NM U.S.A.
245 L7 San Andrés Tuxtla Mex.
246 F8 San Ángel Col.
237 E10 San Angelo TX U.S.A.
206 D3 Sanankoroba Mali
240 J4 San Anselmo CA U.S.A.
182 G2 San Antolín Spain
244 G4 San Antón de los Martinez Mex.
258 D3 San Antonio Catamarca Arg.
260 D3 San Antonio San Luis Arg.
242 □O9 San Antonio Belize
252 D3 San Antonio Bol.
258 C2 San Antonio Atacama Chile
260 B3 San Antonio Valparaíso Chile
242 □P10 San Antonio Hond.
244 G2 San Antonio San Luis Potosí Mex.
245 H2 San Antonio Tamaulipas Mex.
250 C5 San Antonio Peru
92 C4 San Antonio Luzon Phil.
187 C8 San Antonio Spain
261 I2 San Antonio Uru.
239 K10 San Antonio NM U.S.A.
237 F11 San Antonio TX U.S.A.
240 L6 San Antonio r. CA U.S.A.
237 G11 San Antonio r. TX U.S.A.
247 L8 San Antonio Venez.
261 I5 San Antonio, Cabo c. Arg.
246 A3 San Antonio, Cabo c. Cuba
187 F10 San Antonio, Cabo de c. Spain
240 O7 San Antonio, Mount CA U.S.A.
183 K2 San Antonio, Punta de pt Spain
92 A7 San Antonio Bay Palawan Phil.
261 H4 San Antonio de Areco Arg.
250 D3 San Antonio de Caparo Venez.
247 L8 San Antonio del Golfo Venez.
242 A2 San Antonio del Mar Mex.
258 D2 San Antonio de los Cobres Arg.
242 □P10 San Antonio de Oriente Hond.
207 G7 San Antonio de Palé Equat. Guinea
251 E2 San Antonio de Tamanaco Venez.
245 H5 San Antonio Escabedo Mex.
259 D6 San Antonio Este Arg.
245 I2 San Antonio Nogalar Mex.
259 D6 San Antonio Oeste Arg.
245 I3 San Antonio Rayón Mex.
240 L6 San Antonio Reservoir CA U.S.A.
245 H4 San Antonio Tancoyol Mex.
161 H10 Sanary-sur-Mer France
183 O3 San Asensio Spain
78 □4a Sanat i. Chuuk Micronesia
234 D4 Sanatoga PA U.S.A.
261 H6 San Augustín Arg.
260 D2 San Augustín de Valle Fértil Arg.
237 H10 San Augustine TX U.S.A.
125 N4 Sanāw Oman
125 J7 Sanaw Yemen
116 F8 Sanawad Madh. Prad. India
123 N6 Sanawan Pak.
245 K9 San Baltasar Loxicha Mex.
244 G3 San Bartolo Mex.
216 □3c San Bartolomé Lanzarote Canary Is
183 K9 San Bartolomé de las Abiertas Spain
184 E6 San Bartolomé de la Torre Spain
183 K7 San Bartolomé de Pinares Spain
216 □3f San Bartolomé de Tirajana Gran Canaria Canary Is
193 O5 San Bartolomeo in Galdo Italy
245 H6 San Bartolo Morelos Mex.
245 I5 San Bartolo Tutotepec Mex.
260 E3 San Basilio Arg.
192 C8 San Basilio Sardegna Italy
San Baudillo de Llobregat Cataluña Spain see Sant Boi de Llobregat
193 L2 San Benedetto del Tronto Italy
191 J5 San Benedetto Po Italy
228 D7 San Benedicto, Isla i. Mex.
243 O9 San Benito Guat.
185 J3 San Benito Spain
237 G12 San Benito TX U.S.A.
240 K5 San Benito r. CA U.S.A.
184 E3 San Benito de la Contienda Spain
240 L5 San Benito Mountain CA U.S.A.
240 O7 San Bernardino CA U.S.A.
190 G3 San Bernardino, Passo di pass Switz.
241 O7 San Bernardino Mountains CA U.S.A.
92 E5 San Bernardino Strait Phil.
261 I5 San Bernardo Arg.
260 B3 San Bernardo Chile
242 G5 San Bernardo Mex.
244 B2 San Bernardo de Milipas Chico Mex.
103 J11 Sanbe-san vol. Japan
191 M4 San Biagio di Callalta Italy
194 F8 San Biago Platani Sicilia Italy
258 D3 San Blas Arg.
244 B4 San Blas Nayarit Mex.
242 E4 San Blas Sinaloa Mex.
242 □T13 San Blas, Archipiélago de is Panama
231 E11 San Blas, Cape FL U.S.A.
242 □T13 San Blas, Cordillera de mts Panama
195 □ San Blas, Il-Bajja ta' b. Gozo Malta
191 K5 San Bonifacio Italy
252 D3 San Borja Bol.
236 H4 Sanborn IA U.S.A.
233 □N5 Sanbornville NH U.S.A.
Sanbu Guangdong China see Kaiping
105 L4 Sanbu Japan
243 I4 San Buenaventura Mex.
213 G3 Sança Moz.
191 M2 San Candido Italy
186 E4 San Caprasio hill Spain
260 E2 San Carlos Córdoba Arg.
260 C3 San Carlos Mendoza Arg.
258 D2 San Carlos Salta Arg.
260 B5 San Carlos Chile
San Carlos Equat. Guinea see Luba
243 I3 San Carlos Coahuila Mex.
245 I1 San Carlos Tamaulipas Mex.
242 □Q12 San Carlos Nic.
253 F5 San Carlos Para.
253 F5 San Carlos r. Para.
92 C4 San Carlos Luzon Phil.
92 D6 San Carlos Negros Phil.
258 G4 San Carlos Uru.
241 V8 San Carlos AZ U.S.A.
250 E4 San Carlos Amazonas Venez.
250 E3 San Carlos Apure Venez.
250 D2 San Carlos Cojedes Venez.
261 G2 San Carlos Centro Arg.
259 C6 San Carlos de Bariloche Arg.
261 G5 San Carlos de Bolívar Arg.
San Carlos de la Rápita Spain see Sant Carles de la Ràpita
185 M3 San Carlos del Valle Spain
250 D2 San Carlos del Zulia Venez.
241 V8 San Carlos Indian Reservation res. AZ U.S.A.
241 V8 San Carlos Lake AZ U.S.A.
261 G2 San Carlos Sur Arg.
192 H2 San Casciano dei Bagni Italy
191 K8 San Casciano in Val di Pesa Italy
195 O3 San Cataldo Puglia Italy
194 F9 San Cataldo Sicilia Italy
261 H6 San Cayetano Arg.
182 I5 San Cebrián de Castro Spain
San Celoni Spain see Sant Celoni
160 B2 Sancergues France
160 B2 Sancerre France
160 B2 Sancerrois, Collines du hills France
195 O3 San Cesario di Lecce Italy
160 J2 Sancey-le-Grand France
106 I9 Sancha Gansu China
107 L7 Sancha Shanxi China
Sanchahe Jilin China see Fuyu
108 F5 Sancha He r. Guizhou China
110 D7 Sanchakou Xinjiang China
156 C7 Sancheville France
245 N7 Sánchez Magallanes Mex.
116 F8 Sanchi Madh. Prad. India
183 K7 Sanchidrián Spain
96 F4 San Chien Pau mt. Laos
244 F7 Sanchiqueo Mex.
193 Q6 San Chirico Nuovo Italy
193 Q7 San Chirico Raparo Italy
184 E6 Sancho, Embalse de resr Spain
116 C7 Sanchor Rajasthan India
107 L8 Sanchuan He r. China
134 I4 Sanchursk Rus. Fed.
182 E4 San Cibrão das Viñas Spain
194 E8 San Cipirello Sicilia Italy
193 M6 San Cipriano d'Aversa Italy
245 H4 San Ciro de Acosta Mex.
260 B4 San Clemente Chile
185 O2 San Clemente Spain
240 O8 San Clemente CA U.S.A.
185 N5 San Clemente, Embalse de resr Spain
261 I5 San Clemente del Tuyú Arg.
240 N9 San Clemente Island CA U.S.A.
Sanclêr Wales U.K. see St Clears
182 F4 San Clodio Spain
160 B3 Sancoins France
92 F7 Sanco Point Mindanao Phil.
258 F2 San Cosme Arg.
182 F1 San Cosme Spain
193 Q7 San Costantino Albanese Italy
191 O8 San Costanzo Italy
243 N10 San Crisóbal Verapez Guat.
261 G2 San Cristóbal Arg.
252 D5 San Cristóbal Potosí Bol.
253 E3 San Cristóbal Santa Cruz Bol.
250 C5 San Cristóbal Col.
246 H4 San Cristóbal Dom. Rep.
245 I5 San Cristóbal Hidalgo Mex.
244 F4 San Cristóbal Jalisco Mex.
78 □6 San Cristobal i. Solomon Is
250 C3 San Cristóbal Venez.
250 □ San Cristóbal, Isla i. Islas Galápagos Ecuador
242 □P11 San Cristóbal, Volcán vol. Nic.
San Cristóbal de Cea Spain see Cea
182 I4 San Cristóbal de Entreviñas Spain
244 D4 San Cristóbal de la Barranca Mex.
216 □3a San Cristóbal de la Laguna Tenerife Canary Is
243 M9 San Cristóbal de las Casas Mex.
183 K6 San Cristóbal de la Vega Spain
241 S9 San Cristobal Wash watercourse AZ U.S.A.
193 P6 San Croce, Monte mt. Italy
184 G8 Sancti Petri, Isla i. Spain
261 F3 Sancti Spíritu Arg.
246 D3 Sancti Spíritus Cuba
246 D3 Sancti Spíritus prov. Cuba
182 H7 Sancti-Spíritus Spain
185 I3 Sancti-Spíritus Spain
157 K5 Sancy France
142 C2 Sand Norway
215 K4 Sand r. Free State S. Africa
213 F4 Sand r. Limpopo S. Africa
104 B6 Sanda Japan
100 I7 Sandagou Rus. Fed.
95 I5 Sandai Kalimantan Indon.
146 E12 Sanda Island Scotland U.K.
95 M2 Sandakan Sabah Malaysia
95 M2 Sandakan, Pelabuhan inlet Malaysia
117 L6 Sandakphu Peak Sikkim India
183 N2 Sandamendi Spain
190 E6 San Damiano d'Asti Italy
190 C7 San Damiano Macra Italy
169 K11 Sand am Main Ger.
97 H8 Sândăn Cambodia
141 I6 Sandane Norway
178 H7 San Daniele del Friuli Italy
190 I5 San Daniele Po Italy
197 L9 Sandanski Bulg.
Sandaohezi Xinjiang China see Shawan
206 C3 Sandaré Mali
170 F5 Sandau Ger.
146 L4 Sanday i. Scotland U.K.
146 K4 Sanday Sound sea chan. Scotland U.K.
149 M7 Sandbach Cheshire, England U.K.
169 J10 Sandberg Ger.
214 C8 Sandberg S. Africa
168 L1 Sandby Denmark
114 C7 Sand Cay rf India
140 L4 Sanddøla r. Norway
168 F4 Sande Ger.
141 H6 Sande Sogn og Fjordane Norway
142 G2 Sande Vestfold Norway
182 D6 Sande Port.
142 G2 Sandefjord Norway
142 G2 Sandefjord (Torp) airport Norway
142 B2 Sandeid Norway
82 □3 Sandell Bay S. Pacific Ocean
140 P2 Sandelva Norway
195 K4 San Demetrio Corone Italy
193 L3 San Demetrio ne Vestini Italy
263 D2 Sandercock Nunataks nunataks Antarctica
241 W6 Sanders AZ U.S.A.
171 F7 Sandersdorf Ger.
169 I8 Sandershausen (Niestetal) Ger.
171 E7 Sandersleben Ger.
237 D10 Sanderson TX U.S.A.
231 F9 Sandersville GA U.S.A.
168 J3 Sandesneben Ger.
86 F5 Sandfire Roadhouse W.A. Austr.
142 D2 Sandfloeggi mt. Norway
232 E10 Sand Fork WV U.S.A.
146 K4 Sandgarth Orkney, Scotland U.K.
172 F3 Sandhausen Ger.
146 G13 Sandhead Dumfries and Galloway, Scotland U.K.
236 G2 Sand Hill r. MN U.S.A.
236 D5 Sand Hills NE U.S.A.
140 M3 Sandhornøy i. Norway
151 K5 Sandhurst Bracknell Forest, England U.K.
116 H6 Sandi Uttar Prad. India
252 C3 Sandia Peru
182 E4 Sandiás Spain
242 G3 San Diego Chihuahua Mex.
239 J11 San Diego Chihuahua Mex.
244 G4 San Diego Guanajuato Mex.
240 O9 San Diego CA U.S.A.
237 F12 San Diego TX U.S.A.
259 D9 San Diego, Cabo c. Arg.
242 E2 San Diego, Sierra mts Mex.
245 H6 San Diego Alcalá Mex.
251 E2 San Diego de Cabrutica Venez.
245 H3 San Dieguito Mex.
199 L4 Sandıklı Turkey
116 H6 Sandila Uttar Prad. India
231 □2 Sandilands Village New Prov. Bahamas
156 D8 Sandillon France
87 C8 Sandiman, Mount hill W.A. Austr.
195 □ San Dimitri, Il-Ponta ta' pt Gozo Malta
94 D6 Sanding i. Indon.
245 M9 San Dionisio del Mar Mex.
226 D3 Sand Island WI U.S.A.
134 L2 Sandivey r. Rus. Fed.
170 I5 Sandkrug Ger.
179 K2 Sandl Austria
224 C4 Sand Lake Ont. Can.
223 M5 Sand Lake l. Ont. Can.
142 B3 Sandnes Norway
146 □M2 Sandness Shetland, Scotland U.K.
140 L3 Sandnessjøen Norway
Sandø i. Faroe Is see Sandoy
182 H7 Sando Spain
209 D7 Sandoa Dem. Rep. Congo
175 J5 Sandomierska, Kotlina basin Pol.
175 J5 Sandomierz Pol.
197 N4 Sândominic Romania
193 O3 San Domino, Isola i. Italy
250 B4 Sandoná Col.
195 N3 San Donaci Italy
191 N4 San Donà di Piave Italy
195 O3 San Donato di Lecce Italy
193 Q8 San Donato di Ninea Italy
190 G5 San Donato Milanese Italy
193 L4 San Donato Val di Comino Italy
177 J5 Sándorfalva Hungary
84 F6 Sandover watercourse N.T. Austr.
139 T3 Sandovo Rus. Fed.
263 G2 Sandow, Mount Antarctica
Sandoway Myanmar see Thandwè
151 J6 Sandown Isle of Wight, England U.K.
214 C10 Sandown Bay S. Africa
144 D1 Sandoy i. Faroe Is
140 I5 Sandøy Norway
150 D7 Sandplace Cornwall, England U.K.
238 F2 Sandpoint ID U.S.A.
146 B9 Sandray i. Scotland U.K.
151 L4 Sandridge Hertfordshire, England U.K.
84 G8 Sandringham Qld Austr.
215 P2 Sand River Reservoir Swaziland
176 G6 Šandrovac Croatia
140 N4 Sandsele Sweden
149 P4 Sandsend North Yorkshire, England U.K.
222 D4 Sandspit B.C. Can.
237 G7 Sand Springs OK U.S.A.
240 N2 Sand Springs Salt Flat NV U.S.A.
215 K3 Sandspruit r. S. Africa
168 G4 Sandstedt Ger.
232 H11 Sandston VA U.S.A.
87 E9 Sandstone W.A. Austr.
226 B3 Sandstone MN U.S.A.
240 N7 Sandstone Peak hill CA U.S.A.
241 T9 Sand Tank Mountains AZ U.S.A.
215 M2 Sandton S. Africa
234 E3 Sandts Eddy PA U.S.A.
108 F6 Sandu Guizhou China
109 I6 Sandu Hunan China
114 E5 Sandur Karnataka India
227 L6 Sandusky MI U.S.A.
232 C7 Sandusky OH U.S.A.
232 C7 Sandusky Bay OH U.S.A.
214 C7 Sandveld mts S. Africa
215 J3 Sandveld Nature Reserve S. Africa
214 B2 Sandverhaar Namibia
142 G2 Sandvika Akershus Norway
140 L5 Sandvika Nord-Trøndelag Norway
143 M1 Sandviken Sweden
214 I9 Sandvlakte S. Africa
151 O5 Sandwich Kent, England U.K.
233 O7 Sandwich MA U.S.A.
225 J2 Sandwich Bay Nfld and Lab. Can.
212 B4 Sandwich Bay Namibia
Sandwich Island Vanuatu see Éfaté
Sandwich Islands N. Pacific Ocean see Hawai'ian Islands
117 M8 Sandwip Bangl.
117 M8 Sandwip Channel Bangl.
151 L3 Sandy Bedfordshire, England U.K.
238 I6 Sandy UT U.S.A.
233 □P4 Sandy r. ME U.S.A.
223 K4 Sandy Bay Sask. Can.
185 □ Sandy Bay b. Gibraltar
246 □ Sandy Bay Jamaica
80 I2 Sandy Bay b. North I. N.Z.
82 □3 Sandy Bay b. S. Pacific Ocean
216 □2b Sandy Bay b. St Helena
87 G12 Sandy Bight b. W.A. Austr.
85 N8 Sandy Cape Qld Austr.
83 J9 Sandy Cape Tas. Austr.
84 G5 Sandy Creek r. Qld Austr.
148 H5 Sandygate Isle of Man
235 I2 Sandy Hook CT U.S.A.
232 B10 Sandy Hook KY U.S.A.
235 G4 Sandy Hook pt NJ U.S.A.
86 F3 Sandy Island W.A. Austr.
Sandy Island Rodrigues I. Mauritius see Sables, Île aux
123 J3 Sandykgaçy Turkm.
123 J2 Sandykly Gumy des. Turkm.
222 H4 Sandy Lake Alta Can.
223 M4 Sandy Lake Ont. Can.
223 M4 Sandy Lake l. Ont. Can.
216 □2c Sandy Point Tristan da Cunha S. Atlantic Ocean
247 □2 Sandy Point Town St Kitts and Nevis
231 E9 Sandy Springs GA U.S.A.
232 D10 Sandyville WV U.S.A.
160 G3 Sâne r. France
165 I9 Sanem Lux.
182 I3 San Emiliano Spain
261 G4 San Enrique Arg.
253 F6 San Estanislao Para.
242 □Q10 San Esteban Hond.
245 J3 San Esteban Mex.
242 C3 San Esteban, Isla i. Mex.
245 J6 San Esteban Cuautempan Mex.
183 N5 San Esteban de Gormaz Spain
182 I7 San Esteban de la Sierra Spain
260 B5 San Fabián de Alico Chile
193 P6 San Fele Italy
193 M5 San Felice a Cancello Italy
193 K5 San Felice Circeo Italy
182 G7 San Felices de los Gallegos Spain
191 K6 San Felice sul Panaro Italy
260 B3 San Felipe Chile
242 B2 San Felipe Baja California Mex.
242 F4 San Felipe Chihuahua Mex.
244 F4 San Felipe Guanajuato Mex.
183 Q8 San Felipe mt. Spain
250 D2 San Felipe Venez.
246 B3 San Felipe, Cayos de is Cuba
241 Q8 San Felipe Creek watercourse CA U.S.A.
244 E1 San Felipe de Teyra Mex.
244 E1 San Felipe Nuevo Mercurio Mex.
245 K8 San Felipe Usila Mex.
San Feliú de Guíxols Spain see Sant Feliu de Guíxols
San Feliú de Pallarols Spain see Sant Feliu de Pallerols
San Feliú Sasssera Spain see Sant Feliu Sasserra
252 A6 San Félix, Isla i. Islas de los Desventurados S. Pacific Ocean
195 J7 San Ferdinando Italy
193 Q5 San Ferdinando di Puglia Italy
261 H4 San Fernando Arg.
260 B4 San Fernando Chile
242 B3 San Fernando Baja California Mex.
243 J5 San Fernando Tamaulipas Mex.
92 C3 San Fernando Luzon Phil.
92 C4 San Fernando Luzon Phil.
184 G8 San Fernando Spain
247 □7 San Fernando Trin. and Tob.
240 N7 San Fernando CA U.S.A.
250 E3 San Fernando de Apure Venez.
250 E3 San Fernando de Atabapo Venez.
183 M8 San Fernando de Henares Spain
193 Q9 San Fili Italy
195 I7 San Filippo del Mela Sicilia Italy
182 F6 Sanfins do Douro Port.
141 L5 Sånfjället nationalpark nat. park Sweden
87 C9 Sanford r. W.A. Austr.
231 G11 Sanford FL U.S.A.
233 □O5 Sanford ME U.S.A.
226 J6 Sanford MI U.S.A.
231 H8 Sanford NC U.S.A.
247 □7 San Francique Trin. and Tob.
261 F2 San Francisco Arg.

252 D3 San Francisco Bol.
244 F2 San Francisco San Luis Potosí Mex.
245 H3 San Francisco San Luis Potosí Mex.
242 C2 San Francisco Sonora Mex.
240 J4 San Francisco CA U.S.A.
239 J10 San Francisco r. NM U.S.A.
246 H8 San Francisco Venez.
250 A4 San Francisco, Cabo de c. Ecuador
258 C2 San Francisco, Paso de pass Arg.
242 C4 San Francisco, Sierra mts Mex.
240 J4 San Francisco Bay inlet CA U.S.A.
245 K10 San Francisco Cozoaltepec Mex.
261 G6 San Francisco de Bellocq Arg.
242 G4 San Francisco de Conchos Mex.
258 E3 San Francisco del Chañar Arg.
260 D3 San Francisco del Monte de Oro Arg.
242 G4 San Francisco del Oro Mex.
253 E5 San Francisco del Parapetí Bol.
244 F4 San Francisco del Rincón Mex.
246 H4 San Francisco de Macorís Dom. Rep.
260 B3 San Francisco de Mostazal Chile
259 D8 San Francisco de Paula, Cabo c. Arg.
245 I2 San Francisco el Alto Mex.
242 □O11 San Francisco Gotera El Salvador
187 H10 San Francisco Javier Spain
194 H7 San Fratello Sicilia Italy
190 C6 Sanfront Italy
209 B7 Sanga Angola
209 F6 Sanga Dem. Rep. Congo
260 B3 San Gabriel Chile
250 B4 San Gabriel Ecuador
242 C3 San Gabriel, Punta pt Mex.
245 J7 San Gabriel Chilac Mex.
240 N7 San Gabriel Mountains CA U.S.A.
129 K5 Sängäçal Burnu pt Azer.
Sangachaly Azer. see Sanqaçal
94 F6 Sangaigerong Sumatera Indon.
108 B3 Sa'ngain Xizang China
182 D8 Sangalhos Port.
252 A3 San Gallan, Isla i. Peru
114 F5 Sangam Andhra Prad. India
114 C4 Sangameshwar Mahar. India
114 D3 Sangamner Mahar. India
236 J5 Sangamon r. IL U.S.A.
123 K5 Sangan Afgh.
122 H4 Sangān Khorāsān Iran
122 I4 Sangan Iran
123 I7 Sangān Sīstān va Balūchestān Iran
123 L7 Sangan Pak.
123 K5 Sangān, Kūh-e mt. Afgh.
123 N6 Sangar r. Pak.
131 N3 Sangar Rus. Fed.
183 L7 Sangarcía Spain
206 B4 Sangaréa Guinea
114 F4 Sangareddi Andhra Prad. India
206 B4 Sangarédi Guinea
116 E5 Sangaria Rajasthan India
95 L5 Sangasanga Kalimantan Indon.
92 B9 Sanga Sanga i. Phil.
Sangasso Mali see Zangasso
138 J4 Sangaste Estonia
208 A5 Sangatanga Gabon
156 C2 Sangatte France
192 B8 San Gavino Monreale Sardegna Italy
250 B5 Sangay, Parque Nacional nat. park Ecuador
250 B5 Sangay, Volcán vol. Ecuador
111 K11 Sangba Xizang China
141 M5 Sångbäcken Sweden
122 H4 Sang Bast Iran
207 I5 Sangbé Cameroon
92 C8 Sangboy Islands Phil.
123 I5 Sangbur Afgh.
93 A8 Sangeang i. Indon.
106 I6 Sangejing Nei Mongol China
193 J2 San Gemini Italy
261 G3 San Genaro Arg.
Sangenjo Galicia Spain see Sanxenxo
195 O2 San Gennaro, Capo c. Italy
197 M4 Sângeorgiu de Pădure Romania
197 M3 Sângeorz-Băi Romania
106 B5 Sangequanzi Xinjiang China
197 M4 Sânger Romania
240 M5 Sanger CA U.S.A.
Sângera Moldova see Sîngera
Sângerei Moldova see Sîngerei
233 J6 Sangerfield NY U.S.A.
171 D8 Sangerhausen Ger.
261 F6 San German Arg.
247 □1 San Germán Puerto Rico
161 K7 San Germano Chisone Italy
260 D3 San Gerónimo Arg.
Sang-e Sar Iran see Mehdīshahr
107 N6 Sanggan He r. China
95 M9 Sanggar, Teluk b. Sumbawa Indon.
95 I4 Sanggau Kalimantan Indon.
95 H4 Sanggauledo Kalimantan Indon.
93 D2 Sanggeluhang i. Indon.
107 R8 Sanggou Wan b. China
207 F4 Sangha Burkina
208 B4 Sangha admin. reg. Congo
208 C5 Sangha r. Congo
208 C4 Sangha-Mbaéré pref. C.A.R.
123 M8 Sanghar Pak.
191 K2 San Giacomo, Cima mt. Italy
190 I2 San Giacomo, Lago di l. Italy
250 C3 San Gil Col.
106 D1 Sangilen, Nagor'ye mts Rus. Fed.
195 □ San Ġiljan Malta
191 K9 San Gimignano Italy
123 K5 Sangīn Afgh.
183 R7 San Ginés mt. Spain
193 K1 San Ginesio Italy
193 L5 San Giorgio a Liri Italy
191 N3 San Giorgio della Richinvelda Italy
191 O4 San Giorgio di Nogaro Italy
191 K6 San Giorgio di Piano Italy
195 M3 San Giorgio Ionico Italy
193 N5 San Giorgio la Molara Italy
195 K3 San Giorgio Lucano Italy
193 O7 San Giovanni a Piro Italy
190 H4 San Giovanni Bianco Italy
192 H1 San Giovanni d'Asso Italy
194 F8 San Giovanni Gemini Sicilia Italy
193 K4 San Giovanni Incarico Italy
190 I5 San Giovanni in Croce Italy
195 L5 San Giovanni in Fiore Italy
191 K6 San Giovanni in Persiceto Italy
191 K5 San Giovanni Lupatoto Italy
193 P4 San Giovanni Rotondo Italy
192 B9 San Giovanni Suegiu Sardegna Italy
193 M3 San Giovanni Teatino Italy
191 L8 San Giovanni Valdarno Italy
116 E9 Sangir Mahar. India
93 D2 Sangir i. Indon.
93 D2 Sangir, Kepulauan is Indon.
195 K2 San Giuliano, Lago di l. Italy
190 I8 San Giuliano Terme Italy
194 E8 San Giuseppe Jato Sicilia Italy
194 H2 San Giuseppe Vesuviano Italy
191 M8 San Giustino Italy
106 I3 Sangiyn Dalay Mongolia
106 F2 Sangiyn Dalay Nuur salt l. Mongolia
101 F10 Sangju S. Korea
95 J7 Sangkapura Jawa Indon.
93 A6 Sangkarang, Kepulauan is Indon.
97 F8 Sângke, Stœng r. Cambodia
97 D7 Sangkhla Buri Thai.
95 M4 Sangkulirang Kalimantan Indon.
95 M4 Sangkulirang, Teluk b. Indon.
123 O6 Sangla Pak.
114 D4 Sangli Mahar. India
123 N3 Sanglich Afgh.
183 K2 San Glorio, Puerto de pass Spain
207 H6 Sangmélima Cameroon
116 G4 Sangnam Hima. Prad. India
111 K12 Sangngagqoiling Xizang China
213 F4 Sango Zimbabwe
116 F7 Sangod Rajasthan India
191 L8 San Godenzo Italy
114 D4 Sangole Mahar. India
187 C12 Sangonera r. Spain
240 P7 San Gorgonio Mountain CA U.S.A.
190 F2 San Gottardo, Passo del pass Switz.
93 F2 Sangowo Maluku Indon.
Sangpi Sichuan China see Xiangcheng
108 A4 Sang Qu r. Xizang China
239 K7 Sangre de Cristo Range mts CO U.S.A.
261 F4 San Gregorio Arg.
260 B5 San Gregorio Chile
261 I3 San Gregorio Uru.
258 G4 San Gregorio de Polanca Uru.
193 O6 San Gregorio Magno Italy
193 M5 San Gregorio Matese Italy
247 □7 Sangre Grande Trin. and Tob.
183 K9 Sangrera r. Spain
111 K12 Sangri Xizang China
193 N3 Sangro r. Italy
175 L1 Sangrūda Lith.
108 B2 Sangruma Qinghai China
116 E4 Sangrur Punjab India
111 H12 Sangsang Xizang China
117 M8 Sangu r. Bangl.
222 H4 Sangudo Alta Can.
253 F2 Sangue r. Brazil
183 R3 Sangüesa Spain
190 G5 San Guiliano Milanese Italy
261 G2 San Guillermo Arg.
258 C3 San Guillermo, Parque Nacional nat. park Arg.
186 H4 San Guim de Freixenet Spain
192 B4 Sanguinaires, Îles i. Corse France
163 B7 Sanguinet France
191 K5 Sanguinetto Italy
122 G7 Sangū'īyeh Iran
261 H2 San Gustavo Arg.
123 N2 Sangvor Tajik.
Sangyuan Hebei China see Wuqiao
108 H4 Sangzhi Hunan China
206 D4 Sanhala Côte d'Ivoire
Sanhe Guizhou China see Sandu
107 Q1 Sanhe Nei Mongol China
109 K3 Sanhezhen Anhui China
242 D5 San Hilario Mex.
San Hilario Sacalm Spain see Sant Hilari Sacalm
242 B4 San Hipólito, Punta pt Mex.
203 F2 Sanhūr Egypt
231 F12 Sanibel Island FL U.S.A.
261 H5 San Ignacio Arg.
243 O9 San Ignacio Belize
252 D3 San Ignacio Beni Bol.
252 E4 San Ignacio Santa Cruz Bol.
253 E4 San Ignacio Santa Cruz Bol.
242 C3 San Ignacio Baja California Mex.
242 C4 San Ignacio Baja California Sur Mex.
244 A2 San Ignacio Sinaloa Mex.
242 D2 San Ignacio Sonora Mex.
253 F6 San Ignacio Para.
250 B6 San Ignacio Peru
242 C4 San Ignacio, Laguna l. Mex.
224 E1 Sanikiluaq Nunavut Can.
183 M7 San Ildefonso Spain
92 D3 San Ildefonso Peninsula Luzon Phil.
104 A4 Sanin-kaigan Kokuritsu-kōen nat. park Japan
215 N5 Sanipas pass S. Africa
Sanirajak Nunavut Can. see Hall Beach
260 D3 San Isidro Arg.
245 K10 San Isidro Oaxaca Mex.
245 I1 San Isidro Tamaulipas Mex.
244 E1 San Isidro Zacatecas Mex.
183 J2 San Isidro, Puerto de pass Spain
245 L10 San Isidro Chacalapa Mex.
245 K10 San Isidro del Palmar Mex.
197 K3 Sanislău Romania
170 F2 Sanitz Ger.
202 C3 Sāniyat al Fawākhir well Libya
250 C2 San Jacinto Col.
92 D5 San Jacinto Masbate Phil.
240 P8 San Jacinto CA U.S.A.
240 P8 San Jacinto Peak CA U.S.A.
117 K8 Sanjai r. Jharkhand India
261 H2 San Jaime Arg.
261 H2 San Javier Arg.
252 D3 San Javier Beni Bol.
253 E4 San Javier Santa Cruz Bol.
245 H5 San Javier Mex.
187 D12 San Javier Spain
261 H3 San Javier Uru.
260 B4 San Javier de Loncomilla Chile
123 M6 Sanjawi Pak.
122 C3 Sanjbod Iran
244 G8 San Jerónimo Guerrero Mex.
244 D2 San Jerónimo Zacatecas Mex.
252 B1 San Jerónimo Peru
245 K9 San Jerónimo Taviche Mex.
Sanjiang Guangdong China see Liannan
108 G6 Sanjiang Guangxi China
Sanjiang Guizhou China see Jinping
107 R5 Sanjiangkou Liaoning China
Sanjiaocheng Qinghai China see Haiyan
108 H4 Sanjiaoping Hunan China
109 M4 Sanjie Zhejiang China
103 P9 Sanjō Japan
252 D3 San Joaquín Bol.
245 H5 San Joaquin Mex.
253 F6 San Joaquin Para.
240 L5 San Joaquin CA U.S.A.
240 K3 San Joaquin r. CA U.S.A.
240 L4 San Joaquin Valley CA U.S.A.
237 D8 San Jon NM U.S.A.
186 F6 San Jordi Spain
260 D3 San Jorge San Luis Arg.
261 G2 San Jorge Santa Fé Arg.
78 □6 San Jorge i. Solomon Is
259 D7 San Jorge, Golfo de g. Arg.
San Jorge, Golfo de g. Spain see Sant Jordi, Golf de
184 E3 San Jorge de Alor Spain
260 C3 San José Arg.
250 D4 San José Col.
242 □Q13 San José Costa Rica
244 G1 San Jose Mex.
92 C4 San Jose Luzon Phil.
92 C5 San Jose Mindoro Phil.
92 C5 San Jose Mindoro Phil.
185 O7 San José Andalucía Spain
261 I4 San José dept Uru.
261 I4 San José r. Uru.
240 K4 San Jose CA U.S.A.
239 L9 San Jose NM U.S.A.
239 K9 San Jose watercourse NM U.S.A.
250 E2 San José Venez.
259 D7 San José, Cabo c. Arg.
261 I2 San José, Cuchilla de hills Uru.
259 D6 San José, Golfo g. Arg.
242 D5 San José, Isla i. Mex.
260 C3 San José, Volcán vol. Chile
244 G6 San Jose Allende Mex.
243 N8 San José Carpizo Mex.
244 G4 San José de Alburquerque Mex.
251 F2 San José de Amacuro Venez.
242 F3 San José de Bavicora Mex.
92 C6 San Jose de Buenavista Panay Phil.
253 E4 San José de Chiquitos Bol.
242 D4 San José de Comondú Mex.
261 H2 San José de Feliciano Arg.
244 G3 San José de Gallinas Mex.
244 E3 San Jose de Gracia Mex.
242 C4 San José de Gracia Baja California Sur Mex.
244 D6 San José de Gracia Michoacán Mex.
242 F4 San José de Gracia Sinaloa Mex.
242 D3 San José de Gracia Sonora Mex.
247 K9 San José de Guaribe Venez.
260 C2 San Jose de Jáchal Arg.
242 E5 San Joséde la Brecha Mex.
261 F2 San José de la Dormida Arg.
261 G3 San José de la Esquina Arg.
259 B5 San José de la Mariquina Chile
244 D7 San José de la Montaña Mex.
260 E2 San José de las Salinas Arg.
258 E2 San José del Boquerón Arg.
242 E6 San José del Cabo Mex.
250 C4 San José del Guaviare Col.
260 E3 San José del Morro Arg.
245 J9 San José del Progreso Mex.
184 H7 San José del Valle Spain
260 B3 San José de Maipó Chile
261 I4 San José de Mayo Uru.
246 H4 San José de Ocoa Dom. Rep.
250 D3 San José de Ocuné Col.
239 I12 San José de Primas Mex.
244 G1 San José de Raíces Mex.
244 D1 San José de Reyes Mex.
244 G4 San José Iturbide Mex.
111 D8 Sanju Xinjiang China
260 C2 San Juan Arg.
260 C2 San Juan prov. Arg.
253 E4 San Juan Bol.
216 □3a San Juan Tenerife Canary Is
250 B2 San Juan Col.
250 B3 San Juan r. Col.
242 □R12 San Juan r. Costa Rica/Nic.
246 C3 San Juan mt. Cuba
246 H4 San Juan Dom. Rep.
242 F4 San Juan Chihuahua Mex.
243 I4 San Juan Coahuila Mex.
244 E2 San Juan Zacatecas Mex.
244 E4 San Juan r. Mex.
245 L7 San Juan r. Mex.
252 B3 San Juan Peru
92 E6 San Juan Leyte Phil.
92 F7 San Juan Mindanao Phil.
247 □1 San Juan Puerto Rico
183 O2 San Juan Spain
184 G3 San Juan r. Spain
247 □7 San Juan Trin. and Tob.
240 L6 San Juan r. CA U.S.A.
241 V4 San Juan r. UT U.S.A.
251 E3 San Juan Venez.
247 □1 San Juan, Bahía de b. Puerto Rico
259 E9 San Juan, Cabo c. Arg.
207 H6 San Juan, Cabo c. Equat. Guinea
183 L8 San Juan, Embalse de resr Spain
242 □O11 San Juan, Punta pt El Salvador
185 I7 San Juan, Sierra de hills Spain
245 J8 San Juan Achiutla Mex.
253 F6 San Juan Bautista Para.
252 □ San Juan Bautista S. Pacific Ocean
240 K5 San Juan Bautista CA U.S.A.
245 I9 San Juan Bautista lo de Soto Mex.
245 J8 San Juan Bautista Suchitepec Mex.
245 K7 San Juan Bautista Tuxtepec Mex.
240 O8 San Juan Capistrano CA U.S.A.
242 □P10 San Juancito Hond.
244 B5 San Juan de Abajo Mex.
187 E11 San Juan de Alicante Spain
184 G6 San Juan de Aznalfarache Spain
250 C2 San Juan de Cesar Col.
244 E1 San Juan de Guadalupe Mex.
246 F8 San Juan de Guía, Cabo de c. Col.
259 B6 San Juan dela Costa Chile
186 D3 San Juan de la Peña, Sierra de mts Spain
245 H6 San Juan de las Huertas Mex.
242 □R12 San Juan del Norte Nic.
242 □R12 San Juan del Norte, Bahía de b. Nic.
250 D2 San Juan de los Cayos Venez.
244 E4 San Juan de los Lagos Mex.
250 E2 San Juan de los Morros Venez.
244 D4 San Juan de los Potreros Mex.
184 F6 San Juan del Puerto Spain
242 G5 San Juan del Río Durango Mex.
245 L8 San Juan del Río Oaxaca Mex.
245 H5 San Juan del Río Querétaro Mex.
242 □Q12 San Juan del Sur Nic.
259 E9 San Juan de Salvamento Arg.
245 L8 San Juan Evangelista Mex.
242 C4 San Juanico, Punta pt Mex.
238 C2 San Juan Islands WA U.S.A.
242 F4 San Juanito Mex.
244 A4 San Juanito, Isla i. Mex.
245 J7 San Juan Ixcaquixtla Mex.
243 N10 San Juan Ixcoy Guat.
245 L9 San Juan Lachixila Mex.
245 L8 San Juan Mazatlán Mex.
245 K9 San Juan Mixtepec Mex.
239 K8 San Juan Mountains CO U.S.A.
245 K8 San Juan Tepeuxila Mex.
246 B2 San Juan y Martínez Cuba
111 D8 Sanju He watercourse China
259 D8 San Julián Arg.
244 E4 San Julian Mex.
186 D6 San Just mt. Spain
261 G2 San Justo Arg.
182 H4 San Justo de la Vega Spain
96 C4 Sanka Myanmar
206 C4 Sankanbiaiwa mt. Sierra Leone
206 C4 Sankarani r. Côte d'Ivoire/Guinea
114 E8 Sankarankovil Tamil Nadu India
114 D4 Sankeshwar Karnataka India
117 J8 Sankh r. Jharkhand India
122 G3 Sankhāş Iran
116 E5 Sankhu Rajasthan India
Sankosh r. Bhutan see Sunkosh Chhu
116 I9 Sankra Chhattisgarh India
116 C6 Sankra Rajasthan India
179 M4 Sankt Aegyd am Neuwalde Austria
179 K6 Sankt Andrä Austria
179 O4 Sankt Andrä am Zicksee Austria
169 K7 Sankt Andreasberg Ger.
179 M6 Sankt Anna am Aigen Austria
178 B5 Sankt Anton am Arlberg Austria
179 L4 Sankt Anton an der Jeßnitz Austria
169 D9 Sankt Augustin Ger.
172 E6 Sankt Blasien Ger.
171 G9 Sankt Egidien Ger.
179 K4 Sankt Gallen Austria
190 G1 Sankt Gallen Switz.
190 G1 Sankt Gallen canton Switz.
178 A5 Sankt Gallenkirch Austria
171 E9 Sankt Gangloff Ger.
179 J6 Sankt Georgen am Längsee Austria
179 K3 Sankt Georgen am Walde Austria
179 J3 Sankt Georgen an der Gusen Austria
179 H4 Sankt Georgen im Attergau Austria
179 K6 Sankt Georgen im Lavanttal Austria
172 E5 Sankt Georgen im Schwarzwald Ger.
179 H4 Sankt Gilgen Austria
169 E10 Sankt Goar Ger.
169 E10 Sankt Goarshausen Ger.
Sankt Gotthard Hungary see Szentgotthárd
172 C3 Sankt Ingbert Ger.
179 J6 Sankt Jakob im Rosental Austria
179 M5 Sankt Jakob im Walde Austria
178 F6 Sankt Jakob in Defereggen Austria
179 J5 Sankt Johann am Tauern Austria
178 H5 Sankt Johann im Pongau Austria
179 L6 Sankt Johann im Saggautal Austria
178 G6 Sankt Johann im Walde Austria
178 F4 Sankt Johann in Tirol Austria
172 D2 Sankt Julian Ger.
179 K6 Sankt Kanzian am Klopeiner See Austria
179 J5 Sankt Lambrecht Austria
179 L3 Sankt Leonhard am Forst Austria
179 M2 Sankt Leonhard am Hornerwald Austria
178 C5 Sankt Leonhard im Pitztal Austria
179 H4 Sankt Lorenz Austria
178 H6 Sankt Lorenzen im Gitschtal Austria
178 G6 Sankt Lorenzen im Lesachtal Austria
179 L5 Sankt Lorenzen im Mürztal Austria
179 J5 Sankt Lorenzen ob Murau Austria
179 L5 Sankt Marein im Mürztal Austria
179 J6 Sankt Margareten im Rosental Austria
168 H3 Sankt Margarethen Ger.
179 M5 Sankt Margarethen an der Raab Austria
179 K5 Sankt Margarethen bei Knittelfeld Austria
179 O4 Sankt Margarethen im Burgenland Austria
172 E5 Sankt Märgen Ger.
179 J3 Sankt Marien Austria
179 I3 Sankt Marienkirchen an der Polsenz Austria
179 K2 Sankt Martin Niederösterreich Austria
179 H5 Sankt Martin Salzburg Austria
179 N6 Sankt Martin an der Raab Austria
179 J3 Sankt Martin im Mühlkreis Austria
179 L6 Sankt Martin im Sulmtal Austria
179 N5 Sankt Michael im Burgenland Austria
179 I5 Sankt Michael im Lungau Austria
179 L5 Sankt Michael in Obersteiermark Austria
168 H3 Sankt Michaelisdonn Ger.
190 H2 Sankt Moritz Switz.
190 D3 Sankt Niklaus Switz.
179 L6 Sankt Nikolai im Saustal Austria
179 J5 Sankt Nikolai im Sölktal Austria
179 K2 Sankt Oswald bei Freistadt Austria
179 L6 Sankt Oswald ob Eibiswald Austria
173 O4 Sankt Oswald-Riedlhütte Ger.
179 J4 Sankt Pankraz Austria
178 G3 Sankt Pantaleon Austria
179 K6 Sankt Paul im Lavanttal Austria
172 E5 Sankt Peter Ger.
178 H3 Sankt Peter am Hart Austria
179 J5 Sankt Peter am Kammersberg Austria
179 M6 Sankt Peter am Ottersbach Austria
139 N2 Sankt-Peterburg Rus. Fed.
179 L5 Sankt Peter-Freienstein Austria
179 L6 Sankt Peter im Sulmtal Austria
179 K3 Sankt Peter in der Au Austria
168 G2 Sankt Peter-Ording Ger.
Sankt Petersburg Rus. Fed. see Sankt-Peterburg
179 M3 Sankt Pölten Austria
178 G3 Sankt Radegund Austria
179 M5 Sankt Ruprecht an der Raab Austria
179 K6 Sankt Stefan Austria
179 I6 Sankt Stefan im Gailtal Austria
179 M6 Sankt Stefan im Rosental Austria
179 K5 Sankt Stefan ob Leoben Austria
179 L6 Sankt Stefan ob Stainz Austria
178 G4 Sankt Ulrich am Pillersee Austria
179 J3 Sankt Ulrich bei Steyr Austria
179 J6 Sankt Urban Austria
179 K3 Sankt Valentin Austria
179 M6 Sankt Veit am Vogau Austria
179 J6 Sankt Veit an der Glan Austria
179 M3 Sankt Veit an der Gölsen Austria
178 H5 Sankt Veit im Pongau Austria
178 F6 Sankt Veit in Defereggen Austria
172 C3 Sankt Wendel Ger.
173 M5 Sankt Wolfgang Ger.
179 H4 Sankt Wolfgang im Salzkammergut Austria
116 F2 Sanku Jammu and Kashmir
209 D6 Sankuru r. Dem. Rep. Congo
195 □ San Lawrenz Gozo Malta
253 F5 San Lázaro Para.
242 C5 San Lázaro, Cabo c. Mex.
242 E6 San Lázaro, Sierra de mts Mex.
191 K7 San Lazzaro di Savena Italy
240 J4 San Leandro CA U.S.A.
191 M8 San Leo Italy
194 F8 San Leonardo r. Sicilia Italy
183 N5 San Leonardo de Yagüe Spain
191 K2 San Leonardo in Passiria Italy
126 I5 Şanlıurfa Turkey
128 H1 Şanlıurfa prov. Turkey
258 F3 San Lorenzo Corrientes Arg.
261 G3 San Lorenzo Santa Fé Arg.
252 D3 San Lorenzo Beni Bol.
252 D2 San Lorenzo Pando Bol.
252 D5 San Lorenzo Tarija Bol.
250 B4 San Lorenzo Ecuador
242 □P11 San Lorenzo Hond.
195 J8 San Lorenzo Italy
242 F3 San Lorenzo Mex.
252 C2 San Lorenzo Peru
183 O4 San Lorenzo mt. Spain
250 A5 San Lorenzo, Cabo c. Ecuador
192 D9 San Lorenzo, Capo c. Sardegna Italy
259 B7 San Lorenzo, Cerro mt. Arg./Chile
242 C3 San Lorenzo, Isla i. Mex.
252 A3 San Lorenzo, Isla i. Peru
190 D8 San Lorenzo al Mare Italy
193 Q8 San Lorenzo Bellizzi Italy
245 K8 San Lorenzo Cacaotepec Mex.
185 L4 San Lorenzo de Calatrava Spain
183 L7 San Lorenzo de El Escorial Spain
183 P9 San Lorenzo de la Parrilla Spain
San Lorenzo de Morunys Spain see Sant Llorenç de Morunys
191 L2 San Lorenzo di Sebato Italy
191 N8 San Lorenzo in Campo Italy
192 H2 San Lorenzo Nuovo Italy
195 K7 San Luca Italy
184 G7 Sanlúcar de Barrameda Spain
184 E6 Sanlúcar de Guadiana Spain
184 G6 Sanlúcar la Mayor Spain
252 D5 San Lucas Bol.
242 C4 San Lucas Baja California Sur Mex.
242 E6 San Lucas Baja California Sur Mex.
244 G7 San Lucas Michoacán Mex.
242 E6 San Lucas, Cabo c. Mex.
250 C3 San Lucas, Serranía de mts Col.
193 Q9 San Lucido Italy
260 D3 San Luis Arg.
260 D3 San Luis prov. Arg.
252 D2 San Luís Brazil
246 F3 San Luis Cuba
243 O9 San Luis Guat.
244 G8 San Luis Guerrero Mex.
245 M8 San Luis Veracruz Mex.
250 C5 San Luis Peru
241 R9 San Luis AZ U.S.A.
241 U9 San Luis AZ U.S.A.
239 L8 San Luis CO U.S.A.
250 D2 San Luis Venez.
242 B3 San Luís, Isla i. Mex.
241 R9 San Luis, Mesa de plat. Mex.
260 D3 San Luis, Sierra de mts Arg.
245 I9 San Luis Acatlán Mex.
245 K9 San Luis Amatlán Mex.
244 G4 San Luis de la Paz Mex.
258 F2 San Luis del Palmar Arg.
242 D5 San Luis Gonzaga Mex.
242 C2 San Luisito Mex.
240 L6 San Luis Obispo CA U.S.A.
240 L6 San Luis Obispo Bay CA U.S.A.
242 □O10 San Luis Pajón Hond.
244 G3 San Luis Potosí Mex.
244 G3 San Luis Potosí state Mex.
240 K4 San Luis Reservoir CA U.S.A.
242 B1 San Luis Río Colorado Mex.
192 B8 Sanluri Sardegna Italy
191 M2 San Maddalena Vallalta Italy
182 E4 San Mamede, Serra do mts Spain
183 K4 San Mamés de Campos Spain
193 Q9 San Mango d'Aquino Italy
261 H5 San Manuel Arg.
260 B3 San Manuel Chile
241 V9 San Manuel AZ U.S.A.
191 O8 San Marcello Italy
191 J7 San Marcello Pistoiese Italy
242 D5 San Marcial, Punta pt Mex.
192 A8 San Marco, Capo c. Sardegna Italy
194 E9 San Marco, Capo c. Sicilia Italy
193 Q8 San Marco Argentano Italy
194 H7 San Marco d'Alunzio Sicilia Italy
193 N5 San Marco dei Cavoti Italy
193 P4 San Marco in Lamis Italy
260 B2 San Marcos Chile
250 C2 San Marcos Col.
243 N10 San Marcos Guat.
242 □P11 San Marcos Hond.
245 H9 San Marcos Guerrero Mex.
244 C5 San Marcos Jalisco Mex.
252 A1 San Marcos Peru
182 D2 San Marcos Spain
240 O8 San Marcos CA U.S.A.
237 G11 San Marcos TX U.S.A.
237 G11 San Marcos r. TX U.S.A.
242 C4 San Marcos, Isla i. Mex.
191 M8 San Marino country Europe
191 M8 San Marino San Marino
262 T2 San Martín research stn Antarctica
258 D3 San Martín Catamarca Arg.
260 C3 San Martín Mendoza Arg.
253 E3 San Martín r. Bol.
245 I6 San Martín Mex.
252 A1 San Martín dept Peru
177 K4 Sânmartin Romania
186 A1 San Martin Spain
187 F10 San Martín, Cabo de c. Spain
259 B8 San Martín, Lago l. Arg./Chile
245 L7 San Martín, Volcán vol. Mex.
245 I4 San Martín Chalchicuautla Mex.
244 D4 San Martin de Bolaños Mex.
183 M8 San Martín de la Vega Spain
183 J8 San Martín de la Vega del Alberche Spain
259 C6 San Martín de los Andes Arg.
183 J8 San Martin del Pimpollar Spain
183 L9 San Martín de Montalbán Spain
183 K9 San Martín de Pusa Spain
183 Q3 San Martin de Unx Spain
183 L8 San Martín de Valdeiglesias Spain
244 D5 San Martín Hidalgo Mex.
191 K5 San Martino Buon Albergo Italy
191 L3 San Martino di Castrozza Italy
192 C2 San-Martino-di-Lota Corse France
191 L4 San Martino di Lupari Italy
191 L5 San Martino di Venezze Italy
191 L2 San Martino in Badia Italy
191 K2 San Martino in Passiria Italy
193 O4 San Martino in Pensilis Italy
250 D5 San Mateo Peru
San Mateo Spain see Sant Mateu
240 J4 San Mateo CA U.S.A.
251 E2 San Mateo Venez.
186 D4 San Mateo de Gállego Spain
243 N10 San Mateo Ixtatán Guat.
253 F4 San Matías Bol.
259 D6 San Matías, Golfo g. Arg.
250 E2 San Mauricio Venez.
194 G8 San Mauro Castelverde Sicilia Italy
193 Q7 San Mauro Forte Italy
191 M7 San Mauro Pascoli Italy
190 D5 San Mauro Torinese Italy
109 M4 Sanmen Zhejiang China
193 P4 San Menaio Italy
109 M4 Sanmen Wan b. China
107 L9 Sanmenxia Henan China
191 N4 San Michele al Tagliamento Italy
190 D7 San Michele Mondovì Italy
195 N2 San Michele Salentino Italy
258 F3 San Miguel Corrientes Arg.
260 D3 San Miguel San Juan Arg.
253 E4 San Miguel Bol.
252 E3 San Miguel r. Bol.
250 C4 San Miguel r. Col.
242 □O11 San Miguel El Salvador
244 B3 San Miguel Mex.
242 □T13 San Miguel Panama
252 B3 San Miguel Peru
92 C5 San Miguel Luzon Phil.
San Miguel Spain see Sant Miquel de Balansat
240 L6 San Miguel CA U.S.A.
239 J7 San Miguel r. CO U.S.A.
251 E2 San Miguel Venez.
92 D5 San Miguel Bay Luzon Phil.
245 K9 San Miguel Coatlán Mex.
216 □3a San Miguel de Abona Tenerife Canary Is
244 G5 San Miguel de Allende Mex.
183 L6 San Miguel de Arroyo Spain
183 M6 San Miguel de Bernuy Spain
244 B1 San Miguel de Cruces Mex.
244 G5 San Miguel Deheti Mex.
242 D3 San Miguel de Horcasitas r. Mex.
252 D3 San Miguel de Huachi Bol.
244 C5 San Miguel de la Sierra Mex.
261 H4 San Miguel del Monte Arg.
245 K10 San Miguel del Puerto Mex.
187 D12 San Miguel de Salinas Spain
258 D2 San Miguel de Tucumán Arg.
254 C5 San Miguel do Araguaia Brazil
244 E4 San Miguel el Alto Mex.
240 L7 San Miguel Island CA U.S.A.
92 B8 San Miguel Islands Phil.
244 G2 San Miguelito Mex.
242 □T13 San Miguelito Panama
244 G5 San Miguel Octopan Mex.
245 K9 San Miguel Sola de Vega Mex.
245 H8 San Miguel Tecuixiapan Mex.
183 N4 San Millán mt. Spain
183 O4 San Millán de la Cogolla Spain
109 K5 Sanming Fujian China
191 J8 San Miniato Italy
175 J5 Sanna r. Pol.
104 B5 Sannan Japan
92 C4 San Narciso Luzon Phil.
215 K5 Sannaspos S. Africa
195 □ Sannat Gozo Malta
190 F5 Sannazzaro de'Burgondi Italy
114 D5 Sanndatti Karnataka India
Sanndraigh i. Scotland U.K. see Sandray
123 L7 Sanni Pak.
195 L2 Sannicandro di Bari Italy
193 P4 Sannicandro Garganico Italy
195 O3 Sannicola Italy
193 P3 San Nicola, Isole is Italy
195 L5 San Nicola dell'Alto Italy
192 C3 San-Nicolao Corse France
260 A5 San Nicolás Chile
245 I9 San Nicolás Guerrero Mex.
245 I1 San Nicolás Tamaulipas Mex.
244 B6 San Nicolás r. Mex.
250 D5 San Nicolás Peru
92 C3 San Nicolas Luzon Phil.
252 B3 San Nicolás, Bahía b. Peru
244 G5 San Nicolás de los Agustinos Mex.
261 G3 San Nicolás de los Arroyos Arg.
242 G5 San Nicolás del Presidio Mex.
184 H4 San Nicolás del Puerto Spain
216 □3f San Nicolás de Tolentino Gran Canaria Canary Is
239 E10 San Nicolas Island CA U.S.A.
244 G3 San Nicolás Tolentino Mex.
196 I4 Sânnicolau Mare Romania
191 L6 San Nicolò Italy
192 B8 San Nicolò d'Arcidano Sardegna Italy
192 C9 San Nicolò Gerrei Sardegna Italy
215 J2 Sannieshof S. Africa
175 H3 Sanniki Pol.
193 N4 Sannio, Monti del mts Italy
206 C5 Sanniquellie Liberia
102 S6 Sannohe Japan
105 K3 Sano Japan
258 D3 Sañogasta, Sierra de mts Arg.
175 K6 Sanok Pol.
250 C2 San Onofre Col.
259 D9 San Pablo Arg.
252 D5 San Pablo Potosí Bol.
253 E3 San Pablo Santa Cruz Bol.
253 E3 San Pablo r. Bol.
250 D3 San Pablo Col.
245 H5 San Pablo Mex.
92 C4 San Pablo Luzon Phil.
240 J4 San Pablo CA U.S.A.
183 L9 San Pablo de los Montes Spain
San Pablo de Manta Ecuador see Manta
191 K2 San Pancrazio Italy
195 N3 San Pancrazio Salentino Italy
178 B8 San Paolo, Isola i. Italy
193 O4 San Paolo di Civitate Italy
195 □ San Pawl, Gżejjer ta' is Malta
195 □ San Pawl il-Baħar Malta
195 □ San Pawl-il-Baħar, Il-Bajja ta' b. Malta
261 H3 San Pedro Buenos Aires Arg.
258 D2 San Pedro Catamarca Arg.
260 E2 San Pedro Córdoba Arg.
258 D2 San Pedro Jujuy Arg.
258 G2 San Pedro Misiones Arg.
243 P9 San Pedro Belize
252 D3 San Pedro Beni Bol.
253 E4 San Pedro Santa Cruz Bol.
252 D4 San Pedro r. Bol.
260 B3 San Pedro Santiago Chile
260 B3 San Pedro Valparaíso Chile
206 D5 San-Pédro Côte d'Ivoire
246 D3 San Pedro r. Cuba
242 D6 San Pedro Baja California Sur Mex.
242 F3 San Pedro Chihuahua Mex.
244 B4 San Pedro r. Mex.
239 L12 San Pedro r. Mex.
252 C2 San Pedro Peru
92 C5 San Pedro Mindoro Phil.
185 O3 San Pedro Spain
261 I4 San Pedro Uru.
241 V9 San Pedro watercourse AZ U.S.A.
242 □R13 San Pedro, Punta pt Costa Rica
184 E1 San Pedro, Sierra de mts Spain
244 F4 San Pedro Almoloyan Mex.
244 C4 San Pedro Analco Mex.
245 K9 San Pedro Apóstol Mex.
243 N10 San Pedro Carchá Guat.
240 N8 San Pedro Channel CA U.S.A.
185 J8 San Pedro de Alcántara Spain
250 D3 San Pedro de Arimena Col.
252 C5 San Pedro de Atacama Chile
182 H4 San Pedro de Ceque Spain
239 J12 San Pedro de la Cueva Mex.
183 K7 San Pedro del Arroyo Spain
242 H5 San Pedro de las Colonias Mex.
183 J5 San Pedro de Latarce Spain
250 B6 San Pedro de Lloc Peru
253 F6 San Pedro del Paraná Para.
187 D12 San Pedro del Pinatar Spain
183 M2 San Pedro del Romeral Spain
247 I4 San Pedro de Macorís Dom. Rep.
182 I7 San Pedro de Rozados Spain
253 F6 San Pedro de Ycuamandyyú Para.
245 K9 San Pedro el Alto Mex.
242 D3 San Pedro el Saucito Mex.
183 P4 San Pedro Manrique Spain
242 B2 San Pedro Martir, Parque Nacional nat. park Mex.
245 J10 San Pedro Mixtepec Mex.
242 □O10 San Pedro Sula Hond.
177 J5 Sânpetru Mare Romania
191 K8 San Piero a Sieve Italy
195 H7 San Piero Patti Sicilia Italy
195 I6 San Pietro Isole Lipari Italy
192 A9 San Pietro, Isola di i. Sardegna Italy
178 G6 San Pietro di Cadore Italy
191 J4 San Pietro in Cariano Italy
191 K6 San Pietro in Casale Italy
195 O3 San Pietro Vernotico Italy
241 U2 San Pitch r. UT U.S.A.
190 I6 San Polo d'Enza Italy
191 K6 San Prospero Italy
106 G7 Sanpu Gansu China
129 K5 Sanqaçal Azer.
146 I12 Sanquhar Dumfries and Galloway, Scotland U.K.
250 B4 Sanquianga, Parque Nacional nat. park Col.
186 F4 San Quilez mt. Spain
242 A2 San Quintín, Cabo c. Mex.
192 H1 San Quirico d'Orcia Italy
260 C4 San Rafael Arg.
253 E4 San Rafael Bol.
260 B4 San Rafael Chile
250 D3 San Rafael Col.
244 F2 San Rafael San Luis Potosí Mex.
245 K5 San Rafael Veracruz Mex.
240 J4 San Rafael CA U.S.A.
241 V3 San Rafael r. UT U.S.A.
250 D2 San Rafael Venez.
San Rafael del Moján Venez. see San Rafael
242 □P11 San Rafael del Norte Nic.
186 F6 San Rafael del Río Spain
247 I4 San Rafael del Yuma Dom. Rep.
241 V3 San Rafael Knob mt. UT U.S.A.
240 L7 San Rafael Mountains CA U.S.A.
185 J5 San Rafael Navallana, Embalse de resr Spain
260 D2 San Ramón Arg.
252 D3 San Ramón Beni Bol.
253 E4 San Ramón Santa Cruz
245 I2 San Ramón Mex.
261 J4 San Ramón Uru.
109 K6 Sanrao Guangdong Chir
190 D8 San Remo Italy
235 I3 San Remo NY U.S.A.
102 S7 Sanriku Japan
237 E11 San Rodrigo watercourse
261 G6 San Román Arg.
182 F3 San Román Spain
250 D1 San Román, Cabo c. Ve
183 K4 San Román de la Cuba
183 K8 San Román de los Mor Spain
185 I8 San Roque Andalucía Sp
182 C2 San Roque Galicia Spai
182 D4 San Roque Galicia Spai
242 B4 San Roque, Punta pt M
193 O7 San Rufo Italy
237 F10 San Saba TX U.S.A.
237 F10 San Saba r. TX U.S.A.
163 I6 Sansac-de-Marmiesse France
San Sadurniño Spain se Avenida do Marqués de Figueroa
260 E2 San Salano Arg.
245 J6 San Salavador el Seco
206 B4 Sansalé Guinea
261 H2 San Salvador Arg.
246 F1 San Salvador i. Bahama
243 O11 San Salvador El Salvad
245 H1 San Salvador Mex.
250 D5 San Salvador Peru
261 H3 San Salvador r. Uru.
250 □ San Salvador, Isla i. Isla Galápagos Ecuador
183 L3 San Salvador de Cantamunda Spain
258 D2 San Salvador de Jujuy
192 A8 San Salvatore Sardegna
190 F6 San Salvatore Monferr Italy
193 M5 San Salvatore Telesino
193 N3 San Salvo Italy
207 F3 Sansané Haoussa Nige
207 F4 Sansanné-Mango Togo
259 C9 San Sebastián Arg.
244 C5 San Sebastián Mex.
247 □1 San Sebastián Puerto
182 D3 San Sebastián hill Spai
259 C9 San Sebastián, Bahía b. Arg.
182 G4 San Sebastián, Embals resr Spain
216 □3a San Sebastián de la G La Gomera Canary Is
183 M7 San Sebastián de los Spain
245 K9 San Sebastián Río Hor Mex.
245 J7 San Sebastián Zinacat Mex.
190 I6 San Secondo Parmens
191 M8 Sansepolcro Italy
192 H3 San Severa Italy
193 Q7 San Severino Lucano
191 O9 San Severino Marche
193 O4 San Severo Italy
109 M5 Sansha Fujian China
252 C2 San Silvestre Bol.
250 D2 San Silvestre Venez.
241 W9 San Simon AZ U.S.A.
188 F3 Sanski Most Bos.-Herz
183 P3 Sansol Spain
80 J7 Sanson North I. N.Z.
Sansoral Islands Palau Sonsorol Islands
193 Q8 San Sosti Italy
192 C9 San Sperate Sardegna
195 L1 San Spirito Italy
247 □2 Sans Toucher mt. Guac
108 G5 Sansui Guizhou China
252 A2 Santa Peru
252 A2 Santa r. Peru
256 C4 Santa Adélia Brazil
184 G2 Santa Amalia Spain
243 O9 Santa Amelia Guat.
261 I2 Santa Ana Entre Ríos A
258 D2 Santa Ana Tucumán Arg
252 D3 Santa Ana La Paz Bol.
253 E4 Santa Ana Santa Cruz B
253 F4 Santa Ana Santa Cruz B
243 O10 Santa Ana El Salvador
78 □1 Santa Ana Guam
245 H6 Santa Ana México Mex.
244 G1 Santa Ana Nuevo León
242 D2 Santa Ana Sonora Mex.
78 □6 Santa Ana i. Solomon Is
185 P3 Santa Ana Spain
183 L8 Santa Ana hill Spain
240 O8 Santa Ana CA U.S.A.
186 G4 Santa Ana, Embassam resr Spain
183 K9 Santa Ana de Pusa Sp
252 D3 Santa Ana de Yacuma
261 H3 Santa Anita Arg.
242 E6 Santa Anita Baja Califor Mex.
244 D5 Santa Anita Jalisco Mex
237 F10 Santa Anna TX U.S.A.
216 □1a Santa Bárbara Terceira
253 F3 Santa Bárbara Mato Gr Brazil
257 F3 Santa Bárbara Minas G Brazil
260 A5 Santa Bárbara Chile
Santa Bárbara Cuba se La Demajagua
242 □O10 Santa Bárbara Hond.
242 G4 Santa Bárbara Chihuah Mex.
244 E4 Santa Bárbara Jalisco
186 G6 Santa Bàrbara Spain
187 C10 Santa Bárbara mt. Spa
185 N6 Santa Bárbara mt. Spa
240 M7 Santa Barbara CA U.S.
250 E4 Santa Bárbara Amazon Venez.
250 D3 Santa Bárbara Barinas
257 H2 Santa Bárbara, Ilha i.
216 □1a Santa Barbara, Serra Terceira Azores
255 B7 Santa Bárbara, Serra Brazil
240 L7 Santa Barbara Channe CA U.S.A.
184 E5 Santa Bárbara de Cas
184 D5 Santa Bárbara de Pad Port.
256 D5 Santa Bárbara d'Oeste
255 B9 Santa Barbara do Sul
240 M8 Santa Barbara Island CA U.S.A.
261 I3 Santa Bernardina Uru.
216 □3f Santa Brígida Gran Car Canary Is
183 Q4 Santacara Spain
260 E3 Santa Catalina Arg.
258 C2 Santa Catalina Chile
242 □S13 Santa Catalina Panam
78 □6 Santa Catalina i. Solon
251 F2 Santa Catalina Venez.
240 O8 Santa Catalina, Gulf o U.S.A.
242 D5 Santa Catalína, Isla i.
182 C2 Santa Catalina de Arm Spain
240 N8 Santa Catalina Island CA U.S.A.
255 C8 Santa Catarina state B
242 B3 Santa Catarina Baja Ca Mex.
243 I5 Santa Catarina Nuevo Mex.
245 H4 Santa Catarina San Lu Potosí Mex.
245 I9 Santa Catarina r. Mex.
247 □10 Santa Catarina Curaça Neth. Antilles
184 C4 Santa Catarina Port.
255 C8 Santa Catarina, Ilha d' i. Brazil
195 L6 Santa Caterina dello I Italy
192 B7 Santa Caterina di Pitt Sardegna Italy
245 J9 Santa Caterina Juquil
194 G8 Santa Caterina Villarn Sicilia Italy
195 O3 Santa Cesarea Terme

Santa Cilia de Jaca Spain
Santa Clara Chile
Santa Clara Col.
Santa Clara Cuba
Santa Clara Chihuahua Mex.
Santa Clara Durango Mex.
Santa Clara r. Mex.
Santa Clara r. Mex.
Santa Clara CA U.S.A.
Santa Clara UT U.S.A.
Santa Clara r. CA U.S.A.
Santa Clara, Barragem de resr Port.
Santa Clara, Isla i. S. Pacific Ocean
Santa Clara-a-Nova Port.
Santa Clara-a-Velha Port.
Santa Clara de Buena Vista Arg.
Santa Clara de Louredo Port.
Santa Clara de Saguier Arg.
Santa Clarita CA U.S.A.
Santa Clotilde Peru
Santa Coloma de Farners Spain
Santa Coloma de Gramanet Spain
Santa Coloma de Queralt Spain
Santa Colomba de Somoza Spain
Santa Columba de Curueño Spain
Santa Comba Angola see Waku-Kungo
Santa Comba Dão Port.
Santa Comba de Rossas Port.
Santa Cristina d'Aro Spain
Santa Cristina de la Polvorosa Spain
Santa Croce, Capo c. Sicilia Italy
Santa Croce Camerina Sicilia Italy
Santa Croce del Sannio Italy
Santa Croce di Magliano Italy
Santa Croce sull'Arno Italy
Santa Cruz Arg.
Santa Cruz prov. Arg.
Santa Cruz r. Arg.
Santa Cruz Aruba
Santa Cruz Bol.
Santa Cruz dept Bol.
Santa Cruz Amazonas Brazil
Santa Cruz Espírito Santo Brazil
Santa Cruz Pará Brazil
Santa Cruz Pará Brazil
Santa Cruz Rio Grande do Norte Brazil
Santa Cruz Chile
Santa Cruz Costa Rica
Santa Cruz Jamaica
Santa Cruz Madeira
Santa Cruz Nayarit Mex.
Santa Cruz Nayarit Mex.
Santa Cruz Sonora Mex.
Santa Cruz Peru
Santa Cruz Luzon Phil.
Santa Cruz Luzon Phil.
Santa Cruz Luzon Phil.
Santa Cruz Port.
Santa Cruz mt. Spain
Santa Cruz CA U.S.A.
Santa Cruz watercourse AZ U.S.A.
Santa Cruz Venez.
Santa Cruz, Isla i. Islas Galápagos Ecuador
Santa Cruz, Isla i. Mex.
Santa Cruz, Puerto inlet Arg.
Santa Cruz, Sierra de mts Spain
Santa Cruz Barillas Guat.
Santa Cruz Cabrália Brazil
Santa Cruz das Palmeiras Brazil
Santa Cruz da Tapa Port.
Santa Cruz de Bezana Spain
Santa Cruz de Campézo Spain
Santa Cruz de Goiás Brazil
Santa Cruz de la Palma La Palma Canary Is
Santa Cruz de la Serós Spain
Santa Cruz de las Flores Mex.
Santa Cruz de la Sierra Spain
Santa Cruz de la Zarza Spain
Santa Cruz del Quiché Guat.
Santa Cruz del Retamar Spain
Santa Cruz del Sur Cuba
Santa Cruz de Moya Spain
Santa Cruz de Mudela Spain
Santa Cruz de Tenerife Tenerife Canary Is
Santa Cruz de Yojoa Hond.
Santa Cruz do Rio Pardo Brazil
Santa Cruz do Sul Brazil
Santa Cruz Huatulco Mex.
Santa Cruz Island CA U.S.A.
Santa Cruz Islands Solomon Is
Santa Cruz Mountains hills Jamaica
Santa de Enol, Peña mt. Spain
Santadi Sardegna Italy
Santa Domenica Talao Italy
Santa Domenica Vittoria Sicilia Italy
Santa Efigênia de Minas Brazil
Santa Elena Buenos Aires Arg.
Santa Elena Córdoba Arg.
Santa Elena Entre Ríos Arg.
Santa Elena Bol.
Santa Elena Peru
Santa Elena Spain
Santa Elena Venez.
Santa Elena, Cabo c. Costa Rica
Santa Elena, Punta pt Ecuador
Santa Elena de Jamuz Spain
Santa Eleonara Arg.
Santa Elisabetta Sicilia Italy
Santaella Spain
Santa Engracia Spain
Santa Eudóxia Brazil
Santa Eufemia Arg.
Santa Eufemia Spain
Santa Eufemia, Golfo di g. Italy
Santa Eugenia Galicia Spain see Santa Uxía de Ribeira
Santa Eulalia Mex.
Santa Eulália Port.
Santa Eulalia Aragón Spain
Santa Eulalia Asturias Spain
Santa Eulalia Asturias Spain
Santa Eulalia del Río Spain
Santa Eulalia de Oscos Spain
Santa Eulàlia de Riuprimer Spain
Santa Fé Arg.
Santa Fé prov. Arg.
Santa Fé Cuba
Santa Fé Panama
Santa Fe Phil.
Santa Fé Spain
Santa Fe NM U.S.A.
Santa Fé, Isla i. Islas Galápagos Ecuador
Santa Fé de Bogotá Col. see Bogotá
Santa Fé de Minas Brazil
Santa Fé do Sul Brazil
Santa Filomena Brazil
Santa Fiora Italy
Sant'Agata de'Goti Italy
Sant'Agata del Bianco Italy
Sant'Agata di Esaro Italy
Sant'Agata di Militello Sicilia Italy
Sant'Agata di Puglia Italy
Sant'Agata Feltria Italy
Santa Gertrudis Mex.
192 B8 Santa Giusta Sardegna Italy
192 B8 Santa Giusta, Stagno di l. Sardegna Italy
191 M3 Santa Giustina Italy
191 K6 Sant'Agostino Italy
254 D2 Santa Helena Brazil
256 B2 Santa Helena de Goiás Brazil
108 E3 Santai Sichuan China
110 E4 Santai Xinjiang China
110 I4 Santai Xinjiang China
108 C5 Santai Yunnan China
254 F5 Santa Inês Bahia Brazil
254 D2 Santa Inês Maranhão Brazil
245 K9 Santa Ines Mex.
259 B9 Santa Inés, Isla i. Chile
184 D5 Santa Iria Port.
260 D5 Santa Isabel La Pampa Arg.
261 G3 Santa Isabel Santa Fé Arg.
252 D5 Santa Isabel Bol.
253 E3 Santa Isabel Brazil
250 B5 Santa Isabel Ecuador
Santa Isabel Equat. Guinea see Malabo
245 N9 Santa Isabel Mex.
250 C6 Santa Isabel Peru
247 □1 Santa Isabel Puerto Rico
78 □6 Santa Isabel i. Solomon Is
254 E2 Santa Isabel, Ilha Grande de i. Brazil
242 B2 Santa Isabel, Sierra mts Mex.
252 B4 Santa Isabel de Sihuas Peru
256 A5 Santa Isabel do Ivaí Brazil
260 A5 Santa Juana Chile
256 D3 Santa Juliana Brazil
184 C2 Santa Justa Port.
247 □10 Santa Krus Curaçao Neth. Antilles
191 M6 Sant'Alberto Italy
182 F5 Santalha Port.
186 F3 Santa Liestra y San Quílez Spain
116 C8 Santalpur Gujarat India
191 J9 Santa Luce Italy
261 G3 Santa Lucia Arg.
252 C5 Santa Lucia Chile
Santa Lucía Cuba see Rafael Freyre
250 B5 Santa Lucía Ecuador
243 N10 Santa Lucia Guat.
192 D6 Santa Lucia Sardegna Italy
261 I4 Santa Lucia Uru.
261 I4 Santa Lucia r. Uru.
185 K6 Santa Lucía, Cerro de mt. Spain
261 F3 Santa Lucia, Lago l. Arg.
244 C3 Santa Lucia de la Sierra Mex.
195 I7 Santa Lucia del Mela Sicilia Italy
182 C3 Santa Lucía de Moraña Spain
216 □3f Santa Lucía de Tirajana Gran Canaria Canary Is
240 K5 Santa Lucia Range mts CA U.S.A.
261 G5 Santa Luisa Arg.
216 □1c Santa Luzia Pico Azores
254 D3 Santa Luzia Maranhão Brazil
254 F3 Santa Luzia Paraíba Brazil
206 □ Santa Luzia i. Cape Verde
184 C5 Santa Luzia Beja Port.
184 D6 Santa Luzia Faro Port.
261 F4 Santa Magdalena Arg.
187 F7 Santa Magdalena de Pulpís Spain
192 C5 Santa-Manza, Golfe de b. Corse France
197 P3 Santa Mare Romania
187 L8 Santa Margalida Spain
186 I4 Santa Margarida de Montbui Spain
184 C4 Santa Margarida do Sádão Port.
258 E3 Santa Margarita Arg.
240 L6 Santa Margarita CA U.S.A.
242 D5 Santa Margarita, Isla i. Mex.
194 E8 Santa Margherita di Belice Sicilia Italy
190 G7 Santa Margherita Ligure Italy
258 D2 Santa María Arg.
216 □1 Santa Maria i. Azores
252 E3 Santa María Bol.
251 F5 Santa Maria Amazonas Brazil
251 G5 Santa Maria Amazonas Brazil
251 H5 Santa Maria Pará Brazil
255 B9 Santa Maria Rio Grande do Sul Brazil
258 G3 Santa Maria r. Brazil
206 □ Santa Maria Cape Verde
243 N8 Santa María Mex.
242 F2 Santa María r. Mex.
244 H4 Santa María r. Mex.
186 D3 Santa María Spain
187 D8 Santa María mt. Spain
184 G6 Santa María r. Spain
190 I2 Santa Maria Switz.
240 L7 Santa Maria CA U.S.A.
241 S7 Santa Maria r. AZ U.S.A.
250 E3 Santa María Venez.
258 G4 Santa María, Cabo c. Uru.
213 G5 Santa Maria, Cabo de c. Moz.
184 D7 Santa Maria, Cabo de c. Port.
231 J14 Santa Maria, Cape Bahamas
246 D2 Santa María, Cayo i. Cuba
255 D5 Santa Maria, Chapadão de hills Brazil
258 B5 Santa María, Isla i. Chile
250 □ Santa María, Isla i. Islas Galápagos Ecuador
192 C5 Santa Maria, Isola i. Sardegna Italy
252 B3 Santa María, Punta pt Peru
254 D5 Santa Maria, Serra de hills Brazil
260 C5 Santa María, Volcán vol. Arg.
245 H6 Santa María Ajoloapan Mex.
193 M5 Santa Maria Capua Vetere Italy
254 F4 Santa Maria da Boa Vista Brazil
182 C7 Santa Maria da Feira Port.
254 C4 Santa Maria das Barreiras Brazil
256 C5 Santa Maria da Serra Brazil
254 D5 Santa Maria da Vitória Brazil
183 M2 Santa María de Cayón Spain
242 F4 Santa María de Cuevas Mex.
245 H3 Santa María de Guadalupe Mex.
216 □3f Santa María de Guía Gran Canaria Canary Is
244 C3 Santa María de Huazamota Mex.
183 P6 Santa María de Huertas Spain
251 E2 Santa María de Ipire Venez.
183 J7 Santa María del Berrocal Spain
183 M4 Santa María del Campo Spain
183 P9 Santa María del Campo Rus Spain
193 P8 Santa Maria del Cedro Italy
190 G6 Santa Maria della Versa Italy
245 J7 Santa María del Monte Mex.
242 G5 Santa María del Oro Mex.
244 C4 Santa María del Oro Mex.
182 I4 Santa María del Páramo Spain
244 F2 Santa María del Refugio Mex.
244 G4 Santa María del Río Mex.
183 P7 Santa María del Val Spain
185 P6 Santa María de Nieva Spain
185 O5 Santa María de Nieva, Puerto de pass Spain
193 N7 Santa Maria di Castellabate Italy
195 O4 Santa Maria di Leuca, Capo c. Italy
194 H8 Santa Maria di Licodia Sicilia Italy
192 C2 Santa-Maria-di-Lota Corse France
191 M4 Santa Maria di Sala Italy
257 G2 Santa Maria do Salto Brazil
257 F3 Santa Maria do Suaçuí Brazil
245 L9 Santa María Ecatepec Mex.
245 K10 Santa María Huatulco Mex.
78 □5 Santa María Island Vanuatu
245 J8 Santa María Ixcatlán Mex.
183 L6 Santa María la Real de Nieva Spain
257 F4 Santa Maria Madalena Brazil
190 E3 Santa Maria Maggiore Italy
241 T7 Santa Maria Mountains AZ U.S.A.
192 D8 Santa Maria Navarrese Sardegna Italy
190 G3 Santa Maria Rezzonico Italy
192 B4 Santa-Maria-Siché Corse France
245 K8 Santa María Tlalixtac Mex.
245 J9 Santa María Zaniza Mex.
245 K9 Santa María Zoquitlán Mex.
193 P7 Santa Marina Italy
182 I3 Santa Marina del Rey Spain
194 H6 Santa Marina Salina Isole Lipari Italy
192 H3 Santa Marinella Italy
250 C2 Santa Marta Col.
185 O2 Santa Marta Castilla-La Mancha Spain
184 F3 Santa Marta Extremadura Spain
209 B8 Santa Marta, Cabo de c. Angola
Santa Marta, Serra de mts Brazil see Divisões, Serra das
182 I7 Santa Marta de Tormes Spain
255 C9 Santa Marta Grande, Cabo de c. Brazil
245 M7 Santa Martha, Cerro mt. Mex.
Santa Maura i. Greece see Lefkada
192 B2 Sant'Ambroggio Corse France
240 N7 Santa Monica CA U.S.A.
239 H13 Santa Monica, Pico mt. Mex.
240 N8 Santa Monica Bay CA U.S.A.
240 N7 Santa Monica Mountains National Recreation Area park CA U.S.A.
95 L5 Santan Kalimantan Indon.
250 E4 Santana Amazonas Brazil
254 E5 Santana Bahia Brazil
256 B3 Santana r. Brazil
184 □ Santana Madeira
182 C8 Santana Coimbra Port.
184 D4 Santana Évora Port.
184 A4 Santana Setúbal Port.
197 J4 Sântana Romania
255 B9 Santana da Boa Vista Brazil
184 C5 Santana da Serra Port.
184 D5 Santana de Cambas Port.
254 E2 Santana do Acarau Brazil
254 C4 Santana do Araguaia Brazil
184 C3 Santana do Campo Port.
254 F3 Santana do Cariri Brazil
255 B9 Santana do Livramento Brazil
184 C3 Santana do Mato Port.
257 F3 Santana do Paraíso Brazil
194 G2 Sant'Anastasia Italy
193 J2 Sant'Anatolia di Narco Italy
250 B4 Santander Col.
250 C3 Santander dept Col.
183 M2 Santander Spain
183 L2 Santander prov. Spain
183 M2 Santander, Bahía de b. Spain
195 N3 Sant'Andrea, Isola i. Italy
195 L6 Sant'Andrea Apostolo dello Ionio Italy
192 C9 Sant'Andrea Frius Sardegna Italy
177 K4 Sântandrei Romania
240 K4 Santa Nella CA U.S.A.
195 K6 Sant'Angelo Italy
193 N5 Sant'Angelo a Cupola Italy
193 O7 Sant'Angelo a Fasanella Italy
193 O6 Sant'Angelo dei Lombardi Italy
191 N8 Sant'Angelo in Lizzola Italy
191 M8 Sant'Angelo in Vado Italy
190 G5 Sant'Angelo Lodigiano Italy
106 C4 Santanghu Xinjiang China
Santanilla, Islas is Caribbean Sea see Cignes, Islas del
194 D8 Santa Ninfa Sicilia Italy
241 U8 Santan Mountain hill AZ U.S.A.
257 G5 Sant'Anna, Ilha de i. Brazil
192 B9 Sant'Anna Arresi Sardegna Italy
192 A9 Sant'Antioco Sardegna Italy
192 A9 Sant'Antioco, Isola di i. Sardegna Italy
187 H10 Sant Antoni de Portmany Spain
192 C6 Sant'Antonio di Gallura Sardegna Italy
192 A8 Sant'Antonio di Santadi Sardegna Italy
Santañy Spain see Santanyí
187 L9 Santanyí Spain
183 L8 Santa Olalla Spain
182 G8 Santa Olalla hill Spain
186 I5 Santa Oliva Spain
184 G5 Santa Ollala del Cala Spain
195 I9 Santa Panagia, Capo c. Sicilia Italy
186 K3 Santa Pau Spain
240 M7 Santa Paula CA U.S.A.
115 H3 Santapilly Andhra Prad. India
187 D11 Santa Pola Spain
187 E11 Santa Pola, Cabo de c. Spain
241 U2 Santaquin UT U.S.A.
254 E3 Santa Quitéria Brazil
182 E7 Santar Port.
193 Q7 Sant'Arcangelo Italy
191 M7 Santarcangelo di Romagna Italy
261 F4 Santa Regina Arg.
251 H5 Santarém Brazil
184 B2 Santarém Port.
184 B2 Santarém admin. dist. Port.
246 D2 Santaren Channel Bahamas
253 F1 Santa Rita Mato Grosso Brazil
254 G3 Santa Rita Paraíba Brazil
250 C4 Santa Rita Col.
78 □1 Santa Rita Guam
243 I4 Santa Rita Coahuila Mex.
244 G1 Santa Rita Nuevo León Mex.
250 E2 Santa Rita Guárico Venez.
246 H8 Santa Rita Zulia Venez.
254 D4 Santa Rita de Cassia Brazil
256 A2 Santa Rita do Araguaia Brazil
256 A4 Santa Rita do Pardo Brazil
257 E5 Santa Rita do Sapucaí Brazil
250 D5 Santa Rita do Weil Brazil
258 F3 Santa Rosa Corrientes Arg.
261 E5 Santa Rosa La Pampa Arg.
260 C3 Santa Rosa Mendoza Arg.
259 D6 Santa Rosa Río Negro Arg.
258 D2 Santa Rosa Salta Arg.
252 D3 Santa Rosa Bol.
252 C2 Santa Rosa Acre Brazil
255 B8 Santa Rosa Rio Grande do Sul Brazil
250 D4 Santa Rosa Col.
250 B5 Santa Rosa Ecuador
244 G6 Santa Rosa Michoacán Mex.
244 G1 Santa Rosa Nuevo León Mex.
243 O8 Santa Rosa Quintana Roo Mex.
245 I4 Santa Rosa San Luis Potosí Mex.
245 J1 Santa Rosa Tamaulipas Mex.
253 F6 Santa Rosa Para.
250 C5 Santa Rosa Loreto Peru
252 C3 Santa Rosa Puno Peru
261 I4 Santa Rosa Uru.
240 J3 Santa Rosa CA U.S.A.
239 L9 Santa Rosa NM U.S.A.
250 E4 Santa Rosa Amazonas Venez.
251 E2 Santa Rosa Anzoátegui Venez.
250 E3 Santa Rosa Apure Venez.
78 □1 Santa Rosa, Mount Guam
241 P8 Santa Rosa and San Jacinto Mountains National Monument nat. park CA U.S.A.
242 □O10 Santa Rosa de Copán Hond.
253 E4 Santa Rosa de la Roca Bol.
260 E3 Santa Rosa del Conlara Arg.
253 E4 Santa Rosa del Palmar Bol.
261 F2 Santa Rosa del Río Primero Arg.
250 C3 Santa Rosa de Osos Col.
250 B4 Santa Rosa de Sucumbio Ecuador
252 D3 Santa Rosa de Vigo Bol.
256 D4 Santa Rosa de Viterbo Brazil
240 L8 Santa Rosa Island CA U.S.A.
244 G5 Santa Rosa Jauregui Mex.
242 C4 Santa Rosalía Mex.
241 P8 Santa Rosa Mountains CA U.S.A.
238 F6 Santa Rosa Range mts NV U.S.A.
241 T8 Santa Rosa Wash watercourse AZ U.S.A.
193 O7 Sant'Arsenio Italy
195 L5 Santa Severina Italy
183 J4 Santas Martas Spain
191 L8 Santa Sofia Italy
184 C3 Santa Sofia Port.
184 D3 Santa Susana Évora Port.
184 C4 Santa Susana Setúbal Port.
258 E2 Santa Sylvina Arg.
261 G3 Santa Teresa Arg.
84 E8 Santa Teresa N.T. Austr.
257 G3 Santa Teresa Brazil
254 C4 Santa Teresa r. Brazil
244 C1 Santa Teresa Durango Mex.
244 C3 Santa Teresa Nayarit Mex.
243 K5 Santa Teresa Tamaulipas Mex.
247 J8 Santa Teresa Venez.
182 I7 Santa Teresa, Embalse de resr Spain
Santa Teresa Aboriginal Land res. N.T. Austr. see Ltyentye Apurte Aboriginal Land
192 C5 Santa Teresa di Gallura Sardegna Italy
195 I8 Santa Teresa di Riva Sicilia Italy
261 I5 Santa Teresita Arg.
254 C4 Santa Terezinha Brazil
177 L4 Santău Romania
216 □3a Santa Úrsula Tenerife Canary Is
182 C3 Santa Uxía de Ribeira Galicia Spain
195 I8 Santa Venerina Sicilia Italy
256 B3 Santa Vitória Brazil
184 C5 Santa Vitória Port.
184 D3 Santa Vitória do Ameixial Port.
258 G4 Santa Vitória do Palmar Brazil
192 C8 Santa Vittoria, Monte mt. Sardegna Italy
240 L7 Santa Ynez r. CA U.S.A.
Santa Ysabel i. Solomon Is see Santa Isabel
186 K4 Sant Benet mt. Spain
186 J5 Sant Boi de Llobregat Spain
186 G6 Sant Carles de la Ràpita Spain
186 J4 Sant Celoni Spain
186 J5 Sant Cugat del Vallès Spain
158 C4 Santec France
240 P9 Santee CA U.S.A.
231 H9 Santee r. SC U.S.A.
193 L2 Sant'Egidio alla Vibrata Italy
192 C9 Sant'Elia, Capo c. Sardegna Italy
193 N4 Sant'Elia a Pianisi Italy
193 L4 Sant Elia Fiumerapido Italy
187 J8 Sant Elm Spain
242 A2 San Telmo Mex.
184 F5 San Telmo Spain
191 P9 Sant'Elpidio a Mare Italy
192 D6 San Teodoro Sardegna Italy
189 F5 Santeramo in Colle Italy
191 L6 Santerno r. Italy
156 D4 Santerre reg. France
183 K3 Santervás de la Vega Spain
186 H5 Santes Creus Spain
195 J7 Sant'Eufemia d'Aspromonte Italy
186 L4 Sant Feliu de Guíxols Spain
186 K3 Sant Feliu de Pallerols Spain
186 J4 Sant Feliu Sasserra Spain
190 E5 Santhià Italy
186 K4 Sant Hilari Sacalm Spain
186 J3 Sant Hipòlit de Voltregà Spain
255 B9 Santiago Brazil
206 □ Santiago i. Cape Verde
260 B3 Santiago Chile
260 B3 Santiago admin. reg. Chile
246 H4 Santiago Dom. Rep.
242 E6 Santiago Baja California Sur Mex.
244 C6 Santiago Colima Mex.
243 I5 Santiago Nuevo León Mex.
244 B1 Santiago r. Mex.
242 □S13 Santiago Panama
253 F6 Santiago Para.
252 B3 Santiago Peru
250 B6 Santiago r. Peru
92 C3 Santiago Luzon Phil.
259 B8 Santiago, Cabo c. Chile
242 □S13 Santiago, Cerro mt. Panama
244 B4 Santiago, Río Grande de r. Mex.
253 F4 Santiago, Sierra de hills Bol.
245 L9 Santiago Astata Mex.
182 F9 Santiago de Alcántara Spain
185 K5 Santiago de Calatrava Spain
250 B6 Santiago de Cao Peru
Santiago de Carbajo Spain see Santiago de Alcántara
182 C3 Santiago de Compostela Spain
182 D4 Santiago de Covelo Spain
246 F3 Santiago de Cuba Cuba
185 N4 Santiago de la Espada Spain
245 J5 Santiago de la Peña Mex.
187 D12 Santiago de la Ribera Spain
182 H9 Santiago del Campo Spain
258 D2 Santiago del Estero Arg.
261 F1 Santiago del Estero prov. Arg.
Santiago de los Caballeros Dom. Rep. see Santiago
216 □3a Santiago del Teide Tenerife Canary Is
250 B5 Santiago de Méndez Ecuador
252 C3 Santiago de Pacaguaras Bol.
184 B4 Santiago do Cacém Port.
184 C3 Santiago do Escoural Port.
244 B4 Santiago Ixcuintla Mex.
245 J9 Santiago Ixtayutla Mex.
245 I8 Santiago Juxtlahuaca Mex.
245 J9 Santiago Minas Mex.
245 J8 Santiago Mitlatengo Mex.
240 O8 Santiago Peak CA U.S.A.
261 F2 Santiago Temple Arg.
245 L8 Santiago Tutla Mex.
245 L7 Santiago Tuxtla Mex.
261 I4 Santiago Vazquez Uru.
244 C1 Santiaguillo, Laguna de l. Mex.
182 I8 Santibáñez de Béjar Spain
183 K3 Santibáñez de la Peña Spain
182 I7 Santibáñez de la Sierra Spain
182 H4 Santibáñez de Vidriales Spain
182 H8 Santibáñez el Bajo Spain
183 M4 Santibáñez Zarzaguda Spain
244 F1 San Tiburcio Mex.
93 B3 Santigi Sulawesi Indon.
93 B3 Santiki, Tanjung pt Indon.
190 I6 Sant'Ilario d'Enza Italy
183 L2 Santillana Spain
183 M7 Santillana, Embalse de resr Spain
250 D2 San Timoteo Venez.
184 G6 Santiponce Spain
Santipur W. Bengal India see Shantipur
190 G1 Säntis mt. Switz.
185 M4 Santisteban del Puerto Spain
183 K6 Santiuste de San Juan Bautista Spain
182 I6 Santiz Spain
186 □ Sant Jaime Mediterráneo Spain
186 G6 Sant Jaume d'Enveja Spain
186 □ Sant Joan Spain
187 I9 Sant Joan de Labritja Spain
186 J3 Sant Joan de les Abadesses Spain
186 I4 Sant Joan de Vilatorrada Spain
186 G6 Sant Jordi, Golf de g. Spain
187 H10 Sant Josep de sa Talaia Illes Balears Spain
186 I3 Sant Julià de Lòria Andorra
186 I3 Sant Llorenç de Morunys Spain
186 I4 Sant Llorenç de Munt, Parc Natural del nature res. Spain
187 L8 Sant Llorenç des Cardassar Spain
186 □ Sant Lluís Spain
186 I4 Sant Martí de Tous Spain
186 I5 Sant Martí Sarroca Spain
186 F7 Sant Mateu Spain
187 H9 Sant Miquel de Balansat Spain
104 A5 Santō Hyōgo Japan
104 D5 Santō Shiga Japan
184 E3 Santo Aleixo Port.
184 E4 Santo Aleixo da Restauração Port.
216 □1c Santo Amaro Pico Azores
216 □1c Santo Amaro São Jorge Azores
254 F5 Santo Amaro Brazil
257 G4 Santo Amaro de Campos Brazil
256 B4 Santo Anastácio Brazil
256 A4 Santo Anastácio r. Brazil
256 D5 Santo André Brazil
184 B4 Santo André Port.
184 B4 Santo André, Lagoa de lag. Port.
255 B9 Santo Angelo Brazil
216 □1c Santo Antão São Jorge Azores
206 □ Santo Antão i. Cape Verde
182 C3 Santo Antoniño Spain
216 □1c Santo António Pico Azores
216 □1b Santo António São Miguel Azores
251 F5 Santo Antônio Amazonas Brazil
254 D3 Santo Antônio Maranhão Brazil
254 G3 Santo Antônio Rio Grande do Norte Brazil
257 F3 Santo Antônio r. Brazil
207 G6 Santo António São Tomé and Príncipe
257 H2 Santo Antônio, Ponta pt Brazil
256 B2 Santo Antônio da Barra Brazil
251 H5 Santo Antônio da Cachoeira Brazil
256 B5 Santo Antônio da Platina Brazil
254 F5 Santo Antônio de Jesus Brazil
253 F3 Santo Antônio de Leverger Brazil
257 F4 Santo Antônio de Pádua Brazil
257 E4 Santo Antônio do Amparo Brazil
250 E5 Santo Antônio do Içá Brazil
257 G2 Santo Antônio do Jacinto Brazil
257 E4 Santo Antônio do Monte Brazil
256 D2 Santo Antônio do Rio Verde Brazil
184 A3 Santo António dos Cavaleiros Port.
Santo António do Zaire Angola see Soyo
253 F4 Santo Corazón Bol.
191 M3 Santo Croce, Lago di l. Italy
261 I5 Santo Domingo Arg.
260 B3 Santo Domingo Chile
246 C2 Santo Domíngo Cuba
246 I4 Santo Domingo Dom. Rep.
243 O10 Santo Domingo Guat.
242 B3 Santo Domingo Baja California Mex.
242 D5 Santo Domingo Baja California Sur Mex.
245 M9 Santo Domingo Oaxaca Mex.
244 F2 Santo Domingo San Luis Potosí Mex.
245 K7 Santo Domingo r. Mex.
242 □Q11 Santo Domingo Nic.
252 C3 Santo Domingo Peru
186 D3 Santo Domingo mt. Spain
Santo Domingo country West Indies see Dominican Republic
Santo Domingo de Garafía La Palma Canary Is see Garafía
183 O4 Santo Domingo de la Calzada Spain
245 K10 Santo Domingo de Morelos Mex.
183 N5 Santo Domingo de Silos Spain
245 K9 Santo Domingo Ozolotepec Mex.
245 L9 Santo Domingo Petapa Mex.
239 K9 Santo Domingo Pueblo NM U.S.A.
245 L9 Santo Domingo Tehuantepec Mex.
257 G4 Santo Eduardo Brazil
184 D6 Santo Estêvão Faro Port.
184 B3 Santo Estêvão Santarém Port.
182 F4 Santo Estevo, Encoro de resr Spain
80 J7 Santoft North I. N.Z.
257 E3 Santo Hipólito Brazil
254 E4 Santo Inácio Bahia Brazil
256 B5 Santo Inácio Paraná Brazil
184 B3 Santo Isidro de Pegões Port.
251 E2 San Tomé Venez.
187 C11 Santomera Spain
187 C11 Santomera, Embalse de resr Spain
193 L2 Sant Omero Italy
183 N2 Santoña Spain
100 E7 Santong He r. China
92 E6 Santo Niño i. Phil.
195 K6 Sant'Onofrio Italy
194 H9 Santo Pietro Sicilia Italy
192 C2 Santo-Pietro-di-Tenda Corse France
192 C3 Santo-Pietro-di-Venaco Corse France
199 G6 Santorini i. Greece
256 D5 Santos Brazil
185 I4 Santos, Sierra de los hills Spain
257 F4 Santos Dumont Brazil
252 D2 Santos Mercado Bol.
264 F7 Santos Plateau sea feature S. Atlantic Ocean
190 E6 Santo Stefano Belbo Italy
191 N2 Santo Stefano di Cadore Italy
194 G7 Santo Stefano di Camastra Sicilia Italy
190 H7 Santo Stefano di Magra Italy
194 E8 Santo Stefano Quisquina Sicilia Italy
191 N4 Santo Stino di Livenza Italy
182 D6 Santo Tirso Port.
239 K12 Santo Tomás Chihuahua Mex.
239 H11 Santo Tomás Sonora Mex.
242 □P11 Santo Tomás Nic.
252 B3 Santo Tomás Peru
258 F3 Santo Tomé Corrientes Arg.
261 G2 Santo Tomé Santa Fé Arg.
185 M4 Santo Tomé Spain
182 I5 Santovenia Spain
186 I5 Sant Pere de Ribes Spain
186 J3 Sant Pere de Torelló Spain
186 L3 Sant Pere Pescador Spain
164 G4 Santpoort Neth.
186 J3 Sant Privat d'en Bas Spain
186 I5 Sant Quintí de Mediona Spain
116 D8 Santrampur Gujarat India
186 I5 Sant Sadurní d'Anoia Spain
187 L9 Sant Salvador, Puig de hill Spain
182 I2 Santullano Spain
192 B7 Santu Lussurgiu Sardegna Italy
195 □ San Tumas, Il-Bajja ta' b. Malta
Santurce País Vasco Spain see Santurtzi
183 O4 Santurde Spain
183 N2 Santurtzi Spain
186 I4 Sant Vincenç de Castellet Spain
241 S5 Sanup Plateau AZ U.S.A.
259 B7 San Valentín, Cerro mt. Chile
178 F8 San Vendemiano Italy
192 B7 San Vero Milis Sardegna Italy
261 G2 San Vicente Arg.
252 D5 San Vicente Bol.
260 B4 San Vicente Chile
242 □O11 San Vicente El Salvador
242 A2 San Vicente Baja California Mex.
244 G1 San Vicente San Luis Potosí Mex.
92 D2 San Vicente Luzon Phil.
183 K8 San Vicente, Sierra de mts Spain
184 E2 San Vicente de Alcántara Spain
183 P3 San Vicente de Arana Spain
252 A3 San Vicente de Cañete Peru
San Vicente de Castellet Spain see Sant Vincenç de Castellet
183 L2 San Vicente de la Barquera Spain
183 O3 San Vicente de la Sonsierra Spain
250 C4 San Vicente del Caguán Col.
187 D11 San Vicente del Raspeig Spain
183 K6 San Vicente de Palacio Spain
183 M2 San Vicente de Toranzo Spain
245 I4 San Vicente Tancuayalab Mex.
182 C3 San Vicenzo Spain
191 O9 San Vicino, Monte mt. Italy
261 H2 San Victor Arg.
160 E3 Sanvignes-les-Mines France
244 G8 San Vincente de Benitez Mex.
195 I6 San Vincenzo Isole Lipari Italy
192 F1 San Vincenzo Toscana Italy
182 H5 San Vitero Spain
192 D9 San Vito Sardegna Italy
194 D7 San Vito, Capo c. Sicilia Italy
195 M3 San Vito, Capo c. Italy
191 N4 San Vito al Tagliamento Italy
193 M3 San Vito Chietino Italy
195 N2 San Vito dei Normanni Italy
191 M3 San Vito di Cadore Italy
194 D7 San Vito lo Capo Sicilia Italy
193 J4 San Vito Romano Italy
195 K6 San Vito sullo Ionio Italy
105 K3 Sanwa Ibaraki Japan
105 H1 Sanwa Niigata Japan
116 E8 Sanwer Madh. Prad. India
182 C4 Sanxenxo Spain
108 G9 Sanya Hainan China
250 D4 San Yanaro Col.
213 F3 Sanyati r. Zimbabwe
107 K9 Sanyuan Shaanxi China
123 J3 S. A. Nyýazow Adyndaky Turkm.
193 P7 Sanza Italy
209 C6 Sanza Pombo Angola
182 I6 Sanzoles Spain
96 F5 Sao, Phou mt. Laos
184 C6 São Barnabé Port.
216 □1a São Bartolomeu Terceira Azores
256 D2 São Bartolomeu r. Brazil
184 D2 São Bartolomeu Port.
184 B4 São Bartolomeu da Serra Port.
184 C6 São Bartolomeu de Messines Port.
254 E3 São Benedito Brazil
216 □1a São Bento Terceira Azores
252 D1 São Bento Amazonas Brazil
254 D2 São Bento Maranhão Brazil
251 F4 São Bento Roraima Brazil
256 B6 São Bento do Amparo Brazil
254 G3 São Bento do Norte Brazil
254 E2 São Bernardo Brazil
256 D5 São Bernardo do Campo Brazil
253 F7 São Borja Brazil
184 D5 São Brás Port.
184 D6 São Brás de Alportel Port.
184 C4 São Brás do Regedouro Port.
216 □1c São Caetano Pico Azores
252 D2 São Carlos Rondônia Brazil
253 E2 São Carlos Rondônia Brazil
255 B8 São Carlos Santa Catarina Brazil
256 D5 São Carlos São Paulo Brazil
182 E6 São Cosmado Port.
184 C4 São Cristóvão Port.
184 B4 São Cristóvão r. Port.
254 D5 São Desidério Brazil
254 D5 São Domingos Brazil
256 A4 São Domingos r. Brazil
256 B3 São Domingos r. Brazil
184 B5 São Domingos Port.
257 G3 São Domingos do Norte Brazil
184 C2 São Facundo Port.
257 E1 São Felipe, Serra de hills Brazil
254 F5 São Félix Bahia Brazil
254 C4 São Félix Mato Grosso Brazil
251 I6 São Félix Pará Brazil
182 C6 São Félix da Marinha Port.
257 G4 São Fidélis Brazil
206 □ São Filipe Cape Verde
252 C2 São Francisco Acre Brazil
251 F6 São Francisco Amazonas Brazil
257 E1 São Francisco Minas Gerais Brazil
257 E1 São Francisco r. Brazil
252 D2 São Francisco r. Brazil
255 C8 São Francisco, Ilha de i. Brazil
184 B4 São Francisco da Serra Port.
255 B9 São Francisco de Assis Brazil
256 C1 São Francisco de Goiás Brazil
255 C9 São Francisco de Paula Brazil
256 C3 São Francisco de Sales Brazil
254 E3 São Francisco do Maranhão Brazil
255 C8 São Francisco do Sul Brazil
255 B9 São Gabriel Brazil
257 G3 São Gabriel da Palha Brazil
184 C3 São Geraldo Port.
257 F5 São Gonçalo Brazil
257 E3 São Gonçalo do Abaeté Brazil
257 E3 São Gonçalo do Pará Brazil
257 E4 São Gonçalo do Sapucaí Brazil
257 E3 São Gotardo Brazil
184 D3 São Gregório Port.
211 B7 Sao Hill Tanz.
182 C7 São Jacinto Port.
256 B5 São Jerônimo da Serra Brazil
216 □1c São João Pico Azores
250 E5 São João Brazil
254 D2 São João, Ilhas de is Brazil
253 E2 São João, Serra de hills Brazil
254 D5 São João da Aliança Brazil
257 G4 São João da Barra Brazil
256 D4 São João da Boa Vista Brazil
182 D7 São João da Madeira Port.
182 F6 São João da Pesqueira Port.
257 E1 São João da Ponte Brazil
256 B4 São João das Duas Pontas Brazil
257 E4 São João del Rei Brazil
257 F5 São João de Meriti Brazil
182 E7 São João de Tarouca Port.
254 C3 São João do Araguaia Brazil
256 A5 São João do Caiuá Brazil
182 D8 São João do Campo Port.
254 F3 São João do Cariri Brazil
255 E5 São João do Paraíso Brazil
254 E4 São João do Piauí Brazil
184 D5 São João dos Caldeireiros Port.
254 E3 São João dos Patos Brazil
209 B8 São João do Sul Angola
257 F3 São João Evangelista Brazil
257 F4 São João Nepomuceno Brazil
250 E4 São Joaquim Amazonas Brazil
255 C9 São Joaquim Santa Catarina Brazil
256 D4 São Joaquim da Barra Brazil
216 □1c São Jorge i. Azores
184 □ São Jorge Madeira
216 □1c São Jorge, Canal de sea chan. Azores
São Jorge da Mina Ghana see Elmina
256 A5 São Jorge do Ivaí Brazil
250 E5 São José Amazonas Brazil
255 C8 São José Santa Catarina Brazil
256 D4 São José da Boa Vista Brazil
184 C2 São José da Lamarosa Port.
251 F4 São José do Anauá Brazil
257 E5 São José do Barreiro Brazil
254 F3 São José do Belmonte Brazil
257 G4 São José do Calçado Brazil
257 G3 São José do Divino Brazil
254 F3 São José do Egito Brazil
257 F3 São José do Jacurí Brazil
258 G4 São José do Norte Brazil
254 E3 São José do Peixe Brazil
256 D4 São José do Rio Pardo Brazil
256 C4 São José do Rio Preto Brazil
257 E5 São José dos Campos Brazil
256 B4 São José dos Dourados r. Brazil
255 C8 São José dos Pinhais Brazil
182 F5 São Julião de Montenegro Port.
253 G4 São Lourenço Mato Grosso Brazil
257 E5 São Lourenço Minas Gerais Brazil
253 F4 São Lourenço r. Brazil
253 F4 São Lourenço, Pantanal de marsh Brazil
184 □ São Lourenço, Ponta de pt Madeira
184 D3 São Lourenço de Mamporcão Port.
258 H3 São Lourenço do Sul Brazil
209 C7 São Lucas Angola
254 D2 São Luís Brazil
251 G6 São Luís Brazil
184 B5 São Luís Port.
252 D1 São Luís de Cassianã Brazil
256 B2 São Luís de Montes Belos Brazil
257 E5 São Luís do Paraitinga Brazil
254 G4 São Luís do Quitunde Brazil
255 B9 São Luís Gonzaga Brazil
184 E2 São Mamede, Serra de mts Port.
184 C4 São Mamede do Sádão Port.
184 D4 São Manços Port.
256 C5 São Manuel Brazil
250 E4 São Marceline Brazil
256 D3 São Marcos r. Brazil
254 D2 São Marcos, Baía de b. Brazil
184 D5 São Marcos da Ataboeira Port.
184 C6 São Marcos da Serra Port.
184 D4 São Marcos do Campo Port.
251 G6 São Martinho Brazil
182 D8 São Martinho da Cortiça Port.
184 C5 São Martinho das Amoreiras Port.
182 H5 São Martinho de Angueira Port.
182 B9 São Martinho do Porto Port.
216 □1c São Mateus Pico Azores
216 □1a São Mateus Terceira Azores
257 H3 São Mateus Brazil
257 H3 São Mateus r. Brazil
255 C8 São Mateus do Sul Brazil
184 D4 São Matias Port.
216 □1b São Miguel i. Azores
256 D2 São Miguel r. Brazil
182 E9 São Miguel hill Port.
256 D5 São Miguel Arcanjo Brazil
255 B9 São Miguel das Missões tourist site Brazil
182 F8 São Miguel de Acha Port.
184 D3 São Miguel de Machede Port.
184 C2 São Miguel de Rio Torto Port.
184 D5 São Miguel do Pinheiro Port.
254 E3 São Miguel do Tapuio Brazil
247 I4 Saona, Isla i. Dom. Rep.
191 N9 Saonda r. Italy
217 □3a Saondzou mt. Njazidja Comoros
160 I2 Saône France
157 L7 Saône r. France
160 F3 Saône-et-Loire dept France
116 G9 Saoner Mahar. India
São Nicolau Angola see Bentiaba
253 G7 São Nicolau Brazil
206 □ São Nicolau i. Cape Verde
256 D5 São Paulo Brazil
256 C5 São Paulo state Brazil
250 D5 São Paulo de Olivença Brazil
251 G6 São Pedro Amazonas Brazil
256 B3 São Pedro Mato Grosso do Sul Brazil
253 E2 São Pedro Rondônia Brazil
256 D5 São Pedro São Paulo Brazil
257 F5 São Pedro da Aldeia Brazil
184 A2 São Pedro da Cadeira Port.
182 F5 São Pedro de Agostem Port.
182 B9 São Pedro de Muel Port.
184 D6 São Pedro de Solis Port.
184 E4 São Pedro do Corval Port.
252 D2 São Pedro do Desterro Brazil
256 B5 São Pedro do Ivaí Brazil
255 B9 São Pedro do Sul Brazil
182 D7 São Pedro do Sul Port.
264 H5 São Pedro e São Paulo is N. Atlantic Ocean
São Pires r. Brazil see Teles Pires
254 D3 São Raimundo das Mangabeiras Brazil
254 E4 São Raimundo Nonato Brazil
161 L9 Saorge France
104 E5 Saori Japan
250 E6 São Romão Amazonas Brazil
257 E2 São Romão Minas Gerais Brazil
184 E3 São Romão Évora Port.
182 E8 São Romão Guarda Port.
184 C4 São Romão do Sado Port.
216 □1c São Roque Pico Azores
256 D5 São Roque Brazil
256 D4 São Roque de Minas Brazil
São Salvador Angola see M'banza Congo
São Salvador do Congo Angola see M'banza Congo
216 □1a São Sebastião Terceira Azores
252 C1 São Sebastião Amazonas Brazil
251 H6 São Sebastião Pará Brazil
253 E2 São Sebastião Rondônia Brazil
257 E5 São Sebastião São Paulo Brazil
257 E5 São Sebastião, Ilha do i. Brazil
256 B5 São Sebastião da Amoreira Brazil
251 I5 São Sebastião da Boa Vista Brazil
251 F6 São Sebastião de Tapuru Brazil
256 D4 São Sebastião do Paraíso Brazil
255 B9 São Sepé Brazil
182 C8 São Silvestre Port.
253 F5 São Simão Mato Grosso do Sul Brazil
256 B3 São Simão Minas Gerais Brazil
256 D4 São Simão São Paulo Brazil
256 B3 São Simão, Barragem de resr Brazil
256 C3 São Simão, Represa de resr Brazil
93 E3 Sao-Siu Maluku Indon.
184 B5 São Teotónio Port.
257 E4 São Tiago Brazil
São Tiago i. Cape Verde see Santiago
207 G6 São Tomé São Tomé and Príncipe
207 G6 São Tomé i. São Tomé and Príncipe
257 G5 São Tomé, Cabo de c. Brazil
207 G6 São Tomé, Pico de mt. São Tomé and Príncipe
207 G6 São Tomé and Príncipe country Africa
184 B3 São Torcato hill Port.
161 G7 Saou France
204 E3 Saoura, Oued watercourse Alg.
256 D5 São Vicente Brazil
206 □ São Vicente i. Cape Verde
184 □ São Vicente Madeira
184 E3 São Vicente Portalegre Port.
182 F5 São Vicente Vila Real Port.

184 B6 São Vicente, Cabo de c. Port.
182 E8 São Vicente da Beira Port.
254 D2 São Vicente Ferrer Brazil
177 K4 Sáp Hungary
Sápai Greece see Sapes
94 C5 Sapako Indon.
184 E6 Sapal de Castro Marim e Vila Real de Santo António, Reserva Natural do nature res. Spain
252 B3 Sapallanga Peru
199 L2 Sapanca Turkey
199 L2 Sapanca Gölü l. Turkey
254 D4 Sapão r. Brazil
122 H1 Saparmyrat Türkmenbaşy Turkm.
93 F5 Saparua Maluku Indon.
93 F5 Saparua i. Maluku Indon.
151 J2 Sapcote Leicestershire, England U.K.
93 A8 Sape, Selat sea chan. Indon.
95 M9 Sape, Teluk b. Sumbawa Indon.
207 G5 Sapele Nigeria
199 G1 Sapes Greece
199 K3 Şaphane Turkey
192 C6 Sa Pianedda, Monte hill Italy
198 C6 Sapienza i. Greece
242 □T14 Sapo, Serranía del mts Panama
187 L8 Sa Pobla Spain
195 I7 Saponara Sicilia Italy
206 C5 Sapo National Park Liberia
256 B5 Sapopema Brazil
138 G8 Sapotskin Belarus
206 E4 Sapouy Burkina
139 X8 Sapozhok Rus. Fed.
236 F5 Sappa Creek r. NE U.S.A.
191 N2 Sappada Italy
231 □1 Sapphire Bay Bermuda
102 S3 Sapporo Japan
117 L9 Saptamukhi r. India
256 C4 Sapucai r. Brazil
257 E4 Sapucaí r. Brazil
251 G5 Sapucaia Brazil
95 K8 Sapudi i. Indon.
237 G7 Sapulpa OK U.S.A.
95 J8 Sapulu Jawa Indon.
95 L2 Sapulut Sabah Malaysia
124 F2 Sāq, Jabal hill Saudi Arabia
122 H5 Sāqī Iran
221 M2 Saqqaq Greenland
122 B3 Saqqez Iran
124 F7 Saqr Saudi Arabia
129 D3 Saqulia Georgia
117 L7 Sara Bangl.
122 B3 Sarā Iran
122 B3 Sarāb Āžarbāyjān-e Sharqī Iran
122 H5 Sarāb Khorāsān Iran
127 M7 Sarābe Meymeh Iran
128 B9 Sarābīţ al Khādim tourist site Egypt
97 E7 Sara Buri Thai.
140 Q1 Saraby Norway
251 G5 Saracá, Lago l. Brazil
195 L4 Saraceno r. Italy
194 D7 Saraceno, Punta del pt Sicilia Italy
179 N7 Saračinec Croatia
116 C9 Saradiya Gujarat India
202 C6 Saraf Doungous Chad
Saragossa Spain see Zaragoza
123 I3 Saragt Turkm.
250 B5 Saraguro Ecuador
123 L5 Sarai Afgh.
135 H5 Sarai Rus. Fed.
117 J8 Saraikela Jharkhand India
123 O6 Sarai Sidhu Pak.
140 S4 Säräisniemi Fin.
188 G4 Sarajevo Bos.-Herz.
85 L7 Saraji Qld Austr.
123 I3 Sarakhs Iran
198 E4 Sarakiniko, Akrotirio pt Greece
198 F4 Sarakino i. Greece
120 G2 Saraktash Rus. Fed.
237 K10 Saraland AL U.S.A.
120 F3 Saralzhin Kazakh.
117 O7 Saramati mt. India/Myanmar
250 B6 Sarameriza Peru
163 F8 Saramon France
156 C8 Saran France
121 O3 Saran' Kazakh.
95 I5 Saran, Gunung mt. Indon.
233 L4 Saranac r. NY U.S.A.
233 K4 Saranac Lake NY U.S.A.
177 K4 Sáránd Hungary
198 B3 Sarandë Albania
256 B5 Sarandi Paraná Brazil
255 B8 Sarandi Rio Grande do Sul Brazil
Sarandib country Asia see Sri Lanka
258 G4 Sarandí del Yí Uru.
261 I3 Sarandí de Navarro Uru.
261 I3 Sarandí Grande Uru.
92 E9 Sarangani i. Phil.
92 E9 Sarangani Bay Mindanao Phil.
92 E9 Sarangani Islands Phil.
92 E9 Sarangani Strait Phil.
117 I9 Sarangarh Chhattisgarh India
116 F8 Sarangpur Madh. Prad. India
135 I5 Saransk Rus. Fed.
Sara-Ostrov Azer. see Närimanabad
207 H4 Sara Peak Nigeria
96 D5 Saraphi Thai.
134 K4 Sarapul Rus. Fed.
128 E3 Sarāqib Syria
231 F12 Sarasota FL U.S.A.
116 C8 Saraswati r. Gujarat India
136 H7 Sărata r. Moldova
197 O6 Sărata r. Romania
136 I7 Sarata Ukr.
136 I8 Sarata r. Ukr.
136 H6 Sărătenii Vechi Moldova
240 J4 Saratoga CA U.S.A.
238 K6 Saratoga WY U.S.A.
233 L5 Saratoga Lake NY U.S.A.
233 L5 Saratoga Springs NY U.S.A.
95 I4 Saratok Sarawak Malaysia
120 A2 Saratov Rus. Fed.
Saratov Oblast admin. div. Rus. Fed. see Saratovskaya Oblast'
129 A1 Saratovskaya Rus. Fed.
120 B2 Saratovskaya Oblast' admin. div. Rus. Fed.
120 B1 Saratovskoye Vodokhranilishche resr Rus. Fed.
199 G3 Saratsina, Akrotirio pt Lesvos Greece
123 J8 Saravan Iran
92 D6 Saravia Negros Phil.
97 D8 Sarawa r. Myanmar
95 I4 Sarawak state Malaysia
129 K5 Saray Azer.
126 C3 Saray Turkey
206 C4 Saraya Guinea
206 C3 Saraya Senegal
128 D3 Şarāyā Syria
199 K4 Saraycık Turkey
199 J5 Sarayköy Turkey
199 I2 Saraylar Turkey
126 F4 Sarayönü Turkey
123 I8 Sarbāz Iran
123 I9 Sarbāz r. Iran
123 I8 Sarbāz reg. Iran
197 N6 Sârbeni Romania
117 M6 Sarbhang Bhutan
177 L4 Sârbi Romania
122 H5 Sarbīsheh Iran
177 H5 Sárbogárd Hungary
174 F1 Sarbsko, Jezioro lag. Pol.
106 A3 Sarbulak Xinjiang China
191 J4 Sarca r. Italy
178 C7 Sarca di Genova r. Italy
156 D6 Sarcelles France
122 C3 Sarcham Iran
129 F4 Sarch'apet Armenia
192 B8 Sarcidano reg. Sardegna Italy
258 C3 Sarco Chile
111 E12 Sarda r. India/Nepal
116 H5 Sarda r. Nepal
123 N3 Sard Āb pass Afgh.
123 I8 Sardāb Iran
184 B5 Sardão, Cabo c. Port.
192 B8 Sardara Sardegna Italy
116 E8 Sardarpur Madh. Prad. India
116 E5 Sardarshahr Rajasthan India
122 A3 Sar Dasht Iran
122 C5 Sardasht Khūzestān Iran
122 D6 Sardasht Khūzestān Iran
192 C7 Sardegna admin. reg. Italy
192 A7 Sardegna i. Sardegna Italy
Sardica Bulg. see Sofiya
176 G3 Šardice Czech Rep.
216 □3f Sardina Gran Canaria Canary Is
216 □3f Sardina, Punta de pt Gran Canaria Canary Is
250 C2 Sardinata Col.
242 □Q12 Sardinia Costa Rica
Sardinia i. Sardegna Italy see Sardegna
185 L4 Sardinilla r. Spain
237 K8 Sardis MS U.S.A.
232 E9 Sardis WV U.S.A.
237 K8 Sardis Lake resr MS U.S.A.
182 D9 Sardoal Port.
127 M5 Sardrūd Iran
163 A9 Sare France
125 J3 Sareb, Rās as pt U.A.E.
123 L4 Sar-e Būm Afgh.
140 N3 Sareks nationalpark nat. park Sweden
140 N3 Sarektjåkkå mt. Sweden
95 K5 Sarempaka, Gunung mt. Indon.
187 K8 S'Arenal Spain
191 K2 Sarentino Italy
123 K3 Sar-e Pol Afgh.
123 L4 Sar-e Pol Afgh.
123 L3 Sar-e Pol prov. Afgh.
127 L6 Sar-e Pol-e Žahāb Iran
Sar Eskandar Iran see Hashtrud
190 C4 Sareva r. Italy
122 F6 Sare Yazd Iran
123 O2 Sarez, Kŭli l. Tajik.
Sarezskoye Ozero l. Tajik. see Sarez, Kŭli
190 G1 Sargans Switz.
264 E4 Sargasso Sea Atlantic Ocean
250 C5 Sargentu Loros Peru
123 O5 Sargodha Pak.
208 C2 Sarh Chad
122 I7 Sarhad reg. Iran
206 D4 Sarhala Côte d'Ivoire
204 D3 Sarhro, Jbel mt. Morocco
122 E3 Sārī Iran
199 I7 Saria i. Karpathos Greece
242 D2 Sáric Mex.
199 L2 Sarıcakaya Turkey
129 B7 Sarıcan Turkey
197 Q6 Sarichioi Romania
129 E6 Sarıçiçek Dağı mt. Turkey
192 B3 Sari-d'Orcino Corse France
182 I3 Sariegos Spain
91 K3 Sarigan i. N. Mariana Is
129 C5 Sarıgöl Artvin Turkey
199 J4 Sarıgöl Manisa Turkey
199 M5 Sarıdris Turkey
127 K3 Sarıkamış Turkey
128 B2 Sarıkavak Turkey
95 I3 Sarikei Sarawak Malaysia
199 I5 Sarıkemer Turkey
199 I2 Sarıköy Turkey
Sarikŭl, Qatorkŭhi mts China/Tajik. see Sarykol Range
116 G7 Sarila Uttar Prad. India
94 □ Sarimbun Reservoir Sing.
85 L6 Sarina Qld Austr.
186 E4 Sariñena Spain
210 D4 Sarinleev Somalia
Sarıoğlan Turkey see Belören
129 D6 Sarıpınar Turkey
122 F3 Sāri Qamīsh Iran
Sariqamish Kuli salt l. Turkm./Uzbek. see Sarykamyshskoye Ozero
202 C4 Sarīr Tibesti des. Libya
202 D3 Sarir Water Wells Field Libya
117 L7 Sarishabari Bangl.
129 B4 Sarısu Turkey
129 J5 Sarısu Gölü l. Azer.
237 G12 Sarita TX U.S.A.
128 A2 Sarıveliler Turkey
101 D9 Sariwŏn N. Korea
129 I6 Sarıxanlı Azer.
199 M2 Sarıyar Turkey
199 K1 Sarıyer Turkey
126 H4 Sarız Turkey
158 G3 Sark i. Channel Is
177 K5 Sarkad Hungary
177 K5 Sarkadkeresztúr Hungary
121 R5 Sarkand Kazakh.
116 C6 Sarkari Tala Rajasthan India
177 H4 Sárkeresztes Hungary
177 H4 Sárkeresztúr Hungary
126 E4 Şarkikaraağaç Turkey
141 Q6 Särkisalo Fin.
126 H4 Şarkışla Turkey
199 I2 Şarköy Turkey
123 L7 Sarlath Range mts Afgh./Pak.
163 G6 Sarlat-la-Canéda France
122 F2 Şarlawuk Turkm.
179 I2 Sarleinsbach Austria
162 F5 Sarliac-sur-l'Isle France
129 E2 Sarmakovo Rus. Fed.
123 K5 Sarmalan Afgh.
134 K5 Sarmanovo Rus. Fed.
197 K3 Sărmăşag Romania
197 M4 Sărmaşu Romania
195 K3 Sarmento r. Italy
91 I7 Sarmi Papua Indon.
259 C7 Sarmiento Arg.
141 L6 Särna Sweden
182 E9 Sarnadas do Ródão Port.
175 K3 Sarnaki Pol.
193 K1 Sarnano Italy
138 E4 Sārnate Latvia
117 I7 Sarnath Uttar Prad. India
122 B5 Sarneh Iran
190 E2 Sarnen Switz.
190 E2 Sarner See l. Switz.
Sarni Madh. Prad. India see Amla
224 D5 Sarnia Ont. Can.
190 H4 Sarnico Italy
193 N6 Sarno Italy
174 E4 Sarnowa Pol.
136 F2 Sarny Ukr.
93 B5 Saroako Sulawesi Indon.
139 S3 Sarogozha r. Rus. Fed.
94 E6 Sarolangun Sumatera Indon.
102 U2 Saroma-ko l. Japan
226 C4 Sarona WI U.S.A.
198 E5 Saronikos Kolpos g. Greece
190 G4 Saronno Italy
177 H4 Sárosd Hungary
199 H2 Saros Körfezi b. Turkey
177 K3 Sárospatak Hungary
116 D7 Sarotra Gujarat India
135 H5 Sarova Rus. Fed.
177 H3 Šarovce Slovakia
170 H3 Sarow Ger.
123 M4 Sarowbī Afgh.
135 I6 Sarpa, Ozero l. Rus. Fed.
135 I7 Sarpa, Ozero l. Rus. Fed.
Sarpan i. N. Mariana Is see Rota
92 □ Sar Passage Palau
196 I9 Šar Planina mts Macedonia/Yugo.
142 H2 Sarpsborg Norway
Sarqant Kazakh. see Sarkand
192 C9 Sarrabus reg. Sardegna Italy
183 M4 Sarracín Spain
186 H5 Sarral Spain
157 N6 Sarralbe France
163 C9 Sarrance France
163 E10 Sarrancolin France
161 B7 Sarrans, Barrage de dam France
182 E5 Sarraquinhos Port.
161 F6 Sarras France
157 N5 Sarre r. France
190 C4 Sarre Italy
151 O5 Sarre Kent, England U.K.
Sarreal Spain see Sarral
182 E4 Sarreaus Spain
157 N6 Sarre Blanche r. France
157 N6 Sarrebourg France
157 N5 Sarreguemines France
177 H4 Sarreti park Hungary
177 K4 Sárrétudvari Hungary
157 N6 Sarre-Union France
182 F3 Sarria Spain
186 K3 Sarrià de Ter Spain
161 F8 Sarrians France
187 D7 Sarrión Spain
206 D3 Sarro Mali
186 G5 Sarroca de Lleida Spain
192 C9 Sarròch Sardegna Italy
179 O4 Sarród Hungary
192 B3 Sarrola-Carcopino Corse France
163 D8 Sarron France
156 H6 Sarry France
134 L4 Sars Rus. Fed.
191 M8 Sarsina Italy
162 I4 Sarssonne r. France
169 I6 Sarstedt Ger.
177 H5 Sárszentágota Hungary
177 H4 Sárszentmihály Hungary
165 I7 Sart Belgium
183 P4 Sartaguda Spain
137 Q6 Sartana Ukr.
123 N8 Sartanahu Pak.
192 H2 Sarteano Italy
192 B4 Sartène Corse France
159 L6 Sarthe dept France
159 J6 Sarthe r. France
198 E2 Sarti Greece
129 G4 Sart'ichala Georgia
158 I4 Sartilly France
138 E6 Sartininkai Lith.
106 A3 Sartokay Xinjiang China
Sartu Heilong. China see Daqing
177 J4 Sarud Hungary
122 D4 Sarud, Rūdkhāneh-ye r. Iran
102 T4 Saru-gawa r. Japan
199 I4 Saruhanlı Turkey
192 C7 Sarule Sardegna Italy
123 L8 Saruna Pak.
123 L8 Saruna r. Pak.
116 D5 Sarupsar Rajasthan India
122 C4 Saruq Iran
129 F6 Şārur Azer.
123 J6 Saru Tara tourist site Afgh.
125 O2 Sarvāb Iran
122 B4 Sarvābād Iran
Sarvani Georgia see Marneuli
176 F4 Sárvár Hungary
122 E7 Sarvestān Iran
186 E2 Sarvisé Spain
196 G4 Sárvíz r. Romania
177 H5 Sárvíz-malomcsatorna canal Hungary
116 E6 Sarwar Rajasthan India
114 C3 Sarya r. India
121 M7 Saryagash Kazakh.
138 K6 Sar"yanka r. Belarus/Latvia
120 I4 Sarybasat Kazakh.
121 O7 Sary-Bulak Kyrg.
Sarydhaz r. Kyrg. see Sary-Jaz
Sarydzhas Kazakh. see Saryzhaz
Sarygamysh Köli salt l. Turkm./Uzbek. see Sarykamyshskoye Ozero
Sary-Ishikotrau, Peski des. Kazakh. see Saryyesik-Atyrau, Peski
121 R6 Sary-Jaz r. Kyrg.
120 E5 Sarykamys Atyrauskaya Oblast' Kazakh.
121 L3 Sarykamys Karagandinskaya Oblast' Kazakh.
122 G1 Sarykamyshskoye Ozero salt l. Turkm./Uzbek.
121 N6 Sarykemer Kazakh.
121 P2 Sarykiyak Kazakh.
120 K1 Sarykol' Kazakh.
123 P2 Sarykol Range mts China/Tajik.
121 P5 Sarykomey Kazakh.
120 K2 Sarymoyyn, Ozero salt l. Kazakh.
121 R5 Saryozek Kazakh.
Saryqamys Kazakh. see Sarykamys
121 O4 Saryshagan Kazakh.
121 L5 Sarysu watercourse Kazakh.
129 H2 Sarysu Rus. Fed.
120 D5 Sarytash Kazakh.
121 O8 Sary-Tash Kyrg.
121 Q7 Saryter, Gora mt. Kyrg.
120 D2 Saryumir Kazakh.
123 J3 Saryýazy Suw Howdany resr Turkm.
121 P5 Saryyesik-Atyrau, Peski des. Kazakh.
Saryzhal Kazakh. see Sarzhal
121 R6 Saryzhaz Kazakh.
190 H7 Sarzana Italy
158 F6 Sarzeau France
182 E9 Sarzedas Port.
120 D6 Sarzha Kazakh.
121 R3 Sarzhal Kazakh.
241 U10 Sasabe AZ U.S.A.
210 D2 Sasabeneh Eth.
94 C4 Sasak Sumatera Indon.
183 L4 Sasamón Spain
78 □6 Sasamungga Choiseul Solomon Is
93 A8 Sasar, Tanjung pt Sumba Indon.
117 J7 Sasaram Bihar India
78 □6 Sasari, Mount Sta Isabel Solomon Is
104 B5 Sasayama Japan
172 D5 Sasbach Baden-Württemberg Ger.
172 E4 Sasbach Baden-Württemberg Ger.
172 E4 Sasbachwalden Ger.
137 L3 Saschnivka Ukr.
177 H5 Sásd Hungary
103 G13 Sasebo Japan
175 I2 Sasek Wielki, Jezioro l. Pol.
105 K3 Sashima Japan
137 L5 Sasivka Ukr.
223 J4 Saskatchewan prov. Can.
223 K4 Saskatchewan r. Man./Sask. Can.
222 J5 Saskatchewan Landing Provincial Park Sask. Can.
223 J4 Saskatoon Sask. Can.
131 M2 Saskylakh Rus. Fed.
242 □Q11 Saslaya mt. Nic.
242 □Q11 Saslaya, Parque Nacional nat. park Nic.
136 I1 Sasnovy Bor Belarus
215 L2 Sasolburg S. Africa
135 H5 Sasovo Rus. Fed.
222 H2 Sass r. N.W.T. Can.
234 D6 Sassafras MD U.S.A.
206 D5 Sassandra Côte d'Ivoire
206 D5 Sassandra r. Côte d'Ivoire
193 P7 Sassano Italy
192 B6 Sassari Sardegna Italy
192 B6 Sassari prov. Sardegna Italy
190 E7 Sassello Italy
170 H2 Sassen Ger.
161 H6 Sassenage France
169 F7 Sassenberg Ger.
164 G4 Sassenheim Neth.
192 F1 Sassetta Italy
170 I1 Sassnitz Ger.
191 M8 Sassocorvaro Italy
190 G3 Sasso della Paglia mt. Switz.
191 K7 Sasso di Castro mt. Italy
191 N9 Sassoferrato Italy
191 L2 Sasso Lungo mt. Italy
191 K7 Sasso Marconi Italy
191 L2 Sass Rigais mt. Italy
206 C5 Sass Town Liberia
191 J6 Sassuolo Italy
186 E5 Sástago Spain
176 G3 Šaštín-Stráže Slovakia
121 N6 Sastobe Kazakh.
261 G2 Sastre Arg.
114 D3 Sasvad Mahar. India
165 E6 Sas Van Gent Neth.
137 K7 Sasyk r. Ukr.
137 M8 Sasyk, Ozero l. Ukr.
121 S4 Sasykkol', Ozero l. Kazakh.
135 I7 Sasykoli Rus. Fed.
Sasyqköl l. Kazakh. see Sasykkol', Ozero
206 C3 Satadougou Mali
Satahual i. Micronesia see Satawal
206 D5 Satama-Sokoura Côte d'Ivoire
103 H16 Sata-misaki c. Japan
116 E9 Satana Mahar. India
136 F4 Sataniv Ukr.
182 E7 Satão Port.
78 □2 Satapuala Samoa
114 D4 Satara Mahar. India
213 F5 Satara S. Africa
78 □2 Sataua Samoa
91 K5 Satawal i. Micronesia
Sätbaev Kazakh. see Satpayev
196 J5 Satchinez Romania
208 D3 Satéma C.A.R.
95 L8 Satengar i. Indon.
143 L1 Säter Sweden
242 F4 Satevó Mex.
239 K13 Satevo r. Mex.
240 M7 Saticoy CA U.S.A.
140 O3 Satihaure l. Sweden
231 G10 Satilla r. GA U.S.A.
161 F6 Satillieu France
135 H5 Satinka Rus. Fed.
252 B2 Satipo Peru
206 D4 Satiri Burkina
Satırlar Turkey see Yeşilova
130 G4 Satka Rus. Fed.
117 N9 Satkania Bangl.
129 E4 Sat'khe Georgia
117 L8 Satkhira Bangl.
Satluj r. India/Pak. see Sutlej
114 F3 Satmala Range hills India
116 H7 Satna Madh. Prad. India
160 G5 Satolas airport France
105 L2 Satomi Japan
95 L9 Satonda i. Indon.
177 K3 Sátoraljaújhely Hungary
188 E3 Satorina mt. Croatia
170 E3 Satow Ger.
121 L3 Satpayev Karagandinskaya Oblast' Kazakh.
121 L4 Satpayev Karagandinskaya Oblast' Kazakh.
116 E9 Satpura Range mts India
193 P6 Satriano di Lucania Italy
138 F6 Šatrijos kalnis hill Lith.
168 I1 Satrup Ger.
103 H15 Satsuma-hantō pen. Japan
102 U4 Satsunai-gawa r. Japan
97 E8 Sattahip Thai.
140 S3 Sattanen Fin.
105 K3 Satte Japan
178 A5 Satteins Austria
173 I3 Satteldorf Ger.
114 G4 Sattenapalle Andhra Prad. India
96 B5 Satthwa Myanmar
116 F2 Satti Jammu and Kashmir
179 J3 Sattledt Austria
179 J6 Sattnitz reg. Austria
95 K6 Satui Kalimantan Indon.
197 K3 Satu Mare Romania
177 L4 Satu Mare county Romania
97 E11 Satun Thai.
102 □F18 Satunan-shotō is Japan
78 □2 Satupa'itea Samoa
261 F2 Saturnino M. Laspiur Arg.
116 F8 Satwas Madh. Prad. India
186 J4 Sau, Pantà de resr Spain
179 K6 Saualpe mts Austria
142 C2 Sauanuten mt. Norway
95 K8 Saubi i. Indon.
163 B8 Saubusse France
177 L4 Săuca Romania
183 O6 Saúca Spain
163 C6 Saucats France
261 H2 Sauce Arg.
261 G6 Sauce r. Arg.
237 E13 Sauceda Mex.
241 T9 Sauceda Mountains AZ U.S.A.
261 H2 Sauce de Luna Arg.
261 I2 Saucedo Uru.
182 G6 Saucelle, Embalse de resr Port./Spain
242 G3 Saucillo Mex.
161 C9 Sauclières France
142 C2 Sauda Norway
121 M6 Saudakent Kazakh.
140 □D1 Sauðárkrókur Iceland
118 E5 Saudi Arabia country Asia
138 H2 Saue Estonia
168 I4 Sauensiek Ger.
157 P6 Sauer r. France
173 L6 Sauerlach Ger.
169 E8 Sauerland reg. Ger.
253 F3 Sauêruiná r. Brazil
92 E8 Saug r. Mindanao Phil.
138 H3 Sauga r. Estonia
226 H7 Saugatuck MI U.S.A.
235 I2 Saugatuck Reservoir CT U.S.A.
224 D4 Saugeen r. Ont. Can.
233 L6 Saugerties NY U.S.A.
149 L7 Saughall Cheshire, England U.K.
163 C7 Saugnacq-et-Muret France
161 D7 Saugues France
Sāūjbolāgh Iran see Mahābād
258 D2 Saujil Arg.
162 C4 Saujon France
138 I5 Saukas ezers l. Latvia
236 H3 Sauk Center MN U.S.A.
226 E6 Sauk City WI U.S.A.
251 H4 Saül Fr. Guiana
147 K4 Saul Northern Ireland U.K.
163 G10 Saula, Port de pass Spain
142 E2 Sauland Norway
161 F7 Saulce-sur-Rhône France
157 M7 Saulcy-sur-Meurthe France
172 G6 Sauldorf Ger.
162 G1 Sauldre r. France
172 H5 Saulgau Ger.
162 F3 Saulgé France
173 K6 Saulgrub Ger.
172 E2 Saulheim Ger.
160 E2 Saulieu France
138 H4 Saulkrasti Latvia
157 L6 Saulnois reg. France
161 G8 Sault France
163 C8 Sault-de-Navailles France
156 H5 Sault-lès-Rethel France
224 C4 Sault Sainte Marie Ont. Can.
227 J3 Sault Sainte Marie MI U.S.A.
157 L8 Saulx France
157 I6 Saulx r. France
157 M8 Saulxures-sur-Moselotte France
160 B3 Saulzais-le-Potier France
121 M1 Saumalkol' Kazakh.
85 N6 Saumarez Reef Coral Sea Is Terr. Austr.
91 H8 Saumlakki Maluku Indon.
163 B6 Saumos France
162 D1 Saumur France
159 K7 Saumurois reg. France
140 S3 Saunavaara Fin.
84 C2 Saunders, Mount hill N.T. Austr.
262 O1 Saunders Coast Antarctica
150 C4 Saundersfoot Pembrokeshire, Wales U.K.
259 E8 Saunders Island Falkland Is
249 G7 Saunders Island S. Sandwich Is
226 F9 Saunemin IL U.S.A.
97 D10 Saung Thai.
96 C2 Saungka Myanmar
233 J5 Sauquoit NY U.S.A.
121 U4 Saur, Khrebet mts China/Kazakh.
120 D5 Saura Kazakh.
163 H10 Saurat France
138 H5 Saurieši Latvia
209 D7 Saurimo Angola
191 N3 Sauris Italy
191 N3 Sauris, Lago di l. Italy
193 Q7 Sauro r. Italy
179 L6 Sausal hills Austria
240 J4 Sausalito CA U.S.A.
116 G9 Sausar Madh. Prad. India
161 G10 Sausset-les-Pins France
160 F2 Saussy France
93 B4 Sausu Sulawesi Indon.
209 C7 Sautar Angola
178 C5 Sautens Austria
163 D6 Sauternes France
247 □6 Sauteurs Grenada
158 H7 Sautron France
163 D9 Sauvagnon France
161 D9 Sauve France
161 C8 Sauveterre, Causse de plat. France
163 C9 Sauveterre-de-Béarn France
163 D6 Sauveterre-de-Guyenne France
163 I7 Sauveterre-de Rouergue France
163 G6 Sauveterre-la-Lémance France
162 H4 Sauviat-sur-Vige France
160 C3 Sauvigny-les-Bois France
141 Q6 Sauvo Fin.
164 K2 Sauwerd Neth.
160 C5 Sauxillanges France
260 A4 Sauzal Maule Chile
260 B4 Sauzal O'Higgins Chile
244 C1 Sauz de Arriba Mex.
163 G7 Sauzet France
162 E3 Sauzé-Vaussais France
158 E7 Sauzon France
167 J6 Sava r. Europe
242 □P10 Savá Hond.
195 N3 Sava Italy
179 K7 Sava Slovenia
234 B6 Savage MD U.S.A.
83 J9 Savage River Tas. Austr.
78 □2 Savai'i i. Samoa
135 H6 Savala r. Rus. Fed.
207 F5 Savalou Benin
Savanat Iran see Eşţahbān
225 G3 Savane r. Que. Can.
213 G3 Savane Moz.
247 □9 Savaneta Aruba
236 J4 Savanna IL U.S.A.
231 G9 Savannah GA U.S.A.
236 H6 Savannah MO U.S.A.
232 C8 Savannah OH U.S.A.
237 K8 Savannah TN U.S.A.
231 G9 Savannah r. GA/SC U.S.A.
246 E1 Savannah Sound Eleuthera Bahamas
96 G6 Savannakhét Laos
246 □ Savanna-la-Mar Jamaica
226 D1 Savanne Ont. Can.
224 B3 Savant Lake Ont. Can.
224 B3 Savant Lake l. Ont. Can.
Savantvadi Mahar. India see Vadi
114 D5 Savanur Karnataka India
140 P5 Sävar Sweden
197 K4 Săvârşin Romania
140 P4 Sävast Sweden
199 I3 Savaştepe Turkey
179 N7 Savci Slovenia
207 F4 Savè Benin
163 G8 Save r. France
213 G4 Save Moz.
213 G4 Save r. Moz./Zimbabwe
122 D4 Sāveh Iran
195 L5 Savelli Italy
206 E4 Savelugu Ghana
191 K7 Savena r. Italy
158 H7 Savenay France
197 O3 Săveni Romania
163 H9 Saverdun France
251 G3 Saveretik Guyana
157 N6 Saverne France
140 T5 Saviaho Fin.
156 G7 Savières France
190 D6 Savigliano Italy
162 F5 Savignac-les-Églises France
193 O5 Savignano Irpino Italy
191 M7 Savignano sul Rubicone Italy
159 L5 Savigné-l'Évêque France
160 E5 Savigneux France
160 B2 Savigny-en-Sancerre France
160 F2 Savigny-lès-Beaune France
159 M6 Savigny-sur-Braye France
156 D6 Savigny-sur-Orge France
161 I7 Savines-le-Lac France
197 O4 Săvineşti Romania
139 O8 Savinichy Belarus
188 E2 Savinja r. Slovenia
120 B2 Savinka Rus. Fed.
139 Y5 Savino Rus. Fed.
134 L3 Savinobor Rus. Fed.
134 H3 Savinskiy Rus. Fed.
139 W6 Savinskoye Rus. Fed.
191 M7 Savio r. Italy
141 S6 Savitaipale Fin.
114 C3 Savitri r. India
143 N2 Sävja Sweden
199 L5 Savköy Turkey
196 H8 Šavnik Montenegro
78 □6 Savo i. Solomon Is
190 H2 Savognin Switz.
193 P6 Savoia di Lucania Italy
160 J6 Savoie dept France
160 I4 Savoie reg. France
156 H8 Savoisy France
190 E7 Savona Italy
190 E7 Savona prov. Italy
193 L5 Savone r. Italy
141 T6 Savonlinna Fin.
140 T5 Savonranta Fin.
220 A3 Savoonga AK U.S.A.
Savoy reg. France see Savoie
139 Q1 Savozero, Ozero l. Rus. Fed.
136 J5 Savran' Ukr.
136 J5 Savranka r. Ukr.
127 K3 Şavşat Turkey
143 K4 Sävsjö Sweden
93 B9 Savu i. Indon.
191 O5 Savudrija Croatia
188 D3 Savudrija, Rt pt Croatia
140 T3 Savukoski Fin.
127 J5 Savur Turkey
79 □7 Savusavu Vanua Levu Fiji
79 □7 Savusavu Bay Vanua Levu Fiji
Savu Sea Indon. see Sawu, Laut
212 E3 Savute r. Botswana
212 E3 Savuti Botswana
193 Q9 Savuto r. Italy
107 P1 Savvo-Borzya Rus. Fed.
137 L2 Savynky Ukr.
137 Q4 Savyntsi Ukr.
96 B4 Saw Myanmar
94 D5 Sawahlunto Sumatera Indon.
93 F5 Sawai, Teluk b. Seram Indon.
116 F7 Sawai Madhopur Rajasthan India
79 □7 Sawaleke Fiji
95 K5 Sawan Kalimantan Indon.
96 C1 Sawan Myanmar
96 D6 Sawankhalok Thai.
116 E7 Sawar Rajasthan India
105 M4 Sawara Japan
103 P9 Sawasaki-bana pt Japan
102 P9 Sawata Japan
239 K7 Sawatch Range mts CO U.S.A.
151 M4 Sawbridgeworth Hertfordshire, England U.K.
202 B2 Sawdā', Jabal as hills Libya
147 H3 Sawel Mountain hill Northern Ireland U.K.
203 F3 Sawhāj Sawhāj Egypt
97 D9 Sawi, Ao b. Thai.
175 L4 Sawin Pol.
206 E4 Sawla Ghana
213 F3 Sawmills Zimbabwe
96 C3 Sawn Yunnan China
125 M6 Şawqirah, Ghubbat b. Oman
125 M6 Şawqirah, Ra's c. Oman
Şawqirah Bay Oman see Şawqirah, Ghubbat
151 M3 Sawston Cambridgeshire, England U.K.
83 N4 Sawtell N.S.W. Austr.
226 C2 Sawtooth Mountains hills MN U.S.A.
238 G4 Sawtooth Range mts ID U.S.A.
238 D2 Sawtooth Range mts WA U.S.A.
151 L3 Sawtry Cambridgeshire, England U.K.
93 B9 Sawu Indon.
Sawu i. Indon. see Savu
93 B8 Sawu, Laut sea Indon.
187 D10 Sax Spain
146 □O1 Saxa Vord hill Scotland U.K.
85 H5 Saxby r. Qld Austr.
179 K3 Saxen Austria
149 P7 Saxilby Lincolnshire, England U.K.
222 D4 Saxman AK U.S.A.
151 O3 Saxmundham Suffolk, England U.K.
140 M4 Saxnäs Sweden
190 C3 Saxon Switz.
Saxony land Ger. see Sachsen
Saxony-Anhalt land Ger. see Sachsen-Anhalt
151 O2 Saxthorpe Norfolk, England U.K.
232 A12 Saxton KY U.S.A.
232 G8 Saxton PA U.S.A.
206 D3 Say Mali
207 F3 Say Niger
108 C2 Saya Sichuan China
104 E5 Saya Japan
128 D3 Şāyā Syria
Sayabouri Laos see Xaignabouli
93 F3 Sayafi i. Maluku Indon.
182 H6 Sayago reg. Spain
121 Q4 Sayak Kazakh.
114 F8 Sayalkudi Tamil Nadu India
207 I3 Sayam well Niger
105 J4 Sayama Japan
252 A2 Sayán Peru
93 F3 Sayang i. Papua Indon.
98 F1 Sayano-Shushenskoye Vodokhranilishche resr Rus. Fed.
Sayaq Kazakh. see Sayak
123 J2 Saýat Turkm.
183 O8 Sayatón Spain
243 N9 Sayaxché Guat.
171 H9 Sayda Ger.
Sayda Lebanon see Saïda
162 D6 Saye r. France
122 F6 Sāyen Iran
128 D1 Saygeçit Turkey
123 L4 Sayghān Afgh.
124 G7 Şayḩ well Yemen
125 M5 Şayḩ al Aḩmar reg. Oman
125 J8 Sayḩūt Yemen
129 H6 Şayıflı Azer.
108 D5 Sayingpan Yunnan China
120 B3 Saykhin Kazakh.
210 D2 Saylac Somalia
Saylan country Asia see Sri Lanka
234 E3 Saylorsburg PA U.S.A.
110 I2 Saylyugem, Khrebet mts Rus. Fed.
107 L4 Saynshand Mongolia
106 D3 Sayn-Ust Mongolia
Sayot Turkm. see Saýat
Say-Ötesh Kazakh. see Say-Utes
128 F5 Şayqal, Baḩr imp. l. Syria
Şayqyn Kazakh. see Saykhin
110 E4 Sayram Hu salt l. China
121 N6 Sayramskiy, Pik mt. Uzbek.
237 F8 Sayre OK U.S.A.
227 R8 Sayre PA U.S.A.
235 G4 Sayreville NJ U.S.A.
123 L3 Sayrob Uzbek.
106 D5 Saysu Xinjiang China
244 D6 Sayula Jalisco Mex.
245 M8 Sayula Veracruz Mex.
244 D6 Sayula, Laguna de imp. l. Mex.
125 I7 Say'ūn Yemen
120 E5 Say-Utes Kazakh.
235 I3 Sayville NY U.S.A.
222 E5 Sayward B.C. Can.
125 M6 Sayy well Oman
Sayyod Turkm. see Saýat
198 A2 Sazan i. Albania
176 D2 Sázava r. Czech Rep.
120 C4 Sazdy Kazakh.
134 L4 Sazhino Rus. Fed.
137 P3 Sazhnoye Rus. Fed.
217 □3b Sazile, Pointe pt Mayotte
123 O4 Sazin Pak.
139 S2 Sazonovo Rus. Fed.
Saztöbe Kazakh. see Sastobe
205 E3 Sbaa Alg.
205 H2 Sbeitla Tunisia
87 F12 Scaddan W.A. Austr.
158 D5 Scaër France
193 M3 Scafa Italy
149 K5 Scafell Pike hill England U.K.
234 B6 Scaggsville MD U.S.A.
194 G9 Scala, Monte della hill Italy
146 D10 Scalasaig Argyll and Bute, Scotland U.K.
149 Q5 Scalby North Yorkshire, England U.K.
149 K2 Scald Law hill Scotland U.K.
193 P8 Scalea Italy
193 P8 Scalea, Capo c. Italy
195 I7 Scaletta Zanclea Sicilia Italy
146 □N2 Scalloway Shetland, Scotland U.K.
Scalpaigh, Eilean i. Western Isles, Scotland U.K. see Scalpay
146 E8 Scalpay i. Highland, Scotland U.K.
146 C7 Scalpay i. Western Isles, Scotland U.K.
147 H2 Scalp Mountain hill Ireland
83 L9 Scamander Tas. Austr.
161 E9 Scamandre, Étang de lag. France
220 B3 Scammon Bay AK U.S.A.
149 P7 Scampton Lincolnshire, England U.K.
195 L5 Scandale Italy
193 K2 Scandarello, Lago di l. Italy
191 J6 Scandiano Italy
191 K8 Scandicci Italy
193 J3 Scandriglia Italy
Scania reg. Sweden see Skåne
193 L4 Scanno Italy
193 L4 Scanno, Lago di l. Italy
192 B7 Scano di Montiferro Sardegna Italy
192 G2 Scansano Italy
197 P6 Scânteia Romania
195 L3 Scanzano Jonico Italy
146 K5 Scapa Orkney, Scotland U.K.
146 J5 Scapa Flow inlet Scotland U.K.
146 I6 Scaraben hill Scotland U.K.
146 E10 Scarba i. Scotland U.K.
224 E5 Scarborough Ont. Can.
247 □5 Scarborough Trin. and Tob.
149 Q5 Scarborough North Yorkshire, England U.K.
90 E3 Scarborough Shoal sea feature S. China Sea
232 D11 Scarbro WV U.S.A.
191 M6 Scardovari Italy
81 G9 Scargill South I. N.Z.
147 B9 Scariff Island Ireland
146 C9 Scarinish Argyll and Bute, Scotland U.K.
149 L6 Scarisbrick Lancashire, England U.K.
234 D4 Scarlets Mill PA U.S.A.
192 F2 Scarlino Italy
146 B6 Scarp i. Scotland U.K.
Scarpanto i. Greece see Karpathos
156 F2 Scarpe r. France
191 K8 Scarperia Italy
147 E7 Scarriff Ireland
235 H2 Scarsdale NY U.S.A.
147 J4 Scarva Northern Ireland U.K.
225 J4 Scaterie Island N.S. Can.
194 B10 Scauri Sicilia Italy
146 D8 Scavaig, Loch b. Scotland U.K.
179 N6 Ščavnica r. Slovenia
94 G1 Scawfell Shoal sea feature S. China Sea
82 E5 Sceale Bay S.A. Austr.
188 F4 Šćedro i. Croatia
193 N3 Scerni Italy
157 K8 Scey-sur-Saône-et-St-Albin France
172 G2 Schaafheim Ger.
168 I1 Schaalby Ger.
168 K4 Schaale r. Ger.
168 K3 Schaalsee l. Ger.
168 K3 Schaalsee park Ger.
172 H7 Schaan Liechtenstein
164 I4 Schaarsbergen Neth.
168 I2 Schacht-Audorf Ger.
234 C4 Schaefferstown PA U.S.A.
165 F7 Schaerbeek Belgium
165 J7 Schaesberg Neth.
190 F1 Schaffhausen Switz.
190 F1 Schaffhausen canton Switz.
168 H1 Schafflund Ger.
168 H2 Schafstedt Ger.
173 K6 Schäftlarn Ger.
164 G3 Schagen Neth.
164 G3 Schagerbrug Neth.
164 I5 Schaijk Neth.
212 C5 Schakalskuppe Namibia
178 H3 Schalchen Austria
171 D10 Schalkau Ger.
164 J4 Schalkhaar Neth.
169 E8 Schalksmühle Ger.
172 D6 Schallstadt Ger.
190 G1 Schänis Switz.
122 I6 Schao watercourse Afgh./Iran
169 E6 Schapen Ger.
170 H1 Schaprode Ger.
168 K2 Scharbeutz Ger.
179 H2 Schardenberg Austria
179 H3 Schärding Austria
178 H5 Schareck mt. Austria
164 E5 Scharendijke Neth.
178 E4 Scharfreiter mt. Austri
168 F3 Scharhörn sea feature
171 J6 Scharmützelsee l. Ger
168 K4 Scharnebeck Ger.
164 I2 Scharnegoutum Neth.
178 D5 Scharnitz Austria
179 I4 Scharnstein Austria
168 E4 Scharrel (Oldenburg)
169 C10 Scharteberg hill Ger.
164 H3 Scharwoude Neth.
168 K2 Schashagen Ger.
179 O4 Schattendorf Austria
226 F7 Schaumburg IL U.S.A.
173 I2 Schebheim Ger.
173 M6 Schechen Ger.
169 I8 Scheden Ger.
164 K2 Scheemda Neth.
172 G5 Scheer Ger.
168 H4 Scheeßel Ger.
178 H4 Scheffau am Tenneng Austria
178 F4 Scheffau am Wilden K Austria
225 H2 Schefferville Nfld and Can.
172 G3 Schefflenz Ger.
191 N9 Scheggia e Pascelupo
193 J2 Scheggino Italy
179 L3 Scheibbs Austria
179 N4 Scheiblingkirchen Aus
172 H6 Scheidegg Ger.
179 J5 Scheifling Austria
173 I2 Scheinfeld Ger.
172 H5 Schelklingen Ger.
241 R3 Schell Creek Range m NV U.S.A.
165 F6 Schelle Belgium
169 J6 Schellerten Ger.
168 J2 Schellhorn Ger.
232 G8 Schellsburg PA U.S.A.
240 J3 Schellville CA U.S.A.
172 H5 Schemmerhofen Ger.
233 L6 Schenectady NY U.S.A.
168 H2 Schenefeld Schleswig- Ger.
168 I3 Schenefeld Schleswig- Ger.
179 J2 Schenkenfelden Austr
172 E5 Schenkenzell Ger.
169 I9 Schenklengsfeld Ger.
169 C7 Schermbeck Ger.
171 E6 Schermen Ger.
164 G3 Schermerhorn Neth.
169 K8 Schernberg Ger.
173 K4 Schernfeld Ger.
165 G7 Scherpenheuvel Belgi
164 H4 Scherpenzeel Neth.
237 F11 Schertz TX U.S.A.
157 N7 Scherwiller France
190 G1 Scherzingen Switz.
178 A5 Schesaplana mt. Austria
173 K2 Scheßlitz Ger.
173 K5 Scheyern Ger.
191 M3 Schiara, Monte mt. Ita
193 M4 Schiavi di Abruzzo Ita
164 F5 Schiedam Neth.
169 H7 Schieder-Schwalenbe
179 J6 Schiefling am See Au
146 H9 Schiehallion mt. Scotland U.K.
165 J9 Schieren Lux.
169 K7 Schierke Ger.
173 M4 Schierling Ger.
164 J2 Schiermonnikoog Net
164 J1 Schiermonnikoog i. N
164 J1 Schiermonnikoog Nat Park nat. park Neth.
190 H2 Schiers Switz.
168 G3 Schiffdorf Ger.
172 E3 Schifferstadt Ger.
165 J9 Schifflange Lux.
172 C3 Schiffweiler Ger.
164 H5 Schijndel Neth.
165 G6 Schilde Belgium
168 K4 Schilde r. Ger.
164 K2 Schildmeer l. Neth.
170 H5 Schildow Ger.
164 K2 Schildwolde-Hellum N
172 B2 Schillingen Ger.
173 I3 Schillingsfürst Ger.
190 I3 Schilpario Italy
172 E5 Schiltach Ger.
173 K5 Schiltberg Ger.
157 O6 Schiltigheim France
198 E4 Schimatari Greece
165 I7 Schinnen Neth.
165 I7 Schinveld Neth.
191 K4 Schio Italy
164 J4 Schipbeek r. Neth.
164 G4 Schiphol airport Neth.
171 I7 Schipkau Ger.
157 N7 Schirmeck France
173 M2 Schirmitz Ger.
171 F10 Schirnding Ger.
197 P3 Schitu Duca Romania
198 C6 Schiza i. Greece
171 F8 Schkeuditz Ger.
171 E8 Schkölen Ger.
171 G7 Schköna Ger.
171 E8 Schkopau Ger.
171 I7 Schlabendorf Ger.
169 K6 Schladen Ger.
179 I5 Schladming Austria
179 I5 Schladminger Tauern Austria
168 K3 Schlagsdorf Ger.
169 G7 Schlangen Ger.
169 F10 Schlangenbad Ger.
171 D6 Schlanstedt Ger.
173 M6 Schleching Ger.
178 E5 Schlegeisspeicher l. A
168 J1 Schlei r. Ger.
169 B9 Schleiden Ger.
171 K7 Schleife Ger.
179 N3 Schleinbach Austria
190 E1 Schleitheim Switz.
171 E9 Schleiz Ger.
171 G9 Schlema Ger.
171 I6 Schlepzig Ger.
Schlesien reg. Europe Silesia
168 I1 Schleswig Ger.
168 I2 Schleswig-Holstein la
168 G2 Schleswig-Holsteinisc Wattenmeer, National nat. park Ger.
171 G9 Schlettau Ger.
169 K9 Schleusingen Ger.
171 H7 Schlieben Ger.
172 D6 Schliengen Ger.
172 H6 Schlier Ger.
179 J4 Schlierbach Austria
190 E1 Schlieren Switz.
173 L6 Schliersee Ger.
173 L6 Schliersee l. Ger.
178 A5 Schlins Austria
178 E5 Schlitters Austria
169 I9 Schlitz Ger.
169 G7 Schloss Holte-Stuker Ger.
190 D2 Schlosswil Switz.
169 K8 Schlotheim Ger.
172 E6 Schluchsee Ger.
172 E6 Schluchsee l. Ger.
157 N7 Schlucht, Col de la pa France
169 I10 Schlüchtern Ger.
Schlüsselburg Rus. Fe Shlissel'burg
173 J2 Schlüsselfeld Ger.
168 I3 Schmalfeld Ger.
169 F8 Schmallenberg Ger.
172 B3 Schmelz Ger.
173 M3 Schmidgaden Ger.
173 L3 Schmidmühlen Ger.
Schmidt Island Rus. F Shmidta, Ostrov
214 I4 Schmidtsdrif S. Africa
171 I9 Schmiedeberg Ger.
178 E5 Schmirn Austria
178 G5 Schmittenhöhe mt. Au
170 J4 Schmölln Brandenburg
171 F9 Schmölln Thüringen Ge
173 L2 Schnabelwaid Ger.
170 E4 Schnackenburg Ger.
173 M5 Schnaitsee Ger.

Schnaittach Ger.
Schnaittenbach Ger.
Schnebelhorn mt. Switz.
Schnecksville PA U.S.A.
Schneeberg Ger.
Schnega Ger.
Schneidemühl Pol. see Piła
Schneidlingen Ger.
Schneifel hills Ger.
Schneizlreuth Ger.
Schnelldorf Ger.
Schneverdingen Ger.
Schnürpflingen Ger.
Schobüll Ger.
Schœlcher Martinique
Schoemanskloof pass S. Africa
Schoenberg Belgium
Schofield WI U.S.A.
Schofield Barracks military base HI U.S.A.
Schoharie NY U.S.A.
Schokland tourist site Neth.
Scholen Ger.
Scholes West Yorkshire, England U.K.
Schollene Ger.
Schöllkrippen Ger.
Schöllnach Ger.
Schombee S. Africa
Schömberg Baden-Württemberg Ger.
Schömberg Baden-Württemberg Ger.
Schönaich Ger.
Schönau Baden-Württemberg Ger.
Schönau Bayern Ger.
Schönau am Königssee Ger.
Schönau im Schwarzwald Ger.
Schönbach Austria
Schönberg Bayern Ger.
Schönberg Brandenburg Ger.
Schönberg Mecklenburg-Vorpommern Ger.
Schönberg Schleswig-Holstein Ger.
Schönberg (Holstein) Ger.
Schönberg am Kamp Austria
Schönbergerstrand Ger.
Schönberg im Stubaital Austria
Schönborn Ger.
Schönbrunn Ger.
Schönbuch reg. Ger.
Schönbuch, Naturpark nature res. Ger.
Schönburg Ger.
Schondra Ger.
Schönebeck Ger.
Schönebeck (Elbe) Ger.
Schöneck Ger.
Schönecken Ger.
Schönefeld Ger.
Schönefeld airport Ger.
Schöneiche Berlin Ger.
Schönenberg-Kübelberg Ger.
Schönermark Brandenburg Ger.
Schönermark Brandenburg Ger.
Schönewalde Ger.
Schönewörde Ger.
Schönfeld Ger.
Schongau Ger.
Schönhausen Ger.
Schönheide Ger.
Schöningen Ger.
Schönkirchen Ger.
Schönsee Ger.
Schönstedt Ger.
Schöntal Ger.
Schönthal Ger.
Schonungen Ger.
Schönwald Ger.
Schönwalde Brandenburg Ger.
Schönwalde Brandenburg Ger.
Schönwalde Brandenburg Ger.
Schönwalde am Bungsberg Ger.
Schönwies Austria
Schoodic Lake ME U.S.A.
Schoodic Point ME U.S.A.
Schoolcraft MI U.S.A.
Schoondijke Neth.
Schoonebeek Neth.
Schoonhoven Neth.
Schoonoord Neth.
Schoorl Neth.
Schopfheim Ger.
Schöpfl hill Austria
Schopfloch Ger.
Schöppenstedt Ger.
Schoppernau Austria
Schöppingen Ger.
Schorfheide reg. Ger.
Schörfling am Attersee Austria
Schorndorf Baden-Württemberg Ger.
Schorndorf Bayern Ger.
Schortens Ger.
Schoten Belgium
Schotten Ger.
Schouten Island Tas. Austr.
Schouten Islands P.N.G.
Schrader r. PA U.S.A.
Schramberg Ger.
Schrankogel mt. Austria
Schraplau Ger.
Schrecksbach Ger.
Schreiber Ont. Can.
Schrems Austria
Schrepkow Ger.
Schriesheim Ger.
Schrobenhausen Ger.
Schröder Austria
Schroon Lake NY U.S.A.
Schroon Lake l. NY U.S.A.
Schröttersburg Pol. see Płock
Schrozberg Ger.
Schruns Austria
Schübelbach Switz.
Schuby Ger.
Schulenberg im Oberharz Ger.
Schulenburg TX U.S.A.
Schuler Alta Can.
Schull Ireland
Schultz Lake Nunavut Can.
Schulzendorf Ger.
Schulzendorf bei Eichwalde Ger.
Schüpfheim Switz.
Schurwald for. Ger.
Schurz NV U.S.A.
Schussen r. Ger.
Schutter r. Ger.
Schutter r. Ger.
Schuttertal Ger.
Schutterwald Ger.
Schüttorf Ger.
Schuyler NE U.S.A.
Schuyler Lake NY U.S.A.
Schuylerville NY U.S.A.
Schuylkill r. PA U.S.A.
Schuylkill County county PA U.S.A.
Schuylkill Haven PA U.S.A.
Schwaan Ger.
Schwabach Ger.
Schwaben admin. reg. Ger.
Schwäbische Alb mts Ger.
Schwäbisch-Fränkischer Wald, Naturpark nature res. Ger.
Schwäbisch Gmünd Ger.
Schwäbisch Hall Ger.
Schwabmünchen Ger.
Schwabstedt Ger.
Schwaförden Ger.
Schwaig bei Nürnberg Ger.
Schwaigern Ger.
Schwalbach Ger.
Schwallungen Ger.
Schwalm r. Ger.
Schwalmstadt-Treysa Ger.
Schwalmstadt-Ziegenhain Ger.
Schwanberg Austria
Schwanden Switz.
Schwandorf Ger.
Schwanebeck Brandenburg Ger.
171 D7 Schwanebeck Sachsen-Anhalt Ger.
179 I3 Schwanenstadt Austria
95 J5 Schwaner, Pegunungan mts Indon.
168 G4 Schwanewede Ger.
173 J6 Schwangau Ger.
168 K4 Schwanheide Ger.
168 I1 Schwansen reg. Ger.
173 K3 Schwanstetten Ger.
168 H5 Schwarme Ger.
168 I5 Schwarmstedt Ger.
263 D2 Schwartz Range mts Antarctica
170 G4 Schwarz Ger.
169 K9 Schwarza Ger.
172 E6 Schwarza r. Ger.
171 D9 Schwarza r. Ger.
178 A5 Schwarzach Austria
173 N4 Schwarzach Ger.
173 K4 Schwarzach r. Ger.
173 M3 Schwarzach r. Ger.
178 H5 Schwarzach im Pongau Austria
179 M4 Schwarzau im Gebirge Austria
171 G7 Schwarze Elster r. Ger.
173 M4 Schwarze Laber r. Ger.
179 L2 Schwarzenau Austria
179 N4 Schwarzenbach Austria
171 E10 Schwarzenbach am Wald Ger.
171 E10 Schwarzenbach an der Saale Ger.
168 J3 Schwarzenbek Ger.
171 G9 Schwarzenberg Ger.
169 H9 Schwarzenborn Ger.
173 K3 Schwarzenbruck Ger.
190 C2 Schwarzenburg Switz.
173 M3 Schwarzenfeld Ger.
178 E5 Schwarzenstein mt. Austria/Italy
171 J7 Schwarze Pumpe Ger.
173 M3 Schwarzer Bach r. Ger.
169 B10 Schwarzer Mann hill Ger.
173 N3 Schwarzer Regen r. Ger.
171 K8 Schwarzer Schöps r. Ger.
191 P1 Schwarzersee l. Austria
171 I8 Schwarzheide Ger.
173 M3 Schwarzhofen Ger.
178 D5 Schwarzhorn mt. Austria
190 E2 Schwarzhorn mt. Switz.
212 C5 Schwarzrand mts Namibia
173 N3 Schwarzriegel mt. Ger.
172 E6 Schwarzwald mts Ger.
178 E5 Schwaz Austria
179 N3 Schwechat Austria
168 J2 Schwedeneck Ger.
170 J4 Schwedt an der Oder Ger.
172 E3 Schwegenheim Ger.
168 F4 Schwei (Stadland) Ger.
168 F4 Schweiburg Ger.
172 B2 Schweich Ger.
172 D3 Schweigen-Rechtenbach Ger.
157 O6 Schweighouse-sur-Moder France
169 J9 Schweina Ger.
169 J10 Schweinfurt Ger.
171 H7 Schweinitz Ger.
170 G4 Schweinrich Ger.
173 L4 Schweitenkirchen Ger.
Schweiz country Europe see Switzerland
215 J3 Schweizer-Reneke S. Africa
169 D8 Schwelm Ger.
178 E5 Schwendau Austria
172 H5 Schwendi Ger.
172 F5 Schwenningen Baden-Württemberg Ger.
172 F5 Schwenningen Baden-Württemberg Ger.
171 I8 Schwepnitz Ger.
170 D3 Schwerin Ger.
170 D3 Schweriner See l. Ger.
170 D3 Schweriner Seenlandschaft park Ger.
168 H5 Schweringen Ger.
179 K3 Schwertberg Austria
169 E8 Schwerte Ger.
172 F3 Schwetzingen Ger.
170 I3 Schwichtenberg Ger.
172 G4 Schwieberdingen Ger.
171 J6 Schwielochsee l. Ger.
170 D5 Schwiesau Ger.
173 M5 Schwindegg Ger.
168 H3 Schwinge r. Ger.
170 G3 Schwinkendorf Ger.
178 F4 Schwoich Austria
172 D6 Schwörstadt Ger.
190 F1 Schwyz Switz.
190 F1 Schwyz canton Switz.
194 E8 Sciacca Sicilia Italy
194 H10 Scicli Sicilia Italy
156 B4 Scie r. France
160 I4 Sciez France
195 K5 Scigliano Italy
191 L3 Sciliar, Parco Naturale dello nature res. Italy
195 J7 Scilla Italy
Scilly, Île atoll Arch. de la Société Fr. Polynesia see Manuae
150 □ Scilly, Isles of England U.K.
174 E4 Ścinawa Pol.
174 E5 Ścinawka r. Pol.
232 D8 Scio OH U.S.A.
160 J4 Scionzier France
234 E3 Sciota PA U.S.A.
232 C10 Scioto r. OH U.S.A.
241 T2 Scipio UT U.S.A.
150 C4 Scleddau Pembrokeshire, Wales U.K.
238 L2 Scobey MT U.S.A.
Scodra Albania see Shkodër
241 U2 Scofield Reservoir UT U.S.A.
192 F2 Scoglia dello Sparviero i. Italy
194 G10 Scoglitti Sicilia Italy
195 H7 Scolaticci Isole Lipari Italy
151 O3 Scole Norfolk, England U.K.
191 J7 Scoltenna r. Italy
83 M5 Scone N.S.W. Austr.
146 J10 Scone Perth and Kinross, Scotland U.K.
146 D8 Sconser Highland, Scotland U.K.
190 E4 Scopello Italy
193 K3 Scoppito Italy
159 L8 Scorbé-Clairvaux France
194 H9 Scordia Sicilia Italy
221 P2 Scoresby Land reg. Greenland
Scoresbysund Greenland see Ittoqqortoormiit
Scoresby Sund sea chan. Greenland see Kangertittivaq
158 E6 Scorff r. France
197 M6 Scornicești Romania
Scorno, Punta dello pt Sardegna Italy see Caprara, Punta
87 I12 Scorpion Bight b. W.A. Austr.
195 O3 Scorrano Italy
149 N5 Scorton North Yorkshire, England U.K.
191 M4 Scorzè Italy
148 D5 Scotch Corner Ireland
149 N5 Scotch Corner North Yorkshire, England U.K.
235 G3 Scotch Plains NJ U.S.A.
264 F9 Scotia Ridge sea feature S. Atlantic Ocean
265 B9 Scotia Ridge sea feature S. Atlantic Ocean
264 G9 Scotia Sea S. Atlantic Ocean
227 N6 Scotland Ont. Can.
146 I8 Scotland admin. div. U.K.
233 I10 Scotland MD U.S.A.
234 E2 Scotrun PA U.S.A.
147 H4 Scotshouse Ireland
225 G4 Scotstown Que. Can.
84 B2 Scott, Cape N.T. Austr.
222 D5 Scott, Cape B.C. Can.
237 G9 Scott, Mount hill OK U.S.A.
263 L1 Scott Base research stn Antarctica
215 O6 Scottburgh S. Africa
236 E6 Scott City KS U.S.A.
263 K1 Scott Coast Antarctica
149 P7 Scotter Lincolnshire, England U.K.
262 N1 Scott Glacier Antarctica
263 G2 Scott Glacier Antarctica
221 K2 Scott Inlet Nunavut Can.
146 K11 Scottish Borders admin. div. Scotland U.K.
263 L2 Scott Island Antarctica
222 D5 Scott Islands B.C. Can.
223 J3 Scott Lake Sask. Can.
263 D2 Scott Mountains Antarctica
149 N5 Scotton North Yorkshire, England U.K.
151 O2 Scottow Norfolk, England U.K.
80 G1 Scott Point North I. N.Z.
86 G3 Scott Reef W.A. Austr.
236 D5 Scottsbluff NE U.S.A.
231 D8 Scottsboro AL U.S.A.
230 E6 Scottsburg IN U.S.A.
83 K9 Scottsdale Tas. Austr.
241 U8 Scottsdale AZ U.S.A.
247 □2 Scotts Head Dominica
230 D7 Scottsville KY U.S.A.
232 G11 Scottsville VA U.S.A.
226 H6 Scottville MI U.S.A.
146 F6 Scourie Highland, Scotland U.K.
146 □N3 Scousburgh Shetland, Scotland U.K.
146 I5 Scrabster Highland, Scotland U.K.
234 D2 Scranton PA U.S.A.
147 C6 Screeb Ireland
147 G6 Screggan Ireland
147 F4 Scribbagh Northern Ireland U.K.
146 D10 Scridain, Loch inlet Scotland U.K.
190 F5 Scrivia r. Italy
224 E4 Scugog, Lake Ont. Can.
149 P6 Scunthorpe North Lincolnshire, England U.K.
190 I2 Scuol Switz.
Scupi Macedonia see Skopje
193 K3 Scurcola Marsicana Italy
146 B8 Scurrival Point Scotland U.K.
Scutari Albania see Shkodër
196 H8 Scutari, Lake Albania/Montenegro
232 H12 Seaboard NC U.S.A.
234 E5 Seabrook NJ U.S.A.
87 E11 Seabrook, Lake salt flat W.A. Austr.
197 M6 Seaca Romania
151 M6 Seaford East Sussex, England U.K.
233 J10 Seaford DE U.S.A.
227 M6 Seaforth Ont. Can.
246 □ Seaforth Jamaica
146 C7 Seaforth, Loch inlet Scotland U.K.
149 O4 Seaham Durham, England U.K.
92 A6 Seahorse Bank sea feature Phil.
149 N2 Seahouses Northumberland, England U.K.
234 F6 Sea Isle City NJ U.S.A.
223 M3 Seal r. Man. Can.
214 H10 Seal, Cape S. Africa
83 I6 Sea Lake Vic. Austr.
262 X2 Seal Bay Antarctica
216 □2c Seal Bay Tristan da Cunha S. Atlantic Ocean
246 H3 Seal Cays is Turks and Caicos Is
233 □S4 Seal Cove N.B. Can.
225 J3 Seal Cove Nfld and Lab. Can.
146 F7 Sealga, Loch na l. Scotland U.K.
233 □Q5 Seal Island ME U.S.A.
225 I2 Seal Lake Nfld and Lab. Can.
223 I1 Seal Lake N.W.T. Can.
215 I10 Seal Point S. Africa
237 G11 Sealy TX U.S.A.
232 B10 Seaman OH U.S.A.
241 Q4 Seaman Range mts NV U.S.A.
149 Q5 Seamer North Yorkshire, England U.K.
148 H2 Seamill North Ayrshire, Scotland U.K.
182 C5 Seara Port.
241 R6 Searchlight NV U.S.A.
237 J8 Searcy AR U.S.A.
240 O6 Searles Lake CA U.S.A.
233 □Q4 Searsport ME U.S.A.
149 K5 Seascale Cumbria, England U.K.
240 K5 Seaside CA U.S.A.
238 C4 Seaside OR U.S.A.
235 G5 Seaside Park NJ U.S.A.
149 J4 Seaton Cumbria, England U.K.
150 F6 Seaton Devon, England U.K.
149 N3 Seaton Delaval Northumberland, England U.K.
263 D2 Seaton Glacier Antarctica
149 O3 Seaton Sluice Northumberland, England U.K.
238 C3 Seattle WA U.S.A.
222 B2 Seattle, Mount Can./U.S.A.
215 J10 Sea View S. Africa
151 J6 Seaview Isle of Wight, England U.K.
85 J5 Seaview Range mts Qld Austr.
234 F6 Seaville NJ U.S.A.
81 H9 Seaward Kaikoura Range mts South I. N.Z.
93 B9 Seba Indon.
242 □P11 Sebaco Nic.
233 □O5 Sebago Lake ME U.S.A.
95 L5 Sebakung Kalimantan Indon.
182 C8 Sebal Port.
95 J6 Sebangan, Teluk b. Indon.
94 F4 Sebangka i. Indon.
Sebastea Turkey see Sivas
231 G12 Sebastian FL U.S.A.
261 F2 Sebastián Elcano Arg.
242 B3 Sebastián Vizcaíno, Bahía b. Mex.
233 □P4 Sebasticook r. ME U.S.A.
233 □P4 Sebasticook Lake ME U.S.A.
Sebastopol Ukr. see Sevastopol'
240 J3 Sebastopol CA U.S.A.
95 L2 Sebatik i. Indon.
95 J3 Sebauh Sarawak Malaysia
95 I5 Sebayan, Bukit mt. Indon.
161 B8 Sébazac-Concourès France
207 F3 Sebba Burkina
142 F5 Sebbersund Denmark
203 H6 Sebderat Eritrea
205 E2 Sebdou Alg.
206 C3 Sébékoro Mali
126 E3 Seben Turkey
Sebenico Croatia see Šibenik
Sebennytos Egypt see Samannūd
197 L5 Sebeș Romania
197 L4 Sebeș r. Romania
94 F7 Sebesi i. Indon.
177 J5 Sebes-Körös r. Hungary
227 K6 Sebewaing MI U.S.A.
138 L5 Sebezh Rus. Fed.
126 I3 Şebinkarahisar Turkey
197 K4 Sebiș Romania
139 U3 Sebla r. Rus. Fed.
94 E6 Seblat, Gunung mt. Indon.
171 J9 Sebnitz Ger.
233 □Q3 Seboeis ME U.S.A.
233 □Q3 Seboeis Lake ME U.S.A.
233 □P3 Seboomook Lake ME U.S.A.
232 H12 Sebrell VA U.S.A.
231 G12 Sebring FL U.S.A.
135 H6 Sebrovo Rus. Fed.
95 L6 Sebuku i. Indon.
95 L2 Sebuku r. Indon.
95 L3 Sebuku, Teluk b. Indon.
95 L2 Sebuku-Sembakung, Taman Nasional nat. park Kalimantan Indon.
95 I4 Sebuyau Sarawak Malaysia
186 F7 Sec, Riu r. Spain
260 D5 Seca, Pampa plain Arg.
196 I5 Sečanj Vojvodina Serbia
182 D8 Secarias Port.
177 K6 Secaș Romania
197 L4 Secaș r. Romania
242 □S14 Secas, Islas is Panama
191 K5 Secchia r. Italy
210 C3 Seccia mts Eth.
175 H5 Secemin Pol.
222 F5 Sechelt B.C. Can.
135 I5 Sechenovo Rus. Fed.
250 A6 Sechura Peru
250 A6 Sechura, Bahía de b. Peru
250 A6 Sechura, Desierto de des. Peru
172 G3 Seckach Ger.
179 K5 Seckau Austria
179 K5 Seckauer Alpen mts Austria
156 F2 Seclin France
162 D2 Secondigny France
233 □N3 Second Lake NH U.S.A.
241 V6 Second Mesa AZ U.S.A.
234 B4 Second Mountain ridge PA U.S.A.
206 □ Secos, Ilhéus is Cape Verde
177 K3 Sečovce Slovakia
81 A12 Secretary Island South I. N.Z.
215 N2 Secunda S. Africa
114 F4 Secunderabad Andhra Prad. India
252 D3 Sécure r. Bol.
177 J5 Secusigiu Romania
138 I4 Seda Latvia
138 I4 Seda r. Latvia
138 F5 Seda Lith.
184 D2 Seda Port.
184 C3 Seda r. Port.
236 I6 Sedalia MO U.S.A.
114 E4 Sedam Karnataka India
82 G6 Sedan S.A. Austr.
157 I4 Sedan France
237 G7 Sedan KS U.S.A.
85 H5 Sedan Dip Qld Austr.
183 M3 Sedano Spain
149 L5 Sedbergh Cumbria, England U.K.
81 I8 Seddon South I. N.Z.
81 F8 Seddonville South I. N.Z.
199 H2 Seddülbahir Turkey
128 C8 Sedé Boqer Israel
122 E6 Sedeh Fārs Iran
122 H5 Sedeh Khorāsān Iran
161 H8 Séderon France
128 C7 Sederot Israel
149 O4 Sedgefield Durham, England U.K.
223 I4 Sedgewick Alta Can.
150 H2 Sedgley West Midlands, England U.K.
233 □Q4 Sedgwick ME U.S.A.
206 B3 Sédhiou Senegal
191 M3 Sedico Italy
192 B7 Sedilo Sardegna Italy
192 B6 Sedini Sardegna Italy
176 G6 Sedlarica Croatia
176 D2 Sedlčany Czech Rep.
176 D2 Sedlec Prčice Czech Rep.
Sedlets Pol. see Siedlce
177 K3 Sedlice Slovakia
171 J7 Sedlitz Ger.
171 J9 Sedlo hill Czech Rep.
136 E2 Sedlyshche Ukr.
128 D7 Sedom Israel
241 U7 Sedona AZ U.S.A.
Sedovo Ukr. see Syedove
205 G1 Sédrata Alg.
190 H4 Sedrina Italy
95 L4 Sedulang Kalimantan Indon.
138 G6 Šeduva Lith.
175 H4 Sędziejowice Pol.
174 G3 Sędzin Pol.
175 I5 Sędziszów Pol.
175 J5 Sędziszów Małopolski Pol.
178 H5 See Salzburg Austria
178 B5 See Tirol Austria
159 I4 Sée r. France
172 E4 Seebach Baden-Württemberg Ger.
169 J9 Seebach Thüringen Ger.
179 K7 Seeberg pass Austria/Slovenia
169 K9 Seebergen Ger.
179 I6 Seeboden Austria
173 M6 Seebruck Ger.
169 J7 Seeburg Ger.
168 J2 Seedorf Schleswig-Holstein Ger.
168 K3 Seedorf Schleswig-Holstein Ger.
173 K5 Seefeld Bayern Ger.
170 I5 Seefeld Brandenburg Ger.
168 F4 Seefeld (Stadland) Ger.
178 D5 Seefeld in Tirol Austria
147 G8 Seefin hill Ireland
173 J6 Seeg Ger.
171 G7 Seegrehna Ger.
170 I4 Seehausen Brandenburg Ger.
171 D6 Seehausen Sachsen-Anhalt Ger.
170 E5 Seehausen (Altmark) Ger.
173 K6 Seehausen am Staffelsee Ger.
212 C5 Seeheim Namibia
172 F2 Seeheim-Jugenheim Ger.
178 H4 Seekirchen am Wallersee Austria
214 G9 Seekoegat S. Africa
215 I6 Seekoei r. S. Africa
215 N3 Seekoevlei Nature Reserve S. Africa
172 D5 Seelbach Ger.
241 Q9 Seeley CA U.S.A.
262 R1 Seelig, Mount Antarctica
171 F9 Seelingstädt Ger.
170 J5 Seelow Ger.
169 I6 Seelze Ger.
173 M6 Seeon Ger.
190 F1 Seerücken val. Switz.
159 L4 Sées France
169 J7 Seesen Ger.
173 K6 Seeshaupt Ger.
179 J5 Seetaler Alpen mts Austria
179 I5 Seethal Austria
168 J4 Seevetal Ger.
179 I4 Seewalchen am Attersee Austria
179 L4 Seewiesen Austria
179 P4 Seewinkel reg. Austria
160 J5 Séez France
206 C4 Sefadu Sierra Leone
199 H4 Seferihisar Turkey
206 C3 Séféto Mali
122 C5 Sefid, Kūh-e mt. Iran
122 D6 Sefid, Kūh-e mts Iran
122 D5 Sefid Dasht Iran
213 E4 Sefophe Botswana
204 D2 Sefrou Morocco
81 E10 Sefton, Mount South I. N.Z.
163 I7 Ségala reg. France
206 C3 Ségala Mali
141 K6 Segalstad Norway
95 M2 Segama r. Malaysia
94 E3 Segamat Malaysia
180 E5 Segangane Morocco
197 L6 Şegarcea Romania
186 H4 Segarra reg. Spain
207 F4 Ségbana Benin
210 C3 Segen Wenz watercourse Eth.
211 C6 Segera Tanz.
93 A6 Segeri Sulawesi Indon.
176 G5 Segesd Hungary
134 F3 Segezha Rus. Fed.
205 F2 Seggeur, Oued watercourse Alg.
192 H2 Seggiano Italy
78 □6 Seghe New Georgia Is Solomon Is
123 N3 Seghnān Afgh.
121 L5 Segiz, Ozera lakes Kazakh.
190 H3 Segl, Lago da l. Switz.
158 E5 Séglien France
193 K4 Segni Italy
Segontia Gwynedd, Wales U.K. see Caernarfon
Segontium Gwynedd, Wales U.K. see Caernarfon
162 D4 Segonzac France
187 E8 Segorbe Spain
206 D3 Ségou Mali
206 D3 Ségou admin. reg. Mali
250 C3 Segovia Col.
Segovia r. Hond./Nic. see Coco
183 L7 Segovia Spain
183 L6 Segovia prov. Spain
134 F3 Segozerskoye, Ozero resr Rus. Fed.
159 J6 Segré France
186 F5 Segre r. Spain
159 J6 Segréen reg. France
186 G4 Segrià reg. Spain
159 L5 Ségrie France
220 A4 Seguam Island AK U.S.A.
207 I1 Séguédine Niger
206 D5 Séguéla Côte d'Ivoire
206 D3 Séguéla Mali
206 D4 Séguélon Côte d'Ivoire
206 E3 Séguénéga Burkina
261 G3 Seguí Arg.
237 G11 Seguin TX U.S.A.
261 F2 Segundo r. Arg.
161 B8 Ségur France
182 G9 Segura Port.
185 N4 Segura r. Spain
185 N5 Segura, Sierra de mts Spain
185 N4 Segura de la Sierra Spain
184 F4 Segura de León Spain
186 D6 Segura de los Baños Spain
183 K8 Segurilla Spain
212 D4 Sehithwa Botswana
215 N5 Sehlabathebe Lesotho
215 N5 Sehlabathebe National Park Lesotho
169 J6 Sehlde Ger.
169 I6 Sehnde Ger.
93 D4 Seho i. Indon.
116 F8 Sehore Madh. Prad. India
123 L8 Sehwan Pak.
182 E8 Seia Port.
236 D6 Seibert CO U.S.A.
158 H6 Seiche r. France
159 K6 Seiches-sur-le-Loir France
104 A7 Seidan Japan
179 L5 Seiersberg Austria
140 K4 Seierstad Norway
171 K9 Seifhennersdorf Ger.
150 H2 Seighford Staffordshire, England U.K.
161 B8 Seigne, Mont mt. France
225 G3 Seignelay r. Que. Can.
156 G8 Seignelay France
190 B1 Seignelégier Switz.
163 B8 Seignosse France
104 C6 Seika Japan
96 B4 Seikphyu Myanmar
146 E10 Seil i. Scotland U.K.
140 Q1 Seiland i. Norway
162 H5 Seilhac France
237 F7 Seiling OK U.S.A.
161 J9 Seillans France
160 F3 Seille r. France
157 L5 Seille r. France
165 H8 Seilles Belgium
138 F7 Šeimena r. Lith.
158 B5 Sein, Île de i. France
104 G5 Seinaiji Japan
140 Q5 Seinäjoki Fin.
224 B3 Seine r. Ont. Can.
156 B5 Seine r. France
159 J3 Seine, Baie de b. France
160 F2 Seine, Sources de la France
156 F7 Seine, Val de val. France
156 F6 Seine-et-Marne dept France
Seine-Inférieure dept France see Seine-Maritime
156 A4 Seine-Maritime dept France
159 P4 Seine-St-Denis dept France
197 L3 Seini Romania
173 I2 Seinsheim Ger.
95 K5 Seipinang Kalimantan Indon.
175 L1 Seira l. Lith.
186 F3 Seira Spain
175 L1 Seirijai Lith.
175 L1 Seirijis l. Lith.
163 F9 Seissan France
Seistan reg. Iran see Sīstān
179 K3 Seitenstetten Austria
177 J5 Şeitin Romania
141 Q6 Seitsemisen kansallispuisto nat. park Fin.
258 G3 Seival Brazil
104 D7 Seiwa Japan
163 G10 Seix France
184 □ Seixal Madeira
184 A3 Seixal Port.
182 C5 Seixas Port.
184 B6 Seixe r. Port.
182 E8 Seixo da Beira Port.
95 L6 Sejaka Kalimantan Indon.
95 H4 Sejangkung Kalimantan Indon.
142 H6 Sejerby Denmark
142 H6 Sejerø i. Denmark
142 H6 Sejerø Bugt b. Denmark
175 L1 Sejny Pol.
95 I4 Sekadau Kalimantan Indon.
94 F5 Sekanak, Teluk b. Indon.
95 L3 Sekatak Bengara Kalimantan Indon.
94 E6 Sekayu Sumatera Indon.
177 K3 Sekčov r. Slovakia
Seke Sichuan China see Sêrtar
211 B5 Seke Tanz.
209 B6 Seke-Banza Dem. Rep. Congo
211 B6 Sekenke Tanz.
78 □4b Sekeren Iap Pohnpei Micronesia
104 E5 Seki Gifu Japan
104 D6 Seki Mie Japan
199 K6 Seki Turkey
199 K6 Seki r. Turkey
102 □B21 Sekibi-sho i. Nansei-shotō Japan
94 F7 Sekicau, Gunung vol. Indon.
104 E2 Sekidō-san hill Japan
104 D5 Sekigahara Japan
105 K3 Sekijō Japan
105 K3 Sekiyado Japan
212 D5 Sekoma Botswana
206 E5 Sekondi Ghana
210 C1 Sek'ot'a Eth.
175 J6 Sękowa Pol.
Sekseüil Kazakh. see Saksaul'skiy
123 I6 Sekūheh Iran
95 H4 Sekura Kalimantan Indon.
217 □2b Sel, Pointe au pt Mahé Seychelles
Şela Rus. Fed. see Shali
210 C2 Šela Dingay Eth.
94 D6 Selagan r. Indon.
238 D3 Selah WA U.S.A.
95 H4 Selakau Kalimantan Indon.
95 I3 Selalang Sarawak Malaysia
94 D3 Selangor state Malaysia
192 C9 Selargius Sardegna Italy
93 G8 Selaru i. Maluku Indon.
95 K7 Selatan, Tanjung pt Indon.
94 E4 Selatpanjang Sumatera Indon.
150 F2 Selattyn Shropshire, England U.K.
220 B3 Selawik AK U.S.A.
183 M2 Selaya Spain
171 F10 Selb Ger.
178 G5 Selbhorn mt. Austria
171 E10 Selbitz Ger.
142 A2 Selbjørnsfjorden sea chan. Norway
140 K5 Selbu Norway
149 O6 Selby North Yorkshire, England U.K.
236 E3 Selby SD U.S.A.
233 J10 Selbyville DE U.S.A.
191 R5 Selce Croatia
199 I5 Selçuk Turkey
236 E6 Selden KS U.S.A.
220 C4 Seldovia AK U.S.A.
93 G4 Sele Papua Indon.
193 N7 Sele r. Italy
93 G4 Sele, Selat sea chan. Papua Indon.
213 E4 Selebi-Phikwe Botswana
Selebi-Pikwe Botswana see Selebi-Phikwe
197 J9 Selečka Planina mts Macedonia
192 C8 Selegas Sardegna Italy
192 C6 S'Elema r. Sardegna Italy
100 F2 Selemdzha r. Rus. Fed.
100 G2 Selemdzhinsk Rus. Fed.
100 H2 Selemdzhinskiy Khrebet mts Rus. Fed.
199 J4 Selendi Turkey
106 J1 Selenduma Rus. Fed.
106 J1 Selenga r. Rus. Fed. alt. Selenge Mörön (Mongolia)
208 C5 Selenge Dem. Rep. Congo
106 G2 Selenge Mongolia
106 J2 Selenge prov. Mongolia
106 J1 Selenge Mörön r. Mongolia
198 A2 Selenicë Albania
168 J2 Selent Ger.
168 J2 Selenter See l. Ger.
111 F11 Sêlêpug Xizang China
157 N7 Sélestat France
94 □ Seletar Sing.
94 □ Seletar, Pulau i. Sing.
94 □ Seletar Reservoir Sing.
121 O1 Seletinskoye Kazakh.
Selety r. Kazakh. see Sileti
Seletyteniz, Oz. salt l. Kazakh. see Siletiteniz, Ozero
Seleucia Turkey see Silifke
Seleucia Pieria Turkey see Samandağı
177 K5 Seleuș Romania
138 L1 Seleznevo Rus. Fed.
139 O6 Selezni Rus. Fed.
140 □C2 Selfoss Iceland
236 E2 Selfridge ND U.S.A.
100 I4 Sel'gon Stantsiya Rus. Fed.
134 J3 Selib Rus. Fed.
206 B3 Sélibabi Maur.
139 R9 Selichnya Rus. Fed.
Selidovo Ukr. see Selydove
169 G10 Seligenstadt Ger.
139 Q4 Seliger, Ozero l. Rus. Fed.
241 T6 Seligman AZ U.S.A.
100 J3 Selikhino Rus. Fed.
208 D3 Sélim C.A.R.
129 D5 Selim Turkey
203 F4 Selîma Oasis Sudan
95 J4 Selimbau Kalimantan Indon.
199 I5 Selimiye Turkey
206 C4 Sélingué, Lac de l. Mali
206 C3 Selinnkegni Mali
198 D4 Selinountas r. Greece
234 B3 Selinsgrove PA U.S.A.
139 Q5 Selishche Rus. Fed.
135 H5 Selishchi Rus. Fed.
120 B4 Selitrennoye Rus. Fed.
95 G6 Seliu i. Indon.
139 Q5 Selizharovo Rus. Fed.
141 H5 Selje Norway
142 E2 Seljord Norway
142 E2 Seljordsvatnet l. Norway
171 D7 Selke r. Ger.
223 L5 Selkirk Man. Can.
146 K11 Selkirk Scottish Borders, Scotland U.K.
222 G4 Selkirk Mountains B.C. Can.
140 R1 Selkopp Norway
Şelkovski Rus. Fed. see Shelkovskaya
187 E10 Sella Spain
183 J2 Sella r. Spain
193 N5 Sella Canala pass Italy
193 P7 Sella Cessula pass Italy
193 M5 Sella del Perrone pass Italy
149 K5 Sellafield Cumbria, England U.K.
146 □N1 Sellafirth Shetland, Scotland U.K.
193 J2 Sellano Italy
234 E4 Sellersville PA U.S.A.
162 H1 Selles-St-Denis France
159 O7 Selles-sur-Cher France
85 K6 Sellheim r. Qld Austr.
198 F7 Sellia Kriti Greece
195 L6 Sellia Marina Italy
160 H3 Sellières France
170 I2 Sellin, Ostseebad Ger.
151 N5 Sellindge Kent, England U.K.
164 L3 Sellingen Neth.
Sellore Island Myanmar see Saganthit Kyun
178 D5 Sellrain Austria
241 U10 Sells AZ U.S.A.
177 G6 Sellye Hungary
169 D7 Selm Ger.
231 D9 Selma AL U.S.A.
240 M5 Selma CA U.S.A.
237 K8 Selmer TN U.S.A.
184 D4 Selmes Port.
175 K2 Selmęt Wielki, Jezioro l. Pol.
182 G3 Selmo r. Spain
168 K3 Selmsdorf Ger.
Selmunett, Gżejjer is Malta see San Pawl, Gżejjer ta'
156 B8 Selommes France
95 L9 Selong Lombok Indon.
160 G1 Selongey France
161 I8 Selonnet France
215 N1 Selonsrivier S. Africa
206 C4 Sélouma Guinea
222 C2 Selous, Mount Y.T. Can.
211 C7 Selous Game Reserve nature res. Tanz.
170 E3 Selow Ger.
122 I7 Selseleh-ye Pīr Shūrān mts Iran
149 M4 Selset Reservoir England U.K.
151 K6 Selsey West Sussex, England U.K.
151 K6 Selsey Bill hd England U.K.
168 H4 Selsingen Ger.
169 E9 Selters (Westerwald) Ger.
139 R8 Sel'tso Bryanskaya Oblast' Rus. Fed.
139 R8 Sel'tso Bryanskaya Oblast' Rus. Fed.
134 K4 Selty Rus. Fed.
157 P6 Seltz France
95 G2 Seluan i. Indon.
Selukwe Zimbabwe see Shurugwi
159 I4 Sélune r. France
258 E3 Selva Arg.
195 M2 Selva Italy
187 K8 Selva Spain
186 C3 Selva mt. Spain
186 K4 Selva reg. Spain
191 L2 Selva dei Molini Italy
191 K4 Selva di Progno Italy
178 E6 Selva di Val Gardena Italy
204 B3 Selvagens, Ilhas is Madeira
127 L5 Selvānā Iran
260 A6 Selva Obscura Chile
250 D6 Selvas reg. Brazil
191 L5 Selvazzano Dentro Italy
190 H4 Selvino Italy
256 B4 Selviria Brazil
238 G3 Selway r. ID U.S.A.
223 J2 Selwyn Lake N.W.T./Sask. Can.
222 D1 Selwyn Mountains N.W.T./Y.T. Can.
84 G6 Selwyn Range hills Qld Austr.
136 E6 Selyatyn Ukr.
137 Q5 Selydove Ukr.
172 E2 Selz r. Ger.
179 J4 Selzthal Austria
163 I8 Sémalens France
198 A2 Seman r. Albania
94 F7 Semangka, Teluk b. Indon.
95 I8 Semarang Jawa Indon.
95 H4 Sematan Sarawak Malaysia
93 C9 Semau i. Indon.
95 L5 Semayang, Danau l. Indon.
161 D6 Sembadel France
95 L3 Sembakung r. Indon.
94 □ Sembawang Sing.
94 □ Sembawang, Sungai r. Sing.
208 B4 Sembé Congo
159 M6 Semblançay France
190 C3 Sembrancher Switz.
127 L5 Şemdinli Turkey
163 E9 Séméac France
160 D3 Sémelay France
Semendire Serbia see Smederevo
209 C5 Semendua Dem. Rep. Congo
139 V4 Semendyayevo Rus. Fed.
197 K5 Semenic, Vârful mt. Romania
137 L1 Semenivka Chernihivs'ka Oblast' Ukr.
137 P5 Semenivka Kharkivs'ka Oblast' Ukr.
137 K3 Semenivka Kyivs'ka Oblast' Ukr.
137 M4 Semenivka Poltavs'ka Oblast' Ukr.
120 F1 Semenkino Rus. Fed.
137 T2 Semeno-Aleksandrovka Rus. Fed.
134 I4 Semenov Rus. Fed.
Semenovka Ukr. see Semenivka
139 S6 Semenovskoye Rus. Fed.
94 J9 Semeru, Gunung vol. Indon.
Semey Kazakh. see Semipalatinsk
124 D8 Semhar prov. Eritrea
137 S6 Semibalki Rus. Fed.
139 W4 Semibratovo Rus. Fed.
182 D8 Semide Port.
137 R2 Semidesyatnoye Rus. Fed.
220 C4 Semidi Islands AK U.S.A.
134 H4 Semigorodnyaya Rus. Fed.
135 H7 Semikarakorsk Rus. Fed.
135 G6 Semiluki Rus. Fed.
176 E1 Semily Czech Rep.
195 J7 Seminara Italy
160 H4 Semine r. France
238 K5 Seminoe Reservoir WY U.S.A.
237 D9 Seminole TX U.S.A.
231 E10 Seminole, Lake FL/GA U.S.A.
121 U2 Seminskiy Khrebet mts Rus. Fed.
139 X7 Semion Rus. Fed.
100 B2 Semiozernyy Rus. Fed.
121 S2 Semipalatinsk Kazakh.
121 L1 Semipolka Kazakh.
92 C5 Semirara i. Phil.
92 C6 Semirara Islands Phil.
122 D6 Semīrom Iran
220 A4 Semisopochnoi Island AK U.S.A.
95 I4 Semitau Kalimantan Indon.
121 R2 Semiyarka Kazakh.
121 P2 Semizbuga Kazakh.
Semizbughy Kazakh. see Semizbuga
139 V5 Semkhoz Rus. Fed.
Sem Kolodezey Ukr. see Lenine
196 I4 Semlac Romania
139 Q6 Semlevo Smolenskaya Oblast' Rus. Fed.
139 Q6 Semlevo Smolenskaya Oblast' Rus. Fed.
208 F4 Semliki r. Dem. Rep. Congo/Uganda
170 G2 Semlow Ger.
169 K6 Semmenstedt Ger.
122 E4 Semnān Iran
122 D4 Semnān prov. Iran
122 E5 Semnān va Dāmghān reg. Iran
106 G8 Sêmnyi Qinghai China
165 G9 Semois r. Belgium
165 G9 Semois, Vallée de la val. Belgium/France
215 M5 Semonkong Lesotho
157 J7 Semoutiers-Montsaon France
190 E1 Sempach Switz.
190 E1 Sempacher See l. Switz.
179 I8 Šempeter Slovenia
95 M2 Semporna Sabah Malaysia
192 H2 Semproniano Italy
173 L5 Sempt r. Ger.
95 J9 Sempu i. Indon.
179 L5 Semriach Austria
177 K3 Šemša Slovakia
251 H6 Sem Tripa Brazil
139 Q9 Semtsy Rus. Fed.
160 E2 Semur-en-Auxois France
160 E4 Semur-en-Brionnais France
162 C4 Semussac France
Semyonovskoye Arkhangel'skaya Oblast' Rus. Fed. see Bereznik
Semyonovskoye Kostromskaya Oblast' Rus. Fed. see Ostrovskoye
134 I2 Semzha Rus. Fed.
97 G8 Sên, Stœng r. Cambodia
252 D2 Sena Bol.
122 D7 Senā Iran
177 K3 Seňa Slovakia
186 E4 Sena Spain
256 C2 Senador Canedo Brazil
254 F3 Senador Pompeu Brazil
203 H6 Senafe Eritrea
191 L3 Senaiga r. Italy
95 L1 Senaja Sabah Malaysia
129 D3 Senaki Georgia
191 J2 Senales Italy
191 J2 Senales, Val di val. Italy
192 C6 Senalonga, Punta mt. Italy
252 C2 Sena Madureira Brazil
114 G9 Senanayake Samudra l. Sri Lanka
209 D9 Senanga Zambia
95 I4 Senaning Kalimantan Indon.
156 C4 Senarpont France
161 G9 Sénas France
237 K8 Senatobia MS U.S.A.
187 K8 Sencelles Spain
137 M3 Sencha Ukr.
179 J7 Šenčur Slovenia
103 H15 Sendai Kagoshima Japan
102 R8 Sendai Miyagi Japan
103 H15 Sendai-gawa r. Japan
102 S8 Sendai-wan b. Japan
215 K2 Sendelingsfontein S. Africa
173 I5 Senden Bayern Ger.
169 D7 Senden Nordrhein-Westfalen Ger.
169 E7 Sendenhorst Ger.
182 H6 Sendim Bragança Port.
182 D6 Sendim Porto Port.
111 L11 Sêndo Xizang China
197 P5 Şendreni Romania
95 I5 Senduruhan Kalimantan Indon.
158 F6 Séné France
206 E5 Sene r. Ghana
94 D3 Senebui, Tanjung pt Indon.
176 G3 Senec Slovakia
226 F8 Seneca IL U.S.A.
236 G6 Seneca KS U.S.A.
238 E4 Seneca OR U.S.A.
232 F7 Seneca PA U.S.A.
232 I6 Seneca Lake NY U.S.A.
232 F10 Seneca Rocks WV U.S.A.
232 D9 Senecaville Lake OH U.S.A.
165 F7 Seneffe Belgium
206 B3 Senegal country Africa
206 A2 Sénégal r. Maur./Senegal
192 B7 Seneghe Sardegna Italy
100 J1 Seneka, Mys hd Rus. Fed.
215 L4 Senekal S. Africa
185 O6 Senes Spain
192 D7 Senes, Monte hill Italy
192 B4 Senetosa, Capu di c. Corse France
226 I3 Seney MI U.S.A.
226 H3 Seney National Wildlife Refuge nature res. MI U.S.A.
161 I9 Senez France
179 M3 Senftenberg Austria
171 J7 Senftenberg Ger.
211 B8 Senga Malawi
211 A7 Senga Hill Zambia
116 G6 Sengar r. India
95 L4 Sengata Kalimantan Indon.
111 E11 Sêngdoi Xizang China
173 K3 Sengenthal Ger.
211 B5 Sengerema Tanz.
256 C6 Sengés Brazil
134 J1 Sengeyskiy, Ostrov i. Rus. Fed.
135 J5 Sengiley Rus. Fed.
Sengirli, Mys pt Kazakh. see Syngyrli, Mys
111 G11 Sêngli Co l. Xizang China
163 F10 Sengouagnet France
179 J4 Sengsengebirge mts Austria
259 C7 Senguerr r. Arg.
213 F3 Sengwa r. Zimbabwe
124 D8 Senhit prov. Eritrea
184 E2 Senhora do Rosário Port.
254 E4 Senhor do Bonfim Brazil
176 G3 Senica Slovakia
176 G2 Senice na Hané Czech Rep.
191 O8 Senigallia Italy
260 C6 Senillosa Arg.
191 M6 Senio r. Italy
199 L4 Senirkent Turkey
192 B8 Senis Sardegna Italy
193 Q7 Senise Italy
188 E3 Senj Croatia
140 N2 Senja i. Norway
140 N2 Senjehopen Norway
104 C7 Senjōga-dake mt. Japan
105 H4 Senjōga-dake mt. Japan
102 □A21 Senkaku-shotō is Japan
127 K3 Şenkaya Turkey
134 J2 Šen'kina Rus. Fed.
206 C4 Senko Guinea
209 E9 Senkobo Zambia
137 Q4 Sen'kove Ukr.
139 N6 Sen'kovo Rus. Fed.
128 E2 Şenköy Turkey
214 H1 Senlac S. Africa
100 G7 Senlin Shan mt. Jilin China
156 E5 Senlis France
97 H8 Senmonorom Cambodia
104 B7 Sennan Japan
203 G6 Sennar Sudan
203 G6 Sennar state Sudan
192 B7 Sennariolo Sardegna Italy
137 Q8 Sennaya Rus. Fed.
169 G7 Senne reg. Ger.
160 F3 Sennecey-le-Grand France
160 G2 Sennecey-lès-Dijon France
150 □ Sennen Cornwall, England U.K.
224 E3 Senneterre Que. Can.
171 E7 Sennewitz Ger.
Senno Belarus see Syanno
105 I2 Sennokura-yama mt. Japan
192 B6 Sennori Sardegna Italy
190 G1 Sennwald Switz.

150 E4 Sennybridge Powys, Wales U.K.
177 I3 Senohrad Slovakia
156 F7 Sénonais reg. France
156 B6 Senonches France
157 M7 Senones France
192 C8 Senorbì Sardegna Italy
163 H8 Senouillac France
161 C6 Senouire r. France
179 L7 Senovo Slovenia
179 J8 Senožeče Slovenia
215 L6 Senqu r. Lesotho
156 F7 Sens France
158 H5 Sens-de-Bretagne France
156 F3 Sensée, Canal de la r. France
242 □O11 Sensuntepeque El Salvador
196 I5 Senta Vojvodina Serbia
121 T3 Sentas Kazakh.
163 F10 Sentein France
163 G10 Sentenac-d'Oust France
186 G3 Senterada Spain
179 M6 Šentilj Slovenia
241 S9 Sentinel AZ U.S.A.
193 N4 Sentinella, Colle della hill Italy
222 F4 Sentinel Peak B.C. Can.
262 S1 Sentinel Range mts Antarctica
Sentinum Italy see Sassoferrato
244 B4 Sentispac Mex.
179 L8 Šentjernej Slovenia
179 L7 Šentjur pri Celju Slovenia
94 □ Sentosa i. Sing.
157 I5 Senuc France
95 L4 Senyiur Kalimantan Indon.
177 K4 Sényő Hungary
129 C5 Senyurt Turkey
127 J5 Şenyurt Turkey
103 I12 Senzaki Japan
103 J14 Sen-zaki pt Japan
171 I6 Senzig Ger.
Seo de Urgell Spain see Le Seu d'Urgell
190 E1 Seon Switz.
116 I9 Seonath r. India
116 G6 Seondha Madh. Prad. India
116 G8 Seoni Madh. Prad. India
116 G8 Seoni Chhapara Madh. Prad. India
116 F8 Seoni-Malwa Madh. Prad. India
117 I9 Seorinarayan Chhattisgarh India
Seoul S. Korea see Sŏul
163 F7 Séoune r. France
95 K8 Sepanjang i. Indon.
80 G7 Separation Point South I. N.Z.
86 G7 Separation Well W.A. Austr.
122 B4 Separ Shāhābād Iran
95 L4 Sepasu Kalimantan Indon.
252 D1 Sepatini r. Brazil
95 I4 Sepauk Kalimantan Indon.
257 E5 Sepetiba, Baía de b. Brazil
91 J7 Sepik r. P.N.G.
95 M4 Sepinang Kalimantan Indon.
95 K3 Seping r. Malaysia
193 N5 Sepino Italy
101 E9 Sep'o N. Korea
174 F2 Sępólno Krajeńskie Pol.
174 E2 Sępolno Wielkie Pol.
117 O6 Sepon Assam India
253 F3 Sepotuba r. Brazil
117 N6 Seppa Arun. Prad. India
160 K1 Seppois-le-Bas France
197 J4 Şepreuş Romania
160 B3 Septaine reg. France
161 G10 Septèmes-les-Vallons France
156 C6 Septeuil France
163 H7 Septfonds France
225 H3 Sept-Îles Que. Can.
158 E4 Sept-Îles, Réserve Naturelle des nature res. France
225 H3 Sept-Îles-Port-Cartier, Réserve Faunique de nature res. Que. Can.
160 H4 Septmoncel France
182 H7 Sepulcro-Hilario Spain
183 M6 Sepúlveda Spain
212 D3 Sepupa Botswana
94 F7 Seputih r. Indon.
191 N3 Sequals Italy
231 E8 Sequatchie r. TN U.S.A.
261 I2 Sequeira Uru.
182 F4 Sequeiros, Embalse de resr Spain
182 H7 Sequeros Spain
183 J5 Sequillo r. Spain
240 N5 Sequoia National Park CA U.S.A.
124 D8 Serae prov. Eritrea
129 B6 Şerafettin Dağları mts Turkey
135 H6 Serafimovich Rus. Fed.
156 H4 Seraincourt France
165 I7 Seraing Belgium
Sêraitang Qinghai China see Baima
93 F5 Seram i. Maluku Indon.
93 G5 Seram, Laut sea Indon.
160 H5 Séran r. France
94 G8 Serang Jawa Indon.
94 □ Serangoon, Pulau i. Sing.
94 □ Serangoon, Sungai r. Sing.
94 □ Serangoon Harbour b. Sing.
161 D9 Séranne, Montagne de la ridge France
161 J9 Séranon France
94 □ Serapong, Mount hill Sing.
95 H3 Serasan i. Indon.
95 H3 Serasan, Selat sea chan. Indon.
190 I8 Seravezza Italy
93 A8 Seraya i. Indon.
95 H3 Seraya i. Indon.
94 □ Seraya, Pulau reg. Sing.
196 I6 Serbia country Europe
111 I10 Sêrbug Co l. Xizang China
136 G4 Serbynivtsi Ukr.
111 L11 Sêrca Xizang China
129 B6 Serçelik Dağı mts Turkey
117 N8 Serchhip Mizoram India
191 I8 Serchio r. Italy
122 G2 Serdar Turkm.
192 C9 Serdiana Sardegna Italy
Serdica Bulg. see Sofiya
210 D2 Serdo Eth.
135 I5 Serdoba r. Rus. Fed.
135 I5 Serdobsk Rus. Fed.
134 K3 Serebryanka Rus. Fed.
137 M8 Serebryanka Ukr.
121 T3 Serebryansk Kazakh.
139 V7 Serebryanyye Prudy Rus. Fed.
177 G3 Sereď Slovakia
139 S6 Sereda Moskovskaya Oblast' Rus. Fed.
139 X4 Sereda Yaroslavskaya Oblast' Rus. Fed.
139 S7 Seredeyskiy Rus. Fed.
138 L3 Seredka Rus. Fed.
139 W6 Serednikovo Rus. Fed.
136 J7 Seredniy Kuyal'nyk r. Ukr.
206 C4 Sérédou Guinea
137 N1 Seredyna-Buda Rus. Fed.
136 B5 Seredyne Ukr.
126 F4 Şereflikoçhisar Turkey
177 H4 Seregélyes Hungary
190 G4 Seregno Italy
162 G4 Séreilhac France
156 G8 Serein r. France
94 D3 Seremban Malaysia
185 I3 Serena, Embalse de la resr Spain
211 B5 Serengeti National Park Tanz.
211 B5 Serengeti Plain Tanz.
209 F8 Serenje Zambia
158 F6 Sérent France
210 B4 Serere Uganda
136 E5 Seret r. Ukr.
134 H5 Serezha r. Rus. Fed.
139 N5 Serezha r. Rus. Fed.
178 C5 Serfaus Austria
134 L4 Ser'ga Rus. Fed.
134 I5 Sergach Rus. Fed.
139 X5 Sergeikha Rus. Fed.
107 N2 Sergelen Dornod Mongolia
107 L3 Sergelen Sühbaatar Mongolia
197 P9 Sergen Turkey
121 M2 Sergeyevka Akmolinskaya Oblast' Kazakh.
121 L1 Sergeyevka Severnyy Kazakhstan Kazakh.
137 S3 Sergeyevka Rus. Fed.
156 F7 Sergines France
130 H3 Sergino Rus. Fed.
254 F4 Sergipe state Brazil
139 V5 Sergiyev Posad Rus. Fed.
135 J5 Sergiyevsk Rus. Fed.
Sergiyevskiy Rus. Fed. see Fakel
139 V8 Sergiyevskoye Lipetskaya Oblast' Rus. Fed.
139 U9 Sergiyevskoye Orlovskaya Oblast' Rus. Fed.
190 H5 Sergnano Italy
Sergo Ukr. see Stakhanov
129 I3 Sergokala Rus. Fed.
106 F8 Serh Qinghai China
123 J4 Serhetabat Turkm.
137 L3 Serhiyivka Chernihivs'ka Oblast' Ukr.
137 N7 Serhiyivka Khersons'ka Oblast' Ukr.
136 J6 Serhiyivka Odes'ka Oblast' Ukr.
136 J7 Serhiyivka Odes'ka Oblast' Ukr.
137 N2 Serhiyivka Sums'ka Oblast' Ukr.
95 K2 Seria Brunei
95 I4 Serian Sarawak Malaysia
190 H4 Seriate Italy
94 G7 Seribu, Kepulauan is Indon.
94 C3 Seribudolok Sumatera Indon.
156 C5 Sérifontaine France
198 F5 Serifos Serifos Greece
198 F5 Serifos i. Greece
198 F5 Serifou, Steno sea chan. Greece
161 C10 Sérignan France
161 F8 Sérignan-du-Comtat France
225 G2 Sérigny r. Que. Can.
225 G2 Sérigny, Lac l. Que. Can.
199 M6 Serik Turkey
110 C7 Serikbuya Xinjiang China
93 E5 Serikkembelo Seram Indon.
190 H4 Serina Italy
213 □J3 Sèrinama Madag.
251 I6 Seringa, Serra da hills Brazil
86 G2 Seringapatam Reef W.A. Austr.
199 K5 Serinhisar Turkey
129 C7 Serinova Turkey
128 E2 Serinyol Turkey
190 H5 Serio r. Italy
190 H5 Serio, Parco del park Italy
Sêrkang Xizang China see Nyainrong
136 E2 Serkhiv Ukr.
205 G5 Serkout mt. Alg.
Serle atoll Arch. des Tuamotu Fr. Polynesia see Pukarua
156 D7 Sermaises France
157 I6 Sermaize-les-Bains France
192 C3 Sermano Corse France
93 F8 Sermata i. Maluku Indon.
93 F8 Sermata, Kepulauan is Maluku Indon.
197 K9 Sermenin Macedonia
221 L2 Sermersuaq glacier Greenland
221 M2 Sermersuaq glacier Greenland
191 K6 Sermide Italy
160 C3 Sermoise-sur-Loire France
193 K4 Sermoneta Italy
160 F3 Sermoyer France
138 I4 Sērmūkši Latvia
182 F7 Sernancelhe Port.
177 L3 Serne r. Ukr.
175 K4 Serniki Pol.
171 F7 Serno Ger.
135 J5 Sernovodsk Rus. Fed.
134 J4 Sernur Rus. Fed.
136 F2 Sernyky Ukr.
Sernyy Zavod Turkm. see Kükürtli
174 G2 Serock Kujawsko-Pomorskie Pol.
175 J3 Serock Mazowieckie Pol.
Sero Colorado Aruba see Seroe Colorado
261 G3 Serodino Arg.
247 □9 Seroe Colorado Aruba
135 I7 Seroglazka Rus. Fed.
185 O6 Serón Spain
183 P6 Serón de Nájima Spain
183 L7 Serones, Embalse de resr Spain
212 D3 Seronga Botswana
164 E5 Serooskerke Neth.
186 F5 Seròs Spain
205 G4 Serouenout well Alg.
130 H4 Serov Rus. Fed.
212 E4 Serowe Botswana
184 D5 Serpa Port.
Serpa Pinto Angola see Menongue
225 G3 Serpent r. Que. Can.
206 C3 Serpent, Vallée du watercourse Mali
192 D9 Serpentara, Isola i. Sardegna Italy
87 C12 Serpentine r. W.A. Austr.
82 B3 Serpentine Lakes salt flat S.A. Austr.
247 M9 Serpent's Mouth sea chan. Trin. and Tob./Venez.
139 S7 Serpeysk Rus. Fed.
182 D8 Serpins Port.
187 E10 Serpis r. Spain
136 I7 Serpneve Ukr.
139 U7 Serpukhov Rus. Fed.
157 K8 Serqueux France
159 M3 Serquigny France
257 G4 Serra Brazil
192 A6 Serra r. Italy
187 E8 Serra Spain
193 O4 Serracapriola Italy
183 K6 Serrada Spain
257 E5 Serra da Bocaina, Parque Nacional da nat. park Brazil
256 D4 Serra da Canastra, Parque Nacional da nat. park Brazil
254 E4 Serra da Capivara, Parque Nacional da nat. park Brazil
252 D2 Serra da Cutia, Parque Nacional nat. park Brazil
182 E8 Serra da Estrela, Parque Natural da nature res. Port.
254 C5 Serra da Mesa, Represa resr Brazil
251 F4 Serra da Mociade, Parque Nacional da nat. park Brazil
254 E4 Serra das Confusões, Parque Nacional da nat. park Brazil
191 O8 Serra de'Conti Italy
193 Q6 Serra del Corvo, Lago di l. Italy
180 C3 Serra de São Mamede, Parque Natural da nature res. Port.
194 F9 Serradifalco Sicilia Italy
192 B4 Serra-di-Ferro Corse France
182 H9 Serradilla Spain
182 H7 Serradilla del Arroyo Spain
252 B2 Serra do Divisor, Parque Nacional da nat. park Brazil
251 H4 Serra do Navio Brazil
257 G2 Serra dos Aimorés Brazil
256 D3 Serra do Salitre Brazil
Sérrai Greece see Serres
192 B9 Serramanna Sardegna Italy
191 J7 Serramazzoni Italy
256 D4 Serrana Brazil
246 C6 Serrana Bank sea feature Caribbean Sea
251 E4 Serranía de la Neblina, Parque Nacional nat. park Venez.
246 D6 Serranilla Bank sea feature Caribbean Sea
183 K8 Serranillos Spain
261 F4 Serrano Arg.
259 B8 Serrano i. Chile
256 A3 Serranópolis Brazil
Serraria, Ilha i. Brazil see Queimada, Ilha
190 F6 Serra Riccò Italy
195 K6 Serra San Bruno Italy
191 O9 Serra San Quirico Italy
182 C9 Serras de Aire e Candeeiros, Parque Natural das nature res. Port.
254 F3 Serra Talhada Brazil
191 M8 Serravalle San Marino
193 J1 Serravalle di Chienti Italy
190 F6 Serravalle Scrivia Italy
156 F4 Serre r. France
193 O6 Serre Italy
160 H2 Serre, Massif de la hills France
161 J7 Serre-Chevalier France
182 I9 Serrejón Spain
192 B9 Serrenti Sardegna Italy
161 I8 Serre-Ponçon, Lac de l. France
Serrera, Pic de la mt. Andorra see Serrère, Pic de
186 I2 Serrère, Pic de mt. Andorra
161 H8 Serres France
198 E1 Serres Greece
163 D9 Serres-Castet France
216 □1a Serreta Terceira Azores
260 E2 Serrezuela Arg.
192 C8 Serri Sardegna Italy
192 B3 Serriera Corse France
160 G5 Serrière-de-Briord France
161 F6 Serrières France
172 B2 Serrig Ger.
254 F4 Serrinha Brazil
254 F3 Serrita Brazil
257 F3 Sêrro Brazil
183 J8 Serrota mt. Spain
162 E4 Sers France
189 B7 Sers Tunisia
195 L5 Sersale Italy
182 D9 Sertã Port.
254 F4 Sertânia Brazil
256 B5 Sertanópolis Brazil
256 A3 Sertão de Camapuã reg. Brazil
256 D4 Sertãozinho Brazil
108 C2 Sêrtar Sichuan China
128 B2 Sertavul Geçidi pass Turkey
207 H5 Serti Nigeria
139 N1 Sertolovo Rus. Fed.
93 G7 Serua vol. Maluku Indon.
94 C2 Seruai Sumatera Indon.
91 I7 Serui Papua Indon.
213 E4 Serule Botswana
95 H5 Serutu i. Indon.
95 J6 Seruyan r. Indon.
138 K7 Servach r. Belarus
157 M8 Servance France
161 C7 Serverette France
198 D2 Servia Greece
161 C10 Servian France
193 K1 Servigliano Italy
158 I5 Servon-sur-Vilaine France
160 J5 Servoz France
93 E8 Serwaru Maluku Indon.
106 D9 Sêrwolungwa Qinghai China
108 B2 Sêrxü Sichuan China
156 H4 Sery France
Seryítsi i. Limnos Greece see Sideritis
186 E4 Sesa Spain
95 L3 Sesayap Kalimantan Indon.
95 L3 Sesayap r. Indon.
208 E4 Sese Dem. Rep. Congo
203 F4 Sese Sudan
224 B3 Seseganaga Lake Ont. Can.
227 N1 Sesekinika Ont. Can.
Sesel country Indian Ocean see Seychelles
183 M8 Seseña Spain
93 E4 Sesepe Maluku Indon.
212 B3 Sesfontein Namibia
114 F5 Seshachalam Hills India
139 Q8 Seshcha Rus. Fed.
209 E9 Sesheke Zambia
190 F5 Sesia r. Italy
184 A4 Sesimbra Port.
140 Q4 Seskar Furö i. Sweden
199 I6 Sesklio i. Greece
183 P4 Sesma Spain
102 □1 Sesoko Okinawa Japan
102 □1 Sesoko-jima i. Okinawa Japan
114 B6 Sesostris Bank sea feature India
187 H10 S'Espalmador i. Spain
187 I10 S'Espardell i. Spain
209 D8 Sessa Angola
193 L5 Sessa Aurunca Italy
193 O7 Sessa Cilento Italy
187 L9 Ses Salines Spain
190 E4 Sessera r. Italy
169 K10 Seßlach Ger.
190 H7 Sesta Godano Italy
187 K9 S'Estanyol de Migjorn Spain
183 O2 Sestao Spain
191 M8 Sestino Italy
191 M2 Sesto Italy
191 N4 Sesto al Reghena Italy
190 F4 Sesto Calende Italy
193 M5 Sesto Campano Italy
191 K8 Sesto Fiorentino Italy
175 L1 Šeštokai Lith.
191 J7 Sestola Italy
190 G4 Sesto San Giovanni Italy
139 U5 Sestra r. Rus. Fed.
190 B6 Sestriere Italy
190 G7 Sestri Levante Italy
138 M1 Sestroretsk Rus. Fed.
188 E3 Sestrunj i. Croatia
192 C9 Sestu Sardegna Italy
138 F6 Šešupė r. Lith./Rus. Fed.
188 F3 Sesvete Croatia
186 G4 Set r. Spain
96 H7 Set, Phou mt. Laos
102 Q4 Setana Japan
235 I3 Setauket NY U.S.A.
161 D10 Sète France
256 D6 Sete Barras Brazil
138 I6 Šetekšna r. Lith.
257 E3 Sete Lagoas Brazil
185 I7 Setenil Spain
140 O2 Setermoen Norway
142 D2 Setesdal val. Norway
102 □G18 Seteuchi Nansei-shotō Japan
168 J3 Seth Ger.
Seti Georgia see Mestia
116 H5 Seti r. Nepal
117 J6 Seti r. Nepal
Setia Italy see Sezze
205 G1 Sétif Alg.
183 Q7 Setiles Spain
203 G6 Setit r. Africa
104 F5 Seto Japan
103 J13 Seto-naikai sea Japan
104 A7 Seto-naikai Kokuritsu-kōen nat. park Japan
96 B6 Setsan Myanmar
191 K7 Setta r. Italy
204 D2 Settat Morocco
208 A5 Setté Cama Gabon
192 C9 Sette Fratelli, Monte dei mt. Sardegna Italy
190 E7 Settepani, Monte mt. Italy
190 D5 Settimo Torinese Italy
190 D4 Settimo Vittone Italy
149 M5 Settle North Yorkshire, England U.K.
84 G4 Settlement Creek r. Qld Austr.
216 □2c Settlement of Edinburgh Tristan da Cunha S. Atlantic Ocean
160 E2 Settons, Lac des l. France
257 F2 Setúbal r. Brazil
184 B3 Setúbal Port.
184 B4 Setúbal admin. dist. Port.
184 A4 Setúbal, Baía de b. Port.
261 G2 Setúbal, Laguna l. Arg.
257 F2 Setubinha Brazil
Seu i. Vanuatu see Hiu
173 L3 Seubersdorf in der Oberpfalz Ger.
162 C4 Seudre r. France
162 C4 Seugne r. France
192 C8 Seui Sardegna Italy
157 J6 Seuil-d'Argonne France
223 M5 Seul, Lac l. Ont. Can.
226 I4 Seul Choix Point MI U.S.A.
94 A2 Seulimeum Sumatera Indon.
169 J7 Seulingen Ger.
159 K3 Seulles r. France
192 C8 Seulo Sardegna Italy
160 G2 Seurre France
137 N1 Sev r. Rus. Fed.
186 J4 Seva Spain
129 F5 Sevan Armenia
Sevan, Lake Armenia see Sevana Lich
Sevan, Ozero l. Armenia see Sevana Lich
129 G5 Sevana Lich l. Armenia
252 D4 Sevaruyo Bol.
137 M9 Sevastopol' Ukr.
149 P5 Seven r. England U.K.
147 E9 Seven Heads Ireland
Seven Islands Que. Can. see Sept-Îles
225 I1 Seven Islands Bay Nfld and Lab. Can.
87 D7 Seven Mile Creek r. W.A. Austr.
215 O5 Sevenoaks S. Africa
151 M5 Sevenoaks Kent, England U.K.
150 E4 Seven Sisters Neath Port Talbot, Wales U.K.
150 □ Seven Stones is England U.K.
85 M8 Seventeen Seventy Qld Austr.
Seventy Mile House B.C. Can. see 70 Mile House
165 J6 Sevenum Neth.
234 B5 Seven Valleys PA U.S.A.
182 E6 Sever Port.
161 C8 Sévérac-le-Château France
182 D7 Sever do Vouga Port.
176 F6 Severin Croatia
255 B9 Severino Ribeiro Brazil
139 V6 Severka r. Rus. Fed.
83 M3 Severn r. N.S.W. Austr.
224 C2 Severn r. Ont. Can.
81 H9 Severn mt. South I. N.Z.
214 G2 Severn S. Africa
150 H4 Severn r. England/Wales U.K.
234 B6 Severn MD U.S.A.
232 H12 Severn NC U.S.A.
234 C7 Severn r. MD U.S.A.
234 B6 Severna Park MD U.S.A.
134 H2 Severnaya Dvina r. Rus. Fed.
134 L3 Severnaya Mylva r. Rus. Fed.
129 F2 Severnaya Osetiya-Alaniya, Respublika aut. rep. Rus. Fed.
130 H3 Severnaya Sos'va r. Rus. Fed.
131 L1 Severnaya Zemlya is Rus. Fed.
150 G4 Severn Beach South Gloucestershire, England U.K.
224 B2 Severn Lake Ont. Can.
135 K5 Severnoye Rus. Fed.
224 B2 Severn River Provincial Park Ont. Can.
137 P3 Severnyy Belgorodskaya Oblast' Rus. Fed.
139 U5 Severnyy Moskovskaya Oblast' Rus. Fed.
134 J1 Severnyy Nenetskiy Avtonomnyy Okrug Rus. Fed.
134 N2 Severnyy Respublika Komi Rus. Fed.
175 H1 Severnyy, Mys pt Rus. Fed.
100 L1 Severnyy, Zaliv b. Rus. Fed.
131 S3 Severnyy Anyuyskiy Khrebet mts Rus. Fed.
122 E2 Severnyy Aul Turkm.
138 L1 Severnyy Berezovyy, Ostrov i. Rus. Fed.
120 G4 Severnyy Chink Ustyurta esc. Kazakh.
121 M1 Severnyy Kazakhstan admin. div. Kazakh.
134 K4 Severnyy Kommunar Rus. Fed.
129 C2 Severnyy Priyut Rus. Fed.
Severnyy Suchan Rus. Fed. see Uglekamensk
134 L3 Severnyy Ural mts Rus. Fed.
99 I1 Severobaykal'sk Rus. Fed.
131 M4 Severo-Baykal'skoye Nagor'ye mts Rus. Fed.
110 H1 Severo-Chuyskiy Khrebet mts Rus. Fed.
Severodonetsk Ukr. see Syeverodonets'k
134 G2 Severodvinsk Rus. Fed.
Severo-Kazakhstanskaya Oblast' admin. div. Kazakh. see Severnyy Kazakhstan
131 Q4 Severo-Kuril'sk Kuril'skiye O-va Rus. Fed.
140 V2 Severomorsk Rus. Fed.
134 G3 Severoonezhsk Rus. Fed.
Severo-Osetinskaya A.S.S.R. aut. rep. Rus. Fed. see Severnaya Osetiya-Alaniya, Respublika
129 F3 Severo-Osetinskiy Zapovednik nature res. Rus. Fed.
100 M2 Severo-Sakhalinskaya Ravnina plain Rus. Fed.
131 L2 Severo-Sibirskaya Nizmennost' lowland Rus. Fed.
134 L3 Severoural'sk Rus. Fed.
131 K3 Severo-Yeniseyskiy Rus. Fed.
139 V7 Severo-Zadonsk Rus. Fed.
Seversk Ukr. see Sivers'k
135 G7 Severskaya Rus. Fed.
135 H7 Severskiy Donets r. Rus. Fed.
Severskiy Donets r. Ukr. see Sivers'kyy Donets'
158 I3 Sèves r. France
155 I4 Seveso Italy
190 G5 Seveso r. Italy
179 K1 Ševětín Czech Rep.
140 T2 Sevettijärvi Fin.
192 B3 Sevi, Col de pass France
241 T3 Sevier UT U.S.A.
241 T2 Sevier r. UT U.S.A.
241 U2 Sevier Bridge Reservoir UT U.S.A.
241 T2 Sevier Desert UT U.S.A.
241 S3 Sevier Lake UT U.S.A.
231 F8 Sevierville TN U.S.A.
158 G5 Sévignac France
163 D9 Sévignacq France
156 H4 Sévigny-Waleppe France
250 C3 Sevilla Col.
184 H6 Sevilla Spain
184 H5 Sevilla prov. Spain
183 L8 Sevilla la Nueva Spain
Seville Spain see Sevilla
183 K9 Sevilleja de la Jara Spain
261 I5 Sevingé Arg.
197 N7 Sevlievo Bulg.
Sevlyush Ukr. see Vynohradiv
188 E2 Sevnica Slovenia
196 H7 Sevojno Serbia
162 A1 Sèvre Nantaise r. France
162 B3 Sèvre Niortaise r. France
160 I5 Sévrier France
160 G3 Sevron r. France
137 N1 Sevsk Rus. Fed.
111 I10 Sêwa Xizang China
114 D3 Sewand r. India
116 E5 Sewani Haryana India
220 D3 Seward AK U.S.A.
226 E7 Seward IL U.S.A.
236 G5 Seward NE U.S.A.
232 F8 Seward PA U.S.A.
262 T2 Seward Mountains Antarctica
220 B3 Seward Peninsula AK U.S.A.
260 B4 Sewell Chile
234 E5 Sewell NJ U.S.A.
222 C4 Sewell Inlet B.C. Can.
172 D5 Sexau Ger.
Sexi Spain see Almuñécar
222 G4 Sexsmith Alta Can.
242 G4 Sextín Mex.
242 G5 Sextín r. Mex.
105 J5 Seya Japan
123 J5 Seyah Band Koh mts Afgh.
130 I2 Seyakha Rus. Fed.
243 N8 Seybaplaya Mex.
217 □2 Seychelles country Indian Ocean
163 E6 Seyches France
171 G7 Seyda Ger.
199 M3 Seydi r. Turkey
123 J2 Seýdi Turkm.
126 E5 Seydişehir Turkey
140 □F1 Seyðisfjörður Iceland
158 H3 Seye r. France
126 G4 Seyfe Gölü salt flat Turkey
Seyhan Turkey see Adana
126 G5 Seyhan r. Turkey
128 D1 Seyhan Barajı resr Turkey
129 H5 Seyidlär Azer.
199 L3 Seyitgazi Turkey
199 K3 Seyitömer Turkey
137 Q2 Seym Rus. Fed.
137 N2 Seym r. Rus. Fed./Ukr.
131 Q3 Seymchan Rus. Fed.
199 J1 Seymen Turkey
83 J7 Seymour Vic. Austr.
215 K8 Seymour S. Africa
235 I2 Seymour CT U.S.A.
230 E6 Seymour IN U.S.A.
237 F9 Seymour TX U.S.A.
222 E5 Seymour Inlet B.C. Can.
84 D8 Seymour Range mts N.T. Austr.
161 I8 Seyne France
161 E8 Seynes France
160 I5 Seynod France
Seypan i. N. Mariana Is see Saipan
160 H5 Seyssel France
163 G8 Seysses France
160 F5 Seysseuel France
161 H6 Seyssins France
197 P9 Seytan r. Turkey
123 M4 Seyyedābād Afgh.
188 D3 Sežana Slovenia
156 G6 Sézanne France
215 O6 Sezela S. Africa
139 R6 Sezha r. Rus. Fed.
176 D2 Sezimovo Ústí Czech Rep.
193 K5 Sezze Italy
199 G7 Sfaka Kriti Greece
197 N5 Sfântu Gheorghe Covasna Romania
197 R6 Sfântu Gheorghe Tulcea Romania
197 R5 Sfântu Gheorghe, Braţul watercourse Romania
197 R6 Sfântu Gheorghe-Palade-Perişor nature res. Romania
205 H2 Sfax Tunisia
198 D2 Sfendami Greece
192 D8 Sferracavallo, Capo c. Sardegna Italy
198 D2 Sfikias, Limni resr Greece
Sfîntu Gheorghe Romania see Sfântu Gheorghe
Sgiersch Pol. see Zgierz
146 D6 Sgiogarstaigh Western Isles, Scotland U.K.
146 F7 Sgorr Ruadh hill Scotland U.K.
164 G5 's-Gravendeel Neth.
164 F4 's-Gravenhage Neth.
165 E6 's-Gravenpolder Neth.
165 I7 's-Gravenvoeren Belgium
164 F5 's-Gravenzande Neth.
193 K4 Sgurgola Italy
146 F8 Sgurr a' Chaorachain mt. Scotland U.K.
146 G8 Sgurr a' Choire Ghlais mt. Scotland U.K.
146 D8 Sgurr Alasdair hill Scotland U.K.
146 G7 Sgurr a' Mhuilinn hill Scotland U.K.
146 F9 Sgurr Dhomhnuill hill Scotland U.K.
146 F8 Sgurr Fhuaran mt. Scotland U.K.
146 E7 Sgurr Mhòr hill Scotland U.K.
146 F7 Sgurr Mòr mt. Scotland U.K.
146 F8 Sgurr na Ciche mt. Scotland U.K.
129 G2 Shaami-Yurt Rus. Fed.
107 K9 Shaanxi prov. China
Shaartuz Tajik. see Shahrtuz
125 I3 Sha'b, Jabal ash hills Saudi Arabia
Shaba prov. Dem. Rep. Congo see Katanga
123 L7 Shaban Pak.
Shabani Zimbabwe see Zvishavane
137 R9 Shabanovskoye Rus. Fed.
Shabbaz Uzbek. see Beruniy
210 E4 Shabeellaha Dhexe admin. reg. Somalia
210 D4 Shabeellaha Hoose admin. reg. Somalia
135 G7 Shabel'sk Rus. Fed.
122 A2 Shabestar Iran
197 Q7 Shabla Bulg.
197 Q7 Shabla, Nos pt Bulg.
139 S9 Shablykino Rus. Fed.
225 H2 Shabogamo Lake Nfld and Lab. Can.
208 E5 Shabunda Dem. Rep. Congo
124 H8 Shabwah Yemen
124 H8 Shabwah governorate Yemen
110 C7 Shache Xinjiang China
Shacheng Hebei China see Huailai
263 L1 Shackleton Coast Antarctica
263 M1 Shackleton Glacier Antarctica
263 G2 Shackleton Ice Shelf Antarctica
262 V1 Shackleton Range mts Antarctica
124 E5 Shadād Saudi Arabia
123 L8 Shadadkot Pak.
108 G4 Shadaogou Hubei China
96 C5 Shadaw Myanmar
232 C9 Shade OH U.S.A.
122 C6 Shādegān Iran
234 D2 Shades Glen PA U.S.A.
123 L7 Shadihar Pak.
122 E7 Shādkām watercourse Iran
130 H4 Shadrinsk Rus. Fed.
Shadwan Island Egypt see Shākir, Jazīrat
232 G10 Shadwell VA U.S.A.
238 C5 Shady Grove OR U.S.A.
234 B7 Shady Side MD U.S.A.
232 D11 Shady Spring WV U.S.A.
226 H9 Shafer, Lake IN U.S.A.
263 K2 Shafer Peak Antarctica
122 G3 Shafi'abad Iran
Shafirkan Uzbek. see Shofirkon
120 F1 Shafranovo Rus. Fed.
Shafrikan Uzbek. see Shofirkon
240 M6 Shafter CA U.S.A.
150 H5 Shaftesbury Dorset, England U.K.
81 E12 Shag r. South I. N.Z.
224 C2 Shagamu r. Ont. Can.
207 F5 Shagamu Nigeria
120 G4 Shagan watercourse Kazakh.
121 R2 Shagan watercourse Kazakh.
107 L7 Shagedu Nei Mongol China
220 C3 Shageluk AK U.S.A.
124 C2 Shaghab oasis Saudi Arabia
Shaghan Kazakh. see Chagan
Shaghyray Üstirti plat. Kazakh. see Shagyray, Plato
120 H6 Shag'irlik Uzbek.
121 N1 Shaglyteniz, Ozero l. Kazakh.
81 E12 Shag Point South I. N.Z.
249 G7 Shag Rocks is S. Georgia
120 G4 Shagyray, Plato plat. Kazakh.
114 F4 Shahabad Andhra Prad. India
116 F4 Shahabad Haryana India
114 E4 Shahabad Karnataka India
116 F7 Shahabad Rajasthan India
116 H6 Shahabad Uttar Prad. India
Shāhābād Āzarbāyjān-e Gharbī Iran see Showt
122 G7 Shāhābād Kermān Iran
Shāhābād Kermānshāh Iran see Eslāmābād-e Gharb
116 E9 Shahada Mahar. India
94 D3 Shah Alam Malaysia
123 J8 Shahana Pak.
114 D5 Shahapur Karnataka India
114 C3 Shahapur Mahar. India
128 E6 Shahbā' Syria
123 L9 Shahbandar Pak.
122 C3 Shahbanu Farah Dam Iran
123 K8 Shahbaz Kalat Pak.
117 M8 Shahbazpur sea chan. Bangl.
123 L9 Shahbeg Pak.
123 L9 Shah Bilawal Pak.
122 G6 Shahdād Iran
123 M9 Shahdadpur Pak.
116 H8 Shahdol Madh. Prad. India
123 P6 Shahdura Pak.
108 G3 Shahe Chongqing China
107 P8 Shahe Shandong China
107 N8 Sha He r. China
Shahejie Jiangxi China see Jiujiang
Shahepu Gansu China see Linze
Shahezhen Gansu China see Linze
Shahezhen Jiangxi China see Jiujiang
123 L4 Shah Fuladi mt. Afgh.
117 I6 Shahganj Uttar Prad. India
116 G7 Shahgarh Madh. Prad. India
116 B6 Shahgarh Rajasthan India
202 D1 Shaḥḥāt Libya
123 O6 Shah Hussain Pak.
123 J9 Shahid, Ras pt Pak.
Shāhīn Dezh Iran see Sa'īndezh
123 K7 Shah Ismail Afgh.
116 F6 Shahjahanpur Rajasthan India
116 G6 Shahjahanpur Uttar Prad. India
122 H3 Shāh Jehān, Kūh-e mts Iran
123 L5 Shāh Jūy Afgh.
122 H6 Shāh Kūh mt. Iran
127 P6 Shahmīrzād Iran
107 Q6 Shahousuo Liaoning China
Shāh Pasand Iran see Āzād Shahr
114 E4 Shahpur Karnataka India
116 F8 Shahpur Madh. Prad. India
116 F9 Shahpur Madh. Prad. India
116 G8 Shahpur Madh. Prad. India
116 H8 Shahpur Madh. Prad. India
Shāhpūr Iran see Salmās
123 M7 Shahpur Balochistan Pak.
123 O5 Shahpur Punjab Pak.
123 M8 Shahpur Sindh Pak.
116 G8 Shahpura Madh. Prad. India
116 H8 Shahpura Madh. Prad. India
116 E7 Shahpura Rajasthan India
125 J6 Shahr oasis Saudi Arabia
123 K4 Shahrak Afgh.
122 I5 Shāhrakht Iran
124 F6 Shahrān reg. Saudi Arabia
122 F6 Shahr-e Bābak Iran
122 D5 Shahr-e Kord Iran
122 I4 Shahr-e Now Iran
123 L6 Shahr-e Şafā Afgh.
122 D5 Shahrezā Iran
123 L6 Shahrig Pak.
121 O7 Shahrihon Uzbek.
121 L8 Shahrisabz Uzbek.
123 M2 Shahriston Tajik.
122 D4 Shahr Rey Iran
123 N7 Shahr Sultan Pak.
123 M3 Shahrtuz Tajik.
Shāhrūd Iran see Emāmrūd
122 C3 Shāhrūd, Rūdkhāneh-ye r. Iran
122 F4 Shahrud Bustam reg. Iran
122 H7 Shāh Savārān, Kūh-e mts Iran
Shāh Taqī Iran see Emām Taqī
123 K7 Shah Umar Pak.
123 M6 Shaighalu Pak.
123 K7 Shaikh Husain mt. Pak.
128 F4 Shā'īr, Jabal mts Syria
128 C9 Sha'īrah, Jabal mt. Egypt
117 M7 Shaistaganj Bangl.
125 I3 Shaj'ah, Jabal hill Saudi Arabia
116 F8 Shajapur Madh. Prad. India
101 D8 Shajianzi Liaoning China
104 C7 Shakaga-dake mt. Japan
122 B3 Shakar Bolāghī Iran
215 P5 Shakaskraal S. Africa
215 P5 Shakaville S. Africa
212 D3 Shakawe Botswana
224 B3 Shakespeare Island Ont. Can.
Shakh Khatlon Tajik. see Shoh
Shakhagach Azer. see Şahağac
Shakhbuz Azer. see Şahbuz
122 H5 Shākhen Iran
137 P3 Shakhovo Rus. Fed.
139 S5 Shakhovskaya Rus. Fed.
Shakhrisabz Uzbek. see Shahrisabz
Shakhristan Tajik. see Shahriston
124 E8 Shakhs, Ras pt Eritrea
137 R5 Shakhtars'k Ukr.
Shakhtersk Ukr. see Shakhtars'k
Shakhterskoye Ukr. see Pershotravens'k
121 O3 Shakhtinsk Kazakh.
120 H3 Shakhty Kazakh.
Shakhty Respublika Buryatiya Rus. Fed. see Gusinoozersk
135 H7 Shakhty Rostovskaya Oblast' Rus. Fed.
Shakhtyorsk Ukr. see Shakhtars'k
Shakhtyorskoye Ukr. see Pershotravens'k
134 I4 Shakhun'ya Rus. Fed.
207 F4 Shaki Nigeria
203 G3 Shākir, Jazīrat i. Egypt
236 I3 Shakopee MN U.S.A.
102 R3 Shakotan-hantō pen. Japan
102 R3 Shakotan-misaki c. Japan
109 I6 Shakou Guangdong China
202 A1 Shakshūk Libya
210 C3 Shala Hāyk' l. Eth.
134 H3 Shalakusha Rus. Fed.
122 D5 Shālamzār Iran
109 H8 Shalang Guangdong China
129 I4 Shalbuzdag, Gora mt. Rus. Fed.
121 R2 Shalday Kazakh.
151 J6 Shalfleet Isle of Wight, England U.K.
151 K5 Shalford Surrey, England U.K.
121 N4 Shalginskiy Kazakh.
Shalgiya Kazakh. see Shalginskiy
129 G2 Shali Rus. Fed.
106 C8 Shaliangzi Qinghai China
125 L6 Shalim Oman
Shaliuhe Qinghai China see Gangca
116 G4 Shalkar Hima. Prad. India
120 H4 Shalkar Aktyubinskaya Oblast' Kazakh.
Shalkar Kazakh. see Chelkar
120 D2 Shalkar, Ozero salt l. Kazakh.
120 I2 Shalkar Karashatau salt l. Kazakh.
120 I2 Shalkar-Yega-Kara, Ozero l. Rus. Fed.
Shalqar Aktyubinskaya Oblast' Kazakh. see Shalkar
Shalqar Zapadnyy Kazakhstan Kazakh. see Chelkar
Shalqar Köli salt l. Kazakh. see Shalkar, Ozero
Shalqīya Kazakh. see Shalginskiy
122 D3 Shaltrak Iran
108 B3 Shaluli Shan mts Sichuan China
117 P5 Shaluni mt. Arun. Prad. India
134 L4 Shalya Rus. Fed.
137 N2 Shalyhyne Ukr.
119 H5 Shām, Jabal mt. Oman
211 B6 Shama r. Tanz.
128 A8 Shamāl Sīnā' governorate Egypt
123 L6 Shamalzā'ī Afgh.
134 L4 Shamary Rus. Fed.
124 F1 Shāmat al Akbād des. Saudi Arabia
223 M3 Shamattawa Man. Can.
224 C2 Shamattawa r. Ont. Can.
139 O7 Shamava Belarus
122 C5 Shambār Iran
210 A3 Shambe Sudan
210 C2 Shambu Eth.
209 D6 Shambuanda Dem. Rep. Congo
109 □ Sham Chun r. Guangdong/H.K. China
116 E7 Shamgarh Madh. Prad. India
Shamgong Bhutan see Shemgang
122 G8 Shamīl Iran
129 H3 Shamil'kala Rus. Fed.
125 K4 Shamis U.A.E.
129 I2 Shamkhal Rus. Fed.
Shamkhor Azer. see Şämkir
124 F2 Shammar, Jabal reg. Saudi Arabia
234 B3 Shamokin PA U.S.A.
234 B3 Shamokin Dam PA U.S.A.
139 Q1 Shamoksha Rus. Fed.
136 I4 Shamrayivka Ukr.
237 E8 Shamrock TX U.S.A.
213 F3 Shamva Zimbabwe
215 K9 Shamwari Game Rese… nature res. S. Africa
96 D4 Shan state Myanmar
Shancheng Fujian Chin… Nanjing
Shancheng Shandong … see Shanxian
123 I6 Shand Afgh.
122 I7 Shāndak Iran
106 G7 Shandan Gansu China
106 G7 Shandan He r. Gansu C…
107 O6 Shandian He r. China
122 H3 Shandiz Iran
107 O8 Shandong prov. China
107 Q8 Shandong Bandao per…
137 K4 Shandra Ukr.
127 L7 Shandrūkh Iraq
123 O3 Shandur Pass Pak.
234 D4 Shanesville PA U.S.A.
213 F3 Shangani Zimbabwe
213 E3 Shangani r. Zimbabwe
108 B2 Shang Boingor Qingha…
109 J2 Shangcai Henan China
108 G6 Shangchao Guangxi Ch…
109 J3 Shangcheng Henan Ch…
111 I12 Shang Chu r. China
109 I8 Shangchuan Dao i. Guangdong China
Shangchuankou Qingh… China see Minhe
107 M6 Shangdu Nei Mongol C…
100 F5 Shangganling Heilong.
109 J4 Shanggao Jiangxi China
109 M3 Shanghai Shanghai Chi…
109 M3 Shanghai mun. China
109 K6 Shanghang Fujian Chin…
107 O8 Shanghe Shandong Ch…
101 D8 Shanghekou Liaoning …
Shangji Henan China se… Xichuan
Shangjie Yunnan China… Yangbi
108 H2 Shangjin Hubei China
108 B2 Shang Kongma Qingha…
107 Q1 Shangkuli Nei Mongol …
108 G2 Shangluo Shaanxi Chin…
Shangmei Hunan China… Xinhua
108 H2 Shangnan Shaanxi Chi…
209 D9 Shangombo Zambia
Shangpai Anhui China … Feixi
Shangpai Yunnan China… Fugong
Shangpaihe Anhui Chin… Feixi
107 N9 Shangqiu Henan China
109 K4 Shangrao Jiangxi China
110 F3 Shangsanshilipu Xinjia… China
109 J2 Shangshui Henan Chin…
108 G7 Shangsi Guangxi China
Shangtang Zhejiang Ch… Yongjia
109 J6 Shangyou Jiangxi China
110 E6 Shangyou Shuiku resr…
109 M3 Shangyu Zhejiang China
108 A4 Shang Zayü Xizang Chi…
100 E6 Shangzhi Heilong. Chin…
Shangzhou Shaanxi Ch… Shangluo
107 P6 Shanhaiguan Hebei Ch…
Shanhe Gansu China se… Zhengning
100 E6 Shanhetun Heilong. Ch…
175 M3 Shani Belarus
207 I4 Shani Nigeria
129 F3 Shani, Mt'a Georgia/Ru…
151 J6 Shanklin Isle of Wight, England U.K.
108 G8 Shankou Guangxi China
109 H4 Shankou Hunan China
106 D5 Shankou Xinjiang China
80 J7 Shannon North I. N.Z.
147 E7 Shannon airport Ireland
147 E7 Shannon est. Ireland
147 E7 Shannon r. Ireland
215 K5 Shannon S. Africa
226 E7 Shannon IL U.S.A.
147 C7 Shannon, Mouth of the… Ireland
87 D13 Shannon National Par… W.A. Austr.
221 Q2 Shannon Ø i. Greenland
96 C4 Shan Plateau Myanmar
106 B5 Shanshan Xinjiang Chin…
106 B5 Shanshanzhan Xinjiang…
Shansi prov. China see …
131 O4 Shantarskiye Ostrova Rus. Fed.
109 □J7 Shan Tei Tong hill H.K. …
Shan Teng hill H.K. Chi… Victoria Peak
117 L8 Shantipur W. Bengal In…
148 D5 Shantonagh Ireland
109 K7 Shantou Guangdong Ch…
Shantung prov. China s… Shandong
147 F4 Shanvus Ireland
109 J7 Shanwei Guangdong Ch…
107 L7 Shanxi prov. China
107 O9 Shanxian Shandong Chi…
139 S7 Shanya r. Rus. Fed.
108 G2 Shanyang Shaanxi Chin…
107 M7 Shanyin Shanxi China
109 H5 Shaodong Hunan China
109 I6 Shaoguan Guangdong …
109 I5 Shaoshan Hunan China
109 K5 Shaowu Fujian China
109 M3 Shaoxing Zhejiang Chin…
109 H5 Shaoyang Hunan China
109 H5 Shaoyang Hunan China
149 L4 Shap Cumbria, England …
109 H8 Shapa Guangdong Chin…
209 D6 Shapembe Dem. Rep. …
Shaping Sichuan China… Ebian
146 K4 Shapinsay i. Scotland U…
146 K4 Shapinsay Sound sea … Scotland U.K.
139 O2 Shapki Rus. Fed.
134 K2 Shapkina r. Rus. Fed.
137 L2 Shapovalivka Ukr.
139 R1 Shapsha Rus. Fed.
110 I1 Shapshal'skiy Khrebet … Rus. Fed.
137 R9 Shapsugskaya Rus. Fe…
137 R9 Shapsugskoye Vodokhranilishche resr Rus. Fed.
138 M7 Shapyalyevichy Belarus
110 I4 Shaqiuhe Xinjiang China
202 E6 Shaqq el Giefer, Wadi watercourse Sudan
202 E6 Shaqq el Khadir Sudan
124 G3 Shaqrā' Saudi Arabia
110 F4 Shaquanzi Xinjiang Chi…
121 S3 Shar Kazakh.
124 B2 Shār, Jabal mt. Saudi A…
127 K8 Sharaf well Iraq
202 E6 Sharafa Sudan
127 L4 Sharaf-Khāneh Iran
107 J1 Sharalday Rus. Fed.
123 M5 Sharan Afgh.
134 K5 Sharan Rus. Fed.
134 I4 Sharanga Rus. Fed.
123 M6 Sharan Jogizai Pak.
139 U6 Sharapovo Rus. Fed.
128 G2 Sharaqraq Syria
138 H9 Sharashova Belarus
128 B10 Sharātīb, Ra's pt Egypt
147 G6 Sharavogue Ireland
128 E10 Sharawrā, Jabal hills Saudi Arabia
128 E10 Sharawrā', Qā' salt pan Saudi Arabia
Sharbaqty Kazakh. see Shcherbakty
125 M7 Sharbithāt, Ra's c. Oma…
106 C2 Sharbulag Mongolia
121 S1 Sharchino Rus. Fed.
121 L7 Shardara Kazakh.
Shardara Bögeni resr Kazakh./Uzbek. see Chardarinskoye Vodokhranilishche
123 P4 Shardi Pak.
106 D3 Sharga Govĭ-Altay Mong…
106 F2 Sharga Hövsgöl Mongoli…
Shargorod Ukr. see Sha…

Sharg'un Uzbek.
Sharhorod Ukr.
Sharhulsan Mongolia
Shari r. Cameroon/Chad see Chari
Shari Japan
Shārī, Buḩayrat imp. l. Iraq
Shari-dake vol. Japan
Sharīfah Syria
Sharīrah Pass Egypt
Sharivka Kharkivs'ka Oblast' Ukr.
Sharivka Luhans'ka Oblast' Ukr.
Sharivtsek, Pereval pass Georgia/Rus. Fed.
Sharjah U.A.E. see Ash Shāriqah
Sharka-leb La pass Xizang China
Sharkan Rus. Fed.
Sharkawshchyna Belarus
Shark Bay W.A. Austr.
Shark Fin Bay Palawan Phil.
Sharkhāt Yemen
Shark Reef Coral Sea Is Terr. Austr.
Shark River Hills NJ U.S.A.
Sharlawuk Turkm. see Şarlawuk
Sharlyk Rus. Fed.
Sharmah Saudi Arabia
Sharm ash Shaykh Egypt
Sharo-Argun r. Rus. Fed.
Sharon PA U.S.A.
Sharon WI U.S.A.
Sharon, Plain of Israel see HaSharon
Sharon Springs KS U.S.A.
Sharonville OH U.S.A.
Sharoy Rus. Fed.
Sharpe, Lake salt flat W.A. Austr.
Sharpe Lake Man. Can.
Sharpness Gloucestershire, England U.K.
Sharp Peak hill H.K. China see Nam She Tsim
Sharpsburg MD U.S.A.
Sharpsburg OH U.S.A.
Sharqat Iraq see Ash Sharqāţ
Sharqī, Jabal ash mts Lebanon/Syria
Sharqiy Ustyurt Chink esc. Uzbek.
Sharqpur Pak.
Shartlesville PA U.S.A.
Sharur Azer. see Şărur
Shar Us Gol r. Mongolia
Shary well Saudi Arabia
Shar'ya Rus. Fed.
Shar'ya r. Rus. Fed.
Sharyn Kazakh. see Charyn
Shasha Nigeria
Shashe Botswana
Shashe r. Botswana/Zimbabwe
Shashe Dam resr Botswana
Shashemenē Eth.
Shashi Hubei China see Jingzhou
Shashubay Kazakh.
Shasta, Mount vol. CA U.S.A.
Shasta Lake CA U.S.A.
Shatalovka Rus. Fed.
Shatalovo Rus. Fed.
Sha Tau Kok Hoi inlet H.K. China
Shāţi', Wādī ash watercourse Libya
Shatili Georgia
Shatilki Belarus see Svyetlahorsk
Sha Tin H.K. China
Sha Tin Hoi b. H.K. China
Shatki Rus. Fed.
Shaţnat as Salmās, Wādī watercourse Syria
Sha Tong Hau Shan i. H.K. China
Shatoy Rus. Fed.
Shatsk Rus. Fed.
Shats'k Ukr.
Shats'k nat. park Ukr.
Shaţţ, Ra's osh pt Iran
Shaţţ al 'Arab r. Iran/Iraq
Shaţţ al Gharrāf r. Iraq
Shattuck OK U.S.A.
Shatura Rus. Fed.
Shaturtorf Rus. Fed.
Shaubak Jordan see Ash Shawbak
Shāūildir Kazakh. see Shaul'der
Shaul'der Kazakh.
Shaunavon Sask. Can.
Shaverki Rus. Fed.
Shaver Lake CA U.S.A.
Shavers Fork r. WV U.S.A.
Shavi Klde, Mt'a Georgia/Rus. Fed.
Shavington Cheshire, England U.K.
Shaw Arg.
Shaw r. W.A. Austr.
Shaw Greater Manchester, England U.K.
Shawan Xinjiang China
Shawan MD U.S.A.
Shawangunk Kill r. NY U.S.A.
Shawangunk Mountains hills NY U.S.A.
Shawano WI U.S.A.
Shawano Lake WI U.S.A.
Shawāq well Saudi Arabia
Shawbost Western Isles, Scotland U.K.
Shawhan KY U.S.A.
Shawnee OK U.S.A.
Shawnee WY U.S.A.
Shawsville VA U.S.A.
Sha Xi r. China
Shaxian Fujian China
Shayan Kazakh.
Shayang Hubei China
Shaybārā i. Saudi Arabia
Shayboveyem r. Rus. Fed.
Shay Gap W.A. Austr.
Shaykh, Jabal ash mt. Lebanon/Syria see Hermon, Mount
Shaykh, Wādī ash watercourse Egypt
Shaykh Jūwī Iraq
Shaykh Miskīn Syria
Shaykh Sa'd Iraq
Shaykovka Rus. Fed.
Shaytanka r. Ukr.
Shayţūr Iran
Shayzar Syria
Shāzand Iran
Shazaoyuan Gansu China
Shaẓāẓ, Jabal mt. Saudi Arabia
Shazud Tajik.
Shchara r. Belarus
Shcharchova Belarus
Shchastya Ukr.
Shchebetovka Ukr.
Shcheglovka Rus. Fed.
Shchekino Rus. Fed.
Shchekychyn Ukr.
Shchelkanovo Rus. Fed.
Shchelkovo Rus. Fed.
Shchel'yayur Rus. Fed.
Shcherbakov Rus. Fed. see Rybinsk
Shcherbakty Kazakh.
Shcherbani Ukr.
Shcherbinovka Ukr. see Dzerzhyns'k
Shchetinskoye Rus. Fed.
Shchigry Rus. Fed.
Shcholkine Ukr.
Shchomyslitsa Belarus
Shchors Ukr.
Shchors'k Ukr.
Shchuchin Belarus see Shchuchyn
Shchuchinsk Kazakh.
Shchuch'ye Rus. Fed.
Shchuchyn Belarus
Shchuger r. Rus. Fed.
136 C4 Shchyrets' Ukr.
138 L8 Shchytkavichy Belarus
251 G4 Shea Guyana
121 U2 Shebalino Rus. Fed.
226 D1 Shebandowan Lakes Ont. Can.
135 G6 Shebekino Rus. Fed.
123 K3 Sheberghān Afgh.
226 G6 Sheboygan WI U.S.A.
137 R9 Shebsh r. Rus. Fed.
207 H4 Shebshi Mountains Nigeria
100 L5 Shebunino Sakhalin Rus. Fed.
Shecheng Hebei China see Shexian
225 H4 Shediac N.B. Can.
222 E4 Shedin Peak B.C. Can.
129 B1 Shedok Rus. Fed.
147 H5 Sheelin, Lough l. Ireland
147 G2 Sheep Haven b. Ireland
215 O2 Sheepmoor S. Africa
241 Q5 Sheep Peak NV U.S.A.
164 J5 's-Heerenberg Neth.
151 M4 Sheering Essex, England U.K.
151 N5 Sheerness Kent, England U.K.
225 I4 Sheet Harbour N.S. Can.
128 D6 Shefar'am Israel
81 G10 Sheffield South I. N.Z.
149 O7 Sheffield South Yorkshire, England U.K.
231 D8 Sheffield AL U.S.A.
226 E8 Sheffield IL U.S.A.
232 F7 Sheffield PA U.S.A.
237 E10 Sheffield TX U.S.A.
225 J3 Sheffield Lake Nfld and Lab. Can.
151 L3 Shefford Bedfordshire, England U.K.
123 K6 Shegah Afgh.
116 F9 Shegaon Mahar. India
134 J2 Shegmas Rus. Fed.
227 M4 Sheguiandah Ont. Can.
210 D3 Shēh Husēn Eth.
108 E3 Shehong Sichuan China
147 D9 Shehy Mountains hills Ireland
Sheikh, Jebel esh mt. Lebanon/Syria see Hermon, Mount
Sheikh Othman Yemen see Ash Shaykh 'Uthman
123 P6 Sheikhupura Pak.
224 C3 Shekak r. Ont. Can.
122 F5 Shekār Āb Iran
116 E6 Shekhawati reg. India
Shekhem West Bank see Nāblus
137 T1 Shekhman' Rus. Fed.
Sheki Azer. see Şäki
109 □I7 Shekka Ch'ün-Tao is H.K. China
109 □I7 Shek Kwu Chau i. H.K. China
109 □I7 Shek Pik resr H.K. China
Shek Pik Reservoir H.K. China see Shek Pik
134 G4 Sheksna Rus. Fed.
134 G4 Sheksninskoye Vodokhranilishche resr Rus. Fed.
109 □J7 Shek Uk Shan mt. H.K. China
111 K11 Shela Xizang China
121 T1 Shelabolikha Rus. Fed.
123 I7 Shelag watercourse Afgh./Iran
131 S2 Shelagskiy, Mys pt Rus. Fed.
232 C11 Shelbiana KY U.S.A.
236 I6 Shelbina MO U.S.A.
230 D6 Shelburn IN U.S.A.
225 H5 Shelburne N.S. Can.
227 N5 Shelburne Ont. Can.
85 I1 Shelburne Bay Qld Austr.
233 M6 Shelburne Falls MA U.S.A.
226 H6 Shelby MI U.S.A.
237 J9 Shelby MS U.S.A.
238 I2 Shelby MT U.S.A.
231 G8 Shelby NC U.S.A.
232 C8 Shelby OH U.S.A.
236 K6 Shelbyville IL U.S.A.
230 E6 Shelbyville IN U.S.A.
236 I6 Shelbyville MO U.S.A.
231 D8 Shelbyville TN U.S.A.
236 K6 Shelbyville, Lake IL U.S.A.
215 J9 Sheldon S. Africa
236 H4 Sheldon IA U.S.A.
226 G9 Sheldon IL U.S.A.
226 D4 Sheldon WI U.S.A.
238 E6 Sheldon National Wildlife Refuge nature res. NV U.S.A.
233 M4 Sheldon Springs VT U.S.A.
225 H3 Sheldrake Que. Can.
Shelek Kazakh. see Chilik
136 J6 Shelekhove Ukr.
131 Q3 Shelikhova, Zaliv g. Rus. Fed.
220 C4 Shelikof Strait AK U.S.A.
129 H2 Shelkovskaya Rus. Fed.
238 K4 Shell WY U.S.A.
146 C6 Shell, Loch inlet Scotland U.K.
223 J4 Shellbrook Sask. Can.
238 H5 Shelley ID U.S.A.
83 M6 Shellharbour N.S.W. Austr.
223 J4 Shell Lake Sask. Can.
226 C4 Shell Lake WI U.S.A.
87 I10 Shell Lakes salt flat W.A. Austr.
240 I1 Shell Mountain CA U.S.A.
138 N3 Shelon' r. Rus. Fed.
Shelter Bay Que. Can. see Port-Cartier
235 K2 Shelter Island NY U.S.A.
235 K2 Shelter Island i. NY U.S.A.
235 K2 Shelter Island Heights NY U.S.A.
235 K2 Shelter Island Sound str. NY U.S.A.
81 C14 Shelter Point Stewart I. N.Z.
235 I2 Shelton CT U.S.A.
238 C3 Shelton WA U.S.A.
134 F3 Sheltozero Rus. Fed.
Shelyakino Rus. Fed. see Sovetskoye
122 D3 Shem Iran
Shemakha Azer. see Şamaxı
207 H4 Shemankar r. Nigeria
139 R1 Shemenichi Rus. Fed.
117 M6 Shemgang Bhutan
129 D4 Shemok'medi Georgia
121 S2 Shemonaikha Kazakh.
134 J4 Shemordan Rus. Fed.
135 I5 Shemursha Rus. Fed.
135 I5 Shemysheyka Rus. Fed.
236 H5 Shenandoah IA U.S.A.
227 R9 Shenandoah PA U.S.A.
232 G10 Shenandoah VA U.S.A.
232 H9 Shenandoah r. VA U.S.A.
232 F10 Shenandoah Mountains VA/WV U.S.A.
232 G10 Shenandoah National Park VA U.S.A.
109 K7 Shen'ao Guangdong China
120 I3 Shenbertal Kazakh.
107 M7 Shenchi Shanxi China
207 H4 Shendam Nigeria
203 G5 Shendi Sudan
100 H5 Shending Shan hill Heilong. China
206 B5 Shenge Sierra Leone
121 Q5 Shengel'dy Almatinskaya Oblast' Kazakh.
120 I5 Shengel'dy Kyzylordinskaya Oblast' Kazakh.
Shenggeldy Kazakh. see Shengel'dy
196 H9 Shëngjin Albania
109 J3 Shengli Hubei China
110 H5 Shengli Daban pass Xinjiang China
Shengli Feng mt. China/Kyrg. see Jengish Chokusu
110 D6 Shengli Qichang Xinjiang China
110 E6 Shengli Shibachang Xinjiang China
Shengrenjian Shanxi China see Pinglu
109 N3 Shengsi Zhejiang China
109 N3 Shengsi Liedao is China
Shengxian Zhejiang China see Shengzhou
109 M4 Shengzhou Zhejiang China
101 C14 Shenjiamen Zhejiang China
196 H9 Shënkoll Albania
134 H3 Shenkursk Rus. Fed.
107 L7 Shenmu Shaanxi China
108 H3 Shennongjia Hubei China
109 J2 Shenqiu Henan China
100 F5 Shenshu Heilong. China
Shensi prov. China see Shaanxi
151 I2 Shenstone Staffordshire, England U.K.
135 J5 Shentala Rus. Fed.
87 G10 Shenton, Mount hill W.A. Austr.
Shenxian Hebei China see Shenzhou
107 N8 Shenxian Shandong China
107 R6 Shenyang Liaoning China
109 J7 Shenzhen Guangdong China
109 □I7 Shenzhen Wan b. H.K. China
107 N8 Shenzhou Hebei China
116 D7 Sheoganj Rajasthan India
116 F7 Sheopur Madh. Prad. India
262 P2 Shepard Island Antarctica
136 G3 Shepetivka Ukr.
Shepetovka Ukr. see Shepetivka
232 A5 Shepherd MI U.S.A.
78 □5 Shepherd Islands Vanuatu
83 J7 Shepparton Vic. Austr.
151 L5 Shepperton Surrey, England U.K.
151 N5 Sheppey, Isle of i. England U.K.
234 C3 Sheppton PA U.S.A.
151 J2 Shepshed Leicestershire, England U.K.
137 M1 Sheptaky Ukr.
150 G5 Shepton Mallet Somerset, England U.K.
137 O2 Sheptukhovka Rus. Fed.
109 I2 Sheqi Henan China
208 E2 Sherab Sudan
Sherabad Uzbek. see Sherobod
221 J2 Sherard, Cape Nunavut Can.
123 I5 Sher Bakhsh Afgh.
215 I7 Sherborne S. Africa
150 G6 Sherborne Dorset, England U.K.
151 J5 Sherborne St John Hampshire, England U.K.
206 B5 Sherbro Island Sierra Leone
225 I4 Sherbrooke N.S. Can.
225 G4 Sherbrooke Que. Can.
149 N4 Sherburn Durham, England U.K.
233 J6 Sherburne NY U.S.A.
149 O6 Sherburn in Elmet North Yorkshire, England U.K.
147 I5 Shercock Ireland
202 C4 Sherda well Chad
151 L5 Shere Surrey, England U.K.
203 G5 Shereiq Sudan
116 D6 Shergarh Rajasthan India
117 J7 Sherghati Bihar India
237 I8 Sheridan AR U.S.A.
238 K4 Sheridan WY U.S.A.
221 L1 Sheridan, Cape Nunavut Can.
149 O5 Sheriff Hutton North Yorkshire, England U.K.
82 E5 Sheringa S.A. Austr.
151 O2 Sheringham Norfolk, England U.K.
130 H3 Sherkaly Rus. Fed.
123 L7 Sher Khan Qala Afgh.
147 D10 Sherkin Island Ireland
86 D6 Sherlock r. W.A. Austr.
107 O1 Sherlovaya Gora Rus. Fed.
232 F6 Sherman NY U.S.A.
237 G9 Sherman TX U.S.A.
233 □Q3 Sherman Mills ME U.S.A.
241 Q1 Sherman Mountain NV U.S.A.
121 L9 Sherobod Uzbek.
139 O7 Sherovichi Rus. Fed.
117 M7 Sherpur Dhaka Bangl.
117 L7 Sherpur Rajshahi Bangl.
116 E1 Sher Qila Jammu and Kashmir
223 K4 Sherridon Man. Can.
150 H4 Sherston Wiltshire, England U.K.
114 E8 Shertally Kerala India
164 H5 's-Hertogenbosch Neth.
232 A7 Sherwood OH U.S.A.
81 E10 Sherwood Downs South I. N.Z.
149 O7 Sherwood Forest reg. England U.K.
223 K2 Sherwood Lake N.W.T. Can.
100 F3 Sheryshevo Rus. Fed.
227 L4 Sheshegwaning Ont. Can.
122 G3 Sheshtamad Iran
222 D3 Sheslay B.C. Can.
222 C3 Sheslay r. B.C. Can.
134 J4 Shestakovo Kirovskaya Oblast' Rus. Fed.
137 T3 Shestakovo Voronezhskaya Oblast' Rus. Fed.
139 V4 Shestikhino Rus. Fed.
137 M6 Shestirnya Ukr.
236 H3 Shetek, Lake MN U.S.A.
223 L3 Shethanei Lake Man. Can.
146 □O2 Shetland admin. div. Scotland U.K.
144 G1 Shetland Islands Scotland U.K.
120 E5 Shetpe Kazakh.
235 K1 Shetucket r. CT U.S.A.
109 □J7 Sheung Shui H.K. China
109 □J7 Sheung Sze Mun sea chan. H.K. China
109 □J7 Sheung Yue Ho r. H.K. China
114 F7 Shevaroy Hills India
137 N5 Shevchenkivka Ukr.
Shevchenko Kazakh. see Aktau
120 I4 Shevchenko, Zaliv l. Kazakh.
137 K4 Shevchenkove Cherkas'ka Oblast' Ukr.
137 Q4 Shevchenkove Kharkivs'ka Oblast' Ukr.
137 M2 Shevchen Kove Ukr.
Shevchenkovo Ukr. see Dolyns'ka
114 D3 Shevgaon Mahar. India
100 H1 Shevli r. Rus. Fed.
210 B3 Shewa Gīmīra Eth.
109 L4 Shexian Anhui China
107 M8 Shexian Hebei China
131 M3 Sheya Rus. Fed.
109 M2 Sheyang Jiangsu China
134 H4 Sheybukhta Rus. Fed.
236 F2 Sheyenne ND U.S.A.
236 G2 Sheyenne r. ND U.S.A.
139 O5 Sheykino Rus. Fed.
127 O8 Sheykkī Iran
117 I5 Shey Phoksundo National Park Nepal
146 D7 Shiant, Sound of str. Scotland U.K.
146 D7 Shiant Islands Scotland U.K.
131 Q5 Shiashkotan, Ostrov i. Kuril'skiye O-va Rus. Fed.
227 K6 Shiawassee r. MI U.S.A.
105 I5 Shibakawa Japan
125 I8 Shibām Yemen
106 D6 Shibandong Jing well China
106 F6 Shiban Jing well China
106 E7 Shibaocheng Gansu China
123 M4 Shībar, Kowtal-e pass Afgh.
102 Q9 Shibata Japan
105 L4 Shibayama Japan
104 D3 Shibayama-gata l. Japan
100 D2 Shibazhan Heilong. China
102 T2 Shibetsu Hokkaidō Japan
102 W3 Shibetsu Hokkaidō Japan
203 F2 Shibīn al Kawm Egypt
108 G5 Shibing Guizhou China
224 B2 Shibogama Lake Ont. Can.
Shibotsu-jima i. Kuril'skiye O-va Rus. Fed. see Zelenyy, Ostrov
105 J3 Shibukawa Japan
103 I15 Shibushi Japan
103 I15 Shibushi-wan b. Japan
105 I2 Shibu-tōge pass Japan
105 J2 Shibutsu-san mt. Japan
Shicheng Fujian China see Zhouning
109 K5 Shicheng Jiangxi China
107 R7 Shicheng Dao i. China
105 H5 Shichimen-zan mt. Japan
102 S6 Shichinohe Japan
227 R8 Shickshinny PA U.S.A.
Shicun Shanxi China see Xiangfen
128 G7 Shidād al Mismā' hill Saudi Arabia
107 R8 Shidao Shandong China
107 R8 Shidao Wan b. China
121 P1 Shiderti r. Kazakh.
108 B6 Shidian Yunnan China
Shidian Yunnan China see Changning
103 L12 Shido Japan
Shidongsi Gansu China see Gaolan
123 N3 Shidud Afgh.
146 E9 Shiel, Loch l. Scotland U.K.
146 F8 Shiel Bridge Highland, Scotland U.K.
84 F2 Shield, Cape N.T. Austr.
146 E7 Shieldaig Highland, Scotland U.K.
149 J2 Shieldhill Falkirk, Scotland U.K.
Shīeli Kazakh. see Chiili
124 B1 Shifa, Jabal ash mts Saudi Arabia
108 E3 Shifang Sichuan China
150 H2 Shifnal Shropshire, England U.K.
105 G3 Shiga Nagano Japan
104 C5 Shiga Shiga Japan
104 C5 Shiga pref. Japan
116 E2 Shigar Jammu and Kashmir
104 D6 Shigaraki Japan
Shigatse Xizang China see Xigazê
114 D5 Shiggaon Karnataka India
110 L6 Shigong Gansu China
120 C1 Shigony Rus. Fed.
107 L6 Shiguai Nei Mongol China
Shiguaigou Nei Mongol China see Shiguai
125 K7 Shiḩan Yemen
125 K7 Shiḩan, Wādīal r. Oman
110 H4 Shihezi Xinjiang China
Shihkiachwang Hebei China see Shijiazhuang
210 E2 Shiikh Somalia
196 H9 Shijak Albania
Shijiao Guangdong China see Fogang
107 N7 Shijiazhuang Hebei China
109 L3 Shijiu Hu l. China
Shijiusuo Shandong China see Rizhao
104 E1 Shika Japan
102 R4 Shikabe Japan
224 B3 Shikag Lake Ont. Can.
108 G8 Shikang Guangxi China
123 J7 Shikar r. Pak.
114 D5 Shikarpur Karnataka India
123 M8 Shikarpur Pak.
109 I6 Shikengkong mt. Guangdong China
120 B1 Shikhany Rus. Fed.
105 K4 Shiki Japan
105 J7 Shikine-jima i. Japan
105 I4 Shikishima Japan
116 G6 Shikohabad Uttar Prad. India
103 K13 Shikoku i. Japan
103 J13 Shikoku-sanchi mts Japan
99 Q3 Shikotan, Ostrov i. Kuril'skiye O-va Rus. Fed.
Shikotan-tō i. Kuril'skiye O-va Rus. Fed. see Shikotan, Ostrov
102 S4 Shikotsu vol. Japan
102 R4 Shikotsu-Tōya Kokuritsu-kōen nat. park Japan
149 N3 Shilbottle Northumberland, England U.K.
120 H2 Shil'da Rus. Fed.
149 N4 Shildon Durham, England U.K.
134 I2 Shilega Rus. Fed.
107 P9 Shilianghe Shuiku resr China
117 L6 Shiliguri W. Bengal India
108 D6 Shilin Yunnan China
109 I3 Shilipu Hubei China
Shiliu Hainan China see Changjiang
116 G3 Shilla mt. Jammu and Kashmir
146 B7 Shillay i. Scotland U.K.
147 I7 Shillelagh Ireland
227 N1 Shillington Ont. Can.
234 D4 Shillington PA U.S.A.
128 C6 Shillo r. Israel
117 M7 Shillong Meghalaya India
120 C2 Shil'naya Balka Kazakh.
234 E6 Shiloh NJ U.S.A.
232 C8 Shiloh OH U.S.A.
107 L8 Shilou Shanxi China
135 H5 Shilovo Ryazanskaya Oblast' Rus. Fed.
139 V8 Shilovo Tul'skaya Oblast' Rus. Fed.
Shilüüstey Mongolia see Balgatay
104 E7 Shima Japan
105 I2 Shima spring Japan
103 H14 Shimabara Japan
103 H14 Shimabara-wan b. Japan
105 H6 Shimada Japan
104 D6 Shimagahara Japan
104 D7 Shima-hantō pen. Japan
102 R4 Shimamaki Japan
104 C6 Shimamoto Japan
103 J12 Shimane pref. Japan
103 J11 Shimane-hantō pen. Japan
100 E2 Shimanovsk Rus. Fed.
210 E2 Shimbiris mt. Somalia
210 D4 Shimbirre waterhole Kenya
109 H4 Shimen Hunan China
Shimen Yunnan China see Yunlong
108 D4 Shimian Sichuan China
104 D3 Shimizu Fukui Japan
102 T3 Shimizu Hokkaidō Japan
105 H5 Shimizu Shizuoka Japan
105 I5 Shimizu Shizuoka Japan
104 B7 Shimizu Wakayama Japan
116 F4 Shimla Hima. Prad. India
Shimminato Japan see Shinminato
104 F2 Shimo Japan
105 H5 Shimobe Japan
105 I6 Shimoda Japan
105 K3 Shimodate Japan
105 L4 Shimofusa Japan
114 D6 Shimoga Karnataka India
105 K1 Shimogō Japan
104 C7 Shimoichi Japan
105 G5 Shimojō Japan
102 T2 Shimokawa Japan
102 R5 Shimokita-hantō pen. Japan
104 C7 Shimokitayama Japan
103 G15 Shimo-Koshiki-jima i. Japan
211 C6 Shimoni Kenya
105 I3 Shimonita Japan
103 H13 Shimonoseki Japan
105 H3 Shimosuwa Japan
104 B7 Shimotsu Japan
105 K3 Shimotsuma Japan
104 F5 Shimoyama Japan
114 E6 Shimsha r. India
116 E1 Shimshal Jammu and Kashmir
139 N3 Shimsk Rus. Fed.
105 J3 Shin Japan
146 G6 Shin, Loch l. Scotland U.K.
Shināfīyah Iraq see Ash Shanāfīyah
Shinan Guangxi China see Xingye
105 H2 Shinano Japan
104 D5 Shin-asahi Japan
102 □H16 Shin-dake vol. Japan
123 J5 Shīndand Afgh.
151 K5 Shinfield Wokingham, England U.K.
209 F8 Shingana Dem. Rep. Congo
96 C1 Shingbwiyang Myanmar
96 C1 Shing-gai Myanmar
123 P3 Shinghshal Pass Pak.
232 G7 Shinglehouse PA U.S.A.
226 H3 Shingleton MI U.S.A.
Shing Mun Reservoir H.K. China see Ngan Hei Shui Tong
121 S4 Shingozha Kazakh.
103 N13 Shingū Japan
213 F4 Shingwedzi S. Africa
149 M7 Shining Tor hill England U.K.
227 M2 Shining Tree Ont. Can.
102 R8 Shinjō Japan
123 L6 Shīnkāy Afgh.
123 M5 Shīnkay Ghar mts Afgh.
104 F2 Shinminato Japan
103 I12 Shinnan-yō Japan
123 L6 Shin Narai Thana Afgh.
235 K3 Shinnecock Bay NY U.S.A.
146 H6 Shinness Lodge Highland, Scotland U.K.
232 E9 Shinnston WV U.S.A.
104 E6 Shino-jima i. Japan
105 H2 Shinonoi Japan
123 N4 Shinpokh Pak.
147 G7 Shinrone Ireland
104 E5 Shinsei Japan
128 E4 Shinshār Syria
104 F6 Shinshiro Japan
105 H2 Shinshūshin Japan
105 I3 Shintō Japan
102 T3 Shintoku Japan
105 L4 Shintone Japan
129 H6 Shinuhayr Armenia
211 B5 Shinyanga Tanz.
211 B5 Shinyanga admin. reg. Tanz.
104 E2 Shio Japan
105 K2 Shiobara Japan
102 S8 Shiogama Japan
105 G3 Shiojiri Japan
102 □B22 Shiokawa Nansei-shotō Japan
105 H4 Shiomi-dake mt. Japan
103 M13 Shiono-misaki c. Japan
105 K2 Shioya Japan
105 M1 Shioya-zaki pt Japan
105 I1 Shiozawa Japan
109 K3 Shipai Anhui China
233 K9 Ship Bottom NJ U.S.A.
246 E1 Ship Chan Cay i. Bahamas
197 N8 Shipchenski Prokhod pass Bulg.
139 V4 Shipilovo Rus. Fed.
108 D7 Shiping Yunnan China
111 D11 Shipki Pass China/India
151 K5 Shiplake Oxfordshire, England U.K.
149 N6 Shipley West Yorkshire, England U.K.
232 G11 Shipman VA U.S.A.
225 H4 Shippegan N.B. Can.
225 H4 Shippegan Island N.B. Can.
232 H8 Shippensburg PA U.S.A.
232 F7 Shippenville PA U.S.A.
104 E5 Shippō Japan
241 X5 Shiprock NM U.S.A.
241 X5 Shiprock Peak NM U.S.A.
151 I3 Shipston on Stour Warwickshire, England U.K.
149 O5 Shipton North Yorkshire, England U.K.
150 G2 Shipton Shropshire, England U.K.
151 I4 Shipton-under-Wychwood Oxfordshire, England U.K.
Shipu Shaanxi China see Huanglong
109 M4 Shipu Zhejiang China
131 R4 Shipunskiy, Mys hd Rus. Fed.
108 G5 Shiqian Guizhou China
Shiqiao Guangdong China see Panyu
Shiqizhen Guangdong China see Zhongshan
124 H7 Shiqqat al Kharītah des. Saudi Arabia
108 G2 Shiquan Shaanxi China
116 G3 Shiquan He r. China conv. Indus
Shiquanhe Xizang China see Ali
108 G2 Shiquan Shuiku resr China
124 F3 Shi'r, Jabal hill Saudi Arabia
146 F10 Shira r. Scotland U.K.
125 K3 Shirā'awh i. Qatar
122 C2 Shīrābād Iran
105 K6 Shirahama Chiba Japan
103 M13 Shirahama Wakayama Japan
104 D6 Shirai-san hill Japan
102 R5 Shirakami-misaki pt Japan
105 L1 Shirakawa Fukushima Japan
104 E3 Shirakawa Gifu Japan
104 F4 Shirakawa Gifu Japan
104 F3 Shirake-mine mt. Japan
105 L5 Shirako Japan
104 G5 Shirakura-yama mt. Japan
104 B7 Shirama-yama hill Japan
104 E3 Shiramine Japan
105 H4 Shirane Japan
105 H4 Shirane-san mt. Japan
105 I2 Shirane-san mt. Japan
105 J2 Shirane-san vol. Japan
102 V4 Shiranuka Japan
102 S4 Shiraoi Japan
105 J2 Shirasawa Japan
262 O1 Shirase Coast Antarctica
263 C2 Shirase Glacier Antarctica
102 U3 Shirataki Japan
211 B5 Shirati Tanz.
122 E7 Shīrāz Iran
126 E8 Shirbīn Egypt
211 B8 Shire r. Malawi
149 O7 Shirebrook Derbyshire, England U.K.
107 M4 Shireet Mongolia
122 B3 Shīreh Jīn Iran
150 G4 Shirenewton Monmouthshire, Wales U.K.
102 V3 Shiretoko-hantō pen. Japan
102 W2 Shiretoko Kokuritsu-kōen nat. park Japan
102 W2 Shiretoko-misaki c. Japan
123 K8 Shireza Pak.
121 M7 Shirin Uzbek.
123 L6 Shirinab r. Pak.
123 K3 Shīrīn Tagāb Afgh.
102 R5 Shiriuchi Japan
102 S5 Shiriya-zaki c. Japan
120 G4 Shirkala reg. Kazakh.
122 F6 Shīr Kūh mt. Iran
149 O7 Shirland Derbyshire, England U.K.
235 J3 Shirley NY U.S.A.
185 □ Shirley Cove b. Gibraltar
105 L4 Shiroi Japan
102 R9 Shiroishi Japan
105 G5 Shirokura-yama mt. Japan
102 Q9 Shirone Japan
207 G4 Shiroro Reservoir Nigeria
104 E4 Shirotori Japan
104 G2 Shirouma-dake mt. Japan
105 J4 Shiroyama Japan
116 E9 Shirpur Mahar. India
106 E5 Shirten Holoy Gobi des. China
122 G3 Shīrvān Iran
106 B5 Shisanjianfang Xinjiang China
100 D3 Shisanzhan Heilong. China
215 P3 Shiselweni admin. dist. Swaziland
220 B4 Shishaldin Volcano AK U.S.A.
Shisha Pangma mt. Xizang China see Xixabangma Feng
103 L13 Shishikui Japan
Shishkaya Armenia see Geghamasar
109 I4 Shishou Hubei China
105 L4 Shisui Japan
109 K3 Shitai Anhui China
109 I6 Shitan Guangdong China
109 M4 Shitang Zhejiang China
106 J7 Shitanjing Ningxia China
104 G5 Shitara Japan
203 I1 Shithāthah Iraq
100 D7 Shitoukoumen Shuiku resr Jilin China
116 C6 Shiv Rajasthan India
131 R4 Shiveluch, Sopka vol. Rus. Fed.
116 F7 Shivpuri Madh. Prad. India
128 C8 Shivta tourist site Israel
241 S4 Shivwits UT U.S.A.
241 S5 Shivwits Plateau AZ U.S.A.
123 N3 Shiwal l. Afgh.
107 K8 Shiwan Shaanxi China
108 F8 Shiwan Dashan mts China
96 H3 Shiwan Dashan mts China
211 A7 Shiwa Ngandu Zambia
109 J6 Shixing Guangdong China
108 H2 Shiyan Hubei China
108 G4 Shizhu Chongqing China
107 J9 Shizi Gansu China
Shizilu Shandong China see Junan
109 L3 Shizipu Anhui China
108 D6 Shizong Yunnan China
102 S8 Shizugawa Japan
106 J7 Shizuishan Ningxia China
106 J7 Shizuishanzhan Ningxia China
102 R7 Shizukuishi Japan
102 T4 Shizunai Japan
105 H6 Shizuoka Japan
105 H6 Shizuoka pref. Japan
196 I8 Shkëlzenit, Maja e mt. Albania
129 E3 Shkhara mt. Georgia/Rus. Fed.
136 C4 Shklo Ukr.
Shklov Belarus see Shklow
139 N7 Shklow Belarus
136 E3 Shklyn' Ukr.
129 E3 Shk'meri Georgia
196 H8 Shkodër Albania
Shkodrës, Liqeni i l. Albania/Montenegro see Scutari, Lake
196 H9 Shkumbin r. Albania
137 S7 Shkurinskaya Rus. Fed.
136 E2 Shlapan' Ukr.
139 R4 Shlina r. Rus. Fed.
139 Q4 Shlino, Ozero l. Rus. Fed.
139 O2 Shlissel'burg Rus. Fed.
131 K1 Shmidta, Ostrov i. Rus. Fed.
100 M1 Shmidta, Poluostrov pen. Sakhalin Rus. Fed.
138 L4 Shmoylovo Rus. Fed.
138 L6 Sho, Vozyera l. Belarus
83 L6 Shoalhaven r. N.S.W. Austr.
223 K5 Shoal Lake Man. Can.
223 K4 Shoal Lake Sask. Can.
230 D6 Shoals IN U.S.A.
85 M7 Shoalwater Bay Qld Austr.
103 K12 Shōbara Japan
103 L12 Shōdo-shima i. Japan
151 N4 Shoeburyness Southend, England U.K.
234 D3 Shoemakersville PA U.S.A.
120 K7 Shofirkon Uzbek.
104 F2 Shōgawa Japan
104 F2 Shō-gawa r. Japan
122 H3 Shoghlābād Iran
123 M3 Shoh Khatlon Tajik.
Shohi Pass Pak. see Tal Pass
234 F2 Shohola PA U.S.A.
102 S3 Shokanbetsu-dake mt. Japan
104 E3 Shōkawa Japan
102 U2 Shokotsu-gawa r. Japan
Shokpar Kazakh. see Chokpar
139 U1 Shola r. Rus. Fed.
121 M6 Sholakkorgan Kazakh.
120 K2 Sholaksay Kazakh.
Sholapur Mahar. India see Solapur
Sholaqorghan Kazakh. see Sholakkorgan
Sholaqsay Kazakh. see Sholaksay
86 C6 Sholl Island W.A. Austr.
134 F2 Shomba r. Rus. Fed.
120 H4 Shomishkol' Kazakh.
134 J3 Shomvukva Rus. Fed.
104 F2 Shōmyō-gawa r. Japan
146 E9 Shona, Eilean i. Scotland U.K.
264 J9 Shona Ridge sea feature S. Atlantic Ocean
117 M6 Shongar Bhutan
Shonzha Kazakh. see Chundzha
139 W4 Shopsha Rus. Fed.
148 E4 Shoptown Northern Ireland U.K.
120 G4 Shoptykol' Aktyubinskaya Oblast' Kazakh.
121 P2 Shoptykol' Pavlodarskaya Oblast' Kazakh.
Shoqpar Kazakh. see Chokpar
116 F3 Shor Hima. Prad. India
123 L7 Shoran Pak.
114 E7 Shoranur Kerala India
123 K9 Shorap Pak.
114 E4 Shorapur Karnataka India
123 K6 Shorawak reg. Afgh.
121 L9 Sho'rchi Uzbek.
235 G4 Shore Acres NJ U.S.A.
151 M5 Shoreham Kent, England U.K.
151 L6 Shoreham-by-Sea West Sussex, England U.K.
Shorghun Uzbek. see Sharg'un
123 O6 Shorkot Pak.
122 G1 Shorkozakhly, Solonchak salt flat Turkm.
123 P2 Shorkŭl l. Tajik.
Shornaq Kazakh. see Chernak
212 D3 Shorobe Botswana
121 N2 Shortandy Kazakh.
123 L3 Shor Tepe Afgh.
78 □6 Shortland Island Solomon Is
78 □6 Shortland Islands Solomon Is
232 H6 Shortsville NY U.S.A.
Shosambetsu Japan see Shosanbetsu
102 S2 Shosanbetsu Japan
139 T5 Shosha r. Rus. Fed.
241 P6 Shoshone CA U.S.A.
238 G5 Shoshone ID U.S.A.
238 J4 Shoshone r. WY U.S.A.
238 I4 Shoshone Lake WY U.S.A.
240 O2 Shoshone Mountains NV U.S.A.
241 P5 Shoshone Peak NV U.S.A.
212 E4 Shoshong Botswana
238 J5 Shoshoni WY U.S.A.
137 M2 Shostka Ukr.
137 M2 Shostka r. Ukr.
151 O4 Shotley Gate Suffolk, England U.K.
122 F5 Shotoran, Chashmeh-ye well Iran
123 K4 Shotor Khūn pass Afgh.
150 F1 Shotton Flintshire, Wales U.K.
146 I11 Shotts North Lanarkshire, Scotland U.K.
Shouchun Anhui China see Shouxian
107 P8 Shouguang Shandong China
109 K2 Shouxian Anhui China
107 M8 Shouyang Shanxi China
108 G2 Shouyang Shan mt. Shaanxi China
105 J2 Shōwa Japan
203 G6 Showak Sudan
241 V7 Show Low AZ U.S.A.
129 F6 Showt Iran
134 I2 Shoyna Rus. Fed.
135 H7 Shpakovskoye Rus. Fed.
137 K4 Shpola Ukr.
136 H5 Shpykiv Ukr.
136 I3 Shpyli Ukr.
Shqipërisë, Republika e country Europe see Albania
137 L3 Shramkivka Ukr.
232 C8 Shreve OH U.S.A.
237 I9 Shreveport LA U.S.A.
150 G2 Shrewsbury Shropshire, England U.K.
235 G4 Shrewsbury NJ U.S.A.
234 B5 Shrewsbury PA U.S.A.
151 I5 Shrewton Wiltshire, England U.K.
148 F5 Shrigley Northern Ireland U.K.
114 D3 Shrigonda Mahar. India
Shri Lanka country Asia see Sri Lanka
116 C6 Shri Mohangarh Rajasthan India
117 L8 Shrirampur W. Bengal India
114 E6 Shrirangapattana Karnataka India
151 I4 Shrivenham Oxfordshire, England U.K.
150 G2 Shropshire admin. div. England U.K.
235 H2 Shrub Oak NY U.S.A.
Shtefan-Vode Moldova see Ştefan Vodă
196 I10 Shtërmen Albania
196 I8 Shtiqën Albania
137 M8 Shtormove Ukr.
121 O6 Shu Kazakh.
125 K9 Shu'ab, Ghubbat b. Suquţrā Yemen
125 K9 Shu'ab, Ra's pt Suquţrā Yemen
127 M8 Shu'aiba Iraq
108 D2 Shuajingsi Sichuan China
129 D4 Shuakhevi Georgia
108 C6 Shuangbai Yunnan China
Shuangcheng Fujian China see Zherong
100 E6 Shuangcheng Heilong. China
109 I3 Shuanghe Hubei China
108 F3 Shuanghechang Sichuan China
100 G4 Shuanghedagang Heilong. China
111 H10 Shuanghu Xizang China
Shuanghuyu Shaanxi China see Zizhou
Shuangjiang Guizhou China see Jiangkou
Shuangjiang Hunan China see Tongdao
108 B7 Shuangjiang Yunnan China
Shuangjiang Yunnan China see Eshan
107 R5 Shuangliao Jilin China
109 H6 Shuangpai Hunan China
107 P6 Shuangshanzi Hebei China
Shuangshipu Shaanxi China see Fengxian
100 D7 Shuangyang Jilin China
100 G5 Shuangyashan Heilong. China
Shuangzhong Jiangxi China see Hukou
125 J7 Shu'ayt, Wādī r. Yemen
120 G3 Shubarkuduk Kazakh.
120 G3 Shubarshi Kazakh.
128 G8 Shubayḩ well Saudi Arabia
124 F3 Shubayrimah Saudi Arabia
118 C3 Shubrā al Khaymah Egypt
124 G3 Shubrāmīyāh Saudi Arabia
124 F4 Shubrāmīyāh well Saudi Arabia
109 K3 Shucheng Anhui China
250 C6 Shucushuyacu Peru
110 B7 Shufu Xinjiang China
96 A2 Shuganu Manipur India
123 N3 Shughnon, Qatorkŭhi mts Tajik.
Shugnanskiy Khrebet mts Tajik. see Shughnon, Qatorkŭhi
139 R2 Shugozero Rus. Fed.
130 H3 Shugur Rus. Fed.
107 P9 Shu He r. China
Shuicheng Guizhou China see Lupanshui
Shuiding Xinjiang China see Huocheng
Shuidong Guangdong China see Dianbai
Shuihu Anhui China see Changfeng
109 L5 Shuiji Fujian China
Shuiji Shandong China see Laixi
108 E2 Shuijing Sichuan China
111 J10 Shuijingkuang Qinghai China
109 J7 Shuikou Guangdong China
109 H6 Shuikou Hunan China
108 F7 Shuikouguan Guangxi China
109 I5 Shuikoushan Hunan China
Shuiluocheng Gansu China see Zhuanglang
106 I8 Shuiquan Gansu China
106 G7 Shuiquanzi Gansu China
108 C5 Shuituo He r. Sichuan China
Shuizhai Guangdong China see Wuhua
111 J8 Shuizhan Qinghai China
123 N7 Shujaabad Pak.
100 E6 Shulan Jilin China
110 C7 Shule Xinjiang China
110 M6 Shulehe Gansu China
106 C6 Shule He r. China
106 E7 Shule Nanshan mts China
137 T1 Shul'gino Rus. Fed.
137 R4 Shul'hynka Ukr.
107 L6 Shulinzhao Nei Mongol China
Shul'mak Tajik. see Novobod
Shulu Hebei China see Xinji
139 O2 Shum Rus. Fed.
220 B4 Shumagin Islands AK U.S.A.
137 P2 Shumakovo Rus. Fed.
120 H6 Shumanay Uzbek.
102 T2 Shumarinai-ko l. Japan
212 E3 Shumba Zimbabwe
197 O7 Shumen Bulg.
197 O7 Shumensko Plato nat. park Bulg.
134 I5 Shumerlya Rus. Fed.
130 H4 Shumikha Rus. Fed.
138 M6 Shumilina Belarus
131 Q4 Shumshu, Ostrov i. Kuril'skiye O-va Rus. Fed.
136 F3 Shums'k Ukr.
139 P8 Shumyachi Rus. Fed.
121 O4 Shunak, Gora mt. Kazakh.
128 D7 Shūnat Nimrīn Jordan
109 I7 Shunde Guangdong China
139 X4 Shunga Rus. Fed.
220 C3 Shungnak AK U.S.A.
234 B1 Shunk PA U.S.A.
Shunling Hunan China see Ningyuan
129 I3 Shunudag, Gora mt. Rus. Fed.
107 O6 Shunyi Beijing China
108 F7 Shuolong Guangxi China
Shuoxian Shanxi China see Shuozhou
107 M7 Shuozhou Shanxi China
124 G7 Shuqqat Najrān depr. Saudi Arabia
124 G9 Shuqrah Yemen
122 E7 Shūr r. Iran
122 F7 Shūr r. Iran
122 I4 Shūr r. Iran
122 I6 Shūr r. Iran
122 E7 Shūr watercourse Iran
122 F6 Shūr watercourse Iran
122 F8 Shūr watercourse Iran
122 H5 Shur watercourse Iran
122 E4 Shūr, Chāh-e well Iran
122 G6 Shūr, Rūd-e watercourse Iran
122 D5 Shūrāb Chahār Maḩāll va Bakhtīārī Iran
122 D4 Shūr Āb Iran
122 G5 Shūrāb Khorāsān Iran
122 F5 Shūrāb Yazd Iran
122 F6 Shūr Āb watercourse Iran
Shurab Tajik. see Shŭrob
122 E5 Shureghestan Iran
129 I6 Shurestān Iran
122 H7 Shūr Gaz Iran
129 I6 Shūr Gol Iran
102 □1 Shuri Okinawa Japan
122 E6 Shūrjestān Iran
134 J4 Shurma Rus. Fed.
123 N1 Shŭrob Tajik.
122 I7 Shūrū Iran
213 F3 Shurugwi Zimbabwe
127 L8 Shuruppak tourist site Iraq
122 I6 Shusf Iran
122 C5 Shūsh Iran
Shusha Azer. see Şuşa
198 A2 Shushicë r. Albania
122 C5 Shushtar Iran
139 S6 Shustikovo Rus. Fed.
137 O2 Shustovo Rus. Fed.
222 G5 Shuswap Lake B.C. Can.
125 K4 Shutfah, Qalamat well Saudi Arabia
128 F7 Shuwaysh, Tall ash hill Jordan
139 Y5 Shuya Ivanovskaya Oblast' Rus. Fed.
134 F3 Shuya Respublika Kareliya Rus. Fed.
220 C4 Shuyak Island AK U.S.A.
107 P9 Shuyang Jiangsu China
134 H4 Shuyskoye Rus. Fed.
105 I6 Shuzenji Japan
139 U7 Shvartsevskiy Rus. Fed.
96 B5 Shwebandaw Myanmar
96 B3 Shwebo Myanmar
96 B5 Shwedaung Myanmar
96 B2 Shwedwin Myanmar
96 C6 Shwegun Myanmar
96 C6 Shwegyin Myanmar
96 B6 Shwelaung r. Myanmar
96 C3 Shweli r. Myanmar
96 C4 Shwenyaung Myanmar
96 C3 Shweudaung mt. Myanmar
136 F4 Shybena Ukr.
121 N5 Shyganak Kazakh.
Shyghanaq Kazakh. see Chiganak
Shyghys Qazaqstan Oblysy admin. div. Kazakh. see Vostochnyy Kazakhstan
Shyghys-Qongyrat Kazakh. see Shygys Konyrat
121 P4 Shygys Konyrat Kazakh.
121 M6 Shymkent Kazakh.
Shynggyrlaū Kazakh. see Chingirlau
Shyngqozha Kazakh. see Shingozha
116 E2 Shyok r. India
116 G2 Shyok Jammu and Kashmir
137 Q4 Shypuvate Ukr.
137 M6 Shyroke Dnipropetrovs'ka Oblast' Ukr.
137 N8 Shyroke Respublika Krym Ukr.

Sitamau *Madh. Prad.* India
Sitampiky Madag.
Sitangkai Phil.
Sitaniec Pol.
Sitapur *Uttar Prad.* India
Šitbořice Czech Rep.
Siteia *Kriti* Greece
Siteki Swaziland
Sitges Spain
Sithonias, Chersonisos *pen.* Greece
Sitía *Kriti* Greece *see* **Siteia**
Sitian *Xinjiang* China
Sitila Moz.
Siting *Guizhou* China
Sítio da Abadia Brazil
Sítio do Mato Brazil
Sitjar, Embalse de *resr* Spain
Sitka *AK* U.S.A.
Sitkówka-Nowiny Pol.
Sitlaha *Madh. Prad.* India
Sitnica *r.* Serbia
Sitno *mt.* Slovakia
Sitnya *r.* Rus. Fed.
Sitrah *oasis* Egypt
Sitsyenyets Belarus
Sittang *r.* Myanmar *see* Sittaung
Sittard Neth.
Sittaung Myanmar
Sittaung *r.* Myanmar
Sittensen Ger.
Sitter *r.* Ger.
Sittersdorf Austria
Sittingbourne S. Africa
Sittingbourne *Kent, England* U.K.
Sittoung *r.* Myanmar *see* Sittaung
Sittwe Myanmar
Situbondo *Jawa* Indon.
Sitzendorf Ger.
Sitzendorf an der Schmida Austria
Sitzenroda Ger.
Siu A Chau *i. H.K.* China
Siumpu *i.* Indon.
Si'umu Samoa
Siuna Nic.
Siuntio Fin.
Siurgus Donigala *Sardegna* Italy
Siuri *W. Bengal* India
Siva Rus. Fed.
Sivac *Vojvodina* Serbia
Sivaganga *Tamil Nadu* India
Sivakasi *Tamil Nadu* India
Sivaki Rus. Fed.
Sivand Iran
Sivas Turkey
Sivaslı Turkey
Sivé Maur.
Siverek Turkey
Sīvers *l.* Latvia
Sivers'k Ukr.
Siverskiy Rus. Fed.
Sivers'kyy Donets' *r.* Rus. Fed. *see* **Severskiy Donets**
Sivers'kyy Donets' *r.* Ukr.
Sivka-Voynylivs'ka Ukr.
Sivomaskinskiy Rus. Fed.
Sivrice Turkey
Sivrihisar Turkey
Sivry Belgium
Sivry-sur-Meuse France
Sivukile S. Africa
Siwa *Sulawesi* Indon.
Sīwah Egypt
Sīwah, Wāḥāt *oasis* Egypt
Siwalik Range *mts* India/Nepal
Siwan *Bihar* India
Siwana *Rajasthan* India
Siwa Oasis Egypt *see* Sīwah, Wāḥāt
Şıxarx Azer.
Six Cross Roads Barbados
Six-Fours-les-Plages France
Sixian *Anhui* China
Six Lakes *MI* U.S.A.
Sixmilebridge Ireland
Sixmilecross *Northern Ireland* U.K.
Sixt, Réserve Naturelle de *nature res.* France
Sixt-Fer-à-Cheval France
Siyabuswa S. Africa
Siyah Rud Iran
Siyang *Guangxi* China *see* Shangsi
Siyang *Jiangsu* China
Siyathemba S. Africa
Siyathuthuka S. Africa
Siyäzän Azer.
Siyitang *Nei Mongol* China
Sīyunī Iran
Sizandro *r.* Port.
Sizewell *Suffolk, England* U.K.
Siziwang Qi *Nei Mongol* China *see* **Ulan Hua**
Sizun France
Sizyabsk Rus. Fed.
Sjælland *i.* Denmark
Sjaunja naturreservat *nature res.* Sweden
Sjenica Serbia
Sjoa Norway
Sjöbo Sweden
Sjøholt Norway
Sjona *sea chan.* Norway
Sjoutnäset Sweden
Sjøvegan Norway
Sjulsmark Sweden
Sjuøyane *is* Svalbard
Skäckerfjällen *mts* Sweden
Skadarsko Jezero *nat. park* Montenegro
Skadovs'k Ukr.
Skælsør Denmark
Skærbæk Denmark
Skærfjorden *inlet* Greenland
Skaftafell *nat. park* Iceland
Skaftafell *nat. park* Iceland
Skaftárós *r. mouth* Iceland
Skagafjörður *inlet* Iceland
Skagaheiði *reg.* Iceland
Skagen Denmark
Skagen *nature res.* Denmark
Skagern *l.* Sweden
Skagerrak *str.* Denmark/Norway
Skagit *r. WA* U.S.A.
Skagit Mountain *B.C.* Can.
Skagway *AK* U.S.A.
Skaidi Norway
Skaidiškės Lith.
Skaill *Orkney, Scotland* U.K.
Skaill *Orkney, Scotland* U.K.
Skala *Notio Aigaio* Greece
Skala *Peloponnisos* Greece
Skała Pol.
Skala Kallonis *Lesvos* Greece
Skaland Norway
Skala-Podil's'ka Ukr.
Skälderviken *b.* Sweden
Skalice Czech Rep.
Skalistyy Khrebet *reg.* Rus. Fed.
Skalité Slovakia
Skallelv Norway
Skalmodal Sweden
Skalná Czech Rep.
Skals *r.* Denmark
Skalyste Ukr.
Skanderborg Denmark
Skåne *county* Sweden
Skåne *reg.* Sweden
Skaneateles *NY* U.S.A.
Skaneateles Lake *NY* U.S.A.
Skånevik Norway
Skånevikfjorden *sea chan.* Norway
Skansholm Sweden
Skantzoura *i.* Greece
Skąpe Pol.
Skara Sweden
Skara Brae *tourist site Scotland* U.K.
Skarberget Norway
Škarda *i.* Croatia

Skardarsko Jezero *l.* Albania/Montenegro *see* **Scutari, Lake**
85 I1 **Skardon** *r. Qld* Austr.
116 E2 **Skardu** Jammu and Kashmir
142 C2 **Skare** Norway
142 C3 **Skåreheia** *mt.* Norway
141 P7 **Skärgårdshavets nationalpark** *nat. park* Fin.
142 H4 **Skärhamn** Sweden
142 H1 **Skarnes** Norway
168 J1 **Skarø** *i.* Denmark
136 H2 **Skarodnaye** Belarus
143 N1 **Skärplinge** Sweden
141 L5 **Skärsjövålen** Sweden
141 J5 **Skarstind** *mt.* Norway
174 G1 **Skarszewy** Pol.
141 J5 **Skarvedalseggen** *mt.* Norway
140 N4 **Skarvsjöby** Sweden
175 J4 **Skaryszew** Pol.
136 F4 **Skarzhyntsi** Ukr.
175 I4 **Skarżysko-Kamienna** Pol.
142 I1 **Skasberget** *hill* Norway
142 I1 **Skasen** *l.* Norway
138 F6 **Skaudvilė** Lith.
140 P3 **Skaulo** Sweden
142 D1 **Skaupsjøen-Hardangerjøkulen** *park* Norway
142 E5 **Skave** Denmark
146 □O2 **Skaw** *Shetland, Scotland* U.K.
175 H5 **Skawa** *r.* Pol.
175 H6 **Skawina** Pol.
204 B4 **Skaymat** Western Sahara
143 O2 **Skebobruk** Sweden
143 L3 **Skeda udde** Sweden
143 O2 **Skedviken** *l.* Sweden
143 L2 **Skedvisjön** *l.* Sweden
222 D4 **Skeena** *r. B.C.* Can.
222 D3 **Skeena Mountains** *B.C.* Can.
149 R7 **Skegness** *Lincolnshire, England* U.K.
140 □E2 **Skeiðarársandur** *sand area* Iceland
146 □N2 **Skeld** *Shetland, Scotland* U.K.
146 □N2 **Skelda Ness** *hd Scotland* U.K.
168 I1 **Skelde** Denmark
212 B3 **Skeleton Coast Game Park** *nature res.* Namibia
140 P4 **Skellefteå** Sweden
140 P4 **Skellefteälven** *r.* Sweden
140 P4 **Skelleftebukten** *b.* Sweden
140 P4 **Skelleftehamn** Sweden
147 A9 **Skellig Rocks** *is* Ireland
149 L6 **Skelmersdale** *Lancashire, England* U.K.
146 G11 **Skelmorlie** *North Ayrshire, Scotland* U.K.
149 P4 **Skelton** *Redcar and Cleveland, England* U.K.
Skelton-in-Cleveland *England* U.K. *see* **Skelton**
150 G4 **Skenfrith** *Monmouthshire, Wales* U.K.
175 H3 **Skępe** Pol.
141 N5 **Skeppshamn** Sweden
214 G4 **Skerpioenpunt** S. Africa
146 H5 **Skerray** *Highland, Scotland* U.K.
147 J5 **Skerries** Ireland
150 E4 **Sketty** *Swansea, Wales* U.K.
136 B4 **Skhidni Beskydy** *mts* Pol./Ukr.
136 B4 **Skhidni Karpaty** *mts* Ukr.
175 L6 **Skhidnytsya** Ukr.
Skhimatárion Greece *see* Schimatari
205 H2 **Skhira** Tunisia
Skhíza *i.* Greece *see* **Schiza**
142 G2 **Ski** Norway
198 E3 **Skiathos** Greece
198 E3 **Skiathos** *i.* Greece
147 D9 **Skibbereen** Ireland
140 P2 **Skibotn** Norway
138 H8 **Skidal'** Belarus
149 K4 **Skiddaw** *hill England* U.K.
222 D4 **Skidegate Mission** *B.C.* Can.
Skidel' Belarus *see* **Skidal'**
234 C6 **Skidmore** *MD* U.S.A.
138 I6 **Skiemonys** Lith.
142 F2 **Skien** Norway
175 L5 **Skierbieszów** Pol.
175 I4 **Skierniewice** Pol.
141 P6 **Skiftet** *sea chan.* Fin.
205 G1 **Skikda** Alg.
138 K4 **Šķilbēni** Latvia
198 B5 **Skinari, Akrotirio** *pt Zakynthos* Greece
143 L2 **Skinnskatteberg** Sweden
116 F3 **Skio** Jammu and Kashmir
146 F11 **Skipness** *Argyll and Bute, Scotland* U.K.
234 E4 **Skippack** *PA* U.S.A.
149 Q6 **Skipsea** *East Riding of Yorkshire, England* U.K.
214 E10 **Skipskop** S. Africa
83 I7 **Skipton** *Vic.* Austr.
149 M6 **Skipton** *North Yorkshire, England* U.K.
234 C7 **Skipton** *MD* U.S.A.
149 Q6 **Skirlaugh** *East Riding of Yorkshire, England* U.K.
Skiropoúla *i.* Greece *see* Skyropoula
Skíros *i.* Greece *see* **Skyros**
142 F5 **Skive** Denmark
175 K3 **Skiwy Duże** Pol.
140 □E1 **Skjálfandafljót** *r.* Iceland
140 □E1 **Skjálfandi** *b.* Iceland
140 M3 **Skjelatinden** *mt.* Norway
140 L4 **Skjellbreid** Norway
142 G1 **Skjellinhovde** *hill* Norway
142 C1 **Skjemmene** *mt.* Norway
142 D3 **Skjerkeknuten** *hill* Norway
142 E6 **Skjern** Denmark
142 E6 **Skjern** *r.* Denmark
140 K4 **Skjern** Norway
140 M3 **Skjerstadejorden** *inlet* Norway
140 P1 **Skjervøy** Norway
141 I6 **Skjolden** Norway
168 J1 **Skjoldnæs** *pen.* Denmark
198 D3 **Sklithro** Greece
139 U4 **Sknyatino** Rus. Fed.
Skobelev Uzbek. *see* **Farg'ona**
121 O8 **Skobeleva, Pik** *mt.* Kyrg.
179 L8 **Škocjan** Slovenia
179 I8 **Škocjanske Jame** *tourist site* Slovenia
174 G6 **Skoczów** Pol.
215 J10 **Skoenmakerskop** S. Africa
188 E2 **Škofja Loka** Slovenia
179 K8 **Škofljica** Slovenia
141 N6 **Skog** Sweden
140 R2 **Skoganvarri** Norway
140 T2 **Skogfoss** Norway
143 L5 **Skoghult** Sweden
150 B4 **Skokholm Island** *Wales* U.K.
174 F3 **Skoki** Pol.
226 G7 **Skokie** *IL* U.S.A.
120 I3 **Skol'** Kazakh.
136 C4 **Skole** Ukr.
143 L2 **Sköllersta** Sweden
175 J6 **Skołyszyn** Pol.
150 B4 **Skomer Island** *Wales* U.K.
174 G4 **Skomlin** Pol.
140 K3 **Skomvær** *is* Norway
215 K3 **Skoonspruit** *r.* S. Africa
198 E3 **Skopelos** Greece
198 E3 **Skopelos** *i.* Greece
198 G4 **Skopelos** *i.* Greece
198 G3 **Skopia** *hill Limnos* Greece
139 W8 **Skopin** Rus. Fed.
196 J9 **Skopje** Macedonia
Skoplje Macedonia *see* Skopje
144 D1 **Skopunarfjørður** *sea chan.* Faroe Is
174 G2 **Skórcz** Pol.
135 G6 **Skorodnoye** Rus. Fed.
174 F5 **Skorogoszcz** Pol.
174 F5 **Skoroszyce** Pol.
140 L4 **Skorovatn** Norway
144 J1 **Skorpa** *i.* Norway
142 F5 **Skørping** Denmark
175 K3 **Skórzec** Pol.
174 F3 **Skorzęcińskie, Jezioro** *l.* Pol.
198 E1 **Skotoussa** Greece
142 I2 **Skotterud** Norway
198 E1 **Skoutari** Greece
199 H3 **Skoutaros** *Lesvos* Greece
143 J3 **Skövde** Sweden
100 C2 **Skovorodino** Rus. Fed.
233 □P4 **Skowhegan** *ME* U.S.A.

142 F2 **Skrimfjell** *hill* Norway
138 I5 **Skrīveri** Latvia
188 D2 **Škrlatica** *mt.* Slovenia
175 J2 **Skroda** *r.* Pol.
140 P3 **Skröven** Sweden
138 F5 **Skrunda** Latvia
175 H3 **Skrwa** *r.* Pol.
175 H2 **Skrwilno** Pol.
139 N6 **Skrydlyeva** Belarus
174 E2 **Skrzatusz** Pol.
175 G6 **Skrzyczne** *mt.* Pol.
175 I4 **Skrzyńsko** Pol.
175 J6 **Skrzyszów** Pol.
142 B2 **Skudeneshavn** Norway
215 K1 **Skuinsdrif** S. Africa
222 C2 **Skukum, Mount** *Y.T.* Can.
213 F5 **Skukuza** S. Africa
140 O5 **Skuleskogens nationalpark** *nat. park* Sweden
241 P5 **Skull Peak** *NV* U.S.A.
241 T7 **Skull Valley** *AZ* U.S.A.
214 B6 **Skulpfonteinpunt** *pt* S. Africa
174 G3 **Skulsk** Pol.
143 M2 **Skultuna** Sweden
236 J5 **Skunk** *r. IA* U.S.A.
138 E5 **Skuodas** Lith.
139 U7 **Skuratovskiy** Rus. Fed.
142 J6 **Skurup** Sweden
197 L7 **Skŭt** *r.* Bulg.
143 N1 **Skutskär** Sweden
140 M2 **Skutvik** Norway
144 D1 **Skúvoy** *i.* Faroe Is
175 M6 **Skvaryava** Ukr.
136 I4 **Skvyra** Ukr.
174 D3 **Skwierzyna** Pol.
177 H3 **Skýcov** Slovakia
198 D2 **Skydra** Greece
146 D8 **Skye** *i. Scotland* U.K.
142 C3 **Skykula** *hill* Norway
259 B9 **Skyring, Seno** *b.* Chile
198 F4 **Skyropoula** *i.* Greece
198 F4 **Skyros** *Skyros* Greece
198 F4 **Skyros** *i.* Greece
234 E2 **Skytop** *PA* U.S.A.
262 S1 **Skytrain Ice Rise** Antarctica
138 K6 **Slabodka** Belarus
175 I5 **Słaboszów** Pol.
234 C3 **Slabtown** *PA* U.S.A.
234 F4 **Slack Woods** *NJ* U.S.A.
Sládečkovce Slovakia *see* Močenok
137 R7 **Sladkiy, Liman** *salt l.* Rus. Fed.
144 D1 **Slættaratindur** *hill* Faroe Is
142 H6 **Slagelse** Denmark
164 K3 **Slagharen** Neth.
140 O4 **Slagnäs** Sweden
149 M6 **Slaidburn** *Lancashire, England* U.K.
146 I11 **Slamannan** *Falkirk, Scotland* U.K.
95 H8 **Slamet, Gunung** *vol.* Indon.
177 J3 **Slaná** *r.* Slovakia
147 I5 **Slane** Ireland
177 K3 **Slanec** Slovakia
147 I8 **Slaney** *r.* Ireland
197 N5 **Slănic** Romania
197 O5 **Slănic** *r.* Romania
197 O4 **Slănic Moldova** Romania
177 K3 **Slanské vrchy** *mts* Slovakia
138 L2 **Slantsy** Rus. Fed.
176 D1 **Slaný** Czech Rep.
179 I7 **Slap** Slovenia
138 G6 **Šlapaberžė** Lith.
176 F2 **Šlapanice** Czech Rep.
188 E4 **Slapovi Krke** *nat. park* Croatia
135 H6 **Slashchevskaya** Rus. Fed.
85 K5 **Slashers Reefs** *Qld* Austr.
Śląsk *reg.* Europe *see* **Silesia**
174 F4 **Śląska, Nizina** *lowland* Pol.
175 G5 **Śląska, Wyżyna** *hills* Pol.
174 G5 **Śląskie** *prov.* Pol.
234 E3 **Slateford** *PA* U.S.A.
235 G2 **Slate Hill** *NY* U.S.A.
224 C3 **Slate Islands** *Ont.* Can.
86 J5 **Slatey** *watercourse W.A.* Austr.
188 F3 **Slatina** Croatia
197 M6 **Slatina** Romania
177 I3 **Slatina** *r.* Slovakia
197 K5 **Slatina-Timiş** Romania
234 D3 **Slatington** *PA* U.S.A.
176 G2 **Slatinice** Czech Rep.
232 E10 **Slaty Fork** *WV* U.S.A.
137 P3 **Slatyne** Ukr.
131 R3 **Slautnoye** Rus. Fed.
100 F2 **Slava** Rus. Fed.
222 H2 **Slave** *r. Alta/N.W.T.* Can.
207 F5 **Slave Coast** Africa
222 H4 **Slave Lake** *Alta* Can.
222 H2 **Slave Point** *N.W.T.* Can.
Slavgorod Belarus *see* Slawharad
121 R1 **Slavgorod** Rus. Fed.
Slavgorod Ukr. *see* **Slavhorod**
137 O5 **Slavhorod** *Dnipropetrovs'ka Oblast'* Ukr.
137 O3 **Slavhorod** *Sums'ka Oblast'* Ukr.
177 G2 **Slavičín** Czech Rep.
197 K7 **Slavinja** Serbia
138 M4 **Slavkovichi** Rus. Fed.
176 B1 **Slavkovský les** *for.* Czech Rep.
176 F2 **Slavkov u Brna** Czech Rep.
191 P4 **Slavnik** *mt.* Slovenia
139 T5 **Slavnoye** Rus. Fed.
Slavonia *reg.* Croatia *see* Slavonija
176 E3 **Slavonice** Czech Rep.
188 F3 **Slavonija** *reg.* Croatia
Slavonska Požega Croatia *see* Požega
188 G3 **Slavonski Brod** Croatia
177 J3 **Slavošovce** Slovakia
138 E6 **Slavsk** Rus. Fed.
136 F3 **Slavuta** Ukr.
136 J2 **Slavutych** Ukr.
Slavyanka Kazakh. *see* Myrzakent
100 G7 **Slavyanka** Rus. Fed.
197 M7 **Slavyanovo** Bulg.
Slavyansk Ukr. *see* Slov"yans'k
Slavyanskaya Rus. Fed. *see* Slavyansk-na-Kubani
135 G7 **Slavyansk-na-Kubani** Rus. Fed.
174 E4 **Sława** Pol.
175 L4 **Sławatycze** Pol.
174 F2 **Sławęcin** Pol.
139 O8 **Slawharad** Belarus
174 F2 **Sławianowskie Wielkie, Jezioro** *l.* Pol.
143 M7 **Sławno** Pol.
174 D2 **Sławoborze** Pol.
174 E4 **Sławskie, Jezioro** *l.* Pol.
174 E1 **Sławsko** Pol.
236 H4 **Slayton** *MN* U.S.A.
149 Q7 **Slea** *r. England* U.K.
149 Q7 **Sleaford** *Lincolnshire, England* U.K.
82 E6 **Sleaford Bay** *S.A.* Austr.
147 B8 **Slea Head** Ireland
146 E8 **Sleat** *pen. Scotland* U.K.
146 D8 **Sleat, Point of** *Scotland* U.K.
146 E8 **Sleat, Sound of** *sea chan. Scotland* U.K.
223 J4 **Sled Lake** *Sask.* Can.
149 P5 **Sledmere** *East Riding of Yorkshire, England* U.K.
116 H8 **Sleemanabad** *Madh. Prad.* India
164 K3 **Sleen** Neth.
224 E1 **Sleeper Islands** *Nunavut* Can.
226 H5 **Sleeping Bear Dunes National Lakeshore** *nature res. MI* U.S.A.
226 H5 **Sleeping Bear Point** *MI* U.S.A.
109 □J7 **Sleep Island** *H.K.* China
164 G5 **Sleeuwijk** Neth.
149 P5 **Sleights** *North Yorkshire, England* U.K.
95 I8 **Sleman** Indon.
175 H6 **Ślemień** Pol.
129 G2 **Sleptsovskaya** Rus. Fed.
174 G3 **Ślesin** Pol.
262 W1 **Slessor Glacier** Antarctica
174 E5 **Ślęża** *hill* Pol.
174 E4 **Ślęża** *r.* Pol.
176 F1 **Ślężański Park Krajobrazowy** Pol.
Slezsko *reg.* Europe *see* Silesia

177 I3 **Sliač** Slovakia
241 X3 **Slick Rock** *CO* U.S.A.
237 K10 **Slidell** *LA* U.S.A.
233 K7 **Slide Mountain** *NY* U.S.A.
141 J6 **Slidre** Norway
164 G5 **Sliedrecht** Neth.
195 □ **Sliema** Malta
147 B8 **Slievanea** *hill* Ireland
147 G4 **Slieve Anierin** *hill* Ireland
147 G7 **Slieveardagh Hills** Ireland
147 E6 **Slieve Aughty Mountains** *hills* Ireland
147 H4 **Slieve Beagh** *hill* Ireland/U.K.
147 E7 **Slieve Bernagh** *hills* Ireland
147 G7 **Slieve Bloom Mountains** *hills* Ireland
147 D7 **Slievecallan** *hill* Ireland
147 C4 **Slieve Car** *hill* Ireland
147 K4 **Slieve Donard** *hill Northern Ireland* U.K.
147 F7 **Slievefelim Mountains** *hills* Ireland
148 D4 **Slieve Gallion** *hill Northern Ireland* U.K.
147 D5 **Slieve Gamph** *hills* Ireland
147 F7 **Slievekimalta** *hill* Ireland
147 H3 **Slievekirk** *hill Northern Ireland* U.K.
147 B8 **Slieve Mish Mountains** *hills* Ireland
147 B9 **Slieve Miskish Mountains** *hills* Ireland
147 G4 **Slievenakilla** *hill* Ireland
147 G8 **Slievenamon** *hill* Ireland
148 B5 **Slieve Rushen** *hill Northern Ireland* U.K.
147 F3 **Slieve Snaght** *hill* Ireland
147 H2 **Slieve Snaght** *hill* Ireland
146 D8 **Sligachan** *Highland, Scotland* U.K.
Sligeach Ireland *see* **Sligo**
147 F4 **Sligo** Ireland
147 E4 **Sligo** *county* Ireland
232 F7 **Sligo** *PA* U.S.A.
147 E4 **Sligo Bay** Ireland
175 K2 **Ślina** *r.* Pol.
151 L5 **Slinfold** *West Sussex, England* U.K.
164 J4 **Slinge** *r.* Neth.
146 F7 **Slioch** *hill Scotland* U.K.
137 L4 **Sliporid** *r.* Ukr.
80 J4 **Slipper Island** *North I.* N.Z.
232 E7 **Slippery Rock** *PA* U.S.A.
143 O4 **Slite** *Gotland* Sweden
138 F4 **Slīteres rezervāts** *nature res.* Latvia
197 O8 **Sliven** Bulg.
197 L8 **Slivnitsa** Bulg.
197 O7 **Slivo Pole** Bulg.
174 G2 **Śliwice** Pol.
188 E3 **Sljeme** *mt.* Croatia
177 G3 **Slňava** *l.* Slovakia
241 Q6 **Sloan** *NV* U.S.A.
240 L2 **Sloat** *CA* U.S.A.
235 G2 **Sloatsburg** *NY* U.S.A.
136 I6 **Slobidka** Ukr.
134 I3 **Sloboda** *Arkhangel'skaya Oblast'* Rus. Fed.
Sloboda *Respublika Komi* Rus. Fed. *see* **Ezhva**
Sloboda *Smolenskaya Oblast'* Rus. Fed. *see* **Przheval'skoye**
135 H6 **Sloboda** *Voronezhskaya Oblast'* Rus. Fed.
137 M2 **Sloboda** Ukr.
134 J3 **Slobodchikovo** Rus. Fed.
139 R7 **Slobodka** Rus. Fed.
134 J4 **Slobodskoy** Rus. Fed.
Slobodzeya Moldova *see* Slobozia
136 I7 **Slobozia** Moldova
197 P6 **Slobozia** Romania
197 P5 **Slobozia Bradului** Romania
222 G5 **Slocan** *B.C.* Can.
164 K2 **Slochteren** Neth.
175 I5 **Słomniki** Pol.
138 I8 **Slonim** Belarus
137 Q3 **Slonovka** Rus. Fed.
174 D2 **Słonowice** Pol.
174 C3 **Słońsk** Pol.
164 G3 **Slootdorp** Neth.
164 I3 **Sloten** Neth.
164 I3 **Slotermeer** *l.* Neth.
151 K4 **Slough** *Slough, England* U.K.
151 K4 **Slough** *admin. div. England* U.K.
176 F2 **Sloupnice** Czech Rep.
137 M2 **Slout** Ukr.
177 I3 **Slovakia** *country* Europe
136 H2 **Slovechna** *r.* Ukr.
136 H2 **Slovechne** Ukr.
188 E2 **Slovenia** *country* Europe
Slovenija *country* Europe *see* Slovenia
188 E2 **Slovenj Gradec** Slovenia
188 E2 **Slovenska Bistrica** Slovenia
177 J2 **Slovenská Ves** Slovakia
188 E2 **Slovenske Gorice** *hills* Slovenia
179 L7 **Slovenske Konjice** Slovenia
177 K3 **Slovenské Nové Mesto** Slovakia
177 I3 **Slovenské Rudohorie** *mts* Slovakia
Slovensko *country* Europe *see* Slovakia
177 J3 **Slovenský kras** *mts* Slovakia
177 J3 **Slovenský kras** *park* Slovakia
177 J3 **Slovenský raj** *nat. park* Slovakia
177 J3 **Slovinky** Slovakia
175 M6 **Slovita** Ukr.
137 P5 **Slov"yanka** Ukr.
137 Q4 **Slov"yanohirs'k** Ukr.
137 R5 **Slov"yanoserbs'k** Ukr.
137 Q5 **Slov"yans'k** Ukr.
137 M8 **Slov"yans'ke** Ukr.
136 I2 **Slovyechna** *r.* Belarus
175 H4 **Słowik** Pol.
143 N7 **Słowiński Park Narodowy** *nat. park* Pol.
174 C3 **Słubice** *Lubuskie* Pol.
175 H3 **Słubice** *Mazowieckie* Pol.
138 K9 **Sluch** *r.* Belarus
136 F2 **Sluch** *r.* Ukr.
191 J2 **Sluderno** Italy
134 L4 **Sludka** *Permskaya Oblast'* Rus. Fed.
134 J4 **Sludka** *Respublika Komi* Rus. Fed.
165 D6 **Sluis** Neth.
165 E6 **Sluiskil** Neth.
176 D1 **Šluknov** Czech Rep.
176 G2 **Slunečná** *hill* Czech Rep.
97 H9 **S'Lung, B'Nom** *mt.* Vietnam
188 E3 **Slunj** Croatia
174 F3 **Słupca** Pol.
175 J5 **Słupcza** Pol.
175 H4 **Słupia** *Łódzkie* Pol.
175 H5 **Słupia** *Świętokrzyskie* Pol.
175 I4 **Słupia** *Świętokrzyskie* Pol.
143 M7 **Słupia** *r.* Pol.
175 H3 **Słupno** Pol.
143 N7 **Słupsk** Pol.
140 N4 **Slussfors** Sweden
174 G4 **Słuszków** Pol.
138 K8 **Slutsk** Belarus
138 F6 **Šlyna** *r.* Lith.
147 B6 **Slyne Head** Ireland
98 H1 **Slyudyanka** Rus. Fed.
237 I9 **Smackover** *AR* U.S.A.
162 B2 **Smagne** *r.* France
146 K11 **Smailholm** *Scottish Borders, Scotland* U.K.
143 K4 **Småland** *reg.* Sweden
142 H6 **Smålandsfarvandet** *sea chan.* Denmark
142 J4 **Smålandsstenar** Sweden
151 J2 **Smalley** *Derbyshire, England* U.K.
233 □P5 **Small Point** *ME* U.S.A.
225 H2 **Smallwood Reservoir** *Nfld and Lab.* Can.
139 N6 **Smalowka** Belarus
175 M3 **Smalyanitsa** Belarus
138 L7 **Smalyavichy** Belarus
175 I4 **Smardzewice** Pol.
174 D3 **Smardzewo** Pol.
174 D2 **Smardzko** Pol.
138 J7 **Smarhon'** Belarus
179 M7 **Šmarje pri Jelšah** Slovenia
179 L8 **Šmarjeta** Slovenia

179 L7 **Šmartinsko jezero** *l.* Slovenia
223 J2 **Smart Lake** *N.W.T.* Can.
179 K7 **Šmartno** *Mozirje* Slovenia
179 L7 **Šmartno** *Slovenj Gradec* Slovenia
214 H6 **Smartt Syndicate Dam** *resr* S. Africa
162 E2 **Smarves** France
223 J4 **Smeaton** *Sask.* Can.
171 J10 **Smečno** Czech Rep.
176 D1 **Smědá** *r.* Czech Rep.
143 M5 **Smedby** Sweden
196 I6 **Smederevo** Serbia
196 I6 **Smederevska Palanka** Serbia
197 O5 **Smeeni** Romania
151 N5 **Smeeth** *Kent, England* U.K.
Smela Ukr. *see* **Smila**
140 U1 **Smelror** Norway
232 G7 **Smethport** *PA* U.S.A.
151 I3 **Smethwick** *West Midlands, England* U.K.
174 G2 **Smętowo Graniczne** Pol.
176 E1 **Smidary** Czech Rep.
175 M4 **Smidyn** Ukr.
174 E3 **Śmigiel** Pol.
137 K4 **Smila** Ukr.
138 L8 **Smilavichy** Belarus
164 J3 **Smilde** Neth.
137 M3 **Smile** Ukr.
136 G3 **Smilka** *r.* Ukr.
174 E2 **Śmiłowo** Pol.
138 I4 **Smiltene** Latvia
138 F5 **Smiltiņu kalns** *hill* Latvia
140 M2 **Smines** Norway
176 E1 **Smiřice** Czech Rep.
121 M1 **Smirnovo** Kazakh.
Smirnovskiy Kazakh. *see* Smirnovo
100 M4 **Smirnykh** *Sakhalin* Rus. Fed.
222 H4 **Smith** *Alta* Can.
238 I3 **Smith** *r. MT* U.S.A.
232 F12 **Smith** *r. VA* U.S.A.
220 F3 **Smith Arm** *b. N.W.T.* Can.
220 C2 **Smith Bay** *AK* U.S.A.
147 H4 **Smithborough** Ireland
236 F6 **Smith Center** *KS* U.S.A.
222 E4 **Smithers** *B.C.* Can.
222 E4 **Smithers Landing** *B.C.* Can.
215 K6 **Smithfield** S. Africa
231 H8 **Smithfield** *NC* U.S.A.
238 I6 **Smithfield** *UT* U.S.A.
232 I12 **Smithfield** *VA* U.S.A.
262 Q1 **Smith Glacier** Antarctica
262 T2 **Smith Island** Antarctica
221 K3 **Smith Island** *Nunavut* Can.
115 M6 **Smith Island** *Andaman & Nicobar Is* India
233 I10 **Smith Island** *MD* U.S.A.
233 J11 **Smith Island** *VA* U.S.A.
237 K7 **Smithland** *KY* U.S.A.
232 F11 **Smith Mountain Lake** *VA* U.S.A.
84 C1 **Smith Point** *N.T.* Austr.
222 E3 **Smith River** *B.C.* Can.
232 H9 **Smithsburg** *MD* U.S.A.
224 E4 **Smiths Falls** *Ont.* Can.
86 □1 **Smithson Bight** *b.* Christmas I.
221 K2 **Smith Sound** *sea chan.* Can./Greenland
83 J9 **Smithton** *Tas.* Austr.
83 N4 **Smithtown** *N.S.W.* Austr.
235 I3 **Smithtown** *NY* U.S.A.
235 G6 **Smithville** *NJ* U.S.A.
237 H8 **Smithville** *OK* U.S.A.
231 E8 **Smithville** *TN* U.S.A.
232 D9 **Smithville** *WV* U.S.A.
214 I9 **Smitskraal** S. Africa
177 J3 **Smižany** Slovakia
140 □F1 **Smjörfjöll** *mts* Iceland
240 M1 **Smoke Creek Desert** *NV* U.S.A.
222 G3 **Smoky** *r. Alta* Can.
82 D5 **Smoky Bay** *S.A.* Austr.
82 D5 **Smoky Bay** *b. S.A.* Austr.
83 N4 **Smoky Cape** *N.S.W.* Austr.
84 G7 **Smoky Creek** *watercourse Qld* Austr.
224 D3 **Smoky Falls** *Ont.* Can.
236 E6 **Smoky Hill** *r. KS* U.S.A.
236 E6 **Smoky Hill, North Fork** *r. KS* U.S.A.
228 G3 **Smoky Hills** *KS* U.S.A.
236 F6 **Smoky Hills** *KS* U.S.A.
223 H4 **Smoky Lake** *Alta* Can.
238 G5 **Smoky Mountains** *ID* U.S.A.
140 I5 **Smøla** *i.* Norway
174 F1 **Smołdzino** Pol.
120 C2 **Smolenka** Rus. Fed.
139 P7 **Smolensk** Rus. Fed.
139 Q7 **Smolenskaya Oblast'** *admin. div.* Rus. Fed.
Smolensk Oblast *admin. div.* Rus. Fed. *see* Smolenskaya **Oblast'**
139 P7 **Smolensko-Moskovskaya Vozvyshennost'** *hills* Rus. Fed.
121 U1 **Smolenskoye** Rus. Fed.
Smolevichi Belarus *see* Smalyavichy
174 F4 **Smolice** Pol.
198 B2 **Smolikas** *mt.* Greece
137 K5 **Smoline** Ukr.
142 I2 **Smolmark** Sweden
170 K5 **Smolnica** Pol.
177 J3 **Smolník** Slovakia
197 M9 **Smolyan** Bulg.
100 H7 **Smolyoninovo** Rus. Fed.
224 D3 **Smooth Rock Falls** *Ont.* Can.
224 B3 **Smoothrock Lake** *Ont.* Can.
223 J4 **Smoothstone Lake** *Sask.* Can.
140 R1 **Smørfjord** Norway
Smorgon' Belarus *see* Smarhon'
139 P9 **Smotrova Buda** Rus. Fed.
136 F5 **Smotrych** Ukr.
137 L3 **Smotryky** Ukr.
176 G1 **Smrk** *mt.* Czech Rep.
171 L9 **Smrk** *mt.* Czech Rep.
137 K2 **Smyach** Ukr.
197 P7 **Smyadovo** Bulg.
142 J6 **Smygehamn** Sweden
136 E3 **Smyha** Ukr.
175 I4 **Smyków** Pol.
262 S2 **Smyley Island** Antarctica
Smyrna Turkey *see* **İzmir**
234 D6 **Smyrna** *DE* U.S.A.
231 E9 **Smyrna** *GA* U.S.A.
231 D8 **Smyrna** *TN* U.S.A.
234 D6 **Smyrna** *r. DE* U.S.A.
233 □Q2 **Smyrna Mills** *ME* U.S.A.
259 B8 **Smyth, Canal** *sea chan.* Chile
140 □F1 **Snæfell** *mt.* Iceland
148 I5 **Snaefell** *hill* Isle of Man
140 □B1 **Snæfellsjökull** *ice cap* Iceland
140 □B1 **Snæfellsnes** *pen.* Iceland
222 A2 **Snag** *Y.T.* Can.
149 P5 **Snainton** *North Yorkshire, England* U.K.
149 O6 **Snaith** *East Riding of Yorkshire, England* U.K.
236 E4 **Snake** *r. NE* U.S.A.
238 E3 **Snake** *r.* U.S.A.
84 B3 **Snake Creek** *r. N.T.* Austr.
241 R2 **Snake Range** *mts NV* U.S.A.
222 F3 **Snake River** *B.C.* Can.
238 G5 **Snake River Plain** *ID* U.S.A.
Snap Point *Andros* Bahamas *see* **Cistern Point**
222 G2 **Snare** *r. N.W.T.* Can.
222 H1 **Snare Lake** *N.W.T.* Can.
223 J3 **Snare Lake** *Sask.* Can.
Snare Lakes *N.W.T.* Can. *see* **Wekweti**
77 G6 **Snares Islands** N.Z.
140 L4 **Snåsa** Norway
140 L4 **Snåsvatn** *l.* Norway
232 B12 **Sneedville** *TN* U.S.A.
164 I2 **Sneek** Neth.
164 I2 **Sneekermeer** *l.* Neth.
147 C9 **Sneem** Ireland
214 D8 **Sneeuberg** *mt.* S. Africa
214 I7 **Sneeuberge** *mts* S. Africa
225 I2 **Snegamook Lake** *Nfld and Lab.* Can.
Snegurovka Ukr. *see* **Tetiyiv**
240 L4 **Snelling** *CA* U.S.A.
138 E5 **Snēpele** Latvia
151 N2 **Snettisham** *Norfolk, England* U.K.
139 T8 **Snezhed'** *r.* Rus. Fed.
130 J3 **Snezhnogorsk** Rus. Fed.

100 E1 **Snezhnogorskiy** Rus. Fed.
Snezhnoye Ukr. *see* **Snizhne**
176 E1 **Sněžka** *mt.* Czech Rep.
188 E3 **Snežnik** *mt.* Slovenia
175 J2 **Śniadowo** Pol.
175 J2 **Śniardwy, Jezioro** *l.* Pol.
Sniečkus Lith. *see* **Visaginas**
Snieżka *mt.* Czech Rep. *see* Sněžka
176 F1 **Śnieżnicki Park Krajobrazowy** Pol.
174 E5 **Śnieżnik** *mt.* Pol.
137 L6 **Snihurivka** Ukr.
177 L3 **Snina** Slovakia
151 I3 **Snitterfield** *Warwickshire, England* U.K.
137 M3 **Snityn** Ukr.
137 R5 **Snizhne** Ukr.
146 D7 **Snizort, Loch** *b. Scotland* U.K.
141 J5 **Snøhetta** *mt.* Norway
238 C3 **Snohomish** *WA* U.S.A.
142 C2 **Snønuten** *mt.* Norway
139 Q8 **Snopot'** *r.* Rus. Fed.
Snoul Cambodia *see* **Snuŏl**
137 K2 **Snov** *r.* Ukr.
137 P2 **Snova** *r.* Rus. Fed.
139 V9 **Snova** *r.* Rus. Fed.
Snovsk Ukr. *see* **Shchors**
138 J8 **Snow** Belarus
223 K2 **Snowbird Lake** *N.W.T.* Can.
222 G5 **Snowcrest Mountain** *B.C.* Can.
81 C12 **Snowdon** *mt. South I.* N.Z.
150 D1 **Snowdon** *mt. Wales* U.K.
150 E2 **Snowdonia National Park** *Wales* U.K.
Snowdrift *N.W.T.* Can. *see* **Łutselk'e**
223 I2 **Snowdrift** *r. N.W.T.* Can.
241 V7 **Snowflake** *AZ* U.S.A.
233 J10 **Snow Hill** *MD* U.S.A.
231 I8 **Snow Hill** *NC* U.S.A.
223 K4 **Snow Lake** *Man.* Can.
82 G5 **Snowtown** *S.A.* Austr.
238 H6 **Snowville** *UT* U.S.A.
83 L7 **Snowy** *r. N.S.W./Vic.* Austr.
233 K5 **Snowy Mountain** *NY* U.S.A.
83 K7 **Snowy Mountains** *N.S.W.* Austr.
83 L7 **Snowy River National Park** *Vic.* Austr.
138 K6 **Snudy, Vozyera** *l.* Belarus
246 G2 **Snug Corner** *Acklins I.* Bahamas
225 K2 **Snug Harbour** *Nfld and Lab.* Can.
227 N4 **Snug Harbour** *Ont.* Can.
97 H8 **Snuŏl** Cambodia
136 E5 **Snyatyn** Ukr.
237 F8 **Snyder** *OK* U.S.A.
237 E9 **Snyder** *TX* U.S.A.
234 A3 **Snyder County** *county PA* U.S.A.
234 D3 **Snyders** *PA* U.S.A.
214 E7 **Snyderspoort** *pass* S. Africa
139 T8 **Snykhovo** Rus. Fed.
136 H4 **Snyvoda** *r.* Ukr.
93 F5 **Soabuwe** *Seram* Indon.
213 □J3 **Soahany** Madag.
Soaigh *i. Western Isles, Scotland* U.K. *see* **Soay**
146 D10 **Soa Island** *Scotland* U.K.
182 D5 **Soajo** Port.
81 B12 **Soaker, Mount** *South I.* N.Z.
213 □J3 **Soalala** Madag.
182 D6 **Soalhães** Port.
182 F8 **Soalheira** Port.
213 □J4 **Soamanonga** Madag.
190 D5 **Soana** *r.* Italy
213 □K3 **Soanierana-Ivongo** Madag.
101 E11 **Soan-kundo** *is* S. Korea
191 M9 **Soara** *r.* Italy
250 C3 **Soata** Col.
191 K5 **Soave** Italy
213 □J3 **Soavinandriana** Madag.
146 D8 **Soay** *i. Highland, Scotland* U.K.
146 □1 **Soay** *i. Western Isles, Scotland* U.K.
136 I5 **Sob** *r.* Ukr.
207 H4 **Soba** Nigeria
101 E11 **Sobaek-sanmaek** *mts* S. Korea
101 F10 **Sobaek-san National Park** S. Korea
209 C8 **Soba Matias** Angola
210 A2 **Sobat** *r.* Sudan
105 H5 **Sobatsubu-yama** *mt.* Japan
182 E4 **Sober** Spain
176 D2 **Soběslav** Czech Rep.
91 J7 **Sobger** *r. Papua* Indon.
116 G8 **Sobhapur** *Madh. Prad.* India
136 C2 **Sobiborski Park Krajobrazowy** Pol.
139 X6 **Sobinka** Rus. Fed.
139 V6 **Sobolevo** Rus. Fed.
175 J4 **Sobolew** Pol.
103 I14 **Sobo-san** *mt.* Japan
175 H3 **Sobota** Pol.
179 L6 **Soboth** Austria
176 G1 **Sobotín** Czech Rep.
176 G3 **Sobotište** Slovakia
176 E1 **Sobotka** Czech Rep.
174 E5 **Sobótka** *Dolnośląskie* Pol.
175 J5 **Sobótka** *Świętokrzyskie* Pol.
174 F4 **Sobótka** *Wielkopolskie* Pol.
174 G1 **Sobowidz** Pol.
182 G4 **Sobradelo** Spain
256 D1 **Sobradinho** Brazil
254 E4 **Sobradinho, Barragem de** *resr* Brazil
254 E4 **Sobrado** *Bahia* Brazil
251 H6 **Sobrado** *Pará* Brazil
182 D2 **Sobrado** *Galicia* Spain
182 D4 **Sobrado** *Galicia* Spain
250 D7 **Sobral** *Acre* Brazil
254 E2 **Sobral** *Ceará* Brazil
182 D8 **Sobral** Port.
184 E4 **Sobral da Adiça** Port.
184 A2 **Sobral de Monte Agraço** Port.
182 E8 **Sobral do Campo** Port.
177 L3 **Sobrance** Slovakia
116 E4 **Sobraon** *Punjab* India
186 E3 **Sobrarbe** *reg.* Spain
182 D6 **Sobreira** Port.
182 E9 **Sobreira Formosa** Port.
183 N3 **Sobrón, Embalse de** *resr* Spain
104 E5 **Sobue** Japan
168 J1 **Søby** Denmark
137 M2 **Sobych** Ukr.
Soča *r.* Italy *see* **Isonzo**
179 I7 **Soča** Slovenia
188 D3 **Soča** *r.* Slovenia
191 N3 **Socchieve** Italy
191 P5 **Sočerga** Slovenia
175 I3 **Sochaczew** Pol.
129 A2 **Sochi** Rus. Fed.
175 I3 **Sochocin** Pol.
101 E10 **Sŏch'ŏn** S. Korea
198 E2 **Sochos** Greece
79 □9 **Société, Archipel de la** *is* Fr. Polynesia
Society Islands Fr. Polynesia *see* **Société, Archipel de la**
177 K5 **Socodor** Romania
196 J6 **Socol** Romania
252 C6 **Socompa** Chile
177 L4 **Socond** Romania
Soconusco, Sierra de *mts* Mex. *see* **Madre de Chiapas, Sierra**
256 D5 **Socorro** Brazil
250 C3 **Socorro** Col.
239 K9 **Socorro** *NM* U.S.A.
228 D7 **Socorro, Isla** *i.* Mex.
250 B6 **Socota** Peru
Socotra *i.* Yemen *see* **Suquṭrá**
185 P4 **Socovos** Spain
97 H10 **Soc Trăng** Vietnam
185 N2 **Socuéllamos** Spain
240 M6 **Soda Lake** *CA* U.S.A.
241 P6 **Soda Lake** *CA* U.S.A.
140 S3 **Sodankylä** Fin.
111 D9 **Soda Plains** Aksai Chin
116 G8 **Sodarpur** *Madh. Prad.* India
238 I5 **Soda Springs** *ID* U.S.A.
105 K5 **Sodegaura** Japan
143 M5 **Söderåkra** Sweden
143 L1 **Söderbärke** Sweden
143 O1 **Söderboda** Sweden
143 N1 **Söderfors** Sweden

141 N6 **Söderhamn** Sweden
143 M3 **Söderköping** Sweden
143 M2 **Södermanland** *county* Sweden
168 J4 **Soderstorf** Ger.
143 N2 **Södertälje** Sweden
203 F6 **Sodiri** Sudan
214 H6 **Sodium** S. Africa
210 C3 **Sodo** Eth.
143 L1 **Södra Barken** *l.* Sweden
143 N2 **Södra Björkfjärden** *b.* Sweden
143 M3 **Södra Finnö** *i.* Sweden
140 P5 **Södra gloppet** *b.* Fin.
141 O6 **Södra Kvarken** *str.* Fin./Sweden
143 L4 **Södra Vi** Sweden
179 K8 **Sodražica** Slovenia
232 H5 **Sodus** *NY* U.S.A.
215 Q3 **Sodwana Bay** S. Africa
215 Q3 **Sodwana Bay National Park** S. Africa
93 D8 **Soë** *Timor* Indon.
214 B6 **Soebatsfontein** S. Africa
213 F4 **Soekmekaar** S. Africa
138 F3 **Soela väin** *sea chan.* Estonia
Soerabaia *Jawa* Indon. *see* Surabaya
165 I6 **Soerendonk** Neth.
169 F7 **Soest** Ger.
164 H4 **Soest** Neth.
168 E4 **Soeste** *r.* Ger.
215 K4 **Soetdoring Nature Reserve** S. Africa
214 D10 **Soetendalsvlei** *l.* S. Africa
198 D3 **Sofades** Greece
83 L5 **Sofala** *N.S.W.* Austr.
213 G4 **Sofala** Moz.
213 G3 **Sofala** *prov.* Moz.
213 G4 **Sofala, Baía de** *b.* Moz.
Sofia Bulg. *see* **Sofiya**
213 □J2 **Sofia** *r.* Madag.
198 E5 **Sofiko** Greece
197 L8 **Sofiya** Bulg.
Sofiyevka Ukr. *see* **Vil'nyans'k**
137 M5 **Sofiyivka** Ukr.
100 H2 **Sofiysk** *Khabarovskiy Kray* Rus. Fed.
100 K3 **Sofiysk** *Khabarovskiy Kray* Rus. Fed.
140 U4 **Sofporog** Rus. Fed.
199 H6 **Sofrana** *i.* Greece
139 U5 **Sofrino** Rus. Fed.
177 K5 **Şofronea** Romania
128 A2 **Šofta Kalesi** *tourist site* Turkey
103 R17 **Sōfu-gan** *i.* Japan
111 K11 **Sog** *Xizang* China
250 C3 **Sogamoso** Col.
129 A5 **Soğanlı Dağları** *mts* Turkey
129 B5 **Soğanlı Geçidi** *pass* Turkey
110 H6 **Sogat** *Xinjiang* China
100 H3 **Sogda** Rus. Fed.
168 E5 **Sögel** Ger.
123 M2 **Soghd** *admin. div.* Tajik.
111 E9 **Sogma** *Xizang* China
111 D10 **Sogmai** *Xizang* China
142 D3 **Søgne** Norway
141 H6 **Sognefjorden** *inlet* Norway
141 I6 **Sogn og Fjordane** *county* Norway
131 N2 **Sogo** Rus. Fed.
92 E6 **Sogod** *Leyte* Phil.
92 E6 **Sogod Bay** *Leyte* Phil.
210 C4 **Sogo Hills** Kenya
202 B6 **Sogolle** *well* Chad
106 G5 **Sogo Nur** *l. Nei Mongol* China
111 K10 **Sog Qu** *r. Xizang* China
129 F6 **Soğuksu** Turkey
199 L2 **Söğüt** Turkey
199 J3 **Söğütcük** Turkey
199 K5 **Söğüt Dağı** *mts* Turkey
129 B7 **Söğütlü** Turkey
101 E12 **Sŏgwip'o** S. Korea
122 D5 **Soh** Iran
Sohâg *Sawhāj* **Egypt** *see* Sawhāj
116 G8 **Sohagpur** *Madh. Prad.* India
151 M3 **Soham** *Cambridgeshire, England* U.K.
123 N5 **Sohan** *r.* Pak.
91 L8 **Sohano** P.N.G.
Sohar Oman *see* **Şuḥār**
123 O5 **Sohawa** Pak.
165 H8 **Soheit-Tinlot** Belgium
117 I9 **Sohela** *Orissa* India
171 K8 **Sohland am Rotstein** Ger.
169 J6 **Söhlde** Ger.
116 F5 **Sohna** *Haryana* India
97 D7 **Sohng Gwe, Khao** *hill* Myanmar/Thai.
123 J8 **Sohrag** Pak.
172 C2 **Sohren** Ger.
156 H2 **Soignes, Forêt de** *for.* Belgium
165 F7 **Soignies** Belgium
108 A3 **Soila** *Xizang* China
177 L5 **Şoimi** Romania
160 H1 **Soing** France
159 O7 **Soings-en-Sologne** France
140 R5 **Soini** Fin.
169 I9 **Soisberg** *hill* Ger.
156 F5 **Soissons** France
260 D4 **Soitue** Arg.
156 G6 **Soizy-aux-Bois** France
103 K12 **Sōja** Japan
116 D7 **Sojat** *Rajasthan* India
116 D7 **Sojat Road** *Rajasthan* India
175 K5 **Sójkowa** Pol.
92 D7 **Sojoton Point** *Negros* Phil.
179 O6 **Söjtör** Hungary
135 J5 **Sok** *r.* Rus. Fed.
105 K4 **Sōka** Japan
136 D3 **Sokal'** Ukr.
101 F9 **Sokch'o** S. Korea
199 I5 **Söke** Turkey
209 E7 **Sokele** Dem. Rep. Congo
107 L2 **Sokhondo, Gora** *mt.* Rus. Fed.
106 I1 **Sokhor, Gora** *mt.* Rus. Fed.
Sokhós Greece *see* **Sochos**
129 C2 **Sokhumi** Georgia
129 C3 **Sokhumi-Babushara** *airport* Georgia
Sokiryany Ukr. *see* **Sokyryany**
103 G11 **Sŏkkuram Grotto** *tourist site* S. Korea
142 F1 **Sokna** Norway
140 K5 **Soknedal** Norway
197 J7 **Sokobanja** Serbia
207 F4 **Sokodé** Togo
Soko Islands *H.K.* China *see* **Shekka Ch'ün-Tao**
100 M5 **Sokol** *Sakhalin* Rus. Fed.
134 H4 **Sokol** *Vologodskaya Oblast'* Rus. Fed.
188 G4 **Sokolac** Bos.-Herz.
175 L2 **Sokolany** Pol.
136 J4 **Sokolivka** *Cherkas'ka Oblast'* Ukr.
175 M5 **Sokolivka** *L'vivs'ka Oblast'* Ukr.
175 L2 **Sokółka** Pol.
175 K1 **Sokółki** Pol.
179 O1 **Sokolnice** Czech Rep.
139 V7 **Sokol'niki** *Tul'skaya Oblast'* Rus. Fed.
139 R5 **Sokol'niki** *Tverskaya Oblast'* Rus. Fed.
206 D3 **Sokolo** Mali
137 N7 **Sokolohirne** Ukr.
176 B1 **Sokolov** Czech Rep.
137 N4 **Sokolova Balka** Ukr.
179 O7 **Sokolovac** Croatia
121 M1 **Sokolovka** Kazakh.
137 Q3 **Sokolovka** Rus. Fed.
121 U1 **Sokolovo** Rus. Fed.
137 S6 **Sokolovo-Kundryuchenskiy** Rus. Fed.
175 K5 **Sokołów Małopolski** Pol.
175 K3 **Sokołow Podlaski** Pol.
140 U3 **Sokolozero, Ozero** *l.* Rus. Fed.
134 H4 **Sokol'skoye** Rus. Fed.
175 K3 **Sokoły** Pol.
206 A3 **Sokone** Senegal
177 G4 **Sokorópátka** Hungary
140 T2 **Sokosti** *hill* Fin.
207 G3 **Sokoto** Nigeria
207 G4 **Sokoto** *r.* Nigeria
207 G3 **Sokoto** *state* Nigeria
206 C4 **Sokourala** Guinea
136 G5 **Sokyryany** Ukr.
175 K5 **Sól** Pol.

Soutpan S. Africa
Soutpansberg mts S. Africa
Souttouf, Adrar mts Western Sahara
Souvigny France
Sovarnuten mt. Norway
Sovata Romania
Soveja Romania
Soven Arg.
Soverato Italy
Soveria Corse France
Soveria Mannelli Italy
Sovet Kyrg.
Sovet Tajik.
Sovetabad Uzbek. see Xonobod
Sovetashen Armenia see Zangakatun
Sovetsk Kaliningradskaya Oblast' Rus. Fed.
Sovetsk Kirovskaya Oblast' Rus. Fed.
Sovetsk Tul'skaya Oblast' Rus. Fed.
Sovetskaya Krasnodarskiy Kray Rus. Fed.
Sovetskaya Stavropol'skiy Kray Rus. Fed.
Sovetskaya Gavan' Rus. Fed.
Sovetskiy Kyrg. see Sovet
Sovetskiy Khanty-Mansiyskiy Avtonomnyy Okrug Rus. Fed.
Sovetskiy Leningradskaya Oblast' Rus. Fed.
Sovetskiy Respublika Komi Rus. Fed.
Sovetskiy Respublika Mariy El Rus. Fed.
Sovetskiy Tajik. see Sovet
Sovetskoye Belgorodskaya Oblast' Rus. Fed.
Sovetskoye Chechenskaya Respublika Rus. Fed. see Shatoy
Sovetskoye Kabardino-Balkarskaya Respublika Rus. Fed. see Kashkhatau
Sovetskoye Respublika Dagestan Rus. Fed. see Khebda
Sovetskoye Saratovskaya Oblast' Rus. Fed.
Sovetskoye Stavropol'skiy Kray Rus. Fed. see Zelenokumsk
Soviči Bos.-Herz.
Sovicille Italy
Sovpol'ye Rus. Fed.
Sovyets'kyy Ukr.
Sowa Botswana
Sowa Sichuan China
Sōwa Japan
Sowa Pan salt pan Botswana
Sowerby North Yorkshire, England U.K.
Sowerby Bridge West Yorkshire, England U.K.
Soweto S. Africa
Sowno Zachodniopomorskie Pol.
Sowno Zachodniopomorskie Pol.
So'x Tajik.
Sōya-kaikyō str. Japan/Rus. Fed. see La Pérouse Strait
Soyaló Mex.
Sōya-misaki c. Japan
Soyana r. Rus. Fed.
Soyang-ho l. S. Korea
Soyaux France
Sōya-wan b. Japan
Soye France
Soyen Ger.
Soylan Armenia see Vayk'
Soyma r. Rus. Fed.
Soyo Angola
Soyons France
Soyopa Mex.
Soyuqbulaq Azer.
Sozaq Kazakh. see Suzak
Sozh r. Europe
Sozimskiy Rus. Fed.
Sozopol Bulg.
Spa Belgium
Spaatz Island Antarctica
Spabrücken Ger.
Spadafora Sicilia Italy
Spahnharrenstätte Ger.
Spaichingen Ger.
Spain country Europe
Spalato Croatia see Split
Spalatum Croatia see Split
Spalding S.A. Austr.
Spalding Lincolnshire, England U.K.
Spálené Poříčí Czech Rep.
Spalt Ger.
Spangenberg Ger.
Span Head hill England U.K.
Spaniard's Bay Nfld and Lab. Can.
Spanish Ont. Can.
Spanish r. Ont. Can.
Spanish Fork UT U.S.A.
Spanish Guinea country Africa see Equatorial Guinea
Spanish Netherlands country Europe see Belgium
Spanish Point pt Antigua and Barbuda
Spanish Point pt Bermuda
Spanish Point Ireland
Spanish Sahara terr. Africa see Western Sahara
Spanish Town Jamaica
Spanish Wells Eleuthera Bahamas
Spantekow Ger.
Sparagio, Monte mt. Italy
Sparanise Italy
Spargi, Isola i. Sardegna Italy
Sparks NV U.S.A.
Sparlingville MI U.S.A.
Sparrow Bush NY U.S.A.
Sparta Greece see Sparti
Spartà Sicilia Italy
Sparta GA U.S.A.
Sparta MI U.S.A.
Sparta NC U.S.A.
Sparta NJ U.S.A.
Sparta TN U.S.A.
Sparta WI U.S.A.
Spartanburg SC U.S.A.
Spartansburg PA U.S.A.
Spartel, Cap c. Morocco
Sparti Greece
Spartivento, Capo c. Sardegna Italy
Spartivento, Capo c. Italy
Sparwood B.C. Can.
Spas-Demensk Rus. Fed.
Spas'ke Ukr.
Spas-Klepiki Rus. Fed.
Spas'ko-Mykhaylivka Ukr.
Spasove Ukr.
Spass Rus. Fed.
Spassk Rus. Fed.
Spasskaya Guba Rus. Fed.
Spasskaya Polist' Rus. Fed.
Spassk-Dal'niy Rus. Fed.
Spasskoye Kazakh.
Spasskoye-Lutovinovo Rus. Fed.
Spassk-Ryazanskiy Rus. Fed.
Spas-Ugol Rus. Fed.
Spatha, Akrotirio pt Kriti Greece
Spathi, Akrotirio pt Kythira Greece
Spatsizi Plateau Wilderness Provincial Park B.C. Can.
Spay Ger.
Spean Bridge Highland, Scotland U.K.
Spearfish SD U.S.A.
Spearman TX U.S.A.
Specchia Italy
Speculator NY U.S.A.
Speen West Berkshire, England U.K.
Speer mt. Switz.
223 J4 Speers Sask. Can.
216 □2b Speery Island St Helena
172 B2 Speicher Ger.
179 H5 Speicher Sameralm l. Austria
173 L2 Speichersdorf Ger.
247 □4 Speightstown Barbados
179 L5 Speikkogel mt. Austria
211 B5 Speke Gulf Tanz.
169 D6 Spelle Ger.
193 J2 Spello Italy
146 E10 Spelve, Loch inlet Scotland U.K.
Spence Bay Nunavut Can. see Taloyoak
236 H4 Spencer IA U.S.A.
238 H4 Spencer ID U.S.A.
230 D6 Spencer IN U.S.A.
233 N6 Spencer MA U.S.A.
236 F4 Spencer NE U.S.A.
227 R7 Spencer NY U.S.A.
232 E12 Spencer VA U.S.A.
232 D10 Spencer WV U.S.A.
82 F6 Spencer, Cape S.A. Austr.
222 B3 Spencer, Cape AK U.S.A.
220 B5 Spencer, Point AK U.S.A.
212 B5 Spencer Bay Namibia
82 F6 Spencer Gulf est. S.A. Austr.
233 □O3 Spencer Lake ME U.S.A.
84 B3 Spencer Range hills N.T. Austr.
84 D2 Spencer Range hills N.T. Austr.
222 F5 Spences Bridge B.C. Can.
169 F6 Spenge Ger.
149 N4 Spennymoor Durham, England U.K.
81 G9 Spenser Mountains South I. N.Z.
198 D4 Spercheios r. Greece
171 H6 Sperenberg Ger.
142 G1 Sperillen l. Norway
Sperkhiós r. Greece see Spercheios
194 G8 Sperlinga Sicilia Italy
193 K5 Sperlonga Italy
197 M3 Spermezeu Romania
192 A10 Sperone, Capo c. Sardegna Italy
147 H3 Sperrin Mountains hills Northern Ireland U.K.
232 G10 Sperryville VA U.S.A.
169 H11 Spessart reg. Ger.
234 C6 Spesutie Island MD U.S.A.
Spétsai i. Greece see Spetses
198 E5 Spetses Greece
198 E5 Spetses i. Greece
146 J7 Spey r. Scotland U.K.
146 J7 Spey Bay Moray, Scotland U.K.
172 E3 Speyer Ger.
247 □5 Speyside Trin. and Tob.
123 L7 Spezand Pak.
158 D5 Spézet France
193 Q8 Spezzano Albanese Italy
Spice Islands Indon. see Maluku
175 K4 Spiczyn Pol.
147 D6 Spiddal Ireland
173 O4 Spiegelau Ger.
168 E3 Spiekeroog Ger.
168 E3 Spiekeroog i. Ger.
179 K5 Spielberg bei Knittelfeld Austria
179 M6 Spielfeld Austria
172 C3 Spiesen-Elversberg Ger.
190 D2 Spiez Switz.
190 E6 Spigno Monferrato Italy
193 L5 Spigno Saturnia Italy
164 K2 Spijk Neth.
164 F5 Spijkenisse Neth.
129 A6 Spikör Geçidi pass Turkey
191 K6 Spilamberto Italy
199 I4 Spil Dağı Milli Parkı nat. park Turkey
198 F7 Spili Kriti Greece
191 N3 Spilimbergo Italy
195 J6 Spilinga Italy
149 R7 Spilsby Lincolnshire, England U.K.
193 Q6 Spinazzola Italy
123 L6 Spīn Būldak Afgh.
157 K5 Spincourt France
191 M5 Spinea Italy
193 L2 Spinetoli Italy
234 E4 Spinnerstown PA U.S.A.
195 □ Spinola, Ix-Xatt ta' b. Malta
193 P7 Spinoso Italy
123 M7 Spintangi Pak.
177 L4 Spinuș Romania
123 N5 Spinwam Pak.
215 N4 Spioenkop Dam Nature Reserve S. Africa
236 H4 Spirit Lake IA U.S.A.
238 F2 Spirit Lake ID U.S.A.
223 J4 Spiritwood Sask. Can.
139 R4 Spirovo Rus. Fed.
176 G6 Špišić-Bukovica Croatia
178 B6 Spiss Austria
177 J2 Spišská Belá Slovakia
177 J3 Spišská Nová Ves Slovakia
177 J2 Spišská Stará Ves Slovakia
177 J3 Spišské Podhradie Slovakia
177 J3 Spišské Vlachy Slovakia
177 J3 Spišský Hrad Slovakia
177 J2 Spišský Štvrtok Slovakia
129 F5 Spitak Armenia
179 J4 Spital am Pyhrn Austria
179 M4 Spital am Semmering Austria
116 G4 Spiti r. India
86 E6 Spit Point W.A. Austr.
140 □ Spitsbergen i. Svalbard
214 G9 Spitskop mt. S. Africa
215 J7 Spitskopvlei S. Africa
138 K3 Spitsyno Rus. Fed.
179 H6 Spittal an der Drau Austria
146 J9 Spittal of Glenshee Perth and Kinross, Scotland U.K.
231 □1 Spittal Pond Bermuda
179 L3 Spitz Austria
Spitzbergen i. Svalbard see Spitsbergen
178 G6 Spitzkofel mt. Austria
190 G1 Spitzmeilen mt. Switz.
137 R4 Spivakivka Ukr.
151 O2 Spixworth Norfolk, England U.K.
142 E5 Spjald Denmark
188 F4 Split Croatia
223 L3 Split Lake Man. Can.
223 L3 Split Lake l. Man. Can.
190 G2 Spluga, Passo dello pass Italy/Switz.
190 G2 Splügen Switz.
136 H4 Spodakhy Ukr.
179 J7 Spodnja Idrija Slovenia
179 M6 Spodnje Hoče Slovenia
168 K1 Spodsbjerg Denmark
149 O6 Spofforth North Yorkshire, England U.K.
238 F3 Spokane WA U.S.A.
238 E3 Spokane r. WA U.S.A.
238 E3 Spokane Indian Reservation res. WA U.S.A.
129 C1 Spokoynaya Rus. Fed.
190 I2 Spöl r. Italy
Spoletium Italy see Spoleto
193 J2 Spoleto Italy
193 M3 Spoltore Italy
191 J2 Spondigna Italy
165 H8 Spontin Belgium
226 D9 Spoon r. IL U.S.A.
226 C4 Spooner WI U.S.A.
171 F8 Spora Ger.
170 E4 Spornitz Ger.
234 C4 Sporting Hill PA U.S.A.
246 D4 Spot Bay Cayman Is
190 E7 Spotorno Italy
235 G4 Spotswood NJ U.S.A.
232 H10 Spotsylvania VA U.S.A.
238 L4 Spotted Horse WY U.S.A.
227 L3 Spragge Ont. Can.
238 D5 Sprague r. OR U.S.A.
172 H4 Spraitbach Ger.
168 K5 Sprakensehl Ger.
222 F4 Spranger, Mount B.C. Can.
90 D5 Spratly Island S. China Sea
90 D4 Spratly Islands S. China Sea
238 E4 Spray OR U.S.A.
226 F4 Spread Eagle WI U.S.A.
188 G3 Spreča r. Bos.-Herz.
171 H5 Spree r. Ger.
171 I6 Spreenhagen Ger.
171 J7 Spreewald park Ger.
171 I6 Spreewald reg. Ger.
172 E7 Spreitenbach Switz.
171 J7 Spremberg Ger.
172 D2 Sprendlingen Ger.
191 M4 Spresiano Italy
190 H3 Spriana Italy
165 I7 Sprimont Belgium
237 H7 Spring r. MO U.S.A.
227 L4 Spring Bay Ont. Can.
214 B5 Springbok S. Africa
234 D4 Spring City PA U.S.A.
241 U2 Spring City UT U.S.A.
84 F5 Spring Creek r. N.T. Austr.
85 H8 Spring Creek watercourse Qld Austr.
236 E5 Spring Creek r. NE U.S.A.
225 K3 Springdale Nfld and Lab. Can.
237 H7 Springdale AR U.S.A.
169 I6 Springe Ger.
239 L8 Springer NM U.S.A.
241 W7 Springerville AZ U.S.A.
81 F10 Springfield South I. N.Z.
147 G4 Springfield Northern Ireland U.K.
237 D7 Springfield CO U.S.A.
231 G9 Springfield GA U.S.A.
238 H5 Springfield ID U.S.A.
236 K6 Springfield IL U.S.A.
230 E7 Springfield KY U.S.A.
233 M6 Springfield MA U.S.A.
233 □Q3 Springfield ME U.S.A.
236 H3 Springfield MN U.S.A.
237 I7 Springfield MO U.S.A.
232 B9 Springfield OH U.S.A.
238 C4 Springfield OR U.S.A.
234 E5 Springfield PA U.S.A.
231 D7 Springfield TN U.S.A.
233 M5 Springfield VT U.S.A.
232 G9 Springfield WV U.S.A.
215 J6 Springfontein S. Africa
251 G3 Spring Garden Guyana
235 G1 Spring Glen NY U.S.A.
234 B3 Spring Glen PA U.S.A.
241 V2 Spring Glen UT U.S.A.
226 D6 Spring Green WI U.S.A.
226 C6 Spring Grove MN U.S.A.
234 B5 Spring Grove PA U.S.A.
232 I11 Spring Grove VA U.S.A.
225 H4 Springhill N.S. Can.
231 F11 Spring Hill FL U.S.A.
146 I12 Springholm Dumfries and Galloway, Scotland U.K.
222 F5 Springhouse B.C. Can.
226 H6 Spring Lake MI U.S.A.
235 G4 Spring Lake Heights NJ U.S.A.
241 Q5 Spring Mountains NV U.S.A.
226 J7 Springport MI U.S.A.
215 M2 Springs S. Africa
235 K2 Springs NY U.S.A.
81 G9 Springs Junction South I. N.Z.
85 L8 Springsure Qld Austr.
234 E5 Springton Reservoir PA U.S.A.
85 H7 Springvale Qld Austr.
215 K8 Spring Valley S. Africa
240 P9 Spring Valley CA U.S.A.
226 B6 Spring Valley MN U.S.A.
235 G2 Spring Valley NY U.S.A.
226 B5 Spring Valley WI U.S.A.
236 F4 Springview NE U.S.A.
240 N5 Springville CA U.S.A.
232 G6 Springville NY U.S.A.
234 D1 Springville PA U.S.A.
241 U1 Springville UT U.S.A.
232 H6 Springwater NY U.S.A.
149 Q6 Sproatley East Riding of Yorkshire, England U.K.
169 D8 Sprockhövel Ger.
151 O2 Sprowston Norfolk, England U.K.
222 H4 Spruce Grove Alta Can.
232 F10 Spruce Knob mt. WV U.S.A.
241 X3 Spruce Mountain CO U.S.A.
241 R1 Spruce Mountain NV U.S.A.
234 F3 Spruce Run Reservoir NJ U.S.A.
164 G5 Sprundel Neth.
234 B5 Spry PA U.S.A.
195 L4 Spulico, Capo c. Italy
149 R6 Spurn Head England U.K.
220 C5 Spurr, Mount vol. AK U.S.A.
222 F5 Spuzzum B.C. Can.
175 J2 Spychowo Pol.
222 F5 Squamish B.C. Can.
222 F5 Squamish r. B.C. Can.
233 N5 Squam Lake NH U.S.A.
233 □Q2 Squapan Lake ME U.S.A.
191 K5 Squaranto r. Italy
233 □Q1 Square Lake ME U.S.A.
195 L6 Squillace Italy
195 L6 Squillace, Golfo di g. Italy
195 O3 Squinzano Italy
232 D11 Squire WV U.S.A.
87 I9 Squires, Mount hill W.A. Austr.
95 I8 Sragen Jawa Indon.
196 I8 Srbica Kosovo Serbia
Srbija country Europe see Serbia
Srbinje Bos.-Herz. see Foča
Srbobran Bos.-Herz. see Donji Vakuf
196 H5 Srbobran Vojvodina Serbia
97 F9 Srê Âmběl Cambodia
197 P6 Srebărna tourist site Bulg.
188 G3 Srebrenica Bos.-Herz.
197 P8 Sredets Burgas Bulg.
Sredets Sofiya-Grad Bulg. see Sofiya
197 P8 Sredetska Reka r. Bulg.
131 Q4 Sredinnyy Khrebet mts Rus. Fed.
179 N7 Središče Slovenia
197 P7 Sredishte Bulg.
197 L8 Sredna Gora mts Bulg.
100 E3 Srednebelaya Rus. Fed.
131 Q3 Srednekolymsk Rus. Fed.
139 T7 Sredne-Russkaya Vozvyshennost' hills Rus. Fed.
131 M3 Sredne-Sibirskoye Ploskogor'ye plat. Rus. Fed.
140 U4 Sredneye Kuyto, Ozero l. Rus. Fed.
137 S2 Sredniy Ikorets Rus. Fed.
100 H3 Sredniy Urgal Rus. Fed.
191 Q5 Srednja Vrata, Kanal sea chan. Croatia
197 M8 Srednogorie Bulg.
135 I6 Srednyaya Akhtuba Rus. Fed.
97 H8 Sre Khtum Cambodia
174 F3 Śrem Pol.
196 H5 Srem reg. Serbia
196 H6 Sremska Mitrovica Vojvodina Serbia
97 G8 Srê Noy Cambodia
97 H8 Srêpok, Tônlé r. Cambodia
99 K1 Sretensk Rus. Fed.
95 I4 Sri Aman Sarawak Malaysia
137 L3 Sribne Ukr.
114 G6 Sriharikota Island India
114 F9 Sri Jayewardenepura Kotte Sri Lanka
115 I3 Srikakulam Andhra Prad. India
114 F6 Sri Kalahasti Andhra Prad. India
114 G9 Sri Lanka country Asia
116 E6 Sri Madhopur Rajasthan India
117 M7 Srimangal Bangl.
116 G4 Srinagar Uttaranchal India
116 E2 Srinagar Jammu and Kashmir India
114 D6 Sringeri Karnataka India
114 G9 Sri Pada mt. Sri Lanka
114 F7 Srirangam Tamil Nadu India
114 F4 Srisailam Andhra Prad. India
114 E8 Srivaikuntam Tamil Nadu India
114 C3 Srivardhan Mahar. India
114 E8 Srivilliputtur Tamil Nadu India
188 F3 Srnetica mts Bos.-Herz.
188 G3 Srnice Bos.-Herz.
175 J1 Srockowo Pol.
174 E4 Środa Śląska Pol.
174 F3 Środa Wielkopolska Pol.
174 E3 Środkowy Kanał Obry canal Pol.
146 G8 Sròn a' Choire Ghairbh hill Scotland U.K.
121 U1 Srostki Rus. Fed.
196 I5 Srpska Crnja Vojvodina Serbia
Srpska Kostajnica Bos.-Herz. see Bosanska Kostajnica
Srpski Brod Bos.-Herz. see Bosanski Brod
196 I5 Srpski Itebej Vojvodina Serbia
115 H3 Srungavarapukota Andhra Prad. India
139 W9 Sselki Rus. Fed.
214 E3 Staansaam S. Africa
85 H4 Staaten r. Qld Austr.
85 I4 Staaten River National Park Qld Austr.
179 N2 Staatz Austria
140 R1 Stabbursdalen Nasjonalpark nat. park Norway
170 D2 Staberhuk c. Ger.
165 F6 Stabroek Belgium
Stabroek Guyana see Georgetown
176 C2 Stachy Czech Rep.
146 F6 Stac Pollaidh hill Scotland U.K.
Stac Polly hill Scotland U.K. see Stac Pollaidh
226 B4 Stacy MN U.S.A.
226 B6 Stacyville IA U.S.A.
168 H3 Stade Ger.
173 N6 Stadelhorn mt. Ger.
165 D7 Staden Belgium
168 K5 Stadensen Ger.
151 J4 Stadhampton Oxfordshire, England U.K.
Stadhlaigearraidh Scotland U.K. see Stilligarry
141 L6 Städjan-Nipfjällets naturreservat nature res. Sweden
179 I3 Stadl-Paura Austria
164 K3 Stadskanaal Neth.
164 K2 Stadskanaal canal Neth.
169 H9 Stadtallendorf Ger.
173 J5 Stadtbergen Ger.
169 H6 Stadthagen Ger.
171 D9 Stadtilm Ger.
169 C10 Stadtkyll Ger.
169 J10 Stadtlauringen Ger.
169 J9 Stadtlengsfeld Ger.
169 C7 Stadtlohn Ger.
169 I7 Stadtoldendorf Ger.
172 G2 Stadtprozelten Ger.
171 E9 Stadtroda Ger.
179 N5 Stadtschlaining Austria
171 E10 Stadtsteinach Ger.
168 H1 Stadum Ger.
190 F1 Stäfa Switz.
146 D10 Staffa i. Scotland U.K.
171 D10 Staffelberg hill Ger.
157 N8 Staffelfelden France
173 K6 Staffelsee l. Ger.
169 K10 Staffelstein Ger.
168 G5 Staffhorst Ger.
146 D7 Staffin Highland, Scotland U.K.
146 D7 Staffin Bay Scotland U.K.
191 O9 Staffolo Italy
190 G5 Staffora r. Italy
150 H2 Stafford Staffordshire, England U.K.
232 H10 Stafford VA U.S.A.
246 E1 Stafford Creek Andros Bahamas
150 H2 Staffordshire admin. div. England U.K.
215 N6 Stafford's Post S. Africa
233 M7 Stafford Springs CT U.S.A.
95 L6 Stagen Kalimantan Indon.
222 H2 Stagg Lake N.W.T. Can.
147 C4 Stags of Broad Haven is Ireland
173 P2 Štěhlavy Czech Rep.
232 F8 Stahlstown PA U.S.A.
171 H6 Stahnsdorf Ger.
179 K7 Stahovica Slovenia
138 H4 Staicele Latvia
172 H5 Staig Ger.
193 O4 Staina r. Italy
179 J4 Stainach Austria
149 N4 Staindrop Durham, England U.K.
151 K5 Staines Surrey, England U.K.
149 M5 Stainforth North Yorkshire, England U.K.
149 O6 Stainforth South Yorkshire, England U.K.
149 Q5 Staintondale North Yorkshire, England U.K.
157 J6 Stainville France
179 L6 Stainz Austria
195 K8 Staìti Italy
177 L3 Stakčín Slovakia
146 G11 Stake, Hill of Scotland U.K.
137 R5 Stakhanov Ukr.
137 M8 Stakhanovka Ukr.
Stakhanovo Rus. Fed. see Zhukovskiy
150 H6 Stalbridge Dorset, England U.K.
190 D3 Stalden Switz.
168 L1 Ståldyb sea chan. Denmark
151 P2 Stalham Norfolk, England U.K.
Stalin Bulg. see Varna
Stalinabad Tajik. see Dushanbe
Stalingrad Rus. Fed. see Volgograd
Stalingradskaya Oblast' admin. div. Rus. Fed. see Volgogradskaya Oblast'
Staliniri Georgia see Ts'khinvali
Stalino Ukr. see Donets'k
Stalino Uzbek. see Shahrihon
Stalinogorsk Rus. Fed. see Novomoskovsk
Stalinogród Pol. see Katowice
Stalinsk Rus. Fed. see Novokuznetsk
178 H6 Stall Austria
143 N2 Stallarholmen Sweden
179 L5 Stallhofen Austria
149 M5 Stalling Busk North Yorkshire, England U.K.
173 N3 Stallwang Ger.
175 K5 Stalowa Wola Pol.
197 O5 Stâlpu Romania
215 L9 Stalwart Point S. Africa
149 M7 Stalybridge Greater Manchester, England U.K.
197 M8 Stamboliyski Bulg.
85 I6 Stamford Qld Austr.
151 L2 Stamford Lincolnshire, England U.K.
233 L7 Stamford CT U.S.A.
233 K6 Stamford NY U.S.A.
237 F9 Stamford TX U.S.A.
149 P6 Stamford Bridge East Riding of Yorkshire, England U.K.
149 N3 Stamfordham Northumberland, England U.K.
171 E10 Stammbach Ger.
173 K4 Stammham Ger.
Stampalia i. Greece see Astypalaia
212 C5 Stampriet Namibia
178 C5 Stams Austria
173 N3 Stamsried Ger.
140 L2 Stamsund Norway
147 J5 Stamullen Ireland
232 G10 Stanardsville VA U.S.A.
236 H5 Stanberry MO U.S.A.
262 W1 Stancomb-Wills Glacier Antarctica
222 H5 Standard Alta Can.
164 G5 Standdaarbuiten Neth.
215 N2 Standerton S. Africa
236 E3 Standing Rock Indian Reservation res. ND/SD U.S.A.
149 L6 Standish Greater Manchester, England U.K.
227 K6 Standish MI U.S.A.
151 M4 Standon Hertfordshire, England U.K.
148 J2 Stane North Lanarkshire, Scotland U.K.
197 M6 Stănești Romania
241 U9 Stanfield AZ U.S.A.
214 D10 Stanford S. Africa
230 E7 Stanford KY U.S.A.
238 I3 Stanford MT U.S.A.
151 M4 Stanford-le-Hope Thurrock, England U.K.
143 O4 Stånga Gotland Sweden
143 M4 Stångån r. Sweden
140 T1 Stáŋganasčohkka hill Norway
215 P5 Stanger S. Africa
140 J5 Stangvikfjorden inlet Norway
151 N2 Stanhoe Norfolk, England U.K.
149 M4 Stanhope Durham, England U.K.
234 F3 Stanhope NJ U.S.A.
197 Q4 Stănilești Romania
175 K4 Stanin Pol.
196 H5 Stanišić Vojvodina Serbia
Stanislav Ivano-Frankivs'ka Oblast' Ukr. see Ivano-Frankivs'k
137 L7 Stanislav Khersons'ka Oblast' Ukr.
175 M5 Stanislavchyk Ukr.
175 J3 Stanisławów Pol.
197 N3 Stânișoarei, Munții mts Romania
179 I8 Štanjel Slovenia
Stanke Dimitrov Bulg. see Dupnitsa
176 C2 Staňkov Czech Rep.
83 J9 Stanley Tas. Austr.
233 □S2 Stanley N.B. Can.
109 □J7 Stanley H.K. China
259 F8 Stanley Falkland Is
149 N4 Stanley Durham, England U.K.
146 J10 Stanley Perth and Kinross, Scotland U.K.
238 G4 Stanley ID U.S.A.
236 D1 Stanley ND U.S.A.
232 G10 Stanley VA U.S.A.
226 D5 Stanley WI U.S.A.
Stanley, Chutes waterfall Dem. Rep. Congo see Boyoma, Chutes
84 C7 Stanley, Mount hill N.T. Austr.
83 J9 Stanley, Mount hill Tas. Austr.
Stanley, Mount Dem. Rep. Congo/Uganda see Margherita Peak
Stanley Falls Dem. Rep. Congo see Boyoma, Chutes
114 E7 Stanley Reservoir India
Stanleyville Dem. Rep. Congo see Kisangani
213 F4 Stanmore Zimbabwe
Stann Creek Belize see Dangriga
149 N3 Stannington Northumberland, England U.K.
174 D2 Stanomino Pol.
198 C4 Stanos Greece
139 V9 Stanovaya Rus. Fed.
139 W8 Stanovaya Ryasa r. Rus. Fed.
171 G10 Stanovice, Vodní nádrž resr Czech Rep.
139 V9 Stanovoye Rus. Fed.
131 M4 Stanovoye Nagor'ye mts Rus. Fed.
131 N4 Stanovoy Khrebet mts Rus. Fed.
139 T9 Stanovoy Kolodez' Rus. Fed.
178 E5 Stans Austria
190 E2 Stans Switz.
82 F6 Stansbury S.A. Austr.
86 J6 Stansmore Range hills W.A. Austr.
151 M4 Stansted Mountfitchet Essex, England U.K.
83 M3 Stanthorpe Qld Austr.
151 N3 Stanton Suffolk, England U.K.
234 D5 Stanton DE U.S.A.
232 B11 Stanton KY U.S.A.
226 I6 Stanton MI U.S.A.
236 E2 Stanton ND U.S.A.
236 G5 Stanton NE U.S.A.
237 E9 Stanton TX U.S.A.
139 V9 Stantsiya Babarykino Rus. Fed.
139 U8 Stantsiya Skuratovo Rus. Fed.
Stantsiya-Yakkabag Uzbek. see Yakkabog'
151 N4 Stanway Essex, England U.K.
137 S5 Stanychno-Luhans'ke Ukr.
178 C5 Stanzach Austria
179 M5 Stanz im Mürztal Austria
168 K4 Stapel Ger.
169 K7 Stapelburg Ger.
168 J3 Stapelfeld Ger.
164 J3 Staphorst Neth.
151 J2 Stapleford Nottinghamshire, England U.K.
151 N5 Staplehurst Kent, England U.K.
236 H2 Staples MN U.S.A.
236 E5 Stapleton NE U.S.A.
175 I4 Stąporków Pol.
85 J5 Star r. Qld Austr.
139 R8 Star' Rus. Fed.
137 K3 Stara Basan' Ukr.
177 H2 Stará Bystrica Slovakia
136 G3 Stara Chortoryya Ukr.
175 J4 Starachowice Pol.
176 D2 Stará Huť Czech Rep.
137 M1 Stara Huta Ukr.
174 G2 Stara Kiszewa Pol.
175 K3 Stara Kornica Pol.
136 H3 Stara Kotel'nya Ukr.
174 E2 Stara Łubianka Pol.
177 J2 Stará Ľubovňa Slovakia
177 I6 Stara Moravica Vojvodina Serbia
191 R6 Stara Novalja Croatia
176 E1 Stará Paka Czech Rep.
196 I6 Stara Pazova Vojvodina Serbia
197 K7 Stara Planina mts Bulg./Yugo.
179 O8 Stara Plošćica Croatia
170 J5 Stara Rudnica Pol.
175 K6 Stara Sil' Ukr.
177 G3 Stará Turá Slovakia
136 G5 Stara Ushytsya Ukr.
179 M8 Stara vas-Bizeljsko Slovenia
136 D2 Stara Vyzhivka Ukr.
175 K5 Stara Wieś Pol.
Staraya Barda Rus. Fed. see Krasnogorskoye
137 T2 Staraya Chigla Rus. Fed.
137 S3 Staraya Kalitva Rus. Fed.
120 B1 Staraya Kulatka Rus. Fed.
120 B2 Staraya Poltavka Rus. Fed.
139 O4 Staraya Russa Rus. Fed.
139 O5 Staraya Toropa Rus. Fed.
135 J5 Staraya Tumba Rus. Fed.
197 N8 Stara Zagora Bulg.
136 E5 Stara Zhadova Ukr.
267 I6 Starbuck Island Kiribati
137 P6 Starchenkove Ukr.
197 O5 Starchiojd Romania
237 J9 Star City AR U.S.A.
226 H9 Star City IN U.S.A.
85 J3 Starcke National Park Qld Austr.
150 F6 Starcross Devon, England U.K.
137 M8 Stare, Ozero l. Ukr.
174 G5 Stare Budkowice Pol.
179 M1 Stařeč Czech Rep.
174 C2 Stare Czarnowo Pol.
174 D2 Stare Dąbrowa Pol.
175 K2 Stare Dolistowo Pol.
175 K3 Stare Hołowczyce Pol.
171 J9 Staré Křečany Czech Rep.
174 D3 Stare Kurowo Pol.
176 F1 Staré Město Czech Rep.
174 G3 Stare Miasto Pol.
175 H1 Stare Pole Pol.
136 D4 Stare Selo Ukr.
174 E4 Stare Strącze Pol.
Stargard in Pommern Pol. see Stargard Szczeciński
174 D2 Stargard Szczeciński Pol.
177 I3 Star Huta Slovakia
191 R6 Starigrad Croatia
175 M4 Stari Koshary Ukr.
191 R4 Stari Log Slovenia
177 L2 Starina, Vodná nádrž resr Slovakia
136 J3 Stari Petrivtsi Ukr.
196 I7 Stari Ras and Sopoćani tourist site Serbia
191 Q4 Stari Trg Slovenia
139 R5 Staritsa Rus. Fed.
120 H3 Star Karabutak Kazakh.
231 F11 Starke FL U.S.A.
171 F9 Starkenberg Ger.
232 F11 Starkey VA U.S.A.
80 □ Star Keys is Chatham Is S. Pacific Ocean
139 X6 Starkovo Rus. Fed.
237 K9 Starkville MS U.S.A.
233 J4 Star Lake NY U.S.A.
Starling Inlet H.K. China see Sha Tau Kok Hoi
173 K6 Starnberg Ger.
173 K6 Starnberger See l. Ger.
110 F1 Staroaleyskoye Rus. Fed.
Starobel'sk Ukr. see Starobil's'k
137 R6 Starobesheve Ukr.
137 R6 Starobeshivs'ke Vodoskhovyshche resr Ukr.
137 R4 Starobil's'k Ukr.
138 K9 Starobin Belarus
137 O6 Starobohdanivka Ukr.
137 R7 Staroderevyankovskaya Rus. Fed.
139 P9 Starodub Rus. Fed.
174 D2 Starogard Pol.
174 G2 Starogard Gdański Pol.
129 H2 Starogladkovskaya Rus. Fed.
Starokonstantinov Ukr. see Starokostyantyniv
136 G4 Starokostyantyniv Ukr.
136 I7 Starokozache Ukr.
139 W7 Staroletovo Rus. Fed.
137 S8 Staroleushkovskaya Rus. Fed.
135 G7 Starominskaya Rus. Fed.
137 P6 Staromlynivka Ukr.
137 R8 Staronizhestebliyevskaya Rus. Fed.
197 P8 Staro Oryakhovo Bulg.
137 Q2 Starooskol'skoye Vodokhranilishche resr Rus. Fed.
197 M8 Starosel Bulg.
197 O7 Staro Selo Bulg.
139 X8 Staroseslavino Rus. Fed.
135 G7 Staroshcherbinovskaya Rus. Fed.
174 C4 Starosiedle Pol.
120 G1 Starosubkhangulovo Rus. Fed.
137 Q8 Starotitarovskaya Rus. Fed.
137 O4 Starovirivka Ukr.
175 H4 Starowa Góra Pol.
134 H4 Staroye Rus. Fed.
135 I5 Staroye Drozhzhanoye Rus. Fed.
139 Q6 Staroye Istomino Rus. Fed.
139 T5 Staroye Melkovo Rus. Fed.
139 T3 Staroye Sandovo Rus. Fed.
175 M3 Staroye Syalo Brestskaya Voblasts' Belarus
138 M6 Staroye Syalo Vitsyebskaya Voblasts' Belarus
135 H5 Staroyur'yevo Rus. Fed.
139 W7 Starozhilovo Rus. Fed.
175 H3 Staroźreby Pol.
240 N1 Star Peak NV U.S.A.
150 E7 Start Bay England U.K.
149 N4 Startforth Durham, England U.K.
150 E7 Start Point England U.K.
Starve Island Kiribati see Starbuck Island
175 H2 Stary Dzierzgoń Pol.
177 L1 Stary Dzików Pol.
177 G2 Starý Jičín Czech Rep.
174 D4 Stary Kisielin Pol.
175 H3 Stary Kobrzyniec Pol.
175 K5 Stary Majdan Pol.
138 K7 Starynki Belarus
138 M6 Starynovichy Belarus
176 C2 Starý Plzenec Czech Rep.
175 I6 Stary Sącz Pol.
177 J2 Starý Smokovec Slovakia
175 J3 Stary Szelków Pol.
175 H2 Stary Targ Pol.
177 H3 Starý Tekov Slovakia
137 P3 Starytsya Ukr.
175 K4 Stary Uścimów Pol.
138 L8 Staryya Darohi Belarus
136 E2 Staryya Chortoryys'k Ukr.
139 X5 Staryy Dvor Rus. Fed.
Staryye Dorogi Belarus see Staryya Darohi
137 K1 Staryye Yurkovichi Rus. Fed.
131 L2 Staryy Kayak Rus. Fed.
137 Q6 Staryy Krym Donets'ka Oblast' Ukr.
137 O8 Staryy Krym Respublika Krym Ukr.
129 E2 Staryy Lesken Rus. Fed.
130 I3 Staryy Nadym Rus. Fed.
136 E4 Staryy Oleksynets' Ukr.
135 G6 Staryy Oskol Rus. Fed.
136 G4 Staryy Ostropil' Ukr.
Staryy Salavan Rus. Fed. see Novocheremshansk
137 P3 Staryy Saltiv Ukr.
136 B4 Staryy Sambir Ukr.
Staryy Sambor Ukr. see Staryy Sambir
129 I2 Staryy Terek r. Rus. Fed.
174 G1 Starzyno Pol.
137 N4 Stasi Ukr.
171 E7 Staßfurt Ger.
175 J5 Staszów Pol.
232 H8 State College PA U.S.A.
237 K10 State Line MS U.S.A.
Staten Island Arg. see Estados, Isla de los
235 G3 Staten Island NY U.S.A.
231 F10 Statenville GA U.S.A.
231 G9 Statesboro GA U.S.A.
231 G8 Statesville NC U.S.A.
142 F2 Stathelle Norway
203 G4 Station No. 6 Sudan
203 G5 Station No. 10 Sudan
221 Q1 Station Nord Greenland
235 G3 Statue of Liberty tourist site NJ U.S.A.
179 L3 Statzberg hill Austria
179 M3 Statzendorf Austria
136 H6 Stăuceni Moldova
171 H8 Stauchitz Ger.
172 D6 Staufen im Breisgau Ger.
173 J5 Staufersberg hill Ger.
150 H4 Staunton Gloucestershire, England U.K.
232 F10 Staunton VA U.S.A.
171 I7 Staupitz Ger.
142 B3 Stavanger Norway
81 F10 Staveley South I. N.Z.
149 O7 Staveley Derbyshire, England U.K.
165 I8 Stavelot Belgium
164 F5 Stavenisse Neth.
142 G3 Stavern Norway
197 M7 Stavertsi Bulg.
136 J6 Stavkove Ukr.
175 M4 Stavky Ukr.
177 L3 Stavne Ukr.
164 H3 Stavoren Neth.
199 G5 Stavri, Akrotirio pt Naxos Greece
198 C5 Stavrodromi Greece
135 H7 Stavropol' Rus. Fed.
121 L1 Stavropolka Kazakh.
Stavropol Kray admin. div. Rus. Fed. see Stavropol'skiy Kray
Stavropol'-na-Volge Rus. Fed. see Tol'yatti
135 H7 Stavropol'skaya Vozvyshennost' hills Rus. Fed.
129 E1 Stavropol'skiy Kray admin. div. Rus. Fed.
198 D2 Stavros Kentriki Makedonia Greece
198 E2 Stavros Kentriki Makedonia Greece
198 F7 Stavros, Akrotirio pt Kriti Greece
198 F1 Stavroupoli Greece
170 K5 Staw Pol.
139 O9 Stawbun Belarus
83 I7 Stawell Vic. Austr.
85 I6 Stawell r. Qld Austr.
175 I2 Stawiguda Pol.
175 K2 Stawiski Pol.
174 G4 Stawiszyn Pol.
167 I3 Stawki, Park Krajobrazowy Pol.
149 Q5 Staxton North Yorkshire, England U.K.
139 S8 Stayki Rus. Fed.
136 J3 Stayky Ukr.
227 N5 Stayner Ont. Can.
238 C4 Stayton OR U.S.A.
215 N4 Steadville S. Africa
240 M2 Steamboat NV U.S.A.
238 K6 Steamboat Springs CO U.S.A.
175 I2 Stębark Pol.
220 B3 Stebbins AK U.S.A.
137 K4 Stebliv Ukr.
175 L6 Stebnyk Ukr.
195 L6 Steccato Italy
176 D2 Štěchovice Czech Rep.
170 F5 Stechow Ger.
190 F1 Steckborn Switz.
168 E3 Stedesdorf Ger.
171 E8 Stedten Ger.
164 K2 Stedum Neth.
178 B5 Steeg Austria
214 I3 Steekdorings S. Africa
224 C3 Steel r. Ont. Can.
236 F2 Steele ND U.S.A.
262 T2 Steele Island Antarctica
82 □1 Steel's Point Norfolk I.
234 B4 Steelton PA U.S.A.
236 J7 Steelville MO U.S.A.
222 G3 Steen r. Alta Can.
164 F5 Steenbergen Neth.
164 J4 Steenderen Neth.
215 O1 Steenkampsberge mts S. Africa
222 G3 Steen River Alta Can.
238 E5 Steens Mountain OR U.S.A.
Steenstrup Gletscher glacier Greenland see Sermersuaq
156 E2 Steenvoorde France
164 J3 Steenwijk Neth.
150 F5 Steep Holm i. England U.K.
149 R7 Steeping r. England U.K.
151 K4 Steeple Claydon Buckinghamshire, England U.K.
87 B9 Steep Point W.A. Austr.
149 N6 Steeton West Yorkshire, England U.K.
179 O8 Štefanje Croatia
176 G3 Štefanov Slovakia
198 D3 Stefanovikeio Greece
263 D2 Stefansson Bay Antarctica
221 H2 Stefansson Island Nunavut Can.
136 I7 Ștefan Vodă Moldova
197 P6 Ștefan Vodă Romania
190 D2 Steffisburg Switz.
139 V9 Stegalovka Rus. Fed.
173 J2 Stegaurath Ger.
142 I7 Stege Denmark
170 F1 Stege Bugt b. Denmark
171 E6 Stegelitz Ger.
170 F1 Stege Nor lag. Denmark
179 N5 Stegersbach Austria
164 J3 Steggerda Neth.
Stegi Swaziland see Siteki
175 H1 Stegny Pol.
139 O7 Stegrimovo Rus. Fed.
197 K4 Ștei Romania
179 L5 Steiermark land Austria
173 I2 Steigerwald mts Ger.
173 J2 Steigerwald park Ger.
215 P3 Steilrand S. Africa
168 H5 Steimbke Ger.
173 K3 Stein Ger.
165 I7 Stein Neth.
172 D6 Stein Switz.
172 E6 Steina r. Ger.
172 E5 Steinach Baden-Württemberg Ger.
173 N4 Steinach Bayern Ger.
171 D10 Steinach Thüringen Ger.
178 D5 Steinach am Brenner Austria
179 L3 Steinakirchen am Forst Austria
190 F1 Stein am Rhein Switz.
140 □D2 Steinar Iceland
168 G3 Steinau Ger.
169 H10 Steinau an der Straße Ger.
223 L5 Steinbach Man. Can.
171 H9 Steinbach Ger.
169 G10 Steinbach (Taunus) Ger.
179 I4 Steinbach am Attersee Austria
171 D10 Steinbach am Wald Ger.
179 J4 Steinbach an der Steyr Austria
173 M3 Steinberg Bayern Ger.
168 I1 Steinberg Schleswig-Holstein Ger.
168 I1 Steinbergkirche Ger.
168 J3 Steinburg Ger.
179 J6 Steindorf am Ossiacher See Austria
172 D6 Steinen Ger.
178 G4 Steinernes Meer mts Austria
178 H6 Steinfeld Austria
172 H2 Steinfeld Bayern Ger.
172 E3 Steinfeld Rheinland-Pfalz Ger.
168 F5 Steinfeld (Oldenburg) Ger.
165 I9 Steinfort Lux.
169 D6 Steinfurt Ger.
173 J6 Steingaden Ger.
170 G2 Steinhagen Mecklenburg-Vorpommern Ger.
169 F6 Steinhagen Nordrhein-Westfalen Ger.
212 C4 Steinhausen Namibia
171 D10 Steinheid Ger.
169 H7 Steinheim Ger.
173 I4 Steinheim am Albuch Ger.
172 G4 Steinheim an der Murr Ger.
171 J6 Steinhöfel Ger.
173 M5 Steinhöring Ger.
168 J5 Steinhorst Niedersachsen Ger.
168 J3 Steinhorst Schleswig-Holstein Ger.
169 H6 Steinhuder Meer l. Ger.
168 H5 Steinhuder Meer, Naturpark nature res. Ger.
171 J8 Steinigtwolmsdorf Ger.
168 I3 Steinkirchen Ger.
140 K4 Steinkjer Norway
169 G10 Steinkopf hill Ger.
214 B5 Steinkopf S. Africa
171 K6 Steinsdorf Ger.
173 I3 Steinsfeld Ger.
142 B1 Steinsland Norway
172 D3 Steinwenden Ger.
171 D10 Steinwiesen Ger.
172 F6 Steißlingen Ger.
214 H7 Stekaar S. Africa
165 F6 Stekene Belgium
191 K8 Stella r. Italy
191 O4 Stella r. Italy
215 I2 Stella S. Africa
246 F2 Stella Maris Long I. Bahamas
217 □1c Stella Matutina Réunion
168 J4 Stelle Ger.
214 C9 Stellenbosch S. Africa
164 F5 Stellendam Neth.
192 C2 Stello, Monte mt. Corse France
190 I3 Stelvio, Parco Nazionale dello nat. park Italy
190 I2 Stelvio, Passo dello pass Italy
168 I4 Stemmen Ger.
169 F6 Stemshorn Ger.
174 E5 Stěnava r. Pol.
157 J5 Stenay France
143 M4 Stenbo Sweden
170 E5 Stendal Ger.
138 F4 Stende Latvia
143 J4 Stengårdshultasjön l. Sweden
143 N2 Stenhamra Sweden
Stenhouse, Mount hill H.K. China see Shan Tei Tong
146 I10 Stenhousemuir Falkirk, Scotland U.K.
191 J3 Stenico Italy
142 I6 Stenløse Denmark
146 □M2 Stenness Shetland, Scotland U.K.
146 J4 Stenness, Loch of l. Scotland U.K.
198 D5 Steno Greece
173 O2 Štěnovice Czech Rep.
143 K6 Stenshuvuds nationalpark nat. park Sweden
142 I7 Stensved Denmark
146 K11 Stenton East Lothian, Scotland U.K.
140 N3 Stenudden Sweden
142 H3 Stenungsund Sweden
175 M5 Stenyatyn Ukr.
136 D3 Stenzharychi Ukr.
Steornabhagh Western Isles, Scotland U.K. see Stornoway
136 F2 Stepan' Ukr.
Stepanakert Azer. see Xankändi
129 F4 Step'anavan Armenia
137 L2 Stepanivka Chernihivs'ka Oblast' Ukr.
137 R6 Stepanivka Donets'ka Oblast' Ukr.
136 F3 Stepanivka Khmel'nyts'ka Oblast' Ukr.
137 N3 Stepanivka Sums'ka Oblast' Ukr.

137 O7 **Stepanivka Persha** Ukr.
120 G2 **Stepanovka** Kazakh.
139 V6 **Stepanshchino** Rus. Fed.
139 T5 **Stepantsevo** Rus. Fed.
147 J6 **Stepaside** Ireland
168 K3 **Stepenitz** *r.* Ger.
173 M6 **Stephanskirchen** Ger.
173 N4 **Stephansposching** Ger.
236 G1 **Stephen** *MN* U.S.A.
83 I5 **Stephens** *watercourse* *N.S.W.* Austr.
80 H7 **Stephens, Cape** *South I.* N.Z.
234 F3 **Stephensburg** *NJ* U.S.A.
232 G9 **Stephens City** *VA* U.S.A.
83 H4 **Stephens Creek** *N.S.W.* Austr.
222 D4 **Stephens Island** *B.C.* Can.
223 M3 **Stephens Lake** *Man.* Can.
226 G4 **Stephenson** *MI* U.S.A.
262 T2 **Stephenson, Mount** Antarctica
225 J3 **Stephenville** *Nfld and Lab.* Can.
237 F9 **Stephenville** *TX* U.S.A.
137 R8 **Stepnaya** Rus. Fed.
137 M1 **Stepne** Ukr.
235 I2 **Stepney** *CT* U.S.A.
174 C2 **Stepnica** Pol.
121 O1 **Stepnogorsk** Kazakh.
137 O6 **Stepnohirs'k** Ukr.
121 O6 **Stepnoy** Kyrg.
Stepnoy Rus. Fed. *see* **Elista**
120 I1 **Stepnoye** *Chelyabinskaya Oblast'* Rus. Fed.
120 B2 **Stepnoye** *Saratovskaya Oblast'* Rus. Fed.
129 F1 **Stepnoye** *Stavropol'skiy Kray* Rus. Fed.
121 N1 **Stepnyak** Kazakh.
196 I6 **Stepojevac** Serbia
78 □2 **Steps Point** American Samoa
139 S5 **Stepurino** Rus. Fed.
175 K3 **Sterdyń-Osada** Pol.
198 E4 **Sterea Ellada** *admin. reg.* Greece
215 N4 **Sterkfontein Dam** *resr* S. Africa
215 L6 **Sterkspruit** S. Africa
215 K7 **Sterkstroom** S. Africa
175 J1 **Sterławki-Wielkie** Pol.
223 I1 **Sterlet Lake** *N.W.T.* Can.
120 F1 **Sterlibashevo** Rus. Fed.
214 F7 **Sterling** S. Africa
236 D5 **Sterling** *CO* U.S.A.
235 L1 **Sterling** *CT* U.S.A.
226 E8 **Sterling** *IL* U.S.A.
236 F6 **Sterling** *KS* U.S.A.
227 J5 **Sterling** *MI* U.S.A.
236 E2 **Sterling** *ND* U.S.A.
241 U2 **Sterling** *UT* U.S.A.
237 E10 **Sterling City** *TX* U.S.A.
227 K7 **Sterling Heights** *MI* U.S.A.
120 F1 **Sterlitamak** Rus. Fed.
191 P5 **Sterna** Croatia
198 D5 **Sterna** Greece
170 E3 **Sternberg** Ger.
176 G2 **Šternberk** Czech Rep.
168 I1 **Sterup** Ger.
161 F10 **Stes Maries, Golfe des** *b.* France
161 E10 **Stes-Maries-de-la-Mer** France
174 E3 **Stęszew** Pol.
176 D1 **Štětí** Czech Rep.
137 L4 **Stetsivka** Ukr.
137 N2 **Stets'kivka** Ukr.
172 G5 **Stetten am kalten Markt** Ger.
Stettin Pol. *see* **Szczecin**
Stettiner Haff *b.* Ger. *see* **Oderhaff**
238 H1 **Stettler** *Alta* Can.
232 E8 **Steubenville** *OH* U.S.A.
179 J6 **Steuerberg** Austria
171 F7 **Steutz** Ger.
151 L4 **Stevenage** *Hertfordshire, England* U.K.
80 G7 **Stevens, Mount** *South I.* N.Z.
238 D4 **Stevenson** *WA* U.S.A.
82 E2 **Stevenson Creek** *watercourse* *S.A.* Austr.
223 L4 **Stevenson Lake** *Man.* Can.
226 E5 **Stevens Point** *WI* U.S.A.
146 G11 **Stevenston** *North Ayrshire, Scotland* U.K.
220 D3 **Stevens Village** *AK* U.S.A.
234 C7 **Stevensville** *MD* U.S.A.
226 H7 **Stevensville** *MI* U.S.A.
227 R8 **Stevensville** *PA* U.S.A.
262 O1 **Steventon Island** Antarctica
142 I6 **Stevns Klint** *cliff* Denmark
85 I3 **Stewart** *r.* *Qld* Austr.
222 D4 **Stewart** *B.C.* Can.
222 B2 **Stewart** *r.* *Y.T.* Can.
240 U8 **Stewart** *NV* U.S.A.
84 E1 **Stewart, Cape** *N.T.* Austr.
259 C9 **Stewart, Isla** *i.* Chile
222 B2 **Stewart Crossing** *Y.T.* Can.
81 B14 **Stewart Island** N.Z.
81 B14 **Stewart Island** *nature res.* *Stewart I.* N.Z.
78 □6 **Stewart Islands** Solomon Is
221 J3 **Stewart Lake** *Nunavut* Can.
146 G11 **Stewarton** *East Ayrshire, Scotland* U.K.
240 I3 **Stewarts Point** *CA* U.S.A.
147 I3 **Stewartstown** *Northern Ireland* U.K.
234 B5 **Stewartstown** *PA* U.S.A.
246 □ **Stewart Town** Jamaica
223 J5 **Stewart Valley** *Sask.* Can.
226 B6 **Stewartville** *MN* U.S.A.
225 I4 **Stewiacke** *N.S.* Can.
168 H5 **Steyerberg** Ger.
151 L6 **Steyning** *West Sussex, England* U.K.
215 L3 **Steynrus** S. Africa
215 J7 **Steynsburg** S. Africa
179 J3 **Steyr** Austria
179 J4 **Steyr** *r.* Austria
179 J3 **Steyregg** Austria
214 I9 **Steytlerville** S. Africa
175 J4 **Stężyca** *Lubelskie* Pol.
174 F1 **Stężyca** *Pomorskie* Pol.
191 L8 **Stia** Italy
177 H3 **Štiavnické vrchy** *mts* Slovakia
177 H3 **Štiavnické vrchy** *park* Slovakia
177 H2 **Štiavnik** Slovakia
150 D6 **Stibb Cross** *Devon, England* U.K.
149 M2 **Stichill** *Scottish Borders, Scotland* U.K.
149 R7 **Stickney** *Lincolnshire, England* U.K.
169 K7 **Stiege** Ger.
164 I2 **Stiens** Neth.
191 L6 **Stienta** Italy
Stif Alg. *see* **Sétif**
237 H8 **Stigler** *OK* U.S.A.
193 Q7 **Stigliano** Italy
195 K7 **Stignano** Italy
143 M3 **Stigtomta** Sweden
222 C3 **Stikine** *r.* *B.C.* Can.
222 D3 **Stikine Plateau** *B.C.* Can.
222 C3 **Stikine Ranges** *mts* *B.C.* Can.
142 G2 **Stikkvasskollen** *hill* Norway
214 F10 **Stilbaai** S. Africa
214 F10 **Stilbaai** *b.* S. Africa
226 F5 **Stiles** *WI* U.S.A.
215 K2 **Stilfontein** S. Africa
Stilís Greece *see* **Stylida**
146 B8 **Stilligarry** *Western Isles, Scotland* U.K.
149 O5 **Stillington** *North Yorkshire, England* U.K.
234 C6 **Still Pond** *MD* U.S.A.
226 B4 **Stillwater** *MN* U.S.A.
237 G7 **Stillwater** *OK* U.S.A.
238 J4 **Stillwater** *r.* *MT* U.S.A.
240 N2 **Stillwater National Wildlife Refuge** *nature res.* *NV* U.S.A.
240 N2 **Stillwater Range** *mts* *NV* U.S.A.
195 K7 **Stilo** Italy
195 L7 **Stilo, Punta** *pt* Italy
188 F4 **Štilt** *mt.* Bos.-Herz.
151 L3 **Stilton** *Cambridgeshire, England* U.K.
237 H8 **Stilwell** *OK* U.S.A.
196 J8 **Štimlje** *Kosovo* Serbia
173 I3 **Stimpfach** Ger.
263 E2 **Stinear, Mount** Antarctica
197 Q3 **Stînga Nistrului** *reg.* Moldova
237 E8 **Stinnett** *TX* U.S.A.
192 A6 **Stintino** *Sardegna* Italy
193 O7 **Stio** Italy
197 K9 **Štip** Macedonia
188 E3 **Stipanov Grič** *mt.* Croatia
157 M5 **Stiring-Wendel** France
84 D6 **Stirling** *N.T.* Austr.
227 Q5 **Stirling** *Ont.* Can.
146 I10 **Stirling** *Stirling, Scotland* U.K.
146 H10 **Stirling** *admin. div.* *Scotland* U.K.
235 G3 **Stirling** *NJ* U.S.A.
87 D11 **Stirling, Mount** *hill* *W.A.* Austr.
84 B4 **Stirling Creek** *r.* *N.T.* Austr.
82 F5 **Stirling North** *S.A.* Austr.
87 D13 **Stirling Range** *mts* *W.A.* Austr.
87 D13 **Stirling Range National Park** *W.A.* Austr.
190 I6 **Stirone** *r.* Italy
232 C11 **Stirrat** *WV* U.S.A.
150 B7 **Stithians** *Cornwall, England* U.K.
177 J3 **Štítnik** Slovakia
227 S4 **Stittsville** *Ont.* Can.
176 F2 **Štíty** Czech Rep.
191 Q6 **Štivan** Croatia
191 L4 **Stizzon** *r.* Italy
140 Q1 **Stjernøya** *i.* Norway
140 K5 **Stjørdalshalsen** Norway
146 G9 **Stob Choire Claurigh** *mt.* *Scotland* U.K.
146 G9 **Stob Ghabhar** *mt.* *Scotland* U.K.
175 J6 **Stobnica** *r.* Pol.
174 F5 **Stobrawa** *r.* Pol.
176 C1 **Stochov** Czech Rep.
151 M4 **Stock** *Essex, England* U.K.
157 M6 **Stock, Étang du** *l.* France
172 G6 **Stockach** Ger.
151 J5 **Stockbridge** *Hampshire, England* U.K.
227 J7 **Stockbridge** *MI* U.S.A.
168 K3 **Stockelsdorf** Ger.
179 I6 **Stockenboi** Austria
179 N3 **Stockerau** Austria
234 E3 **Stockertown** *PA* U.S.A.
171 D10 **Stockheim** Ger.
143 O2 **Stockholm** Sweden
143 N2 **Stockholm** *county* Sweden
233 □Q1 **Stockholm** *ME* U.S.A.
235 F2 **Stockholm** *NJ* U.S.A.
190 D2 **Stockhorn** *mt.* Switz.
83 K6 **Stockinbingal** *N.S.W.* Austr.
179 M6 **Stocking** Austria
149 M7 **Stockport** *Greater Manchester, England* U.K.
149 N7 **Stocksbridge** *South Yorkshire, England* U.K.
168 H5 **Stöckse** Ger.
149 N4 **Stocksfield** *Northumberland, England* U.K.
149 M5 **Stocks Reservoir** *England* U.K.
264 G6 **Stocks Seamount** *sea feature* S. Atlantic Ocean
172 G2 **Stockstadt am Main** Ger.
172 E2 **Stockstadt am Rhein** Ger.
240 K4 **Stockton** *CA* U.S.A.
226 D7 **Stockton** *IL* U.S.A.
236 F6 **Stockton** *KS* U.S.A.
237 I7 **Stockton** *MO* U.S.A.
234 F4 **Stockton** *NJ* U.S.A.
241 T1 **Stockton** *UT* U.S.A.
149 L7 **Stockton Heath** *Warrington, England* U.K.
226 D3 **Stockton Island** *WI* U.S.A.
237 I7 **Stockton Lake** *MO* U.S.A.
149 O4 **Stockton-on-Tees** *Stockton-on-Tees, England* U.K.
149 O4 **Stockton-on-Tees** *admin. div.* *England* U.K.
237 D10 **Stockton Plateau** *TX* U.S.A.
233 □Q4 **Stockton Springs** *ME* U.S.A.
236 E5 **Stockville** *NE* U.S.A.
175 J3 **Stoczek** Pol.
175 J4 **Stoczek Łukowski** Pol.
176 C2 **Stod** Czech Rep.
141 N5 **Stöde** Sweden
139 P7 **Stodolishche** Rus. Fed.
97 G8 **Stœng Trêng** Cambodia
146 F6 **Stoer** *Highland, Scotland* U.K.
146 F6 **Stoer, Point of** *Scotland* U.K.
215 N1 **Stoffberg** S. Africa
196 I9 **Stogovo Planina** *mts* Macedonia
150 F5 **Stogursey** *Somerset, England* U.K.
179 M8 **Stojdraga** Croatia
179 M7 **Stojnci** Slovenia
151 K3 **Stoke Albany** *Northamptonshire, England* U.K.
151 O3 **Stoke Ash** *Suffolk, England* U.K.
151 N4 **Stoke-by-Nayland** *Suffolk, England* U.K.
151 O2 **Stoke Holy Cross** *Norfolk, England* U.K.
151 K4 **Stoke Mandeville** *Buckinghamshire, England* U.K.
151 K4 **Stokenchurch** *Buckinghamshire, England* U.K.
150 E7 **Stokenham** *Devon, England* U.K.
149 M7 **Stoke-on-Trent** *Stoke-on-Trent, England* U.K.
149 M7 **Stoke-on-Trent** *admin. div.* *England* U.K.
151 K4 **Stoke Poges** *Buckinghamshire, England* U.K.
150 H3 **Stoke Prior** *Worcestershire, England* U.K.
81 I8 **Stokes, Mount** *South I.* N.Z.
150 G3 **Stokesay** *Shropshire, England* U.K.
87 F12 **Stokes Inlet** *W.A.* Austr.
149 O5 **Stokesley** *North Yorkshire, England* U.K.
83 I9 **Stokes Point** *Tas.* Austr.
84 C4 **Stokes Range** *hills* *N.T.* Austr.
150 F6 **Stoke St Mary** *Somerset, England* U.K.
150 G6 **Stoke sub Hamdon** *Somerset, England* U.K.
81 I8 **Stokes Valley** *North I.* N.Z.
136 E2 **Stokhid** *r.* Ukr.
168 L1 **Stokkemarke** Denmark
140 □C2 **Stokkseyri** Iceland
140 L3 **Stokkvågen** Norway
140 M2 **Stokmarknes** Norway
176 E2 **Štoky** Czech Rep.
197 K6 **Stol** *mt.* Serbia
179 H7 **Stol** *mt.* Slovenia
188 F4 **Stolac** Bos.-Herz.
169 K7 **Stolberg (Harz) Kurort** Ger.
169 B9 **Stolberg (Rheinland)** Ger.
121 U2 **Stolboukha** *Vostochnyy Kazakhstan* Kazakh.
121 U3 **Stolboukha** *Vostochnyy Kazakhstan* Kazakh.
130 G2 **Stolbovoy** *Novaya Zemlya* Rus. Fed.
131 O2 **Stolbovoy, Ostrov** *i.* *Novosibirskiye O-va* Rus. Fed.
Stolbtsy Belarus *see* **Stowbtsy**
174 F2 **Stołczno** Pol.
177 J3 **Stolica** *mt.* Slovakia
188 G3 **Stolice** *hill* Bos.-Herz.
136 F2 **Stolin** Belarus
171 G9 **Stollberg** Ger.
168 F3 **Stollhamm (Butjadingen)** Ger.
174 G2 **Stolno** Pol.
Stolp Pol. *see* **Słupsk**
170 J5 **Stolpe** *Brandenburg* Ger.
168 J2 **Stolpe** *Schleswig-Holstein* Ger.
171 J8 **Stolpen** Ger.
141 I6 **Stolsheimen** *park* Norway
141 J6 **Stolsvatnet** *l.* Norway
216 □2c **Stoltenhoff Island** *Tristan da Cunha* S. Atlantic Ocean
164 G5 **Stolwijk** Neth.
169 H5 **Stolzenau** Ger.
214 B8 **Stompneusbaai** S. Africa
193 Q1 **Stončica, Rt** *pt* Croatia
150 H4 **Stone** *Gloucestershire, England* U.K.
151 M5 **Stone** *Kent, England* U.K.
150 H2 **Stone** *Staffordshire, England* U.K.
232 E7 **Stoneboro** *PA* U.S.A.
140 □ **Stonebreen** *glacier* Svalbard
224 E4 **Stonecliffe** *Ont.* Can.
Stonecutters' Island *pen.* *H.K.* China *see* **Ngong Shuen Chau**
236 D5 **Stoneham** *CO* U.S.A.
234 F6 **Stone Harbor** *NJ* U.S.A.
146 L9 **Stonehaven** *Aberdeenshire, Scotland* U.K.
85 I8 **Stonehenge** *Qld* Austr.
151 I5 **Stonehenge** *tourist site* *England* U.K.
150 H4 **Stonehouse** *Gloucestershire, England* U.K.
146 I11 **Stonehouse** *South Lanarkshire, Scotland* U.K.
226 C4 **Stone Lake** *WI* U.S.A.
222 E3 **Stone Mountain Provincial Park** *B.C.* Can.
233 K7 **Stone Ridge** *NY* U.S.A.
232 F12 **Stoneville** *NC* U.S.A.
223 L5 **Stonewall** *Man.* Can.
237 G8 **Stonewall** *OK* U.S.A.
227 O6 **Stoney Creek** *Ont.* Can.
234 D4 **Stoney Creek Mills** *PA* U.S.A.
147 H7 **Stoneyford** Ireland
146 G13 **Stoneykirk** *Dumfries and Galloway, Scotland* U.K.
227 L7 **Stoney Point** *Ont.* Can.
215 M7 **Stoneyride** S. Africa
142 B2 **Stong** Norway
144 J1 **Stongfjorden** Norway
235 L2 **Stonington** *CT* U.S.A.
233 □Q4 **Stonington** *ME* U.S.A.
211 C5 **Stony Athi** Kenya
146 □M3 **Stonybreck** *Shetland, Scotland* U.K.
235 I3 **Stony Brook** *NY* U.S.A.
234 B5 **Stony Brook** *PA* U.S.A.
235 J2 **Stony Creek** *CT* U.S.A.
232 H12 **Stony Creek** *VA* U.S.A.
240 J2 **Stony Gorge Reservoir** *CA* U.S.A.
246 □ **Stony Hill** Jamaica
216 □2c **Stonyhill Point** *Tristan da Cunha* S. Atlantic Ocean
223 L3 **Stony Lake** *Man.* Can.
222 H4 **Stony Plain** *Alta* Can.
233 I5 **Stony Point** *NY* U.S.A.
223 J3 **Stony Rapids** *Sask.* Can.
151 K3 **Stony Stratford** *Milton Keynes, England* U.K.
179 O4 **Stoob** Austria
224 D2 **Stooping** *r.* *Ont.* Can.
179 L8 **Stopiče** Slovenia
175 J1 **Stopki** Pol.
175 I5 **Stopnica** Pol.
168 H3 **Stör** *r.* Ger.
142 E5 **Stora** *r.* Denmark
143 L2 **Storå** Sweden
143 M5 **Stora Alvaret** *pen.* Sweden
143 M4 **Stora Askö** *i.* Sweden
142 I2 **Stora Bör** *l.* Sweden
142 I2 **Stora Gla** *l.* Sweden
142 I4 **Stora Horredssjön** *l.* Sweden
142 H3 **Stora Le** *l.* Sweden
140 O3 **Stora Lulevatten** *l.* Sweden
143 P2 **Stora Nassa naturreservat** *nature res.* Sweden
140 N3 **Stora Sjöfallets nationalpark** *nat. park* Sweden
140 O4 **Storavan** *l.* Sweden
141 L6 **Storbäcken** Sweden
141 K6 **Storbekkfjellet** *mt.* Norway
141 L6 **Storbo** Sweden
142 B2 **Stord** *i.* Norway
140 I5 **Stordal** Norway
141 K6 **Store** *mt.* Norway
179 L7 **Štore** Slovenia
142 G6 **Store Bælt** *sea chan.* Denmark
142 B1 **Storebø** Norway
170 F1 **Store Damme** Denmark
142 I6 **Store Heddinge** Denmark
141 J6 **Store Jukleeggi** *mt.* Norway
221 Q2 **Store Koldewey** *i.* Greenland
140 P2 **Store Lenangstind** *mt.* Norway
140 Q1 **Storelv** Norway
140 T1 **Store Molvik** Norway
143 J4 **Store Moss nationalpark** *nat. park* Sweden
140 K5 **Støren** Norway
142 D2 **Store Nup** *mt.* Norway
168 J1 **Store Rise** Denmark
142 B1 **Store Sotra** *i.* Norway
142 D2 **Store Urevatnet** *l.* Norway
143 N1 **Storfjärden** *l.* Sweden
140 S1 **Storfjordbotn** Norway
140 □ **Storfjorden** *sea chan.* Svalbard
143 K2 **Storfors** Sweden
140 M3 **Storforshei** Norway
179 I8 **Štorje** Slovenia
140 M4 **Storjola** Sweden
140 M3 **Storjord** Norway
140 N4 **Storjuktan** *l.* Sweden
142 D3 **Storkarshei** *hill* Norway
221 H2 **Storkerson Peninsula** *Nunavut* Can.
171 I6 **Storkow** Ger.
168 J3 **Stormarn** *reg.* Ger.
83 K10 **Storm Bay** *Tas.* Austr.
215 K7 **Stormberg** S. Africa
215 K6 **Stormberg** *mt.* S. Africa
215 K6 **Stormberg** *r.* S. Africa
215 K7 **Stormberge** *mts* S. Africa
236 H4 **Storm Lake** *IA* U.S.A.
214 H9 **Stormsrivier** S. Africa
193 P5 **Stornara** Italy
193 P5 **Stornarella** Italy
146 D6 **Stornoway** *Western Isles, Scotland* U.K.
191 J4 **Storo** Italy
143 O2 **Storö-Bockö-Lökaöns naturreservat** *nature res.* Sweden
140 □ **Storøya** *i.* Svalbard
139 P1 **Storozhenskiy, Mys** *pt* Rus. Fed.
134 K3 **Storozhevsk** Rus. Fed.
139 P1 **Storozhno** Rus. Fed.
136 E5 **Storozhynets'** Ukr.
151 L6 **Storrington** *West Sussex, England* U.K.
142 E2 **Stor-Roan** *mt.* Norway
233 M7 **Storrs** *CT* U.S.A.
140 N4 **Storseleby** Sweden
142 H1 **Storsjøen** *l.* Norway
143 M1 **Storsjön** *l.* Sweden
140 M5 **Storsjön** *l.* Sweden
143 N2 **Storsjön** *l.* Sweden
140 J5 **Storskarhø** *mt.* Norway
140 M4 **Storskog** Sweden
140 P2 **Storslett** Norway
142 G7 **Storstrøm** *county* Denmark
142 H7 **Storstrømmen** *sea chan.* Denmark
140 P4 **Storsund** Sweden
151 M4 **Stort** *r.* *England* U.K.
164 H2 **Stortemelk** *sea chan.* Neth.
140 N4 **Storuman** Sweden
140 N4 **Storuman** *l.* Sweden
140 L5 **Storvigelen** *mt.* Norway
143 M1 **Storvik** Sweden
140 N4 **Storvindeln** *l.* Sweden
142 G4 **Storvorde** Denmark
143 N2 **Storvreta** Sweden
238 K4 **Story** *WY* U.S.A.
196 I2 **Štós** Slovakia
259 B8 **Stosch, Isla** *i.* Chile
171 E8 **Stößen** Ger.
179 M3 **Stössing** Austria
151 L3 **Stotfold** *Bedfordshire, England* U.K.
173 J6 **Stötten am Auerberg** Ger.
171 D8 **Stotternheim** Ger.
234 C4 **Stouchsburg** *PA* U.S.A.
223 K5 **Stoughton** *Sask.* Can.
165 I8 **Stoumont** Belgium
97 G8 **Stoŭng, Stœng** *r.* Cambodia
150 I6 **Stour** *r.* *Dorset, England* U.K.
151 O4 **Stour** *r.* *Essex/Suffolk, England* U.K.
151 O5 **Stour** *r.* *Kent, England* U.K.
151 I3 **Stour** *r.* *Oxfordshire/Warwickshire, England* U.K.
150 H3 **Stourbridge** *West Midlands, England* U.K.
150 H3 **Stourport-on-Severn** *Worcestershire, England* U.K.
223 M4 **Stout Lake** *Ont.* Can.
146 K11 **Stow** *Scottish Borders, Scotland* U.K.
138 J8 **Stowbtsy** Belarus
234 D4 **Stowe** *PA* U.S.A.
174 F1 **Stowięcino** Pol.
151 N3 **Stowmarket** *Suffolk, England* U.K.
151 I4 **Stow-on-the-Wold** *Gloucestershire, England* U.K.
136 D3 **Stoyaniv** Ukr.
100 G2 **Stoyba** Rus. Fed.
175 K1 **Stożne** Pol.
191 M5 **Stra** Italy
171 G7 **Straach** Ger.
215 K1 **Straatsdrif** S. Africa
147 H3 **Strabane** *Northern Ireland* U.K.
175 L3 **Strabla** Pol.
146 K8 **Strachan** *Aberdeenshire, Scotland* U.K.
146 F10 **Strachur** *Argyll and Bute, Scotland* U.K.
175 M1 **Stračiūnai** Lith.
168 E4 **Strackholt (Großefehn)** Ger.
174 E2 **Strączno** Pol.
147 H6 **Stradbally** Ireland
151 O3 **Stradbroke** *Suffolk, England* U.K.
190 G5 **Stradella** Italy
179 M6 **Straden** Austria
151 N3 **Stradishall** *Suffolk, England* U.K.
147 H5 **Stradone** Ireland
151 M2 **Stradsett** *Norfolk, England* U.K.
169 B8 **Straelen** Ger.
83 J10 **Strahan** *Tas.* Austr.
241 U4 **Straight Cliffs** *ridge* *UT* U.S.A.
165 H9 **Straimont** Belgium
176 C2 **Strakonice** Czech Rep.
197 O8 **Straldzha** Bulg.
179 M5 **Strallegg** Austria
146 I9 **Straloch** *Perth and Kinross, Scotland* U.K.
170 H2 **Stralsund** Ger.
190 D5 **Strambino** Italy
165 I6 **Stramproy** Neth.
214 C10 **Strand** S. Africa
140 I5 **Stranda** Norway
142 D1 **Strandavatnet** *l.* Norway
168 J2 **Strande** Ger.
147 E4 **Strandhill** Ireland
231 H12 **Strangers Cay** *i.* Bahamas
147 K4 **Strangford** *Northern Ireland* U.K.
147 K4 **Strangford Lough** *inlet* *Northern Ireland* U.K.
143 N2 **Strängnäs** Sweden
193 K4 **Strangolagalli** Italy
84 D3 **Strangways** *r.* *N.T.* Austr.
84 E7 **Strangways Range** *mts* *N.T.* Austr.
177 G3 **Strání** Czech Rep.
147 J2 **Stranocum** *Northern Ireland* U.K.
147 G3 **Stranorlar** Ireland
146 F13 **Stranraer** *Dumfries and Galloway, Scotland* U.K.
194 D8 **Strasatti** *Sicilia* Italy
157 O6 **Strasbourg** France
170 I4 **Strasburg** Ger.
232 D8 **Strasburg** *OH* U.S.A.
234 C5 **Strasburg** *PA* U.S.A.
232 G10 **Strasburg** *VA* U.S.A.
136 H6 **Strășeni** Moldova
Strasheny Moldova *see* **Strășeni**
173 P2 **Strašice** Czech Rep.
172 G5 **Straßberg** *Baden-Württemberg* Ger.
171 D7 **Straßberg** *Sachsen-Anhalt* Ger.
179 J6 **Straßburg** Austria
Strassburg France *see* **Strasbourg**
165 J9 **Strassen** Lux.
179 L5 **Straßengel** Austria
169 E9 **Straßenhaus** Ger.
179 O3 **Strasshof an der Norbahn** Austria
173 N4 **Straßkirchen** Ger.
178 H4 **Straßwalchen** Austria
151 J5 **Stratfield Mortimer** *West Berkshire, England* U.K.
224 D5 **Stratford** *Ont.* Can.
80 I6 **Stratford** *North I.* N.Z.
147 I7 **Stratford** Ireland
240 M5 **Stratford** *CA* U.S.A.
235 I2 **Stratford** *CT* U.S.A.
237 D7 **Stratford** *TX* U.S.A.
226 D5 **Stratford** *WI* U.S.A.
151 I3 **Stratford-upon-Avon** *Warwickshire, England* U.K.
82 G6 **Strathalbyn** *S.A.* Austr.
146 H11 **Strathaven** *South Lanarkshire, Scotland* U.K.
148 I2 **Strathblane** *Stirling, Scotland* U.K.
146 K8 **Strathbogie** *reg.* *Scotland* U.K.
146 G7 **Strathcarron** *val.* *Scotland* U.K.
263 G2 **Strathcona, Mount** Antarctica
222 E5 **Strathcona Provincial Park** *B.C.* Can.
146 G7 **Strathconon** *val.* *Scotland* U.K.
146 H8 **Strath Dearn** *val.* *Scotland* U.K.
146 J8 **Strathdon** *Aberdeenshire, Scotland* U.K.
146 H10 **Strath Earn** *val.* *Scotland* U.K.
146 H6 **Strath Fleet** *val.* *Scotland* U.K.
146 G8 **Strathglass** *val.* *Scotland* U.K.
83 K10 **Strathgordon** *Tas.* Austr.
146 I6 **Strath Halladale** *val.* *Scotland* U.K.
222 H5 **Strathmore** *Alta* Can.
146 G5 **Strathmore** *r.* *Scotland* U.K.
240 M5 **Strathmore** *CA* U.S.A.
222 F4 **Strathnaver** *B.C.* Can.
146 H6 **Strathnaver** *val.* *Scotland* U.K.
146 I6 **Strath of Kildonan** *val.* *Scotland* U.K.
146 G7 **Strathpeffer** *Highland, Scotland* U.K.
227 M7 **Strathroy** *Ont.* Can.
146 I8 **Strathspey** *val.* *Scotland* U.K.
146 I9 **Strath Tay** *val.* *Scotland* U.K.
146 I5 **Strathy** *Highland, Scotland* U.K.
146 H5 **Strathy Point** *Scotland* U.K.
146 H10 **Strathyre** *Stirling, Scotland* U.K.
198 E2 **Stratoni** Greece
199 J5 **Stratonıkeıa** *tourist site* Turkey
198 C4 **Stratos** Greece
150 C6 **Stratton** *Cornwall, England* U.K.
233 □O3 **Stratton** *ME* U.S.A.
233 M5 **Stratton Mountain** *VT* U.S.A.
151 I4 **Stratton St Margaret** *Swindon, England* U.K.
173 N4 **Straubing** Ger.
140 M2 **Straume** Norway
140 M3 **Straumen** *Nordland* Norway
140 M3 **Straumen** *Nordland* Norway
140 □B1 **Straumnes** *pt* Iceland
171 J7 **Straupitz** Ger.
170 I5 **Strausberg** Ger.
169 K8 **Straußfurt** Ger.
234 C3 **Strausstown** *PA* U.S.A.
241 U7 **Strawberry** *AZ* U.S.A.
238 E4 **Strawberry Mountain** *OR* U.S.A.
241 U1 **Strawberry Reservoir** *UT* U.S.A.
175 I5 **Strawczyn** Pol.
226 F9 **Strawn** *IL* U.S.A.
197 K8 **Straža** *mt.* Macedonia
197 N7 **Strazhitsa** Bulg.
176 D2 **Stráž nad Nežárkou** Czech Rep.
171 L9 **Stráž nad Nisou** Czech Rep.
179 I2 **Strážný** Czech Rep.
176 C2 **Strážov** Czech Rep.
177 H3 **Strážov** *mt.* Slovakia
171 K9 **Stráž pod Ralskem** Czech Rep.
177 K3 **Strážske** Slovakia
82 E5 **Streaky Bay** *S.A.* Austr.
82 E5 **Streaky Bay** *b.* *S.A.* Austr.
147 G6 **Streamstown** Ireland
151 J4 **Streatley** *West Berkshire, England* U.K.
226 F8 **Streator** *IL* U.S.A.
176 D2 **Středočeský kraj** *admin. reg.* Czech Rep.
168 F4 **Streek** Ger.
150 G5 **Street** *Somerset, England* U.K.
197 L6 **Strehaia** Romania
171 H8 **Strehla** Ger.
197 L5 **Strei** *r.* Romania
87 G11 **Streich Mound** *hill* *W.A.* Austr.
177 H4 **Strekov** Slovakia
176 C2 **Střela** *r.* Czech Rep.
197 M8 **Strelcha** Bulg.
137 R1 **Strelets** Rus. Fed.
137 P3 **Streletskoye** Rus. Fed.
176 F2 **Střelice** Czech Rep.
137 R2 **Strelitsa** Rus. Fed.
131 Q3 **Strelka** Rus. Fed.
139 R1 **Strelkovo** Rus. Fed.
86 E6 **Strelley** *W.A.* Austr.
86 E6 **Strelley** *r.* *W.A.* Austr.
86 E6 **Strelley Aboriginal Reserve** *W.A.* Austr.
134 G2 **Strel'na** *r.* Rus. Fed.
179 N5 **Strem** Austria
191 J3 **Strembo** Italy
171 F5 **Stremme** *r.* Ger.
136 H3 **Stremyhorod** Ukr.
138 I4 **Strenči** Latvia
179 K3 **Strengberg** Austria
178 B5 **Strengen** Austria
149 O5 **Strensall** *York, England* U.K.
175 M5 **Streptiv** Ukr.
190 F4 **Stresa** Italy
149 M7 **Stretford** *Greater Manchester, England* U.K.
151 M3 **Stretham** *Cambridgeshire, England* U.K.
151 I2 **Stretton** *Staffordshire, England* U.K.
169 J10 **Streu** *r.* Ger.
169 K10 **Streufdorf** Ger.
144 D1 **Streymoy** *i.* Faroe Is
130 I3 **Strezhevoy** Rus. Fed.
176 B2 **Stříbro** Czech Rep.
146 L7 **Strichen** *Aberdeenshire, Scotland* U.K.
91 J8 **Strickland** *r.* P.N.G.
191 L3 **Strigno** Italy
179 N6 **Štrigova** Croatia
164 G5 **Strijen** Neth.
137 P3 **Strilechna** Ukr.
176 E2 **Strimilov** Czech Rep.
198 E1 **Strimoniko** Greece
Strimonikón Greece *see* Strimoniko
148 G2 **Striven, Loch** *inlet* *Scotland* U.K.
188 G3 **Strizivojna** Croatia
179 M8 **Strmec** Croatia
169 K7 **Ströbeck** Ger.
179 H4 **Strobl** Austria
259 E6 **Stroeder** Arg.
198 C5 **Strofades** *i.* Greece
173 L5 **Strogen** *r.* Ger.
137 M7 **Strohanivka** Ukr.
168 G5 **Ströhen** Ger.
136 H6 **Stroiești** Moldova
137 P3 **Stroitel'** Rus. Fed.
147 F5 **Strokestown** Ireland
170 I4 **Strom** *r.* Ger.
146 J5 **Stroma, Island of** *Scotland* U.K.
143 N1 **Strömaren** *l.* Sweden
141 N6 **Strömbacka** Sweden
172 D2 **Stromberg** Ger.
172 F3 **Stromberg-Heuchelberg, Naturpark** *nature res.* Ger.
195 I6 **Stromboli, Isola** *i.* *Isole Lipari* Italy
195 I6 **Strombolicchio, Isola** *i.* *Isole Lipari* Italy
146 E8 **Stromeferry** *Highland, Scotland* U.K.
259 □ **Stromness** S. Georgia
146 J5 **Stromness** *Orkney, Scotland* U.K.
141 N6 **Strömsbruk** Sweden
236 G5 **Stromsburg** *NE* U.S.A.
140 O2 **Strømsmoen** Norway
142 H3 **Strömstad** Sweden
140 M5 **Strömsund** Sweden
193 J3 **Stroncone** Italy
190 I5 **Strone** *r.* Italy
146 G11 **Strone** *Argyll and Bute, Scotland* U.K.
237 I9 **Strong** *AR* U.S.A.
195 M5 **Strongoli** Italy
232 D7 **Strongsville** *OH* U.S.A.
174 E5 **Stronie Śląskie** Pol.
146 K4 **Stronsay** *i.* *Scotland* U.K.
146 K4 **Stronsay Firth** *sea chan.* *Scotland* U.K.
179 N2 **Stronsdorf** Austria
146 E9 **Strontian** *Highland, Scotland* U.K.
177 K2 **Stropkov** Slovakia
176 D3 **Stropnice** *r.* Czech Rep.
190 E5 **Stroppiana** Italy
190 C6 **Stroppo** Italy
150 H4 **Stroud** *Gloucestershire, England* U.K.
83 M5 **Stroud Road** *N.S.W.* Austr.
234 E3 **Stroudsburg** *PA* U.S.A.
Stroyentsy Moldova *see* **Stroiești**
175 H6 **Stróża** Pol.
168 E4 **Strücklingen (Saterland)** Ger.
142 E5 **Struer** Denmark
196 I9 **Struga** Macedonia
174 F3 **Struga** *r.* Pol.
138 M3 **Strugi-Krasnyye** Rus. Fed.
139 P8 **Strugovskaya Buda** Rus. Fed.
214 E10 **Struis Bay** S. Africa
214 E10 **Struis Bay** *b.* S. Africa
147 H3 **Strule** *r.* *Northern Ireland* U.K.
173 J2 **Strullendorf** Ger.
197 L9 **Struma** *r.* Bulg.
150 B3 **Strumble Head** *Wales* U.K.
198 E1 **Strumeshnitsa** *r.* Bulg.
197 K9 **Strumica** Macedonia
197 K9 **Strumica** *r.* Macedonia
174 G6 **Strumień** Pol.
177 L3 **Strumkivka** Ukr.
139 V5 **Strunino** Rus. Fed.
179 J1 **Strunkovice nad Blanicí** Czech Rep.
169 J8 **Struth** Ger.
232 E7 **Struthers** *OH* U.S.A.
197 M8 **Stryama** *r.* Bulg.
214 H5 **Strydenburg** S. Africa
215 J2 **Strydpoort** S. Africa
175 H4 **Stryków** Pol.
198 E2 **Strymonas** *r.* Greece
141 I6 **Stryn** Norway
168 K1 **Strynø** *i.* Denmark
136 E5 **Strypa** *r.* Ukr.
136 J6 **Stryukove** Ukr.
136 C4 **Stryy** Ukr.
136 D4 **Stryy** *r.* Ukr.
136 H4 **Stryzhavka** Ukr.
174 F3 **Strzałkowo** Pol.
174 G5 **Strzebień** Pol.
175 I3 **Strzegocin** Pol.
174 E5 **Strzegom** Pol.
174 E4 **Strzegomka** *r.* Pol.
175 I3 **Strzegowo** Pol.
175 H3 **Strzelce** Pol.
174 D3 **Strzelce Krajeńskie** Pol.
174 G5 **Strzelce Opolskie** Pol.
175 H4 **Strzelce Wielkie** Pol.
84 D6 **Strzelecki, Mount** *hill* *N.T.* Austr.
82 G3 **Strzelecki Creek** *watercourse* *S.A.* Austr.
82 G3 **Strzelecki Regional Reserve** *nature res.* *S.A.* Austr.
174 F5 **Strzeleczki** Pol.
174 F5 **Strzelin** Pol.
174 G3 **Strzelno** Pol.
174 G1 **Strzepcz** Pol.
175 J6 **Strzyżów** Pol.
157 J8 **Sts-Geosmes** France
136 G1 **Stsvina** *r.* Belarus
85 M9 **Stuart** *r.* *Qld* Austr.
231 G12 **Stuart** *FL* U.S.A.
236 H5 **Stuart** *IA* U.S.A.
236 F4 **Stuart** *NE* U.S.A.
232 E12 **Stuart** *VA* U.S.A.
84 D7 **Stuart Bluff Range** *mts* *N.T.* Austr.
146 L7 **Stuartfield** *Aberdeenshire, Scotland* U.K.
222 E4 **Stuart Lake** *B.C.* Can.
81 B12 **Stuart Mountains** *South I.* N.Z.
82 E3 **Stuart Range** *hills* *S.A.* Austr.
232 F10 **Stuarts Draft** *VA* U.S.A.
178 D5 **Stubaier Alpen** *mts* Austria
178 D5 **Stubaital** *val.* Austria
179 K5 **Stubalpe** *mt.* Austria
168 H1 **Stubbæk** Denmark
170 F1 **Stubbekøbing** Denmark
168 G4 **Stubben** Ger.
170 I1 **Stubbenkammer** *hd* Ger.
86 □1 **Stubbings Point** Christmas I.
151 J6 **Stubbington** *Hampshire, England* U.K.
247 □3 **Stubbs** St Vincent
179 M5 **Stubenberg** Austria
196 J7 **Stubica** Serbia
196 I6 **Stubline** Serbia
175 K6 **Stubno** Pol.
Stuchka Latvia *see* **Aizkraukle**
174 D2 **Stuchowo** Pol.
Stučka Latvia *see* **Aizkraukle**
176 E2 **Studená** Czech Rep.
136 H5 **Studena** Ukr.
179 I2 **Studená Vltava** *r.* Czech Rep.
196 I7 **Studenica** *tourist site* Serbia
170 F5 **Stüdenitz** Ger.
177 H2 **Studénka** Czech Rep.
197 N9 **Studen Kladenets, Yazovir** *resr* Bulg.
137 Q1 **Studenoye** Rus. Fed.
136 G2 **Studenytsya** *r.* Ukr.
151 K4 **Studham** *Bedfordshire, England* U.K.
81 F11 **Studholme Junction** *South I.* N.Z.
176 G3 **Studienka** Slovakia
214 I9 **Studis** S. Africa
151 I6 **Studland** *Dorset, England* U.K.
151 I3 **Studley** *Warwickshire, England* U.K.
143 N3 **Studsvik** Sweden
134 B3 **Studsviken** Sweden
237 D11 **Study Butte** *TX* U.S.A.
174 F1 **Studzienice** Pol.
140 M5 **Stugun** Sweden
178 G5 **Stuhlfelden** Austria
172 E6 **Stühlingen** Ger.
136 J3 **Stuhna** *r.* Ukr.
168 G4 **Stuhr** Ger.
223 M4 **Stull Lake** *Man./Ont.* Can.
171 H6 **Stülpe** Ger.
197 N3 **Stulpicani** Romania
178 E5 **Stumm** Austria
223 L6 **Stump Lake** *ND* U.S.A.
Stung Treng Cambodia *see* **Stœng Trêng**
223 M4 **Stupart** *r.* *Man.* Can.
176 G3 **Stupava** Slovakia
139 V7 **Stupino** Rus. Fed.
193 Q1 **Stupišće, Rt** *pt* Croatia
175 I2 **Stupsk** Pol.
190 E5 **Stura** *r.* Italy
190 C5 **Stura di Ala** *r.* Italy
190 D6 **Stura di Demonte** *r.* Italy
161 K6 **Stura di Val Grande** *r.* Italy
190 C5 **Stura di Viù** *r.* Italy
263 K2 **Sturge Island** Antarctica
224 E4 **Sturgeon** *r.* *Ont.* Can.
223 J4 **Sturgeon** *r.* *Sask.* Can.
226 H4 **Sturgeon** *r.* *MI* U.S.A.
226 C1 **Sturgeon, Lake** *Ont.* Can.
223 L4 **Sturgeon Bay** *b.* *Man.* Can.
226 G5 **Sturgeon Bay** *WI* U.S.A.
226 J4 **Sturgeon Bay** *b.* *MI* U.S.A.
226 G5 **Sturgeon Bay Canal** *lake channel* *WI* U.S.A.
224 E4 **Sturgeon Falls** *Ont.* Can.
227 P5 **Sturgeon Lake** *Ont.* Can.
224 B3 **Sturgeon Lake** *Ont.* Can.
230 D7 **Sturgis** *KY* U.S.A.
226 I8 **Sturgis** *MI* U.S.A.
236 D3 **Sturgis** *SD* U.S.A.
190 G7 **Sturla** *r.* Italy
188 E3 **Šturlić** Bos.-Herz.
150 H6 **Sturminster Newton** *Dorset, England* U.K.
177 H4 **Štúrovo** Slovakia
151 O5 **Sturry** *Kent, England* U.K.
83 H3 **Sturt, Mount** *hill* *N.S.W.* Austr.
82 F6 **Sturt Bay** *S.A.* Austr.
86 J5 **Sturt Creek** *W.A.* Austr.
86 I5 **Sturt Creek** *watercourse* *W.A.* Austr.
226 G7 **Sturtevant** *WI* U.S.A.
83 H3 **Sturt National Park** *N.S.W.* Austr.
84 D4 **Sturt Plain** *N.T.* Austr.
82 H3 **Sturt Stony Desert** *Qld* Austr.
157 O5 **Sturzelbronn** France
215 L8 **Stutterheim** S. Africa
172 G4 **Stuttgart** Ger.
172 H3 **Stuttgart** *admin. reg.* Ger.
237 J8 **Stuttgart** *AR* U.S.A.
Stutthof Pol. *see* **Sztutowo**
169 K9 **Stützerbach** Ger.
136 G2 **Stvyha** *r.* Ukr.
140 □B1 **Stykkishólmur** Iceland
137 Q6 **Styla** Ukr.
198 D4 **Stylida** Greece
136 F1 **Styr** *r.* Belarus/Ukr.
Styria *land* Austria *see* **Steiermark**
257 G3 **Suaçuí Grande** *r.* Brazil
93 D8 **Suai** East Timor
95 J3 **Suai** *Sarawak* Malaysia
250 C3 **Suaita** Col.
203 H5 **Suakin** Sudan
124 D6 **Suakin Archipelago** *is* Sudan
203 H5 **Suakin Archipelago** *is* Sudan
209 D6 **Suana** Dem. Rep. Congo
183 L2 **Suances** Spain
109 M6 **Suao** Taiwan
242 E3 **Suaqui Grande** Mex.
203 H5 **Suara, Mount** Eritrea
261 G2 **Suardi** Arg.
250 B4 **Suárez** Col.
129 L1 **Suat** Kazakh.
251 E2 **Suata** Venez.
78 □6 **Suavanao** *Sta Isabel* Solomon Is
138 H6 **Subačius** Lith.
95 G8 **Subang** *Jawa* Indon.
117 M6 **Subankhata** *Assam* India
111 L13 **Subansiri** *r.* India
117 K9 **Subarnarekha** *r.* *W. Bengal* India
122 C4 **Sūbāshī** Iran
199 J1 **Subaşı** *İstanbul* Turkey
199 I4 **Subaşı** *İzmir* Turkey
193 J1 **Subasio, Monte** *mt.* Italy
138 I5 **Subate** Latvia
125 H2 **Subay** *reg.* Saudi Arabia
124 F4 **Subay, 'Irq** *des.* Saudi Arabia
126 I8 **Şubayḩah** Saudi Arabia
124 G9 **Şubayḩī** *reg.* Yemen
191 L8 **Subbiano** Italy
197 N4 **Subcetate** Romania
110 L7 **Subei** *Gansu* China
Subeita *tourist site* Israel *see* **Shivta**
179 H3 **Suben** Austria
193 K4 **Subiaco** Italy
95 H3 **Subi Besar** *i.* Indon.
95 H3 **Subi Kecil** *i.* Indon.
174 G1 **Subkowy** Pol.
237 E7 **Sublette** *KS* U.S.A.
196 H4 **Subotica** *Vojvodina* Serbia
203 I6 **Subucle** *mt.* Eritrea
211 B5 **Subugo** *mt.* Kenya
177 H2 **Sučany** Slovakia
162 H5 **Suc-au-May** *hill* France
234 F3 **Succasunna** *NJ* U.S.A.
240 N5 **Success, Lake** *CA* U.S.A.
190 I7 **Succiso, Alpi di** *mts* Italy
197 O3 **Suceava** Romania
197 N3 **Suceava** *r.* Romania
158 H7 **Sucé-sur-Erdre** France
175 H6 **Sucha Beskidzka** Pol.
175 H1 **Suchacz** Pol.
177 G3 **Suchá Loz** Czech Rep.
174 D2 **Suchań** Pol.
Suchan Rus. Fed. *see* **Partizansk**
100 H7 **Suchan** *r.* Rus. Fed.
176 E2 **Suchdol** Czech Rep.
176 D3 **Suchdol nad Lužnicí** Czech Rep.
175 I4 **Suchedniów** Pol.
167 J3 **Suchedniowsko-Oblęgorski Park Krajobrazowy** Pol.
190 A2 **Suchet, Mont** *mt.* Switz.
244 D2 **Suchil** Mex.
175 L2 **Suchowola** Pol.
175 K3 **Suchożebry** Pol.
247 □1 **Sucia, Bahía** *b.* Puerto Rico
187 D12 **Sucina** Spain
250 B3 **Sucio** *r.* Col.
197 M3 **Suciu de Sus** Romania
147 F6 **Suck** *r.* Ireland
227 N3 **Sucker Creek Landing** *Ont.* Can.
170 E4 **Suckow** Ger.
252 D4 **Sucre** Bol.
250 C2 **Sucre** *dept* Col.
251 F2 **Sucre** *state* Venez.
250 D3 **Sucuaro** Col.
250 B5 **Sucumbíos** *prov.* Ecuado
251 G6 **Sucunduri** *r.* Brazil
256 B4 **Sucuriú** *r.* Brazil
Suczawa Romania *see* Suceava
207 H6 **Sud** *prov.* Cameroon
78 □5 **Sud, Grand Récif du** *rf* New Caledonia
217 □3a **Sud, Pointe** *pt* *Njazidja* Comoros
217 □2b **Sud, Pointe du** *c.* *Mahé* Seychelles
217 □3b **Sud, Récif du** *rf* Mayotte
233 L3 **Sud, Rivière du** *r.* *Que.* C
139 U2 **Suda** Rus. Fed.
139 U2 **Suda** *r.* Rus. Fed.
137 N9 **Sudak** Ukr.
105 H4 **Sudama** Japan
203 F6 **Sudan** *country* Africa
134 H4 **Suday** Rus. Fed.
124 G3 **Sudayr** *reg.* Saudi Arabia
127 L8 **Sudayr, Sha'īb** *watercou* Iraq
139 U9 **Sudbishchi** Rus. Fed.
120 E1 **Sud'bodarovka** Rus. Fed
224 D4 **Sudbury** *Ont.* Can.
151 I2 **Sudbury** *Derbyshire, England* U.K.
151 N3 **Sudbury** *Suffolk, England*
210 A3 **Sudd** *swamp* Sudan
169 D6 **Suddendorf** Ger.
251 G3 **Suddie** Guyana
168 K4 **Sude** *r.* Ger.
168 G2 **Süden** Ger.
168 I1 **Süderbrarup** Ger.
168 J5 **Suderburg** Ger.
168 J4 **Südergellersen** Ger.
168 H2 **Süderhastedt** Ger.
168 G1 **Süderlügum** Ger.
168 G2 **Süderoog** *i.* Ger.
168 F2 **Süderoogsand** *i.* Ger.
168 H2 **Süderstapel** Ger.
Sudest Island P.N.G. *see* **Tagula Island**
Sudetenland *mts* Czech Rep./Pol. *see* **Sude**
174 D5 **Sudety** *mts* Czech Rep./P
168 G2 **Südfall** *i.* Ger.
139 R8 **Sudimir** Rus. Fed.
139 Y4 **Sudislavl'** Rus. Fed.
209 F5 **Sud-Kivu** *prov.* Dem. Rep. Congo
234 D6 **Sudlersville** *MD* U.S.A.
169 C7 **Südlohn** Ger.
168 D5 **Süd-Nord-Kanal** *canal* G
184 B6 **Sudoeste Alentejano e Vicentina, Parque Natur** *nature res.* Port.
139 X6 **Sudogda** Rus. Fed.
139 X5 **Sudogda** *r.* Rus. Fed.
176 G3 **Sudoměřice** Czech Rep.
138 M4 **Sudomskiye Vysoty** *hills* Rus. Fed.
139 Q9 **Sudost'** *r.* Rus. Fed.
207 H5 **Sud-Ouest** *prov.* Camero
217 □1b **Sud Ouest, Pointe** *pt* Mauritius
136 C4 **Sudova Vyshnya** Ukr.
179 N7 **Sudovec** Croatia
203 G2 **Sudr** Egypt
Südtirol *prov.* Italy *see* **Bolzano**
129 I4 **Sudur** Azer.
129 B6 **Sudurağı** Turkey
140 □B1 **Suðurland** *constituency* Iceland
130 A3 **Suðuroy** *i.* Faroe Is
144 D1 **Suðuroy** *i.* Faroe Is
144 D1 **Suðuroyarfjørður** *sea cha* Faroe Is
168 G5 **Sudwalde** Ger.
137 O2 **Sudzha** Rus. Fed.
137 O2 **Sudzha** *r.* Rus. Fed.
208 F3 **Sue** *watercourse* Sudan
187 E9 **Sueca** Spain
197 M8 **Sŭedinenie** Bulg.
192 C8 **Suelli** *Sardegna* Italy
217 □2b **Suète, Île du** *i.* *Inner Islan* Seychelles
183 J2 **Sueva, Reserva Naciona** *nature res.* Spain
156 B8 **Suèvres** France
231 □1 **Sue Wood Bay** Bermuda
Suez Egypt *see* **As Suway**
Suez, Gulf of Egypt *see* **Suways, Khalīj as**
Suez Bay Egypt *see* **Qulzum, Baḩr al**
Suez Canal Egypt *see* **Suways, Qanāt as**
124 E4 **Şufaynah** Saudi Arabia
235 G2 **Suffern** *NY* U.S.A.
151 N3 **Suffolk** *admin. div.* *England*
232 I12 **Suffolk** *VA* U.S.A.
235 J3 **Suffolk County** *county* *NY* U.S.A.
122 A2 **Sūfiān** Iran
Sufi-Kurgan Kyrg. *see* **Sopu-Korgon**
129 E3 **Sugan, Gora** *mt.* Rus. Fec
226 E7 **Sugar** *r.* *WI* U.S.A.
226 F4 **Sugarbush Hill** *WI* U.S.A.
232 C9 **Sugar Grove** *OH* U.S.A.
235 G2 **Sugar Loaf** *NY* U.S.A.
147 C9 **Sugarloaf Mountain** *hill* Ireland
233 □O3 **Sugarloaf Mountain** *ME* U.
83 N5 **Sugarloaf Point** *N.S.W.* A
216 □2b **Sugar Loaf Point** St Hele
234 D2 **Sugar Notch** *PA* U.S.A.
234 C1 **Sugar Run** *PA* U.S.A.
104 E7 **Suga-shima** *i.* Japan
92 F6 **Sugbuhan Point** Phil.
173 I2 **Sugenheim** Ger.
Süget *Xinjiang* China *see* **S**
94 E4 **Sugi** *i.* Indon.
110 C7 **Sugun** *Xinjiang* China
95 L1 **Sugut** *r.* Malaysia
95 L1 **Sugut, Tanjung** *pt* Malays
197 N7 **Suhaia** Romania
110 K7 **Suhai Hu** *l.* *Qinghai* China
106 J6 **Suhai Obo** *Nei Mongol* Ch
106 I7 **Suhait** *Nei Mongol* China
Sūhāj Egypt *see* **Sawhāj**
179 K8 **Suha Krajina** *reg.* Sloveni
125 M3 **Şuḩār** Oman
197 O2 **Suharău** Romania
128 B8 **Suhaymī, Wādī as** *watercourse* Egypt
106 J1 **Sühbaatar** Mongolia
107 M3 **Sühbaatar** *prov.* Mongolia
114 C7 **Suheli Par** *i.* India
179 J8 **Suhi vrh** *mt.* Slovenia
169 K9 **Suhl** Ger.
168 K5 **Suhlendorf** Ger.
188 F3 **Suhopolje** Croatia
172 E7 **Suhr** Switz.
124 G4 **Suhul** *reg.* Saudi Arabia
125 K4 **Suhūl al Kidan** *plain* Saudi Arabia
206 E5 **Suhum** Ghana
199 L4 **Şuhut** Turkey
123 M7 **Sui** Pak.
97 D10 **Sui, Laem** *pt* Thai.
254 B4 **Suiá Missur** *r.* Brazil
Sui'an *Fujian* China *see* **Zhangpu**
100 G5 **Suibin** *Heilong.* China
109 L4 **Suichang** *Zhejiang* China
Suicheng *Fujian* China *see* **Jianning**
Suicheng *Guangdong* Chir *see* **Suixi**
109 J5 **Suichuan** *Jiangxi* China
Suid-Afrika *country* Africa **South Africa, Republic of**
107 L8 **Suide** *Shaanxi* China
182 D3 **Suído, Serra do** *mts* Spai
Suidzhikurmsy Turkm. *see* **Madaw**
100 G6 **Suifenhe** *Heilong.* China
100 G7 **Suifen He** *r.* China
105 L2 **Suifu** Japan
116 C7 **Suigam** *Gujarat* India
104 C4 **Suigetsu-ko** *l.* Japan
105 L3 **Suigō-Tsukuba Kokutei-k** *park* Japan

Suihua Heilong. China
Suijiang Yunnan China
Suileng Heilong. China
Suilly-la-Tour France
Suilven hill Scotland U.K.
Suining Hunan China
Suining Jiangsu China
Suining Sichuan China
Suipacha Arg.
Suipacha Bol.
Suiping Henan China
Suippe r. France
Suippes France
Suir r. Ireland
Suisse country Europe see Switzerland
Suisse Normande reg. France
Suita Japan
Suiti Burunu pt Azer.
Suitland MD U.S.A.
Suixi Anhui China
Suixi Guangdong China
Suixian Henan China
Suixian Hubei China see Suizhou
Suiyang Guizhou China
Suiyang Henan China
Suizhai Henan China see Xiangcheng
Suizhong Liaoning China
Suizhou Hubei China
Suj Nei Mongol China
Sujangarh Rajasthan India
Sujawal Pak.
Suk atoll Micronesia see Pulusuk
Sukabumi Jawa Indon.
Sukadana Kalimantan Indon.
Sukadana Sumatera Indon.
Sukadana, Teluk b. Indon.
Sukagawa Japan
Sukanegara Jawa Indon.
Sukaraja Kalimantan Indon.
Sukaramai Kalimantan Indon.
Sukarnapura Papua Indon. see Jayapura
Sukarno, Puntjak mt. Papua Indon. see Jaya, Puncak
Sukau Sabah Malaysia
Suket Rajasthan India
Sukeva Fin.
Sukhanovka Rus. Fed.
Sukhary Belarus
Sukhinichi Rus. Fed.
Sukhi Yaly r. Ukr.
Sukhodil Ukr.
Sukhodol'skiy Rus. Fed.
Sukhodol'skoye, Ozero l. Rus. Fed.
Sukhodrev r. Rus. Fed.
Sukhoivanovka Ukr. see Stepnohirs'k
Sukhokumskiy Kanal canal Rus. Fed.
Sukhona r. Rus. Fed.
Sukhothai Thai.
Sukhotino Rus. Fed.
Sukhoverkovo Rus. Fed.
Sukhumi Georgia see Sokhumi
Sukhum-Kale Georgia see Sokhumi
Sukhyy Torets' r. Ukr.
Sukhyy Yelanets' Ukr.
Sukkertoppen Greenland see Maniitsoq
Sukkozero Rus. Fed.
Sukkur Pak.
Sukkur Barrage Pak.
Sukma Chhattisgarh India
Sūknah Libya
Sukolilo Jawa Indon.
Sükösd Hungary
Sukow Ger.
Sukpay Rus. Fed.
Sukpay r. Rus. Fed.
Sukri r. India
Sukri r. India
Sukromlya Rus. Fed.
Sukromny Rus. Fed.
Sukses Namibia
Suksun Rus. Fed.
Suktel r. India
Sukumo Japan
Sukumo-wan b. Japan
Sukun i. Indon.
Şükürbäyli Azer.
Sul, Canal do sea chan. Brazil
Sul, Pico do mt. Brazil
Sula i. Norway
Sula r. Rus. Fed.
Sula r. Ukr.
Sula, Kepulauan is Indon.
Sulabesi i. Indon.
Sulaiman Range mts Pak.
Sulak Rus. Fed.
Sulak r. Rus. Fed.
Sūlār Iran
Sula Sgeir i. Scotland U.K.
Sulasih, Gunung vol. Indon.
Sulat i. Indon.
Sulat Samar Phil.
Sulawesi i. Indon.
Sulawesi Barat prov. Indon.
Sulawesi Selatan prov. Indon.
Sulawesi Tengah prov. Indon.
Sulawesi Tenggara prov. Indon.
Sulawesi Utara prov. Indon.
Sulaymān Beg Iraq
Sulaymānīyah Iraq see As Sulaymānīyah
Sulayyimah Saudi Arabia
Sulci Sardegna Italy see Sant'Antioco
Sulcis Sardegna Italy see Sant'Antioco
Sulcis reg. Sardegna Italy
Suldalsvatnet l. Norway
Sulechów Pol.
Sulęcin Pol.
Sulęcinek Pol.
Sulęczyno Pol.
Suledeh Iran
Suleja Nigeria
Sulejów Pol.
Sulejówek Pol.
Sulejowskie, Jezioro l. Pol.
Suleman, Teluk b. Indon.
Su Lernu r. Italy
Sule Skerry i. Scotland U.K.
Sule Stack i. Scotland U.K.
Süleymanlı Kahramanmaraş Turkey
Süleymanlı Manisa Turkey
Suliki Sumatera Indon.
Sulików Pol.
Sulima Sierra Leone
Sulina Romania
Sulina, Braţul watercourse Romania
Sulingen Ger.
Sulin Gol r. Qinghai China
Suliskongen mt. Norway
Suliszewo Pol.
Sulitjelma Norway
Sulkava Fin.
Sułkowice Pol.
Sulla-Chubutla r. Rus. Fed.
Sullana Peru
Sullane r. Ireland
Süller Turkey
Sullington West Sussex, England U.K.
Sullivan IL U.S.A.
Sullivan IN U.S.A.
Sullivan MO U.S.A.
Sullivan Bay B.C. Can.
Sullivan County county NY U.S.A.
Sullivan County county PA U.S.A.
Sullivan Island Myanmar see Lanbi Kyun
Sullivan Lake Alta Can.
Sullom Voe inlet Scotland U.K.
Sully Que. Can.
Sully France
Sully Vale of Glamorgan, Wales U.K.
Sully-sur-Loire France
179 M6 Sulm r. Austria
175 H4 Sulmierzyce Łódzkie Pol.
174 F4 Sulmierzyce Wielkopolskie Pol.
Sulmo Italy see Sulmona
193 L3 Sulmona Italy
158 F6 Sulniac France
78 □6 Sulofoloa Malaita Solomon Is
197 O9 Süloğlu Turkey
175 H5 Sułoszowa Pol.
174 F4 Sułów Dolnośląskie Pol.
175 K5 Sułów Lubelskie Pol.
237 I10 Sulphur LA U.S.A.
237 G8 Sulphur OK U.S.A.
237 H9 Sulphur r. TX U.S.A.
237 D9 Sulphur Draw watercourse TX U.S.A.
237 H9 Sulphur Springs TX U.S.A.
237 E9 Sulphur Springs Draw watercourse NM/TX U.S.A.
224 D4 Sultan Ont. Can.
202 D2 Sultan Libya
123 J7 Sultan, Koh-i- mts Pak.
Sultanabad Andhra Prad. India see Osmannagar
Sultanabad Iran see Arāk
199 K2 Sultanbeyli Turkey
199 M4 Sultandağı Turkey
126 F4 Sultanhanı Turkey
199 J5 Sultanhisar Turkey
199 H2 Sultaniça Turkey
Sultanıye Turkey see Karapınar
116 I6 Sultanpur Uttar Prad. India
123 I1 Sultansandzharskoye Vodokhranilishche resr Turkm.
129 D1 Sultanskoye Rus. Fed.
209 E6 Sulu Dem. Rep. Congo
92 E6 Suluan i. Phil.
92 D8 Sulu Archipelago is Phil.
126 F4 Sülüklü Turkey
121 M8 Sülüktü Kyrg.
117 N6 Sulung Arun. Prad. India
202 D1 Sulunṭah Libya
202 D2 Sulūq Libya
114 G6 Suluru Andhra Prad. India
266 C5 Sulu Sea N. Pacific Ocean
129 J5 Sulut Azer.
225 F1 Suluvvaulik, Lac l. Que. Can.
137 K3 Sulymivka Ukr.
Sulyukta Kyrg. see Sülüktü
178 A5 Sulz Austria
173 K3 Sulz r. Ger.
173 I3 Sulzach r. Ger.
172 F5 Sulz am Neckar Ger.
173 O4 Sulzbach r. Ger.
172 G2 Sulzbach am Main Ger.
172 G3 Sulzbach an der Murr Ger.
172 H4 Sulzbach-Laufen Ger.
173 L2 Sulzbach-Rosenberg Ger.
172 C3 Sulzbach/Saar Ger.
178 A4 Sulzberg Austria
173 I6 Sulzberg Ger.
262 N1 Sulzberger Bay Antarctica
172 D6 Sulzburg Ger.
169 K10 Sulzdorf an der Lederhecke Ger.
173 K5 Sulzemoos Ger.
172 F3 Sulzfeld Baden-Württemberg Ger.
169 J10 Sulzfeld Bayern Ger.
173 I2 Sulzheim Ger.
169 J10 Sulzthal Ger.
104 B6 Suma Japan
250 B5 Sumaco, Volcán vol. Ecuador
196 I6 Šumadija reg. Serbia
125 N4 Sumāil Oman
93 C3 Sumalata Sulawesi Indon.
210 D3 Sumalē admin. reg. Eth.
258 E3 Sumampa Arg.
95 L1 Sumangat, Tanjung pt Malaysia
250 C4 Sumapaz, Parque Nacional nat. park Col.
122 A5 Sūmār Iran
164 J2 Sumar Neth.
94 C3 Sumatera i. Indon.
94 D5 Sumatera Barat prov. Indon.
94 E6 Sumatera Selatan prov. Indon.
94 C3 Sumatera Utara prov. Indon.
Sumatra i. Indon. see Sumatera
253 E1 Sumaúma Brazil
176 C2 Šumava mts Czech Rep.
176 C2 Šumava nat. park Czech Rep.
78 □1 Sumay Guam
93 B8 Sumba i. Indon.
208 C4 Sumba, Île i. Dem. Rep. Congo
93 A8 Sumba, Selat sea chan. Indon.
122 F3 Sumbar r. Turkm.
93 A8 Sumbawa i. Indon.
95 L9 Sumbawabesar Sumbawa Indon.
211 A6 Sumbawanga Tanz.
252 C3 Sumbay Peru
209 B7 Sumbe Angola
94 D6 Sumbing, Gunung vol. Indon.
209 F7 Sumbu Zambia
209 F7 Sumbu National Park Zambia
146 □N3 Sumburgh Shetland, Scotland U.K.
146 □N3 Sumburgh Head Scotland U.K.
206 C5 Sumbuya Sierra Leone
134 J4 Sumchino Rus. Fed.
111 D9 Sumdo Aksai Chin
108 C4 Sumdo Sichuan China
222 C3 Sumdum AK U.S.A.
222 C3 Sumdum, Mount AK U.S.A.
254 F3 Sumé Brazil
179 N8 Šumećani Croatia
95 G8 Sumedang Jawa Indon.
122 C3 Sume'eh Sarā Iran
176 G5 Sümeg Hungary
208 E2 Sumeih Sudan
161 D9 Sumène France
95 J8 Sumenep Jawa Indon.
116 D7 Sumerpur Rajasthan India
Sumgait Azer. see Sumqayıt
177 J3 Šumiac Slovakia
103 R15 Sumisu-jima i. Japan
190 D1 Sumiswald Switz.
107 N2 Sümiyn Bulag Mongolia
102 □G18 Sumiyō Nansei-shotō Japan
127 K5 Summēl Iraq
224 B2 Summer Beaver Ont. Can.
149 N5 Summer Bridge North Yorkshire, England U.K.
212 C4 Summerdown Namibia
225 K3 Summerford Nfld and Lab. Can.
147 I6 Summerhill Ireland
226 H4 Summer Island MI U.S.A.
146 E6 Summer Isles Scotland U.K.
222 G5 Summerland B.C. Can.
225 I4 Summerside P.E.I. Can.
232 E10 Summersville WV U.S.A.
232 E10 Summersville Lake WV U.S.A.
231 E8 Summerville GA U.S.A.
231 G9 Summerville SC U.S.A.
80 K7 Summit hill North I. N.Z.
235 G3 Summit NJ U.S.A.
236 G3 Summit SD U.S.A.
234 D3 Summit Hill PA U.S.A.
222 E3 Summit Lake B.C. Can.
222 F4 Summit Lake B.C. Can.
241 P2 Summit Mountain NV U.S.A.
239 K8 Summit Peak CO U.S.A.
234 C3 Summit Station PA U.S.A.
179 M2 Šumná Czech Rep.
111 D9 Sumnal Aksai Chin
81 G10 Sumner South I. N.Z.
237 J9 Sumner MS U.S.A.
81 G9 Sumner, Lake South I. N.Z.
222 C3 Sumner Strait AK U.S.A.
105 J1 Sumon Japan
103 Q9 Sumon-dake mt. Japan
104 A7 Sumoto Japan
93 A6 Sumpangbinangae Sulawesi Indon.
176 F2 Šumperk Czech Rep.
96 C1 Sumprabum Myanmar
Sumpu Japan see Shizuoka
129 K5 Sumqayıt Azer.
129 K5 Sumqayıt r. Azer.
123 N8 Sumrahu Pak.
121 N7 Sumsar Kyrg.
137 M2 Sums'ka Oblast' admin. div. Ukr.
Sumskaya Oblast' admin. div. Ukr. see Sums'ka Oblast'
134 F2 Sumskiy Posad Rus. Fed.
168 K4 Sumte Ger.
231 G9 Sumter SC U.S.A.
116 F2 Sumur Jammu and Kashmir
176 G2 Šumvald Czech Rep.
190 F2 Sumvitg Switz.
111 E9 Sumxi Xizang China
137 N3 Sumy Ukr.
Sumy Oblast admin. div. Ukr. see Sums'ka Oblast'
108 A4 Sumzom Xizang China
238 I3 Sun r. MT U.S.A.
134 J4 Suna Rus. Fed.
102 S3 Sunagawa Japan
116 F7 Sunaj Madh. Prad. India
116 E4 Sunam Punjab India
117 M7 Sunamganj Bangl.
104 E5 Sunami Japan
106 F7 Sunan Gansu China
101 D9 Sunan N. Korea
146 E9 Sunart, Loch inlet Scotland U.K.
177 J2 Šuňava Slovakia
125 L4 Şunaynah Oman
186 B1 Sunbilla Spain
122 A4 Sunbula Kuh mts Iran
238 I2 Sunburst MT U.S.A.
83 J7 Sunbury Vic. Austr.
151 L5 Sunbury Surrey, England U.K.
232 C8 Sunbury OH U.S.A.
227 R9 Sunbury PA U.S.A.
261 G2 Sunchales Arg.
173 M4 Sünching Ger.
253 E6 Suncho Corral Arg.
101 D9 Sunch'ŏn N. Korea
101 E11 Sunch'ŏn S. Korea
215 L1 Sun City S. Africa
241 T8 Sun City AZ U.S.A.
240 O8 Sun City CA U.S.A.
233 N5 Suncook NH U.S.A.
177 L5 Şuncuiuş Romania
138 D1 Sund Åland Fin.
94 F8 Sunda, Selat str. Indon.
Sunda Kalapa Jawa Indon. see Jakarta
238 L4 Sundance WY U.S.A.
117 L9 Sundarbans coastal area Bangl./India
117 L9 Sundarbans National Park Bangl./India
117 J8 Sundargarh Orissa India
116 F4 Sundarnagar Hima. Prad. India
265 L4 Sunda Shelf sea feature Indian Ocean
Sunda Strait Indon. see Sunda, Selat
Sunda Trench sea feature Indian Ocean see Java Trench
214 J9 Sundays r. Eastern Cape S. Africa
215 O4 Sundays r. KwaZulu-Natal S. Africa
86 G4 Sunday Strait W.A. Austr.
261 F4 Sundblad Arg.
142 B2 Sunde Hordaland Norway
140 J5 Sunde Sør-Trøndelag Norway
149 O4 Sunderland Tyne and Wear, England U.K.
169 F8 Sundern (Sauerland) Ger.
160 K1 Sundgau reg. France
169 K8 Sundhausen Ger.
199 L3 Sündiken Dağları mts Turkey
209 B6 Sundi-Mamba Dem. Rep. Congo
222 H5 Sundre Alta Can.
224 E4 Sundridge Ont. Can.
142 F5 Sunds Denmark
142 E2 Sundsli Norway
141 N5 Sundsvall Sweden
129 J5 Sündü Azer.
215 P5 Sundumbili S. Africa
107 L2 Sunduyka Rus. Fed.
116 F7 Sunel Rajasthan India
211 C6 Sunga Tanz.
94 E4 Sungaiapit Sumatera Indon.
95 I4 Sungai Ayak Kalimantan Indon.
94 E4 Sungaiguntung Sumatera Indon.
94 E4 Sungaikabung Sumatera Indon.
95 H5 Sungaikakap Kalimantan Indon.
94 G5 Sungailiat Sumatera Indon.
94 D6 Sungaipenuh Sumatera Indon.
94 D2 Sungai Petani Malaysia
95 H4 Sungaipinyuh Kalimantan Indon.
94 G6 Sungaiselan Indon.
94 □ Sungai Tuas Basin dock Sing.
Sungari r. China see Songhua Jiang
94 □ Sungei Seletar Reservoir Sing.
93 A6 Sungguminasa Sulawesi Indon.
203 F6 Sungikai Sudan
Sungkiang Shanghai China see Songjiang
109 □J7 Sung Kong i. H.K. China
213 G3 Sungo Moz.
Sungqu Sichuan China see Songpan
94 F6 Sungsang Sumatera Indon.
129 D4 Süngülü Turkey
197 O8 Sungurlare Bulg.
126 G3 Sungurlu Turkey
192 B7 Suni Sardegna Italy
188 F3 Sunja Croatia
121 O5 Sunkar, Gora mt. Kazakh.
117 L7 Sunkosh Chhu r. Bhutan
117 K6 Sun Kosi r. Nepal
137 L4 Sunky Ukr.
169 J9 Sünna Ger.
142 C1 Sunndal Norway
140 J5 Sunndalsøra Norway
142 J2 Sunne Sweden
141 H6 Sunnfjord reg. Norway
151 K5 Sunninghill Windsor and Maidenhead, England U.K.
241 V2 Sunnyside UT U.S.A.
238 E3 Sunnyside WA U.S.A.
240 J4 Sunnyvale CA U.S.A.
105 K6 Suno-saki pt Japan
226 E6 Sun Prairie WI U.S.A.
253 F4 Sunsas, Sierra de hills Bol.
240 □C12 Sunset Beach HI U.S.A.
222 G4 Sunset House Alta Can.
Sunset Peak hill H.K. China see Tai Tung Shan
Sunshine Island H.K. China see Chau Kung To
131 M3 Suntar Rus. Fed.
123 J9 Suntsar Pak.
210 C2 Suntu Eth.
238 G5 Sun Valley ID U.S.A.
101 D10 Sunwi-do i. N. Korea
100 E4 Sunwu Heilong. China
206 E5 Sunyani Ghana
129 H2 Sunzha r. Rus. Fed.
140 T2 Suojanperä Fin.
140 R5 Suolahti Fin.
134 E2 Suolijärvet l. Fin.
Suoločielgi Fin. see Saariselkä
140 Q2 Suoluvuobmi Norway
141 S6 Suomenniemi Fin.
226 E1 Suomi Ont. Can.
Suomi country Europe see Finland
138 G1 Suomusjärvi Fin.
140 T4 Suomussalmi Fin.
103 I13 Suō-nada b. Japan
140 S5 Suonenjoki Fin.
97 G9 Suŏng Cambodia
96 F5 Suong r. Laos
140 S5 Suontee Fin.
140 S5 Suontienselkä l. Fin.
134 F3 Suoyarvi Rus. Fed.
Suozhen Shandong China see Huantai
114 D5 Supa Karnataka India
241 T5 Supai AZ U.S.A.
117 K6 Supaul Bihar India
163 F10 Superbagnères France
156 G6 Superbe r. France
160 B5 Superbesse France
161 H7 Superdévoluy France
241 U8 Superior AZ U.S.A.
238 G3 Superior MT U.S.A.
236 F5 Superior NE U.S.A.
226 B3 Superior WI U.S.A.
245 M9 Superior, Laguna lag. Mex.
226 G2 Superior, Lake Can./U.S.A.
191 J5 Superiore, Lago l. Italy
161 B6 Superlioran France
191 R6 Supertarska Draga Croatia
188 F4 Supetar Croatia
97 E7 Suphan Buri Thai.
127 K4 Süphan Dağı mt. Turkey
193 K4 Supino Italy
91 I7 Supiori i. Papua Indon.
137 K4 Supiy r. Ukr.
177 L4 Suplacu de Barcău Romania
139 R8 Suponevo Rus. Fed.
169 K6 Süpplingen Ger.
262 V1 Support Force Glacier Antarctica
175 L2 Supraśl Pol.
175 K2 Supraśl r. Pol.
129 C3 Sup'sa r. Georgia
101 D8 Supung N. Korea
177 L4 Supur Romania
124 G7 Sūq al Inān Yemen
124 E5 Sūq ar Rubū' Saudi Arabia
127 M8 Sūq ash Shuyūkh Iraq
109 L2 Suqian Jiangsu China
124 D3 Sūq Suwayq Saudi Arabia
125 L9 Suquṭrá i. Yemen
173 N6 Sur r. Ger.
206 E4 Sur r. Ghana
177 H4 Súr Hungary
125 N4 Şūr Oman
240 K5 Sur, Point CA U.S.A.
261 I5 Sur, Punta pt Arg.
135 I5 Sura Rus. Fed.
120 B1 Sura r. Rus. Fed.
129 K5 Şuraabad Azer.
123 L7 Surab Pak.
95 J8 Surabaya Jawa Indon.
123 K7 Surai Pak.
117 I8 Surajpur Chhattisgarh India
122 H9 Sūrak Iran
95 I8 Surakarta Jawa Indon.
93 A4 Suramana Sulawesi Indon.
197 M5 Şura Mare Romania
160 G4 Suran r. France
123 I8 Sūrān Iran
128 E3 Şūrān Syria
177 H3 Šurany Slovakia
210 D3 Surar Eth.
251 F6 Surára Brazil
85 L9 Surat Qld Austr.
116 D9 Surat Gujarat India
116 D5 Suratgarh Rajasthan India
97 D10 Surat Thani Thai.
175 K3 Suraż Pol.
139 N6 Surazh Belarus
139 P8 Surazh Rus. Fed.
173 N6 Surberg Ger.
85 K7 Surbiton Qld Austr.
195 O3 Surbo Italy
127 L6 Sūrdāsh Iraq
197 P5 Surdila-Greci Romania
197 L3 Surduc Romania
197 K8 Surdulica Serbia
172 B2 Sûre r. Ger./Lux.
165 I9 Sûre, Vallée de la val. Lux.
116 C8 Surendranagar Gujarat India
242 □R13 Suretka Costa Rica
240 L7 Surf CA U.S.A.
235 G5 Surf City NJ U.S.A.
151 L2 Surfleet Lincolnshire, England U.K.
116 D9 Surgana Mahar. India
162 C3 Surgères France
246 B2 Surgidero de Batabanó Cuba
130 I3 Surgut Rus. Fed.
164 J2 Surhuizum Neth.
Suri W. Bengal India see Siuri
186 I4 Súria Spain
114 F4 Suriapet Andhra Prad. India
103 □3 Suribachi-yama hill Iō-jima Japan
190 C4 Surier Italy
92 E7 Surigao Mindanao Phil.
92 E6 Surigao Strait Phil.
250 C4 Surimena Col.
97 F7 Surin Thai.
217 □1b Surinam Mauritius
Surinam country S. America see Suriname
251 G3 Suriname country S. America
251 H3 Suriname r. Suriname
97 C10 Surin Nua, Ko i. Thai.
250 D3 Suripá Venez.
127 P6 Surkhābād Iran
121 L9 Surkhandar'ya r. Uzbek.
Surkhandarya Oblast admin. div. Uzbek. see Surxondaryo
123 K6 Surkhduz Afgh.
116 H5 Surkhet Nepal
123 M2 Surkhob r. Tajik.
Surkhondaryo r. Uzbek. see Surkhandar'ya
Surkhondaryo Wiloyati admin. div. Uzbek. see Surxondaryo
122 E6 Surmāq Iran
156 G5 Surmelin r. France
127 J3 Sürmene Turkey
140 J5 Surnadalsøra Norway
197 N8 Sŭrnevo Bulg.
135 H6 Surovikino Rus. Fed.
222 C3 Surprise B.C. Can.
78 □5 Surprise, Île i. New Caledonia
222 C3 Surprise Lake B.C. Can.
124 F4 Surrah, Nafūd as des. Saudi Arabia
184 D2 Surrazala r. Port.
222 F5 Surrey B.C. Can.
246 □ Surrey reg. Jamaica
151 L5 Surrey admin. div. England U.K.
190 E1 Sursee Switz.
190 F2 Surselva reg. Switz.
137 N5 Surs'ko-Mykhaylivka Ukr.
135 I5 Surskoye Rus. Fed.
202 C2 Surt Libya
202 C2 Surt, Khalīj g. Libya
140 □C2 Surtsey i. Iceland
122 G8 Sūrū Hormozgan Iran
122 H9 Sūrū Sīstān va Balūchestān Iran
197 M5 Suru, Vârful mt. Romania
254 C2 Surubiú r. Brazil
126 I5 Suruç Turkey
210 E2 Surud, Raas pt Somalia
Surud Ad mt. Somalia see Shimbiris
105 H6 Suruga-wan b. Japan
94 E6 Surulangun Sumatera Indon.
251 F4 Surumú r. Brazil
92 F8 Surup Mindanao Phil.
156 E5 Survilliers France
168 E5 Surwold Ger.
121 L9 Surxondaryo admin. div. Uzbek.
Suryapet Andhra Prad. India see Suriapet
160 E5 Sury-le-Comtal France
158 F6 Surzur France
129 H6 Şuşa Azer.
142 H6 Suså r. Denmark
190 C5 Susa Italy
103 I12 Susa Japan
190 B5 Susa, Valle di val. Italy
188 F4 Sušac i. Croatia
Susah Tunisia see Sousse
191 Q6 Susak Croatia
188 E3 Susak i. Croatia
103 K13 Susaki Japan
103 M13 Susami Japan
Susamyr Kyrg. see Suusamyr
233 I11 Susan VA U.S.A.
122 C6 Sūsangerd Iran
100 L2 Susanino Khabarovskiy Kray Rus. Fed.
134 H4 Susanino Kostromskaya Oblast' Rus. Fed.
240 L1 Susanville CA U.S.A.
190 I2 Susch Switz.
136 G2 Suschany Ukr.
191 M4 Susegana Italy
126 I3 Suşehri Turkey
168 K2 Süsel Ger.
197 N7 Sushitsa Bulg.
107 L9 Sushui He r. China
176 C2 Sušice Czech Rep.
175 L5 Susiec Pol.
138 L5 Šuškova Latvia
116 F8 Susner Madh. Prad. India
97 D11 Suso Thai.
183 O4 Suso, Monasterio de tourist site Spain
105 H2 Susobana-gawa r. Japan
109 K3 Susong Anhui China
105 I5 Susono Japan
186 K4 Susqueda, Pantà de resr Spain
233 J7 Susquehanna PA U.S.A.
227 R9 Susquehanna r. PA U.S.A.
232 I8 Susquehanna, West Branch r. PA U.S.A.
258 D1 Susques Arg.
172 H4 Süßen Ger.
225 H4 Sussex N.B. Can.
234 F2 Sussex NJ U.S.A.
232 H12 Sussex VA U.S.A.
234 F2 Sussex County county NJ U.S.A.
168 G5 Süstedt Ger.
165 I6 Susteren Neth.
244 D3 Susticacán Mex.
191 K5 Sustinente Italy
168 D5 Sustrum Ger.
222 E3 Sustut Provincial Park B.C. Can.
93 B5 Susua Sulawesi Indon.
78 □6 Susubona Sta Isabel Solomon Is
78 □6 Susuka Choiseul Solomon Is
95 L2 Susul Sabah Malaysia
131 P3 Susuman Rus. Fed.
93 E2 Susupu Halmahera Indon.
199 J3 Susurluk Turkey
129 E5 Susuz Turkey
138 G6 Šušvė r. Lith.
175 H2 Susz Pol.
116 F3 Sutak Jammu and Kashmir
106 C3 Sutay Uul mt. Mongolia
199 L5 Sütçüler Turkey
194 F8 Sutera Sicilia Italy
83 M6 Sutherland N.S.W. Austr.
214 E8 Sutherland S. Africa
146 H6 Sutherland reg. Scotland U.K.
236 E5 Sutherland NE U.S.A.
232 H11 Sutherland VA U.S.A.
87 H9 Sutherland Range hills W.A. Austr.
188 G4 Sutjeska nat. park Bos.-Herz.
116 C5 Sutlej r. India/Pak.
138 G2 Sutlepa meri l. Estonia
128 B2 Sütlüce İçel Turkey
197 P9 Sütlüce Kırklareli Turkey
192 I3 Sutri Italy
240 K2 Sutter CA U.S.A.
240 L3 Sutter Creek CA U.S.A.
151 L2 Sutterton Lincolnshire, England U.K.
233 M3 Sutton Que. Can.
224 D2 Sutton r. Ont. Can.
81 E12 Sutton South I. N.Z.
151 M3 Sutton Cambridgeshire, England U.K.
236 G5 Sutton NE U.S.A.
232 E10 Sutton WV U.S.A.
151 M2 Sutton Bridge Lincolnshire, England U.K.
151 I2 Sutton Coldfield West Midlands, England U.K.
151 J4 Sutton Courtenay Oxfordshire, England U.K.
149 O7 Sutton in Ashfield Nottinghamshire, England U.K.
224 C2 Sutton Lake Ont. Can.
232 E10 Sutton Lake WV U.S.A.
149 O5 Sutton-on-the-Forest North Yorkshire, England U.K.
149 P7 Sutton on Trent Nottinghamshire, England U.K.
151 N5 Sutton Valence Kent, England U.K.
85 K6 Suttor r. Qld Austr.
102 R4 Suttsu Japan
220 C4 Sutwik Island AK U.S.A.
100 H3 Sutyr' r. Rus. Fed.
136 H4 Sutysky Ukr.
78 □6 Su'u Malaita Solomon Is
107 J4 Suugant Mongolia
78 □6 Su'uholo Solomon Is
215 J7 Suurberg mt. S. Africa
215 J9 Suurberg mts S. Africa
214 E10 Suurbraak S. Africa
138 I3 Suure-Jaani Estonia
138 F3 Suuremõisa Estonia
138 F3 Suur katel b. Estonia
138 G2 Suur-Pakri i. Estonia
138 I2 Suurpea Estonia
138 G3 Suur väin sea chan. Estonia
121 O6 Suusamyr Kyrg.
79 □7a Suva Viti Levu Fiji
Suvalki Pol. see Suwałki
196 I8 Suva Reka Kosovo Serbia
129 F6 Suveren Turkey
192 F1 Suvereto Italy
193 Q10 Suvero, Capo c. Italy
191 K7 Suviano, Lago di l. Italy
Suvorov atoll Cook Is see Suwarrow
136 H8 Suvorov Moldova
139 T7 Suvorov Rus. Fed.
137 M6 Suvorove Dnipropetrovs'ka Oblast' Ukr.
136 H8 Suvorove Odes'ka Oblast' Ukr.
197 P7 Suvorovo Bulg.
Suvorovo Moldova see Ştefan Vodă
129 D1 Suvorovskaya Rus. Fed.
137 M8 Suvorovs'ke Ukr.
105 H3 Suwa Japan
105 H3 Suwa-ko l. Japan
95 K5 Suwakong Kalimantan Indon.
175 K1 Suwałki Pol.
96 F7 Suwannaphum Thai.
231 F11 Suwannee r. FL U.S.A.
102 □G17 Suwanose-jima i. Nansei-shotō Japan
95 L4 Suwaran, Gunung mt. Indon.
81 □2 Suwarrow atoll Cook Is
128 D6 Suwayliḥ Jordan
127 L7 Suwayqīyah, Hawr as imp. l. Iraq
127 J8 Suwayr well Saudi Arabia
203 G2 Suways, Khalīj as g. Egypt
203 G2 Suways, Qanāt as canal Egypt
128 C10 Suweihil pt Saudi Arabia
Suweilih Jordan see Suwayliḥ
Suweis, Khalîg el g. Egypt see Suways, Khalīj as
101 E10 Suwŏn S. Korea
106 D7 Suxik Qinghai China
108 G7 Suxu Guangxi China
121 S3 Suykbulak Kazakh.
250 A6 Suyo Peru
Sūyqbulaq Kazakh. see Suykbulak
124 F9 Suyūl Ḥanīsh i. Yemen
129 I1 Suyutkina Kosa Rus. Fed.
129 I1 Suyutkina Kosa, Mys pt Rus. Fed.
120 E7 Suz, Mys pt Kazakh.
122 G8 Sūzā Iran
121 M5 Suzak Kazakh.
105 H2 Suzaka Japan
139 X5 Suzdal' Rus. Fed.
161 F8 Suze-la-Rousse France
137 N1 Suzemka Rus. Fed.
109 K2 Suzhou Anhui China
Suzhou Gansu China see Jiuquan
109 M3 Suzhou Jiangsu China
101 D8 Suzi He r. China
103 O9 Suzu Japan
104 E6 Suzuka Japan
104 E6 Suzuka-gawa r. Japan
104 D5 Suzuka Kokutei-kōen park Japan
104 D6 Suzuka-sanmyaku mts Japan
103 O9 Suzu-misaki pt Japan
191 J6 Suzzara Italy
141 M6 Svabensverk Sweden
140 S1 Sværholthalvøya pen. Norway
140 □ Svalbard terr. Arctic Ocean
197 O7 Svalenik Bulg.
142 H6 Svallerup Denmark
136 B5 Svalyava Ukr.
143 O2 Svanberga Sweden
129 D3 Svanet'is K'edi hills Georgia
143 K5 Svängsta Sweden
140 Q3 Svanstein Sweden
137 N2 Svapa r. Rus. Fed.
140 P3 Svappavaara Sweden
139 P4 Svapushcha Rus. Fed.
176 C3 Švarcenberský kanál canal Czech Rep.
143 L1 Svärdsjö Sweden
142 F2 Svarstad Norway
138 I1 Svarta r. Fin.
143 K2 Svartå Sweden
143 K2 Svartälven r. Sweden
143 J1 Svartån r. Sweden
143 M2 Svartån r. Sweden
140 Q3 Svartbyn Sweden
Svartenhuk Halvø pen. Greenland see Sigguup Nunaa
142 C2 Svartevatn l. Norway
140 P3 Svartlä Sweden
143 P2 Svartlögafjärden b. Sweden
136 F2 Svarytsevychi Ukr.
171 G10 Svatava Czech Rep.
144 J1 Svatjell hill Norway
179 P2 Svatobořice-Mistřín Czech Rep.
137 R4 Svatove Ukr.
177 K3 Svätuše Slovakia
176 G3 Svätý Jur Slovakia
177 H4 Svätý Peter Slovakia
97 G9 Svay Riĕng Cambodia
140 □ Sveagruva Svalbard
134 I4 Svecha Rus. Fed.
138 I6 Svėdasai Lith.
141 M5 Sveg Sweden
141 M5 Svegsjön l. Sweden
142 B2 Sveio Norway
138 J4 Sveķi Latvia
138 E6 Švėkšna Lith.
141 H6 Svelgen Norway
140 J5 Svellingen Norway
137 N1 Sven' Rus. Fed.
138 I6 Švenčionėliai Lith.
138 J6 Švenčionys Lith.
142 G6 Svendborg Denmark
142 J4 Svenljunga Sweden
140 □ Svenskøya i. Svalbard
140 M5 Svenstavik Sweden
175 L1 Šventežeris Lith.
138 H6 Šventoji r. Lith.
100 C2 Sverbeyevo Rus. Fed.
139 S6 Sverchkovo Rus. Fed.
135 I6 Sverdlovo Rus. Fed.
Sverdlovsk Rus. Fed. see Yekaterinburg
137 S5 Sverdlovs'k Ukr.
134 M4 Sverdlovskaya Oblast' admin. div. Rus. Fed.
Sverdlovsk Oblast admin. div. Rus. Fed. see Sverdlovskaya Oblast'
221 I2 Sverdrup Channel Nunavut Can.
221 I2 Sverdrup Islands Nunavut Can.
Sverige country Europe see Sweden
Švermovo Slovakia see Telgárt
137 M2 Svesa Ukr.
197 O7 Sveshtari, Tomb of tourist site Bulg.
188 E4 Sveta Andrija i. Croatia
179 O7 Sveta Marija Croatia
138 G5 Švėtė r. Lith.
191 R6 Sveti Damjan, Rt pt Croatia
191 R6 Sveti Grgur i. Croatia
Sveti Ivan Zelina Croatia see Zelina
188 F4 Sveti Jure mt. Croatia
197 J9 Sveti Nikole Macedonia
176 G1 Světlá Hora Czech Rep.
176 E2 Světlá nad Sázavou Czech Rep.
100 K5 Svetlaya Rus. Fed.
100 M4 Svetlodarskoye Sakhalin Rus. Fed.
Svetlogorsk Belarus see Svyetlahorsk
138 D7 Svetlogorsk Kaliningradskaya Oblast' Rus. Fed.
130 J3 Svetlogorsk Krasnoyarskiy Kray Rus. Fed.
135 H7 Svetlograd Rus. Fed.
134 K4 Svetlopolyansk Rus. Fed.
Svetlovodsk Ukr. see Svitlovods'k
138 D7 Svetlyy Kaliningradskaya Oblast' Rus. Fed.
120 I2 Svetlyy Orenburgskaya Oblast' Rus. Fed.
135 I6 Svetlyy Yar Rus. Fed.
138 L1 Svetogorsk Leningradskaya Oblast' Rus. Fed.
Svetogorsk Respublika Dagestan Rus. Fed. see Shamil'kala
Svetozarevo Serbia see Jagodina
196 H5 Svetozar Miletić Vojvodina Serbia
138 H4 Svētupe r. Latvia
191 P5 Svetvinčenat Croatia
140 □E1 Svíahnúkar vol. Iceland
136 D4 Svicha r. Ukr.
177 K2 Svidník Slovakia
176 C2 Švihov Czech Rep.
138 G3 Sviibi Estonia
188 F4 Svilaja mts Croatia
196 J6 Svilajnac Serbia
197 O9 Svilengrad Bulg.
197 K6 Svinecea Mare, Vârful mt. Romania
177 K2 Svinia Slovakia
177 H3 Svinná Slovakia
142 H6 Svinninge Denmark
Svinø i. Faroe Is see Svínoy
144 D1 Svínoy i. Faroe Is
138 J7 Svir Belarus
139 S1 Svir' r. Rus. Fed.
138 J7 Svir, Vozyera l. Belarus
139 P1 Sviritsa Rus. Fed.
139 P1 Svirskaya Guba b. Rus. Fed.
139 Q1 Svir'stroy Rus. Fed.
175 M6 Svirzh r. Ukr.
197 N7 Svishtov Bulg.
138 H8 Svislach Hrodzyenskaya Voblasts' Belarus
138 K8 Svislach Minskaya Voblasts' Belarus
175 M2 Svislach r. Belarus
138 L8 Svislach r. Belarus
138 L8 Svislach r. Belarus
Svisloch r. Belarus see Svislach
177 J2 Svit Slovakia
176 F3 Svitava r. Czech Rep.
176 F2 Svitavy Czech Rep.
137 R5 Svitlodars'k Ukr.
137 N5 Svitlohirs'ke Ukr.
137 M4 Svitlovods'k Ukr.
175 L4 Svityaz' Ukr.
190 I2 Svizzer, Parc Naziunal nat. park Switz.
Svizzera country Europe see Switzerland
138 E7 Svoboda Kaliningradskaya Oblast' Rus. Fed.
137 P2 Svoboda Kurskaya Oblast' Rus. Fed.
176 E1 Svoboda nad Úpou Czech Rep.
100 F3 Svobodnyy Rus. Fed.
129 E1 Svobody Rus. Fed.
197 L8 Svoge Bulg.
138 L6 Svol'nya r. Belarus
140 M2 Svolvær Norway
176 F2 Svratka Czech Rep.
176 F2 Svratka r. Czech Rep.
177 H2 Svrčinovec Slovakia
197 K7 Svrljig Serbia
197 K7 Svrljiške Planine mts Serbia
138 J7 Svyantsyanskiya Hrady hills Belarus
Svyatogorovskiy Rudnik Ukr. see Dobropillya
139 X6 Svyatoye, Ozero l. Rus. Fed.
134 J2 Svyatoy Nos, Mys c. Rus. Fed.
139 O9 Svyatsk Rus. Fed.
138 M9 Svyetlahorsk Belarus
137 M1 Svyha r. Ukr.
136 D3 Svynya r. Ukr.
136 F3 Svyten'ka r. Ukr.
123 O4 Swabi Pak.
151 I2 Swadlincote Derbyshire, England U.K.
215 J8 Swaershoek S. Africa
215 J8 Swaershoekpas pass S. Africa
151 N2 Swaffham Norfolk, England U.K.
85 N6 Swain Reefs Qld Austr.
231 F9 Swainsboro GA U.S.A.
77 I3 Swains Island atoll American Samoa
212 B4 Swakop watercourse Namibia
212 B4 Swakopmund Namibia
149 O5 Swale r. England U.K.
78 □6 Swallow Islands Santa Cruz Is Solomon Is
165 J6 Swalmen Neth.
114 E5 Swamihalli Karnataka India
225 G1 Swampy r. Que. Can.
87 C11 Swan r. W.A. Austr.
223 K4 Swan r. Man./Sask. Can.
224 D2 Swan r. Ont. Can.
148 C8 Swan Ireland
151 I6 Swanage Dorset, England U.K.
209 E7 Swana-Mume Dem. Rep. Congo
232 E10 Swandale WV U.S.A.
214 H9 Swanepoelspoort mt. S. Africa
83 I6 Swan Hill Vic. Austr.
222 H4 Swan Hills Alta Can.
Swan Islands see Cisne, Islas del
222 D4 Swan Lake l. B.C. Can.
223 K4 Swan Lake l. Man. Can.
234 F1 Swan Lake NY U.S.A.
236 H3 Swan Lake l. MN U.S.A.
151 M5 Swanley Kent, England U.K.
147 G4 Swanlinbar Ireland
81 G10 Swannanoa South I. N.Z.
231 I8 Swanquarter NC U.S.A.
231 I8 Swanquarter National Wildlife Refuge nature res. NC U.S.A.
82 G6 Swan Reach S.A. Austr.
223 K4 Swan River Man. Can.
226 A2 Swan River MN U.S.A.
148 D5 Swan's Cross Roads Ireland
83 L10 Swansea Tas. Austr.
150 E4 Swansea Swansea, Wales U.K.
150 E4 Swansea admin. div. Wales U.K.
150 E4 Swansea Bay Wales U.K.
233 □Q4 Swans Island ME U.S.A.
240 J4 Swanton CA U.S.A.
233 L4 Swanton VT U.S.A.
151 N2 Swanton Morley Norfolk, England U.K.
174 G1 Swarożyn Pol.
215 N6 Swartberg S. Africa
214 D10 Swartberg mt. S. Africa
214 F9 Swartbergpas pass S. Africa
214 B6 Swartdoorn r. S. Africa
234 E5 Swarthmore PA U.S.A.
215 L8 Swart Kei r. S. Africa
214 E6 Swartkolkvloer salt pan S. Africa
215 J9 Swartkops S. Africa
215 J9 Swartkops r. S. Africa
Swart Nossob watercourse Namibia see Black Nossob
215 K2 Swartplaas S. Africa
214 H4 Swartputs S. Africa
214 D2 Swartput se Pan salt pan Namibia
215 K1 Swartruggens S. Africa
215 K1 Swartruggens mts S. Africa
234 F2 Swartswood NJ U.S.A.
234 F2 Swartswood Lake NJ U.S.A.
215 P3 Swart Umfolozi S. Africa
227 K7 Swartz Creek MI U.S.A.
174 F3 Swarzędz Pol.
241 S2 Swasey Peak UT U.S.A.
227 N1 Swastika Ont. Can.
123 N4 Swat r. Pak.
234 B4 Swatara Creek r. PA U.S.A.
123 O4 Swat Kohistan reg. Pak.
Swatow Guangdong China see Shantou
148 D4 Swatragh Northern Ireland U.K.
151 I6 Sway Hampshire, England U.K.
215 P2 Swaziland country Africa
141 M6 Sweden country Europe
234 E5 Swedesboro NJ U.S.A.
84 G4 Sweers Island Qld Austr.
232 F11 Sweet Briar VA U.S.A.
238 C4 Sweet Home OR U.S.A.
232 E11 Sweet Springs WV U.S.A.
234 C2 Sweet Valley PA U.S.A.
237 E9 Sweetwater TX U.S.A.
238 K5 Sweetwater r. WY U.S.A.
238 J5 Sweetwater Station WY U.S.A.
214 E10 Swellendam S. Africa
215 L7 Swempoort S. Africa
175 I2 Świątki Pol.
174 G1 Świbno Pol.
175 J3 Świder r. Pol.
174 E5 Świdnica Dolnośląskie Pol.
174 D4 Świdnica Lubuskie Pol.
175 K4 Świdnik Pol.
174 D2 Świdwin Pol.
174 E5 Świebodzice Pol.
174 D3 Świebodzin Pol.
174 G2 Świecie Pol.
174 E4 Święciechowa Pol.
175 H2 Świecie nad Osą Pol.
171 K6 Świecko Pol.
175 H2 Świedziebnia Pol.
174 G2 Świekatowo Pol.
174 D5 Świeradów-Zdrój Pol.
175 I3 Świercze Pol.
174 F5 Świerczów Pol.
174 G5 Świerklaniec Pol.
174 D4 Świerzawa Pol.
174 E1 Świerzenko Pol.
174 C2 Świerzno Pol.
174 E1 Świeszyno Pol.
175 J2 Świętajno Warmińsko-Mazurskie Pol.
175 K1 Świętajno Warmińsko-Mazurskie Pol.
175 I5 Świętokrzyskie prov. Pol.
175 I5 Świętokrzyskie, Góry hills Pol.
175 I5 Świętokrzyski Park Narodowy nat. park Pol.
233 □O4 Swift r. ME U.S.A.
223 J5 Swift Current Sask. Can.
223 J5 Swiftcurrent Creek r. Sask. Can.
164 I3 Swifterbant Neth.
234 E2 Swiftwater PA U.S.A.
148 B4 Swilly r. Ireland
147 G2 Swilly, Lough inlet Ireland
151 I4 Swindon Swindon, England U.K.
151 I4 Swindon admin. div. England U.K.
149 P6 Swinefleet East Riding of Yorkshire, England U.K.
151 L2 Swineshead Lincolnshire, England U.K.
147 E5 Swinford Ireland
234 F1 Swinging Bridge Reservoir NY U.S.A.
174 G3 Świnice Warckie Pol.
215 J4 Swinkpan imp. l. S. Africa
175 H6 Świnna Pol.
174 C2 Świnoujście Pol.
146 L11 Swinton Scottish Borders, Scotland U.K.
149 O7 Swinton South Yorkshire, England U.K.
Swiss Confederation country Europe see Switzerland
Świstocz r. Belarus see Svislach
190 E2 Switzerland country Europe
Swnt Enlli sea chan. Wales U.K. see Bardsey Sound
174 C2 Swobnica Pol.
147 J6 Swords Ireland
85 H6 Swords Range hills Qld Austr.
174 F2 Swornegacie Pol.
234 D2 Swoyerville PA U.S.A.
138 M7 Syalyava, Vozyera l. Belarus
175 M3 Syalyets Brestskaya Voblasts' Belarus
139 N8 Syalyets Mahilyowskaya Voblasts' Belarus
138 H9 Syalyets Vodaskhovishcha resr Belarus
134 F3 Syamozero, Ozero l. Rus. Fed.
134 H3 Syamzha Rus. Fed.
117 I5 Syang Nepal
138 M7 Syanno Belarus

Tambach Kenya
Tambach-Dietharz Ger.
Tambacounda Senegal
Tamba-kōchi plat. Japan see Tanba-kōchi
Tambalongang i. Indon.
Tambangmunjul Kalimantan Indon.
Tambangsawah Sumatera Indon.
Tambankulu Swaziland
Tambao Burkina
Tambaoura, Falaise de esc. Mali
Tambaqui Brazil
Tambara Moz.
Tambar Springs N.S.W. Austr.
Tambau Brazil
Tambawel Nigeria
Tambea Sulawesi Indon.
Tambelan, Kepulauan is Indon.
Tambelan Besar i. Indon.
Tambellup W.A. Austr.
Tamberías Arg.
Tamberu Jawa Indon.
Tambillo, Cerro mt. Arg.
Tambisan Sabah Malaysia
Tambo Qld Austr.
Tambo r. Vic. Austr.
Tambo r. Peru
Tambobamba Peru
Tambo de Mora Peru
Tambo Grande Peru
Tambohorano Madag.
Tamboli Sulawesi Indon.
Tambopata r. Peru
Tambor Angola
Tambor Mex.
Tambora, Gunung vol. Sumbawa Indon.
Tambores Uru.
Tamboril Brazil
Tamboryacu r. Peru
Tamboura C.A.R.
Tambov Rus. Fed.
Tambovka Georgia
Tambovka Rus. Fed.
Tambov Oblast admin. div. Rus. Fed. see Tambovskaya Oblast'
Tambovskaya Oblast' admin. div. Rus. Fed.
Tambre r. Spain
Tambu, Teluk b. Indon.
Tambulan Sulawesi Indon.
Tambulanan, Bukit hill Malaysia
Tambunan Sabah Malaysia
Tambura Sudan
Tambuyukon, Gunung mt. Malaysia
Tâmchekkeț Maur.
Tamdy Kazakh.
Tamdybulak Uzbek. see Tomdibuloq
Tame Col.
Tâmega r. Port.
Tamel Aike Arg.
Tamelos, Akrotirio pt Kea Greece
Tamenghest Alg. see Tamanrasset
Tamenglong Manipur India
Tamerlanovka Kazakh. see Temirlanovka
Tamesna reg. Niger
Tamgak, Adrar mt. Niger
Tamgué, Massif du mt. Guinea
Tamia Madh. Prad. India
Tamiahua Mex.
Tamiahua, Laguna de lag. Mex.
Tamiami Canal FL U.S.A.
Tamiang r. Indon.
Tamiang, Ujung pt Indon.
Tamil Nadu state India
Tamiment PA U.S.A.
Taminglayang Kalimantan Indon.
Tamins Switz.
Tamirin Gol r. Mongolia
Tamiš r. Serbia
Tamitatoala r. Brazil
Tamitsa Rus. Fed.
Ţāmīyah Egypt
Tamīyah, Jabal hill Saudi Arabia
Tamjit well Niger
Tamkamys Kazakh.
Tamkuhi Uttar Prad. India
Tam Ky Vietnam
Tamlelt, Plaine de plain Morocco
Tamluk W. Bengal India
Tamm Ger.
Tammaro r. Italy
Tammarvi r. Nunavut Can.
Tammela Etelä-Suomi Fin.
Tammela Oulu Fin.
Tammensiel Ger.
Tammerfors Fin. see Tampere
Tammio i. Fin.
Tammisaaren Saariston Kansallispuisto nat. park Fin. see Ekenäskärgårds nationalpark
Tammisaari Fin. see Ekenäs
Tammispää Estonia
Tämnaren l. Sweden
Tamnava r. Serbia
Tamnay-en-Bazois France
Támoga r. Spain
Tamou Niger
Tamou, Réserve Totale de Faune de nature res. Niger
Tampa FL U.S.A.
Tampa Bay FL U.S.A.
Tampacán Mex.
Tampamolón Mex.
Tampang Sumatera Indon.
Tampere Fin.
Tampico Mex.
Tampico el Alto Mex.
Tampin Malaysia
Tampines Sing.
Tampines, Sungai r. Sing.
Tampo Sulawesi Indon.
Tam Quan Vietnam
Tamrah Saudi Arabia
Tamsagbulag Mongolia
Tamsag Muchang Nei Mongol China
Tamsalu Estonia
Tamshiyacu Peru
Tamsweg Austria
Tamu Myanmar
Tamuín Mex.
Tamuning Guam
Tamur r. Nepal
Tamurejo Spain
Tamworohi Pohnpei Micronesia
Tamworth N.S.W. Austr.
Tamworth Staffordshire, England U.K.
Tan Kazakh.
Tana r. Fin./Norway see Tenojoki
Tana r. Kenya
Tana Madag. see Antananarivo
Tana i. Vanuatu see Tanna
Tana, Lake Eth. see T'ana Hāyk'
Tanabe Japan
Tanabi Brazil
Tana Bru Norway
Tanafjorden inlet Norway
Tanaga vol. AK U.S.A.
Tanaga Island AK U.S.A.
Tanagro r. Italy
Tanagura Japan
Tanah, Tanjung pt Indon.
T'ana Hāyk' l. Eth.
Tanahbala i. Indon.
Tanahgrogot Kalimantan Indon.
Tanahjampea i. Indon.
Tanahmasa i. Indon.
Tanahmerah Kalimantan Indon.
Tanah Merah Malaysia
94 D4 Tanahputih Sumatera Indon.
94 D2 Tanah Rata Malaysia
93 A6 Tanakeke i. Indon.
116 H5 Tanakpur Uttaranchal India
93 A5 Tanambung Sulawesi Barat Indon.
84 B5 Tanami N.T. Austr.
84 C5 Tanami Desert N.T. Austr.
84 B6 Tanami Downs Aboriginal Land res. N.T. Austr.
97 H9 Tân An Vietnam
220 C3 Tanana AK U.S.A.
Tananarive Madag. see Antananarivo
213 □I4 Tanandava Madag.
125 I2 Tanāqīb, Ra's pt Saudi Arabia
190 F5 Tanaro r. Italy
150 F2 Tanat r. Wales U.K.
92 E6 Tanauan Leyte Phil.
192 D6 Tanaunella Sardegna Italy
79 □7a Tanavuso Point Viti Levu Fiji
104 B5 Tanba Japan
104 B5 Tanba-kōchi plat. Japan
85 H8 Tanbar Qld Austr.
107 P9 Tanbu Shandong China
159 L3 Tancarville France
Tancheng Fujian China see Pingtan
107 P9 Tancheng Shandong China
101 F8 Tanch'ŏn N. Korea
244 E6 Tancítaro Mex.
244 E6 Tancítaro, Cerro de mt. Mex.
245 N8 Tancochapa r. Mex.
206 E5 Tanda Côte d'Ivoire
116 E4 Tanda Punjab India
116 G5 Tanda Uttar Prad. India
117 I6 Tanda Uttar Prad. India
141 L6 Tandådalen Sweden
92 F7 Tandag Mindanao Phil.
197 P6 Ţăndărei Romania
209 C9 Tandaué Angola
95 L1 Tandek Sabah Malaysia
173 K5 Tandern Ger.
116 F3 Tandi Hima. Prad. India
261 H5 Tandil Arg.
261 H5 Tandil, Sierra del hills Arg.
208 C2 Tandjilé pref. Chad
123 M9 Tando Adam Pak.
123 M9 Tando Alahyar Pak.
123 M9 Tando Bago Pak.
123 M9 Tando Muhammmad Khan Pak.
83 I5 Tandou Lake imp. l. N.S.W. Austr.
147 J4 Tandragee Northern Ireland U.K.
141 M6 Tandsjöborg Sweden
92 C9 Tandubatu i. Phil.
116 H9 Tandula r. India
114 E4 Tandur Andhra Prad. India
114 F3 Tandur Andhra Prad. India
123 L7 Tanduri Pak.
80 K5 Taneatua North I. N.Z.
102 □H16 Tanega-shima i. Japan
102 S6 Taneichi Japan
96 D5 Tanen Taunggyi mts Thai.
93 E4 Taneti i. Maluku Indon.
175 K5 Tanew r. Pol.
234 A5 Taneytown MD U.S.A.
205 E5 Tanezrouft reg. Alg./Mali
205 E5 Tanezrouft Tan-Ahenet reg. Alg.
128 G5 Ţanf, Jabal aţ hill Syria
122 H9 Tang Iran
148 B6 Tang Ireland
122 H9 Tang, Ra's-e pt Iran
107 L1 Tanga Rus. Fed.
211 C6 Tanga Tanz.
211 C6 Tanga admin. reg. Tanz.
80 I3 Tangaehe North I. N.Z.
117 L7 Tangail Bangl.
213 □J4 Tangainony Madag.
91 L7 Tanga Islands P.N.G.
114 G9 Tangalla Sri Lanka
244 E6 Tangamandapio Mex.
244 E6 Tangancícuaro de Arista Mex.
Tanganyika country Africa see Tanzania
211 A6 Tanganyika, Lake Africa
122 F3 Tangar Iran
255 C8 Tangará Brazil
78 □6 Tangarare Guadalcanal Solomon Is
208 C2 Tangaray Chad
114 E8 Tangasseri Kerala India
108 D5 Tangdan Yunnan China
111 K11 Tangdê Xizang China
Tangdukou Hunan China see Shaoyang
127 P9 Tang-e Kalleh Iran
122 F3 Tangeli Iran
142 H1 Tangen Norway
263 D2 Tange Promontory hd Antarctica
204 D2 Tanger Morocco
180 D5 Tanger prov. Morocco
94 G8 Tangerang Jawa Indon.
171 E6 Tangerhütte Ger.
170 E5 Tangermünde Ger.
180 D5 Tanger-Tétouan prov. Morocco
122 H8 Tang-e Sarkheh Iran
106 F8 Tanggarma Qinghai China
111 J11 Tanggo Xizang China
108 D2 Tanggor Sichuan China
107 O7 Tanggu Tianjin China
106 C9 Tanggulashan Qinghai China
111 J10 Tanggula Shan mt. Qinghai/Xizang China
111 I10 Tanggula Shan mts Xizang China
111 J10 Tanggula Shankou pass Xizang China
111 G12 Tangguo Xizang China
107 O7 Tanghai Hebei China
109 I2 Tanghe Henan China
109 I2 Tang He r. China
123 N4 Tangi Pak.
Tangier Morocco see Tanger
233 I11 Tangier Island VA U.S.A.
80 J7 Tangimoana North I. N.Z.
93 B5 Tangkelemboko, Gunung mt. Indon.
94 F7 Tangkittebak, Gunung mt. Indon.
111 I13 Tang La pass Xizang China
96 A1 Tangla Assam India
108 B2 Tanglag Qinghai China
94 □ Tanglin Sing.
111 L11 Tangmai Xizang China
106 G9 Tangnag Qinghai China
104 B4 Tango Japan
85 J6 Tangorin Qld Austr.
111 H11 Tangra Yumco salt l. China
94 A2 Tangse Sumatera Indon.
Tangshan Guizhou China see Shiqian
107 P7 Tangshan Hebei China
168 J3 Tangstedt Ger.
Tangsyq Kazakh. see Tansyk
96 C3 Tangte mt. Myanmar
92 D7 Tangub Mindanao Phil.
92 D6 Tangub Negros Phil.
207 F4 Tanguieta Benin
108 H5 Tangwan Hunan China
100 F4 Tangwanghe Heilong. China
100 F5 Tangwang He r. China
107 N7 Tangxian Hebei China
109 I3 Tangxianzhen Hubei China
96 D3 Tang-yan Myanmar
108 G4 Tangyan He r. China
107 N9 Tangyin Henan China
100 F5 Tangyuan Heilong. China
254 E5 Tanhaçu Brazil
140 S3 Tanhua Fin.
245 J4 Tanhuijo, Arrecife rf Mex.
97 G9 Tani Cambodia
108 A3 Taniantaweng Shan mts Xizang China
105 I2 Tanigawa-dake mt. Japan
104 E4 Tanigumi Japan
91 H8 Tanimbar, Kepulauan is Indon.
160 J4 Taninges France
Taninthari Myanmar see Tenasserim
Tanintharyi Myanmar see Tenasserim
Tanintharyi admin. div. Myanmar see Tenasserim
Taninthayi Myanmar see Tenasserim
93 F5 Taniwel Seram Indon.
103 H15 Taniyama Japan
Tanjah Morocco see Tanger
92 D7 Tanjay Negros Phil.
106 H8 Tanjiajing Gansu China
Tanjore Tamil Nadu India see Thanjavur
95 K6 Tanjung Kalimantan Indon.
94 F5 Tanjung Sumatera Indon.
94 C3 Tanjungbalai Sumatera Indon.
94 E4 Tanjungbalai Sumatera Indon.
93 E5 Tanjungbaliha Maluku Indon.
95 M3 Tanjungbatu Kalimantan Indon.
94 E4 Tanjungbatu Sumatera Indon.
95 M4 Tanjungbuayabuaya, Pulau i. Indon.
94 E6 Tanjungenim Sumatera Indon.
95 L6 Tanjunggaru Kalimantan Indon.
Tanjungkarang-Telukbetung Sumatera Indon. see Bandar Lampung
95 G6 Tanjungpandan Indon.
94 F4 Tanjungpinang Indon.
94 C3 Tanjungpura Sumatera Indon.
95 J6 Tanjung Puting, Taman Nasional nat. park Indon.
94 F6 Tanjungraja Sumatera Indon.
95 L3 Tanjungredeb Kalimantan Indon.
95 H5 Tanjungsaleh i. Indon.
95 H5 Tanjungsatai Kalimantan Indon.
95 L3 Tanjungselor Kalimantan Indon.
123 N5 Tank Pak.
116 C8 Tankara Gujarat India
140 S2 Tankavaara Fin.
116 D9 Tankhala Gujarat India
106 I1 Tankhoy Rus. Fed.
116 G2 Tanktse Jammu and Kashmir
214 D8 Tankwa r. S. Africa
214 D8 Tankwa-Karoo National Park S. Africa
245 H4 Tanlacut Mex.
245 I4 Tanlajas Mex.
156 H8 Tanlay France
96 B5 Tanlwe r. Myanmar
173 N5 Tann Ger.
169 J9 Tann (Rhon) Ger.
171 E10 Tanna Ger.
78 □5 Tanna i. Vanuatu
146 K9 Tannadice Angus, Scotland U.K.
104 B5 Tannan Japan
141 L5 Tännäs Sweden
160 D2 Tannay Bourgogne France
157 I4 Tannay Champagne-Ardenne France
169 K7 Tanne Ger.
Tannenberg Pol. see Stębark
222 G5 Tanner, Mount B.C. Can.
161 J9 Tanneron France
234 E2 Tannersville PA U.S.A.
173 M2 Tännesberg Ger.
173 I4 Tannhausen Ger.
178 C5 Tannheim Austria
173 I6 Tannheim Ger.
178 B4 Tannheimer Gebirge mts Austria/Ger.
140 R4 Tannila Fin.
142 G4 Tannis Bugt b. Denmark
Tannoa i. Vanuatu see Tongoa
171 D9 Tannroda Ger.
85 M7 Tannum Sands Qld Austr.
106 B1 Tannu-Ola, Khrebet mts Rus. Fed.
Tannu Tuva aut. rep. Rus. Fed. see Tyva, Respublika
103 I15 Tano Japan
92 D7 Tañon Strait Phil.
116 C6 Tanot Rajasthan India
207 H3 Tanout Niger
174 C2 Tanowo Pol.
245 I4 Tanquian Mex.
117 I6 Tansen Nepal
109 M6 Tanshui Taiwan
206 D3 Tansilla Burkina
149 N7 Tansley Derbyshire, England U.K.
121 R4 Tansyk Kazakh.
203 F2 Ţanţā Egypt
96 C5 Tantabin Pegu Myanmar
96 B3 Tantabin Sagaing Myanmar
96 B6 Tantabin Yangôn Myanmar
204 C3 Tan-Tan Morocco
82 H7 Tantanoola S.A. Austr.
104 A5 Tantō Japan
157 L7 Tantonville France
170 J4 Tantow Ger.
245 I4 Tantoyuca Mex.
116 F6 Tantpur Uttar Prad. India
107 R3 Tantu Jilin China
114 G4 Tanuku Andhra Prad. India
105 K3 Tanuma Japan
84 E4 Tanumbirini N.T. Austr.
142 H3 Tanumshede Sweden
176 E1 Tanvald Czech Rep.
204 B5 Tanwakka, Sabkhat well Western Sahara
96 I3 Tanxu Guangxi China
137 R4 Tanyushivka Ukr.
211 B6 Tanzania country Africa
105 J5 Tanzawa-Ōyama Kokutei-kōen park Japan
222 D3 Tanzilla r. B.C. Can.
216 □3c Tao Lanzarote Canary Is
97 D9 Tao, Ko i. Thai.
Tao'an Jilin China see Taonan
Taobh Tuath Western Isles, Scotland U.K. see Northton
Taocheng Fujian China see Yongchun
Taocheng Guangdong China see Daxin
109 H6 Taochuan Hunan China
107 Q8 Taocun Shandong China
Taodeni Mali see Taoudenni
107 R4 Tao'er He r. China
106 H9 Tao He r. China
Taohong Hunan China see Longhui
Taohuajiang Hunan China see Taojiang
Taohuaping Hunan China see Longhui
109 I4 Taojiang Hunan China
Taolanaro Madag. see Tôlañaro
106 J7 Taole Ningxia China
107 R4 Taonan Jilin China
195 I8 Taormina Sicilia Italy
239 L8 Taos NM U.S.A.
207 F2 Taouârdeï well Mali
204 E5 Taoudenni Mali
204 D2 Taounate Morocco
205 E5 Taounnant well Mali
204 E2 Taourirt Morocco
204 D3 Taouz Morocco
109 K6 Taoxi Fujian China
Taoyang Gansu China see Lintao
109 H4 Taoyuan Hunan China
109 M6 T'aoyüan Taiwan
Taozhou Anhui China see Guangde
138 I2 Tapa Estonia
92 C9 Tapaan Passage Phil.
243 M10 Tapachula Mex.
78 □2 Tapaga Point Samoa
94 D2 Tapah Malaysia
251 H5 Tapajós r. Brazil
94 B3 Tapaktuan Sumatera Indon.
244 D6 Tapalpa Mex.
261 G5 Tapalqué Arg.
94 D6 Tapan Sumatera Indon.
Tapan Turkey see Mansurlu
251 H3 Tapanahoni r. Suriname
245 M9 Tapanatepec Mex.
94 C4 Tapanuli, Teluk b. Indon.
251 H5 Tapará, Ilha Grande do i. Brazil
251 H5 Tapara, Serra do hills Brazil
93 E4 Tapat i. Maluku Indon.
251 E6 Tapauá Brazil
251 E6 Tapauá r. Brazil
81 G8 Tapawera South I. N.Z.
255 B9 Tapera Rio Grande do Sul Brazil
251 F5 Tapera Roraima Brazil
259 C7 Tapera Chile
253 E3 Tapera Pesoe Brazil
254 F5 Taperoá Brazil
255 C9 Tapes Brazil
206 C5 Tapeta Liberia
173 J4 Tapfheim Ger.
116 D9 Tapi r. India
97 D10 Ta Pi, Mae Nam r. Thai.
253 F4 Tapia, Sierra de hills Bol.
182 G1 Tapia de Casariego Spain
259 C8 Tapi Aike Arg.
92 D8 Tapiantana i. Phil.
Tapiau Rus. Fed. see Gvardeysk
250 C6 Tapiche r. Peru
243 M9 Tapijulapa Mex.
95 I5 Tapinbini Kalimantan Indon.
177 J4 Tápió r. Hungary
177 I4 Tápióbicske Hungary
256 D2 Tapiocanga, Chapada do hills Brazil
177 I4 Tápiógyörgye Hungary
177 I4 Tápióság Hungary
177 I4 Tápiószecső Hungary
177 I4 Tápiószele Hungary
177 I4 Tápiószőlős Hungary
256 D3 Tapira Minas Gerais Brazil
256 A5 Tapira Paraná Brazil
254 D5 Tapiracanga Brazil
256 D5 Tapiraí Brazil
253 H2 Tapirapé r. Brazil
251 E4 Tapirapecó, Sierra mts Brazil/Venez.
253 F3 Tapirapuã Brazil
94 E2 Tapis, Gunung mt. Malaysia
242 E4 Tapisuelas Mex.
176 F4 Táplánszentkereszt Hungary
117 K6 Taplejung Nepal
109 □J7 Tap Mun Chau i. H.K. China
207 F3 Tapoa watercourse Burkina
208 B2 Tapol Chad
176 G5 Tapolca Hungary
96 D4 Ta-pom Myanmar
146 K8 Tap o' Noth hill Scotland U.K.
232 I11 Tappahannock VA U.S.A.
116 F5 Tappal Uttar Prad. India
95 M6 Tappalang Sulawesi Indon.
235 H2 Tappan NY U.S.A.
232 D8 Tappan Lake OH U.S.A.
122 D4 Tappeh, Kūh-e hill Iran
102 R5 Tappi-zaki pt Japan
129 H5 Tap Qaraqoyunlu Azer.
Taprobane country Asia see Sri Lanka
176 G5 Tapsony Hungary
100 B2 Taptugary Rus. Fed.
79 □8a Tapu, Motu i. Tonga
81 H8 Tapuaenuku mt. South I. N.Z.
92 C9 Tapul Phil.
92 C9 Tapul Group is Phil.
94 C4 Tapulonanjing mt. Indon.
94 D4 Tapung r. Indon.
251 F6 Tapurú Brazil
251 E5 Tapurucuara Brazil
78 □2 Taputapu, Cape American Samoa
Taputeouea atoll Gilbert Is Kiribati see Tabiteuea
124 G9 Taqar mt. Yemen
122 E6 Ţāqestān, Chāh-e well Iran
127 L6 Ţaqţaq Iraq
255 C9 Taquara Brazil
256 A1 Taquaral, Serra do hills Brazil
253 F4 Taquarí r. Brazil
253 F4 Taquarí, Pantanal do marsh Brazil
256 C4 Taquaritinga Brazil
256 C5 Taquarituba Brazil
256 A4 Taquaruçu r. Brazil
260 B5 Taquimilán Arg.
177 I4 Tar Hungary
147 G8 Tar r. Ireland
85 M9 Tara Qld Austr.
196 H7 Tara r. Montenegro
196 H7 Tara nat. park Montenegro
147 I5 Tara, Hill of Ireland
207 H4 Taraba r. Nigeria
207 H4 Taraba state Nigeria
256 B5 Tarabaí Brazil
252 D4 Tarabuco Bol.
202 B1 Ţarābulus Libya
183 N7 Taracena Spain
136 H8 Taraclia Moldova
252 C3 Taraco Peru
250 D4 Taracua Brazil
80 K6 Taradale North I. N.Z.
161 I10 Taradeau France
202 B3 Tarāghin Libya
123 N9 Tar Ahmad Rind Pak.
117 L6 Tarai reg. India
Taraíra r. Brazil see Traíra
252 E5 Tarairí Bol.
216 □3b Tarajalejo Fuerteventura Canary Is
95 L3 Tarakan Kalimantan Indon.
95 L3 Tarakan i. Indon.
123 L5 Tarakki reg. Afgh.
199 L2 Taraklı Turkey
Tarakliya Moldova see Taraclia
77 I3 Tarakua Fiji
102 X3 Taraku-shima i. Kuril'skiye O-va Rus. Fed.
83 L6 Taralga N.S.W. Austr.
102 □B22 Tarama-jima i. Nansei-shotō Japan
182 F2 Taramundi Spain
138 C7 Taran, Mys pt Rus. Fed.
116 F8 Tarana Madh. Prad. India
116 E5 Taranagar Rajasthan India
80 H6 Taranaki admin. reg. North I. N.Z.
80 I6 Taranaki, Mount vol. North I. N.Z.
183 N8 Tarancón Spain
137 L3 Tarandyntsi Ukr.
80 I2 Taranga Island North I. N.Z.
114 F7 Tarangambadi Tamil Nadu India
208 C2 Tarangara Chad
211 C6 Tarangire National Park Tanz.
Tarangul l. Kazakh. see Tarankol', Ozero
121 M1 Tarankol', Ozero l. Kazakh.
120 J1 Taranovskoye Kazakh.
146 B7 Taransay i. Scotland U.K.
195 M3 Taranto Italy
195 M2 Taranto prov. Italy
195 M3 Taranto, Golfo di g. Italy
176 G5 Tarany Hungary
252 C4 Tarapacá admin. reg. Chile
250 D5 Tarapacá Col.
78 □6 Tarapaina Malaita Solomon Is
250 B6 Tarapoto Peru
160 E5 Tarare France
261 I4 Tarariras Uru.
80 J7 Tararua Forest Park nature res. North I. N.Z.
81 J7 Tararua Range mts North I. N.Z.
Tarasaigh i. Scotland U.K. see Taransay
161 F9 Tarascon France
163 H10 Tarascon-sur-Ariège France
136 F5 Tarashany Ukr.
136 J4 Tarashcha Ukr.
122 G5 Tarasht Iran
137 M7 Tarasivka Khersons'ka Oblast' Ukr.
137 M7 Tarasivka Khersons'ka Oblast' Ukr.
137 L5 Tarasivka Kirovohrads'ka Oblast' Ukr.
137 R4 Tarasivka Luhans'ka Oblast' Ukr.
134 I2 Tarasovo Rus. Fed.
135 H6 Tarasovskiy Rus. Fed.
205 H4 Tarat Alg.
252 C4 Tarata Peru
252 C2 Tarauacá Brazil
250 D6 Tarauacá r. Brazil
79 □9a Taravao Tahiti Fr. Polynesia
79 □9a Taravao, Baie de b. Tahiti Fr. Polynesia
79 □9a Taravao, Isthme de isth. Tahiti Fr. Polynesia
191 P3 Taravisio, Foresta di Italy
192 B4 Taravo r. Corse France
77 H1 Tarawa atoll Kiribati
80 K6 Tarawera North I. N.Z.
80 K5 Tarawera, Lake North I. N.Z.
80 K5 Tarawera, Mount vol. North I. N.Z.
121 N6 Taraz Kazakh.
183 Q5 Tarazona Spain
185 P2 Tarazona de la Mancha Spain
121 S4 Tarbagatay Kazakh.
107 J1 Tarbagatay Rus. Fed.
121 S4 Tarbagatay, Khrebet mts Kazakh.
146 I7 Tarbat Ness pt Scotland U.K.
187 E10 Tárbena Spain
147 D7 Tarbert Ireland
146 E11 Tarbert Argyll and Bute, Scotland U.K.
146 F11 Tarbert Argyll and Bute, Scotland U.K.
146 C7 Tarbert Western Isles, Scotland U.K.
146 D11 Tarbert, Loch inlet Scotland U.K.
163 E9 Tarbes France
146 G10 Tarbet Argyll and Bute, Scotland U.K.
146 H11 Tarbolton South Ayrshire, Scotland U.K.
231 I8 Tarboro NC U.S.A.
177 L5 Tărcaia Romania
177 K3 Tarcal Hungary
177 L4 Tarcea Romania
191 O3 Tarcento Italy
82 E4 Tarcoola S.A. Austr.
83 K4 Tarcoon N.S.W. Austr.
82 D2 Tarcoonyinna watercourse S.A. Austr.
197 K5 Ţarcului, Munţii mts Romania
83 K6 Tarcutta N.S.W. Austr.
175 I4 Tarczyn Pol.
158 H4 Tard r. France
183 M4 Tardajos Spain
183 O5 Tardelcuende Spain
156 F5 Tardenois reg. France
162 J3 Tardes r. France
163 C9 Tardets-Sorholus France
186 D4 Tardienta Spain
162 E4 Tardoire r. France
100 K4 Tardoki-Yani, Gora mt. Rus. Fed.
83 N4 Taree N.S.W. Austr.
210 B2 Tareifing Sudan
83 I4 Tarella N.S.W. Austr.
140 Q3 Tärendö Sweden
244 F5 Tarengo Mex.
207 F2 Tarenkat well Mali
Tarentum Italy see Taranto
244 F6 Taretán Mex.
131 K2 Tareya Rus. Fed.
125 J4 Ţarfā', Baţn aţ depr. Saudi Arabia
124 F7 Ţarfā, Ra's aţ pt Saudi Arabia
204 B4 Tarfaya Morocco
146 K9 Tarfside Angus, Scotland U.K.
207 G2 Targa well Niger
Targan Heilong. China see Talin Hiag
Targan Kazakh. see Targyn
238 I4 Targhee Pass ID U.S.A.
163 D6 Targon France
197 N6 Târgovişte Romania
174 F3 Targowa Górka Pol.
197 P5 Târgu Bujor Romania
197 L6 Târgu Cărbuneşti Romania
197 O3 Târgu Frumos Romania
204 D2 Targuist Morocco
197 L5 Târgu Jiu Romania
197 L3 Târgu Lăpuş Romania
197 M4 Târgu Mureş Romania
197 O3 Târgu Neamţ Romania
197 O4 Târgu Ocna Romania
197 O4 Târgu Secuiesc Romania
111 G12 Targyailing Xizang China
121 T3 Targyn Kazakh.
122 B5 Tarhān Iran
204 D3 Tarhbalt Morocco
Tarhmanant well Mali see Taghmanant
177 K5 Tarhos Hungary
202 B1 Tarhūnah Libya
91 J8 Tari P.N.G.
107 K7 Tarian Gol Nei Mongol China
124 F6 Tarib, Wādī watercourse Saudi Arabia
125 K3 Tarif U.A.E.
184 H8 Tarifa Spain
184 H8 Tarifa, Punta de pt Spain
92 D3 Tarigtig Point Luzon Phil.
252 D5 Tarija Bol.
252 D5 Tarija dept Bol.
114 D6 Tarikere Karnataka India
91 I7 Tariku r. Papua Indon.
110 F6 Tarim Xinjiang China
125 I7 Tarīm Yemen
Tarim Basin China see Tarim Pendi
211 B5 Tarime Tanz.
110 H6 Tarim He r. China
110 H6 Tarim Liuchang Xinjiang China
244 G5 Tarimoro Mex.
110 E7 Tarim Pendi basin China
110 H6 Tarim Qichang Xinjiang China
253 E5 Taringuiti Bol.
123 K5 Tarīn Kowt Afgh.
91 I7 Taritatu r. Papua Indon.
Taritipan Sabah Malaysia see Tandek
177 H4 Tarján Hungary
215 J8 Tarka r. S. Africa
207 G3 Tarka, Vallée de watercourse Niger
177 G4 Tárkány Hungary
215 K8 Tarkastad S. Africa
137 P8 Tarkhan, Mys pt Ukr.
137 L8 Tarkhankut, Mys pt Ukr.
129 I3 Tarki Rus. Fed.
236 H5 Tarkio MO U.S.A.
130 I3 Tarko-Sale Rus. Fed.
206 E5 Tarkwa Ghana
92 C4 Tarlac Luzon Phil.
92 C3 Tarlac r. Luzon Phil.
121 R4 Tarlauly Kazakh.
149 L6 Tarleton Lancashire, England U.K.
83 L6 Tarlo River National Park N.S.W. Austr.
232 C9 Tarlton OH U.S.A.
142 E6 Tarm Denmark
252 B2 Tarma Junín Peru
250 D5 Tarma Loreto Peru
117 L5 Tarmar Xizang China
168 H4 Tarmstedt Ger.
163 I8 Tarn dept France
161 B8 Tarn r. France
161 C8 Tarn, Gorges du France
177 I4 Tarna r. Hungary
183 J2 Tarna, Puerto de pass Spain
140 M4 Tärnaby Sweden
123 K6 Tarnak r. Afgh.
177 J3 Tarnalelesz Hungary
177 J4 Tarnaméra Hungary
177 J4 Tarnaőrs Hungary
177 J4 Tarnaszentmiklós Hungary
197 L4 Târnava Mare r. Romania
197 L4 Târnava Mică r. Romania
197 M4 Târnăveni Romania
175 K5 Tarnawa Duża Pol.
175 L5 Tarnawatka Pol.
163 G7 Tarn-et-Garonne dept France
175 K6 Tarnica mt. Pol.
175 J5 Tarnobrzeg Pol.
175 K5 Tarnogród Pol.
134 H3 Tarnogskiy Gorodok Rus. Fed.
177 H4 Tárnok Hungary
Tarnopol Ukr. see Ternopil'
163 B8 Tarnos France
175 L5 Tarnoszyn Pol.
177 K5 Târnova Arad Romania
197 K5 Târnova Caraş-Severin Romania
170 F3 Tarnow Ger.
174 C3 Tarnów Lubuskie Pol.
175 I5 Tarnów Małopolskie Pol.
175 J6 Tarnowiec Pol.
Tarnowitz Pol. see Tarnowskie Góry
174 E2 Tarnówka Pol.
174 E3 Tarnowo Podgórne Pol.
174 G5 Tarnów Opolski Pol.
174 G5 Tarnowskie Góry Pol.
140 M3 Tårnvik Norway
190 I6 Taro r. Italy
102 S7 Tarō Japan
111 F11 Taro Co salt l. China
122 F7 Ţārom Iran
137 N5 Taroms'ke Ukr.
163 D8 Taron-Sadirac-Viellenave France
85 L8 Taroom Qld Austr.
105 J2 Tarō-san mt. Japan
182 E6 Tarouca Port.
204 C3 Taroudannt Morocco
182 D6 Tarouquela Port.
168 H1 Tarp Ger.
177 L3 Tarpa Hungary
84 F5 Tarpaulin Swamp N.T. Austr.
82 H7 Tarpeena S.A. Austr.
231 F11 Tarpon Springs FL U.S.A.
149 L7 Tarporley Cheshire, England U.K.
175 L1 Tarprubežiai Lith.
246 E1 Tarpum Bay Eleuthera Bahamas
122 D5 Tarq Iran
122 D6 Tarqān Iran
192 H3 Tarquinia Italy
192 H3 Tarquinia Lido Italy
Tarquinii Italy see Tarquinia
84 E5 Tarrabool Lake salt flat N.T. Austr.
Tarracina Italy see Terracina
Tarraco Spain see Tarragona
206 □ Tarrafal Santiago Cape Verde
186 H5 Tarragona Spain
186 G5 Tarragona prov. Spain
83 K10 Tarraleah Tas. Austr.
83 K5 Tarran Hills N.S.W. Austr.
84 G4 Tarrant Point Qld Austr.
81 D11 Tarras South I. N.Z.
Tarrasa Spain see Terrassa
186 H4 Tàrrega Spain
146 I7 Tarrel Highland, Scotland U.K.
178 C5 Tarrenz Austria
182 D2 Tarrio Spain
186 H4 Tarroja de Segarra Spain
235 H2 Tarrytown NY U.S.A.
142 H7 Tårs Denmark
193 Q8 Tarsia Italy
202 C4 Tarso Ahon mt. Chad
202 C4 Tarso Emissi mt. Chad
202 C4 Tarso Kobour mt. Chad
126 G5 Tarsus Turkey
128 C2 Tarsus r. Turkey
170 E1 Tårs Vig b. Denmark
111 K8 Tart Qinghai China
122 E1 Tarta Turkm.
258 E1 Tartagal Salta Arg.
258 F3 Tartagal Santa Fé Arg.
175 M5 Tartakiv Ukr.
129 H5 Tärtär Azer.
129 H5 Tärtär r. Azer.
129 I5 Tärtär r. Azer.
191 M5 Tartaro r. Italy
163 C8 Tartas France
138 J3 Tartu Estonia
128 D4 Ţarţūs Syria
128 E3 Ţarţūs governorate Syria
104 E5 Tarui Japan
Tarumae-san vol. Japan see Shikotsu
257 G3 Tarumirim Brazil
103 H15 Tarumizu Japan
129 H1 Tarumovka Rus. Fed.
96 C1 Tarung Hka r. Myanmar
139 U7 Tarusa Rus. Fed.
139 U7 Tarusa r. Rus. Fed.
125 J2 Tārūt Saudi Arabia
97 D11 Tarutao, Ko i. Thai.
97 D11 Tarutao National Park Thai.
94 C3 Tarutung Sumatera Indon.
136 I7 Tarutyne Ukr.
146 L8 Tarves Aberdeenshire, Scotland U.K.
149 L7 Tarvin Cheshire, England U.K.
191 P2 Tarvisio Italy
Tarvisium Italy see Treviso
253 E3 Tarvo Bol.
195 □ Tarxien Malta
106 F1 Tarys-Arzhan Rus. Fed.
122 G6 Tarz Iran
121 O4 Tasaral Kazakh.
202 B3 Tasāwah Libya
120 K5 Tasbuget Kazakh.
190 D3 Täsch Switz.
224 E3 Taschereau Que. Can.
222 F5 Taseko Mountain B.C. Can.
205 F4 Tasendjanet, Oued watercourse Alg.
114 D4 Tasgaon Mahar. India
129 A5 Taşgeçit Turkey
137 N4 Tashan' r. Ukr.
Tashauz Turkm. see Daşoguz
Tashauzskaya Oblast' admin. div. Turkm. see Daşoguz
121 Q7 Tash-Bashat Kyrg.
136 H8 Tashbunar r. Ukr.
106 D6 Tashi Gansu China
Tashi Chho Bhutan see Thimphu
117 M6 Tashigang Bhutan
Tashino Rus. Fed. see Pervomaysk
129 F4 Tashir Armenia
122 E7 Tashk, Daryācheh-ye l. Iran
Tashkent Uzbek. see Toshkent
Tashkent Oblast admin. div. Uzbek. see Toshkent
121 O7 Tash-Kömür Kyrg.
Tash-Kumyr Kyrg. see Tash-Kömür
120 E2 Tashla Rus. Fed.
137 K4 Tashlyk Ukr.
Tāshqurghān Afgh. see Kholm
225 F1 Tasialujjuaq, Lac l. Que. Can.
224 F1 Tasiat, Lac l. Que. Can.
221 O3 Tasiilap Karra c. Greenland
Tasiilaq Greenland see Ammassalik
95 H8 Tasikmalaya Jawa Indon.
128 D6 Tasīl Syria
168 K1 Tåsinge i. Denmark
225 G1 Tasiujaq Que. Can.
221 M2 Tasiusaq Greenland
140 M4 Tåsjö Sweden
207 H3 Task well Niger
128 B1 Taşkale Turkey
129 E6 Taşkapı Turkey
128 A2 Taşkent Turkey
207 H3 Tasker Niger
121 S4 Taskesken Kazakh.
129 B5 Taşkıran Turkey
126 G3 Taşköprü Turkey
127 K4 Taşlıçay Turkey
129 E5 Taşlıoğul Turkey
81 H8 Tasman South I. N.Z.
81 G8 Tasman admin. reg. South I. N.Z.
81 E11 Tasman r. South I. N.Z.
81 E10 Tasman, Mount South I. N.Z.
266 F8 Tasman Abyssal Plain sea feature Austr.
265 O7 Tasman Basin sea feature Tasman Sea
81 H8 Tasman Bay South I. N.Z.
83 K10 Tasman Head Tas. Austr.
83 J10 Tasmania state Austr.
81 G8 Tasman Mountains South I. N.Z.
83 L10 Tasman Peninsula Tas. Austr.
77 H6 Tasman Sea S. Pacific Ocean
197 K3 Tăşnad Romania
121 O6 Tasotkel'skoye Vodokhranilishche resr Kazakh.
126 H3 Taşova Turkey
177 I4 Tass Hungary
148 D5 Tassagh Northern Ireland U.K.
207 G2 Tassara Niger
207 G2 Tassa Takorat well Niger
205 F4 Tassedjefit, Erg des. Alg.
160 F2 Tasselot, Mont hill France
207 F3 Tasserest well Mali
208 A5 Tassi Gabon
224 F1 Tassialouc, Lac l. Que. Can.
205 G5 Tassili du Hoggar plat. Alg.
205 G4 Tassili n'Ajjer plat. Alg.
160 F5 Tassin-la-Demi-Lune France
186 F5 Tastavíns r. Spain
131 N3 Tas-Tumus Rus. Fed.
121 M5 Tasty Kazakh.
121 L2 Tasty-Taldy Kazakh.
222 C4 Tasu B.C. Can.
128 B2 Taşucu Turkey
122 A2 Tasūj Iran
131 M3 Tas-Yuryakh Rus. Fed.
177 G5 Taszár Hungary
177 H4 Tát Hungary
177 H4 Tata Hungary
204 D3 Tata Morocco
79 □9a Tataa, Pointe pt Tahiti Fr. Polynesia
93 C4 Tataba Sulawesi Indon.
177 H4 Tatabánya Hungary
177 I5 Tataháza Hungary
245 M7 Tatahuicapan Mex.
106 D8 Tatalin Gol r. Qinghai China
245 J9 Tataltepec Mex.
225 I4 Tatamagouche N.S. Can.
93 D8 Tatamailau, Foho mt. East Timor
78 □6 Tatamba Sta Isabel Solomon Is
117 K8 Tatanagar Jharkhand India
205 H2 Tataouine Tunisia
136 I8 Tatarbunary Ukr.
138 L8 Tatarka Belarus
137 O5 Tatarka r. Ukr.
199 L4 Tatarlı Afyon Turkey
128 E1 Tatarlı Osmaniye Turkey
116 F6 Tatarpur Rajasthan India
130 I4 Tatarsk Novosibirskaya Oblast' Rus. Fed.
139 O7 Tatarsk Smolenskaya Oblast' Rus. Fed.
Tatarskaya A.S.S.R. aut. rep. Rus. Fed. see Tatarstan, Respublika
100 L3 Tatarskiy Proliv str. Rus. Fed.
134 J5 Tatarstan, Respublika aut. rep. Rus. Fed.
Tatar Strait Rus. Fed. see Tatarskiy Proliv
177 I4 Tatárszentgyörgy Hungary
197 O3 Tătăruşi Romania
79 □9a Tatatua, Pointe pt Tahiti Fr. Polynesia
95 J3 Tatau Sarawak Malaysia
122 A3 Tatavi r. Iran
129 I2 Tatayurt Rus. Fed.
85 I4 Tate r. Qld Austr.
105 K3 Tatebayashi Japan
104 D4 Tateishi-misaki pt Japan
105 K1 Tateiwa Japan
105 H3 Tateshina Japan
105 H3 Tateshina-yama mt. Japan
105 K6 Tateyama Chiba Japan
104 F2 Tateyama Toyama Japan
104 G2 Tate-yama vol. Japan
222 G2 Tathlina Lake N.W.T. Can.
124 F6 Tathlīth Saudi Arabia
124 G5 Tathlīth, Wādī watercourse Saudi Arabia
83 L7 Tathra N.S.W. Austr.
213 E4 Tati Botswana
206 B2 Tâtîlt well Maur.
168 G2 Tating Ger.
223 L2 Tatinnai Lake Nunavut Can.
120 A2 Tatishchevo Rus. Fed.
96 C4 Tatkon Myanmar
222 E5 Tatla Lake B.C. Can.
222 E5 Tatla Lake l. B.C. Can.
222 E3 Tatlatui Provincial Park B.C. Can.
222 E5 Tatlayoko Lake B.C. Can.
129 G4 Tatlı Azer.
223 N3 Tatnam, Cape Man. Can.
105 I4 Tatomi Japan
Tatra Mountains Pol./Slovakia see Tatry
111 G7 Tatrang Xinjiang China
177 J2 Tatranská Javorina Slovakia
177 J2 Tatranský nat. park Slovakia
175 H6 Tatry mts Pol./Slovakia
175 H6 Tatrzański Park Narodowy nat. park Pol.
222 B3 Tatshenshini r. B.C. Can.
222 B3 Tatshenshini-Alsek Provincial Wilderness Park B.C. Can.
135 H6 Tatsinskiy Rus. Fed.
103 L12 Tatsuno Hyōgo Japan
105 G4 Tatsuno Nagano Japan
104 E3 Tatsunokuchi Japan
104 E1 Tatsuruhama Japan
105 G6 Tatsuyama Japan
123 L9 Tatta Pak.
149 Q7 Tattershall Lincolnshire, England U.K.
121 O6 Tatti Kazakh.
Tatty Kazakh. see Tatti
80 I5 Tatu hill North I. N.Z.
256 D5 Tatuí Brazil
222 E4 Tatuk Mountain B.C. Can.
138 H5 Tatula r. Lith.
237 D9 Tatum NM U.S.A.
237 H9 Tatum TX U.S.A.
127 K4 Tatvan Turkey
78 □2 Ta'u i. American Samoa
142 B2 Tau Norway
79 □8a Tau i. Tonga
254 E3 Taua Brazil
78 □4b Tauak Passage Pohnpei Micronesia
251 F5 Tauapeçaçu Brazil
251 F6 Tauariã Brazil
257 E5 Taubaté Brazil
171 H8 Taubenheim Ger.
172 H2 Tauber r. Ger.
172 H2 Tauberbischofsheim Ger.
172 H3 Taubergrund reg. Ger.
171 F8 Taucha Ger.
171 J6 Tauche Ger.
120 D5 Tauchik Kazakh.
171 J7 Tauer Ger.
173 L5 Taufkirchen Bayern Ger.
173 M5 Taufkirchen Bayern Ger.
173 M5 Taufkirchen (Vils) Ger.
169 H9 Taufstein hill Ger.
80 K5 Tauhara mt. North I. N.Z.
80 I3 Tauhoa North I. N.Z.
251 G4 Tauini r. Brazil
121 P5 Taukum, Peski des. Kazakh.
158 D4 Taulé France
161 F8 Taulignan France
80 J5 Taumarunui North I. N.Z.
252 B2 Taumaturgo Brazil
253 G5 Taunay Brazil
215 I3 Taung S. Africa
96 C7 Taungbon Myanmar
96 B4 Taungdwingyi Myanmar
96 C4 Taunggyi Myanmar
96 C4 Taunglau Myanmar
96 C5 Taung-ngu Myanmar
96 C6 Taungnyo Range mts Myanmar
96 B4 Taungtha Myanmar
96 B5 Taungup Myanmar
123 N6 Taunsa Pak.
150 F5 Taunton Somerset, England U.K.
233 N7 Taunton MA U.S.A.
169 E10 Taunus hills Ger.
80 □ Taupeka Point Chatham Is S. Pacific Ocean
80 J4 Taupiri North I. N.Z.
179 J4 Tauplitz Austria
80 K5 Taupo North I. N.Z.
80 J5 Taupo, Lake North I. N.Z.
138 F6 Tauragė Lith.
138 E6 Tauralaukis Lith.
250 C3 Tauramena Col.
80 K4 Tauranga North I. N.Z.
Taurasia Italy see Torino
224 F4 Taureau, Réservoir resr Que. Can.
195 K7 Taurianova Italy
80 I2 Taurikura North I. N.Z.
162 G4 Taurion r. France
195 O4 Taurisano Italy
Tauriuiná r. Brazil see Verde
80 H2 Tauroa Point North I. N.Z.
Taurus Mountains Turkey see Toros Dağları
Taūshyq Kazakh. see Tauchik
186 C4 Tauste Spain
177 K5 Tăuţ Romania
163 J10 Tautavel France
158 I3 Taute r. France
171 E9 Tautenhain Ger.
177 L4 Tăuteu Romania
79 □9a Tautira Tahiti Fr. Polynesia
160 B5 Tauves France
80 M5 Tauwhareparae North I. N.Z.
131 Q4 Tauyskaya Guba g. Rus. Fed.
Tauz Azer. see Tovuz
192 B3 Tavaco Corse France
191 O3 Tavagnacco Italy
196 H4 Tavankut Vojvodina Serbia

190 C1 Tavannes Switz.
159 L7 Tavant France
231 G11 Tavares FL U.S.A.
191 K8 Tavarnelle Val di Pesa Italy
199 K5 Tavas Turkey
Tavastehus Fin. see Hämeenlinna
160 G2 Tavaux France
130 H4 Tavda Rus. Fed.
182 D8 Taveiro Port.
161 F8 Tavel France
140 P4 Tavelsjö Sweden
151 O2 Taverham Norfolk, England U.K.
195 L5 Taverna Italy
160 E2 Tavernay France
122 F1 Tavernelle Italy
161 I9 Tavernes France
187 E9 Tavernes de la Valldigna Spain
150 C4 Tavernspite Pembrokeshire, Wales U.K.
156 D5 Taverny France
190 H7 Taverone r. Italy
186 J4 Tavertet Spain
79 □7 Taveuni i. Fiji
195 O4 Taviano Italy
192 D3 Tavignano r. Corse France
129 H7 Tavīl Iran
123 N2 Tavildara Tajik.
193 O4 Taviolere plain Italy
184 D6 Tavira Port.
184 D6 Tavira, Ilha de i. Port.
226 N6 Tavistock Ont. Can.
150 D6 Tavistock Devon, England U.K.
193 M3 Tavo r. Italy
192 D6 Tavolara, Isola i. Sardegna Italy
121 Q1 Tavolzhan Kazakh.
182 E6 Távora r. Spain
97 D7 Tavoy Myanmar
97 D8 Tavoy r. mouth Myanmar
Tavoy Island Myanmar see Mali Kyun
97 D8 Tavoy Point Myanmar
121 T2 Tavricheskoye Kazakh.
Tavril Kazakh. see Tavricheskoye
137 M7 Tavriys'k Ukr.
199 K3 Tavşanlı Turkey
79 □7a Tavua Viti Levu Fiji
79 □7a Tavua i. Fiji
79 □7 Tavuki Kadavu Fiji
191 N8 Tavullia Italy
129 G4 Tavush r. Armenia
150 D7 Tavy r. England U.K.
150 D5 Taw r. England U.K.
124 G5 Tawa, Jabal at hill Saudi Arabia
81 I8 Tawa North I. N.Z.
95 L2 Tawai, Bukit mt. Malaysia
237 H9 Tawakoni, Lake TX U.S.A.
84 E3 Tawallah Range hills N.T. Austr.
117 M6 Tawang Arun. Prad. India
78 □6 Tawaraha San Cristobal Solomon Is
104 C6 Tawaramoto Japan
78 □6 Tawarogha San Cristobal Solomon Is
227 K5 Tawas Bay MI U.S.A.
227 K5 Tawas City MI U.S.A.
95 L2 Tawau Sabah Malaysia
95 L2 Tawau, Teluk b. Malaysia
203 G3 Ṭawd Egypt
Tawè Myanmar see Tavoy
150 E4 Tawe r. Wales U.K.
202 E6 Taweisha Sudan
172 B2 Tawern Ger.
80 K5 Tawhiuau mt. North I. N.Z.
116 E3 Tawi r. India
125 L3 Ṭawī Ḩafīr well U.A.E.
202 E6 Tawila Sudan
124 A2 Ṭawīlah, Juzur is Egypt
Ṭawīla Islands Egypt see Ṭawīlah, Juzur
125 L3 Ṭawī Murra well U.A.E.
92 B9 Tawitawi i. Phil.
96 C2 Tawmaw Myanmar
100 M7 Tawu Taiwan
245 H7 Taxco Mex.
178 G5 Taxenbach Austria
120 H6 Taxiatosh Uzbek.
123 O5 Taxila tourist site Pak.
111 B8 Taxkorgan Xinjiang China
120 I6 Taxtako'pir Uzbek.
222 C2 Tay r. Y.T. Can.
146 J10 Tay r. Scotland U.K.
146 J10 Tay, Firth of est. Scotland U.K.
87 F12 Tay, Lake salt flat W.A. Austr.
146 H10 Tay, Loch l. Scotland U.K.
252 A2 Tayabamba Peru
92 C5 Tayabas Bay Luzon Phil.
95 I4 Tayan Kalimantan Indon.
134 F1 Taybola Rus. Fed.
120 F3 Tayeeglow Somalia
199 H2 Tayfur Turkey
130 J4 Tayga Rus. Fed.
122 D4 Tāygān Iran
106 E3 Taygan Mongolia
198 D5 Taygetos mts Greece
146 E11 Tayinloan Argyll and Bute, Scotland U.K.
136 J7 Tayirove Ukr.
100 I1 Taykanskiy Khrebet mts Rus. Fed.
222 F3 Taylor B.C. Can.
241 V7 Taylor AZ U.S.A.
236 F5 Taylor NE U.S.A.
234 D2 Taylor PA U.S.A.
237 G10 Taylor TX U.S.A.
239 K7 Taylor r. CO U.S.A.
81 F10 Taylor, Mount South I. N.Z.
239 K9 Taylor, Mount NM U.S.A.
234 D6 Taylors Bridge DE U.S.A.
148 B7 Taylor's Cross Ireland
220 E6 Taylorsville KY U.S.A.
234 A6 Taylorsville MD U.S.A.
231 G8 Taylorsville NC U.S.A.
235 G3 Taylortown NJ U.S.A.
236 K6 Taylorville IL U.S.A.
124 D2 Taymā' Saudi Arabia
233 □S2 Taymouth N.B. Can.
131 K3 Taymura r. Rus. Fed.
131 L2 Taymyr, Ozero l. Rus. Fed.
131 J2 Taymyr, Poluostrov pen. Rus. Fed.
Taymyr Peninsula Rus. Fed. see Taymyr, Poluostrov
97 H9 Tây Ninh Vietnam
146 F10 Taynuilt Argyll and Bute, Scotland U.K.
244 B1 Tayoltita Mex.
120 D3 Taypak Kazakh.
Taypaq Kazakh. see Taypak
146 K10 Tayport Fife, Scotland U.K.
131 K4 Tayshet Rus. Fed.
120 E3 Taysoygan, Peski des. Kazakh.
Tayspun tourist site Iraq see Ctesiphon
199 J4 Taytan Turkey
92 C4 Taytay Luzon Phil.
92 B6 Taytay Palawan Phil.
92 B6 Taytay Bay Palawan Phil.
92 E6 Taytay Point Leyte Phil.
95 I8 Tayu Jawa Indon.
100 D3 Tayuan Heilong. China
148 F1 Tayvallich Argyll and Bute, Scotland U.K.
122 I4 Tayyebād Iran
128 C10 Tayyib al Ism Saudi Arabia
121 M1 Tayynsha Kazakh.
130 I3 Taz r. Rus. Fed.
204 E2 Taza Morocco
180 D5 Taza-Al Hoceima-Taounate prov. Morocco
Taza-Bazar Uzbek. see Shumanay
216 □3d Tazacorte La Palma Canary Is
129 H5 Tāzākānd Azer.
127 L6 Tāza Khurmātū Iraq
105 G3 Tazawa Japan
102 R7 Tazawa-ko l. Japan
96 B3 Taze Myanmar
122 B2 Tazeh Kand Azer.
129 I6 Tāzeh Kand-e Angūt Iran
204 D3 Tazenakht Morocco
232 B12 Tazewell TN U.S.A.
232 D11 Tazewell VA U.S.A.
223 I2 Tazin r. N.W.T./Sask. Can.
223 I3 Tazin Lake Sask. Can.
202 D3 Tāzirbū Libya
202 D3 Tazirbu Water Wells Field Libya
207 H2 Tazizilet well Niger
177 I5 Tázlár Hungary
197 O4 Tazlău Romania
197 O4 Tazlău r. Romania
189 C7 Tazoghrane Tunisia
207 H2 Tazolé well Niger
183 J1 Tazones Spain
205 E5 Tazouikert hill Mali
130 I3 Tazovskaya Guba sea chan. Rus. Fed.
130 I3 Tazovskiy Rus. Fed.
205 G5 Tazrouk Alg.
204 D3 Tazzarine Morocco
204 E2 Tazzouguert Morocco
Tbessa Alg. see Tébessa
129 F4 T'bilisi Georgia
135 H7 Tbilisskaya Rus. Fed.
207 I5 Tchabal Gangdaba mt. Cameroon
207 I5 Tchabal Mbabo mt. Cameroon
Tchad country Africa see Chad
207 F4 Tchamba Togo
207 F4 Tchaourou Benin
207 F5 Tchetti Benin
208 A5 Tchibanga Gabon
207 G2 Tchidoutene watercourse Niger
202 C5 Tchié well Chad
202 B4 Tchigaï, Plateau du Niger
209 B8 Tchihepepe Angola
209 C8 Tchikala-Tcholohanga Angola
208 C5 Tchikapika Congo
209 B8 Tchindjenje Angola
207 H3 Tchin Garaguene well Niger
207 G3 Tchin-Tabaradene Niger
207 I4 Tcholliré Cameroon
207 H2 Tchou-m-Adegdeg well Niger
143 O7 Tczew Pol.
97 H8 Te, Prêk r. Cambodia
250 E5 Tea r. Brazil
182 D4 Tea r. Spain
244 B3 Teacapán Mex.
87 F8 Teague, Lake salt flat W.A. Austr.
79 □9a Teahupoo Tahiti Fr. Polynesia
81 □3 Te Aiti Point Rarotonga Cook Is
146 K9 Tealing Angus, Scotland U.K.
81 B12 Te Anau South I. N.Z.
81 B12 Te Anau, Lake South I. N.Z.
235 G3 Teaneck NJ U.S.A.
80 I5 Te Anga North I. N.Z.
193 M5 Teano Italy
87 D8 Teano Range mts W.A. Austr.
Teanum Sidicinum Italy see Teano
243 M9 Teapa Mex.
80 M4 Te Araroa North I. N.Z.
196 J8 Tearce Macedonia
80 J4 Te Aroha North I. N.Z.
80 J4 Te Aroha, Mount hill North I. N.Z.
Teate Italy see Chieti
79 □9a Teavaro Moorea Fr. Polynesia
80 J5 Te Awamutu North I. N.Z.
185 J7 Teba Spain
183 P9 Teba r. Spain
207 G3 Tébarat Niger
95 H4 Tebas Kalimantan Indon.
149 L5 Tebay Cumbria, England U.K.
95 I4 Tebedu Sarawak Malaysia
129 C2 Teberda Rus. Fed.
129 C2 Teberda r. Rus. Fed.
129 C2 Teberdinskiy Zapovednik nature res. Rus. Fed.
223 L2 Tebesjuak Lake Nunavut Can.
205 H2 Tébessa Alg.
205 H2 Tébessa, Monts de mts Alg.
253 F6 Tebicuary Para.
253 F6 Tebicuary r. Para.
94 C3 Tebingtinggi Sumatera Indon.
94 E6 Tebingtinggi Sumatera Indon.
94 E5 Tebo r. Indon.
189 B7 Tébourba Tunisia
189 B7 Teboursouk Tunisia
129 G3 Tebulos Mt'a Georgia/Rus. Fed.
244 D6 Tecalitlán Mex.
245 I6 Tecamac Mex.
245 J7 Tecamachalco Mex.
245 J7 Tecamachalco Nogales Mex.
242 I3 Tecate Mex.
128 C2 Tece Turkey
163 K10 Tech r. France
178 H6 Techendorf Austria
206 E5 Techiman Ghana
197 Q6 Techirghiol Romania
259 C6 Tecka Arg.
259 C6 Tecka r. Arg.
169 E6 Tecklenburger Land reg. Ger.
142 J6 Teckomatorp Sweden
245 I6 Tecocomulca Mex.
243 O7 Tecoh Mex.
244 C5 Tecolotlán Mex.
245 K5 Tecolutla Mex.
244 D7 Tecomán Mex.
245 H9 Tecomate, Laguna lag. Mex.
245 I7 Tecomatlán Mex.
241 P6 Tecopa CA U.S.A.
242 E3 Tecoripa Mex.
244 G8 Tecpan Mex.
244 B3 Técpan r. Mex.
244 B3 Tecuala Mex.
244 B5 Tecuán Jalisco Mex.
244 C6 Tecuán Jalisco Mex.
197 P5 Tecuci Romania
227 K8 Tecumseh MI U.S.A.
236 G5 Tecumseh NE U.S.A.
210 D3 Ted Somalia
202 C4 Tédogora watercourse Chad
104 D3 Tedori-gawa r. Japan
122 H3 Tedzhenstroy Turkm.
241 W5 Teec Nos Pos AZ U.S.A.
214 F8 Teekloof Pass S. Africa
106 G2 Teel Mongolia
110 J1 Teeli Rus. Fed.
219 Q4 Teemore Northern Ireland U.K.
147 B9 Teeranearagh Ireland
149 O4 Tees r. England U.K.
149 O4 Tees Bay England U.K.
149 M4 Teesdale val. England U.K.
227 M5 Teeswater Ont. Can.
Teet'lit Zhen N.W.T. Can. see Fort McPherson
148 D6 Teevurcher Ireland
81 □1 Te Fakanava i. Tokelau
251 E5 Tefé Brazil
251 E5 Tefé r. Brazil
251 E5 Tefé, Lago l. Brazil
205 G4 Tefedest mts Alg.
199 K5 Tefenni Turkey
207 F2 Téfoûlet well Mali
95 H8 Tegal Jawa Indon.
170 H5 Tegel airport Ger.
165 J6 Tegelen Neth.
173 M3 Tegernheim Ger.
173 L6 Tegernsee Ger.
173 L6 Tegernsee l. Ger.
193 P7 Teggiano Italy
207 G4 Tegina Nigeria
94 F7 Tegineneng Sumatera Indon.
177 K4 Téglás Hungary
190 I3 Teglio Italy
191 M3 Tegnås r. Italy
78 □5 Tégua i. Vanuatu
242 □P10 Tegucigalpa Hond.
216 □3a Teguise Tenerife Canary Is
207 G2 Teguidda-n-Tessoumt Niger
216 □3c Teguise Lanzarote Canary Is
240 N6 Tehachapi CA U.S.A.
240 N6 Tehachapi Mountains CA U.S.A.
240 N6 Tehachapi Pass CA U.S.A.
80 I3 Te Hana North I. N.Z.
80 K6 Te Hauke North I. N.Z.
223 M1 Tehek Lake Nunavut Can.
Teheran Iran see Tehrān
223 M1 Tehery Lake Nunavut Can.
206 E4 Téhini Côte d'Ivoire
93 F5 Tehoru Seram Indon.
128 D4 Tehrān Iran
122 D4 Tehrān prov. Iran
Tehri Madh. Prad. India see Tikamgarh
116 G4 Tehri Uttaranchal India
245 J7 Tehuacán Mex.
245 I9 Tehuantepec r. Mex.
243 L10 Tehuantepec, Golfo de g. Mex.
Tehuantepec, Gulf of Mex. see Tehuantepec, Golfo de
245 M8 Tehuantepec, Istmo de isth. Mex.
267 M5 Tehuantepec Ridge sea feature N. Pacific Ocean
245 I7 Tehuitzingo Mex.
245 I9 Tehuixtepec Mex.
81 J8 Te Humenga Point North I. N.Z.
171 E7 Teicha Ger.
171 F9 Teichwolframsdorf Ger.
138 J5 Teiču rezervāts nature res. Latvia
216 □3a Teide, Parque Nacional del nat. park Tenerife Canary Is
216 □3a Teide, Pico del vol. Tenerife Canary Is
150 C3 Teifi r. Wales U.K.
150 E6 Teign r. England U.K.
150 F6 Teignmouth Devon, England U.K.
158 E7 Teignouse, Passage de la str. France
158 H6 Teillay France
163 I8 Teillet France
102 □1 Teima Okinawa Japan
173 N6 Teisendorf Ger.
207 F2 Teïskot well Mali
173 O3 Teisnach Ger.
161 B7 Teissières-lès-Bouliès France
169 J8 Teistungen Ger.
245 K9 Teitipac Mex.
197 N6 Teiu Romania
197 L4 Teiuș Romania
254 F3 Teixeira Brazil
Teixeira da Silva Angola see Bailundo
257 H2 Teixeira de Freitas Brazil
Teixeira de Sousa Angola see Luau
257 F4 Teixeiras Brazil
256 B6 Teixeira Soares Brazil
182 D2 Teixeiro Spain
182 F8 Teixoso Port.
182 F6 Teja r. Port.
183 Q8 Tejadillos Spain
183 P5 Tejado Spain
95 K9 Tejakula Bali Indon.
245 K6 Tejar Mex.
216 □3f Tejeda Gran Canaria Canary Is
182 I8 Tejeda de Tiétar Spain
185 L7 Tejeda y Almijara, Sierra de nature res. Spain
122 I3 Tejen Turkm.
123 I3 Tejen r. Turkm.
117 M8 Tejgaon Bangl.
207 H3 Tejira well Niger
184 B3 Tejo r. Port.
alt. Tajo (Spain), conv. Tagus
184 E1 Tejo Internacional, Parque Natural do nature res. Port.
244 D7 Tejupan, Punta pt Mex.
244 G7 Tejupilco Mex.
80 L4 Te Kaha North I. N.Z.
80 L4 Te Kaha Point North I. N.Z.
80 G1 Te Kao North I. N.Z.
81 E11 Tekapo r. South I. N.Z.
81 E10 Tekapo, Lake South I. N.Z.
117 J7 Tekari Bihar India
105 H5 Tekari-dake mt. Japan
81 J8 Te Kaukau Point North I. N.Z.
80 J4 Te Kauwhata North I. N.Z.
243 O7 Tekax Mex.
121 M6 Teke Kazakh.
197 O9 Teke r. Turkey
121 O1 Teke, Ozero salt l. Kazakh.
128 D2 Tekebaşı Turkey
120 I3 Tekeli Aktyubinskaya Oblast' Kazakh.
121 R5 Tekeli Almatinskaya Oblast' Kazakh.
110 E5 Tekes Xinjiang China
121 S6 Tekes Kazakh.
110 F5 Tekes He r. China
203 H6 Tekezē Wenz r. Eritrea/Eth.
111 E8 Tekiliktag mt. Xinjiang China
100 H4 Tekin Rus. Fed.
199 I2 Tekirdağ Turkey
199 I1 Tekirdağ prov. Turkey
199 L6 Tekirova Turkey
114 G3 Tekka Mahar. India
115 I3 Tekkali Andhra Prad. India
129 A5 Tekke Turkey
127 J4 Tekman Turkey
117 N9 Teknaf Bangl.
129 B5 Tekneciler Turkey
81 G9 Tekoa, Mount South I. N.Z.
94 □ Tekong Kechil, Pulau i. Sing.
226 J7 Tekonsha MI U.S.A.
80 H3 Te Kopuru North I. N.Z.
81 □3 Te Kou hill Rarotonga Cook Is
205 F5 Tekouiat, Oued watercourse Alg.
80 J4 Te Kowhai North I. N.Z.
202 D5 Tékro well Chad
128 H2 Tektek Dağları hills Turkey
93 C4 Teku Sulawesi Indon.
80 J5 Te Kuiti North I. N.Z.
117 I9 Tel r. India
209 F8 Tela Dem. Rep. Congo
242 □P10 Tela Hond.
81 □1 Te Lafu i. Tokelau
81 □1 Te Lafu i. Tokelau
205 E2 Télagh Alg.
175 K3 Telaki Pol.
94 F4 Telan i. Indon.
Telanaipura Sumatera Indon. see Jambi
111 K9 Telashi Hu salt l. Qinghai China
207 F2 Télataï Mali
175 L5 Telatyn Pol.
129 G4 T'elavi Georgia
128 C6 Tel Aviv-Yafo Israel
176 E2 Telč Czech Rep.
243 O7 Telchac Puerto Mex.
139 T8 Tel'ch'ye Rus. Fed.
197 M3 Telciu Romania
168 K4 Teldau Ger.
216 □3f Telde Gran Canaria Canary Is
208 D4 Tele r. Dem. Rep. Congo
206 E2 Télé, Lac l. Mali
197 N5 Teleajen r. Romania
196 H5 Telečka Vojvodina Serbia
95 J6 Telegapulang Kalimantan Indon.
194 E8 Telegrafo, Pizzo hill Italy
222 D3 Telegraph Creek B.C. Can.
177 J5 Telekgerendás Hungary
Telekhany Belarus see Tsyelyakhany
79 □8 Teleki Tonga atoll Tonga
79 □8 Teleki Vavu'u atoll Tonga
137 S1 Telelyuy Rus. Fed.
256 B6 Telêmaco Borba Brazil
142 E2 Telemark county Norway
260 E5 Telén Arg.
95 L4 Telen r. Indon.
Teleneshty Moldova see Telenești
136 H6 Telenești Moldova
122 I9 Teleng Iran
197 N7 Teleorman r. Romania
205 G4 Telertheba, Djebel mt. Alg.
240 O5 Telescope Peak CA U.S.A.
247 □6 Telescope Point Grenada
193 N5 Telese Italy
253 F1 Teles Pires r. Brazil
129 H3 Teletl' Rus. Fed.
86 G6 Telfer Mining Centre W.A. Austr.
150 H2 Telford Telford and Wrekin, England U.K.
234 E4 Telford PA U.S.A.
150 H2 Telford and Wrekin admin. div. England U.K.
178 D5 Telfs Austria
177 J3 Telgárt Slovakia
158 C5 Telgruc-sur-Mer France
169 E7 Telgte Ger.
182 E8 Telhado Port.
242 □P11 Telica, Volcán vol. Nic.
204 E5 Telîg well Mali
206 B4 Télimélé Guinea
202 D5 Télissour well Chad
245 K8 Telixtlahuaca Mex.
202 E6 Teljo, Jebel mt. Sudan
222 E4 Telkwa B.C. Can.
157 K4 Tellancourt France
194 I10 Tellaro r. Sicilia Italy
Tell Atlas mts Alg. see Atlas Tellien
220 B3 Teller AK U.S.A.
Tell es-Sultan West Bank see Jericho
114 D7 Tellicherry Pondicherry India
165 H8 Tellin Belgium
168 H2 Tellingstedt Ger.
129 C5 Telli Tepe mt. Turkey
250 C4 Tello Col.
136 J7 Tellodar Ukr.
127 M8 Telloh Iraq
239 K8 Telluride CO U.S.A.
137 R6 Tel'manove Ukr.
Tel'mansk Turkm. see Gubadag
128 D6 Tel Megiddo tourist site Israel
106 E2 Telmen Nuur salt l. Mongolia
179 O1 Telnice Czech Rep.
94 C5 Telo Indon.
159 L6 Teloché France
182 E6 Telões Port.
245 H7 Teloloapán Mex.
Telo Martius France see Toulon
81 □1 Te Loto i. Tokelau
134 L3 Tel'pos-Iz, Gora mt. Rus. Fed.
259 D6 Telsen Arg.
138 F6 Telšiai Lith.
192 C6 Telti Sardegna Italy
171 H6 Teltow Ger.
Teluk Anson Malaysia see Teluk Intan
Telukbajur Sumatera Indon. see Telukbayur
95 H5 Telukbatang Kalimantan Indon.
94 D5 Telukbayur Sumatera Indon.
Telukbetung Sumatera Indon. see Bandar Lampung
94 B4 Telukdalam Indon.
94 D2 Teluk Intan Malaysia
94 D5 Telukkuantan Sumatera Indon.
95 H5 Telukmelano Kalimantan Indon.
94 G8 Teluknaga Jawa Indon.
95 H5 Telukpakedai Kalimantan Indon.
114 G9 Telulla Sri Lanka
139 U9 Telyazh'ye Rus. Fed.
207 F5 Tema Ghana
244 E4 Temacapulín Mex.
79 □9a Temae, Lac l. Moorea Fr. Polynesia
227 O2 Temagami Ont. Can.
224 E4 Temagami Lake Ont. Can.
95 H4 Temaju i. Indon.
81 □3 Te Manga hill Rarotonga Cook Is
95 I8 Temanggung Jawa Indon.
245 J4 Temapache Mex.
80 I6 Te Mapou hill North I. N.Z.
111 I10 Têmarxung Xizang China
245 K7 Temascal Mex.
244 G6 Temascaltepec de González Mex.
80 I4 Te Mata North I. N.Z.
79 □9 Tematangi atoll Arch. des Tuamotu Fr. Polynesia
243 O7 Temax Mex.
215 M1 Temba S. Africa
91 I7 Tembagapura Papua Indon.
215 Q2 Tembe r. Moz.
215 Q2 Tembe Elephant Park nature res. S. Africa
131 K3 Tembenchi r. Rus. Fed.
94 E5 Tembesi r. Indon.
94 E5 Tembilahan Sumatera Indon.
215 M2 Tembisa S. Africa
183 N9 Tembleque Spain
209 C6 Tembo Aluma Angola
209 C6 Tembo Falls Angola/Dem. Rep. Congo
Tembué Moz. see Chifunde
215 M7 Tembuland reg. S. Africa
211 B7 Tembwe Zambia
150 H3 Teme r. England U.K.
240 O8 Temecula CA U.S.A.
126 F4 Temelli Turkey
106 E1 Temenchula, Gora mt. Rus. Fed.
94 D2 Temengor, Tasik resr Malaysia
179 L8 Temenica r. Slovenia
196 H5 Temerin Vojvodina Serbia
94 E3 Temerluh Malaysia
94 E2 Temiang, Bukit mt. Malaysia
122 C5 Temīleh Iran
91 H7 Teminabuan Papua Indon.
120 G3 Temir Aktyubinskaya Oblast' Kazakh.
Temir Yuzhnyy Kazakhstan Kazakh. see Timur
Temirlan Kazakh. see Temirlanovka
121 M6 Temirlanovka Kazakh.
121 O2 Temirtau Kazakh.
225 F3 Témiscamie r. Que. Can.
225 F3 Témiscamie, Lac l. Que. Can.
224 E4 Témiscaming Que. Can.
224 E4 Témiscamingue, Lac l. Ont./Que. Can.
225 G4 Témiscouata, Lac l. Que. Can.
94 F4 Temiyang i. Indon.
139 R6 Temkino Rus. Fed.
83 J9 Temma Tas. Austr.
140 R4 Temmes Fin.
135 H5 Temnikov Rus. Fed.
192 A7 Temo r. Sardegna Italy
79 □9 Temoe atoll Arch. des Tuamotu Fr. Polynesia
83 K6 Temora N.S.W. Austr.
242 F3 Temósachic Mex.
241 U8 Tempe AZ U.S.A.
93 A6 Tempe, Danau l. Indon.
84 D8 Tempe Downs N.T. Austr.
171 H6 Tempelhof airport Ger.
250 C5 Tempestad Peru
94 E5 Tempino Sumatera Indon.
192 C6 Tempio Pausania Sardegna Italy
226 I5 Temple MI U.S.A.
234 D4 Temple PA U.S.A.
237 G10 Temple TX U.S.A.
156 H7 Temple, Lac du resr France
150 D3 Temple Bar Ceredigion, Wales U.K.
85 I2 Temple Bay Qld Austr.
123 M7 Temple Dera Pak.
147 F7 Templederry Ireland
151 O5 Temple Ewell Kent, England U.K.
147 D8 Templeglentan Ireland
147 G7 Templemore Ireland
147 C9 Templenoe Ireland
147 J3 Templepatrick Northern Ireland U.K.
92 A6 Templer Bank sea feature Phil.
149 L4 Temple Sowerby Cumbria, England U.K.
84 G6 Templeton watercourse Qld Austr.
81 G10 Templeton South I. N.Z.
150 C4 Templeton Pembrokeshire, Wales U.K.
240 L6 Templeton CA U.S.A.
147 G7 Templetouhy Ireland
156 F2 Templeuve France
170 I4 Templin Ger.
147 H4 Tempo Northern Ireland U.K.
245 I4 Tempoal Mex.
245 I4 Tempoal r. Mex.
209 C8 Tempué Angola
106 F8 Têmpung Qinghai China
139 U5 Tempy Rus. Fed.
135 G7 Temryuk Rus. Fed.
135 G7 Temryukskiy Zaliv b. Rus. Fed.
165 F6 Temse Belgium
197 K7 Temska Serbia
190 I3 Temù Italy
260 A6 Temuco Chile
81 F11 Temuka South I. N.Z.
Temuli Sichuan China see Butuo
78 □4b Temwen i. Pohnpei Micronesia
78 □4b Temwetemwensekir hill Pohnpei Micronesia
120 H1 Temyasovo Rus. Fed.
250 B5 Tena Ecuador
186 E2 Tena, Valle de val. Spain
243 N7 Tenabo Mex.
240 P1 Tenabo, Mount NV U.S.A.
244 C6 Tenacatita Mex.
206 E3 Ténado Burkina
235 H3 Tenafly NJ U.S.A.
138 G1 Tenala Fin.
114 G4 Tenali Andhra Prad. India
244 C5 Tenamaxtlán Mex.
228 G7 Tenancingo Mex.
245 H6 Tenango México Mex.
245 L9 Tenango Oaxaca Mex.
79 □9 Tenarunga atoll Arch. des Tuamotu Fr. Polynesia
97 D8 Tenasserim Myanmar
97 D8 Tenasserim admin. div. Myanmar
97 D8 Tenasserim r. Myanmar
160 H5 Tenay France
164 K2 Ten Boer Neth.
150 G3 Tenbury Wells Worcestershire, England U.K.
150 C4 Tenby Pembrokeshire, Wales U.K.
227 K3 Tenby Bay Ont. Can.
161 E6 Tence France
177 I1 Tenczyński Park Krajobrazowy Pol.
210 D2 Tendaho Eth.
155 H4 Tende France
190 D7 Tende, Col de pass France/Italy
115 M8 Ten Degree Channel Andaman & Nicobar Is India
203 F6 Tendelti Sudan
206 B2 Te-n-Dghâmcha, Sebkhet salt marsh Maur.
183 O7 Tendilla Spain
102 R8 Tendō Japan
204 E2 Tendrara Morocco
190 A2 Tendre, Mont mt. Switz.
137 K7 Tendrivs'ka Kosa, Ostriv i. Ukr.
137 K7 Tendrivs'ka Zatoka b. Ukr.
159 O8 Tendu France
116 G8 Tendukheda Madh. Prad. India
129 E6 Tendürek Dağı mt. Turkey
206 C4 Téné r. Guinea
Tenedos i. Turkey see Bozcaada
105 L1 Ten-ei Japan
206 D3 Ténenkou Mali
138 E6 Tenenys r. Lith.
207 H2 Ténéré, Erg du des. Niger
207 H1 Ténéré du Tafassâsset des. Niger
216 □3a Tenerife i. Canary Is
205 F1 Ténès Alg.
197 O8 Tenevo Bulg.
96 C5 Teng, Nam r. Myanmar
95 L8 Tengah, Kepulauan is Indon.
94 □ Tengah, Sungai r. Sing.
93 C8 Tengahdai Flores Indon.
Tengcheng Guangxi China see Tengxian
108 B6 Tengchong Yunnan China
120 E6 Tenge Kazakh.
94 □ Tengeh Reservoir Sing.
177 H5 Tengelic Hungary
172 F6 Tengen Ger.
78 □6 Te Nggano lag. Rennell Solomon Is
95 L5 Tenggarong Kalimantan Indon.
106 I8 Tengger Els Nei Mongol China
106 I7 Tengger Shamo des. Nei Mongol China
94 E2 Tenggul i. Malaysia
121 M2 Tengiz, Ozero salt l. Kazakh.
108 G9 Tengqiao Hainan China
206 D4 Tengréla Côte d'Ivoire
135 H5 Ten'gushevo Rus. Fed.
108 H7 Tengxian Guangxi China
Tengxian Shandong China see Tengzhou
107 O9 Tengzhou Shandong China
161 J8 Ténibre, Mont mt. France/Italy
253 E5 Teniente Enciso, Parque Nacional nat. park Para.
Teniente Jubany research stn Antarctica see Jubany
261 F6 Teniente Origone Arg.
231 F11 Tenille FL U.S.A.
172 D5 Teningen Ger.
206 A2 Te-n-Ioubrar, Sebkhet salt marsh Maur.
245 J5 Tenixtepec Mex.
120 K1 Teniz, Ozero l. Kazakh.
177 J4 Tenk Hungary
114 E8 Tenkasi Tamil Nadu India
104 C7 Tenkawa Japan
209 E7 Tenke Dem. Rep. Congo
131 P2 Tenkeli Rus. Fed.
134 J5 Ten'ki Rus. Fed.
206 E4 Tenkodogo Burkina
87 F8 Ten Mile Lake salt flat W.A. Austr.
225 J3 Ten Mile Lake Nfld and Lab. Can.
191 P9 Tenna r. Italy
84 E5 Tennant Creek N.T. Austr.
172 E5 Tennenbronn Ger.
178 H4 Tennengau val. Austria
178 H5 Tennengebirge mts Austria
235 G4 Tennent NJ U.S.A.
237 K7 Tennessee r. U.S.A.
232 B12 Tennessee state U.S.A.
239 K7 Tennessee Pass CO U.S.A.
165 I8 Tenneville Belgium
140 N2 Tennevoll Norway
140 L3 Tennholmfjorden sea chan. Norway
140 T3 Tenniöjoki r. Fin./Rus. Fed.
260 B4 Teno Chile
260 B4 Teno r. Chile
216 □3a Teno, Punta de pt Tenerife Canary Is
245 K6 Tenochtitlán Mex.
140 T1 Tenojoki r. Fin./Norway
95 K2 Tenom Sabah Malaysia
243 N9 Tenosique Mex.
104 E5 Tenpaku Japan
104 C6 Tenri Japan
105 G5 Tenryū Nagano Japan
105 G6 Tenryū Shizuoka Japan
105 G5 Tenryū-gawa r. Japan
105 G5 Tenryū-Okumikawa Kokutei-kōen park Japan
238 K4 Ten Sleep WY U.S.A.
93 B4 Tenteno Sulawesi Indon.
151 N5 Tenterden Kent, England U.K.
83 N3 Tenterfield N.S.W. Austr.
231 G13 Ten Thousand Islands FL U.S.A.
223 J2 Tent Lake N.W.T. Can.
93 B3 Tentolomatinan, Gunung mt. Indon.
184 G4 Tentudia mt. Spain
182 C8 Tentúgal Port.
158 H7 Tenu r. France
177 G4 Tényő Hungary
244 E4 Teocaltiche Mex.
245 K6 Teocelo Mex.
244 D5 Teocuitatlán de Corona Mex.
261 G4 Teodelina Arg.
192 D6 Teodoro, Stagno di lag. Sardegna Italy
244 A3 Teodoro Beltrán Mex.
256 A5 Teodoro Sampaio Brazil
260 A6 Teodoro Schmidt Chile
257 G2 Teófilo Otôni Brazil
136 F4 Teofipol' Ukr.
92 C8 Teomabal i. Phil.
80 □ Te One Chatham Is S. Pacific Ocean
116 H7 Teonthar Madh. Prad. India
243 M9 Teopisca Mex.
193 O6 Teora Italy
245 I6 Teotihuacán tourist site Mex.
245 J7 Teotitlán Mex.
245 K8 Teotitlán del Valle Mex.
206 E5 Tepa Ghana
93 F7 Tepa Maluku Indon.
242 E3 Tepache Mex.
80 G1 Te Paki North I. N.Z.
244 E6 Tepalcatepec Mex.
244 E7 Tepalcatepec r. Mex.
245 I7 Tepalcingo Mex.
81 □4 Tepa Point Niue
140 R3 Tepasto Fin.
245 H5 Tepatepec Mex.
244 E5 Tepatitlán Mex.
177 K4 Tépe Hungary
245 J7 Tepeaca Mex.
245 I6 Tepeapulco Mex.
244 D4 Tepechitlán Mex.
199 J1 Tepecik Turkey
245 J2 Tepeguajes Mex.
244 A1 Tepehuaje Mex.
242 G5 Tepehuanes Mex.
245 H6 Tepeji Mex.
Tepeköy Turkey see Karakoçan
198 B2 Tepelenë Albania
245 J8 Tepelmeme de Morelos Mex.
176 B2 Tepelská vrchovina hills Czech Rep.
251 F4 Tepequem, Serra mts Brazil
213 H2 Tepere Moz.
244 F4 Tepetates Mex.
244 D3 Tepetengo Mex.
244 G8 Tepetixtla Mex.
245 J4 Tepetzintla Mex.
245 J7 Tepexi de Rodriguez Mex.
245 J6 Tepeyahualco Mex.
95 L4 Tepianlangsat Kalimantan Indon.
244 C4 Tepic Mex.
81 F10 Te Pirita South I. N.Z.
176 B2 Teplá Czech Rep.
176 B1 Teplá r. Czech Rep.
176 C3 Teplá Vltava r. Czech Rep.
134 L4 Teplaya Gora Rus. Fed.
137 S5 Teple Ukr.
129 F3 Tepli, Gora mt. Rus. Fed.
176 C1 Teplice Czech Rep.
177 J3 Teplička Slovakia
137 M8 Teplivka Ukr.
134 K3 Teplogorka Rus. Fed.
139 V8 Teploye Lipetskaya Oblast' Rus. Fed.
139 U8 Teploye Tul'skaya Oblast' Rus. Fed.
136 I5 Teplyk Ukr.
242 C3 Tepopa, Punta pt Mex.
245 J8 Teposcolula Mex.
245 H7 Tepoztlan Mex.
193 J5 Teppia r. Italy
80 K4 Te Puke North I. N.Z.
80 K4 Te Puna North I. N.Z.
244 G6 Tepuxtepec Mex.
244 D5 Tequila Mex.
244 D5 Tequila, Volcán de vol. Mex.
245 L9 Tequisistlán Mex.
245 L9 Tequisistlán r. Mex.
245 H5 Tequisquiapán Mex.
245 J6 Tequixquitla Mex.
245 J7 Tequixtépec Mex.
207 F3 Téra Niger
184 C3 Tera r. Port.
182 I5 Tera r. Spain
164 G4 Ter Aar Neth.
80 J4 Te Rahu North I. N.Z.
104 D3 Terai Japan
210 A3 Terakeka Sudan
116 F2 Teram Kangri mt. China/Jammu and Kashmir
193 L2 Teramo Italy
193 L2 Teramo prov. Italy
83 I8 Terang Vic. Austr.
80 J4 Te Rapa North I. N.Z.
164 L3 Ter Apel Neth.
123 M7 Teratani r. Pak.
175 L5 Teratyn Pol.
81 I8 Terawhiti, Cape North I. N.Z.
93 F7 Terbang Selatan i. Maluku Indon.
93 F7 Terbang Utara i. Maluku Indon.
164 J5 Terborg-Silvolde Neth.
139 V9 Terbuny Rus. Fed.
Tercan Erzincan Turkey see Otlukbeli
127 J4 Tercan Erzincan Turkey
129 B6 Tercan Barajı resr Turkey
216 □1a Terceira i. Azores
261 F3 Tercero r. Arg.
163 B8 Tercis-les-Bains France
190 G5 Terdoppio r. Italy
139 S8 Tereben' Rus. Fed.
177 L4 Terebești Romania
136 C5 Tereblya r. Ukr.
136 E4 Terebovlya Ukr.
139 V7 Terebush Rus. Fed.
197 K5 Teregova Romania
Terek r. Georgia see Tergi
129 F2 Terek Rus. Fed.
127 M2 Terek r. Rus. Fed.
106 D1 Tere-Khol' Rus. Fed.
106 E1 Tere-Khol', Ozero l. Rus. Fed.
129 G1 Terekli-Mekteb Rus. Fed.
121 N7 Terek-Say Kyrg.
110 G1 Terektinskiy Khrebet mts Rus. Fed.
121 M3 Terekty Karagandinskaya Oblast' Kazakh.
121 U3 Terekty Vostochnyy Kazakhstan Kazakh.
177 J6 Teremia Mare Romania
184 E3 Terena Port.
135 J5 Teren'ga Rus. Fed.
94 E2 Terengganu r. Malaysia
94 E2 Terengganu state Malaysia
Terengözek Kazakh. see Terenozek
255 B7 Terenos Brazil
120 K5 Terenozek Kazakh.
120 H2 Terensay Rus. Fed.
95 H5 Terentang Kalimantan Indon.
95 L5 Terentang, Pulau i. Indon.
147 J6 Terenure Ireland
Teren-Uzyak Kazakh. see Terenozek
256 B6 Teresa Cristina Brazil
187 C9 Teresa de Cofrentes Spain
217 □2b Térèse, Île i. Inner Islands Seychelles
120 B2 Tereshka r. Rus. Fed.
175 I3 Teresin Pol.
254 E3 Teresina Brazil
250 D4 Teresita Col.
257 F5 Teresópolis Brazil
175 L3 Terespol Pol.
115 M8 Teressa Island Andaman & Nicobar Is India
136 C5 Teresva Ukr.
136 C6 Teresva r. Ukr.
175 K5 Tereszpol-Zaorenda Pol.
176 D1 Terezín Czech Rep.
176 G6 Terezino Polje Croatia
136 J4 Terezyne Ukr.
178 E5 Terfens Austria
181 F5 Terga Alg.
184 D5 Terges r. Port.
Tergeste Italy see Trieste
129 F3 Tergi r. Georgia
156 F4 Tergnier France
191 M5 Tergola r. Italy
192 B6 Tergu Sardegna Italy
106 D7 Tergun Daba Shan mts Qinghai China
164 G5 Terheijden Neth.
106 F2 Terhiyn Tsagaan Nuur l. Mongolia
134 F1 Teriberka Rus. Fed.
138 K3 Terikeste Estonia
111 I11 Tering Xizang China
121 L2 Terisakkan r. Kazakh.
204 B5 Terjît well Maur.
129 F3 Terk Rus. Fed.
175 K6 Terka Pol.
210 D3 Terka Reba Eth.
202 D5 Terkezi well Chad
191 K2 Terlano Italy
237 D11 Terlingua Creek r. TX U.S.A.
193 R5 Terlizzi Italy
203 I6 Terma, Ras pt Eritrea
136 I2 Termakhivka Ukr.
260 B5 Termas de Chillán Chile
260 B4 Termas de Flaco Chile
261 I2 Termas del Arapey Uru.
260 B6 Termas de Pemehue Chile
260 B2 Termas de Socos Chile
260 B6 Termas de Tolhuaca Chile
260 C3 Termas de Villavicencio Arg.
126 H3 Terme Turkey
193 P9 Terme Luigiane Italy
186 G4 Térmens Spain
163 J9 Termes France
199 L6 Termessos Milli Parkı nat. park Turkey
Termez Uzbek. see Termiz
161 J6 Termignon France
87 F13 Termination Island W.A. Austr.
156 C7 Terminiers France
194 F8 Termini Imerese Sicilia
194 F7 Termini Imerese, Golfo Sicilia Italy
193 J3 Terminillo, Monte mt.
243 N8 Términos, Laguna de lag. Mex.
207 H2 Termit well Niger
207 H2 Termit, Massif de hill
207 H3 Termit-Kaoboul Niger
121 L9 Termiz Uzbek.
193 N4 Termoli Italy
147 G2 Termon Ireland
Termonde Belgium see Dendermonde
148 E6 Termonfeckin Ireland
150 G2 Tern r. England U.K.
137 N3 Tern r. Ukr.
164 I2 Ternaard Neth.
93 E3 Ternate Maluku Indon.
93 E3 Ternate i. Maluku Indon.
217 □2b Ternay, La Passe sea c Inner Islands Seychelles
Ternay Pass sea chan. Islands Seychelles see Ternay, La Passe
179 J4 Ternberg Austria
165 E6 Terneuzen Neth.
100 J6 Terney Rus. Fed.
193 J2 Terni Italy
193 I2 Terni prov. Italy
160 E3 Ternin r. France
179 N4 Ternitz Austria
137 P5 Ternivka Dnipropetrovs' Oblast' Ukr.
137 L6 Ternivka Mykolayivs'ka Oblast' Ukr.
137 M9 Ternivka Respublika Kry
136 I5 Ternivka Vinnyts'ka Obla
156 D3 Ternois reg. France
156 D3 Ternoise r. France
136 E4 Ternopil' Ukr.
Ternopil Oblast admin. Ukr. see Ternopils'ka Ob
136 E4 Ternopils'ka Oblast' admin. div. Ukr.
Ternopol' Ukr. see Tern
Ternopol Oblast admin. Ukr. see Ternopils'ka Ob
Ternopol'skaya Oblast' admin. div. Ukr. see Ternopils'ka Oblast'
135 H6 Ternovka Rus. Fed.
Ternovka Ukr. see Terni
137 P6 Ternuvate Ukr.
137 Q4 Terny Donets'ka Oblast'
137 M3 Terny Sums'ka Oblast' U
216 □3f Teror Gran Canaria Cana
82 G5 Terowie S.A. Austr.
100 N4 Terpeniya, Mys c. Sakh Rus. Fed.
100 N4 Terpeniya, Poluostrov Rus. Fed.
100 M4 Terpeniya, Zaliv g. Sak Rus. Fed.
232 F9 Terra Alta WV U.S.A.
240 M6 Terra Bella CA U.S.A.
256 A5 Terra Boa Brazil
257 F2 Terra Branca Brazil
222 D4 Terrace B.C. Can.
224 C3 Terrace Bay Ont. Can.
216 □1a Terra Chã Terceira Azor
193 K5 Terracina Italy
193 K5 Terracina, Golfo di b. I
Terradas Spain see Terr
186 K3 Terrades Spain
186 G3 Terradets, Pantà de re Spain
214 H1 Terra Firma S. Africa
140 L4 Terråk Norway
192 B8 Terralba Sardegna Italy
263 K1 Terra Nova Bay Antarct
195 K4 Terranova da Sibari Ita
193 Q8 Terranova di Pollino Ita
225 K3 Terra Nova National P Nfld and Lab. Can.
191 L8 Terranuova Braccioli
251 G6 Terra Preta Brazil
256 A5 Terra Rica Brazil
182 D5 Terras do Bouro Port.
194 E7 Terrasini Sicilia Italy
186 J4 Terrassa Spain
162 G5 Terrasson-Lavilledieu
163 F8 Terraube France
195 L5 Terravecchia Italy
242 F3 Terrazas Mex.
Terre Adélie reg. Antar see Adélie Land
237 J11 Terrebonne Bay LA U.S
247 □2 Terre de Bas i. Guadelo
247 □2 Terre de Haut i. Guade
230 D6 Terre Haute IN U.S.A.
234 C4 Terre Hill PA U.S.A.
237 G9 Terrell TX U.S.A.
157 K8 Terre-Natale France
245 J6 Terrenate Mex.
225 K4 Terrenceville Nfld and La
160 E2 Terre Plaine plain Fran
242 F3 Terrero Mex.
Terres Australes et Antarctiques Français Indian Ocean see French Southern and Antarctic
191 J8 Terricciola Italy
183 R8 Terriente Spain
185 I7 Terril mt. Spain
148 C6 Terrin Ireland
185 N3 Terrinches Spain
149 P5 Terrington North Yorksh England U.K.
151 M2 Terrington St Clement Norfolk, England U.K.
157 M8 Territoire de Belfort de France
163 H6 Terrou France
184 A3 Terrugem Lisboa Port.
184 E3 Terrugem Portalegre Po
238 L3 Terry MT U.S.A.
235 I1 Terryville CT U.S.A.
235 I3 Terryville NY U.S.A.
135 I6 Tersa r. Rus. Fed.
Tersakkan r. Kazakh. se Terisakkan
164 H2 Terschelling i. Neth.
Terskey Alatau, Khreb Kyrg. see Terskey Ala-To
121 Q7 Terskey Ala-Too mts Ky
134 G2 Terskiy Bereg coastal a Rus. Fed.
129 F1 Tersko-Kumskiy Kanal Rus. Fed.
137 O6 Tersyanka Ukr.
192 D8 Tertenia Sardegna Italy
Terter Azer. see Tärtär
168 G2 Tertius i. Ger.
156 F4 Tertry France
187 C7 Teruel Spain
183 Q7 Teruel prov. Spain
138 H1 Tervakoski Fin.
197 P7 Tervel Bulg.
159 J8 Terves France
140 S5 Tervo Fin.
140 R3 Tervola Fin.
139 T5 Teryayevo Rus. Fed.
177 H4 Tés Hungary
191 M3 Tesa r. Italy
188 F3 Tešanj Bos.-Herz.
163 G7 Tescou r. France
245 L7 Tesechoacán r. Mex.
177 G3 Tešedíkovo Slovakia
216 □3b Tesejerague Fuertevent Canary Is
203 H6 Teseney Eritrea
191 L3 Tesero Italy
135 H5 Tesha r. Rus. Fed.
220 C2 Teshekpuk Lake AK U.
207 E5 Teshi Ghana
102 V3 Teshikaga Japan
102 S2 Teshio Japan
102 T3 Teshio-dake mt. Japan
102 S2 Teshio-gawa r. Japan
102 S2 Teshio-sanchi mts Japa
242 E4 Tesia Mex.
197 J7 Tešica Serbia
191 K2 Tesimo Italy
191 L5 Tesina r. Italy
244 D5 Tesistán Mex.
106 C1 Tesiyn Gol r. Mongolia
183 M3 Tesla, Sierra de la mts
188 F3 Teslić Bos.-Herz.
222 C2 Teslin Y.T. Can.

Teslin *r. Y.T.* Can.
Teslin Lake *B.C./Y.T.* Can.
Teslui *r.* Romania
Teso Santo *hill* Spain
Tesouro Brazil
Tesovo-Netyl'skiy Rus. Fed.
Tesovskiy Rus. Fed.
Tespe Ger.
Tessalit Mali
Tessaoua Niger
Tessé-la-Madeleine France
Tessenderlo Belgium
Tesséroukane *well* Niger
Tessin Ger.
Tessin *canton* Switz. *see* Ticino
Tessolo Moz.
Tesson France
Tessoûnfat *well* Mali
Tessy-sur-Vire France
Test *r. England* U.K.
Testa, Capo *c. Sardegna* Italy
Testa del Gargano Italy
Testa dell'Acqua *Sicilia* Italy
Testeiro, Montes do *mts* Spain
Testelt Belgium
Testillos *r.* Spain
Testour Tunisia
Têt *r.* France
Tét Hungary
Tetachuck Lake *B.C.* Can.
Tetagouche *r. N.B.* Can.
Tetas, Punta *pt* Chile
Tetbury *Gloucestershire, England* U.K.
Teţchea Romania
Tete Moz.
Tete *prov.* Moz.
Tête de l'Enchastraye *mt.* France/Italy
Tête de l'Estrop *mt.* France
Tête de Soulaure *mt.* France
Tête des Toillies *mt.* Italy
Tetehosi Indon.
Tête Jaune Cache *B.C.* Can.
Te Teko *North I.* N.Z.
Tetela Mex.
Tetela de Ocampo Mex.
Tetela de Volcán Mex.
Tetepare *i. New Georgia Is* Solomon Is
Teteringen Neth.
Teteriv *r.* Ukr.
Teterow Ger.
Tetétlen Hungary
Teteven Bulg.
Tetford *Lincolnshire, England* U.K.
Teti *Sardegna* Italy
Tetillas Mex.
Tetiyev Ukr. *see* **Tetiyiv**
Tetiyiv Ukr.
Tetkino Rus. Fed.
Tetney *Lincolnshire, England* U.K.
Teton *r. MT* U.S.A.
Teton Range *mts WY* U.S.A.
Tétouan Morocco
Tétouan *prov.* Morocco
Tetovo Macedonia
Tetpur *Gujarat* India
Tetrino Rus. Fed.
Tettau Ger.
Tettens Ger.
Tettnang Ger.
Tetuán Morocco *see* **Tétouan**
Tetufera *mt. Tahiti* Fr. Polynesia
Tetulia Bangl.
Tetulia *sea chan.* Bangl.
Tetyń Pol.
Tetyukhe Rus. Fed. *see* **Dal'negorsk**
Tetyukhe-Pristan' Rus. Fed. *see* **Rudnaya Pristan'**
Tetyushi Rus. Fed.
Teublitz Ger.
Teuchern Ger.
Teuchezhsk Rus. Fed. *see* **Adygeysk**
Teuchi Japan
Teuco *r.* Arg.
Teufelsbach Namibia
Teufels Moor *reg.* Ger.
Teufen Switz.
Teufenbach Austria
Teulada *Sardegna* Italy
Teulada Spain
Teulada, Capo *c. Sardegna* Italy
Teulada, Golfo di *b. Sardegna* Italy
Teul de González Ortega Mex.
Teun *vol. Maluku* Indon.
Teunom *Sumatera* Indon.
Teunom *r.* Indon.
Teunz Ger.
Teupitz Ger.
Teupitz-Köriser Seengebiet *park* Ger.
Teuri-tō *i.* Japan
Teuschnitz Ger.
Teustepe Nic.
Teutoburger Wald *hills* Ger.
Teutschenthal Ger.
Teuva Fin.
Tevel Hungary
Tevere *r.* Italy
Teverone *r.* Italy
Teverya Israel
Teviot *South I.* N.Z.
Teviot S. Africa
Teviot *r. Scotland* U.K.
Teviotdale *val. Scotland* U.K.
Teviothead *Scottish Borders, Scotland* U.K.
Te Waewae *South I.* N.Z.
Te Waewae Bay *South I.* N.Z.
Tewah *Kalimantan* Indon.
Te Waiponamu *i.* N.Z. *see* **South Island**
Tewane Botswana
Tewantin *Qld* Austr.
Teweh *r.* Indon.
Te Wera *North I.* N.Z.
Te Wera *North I.* N.Z.
Te Whaiti *North I.* N.Z.
Te Whanga Lagoon *Chatham Is* S. Pacific Ocean
Te Wharau *North I.* N.Z.
Tewkesbury *Gloucestershire, England* U.K.
Tewli Belarus
Têwo *Gansu* China
Têwo *Sichuan* China
Texa *i. Scotland* U.K.
Texarkana *AR* U.S.A.
Texarkana *TX* U.S.A.
Texas *Qld* Austr.
Texas *state* U.S.A.
Texas City *TX* U.S.A.
Texcoco Mex.
Texel *i.* Neth.
Texhoma *OK* U.S.A.
Texistepec Mex.
Texmelucan Mex.
Texoma, Lake *OK/TX* U.S.A.
Teyateyaneng Lesotho
Teyjat France
Teykovo Rus. Fed.
Teynham *Kent, England* U.K.
Teyssieu France
Teyssonne *r.* France
Teyvareh Afgh.
Teza *r.* Rus. Fed.
Teza S. Africa
Teziutlán Mex.
Tezoatlán Mex.
Tezonapa Mex.
Tezontepec Mex.
Tezpur *Assam* India
Tezu *Arun. Prad.* India
Tfaritiy Western Sahara
Tha, Nam *r.* Laos
Tha-anne *r. Nunavut* Can.
Thabana-Ntlenyana *mt.* Lesotho
Thaba Nchu S. Africa
Thabankulu *mt.* S. Africa
Thaba Putsoa *mt.* Lesotho
215 L6 **Thaba Putsoa** *mts* S. Africa
215 M5 **Thaba-Tseka** Lesotho
213 E5 **Thabazimbi** S. Africa
96 C3 **Thabeikkyin** Myanmar
97 F7 **Thab Lan National Park** Thai.
96 F6 **Tha Bo** Laos
215 K3 **Thabong** S. Africa
161 J6 **Thabor, Mont** *mt.* France
96 C4 **Thabyedaung** Myanmar
96 G4 **Thac Ba, Hô** *l.* Vietnam
96 B5 **Thade** *r.* Myanmar
124 G3 **Thādiq** Saudi Arabia
97 D8 **Thagyettaw** Myanmar
Tha Hin Thai. *see* **Lop Buri**
96 H4 **Thai Binh** Vietnam
96 E6 **Thailand** *country* Asia
97 E9 **Thailand, Gulf of** Asia
97 D10 **Thai Muang** Thai.
96 G4 **Thai Nguyên** Vietnam
125 I2 **Thaj** Saudi Arabia
96 G6 **Thakèk** Laos
117 L6 **Thakurgaon** Bangl.
116 H9 **Thakurtola** *Chhattisgarh* India
169 J9 **Thal** Ger.
123 N5 **Thal** Pak.
205 H2 **Thala** Tunisia
Thalabarivat Cambodia *see* **Phumĭ Thalabârĭvăt**
97 D10 **Thalang** Thai.
Thalassery *Pondicherry* India *see* **Tellicherry**
128 A8 **Thalāthah** Egypt
173 K3 **Thalbach** *r.* Ger.
123 N6 **Thal Desert** Pak.
171 D7 **Thale (Harz)** Ger.
172 D3 **Thaleischweiler-Fröschen** Ger.
172 B2 **Thalfang** Ger.
178 H4 **Thalgau** Austria
171 F7 **Thalheim** Ger.
179 J3 **Thalheim bei Wels** Austria
96 E6 **Tha Li** Thai.
Thaliparamba *Kerala* India *see* **Taliparamba**
83 L3 **Thallon** *Qld* Austr.
171 G8 **Thallwitz** Ger.
173 K3 **Thalmässing** Ger.
173 M4 **Thalmassing** Ger.
123 K7 **Thalo** Pak.
190 F1 **Thalwil** Switz.
202 C3 **Thamad Bū Hashīshah** *well* Libya
212 E5 **Thamaga** Botswana
124 H2 **Thāmām, 'Irq ath** *des.* Saudi Arabia
124 G9 **Thamar, Jabal** *mt.* Yemen
125 L7 **Thamarīt** Oman
151 K4 **Thame** *Oxfordshire, England* U.K.
151 J4 **Thame** *r. England* U.K.
227 L7 **Thames** *r. Ont.* Can.
80 J4 **Thames** *North I.* N.Z.
151 N5 **Thames** *est. England* U.K.
151 M5 **Thames** *r. England* U.K.
235 K2 **Thames** *r. CT* U.S.A.
80 J3 **Thames, Firth of** *b. North I.* N.Z.
Thamesdown *admin. div. England* U.K. *see* **Swindon**
227 N6 **Thamesford** *Ont.* Can.
227 M7 **Thamesville** *Ont.* Can.
169 K8 **Thamsbrück** Ger.
125 I7 **Thamūd** Yemen
Thamugadi *tourist site* Alg. *see* **Timgad**
Thana *Mahar.* India *see* **Thane**
116 F6 **Thana Ghazi** *Rajasthan* India
96 C6 **Thanatpin** Myanmar
96 C7 **Thanbyuzayat** Myanmar
96 C5 **Thandaung** Myanmar
116 E8 **Thandla** *Madh. Prad.* India
96 B5 **Thandwè** Myanmar
114 C3 **Thane** *Mahar.* India
151 O5 **Thanet, Isle of** *pen. England* U.K.
116 C8 **Thangadh** *Gujarat* India
86 G5 **Thangoo** *W.A.* Austr.
85 M8 **Thangool** *Qld* Austr.
116 G3 **Thangra** Jammu and Kashmir
96 G5 **Thanh Hoa** Vietnam
114 F7 **Thanjavur** *Tamil Nadu* India
97 D10 **Than Kyun** *i.* Myanmar
Thanlwin *r.* Myanmar *see* **Salween**
96 C6 **Thanlyin** Myanmar
157 N8 **Thann** France
173 I5 **Thannhausen** Ger.
123 L9 **Thano Bula Khan** Pak.
108 D8 **Than Uyên** Vietnam
212 D3 **Thaoge** *r.* Botswana
223 L2 **Thaolintoa Lake** *Nunavut* Can.
157 L7 **Thaon-les-Vosges** France
96 E6 **Tha Pla** Thai.
97 D10 **Thap Put** Thai.
Thapsacus Syria *see* **Dibsī**
97 D9 **Thap Sakae** Thai.
116 C8 **Thara** *Gujarat* India
97 D8 **Tharabwin** Myanmar
116 C7 **Tharad** *Gujarat* India
210 C5 **Tharaka** Kenya
171 I9 **Tharandt** Ger.
164 I4 **'t Harde** Neth.
116 B7 **Thar Desert** India/Pak.
85 I9 **Thargomindah** *Qld* Austr.
96 B6 **Tharrawaw** Myanmar
184 E5 **Tharsis** Spain
127 K7 **Tharthār, Buḥayrat ath** *l.* Iraq
125 L4 **Tharwāniyyah** U.A.E.
97 D10 **Tha Sala** Thai.
198 F2 **Thasopoula** *i.* Greece
198 F2 **Thasos** *Thasos* Greece
198 F2 **Thasos** *i.* Greece
151 J5 **Thatcham** *West Berkshire, England* U.K.
241 W9 **Thatcher** *AZ* U.S.A.
198 B2 **Thatë, Mali i** *mt.* Albania
96 H3 **Thât Khê** Vietnam
96 C6 **Thaton** Myanmar
161 D10 **Thau, Bassin de** *lag.* France
160 B3 **Thaumiers** France
96 B2 **Thaungdut** Myanmar
96 C6 **Thaungyin** *r.* Myanmar/Thai.
178 D5 **Thaur** Austria
96 G6 **Tha Uthen** Thai.
128 D9 **Thawr, Jabal** *mt.* Jordan
151 M4 **Thaxted** *Essex, England* U.K.
179 L2 **Thaya** Austria
179 M2 **Thaya** *r.* Austria/Czech Rep.
96 B6 **Thayawadi** Myanmar
97 C8 **Thayawthadangyi Kyun** *i.* Myanmar
96 B5 **Thayetmyo** Myanmar
96 C2 **Thayetta** Myanmar
190 F1 **Thayngen** Switz.
96 B5 **Thazi** *Magwe* Myanmar
96 C4 **Thazi** *Mandalay* Myanmar
80 K3 **The Aldermen Islands** *North I.* N.Z.
246 □ **The Alley** Jamaica
241 T9 **Theba** *AZ* U.S.A.
Thebacha *N.W.T.* Can. *see* **Fort Smith**
Thebae *tourist site* Egypt *see* **Thebes**
229 K6 **The Bahamas** *country* West Indies
203 G3 **Thebes** *tourist site* Egypt
Thebes Greece *see* **Thiva**
246 E1 **The Bluff** *Eleuthera* Bahamas
216 □2b **The Briars** St Helena
151 P2 **The Broads** *nat. park England* U.K.
The Brothers *is H.K.* China *see* **Tai Siu Mo To**
The Brothers *is* Yemen *see* **Al Ikhwān**
149 L5 **The Calf** *hill England* U.K.
85 N1 **The Calvados Chain** *is* P.N.G.
149 M3 **The Cheviot** *hill England* U.K.
246 □ **The Cockpit Country** *hills* Jamaica
82 G6 **The Coorong** *inlet S.A.* Austr.
247 □4 **The Crane** Barbados
231 □1 **The Crawl** *pt* Bermuda
148 D7 **The Curragh** *lowland* Ireland
238 D4 **The Dalles** *OR* U.S.A.
236 E4 **Thedford** *NE* U.S.A.
148 D4 **The Diamond** *Northern Ireland* U.K.
168 H5 **Thedinghausen** Ger.
84 F1 **The English Company's Islands** *N.T.* Austr.
83 M5 **The Entrance** *N.S.W.* Austr.
214 D10 **Theewaterskloof Dam** *resr* S. Africa
146 □M1 **The Faither** *stack Scotland* U.K.
151 L2 **The Fens** *reg. England* U.K.
80 □ **The Forty Fours** *is Chatham Is* S. Pacific Ocean
206 A3 **The Gambia** *country* Africa
146 H12 **The Glenkens** *val. Scotland* U.K.
83 I7 **The Grampians** *mts Vic.* Austr.
84 C6 **The Granites** *hill N.T.* Austr.
The Great Oasis Egypt *see* **Khārijah, Wāḥāt al**
247 □3 **The Grenadines** *is* St Vincent
125 J1 **The Gulf** Asia
The Hague Neth. *see* **'s-Gravenhage**
147 J7 **The Harrow** Ireland
215 M8 **The Haven** S. Africa
80 □ **The Horns** *hill Chatham Is* S. Pacific Ocean
214 H7 **The Horseshoe** *mt.* S. Africa
81 E11 **The Hunters Hills** *South I.* N.Z.
159 P7 **Theillay** France
97 D9 **Theinkun** Myanmar
96 C6 **Theinzeik** Myanmar
171 F8 **Theißen** Ger.
158 F6 **Theix** France
81 B12 **The Key** *South I.* N.Z.
223 I2 **Thekulthili Lake** *N.W.T.* Can.
83 K7 **The Lakes National Park** *Vic.* Austr.
156 C5 **Thelle** *reg.* France
223 L1 **Thelon** *r. N.W.T./Nunavut* Can.
223 K1 **Thelon Game Sanctuary** *nature res. Nunavut* Can.
150 G2 **The Long Mynd** *hills England* U.K.
148 D4 **The Loup** *Northern Ireland* U.K.
85 J5 **The Lynd Junction** *Qld* Austr.
146 H13 **The Machars** *reg. Scotland* U.K.
147 K3 **The Maidens** *is Northern Ireland* U.K.
169 K9 **Themar** Ger.
214 I8 **Thembalesizwe** S. Africa
215 N3 **Thembalihle** S. Africa
146 D6 **The Minch** *sea chan. Scotland* U.K.
163 H6 **Thémines** France
147 B4 **The Mullet** *b.* Ireland
150 E4 **The Mumbles** *Swansea, Wales* U.K.
231 □1 **The Narrows** *sea chan.* Bermuda
247 □2 **The Narrows** *str.* St Kitts and Nevis
159 N8 **Thenay** France
The Naze *c.* Norway *see* **Lindesnes**
151 O4 **The Naze** *pt England* U.K.
81 C13 **The Neck** *pen. Stewart I.* N.Z.
151 I6 **The Needles** *stack England* U.K.
159 K8 **Thénezay** France
116 G8 **Theni** *Madh. Prad.* India
205 F2 **Theniet El Had** Alg.
162 G5 **Thenon** France
146 K4 **The North Sound** *sea chan. Scotland* U.K.
84 C6 **Theo, Mount** *hill N.T.* Austr.
146 D11 **The Oa** *pen. Scotland* U.K.
85 M8 **Theodore** *Qld* Austr.
223 K5 **Theodore** *Sask.* Can.
253 E1 **Theodore Roosevelt** *r.* Brazil
241 U8 **Theodore Roosevelt Lake** *AZ* U.S.A.
236 D2 **Theodore Roosevelt National Park** *ND* U.S.A.
Theodosia Ukr. *see* **Feodosiya**
82 D2 **The Officer Creek** *watercourse S.A.* Austr.
149 K5 **The Old Man of Coniston** *hill England* U.K.
159 P7 **Théols** *r.* France
161 J9 **Théoule-sur-Mer** France
147 D8 **The Paps** *hill* Ireland
223 K4 **The Pas** *Man.* Can.
216 □2a **The Peak** *hill Ascension* S. Atlantic Ocean
147 G8 **The Pike** Ireland
Thera *i.* Greece *see* **Santorini**
156 D5 **Thérain** *r.* France
81 C12 **The Remarkables** *mts South I.* N.Z.
169 J10 **Theres** Ger.
233 J4 **Theresa** *NY* U.S.A.
85 L7 **Theresa Creek** *r. Qld* Austr.
Thérèse Island *Inner Islands* Seychelles *see* **Térèse, Île**
146 F13 **The Rinns of Galloway** *pen. Scotland* U.K.
199 G2 **Therma** *Samothraki* Greece
198 D2 **Thermaïkos Kolpos** *g.* Greece
198 E2 **Thermi** Greece
198 C4 **Thermo** Greece
Thérmon Greece *see* **Thermo**
238 J5 **Thermopolis** *WY* U.S.A.
198 D4 **Thermopyles** Greece
83 K6 **The Rock** *N.S.W.* Austr.
185 □ **The Rock** *hill* Gibraltar
156 D2 **Thérouanne** France
246 □ **The Salt Ponds** *lakes* Jamaica
86 □1 **The Settlement** Christmas I.
147 B8 **The Seven Hogs** *is* Ireland
147 J3 **The Sheddings** *Northern Ireland* U.K.
220 F2 **Thesiger Bay** *N.W.T.* Can.
The Sisters *is Inner Islands* Seychelles *see* **Les Sœurs**
80 □ **The Sisters** *is Chatham Is* S. Pacific Ocean
The Skaw *spit* Denmark *see* **Grenen**
The Slot *sea chan.* Solomon Is *see* **New Georgia Sound**
146 □L2 **The Sneug** *hill Scotland* U.K.
151 J6 **The Solent** *str. England* U.K.
198 B3 **Thesprotiko** Greece
198 C3 **Thessalia** *admin. reg.* Greece
224 D4 **Thessalon** *Ont.* Can.
Thessalonica Greece *see* **Thessaloniki**
198 D2 **Thessaloniki** Greece
Thessaly *admin. reg.* Greece *see* **Thessalia**
151 N5 **The Stocks** *Kent, England* U.K.
146 D7 **The Storr** *hill Scotland* U.K.
151 N5 **The Swale** *sea chan. England* U.K.
151 N3 **Thet** *r. England* U.K.
92 B7 **The Teeth** *mt. Palawan* Phil.
148 F5 **The Temple** *Northern Ireland* U.K.
87 F10 **The Terraces** *hills W.A.* Austr.
151 N3 **Thetford** *Norfolk, England* U.K.
225 G4 **Thetford Mines** *Que.* Can.
81 E10 **The Thumbs** *mt. South I.* N.Z.
96 B7 **Thetkethaung** *r.* Myanmar
96 C2 **The Triangle** *mts* Myanmar
146 H10 **The Trossachs** *hills Scotland* U.K.
82 E4 **The Twins** *S.A.* Austr.
96 G5 **Theun** *r.* Laos
215 K4 **Theunissen** S. Africa
165 I7 **Theux** Belgium
Theva-i-Ra *rf* Fiji *see* **Ceva-i-Ra**
247 L4 **The Valley** Anguilla
82 D5 **Thevenard** *S.A.* Austr.
86 C6 **Thevenard Island** *W.A.* Austr.
225 G1 **Thévenet, Lac** *l. Que.* Can.
Theveste Alg. *see* **Tébessa**
151 M2 **The Wash** *b. England* U.K.
151 M5 **The Weald** *reg. England* U.K.
237 H10 **The Woodlands** *TX* U.S.A.
The Wrekin *admin. div. England* U.K. *see* **Telford and Wrekin**
163 D9 **Thèze** *Aquitaine* France
161 H8 **Thèze** *Provence-Alpes-Côte d'Azur* France
Thíamis *r.* Greece *see* **Kalamas**
157 K6 **Thiaucourt-Regniéville** France
159 L3 **Thiberville** France
156 H6 **Thibie** France
237 J11 **Thibodaux** *LA* U.S.A.
223 L4 **Thicket Portage** *Man.* Can.
156 I6 **Thiéblemont-Farémont** France
236 G1 **Thief River Falls** *MN* U.S.A.
Thiel Neth. *see* **Tiel**
190 B2 **Thielle** *r.* Switz.
235 G2 **Thiells** *NY* U.S.A.
262 R1 **Thiel Mountains** Antarctica
238 C5 **Thielsen, Mount** *OR* U.S.A.
Thielt Belgium *see* **Tielt**
191 K4 **Thiene** Italy
156 G4 **Thiérache** *reg.* France
173 J4 **Thierhaupten** Ger.
190 B2 **Thierrens** Switz.
160 D5 **Thiers** France
178 F4 **Thiersee** Austria
171 F10 **Thiersheim** Ger.
157 J5 **Thierville-sur-Meuse** France
206 A3 **Thiès** Senegal
192 B6 **Thiesi** *Sardegna* Italy
170 I2 **Thießow** Ger.
161 B6 **Thiézac** France
211 C5 **Thika** Kenya
Thikombia *i.* Fiji *see* **Cikobia**
114 C9 **Thiladhunmathi Atoll** Maldives
206 B3 **Thilogne** Senegal
Thimbu Bhutan *see* **Thimphu**
156 B6 **Thimert-Gâtelles** France
117 L6 **Thimphu** Bhutan
140 □C1 **Thingvallavatn (Þingvallavatn)** *l.* Iceland
140 □C1 **Thingvellir (Þingvellir)** Iceland
140 C1 **Thingvellir (Þingvellir)** *nat. park* Iceland
156 I4 **Thin-le-Moutier** France
78 □5 **Thio** New Caledonia
157 L5 **Thionville** France
Thira *i.* Greece *see* **Santorini**
198 G6 **Thirasia** *i.* Greece
149 K4 **Thirlmere** *resr England* U.K.
159 M5 **Thiron Gardais** France
156 B7 **Thironne** *r.* France
116 F4 **Thirrach** *Hima. Prad.* India
149 O5 **Thirsk** *North Yorkshire, England* U.K.
87 F12 **Thirsty, Mount** *hill W.A.* Austr.
223 L2 **Thirty Mile Lake** *Nunavut* Can.
Thiruvananthapuram *Kerala* India *see* **Trivandrum**
114 F7 **Thiruvarur** *Tamil Nadu* India
Thiruvattiyur *Tamil Nadu* India *see* **Tiruvottiyur**
160 I2 **Thise** France
198 F1 **Thissavros, Techniti Limni** *resr* Greece
142 E5 **Thisted** Denmark
140 □F1 **Thistilfjörður (Þistilfjörður)** *b.* Iceland
222 B2 **Thistle Creek** *Y.T.* Can.
82 F6 **Thistle Island** *S.A.* Austr.
223 I1 **Thistle Lake** *Nunavut* Can.
96 B3 **Thityabin** Myanmar
198 E4 **Thiva** Greece
Thívai Greece *see* **Thiva**
156 B7 **Thivars** France
162 F5 **Thiviers** France
160 E4 **Thizy** France
140 □C2 **Thjórsá (Þjórsá)** *r.* Iceland
223 M2 **Thlewiaza** *r. Nunavut* Can.
223 I2 **Thoa** *r. N.W.T.* Can.
161 I8 **Thoard** France
97 F10 **Thô Chu, Đao** *i.* Vietnam
96 D6 **Thoen** Thai.
96 E5 **Thoeng** Thai.
213 F4 **Thohoyandou** S. Africa
160 H4 **Thoirette** France
156 C6 **Thoiry** *Île-de-France* France
160 H4 **Thoiry** *Rhône-Alpes* France
160 F4 **Thoissey** France
160 E2 **Thoisy-la-Berchère** France
164 F5 **Tholen** Neth.
164 F5 **Tholen** *i.* Neth.
172 C3 **Tholey** Ger.
156 F7 **Tholon** *r.* France
87 D8 **Thomas** *r. W.A.* Austr.
84 F9 **Thomas, Lake** *salt flat S.A.* Austr.
168 K4 **Thomasburg** Ger.
236 I6 **Thomas Hill Reservoir** *MO* U.S.A.
221 I1 **Thomas Hubbard, Cape** *Nunavut* Can.
240 P8 **Thomas Mountain** *CA* U.S.A.
235 I1 **Thomaston** *CT* U.S.A.
231 E9 **Thomaston** *GA* U.S.A.
233 □P4 **Thomaston** *ME* U.S.A.
233 □R3 **Thomaston Corner** *N.B.* Can.
147 H7 **Thomastown** Ireland
231 D10 **Thomasville** *AL* U.S.A.
231 F10 **Thomasville** *GA* U.S.A.
231 G8 **Thomasville** *NC* U.S.A.
165 J8 **Thommen** Belgium
246 H4 **Thomonde** Haiti
223 L4 **Thompson** *Man.* Can.
222 F5 **Thompson** *r. B.C.* Can.
226 H4 **Thompson** *MI* U.S.A.
241 W3 **Thompson** *UT* U.S.A.
236 I6 **Thompson** *r. MO* U.S.A.
238 G3 **Thompson Falls** *MT* U.S.A.
239 L9 **Thompson Peak** *NM* U.S.A.
Thompson's Falls Kenya *see* **Nyahururu**
222 E5 **Thompson Sound** *B.C.* Can.
81 A12 **Thompson Sound** *inlet South I.* N.Z.
234 A3 **Thompsontown** *PA* U.S.A.
233 M7 **Thompsonville** *CT* U.S.A.
85 I8 **Thomson** *watercourse Qld* Austr.
231 F9 **Thomson** *GA* U.S.A.
226 D8 **Thomson** *IL* U.S.A.
81 C11 **Thomson Mountains** *South I.* N.Z.
97 E8 **Thon Buri** Thai.
116 F3 **Thondhe** Jammu and Kashmir
160 I5 **Thônes** France
96 C6 **Thongwa** Myanmar
157 J7 **Thonnance-lès-Joinville** France
223 I1 **Thonokied Lake** *N.W.T.* Can.
160 I4 **Thonon-les-Bains** France
161 J8 **Thorame-Basse** France
161 J8 **Thorame-Haute** France
161 D7 **Thoras** France
163 I8 **Thoré** *r.* France
239 J9 **Thoreau** *NM* U.S.A.
159 M6 **Thoré-la-Rochette** France
161 J9 **Thorenc** France
160 I5 **Thorens-Glières** France
222 H4 **Thorhild** *Alta* Can.
156 F7 **Thorigny-sur-Oreuse** France
140 □D1 **Thórisvatn (Þórisvatn)** *l.* Iceland
179 L4 **Thörl** Austria
165 I6 **Thorn** Neth.
Thorn Pol. *see* **Toruń**
149 O4 **Thornaby-on-Tees** *Stockton-on-Tees, England* U.K.
226 I7 **Thornapple** *r. MI* U.S.A.
81 C13 **Thornbury** *South I.* N.Z.
150 G4 **Thornbury** *South Gloucestershire, England* U.K.
227 O3 **Thorne** *Ont.* Can.
149 P6 **Thorne** *South Yorkshire, England* U.K.
240 N3 **Thorne** *NV* U.S.A.
222 C4 **Thorne Bay** *AK* U.S.A.
151 L2 **Thorney** *Peterborough, England* U.K.
149 Q6 **Thorngumbald** *East Riding of Yorkshire, England* U.K.
146 I12 **Thornhill** *Dumfries and Galloway, Scotland* U.K.
148 I1 **Thornhill** *Stirling, Scotland* U.K.
234 D2 **Thornhurst** *PA* U.S.A.
149 O4 **Thornley** *Durham, England* U.K.
84 G5 **Thornton** *r. Qld* Austr.
146 J10 **Thornton** *Fife, Scotland* U.K.
149 L6 **Thornton** *Lancashire, England* U.K.
226 F5 **Thornton** *WI* U.S.A.
149 P5 **Thornton Dale** *North Yorkshire, England* U.K.
235 H2 **Thornwood** *NY* U.S.A.
227 O6 **Thorold** *Ont.* Can.
226 D5 **Thorp** *WI* U.S.A.
81 G8 **Thorpe** *South I.* N.Z.
151 O4 **Thorpe-le-Soken** *Essex, England* U.K.
151 O2 **Thorpe Market** *Norfolk, England* U.K.
151 P3 **Thorpeness** *Suffolk, England* U.K.
151 O2 **Thorpe St Andrew** *Norfolk, England* U.K.
222 H4 **Thorsby** *Alta* Can.
Thorshavn Faroe Is *see* **Tórshavn**
Thorshavnfjella *reg.* Antarctica *see* **Thorshavnheiane**
263 B2 **Thorshavnheiane** *reg.* Antarctica
140 □F1 **Thórshöfn (Þórshöfn)** Iceland
140 □E1 **Thorvaldsfell (Þorvaldsfell)** *vol.* Iceland
215 L5 **Thota-ea-Moli** Lesotho
159 K7 **Thouarcé** France
158 I7 **Thouaré-sur-Loire** France
162 D2 **Thouars** France
117 N7 **Thoubal** *Manipur* India
162 D1 **Thouet** *r.* France
86 E6 **Thouin, Cape** *pt W.A.* Austr.
156 E5 **Thourotte** France
Thourout Belgium *see* **Torhout**
227 R5 **Thousand Islands** Can./U.S.A.
241 U3 **Thousand Lake Mountain** *UT* U.S.A.
240 N7 **Thousand Oaks** *CA* U.S.A.
241 P8 **Thousand Palms** *CA* U.S.A.
232 B11 **Thousandsticks** *KY* U.S.A.
234 B6 **T. Howard Duckett Reservoir** *MD* U.S.A.
197 O9 **Thrace** *reg.* Turkey
Thraki *reg.* Turkey *see* **Thrace**
198 F2 **Thrakiko Pelagos** *sea* Greece
151 K3 **Thrapston** *Northamptonshire, England* U.K.
83 L7 **Thredbo** *N.S.W.* Austr.
234 F3 **Three Bridges** *NJ* U.S.A.
147 C10 **Three Castle Head** Ireland
Three Fathoms Cove *b. H.K.* China *see* **Kei Ling Ha Hoi**
238 I4 **Three Forks** *MT* U.S.A.
108 G3 **Three Gorges Dam Project** *resr* China
83 J9 **Three Hummock Island** *Tas.* Austr.
80 G1 **Three Kings Islands** *North I.* N.Z.
226 E4 **Three Lakes** *WI* U.S.A.
226 H8 **Three Oaks** *MI* U.S.A.
96 D7 **Three Pagodas Pass** Myanmar/Thai.
241 U9 **Three Points** *AZ* U.S.A.
206 E5 **Three Points, Cape** Ghana
240 N5 **Three Rivers** *CA* U.S.A.
226 I8 **Three Rivers** *MI* U.S.A.
237 F11 **Three Rivers** *TX* U.S.A.
214 H7 **Three Sisters** S. Africa
238 D4 **Three Sisters** *mt. OR* U.S.A.
78 □6 **Three Sisters Islands** Solomon Is
87 C10 **Three Springs** *W.A.* Austr.
149 K4 **Threlkeld** *Cumbria, England* U.K.
149 M5 **Threshfield** *North Yorkshire, England* U.K.
Thrissur *Kerala* India *see* **Trichur**
237 F9 **Throckmorton** *TX* U.S.A.
234 D2 **Throop** *PA* U.S.A.
149 N3 **Thropton** *Northumberland, England* U.K.
87 H9 **Throssell, Lake** *salt flat W.A.* Austr.
86 F6 **Throssel Range** *hills W.A.* Austr.
146 J6 **Thrumster** *Highland, Scotland* U.K.
150 H4 **Thrupp** *Gloucestershire, England* U.K.
85 K9 **Thrushton National Park** *Qld* Austr.
149 O7 **Thrybergh** *South Yorkshire, England* U.K.
211 D5 **Thua** *watercourse* Kenya
96 H6 **Thuân An** Vietnam
97 G10 **Thư Ba** Vietnam
96 I6 **Thu Bôn, Sông** *r.* Vietnam
223 I2 **Thubun Lakes** *N.W.T.* Can.
97 H9 **Thu Dâu Môt** Vietnam
83 L6 **Thuddungra** *N.S.W.* Austr.
97 H9 **Thu Đuc** Vietnam
163 I10 **Thuès-entre-Valls** France
161 E7 **Thueyts** France
165 F8 **Thuin** Belgium
169 E6 **Thuine** Ger.
163 J10 **Thuir** France
210 B2 **Thul** Sudan
210 A2 **Thul** *watercourse* Sudan
128 H3 **Thulaythawāt Gharbī, Jabal** *hill* Syria
169 I10 **Thulba** *r.* Ger.
Thule Greenland *see* **Qaanaaq**
213 F4 **Thuli** Zimbabwe
213 F4 **Thuli** *r.* Zimbabwe
Thulusdhoo *N. Male* Maldives *see* **Thulusdhu**
113 □1 **Thulusdhu** *N. Male* Maldives
171 G9 **Thum** Ger.
190 D2 **Thun** Switz.
85 I8 **Thunda** *Qld* Austr.
87 D10 **Thundelarra** *W.A.* Austr.
224 B3 **Thunder Bay** *Ont.* Can.
224 B3 **Thunder Bay** *b. Ont.* Can.
227 K4 **Thunder Bay** *b. MI* U.S.A.
223 J5 **Thunder Creek** *r. Sask.* Can.
246 C5 **Thunder Knoll** *sea feature* Caribbean Sea
151 N4 **Thundersley** *Essex, England* U.K.
190 D2 **Thuner See** *l.* Switz.
172 H2 **Thüngen** Ger.
172 H2 **Thüngersheim** Ger.
96 E6 **Thung Salaeng Luang National Park** Thai.
97 D10 **Thung Song** Thai.
97 D11 **Thung Wa** Thai.
96 D7 **Thung Yai Naresuan Wildlife Reserve** *nature res.* Thai.
157 N7 **Thur** *r.* France
190 F1 **Thur** *r.* Switz.
80 J7 **Thuraua** *North I.* N.Z.
149 O7 **Thurcroft** *South Yorkshire, England* U.K.
159 L8 **Thuré** France
160 C5 **Thuret** France
160 G3 **Thurey** France
190 G1 **Thurgau** *canton* Switz.
178 A5 **Thüringen** Austria
169 K8 **Thüringen** *land* Ger.
171 D8 **Thüringer Becken** *reg.* Ger.
169 J9 **Thüringer Wald** *mts* Ger.
169 K9 **Thüringer Wald** *park* Ger.
Thuringia *land* Ger. *see* **Thüringen**
Thuringian Forest *mts* Ger. *see* **Thüringer Wald**
160 F5 **Thurins** France
170 G3 **Thürkow** Ger.
151 L2 **Thurlby** *Lincolnshire, England* U.K.
147 G7 **Thurles** Ireland
171 G9 **Thurm** Ger.
173 O4 **Thurmansbang** Ger.
232 H9 **Thurmont** *MD* U.S.A.
178 F5 **Thurn, Pass** Austria
171 D10 **Thurnau** Ger.
149 O6 **Thurnscoe** *South Yorkshire, England* U.K.
151 M4 **Thurrock** *admin. div. England* U.K.
149 K4 **Thursby** *Cumbria, England* U.K.
85 I1 **Thursday Island** *Qld* Austr.
233 J3 **Thurso** *Que.* Can.
146 I5 **Thurso** *Highland, Scotland* U.K.
146 I5 **Thurso** *r. Scotland* U.K.
146 I5 **Thurso Bay** *Scotland* U.K.
151 N3 **Thurston** *Suffolk, England* U.K.
262 R2 **Thurston Island** Antarctica
Thurston Peninsula *i.* Antarctica *see* **Thurston Island**
151 O2 **Thurton** *Norfolk, England* U.K.
159 K4 **Thury-Harcourt** France
190 G2 **Thusis** Switz.
169 I6 **Thüster Berg** *hill* Ger.
160 H5 **Thusy** France
149 M5 **Thwaite** *North Yorkshire, England* U.K.
262 Q1 **Thwaites Glacier Tongue** Antarctica
142 E5 **Thy** *reg.* Denmark
Thyatira Turkey *see* **Akhisar**
142 E5 **Thyborøn** Denmark
160 J4 **Thyez** France
85 I9 **Thylungra** *Qld* Austr.
199 H5 **Thymaina** *i.* Greece
156 B6 **Thymerais** *reg.* France
211 B8 **Thyolo** Malawi
206 E4 **Thyou** *Boulkiemde* Burkina
Thyou *Yatenga* Burkina *see* **Tiou**
173 P4 **Thyrnau** Ger.
Thysville Dem. Rep. Congo *see* **Mbanza-Ngungu**
122 G8 **Tīāb** Iran
252 C4 **Tiahuanaco** Bol.
246 H8 **Tía Juana** Venez.
192 C7 **Tiana** *Sardegna* Italy
106 F6 **Tiancang** *Gansu* China
109 L2 **Tianchang** *Anhui* China
106 F7 **Tiancheng** *Gansu* China
Tiancheng *Hubei* China *see* **Chongyang**
107 J8 **Tianchi** *Gansu* China
Tianchi *Sichuan* China *see* **Lezhi**
108 F7 **Tiandeng** *Guangxi* China
Tiandiba *Sichuan* China *see* **Jinyang**
108 F7 **Tiandong** *Guangxi* China
108 F6 **Tian'e** *Guangxi* China
129 F3 **T'ianet'i** Georgia
109 K4 **Tianfanjie** *Jiangxi* China
206 B3 **Tiângol Lougguéré** *watercourse* Senegal
254 E2 **Tianguá** Brazil
245 I5 **Tianguistengo** Mex.
107 O7 **Tianjin** *Tianjin* China
107 O7 **Tianjin** *mun.* China
106 F8 **Tianjun** *Qinghai* China
206 B3 **Tiankoye** Senegal
108 F6 **Tianlin** *Guangxi* China
109 I3 **Tianmen** *Hubei* China
109 L3 **Tianmu Shan** *mts* China
100 F7 **Tianqiaoling** *Jilin* China
108 D3 **Tianquan** *Sichuan* China
107 Q5 **Tianshan** *Nei Mongol* China
Tian Shan *mts* China/Kyrg. *see* **Tien Shan**
101 D8 **Tianshifu** *Liaoning* China
106 I9 **Tianshui** *Gansu* China
106 J8 **Tianshuibu** *Gansu* China
111 D9 **Tianshuihai** Aksai Chin
110 L6 **Tianshuijing** *Gansu* China
109 M4 **Tiantai** *Zhejiang* China
107 O5 **Tiantaiyong** *Nei Mongol* China
Tiantang *Anhui* China *see* **Yuexi**
108 F7 **Tianyang** *Guangxi* China
Tianyi *Nei Mongol* China *see* **Ningcheng**
Tianzhen *Shandong* China *see* **Gaoqing**
107 N6 **Tianzhen** *Shanxi* China
Tianzhou *Guangxi* China *see* **Tianyang**
106 H8 **Tianzhu** *Gansu* China
108 G5 **Tianzhu** *Guizhou* China
79 □9a **Tiarei** *Tahiti* Fr. Polynesia
205 F2 **Tiaret** Alg.
205 H3 **Tiaret** *well* Tunisia
78 □5 **Tiari** New Caledonia
85 N8 **Tiaro** *Qld* Austr.
216 □3c **Tías** *Lanzarote* Canary Is
206 D5 **Tiassalé** Côte d'Ivoire
78 □2 **Ti'avea** Samoa
Tibabar *Sabah* Malaysia *see* **Tambunan**
256 B6 **Tibagi** Brazil
256 B5 **Tibagi** *r.* Brazil
Tibaji *r.* Brazil *see* **Tibagi**
127 K7 **Tibal, Wādī** *watercourse* Iraq
250 C3 **Tibaná** Col.
207 I5 **Tibati** Cameroon
123 N7 **Tibba** Pak.
146 I10 **Tibbermore** *Perth and Kinross, Scotland* U.K.
206 C4 **Tibé, Pic de** *mt.* Guinea
Tiber *r.* Italy *see* **Tevere**
205 F3 **Tiberghamine** Alg.
204 B5 **Tiberguent** *well* Maur.
Tiberias Israel *see* **Teverya**
238 I2 **Tiber Reservoir** *MT* U.S.A.
202 C4 **Tibesti** *mts* Chad
Tibet *aut. reg.* China *see* **Xizang Zizhiqu**
Tibet, Plateau of *Xizang* China *see* **Qingzang Gaoyuan**
187 D10 **Tibi** Spain
187 D11 **Tibi, Embalse de** *resr* Spain
207 G3 **Tibiri** Niger
197 M4 **Ţibleş, Vârful** *mt.* Romania
251 G3 **Tiboku Falls** Guyana
177 J4 **Tibolddaróc** Hungary
83 I3 **Tibooburra** *N.S.W.* Austr.
177 L4 **Tiborszállás** Hungary
117 I5 **Tibrikot** Nepal
143 K3 **Tibro** Sweden
149 O7 **Tibshelf** *Derbyshire, England* U.K.
250 B3 **Tibuga, Ensenada** *b.* Col.
Tibur Italy *see* **Tivoli**
242 C3 **Tiburón, Isla** *i.* Mex.
92 D5 **Ticao** *i.* Phil.
151 M5 **Ticehurst** *East Sussex, England* U.K.
197 O7 **Ticha** *r.* Bulg.
197 K8 **Tichak** *mt.* Bulg.
Tichau Pol. *see* **Tychy**
227 R5 **Tichborne** *Ont.* Can.
225 F3 **Tichégami** *r. Que.* Can.
207 F2 **Tichet** *well* Mali
206 C2 **Tîchît** Maur.
204 B5 **Tichla** Western Sahara
190 G5 **Ticino** *r.* Italy/Switz.
190 F3 **Ticino** *canton* Switz.
Ticinum Italy *see* **Pavia**
149 O7 **Tickhill** *South Yorkshire, England* U.K.
197 L6 **Ţicleni** Romania
233 L5 **Ticonderoga** *NY* U.S.A.
243 O7 **Ticul** Mex.
Ticumbia *i.* Fiji *see* **Cikobia**
143 J3 **Tidaholm** Sweden
143 K3 **Tidan** Sweden
143 J3 **Tidan** *r.* Sweden
96 A3 **Tiddim** Myanmar
168 K5 **Tiddische** Ger.
115 M9 **Tiden** *Andaman & Nicobar Is* India
150 G4 **Tidenham** *Gloucestershire, England* U.K.
205 F5 **Tideridjaounine, Adrar** *mts* Alg.
149 N7 **Tideswell** *Derbyshire, England* U.K.
205 F4 **Tidikelt, Plaine du** *plain* Alg.
232 F7 **Tidioute** *PA* U.S.A.
207 F2 **Tidjerouene** *well* Mali
206 C2 **Tidjikja** Maur.
190 H5 **Tidone** *r.* Italy
93 E3 **Tidore** *i. Maluku* Indon.
204 B5 **Tidsit, Sabkhet** *salt pan* Western Sahara
151 I5 **Tidworth** *Wiltshire, England* U.K.
163 A10 **Tiebas** Spain
206 D5 **Tiébissou** Côte d'Ivoire
202 C4 **Tiéboro** Chad
110 G3 **Tiechanggou** *Xinjiang* China
183 J5 **Tiedra** Spain
Tiefa *Liaoning* China *see* **Diaobingshan**
173 M4 **Tiefenbach** *Bayern* Ger.
173 N3 **Tiefenbach** *Bayern* Ger.
173 O4 **Tiefenbach** *Bayern* Ger.
172 F4 **Tiefenbronn** Ger.
190 H2 **Tiefencastel** Switz.
170 I5 **Tiefensee** Ger.
164 H5 **Tiel** Neth.
206 B3 **Tiel** Senegal
165 G6 **Tielen** Belgium
100 E5 **Tieli** *Heilong.* China
107 R5 **Tieling** *Liaoning* China
111 D9 **Tielongtan** Aksai Chin
165 D7 **Tielt** Belgium
206 D4 **Tiémé** Côte d'Ivoire
206 C5 **Tiene** Liberia
165 G7 **Tienen** Belgium
172 E6 **Tiengen** Ger.
110 C6 **Tien Shan** *mts* China/Kyrg.
Tien Shan Oblast *admin. div.* Kyrg. *see* **Naryn**
Tientsin *Tianjin* China *see* **Tianjin**
Tientsin *mun.* China *see* Tianjin
96 H4 **Tiên Yên** Vietnam
191 J6 **Tiepido** *r.* Italy
159 K6 **Tiercé** France
215 K4 **Tierfontein** S. Africa
183 Q5 **Tierga** Spain
143 N1 **Tierp** Sweden
258 C2 **Tierra Amarilla** Chile
239 K8 **Tierra Amarilla** *NM* U.S.A.
244 G4 **Tierrablanca** Mex.
245 K7 **Tierra Blanca** Mex.
250 C6 **Tierra Blanca** Peru
245 H8 **Tierra Colorada** Mex.
259 D9 **Tierra del Fuego** *prov.* Arg.
259 C9 **Tierra del Fuego, Isla Grande de** *i.* Arg./Chile
259 D9 **Tierra del Fuego, Parque Nacional** *nat. park* Arg.
250 B4 **Tierradentro, Parque Arqueológico Nacional** *tourist site* Col.
250 B2 **Tierralta** Col.
216 □3c **Tierra Negra, Punta de** *pt Lanzarote* Canary Is
244 G4 **Tierranueva** Mex.
183 Q7 **Tierzo** Spain
185 I5 **Tiesa** *hill* Spain
179 M6 **Tieschen** Austria
182 I9 **Tiétar** *r.* Spain
183 J8 **Tiétar, Valle de** *val.* Spain
256 D5 **Tietê** Brazil
256 B4 **Tietê** *r.* Brazil
82 D2 **Tieyon** *S.A.* Austr.
159 I7 **Tiffauges** France
232 B7 **Tiffin** *OH* U.S.A.
Tiflis Georgia *see* **T'bilisi**
93 E3 **Tifore** *i. Maluku* Indon.
231 F10 **Tifton** *GA* U.S.A.
93 E5 **Tifu** *Buru* Indon.
95 K2 **Tiga** *i.* Malaysia
78 □5 **Tiga** *i. Îles Loyauté* New Caledonia
215 K2 **Tigane** S. Africa
197 N7 **Ţigăneşti** Romania
94 E5 **Tigapuluh, Pegunungan** *mts* Indon.
120 D5 **Tigen** Kazakh.
122 I8 **Tīgh Āb** Iran
136 H8 **Tigheciului, Dealurile** *hills* Moldova
136 I7 **Tighina** Moldova
136 G6 **Ţîghira** Moldova
146 F11 **Tighnabruaich** *Argyll and Bute, Scotland* U.K.
121 T2 **Tigiretskiy Khrebet** *mts* Kazakh./Rus. Fed.
117 J9 **Tigiria** *Orissa* India
191 J4 **Tignale** Italy
207 I5 **Tignère** Cameroon
160 J6 **Tignes** France
225 H4 **Tignish** *P.E.I.* Can.
139 O2 **Tigoda** *r.* Rus. Fed.
206 D2 **Tigoumatene** *well* Mali
Tigranocerta Turkey *see* **Siirt**
210 C1 **Tigray** *admin. reg.* Eth.
261 H4 **Tigre** Arg.
250 C6 **Tigre** *r.* Ecuador/Peru
245 J3 **Tigre** *r.* Mex.
245 H2 **Tigre, Cerro del** *mt.* Mex.
260 C2 **Tigre, Sierra** *mts* Arg.
127 M8 **Tigris** *r.* Asia
alt. **Dicle (Turkey)**
alt. **Dijlah, Nahr (Iraq/Syria)**
123 M3 **Tigrovaya Balka Zapovednik** *nature res.* Tajik.
205 F4 **Tiguelguemine** *well* Alg.
206 B2 **Tiguent** Maur.
204 C4 **Tiguesmat** *hills* Maur.
202 C5 **Tigui** Chad
207 G2 **Tiguidit, Falaise de** *esc.* Niger
206 D2 **Tiguîguil** *well* Maur.
205 H6 **Tiguir** *well* Niger
156 D8 **Tigy** France
204 C3 **Tigzerte, Oued** *watercourse* Morocco
203 G2 **Tīh, Jabal at** *plat.* Egypt
124 F7 **Tihāmah** *reg.* Saudi Arabia
177 G5 **Tihany** Hungary
177 G5 **Tihany** *park* Hungary
205 F4 **Tihatimine** *well* Alg.
205 G4 **Tihodaïne, Erg** *des.* Alg.
245 J5 **Tihuatlán** Mex.
252 D3 **Tijamuchi** *r.* Bol.
116 F6 **Tijara** *Rajasthan* India
216 □3d **Tijarafe** *La Palma* Canary Is
202 A1 **Tijī** Libya
204 B5 **Tijirît** *reg.* Maur.
164 I2 **Tijnje** Neth.
185 O6 **Tíjola** Spain
242 A1 **Tijuana** Mex.
255 C8 **Tijucas** Brazil
255 C8 **Tijucas, Baía de** *b.* Brazil
256 B3 **Tijuco** *r.* Brazil
Tika *i. Îles Loyauté* New Caledonia *see* **Tiga**
243 O9 **Tikal** *tourist site* Guat.
243 O9 **Tikal, Parque Nacional** *nat. park* Guat.
116 G7 **Tikamgarh** *Madh. Prad.* India
110 H6 **Tikanlik** *Xinjiang* China
220 C4 **Tikchik Lake** *AK* U.S.A.
137 S3 **Tikhaya Sosna** *r.* Rus. Fed.
Tikherón Greece *see* **Tychero**
139 V3 **Tikhmenevo** Rus. Fed.
139 T7 **Tikhonova Pustyn'** Rus. Fed.
135 H7 **Tikhoretsk** Rus. Fed.
140 U4 **Tikhtozero** Rus. Fed.
139 Q2 **Tikhvin** Rus. Fed.
139 Q2 **Tikhvinka** *r.* Rus. Fed.
139 Q2 **Tikhvinskaya Gryada** *ridge* Rus. Fed.
267 K7 **Tiki Basin** *sea feature* Pacific Ocean
207 G2 **Tikiktene** *well* Niger
Tikirarjuaq *Nunavut* Can. *see* **Whale Cove**
80 M4 **Tikitiki** *North I.* N.Z.
79 □7a **Tikituru** *mt. Viti Levu* Fiji
140 R5 **Tikkakoski** Fin.
138 I1 **Tikkurila** Fin.
129 F6 **Tīkmeh-ye Bālā** Iran
80 K6 **Tikokino** *North I.* N.Z.
77 G3 **Tikopia** *i.* Solomon Is
127 K6 **Tikrīt** Iraq
116 F2 **Tikse** Jammu and Kashmir
140 V3 **Tiksheozero, Ozero** *l.* Rus. Fed.
131 N2 **Tiksi** Rus. Fed.
Tikumbia *i.* Fiji *see* **Cikobia**
Tikus *i.* Cocos Is *see* **Direction Island**
197 J9 **Tikveš Ezero** *l.* Macedonia
215 J3 **Tikwana** S. Africa
116 H5 **Tila** *r.* Nepal
117 J7 **Tilaiya Reservoir** India
260 B3 **Tilama** Chile
93 C3 **Tilamuta** *Sulawesi* Indon.
122 F3 **Tilavar** Iran
128 F2 **Tilbeşar Ovasi** *plain* Turkey
85 J9 **Tilbooroo** *Qld* Austr.
164 H5 **Tilburg** Neth.
227 L7 **Tilbury** *Ont.* Can.
151 M5 **Tilbury** *Thurrock, England* U.K.
258 D1 **Tilcara** Arg.
82 H3 **Tilcha** *S.A.* Austr.
160 G1 **Til-Châtel** France
237 F11 **Tilden** *TX* U.S.A.
197 K3 **Tileagd** Romania
151 J5 **Tilehurst** *Reading, England* U.K.
207 G3 **Tilemsès** Niger
207 F2 **Tîlemsi, Vallée du** *watercourse* Mali
233 I10 **Tilghman** *MD* U.S.A.
163 C8 **Tilh** France
116 G6 **Tilhar** *Uttar Prad.* India
205 F4 **Tilia, Oued** *watercourse* Alg.
Tiligulo-Berezanka Ukr. *see* **Berezanka**
Tilimsen Alg. *see* **Tlemcen**
96 B4 **Tilin** Myanmar
260 E3 **Tilisarao** Arg.
149 M2 **Till** *r. England* U.K.
207 F3 **Tillabéri** Niger
207 F3 **Tillabéri** *dept* Niger
163 E9 **Tillac** France
238 C4 **Tillamook** *OR* U.S.A.
115 M8 **Tillanchong Island** *Andaman & Nicobar Is* India
160 G2 **Tille** *r.* France
171 D8 **Tilleda (Kyffhäuser)** Ger.

223 I5 **Tilley** Alta Can.
207 G2 **Tillia** Niger
146 I10 **Tillicoultry** Clackmannanshire, Scotland U.K.
156 B6 **Tillières-sur-Avre** France
156 I5 **Tilly-et-Bellay** France
224 D5 **Tillsonburg** Ont. Can.
146 K8 **Tillyfourie** Aberdeenshire, Scotland U.K.
159 J3 **Tilly-sur-Seulles** France
207 F3 **Tiloa** Niger
Tilogne Senegal see **Thilogne**
252 C5 **Tilomonte** Chile
116 E6 **Tilonia** Rajasthan India
199 I6 **Tilos** i. Greece
117 J7 **Tilothu** Bihar India
83 J4 **Tilpa** N.S.W. Austr.
205 F2 **Tilrhemt** Alg.
138 K5 **Tilsa** r. Latvia
Tilsit Rus. Fed. see **Sovetsk**
149 L7 **Tilston** Cheshire, England U.K.
149 I9 **Tilt** r. Scotland U.K.
260 B3 **Tiltil** Chile
134 M2 **Til'tim** Rus. Fed.
233 N5 **Tilton** NH U.S.A.
93 B4 **Tilu, Bukit** mt. Indon.
138 K5 **Tilža** Latvia
135 G6 **Tim** Rus. Fed.
137 Q1 **Tim** r. Rus. Fed.
203 F3 **Timā** Egypt
203 I6 **Timā** Yemen
94 □ **Timah, Bukit** hill Sing.
148 C8 **Timahoe** Ireland
114 C7 **Timakara** i. India
253 F5 **Timane** r. Para.
216 □3c **Timanfaya** vol. Lanzarote Canary Is
216 □3c **Timanfaya, Parque Nacional de** nat. park Lanzarote Canary Is
134 J2 **Timanskiy Kryazh** ridge Rus. Fed.
127 K4 **Timar** Turkey
81 F11 **Timaru** South I. N.Z.
120 D1 **Timashevo** Rus. Fed.
135 G7 **Timashevsk** Rus. Fed.
Timashevskaya Rus. Fed. see **Timashevsk**
191 O2 **Timau** Italy
Timbákion Kriti Greece see **Tympaki**
237 J11 **Timbalier Bay** LA U.S.A.
254 G3 **Timbaúba** Brazil
206 C2 **Timbedgha** Maur.
84 C3 **Timber Creek** N.T. Austr.
236 E3 **Timber Lake** SD U.S.A.
241 P4 **Timber Mountain** NV U.S.A.
232 G10 **Timberville** VA U.S.A.
250 B4 **Timbiquí** Col.
206 C4 **Timbo** Guinea
83 I8 **Timboon** Vic. Austr.
213 H3 **Timbué, Ponta** pt Moz.
Timbuktu Mali see **Tombouctou**
95 M2 **Timbun Mata** i. Malaysia
179 I3 **Timelkam** Austria
207 E2 **Timétrine** Mali
206 E2 **Timétrine** reg. Mali
Timfi mts Greece see **Tymfi**
205 G2 **Timgad** tourist site Alg.
207 H2 **Timia** Niger
205 F5 **Timiaouine** Alg.
205 F3 **Timimoun** Alg.
198 F2 **Timiou Prodromou, Akrotirio** pt Greece
206 A2 **Timirist, Râs** pt Maur.
121 L1 **Timiryazev** Kazakh.
121 I1 **Timiryazevo** Kazakh.
177 K6 **Timiș** county Romania
197 I5 **Timiș** r. Romania
Timiskaming, Lake Ont./Que. Can. see **Témiscamingue, Lac**
196 J5 **Timișoara** Romania
196 I5 **Timișului, Câmpia** plain Romania
Timkovichi Belarus see **Tsimkavichy**
207 G2 **Ti-m-Meghsoi** watercourse Niger
178 D6 **Timmelsjoch** pass Austria/Italy
168 K3 **Timmendorfer Strand** Ger.
224 D3 **Timmins** Ont. Can.
226 D4 **Timms Hill** WI U.S.A.
Timoé atoll Arch. des Tuamotu Fr. Polynesia see **Temoe**
196 K6 **Timok** r. Serbia
139 T2 **Timokhino** Rus. Fed.
147 E9 **Timoleague** Ireland
254 E3 **Timon** Brazil
192 H3 **Timone** r. Italy
236 B4 **Timonium** MD U.S.A.
93 E8 **Timor** i. Indon.
76 C3 **Timor Sea** Austr./Indon.
Timor Timur country Asia see **East Timor**
139 T1 **Timoshino** Rus. Fed.
261 F4 **Timote** Arg.
257 F3 **Timóteo** Brazil
205 E3 **Timoudi** Alg.
93 D4 **Timpaus** i. Indon.
87 G8 **Timperley Range** hills W.A. Austr.
141 N5 **Timrå** Sweden
128 A8 **Timsāḩ, Buḩayrat at** l. Egypt
150 H5 **Timsbury** Bath and North East Somerset, England U.K.
231 D8 **Tims Ford Lake** TN U.S.A.
146 B6 **Timsgearraidh** Western Isles, Scotland U.K.
134 K3 **Timsher** Rus. Fed.
134 K3 **Timshor** r. Rus. Fed.
121 M6 **Timur** Kazakh.
116 F8 **Timurni Muafi** Madh. Prad. India
124 F2 **Tin, Jabal** hill Saudi Arabia
202 D1 **Tin, Ra's at** pt Libya
191 L2 **Tina** r. Italy
215 N7 **Tina** r. S. Africa
206 E2 **Ti-n-Aba** well Mali
128 G2 **Tinah** Syria
128 A7 **Tinah, Khalīj at** b. Egypt
148 E8 **Tinahely** Ireland
183 O8 **Tinajas** Spain
216 □3c **Tinajo** Lanzarote Canary Is
182 E9 **Tinalhas** Port.
207 A3 **Tin Alkoum** Libya
207 F2 **Ti-n-Amâssine** well Mali
205 G5 **Tin Amzi, Oued** watercourse Alg.
250 D2 **Tinaquillo** Venez.
207 F2 **Ti-n-Azabo** well Mali
204 C5 **Ti-n-Bessaïs** well Maur.
206 E2 **Ti-n-Boukri** well Mali
177 K5 **Tinca** Romania
85 N8 **Tin Can Bay** Qld Austr.
159 J4 **Tinchebray** France
205 E5 **Ti-n-Didine** well Mali
114 F6 **Tindivanam** Tamil Nadu India
204 C4 **Tindouf** Alg.
144 D1 **Tindur** hill Faroe Is
202 D6 **Tiné** Chad
206 E2 **Ti-n-Echeri** well Mali
206 E2 **Ti-n-Edrine** well Mali
161 K9 **Tinée** r. France
182 H2 **Tineo** Spain
207 F3 **Ti-n-Eratilene** well Mali
204 D3 **Tinerhir** Morocco
207 F2 **Ti-n-Essako** Mali
206 E2 **Ti-n-Etissane** well Mali
204 D3 **Tinfouchy** Alg.
151 J4 **Tingewick** Buckinghamshire, England U.K.
94 F3 **Tinggi** i. Malaysia
202 A2 **Tingharat, Hammādat** des. Libya
206 C4 **Tingi Mountains** Sierra Leone
Tingis Morocco see **Tanger**
109 K6 **Ting Jiang** r. China
96 C1 **Tingkawk Sakan** Myanmar
142 F7 **Tinglev** Denmark
252 B2 **Tingo María** Peru
Tingrela Côte d'Ivoire see **Tengréla**
111 H12 **Tingri** Xizang China
143 K5 **Tingsryd** Sweden
143 O4 **Tingstäde** Gotland Sweden
143 O4 **Tingstädeträsk** l. Gotland Sweden
244 E6 **Tingüindín** Mex.
260 B4 **Tinguiririca** Chile
260 B4 **Tinguiririca, Volcán** vol. Chile
142 D3 **Tingvatn** Norway
140 J5 **Tingvoll** Norway
146 J4 **Tingwall** Orkney, Scotland U.K.
Tingzhou Fujian China see **Changting**
254 F5 **Tinharé, Ilha de** i. Brazil
182 F6 **Tinhela** r. Port.
96 G5 **Tinh Gia** Vietnam
91 K4 **Tinian** i. N. Mariana Is
206 B2 **Tiniéré** well Maur.
250 C4 **Tinigua, Parque Nacional** nat. park Col.
Tini Heke is N.Z. see **Snares Islands**
80 L5 **Tiniroto** North I. N.Z.
188 G3 **Tinja** r. Bos.-Herz.
191 P5 **Tinjan** Croatia
95 K2 **Tinjar** r. Malaysia
94 F8 **Tinjil** i. Indon.
206 C4 **Tinkisso** r. Guinea
137 L4 **Tin'ky** Ukr.
81 H9 **Tinline, Mount** South I. N.Z.
205 H5 **Ti-n-Merzouga** des. Alg.
142 E2 **Tinn** Norway
142 F2 **Tinne** r. Norway
Tinnelvelly Tamil Nadu India see **Tirunelveli**
142 E2 **Tinnsjø** l. Norway
177 H4 **Tinnye** Hungary
190 H7 **Tino, Isola del** i. Italy
261 F2 **Tinoco** Arg.
258 D3 **Tinogasta** Arg.
93 B3 **Tinompo** Sulawesi Indon.
198 G5 **Tinos** Tinos Greece
198 G5 **Tinos** i. Greece
185 K6 **Tiñosa** mt. Spain
183 K7 **Tiñosillos** Spain
187 C12 **Tiñoso, Cabo** c. Spain
156 G5 **Tinqueux** France
205 G5 **Ti-n-Rerhoh** well Alg.
205 G3 **Tinrhert, Plateau du** Alg.
109 □I7 **Tin Shui Wai** H.K. China
207 F2 **Ti-n-Srir** well Mali
117 O6 **Tinsukia** Assam India
222 E4 **Tintagel** B.C. Can.
150 C6 **Tintagel** Cornwall, England U.K.
206 C2 **Ţînţâne** Maur.
205 G5 **Ti-n-Tarabine** well Alg.
205 G5 **Ti-n-Tarabine, Oued** watercourse Alg.
206 E2 **Ti-n-Tehoun** well Mali
205 F4 **Tintejert, Adrar** mt. Alg.
158 H5 **Tinténiac** France
150 G4 **Tintern Parva** Monmouthshire, Wales U.K.
207 F2 **Ti-n-Tersi** well Mali
165 I9 **Tintigny** Belgium
258 E2 **Tintina** Arg.
82 H6 **Tintinara** S.A. Austr.
184 F6 **Tinto** r. Spain
149 J2 **Tinto** hill Scotland U.K.
Tin Tounnant well Mali see **Taounnant**
81 K7 **Tinui** North I. N.Z.
137 M9 **Tinyste** Ukr.
207 F2 **Ti-n-Zaouâtene** Mali
236 D1 **Tioga** ND U.S.A.
232 H7 **Tioga** PA U.S.A.
232 H6 **Tioga** r. PA U.S.A.
234 A1 **Tioga County** county PA U.S.A.
94 F3 **Tioman** i. Malaysia
227 L1 **Tionaga** Ont. Can.
191 K5 **Tione** r. Italy
191 J3 **Tione di Trento** Italy
232 F7 **Tionesta** PA U.S.A.
206 C3 **Tioribougou** Mali
206 E3 **Tiou** Burkina
205 E5 **Tiouararène** well Mali
235 J6 **Tioughnioga** r. NY U.S.A.
205 F1 **Tipasa** Alg.
Tiphsah Syria see **Dibsī**
242 □P11 **Tipitapa** Nic.
226 F4 **Tipler** WI U.S.A.
230 D5 **Tippecanoe** r. IN U.S.A.
147 F8 **Tipperary** Ireland
147 G7 **Tipperary** county Ireland
117 K6 **Tipta Bhanjyang** pass Nepal
240 M5 **Tipton** CA U.S.A.
236 J5 **Tipton** IA U.S.A.
236 I6 **Tipton** MO U.S.A.
241 R6 **Tipton, Mount** AZ U.S.A.
237 K7 **Tiptonville** TN U.S.A.
232 D11 **Tiptop** VA U.S.A.
224 C3 **Tip Top Hill** Ont. Can.
151 N4 **Tiptree** Essex, England U.K.
114 E6 **Tiptur** Karnataka India
114 E6 **Tipturi** Karnataka India
Tipturi Karnataka India see **Tiptur**
252 C3 **Tipuani** Bol.
244 G7 **Tiquicheo** Mex.
250 D4 **Tiquié** r. Brazil
243 N10 **Tiquisate** Guat.
254 D3 **Tiracambu, Serra do** hills Brazil
205 F5 **Tirahart, Oued** watercourse Alg.
122 D5 **Tirān** Iran
124 B2 **Tirān** i. Saudi Arabia
Tirana Albania see **Tiranë**
196 H9 **Tiranë** Albania
161 D6 **Tiranges** France
190 I3 **Tirano** Italy
207 G2 **Tiraouene** well Niger
127 O6 **Tirap** Arun. Prad. India
124 F2 **Ţirāq, Jāl aţ** hills Saudi Arabia
206 E2 **Tiraraouine** well Mali
82 G2 **Tirari Desert** S.A. Austr.
136 I7 **Tiraspol** Moldova
80 J4 **Tirau** North I. N.Z.
80 K7 **Tiraumea** North I. N.Z.
212 C5 **Tiraz Mountains** Namibia
199 I4 **Tire** Turkey
177 L4 **Tiream** Romania
146 C10 **Tiree** i. Scotland U.K.
205 F5 **Tirek** well Alg.
205 F5 **Tirest** well Mali
146 C7 **Tirga Mòr** hill Scotland U.K.
183 O3 **Tirgo** Spain
Tîrgoviște Romania see **Târgoviște**
Tîrgu Bujor Romania see **Târgu Bujor**
Tîrgu Cărbunești Romania see **Târgu Cărbunești**
Tîrgu Frumos Romania see **Târgu Frumos**
Tîrgu Jiu Romania see **Târgu Jiu**
Tîrgu Lăpuș Romania see **Târgu Lăpuș**
Tîrgu Mureș Romania see **Târgu Mureș**
Tîrgu Neamț Romania see **Târgu Neamț**
Tîrgu Ocna Romania see **Târgu Ocna**
Tîrgu Secuiesc Romania see **Târgu Secuiesc**
116 G3 **Tiri** Jammu and Kashmir
123 L7 **Tiri** Pak.
123 N3 **Tirich Mir** mt. Pak.
185 O3 **Tiriez** Spain
186 F7 **Tirig** Spain
195 L6 **Tiriolo** Italy
244 F6 **Tiripetío** Mex.
205 F5 **Tirirrine, Oued** watercourse Alg.
204 C5 **Tiris Zemmour** admin. reg. Maur.
138 F5 **Tirkšliai** Lith.
Tirlemont Belgium see **Tienen**
120 H1 **Tirlyanskiy** Rus. Fed.
114 E3 **Tirna** r. India
Tîrnăveni Romania see **Târnăveni**
Tirnavos Greece see **Tyrnavos**
Tîrnova Romania see **Târnova**
185 I3 **Tiro** hill Spain
116 G9 **Tirodi** Madh. Prad. India
178 D5 **Tirol** land Austria
183 O3 **Tirón** r. Spain
81 L5 **Tironia** North I. N.Z.
257 E3 **Tiros** Brazil
208 D2 **Tiroungoulou** C.A.R.
171 F10 **Tirpersdorf** Ger.
190 I8 **Tirrenia** Italy
Tirreno, Mare sea France/Italy see **Tyrrhenian Sea**
173 M2 **Tirschenreuth** Ger.
192 B8 **Tirso** r. Sardegna Italy
142 G5 **Tirstrup** Denmark
185 K3 **Tirteafuera** Spain
185 K3 **Tirteafuera** r. Spain
114 D6 **Tirthahalli** Karnataka India
117 K9 **Tirtol** Orissa India
114 F8 **Tiruchchendur** Tamil Nadu India
114 F7 **Tiruchchirappalli** Tamil Nadu India
114 E7 **Tiruchengodu** Tamil Nadu India
114 F7 **Tirukkoyilur** Tamil Nadu India
114 F8 **Tirumangalam** Tamil Nadu India
114 E8 **Tirunelveli** Tamil Nadu India
252 B1 **Tiruntán** Peru
114 F6 **Tirupati** Andhra Prad. India
114 F6 **Tiruppattur** Tamil Nadu India
114 F7 **Tiruppattur** Tamil Nadu India
114 F7 **Tiruppur** Tamil Nadu India
114 F6 **Tiruttani** Andhra Prad. India
114 F7 **Tiruturaippundi** Tamil Nadu India
114 F6 **Tiruvallur** Tamil Nadu India
114 F6 **Tiruvannamalai** Tamil Nadu India
114 F6 **Tiruvettipuram** Tamil Nadu India
114 G6 **Tiruvottiyur** Tamil Nadu India
86 H6 **Tiru Well** W.A. Austr.
198 E5 **Tiryns** tourist site Greece
138 J4 **Tirza** r. Latvia
197 J7 **Tisa** r. Serbia
alt. **Tisza** (Hungary),
alt. **Tysa** (Ukraine)
114 E8 **Tisaiyanvilai** Tamil Nadu India
143 L2 **Tisaren** l. Sweden
197 O5 **Tisău** Romania
150 H5 **Tisbury** Wiltshire, England U.K.
216 □3b **Tiscamanita** Fuerteventura Canary Is
185 M5 **Tiscar, Puerto de** pass Spain
223 J4 **Tisdale** Sask. Can.
237 G8 **Tishomingo** OK U.S.A.
175 I1 **Tishono** Rus. Fed.
176 G2 **Tišice** Czech Rep.
128 E6 **Tisiyah** Syria
205 H5 **Tiska, Mont** mt. Alg.
143 L3 **Tisnaren** l. Sweden
176 F2 **Tišnov** Czech Rep.
177 I3 **Tisovec** Slovakia
114 G9 **Tissamaharama** Sri Lanka
205 F2 **Tissemsilt** Alg.
192 B6 **Tissi** Sardegna Italy
117 L7 **Tista** r. India
177 J5 **Tisza** r. Hungary
alt. **Tisa** (Serbia),
alt. **Tysa** (Ukraine)
177 I5 **Tiszaalpár** Hungary
177 L3 **Tiszabecs** Hungary
177 L3 **Tiszabezdéd** Hungary
177 J4 **Tiszabő** Hungary
177 J4 **Tiszabura** Hungary
177 K4 **Tiszacsege** Hungary
177 J4 **Tiszaderzs** Hungary
177 K3 **Tiszadob** Hungary
177 K3 **Tiszadobi arter** nature res. Hungary
177 K3 **Tiszaeszlár** Hungary
177 J5 **Tiszaföldvár** Hungary
177 K4 **Tiszafüred** Hungary
Tiszafüredi Madárrezervátum nature res. Hungary
177 J4 **Tiszaigar** Hungary
177 J4 **Tiszajenő** Hungary
177 K3 **Tiszakarád** Hungary
177 J5 **Tiszakécske** Hungary
177 L3 **Tiszakerecseny** Hungary
177 J4 **Tiszakeszi** Hungary
177 K3 **Tiszalök** Hungary
177 K3 **Tiszalúc** Hungary
177 K3 **Tiszanagyfalu** Hungary
177 J4 **Tiszanána** Hungary
177 J4 **Tiszántúl** reg. Hungary
177 J5 **Tiszaörs** Hungary
177 J4 **Tiszapüspöki** Hungary
177 J4 **Tiszaroff** Hungary
177 J4 **Tiszasas** Hungary
177 L3 **Tiszaszentmárton** Hungary
177 J5 **Tiszasziget** Hungary
177 K3 **Tiszatelek** Hungary
177 K3 **Tiszatelek-Tiszabercel** nature res. Hungary
177 J4 **Tiszatenyő** Hungary
177 J5 **Tiszaug** Hungary
177 K4 **Tiszaújváros** Hungary
177 K4 **Tiszavasvári** Hungary
205 F4 **Tit** Adrar Alg.
205 G5 **Tit** Tamanrasset Alg.
117 O6 **Titabar** Assam India
187 C8 **Titaguas** Spain
263 K1 **Titan Dome** ice feature Antarctica
206 E3 **Titao** Burkina
137 T4 **Titarevka** Rus. Fed.
198 D3 **Titarisios** r. Greece
131 N2 **Tit-Ary** Rus. Fed.
Titawin Morocco see **Tétouan**
206 B4 **Tite** Guinea-Bissau
196 I5 **Titel** Vojvodina Serbia
193 M5 **Titerno** r. Italy
123 O4 **Tithwal** Pak.
252 C3 **Titicaca, Lago** l. Bol./Peru
Titicaca, Lake Bol./Peru see **Titicaca, Lago**
235 H2 **Titicus** CT U.S.A.
81 B14 **Titi Islands** Stewart I. N.Z.
81 □3 **Titikaveka** Rarotonga Cook Is
172 E6 **Titisee** Ger.
Tititea mt. South I. N.Z. see **Aspiring, Mount**
117 I9 **Titlagarh** Orissa India
190 E2 **Titlis** mt. Switz.
193 P6 **Tito** Italy
Titograd Montenegro see **Podgorica**
188 E3 **Titova Korenica** Croatia
Titova Mitrovica Kosovo Serbia see **Kosovska Mitrovica**
188 F3 **Titov Drvar** Bos.-Herz.
140 U2 **Titovka** r. Rus. Fed.
Titovo Užice Serbia see **Užice**
Titovo Velenje Slovenia see **Velenje**
Titov Veles Macedonia see **Veles**
Titov Vrbas Vojvodina Serbia see **Vrbas**
140 J5 **Titran** Norway
84 D7 **Ti Tree** N.T. Austr.
227 K6 **Tittabawassee** r. MI U.S.A.
173 K4 **Titting** Ger.
173 O4 **Tittling** Ger.
173 N5 **Tittmoning** Ger.
197 N6 **Titu** Romania
183 M8 **Titulcia** Spain
208 E4 **Titule** Dem. Rep. Congo
231 G11 **Titusville** FL U.S.A.
232 F7 **Titusville** PA U.S.A.
109 □J7 **Tiu Chung Chau** i. H.K. China
146 D6 **Tiumpan Head** Scotland U.K.
211 C5 **Tiva** watercourse Kenya
116 D6 **Tivari** Rajasthan India
196 G8 **Tivat** Montenegro
143 K3 **Tiveden nationalpark** nat. park Sweden
186 G6 **Tivenys** Spain
227 M5 **Tiverton** Ont. Can.
150 F6 **Tiverton** Devon, England U.K.
Tivisa Spain see **Tivissa**
186 G5 **Tivissa** Spain
193 J4 **Tivoli** Italy
208 D2 **Tiwal, Wadi** watercourse Sudan
252 C4 **Tiwanaku** tourist site Bol.
125 N4 **Ţīwī** Oman
84 C1 **Tiwi Aboriginal Land** res. N.T. Austr.
93 C6 **Tiworo, Selat** sea chan. Indon.
243 O7 **Tixkokob** Mex.
245 H8 **Tixtla** Mex.
210 C2 **Tiya** tourist site Eth.
128 F8 **Tiyās** Syria
244 D5 **Tizapán el Alto** Mex.
245 I6 **Tizayuca** Mex.
204 C3 **Tizi Mighert** pass Morocco
243 O7 **Tizimín** Mex.
204 C3 **Tizi-n-Test** pass Morocco
204 C3 **Tizi-n-Tichka** pass Morocco
205 G1 **Tizi Ouzou** Alg.
111 C7 **Tiznap He** r. China
204 C3 **Tiznit** Morocco
242 H5 **Tizoc** Mex.
204 E2 **Tiztoutine** Morocco
192 B4 **Tizzano** Corse France
140 O3 **Tjaktjajaure** l. Sweden
143 L3 **Tjällmo** Sweden
140 O3 **Tjåmotis** Sweden
215 P1 **Tjaneni** Swaziland
140 O4 **Tjappsåive** Sweden
140 M4 **Tjärmyrberget** Sweden
140 P3 **Tjautas** Sweden
140 N3 **Tjeggelvas** l. Sweden
144 J1 **Tjeldstø** Norway
164 I3 **Tjeukemeer** l. Neth.
Tjirebon Jawa Indon. see **Cirebon**
87 H8 **Tjirrkarli Aboriginal Reserve** W.A. Austr.
Tjolotjo Zimbabwe see **Tsholotsho**
142 G2 **Tjøme** Norway
142 C3 **Tjorhom** Norway
142 H3 **Tjörn** i. Sweden
140 □1 **Tjörnes** pen. Iceland
140 L4 **Tjøtta** Norway
Tjumen' Rus. Fed. see **Tyumen'**
143 K5 **Tjurken** l. Sweden
140 □ **Tjuvfjorden** b. Svalbard
Tkibuli Georgia see **Tqibuli**
Tkvarcheli Georgia see **Tqvarch'eli**
244 E4 **Tlachichila** Mex.
245 I5 **Tlachichilo** Mex.
245 I8 **Tlacoapa** Mex.
245 K9 **Tlacolula** Mex.
245 L9 **Tlacolulita** Mex.
245 L7 **Tlacotalpán** Mex.
245 H6 **Tlacotenco** Mex.
245 H8 **Tlacotepec** Mex.
244 G8 **Tlacotepec, Cerro** mt. Mex.
245 I5 **Tlacuilotepec** Mex.
242 H4 **Tlahualilo** Mex.
245 I6 **Tlahuapan** Mex.
244 D5 **Tlajomulco** Mex.
244 G7 **Tlalchapa** Mex.
245 J6 **Tlalchichuca** Mex.
245 K7 **Tlalixcoyan** Mex.
245 I8 **Tlalixtaquilla** Mex.
245 I6 **Tlalmanalco** Mex.
245 H6 **Tlalnepantla** Mex.
245 H6 **Tlálpan** Mex.
244 G6 **Tlalpujahua** Mex.
244 D4 **Tlaltenango de Sánchez Román** Mex.
245 H7 **Tlaltizapan** Mex.
245 I7 **Tlancualpican** Mex.
245 I8 **Tlapa** Mex.
245 J6 **Tlapacoyan** Mex.
245 I7 **Tlapaneco** r. Mex.
244 G7 **Tlapehuala** Mex.
244 D5 **Tlaquepaque** Mex.
245 J7 **Tlaquilpa** Mex.
245 I6 **Tlaxcala** Mex.
245 I6 **Tlaxcala** state Mex.
245 I6 **Tlaxco** Mex.
245 H5 **Tlaxcoapán** Mex.
245 J8 **Tlaxiaco** Mex.
222 D4 **Tl'ell** B.C. Can.
205 E2 **Tlemcen** Alg.
174 G2 **Tleń** Pol.
180 D5 **Tleta Rissana** Morocco
215 K2 **Tlhabologang** S. Africa
214 H4 **Tlhakalatlou** S. Africa
214 I2 **Tlhakgameng** S. Africa
215 M4 **Tlholong** S. Africa
177 H3 **Tlmače** Slovakia
129 H3 **Tlokh** Rus. Fed.
212 E5 **Tlokweng** Botswana
175 H3 **Tłuchowo** Pol.
173 O2 **Tlučná** Czech Rep.
136 E5 **Tlumach** Ukr.
174 F6 **Tlumačov** Czech Rep.
175 J3 **Tłuszcz** Pol.
129 H3 **Tlyadal** Rus. Fed.
129 H3 **Tlyarata** Rus. Fed.
137 S9 **Tlyustenkhabl'** Rus. Fed.
139 S5 **T'ma** r. Rus. Fed.
202 B3 **Tmassah** Libya
204 B5 **Tmeïmîchât** Maur.
97 G9 **Tnaôt, Prêk** r. Cambodia
136 G3 **Tnya** r. Ukr.
96 C6 **To** r. Myanmar
246 F3 **Toa** r. Cuba
247 □1 **Toa Alta** Puerto Rico
146 □N3 **Toab** Shetland, Scotland U.K.
247 □1 **Toa Baja** Puerto Rico
222 E3 **Toad** r. B.C. Can.
222 E3 **Toad River** B.C. Can.
92 □ **Toagel Mlungui** Palau
177 I4 **Tóalmás** Hungary
213 □K3 **Toamasina** Madag.
213 □K3 **Toamasina** prov. Madag.
147 E9 **Toames** Ireland
241 R1 **Toana** mts NV U.S.A.
191 J7 **Toano** Italy
232 I11 **Toano** VA U.S.A.
79 □9a **Toanoano** Tahiti Fr. Polynesia
94 □ **Toa Payoh** Sing.
232 E12 **Toast** NC U.S.A.
80 L5 **Toatoa** North I. N.Z.
203 G4 **To Awai** well Sudan
260 E5 **Toay** Arg.
108 A3 **Toba** Xizang China
169 K8 **Toba** Ger.
104 E7 **Toba** Japan
94 C3 **Toba, Danau** l. Indon.
Toba, Lake Indon. see **Toba, Danau**
123 L6 **Toba and Kakar Ranges** mts Pak.
247 □5 **Tobago** i. Trin. and Tob.
222 E5 **Toba Inlet** B.C. Can.
213 F4 **Tobane** Botswana
185 P3 **Tobarra** Spain
258 E3 **Tobas** Arg.
123 O6 **Toba Tek Singh** Pak.
179 L6 **Tobelbad** Austria
93 E3 **Tobelo** Halmahera Indon.
147 I3 **Tobermore** Northern Ireland U.K.
85 I9 **Tobermory** Qld Austr.
224 D4 **Tobermory** Ont. Can.
146 D9 **Tobermory** Argyll and Bute, Scotland U.K.
146 E10 **Toberonochy** Argyll and Bute, Scotland U.K.
102 S3 **Tōbetsu** Japan
91 H6 **Tobi** i. Palau
209 B7 **Tobias** Angola
254 F4 **Tobias Barreto** Brazil
103 □ **Tobishi-hana** c. Iō-jima Japan
86 H6 **Tobin, Lake** salt flat W.A. Austr.
240 O1 **Tobin, Mount** NV U.S.A.
223 K4 **Tobin Lake** Sask. Can.
225 H4 **Tobique** r. N.B. Can.
104 E5 **Tobishima** Japan
102 Q7 **Tobi-shima** i. Japan
94 G6 **Toboali** Indon.
120 M1 **Tobol** Kazakh.
120 M1 **Tobol** r. Kazakh./Rus. Fed.
130 H4 **Tobol'sk** Rus. Fed.
78 □6 **Tobona Island** Solomon Is
92 D6 **Toboso** Negros Phil.
Tobruk Libya see **Tubruq**
134 K1 **Tobseda** Rus. Fed.
105 H3 **Tōbu** Japan
234 E2 **Tobyhanna** PA U.S.A.
Tobyl Kazakh. see **Tobol**
Tobyl r. Kazakh./Rus. Fed. see **Tobol**
Tobylzhan Kazakh. see **Tavolzhan**
134 J2 **Tobysh** r. Rus. Fed.
252 A2 **Tocache Nuevo** Peru
162 E5 **Tocane-St-Apre** France
254 D3 **Tocantinópolis** Brazil
251 G6 **Tocantins** r. Brazil
251 I5 **Tocantins** r. Brazil
254 C4 **Tocantins** state Brazil
231 F8 **Toccoa** GA U.S.A.
193 L3 **Tocco da Casauria** Italy
190 E4 **Toce** r. Italy
182 C8 **Tocha** Port.
123 N5 **Tochi** r. Pak.
105 K3 **Tochigi** Japan
105 J2 **Tochigi** pref. Japan
245 I7 **Tochimilzoco** Mex.
103 P9 **Tochio** Japan
142 H2 **Töcksfors** Sweden
247 □7 **Toco** Trin. and Tob.
242 □P10 **Tocoa** Hond.
185 L6 **Tocón** Spain
252 C5 **Tocopilla** Chile
252 D5 **Tocorpuri, Cerros de** mts Bol./Chile
83 J6 **Tocumwal** N.S.W. Austr.
247 I8 **Tocuyo de la Costa** Venez.
175 K3 **Toczna** r. Pol.
222 G5 **Tod, Mount** B.C. Can.
105 K4 **Toda** Japan
116 F6 **Toda Bhim** Rajasthan India
116 E6 **Toda Rai Singh** Rajasthan India
261 G4 **Todd** Arg.
84 E8 **Todd** watercourse N.T. Austr.
151 K4 **Toddington** Bedfordshire, England U.K.
151 I4 **Toddington** Gloucestershire, England U.K.
233 □S2 **Todd Mountain** hill N.B. Can.
87 I8 **Todd Range** hills W.A. Austr.
235 H2 **Toddville** NY U.S.A.
90 F7 **Todeli** Maluku Indon.
168 J3 **Todesfelde** Ger.
116 D7 **Todgarh** Rajasthan India
193 I2 **Todi** Italy
190 F2 **Todi** mt. Switz.
149 M6 **Todmorden** West Yorkshire, England U.K.
110 F4 **Todog** Xinjiang China
102 T7 **Todoga-saki** pt Japan
102 S5 **Todohokke** Japan
Todok Xinjiang China see **Todog**
257 G2 **Todos os Santos** r. Brazil
252 D4 **Todos Santos** Bol.
242 D6 **Todos Santos** Mex.
240 P10 **Todos Santos, Isla** i. Mex.
122 F8 **Todrūyeh** Iran
172 D6 **Todtmoos** Ger.
172 D6 **Todtnau** Ger.
147 D10 **Toe Head** Ireland
146 B7 **Toe Head** Scotland U.K.
104 G5 **Tōei** Japan
96 D7 **Toe Jaga, Khao** hill Thai.
182 E4 **Toén** Spain
206 E3 **Toéni** Burkina
81 C13 **Toetoes Bay** South I. N.Z.
222 H4 **Tofield** Alta Can.
222 E5 **Tofino** B.C. Can.
146 □N2 **Toft** Shetland, Scotland U.K.
143 L1 **Toftan** l. Sweden
226 D2 **Tofte** MN U.S.A.
143 K2 **Toften** l. Sweden
142 F6 **Toftlund** Denmark
79 □8 **Tofua** i. Tonga
104 F3 **Toga** Japan
232 G11 **Toga** VA U.S.A.
78 □5 **Toga** i. Vanuatu
105 L4 **Tōgane** Japan
111 E9 **Togatax** Xinjiang China
208 C3 **Togbo** C.A.R.
210 E2 **Togdheer** admin. reg. Somalia
190 G1 **Toggenburg** reg. Switz.
147 D9 **Togher** Cork Ireland
147 J5 **Togher** Louth Ireland
147 G6 **Togher** Offaly Ireland
104 E1 **Togi** Japan
220 B4 **Togiak** AK U.S.A.
93 B4 **Togian** i. Indon.
93 B4 **Togian, Kepulauan** is Indon.
173 N5 **Töging am Inn** Ger.
Togliatti Rus. Fed. see **Tol'yatti**
207 F4 **Togo** country Africa
104 F5 **Tōgō** Aichi Japan
103 I14 **Tōgō** Miyazaki Japan
226 A2 **Togo** MN U.S.A.
111 J7 **Tograsay He** r. China
106 C3 **Tögrög** Mongolia
107 M6 **Togrog Ul** Nei Mongol China
149 N3 **Togston** Northumberland, England U.K.
107 L6 **Togtoh** Nei Mongol China
111 K9 **Togton He** r. China
130 J4 **Toguchin** Rus. Fed.
105 H3 **Togura** Japan
120 I4 **Toguz** Kazakh.
210 D2 **Tog Wajaale** Somalia
203 H5 **Tohamiyam** Sudan
116 E5 **Tohana** Haryana India
241 X6 **Tohatchi** NM U.S.A.
95 J4 **Tohenbatu** mt. Malaysia
79 □9a **Tohiea** mt. Moorea Fr. Polynesia
140 U5 **Tohmajärvi** Fin.
140 U5 **Tohmajärvi** l. Fin.
104 D5 **Tohoku** Japan
140 R5 **Toholampi** Fin.
106 I6 **Tohom** Nei Mongol China
107 K4 **Töhöm** Mongolia
241 T9 **Tohono O'Odham (Papago) Indian Reservation** res. AZ U.S.A.
207 F5 **Tohoun** Togo
102 S5 **Toi** Hokkaidō Japan
105 I6 **Toi** Shizuoka Japan
78 □2 **To'iave'a** mt. Samoa
111 I11 **Toiba** Xizang China
115 M7 **Toibalewe** Andaman & Nicobar Is India
104 E2 **Toide** Japan
141 Q6 **Toijala** Fin.
93 C4 **Toili** Sulawesi Indon.
103 I15 **Toi-misaki** pt Japan
78 □6 **Toimonapu** P.N.G.
104 E5 **Toin** Japan
93 D9 **Toineke** Timor Indon.
190 E7 **Toirano** Italy
141 S5 **Toivakka** Fin.
81 □4 **Toi Village** Niue
240 O2 **Toiyabe Range** mts NV U.S.A.
93 B4 **Toja** Sulawesi Indon.
Tojikiston country Asia see **Tajikistan**
123 N2 **Tojikobod** Tajik.
103 K12 **Tōjō** Hiroshima Japan
104 B6 **Tōjō** Hyōgo Japan
120 E1 **Tok** r. Rus. Fed.
220 D3 **Tok** AK U.S.A.
102 U4 **Tokachi-gawa** r. Japan
104 E5 **Tōkai** Aichi Japan
105 M3 **Tōkai** Ibaraki Japan
177 K3 **Tokaj** Hungary
177 K3 **Tokaj-Bodrog-Zug** park Hungary
93 B4 **Tokala, Gunung** mt. Indon.
105 I1 **Tōkamachi** Japan
81 C13 **Tokanui** South I. N.Z.
203 H5 **Tokar** Sudan
81 E11 **Tokarahi** South I. N.Z.
102 □G18 **Tokara-rettō** is Japan
121 O2 **Tokarevka** Kazakh.
135 H6 **Tokarevka** Rus. Fed.
139 R1 **Tokari** Rus. Fed.
175 I5 **Tokarnia** Pol.
137 O8 **Tokaryeve** Ukr.
102 □E20 **Tokasiki-jima** i. Nansei-shotō Japan
126 H3 **Tokat** Turkey
80 H3 **Tokatoka** North I. N.Z.
80 I3 **Tokatu Point** North I. N.Z.
137 U2 **Tokay** r. Rus. Fed.
101 E10 **Tŏkchok-to** i. S. Korea
101 E9 **Tŏkch'ŏn** N. Korea
Tokdo i. N. Pacific Ocean see **Liancourt Rocks**
81 □1 **Tokelau** terr. S. Pacific Ocean
T'okhluja Armenia see **Drakhtik**
Tokhtamysh Tajik. see **Tŭkhtamish**
104 F5 **Toki** Japan
105 J3 **Tokigawa** Japan
104 E5 **Toki-gawa** r. Japan
Tokkuztara Xinjiang China see **Gongliu**
129 B6 **Toklular** Turkey
137 O6 **Tokmachka** r. Ukr.
Tokmak Kyrg. see **Tokmok**
137 O6 **Tokmak** Ukr.
121 P6 **Tokmok** Kyrg.
177 H4 **Tokod** Hungary
80 M5 **Tokomaru Bay** North I. N.Z.
104 E6 **Tokoname** Japan
80 J5 **Tokoroa** North I. N.Z.
102 V2 **Tokoro-gawa** r. Japan
105 J4 **Tokorozawa** Japan
202 D5 **Tokou** well Chad
206 C4 **Tokounou** Guinea
215 M2 **Tokoza** S. Africa
Tokrau watercourse Kazakh. see **Tokyrau**
Toksu Xinjiang China see **Xinhe**
110 I5 **Toksun** Xinjiang China
Tok-tō i. N. Pacific Ocean see **Liancourt Rocks**
121 O7 **Toktogul** Kyrg.
Toktogul'skoye Vodokhranilishche resr Kyrg. see **Toktogul Suu Saktagychy**
121 O7 **Toktogul Suu Saktagychy** resr Kyrg.
Tokto-ri i. N. Pacific Ocean see **Liancourt Rocks**
121 T5 **Tokty** Kazakh.
77 I3 **Tokû** i. Tonga
79 □8 **Tokulu** atoll Tonga
102 □G19 **Tokunoshima** Nansei-shotō Japan
102 □F19 **Toku-no-shima** i. Nansei-shotō Japan
100 H2 **Tokur** Rus. Fed.
104 A7 **Tokushima** Japan
103 L13 **Tokushima** pref. Japan
103 I12 **Tokuyama** Japan
Tokwe r. Zimbabwe see **Tugwi**
105 K4 **Tōkyō** Japan
105 J5 **Tōkyō** mun. Japan
105 K4 **Tōkyō-wan** b. Japan
121 P4 **Tokyrau** watercourse Kazakh.
101 E11 **Tokyu-san National Park** S. Korea
123 L4 **Tokzār** Afgh.
78 □4a **Tol** i. Chuuk Micronesia
80 M5 **Tolaga Bay** North I. N.Z.
213 □J5 **Tôlañaro** Madag.
258 D2 **Tolar, Cerro** mt. Arg.
146 D6 **Tolastadh Úr** Western Isles, Scotland U.K.
183 K7 **Tolbaños** Spain
120 F1 **Tolbazy** Rus. Fed.
164 J2 **Tolbert** Neth.
106 B2 **Tolbo** Mongolia
Tolbukhin Bulg. see **Dobrich**
139 X4 **Tolbukhino** Rus. Fed.
100 D2 **Tolbuzino** Rus. Fed.
262 T1 **Tolchin, Mount** Antarctica
177 K3 **Tolcsva** Hungary
242 □S13 **Tolé** Panama
121 O6 **Tole Bi** Kazakh.
250 C6 **Toledo** Amazonas Brazil
255 B8 **Toledo** Paraná Brazil
258 C2 **Toledo** Chile
183 L9 **Toledo** Spain
183 L9 **Toledo** prov. Spain
236 I5 **Toledo** IA U.S.A.
236 K6 **Toledo** IL U.S.A.
232 B7 **Toledo** OH U.S.A.
238 C4 **Toledo** OR U.S.A.
183 K9 **Toledo, Montes de** mts Spain
237 I10 **Toledo Bend Reservoir** LA/TX U.S.A.
191 O9 **Tolentino** Italy
Toletum Spain see **Toledo**
192 H3 **Tolfa** Italy
85 J4 **Tolga** Qld Austr.
141 K5 **Tolga** Norway
260 B6 **Tolhuaca, Parque Nacional** nat. park Chile
110 F4 **Toli** Xinjiang China
213 □I4 **Toliara** Madag.
213 □J4 **Toliara** prov. Madag.
250 C4 **Tolima** dept Col.
244 D6 **Tolimán** Jalisco Mex.
245 H5 **Tolimán** Querétaro Mex.
93 B3 **Tolitoli** Sulawesi Indon.
168 I1 **Tolk** Ger.
130 J3 **Tol'ka** Rus. Fed.
142 I4 **Tolken** l. Sweden
143 P7 **Tolkmicko** Pol.
164 I3 **Tollebeek** Neth.
170 H3 **Tollense** r. Ger.
170 H4 **Tollensesee** l. Ger.
170 H4 **Tollensesee-Becken** park Ger.
151 N4 **Tollesbury** Essex, England U.K.
151 N4 **Tolleshunt D'Arcy** Essex, England U.K.
241 T8 **Tolleson** AZ U.S.A.
120 K8 **Tollimarjon** Uzbek.
193 M3 **Tollo** Italy
142 H6 **Tølløse** Denmark
138 M3 **Tolmachevo** Rus. Fed.
191 O3 **Tolmezzo** Italy
188 D2 **Tolmin** Slovenia
177 H5 **Tolna** Hungary
177 H5 **Tolna** county Hungary
177 H5 **Tolnai-hegyhát** hills Hungary
177 H5 **Tolnanémedi** Hungary
208 C5 **Tolo** Dem. Rep. Congo
242 □P10 **Toloa Creek** Hond.
Tolo Channel H.K. China see **Chek Mun Hoi Hap**
Tolochin Belarus see **Talachyn**
Tolo Harbour b. H.K. China see **Tai Po Hoi**
140 S2 **Tolonen** Fin.
93 F3 **Tolonuu** i. Maluku Indon.
Tolosa France see **Toulouse**
184 D2 **Tolosa** Port.
186 A1 **Tolosa** Spain
185 J7 **Tolox** Spain
139 Y4 **Tolpygino** Rus. Fed.
101 E11 **Tolsan-do** i. S. Korea
227 K4 **Tolsmaville** Ont. Can.
146 D6 **Tolsta Head** Scotland U.K.
131 Q4 **Tolstoy, Mys** c. Rus. Fed.
259 B5 **Toltén** Chile
250 C2 **Tolú** Col.
245 H6 **Toluca** Mex.
186 G3 **Tolva** Spain
140 U3 **Tolvand, Ozero** l. Rus. Fed.
193 Q6 **Tolve** Italy
193 Q6 **Tolve** r. Italy
135 J5 **Tol'yatti** Rus. Fed.
120 J2 **Tolybay** Kazakh.
163 E7 **Tolzac** r. France
100 E3 **Tom'** r. Rus. Fed.
206 E3 **Toma** Burkina
104 B7 **Tomaga-shima** i. Japan
104 A7 **Tomagashima-suidō** sea chan. Japan
226 D6 **Tomah** WI U.S.A.
226 E4 **Tomahawk** WI U.S.A.
137 N6 **Tomakivka** r. Ukr.
102 S4 **Tomakomai** Japan
240 J3 **Tomales** CA U.S.A.
102 S2 **Tomamae** Japan
95 K2 **Tomani** Sabah Malaysia
79 □7a **Tomanivi** mt. Viti Levu Fiji
251 F5 **Tomar** Brazil
182 D9 **Tomar** Port.
102 R3 **Tomari** Japan
100 M5 **Tomari** Sakhalin Rus. Fed.
129 E5 **Tomarlı** Turkey
198 B3 **Tomaros** mt. Greece
137 P3 **Tomarovka** Rus. Fed.
126 G4 **Tomarza** Turkey
252 D4 **Tomás Barron** Bol.
261 I2 **Tomás Gomensoro** Uru.
136 G2 **Tomashhorod** Rivnens'ka Oblast' Ukr.
136 G2 **Tomashhorod** Rivnens'ka Oblast' Ukr.
136 H5 **Tomashpil'** Ukr.
176 G3 **Tomášov** Slovakia
177 I3 **Tomášovce** Slovakia
175 L5 **Tomaszów Lubelski** Pol.
175 I4 **Tomaszów Mazowiecki** Pol.
146 I8 **Tomatin** Highland, Scotland U.K.
244 B6 **Tomatlán** Mex.
252 D5 **Tomave** Bol.
256 C5 **Tomazina** Brazil
254 E4 **Tombador, Serra do** hills Brazil
253 F3 **Tombador, Serra do** hills Brazil
217 □1b **Tombeau Bay** Mauritius
163 E6 **Tombebœf** France
231 D10 **Tombigbee** r. AL U.S.A.
215 N7 **Tombo** S. Africa
259 D7 **Tombo, Punta** pt Arg.
209 B6 **Tomboco** Angola
257 F4 **Tombos** Brazil
206 E2 **Tombouctou** Mali
206 E2 **Tombouctou** admin. reg. Mali
80 G1 **Tom Bowling Bay** North I. N.Z.
210 B4 **Tombs of Buganda Kings** tourist site Uganda
241 V10 **Tombstone** AZ U.S.A.
209 A8 **Tombua** Angola
213 E4 **Tom Burke** S. Africa
120 K7 **Tomdibuloq** Uzbek.
120 K7 **Tomditov tog'lari** hills
Tomditow Toghi hills U
see **Tomditov tog'lari**
258 B5 **Tomé** Chile
213 G4 **Tome** Moz.
93 C6 **Tomea** i. Indon.
143 J6 **Tomelilla** Sweden
185 M2 **Tomelloso** Spain
121 L6 **Tomenaryk** Kazakh.
177 L5 **Tomești** Hunedoara Ror
177 L6 **Tomești** Timiș Romania
Tomi Romania see **Cons**
175 H6 **Tomice** Pol.
102 □1 **Tomigusuku** Okinawa J
104 E5 **Tomika** Japan
227 O3 **Tomiko** Ont. Can.
252 D4 **Tomina** Bol.
206 B3 **Tominé** r. Guinea
83 L5 **Tomingley** N.S.W. Austr
93 B4 **Tomini, Teluk** g. Indon.
206 D3 **Tominian** Mali
146 J8 **Tomintoul** Moray, Scotlar
102 S9 **Tomioka** Fukushima Jap
105 I3 **Tomioka** Gunma Japan
105 L4 **Tomisato** Japan
188 F4 **Tomislavgrad** Bos.-Her
105 K5 **Tomiura** Japan
105 G5 **Tomiyama** Aichi Japan
105 K5 **Tomiyama** Chiba Japan
105 H5 **Tomizawa** Japan
235 H2 **Tomkins Cove** NY U.S.
82 B2 **Tomkinson Ranges** mt
S.A. Austr.
142 E4 **Tommerby Fjord** l. Den
140 M3 **Tømmerneset** Norway
131 N4 **Tommot** Rus. Fed.
146 J8 **Tomnavoulin** Moray, Scotland U.K.
250 E4 **Tomo** Col.
250 E3 **Tomo** r. Col.
105 L3 **Tomobe** Japan
242 F3 **Tomóchic** Mex.
208 B4 **Tomori** C.A.R.
198 B2 **Tomorit, Maja e** mt. Alb
111 J7 **Tomorlog** Qinghai China
107 M6 **Tomortei** Nei Mongol Ch
177 I5 **Tompa** Hungary
93 B5 **Tompira** Sulawesi Indon
93 A4 **Tompo** Sulawesi Indon.
131 O3 **Tompo** Rus. Fed.
86 D7 **Tom Price** W.A. Austr.
111 H11 **Tomra** Xizang China
235 G5 **Toms** r. NJ U.S.A.
123 L2 **Tomshush** Uzbek.
130 J4 **Tomsk** Rus. Fed.
86 □1 **Tom's Ridge** Christmas
233 K9 **Toms River** NJ U.S.A.
143 K4 **Tomtabacken** hill Swec
131 P3 **Tomtor** Rus. Fed.
128 C2 **Tömük** Turkey
102 T3 **Tomuraushi-yama** mt.
Tomur Feng mt. China/
see **Jengish Chokusu**
129 F1 **Tomuzlovka** r. Rus. Fed
220 D3 **Tom White, Mount** AK
137 L7 **Tomyna Balka** Ukr.
186 J4 **Tona** Spain
102 □E20 **Tonaki-jima** i. Nansei-s
Japan
245 N9 **Tonalá** Chiapas Mex.
244 D5 **Tonala** Mex.
245 J8 **Tonalá** Oaxaca Mex.
245 M7 **Tonalá** Veracruz Mex.
245 H7 **Tonalapa de Rio** Mex.
191 J3 **Tonale, Passo di** pass
104 E2 **Tonami** Japan
250 E5 **Tonantins** Brazil
192 C7 **Tonara** Sardegna Italy
238 E2 **Tonasket** WA U.S.A.
251 H3 **Tonate** Fr. Guiana
232 G5 **Tonawanda** NY U.S.A.
244 D6 **Tonaya** Mex.
Tonb-e Bozorg, Jazīre
The Gulf see **Greater Tu**
Tonb-e Kūchek, Jazīre
The Gulf see **Lesser Tur**
151 M5 **Tonbridge** Kent, Englan
182 D7 **Tonda** Port.
104 C7 **Tondabayashi** Japan
93 D3 **Tondano** Sulawesi Indo
182 D7 **Tondela** Port.
142 E7 **Tønder** Denmark
114 F8 **Tondi** Tamil Nadu India
105 J2 **Tone** Gunma Japan
105 L4 **Tone** Ibaraki Japan
150 G5 **Tone** r. England U.K.
140 □ **Tonefjellet** hill Svalbard
105 M4 **Tone-gawa** r. Japan
262 Q1 **Toney Mountain** Antarc
191 K4 **Tonezza del Cimone** It
207 H5 **Tonga** Cameroon
79 □8 **Tonga** country S. Pacific
210 A2 **Tonga** Sudan
215 P5 **Tongaat** S. Africa
109 L6 **Tong'an** Fujian China
209 E9 **Tonga Plateau** Zambia
80 I5 **Tongaporutu** North I. N
Tongareva atoll Cook Is
Penrhyn
80 J6 **Tongariro** vol. North I. N
80 J6 **Tongariro National Par**
North I. N.Z.
79 □8a **Tongatapu** i. Tonga
79 □8a **Tongatapu Group** is To
266 H7 **Tonga Trench** sea featu
S. Pacific Ocean
109 I2 **Tongbai** Henan China
109 I2 **Tongbai Shan** mts Chir
109 K3 **Tongcheng** Anhui China
109 I4 **Tongcheng** Hubei China
Tongcheng Shandong C
see **Dong'e**
101 E9 **T'ongch'ŏn** N. Korea
107 K9 **Tongchuan** Shaanxi Chi
Tongchuan Sichuan Ch
Santai
108 G5 **Tongdao** Hunan China
106 G9 **Tongde** Qinghai China
101 E10 **Tongduch'ŏn** S. Korea
165 H7 **Tongeren** Belgium
109 J4 **Tonggu** Jiangxi China
107 L9 **Tongguan** Shaanxi Chin
110 E7 **Tongguzbasti** Xinjiang C
108 H9 **Tonggu Zui** pt China
101 F10 **Tonghae** S. Korea
108 D6 **Tonghai** Yunnan China
100 F6 **Tonghe** Heilong. China
101 D8 **Tonghua** Jilin China
101 D8 **Tonghua** Jilin China
Tongi Bangl. see **Tungi**
100 H5 **Tongjiang** Heilong. Chin
108 F3 **Tongjiang** Sichuan Chin
100 C7 **Tongjiangkou** Liaoning
101 E9 **Tongjosŏn-man** b. N. K
100 E5 **Tongken He** r. China
96 I4 **Tongking, Gulf of** China/Vietnam
93 B4 **Tongko** Sulawesi Indon.
146 H13 **Tongland** Dumfries and Galloway, Scotland U.K.
Tongle Guangxi China se
107 R5 **Tongliao** Nei Mongol Ch
109 K3 **Tongling** Anhui China
109 K3 **Tongling** Anhui China
109 L4 **Tonglu** Zhejiang China
109 I5 **Tongmu** Jiangxi China
103 G11 **Tongnae** S. Korea
83 I4 **Tongo** N.S.W. Austr.
78 □5 **Tongoa** i. Vanuatu
213 □J4 **Tongobory** Madag.
260 B2 **Tongoi, Bahía** b. Chile
83 I4 **Tongo Lake** salt flat N.S.W. Austr.
260 B2 **Tongoy** Chile
Tongquan Yunnan China
Malong
92 C8 **Tongquil** i. Phil.
108 G5 **Tongren** Guizhou China
106 G9 **Tongren** Qinghai China
Tongres Belgium see **Tongeren**
117 M6 **Tongsa** Bhutan
Tongshan Jiangsu China
Xuzhou
Tongshi Hainan China se
Wuzhishan
108 G9 **Tongshi** Hainan China
96 D4 **Tongta** Myanmar
106 C9 **Tongtian He** r. Qinghai C
111 M10 **Tongtian He** r. Qinghai C

Tongtian He r. China
alt. Chang Jiang,
alt. Jinsha Jiang,
conv. Yangtze,
long Yangtze Kiang
Tongue Highland, Scotland U.K.
Tongue r. MT U.S.A.
Tongue of Arabat spit Ukr. see Arabats'ka Strilka, Kosa
Tongue of the Ocean sea chan. Bahamas
Tongue River Reservoir MT U.S.A.
Tongwei Gansu China
Tongxiang Zhejiang China
Tongxin Ningxia China
T'ongyŏng S. Korea
Tongyu Jilin China
Tongzhou Beijing China
Tongzhou Jiangsu China
Tongzi Guizhou China
Tonhil Mongolia see Dzüyl
Tonica IL U.S.A.
Tónichi Mex.
Tonila Mex.
Tonj Sudan
Tonj watercourse Sudan
Tonk Rajasthan India
Tonkābon Iran
Tonkawa OK U.S.A.
Tonkin reg. Vietnam
Tonkino Rus. Fed.
Tônle Repou r. Laos
Tônlé Sab l. Cambodia
Tônlé San r. Cambodia
Tonle Sap l. Cambodia see Tônlé Sab
Tonna Neath Port Talbot, Wales U.K.
Tonnay-Boutonne France
Tonnay-Charente France
Tonneins France
Tonnerre France
Tonnerrois reg. France
Tönning Ger.
Tōno Fukushima Japan
Tōno Iwate Japan
Tonoas i. Chuuk Micronesia
Tonopah AZ U.S.A.
Tonopah NV U.S.A.
Tonoshō Chiba Japan
Tonoshō Kagawa Japan
Tonosí Panama
Tons r. India
Tønsberg Norway
Tonshalovo Rus. Fed.
Tonstad Norway
Tontal, Sierra mts Arg.
Tontelbos S. Africa
Tonto r. Mex.
Tonto Basin AZ U.S.A.
Tonto Creek watercourse AZ U.S.A.
Tonumea atoll Tonga
Tonvarjeh Iran
Tonyezh Belarus
Tonyrefail Rhondda Cynon Taff, Wales U.K.
Tonzang Myanmar
Tonzi Myanmar
Toobeah Qld Austr.
Toobli Liberia
Toodyay W.A. Austr.
Tooele UT U.S.A.
Toogoolawah Qld Austr.
Tooleybuc N.S.W. Austr.
Tooligie S.A. Austr.
Toolonga Nature Reserve W.A. Austr.
Tooma r. N.S.W. Austr.
Toomebridge Northern Ireland U.K.
Toompine Qld Austr.
Toora Vic. Austr.
Tooraweenah N.S.W. Austr.
Toorberg mt. S. Africa
Toormore Ireland
Toowoomba Qld Austr.
Tooxin Somalia
Top Afgh.
Topador Uru.
Topalapa del Sur Mex.
Topalki Rus. Fed.
Topana Romania
Topares Spain
Topaze, Baie b. Rodrigues I. Mauritius
Topaz Lake NV U.S.A.
Topchikha Rus. Fed.
Töpchin Ger.
Topchyne Ukr.
Topcliffe North Yorkshire, England U.K.
Topçu Dağı mt. Turkey
Top Dağı mt. Turkey
Topeka KS U.S.A.
Töpen Ger.
Topia Mex.
Topino r. Italy
Topkanovo Rus. Fed.
Topki Rus. Fed.
Topla reg. Madh. Prad. India
Topľa r. Slovakia
Toplana, Gunung mt. Seram Indon.
Topley B.C. Can.
Topley Landing B.C. Can.
Toplica r. Serbia
Toplița Harghita Romania
Toplița Hunedoara Romania
Töplitz Ger.
Toplitzsee l. Austria
Topo São Jorge Azores
Topo, Ilhéu do i. Azores
Topo, Serra do mt. São Jorge Azores
Topocalma, Punta pt Chile
Topock AZ U.S.A.
Topoľčany Slovakia
Topoľčianky Slovakia
Topoli Kazakh.
Topólka Pol.
Topolná Czech Rep.
Topolnitsa r. Bulg.
Topolobampo Mex.
Topolog Romania
Topolog r. Romania
Topolovățu Mare Romania
Topoloveni Romania
Topolovgrad Bulg.
Topolšica Slovenia
Toporec Slovakia
Toporów Pol.
Topory Ukr.
Toporyshche Ukr.
Toporzyk Pol.
Topozero, Ozero l. Rus. Fed.
Toppenish WA U.S.A.
Topraisar Romania
Toprakkale Ağrı Turkey
Toprakkale Erzurum Turkey
Toprakkale Osmaniye Turkey
Topraklık Turkey
Topsfield ME U.S.A.
Topsham Devon, England U.K.
Toptepe Turkey
Topton PA U.S.A.
Topuni North I. N.Z.
Toquepala Peru
Toqyraū watercourse Kazakh. see Tokyrau
Tor Eth.
Tor, Noguera de r. Spain
Tora Dem. Rep. Congo
Torá Spain
Torağay Dağı hill Azer.
Torahime Japan
Toral de los Guzmanes Spain
Toral de los Vados Spain
Toraman Turkey see Haliļçavuş
Toranggekuduk Xinjiang China
Torano Castello Italy
Torata Peru
Tor Baldak mt. Afgh.
Torbalı Turkey
Torbat-e Heydarīyeh Iran
Torbat-e Jām Iran
Torbay admin. div. England U.K.
Tor Bay England U.K.
Torbay Bay W.A. Austr.
135 H5 Torbeyevo Respublika Mordoviya Rus. Fed.
139 R6 Torbeyevo Smolenskaya Oblast' Rus. Fed.
185 J7 Torcal de Antequera park Spain
186 C5 Torcas, Embalse de las resr Spain
223 K4 Torch r. Sask. Can.
193 O7 Torchiara Italy
195 O3 Torchiarolo Italy
139 X5 Torchino Rus. Fed.
136 E3 Torchyn Ukr.
183 L9 Torcón r. Spain
183 L9 Torcón, Embalse del resr Spain
160 E3 Torcy France
156 B4 Torcy-le-Petit France
177 H4 Tordas Hungary
183 J5 Tordehumos Spain
186 K4 Tordera Spain
183 K5 Tordesillas Spain
183 Q7 Tordesilos Spain
183 P9 Tórdiga, Puerto de pass Spain
193 L2 Tordino r. Italy
140 Q4 Töre Sweden
146 H7 Tore Highland, Scotland U.K.
143 K3 Töreboda Sweden
170 E1 Toreby Denmark
142 I5 Torekov Sweden
193 N4 Torella del Sannio Italy
187 D11 Torellano Spain
140 □ Torell Land reg. Svalbard
186 J3 Torelló Spain
164 I4 Torenberg hill Neth.
182 G3 Toreno Spain
93 C5 Toreo Sulawesi Indon.
80 L4 Torere North I. N.Z.
Toretam Kazakh. see Baykonyr
106 I1 Torey Rus. Fed.
137 R5 Torez Ukr.
150 F4 Torfaen admin. div. Wales U.K.
Torga i. Vanuatu see Toga
171 G7 Torgau Ger.
170 J3 Torgelow Ger.
Torghay Kazakh. see Turgay
193 I1 Torgiano Italy
120 B2 Torgun r. Rus. Fed.
143 L5 Torhamn Sweden
165 D6 Torhout Belgium
136 E3 Torhovytsya Ukr.
138 H3 Tori Estonia
117 J8 Tori Jharkhand India
210 A3 Tori r. Sudan
105 L4 Toride Japan
105 H1 Torigakubi-misaki pt Japan
159 J3 Torigni-sur-Vire France
104 E3 Torigoe Japan
105 G4 Torii-tōge pass Japan
105 H3 Torii-tōge pass Japan
183 N7 Torija Spain
105 I2 Torikabuto-yama mt. Japan
188 G4 Torine pass Bos.-Herz.
190 D5 Torino Italy
190 D5 Torino prov. Italy
193 N3 Torino di Sangro Italy
103 R16 Tori-shima i. Japan
210 B3 Torit Sudan
195 L2 Toritto Italy
256 A2 Torixoréu Brazil
104 E2 Toriya Japan
122 B3 Torkamān Iran
123 J4 Torkestān, Band-e mts Afgh.
123 N5 Torkhan Pak.
139 N3 Torkovichi Rus. Fed.
186 E2 Torla Spain
138 J3 Torma Estonia
140 S2 Törmänen Fin.
86 G4 Torment, Point W.A. Austr.
182 H6 Tormes r. Spain
187 C7 Tormón Spain
146 F11 Tormore North Ayrshire, Scotland U.K.
183 K7 Tornadizos de Ávila Spain
222 H5 Tornado Mountain Alta/B.C. Can.
185 N5 Tornajuelos mt. Spain
177 J3 Tornaľa Slovakia
182 I8 Tornavacas Spain
182 I8 Tornavacas, Puerto de pass Spain
149 P6 Torne r. England U.K.
Torneå Fin. see Tornio
140 R4 Torneälven r. Sweden
185 K2 Torneros, Sierra de los mts Spain
168 I3 Tornesch Ger.
140 O2 Torneträsk Sweden
140 O2 Torneträsk l. Sweden
Torngat, Monts mts Nfld and Lab./Que. Can. see Torngat Mountains
225 H1 Torngat Mountains Nfld and Lab./Que. Can.
196 H7 Tornik mt. Serbia
140 R4 Tornio Fin.
177 I6 Tornjoš Vojvodina Serbia
190 G4 Torno Italy
183 R7 Tornos Spain
170 H4 Tornow Ger.
261 F6 Tornquist Arg.
177 L3 Tornyospálca Hungary
207 H4 Toro Nigeria
183 J5 Toro Spain
143 N3 Torö i. Sweden
259 B8 Toro, Lago del l. Chile
244 F1 Toro, Pico del mt. Mex.
260 B3 Toro, Punta pt Chile
93 C6 Torobuku Sulawesi Indon.
207 F3 Torodi Niger
177 H4 Törökbálint Hungary
177 J4 Törökszentmiklós Hungary
100 I1 Torom Rus. Fed.
224 E5 Toronto Ont. Can.
232 E8 Toronto OH U.S.A.
234 F1 Toronto Reservoir NY U.S.A.
179 O5 Torony Hungary
139 O5 Toropatsa Rus. Fed.
241 P8 Toro Peak CA U.S.A.
139 O5 Toropets Rus. Fed.
202 C6 Tororo Chad
210 B4 Tororo Uganda
126 F5 Toros Dağları mts Turkey
138 L4 Toroshino Rus. Fed.
183 K5 Torozos, Montes de reg. Spain
192 D6 Torpè Sardegna Italy
146 K8 Torphins Aberdeenshire, Scotland U.K.
150 D7 Torpoint Cornwall, England U.K.
255 B9 Torquato Severo Brazil
83 J8 Torquay Vic. Austr.
150 E7 Torquay Torbay, England U.K.
183 L4 Torquemada Spain
147 J2 Torr Northern Ireland U.K.
185 L2 Torralba de Calatrava Spain
192 B6 Torralba Sardegna Italy
183 P8 Torralba Spain
186 D4 Torralba de Aragón Spain
183 O5 Torralba de El Burgo Spain
183 R7 Torralba de los Sisones Spain
183 J9 Torralba de Oropesa Spain
240 N8 Torrance CA U.S.A.
184 C4 Torrão Port.
182 E8 Torre mt. Port.
193 M6 Torre Annunziata Italy
193 J5 Torre Astura cliff Italy
187 C7 Torrebaja Spain
183 O5 Torreblacos Spain
187 F7 Torreblanca Spain
242 B1 Torre Blanco, Cerro mt. Mex.
185 L5 Torreblascopedro Spain
193 N4 Torrebruna Italy
183 L7 Torrecaballeros Spain
185 J4 Torrecampo Spain
195 M2 Torre Canne Italy
185 M5 Torre-Cardela Spain
195 O2 Torre Cavallo, Capo di c. Italy
183 K2 Torrecerredo mt. Spain
192 G3 Torre Ciana, Punta di pt Italy
185 J7 Torrecilla mt. Spain
183 K9 Torrecilla de la Jara Spain
183 J6 Torrecilla de la Orden Spain
186 C6 Torrecilla del Rebollar Spain
183 O4 Torrecilla en Cameros Spain
182 I9 Torrecillas de la Tiesa Spain
193 N5 Torrecuso Italy
184 C3 Torre da Gadanha Port.
184 D2 Torre das Vargens Port.
185 K2 Torre de Abraham, Embalse de la resr Spain
186 I3 Torre de Cadí mt. Spain
182 F5 Torre de Dona Chama Port.
182 D7 Torredeita Port.
185 M3 Torre de Juan Abad Spain
184 H6 Torre del Águila, Embalse de la resr Spain
182 H3 Torre del Bierzo Spain
183 N7 Torre del Burgo Spain
185 L5 Torre del Campo Spain
193 M6 Torre del Greco Italy
190 I8 Torre della Meloria i. Italy
185 K7 Torre del Mar Spain
195 N4 Torre del Pizzo pt Italy
186 H5 Torredembarra Spain
184 F3 Torre de Miguel Sesmero Spain
182 F6 Torre de Moncorvo Port.
193 L3 Torre de'Passeri Italy
185 L5 Torredonjimeno Spain
182 F7 Torre do Terrenho Port.
182 H6 Torregamones Spain
186 G4 Torregrossa Spain
183 L6 Torreiglesias Spain
182 C7 Torreira Port.
182 H9 Torrejoncillo Spain
183 O8 Torrejoncillo del Rey Spain
183 N8 Torrejón de Ardoz Spain
183 N7 Torrejón del Rey Spain
182 I9 Torrejón el Rubio Spain
182 I9 Torrejón-Tajo, Embalse de resr Spain
182 I9 Torrejón-Tiétar, Embalse de resr Spain
186 C6 Torrelacarcel Spain
183 M7 Torrelaguna Spain
183 Q5 Torrelapaja Spain
183 L2 Torrelavega Spain
183 Q5 Torrellas Spain
186 I5 Torrelles de Foix Spain
183 J5 Torrelobatón Spain
183 M7 Torrelodones Spain
193 O4 Torremaggiore Italy
187 E10 Torremanzanas-La Torre de les Macanes Spain
184 F3 Torremayor Spain
184 G3 Torremegía Spain
193 P4 Torre Mileto Italy
184 G2 Torremocha Spain
185 J7 Torremolinos Spain
187 F7 Torrenostra Spain
82 F4 Torrens, Lake imp. l. S.A. Austr.
85 J6 Torrens Creek Qld Austr.
85 J7 Torrens Creek watercourse Qld Austr.
258 F3 Torrent Arg.
187 E9 Torrent Spain
Torrente Valencia Spain see Torrent
186 F5 Torrente del Cinca Spain
185 M3 Torrenueva Spain
190 H9 Torre Nuovo Scalo Italy
242 H5 Torreón Mex.
184 G2 Torreorgaz Spain
193 O7 Torre Orsaia Italy
187 D12 Torre-Pacheco Spain
185 K5 Torreparedones hill Spain
190 C6 Torre Pellice Italy
185 M4 Torreperogil Spain
255 C9 Torres Brazil
242 D3 Torres Mex.
185 L5 Torres Spain
185 L5 Torres r. Spain
182 I1 Torres, Cabo c. Spain
183 M5 Torresandino Spain
195 O4 Torre San Giovanni Italy
193 L5 Torre Sant'Agostino cliff Italy
195 N3 Torre Santa Susanna Italy
185 N4 Torres de Albánchez Spain
186 C4 Torres de Berrellén Spain
183 N8 Torres de la Alameda Spain
182 I5 Torres del Carrizal Spain
259 B8 Torres del Paine, Parque Nacional nat. park Chile
186 G4 Torres de Segre Spain
78 □5 Torres Islands Vanuatu
182 I6 Torresmenudas Spain
184 B2 Torres Novas Port.
76 E2 Torres Strait Qld Austr.
184 A2 Torres Vedras Port.
193 P6 Torretta, Monte mt. Italy
186 E6 Torrevelilla Spain
187 D12 Torrevieja Spain
241 U3 Torrey UT U.S.A.
193 K4 Torrice Italy
195 N3 Torricella Italy
193 J3 Torricella in Sabina Italy
193 M3 Torricella Peligna Italy
193 L2 Torricella Sicura Italy
190 F3 Torricella Taverne Switz.
183 J9 Torrico Spain
184 F2 Torrico de San Pedro hill Spain
191 J4 Torri del Benaco Italy
150 D6 Torridge r. England U.K.
146 E7 Torridon Highland, Scotland U.K.
146 E7 Torridon, Loch b. Scotland U.K.
190 G6 Torriglia Italy
193 J3 Torri in Sabina Italy
187 D7 Torrijas Spain
183 Q6 Torrijo Spain
183 L9 Torrijos Spain
146 D8 Torrin Highland, Scotland U.K.
233 L7 Torrington CT U.S.A.
238 L5 Torrington WY U.S.A.
256 C5 Torrinha Brazil
192 H1 Torrita di Siena Italy
184 B4 Torroal Port.
186 L3 Torroella de Montgrí Spain
140 L5 Torrön l. Sweden
138 G1 Torronsuon kansallispuisto nat. park Fin.
185 L7 Torrox Spain
185 L7 Torrox, Punta de pt Spain
183 O9 Torrubia del Campo Spain
183 P5 Torrubia de Soria Spain
143 K2 Torrvarpen l. Sweden
117 L6 Torsa Chhu r. Bhutan
142 G1 Torsæterkampen hill Norway
168 H1 Tørsbøl Denmark
142 J1 Torsby Sweden
143 M2 Torshälla Sweden
144 D1 Tórshavn Faroe Is
143 J3 Torsö i. Sweden
140 O1 Torsvåg Norway
177 I4 Törtel Hungary
158 F3 Torteval Channel Is
241 U8 Tortilla Flat AZ U.S.A.
120 I7 To'rtko'l Uzbek.
Törtköl Uzbek. see To'rtko'l
121 P2 Tortkuduk Kazakh.
194 F8 Torto r. Sicilia Italy
247 K4 Tortola i. Virgin Is (U.K.)
183 N7 Tórtola de Henares Spain
183 L5 Tórtoles de Esgueva Spain
192 D8 Tortolì Sardegna Italy
197 Q6 Tortomanu Romania
190 F6 Tortona Italy
193 P8 Tortora Italy
193 L2 Tortoreto Italy
194 H7 Tortorici Sicilia Italy
186 G6 Tortosa Spain
182 E8 Tortozendo Port.
246 G3 Tortue, Île de la i. Haiti
183 Q7 Tortuera Spain
245 I3 Tortuga, Laguna l. Mex.
261 G3 Tortugas Arg.
242 □R12 Tortuguero, Parque Nacional nat. park Costa Rica
127 J3 Tortum Turkey
121 Q6 Toru-Aygyr Kyrg.
122 F4 Torūd Iran
93 B4 Torue Sulawesi Indon.
Torugart, Pereval pass China/Kyrg. see Turugart Pass
126 I3 Torul Turkey
174 G2 Toruń Pol.
138 I3 Tõrva Estonia
193 I4 Tor Vaianica Italy
149 K5 Torver Cumbria, England U.K.
185 M7 Torvizcón Spain
141 I5 Torvløysa mt. Norway
140 N4 Torvsjö Sweden
147 F2 Tory Island Ireland
177 J2 Torysa Slovakia
177 K3 Torysa r. Slovakia
147 F2 Tory Sound sea chan. Ireland
139 R5 Torzhkovskaya Gryada hills Rus. Fed.
139 R4 Torzhok Rus. Fed.
174 D3 Torzym Pol.
103 K13 Tosa Japan
191 J3 Tosa, Cima mt. Italy
103 J14 Tosashimizu Japan
103 K13 Tosa-wan b. Japan
103 K13 Tosa-yamada Japan
140 L4 Tosbotn Norway
214 H1 Tosca S. Africa
242 D5 Tosca, Punta pt Mex.
146 E8 Toscaig Highland, Scotland U.K.
191 K9 Toscana admin. reg. Italy
192 D2 Toscano, Arcipelago is Italy
191 J4 Toscolano-Maderno Italy
140 L4 Tosenfjorden inlet Norway
104 E6 Tōshi-jima i. Japan
105 J6 To-shima i. Japan
102 S6 Tōshima-yama mt. Japan
121 M7 Toshkent Toshkent Uzbek.
121 M7 Toshkent admin. div. Uzbek.
Toshkent Wiloyati admin. div. Uzbek. see Toshkent
139 N2 Tosno Rus. Fed.
106 E8 Toson Hu l. Qinghai China
106 F2 Tosontsengel Mongolia
190 F1 Töss r. Switz.
186 K4 Tossa Spain
163 B8 Tosse France
193 L2 Tossicia Italy
149 M5 Tosside Lancashire, England U.K.
258 E3 Tostado Arg.
138 G3 Tõstamaa Estonia
168 I4 Tostedt Ger.
182 B2 Tosto, Cabo c. Spain
103 H13 Tosu Japan
126 G3 Tosya Turkey
177 J4 Tószeg Hungary
174 G5 Toszek Pol.
187 C12 Totana Spain
114 G9 Totapola mt. Sri Lanka
81 E12 Totara South I. N.Z.
80 G7 Totaranui South I. N.Z.
244 D4 Totatiche Mex.
212 D4 Toteng Botswana
172 D5 Totenkopf hill Ger.
156 B4 Tôtes France
179 I4 Totes Gebirge mts Austria
78 □4a Totiw i. Chuuk Micronesia
151 I6 Totland Isle of Wight, England U.K.
134 H4 Tot'ma Rus. Fed.
150 E7 Totnes Devon, England U.K.
251 G3 Totness Suriname
245 K9 Totolapan Mex.
245 L9 Totolapilla Mex.
245 J7 Totoltepec Mex.
134 H4 Totomitsa Rus. Fed.
243 N10 Totonicapán Guat.
252 D4 Totora Bol.
260 D2 Totoral Arg.
258 C2 Totoral Chile
258 D3 Totoralejos Arg.
261 G3 Totoras Arg.
206 C5 Totota Liberia
244 E5 Tototlán Mex.
79 □7 Totoya i. Fiji
120 E1 Totskoye Rus. Fed.
105 K5 Totsuka Japan
104 C7 Totsukawa Japan
104 C8 Totsu-kawa r. Japan
176 F5 Tótszentmárton Hungary
176 F5 Tótszerdahely Hungary
151 J6 Totton Hampshire, England U.K.
103 L11 Tottori Japan
103 K11 Tottori pref. Japan
245 K6 Totutla Mex.
177 G4 Tótvázsony Hungary
207 G1 Touâret well Niger
206 D4 Touba Côte d'Ivoire
206 B3 Touba Senegal
204 D3 Toubkal, Jbel mt. Morocco
204 D3 Toubkal, Parc National nat. park Morocco
207 I5 Touboro Cameroon
182 F6 Touça Port.
163 G8 Touch r. France
238 E3 Touchet r. WA U.S.A.
156 F8 Toucy France
106 I7 Toudaohu Nei Mongol China
204 B5 Toueïrma well Maur.
206 E2 Touérât well Mali
163 G7 Touffailles France
204 D4 Toufourine well Mali
206 E3 Tougan Burkina
163 F8 Touget France
205 G2 Touggourt Alg.
206 E3 Tougouri Burkina
207 G3 Tougoutaou well Niger
206 C4 Tougué Guinea
78 □5 Touho New Caledonia
206 C2 Touijinet well Maur.
206 C3 Touil Maur.
206 C3 Toukoto Mali
207 F4 Toukountouna Benin
157 K6 Toul France
206 C5 Toulépleu Côte d'Ivoire
206 E3 Toulfé Burkina
109 M7 Touliu Taiwan
225 G3 Toulnustouc r. Que. Can.
161 H10 Toulon France
226 E8 Toulon IL U.S.A.
160 C3 Toulon-sur-Allier France
160 E3 Toulon-sur-Arroux France
163 J10 Toulouges France
207 G2 Toulouk well Niger
163 G8 Toulouse France
207 G3 Toumbélaga well Niger
202 B4 Toummo well Niger
206 D5 Toumodi Côte d'Ivoire
206 D4 Touna Mali
204 D3 Tounassine, Hamada des. Alg.
207 G3 Tounfaminir well Niger
207 I4 Toungo Nigeria
108 H6 Toupai Guangxi China
159 L3 Touques France
159 L3 Touques r. France
206 D5 Toura, Monts mt. Côte d'Ivoire
162 E1 Touraine reg. France
159 L7 Touraine, Val de val. France
108 D9 Tourakom Laos
Tourane Vietnam see Đa Năng
204 C4 Tourassine well Maur.
202 B6 Tourba Chad
158 D5 Tourch France
156 F2 Tourcoing France
161 K9 Tourette-sur-Loup France
223 J1 Tourgis Lake Nunavut Can.
182 B2 Touriñán, Cabo c. Spain
198 D5 Tourkovigla, Akrotirio pt Greece
158 H2 Tourlaville France
147 D5 Tourmakeady Ireland
163 E10 Tourmalet, Col du pass France
160 E5 Tour Matagrin hill France
165 D7 Tournai Belgium
161 K8 Tournairet, Mont mt. France
156 E6 Tournan-en-Brie France
252 B2 Tournavista Peru
163 E9 Tournay France
205 H5 Tourndo, Oued watercourse Alg./Niger
163 F8 Tournecoupe France
163 G8 Tournefeuille France
163 F7 Tournon-d'Agenais France
159 M8 Tournon-St-Martin France
161 F6 Tournon-sur-Rhône France
160 F3 Tournus France
156 C5 Tourny France
182 E7 Touro Port.
255 A9 Touro Passo Brazil
254 G3 Touros Brazil
207 I4 Touroua Cameroon
159 M4 Tourouvre France
161 K9 Tourrette-Levens France
162 F1 Tours France
156 I4 Tourteron France
162 G5 Tourtoirac France
161 H10 Tourves France
156 C7 Toury France
187 D9 Tous, Embalse de resr Spain
206 D4 Toussiana Burkina
202 C4 Toussidé, Pic mt. Chad
208 D2 Toussoro, Mont mt. C.A.R.
100 D6 Toutai Heilong. China
184 E4 Toutalga r. Port.
82 □3 Toutcher, Cape S. Pacific Ocean
158 H8 Touvois France
214 F9 Touws r. S. Africa
214 E9 Touwsrivier S. Africa
176 B1 Toužim Czech Rep.
106 I3 Töv prov. Mongolia
176 G2 Tovačov Czech Rep.
250 D2 Tovar Venez.
139 S7 Tovarkovo Rus. Fed.
139 V8 Tovarkovskiy Rus. Fed.
177 K3 Tovarné Slovakia
188 G3 Tovarnik Croatia
151 K3 Tove r. England U.K.
178 C7 Tovel, Lago di l. Italy
Tovil'-Dora Tajik. see Tavildara
136 E5 Tovste Ukr.
79 □7 Tovu Fiji
129 G5 Tovuz Azer.
Tovuzçay r. Armenia see Tavush
235 G3 Towaco NJ U.S.A.
102 S6 Towada Japan
102 R7 Towada-Hachimantai Kokuritsu-kōen nat. park Japan
102 S6 Towada-ko l. Japan
80 I2 Towai North I. N.Z.
251 G3 Towakaima Guyana
131 U3 Towak Mountain hill AK U.S.A.
227 R8 Towanda PA U.S.A.
234 C1 Towanda Creek r. PA U.S.A.
241 X4 Towaoc CO U.S.A.
93 B6 Towari Sulawesi Indon.
151 K3 Towcester Northamptonshire, England U.K.
147 E9 Tower Ireland
226 B2 Tower MN U.S.A.
234 B3 Tower City PA U.S.A.
85 J7 Towerhill Creek watercourse Qld Austr.
Tower Island Islas Galápagos Ecuador see Genovesa, Isla
81 B13 Tower Peak South I. N.Z.
149 N4 Tow Law Durham, England U.K.
234 F7 Town Bank NJ U.S.A.
236 E1 Towner ND U.S.A.
146 I13 Townhead of Greenlaw Dumfries and Galloway, Scotland U.K.
146 J10 Townhill Fife, Scotland U.K.
84 E3 Towns r. N.T. Austr.
234 D6 Townsend DE U.S.A.
233 N6 Townsend MA U.S.A.
238 I3 Townsend MT U.S.A.
234 F6 Townsends Inlet NJ U.S.A.
85 M7 Townshend Island Qld Austr.
85 K5 Townsville Qld Austr.
93 B5 Towori, Teluk b. Indon.
210 B3 Towot Sudan
123 J4 Towraghondi Afgh.
123 N4 Towr Kham Afgh.
234 B6 Towson MD U.S.A.
93 B5 Towuti, Danau l. Indon.
150 E1 Towyn Conwy, Wales U.K.
Towyn Gwynedd, Wales U.K. see Tywyn
110 E6 Toxkan He r. China
240 N1 Toy NV U.S.A.
237 D10 Toyah TX U.S.A.
102 S4 Tōya-ko l. Japan
104 F2 Toyama Japan
104 F2 Toyama pref. Japan
104 F2 Toyama-wan b. Japan
106 G9 Toyêma Qinghai China
136 D2 Toykut Ukr.
103 K13 Tōyo Japan
104 F5 Toyoake Japan
105 G6 Toyoda Japan
103 K12 Toyohama Japan
104 F6 Toyohashi Japan
104 F6 Toyokawa Japan
104 F6 Toyo-kawa r. Japan
104 B6 Toyonaka Japan
104 G5 Toyone Japan
105 H2 Toyono Nagano Japan
104 B6 Toyono Ōsaka Japan
104 A4 Toyooka Hyōgo Japan
105 G4 Toyooka Nagano Japan
105 G6 Toyooka Shizuoka Japan
102 Q9 Toyosaka Japan
105 G3 Toyoshina Japan
104 F5 Toyota Japan
102 S1 Toyotomi Japan
104 E5 Toyoyama Japan
140 Q5 Töysä Fin.
121 M7 To'ytepa Uzbek.
Tozal del Orri mt. Spain see Orri, Tossal de l'
Tozanlı Turkey see Almus
111 F9 Tozê Kangri mt. Xizang China
205 H2 Tozeur Tunisia
129 I4 Tpig Rus. Fed.
129 D3 Tqibuli Georgia
129 C3 Tqvarch'eli Georgia
182 F2 Trabada Spain
96 H4 Tra Ban, Đao i. Vietnam
182 H6 Trabanca Spain
182 H5 Trabazos Spain
194 F8 Trabia Sicilia Italy
174 G1 Trąbki Wielkie Pol.
128 D4 Trâblous Lebanon
179 K5 Traboch Austria
197 K9 Trabotivište Macedonia
192 A5 Trabuccato, Punta pt Sardegna Italy
127 I3 Trabzon Turkey
129 A5 Trabzon prov. Turkey
194 C10 Tracino Sicilia Italy
233 □S3 Tracy N.B. Can.
240 K4 Tracy CA U.S.A.
236 H3 Tracy MN U.S.A.
160 B2 Tracy-sur-Loire France
190 F4 Tradate Italy
169 G8 Traddelkopf hill Ger.
226 B4 Trade Lake WI U.S.A.
237 K7 Tradewater r. KY U.S.A.
224 B3 Trading r. Ont. Can.
140 L3 Træna i. Norway
140 L3 Trænfjorden sea chan. Norway
236 I4 Traer IA U.S.A.
184 G8 Trafalgar, Cabo c. Spain
222 D2 Traffic Mountain Y.T. Can.
183 Q8 Tragacete Spain
185 O4 Tragoncillo mt. Spain
199 G5 Tragonisi i. Greece
179 K3 Tragwein Austria
197 N7 Traian Romania
177 L6 Traian Vuia Romania
183 Q7 Traid Spain
260 A6 Traiguén Chile
186 F6 Traiguera Spain
222 G5 Trail B.C. Can.
237 F8 Trail OK U.S.A.
146 E11 Tràille, Rubha na pt Scotland U.K.
Traill Island Greenland see Traill Ø
221 P2 Traill Ø i. Greenland
173 L4 Train Ger.
156 F7 Traînel France
234 E5 Trainer PA U.S.A.
156 D8 Traînou France
254 F4 Traipu Brazil
250 D5 Traíra r. Brazil
256 D2 Trairas r. Brazil
254 F2 Trairi Brazil
179 M3 Traisen Austria
179 M3 Traisen r. Austria
179 N3 Traiskirchen Austria
179 M3 Traismauer Austria
173 N3 Traitsching Ger.
257 F5 Trajano de Morais Brazil
Trajectum Neth. see Utrecht
214 H9 Traka r. S. Africa
138 H7 Trakai Lith.
141 R9 Trakai nat. park Lith.
Trakiya reg. Turkey see Thrace
134 J3 Trakt Rus. Fed.
Trakya reg. Turkey see Thrace
147 C8 Tralee Ireland
147 C8 Tralee Bay Ireland
Trá Li Ireland see Tralee
183 Q8 Tramacastilla Spain
192 A6 Tramariglio Sardegna Italy
187 C7 Tramascastiel Spain
192 B7 Tramatza Sardegna Italy
191 L7 Tramazzo r. Italy
172 C7 Tramelan Switz.
163 E10 Tramezaïgues France
Trá Mhór Ireland see Tramore
232 C11 Trammel VA U.S.A.
178 G7 Tramonti, Lago dei l. Italy
191 N3 Tramonti di Sopra Italy
178 G7 Tramonti di Sotto Italy
147 H8 Tramore Ireland
187 J8 Tramuntana, Serra de mts Spain
193 P7 Tramutola Italy
143 K3 Tranås Sweden
142 G5 Tranbjerg Denmark
258 D2 Trancas Arg.
185 N4 Tranco de Beas, Embalse del resr Spain
257 H2 Trancoso Brazil
182 F7 Trancoso Port.
142 G6 Tranebjerg Denmark
142 J4 Tranemo Sweden
146 K11 Tranent East Lothian, Scotland U.K.
97 D11 Trang Thai.
91 H8 Trangan i. Indon.
83 K5 Trangie N.S.W. Austr.
193 Q5 Trani Italy
156 I7 Trannes France
96 F5 Trân Ninh, Cao Nguyên plat. Laos
213 □J5 Tranoroa Madag.
213 □J5 Tranovaho Madag.
183 Q6 Tranquera, Embalse de la resr Spain
258 G3 Tranqueras Uru.
260 B3 Tranquilla Chile
158 H5 Trans France
263 K2 Transantarctic Mountains Antarctica
223 H5 Trans Canada Highway Can.
Transcarpathian Oblast admin. div. Ukr. see Zakarpats'ka Oblast'
223 L5 Transcona Man. Can.
161 I9 Trans-en-Provence France
245 H6 Transfiguracion Mex.
197 M4 Transilvaniei, Podişul plat. Romania
141 L6 Transtrand Sweden
Transylvanian Alps mts Romania see Carpaţii Meridionali
Transylvanian Basin plat. Romania see Transilvaniei, Podişul
146 I6 Trantlemore Highland, Scotland U.K.
97 G10 Tra Ôn Vietnam
194 D7 Trapani Sicilia Italy
194 D8 Trapani prov. Sicilia Italy
Trapezus Turkey see Trabzon
260 D3 Trapiche Arg.
234 E4 Trappe PA U.S.A.
168 J2 Trappenkamp Ger.
238 G4 Trapper Peak MT U.S.A.
156 D6 Trappes France
255 B9 Trapua r. Brazil
83 K8 Traralgon Vic. Austr.
172 C2 Trarbach Ger.
143 J5 Traryd Sweden
206 B2 Trarza admin. reg. Maur.
193 L4 Trasacco Italy
197 L4 Trascăului, Munţii mts Romania
Trashigang Bhutan see Tashigang
192 I1 Trasimeno, Lago l. Italy
182 E4 Trasmiras Spain
182 F5 Trás-os-Montes reg. Port.
192 G2 Trasubbie r. Italy
183 P9 Trasvase, Canal de Spain
97 F8 Trat Thai.
192 B9 Tratalias Sardegna Italy
179 M6 Trate Slovenia
179 J3 Traun Austria
179 J3 Traun r. Austria
173 N5 Traun r. Ger.
173 N6 Traunreut Ger.
179 I4 Traunsee l. Austria
179 L3 Traunstein Austria
173 N6 Traunstein Ger.
138 H6 Traupis Lith.
179 O3 Trautmannsdorf an der Leitha Austria
191 R4 Trava Slovenia
190 I4 Travagliato Italy
182 D8 Travanca do Mondego Port.
182 D7 Travassô Port.
182 E7 Travassós de Cima Port.
168 K3 Trave r. Ger.
83 I5 Travellers Lake imp. l. N.S.W. Austr.
168 K3 Travemünde Ger.
168 J3 Travenbrück Ger.
190 B2 Travers Switz.
81 G9 Travers, Mount South I. N.Z.
249 G7 Traversay Islands S. Sandwich Is
226 I5 Traverse City MI U.S.A.
190 I6 Traversetolo Italy
257 G4 Travessão Brazil
191 L3 Travignolo r. Italy
97 H10 Tra Vinh Vietnam
237 F10 Travis, Lake TX U.S.A.
188 F3 Travnik Bos.-Herz.
192 C4 Travo r. Corse France
190 H6 Travo Italy
147 B4 Trawmore Bay Ireland
150 E2 Trawsfynydd Gwynedd, Wales U.K.
150 E2 Trawsfynydd, Llyn resr Wales U.K.
87 D11 Trayning W.A. Austr.
188 E2 Trbovlje Slovenia
97 G10 Tre, Hon i. Vietnam
147 D5 Trean Ireland
246 □ Treasure Beach Jamaica
78 □6 Treasury Islands Solomon Is
177 G3 Trebatice Slovakia
171 J6 Trebatsch Ger.
190 H5 Trebbia r. Italy
171 H6 Trebbin Ger.
188 G4 Trebebvić nat. park Bos.-Herz.
170 D5 Trebel Ger.
170 H3 Trebel r. Ger.
171 F8 Treben Ger.
176 C1 Třebenice Czech Rep.
170 I4 Trebenow Ger.
163 I9 Trèbes France
179 I6 Trebesing Austria
158 D4 Trébeurden France
176 E2 Třebíč Czech Rep.
188 G4 Trebinje Bos.-Herz.
195 L4 Trebisacce Italy
188 F4 Trebišnjica r. Bos.-Herz.
177 K3 Trebišov Slovakia
171 G7 Trebitz Ger.
188 F4 Trebižat r. Bos.-Herz.
Trebizond Turkey see Trabzon
188 E3 Trebnje Slovenia
261 F4 Trebolares Arg.
182 E3 Trebolle Spain
176 D2 Třeboň Czech Rep.
85 K5 Trebonne Qld Austr.
176 D2 Třeboňsko park Czech Rep.
158 C5 Tréboul France
171 G8 Trebsen Ger.
184 G7 Trebujena Spain
172 E2 Trebur Ger.
150 E4 Trecastle Powys, Wales U.K.
190 F5 Trecate Italy
193 P7 Trecchina Italy
191 K5 Trecenta Italy
150 F4 Tredegar Blaenau Gwent, Wales U.K.
151 I3 Tredington Warwickshire, England U.K.
191 L7 Tredozio Italy
148 C5 Treehoo Ireland
114 C7 Tree Island India
168 H2 Treene r. Ger.
Trefaldwyn Powys, Wales U.K. see Montgomery
Trefdraeth Wales U.K. see Newport
150 E2 Trefeglwys Powys, Wales U.K.
179 I6 Treffen Austria
158 C6 Treffiagat France
160 G4 Treffort-Cuisiat France
169 J8 Treffurt Ger.
Treffynnon Flintshire, Wales U.K. see Holywell
150 E1 Trefriw Conwy, Wales U.K.
Tref-y-clawdd Wales U.K. see Knighton
Trefynwy Monmouthshire, Wales U.K. see Monmouth
150 E3 Tregaron Ceredigion, Wales U.K.
158 D4 Trégastel France
191 K4 Tregnago Italy
226 C4 Trego WI U.S.A.
150 C7 Tregony Cornwall, England U.K.
158 E4 Trégorrois reg. France
85 M4 Tregosse Islets and Reefs Coral Sea Is Terr. Austr.
260 A5 Treguaco Chile
158 F5 Trégueux France
158 E4 Tréguier France
158 D6 Trégunc France
150 F2 Tregynon Powys, Wales U.K.
140 O5 Trehörningsjö Sweden
168 H1 Treia Ger.
191 O9 Treia Italy
146 G9 Treig, Loch l. Scotland U.K.
162 H4 Treignac France
160 C1 Treigny France
Treinta de Agosto Arg. see 30 de Agosto
258 G4 Treinta y Tres Uru.
169 D10 Treis Ger.
182 H2 Treisa, Peña mt. Spain
140 □ Tre Kroner mt. Svalbard
246 □ Trelawny parish Jamaica
159 K7 Trélazé France
150 D4 Trelech Carmarthenshire, Wales U.K.
259 D6 Trelew Arg.
162 F5 Trélissac France
158 G5 Trélivan France
142 J6 Trelleborg Sweden
156 H3 Trélon France
197 K7 Trem mt. Serbia
150 D2 Tremadog Gwynedd, Wales U.K.
150 D2 Tremadog Bay Wales U.K.
224 F4 Tremblant, Mont hill Que. Can.
158 I5 Tremblay France
156 B6 Tremblay-les-Villages France
217 □1c Tremblet Réunion
222 E4 Trembleur Lake B.C. Can.
183 Q7 Tremedal, Sierra del mts Spain
182 H6 Tremedal de Tormes Spain
165 G7 Tremelo Belgium
159 J7 Trémentines France
184 B2 Tremês Port.
158 D6 Tréméven France
190 G4 Tremezzo Italy
193 P3 Tremiti, Isole is Italy
138 M9 Tremlya r. Belarus
163 F6 Trémolat France
227 R9 Tremont PA U.S.A.
238 H6 Tremonton UT U.S.A.
176 C2 Třemošná Czech Rep.
176 E2 Třemošnice Czech Rep.
161 B8 Trémouilles France
186 G3 Tremp Spain
226 C5 Trempealeau r. WI U.S.A.
168 J3 Tremsbüttel Ger.
150 B7 Trenance Cornwall, England U.K.
226 H3 Trenary MI U.S.A.
225 F4 Trenche r. Que. Can.
177 H3 Trenčianska Turná Slovakia
177 G3 Trenčianske Stankovce Slovakia
177 H3 Trenčianske Teplice Slovakia
177 H3 Trenčiansky kraj admin. reg. Slovakia
177 H3 Trenčín Slovakia
169 H7 Trendelburg Ger.
261 E4 Trenel Arg.
97 F8 Trêng Cambodia
95 I9 Trenggalek Jawa Indon.
Trengganu state Malaysia see Terengganu
261 F4 Trenque Lauquén Arg.
163 C7 Trensacq France
170 H1 Trent Ger.
Trent Italy see Trento
149 P6 Trent r. Dorset, England U.K.
Trent r. England U.K. see Piddle
179 I7 Trenta Slovenia
163 F7 Trentels France
191 K3 Trentino-Alto Adige admin. reg. Italy
191 K3 Trento Italy
191 K3 Trento prov. Italy
193 M6 Trentola-Ducenta Italy
224 E4 Trenton Ont. Can.
231 F11 Trenton FL U.S.A.
231 E8 Trenton GA U.S.A.
236 I5 Trenton MO U.S.A.
231 I8 Trenton NC U.S.A.
236 E5 Trenton NE U.S.A.
234 F4 Trenton NJ U.S.A.
237 K8 Trenton TN U.S.A.
156 B6 Tréon France
150 E4 Treorchy Rhondda Cynon Taff, Wales U.K.
84 C1 Trepang Bay N.T. Austr.
225 K4 Trepassey Nfld and Lab. Can.
137 L5 Trepivka Ukr.
171 K6 Treppeln Ger.
160 G5 Trept France
195 O3 Trepuzzi Italy
192 H1 Trequanda Italy
190 F3 Tresa r. Italy
261 F4 Tres Algarrobas Arg.
190 H7 Tresana Italy
261 I3 Tres Arboles Uru.
261 G6 Tres Arroyos Arg.
256 B6 Três Bicos Brazil
261 H3 Tres Bocas Arg.
261 I3 Tres Bocas Uru.
251 F6 Três Casas Brazil
259 D8 Tres Cerros Arg.
234 D3 Tresckow PA U.S.A.
161 H8 Trescléoux France
150 □ Tresco i. England U.K.
257 E4 Três Corações Brazil
190 H4 Trescore Balneario Italy
258 D1 Tres Cruces Arg.
258 C3 Tres Cruces Chile
190 I3 Tresenda Italy
250 C4 Tres Esquinas Col.
261 I4 Tres Esquinas Uru.
Tres Forcas, Cabo c. Morocco see Trois Fourches, Cap des
146 D10 Treshnish Isles Scotland U.K.
191 L6 Tresigallo Italy
190 J3 Tre Signori, Corno dei mt. Italy
256 B4 Três Irmãos, Represa resr Brazil
258 E2 Tres Isletas Arg.
196 J8 Treska r. Macedonia
138 K4 Treski Estonia
256 B4 Três Lagoas Brazil
259 C8 Tres Lagos Arg.
261 F5 Tres Lomas Arg.
183 L2 Tres Mares, Pico mt. Spain
257 E3 Três Marias Brazil
257 E3 Três Marias, Represa resr Brazil
251 E2 Tres Matas Venez.
259 B7 Tres Montes, Península pen. Chile
192 B7 Tresnuraghes Sardegna Italy
183 N3 Trespaderne Spain
245 H9 Tres Palos Guerrero Mex.
245 I1 Tres Palos Tamaulipas Mex.
245 H9 Tres Palos, Laguna lag. Mex.
239 K12 Tres Picachos, Sierra mts Mex.
261 F6 Tres Picos Arg.
259 C6 Tres Picos mt. Arg.
243 M10 Tres Picos Mex.
261 G6 Tres Picos, Cerro mt. Arg.
245 N9 Tres Picos, Cerro mt. Mex.
239 L8 Tres Piedras NM U.S.A.
240 K5 Tres Pinos CA U.S.A.
257 E4 Três Pontas Brazil
256 C6 Tres Pontões, Pico mt. Brazil
260 C3 Tres Porteñas Arg.
258 C2 Tres Puentes Chile
259 D7 Tres Puntas, Cabo c. Arg.
256 D3 Três Ranchos Brazil
257 F5 Três Rios Brazil
146 I9 Tressait Perth and Kinross, Scotland U.K.
261 H4 Tres Sargentos Arg.
160 H5 Tresserve France
176 E2 Třešť Czech Rep.
193 N4 Treste r. Italy
139 Q4 Trestino Rus. Fed.
139 S4 Trestna Rus. Fed.
250 D6 Três Unidos Brazil
245 K7 Tres Valles Mex.
245 L7 Tres Zapotes tourist site Mex.

150 F4 **Tretower** *Powys, Wales* U.K.
161 H10 **Trets** France
141 K6 **Tretten** Norway
173 J4 **Treuchtlingen** Ger.
171 F9 **Treuen** Ger.
171 G6 **Treuenbrietzen** Ger.
142 E2 **Treungen** Norway
158 F5 **Trévé** France
185 M7 **Trevélez** Spain
185 M7 **Trevélez** *r.* Spain
259 C6 **Trevelín** Arg.
157 J6 **Tréveray** France
161 C8 **Trèves** France
Treves Ger. *see* **Trier**
193 J2 **Trevi** Italy
183 N3 **Treviana** Spain
159 J3 **Trévières** France
190 H4 **Treviglio** Italy
192 I3 **Trevignano Romano** Italy
160 J2 **Trévillers** France
183 O3 **Treviño** Spain
191 M4 **Treviso** Italy
191 M4 **Treviso** *airport* Italy
191 M4 **Treviso** *prov.* Italy
182 F6 **Trevões** Port.
Trevor Point *pt Inner Islands* Seychelles *see* **Grande Barbe, Pointe**
234 B3 **Trevorton** *PA* U.S.A.
234 F4 **Trevose** *PA* U.S.A.
150 B6 **Trevose Head** *England* U.K.
160 F5 **Trévoux** France
234 D3 **Trexlertown** *PA* U.S.A.
261 G2 **Trezanos Pinto** Arg.
160 D4 **Trézelles** France
197 K8 **Trgovište** Serbia
176 D3 **Trhové Sviny** Czech Rep.
177 K3 **Trhovište** Slovakia
83 K10 **Triabunna** *Tas.* Austr.
182 F3 **Triacastela** Spain
234 A6 **Triadelphia Reservoir** *MD* U.S.A.
162 B3 **Triaize** France
84 F2 **Trial Bay** *N.T.* Austr.
129 F4 **T'rialet'i** Georgia
129 E4 **T'rialet'is K'edi** *hills* Georgia
97 H9 **Tri An, Hô** *resr* Vietnam
Triánda *Rodos* Greece *see* **Trianta**
232 H10 **Triangle** *VA* U.S.A.
213 F4 **Triangle** Zimbabwe
199 H6 **Tria Nisia** *i.* Greece
199 J6 **Trianta** *Rodos* Greece
123 N5 **Tribal Areas** *admin. div.* Pak.
191 R5 **Tribalj** Croatia
177 H3 **Tribeč** *mts* Slovakia
158 I3 **Tribehou** France
172 E5 **Triberg im Schwarzwald** Ger.
100 M1 **Tri Brata, Gora** *hill Sakhalin* Rus. Fed.
170 G2 **Tribsees** Ger.
85 J4 **Tribulation, Cape** *Qld* Austr.
236 E6 **Tribune** *KS* U.S.A.
260 B5 **Tricao Malal** Arg.
193 Q6 **Tricarico** Italy
195 O4 **Tricase** Italy
191 O3 **Tricesimo** Italy
191 M3 **Trichiana** Italy
Trichinopoly *Tamil Nadu* India *see* **Tiruchchirappalli**
198 C4 **Trichonida, Limni** *l.* Greece
114 E7 **Trichur** *Kerala* India
156 E4 **Tricot** France
83 J5 **Trida** *N.S.W.* Austr.
Tridentum Italy *see* **Trento**
171 F10 **Triebel** *r.* Ger.
179 J4 **Trieben** Austria
171 F9 **Triebes** Ger.
156 C5 **Trie-Château** France
192 D7 **Triei** *Sardegna* Italy
172 E7 **Triengen** Switz.
172 B2 **Trier** Ger.
172 B2 **Trierweiler** Ger.
191 P4 **Trieste** Italy
191 P4 **Trieste** *prov.* Italy
Trieste, Golfo di *g.* Europe *see* **Trieste, Gulf of**
188 D3 **Trieste, Gulf of** Europe
191 O4 **Trieste-Ronchi dei Legionari** *airport* Italy
163 E9 **Trie-sur-Baïse** France
157 K5 **Trieux** France
158 E4 **Trieux** *r.* France
173 O5 **Triftern** Ger.
184 D4 **Trigaches** Port.
161 I9 **Trigance** France
195 L1 **Triggiano** Italy
179 I7 **Triglav** *mt.* Slovenia
188 D2 **Triglavski narodni park** *nat. park* Slovenia
170 F4 **Triglitz** Ger.
158 G7 **Trignac** France
193 N3 **Trigno** *r.* Italy
216 □1c **Trigo, Monte** *hill São Jorge* Azores
156 E8 **Triguères** France
184 F6 **Trigueros** Spain
183 K5 **Trigueros del Valle** Spain
198 C3 **Trikala** Greece
198 D3 **Trikeriou, Diavlos** *sea chan.* Greece
Tríkkala Greece *see* **Trikala**
Trikomo Cyprus *see* **Trikomon**
128 B3 **Trikomon** Cyprus
91 I7 **Trikora, Puncak** *mt. Papua* Indon.
198 D4 **Trikorfo** *mt.* Greece
188 F4 **Trilj** Croatia
261 F4 **Trill** Arg.
147 H4 **Trillick** *Northern Ireland* U.K.
183 O7 **Trillo** Spain
198 D5 **Trilofo** Greece
116 F3 **Triloknath** *Hima. Prad.* India
156 E6 **Trilport** France
147 I5 **Trim** Ireland
149 O4 **Trimdon** *Durham, England* U.K.
151 O4 **Trimley St Mary** *Suffolk, England* U.K.
190 H2 **Trimmis** Switz.
86 C6 **Trimouille Island** *W.A.* Austr.
150 D4 **Trimsaran** *Carmarthenshire, Wales* U.K.
242 D2 **Trincheras** Mex.
114 G8 **Trincomalee** Sri Lanka
256 C2 **Trindade** Brazil
184 D5 **Trindade** *Beja* Port.
182 F6 **Trindade** *Bragança* Port.
264 H7 **Trindade, Ilha da** *i.* S. Atlantic Ocean
177 H2 **Třinec** Czech Rep.
151 K4 **Tring** *Hertfordshire, England* U.K.
198 C3 **Tringia** *mt.* Greece
252 D3 **Trinidad** Bol.
246 D3 **Trinidad** Cuba
245 L8 **Trinidad** *r.* Mex.
247 □7 **Trinidad** *i.* Trin. and Tob.
261 I3 **Trinidad** Uru.
239 L8 **Trinidad** *CO* U.S.A.
259 B8 **Trinidad, Golfo** *b.* Chile
261 G6 **Trinidad, Isla** *i.* Arg.
247 M8 **Trinidad and Tobago** *country* West Indies
194 D8 **Trinità, Lago della** *l. Sicilia* Italy
192 B6 **Trinità d'Agultu** *Sardegna* Italy
193 Q5 **Trinitapoli** Italy
237 H10 **Trinity** *TX* U.S.A.
238 C6 **Trinity** *r. CA* U.S.A.
237 H11 **Trinity** *r. TX* U.S.A.
237 G9 **Trinity, West Fork** *r. OK* U.S.A.
85 J4 **Trinity Bay** *Qld* Austr.
225 K4 **Trinity Bay** *Nfld and Lab.* Can.
247 □7 **Trinity Hills** Trin. and Tob.
220 C4 **Trinity Islands** *AK* U.S.A.
240 M1 **Trinity Range** *mts NV* U.S.A.
115 M8 **Trinkat Island** *Andaman & Nicobar Is* India
124 C6 **Trinkitat** Sudan
190 E5 **Trino** Italy
178 D5 **Trins** Austria
182 F7 **Trinta** Port.
232 C8 **Trinway** *OH* U.S.A.
170 G2 **Trinwillershagen** Ger.
217 □1b **Triolet** Mauritius
183 K3 **Triollo** Spain
193 P4 **Triolo** *r.* Italy
195 L4 **Trionto** *r.* Italy
195 L4 **Trionto, Capo** *c.* Italy
190 D8 **Triora** Italy
162 I5 **Triouzoune, Lac de la** *l.* France
94 B3 **Tripa** *r.* Indon.
170 D4 **Tripkau** Ger.
198 D5 **Tripoli** Greece
Tripoli Lebanon *see* **Trâblous**
Tripoli Libya *see* **Ţarābulus**
Trípolis Greece *see* **Tripoli**
Tripolis Lebanon *see* **Trâblous**
202 B2 **Tripolitania** *reg.* Libya
198 C5 **Tripotama** Greece
172 D3 **Trippstadt** Ger.
171 E9 **Triptis** Ger.
114 E8 **Tripunittura** *Kerala* India
117 M8 **Tripura** *state* India
178 C5 **Trisanna** *r.* Austria
168 G2 **Trischen** *i.* Ger.
178 G6 **Tristach** Austria
216 □2c **Tristan da Cunha** *i.* S. Atlantic Ocean
206 B4 **Tristao, Îles** *is* Guinea
184 □ **Tristão, Ponta do** *pt* Madeira
178 H6 **Tristenspitze** *mt.* Austria
116 G4 **Trisul** *mt. Uttaranchal* India
225 K3 **Triton** *Nfld and Lab.* Can.
90 D3 **Triton Island** *atoll* Paracel Is
168 J3 **Trittau** Ger.
172 B2 **Trittenheim** Ger.
254 F3 **Triunfo** *Pernambuco* Brazil
252 D2 **Triunfo** *Rondônia* Brazil
242 □P11 **Triunfo** Hond.
114 E8 **Trivandrum** *Kerala* India
193 N4 **Trivento** Italy
190 E4 **Trivero** Italy
190 E6 **Triversa** *r.* Italy
193 P6 **Trivigno** Italy
161 B6 **Trizac** France
198 E5 **Trizina** Greece
177 G2 **Trnava** Czech Rep.
177 G3 **Trnava** Slovakia
177 H3 **Trnavá Hora** Slovakia
177 G3 **Trnavský kraj** *admin. reg.* Slovakia
179 N7 **Trnovec Bartolovečki** Croatia
179 I8 **Trnovski gozd** *mts* Slovenia
159 K3 **Troarn** France
171 H7 **Tröbitz** Ger.
91 L8 **Trobriand Islands** P.N.G.
172 G5 **Trochtelfingen** Ger.
222 H5 **Trochu** *Alta* Can.
141 N6 **Trödje** Sweden
182 C6 **Trofa** Port.
179 L5 **Trofaiach** Austria
140 L4 **Trofors** Norway
188 F4 **Trogir** Croatia
178 H6 **Trogkofel** *mt.* Austria/Italy
188 F4 **Troglav** *mt.* Croatia
142 H2 **Trøgstad** Norway
193 O5 **Troia** Italy
184 B4 **Tróia** Port.
194 H8 **Troina** *Sicilia* Italy
194 H8 **Troina** *r. Sicilia* Italy
169 D9 **Troisdorf** Ger.
157 N6 **Troisfontaines** France
204 E2 **Trois Fourches, Cap des** *c.* Morocco
225 G3 **Trois-Pistoles** *Que.* Can.
165 I8 **Trois-Ponts** Belgium
225 F4 **Trois-Rivières** *Que.* Can.
247 □2 **Trois-Rivières** Guadeloupe
163 G10 **Trois Seigneurs, Pic des** *mt.* France
156 D5 **Troissereux** France
160 C3 **Trois-Vèvres** France
165 J8 **Troisvierges** Lux.
130 H3 **Troitsa** *Khanty-Mansiyskiy Avtonomnyy Okrug* Rus. Fed.
139 X7 **Troitsa** *Ryazanskaya Oblast'* Rus. Fed.
120 I1 **Troitsk** *Chelyabinskaya Oblast'* Rus. Fed.
139 U6 **Troitsk** *Moskovskaya Oblast'* Rus. Fed.
137 Q2 **Troitskiy** *Belgorodskaya Oblast'* Rus. Fed.
Troitskiy *Moskovskaya Oblast'* Rus. Fed. *see* **Troitsk**
134 L3 **Troitsko-Pechorsk** Rus. Fed.
121 U1 **Troitskoye** *Altayskiy Kray* Rus. Fed.
100 J4 **Troitskoye** *Khabarovskiy Kray* Rus. Fed.
120 E1 **Troitskoye** *Orenburgskaya Oblast'* Rus. Fed.
120 G1 **Troitskoye** *Respublika Bashkortostan* Rus. Fed.
135 I7 **Troitskoye** *Respublika Kalmykiya-Khalm'g-Tangch* Rus. Fed.
246 □ **Troja** Jamaica
174 G5 **Troja** *r.* Pol.
179 K7 **Trojane** Slovenia
143 O7 **Trójmiejski Park Krajobrazowy** Pol.
262 X2 **Troll** *research stn* Antarctica
202 B6 **Trolla** *well* Chad
142 I3 **Trollhättan** Sweden
140 J5 **Trollheimen** *park* Norway
251 G5 **Trombetas** *r.* Brazil
217 □1 **Tromelin, Île** *i.* Indian Ocean
Tromelin Island Micronesia *see* **Fais**
190 F5 **Tromello** Italy
260 B5 **Tromen, Volcán** *vol.* Arg.
146 H8 **Tromie** *r. Scotland* U.K.
170 H1 **Tromper Wiek** *b.* Ger.
215 J6 **Trompsburg** S. Africa
140 O2 **Troms** *county* Norway
140 O2 **Tromsø** Norway
240 O6 **Trona** *CA* U.S.A.
259 C6 **Tronador, Monte** *mt.* Arg.
160 B3 **Tronçais, Forêt de** *for.* France
182 F5 **Tronco** Port.
244 E3 **Troncoso** Mex.
140 K5 **Trondheim** Norway
140 J5 **Trondheimsfjorden** *sea chan.* Norway
140 J5 **Trondheimsleia** *sea chan.* Norway
150 E6 **Troney** *r. England* U.K.
Trongsa Bhutan *see* **Tongsa**
117 M6 **Trongsa Chhu** *r.* Bhutan
193 L2 **Tronto** *r.* Italy
157 J6 **Tronville-en-Barrois** France
190 E5 **Tronzano Vercellese** Italy
159 M6 **Troo** France
128 A4 **Troödos** Cyprus
128 A4 **Troödos, Mount** Cyprus
128 A4 **Troödos Mountains** Cyprus
146 G11 **Troon** *South Ayrshire, Scotland* U.K.
198 C5 **Tropaia** Greece
139 S6 **Troparevo** Rus. Fed.
251 G6 **Tropas** *r.* Brazil
195 J6 **Tropea** Italy
254 D5 **Tropeiros, Serra dos** *hills* Brazil
241 T4 **Tropic** *UT* U.S.A.
147 G4 **Trory** *Northern Ireland* U.K.
134 K2 **Trosh** Rus. Fed.
139 S9 **Trosna** Rus. Fed.
171 G7 **Trossin** Ger.
172 F5 **Trossingen** Ger.
139 P9 **Trostan'** Rus. Fed.
147 J2 **Trostan** *hill Northern Ireland* U.K.
173 L1 **Tröstau** Ger.
173 N5 **Trostberg** Ger.
137 N3 **Trostyanets'** *Sums'ka Oblast'* Ukr.
136 I5 **Trostyanets'** *Vinnyts'ka Oblast'* Ukr.
136 E3 **Trostyanets'** *Volyns'ka Oblast'* Ukr.
146 D7 **Trotternish** *hills Scotland* U.K.
197 O4 **Trotuş** *r.* Romania
163 E10 **Troumouse, Cirque de** *corrie* France/Spain
146 L7 **Troup Head** *Scotland* U.K.
233 □S1 **Trousers Lake** *N.B.* Can.
222 E3 **Trout** *r. B.C.* Can.
222 G2 **Trout** *r. N.W.T.* Can.
149 L5 **Troutbeck** *Cumbria, England* U.K.
227 O4 **Trout Creek** *Ont.* Can.
226 E3 **Trout Creek** *MI* U.S.A.
232 D12 **Trout Dale** *VA* U.S.A.
222 H3 **Trout Lake** *Alta* Can.
222 F2 **Trout Lake** *N.W.T.* Can.
222 F2 **Trout Lake** *l. N.W.T.* Can.
223 M5 **Trout Lake** *l. Ont.* Can.
226 I3 **Trout Lake** *MI* U.S.A.
226 E3 **Trout Lake** *l. WI* U.S.A.
225 J3 **Trout River** *Nfld and Lab.* Can.
227 Q8 **Trout Run** *PA* U.S.A.
232 F11 **Troutville** *VA* U.S.A.
159 L3 **Trouville-sur-Mer** France
159 P7 **Trouy** France
182 D9 **Troviscal** Port.
150 H5 **Trowbridge** *Wiltshire, England* U.K.
83 J9 **Trowutta** *Tas.* Austr.
246 □ **Troy** Jamaica
Troy *tourist site* Turkey *see* **Truva**
231 E10 **Troy** *AL* U.S.A.
236 H6 **Troy** *KS* U.S.A.
227 K7 **Troy** *MI* U.S.A.
236 J6 **Troy** *MO* U.S.A.
238 G2 **Troy** *MT* U.S.A.
231 H8 **Troy** *NC* U.S.A.
233 M6 **Troy** *NH* U.S.A.
233 L6 **Troy** *NY* U.S.A.
232 A8 **Troy** *OH* U.S.A.
227 R8 **Troy** *PA* U.S.A.
197 M8 **Troyan** Bulg.
136 H3 **Troyaniv** Ukr.
136 J5 **Troyanka** Ukr.
139 V9 **Troyekurovo** *Lipetskaya Oblast'* Rus. Fed.
139 W8 **Troyekurovo** *Lipetskaya Oblast'* Rus. Fed.
139 U8 **Troyekurovo** *Tul'skaya Oblast'* Rus. Fed.
156 H7 **Troyes** France
137 R4 **Troyits'ke** *Luhans'ka Oblast'* Ukr.
136 J6 **Troyits'ke** *Odes'ka Oblast'* Ukr.
137 L6 **Troyits'ko-Safonove** Ukr.
240 P7 **Troy Lake** *CA* U.S.A.
157 J5 **Troyon** France
241 Q3 **Troy Peak** *NV* U.S.A.
176 G2 **Tršice** Czech Rep.
179 I8 **Trstelj** *hill* Slovenia
177 I2 **Trstená** Slovakia
196 J7 **Trstenik** Serbia
177 G3 **Trstice** Slovakia
176 G3 **Trstín** Slovakia
84 F1 **Truant Island** *N.T.* Austr.
139 Q9 **Trubchevsk** Rus. Fed.
139 W9 **Trubetchino** Rus. Fed.
182 I2 **Trubia** Spain
182 I2 **Trubia** *r.* Spain
137 K3 **Trubizh** *r.* Ukr.
161 C7 **Truc de la Garde** *mt.* France
Truc Giang Vietnam *see* **Bên Tre**
182 H4 **Truchas** Spain
157 O6 **Truchtersheim** France
Trucial Coast *country* Asia *see* **United Arab Emirates**
Trucial States *country* Asia *see* **United Arab Emirates**
240 L2 **Truckee** *CA* U.S.A.
139 Q4 **Trud** Rus. Fed.
120 B5 **Trudfront** Rus. Fed.
Trudovoy Kazakh. *see* **Novoishimskiy**
Trudovoy Rus. Fed. *see* **Yusta**
100 H7 **Trudovoye** Rus. Fed.
139 U9 **Trudy** *r.* Rus. Fed.
84 C7 **Truer Range** *hills N.T.* Austr.
134 I2 **Trufanovo** Rus. Fed.
227 P2 **Truite, Lac à la** *l. Que.* Can.
184 G3 **Trujillanos** Spain
242 □Q10 **Trujillo** Hond.
252 A2 **Trujillo** Peru
184 H2 **Trujillo** Spain
250 D2 **Trujillo** Venez.
250 D2 **Trujillo** *state* Venez.
Trujillo, Monte *mt.* Dom. Rep. *see* **Duarte, Pico**
247 □1 **Trujillo Alto** Puerto Rico
Truk *is* Micronesia *see* **Chuuk**
172 D3 **Trulben** Ger.
150 F6 **Trull** *Somerset, England* U.K.
237 J8 **Trumann** *AR* U.S.A.
232 I6 **Trumansburg** *NY* U.S.A.
235 I2 **Trumbull** *CT* U.S.A.
241 S5 **Trumbull, Mount** *AZ* U.S.A.
94 B3 **Trumon** *Sumatera* Indon.
151 M3 **Trumpington** *Cambridgeshire, England* U.K.
197 K8 **Trŭn** Bulg.
159 L4 **Trun** France
190 F2 **Trun** Switz.
197 L8 **Trŭna** *mt.* Bulg.
83 K5 **Trundle** *N.S.W.* Austr.
96 H3 **Trung Khanh** Vietnam
97 H10 **Trưng Lơn, Hon** *i.* Vietnam
97 H10 **Trưng Nho, Hon** *i.* Vietnam
Truong Sa *is* S. China Sea *see* **Spratly Islands**
225 I4 **Truro** *N.S.* Can.
150 B7 **Truro** *Cornwall, England* U.K.
95 K2 **Trusan** *Sarawak* Malaysia
95 K2 **Trusan** *r.* Malaysia
197 P3 **Truşeşti** Romania
169 J9 **Trusetal** Ger.
196 H9 **Trush** Albania
137 L4 **Trushivtsi** Ukr.
136 C4 **Truskavets'** Ukr.
147 F4 **Truskmore** *hill* Ireland
95 L2 **Trus Madi, Gunung** *mt.* Malaysia
197 M7 **Trŭstenik** Bulg.
222 F3 **Trutch** *B.C.* Can.
222 F3 **Trutch Creek** *r. B.C.* Can.
239 K10 **Truth or Consequences** *NM* U.S.A.
176 E1 **Trutnov** Czech Rep.
199 H3 **Truva** *tourist site* Turkey
161 B7 **Truyère** *r.* France
161 B7 **Truyère, Gorges de la** France
139 S3 **Truzhenik** Rus. Fed.
197 N8 **Tryavna** Bulg.
198 C4 **Tryfos** Greece
168 K1 **Tryggelev** Denmark
198 C3 **Trygona** Greece
175 K5 **Tryńcza** Pol.
236 E5 **Tryon** *NE* U.S.A.
80 J3 **Tryphena Harbour** *North I.* N.Z.
198 F7 **Trypiti, Akrotirio** *pt Kriti* Greece
198 F3 **Trypiti, Akrotirio** *pt* Greece
141 L6 **Trysil** Norway
141 L6 **Trysilelva** *r.* Norway
141 L6 **Trysilfjellet** *mt.* Norway
138 F5 **Tryškiai** Lith.
188 E3 **Tržac** Bos.-Herz.
175 J3 **Trzcianka** *Mazowieckie* Pol.
174 E2 **Trzcianka** *Wielkopolskie* Pol.
175 K2 **Trzcianne** Pol.
174 D3 **Trzciel** Pol.
174 G4 **Trzcinica** Pol.
174 D1 **Trzebiatów** Pol.
174 C4 **Trzebiel** Pol.
174 F1 **Trzebielino** Pol.
175 K4 **Trzebieszów** Pol.
174 C2 **Trzebież** Pol.
175 H5 **Trzebinia** Pol.
174 F4 **Trzebnica** Pol.
175 K5 **Trzebośnica** *r.* Pol.
174 F3 **Trzemeszno** Pol.
174 D3 **Trzemeszyno Lubuskie** Pol.
175 L3 **Trześcianka** Pol.
175 J6 **Trześniów** Pol.
175 J5 **Trześniówka** *r.* Pol.
175 L5 **Trzeszczany Pierwsze** Pol.
188 E2 **Tržič** Slovenia
179 K7 **Trzin** Slovenia
174 C3 **Trzrcińsko-Zdrój** Pol.
175 H5 **Trzyciąż** Pol.
175 K5 **Trzydnik Duży** Pol.
106 A2 **Tsagaannuur** *Bayan-Ölgiy* Mongolia
107 P3 **Tsagaannuur** *Dornod* Mongolia
106 D3 **Tsagaan Nuur** *salt l.* Mongolia
106 E3 **Tsagaan-Olom** Mongolia
107 M2 **Tsagaan Ovoo** Mongolia
106 G4 **Tsagaan-Ovoo** Mongolia
Tsagaan-Uul Mongolia *see* **Sharga**
135 I7 **Tsagan Aman** Rus. Fed.
135 I7 **Tsagan-Nur** Rus. Fed.
129 D3 **Ts'ageri** Georgia
Tsaidam Basin China *see* **Qaidam Pendi**
129 I4 **Tsakhur** Rus. Fed.
129 B2 **Tsakhvoa, Gora** *mt.* Rus. Fed.
140 P2 **Tsåktso** *mt.* Sweden
129 D3 **Tsalenjikha** Georgia
208 B5 **Tsama I** Congo
217 □3a **Tsangadjou** *Njazidja* Comoros
140 M3 **Tsangatjåkkå** *mt.* Sweden
212 D4 **Tsao** Botswana
213 □J3 **Tsaramandroso** Madag.
213 □J3 **Tsaratanana** Madag.
213 □K2 **Tsaratanana, Massif du** *mts* Madag.
197 P8 **Tsarevo** Bulg.
139 R6 **Tsarevo-Zaymishche** Rus. Fed.
Tsaribrod Serbia *see* **Dimitrovgrad**
197 M8 **Tsarimir** Bulg.
Tsaritsyn Rus. Fed. *see* **Volgograd**
137 N5 **Tsarychanka** Ukr.
135 I6 **Tsatsa** Rus. Fed.
215 M6 **Tsatsana** *mt.* S. Africa
109 □J7 **Tsat Tsze Mui** *pt H.K.* China
212 B5 **Tsaukaib** Namibia
211 C5 **Tsavo** Kenya
211 C5 **Tsavo East National Park** Kenya
211 C5 **Tsavo West National Park** Kenya
215 L7 **Tsazo** S. Africa
178 A5 **Tschagguns** Austria
171 K7 **Tschernitz** Ger.
212 E3 **Tsebanana** Botswana
129 C2 **Tsebelda** Georgia
106 D4 **Tseel** Mongolia
Tsefat Israel *see* **Ẕefat**
135 H7 **Tselina** Rus. Fed.
121 U1 **Tselinnoye** Rus. Fed.
120 I2 **Tselinnyy** Rus. Fed.
Tselinograd Kazakh. *see* **Astana**
Tselinogradskaya Oblast' *admin. div.* Kazakh. *see* **Akmolinskaya Oblast'**
Tsementnyy Rus. Fed. *see* **Fokino**
106 G2 **Tsengel** Mongolia
134 I2 **Tsenogora** Rus. Fed.
197 M8 **Tsentralen Balkan** *nat. park* Bulg.
139 P5 **Tsentral'noolesnoy Zapovednik** *nature res.* Rus. Fed.
134 J4 **Tsentral'nyy** *Kirovskaya Oblast'* Rus. Fed.
Tsentral'nyy *Moskovskaya Oblast'* Rus. Fed. *see* **Radovitskiy**
139 W8 **Tsentral'nyy** *Ryazanskaya Oblast'* Rus. Fed.
139 N6 **Tserkovishche** Rus. Fed.
197 L7 **Tserovo** Bulg.
212 C5 **Tses** Namibia
106 C3 **Tsetsegnuur** Mongolia
212 D4 **Tsetseng** Botswana
106 G3 **Tsetserleg** *Arhangay* Mongolia
Tsetserleg *Hövsgöl* Mongolia *see* **Halban**
109 □J7 **Tseung Kwan O** *H.K.* China
207 F5 **Tsévié** Togo
208 F4 **Tsha** Dem. Rep. Congo
212 D5 **Tshabong** Botswana
Tshad *country* Africa *see* **Chad**
209 D7 **Tshala** Dem. Rep. Congo
135 G7 **Tshchikskoye Vodokhranilishche** *resr* Rus. Fed.
209 B6 **Tshela** Dem. Rep. Congo
209 C6 **Tshene** Dem. Rep. Congo
213 E4 **Tshesebe** Botswana
209 D6 **Tshibala** Dem. Rep. Congo
209 D6 **Tshibuka** Dem. Rep. Congo
209 D7 **Tshibwika** Dem. Rep. Congo
214 I1 **Tshidilamolomo** Botswana
209 D6 **Tshikapa** Dem. Rep. Congo
209 D6 **Tshikapa** *r.* Dem. Rep. Congo
209 D6 **Tshilenge** Dem. Rep. Congo
209 F6 **Tshimbo** Dem. Rep. Congo
209 D6 **Tshimbulu** Dem. Rep. Congo
215 K2 **Tshing** S. Africa
213 F4 **Tshipise** S. Africa
209 D6 **Tshisenge** Dem. Rep. Congo
209 D7 **Tshitanzu** Dem. Rep. Congo
209 D6 **Tshitupa** Dem. Rep. Congo
209 D6 **Tshiumbe** *r.* Angola/Dem. Rep. Congo
209 E6 **Tshofa** Dem. Rep. Congo
213 F5 **Tshokwane** S. Africa
213 E3 **Tsholotsho** Zimbabwe
209 E6 **Tshongwe** Dem. Rep. Congo
212 D4 **Tshootsha** Botswana
208 D5 **Tshuapa** *r.* Dem. Rep. Congo
208 C5 **Tshumbiri** Dem. Rep. Congo
Tshwane S. Africa *see* **Pretoria**
213 □J3 **Tsiazonano** *mt.* Madag.
197 L7 **Tsibritsa** *r.* Bulg.
220 E3 **Tsiigehtchic** *N.W.T.* Can.
134 J2 **Tsil'ma** *r.* Rus. Fed.
138 J8 **Tsimkavichy** Belarus
135 H7 **Tsimlyansk** Rus. Fed.
135 H7 **Tsimlyanskoye Vodokhranilishche** *resr* Rus. Fed.
100 K3 **Tsimmermanovka** Rus. Fed.
Tsinan *Shandong* China *see* **Jinan**
214 H3 **Tsineng** S. Africa
Tsinghai *prov.* China *see* **Qinghai**
217 □3b **Tsingoni** Mayotte
109 □I7 **Tsing Shan** *hill H.K.* China
109 □I7 **Tsing Shan Wan** *b. H.K.* China
109 □J7 **Tsing Shui Wan** *b. H.K.* China
Tsingtao *Shandong* China *see* **Qingdao**
213 □J3 **Tsingy de Bemaraha, Réserve** *nature res.* Madag.
109 □J7 **Tsing Yi** *i. H.K.* China
217 □3a **Tsinimouapanga** *Njazidja* Comoros
Tsining *Nei Mongol* China *see* **Jining**
213 □J3 **Tsinjomay** *mt.* Madag.
212 C3 **Tsintsabis** Namibia
213 □J5 **Tsiombe** Madag.
129 E4 **Tsip'a** Georgia
213 □J3 **Tsiroanomandidy** Madag.
129 C4 **Tsiskara Nakrdzali** *nature res.* Georgia
Tsiteli Tskaro Georgia *see* **Dedop'listsqaro**
213 □J4 **Tsitondroina** Madag.
Tsitsihar *Heilong.* China *see* **Qiqihar**
214 H10 **Tsitsikamma Forest and Coastal National Park** S. Africa
222 E4 **Tsitsutl Peak** *B.C.* Can.
129 C3 **Ts'ivi** *r.* Georgia
129 G4 **Ts'ivi, Mt'a** Georgia
134 I5 **Tsivil'sk** Rus. Fed.
Tskhakaia Georgia *see* **Senaki**
Tskhaltubo Georgia *see* **Tsqaltubo**
129 E3 **Ts'khinvali** Georgia
129 F4 **Ts'khneti** Georgia
138 K9 **Tsna** *r.* Belarus
135 H5 **Tsna** *r.* Rus. Fed.
139 R4 **Tsna** *r.* Rus. Fed.
139 W6 **Tsna** *r.* Rus. Fed.
129 G4 **Tsnori** Georgia
212 D3 **Tsodilo Hills** Botswana
116 G3 **Tsokar Chumo** *l.* Jammu and Kashmir
215 M7 **Tsolo** S. Africa
215 L8 **Tsomo** S. Africa
215 L8 **Tsomo** *r.* S. Africa
139 T9 **Tson** *r.* Rus. Fed.
Tsona *Xizang* China *see* **Cona**
199 G2 **Tsopan** *hill* Greece
198 C2 **Tsotili** Greece
129 G5 **Tsovinar** Armenia
129 D3 **Tsqaltubo** Georgia
104 E6 **Tsu** Japan
103 P9 **Tsubame** Japan
104 E2 **Tsubata** Japan
102 V3 **Tsubetsu** Japan
105 L3 **Tsuchiura** Japan
104 D6 **Tsuchiyama** Japan
129 I3 **Tsudakhar** Rus. Fed.
109 □J7 **Tsuen Wan** *H.K.* China
105 K3 **Tsuga** Japan
102 R5 **Tsugarū-kaikyō** *str.* Japan
Tsugaru Strait Japan *see* **Tsugarū-kaikyō**
104 C6 **Tsuge** Japan
104 G5 **Tsugu** Japan
104 F4 **Tsukechi** Japan
102 □1 **Tsuken-jima** *i. Okinawa* Japan
104 D6 **Tsukigase** Japan
102 S3 **Tsukigata** Japan
105 I2 **Tsukiyono** Japan
105 L3 **Tsukuba** Japan
104 F6 **Tsukude** Japan
105 J4 **Tsukui** Japan
103 I13 **Tsukumi** Japan
106 I3 **Tsul-Ulaan** Mongolia
105 I2 **Tsumagoi** Japan
136 E3 **Tsuman'** Ukr.
212 C3 **Tsumeb** Namibia
105 I6 **Tsumeki-zaki** *pt* Japan
212 C4 **Tsumis Park** Namibia
212 D3 **Tsumkwe** Namibia
104 A7 **Tsuna** Japan
105 I1 **Tsunan** Japan
104 C4 **Tsunega-misaki** *pt* Japan
103 H12 **Tsuno-shima** *i.* Japan
129 H3 **Tsurib** Rus. Fed.
105 I4 **Tsuru** Japan
104 D4 **Tsuruga** Japan
104 C4 **Tsuruga-wan** *b.* Japan
104 E3 **Tsurugi** Japan
104 G2 **Tsurugi-dake** *mt.* Japan
103 L13 **Tsurugi-san** *mt.* Japan
Tsurukhaytuy Rus. Fed. *see* **Priargunsk**
103 J14 **Tsurumi-zaki** *pt* Japan
102 Q8 **Tsuruoka** Japan
104 E5 **Tsushima** Japan
103 G12 **Tsushima** *is* Japan
Tsushima-kaikyō *str.* Japan/S. Korea *see* **Korea Strait**
103 I12 **Tsuwano** Japan
103 L11 **Tsuyama** Japan
197 L9 **Tsvetino** Bulg.
137 K4 **Tsvitkove** Ukr.
137 L5 **Tsvitne** Ukr.
212 D4 **Tswaane** Botswana
215 J4 **Tswaraganang** S. Africa
215 J3 **Tswelelang** S. Africa
136 I4 **Tsybuliv** Ukr.
138 I9 **Tsyelyakhany** Belarus
137 K1 **Tsyerakhowka** Belarus
Tsygira Moldova *see* **Ţighira**
222 E5 **Ts'yl-os Provincial Park** *B.C.* Can.
139 O7 **Tsyomny Lyes** Belarus
140 V2 **Tsyp-Navolok** Rus. Fed.
175 N4 **Tsyr** *r.* Ukr.
137 L7 **Tsyurupyns'k** Ukr.
Tthedzeh Koe *N.W.T.* Can. *see* **Wrigley**
Tthenaagoo *N.W.T.* Can. *see* **Nahanni Butte**
209 C5 **Tua** Dem. Rep. Congo
182 F6 **Tua** *r.* Port.
94 F7 **Tua, Tanjung** *pt* Indon.
80 I4 **Tuakau** *North I.* N.Z.
91 H8 **Tual** *Maluku* Indon.
129 H6 **Tū 'Ālī-ye Soflá** Iran
147 E5 **Tuam** Ireland
81 H8 **Tuamarina** *South I.* N.Z.
147 E7 **Tuamgraney** Ireland
79 □9 **Tuamotu, Archipel des** *is* Fr. Polynesia
Tuamotu Islands Fr. Polynesia *see* **Tuamotu, Archipel des**
96 F4 **Tuân Giao** Vietnam
94 B3 **Tuangku** *i.* Indon.
81 □4 **Tuapa** Niue
81 D13 **Tuapeka Mouth** *South I.* N.Z.
129 A1 **Tuapse** Rus. Fed.
95 L1 **Tuaran** *Sabah* Malaysia
94 □ **Tuas** Sing.
78 □2 **Tuasivi** Samoa
81 B13 **Tuatapere** *South I.* N.Z.
146 D9 **Tuath, Loch** *sea chan. Scotland* U.K.
146 D6 **Tuath, Loch a'** *b. Scotland* U.K.
241 U5 **Tuba City** *AZ* U.S.A.
93 F4 **Tubalai** *i. Maluku* Indon.
95 J8 **Tuban** *Jawa* Indon.
255 C9 **Tubarão** Brazil
126 I8 **Tubarjal** Saudi Arabia
128 D6 **Ţūbās** West Bank
95 J3 **Tubau** *Sarawak* Malaysia
92 B7 **Tubbataha Reefs** Phil.
147 E4 **Tubbercurry** Ireland
164 K4 **Tubbergen** Neth.
148 B8 **Tubbrid** Ireland
209 D6 **Tubeya** Dem. Rep. Congo
92 C8 **Tubigan** *i.* Phil.
183 M3 **Tubilla del Agua** Spain
172 G4 **Tübingen** Ger.
172 H5 **Tübingen** *admin. reg.* Ger.
120 H1 **Tubinskiy** Rus. Fed.
165 F7 **Tubize** Belgium
206 C5 **Tubmanburg** Liberia
207 G4 **Tubo** *r.* Nigeria
92 D7 **Tubod** *Mindanao* Phil.
77 I3 **Tubou** Fiji
190 I2 **Tubre** Italy
86 C6 **Tubridgi Point** *W.A.* Austr.
202 D1 **Tubruq** Libya
95 L3 **Tubu** *r.* Indon.
79 □9 **Tubuai** *i. Îs Australes* Fr. Polynesia
Tubuai Islands Fr. Polynesia *see* **Australes, Îles**
242 D2 **Tubutama** Mex.
247 I8 **Tucacas** Venez.
251 F5 **Tucandera** Brazil
238 E3 **Tucannon** *r. WA* U.S.A.
254 F4 **Tucano** Brazil
260 B5 **Tucapel** Chile
253 F4 **Tucavaca** Bol.
253 F4 **Tucavaca** *r.* Bol.
163 J10 **Tuchan** France
170 F4 **Tüchen** Ger.
171 F6 **Tuchheim** Ger.
222 D2 **Tuchitua** *Y.T.* Can.
139 T6 **Tuchkovo** Rus. Fed.
171 I10 **Tuchlovice** Czech Rep.
222 F3 **Tuchodi** *r. B.C.* Can.
174 F2 **Tuchola** Pol.
174 G2 **Tucholskie, Bory** *for.* Pol.
167 H2 **Tucholski Park Krajobrazowy** Pol.
174 F1 **Tuchomie** Pol.
175 J6 **Tuchów** Pol.
175 K4 **Tuchowicz** Pol.
136 F3 **Tuchyn** Ukr.
234 F6 **Tuckahoe** *NJ* U.S.A.
235 K3 **Tuckahoe** *NY* U.S.A.
234 F6 **Tuckahoe** *r. NJ* U.S.A.
234 D7 **Tuckahoe Creek** *r. MD* U.S.A.
87 E9 **Tuckanarra** *W.A.* Austr.
263 L2 **Tucker Glacier** Antarctica
231 □1 **Tucker's Town** Bermuda
235 G5 **Tuckerton** *NJ* U.S.A.
234 D4 **Tuckerton** *PA* U.S.A.
Tucopia *i.* Solomon Is *see* **Tikopia**
157 K5 **Tucquegnieux** France
241 V9 **Tucson** *AZ* U.S.A.
241 U9 **Tucson Mountains** *AZ* U.S.A.
225 H1 **Tuctuc** *r. Que.* Can.
Tucumán Arg. *see* **San Miguel de Tucumán**
258 D2 **Tucumán** *prov.* Arg.
237 D8 **Tucumcari** *NM* U.S.A.
260 C2 **Tucunuco** Arg.
251 H6 **Tucuparé** Brazil
251 F2 **Tucupita** Venez.
250 C2 **Tucuracas** Col.
251 I5 **Tucuruí** Brazil
251 I6 **Tucuruí, Represa** *resr* Brazil
175 L4 **Tuczna** Pol.
174 E2 **Tuczno** Pol.
142 H6 **Tudeå** *r.* Denmark
183 Q4 **Tudela** Spain
183 K5 **Tudela de Duero** Spain
Tuder Italy *see* **Todi**
197 O3 **Tudora** Romania
197 P5 **Tudor Vladimirescu** Romania
139 Q5 **Tudovka** *r.* Rus. Fed.
138 J2 **Tudu** Estonia
138 K2 **Tudulinna** Estonia
150 C2 **Tudweiliog** *Gwynedd, Wales* U.K.
187 C8 **Tuejar** Spain
182 F5 **Tuela** *r.* Port.
109 □I7 **Tuen Mun** *H.K.* China
191 K3 **Tuenno** Italy
117 O6 **Tuensang** *Nagaland* India
251 I5 **Tueré** *r.* Brazil
182 I4 **Tuerto** *r.* Spain
139 X3 **Tufanovo** Rus. Fed.
125 I2 **Ţufayḩ** Saudi Arabia
159 M5 **Tuffé** France
91 K8 **Tufi** P.N.G.
267 J2 **Tufts Abyssal Plain** *sea feature* N. Pacific Ocean
Tuga *i.* Vanuatu *see* **Tégua**
215 P5 **Tugela** *r.* S. Africa
215 M4 **Tugela Falls** S. Africa
215 O4 **Tugela Ferry** S. Africa
Tūghyl Kazakh. *see* **Tugyl**
111 K11 **Tuglung** *Xizang* China
92 E6 **Tugnug Point** *Samar* Phil.
108 C5 **Tuguancun** *Yunnan* China
93 A3 **Tuguan Maputi** *i.* Indon.
92 F8 **Tugubun Point** *Mindanao* Phil.
92 C3 **Tuguegarao** *Luzon* Phil.
100 J2 **Tugur** Rus. Fed.
100 J2 **Tugurskiy Zaliv** *b.* Rus. Fed.
213 F4 **Tugwi** *r.* Zimbabwe
121 U4 **Tugyl** Kazakh.
107 P8 **Tuhai He** *r.* China
94 B4 **Tuhemberua** Indon.
96 D1 **Tuhtong** Myanmar
182 C4 **Tui** Spain
252 D3 **Tuichi** *r.* Bol.
192 B8 **Tuili** *Sardegna* Italy
117 N8 **Tuilianpui** *r.* Bangl./India
216 □3b **Tuineje** *Fuerteventura* Canary Is
214 E5 **Tuins** *watercourse* S. Africa
138 H4 **Tūja** Latvia
122 G8 **Tūjak** Iran
Tujiabu *Jiangxi* China *see* **Yongxiu**
94 F5 **Tujuh, Kepulauan** *is* Indon.
95 L3 **Tujung** *Kalimantan* Indon.
120 G1 **Tukan** Rus. Fed.
93 C6 **Tukangbesi, Kepulauan** *is* Indon.
224 E1 **Tukarak Island** *Nunavut* Can.
210 E2 **Tukayel** Eth.
138 I9 **Tukhavichy** Belarus
125 I4 **Ţukhmān, Banī** *reg.* Saudi Arabia
136 C5 **Tukhol'ka** Ukr.
123 P3 **Tŭkhtamish** Tajik.
80 K6 **Tukituki** *r. North I.* N.Z.
202 D1 **Tūkrah** Libya
220 E3 **Tuktoyaktuk** *N.W.T.* Can.
220 F3 **Tuktut Nogait National Park** *N.W.T.* Can.
138 G5 **Tukums** Latvia
95 I5 **Tukung, Bukit** *mt.* Indon.
100 E1 **Tukuringra, Khrebet** *mts* Rus. Fed.
129 G1 **Tukuy-Mekteb** Rus. Fed.
211 B7 **Tukuyu** Tanz.
78 □2 **Tula** American Samoa
192 B6 **Tula** *Sardegna* Italy
210 C5 **Tula** *watercourse* Kenya
245 H5 **Tula** *Hidalgo* Mex.
245 H2 **Tula** *Tamaulipas* Mex.
245 H5 **Tula** *r.* Mex.
139 U7 **Tula** Rus. Fed.
Tulach Mhór Ireland *see* **Tullamore**
78 □6 **Tulaghi** Solomon Is
111 K8 **Tulagt Ar Gol** *r.* China
260 B2 **Tulahuén** Chile
106 F7 **Tulai** *Qinghai* China
106 E7 **Tulai Nanshan** *mts* China
106 E7 **Tulai Shan** *mts* China
123 J5 **Tulak** Afgh.
263 D2 **Tula Mountains** Antarctica
245 I5 **Tulancingo** Mex.
94 F7 **Tulangbawang** *r.* Indon.
Tula Oblast *admin. div.* Rus. Fed. *see* **Tul'skaya Oblast'**
240 M5 **Tulare** *CA* U.S.A.
240 M6 **Tulare Lake Bed** *CA* U.S.A.
239 L10 **Tularosa** *NM* U.S.A.
114 H3 **Tulasi** *mt. Madh. Prad./Orissa* India
168 K5 **Tülau** Ger.
175 I2 **Tuławki** Pol.
214 D9 **Tulbagh** S. Africa
179 N3 **Tulbing** Austria
177 K5 **Tulca** Romania
250 B4 **Tulcán** Ecuador
174 F3 **Tulce** Pol.
197 Q5 **Tulcea** Romania
Tul'chin Ukr. *see* **Tul'chyn**
136 H5 **Tul'chyn** Ukr.
245 I7 **Tulcingo** Mex.
240 M5 **Tule** *r. CA* U.S.A.
246 G8 **Tulé** Venez.
Tuléar Madag. *see* **Toliara**
122 E4 **Tuleh** Iran
93 F5 **Tulehu** *Maluku* Indon.
238 D6 **Tulelake** *CA* U.S.A.
223 L2 **Tulemalu Lake** *Nunavut* Can.
107 Q4 **Tule Mod** *Nei Mongol* China
161 F8 **Tulette** France
176 F5 **Tulfás** *r.* Hungary
178 E5 **Tulfes** Austria
197 N4 **Tulgheş** Romania
237 E8 **Tulia** *TX* U.S.A.
107 Q1 **Tulihe** *Nei Mongol* China
174 G3 **Tuliszków** Pol.
222 E1 **Tulita** *N.W.T.* Can.
114 E3 **Tuljapur** *Mahar.* India
128 D6 **Ţūlkarm** West Bank
147 E7 **Tulla** Ireland
147 F4 **Tullaghan** Ireland
231 D8 **Tullahoma** *TN* U.S.A.
83 K5 **Tullamore** *N.S.W.* Austr.
147 H6 **Tullamore** Ireland
148 C8 **Tullaroan** Ireland
162 H5 **Tulle** France
168 K1 **Tullebølle** Denmark
83 K5 **Tullibigeal** *N.S.W.* Austr.
161 G6 **Tullins** France
179 N3 **Tulln** Austria
179 M3 **Tullner Feld** *plain* Austria
240 L4 **Tullock Lake** *CA* U.S.A.
237 I10 **Tullos** *LA* U.S.A.
147 I7 **Tullow** Ireland
85 K4 **Tully** *Qld* Austr.
147 G4 **Tully** *Northern Ireland* U.K.
147 H4 **Tully** *Northern Ireland* U.K.
147 J5 **Tullyallen** Ireland
147 G4 **Tullybrack** *hill Northern Ireland* U.K.
147 I8 **Tullycanna** Ireland
85 J4 **Tully Falls** *Qld* Austr.
147 I3 **Tullyhogue** *Northern Ireland* U.K.
234 F4 **Tullytown** *PA* U.S.A.
147 H4 **Tullyvin** Ireland
147 F3 **Tullyvoos** Ireland
197 O5 **Tulnici** Romania
140 V2 **Tuloma** *r.* Rus. Fed.
140 U5 **Tulos** Rus. Fed.
175 I3 **Tułowice** *Mazowieckie* Pol.
174 F5 **Tułowice** *Opolskie* Pol.
134 L3 **Tulpan** Rus. Fed.
140 T3 **Tulppio** Fin.
237 H7 **Tulsa** *OK* U.S.A.
222 C3 **Tulsequah** *B.C.* Can.
116 I5 **Tulsipur** Nepal
147 F5 **Tulsk** Ireland
139 U8 **Tul'skaya Oblast'** *admin. div.* Rus. Fed.
129 B1 **Tul'skiy** Rus. Fed.
121 P1 **Tul'skoye** Kazakh.
250 B3 **Tuluá** Col.
210 C2 **Tulu Bolo** Eth.
197 Q5 **Tuluceşti** Romania
210 C3 **Tulu Dimtu** *mt.* Eth.
220 B3 **Tuluksak** *AK* U.S.A.
128 F6 **Tulūl al Ashāqif** *hills* Jordan
243 P7 **Tulum** *tourist site* Mex.
260 C2 **Tulum, Valle de** *val.* Arg.
98 H1 **Tulun** Rus. Fed.
95 I9 **Tulungagung** *Jawa* Indon.
Tulusdu *N. Male* Maldives *see* **Thulusdhu**
251 F4 **Tulu-Tuloi, Serra** *hills* Brazil
210 B2 **Tulu Welel** *mt.* Eth.
134 K4 **Tulva** *r.* Rus. Fed.
175 M4 **Tulychiv** Ukr.
137 M2 **Tulyholove** Ukr.
242 □Q11 **Tuma** *r.* Nic.
139 X6 **Tuma** Rus. Fed.
250 B4 **Tumaco** Col.
215 L2 **Tumahole** S. Africa
111 J10 **Tumain** *Xizang* China
120 C4 **Tumak** Rus. Fed.
122 I4 **Tūmān Āqā** Iran
Tuman-gang *r.* Asia *see* **Tumen Jiang**
Tumannaya *r.* Asia *see* **Tumen Jiang**
134 F1 **Tumannyy** Rus. Fed.
139 R6 **Tumanovo** Rus. Fed.
131 S3 **Tumanskiy** Rus. Fed.
Tumasik Sing. *see* **Singa**
251 G3 **Tumatumari** Guyana
139 R1 **Tumazy** Rus. Fed.
106 G8 **Tumba** *Qinghai* China
209 D5 **Tumba** Dem. Rep. Congo
143 N2 **Tumba** Sweden
208 C5 **Tumba, Lac** *l.* Dem. Rep. Congo
95 J5 **Tumbangmiri** *Kalimantan* Indon.
95 J5 **Tumbangsamba** *Kalimar* Indon.
95 J5 **Tumbangsenamang** *Kalimantan* Indon.
95 I5 **Tumbangtiti** *Kalimantan*
92 E8 **Tumbao** *Mindanao* Phil.
192 A5 **Tumbarino, Punta** *pt Sardegna* Italy
83 L6 **Tumbarumba** *N.S.W.* Au
250 A5 **Tumbes** Peru
250 A5 **Tumbes** *dept* Peru
244 E7 **Tumbiscatio** Mex.
222 F4 **Tumbler Ridge** *B.C.* Can
Tumbou Fiji *see* **Tubou**
82 F6 **Tumby Bay** *S.A.* Austr.
140 U3 **Tumcha** *r.* Fin./Rus. Fed.
Tumd Youqi *Nei Mongol* *see* **Salaqi**
Tumd Zuoqi *Nei Mongol* *see* **Qasq**
100 F7 **Tumen** *Jilin* China
108 H2 **Tumen** *Shaanxi* China
100 G7 **Tumen Jiang** *r.* Asia
251 F3 **Tumeremo** Venez.
251 F3 **Tumereng** Guyana
92 B9 **Tumindao** *i.* Phil.
257 G3 **Tumiritinga** Brazil
114 E6 **Tumkur** *Karnataka* India
117 K6 **Tumlingtar** Nepal
146 I9 **Tummel, Loch** *l. Scotlan*
146 H9 **Tummel Bridge** *Perth ar Kinross, Scotland* U.K.
202 B4 **Tummo, Mountains of** Libya/Niger
100 L4 **Tumnin** *r.* Rus. Fed.
78 □1 **Tumon Bay** Guam
123 J8 **Tump** Pak.
95 K5 **Tumpah** *Kalimantan* Indo
94 E1 **Tumpat** Malaysia
97 F8 **Tumpôr, Phnum** *mt.* Cambodia
93 C4 **Tumpu, Gunung** *mt.* Ind
93 C4 **Tumputiga, Gunung** *mt.* Indon.
116 G9 **Tumsar** *Mahar.* India
206 E4 **Tumu** Ghana
251 G4 **Tumucumaque, Serra** *h* Brazil
115 H3 **Tumudibandh** *Orissa* Inc
182 H9 **Tumuja** *r.* Spain
252 D3 **Tumupasa** Bol.
Tumur Kazakh. *see* **Timu**
110 E6 **Tumushuke** *Xinjiang* Chi
252 D5 **Tumusla** Bol.
83 L6 **Tumut** *N.S.W.* Austr.
134 K5 **Tumutuk** Rus. Fed.
206 E4 **Tuna** Ghana
247 □1 **Tuna, Punta** *pt* Puerto F
92 E8 **Tuna Bay** *Mindanao* Phil.
143 L1 **Tuna-Hästberg** Sweden
247 □7 **Tunapuna** Trin. and Tob.
246 D3 **Tunas de Zaza** Cuba
Ţunb al Kubrá *i.* The Gu Greater Tunb
Ţunb aş Şughrá *i.* The *see* **Lesser Tunb**
151 M5 **Tunbridge Wells, Royal** *England* U.K.
199 K3 **Tunçbilek** Turkey
126 I4 **Tunceli** Turkey
129 A6 **Tunceli** *prov.* Turkey
108 H9 **Tunchang** *Hainan* China
129 D4 **Tunçoluk** Turkey
83 N5 **Tuncurry** *N.S.W.* Austr.
111 D13 **Tundla** *Uttar Prad.* India
203 F5 **Tundubai** *well* Sudan
211 B7 **Tunduma** Tanz.
207 H4 **Tundun-Wada** Nigeria
211 C7 **Tunduru** Tanz.
197 O9 **Tundzha** *r.* Bulg.
142 I6 **Tune** Denmark
Tunes Tunisia *see* **Tunis**
207 H4 **Tunga** Nigeria
146 D6 **Tunga** *Western Isles, Scotland* U.K.
114 F5 **Tungabhadra** *r.* India
114 E5 **Tungabhadra Reservoir**
210 A2 **Tungaru** Sudan
92 D8 **Tungawan** *Mindanao* Ph
109 □I7 **Tung Chung** *H.K.* China
109 □I7 **Tung Chung Wan** *b. H.K* China
117 M8 **Tungi** Bangl.
95 M2 **Tungku** *Sabah* Malaysia
242 □Q11 **Tungla** Nic.
109 □J7 **Tung Lung Chau** *i. H.K.*
Tung Lung Island *H.K.* *see* **Tung Lung Chau**
140 □D1 **Tungnaá** *r.* Iceland
100 M2 **Tungor** *Sakhalin* Rus. Fe
140 U4 **Tungozero** Rus. Fed.
109 □J7 **Tung Pok Liu Hoi Hap** *sea chan. H.K.* China
222 D2 **Tungsten** *N.W.T.* Can.
134 F2 **Tunguda** Rus. Fed.
95 J4 **Tungun, Bukit** *mt.* Indor
109 □J7 **Tung Wan** *b. H.K.* China
115 H4 **Tuni** *Andhra Prad.* India
122 H5 **Tūnī, Chāh-e** *well* Iran
237 J8 **Tunica** *MS* U.S.A.
172 F5 **Tuningen** Ger.
227 N1 **Tunis** *Ont.* Can.
205 H1 **Tunis** Tunisia
205 H1 **Tunis, Golfe de** *g.* Tunis
205 H2 **Tunisia** *country* Africa
250 C3 **Tunja** Col.
234 D1 **Tunkhannock** *PA* U.S.A.
242 □Q11 **Tunki** Nic.
107 M8 **Tunliu** *Shanxi* China
226 D5 **Tunnel City** *WI* U.S.A.
87 E8 **Tunnel Creek** *watercou* *W.A.* Austr.
232 F9 **Tunnelton** *WV* U.S.A.
142 E1 **Tunnhovd** Norway
142 E1 **Tunnhovdfjorden** *l.* Nor
140 L4 **Tunnsjøen** *l.* Norway
139 X4 **Tunoshna** Rus. Fed.
151 O3 **Tunstall** *Suffolk, Englanc*
173 M6 **Tuntenhausen** Ger.
140 T3 **Tuntsa** Fin.
225 H1 **Tunulic** *r. Que.* Can.
220 B3 **Tununak** *AK* U.S.A.
225 I1 **Tunungayualok Island** *Nfld and Lab.* Can.
260 C3 **Tunuyán** Arg.
260 D4 **Tunuyán** *r.* Arg.
260 C3 **Tunuyán, Sierra de** *mts*
260 D3 **Tunuyán, Travesía** *des.*
Tunxi *Anhui* China *see* **Huangshan**
177 L4 **Tunyogmatolcs** Hungar
Tuodian *Yunnan* China *s* **Shuangbai**
109 K2 **Tuo He** *r.* China
Tuojiang *Hunan* China *se* **Fenghuang**
Tuojiang *Hunan* China *se* **Jianghua**
108 E4 **Tuo Jiang** *r. Sichuan* Chi
97 G9 **Tuŏl Khpos** Cambodia
240 L4 **Tuolumne** *CA* U.S.A.
240 K4 **Tuolumne** *r. CA* U.S.A.
240 M4 **Tuolumne Meadows** *CA*
192 H1 **Tuoma** *r.* Italy
108 E6 **Tuoniang Jiang** *r. Guan* China
Tuoputiereke *Xinjiang* C *see* **Jeminay**
191 M9 **Tuoro sul Trasimeno** Ita
Tuotuoheyan *Qinghai* C *see* **Tanggulashan**
121 R6 **Tüp** Kyrg.
256 B4 **Tupã** Brazil
256 C3 **Tupaciguara** Brazil
122 B3 **Tūp Āghāj** Iran
Tupai *i.* Fr. Polynesia *see* **Motu Iti**
251 F5 **Tupanaóca** Brazil

Tupanciretã Brazil
Tupelo *MS* U.S.A.
Tupesy Czech Rep.
Tupinambarama, Ilha *i.* Brazil
Tupi Paulista Brazil
Tupiratins Brazil
Tupiza Bol.
Tuplice Pol.
Tupper *B.C.* Can.
Tupper Lake *NY* U.S.A.
Tupper Lake *l. NY* U.S.A.
Tüpqaraghan Tübegi *pen.* Kazakh. *see* **Mangyshlak, Poluostrov**
Tupungato Arg.
Tupungato, Cerro *mt.* Arg./Chile
Tuqayyid *well* Iraq
Tuquan *Nei Mongol* China
Túquerres Col.
Tur *r.* Romania
Tura *Xinjiang* China
Tura Hungary
Tura *Meghalaya* India
Tura Rus. Fed.
Turabah *Ḥā'il* Saudi Arabia
Turabah *Makkah* Saudi Arabia
Turabah, Wādī *watercourse* Saudi Arabia
Turagua, Serranía *mt.* Venez.
Turaiyur *Tamil Nadu* India
Turakina *North I.* N.Z.
Turakina *r. North I.* N.Z.
Turakirae Head *North I.* N.Z.
Turan Iran
Turana, Khrebet *mts* Rus. Fed.
Turangi *North I.* N.Z.
Turan Lowland Asia
Turano *r.* Italy
Turanskaya Nizmennost' *lowland* Asia *see* **Turan Lowland**
Ţurāq al 'Ilab *hills* Syria
Turar Ryskulov Kazakh.
Turaw Belarus
Ţurayf Saudi Arabia
Ţurayf *well* Saudi Arabia
Ţurayf, Kutayfat *vol.* Saudi Arabia
Turba Estonia
Turbaco Col.
Turbacz *mt.* Pol.
Turbanovo Rus. Fed.
Turbat Pak.
Turbenthal Switz.
Turbio *r.* Mex.
Turbiv Ukr.
Turbo Col.
Turbotville *PA* U.S.A.
Türchlwand *mt.* Austria
Turcia Spain
Turčianske Teplice Slovakia
Turckheim France
Turco Bol.
Turda Romania
Turdey Rus. Fed.
Turdine *r.* France
Turee Creek *r. W.A.* Austr.
Turégano Spain
Türeh Iran
Turek Pol.
Turenki Fin.
Turew Pol.
Turfan *Xinjiang* China *see* **Turpan**
Turfan Depression China *see* **Turpan Pendi**
Turgay *Akmolinskaya Oblast'* Kazakh.
Turgay *Kostanayskaya Oblast'* Kazakh.
Turgay *r.* Kazakh.
Turgayskaya Dolina *val.* Kazakh.
Turgayskaya Stolovaya Strana *reg.* Kazakh.
Türgen Uul *mt.* Mongolia
Türgen Uul *mts* Mongolia
Turgeon *r. Ont./Que.* Can.
Tŭrgovishte Bulg.
Turgut *Konya* Turkey
Turgut *Muğla* Turkey
Turgutalp Turkey
Turgutlu Turkey
Turgutreis Turkey
Turhal Turkey
Turhenyevka Ukr.
Türi Estonia
Turi Italy
Turia *r.* Spain
Turiaçu Brazil
Turiaçu *r.* Brazil
Turiaçu, Baía de *b.* Brazil
Turiamo Venez.
Turiani Tanz.
Turie Slovakia
Turiec *r.* Slovakia
Turin *Alta* Can.
Turin Italy *see* **Torino**
Turinsk Rus. Fed.
Turís Spain
Turiya *r.* Ukr.
Turiy Rog Rus. Fed.
Turiys'k Ukr.
Türje Hungary
Turka Rus. Fed.
Turka Ukr.
Turkana, Lake *salt l.* Eth./Kenya
Türkeli Turkey
Türkeli Adası *i.* Turkey
Türkenfeld Ger.
Turkestan Kazakh.
Turkestan Range *mts* Asia
Túrkeve Hungary
Turkey *country* Asia/Europe
Turkey *KY* U.S.A.
Turkey *r. IA* U.S.A.
Turkey Creek *W.A.* Austr.
Türkheim Ger.
Turki Rus. Fed.
Türkistan Kazakh. *see* **Turkestan**
Türkmenabat *Lebapskaya Oblast'* Turkm.
Turkmen Adasy *i.* Turkm. *see* **Ogurjaly Adasy**
Türkmen Aylagy *b.* Turkm. *see* **Türkmen Aýlagy**
Türkmen Aýlagy *b.* Turkm.
Türkmenbaşy Turkm.
Türkmenbaşy Aýlagy *b.* Turkm.
Türkmenbaşy Döwlet Gorugy *nature res.* Turkm.
Türkmen Dağı *mt.* Turkey
Türkmengala Turkm.
Turkmenistan *country* Asia
Turkmeniya *country* Asia *see* **Turkmenistan**
Turkmen-Kala Turkm. *see* **Türkmengala**
Turkmenkarakul' Turkm.
Türkmenostan *country* Asia *see* **Turkmenistan**
Turkmenskaya S.S.R. *country* Asia *see* **Turkmenistan**
Türkoğlu Turkey
Turkova Belarus
Turks and Caicos Islands *terr.* West Indies
Turks Island Passage Turks and Caicos Is
Turks Islands Turks and Caicos Is
Turku Fin.
Turkwel *watercourse* Kenya
Turleque Spain
Turlock *CA* U.S.A.
Turlock Lake *CA* U.S.A.
Turlough *Clare* Ireland
Turlough *Mayo* Ireland
Turmalina Brazil
Turmus, Wādī at *watercourse* Saudi Arabia
Turnagain *r. B.C.* Can.
Turnagain, Cape *North I.* N.Z.
Turnalı Turkey
Turňa nad Bodvou Slovakia
Turnau Austria
146 G12 **Turnberry** *South Ayrshire, Scotland* U.K.
81 C12 **Turnbull, Mount** *South I.* N.Z.
241 V8 **Turnbull, Mount** *AZ* U.S.A.
243 P9 **Turneffe Islands** *atoll* Belize
86 E6 **Turner** *r. W.A.* Austr.
87 E8 **Turner** *watercourse W.A.* Austr.
227 K5 **Turner** *MI* U.S.A.
86 J4 **Turner River** *W.A.* Austr.
151 L5 **Turners Hill** *West Sussex, England* U.K.
206 B5 **Turner's Peninsula** Sierra Leone
222 H5 **Turner Valley** *Alta* Can.
165 G6 **Turnhout** Belgium
179 N6 **Turnišče** Slovenia
179 M4 **Türnitz** Austria
223 I3 **Turnor Lake** *Sask.* Can.
223 I3 **Turnor Lake** *l. Sask.* Can.
176 E1 **Turnov** Czech Rep.
Tŭrnovo Bulg. *see* **Veliko Tŭrnovo**
197 M7 **Turnu Măgurele** Romania
Turnu Severin Romania *see* **Drobeta-Turnu Severin**
175 K5 **Turobin** Pol.
83 L5 **Turon** *r. N.S.W.* Austr.
185 J7 **Turón** *r.* Spain
Turones France *see* **Tours**
188 E3 **Turopolje** *plain* Croatia
175 J2 **Turośl** *Podlaskie* Pol.
175 J2 **Turośl** *Warmińsko-Mazurskie* Pol.
134 H4 **Turovets** Rus. Fed.
139 U7 **Turovo** Rus. Fed.
175 K4 **Turów** Pol.
138 L6 **Turowlya** Belarus
174 E2 **Turowo** Pol.
110 I5 **Turpan** *Xinjiang* China
110 I5 **Turpan Pendi** *depr.* China
110 I5 **Turpan Zhan** *Xinjiang* China
184 B2 **Turquel** Port.
179 I6 **Turrach** Austria
179 I6 **Turracher Höhe** *pass* Austria
185 P6 **Turre** Spain
242 □R13 **Turrialba** Costa Rica
161 I8 **Turriers** France
146 L7 **Turriff** *Aberdeenshire, Scotland* U.K.
Turris Libisonis *Sardegna* Italy *see* **Porto Torres**
127 L7 **Tursāq** Iraq
195 K3 **Tursi** Italy
136 D2 **Turs'kyy Kanal** *canal* Ukr.
197 L3 **Turţ** Romania
226 D3 **Turtle Flambeau Flowage** *resr WI* U.S.A.
223 I4 **Turtleford** *Sask.* Can.
85 M4 **Turtle Island** *Coral Sea Is Terr.* Austr.
Turtle Island Fiji *see* **Vatoa**
92 B8 **Turtle Islands** Phil.
206 B5 **Turtle Islands** Sierra Leone
223 I4 **Turtle Lake** *l. Sask.* Can.
226 B4 **Turtle Lake** *WI* U.S.A.
140 Q3 **Turtola** Fin.
121 P7 **Turugart Pass** China/Kyrg.
Turugart Shankou *pass* China/Kyrg. *see* **Turugart Pass**
130 J3 **Turukhansk** Rus. Fed.
177 M4 **Turulung** Romania
251 G4 **Turuna** *r.* Brazil
128 D1 **Turunçlu** Turkey
199 L6 **Turunçova** Turkey
120 G5 **Turush** Kazakh.
114 E5 **Turuvanur** *Karnataka* India
256 B2 **Turvelândia** Brazil
255 C9 **Turvo** Brazil
256 B2 **Turvo** *r.* Brazil
256 C3 **Turvo** *r.* Brazil
256 C5 **Turvo** *r.* Brazil
177 L3 **Tur"ya** *r.* Ukr.
177 L3 **Tur"ya-Bystra** Ukr.
129 I5 **Türyançay** Azer.
129 I5 **Türyançay** *r.* Azer.
129 I5 **Türyançay Qoruğu** *nature res.* Azer.
177 L3 **Tur"ya-Polyana** Ukr.
136 C4 **Tur"ye** Ukr.
177 L3 **Tur"yi Remety** Ukr.
136 D3 **Turynka** Ukr.
175 I2 **Turza Wielka** Pol.
177 H2 **Turzovka** Slovakia
122 H3 **Ţūs** Iran
185 O4 **Tús** *r.* Spain
194 G8 **Tusa** *Sicilia* Italy
194 G7 **Tusa** *r. Sicilia* Italy
241 T6 **Tusayan** *AZ* U.S.A.
231 D9 **Tuscaloosa** *AL* U.S.A.
192 H3 **Tuscania** Italy
Tuscany *admin. reg.* Italy *see* **Toscana**
232 D8 **Tuscarawas** *r. OH* U.S.A.
234 C3 **Tuscarora** *PA* U.S.A.
232 H8 **Tuscarora Mountains** *hills PA* U.S.A.
236 K6 **Tuscola** *IL* U.S.A.
237 F9 **Tuscola** *TX* U.S.A.
231 D8 **Tuscumbia** *AL* U.S.A.
236 I6 **Tuscumbia** *MO* U.S.A.
122 G4 **Tusharīk** Iran
137 P2 **Tuskar'** *r.* Rus. Fed.
231 E9 **Tuskegee** *AL* U.S.A.
197 N4 **Tuşnad** Romania
173 J5 **Tussenhausen** Ger.
232 G8 **Tussey Mountains** *hills PA* U.S.A.
173 N5 **Tüßling** Ger.
226 I5 **Tustin** *MI* U.S.A.
175 J5 **Tuszów Narodowy** Pol.
175 J5 **Tuszyma** Pol.
175 H4 **Tuszyn** Pol.
122 F5 **Tūt** Iran
127 K4 **Tutak** Turkey
122 H8 **Tūtān** Iran
139 W4 **Tutayev** Rus. Fed.
151 I2 **Tutbury** *Staffordshire, England* U.K.
Tutera Spain *see* **Tudela**
123 N5 **Tutia Khel** Pak.
114 F8 **Tuticorin** *Tamil Nadu* India
95 K3 **Tutoh** *r.* Malaysia
95 K2 **Tutong** Brunei
197 P4 **Tutova** *r.* Romania
170 H3 **Tutow** Ger.
197 O6 **Tutrakan** Bulg.
150 G4 **Tutshill** *Gloucestershire, England* U.K.
236 G6 **Tuttle Creek Reservoir** *KS* U.S.A.
234 F2 **Tuttles Corner** *NJ* U.S.A.
172 F6 **Tuttlingen** Ger.
221 P2 **Tuttut Nunaat** *reg.* Greenland
93 E8 **Tutuala** East Timor
211 B6 **Tutubu** Tanz.
78 □2 **Tutuila** *i.* American Samoa
80 I2 **Tutukaka** *North I.* N.Z.
213 E4 **Tutume** Botswana
250 B3 **Tutunendo** Col.
252 C4 **Tutupaca, Volcán** *vol.* Peru
81 J8 **Tuturumuri** *North I.* N.Z.
245 J9 **Tututepec** Mex.
173 K6 **Tutzing** Ger.
170 H3 **Tützpatz** Ger.
106 I2 **Tuul Gol** *r.* Mongolia
138 H1 **Tuulos** Fin.
101 E8 **Tuun-bong** *mt.* N. Korea
140 U5 **Tuupovaara** Fin.
140 T5 **Tuusniemi** Fin.
141 R6 **Tuusula** Fin.
Tuva *aut. rep.* Rus. Fed. *see* **Tyva, Respublika**
77 H2 **Tuvalu** *country* S. Pacific Ocean
77 I4 **Tuvana-i-Colo** *i.* Fiji
77 I4 **Tuvana-i-Ra** *i.* Fiji
Tuvana-i-Tholo *i.* Fiji *see* **Tuvana-i-Colo**
142 H4 **Tuve** Sweden
262 S2 **Tuve, Mount** *hill* Antarctica
Tuvinskaya A.S.S.R. *aut. rep.* Rus. Fed. *see* **Tyva, Respublika**
79 □7a **Tuvutau** *mt. Viti Levu* Fiji
95 L4 **Tuwau** *r.* Indon.
124 G2 **Tuwayq, Jabal** *hills* Saudi Arabia
124 G5 **Tuwayq, Jabal** *mts* Saudi Arabia
124 D3 **Ţuwayrah** Saudi Arabia
128 D9 **Ţuwayyil al Ḥājj** *mt.* Jordan
128 E8 **Ţuwayyil ash Shihāq** *mt.* Jordan
124 D4 **Tuwwal** Saudi Arabia
244 D6 **Tuxcacuesco** Mex.
235 G2 **Tuxedo Park** *NY* U.S.A.
178 E5 **Tuxer Gebirge** *mts* Austria
149 P7 **Tuxford** *Nottinghamshire, England* U.K.
244 D6 **Tuxpan** *Jalisco* Mex.
244 B4 **Tuxpan** *Nayarit* Mex.
245 J5 **Tuxpan** *Veracruz* Mex.
245 J4 **Tuxpan, Arrecife** *rf* Mex.
243 M9 **Tuxtla Gutiérrez** Mex.
Túy *Galicia* Spain *see* **Tui**
247 K8 **Tuy** *r.* Venez.
222 D3 **Tuya Lake** *B.C.* Can.
97 H8 **Tuy Đưc** Vietnam
96 G4 **Tuyên Quang** Vietnam
129 D5 **Tuygun** Turkey
97 I8 **Tuy Hoa** Vietnam
135 K5 **Tuymazy** Rus. Fed.
122 C4 **Tūysarkān** Iran
Tŭytepa Uzbek. *see* **To'ytepa**
121 R6 **Tuyuk** Kazakh.
Tuz, Lake *salt l.* Turkey *see* **Tuz Gölü**
244 G7 **Tuzantla** *r.* Mex.
126 F4 **Tuz Gölü** *salt l.* Turkey
197 N8 **Tŭzha** Bulg.
134 I4 **Tuzha** Rus. Fed.
196 H8 **Tuzi** Montenegro
127 L6 **Tuz Khurmātū** Iraq
188 G3 **Tuzla** Bos.-Herz.
197 Q6 **Tuzla** Romania
126 G5 **Tuzla** Turkey
127 J4 **Tuzla** *r.* Turkey
135 H7 **Tuzlov** *r.* Rus. Fed.
129 E5 **Tuzluca** Turkey
179 N7 **Tužno** Croatia
96 B2 **Tuzu** *r.* Myanmar
202 C4 **Tuzugu** *well* Libya
142 I4 **Tvååker** Sweden
140 O4 **Tvärålund** Sweden
176 F2 **Tvarožná** Czech Rep.
142 E3 **Tvedestrand** Norway
142 B1 **Tveitakvitingen** *mt.* Norway
139 S5 **Tver'** Rus. Fed.
Tver Oblast *admin. div.* Rus. Fed. *see* **Tverskaya Oblast'**
129 A1 **Tverskaya** Rus. Fed.
139 S4 **Tverskaya Oblast'** *admin. div.* Rus. Fed.
139 S5 **Tvertsa** *r.* Rus. Fed.
144 D1 **Tvøroyri** Faroe Is
138 L3 **Tvorozhkovo** Rus. Fed.
179 O2 **Tvrdonice** Czech Rep.
177 I2 **Tvrdošín** Slovakia
197 N8 **Tvŭrditsa** Bulg.
240 L3 **Twain Harte** *CA* U.S.A.
174 F4 **Twardogóra** Pol.
146 J4 **Twatt** *Orkney, Scotland* U.K.
227 Q5 **Tweed** *Ont.* Can.
149 M2 **Tweed** *r. England/Scotland* U.K.
146 J11 **Tweeddale** *val. Scotland* U.K.
164 K3 **Tweede Exloërmond** Neth.
83 N3 **Tweed Heads** *N.S.W.* Austr.
223 I4 **Tweedie** *Alta* Can.
149 M2 **Tweedmouth** *Northumberland, England* U.K.
146 J11 **Tweedsmuir** *Scottish Borders, Scotland* U.K.
222 E4 **Tweedsmuir Provincial Park** *B.C.* Can.
214 D8 **Tweefontein** S. Africa
215 M3 **Tweeling** S. Africa
212 C5 **Twee Rivier** Namibia
214 E2 **Twee Rivieren** Botswana
215 L5 **Tweespruit** S. Africa
164 J4 **Twello** Neth.
164 K4 **Twente** *reg.* Neth.
164 J4 **Twentekanaal** *canal* Neth.
241 P7 **Twentynine Palms** *CA* U.S.A.
208 C5 **Tweya** Dem. Rep. Congo
225 K3 **Twillingate** *Nfld and Lab.* Can.
240 L3 **Twin Bridges** *CA* U.S.A.
238 H4 **Twin Bridges** *MT* U.S.A.
237 E10 **Twin Buttes Reservoir** *TX* U.S.A.
225 H2 **Twin Falls** *Nfld and Lab.* Can.
238 G5 **Twin Falls** *ID* U.S.A.
209 F7 **Twingi** Zambia
86 I6 **Twin Heads** *hill W.A.* Austr.
234 F2 **Twin Lakes** *PA* U.S.A.
233 N4 **Twin Mountain** *NH* U.S.A.
240 L2 **Twin Peak** *CA* U.S.A.
87 D13 **Twin Peaks** *hill W.A.* Austr.
232 D7 **Twinsburg** *OH* U.S.A.
82 G3 **Twins Creek** *watercourse S.A.* Austr.
238 D2 **Twisp** *WA* U.S.A.
168 D5 **Twist** Ger.
169 G8 **Twiste (Twistetal)** Ger.
168 G5 **Twistringen** Ger.
240 L6 **Twitchen Reservoir** *CA* U.S.A.
222 D1 **Twitya** *r. N.W.T.* Can.
81 E11 **Twizel** *South I.* N.Z.
216 □2a **Two Boats Village** *Ascension* S. Atlantic Ocean
237 D6 **Two Butte Creek** *r. CO* U.S.A.
226 C2 **Two Harbors** *MN* U.S.A.
223 I4 **Two Hills** *Alta* Can.
148 B8 **Twomileborris** Ireland
147 H6 **Two Mile Bridge** Ireland
226 G5 **Two Rivers** *WI* U.S.A.
174 G5 **Tworóg** Pol.
151 J5 **Twyford** *Hampshire, England* U.K.
151 K5 **Twyford** *Wokingham, England* U.K.
146 H13 **Twynholm** *Dumfries and Galloway, Scotland* U.K.
Tyachev Ukr. *see* **Tyachiv**
136 C5 **Tyachiv** Ukr.
137 M7 **Tyahynka** Ukr.
Tyan' Shan' *mts* China/Kyrg. *see* **Tien Shan**
Tyanshanskaya Oblast' *admin. div.* Kyrg. *see* **Naryn**
96 A3 **Tyao** *r.* India/Myanmar
137 L4 **Tyasmyn** *r.* Ukr.
102 X2 **Tyatya, Vulkan** *vol.* Rus. Fed.
199 H1 **Tychero** Greece
174 E2 **Tychówko** Pol.
174 E2 **Tychowo** Pol.
174 G5 **Tychy** Pol.
175 K6 **Tyczyn** Pol.
140 K5 **Tydal** Norway
148 C5 **Tydavnet** Ireland
Tyddewi *Pembrokeshire, Wales* U.K. *see* **St David's**
232 F10 **Tygart Valley** *WV* U.S.A.
100 E2 **Tygda** Rus. Fed.
100 E2 **Tygda** *r.* Rus. Fed.
147 I4 **Tyholland** Ireland
141 J6 **Tyinkrysset** Norway
137 L2 **Tykhonovychi** Ukr.
175 K2 **Tykocin** Pol.
175 J6 **Tylawa** Pol.
237 H9 **Tyler** *TX* U.S.A.
237 J10 **Tylertown** *MS* U.S.A.
136 K7 **Tylihul** *r.* Ukr.
100 I2 **Tyl'skiy Khrebet** *mts* Rus. Fed.
100 M3 **Tym'** *r. Sakhalin* Rus. Fed.
175 I6 **Tymbark** Pol.
137 L4 **Tymchenky** Ukr.
198 B2 **Tymfi** *mts* Greece
174 D1 **Tymień** Pol.
137 R4 **Tymonove** Ukr.
137 L1 **Tymonovychi** Ukr.
137 O6 **Tymoshivka** Ukr.
100 M3 **Tymovskoye** *Sakhalin* Rus. Fed.
174 E4 **Tymowa** Pol.
198 F7 **Tympaki** *Kriti* Greece
164 K2 **Tynaarlo** Neth.
148 D5 **Tynan** *Northern Ireland* U.K.
131 N4 **Tynda** Rus. Fed.
236 G4 **Tyndall** *SD* U.S.A.
Tyndinskiy Rus. Fed. *see* **Tynda**
146 G10 **Tyndrum** *Stirling, Scotland* U.K.
146 K10 **Tyne** *r. Scotland* U.K.
149 O4 **Tyne and Wear** *admin. div. England* U.K.
176 E1 **Týnec nad Labem** Czech Rep.
176 D2 **Týnec nad Sázavou** Czech Rep.
149 O3 **Tynemouth** *Tyne and Wear, England* U.K.
233 N6 **Tyngsboro** *MA* U.S.A.
143 J1 **Tyngsjö** Sweden
176 F1 **Týniště nad Orlicí** Czech Rep.
136 J4 **Tynivka** Ukr.
176 D2 **Týn nad Vltavou** Czech Rep.
136 F2 **Tynne** Ukr.
141 K5 **Tynset** Norway
Tyr Lebanon *see* **Soûr**
Tyras Ukr. *see* **Bilhorod-Dnistrovs'kyy**
175 K6 **Tyrawa Wołoska** Pol.
Tyre Lebanon *see* **Soûr**
262 S1 **Tyree, Mount** Antarctica
148 F5 **Tyrella** *Northern Ireland* U.K.
143 O2 **Tyresö** Sweden
143 O2 **Tyresta nationalpark** *nat. park* Sweden
142 G1 **Tyrifjorden** *l.* Norway
173 N5 **Tyrlaching** Ger.
100 H3 **Tyrma** Rus. Fed.
100 G3 **Tyrma** *r.* Rus. Fed.
140 R4 **Tyrnävä** Fin.
198 D3 **Tyrnavos** Greece
139 W7 **Tyrnovo** Rus. Fed.
129 D2 **Tyrnyauz** Rus. Fed.
Tyrol *land* Austria *see* **Tirol**
147 H3 **Tyrone** *county Northern Ireland* U.K.
239 J10 **Tyrone** *NM* U.S.A.
232 G8 **Tyrone** *PA* U.S.A.
83 I6 **Tyrrell** *r. Vic.* Austr.
83 I6 **Tyrrell, Lake** *dry lake Vic.* Austr.
223 J2 **Tyrrell Lake** *N.W.T.* Can.
147 H6 **Tyrrellspass** Ireland
189 C5 **Tyrrhenian Sea** France/Italy
Tyrus Lebanon *see* **Soûr**
136 A5 **Tysa** *r.* Ukr. *alt.* **Tisa (Serbia),** *alt.* **Tisza (Hungary)**
136 D5 **Tysmenytsya** Ukr.
142 B2 **Tysnesøy** *i.* Norway
241 R8 **Tyson Wash** *watercourse AZ* U.S.A.
142 B1 **Tysse** Norway
144 J1 **Tyssebotnen** Norway
142 C1 **Tyssedal** Norway
142 H6 **Tystrup-Bavelse** *nature res.* Denmark
175 L5 **Tyszowce** Pol.
150 E5 **Tythegston** *Bridgend, Wales* U.K.
164 I2 **Tytsjerk** Neth.
138 G6 **Tytuvėnai** Lith.
129 I2 **Tyube** Rus. Fed.
131 P3 **Tyubelyakh** Rus. Fed.
120 D5 **Tyub-Karagan, Mys** *pt* Kazakh.
129 L1 **Tyub-Karagan, Poluostrov** *pen.* Kazakh.
130 I4 **Tyukalinsk** Rus. Fed.
120 C5 **Tyulen'i Ostrova** *is* Kazakh.
Tyuleniy, Mys *pt* Azer. *see* **Suiti Burunu**
129 I1 **Tyuleniy, Ostrov** *i.* Rus. Fed.
120 G1 **Tyul'gan** Rus. Fed.
134 L4 **Tyul'kino** Rus. Fed.
130 H4 **Tyumen'** Rus. Fed.
Tyumen'-Aryk Kazakh. *see* **Tomenaryk**
121 S1 **Tyumentsevo** Rus. Fed.
131 N3 **Tyung** *r.* Rus. Fed.
120 K1 **Tyuntyugur** Kazakh.
Tyup Kyrg. *see* **Tüp**
Tyuratam Kazakh. *see* **Baykonyr**
140 V2 **Tyuva-Guba** Rus. Fed.
123 I1 **Tyuyamuyunskoye Vodokhranilishche** *resr* Turkm./Uzbek.
106 E1 **Tyva, Respublika** *aut. rep.* Rus. Fed.
136 H4 **Tyvriv** Ukr.
174 C2 **Tywa** *r.* Pol.
150 C7 **Tywardreath** *Cornwall, England* U.K.
150 D4 **Tywi** *r. Wales* U.K.
150 D2 **Tywyn** *Gwynedd, Wales* U.K.
213 F4 **Tzaneen** S. Africa
198 F5 **Tzia** *i.* Greece
243 O7 **Tzucacab** Mex.
164 I2 **Tzummarum** Neth.

U

251 F3 **Uacauyén** Venez.
Uaco Congo Angola *see* **Waku-Kungo**
78 □2 **Uafato** Samoa
79 □9 **Ua Huka** *i.* Fr. Polynesia
250 D4 **Uainambi** Brazil
Ualan *atoll* Micronesia *see* **Kosrae**
Ūālīkhanov Kazakh. *see* **Valikhanovo**
209 D9 **Uamanda** Angola
213 H3 **Uape** Moz.
Ua Pou *i.* Fr. Polynesia *see* **Ua Pu**
79 □9 **Ua Pu** *i.* Fr. Polynesia
251 E5 **Uara** Brazil
Uarc, Ras *c.* Morocco *see* **Trois Fourches, Cap des**
251 G6 **Uari** Brazil
251 E5 **Uarini** Brazil
87 C7 **Uaroo** *W.A.* Austr.
250 D4 **Uaruma** Brazil
251 E3 **Uasadi-jidi, Sierra** *mts* Venez.
251 F4 **Uatatás** *r.* Brazil
251 G5 **Uatumã** *r.* Brazil
254 F4 **Uauá** Brazil
250 E5 **Uaupés** Brazil
250 E4 **Uaupés** *r.* Brazil
243 O9 **Uaxactún** Guat.
124 G5 **U'ayfirah** *well* Saudi Arabia
128 G8 **U'aylī, Wādī al** *watercourse* Saudi Arabia
124 G1 **U'aywij** *well* Saudi Arabia
127 K9 **U'aywij, Wādī al** *watercourse* Saudi Arabia
196 I6 **Ub** Serbia
257 F4 **Ubá** Brazil
121 S2 **Uba** *r.* Kazakh.
169 B9 **Übach-Palenberg** Ger.
120 K1 **Ubagan** *r.* Kazakh.
257 E2 **Ubaí** Brazil
202 E6 **Ubaid** *well* Sudan
254 F5 **Ubaitaba** Brazil
124 F8 **'Ubāl** Yemen
208 C5 **Ubangi** *r.* C.A.R./Dem. Rep. Congo
Ubangi-Shari *country* Africa *see* **Central African Republic**
257 F3 **Ubaporanga** Brazil
136 H1 **Ubarts** *r.* Belarus
250 C3 **Ubate** Col.
257 E5 **Ubatuba** Brazil
123 M7 **Ubauro** Pak.
161 I8 **Ubaye** *r.* France
127 K7 **Ubayyiḍ, Wādī al** *watercourse* Iraq/Saudi Arabia
103 I13 **Ube** Japan
185 M4 **Úbeda** Spain
211 C6 **Ubenazomozi** Tanz.
256 D3 **Uberaba** Brazil
256 C4 **Uberaba** *r.* Brazil
172 B3 **Überherrn** Ger.
256 C3 **Uberlândia** Brazil
172 G6 **Überlingen** Ger.
172 G6 **Überlinger See** *l.* Ger.
173 M6 **Übersee** Ger.
94 □ **Ubin, Pulau** *i.* Sing.
182 I2 **Ubiña, Peña** *mt.* Spain
137 R9 **Ubinskaya** Rus. Fed.
130 J4 **Ubinskoye, Ozero** *l.* Rus. Fed.
256 A6 **Ubiratâ** Brazil
227 L6 **Ubly** *MI* U.S.A.
137 Q2 **Ublya** *r.* Rus. Fed.
96 F6 **Ubolratna Reservoir** Thai.
215 Q3 **Ubombo** S. Africa
208 E5 **Ubondo** Dem. Rep. Congo
96 G7 **Ubon Ratchathani** Thai.
208 F3 **Ubori** Sudan
136 G2 **Ubort'** *r.* Ukr.
100 I6 **Ubovka** Rus. Fed.
161 J9 **Ubraye** France
185 I7 **Ubrique** Spain
172 F3 **Ubstadt-Weiher** Ger.
208 E5 **Ubundu** Dem. Rep. Congo
261 F3 **Ucacha** Arg.
123 J2 **Üçajy** Turkm.
129 I5 **Ucar** Azer.
128 A2 **Uçarı** Turkey
252 B2 **Ucayali** *dept* Peru
250 C6 **Ucayali** *r.* Peru
192 B3 **Ucciani** *Corse* France
165 F7 **Uccle** Belgium
183 N7 **Uceda** Spain
161 E7 **Ucel** France
183 N5 **Ucero** Spain
183 N5 **Ucero** *r.* Spain
123 N7 **Uch** Pak.
182 C5 **Ucha** Port.
Üchajy Turkm. *see* **Üçajy**
122 D3 **Ūchān** Iran
121 S4 **Ucharal** Kazakh.
161 F8 **Uchaux** France
105 M1 **Uchigō** Japan
105 L3 **Uchihara** Japan
103 J13 **Uchiko** Japan
105 H3 **Uchimura-gawa** *r.* Japan
104 E2 **Uchinada** Japan
103 I15 **Uchinoura** Japan
104 B7 **Uchita** Japan
103 O9 **Uchiura** Japan
102 R4 **Uchiura-wan** *b.* Japan
105 I3 **Uchiyama-tōge** *pass* Japan
252 A2 **Uchiza** Peru
160 F3 **Uchizy** France
129 D2 **Uchkeken** Rus. Fed.
Uchkuduk Uzbek. *see* **Uchquduq**
129 D2 **Uchkulan** Rus. Fed.
120 J6 **Uchquduq** Uzbek.
121 L7 **Uchquloch** Uzbek.
Uchsay Uzbek. *see* **Uchsoy**
120 H6 **Uchsoy** Uzbek.
169 G6 **Uchte** Ger.
170 E5 **Uchte** *r.* Ger.
169 J10 **Üchtelhausen** Ger.
123 L9 **Uchto** *r.* Pak.
170 E5 **Uchtspringe** Ger.
131 O4 **Uchur** *r.* Rus. Fed.
183 L4 **Ucieza** *r.* Spain
157 L5 **Uckange** France
170 J2 **Ückeritz** Ger.
170 I4 **Uckermark** *reg.* Ger.
151 M6 **Uckfield** *East Sussex, England* U.K.
171 I7 **Uckro** Ger.
183 O9 **Uclés** Spain
222 E5 **Ucluelet** *B.C.* Can.
129 B6 **Üçpınar** *Erzincan* Turkey
128 A1 **Üçpınar** *Konya* Turkey
238 K4 **Ucross** *WY* U.S.A.
100 I1 **Uda** *r.* Rus. Fed.
137 P4 **Uda** *r.* Ukr.
129 G4 **Udabno** Georgia
129 G4 **Udabno, Mt'a** *hill* Georgia
135 I7 **Udachnoye** Rus. Fed.
131 M3 **Udachnyy** Rus. Fed.
114 E7 **Udagamandalam** *Tamil Nadu* India
116 D7 **Udaipur** *Rajasthan* India
116 E6 **Udaipur** *Rajasthan* India
117 M8 **Udaipur** *Tripura* India
116 G8 **Udaipura** *Madh. Prad.* India
117 K6 **Udaipur Garhi** Nepal
175 L4 **Udal** *r.* Pol.
117 N6 **Udalguri** *Assam* India
174 E4 **Udanin** Pol.
117 I9 **Udanti** *r.* India/Myanmar
261 H5 **Udaquilla** Arg.
129 D1 **Udarnyy** Rus. Fed.
177 K3 **Udava** *r.* Slovakia
177 K3 **Udavské** Slovakia
114 G9 **Uda Walawe Reservoir** Sri Lanka
137 M3 **Uday** *r.* Ukr.
114 F5 **Udayagiri** *Andhra Prad.* India
115 I3 **Udayagiri** *Orissa* India
125 I4 **'Udaynān** *well* Saudi Arabia
143 J1 **Uddeholm** Sweden
164 I4 **Uddel** Neth.
142 H3 **Uddevalla** Sweden
148 I2 **Uddingston** *South Lanarkshire, Scotland* U.K.
146 I11 **Uddington** *South Lanarkshire, Scotland* U.K.
140 N4 **Uddjaure** *l.* Sweden
129 D4 **Ude** Georgia
125 J3 **'Udeid, Khōr al** *inlet* Qatar
164 I5 **Uden** Neth.
164 H5 **Udenhout** Neth.
169 J8 **Uder** Ger.
178 E5 **Uderns** Austria
169 C10 **Üdersdorf** Ger.
114 E3 **Udgir** *Mahar.* India
Udhagamandalam *Tamil Nadu* India *see* **Udagamandalam**
116 E3 **Udhampur** Jammu and Kashmir
177 H2 **Udiča** Slovakia
134 I3 **Udimskiy** Rus. Fed.
191 O3 **Udine** Italy
191 N3 **Udine** *prov.* Italy
116 D6 **Udit** *Rajasthan* India
225 I2 **Udjuktok Bay** *Nfld and Lab.* Can.
Udmalaippettai *Tamil Nadu* India *see* **Udumalaippettai**
Udmurtia *aut. rep.* Rus. Fed. *see* **Udmurtskaya Respublika**
Udmurtskaya A.S.S.R. *aut. rep.* Rus. Fed. *see* **Udmurtskaya Respublika**
134 K4 **Udmurtskaya Respublika** *aut. rep.* Rus. Fed.
129 C1 **Udobnaya** Rus. Fed.
131 M4 **Udokan, Khrebet** *mts* Rus. Fed.
139 S4 **Udomlya** Rus. Fed.
105 J7 **Udone-jima** *i.* Japan
96 F6 **Udon Thani** Thai.
174 F1 **Udorpie** Pol.
78 □4a **Udot** *i. Chuuk* Micronesia
182 C4 **Udra, Cabo** *c.* Spain
175 L5 **Udrycze** Pol.
100 I1 **Udskoye** Rus. Fed.
114 E7 **Udumalaippettai** *Tamil Nadu* India
114 D6 **Udupi** *Karnataka* India
137 P3 **Udy** Ukr.
100 K2 **Udyl', Ozero** *l.* Rus. Fed.
Udzharma Georgia *see* **Ujarma**
Udzhary Azer. *see* **Ucar**
Uéa *atoll Îles Loyauté* New Caledonia *see* **Ouvéa**
171 H7 **Uebigau** Ger.
93 B4 **Uëbonti** *Sulawesi* Indon.
170 J3 **Uecker** *r.* Ger.
170 J3 **Ueckermünde** Ger.
105 H3 **Ueda** Japan
173 J2 **Uehlfeld** Ger.
169 K6 **Uehrde** Ger.
93 B4 **Uekuli** *Sulawesi* Indon.
208 D3 **Uele** *r.* Dem. Rep. Congo
131 U3 **Uelen** Rus. Fed.
131 T3 **Uel'kal'** Rus. Fed.
169 C6 **Uelsen** Ger.
168 K5 **Uelzen** Ger.
105 I3 **Ueno** *Gunma* Japan
104 D6 **Ueno** *Mie* Japan
105 J4 **Uenohara** Japan
208 E4 **Uere** *r.* Dem. Rep. Congo
190 D2 **Uetendorf** Switz.
168 I3 **Uetersen** Ger.
172 H2 **Uettingen** Ger.
169 J6 **Uetze** Ger.
134 K5 **Ufa** Rus. Fed.
134 L5 **Ufa** *r.* Rus. Fed.
150 F6 **Uffculme** *Devon, England* U.K.
173 I2 **Uffenheim** Ger.
173 K6 **Uffing am Staffelsee** Ger.
193 O5 **Ufita** *r.* Italy
169 K7 **Uftrungen** Ger.
134 I3 **Uftyuga** *r.* Rus. Fed.
212 B4 **Ugab** *watercourse* Namibia
138 F4 **Ugāle** Latvia
211 A6 **Ugalla** *r.* Tanz.
211 A6 **Ugalla River Game Reserve** *nature res.* Tanz.
210 B4 **Uganda** *country* Africa
188 F3 **Ugar** *r.* Bos.-Herz.
183 O2 **Ugarana** Spain
260 C3 **Ugarteche** Arg.
150 E7 **Ugborough** *Devon, England* U.K.
168 H1 **Uge** Denmark
195 O4 **Ugento** Italy
142 B1 **Uggdal** Norway
142 G4 **Uggerby** *r.* Denmark
195 O3 **Uggiano la Chiesa** Italy
207 G5 **Ughelli** Nigeria
215 M7 **Ugie** S. Africa
Ugi Island Solomon Is *see* **Uki Island**
185 M7 **Ugíjar** Spain
122 I8 **Ūgīnak** Iran
160 I5 **Ugine** France
100 M4 **Uglegorsk** *Sakhalin* Rus. Fed.
100 H7 **Uglekamensk** Rus. Fed.
134 L4 **Ugleural'skiy** Rus. Fed.
139 V4 **Uglich** Rus. Fed.
188 E3 **Ugljan** *i.* Croatia
139 Q3 **Uglovka** Rus. Fed.
100 F3 **Uglovoye** *Amurskaya Oblast'* Rus. Fed.
100 H7 **Uglovoye** *Primorskiy Kray* Rus. Fed.
121 S2 **Uglovskoye** Rus. Fed.
177 G4 **Ugod** Hungary
Ugodskiy Zavod Rus. Fed. *see* **Zhukovo**
131 P3 **Ugol'noye** Rus. Fed.
Ugolnyy Rus. Fed. *see* **Beringovskiy**
129 E2 **Ugol'nyy** Rus. Fed.
131 S3 **Ugol'nyye Kopi** Rus. Fed.
139 R7 **Ugra** Rus. Fed.
139 T7 **Ugra** *r.* Rus. Fed.
197 M7 **Ugŭrchin** Bulg.
199 G2 **Uğurlu** *Gökeada* Turkey
130 I3 **Ugut** Rus. Fed.
137 M8 **Ugutne** Ukr.
177 K3 **Uh** *r.* Slovakia
183 Q3 **Uharte-Arakil** Spain
179 O2 **Uherčice** Czech Rep.
107 L6 **Uher Hudag** *Nei Mongol* China
175 L4 **Uherka** *r.* Pol.
176 G2 **Uherské Hradiště** Czech Rep.
177 G2 **Uherský Brod** Czech Rep.
172 H4 **Uhingen** Ger.
176 C2 **Úhlava** *r.* Czech Rep.
172 G6 **Uhldingen** Ger.
176 E2 **Uhlířské Janovica** Czech Rep.
171 D9 **Uhlstädt** Ger.
136 C3 **Uhniv** Ukr.
232 D8 **Uhrichsville** *OH* U.S.A.
177 H3 **Uhrovec** Slovakia
137 O3 **Uhroyidy** Ukr.
171 D6 **Uhrsleben** Ger.
171 K8 **Uhyst** Ger.
254 E4 **Uibaí** Brazil
Uibhist a' Deas *i. Scotland* U.K. *see* **South Uist**
Uibhist a' Tuath *i. Scotland* U.K. *see* **North Uist**
171 E8 **Uichteritz** Ger.
146 D7 **Uig** *Highland, Scotland* U.K.
209 B6 **Uíge** Angola
209 B6 **Uíge** *prov.* Angola
79 □8 **'Uiha** Tonga
101 E10 **Ŭijŏngbu** S. Korea
101 D8 **Ŭiju** N. Korea
120 F3 **Uil** Kazakh.
120 E3 **Uil** *r.* Kazakh.
129 E3 **Uilpata, Gora** *mt.* Rus. Fed.
140 U5 **Uimaharju** Fin.
241 S5 **Uinkaret Plateau** *AZ* U.S.A.
134 L4 **Uinskoye** Rus. Fed.
238 J6 **Uinta** *r. CO* U.S.A.
241 W1 **Uintah and Ouray Indian Reservation** *res. UT* U.S.A.
238 I6 **Uinta Mountains** *UT* U.S.A.
212 B4 **Uis Mine** Namibia
215 J9 **Uitenhage** S. Africa
164 G3 **Uitgeest** Neth.
164 G4 **Uithoorn** Neth.
164 K2 **Uithuizen** Neth.
164 K2 **Uithuizermeeden** Neth.
214 C5 **Uitkyk** S. Africa
214 E3 **Uitsakpan** *salt pan* S. Africa
214 D8 **Uitspankraal** S. Africa
225 I1 **Uivak, Cape** *Nfld and Lab.* Can.
177 J6 **Uivar** Romania
129 G4 **Ujarma** Georgia
175 H4 **Ujazd** *Łódzkie* Pol.
174 G5 **Ujazd** *Opolskie* Pol.
177 G2 **Újezd** Czech Rep.
176 F2 **Újezd u Brna** Czech Rep.
177 K4 **Újfehértó** Hungary
116 G6 **Ujhani** *Uttar Prad.* India
177 I4 **Újhartyán** Hungary
104 C6 **Uji** Japan
104 C6 **Uji-gawa** *r.* Japan
103 G15 **Uji-guntō** *is* Japan
105 K2 **Ujiie** Japan
104 C6 **Ujitawara** Japan
Ujiyamada Japan *see* **Ise**
116 E8 **Ujjain** *Madh. Prad.* India
177 L3 **Újkenéz** Hungary
176 F4 **Újkér** Hungary
177 K5 **Újkígyós** Hungary
177 K4 **Újléta** Hungary
95 K4 **Ujohbilang** *Kalimantan* Indon.
86 □2 **Ujong Tanjong** *pt* Cocos Is
177 H6 **Újpetre** Hungary
174 E2 **Ujście** Pol.
175 H6 **Ujsoły** Pol.
177 K5 **Újszalonta** Hungary
177 J4 **Újszász** Hungary
177 J5 **Újszentiván** Hungary
177 K4 **Újszentmargita** Hungary
177 I4 **Újszilvás** Hungary
177 K4 **Újtikos** Hungary
176 F5 **Újudvar** Hungary
94 F8 **Ujung Kulon, Taman Nasional** *nat. park* Indon.
Ujung Pandang *Sulawesi* Indon. *see* **Makassar**
Újvidék *Vojvodina* Serbia *see* **Novi Sad**
102 □1 **Uka** *Okinawa* Japan
116 D9 **Ukal Sagar** *l.* India
207 G4 **Ukata** Nigeria
104 F1 **Ukawa** Japan
124 G2 **'Ukayrishah** *well* Saudi Arabia
102 □G19 **Uke-jima** *i. Nansei-shotō* Japan
211 B5 **Ukerewe Island** Tanz.
215 N5 **uKhahlamba-Drakensberg Park** *nat. park* S. Africa
127 K7 **Ukhaydir** *tourist site* Iraq
124 G7 **Ukhdūd** *tourist site* Saudi Arabia
Ukhimath *Uttaranchal* India *see* **Okhimath**
135 H5 **Ukholovo** Rus. Fed.
175 M4 **Ukhovets'k** Ukr.
117 O7 **Ukhrul** *Manipur* India
Ukhta *Respublika Kareliya* Rus. Fed. *see* **Kalevala**
134 K3 **Ukhta** *Respublika Komi* Rus. Fed.
134 K3 **Ukhta** *r.* Rus. Fed.
138 M7 **Ukhvala** Belarus
83 N3 **Uki** *N.S.W.* Austr.
240 I2 **Ukiah** *CA* U.S.A.
238 E4 **Ukiah** *OR* U.S.A.
78 □6 **Uki Island** Solomon Is
211 B6 **Ukimbo** Tanz.
221 M2 **Ukkusissat** Greenland
174 D2 **Ukleja** *r.* Pol.
138 H6 **Ukmergė** Lith.
139 S8 **Ukolitsa** Rus. Fed.
136 K4 **Ukraine** *country* Europe
Ukrainka *Kyivs'ka Oblast'* Ukr. *see* **Ukrayinka**
Ukrainka *Respublika Krym* Ukr. *see* **Ukrayinka**
Ukrainskaya S.S.R. *country* Europe *see* **Ukraine**
Ukrainskoye Ukr. *see* **Ukrayins'ke**
Ukrayina *country* Europe *see* **Ukraine**
136 J3 **Ukrayinka** *Kyivs'ka Oblast'* Ukr.
137 N9 **Ukrayinka** *Respublika Krym* Ukr.
137 L3 **Ukrayins'ke** Ukr.
188 F3 **Ukrina** *r.* Bos.-Herz.
209 B7 **Uku** Angola
103 G13 **Uku-jima** *i.* Japan
209 B8 **Ukuma** Angola
212 D4 **Ukwi** Botswana
111 C11 **Ul** *r.* India
138 M6 **Ula** Belarus
138 M6 **Ula** *r.* Belarus
175 M1 **Ūla** *r.* Lith.
199 J5 **Ula** Turkey
106 J3 **Ulaanbaatar** Mongolia
106 J3 **Ulaanbaatar** *mun.* Mongolia
107 K3 **Ulaan-Ereg** Mongolia
106 C2 **Ulaangom** Mongolia
106 I3 **Ulaanhudag** Mongolia
106 H4 **Ulaan Nuur** *salt l.* Mongolia
106 G3 **Ulaan-Uul** *Bayanhongor* Mongolia
107 L4 **Ulaan-Uul** *Dornogovĭ* Mongolia
83 L5 **Ulan** *N.S.W.* Austr.
107 K7 **Ulan** *Nei Mongol* China
106 F8 **Ulan** *Qinghai* China
Ulan Bator Mongolia *see* **Ulaanbaatar**
121 N5 **Ulanbel'** Kazakh.
106 J6 **Ulan Buh Shamo** *des.* China
135 I7 **Ulan Erge** Rus. Fed.
Ulanhad *Nei Mongol* China *see* **Chifeng**
107 R3 **Ulanhot** *Nei Mongol* China
107 L6 **Ulan Hua** *Nei Mongol* China
136 H4 **Ulaniv** Ukr.
135 I7 **Ulan-Khol** Rus. Fed.
110 H5 **Ulanlinggi** *Xinjiang* China
175 K4 **Ulan-Majorat** Pol.
106 I7 **Ulan Mod** *Nei Mongol* China
137 N2 **Ulanove** Ukr.
175 K5 **Ulanów** Pol.
106 I6 **Ulan Suhai** *Nei Mongol* China
107 K6 **Ulansuhai Nur** *l.* China
106 G6 **Ulan Tohoi** *Nei Mongol* China
98 I1 **Ulan-Ude** Rus. Fed.
111 J9 **Ulan Ul Hu** *l.* China
260 D2 **Ulapes** Arg.
260 D2 **Ulapes, Sierra** *mts* Arg.
126 H4 **Ulaş** *Sivas* Turkey
199 I1 **Ulaş** *Tekirdağ* Turkey
192 D8 **Ulassai** *Sardegna* Italy
110 H5 **Ulastai** *Xinjiang* China
78 □6 **Ulawa Island** Solomon Is
211 C6 **Ulaya** Tanz.
124 H4 **Ulayyah** *reg.* Saudi Arabia
121 T2 **Ul'ba** Kazakh.
100 J2 **Ul'banskiy Zaliv** *b.* Rus. Fed.
238 K3 **UL Bend National Wildlife Refuge** *nature res. MT* U.S.A.
Ülbi Kazakh. *see* **Ul'ba**
138 H5 **Ulbroka** Latvia
146 J6 **Ulbster** *Highland, Scotland* U.K.
149 Q6 **Ulceby** *North Lincolnshire, England* U.K.
101 F10 **Ulchin** S. Korea
196 H9 **Ulcinj** Montenegro
214 I4 **Ulco** S. Africa
142 F6 **Uldum** Denmark
107 L2 **Uldz** Mongolia
107 N2 **Uldz** *r.* Mongolia
Uleåborg Fin. *see* **Oulu**
Ulebsechel *i.* Palau *see* **Auluptagel**
142 F2 **Ulefoss** Norway
78 □5 **Uléi** Vanuatu
185 O6 **Uleila del Campo** Spain
106 I1 **Ulekchin** Rus. Fed.
138 J3 **Ülenurme** Estonia
107 M1 **Ulety** Rus. Fed.
175 K4 **Ułęż** Pol.
142 E5 **Ulfborg** Denmark
142 E5 **Ulfborg Vind** *nature res.* Denmark
Ulflingen Lux. *see* **Troisvierges**
164 J5 **Ulft** Neth.
107 P4 **Ulgain Gol** *r.* China
149 N3 **Ulgham** *Northumberland, England* U.K.
121 L2 **Ul'gili** Kazakh.
114 C3 **Ulhasnagar** *Mahar.* India
175 L5 **Ulhówek** Pol.
129 G4 **Ulianovka** Georgia
107 O4 **Uliastai** *Nei Mongol* China
106 E3 **Uliastay** Mongolia
Uliatea *i. Arch. de la Société* Fr. Polynesia *see* **Raiatea**
177 L3 **Ulič** Slovakia
165 G6 **Ulicoten** Neth.
Ulie *atoll* Micronesia *see* **Woleai**
78 □3b **Uliga** *i. Majuro* Marshall Is
208 E5 **Ulindi** *r.* Dem. Rep. Congo
134 F1 **Ulita** *r.* Rus. Fed.
91 I4 **Ulithi** *atoll* Micronesia
Uljanovsk Rus. Fed. *see* **Ul'yanovsk**
120 J3 **Ul'kayak** *r.* Kazakh.
121 N1 **Ul'ken-Karoy, Ozero** *salt l.* Kazakh.
Ülkenözen *r.* Kazakh./Rus. Fed. *see* **Bol'shoy Uzen'**
121 P6 **Ul'ken Sulutor** Kazakh.
Ülken Vladīmīrovka Kazakh. *see* **Bol'shaya Vladimirovka**
182 C3 **Ulla** *r.* Spain
83 M6 **Ulladulla** *N.S.W.* Austr.
146 F7 **Ullapool** *Highland, Scotland* U.K.
142 I4 **Ullared** Sweden
140 P3 **Ullatti** Sweden
252 C3 **Ulla Ulla, Parque Nacional** *nat. park* Bol.
87 D7 **Ullawarra Aboriginal Reserve** *W.A.* Austr.
186 F6 **Ulldecona** Spain
186 G5 **Ulldemolins** Spain
142 G6 **Ullerslev** Denmark
177 I5 **Üllés** Hungary
149 O6 **Ulleskelf** *North Yorkshire, England* U.K.
262 S1 **Ullmer, Mount** Antarctica
252 C4 **Ulloma** Bol.
140 O2 **Ullsfjorden** *sea chan.* Norway
149 L4 **Ullswater** *l. England* U.K.
129 J3 **Ulluchay** *r.* Rus. Fed.
101 G10 **Ullŭng-do** *i.* S. Korea
172 H5 **Ulm** Ger.
100 F3 **Ul'ma** *r.* Rus. Fed.
169 H10 **Ulmbach** Ger.
184 B2 **Ulme** *r.* Port.
169 C10 **Ulmen** Ger.
197 O6 **Ulmeni** *Călărași* Romania
197 L3 **Ulmeni** *Maramureș* Romania
188 G4 **Ulog** Bos.-Herz.
213 G2 **Ulongue** Moz.
82 G2 **Uloowaranie, Lake** *salt flat S.A.* Austr.
149 K5 **Ulpha** *Cumbria, England* U.K.
142 J4 **Ulricehamn** Sweden
179 I2 **Ulrichsberg** Austria
169 H9 **Ulrichstein** Ger.
164 J2 **Ulrum** Neth.
101 F11 **Ulsan** S. Korea
140 J5 **Ulsberg** Norway
146 □N1 **Ulsta** *Shetland, Scotland* U.K.
142 G4 **Ulsted** Denmark
140 H5 **Ulsteinvik** Norway
147 H3 **Ulster** *reg.* Ireland/U.K.
227 R8 **Ulster** *PA* U.S.A.
235 G1 **Ulster County** *county NY* U.S.A.
246 □ **Ulster Spring** Jamaica
83 I6 **Ultima** *Vic.* Austr.
252 B1 **Ultraoriental, Cordillera** *mts* Peru
183 Q3 **Ultzama** *r.* Spain
186 B1 **Ultzama, Valle de** *val.* Spain
93 D2 **Ulu** *Sulawesi* Indon.
210 B2 **Ulu** Sudan
242 □P10 **Ulúa** *r.* Hond.
129 C5 **Ulubağ** Turkey
199 J2 **Ulubat Gölü** *l.* Turkey
199 K4 **Ulubey** Turkey
199 L4 **Uluborlu** Turkey
199 K2 **Uludağ** *mt.* Turkey
199 K2 **Uludağ Milli Parkı** *nat. park* Turkey
Ulugqat *Xinjiang* China *see* **Wuqia**
94 D3 **Ulu Kali, Gunung** *mt.* Malaysia
129 C7 **Ulukaya** Turkey
126 G5 **Ulukışla** Turkey
199 L4 **Uluköy** Turkey
215 P4 **Ulundi** S. Africa
110 H3 **Ulungur He** *r.* China
110 H3 **Ulungur Hu** *l.* China
240 □E13 **'Ulupalakua** *HI* U.S.A.
94 □ **Ulu Pandan** Sing.
Uluqsaqtuua *N.W.T.* Can. *see* **Holman**
84 C8 **Uluṟu** *hill N.T.* Austr.
84 C8 **Uluṟu-Kata Tjuṯa National Park** *N.T.* Austr.
199 J3 **Ulus Dağı** *mt.* Turkey
Ulutau Kazakh. *see* **Ulytau**

95 K2 Ulu Temburong National Park Brunei
146 D10 Ulva i. Scotland U.K.
Ulvéah i. Vanuatu see Lopévi
140 □ Ulvebreen glacier Svalbard
142 B2 Ulvenåso mt. Norway
164 G5 Ulvenhout Neth.
149 K5 Ulverston Cumbria, England U.K.
83 K9 Ulverstone Tas. Austr.
142 C1 Ulvik Norway
141 N5 Ulvsjön Sweden
139 U3 Ul'yanikha Rus. Fed.
139 V6 Ul'yanino Rus. Fed.
137 K6 Ulyanivka Mykolayivs'ka Oblast' Ukr.
137 N3 Ulyanivka Sums'ka Oblast' Ukr.
Ūl'yanov Kazakh. see Ul'yanovskiy
139 N2 Ul'yanovka Rus. Fed.
136 J5 Ul'yanovka Kirovohrads'ka Oblast' Ukr.
137 L3 Ul'yanovka Poltavs'ka Oblast' Ukr.
138 F7 Ul'yanovo Kaliningradskaya Oblast' Rus. Fed.
139 S8 Ul'yanovo Kaluzhskaya Oblast' Rus. Fed.
135 J5 Ul'yanovsk Rus. Fed.
135 I5 Ul'yanovskaya Oblast' admin. div. Rus. Fed.
121 O2 Ul'yanovskiy Kazakh.
Ulyanovsk Oblast admin. div. Rus. Fed. see Ul'yanovskaya Oblast'
Ul'yanovskoye Kazakh. see Ul'yanovskiy
107 O1 Ulyatuy Rus. Fed.
237 E7 Ulysses KS U.S.A.
232 C11 Ulysses KY U.S.A.
121 L3 Ulytau Kazakh.
121 L4 Ulytau, Gory mts Kazakh.
120 J3 Uly-Zhylanshyk r. Kazakh.
100 B2 Uma Rus. Fed.
188 D3 Umag Croatia
252 D4 Umala Bol.
100 H3 Umaltinskiy Rus. Fed.
'Umān country Asia see Oman
243 O7 Umán Mex.
78 □4a Uman i. Chuuk Micronesia
136 J5 Uman' Ukr.
258 C3 Umango, Cerro mt. Arg.
123 K7 Umarao Pak.
128 E7 'Umarī, Qā' al salt pan Jordan
116 H8 Umaria Madh. Prad. India
114 E3 Umarkhed Mahar. India
114 H3 Umarkot Orissa India
123 M9 Umarkot Pak.
82 G2 Umaroona, Lake salt flat S.A. Austr.
116 D9 Umarpada Gujarat India
78 □1 Umatac Guam
238 E4 Umatilla OR U.S.A.
92 E7 Umayan r. Mindanao Phil.
124 G9 'Umayrah, Khawr al b. Yemen
125 M5 'Umayrī, Wādī watercourse Oman
134 F2 Umba Rus. Fed.
233 □N4 Umbagog Lake NH U.S.A.
84 F2 Umbakumba N.T. Austr.
84 D8 Umbeara N.T. Austr.
208 E2 Umbelasha watercourse Sudan
93 C5 Umbele i. Indon.
150 E6 Umberleigh Devon, England U.K.
191 M9 Umbertide Italy
91 K8 Umboi i. P.N.G.
81 D12 Umbrella Mountains South I. N.Z.
246 □ Umbrella Point Jamaica
191 M9 Umbria admin. reg. Italy
195 L5 Umbriatico Italy
215 P5 Umdloti Beach S. Africa
213 F3 Ume r. Zimbabwe
140 P5 Umeå Sweden
140 P5 Umeälven r. Sweden
93 F4 Umera Maluku Indon.
135 H5 Umet Rus. Fed.
215 Q4 Umfolozi r. S. Africa
215 P4 Umfolozi Game Reserve nature res. S. Africa
140 M4 Umfors Sweden
223 M5 Umfreville Lake Man./Ont. Can.
Umfuli r. Zimbabwe see Mupfure
215 O6 Umgababa S. Africa
215 P5 Umgeni r. S. Africa
125 H1 Umgharah Kuwait
215 P5 Umhali S. Africa
178 C5 Umhausen Austria
215 P5 Umhlanga Rocks S. Africa
215 Q4 Umhlatuzi Lagoon S. Africa
182 C3 Umia r. Spain
105 G1 Umi-gawa r. Japan
221 N3 Umiiviip Kangertiva inlet Greenland
240 □F14 'Umikoa HI U.S.A.
220 H3 Umingmaktok Nunavut Can.
120 D6 Umirzak Kazakh.
224 E1 Umiujaq Que. Can.
172 D5 Umkirch Ger.
215 O6 Umkomaas S. Africa
215 O6 Umkomaas r. S. Africa
215 O5 Umlazi S. Africa
127 L8 Umma tourist site Iraq
128 D6 Umm ad Daraj, Jabal mt. Jordan
128 F4 Umm al 'Amad Syria
124 D4 Umm al Birak Saudi Arabia
128 D9 Umm al Hashīm, Jabal mt. Jordan
124 G2 Umm al Jamājim well Saudi Arabia
Umm al Qaiwain U.A.E. see Umm al Qaywayn
125 L3 Umm al Qaywayn U.A.E.
170 H2 Ummanz i. Ger.
128 F9 Umm ar Raqabah, Khabrat imp. l. Saudi Arabia
125 L5 Umm as Samīm salt flat Oman
124 E2 Umm at Qalbān Saudi Arabia
125 L4 Umm az Zumūl well Oman
125 J3 Umm Bāb Qatar
202 E6 Umm Badr Sudan
202 F6 Umm Bel Sudan
128 B10 Umm Bujmah Egypt
203 F6 Umm Dam Sudan
172 H5 Ummendorf Ger.
202 C2 Umm Farud Libya
203 G4 Umm Gerifat waterhole Sudan
124 C2 Umm Ḥarb Saudi Arabia
208 F2 Umm Heitan Sudan
202 E6 Umm Keddada Sudan
124 C3 Umm Lajj Saudi Arabia
128 C9 Umm Mafrūḍ, Jabal mt. Egypt
124 D4 Umm Mukhbār, Jabal hill Saudi Arabia
128 G9 Umm Nukhaylah hill Saudi Arabia
128 D10 Umm Nukhaylah well Saudi Arabia
127 M8 Umm Qaṣr Iraq
203 F5 Umm Qurein well Sudan
124 B2 Umm Quṣūr i. Saudi Arabia
203 G5 Umm Rumeila well Sudan
203 F6 Umm Ruwaba Sudan
202 E2 Umm Sa'ad Libya
125 J3 Umm Sa'id Qatar
203 F6 Umm Saiyala Sudan
125 J3 Umm Ṣalāl 'Alī Qatar
124 D4 Umm Samā Saudi Arabia
128 D9 Umm Saysabān, Jabal mt. Jordan
128 E9 Umm Shaitiya well Jordan
128 B10 Umm Shawmar, Jabal mt. Egypt
203 F6 Umm Shugeira Sudan
128 A10 Umm Tināṣṣib, Jabal mt. Egypt
124 C3 Umm Urūmah i. Saudi Arabia
128 G7 Umm Wa'āl hill Saudi Arabia
124 G4 Umm Wazīr well Saudi Arabia
128 A10 Umm Zanātīr mt. Egypt
220 B4 Umnak Island AK U.S.A.
96 D7 Um Phang Wildlife Reserve nature res. Thai.
213 H2 Umpilua Moz.
238 B5 Umpqua r. OR U.S.A.
209 C8 Umpulo Angola
199 M3 Umraniye Turkey
116 G9 Umred Mahar. India
114 C1 Umreth Gujarat India
Umtali Zimbabwe see Mutare
215 O7 Umtamvuna r. S. Africa
215 M7 Umtata S. Africa
215 N7 Umtata r. S. Africa
215 M7 Umtata Dam resr S. Africa
215 O6 Umtentweni S. Africa
207 G5 Umuahia Nigeria
256 A5 Umuarama Brazil
129 H5 Umudlu Azer.
129 C5 Umudum Turkey
199 H2 Umurbey Turkey
199 J3 Umurlar Turkey
80 J7 Umutoi North I. N.Z.
215 P5 Umvoti r. S. Africa
Umvukwes Zimbabwe see Mvurwi
Umvuma Zimbabwe see Mvuma
215 N7 Umzimhlava r. S. Africa
215 N6 Umzimkulu S. Africa
215 O6 Umzimkulu r. S. Africa
215 N7 Umzimvubu r. S. Africa
Umzingwani r. Zimbabwe see Mzingwani
215 O6 Umzinto S. Africa
215 O6 Umzumbe S. Africa
139 N6 Una Belarus
188 F3 Una r. Bos.-Herz./Croatia
255 F5 Una Brazil
254 G4 Una r. Brazil
116 F4 Una Hima. Prad. India
183 Q8 Uña Spain
81 G9 Una, Mount South I. N.Z.
128 E9 'Unāb, Jabal al hill Jordan
128 E8 'Unāb, Wādī al watercourse Jordan
188 F3 Unac r. Bos.-Herz.
182 H4 Uña de Quintana Spain
233 J6 Unadilla NY U.S.A.
233 J6 Unadilla r. NY U.S.A.
256 D2 Unaí Brazil
105 M4 Unakami Japan
220 B3 Unalakleet AK U.S.A.
220 B4 Unalaska AK U.S.A.
220 B4 Unalaska Island AK U.S.A.
211 B8 Unango Moz.
176 F3 Únanov Czech Rep.
146 F6 Unapool Highland, Scotland U.K.
140 R3 Unari Fin.
93 B4 Unauna i. Indon.
136 J3 Unava r. Ukr.
128 D8 'Unayzah Jordan
124 F2 'Unayzah Saudi Arabia
126 I7 'Unayzah, Jabal hill Iraq
104 G2 Unazuki Japan
186 C3 Uncastillo Spain
116 H7 Unchahra Madh. Prad. India
241 X3 Uncompahgre Plateau CO U.S.A.
85 J5 Undara National Park Qld Austr.
143 K3 Unden l. Sweden
215 N5 Underberg S. Africa
83 H6 Underbool Vic. Austr.
140 L5 Undersåker Sweden
236 E2 Underwood ND U.S.A.
172 G5 Undingen Ger.
135 J5 Undory Rus. Fed.
93 B9 Undu, Tanjung pt Sumba Indon.
163 B10 Undués de Lerda Spain
93 G5 Undur Seram Indon.
138 E3 Undva Estonia
150 G4 Undy Monmouthshire, Wales U.K.
139 P9 Unecha Rus. Fed.
139 O9 Unecha r. Rus. Fed.
251 E5 Uneiuxi r. Brazil
220 B4 Unga Island AK U.S.A.
83 K5 Ungarie N.S.W. Austr.
82 F6 Ungarra S.A. Austr.
Ungava, Baie d' b. Que. Can. see Ungava Bay
221 K3 Ungava, Péninsule d' pen. Que. Can.
225 H1 Ungava Bay Que. Can.
Ungava Peninsula Que. Can. see Ungava, Péninsule d'
Ungeny Moldova see Ungheni
173 I5 Ungerhausen Ger.
100 G7 Unggi N. Korea
136 G6 Ungheni Moldova
197 M4 Ungheni Romania
213 G4 Unguana Moz.
Unguja i. Tanz. see Zanzibar Island
Unguja North admin. reg. Tanz. see Zanzibar North
Unguja South admin. reg. Tanz. see Zanzibar South
Unguja West admin. reg. Tanz. see Zanzibar West
197 M3 Ungurași Romania
122 H2 Unguz, Solonchakovyye Vpadiny salt flat Turkm.
122 H1 Üngüz Angyrsyndaky Garagum des. Turkm.
Ungvár Ukr. see Uzhhorod
211 D5 Ungwana Bay Kenya
182 E8 Unhais da Serra Port.
182 E8 Unhais-o-Velho Port.
171 J10 Unhošť Czech Rep.
134 J4 Uni Rus. Fed.
252 C2 União Acre Brazil
256 B3 União Minas Gerais Brazil
254 E3 União Piauí Brazil
255 C8 União da Vitória Brazil
251 F5 União do Marará Brazil
254 G4 União dos Palmares Brazil
116 F7 Uniara Rajasthan India
216 □2a Unicorn Point Ascension S. Atlantic Ocean
176 G2 Uničov Czech Rep.
174 G4 Uniejów Pol.
161 E6 Unieux France
191 Q6 Unije Croatia
188 E3 Unije i. Croatia
220 B4 Unimak Island AK U.S.A.
176 G3 Unín Slovakia
251 F5 Unini r. Brazil
252 B2 Unini Peru
260 E4 Unión Arg.
253 F6 Unión Para.
233 □P4 Union ME U.S.A.
236 J6 Union MO U.S.A.
235 G3 Union NJ U.S.A.
238 F4 Union OR U.S.A.
231 G8 Union SC U.S.A.
232 E11 Union WV U.S.A.
259 E5 Unión, Bahía b. Arg.
241 T7 Union, Mount AZ U.S.A.
235 G4 Union Beach NJ U.S.A.
234 A5 Union Bridge MD U.S.A.
232 A8 Union City OH U.S.A.
232 F7 Union City PA U.S.A.
237 K7 Union City TN U.S.A.
235 G3 Union County county NJ U.S.A.
234 A3 Union County county PA U.S.A.
214 H9 Uniondale S. Africa
234 E1 Union Dale PA U.S.A.
246 C2 Unión de Reyes Cuba
244 C6 Unión de Tula Mex.
147 D9 Unionhall Ireland
245 M9 Unión Hidalgo Mex.
247 □3 Union Island St Vincent
234 E6 Union Lake NJ U.S.A.
231 E9 Union Springs AL U.S.A.
232 I6 Union Springs NY U.S.A.
231 D9 Uniontown AL U.S.A.
232 F9 Uniontown PA U.S.A.
217 □1b Union Vale Mauritius
240 L3 Union Valley Reservoir CA U.S.A.
235 J1 Unionville CT U.S.A.
227 K6 Unionville MI U.S.A.
236 I5 Unionville MO U.S.A.
240 N1 Unionville NV U.S.A.
234 F2 Unionville NY U.S.A.
234 D5 Unionville PA U.S.A.
232 H10 Unionville VA U.S.A.
174 G2 Unisław Pol.
125 K4 United Arab Emirates country Asia
United Arab Republic country Africa see Egypt
145 G4 United Kingdom country Europe
United Provinces state India see Uttar Pradesh
228 G3 United States of America country N. America
221 L1 United States Range mts Nunavut Can.
191 M7 Uniti r. Italy
223 I4 Unity Sask. Can.
238 E4 Unity OR U.S.A.
234 B2 Unityville PA U.S.A.
183 Q8 Universales, Montes reg. Spain
212 B4 Unjab watercourse Namibia
116 D8 Unjha Gujarat India
169 D9 Unkel Ger.
178 G4 Unken Austria
172 H5 Unlingen Ger.
169 E7 Unna Ger.
116 H6 Unnao Uttar Prad. India
169 E9 Unnau Ger.
104 E2 Unoke Japan
101 D9 Ŭnp'a N. Korea
261 E2 Unquillo Arg.
101 D8 Unsan N. Korea
101 E9 Ŭnsan N. Korea
129 E7 Ünseli Turkey
146 □O1 Unst i. Scotland U.K.
149 O7 Unstone Derbyshire, England U.K.
171 E8 Unstrut r. Ger.
171 E8 Unstrut-Trias-Land park Ger.
117 I7 Untari Jharkhand India
102 □1 Unten Okinawa Japan
197 O3 Unțeni Romania
190 F1 Unterägeri Switz.
173 K6 Unterammergau Ger.
169 I9 Unterbreizbach Ger.
173 J6 Unterdießen Ger.
173 N5 Unterdietfurt Ger.
170 F5 Untere Havel park Ger.
190 I2 Unter Engadin reg. Switz.
170 J5 Unteres Odertal, Nationalpark nat. park Ger.
170 J5 Unteres Odertal, Nationalpark nat. park Ger.
169 I10 Unterfranken admin. reg. Ger.
173 P4 Untergriesbach Ger.
173 L5 Unterhaching Ger.
178 D5 Unter Inn Thal val. Austria
190 E1 Unterkulm Switz.
179 N6 Unterlamm Austria
168 J5 Unterlüß Ger.
169 J9 Untermaßfeld Ger.
173 J5 Untermeitingen Ger.
169 K10 Untermerzbach Ger.
172 H3 Untermünkheim Ger.
173 N5 Unterneukirchen Ger.
173 I2 Unterpleichfeld Ger.
173 M5 Unterreit Ger.
190 F2 Unterschächen Switz.
173 L5 Unterschleißheim Ger.
173 I4 Unterschneidheim Ger.
172 G6 Untersee l. Ger./Switz.
169 K10 Untersiemau Ger.
171 E10 Untersteinach Ger.
173 J6 Unterthingau Ger.
170 I4 Unterueckersee l. Ger.
179 K3 Unterweißenbach Austria
171 D9 Unterwellenborn Ger.
173 M6 Unterwössen Ger.
129 H3 Untsukul' Rus. Fed.
251 E4 Unturán, Sierra de mts Venez.
222 D3 Unuk r. Can./U.S.A.
106 B9 Unuli Horog Qinghai China
156 B7 Unverre France
134 L3 Un'ya r. Rus. Fed.
103 H14 Unzen-Amakusa Kokuritsu-kōen nat. park Japan
134 I4 Unzha Rus. Fed.
183 Q3 Unzué Spain
102 □A21 Uoturi-shima i. Nansei-shotō Japan
104 F2 Uozu Japan
176 E1 Úpa r. Czech Rep.
139 T7 Upa r. Rus. Fed.
241 V1 Upalco UT U.S.A.
117 J8 Upar Ghat reg. Chhattisgarh India
251 F2 Upata Venez.
151 I5 Upavon Wiltshire, England U.K.
209 E7 Upemba, Lac l. Dem. Rep. Congo
209 E7 Upemba, Parc National de l' nat. park Dem. Rep. Congo
117 K8 Uperbada Orissa India
221 M2 Upernavik Greenland
221 M2 Upernavik Kujalleq Greenland
168 D3 Upgant-Schott Ger.
92 E8 Upi Mindanao Phil.
250 C3 Upía r. Col.
176 F1 Úpice Czech Rep.
214 F4 Upington S. Africa
141 R6 Upinniemi Fin.
240 O7 Upland CA U.S.A.
116 C9 Upleta Gujarat India
129 F4 Up'lists'ikhe Georgia
150 G6 Uplyme Devon, England U.K.
80 J6 Upokongaro North I. N.Z.
140 U3 Upoloksha Rus. Fed.
78 □2 'Upolu i. Samoa
240 □F13 'Upolu Point HI U.S.A.
129 C1 Upornaya Rus. Fed.
238 D6 Upper Alkali Lake CA U.S.A.
232 B8 Upper Arlington OH U.S.A.
222 G5 Upper Arrow Lake B.C. Can.
Upper Austria land Austria see Oberösterreich
146 D6 Upper Bayble Western Isles, Scotland U.K.
234 E3 Upper Black Eddy PA U.S.A.
146 J6 Upper Camster Highland, Scotland U.K.
150 F3 Upper Chapel Powys, Wales U.K.
Upper Chindwin Myanmar see Mawlaik
151 J5 Upper Clatford Hampshire, England U.K.
234 C5 Upper Crossroads MD U.S.A.
234 E5 Upper Darby PA U.S.A.
206 E4 Upper East admin. reg. Ghana
222 F4 Upper Fraser B.C. Can.
151 J4 Upper Heyford Oxfordshire, England U.K.
81 J8 Upper Hutt North I. N.Z.
226 C6 Upper Iowa r. IA U.S.A.
233 □R2 Upper Kent N.B. Can.
238 D5 Upper Klamath Lake OR U.S.A.
146 J8 Upper Knockando Moray, Scotland U.K.
147 I3 Upperlands Northern Ireland U.K.
222 D2 Upper Liard Y.T. Can.
147 G4 Upper Lough Erne l. Northern Ireland U.K.
224 A3 Upper Manitou Lake Ont. Can.
247 □7 Upper Manzanilla Trin. and Tob.
234 B7 Upper Marlboro MD U.S.A.
227 Q5 Upper Mazinaw Lake Ont. Can.
238 J3 Upper Missouri Breaks National Monument nat. park MT U.S.A.
210 B2 Upper Nile state Sudan
235 H2 Upper Nyack NY U.S.A.
94 □ Upper Peirce Reservoir Sing.
226 E9 Upper Preoria Lake IL U.S.A.
236 H1 Upper Red Lake MN U.S.A.
232 B8 Upper Sandusky OH U.S.A.
233 K4 Upper Saranac Lake NY U.S.A.
Upper Seal Lake Que. Can. see Iberville, Lac d'
81 G8 Upper Takaka South I. N.Z.
151 I2 Upper Tean Staffordshire, England U.K.
Upper Tunguska r. Rus. Fed. see Angara
Upper Volta country Africa see Burkina
114 D6 Uppinangadi Karnataka India
151 K2 Uppingham Rutland, England U.K.
143 N2 Uppland reg. Sweden
143 N1 Upplanda Sweden
143 N2 Upplands-Väsby Sweden
143 N2 Uppsala Sweden
143 N1 Uppsala county Sweden
117 I8 Uprara Chhattisgarh India
224 B3 Upsala Ont. Can.
116 F3 Upshi Jammu and Kashmir
226 D3 Upson WI U.S.A.
85 K5 Upstart, Cape Qld Austr.
85 K5 Upstart Bay Qld Austr.
150 H6 Upton Dorset, England U.K.
233 N6 Upton MA U.S.A.
150 H4 Upton St Leonards Gloucestershire, England U.K.
150 H3 Upton upon Severn Worcestershire, England U.K.
128 D8 'Uqayqah, Wādī watercourse Jordan
128 F3 'Uqayribāt Syria
127 M9 Uqlat al 'Udhaybah well Iraq
124 F3 'Uqlat aṣ Ṣuqūr Saudi Arabia
Uqsuqtuq Nunavut Can. see Gjoa Haven
Uqturpan Xinjiang China see Wushi
127 M8 Ur tourist site Iraq
250 B2 Urabá, Golfo de b. Col.
Uracas vol. N. Mariana Is see Farallon de Pajaros
Urad Qianqi Nei Mongol China see Xishanzui
Urad Zhongqi Nei Mongol China see Haliut
122 G6 Ūrāf Iran
146 □N2 Urafirth Shetland, Scotland U.K.
105 K6 Uraga-suidō sea chan. Japan
105 H1 Uragawara Japan
190 H4 Urago d'Oglio Italy
140 V2 Ura-Guba Rus. Fed.
102 U4 Urahoro Japan
256 B5 Uraí Brazil
176 F4 Uraiújfalu Hungary
114 E7 Urakam Kerala India
102 T4 Urakawa Japan
83 K5 Ural hill N.S.W. Austr.
120 D4 Ural r. Kazakh./Rus. Fed.
83 M4 Uralla N.S.W. Austr.
Ural Mountains Rus. Fed. see Ural'skiy Khrebet
100 F2 Uralovka Rus. Fed.
120 D2 Ural'sk Kazakh.
Ural'skaya Oblast' admin. div. Kazakh. see Zapadnyy Kazakhstan
Ural'skiye Gory mts Rus. Fed. see Ural'skiy Khrebet
134 L2 Ural'skiy Khrebet mts Rus. Fed.
211 B6 Urambo Tanz.
114 C3 Uran Mahar. India
83 K6 Urana N.S.W. Austr.
83 K6 Urana, Lake N.S.W. Austr.
84 G6 Urandangi Qld Austr.
254 E5 Urandi Brazil
223 I3 Uranium City Sask. Can.
83 K6 Uranquinty N.S.W. Austr.
84 E3 Urapunga N.T. Austr.
84 E7 Urapuntja N.T. Austr.
251 F4 Uraricoera Brazil
251 F4 Uraricoera r. Brazil
Urartu country Asia see Armenia
192 B8 Uras Sardegna Italy
102 □1 Urasoe Okinawa Japan
Ura-Tyube Tajik. see Ŭroteppa
114 E5 Uravakonda Andhra Prad. India
241 X3 Uravan CO U.S.A.
105 K4 Urawa Japan
130 H3 Uray Rus. Fed.
105 K4 Urayasu Japan
128 C8 'Urayf an Nāqah, Jabal hill Egypt
125 I3 Uray'irah Saudi Arabia
124 F3 'Urayq, Nafūd al des. Saudi Arabia
124 G2 'Urayq ad Duḥūl des. Saudi Arabia
124 H2 'Urayq Sāqān des. Saudi Arabia
174 E4 Uraz Pol.
135 I5 Urazovka Rus. Fed.
135 G6 Urazovo Rus. Fed.
169 E9 Urbach Ger.
236 K5 Urbana IL U.S.A.
226 I9 Urbana IN U.S.A.
232 B8 Urbana OH U.S.A.
191 N8 Urbania Italy
254 E2 Urbano Santos Brazil
169 E10 Urbar Ger.
183 P3 Urbasa, Sierra de mts Spain
190 F7 Urbe Italy
183 M4 Urbel r. Spain
83 N3 Urbenville N.S.W. Austr.
172 F2 Urberach Ger.
191 N8 Urbino Italy
192 C3 Urbino, Étang d' lag. Corse France
Urbinum Italy see Urbino
183 O4 Urbión mt. Spain
183 O4 Urbión, Picos de mts Spain
191 O9 Urbisaglia Italy
160 D4 Urbise France
Urbs Vetus Italy see Orvieto
176 G2 Určice Czech Rep.
252 C3 Urcos Peru
163 B9 Urcuit France
120 B3 Urda Kazakh.
185 L2 Urda Spain
261 G5 Urdampolleta Arg.
186 B1 Urdax-Urdazuli Spain
Ur'devarri hill Fin./Norway see Urtivaara
261 H3 Urdinarrain Arg.
134 J3 Urdoma Rus. Fed.
172 E7 Urdorf Switz.
163 C10 Urdos France
106 G3 Urd Tamir Gol r. Mongolia
183 O3 Urduña Spain
129 L1 Urdyuk, Mys pt Kazakh.
134 J2 Urdyuzhskoye, Ozero l. Rus. Fed.
121 S4 Urdzhar Kazakh.
149 O5 Ure r. England U.K.
138 K9 Urechcha Belarus
197 P4 Urechești Romania
134 I4 Uren' Rus. Fed.
130 I3 Urengoy Rus. Fed.
142 D2 Urenosi mt. Norway
80 I5 Urenui North I. N.Z.
78 □5 Uréparapara i. Vanuatu
163 B9 Urepel France
242 D3 Ures Mex.
104 D6 Ureshino Japan
164 J2 Ureterp Neth.
80 L5 Urewera National Park North I. N.Z.
Urfa Turkey see Şanlıurfa
169 B9 Urft r. Ger.
Urga Mongolia see Ulaanbaatar
100 H3 Urgal r. Rus. Fed.
120 I7 Urganch Uzbek.
199 I4 Urganlı Turkey
186 H4 Urgell, Canal d' Spain
Urgench Uzbek. see Urganch
126 G4 Ürgüp Turkey
121 L8 Urgut Uzbek.
110 G3 Urho Xinjiang China
140 S2 Urho Kekkosen kansallispuisto nat. park Fin.
192 B6 Uri Sardegna Italy
116 E2 Uri Jammu and Kashmir
190 F2 Uri canton Switz.
81 F9 Uriah, Mount South I. N.Z.
183 O3 Uribarri-Ganboa, Embalse de resr Spain
250 C2 Uribia Col.
261 F5 Uriburu Arg.
146 L8 Urie r. Scotland U.K.
100 G4 Uril Rus. Fed.
157 L7 Uriménil France
244 E6 Uripitijuata, Cerro mt. Mex.
242 F4 Urique Mex.
239 K13 Urique r. Mex.
190 F2 Uri-Rotstock mt. Switz.
83 I3 Urisino N.S.W. Austr.
137 R1 Uritskoye Rus. Fed.
210 C1 Urī Wenz r. Eth.
105 L3 Urizura Japan
141 Q6 Urjala Fin.
164 I3 Urk Neth.
100 D1 Urkan Rus. Fed.
100 E2 Urkan r. Rus. Fed.
129 I3 Urkarakh Rus. Fed.
177 G4 Úrkút Hungary
210 D4 Urkut Somalia
199 H4 Urla Turkey
197 O6 Urlați Romania
147 G7 Urlingford Ireland
197 N7 Urlui r. Romania
107 J1 Urluk Rus. Fed.
128 E2 Urmā aṣ Ṣughrá Syria
111 H11 Urmai Xizang China
128 E6 'Urmān Syria
134 I5 Urmary Rus. Fed.
123 M2 Urmetan Tajik.
100 I4 Urmi r. Rus. Fed.
Urmia Iran see Orūmīyeh
Urmia, Lake salt l. Iran see Orūmīyeh, Daryācheh-ye
157 O3 Urmitz Ger.
149 M7 Urmston Greater Manchester, England U.K.
109 □I7 Urmston Road sea chan. H.K. China
190 G1 Urnäsch Switz.
186 A1 Urola r. Spain
207 G5 Uromi Nigeria
196 J8 Uroševac Kosovo Serbia
134 F3 Urosozero Rus. Fed.
123 M2 Ŭroteppa Tajik.
137 N8 Urozhayne Ukr.
129 F2 Urozhaynoye Rus. Fed.
183 P3 Urquilla, Sierra de mts Spain
183 N4 Urquiza, Embalse de resr Spain
184 E2 Urra Port.
186 E5 Urrea de Gaén Spain
186 C4 Urrea de Jalón Spain
260 E6 Urre Lauquén, Laguna l. Arg.
163 B10 Urriés Spain
182 F6 Urros Port.
183 R3 Urroz Spain
111 H11 Urru Co salt l. China
163 A9 Urrugne France
183 O3 Urrúnaga, Embalse de resr Spain
Ursat'yevskaya Uzbek. see Xovos
173 I5 Ursberg Ger.
173 L3 Ursensollen Ger.
139 X6 Urshel'skiy Rus. Fed.
245 I3 Úrsulo Galván Mex.
245 K6 Úrsulo Galván Mex.
163 B9 Ursuya, Mont hill France
175 L4 Urszulin Pol.
163 B9 Urt France
106 G5 Urt Mongolia
120 H1 Urtazym Rus. Fed.
190 C1 Urtenen Switz.
140 Q2 Urtivaara hill Fin./Norway
111 K8 Urt Moron Qinghai China
106 C8 Urt Moron r. Qinghai China
242 E4 Uruáchic Mex.
254 C5 Uruaçu Brazil
253 H3 Uruana Brazil
239 F11 Uruapan Baja California Mex.
244 E6 Uruapan Michoacán Mex.
252 B3 Urubamba Peru
251 E5 Urubaxi r. Brazil
251 G5 Urubu r. Brazil
256 B4 Urubupungá, Salto do waterfall Brazil
251 G5 Urucara Brazil
139 Q9 Uruch'ye Rus. Fed.
251 F6 Urucu r. Brazil
254 D3 Uruçuí Brazil
254 D4 Uruçuí, Serra do hills Brazil
257 E2 Urucuia Brazil
257 E2 Urucuia r. Brazil
254 D3 Uruçui Preto r. Brazil
253 F4 Urucum Brazil
251 G5 Urucurituba Brazil
183 J5 Urueña Spain
104 G5 Urugi Japan
261 H3 Uruguai r. Brazil alt. Uruguay (Arg./Uru.)
258 F3 Uruguaiana Brazil
255 B8 Uruguay r. Arg./Uru. alt. Uruguai (Brazil)
258 G4 Uruguay country S. America
Uruk tourist site Iraq see Erech
129 F2 Urukh r. Rus. Fed.
92 □ Urukthapel i. Palau
Urumchi Xinjiang China see Ürümqi
110 H5 Ürümqi Xinjiang China
Urundi country Africa see Burundi
83 N4 Urunga N.S.W. Austr.
78 □1 Uruno Point Guam
129 C2 Urup Rus. Fed.
129 C1 Urup r. Rus. Fed.
131 Q5 Urup, Ostrov i. Kuril'skiye O-va Rus. Fed.
253 E2 Urupá r. Brazil
123 Q1 Uru Pass China/Kyrg.
256 C4 Urupês Brazil
Urupskaya Rus. Fed. see Sovetskaya
124 H6 'Urūq al Awārik des. Saudi Arabia
125 L4 'Urūq ash Shaybah des. Saudi Arabia
193 O4 Ururi Italy
100 C1 Urusha Rus. Fed.
100 C2 Urusha r. Rus. Fed.
129 G2 Urus-Martan Rus. Fed.
135 K5 Urussu Rus. Fed.
256 C2 Urutaí Brazil
80 I5 Uruti North I. N.Z.
81 K8 Uruti Point North I. N.Z.
211 A6 Uruwira Tanz.
123 L5 Urūzgān prov. Afgh.
129 E2 Urvan' Rus. Fed.
158 H2 Urville Nacqueville France
121 V3 Uryl' Kazakh.
102 S3 Uryū Japan
102 S3 Uryū-gawa r. Japan
100 B2 Uryumkan r. Rus. Fed.
100 B2 Uryupino Rus. Fed.
135 H6 Uryupinsk Rus. Fed.
184 C5 Urza hill Port.
175 K5 Urzędów Pol.
216 □1c Urzelina São Jorge Azores
Ürzhar Kazakh. see Urdzhar
134 J4 Urzhum Rus. Fed.
197 O6 Urziceni Ialomița Romania
177 L4 Urziceni Satu Mare Romania
137 Q7 Urzuf Ukr.
192 D7 Urzulei Sardegna Italy
160 C2 Urzy France
138 L8 Usa r. Belarus
103 I13 Usa Japan
120 C1 Usa r. Rus. Fed.
134 L2 Usa r. Rus. Fed.
92 C9 Usada i. Phil.
184 G4 Usagre Spain
199 K4 Uşak Turkey
199 K4 Uşak prov. Turkey
212 B4 Usakos Namibia
211 C6 Usambara Mountains Tanz.
211 B7 Usangu Flats plain Tanz.
263 K2 Usarp Mountains Antarctica
259 F8 Usborne, Mount hill Falkland Is
196 I7 Ušće Serbia
169 I8 Uschlag (Staufenberg) Ger.
175 J6 Uście Gorlickie Pol.
175 I5 Uście Solne Pol.
190 G7 Uscio Italy
170 I3 Usedom Ger.
170 J3 Usedom i. Ger.
87 B9 Useless Loop W.A. Austr.
192 B8 Usellus Sardegna Italy
210 B5 Usengi Kenya
187 E7 Useras Spain
124 D5 Usfān Saudi Arabia
138 I8 Usha r. Belarus
138 L8 Usha r. Belarus
Ushachi Belarus see Ushachy
138 L6 Ushachy Belarus
130 I1 Ushakova, Ostrov i. Rus. Fed.
121 T3 Ushanovo Kazakh.
Ushant i. France see Ouessant, Île d'
Üsharal Kazakh. see Ucharal
121 N6 Usharal Kazakh.
149 N4 Ushaw Moor Durham, England U.K.
124 G3 Ushayqir Saudi Arabia
124 E5 'Ushayrah Saudi Arabia
129 D2 Ushba, Mt'a Georgia
138 M6 Ushcha r. Rus. Fed.
139 O9 Ushcherp'ye Rus. Fed.
105 M4 Ushibori Japan
103 H14 Ushibuka Japan
105 L3 Ushiku Japan
104 C8 Ushimawashi-yama mt. Japan
211 A5 Ushirombo Tanz.
137 N6 Ushkalka Ukr.
134 M3 Ushma Rus. Fed.
120 E6 Ushtagan Kazakh.
121 Q5 Ushtobe Kazakh.
Ush-Tyube Kazakh. see Ushtobe
259 C9 Ushuaia Arg.
136 G5 Ushytsya r. Ukr.
138 F4 Uši Latvia
254 B3 Usina Brazil
169 G10 Usingen Ger.
192 B6 Usini Sardegna Italy
134 L2 Usinsk Rus. Fed.
150 G4 Usk Monmouthshire, Wales U.K.
150 G4 Usk r. Wales U.K.
117 I6 Uska Uttar Prad. India
138 K8 Uskhodni Belarus
Uskoplje Bos.-Herz. see Gornji Vakuf
150 E4 Usk Reservoir Wales U.K.
199 K1 Üsküdar Turkey
197 P9 Üsküp Turkey
169 I7 Uslar Ger.
176 C2 Úslava r. Czech Rep.
138 F4 Usma Latvia
139 W9 Usman' Rus. Fed.
139 W9 Usman' r. Rus. Fed.
138 F4 Usmas ezers l. Latvia
121 L8 Usmat Uzbek.
Usmet Uzbek. see Usmat
139 O6 Usmyn' Rus. Fed.
260 D2 Usno Arg.
183 J9 Uso r. Spain
134 J3 Usogorsk Rus. Fed.
211 B6 Usoke Tanz.
134 L4 Usol'ye Rus. Fed.
98 H1 Usol'ye-Sibirskoye Rus. Fed.
188 G3 Usora r. Bos.-Herz.
176 G2 Úsov Czech Rep.
137 N1 Usozha r. Rus. Fed.
137 O1 Usozha r. Rus. Fed.
260 C3 Uspallata Arg.
137 P6 Uspenivka Ukr.
121 Q1 Uspenka Kazakh.
137 R6 Uspenka Donets'ka Oblast' Ukr.
137 M5 Uspenka Kirovohrads'ka Oblast' Ukr.
137 M2 Uspenka Sums'ka Oblast' Ukr.
100 E2 Uspenovka Rus. Fed.
121 O3 Uspenskiy Kazakh.
135 H7 Uspenskoye Krasnodarskiy Kray Rus. Fed.
139 N5 Uspenskoye Pskovskaya Oblast' Rus. Fed.
134 H4 Uspen'ye Rus. Fed.
164 K2 Usquert Neth.
192 C9 Ussana Sardegna Italy
192 C8 Ussassai Sardegna Italy
161 K6 Usseglio Italy
161 B6 Ussel Auvergne France
162 I4 Ussel Limousin France
160 H5 Usses r. France
162 F3 Usson-du-Poitou France
161 D6 Usson-en-Forez France
100 I4 Ussuri r. Rus. Fed.
100 G7 Ussuriysk Rus. Fed.
134 I4 Usta r. Rus. Fed.
Ust'-Abakanskoye Rus. Fed. see Abakan
134 I3 Ust'-Alekseyevo Rus. Fed.
123 M7 Usta Muhammad Pak.
163 B9 Ustaritz France
Ust'-Balyk Rus. Fed. see Nefteyugansk
99 I1 Ust'-Barguzin Rus. Fed.
134 L4 Ust'-Dolgaya Rus. Fed.
138 M5 Ust'-Dolyssy Rus. Fed.
135 H7 Ust'-Donetskiy Rus. Fed.
129 C1 Ust'-Dzheguta Rus. Fed.
Ust'-Dzhegutinskaya Rus. Fed. see Ust'-Dzheguta
176 C1 Ústecký kraj admin. reg. Czech Rep.
176 D1 Úštěk Czech Rep.
190 F1 Uster Switz.
142 D1 Ustevatn l. Norway
194 E6 Ustica Sicilia Italy
194 E6 Ustica, Isola di i. Sicilia Italy
131 L4 Ust'-Ilimsk Rus. Fed.
131 L4 Ust'-Ilimskiy Vodokhranilishche resr Rus. Fed.
107 M1 Ust'-Ilya Rus. Fed.
134 L3 Ust'-Ilych Rus. Fed.
176 D1 Ústí nad Labem Czech Rep.
176 F2 Ústí nad Orlicí Czech Rep.
Ustinov Rus. Fed. see Izhevsk
Ustirt plat. Kazakh./Uzbek. see Ustyurt Plateau
143 M7 Ustka Pol.
121 T1 Ust'-Kalmanka Rus. Fed.
131 R4 Ust'-Kamchatsk Rus. Fed.
121 T3 Ust'-Kamenogorsk Kazakh.
110 G1 Ust'-Kan Rus. Fed.
100 A2 Ust'-Karsk Rus. Fed.
110 G1 Ust'-Koksa Rus. Fed.
134 K3 Ust'-Kulom Rus. Fed.
131 L4 Ust'-Kut Rus. Fed.
131 O2 Ust'-Kuyga Rus. Fed.
135 G7 Ust'-Labinsk Rus. Fed.
Ust'-Labinskaya Rus. Fed. see Ust'-Labinsk
100 B2 Ust'-Lubiya Rus. Fed.
138 L2 Ust'-Luga Rus. Fed.
134 L2 Ust'-Lyzha Rus. Fed.
134 M3 Ust'-Man'ya Rus. Fed.
131 O3 Ust'-Maya Rus. Fed.
Ust'-Mongunay Rus. Fed. see Primorskiy
130 J3 Ust'-Munduyka Rus. Fed.
134 K3 Ust'-Nem Rus. Fed.
131 P3 Ust'-Nera Rus. Fed.
134 J3 Ust'-Ocheya Rus. Fed.
131 M2 Ust'-Olenek Rus. Fed.
131 P3 Ust'-Omchug Rus. Fed.
98 H1 Ust'-Ordynskiy Rus. Fed.
98 H1 Ust'-Ordynskiy Buryatskiy Avtonomnyy Okrug admin. div. Rus. Fed.
163 G10 Ustou France
130 J3 Ust'-Port Rus. Fed.
197 O8 Ustrem Bulg.
174 G6 Ustroń Pol.
174 D1 Ustronie Morskie Pol.
175 K6 Ustrzyki Dolne Pol.
139 Q1 Ust'-Sara Rus. Fed.
134 H3 Ust'-Shonosha Rus. Fed.
134 K2 Ust'-Tsil'ma Rus. Fed.
110 H1 Ust'-Ulagan Rus. Fed.
134 L3 Ust'-Uls Rus. Fed.
100 H3 Ust'-Umalta Rus. Fed.
134 L3 Ust'-Unya Rus. Fed.
134 I3 Ust'-Ura Rus. Fed.
100 H3 Ust'-Urgal Rus. Fed.
100 B2 Ust'-Urov Rus. Fed.
134 L2 Ust'-Usa Rus. Fed.
120 J1 Ust'-Uyskoye Kazakh.
134 H3 Ust'-Vayen'ga Rus. Fed.
134 L2 Ust'-Voya Rus. Fed.
134 I3 Ust'-Vyyskaya Rus. Fed.
134 H3 Ust'ya r. Rus. Fed.
131 O2 Ust'-Yansk Rus. Fed.
139 O5 Ust'ye Tverskaya Oblast' Rus. Fed.
134 G4 Ust'ye Vologodskaya Oblast' Rus. Fed.
134 H4 Ust'ye Vologodskaya Oblast' Rus. Fed.
139 W4 Ust'ye Yaroslavskaya Oblast' Rus. Fed.
139 W4 Ust'ye r. Rus. Fed.
139 S3 Ust'ye-Kirovskoye Rus. Fed.
136 D3 Ustyluh Ukr.
137 L6 Ustynivka Ukr.
Ustyurt, Plato plat. Kazakh./Uzbek. see Ustyurt Plateau
120 G6 Ustyurt Plateau Kazakh./Uzbek.
Ustyurt Platosi plat. Kazakh./Uzbek. see Ustyurt Plateau
139 S3 Ustyutskoye Rus. Fed.
139 T3 Ustyuzhna Rus. Fed.
110 G4 Usu Xinjiang China
93 C9 Usu i. Indon.
105 H3 Usuda Japan
129 I4 Usukhchay Rus. Fed.
103 I13 Usuki Japan
242 □O11 Usulután El Salvador
243 M8 Usumacinta r. Guat./Me[x.]
Usumbura Burundi see Bujumbura
95 K3 Usun Apau, Dataran Ti[nggi] plat. Malaysia
186 A1 Usurbil Spain
175 H6 Úšust mt. Pol.
215 Q2 Usutu r. Africa
134 L4 Us'va Rus. Fed.
139 N6 Usvyaty Rus. Fed.
138 M7 Usvyeyka r. Belarus
175 I6 Uszew Pol.
177 H5 Uszód Hungary
175 I5 Uszwica r. Pol.
91 I7 Uta Papua Indon.
93 F3 Uta i. Maluku Indon.
192 B9 Uta Sardegna Italy
241 U2 Utah state U.S.A.
241 U1 Utah Lake UT U.S.A.
140 S4 Utajärvi Fin.
95 L9 Utan Sumbawa Indon.
104 C7 Utano Japan
168 D3 Utarp Ger.
Utashinai Kuril'skiye O-va Rus. Fed. see Yuzhno-Ku[ril'sk]
106 H1 Utata Rus. Fed.
79 □8 'Uta Vava'u Vava'u Gp To[nga]
124 E4 'Utaybah reg. Saudi Arab[ia]
128 E5 'Utaybah, Buḥayrat al i[mp. l.] Syria
128 B10 Utayrtīr ad Dahamī, Ja[bal] mt. Egypt
125 I2 Utayyiq Saudi Arabia
142 B2 Utbjoa Norway
186 D4 Utebo Spain
237 D8 Ute Creek r. NM U.S.A.
161 K9 Utelle France
209 D9 Utembo r. Angola
241 X4 Ute Mountain Indian Reservation res. CO/NM U[.S.A.]
138 I6 Utena Lith.
100 B1 Uteni Rus. Fed.
116 C7 Uterlai Rajasthan India
168 F1 Utersum Ger.
211 C7 Utete Tanz.
116 F6 Utgir Rajasthan India
96 E7 Uthai Thani Thai.
123 L9 Uthal Pak.
169 K8 Uthleben Ger.
168 G4 Uthlede Ger.
128 F4 'Uthmānīyah Syria
97 D7 U Thong Thai.
96 G7 Uthumphon Phisai Thai.
253 F3 Utiariti Brazil
227 K7 Utica MI U.S.A.
237 J9 Utica MS U.S.A.
233 J5 Utica NY U.S.A.
232 C8 Utica OH U.S.A.
187 C8 Utiel Spain
222 H4 Utikuma Lake Alta Can.
242 □P9 Utila Hond.
254 E5 Utinga r. Brazil
141 I6 Utladalen park Norway
143 L5 Utlängan i. Sweden
215 J3 Utlwanang S. Africa
137 N7 Utlyuks'kyy Lyman b. U[kr.]
103 H14 Uto Japan
143 O3 Utö i. Sweden
84 E7 Utopia N.T. Austr.
260 E5 Utracán Arg.
175 I3 Utrata r. Pol.
116 I6 Utraula Uttar Prad. India
164 H4 Utrecht Neth.
164 H4 Utrecht prov. Neth.
215 O3 Utrecht S. Africa
184 H6 Utrera Spain
184 F4 Utrera, Peña hill Spain
186 D6 Utrillas Spain
177 I6 Utrine Vojvodina Serbia
138 L4 Utroya r. Rus. Fed.
142 A2 Utsira Norway
140 S2 Utsjoki Fin.
140 M2 Utskor Norway
105 G4 Utsugi-dake mt. Japan
105 K2 Utsunomiya Japan
135 I7 Utta Rus. Fed.
114 F6 Uttangarai Tamil Nadu In[dia]
96 E6 Uttaradit Thai.
Uttarakhand state India [see] Uttaranchal
116 G4 Uttaranchal state India
116 G4 Uttarkashi Uttaranchal In[dia]
116 G6 Uttar Pradesh state Indi[a]
178 H3 Uttendorf Oberösterreich Austria
178 G5 Uttendorf Salzburg Austr[ia]
173 K2 Uttenreuth Ger.
172 H5 Uttenweiler Ger.
168 L1 Utterslev Denmark
173 K5 Utting am Ammersee G[er.]
151 I2 Uttoxeter Staffordshire, England U.K.
Uttranchal state India se[e] Uttaranchal
Utu Xinjiang China see Miao'ergou
247 □1 Utuado Puerto Rico
110 H3 Utubulak Xinjiang China
79 □9a Utuofai Tahiti Fr. Polynes[ia]
78 □6 Utupua i. Santa Cruz Is Solomon Is
120 E2 Utva r. Kazakh.
170 H3 Utzedel Ger.
138 H3 Uulu Estonia
221 L2 Uummannaq Avanersuaq Greenland
221 M2 Uummannaq Kitaa Green[land]
221 M2 Uummannaq Fjord inlet Greenland
Uummannarsuaq c. Greenland see Nunap Isu[a]
140 R5 Uurainen Fin.
106 B1 Üüreg Nuur salt l. Mongo[lia]
106 G1 Üür Gol r. Mongolia
Uusikaarlepyy Fin. see Nykarleby
141 P6 Uusikaupunki Fin.
212 B3 Uutapi Namibia
250 D4 Uva r. Col.
134 K4 Uva Rus. Fed.
196 H7 Uvac r. Bos.-Herz./Monte[negro]
237 F11 Uvalde TX U.S.A.
176 D1 Úvaly Czech Rep.
139 N9 Uvaravichy Belarus
139 S6 Uvarovka Rus. Fed.
135 H6 Uvarovo Rus. Fed.
Uvéa atoll Îles Loyauté New Caledonia see Ouvéa
120 I1 Uvel'ka r. Rus. Fed.
139 R3 Uver' r. Rus. Fed.
161 J8 Uvernet-Fours France
211 A6 Uvinza Tanz.
209 F5 Uvira Dem. Rep. Congo
139 Y5 Uvod' r. Rus. Fed.
215 O6 Uvongo S. Africa
106 C2 Uvs prov. Mongolia
106 C1 Uvs Nuur salt l. Mongolia
103 J13 Uwa Japan
103 J13 Uwajima Japan
103 J13 Uwa-kai b. Japan
125 M4 'Uwayfī Oman
124 E3 'Uwayja well Saudi Arabi[a]
202 B2 'Uwaynāt Wannīn Libya
124 C2 'Uwayriḍ, Ḥarrat al lava Saudi Arabia
128 G8 Uwaysiṭ well Saudi Arabi[a]
202 E4 Uweinat, Jebel mt. Suda[n]
211 B7 Uwemba Tanz.
94 G4 Uwi i. Indon.
227 O5 Uxbridge Ont. Can.
151 L4 Uxbridge Greater London England U.K.
160 E3 Uxeau France
169 C10 Üxheim Ger.
107 K7 Uxin Ju Nei Mongol Chin[a]
Uxin Qi Nei Mongol China [see] Dabqig
251 H6 Uxituba Brazil
243 O7 Uxmal tourist site Mex.
245 M8 Uxpanapa r. Mex.
110 H5 Uxxaktal Xinjiang China
120 J1 Uy r. Rus. Fed.
120 I5 Uyaly Kazakh.
Uyaly, Ozero l. Kazakh. s[ee] Koshkarkol', Ozero
129 A7 Uyandık Turkey
131 K4 Uyar Rus. Fed.

114 F6 Vayalpad Andhra Prad. India
Vayenga Rus. Fed. see Severomorsk
130 G2 Vaygach, Ostrov i. Rus. Fed.
114 E7 Vayittiri Kerala India
129 G6 Vayk' Armenia
140 S2 Väylä Fin.
162 H6 Vayrac France
162 F4 Vayres France
256 D2 Vazante Brazil
Vazáš Sweden see Vittangi
129 G5 Vazashen Armenia
177 I2 Važec Slovakia
139 R1 Vazhinka r. Rus. Fed.
129 G4 Vaziani Georgia
213 □J3 Vazobe mt. Madag.
261 G6 Vázquez Arg.
139 R6 Vazuza r. Rus. Fed.
139 R6 Vazuzskoye Vodokhranilishche resr Rus. Fed.
176 D3 Včelná Czech Rep.
Veaikevárri Sweden see Svappavaara
97 F8 Veal Vêng Cambodia
160 E5 Veauche France
142 J6 Veberöd Sweden
140 P4 Vebomark Sweden
161 D8 Vebron France
190 I8 Vecchiano Italy
177 K3 Vechec Slovakia
169 J6 Vechelde Ger.
164 J3 Vecht r. Neth. alt. Vechte (Germany)
168 F5 Vechta Ger.
169 C5 Vechte r. Ger. alt. Vecht (Neth.)
216 □3f Vecindario Gran Canaria Canary Is
182 I7 Vecinos Spain
169 K7 Veckenstedt Ger.
169 I8 Veckerhagen (Reinhardshagen) Ger.
138 G5 Vecmikeļi Latvia
177 I4 Vecsés Hungary
176 E2 Vectec hill Czech Rep.
138 H5 Vecumnieki Latvia
Vedana Rus. Fed. see Vedeno
114 F7 Vedaranniyam Tamil Nadu India
114 E7 Vedasandur Tamil Nadu India
142 I4 Veddige Sweden
197 M6 Vedea Argeș Romania
197 N7 Vedea Giurgiu Romania
197 N7 Vedea r. Romania
191 M4 Vedelago Italy
161 F9 Vedène France
129 H3 Vedeno Rus. Fed.
143 L2 Vedevåg Sweden
129 F6 Vedi Armenia
261 G4 Vedia Arg.
134 F3 Vedlozero Rus. Fed.
137 S5 Vedmezha r. Ukr.
182 D3 Vedra Spain
187 H10 Vedrà, Illa de es i. Spain
161 C6 Védrines-St-Loup France
136 J1 Vedrych r. Belarus
137 S2 Veduga r. Rus. Fed.
164 K2 Veendam Neth.
164 I4 Veenendaal Neth.
164 J2 Veenhuizen Neth.
168 D4 Veenhusen Ger.
164 K3 Veenoord Neth.
146 □N2 Veensgarth Shetland, Scotland U.K.
164 I2 Veenwouden Neth.
164 E5 Veere Neth.
168 H4 Veerse r. Ger.
164 E5 Veerse Meer resr Neth.
140 L4 Vefsnfjord sea chan. Norway
140 K4 Vega i. Norway
237 D8 Vega TX U.S.A.
247 □1 Vega Alta Puerto Rico
247 □1 Vega Baja Puerto Rico
182 I3 Vegacervera Spain
245 K5 Vega de Alatorre Mex.
182 G3 Vega de Espinareda Spain
182 F2 Vegadeo Spain
183 M2 Vega de Pas Spain
216 □3f Vega de San Mateo Gran Canaria Canary Is
182 I6 Vega de Tirados Spain
182 G3 Vega de Valcarce Spain
183 J5 Vega de Valdetronco Spain
183 M6 Veganzones Spain
142 E3 Vegar l. Norway
182 H3 Vegarienza Spain
142 E3 Vegarshei Norway
183 J3 Vegas del Condado Spain
183 L7 Vegas de Matute Spain
164 I5 Veghel Neth.
195 N3 Veglie Italy
198 C2 Vegoritida, Limni l. Greece
159 K6 Vègre r. France
223 H4 Vegreville Alta Can.
252 A2 Végueta Peru
138 K1 Vehkalahti Fin.
170 F4 Vehlow Ger.
141 P6 Vehmaa Fin.
123 N6 Vehoa Pak.
123 N6 Vehoa r. Pak.
140 S1 Veidneset Norway
159 M7 Veigné France
160 I4 Veigy-Foncenex France
169 K10 Veilsdorf Ger.
Veinticinco de Mayo Buenos Aires Arg. see 25 de Mayo
Veinticinco de Mayo La Pampa Arg. see 25 de Mayo
Veinticinco de Mayo Mendoza Arg. see 25 de Mayo
Veinticinco de Mayo Uru. see 25 de Mayo
251 H5 Veiros Brazil
184 D3 Veiros Port.
123 M9 Veirwaro Pak.
175 L1 Veisiejai l. Lith.
138 G7 Veisiejis Lith.
173 J2 Veitsbronn Ger.
179 M4 Veitsch Austria
179 L4 Veitsch mt. Austria
172 H2 Veitshöchheim Ger.
140 R4 Veitsiluoto Fin.
138 E6 Veiviržas r. Lith.
192 I3 Vejano Italy
142 F6 Vejen Denmark
184 H8 Vejer de la Frontera Spain
142 F6 Vejle Denmark
142 F6 Vejle county Denmark
173 O2 Vejprnice Czech Rep.
176 C1 Vejprty Czech Rep.
168 J1 Vejsnæs Nakke pt Denmark
250 C1 Vela, Cabo de la c. Col.
116 D9 Velachha Gujarat India
183 K9 Velada Spain
188 F4 Vela Luka Croatia
183 O6 Velamazán Spain
242 H5 Velardena Mex.
216 □1c Velas São Jorge Azores
242 □Q12 Vèlas, Cabo c. Costa Rica
245 I3 Velasco Mex.
258 D3 Velasco, Sierra de mts Arg.
113 □1 Velassary i. S. Male Maldives
177 K3 Veľaty Slovakia
161 G9 Velaux France
188 E3 Vela Vrata, Kanal sea chan. Croatia
161 D6 Velay reg. France
122 E8 Velāyat Iran
258 G4 Velázquez Uru.
169 D8 Velbert Ger.
173 L3 Velburg Ger.
197 K8 Velbŭzhdki Prokhod pass Macedonia
214 C8 Velddrif S. Africa
165 D6 Veldegem Belgium
173 L2 Velden Bayern Ger.
173 M5 Velden Bayern Ger.
165 J6 Velden Neth.
179 J6 Velden am Wörther See Austria
165 H6 Veldhoven Neth.
114 E5 Veldurti Andhra Prad. India
188 E3 Velebit mts Croatia
188 E3 Velebitski Kanal sea chan. Croatia
185 O6 Velefique Spain
197 P8 Veleka r. Bulg.
169 C7 Velen Ger.
177 H4 Velence Hungary
177 H4 Velencei-tó l. Hungary
188 E2 Velenje Slovenia
197 J9 Veles Macedonia
196 H9 Velës, Mali i mt. Albania
176 D3 Velešín Czech Rep.
191 Q6 Vele Srakane i. Croatia
185 M6 Veleta, Pico mt. Spain
188 F4 Velež mts Bos.-Herz.
250 C3 Vélez Col.
185 O5 Vélez-Blanco Spain
185 M7 Vélez de Benaudalla Spain
185 K7 Vélez-Málaga Spain
185 O5 Vélez-Rubio Spain
140 L4 Velfjorden inlet Norway
170 G2 Velgast Ger.
256 D3 Velhas r. Brazil
257 E2 Velhas r. Brazil
Velibaba Turkey see Aras
135 I7 Velichayevskoye Rus. Fed.
136 E4 Velika Berezovytsya Ukr.
196 J7 Velika Drenova Serbia
188 F3 Velika Gorica Croatia
136 E2 Velika Hlusha Ukr.
188 E3 Velika Kapela mts Croatia
188 E3 Velika Kladuša Bos.-Herz.
188 F3 Velika Mlaka Croatia
196 J6 Velika Morava canal Serbia
136 F2 Velika Ozera Ukr.
176 G6 Velika Pisanica Croatia
196 J6 Velika Plana Serbia
179 K8 Velika Račna Slovenia
179 K7 Velika Rogatec mt. Slovenia
134 J4 Velikaya Rus. Fed.
134 J4 Velikaya r. Rus. Fed.
131 S3 Velikaya r. Rus. Fed.
138 L4 Velikaya r. Rus. Fed.
134 F3 Velikaya Guba Rus. Fed.
100 J6 Velikaya Kema Rus. Fed.
Velikaya Novoselka Ukr. see Velyka Novosilka
137 L1 Velikaya Topal' Rus. Fed.
179 K8 Velike Lašče Slovenia
188 F4 Veliki Drvenik i. Croatia
176 G6 Veliki Grđevac Croatia
196 J7 Veliki Jastrebac mts Serbia
136 E4 Veliki Kunynets' Ukr.
197 O7 Veliki Preslav Bulg.
188 E3 Veliki Risnjak mt. Croatia
197 J7 Veliki Šiljegovac Serbia
197 K8 Veliki Strešer mt. Serbia
196 I6 Veliki Šturac mt. Serbia
139 N5 Velikiye Luki Rus. Fed.
137 K2 Velikiy Lystven Ukr.
136 C4 Velikiy Lyubin' Ukr.
139 O3 Velikiy Novgorod Rus. Fed.
134 I3 Velikiy Ustyug Rus. Fed.
137 T3 Velikoarkhangel'skoye Rus. Fed.
139 X6 Velikodvorskiy Rus. Fed.
137 Q3 Velikomikhaylovka Rus. Fed.
114 F5 Velikonda Range hills India
139 Q4 Velikooktyabr'skiy Rus. Fed.
176 F6 Veliko Trojstvo Croatia
197 N7 Veliko Tŭrnovo Bulg.
129 D4 Veliköy Turkey
139 T2 Velikoye Vologodskaya Oblast' Rus. Fed.
139 W4 Velikoye Yaroslavskaya Oblast' Rus. Fed.
139 X6 Velikoye, Ozero l. Ryazanskaya Oblast' Rus. Fed.
139 T4 Velikoye, Ozero l. Tverskaya Oblast' Rus. Fed.
186 F4 Velilla de Cinca Spain
186 E5 Velilla de Ebro Spain
Velilla de Guardo Spain see Velilla del Río Carrión
183 K3 Velilla del Río Carrión Spain
185 L6 Velillas r. Spain
188 E3 Veli Lošinj Croatia
196 G8 Velimlje Montenegro
163 E6 Vélines France
206 B3 Vélingara Kolda Senegal
206 B3 Vélingara Louga Senegal
197 M8 Velingrad Bulg.
193 J2 Velino r. Italy
193 K3 Velino, Monte mt. Italy
138 G6 Veliuona Lith.
139 O6 Velizh Rus. Fed.
176 F2 Velká Bíteš Czech Rep.
176 D1 Velká Dobrá Czech Rep.
177 K2 Veľká Domaša, Vodná nádrž resr Slovakia
177 H3 Veľká Fatra mts Slovakia
177 I3 Veľká Fatra park Slovakia
176 G2 Velká Haná r. Czech Rep.
173 N2 Velká Hleďsebe Czech Rep.
177 G3 Velká Javořina hill Czech Rep./Slovakia
177 K2 Veľká Javořina mt. Slovakia
177 H3 Veľká Lehota Slovakia
177 H2 Veľká Lúka mt. Slovakia
177 I3 Veľká nad Ipľom Slovakia
177 H2 Velká Polom Czech Rep.
Veľká Rača mt. Pol./Slovakia see Wielka Racza
176 F3 Velké Bílovice Czech Rep.
171 J9 Velké Březno Czech Rep.
177 L3 Veľké Kapušany Slovakia
177 H2 Velké Karlovice Czech Rep.
179 P2 Veľké Leváre Slovakia
176 G1 Velké Losiny Czech Rep.
177 H3 Veľké Lovce Slovakia
177 H4 Veľké Ludince Slovakia
176 F2 Velké Meziříčí Czech Rep.
176 F3 Velké Němčice Czech Rep.
176 F3 Velké Pavlovice Czech Rep.
177 G3 Veľké Rípňany Slovakia
177 L3 Veľké Trakany Slovakia
177 H3 Veľké Uherce Slovakia
138 E1 Velkua Fin.
177 J3 Veľký Blh Slovakia
177 H3 Veľký Ďur Slovakia
177 H2 Veľký Javorník mt. Slovakia
177 I2 Veľký Kriváň mt. Slovakia
177 I3 Veľký Krtíš Slovakia
177 H3 Veľký Kýr Slovakia
177 G3 Velký Lopeník hill Czech Rep.
177 G4 Veľký Meder Slovakia
177 K2 Veľký Šariš Slovakia
177 H3 Veľký Tribeč hill Slovakia
176 G2 Velký Týnec Czech Rep.
176 B2 Velký Zvon hill Czech Rep.
179 J6 Vellach r. Austria
78 □6 Vella Gulf sea chan. New Georgia Is Solomon Is
168 K4 Vellahn Ger.
78 □6 Vella Lavella i. New Georgia Is Solomon Is
114 F7 Vellar r. India
172 H3 Vellberg Ger.
182 E4 Velle, Embalse de resr Spain
193 J4 Velletri Italy
160 J2 Vellevans France
160 H1 Vellexon-Queutrey-et-Vaudey France
142 J6 Vellinge Sweden
183 O8 Vellisca Spain
169 I8 Vellmar Ger.
114 F6 Vellore Tamil Nadu India
186 F2 Vellos r. Spain
131 K3 Vel'mo r. Rus. Fed.
198 D5 Velo Greece
157 J4 Velosnes France
165 H7 Velp r. Belgium
164 I5 Velp Neth.
169 K6 Velpke Ger.
134 H3 Vel'sk Rus. Fed.
Velsuna Italy see Orvieto
134 J1 Vel't Rus. Fed.
170 H5 Velten Ger.
169 K6 Veltheim (Ohe) Ger.
176 D1 Veltrusy Czech Rep.
191 L2 Velturno Italy
164 H4 Veluwe reg. Neth.
164 I4 Veluwemeer l. Neth.
164 I4 Veluwezoom, Nationaal Park nat. park Neth.
236 E1 Velva ND U.S.A.
176 D1 Velvary Czech Rep.
198 D2 Velventos Greece
139 P4 Vel'ye, Ozero l. Rus. Fed.
137 L4 Velyka Andrusivka Ukr.
137 P4 Velyka Babka Ukr.
137 M4 Velyka Bahachka Ukr.
137 N6 Velyka Bilozerka Ukr.
137 N6 Velyka Bilozerka r. Ukr.
137 L4 Velyka Burimka Ukr.
136 J3 Velyka Dymerka Ukr.
175 L6 Velyka Horozhanna Ukr.
136 H5 Velyka Kisnytsya Ukr.
137 P4 Velyka Komyshuvakha Ukr.
177 M3 Velyka Kopanya Ukr.
137 K7 Velyka Korenykha Ukr.
137 M6 Velyka Kostromka Ukr.
137 M6 Velyka Lepetykha Ukr.
136 I6 Velyka Mykhaylivka Ukr.
137 P6 Velyka Novosilka Ukr.
137 M6 Velyka Oleksandrivka Ukr.
137 O3 Velyka Pysarivka Ukr.
137 N4 Velyka Rublivka Ukr.
137 L5 Velyka Severynka Ukr.
136 G3 Velyka Tsvilya Ukr.
137 J5 Velyka Vys' r. Ukr.
137 K5 Velyka Vyska Ukr.
137 N6 Velyka Znam"yanka Ukr.
177 L3 Velyki Kom"yaty Ukr.
137 L7 Velyki Kopani Ukr.
136 H4 Velyki Korovyntsi Ukr.
137 M4 Velyki Krynky Ukr.
177 L3 Velyki Luchky Ukr.
136 D3 Velyki Mosty Ukr.
137 M3 Velyki Sorochyntsi Ukr.
137 L4 Velykiy Khutir Ukr.
136 J7 Velykiy Kuyal'nyk r. Ukr.
137 M2 Velykiy Sambir Ukr.
136 J7 Velykodolyns'ke Ukr.
137 O5 Velykomykhaylivka Dnipropetrovs'ka Oblast' Ukr.
137 P6 Velykomykhaylivka Dnipropetrovs'ka Oblast' Ukr.
137 O5 Velykooleksandrivka Ukr.
137 K6 Velykoserbulivka Ukr.
136 B5 Velykyy Bereznyy Ukr.
137 Q3 Velykyy Burluk Ukr.
136 D6 Velykyy Bychkiv Ukr.
Velykyy Tokmak Ukr. see Tokmak
134 K3 Vel'yu r. Rus. Fed.
114 F3 Vemalwada Andhra Prad. India
264 J8 Vema Seamount sea feature S. Atlantic Ocean
265 I5 Vema Trench sea feature Indian Ocean
114 E8 Vembanad Lake India
177 H5 Véménd Hungary
100 M5 Vemor'ye Sakhalin Rus. Fed.
114 F5 Vempalle Andhra Prad. India
142 I6 Ven i. Sweden
192 C3 Venaco Corse France
244 F3 Venado Mex.
242 □R12 Venados, Isla del i. Nic.
245 I5 Venados r. Mex.
261 G3 Venado Tuerto Arg.
193 M5 Venafro Italy
251 F3 Venamo r. Venez. alt. Wenamu (Guyana)
251 F3 Venamo, Cerro mt. Venez.
158 H8 Venansault France
160 E1 Venarey-les-Laumes France
190 D5 Venaria Italy
193 K2 Venarotta Italy
161 K7 Venasca Italy
161 K9 Vence France
251 F6 Vencedor Brazil
256 C5 Venceslau Bráz Brazil
183 M6 Vencías, Embalse de las resr Spain
138 H7 Venciūnai Lith.
191 L5 Venda, Monte hill Italy
184 A3 Venda do Pinheiro Port.
257 G4 Venda Nova Brazil
182 E5 Venda Nova, Barragem de resr Port.
161 D9 Vendargues France
184 B3 Vendas de Azeitão Port.
184 C3 Vendas Novas Port.
160 C4 Vendat France
162 B5 Vendays-Montalivet France
158 I8 Vendée dept France
162 C3 Vendée r. France
157 O6 Vendenheim France
159 L8 Vendeuvre-du-Poitou France
156 H7 Vendeuvre-sur-Barse France
195 I10 Vendicari, Isola i. Sicilia Italy
134 I3 Vendinga Rus. Fed.
184 D4 Vendinha Port.
159 N8 Vendœuvres France
156 B8 Vendôme France
184 G4 Vendoval r. Spain
Vendrell Spain see El Vendrell
136 G5 Vendychany Ukr.
250 C4 Venecia Col.
244 G2 Venegas Mex.
161 G9 Venelles France
163 I8 Vénès France
191 M5 Veneta, Laguna lag. Italy
Venetia Italy see Venezia
191 L5 Veneto admin. reg. Italy
139 V7 Venev Rus. Fed.
191 M5 Venezia Italy
191 N4 Venezia prov. Italy
Venezia, Golfo di g. Europe see Venice, Gulf of
251 E3 Venezuela country S. America
250 D2 Venezuela, Golfo de g. Venez.
264 E4 Venezuelan Basin sea feature S. Atlantic Ocean
114 C5 Vengurla Mahar. India
164 H3 Venhuizen Neth.
182 I6 Venialbo Spain
220 C4 Veniaminof Volcano AK U.S.A.
Venice Italy see Venezia
231 F12 Venice FL U.S.A.
237 K11 Venice LA U.S.A.
188 D3 Venice, Gulf of Europe
190 H3 Venina r. Italy
160 F5 Vénissieux France
156 F5 Venizel France
141 L6 Venjan Sweden
114 F6 Venkatagiri Andhra Prad. India
114 G3 Venkatapalem Orissa India
114 G3 Venkatapuram Andhra Prad. India
165 J6 Venlo Neth.
142 D3 Vennesla Norway
142 E5 Venø Bugt b. Denmark
193 P6 Venosa Italy
193 P5 Venosa r. Italy
191 I2 Venosta, Val val. Italy
156 G8 Venoy France
164 I5 Venray Neth.
178 C6 Vent Austria
79 □9 Vent, Îles du is Arch. de la Société Fr. Polynesia
138 F5 Venta r. Latvia/Lith.
138 F5 Venta Lith.
161 G9 Ventabren France
161 K9 Ventabren, Mont mt. France
183 L5 Venta de Baños Spain
185 K4 Venta del Charco Spain
187 C9 Venta del Moro Spain
185 M4 Venta de los Santos Spain
182 I1 Venta las Ranas Spain
261 F6 Ventana, Sierra de la hills Arg.
258 E5 Ventana, Sierra de la mts Arg.
256 B6 Ventania Brazil
182 G2 Venta Nueva Spain
185 L6 Ventas de Huelma Spain
185 K7 Ventas de Zafarraya Spain
161 H8 Ventavon France
215 L4 Ventersburg S. Africa
215 K2 Ventersdorp S. Africa
215 L2 Venterskroon S. Africa
215 J6 Venterstad S. Africa
161 D7 Venteuges France
192 C5 Ventilegne, Golfe de b. Corse France
190 D8 Ventimiglia Italy
192 C4 Ventiseri Corse France
259 C6 Ventisquero mt. Arg.
151 J6 Ventnor Isle of Wight, England U.K.
235 G6 Ventnor City NJ U.S.A.
193 K6 Ventotene, Isola i. Italy
161 G8 Ventoux, Mont mt. France
170 E3 Ventschow Ger.
138 E4 Ventspils Latvia
251 E3 Ventuari r. Venez.
240 M7 Ventura CA U.S.A.
79 □9a Vénus, Pointe pt Tahiti Fr. Polynesia
83 J8 Venus Bay Vic. Austr.
Venusia Italy see Venosa
244 D6 Venustiano Mex.
245 N9 Venustiano Carranza Chiapas Mex.
245 J5 Venustiano Carranza Puebla Mex.
243 I4 Venustiano Carranza, Presa resr Mex.
192 C3 Venzolasca Corse France
191 O3 Venzone Italy
176 F4 Vép Hungary
137 N3 Vepryk Ukr.
139 R1 Vepsovskaya Vozvyshennost' hills Rus. Fed.
258 E3 Vera Arg.
185 P6 Vera Spain
253 F6 Verá, Lago l. Para.
252 D2 Vera Cruz Amazonas Brazil
256 C5 Vera Cruz São Paulo Brazil
245 K6 Veracruz Mex.
Vera Cruz Mex. see Veracruz
245 J5 Veracruz state Mex.
184 D4 Vera Cruz Port.
234 E3 Vera Cruz PA U.S.A.
186 D2 Veral r. Spain
255 C9 Veranópolis Brazil
116 C9 Veraval Gujarat India
261 G2 Vera y Pintado Arg.
136 E3 Verba Rivnens'ka Oblast' Ukr.
136 D3 Verba Volyns'ka Oblast' Ukr.
190 F4 Verbania Italy
235 H1 Verbank NY U.S.A.
190 E3 Verbano-Cusio-Ossola prov. Italy
156 E5 Verberie France
193 P8 Verbicaro Italy
190 C3 Verbier Switz.
139 U5 Verbilki Rus. Fed.
137 L5 Verblyuzhka Ukr.
137 O6 Verbove Ukr.
136 E4 Verbovets' Ukr.
135 H5 Verbovskiy Rus. Fed.
137 N7 Verby Ukr.
190 G3 Verceia Italy
190 E5 Vercelli Italy
190 E5 Vercelli prov. Italy
160 I2 Vercel-Villedieu-le-Camp France
170 G3 Verchen Ger.
161 G7 Vercors reg. France
161 G7 Vercors, Parc Naturel Régional du nature res. France
Vercovicium tourist site England U.K. see Housesteads
179 J8 Verd Slovenia
139 X8 Verda r. Rus. Fed.
161 I8 Verdaches France
140 K5 Verdalsøra Norway
259 D6 Verde r. Arg.
256 B2 Verde r. Brazil
256 B3 Verde r. Brazil
256 B4 Verde r. Brazil
256 C3 Verde r. Brazil
256 D2 Verde r. Brazil
257 E4 Verde r. Brazil
254 E4 Verde r. Brazil
253 F3 Verde r. Brazil
253 G2 Verde r. Brazil
244 D5 Verde r. Aguascalientes/Jalisco Mex.
242 F4 Verde r. Chihuahua/Durango Mex.
245 I9 Verde r. Guerrero/Oaxaca Mex.
245 H4 Verde r. Mex.
245 J10 Verde r. Mex.
253 F5 Verde r. Para.
185 L7 Verde r. Spain
185 M6 Verde r. Spain
241 U8 Verde r. AZ U.S.A.
Verde, Cabo c. Senegal see Vert, Cap
261 F6 Verde, Península pen. Arg.
257 F1 Verde Grande r. Brazil
92 C5 Verde Island Passage Phil.
168 H5 Verden (Aller) Ger.
254 E5 Verde Pequeno r. Brazil
240 M2 Verdi NV U.S.A.
237 H8 Verdigris r. KS U.S.A.
198 C3 Verdikoussa Greece
256 B2 Verdinho r. Brazil
256 B3 Verdinho, Serra do mts Brazil
245 H2 Verdolaga Mex.
161 H9 Verdon r. France
161 I9 Verdon, Grand Canyon du gorge France
182 C4 Verdugo r. Spain
157 J5 Verdun France
163 G8 Verdun-sur-Garonne France
160 G3 Verdun-sur-le-Doubs France
194 E9 Verdura r. Sicilia Italy
175 L1 Verebiejai Lith.
215 L2 Vereeniging S. Africa
137 L4 Veremiyivka Ukr.
215 N1 Verena S. Africa
224 E4 Vérendrye, Réserve Faunique de la nature res. Que. Can.
177 I4 Veresegyház Hungary
134 K4 Vereshchagino Rus. Fed.
137 K2 Veresoch Ukr.
139 T4 Verestovo, Ozero l. Rus. Fed.
139 T6 Vereya Rus. Fed.
139 W6 Vereyka Rus. Fed.
163 H7 Verfeil Midi-Pyrénées France
163 H8 Verfeil Midi-Pyrénées France
206 B4 Verga, Cap c. Guinea
261 I4 Vergara Arg.
Vergara Spain see Bergara
258 G4 Vergara Uru.
191 K7 Vergato Italy
157 M6 Vergaville France
214 I1 Vergeleë S. Africa
85 I8 Vergemont Creek watercourse Qld Austr.
233 L4 Vergennes VT U.S.A.
186 L3 Verges Spain
161 E9 Vergèze France
191 M8 Verghereto Italy
156 G8 Vergigny France
198 D2 Vergina Greece
192 B3 Vergio, Col de pass France
161 C6 Vergongheon France
162 F5 Vergt France
137 L4 Verhuny Cherkas'ka Oblast' Ukr.
137 M4 Verhuny Poltavs'ka Oblast' Ukr.
Véria Greece see Veroia
139 V5 Verigino Rus. Fed.
182 F5 Verín Spain
172 G5 Veringenstadt Ger.
Verin T'alin Armenia see T'alin
138 K3 Veriora Estonia
256 C3 Veríssimo Brazil
Veríssimo Sarmento Angola see Camissombo
215 K4 Verkeerdevlei S. Africa
137 N5 Verkhivtseve Ukr.
120 G1 Verkhne-Avzyan Rus. Fed.
137 Q9 Verkhnebakanskiy Rus. Fed.
121 T2 Verkhne-berezovskiy Kazakh.
Verkhnedneprovsk Ukr. see Verkhn'odniprovs'k
139 Q7 Verkhnedneprovskiy Rus. Fed.
130 J3 Verkhneimbatsk Rus. Fed.
134 L2 Verkhnekolvinsk Rus. Fed.
139 S6 Verkhneruzskoye Vodokhranilishche resr Rus. Fed.
134 I4 Verkhnespasskoye Rus. Fed.
140 U2 Verkhnetulomskiy Rus. Fed.
140 U2 Verkhnetulomskoye Vodokhranilishche resr Rus. Fed.
137 R2 Verkhneturovo Rus. Fed.
120 H1 Verkhneural'sk Rus. Fed.
131 N3 Verkhnevilyuysk Rus. Fed.
139 P4 Verkhnevolzhskoye Vodokhranilishche resr Rus. Fed.
134 K5 Verkhneyarkeyevo Rus. Fed.
140 U4 Verkhneye Kuyto, Ozero l. Rus. Fed.
100 F1 Verkhnezeysk Rus. Fed.
131 Q3 Verkhniy At-Uryakh Rus. Fed.
129 D2 Verkhniy Baksan Rus. Fed.
135 I6 Verkhniy Baskunchak Rus. Fed.
137 P4 Verkhniy Byshkyn Ukr.
129 F2 Verkhniye Achaluki Rus. Fed.
Verkhniye Kholokhory Moldova see Halahora de Sus
139 O6 Verkhniye Koshevichi Rus. Fed.
139 O6 Verkhniye Mokhovichi Rus. Fed.
129 F3 Verkhniy Fiagdon Rus. Fed.
Verkhniy Karabulag Georgia see Zemo Qarabulakhi
139 V9 Verkhniy Lomovets Rus. Fed.
135 H6 Verkhniy Mamon Rus. Fed.
Verkhniy Naur Rus. Fed. see Lakkha-Nevre
137 N6 Verkhniy Rohachyk Ukr.
134 J1 Verkhniy Shar Rus. Fed.
107 K1 Verkhniy Shergol'dzhin Rus. Fed.
134 K4 Verkhniy Tatyshly Rus. Fed.
137 P6 Verkhniytokmak Ukr.
107 M2 Verkhniy Ul'khun Rus. Fed.
134 F2 Verkhniy Vyalozerskiy Rus. Fed.
137 N5 Verkhn'odniprovs'k Ukr.
136 J5 Verkhnyachka Ukr.
175 M6 Verkhnya Lypytsya Ukr.
137 N3 Verkhnya Syrovatka Ukr.
137 O5 Verkhnya Tersa r. Ukr.
136 C5 Verkhnya Vysots'ke Ukr.
177 L3 Verkhnya Vyznytsya Ukr.
129 E2 Verkhnyaya Balkariya Rus. Fed.
177 L2 Verkhnya Yablun'ka Ukr.
137 Q2 Verkhnyaya Grayvoronka Rus. Fed.
134 M2 Verkhnyaya Inta Rus. Fed.
135 G6 Verkhnyaya Khava Rus. Fed.
129 D2 Verkhnyaya Mara Rus. Fed.
131 R3 Verkhnyaya Pakhachi Rus. Fed.
137 T2 Verkhnyaya Plavitsa Rus. Fed.
131 K2 Verkhnyaya Taymyra r. Rus. Fed.
129 C2 Verkhnyaya Teberda Rus. Fed.
137 T2 Verkhnyaya Tishanka Rus. Fed.
137 T2 Verkhnyaya Toyda Rus. Fed.
134 I3 Verkhnyaya Toyma Rus. Fed.
139 U4 Verkhnyaya Troitsa Rus. Fed.
Verkhnyaya Tunguska r. Rus. Fed. see Angara
136 C4 Verkhnye Syn'ovydne Ukr.
134 J4 Verkhoramen'ye Rus. Fed.
137 M9 Verkhorichchya Ukr.
134 J4 Verkhoshizhem'ye Rus. Fed.
137 N3 Verkhosulka Ukr.
139 Z1 Verkhovazh'ye Rus. Fed.
Verkhovina Ukr. see Verkhovyna
139 U9 Verkhov'ye Rus. Fed.
136 D5 Verkhovyna Ukr.
131 N2 Verkhoyanskiy Khrebet mts Rus. Fed.
121 T2 Verkhuba Kazakh.
175 N4 Verkhy Ukr.
138 H7 Verknė r. Lith.
134 I3 Verkola Rus. Fed.
215 N3 Verkykerskop S. Africa
169 G7 Verl Ger.
165 H7 Verlaine Belgium
214 E8 Verlatekloof pass S. Africa
140 □ Verlegenhuken pt Svalbard
140 J5 Verma Norway
214 F10 Vermaaklikheid S. Africa
156 F4 Vermand France
156 F4 Vermandois reg. France
256 B5 Vermelha, Serra hills Brazil
254 C3 Vermelho r. Brazil
254 D3 Vermelho r. Brazil
253 H3 Vermelho r. Brazil
156 G8 Vermenton France
197 J5 Vermeș Romania
191 J3 Vermiglio Italy
223 I4 Vermilion Alta Can.
232 C7 Vermilion OH U.S.A.
226 E8 Vermilion r. IL U.S.A.
237 J11 Vermilion Bay LA U.S.A.
241 T5 Vermilion Cliffs esc. AZ U.S.A.
241 T4 Vermilion Cliffs esc. UT U.S.A.
239 H8 Vermilion Cliffs National Monument nat. park AZ U.S.A.
226 B2 Vermilion Lake MN U.S.A.
226 B2 Vermilion Range hills MN U.S.A.
236 G4 Vermillion SD U.S.A.
236 G4 Vermillion r. SD U.S.A.
236 G4 Vermillion, East Fork r. SD U.S.A.
223 M5 Vermillion Bay Ont. Can.
230 K2 Vermillion r. Que. Can.
198 C2 Vermio mt. Greece
182 G7 Vermiosa Port.
182 C9 Vermoil Port.
247 □3 Vermont St Vincent
233 M4 Vermont state U.S.A.
262 T2 Vernadsky research stn Antarctica
191 J2 Vernago, Lago di l. Italy
163 H10 Vernajoul France
238 J6 Vernal UT U.S.A.
190 D7 Vernante Italy
159 L7 Vernantes France
190 C3 Vernayaz Switz.
159 J6 Vern-d'Anjou France
224 D4 Verner Ont. Can.
176 D1 Verneřice Czech Rep.
163 G9 Vernet France
163 I10 Vernet-les-Bains France
159 M4 Verneuil-sur-Avre France
162 G4 Verneuil-sur-Vienne France
214 F5 Verneuk Pan salt pan S. Africa
190 A3 Vernier Switz.
191 K7 Vernio Italy
163 H9 Verniolle France
198 C2 Verno mt. Greece
195 O3 Vernole Italy
222 G5 Vernon B.C. Can.
156 B5 Vernon France
237 K9 Vernon AL U.S.A.
230 E6 Vernon IN U.S.A.
235 G2 Vernon NJ U.S.A.
237 F8 Vernon TX U.S.A.
241 T1 Vernon UT U.S.A.
87 E8 Vernon, Mount hill W.A. Austr.
84 C2 Vernon Islands N.T. Austr.
156 B6 Vernouillet France
161 F7 Vernoux-en-Vivarais France
234 F3 Vernoy NJ U.S.A.
100 F3 Vernoye Rus. Fed.
158 H5 Vern-sur-Seiche France
157 L5 Verny France
Vernyy Kazakh. see Almaty
192 B3 Vero Corse France
186 F4 Vero r. Spain
231 G12 Vero Beach FL U.S.A.
177 I4 Verőcemaros Hungary
198 D2 Veroia Greece
190 I5 Verolanuova Italy
193 K4 Veroli Italy
156 F7 Véron France
191 J5 Verona Italy
191 K5 Verona prov. Italy
232 F10 Verona VA U.S.A.
226 E7 Verona WI U.S.A.
261 I4 Verónica Arg.
160 E4 Verosvres France
177 J4 Verpelét Hungary
235 H2 Verplanck NY U.S.A.
82 F5 Verran S.A. Austr.
190 D4 Verres Italy
162 F3 Verrières France
193 M4 Verrino r. Italy
190 E6 Versa r. Italy
190 G5 Versa r. Italy
191 O4 Versa r. Italy
156 D6 Versailles France
230 E6 Versailles IN U.S.A.
230 E6 Versailles KY U.S.A.
236 I6 Versailles MO U.S.A.
232 A8 Versailles OH U.S.A.
252 E3 Versalles Bol.
Versec Vojvodina Serbia see Vršac
138 H7 Verseka r. Lith.
160 H3 Vers-en-Montage France
137 L4 Vershatsi Ukr.
169 F6 Versmold Ger.
190 A3 Versoix Switz.
161 B9 Versols-et-Lapeyre France
159 K3 Verson France
161 F9 Vers-Pont-du-Gard France
163 C7 Vert France
163 G6 Vert r. France
206 A3 Vert, Cap c. Senegal
225 G3 Vert, Île i. Que. Can.
160 C5 Vertaizon France
162 E5 Verteillac France
254 C4 Vertentes r. Brazil
177 H4 Vértesacsa Hungary
177 H4 Vértesboglár Hungary
177 H4 Vertesi park Hungary
163 E7 Verteuil-d'Agenais France
162 E4 Verteuil-sur-Charente France
162 C5 Vertheuil France
246 D3 Vertientes Cuba
137 K2 Vertiyivka Ukr.
261 F4 Vertiz Arg.
156 C3 Verton France
191 J2 Vertona, Cima mt. Italy
158 I7 Vertou France
156 H6 Vertus France
191 M8 Verucchio Italy
215 P5 Verulam S. Africa
Verulamium Hertfordshire, England U.K. see St Albans
165 I7 Verviers Belgium
156 G4 Vervins France
178 A5 Verwallgruppe mts Austria
Verwoerdburg S. Africa see Centurion
223 J5 Verwood Sask. Can.
151 I6 Verwood Dorset, England U.K.
Veryína Greece see Vergina
159 J6 Verzée r. France
156 H5 Verzenay France
195 L5 Verzino Italy
190 C6 Verzuolo Italy
156 H5 Verzy France
140 S5 Vesanto Fin.
192 C3 Vescovato Corse France
190 I5 Vescovato Italy
165 I7 Vesdre r. Belgium
176 G5 Vése Hungary
130 G4 Veselaya, Gora mt. Rus. Fed.
137 N6 Vesele Ukr.
139 T6 Veselevo Rus. Fed.
197 N7 Veselina r. Bulg.
176 D2 Veselí nad Lužnicí Czech Rep.
176 G3 Veselí nad Moravou Czech Rep.
137 L6 Veselivka Kirovohrads'ka Oblast' Ukr.
136 H3 Veselivka Zhytomyrs'ka Oblast' Ukr.
137 R6 Veselo-Voznesenka Rus. Fed.
135 H7 Veselovskoye Vodokhranilishche resr Rus. Fed.
121 S2 Veseloyarsk Rus. Fed.
137 R3 Veseloye Rus. Fed.
137 K3 Veselynivka Ukr.
137 K6 Veselynove Ukr.
135 H7 Veselyy Rus. Fed.
120 K1 Veselyy Podol Kazakh.
156 B6 Vesgre r. France
135 H6 Veshenskaya Rus. Fed.
134 H2 Veshkoma Rus. Fed.
141 R6 Vesijärvi l. Fin.
190 E6 Vesime Italy
156 F5 Vesle r. France
134 K3 Veslyana r. Rus. Fed.
Vesontio France see Besançon
160 I1 Vesoul France
190 F5 Vespolate Italy
100 I7 Vesselyy Yar Rus. Fed.
165 H6 Vessem Neth.
142 D3 Vest-Agder county Norway
140 L2 Vesterålen is Norway
140 L2 Vesterålsfjorden sea chan. Norway
168 L1 Vesterby Denmark
170 E1 Vestermark Denmark
168 I1 Vester Sottrup Denmark
140 S1 Vestertana Norway
140 □B1 Vestfirðir constituency Iceland
142 E2 Vestfjorddalen val. Norway
140 L3 Vestfjorden sea chan. Norway
142 G2 Vestfold county Norway
263 F2 Vestfold Hills Antarctica
140 □ Vestfonna ice cap Svalbard
256 B4 Véstia Brazil
144 D1 Vestmanna Faroe Is
140 □C2 Vestmannaeyjar is Iceland
140 I5 Vestnes Norway
190 I4 Vestone Italy
140 T1 Vestre Jakobselv Norway
142 H6 Vestsjælland county Denmark
262 X2 Veststraumen Glacier Antarctica
140 □B1 Vesturland constituency Iceland
140 L2 Vestvågøy i. Norway
161 K9 Vésubie r. France
193 M6 Vesuvio vol. Italy
193 M6 Vesuvio, Parco Nazionale del nat. park Italy
Vesuvius vol. Italy see Vesuvio
139 U3 Ves'yegonsk Rus. Fed.
176 G4 Veszkény Hungary
177 G4 Veszprém Hungary
176 G4 Veszprém county Hungary
177 G4 Veszprémvarsány Hungary
177 K5 Vésztő Hungary
215 J3 Vet r. S. Africa
79 □7 Vetauua i. Fiji
140 Q5 Veteli Fin.
223 I4 Veteran Alta Can.
196 H5 Veternik Vojvodina Serbia
156 C5 Vétheuil France
177 L4 Vetiș Romania
143 L4 Vetlanda Sweden
141 I6 Vetlefjorden Norway
134 I4 Vetluga Rus. Fed.
134 I4 Vetluga r. Rus. Fed.
130 F4 Vetluzhskiy Kostromskaya Oblast' Rus. Fed.
134 I4 Vetluzhskiy Nizhegorodskaya Oblast' Rus. Fed.
136 E2 Vetly Ukr.
139 Q8 Vet'ma r. Rus. Fed.
197 O7 Vetovo Bulg.
192 I3 Vetralla Italy
197 P8 Vetren Bulg.
197 Q4 Vetrișoaia Romania
176 D3 Větřní Czech Rep.
171 J7 Vetschau Ger.
140 S2 Vetsikko Fin.
140 P3 Vettasjärvi Sweden
169 D9 Vettelschoss Ger.
190 I7 Vetto Italy
193 K2 Vettore, Monte mt. Italy
159 L7 Veude r. France
159 M2 Veules-les-Roses France
159 M2 Veulettes-sur-Mer France
165 C6 Veurne Belgium
230 E6 Vevay IN U.S.A.
210 B3 Veveno r. Sudan
190 B3 Vevey Switz.
190 C3 Vex Switz.
156 C5 Vexin Français reg. France
156 B5 Vexin Normand reg. France
135 G6 Veydelevka Rus. Fed.
160 F4 Veyle r. France
161 H7 Veynes France
160 D3 Veynon r. France
241 S4 Veyo UT U.S.A.
160 C5 Veyre-Monton France
160 I5 Veyrier-du-Lac France
122 C6 Veys Iran
138 E6 Vėžaičiai Lith.
160 D2 Vézelay France
157 L7 Vézelise France
161 E8 Vézénobres France
162 F6 Vézère r. France
134 K3 Vezhayu Rus. Fed.
197 M8 Vezhen mt. Bulg.
159 J7 Vezins France
161 B8 Vézins-de-Lévézou France
199 K2 Vezirhan Turkey
126 G3 Vezirköprü Turkey
157 L6 Vezouze r. France
190 I3 Vezza d'Oglio Italy
178 E7 Vezzana, Cima della mt. Italy
192 C3 Vezzani Corse France
191 K3 Vezzano Italy
213 F4 Vhembe Dongola National Park nature res. S. Africa
206 C5 Via r. Liberia
252 C4 Viacha Bol.
191 J6 Viadana Italy
182 E5 Viade de Baixo Port.
161 K9 Vial, Mont mt. France
161 B8 Viala du Tarn France
Vialar Alg. see Tissemsilt
161 D8 Vialas France
261 G2 Viale Arg.
255 C9 Viamao Brazil
261 F3 Viamonte Córdoba Arg.
259 D9 Viamonte Tierra del Fueg[o]
209 B7 Viana Angola
257 G4 Viana Espírito Santo Braz[il]
254 D2 Viana Maranhão Brazil
183 P3 Viana Spain
183 K5 Viana de Cega Spain
Viana del Bollo Spain se[e] Viana do Bolo
184 D4 Viana do Alentejo Port.
182 F4 Viana do Bolo Spain
182 C5 Viana do Castelo Port.
182 D5 Viana do Castelo admin. Port.
165 J9 Vianden Lux.
161 B9 Viane France
164 H5 Vianen Neth.
96 F6 Viangchan Laos
96 E4 Viangphoukha Laos
163 E7 Vianne France
199 G7 Viannos Kriti Greece
182 D2 Viaño Pequeno Spain
256 C2 Vianópolis Brazil
185 O3 Vianos Spain
184 H5 Viar r. Spain
190 I8 Viareggio Italy
156 D5 Viarmes France
161 C10 Vias France
182 C6 Viatodos Port.
182 C7 Viator Spain
163 H7 Viaur r. France
163 I6 Viazac France
193 P7 Vibonati Italy
185 K5 Víboras r. Spain
142 F5 Viborg Denmark
142 F5 Viborg county Denmark
Viborg Rus. Fed. see Vyb[org]
195 K6 Vibo Valentia Italy
195 K6 Vibo Valentia prov. Italy
159 M5 Vibraye France
186 J4 Vic Spain
162 H5 Vic, Roche de hill France
242 D4 Vicam Mex.
185 N7 Vícar Spain
194 F8 Vicari Sicilia Italy
148 C7 Vicarstown Ireland
191 K8 Vicchio Italy
163 H10 Vicdessos France
163 H10 Vicdessos r. France
Viçe Turkey see Fındıklı
Vicecomodoro Marambi[o] research stn Antarctica se[e] Marambio
163 E9 Vic-en-Bigorre France
240 N8 Vicente, Point CA U.S.A.
261 H4 Vicente Casares Arg.
260 D4 Vicente Dupuy Arg.
242 A2 Vicente Guerrero Baja California Mex.
244 D2 Vicente Guerrero Durango
245 N7 Vicente Guerrero Tabasco
245 I6 Vicente Guerrero Tlaxcala
245 K7 Vicente y Camalote Mex[.]
191 L4 Vicenza Italy
191 K4 Vicenza prov. Italy
163 E8 Vic-Fezensac France
Vich Spain see Vic
250 D3 Vichada dept Col.
250 E3 Vichada r. Col.
258 G3 Vichadero Uru.
245 I3 Vichinchijol Nuevo Mex.
134 H4 Vichuga Rus. Fed.
260 A4 Vichuquén Chile
160 C4 Vichy France
237 F7 Vici OK U.S.A.
186 E3 Vicién Spain
149 K5 Vickerstown Cumbria, England U.K.
241 S8 Vicksburg AZ U.S.A.
226 I7 Vicksburg MI U.S.A.
237 J9 Vicksburg MS U.S.A.
234 B3 Vicksburg PA U.S.A.
160 C5 Vic-le-Comte France
192 B3 Vico Corse France
192 I3 Vico, Lago di l. Italy
193 P4 Vico del Gargano Italy
193 M6 Vico Equense Italy
190 D7 Vicoforte Italy
193 K4 Vico nel Lazio Italy
183 Q6 Vicort, Sierra de mts Spa[in]
254 F4 Viçosa Alagoas Brazil
257 F4 Viçosa Minas Gerais Brazi[l]
193 J3 Vicovaro Italy
197 N3 Vicovu de Sus Romania
159 P8 Vicq-Exemplet France
162 G4 Vicq-sur-Breuilh France
156 F5 Vic-sur-Aisne France
161 B7 Vic-sur-Cère France
157 M6 Vic-sur-Seille France
263 C2 Victor, Mount Antarctica
168 D4 Victorbur (Südbrookmer[land]) Ger.
82 G6 Victor Harbor S.A. Austr.
261 G3 Victoria Arg.
261 H3 Victoria r. Arg.
84 C3 Victoria r. N.T. Austr.
83 J7 Victoria state Austr.
Victoria Cameroon see Li[mbe]
222 F5 Victoria B.C. Can.
260 A6 Victoria Araucanía Chile
259 C9 Victoria Magallanes y Antá[rtica] Chilena Chile
247 □6 Victoria Grenada
242 □P10 Victoria Hond.
Victoria Malaysia see Lab[uan]
195 □ Victoria Gozo Malta
244 G4 Victoria Mex.
92 C4 Victoria Luzon Phil.
197 P6 Victoria Brăila Romania
197 M5 Victoria Brașov Romania
217 □2b Victoria Mahé Seychelles
247 □7 Victoria county Trin. and T[obago]
237 G11 Victoria TX U.S.A.
232 G12 Victoria VA U.S.A.
259 B7 Victoria, Isla i. Chile
210 B4 Victoria, Lake Africa
82 H5 Victoria, Lake N.S.W. Aus[tr.]
Victoria, Mount Viti Levu [Fiji] see Tomanivi
96 A4 Victoria, Mount Myanmar
81 G9 Victoria, Mount South I. N[.Z.]
91 K8 Victoria, Mount P.N.G.
221 K2 Victoria and Albert Mountains Nunavut Can.
209 E9 Victoria Falls waterfall Zambia/Zimbabwe
212 E3 Victoria Falls Zimbabwe
212 E3 Victoria Falls National Pa[rk] Zimbabwe
221 N1 Victoria Fjord inlet Greenl[and]
81 G8 Victoria Forest Park nature res. South I. N.Z.
Victoria Harbour sea cha[n.] H.K. China see Hong Kong Harbour
217 □2b Victoria Harbour b. Mahé Seychelles
220 H2 Victoria Island N.W.T./Nunavut Can.
225 J3 Victoria Lake Nfld and Lab.
263 K2 Victoria Land coastal area Antarctica
109 □J7 Victoria Peak hill H.K. Chi[na]
82 □3 Victoria Point S. Pacific Ocean
81 G9 Victoria Range mts South I. N.Z.
84 C3 Victoria River N.T. Austr.
84 C4 Victoria River Downs N.T. Austr.
80 H2 Victoria Valley North I. N.Z.
225 G4 Victoriaville Que. Can.
214 H7 Victoria West S. Africa
260 E5 Victorica Arg.
250 E4 Victorino Venez.
244 E3 Víctor Rosales Mex.
240 O7 Victorville CA U.S.A.
177 K6 Victor Vlad Delamarina Romania
232 I5 Victory NY U.S.A.
84 D8 Victory Downs N.T. Austr.
260 B2 Vicuña Chile
260 E3 Vicuña Mackenna Arg.
182 H9 Vid, Río de la r. Spain
182 E5 Vidago Port.
184 A2 Vidais Port.
259 B8 Vidal, Isla i. Chile
237 J10 Vidalia LA U.S.A.
241 R7 Vidal Junction CA U.S.A.
138 G9 Vidamlya Belarus

Vidángoz Spain
Vidauban France
Viddalba Sardegna Italy
Videbæk Denmark
Videira Brazil
Videla Arg.
Videle Romania
Videm Gornja Radgona Slovenia
Videm Grosuplje Slovenia
Videmonte Port.
Viden mt. Bulg.
Viderø i. Faroe Is see Viðoy
Vidgiriu kalnas hill Lith.
Vidigueira Port.
Vidima r. Bulg.
Vidin Bulg.
Vidiná Slovakia
Vidio, Cabo c. Spain
Vidisha Madh. Prad. India
Vidlin Shetland, Scotland U.K.
Vidlitsa Rus. Fed.
Vidmyr nature res. Norway
Vidnava Czech Rep.
Vidnoye Rus. Fed.
Vidöstern l. Sweden
Vidourle r. France
Vidova Gora hill Croatia
Vidovec Croatia
Viðoy i. Faroe Is
Vidra Romania
Vidreras Spain see Vidrieres
Vidrieres Spain
Vidsel Sweden
Viduklė Lith.
Viduša mts Bos.-Herz.
Vidzemes centrālā augstiene hills Latvia
Vidzy Belarus
Vie r. France
Vie r. France
Viechtach Ger.
Viečiūnai Lith.
Viedgesville S. Africa
Viedma Arg.
Viedma, Lago l. Arg.
Viehberg mt. Austria
Vieille-Brioude France
Vieillevigne France
Vieira de Leiria Port.
Vieira do Minho Port.
Viejo r. Mex.
Viejo, Cerro mt. Mex.
Viekšniai Lith.
Vielank Ger.
Vielha Spain
Viella France
Viella Spain see Vielha
Vielle-Aure France
Vielle-St-Girons France
Vielmur-sur-Agout France
Vielsalm Belgium
Vielverge France
Vienenburg Ger.
Vienna Austria see Wien
Vienna GA U.S.A.
Vienna IL U.S.A.
Vienna MD U.S.A.
Vienna MO U.S.A.
Vienna NJ U.S.A.
Vienna WV U.S.A.
Vienne France
Vienne dept France
Vienne r. France
Vienne-le-Château France
Vientiane Laos see Viangchan
Viento, Cordillera del mts Arg.
Viento, Puerto del pass Spain
Vieques i. Puerto Rico
Vière r. France
Viereck Ger.
Vieremä Fin.
Viereth-Trunstadt Ger.
Vierkirchen Ger.
Vierlingsbeek Neth.
Viernau Ger.
Viernheim Ger.
Vierraden Ger.
Viersen Ger.
Vierville-sur-Mer France
Vierwaldstätter See l. Switz.
Vierzon France
Viesca Mex.
Viesecke Ger.
Vieselbach Ger.
Viesīte Latvia
Vieste Italy
Viešvilės rezervatas nature res. Lith.
Vietas Sweden
Viet Nam country Asia see Vietnam
Vietnam country Asia
Viêt Quang Vietnam
Vietri di Potenza Italy
Vietri sul Mare Italy
Viêt Tri Vietnam
Vieux-Boucau-les-Bains France
Vieux-Bourg Guadeloupe
Vieux Chaillol mt. France
Vieux-Charmont France
Vieux Comptoir, Lac du l. Que. Can.
Vieux-Condé France
Vieux-Fort Que. Can.
Vieux-Fort Guadeloupe
Vieux Fort St Lucia
Vieux-Fort, Pointe de pt Guadeloupe
Vieux-Habitants Guadeloupe
Vieux Poste, Pointe du pt Que. Can.
Vievis Lith.
Viewpark North Lanarkshire, Scotland U.K.
Vieytes Arg.
Vif France
Vigala r. Estonia
Vigan Luzon Phil.
Vigarano Mainarda Italy
Vigasio Italy
Vigaun Austria
Vigeois France
Vigevano Italy
Viggianello Corse France
Viggianello Italy
Viggiano Italy
Viggiù Italy
Vigia Brazil
Vigia hill Port.
Vigia, Barragem da resr Port.
Vigía, Cabo c. Arg.
Vigía Chico Mex.
Vígľaš Slovakia
Viglio, Monte mt. Italy
Vignacourt France
Vignale Monferrato Italy
Vignanello Italy
Vignemale mt. France
Vigneulles-lès-Hattonchâtel France
Vignoble reg. France
Vignola Italy
Vignola r. Italy
Vignola Mare l'Agnata Sardegna Italy
Vignory France
Vigny France
Vigo Spain
Vigo, Ría de est. Spain
Vigo di Cadore Italy
Vigo di Fassa Italy
Vigone Italy
Vigonza Italy
Vigo Rendena Italy
Vigors, Mount W.A. Austr.
Vigsø Bugt b. Denmark
Viguzzolo Italy
Vigy France
Vihanti Fin.
Vihari Pak.
Vihiers France
Vihorlat mt. Slovakia
Vihorlat park Slovakia
Vihorlatské vrchy mts Slovakia
Vihterpalu r. Estonia
Vihti Fin.
Viiala Fin.
Viile Satu Mare Romania
Viipuri Rus. Fed. see Vyborg
140 S3 Viirinkylä Fin.
177 L4 Viișoara Romania
140 R5 Viitasaari Fin.
138 K4 Viitka Estonia
116 D5 Vijainagar Rajasthan India
116 D8 Vijapur Gujarat India
114 C4 Vijayadurg Mahar. India
Vijayanagar Karnataka India see Hampi
114 E8 Vijayapati Tamil Nadu India
114 G4 Vijayawada Andhra Prad. India
140 □D2 Vík Iceland
140 L4 Vik Norway
140 S3 Vikajärvi Fin.
114 E4 Vikarabad Andhra Prad. India
143 M3 Vikbolandet pen. Sweden
142 B2 Vikedal Norway
Vikeke East Timor see Viqueque
143 K3 Viken l. Sweden
142 F2 Vikersund Norway
142 B2 Vikevåg Norway
139 O7 Vikhra r. Rus. Fed.
197 L9 Vikhren mt. Bulg.
223 I4 Viking Alta Can.
140 K4 Vikna i. Norway
177 I2 Vikolínec Slovakia
198 B3 Vikou-Aoou, Ethnikos Drymos nat. park Greece
141 I6 Vikøyri Norway
140 O2 Vikran Norway
175 L1 Viktarinas Lith.
136 J6 Viktorivka Ukr.
Viktorovka Kazakh. see Taranovskoye
171 D7 Viktorshöhe hill Ger.
182 D5 Vila Spain
Vila Vanuatu see Port Vila
Vila Alferes Chamusca Moz. see Guija
184 D4 Vila Alva Port.
Vila Arriaga Angola see Bibala
184 □ Vila Baleira Madeira
250 D5 Vila Bittencourt Brazil
182 G8 Vila Boa Port.
184 E3 Vila Boim Port.
251 G6 Vila Braga Brazil
Vila Bugaço Angola see Camanongue
Vila Cabral Moz. see Lichinga
182 D6 Vila Caiz Port.
Vila Caldas Xavier Moz. see Muende
252 D4 Vilacaya Bol.
182 C6 Vila Chã Port.
182 E7 Vila Chã de Sá Port.
182 D6 Vila Chão do Marão Port.
Vila Coutinho Moz. see Ulongue
182 E7 Vila Cova à Coelheira Port.
182 D6 Vila Cova da Lixa Port.
186 I3 Vilada Spain
186 L3 Viladamat Spain
Vila da Ponte Angola see Kuvango
182 E5 Vila da Ponte Port.
216 □1a Vila da Praia da Vitória Terceira Azores
206 □ Vila da Ribeira Brava Cape Verde
Vila de Aljustrel Angola see Cangamba
Vila de Almoster Angola see Chiange
186 J5 Viladecans Spain
182 D3 Vila de Cruces Spain
Vila de João Belo Moz. see Xai-Xai
Vila de Junqueiro Moz. see Gurué
261 F1 Vila de María Arg.
Vilademat Spain see Viladamat
182 D9 Vila de Rei Port.
213 G3 Vila de Sena Moz.
Vila de Trego Morais Moz. see Chókwé
184 B6 Vila do Bispo Port.
182 C6 Vila do Conde Port.
186 J4 Viladrau Spain
187 E7 Vilafamés Spain
186 K3 Vilafant Spain
184 E3 Vila Fernando Port.
216 □3a Vilaflor Tenerife Canary Is
182 F6 Vila Flor Port.
Vila Fontes Moz. see Caia
216 □1b Vila Franca, Ilhéu de i. Azores
182 F7 Vila Franca das Naves Port.
187 L8 Vilafranca de Bonany Spain
186 I5 Vilafranca del Penedès Spain
184 B3 Vila Franca de Xira Port.
216 □1b Vila Franca do Campo São Miguel Azores
182 C3 Vilagarcía de Arousa Spain
213 G5 Vila Gomes da Costa Moz.
Vila Gouveia Moz. see Catandica
182 D2 Vilagudín, Encoro de resr Spain
158 G6 Vilaine r. France
186 L3 Vilajuiga Spain
138 K4 Viļaka Latvia
182 E2 Vilalba Spain
186 J3 Vilallonga Spain
Vila Luísa Moz. see Marracuene
Vila Marechal Carmona Angola see Uíge
182 F4 Vilamartín Spain
187 D8 Vilamarxant Spain
260 A5 Vila Mercedes Chile
Vila Miranda Moz. see Macaloge
184 B2 Vila Moreira Port.
184 C6 Vilamoura Port.
252 D2 Vila Murtinho Brazil
182 B2 Vilán, Cabo c. Spain
213 □J3 Vilanandro, Tanjona pt Madag.
213 G4 Vilanculos Moz.
138 J5 Viļāni Latvia
184 A3 Vila Nogueira de Azeitão Port.
Vila Nova Angola see Tchikala-Tcholohanga
216 □1a Vila Nova Terceira Azores
182 F2 Vilanova Spain
184 C4 Vila Nova da Baronia Port.
213 G3 Vila Nova da Fronteira Moz.
187 F7 Vilanova d'Alcolea Spain
182 C8 Vila Nova de Anços Port.
182 C3 Vilanova de Arousa Spain
Vilanova de Castelló Spain see Villanueva de Castellón
182 C5 Vila Nova de Cerveira Port.
182 C6 Vila Nova de Famalicão Port.
182 F6 Vila Nova de Foz Coa Port.
182 C6 Vila Nova de Gaia Port.
186 H4 Vilanova de L'Aguda Spain
186 H4 Vilanova de Meià Spain
182 C9 Vila Nova de Ourém Port.
182 E7 Vila Nova de Paiva Port.
182 D8 Vila Nova de Poiares Port.
184 E5 Vila Nova de São Bento Port.
Vila Nova do Seles Angola see Uku
186 I5 Vilanova i la Geltrú Spain
206 □ Vila Nova Sintra Cape Verde
Vila Paiva de Andrada Moz. see Gorongosa
Vila Pery Moz. see Chimoio
182 E8 Vila Pouca da Beira Port.
182 E5 Vila Pouca de Aguiar Port.
182 C5 Vila Praia de Âncora Port.
182 F7 Vilar, Barragem de resr Port.
182 F5 Vilarandelo Port.
182 E4 Vilarchao Spain
182 D5 Vilar da Veiga Port.
182 C6 Vilar de Andorinho Port.
182 E4 Vilar de Barrio Spain
182 E4 Vilar de Santos Spain
182 F5 Vilardevós Spain
182 E6 Vila Real Port.
182 E5 Vila Real admin. dist. Port.
184 E6 Vila Real de Santo António Port.
182 F5 Vilarelho da Raia Port.
182 G7 Vilar Formoso Port.
182 F6 Vilarinho da Castanheira Port.
182 C8 Vilarinho do Bairro Port.
182 F4 Vilariño de Conso Spain
186 H5 Vila-rodona Spain
184 D4 Vila Ruiva Port.
Vilas i. S. Male Maldives see Velassary
Vila Salazar Angola see N'dalatando
Vila Salazar Zimbabwe see Sango
129 J6 Viläşçay r. Azer.
182 C5 Vila Seca Port.
186 H5 Vilaseca de Solcina Spain
Vila Teixeira de Sousa Angola see Luau
261 G2 Vila Trinidad Arg.
114 E8 Vilavankod Tamil Nadu India
251 I4 Vila Velha Amapá Brazil
257 G4 Vila Velha Espírito Santo Brazil
182 E9 Vila Velha de Ródão Port.
182 D5 Vila Verde Braga Port.
182 C8 Vila Verde Coimbra Port.
182 E6 Vila Verde Vila Real Port.
182 F5 Vila Verde da Raia Port.
184 E5 Vila Verde de Ficalho Port.
184 E3 Vila Viçosa Port.
252 B3 Vilcabamba, Cordillera mts Peru
252 C3 Vilcanota, Cordillera de mts Peru
136 I2 Vil'cha Ukr.
130 H1 Vil'cheka, Zemlya i. Zemlya Frantsa-Iosifa Rus. Fed.
185 M4 Vilches Spain
260 A6 Vilcun Chile
134 I3 Viled' r. Rus. Fed.
261 H4 Vilela Arg.
Vileyka Belarus see Vilyeyka
134 L3 Vil'gort Permskaya Oblast' Rus. Fed.
134 J3 Vil'gort Respublika Komi Rus. Fed.
140 N4 Vilhelmina Sweden
253 E3 Vilhena Brazil
Viligili i. N. Male Maldives see Vilingli
137 M9 Viline Ukr.
113 □1 Vilingli i. N. Male Maldives
113 □1 Vilingli i. N. Male Maldives
138 I7 Viliya r. Belarus/Lith.
136 F3 Viliya r. Ukr.
138 I3 Viljandi Estonia
214 D10 Viljoenshof S. Africa
215 K3 Viljoenskroon S. Africa
138 G7 Vilkaviškis Lith.
137 S5 Vil'khova r. Ukr.
138 G6 Vilkija Lith.
130 I2 Vil'kitskogo, Ostrov i. Rus. Fed.
131 K2 Vil'kitskogo, Proliv str. Rus. Fed.
252 D5 Villa Abecia Bol.
260 C2 Villa Aberastain Arg.
193 J4 Villa Adriana tourist site Italy
242 F2 Villa Ahumada Mex.
261 F6 Villa Alba Arg.
260 B4 Villa Alegre Chile
260 B3 Villa Alemana Chile
245 K8 Villa Alta Mex.
246 H4 Villa Altagracia Dom. Rep.
258 F3 Villa Ana Arg.
261 G3 Villa Ángela Arg.
258 E2 Villa Ángela Arg.
244 G5 Villa Apaseo El Alto Mex.
261 F6 Villa Atlántica Arg.
260 D4 Villa Atuel Arg.
245 J5 Villa Ávila Camacho Mex.
245 L7 Villa Azueta Mex.
191 K5 Villa Bartolomea Italy
194 E7 Villabate Sicilia Italy
252 D2 Villa Bella Bol.
Villa Bens Morocco see Tarfaya
258 E2 Villa Berthet Arg.
184 E6 Villablanca Spain
182 H3 Villablino Spain
186 A1 Villabona Spain
183 J5 Villabrágima Spain
183 J6 Villabuena del Puente Spain
162 G5 Villac France
261 G4 Villa Cañás Arg.
183 N9 Villacañas Spain
190 I4 Villa Carcina Italy
260 E2 Villa Carlos Paz Arg.
185 M4 Villacarrillo Spain
261 F5 Villa Castelar Arg.
195 M2 Villa Castelli Italy
183 L7 Villacastín Spain
179 I6 Villach Austria
192 B9 Villacidro Sardegna Italy
183 O5 Villaciervos Spain
Villa Cisneros Western Sahara see Ad Dakhla
Villa Cisneros, Ría de b. Western Sahara see Río de Oro, Bahía de
243 M10 Villa Comaltitlán Mex.
261 F2 Villa Concepción del Tío Arg.
183 N8 Villaconejos Spain
183 P8 Villaconejos de Trabaque Spain
261 G3 Villa Constitución Arg.
244 D5 Villa Corona Mex.
242 G4 Villa Coronado Mex.
243 M9 Villa Corzo Mex.
260 E2 Villa Cura Brochero Arg.
261 G3 Villada Arg.
183 K4 Villada Spain
190 H4 Villa d'Almè Italy
244 D6 Villa de Álvarez Mex.
244 E2 Villa de Cos Mex.
250 E2 Villa de Cura Venez.
243 N8 Villa de Guadalupe Campeche Mex.
244 G2 Villa de Guadalupe San Luis Potosí Mex.
260 E3 Villa del Carmen Arg.
183 L8 Villa del Prado Spain
244 G5 Villa del Pueblito Mex.
185 K5 Villa del Río Spain
261 F2 Villa del Rosario Arg.
260 C2 Villa del Salvador Arg.
261 E2 Villa del Totoral Arg.
182 H5 Villadepera Spain
187 C9 Villa de Ves Spain
261 G3 Villa Diego Arg.
183 L3 Villadiego Spain
260 E2 Villa Dolores Arg.
261 H3 Villa Domínguez Arg.
191 L5 Villadose Italy
190 E3 Villadossola Italy
186 C5 Villadoz Spain
260 C6 Villa El Chocón Arg.
183 K3 Villaeles de Valdavia Spain
261 H3 Villa Elisa Arg.
261 G3 Villa Eloisa Arg.
244 F6 Villa Escalante Mex.
183 O9 Villaescusa de Haro Spain
183 N4 Villaescusa la Sombría Spain
182 I5 Villafáfila Spain
183 R6 Villafeliche Spain
243 M9 Villa Flores Mex.
183 J6 Villaflores Spain
253 F6 Villa Florida Para.
183 Q4 Villafranca Spain
190 E6 Villafranca d'Asti Italy
185 J5 Villafranca de Córdoba Spain
186 D4 Villafranca de Ebro Spain
182 G3 Villafranca del Bierzo Spain
186 C6 Villafranca del Campo Spain
186 E7 Villafranca del Cid Spain
184 G3 Villafranca de los Barros Spain
185 M2 Villafranca de los Caballeros Spain
Villafranca del Penedès Spain see Vilafranca del Penedès
191 J5 Villafranca di Verona Italy
190 H7 Villafranca in Lunigiana Italy
183 N4 Villafranca-Montes de Oca Spain
195 I7 Villafranca Tirrena Sicilia Italy
191 J5 Villafranca Veronese airport Italy
184 G6 Villafranco del Guadalquivir Spain
194 E8 Villafrati Sicilia Italy
183 J5 Villafrechos Spain
183 M5 Villafruela Spain
183 L5 Villafuerte Spain
Villagarcía de Arosa Spain see Vilagarcía de Arousa
183 J5 Villagarcía de Campos Spain
184 G4 Villagarcía de la Torre Spain
185 P2 Villagarcía del Llano Spain
260 D3 Villa General Roca Arg.
261 I5 Villa Gesell Arg.
195 L5 Villagio Mancuso Italy
184 G3 Villagonzalo Spain
261 G3 Villa Governador Gálvez Arg.
245 H1 Villagrán Mex.
192 D8 Villagrande Strisaili Sardegna Italy
261 H2 Villaguay Arg.
244 D4 Villa Guerrero Mex.
258 F3 Villa Guillermina Arg.
185 J4 Villaharta Spain
253 F6 Villa Hayes Para.
243 M8 Villahermosa Mex.
185 N3 Villahermosa Spain
187 E7 Villahermosa del Río Spain
261 H2 Villa Hernandarias Arg.
183 L4 Villaherreros Spain
244 E4 Villa Hidalgo Jalisco Mex.
244 B4 Villa Hidalgo Nayarit Mex.
244 G3 Villa Hidalgo San Luis Potosí Mex.
239 J11 Villa Hidalgo Sonora Mex.
183 M4 Villahizán Spain
183 M4 Villahoz Spain
260 E4 Villa Huidobro Arg.
156 I8 Villaines-en-Duesmois France
159 K5 Villaines-la-Juhel France
159 K6 Villaines-sous-Malicorne France
242 D5 Villa Insurgentes Mex.
261 F6 Villa Iris Arg.
187 E10 Villajoyosa-La Vila Joíosa Spain
244 B4 Villa Juárez Nayarit Mex.
244 G3 Villa Juárez San Luis Potosí Mex.
191 K4 Villa Lagarina Italy
193 L4 Villalago Italy
183 J5 Villalar de los Comuneros Spain
193 L4 Villa Latina Italy
245 M7 Villa La Venta Mex.
245 J5 Villa Lázaro Cárdenas Mex.
194 F8 Villalba Sicilia Italy
247 □1 Villalba Puerto Rico
183 M5 Villalba de Duero Spain
183 K3 Villalba de Guardo Spain
184 G6 Villalba del Alcor Spain
183 P8 Villalba de la Sierra Spain
183 K5 Villalba de los Alcores Spain
184 F3 Villalba de los Barros Spain
183 O8 Villalba del Rey Spain
186 F5 Villalba dels Arcs Spain
183 O3 Villalba de Rioja Spain
182 H5 Villalcampo Spain
182 H6 Villalcampo, Embalse de resr Spain
183 K4 Villalcázar de Sirga Spain
243 I4 Villaldama Mex.
183 Q6 Villalengua Spain
185 O2 Villalgordo del Júcar Spain
183 P9 Villalgordo del Marquesado Spain
261 H4 Villa Lía Arg.
261 H3 Villa Lila Arg.
193 M5 Villa Literno Italy
183 J5 Villalobos Spain
183 J4 Villalón de Campos Spain
259 E5 Villalonga Arg.
187 E10 Villalonga Spain
183 J5 Villalpando Spain
185 P2 Villalpardo Spain
183 M8 Villaluenga de la Sagra Spain
183 K4 Villalumbroso Spain
244 F6 Villa Madero Mex.
245 H1 Villa Mainero Mex.
185 P2 Villamalea Spain
182 I4 Villamañán Spain
182 I4 Villamandos Spain
185 N3 Villamanrique Spain
184 G6 Villamanrique de la Condesa Spain
183 L8 Villamanta Spain
192 B8 Villamar Sardegna Italy
Villamarchante Spain see Vilamarxant
261 G4 Villa María Arg.
261 F3 Villa María Córdoba Arg.
261 G2 Villa María Entre Ríos Arg.
261 H2 Villa María Grande Arg.
252 D5 Villa Martín Bol.
184 H7 Villamartín Spain
183 K4 Villamartín de Campos Spain
192 B9 Villamassargia Sardegna Italy
258 E2 Villa Matoque Arg.
182 I7 Villamayor Spain
185 K3 Villamayor de Calatrava Spain
183 J5 Villamayor de Campos Spain
183 O9 Villamayor de Santiago Spain
183 L4 Villamayor de Treviño Spain
162 F5 Villamblard France
183 L4 Villamediana Spain
183 P4 Villamediana de Iregua Spain
182 H3 Villamejil Spain
260 C2 Villa Mercedes Arg.
260 E3 Villa Mercedes San Luis Arg.
184 H2 Villamesías Spain
182 G8 Villamiel Spain
190 I7 Villa Minozzo Italy
252 E5 Villa Montes Bol.
182 I6 Villamor de los Escuderos Spain
244 F5 Villa Morelos Mex.
183 M9 Villamuelas Spain
183 L5 Villamuriel de Cerrato Spain
163 D7 Villandraut France
195 N2 Villanova Italy
190 E7 Villanova d'Albenga Italy
190 D6 Villanova d'Asti Italy
193 O5 Villanova del Battista Italy
192 C8 Villanovafranca Sardegna Italy
192 A6 Villanova Monteleone Sardegna Italy
192 B8 Villanova Truschedu Sardegna Italy
192 C8 Villanova Tulo Sardegna Italy
190 G5 Villanterio Italy
186 D2 Villanúa Spain
183 K5 Villanubla Spain
261 F3 Villa Nueva Córdoba Arg.
260 C3 Villa Nueva Mendoza Arg.
250 C2 Villanueva Col.
244 E3 Villanueva Mex.
Villanueva Spain see Vilanova
183 O9 Villanueva de Alcardete Spain
Villanueva de Alcolea Spain see Vilanova d'Alcolea
183 P7 Villanueva de Alcorón Spain
185 K6 Villanueva de Algaidas Spain
183 M4 Villanueva de Argaño Spain
Villanueva de Arosa Spain see Vilanova de Arousa
183 M9 Villanueva de Bogas Spain
183 O4 Villanueva de Cameros Spain
187 E9 Villanueva de Castellón Spain
185 J4 Villanueva de Córdoba Spain
186 D4 Villanueva de Gállego Spain
183 K7 Villanueva de Gómez Spain
183 M8 Villanueva de la Cañada Spain
185 J7 Villanueva de la Concepción Spain
185 N3 Villanueva de la Fuente Spain
185 P2 Villanueva de la Jara Spain
185 L4 Villanueva de la Reina Spain
185 M4 Villanueva del Arzobispo Spain
184 E5 Villanueva de las Cruces Spain
184 H3 Villanueva de la Serena Spain
182 H8 Villanueva de la Sierra Spain
185 M5 Villanueva de las Torres Spain
183 J8 Villanueva de la Vera Spain
183 J5 Villanueva del Campo Spain
185 J4 Villanueva del Duque Spain
184 E4 Villanueva del Fresno Spain
184 E5 Villanueva de los Castillejos Spain
185 N3 Villanueva de los Infantes Spain
185 I4 Villanueva del Rey Spain
187 C11 Villanueva del Río Segura Spain
184 H5 Villanueva del Río y Minas Spain
185 K7 Villanueva del Rosario Spain
185 K6 Villanueva del Trabuco Spain
185 L3 Villanueva de San Carlos Spain
185 I6 Villanueva de San Juan Spain
185 K6 Villanueva de Tapia Spain
183 N3 Villanueva de Valdegovia Spain
Villanueva-y-Geltrú Spain see Vilanova i la Geltrú
183 K3 Villanuño de Valdavia Spain
177 H6 Villány Hungary
177 H6 Villányi-hegység ridge Hungary
258 F3 Villa Ocampo Arg.
242 G4 Villa Ocampo Mex.
259 B8 Villa O'Higgins Chile
258 E3 Villa Ojo de Agua Arg.
253 F6 Villa Oliva Para.
Villa O. Pereyra Mex. see Villa Orestes Pereyra
191 P4 Villa Opicina Italy
242 G4 Villa Orestes Pereyra Mex.
252 D4 Villa Oropeza Bol.
185 N3 Villapalacios Spain
192 B9 Villaperuccio Sardegna Italy
239 J12 Villa Pesqueira Mex.
195 K4 Villapiana Italy
195 K4 Villapiana Lido Italy
191 K6 Villa Poma Italy
160 D3 Villapourçon France
260 B4 Villa Prat Chile
192 D9 Villaputzu Sardegna Italy
182 I4 Villaquejida Spain
182 I3 Villaquilambre Spain
252 D4 Villar Bol.
182 I6 Villaralbo Spain
185 J4 Villaralto Spain
261 G3 Villa Ramírez Arg.
183 M3 Villarcayo Spain
161 I6 Villar-d'Arêne France
161 H6 Villard-Bonnot France
161 H6 Villard-de-Lans France
185 P3 Villar de Chinchilla Spain
182 G7 Villar de Ciervo Spain
182 H5 Villardeciervos Spain
183 J5 Villardefrades Spain
187 D8 Villar del Arzobispo Spain
182 G7 Villar de la Yegua Spain
182 H6 Villar del Buey Spain
183 Q8 Villar del Cobo Spain
183 Q9 Villar del Humo Spain
182 G3 Villar de los Barrios Spain
186 C5 Villar de los Navarros Spain
183 J9 Villar del Pedroso Spain
184 F2 Villar del Rey Spain
183 R7 Villar del Salz Spain
183 P8 Villar de Olalla Spain
182 H6 Villar de Peralonso Spain
184 H2 Villar de Rena Spain
183 O4 Villar de Torre Spain
185 K5 Villardompardo Spain
187 E8 Villareal Spain
Villareal Spain see Villareal
Villareal de los Infantes Spain see Villareal
261 F3 Villa Reducción Arg.
260 D6 Villa Regina Arg.
183 O9 Villarejo de Fuentes Spain
183 K9 Villarejo de Montalbán Spain
182 I4 Villarejo de Orbigo Spain
183 N8 Villarejo de Salvanés Spain
191 J3 Villa Rendena Italy
183 J3 Villarente Spain
182 I6 Villares de la Reina Spain
253 F6 Villa Rey Para.
260 E3 Villa Reynolds Arg.
185 L5 Villargordo Spain
182 H6 Villarino de los Aires Spain
186 D6 Villarluengo Spain
194 G9 Villa Romana del casale tourist site Italy
194 G8 Villarosa Sicilia Italy
186 C6 Villarquemado Spain
183 K4 Villarramiel Spain
186 C5 Villarreal de Huerva Spain
260 A6 Villarrica Chile
253 F6 Villarrica Para.
260 A6 Villarrica, Lago l. Chile
260 B6 Villarrica, Parque Nacional nat. park Chile
182 I5 Villarrín de Campos Spain
185 N2 Villarrobledo Spain
185 N4 Villarrodrigo Spain
183 P4 Villarroya Spain
186 D6 Villarroya de los Pinares Spain
185 L2 Villarrubia de los Ojos Spain
183 N9 Villarrubia de Santiago Spain
183 O9 Villarrubio Spain
261 H4 Villars Arg.
162 F5 Villars Aquitaine France
161 E6 Villars Rhône-Alpes France
161 J7 Villar-St-Pancrace France
183 P9 Villars del Saz Spain
160 J2 Villars-lès-Blamont France
160 G5 Villars-les-Dombes France
161 K9 Villars-sur-Var France
185 P2 Villarta Spain
185 J2 Villarta de los Montes Spain
185 M2 Villarta de San Juan Spain
234 F6 Villas NJ U.S.A.
Villasalazar Zimbabwe see Sango
192 C9 Villasalto Sardegna Italy
180 E1 Villasana de Mena Spain
183 L4 Villasandino Spain
195 J7 Villa San Giovanni Italy
261 H3 Villa San José Arg.
Villa Sanjurjo Morocco see Al Hoceima
261 H3 Villa San Marcial Arg.
258 D3 Villa San Martin Arg.
193 M4 Villa Santa Maria Italy
260 D2 Villa Santa Rita de Catuna Arg.
260 C2 Villa Santa Rosa Arg.
183 N2 Villasante de Montija Spain
191 N3 Villa Santina Italy
260 E4 Villa Sarmiento Arg.
183 L4 Villasarracino Spain
261 F4 Villa Sauze Arg.
163 I9 Villasavary France
183 O6 Villasayas Spain
261 I3 Villasboas Uru.
182 G6 Villasbuenas Spain
182 H6 Villasdardo Spain
182 H3 Villaseca de Laciana Spain
183 M9 Villaseca de la Sagra Spain
182 H6 Villaseco de los Gamitos Spain
182 H6 Villaseco de los Reyes Spain
182 I6 Villaseco del Pan Spain
183 M9 Villasequilla de Yepes Spain
252 D4 Villa Serrano Bol.
192 D9 Villasimius Sardegna Italy
195 I9 Villasmundo Sicilia Italy
192 B9 Villasor Sardegna Italy
192 B9 Villaspeciosa Sardegna Italy
182 G8 Villasrubias Spain
187 C7 Villastar Spain
183 N4 Villasur de Herreros Spain
183 N9 Villatobas Spain
183 J7 Villatoro Spain
187 C9 Villatoya Spain
261 E2 Villa Tulumba Arg.
183 J3 Villaturiel Spain
183 K4 Villaumbrales Spain
258 C3 Villa Unión Arg.
243 I3 Villa Unión Coahuila Mex.
244 C2 Villa Unión Durango Mex.
244 A2 Villa Unión Sinaloa Mex.
192 B8 Villaurbana Sardegna Italy
261 G2 Villa Urquiza Arg.
260 E4 Villa Valeria Arg.
193 L4 Villavallelonga Italy
246 H4 Villa Vasquez Dom. Rep.
183 O4 Villavelayo Spain
216 □3b Villaverde Fuerteventura Canary Is
192 B8 Villa Verde Sardegna Italy
185 N4 Villaverde de Guadalimar Spain
184 H5 Villaverde del Río Spain
187 A8 Villaverde y Pasaconsol Spain
190 F6 Villavernia Italy
250 C3 Villavicencio Col.
183 J2 Villaviciosa Spain
183 J1 Villaviciosa, Ría de inlet Spain
185 I4 Villaviciosa de Córdoba Spain
183 M8 Villaviciosa de Odón Spain
244 D7 Villa Victoria Mex.
187 E8 Villavieja Spain
183 M6 Villavieja del Lozoya Spain
182 H7 Villavieja de Yeltes Spain
252 D4 Villa Viscarra Bol.
183 L5 Villaviudas Spain
182 G2 Villayón Spain
183 K3 Villazanzo de Valderaduey Spain
252 D5 Villazon Bol.
157 N7 Villé France
160 G5 Villebois France
162 E5 Villebois-Lavalette France
163 G8 Villebrumier France
163 E9 Villecomtal-sur-Arros France
160 G1 Villecomte France
161 I9 Villecroze France
161 B10 Villedaigne France
244 F3 Ville de Ramos Mex.
244 G4 Ville de Reyes Mex.
159 I7 Villedieu-la-Blouère France
158 I4 Villedieu-les-Poêles France
159 O8 Villedieu-sur-Indre France
192 C2 Ville-di-Pietrabugno Corse France
159 M6 Villedômer France
156 G5 Ville-en-Tardenois France
162 E3 Villefagnan France
160 G5 Villefontaine France
161 D8 Villefort France
156 F8 Villefranche Bourgogne France
163 F9 Villefranche Midi-Pyrénées France
163 I8 Villefranche-d'Albigeois France
160 B4 Villefranche-d'Allier France
163 I10 Villefranche-de-Conflent France
163 H9 Villefranche-de-Lauragais France
162 E6 Villefranche-de-Lonchat France
161 B8 Villefranche-de-Panat France
163 I7 Villefranche-de-Rouergue France
163 G6 Villefranche-du-Périgord France
159 O7 Villefranche-sur-Cher France
161 K9 Villefranche-sur-Mer France
160 F5 Villefranche-sur-Saône France
163 B9 Villefranque France
183 L4 Villegas Spain
244 E3 Ville Juarez Mex.
187 C7 Villel Spain
244 G4 Villela Mex.
161 G9 Villelaure France
156 E8 Villemandeur France
227 O2 Ville-Marie Que. Can.
Ville-Marie Que. Can. see Montréal
156 G7 Villemaur-sur-Vanne France
227 P1 Villemontel Que. Can.
156 H7 Villemorien France
163 I9 Villemoustaussou France
163 H8 Villemur-sur-Tarn France
187 D10 Villena Spain
156 G6 Villenauxe-la-Grande France
163 C6 Villenave-d'Ornon France
163 I7 Villeneuve Midi-Pyrénées France
161 H9 Villeneuve Provence-Alpes-Côte d'Azur France
160 F4 Villeneuve Rhône-Alpes France
190 B3 Villeneuve Switz.
156 G7 Villeneuve-au-Chemin France
161 C6 Villeneuve-d'Allier France
156 F2 Villeneuve-d'Ascq France
161 F7 Villeneuve-de-Berg France
163 D8 Villeneuve-de-Marsan France
163 F9 Villeneuve-de-Rivière France
163 H10 Villeneuve-d'Olmes France
163 H9 Villeneuve-du-Paréage France
156 F7 Villeneuve-la-Guyard France
156 G7 Villeneuve-l'Archevêque France
161 F9 Villeneuve-lès-Avignon France
161 C10 Villeneuve-lès-Béziers France
161 D9 Villeneuve-lès-Maguelone France
161 K9 Villeneuve-Loubet France
156 F5 Villeneuve-St-Germain France
160 C3 Villeneuve-sur-Allier France
163 F7 Villeneuve-sur-Lot France
156 F7 Villeneuve-sur-Yonne France
163 G8 Villeneuve-Tolosane France
163 H9 Villenouvelle France
163 I9 Villepinte France
237 I10 Ville Platte LA U.S.A.
159 M2 Villequier France
161 B7 Villercomtal France
163 F6 Villeréal France
160 E5 Villerest France
160 E5 Villerest, Barrage de dam France
183 K5 Villerías Spain
161 B10 Villerouge-Termenès France
159 J3 Villers-Bocage Basse-Normandie France
156 D4 Villers-Bocage Picardie France
156 E4 Villers-Bretonneux France
156 E4 Villers-Carbonnel France
156 F5 Villers-Cotterêts France
156 A4 Villers-Écalles France
157 I5 Villers-en-Argonne France
160 I1 Villersexel France
160 H2 Villers-Farlay France
165 H7 Villers-le-Bouillet Belgium
160 J2 Villers-le-lac France
157 L6 Villers-lès-Nancy France
156 F3 Villers-Outréaux France
165 B10 Villers-St-Paul France
156 I4 Villers-Semeuse France
190 C2 Villers-sur-Glâne Switz.
159 K3 Villers-sur-Mer France
157 J5 Villers-sur-Meuse France
157 K5 Villerupt France
159 L3 Villerville France
156 H7 Villery France
156 H6 Villeseneux France
161 G8 Villes-sur-Auzon France
157 I5 Ville-sur-Tourbe France
253 F6 Villeta Para.
193 L4 Villetta Barrea Italy
160 G5 Villette-d'Anthon France
160 F5 Villeurbanne France
161 D9 Villeveyrac France
161 F6 Villevocance France
244 G3 Ville Zaragoza Mex.
260 C2 Villicun, Sierra mts Arg.
160 F4 Villié-Morgon France
215 M3 Villiers S. Africa
159 J6 Villiers-Charlemagne France
214 D9 Villiersdorp S. Africa
157 I6 Villiers-en-Lieu France
162 C3 Villiers-en-Plaine France
156 D5 Villiers-le-Bel France
157 J7 Villiers-le-Sec France
156 F8 Villiers-St-Benoît France
156 F6 Villiers-St-Georges France
147 G8 Villierstown Ireland
160 G5 Villieu-Loyes-Mollon France
172 E5 Villingen Ger.
172 F5 Villingendorf Ger.
169 F10 Villmar Ger.
183 K4 Villoldo Spain
183 Q9 Villora Spain
183 Q9 Villora r. Spain
191 M4 Villorba Italy
190 G4 Villoresi, Canale canal Italy
183 J7 Villoria Spain
183 J6 Villoruela Spain
157 J6 Villotte-sur-Aire France
185 H1 Villuercas, Sierra de las mts Spain
114 F7 Villupuram Tamil Nadu India
170 I2 Vilm i. Ger.
177 K3 Vilmány Hungary
223 I4 Vilna Alta Can.
Vilna Lith. see Vilnius
144 J1 Vilnesfjorden inlet Norway
138 I7 Vilnius Lith.
137 N5 Vil'nohirs'k Ukr.
137 O6 Vil'nyans'k Ukr.
186 K4 Viloví d'Onyar Spain
141 R5 Vilppula Fin.
178 C4 Vils Austria
173 L3 Vils r. Ger.
173 O4 Vils r. Ger.
138 E3 Vilsandi i. Estonia
138 E3 Vilsandi nature res. Estonia
173 M5 Vilsbiburg Ger.
173 L2 Vilseck Ger.
137 K4 Vil'shana Cherkas'ka Oblast' Ukr.
137 L3 Vil'shana Chernihivs'ka Oblast' Ukr.
137 Q4 Vil'shana Kharkivs'ka Oblast' Ukr.
136 J5 Vil'shanka Kirovohrads'ka Oblast' Ukr.
136 H5 Vil'shanka Vinnyts'ka Oblast' Ukr.
136 H3 Vil'shanka Zhytomyrs'ka Oblast' Ukr.
173 O4 Vilshofen Ger.
142 E5 Vilsund Vest Denmark
Viluppuram Tamil Nadu India see Villupuram
138 K4 Viluste Estonia
182 G6 Vilvestre Spain
165 F7 Vilvoorde Belgium
138 J7 Vilyeyka Belarus
138 K7 Vilyeyskaye Vodaskhovishcha l. Belarus
131 N3 Vilyuy r. Rus. Fed.
131 M3 Vilyuyskoye Vodokhranilishche resr Rus. Fed.
209 F8 Vimbe mt. Zambia
186 H5 Vimbodi Spain
184 A2 Vimeiro Port.
190 G4 Vimercate Italy
156 C3 Vimeu reg. France
182 B2 Vimianzo Spain
184 D3 Vimieiro Port.
182 G5 Vimioso Port.
143 L4 Vimmerby Sweden
156 E8 Vimory France
159 L4 Vimoutiers France
140 Q5 Vimpeli Fin.
176 C2 Vimperk Czech Rep.
207 I5 Vina r. Cameroon
240 J2 Vina CA U.S.A.
186 D5 Vinaceite Spain
260 B3 Viña del Mar Chile
190 C7 Vinadio Italy
186 G5 Vinaixa Spain
246 B2 Viñales Cuba
246 E4 Viñales Valley tourist site Cuba
233 □Q4 Vinalhaven ME U.S.A.
233 Q4 Vinalhaven Island ME U.S.A.
187 D11 Vinalopó r. Spain
213 □K2 Vinanivao Madag.
171 J10 Vinařice Czech Rep.
78 □6 Vinarori, Mount New Georgia Is Solomon Is
186 F7 Vinaròs Spain
Vinaroz Spain see Vinaròs
161 C10 Vinassan France
161 G6 Vinay France
245 J5 Vinazco r. Mex.
163 J10 Vinça France
225 F2 Vincelotte, Lac l. Que. Can.
217 □1c Vincendo Réunion
230 D6 Vincennes IN U.S.A.
263 H2 Vincennes Bay Antarctica
82 □1 Vincent, Point Norfolk I.
234 F5 Vincentown NJ U.S.A.
250 B5 Vinces r. Ecuador
157 L7 Vincey France
193 N5 Vinchiaturo Italy
258 C3 Vinchina Arg.
252 B3 Vinchos Peru
191 J8 Vinci Italy
168 J1 Vindeballe Denmark
140 O5 Vindelälven r. Sweden
140 M3 Vindelfjällens naturreservat nature res. Sweden
140 O4 Vindeln Sweden
142 E5 Vinderup Denmark
116 E8 Vindhya Range hills Madh. Prad. India
Vindobona Austria see Wien
186 G5 Vinebre Spain
234 E6 Vineland NJ U.S.A.
159 N6 Vineuil Centre France
159 O8 Vineuil Centre France
215 K6 Vineyard S. Africa
196 J4 Vinga Romania
196 J4 Vingăi, Câmpia plain Romania
143 L2 Vingåker Sweden
160 G2 Vingeanne r. France
163 J10 Vingrau France
96 G5 Vinh Vietnam
182 G5 Vinhais Port.
182 G5 Vinhas Port.
96 G3 Vinh Loc Vietnam
97 G9 Vinh Long Vietnam
96 H4 Vinh Thưc, Đao i. Vietnam
96 G4 Vinh Yên Vietnam
179 N7 Vinica Croatia
197 K9 Vinica Macedonia
177 I3 Vinica Slovakia
176 G3 Viničné Slovakia
179 O1 Viničné Šumice Czech Rep.
183 O4 Viniegra de Arriba Spain
237 H7 Vinita OK U.S.A.
116 B8 Vinjhan Gujarat India
Vînju Mare Romania see Vânju Mare
136 G4 Vin'kivtsi Ukr.
188 G3 Vinkovci Croatia
Vinland i. Nfld and Lab. Can. see Newfoundland
177 K3 Vinné Slovakia
138 J2 Vinni Estonia
172 D3 Vinningen Ger.
Vinnitsa Ukr. see Vinnytsya
Vinnitsa Oblast admin. div. Ukr. see Vinnyts'ka Oblast'
Vinnitskaya Oblast' admin. div. Ukr. see Vinnyts'ka Oblast'
139 R1 Vinnitsy Rus. Fed.
136 G5 Vinnyts'ka Oblast' admin. div. Ukr.
136 H4 Vinnytsya Ukr.
Vinnytsya Oblast admin. div. Ukr. see Vinnyts'ka Oblast'
182 I6 Vino, Tierra del reg. Spain
177 H3 Vinodol Slovakia
Vinogradov Ukr. see Vynohradiv
139 V6 Vinogradovo Rus. Fed.
177 G3 Vinohrady nad Váhom Slovakia
143 L2 Vinön i. Sweden
161 H9 Vinon-sur-Verdon France
161 G8 Vinsobres France
262 S1 Vinson Massif mt. Antarctica
141 J6 Vinstra Norway
92 C2 Vintar Luzon Phil.
236 I4 Vinton IA U.S.A.
185 K7 Viñuela, Embalse de la resr Spain
183 N7 Viñuelas Spain
183 O5 Vinuesa Spain
114 F4 Vinukonda Andhra Prad. India
209 B5 Vinza Congo
170 E5 Vinzelberg Ger.
168 H1 Viöl Ger.
186 D3 Violada, Llanos de la plain Spain
160 E5 Violay France
161 F8 Violès France
Violeta Cuba see Primero de Enero
86 I4 Violet Valley Aboriginal Reserve W.A. Austr.
161 D9 Viols-le-Fort France
214 B4 Vioolsdrif S. Africa
156 D5 Viosne r. France

179 I8 **Vipava** Slovenia
179 I8 **Vipava** *r.* Slovenia
211 B8 **Viphya Mountains** Malawi
191 K2 **Vipiteno** Italy
170 G4 **Vipperow** Ger.
93 E8 **Viqueque** East Timor
188 E3 **Vir** *i.* Croatia
179 K7 **Vir** Slovenia
92 E5 **Virac** Phil.
92 E5 **Virac Point** Phil.
256 C4 **Viradouro** Brazil
116 D8 **Viramgam** *Gujarat* India
127 I5 **Viranşehir** Turkey
114 D6 **Virarajendrapet** *Karnataka* India
123 N9 **Virawah** Pak.
138 M6 **Virawlya** Belarus
163 E6 **Virazeil** France
138 G5 **Vircava** *r.* Latvia/Lith.
86 D6 **Virchow, Mount** *hill W.A.* Austr.
Virdáánjarga Fin. *see* **Virtaniemi**
223 K5 **Virden** *Man.* Can.
159 J4 **Vire** France
159 I3 **Vire** *r.* France
209 B8 **Virei** Angola
156 I3 **Vireux-Molhain** France
156 I3 **Vireux-Wallerand** France
156 H7 **Virey-sous-Bar** France
257 F2 **Virgem da Lapa** Brazil
178 F5 **Virgen** Austria
185 O6 **Virgen, Puerto de la** *pass* Spain
183 Q5 **Virgen, Sierra de la** *mts* Spain
259 C9 **Vírgenes, Cabo** *c.* Arg.
178 F5 **Virgental** *val.* Austria
232 G12 **Virgilina** *VA* U.S.A.
241 R5 **Virgin** *r. AZ* U.S.A.
227 O1 **Virginatown** *Ont.* Can.
247 K4 **Virgin Gorda** *i.* Virgin Is (U.K.)
147 H5 **Virginia** Ireland
215 K4 **Virginia** S. Africa
226 B2 **Virginia** *MN* U.S.A.
232 G11 **Virginia** *state* U.S.A.
233 J12 **Virginia Beach** *VA* U.S.A.
238 I4 **Virginia City** *MT* U.S.A.
240 M2 **Virginia City** *NV* U.S.A.
222 E2 **Virginia Falls** *N.W.T.* Can.
151 K5 **Virginia Water** *Surrey, England* U.K.
247 K4 **Virgin Islands (U.K.)** *terr.* West Indies
247 K4 **Virgin Islands (U.S.A.)** *terr.* West Indies
241 R5 **Virgin Mountains** *AZ* U.S.A.
257 F3 **Virginópolis** Brazil
160 G4 **Viriat** France
160 G6 **Virieu** France
160 H5 **Virieu-le-Grand** France
160 E5 **Virigneux** France
160 H5 **Virignin** France
161 G6 **Viriville** France
138 H1 **Virkkala** Fin.
140 S5 **Virmasvesi** *l.* Fin.
97 H8 **Virôchey** Cambodia
165 G8 **Viroin** *r.* Belgium
141 S6 **Virolahti** Fin.
226 D6 **Viroqua** *WI* U.S.A.
188 F3 **Virovitica** Croatia
138 F4 **Virpe** Latvia
141 Q5 **Virrat** Fin.
143 L4 **Virserum** Sweden
140 T2 **Virtaniemi** Fin.
165 I9 **Virton** Belgium
138 G3 **Virtsu** Estonia
252 A2 **Virú** Peru
251 F4 **Viruá, Parque Nacional do** *nat. park* Brazil
114 E8 **Virudhunagar** *Tamil Nadu* India
208 F5 **Virunga, Parc National des** *nat. park* Dem. Rep. Congo
138 F5 **Virvytė** *r.* Lith.
160 H4 **Viry** *Franche-Comté* France
160 I4 **Viry** *Rhône-Alpes* France
156 F4 **Viry-Noureuil** France
188 F4 **Vis** Croatia
188 F4 **Vis** *i.* Croatia
161 C9 **Vis, Gorges de la** France
138 J6 **Visaginas** Lith.
Visakhapatnam *Andhra Prad.* India *see* **Vishakhapatnam**
78 □6 **Visale** *Guadalcanal* Solomon Is
240 M5 **Visalia** *CA* U.S.A.
161 F8 **Visan** France
197 P5 **Vişani** Romania
114 D3 **Visapur** *Mahar.* India
116 C9 **Visavadar** *Gujarat* India
92 E6 **Visayan Islands** Phil.
92 D6 **Visayan Sea** Phil.
168 F5 **Visbek** Ger.
168 G1 **Visby** Denmark
143 O4 **Visby** *Gotland* Sweden
257 F4 **Visconde do Rio Branco** Brazil
221 G2 **Viscount Melville Sound** *sea chan. N.W.T./Nunavut* Can.
165 I7 **Visé** Belgium
130 I2 **Vise, Ostrov** *i.* Rus. Fed.
188 G4 **Višegrad** Bos.-Herz.
191 N7 **Viserba** Italy
254 D2 **Viseu** Brazil
182 E7 **Viseu** Port.
182 E7 **Viseu** *admin. dist.* Port.
197 M3 **Vişeu** *r.* Romania
197 M3 **Vişeu de Sus** Romania
191 R5 **Viševica** *mt.* Croatia
115 H4 **Vishakhapatnam** *Andhra Prad.* India
197 O9 **Vishegrad** *hill* Bulg.
134 K3 **Vishera** *r.* Rus. Fed.
134 L4 **Vishera** *r.* Rus. Fed.
139 O3 **Vishera** *r.* Rus. Fed.
135 H5 **Vishnevoye** Rus. Fed.
Vishnevoye Ukr. *see* **Vyshneve**
138 J7 **Vishnyeva** Belarus
186 C6 **Visiedo** Spain
138 K4 **Vīsikums** Latvia
134 L4 **Visim** Rus. Fed.
197 N6 **Vişina** Romania
143 K3 **Visingsö** *i.* Sweden
142 I4 **Viskan** *r.* Sweden
138 J5 **Viški** Latvia
188 F4 **Viški Kanal** *sea chan.* Croatia
143 K5 **Vislanda** Sweden
116 D8 **Visnagar** *Gujarat* India
179 K8 **Višnja Gora** Slovenia
171 L9 **Višňová** Czech Rep.
176 F3 **Višňové** Czech Rep.
177 H2 **Višňové** Slovakia
190 C6 **Viso, Monte** *mt.* Italy
185 L3 **Viso del Marqués** Spain
188 G4 **Visoko** Bos.-Herz.
190 F6 **Visone** Italy
177 J4 **Visonta** Hungary
190 D3 **Visp** Switz.
215 J7 **Visrivier** S. Africa
161 D6 **Vissac-Auteyrac** France
114 G4 **Vissannapeta** *Andhra Prad.* India
143 L5 **Visselfjärda** Sweden
168 I5 **Visselhövede** Ger.
143 K5 **Vissjön** *l.* Sweden
193 K2 **Visso** Italy
190 D3 **Vissoie** Switz.
240 O8 **Vista** *CA* U.S.A.
235 H2 **Vista** *NY* U.S.A.
250 D4 **Vista Alegre** *Amazonas* Brazil
250 D6 **Vista Alegre** *Amazonas* Brazil
251 F6 **Vista Alegre** *Amazonas* Brazil
253 F4 **Vista Alegre** *Mato Grosso do Sul* Brazil
251 F4 **Vista Alegre** *Roraima* Brazil
187 E7 **Vistabella del Maestrazgo** Spain
260 C3 **Vista Flores** Arg.
245 J2 **Vista Hermosa** Mex.
240 M6 **Vista Lake** *CA* U.S.A.
142 J2 **Visten** *l.* Sweden
198 G1 **Vistonida, Limni** *lag.* Greece
Vistula *r.* Pol. *see* **Wisła**
138 F7 **Vištytis** Lith.
175 K1 **Vištytis** *l.* Lith./Rus. Fed.
137 L6 **Visun'** *r.* Ukr.
117 O7 **Viswema** *Nagaland* India
177 J4 **Visznek** Hungary
197 M7 **Vit** *r.* Bulg.
250 E3 **Vita** *r.* Col.
194 D8 **Vita** *Sicilia* Italy
192 E2 **Vita, Capo** *c.* Italy
123 M7 **Vitakri** Pak.
196 G7 **Vitao** *mt.* Montenegro
177 J3 **Vít'az** Slovakia
Vitebsk Belarus *see* **Vitsyebsk**
Vitebskaya Oblast' *admin. div.* Belarus *see* **Vitsyebskaya Voblasts'**
Vitebsk Oblast *admin. div.* Belarus *see* **Vitsyebskaya Voblasts'**
192 I3 **Viterbo** Italy
192 H3 **Viterbo** *prov.* Italy
157 L6 **Viterne** France
188 F3 **Vitez** Bos.-Herz.
188 G4 **Vitez** *pass* Bos.-Herz.
252 D5 **Vitichi** Bol.
182 H6 **Vitigudino** Spain
79 □7a **Viti Levu** *i.* Fiji
99 K1 **Vitim** *r.* Rus. Fed.
99 J1 **Vitimskoye Ploskogor'ye** *plat.* Rus. Fed.
196 J8 **Vitina** *Kosovo* Serbia
179 L2 **Vitis** Austria
177 G2 **Vítkov** Czech Rep.
179 O4 **Vitnyéd** Hungary
78 □6 **Vito** P.N.G.
197 J9 **Vitolište** Macedonia
196 I8 **Vitomirica** *Kosovo* Serbia
252 C4 **Vitor** Peru
252 B4 **Vitor** *r.* Peru
192 I3 **Vitorchiano** Italy
257 G4 **Vitória** *Espírito Santo* Brazil
251 H5 **Vitória** *Pará* Brazil
Vitoria Spain *see* **Vitoria-Gasteiz**
183 O3 **Vitoria** *airport* Spain
183 O3 **Vitoria, Montes de** *mts* Spain
255 E5 **Vitória da Conquista** Brazil
183 O3 **Vitoria-Gasteiz** Spain
264 G7 **Vitória Seamount** *sea feature* S. Atlantic Ocean
197 L8 **Vitosha** *nat. park* Bulg.
195 M5 **Vitravo** *r.* Italy
158 I5 **Vitré** France
157 K8 **Vitrey-sur-Mance** France
161 G10 **Vitrolles** France
156 E3 **Vitry-en-Artois** France
156 I6 **Vitry-en-Perthois** France
156 H6 **Vitry-la-Ville** France
156 I6 **Vitry-le-François** France
160 D3 **Vitry-sur-Loire** France
156 D6 **Vitry-sur-Seine** France
136 I2 **Vits'** *r.* Belarus
139 N6 **Vitsyebsk** Belarus
138 L6 **Vitsyebskaya Voblasts'** *admin. div.* Belarus
140 P3 **Vittangi** Sweden
160 F2 **Vitteaux** France
157 K7 **Vittel** France
194 H10 **Vittoria** *Sicilia* Italy
Vittoriosa Malta *see* **Birgu**
191 M4 **Vittorio Veneto** Italy
193 M5 **Vitulazio** Italy
137 Q8 **Vityazevo** Rus. Fed.
137 Q8 **Vityazevskiy Liman** *lag.* Rus. Fed.
171 E8 **Vitzenburg** Ger.
187 E8 **Viuda, Rambla de la** *r.* Spain
160 I4 **Viuz-en-Sallaz** France
161 E7 **Vivarais, Monts du** *mts* France
192 C3 **Vivario** *Corse* France
137 R4 **Vivcharove** Ukr.
182 E1 **Viveiro** Spain
182 E1 **Viveiro, Ría de** *est.* Spain
186 D6 **Vivel del Río Martín** Spain
187 D8 **Viver** Spain
261 F4 **Vivero** Arg.
Vivero Spain *see* **Viveiro**
161 D6 **Viverols** France
190 E5 **Viverone, Lago di** *l.* Italy
185 N3 **Viveros** Spain
237 I9 **Vivian** *LA* U.S.A.
157 I4 **Vivier-au-Court** France
161 F8 **Viviers** France
163 I6 **Viviez** France
161 E9 **Viv-le-Fesq** France
213 F4 **Vivo** S. Africa
179 K7 **Vivodnik** *mt.* Slovenia
162 E3 **Vivonne** France
261 I5 **Vivoratá** Arg.
242 □R10 **Vivorillo, Cayos** *is* Hond.
156 I8 **Vix** *Bourgogne* France
162 C3 **Vix** *Pays de la Loire* France
175 M5 **Viynytsya** Ukr.
137 O5 **Viys'kove** Ukr.
136 F4 **Viytivtsi** Ukr.
Vizagapatam *Andhra Prad.* India *see* **Vishakhapatnam**
242 C4 **Vizcaíno, Desierto de** *des.* Mex.
242 B4 **Vizcaíno, Sierra** *mts* Mex.
183 O2 **Vizcaya** *prov.* Spain
126 C3 **Vize** Turkey
160 E5 **Vizézy** *r.* France
134 I2 **Vizhas** Rus. Fed.
134 I2 **Vizhas** *r.* Rus. Fed.
175 L6 **Vizhomlya** Ukr.
115 H3 **Vizianagaram** *Andhra Prad.* India
161 H6 **Vizille** France
191 P5 **Vižinada** Croatia
134 J3 **Vizinga** Rus. Fed.
197 P5 **Viziru** Romania
177 G2 **Vizovice** Czech Rep.
177 I3 **Vizslás** Hungary
177 K3 **Vizsoly** Hungary
194 H9 **Vizzini** *Sicilia* Italy
252 C3 **V. J. José Perez** Bol.
198 A2 **Vjosë** *r.* Albania
165 G7 **Vlaams-Brabant** *prov.* Belgium
164 F5 **Vlaardingen** Neth.
198 B4 **Vlachata** *Kefallonia* Greece
198 D5 **Vlachokerasia** Greece
179 I1 **Vlachovo Březí** Czech Rep.
177 L5 **Vlădeasa, Munții** *mts* Romania
197 K4 **Vlădeasa, Vârful** *mt.* Romania
197 K8 **Vladičin Han** Serbia
129 F2 **Vladikavkaz** Rus. Fed.
100 I7 **Vladimir** *Primorskiy Kray* Rus. Fed.
139 X5 **Vladimir** *Vladimirskaya Oblast'* Rus. Fed.
177 K5 **Vladimirescu** Romania
100 H7 **Vladimiro-Aleksandrovskoye** Rus. Fed.
Vladimir Oblast *admin. div.* Rus. Fed. *see* **Vladimirskaya Oblast'**
120 K1 **Vladimirovka** *Kostanayskaya Oblast'* Kazakh.
120 D2 **Vladimirovka** *Zapadnyy Kazakhstan* Kazakh.
100 M3 **Vladimirovka** *Sakhalinskaya Oblast'* Rus. Fed.
129 F1 **Vladimirovka** *Stavropol'skiy Kray* Rus. Fed.
197 L7 **Vladimirovo** Bulg.
100 M4 **Vladimirovo** Rus. Fed.
Vladimirovskiy Kazakh. *see* **Vladimirovka**
139 X6 **Vladimirskaya Oblast'** *admin. div.* Rus. Fed.
139 Q6 **Vladimirskiy Tupik** Rus. Fed.
Vladimir-Volynskiy Ukr. *see* **Volodymyr-Volyns'kyy**
176 E2 **Vladislav** Czech Rep.
100 G7 **Vladivostok** Rus. Fed.
134 G4 **Vladychnoye** Rus. Fed.
164 L2 **Vlagtwedde** Neth.
197 N4 **Vlăhița** Romania
197 J8 **Vlajna** *mt.* Serbia
Vlakhokerassía Greece *see* **Vlachokerasia**
188 G3 **Vlasenica** Bos.-Herz.
196 H6 **Vlašić Planina** *mts* Serbia
176 D2 **Vlašim** Czech Rep.
137 M4 **Vlasivka** Ukr.
197 K8 **Vlasotince** Serbia
Vlasova-Ayuta Rus. Fed. *see* **Ayutinskiy**
139 W6 **Vlasovo** Rus. Fed.
100 L2 **Vlas'yevo** Rus. Fed.
139 P8 **Vlazovichi** Rus. Fed.
177 G3 **Vlčany** Slovakia
164 J3 **Vledder** Neth.
214 F10 **Vleesbaai** *b.* S. Africa
214 F9 **Vleiland** S. Africa
164 H4 **Vleuten** Neth.
164 G2 **Vlieland** *i.* Neth.
164 H5 **Vlijmen** Neth.
165 E6 **Vlissingen** Neth.
198 A2 **Vlorë** Albania
198 A2 **Vlorës, Gjiri i** *b.* Albania
169 G6 **Vlotho** Ger.
Vlotslavsk Pol. *see* **Włocławek**
176 D1 **Vltava** *r.* Czech Rep.
179 J7 **Vnanje Gorice** Slovenia
139 T2 **Vnina** *r.* Rus. Fed.
120 K7 **Vobkent** Uzbek.
171 F7 **Vockerode** Ger.
179 I3 **Vöcklabruck** Austria
179 H3 **Vöcklamarkt** Austria
177 G3 **Voderady** Slovakia
191 Q5 **Vodice** *Istra* Croatia
188 E4 **Vodice** *Šibenik* Croatia
134 G3 **Vodlozero, Ozero** *l.* Rus. Fed.
176 D2 **Vodňany** Czech Rep.
188 D3 **Vodnjan** Croatia
Vodopyanovo Rus. Fed. *see* **Donskoye**
146 □N2 **Voe** *Shetland, Scotland* U.K.
215 J9 **Voël** *r.* S. Africa
169 C7 **Voerde (Niederrhein)** Ger.
165 I7 **Voerendaal** Neth.
142 G4 **Voerså** Denmark
207 F5 **Vogan** Togo
164 G4 **Vogelenzang** Neth.
157 O7 **Vogelgrun** France
Vogelkop Peninsula *Papua* Indon. *see* **Doberai, Jazirah**
207 H4 **Vogel Peak** Nigeria
170 H4 **Vogelsang** Ger.
169 G10 **Vogelsberg** *hills* Ger.
171 I6 **Vogelsdorf** Ger.
157 O7 **Vogelsheim** France
172 D3 **Vogelweh** Ger.
190 G6 **Voghera** Italy
191 L6 **Voghiera** Italy
129 H6 **Voghji** *r.* Armenia
140 J5 **Vognill** Norway
188 G4 **Vogošća** Bos.-Herz.
172 H6 **Vogt** Ger.
173 M6 **Vogtareuth** Ger.
171 F10 **Vogtland** *reg.* Ger.
161 E7 **Vogüé** France
78 □5 **Voh** New Caledonia
173 L4 **Vohburg an der Donau** Ger.
Vohémar Madag. *see* **Iharaña**
173 M2 **Vohenstrauß** Ger.
Vohibinany Madag. *see* **Ampasimanolotra**
213 □J4 **Vohilava** *Fianarantsoa* Madag.
213 □K4 **Vohilava** *Fianarantsoa* Madag.
Vohimarina Madag. *see* **Iharaña**
213 □J5 **Vohimena, Tanjona** *c.* Madag.
213 □J4 **Vohipeno** Madag.
213 □K4 **Vohitrandriana** Madag.
169 G8 **Vöhl** Ger.
138 I3 **Võhma** Estonia
172 E5 **Vöhrenbach** Ger.
172 F5 **Vöhringen** *Baden-Württemberg* Ger.
173 I5 **Vöhringen** *Bayern* Ger.
211 C5 **Voi** Kenya
157 K6 **Void-Vacon** France
171 D8 **Voigtstedt** Ger.
141 S6 **Voikoski** Fin.
157 I6 **Voillecomte** France
197 L5 **Voineasa** Romania
197 P3 **Voineşti** Romania
206 C4 **Voinjama** Liberia
139 T8 **Voin Pervyy** Rus. Fed.
161 H6 **Voiron** France
156 C6 **Voise** *r.* France
225 I1 **Voisey Bay** *Nfld and Lab.* Can.
160 H3 **Voiteur** France
179 L5 **Voitsberg** Austria
177 K3 **Vojčice** Slovakia
142 F6 **Vojens** Denmark
140 N4 **Vojmsjön** *l.* Sweden
Vojnice Slovakia *see* **Bátorove Kosihy**
179 L7 **Vojnik** Slovenia
196 H5 **Vojvodina** *prov.* Serbia
138 K2 **Voka** Estonia
177 H6 **Vokány** Hungary
134 I4 **Vokhma** Rus. Fed.
140 U4 **Voknavolok** Rus. Fed.
207 I4 **Voko** Cameroon
134 K3 **Vol'** *r.* Rus. Fed.
176 C3 **Volary** Czech Rep.
Volaterrae Italy *see* **Volterra**
238 L4 **Volborg** *MT* U.S.A.
258 D1 **Volcán** Arg.
252 D5 **Volcán, Cerro** *vol.* Bol.
260 B2 **Volcán, Cerro del** *vol.* Chile
261 H5 **Volcán, Sierra del** *hills* Arg.
242 □R13 **Volcán Barú, Parque Nacional** *nat. park* Panama
Volcano Bay Japan *see* **Uchiura-wan**
240 □F14 **Volcano House** *HI* U.S.A.
Volcano Islands N. Pacific Ocean *see* **Kazan-rettō**
161 B6 **Volcans d'Auvergne, Parc Naturel Régional des** *nature res.* France
Volchansk Ukr. *see* **Vovchans'k**
139 O8 **Volchas** *r.* Belarus
121 S1 **Volchikha** Rus. Fed.
139 S4 **Volchina** *r.* Rus. Fed.
139 P1 **Volchiy Nos, Mys** *pt* Rus. Fed.
137 T1 **Volchki** Rus. Fed.
141 I5 **Volda** Norway
134 K3 **Vol'dino** Rus. Fed.
173 P2 **Volduchy** Czech Rep.
164 H4 **Volendam** Neth.
232 F12 **Volens** *VA* U.S.A.
139 V4 **Volga** Rus. Fed.
139 V4 **Volga** *r.* Rus. Fed.
Volga Upland *hills* Rus. Fed. *see* **Privolzhskaya Vozvyshennost'**
135 H7 **Volgodonsk** Rus. Fed.
135 I6 **Volgograd** Rus. Fed.
Volgograd Oblast *admin. div.* Rus. Fed. *see* **Volgogradskaya Oblast'**
135 I6 **Volgogradskaya Oblast'** *admin. div.* Rus. Fed.
135 I6 **Volgogradskoye Vodokhranilishche** *resr* Rus. Fed.
139 Y4 **Volgorechensk** Rus. Fed.
Volhynia *admin. div.* Ukr. *see* **Volyns'ka Oblast'**
136 I7 **Volintiri** Moldova
199 G4 **Volissos** *Chios* Greece
79 □7a **Volivoli Point** *Viti Levu* Fiji
173 I2 **Volkach** Ger.
173 I2 **Volkach** *r.* Ger.
179 K6 **Völkermarkt** Austria
172 F6 **Volkertshausen** Ger.
190 F1 **Volketswil** Switz.
139 P2 **Volkhov** Rus. Fed.
139 P1 **Volkhov** *r.* Rus. Fed.
139 P1 **Volkhovskaya Guba** *b.* Rus. Fed.
139 O3 **Volkhovskiy** Rus. Fed.
172 B3 **Völklingen** Ger.
169 H8 **Volkmarsen** Ger.
Volkovichi Belarus *see* **Vawkavichy**
139 N7 **Volkovo** Rus. Fed.
Volkovysk Belarus *see* **Vawkavysk**
Volkovyskiye Vysoty *hills* Belarus *see* **Vawkavyskaye Wzvyshsha**
215 N3 **Volksrust** S. Africa
171 E7 **Volkstedt** Ger.
168 D4 **Völlen** Ger.
164 I3 **Vollenhove** Neth.
168 G4 **Vollersode** Ger.
160 D5 **Vollore-Montagne** France
157 N5 **Volmunster** France
160 F2 **Volnay** France
Vol'nogorsk Ukr. *see* **Vil'nohirs'k**
100 G7 **Vol'no-Nadezhdinskoye** Rus. Fed.
137 Q6 **Volnovakha** Ukr.
121 N1 **Vol'noye** Rus. Fed.
Vol'nyansk Ukr. *see* **Vil'nyans'k**
131 K2 **Volochanka** Rus. Fed.
100 I4 **Volochayevka-Vtoraya** Rus. Fed.
Volochisk Ukr. *see* **Volochys'k**
136 F4 **Volochys'k** Ukr.
136 I4 **Volodarka** Ukr.
175 J1 **Volodarovka** Rus. Fed.
137 Q6 **Volodars'ke** Ukr.
120 C4 **Volodarskiy** Rus. Fed.
Volodarskoye Kazakh. *see* **Saumalkol'**
136 H3 **Volodars'k-Volyns'kyy** Ukr.
136 F2 **Volodymyrets'** Ukr.
137 L6 **Volodymyrivka** Ukr.
136 D3 **Volodymyr-Volyns'kyy** Ukr.
134 G4 **Vologda** Rus. Fed.
Vologda Oblast *admin. div.* Rus. Fed. *see* **Vologodskaya Oblast'**
157 M7 **Vologne** *r.* France
139 Y2 **Vologodskaya Oblast'** *admin. div.* Rus. Fed.
137 Q3 **Volokhivka** Ukr.
137 P4 **Volokhiv Yar** Ukr.
139 S5 **Volokolamsk** Rus. Fed.
135 G6 **Volokonovka** Rus. Fed.
134 J2 **Volokovaya** Rus. Fed.
161 I8 **Volonne** France
214 G4 **Volop** S. Africa
198 D3 **Volos** Greece
175 L6 **Voloshcha** Ukr.
137 S5 **Voloshino** Rus. Fed.
134 H3 **Voloshka** Rus. Fed.
137 Q4 **Volos'ka Balakliya** Ukr.
137 P4 **Volos'ka Balakliyka** *r.* Ukr.
138 M2 **Volosovo** Rus. Fed.
177 L3 **Volosyanka** Ukr.
139 N4 **Volot** Rus. Fed.
137 R3 **Volotovo** Rus. Fed.
136 C5 **Volovets'** Ukr.
135 G5 **Volovo** *Lipetskaya Oblast'* Rus. Fed.
139 V8 **Volovo** *Tul'skaya Oblast'* Rus. Fed.
177 J3 **Volovské vrchy** *mts* Slovakia
139 R7 **Voloye** Rus. Fed.
Volozhin Belarus *see* **Valozhyn**
178 F8 **Volpago del Mòntello** Italy
190 F6 **Volpedo** Italy
190 D5 **Volpiano** Italy
171 D6 **Völpke** Ger.
178 D5 **Völs** Austria
170 H3 **Völschow** Ger.
192 H2 **Volsini, Monti** *mts* Italy
Volsinii Italy *see* **Orvieto**
120 B1 **Vol'sk** Rus. Fed.
214 H9 **Volstruisleegte** S. Africa
214 G6 **Volstruispoort** *pass* S. Africa
207 F5 **Volta** *admin. reg.* Ghana
207 F5 **Volta** *r.* Ghana
207 F5 **Volta, Lake** *resr* Ghana
86 H3 **Voltaire, Cape** *W.A.* Austr.
Volta Noire *r.* Africa *see* **Black Volta**
257 E5 **Volta Redonda** Brazil
Volta Rouge *r.* Burkina/Ghana *see* **Nazinon**
191 J9 **Volterra** Italy
169 E6 **Voltlage** Ger.
183 K6 **Voltoya** *r.* Spain
193 O5 **Volturara Appula** Italy
194 H2 **Volturara Irpina** Italy
193 O5 **Volturino** Italy
193 P7 **Volturino, Monte** *mt.* Italy
193 L5 **Volturno** *r.* Italy
204 D2 **Volubilis** *tourist site* Morocco
197 O6 **Voluntari** Romania
259 F8 **Volunteer Point** Falkland Is
235 L1 **Voluntown** *CT* U.S.A.
198 E2 **Volvi, Limni** *l.* Greece
160 C5 **Volvic** France
161 H9 **Volx** France
175 L3 **Volya** Belarus
137 S2 **Volya** Rus. Fed.
134 M3 **Vol'ya** *r.* Rus. Fed.
175 L6 **Volya Arlamivs'ka** Ukr.
176 C2 **Volyně** Czech Rep.
176 C2 **Volyňka** *r.* Czech Rep.
137 L2 **Volynka** Ukr.
Volyn Oblast *admin. div.* Ukr. *see* **Volyns'ka Oblast'**
136 D2 **Volyns'ka Oblast'** *admin. div.* Ukr.
Volynskaya Oblast' *admin. div.* Ukr. *see* **Volyns'ka Oblast'**
136 F4 **Volytsya** Ukr.
136 F4 **Volytsya Druha** Ukr.
134 J5 **Volzhsk** Rus. Fed.
120 D1 **Volzhskiy** *Samarskaya Oblast'* Rus. Fed.
135 I6 **Volzhskiy** *Volgogradskaya Oblast'* Rus. Fed.
79 □7a **Voma** *mts Viti Levu* Fiji
193 M2 **Vomano** *r.* Italy
79 □7a **Vomo** *i.* Fiji
178 E5 **Vomp** Austria
78 □6 **Vonavona** *i. New Georgia Is* Solomon Is
223 J4 **Vonda** *Sask.* Can.
134 I4 **Vondanka** Rus. Fed.
213 □J4 **Vondrozo** Madag.
134 H2 **Vonga** Rus. Fed.
160 G2 **Vonges** France
198 B4 **Vonitsa** Greece
160 F4 **Vonnas** France
138 K3 **Võnnu** Estonia
139 R1 **Vonozero** Rus. Fed.
114 F5 **Vontimitta** *Andhra Prad.* India
176 G5 **Vonyarcvashegy** Hungary
164 F4 **Voorburg** Neth.
233 L6 **Voorheesville** *NY* U.S.A.
164 F4 **Voorschoten** Neth.
164 J4 **Voorst** Neth.
164 I4 **Voorthuizen** Neth.
138 G2 **Voosi kurk** *sea chan.* Estonia
139 P7 **Vop'** *r.* Rus. Fed.
140 □F1 **Vopnafjörður** Iceland
140 □F1 **Vopnafjörður** *b.* Iceland
140 Q5 **Vörå** Fin.
179 K4 **Voralm** *mt.* Austria
138 L6 **Voran'** Belarus
138 I7 **Voranava** Belarus
178 A5 **Vorarlberg** *land* Austria
134 J4 **Vorchanka** Rus. Fed.
179 I3 **Vorchdorf** Austria
164 J4 **Vorden** Neth.
179 K4 **Vordernberg** Austria
190 H1 **Vorderrhein** *r.* Switz.
142 H6 **Vordingborg** Denmark
169 K6 **Vordorf** Ger.
196 H9 **Vorë** Albania
198 B2 **Voreia Pindos** *mts* Greece
198 B4 **Voreies Echinades** *i.* Greece
198 E3 **Voreies Sporades** *is* Greece
199 G3 **Voreio Aigaio** *admin. reg.* Greece
198 E4 **Voreios Evvoïkos Kolpos** *sea chan.* Greece
134 F3 **Vorenzha** Rus. Fed.
161 H6 **Voreppe** France
161 D6 **Vorey** France
139 P8 **Vorga** Rus. Fed.
134 M2 **Vorgashor** Rus. Fed.
Voríai Sporádhes *is* Greece *see* **Voreies Sporades**
Vorία Píndhos *mts* Greece *see* **Voreia Pindos**
264 J1 **Voring Plateau** *sea feature* N. Atlantic Ocean
117 O5 **Vorjing** *mt. Arun. Prad.* India
134 N2 **Vorkuta** Rus. Fed.
142 H1 **Vorma** *r.* Norway
142 C2 **Vormedalsheia** *park* Norway
138 G2 **Vormsi** *i.* Estonia
142 H1 **Vormsund** Norway
139 W9 **Vorob'yevka** *Lipetskaya Oblast'* Rus. Fed.
135 H6 **Vorob'yevka** *Voronezhskaya Oblast'* Rus. Fed.
137 M1 **Vorob"yivka** Ukr.
137 M8 **Vorobyove** Ukr.
130 J3 **Vorogovo** Rus. Fed.
136 D5 **Vorokhta** Ukr.
197 O3 **Vorona** Romania
135 H6 **Vorona** *r.* Rus. Fed.
135 G6 **Voronezh** Rus. Fed.
139 W9 **Voronezh** *r.* Rus. Fed.
Voronezh Oblast *admin. div.* Rus. Fed. *see* **Voronezhskaya Oblast'**
135 H6 **Voronezhskaya Oblast'** *admin. div.* Rus. Fed.
135 G6 **Voronezhskiy Zapovednik** *nature res.* Rus. Fed.
137 S2 **Voronezhskoye Vodokhranilishche** *resr* Rus. Fed.
137 M2 **Voronizh** Ukr.
137 M3 **Voron'ky** Ukr.
136 F2 **Voronky** Ukr.
137 L1 **Voronok** Rus. Fed.
134 H2 **Voronov, Mys** *pt* Rus. Fed.
139 P1 **Voronov, Mys** *pt* Rus. Fed.
139 U6 **Voronovo** Rus. Fed.
136 H4 **Voronovytsya** Ukr.
135 H6 **Vorontsovka** Rus. Fed.
138 L4 **Vorontsovo** Rus. Fed.
Vorontsovo-Aleksandrovskoye Rus. Fed. *see* **Zelenokumsk**
136 D4 **Voronyaky** *hills* Ukr.
134 H4 **Voron'ye** Rus. Fed.
Voroshilov Rus. Fed. *see* **Ussuriysk**
Voroshilovgrad Ukr. *see* **Luhans'k**
Voroshilovsk Rus. Fed. *see* **Stavropol'**
Voroshilovsk Ukr. *see* **Alchevs'k**
121 S5 **Vorota** *val.* Kazakh.
129 H6 **Vorotan** *r.* Armenia
139 Q6 **Vorot'kovo** Rus. Fed.
134 I4 **Vorotynets** Rus. Fed.
139 T7 **Vorotynsk** Rus. Fed.
129 D1 **Vorovskolesskaya** Rus. Fed.
137 N2 **Vorozhba** *Sums'ka Oblast'* Ukr.
137 N3 **Vorozhba** *Sums'ka Oblast'* Ukr.
170 G2 **Vorpommersche Boddenlandschaft, Nationalpark** *nat. park* Ger.
263 B2 **Vorposten Peak** Antarctica
173 K2 **Vorra** Ger.
179 M5 **Vorsau** Austria
165 G6 **Vorselaar** Belgium
135 F6 **Vorskla** *r.* Rus. Fed.
137 O3 **Vorsklitsa** *r.* Rus. Fed./Ukr.
165 H6 **Vorst** Belgium
214 H1 **Vorstershoop** S. Africa
177 L5 **Vorța** Romania
263 B2 **Vørterkaka Nunatak** *mt.* Antarctica
138 I3 **Võrtsjärv** *l.* Estonia
138 K4 **Võru** Estonia
123 N2 **Vorukh** Tajik.
168 H4 **Vorwerk** Ger.
139 R7 **Vorya** *r.* Rus. Fed.
136 J3 **Vorzel'** Ukr.
175 M4 **Vosa** Belarus
214 G6 **Vosburg** S. Africa
123 M3 **Vose** Tajik.
179 N3 **Vösendorf** Austria
157 L7 **Vosges** *dept* France
157 M8 **Vosges** *mts* France
157 O6 **Vosges du Nord, Parc Naturel Régional des** *nature res.* France
139 W4 **Voshchazhnikovo** Rus. Fed.
129 G4 **Voskevan** Armenia
137 N8 **Voskhod** Ukr.
139 V6 **Voskresensk** Rus. Fed.
137 L6 **Voskresens'ke** Ukr.
139 V8 **Voskresenskoye** *Lipetskaya Oblast'* Rus. Fed.
134 I4 **Voskresenskoye** *Nizhegorodskaya Oblast'* Rus. Fed.
120 G1 **Voskresenskoye** *Respublika Bashkortostan* Rus. Fed.
139 U7 **Voskresenskoye** *Tul'skaya Oblast'* Rus. Fed.
139 U2 **Voskresenskoye** *Vologodskaya Oblast'* Rus. Fed.
139 U4 **Voskresenskoye** *Yaroslavskaya Oblast'* Rus. Fed.
160 F2 **Vosne-Romanée** France
141 I6 **Voss** Norway
165 G6 **Vosselaar** Belgium
139 N1 **Vossinansari, Ostrov** *i.* Rus. Fed.
134 G1 **Vostochnaya Litsa** Rus. Fed.
Vostochno-Kazakhstanskaya Oblast' *admin. div.* Kazakh. *see* **Vostochnyy Kazakhstan**
Vostochno-Kounradskiy Kazakh. *see* **Shygys Konyrat**
100 M3 **Vostochno-Sakhalinskiy Gory** *mts Sakhalin* Rus. Fed.
131 P2 **Vostochno-Sibirskoye More** *sea* Rus. Fed.
134 F2 **Vostochnoye Munozero** Rus. Fed.
134 K4 **Vostochnyy** *Kirovskaya Oblast'* Rus. Fed.
100 M4 **Vostochnyy** *Sakhalin* Rus. Fed.
137 Q8 **Vostochnyy, Liman** *l.* Rus. Fed.
121 U3 **Vostochnyy Kazakhstan** *admin. div.* Kazakh.
98 F1 **Vostochnyy Sayan** *mts* Rus. Fed.
100 I5 **Vostok** *Primorskiy Kray* Rus. Fed.
Vostok *Sakhalin* Rus. Fed. *see* **Neftegorsk**
100 I6 **Vostretsovo** Rus. Fed.
134 I3 **Vostroye** Rus. Fed.
138 I2 **Võsu** Estonia
176 D2 **Votice** Czech Rep.
134 K4 **Votkinsk** Rus. Fed.
134 K4 **Votkinskoye Vodokhranilishche** *resr* Rus. Fed.
142 E1 **Votna** *r.* Norway
256 D5 **Votorantim** Brazil
139 P6 **Votrya** *r.* Rus. Fed.
78 □5 **Vot Tandé** *i.* Vanuatu
79 □7 **Votua** *Vanua Levu* Fiji
256 C4 **Votuporanga** Brazil
199 J6 **Voudi, Akrotirio** *pt Rodos* Greece
162 I3 **Voueize** *r.* France
Vouga Angola *see* **Cunhinga**
182 C7 **Vouga** *r.* Port.
160 F2 **Vougeot** France
160 H4 **Vouglans, Lac de** *l.* France
162 D3 **Vouillé** *Poitou-Charentes* France
162 E2 **Vouillé** *Poitou-Charentes* France
198 E5 **Voula** Greece
156 I8 **Voulaines-les-Templiers** France
156 E7 **Voulx** France
162 E2 **Vouneuil-sous-Biard** France
159 M8 **Vouneuil-sur-Vienne** France
209 A5 **Voungou** Gabon
198 C2 **Vourinos** *mt.* Greece
160 D1 **Voutenay-sur-Cure** France
162 G5 **Voutezac** France
162 C2 **Vouvant** France
159 M7 **Vouvray** France
190 B3 **Vouvry** Switz.
182 D7 **Vouzela** Port.
156 I5 **Vouziers** France
156 D8 **Vouzon** France
137 O5 **Vovcha** *r.* Ukr.
137 P3 **Vovcha** *r.* Ukr.
137 P3 **Vovchans'k** Ukr.
137 M3 **Vovchyk** Ukr.
156 C7 **Voves** France
136 G4 **Vovk** *r.* Ukr.
136 F3 **Vovkoshiv** Ukr.
136 G4 **Vovkovyntsi** Ukr.
208 E3 **Vovodo** *r.* C.A.R.
138 G9 **Vowchyn** Belarus
141 M6 **Voxna** Sweden
141 N6 **Voxnan** *r.* Sweden
134 J4 **Voya** *r.* Rus. Fed.
236 I1 **Voyageurs National Park** *MN* U.S.A.
137 K5 **Voyevods'ke** Ukr.
140 U4 **Voynitsa** Rus. Fed.
175 M6 **Voynyliv** Ukr.
Vöyri Fin. *see* **Vörå**
134 K2 **Voyvozh** *Respublika Komi* Rus. Fed.
134 K3 **Voyvozh** *Respublika Komi* Rus. Fed.
78 □6 **Voza** *Choiseul* Solomon Is
139 T5 **Vozdvizhenskoye** *Moskovskaya Oblast'* Rus. Fed.
139 V5 **Vozdvizhenskoye** *Moskovskaya Oblast'* Rus. Fed.
139 W7 **Vozha** *r.* Rus. Fed.
134 G3 **Vozhe, Ozero** *l.* Rus. Fed.
134 H3 **Vozhega** Rus. Fed.
134 J2 **Vozhgora** Rus. Fed.
183 Q5 **Vozmediano** Spain
121 N1 **Voznesenka** Kazakh.
137 K6 **Voznesens'k** Ukr.
129 C1 **Voznesenskaya** *Krasnodarskiy Kray* Rus. Fed.
129 F2 **Voznesenskaya** *Respublika Ingushetiya* Rus. Fed.
137 K6 **Voznesens'ke** Ukr.
135 H5 **Voznesenskoye** Rus. Fed.
139 Y5 **Voznesen'ye** *Ivanovskaya Oblast'* Rus. Fed.
139 S1 **Voznesen'ye** *Leningradskaya Oblast'* Rus. Fed.
120 H5 **Vozrojdenie** Uzbek.
120 H5 **Vozrozhdenya Island** *pen.* Uzbek.
137 L6 **Vozsiyats'ke** Ukr.
121 N1 **Vozvyshenka** Kazakh.
Vozvyshenskiy Kazakh. *see* **Vozvyshenka**
100 F3 **Vozzhayevka** Rus. Fed.
142 F4 **Vrå** Denmark
197 M8 **Vrabevo** Bulg.
177 H3 **Vráble** Slovakia
198 B5 **Vrachionas** *hill Zakynthos* Greece
198 C4 **Vrachnaiika** Greece
142 E2 **Vrådal** Norway
136 J6 **Vradiyivka** Ukr.
Vrakhiónas Óros *hill Zakynthos* Greece *see* **Vrachionas**
Vrakhnaíika Greece *see* **Vrachnaiika**
188 F4 **Vran** *mt.* Bos.-Herz.
197 O7 **Vrana** *r.* Bulg.
100 H7 **Vrangel'** Rus. Fed.
100 K1 **Vrangelya, Mys** *pt* Rus. Fed.
131 T2 **Vrangelya, Ostrov** *i.* Rus. Fed.
142 H4 **Vrångö naturreservat** *nature res.* Sweden
188 G3 **Vranjak** Bos.-Herz.
197 J8 **Vranje** Serbia
197 K8 **Vranjska Banja** Serbia
176 E3 **Vranov, Vodní nádrž** *resr* Czech Rep.
179 O2 **Vranovice** Czech Rep.
177 K3 **Vranov nad Topľou** Slovakia
179 K7 **Vransko** Slovenia
191 Q6 **Vransko Jezero** *l.* Croatia
196 D7 **Vransko Jezero** *l.* Croatia
196 I9 **Vrapčište** Macedonia
198 F2 **Vrasidas, Akrotirio** *pt* Greece
197 K7 **Vratarnica** Serbia
197 O8 **Vratnik** *pass* Bulg.
197 L7 **Vratsa** Bulg.
188 F3 **Vrbanja** *r.* Bos.-Herz.
188 F3 **Vrbas** *r.* Bos.-Herz.
196 H5 **Vrbas** *Vojvodina* Serbia
177 J5 **Vrbica** *Vojvodina* Serbia
191 R5 **Vrbnik** Croatia
176 G1 **Vrbno pod Pradědem** Czech Rep.
177 J2 **Vrbov** Slovakia
176 G3 **Vrbovce** Slovakia
177 G3 **Vrbové** Slovakia
188 F3 **Vrbovec** Croatia
188 E3 **Vrbovsko** Croatia
176 E1 **Vrchlabí** Czech Rep.
157 K7 **Vrécourt** France
215 N3 **Vrede** S. Africa
215 L2 **Vredefort** S. Africa
169 C6 **Vreden** Ger.
214 B8 **Vredenburg** S. Africa
214 C7 **Vredendal** S. Africa
214 D3 **Vredeshoop** Namibia
251 G3 **Vreed-en-Hoop** Guyana
164 H4 **Vreeland** Neth.
168 E5 **Vrees** Ger.
182 E6 **Vreia de Jales** Port.
196 I8 **Vrela** *Kosovo* Serbia
179 J8 **Vremščica** *mt.* Slovenia
165 G9 **Vresse** Belgium
188 E3 **Vrhnika** Slovenia
114 F7 **Vriddhachalam** *Tamil Nadu* India
164 K2 **Vries** Neth.
164 K4 **Vriezenveen** Neth.
143 K4 **Vrigstad** Sweden
160 B1 **Vrille** *r.* France
111 C13 **Vrindavan** *Uttar Prad.* India
123 N3 **Vrist** Afgh.
143 J3 **Vristulven** *l.* Sweden
156 I5 **Vrizy** France
196 I7 **Vrnjačka Banja** Serbia
214 D9 **Vrolijkheid Nature Reserve** S. Africa
156 C3 **Vron** France
164 K4 **Vroomshoop** Neth.
198 B3 **Vrosina** Greece
176 C1 **Vroutek** Czech Rep.
164 E5 **Vrouwenpolder** Neth.
196 H9 **Vrrin** Albania
196 J5 **Vršac** *Vojvodina* Serbia
191 P5 **Vrsar** Croatia
179 I8 **Vrtojba** Slovenia
215 I2 **Vryburg** S. Africa
215 O3 **Vryheid** S. Africa
173 O2 **Všeruby** Czech Rep.
171 K10 **Všetaty** Czech Rep.
177 G2 **Vsetín** Czech Rep.
220 B4 **Vsevidof, Mount** *vol. AK* U.S.A.
139 N1 **Vsevolozhsk** Rus. Fed.
137 O4 **Vshyva** *r.* Ukr.
139 R7 **Vskhody** Rus. Fed.
177 H3 **Vtáčnik** *mt.* Slovakia
177 H3 **Vtáčnik** *mts* Slovakia
160 H4 **Vuache, Montagne de** *mt.* France
79 □7 **Vuaqava** *i.* Fiji
108 E8 **Vu Ban** Vietnam
197 M9 **Vŭcha** *r.* Bulg.
188 G3 **Vučica** *r.* Croatia
196 I8 **Vučitrn** *Kosovo* Serbia
197 J8 **Vučje** Serbia
164 H5 **Vught** Neth.
137 Q6 **Vuhledar** Ukr.
137 R5 **Vuhlehirs'k** Ukr.
188 G3 **Vuka** *r.* Croatia
188 G3 **Vukovar** Croatia
134 L3 **Vuktyl'** Rus. Fed.
215 N3 **Vukuzakhe** S. Africa
222 H5 **Vulcan** *Alta* Can.
197 L5 **Vulcan** Romania
136 H8 **Vulcănești** Moldova
Vulcan Island P.N.G. *see* **Manam Island**
194 H7 **Vulcano, Isola** *i. Isole Lipari* Italy
197 L7 **Vŭlchedrŭm** Bulg.
197 P7 **Vŭlchidol** Bulg.
193 O4 **Vulgano** *r.* Italy
96 G5 **Vu Liêt** Vietnam
Vulkaneshty Moldova *see* **Vulcănești**
137 O8 **Vulkanivka** Ukr.
193 P6 **Vulture, Monte** *mt.* Italy
241 S8 **Vulture Mountains** *AZ* U.S.A.
97 H9 **Vung Tau** Vietnam
79 □7a **Vunidawa** *Viti Levu* Fiji
Vunindawa *Viti Levu* **Fiji** *see* **Vunidawa**
220 E3 **Vuntut National Park** *Y.T.* Can.
138 J1 **Vuohijärvi** Fin.
141 S6 **Vuohijärvi** *l.* Fin.
140 T4 **Vuokatti** Fin.
138 N1 **Vuoksa** *r.* Rus. Fed.
138 M1 **Vuoksa, Ozero** *l.* Rus. Fed.
138 L1 **Vuoksi** *r.* Fin.
140 S4 **Vuolijoki** Fin.
140 P3 **Vuollerim** Sweden
140 O3 **Vuolvojaure** *l.* Sweden
140 S3 **Vuostimo** Fin.
140 S2 **Vuotso** Fin.
78 □6 **Vuranimala** Solomon Is
197 O8 **Vŭrbitsa** Bulg.
197 M5 **Vurpær** Romania
197 L7 **Vŭrshets** Bulg.
138 K6 **Vustsye** Belarus
197 P4 **Vutcani** Romania
114 G4 **Vuyyuru** *Andhra Prad.* India
179 L6 **Vuzenica** Slovenia
136 D3 **Vuzlove** *L'vivs'ka Oblast'* Ukr.
136 B5 **Vuzlove** *Zakarpats'ka Oblast'* Ukr.
138 J7 **Vuzlyanka** *r.* Belarus
120 J1 **Vvedenka** Kazakh.
139 Y5 **Vveden'ye** Rus. Fed.
211 B7 **Vwawa** Tanz.
211 B7 **Vwaza Game Reserve** *nature res.* Malawi
137 P7 **Vyacheslavka** Ukr.
175 M2 **Vyalikaya Byerastavitsa** Belarus
138 H8 **Vyalikaya Mazheykava** Belarus
138 M8 **Vyalikiya Bortniki** Belaru
138 J8 **Vyalikiya Zhukhavichy** Belarus
139 N2 **Vyal'ye, Ozero** *l.* Rus. Fe
116 D9 **Vyara** *Gujarat* India
139 N6 **Vyarechcha** Belarus
138 G9 **Vyarkhovichy** Belarus
Vyarkhowye Belarus *see*
138 L9 **Vyatchyn** Belarus
Vyatka Rus. Fed. *see* **Kiro**
134 J5 **Vyatka** *r.* Rus. Fed.
134 J4 **Vyatskiye Polyany** Rus. F
139 X4 **Vyatskoye** Rus. Fed.
138 M5 **Vyaz** Rus. Fed.
100 I5 **Vyazemskiy** Rus. Fed.
139 R6 **Vyaz'ma** Rus. Fed.
139 Q6 **Vyaz'ma** *r.* Rus. Fed.
134 H4 **Vyazniki** Rus. Fed.
135 I6 **Vyazovka** *Astrakhanskaya Oblast'* Rus. Fed.
120 A2 **Vyazovka** *Saratovskaya O* Rus. Fed.
120 B1 **Vyazovka** *Saratovskaya O* Rus. Fed.
135 H6 **Vyazovka** *Volgogradskaya Oblast'* Rus. Fed.
139 W8 **Vyazovo** Rus. Fed.
137 P2 **Vyazovoye** Rus. Fed.
138 L1 **Vyborg** Rus. Fed.
138 L1 **Vyborgskiy Zaliv** *b.* Rus.
134 I3 **Vychegda** *r.* Rus. Fed.
134 I3 **Vychegodskiy** Rus. Fed.
177 I2 **Východná** Slovakia
177 L2 **Východné Karpaty** *park* Slovakia
175 M1 **Vydeniai** Lith.
175 N4 **Vyderta** Ukr.
175 M4 **Vydranytsya** Ukr.
106 I1 **Vydrino** Rus. Fed.
175 M4 **Vydrychi** Ukr.
139 O8 **Vyeramyeyki** Belarus
138 K6 **Vyerkhnyadzvinsk** Belaru
139 O9 **Vyetka** Belarus
138 L6 **Vyetryna** Belarus
139 R8 **Vygonichi** Rus. Fed.
134 F3 **Vygozero, Ozero** *l.* Rus. F
136 E1 **Vyhanashchy** Belarus
177 H3 **Vyhne** Slovakia
135 H5 **Vyksa** Rus. Fed.
160 I1 **Vy-lès-Lure** France
136 I8 **Vylkove** Ukr.
136 B5 **Vylok** Ukr.
134 J3 **Vym'** *r.* Rus. Fed.
136 D4 **Vynnyky** Ukr.
136 C5 **Vynohradiv** Ukr.
137 M5 **Vynohradivka** Ukr.
137 K6 **Vynohradne** Ukr.
137 L7 **Vynohradove** *Khersons'ka Oblast'* Ukr.
137 M8 **Vynohradove** *Respublika Krym* Ukr.
114 E7 **Vypin Island** India
139 Q4 **Vypolzovo** Rus. Fed.
137 M3 **Vyrishal'ne** Ukr.
139 N2 **Vyritsa** Rus. Fed.
150 F2 **Vyrnwy, Lake** *Wales* U.K.
137 N2 **Vyry** Ukr.
135 G7 **Vyselki** Rus. Fed.
136 J3 **Vyshcha Dubechnya** Ukr.
137 Q4 **Vyshche Solone** Ukr.
137 N6 **Vyshchetarasivka** Ukr.
139 X7 **Vyshgorod** Rus. Fed.
138 K4 **Vyshgorodok** Rus. Fed.
136 J3 **Vyshhorod** Ukr.
136 B5 **Vyshka** Ukr.
139 O9 **Vyshkov** Rus. Fed.
136 C5 **Vyshkove** Ukr.
139 S4 **Vyshkovo** Rus. Fed.
137 M5 **Vyshneve** *Dnipropetrovs'k Oblast'* Ukr.
136 J3 **Vyshneve** *Kyivs'ka Oblast'*
139 R5 **Vyshnevolotskaya Gryad** *ridge* Rus. Fed.
139 R4 **Vyshnevolotskoye Vodokhranilishche** *resr* Rus. Fed.
137 Q1 **Vyshneye-Ol'shanoye** Rus. Fed.
175 M4 **Vyshniv** Ukr.
136 E4 **Vyshnivets'** Ukr.
139 R4 **Vyshniy-Volochek** Rus. Fe
136 C4 **Vyshnya** *r.* Ukr.
137 M4 **Vyshnyaky** Ukr.
139 N4 **Vyskod'** Rus. Fed.
176 G2 **Vyškov** Czech Rep.
177 K2 **Vyšný Mirošov** Slovakia
177 K2 **Vyšný Orlík** Slovakia
176 E2 **Vysočina** *admin. reg.* Czech Rep.
176 D3 **Vysoká** *mt.* Czech Rep.
176 G3 **Vysoká** *hill* Slovakia
136 H3 **Vysoka Pich** Ukr.
176 F3 **Vysoká pri Morave** Slova
138 G9 **Vysokaye** *Brestskaya Vobl* Belarus
139 N7 **Vysokaye** *Vitsyebskaya Voblasts'* Belarus
137 M7 **Vysoke** Ukr.
176 F2 **Vysoké Mýto** Czech Rep.
139 T7 **Vysokinichi** Rus. Fed.
100 K3 **Vysokogorniy** Rus. Fed.
137 Q5 **Vysokopillya** *Donets'ka Oblast'* Ukr.
137 O4 **Vysokopillya** *Kharkivs'ka Oblast'* Ukr.
137 M6 **Vysokopillya** *Khersons'ka Oblast'* Ukr.
139 V4 **Vysokovo** Rus. Fed.
139 T5 **Vysokovsk** Rus. Fed.
Vysokoye Belarus *see* **Vysokaye**
139 R5 **Vysokoye** Rus. Fed.
138 L1 **Vysotsk** Rus. Fed.
136 F2 **Vysots'k** Ukr.
179 J2 **Vyšší Brod** Czech Rep.
136 I2 **Vystupovychi** Ukr.
139 T1 **Vytegra** Rus. Fed.
131 R3 **Vyvenka** Rus. Fed.
134 I3 **Vyya** *r.* Rus. Fed.
136 D2 **Vyzhivka** *r.* Ukr.
136 E5 **Vyzhnytsya** Ukr.
138 I6 **Vyžuona** *r.* Lith.
175 I1 **Vzmor'ye** Rus. Fed.

W

206 E4 **Wa** Ghana
168 I1 **Waabs** Ger.
210 D4 **Waajid** Somalia
169 J7 **Waake** Ger.
173 L6 **Waakirchen** Ger.
173 J6 **Waal** Ger.
164 G5 **Waal** *r.* Neth.
165 H6 **Waalre** Neth.
164 H5 **Waalwijk** Neth.
84 F5 **Waanyi/Garawa Aborigina Land** *res. N.T.* Austr.
164 G3 **Waarland** Neth.
165 E6 **Waarschoot** Belgium
165 F6 **Waasmunster** Belgium
210 B2 **Waat** Sudan
91 J8 **Wabag** P.N.G.
224 B3 **Wabakimi Lake** *Ont.* Can.
224 B3 **Wabakimi Provincial Park** *Ont.* Can.
125 M4 **Wabal** *well* Oman
222 H4 **Wabamun** *Alta* Can.
222 H4 **Wabamun Lake** *Alta* Can.
222 H3 **Wabasca** *r. Alta* Can.
222 H4 **Wabasca-Desmarais** *Alta* C
230 E5 **Wabash** *IN* U.S.A.
232 A8 **Wabash** *OH* U.S.A.
236 K7 **Wabash** *r. IN* U.S.A.
226 B5 **Wabasha** *MN* U.S.A.
224 C3 **Wabassi** *r. Ont.* Can.
227 J1 **Wabatongushi Lake** *Ont.*
210 D3 **Wabē Gestro** *r.* Eth.

3 Wabē Mena r. Eth.
4 Wabeno WI U.S.A.
8 Wabern Ger.
3 Wabē Shebelē Wenz r. Eth.
3 Wabigoon Lake Ont. Can.
3 Wabowden Man. Can.
2 Wabrah well Saudi Arabia
2 Wąbrzeźno Pol.
2 Wabu Anhui China
2 Wabuk Point Ont. Can.
2 Wabush Nfld and Lab. Can.
2 Wabush Lake Nfld and Lab. Can.
9 Waccamaw r. SC U.S.A.
8 Waccamaw, Lake NC U.S.A.
11 Waccasassa Bay FL U.S.A.
11 Wachapreague VA U.S.A.
3 Wachau reg. Austria
3 Wachenheim an der Weinstraße Ger.
5 Wachi Japan
5 Wach'īlē Eth.
5 Wachow Ger.
6 Wachtebeke Belgium
10 Wächtersbach Ger.
6 Wachusett Reservoir MA U.S.A.
2 Wacken Ger.
3 Wackersdorf Ger.
3 Waco Que. Can.
10 Waco TX U.S.A.
3 Waconda Lake KS U.S.A.
5 Wacouta MN U.S.A.
8 Wad Pak.
5 Wada Japan
6 Wada'a Sudan
6 Wada-misaki pt Japan
3 Wada-tōge pass Japan
3 Wada Wadalla Aboriginal Land res. N.T. Austr.
5 Wadayama Japan
6 Wad Banda Sudan
7 Wadbilliga National Park N.S.W. Austr.
2 Waddān Libya
2 Waddān, Jabal hills Libya
8 Waddell Dam AZ U.S.A.
2 Waddeneilanden is Neth.
2 Wadden Islands Neth. see Waddeneilanden
3 Waddenzee sea chan. Neth.
3 Waddesdon Buckinghamshire, England U.K.
4 Waddeweitz Ger.
5 Waddikee S.A. Austr.
7 Waddington Lincolnshire, England U.K.
5 Waddington, Mount B.C. Can.
4 Waddingtown Ireland
4 Waddinxveen Neth.
8 Waddy Point Qld Austr.
6 Wadebridge Cornwall, England U.K.
2 Wadega Sudan
5 Wadena Sask. Can.
5 Wadena MN U.S.A.
7 Wad en Nail Sudan
3 Wadenswil Switz.
2 Wadern Ger.
2 Wadersloh Ger.
8 Wadesboro NC U.S.A.
2 Wadeye N.T. Austr.
3 Wadgaon Mahar. India
3 Wadgaon Mahar. India
3 Wadgassen Ger.
5 Wad Hamid Sudan
2 Wad Hassib Sudan
15 Wadhurst East Sussex, England U.K.
8 Wadhwan Gujarat India
Wadhwan Gujarat India see Surendranagar
4 Wadi Karnataka India
2 Wadian Henan China
7 Wādī as Sīr Jordan
10 Wādī Fayrān Egypt
Wādī Gimāl Island Egypt see Wādī Jimāl, Jazīrat
4 Wadi Halfa Sudan
4 Wādī Ḩammah Saudi Arabia
4 Wādī Jimāl, Jazīrat i. Egypt
5 Wādī Mūsá Jordan
5 Wading r. NJ U.S.A.
3 Wading River NY U.S.A.
4 Wadlew Pol.
6 Wad Medani Sudan
F19 Wadomari Nansei-shotō Japan
6 Wadowice Pol.
5 Wadowice Górne Pol.
2 Wadsworth NV U.S.A.
7 Wadsworth OH U.S.A.
Wadu i. S. Male Maldives see Vaadhu
Wadu Channel Maldives see Vaadhu Channel
10 Waenhuiskrans S. Africa
1 Waesche, Mount Antarctica
7 Wafangdian Liaoning China
5 Wafania Dem. Rep. Congo
Wafra Kuwait see Al Wafrah
7 Waga-gawa r. Japan
4 Wagah Punjab India
2 Wagait Aboriginal Land res. N.T. Austr.
3 Waganiec Pol.
5 Wagenfeld Ger.
5 Wagenhoff Ger.
5 Wageningen Neth.
3 Wageningen Suriname
6 Wager Bay Nunavut Can.
6 Wagga Wagga N.S.W. Austr.
9 Waghai Gujarat India
7 Waghäusel Ger.
3 Wagiman Aboriginal Land res. N.T. Austr.
12 Wagin W.A. Austr.
6 Waging am See Ger.
6 Waginger See l. Ger.
6 Wägitaler See l. Switz.
4 Waglisla B.C. Can.
4 Wagner Brazil
4 Wagner SD U.S.A.
7 Wagoner OK U.S.A.
6 Wagon Mound NM U.S.A.
8 Wagrain Austria
2 Wagrien reg. Ger.
3 Wągrowiec Pol.
5 Wah Pak.
5 Wahai Seram Indon.
5 Wahala Togo
2 Wāḥāt Jālū Libya
2 Wahda state Sudan
2 Wahemen, Lac l. Que. Can.
C12 Wahiawā HI U.S.A.
5 Wahībah, Ramlat al des. Oman
Wahlenbergfjorden inlet Svalbard
8 Wahlhausen Ger.
7 Wahlsdorf Ger.
3 Wahlstedt Ger.
3 Wahoo NE U.S.A.
2 Wahpeton ND U.S.A.
Wahran Alg. see Oran
5 Wahrenholz Ger.
3 Wah Wah Mountains UT U.S.A.
4 Wai Mahar. India
D12 Waiāhole HI U.S.A.
E13 Waiakoa HI U.S.A.
B11 Wai'ale'ale mt. HI U.S.A.
C12 Wai'ale'e HI U.S.A.
C12 Waialua HI U.S.A.
C12 Waialua Bay HI U.S.A.
C12 Wai'anae HI U.S.A.
C12 Wai'anae Range mts HI U.S.A.
M4 Waiapu r. North I. N.Z.
K7 Waiaruhe North I. N.Z.
L9 Waiau South I. N.Z.
L5 Waiau r. North I. N.Z.
B13 Waiau r. South I. N.Z.
H9 Waiau r. South I. N.Z.
G4 Waiblingen Ger.
F3 Waibstadt Ger.
N2 Waidhaus Ger.
K4 Waidhofen Ger.
L2 Waidhofen an der Thaya Austria
K4 Waidhofen an der Ybbs Austria
F4 Waigama Papua Indon.
G4 Waigeo i. Papua Indon.
I2 Waigolshausen Ger.
81 E11 Waihao Downs South I. N.Z.
80 H1 Waiharara North I. N.Z.
80 J4 Waiharoa North I. N.Z.
80 J3 Waiheke Island North I. N.Z.
80 J4 Waihi North I. N.Z.
80 J4 Waihi Beach North I. N.Z.
81 C14 Waihi Estuary North I. N.Z.
81 E13 Waihola, Lake South I. N.Z.
80 J4 Waihou r. North I. N.Z.
80 L6 Waihua North I. N.Z.
208 E5 Waika Dem. Rep. Congo
93 A8 Waikabubak Sumba Indon.
81 C12 Waikaia South I. N.Z.
81 C12 Waikaia r. South I. N.Z.
81 D12 Waikaka South I. N.Z.
81 J7 Waikanae North I. N.Z.
240 □E13 Waikāne HI U.S.A.
240 □E13 Waikapu HI U.S.A.
80 J4 Waikare, Lake North I. N.Z.
80 L5 Waikareiti, Lake North I. N.Z.
80 K5 Waikaremoana, Lake North I. N.Z.
80 I4 Waikaretu North I. N.Z.
81 G9 Waikari South I. N.Z.
80 I4 Waikato admin. reg. North I. N.Z.
80 I4 Waikato r. North I. N.Z.
81 D13 Waikawa South I. N.Z.
80 L4 Waikawa Point North I. N.Z.
80 J5 Waikeria North I. N.Z.
82 G6 Waikerie S.A. Austr.
240 □F14 Waiki'i HI U.S.A.
240 □D12 Waikīkī Beach HI U.S.A.
80 K5 Waikirikiri North I. N.Z.
93 C8 Waikilibang Flores Indon.
81 D13 Waikoikoi South I. N.Z.
80 L6 Waikokopa North I. N.Z.
81 E12 Waikouaiti South I. N.Z.
79 □7a Wailotua Viti Levu Fiji
240 □B11 Wailua HI U.S.A.
240 □E13 Wailua HI U.S.A.
240 □E13 Wailuku HI U.S.A.
81 C13 Waimahaka South I. N.Z.
81 G10 Waimakariri r. South I. N.Z.
80 L5 Waimana North I. N.Z.
240 □D12 Waimānalo HI U.S.A.
240 □D12 Waimānalo Beach HI U.S.A.
81 F8 Waimangaroa South I. N.Z.
80 K6 Waimarama North I. N.Z.
81 F8 Waimarie South I. N.Z.
81 F11 Waimate South I. N.Z.
80 H2 Waimatenui North I. N.Z.
80 I3 Waimauku North I. N.Z.
240 □E12 Waimea HI U.S.A.
240 □C12 Waimea HI U.S.A.
240 □F13 Waimea HI U.S.A.
240 □C12 Waimea Bay HI U.S.A.
93 B5 Waimenda Sulawesi Indon.
165 J8 Waimes Belgium
173 I5 Wain Ger.
232 F6 Wainfleet Ont. Can.
149 R7 Wainfleet All Saints Lincolnshire, England U.K.
114 F3 Wainganga r. India
93 B8 Waingapu Sumba Indon.
81 J7 Waingawa North I. N.Z.
150 C6 Wainhouse Corner Cornwall, England U.K.
251 G2 Waini Point Guyana
81 F11 Wainono Lagoon South I. N.Z.
223 I4 Wainwright Alta Can.
220 C2 Wainwright AK U.S.A.
80 L5 Waioeka r. North I. N.Z.
80 I2 Waiotira North I. N.Z.
80 J6 Waiouru North I. N.Z.
80 J4 Waipa r. North I. N.Z.
81 D13 Waipahi South I. N.Z.
240 □C12 Waipahu HI U.S.A.
80 L5 Waipaoa r. North I. N.Z.
81 C13 Waipapa Point South I. N.Z.
81 G10 Waipara South I. N.Z.
80 K6 Waipawa North I. N.Z.
80 I4 Waipipi North I. N.Z.
80 I2 Waipu North I. N.Z.
80 K6 Waipukurau North I. N.Z.
80 K5 Wairakei North I. N.Z.
81 J8 Wairarapa, Lake North I. N.Z.
81 I8 Wairau r. South I. N.Z.
81 H8 Wairau Valley South I. N.Z.
80 L5 Wairoa North I. N.Z.
80 I3 Wairoa r. North I. N.Z.
80 L6 Wairoa r. North I. N.Z.
93 C8 Wairunu Flores Indon.
93 G7 Waisai Papua Indon.
173 K2 Waischenfeld Ger.
120 H6 Waishe Zhejiang China
80 K5 Waitahanui North I. N.Z.
81 D12 Waitahuna South I. N.Z.
80 J4 Waitakaruru North I. N.Z.
81 F11 Waitaki South I. N.Z.
81 F11 Waitaki r. South I. N.Z.
80 □ Waitangi Chatham Is S. Pacific Ocean
81 E10 Waitangitaona r. South I. N.Z.
80 I5 Waitara North I. N.Z.
81 E12 Waitati South I. N.Z.
82 □3 Waite, Mount hill S. Pacific Ocean
84 E7 Waite River N.T. Austr.
80 J4 Waitoa North I. N.Z.
80 J5 Waitomo Caves North I. N.Z.
80 I6 Waitotara North I. N.Z.
80 I6 Waitotara r. North I. N.Z.
238 E3 Waitsburg WA U.S.A.
80 I4 Waiuku North I. N.Z.
81 D13 Waiwera South South I. N.Z.
93 F5 Waiya Seram Indon.
109 L5 Waiyang Fujian China
79 □7 Waiyevo Taveuni Fiji
179 I3 Waizenkirchen Austria
124 G6 Wajid, Jabal al hills Saudi Arabia
103 L13 Wajiki Japan
103 N9 Wajima Japan
210 D4 Wajir Kenya
208 D4 Waka Équateur Dem. Rep. Congo
208 D5 Waka Équateur Dem. Rep. Congo
93 B8 Waka Flores Indon.
93 E5 Waka, Tanjung pt Indon.
227 L2 Wakami Lake Ont. Can.
81 H8 Wakapuaka South I. N.Z.
103 L11 Wakasa Japan
104 C4 Wakasa-wan b. Japan
104 C4 Wakasa-wan Kokutei-kōen park Japan
81 C12 Wakatipu, Lake South I. N.Z.
93 C6 Wakatobi, Taman Nasional nat. park Indon.
227 K3 Wakatoma Lake Ont. Can.
223 J4 Wakaw Sask. Can.
79 □7 Wakaya i. Fiji
84 F5 Wakaya Aboriginal Land res. N.T. Austr.
104 B7 Wakayama Japan
104 B8 Wakayama pref. Japan
102 S8 Wakayanagi Japan
Wake Atoll N. Pacific Ocean see Wake Island
236 F6 WaKeeney KS U.S.A.
227 S4 Wakefield Que. Can.
246 □ Wakefield Jamaica
81 H8 Wakefield South I. N.Z.
149 N6 Wakefield West Yorkshire, England U.K.
226 E3 Wakefield MI U.S.A.
232 B10 Wakefield OH U.S.A.
234 C5 Wakefield PA U.S.A.
233 N7 Wakefield RI U.S.A.
232 I12 Wakefield VA U.S.A.
Wakeham Que. Can. see Kangiqsujuaq
75 F2 Wake Island N. Pacific Ocean
96 B6 Wakema Myanmar
123 O3 Wakhan reg. Afgh.
103 L12 Waki Japan
102 R5 Wakinosawa Japan
124 D8 Wakiro watercourse Eritrea
210 B4 Wakiso Uganda
102 S1 Wakkanai Japan
215 O3 Wakkerstroom S. Africa
83 J6 Wakool N.S.W. Austr.
83 I6 Wakool r. N.S.W. Austr.
225 H2 Wakuach, Lac l. Que. Can.
209 B7 Waku-Kungo Angola
102 S8 Wakuya Japan
224 D3 Wakwayowkastic r. Ont. Can.
78 □6 Walade Solomon Is
86 F7 Walagunya Aboriginal Reserve W.A. Austr.
114 F6 Walajapet Tamil Nadu India
171 D6 Walbeck Ger.
151 P3 Walberswick Suffolk, England U.K.
174 E5 Wałbrzych Pol.
169 I8 Walburg Ger.
83 M4 Walcha N.S.W. Austr.
173 K6 Walchensee l. Ger.
178 F4 Walchsee Austria
178 F4 Walchsee l. Austria
168 D5 Walchum Ger.
238 K6 Walcott WY U.S.A.
86 H4 Walcott Inlet W.A. Austr.
165 F8 Walcourt Belgium
174 E2 Wałcz Pol.
172 G6 Wald Baden-Württemberg Ger.
173 M3 Wald Bayern Ger.
172 F7 Wald Switz.
172 D2 Waldachtal Ger.
179 K3 Waldaist r. Austria
172 D2 Waldböckelheim Ger.
169 D9 Waldbreitbach Ger.
169 E9 Waldbröl Ger.
172 H2 Waldbrunn Ger.
169 F9 Waldbrunn-Lahr Ger.
172 H6 Waldburg Ger.
87 D8 Waldburg Range mts W.A. Austr.
171 I7 Walddrehna Ger.
169 H8 Waldeck Ger.
179 N4 Waldegg Austria
235 G1 Walden NY U.S.A.
172 G4 Waldenbuch Ger.
172 H3 Waldenburg Baden-Württemberg Ger.
171 G9 Waldenburg Sachsen Ger.
Waldenburg Pol. see Wałbrzych
190 D1 Waldenburg Switz.
173 M3 Walderbach Ger.
173 M2 Waldershof Ger.
151 N5 Walderslade Medway, England U.K.
172 D3 Waldfischbach-Burgalben Ger.
179 L2 Waldhausen Austria
179 K3 Waldhausen im Strudengau Austria
171 H8 Waldheim Ger.
179 J3 Walding Austria
169 I8 Waldkappel Ger.
172 D5 Waldkirch Ger.
173 P4 Waldkirchen Ger.
173 M5 Waldkraiburg Ger.
172 F2 Wald-Michelbach Ger.
172 C3 Waldmohr Ger.
173 N3 Waldmünchen Ger.
231 F11 Waldo FL U.S.A.
226 G6 Waldo WI U.S.A.
233 □P4 Waldoboro ME U.S.A.
150 D6 Waldon r. England U.K.
232 I10 Waldorf MD U.S.A.
174 G2 Wałdowo-Szlacheckie Pol.
238 B4 Waldport OR U.S.A.
172 B2 Waldrach Ger.
237 H8 Waldron AR U.S.A.
226 J8 Waldron MI U.S.A.
263 H2 Waldron, Cape Antarctica
171 F10 Waldsassen Ger.
172 E6 Waldshut Ger.
190 G1 Waldstatt Switz.
172 H4 Waldstetten Baden-Württemberg Ger.
173 I5 Waldstetten Bayern Ger.
173 M2 Waldthurn Ger.
179 L3 Waldviertel reg. Austria
93 C4 Walea, Selat sea chan. Indon.
93 C4 Waleabahi i. Indon.
93 C4 Waleakodi i. Indon.
87 D11 Walebing W.A. Austr.
108 C4 Walêg Sichuan China
190 G1 Walenstadt Switz.
150 E3 Wales admin. div. U.K.
206 E4 Walewale Ghana
165 J9 Walferdange Lux.
83 L4 Walgett N.S.W. Austr.
262 Q1 Walgreen Coast Antarctica
226 H6 Walhalla MI U.S.A.
236 G1 Walhalla ND U.S.A.
231 F8 Walhalla SC U.S.A.
123 M7 Walhar Pak.
208 F5 Walikale Dem. Rep. Congo
87 C10 Walkaway W.A. Austr.
170 G3 Walkendorf Ger.
169 K7 Walkenried Ger.
84 E2 Walker r. N.T. Austr.
84 D8 Walker watercourse N.T. Austr.
226 I6 Walker MI U.S.A.
236 H2 Walker MN U.S.A.
240 N3 Walker r. NV U.S.A.
214 D10 Walker Bay S. Africa
231 H12 Walker Cay i. Bahamas
85 H4 Walker Creek r. Qld Austr.
223 L4 Walker Lake l. Man. Can.
240 N3 Walker Lake NV U.S.A.
240 N3 Walker Lake l. NV U.S.A.
262 R2 Walker Mountains Antarctica
240 N3 Walker River Indian Reservation res. NV U.S.A.
232 H9 Walkersville MD U.S.A.
232 E10 Walkersville WV U.S.A.
227 M5 Walkerton Ont. Can.
226 H8 Walkerton IN U.S.A.
235 G1 Walker Valley NY U.S.A.
236 D3 Wall SD U.S.A.
87 D7 Wall, Mount hill W.A. Austr.
87 B10 Wallabi Group is W.A. Austr.
85 H3 Wallaby Island Qld Austr.
238 F3 Wallace ID U.S.A.
231 I8 Wallace NC U.S.A.
236 E5 Wallace NE U.S.A.
232 C12 Wallace VA U.S.A.
224 D5 Wallaceburg Ont. Can.
81 C13 Wallacetown South I. N.Z.
86 F5 Wallal Downs W.A. Austr.
87 D11 Wallambin, Lake salt flat W.A. Austr.
83 M3 Wallangarra Qld Austr.
82 F5 Wallaroo S.A. Austr.
149 K7 Wallasey Merseyside, England U.K.
85 M8 Wallaville Qld Austr.
238 E3 Walla Walla WA U.S.A.
172 F3 Walldorf Baden-Württemberg Ger.
172 F1 Walldorf Hessen Ger.
169 J9 Walldorf Thüringen Ger.
172 G2 Walldürn Ger.
214 B6 Wallekraal S. Africa
83 L6 Wallendbeen N.S.W. Austr.
171 D10 Wallenfels Ger.
234 E2 Wallenpaupack, Lake PA U.S.A.
190 G1 Wallensee l. Switz.
173 N4 Wallerfing Ger.
179 O4 Wallern im Burgenland Austria
173 N4 Wallersdorf Ger.
178 H4 Wallersee l. Austria
173 I4 Wallerstein Ger.
173 K6 Wallgau Ger.
173 I3 Wallhausen Baden-Württemberg Ger.
172 D2 Wallhausen Rheinland-Pfalz Ger.
80 K7 Wallingford North I. N.Z.
151 J4 Wallingford Oxfordshire, England U.K.
235 J2 Wallingford CT U.S.A.
233 M5 Wallingford VT U.S.A.
Wallis canton Switz. see Valais
77 I3 Wallis, Îles is Wallis and Futuna Is
77 I3 Wallis and Futuna Islands terr. S. Pacific Ocean
172 F7 Wallisellen Switz.
Wallis et Futuna, Îles terr. S. Pacific Ocean see Wallis and Futuna Islands
Wallis Islands Wallis and Futuna Is see Wallis, Îles
235 G1 Wallkill NY U.S.A.
235 H1 Wallkill r. NY U.S.A.
233 J11 Wallops Island VA U.S.A.
238 F4 Wallowa OR U.S.A.
238 F4 Wallowa Mountains OR U.S.A.
146 □M2 Walls Shetland, Scotland U.K.
168 H1 Wallsbüll Ger.
149 N4 Wallsend Tyne and Wear, England U.K.
83 K9 Walls of Jerusalem National Park Tas. Austr.
170 D5 Wallstawe Ger.
169 F10 Walluf Ger.
238 E3 Wallula WA U.S.A.
85 L9 Wallumbilla Qld Austr.
123 J5 Walma Afgh.
151 O5 Walmer Kent, England U.K.
223 I2 Walmsley Lake N.W.T. Can.
149 K5 Walney, Isle of i. England U.K.
226 E8 Walnut IL U.S.A.
232 H8 Walnut Bottom PA U.S.A.
240 J4 Walnut Creek CA U.S.A.
236 F6 Walnut Creek r. KS U.S.A.
240 K3 Walnut Grove CA U.S.A.
234 D3 Walnutport PA U.S.A.
236 J7 Walnut Ridge AR U.S.A.
117 P5 Walong Arun. Prad. India
171 K7 Walowice Pol.
173 L5 Walpertskirchen Ger.
87 D13 Walpole W.A. Austr.
233 M5 Walpole NH U.S.A.
78 □5 Walpole, Île i. New Caledonia
175 J2 Wałpusza r. Pol.
178 G4 Wals Austria
151 I2 Walsall West Midlands, England U.K.
173 J2 Walsdorf Ger.
239 L8 Walsenburg CO U.S.A.
85 I4 Walsh r. Qld Austr.
237 D7 Walsh CO U.S.A.
170 G5 Walsleben Ger.
151 M2 Walsoken Cambridgeshire, England U.K.
168 I5 Walsrode Ger.
175 H1 Walsza r. Pol.
115 H4 Waltair Andhra Prad. India
173 I6 Waltenhofen Ger.
231 G9 Walterboro SC U.S.A.
231 E10 Walter F. George Reservoir AL/GA U.S.A.
237 F8 Walters OK U.S.A.
169 K9 Waltershausen Ger.
83 M1 Walter's Range hills Qld Austr.
237 K9 Walthall MS U.S.A.
227 R4 Waltham Que. Can.
149 Q6 Waltham North East Lincolnshire, England U.K.
233 N6 Waltham MA U.S.A.
233 □Q4 Waltham ME U.S.A.
151 M4 Waltham Abbey Essex, England U.K.
151 K2 Waltham on the Wolds Leicestershire, England U.K.
173 K4 Walting Ger.
226 H9 Walton IN U.S.A.
233 J6 Walton NY U.S.A.
232 D10 Walton WV U.S.A.
246 D5 Walton Bank sea feature Jamaica
151 L5 Walton-on-Thames Surrey, England U.K.
151 O4 Walton on the Naze Essex, England U.K.
Walvisbaai Namibia see Walvis Bay
212 B4 Walvis Bay Namibia
212 B4 Walvis Bay b. Namibia
264 I8 Walvis Ridge sea feature S. Atlantic Ocean
87 E11 Walyahmoing hill W.A. Austr.
123 N4 Wama Afgh.
210 A4 Wamala, Lake Uganda
209 E6 Wamaza Dem. Rep. Congo
208 D5 Wamba Équateur Dem. Rep. Congo
208 E4 Wamba Orientale Dem. Rep. Congo
209 C5 Wamba r. Dem. Rep. Congo
207 H4 Wamba Nigeria
183 K5 Wamba Spain
84 C3 Wambardi Aboriginal Land res. N.T. Austr.
236 G6 Wamego KS U.S.A.
91 I7 Wamena Papua Indon.
211 C6 Wami r. Tanz.
93 E5 Wamlana Buru Indon.
84 E4 Wampaya Aboriginal Land res. Qld Austr.
242 □Q10 Wampusirpi Hond.
238 K6 Wamsutter WY U.S.A.
93 E5 Wamulan Buru Indon.
123 M5 Wana Pak.
83 J3 Wanaaring N.S.W. Austr.
81 D11 Wanaka South I. N.Z.
81 D11 Wanaka, Lake South I. N.Z.
235 G4 Wanamassa NJ U.S.A.
234 C2 Wanamie PA U.S.A.
109 J5 Wan'an Jiangxi China
224 D4 Wanapitei Lake Ont. Can.
235 G2 Wanaque NJ U.S.A.
235 G2 Wanaque Reservoir NJ U.S.A.
93 C6 Wanasabari Sulawesi Indon.
82 H6 Wanbi S.A. Austr.
108 C5 Wanbi Yunnan China
81 E12 Wanbrow, Cape South I. N.Z.
231 J8 Wanchese NC U.S.A.
93 C6 Wanci Sulawesi Indon.
258 G2 Wanda Arg.
87 C10 Wandana Nature Reserve W.A. Austr.
100 H6 Wanda Shan mts China
223 H4 Wandering River Alta Can.
169 K9 Wandersleben Ger.
168 H1 Wanderup Ger.
108 B6 Wanding Yunnan China
Wandingzhen Yunnan China see Wanding
Wandiwash Tamil Nadu India see Vandavasi
81 H9 Wandle Downs South I. N.Z.
170 H5 Wandlitz Ger.
101 E11 Wando S. Korea
85 L9 Wandoan Qld Austr.
151 L5 Wandsworth Greater London, England U.K.
179 L3 Wang Austria
96 D6 Wang, Mae Nam r. Thai.
208 F4 Wanga Dem. Rep. Congo
80 J6 Wanganui North I. N.Z.
80 I6 Wanganui r. North I. N.Z.
81 E10 Wanganui r. South I. N.Z.
83 K7 Wangaratta Vic. Austr.
82 E6 Wangary S.A. Austr.
109 F2 Wangcang Sichuan China
109 I4 Wangcheng Hunan China
107 Q8 Wangcun Shandong China
Wangda Xizang China see Zogang
111 I12 Wangdain Xizang China
117 L6 Wangdi Phodrang Bhutan
107 N7 Wangdu Hebei China
169 I7 Wangelnstedt Ger.
168 K2 Wangels Ger.
190 D1 Wangen Switz.
172 H6 Wangen im Allgäu Ger.
168 E3 Wangerooge Ger.
168 E3 Wangerooge i. Ger.
93 B9 Wanggamet, Gunung mt. Sumba Indon.
106 E8 Wang Gaxun Qinghai China
Wanggezhuang Shandong China see Jiaonan
108 E2 Wangguan Gansu China
190 F1 Wängi Switz.
93 C6 Wangiwangi i. Indon.
109 K3 Wangjiang Anhui China
107 K8 Wangjiawan Shaanxi China
242 □Q10 Wangkibila Hond.
100 E5 Wangkui Heilong. China
178 C5 Wängle Austria
Wang Mai Khon Thai. see Sawankhalok
108 G7 Wangmao Guangxi China
108 F6 Wangmo Guizhou China
Wangolodougou Côte d'Ivoire see Ouangolodougou
100 F7 Wangqing Jilin China
Wangying Jiangsu China see Huaiyin
222 G4 Wanham Alta Can.
251 H3 Wanhatti Suriname
96 B4 Wan Hsa-la Myanmar
208 E4 Wanie-Rukula Dem. Rep. Congo
84 C3 Wanimiyn Aboriginal Land res. N.T. Austr.
87 F9 Wanjarri Nature Reserve W.A. Austr.
116 C8 Wankaner Gujarat India
168 J2 Wankendorf Ger.
Wankie Zimbabwe see Hwange
210 E4 Wanlaweyn Somalia
168 G3 Wanna Ger.
87 J10 Wanna Lakes salt flat W.A. Austr.
87 C11 Wanneroo W.A. Austr.
109 K4 Wannian Jiangxi China
108 H9 Wanning Hainan China
104 E5 Wanouchi Japan
164 I5 Wanroij Neth.
107 L9 Wanrong Shanxi China
108 G5 Wanshan Guizhou China
109 I8 Wanshan Qundao is Guangdong China
171 E8 Wansleben am See Ger.
80 K7 Wanstead North I. N.Z.
151 J4 Wantage Oxfordshire, England U.K.
235 H3 Wantagh NY U.S.A.
227 N3 Wanup Ont. Can.
108 G3 Wanxian Chongqing China
108 G2 Wanyuan Sichuan China
109 J4 Wanzai Jiangxi China
165 H7 Wanze Belgium
Wanzhi Anhui China see Wuhu
232 A8 Wapakoneta OH U.S.A.
223 J4 Wapawekka Lake Sask. Can.
164 J4 Wapenveld Neth.
175 H2 Wąpiersk Pol.
224 B3 Wapikaimaski Lake Ont. Can.
224 B2 Wapikopa Lake Ont. Can.
222 G4 Wapiti r. Alta Can.
175 I2 Waplewo Pol.
174 D2 Wapnica Pol.
174 F3 Wapno Pol.
93 E5 Wapotih Buru Indon.
237 J7 Wappapello Lake resr MO U.S.A.
235 H1 Wappinger Creek r. NY U.S.A.
235 H1 Wappingers Falls NY U.S.A.
236 J5 Wapsipinicon r. IA U.S.A.
221 I4 Wapusk National Park Man. Can.
108 D2 Waqên Sichuan China
128 E7 Waqf aş Şawwān, Jibāl hills Jordan
127 K8 Wāqişah well Iraq
125 I4 Waqr well Saudi Arabia
124 G7 Waqr Maryamah well Yemen
232 D11 War WV U.S.A.
104 F4 Wara Japan
208 F2 Warab Sudan
208 F2 Warab state Sudan
105 K4 Warabi Japan
210 D4 Waradi waterhole Kenya
123 L8 Warah Pak.
87 J9 Warakurna-Wingellina-Irrunytju Aboriginal Reserve W.A. Austr.
210 E3 Warandab Eth.
114 F4 Warangal Andhra Prad. India
116 H9 Waraseoni Madh. Prad. India
83 J9 Waratah Tas. Austr.
125 I1 Warbah, Jazīrat i. Iraq
169 K6 Warberg Ger.
151 L3 Warboys Cambridgeshire, England U.K.
85 I8 Warbreccan Qld Austr.
222 H4 Warburg Alta Can.
169 H8 Warburg Ger.
169 H8 Warburger Börde reg. Ger.
83 J7 Warburton Vic. Austr.
87 I9 Warburton W.A. Austr.
82 F2 Warburton watercourse S.A. Austr.
215 O2 Warburton S. Africa
87 I9 Warburton Aboriginal Reserve W.A. Austr.
223 I2 Warburton Bay N.W.T. Can.
87 I8 Warburton Range hills W.A. Austr.
123 O5 Warcha Pak.
165 I8 Warche r. Belgium
149 M4 Warcop Cumbria, England U.K.
157 K5 Warcq France
85 K9 Ward watercourse Qld Austr.
81 I8 Ward South I. N.Z.
262 T2 Ward, Mount Antarctica
81 B12 Ward, Mount South I. N.Z.
81 D10 Ward, Mount South I. N.Z.
123 M4 Wardag prov. Afgh.
82 F6 Wardang Island S.A. Austr.
210 D4 Wardeglo waterhole Kenya
215 M3 Warden S. Africa
168 F4 Wardenburg Ger.
116 G9 Wardha Mahar. India
114 F3 Wardha r. India
146 J5 Ward Hill Scotland U.K.
195 □ Wardija, Il-Ponta tal- pt Gozo Malta
195 □ Wardija Ridge Malta
151 J3 Wardington Oxfordshire, England U.K.
146 □N2 Ward of Bressay hill Scotland U.K.
170 F3 Wardow Ger.
149 L5 Ward's Stone hill England U.K.
222 E3 Ware B.C. Can.
151 L4 Ware Hertfordshire, England U.K.
233 M6 Ware MA U.S.A.
165 D7 Waregem Belgium
150 H6 Wareham Dorset, England U.K.
233 O7 Wareham MA U.S.A.
165 H7 Waremme Belgium
170 G3 Waren Ger.
169 E7 Warendorf Ger.
164 K2 Warffum Neth.
Wargili i. S. Male Maldives see Vaagali
85 M7 Warginburra Peninsula Qld Austr.
Wargla Alg. see Ouargla
151 K5 Wargrave Wokingham, England U.K.
210 E2 War Gunbi waterhole Somalia
83 M3 Warialda N.S.W. Austr.
123 L10 Wari Creek inlet Pak.
85 M1 Wari Island P.N.G.
170 E3 Warin Ger.
96 G7 Warin Chamrap Thai.
147 J4 Waringstown Northern Ireland U.K.
149 M3 Wark Northumberland, England U.K.
175 J4 Warka Pol.
80 I3 Warkworth North I. N.Z.
149 N3 Warkworth Northumberland, England U.K.
210 E2 War Idaad Somalia
Warli Sichuan China see Walêg
151 L5 Warlingham Surrey, England U.K.
156 E3 Warloy-Baillon France
174 G2 Warlubie Pol.
223 J4 Warman Sask. Can.
212 C6 Warmbad Namibia
173 L2 Warmensteinach Ger.
156 H5 Warmeriville France
214 D3 Warmfontein Namibia
143 Q7 Warmia reg. Pol.
151 J3 Warmington Warwickshire, England U.K.
175 I2 Warmińsko-Mazurskie prov. Pol.
150 H5 Warminster Wiltshire, England U.K.
234 E4 Warminster PA U.S.A.
164 G4 Warmond Neth.
169 G6 Warmsen Ger.
241 P3 Warm Springs NV U.S.A.
232 F10 Warm Springs VA U.S.A.
238 D4 Warm Springs Indian Reservation res. OR U.S.A.
214 E9 Warmwaterberg S. Africa
214 E9 Warmwaterberg mts S. Africa
170 F2 Warnemünde Ger.
223 H5 Warner Alta Can.
233 N5 Warner NH U.S.A.
238 E5 Warner Lakes OR U.S.A.
238 D6 Warner Mountains CA U.S.A.
231 F9 Warner Robins GA U.S.A.
240 P8 Warner Springs CA U.S.A.
253 E4 Warnes Bol.
165 C7 Warneton Belgium
173 L6 Warngau Ger.
151 L5 Warnham West Sussex, England U.K.
174 C2 Warnice Zachodniopomorskie Pol.
170 K5 Warnice Zachodniopomorskie Pol.
174 E2 Warnino Pol.
170 E3 Warnow Ger.
170 F2 Warnow r. Ger.
164 J4 Warnsveld Neth.
114 E3 Waronda Mahar. India
87 C12 Waroona W.A. Austr.
116 G9 Warora Mahar. India
168 H5 Warpe Ger.
85 M9 Warra Qld Austr.
84 E6 Warrabri Aboriginal Land res. N.T. Austr.
83 I7 Warracknabeal Vic. Austr.
83 M6 Warragamba Reservoir N.S.W. Austr.
83 J8 Warragul Vic. Austr.
82 G3 Warrakalanna, Lake salt flat S.A. Austr.
235 I1 Warramaug, Lake CT U.S.A.
82 E5 Warramboo S.A. Austr.
87 D10 Warramboo hill W.A. Austr.
83 K4 Warrambool r. N.S.W. Austr.
82 F2 Warrandirinna, Lake salt flat S.A. Austr.
83 J7 Warrandyte Vic. Austr.
86 F6 Warrawagine W.A. Austr.
83 J4 Warrego r. N.S.W./Qld Austr.
85 J8 Warrego Range hills Qld Austr.
83 K4 Warren N.S.W. Austr.
87 C13 Warren r. W.A. Austr.
227 N3 Warren Ont. Can.
237 I9 Warren AR U.S.A.
226 E7 Warren IL U.S.A.
226 I9 Warren IN U.S.A.
227 K7 Warren MI U.S.A.
236 G1 Warren MN U.S.A.
232 E7 Warren OH U.S.A.
232 F7 Warren PA U.S.A.
234 F3 Warren County county NJ U.S.A.
235 G5 Warren Grove NJ U.S.A.
Warren Hastings Island Palau see Merir
222 C4 Warren Island AK U.S.A.
147 J4 Warrenpoint Northern Ireland U.K.
226 D5 Warrens WI U.S.A.
236 I6 Warrensburg MO U.S.A.
233 L5 Warrensburg NY U.S.A.
234 B2 Warrensville PA U.S.A.
215 I4 Warrenton S. Africa
231 F9 Warrenton GA U.S.A.
236 J6 Warrenton MO U.S.A.
231 H7 Warrenton NC U.S.A.
232 H10 Warrenton VA U.S.A.
207 G5 Warri Nigeria
87 D10 Warriedar hill W.A. Austr.
82 F3 Warriners Creek watercourse S.A. Austr.
81 E12 Warrington South I. N.Z.
149 L7 Warrington Warrington, England U.K.
149 L7 Warrington admin. div. England U.K.
231 D10 Warrington FL U.S.A.
82 G4 Warriota watercourse S.A. Austr.
83 I8 Warrnambool Vic. Austr.
236 H1 Warroad MN U.S.A.
82 E6 Warrow S.A. Austr.
83 L4 Warrumbungle National Park N.S.W. Austr.
84 D1 Warruwi N.T. Austr.
83 H3 Warry Warry watercourse Qld Austr.
Warsaw Pol. see Warszawa
226 C9 Warsaw IL U.S.A.
230 E5 Warsaw IN U.S.A.
230 E6 Warsaw KY U.S.A.
236 I6 Warsaw MO U.S.A.
232 G6 Warsaw NY U.S.A.
232 I11 Warsaw VA U.S.A.
179 J4 Warscheneck mt. Austria
210 E4 Warshiikh Somalia
168 D4 Warsingsfehn Ger.
149 N7 Warslow Staffordshire, England U.K.
169 F8 Warstein Ger.
175 J3 Warszawa Pol.
174 E1 Warszkowo Pol.
174 G4 Warta Pol.
174 C3 Warta r. Pol.
174 D4 Warta Bolesławiecka Pol.
174 G3 Warta-Gopło, Kanał canal Pol.
179 J4 Wartberg an der Krems Austria
231 E7 Wartburg TN U.S.A.
171 B9 Wartburg, Schloss tourist site Ger.
171 B9 Wartburg Schloß tourist site Ger.
173 L5 Wartenberg Ger.
169 H9 Wartenberg-Angersbach Ger.
178 B5 Warth Austria
172 H5 Warthausen Ger.
170 J4 Wartin Ger.
175 H4 Wartkowice Pol.
169 I10 Wartmannsroth Ger.
149 L5 Warton Lancashire, England U.K.
95 L5 Waru Kalimantan Indon.
116 G9 Warud Mahar. India
84 E5 Warumungu Aboriginal Land res. N.T. Austr.
83 N3 Warwick Qld Austr.
151 I3 Warwick Warwickshire, England U.K.
234 D6 Warwick MD U.S.A.
235 G2 Warwick NY U.S.A.
233 N7 Warwick RI U.S.A.
149 L4 Warwick Bridge Cumbria, England U.K.
84 F3 Warwick Channel N.T. Austr.
151 I3 Warwickshire admin. div. England U.K.
108 C4 Warzhong Sichuan China
222 H5 Wasa B.C. Can.
227 N5 Wasaga Beach Ont. Can.
207 G4 Wasagu Nigeria
241 U2 Wasatch Range mts UT U.S.A.
215 O4 Wasbank S. Africa
168 I2 Wasbek Ger.
146 J4 Wasbister Orkney, Scotland U.K.
169 K6 Wasbüttel Ger.
223 J5 Wascana Creek r. Sask. Can.
172 H4 Wäschenbeuren Ger.
240 M6 Wasco CA U.S.A.
226 C3 Wascott WI U.S.A.
236 I3 Waseca MN U.S.A.
223 I3 Wasekamio Lake Sask. Can.
175 J3 Wąsewo Pol.
251 G3 Washado Suriname
123 J8 Washap Pak.
226 E9 Washburn IL U.S.A.
233 □Q2 Washburn ME U.S.A.
236 E2 Washburn ND U.S.A.
232 B12 Washburn TN U.S.A.
226 D3 Washburn WI U.S.A.
104 E4 Washiga-take mt. Japan
116 F9 Washim Mahar. India
225 F3 Washimeska r. Que. Can.
260 E3 Washington Arg.
149 N4 Washington Tyne and Wear, England U.K.
235 I1 Washington CT U.S.A.
234 A7 Washington DC U.S.A.
231 F9 Washington GA U.S.A.
236 J5 Washington IA U.S.A.
226 E9 Washington IL U.S.A.
230 D6 Washington IN U.S.A.
236 G6 Washington KS U.S.A.
232 B10 Washington KY U.S.A.
231 I8 Washington NC U.S.A.
233 M5 Washington NH U.S.A.
234 F3 Washington NJ U.S.A.
232 E8 Washington PA U.S.A.
241 S4 Washington UT U.S.A.
232 G10 Washington VA U.S.A.
238 D3 Washington state U.S.A.
263 L2 Washington, Cape Antarctica
233 N4 Washington, Mount NH U.S.A.
232 B9 Washington Court House OH U.S.A.
234 F4 Washington Crossing NJ U.S.A.
235 I1 Washington Depot CT U.S.A.
234 A6 Washington Grove MD U.S.A.
226 H4 Washington Island WI U.S.A.
226 H4 Washington Island i. WI U.S.A.
221 L2 Washington Land reg. Greenland
235 G2 Washingtonville NY U.S.A.
234 B2 Washingtonville PA U.S.A.
123 J5 Washir Afgh.
237 G8 Washita r. OK U.S.A.
83 N3 Washpool National Park N.S.W. Austr.
238 E3 Washtucna WA U.S.A.
123 K8 Washuk Pak.
114 D3 Wasi Mahar. India
125 H3 Wasī' Saudi Arabia
125 J4 Wasī' well Saudi Arabia
156 H4 Wasigny France
175 L2 Wasilków Pol.
220 D3 Wasilla AK U.S.A.
207 F4 Wasinmi Nigeria
93 E7 Wasiri Maluku Indon.
93 E5 Wasisi Buru Indon.
128 C9 Wāsiţ Egypt
127 L7 Wāsiţ governorate Iraq
127 M7 Wasit tourist site Iraq
125 M4 Wāsiţ Oman
124 D4 Wāsiţah Saudi Arabia
224 E3 Waskaganish Que. Can.
223 L3 Waskaiowaka Lake Man. Can.
222 H4 Waskatenau Alta Can.
174 E4 Wąsosz Dolnośląskie Pol.
175 K2 Wąsosz Podlaskie Pol.
174 E3 Wąsowo Pol.
242 □Q10 Waspán Nic.
164 G5 Waspik Neth.
149 O5 Wass North Yorkshire, England U.K.
206 B3 Wassadou Senegal
102 T2 Wassamu Japan
165 H7 Wasseiges Belgium
157 N6 Wasselonne France
190 F2 Wassen Switz.
164 F4 Wassenaar Neth.
169 B8 Wassenberg Ger.
212 C5 Wasser Namibia
173 I4 Wasseralfingen Ger.
173 M5 Wasserburg am Inn Ger.
169 I10 Wasserkuppe hill Ger.
169 K7 Wasserleben Ger.
172 B2 Wasserliesch Ger.
169 J10 Wasserlosen Ger.
173 J3 Wassertrüdingen Ger.
156 G3 Wassigny France
206 B4 Wassou Guinea
240 N3 Wassuk Range mts NV U.S.A.
157 I6 Wassy France
124 D4 Wasta Saudi Arabia
149 K5 Wast Water l. England U.K.
169 J9 Wasungen Ger.
224 E3 Waswanipi, Lac l. Que. Can.
227 N1 Watabeag Lake Ont. Can.
93 B4 Watambayoli Sulawesi Indon.
93 B6 Watampone Sulawesi Indon.
93 A6 Watansoppeng Sulawesi Indon.
223 I4 Watapi Lake Sask. Can.
104 E7 Watarai Japan
105 K3 Watarase-gawa r. Japan
84 C8 Watarrka National Park N.T. Austr.
105 H2 Watauchi Japan
232 C12 Watauga r. TN U.S.A.
96 D5 Wat Chan Thai.
150 F5 Watchet Somerset, England U.K.
149 L5 Watchgate Cumbria, England U.K.
235 L2 Watch Hill Point RI U.S.A.
Watenstadt-Salzgitter Ger. see Salzgitter
151 M3 Waterbeach Cambridgeshire, England U.K.
212 C4 Waterberg Namibia
212 C4 Waterberg Plateau Game Park nature res. Namibia
233 L7 Waterbury CT U.S.A.
233 M4 Waterbury VT U.S.A.
223 J3 Waterbury Lake Sask. Can.
246 E2 Water Cays i. Bahamas
227 O6 Waterdown Ont. Can.
231 G9 Wateree r. SC U.S.A.
222 C4 Waterfall AK U.S.A.
82 □3 Waterfall Lake S. Pacific Ocean
147 H8 Waterford Ireland
147 G8 Waterford county Ireland
215 J9 Waterford S. Africa
240 L4 Waterford CA U.S.A.
235 K2 Waterford CT U.S.A.
232 F7 Waterford PA U.S.A.
147 I8 Waterford Harbour Ireland
234 F5 Waterford Works NJ U.S.A.
150 B7 Watergate Bay England U.K.
223 J4 Waterhen r. Sask. Can.
223 L4 Waterhen Lake Man. Can.
84 D3 Waterhouse r. N.T. Austr.
84 D8 Waterhouse Range mts N.T. Austr.
164 F4 Wateringen Neth.
165 E6 Waterland-Oudeman Belgium
84 B4 Waterloo N.T. Austr.
165 F7 Waterloo Belgium
224 D5 Waterloo Ont. Can.
206 B4 Waterloo Sierra Leone
247 □7 Waterloo Trin. and Tob.
236 I4 Waterloo IA U.S.A.
236 J6 Waterloo IL U.S.A.
234 B6 Waterloo MD U.S.A.
232 I6 Waterloo NY U.S.A.
226 F6 Waterloo WI U.S.A.
151 J6 Waterlooville Hampshire, England U.K.
226 F8 Waterman IL U.S.A.
235 K3 Watermill NY U.S.A.
149 K2 Water of Leith r. Scotland U.K.
146 G9 Water of Tulla r. Scotland U.K.
151 I2 Water Orton Warwickshire, England U.K.
213 F4 Waterpoort S. Africa
147 H3 Waterside Northern Ireland U.K.
226 E3 Watersmeet MI U.S.A.
222 H5 Waterton Lakes National Park B.C. Can.
222 H5 Waterton Park Alta Can.
235 I1 Watertown CT U.S.A.
233 J5 Watertown NY U.S.A.
236 G3 Watertown SD U.S.A.
226 F6 Watertown WI U.S.A.
215 M2 Waterval r. S. Africa
215 O1 Waterval Boven S. Africa
82 G5 Watervale S.A. Austr.
237 K8 Water Valley MS U.S.A.
147 B9 Waterville Ireland
233 □P4 Waterville ME U.S.A.
232 B7 Waterville OH U.S.A.
238 D3 Waterville WA U.S.A.
233 L6 Watervliet NY U.S.A.
95 I8 Wates Indon.
227 M7 Watford Ont. Can.
151 L4 Watford Hertfordshire, England U.K.
236 D2 Watford City ND U.S.A.
223 K3 Wathaman r. Sask. Can.
223 K3 Wathaman Lake Sask. Can.
87 D11 Watheroo W.A. Austr.
87 C11 Watheroo National Park W.A. Austr.
222 G4 Watino Alta Can.
128 C9 Watīr, Wādī watercourse Egypt
232 I6 Watkins Glen NY U.S.A.
231 F9 Watkinsville GA U.S.A.
Watling Island Bahamas see San Salvador
151 J4 Watlington Oxfordshire, England U.K.
237 F8 Watonga OK U.S.A.
93 F3 Watowato, Bukit mt. Halmahera Indon.
223 J5 Watrous Sask. Can.
239 L9 Watrous NM U.S.A.
208 F4 Watsa Dem. Rep. Congo
226 G9 Watseka IL U.S.A.
208 D5 Watsi Kengo Dem. Rep. Congo
85 H2 Watson r. Qld Austr.
223 J4 Watson Sask. Can.
262 P1 Watson Escarpment Antarctica
222 D2 Watson Lake Y.T. Can.
234 B2 Watsontown PA U.S.A.
240 K5 Watsonville CA U.S.A.
87 I9 Watt, Mount hill W.A. Austr.

Whiddon Down Devon, England U.K.
Whiddy Island Ireland
Whim Creek W.A. Austr.
Whimple Devon, England U.K.
Whinham, Mount S.A. Austr.
Whippany NJ U.S.A.
Whirinaki Forest Park nature res. North I. N.Z.
Whiskey Jack Lake Man. Can.
Whispering Pines CA U.S.A.
Whistleduck Creek watercourse N.T. Austr.
Whistler B.C. Can.
Whitbourne Nfld and Lab. Can.
Whitburn West Lothian, Scotland U.K.
Whitby Ont. Can.
Whitby North Yorkshire, England U.K.
Whitchurch Buckinghamshire, England U.K.
Whitchurch Cardiff, Wales U.K.
Whitchurch Hampshire, England U.K.
Whitchurch Shropshire, England U.K.
Whitchurch-Stouffville Ont. Can.
Whitcombe, Mount South I. N.Z.
White r. Ont. Can.
White r. Can./U.S.A.
White r. Jamaica
White r. AR U.S.A.
White r. AR U.S.A.
White r. CO U.S.A.
White r. IN U.S.A.
White r. MI U.S.A.
White r. NV U.S.A.
White r. SD U.S.A.
White r. VT U.S.A.
White r. WI U.S.A.
White watercourse AZ U.S.A.
White watercourse TX U.S.A.
White, East Fork r. IN U.S.A.
White, Lake salt flat N.T. Austr.
White, North Fork r. MO U.S.A.
Whiteadder Water r. Scotland U.K.
White Bay Nfld and Lab. Can.
White Butte mt. ND U.S.A.
White Canyon UT U.S.A.
Whitechurch Cork Ireland
Whitechurch Waterford Ireland
White Cliffs N.S.W. Austr.
White Cloud MI U.S.A.
Whitecoomb mt. South I. N.Z.
White Coomb hill Scotland U.K.
Whitecourt Alta Can.
Whitecraig East Lothian, Scotland U.K.
Whitecross Northern Ireland U.K.
White Deer PA U.S.A.
White Earth Indian Reservation res. MN U.S.A.
Whiteface Lake MN U.S.A.
Whiteface Mountain NY U.S.A.
Whitefield NH U.S.A.
Whitefish Ont. Can.
Whitefish r. N.W.T. Can.
Whitefish MT U.S.A.
Whitefish r. MI U.S.A.
Whitefish Bay WI U.S.A.
Whitefish Lake N.W.T. Can.
Whitefish Lake Ont. Can.
Whitefish Point MI U.S.A.
Whiteford MD U.S.A.
Whitegate Clare Ireland
Whitegate Cork Ireland
White Hall Ireland
Whitehall Ireland
Whitehall Orkney, Scotland U.K.
White Hall IL U.S.A.
White Hall MD U.S.A.
Whitehall MI U.S.A.
Whitehall MT U.S.A.
Whitehall NY U.S.A.
Whitehall OH U.S.A.
White Hall PA U.S.A.
Whitehall PA U.S.A.
Whitehall WI U.S.A.
Whitehaven Cumbria, England U.K.
White Haven PA U.S.A.
Whitehead Northern Ireland U.K.
White Hill N.S. Can.
Whitehill Hampshire, England U.K.
Whitehills Aberdeenshire, Scotland U.K.
Whitehorse Y.T. Can.
White Horse NJ U.S.A.
White Horse, Vale of val. England U.K.
White Horses Jamaica
Whitehouse NJ U.S.A.
White House Station NJ U.S.A.
White Island Antarctica
White Island North I. N.Z. see **Whakaari**
White Kei r. S. Africa
White Lake salt flat W.A. Austr.
White Lake l. Ont. Can.
White Lake l. Ont. Can.
White Lake NY U.S.A.
White Lake l. LA U.S.A.
White Lake l. MI U.S.A.
Whitemark Tas. Austr.
White Mills PA U.S.A.
White Mountain Peak CA U.S.A.
White Mountains NH U.S.A.
White Mountains National Park Qld Austr.
Whitemouth r. Man. Can.
Whitemouth Lake Man. Can.
Whitemud r. Alta Can.
Whiten Head Scotland U.K.
White Nile state Sudan
White Nile r. Sudan/Uganda
alt. **Abiad, Bahr el,**
alt. **Jebel, Bahr el**
White Nile Dam Sudan
White Nossob watercourse Namibia
White Oak KY U.S.A.
White Otter Lake Ont. Can.
White Pass Can./U.S.A.
White Pigeon MI U.S.A.
White Pine MI U.S.A.
White Pine Range mts NV U.S.A.
White Plains NY U.S.A.
Whiterashes Aberdeenshire, Scotland U.K.
White River Ont. Can.
Whiteriver AZ U.S.A.
White River SD U.S.A.
White River Junction VT U.S.A.
White River National Wildlife Refuge nature res. AR U.S.A.
White River Valley NV U.S.A.
White Rock Peak NV U.S.A.
White Russia country Europe see **Belarus**
Whitesail Lake B.C. Can.
White Salmon WA U.S.A.
Whitesand r. Alta/N.W.T. Can.
Whitesand r. Sask. Can.
White Sands National Monument nat. park NM U.S.A.
Whitesboro NJ U.S.A.
Whitesboro NY U.S.A.
Whitesburg KY U.S.A.
White Sea Rus. Fed. see **Beloye More**
Whiteshell Provincial Park Man. Can.
White Stone VA U.S.A.
White Sulphur Springs MT U.S.A.
White Sulphur Springs WV U.S.A.
Whites Valley PA U.S.A.
Whitesville WV U.S.A.
White Umfolozi r. S. Africa
Whiteville NC U.S.A.
206 E4 **White Volta** watercourse Burkina/Ghana
alt. **Nakambé,**
alt. **Nakanbe,**
alt. **Volta Blanche**
206 E4 **White Volta** r. Ghana
240 P8 **White Water** CA U.S.A.
241 X3 **Whitewater** CO U.S.A.
226 F7 **Whitewater** WI U.S.A.
239 J10 **Whitewater Baldy** mt. NM U.S.A.
224 B3 **Whitewater Lake** Ont. Can.
82 C4 **White Well** S.A. Austr.
236 E6 **White Woman Creek** r. KS U.S.A.
85 I6 **Whitewood** Qld Austr.
223 K5 **Whitewood** Sask. Can.
83 K7 **Whitfield** Vic. Austr.
151 O5 **Whitfield** Kent, England U.K.
150 F1 **Whitford** Flintshire, Wales U.K.
150 D4 **Whitford Point** Wales U.K.
146 H13 **Whithorn** Dumfries and Galloway, Scotland U.K.
80 J3 **Whitianga** North I. N.Z.
233 □R4 **Whiting** ME U.S.A.
235 G5 **Whiting** NJ U.S.A.
226 E5 **Whiting** WI U.S.A.
146 F12 **Whiting Bay** North Ayrshire, Scotland U.K.
150 C4 **Whitland** Carmarthenshire, Wales U.K.
149 O3 **Whitley Bay** Tyne and Wear, England U.K.
231 E7 **Whitley City** KY U.S.A.
234 E5 **Whitman Square** NJ U.S.A.
231 G8 **Whitmire** SC U.S.A.
215 M7 **Whitmore** S. Africa
262 Q1 **Whitmore Mountains** Antarctica
151 I3 **Whitnash** Warwickshire, England U.K.
227 P4 **Whitney** Ont. Can.
237 G10 **Whitney, Lake** TX U.S.A.
240 N5 **Whitney, Mount** CA U.S.A.
233 J6 **Whitney Point** NY U.S.A.
150 D7 **Whitsand Bay** England U.K.
151 O5 **Whitstable** Kent, England U.K.
85 L6 **Whitsunday Group** is Qld Austr.
85 L6 **Whitsunday Island** Qld Austr.
85 L6 **Whitsunday Island National Park** Qld Austr.
85 L6 **Whitsunday Passage** Qld Austr.
Whitsun Island Vanuatu see **Pentecost Island**
227 K5 **Whittemore** MI U.S.A.
240 N8 **Whittier** CA U.S.A.
149 N3 **Whittingham** Northumberland, England U.K.
150 F2 **Whittington** Shropshire, England U.K.
84 D5 **Whittington Range** hills N.T. Austr.
83 J7 **Whittlesea** Vic. Austr.
215 K8 **Whittlesea** S. Africa
151 L2 **Whittlesey** Cambridgeshire, England U.K.
226 D4 **Whittlesey** WI U.S.A.
226 D3 **Whittlesey, Mount** hill WI U.S.A.
83 K6 **Whitton** N.S.W. Austr.
85 H8 **Whitula** watercourse Qld Austr.
149 M6 **Whitworth** Lancashire, England U.K.
223 J2 **Wholdaia Lake** N.W.T. Can.
241 T9 **Why** AZ U.S.A.
82 F5 **Whyalla** S.A. Austr.
Whydah Benin see **Ouidah**
96 D6 **Wiang Kosai National Park** Thai.
96 D5 **Wiang Pa Pao** Thai.
96 E5 **Wiang Sa** Thai.
175 K6 **Wiar** r. Pol.
175 J2 **Wiartel** Pol.
224 D4 **Wiarton** Ont. Can.
206 E4 **Wiasi** Ghana
174 F3 **Wiatrowo** Pol.
206 E5 **Wiawso** Ghana
146 B8 **Wiay** i. Scotland U.K.
174 F5 **Wiązów** Pol.
238 L3 **Wibaux** MT U.S.A.
210 C2 **Wich'alē** Eth.
165 E6 **Wichelen** Belgium
237 G7 **Wichita** KS U.S.A.
237 F8 **Wichita** r. TX U.S.A.
237 F9 **Wichita Falls** TX U.S.A.
237 F8 **Wichita Mountains** OK U.S.A.
237 F8 **Wichita Mountains National Wildlife Refuge** nature res. OK U.S.A.
146 J6 **Wick** Highland, Scotland U.K.
150 H5 **Wick** South Gloucestershire, England U.K.
150 E5 **Wick** Vale of Glamorgan, Wales U.K.
151 K6 **Wick** West Sussex, England U.K.
146 J6 **Wick** r. Scotland U.K.
169 E7 **Wickede** airport Ger.
169 E8 **Wickede (Ruhr)** Ger.
241 T8 **Wickenburg** AZ U.S.A.
87 D12 **Wickepin** W.A. Austr.
237 H8 **Wickes** AR U.S.A.
151 N4 **Wickford** Essex, England U.K.
86 D6 **Wickham** W.A. Austr.
84 C4 **Wickham** r. N.T. Austr.
151 J6 **Wickham** Hampshire, England U.K.
83 I8 **Wickham, Cape** Tas. Austr.
84 B4 **Wickham, Mount** hill N.T. Austr.
151 O3 **Wickham Market** Suffolk, England U.K.
237 K7 **Wickliffe** KY U.S.A.
147 J7 **Wicklow** Ireland
147 J6 **Wicklow** county Ireland
147 K7 **Wicklow Head** Ireland
147 I7 **Wicklow Mountains** Ireland
147 J6 **Wicklow Mountains National Park** Ireland
174 F1 **Wicko** Pol.
143 M7 **Wicko, Jezioro** lag. Pol.
150 H4 **Wickwar** South Gloucestershire, England U.K.
234 B3 **Wiconisco** PA U.S.A.
234 B3 **Wiconisco Creek** r. PA U.S.A.
174 G4 **Widawa** Pol.
174 E4 **Widawa** r. Pol.
175 G4 **Widawka** r. Pol.
85 N8 **Wide Bay** Qld Austr.
150 E6 **Widecombe in the Moor** Devon, England U.K.
146 J4 **Wide Firth** sea chan. Scotland U.K.
87 K8 **Wide Gum** watercourse S.A. Austr.
263 B2 **Widerøe, Mount** Antarctica
151 M4 **Widford** Hertfordshire, England U.K.
85 J9 **Widgeegoara** watercourse Qld Austr.
87 F11 **Widgiemooltha** W.A. Austr.
93 F4 **Widi, Kepulauan** is Maluku Indon.
190 H1 **Widnau** Switz.
149 L7 **Widnes** Halton, England U.K.
101 E11 **Wi-do** i. S. Korea
174 C2 **Widuchowa** Pol.
174 F2 **Więcbork** Pol.
170 G2 **Wieck am Darß** Ger.
175 I2 **Wieczfnia Kościelna** Pol.
174 G2 **Wieczno, Jezioro** l. Pol.
169 D10 **Wied** r. Ger.
169 K7 **Wieda** Ger.
171 G9 **Wiederau** Ger.
171 F8 **Wiederitzsch** Ger.
195 □ **Wied Il-Għajn** Malta
171 J8 **Wiednitz** Ger.
168 F4 **Wiefelstede** Ger.
171 D8 **Wiehe** Ger.
169 F6 **Wiehengebirge** hills Ger.
169 E9 **Wiehl** Ger.
170 H1 **Wiek** Ger.
174 G5 **Większyce** Pol.
175 I2 **Wielbark** Pol.
174 E3 **Wieleń** Pol.
173 K6 **Wielenbach** Ger.
175 H3 **Wielgie** Pol.
174 E3 **Wielichowo** Pol.
175 I6 **Wieliczka** Pol.
175 K2 **Wieliczki** Pol.
174 E2 **Wielimie, Jezioro** l. Pol.
174 G2 **Wielka Nieszawka** Pol.
177 H2 **Wielka Racza** mt. Pol./Slovakia
175 K6 **Wielka Rawka** mt. Pol.
174 E5 **Wielka Sowa** mt. Pol.
175 L5 **Wielkie Oczy** Pol.
175 H2 **Wielkie Partęczyny, Jezioro** l. Pol.
174 G1 **Wielki Klincz** Pol.
174 F4 **Wielkopolska, Nizina** lowland Pol.
174 F3 **Wielkopolskie** prov. Pol.
174 F3 **Wielkopolskie, Pojezierze** reg. Pol.
174 E3 **Wielkopolski Park Narodowy** nat. park Pol.
175 J6 **Wielopole Skrzyńskie** Pol.
174 G5 **Wielowieś** Pol.
165 D7 **Wielsbeke** Belgium
174 G4 **Wieluń** Pol.
168 I3 **Wiemersdorf** Ger.
179 N3 **Wien** Austria
179 N3 **Wien** land Austria
179 L4 **Wienerbruck** Austria
179 N3 **Wiener Neudorf** Austria
179 N4 **Wiener Neustadt** Austria
179 N3 **Wiener Wald** mts Austria
168 J5 **Wienhausen** Ger.
175 I4 **Wieniawa** Pol.
174 G3 **Wieniec** Pol.
179 L3 **Wiensberg** mt. Austria
170 D5 **Wiepke** Ger.
175 H6 **Wieprz** Pol.
175 J4 **Wieprz** r. Pol.
143 M7 **Wieprza** r. Pol.
175 L4 **Wieprz-Krzna, Kanał** canal Pol.
175 K3 **Wiercień Duży** Pol.
164 K4 **Wierden** Neth.
168 K5 **Wieren** Ger.
164 G3 **Wieringermeer Polder** Neth.
164 H3 **Wieringerwerf** Neth.
172 F4 **Wiernsheim** Ger.
174 G4 **Wieruszów** Pol.
175 L4 **Wierzbica** Lubelskie Pol.
175 J4 **Wierzbica** Mazowieckie Pol.
174 F4 **Wierzbica Górna** Pol.
174 D2 **Wierzbięcin** Pol.
174 G3 **Wierzbinek** Pol.
174 F5 **Wierzbnik** Pol.
175 L2 **Wierzchlesie** Pol.
174 G3 **Wierzchosławice** Kujawsko-Pomorskie Pol.
175 I5 **Wierzchosławice** Małopolskie Pol.
174 E2 **Wierzchowo** Zachodniopomorskie Pol.
174 E2 **Wierzchowo** Zachodniopomorskie Pol.
174 E2 **Wierzchowo, Jezioro** l. Pol.
174 G1 **Wierzchucino** Pol.
174 G2 **Wierzyca** r. Pol.
179 L6 **Wies** Austria
173 J6 **Wies** Ger.
171 G9 **Wiesa** Ger.
173 M2 **Wiesau** Ger.
169 F10 **Wiesbaden** Ger.
172 D6 **Wiese** r. Ger.
179 L3 **Wieselburg** Austria
179 N4 **Wiesen** Austria
169 H10 **Wiesen** Ger.
190 H2 **Wiesen** Switz.
171 K6 **Wiesenau** Ger.
171 F6 **Wiesenburg** Ger.
173 N3 **Wiesenfelden** Ger.
172 H4 **Wiesensteig** Ger.
173 M3 **Wiesent** Ger.
173 K2 **Wiesent** r. Ger.
173 K2 **Wiesenthau** Ger.
173 I2 **Wiesentheid** Ger.
173 K2 **Wiesenttal** Ger.
178 E5 **Wiesing** Austria
168 H4 **Wiesle** r. Ger.
172 F3 **Wiesloch** Ger.
179 N4 **Wiesmath** Austria
168 E4 **Wiesmoor** Ger.
234 D3 **Wiessport** PA U.S.A.
168 D5 **Wietmarschen** Ger.
175 I5 **Wietrzychowice** Pol.
168 I5 **Wietze** Ger.
169 I5 **Wietze** r. Ger.
168 H5 **Wietzen** Ger.
168 I5 **Wietzendorf** Ger.
143 O7 **Wieżyca** hill Pol.
149 L6 **Wigan** Greater Manchester, England U.K.
173 I6 **Wiggensbach** Ger.
237 K10 **Wiggins** MS U.S.A.
202 C3 **Wigh, Ramlat al** des. Libya
145 G6 **Wight, Isle of** i. England U.K.
175 L1 **Wigierski Park Narodowy** nat. park Pol.
150 G3 **Wigmore** Herefordshire, England U.K.
223 J2 **Wignes Lake** N.W.T. Can.
175 L1 **Wigry, Jezioro** l. Pol.
151 J2 **Wigston** Leicestershire, England U.K.
149 K4 **Wigton** Cumbria, England U.K.
146 H13 **Wigtown** Dumfries and Galloway, Scotland U.K.
146 H13 **Wigtown Bay** Scotland U.K.
164 I5 **Wijchen** Neth.
140 □ **Wijdefjorden** inlet Svalbard
174 E4 **Wijewo** Pol.
164 J4 **Wijhe** Neth.
164 G4 **Wijk aan Zee** Neth.
164 H5 **Wijk bij Duurstede** Neth.
164 H5 **Wijk en Aalburg** Neth.
165 G6 **Wijnegem** Belgium
164 J2 **Wijnjewoude** Neth.
241 S7 **Wikieup** AZ U.S.A.
210 C1 **Wik'ro** Eth.
227 M4 **Wikwemikong** Ont. Can.
190 G1 **Wil** Switz.
175 H6 **Wilamowice** Pol.
236 G5 **Wilber** NE U.S.A.
81 F10 **Wilberforce** r. South I. N.Z.
84 F1 **Wilberforce, Cape** N.T. Austr.
238 E3 **Wilbur** WA U.S.A.
173 I3 **Wilburgstetten** Ger.
237 H8 **Wilburton** OK U.S.A.
83 I4 **Wilcannia** N.S.W. Austr.
232 G7 **Wilcox** PA U.S.A.
Wilczek Land i. Zemlya Frantsa-Iosifa Rus. Fed. see **Vil'cheka, Zemlya**
175 H1 **Wilczęta** Pol.
174 G3 **Wilczogóra** Pol.
174 G3 **Wilczyn** Pol.
179 K4 **Wildalpen** Austria
179 L4 **Wildalpener Salzatal** nature res. Austria
171 I6 **Wildau** Ger.
172 F4 **Wildberg** Baden-Württemberg Ger.
170 G5 **Wildberg** Brandenburg Ger.
170 H3 **Wildberg** Mecklenburg-Vorpommern Ger.
223 K4 **Wildcat Hill Provincial Wilderness Park** nature res. Sask. Can.
240 P3 **Wildcat Peak** NV U.S.A.
215 N7 **Wild Coast** S. Africa
169 J9 **Wildeck-Obersuhl** Ger.
169 J9 **Wildeck-Richelsdorf** Ger.
169 J7 **Wildemann** Ger.
179 N2 **Wildendürnbach** Austria
171 G9 **Wildenfels** Ger.
214 G9 **Wilderness** S. Africa
232 H10 **Wilderness** VA U.S.A.
214 G10 **Wilderness National Park** S. Africa
168 F5 **Wildeshausen** Ger.
169 I10 **Wildflecken** Ger.
226 E1 **Wild Goose** Ont. Can.
222 G4 **Wildhay** r. Alta Can.
190 C3 **Wildhorn** mt. Switz.
239 L11 **Wild Horse Draw** r. TX U.S.A.
236 E5 **Wild Horse Hill** mt. NE U.S.A.
179 M6 **Wildon** Austria
173 I6 **Wildpoldsried** Ger.
236 G2 **Wild Rice** r. MN U.S.A.
236 G2 **Wild Rice** r. ND U.S.A.
226 B3 **Wild Rice Lake** MN U.S.A.
178 G5 **Wildseeloder** mt. Austria
178 G3 **Wildshut** Austria
178 C6 **Wildspitze** mt. Austria
222 H4 **Wildwood** Alta Can.
231 F11 **Wildwood** FL U.S.A.
234 F7 **Wildwood** NJ U.S.A.
234 F7 **Wildwood Crest** NJ U.S.A.
236 D6 **Wiley** CO U.S.A.
232 G9 **Wiley Ford** WV U.S.A.
175 J4 **Wilga** Pol.
175 J4 **Wilga** r. Pol.
215 M3 **Wilge** r. Free State S. Africa
215 N1 **Wilge** r. S. Africa
82 E4 **Wilgena** S.A. Austr.
91 J8 **Wilhelm, Mount** P.N.G.
251 G4 **Wilhelmina Gebergte** mts Suriname
164 H6 **Wilhelmina Kanaal** canal Neth.
140 □ **Wilhelmøya** i. Svalbard
Wilhelm-Pieck-Stadt Ger. see **Guben**
179 M3 **Wilhelmsburg** Austria
170 I3 **Wilhelmsburg** Ger.
172 G6 **Wilhelmsdorf** Ger.
168 F3 **Wilhelmshaven** Ger.
212 C4 **Wilhelmstal** Namibia
171 D10 **Wilhelmsthal** Ger.
179 J3 **Wilhering** Austria
173 J3 **Wilhermsdorf** Ger.
113 □2 **Wilingili** i. Addu Atoll Maldives
171 G9 **Wilkau-Haßlau** Ger.
234 D2 **Wilkes-Barre** PA U.S.A.
231 G7 **Wilkesboro** NC U.S.A.
263 I2 **Wilkes Coast** Antarctica
263 I2 **Wilkes Land** reg. Antarctica
223 I4 **Wilkie** Sask. Can.
232 F8 **Wilkinsburg** PA U.S.A.
262 T2 **Wilkins Coast** Antarctica
262 T2 **Wilkins Ice Shelf** Antarctica
82 D3 **Wilkinson Lakes** salt flat S.A. Austr.
147 I5 **Wilkinstown** Ireland
175 K4 **Wilkołaz Pierwszy** Pol.
175 J4 **Wilków** Lubelskie Pol.
174 F4 **Wilków** Opolskie Pol.
174 D3 **Wilkowo** Pol.
222 D3 **Will, Mount** B.C. Can.
238 C4 **Willamette** r. OR U.S.A.
150 F6 **Willand** Devon, England U.K.
83 J5 **Willandra Billabong** watercourse N.S.W. Austr.
83 J5 **Willandra National Park** N.S.W. Austr.
238 B3 **Willapa Bay** WA U.S.A.
242 D3 **Willard** Mex.
239 K9 **Willard** NM U.S.A.
232 C7 **Willard** OH U.S.A.
233 J10 **Willards** MD U.S.A.
149 K7 **Willaston** Cheshire, England U.K.
241 W9 **Willcox** AZ U.S.A.
241 W9 **Willcox Playa** salt flat AZ U.S.A.
169 H7 **Willebadessen** Ger.
165 F6 **Willebroek** Belgium
215 L4 **Willem Pretorius Game Reserve** nature res. S. Africa
164 F5 **Willemstad** Neth.
247 □10 **Willemstad** Curaçao Neth. Antilles
84 C3 **Willeroo** N.T. Austr.
223 I3 **William** r. Sask. Can.
83 I7 **William, Mount** Vic. Austr.
87 C7 **Williambury** W.A. Austr.
82 F3 **William Creek** S.A. Austr.
223 L4 **William Lake** Man. Can.
87 D12 **Williams** W.A. Austr.
85 H6 **Williams** r. Qld Austr.
87 D12 **Williams** r. W.A. Austr.
241 T6 **Williams** AZ U.S.A.
240 J2 **Williams** CA U.S.A.
236 I5 **Williamsburg** IA U.S.A.
232 A12 **Williamsburg** KY U.S.A.
226 I5 **Williamsburg** MI U.S.A.
232 A9 **Williamsburg** OH U.S.A.
232 G8 **Williamsburg** PA U.S.A.
232 I11 **Williamsburg** VA U.S.A.
246 □ **Williamsfield** Jamaica
246 D1 **Williams Island** Bahamas
222 F4 **Williams Lake** B.C. Can.
225 H1 **William Smith, Cap** c. Que. Can.
232 H5 **Williamson** NY U.S.A.
232 C11 **Williamson** WV U.S.A.
230 D5 **Williamsport** IN U.S.A.
232 B9 **Williamsport** OH U.S.A.
227 Q8 **Williamsport** PA U.S.A.
227 J7 **Williamston** MI U.S.A.
231 I8 **Williamston** NC U.S.A.
233 L6 **Williamstown** MA U.S.A.
234 F5 **Williamstown** NJ U.S.A.
233 J5 **Williamstown** NY U.S.A.
234 B3 **Williamstown** PA U.S.A.
232 D9 **Williamstown** WV U.S.A.
169 C8 **Willich** Ger.
247 □2 **Willikies** Antigua and Barbuda
233 M7 **Willimantic** CT U.S.A.
235 K1 **Willimantic** r. CT U.S.A.
234 F4 **Willingboro** NJ U.S.A.
151 M6 **Willingdon** East Sussex, England U.K.
169 G8 **Willingen (Upland)** Ger.
151 M3 **Willingham** Cambridgeshire, England U.K.
Willingili i. N. Male Maldives see **Vilingli**
169 H9 **Willingshausen** Ger.
151 I2 **Willington** Derbyshire, England U.K.
190 E1 **Willisau** Switz.
85 M4 **Willis Group** atolls Coral Sea Is Terr. Austr.
259 □ **Willis Islands** S. Georgia
214 E7 **Williston** S. Africa
231 F11 **Williston** FL U.S.A.
236 D1 **Williston** ND U.S.A.
231 G9 **Williston** SC U.S.A.
222 F4 **Williston Lake** B.C. Can.
150 F5 **Williton** Somerset, England U.K.
240 I2 **Willits** CA U.S.A.
83 N4 **Willi Willi National Park** N.S.W. Austr.
236 H3 **Willmar** MN U.S.A.
222 G4 **Willmore Wilderness Provincial Park** Alta Can.
82 F4 **Willochra** watercourse S.A. Austr.
149 R7 **Willoughby** Lincolnshire, England U.K.
232 D7 **Willoughby** OH U.S.A.
233 M4 **Willoughby, Lake** VT U.S.A.
222 F4 **Willow** r. B.C. Can.
241 R6 **Willow Beach** AZ U.S.A.
223 J5 **Willow Bunch** Sask. Can.
222 H5 **Willow Creek** r. Alta Can.
238 C6 **Willow Creek** CA U.S.A.
238 D4 **Willow Creek** r. OR U.S.A.
241 W1 **Willow Creek** r. UT U.S.A.
234 D6 **Willow Grove** DE U.S.A.
234 E4 **Willow Grove** PA U.S.A.
232 H8 **Willow Hill** PA U.S.A.
222 G2 **Willow Lake** N.W.T. Can.
222 F2 **Willowlake** r. N.W.T. Can.
214 H9 **Willowmore** S. Africa
84 D6 **Willowra** N.T. Austr.
Willowra Aboriginal Land Trust res. N.T. Austr. see **Wirliyajarrayi Aboriginal Land Trust**
226 E4 **Willow Reservoir** WI U.S.A.
240 J2 **Willows** CA U.S.A.
237 J7 **Willow Springs** MO U.S.A.
234 C5 **Willow Street** PA U.S.A.
215 M8 **Willowvale** S. Africa
86 J6 **Wills, Lake** salt flat W.A. Austr.
84 H7 **Wills Creek** watercourse Qld Austr.
172 D4 **Willstätt** Ger.
82 G6 **Willunga** S.A. Austr.
231 E10 **Wilma** FL U.S.A.
170 I4 **Wilmersdorf** Brandenburg Ger.
171 J7 **Wilmersdorf** Brandenburg Ger.
82 G5 **Wilmington** S.A. Austr.
234 D5 **Wilmington** DE U.S.A.
231 I8 **Wilmington** NC U.S.A.
232 B9 **Wilmington** OH U.S.A.
233 M6 **Wilmington** VT U.S.A.
231 G9 **Wilmington Island** GA U.S.A.
149 M7 **Wilmslow** Cheshire, England U.K.
164 G4 **Wilnis** Neth.
Wilno Lith. see **Vilnius**
169 F9 **Wilnsdorf** Ger.
164 J4 **Wilp** Neth.
114 G8 **Wilpattu National Park** Sri Lanka
82 G4 **Wilpena** watercourse S.A. Austr.
171 I8 **Wilsdruff** Ger.
168 I4 **Wilseder Berg** hill Ger.
170 I4 **Wilsickow** Ger.
86 J4 **Wilson** r. W.A. Austr.
85 I9 **Wilson** watercourse Qld Austr.
Wilson atoll Micronesia see **Ifalik**
236 F6 **Wilson** KS U.S.A.
226 C6 **Wilson** MN U.S.A.
231 I8 **Wilson** NC U.S.A.
232 G5 **Wilson** NY U.S.A.
234 E3 **Wilson** PA U.S.A.
221 J3 **Wilson, Cape** Nunavut Can.
239 K8 **Wilson, Mount** CO U.S.A.
241 R3 **Wilson, Mount** NV U.S.A.
238 D4 **Wilson, Mount** OR U.S.A.
84 C5 **Wilson Creek** watercourse N.T. Austr.
263 K2 **Wilson Hills** Antarctica
240 N5 **Wilsonia** CA U.S.A.
231 D8 **Wilson Lake** resr AL U.S.A.
232 H11 **Wilsons** VA U.S.A.
83 K8 **Wilson's Promontory** pen. Vic. Austr.
83 K8 **Wilson's Promontory National Park** Vic. Austr.
168 H4 **Wilstedt** Ger.
168 H3 **Wilster** Ger.
168 C5 **Wilsum** Ger.
179 O2 **Wiltersdorf** Austria
171 J8 **Wilthen** Ger.
172 B2 **Wiltingen** Ger.
84 E3 **Wilton** r. N.T. Austr.
151 I5 **Wilton** Wiltshire, England U.K.
235 I2 **Wilton** CT U.S.A.
233 □O4 **Wilton** ME U.S.A.
236 E2 **Wilton** ND U.S.A.
233 N6 **Wilton** NH U.S.A.
150 I5 **Wiltshire** admin. div. England U.K.
165 I9 **Wiltz** Lux.
87 F9 **Wiluna** W.A. Austr.
150 F5 **Wimbleball Lake** England U.K.
80 K7 **Wimbledon** North I. N.Z.
151 M2 **Wimblington** Cambridgeshire, England U.K.
151 I6 **Wimborne Minster** Dorset, England U.K.
156 C2 **Wimereux** France
171 E7 **Wimmelburg** Ger.
83 H7 **Wimmera** r. Vic. Austr.
190 D2 **Wimmis** Switz.
179 N4 **Wimpassing** Austria
Wina r. Cameroon see **Vina**
230 D5 **Winamac** IN U.S.A.
210 B5 **Winam Gulf** Kenya
85 J9 **Winbin** watercourse Qld Austr.
215 L4 **Winburg** S. Africa
214 G3 **Wincanton** S. Africa
150 H5 **Wincanton** Somerset, England U.K.
151 I4 **Winchcombe** Gloucestershire, England U.K.
151 N6 **Winchelsea** East Sussex, England U.K.
233 M6 **Winchendon** MA U.S.A.
172 A2 **Wincheringen** Ger.
233 J3 **Winchester** Ont. Can.
81 F11 **Winchester** South I. N.Z.
151 J5 **Winchester** Hampshire, England U.K.
236 J6 **Winchester** IL U.S.A.
230 E5 **Winchester** IN U.S.A.
232 A11 **Winchester** KY U.S.A.
233 M6 **Winchester** NH U.S.A.
231 D8 **Winchester** TN U.S.A.
232 G9 **Winchester** VA U.S.A.
165 I8 **Wincrange** Lux.
220 E3 **Wind** r. Y.T. Can.
238 J5 **Wind** r. WY U.S.A.
175 J1 **Winda** Pol.
82 F4 **Windabout, Lake** salt flat S.A. Austr.
173 K5 **Windach** Ger.
Windau Latvia see **Ventspils**
232 G8 **Windber** PA U.S.A.
236 D4 **Wind Cave National Park** SD U.S.A.
168 I2 **Windeby** Ger.
231 F9 **Winder** GA U.S.A.
149 L5 **Windermere** Cumbria, England U.K.
149 L5 **Windermere** l. England U.K.
172 D2 **Windesheim** Ger.
234 E3 **Windgap** PA U.S.A.
169 D9 **Windhagen** Ger.
222 C3 **Windham** AK U.S.A.
235 K1 **Windham** CT U.S.A.
232 D7 **Windham** OH U.S.A.
169 J7 **Windhausen** Ger.
212 C4 **Windhoek** Namibia
87 G9 **Windidda Aboriginal Reserve** W.A. Austr.
221 I4 **Windigo** r. Ont. Can.
224 B2 **Windigo Lake** Ont. Can.
179 L2 **Windigsteig** Austria
173 M2 **Windischeschenbach** Ger.
179 J4 **Windischgarsten** Austria
146 K11 **Windlestraw Law** hill Scotland U.K.
148 D7 **Windmill** Ireland
185 □ **Windmill Hill Flats** Gibraltar
239 L10 **Wind Mountain** NM U.S.A.
236 H4 **Windom** MN U.S.A.
85 I8 **Windorah** Qld Austr.
173 O4 **Windorf** Ger.
241 W6 **Window Rock** AZ U.S.A.
226 G7 **Wind Point** WI U.S.A.
232 E9 **Wind Ridge** PA U.S.A.
238 J5 **Wind River Indian Reservation** res. WY U.S.A.
238 J5 **Wind River Range** mts WY U.S.A.
151 J4 **Windrush** r. England U.K.
263 G2 **Winds, Bay of** Antarctica
173 J3 **Windsbach** Ger.
83 M5 **Windsor** N.S.W. Austr.
225 H4 **Windsor** N.S. Can.
224 D5 **Windsor** Ont. Can.
225 F4 **Windsor** Que. Can.
151 K5 **Windsor** Windsor and Maidenhead, England U.K.
233 M7 **Windsor** CT U.S.A.
231 I7 **Windsor** NC U.S.A.
234 F4 **Windsor** NJ U.S.A.
233 J6 **Windsor** NY U.S.A.
234 B5 **Windsor** PA U.S.A.
232 I12 **Windsor** VA U.S.A.
233 M5 **Windsor** VT U.S.A.
151 K5 **Windsor and Maidenhead** admin. div. England U.K.
233 M6 **Windsor Dam** MA U.S.A.
233 M7 **Windsor Locks** CT U.S.A.
214 I4 **Windsorton** S. Africa
85 H9 **Windula** watercourse Qld Austr.
247 □3 **Windward** Grenada
247 M6 **Windward Islands** Caribbean Sea
Windward Islands Arch. de la Société Fr. Polynesia see **Vent, Îles du**
246 F4 **Windward Passage** Cuba/Haiti
87 C13 **Windy Harbour** W.A. Austr.
223 I4 **Winefred Lake** Alta Can.
231 D9 **Winfield** AL U.S.A.
237 G7 **Winfield** KS U.S.A.
232 D10 **Winfield** WV U.S.A.
150 G5 **Winford** North Somerset, England U.K.
151 K4 **Wing** Buckinghamshire, England U.K.
149 O4 **Wingate** Durham, England U.K.
84 C3 **Wingate Mountains** hills N.T. Austr.
235 H1 **Wingdale** NY U.S.A.
83 M4 **Wingen** N.S.W. Austr.
165 D6 **Wingene** Belgium
157 N6 **Wingen-sur-Moder** France
169 J8 **Wingerode** Ger.
83 N4 **Wingham** N.S.W. Austr.
224 D5 **Wingham** Ont. Can.
151 O5 **Wingham** Kent, England U.K.
156 E3 **Wingles** France
168 H3 **Wingst** Ger.
173 N5 **Winhöring** Ger.
93 D8 **Wini** East Timor
86 G7 **Winifred, Lake** salt flat W.A. Austr.
261 E5 **Winifreda** Arg.
78 □4a **Winion, Mochun** sea chan. Chuuk Micronesia
224 C2 **Winisk** Ont. Can.
224 C2 **Winisk** r. Ont. Can.
224 C2 **Winisk Lake** Ont. Can.
224 C2 **Winisk River Provincial Park** Ont. Can.
96 C7 **Winkana** Myanmar
214 D8 **Winkelhaaks** r. S. Africa
173 K3 **Winkelhaid** Ger.
241 V9 **Winkelman** AZ U.S.A.
215 K3 **Winkelpos** S. Africa
168 G5 **Winkelsett** Ger.
151 K5 **Winkfield** Bracknell Forest, England U.K.
173 M3 **Winklarn** Ger.
150 E6 **Winkleigh** Devon, England U.K.
223 L5 **Winkler** Man. Can.
178 G6 **Winklern** Austria
179 J5 **Winklern bei Oberwölz** Austria
238 C3 **Winlock** WA U.S.A.
84 C8 **Winnalls Ridge** N.T. Austr.
206 E5 **Winneba** Ghana
236 H4 **Winnebago** MN U.S.A.
226 F5 **Winnebago, Lake** WI U.S.A.
236 G4 **Winnebago Indian Reservation** res. NE U.S.A.
84 C5 **Winnecke Creek** watercourse N.T. Austr.
226 F5 **Winneconne** WI U.S.A.
238 F6 **Winnemucca** NV U.S.A.
240 M1 **Winnemucca Lake** NV U.S.A.
172 G4 **Winnenden** Ger.
236 E4 **Winner** SD U.S.A.
151 K5 **Winnersh** Wokingham, England U.K.
168 H2 **Winnert** Ger.
238 J3 **Winnett** MT U.S.A.
237 I10 **Winnfield** LA U.S.A.
236 H2 **Winnibigoshish, Lake** MN U.S.A.
175 I3 **Winnica** Pol.
237 H11 **Winnie** TX U.S.A.
87 C7 **Winning** W.A. Austr.
169 E10 **Winningen** Rheinland-Pfalz Ger.
171 D7 **Winningen** Sachsen-Anhalt Ger.
223 L5 **Winnipeg** Man. Can.
223 L5 **Winnipeg** r. Man./Ont. Can.
223 L5 **Winnipeg, Lake** Man. Can.
223 L5 **Winnipegosis** Man. Can.
223 K4 **Winnipegosis, Lake** Man. Can.
233 N5 **Winnipesaukee, Lake** NH U.S.A.
237 J9 **Winnsboro** LA U.S.A.
231 G8 **Winnsboro** SC U.S.A.
237 H9 **Winnsboro** TX U.S.A.
172 D2 **Winnweiler** Ger.
241 U6 **Winona** AZ U.S.A.
226 F3 **Winona** MI U.S.A.
226 C5 **Winona** MN U.S.A.
237 J7 **Winona** MO U.S.A.
237 K9 **Winona** MS U.S.A.
233 L4 **Winooski** VT U.S.A.
233 L4 **Winooski** r. VT U.S.A.
164 L2 **Winschoten** Neth.
150 G5 **Winscombe** North Somerset, England U.K.
168 I5 **Winsen (Aller)** Ger.
168 J4 **Winsen (Luhe)** Ger.
149 L7 **Winsford** Cheshire, England U.K.
174 E4 **Wińsko** Pol.
150 H5 **Winsley** Wiltshire, England U.K.
151 K4 **Winslow** Buckinghamshire, England U.K.
241 V6 **Winslow** AZ U.S.A.
233 □P4 **Winslow** ME U.S.A.
234 F5 **Winslow** NJ U.S.A.
233 L7 **Winsted** CT U.S.A.
149 N4 **Winston** Durham, England U.K.
231 G7 **Winston-Salem** NC U.S.A.
164 I2 **Winsum** Friesland Neth.
164 K2 **Winsum** Groningen Neth.
226 C4 **Winter** WI U.S.A.
169 G8 **Winterberg** Ger.
215 K8 **Winterberg** mts S. Africa
150 G4 **Winterbourne** South Gloucestershire, England U.K.
150 G6 **Winterbourne Abbas** Dorset, England U.K.
170 D5 **Winterfeld** Ger.
233 □Q4 **Winter Harbor** ME U.S.A.
231 G11 **Winter Haven** FL U.S.A.
172 G5 **Winterlingen** Ger.
231 G11 **Winter Park** FL U.S.A.
233 □Q4 **Winterport** ME U.S.A.
240 K3 **Winters** CA U.S.A.
237 F10 **Winters** TX U.S.A.
171 F8 **Wintersdorf** Ger.
236 H5 **Winterset** IA U.S.A.
234 C6 **Winters Run** r. MD U.S.A.
234 B5 **Winterstown** PA U.S.A.
164 K5 **Winterswijk** Neth.
190 F1 **Winterthur** Switz.
215 N4 **Winterton** S. Africa
149 P6 **Winterton** North Lincolnshire, England U.K.
215 M1 **Winterveld** S. Africa
233 □Q2 **Winterville** ME U.S.A.
235 K2 **Winthrop** CT U.S.A.
233 □P4 **Winthrop** ME U.S.A.
85 I7 **Winton** Qld Austr.
231 □2 **Winton** New Prov. Bahamas
81 C13 **Winton** South I. N.Z.
149 M5 **Winton** Cumbria, England U.K.
231 I7 **Winton** NC U.S.A.
172 B2 **Wintrich** Ger.
157 N7 **Wintzenheim** France
151 L3 **Winwick** Cambridgeshire, England U.K.
169 I7 **Winzenburg** Ger.
179 N4 **Winzendorf** Austria
173 O4 **Winzer** Ger.
171 D8 **Wipper** r. Ger.
169 K8 **Wipperdorf** Ger.
169 D8 **Wipperfürth** Ger.
168 D5 **Wippingen** Ger.
171 D7 **Wippra Kurort** Ger.
178 D5 **Wipptal** val. Austria
94 F6 **Wiralaga** Sumatera Indon.
168 D4 **Wirdumer (Wirdum)** Ger.
169 E10 **Wirges** Ger.
149 N7 **Wirksworth** Derbyshire, England U.K.
84 D6 **Wirliyajarrayi Aboriginal Land Trust** res. N.T. Austr.
82 G5 **Wirrabara** S.A. Austr.
149 K7 **Wirral** pen. England U.K.
82 F4 **Wirraminna** S.A. Austr.
82 H7 **Wirrega** S.A. Austr.
82 E3 **Wirrida, Lake** salt flat S.A. Austr.
83 N4 **Wirrikimbe National Park** N.S.W. Austr.
82 E5 **Wirrulla** S.A. Austr.
171 E10 **Wirsberg** Ger.
78 □4a **Wisas** i. Chuuk Micronesia
151 M2 **Wisbech** Cambridgeshire, England U.K.
233 □P4 **Wiscasset** ME U.S.A.
168 H3 **Wischhafen** Ger.
226 C6 **Wisconsin** r. WI U.S.A.
236 K3 **Wisconsin** state U.S.A.
226 E6 **Wisconsin, Lake** WI U.S.A.
226 E6 **Wisconsin Dells** WI U.S.A.
226 E5 **Wisconsin Rapids** WI U.S.A.
232 C12 **Wise** VA U.S.A.
146 I11 **Wishaw** North Lanarkshire, Scotland U.K.
236 F2 **Wisher** ND U.S.A.
210 F3 **Wisil Dabarow** Somalia
149 O5 **Wiske** r. England U.K.
175 I3 **Wiskitki** Pol.
174 G6 **Wisła** Pol.
143 O7 **Wisła** r. Pol.
143 P7 **Wiślana, Mierzeja** spit Pol.
143 P7 **Wiślany, Zalew** b. Pol.
175 I5 **Wiślica** Pol.
175 K5 **Wisłok** r. Pol.
175 J5 **Wisłoka** r. Pol.
170 D3 **Wismar** Ger.
170 D2 **Wismarbucht** b. Ger.
237 J10 **Wisner** LA U.S.A.
175 K3 **Wiśniew** Pol.
175 I2 **Wiśniewo** Pol.
175 I6 **Wiśniowa** Pol.
156 C2 **Wissant** France
157 O5 **Wissembourg** France
169 E9 **Wissen** Ger.
226 C5 **Wissota Lake** WI U.S.A.
150 G3 **Wistanstow** Shropshire, England U.K.
222 E4 **Wistaria** B.C. Can.
149 M7 **Wistaston** Cheshire, England U.K.
168 I4 **Wistedt** Ger.
175 K6 **Wisznia** r. Pol.
174 F4 **Wisznia Mała** Pol.
175 L4 **Wisznice** Pol.
215 N1 **Witbank** S. Africa
212 C5 **Witbooisvlei** Namibia
214 E2 **Witdraai** S. Africa
151 N4 **Witham** Essex, England U.K.
151 M2 **Witham** r. England U.K.
233 L4 **Witherbee** NY U.S.A.
150 E6 **Witheridge** Devon, England U.K.
149 R6 **Withernsea** East Riding of Yorkshire, England U.K.
231 F10 **Withlacoochee** r. FL U.S.A.
231 F11 **Withlacoochee** r. FL U.S.A.
82 E2 **Witjira National Park** S.A. Austr.
215 N3 **Witkoppies** mt. S. Africa
174 F3 **Witkowo** Wielkopolskie Pol.
174 D2 **Witkowo** Zachodniopomorskie Pol.
215 J7 **Witkransnek** pass S. Africa
151 K5 **Witley** Surrey, England U.K.
164 H2 **Witmarsum** Neth.
215 J8 **Witmos** S. Africa
215 M1 **Witnek** S. Africa
151 J4 **Witney** Oxfordshire, England U.K.
174 C3 **Witnica** Lubuskie Pol.
174 C3 **Witnica** Zachodniopomorskie Pol.
175 H3 **Witonia** Pol.
174 F2 **Witosław** Pol.
214 I5 **Witput** S. Africa
215 P1 **Witrivier** S. Africa
156 H5 **Witry-lès-Reims** France
214 G4 **Witsand Nature Reserve** S. Africa
168 F1 **Wittdün** Ger.
214 G9 **Witteberg** mt. Eastern Cape S. Africa
215 M4 **Witteberg** mt. Free State S. Africa
215 L6 **Witteberg** mts S. Africa
214 E9 **Witteberge** mts S. Africa
157 N8 **Wittelsheim** France
169 D8 **Witten** Ger.
172 G7 **Wittenbach** Switz.
Wittenberg Ger. see **Lutherstadt Wittenberg**
226 E5 **Wittenberg** WI U.S.A.
170 E5 **Wittenberge** Ger.
170 D3 **Wittenburg** Ger.
170 D3 **Wittenförden** Ger.
170 H2 **Wittenhagen** Ger.
157 N8 **Wittenheim** France
86 E7 **Wittenoom** W.A. Austr.
Wittenoom Gorge W.A. Austr. see **Wittenoom**
168 I2 **Wittensee** l. Ger.
247 □8 **Witte Pan** salt l. Bonaire Neth. Antilles
151 L2 **Wittering** Peterborough, England U.K.
171 G9 **Wittgensdorf** Ger.
95 L2 **Witti, Banjaran** mts Malaysia
173 N5 **Wittibreut** Ger.
171 J8 **Wittichenau** Ger.
172 H2 **Wittighausen** Ger.
168 K5 **Wittingen** Ger.
173 I4 **Wittislingen** Ger.
172 B2 **Wittlich** Ger.
234 C7 **Wittman** MD U.S.A.
169 K6 **Wittmar** Ger.
168 E3 **Wittmund** Ger.
149 N4 **Witton Gilbert** Durham, England U.K.
170 H1 **Wittow** pen. Ger.
170 F4 **Wittstock** Ger.
211 D5 **Witu** Kenya
91 K7 **Witu Islands** P.N.G.
212 C4 **Witvlei** Namibia
215 L2 **Witwatersberg** mts S. Africa
215 K2 **Witwatersrand** mts S. Africa
169 I8 **Witzenhausen** Ger.
168 J3 **Witzhave** Ger.
170 E3 **Witzin** Ger.
168 G2 **Witzwort** Ger.
150 F5 **Wiveliscombe** Somerset, England U.K.
151 N4 **Wivenhoe** Essex, England U.K.
85 N9 **Wivenhoe, Lake** Qld Austr.
175 K1 **Wiżajny** Pol.
156 D2 **Wizernes** France
175 K2 **Wizna** Pol.
175 I3 **Wkra** r. Pol.
174 G3 **Władysławów** Pol.
143 O7 **Władysławowo** Pol.
174 D4 **Wleń** Pol.
175 H3 **Włocławek** Pol.
175 L4 **Włodawa** Pol.
175 L4 **Włodawka** r. Pol.
175 H5 **Włodowice** Pol.
174 F5 **Włodzienin** Pol.
175 H4 **Włodzimierzów** Pol.
174 E4 **Włoszakowice** Pol.
175 H5 **Włoszczowa** Pol.
170 E4 **Wöbbelin** Ger.
Wobkent Uzbek. see **Vobkent**
233 □O3 **Woburn** Que. Can.
151 K4 **Woburn** Bedfordshire, England U.K.
151 K3 **Woburn Sands** Milton Keynes, England U.K.
83 K7 **Wodonga** Vic. Austr.
175 J3 **Wodynie** Pol.
175 H4 **Wodzierady** Pol.
175 I5 **Wodzisław** Pol.
174 G5 **Wodzisław Śląski** Pol.
164 G4 **Woerden** Neth.
157 O6 **Wœrth** France
157 J5 **Wœvre, Forêt de** for. France
157 K5 **Woëvre, Plaine de la** plain France
164 H3 **Wognum** Neth.
208 F3 **Wohko** watercourse Sudan
190 E1 **Wohlen** Aargau Switz.
190 C2 **Wohlen** Bern Switz.
171 D8 **Wohlmirstedt** Ger.
263 A2 **Wohlthat Mountains** Antarctica
168 J3 **Wohltorf** Ger.
169 G9 **Wohra** r. Ger.
168 H2 **Wöhrden** Ger.
175 K4 **Wohyń** Pol.
108 B2 **Woinbo** Sichuan China
157 L5 **Woippy** France
175 J6 **Wojaszówka** Pol.
175 J5 **Wojciechowice** Pol.
175 K4 **Wojcieszków** Pol.
174 D5 **Wojcieszów** Pol.
174 G3 **Wójcin** Pol.
78 □3b **Woje Majuro** i. Majuro Marshall Is
Wōjjā atoll Marshall Is see **Wotje**
175 H5 **Wojkowice** Pol.
175 I6 **Wojnicz** Pol.
174 F2 **Wojnowo** Pol.
175 L5 **Wojsławice** Pol.
175 L5 **Wojsławka** r. Pol.
91 H8 **Wokam** i. Indon.
100 F5 **Woken He** r. China
117 O6 **Wokha** Nagaland India
151 K5 **Woking** Surrey, England U.K.
85 I7 **Wokingham** watercourse Qld Austr.
151 K5 **Wokingham** Wokingham, England U.K.
151 K5 **Wokingham** admin. div. England U.K.
83 M4 **Woko National Park** N.S.W. Austr.
170 H4 **Wokuhl** Ger.
175 H3 **Wola** Pol.
175 J4 **Wola Mysłowska** Pol.

X

Xiro *hill* Greece
Xirokampo Greece
Xiruá *r.* Brazil
Xisa *Yunnan* China *see* **Xichou**
Xishanzui *Nei Mongol* China
Xishuangbanna *reg. Yunnan* China
Xishuanghe *Shandong* China *see* **Kenli**
Xishui *Guizhou* China
Xishui *Hubei* China
Xistral, Serra do *mts* Spain
Xi Taijnar Hu *l. Qinghai* China
Xitieshan *Qinghai* China
Xitla Mex.
Xitole Guinea-Bissau
Xiucaiwan *Chongqing* China *see* **Fengdu**
Xiugu *Jiangxi* China *see* **Jinxi**
Xi Ujimqin Qi *Nei Mongol* China *see* **Bayan Ul Hot**
Xiuning *Anhui* China
Xiushan *Chongqing* China
Xiushan *Yunnan* China *see* **Tonghai**
Xiushui *Jiangxi* China
Xiu Shui *r.* China
Xiuwen *Guizhou* China
Xiuwu *Henan* China
Xiuyan *Liaoning* China
Xiuyan *Shaanxi* China *see* **Qingjian**
Xiuying *Hainan* China
Xiva Uzbek.
Xiwanzi *Hebei* China *see* **Chongli**
Xiwu *Qinghai* China
Xixabangma Feng *mt. Xizang* China
Xixia *Henan* China
Xixian *Henan* China
Xixian *Shanxi* China
Xixiang *Shaanxi* China
Xixiu *Guizhou* China *see* **Anshun**
Xixón Spain *see* **Gijón-Xixón**
Xiyang *Shanxi* China
Xiyang Dao *i.* China
Xiyang Jiang *r. Yunnan* China
Xiying *Gansu* China
Xizang *aut. reg.* China *see* **Xizang Zizhiqu**
Xizang Gaoyuan *plat. Xizang* China *see* **Qingzang Gaoyuan**
Xizang Zizhiqu *aut. reg.* China
Xizhong Dao *i.* China
Xızı Azer.
Xobando *Xizang* China
Xocalı Azer.
Xocavänd Azer.
Xochiapa Mex.
Xochiatiapan Mex.
Xochicalco *tourist site* Mex.
Xochimilco Mex.
Xochistlahuaca Mex.
Xodoto, Akrotirio *pt* Greece
Xoi *Xizang* China *see* **Qüxü**
Xo'jadavlat Uzbek.
Xo'japiryox tog'i *mt.* Uzbek.
Xo'jayli *Qoraqalpog'iston Respublikasi* Uzbek.
Xoka *Xizang* China
Xolobe S. Africa
Xol Qarabucaq Azer.
Xonacatlán Mex.
Xonobod Uzbek.
Xonqa Uzbek.
Xonrupt France *see* **Xonrupt-Longemer**
Xonrupt-Longemer France
Xonxa Dam S. Africa
Xo Qu *r. Sichuan* China
Xorazm *admin. div.* Uzbek.
Xorkol *Xinjiang* China
Xortang *Xinjiang* China
Xosrov Azer.
Xove Spain
Xovos Uzbek.
Xuancheng *Anhui* China
Xuan'en *Hubei* China
Xuanhan *Sichuan* China
Xuanhua *Hebei* China
Xuân Lôc Vietnam
Xuanwei *Yunnan* China
Xuanzhou *Anhui* China *see* **Xuancheng**
Xubín Spain
Xuchang *Henan* China
Xuchang *Henan* China
Xucheng *Guangdong* China *see* **Xuwen**
Xudat Azer.
Xuddur Somalia
Xudun Somalia
Xueba *Xizang* China
Xuefeng *Fujian* China *see* **Mingxi**
Xuefeng Shan *mts* China
Xuehua Shan *hill Shanxi* China
Xuejiawan *Nei Mongol* China
Xue Shan *mts Yunnan* China
Xugin Gol *r. Qinghai* China
Xugou *Jiangsu* China
Xugui *Nei Mongol* China
Xugui *Qinghai* China
Xuguit Qi *Nei Mongol* China *see* **Yakeshi**
Xujiang *Jiangxi* China *see* **Guangchang**
Xulun Hobot Qagan Qi *Nei Mongol* China *see* **Qagan Nur**
Xulun Hoh Qi *Nei Mongol* China *see* **Dund Hot**
Xundian *Yunnan* China
Xungba *Xizang* China *see* **Xangdoring**
Xungmai *Xizang* China
Xung Qu *r. Xizang* China
Xungru *Xizang* China
Xunhe *Heilong.* China
Xun He *r.* China
Xun He *r.* China
Xunhua *Qinghai* China
Xun Jiang *r.* China
Xunke *Heilong.* China
Xunqueira de Ambía Spain
Xunwu *Jiangxi* China
Xunxian *Henan* China
Xunyang *Shaanxi* China
Xunyi *Shaanxi* China
Xupu *Hunan* China
Xurgan *Qinghai* China
Xuru Co *salt l.* China
Xushui *Hebei* China
Xuwen *Guangdong* China
Xuyang *Sichuan* China *see* **Rongxian**
Xuyi *Jiangsu* China
Xuyong *Sichuan* China
Xuzhou *Jiangsu* China
Xylagani Greece
Xylokastro Greece
Xyloupoli Greece

Yaamba *Qld* Austr.
Ya'an *Sichuan* China
Yaapeet *Vic.* Austr.
Yaba *Maluku* Indon.
Yabanabat Turkey *see* **Kızılcahamam**
Yabassi Cameroon
Yabbenohr *i. Kwajalein* Marshall Is
Yabēlo Eth.
Yabēlo Wildlife Sanctuary *nature res.* Eth.
Yabia Dem. Rep. Congo
Yablanitsa Bulg.
Yablanovo Bulg.
Yablochnoye Rus. Fed.
Yablonovets Rus. Fed.
Yablonovskiy Rus. Fed.
Yablonovyy Khrebet *mts* Rus. Fed.
Yabluniv Ukr.
137 K4 **Yablunivka** Ukr.
207 G3 **Yabo** Nigeria
106 H7 **Yabrai Shan** *mts* China
106 H7 **Yabrai Yanchang** *Nei Mongol* China
125 I4 **Yabrīn** *reg.* Saudi Arabia
128 E5 **Yabrūd** Syria
104 A5 **Yabu** Japan
247 □1 **Yabucoa** Puerto Rico
247 □1 **Yabucoa, Puerto** *b.* Puerto Rico
105 L1 **Yabuki** Japan
100 F6 **Yabuli** *Heilong.* China
136 H3 **Yabunets'** Ukr.
250 C5 **Yabuyanos** Peru
105 J3 **Yabuzukahon** Japan
Yacha *Hainan* China *see* **Baisha**
108 G9 **Yacheng** *Hainan* China
108 F5 **Yachi He** *r.* China
105 L4 **Yachimata** Japan
105 L4 **Yachiyo** *Chiba* Japan
105 K3 **Yachiyo** *Ibaraki* Japan
255 A8 **Yaciretá, Isla** *i.* Para.
83 K7 **Yackandandah** *Vic.* Austr.
252 E5 **Yacuiba** Bol.
250 E3 **Yacurai** Venez.
258 F2 **Yacyretá Apipé, Embalse** *resr* Arg./Para.
208 B3 **Yadé, Massif du** *mts* C.A.R.
114 E4 **Yadgir** *Karnataka* India
114 E5 **Yadiki** *Andhra Prad.* India
231 G8 **Yadkin** *r. NC* U.S.A.
231 G7 **Yadkinville** *NC* U.S.A.
111 I13 **Yadong** *Xizang* China
134 I5 **Yadrin** Rus. Fed.
79 □7 **Yadua** *i.* Fiji
102 □A22 **Yaeyama-rettō** *is* Japan
Yafa Israel *see* **Tel Aviv-Yafo**
202 B1 **Yafran** Libya
206 E4 **Yagaba** Ghana
Yagaing *state* Myanmar *see* **Arakan**
102 □1 **Yagaji-jima** *i. Okinawa* Japan
103 G14 **Yagami** Japan
106 H6 **Yagan** *Nei Mongol* China
199 I3 **Yağcılı** Turkey
Yağda Turkey *see* **Erdemli**
264 E9 **Yaghan Basin** *sea feature* S. Atlantic Ocean
104 C5 **Yagi** Japan
102 S2 **Yagishiri-tō** *i.* Japan
128 D1 **Yağızlar** Turkey
106 F8 **Yagkêng** *Qinghai* China
129 E5 **Yağlıca Dağı** *mt.* Turkey
134 E3 **Yaglyayarvi** Rus. Fed.
122 F2 **Yagman** Turkm.
129 E6 **Yağmurlu** *r.* Turkey
139 U3 **Yagnitsa** Rus. Fed.
244 B4 **Yago** Mex.
197 N8 **Yagoda** Bulg.
120 A2 **Yagodnaya Polyana** Rus. Fed.
139 S8 **Yagodnoye** *Kaluzhskaya Oblast'* Rus. Fed.
131 P3 **Yagodnoye** *Magadanskaya Oblast'* Rus. Fed.
100 K3 **Yagodnyy** Rus. Fed.
Yagotin Ukr. *see* **Yahotyn**
207 I4 **Yagoua** Cameroon
111 F11 **Yagra** *Xizang* China
106 D9 **Yagradagzê Shan** *mt. Qinghai* China
246 D2 **Yaguajay** Cuba
Yaguarón *r.* Brazil/Uru. *see* **Jaguarão**
250 D5 **Yaguas** *r.* Peru
97 E11 **Yaha** Thai.
104 E6 **Yahagi-gawa** *r.* Japan
208 D4 **Yahila** Dem. Rep. Congo
222 G5 **Yahk** *B.C.* Can.
136 I6 **Yahorlyk** *r.* Ukr.
137 K3 **Yahotyn** Ukr.
244 E4 **Yahualica** Mex.
208 D4 **Yahuma** Dem. Rep. Congo
118 D2 **Yahyalı** Turkey
123 M6 **Yahya Wana** Afgh.
97 D8 **Yai, Khao** *mt.* Thai.
105 K2 **Yaita** Japan
216 □3c **Yaiza** *Lanzarote* Canary Is
105 H6 **Yaizu** Japan
108 C3 **Yajiang** *Sichuan* China
208 C3 **Yaka** C.A.R.
128 E2 **Yakacık** Turkey
128 D2 **Yakapınar** Turkey
110 H7 **Yakatograk** *Xinjiang* China
123 K5 **Yak Dar** Afgh.
104 G3 **Yake-dake** *vol.* Japan
107 Q2 **Yakeshi** *Nei Mongol* China
122 G4 **Yakhab** *waterhole* Iran
123 K6 **Yakhehal** Afgh.
136 F4 **Yakhivtsi** Ukr.
137 M3 **Yakhnyky** Ukr.
139 U5 **Yakhroma** Rus. Fed.
238 D3 **Yakima** *WA* U.S.A.
238 E3 **Yakima** *r. WA* U.S.A.
238 D3 **Yakima Indian Reservation** *res. WA* U.S.A.
122 E5 **Yakinish** Iran
121 L8 **Yakkabog'** Uzbek.
123 J7 **Yakmach** Pak.
206 E3 **Yako** Burkina
222 B3 **Yakobi Island** *AK* U.S.A.
208 D3 **Yakoma** Dem. Rep. Congo
197 L8 **Yakoruda** Bulg.
137 P4 **Yakovenkove** Ukr.
100 H6 **Yakovlevka** Rus. Fed.
137 P3 **Yakovlevo** Rus. Fed.
134 K4 **Yakskur-Bod'ya** Rus. Fed.
102 R4 **Yakumo** Japan
104 A5 **Yakuno** Japan
102 □H16 **Yaku-shima** *i.* Japan
220 E4 **Yakutat** *AK* U.S.A.
220 D4 **Yakutat Bay** *AK* U.S.A.
131 N3 **Yakutsk** Rus. Fed.
137 O7 **Yakymivka** Ukr.
206 E4 **Yala** Ghana
210 B4 **Yala** Kenya
114 G9 **Yala** Sri Lanka
97 E11 **Yala** Thai.
111 H12 **Yalai** *Xizang* China
108 C3 **Yalakan** *Sichuan* China
199 K2 **Yalakdere** Turkey
129 J4 **Yalama** Azer.
128 A2 **Yalan Dünya Mağarası** *tourist site* Turkey
82 C4 **Yalata Aboriginal Lands** *res. S.A.* Austr.
81 G10 **Yaldhurst** *South I.* N.Z.
222 F5 **Yale** *B.C.* Can.
227 L6 **Yale** *MI* U.S.A.
208 E4 **Yaleko** Dem. Rep. Congo
206 E3 **Yalgo** Burkina
87 D10 **Yalgoo** *W.A.* Austr.
199 I5 **Yalıkavak** Turkey
197 Q9 **Yalıköy** Turkey
129 C6 **Yalınca** Turkey
208 D3 **Yalinga** C.A.R.
138 M8 **Yalizava** Belarus
243 O7 **Yalkubul, Punta** *pt* Mex.
246 □ **Yallahs** Jamaica
85 J8 **Yalleroi** *Qld* Austr.
87 C12 **Yallingup** *W.A.* Austr.
206 E3 **Yallo** Burkina
83 K8 **Yallourn** *Vic.* Austr.
129 D5 **Yalnızçam Dağları** *mts* Turkey
237 J9 **Yalobusha** *r. MS* U.S.A.
Yalogo Burkina *see* **Yalgo**
208 C3 **Yaloké** C.A.R.
108 C5 **Yalong Jiang** *r. Sichuan* China
199 K2 **Yalova** Turkey
197 R10 **Yalova** *prov.* Turkey
Yaloven' Moldova *see* **Ialoveni**
84 D7 **Yalpirakinu Aboriginal Land** *res. N.T.* Austr.
136 H8 **Yalpuh, Ozero** *l.* Ukr.
Yalpukh *r.* Moldova *see* **Ialpug**
137 Q7 **Yalta** *Donets'ka Oblast'* Ukr.
137 N9 **Yalta** *Respublika Krym* Ukr.
137 N9 **Yaltins'kyy Zapovidnyk** *nature res.* Ukr.
136 G5 **Yaltushkiv** Ukr.
107 R3 **Yalu He** *r.* China
101 D8 **Yalu Jiang** *r.* China/N. Korea
208 D5 **Yalusaka** Dem. Rep. Congo
130 H4 **Yalutorovsk** Rus. Fed.
199 M4 **Yalvaç** Turkey
124 G7 **Yām** *reg.* Saudi Arabia
Yama Ukr. *see* **Sivers'k**
105 M4 **Yamada** *Chiba* Japan
102 S7 **Yamada** *Iwate* Japan
104 F2 **Yamada** *Toyama* Japan
103 H13 **Yamaga** Japan
105 L2 **Yamagata** *Ibaraki* Japan
102 S6 **Yamagata** *Iwate* Japan
105 G3 **Yamagata** *Nagano* Japan
102 R8 **Yamagata** *Yamagata* Japan
102 Q8 **Yamagata** *pref.* Japan
104 G4 **Yamaguchi** *Nagano* Japan
103 I12 **Yamaguchi** *Yamaguchi* Japan
103 I12 **Yamaguchi** *pref.* Japan
105 J5 **Yamakita** Japan
130 H2 **Yamal, Poluostrov** *pen.* Rus. Fed.
100 I2 **Yam Alin', Khrebet** *mts* Rus. Fed.
Yamal Peninsula Rus. Fed. *see* **Yamal, Poluostrov**
104 D3 **Yamanaka** Japan
105 I5 **Yamanaka-ko** *l.* Japan
105 I4 **Yamanashi** Japan
105 H4 **Yamanashi** *pref.* Japan
85 J5 **Yamanie Falls National Park** *Qld* Austr.
Yamankhalinka Kazakh. *see* **Makhambet**
105 I5 **Yamanokako** Japan
105 H2 **Yamanouchi** Japan
106 C6 **Yamansu** *Xinjiang* China
104 F5 **Yamaoka** Japan
107 L1 **Yamarovka** Rus. Fed.
103 L11 **Yamasaki** Japan
104 C6 **Yamashiro** Japan
104 E4 **Yamato** *Gifu* Japan
105 L3 **Yamato** *Ibaraki* Japan
105 J5 **Yamato** *Kanagawa* Japan
102 □G18 **Yamato** *Nansei-shotō* Japan
105 I1 **Yamato** *Niigata* Japan
104 C6 **Yamato-Aogaki Kokutei-kōen** *park* Japan
104 C6 **Yamato-Kōriyama** Japan
104 C6 **Yamatotakada** Japan
105 L2 **Yamatsuri** Japan
104 D6 **Yamazoe** Japan
83 N3 **Yamba** *N.S.W.* Austr.
83 I8 **Yambacoona** *Tas.* Austr.
223 I1 **Yamba Lake** *N.W.T.* Can.
84 C3 **Yambarran Range** *hills N.T.* Austr.
208 B2 **Yamba Tchangsou** Chad
206 B4 **Yambéring** Guinea
250 D4 **Yambi, Mesa de** *hills* Col.
208 F3 **Yambio** Sudan
197 O8 **Yambol** Bulg.
250 B6 **Yambrasbamba** Peru
91 H8 **Yamdena** *i.* Indon.
103 H13 **Yame** Japan
96 C4 **Yamethin** Myanmar
92 C1 **Y'ami** *i.* Phil.
105 L2 **Yamizo-san** *mt.* Japan
114 D4 **Yamkanmardi** *Karnataka* India
Yamkhad Syria *see* **Ḥalab**
138 M4 **Yamkino** Rus. Fed.
138 L3 **Yamm** Rus. Fed.
85 H9 **Yamma Yamma, Lake** *salt flat Qld* Austr.
137 O3 **Yamne** Ukr.
206 D5 **Yamoussoukro** Côte d'Ivoire
137 K5 **Yampil'** *Cherkas'ka Oblast'* Ukr.
136 F4 **Yampil'** *Khmel'nyts'ka Oblast'* Ukr.
137 M2 **Yampil'** *Sums'ka Oblast'* Ukr.
136 H5 **Yampil'** *Vinnyts'ka Oblast'* Ukr.
Yampol' *Cherkas'ka Oblast'* Ukr. *see* **Yampil'**
Yampol' *Khmel'nyts'ka Oblast'* Ukr. *see* **Yampil'**
Yampol' *Sums'ka Oblast'* Ukr. *see* **Yampil'**
Yampol' *Vinnyts'ka Oblast'* Ukr. *see* **Yampil'**
116 H7 **Yamuna** *r.* India
116 F4 **Yamunanagar** *Haryana* India
111 J12 **Yamzho Yumco** *l.* China
207 H4 **Yana** Nigeria
131 O2 **Yana** *r.* Rus. Fed.
82 H7 **Yanac** *Vic.* Austr.
252 B2 **Yanachaga-Chemillen, Parque Nacional** *nat. park* Peru
103 K13 **Yanadani** Japan
102 R9 **Yanagawa** Japan
102 □1 **Yanaha-jima** *i. Okinawa* Japan
103 J13 **Yanai** Japan
114 H4 **Yanam** *Pondicherry* India
107 K8 **Yan'an** *Shaanxi* China
252 C3 **Yanaoca** Peru
Yanaon *Pondicherry* India *see* **Yanam**
134 K4 **Yanaul** Rus. Fed.
139 N6 **Yanavichy** Belarus
250 C5 **Yanayacu** Peru
108 C5 **Yanbian** *Yunnan* China
124 C3 **Yanbu, Sharm** *b.* Saudi Arabia
124 D3 **Yanbu' al Baḩr** Saudi Arabia
124 D3 **Yanbu' an Nakhl** *reg.* Saudi Arabia
231 H7 **Yanceyville** *NC* U.S.A.
107 L8 **Yanchang** *Shaanxi* China
109 M2 **Yancheng** *Jiangsu* China
Yancheng *Shandong* China *see* **Qihe**
Yancheng *Sichuan* China *see* **Jingyan**
87 C11 **Yanchep** *W.A.* Austr.
107 J8 **Yanchi** *Ningxia* China
106 D5 **Yanchi** *Xinjiang* China
110 H3 **Yanchi** *Xinjiang* China
110 L7 **Yanchiwan** *Gansu* China
107 L8 **Yanchuan** *Shaanxi* China
137 P6 **Yanchur** *r.* Ukr.
83 K6 **Yanco** *N.S.W.* Austr.
83 J6 **Yanco Creek** *r. N.S.W.* Austr.
83 H4 **Yanco Glen** *N.S.W.* Austr.
83 J4 **Yanda** *watercourse N.S.W.* Austr.
82 H4 **Yandama Creek** *watercourse S.A.* Austr.
109 M5 **Yandang Shan** *mts* China
Yandao *Sichuan* China *see* **Yingjing**
86 E6 **Yandeyarra Aboriginal Reserve** *W.A.* Austr.
86 E7 **Yandicoogina Mine** *W.A.* Austr.
87 E9 **Yandil** *W.A.* Austr.
85 N9 **Yandina** *Qld* Austr.
78 □6 **Yandina** Solomon Is
208 C5 **Yandja** Dem. Rep. Congo
96 B6 **Yandoon** Myanmar
Yandua *i.* Fiji *see* **Yadua**
106 D5 **Yandun** *Xinjiang* China
139 Q1 **Yanega** Rus. Fed.
206 C4 **Yanfolila** Mali
208 D3 **Yangalia** C.A.R.
208 E4 **Yangambi** Dem. Rep. Congo
111 L11 **Ya'ngamdo** *Xizang* China
111 L11 **Ya'ngamdo** *Xizang* China
206 D3 **Yangasso** Mali
111 J11 **Yangbajain** *Xizang* China
108 B6 **Yangbi** *Yunnan* China
Yangcheng *Guangdong* China *see* **Yangshan**
107 M9 **Yangcheng** *Shanxi* China
Yangchuan *Guizhou* China *see* **Suiyang**
109 H7 **Yangchun** *Guangdong* China
109 J7 **Yangcun** *Guangdong* China
Yangcun *Tianjin* China *see* **Wuqing**
110 I7 **Yangdaxkak** *Xinjiang* China
101 E9 **Yangdok** N. Korea
109 H8 **Yangdong** *Guangdong* China
107 M6 **Yanggao** *Shanxi* China
107 N8 **Yanggu** *Shandong* China
Yanghe *Ningxia* China *see* **Yongning**
107 N6 **Yang He** *r.* China
111 G9 **Yang Hu** *l. Xizang* China
120 I7 **Yangiariq** Uzbek.
Yangibazar Kyrg. *see* **Jangy-Bazar**
111 D9 **Yangi Davan** *pass* Aksai Chin/China
120 K8 **Yangi Nishon** Uzbek.
123 M3 **Yangi Qal'eh** Afgh.
121 L7 **Yangiqishloq** Uzbek.
120 K7 **Yangirabot** Uzbek.
121 M7 **Yangiyo'l** Uzbek.
107 K8 **Yangjialing** *Shaanxi* China
109 H8 **Yangjiang** *Guangdong* China
107 P8 **Yangjiaogou** *Shandong* China
96 C6 **Yangôn** Myanmar
115 O4 **Yangôn** *admin. div.* Myanmar
109 H3 **Yangping** *Hubei* China
107 M8 **Yangquan** *Shanxi* China
107 L8 **Yangquangu** *Shanxi* China
109 I6 **Yangshan** *Guangdong* China
108 H6 **Yangshuo** *Guangxi* China
97 I8 **Yang Sin, Chư** *mt.* Vietnam
96 F6 **Yang Talat** Thai.
108 C6 **Yangtouyan** *Yunnan* China
Yangtze *r. Qinghai* China *see* **Tongtian He**
109 M3 **Yangtze** *r.* China
alt. **Chang Jiang,**
alt. **Jinsha Jiang,**
alt. **Tongtian He,**
long **Yangtze Kiang**
Yangtze, Mouth of the China *see* **Changjiang Kou**
108 E1 **Yanguan** *Gansu* China
183 P4 **Yanguas** Spain
210 D2 **Yangudi Rassa National Park** Eth.
107 P9 **Yangweigang** *Jiangsu* China
109 H8 **Yangxi** *Guangdong* China
108 F2 **Yangxian** *Shaanxi* China
101 F9 **Yangyang** S. Korea
107 N6 **Yangyuan** *Hebei* China
109 L2 **Yangzhou** *Jiangsu* China
Yangzhou *Shaanxi* China *see* **Yangxian**
108 G4 **Yanhe** *Guizhou* China
107 L8 **Yan He** *r.* China
110 I5 **Yanhu** *Xinjiang* China
111 F10 **Yanhu** *Xizang* China
82 E5 **Yaninee, Lake** *salt flat S.A.* Austr.
134 F3 **Yanishpole** Rus. Fed.
140 U5 **Yanis"yarvi, Ozero** *l.* Rus. Fed.
100 F7 **Yanji** *Jilin* China
107 N9 **Yanjin** *Henan* China
108 E4 **Yanjin** *Yunnan* China
Yanjing *Sichuan* China *see* **Yanyuan**
108 B4 **Yanjing** *Xizang* China
Yanjing *Yunnan* China *see* **Yanjin**
207 H4 **Yankara National Park** Nigeria
138 L6 **Yankavichy** Belarus
Yankou *Sichuan* China *see* **Wusheng**
236 G4 **Yankton** *SD* U.S.A.
236 F4 **Yankton Indian Reservation** *res. SD* U.S.A.
129 D1 **Yankul'** Rus. Fed.
129 D1 **Yankul'** *r.* Rus. Fed.
107 N9 **Yanling** *Henan* China
109 I5 **Yanling** *Hunan* China
Yannina Greece *see* **Ioannina**
131 P2 **Yano-Indigirskaya Nizmennost'** *lowland* Rus. Fed.
139 P7 **Yanovo** Rus. Fed.
130 J3 **Yanov-Stan** Rus. Fed.
114 G8 **Yan Oya** *r.* Sri Lanka
110 H5 **Yanqi** *Xinjiang* China
107 N6 **Yanqing** *Beijing* China
125 M4 **Yanqul** Oman
87 C7 **Yanrey** *r. W.A.* Austr.
107 O7 **Yanshan** *Hebei* China
109 K4 **Yanshan** *Jiangxi* China
108 E7 **Yanshan** *Yunnan* China
107 O6 **Yan Shan** *mts* China
107 M9 **Yanshi** *Henan* China
111 K10 **Yanshiping** *Qinghai* China
100 F6 **Yanshou** *Heilong.* China
131 O2 **Yanskiy Zaliv** *g.* Rus. Fed.
83 J3 **Yantabulla** *N.S.W.* Austr.
122 C2 **Yantagh** Iran
107 Q8 **Yantai** *Shandong* China
259 B6 **Yántales, Cerro** *mt.* Chile
137 N8 **Yantarne** Ukr.
138 C7 **Yantarnyy** Rus. Fed.
235 K1 **Yantic** *r. CT* U.S.A.
108 E3 **Yanting** *Sichuan* China
100 E7 **Yantongshan** *Jilin* China
109 M4 **Yantou** *Zhejiang* China
197 N7 **Yantra** *r.* Bulg.
79 □7a **Yanuca** *i.* Fiji
124 F4 **Yanūfī, Jabal al** *hill* Saudi Arabia
Yanutha *i.* Fiji *see* **Yanuca**
108 B5 **Yanwa** *Yunnan* China
108 H4 **Yanxi** *Hunan* China
Yany-Kurgan Kazakh. *see* **Zhanakorgan**
108 C5 **Yanyuan** *Sichuan* China
107 O9 **Yanzhou** *Shandong* China
104 C6 **Yao** Japan
108 C6 **Yao'an** *Yunnan* China
107 K8 **Yaodian** *Shaanxi* China
Yaodu *Anhui* China *see* **Dongzhi**
Yaojie *Gansu* China *see* **Honggu**
109 K4 **Yaoli** *Jiangxi* China
106 E7 **Yaoquanzi** *Gansu* China
104 F5 **Yaotsu** Japan
207 H6 **Yaoundé** Cameroon
Yaoxian *Shaanxi* China *see* **Yaozhou**
97 D10 **Yao Yai, Ko** *i.* Thai.
107 L7 **Yaozhen** *Shaanxi* China
107 K9 **Yaozhou** *Shaanxi* China
91 I5 **Yap** *i.* Micronesia
250 E4 **Yapacana, Parque Nacional** *nat. park* Venez.
252 D3 **Yapacani** *r.* Bol.
206 E4 **Yapei** Ghana
91 I7 **Yapen** *i. Papua* Indon.
91 I7 **Yapen, Selat** *sea chan. Papua* Indon.
258 F3 **Yapeyú** Arg.
235 J3 **Yaphank** *NY* U.S.A.
85 H5 **Yappar** *r. Qld* Austr.
151 K6 **Yapton** *West Sussex, England* U.K.
266 E5 **Yap Trench** *sea feature* N. Pacific Ocean
251 G4 **Yapukarri** Guyana
87 I9 **Yapuparra Aboriginal Reserve** *W.A.* Austr.
242 D4 **Yaqui** *r.* Mex.
134 K4 **Yar** Rus. Fed.
246 E3 **Yara** Cuba
250 D2 **Yaracal** Venez.
250 D2 **Yaracuy** *state* Venez.
Yaradzha Turkm. *see* **Ýarajy**
122 G2 **Ýarajy** Turkm.
85 J8 **Yaraka** *Qld* Austr.
Yarangüme Turkey *see* **Tavas**
134 I4 **Yaransk** Rus. Fed.
Yardan Uzbek. *see* **Yordon**
82 E5 **Yardea** *S.A.* Austr.
199 L6 **Yardımcı Burnu** *pt* Turkey
129 J7 **Yardımlı** Azer.
234 F4 **Yardley** *PA* U.S.A.
111 J12 **Yardoi** *Xizang* China
234 F4 **Yardville** *NJ* U.S.A.
Yardymly Azer. *see* **Yardımlı**
151 P3 **Yare** *r. England* U.K.
134 K3 **Yarega** Rus. Fed.
136 D5 **Yaremcha** Ukr.
77 G2 **Yaren** Nauru
134 J3 **Yarenga** *r.* Rus. Fed.
245 K8 **Yareni** Mex.
134 J3 **Yarensk** Rus. Fed.
137 M4 **Yares'ky** Ukr.
Yargara Moldova *see* **Iargara**
250 C5 **Yari** *r.* Col.
104 G3 **Yariga-take** *mt.* Japan
124 G8 **Yarīm** Yemen
Yarımca Turkey *see* **Körfez**
84 G6 **Yaringa** *watercourse Qld* Austr.
251 H4 **Yaripo** Brazil
207 G3 **Yaris** *well* Niger
247 I8 **Yaritagua** Venez.
Yarkand *Xinjiang* China *see* **Shache**
Yarkant *Xinjiang* China *see* **Shache**
111 D7 **Yarkant He** *r.* China
227 R5 **Yarker** *Ont.* Can.
123 O3 **Yarkhun** *r.* Pak.
87 K11 **Yarle Lakes** *salt flat S.A.* Austr.
197 L8 **Yarlovo** Bulg.
111 L12 **Yarlung Zangbo** *r.* China
alt. **Dihang (India),**
alt. **Jamuna (Bangladesh),**
conv. **Brahmaputra**
149 O4 **Yarm** *Stockton-on-Tees, England* U.K.
136 F4 **Yarmolyntsi** Ukr.
225 H5 **Yarmouth** *N.S.* Can.
151 J6 **Yarmouth** *Isle of Wight, England* U.K.
Yarmouth *Norfolk, England* U.K. *see* **Great Yarmouth**
233 □O5 **Yarmouth** *ME* U.S.A.
128 D6 **Yarmuk** *r.* Asia
241 T7 **Yarnell** *AZ* U.S.A.
151 J4 **Yarnton** *Oxfordshire, England* U.K.
139 X9 **Yarok** Rus. Fed.
139 N6 **Yaromina** Belarus
137 M3 **Yaroshivka** Ukr.
137 M2 **Yaroslavets'** Ukr.
139 R1 **Yaroslavichi** Rus. Fed.
139 W4 **Yaroslavl'** Rus. Fed.
Yaroslavl Oblast *admin. div.* Rus. Fed. *see* **Yaroslavskaya Oblast'**
129 B1 **Yaroslavskaya** Rus. Fed.
139 W4 **Yaroslavskaya Oblast'** *admin. div.* Rus. Fed.
100 H6 **Yaroslavskiy** Rus. Fed.
85 J4 **Yarrabah Aboriginal Reserve** *Qld* Austr.
85 I3 **Yarraden** *Qld* Austr.
83 J7 **Yarra Junction** *Vic.* Austr.
84 C4 **Yarralin Aboriginal Land** *res. N.T.* Austr.
86 C6 **Yarraloola** *W.A.* Austr.
83 K8 **Yarram** *Vic.* Austr.
85 M9 **Yarraman** *Qld* Austr.
83 J7 **Yarrawonga** *Vic.* Austr.
87 C10 **Yarra Yarra Lakes** *salt flat W.A.* Austr.
86 F6 **Yarrie** *W.A.* Austr.
85 J9 **Yarronvale** *Qld* Austr.
85 J6 **Yarrowmere** *Qld* Austr.
117 N5 **Yartö Tra La** *pass Xizang* China
130 J3 **Yartsevo** *Krasnoyarskiy Kray* Rus. Fed.
139 P6 **Yartsevo** *Smolenskaya Oblast'* Rus. Fed.
111 H12 **Yaru** *r.* China
250 C3 **Yarumal** Col.
108 B3 **Yarwa** *Sichuan* China
129 H2 **Yaryk-Aul** Rus. Fed.
108 A4 **Yarzhong** *Xizang* China
Yaş Romania *see* **Iaşi**
209 D5 **Yasa** Dem. Rep. Congo
115 J1 **Yasai** *r. W. Bengal* India
104 B4 **Yasaka** *Kyōto* Japan
105 G3 **Yasaka** *Nagano* Japan
105 L3 **Yasato** Japan
79 □7 **Yasawa** *i.* Fiji
79 □7 **Yasawa Group** *is* Fiji
136 D5 **Yasen'** Ukr.
137 R7 **Yaseni** *r.* Rus. Fed.
197 O7 **Yasenkovo** Bulg.
135 G7 **Yasenskaya** Rus. Fed.
135 H7 **Yashalta** Rus. Fed.
207 G3 **Yashi** Nigeria
207 F4 **Yashikera** Nigeria
123 O3 **Yashilkŭl** *l.* Tajik.
102 R7 **Yashima** Japan
103 J13 **Ya-shima** *i.* Japan
105 H2 **Yashira** Japan
104 A6 **Yashiro** Japan
103 J13 **Yashiro-jima** *i.* Japan
135 K5 **Yashkino** Rus. Fed.
135 I7 **Yashkul'** Rus. Fed.
116 D1 **Yasin** Jammu and Kashmir
Yasinovataya Ukr. *see* **Yasynuvata**
136 D5 **Yasinya** Ukr.
138 K9 **Yaskavichy** Belarus
129 K5 **Yaşma** Azer.
129 K5 **Yaşma Adası** *i.* Azer.
197 P8 **Yasna Polyana** Bulg.
139 U7 **Yasnogorsk** Rus. Fed.
137 Q5 **Yasnohirka** Ukr.
136 J3 **Yasnohorodka** Ukr.
100 F2 **Yasnyy** *Amurskaya Oblast'* Rus. Fed.
120 H2 **Yasnyy** *Orenburgskaya Oblast'* Rus. Fed.
96 G7 **Yasothon** Thai.
83 L6 **Yass** *N.S.W.* Austr.
83 L6 **Yass** *r. N.S.W.* Austr.
Yassı Burnu *c.* Cyprus *see* **Plakoti, Cape**
199 K5 **Yassıhüyük** Turkey
139 N4 **Yasski** Rus. Fed.
129 C6 **Yastıktepe** Turkey
137 Q2 **Yastrebovka** Rus. Fed.
137 N2 **Yastrubyne** Ukr.
104 D5 **Yasu** Japan
103 K13 **Yasuda** Japan
103 K11 **Yasugi** Japan
122 D6 **Yāsūj** Iran
250 C5 **Yasuní, Parque Nacional** *nat. park* Ecuador
105 G5 **Yasuoka** Japan
77 G3 **Yasur** *vol.* Vanuatu
105 H1 **Yasuzuka** Japan
136 F1 **Yasyel'da** *r.* Belarus
137 Q5 **Yasynuvata** Ukr.
207 I1 **Yat** *well* Niger
252 D2 **Yata** *r.* Bol.
208 D2 **Yata** *r.* C.A.R.
199 J5 **Yatağan** Turkey
207 F3 **Yatakala** Niger
208 D2 **Yata-Ngaya, Réserve de Faune de la** *nature res.* C.A.R.
211 C5 **Yata Plateau** Kenya
78 □5 **Yaté** New Caledonia
150 H4 **Yate** *South Gloucestershire, England* U.K.
151 K5 **Yateley** *Hampshire, England* U.K.
222 H2 **Yates** *r. Alta/N.W.T.* Can.
237 H7 **Yates Center** *KS* U.S.A.
223 L2 **Yathkyed Lake** *Nunavut* Can.
83 J5 **Yathong Nature Reserve** *N.S.W.* Austr.
245 I5 **Yatipan** Mex.
208 E4 **Yatolema** Dem. Rep. Congo
104 E5 **Yatomi** Japan
Yatou *Shandong* China *see* **Rongcheng**
187 D9 **Yatova** Spain
136 J5 **Yatran'** *r.* Ukr.
105 H4 **Yatsuga-take** *vol.* Japan
105 H3 **Yatsuga-take-Chūshin-kōgen Kokutei-kōen** *park* Japan
104 F2 **Yatsuo** Japan
103 H14 **Yatsushiro** Japan
103 H14 **Yatsushiro-kai** *b.* Japan
128 D7 **Yaṭṭa** West Bank
150 G5 **Yatton** *North Somerset, England* U.K.
252 B3 **Yauca** Peru
252 B3 **Yauca** *r.* Peru
247 □1 **Yauco** Puerto Rico
252 A2 **Yauli** Peru
250 D5 **Yauna Maloca** Col.
252 C3 **Yauri** Peru
252 B3 **Yauricocha** Peru
245 H7 **Yautepec** *Morelos* Mex.
245 K9 **Yautepec** *Oaxaca* Mex.
109 □J7 **Yau Tong** *b. H.K.* China
252 B3 **Yauyos** Peru
242 □P11 **Yauyupe** Hond.
Yavan Tajik. *see* **Yovon**
250 D6 **Yavari** *r.* Brazil/Peru
alt. **Javari**
242 E4 **Yávaros** Mex.
116 G9 **Yavatmal** *Mahar.* India
252 B3 **Yavero** *r.* Peru
251 E3 **Yaví, Cerro** *mt.* Venez.
137 L6 **Yavkyne** Ukr.
121 M1 **Yavlenka** Kazakh.
175 L6 **Yavora** Ukr.
136 D5 **Yavoriv** *Ivano-Frankivs'ka Oblast'* Ukr.
136 C4 **Yavoriv** *L'vivs'ka Oblast'* Ukr.
140 U2 **Yavr** *r.* Fin./Rus. Fed.
128 F2 **Yavuzlu** Turkey
104 C6 **Yawata** Japan
103 J13 **Yawatahama** Japan
111 F8 **Yawatongguz He** *r.* China
111 F8 **Yawatongguzlangar** *Xinjiang* China
96 B4 **Yaw Chaung** *r.* Myanmar
96 C4 **Yawng-hwe** Myanmar
243 N9 **Yaxchilan** *tourist site* Guat.
Yaxian *Hainan* China *see* **Sanya**
151 L2 **Yaxley** *Cambridgeshire, England* U.K.
129 C7 **Yaygın** Turkey
129 A6 **Yaylabaşı** Turkey
128 E3 **Yayladağı** Turkey
129 B6 **Yayladere** Turkey
129 D6 **Yayladüzü** Turkey
134 L4 **Yayva** Rus. Fed.
96 B3 **Yazagyo** Myanmar
122 F6 **Yazd** Iran
122 F6 **Yazd** *prov.* Iran
122 I5 **Yazdān** Iran
122 E6 **Yazd-e Khvāst** Iran
Yazgulemskiy Khrebet *mts* Tajik. *see* **Yazgulom, Qatorkŭhi**
123 N2 **Yazgulom, Qatorkŭhi** *mts* Tajik.
139 P3 **Yazhelbitsy** Rus. Fed.
126 I4 **Yazıhan** Turkey
199 J5 **Yazıkent** Turkey
199 I6 **Yazıköy** Turkey
199 L5 **Yazır** Turkey
237 J9 **Yazoo** *r. MS* U.S.A.
237 J9 **Yazoo City** *MS* U.S.A.
105 L2 **Yazukami** Japan
134 L3 **Yaz'va** *r.* Rus. Fed.
202 B4 **Ybakoura** *well* Chad
Y Bala *Gwynedd, Wales* U.K. *see* **Bala**
179 L3 **Ybbs** *r.* Austria
179 L3 **Ybbs an der Donau** Austria
179 K4 **Ybbsitz** Austria
253 F6 **Ybycui** Para.
163 C7 **Ychoux** France
162 I5 **Ydes** France
142 F6 **Yding Skovhøj** *hill* Denmark
198 E5 **Ydra** Greece
198 E5 **Ydra** *i.* Greece
198 E5 **Ydras, Kolpos** *sea chan.* Greece
Y Drenewydd *Powys, Wales* U.K. *see* **Newtown**
96 C7 **Ye** Myanmar
96 C7 **Ye** *r.* Myanmar
149 N6 **Yeadon** *West Yorkshire, England* U.K.
150 E7 **Yealmpton** *Devon, England* U.K.
Yebaishou *Liaoning* China *see* **Jianping**
96 B2 **Yebawmi** Myanmar
202 C4 **Yebbi-Bou** Chad
202 C4 **Yebbi-Souma** Chad
183 L9 **Yébenes, Sierra de** *mts* Spain
183 O8 **Yebra** Spain
186 E3 **Yebra de Basa** Spain
111 C8 **Yecheng** *Xinjiang* China
187 C10 **Yecla** Spain
182 H7 **Yecla de Yeltes** Spain
242 E3 **Yécora** Mex.
245 K6 **Yecuautla** Mex.
96 C5 **Yedashe** Myanmar
114 E6 **Yedatore** *Karnataka* India
210 C3 **YeDebub Bihēroch Bihēreseboch na Hizboch** *admin. reg.* Eth.
199 K6 **Yedi Burun Başı** *pt* Turkey
Yedintsy Moldova *see* **Edineţ**
Yedisa Georgia *see* **Edisa**
129 B6 **Yedisu** Turkey
128 D3 **Yeditepe** Turkey
134 I3 **Yedoma** Rus. Fed.
202 C4 **Yedri** *well* Chad
139 Q4 **Yedrovo** Rus. Fed.
138 K6 **Yedy** Belarus
210 D3 **Yeed** Eth.
86 G4 **Yeeda River** *W.A.* Austr.
231 G12 **Yeehaw Junction** *FL* U.S.A.
82 E6 **Yeelanna** *S.A.* Austr.
139 R2 **Yefimovskiy** Rus. Fed.
139 V8 **Yefremov** Rus. Fed.
Yêgainnyin *Qinghai* China *see* **Henan**
207 I2 **Yeggueba** *well* Niger
129 G6 **Yeghegis** *r.* Armenia
129 G6 **Yeghegnadzor** Armenia
129 F5 **Yeghvard** Armenia
121 Q3 **Yegindybulak** Kazakh.
121 M2 **Yegindykol'** Kazakh.
135 H7 **Yegorlyk** *r.* Rus. Fed.
135 H7 **Yegorlykskaya** Rus. Fed.
100 J6 **Yegorova, Mys** *pt* Rus. Fed.
139 Q6 **Yegor'ye** Rus. Fed.
139 W6 **Yegor'yevsk** Rus. Fed.
185 K4 **Yeguas** *r.* Spain
185 K4 **Yeguas, Embalse del** *resr* Spain
185 I6 **Yeguas, Sierra de las** *hills* Spain
260 B4 **Yeguas, Volcán** *vol.* Chile
207 F4 **Yégué** Togo
210 A3 **Yei** Sudan
210 A3 **Yei** *r.* Sudan
109 J3 **Yeji** *Anhui* China
206 E4 **Yeji** Ghana
Yejiaji *Anhui* China *see* **Yeji**
130 H4 **Yekaterinburg** Rus. Fed.
Yekaterinodar Rus. Fed. *see* **Krasnodar**
Yekaterinoslav Ukr. *see* **Dnipropetrovs'k**
100 F3 **Yekaterinoslavka** Rus. Fed.
139 V9 **Yekaterinovka** *Lipetskaya Oblast'* Rus. Fed.
137 R6 **Yekaterinovka** *Rostovskaya Oblast'* Rus. Fed.
135 I5 **Yekaterinovka** *Saratovskaya Oblast'* Rus. Fed.
Yekaterinovskaya Rus. Fed. *see* **Krylovskaya**
129 F2 **Yekatorinogradskaya** Rus. Fed.
Yekhegnadzor Armenia *see* **Yeghegnadzor**
139 Q7 **Yekimovichi** Rus. Fed.
208 D4 **Yekokora** *r.* Dem. Rep. Congo
100 I4 **Yelabuga** *Khabarovskiy Kray* Rus. Fed.
134 J5 **Yelabuga** *Respublika Tatarstan* Rus. Fed.
135 H6 **Yelan'** Rus. Fed.
135 H6 **Yelan'** *r.* Rus. Fed.
135 H6 **Yelan'** *r.* Rus. Fed.
137 K6 **Yelanets'** Ukr.
83 M3 **Yelarbon** *Qld* Austr.
135 H5 **Yelat'ma** Rus. Fed.
122 I2 **Yelbarsli** Turkm.
199 J4 **Yeleğen** Turkey
Yelenovka Ukr. *see* **Zoryns'k**
Yelenovskiye Kar'yery Ukr. *see* **Dokuchayevs'k**
139 S8 **Yelenskiy** Rus. Fed.
139 V9 **Yelets** Rus. Fed.
134 N2 **Yeletskiy** Rus. Fed.
139 Q3 **Yeligovo** Rus. Fed.
106 H9 **Yeliguan** *Gansu* China
206 C3 **Yélimané** Mali
139 W7 **Yelino** Rus. Fed.
137 N5 **Yelizarove** Ukr.
Yelizavetgrad Ukr. *see* **Kirovohrad**
137 R7 **Yelizavetovka** *Rostovskaya Oblast'* Rus. Fed.
137 T3 **Yelizavetovka** *Voronezhskaya Oblast'* Rus. Fed.
131 P4 **Yelizavety, Mys** *c. Sakhalin* Rus. Fed.
131 Q4 **Yelizovo** Rus. Fed.
135 J5 **Yelkhovka** Rus. Fed.
146 □N1 **Yell** *i. Scotland* U.K.
82 D4 **Yellabina Regional Reserve** *nature res. S.A.* Austr.
114 G4 **Yellandu** *Andhra Prad.* India
114 D5 **Yellapur** *Karnataka* India
114 E3 **Yellareddi** *Andhra Prad.* India
226 D6 **Yellow** *r. WI* U.S.A.
87 E11 **Yellowdine** *W.A.* Austr.
234 F3 **Yellow Frame** *NJ* U.S.A.
222 G4 **Yellowhead Pass** *Alta/B.C.* Can.
234 D4 **Yellow House** *PA* U.S.A.
222 H2 **Yellowknife** *N.W.T.* Can.
222 H2 **Yellowknife** *r. N.W.T.* Can.
83 K5 **Yellow Mountain** *hill N.S.W.* Austr.
Yellow River *r.* China *see* **Huang He**
266 D3 **Yellow Sea** N. Pacific Ocean
232 B9 **Yellow Springs** *OH* U.S.A.
236 D2 **Yellowstone** *r. MT* U.S.A.
238 I4 **Yellowstone Lake** *WY* U.S.A.
238 I4 **Yellowstone National Park** U.S.A.
146 □N1 **Yell Sound** *str. Scotland* U.K.
237 I7 **Yellville** *AR* U.S.A.
238 C3 **Yelm** *WA* U.S.A.
185 N4 **Yelmo** *mt.* Spain
135 H5 **Yel'niki** Rus. Fed.
139 Q7 **Yel'nya** Rus. Fed.
134 K4 **Yelovo** Rus. Fed.
129 G6 **Yelp'in** Armenia
136 I2 **Yel'sk** Belarus
121 S4 **Yel'tay** Kazakh.
182 H7 **Yeltes** *r.* Spain
139 Q5 **Yel'tsy** Rus. Fed.
242 □Q10 **Yelucá** *mt.* Nic.
134 J3 **Yelva** *r.* Rus. Fed.
221 J1 **Yelverton Bay** *Nunavut* Can.
207 G4 **Yelwa** *Kebbi* Nigeria
207 H4 **Yelwa** *Plateau* Nigeria
137 P6 **Yelyseyivka** Ukr.
137 L5 **Yelyzavethradka** Ukr.
106 D7 **Yema Nanshan** *mts* China
110 L7 **Yema Shan** *mts* China
106 E9 **Yematan** *Qinghai* China
106 F8 **Yematan** *Qinghai* China
210 C2 **Yembo** Eth.
183 Q9 **Yémeda** Spain
124 G8 **Yemen** *country* Asia
134 H3 **Yemetsk** Rus. Fed.
136 G3 **Yemil'chyne** Ukr.
Yemişenbükü Turkey *see* **Taşova**
Yemmiganur *Andhra Prad.* India *see* **Emmiganuru**
134 H3 **Yemtsa** Rus. Fed.
134 J3 **Yemva** Rus. Fed.
207 I6 **Yen** Cameroon
140 U3 **Yena** Rus. Fed.
207 G5 **Yenagoa** Nigeria
137 R5 **Yenakiyeve** Ukr.
Yenakiyevo Ukr. *see* **Yenakiyeve**
96 B4 **Yenangyat** Myanmar
96 B4 **Yenangyaung** Myanmar
96 B5 **Yenanma** Myanmar
96 G4 **Yên Bai** Vietnam
121 M7 **Yenbekshi** Kazakh.
96 G4 **Yên Châu** Vietnam
83 K6 **Yenda** *N.S.W.* Austr.
207 E4 **Yendi** Ghana
Yêndum *Xizang* China *see* **Zhag'yab**
209 B5 **Yénéganou** Congo
209 C6 **Yenga-Lusundji** Dem. Rep. Congo
96 C4 **Yengan** Myanmar
208 D5 **Yenge** *r.* Dem. Rep. Congo
122 B3 **Yengejeh** Iran
206 C4 **Yengema** Sierra Leone
110 C7 **Yengisar** *Xinjiang* China
110 G6 **Yengisar** *Xinjiang* China
110 H6 **Yengisu** *Xinjiang* China
208 B4 **Yengo** Congo
83 M5 **Yengo National Park** *N.S.W.* Austr.
129 B6 **Yenibaşlar** Turkey
135 F8 **Yeniçağa** Turkey
199 I3 **Yenice** *Çanakkale* Turkey
128 D2 **Yenice** *İçel* Turkey
199 K2 **Yeniceköy** Turkey
126 F4 **Yeniceoba** Turkey
199 I2 **Yeniçiftlik** *Çanakkale* Turkey
199 I1 **Yeniçiftlik** *Tekirdağ* Turkey
129 B7 **Yenidal** Turkey
Yenidamlar Turkey *see* **Demirtaş**
199 J5 **Yenidere** *r.* Turkey
199 H4 **Yenifoça** Turkey
129 G5 **Yeni Göyçä** Azer.
Yenıhan Turkey *see* **Yıldızeli**
199 I5 **Yenihisar** Turkey
Yenije-i-Vardar Greece *see* **Giannitsa**
129 H5 **Yenikänd** Azer.
129 J5 **Yenikänd** Azer.
128 E2 **Yeniköy** *Hatay* Turkey
199 I4 **Yeniköy** *İzmir* Turkey
199 J3 **Yeniköy** *Kütahya* Turkey
199 K4 **Yeniköy** *Kütahya* Turkey
199 H2 **Yenimuhacirköy** Turkey
199 J5 **Yenipazar** *Aydın* Turkey
199 L2 **Yenipazar** *Bilecik* Turkey
199 I4 **Yenişakran** Turkey
Yeniséa Greece *see* **Genisea**
Yenişehir Greece *see* **Larisa**
199 K2 **Yenişehir** Turkey
131 J2 **Yenisey** *r.* Rus. Fed.
131 K4 **Yeniseysk** Rus. Fed.
131 K4 **Yeniseyskiy Kryazh** *ridge* Rus. Fed.
130 I2 **Yeniseyskiy Zaliv** *inlet* Rus. Fed.
106 E9 **Yeniugou** *Qinghai* China
106 F7 **Yeniugou** *Qinghai* China
Yeniyol Turkey *see* **Borçka**
96 G3 **Yên Minh** Vietnam
160 H5 **Yenne** France
135 I7 **Yenotayevka** Rus. Fed.
150 E6 **Yeo** *r. England* U.K.
116 E9 **Yeola** *Mahar.* India
87 H9 **Yeo Lake** *salt flat W.A.* Austr.
87 H10 **Yeo Lake Nature Reserve** *W.A.* Austr.
Yeotmal *Mahar.* India *see* **Yavatmal**
83 L5 **Yeoval** *N.S.W.* Austr.
150 G6 **Yeovil** *Somerset, England* U.K.
150 G5 **Yeovilton** *Somerset, England* U.K.
Yeo Yeo *r. N.S.W.* Austr. *see* **Bland**
242 E3 **Yepachi** Mex.
183 M9 **Yepes** Spain
139 V8 **Yepifan'** Rus. Fed.
85 M7 **Yeppoon** *Qld* Austr.
Yerakaroú Greece *see* **Gerakarou**
135 H5 **Yerakhtur** Rus. Fed.
Yeráki, Ákra *pt Zakynthos* Greece *see* **Gerakas, Akrotirio**
Yerákion Greece *see* **Geraki**
Yeraliyev Kazakh. *see* **Kuryk**
244 F2 **Yerbabuena** Mex.
122 H2 **Yerbent** Turkm.
131 L3 **Yerbogachen** Rus. Fed.
114 F7 **Yercaud** *Tamil Nadu* India
121 O2 **Yerementau, Gory** *hills* Kazakh.
129 F5 **Yerevan** Armenia
121 O2 **Yereymentau** Kazakh.
129 J4 **Yerfi** Azer.
114 E4 **Yergara** *Karnataka* India
135 I7 **Yergeni** *hills* Rus. Fed.
Yergoğu Romania *see* **Giurgiu**
Yeriḩo West Bank *see* **Jericho**
87 F10 **Yerilla** *W.A.* Austr.
240 M3 **Yerington** *NV* U.S.A.
199 J5 **Yerkesik** Turkey
128 A1 **Yerköprü Mağarası** *tourist site* Turkey
126 G4 **Yerköy** Turkey
114 D4 **Yerla** *r.* India
Yermak Kazakh. *see* **Aksu**
100 E2 **Yermakovo** Rus. Fed.
268 A1 **Yermak Plateau** *sea feature* Arctic Ocean
Yermentau Kazakh. *see* **Yereymentau**
135 H5 **Yermish'** Rus. Fed.
134 K2 **Yermitsa** Rus. Fed.
242 G4 **Yermo** Mex.
240 P7 **Yermo** *CA* U.S.A.
139 Y4 **Yermolino** Rus. Fed.
100 B2 **Yerofey Pavlovich** Rus. Fed.
128 C8 **Yeroham** Israel
Yeropótamos *r. Kriti* Greece *see* **Geropotamos**
156 B7 **Yerre** *r.* France
156 D6 **Yerres** *r.* France
134 K2 **Yersa** *r.* Rus. Fed.
164 F6 **Yerseke** Neth.
129 F3 **Yersh** Rus. Fed.
139 R7 **Yershi** Rus. Fed.
139 P8 **Yershichi** Rus. Fed.
120 C2 **Yershov** Rus. Fed.
138 L4 **Yershovo** Rus. Fed.
139 X1 **Yertsevo** Rus. Fed.

252 A2 Yerupaja mt. Peru
Yerushalayim Israel/West Bank see Jerusalem
120 B2 Yeruslan r. Rus. Fed.
159 M2 Yerville France
137 T3 Yeryshevka Rus. Fed.
Yerzhar Uzbek. see Gagarin
186 C2 Yesa Spain
186 C2 Yesa, Embalse de resr Spain
139 R4 Yesenovichi Rus. Fed.
Yeshera Georgia see Eshera
121 Q6 Yesik Kazakh.
121 L2 Yesil' Kazakh.
128 E2 Yeşil Turkey
199 K5 Yeşildere Burdur Turkey
128 F2 Yeşildere Gaziantep Turkey
128 B1 Yeşildere Karaman Turkey
126 G4 Yeşilhisar Turkey
126 H3 Yeşilırmak r. Turkey
128 F1 Yeşilkent Turkey
199 K3 Yeşilköy Turkey
199 K5 Yeşilova Burdur Turkey
Yeşilova Yozgat Turkey see Sorgun
199 L5 Yeşilyayla Turkey
199 J4 Yeşilyurt Turkey
199 K5 Yeşilyuva Turkey
139 W5 Yesiplevo Rus. Fed.
139 O6 Yes'kovo Rus. Fed.
146 J4 Yesnaby Orkney, Scotland U.K.
261 H2 Yeso Arg.
260 B4 Yeso, Cerro mt. Chile
129 D1 Yessentuki Rus. Fed.
129 D1 Yessentukskaya Rus. Fed.
131 L3 Yessey Rus. Fed.
185 O4 Yeste Spain
150 D6 Yes Tor hill England U.K.
128 D5 Yesud HaMa'ala Israel
185 O4 Yetas de Abajo Spain
Yêtatang Xizang China see Baqên
83 M3 Yetman N.S.W. Austr.
96 B3 Ye-U Myanmar
158 G8 Yeu, Île d' i. France
137 S3 Yevdakovo Rus. Fed.
Yevdokimovskoye Rus. Fed. see Krasnogvardeyskoye
Yevlakh Azer. see Yevlax
137 Q1 Yevlanovo Rus. Fed.
129 I5 Yevlax Azer.
137 M8 Yevpatoriya Ukr.
137 M8 Yevpatoriys'kyy, Mys pt Ukr.
160 A2 Yèvre r. France
100 H4 Yevreyskaya Avtonomnaya Oblast' admin. div. Rus. Fed.
139 O6 Yevseyevka Rus. Fed.
137 S3 Yevstratovka Rus. Fed.
137 S5 Yevsuh r. Ukr.
109 I2 Yexian Henan China
Yexian Shandong China see Laizhou
121 Q6 Yeygen'yevka Kazakh.
111 F8 Yeyik Xinjiang China
135 G7 Yeysk Rus. Fed.
137 R7 Yeyskiy Liman inlet Rus. Fed.
137 R7 Yeyskoye Ukreplenie Rus. Fed.
110 G6 Yeyungou Xinjiang China
138 N6 Yezerishche, Ozero l. Belarus/Rus. Fed.
Yezhou Hubei China see Jianshi
134 I2 Yezhuga r. Rus. Fed.
Yezo i. Japan see Hokkaidō
138 M6 Yezyaryshcha Belarus
Y Fali Wales U.K. see Valley
Y Fenni Monmouthshire, Wales U.K. see Abergavenny
158 F5 Yffiniac France
Y Fflint Flintshire, Wales U.K. see Flint
253 G6 Ygatimí Para.
Y Gelli Gandryll Wales U.K. see Hay-on-Wye
163 C8 Ygos-St-Saturnin France
160 B3 Ygrande France
253 G6 Yhú Para.
261 I3 Yí r. Uru.
Yialí i. Greece see Gyali
Yialousa Cyprus see Aigialousa
100 D5 Yi'an Heilong. China
Yianisádha i. Greece see Gianisada
Yiannitsá Greece see Giannitsa
124 E6 Yibā, Wādī watercourse Saudi Arabia
108 E4 Yibin Sichuan China
108 E4 Yibin Sichuan China
111 H10 Yibug Caka salt l. China
109 H3 Yichang Hubei China
Yicheng Henan China see Zhumadian
109 I3 Yicheng Hubei China
107 L9 Yicheng Shanxi China
107 M9 Yichuan Henan China
107 L9 Yichuan Shaanxi China
100 F5 Yichun Heilong. China
109 J5 Yichun Jiangxi China
Yidu Shandong China see Qingzhou
108 B3 Yidun Sichuan China
109 J4 Yifeng Jiangxi China
Yiggêtang Qinghai China see Sêrwolungwa
108 A2 Yiggêtang Qinghai China
199 M2 Yığılca Turkey
129 A6 Yiğitler Turkey
128 E2 Yiğityolu Turkey
78 □1 Yigo Guam
Yigu Guam see Yigo
106 E5 Yihatuoli Gansu China
107 M9 Yi He r. Henan China
107 P9 Yi He r. Shandong China
109 K5 Yihuang Jiangxi China
Yijiang Jiangxi China see Yiyang
107 K9 Yijun Shaanxi China
107 S2 Yilaha Heilong. China
100 F5 Yilan Heilong. China
Yilan Taiwan see Ilan
129 B5 Yıldırım Turkey
126 C3 Yıldız Dağları mts Turkey
126 H4 Yıldızeli Turkey
100 C3 Yilehuli Shan mts China
108 D6 Yiliang Yunnan China
108 E5 Yiliang Yunnan China
111 K8 Yiliping Qinghai China
87 D12 Yilliminning W.A. Austr.
100 D5 Yilong Heilong. China
108 F3 Yilong Sichuan China
Yilong Yunnan China see Shiping
108 D7 Yilong Hu l. China
107 O6 Yimatu He r. China
96 F2 Yimen Yunnan China
100 F6 Yimianpo Heilong. China
107 P2 Yimin He r. China
100 B2 Yimuhe Nei Mongol China
107 P9 Yinan Shandong China
96 C6 Yinbaing Myanmar
Yincheng Jiangxi China see Dexing
106 J7 Yinchuan Ningxia China
87 G11 Yindarlgooda, Lake salt flat W.A. Austr.
84 C4 Yingawunarri Aboriginal Land res. N.T. Austr.
109 I3 Yingcheng Hubei China
100 D7 Yingchengzi Jilin China
109 I6 Yingde Guangdong China
108 G9 Yinggehai Hainan China
Yinggen Hainan China see Qiongzhong
109 K2 Ying He r. China
108 A6 Yingjiang Yunnan China
108 D4 Yingjing Sichuan China
Yingkou Liaoning China see Dashiqiao
107 R6 Yingkou Liaoning China
106 I8 Yingpanshui Ningxia China
109 J3 Yingshan Hubei China
108 F3 Yingshan Sichuan China
109 K2 Yingshang Anhui China
109 K4 Yingtan Jiangxi China
107 N9 Yingtaoyuan Shandong China
207 H5 Yingui Cameroon
107 M7 Yingxian Shanxi China
Yining Jiangxi China see Xiushui
110 E5 Yining Xinjiang China
110 E5 Yining Xinjiang China
84 B6 Yiningarra Aboriginal Land res. N.T. Austr.
108 G5 Yinjiang Guizhou China
109 J5 Yinkengxu Jiangxi China
96 B3 Yinmabin Myanmar
100 D6 Yinma He r. China
96 C6 Yinnyein Myanmar
107 K6 Yin Shan mts China
Yinxian Zhejiang China see Ningbo
Yiófiros r. Kriti Greece see Giofyros
111 L11 Yi'ong Nongchang Xizang China
111 L11 Yi'ong Zangbo r. Xizang China
Yioúra i. Greece see Gioura
108 C6 Yipinglang Yunnan China
199 L4 Yıprak Turkey
Yiquan Guizhou China see Meitan
257 E5 Yira Chapéu, Monte mt. Brazil
111 K10 Yiran Co l. Qinghai China
210 C3 Yirga Alem Eth.
210 C3 Yirga Ch'efē Eth.
210 A3 Yirol Sudan
84 F2 Yirrkala N.T. Austr.
107 P3 Yirshi Nei Mongol China
110 I6 Yirtkuq Bulak spring Xinjiang China
Yirxie Nei Mongol China see Yirshi
Yisa Yunnan China see Honghe
Yishan Guangxi China see Yizhou
Yishan Jiangsu China see Guanyun
107 P8 Yi Shan mt. Shandong China
107 P8 Yi Shan mts China
107 P9 Yishui Shandong China
94 □ Yishun Sing.
207 I1 Yi Tchouma well Niger
Yíthion Greece see Gytheio
Yitiaoshan Gansu China see Jingtai
100 D7 Yitong Jilin China
100 D6 Yitong He r. China
96 C3 Yi Tu, Nam r. Myanmar
107 Q1 Yitulihe Nei Mongol China
106 C5 Yiwanquan Xinjiang China
106 D5 Yiwu Xinjiang China
108 C8 Yiwu Yunnan China
107 Q6 Yiwulü Shan mts China
109 K4 Yixian Anhui China
107 N7 Yixian Hebei China
107 Q6 Yixian Liaoning China
100 D2 Yixiken Heilong. China
109 L3 Yixing Jiangsu China
107 O6 Yixun He r. China
109 I4 Yiyang Hunan China
109 K4 Yiyang Jiangxi China
107 P8 Yiyuan Shandong China
109 I6 Yizhang Hunan China
109 L2 Yizheng Jiangsu China
108 G6 Yizhou Guangxi China
Yizhou Hebei China see Yixian
Yizhou Liaoning China see Yixian
Yizra'el country Asia see Israel
140 R5 Ylä-Keitele l. Fin.
141 T6 Ylämaa Fin.
141 Q6 Yläne Fin.
78 □1 Ylig Bay Guam
140 Q5 Ylihärmä Fin.
140 R4 Yli-Ii Fin.
140 R4 Yli-Kärppä Fin.
140 S4 Ylikiiminki Fin.
140 T3 Yli-Kitka l. Fin.
140 Q5 Ylistaro Fin.
140 Q3 Ylitornio Fin.
140 R4 Ylivieska Fin.
140 R3 Ylläs hill Fin.
150 E2 Y Llethr hill Wales U.K.
141 Q6 Ylöjärvi Fin.
221 P2 Ymer Nunatak Greenland
221 P2 Ymer Ø i. Greenland
156 C7 Ymonville France
143 J3 Ymsen l. Sweden
134 K3 Yndin Rus. Fed.
143 M3 Yngaren l. Sweden
143 K2 Yngen l. Sweden
143 N2 Yngern l. Sweden
121 N3 Yntaly Kazakh.
131 O3 Ynykchanskiy Rus. Fed.
Ynys Enlli i. Wales U.K. see Bardsey Island
Ynys Môn i. Wales U.K. see Anglesey
237 G11 Yoakum TX U.S.A.
207 H4 Yobe state Nigeria
102 R3 Yobetsu-dake vol. Japan
210 D2 Yoboki Djibouti
103 G13 Yobuko Japan
203 H5 Yob Wildlife Reserve nature res. Eritrea
104 B6 Yodo-gawa r. Japan
234 B5 Yoe PA U.S.A.
259 C9 Yogan, Cerro mt. Chile
245 K9 Yogana Mex.
104 D4 Yogo Japan
202 C5 Yogoum well Chad
95 I8 Yogyakarta Indon.
95 I9 Yogyakarta admin. dist. Indon.
222 G5 Yoho National Park B.C. Can.
102 R3 Yoichi Japan
102 S3 Yoichi-dake mt. Japan
111 M9 Yoigilanglêb r. Qinghai China
242 □P10 Yojoa, Lago de l. Hond.
101 E10 Yŏju S. Korea
104 A5 Yōka Japan
207 I6 Yokadouma Cameroon
103 J13 Yokagawara Japan
104 D5 Yōkaichi Japan
105 M4 Yōkaichiba Japan
102 □F18 Yokate-jima i. Nansei-shotō Japan
104 B6 Yokawa Japan
104 E6 Yokkaichi Japan
207 I5 Yoko Cameroon
102 S5 Yokohama Aomori Japan
105 K5 Yokohama Kanagawa Japan
105 I3 Yokokawa Japan
105 L4 Yokoshiba Japan
105 K5 Yokosuka Japan
103 K11 Yokota Japan
102 R7 Yokote Japan
102 R5 Yokotsu-dake mt. Japan
105 J4 Yokoze Japan
116 F3 Yol Hima. Prad. India
207 I4 Yola Nigeria
242 □Q12 Yolaina, Cordillera de mts Nic.
240 J1 Yolla Bolly Middle Eel Wilderness nature res. CA U.S.A.
240 K3 Yolo CA U.S.A.
208 D5 Yolombo Dem. Rep. Congo
Yolöten Turkm. see Ýolöten
123 J3 Ýolöten Turkm.
245 J9 Yolotepec Mex.
245 K8 Yolox Mex.
245 I9 Yoloxóchitl Mex.
243 P7 Yoluk Mex.
96 E7 Yom, Mae Nam r. Thai.
103 □2 Yome-jima i. Japan
105 M1 Yomogida-dake hill Japan
206 C5 Yomou Guinea
129 A5 Yomra Turkey
117 N6 Yomtam Arun. Prad. India
162 B2 Yon r. France
78 □1 Yona Guam
102 □1 Yona Okinawa Japan
102 □1 Yonabaru Okinawa Japan
103 K11 Yonago Japan
102 □A22 Yonaguni-jima i. Nansei-shotō Japan
102 □1 Yonaha-dake hill Okinawa Japan
101 E10 Yŏnan N. Korea
102 R6 Yoneshiro-gawa r. Japan
105 I1 Yone-yama hill Japan
102 R9 Yonezawa Japan
82 G5 Yongala S.A. Austr.
101 E11 Yŏng-am S. Korea
Yong'an Chongqing China see Fengjie
109 K6 Yong'an Fujian China
Yongbei Yunnan China see Yongsheng
106 G7 Yongchang Gansu China
109 K2 Yongcheng Henan China
101 F11 Yŏngch'ŏn S. Korea
108 E4 Yongchuan Chongqing China
109 L6 Yongchun Fujian China
108 B6 Yongde Yunnan China
106 H8 Yongdeng Gansu China
109 K6 Yongding Fujian China
Yongding Yunnan China see Yongren
Yongding Yunnan China see Fumin
107 O7 Yongding He r. China
101 F10 Yŏngdŏk S. Korea
109 J5 Yongfeng Jiangxi China
Yongfeng Jiangxi China see Guangfeng
110 H5 Yongfengqu Xinjiang China
108 G6 Yongfu Guangxi China
101 E11 Yŏnggwang S. Korea
107 L8 Yonghe Shanxi China
101 E9 Yŏnghŭng N. Korea
101 E9 Yŏnghŭng-man b. N. Korea
103 G11 Yŏngil-man b. S. Korea
100 E7 Yongji Jilin China
109 M4 Yongjia Zhejiang China
106 H9 Yongjing Gansu China
Yongjing Guizhou China see Xifeng
Yongjing Liaoning China see Xifeng
107 M8 Yongjin Qu r. China
101 F10 Yŏngju S. Korea
108 B6 Yongkang Yunnan China
109 M4 Yongkang Zhejiang China
108 C3 Yonglaxi Sichuan China
Yongle Shaanxi China see Zhen'an
Yongle Sichuan China see Jiuzhaigou
101 D8 Yongling Liaoning China
107 N8 Yongnian Hebei China
108 G7 Yongning Guangxi China
Yongning Jiangxi China see Tonggu
106 J7 Yongning Ningxia China
Yongning Sichuan China see Xuyong
108 B6 Yongping Yunnan China
Yongqing Gansu China see Qingshui
108 C5 Yongren Yunnan China
101 E11 Yŏngsan-gang r. S. Korea
108 D4 Yongshan Yunnan China
108 C5 Yongsheng Yunnan China
107 K9 Yongshou Shaanxi China
108 G4 Yongshun Hunan China
109 L6 Yongtai Fujian China
101 F10 Yŏngwol S. Korea
Yongxi Guizhou China see Nayong
109 I5 Yongxing Hunan China
109 J5 Yongxing Jiangxi China
107 L7 Yongxing Shaanxi China
109 J4 Yongxiu Jiangxi China
109 H5 Yongzhou Hunan China
233 L8 Yonkers NY U.S.A.
156 G8 Yonne dept France
156 E7 Yonne r. France
206 B3 Yonoféré Senegal
207 I2 Yoo Baba well Niger
250 C3 Yopal Col.
110 C7 Yopurga Xinjiang China
242 F4 Yoquivo Mex.
121 N7 Yordon Uzbek.
116 E3 Yordu Jammu and Kashmir
244 F6 Yoricostío Mex.
105 J3 Yorii Japan
87 D11 York W.A. Austr.
227 O6 York Ont. Can.
223 M4 York r. Man. Can.
149 O6 York York, England U.K.
149 O6 York admin. div. England U.K.
237 K9 York AL U.S.A.
236 G5 York NE U.S.A.
234 B5 York PA U.S.A.
231 G8 York SC U.S.A.
85 I1 York, Cape Qld Austr.
York, Kap c. Greenland see Innaanganeq
149 N5 York, Vale of val. England U.K.
234 B5 York County county PA U.S.A.
85 I2 York Downs Qld Austr.
82 F6 Yorke Peninsula S.A. Austr.
82 F6 Yorketown S.A. Austr.
234 B4 York Haven PA U.S.A.
149 M5 Yorkshire Dales National Park England U.K.
149 P6 Yorkshire Wolds hills England U.K.
234 A4 York Springs PA U.S.A.
223 K5 Yorkton Sask. Can.
232 I11 Yorktown VA U.S.A.
235 H2 Yorktown Heights NY U.S.A.
224 B5 Yorkville IL U.S.A.
242 □P10 Yoro Hond.
104 E5 Yōrō Japan
104 E7 Yoroi-zaki pt Japan
102 □G18 Yoro-jima i. Nansei-shotō Japan
93 F4 Yoronga i. Maluku Indon.
102 □F19 Yoron-tō i. Nansei-shotō Japan
106 J2 Yöröö Gol r. Mongolia
206 D3 Yorosso Mali
240 M4 Yosemite National Park CA U.S.A.
240 M4 Yosemite Village CA U.S.A.
103 J13 Yoshida Ehime Japan
103 J12 Yoshida Hiroshima Japan
105 J3 Yoshida Saitama Japan
105 H6 Yoshida Shizuoka Japan
103 H13 Yoshii Fukuoka Japan
105 I3 Yoshii Gunma Japan
103 L12 Yoshii-gawa r. Japan
105 H1 Yoshikawa Japan
105 M1 Yoshima Japan
104 C7 Yoshino Japan
104 E3 Yoshinodani Japan
104 C7 Yoshino-gawa r. Japan
103 L12 Yoshino-gawa r. Japan
104 D8 Yoshino-Kumano Kokuritsu-kōen nat. park Japan
134 I4 Yoshkar-Ola Rus. Fed.
Yos Sudarso i. Papua Indon. see Dolok, Pulau
101 E11 Yŏsu S. Korea
253 E4 Yotau Bol.
102 R4 Yōtei-zan mt. Japan
105 L4 Yotsukaidō Japan
105 M1 Yotsukura Japan
128 D9 Yotvata Israel
210 E3 Yoube well Eth.
222 E5 Youbou B.C. Can.
111 J7 Youdunzi Qinghai China
147 G9 Youghal Ireland
147 F9 Youghal Bay Ireland
108 G7 You Jiang r. China
149 N7 Youlgreave Derbyshire, England U.K.
107 P8 Youlin Shandong China
208 C5 Youmba Congo
83 L6 Young N.S.W. Austr.
87 F12 Young r. W.A. Austr.
261 I3 Young Uru.
241 V7 Young AZ U.S.A.
80 □ Young, Cape Chatham Is S. Pacific Ocean
82 F4 Younghusband, Lake salt flat S.A. Austr.
82 G6 Younghusband Peninsula S.A. Austr.
263 K2 Young Island Antarctica
80 L5 Young Nicks Head North I. N.Z.
81 D11 Young Range mts South I. N.Z.
223 I5 Youngstown Alta Can.
232 E7 Youngstown OH U.S.A.
232 F7 Youngsville PA U.S.A.
240 J3 Yountville CA U.S.A.
111 J7 Youshashan Qinghai China
108 H4 You Shui r. China
204 C2 Youssoufia Morocco
206 D3 Youvarou Mali
109 L5 Youxi Fujian China
109 I5 Youxian Hunan China
108 G4 Youyang Chongqing China
100 G5 Youyi Heilong. China
110 H2 Youyi Feng mt. China/Rus. Fed.
107 M7 Youyu Shanxi China
123 M2 Yovon Tajik.
83 J3 Yowah watercourse Qld Austr.
87 E8 Yowereena Hill W.A. Austr.
151 I2 Yoxall Staffordshire, England U.K.
151 P3 Yoxford Suffolk, England U.K.
126 G4 Yozgat Turkey
253 G5 Ypé-Jhú Para.
159 L2 Yport France
140 R4 Yppäri Fin.
Ypres West-Vlaanderen Belgium see Ieper
227 K7 Ypsilanti MI U.S.A.
238 C6 Yreka CA U.S.A.
Yrghyz Kazakh. see Irgiz
Yr Wyddfa mt. Wales U.K. see Snowdon
Yr Wyddgrug Flintshire, Wales U.K. see Mold
150 E3 Ysbyty Ystwyth Ceredigion, Wales U.K.
156 E2 Yser r. France alt. IJzer (Belgium)
164 I6 Ysselsteyn Neth.
161 E6 Yssingeaux France
143 J6 Ystad Sweden
150 E4 Ystalyfera Neath Port Talbot, Wales U.K.
150 F1 Ystrad r. Wales U.K.
150 E4 Ystradgynlais Powys, Wales U.K.
150 D3 Ystwyth r. Wales U.K.
121 P6 Ysyk-Ata Kyrg.
Ysyk-Köl Kyrg. see Balykchy
121 R7 Ysyk-Köl admin. div. Kyrg.
121 Q6 Ysyk-Köl salt l. Kyrg.
146 L8 Ythan r. Scotland U.K.
Y Trallwng Powys, Wales U.K. see Welshpool
142 C1 Ytre Samlen b. Norway
Ytre Vinje Norway see Åmot
131 O3 Ytyk-Kyuyel' Rus. Fed.
93 F4 Yu i. Maluku Indon.
128 B8 Yu'alliq, Jabal mt. Egypt
109 H3 Yuan'an Hubei China
107 P5 Yuanbaoshan Nei Mongol China
108 G6 Yuanbao Shan mt. Guangxi China
109 I4 Yuanjiang Hunan China
108 C7 Yuanjiang Yunnan China
108 H4 Yuan Jiang r. Hunan China
108 D7 Yuan Jiang r. Yunnan China
Yuanjiazhuang Shaanxi China see Foping
109 M6 Yüanli Taiwan
107 Q2 Yuanlin Nei Mongol China
108 H4 Yuanling Hunan China
Yuanma Yunnan China see Yuanmou
108 C6 Yuanmou Yunnan China
107 M7 Yuanping Shanxi China
107 L9 Yuanqu Shanxi China
Yuanquan Gansu China see Anxi
Yuanshan Guangdong China see Lianping
106 F7 Yuanshanzi Gansu China
Yuanyang Yunnan China see Xinjie
108 D7 Yuanyang Yunnan China
104 B7 Yuasa Japan
124 B2 Yub'ā i. Saudi Arabia
240 K2 Yuba City CA U.S.A.
102 S3 Yūbari Japan
102 T3 Yūbari-dake mt. Japan
102 T3 Yūbari-sanchi mts Japan
108 F4 Yubei Chongqing China
102 U2 Yūbetsu Japan
102 U2 Yūbetsu-gawa r. Japan
208 E3 Yubu Sudan
240 O7 Yucaipa CA U.S.A.
243 N8 Yucatán pen. Mex.
243 O7 Yucatán state Mex.
243 P6 Yucatan Channel Cuba/Mex.
241 R7 Yucca AZ U.S.A.
241 P5 Yucca Lake NV U.S.A.
241 P7 Yucca Valley CA U.S.A.
129 C7 Yücetepe Turkey
107 N9 Yucheng Henan China
107 O8 Yucheng Shandong China
Yucheng Sichuan China see Ya'an
Yuci Shanxi China see Jinzhong
252 D3 Yucumo Bol.
139 U5 Yudino Moskovskaya Oblast' Rus. Fed.
134 J5 Yudino Respublika Tatarstan Rus. Fed.
134 G4 Yudino Yaroslavskaya Oblast' Rus. Fed.
100 B2 Yudi Shan mt. China
131 O4 Yudoma r. Rus. Fed.
109 J6 Yudu Jiangxi China
Yuecheng Sichuan China see Yuexi
108 F3 Yuechi Sichuan China
Yuelai Heilong. China see Huachuan
107 R4 Yueliang Pao l. China
84 C7 Yuendumu N.T. Austr.
84 C7 Yuendumu Aboriginal Land res. N.T. Austr.
109 □J7 Yuen Long H.K. China
109 M4 Yueqing Zhejiang China
109 K3 Yuexi Anhui China
108 D4 Yuexi Sichuan China
109 I4 Yueyang Hunan China
109 I4 Yueyang Hunan China
Yueyang Sichuan China see Anyue
134 L4 Yug Rus. Fed.
134 I3 Yug r. Rus. Fed.
109 K4 Yugan Jiangxi China
105 J5 Yugawara Japan
111 L9 Yuge Qinghai China
128 B1 Yuğluk Dağı mts Turkey
134 K4 Yugo-Kamskiy Rus. Fed.
Yugo-Osetinskaya Avtonomnaya Oblast' aut. reg. Georgia see Samkhret' Oset'i
130 H3 Yugorsk Rus. Fed.
134 M1 Yugorskiy Poluostrov pen. Rus. Fed.
134 M2 Yugud-Vayskiy Natsional'nyy Park nat. park Rus. Fed.
109 M3 Yuhang Zhejiang China
107 M7 Yu He r. China
Yuhu Yunnan China see Eryuan
109 M4 Yuhuan Zhejiang China
107 O8 Yuhuang Ding mt. Shandong China
105 I5 Yui Japan
87 D9 Yuin W.A. Austr.
109 K4 Yujiang Jiangxi China
108 H7 Yu Jiang r. China
Yujin Sichuan China see Qianwei
131 Q3 Yukagirskoye Ploskogor'ye plat. Rus. Fed.
134 K4 Yukamenskoye Rus. Fed.
129 F7 Yukarı Balçıklı Turkey
199 I3 Yukarıbey Turkey
129 B5 Yukarıcanören Turkey
129 D4 Yukarıgündeş Turkey
129 E5 Yukarıkaragüney Turkey
199 M3 Yukarı Sakarya Ovaları plain Turkey
129 D5 Yukarısarıkamış Turkey
126 G4 Yukarısarıkaya Turkey
138 L5 Yukhavichy Belarus
135 J5 Yukhmachi Rus. Fed.
139 S7 Yukhnov Rus. Fed.
139 N5 Yukhovo Rus. Fed.
209 C5 Yuki Dem. Rep. Congo
103 K12 Yuki Japan
105 K3 Yūki Japan
220 B3 Yukon r. Can./U.S.A.
220 D3 Yukon-Charley Rivers National Preserve nature res. AK U.S.A.
222 B2 Yukon Crossing Y.T. Can.
222 C2 Yukon Territory admin. div. Can.
127 L5 Yüksekova Turkey
103 H13 Yukuhashi Japan
84 C8 Yulara N.T. Austr.
120 G1 Yuldybayevo Rus. Fed.
86 E6 Yule r. W.A. Austr.
85 L9 Yuleba Qld Austr.
231 G10 Yulee FL U.S.A.
110 H6 Yuli Xinjiang China
109 M7 Yüli Taiwan
108 H7 Yulin Guangxi China
108 G9 Yulin Hainan China
107 K7 Yulin Shaanxi China
108 C5 Yulong Xueshan mt. Yunnan China
241 R9 Yuma AZ U.S.A.
236 D5 Yuma CO U.S.A.
241 R9 Yuma Desert AZ U.S.A.
120 G1 Yumaguzino Rus. Fed.
82 D4 Yumbarra Conservation Park nature res. S.A. Austr.
210 A4 Yumbe Uganda
260 A5 Yumbel Chile
208 C5 Yumbi Bandundu Dem. Rep. Congo
208 E5 Yumbi Maniema Dem. Rep. Congo
250 B4 Yumbo Col.
111 G11 Yumco Xizang China
106 E7 Yumen Gansu China
106 E7 Yumendongzhan Gansu China
110 K6 Yumenguan Gansu China
106 E6 Yumenzhen Gansu China
110 F3 Yumin Xinjiang China
106 E4 Yumt Uul mt. Mongolia
128 D2 Yumurtalık Turkey
87 C10 Yuna W.A. Austr.
246 I4 Yuna r. Dom. Rep.
126 E4 Yunak Turkey
137 O2 Yunakivka Ukr.
109 H7 Yunan Guangdong China
109 I7 Yun'an Guangdong China
220 A4 Yunaska Island AK U.S.A.
252 D5 Yunchara Bol.
107 N9 Yuncheng Shandong China
107 L9 Yuncheng Shanxi China
129 C5 Yüncüler Turkey
87 G10 Yundamindera W.A. Austr.
109 I7 Yunfu Guangdong China
252 D4 Yungas reg. Bol.
252 C6 Yungay Antofagasta Chile
260 A5 Yungay Bíobío Chile
252 C4 Yungayo Peru
108 D6 Yungui Gaoyuan plat. Guizhou/Yunnan China
Yunhe Jiangsu China see Pizhou
Yunhe Yunnan China see Heqing
109 L4 Yunhe Zhejiang China
Yunjinghong Yunnan China see Jinghong
108 H7 Yunkai Dashan mts China
84 C7 Yunkanjini Aboriginal Land res. N.T. Austr.
Yunling Fujian China see Yunxiao
108 B5 Yun Ling mts Yunnan China
108 B6 Yunlong Yunnan China
109 I3 Yunmeng Hubei China
108 C6 Yunnan prov. China
137 R5 Yunokomunarivs'k Ukr.
105 J1 Yunotani Japan
103 J11 Yunotsu Japan
185 J7 Yunquera Spain
183 N7 Yunquera de Henares Spain
109 I3 Yun Shui r. China
82 G5 Yunta S.A. Austr.
128 A2 Yunt Dağı mt. Turkey
199 K3 Yunuslar Turkey
109 H7 Yunwu Shan mts China
108 H2 Yunxi Hubei China
Yunxi Sichuan China see Yanting
108 H2 Yunxian Hubei China
108 C6 Yunxian Yunnan China
109 K7 Yunxiao Fujian China
134 M2 Yun'yakha r. Rus. Fed.
108 G3 Yunyang Chongqing China
109 I2 Yunyang Henan China
Yupin Yunnan China see Pingbian
Yuping Guizhou China see Libo
108 G5 Yuping Guizhou China
109 L3 Yuqian Zhejiang China
108 F5 Yuqing Guizhou China
252 D5 Yura Bol.
252 D5 Yura r. Bol.
104 B8 Yura Japan
252 C4 Yura Peru
250 B6 Yuracyacu Peru
104 B5 Yura-gawa r. Japan
102 R4 Yūrappu-dake mt. Japan
137 S3 Yurasovka Rus. Fed.
138 I7 Yuratsishki Belarus
136 I2 Yuravichy Belarus
83 N3 Yuraygir National Park N.S.W. Austr.
111 H9 Yurba Co l. Xizang China
137 Q4 Yurchenkove Ukr.
244 E5 Yurécuaro Mex.
128 D2 Yürekli Turkey
130 J4 Yurga Rus. Fed.
250 B6 Yurimaguas Peru
134 I4 Yurino Rus. Fed.
244 F5 Yuriria Mex.
244 F5 Yuriria, Laguna l. Mex.
129 H1 Yurkovka Rus. Fed.
134 K4 Yurla Rus. Fed.
137 T1 Yurlovka Rus. Fed.
134 I2 Yuroma Rus. Fed.
137 Q8 Yurovka Rus. Fed.
199 I2 Yürük Turkey
111 E7 Yurungkax He r. China
102 W3 Yururi-jima i. Japan
134 J4 Yur'ya Rus. Fed.
134 K2 Yur'yakha r. Rus. Fed.
Yuryev Estonia see Tartu
134 H4 Yur'yevets Ivanovskaya Oblast' Rus. Fed.
139 X5 Yur'yevets Vladimirskaya Oblast' Rus. Fed.
139 W5 Yur'yev-Pol'skiy Rus. Fed.
137 P5 Yur"yivka Dnipropetrovs'ka Oblast' Ukr.
137 P7 Yur"yivka Zaporiz'ka Oblast' Ukr.
242 □P11 Yuscarán Hond.
109 L5 Yushan Fujian China
109 L4 Yushan Jiangxi China
109 M7 Yü Shan mt. Taiwan
109 M4 Yushan Liedao is China
107 M8 Yushe Shanxi China
134 K1 Yushino Rus. Fed.
134 F2 Yushkozero Rus. Fed.
100 E6 Yushu Jilin China
108 A2 Yushu Qinghai China
110 H5 Yushugou Xinjiang China
134 J4 Yushut r. Rus. Fed.
135 I7 Yusta Rus. Fed.
127 J3 Yusufeli Turkey
103 K13 Yusuhara Japan
134 K4 Yus'va Rus. Fed.
107 O9 Yutai Shandong China
Yutan Hunan China see Ningxiang
135 K5 Yutaza Rus. Fed.
107 O7 Yutian Hebei China
111 E8 Yutian Xinjiang China
107 P5 Yutiangao Nei Mongol China
104 G6 Yūtō Japan
Yutpundji Djindiniwirritj res. N.T. Austr. see Roper Bar Aboriginal Land
261 F5 Yutuyaco Arg.
253 F6 Yuty Para.
157 L5 Yutz France
199 K6 Yuva Turkey
129 A5 Yuvacık Turkey
102 □G18 Yuwan-dake hill Nansei-shotō Japan
106 J8 Yuwang Ningxia China
129 I5 Yuxarı Garabağ Kanalı canal Azer.
129 G4 Yuxarı Salahlı Azer.
129 H4 Yuxarı Tala Azer.
Yuxi Guizhou China see Daozhen
109 H3 Yuxi Hubei China
108 D6 Yuxi Yunnan China
108 H3 Yuxiakou Hubei China
107 N7 Yuxian Hebei China
107 M7 Yuxian Shanxi China
109 L3 Yuxikou Anhui China
109 H3 Yuyangguan Hubei China
109 M3 Yuyao Zhejiang China
Yuyue Hubei China see Jiayu
102 Q7 Yuza Japan
102 R7 Yuzawa Japan
129 F5 Yüzbaşılar Turkey
134 H4 Yuzha Rus. Fed.
137 K7 Yuzhne Ukr.
Yuzhno-Alichurskiy, Khrebet mts Tajik. see Alichuri Janubí, Qatorkŭhi
100 M5 Yuzhno-Kamyshovyy Khrebet ridge Sakhalin Rus. Fed.
Yuzhno-Kazakhstanskaya Oblast' admin. div. Kazakh. see Yuzhnyy Kazakhstan
99 Q3 Yuzhno-Kuril'sk Kuril'skiye O-va Rus. Fed.
131 M4 Yuzhno-Muyskiy Khrebet mts Rus. Fed.
100 M5 Yuzhno-Sakhalinsk Sakhalin Rus. Fed.
129 G1 Yuzhno-Sukhokumsk Rus. Fed.
135 E7 Yuzhnoukrayinsk Ukr.
120 I1 Yuzhnoural'sk Rus. Fed.
121 T1 Yuzhnyy Altayskiy Kray Rus. Fed.
175 I1 Yuzhnyy Kaliningradskaya Oblast' Rus. Fed.
Yuzhnyy Respublika Kalmykiya-Khalm'g-Tangch Rus. Fed. see Adyk
135 H7 Yuzhnyy Rostovskaya Oblast' Rus. Fed.
131 Q4 Yuzhnyy, Mys hd Rus. Fed.
121 V3 Yuzhnyy Altay, Khrebet mts Kazakh.
Yuzhnyy Bug r. Ukr. see Pivdennyy Buh
121 M6 Yuzhnyy Kazakhstan admin. div. Kazakh.
120 G1 Yuzhnyy Ural mts Rus. Fed.
106 I9 Yuzhong Gansu China
Yuzhou Hebei China see Yuxian
107 M9 Yuzhou Henan China
Yuzkuduk Uzbek. see Yuzquduq
Yuzovka Ukr. see Donets'k
120 J6 Yuzquduq Uzbek.
104 A7 Yuzuruha-yama hill Japan
158 G5 Yvel r. France
156 C6 Yvelines dept France
190 B2 Yverdon Switz.
159 M2 Yvetot France
158 G5 Yvignac France
165 G8 Yvoir Belgium
160 I4 Yvoire France
190 B2 Yvonand Switz.
96 B4 Ywamun Myanmar
96 C5 Ywathit Myanmar
Y Waun Wales U.K. see Chirk
143 M4 Yxern l. Sweden
143 M3 Yxningen l. Sweden
143 M3 Yxnö i. Sweden
214 C9 Yzerfontein S. Africa
214 C9 Yzerfonteinpunt pt S. Africa
160 C3 Yzeure France
159 M8 Yzeures-sur-Creuse France

Z

204 E2 Za, Oued r. Morocco
245 K9 Zaachila Mex.
214 H9 Zaaimansdal S. Africa
Zaamin Uzbek. see Zomin
165 E6 Zaamslag Neth.
164 G4 Zaandam Neth.
164 G4 Zaandijk Neth.
197 O5 Zăbala r. Romania
196 I5 Žabalj Vojvodina Serbia
127 K5 Zāb al Kabīr, Nahr az r. Iraq
138 K4 Zabalova Latvia
122 G4 Zabānābād Iran
124 C4 Zabarjad, Jazīrat i. Egypt
127 K6 Zāb aş Şaghīr, Nahr az r. Iraq
107 O2 Zabaykal'sk Rus. Fed.
195 □ Żabbar Malta
176 F2 Žabčice Czech Rep.
122 A4 Zab-e Kuchek r. Iran
171 I8 Zabeltitz-Treugeböhla Ger.
208 E4 Zabia Dem. Rep. Congo
175 I3 Żabia Wola Pol.
191 Q4 Zabiče Slovenia
124 F8 Zabīd Yemen
124 F8 Zabīd, Wādī watercourse Yemen
175 J2 Zabiele Pol.
175 J3 Ząbki Pol.
174 E5 Ząbkowice Śląskie Pol.
175 L4 Zabłocie Pol.
175 L2 Zabłudów Pol.
179 O8 Žabno Croatia
175 I5 Żabno Pol.
188 E2 Zabok Croatia
177 H2 Žabokreky Slovakia
123 I6 Zābol Iran
123 I8 Zābolī Iran
136 E5 Zabolotiv Ukr.
136 D2 Zabolottya Ukr.
167 H2 Zaborski Park Krajobrazowy Pol.
139 S2 Zabor'ye Rus. Fed.
170 K4 Żabów Pol.
174 D2 Żabowo Pol.
111 H11 Zabqung Xizang China
197 J4 Zăbrani Romania
129 K5 Zabrat Azer.
206 E4 Zabré Burkina
176 F2 Zábřeh Czech Rep.
174 G5 Zabrze Pol.
123 L5 Zābul prov. Afgh.
120 D4 Zaburun'ye Kazakh.
136 I3 Zabuyannya Ukr.
136 C2 Zabuzhzhya Ukr.
207 F4 Zabzugu Ghana
243 O10 Zacapa Guat.
245 J6 Zacapoaxtla Mex.
244 F6 Zacapu Mex.
244 G7 Zacapuato Mex.
254 C4 Zacarias r. Brazil
243 N8 Zacatal Mex.
244 E3 Zacatecas Mex.
244 E2 Zacatecas state Mex.
242 □O11 Zacatecoluca El Salvador
245 I6 Zacatelco Mex.
245 H7 Zacatepec Morelos Mex.
245 J9 Zacatepec Oaxaca Mex.
245 L8 Zacatepec Oaxaca Mex.
245 J6 Zacatlán Mex.
120 D2 Zachagansk Kazakh.
198 C5 Zacharo Greece
174 F2 Zacharzyn Pol.
173 O4 Zachenberg Ger.
137 O4 Zachepylivka Ukr.
174 D2 Zachodniopomorskie prov. Pol.
244 D5 Zacoalco Mex.
245 H7 Zacualpán Mex.
244 B4 Zacualpan Nayarit Mex.
245 I5 Zacualpan Veracruz Mex.
245 I5 Zacualtipán Mex.
Zacynthus i. Greece see Zakynthos
175 L3 Zaczopki Pol.
204 D2 Zad, Col du pass Morocco
188 E3 Zadar Croatia
188 E3 Zadarski Kanal sea chan. Croatia
136 J2 Zaderiyivka Ukr.
97 D9 Zadetkale Kyun i. Myanmar
97 D10 Zadetkyi Kyun i. Myanmar
97 C7 Zadi Myanmar
111 L10 Zadoi Qinghai China
139 V9 Zadonsk Rus. Fed.
183 O3 Zadorra r. Spain
123 M5 Zadran reg. Afgh.
139 N6 Zadubrowye Belarus
177 G2 Zádveřice Czech Rep.
139 N6 Zadzyetuni Belarus
203 G2 Za'farānah Egypt
128 A9 Za'farānah, Ra's pt Egypt
185 K7 Zafarraya Spain
123 P5 Zafarwal Pak.
Zafer Adaları is Cyprus see Kleides Islands
Zafer Burnu c. Cyprus see Apostolos Andreas, Cape
195 I8 Zafferana Etnea Sicilia Italy
194 F7 Zafferano, Capo c. Sicilia
184 G4 Zafra Spain
183 O9 Zafra de Záncara Spain
183 Q8 Zafrilla Spain
183 Q8 Zafrilla, Sierra de mts Sp…
204 C3 Zag Morocco
179 H7 Žaga Slovenia
174 D4 Żagań Pol.
138 G5 Žagarė Lith.
193 J4 Zagarolo Italy
Zagazig Ash Sharqīyah Eg… see Az Zaqāzīq
129 F4 Zages Georgia
122 G4 Zaghdeh well Iran
122 D4 Zāgheh Iran
122 B4 Zāgheh-ye Bālā Iran
205 H1 Zaghouan Tunisia
189 C7 Zaghouan admin. div. Tun…
175 I5 Zagnańsk Pol.
197 O5 Zagon Romania
198 E3 Zagora Greece
204 D3 Zagora Morocco
179 M7 Zagorje reg. Croatia
191 Q4 Zagorje Slovenia
188 E2 Zagorje ob Savi Slovenia
174 F3 Zagórów Pol.
Zagorsk Rus. Fed. see Sergiyev Posad
175 K6 Zagórz Pol.
185 K6 Zagra Spain
197 M9 Zagrazhden Bulg.
188 E3 Zagreb Croatia
174 D4 Zagrodno Pol.
122 B4 Zagros, Kūhhā-ye mts Ir…
Zagros Mountains Iran s… Zagros, Kūhhā-ye
197 J6 Žagubica Serbia
Zagunao Sichuan China s… Lixian
111 I11 Za'gya Zangbo r. Xizang…
177 J4 Zagyva r. Hungary
177 J4 Zagyvarékas Hungary
136 I3 Zahal'tsi Ukr.
213 □K3 Zahamena, Réserve de nature res. Madag.
185 I7 Zahara Spain
184 H8 Zahara de los Atunes S…
185 I7 Zahara-El Gastor, Emba… de resr Spain
175 M3 Zaharoddzye reg. Belaru…
122 E7 Zāhedān Fārs Iran
122 I7 Zāhedān Sīstān va Balūch… Iran
184 F4 Zahinos Spain
123 N7 Zahir Pir Pak.
128 D5 Zahlé Lebanon
129 G5 Zähmätkänd Azer.
123 J3 Zähmet Turkm.
171 G7 Zahna Ger.
177 L3 Záhony Hungary
177 G2 Záhorovice Czech Rep.
176 F3 Záhorská Ves Slovakia
124 F7 Zahrān Saudi Arabia
123 L7 Zahri Nur Gama Pak.
138 K4 Zaiceva Latvia
183 Q6 Zaida, Laguna de resr S…
186 F4 Zaidín Spain
138 G6 Žaiginys Lith.
124 G5 Zā'in, Jabal hill Saudi Ar…
122 E5 Zaindeh r. Iran
Zainlha Sichuan China se… Xiaojin
Zainsk Rus. Fed. see Novyy Zay
Zair Uzbek. see Zoir
Zaire country Africa see Congo, Democratic Rep… of the
209 B6 Zaire prov. Angola
Zaïre r. Congo/Dem. Rep… Congo see Congo
196 I9 Zajas Macedonia
197 K7 Zaječar Serbia
173 P2 Zaječov Czech Rep.
174 D2 Zajezierze Pol.
213 F4 Zaka Zimbabwe
106 H1 Zakamensk Rus. Fed.
176 F5 Zákány Hungary
177 I5 Zákányszek Hungary
136 C5 Zakarpats'ka Oblast' admin. div. Ukr.
Zakarpatskaya Oblast' admin. div. Ukr. see Zakarpats'ka Oblast'
Zakataly Azer. see Zaqat…
Zakháro Greece see Zac…
139 W7 Zakharovo Rus. Fed.
136 D3 Zakhidnyy Buh r. Ukr.
127 K5 Zākhō Iraq
Zakhodnyaya Dzvina r. Europe see Zapadnaya D…
134 G1 Zakhrebetnoye Rus. Fed…
122 A2 Zakī, Kūh-e mt. Iran
Zákinthos i. Greece see Zakynthos
175 I6 Zakliczyn Pol.
175 K5 Zaklików Pol.
175 H6 Zakopane Pol.
208 C2 Zakouma Chad
208 C2 Zakouma, Parc Nationa… nat. park Chad
199 H7 Zakros Kriti Greece
175 K5 Zakrzew Lubelskie Pol.
175 J4 Zakrzew Mazowieckie Po…
174 G3 Zakrzewo Kujawsko-Pomorskie Pol.
174 F2 Zakrzewo Wielkopolskie …
175 K5 Zakrzówek-Wieś Pol.
176 D1 Zákupy Czech Rep.
222 F5 Zakwaski, Mount B.C. C…
198 B5 Zakynthos Zakynthos Gr…
198 B5 Zakynthos i. Greece
198 B5 Zakynthou, Porthmos sea chan. Greece
209 B6 Zala Angola
111 L11 Zala Xizang China
176 F5 Zala county Hungary
196 F4 Zala r. Romania
176 G5 Zalaapáti Hungary
176 F5 Zalaegerszeg Hungary
176 F5 Zalai-domsag hills Hung…
176 G5 Zalakaros Hungary
176 G5 Zalakomár Hungary
176 F5 Zalalövő Hungary
184 H3 Zalamea de la Serena S…
184 F5 Zalamea la Real Spain
207 H4 Zalanga Nigeria
107 R3 Zalantun Nei Mongol Chi…
176 G5 Zalaszántó Hungary
176 F5 Zalaszentbalázs Hungar…
176 G5 Zalaszentgrót Hungary
176 F5 Zalaszentiván Hungary
176 F5 Zalaszentmihály Hungar…
197 L3 Zalău Romania
177 L4 Zalău r. Romania
176 G5 Zalavár Hungary
138 J7 Zalavas Lith.
175 J4 Załazy Pol.
188 E2 Žalec Slovenia
167 I3 Załęczański Park Krajobrazowy Pol.
139 T9 Zalegoshch' Rus. Fed.
174 F3 Zalesie Kujawsko-Pomorsk…
175 L3 Zalesie Lubelskie Pol.
232 C9 Zaleski OH U.S.A.
139 T3 Zales'ye Rus. Fed.
175 H2 Zalewo Pol.
124 F4 Ẓalim Saudi Arabia
202 D6 Zalingei Sudan
136 E5 Zalishchyky Ukr.
136 E5 Zalissya Ukr.
137 P6 Zaliznychne Ukr.
137 L7 Zaliznyy Port Ukr.
136 E4 Zaliztsi Ukr.
124 D2 Ẓalmā, Jabal aẓ mt. Saudi Arabia
174 F2 Żalno Pol.
202 A1 Zalṭan Libya
202 C2 Zaltan, Jabal hills Libya
164 H5 Zaltbommel Neth.
175 L1 Žaltytis l. Lith.
139 O4 Zaluch'ye Rus. Fed.
136 D2 Zalukhiv Ukr.
129 E2 Zalukokoazhe Rus. Fed.
115 N4 Zalun Myanmar
138 L8 Zaluzhzha Belarus
175 M2 Zal'vyanka r. Belarus
177 L5 Zam Romania
105 J5 Zama Japan
207 F3 Zama Niger
222 G3 Zama City Alta Can.

H7 Zamakh Saudi Arabia
N3 Zamani S. Africa
G4 Zamanti r. Turkey
G5 Zamárdi Hungary
F2 Zamarte Pol.
C4 Zambales Mountains Luzon Phil.
F1 Žamberk Czech Rep.
D8 Zambeze r. Africa alt. Zambezi
D7 Zambezi r. Africa alt. Zambeze
D8 Zambezi Zambia
H3 Zambézia prov. Moz.
E9 Zambezi Escarpment Zambia/Zimbabwe
E3 Zambezi National Park Zimbabwe
E8 Zambia country Africa
D8 Zamboanga Mindanao Phil.
D8 Zamboanga Peninsula Mindanao Phil.
D7 Zamboanguita Negros Phil.
O3 Zambrana Spain
F9 Zambrano Col.
K3 Zambrów Pol.
F2 Zambue Moz.
A4 Zambujal de Cima Port.
B5 Zambujeira do Mar Port.
D2 Zamęcin Pol.
G3 Zamfara state Nigeria
G3 Zamfara watercourse Nigeria
J6 Zamīndāvar reg. Afgh.
Zamkog Sichuan China see Zamtang
B4 Zamlat Amagraj hills Western Sahara
K3 Zamogil'ye Rus. Fed.
H4 Zámoly Hungary
B6 Zamora Ecuador
B6 Zamora r. Ecuador
I5 Zamora Spain
I5 Zamora prov. Spain
E6 Zamora de Hidalgo Mex.
L5 Zamość Lubelskie Pol.
J2 Zamość Mazowieckie Pol.
Zamost'ye Pol. see Zamość
Q6 Zamozhne Ukr.
Zampa-misaki hd Okinawa Japan see Zanpa-misaki
D5 Zamp Dağı mt. Turkey
D5 Zams Austria
C2 Zamtang Sichuan China
D2 Zamuro, Punta pt Venez.
F3 Zamuro, Sierra del mts Venez.
B2 Zamzam, Wādī watercourse Libya
B6 Zaña Peru
B5 Zanaga Congo
M9 Zanatepec Mex.
K5 Zänbil Adası i. Azer.
N10 Záncara r. Spain
Zancle Sicilia Italy see Messina
D11 Zanda Xizang China
D2 Zandamela Moz.
D3 Zanderij Suriname
G6 Zandhoven Belgium
J9 Žandov Czech Rep.
F6 Zandvliet Belgium
G4 Zandvoort Neth.
C9 Zanesville OH U.S.A.
G6 Zangakatun Armenia
D3 Zangasso Mali
Zangelan Azer. see Zängilan
D6 Zangezuri Lerrnashght'a mts Armenia/Azer.
D8 Zangguy Xinjiang China
H6 Zängilan Azer.
F3 Zangla Jammu and Kashmir
G9 Zangsêr Kangri mt. Xizang China
N8 Zanhuang Hebei China
N8 Zani Dem. Rep. Congo
M7 Zani Pak.
Zaniemyśl Pol.
Zanjān Iran
Zanjān prov. Iran
M5 Zanjān Rūd r. Iran
Zanjitas Arg.
Zannah, Jabal aẓ hill U.A.E.
Zannone, Isola i. Italy
Zanpa-misaki hd Okinawa Japan
Zanskar r. India
Zanskar reg. Jammu and Kashmir
Zanskar Mountains India
Zante i. Ionioi Nisoi Greece see Zakynthos
Zante i. Ionioi Nisoi Greece see Zakynthos
Zanthus W.A. Austr.
Zantiébougou Mali
Zanzibar Tanz.
Zanzibar Channel Tanz.
Zanzibar Island Tanz.
Zanzibar North admin. reg. Tanz.
Zanzibar South admin. reg. Tanz.
Zanzibar West admin. reg. Tanz.
Zaohe Jiangsu China
Zaokskiy Rus. Fed.
Zaouia Mornag Tunisia
Zaorejas Spain
Zaoro-Songou C.A.R.
Zaosheng Gansu China
Zaoshi Hubei China
Zaoshi Hunan China
Zaostrov'ye Rus. Fed.
Zaouatallaz Alg.
Zaouet el Kahla Alg. see Bordj Omer Driss
Zaouiet Kounta Alg.
Zaoyang Hubei China
Zaoyangzhan Hubei China
Zaoyuan Xinjiang China
Zaō-zan vol. Japan
Zaozerne Ukr.
Zaozernyy Kazakh.
Zaozernyy Rus. Fed.
Zaozer'ye Rus. Fed.
Zaozhuang Shandong China
Zap r. Turkey
Zapadna Morava r. Serbia
Zapadnaya Dvina r. Europe alt. Daugava (Latvia), alt. Zakhodnyaya Dzvina, conv. Western Dvina
Zapadni Rodopi mts Bulg.
Zapadno-Kazakhstanskaya Oblast' admin. div. Kazakh. see Zapadnyy Kazakhstan
Zapadno-Sakhalinskiy Khrebet mts Rus. Fed.
Zapadno-Sibirskaya Nizmennost' plain Rus. Fed. see Zapadno-Sibirskaya Ravnina
Zapadno-Sibirskaya Ravnina plain Rus. Fed.
Zapadnyy Alamedin, Pik mt. Kyrg.
Zapadnyy Berezovyy, Ostrov i. Rus. Fed.
Zapadnyy Chink Ustyurta esc. Kazakh.
Zapadnyy Chink Ustyurta esc. Kazakh.
Zapadnyy Kazakhstan admin. div. Kazakh.
Zapadnyy Kil'din Rus. Fed.
Zapadnyy Sayan reg. Rus. Fed.
Zapadyntsi Ukr.
Zapala Arg.
Zapallar Chile
Zapałów Pol.
Zapardiel r. Spain
Zapata Arg.
Zapata TX U.S.A.
Zapata, Peninsula de pen. Cuba
Zapatoca Col.
Zapatón r. Spain
Zapatoza, Ciénaga de l. Col.
Zapfendorf Ger.
Zapiga Chile
Zápio Greece see Zappeio
138 M3 Zaplyus'ye Rus. Fed.
197 P4 Zăpodeni Romania
174 G4 Zapolice Pol.
140 U2 Zapolyarnyy Murmanskaya Oblast' Rus. Fed.
134 M2 Zapolyarnyy Respublika Komi Rus. Fed.
138 M3 Zapol'ye Pskovskaya Oblast' Rus. Fed.
139 T2 Zapol'ye Vologodskaya Oblast' Rus. Fed.
244 D5 Zapopan Mex.
137 O6 Zaporizhzhya Ukr.
Zaporizhzhya Oblast admin. div. Ukr. see Zaporiz'ka Oblast'
137 O6 Zaporiz'ka Oblast' admin. div. Ukr.
Zaporozhskaya Oblast' admin. div. Ukr. see Zaporiz'ka Oblast'
139 N1 Zaporozhskoye Rus. Fed.
Zaporozh'ye Ukr. see Zaporizhzhya
Zaporozhye Oblast admin. div. Ukr. see Zaporiz'ka Oblast'
244 D6 Zapotiltic Mex.
244 D6 Zapotitlán Jalisco Mex.
245 J6 Zapotitlán Puebla Mex.
245 J7 Zapotitlán Salinas Mex.
244 D5 Zapotlanejo Mex.
100 H7 Zapovednyy Rus. Fed.
198 D3 Zappeio Greece
171 E7 Zappendorf Ger.
193 P5 Zapponeta Italy
188 E3 Zaprešić Croatia
139 U5 Zaprudnya Rus. Fed.
138 H9 Zaprudy Belarus
111 E10 Zapug Xizang China
175 M6 Zapytiv Ukr.
129 H4 Zaqatala Azer.
129 H4 Zaqatala Qoruğu nature res. Azer.
Zaqāzīq Egypt see Az Zaqāzīq
111 L10 Zaqên Qinghai China
202 C2 Zaqqui Libya
108 A3 Za Qu r. Qinghai China
111 I10 Zaqungngomar mt. Xizang China
Zara Xizang China see Moinda
Zara Croatia see Zadar
126 H4 Zara Turkey
Zarafshan Uzbek. see Zarafshon
123 M2 Zarafshon Tajik.
123 M2 Zarafshon r. Tajik.
120 K7 Zarafshon Uzbek.
121 J8 Zarafshon r. Uzbek.
123 L2 Zarafshon, Qatorkŭhi mts Tajik.
250 C3 Zaragoza Col.
243 I3 Zaragoza Coahuila Mex.
245 H2 Zaragoza Nuevo León Mex.
245 J6 Zaragoza Puebla Mex.
186 D4 Zaragoza Spain
183 R5 Zaragoza prov. Spain
186 D7 Zaragozana mt. Spain
122 G6 Zarand Kermān Iran
122 D4 Zarand Markazī Iran
177 K5 Zărand Romania
197 K4 Zarandului, Munții hills Romania
111 D11 Zarang Xizang China
123 I6 Zaranj Afgh.
174 D2 Zarańsko Pol.
138 J6 Zarasai Lith.
129 K5 Zarat Azer.
183 O2 Zaratamo Spain
183 K5 Zaratán Spain
261 H4 Zárate Arg.
186 A1 Zarautz Spain
139 V7 Zaraysk Rus. Fed.
251 E2 Zaraza Venez.
121 M7 Zarbdor Uzbek.
185 P5 Zarcilla de Ramos Spain
123 K7 Zard Pak.
129 I5 Zärdab Azer.
122 H4 Zardak Iran
122 C5 Zard Kuh mts Iran
175 J2 Zaręby Pol.
175 K3 Zaręby-Kościelne Pol.
134 E2 Zarechensk Rus. Fed.
136 E1 Zarechka Belarus
134 L3 Zarechka Rus. Fed.
139 W8 Zarechnyy Rus. Fed.
139 X7 Zarech'ye Rus. Fed.
122 C4 Zāreh Iran
222 C3 Zarembo Island AK U.S.A.
138 F6 Žarėnai Lith.
124 E2 Zarghat Saudi Arabia
123 M5 Zarghūn Shahr Afgh.
123 L6 Zargun mt. Pak.
123 L4 Zari Afgh.
207 G4 Zaria Nigeria
Zariaspa Afgh. see Balkh
177 L3 Zaricheve Ukr.
137 N8 Zarichne Respublika Krym Ukr.
136 F2 Zarichne Rivnens'ka Oblast' Ukr.
122 F6 Zarīgān Iran
122 A3 Zarīneh Rūd r. Iran
175 H5 Żarki Pol.
174 C4 Żarki Wielkie Pol.
123 J5 Zarmardan Afgh.
129 J5 Zarnava Azer.
122 B5 Zarneh Iran
197 N5 Zărnești Romania
177 H3 Žarnovica Slovakia
175 I4 Żarnów Pol.
175 H5 Żarnowiec Pol.
143 O7 Żarnowieckie, Jezioro l. Pol.
174 E5 Żarów Pol.
168 K3 Zarpen Ger.
Zarqā' Jordan see Az Zarqā'
128 D6 Zarqā', Nahr az r. Jordan
128 D7 Zarqā' Mā'īn, Wādī r. Jordan
122 E7 Zarqān Iran
129 J4 Zärqava Azer.
165 C6 Zarren Belgium
168 K3 Zarrentin Ger.
122 F5 Zarrīn Iran
175 K6 Zarszyn Pol.
122 E6 Zarū Iran
139 Q3 Zarubino Novgorodskaya Oblast' Rus. Fed.
100 G7 Zarubino Primorskiy Kray Rus. Fed.
105 H5 Zaruga-dake mt. Japan
174 D4 Żary Pol.
120 G3 Zarya Oktyabrya Kazakh.
185 I3 Zarza Capilla Spain
184 G3 Zarza de Alange Spain
182 H8 Zarza de Granadilla Spain
183 N8 Zarza de Tajo Spain
185 P5 Zarzadilla de Totana Spain
205 H3 Zarzaïtine Alg.
250 B3 Zarzal Col.
182 G9 Zarza la Mayor Spain
175 K6 Zarzecze Pol.
205 H2 Zarzis Tunisia
183 L7 Zarzuela del Monte Spain
183 L6 Zarzuela del Pinar Spain
182 C2 Zas Spain
138 I5 Zasa Latvia
121 T3 Zashchita Kazakh.
140 U3 Zasheyek Rus. Fed.
Zaskar reg. Jammu and Kashmir see Zanskar
138 L6 Zaskarki Belarus
177 I2 Žaškov Slovakia
138 K8 Zaslawskaye Vodaskhovishcha resr Belarus
138 K7 Zaslawye Belarus
176 E2 Zásmuky Czech Rep.
137 R3 Zasosna Rus. Fed.
175 J5 Zasów Pol.
129 B1 Zassovskaya Rus. Fed.
136 E5 Zastavna Ukr.
215 L6 Zastron S. Africa
175 K3 Zaszków Pol.
128 E6 Za'tarī, Wādī az watercourse Jordan
176 C1 Žatec Czech Rep.
129 G1 Zaterechnyy Rus. Fed.
120 J1 Zatobol'sk Kazakh.
136 J7 Zatoka Ukr.
177 G1 Zátor Czech Rep.
175 H6 Zator Pol.
175 J3 Zatory Pol.
136 D3 Zaturtsi Ukr.
136 I6 Zatyshshya Ukr.
171 G6 Zauche reg. Ger.
245 J6 Zautla Mex.
177 M2 Zavadka Ukr.
177 I3 Závadka nad Hronom Slovakia
263 F2 Zavadovskiy Island Antarctica
261 G4 Zavalía Arg.
261 G3 Zavalla Arg.
237 H10 Zavalla TX U.S.A.
136 J5 Zavallya Ukr.
122 E5 Zavareh Iran
190 G6 Zavattarello Italy
165 F7 Zaventem Belgium
135 H7 Zavetnoye Rus. Fed.
100 L4 Zavety Il'icha Rus. Fed.
188 G3 Zavidovići Bos.-Herz.
139 T5 Zavidovskiy Zapovednik nature res. Rus. Fed.
Zavitaya Rus. Fed. see Zavitinsk
100 F3 Zavitinsk Rus. Fed.
137 N8 Zavit-Lenins'ky Ukr.
176 G3 Závod Slovakia
175 M5 Zavods'ke L'vivs'ka Oblast' Ukr.
136 E4 Zavods'ke Ternopils'ka Oblast' Ukr.
121 U1 Zavodskoy Altayskiy Kray Rus. Fed.
Zavodskoy Respublika Mordoviya Rus. Fed. see Komsomol'skiy
129 F3 Zavodskoy Respublika Severnaya Osetiya-Alaniya Rus. Fed.
197 K7 Zavojsko Jezero resr Serbia
134 H4 Zavolzhsk Rus. Fed.
Zavolzh'ye Rus. Fed. see Zavolzhsk
213 G5 Závora, Ponta pt Moz.
137 K3 Zavorychi Ukr.
138 L6 Zavutstsye Belarus
138 L6 Zavyachellye Belarus
131 Q4 Zav'yalova, Ostrov i. Rus. Fed.
121 S1 Zav'yalovo Rus. Fed.
175 L6 Zavydovychi Ukr.
106 G8 Zawa Qinghai China
111 D8 Zawa Xinjiang China
175 H4 Zawada Łódzkie Pol.
175 L5 Zawada Lubelskie Pol.
174 D4 Zawada Lubuskie Pol.
174 F5 Zawada Opolskie Pol.
175 H5 Zawada Śląskie Pol.
175 K2 Zawady Pol.
174 G5 Zawadzkie Pol.
96 C4 Zawgyi r. Myanmar
175 J5 Zawichost Pol.
174 D4 Zawidów Pol.
175 H3 Zawidz Kościelny Pol.
175 H5 Zawiercie Pol.
202 B3 Zawīlah Libya
128 E3 Zāwīyah, Jabal az hills Syria
202 D2 Zāwiyat Masūs Libya
126 C8 Zāwiyat Shammās pt Egypt
125 L5 Zawlīyah, Jiddat az plain Oman
175 H6 Zawoja Pol.
174 F4 Zawonia Pol.
111 J11 Zaxoi Xizang China
134 J5 Zay r. Rus. Fed.
179 O2 Zaya r. Austria
129 G5 Zäyäm Azer.
129 G4 Zäyämçay r. Azer.
128 E6 Zaydī, Wādī az watercourse Syria
139 N6 Zaykava Belarus
121 U4 Zaysan Kazakh.
Zaysan, Lake Kazakh. see Zaysan, Ozero
121 T3 Zaysan, Ozero l. Kazakh.
137 R5 Zaytseve Ukr.
138 L4 Zaytsevo Rus. Fed.
Zayü Xizang China see Gyigang
108 A4 Zayü Xizang China
108 A4 Zayü Xizang China
129 E2 Zayukovo Rus. Fed.
108 A4 Zayü Qu r. China/India
Zayyr Uzbek. see Zoir
213 □J4 Zazafotsy Madag.
207 G3 Zazagawa Nigeria
205 G6 Zazir, Oued watercourse Alg.
177 I2 Zázrivá Slovakia
136 E4 Zbarazh Ukr.
174 D3 Zbąszyn Pol.
174 D3 Zbąszynek Pol.
174 D3 Zbąszyńskie, Jezioro l. Pol.
175 H2 Zbiczno Pol.
174 G4 Zbiersk Pol.
173 P2 Zbiroh Czech Rep.
174 G2 Zblewo Pol.
175 I5 Zbludowice Pol.
175 J2 Zbójna Pol.
175 H2 Zbójno Pol.
196 H7 Zborište mt. Serbia
136 E4 Zboriv Ukr.
177 K2 Zborov Slovakia
174 F6 Zborovice Czech Rep.
179 N1 Zbraslav Czech Rep.
176 E2 Zbraslavice Czech Rep.
136 F5 Zbruch r. Ukr.
176 C2 Zbůch Czech Rep.
175 K3 Zbuczyn Poduchowny Pol.
137 L7 Zbur"yivka Ukr.
179 N1 Zbýšov Czech Rep.
176 G5 Ždala Croatia
179 P1 Ždánice Czech Rep.
176 F2 Ždánický les for. Czech Rep.
171 L9 Ždár Czech Rep.
176 E2 Žďár nad Sázavou Czech Rep.
176 E2 Žďárské vrchy hills Czech Rep.
176 E2 Zdárské vrchy park Czech Rep.
177 J2 Ždiar Slovakia
176 C2 Zdíkov Czech Rep.
176 E2 Ždírec nad Doubravou Czech Rep.
136 F3 Zdolbuniv Ukr.
Zdolbunov Ukr. see Zdolbuniv
176 G2 Zdounky Czech Rep.
174 G4 Zduńska Wola Pol.
175 H3 Zduny Łódzkie Pol.
174 F4 Zduny Wielkopolskie Pol.
136 J2 Zdvyzh r. Ukr.
175 J6 Zdynia Pol.
174 G4 Zdziechowice Opolskie Pol.
175 K5 Zdziechowice Podkarpackie Pol.
174 G5 Zdzieszowice Pol.
175 K5 Zdziłowice Pol.
175 N3 Zdzitava Belarus
Zealand i. Denmark see Sjælland
123 N3 Zēbāk Afgh.
259 C7 Zeballos mt. Arg.
222 E5 Zeballos B.C. Can.
127 L5 Zēbār Iraq
195 □ Żebbiegħ Malta
195 □ Żebbuġ Gozo Malta
195 □ Żebbuġ Malta
Zebirget Island Egypt see Zabarjad, Jazīrat
174 G5 Zębowice Pol.
173 P2 Žebrák Czech Rep.
182 F9 Zebreira Port.
174 D4 Zebrzydowa Pol.
174 G6 Zebrzydowice Dolne Pol.
231 E9 Zebulon GA U.S.A.
232 C11 Zebulon KY U.S.A.
231 H8 Zebulon NC U.S.A.
191 Q6 Zeča i. Croatia
170 G4 Zechlin Dorf Ger.
170 G4 Zechlinerhütte Ger.
164 J5 Zeddam Neth.
192 B8 Zeddiani Sardegna Italy
165 D6 Zedelgem Belgium
179 I5 Zederhaus Austria
177 I6 Žednik Vojvodina Serbia
165 D6 Zeebrugge Belgium
83 J9 Zeehan Tas. Austr.
164 I5 Zeeland Neth.
164 E5 Zeeland prov. Neth.
226 H7 Zeeland MI U.S.A.
128 C7 Ze'elim Israel
215 K1 Zeerust S. Africa
171 I6 Zeesen Ger.
165 D6 Zeeuwsch-Vlaanderen reg. Neth.
164 I4 Zeewolde Neth.
128 D6 Ẕefat Israel
122 E5 Zefreh Iran
186 A2 Zegama Spain
175 I6 Żegiestów Pol.
175 I6 Żegocina Pol.
175 J3 Zegrzyńskie, Jezioro l. Pol.
170 H5 Zehdenick Ger.
170 F3 Zehna Ger.
171 H8 Zehren Ger.
84 D7 Zeil, Mount N.T. Austr.
169 K10 Zeil am Main Ger.
173 N5 Zeilarn Ger.
138 H5 Žeimelis Lith.
179 N3 Zeiselmauer Austria
164 H4 Zeist Neth.
171 H8 Zeithain Ger.
173 M3 Zeitlarn Ger.
169 I10 Zeitlofs Ger.
171 F8 Zeitz Ger.
195 □ Żejtun Malta
106 G9 Zêkog Qinghai China
110 F5 Zekti Xinjiang China
Zela Turkey see Zile
174 G4 Żelazków Pol.
165 F6 Zele Belgium
175 I4 Żelechlinek Pol.
175 J4 Żelechów Pol.
136 F5 Zelena Chernivets'ka Oblast' Ukr.
136 D5 Zelena Ivano-Frankivs'ka Oblast' Ukr.
136 D5 Zelena Ivano-Frankivs'ka Oblast' Ukr.
188 F4 Zelena Gora mt. Bos.-Herz.
176 G2 Zelená hora tourist site Czech Rep.
121 P1 Zelenaya Roshcha Kazakh.
129 C2 Zelenchukskaya Rus. Fed.
171 K10 Zeleneč Czech Rep.
177 G3 Zeleneč Slovakia
137 P6 Zelene Pole Ukr.
188 G4 Zelengora mts Bos.-Herz.
137 L7 Zelenivka Ukr.
137 N4 Zelenkivka Ukr.
134 I3 Zelennik Rus. Fed.
140 V3 Zelenoborskiy Rus. Fed.
134 J5 Zelenodol'sk Rus. Fed.
137 M6 Zelenodol's'k Ukr.
138 M1 Zelenogorsk Rus. Fed.
139 U5 Zelenograd Rus. Fed.
138 D7 Zelenogradsk Rus. Fed.
136 J6 Zelenohirs'ke Ukr.
129 E1 Zelenokumsk Rus. Fed.
134 I4 Zelentsovo Rus. Fed.
99 Q3 Zelenyy, Ostrov i. Kuril'skiye O-va Rus. Fed.
121 N2 Zelenyy Gay Kazakh.
179 O1 Želešice Czech Rep.
176 E2 Želetava Czech Rep.
176 C2 Železná Ruda Czech Rep.
177 I3 Železné Slovakia
176 E2 Železné hory hills Czech Rep.
179 J7 Železniki Slovenia
176 E1 Železný Brod Czech Rep.
164 J4 Zelhem Neth.
232 E8 Zelienople PA U.S.A.
177 H3 Želiezovce Slovakia
188 F3 Zelina Croatia
106 E8 Zelinggou Qinghai China
196 J9 Želino Macedonia
176 E2 Želivka r. Czech Rep.
176 E2 Želivka, Vodní nádrž resr Czech Rep.
196 I7 Željin mt. Serbia
175 K3 Żelków-Kolonia Pol.
171 E10 Zell Ger.
169 D10 Zell (Mosel) Ger.
169 K9 Zella-Mehlis Ger.
172 E5 Zell am Harmersbach Ger.
178 G5 Zell am See Austria
178 E5 Zell am Ziller Austria
179 I3 Zell an der Pram Austria
179 M2 Zellerndorf Austria
179 L4 Zellerrain pass Austria
178 G5 Zeller See l. Austria
179 H4 Zellersee l. Austria
172 G6 Zellersee l. Ger.
172 D6 Zell im Wiesental Ger.
172 H2 Zellingen Ger.
179 J7 Zell-Pfarre Austria
177 I3 Želovce Slovakia
175 H4 Zelów Pol.
172 C2 Zeltingen-Rachtig Ger.
138 J4 Zeltiņi Latvia
179 K5 Zeltweg Austria
138 H8 Zel'va Belarus
175 M2 Zel'vyenskaye Vodaskhovishcha resr Belarus
165 E6 Zelzate Belgium
138 E6 Žemaičių Naumiestis Lith.
138 E5 Žemaitijos nacionalinis parkas nat. park Lith.
177 H3 Žemberovce Slovakia
138 L7 Zembin Belarus
198 B2 Zemblak Albania
175 K3 Zembrów Pol.
175 H6 Zembrzyce Pol.
197 K8 Zemen Bulg.
197 O4 Zemeș Romania
135 H5 Zemetchino Rus. Fed.
177 G4 Zemianska Olča Slovakia
208 E3 Zémio C.A.R.
170 I3 Zemitz Ger.
137 R2 Zemlyansk Rus. Fed.
172 B2 Zemmer Ger.
129 C3 Zemo Barghebi Georgia
129 E4 Zemo Khveduret'i Georgia
208 E3 Zémongo, Réserve de Faune de nature res. C.A.R.
129 F4 Zemo Qarabulakhi Georgia
177 L3 Zemplénagárd Hungary
177 K3 Zempleni park Hungary
177 K3 Zempléni-hegység hills Hungary
177 L3 Zemplínska šírava l. Slovakia
177 K3 Zemplínska Teplica Slovakia
177 L3 Zemplínske Hámre Slovakia
245 I6 Zempoala Hidalgo Mex.
245 K6 Zempoala Veracruz Mex.
245 L8 Zempoaltépetl, Nudo de mt. Mex.
165 F7 Zemst Belgium
139 P5 Zemtsy Rus. Fed.
196 I6 Zemun Serbia
108 A2 Zênda Sichuan China
109 I7 Zengcheng Guangdong China
100 F7 Zengfeng Shan mt. China
177 H5 Zengő hill Hungary
188 F3 Zenica Bos.-Herz.
128 C8 Ẕenifim watercourse Israel
173 J2 Zenn r. Ger.
150 □ Zennor Cornwall, England U.K.
Zenta Vojvodina Serbia see Senta
103 K12 Zentsūji Japan
123 M4 Zenyeh Afgh.
205 F2 Zenzach Alg.
245 J9 Zenzontepec Mex.
188 G3 Žepče Bos.-Herz.
170 I5 Zepernick Ger.
240 M2 Zephyr Cove NV U.S.A.
231 F11 Zephyrhills FL U.S.A.
111 C7 Zepu Xinjiang China
208 C2 Zérab, Ouadi watercourse Chad
210 A2 Zeraf, Bahr el r. Sudan
Zeravshan Tajik. see Zarafshon
Zeravshan r. Tajik. see Zarafshon
Zeravshan r. Uzbek. see Zarafshon
Zeravshanskiy Khrebet mts Tajik. see Zarafshon, Qatorkŭhi
171 F7 Zerbst Ger.
123 I6 Zereh, Gowd-e depr. Afgh.
123 J7 Zereh, Gowd-e depr. Afgh.
121 M1 Zerenda Kazakh.
172 B2 Zerf Ger.
205 G2 Zeribet el Oued Alg.
177 K5 Zerind Romania
174 F3 Żerków Pol.
190 D3 Zermatt Switz.
190 I2 Zernez Switz.
168 K4 Zernien Ger.
170 F5 Zernitz Ger.
135 H7 Zernograd Rus. Fed.
Zernovoy Rus. Fed. see Zernograd
191 M4 Zero r. Italy
170 I5 Zerpenschleuse Ger.
170 J4 Zerrenthin Ger.
167 I2 Zespół Nadwiślanskich Parków Krajobrazowych Pol.
167 I2 Zespół Nadwiślanskich Parków Krajobrazowych Pol.
Zestafoni Georgia see Zestap'oni
129 E3 Zestap'oni Georgia
186 A1 Zestoa Spain
117 L5 Zêsum Xizang China
196 H8 Zeta r. Montenegro
179 M7 Žetale Slovenia
111 J12 Zêtang Xizang China
197 N4 Zetea Romania
168 E4 Zetel Ger.
171 E9 Zeulenroda Ger.
171 I6 Zeuthen Ger.
168 H4 Zeven Ger.
164 J5 Zevenaar Neth.
164 G5 Zevenbergen Neth.
164 J2 Zevenhuizen Neth.
128 A4 Zevgari, Cape Cyprus
198 D5 Zevgolatio Greece
191 K5 Zevio Italy
100 E2 Zeya Rus. Fed.
100 E3 Zeya r. Rus. Fed.
122 F7 Zeydābād Iran
122 G3 Zeydar Iran
123 J8 Zeydī Iran
122 G7 Zeynalābād Iran
100 E1 Zeyskiy Zapovednik nature res. Rus. Fed.
100 G3 Zeysko-Bureinskaya Vpadina depr. Rus. Fed.
100 E1 Zeyskoye Vodokhranilishche resr Rus. Fed.
Zeytin Burnu c. Cyprus see Elaia, Cape
199 I4 Zeytindağ Turkey
198 B2 Zezë, Maja e mt. Albania
182 D10 Zêzere r. Port.
107 M9 Zezhou Shanxi China
128 D4 Zgharta Lebanon
175 H4 Zgierz Pol.
175 I6 Zgłobice Pol.
179 J7 Zgornje Bitnje Slovenia
179 J7 Zgornje Jezersko Slovenia
179 M6 Zgornji Duplek Slovenia
174 D4 Zgorzelec Pol.
136 G5 Zgurița Moldova
136 D1 Zhabinka Belarus
136 H5 Zhabokrychka Ukr.
Zhabye Ukr. see Verkhovyna
136 H3 Zhad'ky Ukr.
137 L1 Zhadove Ukr.
Zhaggo Sichuan China see Luhuo
108 B2 Zhaglag Sichuan China
108 A3 Zhag'yab Xizang China
Zhahti Koe N.W.T. Can. see Fort Providence
120 I2 Zhailma Kazakh.
121 L2 Zhaksy Kazakh.
121 M3 Zhaksy-Kon watercourse Kazakh.
120 I4 Zhaksykylysh Kazakh.
120 I4 Zhaksykylysh, Ozero salt l. Kazakh.
Zhaksy Sarysu watercourse Kazakh. see Sarysu
Zhalaghash Kazakh. see Dzhalagash
121 R6 Zhalanash Almatinskaya Oblast' Kazakh.
Zhalanash Kostanayskaya Oblast' Kazakh. see Damdy
Zhalgyztöbe Kazakh. see Zhangiztobe
120 C3 Zhalpaktal Kazakh.
Zhalpaqtal Kazakh. see Zhalpaktal
121 M2 Zhaltyr Akmolinskaya Oblast' Kazakh.
121 Q2 Zhaltyr Pavlodarskaya Oblast' Kazakh.
120 D4 Zhaltyr, Ozero l. Kazakh.
138 H8 Zhaludok Belarus
120 J3 Zhamanakkol', Ozero salt l. Kazakh.
120 E4 Zhamansor Kazakh.
121 N4 Zhambyl Karagandinskaya Oblast' Kazakh.
Zhambyl Zhambylskaya Oblast' Kazakh. see Taraz
Zhambyl Oblast admin. div. Kazakh. see Zhambylskaya Oblast'
121 O5 Zhambylskaya Oblast' admin. div. Kazakh.
121 S4 Zhameuka Kazakh.
Zhamo Xizang China see Bomi
121 M4 Zhanabas Kazakh.
121 L6 Zhanakorgan Kazakh.
120 I5 Zhanakurylys Kazakh.
111 J12 Zhanang Xizang China
121 P4 Zhanaortalyk Kazakh.
120 E6 Zhanaozen Kazakh.
121 R6 Zhanatalan Kazakh.
121 M6 Zhanatas Kazakh.
120 I5 Zhanay Kazakh.
120 D4 Zhanbay Kazakh.
100 E4 Zhanbei Heilong. China
Zhangaözen Kazakh. see Zhanaozen
Zhangaqazaly Kazakh. see Ayteke Bi
Zhanga Qazan Kazakh. see Novaya Kazanka
Zhangaqorghan Kazakh. see Zhanakorgan
Zhangatas Kazakh. see Zhanatas
107 N6 Zhangbei Hebei China
Zhangcheng Fujian China see Yongtai
109 K2 Zhangcunpu Anhui China
Zhangdian Shandong China see Zibo
Zhanggu Sichuan China see Danba
100 F5 Zhangguangcai Ling mts China
107 R5 Zhanggutai Liaoning China
107 N8 Zhang He r. China
Zhanghua Taiwan see Changhua
108 G8 Zhanghuang Guangxi China
121 S3 Zhangiztobe Kazakh.
108 F1 Zhangjiachuan Gansu China
108 H4 Zhangjiajie Hunan China
107 N6 Zhangjiakou Hebei China
109 K4 Zhangjialing Jiangxi China
Zhangjiang Hunan China see Taoyuan
Zhangjiapan Shaanxi China see Jingbian
100 C2 Zhangling Heilong. China
109 K2 Zhanglou Anhui China
109 K6 Zhangping Fujian China
109 K6 Zhangpu Fujian China
107 R5 Zhangqiangzhen Liaoning China
107 O8 Zhangqiu Shandong China
109 J4 Zhangshu Jiangxi China
Zhangwan Hubei China see Xiangyang
107 O7 Zhangwei Xinhe r. China
107 R5 Zhangwu Liaoning China
106 I9 Zhangxian Gansu China
106 G7 Zhangye Gansu China
109 K6 Zhangzhou Fujian China
107 M8 Zhangzi Shanxi China
Zhanhe Heilong. China see Zhanbei
100 F4 Zhan He r. China
107 P8 Zhanhua Shandong China
120 B3 Zhanibek Kazakh.
Zhänibek Kazakh. see Zhanibek
108 H8 Zhanjiang Guangdong China
Zhansügirov Kazakh. see Dzhansugurov
120 F4 Zhanterek Kazakh.
108 D6 Zhanyi Yunnan China
109 K7 Zhao'an Fujian China
100 D5 Zhaodong Heilong. China
Zhaoge Henan China see Qixian
108 D4 Zhaojue Sichuan China
109 I4 Zhaoliqiao Hubei China
108 H6 Zhaoping Guangxi China
109 I7 Zhaoqing Guangdong China
Zhaoren Shaanxi China see Changwu
110 E5 Zhaosu Xinjiang China
107 R5 Zhaosutai He r. China
108 D5 Zhaotong Yunnan China
107 N8 Zhaoxian Hebei China
107 O9 Zhaoyang Hu l. China
100 D6 Zhaoyuan Heilong. China
107 Q8 Zhaoyuan Shandong China
Zhaozhen Sichuan China see Jintang
Zhaozhou Hebei China see Zhaoxian
100 D6 Zhaozhou Heilong. China
109 H8 Zhapo Guangdong China
Zhaqsy Kazakh. see Zhaksy
136 H4 Zhar r. Ukr.
121 T4 Zharbulak Kazakh.
138 K7 Zhardzyazhzha Belarus
111 G11 Zhari Namco salt l. China
120 G4 Zharkamys Kazakh.
121 S5 Zharkent Kazakh.
139 P6 Zharkovskiy Rus. Fed.
120 E6 Zharma Mangistauskaya Oblast' Kazakh.
121 S3 Zharma Vostochnyy Kazakhstan Kazakh.
120 E5 Zharmysh-Ondy Kazakh.
121 S4 Zharsuat Kazakh.
Zharyk Kazakh. see Saken Seyfullin
121 S3 Zharyk Kazakh.
136 J4 Zhashkiv Ukr.
Zhashkov Ukr. see Zhashkiv
108 G2 Zhashui Shaanxi China
Zhaslyk Uzbek. see Jasliq
139 P8 Zhastkovo Rus. Fed.
Zhaxi Yunnan China see Weixin
111 G10 Zhaxi Co salt l. China
111 D10 Zhaxigang Xizang China
111 I12 Zhaxigang Xizang China
108 A3 Zhaxizê Xizang China
111 H12 Zhaxizong Xizang China
121 N3 Zhayrem Kazakh.
108 B4 Zhayü Xizang China
Zhayylma Kazakh. see Zhailma
Zhayyq r. Kazakh./Rus. Fed. see Ural
137 O5 Zhdanivka Ukr.
Zhdanov Ukr. see Mariupol'
121 N6 Zhdanovo Kazakh.
139 Q4 Zhdanovo Rus. Fed.
Zhdanovsk Azer. see Beyläqan
137 M3 Zhdany Ukr.
Zhdenevo Ukr. see Zhdeniyevo
136 C5 Zhdeniyevo Ukr.
107 N9 Zhecheng Henan China
Zhedao Yunnan China see Lianghe
108 C3 Zhêhor Sichuan China
109 M4 Zhejiang prov. China
121 P3 Zhekezhal Kazakh.
109 J7 Zhelang Guangdong China
130 H2 Zhelaniya, Mys c. Novaya Zemlya Rus. Fed.
138 K3 Zhelcha r. Rus. Fed.
121 P1 Zhelezinka Kazakh.
138 E7 Zheleznodorozhnyy Kaliningradskaya Oblast' Rus. Fed.
Zheleznodorozhnyy Respublika Komi Rus. Fed. see Yemva
Zheleznodorozhnyy Uzbek. see Qo'ng'irot
139 S9 Zheleznogorsk Rus. Fed.
129 E1 Zheleznovodsk Rus. Fed.
139 U7 Zheleznya Rus. Fed.
Zhelou Guizhou China see Ceheng
121 P5 Zheltorangy Kazakh.
Zheltyye Vody Ukr. see Zhovti Vody
137 N8 Zhelyabovka Ukr.
197 O8 Zhelyu Voyvoda Bulg.
Zhem Kazakh. see Emba
108 G2 Zhen'an Shaanxi China
108 F2 Zhenba Shaanxi China
108 E6 Zhenfeng Guizhou China
108 F4 Zheng'an Guizhou China
107 N7 Zhengding Hebei China
109 L5 Zhenghe Fujian China
Zhengjiakou Hebei China see Gucheng
Zhengjiatun Jilin China see Shuangliao
Zhengkou Hebei China see Gucheng
Zhenglan Qi Nei Mongol China see Dund Hot
106 H8 Zhenglubu Gansu China
107 K9 Zhengning Gansu China
Zhengxiangbai Qi Nei Mongol China see Qagan Nur
109 J2 Zhengyang Henan China
107 M9 Zhengzhou Henan China
109 M4 Zhenhai Zhejiang China
109 L2 Zhenjiang Jiangsu China
Zhenjiang Jiangsu China see Zhenjiang
108 D2 Zhenjiangguan Sichuan China
Zhenkang Yunnan China see Fengwei
108 B7 Zhenkang Yunnan China
107 R4 Zhenlai Jilin China
108 E5 Zhenning Guizhou China
108 G3 Zhenping Shaanxi China
Zhenwudong Shaanxi China see Ansai
107 R4 Zhenxi Jilin China
108 E5 Zhenxiong Yunnan China
Zhenyang Henan China see Zhengyang
107 J9 Zhenyuan Gansu China
108 G5 Zhenyuan Guizhou China
108 C7 Zhenyuan Yunnan China
108 H3 Zhenziling Hubei China
135 H6 Zherdevka Rus. Fed.
139 T8 Zherdevo Rus. Fed.
136 F5 Zherdya Ukr.
137 R5 Zherebets' r. Ukr.
136 I2 Zheriv r. Ukr.
136 I3 Zheriv r. Ukr.
109 L5 Zherong Fujian China
134 J3 Zheshart Rus. Fed.
139 U5 Zhestylevo Rus. Fed.
Zhetibay Kazakh. see Zhetybay
Zhetikara Kazakh. see Zhitikara
Zhetisay Kazakh. see Zhetysay
120 E6 Zhetybay Kazakh.
120 I2 Zhety-Kol', Ozero l. Rus. Fed.
121 M7 Zhetysay Kazakh.
111 H11 Zhêxam Xizang China
109 H4 Zhexi Shuiku resr China
121 L3 Zhezdy Kazakh.
121 L4 Zhezkazgan Karagandinskaya Oblast' Kazakh.
121 L4 Zhezkazgan Karagandinskaya Oblast' Kazakh.
Zhezqazghan Kazakh. see Zhezkazgan
Zhicheng Shandong China see Qingzhou
Zhicheng Zhejiang China see Changxing
139 O6 Zhichitsy Rus. Fed.
107 K8 Zhidan Shaanxi China
111 L10 Zhidoi Qinghai China
131 N3 Zhigansk Rus. Fed.
107 P9 Zhigou Shandong China
120 C1 Zhigulevsk Rus. Fed.
111 J11 Zhigung Xizang China
108 G5 Zhijiang Hunan China
108 E5 Zhijin Guizhou China
139 V7 Zhilevo Rus. Fed.
139 T8 Zhilino Orlovskaya Oblast' Rus. Fed.
137 S4 Zhilino Voronezhskaya Oblast' Rus. Fed.
Zhilong Guangdong China see Yangxi
107 K9 Zhiluozhen Shaanxi China
Zhilyanka Kazakh. see Kargalinskoye
135 I6 Zhirnovsk Rus. Fed.
Zhirnovskiy Rus. Fed. see Zhirnovsk
Zhirnoye Rus. Fed. see Zhirnovsk
139 Q8 Zhiryatino Rus. Fed.
Zhitarovo Bulg. see Vetren
120 I1 Zhitikara Kazakh.
Zhitkovichi Belarus see Zhytkavichy
138 M1 Zhitkovo Rus. Fed.
135 I6 Zhitkur Rus. Fed.
198 A2 Zhitom Albania
Zhitomir Ukr. see Zhytomyr
Zhitomir Oblast admin. div. Ukr. see Zhytomyrs'ka Oblast'
Zhitomirskaya Oblast' admin. div. Ukr. see Zhytomyrs'ka Oblast'
127 M6 Zhivār Iran
139 R8 Zhizdra Rus. Fed.
139 T7 Zhizdra r. Rus. Fed.
139 O5 Zhizhitsa Rus. Fed.
139 O5 Zhizhitskoye, Ozero l. Rus. Fed.
108 B5 Zhiziluo Yunnan China
139 N9 Zhlobin Belarus
Zhmerinka Ukr. see Zhmerynka
136 H4 Zhmerynka Ukr.
123 M6 Zhob Pak.
123 M5 Zhob r. Pak.
138 L7 Zhodzina Belarus
131 Q2 Zhokhova, Ostrov i. Novosibirskiye O-va Rus. Fed.
Zholkva Ukr. see Zhovkva
121 T3 Zholnuskay Kazakh.
121 N2 Zholymbet Kazakh.
Zhong'an Yunnan China see Fuyuan
109 J7 Zhongba Guangdong China
Zhongba Sichuan China see Jiangyou
111 G12 Zhongba Xizang China
Zhongcheng Sichuan China see Xingwen
Zhongcheng Yunnan China see Suijiang
Zhongduo Chongqing China see Youyang
Zhongguo country Asia see China
Zhongguo Renmin Gongheguo country Asia see China
Zhonghe Chongqing China see Xiushan
107 N9 Zhongmou Henan China
106 I8 Zhongning Ningxia China
Zhongping Yunnan China see Huize
106 H8 Zhongpu Gansu China
263 F2 Zhongshan research stn Antarctica
109 I7 Zhongshan Guangdong China
109 H6 Zhongshan Guangxi China
Zhongshan Guizhou China see Lupanshui
Zhongsha Qundao sea feature Paracel Is see Macclesfield Bank
Zhongshu Yunnan China see Luxi
Zhongshu Yunnan China see Luliang
Zhongtai Gansu China see Lingtai
107 L9 Zhongtiao Shan mts China
106 I8 Zhongwei Ningxia China
108 G3 Zhongxian Chongqing China
109 J6 Zhongxin Guangdong China
Zhongxin Yunnan China see Huaping
Zhongxing Jiangsu China see Siyang
109 K3 Zhongxingji Anhui China
108 B1 Zhongxinzhan Qinghai China
107 L8 Zhongyang Shanxi China
100 D3 Zhongyaozhan Heilong. China
108 D6 Zhongyicun Yunnan China
108 H9 Zhongyuan Hainan China
Zhong Yunhe canal China see Da Yunhe
108 E2 Zhongzhai Gansu China
109 N4 Zhongzhai Zhejiang China
Zhongzhou Chongqing China see Zhongxian
175 L4 Zhorany Ukr.
137 M5 Zhorte Ukr.
137 L2 Zhortneve Ukr.
Zhosaly Kyzylordinskaya Oblast' Kazakh. see Dzhusaly
121 Q2 Zhosaly Pavlodarskaya Oblast' Kazakh.
107 O9 Zhoucheng Shandong China
108 F3 Zhou He r. China
106 H7 Zhoujiajing Gansu China
108 F2 Zhoujiaping Shaanxi China
109 J2 Zhoukou Henan China
Zhoukou Sichuan China see Peng'an
107 N7 Zhoukoudian tourist site China
109 L5 Zhouning Fujian China
109 N3 Zhoushan Zhejiang China
109 N3 Zhoushan Dao i. China
109 N3 Zhoushan Qundao is China
107 K9 Zhouzhi Shaanxi China
136 C3 Zhovkva Ukr.
137 M6 Zhovta r. Ukr.
136 J6 Zhovten' Ukr.
137 M5 Zhovti Vody Ukr.
137 Q4 Zhovtneve Kharkivs'ka Oblast' Ukr.
137 N4 Zhovtneve Poltavs'ka Oblast' Ukr.
137 N3 Zhovtneve Sums'ka Oblast' Ukr.
175 M5 Zhovtneve Volyns'ka Oblast' Ukr.
120 I2 Zhualy Kazakh.
107 R7 Zhuanghe Liaoning China
106 I9 Zhuanglang Gansu China
121 M5 Zhuantobe Kazakh.
108 A2 Zhubgyügoin Qinghai China
136 G2 Zhubrovychi Ukr.
107 P9 Zhucheng Shandong China
Zhudong Taiwan see Chutung
106 F8 Zhugkyung Qinghai China
111 K11 Zhugla Xizang China
108 E2 Zhugqu Gansu China
109 I7 Zhuhai Guangdong China
109 M4 Zhuji Zhejiang China
107 L7 Zhujia Chuan r. China
109 I7 Zhu Jiang r. Guangdong China
109 M3 Zhujing Shanghai China
109 I7 Zhukeng Guangdong China
139 P5 Zhukopa r. Rus. Fed.
139 Q8 Zhukovka Rus. Fed.
139 T6 Zhukovo Rus. Fed.
139 V6 Zhukovskiy Rus. Fed.
136 J3 Zhukyn Ukr.
107 N7 Zhulong He r. China
109 J2 Zhumadian Henan China
120 D4 Zhumysker Kazakh.
107 N6 Zhuolu Hebei China
Zhuoyang Henan China see Suiping
107 O7 Zhuozhou Hebei China
107 M6 Zhuozi Nei Mongol China
Zhuozishan Nei Mongol China see Zhuozi
137 T3 Zhuravka Rus. Fed.
137 O8 Zhuravky Ukr.
121 M2 Zhuravlevka Kazakh.
136 D4 Zhuravno Ukr.
137 S8 Zhuravskaya Rus. Fed.
137 L1 Zhurbin Rus. Fed.
137 K3 Zhurivka Ukr.
138 K6 Zhurki Belarus
120 G3 Zhuryn Kazakh.
121 O5 Zhusandala, Step' plain Kazakh.
Zhushan Hubei China see Xuan'en
108 H2 Zhushan Hubei China
108 G2 Zhuxi Hubei China
Zhuyang Sichuan China see Dazhu
109 I5 Zhuzhou Hunan China
109 I5 Zhuzhou Hunan China

175 M5 Zhvyrka Ukr.
136 D4 Zhydachiv Ukr.
120 E2 Zhympity Kazakh.
120 D5 Zhyngyldy Kazakh.
175 N1 Zhyrmuny Belarus
175 N2 Zhyrovichy Belarus
175 M4 Zhyrychi Ukr.
136 G1 Zhytkavichy Belarus
136 H3 Zhytomyr Ukr.
Zhytomyr Oblast *admin. div.* Ukr. *see* Zhytomyrs'ka Oblast'
136 G3 Zhytomyrs'ka Oblast' *admin. div.* Ukr.
136 I4 Zhyvka *r.* Ukr.
138 I8 Zhyzhma *r.* Belarus
206 C4 Ziama *mt.* Guinea
122 D3 Ziārān Iran
122 G3 Ziarat Iran
123 L6 Ziarat Pak.
177 H3 Žiar nad Hronom Slovakia
128 G8 Zibā *salt pan* Saudi Arabia
127 K5 Zībār Iraq
190 I5 Zibello Italy
107 P8 Zibo *Shandong* China
184 B2 Zibreira Port.
192 C4 Zicavo *Corse* France
107 K8 Zichang *Shaanxi* China
Zicheng *Guangdong* China *see* Zijin
173 P3 Žichovice Czech Rep.
170 D5 Zichtauer Berge und Klötzer Forst *park* Ger.
170 D3 Zickhusen Ger.
244 F7 Zicuirán Mex.
179 L7 Zidani Most Slovenia
123 M2 Ziddí Tajik.
123 L8 Zidi Pak.
137 P4 Zid'ky Ukr.
174 F5 Ziębice Pol.
170 E4 Ziegendorf Ger.
171 E9 Ziegenrück Ger.
171 H8 Ziegra Ger.
Ziel, Mount *N.T.* Austr. *see* Zeil, Mount
175 L4 Zielawa *r.* Pol.
174 D1 Zieleniewo *Zachodniopomorskie* Pol.
174 D2 Zieleniewo *Zachodniopomorskie* Pol.
171 E6 Zielitz Ger.
175 I3 Zielkowice Pol.
175 H2 Zielona Pol.
174 F2 Zielona Chocina Pol.
174 D4 Zielona Góra *Lubuskie* Pol.
174 E3 Zielona Góra *Wielkopolskie* Pol.
175 J3 Zielonka Pol.
175 H2 Zieluń Pol.
138 F4 Ziemelkursas augstiene *hills* Latvia
138 K4 Ziemeris Latvia
173 J5 Ziemetshausen Ger.
138 E5 Ziemupe Latvia
169 H8 Zierenberg Ger.
164 E5 Zierikzee Neth.
179 M2 Ziersdorf Austria
170 E4 Zierzow Ger.
171 F6 Ziesar Ger.
203 F2 Ziftá Egypt
96 A4 Zigaing Myanmar
129 A5 Zigana Geçidi *pass* Turkey
111 J10 Zigê Tangco *l.* China
202 D3 Zīghan Libya
191 N4 Zignago, Valle *lag.* Italy
96 B5 Zigon Myanmar
108 E4 Zigong *Sichuan* China
202 B6 Ziguey Chad
Zigui *Hubei* China *see* Guojiaba
108 H3 Zigui *Hubei* China
206 A3 Ziguinchor Senegal
138 K4 Žīguri Latvia
107 P8 Zi He *r.* China
176 C1 Žihle Czech Rep.
244 F7 Zihuaquio Mex.
244 F8 Zihuatanejo Mex.
109 J7 Zijin *Guangdong* China
164 J4 Zijpenberg *hill* Neth.
Ziketan *Qinghai* China *see* Xinghai
139 R8 Zikeyevo Rus. Fed.
128 C6 Zikhron Ya'aqov Israel
120 G1 Zilair Rus. Fed.
138 I4 Zilaiskalns Latvia
126 G3 Zile Turkey
135 L5 Zilim *r.* Rus. Fed.
177 H2 Žilina Slovakia
175 M1 Žilinai Lith.
177 I2 Žilinský kraj *admin. reg.* Slovakia
202 C2 Zillah Libya
178 E5 Ziller *r.* Austria
178 E5 Zillertal *val.* Austria
178 E5 Zillertaler Alpen *mts* Austria
190 G2 Zillis Switz.
169 K7 Zilly Ger.
171 K6 Ziltendorf Ger.
138 L5 Zilupe Latvia
98 H1 Zima Rus. Fed.
177 K5 Zimandu Nou Romania
245 H5 Zimapán Mex.
245 K9 Zimatlán Mex.
209 E9 Zimba Zambia
213 F4 Zimbabwe *country* Africa
Zimbabwe *tourist site* Zimbabwe *see* Great Zimbabwe National Monument
122 A4 Zīmkān, Rūdkhāneh-ye *r.* Iran
Zimmerbude Rus. Fed. *see* Svetlyy
172 F5 Zimmern ob Rottweil Ger.
169 H8 Zimmersrode (Neuental) Ger.
206 C5 Zimmi Sierra Leone
197 N7 Zimnicea Romania
134 G2 Zimniy Bereg *coastal area* Rus. Fed.
135 H7 Zimovniki Rus. Fed.
126 G6 Zimrīn Syria
128 D7 Ẕin *watercourse* Israel
245 M8 Zinapa *r.* Mex.
244 F5 Zináparo Mex.
244 G6 Zinapécuaro Mex.
213 G4 Zinave, Parque Nacional de *nat. park* Moz.
199 L4 Zindan Mağarası *tourist site* Turkey
123 N6 Zindawar Pak.
207 H3 Zinder Niger
207 H3 Zinder *dept* Niger
108 C3 Zindo *Sichuan* China
207 H4 Zing Nigeria
211 C7 Zinga Mulike Tanz.
170 G2 Zingst *reg.* Ger.
170 G2 Zingst am Darß, Ostseebad Ger.
206 E3 Ziniaré Burkina
106 I7 Zinihu *Nei Mongol* China
124 G9 Zinjibār Yemen
137 N3 Zin'kiv Ukr.
173 O3 Žinkovy Czech Rep.
215 P5 Zinkwazi Beach S. Africa
170 I2 Zinnowitz Ger.
139 X5 Zinovo Rus. Fed.
Zinoyevsk Ukr. *see* Kirovohrad
108 B3 Zin Qu *r.* *Sichuan* China
206 D3 Zinzana Mali
247 □2 Zion St Kitts and Nevis
226 G7 Zion *IL* U.S.A.
234 D5 Zion *MD* U.S.A.
234 C3 Zion Grove *PA* U.S.A.
241 S4 Zion National Park *UT* U.S.A.
224 B3 Zionz Lake *Ont.* Can.
111 M10 Zi Qu *r.* *Qinghai* China
108 A2 Ziqudukou *Qinghai* China
122 E3 Zīrab Iran
244 G7 Zirándaro Mex.
179 K5 Zirbitzkogel *mt.* Austria
177 G4 Zirc Hungary
170 J3 Zirchow Ger.
129 D6 Zirekli Turkey
179 J7 Žiri Slovenia
188 E4 Žirje *i.* Croatia
238 K6 Zirkel, Mount *CO* U.S.A.
125 K3 Zirkūh *i.* U.A.E.
178 D5 Zirl Austria
173 J3 Zirndorf Ger.
117 N6 Ziro *Arun. Prad.* India
179 L1 Žirovnice Czech Rep.
123 I7 Zirreh Afgh.
122 D7 Zīr Rūd Iran
109 I4 Zi Shui *r.* China
179 O2 Zistersdorf Austria
244 G6 Zitácuaro Mex.
177 H4 Zitava *r.* Slovakia
196 I5 Žitište *Vojvodina* Serbia
254 D2 Zitiua *r.* Brazil
108 E3 Zitong *Sichuan* China
197 J7 Žitorsđa Serbia
171 K9 Zittau Ger.
171 K9 Zittauer Gebirge *park* Ger.
178 A5 Zitterklapfen *mt.* Austria
171 F6 Zitz Ger.
127 L5 Zīveh Iran
188 G3 Živinice Bos.-Herz.
210 C2 Ziway Hāyk' *l.* Eth.
109 K5 Zixi *Jiangxi* China
109 I6 Zixing *Hunan* China
107 O7 Ziya He *r.* China
Ziyamet Cyprus *see* Leonarisson
120 G2 Ziyanchurino Rus. Fed.
Ziyang *Jiangxi* China *see* Wuyuan
108 G2 Ziyang *Shaanxi* China
108 E3 Ziyang *Sichuan* China
122 G8 Ziyārat Iran
128 C2 Ziyaret Dağı *hill* Turkey
129 A5 Ziyaret Dağı *mt.* Turkey
108 H5 Ziyuan *Guangxi* China
108 F6 Ziyun *Guizhou* China
204 D3 Ziz, Oued *watercourse* Morocco
190 H2 Zizers Switz.
108 E4 Zizhong *Sichuan* China
107 L8 Zizhou *Shaanxi* China
186 A1 Zizurkil Spain
179 N7 Zlatar Croatia
196 H7 Zlatar *mts* Serbia
179 N7 Zlatar-Bistrica Croatia
177 H3 Zlatá Studňa *mt.* Slovakia
176 G1 Zlaté Hory Czech Rep.
177 H3 Zlaté Moravce Slovakia
197 K6 Zlaten Rog Bulg.
196 H7 Zlatibor *mts* Serbia
196 I5 Zlatica *r.* Serbia
197 L4 Zlatna Romania
197 Q7 Zlatni Pyasŭtsi *nat. park* Bulg.
197 N9 Zlatograd Bulg.
130 G4 Zlatoust Rus. Fed.
137 M6 Zlatoustivka *Dnipropetrovs'ka Oblast'* Ukr.
137 Q6 Zlatoustivka *Donets'ka Oblast'* Ukr.
100 H2 Zlatoustovsk Rus. Fed.
177 J3 Zlatý Stôl *mt.* Slovakia
174 G2 Zławieś Wielka Pol.
136 F3 Zlazne Ukr.
179 K8 Žlebič Slovenia
177 G2 Zlín Czech Rep.
177 G2 Zlínský kraj *admin. reg.* Czech Rep.
202 B1 Zlīţan Libya
176 D2 Zliv Czech Rep.
174 E2 Złocieniec Pol.
174 G4 Złoczew Pol.
171 J10 Zlonice Czech Rep.
175 I4 Złota Pol.
174 G3 Złotniki Kujawskie Pol.
174 D4 Złotoryja Pol.
174 F2 Złotów Pol.
174 E5 Złoty Stak Pol.
176 C1 Žlutice Czech Rep.
135 E5 Zlynka Rus. Fed.
137 K5 Zlynka Ukr.
121 T2 Zmeinogorsk Rus. Fed.
174 E4 Żmigród Pol.
191 P5 Žminj Croatia
Zmiyev Ukr. *see* Zmiyiv
139 T9 Zmiyevka Rus. Fed.
197 S5 Zmiyinyy, Ostriv *i.* Ukr.
137 P4 Zmiyiv Ukr.
137 M7 Zmiyivka Ukr.
175 L4 Żmudź Pol.
121 R2 Znamenka Kazakh.
121 R1 Znamenka *Altayskiy Kray* Rus. Fed.
139 S9 Znamenka *Orlovskaya Oblast'* Rus. Fed.
139 R7 Znamenka *Smolenskaya Oblast'* Rus. Fed.
Znamenka Ukr. *see* Znam"yanka
175 J1 Znamensk Rus. Fed.
139 W8 Znamenskoye *Lipetskaya Oblast'* Rus. Fed.
139 S8 Znamenskoye *Orlovskaya Oblast'* Rus. Fed.
137 L5 Znam"yanka Ukr.
137 L5 Znam"yanka Druha Ukr.
Znauri Georgia *see* Qornisi
174 F3 Żnin Pol.
137 M1 Znobivka *r.* Ukr.
137 M1 Znob Novhorods'ke Ukr.
176 F3 Znojmo Czech Rep.
190 G7 Zoagli Italy
214 F9 Zoar S. Africa
122 B4 Zobeyrī Iran
213 G2 Zóbuè Moz.
178 C6 Zoccola, Lago di *l.* Italy
111 E10 Zoco *Xizang* China
129 E3 Zodi Georgia
Zodi-Qornisi Georgia *see* Zodi
164 H5 Zoelen Neth.
165 G6 Zoersel Belgium
207 H6 Zoetéle Cameroon
164 F4 Zoetermeer Neth.
164 F4 Zoeterwoude Neth.
190 D1 Zofingen Switz.
Zogainrawar *Qinghai* China *see* Huashixia
108 A4 Zogang *Xizang* China
190 H4 Zogno Italy
108 B2 Zogqên *Sichuan* China
198 E5 Zografou Greece
122 A4 Zohāb Iran
176 F3 Zohor Slovakia
122 C6 Zohreh *r.* Iran
111 I10 Zoidê Lhai *Xizang* China
108 D2 Zoigê *Sichuan* China
120 H6 Zoir Uzbek.
211 C6 Zoissa Tanz.
116 E2 Zoji La *pass* Jammu and Kashmir
215 K8 Zola S. Africa
191 K6 Zola Predosa Italy
165 H6 Zolder Belgium
191 M3 Zoldo Alto Italy
129 E1 Zolka *r.* Rus. Fed.
175 K5 Żółkiewka-Osada Pol.
170 E3 Zölkow Ger.
190 C1 Zollikofen Switz.
190 F1 Zollikon Switz.
173 L5 Zolling Ger.
Zolochev *Kharkivs'ka Oblast'* Ukr. *see* Zolochiv
Zolochev *L'vivs'ka Oblast'* Ukr. *see* Zolochiv
137 O3 Zolochiv *Kharkivs'ka Oblast'* Ukr.
136 D4 Zolochiv *L'vivs'ka Oblast'* Ukr.
136 E5 Zolota Lypa *r.* Ukr.
100 E1 Zolotaya Gora Rus. Fed.
137 R5 Zolote Ukr.
137 O8 Zolote Pole Ukr.
175 K6 Zolotkovychi Ukr.
136 E4 Zolotnyky Ukr.
137 L4 Zolotonosha Ukr.
120 A2 Zolotoye Rus. Fed.
Zolotoye Ukr. *see* Zolote
135 G5 Zolotukhino Rus. Fed.
136 E5 Zolotyy Potik Ukr.
174 E2 Zółtnica Pol.
175 K5 Żołynia Pol.
213 □J4 Zomandao *r.* Madag.
177 H5 Zomba Hungary
211 B8 Zomba Malawi
Zombor *Vojvodina* Serbia *see* Sombor
165 E6 Zomergem Belgium
121 M8 Zomin Uzbek.
260 C2 Zonda Arg.
106 E8 Zongjiafangzi *Qinghai* China
208 C3 Zongo Dem. Rep. Congo
245 K7 Zongolica Mex.
126 E3 Zonguldak Turkey
199 M1 Zonguldak *prov.* Turkey
109 K3 Zongyang *Anhui* China
108 B4 Zongza *Sichuan* China
106 F7 Zongzhai *Gansu* China
165 H7 Zonhoven Belgium
165 C7 Zonnebeke Belgium
195 □ Żonqor, Il-Ponta taż- *pt* Malta
122 A2 Zonūz Iran
192 C4 Zonza *Corse* France
207 I2 Zoo Baba *well* Niger
245 K8 Zoogocho Mex.
194 H8 Zoppo, Portella dello *pass* Italy
245 I6 Zoquiapán y Anexas, Parque Nacional *nat. park* Mex.
245 J7 Zoquitlán Mex.
174 F5 Żórawina Pol.
171 F7 Zörbig Ger.
129 E6 Zor Dağ *mt.* Turkey
169 K7 Zorge Ger.
206 E3 Zorgho Burkina
Zorgo Burkina *see* Zorgho
Zorinsk Ukr. *see* Zoryns'k
184 H2 Zorita Spain
183 L7 Zorita *r.* Spain
186 E6 Zorita del Maestrazgo Spain
137 N8 Zorkine Ukr.
123 O3 Zorkŭl *l.* Afgh./Tajik.
197 P4 Zorleni Romania
197 J5 Zorlenţu Mare Romania
157 P6 Zorn *r.* France
173 L5 Zorneding Ger.
172 E2 Zornheim Ger.
197 O8 Zornitsa Bulg.
Zornotza *País Vasco* Spain *see* Amorebieta
250 A5 Zorritos Peru
174 G5 Żory Pol.
137 R5 Zoryns'k Ukr.
206 C5 Zorzor Liberia
171 H6 Zossen Ger.
165 E7 Zottegem Belgium
206 C5 Zouan-Hounien Côte d'Ivoire
202 C4 Zouar Chad
107 O9 Zoucheng *Shandong* China
204 B5 Zouérat Maur.
206 D2 Zouina *well* Maur.
106 F7 Zoulang Nanshan *mts* China
107 O8 Zouping *Shandong* China
198 E5 Zourvas, Akrotirio *pt* Greece
109 H4 Zoushi *Hunan* China
164 J2 Zoutkamp Neth.
165 H7 Zoutleeuw Belgium
Zouxian *Shandong* China *see* Zoucheng
122 E5 Zovār Iran
138 L3 Zovka Rus. Fed.
245 J5 Zozocolco de Hidalgo Mex.
179 L7 Zreče Slovenia
196 I5 Zrenjanin *Vojvodina* Serbia
179 O7 Zrinski Topolovac Croatia
188 E3 Zrmanja *r.* Croatia
173 O2 Zruč Czech Rep.
176 E2 Zruč nad Sázavou Czech Rep.
177 K5 Zsadány Hungary
177 K4 Zsáka Hungary
177 H4 Zsámbék Hungary
177 I4 Zsámbok Hungary
177 I5 Zsana Hungary
171 H8 Zschaitz Ger.
171 H9 Zschopau Ger.
171 H8 Zschopau *r.* Ger.
171 F8 Zschortau Ger.
177 G5 Zselic *hills* Hungary
177 G5 Zselicsegi *park* Hungary
123 N3 Zu Afgh.
251 E3 Zuata *r.* Venez.
191 P5 Zub, Rt *pt* Croatia
127 K9 Zubālah, Birkat *waterhole* Saudi Arabia
124 F8 Zubayr, Jazā'ir az *i.* Yemen
177 I2 Zuberec Slovakia
180 E4 Zubia Spain
183 O2 Zubiaur Spain
190 E5 Zubiena Italy
186 B1 Zubieta Spain
186 A1 Zubieta Spain
261 F5 Zubillaga Arg.
183 Q3 Zubiri Spain
139 T8 Zubkovo Rus. Fed.
135 H5 Zubova Polyana Rus. Fed.
135 J5 Zubovka Rus. Fed.
139 S7 Zubovo *Kaluzhskaya Oblast'* Rus. Fed.
139 T1 Zubovo *Vologodskaya Oblast'* Rus. Fed.
136 C4 Zubra *r.* Ukr.
174 D3 Żubrów Pol.
139 R5 Zubtsov Rus. Fed.
187 E7 Zucaina Spain
190 F3 Zucchero, Monte *mt.* Switz.
172 D7 Zuchwil Switz.
178 D6 Zuckerhütl *mt.* Austria
223 J2 Zucker Lake *N.W.T.* Can.
183 P3 Zudaire Spain
170 H2 Zudar Ger.
206 D5 Zuénoula Côte d'Ivoire
186 D4 Zuera Spain
125 L7 Ẓufār *admin. reg.* Oman
184 G5 Zufre Spain
184 G5 Zufre, Embalse de *resr* Spain
190 F1 Zug Switz.
190 F1 Zug *canton* Switz.
186 B1 Zugarramurdi Spain
129 C3 Zugdidi Georgia
190 E1 Zuger See *l.* Switz.
178 C5 Zugspitze *mt.* Austria/Ger.
207 G4 Zugu Nigeria
183 O3 Zuhatzu-Kuartango Spain
185 K5 Zuheros Spain
137 R5 Zuhres Ukr.
164 F5 Zuid-Beijerland Neth.
Zuider Zee *l.* Neth. *see* IJsselmeer
164 F5 Zuid-Holland *prov.* Neth.
164 J2 Zuidhorn Neth.
164 G4 Zuid-Kennemerland Nationaal Park *nat. park* Neth.
164 K2 Zuidlaardermeer *l.* Neth.
164 F5 Zuidland Neth.
164 K2 Zuidlaren Neth.
164 I6 Zuid-Willemsvaart *canal* Neth.
164 J3 Zuidwolde Neth.
165 D6 Zuienkerke Belgium
Zuitai *Gansu* China *see* Kangxian
Zuitaizi *Gansu* China *see* Kangxian
Zuitou *Shaanxi* China *see* Taibai
185 N5 Zújar Spain
185 H2 Zújar *r.* Spain
185 I3 Zújar, Embalse del *resr* Spain
175 L4 Żuków *Lubelskie* Pol.
175 I3 Żuków *Mazowieckie* Pol.
174 D4 Żukowice Pol.
143 O7 Żukowo Pol.
250 D2 Zulia *state* Venez.
106 I8 Zuli He *r.* *Gansu* China
176 G1 Žulová Czech Rep.
169 C9 Zülpich Ger.
165 D7 Zulte Belgium
186 A1 Zumaia Spain
186 A1 Zumarraga Spain
250 B6 Zumba Ecuador
179 L8 Žumberačka Gora *mts* Croatia
213 F2 Zumbo Moz.
226 B5 Zumbro *r.* *MN* U.S.A.
226 B5 Zumbrota *MN* U.S.A.
185 O4 Zumeta *r.* Spain
245 H7 Zumpahuacán Mex.
245 H6 Zumpango Mex.
245 H8 Zumpango del Río Mex.
165 G6 Zundert Neth.
207 G4 Zungeru Nigeria
195 J6 Zungri Italy
107 P6 Zunhua *Hebei* China
241 X6 Zuni *NM* U.S.A.
241 W7 Zuni *watercourse* *AZ/NM* U.S.A.
239 J9 Zuni Mountains *NM* U.S.A.
107 N1 Zun-Torey, Ozero *l.* Rus. Fed.
108 F5 Zunyi *Guizhou* China
108 F5 Zunyi *Guizhou* China
183 R3 Zunzarren Spain
96 I3 Zuo Jiang *r.* China/Vietnam
107 M8 Zuoquan *Shanxi* China
107 M7 Zuoyun *Shanxi* China
190 H2 Zuoz Switz.
188 G3 Županja Croatia
124 E6 Zuqāq *i.* Saudi Arabia
196 I8 Žur *Kosovo* Serbia
134 K4 Zura Rus. Fed.
127 L4 Zūrābād *Āžarbāyjān-e Gharbī* Iran
120 G9 Zurabad Iran
123 I4 Zūrābād *Khorāsān* Iran
122 B5 Zurbāţīyah Iraq
185 O6 Zúrgena Spain
111 J9 Zurhen Ul Shan *mts* China
190 F1 Zürich Switz.
190 F1 Zürich *canton* Switz.
190 F1 Zürichsee *l.* Switz.
123 M5 Zurmat *reg.* Afgh.
129 H5 Zurnabad Azer.
179 P4 Zurndorf Austria
197 P7 Zŭrnevo Bulg.
175 H2 Żuromin Pol.
170 E3 Zurow Ger.
195 □ Żurrieq Malta
207 G4 Zuru Nigeria
190 E1 Zurzach Switz.
Zurzuna Turkey *see* Çıldır
173 J4 Zusam *r.* Ger.
139 T8 Zusha *r.* Rus. Fed.
105 K5 Zushi Japan
173 J5 Zusmarshausen Ger.
170 E3 Züsow Ger.
170 I3 Züssow Ger.
165 I7 Zutendaal Belgium
164 J4 Zutphen Neth.
215 J9 Zuurberg National Park S. Africa
175 L1 Žuvintas *l.* Lith.
138 G7 Žuvinto rezervatas *nature res.* Lith.
202 B1 Zuwārah Libya
137 N8 Zuya *r.* Ukr.
156 D1 Zuydcoote France
134 J4 Zuyevka Rus. Fed.
87 C9 Zuytdorp Nature Reserve *W.A.* Austr.
122 H4 Zūzan Iran
179 K8 Žužemberk Slovenia
196 I8 Zvečan *Kosovo* Serbia
138 H4 Zvejniekciems Latvia
139 T6 Zvenigorod Rus. Fed.
Zvenigorodka Ukr. *see* Zvenyhorodka
136 J4 Zvenyhorodka Ukr.
137 T5 Zverevo Rus. Fed.
197 L7 Zverino Bulg.
120 K1 Zverinogolovskoye Rus. Fed.
198 B2 Zvezdë Albania
188 G3 Zvijezda *mts* Bos.-Herz.
213 F4 Zvishavane Zimbabwe
177 I3 Zvolen Slovakia
197 K8 Zvonce Serbia
188 G3 Zvornik Bos.-Herz.
175 M5 Zvynyache Ukr.
164 J2 Zwaagwesteinde Neth.
179 L6 Zwaring Austria
214 F6 Zwarkop S. Africa
164 J3 Zwartewater *l.* Neth.
164 J3 Zwartsluis Neth.
206 C5 Zwedru Liberia
164 K3 Zweeloo Neth.
172 C3 Zweibrücken Ger.
190 C2 Zweisimmen Switz.
214 D9 Zweletemba S. Africa
215 L8 Zwelitsha S. Africa
171 F8 Zwenkau Ger.
179 M3 Zwentendorf an der Donau Austria
171 H7 Zwethau Ger.
179 L2 Zwettl Austria
179 L2 Zwettl *r.* Austria
165 D7 Zwevegem Belgium
165 D6 Zwevezele Belgium
171 G9 Zwickau Ger.
171 G8 Zwickauer Mulde *r.* Ger.
172 G5 Zwiefalten Ger.
174 D3 Zwierzyn Pol.
175 K5 Zwierzyniec Pol.
173 O3 Zwiesel Ger.
173 N6 Zwiesel *mt.* Ger.
165 F6 Zwijndrecht Belgium
164 G5 Zwijndrecht Neth.
190 D1 Zwingen Switz.
172 F2 Zwingenberg Ger.
168 F4 Zwischenahner Meer *l.* Ger.
178 A5 Zwischenwasser Austria
171 F8 Zwochau Ger.
175 J4 Zwoleń Pol.
164 J3 Zwolle Neth.
171 G9 Zwönitz Ger.
171 F10 Zwota Ger.
134 K4 Zyablovo Rus. Fed.
138 L6 Zyal'ki Belarus
137 N8 Zybyny Ukr.
175 H3 Żychlin Pol.
174 F3 Żydowo *Wielkopolskie* Pol.
174 E1 Żydowo *Zachodniopomorskie* Pol.
175 M3 Zyelyanyevichy Belarus
128 B4 Zygi Cyprus
174 G4 Zygry Pol.
175 M5 Zymne Ukr.
Zymogor'ye Ukr. *see* Zymohir"ya
137 R5 Zymohir"ya Ukr.
137 M8 Zymyne Ukr.
175 I3 Żyrardów Pol.
Zyryan Kazakh. *see* Zyryanovsk
131 Q3 Zyryanka Rus. Fed.
130 J3 Zyryanovo Rus. Fed.
121 U3 Zyryanovsk Kazakh.
175 K4 Żyrzyn Pol.
175 K1 Żytkiejmy Pol.
175 H5 Żytno Pol.
175 H6 Żywiec Pol.
177 I2 Żywiecki Park Krajobrazowy Pol.
174 F5 Żywocice Pol.
Zyyi Cyprus *see* Zygi

ACKNOWLEDGEMENTS

MAPS AND DATA

Maps designed and created by
HarperCollins Reference, Glasgow

Data acknowledgements
Pages 30–31
Land cover map: Developed by the European Commission's Joint Research Centre in association with the United Nations Environmental Programme and the Food and Agriculture Organisation, on behalf of the Global Land Cover 2000 Partnership; edited by Etienne Bartholomé, Alan Belward, Rene Beuchle, Hugh Eva, Steffen Fritz, Andrew Hartley, Philippe Mayaux and Hans-Jurgen Stbig.
© Copyright European Commission, 2004
Digital data and more information available from
http://www.gvm.jrc.it/glc2000/defaultGLC2000.htm
Glc2000.info@jrc.it

Pages 32–33
Population map: Center for International Earth Science Information Network (CIESIN), Columbia University; International Food Policy Research Institute (IFPRI); and World Resources Institute (WRI). 2000. Gridded Population of the World (GPW), Version 3. Palisades, NY: CIESIN, Columbia University. Available at http://sedac.ciesin.columbia.edu/plue/gpw

Pages 262-263: Antarctic Digital Database (versions 1 and 2), © Scientific Committee on Antarctic Research (SCAR), Cambridge (1993, 1998)
Bathymetric data: The GEBCO Digital Atlas published by the British Oceanographic Data Centre on behalf of IOC and IHO, 1994

All mapping in this atlas is generated from Collins Bartholomew digital databases. Collins Bartholomew, the UK's leading independent geographical information supplier, can provide a digital, custom, and premium mapping service to a variety of markets. For further information:
Tel: +44 (0) 141 306 3752
e-mail: collinsbartholomew@harpercollins.co.uk
www.collinsbartholomew.com

The publishers would like to thank all National Survey Departments, Road, Rail and National Park authorities, Statistical Offices and national place name committees throughout the World for their valuable assistance, and in particular the following:

Antarctic Place-Names Committee, FCO, London, UK

Australian Surveying & Land Information Group, Belconnen, Australia

Automobile Association of South Africa, Johannesburg, Republic of South Africa

British Antarctic Survey, Cambridge, UK

BP Amoco PLC, London, UK

British Geological Survey, Keyworth, Nottingham, UK

Chief Directorate: Surveys and Mapping, Mowbray, Republic of South Africa

Commission de toponymie du Québec, Québec, Canada

Dr John Davies, The Royal Observatory, Edinburgh

Defence Geographic and Imagery Intelligence Agency, Geographic Information Group, Tolworth, UK

Federal Survey Division, Lagos, Nigeria

Food and Agriculture Organization of the United Nations, Rome, Italy

Foreign and Commonwealth Office, London, UK

Mr P J M Geelan, London, UK

General Directorate of Highways, Ankara, Turkey

Hydrographic Office, Ministry of Defence, Taunton, UK

Institut Géographique National, Brussels, Belgium

Institut Géographique National, Paris, France

Instituto Brasileiro de Geografia e Estatistica, Rio de Janeiro, Brazil

Instituto Geográfico Nacional, Lima, Peru

Instituto Geográfico Nacional, Madrid, Spain

Instituto Portugués de Cartografia e Cadastro, Lisbon, Portugal

International Atomic Energy Agency, Vienna, Austria

International Boundary Research Unit, University of Durham, UK

International Hydrographic Organization, Monaco

International Union for the Conservation of Nature, Gland, Switzerland and Cambridge, UK

Kort- og Matrikelstyrelsen, Copenhagen, Denmark

Land Information New Zealand, Wellington, New Zealand

Lands and Surveys Department, Kampala, Uganda

H A G Lewis OBE

National Geographic Society, Washington DC, USA

National Library of Scotland, Edinburgh, UK

National Mapping and Resources Information Authority (NAMRIA), Manila, Philippines

National Oceanic and Atmospheric Administration, USA

Permanent Committee on Geographical Names, London, UK

Royal Geographical Society, London, UK

Royal Scottish Geographical Society, Glasgow, UK

Scientific Committee on Antarctic Research, Cambridge, UK

Scott Polar Research Institute, Cambridge, UK

Scottish Office Development Department, Edinburgh, UK

SNCF French Railways, London, UK

Statens Kartverket, Hønefoss, Norway

Survey Department, Singapore

Survey of India, Dehra Dun, India

Survey of Israel, Tel Aviv, Israel

Survey of Kenya, Nairobi, Kenya

Surveyor General, Harare, Zimbabwe

Surveyor General, Ministry of Lands and Natural Resources, Lusaka, Zambia

Surveys and Mapping Branch, Natural Resources, Ottawa, Canada

Surveys and Mapping Division, Dar-es-Salaam, Tanzania

Terralink New Zealand Ltd, Wellington, New Zealand

The Meteorological Office, Bracknell, Berkshire, UK

The National Imagery and Mapping Agency (NIMA), Bethesda, Maryland, USA

The Stationery Office, London, UK

The United States Board on Geographic Names, Washington DC, USA

The United States Department of State, Washington DC, USA

The United States Geological Survey, Earth Science Information Center, Reston, Virginia, USA

United Nations, specialized agencies, New York, USA

Marcel Vârlan, University 'Al. I. Cuza', Iași, Romania

IMAGES AND PHOTOS

Pages 8–19
Remote Sensing Applications Consultants Ltd, 4 Mansfield Park, Medstead, Alton, Hants, GU34 5PZ, UK

Pages 20–21
NRSC Ltd/Science Photo Library

Pages 22–23
The Sun: Jisas/Lockheed/Science Photo Library
Mercury: NASA/Science Photo Library
Venus: NASA/Science Photo Library
Earth: Photo Library International/Science Photo Library
Mars: US Geological Survey/Science Photo Library
Jupiter: NASA/Science Photo Library
Saturn: Space Telescope ScienceInstitute/NASA/Science Photo Library
Uranus: NASA/Science Photo Library
Neptune: NASA/Science Photo Library
Pluto and Charon: Space Telescope Science Institute/NASA/Science Photo Library

Pages 24–25
Bam earthquake: Hasan Sarbakhshian/AP/EMPICS
Montserrat: Bernhard Edmaier/Space Photo Library

Pages 26–27
1: WHF Smith, US National Oceanic and Atmospheric Administration (NOAA), USA
2: A McDonald and C Wunsch, USA
4: NASA/JPL, USA
5: L Talley, USA

Pages 28–29
Cyclone Larry: MODIS/NASA

Pages 30–31
Itapu Dam/Iguaçu Falls: UNEP/USGS
Lake Chad: UNEP/GRID
Images reproduced by kind permission of UNEP

Page 40
PriMetrica Inc., Washington D.C., USA
www.telegeography.com and www.primetrica.com

Pages 42–43
1: © British Museum, London, UK
2: By permission of The British Library, London, UK C.3.d.7
3: Bridgeman Art Library
4: Hereford Cathedral/Bridgeman Art Library
5: E T Archive/The British Library
6: By permission of The British Library, London, UK Maps.4.Tab.8folio1
7 and 8: Reproduced by permission of the Trustees of the National Library of Scotland, Edinburgh, UK
9: Alan Collinson Design/Geoinnovations, Llandudno, UK

Pages 44–45
1: © National Maritime Museum, London
3: IKONOS Image © CRISP 2004
4: Space Imaging, Thornton, Colorado www.spaceimaging.com
5: © Leif Skoogfors/CORBIS
6: Richland County, South Carolina GIS www.richlandmaps.com
7: Courtesy of Garmin Ltd www.garmin.com

Pages 46
Puncak Jaya: Alpine Ascents International Inc.
New Guinea: NASA/Goddard Space Flight Center/USGS
Darling river: Image courtesy of Earth Sciences and Image Analysis Laboratory, NASA Johnson Space Center. STS099-719-87 http://eol.jsc.nasa.gov
Lake Eyre: NASA
Mt Everest: © Alison Wright/CORBIS
Borneo: NASA/Goddard Space Flight Center/USGS
Chang Jiang: Earth Satellite Corporation/Science Photo Library
Aral Sea: U.S. Geological Survey, EROS Data Center, Sioux Falls, SD

Pages 47
El'brus: © Dean Conger/CORBIS
Great Britain: M-SAT LTD/Science Photo Library
Volga: CNES, 1996 Distribution SPOT Image/Science Photo Library
Caspian Sea: MODIS/NASA
Kilimanjaro: Tony Stone Images Ltd
Madagascar: MODIS/NASA
Nile: MODIS/NASA
Lake Victoria: MODIS/NASA

Pages 48–49
Mt McKinley: Tony Stone Images Ltd
Greenland: MODIS/NASA
Mississippi: ASTER/NASA
Lake Superior: Image courtesy of MODIS Rapid Response Project at NASA/GSFC
Cerro Aconcagua: Andes Press Agency
Isla Grande de Tierra del Fuego: MODIS/NASA
Amazonas: NASA
Lago Titicaca: NASA
Vinson Massif: B. Storey/British Antarctic Survey

220-221
222-223
224-225
226-227
NORTH AMERICA
218-219
Chicago
226
240-241
San Francisco
239
Los Angeles
239
238-239
242-243
236-237
New York
234
234-235
Washington
235
232-233
Bermuda
231
New
Providence
231
230-231
244-245
Mexico
245
228-229
242
KEY TO MAP PAGES
228-229
1:9 000 000 and smaller
244-245
1:2 000 000 - 1:4 000 000
246-247
1:5 000 000 - 1:8 000 000
234-235
1:1 000 000 - 1:2 000 000
Inset maps of islands and cities are named.